THE
CORPORATE
DIRECTORY

OF U.S. PUBLIC COMPANIES

BY WALKER'S

2008

Company Profiles and Indexes

WALKER'S RESEARCH
Branford, Connecticut

ISBN: 0-9771690-2-2
Filed with The Library of Congress

Walker's Research
Samantha Nicholas, Publisher
P.O. Box 817, Branford, CT 06405
PHONE: 1-800-913-0382
FAX: 206-274-7203
http://www.walkersresearch.com

TABLE OF CONTENTS

COMPANY PROFILES

INDEXES

INTRODUCTION

THE CORPORATE DIRECTORY of U.S. Public Companies -Walker's Research, provides information on more than 10,000 publicly-held U.S. corporations, including foreign companies offering American Depository Receipts. This **DIRECTORY** supplies financial, management, and stock data in broad company profiles. Seven indexes are featured, allowing quick reference to profile data.

THE CORPORATE DIRECTORY of U.S. Public Companies -Walker's Research, displays general information in each profile, including company name, address, telephone number, Internet World Wide Web address when available, state of incorporation, fiscal year end, and number of employees. In addition, the **DIRECTORY** describes the company's area(s) of business and lists its SIC (Standard Industrial Classification) codes, auditor, stock transfer agent, legal counsel, and DUNS (Data Universal Numbering System) number.

The **DIRECTORY** supplies key elements of corporate stock data, including stock exchange, ticker symbol, 12/24/2007 stock price, number of outstanding shares and shareholders, and shares held by officers and directors.

In addition, corporate structures are identified by displaying names and titles, and when available, age and compensation of officers and directors and the names of individuals, businesses, or family groups that own substantial portions of company stock. Major subsidiaries are also listed.

DIRECTORY profiles provide essential financial data, including up to three years history of sales, net income, and earnings per share. Also included are the most recent year's figures for current assets, gross property, plant and equipment, total assets, current liabilities, total liabilities, total equity, price/earnings ratio, dividend information, and total debt to equity ratio.

Information in the **DIRECTORY** has been compiled from corporate documents filed with the U.S. Securities and Exchange Commission (SEC) and other related company resources.

Each company included in the **DIRECTORY** is publicly owned and trades stock or debentures on the New York or American Stock Exchanges or on NASDAQ (National Association of Securities Dealers Automated Quotation System) or other over-the-counter markets, and (or) has filed a Form 10-K with the SEC.

i

Organization of
THE CORPORATE DIRECTORY
of U.S. Public Companies - WALKER'S

PROFILE ELEMENTS

Company

Company Name: Profiles are arranged alphabetically by company name.

Contact Information: Address, telephone number, Fax and toll-free number of the company's principal office. Internet home pages (when available) are formatted as http://World Wide Web address. Email addresses (when available) are formatted as Email:email address

General Information

Incorporation: State (or country) in which the profiled company is incorporated.

Employees: Number of employees of the company, including full and part-time workers.

Auditor: Name of the accountant or accounting firm that audited the corporation's financial statements.

Stock Agent: Name of the commercial bank or other entity appointed by the company to handle its stocks and securities records.

Legal Counsel: Name of the individual or firm appointed to handle the company's legal matters.

DUNS Number: Data Universal Numbering System number, used to identify each business uniquely.

Stock Data

Closing Price: Last sale or bid price of basic common shares at close of trading on 12/24/2007.

Stock Exchange: Stock exchange on which the company's common stock is traded, abbreviated as follows: NYSE (New York Stock Exchange), AMEX (American Stock Exchange), NDQ (NASDAQ), OTC (Over-The-Counter).

Ticker Symbol: Symbol used in trading the company's common stock.

Outstanding Shares: Indicates number of outstanding shares of common stock, all classes, from the latest available year-end data.

Shares Held by Officers and Directors: Number of shares of common stock held by the company's Officers and Directors as a group.

Shareholders: Total number of reported holders of common shares.

Note: For dividend information, see financial section.

Business Description

Narrative description of the company's area(s) of business.

Primary SIC and Additional SICs: Four-digit Standard Industrial Classification (SIC) code first indicating the company's main line of business by sales then followed by additional codes identifying additional lines of business in which the company engages, in descending order by net sales.

CIK Number: A CIK is the unique number that the SEC's computer system assigns to individuals and corporations who file disclosure documents with the SEC. All new electronic and paper filers, foreign and domestic, receive a CIK number.

Major Subsidiaries: Lists both directly-owned and indirectly-owned subsidiaries of the profiled company.

Officers: Names and titles of Officers of the profiled company, and when available, age and compensation. Titles are abreviated as follows:

CAO	Chief Accounting Officer	CEO	Chief Executive Officer
CFO	Chief Financial Officer	COO	Chief Operating Officer
CIO	Chief Information Officer	CTO	Chief Technology Officer
Exec. VP	Executive Vice President	Pres.	President
Sec.	Corporate Secretary	Chmn.	Chairman

Directors: Names and ages of Directors of the corporation.

Owner(s): Names of individuals, business or family entities able to influence corporate affairs due to substantial stock ownership and/or management position. Includes percent of outstanding shares owned, when available.

Financial Data
Financial data is given in whole figures. Where applicable, clarifying comments may be included. If the profiled company is a foreign registrant and reports its financials in terms of foreign currency, the type of currency is noted.

Fiscal Year End: Ending date of the company's fiscal year.

Latest Annual Data: Fiscal year end data for most recent Sales and Net Income as well as reported balances for Current Assets, Plant and Equipment, Total Assets, Current Liabilities, Total Liabilities and Net Worth.

A tabular listing of figures for Sales, Net Income is provided for up to three years. The E.P.S. is diluted E.P.S. for the recent four quarters unless otherwise noted.

Current Assets: Total current assets, including cash, marketable securities, receivables, and inventory for the latest available year.

Plant, Equipment: Total property, plant and equipment (including property under leases, capital leases and leasehold improvements), after depreciation.

Total Assets: Total current assets plus non-current assets.

Current Liabilities: Total current liabilities, including notes payable, current portion of long-term debt, income taxes, and other current liabilities.

Total Liabilities: Total current liabilities plus non-current and other long-term liabilities.

Net Worth: Total shareholders' equity including both preferred and common stock.

P/E Ratio: Price/Earnings Ratio of the company's common stock based on the listed closing price divided by the most recent four quarters' earnings.

Indicated Annual Dividend: Amount of dividend per share of common stock expected on an annual basis.

Debt/Equity Ratio: Total long-term debt divided by total shareholders' equity.

Efforts have been made to make **THE CORPORATE DIRECTORY of U.S. Public Companies - Walker's** as comprehensive and current as possible. In some cases, however, certain data may not have been available at the time of publication. In those cases, the abbreviation "NA" appears beside the respective heading. For certain textual items, such as Owners and Major Subsidiaries, "NA" is not used; instead, the entire data element is omitted where information is unavailable.

INDEXES

Company Index

Lists companies in alphabetical order with page reference.

Officers & Directors Index

Lists Officers and Directors, followed by the name of the profiled company for which they serve.

Owners Index

Identifies names of individuals, corporate entities, or family groups that own a significant portion of stock of one or more of the profiled companies.

Standard Industrial Classification (SIC) Code Index

Standard Industrial Classification (SIC) Codes are presented in numerical order with the assigned definition. Profiled companies are listed alphabetically under their reported SIC codes.

Subsidiary/Parent Index

Lists subsidiaries alphabetically, followed by the name of its parent company and page number for the parent company profile.

Geographic Index

Lists profiled companies by the state and ZIP code in which they have their principal offices. Companies headquartered in Puerto Rico, the U.S. Virgin Islands, or outside of the United States and territories, are listed under the appropriate country heading at the end of the index.

Stock Exchange/Ticker Symbol Index

Lists profiled companies according to the exchange on which their common shares are traded, in alphabetical order by ticker symbol. The exchanges are in order as follows: AMEX (American Stock Exchange), NDQ (NASDAQ), NYSE (New York Stock Exchange), OTC (Over-The-Counter).

Company Profiles

A B Watley Group Inc

90 Pk. Ave., New York, NY, 10016; *PH:* 1-646-753-9301; *Fax:* 1-212-202-5204; *http://* www.abwatley.com; *Email:* accounts@abwatley.com

General - Incorporation	DE	**Stock**- Price on:12/24/2007	$0.09
Employees	NA	Stock Exchange	OTC
Auditor	Marcum & Kliegman LLP	Ticker Symbol	ABWG
Stk Agt	American Stock Transfer & Trust Co.	Outstanding Shares	NA
Counsel	NA	E.P.S	NA
DUNS No.	NA	Shareholders	NA

Business: The group's principal activity is to provide direct-access trading capabilities and related software to both retail as well as corporate customers. The group markets its proprietary technology, direct-access vertical exchange (dave), to the brokerage and banking industries. This system consists of two applications, namely ultimatetrader and watleytrader, a client-server and a Web-based application respectively. As on 30-Sep-2003, the group had approximately 1,100 customers.

Primary SIC and add'l.: 6719 7375 6211

CIK No: 0001035632

Officers: Robert Malin/Pres.

Financial Data: *Fiscal Year End:*09/30 *Latest Annual Data:* 9/30/2004

Year	Sales	Net Income
2004	$9,515,000	-$4,536,000
2001	$25,472,000	-$21,024,000
2000	$42,753,000	-$9,847,000

Curr. Assets:	$497,000	*Curr. Liab.:*	$11,901,000		
Plant, Equip.:	NA	*Total Liab.:*	$15,942,000	*Indic. Yr. Divd.:*	NA
Total Assets:	$778,000	*Net Worth:*	-$15,164,000	*Debt/ Equity:*	NA

A M Castle & Co

3400 N Wolf Rd., Franklin Park, IL, 60131; *PH:* 1-847-455-7111; *http://* www.amcastle.com

General - Incorporation	MD	**Stock**- Price on:12/24/2007	$36.82
Employees	2,016	Stock Exchange	NDQ
Auditor	Deloitte & Touche LLP	Ticker Symbol	CAS
Stk Agt	American Stock Transfer & Trust Co.	Outstanding Shares	17,450,000
Counsel	Mayer, Brown & Platt	E.P.S	$2.61
DUNS No.	00-693-4004	Shareholders	NA

Business: The group's principal activity is to purchase, store, process and distribute specialty metals and plastics. The group operates in two segments : metals and plastics. Metals segment includes the distribution of carbon, stainless steel and non-ferrous metal products. Plastics segment includes servicing a wide variety of industrial plastics. The group operates service centers in various cities of the United States and Canada, equipped with cutting machinery to shape and fabricate the metals to the customers needs. The group's customers include metal users within the Fortune 500 list of companies. On 01-Jan-2004, the group acquired castle de Mexico, s.a. De c.v.

Primary SIC and add'l.: 5162 5051

CIK No: 0000018172

Subsidiaries: A. M. Castle & Co. (Canada) Inc, A. M. Castle & Co. (Canada) Inc., Advanced Fabricating Technology, LLC, Castle Foundation, Inc., Castle IND MGR, Inc., Castle Metals de Mexico, S.A. de C.V., Castle SPFD, LLC, Datamet, Inc., Hy-Alloy Steels Company, Keystone Services Inc., Keystone Tube Company LLC, KSI, LLC, Metal Express, LLC, Oliver Steel Plate Co., Pacific Metals Company 17 Subsidiaries included in the Index

Officers: Michael H. Goldberg/CEO, Pres./$1,578,768.00, Blain A. Tiffany/VP - Sales, Larry A. Boik/VP - Finance, CFO, Thomas L. Garrett/Pres. - Total Plastics, Inc, Sherry L. Holland/VP, General Counsel, Corp. Sec., Steven Scheinkman/Pres. - Transtar Metals, Paul A. Lisius/VP, GM - Metal Express LLC, Paul J. Winsauer/VP - Human Resources/$435,453.00, Stephen V. Hooks/Exec. VP/$967,153.00, Albert J. Biemer/VP, Tim N. Lafontaine/VP - Marketing, Michael J. Coulson/VP - Global Solutions, Robert R. Hudson/VP - Procurement, Henry J. Veith/Controller, Kevin B. Coughlin/VP - Operations

Directors: John McCartney/Chmn., Robert S. Hamada/Dir., Brian P. Anderson/Dir., Thomas A. Donahoe/Dir., Ann M. Drake/Dir., Pamela Forbes/Dir., William K. Hall/Dir., Patrick J. Herbert/Dir., Michael Simpson/Dir.

Owners: John W. Puth, W. B. & CO., an Illinois partnership, BARCLAYS GLOBAL INVESTORS, NA, Michael Simpson, William K. Hall, Craig R. Wilson, Michael H. Goldberg, Robert S. Hamada, Thomas A. Donahoe, Paul J. Winsauer, Brian P. Anderson, Patrick J. Herbert, Stephen V. Hooks, Lawrence A. Boik, John McCartney *(18 Owners included in Index)*

Financial Data: *Fiscal Year End:*12/31 *Latest Annual Data:* 12/31/2006

Year	Sales	Net Income
2006	$1,177,600,000	$55,119,000
2005	$958,978,000	$38,909,000
2004	$760,997,000	$16,877,000

Curr. Assets:	$391,662,000	*Curr. Liab.:*	$301,078,000	*P/E Ratio:*	12.83
Plant, Equip.:	$70,398,000	*Total Liab.:*	$439,213,000	*Indic. Yr. Divd.:*	NA
Total Assets:	$655,120,000	*Net Worth:*	$215,907,000	*Debt/ Equity:*	NA

A Schulman Inc

3550 W Market St., Akron, OH, 44333; *PH:* 1-330-666-3751; *Fax:* 1-330-668-7204; *http://* www.aschulman.com; *Email:* info@aschulman.com

General - Incorporation	DE	**Stock**- Price on:12/24/2007	$21.59
Employees	2,480	Stock Exchange	NDQ
Auditor	PricewaterhouseCoopers LLP	Ticker Symbol	NA
Stk Agt	National City Bank	Outstanding Shares	26,970,000
Counsel	NA	E.P.S	$0.82
DUNS No.	00-699-8413	Shareholders	NA

Business: The groups principle activity is to supply plastic compounds and resins. The groups product line includes proprietary and custom-formulated engineered plastic compounds, color concentrates and additives. The group operates from United States.

Primary SIC and add'l.: 2821 5162 3087

CIK No: 0000087565

Subsidiaries: A. Schulman AG, A. Schulman Canada Ltd., A. Schulman de Mexico, S.A. de C.V., A. Schulman Europe GmbH, A. Schulman GmbH, A. Schulman Holdings S.r.l, A. Schulman Hungary Kft., A. Schulman International Services N.V., A. Schulman International, Inc., A. Schulman Invision, Inc., A. Schulman Italia S.p.A., A. Schulman Plastics (Dongguan) Ltd., A. Schulman Plastics S.L., A. Schulman Plastics SpA, A. Schulman Plastics, BVBA 29 Subsidiaries included in the Index

Officers: Terry L. Haines/Chmn., CEO, Pres., Ronald G. Andres/58/VP, GM - Engineered Compounds, Gary J. Elek/56/VP, Controller - North America, Jolene Collier/Contact - Sales Reps, Western Regional Sales Office, Alain C. Adam/59/VP - Global Automotive Marketing Development, Paul F. Desantis/44/CFO, VP, Treasurer, Barry A. Rhodes/48/COO, Exec. VP - North America

Directors: Terry L. Haines/Chmn., CEO, Pres., James S. Marlen/66/Dir., Ernest J. Novak/62/Dir., Howard R. Curd/68/Dir., Michael A. McManus/64/Dir., Peggy Miller/70/Dir., Willard R. Holland/Dir., John B. Yasinsky/Dir., David G. Birney/Dir., James A. Karman/Dir., Joseph M. Gingo/Dir., James A. Mitarotonda/Dir.

Owners: Howard R. Curd, David G. Birney, James S. Marlen, Ronald G. Andres, James A. Karman, Barington Companies Offshore Fund, Ltd./8.97%, Michael A. McManus, Ernest J. Novak, John M. Myles, Barclays Global Investors NA/5.08%, Peggy Miller, Joseph M. Gingo, Paul F. DeSantis, Terry L. Haines/1.42%, Ramius Capital Group, L.L.C./7.38% *(22 Owners included in Index)*

Financial Data: *Fiscal Year End:*08/31 *Latest Annual Data:* 8/31/2006

Year	Sales	Net Income
2006	$1,616,386,000	$32,662,000
2005	$1,435,590,000	$32,093,000
2004	$1,241,343,000	$27,906,000

Curr. Assets:	$627,348,000	*Curr. Liab.:*	$223,561,000	*P/E Ratio:*	27.68
Plant, Equip.:	$186,879,000	*Total Liab.:*	$433,969,000	*Indic. Yr. Divd.:*	$0.580
Total Assets:	$843,245,000	*Net Worth:*	$403,492,000	*Debt/ Equity:*	NA

A T Cross Co

1 Albion Rd., Lincoln, RI, 02865; *PH:* 1-401-333-1200; *Fax:* 1-401-334-2861; *http://* www.cross.com; *Email:* consumerre@cross.com

General - Incorporation	RI	**Stock**- Price on:12/24/2007	$11.4
Employees	900	Stock Exchange	AMEX
Auditor	Deloitte & Touche LLP	Ticker Symbol	ATX
Stk Agt	Computershare Ltd.	Outstanding Shares	15,320,000
Counsel	NA	E.P.S	$0.40
DUNS No.	00-120-1508	Shareholders	NA

Business: The group's principal activity is to manufacture and market fine writing instruments. The products include ball-point pens, fountain pens, selectip rolling ball pens and mechanical pencils. The group is an original equipment manufacturer of writing instruments and digital pens that are used with tablet pcs. It also designs and markets desk sets. In Feb 2003, the group launched a new line of business accessories, which includes: pad portfolios, personal digital assistant cases, business card cases, key rings, letter openers, money clips, timepieces, etc. Brand names include cross (R), penatia, omnia and bill blassa. The products are sold to approximately 8,100 active retail and wholesale accounts in the United States, foreign distributors and retailers worldwide. Customers include staples inc, officemax inc and office depot inc. On 23-Apr-2003, the group acquired costa del mar sunglasses, inc.

Primary SIC and add'l.: 5112 3951

CIK No: 0000025793

Subsidiaries: A.T. Cross (Asia Pacific) Limited Hong Kong Branch, A.T. Cross (Asia Pacific) Limited Singapore Branch, A.T. Cross (Asia Pacific) Limited Taiwan Branch, A.T. Cross Benelux B.V., A.T. Cross Company French Branch, A.T. Cross Deutschland GmbH, A.T. Cross Limited, A.T.X. International, Inc., Costa Del Mar Sunglasses, Inc., Cross Company of Japan, Ltd., Cross Retail Ventures, Inc.

Officers: David Whalen/Dir., CEO, Pres./$873,524.00, Gary S. Simpson/Corporate Controller, Tina C. Benik/VP - Legal, Human Resources, Corp. Sec., Kevin F. Mahoney/CFO, Treasurer/$330,886.00, Francesca Martinez-Gonzalez/Exec., International Requests, EMEA, Spain, Monica Brandt/Exec., International Requests, EMEA, Italy, Diane Eeraerts/Exec., International Requests, EMEA, Holland, Belgium, Luxembourg, David Ferreira/Exec., International Requests, Caribbean, Charles S. Mellen/Sr. VP - Global Marketing, Sales/$397,194.00, Charles R. MacDonald/VP - A T Cross Optical Division/$486,422.00, Stephen A. Perreault/VP - Operations/$305,115.00, Joseph V. Bassi/Dir. - Finance, Robin Boss Dorman/VP - Strategic Development, Robert Kim/Exec., International Requests, Asia, Japan, Rudy Lee/Exec., International Requests, Asia, Taiwan *(24 Officers included in Index)*

Directors: David Whalen/Dir., CEO, Pres., Russell A. Boss/69/Chmn., Edward J. Cooney/Dir., Bernard V. Buonanno/Dir., Galal P. Doss/Dir., Bradford R. Boss/Dir., James C. Tappan/Dir., Terrence Murray/Dir., Andrew J. Parsons/Dir.

Owners: David G. Whalen/6.90%, John B. Costello/5.40%, Edward J. Cooney, Bernard V. Buonanno, Edward P. Pieroni/5.40%, Paul A. Silver, Russell A. Boss, Paul A. Silver/6.20%, Galal P. Doss/31.60%, Stephen A. Perreault, Marjorie B. Boss, Edward P. Pieroni, Andrew J. Parsons, Marjorie B. Boss/6.30%, Russell A. Boss/12.80% *(27 Owners included in Index)*

Financial Data: *Fiscal Year End:*12/31 *Latest Annual Data:* 12/30/2006

Year	Sales	Net Income
2006	$139,336,000	$3,287,000
2005	$129,115,000	$384,000

Curr. Assets:	$73,590,000	*Curr. Liab.:*	$23,298,000	*P/E Ratio:*	47.50
Plant, Equip.:	$21,693,000	*Total Liab.:*	$45,716,000	*Indic. Yr. Divd.:*	NA
Total Assets:	$112,893,000	*Net Worth:*	$67,177,000	*Debt/ Equity:*	NA

A.C. Moore Arts & Crafts Inc

333 N Fairfax St., Alexandria, VA, 22314; *PH:* 1-866-342-8802; *http://* www.acmoore.com

General - Incorporation	PA	**Stock**- Price on:12/24/2007	$20.78
Employees	2,109	Stock Exchange	NDQ
Auditor	PricewaterhouseCoopers LLP	Ticker Symbol	ACMR
Stk Agt	StockTrans, Inc.	Outstanding Shares	20,230,000
Counsel	Drake Sommers Loeb Tarshis & Catania	E.P.S	$0.21
DUNS No.	11-627-5330	Shareholders	NA

Business: The group's principal activity is to retail arts, crafts and floral merchandise. The group primarily targets women between the ages of 25 and 55 for its products. The product range is divided into five categories. Art supplies and frames include paints, brushes, canvas, drawing tools, stationery, stencils and frames. Traditional crafts include stitchery, yarn for knitting and rug hooking and cake and

candy making supplies. Floral and accessories include silk and dried flowers. Fashion crafts include t-shirts and sweatshirts and decorative items like patches and rhinestones. Seasonal items include craft making material for all major holidays and seasons. The group had 81 stores in the eastern regions of the United States from new England to the carolinas. The group operate solely in the domestic market.

Primary SIC and add'l.: 5949 6719 5999

CIK No: 0001042809

Officers: Rick A. Lepley/Dir., CEO, Pres./$913,397.00, Marc D. Katz/CFO, Exec. VP/$224,111.00, Roxanne Stankiewicz/VP - Human Resources, Joe Crivelli/Investor Relation Officer, Sandra L. Smith/VP, General Merchandise Mgr., Michael G. Zawoysky/VP - Financial Planning, Analysis, Craig R. Davis/Sr. VP - Merchandising, Marketing/$88,290.00, David M. Frawley/VP - Advertising, Marketing, Robert J. Grimsley/VP - Real Estate, Dennis P. Hodgson/CIO, VP, Daniel C. Maguire/VP - Store Operations, Michael J. Metheny/VP - Supply Chain, Amy Rhoades/VP, General Counsel, Rodney B. Schriver/VP, Controller

Directors: Rick A. Lepley/Dir., CEO, Pres., Michael J. Joyce/Chmn., Neil A. McLachlan/Dir., Thomas S. Rittenhouse/Dir., Lori J. Schafer/Dir., Joseph F. Coradino/Dir.

Owners: Dimensional Fund Advisors LP/5.60%, Lawrence H. Fine/1.10%, S.A.C. Capital Advisors, LLC/8.10%, Highside Capital Management, L.P./7.20%, Wells Fargo & Company/6.90%, Jack Parker/2.60%, Insiders/1.50%, Thomas S. Rittenhouse, Michael J. Joyce, Vardon Capital, LLC/6.30%, Patricia A. Parker, Royce & Associates, LLC/6.40%, Leslie H. Gordon, Lori J. Schafer, Rick A. Lepley *(19 Owners included in Index)*

Financial Data: ***Fiscal Year End:***12/31 ***Latest Annual Data:*** 12/31/2006

Year		Sales		Net Income	
2006		$589,506,000		$2,434,000	
2005		$539,436,000		$10,042,000	
2004		$497,626,000		$16,848,000	
Curr. Assets:	$233,160,000	**Curr. Liab.:**	$74,381,000	**P/E Ratio:**	98.95
Plant, Equip.:	$95,268,000	**Total Liab.:**	$122,059,000	**Indic. Yr. Divd.:**	NA
Total Assets:	$329,837,000	**Net Worth:**	$207,778,000	**Debt/ Equity:**	0.1004

A.D.A.M. Inc

1600 RiverEdge Pkwy., Ste. 100, Atlanta, GA, 30328; ***PH:*** 1-770-980-0888; ***Fax:*** 1-770-955-3088; ***http://*** www.adam.com; ***Email:*** sales@adamcorp.com

General - Incorporation	GA	***Stock***- Price on:12/24/2007	$6.69
Employees	108	Stock Exchange	NDQ
Auditor	Tauber & Balser, P.C	Ticker Symbol	ADAM
Stk Agt	American Stock Transfer & Trust Co.	Outstanding Shares	9,530,000
Counsel	Smith, Gambrell & Russell	E.P.S	$0.21
DUNS No.	78-376-7569	Shareholders	NA

Business: The group's principal activity is to provide health and medical information products. The products of the group are used for learning about health, wellness, disease, treatments, alternative medicine, anatomy, nutrition and general medical reference in both the healthcare and education markets. The group's products contain physician-reviewed text, in-house developed medical graphics and multimedia to create health information that offers a unique visual learning experience. The group provides information on annual licensing agreements to healthcare organizations, Internet websites and educational institutions. The trademark of the group is a.d.a.m.

Primary SIC and add'l.: 7372 7371

CIK No: 0000863650

Subsidiaries: Integrative Medicine Communications Inc., Nidus Information Services Inc.

Officers: Kevin S. Noland/Dir., CEO, Pres./$317,745.00, Tony Lynn/VP - Engineering, Greg Juhn/Sr. VP - Product Strategy, Kyle McNeir/VP - Internet, Product Design, Jim Retel/VP - Sales, Alan Greene/Chief Medical Officer, Meredith Nienkamp/VP - Production, David R. Eltz/Editorial Dir., Kelli A. Stacy/Managing Editor, Health Illustrated Encyclopedia, Mark B. Adams/56/CFO, Sec./$229,154.00, Alan Cohen/41/Pres. - Online Benefits, Inc/$201,618.00, John Gedney/48/COO - Online Benefits, Inc/$201,618.00, James L. Retel/54/VP - Sales, Adam, Inc/$219,387.00, John George/Sr. VP - Sales, Shannon McGuire/VP - Education Sales

Directors: Kevin S. Noland/Dir., CEO, Pres., Robert S. Cramer/Co - Founder, Chmn., Mark Kishel/Dir., Daniel S. Howe/Dir., Clay Scarborough/Dir.

Owners: Mark Kishel/1.10%, Clay E. Scarborough, Kevin S. Noland/3.60%, Daniel S. Howe/1.10%, The Red Oak Fund, LP/5.00%, Robert S. Cramer/12.30%, Capital Source Finance LLC/8.40%, Insiders/1.70%

Financial Data: ***Fiscal Year End:***12/31 ***Latest Annual Data:*** 12/31/2006

Year		Sales		Net Income	
2006		$16,505,000		$2,548,000	
2005		$10,054,000		$7,062,000	
2004		$8,433,000		$1,621,000	
Curr. Assets:	$14,261,000	**Curr. Liab.:**	$11,177,000	**P/E Ratio:**	31.86
Plant, Equip.:	$876,000	**Total Liab.:**	$36,669,000	**Indic. Yr. Divd.:**	NA
Total Assets:	$60,138,000	**Net Worth:**	$23,469,000	**Debt/ Equity:**	0.9548

A.G. Edwards Inc

One N Jefferson Ave., St Louis, MO, 63103; ***PH:*** 1-314-955-3000; ***http://*** www.agedwards.com

General - Incorporation	DE	***Stock***- Price on:12/24/2007	$87.47
Employees	15,338	Stock Exchange	NYSE
Auditor	Deloitte & Touche LLP	Ticker Symbol	AGE
Stk Agt	Bank of New York	Outstanding Shares	76,000,000
Counsel	NA	E.P.S	$4.34
DUNS No.	00-632-9536	Shareholders	NA

Business: The groups principle activity is to provide full- service brokerage services. The group also provides securities and commodities brokerage, asset management, trust services, mutual funds and insurance services to individuals. The group operates from United States.

Primary SIC and add'l.: 6719 6211

CIK No: 0000718482

Subsidiaries: A.G. Edwards & Sons (UK) Limited, A.G. Edwards & Sons, Inc., A.G. Edwards Capital, Inc., A.G. Edwards Hedging Services, Inc., A.G. Edwards Technology Group, Inc., A.G. Edwards Trust Company FSB, A.G.E. Properties, Inc., AGE Capital Holding, Inc., AGE International, Inc., AGE Investments, Inc., Beaumont Insurance Company, Gallatin Asset Management, Inc.

Officers: Robert L. Bagby/64/Chmn., CEO, Pres./$5,049,474.00, Douglas L. Kelly/59/CFO, VP, Corp. Sec., Treasurer/$2,814,803.00, Gene M. Diederich/Exec. VP, Dir. - Branch Division, Brokerage Company/$1,591,105.00, Alfred E. Goldman/Corporate VP, Chief Marketing Strategist, Mary V. Atkin/53/Dir. - Staff, Peter M. Miller/50/Exec. VP, Dir. - Sales, Marketing Division/$1,603,427.00, Paul F. Pautler/62/Exec. VP, Dir. - Capital Markets Division/$2,396,119.00, John C. Parker/48/Exec. VP, Charles J. Galli/67/Sr. VP, Regional Mgr., Joseph G. Porter/47/Assist. Treasurer, Assist. Sec.

Directors: Robert L. Bagby/64/Chmn., CEO, Pres., Ronald J. Kessler/60/Vice Chmn., Vicki B. Escarra/55/Dir., Mark S. Wrighton/58/Dir., Samuel C. Hutchinson/Dir., Eugene E. Carter/66/Dir., Peter B. Madoff/62/Dir.

Owners: Peter B. Madoff, Paul F. Pautler, Insiders/1.50%, E. Eugene Carter, Mark S. Wrighton, Peter M. Miller, Samuel C. Hutchinson, Vicki B. Escarra, Gene M. Diederich, Ronald J. Kessler, Robert L. Bagby, Douglas L. Kelly

Financial Data: ***Fiscal Year End:***02/28 ***Latest Annual Data:*** 2/28/2007

Year		Sales		Net Income	
2007		$3,126,077,000		$331,353,000	
2006		$2,750,766,000		$238,329,000	
2005		$2,611,795,000		$186,474,000	
Curr. Assets:	$3,525,890,000	**Curr. Liab.:**	$1,863,660,000	**P/E Ratio:**	20.15
Plant, Equip.:	$463,526,000	**Total Liab.:**	$3,210,079,000	**Indic. Yr. Divd.:**	$0.800
Total Assets:	$5,312,118,000	**Net Worth:**	$2,102,039,000	**Debt/ Equity:**	0.1016

A.J. Smith Federal Savings Bank

14757 S Cicero Ave., Midlothian, IL, 60445; ***PH:*** 1-708-687-7400; ***Fax:*** 1-708-687-7466; ***http://*** www.ajsmithbank.com; ***Email:*** ajsmithbank@ajsmithbank.com

General - Incorporation	US	***Stock***- Price on:12/24/2007	$25.5
Employees	53	Stock Exchange	OTC
Auditor	Crowe Chizek & Co. LLC	Ticker Symbol	AJSB
Stk Agt	Registrar & Transfer Co	Outstanding Shares	2,130,000
Counsel	NA	E.P.S	$0.39
DUNS No.	NA	Shareholders	NA

Business: The group's principal activities are that of a savings bank. This includes acceptance of deposits from customers and origination of one- to four-family real estate loans, multi-family, commercial real estate and consumer loans. The deposits include demand, now, money market, savings, and term certificate accounts. The group conducts it business through two wholly owned subsidiaries, a. J. Smith federal savings bank and a.j.s. Insurance, llc, which provides insurance and investment services to the general public. At 31-Dec-2003, the group had three offices at midlothian, Illinois and orland park.

Primary SIC and add'l.: 6712 6035

CIK No: 0001144515

Officers: Thomas R. Butkus/Chmn., CEO, Lyn G. Rupich/COO, Pres., Julie Landry/VP, Treasurer, Anthony W. Kopp/Sr. VP - Commercial Lending, Jo Anne Cano/VP, Donna J. Manuel/VP - Loan Operations, Nancy Mehall/Assist. VP, Robert W. Racinowski/Assist. VP, Information Technology Officer, Pamela Favero/CFO, Susan Coleman/Assist. VP, Phyllis Furler/Assist. VP, Tammy Esposito/Coordinator, Gold Club, Claudia Hawkins/Coordinator, Gold Club, Leona Pieczyrak/Coordinator, Gold Club, Elvina Vondrak/Coordinator, Gold Club

Directors: Thomas R. Butkus/Chmn., CEO, Roger L. Aurelio/Dir., Raymond J. Blake/Dir., Edward S. Milen/Dir., Richard Nogal/Dir.

Owners: Lyn G. Rupich/1.72%, Edward S. Milen/0.82%, W. Anthony Kopp/0.87%, Richard J. Nogal/0.30%, AJS Bancorp, MHC/57.60%, Insiders/10.32%, Raymond J. Blake/1.73%, Roger L. Aurelio/1.06%, Thomas R. Butkus/3.65%, Pamela N. Favero/0.17%

Financial Data: ***Fiscal Year End:***12/31 ***Latest Annual Data:*** 12/31/2006

Year		Sales		Net Income	
2006		$14,528,000		$911,000	
2005		$13,884,000		$1,097,000	
2004		$13,670,000		$1,580,000	
Curr. Assets:	$50,359,000	**Curr. Liab.:**	$230,926,000	**P/E Ratio:**	60.71
Plant, Equip.:	$4,342,000	**Total Liab.:**	$237,764,000	**Indic. Yr. Divd.:**	$0.440
Total Assets:	$266,513,000	**Net Worth:**	$28,749,000	**Debt/ Equity:**	NA

A.O. Smith Corp

11270 W Pk. Pl., Milwaukee, WI, 53224; ***PH:*** 1-414-359-4000; ***Fax:*** 1-414-359-4064; ***http://*** www.aosmith.com; ***Email:*** info@aosmith.com

General - Incorporation	DE	***Stock***- Price on:12/24/2007	$40.54
Employees	18,000	Stock Exchange	NYSE
Auditor	Ernst & Young LLP	Ticker Symbol	AOS
Stk Agt	Wells Fargo Bank Minnesota N.A	Outstanding Shares	30,800,000
Counsel	NA	E.P.S	$2.90
DUNS No.	00-608-5815	Shareholders	NA

Business: The groups principle activity is to manufacture water heating equipment and electric motors. The groups products include copper-tube boilers, water systems tanks, hermetic and horsepower motors. The group operates from United States.

Primary SIC and add'l.: 3621 3639

CIK No: 0000091142

Subsidiaries: A. O. Smith (China) Investment Co., Ltd., A. O. Smith (China) Water Heater Co., Ltd., A. O. Smith (Nanjing) Consulting Co., Ltd., A. O. Smith (Shanghai) Consulting Co., Ltd., A. O. Smith Electric Motors (Ireland) Ltd., A. O. Smith Electrical Products (Changzhou) Co., Ltd., A. O. Smith Electrical Products (S.E.A.) Pte Ltd., A. O. Smith Electrical Products (Shenzhen) Co., Ltd., A. O. Smith Electrical Products (Suzhou) Co., Ltd., A. O. Smith Electrical Products (Taizhou) Co., Ltd., A. O. Smith Electrical Products (Yueyang) Co., Ltd., A. O. Smith Electrical Products Limited, A. O. Smith Electrical Products Limited Liability Company, A. O. Smith Enterprises Ltd., A. O. Smith Holdings (Barbados) SRL 33 Subsidiaries included in the Index

Officers: Paul W. Jones/Chmn., CEO/$3,234,375.00, Mark A. Petrarca/Sr. VP - Human Resources, Public Affairs, Christopher L. Mapes/Exec. VP, Pres. - EPC/$858,664.00, Steve W. Rettler/Sr. VP - Corporate Development, Randall S. Bednar/55/Sr. VP - Information Technology, John J. Kita/Sr. VP - Corporate Finance, Controller, Ronald E. Massa/Exec. VP - Corporate Technology, Global Supply Chain/$1,230,551.00, Charles J. Bishop/66/Sr. VP - Corporate Technology, Michael J. Cole/63/Sr. VP - Asia, Ajita G. Rajendra/Exec. VP, Pres. - WPC/$1,181,281.00, Terry M. Murphy/CFO, Exec. VP/$1,629,327.00, David W. Romoser/64/Sr. VP, Sec., General Counsel, James F. Stern/Exec. VP, General Counsel, Sec.

Directors: Paul W. Jones/Chmn., CEO, Idelle K. Wolf/Dir., Mark D. Smith/Dir., Gene C. Wulf/Dir., Ronald D. Brown/Dir., William F. Buehler/Dir., Bruce M. Smith/Dir., Robert J. O'Toole/Dir., Gloster B. Current/Dir., William P. Greubel/Dir.

Owners: Paul W. Jones, Franklin Resources, Inc., Mark D. Smith, Gene C. Wulf, T. Rowe Price Associates, Inc., Dimensional Fund Advisors Inc., Idelle K. Wolf, William F. Buehler, The Vanguard Group, Inc., Ajita G. Rajendra, Christopher L. Mapes, Robert J. OToole, Christopher L. Mapes, Smith Investment Company, Goldman Sachs Asset Management, L.P. *(19 Owners included in Index)*

Financial Data: *Fiscal Year End:*12/31 *Latest Annual Data:* 12/31/2006

Year	Sales	Net Income
2006	$2,161,300,000	$76,500,000
2005	$1,689,200,000	$46,500,000
2004	$1,653,100,000	$35,400,000

Curr. Assets:	$760,000,000	**Curr. Liab.:**	$437,300,000	**P/E Ratio:**	15.24
Plant, Equip.:	$427,200,000	**Total Liab.:**	$1,155,300,000	**Indic. Yr. Divd.:**	$0.720
Total Assets:	$1,839,900,000	**Net Worth:**	$684,600,000	**Debt/ Equity:**	0.6512

A.P. Pharma Inc

123 Saginaw Dr., Redwood City, CA, 94063; **PH:** 1-650-366-2626; **Fax:** 1-650-365-6490; *http://* www.appharma.com

General - Incorporation	DE	**Stock**- Price on:12/24/2007	NA
Employees	36	Stock Exchange	NDQ
Auditor	Ernst & Young LLP	Ticker Symbol	APPA
Stk Agt	Computershare Trust Co	Outstanding Shares	NA
Counsel. Heller Ehrman White & McAuliffe LLP		E.P.S	NA
DUNS No.	10-209-9843	Shareholders	NA

Business: The group's principal activity is to develop patented polymer- based delivery systems that enhance the safety and effectiveness of pharmaceutical compounds. These delivery systems are targeted at pain management, inflammation, oncology and ophthalmology applications. The group is in process of the development of bioerodible injectable and implantable systems under the trade names biochronomer(tm) and bioerodimer(tm). The projects are under feasibility study and will require marketing clearance from the fda before they can be sold in the United States. The group has already developed and commercialized ethical dermatological products by the name retin-a micro and carac.

Primary SIC and add'l.: 6794 2834

CIK No: 0000818033

Subsidiaries: Cardinal Health, Inc

Officers: Gregory Turnbull/Dir., CEO, Pres./$122,068.00, John Barr/Sr. VP - Research, Development/$298,357.00, Michael O'Connell/Dir., CFO, COO/$462,325.00, Sandra Squires/Human Resources, Mike O'Connell/COO, Julian N. Stern/Sec., Stephen Whiteford/VP - Finance/$71,827.00, Anastassios Retzios/VP - Clinical Development

Directors: Gregory Turnbull/Dir., CEO, Pres., Paul Goddard/Chmn., Peter Riepenhausen/Dir., Toby Rosenblatt/Dir., Robert Zerbe/Dir., Michael O'Connell/Dir., CFO, COO, Arthur Taylor/Dir.

Owners: Insiders/2.00%, Toby Rosenblatt, Visium Asset Management, LLC and its affiliates/9.90%, Gregory Turnbull, Paul Goddard, Arthur Taylor, Anastassios Retzios, OrbiMed Advisors, LLC and its affiliates/7.90%, RA Capital Management, LLC and its affiliates/7.90%, Tang Capital Managment, LLC and its affiliates/15.80%, Peter Riepenhausen, Deerfield Management Company, L.P. and its affiliates/7.40%, John Barr, Robert Zerbe, Michael OConnell

Financial Data: *Fiscal Year End:*12/31 *Latest Annual Data:* 12/31/2006

Year	Sales	Net Income
2006	NA	$5,266,000
2005	$5,391,000	-$8,210,000
2004	$5,404,000	-$9,221,000

Curr. Assets:	$16,206,000	**Curr. Liab.:**	$4,192,000		
Plant, Equip.:	$958,000	**Total Liab.:**	$5,192,000	**Indic. Yr. Divd.:**	NA
Total Assets:	$17,251,000	**Net Worth:**	$12,059,000	**Debt/ Equity:**	NA

A21 Inc

7660 Centurion Pkwy., Jacksonville, FL, 32256; **PH:** 1-904-565-0066; **Fax:** 1-904-565-1620; *http://* www.a21group.com; **Email:** a21info@a21group.com

General - Incorporation	TX	**Stock**- Price on:12/24/2007	$0.13
Employees	130	Stock Exchange	OTC
Auditor	BDO Seidman LLP	Ticker Symbol	ATWO
Stk Agt	Transfer Online, Inc.	Outstanding Shares	87,750,000
Counsel	NA	E.P.S	-$0.09
DUNS No.	NA	Shareholders	NA

Business: The groups principle activity is to create content marketplace for the professional creative community. The customers of the group include advertising and design agencies, publishing and media entities and the general public. The group operates through three segments namely corporate, superstock, and artselect. The group operates from the United States. The group's quarterly revenue for September 2007 was 5.39 millions of USD.

Primary SIC and add'l.: 8999 7375

CIK No: 0001074436

Subsidiaries: Ingram Publishing Limited, SuperStock Canada, Inc., SuperStock Limited, SuperStock, Inc.

Officers: John Z. Ferguson/Dir., CEO/$121,559.00, Philip N. Garfinkle/46/Exec. Chmn./$355,289.00, Thomas Costanza/CFO, VP/$205,838.00, Albert H. Pleus/46/Dir., Exec. Advisor/$558,993.00, Bruce D. Slywka/Exec. VP - Sales, Marketing

Directors: John Z. Ferguson/Dir., CEO, Philip N. Garfinkle/46/Exec. Chmn., Albert H. Pleus/46/Dir., Exec. Advisor, Laura B. Sachar/Dir., Donald C. Wiggins/57/Dir., John O. Hallberg/Dir.

Owners: StarVest Partners L.P./18.57%, John Z. Ferguson, Jonathan Gallen/25.94%, John O. Hallberg, Thomas Costanza, Albert H. Pleus/7.95%, Morgan Stanley & Co., Inc./8.04%, Insiders/27.05%, Laura B. Sachar/18.57%, Bruce D. Slywka, Clonure Limited/5.09%, John L. Steffens/5.35%, Luke A. Allen/8.51%

Financial Data: *Fiscal Year End:*12/31 *Latest Annual Data:* 12/31/2006

Year	Sales	Net Income
2006	$19,633,000	-$9,101,000
2005	$9,563,000	-$4,774,000
2004	$7,475,000	-$2,491,000

Curr. Assets:	$9,513,000	**Curr. Liab.:**	$5,213,000		
Plant, Equip.:	$7,300,000	**Total Liab.:**	$32,981,000	**Indic. Yr. Divd.:**	NA
Total Assets:	$34,614,000	**Net Worth:**	$1,633,000	**Debt/ Equity:**	NA

AAA Energy Inc

3841 Amador Way, Reno, NV, 89502; **PH:** 1-775-827-2324

General - Incorporation	NV	**Stock**- Price on:12/24/2007	$1.19
Employees	2	Stock Exchange	OTC
Auditor	Dale Matheson Carr-hilton Labonte LLP	Ticker Symbol	AAAE
Stk Agt	NA	Outstanding Shares	34,270,000
Counsel	NA	E.P.S	-$0.01
DUNS No.	NA	Shareholders	NA

Business: The groups principal activity is to explore minerals. The group operates from the United States and Canada.

Primary SIC and add'l.: 1000

CIK No: 0001304741

Officers: Earl Abbott/64/Dir., CEO, Pres., David Lorge/50/Dir., Sec., Treasurer, Principal Accounting Officer - Principal Financial Ifficer

Directors: Earl Abbott/64/Dir., CEO, Pres., David Lorge/50/Dir., Sec., Treasurer, Principal Accounting Officer - Principal Financial Ifficer

Owners: Earl Abbott/26.26%, Insiders/26.26%, Dennis LaPrairie/26.26%

Financial Data: *Fiscal Year End:*07/31 *Latest Annual Data:* 7/31/2006

Year	Sales	Net Income
2006	NA	-$36,000

Curr. Assets:	$61,000	**Curr. Liab.:**	$28,000		
Plant, Equip.:	NA	**Total Liab.:**	$28,000	**Indic. Yr. Divd.:**	NA
Total Assets:	$61,000	**Net Worth:**	$33,000	**Debt/ Equity:**	0.6590

AAMPRO Group Inc

Formerly: Trident Systems International
1120 Rte. 22 E, Bridgewater, NJ, 08807; **PH:** 1-908-252-0008

General - Incorporation	NV	**Stock**- Price on:12/24/2007	NA
Employees	232	Stock Exchange	NA
Auditor	Bagell, Josephs, Levine & Co. LLC	Ticker Symbol	NA
Stk Agt	Manhattan Transfer Registrar Co	Outstanding Shares	NA
Counsel	NA	E.P.S	-$6.32
DUNS No.	NA	Shareholders	NA

Business: The group's principle activity is to provide employee leases, payroll, benefits and human resource management services to small and middle market businesses in a variety of industries. The group 's services are designed to improve the productivity and profitability of small and medium-sized businesses by relieving business owners and key executives of many employer-related administrative and regulatory burdens and enables them to focus on the core competencies of their businesses.

Primary SIC and add'l.: 7363

CIK No: 0001116139

Subsidiaries: Aampro Pay, AAMPRO Staffing Concepts, Inc, AAMPRO, Inc

Officers: Terri Munkirs/59/Pres. - Aampro Pay, LLC

Owners: John F. Vitale/59.90%, Insiders/59.90%

Financial Data: *Fiscal Year End:*12/31 *Latest Annual Data:* 12/31/2006

Year	Sales	Net Income
2006	$1,860,000	-$1,193,000
2005	$1,811,000	-$978,000
2004	$1,441,000	-$1,689,000

Curr. Assets:	$628,000	**Curr. Liab.:**	$6,039,000		
Plant, Equip.:	$8,000	**Total Liab.:**	$6,039,000	**Indic. Yr. Divd.:**	NA
Total Assets:	$658,000	**Net Worth:**	-$5,381,000	**Debt/ Equity:**	NA

AAON Inc

2425 S Yukon Ave., Tulsa, OK, 74107; **PH:** 1-918-583-2266; **Fax:** 1-918-382-6367; *http://* www.aaon.com

General - Incorporation	NV	**Stock**- Price on:12/24/2007	$30.36
Employees	1,368	Stock Exchange	NDQ
Auditor	Grant Thornton LLP	Ticker Symbol	AAON
Stk Agt	Progressive Transfer Co.	Outstanding Shares	12,450,000
Counsel	Johnson Jones Dornblaser Et Al	E.P.S	$1.83
DUNS No.	19-411-8642	Shareholders	NA

Business: The group's principal activities are to engineer, manufacture and market air conditioners and heating equipment. The products include commercial rooftop air-conditioners, heat recovery equipment, air-conditioning coils and air handling and condensing units. Some of the rooftop products include the rk series, rf series, rl series and ha series. The group also markets commercial water chillers. The products are used in the commercial and industrial new construction and replacement markets. The major customer is wal-Mart stores inc. The operations of the group are conducted mainly in the United States through its subsidiaries aaon inc, an Oklahoma corporation and aaon coil products inc, a Texas corporation. On 05-May-2004 the group acquired air wise inc.

Primary SIC and add'l.: 5078 3585

CIK No: 0000824142

Subsidiaries: AAON Canada Inc, AAON Coil Products, Inc, AAON Properties Inc

Officers: Norman H. Asbjornson/72/Chmn., CEO, Pres./$314,779.00, Kathy I. Sheffield/55/CFO, VP, Treasurer/$165,644.00, David E. Knebel/62/Mgr. - Technology, Training/$165,640.00, Robert G. Fergus/67/VP/$149,841.00, John B. Johnson/74/Dir., Sec.

Directors: Norman H. Asbjornson/72/Chmn., CEO, Pres., Anthony Pantaleoni/68/Dir., Thomas E. Naugle/69/Dir., Jack E. Short/67/Dir., John B. Johnson/74/Dir., Sec., Charles C. Stephenson/71/Dir.

Owners: Jerry E. Ryan, Royce & Associates, LLC/7.50%, Robert G. Fergus, Thompson, Horstmann & Bryant, Inc./6.10%, Scott M. Asbjornson/2.20%, Insiders/28.80%, Kathy I. Sheffield, Charles C. Stephenson/4.10%, Thomas E. Naugle, Jack E. Short, Wellington Management Company, LLP/8.60%, Anthony Pantaleoni, John B. Johnson, Norman H. Asbjornson/19.60%, David E. Knebel

Financial Data: *Fiscal Year End:*12/31 *Latest Annual Data:* 12/31/2006

Year	Sales	Net Income
2006	$231,460,000	$17,133,000
2005	$185,195,000	$11,462,000
2004	$173,267,000	$7,521,000

Curr. Assets:	$70,759,000	**Curr. Liab.:**	$34,403,000	**P/E Ratio:**	16.59
Plant, Equip.:	$59,222,000	**Total Liab.:**	$38,464,000	**Indic. Yr. Divd.:**	$0.400
Total Assets:	$130,056,000	**Net Worth:**	$91,592,000	**Debt/ Equity:**	NA

AAR Corp

1100 N Wood Dale Rd., Wood Dale, IL, 60191; *PH:* 1-630-227-2000; *Fax:* 1-630-227-2039; *http://* www.aarcorp.com

General - Incorporation	DE	**Stock**- Price on:12/24/2007	$33.39
Employees	3,300	Stock Exchange	NYSE
Auditor	KPMG LLP	Ticker Symbol	AIR
Stk Agt	EquiServe Trust Co N.A	Outstanding Shares	37,290,000
Counsel	Schief Hardin & Waite	E.P.S	$1.47
DUNS No.	00-542-5814	Shareholders	NA

Business: The group's principle activity is to supply a products and services to the aviation and aerospace industry. Products and services are sold primarily to commercial, domestic and foreign airlines. The group operates in four segments. Inventory and logistic services include purchase, sale and lease of overhauled and repaired products. Maintenance, repair and overhaul provide a wide range of accessory parts and components for overhaul and exchange of airframe. Manufacturing includes a wide array of containers, pallets and shelters for military and humanitarian rapid deployment activities. Aircraft and engine sales and leasing segment includes the sale or lease of used commercial aircraft, overhauled and repaired commercial aircraft engines. The group's total revenue for year 2007 was 1,061.17 millions of USD.

Primary SIC and add'l.: 7359 5088 3728

CIK No: 0000001750

Subsidiaries: AAR Aircraft & Engine Sales & Leasing, AAR Aircraft Services, Inc., AAR Allen Services, Inc., AAR Engine Services, Inc, AAR International, Inc., AAR Manufacturing Group, Inc, AAR Parts Trading, Inc., AAR Services, Inc.

Officers: David P. Storch/Chmn., CEO/$3,348,400.00, Richard J. Poulton/43/CFO, VP, Treasurer, Kevin Burkhart/Contact - AAR Aircraft Sales, Leasing, Steven Ernsberger/Contact - Technical Services, James Clark/Group VP - Aviation Supply Chain/$1,201,900.00, Timothy Romenesko/COO, Pres./$1,135,200.00, Pat Aherne/Contact - Sales, Marketing, London Office, Harold Kugelman/Contact - Sales, Marketing, Howard Pulsifer/VP, General Counsel, Sec./$864,200.00, Michael Carr/VP - Tax, Peter Chapman/VP - Marketing, Business Development, Michael Cohen/VP - Operations, Engineering, John Johnson/Group VP, Kevin Larson/CIO, VP, David Prusiecki/VP - Defense Programs *(18 Officers included in Index)*

Directors: David P. Storch/Chmn., CEO, Marc J. Walfish/Dir., James E. Goodwin/Dir., Patrick J. Kelly/Dir., Ronald B. Woodard/Dir., James G. Brocksmith/Dir., Michael R. Boyce/Dir., Gerald F. Fitzgerald/Dir., Ronald R. Fogleman/Dir.

Owners: James J. Clark, James G. Brocksmith, Ronald R. Fogleman, Insiders/6.63%, Ronald B. Woodard, Marc J. Walfish, Patrick J. Kelly, Barclays Global/5.16%, FMR Corp./10.98%, Michael R. Boyce, Lord, Abbett & Co. LLC/6.14%, Putnam Investments/5.00%, Howard A. Pulsifer, Mark McDonald, James E. Goodwin *(18 Owners included in Index)*

Financial Data: **Fiscal Year End:**05/31 **Latest Annual Data:** 05/31/2007

Year	**Sales**	**Net Income**
2007	$1,061,169,000	$58,660,000
2006	$897,284,000	$35,163,000
2005	$747,848,000	$15,453,000

Curr. Assets:	$624,454,000	**Curr. Liab.:**	$187,788,000	**P/E Ratio:**	25.88
Plant, Equip.:	$213,380,000	**Total Liab.:**	$556,102,000	**Indic. Yr. Divd.:**	NA
Total Assets:	$978,819,000	**Net Worth:**	$422,717,000	**Debt/ Equity:**	0.5384

Aaron Rents Inc

309 E Paces Ferry Rd. NE, Atlanta, GA, 30305; *PH:* 1-404-231-0011; *Fax:* 1-678-402-3560; *http://* www.aaronrents.com; *Email:* ir@aaronrents.com

General - Incorporation	GA	**Stock**- Price on:12/24/2007	$29.34
Employees	8,400	Stock Exchange	NYSE
Auditor	Ernst & Young LLP	Ticker Symbol	RNT
Stk Agt	Suntrust Bank	Outstanding Shares	54,180,000
Counsel	Kilpatrick Stockton	E.P.S	$1.55
DUNS No.	03-350-1545	Shareholders	NA

Business: The group's principle activities are to rent and sell of residential and office furniture, accessories, consumer electronics and appliances. The group operates through four segments: the sales and lease ownership division offers electronics, residential furniture and appliances to consumers primarily on a monthly payment basis with no credit requirements. The group also provides them with the option of ownership. The rent-to-rent division offers furniture on rent or sale to customers with a temporary need for office or residential merchandise. The furniture industries division manufactures living room and office furniture, lamps and bedding for use by other divisions. The franchise division sells and supports franchises of its sales and lease ownership concept. The group's quarterly revenue for Sep'07 was 359.38 millions of USD.

Primary SIC and add'l.: 5712 7359

CIK No: 0000706688

Subsidiaries: Aaron Investment Company, Aaron Rents, Inc. Puerto Rico

Officers: Charles R. Loudermilk/Chmn., CEO/$2,527,773.00, John Schuerholz/Dir., Exec. VP, GM, Lee Wilder/Primary Investor Relations Officer, Elizabeth L. Gibbs/VP, General Counsel, Mitchell S. Paull/Sr. VP - Merchandising, Logistics, Marc S. Rogovin/VP - Real Estate, Construction, Sales, Lease Ownership Division, Lee B. Landers/CIO, VP - Sales, Lease Ownership Division, Todd K. Evans/VP - Franchising, Aaron's Sales, Lease Ownership Division/$395,771.00, Robert P. Sinclair/VP, Corporate Controller - Sales, Lease Ownership Division, William K. Butler/Dir., Pres. - Aaron's Sales, Lease Ownership Division/$1,870,126.00, Leo Benatar/Dir. - Sr. Partner, Associate Consultant, Robert C. Loudermilk/Dir., COO, Pres./$1,259,683.00, Ray M. Robinson/Dir., Pres., Eduardo Quinones/Pres. - Aaron Rents' Rent, to, Rent Division, Gilbert L. Danielson/Dir., CFO, Exec. VP/$1,242,195.00 *(16 Officers included in Index)*

Directors: Charles R. Loudermilk/Chmn., CEO, Earl Dolive/Vice Chmn. Emeritus, Gilbert L. Danielson/Dir., CFO, Exec. VP, Robert C. Loudermilk/Dir., COO, Pres., Ray M. Robinson/Dir., Pres., David L. Kolb/Dir., Ronald W. Allen/Dir., William K. Butler/Dir., Pres. - Aaron's Sales, Lease Ownership Division, Leo Benatar/Dir. - Sr. Partner, Associate Consultant, John Schuerholz/Dir., Exec. VP, GM, John C. Portman/Dir.

Owners: Ronald W. Allen, David L. Kolb, William K. Butler, Ronald W. Allen, Ray M. Robinson, Gilbert L. Danielson, Leo Benatar, Insiders/7.95%, Robert C. Loudermilk, Todd K. Evans, John C. Portman, Gamco Investors, Inc./5.29%, Charles R. Loudermilk/3.29%, Leo Benatar, Insiders/66.38% *(22 Owners included in Index)*

Financial Data: **Fiscal Year End:**12/31 **Latest Annual Data:** 12/31/2006

Year	**Sales**	**Net Income**
2006	$1,326,592,000	$78,635,000
2005	$1,125,505,000	$57,993,000
2004	$946,480,000	$52,616,000

Curr. Assets:	$664,451,000	**Curr. Liab.:**	$121,829,000	**P/E Ratio:**	18.45
Plant, Equip.:	$170,294,000	**Total Liab.:**	$372,591,000	**Indic. Yr. Divd.:**	$0.060
Total Assets:	$979,606,000	**Net Worth:**	$607,015,000	**Debt/ Equity:**	0.1864

AARX Inc

2250 Candlewood Ln., Akron, OH, 44333; *PH:* 1-330-665-5917; *http://* www.aarx.com

General - Incorporation	DE	**Stock**- Price on:12/24/2007	NA
Employees	NA	Stock Exchange	NA
Auditor	NA	Ticker Symbol	NA
Stk Agt	NA	Outstanding Shares	NA
Counsel	NA	E.P.S	NA
DUNS No.	NA	Shareholders	NA

Business: The groups principle activity is to locate and consummate a merger or acquisition with an unidentified private entity. The group operates from United States.

Primary SIC and add'l.: 6199

CIK No: 0001306299

Aastrom Biosciences Inc

Domino's Farms, Lobby K, 24 Frank Lloyd Wright Dr., Ann Arbor, MI, 48105; *PH:* 1-734-930-5555; *Fax:* 1-734-665-0485; *http://* www.aastrom.com; *Email:* mail@aastrom.com

General - Incorporation	MI	**Stock**- Price on:12/24/2007	$1.41
Employees	59	Stock Exchange	NDQ
Auditor	PricewaterhouseCoopers LLP	Ticker Symbol	ASTM
Stk Agt	Continental Stock Transfer & Trust Co	Outstanding Shares	119,960,000
Counsel	Gray, Cary, Ware & Freidenrich	E.P.S	-$0.15
DUNS No.	78-740-6107	Shareholders	NA

Business: The group's principal activity is to develop human cell therapy for a broad range of medical applications. The group has three product areas in various stages of development: tissue repair cells for immunotherapy and devices for cell production. The tissue repair cell products develops the sc-i and cb-i cells for use in stem cell therapy and the oc cell products for the restoration of bone tissue. The lead device products under development include the aastromreplicelltm system and the dc-i and dcv-i kits for the clinical-scale production of dendritic cells intended for the emerging cancer vaccine market. The aastromreplicelltm system is used by the group to produce its proprietary tissue repair and therapeutic cell products and is sold as an independent product.

Primary SIC and add'l.: 2834 8731

CIK No: 0000887359

Subsidiaries: Aastrom Biosciences GmbH, Aastrom Biosciences SL, Aastrom Biosciences, Ltd.

Officers: George W. Dunbar/Dir., CEO, Pres., Gerald D. Brennan/VP - Administrative - Financial Operations, CFO, Peter C. Alain/Sr. Dir. - Quality Assurance, Ronnda L. Bartel/VP - Research, Development, Elmar R. Burchardt/VP - Medical Affairs, Martin C. Peters/Sr. Dir. - Strategic Marketing, Sheldon A. Schaffer/VP - Corporate Development, Intellectual Property

Directors: George W. Dunbar/Dir., CEO, Pres., Stephen G. Sudovar/Chmn., Alan L. Rubino/Dir., Susan L. Wyant/Dir., Timothy M. Mayleben/Dir., Nelson M. Sims/Dir., Robert L. Zerbe/Dir.

Owners: Gerald D. Brennan, Alan L. Rubino, Elmar R. Burchardt, Robert L. Zerbe, Susan L. Wyant, Stephen G. Sudovar, George W. Dunbar, Timothy M. Mayleben, Insiders, Robert J. Bard, Douglas R. Armstrong/1.60%, Nelson M. Sims

Financial Data: **Fiscal Year End:**06/30 **Latest Annual Data:** 6/30/2006

Year	**Sales**	**Net Income**
2006	$863,000	-$16,475,000
2005	$909,000	-$11,811,000
2004	$1,302,000	-$10,488,000

Curr. Assets:	$43,665,000	**Curr. Liab.:**	$2,539,000		
Plant, Equip.:	$1,216,000	**Total Liab.:**	$2,539,000	**Indic. Yr. Divd.:**	NA
Total Assets:	$44,881,000	**Net Worth:**	$42,342,000	**Debt/ Equity:**	NA

AB Volvo

570 Lexington Ave., 20th Fl., New York, NY, 10022; *PH:* 1-212-418-7400; *Fax:* 1-212-418-7435; *http://* www.volvo.com

General - Incorporation		**Stock**- Price on:12/24/2007	$20.38
Employees	83,187	Stock Exchange	OTC
Auditor	NA	Ticker Symbol	VOLVY
Stk Agt	Morgan ADR Service Center	Outstanding Shares	2,020,000,000
Counsel	NA	E.P.S	$1.13
DUNS No.	NA	Shareholders	NA

Business: The groups principal activity is to provide commercial transport solutions. The products of the group include trucks, buses, and construction equipment. The group operates from the United States.

Primary SIC and add'l.: 6159 3713 3724

CIK No: 0001005639

Officers: Leif Johansson/57/Dir., Pres., CEO - Volvo Group, Jorma Halonen/60/Exec. VP, Satoru Takeuchi/Pres. - Nissan Diesel, Staffan Jufors/57/Pres. - Volvo Truck Corporation, Paul Vikner/59/Pres. - Mack Trucks, Inc, Stefano Chmielewski/56/Pres. - Renault Trucks, Hakan Karlsson/47/Pres. - Volvo Bus Corporation, Tony Helsham/54/Pres. - Volvo Construction Equipment, Goran Gummeson/61/Pres. - Volvo Penta, Olof Persson/Pres. - Volvo Aero Corporation, Salvatore L. Mauro/48/Pres. - Volvo Financial Services, Lars-Goran Moberg/Pres. - Volvo Powertrain, Stefan Johnsson/49/Sr. VP, Per Lojdquist/59/Sr. VP, Eva Persson/55/Dir., Sec., Sr. VP *(17 Officers included in Index)*

Directors: Leif Johansson/57/Dir., Pres., CEO - Volvo Group, Finn Johnsson/62/Chmn., Eva Persson/55/Dir., Sec., Sr. VP, Peter Bijur/66/Dir., Berth Thulin/57/Dir., Ying Yeh/60/Dir., Margareta ohlin/61/Dir., Lars Westerberg/Dir., Per-Olof Eriksson/70/Dir., Tom Hedelius/69/Dir., Philippe Klein/51/Dir., Martin Linder/35/Dir., Olle Ludvigsson/60/Dir., Johnny Ronnkvist/61/Dir., Louis Schweitzer/66/Dir.

Financial Data: **Fiscal Year End:**NA **Latest Annual Data:** 12/31/2006

Year	Sales	Net Income
2006	$37,815,794,000	$2,090,545,000
2005	$30,238,266,000	$1,432,477,000
2004	$31,854,711,000	$2,182,582,000

Curr. Assets:	$19,634,087,000	Curr. Liab.:	$15,474,620,000	P/E Ratio:	53.58
Plant, Equip.:	$8,835,544,000	Total Liab.:	$26,776,770,000	Indic. Yr. Divd.:	$0.720
Total Assets:	$39,174,524,000	Net Worth:	$12,397,754,000	Debt/ Equity:	NA

Abatix Corp

2400 Skyline Dr., Ste. 400, Mesquite, TX, 75149; *PH:* 1-214-381-0322; *Fax:* 1-214-388-0443; *http://* www.abatix.com; *Email:* ir@abatix.com

General - Incorporation.............................DE
Employees 105
Auditor ....KPMG LLP
Stk Agt................... North American Transfer Co
Counsel.............................Bellinger & Dewolf
DUNS No. 10-259-5931

Stock- Price on:12/24/2007 ....$10.55
Stock Exchange...NDQ
Ticker Symbol...ABIX
Outstanding Shares 1,710,000
E.P.S..$0.66
Shareholders..NA

Business: The group's principle activities are to market and distribute industrial safety equipment. The group supplies personal protection and safety equipment and durable and nondurable supplies predominantly to the environmental industry, the industrial safety industry and, combined with tools and tool supplies, to the construction industry. The group maintains sales, distribution and warehouse centers in los angeles, san francisco, Dallas, houston, phoenix, las vegas and seattle. The group's quarterly revenue for Sep'07 was 17.58 millions of USD.

Primary SIC and add'l.: 5085 5084
CIK No: 0000845779
Subsidiaries: International Enviroguard Systems, Inc.
Officers: Terry W. Shaver/Chmn., CEO, Pres./$248,079.00, Gary L. Cox/Dir., COO, Exec. VP/$252,234.00, Frank J. Cinatl/CFO, VP/$173,502.00
Directors: Terry W. Shaver/Chmn., CEO, Pres., Eric A. Young/Dir., Gary L. Cox/Dir., COO, Exec. VP, Donald N. Black/Dir., David A. Cook/Dir.
Owners: Eric A. Young/0.40%, Insiders/49.20%, Terry W. Shaver/30.90%, Gary L. Cox/16.90%, Frank J. Cinatl/1.10%
Financial Data: Fiscal Year End:12/31   Latest Annual Data: 12/31/2006

Year	Sales	Net Income
2006	$66,448,000	$998,000
2005	$70,626,000	$2,084,000
2004	$52,892,000	$214,000

Curr. Assets:	$20,451,000	Curr. Liab.:	$10,364,000	P/E Ratio:	15.98
Plant, Equip.:	$1,433,000	Total Liab.:	$10,377,000	Indic. Yr. Divd.:	NA
Total Assets:	$22,342,000	Net Worth:	$11,965,000	Debt/ Equity:	0.0008

Abaxis Inc

3240 Whipple Rd., Union City, CA, 94587; *PH:* 1-510-675-6500; *Fax:* 1-510-441-6150; *http://* www.abaxis.com; *Email:* abaxis@abaxis.com

General - Incorporation.............................CA
Employees 217
Auditor .... Burr, Pilger & Mayer, LLP
Stk Agt................... Computershare Providence RI
Counsel...............DLA Piper Rudnick Gray Cary
DUNS No. 55-550-3770

Stock- Price on:12/24/2007 ....$21.6
Stock Exchange...NDQ
Ticker Symbol..ABAX
Outstanding Shares 21,420,000
E.P.S..$0.46
Shareholders..NA

Business: The group's principle activities include manufacturing, developing and marketing portable blood analysis systems. This system is used in patient-care setting to provide clinicians with rapid blood constituent measurements. The system performs multiple routine tests on blood, plasma or serum using venous or finger-stick samples. The company's primary product is a system consisting of a compact 6.9 kilogram analyzer and a series of single-use plastic discs, called reagent discs, containing all the chemicals required to perform a panel of up to 12 tests. The products are sold under the trade name vetscan (R), vetscan hmt and piccolo (r). The products cater to the veterinary and human patients. The company operates in the United States, Europe, Asia and Latin America.

Primary SIC and add'l.: 2835
CIK No: 0000881890
Officers: Clinton H. Severson/Chmn., CEO, Pres./$947,216.00, Kenneth P. Aron/VP - Research, Development/$523,481.00, Gerard Cabrera/Area Sales Mgr. - Northeast, Chris Ballinger/Area Sales Mgr. - Southeast, Valdimir E. Ostoich/VP - Government Affairs, VP - Marketing The Pacific Rim/$527,948.00, Brett Stromatt/Area Dir. - Sales, East, Rick Betts/Dir. - Marketing Medical Diagnostics, John Therrien/Area Sales Mgr. - Mid, West, Alberto R. Santa Ines/CFO, VP - Finance/$506,185.00, Christopher Bernard/VP - Marketing, Sales Medical Market, Martin Mulroy/VP - Marketing, Sales, Veterinary Market, Matthew Rapp/US Medical Sales, Western Area Sales Dir., Randy Knick/US Veterinary Sales, Area Sales Dir. - Central US, Bill Wilson/US Veterinary Sales, Area Sales Dir. - Northeast, Andy Koupas/US Veterinary Sales, Area Sales Dir. - West (18 Officers included in Index)
Directors: Clinton H. Severson/Chmn., CEO, Pres., Henk J. Evenhuis/Dir., Prithipal Singh/Dir., Richard J. Bastiani/Dir., Brenton G.A. Hanlon/Dir., Ernest S. Tucker/Dir.
Owners: Alberto R. Santa Ines, Ernest S. Tucker, Richard J. Bastiani, The TCW Group, Inc./5.40%, Prithipal Singh, Kenneth P. Aron, Brown Capital Management, Inc./6.50%, Insiders/7.20%, Clinton H. Severson/3.30%, Lord, Abbett & Co. LLC/6.90%, Vladimir E. Ostoich/2.00%, Henk J. Evenhuis, Brenton G. A. Hanlon, Robert B. Milder, Wasatch Advisors, Inc./10.20%
Financial Data: Fiscal Year End:03/31   Latest Annual Data: 3/31/2007

Year	Sales	Net Income
2007	$86,221,000	$10,073,000
2006	$68,928,000	$7,475,000
2005	$52,758,000	$4,851,000

Curr. Assets:	$87,253,000	Curr. Liab.:	$12,736,000	P/E Ratio:	44.08
Plant, Equip.:	$12,662,000	Total Liab.:	$14,903,000	Indic. Yr. Divd.:	NA
Total Assets:	$102,715,000	Net Worth:	$87,812,000	Debt/ Equity:	NA

Abazias Inc

5214 Sw 91st Ter, Ste. A, Gainesville, FL, 32608; *PH:* 1-352-264-9940; *http://* www.abazias.com; *Email:* webcontact@abazias.com

General - Incorporation ....FL
Employees..6
Auditor .... Malone & Bailey, P.C
Stk Agt.........First American Stock Transfer, Inc.
Counsel..NA
DUNS No. ....NA

Stock- Price on:12/24/2007 ....$2.1
Stock Exchange...OTC
Ticker Symbol...ABZA
Outstanding Shares 2,920,000
E.P.S...-$0.67
Shareholders..NA

Business: The group's principle activity is to provide online retail service of loose diamonds and jewelry settings for diamonds. The company's Web site www.abazias.com showcases over 60,000 diamonds, most of which are independently certified; and more than 100 styles of jewelry, including rings, wedding bands, earrings, necklaces, and bracelets. The group operates from United States.

Primary SIC and add'l.: 5094
CIK No: 0001096208
Subsidiaries: Biologistics, Inc., PBI Acquisition Corp
Officers: Oscar Rodriguez/41/Dir., CEO, Pres., Jesus Diaz/40/Dir., CFO, Aaron Taravella/30/Dir., CIO
Directors: Oscar Rodriguez/41/Dir., CEO, Pres., Jesus Diaz/40/Dir., CFO, Aaron Taravella/30/Dir., CIO
Owners: Rob Rill/5.60%, Strategic Capital Advisors, Inc./4.80%, Oscar Rodriguez/38.40%, Aaron Taravella/4.20%, Jesus Diaz/12.80%, Insiders/58.30%
Financial Data: Fiscal Year End:12/31   Latest Annual Data: 12/31/2006

Year	Sales	Net Income
2006	$4,794,000	-$222,000
2005	$3,058,000	-$435,000
2004	$2,062,000	-$1,013,000

Curr. Assets:	$1,261,000	Curr. Liab.:	$1,256,000		
Plant, Equip.:	$2,000	Total Liab.:	$1,256,000	Indic. Yr. Divd.:	$0.240
Total Assets:	$1,294,000	Net Worth:	$38,000	Debt/ Equity:	NA

ABB Ltd

501 Merritt 7, Norwalk, CT, 06058; *PH:* 1-203-750-2200; *Fax:* 1-203-750-2263; *http://* www.abb.com

General - Incorporation ....Switzerland
Employees 108,000
Auditor ....Ernst & Young AG
Stk Agt...Citibank N.A
Counsel..NA
DUNS No. ....NA

Stock- Price on:12/24/2007 ....$22.54
Stock Exchange...NYSE
Ticker Symbol...ABB
Outstanding Shares 2,190,000,000
E.P.S..$1.06
Shareholders..NA

Business: The group's principal activities are providing power and automation technologies that enable utility and industry customers to improve performance. The activities of the group are organized into 2 core divisions: utilities (modular substations, power systems, utility automation & services) and automation technology (air handling, automotive, building & logistic systems, telecom & manufacturing industries. Non-core activities equity ventures, insurance, structured finance, new venture, building systems and treasury centers.

Primary SIC and add'l.: 1541 3511 3357 3612 3549 2611 3443
CIK No: 0001091587
Subsidiaries: ABB (Pty) Ltd., Gaborone, Abb Ach, Zaventem, ABB AG, Vienna, ABB Australia Pty Limited, Sydney, ABB Avangard AD, Sevlievo, ABB Bomem Inc., Quebec, ABB Bulgaria EOOD, Sofia, ABB Electrica SGPS, Lda., Luanda, ABB Group Holdings Pty. Ltd., Sydney, ABB Group Investment LLP, Sydney, ABB Group Investment Management Pty. Ltd., Sydney, ABB Import & Export Services Ltd., Oranjestad/Aruba (NA), ABB Inc., St. Laurent, Quebec, ABB Ltda., Osasco, ABB Lummus Global Ltda., Osasco 29 Subsidiaries included in the Index
Officers: Fred Kindle/49/CEO, Pres., Ulrich Spiesshofer/44/Exec. - Corporate Development, Jolanta Szczepaniake/Environmental Specialist - Poland, Michel Demare/52/CFO, Bernhard Jucker/54/Exec. - Division, Power Products, Tom Sjoekvist/61/Exec. - Automation Products, Anders Jonsson/58/Exec. - Robotics Division, Adam Roscoe/Group Function, Sustainability Affairs, Markus Kistler/Group Function, Group Internal Audit, Silvio Ghislanzoni/Group Function, Assurance, Internal Control, Alfred Storck/Group Function, Corporate Finance, Taxes, Hannu Kasi/Group Function, Group Planning, Controlling, Haider Rashid/Group Function, Information Systems, Michel Gerber/Head - Investor Relations, Charles J. Salek/Group Functions, Risk Management, Insurance (102 Officers included in Index)
Directors: Hubertus Von Grunberg/Chmn., Hans Ulrich Maerki/62/Dir., Louis R. Hughes/59/Dir., Bernd W. Voss/69/Dir., Roger Agnelli/49/Dir., Jacob Wallenberg/52/Dir., Juergen Dormann/68/Dir., Michel Derosen/57/Dir., Michael Treschow/65/Dir.
Owners: FMR Corporation/5.00%, Investor AB/7.60%
Financial Data: Fiscal Year End:12/31   Latest Annual Data: 12/31/2006

Year	Sales	Net Income
2006	$24,412,000,000	$1,390,000,000
2005	$22,442,000,000	$735,000,000
2004	$20,721,000,000	-$35,000,000

Curr. Assets:	$17,177,000,000	Curr. Liab.:	$12,376,000,000		
Plant, Equip.:	$2,811,000,000	Total Liab.:	$19,104,000,000	Indic. Yr. Divd.:	$0.200
Total Assets:	$25,142,000,000	Net Worth:	$6,038,000,000	Debt/ Equity:	NA

Abbott Laboratories

100 Abbott Pk. Rd., Abbott Park, IL, 60064; *PH:* 1-847-937-6100; *http://* www.abbott.com

General - Incorporation IL
Employees 66,663
Auditor ....Deloitte & Touche LLP
Stk Agt..........................Computershare Trust Co
Counsel..NA
DUNS No. 00-130-7602

Stock- Price on:12/24/2007 ....$54.63
Stock Exchange...NYSE
Ticker Symbol..ABT
Outstanding Shares 1,540,000,000
E.P.S..NA
Shareholders..NA

Business: The groups principle activities include discovering, developing, manufacturing, and selling a broad and diversified line of health care products. The group's products include bacFix,deflox and jevity. The group operates from United States.

Primary SIC and add'l.: 3845 2834 2844 3841
CIK No: 0000001800

Subsidiaries: Abbott (UK) Finance Limited, Abbott (UK) Holdings Limited, Abbott Administration Inc., Abbott AG, Abbott AIE s.r.l., Abbott Asia Holdings Limited, Abbott Australasia Pty. Limited, Abbott AVI s.r.l., Abbott B.V., Abbott Bahamas Overseas Businesses Corporation, Abbott Belgian Pension Fund A.S.B.L., Abbott Bioresearch Center,Inc., Abbott Biotechnology Deutschland GmbH, Abbott Biotechnology Ltd., Abbott Biotechnology Netherlands B.V. 199 Subsidiaries included in the Index

Officers: Miles D. White/Chmn., CEO/$26,915,360.00, Jeffrey R. Binder/44/Sr. VP - Diagnostic Operations, Stephen R. Fussell/51/Sr. VP - Human Resources, Gary E. McCullough/49/Sr. VP - Ross Products, James L. Tyree/Exec. VP - Pharmaceutical Products Group, William G. Dempsey/56/Exec. VP - Pharmaceutical Products Group/$5,471,627.00, Thomas C. Freyman/54/CFO, Exec. VP - Finance/$6,021,479.00, Joseph M. Nemmers/53/Exec. VP - Diagnostic, Animal Health Divisions, Laura J. Schumacher/Exec. VP, General Counsel, Sec., Alesia Watson/Dir. - Public Affairs, US Nutrition, Larry Baumann/Dir. - Public Affairs, International Nutrition, Greg W. Linder/51/VP, Controller, John C. Landgraf/Sr. VP - Global Pharmaceutical Manufacturing, Supply, Richard A. Gonzalez/54/Dir., COO, Pres./$16,713,290.00, Richard W. Ashley/65/Exec. VP - Corporate Development *(36 Officers included in Index)*

Directors: Miles D. White/Chmn., CEO, Samuel C. Scott/Dir., Glenn F. Tilton/Dir., Boone Powell/Dir., Ann W. Reynolds/Dir., Roy S. Roberts/Dir., William D. Smithburg/Dir., David A.L. Owen/Dir., William M. Daley/Dir., Richard A. Gonzalez/54/Dir., COO, Pres., Lord Owen/Dir., Roxanne S. Austin/Dir., James W. Farrell/Dir., Laurance H. Fuller/Dir., Jack M. Greenberg/Dir.

Owners: B. Powell, J. R. Walter, R. S. Austin, H. L. Fuller, H. Liepmann, W. D. Smithburg, W. G. Dempsey, R. A. Gonzalez, T. C. Freyman, G. F. Tilton, M. D. White, R. S. Roberts, Insiders, J. M. Greenberg, W. A. Reynolds *(18 Owners included in Index)*

Financial Data: *Fiscal Year End:*12/31   *Latest Annual Data:* 12/31/2006

Year	Sales	Net Income
2006	$22,476,322,000	$1,716,755,000
2005	$22,337,808,000	$3,372,065,000
2004	$19,680,016,000	$3,235,851,000

Curr. Assets:	$11,281,883,000	**Curr. Liab.:**	$11,951,195,000	**P/E Ratio:** 54.63
Plant, Equip.:	$6,946,435,000	**Total Liab.:**	$22,123,986,000	**Indic. Yr. Divd.:** NA
Total Assets:	$36,178,172,000	**Net Worth:**	$14,054,186,000	**Debt/ Equity:** 0.4568

Abercrombie & Fitch Co

6301 Fitch Path, New York, NY, 10019; ; *http://* www.abercrombie.com;
Email: abercrombie@abercrombie.com

General - Incorporation .... DE	**Stock**- Price on:12/24/2007 ....$74.93
Employees...8,500	Stock Exchange...NYSE
Auditor ....PricewaterhouseCoopers LLP	Ticker Symbol...ANF
Stk Agt....................................National City Bank	Outstanding Shares 88,070,000
Counsel..NA	E.P.S..$4.96
DUNS No. 03-816-3168	Shareholders..NA

Business: The groups principle activity is to operate retail stores. The groups products include shirts, graphic t-shirts, jeans, woven shirts, shorts, including personal care and other accessories for men, women and kids. The groups products are sold under the brand names Abercrombie and Fitch, abercrombie, Hollister and RUEHL brands. The group operates from United States.

Primary SIC and add'l.: 5621 5611 5651

CIK No: 0001018840

Subsidiaries: A&f 2001, Inc., A&F Canada Holding Co., A&F s.r.l., A&F Trademark, Inc., Abercrombie & Fitch (UK)Limited, Abercrombie & Fitch Design Limited, Abercrombie & Fitch Distribution Company, Abercrombie & Fitch Europe SA, Abercrombie & Fitch Fulfillment Company, Abercrombie & Fitch Holding Corporation, Abercrombie & Fitch Hong Kong Limited, Abercrombie & Fitch International, Inc., Abercrombie & Fitch Management Co., Abercrombie & Fitch Procurement Services, LLC, Abercrombie & Fitch Stores, Inc. 25 Subsidiaries included in the Index

Officers: Michael S. Jeffries/63/Chmn., CEO/$26,196,920.00, Diane Chang/52/Exec. VP - Sourcing/$4,218,864.00, Leslee K. Herro/47/Exec. VP - Planning, Allocation/$4,254,934.00, Michael W. Kramer/43/CFO, Exec. VP/$2,387,047.00

Directors: Michael S. Jeffries/63/Chmn., CEO, Archie M. Griffin/53/Dir., James B. Bachmann/65/Dir., John A. Golden/63/Dir., Russell M. Gertmenian/60/Dir., Allan A. Tuttle/68/Dir., Lauren J. Brisky/57/Dir., Edward F. Limato/71/Dir., John W. Kessler/72/Dir., Daniel J. Brestle/Dir.

Owners: Russell M. Gertmenian, Edward F. Limato, Leslee K. Herro, James B. Bachmann, FMR Corp./5.47%, Insiders/8.62%, Lauren J. Brisky, Diane Chang, Allan A. Tuttle, Columbia Wanger Asset Management, L.P./6.77%, Archie M. Griffin, Morgan Stanley/7.00%, Daniel J. Brestle, Michael W. Kramer, James A. Yano *(18 Owners included in Index)*

Financial Data: *Fiscal Year End:*01/28   *Latest Annual Data:* 2/3/2007

Year	Sales	Net Income
2007	$3,318,158,000	$422,186,000
2006	$2,784,711,000	$333,986,000
2005	$2,021,253,000	$216,376,000

Curr. Assets:	$1,092,078,000	**Curr. Liab.:**	$510,627,000	
Plant, Equip.:	$1,092,282,000	**Total Liab.:**	$842,770,000	**Indic. Yr. Divd.:** $0.700
Total Assets:	$2,248,067,000	**Net Worth:**	$1,405,297,000	**Debt/ Equity:** NA

ABF Capital Corp

2 Winthrop Ln., Scarsdale, NY, 10583; *PH:* 1-914-725-5474

General - Incorporation .... DE	**Stock**- Price on:12/24/2007 ....NA
Employees...NA	Stock Exchange...NA
Auditor ....NA	Ticker Symbol...NA
Stk Agt..............Continental Stock Transfer & Trust Co	Outstanding Shares ....NA
Counsel..NA	E.P.S..NA
DUNS No. ....NA	Shareholders..NA

Business: The group's principle activity is to provide financial services. The group operates from United States.

Primary SIC and add'l.: 1381

CIK No: 0000728390

Officers: Adolph Weissman/80/Dir., Pres.

Directors: Adolph Weissman/80/Dir., Pres.

Owners: Insiders/88.40%, Adolph Weissman/88.40%

Abgenix Inc

6701 Kaiser Dr., Fremont, CA, 94555; *PH:* 1-510-608-6500; *http://* www-ext.amgen.com

General - Incorporation .... DE	**Stock**- Price on:12/24/2007 ....$58.61
Employees...20,000	Stock Exchange...NA
Auditor ....Ernst & Young LLP	Ticker Symbol...NA
Stk Agt ..... American Stock Transfer & Trust Co.	Outstanding Shares 1,160,000,000
Counsel.........Wilson Sonsini Goodrich & Rosati	E.P.S..$3.49
DUNS No. 96-019-3530	Shareholders..NA

Business: The group's principal activities are to develop and commercialize fully human monoclonal antibody therapies for cancer and other diseases. The group's technology and integrated product development platform enable rapid generation and selection of product candidates for disease targets appropriate for antibody therapy. It leverages the human antibody technology to build a large and diversified product portfolio. It develops its own proprietary products internally and establishes licensing arrangements with multiple biopharmaceutical collaborators. The group has four products in development: ABX-Il8, ABX-EGF, ABX-MA1 and ABX-PTH in clinical trials. In addition, the group has four customer-developed antibodies generated with xenomouse technology in clinical trials from collaborations at Amgen and Pfizer.

Primary SIC and add'l.: 2834 8731

CIK No: 0001052837

Subsidiaries: Amarin Pharmaceuticals Inc, Amgen and Athletics Merger Sub Inc, Immunex Corporation, Medarex

Financial Data: *Fiscal Year End:*12/31   *Latest Annual Data:* 12/31/2006

Year	Sales	Net Income
2006	$14,268,000,000	$2,950,000,000
2005	$12,430,000,000	$3,674,000,000
2004	$10,550,000,000	$2,363,000,000

Curr. Assets:	$11,712,000,000	**Curr. Liab.:**	$7,022,000,000	**P/E Ratio:** 16.79
Plant, Equip.:	$5,921,000,000	**Total Liab.:**	$14,824,000,000	**Indic. Yr. Divd.:** NA
Total Assets:	$33,788,000,000	**Net Worth:**	$18,964,000,000	**Debt/ Equity:** 0.3761

Abigail Adams National Bancorp Inc

1130 Connecticut Ave. NW, Ste. 200, Washington, DC, 20036; *PH:* 1-202-772-3600;
Fax: 1-202-835-3871; *http://* www.adamsbank.com; *Email:* customerservice@adamsbank.com

General - Incorporation .... DE	**Stock**- Price on:12/24/2007 ....$13.75
Employees...108	Stock Exchange...NDQ
Auditor ....McGladrey & Pullen LLP	Ticker Symbol...AANB
Stk Agt ..... American Stock Transfer & Trust Co.	Outstanding Shares 3,460,000
Counsel.........Luse Gorman Pomerenk & Schick	E.P.S..$1.08
DUNS No. 09-410-8230	Shareholders..NA

Business: The group's principal activity is to provide commercial and retail banking services. It is a bank holding company, which operates through its subsidiary, the Adams National Bank. The commercial banking services include commercial real estate and commercial business loans, cash management services, letter of credit and collateral repurchase agreements. The retail banking services include consumer loans and a variety of deposit account products including transaction, money market, certificates of deposits and individual retirement accounts. The group also offers computer banking and 24 hour telephone banking services, Visa credit card services and custodial services. The customers of the group include individuals, small to medium-sized businesses, professionals, nonprofit organizations and other organizations.

Primary SIC and add'l.: 6021 6712

CIK No: 0000356809

Subsidiaries: Consolidated Bank & Trust Company, The Adams National Bank

Officers: Tonya McCray/Contact - Corporate Office, Joseph Power/Contact - Georgetown Office, Philip Wyse/Contact - Union Station Office, Stephanie Lipscomb/Contact - Dupont Circle Office, Ali Kianersi/Contact - Chinatown Office

Owners: Robert L. Shell/4.30%, Thomas W. Wright, Marianne Steiner, Marshall T. Reynolds/10.70%, Betty J. Serrano, Patricia G. Shannon, Bonita A. Wilson, Jeanne D. Hubbard, Deborah P. Wright/1.10%, Douglas V. Reynolds/1.60%, Sandra C. Ramsey, David M. Glaser, Shirley A. Reynolds/17.20%, Karen E. Troutman, Insiders/13.60% *(18 Owners included in Index)*

Financial Data: *Fiscal Year End:*12/31   *Latest Annual Data:* 12/31/2006

Year	Sales	Net Income
2006	$28,389,000	$3,696,000
2005	$20,372,000	$3,320,000
2004	$15,804,000	$3,602,000

Curr. Assets:	$27,563,000	**Curr. Liab.:**	$365,968,000	**P/E Ratio:** 12.73
Plant, Equip.:	$4,904,000	**Total Liab.:**	$375,320,000	**Indic. Yr. Divd.:** $0.500
Total Assets:	$405,502,000	**Net Worth:**	$30,182,000	**Debt/ Equity:** NA

Abington Community Bancorp Inc

180 Old York Rd., Jenkintown, PA, 19046; *PH:* 1-215-886-8280; *Fax:* 1-215-887-4100;
http:// www.abingtonbankonline.com; *Email:* abington@abingtonbank.com

General - Incorporation .... PA	**Stock**- Price on:12/24/2007 ....$17.64
Employees...114	Stock Exchange...NDQ
Auditor ....Deloitte & Touche LLP	Ticker Symbol...ABBC
Stk Agt ....Registrar & Transfer Co	Outstanding Shares 15,290,000
Counsel..NA	E.P.S..$0.45
DUNS No. ....NA	Shareholders..NA

Business: The group operates through its subsidiaries whose principle activity is to provide financial services. The groups services include commercial real estate mortgage loans, deposit accounts, automobile loans, home equity loans and home equity loans. The group operates from United States.

Primary SIC and add'l.: 6036

CIK No: 0001292898

Subsidiaries: Abington Corp, Abington Savings Bank, ASB Investment Co, Keswick Services II

Officers: Robert W. White/Chmn., CEO, Pres.

Directors: Robert W. White/Chmn., CEO, Pres., Michael F. Czerwonka/Dir., Joseph B. McHugh/Dir., Baron Rowland/Dir. Emeritus, Harold N. Grier/Dir. Emeritus, Robert John Pannepacker/Dir., Stuard A. Graham/Dir. Emeritus, Jane Margraff Kieser/Dir., Price G. Wilson/Dir.

Owners: Michael F. Czerwonka, Robert J. Pannepacker, Edward W. Gormley, Jane Margraff Kieser, Abington Mutual Holding Company/57.10%, Frank Kovalcheck, Robert W. White/1.10%, Insiders/4.60%, Stuard A. Graham, Joseph B. McHugh, Jack J. Sandoski, Price G. Wilson

Financial Data: ***Fiscal Year End:***12/31 ***Latest Annual Data:*** 12/31/2006

Year	Sales	Net Income
2006	$52,695,000	$6,802,000
2005	$42,881,000	$6,302,000
2004	$33,232,000	$4,555,000

Curr. Assets:	$48,931,000	**Curr. Liab.:**	$790,679,000		
Plant, Equip.:	$8,909,000	**Total Liab.:**	$811,084,000	**Indic. Yr. Divd.:**	$0.180
Total Assets:	$925,186,000	**Net Worth:**	$114,102,000	**Debt/ Equity:**	NA

Abiomed Inc

22 Cherry Hill Dr., Danvers, MA, 01923; ***PH:*** 1-978-777-5410; ***Fax:*** 1-978-777-8411; ***http://*** www.abiomed.com

General - Incorporation	DE	**Stock**- Price on:12/24/2007	$11.76
Employees	324	Stock Exchange	NDQ
Auditor	Deloitte & Touche, LLP	Ticker Symbol	ABMD
Stk Agt	American Stock Transfer & Trust Co.	Outstanding Shares	32,440,000
Counsel	Brown, Rudnick, Freed & Gesmer	E.P.S	-$0.95
DUNS No.	05-063-6737	Shareholders	NA

Business: The group's principal activities are to develop, manufacture and market medical products. These products are designed to assist or replace the pumping function of the failing heart. The group manufactures and sells the bvs 5000 bioventricular support system, a temporary heart assist device. Bvs is an advanced heart assist device for the temporary treatment of all patients with failing but potentially recoverable hearts. It also serves a different function than bridge-to-transplant devices, which are intended for long-term use by patients awaiting a heart transplant. The group also conducts research and development relating to other devices to replace or support the pumping function of the heart. The group's trademarks include abiomed, bvs, abiocor, angioflex, abiofit and ab5000. The group operates in the United States.

Primary SIC and add'l.: 3845 3841 8731

CIK No: 0000815094

Subsidiaries: ABD Holding Company, Inc., Abiomed R&d, Inc., Impella CardioSystems, GmbH, Impella CardioSystems, USA, Inc.

Officers: Michael R. Minogue/Chmn., CEO, Pres./$1,826,686.00, Karim Benali/Chief Medical Officer/$523,317.00, John Pristas/Dir. - Clinical Operations, Thorsten Siess/CTO, Liza Heapes/Contact - Media Relations, Dan Raess/Medical Advisor, Paul Krell/GM - Abiomed Europe, David Weber/COO, Christopher MacDonald/Sr. VP - Global Sales, Clinical Applications/$534,120.00, Robert T.V. Kung/Chief Scientific Officer, Sr. VP, William J. Bolt/Sr. VP - Global Quality, Service, Andrew J. Greenfield/VP - Healthcare Solutions/$438,614.00, Daniel J. Sutherby/CFO/$554,526.00, Mary Mologne/Dir. - Healthcare Solutions, Laura Bentley/Hospital Marketing *(16 Officers included in Index)*

Directors: Michael R. Minogue/Chmn., CEO, Pres., Louis E. Lataif/Dir., Desmond H. O'Connell/Dir., Eric A. Rose/Dir., Dorothy E. Puhy/Dir., Henri A. Termeer/Dir., Gerald W. Austen/Dir., Ronald W. Dollens/Dir.

Owners: Desmond H. OConnell, Dorothy E. Puhy, Henri A. Termeer/7.40%, Genzyme Corporation/7.10%, Ronald W. Dollens, Great Point Partners, LLC/4.90%, Michael R. Minogue/1.40%, Christopher D. Macdonald, Essex Woodlands Health Ventures/8.00%, David Gottlieb, Gerald W. Austen, Karim Benali, Daniel J. Sutherby, Andrew J. Greenfield, Louis E. Lataif *(16 Owners included in Index)*

Financial Data: ***Fiscal Year End:***03/31 ***Latest Annual Data:*** 3/31/2007

Year	Sales	Net Income
2007	$50,649,000	-$27,881,000
2006	$43,670,000	-$29,449,000
2005	$38,216,000	-$2,342,000

Curr. Assets:	$46,443,000	**Curr. Liab.:**	$8,739,000		
Plant, Equip.:	$4,824,000	**Total Liab.:**	$9,049,000	**Indic. Yr. Divd.:**	NA
Total Assets:	$78,537,000	**Net Worth:**	$69,488,000	**Debt/ Equity:**	NA

Able Energy Inc

198 Green Pond Rd., Rockaway, NJ, 07866; ***PH:*** 1-973-625-1012; ***Fax:*** 1-973-586-9866; ***http://*** www.ableenergy.com

General - Incorporation	DE	**Stock**- Price on:12/24/2007	$2
Employees	95	Stock Exchange	OTC
Auditor	Simontacchi & Co. LLP	Ticker Symbol	ABLE
Stk Agt	Continental Stock Transfer & Trust Co	Outstanding Shares	NA
Counsel	Gregory D. Frost Esq	E.P.S	NA
DUNS No.	NA	Shareholders	NA

Business: The group's principal activity is the retail distribution of fuel oil, propane gas and diesel fuel. It also provides installation and repair of heating, ventilation, air-conditioning and other home heating equipments. It markets on-road and off-road diesel fuel, gasoline, lubricants and other petrroleum products to commercial customers. The retail fuel oil distribution business and provision of oil burner service for the maintenance, repair and installation of oil burners are conducted through its subsidiaries able oil, able energy New York, inc and able melbourne. The group provides retail distribution of propane gas, propane equipment and related services through its subsidiary able propane. It operates and markets its products in northern New Jersey, melbourne, Florida, warrensburg and New York.

Primary SIC and add'l.: 5984 5983 6794 6719

CIK No: 0001065728

Subsidiaries: Able Energy New York Inc., Able Melbourne Inc., Able Oil Inc., PriceEnergy Inc.

Officers: Christopher P. Westad/54/Acting CEO, Frank Nocito/60/VP - Business Development, John Vrabel/COO, Gregory D. Frost/60/General Counsel, Dir., Jeffrey S. Feld/CFO

Directors: Alan E. Richards/71/Dir., Edward C. Miller/40/Dir., Stephen Chalk/63/Dir., Solange Charas/46/Dir., Gregory D. Frost/60/General Counsel, Dir., Patrick O'Neill/48/Dir., Mark Barbera/49/Dir.

Owners: Alan E. Richards, Mark Barbera, Insiders/33.20%, Edward C. Miller, Christopher P. Westad/1.10%, Steven Chalk, All American Plazas, Inc./31.80%, Solange Charas, Patrick O'Neil, Frank Nocito/31.80%, Gregory D. Frost/31.80%, John L. Vrabel

Financial Data: ***Fiscal Year End:***06/30 ***Latest Annual Data:*** 6/30/2006

Year	Sales	Net Income
2006	$75,093,000	-$6,242,000
2005	$61,947,000	-$2,180,000
2004	$42,882,000	-$89,000

Curr. Assets:	$7,165,000	**Curr. Liab.:**	$7,597,000		
Plant, Equip.:	$4,414,000	**Total Liab.:**	$11,418,000	**Indic. Yr. Divd.:**	NA
Total Assets:	$13,091,000	**Net Worth:**	$1,672,000	**Debt/ Equity:**	2.2852

Able Laboratories Inc

1 Able Dr., Cranbury, NJ, 08512; ***PH:*** 1-609-495-2800; ***http://*** www.ablelabs.com

General - Incorporation	DE	**Stock**- Price on:12/24/2007	NA
Employees	NA	Stock Exchange	NA
Auditor	Wolf & Co. P.C	Ticker Symbol	NA
Stk Agt	American Stock Transfer & Trust Co.	Outstanding Shares	NA
Counsel	Foley, Hoag & Eliot LLP	E.P.S	NA
DUNS No.	60-400-5116	Shareholders	NA

Business: The group's principal activity is to manufacture and distribute generic drug products. Generic drugs are the chemical and therapeutic equivalents of brand-name drugs. The group manufactures and markets prescription generic drugs including tablets, capsules and suppositories. The products of the group are marketed under the brand names esgic plus(R), soma(R), tranxene(R) , lomotil(R), anusol(R), indocin(r)sr, eskalith(R), ritalin(R), metadate-sr(R), nitrostat(R), pyridium(R), phentermine hydrochloride , adipex-p(R), compazine(R), darvocet-n(R) and disalcid(r).on Nov 17,2003 the group acquired assets of liquisource inc.

Primary SIC and add'l.: 2834 8731

CIK No: 0000857171

Officers: Jay Wadekar/Chmn., CEO, Iva Klemick/VP - Compliance, Regulatory Affairs, Robert Weinstein/Dir. - Investor Relations, Andreea C. Cordoba/Investor Contact

Directors: Jay Wadekar/Chmn., CEO, Elliot F. Hahn/Dir.

Ableauctions.com Inc

1963 Lougheed Hwy., Coquitlam, BC, V3K 3T8; ***PH:*** 1-604-521-3369; ***http://*** www.ableauctions.com; ***Email:*** investorrelations@ableauctions.com

General - Incorporation	FL	**Stock**- Price on:12/24/2007	$0.18
Employees	35	Stock Exchange	AMEX
Auditor	Cinnamon, Jang, Willoughby & Co	Ticker Symbol	AAC
Stk Agt	Mellon Trust Co	Outstanding Shares	27,670,000
Counsel	NA	E.P.S	$0.002
DUNS No.	NA	Shareholders	NA

Business: The group's principal activity is to auction a broad range of merchandise and equipment. The group conducts auctions for merchandise and equipment relating to antique, automotive, bakery, broadcasting, chemical, construction, dairy, electronics, energy, food processing, foundry and furniture. It also conducts auctions on high technology, machine tool, metal fabrication, office, paper, pharmaceutical, plastic, printing, restaurant, textile and others. These merchandise and equipment are acquired through bankruptcies, insolvencies and defaults. The auctions are held through auction houses, over the Internet and through the group's Website. During the year 2003, the group acquired rapidfusion technologies inc.

Primary SIC and add'l.: 7389

CIK No: 0001099290

Subsidiaries: 0716590 B.c. Ltd., 652297 B.c. Ltd, Able Auctions (1991) Ltd., Ableauctions.com (Washington) Inc., Icollector International, Ltd., Icollector.com Technologies, Ltd., iTrustee.com International, Ltd., iTrustee.com Technologies Ltd., Jarvis Industries Ltd., Rapidfusion Technologies Inc., Unlimited Closeouts Inc.

Officers: Abdul Ladha/Dir., CEO/$162,000.00

Directors: Abdul Ladha/Dir., CEO, David Vogt/Dir., Barret E.G. Sleeman/Dir., Michael Boyling/Dir.

Owners: Michael Boyling/0.70%, Abdul Ladha/18.70%, Insiders/20.80%, Barrett Sleeman/0.70%, David Vogt

Financial Data: ***Fiscal Year End:***12/31 ***Latest Annual Data:*** 12/31/2006

Year	Sales	Net Income
2006	$6,244,000	$167,000
2005	$5,202,000	$437,000
2004	$5,074,000	$498,000

Curr. Assets:	$7,445,000	**Curr. Liab.:**	$634,000		
Plant, Equip.:	$4,312,000	**Total Liab.:**	$634,000	**Indic. Yr. Divd.:**	NA
Total Assets:	$13,525,000	**Net Worth:**	$12,890,000	**Debt/ Equity:**	NA

ABM Industries Inc

160 Pacific Ave., Ste. 222, San Francisco, CA, 94111; ***PH:*** 1-415-733-4000; ***Fax:*** 1-415-733-7333; ***http://*** www.abm.com; ***Email:*** janitorial@abm.com

General - Incorporation	DE	**Stock**- Price on:12/24/2007	$26.06
Employees	75,000	Stock Exchange	NYSE
Auditor	KPMG LLP	Ticker Symbol	ABM
Stk Agt	Mellon Investor Services LLC	Outstanding Shares	49,750,000
Counsel	Orrick, Herrington & Sutcliffe LLP	E.P.S	$2.09
DUNS No.	00-691-1622	Shareholders	NA

Business: The groups principle activity is to provide facility services for commercial, industrial, institutional and retail facilities. The group operate through five business segments namely janitorial, parking, security, engineering and lighting. The group operates from United States.

Primary SIC and add'l.: 7381 7349 5087 8711 3648 7521

CIK No: 0000771497

Subsidiaries: Abm Cms, Inc., ABM Co. of Boston, ABM Engineering Services Company, ABM Facility Services Company, ABM Janitorial Northern California, ABM Janitorial Northeast, Inc., ABM Janitorial Services Co., Ltd., ABM Janitorial Services, Inc., ABM Mid-Atlantic, Inc., ABM Payroll Service, Inc., ABM Security Services, Inc., ABMI Security Services, Inc., Allied Maintenance Services, Inc., American Building Maintenance Co., American Building Maintenance Co. West 36 Subsidiaries included in the Index

Officers: Henrik C. Slipsager/Dir., CEO, Pres., James P. McClure/Exec. VP, George B. Sundby/CFO, Exec. VP, Steven M. Zaccagnini/Exec. VP, Erin M. Andre/Sr. VP - Human Resources, Linda S. Auwers/Sr. VP, General Counsel, Sec., David L. Farwell/Sr. VP, Chief - Staff, Treasurer, Gary R. Wallace/Sr. VP, Dir. - Business Development, Chief Marketing Officer, Wayne Greenleaf/Assist. VP, Dir. - Employee Benefits, Anna Esquivel/Assist. VP - Human Resources, William Mike Horton/Assist. VP - Compensation, Eric Johnson/VP - Southwest Region, James Lusk/Exec. VP, Anthony P. Piucci/VP - Federal Government, Oded Barlev/Security Contract Administrator - Federal Government

Directors: Henrik C. Slipsager/Dir., CEO, Pres., Maryellen C. Herringer/Chmn., William W. Steele/Dir., Luke S. Helms/Dir., Henry L. Kotkins/Dir., Charles T. Horngren/Dir., Martinn H. Mandles/Dir., Linda L. Chavez/Dir., Theodore T. Rosenberg/Dir.

Owners: Kayne Anderson Rudnick Investment Management LLC/7.70%, Luke S. Helms, Henrik C. Slipsager, Steven M. Zaccagnini, Franklin Advisory Services, LLC/7.30%, Linda S. Auwers, Insiders/14.40%, Martinn H. Mandles, William W. Steele, Maryellen C. Herringer, James P. McClure, Linda L. Chavez, Theodore T. Rosenberg/10.00%, Charles T. Horngren, George B. Sundby *(16 Owners included in Index)*

Financial Data: **Fiscal Year End:**10/31 **Latest Annual Data:** 10/31/2006

Year	Sales	Net Income
2006	$2,792,668,000	$93,205,000
2005	$2,587,761,000	$57,941,000
2004	$2,416,223,000	$30,473,000

Curr. Assets:	$631,741,000	**Curr. Liab.:**	$319,285,000	**P/E Ratio:**	12.47
Plant, Equip.:	$32,185,000	**Total Liab.:**	$475,027,000	**Indic. Yr. Divd.:**	$0.480
Total Assets:	$1,016,274,000	**Net Worth:**	$541,247,000	**Debt/ Equity:**	NA

ABN AMRO Holding

Gustav Mahlerlaan 10, Amsterdam; ; *http://* www.abnamro.com

General - Incorporation	Netherlands	**Stock**- Price on:12/24/2007	$47.49
Employees	107,535	Stock Exchange	NYSE
Auditor	Ernst & Young Accountants	Ticker Symbol	ABN
Stk Agt	Morgan ADR Service Center	Outstanding Shares	1,850,000,000
Counsel	NA	E.P.S.	$3.64
DUNS No.	41-409-4367	Shareholders	NA

Business: The group's principal activity is that of an internationally operating bank which was formed following a merger in 1990 of the two largest publicly quoted banks in the Netherlands namely abn and amro bank; the objective of the group is to provide all kinds of banking services in the Netherlands & abroad. The bank provides worldwide services to certain customer groups in specific fields such as corporate finance, securities, treasury products and facilities, trade and commodity financing, leasing and private banking. The company's principal activities are the provision of a range of private and consumer banking and insurance services through the following divisions: wholesale clients: global investment banking and corporate investment banking activities; consumer & commercial clients: retail, small and medium-sized enterprise clients; private clients & asset management: asset gathering activities of the private banking and fund management businesses.

Primary SIC and add'l.: 6211 6036 6111 6021 6282 6162

CIK No: 0001038727

Subsidiaries: Abn Amro Capital Funding Trust V, Abn Amro Capital Funding Trust Vi, Abn Amro Capital Funding Trust Vii, La Salle Funding LLC

Officers: Rijkman Groenink/58/Group Audit, Group Compliance, Legal, Group Human Resources, Hugh Scott-Barrett/49/CFO - Group Finance, Investor Relations, A. Cairns/Head - Business Unit Transaction Banking, Bob Kramer/MD, Head - ABN Amro Participaties, The Netherlands, Machiel Papousek/Exec. Dir., Head ABN Amro Capital Media - Telecom, Bart Bergstein/Exec. Dir., Head ABN Amro Capital Life Sciences Team, Dies Donker/Head - Investor Relations, Alex Van Leeuwen/Investor Relations Officer - US, Johan Bos/Investor Relations Officer - Sustainability, Agnes Blanco Querido/Investor Relations Analyst, Kim Vissers/Coordinator - Investor Relations, Laetitia Hart/Sec. - Investor Relations

Directors: A. A. Olijslager/64/Vice Chmn. - Supervisory Board, A. C. Martinez/69/Chmn. - Supervisory Board, Huibert Boumeester/48/Member - Managing Board, Piero Overmars/44/Member - Managing Board, Ron Teerlink/47/Member - Managing Board, D. R.J. Baron De Rothschild/66/Member - Supervisory Board, T. A. Maas-De Brouwer/62/Member - Supervisory Board, Lord Sharman/65/Member - Supervisory Board, Rob F. Van Den Bergh/58/Member - Supervisory Board, P. Scaroni/62/Member - Supervisory Board, Wilco Jiskoot/58/Member - Managing Board, Anthony Ruys/61/Member - Supervisory Board, A. M. Llopis Rivas/58/Member - Supervisory Board, Machiel Papousek/Exec. Dir., Head ABN Amro Capital Media - Telecom, Bart Bergstein/Exec. Dir., Head ABN Amro Capital Life Sciences Team *(18 Directors included in Index)*

Owners: Eureko B.V./12.12%, Aviva plc/17.48%, Kempen Capital Management Ltd./15.02%, Fortis Utrecht N.V./16.85%, ING Groep N.V./21.29%, Aegon N.V./14.33%

Financial Data: **Fiscal Year End:**12/31 **Latest Annual Data:** 12/31/2006

Year	Sales	Net Income
2006	$73,711,029,000	$5,889,858,000
2005	$53,964,817,000	$3,399,228,000
2004	$46,423,710,000	$3,853,066,000

Curr. Assets:	$289,465,213,000	**Curr. Liab.:**	$16,722,920,000		
Plant, Equip.:	$8,278,281,000	**Total Liab.:**	$1,272,065,480,000	**Indic. Yr. Divd.:**	$1.880
Total Assets:	$1,309,139,504,000	**Net Worth:**	$37,074,024,000	**Debt/ Equity:**	NA

Abraxas Petroleum Corp

500 N Loop 1604 E, Ste. 100, San Antonio, TX, 78232; *PH:* 1-210-490-4788; *Fax:* 1-210-490-8816; *http://* www.abraxaspetroleum.com

General - Incorporation	NV	**Stock**- Price on:12/24/2007	$4.25
Employees	50	Stock Exchange	AMEX
Auditor	BDO Seidman LLP	Ticker Symbol	ABP
Stk Agt	American Stock Transfer & Trust Co.	Outstanding Shares	42,880,000
Counsel	Jackson Walker LLP	E.P.S.	$1.25
DUNS No.	08-848-2898	Shareholders	NA

Business: The group's principal activities are acquisition, exploration, exploitation and production of crude oil and natural gas. The principal areas of operation are in Texas and western Canada.

Primary SIC and add'l.: 1311 1321 1389 9999

CIK No: 0000867665

Subsidiaries: Abraxas Petroleum Corporation, Associated Energy Corporation, Eastside Coal Company, Inc., Grey Wolf Exploration Inc., Sandia Oil & Gas Corporation, Sandia Operating Corp., Wamsutter Holdings, Inc., Western Associated Energy Corporation

Officers: Robert L.G. Watson/Chmn., CEO, Pres./$457,160.00, Chris E. Williford/Exec. VP, CFO, Treasurer - Accounting, Administration/$313,441.00, Lee T. Billingsley/VP - Exploration/$252,431.00, William H. Wallace/VP - Operations/$248,950.00, Stephen T. Wendel/VP - Land, Marketing, Lease, Royalty Owner Relations/$240,299.00, Barbara M. Stuckey/Investor Relations, Corporate Development, Carol O'Brien/Human Resources

Directors: Robert L.G. Watson/Chmn., CEO, Pres., Scott C. Bartlett/Dir., Franklin A. Burke/Dir., Harold D. Carter/Dir., Ralph F. Cox/Dir., Barry J. Galt/Dir., Dennis E. Logue/Dir., Paul A. Powell/Dir.

Owners: Lee T. Billingsley, Dennis E. Logue, Scott C. Bartlett, Robert L.G. Watson/2.80%, Barry J. Galt, Richard M. Riggs, William H. Wallace, Ralph F. Cox, Paul A. Powell, Insiders/15.40%, Stephen T. Wendel, Chris E. Williford, Franklin A. Burke/8.10%, Harold D. Carter

Financial Data: **Fiscal Year End:**12/31 **Latest Annual Data:** 12/31/2006

Year	Sales	Net Income
2006	$51,723,000	$1,246,000
2005	$48,625,000	$19,117,000
2004	$33,854,000	$11,167,000

Curr. Assets:	$6,753,000	**Curr. Liab.:**	$10,472,000	**P/E Ratio:**	3.40
Plant, Equip.:	$104,957,000	**Total Liab.:**	$139,105,000	**Indic. Yr. Divd.:**	NA
Total Assets:	$117,486,000	**Net Worth:**	-$21,619,000	**Debt/ Equity:**	NA

Absolute Waste Services Inc

141 W Jackson Blvd., Ste. 2182, Chicago, IL, 60604; *PH:* 1-312-427-5457

General - Incorporation	FL	**Stock**- Price on:12/24/2007	$0.0001
Employees	NA	Stock Exchange	NA
Auditor	Pender Newkirk & Co	Ticker Symbol	NA
Stk Agt	Continental Stock Transfer & Trust Co	Outstanding Shares	NA
Counsel	NA	E.P.S.	NA
DUNS No.	NA	Shareholders	NA

Business: The group's principal activity is to develop, manufacture and market evacuated glass spheres. The company is into developing, manufacturing, and marketing insulating materials and coatings using partially evacuated glass microspheres. The group operates solely in the United States of America.

Primary SIC and add'l.: 2899

CIK No: 0001002360

Officers: Thomas F. Duszynski/52/Dir., CEO, CFO

Directors: Thomas F. Duszynski/52/Dir., CEO, CFO

Owners: Augustine Fund, L.P., Insiders, PAC Funding LLC, Thomas F. Duszynski

Financial Data: **Fiscal Year End:**09/30 **Latest Annual Data:** 9/30/2005

Year	Sales	Net Income
2005	NA	-$295,000
2004	NA	-$662,000
2003	$4,163,000	-$686,000

Curr. Assets:	$4,000	**Curr. Liab.:**	$408,000		
Plant, Equip.:	NA	**Total Liab.:**	$636,000	**Indic. Yr. Divd.:**	NA
Total Assets:	$4,000	**Net Worth:**	-$632,000	**Debt/ Equity:**	NA

ABX Air Inc

145 Hunter Dr., Wilmington, OH, 45177; *PH:* 1-937-382-5591; *Fax:* 1-937-383-3838; *http://* www.abxair.com; *Email:* investor.relations@abxair.com

General - Incorporation	DE	**Stock**- Price on:12/24/2007	$6.86
Employees	6,100	Stock Exchange	NDQ
Auditor	Deloitte & Touche LLP	Ticker Symbol	ABXA
Stk Agt	National City Bank	Outstanding Shares	58,680,000
Counsel	NA	E.P.S.	$1.44
DUNS No.	NA	Shareholders	NA

Business: The group's principal activity is to provide air cargo transportation services within the United States and to Canada and Puerto Rico. The group also performs package sorting and handling services and other air cargo transportation related services. It provides acmi services and on-demand charter services, airport-to-airport transportation of freight on a space available basis. It is also a reseller and broker for mcdonnell douglas dc-8, dc-9 and boeing 767 aircraft parts to other customers. As of 31-Mar-2003, group operated and maintained an in-service fleet of one hundred and sixteen aircraft, consisting of twenty-three 767, nineteen dc-8, and seventy-four dc-9 aircraft. The group spun off from airborne inc on of 15-Aug-2003. It acquired one additional boeing 767 aircraft during 2004.

Primary SIC and add'l.: 4512 4522

CIK No: 0000894081

Subsidiaries: ABX Cargo Services, Inc, Airborne FTZ, Inc

Officers: Joseph C. Hete/Dir., CEO, Pres./$2,377,930.00, Quint O. Turner/CFO - Principal Financial, Accounting Officer/$749,205.00, Dennis Manibusan/Sr. VP - Maintenance, Engineering/$1,125,277.00, Robert Morgenfeld/Sr. VP - Flight Operations/$1,188,181.00, Tom Poynter/Sr. VP - Ground Operations, Robert Gray/VP - Regulatory Compliance, Government Affairs, John Jessup/VP - Materials Management, Contracts/$887,326.00, Joe Payne/VP, General Counsel, Sec., Terry Scherz/VP - Maintenance, Brady Templeton/VP - Ground Operations, Beth Huber/Supervisor, Community Relations, James Mastin/Pres., Mary Ellen Diersing/VP, Phil Flowers/Sec., Jana Reser/Treasurer

Directors: Joseph C. Hete/Dir., CEO, Pres., James H. Carey/Chmn., Frederick R. Reed/Dir., Edward P. Smethwick/63/Dir., Randy D. Rademacher/Dir., John D. Geary/Dir., James E. Bushman/Dir., Jeffrey J. Vorholt/Dir.

Owners: Joseph C. Hete, John D. Geary, James H. Carey, Jeffrey J. Vorholt, Quint O. Turner, Frederick R. Reed, Red Mountain Capital Partners LLC/6.20%, James E. Bushman, The Pabrai Investment Funds/8.60%, Dennis A. Manibusan, Robert J. Morgenfeld, Barclays Global Investors, NA/5.30%, Insiders/1.20%, John A. Jessup

Financial Data: **Fiscal Year End:**12/31 **Latest Annual Data:** 12/31/2006

Year	Sales	Net Income
2006	$1,260,361,000	$90,054,000
2005	$1,464,390,000	$30,312,000
2004	$1,202,509,000	$36,973,000

Curr. Assets:	$126,170,000	**Curr. Liab.:**	$144,278,000	**P/E Ratio:**	4.76
Plant, Equip.:	$458,638,000	**Total Liab.:**	$559,588,000	**Indic. Yr. Divd.:**	NA
Total Assets:	$679,798,000	**Net Worth:**	$120,210,000	**Debt/ Equity:**	1.6155

ACA Capital Holdings Inc

140 Broadway, 47th Fl., New York, NY, 10005; *PH:* 1-212-375-2000; *Fax:* 1-212-375-2100; *http://* www.aca.com; *Email:* info@aca.com

General - Incorporation		**Stock**- Price on:12/24/2007	$13.74
Employees	115	Stock Exchange	NYSE
Auditor	NA	Ticker Symbol	ACA
Stk Agt	Mellon Investor Services LLC	Outstanding Shares	36,560,000
Counsel	NA	E.P.S	$1.71
DUNS No.	NA	Shareholders	NA

Business: The group operates through its subsidiaries whose principle activity is to provide financial guaranty insurance products. The groups service is CDO Asset Management. The group operates from the United States. The assets of the group for the year 2006 were $6,038,194 (thousands).

Primary SIC and add'l.: 6726 6351

CIK No: 0001304623

Subsidiaries: ACA ABS 2003-3 Funding, Limited, ACA ABS 2005-1 Funding, Limited, ACA Assurance, Ltd., ACA Capital (Singapore) Pvt. Limited, ACA Capital Management (U.K.) Pvt. Limited, ACA Capital Partners I Master Fund, Ltd., ACA CDS 2001-1, L.L.C., ACA CDS 2002-2, L.L.C., ACA Credit Products - ABN Amro, LLC, ACA Credit Products - Alpha, L.L.C., ACA Credit Products - BA, L.L.C., ACA Credit Products - CA, L.L.C., ACA Credit Products - CAN, L.L.C., ACA Credit Products - CBNA 1, L.L.C., ACA Credit Products - CBNA 2, L.L.C. 87 Subsidiaries included in the Index

Officers: Alan S. Roseman/Dep. Chmn., CEO, Pres., James Rothman/Sr. MD, Head - Asset Management, Edward U. Gilpin/Dir., CFO, Exec. VP, Peter J. Hill/Exec. VP - Public Finance, Brad Larson/MD, Head - Structured Credit, Simon Meers/MD, Head - Alternative Investments Strategy, Adam Willkomm/Treasurer, Maria Carbone/Admin Assist, Head - Public Finance, Sandra Brinkert/MD - Underwriting, Carolyn Edwards-Boyce/Dir. - Underwriting, Emory Dawson/Dir. - Underwriting, Julie Morrone/Dir. - Underwriting, Shelley Stein/Dir. - Underwriting, Loretta Duffy/VP - Underwriting, Kristin Stephens/VP - Underwriting *(35 Officers included in Index)*

Directors: Alan S. Roseman/Dep. Chmn., CEO, Pres., David E. King/Chmn., Edward U. Gilpin/Dir., CFO, Exec. VP, David M. Barse/Dir., John G. Berylson/Dir., Douglas L. Jacobs/Dir., Robert Juneja/Dir., William H. Lacy/Dir., Warren A. Stephens/Dir., Gideon A. Pell/Dir.

Owners: Alan S. Roseman, John G. Berylson, Perry Corp., Chestnut Hill ACA,LLC, Third Avenue Trust, SF Holding Corp., William H. Lacy, Douglas L. Jacobs, James A. Rothman, Insiders, Laura U. Schwartz, Warren A. Stephens, BSMB/ACA LLC, Robert Juneja, David M. Barse *(18 Owners included in Index)*

Financial Data: *Fiscal Year End:*NA *Latest Annual Data:* 12/31/2006

Year	Sales	Net Income
2006	$464,115,000	$58,708,000
2005	$330,594,000	$28,760,000
2004	$193,012,000	-$3,789,000

Curr. Assets:	$458,566,000	**Curr. Liab.:**	$3,006,494,000	**P/E Ratio:**	8.04
Plant, Equip.:	NA	**Total Liab.:**	$5,528,380,000	**Indic. Yr. Divd.:**	NA
Total Assets:	$6,038,194,000	**Net Worth:**	$509,814,000	**Debt/ Equity:**	5.2733

Acacia Research Corp

500 Newport Ctr. Dr., 7th Fl., Newport Beach, CA, 92660; *PH:* 1-949-480-8300; *Fax:* 1-949-480-8301; *http://* www.acaciaresearch.com; *Email:* info@acaciares.com

General - Incorporation	DE	**Stock**- Price on:12/24/2007	$14.68
Employees	33	Stock Exchange	NDQ
Auditor	PricewaterhouseCoopers LLP	Ticker Symbol	ACTG
Stk Agt	U.S. Stock Transfer Corp	Outstanding Shares	28,470,000
Counsel	O'melveny & Myers	E.P.S	-$0.12
DUNS No.	84-544-2326	Shareholders	NA

Business: The group's principal activities are to develop, license and provide products for the media technology and life science sectors. The group operates through two segments: media technologies and life sciences, through its subsidiaries, acacia media technologies group and combimatrix corporation and advanced material sciences, inc respectively. The media technologies segment includes intellectual property related to a television blanking system known as the v-chip, as well as audio and video transmission and receiving systems. The life sciences segment is developing a proprietary biochip array processor system that integrates semiconductor technology with new developments in biotechnology and chemistry.

Primary SIC and add'l.: 3663 3679 8731

CIK No: 0000934549

Subsidiaries: Acacia Global Acquisition Corporation, Acacia Media Technologies Corporation, CombiMatrix Corporation, IP Innovation LLC

Officers: Paul R. Ryan/Chmn., CEO/$612,768.00, Robert L. Harris/Dir., Pres./$606,565.00, Robert A. Berman/COO, General Counsel/$663,838.00, Clayton J. Haynes/CFO, Sr. VP/$354,079.00, Robert Stewart/Sr. VP - Corporate Finance, Dooyong Lee/Exec. VP, Edward J. Treska/Sec.

Directors: Paul R. Ryan/Chmn., CEO, Rigdon Currie/Dir., Fred A. De Boom/Dir., Louis G. Graziadio/Dir., Robert L. Harris/Dir., Pres., Thomas B. Akin/Dir., Edward W. Frykman/Dir., Amit Kumar/Dir., William S. Anderson/Dir.

Financial Data: *Fiscal Year End:*12/31 *Latest Annual Data:* 12/31/2006

Year	Sales	Net Income
2006	$40,565,000	-$25,456,000
2005	$27,607,000	-$18,676,000
2004	$23,925,000	-$4,833,000

Curr. Assets:	$62,006,000	**Curr. Liab.:**	$7,456,000		
Plant, Equip.:	$2,006,000	**Total Liab.:**	$15,295,000	**Indic. Yr. Divd.:**	NA
Total Assets:	$109,604,000	**Net Worth:**	$94,309,000	**Debt/ Equity:**	NA

Acadia Pharmaceuticals Inc

3911 Sorrento Valley Blvd., San Diego, CA, 92121; *PH:* 1-858-558-2871; *Fax:* 1-858-558-2872; *http://* www.acadia-pharm.com; *Email:* info@acadia-pharm.com

General - Incorporation	DE	**Stock**- Price on:12/24/2007	$14.322
Employees	138	Stock Exchange	NDQ
Auditor	PricewaterhouseCoopers LLP	Ticker Symbol	ACAD
Stk Agt	Mellon Investor Services LLC	Outstanding Shares	36,870,000
Counsel	NA	E.P.S	-$1.55
DUNS No.	NA	Shareholders	NA

Business: The group's principal activity is to discover, develop and commercialize small molecule drugs for the treatment of central nervous system disorders. The group presently has five drug programs in clinical and preclinical development.

Primary SIC and add'l.: 2834

CIK No: 0001070494

Subsidiaries: ACADIA Pharmaceuticals A/S, ACADIA Pharmaceuticals AB

Officers: Uli Hacksell/Dir., CEO/$905,104.00, Povl Krogsgaard-Larsen/Scientific Advisor, Bo-Ragnar Tolf/VP - Chemistry, MD - Acadia Pharmaceuticals AB/$460,877.00, Herbert Y. Meltzer/Clinical Advisor, Carol Tamminga/Clinical Advisor, Brian Lundstrom/Sr. VP - Business Development/$431,663.00, Henry Bourne/Scientific Advisor, Paul S. Anderson/Scientific Advisor, Allan I. Levey/Clinical Advisor, Marc G. Caron/Scientific Advisor, Thomas H. Aasen/VP, CFO, Sec., Treasurer/$495,416.00, Roger G. Mills/Exec. VP - Development/$261,905.00, Arvid Carlsson/Scientific Advisor

Directors: Uli Hacksell/Dir., CEO, Leslie L. Iversen/Chmn., Lester J. Kaplan/Dir., Alan G. Walton/Dir., Michael T. Borer/Dir., Gordon Binder/Dir., Torsten Rasmussen/Dir., Mary Ann Gray/Dir.

Owners: Mary Ann Gray, Leslie L. Iversen, Brian Lundstrom, T. Rowe Price Associates, Inc./6.40%, Bo-Ragnar Tolf, Gordon Binder/2.00%, Nomura Phase4 Ventures/9.20%, Torsten Rasmussen, Oxford Bioscience Partners IV affiliates/11.40%, Uli Hacksell/1.70%, Mark R. Brann/1.80%, Sepracor Inc./6.30%, Thomas H. Aasen, Insiders/17.10%, Wellington Management Company, LLP/5.10% *(19 Owners included in Index)*

Financial Data: *Fiscal Year End:*12/31 *Latest Annual Data:* 12/31/2006

Year	Sales	Net Income
2006	$8,133,000	-$45,048,000
2005	$10,956,000	-$34,135,000
2004	$4,604,000	-$25,917,000

Curr. Assets:	$85,783,000	**Curr. Liab.:**	$20,534,000		
Plant, Equip.:	$3,505,000	**Total Liab.:**	$22,385,000	**Indic. Yr. Divd.:**	NA
Total Assets:	$89,544,000	**Net Worth:**	$67,159,000	**Debt/ Equity:**	0.0264

Acadia Realty Trust

1311 Mamaroneck Ave., Ste. 260, White Plains, NY, 10605; *PH:* 1-914-288-8100; *Fax:* 1-914-428-2760; *http://* www.acadiarealty.com

General - Incorporation	MD	**Stock**- Price on:12/24/2007	$26.95
Employees	130	Stock Exchange	NYSE
Auditor	BDO Seidman, LLP	Ticker Symbol	AKR
Stk Agt	Mellon Investor Services LLC	Outstanding Shares	32,130,000
Counsel	NA	E.P.S	$2.04
DUNS No.	NA	Shareholders	NA

Business: The groups principle activities include acquiring and managing commercial retail properties. The groups operates through two segments namely retail properties and multi family properties. The group operates from the United States.

Primary SIC and add'l.: 6798 6798

CIK No: 0000899629

Subsidiaries: 239 Greenwich Associates Limited Partnership, ABR Amboy Road LLC, Acadia 239 Greenwich Avenue, LLC, Acadia 2914 Third Avenue LLC, Acadia Albertsons Investors LLC, Acadia Amherst, LLC, Acadia Atlantic Avenue LLC, Acadia Bartow Avenue, LLC, Acadia Berlin LLC, Acadia Boonton LLC, Acadia Brandywine Condominium, LLC, Acadia Brandywine Subsidiary, LLC, Acadia Brandywine Town Center, LLC, Acadia Chestnut LLC, Acadia Clark-Diversey LLC 127 Subsidiaries included in the Index

Officers: Kenneth F. Bernstein/Dir., CEO, Pres./$1,815,504.00, Lee S. Wielansky/Chmn., CEO - Midland Development Group, Inc., Numa Jerome/Sr. VP, Dir. - Leasing, Joel Braun/Exec. VP, Chief Investment Officer/$805,682.00, Joseph Hogan/Sr. VP, Dir. - Construction/$495,523.00, Robert Masters/Sr. VP, General Counsel, Corp. Sec./$471,186.00, Joseph M. Napolitano/Sr. VP, Chief Administrative Officer, Michael L. Nelsen/Sr. VP, CFO/$417,919.00, Joseph Povinelli/51/Sr. VP, Dir. - Leasing, Robert B. Scholem/Sr. VP, Dir. - Property Management, Jon Grisham/Chief Accounting Officer, Sr. VP, Richard M. Hartmann/VP, Controller, Michael Hurwitz/Dir. - Taxation, Todd Rollins/VP - Asset Management, Larry Schachter/Dir. - Information Technology *(18 Officers included in Index)*

Directors: Kenneth F. Bernstein/Dir., CEO, Pres., Lee S. Wielansky/Chmn., CEO - Midland Development Group, Inc., Alan S. Forman/Dir., Lorrence T. Kellar/Dir., Douglas Crocker/Dir., Suzanne Hopgood/Dir., Wendy Luscombe/Dir.

Owners: Joel Braun, Vanguard Group, Inc./4.95%, Wendy Luscombe, Joseph Hogan, Kenneth F. Bernstein/3.88%, Third Avenue Management LLC/7.95%, Barclays Global Investors, NA/5.70%, Lee S. Wielansky, Morgan Stanley Investment Management, Inc./4.93%, Insiders/5.86%, Alan Forman, Michael Nelsen, Yale University/6.02%, Morgan Stanley/5.36%, Cliffwood Partners, LLC/4.88% *(20 Owners included in Index)*

Financial Data: *Fiscal Year End:*12/31 *Latest Annual Data:* 12/31/2006

Year	Sales	Net Income
2006	$102,693,000	$39,013,000
2005	$83,318,000	$20,626,000
2004	$72,856,000	$19,585,000

Curr. Assets:	$153,069,000	**Curr. Liab.:**	$17,209,000	**P/E Ratio:**	8.04
Plant, Equip.:	$535,167,000	**Total Liab.:**	$610,573,000	**Indic. Yr. Divd.:**	$0.800
Total Assets:	$851,692,000	**Net Worth:**	$241,119,000	**Debt/ Equity:**	NA

Acambis Plc

38 Sidney St., Cambridge, MA, 02139; *PH:* 1-617-761-4200; *Fax:* 1-617-494-1741; *http://* www.acambis.com; *Email:* acambis@acambis.com

General - Incorporation	England And Wales	**Stock**- Price on:12/24/2007	NA
Employees	288	Stock Exchange	NA
Auditor	PricewaterhouseCoopers LLP	Ticker Symbol	NA
Stk Agt	NA	Outstanding Shares	NA
Counsel	Weil, Gotshal & Manges LLP	E.P.S	NA
DUNS No.	NA	Shareholders	NA

Business: The group's principal activities are the research, development, manufacture and sale of vaccines to prevent and treat infectious diseases. Products include vaccines against smallpox, typhoid, yellow fever, Japanese encephalitis, dengue fever, west nile and diarrhoea. The group operates in Europe and North America. In Aug 2003, the group acquired berna products corporation.

Primary SIC and add'l.: 8731 2834

CIK No: 0001073965

Subsidiaries: Acambis Inc, Acambis Research Limited, Berna Products Corporation, Smallpox Biosecurity Limited

Officers: Ian Garland/43/CEO, Jayant Aphale/VP - Operations, Project Management, Elizabeth Jones/37/CFO, Company Sec., Michael Watson/Exec. VP - Research, Development, David Wonnacott/Sr. VP - Regulatory Affairs, Quality Systems, Daniel Fredian/Acting VP - Human Resources, Harold Kleanthous/VP - Research, Joan Fusco/51/Sr. VP - Operations, Paul Giannasca/VP - Development, Lyndsay Wright/VP - Communications, Investor Relations, Clement Lewin/VP - Marketing, Policy, Strategy

Directors: Peter Fellner/64/Chmn., Randal Chase/58/Non Exec. Dir., Ross Graham/60/Non Exec. Dir., William Jenkins/60/Non Exec. Dir., John Lambert/56/Non Exec. Dir., Alan Dalby/71/Non Exec. Dir.

Accelerated Building Concepts Corp

Formerly: K2 Digital Inc
500 Fifth Avenue`, Ste. 1650, New York, NY, 10110; **PH:** 1-212-810-2430

General - Incorporation		Stock - Price on:12/24/2007	
General - Incorporation	DE	Stock - Price on:12/24/2007	$0.056
Employees	1	Stock Exchange	OTC
Auditor	Rothstein, Kass & Co, P.C	Ticker Symbol	KTWO
Stk Agt	Continental Stock Transfer & Trust Co	Outstanding Shares	4,980,000
Counsel	NA	E.P.S.	-$0.005
DUNS No.	88-399-8510	Shareholders	NA

Business: The group's principle activity was to develop and provide digital consulting, communications and design related services including strategic planning, system design, creative design, implementation and performance metrics and analysis. The group is in the process of liquidating assets, collecting accounts receivable and paying creditors. There are no ongoing business operations and remaining revenue sources beyond those few remaining receivables not purchased by iis and not yet collected by the group.

Primary SIC and add'l.: 9999

CIK No: 0001009624

Subsidiaries: Delaware holding company

Officers: Joseph Sorci/Dir., CEO, Bruce Harmon/Interim CFO, Principal Accounting, Financial Officer

Directors: Joseph Sorci/Dir., CEO, Michael W. Hawkins/45/Dir.

Owners: Douglas E. Cleek, Matthew G. de Ganon, David Sklaver, Gary W. Brown/2.00%, Avante Holding Group, Inc./3.00%, Insiders/5.00%

Financial Data: Fiscal Year End: 12/31   **Latest Annual Data:** 12/31/2006

Year	Sales	Net Income
2006	$43,000	-$28,000
2005	NA	-$21,000
2004	$3,000	-$2,000

Curr. Assets:	$96,000	Curr. Liab.:	$125,000		
Plant, Equip.:	NA	Total Liab.:	$125,000	Indic. Yr. Divd.:	NA
Total Assets:	$96,000	Net Worth:	-$29,000	Debt/ Equity:	NA

Accelr8 Technology Corp

7000 N Broadway Bldg. 3 Unit 307, Denver, CO, 80221; **PH:** 1-303-863-8088;
Fax: 1-303-863-1218; **http://** www.accelr8.com

General - Incorporation		Stock - Price on:12/24/2007	
General - Incorporation	CO	Stock - Price on:12/24/2007	$2.35
Employees	13	Stock Exchange	AMEX
Auditor	Anton Collins Mitchell LLP	Ticker Symbol	AXK
Stk Agt	Computershare Trust Co	Outstanding Shares	9,970,000
Counsel	Saul, Ewing, Remick & Saul	E.P.S.	-$0.188
DUNS No.	18-632-8670	Shareholders	NA

Business: The group's principle activity is to provide software tools and consulting services for system modernization solutions for vms legacy systems developed by digital equipment corporation. The consulting services and software conversion tools enable the company's customers to analyze and implement their unix, linux and nt operating systems. The company offers tools that support migration from vms platforms to client or server systems. The company also specializes in the area of biosciences including dna/rna assays, protein-based assays and biosensors. The customers of the company include Fortune 1000 companies and government agencies. The group operates from United States.

Primary SIC and add'l.: 8731 7371 7372 5734

CIK No: 0000727207

Officers: Thomas V. Geimer/Chmn., CEO, CFO, Sec., Marin Kollef/51/Consultant, Ken Emoto/44/Sr. Scientist, Bruce McDonald/Principal Accounting Officer, Charles Greef/Sr. Scientist, Michael J. Lochhead/Sr. Scientist, David C. Howson/Pres., Steven W. Metzger/Sr. Scientist

Directors: Thomas V. Geimer/Chmn., CEO, CFO, Sec., David W. Grainger/Chmn. - Scientific Advisory Board, David Goldberg/Member - Scientific Advisory Board, Scott S. Saavedra/Member - Scientific Advisory Board, Alexander A. Arnold/Dir., Charles E. Gerretson/Dir.

Owners: David Howson/3.28%, Alexander A. Arnold/9.73%, Charles E. Gerretson/1.44%, Insiders/17.29%, Thomas V. Geimer/3.84%

Financial Data: Fiscal Year End: 07/31   **Latest Annual Data:** 7/31/2007

Year	Sales	Net Income
2007	$183,000	-$1,924,000
2006	$213,000	-$3,031,000
2005	$502,000	-$2,091,000

Curr. Assets:	$1,532,000	Curr. Liab.:	$155,000		
Plant, Equip.:	$107,000	Total Liab.:	$1,258,000	Indic. Yr. Divd.:	NA
Total Assets:	$6,138,000	Net Worth:	$4,880,000	Debt/ Equity:	NA

AccelRate Power Systems Inc

1140 W Pender St., Ste. 1370, Vancouver, BC, V6E 4G1; **PH:** 1-604-688-8656;
Fax: 1-604-688-8654; **http://** www.accelrate.com

General - Incorporation		Stock - Price on:12/24/2007	
General - Incorporation	Canada	Stock - Price on:12/24/2007	$0.2
Employees	NA	Stock Exchange	NA
Auditor	NA	Ticker Symbol	NA
Stk Agt	Pacific Corporate Trust Co	Outstanding Shares	NA
Counsel	NA	E.P.S.	NA
DUNS No.	NA	Shareholders	NA

Business: The group's principal activities include commercialization and marketing of patented energy technologies with global applications and its principal products include advanced battery charging technology. The unique and proprietary AccelRate technology can be used with lead-acid, nickel metal hydride (NiMh), nickel cadmium (NiCd), lithium ion (Li-Ion) and other specialty batteries powering equipment large and small, from cell phones to electric vehicles. AccelRate and Hawker Powersource Inc. have signed a license agreement for the manufacturing and marketing of battery chargers throughout North America, incorporating AccelRate's patented technology. The Hawker brand-name of industrial batteries is among the world's largest. The company is a Canadian publicly traded company with headquarters in Vancouver, British Columbia and its laboratory in neighbouring Burnaby, BC.

Primary SIC and add'l.: 3690

CIK No: 0001304658

Officers: Reimar Koch/Dir., CEO, Pres., Vladimir Petrovic/CTO, Pierre C. Gadbois/Pres. - Motive, Reserve Power Division

Directors: Reimar Koch/Dir., CEO, Pres., Caspar Koch/Chmn., Ian M. Adam/Dir., Ronald M. Snyder/Dir.

Accelrys Inc

10188 Telesis Ct., Ste. 100, San Diego, CA, 92121; **PH:** 1-858-799-5000; **Fax:** 1-858-799-5100;
http:// www.accelrys.com

General - Incorporation		Stock - Price on:12/24/2007	
General - Incorporation	DE	Stock - Price on:12/24/2007	$5.85
Employees	479	Stock Exchange	NDQ
Auditor	Ernst & Young LLP	Ticker Symbol	ACCL
Stk Agt	American Stock Transfer & Trust Co.	Outstanding Shares	26,510,000
Counsel	NA	E.P.S.	$0.04
DUNS No.	12-171-5460	Shareholders	NA

Business: The group's principal activity is to design, develop, market and support science- and technology-based products and services. The group operates under two segments: software segment and drug discovery segment. Through accelrys inc the group develops and commercializes molecular modeling, simulation, informatics, and decision support software for the life sciences and materials research markets. Through pharmacopeia drug discovery, inc. It integrates proprietary small molecule combinatorial and medicinal chemistry, high-throughput screening, in-vitro pharmacology, computational methods and informatics to discover and optimize lead compounds. Customers include pharmaceutical, biotechnology, chemical, petroleum and semiconductor companies, governmental institutions and universities. On 30-Apr-2004, the group discontinued pdd operations. On 28-Sep-2004, the group acquired scitegic, inc.

Primary SIC and add'l.: NA

CIK No: 0001002388

Subsidiaries: Accelrys GmbH, Accelrys kk, Accelrys Limited, Accelrys SARL, Accelrys Software Incorporated, Accelrys Software Solutions Pvt., Ltd., Chemical Design Holdings plc, Chemical Design SARL, Oxford Molecular Limited, Oxford Molecular SA, SciTegic, Inc., Synomics Limited, Synopsys Scientific Systems Incorporated, Synopsys Scientific Systems Limited

Officers: Mark J. Emkjer/Dir., CEO, Pres./$1,582,493.00, Judith Ohrn Hicks/VP - Human Resources, William R. Taylor/VP - Corporate Development, Marketing/$483,915.00, Judith Ohrn-Hicks/VP - Human Resources, David Mersten/Sr. VP, General Counsel, Sec., Richard Murphy/Sr. VP - Worldwide Sales, Services/$529,987.00, Katie Hollister/VP - Worldwide Client Services, Nic Austin/VP - Research, Development, Matt Hahn/VP - Platform Strategy, Technology/$573,605.00, Rick Russo/Sr. VP, CFO/$269,453.00, Frank Brown/Chief Science Officer

Directors: Mark J. Emkjer/Dir., CEO, Pres., Kenneth L. Coleman/Chmn., Ricardo B. Levy/Dir., Christopher J. Steffen/Dir., Jeffrey Rodek/Dir.

Owners: Insiders/4.40%, Dimensional Fund Advisors,Inc./7.70%, Group consisting of Paloma International L.P./5.50%, William R. Taylor, Gary E. Costley, Wellington Management Company, LLP./8.80%, Nicholas Austin, Brown Capital Management,Inc./7.40%, Ricardo B. Levy, Federated Investors,Inc./7.30%, David J. Greene and Company, L.L.C./9.50%, Kenneth L. Coleman, Christopher J. Steffen, Rick E. Russo, Richard C.G. Murphy (17 Owners included in Index)

Financial Data: Fiscal Year End: 03/31   **Latest Annual Data:** 3/31/2007

Year	Sales	Net Income
2007	$80,955,000	-$1,525,000
2006	$82,001,000	-$7,739,000
2005	$69,631,000	-$25,172,000

Curr. Assets:	$80,116,000	Curr. Liab.:	$68,270,000		
Plant, Equip.:	$7,860,000	Total Liab.:	$83,547,000	Indic. Yr. Divd.:	NA
Total Assets:	$146,755,000	Net Worth:	$63,208,000	Debt/ Equity:	0.0961

Accentia Biopharmaceuticals Inc

324 S Hyde Pk. Ave., Ste. 350, Tampa, FL, 33606; **PH:** 1-813-864-2554; **Fax:** 1-813-258-6912;
http:// www.accentia.net; **Email:** investors@accentia.net

General - Incorporation		Stock - Price on:12/24/2007	
General - Incorporation	FL	Stock - Price on:12/24/2007	$3.12
Employees	258	Stock Exchange	NDQ
Auditor	Aidman, Piser & Company, P.A.	Ticker Symbol	ABPI
Stk Agt	Wachovia Securities	Outstanding Shares	33,600,000
Counsel	NA	E.P.S.	-$2.21
DUNS No.	NA	Shareholders	NA

Business: The groups principle activities include developing and commercializing therapeutic clinical products. The group products sold under the trade names Flonase(R), Emezine(R) Nasonex(R), Rhinocort Aqua(R), Nasacort AQ(R), and Nasarel(R). The groups operates through two segments namely biopharmaceutical products and services and, specialty pharmaceuticals. Specific customers of the group include Cardinal Health and McKesson Corporation. The group operates from United States and Europe.

Primary SIC and add'l.: 2834 3826 2833 2836

CIK No: 0001310094

Subsidiaries: Accent RX, Inc, TEAMM Pharmaceuticals, Inc

Officers: Francis E. O'Donnell/Chmn., CEO, Steven R. Arikian/Dir., Pres., COO - Product Development, Marketing Services, Alan M. Pearce/Dir., CFO, Samuel S. Duffey/General Counsel

Directors: Francis E. O'Donnell/Chmn., CEO, Steven R. Arikian/Dir., Pres., COO - Product Development, Marketing Services, Alan M. Pearce/Dir., CFO, John P. Dubinsky/Dir., David M. Schubert/Dir., Todd D. Thomason/Dir., Edmund C. King/Dir., William S. Poole/Dir.

Owners: John P. Dubinsky, Timothy D. Ryll/12.40%, Todd D. Thomason, Ronald E. Osman/6.40%, Alan M. Pearce/2.60%, Edmund King, Francis E. ODonnell/14.30%, Steven R. Arikian/3.10%, Samuel S. Duffey, David M. Schubert, Insiders/21.50%, Pharmaceutical Product Development, Inc./12.70%, The Hopkins Capital Group, LLC/13.10%

Financial Data: ***Fiscal Year End:***09/30 ***Latest Annual Data:*** 9/30/2006

Year	Sales	Net Income
2006	$25,058,000	-$43,395,000
2005	$25,195,000	-$44,736,000
2004	$25,936,000	-$23,226,000

Curr. Assets:	$30,117,000	***Curr. Liab.:***	$50,586,000		
Plant, Equip.:	$1,536,000	***Total Liab.:***	$83,577,000	***Indic. Yr. Divd.:***	NA
Total Assets:	$57,136,000	***Net Worth:***	-$26,441,000	***Debt/ Equity:***	NA

Accenture Ltd

1345 Ave. of the Americas, New York, NY, 10105; ***PH:*** 1-917-452-4400; ***Fax:*** 1-917-527-9915; ***http://*** www.accenture.com

General - Incorporation	Bermuda	***Stock***- Price on:12/24/2007	$41.17
Employees	140,000	Stock Exchange	NYSE
Auditor	KPMG LLP	Ticker Symbol	ACN
Stk Agt	National City Bank	Outstanding Shares	593,590,000
Counsel	Appleby Spurling & Kempe	E.P.S	$2.11
DUNS No.	NA	Shareholders	NA

Business: The group's principal activities are to provide management and technology consulting services and solutions to the communications, high technology and media and entertainment industries. The group operates globally with one common brand and business model designed to enable it to serve clients on a consistent basis around the world and has operations in over 110 offices in 48 countries. The group also serves companies related to banking, health services, insurance, consumer goods and services, industrial equipment, pharmaceuticals and medical products, retail transportation and travel services, energy, chemicals, utilities, metals, mining and forest products. The principal markets of the group are North America, western Europe, Japan and Australia.

Primary SIC and add'l.: 7376 8748 8742 7549 7378 7389 8741

CIK No: 0001134538

Subsidiaries: 1021904 Ontario Limited, Accenture, Accenture (Botswana) (PTY)Ltd, Accenture (Iberia) Holdings SL, Accenture (Mauritius) Onshore Ltd, Accenture (Shanghai) Co Ltd, Accenture (South Africa) Pty Ltd, Accenture (UK)Ltd, Accenture A.N.S, Accenture AB, Accenture Africa Ltd, Accenture AG, Accenture Australia Holding B.V, Accenture Australia Holdings ApS, Accenture Australia Holdings Pty Ltd 230 Subsidiaries included in the Index

Officers: William D. Green/Chmn., CEO, Alexander M. Vant Noordende/45/Group CEO - Resources Operating Group, Kevin M. Campbell/Group CEO - Outsourcing, Martin I. Cole/Group CEO - Communications, High Tech, Mark Foster/Group CEO - Management Consulting, Integrated Markets, Karl-Heinz Floether/Group CEO - Systems Integration, Technology, Delivery, Gianfranco Casati/Group CEO - Products, Lisa M. Mascolo/Group CEO - Public Service, Pierre Nanterme/Group CEO - Financial Services, Sander Van't Noordende/Group CEO - Resources, David P. Rowland/Sr. VP - Finance, Roxanne Taylor/Chief Marketing, Communications Officer, Mani Singhal/Business Analyst, Lori L. Lovelace/Exec. Dir., Pamela J. Craig/CFO *(38 Officers included in Index)*

Directors: William D. Green/Chmn., CEO, Mark Moody-Stuart/Dir., Dennis F. Hightower/Dir., Nobuyuki Idei/Dir., William L. Kimsey/Dir., Robert I. Lipp/Dir., Marjorie Magner/Dir., Blythe J. McGarvie/Dir., Wulf Von Schimmelmann/Dir., Dina Dublon/Dir., Lori L. Lovelace/Exec. Dir.

Owners: Robert I. Lipp, Mark Moody-Stuart, Pamela J. Craig, William L. Kimsey, William D. Green, Michael G. McGrath, Pamela J. Craig, William D. Green, Mark Foster, Karl-Heinz Flther, Wellington Management Co. LLP/5.00%, Blythe J. McGarvie, Dennis F. Hightower, Barclays Global Investors, NA et al./8.20%, Wulf von Schimmelmann *(20 Owners included in Index)*

Financial Data: ***Fiscal Year End:***08/31 ***Latest Annual Data:*** 8/31/2006

Year	Sales	Net Income
2006	$18,228,366,000	$973,329,000
2005	$17,094,420,000	$940,474,000
2004	$15,113,582,000	$690,828,000

Curr. Assets:	$7,353,821,000	***Curr. Liab.:***	$5,816,482,000	***P/E Ratio:***	20.08
Plant, Equip.:	$727,692,000	***Total Liab.:***	$7,523,825,000	***Indic. Yr. Divd.:***	$0.420
Total Assets:	$9,418,080,000	***Net Worth:***	$1,894,255,000	***Debt/ Equity:***	0.0022

Access Integrated Technologies Inc

55 Madison Ave., Ste. 300, Morristown, NJ, 07960; ***PH:*** 1-973-290-0080; ***Fax:*** 1-973-290-0081; ***http://*** www.accessitx.com; ***Email:*** info@accessitx.com

General - Incorporation	DE	***Stock***- Price on:12/24/2007	$7
Employees	86	Stock Exchange	NDQ
Auditor	Eisner LLP	Ticker Symbol	AIXD
Stk Agt	American Stock Transfer & Trust Co.	Outstanding Shares	24,510,000
Counsel	Kelley Drye & Warren LLP	E.P.S	-$1.36
DUNS No.	NA	Shareholders	NA

Business: The group's principal activities are to design, build and operate a national platform of carrier-diverse Internet data centers. The group provides software services and technology solutions to the motion picture industry and operating Internet data centers. It operates through two segments: media services, which represents the operations of accessdm and hollywood sw, and data center services, which are comprised of idc operations and managed service offerings. The customers of the group include 20th century fox, paramount pictures, universal studios, mgm, lions gate films, newmarket films, gold circle films, ifc films, first look or overseas film group, brenden theatres, and madstone theatres. The group operates in the United States. In fiscal 2004, the group acquired core technology services and all the asset of boeing digital cinema.

Primary SIC and add'l.: 7372 6719 7374

CIK No: 0001173204

Subsidiaries: Access Digital Media, Inc., ADM Cinema Corporation., Christie/AIX, Inc., Core Technology Services, Inc., FiberSat Global Services Inc., Hollywood Software, Inc., PLX Acquisition Corp.

Officers: Dale A. Mayo/Chmn., CEO, Pres./$1,138,400.00, Chuck Goldwater/Pres. - Accessit Media Services Group, Pres., COO - Christie, AIX, a Division, Accessit/$367,035.00, Gary S. Loffredo/Sr. VP - General Counsel, Sec., Dir./$292,550.00, Jeff Butkovsky/Sr. VP - Managed Services - Accessit/$266,420.00, David Gajda/Sr. VP - International - Accessit, Brian D. Pflug/Sr. VP - Accounting - Finance, Accessit/$233,945.00, Kevin J. Farrell/Sr. VP - Facilities, Dir., Robert Jackovich/CTO - Accessit Software Division, Jim Miller/Pres., COO - Accessit Software Division, Gerd A. Jakuszeit/Sr. VP, GM - Accessit Digital Media Services Division

Directors: Dale A. Mayo/Chmn., CEO, Pres., Gary S. Loffredo/Sr. VP - General Counsel, Sec., Dir., Robert Davidoff/Dir., Robert E. Mulholland/56/Dir., Cary C. Jones/Member - Advisory Board, John L. O'Hara/Member - Advisory Board, Gerald C. Crotty/Dir., Kevin J. Farrell/Sr. VP - Facilities, Dir., Wayne Clevenger/Dir., Brett E. Marks/Dir., Matthew W. Finlay/Dir., Edward H. Herbst/Member - Advisory Board, Harvey Marks/Member - Advisory Board

Owners: Alydar Partners, LLC/5.90%, Kevin J. Farrell/1.10%, Charles Goldwater, Jeff Butkovsky, Gary S. Loffredo, Wayne L. Clevenger/7.70%, Gruber and McBaine Capital Management, LLC/6.10%, William Blair & Company, L.L.C./10.80%, Gerald Crotty, Dale A. Mayo/100.00%, Matthew Finlay/7.70%, Westcliff Capital Management, LLC/5.70%, Cortina Asset Management, LLC/6.50%, Insiders/19.30%, Dale A. Mayo/5.10% *(23 Owners included in Index)*

Financial Data: ***Fiscal Year End:***03/31 ***Latest Annual Data:*** 03/31/2007

Year	Sales	Net Income
2007	$47,110,000	-$25,999,000
2006	$16,795,000	-$16,812,000
2005	$10,651,000	-$6,788,000

Curr. Assets:	$64,469,000	***Curr. Liab.:***	$15,618,000		
Plant, Equip.:	$44,551,000	***Total Liab.:***	$25,466,000	***Indic. Yr. Divd.:***	NA
Total Assets:	$123,947,000	***Net Worth:***	$98,481,000	***Debt/ Equity:***	1.4659

Access National Corp

1800 Robert Fulton Dr., Ste. 310, Reston, VA, 20191; ***PH:*** 1-703-871-2100; ***Fax:*** 1-703-766-3386; ***http://*** www.accessnationalbank.com

General - Incorporation	VA	***Stock***- Price on:12/24/2007	$8.86
Employees	253	Stock Exchange	NDQ
Auditor	BDO Seidman LLP	Ticker Symbol	ANCX
Stk Agt	Registrar & Transfer Co	Outstanding Shares	12,000,000
Counsel	NA	E.P.S	$0.59
DUNS No.	NA	Shareholders	NA

Business: The group's principal activities are to provide a comprehensive range of financial services and products and specializes in providing customized financial services to small and medium sized businesses, professionals, and associated individuals. The group provides its customers with personal customized service utilizing the latest technology and delivery channels.

Primary SIC and add'l.: 6712 6029

CIK No: 0001176316

Subsidiaries: Access National Bank, Access National Capital Trust I, Access National Capital Trust II, Access National Leasing Corporation, Access National Mortgage Corporation, Access National Real Estate LLC, United First Mortgage Corporation

Officers: Michael W. Clarke/Dir., CEO, Pres., Charles Wimer/CFO, Exec. VP, Robert C. Shoemaker/Dir., Exec. VP - Bank, Sheila Linton/Investor Relation Officer

Directors: Michael W. Clarke/Dir., CEO, Pres., Jacques Rebibo/Chmn., James L. Jadlos/Dir., John W. Edgemond/Dir., Thomas M. Kody/Dir., Robert C. Shoemaker/Dir., Exec. VP - Bank, Randolph J. Babbitt/Dir.

Owners: Insiders/28.34%, John W. Edgemond/4.64%, Randolph J. Babbitt/1.88%, Charles Wimer/0.92%, Dean F. Hackemer/1.55%, Thomas M. Kody/3.03%, James L. Jadlos/2.15%, Michael W. Clarke/5.39%, Jacques Rebibo/5.52%, Robert C. Shoemaker/3.27%, Michael Rebibo/6.90%

Financial Data: ***Fiscal Year End:***12/31 ***Latest Annual Data:*** 12/31/2006

Year	Sales	Net Income
2006	$67,571,000	$7,593,000
2005	$59,260,000	$5,897,000
2004	$44,177,000	$3,315,000

Curr. Assets:	$27,365,000	***Curr. Liab.:***	$523,883,000	***P/E Ratio:***	13.63
Plant, Equip.:	$9,598,000	***Total Liab.:***	$582,487,000	***Indic. Yr. Divd.:***	$0.040
Total Assets:	$644,782,000	***Net Worth:***	$62,295,000	***Debt/ Equity:***	0.8513

Access Pharmaceuticals Inc

2600 N Stemmons Fwy., Ste. 176, Dallas, TX, 75207; ***PH:*** 1-214-905-5100; ***Fax:*** 1-214-905-5101; ***http://*** www.accesspharma.com; ***Email:*** akc@accesspharma.com

General - Incorporation	DE	***Stock***- Price on:12/24/2007	$5.15
Employees	9	Stock Exchange	OTC
Auditor	Whitley Penn LLP	Ticker Symbol	ACCP
Stk Agt	American Stock Transfer & Trust Co.	Outstanding Shares	3,540,000
Counsel	Bingham Dana Ltd	E.P.S	-$3.09
DUNS No.	01-061-4386	Shareholders	NA

Business: The group's principal activity is to develop drug delivery systems and advanced polymer technology for application in cancer treatment, dermatology and treatment of oral diseases. It is in the development stage. The group has proprietary patents and rights to seven drug delivery technology platforms: synthetic polymer targeted delivery, vitamin mediated targeted delivery (including oral), bioerodible hydrogel technology, nanoparticles and nanoparticle networks, residerm(R) topical delivery, carbohydrate targeting technology and agents for the prevention and treatment of viral disease, including HIV. The products residerm(R) a gel - zindaclin (TM), aphthasol(R) and aptheal(R) are being marketed currently.

Primary SIC and add'l.: 8731

CIK No: 0000318306

Subsidiaries: Access Pharmaceuticals Australia Pty. Limited, Tacora Corporation, Virologix Corporation

Officers: Stephen R. Seiler/Dir., CEO, Pres., Esteban Cvitkovic/Vice Chmn. - Europe, Phillip Wise/VP - Business Development, Strategy/$182,757.00, Stephen B. Thompson/CFO, VP/$219,320.00, David P. Nowotnik/Sr. VP - Research, Development/$321,504.00

Directors: Stephen R. Seiler/Dir., CEO, Pres., Jeffrey B. Davis/Chmn., Rosemary Mazanet/Vice Chmn., John Kirkwood/Member - Advisory Board, Mace Rothenberg/Member - Advisory Board, Mark Ahn/Dir., Mark J. Alvino/Dir., Herbert H. McDade/Dir., Michael J. Flinn/Dir., Leonard Saltz/Member - Advisory Board, Carlos Becerra/Member - Advisory Board, Maurie Markman/Member - Advisory Board, David Gandara/Member - Advisory Board, Stephen B. Howell/Dir., Member - Advisory Board, Alejandro Yovine/Member - Advisory Board *(17 Directors included in Index)*

Owners: SCO Capital Partners LLC, John J. Meakem, Mark J. Alvino, Stephen B. Howell, Michael J. Flinn, Phillip S. Wise, David P. Nowotnik, Insiders, Jeffery B. Davis, Stephen B. Thompson, Kerry P. Gray, Rosemary Mazanet, Mark Ahn, Herbert H. McDade, Larry N. Feinberg

Financial Data: Fiscal Year End:12/31 Latest Annual Data: 12/31/2006

Year	Sales	Net Income
2006	NA	-$12,874,000
2005	NA	-$1,700,000
2004	$549,000	-$10,238,000

Curr. Assets:	$5,031,000	Curr. Liab.:	$10,813,000		
Plant, Equip.:	$212,000	Total Liab.:	$16,313,000	Indic. Yr. Divd.:	NA
Total Assets:	$6,426,000	Net Worth:	-$9,887,000	Debt/ Equity:	NA

Access Worldwide Communications Inc

1820 N Ft. Myer Dr., 3rd Fl., Arlington, VA, 22209; **PH:** 1-703-292-5210; **Fax:** 1-703-465-8642; **http://** www.accessww.com; **Email:** investor@accessww.com

General - Incorporation	DE	**Stock** - Price on:12/24/2007	$1.05
Employees	1,000	Stock Exchange	OTC
Auditor	Daszkal Bolton LLP	Ticker Symbol	AWWC
Stk Agt	American Stock Transfer & Trust Co.	Outstanding Shares	17,680,000
Counsel	Shapiro, Sontag	E.P.S.	-$0.15
DUNS No.	10-673-3728	Shareholders	NA

Business: The group's principle activity is to provide a variety of sales, education and communication programs in the pharmaceutical, telecommunication and consumer product industries. The group's activities are carried out through two business segments namely pharmaceutical marketing service segment and consumer and business services segment. Pharmaceutical marketing service segment provides outsourced services including medical education and medical publishing to the pharmaceutical and medical industries. Consumer and business services segment provides consumer and multilingual telemarketing services to the telecommunications and consumer products industries. The group's quarterly revenue for September 2007 was 8.18 millions of USD.

Primary SIC and add'l.: 4899 7389

CIK No: 0001048422

Officers: Shawkat Raslan/Chmn., CEO, Pres./$265,396.00, Richard Lyew/CFO, Exec. VP/$227,446.00, Ted Jordan/COO, Exec. VP/$216,246.00, Mark Wright/General Counsel/$132,557.00, Mike Bowling/Dir. - New Business Development

Directors: Shawkat Raslan/Chmn., CEO, Pres., Michael Dornemann/Dir., Frederick Thorne/Dir., Charles Henri Weil/Dir., Carl Tiedemann/Dir., Alfonso Yuchengco/Dir.

Owners: Mark Wright, Insiders/46.30%, Carl Tiedemann/8.60%, Alfonso Yuchengco/3.00%, Charles Henri Weil/6.80%, Georges Andr/2.10%, Orhan Sadik-Khan/5.00%, Shawkat Raslan/17.40%, Frederick Thorne/4.30%, Jared Jordan, Michael Dornemann/9.60%, Richard Lyew

Financial Data: Fiscal Year End:12/31 Latest Annual Data: 12/31/2006

Year	Sales	Net Income
2006	$27,712,000	$2,886,000
2005	$38,922,000	-$4,681,000
2004	$47,467,000	-$1,411,000

Curr. Assets:	$10,756,000	Curr. Liab.:	$6,624,000	P/E Ratio:	4.57
Plant, Equip.:	$3,375,000	Total Liab.:	$12,040,000	Indic. Yr. Divd.:	NA
Total Assets:	$14,860,000	Net Worth:	-$1,180,000	Debt/ Equity:	NA

Accesstel Inc

66 Clinton Rd. , Fairfield, NJ, 07004; **PH:** 1-973-882-8861; **http://** www.globalinvestholdings.com; **Email:** info@globalinvestholdings.com

General - Incorporation	UT	**Stock** - Price on:12/24/2007	$0.007
Employees	NA	Stock Exchange	OTC
Auditor	Robert G. Jeffrey, CPA	Ticker Symbol	ACCS
Stk Agt	NA	Outstanding Shares	NA
Counsel	NA	E.P.S.	NA
DUNS No.	NA	Shareholders	NA

Business: The group's principal activity is to supply broadband wireless, voip and utility meter reading over a wireless and wired broadband network. The group's services are provided primarily in China and the western United States. The wireless network and wireless local loop services provide rapid deployment of phone, facsimile, high-speed data, video and fixed isp connection. The company is currently insolvent and has no business operations.

Primary SIC and add'l.: 7389 4813

CIK No: 0001063293

Financial Data: Fiscal Year End:12/31 Latest Annual Data: 12/31/2004

Year	Sales	Net Income
2004	$6,864,000	$25,000
2003	NA	-$1,811,000
2002	NA	-$170,000

Curr. Assets:	$1,512,000	Curr. Liab.:	$1,683,000		
Plant, Equip.:	NA	Total Liab.:	$1,683,000	Indic. Yr. Divd.:	NA
Total Assets:	$1,671,000	Net Worth:	-$12,000	Debt/ Equity:	NA

ACCO Brands Corp

300 Tower Pkwy., Lincolnshire, IL, 60069; **PH:** 1-847-541-9500; **Fax:** 1-847-484-4492; **http://** www.accobrands.com

General - Incorporation	DE	**Stock** - Price on:12/24/2007	$24.79
Employees	6,846	Stock Exchange	NYSE
Auditor	PricewaterhouseCoopers LLP	Ticker Symbol	ABD
Stk Agt	Wells Fargo Bank, N.a.	Outstanding Shares	53,960,000
Counsel	NA	E.P.S.	$0.14
DUNS No.	NA	Shareholders	NA

Business: The groups principle activities include designing, developing, manufacturing and marketing traditional and computer related office products, supplies, binding and laminating equipment. The products of the group include shredders, indexes, staplers and staples, easels, labels, and clips. The group products sold under the trade names Ibico(R), NOBO(R),Eastlight(R), Marbig(R) and Dox(R). The groups operates through four segments namely office products group, computer products group, commercial IPFG and other. The group operates from United States, the United Kingdom, Australia and Canada. The group's quarterly revenue for September 2007 was 494.70 millions of USD.

Primary SIC and add'l.: 5112

CIK No: 0000712034

Subsidiaries: ACCO Australia Pty. Limited, ACCO Benelux B.V., ACCO Brands Benelux B.V., ACCO Brands Canada Inc., ACCO Brands Europe Holding LP, ACCO Brands Europe Ltd., ACCO Brands International, Inc., ACCO Brands Italia S.r.L., ACCO Brands USA LLC, ACCO Deutschland GmbH& Co. KG, ACCO Development, S.A. de C.V., ACCO Eastlight Limited, ACCO Europe Finance Holdings, LLC, ACCO Europe Finance LP, ACCO Europe International Holdings, LLC 35 Subsidiaries included in the Index

Officers: David D. Campbell/Chmn., CEO, Neal V. Fenwick/CFO, Exec. VP, Dennis L. Chandler/COO, Pres. - Office Products, Boris Elisman/Pres. - Kensington Computer Products Group, John Turner/Pres. - Commercial Laminating Solutions Group, Richard Nelson/VP - Corporate Communications, Thomas P. O'Neill/VP - Finance, Accounting, Chief Accounting Officer, Jennifer Rice/VP - Investor Relations, Steven Rubin/Sr. VP, Sec., General Counsel, Kriss Kirchhoff/Pres. - Document Finishing Group, Marc C. Anderson/Sr. VP - Corporate Development, David L. Kaput/Chief Human Resources Officer, Sr. VP

Directors: David D. Campbell/Chmn., CEO, George V. Bayly/Dir., Patricia O. Ewers/Dir., Thomas G. Hargrove/Dir., Robert J. Keller/Dir., Pierre E. Leroy/Dir., Gordon R. Lohman/Dir., Norman H. Wesley/Dir., Robert H. Jenkins/65/Dir.

Owners: Ariel Capital Management, LLC/14.90%, Dennis L. Chandler, Morgan Stanley/6.20%, David D. Campbell/1.20%, Gordon R. Lohman, Patricia O. Ewers, Boris Elisman, Steven Rubin, George V. Bayly, Norman H. Wesley, Pierre E. Leroy, Thomas P. ONeill, Thomas G. Hargrove, O.S.S. Capital Management LP/5.00%, Insiders/2.10% (18 Owners included in Index)

Financial Data: Fiscal Year End:12/31 Latest Annual Data: 12/31/2006

Year	Sales	Net Income
2006	$1,951,000,000	$7,200,000
2005	$1,487,500,000	$59,500,000

Curr. Assets:	$822,200,000	Curr. Liab.:	$496,100,000	P/E Ratio:	8.04
Plant, Equip.:	$217,200,000	Total Liab.:	$1,465,600,000	Indic. Yr. Divd.:	NA
Total Assets:	$1,849,600,000	Net Worth:	$384,000,000	Debt/ Equity:	2.0841

Accredited Home Lenders Co

15253 Ave. Of Science, San Diego, CA, 92128; **PH:** 1-858-676-2100; **http://** www.accredhome.com

General - Incorporation	DE	**Stock** - Price on:12/24/2007	$13.83
Employees	4,196	Stock Exchange	NDQ
Auditor	Squar, Peterson, LLP	Ticker Symbol	LEND
Stk Agt	U.S. Stock Transfer Corp	Outstanding Shares	25,260,000
Counsel	NA	E.P.S.	-$9.1
DUNS No.	NA	Shareholders	NA

Business: The group's principal activity is to provide mortgage banking services. It originates, finances, sells, securitizes and services non-prime mortgage loans secured by residential real estate. The group focuses on borrowers who do not meet conforming underwriting guidelines due to higher loan-to-value ratios. It originates loans primarily through approved and licensed independent mortgage brokers. As of 31-Dec-2003, the group had a network of 6,800 independent brokers throughout the United States. The group also operates axiom financial services and home funds direct, which originates direct-to-consumer loans.

Primary SIC and add'l.: 6159 6162

CIK No: 0001174735

Subsidiaries: Accredited Home Lenders Canada, Inc, Accredited Home Lenders Funding Corp., Accredited Home Lenders, Inc., Accredited Mortgage Loan REIT Trust, Accredited Processing Services, Inc., Inzura Insurance Services, Inc., Vendor Management Services of Alabama, LLC, Vendor Management Services, LLC

Officers: James A. Konrath/Chmn., CEO, Larry Murphy/CIO, Joseph J. Lydon/Dir., COO, Pres., Michael J. Matthews/Dir. - Non - Prime Production, Joseph F. Weinbrecht/Dir. - Human Resources, Administration, David E. Hertzel/General Counsel, Roxane W. Helstrom/Dir. - Marketing, Jeffrey W. Crawford/Dir. - Operations, Stuart D. Marvin/Exec. VP, Richard W. Howe/Dir. - Corporate Communications, James Voisard/Dir. - Wholesale Operations

Directors: James A. Konrath/Chmn., CEO, Jay A. Meyerson/61/Dir., Michael Thomson/Dir., Benjamin D. Velvin/Dir., Len Allen/Dir., Marc Lipshy/Dir., Catharon Miller/Dir., Leigh Rea/Dir., Joseph J. Lydon/Dir., COO, Pres.

Owners: Gary M. Erickson, Joseph J. Lydon/3.00%, Jeffrey W. Crawford, Stuart D. Marvin, John S. Buchanan, Stephen E. Wall, Farallon Funds/10.00%, Richard T. Pratt, Insiders/12.00%, Silver Point Capital, L.P./5.20%, Jay A. Meyerson, Goldman Sachs Asset Management, L.P./6.00%, James H. Berglund, Jody A. Gunderson, Bowers W. Espy (18 Owners included in Index)

Financial Data: Fiscal Year End:12/31 Latest Annual Data: 12/31/2006

Year	Sales	Net Income
2006	$1,072,212,000	-$205,648,000
2005	$941,418,000	$155,432,000
2004	$660,670,000	$130,778,000

Curr. Assets:	$337,999,000	Curr. Liab.:	$266,056,000	P/E Ratio:	5.58
Plant, Equip.:	$152,119,000	Total Liab.:	$10,694,975,000	Indic. Yr. Divd.:	NA
Total Assets:	$11,349,046,000	Net Worth:	$556,149,000	Debt/ Equity:	13.9750

Accuride Corp

7140 Office Cir., Evansville, IN, 47716; **PH:** 1-812-962-5000; **Fax:** 1-812-962-5400; **http://** www.accuridecorp.com; **Email:** investor@accuridecorp.com

General - Incorporation	DE	**Stock** - Price on:12/24/2007	$15.38
Employees	4,622	Stock Exchange	NYSE
Auditor	Deloitte & Touche LLP	Ticker Symbol	ACW
Stk Agt	American Stock Transfer & Trust Co.	Outstanding Shares	35,000,000
Counsel	NA	E.P.S.	$0.46
DUNS No.	NA	Shareholders	NA

Business: The groups principle activities include manufacturering and supplying commercial vehicle components. The products of the group include Brake Drums, vehicle wheels, truck body and chassis parts and seating assemblies. Specific customers of the group include Freightliner, PACCAR, Volvo and Mack. In January 31, 2005, the group acquired Transportation Technologies Industries, Inc. The group operates from the United States, Canada, and Mexico. The group's quarterly revenue for September 2007 was 220.58 millions of USD.

Primary SIC and add'l.: 3714

CIK No: 0000817979

Subsidiaries: Accuride Canada, Inc., Accuride Cuyahoga Falls, Inc., Accuride de Mexico, S.A. de C.V., Accuride EMI, LLC, Accuride Erie, L.P., Accuride Henderson Limited Liability Company, AKW General Partner, L.L.C., Transportation Technologies Industries, Inc.

Officers: John R. Murphy/57/COO, Pres./$1,423,175.00, David K. Armstrong/CFO, Sr. VP, General Counsel/$820,079.00, Elizabeth I. Hamme/Sr. VP - Human Resources/$725,041.00, Robert L. Nida/Sr. VP - Operations Steel - Aluminum Wheels, Gunite Corporation, Brillion Iron Works, Henry L. Taylor/54/Sr. VP - Sales, Marketing/$692,241.00, Anthony A. Donatelli/Sr. VP - Imperial, Bostrom, Fabco, Richard F. Schomer/Sr. VP - Sales, Marketing, Steven J. Holt/Sr. VP - Strategy, Growth, Technology, Eva Schmitz/Corp. Dir. - Communications

Directors: Terrence J. Keating/Chmn., Mark D. Dalton/Dir., Frederick M. Goltz/37/Dir., James H. Greene/57/Dir., Donald T. Johnson/Dir., Craig H. Muhlhauser/58/Dir., Charles E. Mitchell Rentschler/Dir., Donald C. Roof/Dir., John D. Durrett/Dir., William M. Lasky/Dir.

Owners: Donald C. Roof, Entities affiliated with Stadium Capital Management, LLC/9.50%, John R. Murphy, Caravelle Investment Fund, L.L.C., Frederick M. Goltz, James H. Greene/22.50%, Charles E. Mitchell Rentschler, Elizabeth I. Hamme, Henry L. Taylor, Craig H. Muhlhauser, Terrence J. Keating, Mark D. Dalton/10.10%, KKR 1996 GP L.L.C./22.40%, Entities affiliated with Trimaran InvestmentsII, L.L.C./11.10%, Insiders/33.70% *(19 Owners included in Index)*

Financial Data: *Fiscal Year End:*12/31 *Latest Annual Data:* 12/31/2006

Year	Sales	Net Income
2006	$1,408,155,000	$65,133,000
2005	$1,229,311,000	$51,229,000
2004	$494,008,000	$21,776,000

Curr. Assets:	$398,240,000	**Curr. Liab.:**	$186,899,000	**P/E Ratio:**	18.09
Plant, Equip.:	$300,806,000	**Total Liab.:**	$969,605,000	**Indic. Yr. Divd.:**	NA
Total Assets:	$1,233,187,000	**Net Worth:**	$263,582,000	**Debt/ Equity:**	2.2322

ACE Cash Express Inc

1231 Greenway Dr., Ste. 600, Irving, TX, 75038; ***PH:*** 1-214-550-5000; ***http://*** www.acecashexpress.com

General - Incorporation	TX	**Stock**- Price on:12/24/2007	NA
Employees	NA	Stock Exchange	NDQ
Auditor	Grant Thornton LLP	Ticker Symbol	AACE
Stk Agt	Chase Mellon Shareholder Services LLC	Outstanding Shares	NA
Counsel	Gardere, Wynne Sewell LLP	E.P.S	NA
DUNS No.	13-972-9412	Shareholders	NA

Business: The group's principal activity is to provide retail financial services in the United States. The group also owns, operates, and franchises check-cashing stores in the United States. The services provided by the group include offering short-term consumer loans, selling money orders, providing money transfer services using the moneygram network, bill payment services and other retail financial transaction processing services. The services provided also include cashing payroll checks, government checks and insurance drafts. At 31-Aug-2003 the group's services are offered through a network of 1,168 stores in 36 states and the district of columbia, consisting of 968 company-owned stores and 200 franchised stores.

Primary SIC and add'l.: 6099

CIK No: 0000849116

Subsidiaries: ACE Credit Services, LLC, Ace Funding LLC, Ace Payment Services, Inc., Check Express Finance, Inc., Check Express Florida, Inc., Check Express South Carolina, Inc, Check Express USA, Inc, Check Express, Inc, Check-X-Change Corporation, Q.c.& G. Financial, Inc.

Officers: Jay B. Shipowitz/Dir., CEO, Pres., Eric C. Norrington/Sr. VP - Public Affairs, Ted M. Eades/Sr. VP, General Counsel, Joe B. Edwards/Sr. VP - Information Systems, CIO, Barry M. Barron/COO, Allen J. Klose/Chief Marketing Officer, James E. Gibbs/Sr. VP - Human Resources

Directors: Jay B. Shipowitz/Dir., CEO, Pres., Joseph M. Haggar/Dir., Charles Daniel Yost/Dir., Edward W. Rose/Dir., Matrice Ellis-Kirk/Dir., Marshall B. Payne/Dir., Michael S. Rawlings/Dir., Raymond C. Hemmig/Dir., Rob Allyn/Dir.

ACE COMM Corp

704 Quince Orchard Rd., Ste. 100, Gaithersburg, MD, 20878; ***PH:*** 1-301-721-3000; ***Fax:*** 1-301-721-3001; ***http://*** www.acec.com; ***Email:*** support@acecomm.com

General - Incorporation	MD	**Stock**- Price on:12/24/2007	$1.12
Employees	128	Stock Exchange	OTC
Auditor	Grant Thornton LLP	Ticker Symbol	ACEC
Stk Agt	Mellon Investor Services LLC	Outstanding Shares	18,620,000
Counsel	Venable, Baetjer, Howard & Civiletti	E.P.S	-$0.31
DUNS No.	10-192-0791	Shareholders	NA

Business: The group's principal activity is to develop and market enterprise telemanagement and convergent mediation (TM) solutions to wired and wireless voice, data and Internet communications providers. It's solutions consist of hardware, software and related services, that enable the capture, security, validation, correlation and warehousing of data from network elements and the distribution of data in appropriate formats to oss (operations support s ystems) and bss (business support systems) operations. Convergent mediation (TM) solutions are designed to solve a customer's data needs while protecting their investment in their existing operations support systems and business support systems infrastructure. The customers of the group include government agencies, military organizations, educational institutions and Fortune 1000 companies, for the automation of network operations and management functions. During 2004, the group acquired i3 mobile, inc.

Primary SIC and add'l.: 3572 7373 7372

CIK No: 0001017526

Subsidiaries: ACECOMM Holdings I, ACECOMM Holdings II, ACECOMM Holdings III, ACECOMM Solutions Australia Pty Limited, ACECOMM Solutions UK Limited, Double Helix Solutions Limited, Helix Europe Limited, i3 Mobile, Inc., Solutions ACECOMM Corporation

Officers: Jim Greenwell/Dir., CEO, Pres., Jody Burfening/Investor Relations Contact, Harriet Fried/Investor Relations Contact, Paul G. Casner/70/Dir. - Business Management Consultant, Steven R. Delmar/CFO, Sr. VP, Loretta L. Rivers/Corp. Sec., Harry M. Linowes/Dir. - Business Management Consultant

Directors: Jim Greenwell/Dir., CEO, Pres., George T. Jimenez/72/Chmn., Matthew J. Stover/Dir., Harry M. Linowes/Dir. - Business Management Consultant, Gilbert A. Wetzel/Dir., William J. Grimes/Dir.

Owners: Matthew J. Stover, Gilbert A. Wetzel, Loretta L. Rivers, James W. Greenwell/1.55%, Harry M. Linowes, William J. Grimes, Insiders/14.58%, Steven R. Delmar/1.16%, George T. Jimenez/10.36%, Paul G. Casner

Financial Data: *Fiscal Year End:*06/30 *Latest Annual Data:* 6/30/2006

Year	Sales	Net Income
2006	$26,671,000	$319,000
2005	$19,961,000	-$6,462,000
2004	$13,671,000	-$5,898,000

Curr. Assets:	$13,354,000	**Curr. Liab.:**	$10,247,000		
Plant, Equip.:	$787,000	**Total Liab.:**	$10,264,000	**Indic. Yr. Divd.:**	NA
Total Assets:	$16,361,000	**Net Worth:**	$6,097,000	**Debt/ Equity:**	NA

ACE Ltd

436 Walnut St., Philadelphia, PA, 19106; ***PH:*** 1-215-640-1000; ***Fax:*** 1-215-640-2489; ***http://*** www.acelimited.com; ***Email:*** info@acelimited.com

General - Incorporation	Cayman Islands	**Stock**- Price on:12/24/2007	$62.75
Employees	10,000	Stock Exchange	NYSE
Auditor	PricewaterhouseCoopers LLP	Ticker Symbol	ACE
Stk Agt	Mellon Investor Services LLC	Outstanding Shares	328,600,000
Counsel	Cleary Gottlieb Steen & Hamilton	E.P.S	$7.96
DUNS No.	87-563-6698	Shareholders	NA

Business: The group's principal activity is to provide property and casualty insurance and reinsurance. The group operates through four business segments: the insurance - north American segment comprises p&c insurance, which operates in the us, Bermuda and Canada. The segment writes insurance products including property, liability, professional lines and other specialty lines. The insurance - overseas general includes the operations of ace international and ace global markets. The global reinsurance segment comprises ace tempest re Bermuda, ace tempest re usa, ace tempest re Europe and life reinsurance operations. The financial services segment includes the financial guaranty business of ace guaranty corp and ace capital re international and the financial solutions business in the us and Bermuda. These segments distribute their products through various forms of brokers and agencies.

Primary SIC and add'l.: 6331 6311 9999

CIK No: 0000896159

Subsidiaries: ACE (Barbados) Holdings Limited, Ace (cidr) Limited, Ace (cr) Holdings, Ace (pm) Limited, Ace (rgb) Holdings Limited, ACE American Insurance Company, ACE American Lloyds Insurance, ACE American Reinsurance Company, ACE Asset Management Inc., ACE Australia Holdings Pty Limited, ACE Bermuda Insurance Ltd., ACE Canada Holdings, Inc., ACE Capital II Limited, ACE Capital III Limited, ACE Capital IV Limited 174 Subsidiaries included in the Index

Officers: Evan G. Greenberg/Chmn., CEO, Pres./$11,833,470.00, Brian E. Dowd/Chmn. - ACE Westchester, Chmn. - ACE USA, CEO - Insurance, North America/$3,603,831.00, John Keogh/CEO - ACE Overseas General, John Bassetto/CEO, Pres. - ACE Asia Pacific, Jacques Q. Bonneau/CEO, Pres. - ACE Tempest Re Group, Dennis Crosby/CEO, Pres. - ACE Westchester, Rees Fletcher/CEO, Pres. - ACE Bermuda, Andrew Kendrick/Chmn., CEO - ACE European Group, John Lupica/CEO, Pres. - ACE USA, James E. Wixtead/CEO - ACE Tempest Re USA, Jorge Luis Cazar/CEO, Pres. - ACE Latin America, Barry Jacobson/Pres. - ACE International Life, Rainer Kirchgaessner/Global Corporate Development Officer - ACE Group, Ken Koreyva/Exec. VP, Treasurer - ACE Group, Helen Wilson/Dir. - Investor Relations *(35 Officers included in Index)*

Directors: Evan G. Greenberg/Chmn., CEO, Pres., Brian Duperreault/60/Non - Exec. Chmn., Michael G. Atieh/54/Dir., Bruce L. Crockett/64/Dir., Peter Menikoff/67/Dir., Robert Ripp/66/Dir., Gary M. Stuart/67/Dir., Mary A. Cirillo/Dir., Robert M. Hernandez/63/Dir., John A. Krol/71/Dir., Thomas J. Neff/70/Dir., Dermot F. Smurfit/63/Dir.

Owners: Wellington Management Company, LLP/13.51%, Franklin Resources, Inc./7.38%, Brian Duperreault, Robert Cusumano, Gary Schmalzriedt, Robert M. Hernandez, Peter Menikoff, Paul Medini, Brian E. Dowd, Gary M. Stuart, Insiders, Thomas J. Neff, FMR Corp./9.90%, Barclays Global Investors, NA/8.62%, Evan G. Greenberg *(21 Owners included in Index)*

Financial Data: *Fiscal Year End:*12/31 *Latest Annual Data:* 12/31/2006

Year	Sales	Net Income
2006	$13,328,000,000	$2,305,000,000
2005	$13,088,000,000	$1,028,000,000
2004	$12,320,633,000	$1,152,686,000

Curr. Assets:	$22,767,000,000	**Curr. Liab.:**	$8,516,000,000	**P/E Ratio:**	8.10
Plant, Equip.:	NA	**Total Liab.:**	$52,857,000,000	**Indic. Yr. Divd.:**	$1.080
Total Assets:	$67,135,000,000	**Net Worth:**	$14,278,000,000	**Debt/ Equity:**	0.1309

Ace Marketing & Promotions Inc

457 Rockaway Ave., Valley Stream, NY, 11581; ***PH:*** 1-516-256-7766; ***Fax:*** 1-516-256-7805; ***http://*** www.acemarketing.net; ***Email:*** sales@acemarketing.net

General - Incorporation	NY	**Stock**- Price on:12/24/2007	$1.85
Employees	10	Stock Exchange	OTC
Auditor	Holtz Rubenstein Reminick LLP	Ticker Symbol	AMKT
Stk Agt	Continental Stock Transfer & Trust Co	Outstanding Shares	8,030,000
Counsel	NA	E.P.S	-$0.07
DUNS No.	NA	Shareholders	NA

Business: The group's principal activity is providing services in advertising specialties and promotional products distribution. The group distributes items manufactured by others to their customers typically with the customers' logos on them. Customer categories include large corporations, local schools, universities, financial institutions, hospitals and not-for-profit organizations. The promotional products are a useful, practical, informative, entertaining, and/or decorative item, most often imprinted with the sponsoring advertiser's name, logo, slogan or message, and typically retained and appreciated by the end recipients who receive them, in many cases free of charge in marketing and communication programs. The group is based in Valley Stream, N.Y.

Primary SIC and add'l.: 7310

CIK No: 0001084267

Officers: Dean L. Julia/40/Chmn., CEO, Michael Trepeta/Co - Founder, Dir., Pres., Sean McDonnell/CFO

Directors: Dean L. Julia/40/Chmn., CEO, Michael Trepeta/Co - Founder, Dir., Pres., Scott J. Novack/Co - Founder, Dir.

Owners: Scott Novack/13.10%, Insiders/45.30%, Dean L. Julia/17.50%, Sean McDonnell, Glenwood Capital Corporation/15.30%, Domenico Iannucci/9.70%, Michael D. Trepeta/17.80%

Financial Data: *Fiscal Year End:*12/31 *Latest Annual Data:* 12/31/2006

Year	Sales	Net Income
2006	$4,507,000	-$481,000
2005	$3,423,000	-$683,000

Curr. Assets:	$2,123,000	*Curr. Liab.:*	$497,000		
Plant, Equip.:	$17,000	*Total Liab.:*	$497,000	*Indic. Yr. Divd.:*	NA
Total Assets:	$2,145,000	*Net Worth:*	$1,648,000	*Debt/ Equity:*	NA

Acergy S.A.

10787 Clay Rd., Houston, TX, 77041; *PH:* 1-713-430-1100; *Fax:* 1-713-461-0039; *http://* www.acergy-group.com; *Email:* info@acergy-group.com

General - Incorporation	Luxembourg	*Stock*- Price on:12/24/2007	$21.89
Employees	7,000	Stock Exchange	NDQ
Auditor	Deloitte & Touche LLP	Ticker Symbol	ACGY
Stk Agt	Citibank N.A	Outstanding Shares	194,950,000
Counsel	NA	E.P.S	$1.14
DUNS No.	NA	Shareholders	NA

Business: The groups principle activities include designing, procuring, building, installing and servicing offshore surface and subsurface infrastructure. The groups operates through five segments namely Africa and Mediterranean, Northern Europe and Canada, North America and Mexico, South America, Asia and Middle East, and other. Customers served by the group include oil and gas industry. Specific customers of the group include ChevronTexaco, Total, Statoil, Petrobras, ExxonMobil and BP. The group operates from Africa, Europe, Canada, America, Mexico and other. The group's quarterly revenue for September 2007 was 709.20 millions of USD.

Primary SIC and add'l.: 1389 1382 8711

CIK No: 0000898685

Subsidiaries: Acergy Norway AS, Acergy Services SA, Acergy Shipping Ltd, Acergy Treasury Ltd., Acergy West Africa SASU, Class 3 Shipping Limited

Officers: Tom Ehret/56/Dir., CEO, Stuart Jackson/CFO, Bruno Chabas/COO, Jean-Luc Laloe/Corporate VP - Strategic Planning, Mark Preece/Corporate VP - Business Development, Keith Tipson/Corporate VP - Human Resources, Johan Rasmussen/Corporate VP, General Counsel, Allen Leatt/CTO, Olivier Carre/Regional VP - Africa - Mediterranean, Jeff Champion/Regional VP - Asia - Middle East, Tony Duncan/Regional VP - North America - Mexico, Oyvind Mikaelsen/Regional VP - Northern Europe - Canada, Philippe Lamoure/Regional VP - South America, Brian Leith/VP - Marine Assets

Directors: Tom Ehret/56/Dir., CEO, Mark Woolveridge/Chmn., James B. Hurlock/Dep. Chmn., George H. Doremus/Dir., Frithjof J. Skouveroe/Dir., Trond O. Westlie/Dir., Peter Mason/Dir.

Owners: State Street Bank/8.14%, FMR Corporation/10.36%, Folketrygdfondet/7.69%, Artisan Partners, LP/9.70%, GE Asset Management/9.80%, DWS Investment GmBH/9.90%

Financial Data: Fiscal Year End: 11/30 *Latest Annual Data:* 11/30/2006

Year	Sales	Net Income
2006	$2,124,200,000	$236,700,000
2005	$1,483,300,000	$139,500,000
2004	$1,241,900,000	$5,100,000

Curr. Assets:	$1,403,600,000	*Curr. Liab.:*	$919,500,000	*P/E Ratio:*	53.58
Plant, Equip.:	$645,600,000	*Total Liab.:*	$1,509,500,000	*Indic. Yr. Divd.:*	$0.180
Total Assets:	$2,209,200,000	*Net Worth:*	$699,700,000	*Debt/ Equity:*	NA

Aceto Corp

1 Hollow Ln., Lake Success, NY, 11042; *PH:* 1-516-627-6000; *Fax:* 1-516-627-6093; *http://* www.aceto.com; *Email:* aceto@aceto.com

General - Incorporation	NY	*Stock*- Price on:12/24/2007	$8.77
Employees	216	Stock Exchange	NDQ
Auditor	BDO Seidman, LLP	Ticker Symbol	ACET
Stk Agt	Bank of New York	Outstanding Shares	24,320,000
Counsel	NA	E.P.S	$0.365
DUNS No.	08-052-1768	Shareholders	NA

Business: The group's principal activities are to market, sell and distribute pharmaceutical, fine and industrial chemicals. The group's business is organized into four segments. The agrochemical segment sells herbicides, fungicides and insecticides. The chemicals and colorants segment sells specialty chemicals used in adhesives, coatings and cosmetics, in addition to dyes and pigment intermediates. The health sciences segment sells the active ingredients for generic pharmaceuticals, vitamins and nutritional supplements as well as products used in preparation of pharmaceuticals. The institutional sanitary supplies and other segment sells cleaning solutions, fragrances and deodorants. The group operates in the United States, Europe, Asia- pacific and Australia. Its customers include industrial chemical and pharmaceutical companies. On 05-Jan-2004, the group acquired pharma waldhof.

Primary SIC and add'l.: 5191 5122 5169

CIK No: 0000002034

Subsidiaries: Acci Realty Corp., Aceto (Holding) B.V., Aceto (Hong Kong) Ltd., Aceto (Shanghai) Ltd., Aceto Agricultural Chemical Corporation Limited, Aceto Agricultural Chemicals Corp., Aceto B.V., Aceto Finechem GmbH, Aceto France S.A.S, Aceto Holding GmbH, Aceto Industrial Chemical Corp., Aceto Ltd., Aceto Luxembourg S.a.r.L., Aceto Pharma GmbH - India, Aceto Pharmaceutical (Shanghai) Ltd. 23 Subsidiaries included in the Index

Officers: Leonard S. Schwartz/61/Chmn., CEO, Theodore Ayvas/Dir. - Corporate Communications, Investor Relations, Douglas Roth/CFO, Corp. Sec., Frank Debenedittis/54/Sr. VP, Vincent Miata/55/Sr. VP

Directors: Leonard S. Schwartz/61/Chmn., CEO, Hans C. Noetzli/65/Dir., Albert L. Eilender/63/Dir., Robert A. Wiesen/55/Dir., Ira S. Kallem/58/Dir., Stanley H. Fischer/63/Dir., William N. Britton/61/Dir.

Owners: MAK Capital One L.L.C/5.90%, Douglas Roth, Royce & Associates, LLC/8.90%, Insiders/7.00%, William N. Britton, Vincent Miata, Ira S. Kallem, Albert L. Eilender, Frank DeBenedittis, Michael Feinnan, T. Rowe Price Associates, Inc./6.00%, Stanley H. Fischer, Hans Noetzli, Dimension Fund Advisors, Inc./8.70%, Leonard S. Schwartz/4.20% *(16 Owners included in Index)*

Financial Data: Fiscal Year End: 06/30 *Latest Annual Data:* 06/30/2007

Year	Sales	Net Income
2007	$313,473,000	$10,212,000
2006	$297,130,000	$9,237,000
2005	$313,381,000	$10,015,000

Curr. Assets:	$141,106,000	*Curr. Liab.:*	$36,399,000	*P/E Ratio:*	24.36
Plant, Equip.:	$9,339,000	*Total Liab.:*	$51,307,000	*Indic. Yr. Divd.:*	NA
Total Assets:	$166,592,000	*Net Worth:*	$115,053,000	*Debt/ Equity:*	NA

ACG Holdings Inc

100 Winners Cir., Brentwood, TN, 37027; *PH:* 1-615-377-0377; *http://* www.amcolorgraphics.com

General - Incorporation	DE	*Stock*- Price on:12/24/2007	NA
Employees	NA	Stock Exchange	NA
Auditor	Ernst & Young LLP	Ticker Symbol	NA
Stk Agt	NA	Outstanding Shares	NA
Counsel	NA	E.P.S	NA
DUNS No.	60-789-9903	Shareholders	NA

Business: The group's principle activity is to provide printing services. The business is classified into two main segments namely, commercial printing and premedia services. The commercial printing industry provides publication and sales to retail advertisement inserts, comics, local newspapers, TV guide listings and others. The operations of the group are carried out through nine printing plants in the United States and Canada. The premedia services are conducted through its wholly owned subsidiary, American color division and include capture, manipulation, transmission and distribution of images. The group operates solely in domestic market.

Primary SIC and add'l.: 2759 2752 7389

CIK No: 0000856710

Subsidiaries: American Color Graphics, Inc., American Images of North America, Inc., Sullivan Marketing, Inc., Sullivan Media Corporation

Owners: Patrick W. Kellick/1.80%, Denis S. Longpr/0.50%, The Morgan Stanley Leveraged Equity Fund II, L.P./37.60%, Kathleen A. DeKam/1.40%, Stuart R. Reeve/1.60%, Morgan Stanley Capital Investors, L.P./0.50%, Stephen M. Dyott/9.50%, Insiders/14.50%, First Plaza Group Trust/10.80%, Morgan Stanley Capital Partners III, L.P./14.20%

Achievers Magazine Inc

220 Cambie St., Ste. 400, Vancouver, V6B 2M9; *PH:* 1-604-689-3983

General - Incorporation	NV	*Stock*- Price on:12/24/2007	$0.95
Employees	NA	Stock Exchange	OTC
Auditor	Amisano Hanson	Ticker Symbol	ACMZ
Stk Agt	Empire Stock Transfer Inc.	Outstanding Shares	NA
Counsel	Warren J. Soloski	E.P.S	NA
DUNS No.	NA	Shareholders	NA

Business: The groups principal activity is to operate publishing articles. The group operates from the United States.

Primary SIC and add'l.: 2721

CIK No: 0001284450

Subsidiaries: Achievers Publishing Inc.

Officers: Arto Tavukciyan/49/Dir., CEO, Pres., Sec., Treasurer, Lyndon Grove/74/Dir., VP - Editorial Production, Alexander Ozer/49/VP - Marketing, Promotion

Directors: Arto Tavukciyan/49/Dir., CEO, Pres., Sec., Lyndon Grove/74/Dir., VP - Editorial Production

Owners: Lyndon Grove/9.79%, Arto Tavukciyan/55.59%, Insiders/65.38%

Financial Data: Fiscal Year End: 07/31 *Latest Annual Data:* 7/31/2006

Year	Sales	Net Income
2006	NA	-$139,000

Curr. Assets:	NA	*Curr. Liab.:*	$339,000		
Plant, Equip.:	NA	*Total Liab.:*	$339,000	*Indic. Yr. Divd.:*	NA
Total Assets:	NA	*Net Worth:*	-$339,000	*Debt/ Equity:*	NA

Acies Corp

14 Wall St., Ste 1620, New York, NY, 10005; *PH:* 1-212-931-5188; *Fax:* 1-212-202-6339; *http://* www.aciesinc.com

General - Incorporation	NV	*Stock*- Price on:12/24/2007	$0.045
Employees	13	Stock Exchange	OTC
Auditor	Malone & Bailey, P.C	Ticker Symbol	ACIE
Stk Agt	American Stock Transfer & Trust Co.	Outstanding Shares	51,170,000
Counsel	NA	E.P.S	-$0.023
DUNS No.	NA	Shareholders	NA

Business: The group's principle activity is to provide Internet-based Web design services. The group also provides e-business consulting, business deployment, custom Web site and Web based software development and e-business research and testing services to small and medium-size businesses. The group's services include Web site design, Web site hosting, Web site maintenance, Web and computer programming and search engine placement services. The group markets its products through direct sales. The group's intellectual properties consist of terencenet.com and breakthepattern.com. The group's major customers are America's favorite golf schools and interbasix inc.

Primary SIC and add'l.: 7375

CIK No: 0001138462

Subsidiaries: Acies, Inc.

Officers: Oleg Firer/Chmn., CEO, Pres., Michael H. Steeneck/Sr. VP - Sales, Marketing, Jeffrey A. Tischler/Dir., CFO, Exec. VP, Yakov Shimon/VP - Technology, Data Management

Directors: Oleg Firer/Chmn., CEO, Pres., Jeffrey A. Tischler/Dir., CFO, Exec. VP, Jeffrey D. Klores/Dir., Bonnie W. Wachtel/Dir., William B.G. Scigliano/Dir.

Owners: Jeffrey A. Tischler/6.81%, Yakov Shimon/18.83%, Bristol Investment Fund, Ltd./7.13%, Bonnie K. Wachtel/1.17%, Oleg Firer/21.41%, Insiders/45.83%, Jeffrey D. Klores, Miron Guilliadov/14.50%, William B.G. Scigliano

Financial Data: Fiscal Year End: 03/31 *Latest Annual Data:* 03/31/2007

Year	Sales	Net Income
2007	$11,823,000	-$1,131,000
2006	$8,980,000	-$903,000
2005	$3,920,000	-$3,341,000

Curr. Assets:	$1,051,000	*Curr. Liab.:*	$1,079,000		
Plant, Equip.:	$189,000	*Total Liab.:*	$1,113,000	*Indic. Yr. Divd.:*	NA
Total Assets:	$1,282,000	*Net Worth:*	$169,000	*Debt/ Equity:*	NA

ACL Semiconductors Inc

B24-B27,1/F., Block B, Proficient Industrial Ctr., 6 Wang Kwun Rd., Kowloon; *PH:* 852-27991996; *http://* www.atlantic.com.hk; *Email:* info@atlantic.com.hk

General		Stock	
Incorporation	DE	Price on:12/24/2007	NA
Employees	NA	Stock Exchange	OTC
Auditor	Stonefield Josephson, Inc	Ticker Symbol	ACLO
Stk Agt	American Stock Transfer & Trust Co.	Outstanding Shares	NA
Counsel	Sullivan & Worcester LLP	E.P.S	NA
DUNS No.	NA	Shareholders	NA

Business: The group's principal activities are to distribute electronic components under the samsung brand name. These products comprise of dram and graphic ram, flash, sram and mask rom for the Hong Kong and southern China markets. On 08-Sep-2003 the company formed through reverse merger of Atlantic components ltd.

Primary SIC and add'l.: 5065

CIK No: 0000934445

Subsidiaries: Samsung Electronics H.K. Co., Ltd., Samsung HK

Owners: Chung-Lun Yang/78.90%, Insiders/78.90%

Financial Data: *Fiscal Year End:*12/31 *Latest Annual Data:* 12/31/2005

Year	Sales	Net Income
2005	$110,208,000	$260,000
2004	$133,244,000	-$454,000
2003	$72,673,000	-$1,438,000

Curr. Assets:	$8,349,000	Curr. Liab.:	$8,072,000		
Plant, Equip.:	$102,000	Total Liab.:	$8,072,000	Indic. Yr. Divd.:	NA
Total Assets:	$8,832,000	Net Worth:	$761,000	Debt/ Equity:	NA

Acme Communications Inc

2101 E 4th St., Ste. 202A, Santa Ana, CA, 92705; *PH:* 1-714-245-9499; *Fax:* 1-714-245-9494; *http://* www.acmecommunications.com; *Email:* ir@acmecommunications.co

General		Stock	
Incorporation	DE	Price on:12/24/2007	$4.89
Employees	186	Stock Exchange	NDQ
Auditor	KPMG LLP	Ticker Symbol	ACME
Stk Agt	U.S. Stock Transfer Corp	Outstanding Shares	16,050,000
Counsel	Irell & Manella	E.P.S	$1.05
DUNS No.	NA	Shareholders	NA

Business: The group's principal activity is to own and operate nine broadcast television stations in medium-sized markets across the United States. The group acquires and develops independently owned stations, under-performing stations and construction permits for new stations that have growth potential and demographic profile. The group's programs include the wb network prime time programming, kids' wb, syndicated programming; and local programming. These programs are targeted at younger audiences, in particular, young adults, teens and kids. On 21-Mar-2003, the group sold two of its stations kplr-TV (st. Louis) and kwbp-TV (portland, Oregon).

Primary SIC and add'l.: 6719 4833

CIK No: 0001092013

Subsidiaries: ACME Communications, Inc, Clear Channel Communications, Inc., Emmis Communications Corporation, Tribune Company

Officers: Jamie Kellner/Chmn., Founder, CEO/$258,500.00, Brent Stephenson/VP - Engineering, FCC Compliance, Doug Gealy/Founder, Dir., COO, Pres./$397,170.00, Steve Bailey/VP - Promotion, Tom Allen/Founder, Dir., Exec. VP, CFO/$402,862.00, Sandi Gehring/VP, GM - Daily Buzz, Sharon Weiler/VP, Dir. - Sales, Bob Shaw/VP - Programming, Stan Gill/Station GM, Dan Phillippi/Station GM - Knoxville, WB 20, Steve Shanks/Station GM - Green Bay, Appleton, WB 14, Bill Snider/Station GM - Champaign, Springfield, Decatur, WB 23, Chris Plunkett/Investor Contact, Todd St. Onge/Investor Contact, Jutta Gebauer/Acting Controller *(16 Officers included in Index)*

Directors: Jamie Kellner/Chmn., Founder, CEO, James Collis/Dir., John Conlin/Dir., Michael Corrigan/Dir., Tom Allen/Founder, Dir., Exec. VP, CFO, Brian McNeill/Dir., Frederick Wasserman/53/Dir., Thomas Embrescia/Dir., Doug Gealy/Founder, Dir., COO, Pres.

Owners: West Creek Capital, Inc./7.23%, Frederick Wasserman, Thomas Allen/5.54%, Insiders/25.97%, Edward Danduran, Brian McNeill/7.54%, Jamie Kellner/7.36%, Alta Communications, Inc./Burr, Egan, Deleage & Co., Inc./7.54%, Thomas Embrescia, Dimensional Fund Advisors LP/8.40%, CEA Capital Partners USA, LP/9.57%, John Conlin, Wynnefield Capital Management LLC/16.66%, Michael Corrigan, Gabelli Investors, Inc./6.00% *(16 Owners included in Index)*

Financial Data: *Fiscal Year End:*12/31 *Latest Annual Data:* 12/31/2006

Year	Sales	Net Income
2006	$34,789,000	-$4,179,000
2005	$40,934,000	-$15,945,000
2004	$46,936,000	-$17,547,000

Curr. Assets:	$33,564,000	Curr. Liab.:	$56,198,000	P/E Ratio:	4.29
Plant, Equip.:	$18,508,000	Total Liab.:	$83,814,000	Indic. Yr. Divd.:	$0.500
Total Assets:	$139,244,000	Net Worth:	$55,430,000	Debt/ Equity:	0.2452

Acme United Corp

60 Round Hill Rd., Fairfield, CT, 06824; *PH:* 1-203-254-6060; *Fax:* 1-203-254-6019; *http://* www.acmeunited.com

General		Stock	
Incorporation	CT	Price on:12/24/2007	$15.06
Employees	120	Stock Exchange	AMEX
Auditor	Ernst & Young LLP	Ticker Symbol	ACU
Stk Agt	American Stock Transfer & Trust Co.	Outstanding Shares	3,520,000
Counsel	Brody, Wilkinson & Ober	E.P.S	$1.018
DUNS No.	00-118-0207	Shareholders	NA

Business: The group's principal activities are to manufacture and distribute cutting devices, measuring instruments and safety products for school, office and home use. The products of the group include scissors, shears, rulers, first aid kits and related products. The products are sold to wholesale, contract and retail stationery distributors, office supply super stores, school supplies distributors, drug store retailers and mass market retailers. The group manufactures its products in the United States and Germany and markets in the United States, Germany, Canada and England. On 28-May-2004, the group acquired clauss cutlery.

Primary SIC and add'l.: 5090 3421 5112 2678

CIK No: 0000002098

Subsidiaries: Acme United (Asia Pacific) Limited, Acme United Europe GmbH, Acme United Limited

Officers: Walter C. Johnsen/Chmn., CEO, Pres./$538,093.00, Paul G. Driscoll/VP, CFO, Sec., Treasurer/$254,564.00, Brian S. Olschan/Dir., Exec. VP, COO/$442,052.00, Larry H. Buchtmann/VP - Operations, Technology/$188,182.00, James A. Benkovic/Sr. VP - Global Sales/$251,366.00

Directors: Walter C. Johnsen/Chmn., CEO, Pres., Stevenson E. Ward/Dir., George R. Dunbar/Dir., Brian S. Olschan/Dir., Exec. VP, COO, Susan H. Murphy/Dir., Gary D. Penisten/Dir., Richmond Y. Holden/Dir., Rex L. Davidson/58/Dir., Stephen Spinelli/53/Dir.

Owners: Paul G. Driscoll/1.10%, Brian S. Olschan/3.30%, Walter C. Johnsen/16.90%, Rex L. Davidson, George R. Dunbar/1.35%, James A. Benkovic, Scott R. Asen/10.49%, Stevenson E. Ward, Larry H. Buchtmann/1.56%, Richmond Y. Holden/1.14%, Gary D. Penisten/3.03%, Stephen Spinelli, Insiders/27.94%, Susan M. Murphy

Financial Data: *Fiscal Year End:*12/31 *Latest Annual Data:* 12/31/2006

Year	Sales	Net Income
2006	$56,863,000	$3,886,000
2005	$49,946,000	$2,937,000
2004	$43,381,000	$3,238,000

Curr. Assets:	$31,487,000	Curr. Liab.:	$6,026,000		
Plant, Equip.:	$2,540,000	Total Liab.:	$16,889,000	Indic. Yr. Divd.:	$0.160
Total Assets:	$35,021,000	Net Worth:	$18,131,000	Debt/ Equity:	0.5635

ACNB Corp

16 Lincoln Sq., Gettysburg, PA, 17325; *PH:* 1-717-334-3161; *Fax:* 1-717-334-9319; *http://* www.acnb.com

General		Stock	
Incorporation	PA	Price on:12/24/2007	$18.5
Employees	260	Stock Exchange	OTC
Auditor	Beard Miller Co. LLP	Ticker Symbol	ACNB
Stk Agt	Registrar & Transfer Co	Outstanding Shares	5,710,000
Counsel	NA	E.P.S	$1.29
DUNS No.	16-099-4083	Shareholders	NA

Business: The group's principal activity is to provide consumer, commercial and fiduciary banking services. These services are provided to the individuals, businesses, public entities and community organizations through seventeen offices in adams, cumberland and york counties in Pennsylvania. The services include accepting demand, savings and time deposits and providing secured and unsecured commercial and consumer loans. The group also provides trust services, which include services as executor and trustee under wills and deeds, estate planning services, custodian and agent for various investment companies.

Primary SIC and add'l.: 6712 9999 6021

CIK No: 0000715579

Subsidiaries: A National Banking Association, Adams County National Bank, Pennbanks Insurance Company, Russell Insurance Group, Inc

Officers: Thomas A. Ritter/56/CEO, Pres./$327,967.00, Frank C. Russell/Pres., CEO - Russell Insurance Group, Inc/$267,478.00, Lynda L. Glass/Sec., Treasurer Exec. VP - Assist. Sec./$190,880.00, David W. Cathell/Sr. VP, CFO Principal Financial Officer/$109,222.00

Directors: Richard D. Guise/74/Vice Chmn., Ronald L. Hankey/67/Chmn., Marian B. Schultz/58/Dir., Alan J. Stock/50/Dir., Wayne E. Lau/73/Dir., Jennifer L. Weaver/60/Dir., Harry L. Wheeler/67/Dir., Philip P. Asper/59/Dir., Frank Elsner/47/Dir., Daniel W. Potts/55/Dir.

Owners: Lynda L. Glass, Thomas A. Ritter, James E. Williams, Frank C. Russell, David W. Cathell, Alan J. Stock, Robert W. Miller, Jennifer L. Weaver, James J. Lott, Daniel W. Potts, Frank Elsner, Wayne E. Lau, Harry L. Wheeler, Ronald L. Hankey, Insiders/1.14% *(17 Owners included in Index)*

Financial Data: *Fiscal Year End:*12/31 *Latest Annual Data:* 12/31/2006

Year	Sales	Net Income
2006	$58,199,000	$7,290,000
2005	$51,449,000	$7,376,000
2004	$43,617,000	$9,308,000

Curr. Assets:	$20,656,000	Curr. Liab.:	$729,688,000	P/E Ratio:	14.34
Plant, Equip.:	$14,871,000	Total Liab.:	$887,453,000	Indic. Yr. Divd.:	$0.800
Total Assets:	$964,757,000	Net Worth:	$77,304,000	Debt/ Equity:	NA

Acorda Therapeutics Inc

15 Skyline Dr., Hawthorne, NY, 10532; *PH:* 1-914-347-4300; *Fax:* 1-914-347-4560; *http://* www.acorda.com; *Email:* info@acorda.com

General		Stock	
Incorporation	DE	Price on:12/24/2007	$17.52
Employees	126	Stock Exchange	NDQ
Auditor	KPMG LLP	Ticker Symbol	ACOR
Stk Agt	Registrar & Transfer Co	Outstanding Shares	24,130,000
Counsel	Covington and Burling	E.P.S	-$1.14
DUNS No.	NA	Shareholders	NA

Business: The groups principle activities include identifying, developing and commercializing novel therapies. The products of the group include Zanaflex Capsules, Zanaflex, Fampridine-SR, Neuregulin Program, Remyelinating Antibody Program and Chondroitinase Program. The group products sold under the trade name Zanaflex(R). Customers served by the group include McKesson, Cardinal and Amerisource. Specific customer of the group is TMS Professional Markets Group, LLC. The group operates from the United States. The quarterly revenue of the group for September 2007 was 10.46 millions of USD.

Primary SIC and add'l.: 2834 2833

CIK No: 0001008848

Subsidiaries: MS Research and Development Corp.

Officers: Ron Cohen/Dir., CEO, Pres./$1,411,222.00, Jacqueline C. Bresnahan/Member - Scientific Advisors Network, Mary B. Bunge/Member - Scientific Advisors Network, Carl W. Cotman/Member - Scientific Advisors Network, James Fawcett/Member - Scientific Advisors Network, Martin Grumet/Member - Scientific Advisors Network, Eugene Johnson/Member - Scientific Advisors Network, Mark D. Noble/Member - Scientific Advisors Network, Melitta Schachner/Member - Scientific Advisors Network, Jerry Silver/Member - Scientific Advisors Network, Patrick A. Tresco/Member - Scientific Advisors Network, Mark H. Tuszynski/Member - Scientific Advisors Network, Stephen G. Waxman/Member - Scientific Advisors Network, Wise Young/Dir. - Scientific Advisors Network, Andrew R. Blight/Chief Scientific Officer/$629,042.00 *(24 Officers included in Index)*

Directors: Ron Cohen/Dir., CEO, Pres., Barry Greene/Dir., Sandra Panem/Dir., Barclay A. Phillips/Dir., Lorin J. Randall/Dir., Steven M. Rauscher/Dir., Ian F. Smith/Dir.

Owners: Andrew R. Blight, Lorin J. Randall, Barry Greene, Atlas/Visium Entities/5.10%, Barclay Phillips/2.30%, Third Point Entities/9.50%, Ron Cohen/4.00%, Steven Rauscher, Morgan Stanley Entities/10.90%, Fidelity Entities/7.60%, David Lawrence, Insiders/12.00%, Ridgeback Entities/13.80%, Mary Fisher, Wise Young *(18 Owners included in Index)*

Financial Data: *Fiscal Year End:*12/31 **Latest Annual Data:** 12/31/2006

Year	Sales	Net Income
2006	$27,351,000	-$24,019,000
2005	$5,146,000	-$35,530,000
2004	NA	-$44,741,000

Curr. Assets:	$72,233,000	**Curr. Liab.:**	$38,910,000		
Plant, Equip.:	$1,223,000	**Total Liab.:**	$65,699,000	**Indic. Yr. Divd.:**	NA
Total Assets:	$84,368,000	**Net Worth:**	$18,669,000	**Debt/ Equity:**	0.4825

Acorn Factor Inc

Formerly: Data Systems & Software Inc
4 W Rockland Rd., Montchanin, DE, 19710; *PH:* 1-302-656-1707; *Fax:* 1-302-994-3086; *http://* www.dssiinc.com

General - Incorporation	DE	**Stock** - Price on:12/24/2007	$4.52
Employees	94	Stock Exchange	NDQ
Auditor	Kesselman & Kesselman	Ticker Symbol	ACFN
Stk Agt	American Stock Transfer & Trust Co.	Outstanding Shares	9,590,000
Counsel	Ehrenreich Eilenberg & Krause LLP	E.P.S	-$0.56
DUNS No.	78-587-4041	Shareholders	NA

Business: The group's principal activities are to provide consulting and development services for computer software and systems. The group operates in three segments: computer hardware, energy intelligence solutions and software consulting and development. Computer hardware segment is an authorized dealer and a value-added-reseller of computer hardware. Energy intelligence solutions segment develops and markets load control, data communications and other energy intelligence solutions for electric utilities and their customers. Software consulting and development segment provides consulting and development services for computer software and systems. The group provides its services primarily to customers in Israel and the United States. As a result of the private equity financing transactions and other agreements, effective Apr 1, 2003, comverge is no longer a controlled subsidiary of the company.

Primary SIC and add'l.: 3577 7372 3674 7379 7371 7373

CIK No: 0000880984

Subsidiaries: dsIT Solutions Ltd.

Officers: John A. Moore/Dir., CEO, Pres., Michael Barth/CFO, Sheldon Krause/Sec., General Counsel, Christianna Hannum Miller/Dir. - Communications, Scott Mossbrooks/Contact - Southern US, Comverge, Dave Hyland/Contact - Northern US, Saskatchewan, Manitoba, Ontario, Quebec, Comverge, Dave Lentsch/Contact - Western US, Akaska, Hawaii, Mexico, Central America, Pacific Rim, Comverge, Dick Preston/Contact - Strategic Sales, Comverge, Inc

Directors: John A. Moore/Dir., CEO, Pres., George Morgenstern/Chmn., Samuel Zentman/62/Dir., Richard J. Giacco/56/Dir., Richard Rimer/Dir., Scott Ungerer/Dir., Joseph Musanti/51/Dir.

Owners: George Morgenstern/4.60%, Benny Sela, Michael Barth, Samuel M. Zentman, Richard J. Giacco, Insiders/13.30%, Richard Rimer/1.00%, John A. Moore/7.10%

Financial Data: *Fiscal Year End:*12/31 **Latest Annual Data:** 12/31/2006

Year	Sales	Net Income
2006	$4,117,000	-$6,136,000
2005	$21,864,000	-$1,318,000
2004	$30,113,000	-$1,172,000

Curr. Assets:	$3,603,000	**Curr. Liab.:**	$3,344,000		
Plant, Equip.:	$445,000	**Total Liab.:**	$7,719,000	**Indic. Yr. Divd.:**	NA
Total Assets:	$7,258,000	**Net Worth:**	-$461,000	**Debt/ Equity:**	NA

ACR Group Inc

3200 Wilcrest Dr., Ste. 440, Houston, TX, 77042; *PH:* 1-713-780-8532; *http://* www.acrgroup.com

General - Incorporation	TX	**Stock** - Price on:12/24/2007	$4.87
Employees	483	Stock Exchange	AMEX
Auditor	BDO Seidman LLP	Ticker Symbol	BRR
Stk Agt	Chase Mellon Shareholder Services LLC	Outstanding Shares	12,060,000
Counsel	Robert D. Remy	E.P.S	$0.494
DUNS No.	03-883-9163	Shareholders	NA

Business: The group's principal activity is to supply equipment and parts for heating, ventilation, air conditioning and refrigeration in the southeastern United States, Texas, Nevada, New Mexico, Colorado and California. The supplies and equipment are sold to installing contractors and dealers and other technically trained customers responsible for the installation, repair and maintenance of equipment systems. The group has 45 branch operations in nine states.

Primary SIC and add'l.: 5075 7623 5078

CIK No: 0000711307

Subsidiaries: ACR Supply, LLC, ACR Supply, LP, CAC Distributors, Inc., Contractors Heating and Supply, LP, ETI Texas, Inc., Florida Cooling Supply, Inc., Heating and Cooling Supply, LLC, Lifetime Filter, Inc., Total Supply, Inc., Valley Supply, Inc., West Coast HVAC Supply, Inc., Westbrook GP, LLC

Officers: Alex Trevino/71/Chmn., CEO, Pres., John Forsythe/Pres. - Heating, Cooling Supply, Robert Bodemer/Purchasing Mgr. - Heating, Cooling Supply, Stephen A. Trevino/44/Dir., General Counsel, Sr. VP, Ron Miller/Controller - Contractor's Heating, Supply, LLC, Ralph Dierdorff/Credit Mgr. - Contractor's Heating, Supply, LLC, Steve Blanchard/Acting Mgr. - Contractor's Heating, Supply, LLC, Mike Tucci/Pres. - ACH Supply, Anthony R. Maresca/56/Dir., Sr. VP, CFO, Treasurer, Mike Spradling/Acting Mgr. - ACR Supply, LLC, Mike Knoop/Pres. - Florida Cooling Supply, Inc, Lana Radowick/Controller - Florida Cooling Supply, Inc, Bill Maitland/Credit Mgr. - Florida Cooling Supply, Inc, Ronnie Floyd/Pres. - Total Supply, Inc, Pete Bly/Controller - Total Supply, Inc *(25 Officers included in Index)*

Directors: Alex Trevino/71/Chmn., CEO, Pres., Stephen A. Trevino/44/Dir., General Counsel, Sr. VP, Alan D. Feinsilver/59/Dir., Anthony R. Maresca/56/Dir., Sr. VP, CFO, Treasurer, Thomas J. Reno/65/Dir., Jo E. Shaw/73/Dir., Roland H. St. Cyr/77/Dir., Marshall G. Webb/64/Dir.

Owners: Alan D. Feinsilver/1.60%, Stephen A. Trevino/14.50%, Alex Trevino/15.50%, Roland H. St. Cyr/0.40%, Insiders/28.20%, Thomas J. Reno/0.20%, Anthony R. Maresca/6.40%, DST Investments/10.50%

Financial Data: *Fiscal Year End:*02/28 **Latest Annual Data:** 2/28/2006

Year	Sales	Net Income
2006	$204,312,000	$2,754,000
2005	$199,553,000	$4,211,000
2004	$174,353,000	$2,395,000

Curr. Assets:	$48,292,000	**Curr. Liab.:**	$22,411,000	**P/E Ratio:**	9.86
Plant, Equip.:	$4,461,000	**Total Liab.:**	$45,669,000	**Indic. Yr. Divd.:**	NA
Total Assets:	$58,727,000	**Net Worth:**	$13,058,000	**Debt/ Equity:**	1.3497

Acrex Ventures Ltd

570 Granville St. , Ste. 1400, Vancouver, BC, V6C 3P1; *PH:* 1-604-618-1758; *Fax:* 1-604-687-4212; *http://* www.acrexventures.com; *Email:* info@acrexventures.com

General - Incorporation	BC	**Stock** - Price on:12/24/2007	$0.18
Employees	NA	Stock Exchange	OTC
Auditor	Amisano Hanson	Ticker Symbol	AXVEF
Stk Agt	Computershare Investor Services	Outstanding Shares	NA
Counsel	NA	E.P.S	NA
DUNS No.	NA	Shareholders	NA

Business: The groups principal activity is to explore minerals and natural gas. The group operates through two segments namely British Columbia and Ontario. The group operates from the United States and Canada.

Primary SIC and add'l.: 1081

CIK No: 0001194506

Officers: Malcolm T.J. Powell/CEO, Pres., Carl R. Jonsson/Dir., Sec., CFO

Directors: Frank Lang/Chmn., Robin Merrifield/Dir., Gregory G. Crowe/Dir., Carl R. Jonsson/Dir., Sec., CFO, Arthur G. Troup/Dir.

Owners: Greg Crowe, Malcolm T.J. Powell/4.84%, Carl R. Jonsson/1.02%, Frank A. Lang/1.37%, Arthur G. Troup

Financial Data: *Fiscal Year End:*12/31 **Latest Annual Data:** 12/31/2006

Year	Sales	Net Income
2006	NA	-$930,000
2005	NA	-$535,000
2004	NA	-$699,000

Curr. Assets:	$625,000	**Curr. Liab.:**	$15,000		
Plant, Equip.:	NA	**Total Liab.:**	$15,000	**Indic. Yr. Divd.:**	NA
Total Assets:	$625,000	**Net Worth:**	$610,000	**Debt/ Equity:**	NA

Acrongenomics Inc

1530 9 Ave. SE, Calgary, AB, T2G 0T7; *PH:* 1-800-689-8181; *http://* www.acrongen.com; *Email:* info@acrongen.com

General - Incorporation	NV	**Stock** - Price on:12/24/2007	$0.92
Employees	NA	Stock Exchange	OTC
Auditor	Amisano Hanson	Ticker Symbol	AGNM
Stk Agt	Pacific Stock Transfer Company	Outstanding Shares	NA
Counsel	Clark Wilson LLP	E.P.S	NA
DUNS No.	NA	Shareholders	NA

Business: The groups principal activities include investing and commercializing novel technology platforms concerning the Life Sciences sector. The group operates from the United States.

Primary SIC and add'l.: 2835

CIK No: 0001104502

Subsidiaries: Acrongenomics Hellas S.A

Officers: Dimitri Goundis/Dir., CEO, Manos Topoglidis/33/Dir., CTO, Member - Scientific Advisory Board, Platon Tzouvalis/43/Dir., Pres., Member - Scientific Advisory Board, Ron Lizee/53/Dir., CFO

Directors: Dimitri Goundis/Dir., CEO, Evan Manolis/Dir., Member - Scientific Advisory Board, Andrew De Mello/Member - Scientific Advisory Board, John De Mello/Member - Scientific Advisory Board, Platon Tzouvalis/43/Dir., Pres., Member - Scientific Advisory Board, Ron Lizee/53/Dir., CFO, Manos Topoglidis/33/Dir., CTO, Member - Scientific Advisory Board, Donal Bradley/Member - Scientific Advisory Board

Owners: Ronald Lize, Platon Tzouvalis, Insiders

Financial Data: *Fiscal Year End:*12/31 **Latest Annual Data:** 12/31/2006

Year	Sales	Net Income
2006	NA	-$2,480,000
2005	NA	-$14,154,000
2004	NA	-$1,863,000

Curr. Assets:	$5,000	**Curr. Liab.:**	$190,000		
Plant, Equip.:	NA	**Total Liab.:**	$190,000	**Indic. Yr. Divd.:**	NA
Total Assets:	$5,000	**Net Worth:**	-$185,000	**Debt/ Equity:**	NA

Across America Real Estate Corp

Formerly: Across America Real Estate Development Corp
700 17th St., Ste. 1200, Denver, CO, 80202; *PH:* 1-303-893-1003; *http://* www.aard.us

General - Incorporation	CO	**Stock** - Price on:12/24/2007	$2.85
Employees	17	Stock Exchange	OTC
Auditor	Cordovano & Honeck LLP	Ticker Symbol	AARD
Stk Agt	Corporate Stock Transfer, Inc.	Outstanding Shares	16,040,000
Counsel	NA	E.P.S	-$0.08
DUNS No.	NA	Shareholders	NA

Business: The group's principal activity is to provide 100% financing for rapid retail expansion. The company also provides guidance and create financing solutions in order to increase retail productivity and profit. The company creates relationships with real estate developers, banks, and build-to-suit retailers to target the underserved, profitable niche of the national retail market. The company has helped numerous companies achieve success through property acquisition.

Primary SIC and add'l.: 6500

CIK No: 0001233275

Subsidiaries: 119th and Ridgeview LLC, 53rd and Baseline LLC, AARD-Belle Creek LLC, AARD-Charmar-Olive Branch LLC, AARD-Cypress Sound LLC, AARD-Greeley-Lot 3 LLC, AARD-Stonegate LLC, Aard-tsd-csk Firestone LLC, Across America Financial Services Inc., Across America Real Estate Exchange Inc., CCI Corona LLC, CCI Southeast LLC, Cross Country Properties II LLC, Cross Country Properties III LLC, Eagle Palm I LLC 20 Subsidiaries included in the Index

Officers: Ann L. Schmitt/47/Dir., CEO, Pres., Joni K. Troska/48/Sec., Controller, James W. Creamer/CFO, John Whitson/Mgr. - National Sales, Terry Thompson/Sr. VP - Operations

Directors: Ann L. Schmitt/47/Dir., CEO, Pres., Eric Balzer/Dir., Brent G. Backman/Dir., Joseph Zimlich/Dir.

Owners: Brent G. Backman/67.20%, Sarmat, LLC/20.50%, Ann L. Schmitt, James W. Creamer, Eric Balzer/1.00%, Insiders/69.90%, Joseph Zimlich, Joni K. Troska

Financial Data: Fiscal Year End:12/31 Latest Annual Data: 12/31/2006

Year	Sales	Net Income
2006	$8,460,000	-$736,000
2005	$7,952,000	$78,000
2004	$1,788,000	$26,000

Curr. Assets:	$1,772,000	Curr. Liab.:	$526,000		
Plant, Equip.:	$16,949,000	Total Liab.:	$13,364,000	Indic. Yr. Divd.:	NA
Total Assets:	$19,011,000	Net Worth:	$5,647,000	Debt/ Equity:	3.4146

ACS-Tech80 Ltd

14700 28th Ave. N., Ste. 25, Plymouth, MN, 55447; **PH:** 1-763-559-7669; **Fax:** 1-763-559-0110; **http://** www.acs-tech80.com; **Email:** info@acsmotioncontrol.com

General - Incorporation	Israel	Stock- Price on:12/24/2007	$3.94
Employees	65	Stock Exchange	NDQ
Auditor	Lurie Besikof Lapidus & Co. LLP	Ticker Symbol	ACSEF
Stk Agt	Continental Stock Transfer & Trust Co	Outstanding Shares	3,280,000
Counsel	NA	E.P.S.	-$0.007
DUNS No.	60-016-5450	Shareholders	NA

Business: The group's principle activities include developing and producing fully-digital motion control products utilized in advanced industrial application, medical scanning and imaging systems, semi-conductor manufacturing equipment, electronic testing and inspection stations and high-quality printing machinery. The group operates from United States.

Primary SIC and add'l.: 3670
CIK No: 0001038144
Subsidiaries: ACS-Tech80 Inc., Technology 80 Inc
Owners: Zeev Kirshenboim/27.00%, Jacob Engel/18.40%
Financial Data: Fiscal Year End:12/31 Latest Annual Data: 12/31/2006

Year	Sales	Net Income
2006	$13,503,000	$1,388,000
2005	$11,428,000	$974,000
2004	$14,376,000	$2,253,000

Curr. Assets:	$12,139,000	Curr. Liab.:	$2,666,000	P/E Ratio:	8.10
Plant, Equip.:	$488,000	Total Liab.:	$2,868,000	Indic. Yr. Divd.:	NA
Total Assets:	$15,776,000	Net Worth:	$12,908,000	Debt/ Equity:	NA

ACT Teleconferencing Inc

1526 Cole Blvd., Ste. 300, Golden, CO, 80401; **PH:** 1-303-233-3500; **Fax:** 1-303-238-0096; **http://** www.acttel.com

General - Incorporation	CO	Stock- Price on:12/24/2007	$0.08
Employees	324	Stock Exchange	OTC
Auditor	Hein & Assoc. LLP	Ticker Symbol	ACTT
Stk Agt	Computershare Trust Co	Outstanding Shares	NA
Counsel	Faegre & Benson LLP	E.P.S.	-$0.326
DUNS No.	62-089-1903	Shareholders	NA

Business: The group's principle activity is to provide high quality audio, video, data and Internet based conferencing services to businesses and organizations worldwide. They enable the clients to conduct electronic meetings by linking multiple participants in geographical dispersed locations. The group operates sales and service delivery centers in nine countries. These centers are installed with computer-managed telecommunications equipment known as bridges for audio conferencing and multi-point control units in the case of video conferencing. The group operates in the United Kingdom, the Netherlands, France, Belgium, Germany, Hong Kong, Singapore, Australia and Canada. Major customers of the services are multinationals, banks, law firms, accounting firms, high tech companies and a variety of other businesses. The group's quarterly revenue for March 2007 was 14.25 millions of USD.

Primary SIC and add'l.: 4899
CIK No: 0000918709
Subsidiaries: ACT Business Solutions Limited, ACT Proximity, Inc., ACT Research, Inc., ACT Teleconferencing (Pty) Limited, ACT Teleconferencing Belgium SA, ACT Teleconferencing BV, ACT Teleconferencing Canada Inc., ACT Teleconferencing France SA, ACT Teleconferencing GmbH, ACT Teleconferencing Hong Kong Limited, ACT Teleconferencing Limited, ACT Teleconferencing of Bermuda Limited, ACT Teleconferencing Services, Inc., formerly ACT Capital, Inc., ACT Teleconferencing Singapore PTE Limited, ACT VideoConferencing, Inc., formerly NBS, Inc. 17 Subsidiaries included in the Index
Officers: Peter E. Salas/Executive Chmn., Mark Kelly/CTO, Marina Bogard/Chief Sales, Marketing Officer, Rick Fresia/52/CFO
Directors: Peter E. Salas/Executive Chmn., Michael W. Shepherd/Dir., Carlos P. Salas/Dir., Malcolm M. Aslin/Dir., Clarke H. Bailey/Dir., Naomi Perry/Dir.
Owners: Gene Warren, Mark K. Kelly, Gary Martin Glaser, Malcolm M. Aslin, Insiders, Kenneth J. Knopp, Naomi Perry, William S. Lapp, Insiders, Dolphin Management Inc., Gary Martin Glaser, Peter E. Salas, Malcolm M. Aslin, Dolphin Management Inc., Gerald D. Van Eeckhout (18 Owners included in Index)
Financial Data: Fiscal Year End:12/31 Latest Annual Data: 12/31/2006

Year	Sales	Net Income
2006	$53,621,000	$1,797,000
2005	$50,964,000	-$18,153,000
2004	$53,540,000	-$21,164,000

Curr. Assets:	$13,737,000	Curr. Liab.:	$12,056,000		
Plant, Equip.:	$9,384,000	Total Liab.:	$13,082,000	Indic. Yr. Divd.:	NA
Total Assets:	$24,550,000	Net Worth:	-$11,552,000	Debt/ Equity:	NA

Actel Corp

2061 Stierlin Ct., Mountain View, CA, 94043; **PH:** 1-650-318-4200; **Fax:** 1-650-318-4600; **http://** www.actel.com; **Email:** tech@actel.com

General - Incorporation	CA	Stock- Price on:12/24/2007	$13.99
Employees	565	Stock Exchange	NDQ
Auditor	Ernst & Young LLP	Ticker Symbol	ACTL
Stk Agt	Norwest Bank Minnesota N.A	Outstanding Shares	26,280,000
Counsel	Wilson Sonsini Goodrich & Rosati	E.P.S.	$0.17
DUNS No.	14-822-2045	Shareholders	NA

Business: The group's principal activities are to design, develop and market field programmable gate arrays (FPGAs) and supporting products and services. FPGAs are used by manufacturers of communications, computer, consumer, industrial, military and aerospace and other electronic systems their products and get them to market faster. In support of FPGAs, the group offers asic conversion products, intellectual property (IP) cores, development systems, programming hardware, debugging tool kits and demonstration boards, a web-based resource center and design and programming services. The customers include Abbott Laboratories, Alcatel, Bae Systems, The Boeing Company, Cisco Systems, Inc., Hewlett-Packard Company, Honeywell International Inc., LG Electronics Inc., Lockheed Martin Corporation, Marconi Corporation PLC, Nokia, Nortel Networks Corporation, Raytheon Company, Siemens AG and Varian Medical Systems, Inc.

Primary SIC and add'l.: 3674
CIK No: 0000907687
Subsidiaries: Actel Engineering Eurl, Actel Europe SARL, Actel Europe, Ltd., Actel GmbH, Actel Italia SRL, an corporation, Actel Japan, KK, Actel Pan-Asia Corporation, Actel Pan-Asia, Hong Kong Ltd., Actel Semiconductor Limited, an corporatio
Officers: John C. East/Dir., CEO, Pres., Anand Kumar/Contact Person - Vietnam, Esmat Hamdy/Sr. VP - Technology, Operations, Tanmoy Das/Contact Person - Vietnam, Barbara McArthur/VP - Human Resources, Fares Mubarak/Sr. VP, David Van De Hey/VP, General Counsel, Jon Anderson/VP - Finance, CFO, Tony Farinaro/VP, GM - Design Services, Esam Elashmawi/VP - Software Engineering, Patrizio Piasentin/Contact - France, Edmund Gerstl/Contact Person - Germany, Mauro Ardizzoia/Contact Person - Italy, Sharon Blades/Contact Person - United Kingdom, Jeff Moris/Contact Person - Belgium (42 Officers included in Index)
Directors: John C. East/Dir., CEO, Pres., Robert G. Spencer/Dir., Dan McCranie/Dir., Jim Fiebiger/Dir., Jacob Jacobsson/Dir.
Financial Data: Fiscal Year End:12/31 Latest Annual Data: 12/31/2005

Year	Sales	Net Income
2005	$179,397,000	$7,036,000
2004	$165,536,000	$2,394,000

Curr. Assets:	$233,307,000	Curr. Liab.:	$57,926,000	P/E Ratio:	82.29
Plant, Equip.:	$23,859,000	Total Liab.:	$66,663,000	Indic. Yr. Divd.:	NA
Total Assets:	$339,384,000	Net Worth:	$272,721,000	Debt/ Equity:	NA

Action Products International Inc

1101 N Keller Rd., Ste. E, Orlando, FL, 32810; **PH:** 1-407-481-8007; **Fax:** 1-407-481-2781; **http://** www.apii.com; **Email:** info@apii.com

General - Incorporation	FL	Stock- Price on:12/24/2007	$1.62
Employees	30	Stock Exchange	NDQ
Auditor	Moore Stephens Lovelace P.A	Ticker Symbol	APII
Stk Agt	Registrar & Transfer Co	Outstanding Shares	5,230,000
Counsel	Cohen Berke Bernstein Et Al	E.P.S.	-$0.41
DUNS No.	05-330-2733	Shareholders	NA

Business: The group's principal activity is to design, manufacture and market educational, non-violent toys, books and other educational and entertainment products. These products are sold to toy stores, specialty retailers, education outlets and museums in the United States and all over the world. The group's products are sold under the proprietary brand names such as space voyagers(R), climb@tron(tm), earthlore (R), i dig dinosaurs(R), woodkits (TM), drop zone extreme(tm), and jay jay the jet plane(tm) thomas & friends(tm). The product line includes action figures, play sets and activity kit highlighting on space, dinosaurs, science and nature. The group's services are provided to customers throughout 50 states in the United States and several foreign countries including the United Kingdom, Spain, Canada and Japan.

Primary SIC and add'l.: 3944 5092
CIK No: 0000747435
Subsidiaries: Action Products Canada, Ltd
Officers: Richard Malagodi/48/Pres., COO - Action Toys, Crafts Division
Directors: Cecilia Sternberg/57/Dir.
Owners: Warren Kaplan, Scott Runkel, Insiders, Ronald S. Kaplan, Financial& Investment Management Group, Ltd., Richard S. Malagodi, Barry Render, Ann E.W. Stone, Judith Kaplan
Financial Data: Fiscal Year End:12/31 Latest Annual Data: 12/31/2006

Year	Sales	Net Income
2006	$7,437,000	-$2,715,000
2005	$9,481,000	-$21,000
2004	$9,109,000	-$68,000

Curr. Assets:	$4,249,000	Curr. Liab.:	$2,583,000		
Plant, Equip.:	$1,000,000	Total Liab.:	$2,583,000	Indic. Yr. Divd.:	NA
Total Assets:	$6,750,000	Net Worth:	$4,168,000	Debt/ Equity:	NA

Actions Semiconductor Company Ltd

15-1, NO.1, HIT Rd., Tangjia, Zhuhai, Guangdong, 519085; **PH:** 86-7563392353; **Fax:** 86-7563392251; **http://** www.actions-semi.com; **Email:** investor.relations@actions-semi.com

General - Incorporation	Cayman Islands	Stock- Price on:12/24/2007	$6.21
Employees	422	Stock Exchange	NDQ
Auditor	Deloitte Touche Tohmatsu CPA Ltd	Ticker Symbol	ACTS
Stk Agt	Mellon Investor Services LLC	Outstanding Shares	86,000,000
Counsel	NA	E.P.S.	$0.63
DUNS No.	NA	Shareholders	NA

Business: The groups principle activities include developing and manufacturing personal media players. The products of the group include MP3 SoC, Energy metering SoC, TxRx SoC and Testing solutions. Specific customers of the group include Hong Kong Beta Power Tech, Jess Technology, MCU Power, Power Radio and Sino-Mos Electronic. In the year 2005, the group acquired Hi- Trend Investment Holding Co., Ltd. The group operates from China and Hong Kong. The group's quarterly revenue for September 2007 was 27.04 millions of USD.

Primary SIC and add'l.: 3577 3674 3672

CIK No: 0001342068

Subsidiaries: Actions Microelectronics Co., Ltd., Actions Semiconductor Co., Ltd., Actions Technology (HK) Company Limited

Officers: Nan-Horng Yeh/CEO, Shao Chuan Li/Dir., CTO, Hsiang-Wei Lee/CFO

Directors: Byung-Jin Kang/59/Chmn., Paul Hsiao/Dir., Chiu Tzu-Yin/52/Dir., Fred Chen/Dir., Shao Chuan Li/Dir., CTO, Tzu-Yin Chiu/Dir., Yu-Hsin Casper Lin/Dir., Hui-Dong Tien/49/Dir.

Owners: Tetrad Venture Pte Limited/7.14%, Wang De Liang/1.00%, Zhao Guang Min/3.40%, Rich Dragon Consultants Limited/5.99%, Zhu Wen Ge/1.84%, Wu Zhang Liang/2.02%, Cai Jian Yu/1.54%, Ding Ran, Insiders/10.47%

Financial Data: Fiscal Year End: 12/31   **Latest Annual Data:** 12/31/2006

Year	Sales	Net Income
2006	$171,862,000	$74,561,000
2005	$149,622,000	$73,605,000
2004	$57,257,000	$26,485,000

Curr. Assets:	$225,523,000	Curr. Liab.:	$28,165,000	P/E Ratio:	53.58
Plant, Equip.:	$6,749,000	Total Liab.:	$28,651,000	Indic. Yr. Divd.:	NA
Total Assets:	$237,671,000	Net Worth:	$209,020,000	Debt/ Equity:	NA

ActionView International Inc

221 10th Ave. E , Ste. 103, Vancouver, BC, V5T 4V1; **PH:** 1-604-878-0200; **Fax:** 1-604-879-8224; **http://** www.actionview.ca, **Email:** info@actionview.ca

General - Incorporation	NV	**Stock**- Price on:12/24/2007	$0.0069
Employees	NA	Stock Exchange	OTC
Auditor	Dale Matheson Carr-Hilton LaBonte LLP	Ticker Symbol	AVWI
Stk Agt.	Pacific Stock Transfer Company	Outstanding Shares	NA
Counsel	NA	E.P.S.	NA
DUNS No.	NA	Shareholders	NA

Business: The groups principle activity is to develop a system that provides advertisement. The group products include scrolling sign and pop program. Specific customers of the group include Chuangrun Media Ltd and Open Media Management Pty Ltd. The group operates from United Ara Emirates, Australia, the United States and China. The groups quarterly revenue for September 2007 was 0.06 millions of USD.

Primary SIC and add'l.: 7312

CIK No: 0000789667

Subsidiaries: ActionView Advertising Systems Inc

Officers: Rick Mari/Founder, CEO, Ron McGregor/CFO, Greg McArthur/VP - Business Development

Directors: Rick Mari/Founder, CEO, Christopher Stringer/Chmn.

Owners: Christopher Stringer/9.00%, Rick Mari/15.10%, Insiders/30.50%, Thomas Schulte/6.40%

Financial Data: Fiscal Year End: 12/31   **Latest Annual Data:** 12/31/2006

Year	Sales	Net Income
2006	$87,000	-$1,477,000
2005	$83,000	-$3,291,000
2004	$131,000	-$1,460,000

Curr. Assets:	$56,000	Curr. Liab.:	$1,471,000		
Plant, Equip.:	$0	Total Liab.:	$1,471,000	Indic. Yr. Divd.:	NA
Total Assets:	$56,000	Net Worth:	-$1,416,000	Debt/ Equity:	NA

ACTIS Global Ventures Inc

1905 Aston Ave. Ste. 101, Carlsbad, CA, 92008; **PH:** 1-760-448-2498; **http://** www.actisglobalventures.com; **Email:** ir@actisglobalventures.com

General - Incorporation	NV	**Stock**- Price on:12/24/2007	$0.0016
Employees	NA	Stock Exchange	OTC
Auditor	Squar, Peterson, LLP	Ticker Symbol	AGLV
Stk Agt.	American Stock Transfer & Trust Co.	Outstanding Shares	NA
Counsel	NA	E.P.S.	-$0.008
DUNS No.	NA	Shareholders	NA

Business: The groups principle activity is to market wellness products in the areas of bioenergetics, nutrition and beauty. The group products include Biopro Cell Chip(TM), Biopro Qlink, Bionutratonic(TM), QX-3(TM) and Bioproduce(TM).The group marketed its products under the trade names Channoine(R) , LeanCHOICES(TM) and BIOPRODUCE(TM).The group operates through two segments namely direct sales and direct response television marketing. The group operates from Manila, Soth Africa, Cebu, Davao City , Australia, the United States. The group's quarterly revenue for September 2007 was 3.14 millions of USD.

Primary SIC and add'l.: 5122

CIK No: 0001161461

Officers: Ray W. Grimm/Dir., CEO, CFO, Alfred Hanser/Dir., Pres., Sec.

Directors: Ray W. Grimm/Dir., CEO, CFO, Alfred Hanser/Dir., Pres., Sec., Joseph V. Caracciolo/Dir.

Owners: Joseph V. Caracciolo, Alfred Hanser/3.70%, Ray W. Grimm/21.60%, Insiders/25.72%

Financial Data: Fiscal Year End: 12/31   **Latest Annual Data:** 12/31/2006

Year	Sales	Net Income
2006	$10,543,000	-$5,547,000
2005	$7,755,000	-$3,022,000
2004	$1,918,000	-$3,139,000

Curr. Assets:	$1,018,000	Curr. Liab.:	$10,483,000		
Plant, Equip.:	$201,000	Total Liab.:	$10,574,000	Indic. Yr. Divd.:	NA
Total Assets:	$1,593,000	Net Worth:	-$8,981,000	Debt/ Equity:	NA

Active Power Inc

2128 W Braker Ln., Bldg. 12, Austin, TX, 78758; **PH:** 1-512-836-6464; **Fax:** 1-512-836-4511; **http://** www.activepower.com; **Email:** info@activepower.com

General - Incorporation	DE	**Stock**- Price on:12/24/2007	$1.67
Employees	164	Stock Exchange	NDQ
Auditor	Ernst & Young LLP	Ticker Symbol	ACPW
Stk Agt	American Stock Transfer & Trust CO.	Outstanding Shares	50,100,000
Counsel	NA	E.P.S.	-$0.36
DUNS No.	NA	Shareholders	NA

Business: The group's principle activities include designing and manufacturing power quality products that provide consistent electric power. Its flywheel energy storage system provides low-cost and non-toxic replacement for lead-acid batteries used in conventional power quality installations. The company has developed cleansource, a battery-free power quality system in conjunction with caterpillar that distributes the system under the brand name of cat(R) ups. The products are sold for use in commercial facilities in many different industries that all share a critical need for reliable, high-quality power. The major trademarks of the group are active power, active power + logo, cleansource and making electricity better. They include plastic manufacturers, semiconductor manufacturers, hospitals, credit card processing centers, broadcasters, advanced data centers and electric utilities. The group operates from United States.

Primary SIC and add'l.: 3699

CIK No: 0001044435

Officers: James A. Clishem/Dir., CEO, Pres., Karl Schuetze/VP - Engineering, Uwe Schrader-Hausmann/VP - Technical Services, Michael Chibib/Investor Relations Officer, David Beatty/VP - Engineering/$262,236.00, Derek Jones/Contact - Corporate Communications, Gary Rackow/VP - Americas, Jim Murphy/VP - EMEA, Apac, John K. Penver/CFO, VP - Finance, Sec./$340,483.00, Jason Rubin/VP - Manufacturing, David E. Perkins/CTO, Lisa Brown/VP - Marketing - Customer Service, Corporate Communications/$246,177.00

Directors: James A. Clishem/Dir., CEO, Pres., Benjamin L. Scott/58/Chmn., Richard E. Anderson/43/Dir., Rodney S. Bond/63/Dir., Ake Almgren/61/Dir., Jan H. Lindelow/62/Dir., Brad Boston/54/Dir.

Owners: Brad Boston, Ake Almgren, James A. Clishem/1.58%, David M. Beatty, John K. Penver, Sound Energy Partners, Inc./9.98%, Joseph F. Pinkerton/8.71%, Dawson Herman Capital Management, Inc./8.31%, Benjamin L. Scott, Jan H. Lindelow, Dimensional Fund Advisors LP/5.83%, Richard E. Anderson, Rodney S. Bond, Lisa M. Brown, Insiders/5.22%

Financial Data: Fiscal Year End: 12/31   **Latest Annual Data:** 12/31/2006

Year	Sales	Net Income
2006	NA	NA
2005	NA	NA
2004	NA	NA

Curr. Assets:	$39,153,000	Curr. Liab.:	$7,948,000		
Plant, Equip.:	$7,341,000	Total Liab.:	$7,948,000	Indic. Yr. Divd.:	NA
Total Assets:	$46,726,000	Net Worth:	$38,778,000	Debt/ Equity:	NA

Activecore Technologies Inc

Formerly: IVP Technology Corp
156 Front St. W, Ste. 210, Toronto, ON, M5J 2L6; **PH:** 1-416-252-6200; **http://** www.activecore.com

General - Incorporation	NV	**Stock**- Price on:12/24/2007	NA
Employees	NA	Stock Exchange	OTC
Auditor	Weinberg & Co. P.A	Ticker Symbol	ATVEE
Stk Agt	Pacific Stock Transfer Company	Outstanding Shares	NA
Counsel	NA	E.P.S.	NA
DUNS No.	NA	Shareholders	NA

Business: The group's principal activities are to develop, market, license, publish and distribute software and related products for both the consumer and enterprise marketplaces. The group operates within the enterprise software market sector. It provides software and services which enable the customers to integrate and extend the current systems and data bases, to reach new or existing markets. The group markets their products and services under two trade names activecore technologies and mdi solutions. On 22-Jun-2004, the group acquired twincentric limited.

Primary SIC and add'l.: 7372

CIK No: 0001011601

Subsidiaries: ActiveCore Technologies Limited, Twincentric Limited

Officers: Peter Hamilton/52/Dir., CEO, Russ Hamilton/Customer, Technical Support

Directors: Peter Hamilton/52/Dir., CEO, Stephen Lewis/Dir., Stephen J. Smith/Dir.

Owners: Insiders/24.80%, Debbie Gracie-Smith/5.70%, Efrem Ainsley/0.30%, George Theodore/6.20%, Stephen J. Smith/0.60%, Andrew Wickett/5.70%, Peter J. Hamilton/6.10%, Stephen Lewis/0.50%

Activeworlds Corp

40 Wall St., 58th Fl., Newburyport, NY, 10005; **PH:** 1-212-509-1700; **http://** www.activeworlds.com; **Email:** info@activeworlds.com

General - Incorporation	DE	**Stock**- Price on:12/24/2007	$0.55
Employees	NA	Stock Exchange	OTC
Auditor	Pannell Kerr Forster	Ticker Symbol	AWLD
Stk Agt	Interwest Transfer Company, Inc.	Outstanding Shares	5,320,000
Counsel	Peabody & Arnold	E.P.S.	-$0.09
DUNS No.	NA	Shareholders	NA

Business: The group's principal activity is to provide software products and services that enable the efficient development and delivery of three-dimensional content over the Internet and intranet. The group's technology allows the users to create objects and structures in three-dimensional virtual environments. The three-dimensional technology has a wide range of applications in the entertainment industry, education industry, distance learning and e-commerce. Its software products have been licensed to boeing, centropolis studios, siemens electromedical group, kodak and philips multimedia. It markets its software and related products in the United States, the United Kingdom, scandinavia, Spain, Germany, France, Korea, Brazil, Taiwan, Russia and China. On 10-Jul-2002, the group sold its business to its former management and became inactive. It is currently seeking business opportunities.

Primary SIC and add'l.: 7372 7379

CIK No: 0001089531

Subsidiaries: AWLD, Inc

Officers: Rick Noll/40/Dir., CEO, Pres., Sean Deson/43/CFO, Pres., Treasurer, Sec., Dir.

Directors: Rick Noll/40/Dir., CEO, Pres., J. P. McCormick/45/Chmn., Sean Deson/43/CFO, Pres., Treasurer, Sec., Dir.

Owners: J. P. McCormick/7.50%, Sean Deson/6.90%, Richard F. Noll/7.80%, Michael Gardner/48.30%, Insiders/6.90%

Financial Data: Fiscal Year End:12/31 Latest Annual Data: 12/31/2006

Year	Sales	Net Income
2006	NA	-$649,000
2005	NA	-$652,000
2004	NA	-$133,000

Curr. Assets:	$247,000	**Curr. Liab.:**	$9,000		
Plant, Equip.	NA	**Total Liab.:**	$9,000	**Indic. Yr. Divd.:**	NA
Total Assets:	$247,000	**Net Worth:**	$239,000	**Debt/ Equity:**	NA

ActivIdentity Corp

6623 Dumbarton Cir., Fremont, CA, 94555; **PH:** 1-510-574-0100; **Fax:** 1-510-574-0101; **http://** www.actividentity.com

General - Incorporation	DE	Stock - Price on:12/24/2007	$4.57
Employees	313	Stock Exchange	NDQ
Auditor	BDO Seidman, LLP	Ticker Symbol	ACTI
Stk Agt	Bank of New York	Outstanding Shares	45,710,000
Counsel	NA	E.P.S	-$0.23
DUNS No.	NA	Shareholders	NA

Business: The groups principle activity is to provide digital identity assurance solutions.The products of the group include smart cards, USB tokens, one time password tokens, soft OTP tokens. The group products sold under the trade name ActivClien(TM), SecureLogin(R), 4TRESS(TM), ActivID(TM) and ActivKey(TM). Customers served by the group include enterprise, government, healthcare, and financial services markets. Specific customers of the group include Honeywell International Inc, IBM Global Services, Lenel Systems International Inc, Novell Inc and Sun Microsystems Inc. The group operates from North America, Europe and Asia Pacific. The quarterly revenue of the group for September 2007 was 59.55 millions of USD.

Primary SIC and add'l.: 7372

CIK No: 0001183941

Subsidiaries: A8 Corporation Ltd., ActivCard Developments Pty. Ltd., ActivCard GmbH, ActivCard Ireland Ltd., ActivIdentity (Australia) Pty. Ltd., ActivIdentity (Canada) Inc., ActivIdentity (Hong Kong) Limited, ActivIdentity (Singapore) Pte. Ltd., ActivIdentity (UK) Limited, ActivIdentity Europe S.A. (formerly known as ActivCard S.A.), ActivIdentity K.K., ActivIdentity South Africa (Proprietary) Pty. Ltd., ActivIdentity, Inc., Protocom Consulting Limited, Protocom Development Systems Europe BV 16 Subsidiaries included in the Index

Officers: Thomas Jahn/CEO, Tim Polakowski/Corporate Public Relations Contact, Yves Audebert/Pres., Founder, Chief - Engineering, Mark Lustig/CFO, Isabelle Joulot/EMEA Public Relations Contact, Phil Jacobs/Apac Public Relations Contact, Mahima Patnaik/Investor Relations Contact

Directors: Richard A. Kashnow/Chmn., Jason Hart/Dir., James E. Ousley/Dir., Richard White/Dir., Jim Frankola/Dir.

Owners: Richard White, OZ Management, L.L.C./7.70%, Thomas Jahn, James W. Frankola, James Ousley, Richard Kashnow, Jason Hart/3.40%, Ben Barnes, Mark J. Lustig, Yves Audebert/2.60%, Insiders/7.10%

Financial Data: Fiscal Year End:09/30 Latest Annual Data: 9/30/2006

Year	Sales	Net Income
2006	$53,375,000	-$22,472,000
2005	$42,156,000	-$47,926,000
2004	$26,910,000	-$27,407,000

Curr. Assets:	$150,704,000	**Curr. Liab.:**	$26,549,000		
Plant, Equip.:	$3,612,000	**Total Liab.:**	$31,662,000	**Indic. Yr. Divd.:**	NA
Total Assets:	$200,988,000	**Net Worth:**	$168,953,000	**Debt/ Equity:**	NA

Activision Inc

3100 Ocean Pk. Blvd., Santa Monica, CA, 90405; **PH:** 1-310-255-2000; **Fax:** 1-310-255-2100; **http://** www.activision.com

General - Incorporation	DE	Stock - Price on:12/24/2007	$18.81
Employees	2,125	Stock Exchange	NDQ
Auditor	PricewaterhouseCoopers LLP	Ticker Symbol	ATVI
Stk Agt	Continental Stock Transfer & Trust Co	Outstanding Shares	282,990,000
Counsel	Bryan Cave LLP	E.P.S	$0.49
DUNS No.	09-853-3342	Shareholders	NA

Business: The group's principal activities are to publish, develop and distribute interactive entertainment and leisure software products. The group's products include a variety of game platforms, including pcs, the sony playstation console system and the nintendo 64-console system. The interactive entertainment software is developed primarily for personal computers and the topics include action, adventure, strategy and simulation products. The products are marketed through departmental stores, video rental stores and toy stores. The group has international operations in Canada, the United Kingdom, France, Japan, Australia, Belgium and the Netherlands. In fiscal 2003, the group acquired z-axis ltd, luxoflux corporation and infinity ward.

Primary SIC and add'l.: 6719 7372

CIK No: 0000718877

Subsidiaries: Activision Asia Pacific Holding Pte. Ltd., Activision Beteiligungs GmbH, Activision Canada, Inc., Activision Deutschland GmbH, Activision Europe, Limited, Activision GmbH, Activision International B.V., Activision International Europe, LLC, Activision Italia, S.p.A., Activision Korea, Ltd., Activision Luxembourg S.a.r.l., Activision Productions, Inc., Activision Pty Ltd., Activision Publishing Europe, LLP, Activision Publishing International, Inc. 44 Subsidiaries included in the Index

Officers: Michael Griffith/Pres., CEO - Activision Publishing, Inc/$4,634,089.00, Robert Kotick/Chmn., CEO/$2,844,371.00, Ron Doornink/Dir. - Sr. Advisor, Thomas Tippl/CFO - Activision Publishing, Inc/$3,510,111.00, George Rose/Sr. VP, General Counsel, Sec., Robin Kaminsky/Exec. VP - Publishing/$2,659,668.00, Brian Hodous/Chief Customer Officer - Activision Publishing/$1,251,033.00, Ann Weiser/Chief Human Resources Officer

Directors: Robert Kotick/Chmn., CEO, Brian Kelly/Co - Chmn., Barbara Isgur/Dir., Robert Morgado/Dir., Ron Doornink/Dir. - Sr. Advisor, Robert J. Corti/Dir., Peter J. Nolan/Dir., Richard Sarnoff/Dir.

Owners: Charles J. Huebner, Ronald Doornink, Brian G. Kelly/3.40%, Robert J. Corti, Wellington Management Company, LLP/10.40%, Robert A. Kotick/4.60%, Robin Kaminsky, Robert J. Morgado, Barbara S. Isgur, Brian Hodous, Peter J. Nolan, Richard Sarnoff, Michael J. Griffith, Insiders/9.30%, Thomas Tippl (16 Owners included in Index)

Financial Data: Fiscal Year End:03/31 Latest Annual Data: 3/31/2007

Year	Sales	Net Income
2007	$1,513,012,000	$85,787,000
2006	$1,468,000,000	$41,899,000
2005	$1,405,857,000	$138,335,000

Curr. Assets:	$1,401,233,000	**Curr. Liab.:**	$341,169,000	**P/E Ratio:**	67.18
Plant, Equip.:	$46,540,000	**Total Liab.:**	$382,415,000	**Indic. Yr. Divd.:**	NA
Total Assets:	$1,793,947,000	**Net Worth:**	$1,411,532,000	**Debt/ Equity:**	NA

Actuant Corp

13000 W Silver Spring Dr., Butler, WI, 53007; **PH:** 1-414-352-4160; **Fax:** 1-414-247-5550; **http://** www.actuant.com

General - Incorporation	WI	Stock - Price on:12/24/2007	$59.2
Employees	6,300	Stock Exchange	NYSE
Auditor	PricewaterhouseCoopers LLP	Ticker Symbol	ATU
Stk Agt	National City Bank	Outstanding Shares	27,410,000
Counsel	McDermott Will & Emery	E.P.S	$1.72
DUNS No.	00-658-2779	Shareholders	NA

Business: The group's principal activity is to manufacture and market industrial products and systems. It operates in two business segments: tools and supplies and engineered solutions. The tools and supplies segment markets branded specialized electrical and industrial tools and supplies to hydraulic and electrical wholesale distributors. The customers for the tools and supplies segment include lowe's, ace hardware, the home depot, truserve and w.w. Grainger. The engineered solutions segment designs, manufactures and markets customized motion control systems primarily for original equipment manufacturers. The customers for the engineering solutions segment wilhelm karmann gmbh, fleetwood, monaco, volvo, bertone, jayco, and cts dachsysteme. In Apr 2003, the group acquired shanghai sanxin hydraulic co. Ltd. On 16-Sep-2004, the group acquired yvel s.a.

Primary SIC and add'l.: 3728 3572 3492 3531 3469 3545

CIK No: 0000006955

Subsidiaries: A.W. Sperry Instruments, Inc., Acme Electric Corporation, Acme Electric de Mexico S. De. R.L. de C.V., Acme Electric Mexico Holdings I, Inc., Acme Electric Mexico Holdings II, Inc., Acme Electric MFG de Mexico S. De. R.L. de C.V., Actuant Asia Pte. Ltd., Actuant Australia Ltd., Actuant Canada Corporation, Actuant China Ltd., Actuant Europe CV, Actuant European SarL, Actuant Finance CV, Actuant France SA, Actuant Hydraulic Co. Ltd. 107 Subsidiaries included in the Index

Officers: Robert C. Arzbaecher/Chmn., CEO, Pres., Gustav Boel/Dir., Exec. VP, Mark Goldstein/COO, Andy Lampereur/CFO, Exec. VP, Bill Blackmore/Exec. VP - Actuation Systems, Engineered Products Segments, Brian Kobylinski/Exec. VP - Industrial Segment, Karen Bauer/Dir. - Investor Relations, Karen Yates/Investor Relations Specialist, Chadwick I. Deluka/Corporate Controller, Principal Accounting Officer, Theodore C. Wozniak/50/VP - Business Development

Directors: Robert C. Arzbaecher/Chmn., CEO, Pres., Kathleen J. Hempel/Dir., Larry D. Yost/Dir., Gustav Boel/Dir., Exec. VP, William P. Sovey/Dir., Robert A. Peterson/Dir., Thomas J. Fischer/Dir., William K. Hall/Dir., Dennis K. Williams/Dir.

Owners: Gustav H.P. Boel, Larry D. Yost, T. Rowe Price Associates, Inc./13.40%, Thomas J. Fischer, Capital Research and Management Company/6.40%, William K. Hall, William S. Blackmore, Theodore C. Wozniak, Westfield Capital Management Company Inc./6.10%, Robert A. Peterson, Insiders/4.80%, Andrew G. Lampereur, Kathleen J. Hempel, Mark E. Goldstein, Robert C. Arzbaecher/2.60% (16 Owners included in Index)

Financial Data: Fiscal Year End:08/31 Latest Annual Data: 8/31/2006

Year	Sales	Net Income
2006	$1,201,158,000	$92,588,000
2005	$976,066,000	$71,251,000
2004	$726,851,000	$34,823,000

Curr. Assets:	$390,925,000	**Curr. Liab.:**	$264,394,000	**P/E Ratio:**	19.04
Plant, Equip.:	$94,544,000	**Total Liab.:**	$850,410,000	**Indic. Yr. Divd.:**	$0.040
Total Assets:	$1,213,375,000	**Net Worth:**	$362,965,000	**Debt/ Equity:**	1.4113

Actuate Corp

701 Gateway Blvd., South San Francisco, CA, 94080; **PH:** 1-650-837-2000; **http://** www.actuate.com

General - Incorporation	DE	Stock - Price on:12/24/2007	NA
Employees	582	Stock Exchange	NDQ
Auditor	KPMG LLP	Ticker Symbol	ACTU
Stk Agt	EquiServe Trust Co N.A	Outstanding Shares	60,540,000
Counsel	Gunderson Dettmer	E.P.S	$0.28
DUNS No.	NA	Shareholders	NA

Business: The group's principle activity is to provide an information application software platform. Information applications include business performance management dashboards, information portals as well as business analytic, enterprise reporting and spreadsheet reporting applications.this platform enables large organization and packaged application software vendor to develop and deploy self-service, customer and employee-facing enterprise reporting applications. These applications enable companies to increase their business agility, improve customer and partner relationships, adhere to corporate governance policies and increase revenues. The actuate e.reporting suite 6 product line provides a platform upon which global 9000 and packaged application software vendors create reporting and analytics applications that scale to empower 100 percent of their user community inside and outside the firewall. The group's quarterly revenue for September 2007 was 34.74 millions of USD.

Primary SIC and add'l.: 7372 7371 7373

CIK No: 0001062478

Subsidiaries: Actuate Asia Pacific Pty. Ltd., Actuate Canada Corporation, Actuate Cayman Limited, Actuate France, S.A., Actuate International Corporation, Actuate International Sarl, Actuate Japan Co., Ltd., Actuate Limited, Actuate Pte. Limited, Actuate Software (Shanghai) Co. Ltd., Actuate Software GmbH, Actuate UK Ltd., Nimble Technology, Inc.

Officers: Peter I. Cittadini/Dir., CEO, Pres./$1,458,573.00, Nicolas C. Nierenberg/Chmn., Chief Architect, Daniel A. Gaudreau/Sr. VP - Operations, CFO/$1,033,454.00, Tom McKeever/General Counsel, VP - Corporate Development, Ilene M. Vogt/Sr. VP - Global Field Operations/$686,513.00, Nobby N. Akiha/Sr. VP - Marketing/$405,756.00, Mark A. Coggins/Sr. VP - Engineering/$604,583.00, Thomas P. Ryan/CIO, Sr. VP - Customer Service, Steve Fluin/Sr. VP - Performance Management Division

Directors: Peter I. Cittadini/Dir., CEO, Pres., Nicolas C. Nierenberg/Chmn., Chief Architect, Steven D. Whiteman/Dir., Kenneth E. Marshall/Dir., George B. Beitzel/Dir., Arthur C. Patterson/Dir.

Owners: Heartland Advisors, Inc./6.70%, Nobby N. Akiha, Kenneth E. Marshall, Peter I. Cittadini/8.10%, Mark A. Coggins, Daniel A. Gaudreau/2.00%, Steven D. Whiteman, Ashford Capital Management, Inc./5.30%, Ilene M. Vogt/1.90%, Insiders/18.60%, Arthur A. Patterson/3.10%, Nicolas C. Nierenberg/3.50%, George B. Beitzel, Columbia Wanger Asset Management, L.P./12.30%

Financial Data: *Fiscal Year End:*12/31 *Latest Annual Data:* 12/31/2006

Year	Sales	Net Income
2006	$128,569,000	$13,797,000
2005	$106,401,000	$11,591,000
2004	$104,657,000	$1,298,000

Curr. Assets:	$96,545,000	**Curr. Liab.:**	$59,247,000		
Plant, Equip.:	$4,379,000	**Total Liab.:**	$69,779,000	**Indic. Yr. Divd.:**	NA
Total Assets:	$147,589,000	**Net Worth:**	$77,810,000	**Debt/ Equity:**	0.0005

Acuity Brands Inc

1170 Peachtree St., N.e., Ste. 2400, Atlanta, GA, 30309; *PH:* 1-404-853-1400; *http://* www.acuitybrands.com

General - Incorporation	DE	**Stock**- Price on:12/24/2007	$61.73
Employees	10,600	Stock Exchange	NYSE
Auditor	Ernst & Young LLP	Ticker Symbol	AYI
Stk Agt	Bank of New York	Outstanding Shares	43,440,000
Counsel	NA	E.P.S	$3.37
DUNS No.	NA	Shareholders	NA

Business: The groups principle activity is to provide lighting fixtures. The group provides a broad array of indoor and outdoor lighting fixtures for commercial and institutional, industrial, infrastructure, and residential applications for various markets. The group operates from United States.

Primary SIC and add'l.: 3645 2842 3648

CIK No: 0001144215

Subsidiaries: Acuity Brands Lighting (Hong Kong) Ltd., Acuity Brands Lighting Mexico, S. de R.L. de C.V., Acuity Brands Lighting Operations de Mexico, S. de R.L. de C.V., Acuity Brands Lighting Servicios de Mexico, S. de R.L. de C.V., Acuity Brands Servicios S.A. de C.V., Acuity Enterprise, Inc., Acuity Holdings, Inc., Acuity Insurance (Bermuda) Ltd., Acuity Lighting Group, Inc., Acuity Mexico Holdings, LLC, Acuity Puerto Rico, Inc., Acuity Specialty Products Group, Inc., Acuity Unlimited, Inc., C&G Carandini SA, Castlight de Mexico, S.A. de C.V. 32 Subsidiaries included in the Index

Officers: Vernon J. Nagel/Chmn., CEO, Pres., Kenyon W. Murphy/Exec. VP, Chief Administrative Officer, General Counsel, Richard K. Reece/CFO, Exec. VP, Helen D. Haines/VP, Sec.

Directors: Vernon J. Nagel/Chmn., CEO, Pres., Peter C. Browning/Dir., John L. Clendenin/Dir., Earnest W. Deavenport/Dir., Robert F. McCullough/Dir., Julia B. North/Dir., Ray M. Robinson/Dir., Neil Williams/Dir.

Owners: All directors and executive officers as a group/2.70%, Julia B. North, John L. Clendenin, Richard K. Reece, Peter C. Browning, Robert F. McCullough, John K. Morgan, Neil Williams, Vernon J. Nagel/1.50%, Ray M. Robinson, Wellington Management Company, LLP/5.70%, Kenyon W. Murphy, William A. Holl, Barclays Global Investors, N.A./5.40%

Financial Data: *Fiscal Year End:*08/31 *Latest Annual Data:* 08/31/2007

Year	Sales	Net Income
2007	$2,530,668,000	$148,054,000
2006	$2,393,123,000	$106,562,000
2005	$2,172,854,000	$52,229,000

Curr. Assets:	$737,645,000	**Curr. Liab.:**	$427,794,000	**P/E Ratio:**	21.51
Plant, Equip.:	$215,633,000	**Total Liab.:**	$901,857,000	**Indic. Yr. Divd.:**	$0.600
Total Assets:	$1,444,116,000	**Net Worth:**	$542,259,000	**Debt/ Equity:**	0.6278

AcuNetx Inc

2301 W 205th St., Ste. 102, Torrance, CA, 90501; *PH:* 1-310-328-0477; *Fax:* 1-310-328-0697; *http://* www.acunetx.com; *Email:* contact@acunetx.com

General - Incorporation	NV	**Stock**- Price on:12/24/2007	$0.045
Employees	4	Stock Exchange	OTC
Auditor	Spector & Wong, LLP	Ticker Symbol	ANTX
Stk Agt	Pacific Stock Transfer Company	Outstanding Shares	62,720,000
Counsel	NA	E.P.S	-$0.098
DUNS No.	NA	Shareholders	NA

Business: The groups principle activity is to produce products and technologies for capturing, digital processing and analyzing human eye movements. The group products include neurological diagnostic equipment. Devices designed to test individuals for impaired performance, Orthopedic and craniomaxillofacial surgery, SmartDevice-Connect(TM). The group marketed its products under the trade name SafetyScan(TM) and GenerOs(TM). The group operates from the United States.

Primary SIC and add'l.: 3861 7382 3826 3829 5043 3841 3827

CIK No: 0001097575

Officers: Ronald A. Waldorf/CEO, Pres., Douglas E. MacCarthy/Sr. VP - Operations

Directors: Charles E. Phillips/72/Chmn., Terry R. Knapp/Dir., Robert S. Corrigan/54/Dir.

Owners: Douglas E. MacCarthy/1.10%, Galen Capital Group LLC/6.00%, Robert S. Corrigan/1.30%, Insiders/12.00%, Ronald A. Waldorf/1.60%, Terry R. Knapp/4.10%, Charles E. Phillips/3.80%, Randolph C. Robinson/11.40%

Financial Data: *Fiscal Year End:*12/31 *Latest Annual Data:* 12/31/2006

Year	Sales	Net Income
2006	$2,224,000	-$8,223,000
2005	$1,403,000	-$393,000
2004	$2,085,000	$386,000

Curr. Assets:	$646,000	**Curr. Liab.:**	$1,072,000		
Plant, Equip.:	$30,000	**Total Liab.:**	$1,074,000	**Indic. Yr. Divd.:**	NA
Total Assets:	$1,048,000	**Net Worth:**	-$25,000	**Debt/ Equity:**	NA

Acura Pharmaceuticals Inc

616 N N Ct., Ste. 120, Palatine, IL, 60067; *PH:* 1-847-705-7709; *Fax:* 1-847-705-5399; *http://* acurapharm.com

General - Incorporation	NY	**Stock**- Price on:12/24/2007	$0.99
Employees	13	Stock Exchange	OTC
Auditor	BDO Seidman, LLP	Ticker Symbol	ACPH
Stk Agt	Continental Stock T & T Co.	Outstanding Shares	331,690,000
Counsel	Insurance Carrier	E.P.S	-$0.09
DUNS No.	NA	Shareholders	NA

Business: The group's principal activities are to develop, manufacture and distribute generic drugs and active pharmaceutical ingredients. The group's products include antibiotics, narcotic analgesics, anti-infective and anti-tubercular drugs, antihistamines and antihistaminic decongestants, antitussives and steroids. The group's drug products are marketed in various forms, including liquid and powder preparations, compressed tablets and two-piece, hard-shelled capsules. The generic drug products are marketed by watson to drugstore chains and drug wholesalers. The group has manufacturing facilities in New York and Indiana.

Primary SIC and add'l.: 2834

CIK No: 0000786947

Subsidiaries: Acura Pharmaceutical Technologies, Inc., Axiom Pharmaceutical Corporation

Officers: Andrew D. Reddick/Dir., CEO, Pres., James F. Emigh/VP - Marketing, Administration, Robert A. Seiser/VP, Treasurer, Corporate Controller, Ron J. Spivey/Chief Scientific Officer, Sr. VP, Peter A. Clemens/Sr. VP, CFO, John G. Gilkay/Dir. - EHS, Engineering, Ronald L. Leech/Sr. Dir. Quality Assurance - Quality Control, Analytical Services, Gregory A. Spinner/Dir. - Logistics, Special Projects

Directors: Andrew D. Reddick/Dir., CEO, Pres., Immanuel Thangaraj/Dir., William G. Skelly/Dir., Bruce F. Wesson/Dir., William A. Sumner/Dir., Richard J. Markham/Dir.

Owners: James F. Emigh, Robert A. Seiser, Ron J. Spivey/2.10%, Peter A. Clemens, Andrew D. Reddick/2.60%, William G. Skelly, William A. Sumner, Insiders/5.30%

Financial Data: *Fiscal Year End:*12/31 *Latest Annual Data:* 12/31/2006

Year	Sales	Net Income
2006	NA	-$5,967,000
2005	NA	-$12,075,000
2004	$838,000	-$69,996,000

Curr. Assets:	$467,000	**Curr. Liab.:**	$29,108,000		
Plant, Equip.:	$1,145,000	**Total Liab.:**	$39,899,000	**Indic. Yr. Divd.:**	NA
Total Assets:	$1,619,000	**Net Worth:**	-$38,280,000	**Debt/ Equity:**	NA

Acusphere Inc

500 Arsenal St., Watertown, MA, 02472; *PH:* 1-617-648-8800; *Fax:* 1-617-926-4750; *http://* www.acusphere.com

General - Incorporation	DE	**Stock**- Price on:12/24/2007	$2.23
Employees	116	Stock Exchange	NDQ
Auditor	Deloitte & Touche LLP	Ticker Symbol	ACUS
Stk Agt	American Stock Transfer & Trust Co.	Outstanding Shares	38,480,000
Counsel	Goodwin Procter LLP	E.P.S	-$1.43
DUNS No.	NA	Shareholders	NA

Business: The group's principal activity is to develop new drugs and improved formulations of existing drugs using proprietary porous microparticle technology. The group develops proprietary drug that offers benefits such as improved safety and efficacy, increased patient compliance and greater ease of use. The group's products are in clinical development and are designed to address clinical needs within cardiology, oncology and asthma. The group is a development stage company.

Primary SIC and add'l.: 2834 8731

CIK No: 0001115143

Officers: Sherri C. Oberg/Pres., CEO, Dir., Principal Executive Officer/$765,948.00, Richard Walovitch/Sr. VP - Clinical Research/$338,257.00, David Tuck/Scientific Advisor, William I. Ramage/Executive Consultant, Business Development, Howard Bernstein/Sr. VP - Research, Development/$478,068.00, Michael Picard/Scientific Advisor, Natesa Pandian/Scientific Advisor, Michael R. Slater/Sr. VP - Operations/$327,177.00, John F. Thero/47/Sr. VP, CFO - Principal Financial, Accounting Officer/$569,717.00, Mona Haynes/VP - Marketing, Sales, Eric Huang/Mgr. - Business Development, Dennis Bucceri/65/Sr. VP - Regulatory Affairs

Directors: Sherri C. Oberg/Pres., CEO, Dir., Principal Executive Officer, Garen Bohlin/Dir., Robert S. Langer/Founder, Sandra L. Fenwick/Dir., Derek Lemke-von Ammon/Dir., Frank Baldino/Dir., Martyn Greenacre/Dir.

Owners: Garen Bohlin, Insiders/4.80%, Quaker Capital Management Corporation/8.60%, Richard Walovitch, Howard Bernstein, Frank Baldino, Meditor Group Ltd/7.20%, Sandra Fenwick, Sherri C. Oberg/1.90%, Derek Lemke-Von Ammon, Martyn Greenacre, John F. Thero, Michael R. Slater, Deutsche Bank AG/5.50%, Bank of America Corporation/7.60% *(18 Owners included in Index)*

Financial Data: *Fiscal Year End:*12/31 *Latest Annual Data:* 12/31/2006

Year	Sales	Net Income
2006	$1,781,000	-$61,089,000
2005	$3,429,000	-$44,625,000
2004	$1,714,000	-$29,959,000

Curr. Assets:	$60,591,000	**Curr. Liab.:**	$22,325,000		
Plant, Equip.:	$32,453,000	**Total Liab.:**	$36,373,000	**Indic. Yr. Divd.:**	NA
Total Assets:	$94,822,000	**Net Worth:**	$58,449,000	**Debt/ Equity:**	0.2170

Acxiom Corp

1 Information Way, Ste. 200, Little Rock, AR, 72202; *PH:* 1-501-342-1000; *Fax:* 1-501-342-3913; *http://* www.acxiom.com

General - Incorporation	DE	**Stock**- Price on:12/24/2007	$27.09
Employees	7,100	Stock Exchange	NDQ
Auditor	KPMG LLP	Ticker Symbol	ACXM
Stk Agt	Computershare Shareholder Ser Inc	Outstanding Shares	79,830,000
Counsel	NA	E.P.S	$0.38
DUNS No.	05-196-4047	Shareholders	NA

Business: The group's principal activities are to integrate data, service and technology to create and deliver customer and information management solutions. The group operates in three segments. The services segment provides solutions that integrate and manage customer, consumer, and business data using information management skills and technology. The data and software products segment includes abilitec-enabled solutions that provides the services segment the ability to effectively integrate and manage data. The IT management segment manages technical infrastructure needs of its customers. The services are provided primarily in the United States and the United Kingdom. On 01-Jan-2004, the group acquired Claritas Europe group of companies.

Primary SIC and add'l.: 7375 7372 7379 7374

CIK No: 0000733269

Subsidiaries: Acxiom / Direct Media, Inc., Acxiom / May & Speh, Inc., Acxiom Australia Pty Ltd, Acxiom Canada, Inc., Acxiom CDC, Inc., Acxiom CH, Inc., Acxiom e-Products, Inc., Acxiom European Holdings Ltd., Acxiom Information Security Services, Inc., Acxiom Interim Holdings, Inc., Acxiom RM-Tools, Inc., Acxiom Transportation Services, Inc., Acxiom UWS, Ltd., Digital Impact, Inc., InsightAmerica, Inc. 16 Subsidiaries included in the Index

Officers: David J. Allen/European CEO - Services Division, Jerry C. Jones/Business Development, Legal Leader, Assist. Sec., Terry M. Talley/Chief Technology Leader, Christopher W. Wolf/CFO, Timothy J. Suther/Multi, Industry Client Services Organization Leader - Services Division, Drew A. May/Infobase Organization Leader - Products Division, Thomas N. Mangan/Consulting Organization Leader - Services Division, Katharine Raymond/Investor Relations Officer, Dathan A. Gaskill/Corporate Finance Leader, Treasurer, Catherine L. Hughes/Corporate Governance Officer, Sec., Timothy Watts/Delivery Center Organization Leader, Scott D. Hambuchen/Traditional Services Organization Leader - Services Division, Martin D. Sunde/Infrastructure Management Division Leader, Richard K. Howe/Marketing Organization Leader, Jefferson D. Stalnaker/Financial Services Organization Leader - Services Divison (30 Officers included in Index)

Directors: William T. Dillard/Vice Chmn., Michael J. Durham/57/Chmn., Jeffrey W. Ubben/47/Dir., Stephen M. Patterson/57/Dir., Rodger S. Kline/65/Dir., Chief Administrative Leader, Thomas F. McLarty/62/Dir., Mary L. Good/Dir., Harry C. Gambill/Dir., Halsey R. Wise/43/Dir., Ann Die Hasselmo/64/Dir., William J. Henderson/61/Dir.

Owners: Thomas F. McLarty, James T. Womble/1.90%, Cindy K. Childers, William J. Henderson, Lee L. Hodges, Alex C. Dietz, Jerry C. Jones, Christopher W. Wolf, Rodger S. Kline/3.00%, Halsey R. Wise, Mary L. Good, Ann Die Hasselmo, Richard K. Howe, Insiders/23.30%, Jeffrey W. Ubben/12.80% (21 Owners included in Index)

Financial Data: Fiscal Year End:03/31 **Latest Annual Data:** 3/31/2007

Year	Sales	Net Income
2007	$1,395,136,000	$70,740,000
2006	$1,332,568,000	$64,128,000
2005	$1,223,042,000	$69,718,000

Curr. Assets:	$412,876,000	**Curr. Liab.:**	$387,788,000	**P/E Ratio:**	27.09
Plant, Equip.:	$312,292,000	**Total Liab.:**	$1,134,593,000	**Indic. Yr. Divd.:**	$0.240
Total Assets:	$1,655,904,000	**Net Worth:**	$521,311,000	**Debt/ Equity:**	NA

ADA-ES Inc

8100 SPk. Way, Unit B, Littleton, CO, 80120; **PH:** 1-303-734-1727; **Fax:** 1-303-734-0330; http:// www.adaes.com; **Email:** contactus@adaes.com

General - Incorporation	CO	**Stock** - Price on:12/24/2007	$20.38
Employees	42	Stock Exchange	NDQ
Auditor	Hein & Assoc. LLP	Ticker Symbol	ADES
Stk Agt	Computershare Investor Services LLC	Outstanding Shares	5,640,000
Counsel	NA	E.P.S.	$0.02
DUNS No.	NA	Shareholders	NA

Business: The group's principle activity is to provide environmental technologies and specialty chemicals to the coal burning utility industry. The group also generates revenue from government contracts. The group provides non-toxic chemical conditioners and flue gas conditioning chemicals that offers both technical and economic advantages over the hazardous chemicals. The technology can be used in the cement and petroleum refining industries where emissions need to be controlled. The group has also introduced specialty chemical for utility companies with cyclone furnaces. The group has a government contract to develop a flue gas conditioning agents. The group's quarterly revenue for September 2007 was 5.60 millions of USD.

Primary SIC and add'l.: 3559 6794

CIK No: 0001223112

Subsidiaries: ADA Environment Solutions, LLC, ADA LLC

Officers: Michael Durham/Dir., CEO, Pres., Travis Starns/Mgr. - Mercury Control System Projects, David Graham/Field Services Mgr., Mark H. McKinnies/Dir., CFO, Sr. VP, Catherine Tubman/Contact - Investor Relations, Richard Schlager/VP - Administration, Cam Martin/Dir. - Mercury Control Systems, Sharon Sjostrom/VP - Technology, Beth Turner-Graziano/Human Resources Mgr., Marki Morison-Gille/Office Mgr., Chad Sapp/Engineer II, Robin Stewart/Mgr. - Contract Research & Development, Cody Wilson/Project Engineer - I, Erik Zipp/Field Engineer, Jean C. Bustard/COO (41 Officers included in Index)

Directors: Michael Durham/Dir., CEO, Pres., Jeffrey C. Smith/Chmn., Mark H. McKinnies/Dir., CFO, Sr. VP, Robert H. Lowdermilk/71/Dir., Ronald B. Johnson/Dir., Ramon E. Bisque/Dir., Rollie Peterson/Dir., Duane N. Bloom/Dir., Robert Caruso/Dir., John Eaves/Dir., Derek Johnson/Dir., Richard Swanson/Dir.

Owners: Jeffrey C. Smith, Jonathan S. Barr, Dynamis Advisors LLC/0.09%, John W. Eaves, Richard J. Schlager, Richard Miller, Wellington Management Co. LLP/0.09%, Sharon M. Sjostrom, Ronald B. Johnson, Mazama Capital Management, Inc./0.05%, Insiders, C. Jean Bustard, Michael D. Durham/0.03%, Mark H. McKinnies/0.01%, Rollie J. Peterson

Financial Data: Fiscal Year End:12/31 **Latest Annual Data:** 12/31/2006

Year	Sales	Net Income
2006	$15,488,000	$377,000
2005	$11,028,000	$663,000
2004	$8,417,000	$336,000

Curr. Assets:	$22,439,000	**Curr. Liab.:**	$3,892,000	**P/E Ratio:**	1019.00
Plant, Equip.:	$797,000	**Total Liab.:**	$4,076,000	**Indic. Yr. Divd.:**	NA
Total Assets:	$31,754,000	**Net Worth:**	$27,641,000	**Debt/ Equity:**	NA

Adagio Acquisition I Inc

Formerly: Adagio Acquisition I Inc
535 Madison Ave., 18th Fl., New York, NY, 10022; **PH:** 1-212-418-8573

General - Incorporation	DE	**Stock** - Price on:12/24/2007	NA
Employees	NA	Stock Exchange	NA
Auditor	Raich Ende Malter & Co. LLP	Ticker Symbol	NA
Stk Agt	NA	Outstanding Shares	NA
Counsel	NA	E.P.S.	NA
DUNS No.	NA	Shareholders	NA

Business: The groups principle activity is to provide initial financing services. The group also sets up business to seek the acquisition of, or merger with, an existing company. The group operates from United States.

Primary SIC and add'l.: 6770

CIK No: 0001328999

Adagio Acquisition II Inc

535 Madison Ave., 18th Fl., New York, NY, 10022; **PH:** 1-212-418-8573

General - Incorporation	DE	**Stock** - Price on:12/24/2007	NA
Employees	NA	Stock Exchange	NA
Auditor	Raich Ende Malter & Co. LLP	Ticker Symbol	NA
Stk Agt	Registrar And Transfer Agent	Outstanding Shares	NA
Counsel	NA	E.P.S.	NA
DUNS No.	NA	Shareholders	NA

Business: The group's principal activities are to seek the acquisition of, or merger with, an existing company. The group was organized as a vehicle to investigate and acquire a target company or business seeking the perceived advantages of being a publicly held corporation and, to a lesser extent that desires to employ our funds in its business. The Company will not restrict its potential candidate target companies to any specific business, industry or geographical location and, thus, may acquire any type of business.

Primary SIC and add'l.: 6770

CIK No: 0001329000

Officers: William P. Dioguardi/Dir., Pres., Sec.

Adagio Acquisition III Inc

535 Madison Ave., 18th Fl., New York, NY, 10022; **PH:** 1-212-418-8573

General - Incorporation	DE	**Stock** - Price on:12/24/2007	NA
Employees	NA	Stock Exchange	NA
Auditor	Raich Ende Malter & Co. LLP	Ticker Symbol	NA
Stk Agt	Registrar And Transfer Agent	Outstanding Shares	NA
Counsel	NA	E.P.S.	NA
DUNS No.	NA	Shareholders	NA

Business: The groups principle activity is to seek the acquisition of, or merger with, an existing company. The group operates from United States.

Primary SIC and add'l.: 6770

CIK No: 0001329001

Adams Express Company (The)

7 St. Paul St., Ste. 1140, Baltimore, MD, 21202; **PH:** 1-410-752-5900; **Fax:** 1-410-659-0080; http:// www.adamsexpress.com; **Email:** contact@adamsexpress.com

General - Incorporation	MD	**Stock** - Price on:12/24/2007	$14.99
Employees	NA	Stock Exchange	NYSE
Auditor	Pricewaterhousecoopers LLP	Ticker Symbol	ADX
Stk Agt	American Stock Transfer & Trust Co.	Outstanding Shares	86,080,000
Counsel	NA	E.P.S.	$2.53
DUNS No.	NA	Shareholders	NA

Business: The groups principal activity is to provide financial services. The group operates from the United States. The net assets of the group for the year 2006 were $1,377,418,310.

Primary SIC and add'l.: 6799 6726

CIK No: 0000002230

Officers: Douglas G. Ober/CEO, Joseph M. Truta/63/Pres., Lawrence L. Hooper/55/Chief Compliance Officer, VP, General Counsel, Sec., Maureen A. Jones/60/CFO, VP, Treasurer

Directors: Enrique R. Arzac/66/Dir., Phyllis O. Bonanno/64/Dir., Daniel E. Emerson/83/Dir., Frederic A. Escherich/55/Dir., Roger W. Gale/61/Dir., Thomas H. Lenagh/89/Dir., Kathleen T. McGahran/57/Dir., Craig R. Smith/61/Dir.

Owners: Erik E. Bergstrom, Maureen A. Jones, Joseph M. Truta, Lawrence L. Hooper

Financial Data: Fiscal Year End:12/31 **Latest Annual Data:** 12/31/2006

Year	Sales	Net Income
2006	$185,065,000	$178,524,000
2005	$77,785,000	$44,913,000
2004	$140,616,000	$135,280,000

Curr. Assets:	$51,440,000	**Curr. Liab.:**	$4,315,000	**P/E Ratio:**	18.09
Plant, Equip.:	NA	**Total Liab.:**	$74,417,000	**Indic. Yr. Divd.:**	$1.030
Total Assets:	$1,451,835,000	**Net Worth:**	$1,377,418,000	**Debt/ Equity:**	NA

Adams Golf Inc

2801 E Plano Pkwy., Plano, TX, 75074; **PH:** 1-972-673-9000; **Fax:** 1-972-398-8818; http:// www.adamsgolf.com; **Email:** info@adamsgolf.com

General - Incorporation	DE	**Stock** - Price on:12/24/2007	$2.1
Employees	147	Stock Exchange	OTC
Auditor	KBA Group, LLP	Ticker Symbol	ADGO
Stk Agt	Bank of New York	Outstanding Shares	24,000,000
Counsel	Arter & Hadden	E.P.S.	$0.34
DUNS No.	00-248-5035	Shareholders	NA

Business: The group's principal activity is to design, manufacture, market and distribute golf clubs and provide custom golf club fitting technology. The products are marketed under the brand names tight lies gt irons and i-woods, the tight lies family of fairway woods and drivers, the tom watson signature series of wedges and the gt spec putters. The products are sold to on- and off- course golf shops and selected sporting goods retailers and international distributors. The group offers a variety of different models based on the shape, size and materials used in the club. The group's products are sold throughout the world through a network of 40 independent distributors.

Primary SIC and add'l.: 3949

CIK No: 0001059763

Subsidiaries: Adams Golf GP Corp, Adams Golf Holding Corp., Adams Golf IP, L.P., Adams Golf Japan, Inc., Adams Golf Management Corp, Adams Golf U.K. Limited, Adams Golf, Ltd

Officers: Oliver G. Brewer/45/Inside Dir., CEO, Pres./$786,172.00, Eric T. Logan/42/Sr. VP, CFO/$315,994.00, Patty Walsh/Dir. - Investor Relations

Directors: Oliver G. Brewer/45/Inside Dir., CEO, Pres., B. H. Adams/69/Chmn., Stephen R. Patchin/49/Outside Affiliated Dir., Paul F. Brown/62/Outside Affiliated Dir., Mark R. Mulvoy/67/Dir., Robert D. Rogers/72/Dir., Russell L. Fleischer/41/Dir.

Owners: Mark R. Mulvoy, Joseph R. Gregory, Insiders, Roland E. Casati, John M. Gregory, B. H. Adams, Russell L. Fleischer, SJ Strategic Investments LLC, Oliver G. Brewer, Eric T. Logan, Robert D. Rogers

Financial Data: Fiscal Year End: 12/31   **Latest Annual Data:** 12/31/2006

Year	Sales	Net Income
2006	$76,030,000	$9,000,000
2005	$56,424,000	$3,240,000
2004	$56,762,000	$3,078,000

Curr. Assets:	$49,733,000	**Curr. Liab.:**	$13,734,000	**P/E Ratio:**	6.18
Plant, Equip.:	$719,000	**Total Liab.:**	$13,734,000	**Indic. Yr. Divd.:**	NA
Total Assets:	$55,603,000	**Net Worth:**	$41,869,000	**Debt/ Equity:**	NA

Adams Resources & Energy Inc

4400 Post Oak Pkwy., Ste. 2700, Houston, TX, 77027; **PH:** 1-713-881-3600; **Fax:** 1-713-881-3491; *http://* www.adamsresources.com

General - Incorporation	DE	**Stock**- Price on:12/24/2007	$29.1
Employees	748	Stock Exchange	AMEX
Auditor	Deloitte & Touche LLP	Ticker Symbol	AE
Stk Agt	NA	Outstanding Shares	4,220,000
Counsel	NA	E.P.S.	$3.84
DUNS No.	06-727-3649	Shareholders	NA

Business: The groups principle activities include marketing crude oil, natural gas and petroleum products, tank truck transportation of liquid chemicals, and oil and gas exploration and production. The group operates from United States.

Primary SIC and add'l.: 4213 5172 9999 1311

CIK No: 0000002178

Subsidiaries: Ada Crude Oil Company, Ada Mining Corporation, Ada Resources, Inc., Adams Exploration UK Limited, Adams Resources Exploration Corporation, Adams Resources Marketing GP, Inc., Adams Resources Marketing II, Inc., Adams Resources Marketing, Ltd., Adams Resources UK Limited, Bayou City Pipelines, Inc., Buckley Mining Corporation, CJC Leasing, Inc., Classic Coal Corporation, Gulfmark Energy Marketing, Inc., Gulfmark Energy, Inc. 18 Subsidiaries included in the Index

Officers: K. S. Adams/Chmn., CEO/$385,239.00, James L. Smith/Pres. - Ada Resources, Inc, Richard B. Abshire/CFO, VP/$387,097.00, Frank T. Webster/Dir., COO, Pres./$551,439.00, Tony Gant/Pres. - Adams Resources Marketing, Ltd, Geoffrey L. Griffith/Pres. - Gulfmark Energy, Inc, Claude H. Lewis/Pres. - Service Transport Company, James Brock Moore/Pres. - Adams Resources Exploration Corporation, David B. Hurst/Sec.

Directors: K. S. Adams/Chmn., CEO, E. C. Reinauer/72/Dir., Jack E. Webster/87/Dir., Frank T. Webster/Dir., COO, Pres., William B. Wiener/Dir., Larry E. Bell/60/Dir.

Owners: Jack E. Webster, Richard B. Abshire, William B. Wiener, K. S. Adams/49.30%, E. C. Reinauer, Frank T. Webster, FMR Corp./10.00%, Insiders/50.30%

Financial Data: Fiscal Year End: 12/31   **Latest Annual Data:** 12/31/2006

Year	Sales	Net Income
2006	$2,246,603,000	$10,483,000
2005	$2,364,833,000	$17,641,000
2004	$2,069,788,000	$8,608,000

Curr. Assets:	$241,790,000	**Curr. Liab.:**	$206,582,000	**P/E Ratio:**	15.82
Plant, Equip.:	$43,316,000	**Total Liab.:**	$214,919,000	**Indic. Yr. Divd.:**	$0.470
Total Assets:	$289,287,000	**Net Worth:**	$74,368,000	**Debt/ Equity:**	0.0403

Adams Respiratory Therapeutics Inc

4 Mill Ridge Ln., Mill Ridge Farm, Chester, NJ, 07930; **PH:** 1-908-879-1400; **Fax:** 1-908-879-9191; *http://* www.adamslaboratories.com

General - Incorporation	DE	**Stock**- Price on:12/24/2007	$41.77
Employees	205	Stock Exchange	NDQ
Auditor	Ernst& Young LLP	Ticker Symbol	ARXT
Stk Agt	American Stock Transfer & Trust Co.	Outstanding Shares	35,620,000
Counsel	NA	E.P.S.	$1.17
DUNS No.	NA	Shareholders	NA

Business: The groups principal activities include selling, marketing developing, commercializing and marketing over the counter and prescription pharmaceuticals. The group products sold under the trade names Claritin(R), Robitussin(R), Tylenol(R), Advil(R) and Theraflu(R). Specific customers of the group include CVS, McKesson Corporation, Walgreens, and Wal-Mart. The group operates from the United States. The net sale of the group for the year 2006 was $239,105 (thousands)

Primary SIC and add'l.: 2834

CIK No: 0001319439

Subsidiaries: Adams Respiratory Operations Sub, Inc., Adams Respiratory Operations, Inc., Adams Respiratory Products, Inc.

Officers: Michael J. Valentino/Dir., CEO, Pres., Robert D. Casale/COO, Rita M. O'Connor/CFO, Treasurer, Walter E. Riehemann/Exec. VP, General Counsel, Chief Compliance Officer, Sec., John S. Thievon/Exec. VP - Sales, Corporate Accounting, Peter D. Wentworth/Exec. VP - Human Resources, Helmut H. Albrecht/Sr. VP - Research, Development, Marylou W. Arnett/Sr. VP - Marketing, William P. Fogarty/Sr. VP - Sales, Trade Development, William H. Howard/Sr. VP - New Products, Business Development, David J. Long/Sr. VP - Regulatory Affairs, Thomas L. Long/Sr. VP, GM - Manufacturing Operations, Janet M. Barth/Sr. VP - Investor Relations, Corporate Communications

Directors: Michael J. Valentino/Dir., CEO, Pres., Joan P. Neuscheler/Dir., Kirk K. Calhoun/Dir., John N. Lilly/Dir., Donald J. Liebentritt/Dir., Mark R. Sotir/Dir., Alan W. Dunton/Dir., Jane L. Delgado/Dir.

Owners: Brookside Capital Partners Fund, L.P./5.58%, Alan W. Dunton, FMR Corp./11.63%, Joan P. Neuscheler/1.23%, Michael J. Valentino/1.77%, Ridgeback Capital Investments Ltd./8.20%, TIA-CREFF Investment Management/7.12%, Donald J. Liebentritt, Kirk K. Calhoun, John S. Thievon, John N. Lilly, Walter E. Riehemann, Rita M. OConnor, Harold F. Oberkfell, Insiders/3.48% (18 Owners included in Index)

Financial Data: Fiscal Year End: 06/30   **Latest Annual Data:** 06/30/2007

Year	Sales	Net Income
2007	$331,603,000	$30,529,000
2006	$239,105,000	$46,351,000
2005	$160,210,000	$26,999,000

Curr. Assets:	$167,339,000	**Curr. Liab.:**	$42,411,000	**P/E Ratio:**	53.58
Plant, Equip.:	$19,763,000	**Total Liab.:**	$43,117,000	**Indic. Yr. Divd.:**	NA
Total Assets:	$318,465,000	**Net Worth:**	$275,348,000	**Debt/ Equity:**	NA

Adaptec Inc

691 S Milpitas Blvd., Milpitas, CA, 95035; **PH:** 1-408-945-8600; **Fax:** 1-408-262-2533; *http://* www.adaptec.com

General - Incorporation	DE	**Stock**- Price on:12/24/2007	$3.9
Employees	598	Stock Exchange	NDQ
Auditor	PricewaterhouseCoopers LLP	Ticker Symbol	ADPT
Stk Agt	Registrar & Transfer Co	Outstanding Shares	118,970,000
Counsel	Fenwick & West LLP	E.P.S.	$0.25
DUNS No.	03-335-8581	Shareholders	NA

Business: The group's principal activities are to design, manufacture and market storage access solutions that move, manage and protect critical data and digital content. The group has three segments: storage solutions group, desktop solutions group and storage networking group. The storage solutions group's interface products enable the movement, storage and protection of data across a range of server platforms, direct attached storage servers, san based servers, nas devices and storage subsystems. The desktop solutions group provides i/o connectivity solutions for personal computing platforms and consumer electronic devices. The storage networking group provides storage connectivity solutions for storage devices, fabric switches and nas devices. The group operates in the United States, Singapore and other countries. In fiscal 2004, the group acquired eurologic systems group limited, icp vortex computersysteme gmbh and elipsan limited.

Primary SIC and add'l.: 3572 3577 7373 3674

CIK No: 0000709804

Subsidiaries: Adaptec (India) Pvt. Ltd., Adaptec France SARL, Adaptec GmbH, Adaptec Japan Ltd., Adaptec Mfg. (S) Pte. Ltd., Adaptec UK, Ltd., Elipsan UK Limited, Eurologic Systems Ltd., ICP vortex Computersysteme GmbH

Officers: Subramanian Sundaresh/CEO, Pres., Shirley B. Olerich/VP - Human Resources, Facilities, Marc Lowe/VP - Corporate Development, Dennis R. Debroeck/Corp. Sec., Christopher O'Meara/CFO, VP, Manoj Goyal/VP, GM, John M. Westfield/VP, Corporate Controller, Principal Accounting Officer, John Noellert/VP - Worldwide Sales, Stephen Terlizzi/VP, GM

Directors: Scott D. Mercer/Chmn., Jack L. Howard/47/Dir., John Mutch/52/Dir., John J. Quicke/59/Dir., Douglas E. Van Houweling/Dir., Robert Loarie/Dir., Charles Robel/Dir., Jon Castor/Dir., Joseph S. Kennedy/Dir., Judith O'Brian/Dir.

Owners: Steel Partners II, L.P./14.94%, Christopher G. OMeara, Charles J. Robel, Manoj Goyal, Marcus D. Lowe, Robert J. Loarie, Joseph S. Kennedy, Dimensional Advisors, L.P./6.96%, Judith M. OBrien, Insiders/1.87%, Wellington Management Company, LLP/7.78%, Douglas E. Van Houweling, Russell Johnson, D. Scott Mercer, Jon S. Castor (16 Owners included in Index)

Financial Data: Fiscal Year End: 03/31   **Latest Annual Data:** 3/31/2007

Year	Sales	Net Income
2007	$255,208,000	$30,843,000
2006	$310,145,000	-$148,432,000
2005	$474,990,000	-$145,106,000

Curr. Assets:	$681,268,000	**Curr. Liab.:**	$65,235,000	**P/E Ratio:**	10.00
Plant, Equip.:	$15,852,000	**Total Liab.:**	$293,244,000	**Indic. Yr. Divd.:**	NA
Total Assets:	$715,402,000	**Net Worth:**	$422,158,000	**Debt/ Equity:**	NA

ADB Systems International Ltd

302 The E Mall, Ste. 300, Toronto, ON, M9B 6C7; ; *http://* www.adbsys.com

General - Incorporation	ON	**Stock**- Price on:12/24/2007	$0.106
Employees	NA	Stock Exchange	NA
Auditor	KPMG LLP	Ticker Symbol	NA
Stk Agt	Equity Transfer Services Inc	Outstanding Shares	NA
Counsel	NA	E.P.S.	NA
DUNS No.	NA	Shareholders	NA

Business: The group's principle activities include selling and marketing proprietary and patented Internet technology through simultaneous auctions for customers on behalf of manufacturers, distributors, trustees, banks and third parties, licensing of e-commerce technology and provision of consulting services. The group operates from United States.

Primary SIC and add'l.: 7374 5961

CIK No: 0001079171

Subsidiaries: ADB Syestmer As, ADB Systems USA, Inc

Officers: Jeffrey Lymburner/51/Dir., CEO, Tam Nguyen/Corporate Controller

Directors: Jeffrey Lymburner/51/Dir., CEO, Christopher T. Bulger/51/Chmn., Jim Moskos/45/Dir., Darroch Robertson/56/Dir., Duncan G. Copeland/51/Dir., Dave Gelineau/49/Dir.

Owners: Darroch Robertson, Duncan Copeland, David Gelineau, Christopher T. Bulger, Jeffrey Lymburner/5.00%, Jim Moskos

Financial Data: Fiscal Year End: 12/31   **Latest Annual Data:** 12/31/2006

Year	Sales	Net Income
2006	$921,000	-$1,013,000
2005	$4,955,000	-$2,830,000
2004	$4,093,000	-$4,162,000

Curr. Assets:	$594,000	**Curr. Liab.:**	$2,225,000		
Plant, Equip.:	$69,000	**Total Liab.:**	$2,866,000	**Indic. Yr. Divd.:**	NA
Total Assets:	$757,000	**Net Worth:**	-$2,109,000	**Debt/ Equity:**	NA

ADC Telecommunications Inc

13625 Technology Dr., Eden Prairie, MN, 55344; **PH:** 1-952-938-8080; **Fax:** 1-952-917-1717; *http://* www.adc.com; **Email:** investor@adc.com

General - Incorporation	MN	**Stock**- Price on:12/24/2007	$19.14
Employees	8,600	Stock Exchange	NDQ
Auditor	Ernst & Young LLP	Ticker Symbol	ADCT
Stk Agt	Computershare Investor Services LLC	Outstanding Shares	117,410,000
Counsel	NA	E.P.S.	$0.91
DUNS No.	00-624-9312	Shareholders	NA

Business: The group's principal activitiy is to provide broadband network equipment, software and systems integration services. The group's services enable communications service providers to deliver high-speed Internet, data, video and voice services to consumers and businesses. The group operates in two segments: broadband infrastructure and access business provides network infrastructure products for wireline, cable and wireless communications network applications; digital subscriber line offerings for the telecommunications industry; and Internet protocol based offerings for the cable industry. Integrated solutions business provides system integration services and operations support system software for broadband and, multiservice communications. The group's customers include telephone companies, cable television operators, wireless service providers, broadcasters, governments, businesses, system integrators and communications equipment manufacturers and distributors.

Primary SIC and add'l.: 3661 3679 3663 3669

CIK No: 0000061478

Subsidiaries: ADC (Australia) Technique PTY Limited, ADC (India) Communications &, ADC AS, ADC Beteiligungsgesellschaft mbH, ADC Broadband (Hong Kong) Limited, ADC Broadband Italy S.r.l., ADC Broadband Wireless Group, Inc., ADC Communications (Australia) PTY Limited, ADC Communications (NZ)Ltd., ADC Communications (SEA)Pte. Ltd., ADC Communications (Shanghai), ADC Communications (Thailand) Ltd., ADC Communications (UK)Holding Ltd., ADC Communications (UK)Ltd., ADC Communications Hong Kong Limited 90 Subsidiaries included in the Index

Officers: Robert E. Switz/Dir., CEO, Pres., Michael H. Day/VP - Technology, Strategy, CTO, Mark P. Borman/VP - Investor Relations, Treasurer, Laura N. Owen/VP - Human Resources, Gokul V. Hemmady/47/VP, Bradley V. Crary/VP - Tax, Mary E. Quay/VP - Corporate Services, Axel Kahsnitz/VP - International Sales, Marketing, Customer Service, James G. Mathews/CFO, VP, Stephen C. Mitchell/VP - Americas Sales, Marketing, Customer Service, Hilton M. Nicholson/VP, Pres. - Active Infrastructure, Richard B. Parran/VP, Pres. Professional Services, John Dulin/VP - Asia Pacific Sales, Marketing, Customer Service, Kimberly Hartwell/VP - Americas Sales, Marketing, Customer Service, Steven G. Nemitz/VP, Controller (28 Officers included in Index)

Directors: Robert E. Switz/Dir., CEO, Pres., John A. Blanchard/Chmn., William R. Spivey/Dir., Lois M. Martin/Dir., John D. Wunsch/Dir., Larry W. Wangberg/Dir., Jean-Pierre Rosso/Dir., Kevin J. Gilligan/Dir., James C. Castle/Dir., Mickey P. Foret/Dir., John E. Rehfeld/Dir., John J. Boyle/Dir.

Owners: AllianceBernstein L.P./8.60%, John J. Boyle, Robert E. Switz, Mickey P. Foret, Gokul V. Hemmady, Patrick D. OBrien, John E. Rehfeld, Kevin J. Gilligan, Insiders/2.33%, Jean-Pierre Rosso, William R. Spivey, Lord, Abbett& Co. LLC/10.20%, Jeffrey D. Pflaum, Lois M. Martin, James C. Castle (19 Owners included in Index)

Financial Data: Fiscal Year End:10/31   Latest Annual Data: 10/31/2006

Year	Sales		Net Income
2006	$1,281,900,000		$65,700,000
2005	$1,169,200,000		$110,700,000
2004	$784,300,000		$16,400,000
Curr. Assets:	$942,700,000	Curr. Liab.:	$260,100,000	P/E Ratio:	16.22
Plant, Equip.:	$206,500,000	Total Liab.:	$737,900,000	Indic. Yr. Divd.:	NA
Total Assets:	$1,611,400,000	Net Worth:	$873,500,000	Debt/ Equity:	NA

Addison Davis Diagnostics Inc

143 Triunfo Canyon Rd. , Ste 104, Westlake Village, CA, 91361; **PH:** 1-805-494-7838; *http://* www.addisondavis.com

General - Incorporation	DE	Stock- Price on:12/24/2007	$0.008
Employees	3	Stock Exchange	OTC
Auditor	Armando C. Ibarra CPA	Ticker Symbol	ADSD
Stk Agt	American Stock Transfer & Trust Co.	Outstanding Shares	1,230,000
Counsel	NA	E.P.S.	-$15.324
DUNS No.	NA	Shareholders	NA

Business: The groups principle activity is to provide screening tests. The groups DrugStop screener is used to detect colon cancer and other intestinal diseases. The group operates from United States.

Primary SIC and add'l.: NA

CIK No: 0000932127

Subsidiaries: Nico International, Inc

Financial Data: Fiscal Year End:06/30   Latest Annual Data: 6/30/2005

Year	Sales		Net Income
2005	$5,000		-$3,618,000
2004	$192,000		-$7,161,000
2003	$9,000		-$6,410,000
Curr. Assets:	$618,000	Curr. Liab.:	$1,711,000		
Plant, Equip.:	$20,000	Total Liab.:	$2,930,000	Indic. Yr. Divd.:	NA
Total Assets:	$1,223,000	Net Worth:	-$1,707,000	Debt/ Equity:	NA

Addvantage Technologies Group Inc

1221 E Houston, Broken Arrow, OK, 74012; **PH:** 1-918-251-9121; **Fax:** 1-918-268-7771; *http://* www.addvantagetech.com

General - Incorporation	OK	Stock- Price on:12/24/2007	$4.8
Employees	167	Stock Exchange	NDQ
Auditor	Tullius Taylor Sartain & Sartain LLP	Ticker Symbol	AEY
Stk Agt	The Bank of New York	Outstanding Shares	10,230,000
Counsel	NA	E.P.S.	$0.38
DUNS No.	61-750-1200	Shareholders	NA

Business: The group's principal activity is to sell new, surplus and re-manufactured cable television equipment. The group also provides repair services to its clients and other cable companies. The customers of the group include cable operators, apartment complexes, universities and other entities that distribute broadband signals. The group's products are marketed under two product lines: linegear and headend equipment. Linegear includes active electronics, trunk stations and line extenders and passive equipment such as taps, splitters and directional couplers. The headend equipment segment includes scientific atlanta, blonder tongue, magnavox, general instruments and drake lines of satellite receivers, integrated receiver/decoders, videociphers, demodulators, modulators, amplifiers, equalizers, processors, antennas, and antenna mounts. The group markets its products in North America, South America, Mexico and Pacific Rim.

Primary SIC and add'l.: 3663

CIK No: 0000874292

Subsidiaries: ADDvantage Technologies Group of Missouri, Inc., ADDvantage Technologies Group of Texas, Inc, Jones Broadband International, Inc, NCS Industries, Inc, Tulsat, Tulsat-Atlanta, LLC, a subsidiary of Tulsat, Tulsat-Nebraska, Inc

Officers: Ken Chymiak/Dir., CEO, Pres., Dan Okeefe/CFO, David Burke/Contact - Investor Relations, Lee Roth/Contact - Investor Relations

Directors: Ken Chymiak/Dir., CEO, Pres., David Chymiak/Chmn., Freddie H. Gibson/60/Dir., Henry McCabe/85/Dir., Stephen J. Tyde/59/Dir., Thomas J. Franz/49/Dir., Paul F. Largess/57/Dir., James C. McGill/64/Dir.

Owners: David E. Chymiak, Daniel E. O'Keefe, Susan C. Chymiak, Henry F. McCabe, Insiders, David E. Chymiak/23.70%, Kenneth A. Chymiak, Susan C. Chymiak/20.10%, Insiders/44.40%, Kenneth A. Chymiak/20.10%, Freddie H. Gibson, Stephen J. Tyde

Financial Data: Fiscal Year End:09/30   Latest Annual Data: 9/30/2006

Year	Sales		Net Income
2006	$52,541,000		$4,843,000
2005	$50,273,000		$5,814,000
2004	$47,071,000		$5,814,000
Curr. Assets:	$35,789,000	Curr. Liab.:	$8,728,000	P/E Ratio:	9.06
Plant, Equip.:	$2,538,000	Total Liab.:	$13,395,000	Indic. Yr. Divd.:	NA
Total Assets:	$40,925,000	Net Worth:	$27,531,000	Debt/ Equity:	0.2389

ADE Corp

80 Wilson Way, Westwood, MA, 02090; **PH:** 1-617-467-3500; *http://* www.ade.com

General - Incorporation	MA	Stock- Price on:12/24/2007	$55.34
Employees	5,900	Stock Exchange	NA
Auditor	PricewaterhouseCoopers LLP	Ticker Symbol	NA
Stk Agt	American Stock Transfer & Trust Co.	Outstanding Shares	191,620,000
Counsel	Sullivan & Worcester LLP	E.P.S.	$2.51
DUNS No.	04-827-6679	Shareholders	NA

Business: The group's principal activities are to design, manufacture and market production metrology and inspection systems. The group operates through three segments: ade semiconductor systems group, ade phase shift and ade technologies. The semiconductor systems segment manufactures and markets metrology and inspection systems to the semiconductor wafer and device manufacturing industries. The phase shift segment manufactures and markets high performance, non-contact surface metrology equipment using advanced interferometric technology that provides enhanced yield management to the data storage, semiconductor and optics industries. The technologies segment manufactures and markets high precision magnetic characterization and non-contact dimensional metrology gauging systems primarily for the data storage industry.

Primary SIC and add'l.: 7372 7371 3559

CIK No: 0000884498

Subsidiaries: ADE International Corporation, ADE International GmbH, ADE Optical Systems Corporation, ADE Phase Shift, Inc, ADE Securities Corp, ADE Software Corporation, ADE Technologies, Inc, ATI Foreign Sales Corporation, Japan ADE, Ltd., Phase Shift Technology, Inc.

Officers: Jeffrey Hall/CFO, Kyra Whitten/Sr. Dir. - Corporate Communications

Financial Data: Fiscal Year End:04/30   Latest Annual Data: 6/30/2006

Year	Sales		Net Income
2006	$2,070,627,000		$380,452,000
2005	$2,085,153,000		$466,695,000
2004	$1,496,718,000		$243,701,000
Curr. Assets:	$3,543,243,000	Curr. Liab.:	$1,002,481,000	P/E Ratio:	21.20
Plant, Equip.:	$395,412,000	Total Liab.:	$1,002,481,000	Indic. Yr. Divd.:	$0.480
Total Assets:	$4,575,911,000	Net Worth:	$3,567,991,000	Debt/ Equity:	NA

Adecco

Saegereistrasse 10, Glattbrugg; ; *http://* www.adecco.com; **Email:** investor.relations@adecco.com

General - Incorporation	Switzerland	Stock- Price on:12/24/2007	NA
Employees	35,284	Stock Exchange	NA
Auditor	Ernst & Young AG	Ticker Symbol	NA
Stk Agt	Morgan ADR Service Center	Outstanding Shares	NA
Counsel	NA	E.P.S.	NA
DUNS No.	06-161-8492	Shareholders	NA

Business: The group's principle activity is to supply temporary and permanent staff through employment agencies. The group offers human resource services and staffing solutions in mainstream clerical and industrial areas and is also specializing in accounting, information technology and engineering. In 2002, it increased its operating divisions to four. The group operates from United States.

Primary SIC and add'l.: 7389 7363 7361

CIK No: 0000931496

Subsidiaries: Adecco Travail Temporaire SASU

Officers: Dieter Scheiff/CEO, Ekkehard Kuppel/46/Pres. - Human Capital Solutions, Dominik De Daniel/32/CFO, Jan-Pieter Gommers/42/Pres. - Sales, Marketing, Events, Francois-Xavier Quilici/CIO, Jean-Manuel Bullukian/44/Pres. - Adecco Engineering, Technical, Adecco Information Technology, Philippe Foriel-Destezet/73/Honorary Pres., Klaus J. Jacobs/72/Honorary Pres., Gonzalo Fernandez-Castro/35/Chief Marketing, Business Development Officer, Neil Lebovits/45/Pres. - Adecco Finance, Legal, Christian Vasino/Chief Human Resources Officer, Francois Davy/Country Mgr. - Adecco France, Tig Gilliam/Country Mgr. - Adecco US, Canada, Rene Schuster/Country Mgr. - Adecco UK, Ireland

Directors: Rolf Dorig/Vice Chmn., Jurgen Dormann/68/Chmn., Philippe Marcel/55/Dir., Jakob Baer/64/Dir., David Prince/57/Dir., Thomas O'Neill/63/Dir., Andreas Jacobs/45/Dir., Francis Mer/69/Dir., Peter V. Ueberroth/71/Dir.

Adept Technology Inc

3011 Triad Dr., Livermore, CA, 94551; **PH:** 1-925-245-3400; **Fax:** 1-925-960-0452; *http://* www.adept.com; **Email:** info@adept.com

General - Incorporation	CA	Stock- Price on:12/24/2007	$7.379
Employees	175	Stock Exchange	NDQ
Auditor	Armanino Mckenna LLP	Ticker Symbol	ADEP
Stk Agt	Mellon Investor Services LLC	Outstanding Shares	7,690,000
Counsel	Gibson, Dunn & Crutcher LLP	E.P.S.	-$0.651
DUNS No.	10-277-9337	Shareholders	NA

Business: The group's principal activities are to design, manufacture and market factory automation components and systems. The group operates through three segments: components, solutions and services and support. The components segment provides intelligent automation software and hardware component

products for support and integration into higher level assemblies to internal and external customers. The solutions segment produces an integrated family of process-ready platforms for semiconductor, electronics and precision assembly and other markets driven towards standard offerings. The services and support segment provides support services like giving product usage information, consulting and training on applications to customers. The customers include food, communications, appliance, semiconductor, photonics and life sciences industries. The group operates in the United States, Germany, France, other European countries, Singapore, China and other Asian countries.

Primary SIC and add'l.: 7372 3571 3577 7371

CIK No: 0000865415

Subsidiaries: Adept Global Technologies, Adept Technology Canada Co., Adept Technology Canada Holding Co., Adept Technology GmbH, Adept Technology Holdings Co., Adept Technology International Ltd., Adept Technology S.A.R.L., Meta Control Technologies Inc.

Officers: Robert H. Bucher/Dir., CEO, John Dulchinos/COO, Pres., Gordon Deans/VP - Business Development, Joachim Melis/VP - Worldwide Sales, Dave Pap Rocki/CTO, Lisa Cummins/VP - Finance, CFO

Directors: Robert H. Bucher/Dir., CEO, Michael P. Kelly/Chmn., Richard A. Juelis/Dir., Charles H. Finnie/Dir., Robert J. Majteles/Dir., Herbert J. Martin/Dir., Cary R. Mock/Dir.

Owners: Robert H. Bucher/2.90%, Kopp Investment Advisors, LLC/16.10%, Marxe & Greenhouse/38.20%, Joachim Melis, Charles H. Finnie, Matthew J. Murphy, Jon D. Gruber/12.50%, Insiders/4.60%, John D. Dulchinos, Herbert J. Martin, Richard A. Juelis, Crosslink Capital Inc./12.00%, Cary R. Mock, Michael P. Kelly, Robert J. Majteles

Financial Data: ***Fiscal Year End:*** 06/30 ***Latest Annual Data:*** 6/30/2006

Year	Sales	Net Income
2006	$57,637,000	$538,000
2005	$50,480,000	$1,295,000
2004	$49,084,000	-$7,325,000

Curr. Assets:	$37,687,000	***Curr. Liab.:***	$10,570,000		
Plant, Equip.:	$2,596,000	***Total Liab.:***	$11,003,000	***Indic. Yr. Divd.:***	NA
Total Assets:	$43,692,000	***Net Worth:***	$32,689,000	***Debt/ Equity:***	NA

Adesa Inc

13085 Hamilton Crossing Blvd., Carmel, IN, 46032; ***PH:*** 1-800-923-3725; ***http://*** www.adesa.com

General - Incorporation	DE	***Stock***- Price on:12/24/2007	NA
Employees	7,625	Stock Exchange	NA
Auditor	KPMG LLP	Ticker Symbol	NA
Stk Agt	Mellon Investor Services LLC	Outstanding Shares	NA
Counsel	NA	E.P.S	NA
DUNS No.	NA	Shareholders	NA

Business: The group's princiapl activity is to provide national provider vehicle auction and related vehicle redistribution services for the automotive industry in North America. The group operates a network of 53 used vehicle auctions, 27 salvage auctions and 80 afc loan production offices in the United States and Canada.

Primary SIC and add'l.: 7549

CIK No: 0001281949

Subsidiaries: 3048538 Nova Scotia Company, 3048540 Nova Scotia Company, 504811 Nb Ltd., 51937 Newfoundland & Labrador Limited, 79378 Manitoba Inc., A.D.E. of Ark-La-Tex, Inc., A.D.E. of Knoxville, LLC, ADESA Ark-La-Tex, LLC, ADESA Arkansas, LLC, ADESA Atlanta, LLC, ADESA Auctions Canada Corporation, ADESA Automotive Services, LP, ADESA Birmingham, LLC, ADESA California, LLC, ADESA Canada Corporation 58 Subsidiaries included in the Index

Officers: David G. Gartzke/63/Chmn., CEO, Brenda J. Flayton/52/Exec. VP, Chief Administrative Officer, Scott A. Anderson/42/Controller, Ron Beaver/49/CIO, VP, Curt L. Phillips/51/VP, Cameron C. Hitchcock/46/Exec. VP, Bradley A. Todd/39/Exec. VP, George J. Lawrence/49/Exec. VP, General Counsel, Sec., Jonathan Peisner/48/Treasurer, Angel Rodolfo Sales/58/Dir., COO, Pres., Timothy C. Clayton/53/CFO

Directors: David G. Gartzke/63/Chmn., CEO, Wynn V. Bussmann/66/Dir., Deborah L. Weinstein/47/Dir., Donald C. Wegmiller/68/Dir., Dennis O. Green/66/Dir., Nick Smith/70/Dir., Angel Rodolfo Sales/58/Dir., COO, Pres., Thomas L. Cunningham/61/Dir., Van W. Bussmann/65/Dir.

Owners: Cameron C. Hitchcock, Royce & Associates, LLC/7.19%, Wynn V. Bussmann, Insiders/2.55%, Donald C. Wegmiller, Nick Smith, A. R. Sales, George J. Lawrence, Dennis O. Green, Deborah L. Weinstein, David G. Gartzke/1.18%, Thomas L. Cunningham, Timothy C. Clayton, Bradley A. Todd

Adeza Biomedical Corp

1240 Elko Dr, Sunnyvale, CA, 94089; ***PH:*** 1-408-745-0975; ***http://*** www.adeza.com

General - Incorporation	DE	***Stock***- Price on:12/24/2007	NA
Employees	NA	Stock Exchange	NA
Auditor	Ernst & Young LLP	Ticker Symbol	NA
Stk Agt	Wells Fargo Bank, N.A.	Outstanding Shares	NA
Counsel	NA	E.P.S	NA
DUNS No.	NA	Shareholders	NA

Business: The groups principle activities include designing, developing, manufacturing and marketing products for womens health. The products of the group include E-tegrity Test, Gestiva and TLiIQ System. The group products sold under the trade names Adeza(R), E-tegrity(R) Test, SalEst(R) and FullTerm(TM). The group operates from the United States.

Primary SIC and add'l.: 3825

CIK No: 0000902482

Officers: Emory V. Anderson/54/Dir., CEO, Pres., Mark D. Fischer-Colbrie/51/Sr. VP - Finance, Administration, CFO, Durlin E. Hickok/60/Sr. VP - Medical Affairs, Robert O. Hussa/66/VP - Research, Development, Marian E. Sacco/54/Sr. VP - Sales, Marketing

Directors: Emory V. Anderson/54/Dir., CEO, Pres., Andrew Senyei/Chmn., Craig C. Taylor/Dir., Kathleen D. Laporte/Dir., Michael P. Downey/Dir., Gregory C. Vontz/Dir.

Adherex Technologies Inc

4620 Creekstone Dr., Ste. 200, Durham, NC, 27703; ***PH:*** 1-919-484-8484; ***Fax:*** 1-919-484-8001; ***http://*** www.adherex.com; ***Email:*** info@adherex.com

General - Incorporation	Canada	***Stock***- Price on:12/24/2007	$0.57
Employees	25	Stock Exchange	AMEX
Auditor	PricewaterhouseCoopers LLP	Ticker Symbol	ADH
Stk Agt	Computershare Investor Services LLC	Outstanding Shares	NA
Counsel	NA	E.P.S	-$0.248
DUNS No.	NA	Shareholders	NA

Business: The group's principle activities include discovering and developing novel cancer therapeutics products for cancer treatments. The group provides products including ADH-1 (ExherinTM), Eniluracil and Sodium Thiosulfate (STS). The groups ADH-1 product lead biotechnology compound selectively targets N-cadherin, Eniluracil, dihydropyrimidine dehydrogenase (DPD) inhibitor. The groups specialty pharmaceuticals pipeline protects against the disabling hearing loss that can often result from treatment with platinum-based chemotherapy drugs. The group operates from United States.

Primary SIC and add'l.: 2836

CIK No: 0001211583

Subsidiaries: Adherex, Inc., Oxiquant, Inc

Officers: William P. Peters/Chmn., CEO, Robin J. Norris/Dir., COO, Pres., Brian E. Huber/Chief Scientific Officer, James A. Klein/CFO, Rajesh K. Malik/Chief Medical Officer, Scott D. Murray/Sr. VP - Corporate Development, General Counsel, Sec., Jeffrey Solash/Chief Licensing Officer, Robert Diasio/Assoc.

Directors: William P. Peters/Chmn., CEO, Robin J. Norris/Dir., COO, Pres., William G. Breen/Dir., Claudio G. Bussandri/Dir., Robert W. Butts/Dir., Donald W. Kufe/Dir., Michael G. Martin/Dir., Fred H. Mermelstein/Dir., Peter Morand/Dir., Arthur T. Porter/Dir., Donald Berry/Member - Scientific Advisory Board, Stephen Byers/Member - Scientific Advisory Board, Harold F. Dvorak/Member - Scientific Advisory Board, Emil Frei/Member - Scientific Advisory Board, Robert Herfkens/Member - Scientific Advisory Board *(20 Directors included in Index)*

Owners: Scott D. Murray, Lawrence Asset Management Inc/16.90%, Donald W. Kufe, Peter Morand, Fred H. Mermelstein/1.26%, Southpoint Capital Advisors LP/42.40%, Insiders/4.90%, William P. Peters/2.51%, Michael G. Martin, Robin J. Norris, James A. Klein, Arthur T. Porter, OrbiMed Advisors LLC/10.10%

Financial Data: ***Fiscal Year End:*** 12/31 ***Latest Annual Data:*** 12/31/2006

Year	Sales	Net Income
2006	NA	-$16,440,000
2005	NA	-$13,871,000
2004	NA	-$6,921,000

Curr. Assets:	$5,895,000	***Curr. Liab.:***	$4,695,000		
Plant, Equip.:	$733,000	***Total Liab.:***	$8,999,000	***Indic. Yr. Divd.:***	NA
Total Assets:	$16,584,000	***Net Worth:***	$7,585,000	***Debt/ Equity:***	NA

ADM Tronics Unlimited Inc

224-S Pegasus Ave., Northvale, NJ, 07647; ***PH:*** 1-201-767-6040; ***Fax:*** 1-201-784-0620; ***http://*** www.admtronics.com; ***Email:*** sales@admtronics.com

General - Incorporation	DE	***Stock***- Price on:12/24/2007	$0.27
Employees	19	Stock Exchange	OTC
Auditor	Raich Ende Malter & Co. LLP	Ticker Symbol	ADMT
Stk Agt	Securities Transfer Corp	Outstanding Shares	53,880,000
Counsel	NA	E.P.S	NA
DUNS No.	07-095-2726	Shareholders	NA

Business: The group's principal activity is to produce and market chemical products for industrial users. The group also manufactures, markets and leases medical equipment and devices. The chemical products consist of water-based primers and adhesives; water-based coatings and resins for the printing and packaging industry and water-based chemical additives cosmetic, medical and related adhesives and formulations. The chemical products are sold to customers located in the United States, Australia and Europe. The medical device product line consists of proprietary devices used in the treatment of joint pain, postoperative edema and tinnitus. The medical equipment are sold or leased to customers located in the United States and Asia. Medical equipment and medical devices are manufactured in accordance with customer specification on a contract basis.

Primary SIC and add'l.: 3845 2899 7352 2891

CIK No: 0000849401

Subsidiaries: Ivivi Technologies, Inc., Pegasus Laboratories, Inc., Sonotron Medical Systems, Inc.

Officers: Andre Dimino/Dir., CEO, CFO, Pres., Vincent Di Mino/82/Dir., VP - Production

Directors: Andre Dimino/Dir., CEO, CFO, Pres., David Saloff/55/Dir., Vincent Di Mino/82/Dir., VP - Production, Alfonso Dimino/Founder

Owners: Eugene Stricker/7.90%, Andre' DiMino/40.50%, Vincent DiMino/13.80%, David Saloff, Insiders/44.70%

Financial Data: ***Fiscal Year End:*** 03/31 ***Latest Annual Data:*** 03/31/2007

Year	Sales	Net Income
2007	$1,538,000	-$8,166,000
2006	$1,724,000	-$7,171,000
2005	$1,382,000	-$3,134,000

Curr. Assets:	$1,565,000	***Curr. Liab.:***	$1,258,000		
Plant, Equip.:	$377,000	***Total Liab.:***	$9,439,000	***Indic. Yr. Divd.:***	NA
Total Assets:	$3,240,000	***Net Worth:***	-$6,200,000	***Debt/ Equity:***	NA

Administaff Inc

19001 Crescent Springs Dr., Kingwood, TX, 77339; ***PH:*** 1-281-358-8986; ***Fax:*** 1-281-348-3718; ***http://*** www.administaff.com

General - Incorporation	DE	***Stock***- Price on:12/24/2007	$35.49
Employees	102,375	Stock Exchange	NYSE
Auditor	Ernst & Young LLP	Ticker Symbol	ASF
Stk Agt	Computershare Trust Co	Outstanding Shares	27,810,000
Counsel	Baker & Botts LLP	E.P.S	$1.72
DUNS No.	18-126-2080	Shareholders	NA

Business: The group's principle activity is to provide a comprehensive personnel management system. Services provided includes benefits and payroll administration, health and workers' compensation insurance programs, personnel records management, employer liability management, employee recruiting and selection, employee performance management and employee training and development services to small and medium-sized businesses in selected markets. The group operates throughout the United States. The group has entered into a marketing agreement with American express, under which American express is utilizing its resources and working jointly. The group's quarterly revenue for September 2007 was 383.38 millions of USD.

Primary SIC and add'l.: 8742

CIK No: 0001000753

Subsidiaries: Administaff Business Services,L.P., Administaff Captive Insurance Companies Limited, Administaff Client Services, L.P, Administaff Companies II, L.P, Administaff Companies, Inc, Administaff Enterprises, Inc, Administaff Financial Management Services, Inc, Administaff GP, Inc, Administaff Insurance Services, LLC, Administaff of Texas, Inc, Administaff Partnerships Holding II, Inc, Administaff Partnerships Holding III, Inc, Administaff Partnerships Holding, Inc, Administaff Retirement Services,L.P., Administaff Services, L.P

Officers: Paul J. Sarvadi/Chmn., CEO, Roger L. Gaskamp/VP - Client Selection, Pricing, John H. Spurgin/VP - Legal, General Counsel, Sec., Randall H. McCollum/VP - Strategic Alliances, John Orth/VP - Sales, Gregory R. Clouse/VP - Service Operations, Richard G. Rawson/Dir., Pres., Betty L. Collins/VP - Corporate Human Resources, Jay E. Mincks/Exec. VP - Sales, Marketing, Samuel G. Larson/VP - Enterprise, Technology Solutions, Douglas S. Sharp/VP - Finance, CFO, Treasurer, Steve A. Arizpe/Exec. VP - Client Services, COO, Martin K. Scirratt/VP - Sales, Mark W. Allen/VP - Strategic Planning, Daniel D. Herink/VP - Legal, General Counsel, Sec. *(16 Officers included in Index)*

Directors: Paul J. Sarvadi/Chmn., CEO, Gregory E. Petsch/57/Dir., Austin P. Young/67/Dir., Jack M. Fields/56/Dir., Richard G. Rawson/Dir., Pres., Eli Jones/46/Dir., Paul S. Lattanzio/44/Dir., Michael W. Brown/62/Dir.

Owners: EARNEST Partners, L.L.C/8.90%, Richard G. Rawson/4.90%, Eli Jones, Steve A. Arizpe/1.20%, Paul S. Lattanzio, Insiders/15.90%, Austin P. Young, Paul J. Sarvadi/8.30%, Jack M. Fields, Douglas S. Sharp, Gregory E. Petsch, AXA Financial, Inc./5.30%, Columbia Wanger Asset Management, L.P./8.10%, Jay E. Mincks, Michael W. Brown

Financial Data: ***Fiscal Year End:***12/31 ***Latest Annual Data:*** 12/31/2006

Year	Sales	Net Income
2006	$1,389,464,000	$46,506,000
2005	$1,169,612,000	$29,983,000
2004	$969,527,000	$19,210,000

Curr. Assets:	$415,079,000	***Curr. Liab.:***	$286,678,000	***P/E Ratio:***	21.00
Plant, Equip.:	$81,120,000	***Total Liab.:***	$333,070,000	***Indic. Yr. Divd.:***	$0.440
Total Assets:	$561,515,000	***Net Worth:***	$228,445,000	***Debt/ Equity:***	0.0045

Admiralty Holding Co

Formerly: Ruby Mining Co

3318 Hwy 5 No.504, Douglasville, GA, 30135; ***PH:*** 1-404-348-4728;

http:// www.admiraltycorporation.com

General - Incorporation	CO	***Stock***- Price on:12/24/2007	NA
Employees	3	Stock Exchange	NA
Auditor	Cherry, Bekaert & Holland LLP	Ticker Symbol	NA
Stk Agt	Computershare Trust Co	Outstanding Shares	NA
Counsel	NA	E.P.S	-$0.059
DUNS No.	06-406-8299	Shareholders	NA

Business: The group's principal activity is to develop proprietary detection technology used in locating and recovering valuable cargoes from historic shipwrecks from the 16th, 17th, and 18th centuries. The group uses its in partnership with governments, marine archaeologists and other nautical and maritime experts. The group also conducts historical research on shipwrecks and analyzes the principal issues related to the legalities associated with the shipwreck search. The group also develops technology to detect gold, silver and other precious metals in a salt-water environment.

Primary SIC and add'l.: 8731

CIK No: 0000085684

Subsidiaries: Admiralty Corporation. Pursuant, Admiralty Marine Operations, Ltd

Officers: Herbert C. Leeming/CEO

Financial Data: ***Fiscal Year End:***12/31 ***Latest Annual Data:*** 12/31/2005

Year	Sales	Net Income
2005	$1,000	-$3,252,000
2004	NA	-$2,960,000
2003	NA	-$1,131,000

Curr. Assets:	$1,153,000	***Curr. Liab.:***	$4,978,000		
Plant, Equip.:	$734,000	***Total Liab.:***	$11,233,000	***Indic. Yr. Divd.:***	NA
Total Assets:	$2,516,000	***Net Worth:***	-$8,717,000	***Debt/ Equity:***	NA

Adobe Systems Inc

345 Pk. Ave., San Jose, CA, 95110; ***PH:*** 1-408-536-6000; ***Fax:*** 1-408-537-6000;

http:// www.adobe.com; ***Email:*** adobe@kpcorp.com

General - Incorporation	DE	***Stock***- Price on:12/24/2007	$41.53
Employees	6,082	Stock Exchange	NDQ
Auditor	KPMG LLP	Ticker Symbol	ADBE
Stk Agt	Computershare Investor Services LLC	Outstanding Shares	587,930,000
Counsel	NA	E.P.S	$0.90
DUNS No.	10-209-6559	Shareholders	NA

Business: The groups principle activity is to provide software and services to creative professionals, designers, knowledge workers, high-end consumers, original equipment manufacturers (OEM) and developers. The groups products include Creative Suite(R) 3 Design Premium, Acrobat Connect and Acrobat Family. The group operates through five business segments namely creative solutions, knowledge worker solutions, enterprise and developer solutions, mobile and device solutions, and other. The group operates from United States.

Primary SIC and add'l.: 6794 7379 7372

CIK No: 0000796343

Subsidiaries: Accelio Corporation, Accelio France SA, Accelio UKLtd., Adobe International LLC, Adobe Software Trading Company Limited, Adobe Systems (Schweiz) GmbH, Adobe Systems Benelux BV, Adobe Systems Brasil Limitada, Adobe Systems CanadaInc., Adobe Systems CompanyLtd., Adobe Systems Danmark ApS, Adobe Systems DirectLtd., Adobe Systems Engineering GmbH, Adobe Systems EuropeLtd., Adobe Systems France SAS 33 Subsidiaries included in the Index

Officers: Bruce Chizen/CEO, Kevin Burr/VP - Corporate Communications, Mike Saviage/VP - Investor Relations, Richard T. Rowley/52/VP, Principal Accounting Officer, Ann Lewnes/Sr. VP - Corporate Marketing, Communications, Rob Tarkoff/Sr. VP - Corporate Development, Matt Thompson/Sr. VP - Worldwide Field Operations, Gerri Martin-Flickinger/CIO, Sr. VP, Tom Malloy/Sr. VP, Chief Software Architect - Advanced Technology Labs, John Brennan/Sr. VP - Platform Business Unit, John Loiacono/Sr. VP - Creative Solutions Business Unit, Kevin Lynch/Sr. VP - Platform Business Unit, Chief Software Architect, David Mendels/Sr. VP - Business Productivity, Business Unit, Alan S. Ramadan/Sr. VP - Mobile, Device Solutions Business Unit, Mark Garrett/CFO, Exec. VP *(20 Officers included in Index)*

Directors: Charles M. Geschke/Chmn., John E. Warnock/Chmn., Colleen M. Pouliot/Dir., Robert Sedgewick/Dir., Edward W. Barnholt/Dir., Michael R. Cannon/Dir., James E. Daley/Dir., Delbert W. Yocam/Dir., Robert K. Burgess/Dir., Carol Mills/Dir.

Owners: Randy W. Furr, Delbert W. Yocam, James E. Daley, Shantanu Narayen, Wellington Management Company, LLP/7.04%, PRIMECAP Management Company/7.56%, Robert K. Burgess, Stephen A. Elop, Carol Mills, Insiders/1.68%, Edward W. Barnholt, Prudential Financial, Inc./5.21%, Bruce R. Chizen, Robert Sedgewick, Karen O. Cottle *(21 Owners included in Index)*

Financial Data: ***Fiscal Year End:***12/02 ***Latest Annual Data:*** 12/1/2006

Year	Sales	Net Income
2006	$2,575,300,000	$505,809,000
2005	$1,966,321,000	$602,839,000
2004	$1,666,581,000	$450,398,000

Curr. Assets:	$1,551,029,000	***Curr. Liab.:***	$451,408,000	***P/E Ratio:***	43.72
Plant, Equip.:	$99,675,000	***Total Liab.:***	$535,155,000	***Indic. Yr. Divd.:***	NA
Total Assets:	$1,958,632,000	***Net Worth:***	$1,423,477,000	***Debt/ Equity:***	NA

Adolor Corp

700 Pennsylvania Dr., Exton, PA, 19341; ***PH:*** 1-484-595-1500; ***Fax:*** 1-484-595-1520;

http:// www.adolor.com; ***Email:*** questions@adolor.com

General - Incorporation	DE	***Stock***- Price on:12/24/2007	$3.73
Employees	128	Stock Exchange	NDQ
Auditor	KPMG LLP	Ticker Symbol	ADLR
Stk Agt	StockTrans, Inc.	Outstanding Shares	46,000,000
Counsel	Dechert, Price & Rhoads	E.P.S	-$1.24
DUNS No.	NA	Shareholders	NA

Business: The group's principal activity is to discover, develop and market proprietary pharmaceutical products for the treatment of pain and the side effects that are caused by current pain treatments. The group is in the development stage. The group has a portfolio of small molecule product candidates that are in various stages of development ranging from pre-clinical studies to phase i through phase iii clinical trials. Its product candidate, alvimopan, also known as adl 8-2698, is designed to selectively block the effects of narcotic analgesics on the gastrointestinal tract. It has obtained licenses from kwang dong pharmaceutical co ltd and santen pharmaceutical co ltd of Japan to develop and market dermal formulations of adl 2-1294 in South Korea and north Korea for dermal pain and ophthalmic pain respectively.

Primary SIC and add'l.: 2834 8731

CIK No: 0001076167

Subsidiaries: Adolor Finance LLC

Officers: Michael R. Dougherty/Dir., CEO, Pres./$1,055,512.00, Linda Y. Harver/VP - Regulatory Affairs, Richard M. Woodward/VP - Discovery, David M. Stephon/VP - Quality Assurance, James E. Barrett/65/Sr. VP, Chief Scientific Officer, Pres. - Research/$891,950.00, David Jackson/Sr. VP, Chief Medical Officer/$616,054.00, Robert B. Jones/VP - Strategy, Business Analysis, Kevin G. Taylor/VP - Business Development, Martha Manning/Sr. VP, General Counsel, Sec./$667,253.00, Thomas P. Hess/VP - Finance, CFO/$291,809.00, Randall J. Mack/VP - Project Management, Richard M. Mangano/VP - Clinical Operations, George R. Maurer/VP - Commercial Manufacturing, Scott T. Megaffin/VP - Marketing

Directors: Michael R. Dougherty/Dir., CEO, Pres., David M. Madden/Chmn., Donald E. Nickelson/Dir., Georges Gemayel/Dir., Claude H. Nash/Dir., Robert T. Nelsen/Dir., Armando Anido/50/Dir., Paul Goddard/Dir., George V. Hager/Dir.

Owners: Westfield Capital Management Company, LLC/11.33%, Insiders/7.50%, Thomas Hess, Ziff Asset Management, L.P./9.06%, Armando Anido, James E. Barrett, Franklin Resources, Inc./10.41%, Robert T. Nelsen/2.80%, D.E. Shaw & Co., L.P./8.96%, Claude H. Nash, David Jackson, Roger D. Graham, David M. Madden/1.83%, Martha E. Manning, George V. Hager *(18 Owners included in Index)*

Financial Data: ***Fiscal Year End:***12/31 ***Latest Annual Data:*** 12/31/2006

Year	Sales	Net Income
2006	$15,087,000	-$69,738,000
2005	$15,719,000	-$56,797,000
2004	$25,542,000	-$43,586,000

Curr. Assets:	$193,332,000	***Curr. Liab.:***	$20,202,000		
Plant, Equip.:	$7,022,000	***Total Liab.:***	$47,416,000	***Indic. Yr. Divd.:***	NA
Total Assets:	$200,598,000	***Net Worth:***	$153,181,000	***Debt/ Equity:***	NA

ADSERO Corp

21301 Powerline Rd. , Ste 311, Boca Raton, FL, 33433; ***PH:*** 1-866-643-4040;

http:// www.AdseroCorp.com

General - Incorporation	DE	***Stock***- Price on:12/24/2007	$0.07
Employees	NA	Stock Exchange	OTC
Auditor	Marcum & Kliegman LLP	Ticker Symbol	ADSE
Stk Agt	DGM Bank & Trust Inc	Outstanding Shares	NA
Counsel	NA	E.P.S	NA
DUNS No.	NA	Shareholders	NA

Business: The group's principal activities are to manufacture and markets ink products for imaging consumables market. The products of the group include ink jet and remanufactured laser toner cartridges, inkjet refill kits, remanufactured inkjet cartridges, thermal printer film, impact printer ribbons, bulk ink and a wide range of specialty inks for industrial printer applications. Reink (TM) is a registered trademark of the group. The products are sold to wholesale distributors, original equipment manufactureres and retail office supply stores, both domestically and internationally. On Mar 22, 2004 reink changed its name to adsero corp. It operates in mississauga, ontario.

Primary SIC and add'l.: 2893 3577 3955

CIK No: 0001103544

Subsidiaries: 3091503 Nova Scotia Company, 3091732 Nova Scotia Company, Adsero Canada Corp., Teckn-O-Laser Company, Teckn-O-Laser Global Company, Teckn-O-Laser USA Inc., YAC Corp.

Officers: William Smith/CFO, Sec.

Owners: Westminster Capital Inc/9.17%, Turbon AG/16.41%, Insiders/14.68%, William Smith/0.98%, Wayne Maddever/0.42%, Dynamic Power Hedge Fund/8.57%, Heath Bank and Trust Limited/8.06%, Alain Lachambre/5.85%

Financial Data: Fiscal Year End:12/31 Latest Annual Data: 12/31/2005

Year	Sales	Net Income
2005	$27,841,000	-$7,387,000
2004	NA	-$1,762,000
2003	NA	-$1,627,000

Curr. Assets:	$10,330,000	Curr. Liab.:	$15,350,000		
Plant, Equip.:	$2,120,000	Total Liab.:	$22,208,000	Indic. Yr. Divd.:	NA
Total Assets:	$25,252,000	Net Worth:	$3,044,000	Debt/ Equity:	NA

Adsouth Partners Inc

1515 N Federal Hwy, Ste 418, Boca Raton, FL, 33432; ***PH:*** 1-561-750-0410; ***http://*** www.adsouthpartners.com; ***Email:*** info@adsouthinc.com

General - Incorporation .... NV
Employees 30
Auditor .... Marcum & Kliegman LLP
Stk Agt .... Mountain Share Transfer
Counsel .... NA
DUNS No. .... NA

Stock- Price on:12/24/2007 .... NA
Stock Exchange .... OTC
Ticker Symbol .... ASPR
Outstanding Shares .... NA
E.P.S. .... -$0.657
Shareholders .... NA

Business: The group's principle activity is to provide provision of one plus voice long distance services to the residential and business users throughout the United States. The one plus service enables a caller to make a long distance telephone call without the need to enter a 7 digit carrier code, nor the need to enter a pin (personal identification number) code, which can be as long as 15 digits. The initial markets for this service include California, Pennsylvania and New York. The company provides this service as a reseller, utilizing the infrastructure of a competitive local exchange carrier. In Feb 2004, the company acquired the dermafreshtm product line from think-tek, inc. The group operates from United States.

Primary SIC and add'l.: 4813

CIK No: 0001158235

Subsidiaries: Adsouth, Inc, Dermafresh, Inc., Genco Power Solutions, Inc., Miko Distributors, Inc.

Owners: Harlan I. Press/0.76%, John P. Acunto/46.35%, Loren B. Haynes/0.76%, Insiders/1.52%, John Cammarano/6.41%, Angela E. Acunto/46.35%

Financial Data: Fiscal Year End:12/31 Latest Annual Data: 12/31/2005

Year	Sales	Net Income
2005	$13,314,000	-$669,000
2004	$4,044,000	-$5,811,000
2003	NA	-$70,000

Curr. Assets:	$5,135,000	Curr. Liab.:	$3,294,000		
Plant, Equip.:	$578,000	Total Liab.:	$3,472,000	Indic. Yr. Divd.:	NA
Total Assets:	$6,023,000	Net Worth:	$2,551,000	Debt/ Equity:	NA

Adstar Inc

4553 Glencoe Ave. Ste. 300, Marina del Rey, CA, 90292; ***PH:*** 1-310-577-8255; ***Fax:*** 1-310-577-8266; ***http://*** www.adstar.com; ***Email:*** techsupport@adstar.com

General - Incorporation .... DE
Employees 31
Auditor .... Holtz Rubenstein Reminick LLP
Stk Agt...... American Stock Transfer & Trust Co.
Counsel .... Stoel Rives LLP
DUNS No. .... NA

Stock- Price on:12/24/2007 .... $1.4
Stock Exchange .... NDQ
Ticker Symbol .... ADST
Outstanding Shares 20,210,000
E.P.S. .... -$0.1
Shareholders .... NA

Business: The group's principle activities are to license proprietary software systems and supply related support and maintenance. The group's proprietary software is an integrated suite of applications that electronically connects publishers with the source of their advertising revenue. The group also offers publisher-specific ad-taking Web site service, which is an application service provider (asp). The e-business application suite consists of two products: professional software, which accepts transmissions from classified, advertising agencies and large corporations using advanced Web-based technology and asp Web site technology, which enhances a publication's Web site by enabling the public to execute transactions to purchase classified advertising. These software systems unite large commercial advertising agencies and corporations with sophisticated publishing software systems installed at major metropolitan newspapers. The group's quarterly revenue for September 2007 was 1.18 millions of USD.

Primary SIC and add'l.: 7379 7372

CIK No: 0001091599

Subsidiaries: Edgil Associates, Inc.

Officers: Leslie Bernhard/Dir., CEO, Pres./$202,160.00, Daniel Nadeau/VP - Software Engineering, David Fabrizio/VP - Edgil Operations, Eli Rousso/Dir., CTO, Exec. VP, Sec., Treasurer/$202,160.00, Ed Heinrich/Sr. VP - Technology, Architecture, Jeffrey Baudo/Dir., COO, Sr. VP/$182,115.00, James Linesch/CFO/$163,292.00, William Bernhard/VP - Adstar Operations, Al Cortez/VP - Technical Operations, Ron Stephens/VP - Sales, Phil Lowe/Pres. - International Division

Directors: Leslie Bernhard/Dir., CEO, Pres., Eli Rousso/Dir., CTO, Exec. VP, Sec., Treasurer, Jeffrey Baudo/Dir., COO, Sr. VP, Michael Jackson/Dir., John C. Rudy/Dir., Peter M. Zollman/Dir., Michael Dubreuil/Dir.

Owners: Insiders/8.40%, James Linesch, Eli Rousso/3.20%, Michael Jackson, Leslie Bernhard/3.10%, Jeffrey Baudo/1.20%, Michael Dubreuil, Tribune Company/17.10%, John Rudy, Peter M. Zollman

Financial Data: Fiscal Year End:12/31 Latest Annual Data: 12/31/2006

Year	Sales	Net Income
2006	$5,114,000	-$1,393,000
2005	$5,239,000	-$1,090,000
2004	$4,934,000	-$3,648,000

Curr. Assets:	$3,236,000	Curr. Liab.:	$2,136,000		
Plant, Equip.:	$127,000	Total Liab.:	$2,189,000	Indic. Yr. Divd.:	NA
Total Assets:	$7,560,000	Net Worth:	$5,371,000	Debt/ Equity:	0.0049

Adtran Inc

901 Explorer Blvd., Huntsville, AL, 35806; ***PH:*** 1-256-963-8000; ***Fax:*** 1-256-963-8030; ***http://*** www.adtran.com; ***Email:*** info@adtran.com

General - Incorporation .... DE
Employees 1,601
Auditor .... PricewaterhouseCoopers LLP
Stk Agt .... American Stock Transfer & Trust CO.
Counsel .... James L. North
DUNS No. 14-787-1412

Stock- Price on:12/24/2007 .... $25.7
Stock Exchange .... NDQ
Ticker Symbol .... ADTN
Outstanding Shares 69,050,000
E.P.S. $1.07
Shareholders .... NA

Business: The group's principal activities are to design, manufacture, market and service high-speed network access products. The group operates in two divisions: carrier networks and enterprise networks. The carrier networks segment provides products for use in the service provider's local loop, including central office, remote terminal and customer premises. The enterprise networks segment offers products for use at enterprise headquarters, remote offices and telecommuting locations. The major customers include alltel corp, ingram micro inc, sbc communications inc,at&t corp, bell south corp, ingram micro, inc,qwest communications international, sbc communications, inc, sprint corp, tech data corp, telstra corp & verizon communications, inc. These customers use the group's products to implement high-speed voice and data communications over copper and fiber network infrastructures.

Primary SIC and add'l.: 3661

CIK No: 0000926282

Subsidiaries: ADTRAN Asia-Pacific, Inc., ADTRAN Asia-Pacific,Inc., ADTRAN Canada Inc., ADTRAN Networks GMBH, ADTRAN Networks, PTY. Ltd., Mexico ADTRAN Networks S.A. DE C.V.

Officers: Thomas R. Stanton/Dir., CEO/$912,618.00, James E. Matthews/Sr. VP - Finance, CFO, Treasurer, Sec., Dir./$433,008.00, Robert A. Fredrickson/VP - Carrier Networks Sales/$613,242.00, Kevin W. Schneider/CTO, Jay Wilson/Sr. VP, GM - Carrier Networks Division, Rick Schansman/Sr. VP, GM - Enterprise Networks Division, Michael Foliano/Sr. VP - Global Operations, Cathy Bartels/Contact - Investor Relations, Gayle Ellis/Contact - Investor Relations, Tammie Dodson/Contact - Media Inquiries, Ed Rohlfs/VP - Quality, Don Brannen/Quality Dir., Steve Shipley/Product Qualification Dir., William Powell/Customer Quality Engineer, Chuck Stutler/Supplier Quality Mgr.

Directors: Thomas R. Stanton/Dir., CEO, Mark C. Smith/67/Chmn. - Co - Founder, William L. Marks/64/Dir., James E. Matthews/Sr. VP - Finance, CFO, Treasurer, Sec., Dir., Frank W. Blount/Dir., Fenwick H. Huss/57/Dir., Roy J. Nichols/69/Dir., Balan Nair/41/Dir.

Owners: Mark C. Smith/11.50%, James L. North, Roy J. Nichols, Thomas R. Stanton, Frank W. Blount, Insiders/14.30%, Danny J. Windham, James E. Matthews, Steven L. Harvey, Robert A. Fredrickson, William L. Marks, Fenwick H. Huss

Financial Data: Fiscal Year End:12/31 Latest Annual Data: 12/31/2006

Year	Sales	Net Income
2006	$472,708,000	$78,333,000
2005	$513,215,000	$101,150,000
2004	$454,517,000	$75,141,000

Curr. Assets:	$269,165,000	Curr. Liab.:	$49,529,000	P/E Ratio:	23.80
Plant, Equip.:	$80,194,000	Total Liab.:	$103,702,000	Indic. Yr. Divd.:	$0.360
Total Assets:	$539,658,000	Net Worth:	$435,956,000	Debt/ Equity:	0.1106

Aduddell Industries Inc

1601 NW Exwy., Ste. 1500, Oklahoma City, OK, 73118; ***PH:*** 1-405-692-2300; ***http://*** www.aduddell.com; ***Email:*** contact@aduddell.com

General - Incorporation .... CO
Employees .... NA
Auditor .... Sutton Robinson Freeman & Co., P.C.
Stk Agt .... Jersey Transfer & Trust Co
Counsel .... NA
DUNS No. .... NA

Stock- Price on:12/24/2007 .... $0.52
Stock Exchange .... OTC
Ticker Symbol .... ADDL
Outstanding Shares .... NA
E.P.S. .... NA
Shareholders .... NA

Business: The groups principle activity is to provide commercial roofing services. The groups services include re-roofing, restoration and repair, new roof construction, sheet metal fabrication, waterproofing, and emergency post-event response services. In the year 2006, the group acquired Merit Construction Services. The group operates from the United States.

Primary SIC and add'l.: 1700

CIK No: 0000928373

Subsidiaries: Aduddell Financial Services LLC., Aduddell Restoration and Waterproofing, Inc., Aduddell Roofing, Inc., Enviro and Emergency management Services, Inc., Global Specialty Group, Inc.

Officers: Stan Genega/65/Dir., CEO, Pres./$218,346.00, Timothy Aduddell/53/Chmn., COO/$218,940.00, David Aduddell/44/Vice Chmn., Dir. - Corporate Development/$143,671.00, Falba Woodard/Sec., Reggie Cook/CFO/$121,476.00, Josh Brock/Interim CFO

Directors: Stan Genega/65/Dir., CEO, Pres., Timothy Aduddell/53/Chmn., COO, David Aduddell/44/Vice Chmn., Dir. - Corporate Development, Ron Carte/65/Dir., Jerry Whitlock/56/Dir., Thomas Parrish/58/Dir.

Owners: David Aduddell/6.60%, Doug Bruns, Doug Bruns, Stan Genega, Timothy Aduddell/60.10%, Oklahoma Development Group, LLC/6.70%, Jerry Whitlock/3.20%, Reggie Cook, Thomas Parrish, Ron Carte, Insiders/71.30%

Financial Data: Fiscal Year End:12/31 Latest Annual Data: 12/31/2006

Year	Sales	Net Income
2006	$31,661,000	-$2,891,000
2005	$59,227,000	$9,325,000
2004	$27,828,000	$1,534,000

Curr. Assets:	$19,300,000	Curr. Liab.:	$20,165,000		
Plant, Equip.:	$7,838,000	Total Liab.:	$21,684,000	Indic. Yr. Divd.:	NA
Total Assets:	$33,341,000	Net Worth:	$11,657,000	Debt/ Equity:	NA

Aduromed Industries Inc

Formerly: General Devices Inc
3 Trowbridge Dr., Bethel, CT, 06801; ***PH:*** 1-203-798-1080; ***http://*** www.gendevco.com

General - Incorporation .... DE
Employees 13
Auditor Child, Van Wagoner & Bradshaw, PLLC
Stk Agt ..... American Stock Transfer & Trust Co.
Counsel .... NA
DUNS No. 00-215-9333

Stock- Price on:12/24/2007 .... NA
Stock Exchange .... NA
Ticker Symbol .... NA
Outstanding Shares .... NA
E.P.S. .... -$0.16
Shareholders .... NA

Business: The group invested in the drilling of an oil well in eastern Montana in Jun 2002 and sold the same on 31-Dec-2002. On 02-Jan-2003, the proceeds from the sale were collected.

Primary SIC and add'l.: 1311

CIK No: 0000040528

Subsidiaries: Aduromed Corporation

Officers: Damien R. Tanaka/64/Chmn., CEO, Pres., Kevin T. Dunphy/59/Dir., CFO, Treasurer, Stephen Birch/36/VP - Business Development, Aduromed Corporation, Robert C. Meyer/52/VP - Operation, Marketing - Aduromed Corporation, Timothy R. Hertweck/53/VP - Sales, Aduromed Corporation

Directors: Damien R. Tanaka/64/Chmn., CEO, Pres., Paul Farrell/45/Dir., Kevin T. Dunphy/59/Dir., CFO, Treasurer, Jay S. Bendis/61/Dir., Elan Gandsman/66/Dir., Ronald A. Lamorte/70/Dir.

Owners: Damien R. Tanaka/34.06%, Paul T. Chan/4.45%, Crown Capital Pty Ltd./4.20%, Christopher J. Winners/3.71%, Sherleigh Associates Inc., Norman C. Kristoff/5.95%, Pequot Capital Management, Inc.

Financial Data: ***Fiscal Year End:***12/31 ***Latest Annual Data:*** 12/31/2006

Year	Sales	Net Income
2006	$4,594,000	-$3,282,000
2005	NA	-$1,056,000
2004	$0	-$81,000

Curr. Assets:	$2,917,000	***Curr. Liab.:***	$2,683,000		
Plant, Equip.:	$435,000	***Total Liab.:***	$2,933,000	***Indic. Yr. Divd.:***	NA
Total Assets:	$3,371,000	***Net Worth:***	$438,000	***Debt/ Equity:***	NA

Advance America Cash Advance Centers Inc

135 N Church St., Spartanburg, SC, 29306; ***PH:*** 1-864-342-5600; ***Fax:*** 1-864-342-5612; ***http://*** www.advanceamericacash.com

General - Incorporation	DE	***Stock*** - Price on:12/24/2007	$18.05
Employees	7,000	Stock Exchange	NYSE
Auditor	PricewaterhouseCoopers LLP	Ticker Symbol	AEA
Stk Agt	National City Bank	Outstanding Shares	79,540,000
Counsel	NA	E.P.S	$0.90
DUNS No.	NA	Shareholders	NA

Business: The groups principle activity is to provide payday cash advance services. The groups services include payday advance, deferred presentment, check-cashing, small loan, credit service. The group operates from the United States. The group's quarterly revenue for September 2007 was 133.22 millions of USD.

Primary SIC and add'l.: 6141

CIK No: 0001299704

Subsidiaries: AA Air, LLC, AA Canada Holdings, Inc., AA Challenger, LLC, AAIC, Inc., AARC, Inc., ACSO Michigan, Inc, ACSO of Texas, L.P., Advance America Leasing Services, Inc., Advance America Money.Com, Inc., Advance America Servicing Of Arkansas, Inc., Advance America Servicing Of Georgia, Inc., Advance America Servicing Of Indiana, Inc., Advance America Servicing Of Texas, L.P., Advance America, Cash Advance Centers Of Alabama, Inc., Advance America, Cash Advance Centers Of Alaska, Inc. 84 Subsidiaries included in the Index

Officers: Kenneth E. Compton/Dir., CEO, Pres., John I. Hill/54/Exec. VP, Leigh Anna Hollis/Sec., Patrick J. O'Shaughnessy/Dir., CFO, Exec. VP

Directors: Kenneth E. Compton/Dir., CEO, Pres., George D. Johnson/Chmn., William M. Webster/Vice Chmn., Stephen K. Benjamin/Dir., Robert H. Chapman/Dir., Thomas E. Hannah/Dir., Donovan A. Langford/Dir., Olin W. Nisbet/Dir., Patrick J. O'Shaughnessy/Dir., CFO, Exec. VP

Owners: Olin W. Nisbet, George D. Johnson/13.00%, William M. Webster/2.30%, Insiders/16.30%, AAI/SPJ Trust/5.80%, John I. Hill, Dean L. Buntrock/5.90%, Daniel C. Breeden/1.20%, Stephen K. Benjamin, Donovan A. Langford, Thomas E. Hannah, AAI/GDJ, III Trust/5.80%, Kenneth E. Compton, Robert H. Chapman

Financial Data: ***Fiscal Year End:***12/31 ***Latest Annual Data:*** 12/31/2006

Year	Sales	Net Income
2006	$672,294,000	$70,151,000
2005	$515,006,000	$62,990,000
2004	$570,188,000	$83,055,000

Curr. Assets:	$328,432,000	***Curr. Liab.:***	$68,421,000	***P/E Ratio:***	20.06
Plant, Equip.:	$63,198,000	***Total Liab.:***	$225,195,000	***Indic. Yr. Divd.:***	$0.500
Total Assets:	$525,092,000	***Net Worth:***	$299,897,000	***Debt/ Equity:***	0.1070

Advance Auto Parts Inc

5008 Airport Rd., Roanoke, VA, 24012; ***PH:*** 1-540-362-4911; ***Fax:*** 1-540-561-1448; ***http://*** www.advance-auto.com

General - Incorporation	DE	***Stock*** - Price on:12/24/2007	$41.01
Employees	25,489	Stock Exchange	NYSE
Auditor	Deloitte & Touche LLP	Ticker Symbol	AAP
Stk Agt	Mellon Investor Services LLC	Outstanding Shares	106,460,000
Counsel	NA	E.P.S	$2.24
DUNS No.	NA	Shareholders	NA

Business: The group's principle activity is to distribute automotive products. The group's products include replacement parts, accessories, maintenance items, batteries and automotive fluids for cars and light trucks. The group operates from United States, Puerto Rico and the Virgin Islands.

Primary SIC and add'l.: 5015

CIK No: 0001158449

Subsidiaries: Advance Aircraft Company, Inc., Advance Auto of Puerto Rico, Inc., Advance Merchandising Company, Inc., Advance Stores Company, Incorporated, Advance Trucking Corporation, AdvancePatriot, Inc., Autopart International, Inc., Discount Auto Parts, Inc., Western Auto Supply Company (Western Auto Supply Company operates auto parts stores through two wholly-owned subsidiaries organized in Delaware)

Officers: Jack Brouillard/Interim Chmn., CEO, Pres., Michael N. Coppola/Chmn., CEO, Pres./$3,240,540.00, Donald L. Lockard/Sr. VP - Store Operations, West, Keith A. Oreson/Sr. VP - Human Resources, Kenneth A. Wirth/Sr. VP - Store Operations, Northeast, Jill A. Livesay/Sr. VP, Controller, Tom Merk/Sr. VP - Store Operations, Southeast, Randall A. Young/Sr. VP - Real Estate, Eric M. Margolin/Sr. VP, General Counsel, Sec., David B. Mueller/Exec. VP - Merchandising, Marketing/$1,094,983.00, Kurt R. Schumacher/Sr. VP - Store Operations, Florida, Ralph Castanza/Sr. VP - Store Operations, Michael O. Moore/CFO, Exec. VP/$942,910.00, Jimmie L. Wade/Exec. VP - Business Development/$1,746,148.00, Ricardo S. Coro/Sr. VP - Information Technology, CIO *(20 Officers included in Index)*

Directors: Jack Brouillard/Interim Chmn., CEO, Pres., Michael N. Coppola/Chmn., CEO, Pres., Carlos A. Saladrigas/Dir., Francesca M. Spinelli/Dir., William S. Oglesby/Dir., Lawrence P. Castellani/Dir., Nicholas J. Lahowchic/Dir., Gilbert T. Ray/Dir., Darren R. Jackson/Dir., John C. Brouillard/Dir., William L. Salter/Dir.

Owners: Jimmie L. Wade, T. Rowe Price Associates, Inc./5.30%, William S. Oglesby, Michael O. Moore, Francesca M. Spinelli, Lawrence P. Castellani, William L. Salter, John C. Brouillard, Insiders/2.70%, Darren R. Jackson, Carlos A. Saladrigas, David B. Mueller, Gilbert T. Ray, Paul W. Klasing, Nicholas J. LaHowchic *(16 Owners included in Index)*

Financial Data: ***Fiscal Year End:***12/31 ***Latest Annual Data:*** 12/30/2006

Year	Sales	Net Income
2006	$4,616,503,000	$231,318,000
2005	$4,264,971,000	$234,725,000

Curr. Assets:	$1,547,940,000	***Curr. Liab.:***	$1,141,464,000	***P/E Ratio:***	18.31
Plant, Equip.:	$907,049,000	***Total Liab.:***	$1,622,378,000	***Indic. Yr. Divd.:***	$0.240
Total Assets:	$2,542,149,000	***Net Worth:***	$919,771,000	***Debt/ Equity:***	0.3615

Advance Display Technologies Inc

7334 S Alton Way Ste. F, Centennial, CO, 80112; ***PH:*** 1-303-267-0111; ***Fax:*** 1-303-267-0330; ***http://*** www.gilead.com

General - Incorporation	CO	***Stock*** - Price on:12/24/2007	NA
Employees	5	Stock Exchange	OTC
Auditor	Hein & Assoc. LLP	Ticker Symbol	ADTI
Stk Agt	Mellon Investor Services LLC	Outstanding Shares	26,200,000
Counsel	NA	E.P.S	-$0.13
DUNS No.	14-829-7500	Shareholders	NA

Business: The group's principle activities include developing and manufacturing full color video and other display screen systems. It develops display screen system using a projection light source to send images through a bundle of optical fibers that are evenly disbursed in a matrix pattern forming the viewable screen face. This screen is designed so that the image input by the projector is enlarged many times on the face of the screen. Products are used in video display systems for stadiums and arenas, point-of-purchase advertising in markets such as shopping malls, department stores and supermarkets, as well as in providing information and advertising in locations such as airports, trade shows, race tracks and video billboards. On 30-Nov-2003, the company acquired all of the membership interests in regent theaters, l.l.c. And regent releasing, l.l.c. From regent entertainment partnership, l.p. Of Dallas, Texas. The group operates from United states.

Primary SIC and add'l.: 3651 3993

CIK No: 0000770034

Officers: Matthew W. Shankle/48/Dir., CEO, Pres./$131,154.00, John W. Temple/53/VP - Technical Sales, Dir./$123,797.00, James P. Martindale/45/VP - Manufacturing, Technical Operations

Directors: Matthew W. Shankle/48/Dir., CEO, Pres., John W. Temple/53/VP - Technical Sales, Dir., Lawrence F. Degeorge/64/Dir.

Owners: John W. Temple/4.88%, James P. Martindale/0.36%, G. Schneider Holdings, Co./20.85%, Lawrence F. DeGeorge/69.55%, Bruce H. Etkin/13.70%, Lawrence F. DeGeorge/15.96%, Insiders/22.41%, Lawrence F. DeGeorge/100.00%, Insiders/100.00%, Insiders/70.11%, Matthew W. Shankle/2.33%, John W. Temple/1.09%, William W. Becker/7.90%

Financial Data: ***Fiscal Year End:***06/30 ***Latest Annual Data:*** 6/30/2006

Year	Sales	Net Income
2006	$125,000	-$1,182,000
2005	$104,000	-$760,000
2004	$115,000	-$598,000

Curr. Assets:	$142,000	***Curr. Liab.:***	$1,453,000		
Plant, Equip.:	$49,000	***Total Liab.:***	$1,459,000	***Indic. Yr. Divd.:***	NA
Total Assets:	$191,000	***Net Worth:***	-$1,268,000	***Debt/ Equity:***	NA

Advance Nanotech Inc

600 Lexington Ave. Fl 29, New York, NY, 10022; ***PH:*** 1-212-583-0080; ***http://*** www.advancenanotech.com; ***Email:*** info@advancenanotech.com

General - Incorporation	CO	***Stock*** - Price on:12/24/2007	$0.34
Employees	25	Stock Exchange	OTC
Auditor	Mendoza Berger & Company, LLP	Ticker Symbol	AVNA
Stk Agt	Computershare Trust Co	Outstanding Shares	35,390,000
Counsel	NA	E.P.S	NA
DUNS No.	NA	Shareholders	NA

Business: The groups principle activity is to provide financing and support services to drive the commercialization of nanotechnology related products. The group operates through two segments namely advance display technologies and advance homeland security. The group operates from the United States and the United Kingdom. The groups quarterly revenue for September 2007 was 0.10 millions of USD.

Primary SIC and add'l.: 6799

CIK No: 0000354699

Subsidiaries: Advance Display Technologies PLC, Advance Homeland Security PLC, Advance Nanotech Ltd., Advance Nanotech Singapore Pte. Ltd., Bio-Nano Sensium Tech. Ltd., Cambridge Nanotechnology Ltd., NanoFED Ltd., NanoSolutions Ltd., Owlstone Nanotech Inc., Owlstone Nanotech Ltd., Singular ID Pte. Ltd.

Officers: Tony Goncalves/CEO, Mangnus R.E. Gittins/Co - Founder, Exec. Chmn./$624,444.00, Thomas P. Finn/CFO/$419,921.00, Michael Helmus/Sr. VP - Biopharma/$319,258.00, Gerhard Rebel/Sr. VP - Technology, Michael Jordan/Corporate Advisor, David Clarke/Corporate Advisor, Jonathan Segal/Corporate Advisor, Louis Marx/Corporate Advisor, Larry D. Bouts/Corporate Advisor, Greg Osborn/Corporate Advisor, Timothy Lane/Corporate Advisor, Giles Davies/Science Advisor, Bill Milne/Science Advisor, James Scott/Science Advisor *(16 Officers included in Index)*

Directors: Mangnus R.E. Gittins/Co - Founder, Exec. Chmn., Lee J. Cole/Dir., John Robertson/Dir., Peter Rugg/Dir., Virgil E. Wenger/Dir., Douglas Zorn/59/Dir.

Owners: Lee Cole, Antonio Goncalves, Peter Rugg, Thomas Finn, Michael Helmus, Insiders/3.93%, Magnus Gittins/1.97%, John Robertson, Virgil Wenger

Curr. Assets:	$1,858,000	***Curr. Liab.:***	$4,139,000		
Plant, Equip.:	$351,000	***Total Liab.:***	$11,273,000	***Indic. Yr. Divd.:***	NA
Total Assets:	$4,452,000	***Net Worth:***	-$6,821,000	***Debt/ Equity:***	NA

Advanced Analogic Technologies Inc

830 E Arques Ave., Sunnyvale, CA, 94085; *PH:* 1-408-737-4600; *Fax:* 1-408-737-4611; *http://* www.analogictech.com; *Email:* info@analogictech.com

General - Incorporation	DE	**Stock**- Price on:12/24/2007	$9.55
Employees	252	Stock Exchange	NDQ
Auditor	Deloitte& Touche LLP	Ticker Symbol	AATI
Stk Agt	Mellon Investor Services LLC	Outstanding Shares	44,570,000
Counsel	NA	E.P.S	-$0.13
DUNS No.	NA	Shareholders	NA

Business: The groups principal activities include design and marketing management semiconductors for mobile consumer electronic devices. The groups services include digital music downloads, video downloads, video messaging, video streaming. The product line of the group includes voltage regulation and dc, dc conversion, battery management, display and lighting solutions, interface and power management. The group products sold under the trade names S2Cwire(TM), NanoPowe(TM) and AutoBias(TM). Specific customers of the group include LG Electronics, Inc, Samsung Electronics Co Ltd., Sagem SA, Pantech and Curitel Communications, Inc, Motorola, Inc and Sony Ericsson. In the year October 2006, the group acquired Analog Power Semiconductor Corporation. The group operates from the South Korea, Taiwan, China, Europe, Japan and North America. Of the year 2006, voltage regulation and dc, dc conversion accounted for 21%, battery management 1%, display and lighting solutions 56% and interface and power management 22%.

Primary SIC and add'l.: 3674 3679

CIK No: 0001104042

Subsidiaries: Advanced Analogic Technologies, Advanced Analogic Technologies (France) SARL, Advanced Analogic Technologies Corporation, Advanced Analogic Technologies Holdings, Inc., Advanced Analogic Technologies Japan, Advanced Analogic Technologies(Hong Kong)Ltd., Analog Power Semiconductor (Shanghai) Co., Ltd., Analog Power Semiconductor Corporation

Officers: Richard K. Williams/Dir., CEO, CTO, Pres./$1,144,112.00, Brian R. McDonald/CFO, VP - Worldwide Finance, Sec./$780,867.00, Jun-Wei Chen/VP - Technology/$417,733.00, Kevin D'Angelo/VP - Engineering/$533,911.00, Allen Lam/VP - Worldwide Operations/$535,882.00, Eden Ho/Contact - Direct Sales, China, Rack Ko/Contact - Direct Sales, China, Heather Cha/Contact - Direct Sales, Australia, Bill Compitello/Contact - Direct Sales, Canada, Marja-Liisa Syrjakyka/Contact - Direct Sales, Canada, Gerard Ducrot/Contact - Direct Sales, France, Phil Dewsbury/Contact - Direct Sales, Ireland, Ryoki Chiba/Contact - Direct Sales, Japan, Jan Gripsborn/Contact - Direct Sales, Denmark, John Franz/Contact - Direct Sales, United States *(16 Officers included in Index)*

Directors: Richard K. Williams/Dir., CEO, CTO, Pres., Samuel J. Anderson/Chmn., Thomas C. Weatherford/Dir., Kenneth P. Lawler/Dir., Jaff Lin/Dir., Chandramohan Subramaniam/Dir.

Owners: Battery Ventures Funds/7.30%, Samuel J. Anderson, Insiders/16.30%, Thomas Weatherford, Richard K. Williams/6.10%, Jaff Lin, Allen K. Lam/1.00%, Kevin DAngelo/1.00%, T. Rowe Price Associates, Inc./5.00%, Jun-Wei Chen, Kenneth P. Lawler/7.30%, Brian R. McDonald

Financial Data: ***Fiscal Year End:***12/31 ***Latest Annual Data:*** 12/31/2006

Year	Sales	Net Income
2006	$81,161,000	-$2,082,000
2005	$68,298,000	$2,085,000
2004	$51,345,000	$15,178,000

Curr. Assets:	$130,984,000	**Curr. Liab.:**	$15,070,000		
Plant, Equip.:	$2,812,000	**Total Liab.:**	$15,261,000	**Indic. Yr. Divd.:**	NA
Total Assets:	$161,198,000	**Net Worth:**	$145,937,000	**Debt/ Equity:**	0.0162

Advanced Battery Technologies Inc

21 W 39th St. Rm 2a, New York, NY, 10018; *PH:* 1-212-391-2752; *Fax:* 1-212-391-5751; *http://* www.abat.com; *Email:* sales@zqpt.com

General - Incorporation	DE	**Stock**- Price on:12/24/2007	$2.58
Employees	1,264	Stock Exchange	AMEX
Auditor	Bagell, Josephs, Levine & Co., L.l.c.	Ticker Symbol	GBT
Stk Agt	Continental Stock Transfer & Trust Co	Outstanding Shares	49,630,000
Counsel	NA	E.P.S	$0.14
DUNS No.	NA	Shareholders	NA

Business: The groups principle activities include designing, manufacturing and marketing rechargeable polymer lithium-ion batteries. The group products include rechargeable PLI batteries for mine-use lamps, electric automobiles, motorcycles, cellular phones, notebook computers, walkie-talkies and other personal electronic devices. The group operates from China and the United States. The groups quarterly revenue for September 2007 was 8.57 millions of USD.

Primary SIC and add'l.: 3691

CIK No: 0000745651

Subsidiaries: Cashtech Investment Limited, Heilongjiang ZhongQiang Power-Tech Co

Owners: Zhiguo Fu/15.80%, Insiders/15.80%

Financial Data: ***Fiscal Year End:***12/31 ***Latest Annual Data:*** 12/31/2006

Year	Sales	Net Income
2006	$16,329,000	$5,991,000
2005	$4,223,000	-$158,000
2004	$1,192,000	-$2,350,000

Curr. Assets:	$7,969,000	**Curr. Liab.:**	$981,000	**P/E Ratio:**	18.43
Plant, Equip.:	$12,889,000	**Total Liab.:**	$1,365,000	**Indic. Yr. Divd.:**	NA
Total Assets:	$22,522,000	**Net Worth:**	$21,156,000	**Debt/ Equity:**	0.0181

Advanced Biotherapy Inc

141 W Jackson Blvd., Ste. 2182, Chicago, IL, 60604; *PH:* 1-312-427-1912; *http://* www.advancedbiotherapy.com; *Email:* info@advancedbiotherapy.com

General - Incorporation	DE	**Stock**- Price on:12/24/2007	$0.02
Employees	NA	Stock Exchange	OTC
Auditor	Williams & Webster, P.S	Ticker Symbol	ADVB
Stk Agt	American Stock Transfer & Trust Co.	Outstanding Shares	946,560,000
Counsel	Rutter Hobbs & Davidoff Inc	E.P.S	NA
DUNS No.	NA	Shareholders	NA

Business: The group's principle activities include research and developing on therapeutics for a range of autoimmune diseases based on an anti-cytokine platform technology. The company is a development stage enterprise conducting its research in Maryland. The primary area under consideration is research and development of the treatment of autoimmune diseases in humans, most notably, multiple sclerosis and rheumatoid arthritis. The company's activities have consisted primarily of research, development and non-United States clinical trials.the company has developed drugs through out-licensing or development arrangements that may effectively treat a range of autoimmune diseases. The company conducts its research in Maryland. The company is a development stage enterprise. The group operates from United States.

Primary SIC and add'l.: 8731 2834

CIK No: 0000791833

Subsidiaries: Advanced Biotherapy, Inc

Officers: Christopher W. Capps/25/CEO, Pres., Simon Skurkovich/Founder, Chmn. Emeritus, VP - Research, Development, Joseph A. Bellanti/73/Dir., Scientific Advisor, Thomas J. Pernice/46/Dir., Treasurer, Sec., John L. Drew/CFO, Controller

Directors: Simon Skurkovich/Founder, Chmn. Emeritus, VP - Research, Development, Richard P. Kiphart/66/Chmn., Keith Gregg/44/Dir., Boris Skurkovich/52/Dir., Thomas J. Pernice/46/Dir., Treasurer, Sec., Lawrence Loomis/65/Member - Advisory Board, Edmond F. Buccellato/62/Member - Advisory Board, Joseph A. Bellanti/73/Dir., Scientific Advisor, Matthew Gooch/33/Dir., David Valentine/38/Dir.

Owners: David Valentine, Insiders/86.67%, Joseph A. Bellanti, John R. Capps, Thomas J. Pernice, Christopher W. Capps, Boris Skurkovich/1.12%, Matthew Gooch, Michael P. Krasny/6.56%, Keith Gregg, Richard P. Kiphart/81.46%

Financial Data: ***Fiscal Year End:***12/31 ***Latest Annual Data:*** 12/31/2006

Year	Sales	Net Income
2006	NA	-$7,419,000
2005	NA	-$2,158,000
2004	NA	-$2,441,000

Curr. Assets:	$6,150,000	**Curr. Liab.:**	$112,000		
Plant, Equip.:	$275,000	**Total Liab.:**	$112,000	**Indic. Yr. Divd.:**	NA
Total Assets:	$7,204,000	**Net Worth:**	$7,093,000	**Debt/ Equity:**	NA

Advanced Cell Technology Inc

1201 Harbor Bay Pkwy., Ste. 120, Alameda, CA, 94502; *PH:* 1-510-748-4901; *Fax:* 1-510-748-4950; *http://* www.advancedcell.com; *Email:* info@advancedcell.com

General - Incorporation	DE	**Stock**- Price on:12/24/2007	$0.66
Employees	40	Stock Exchange	OTC
Auditor	Stonefield Josephson, Inc.	Ticker Symbol	ACTC
Stk Agt	Interwest Transfer Company, Inc.	Outstanding Shares	49,470,000
Counsel	NA	E.P.S	-$0.49
DUNS No.	NA	Shareholders	NA

Business: The groups principle activities include developing and commercializing human stem cell technology in the emerging field of regenerative medicine. The groups quarterly revenue for September 2007 was 0.12 millions of USD. The group operates from the United States.

Primary SIC and add'l.: 2836

CIK No: 0001140098

Officers: William M. Caldwell/Chmn., CEO, Robert Lanza/Chief Scientific Officer, Jonathan F. Atzen/Sr. VP, General Counsel, Ivan Wolkind/Sr. VP - Finance, Administration, Chief Accounting Officer, Jonathan H. Dinsmore/Sr. VP - Regulatory, Clinical

Directors: William M. Caldwell/Chmn., CEO, Michael D. West/Dir., Erkki Ruoslahti/Dir., Alan C. Shapiro/Dir., Alan G. Walton/Dir., Ronald M. Green/Member - Ethics Advisory Board, Judith Bernstein/Member - Ethics Advisory Board, Kenneth W. Goodman/Member - Ethics Advisory Board, Jeremy B.A. Green/Member - Ethics Advisory Board, Robert Kaufmann/Member - Ethics Advisory Board, Carol A. Tauer/Member - Ethics Advisory Board, Kier Olsen Devries/Member - Ethics Advisory Board, Gary Rabin/43/Dir.

Owners: Gary Rabin/2.40%, Anthem Ventures Fund, L.P./15.60%, Erkki Ruoslahti, Alan G. Walton, Robert Peabody, Alan C. Shapiro/4.60%, Insiders/20.40%, Robert P. Lanza/2.50%, Michael D. West/5.80%, William M. Caldwell/4.70%, Pedro Huertas/1.70%, Jonathan F. Atzen/1.00%, Ivan Wolkind

Financial Data: ***Fiscal Year End:***12/31 ***Latest Annual Data:*** 12/31/2006

Year	Sales	Net Income
2006	$441,000	-$18,720,000
2005	$395,000	-$9,394,000
2004	$3,000	-$52,000

Curr. Assets:	$9,092,000	**Curr. Liab.:**	$19,036,000		
Plant, Equip.:	$1,082,000	**Total Liab.:**	$46,532,000	**Indic. Yr. Divd.:**	NA
Total Assets:	$16,990,000	**Net Worth:**	-$29,542,000	**Debt/ Equity:**	NA

Advanced Communications Technologies Inc

420 Lexington Ave., New York, NY, 10170; *PH:* 1-646-227-1600; *http://* www.advancedcomtech.net

General - Incorporation	FL	**Stock**- Price on:12/24/2007	$0.0008
Employees	102	Stock Exchange	OTC
Auditor	J.H. Cohn, LLP	Ticker Symbol	ADVC
Stk Agt	American Stock Transfer & Trust Co.	Outstanding Shares	NA
Counsel	Levinson & Lichtman	E.P.S	$0.00
DUNS No.	NA	Shareholders	NA

Business: The group's principal activity is the ownership of the rights to the spectrucell technology including a license and distribution agreement and its investment in advanced communications (Australia). The primary focus of the group is the marketing and distribution of advanced communications (Australia)'s software defined radio based wireless communication product 'spectrucell'. Spectrucell is a wireless software based communications platform that is being developed to offer mobile communications network providers the flexibility of processing and transmitting multiple wireless communication signals through one base station. The group owns the north and south American rights to market and distribute spectrucell.

Primary SIC and add'l.: 7379

CIK No: 0001100820

Subsidiaries: Cyber-Test, Inc., Encompass Group Affiliates, Inc, Hudson Street Investments, LLC, SpectruCell, Inc.

Officers: Wayne I. Danson/Dir., CEO, CFO, Pres., Lisa A. Welton/Pres., CEO - Cyber, Test, Fred Baldwin/Pres., CEO - Vance, Baldwin Electronics, Thomas Sutlive/Sr. VP - Cyber, Test, Robert Coolidge/Sr. VP - Vance, Baldwin Electronics, Steven J. Miller/COO, John E. Donahue/VP, CFO - Online Benefits Inc

Directors: Wayne I. Danson/Dir., CEO, CFO, Pres., Wilbank J. Roche/62/Dir., John G. Ball/69/Dir., John R. Black/44/Dir., Thomas R. Ketteler/65/Dir., William J. Nolan/34/Dir., Gerald E. Wedren/71/Dir.

Owners: Robert Coolidge/56.25%, Insiders/35.35%, Robert Coolidge/1.50%, Steven J. Miller/3.71%, Sankaty entities, John E. Donahue/6.67%, Fred Baldwin/31.25%, Wilbank J. Roche/1.26%, Steven J. Miller/11.16%, Wayne I. Danson/1.24%, Insiders/7.68%, Wayn I. Danson, John E. Donahue/1.86%, Scott Cameron/12.50%, Wilbank J. Roche *(16 Owners included in Index)*

Financial Data: *Fiscal Year End:*06/30 *Latest Annual Data:* 06/30/2007

Year	Sales	Net Income
2007	$9,244,000	-$1,250,000
2006	$9,183,000	-$574,000
2005	$7,522,000	-$736,000

Curr. Assets:	$1,728,000	*Curr. Liab.:*	$4,205,000		
Plant, Equip.:	$262,000	*Total Liab.:*	$7,591,000	*Indic. Yr. Divd.:*	NA
Total Assets:	$5,508,000	*Net Worth:*	-$2,083,000	*Debt/ Equity:*	NA

Advanced Digital Information Corp

11431 Willows Rd. Ne, Redmond, WA, 98073; *PH:* 1-425-881-8004; *http://* www.adic.com

General - Incorporation............WA	**Stock**- Price on:12/24/2007 ....$3.04
Employees 2,320	Stock Exchange..............................NA
Auditor ....PricewaterhouseCoopers LLP	Ticker Symbol..................................NA
Stk Agt...... American Stock Transfer & Trust Co.	Outstanding Shares 199,200,000
Counsel......................Perkins Coie LLP	E.P.S..NA
DUNS No. 10-350-7778	Shareholders....................................NA

Business: The group's principal activity is to provide hardware and software-based data storage solutions to the open systems marketplace. It offers products, which help organizations to effectively capture, protect, manage and archive the increasing amount of complex data. The products are used to store, protect, manage and access data in computer networks based on open systems standards. The open systems storage management software product is a component of a sophisticated data storage system. The group has operations in the United States and Europe.

Primary SIC and add'l.: 7372 3572 3577

CIK No: 0000770403

Subsidiaries: ADIC AG, ADIC Europe SARL, ADIC Germany Beteiligungs GmbH, ADIC Germany GmbH & Co. KG, ADIC Germany Sales & Support GmbH, ADIC International Holdings, ADIC Limited, ADIC Manufacturing, LLCMountaingate Imaging Systems Corporation, Pathlight Technology, Inc.

Financial Data: *Fiscal Year End:*10/31 *Latest Annual Data:* 03/31/2007

Year	Sales	Net Income
2007	$1,016,174,000	-$64,094,000
2006	NA	NA
2005	$794,168,000	-$3,496,000

Curr. Assets:	$386,461,000	*Curr. Liab.:*	$329,450,000		
Plant, Equip.:	$50,241,000	*Total Liab.:*	$871,388,000	*Indic. Yr. Divd.:*	NA
Total Assets:	$1,125,829,000	*Net Worth:*	$254,441,000	*Debt/ Equity:*	1.9552

Advanced Energy Industries Inc

1625 Sharp Point Dr., Fort Collins, CO, 80525; *PH:* 1-970-221-4670; *Fax:* 1-970-407-6550; *http://* www.advanced-energy.com; *Email:* sales.support@aei.com

General - Incorporation............DE	**Stock**- Price on:12/24/2007 ....$23.13
Employees 1,583	Stock Exchange..............................NDQ
Auditor ....Grant Thornton LLP	Ticker Symbol..................................AEIS
Stk Agt...... American Stock Transfer & Trust Co.	Outstanding Shares 45,170,000
Counsel......Thelen Reid & Priest LLP	E.P.S..$1.55
DUNS No. 02-119-2422	Shareholders....................................NA

Business: The group's principal activity is to design and manufacture a group of key components and subsystems primarily for vacuum process systems. The primary products of the group are complex power conversion and control systems. The customers of the group use the products in plasma-based thin-film processing equipment. This equipment is used in the manufacture of semiconductor devices for electronics applications, flat panel displays for hand-held devices, computer and television screens, compact discs, dvds and other digital storage media, optical coatings for architectural glass, eyeglasses and solar panels and industrial laser and medical applications. The group has operations in the United States, Europe and Asia-Pacific.

Primary SIC and add'l.: 3823 3629 3625

CIK No: 0000927003

Officers: Hans-Georg Betz/Dir., CEO, Pres./$1,687,370.00, Yves Hamel/Advanced Energy, Lumbin, France, John D. Pirnot/Corp. Sec., Steve Rhoades/COO, Lawrence Firestone/CFO/$252,238.00, Charles S. Rhoades/47/COO, Exec. VP/$959,595.00, Jim Guilmart/Sr. VP - Sales/$524,017.00, Zach Ward/Direct Sales Representative - British Columbia, Michael Frank/Authorized Regional Representative, British Columbia, Tom Leeland/Authorized Regional Representative, British Columbia, Kim Mast/Customer Quality Contact - British Columbia, Troy Mai/Customer Quality Contact - British Columbia, Reese Puckett/Direct Sales Representative - Manitoba, Mike Berry/Authorized Regional Representative, Maine, Dave Stapleton/Authorized Regional Representative, Pennsylvania *(43 Officers included in Index)*

Directors: Hans-Georg Betz/Dir., CEO, Pres., Douglas S. Schatz/Chmn., Co - Founder, Richard P. Beck/Dir., Trung T. Doan/Dir., Thomas M. Rohrs/Dir., Elwood Spedden/Dir., Joseph R. Bronson/Dir., Barry Z. Posner/Dir.

Owners: Insiders/22.20%, Hans Georg Betz, Joseph R. Bronson, Barry Z. Posner, T. Rowe Price Associates, Inc./6.50%, Charles S. Rhoades, Trung T. Doan, Elwood Spedden, Barclays Global/6.00%, Mark D. Hartman, Douglas S. Schatz/21.00%, James G. Guilmart, Richard P. Beck

Financial Data: *Fiscal Year End:*12/31 *Latest Annual Data:* 12/31/2006

Year	Sales	Net Income
2006	$410,742,000	$88,322,000
2005	$325,482,000	$12,817,000
2004	$395,305,000	-$12,747,000

Curr. Assets:	$300,727,000	*Curr. Liab.:*	$52,929,000	*P/E Ratio:*	12.92
Plant, Equip.:	$33,571,000	*Total Liab.:*	$56,113,000	*Indic. Yr. Divd.:*	NA
Total Assets:	$411,903,000	*Net Worth:*	$355,790,000	*Debt/ Equity:*	0.0004

Advanced Environmental Recycling Tec Inc

914 N Jefferson St., Springdale, AR, 72764; *PH:* 1-479-756-7400; *Fax:* 1-479-756-7410; *http://* www.choicedek.com; *Email:* info@aertinc.com

General - Incorporation .... DE	**Stock**- Price on:12/24/2007 ....$1.73
Employees 664	Stock Exchange..............................NDQ
Auditor ..... Tullius Taylor Sartain & Sartain LLP	Ticker Symbol..................................AERT
Stk Agt...... American Stock Transfer & Trust Co.	Outstanding Shares 47,030,000
Counsel .... Akin, Gump, Strauss, Hauer & Feld LLP	E.P.S..-$0.05
DUNS No. 61-000-8500	Shareholders....................................NA

Business: The group's principal activities are to develop, manufacture and market composite building materials that can be used as an alternative to traditional wood products for exterior applications in building and remodeling homes. The group uses waste wood fiber and reclaimed polyethylene plastics as raw materials. These products are marketed under the trade names lifecycle(R), moistureshield(R), weyerhaeuser choicedek(R) classic, weyerhaeuser choicedek(R) plus and weyerhaeuser choicedek(R) premium. The group's customers primarily consist of a number of regional and national door and window manufacturers, industrial-flooring companies and weyerhaeuser, the group's primary decking customer.

Primary SIC and add'l.: 5039

CIK No: 0000849706

Officers: Joe G. Brooks/52/Chmn., CEO, Pres./$263,162.00, Alford Drinkwater/56/Sr. VP/$114,127.00, Stephen W. Brooks/51/Dir., COO/$150,963.00, Marjorie S. Brooks/72/Dir., Sec., Treasurer, Douglas J. Brooks/48/Sr. VP/$128,324.00, Jim Precht/62/Sr. VP - Sales, Marketing/$167,885.00, Robert A. Thayer/56/Sr. VP, CFO/$188,065.00, Eric E. Barnes/34/Chief Accounting Officer, Controller

Directors: Joe G. Brooks/52/Chmn., CEO, Pres., Melinda Davis/65/Dir., Jim Robason/70/Dir., Sal Miwa/51/Dir., Stephen W. Brooks/51/Dir., COO, Marjorie S. Brooks/72/Dir., Sec., Treasurer, Jerry B. Burkett/51/Dir., Edward P. Carda/67/Dir., Tim W. Kizer/42/Dir., Samuel L. Milbank/67/Dir., Michael M. Tull/53/Dir.

Owners: Jerry B. Burkett, Sal Miwa, Jim Precht, Melinda Davis, Joe G. Brooks/1.90%, Tim W. Kizer, Jerry B. Burkett, Insiders/43.30%, Peter S. Lau, Stephen W. Brooks/2.40%, Alford Drinkwater, Jim Robason, Sal Miwa, Michael M. Tull/1.90%, Edward P. Carda *(18 Owners included in Index)*

Financial Data: *Fiscal Year End:*12/31 *Latest Annual Data:* 12/31/2006

Year	Sales	Net Income
2006	$97,840,000	$1,805,000
2005	$87,313,000	$7,798,000
2004	$63,637,000	$1,268,000

Curr. Assets:	$24,200,000	*Curr. Liab.:*	$27,666,000		
Plant, Equip.:	$37,522,000	*Total Liab.:*	$44,494,000	*Indic. Yr. Divd.:*	NA
Total Assets:	$72,050,000	*Net Worth:*	$27,557,000	*Debt/ Equity:*	0.6056

Advanced ID Corp

6143 4th St. SE, Ste. 14, Calgary, AB, T2H 2H9; *PH:* 1-403-264-6300; *Fax:* 1-403-263-2055; *http://* www.advancedidcorp.com; *Email:* info@avidcanada.com

General - Incorporation ....SD	**Stock**- Price on:12/24/2007 ....$0.36
Employees ....NA	Stock Exchange..............................OTC
Auditor ....Lopez, Blevins, Bork & Assoc. LLP	Ticker Symbol..................................AIDO
Stk Agt...............Signature Stock Transfer, Inc.	Outstanding Shares ....NA
Counsel......................NA	E.P.S..NA
DUNS No. ....NA	Shareholders....................................NA

Business: The group's principal activities are the distributing and marketing of radio frequency identification microchips and scanners. The group supplies over 3,000 organizations such as animal shelters, veterinarians, breeders, government agencies, universities, zoos, research labs and fisheries with rfid devices. The group also provides service to global tracking system for all animals identified with microchips in Canada.

Primary SIC and add'l.: 3679

CIK No: 0001005356

Subsidiaries: Advanced ID Asia Engineering Co. Ltd, AVID Canada Corporation, Universal Pet Care

Officers: Dan Finch/Dir., Pres., CEO - Pneu, Logic, Terry R. Fields/Dir. - Pneu, Logic, Marci Buckland/Contact - Sales, Laren Yeomans/MD - Pneu, Logic Ltd, Gottfried Auer/MD - Advanced ID Asia Engineering Co Ltd, Sudeep Bhargava/VP - Operations, COO - Advanced ID Corporation, Jan Wilke/Contact - Sales, Ken Field/Contact - Sales, Sales Dir. - Pneu, Logic, Advanced ID Products, Sergio Teles/Marketing Executive

Directors: Seymour Kazimirski/Chmn. - Pneu, Logic, Hubert Meier/Dir. - Pneu, Logic

Owners: Seymour Kazimirski/5.50%, Heritage Ventures Ltd./27.10%

Financial Data: *Fiscal Year End:*12/31 *Latest Annual Data:* 12/31/2006

Year	Sales	Net Income
2006	$889,000	-$2,211,000
2005	$1,028,000	-$1,050,000
2004	$896,000	-$1,867,000

Curr. Assets:	$456,000	*Curr. Liab.:*	$376,000		
Plant, Equip.:	$144,000	*Total Liab.:*	$423,000	*Indic. Yr. Divd.:*	NA
Total Assets:	$656,000	*Net Worth:*	$233,000	*Debt/ Equity:*	0.0891

Advanced Life Sciences Holdings Inc

1440 DAve.y Rd., Woodridge, IL, 60517; *PH:* 1-630-739-6744; *Fax:* 1-630-739-6754; *http://* www.advancedlifesciences.com; *Email:* publicrelations@advancedlifesciences.com

General - Incorporation .... DE	**Stock**- Price on:12/24/2007 ....$3.19
Employees 28	Stock Exchange..............................NDQ
Auditor ....Deloitte & Touche LLP	Ticker Symbol..................................ADLS
Stk Agt...............LaSalle Bank N.A	Outstanding Shares 28,290,000
Counsel......................NA	E.P.S..-$1.162
DUNS No. ....NA	Shareholders....................................NA

Business: The groups principle activities include discovering, developing and commercializing novel drugs. The group products sold under the trade name Ketek(R). The group operates from United States.

Primary SIC and add'l.: 2836 2834

CIK No: 0001322734

Officers: Michael T. Flavin/Chmn., CEO - Advanced Life Sciences Inc/$377,069.00, John L. Flavin/Dir., Pres. - Advanced Life Sciences Inc/$313,202.00, Suseelan Pookote/Exec. VP - Corporate Development/$271,515.00, Richard R. Wieland/CFO, Exec. VP/$262,154.00, Ze-Qi Xu/Chief Scientific Officer, Exec. VP/$249,786.00, David A. Eiznhamer/Exec. VP - Clinical Development/$254,036.00, Patrick W. Flavin/Chief Legal Counsel, Michael J. Cogan/VP, Controller, Edward P. Flavin/Primary Investor Relations Officer

Directors: Michael T. Flavin/Chmn., CEO - Advanced Life Sciences Inc, John L. Flavin/Dir., Pres. - Advanced Life Sciences Inc, Rosalie Sagraves/Dir. - Advanced Life Sciences Inc, Thomas V. Thornton/Dir. - Advanced Life Sciences Inc, Terry W. Osborn/Dir. - Advanced Life Sciences Inc, Israel Rubinstein/Dir. - Advanced Life Sciences Inc, Richard Reck/Dir. - Advanced Life Sciences Inc, Scott Meadow/Dir. - Advanced Life Sciences Inc, Theron E. Odlaug/Dir. - Advanced Life Sciences Inc

Owners: Israel Rubinstein, John L. Flavin, Flavin Ventures, LLC, Rosalie Sagraves, Terry W. Osborn, David A. Eiznhamer, Xmark Opportunity Partners, LLC, BVF Partners L.P., Suseelan R. Pookote, R. Richard Wieland, Scott Meadow, Thomas V. Thornton, Richard Reck, Insiders, Abbott Laboratories (18 Owners included in Index)

Financial Data: Fiscal Year End:12/31   Latest Annual Data: 12/31/2006

Year	Sales	Net Income
2006	$40,000	-$20,541,000
2005	$121,000	-$6,444,000
2004	$320,000	-$27,187,000

Curr. Assets:	$30,073,000	Curr. Liab.:	$5,168,000		
Plant, Equip.:	$409,000	Total Liab.:	$9,115,000	Indic. Yr. Divd.:	NA
Total Assets:	$30,510,000	Net Worth:	$21,395,000	Debt/ Equity:	0.0037

Advanced Medical Optics Inc

1700 E St. Andrew Pl., Santa Ana, CA, 92705; **PH:** 1-714-247-8200; **Fax:** 1-714-247-8672; http:// www.allergan.com

General - Incorporation	DE	Stock - Price on:12/24/2007	$33.81
Employees	3,800	Stock Exchange	NYSE
Auditor	PricewaterhouseCoopers, KPMG	Ticker Symbol	EYE
Stk Agt	Wells Fargo Bank, N.A.	Outstanding Shares	59,940,000
Counsel	NA	E.P.S.	-$1.27
DUNS No.	NA	Shareholders	NA

Business: The group's principal activities are to develop, manufacture and market surgical medical devices for eye and eye care products. The activities are carried out through two segments namely: ophthalmic surgical and eye care. The ophthalmic surgical segment develops, manufactures and markets medical devices for the cataract and refractive surgery markets. The eye care division develops, manufactures and markets cleaning, storage and disinfection products for the consumer contact lens market. The customers include surgeons performing cataract surgeries, hospitals, ambulatory surgical centers, optometrists, opticians, ophthalmologists and retailers that sell directly to consumers. On 26-Jun-2004, the group acquired pfizer inc.

Primary SIC and add'l.: 3827 3851

CIK No: 0001168335

Subsidiaries: Advanced Medical Optics Australia Pty Ltd., Advanced Medical Optics India Private Limited, Advanced Medical Optics Norden AB, Advanced Medical Optics Norway ASA, Advanced Medical Optics Spain S.L., Advanced Medical Optics Uppsala AB, Allergan Trading International Limited, AMO (Hangzhou) Co., Ltd., AMO Asia Limited, AMO Belgium BVBA, AMO Brasil Ltda., AMO Canada Company, AMO Denmark ApS, AMO France SAS, AMO Germany GmbH 39 Subsidiaries included in the Index

Officers: James V. Mazzo/Chmn., CEO, Pres., Francine D. Meza/Corporate VP - Human Resources, Richard A. Meier/ECFO, COO, Robert F. Gallagher/Sr. VP, Chief Accounting Officer, Controller, Douglas H. Post/Exec. VP, Pres. - Corneal Refractive Group, Angelo Rago/Sr. VP - Global Customer Services, Sheree L. Aronson/Corporate VP - Corporate Communications, Investor Relations, Marketing Research, Aimee S. Weisner/39/Corporate VP, General Counsel, Sec., Holger Heidrich/Corporate VP, Pres. - EAM, International Government Affairs, Russell C. Trenary/Exec. VP, Pres. - Cataract Refractive Group, Jane E. Rady/Exec. VP - Strategy, Corporate Development, Leonard R. Borrmann/Exec. VP - Research, Development

Directors: James V. Mazzo/Chmn., CEO, Pres., Christopher G. Chavez/Dir., Robert J. Palmisano/Dir., Deborah Dunsire/Dir., Elizabeth H. Davila/Dir., William J. Link/Dir., Michael A. Mussallem/Dir., Deborah J. Neff/Dir., James O. Rollans/Presiding Dir.

Owners: Michael A. Mussallem, Deborah J. Neff, James O. Rollans, Insiders, FMR Corp./14.82%, Holger Heidrich, Jane E. Rady, James V. Mazzo, Elizabeth H. Dvila, Capital Research and Management Company/7.22%, Richard A. Meier, Christopher G. Chavez, Massachusetts Financial Services Company/13.22%, Russell C. Trenary, William R. Grant (16 Owners included in Index)

Financial Data: Fiscal Year End:12/31   Latest Annual Data: 12/31/2006

Year	Sales	Net Income
2006	$997,496,000	$79,471,000
2005	$920,673,000	-$453,197,000
2004	$742,099,000	-$129,370,000

Curr. Assets:	$478,143,000	Curr. Liab.:	$217,453,000	P/E Ratio:	23.98
Plant, Equip.:	$132,756,000	Total Liab.:	$1,297,906,000	Indic. Yr. Divd.:	NA
Total Assets:	$2,013,897,000	Net Worth:	$715,991,000	Debt/ Equity:	1.1528

Advanced Micro Devices Inc

1 AMD Pl., Sunnyvale, CA, 94088; **PH:** 1-408-749-4000; **Fax:** 1-408-982-6164; http:// www.amd.com

General - Incorporation	DE	Stock - Price on:12/24/2007	$13.64
Employees	16,500	Stock Exchange	NYSE
Auditor	Ernst & Young LLP	Ticker Symbol	AMD
Stk Agt	Computershare Investor Services LLC	Outstanding Shares	550,440,000
Counsel	NA	E.P.S.	-$4
DUNS No.	04-863-4059	Shareholders	NA

Business: The group's principle activities include manufacturing and supplying semiconductor products. The groups product lines include desktop processors, notebook processors, server processors, desktop chipsets, notebook chipsets and workstation processors. The groups products sold under the brand name AMD Phenom(TM), AMD Athlon(TM), AMD Sempron(TM), AMD Opteron(TM), Mobile AMD Sempron(TM) and ATI Radeon(TM) Xpress 1100 Series. The group operates from United States.

Primary SIC and add'l.: 3674

CIK No: 0000002488

Subsidiaries: Advanced Micro Devices (Canada) Limited, Advanced Micro Devices (China) Co. Ltd., Advanced Micro Devices (Singapore) Pte. Ltd., Advanced Micro Devices (U.K.) Limited, Advanced Micro Devices Belgium N.V., Advanced Micro Devices Export Sdn. Bhd., Advanced Micro Devices GmbH, Advanced Micro Devices S.A.S., Advanced Micro Devices S.p.A., Advanced Micro Devices Sdn. Bhd., Advanced Micro Devices, AB, Advanced Micro Ltd., Amd (emea) Ltd., AMD (Netherlands) B.V., Amd (us) Holdings, Inc. 36 Subsidiaries included in the Index

Officers: Hector J. Ruiz/Chmn., CEO/$12,848,440.00, Thomas M. McCoy/Exec. VP - Legal Affairs, Chief Administrative Officer/$2,814,492.00, Marty Seyer/Sr. VP - Commercial Segment, William T. Edwards/Sr. VP, Chief Innovation Officer, James D. Fleck/Board Observer, David E. Orton/52/Exec. VP - Visual, Media Businesses, Phil Hester/CTO, Group VP, Derrick R. Meyer/COO, Pres., Henri Richard/Exec. VP, Chief Sales, Marketing Officer/$3,359,320.00, Robert J. Rivet/CFO, Exec. VP/$5,300,158.00, Joe Menard/Corporate VP - Amd's Consumer Business Segment, Richard Bergman/Sr. VP, GM - Graphics Product Group, Mario Rivas/Exec. VP - Computing Products Group, Adrian Hartog/Sr. VP, GM - Global Consumer Electronics Group, Pres. - AMD Canada

Directors: Hector J. Ruiz/Chmn., CEO, Robert B. Palmer/Dir., Frank Clegg/Dir., Morton L. Topfer/Dir., Bruce L. Claflin/Dir., Paulett H. Eberhart/Dir., Michael W. Barnes/Dir., John E. Caldwell/Dir.

Owners: Robert J. Rivet, AXA/5.10%, FMR Corporation/12.93%, Thomas M. McCoy, Paulett H. Eberhart, Michael W. Barnes, Bruce L. Claflin, Capital Research & Management Company/10.36%, Hector J. Ruiz, Derrick R. Meyer, Henri P. Richard, Oppenheimer Funds, Inc./7.73%, Insiders/1.34%, Morton L. Topfer, John E. Caldwell (16 Owners included in Index)

Financial Data: Fiscal Year End:12/25   Latest Annual Data: 12/31/2006

Year	Sales	Net Income
2006	$5,649,000,000	-$166,000,000
2005	$5,847,577,000	$165,483,000
2004	$5,001,435,000	$91,156,000

Curr. Assets:	$3,963,000,000	Curr. Liab.:	$2,852,000,000		
Plant, Equip.:	$3,987,000,000	Total Liab.:	$7,072,000,000	Indic. Yr. Divd.:	NA
Total Assets:	$13,147,000,000	Net Worth:	$342,171,000	Debt/ Equity:	0.7029

Advanced Neuromodulation Systems Inc

6901 Preston Rd., Plano, TX, 75024; **PH:** 1-972-309-8000; http:// www.ans-medical.com

General - Incorporation	TX	Stock - Price on:12/24/2007	$43.02
Employees	11,000	Stock Exchange	NA
Auditor	Ernst & Young LLP	Ticker Symbol	NA
Stk Agt	Computershare Investor Services LLC	Outstanding Shares	338,320,000
Counsel	Hughes & Luce LLP	E.P.S.	$1.53
DUNS No.	02-167-5699	Shareholders	NA

Business: The group's principal activities are to design, develop, manufacture and market advanced implantable neuromodulation devices. The group operates in two business segments: the neuro products and hi-tronics designs and o.e.m. Segment. The neuro products segment designs, develops, manufactures and markets implantable medical devices that are used to manage chronic intractable pain and other disorders of the central nervous system. The hi-tronics designs and o.e.m. Segment provides contract development and o.e.m. Manufacturing of electro-mechanical devices. The group's products are renew(R) radio frequency (rf) system, genesis(R) and genesisxptm implantable pulse generator (ipg) systems and accurx(R) implantable drug pumps. The group markets products to physicians. On 27-Mar-2003, the group acquired certain assets and operations of sun medical, inc., on 4-Sep-2003, comedical, inc. And state of the art medical products on 1-Nov-2003.

Primary SIC and add'l.: 3845 3841

CIK No: 0000351721

Subsidiaries: Advanced Neuromodulation Systems Australia Pty Limited, ANS Germany GmbH, Hi-tronics Designs, Inc., MicroNet Medical, Inc., SPAC Acquisition Corp.

Officers: Denise Landry/Media Contact

Financial Data: Fiscal Year End:12/31   Latest Annual Data: 12/30/2006

Year	Sales	Net Income
2006	$3,302,447,000	$548,251,000
2005	$2,915,280,000	$393,490,000
2004	$2,294,173,000	$409,934,000

Curr. Assets:	$1,941,141,000	Curr. Liab.:	$1,534,382,000	P/E Ratio:	28.30
Plant, Equip.:	$438,416,000	Total Liab.:	$1,961,795,000	Indic. Yr. Divd.:	NA
Total Assets:	$4,844,840,000	Net Worth:	$2,883,045,000	Debt/ Equity:	0.4400

Advanced Optics Electronics Inc

8301 Washington NE, Ste. 5, Albuquerque, NM, 87113; **PH:** 1-505-797-7878; **Fax:** 1-505-858-1871; http:// www.adot.org

General - Incorporation	NV	Stock - Price on:12/24/2007	$0.0001
Employees	6	Stock Exchange	OTC
Auditor	Malone & Bailey, PC	Ticker Symbol	ADOT
Stk Agt	Silver State Transfer & Registrar	Outstanding Shares	16,620,000,000
Counsel	NA	E.P.S.	$0.00
DUNS No.	NA	Shareholders	NA

Business: The groups principal activities include image display and recognition technology. The group products include flat panel displays and Color-Chek. The group operates through two segments namely adot and biomoda.

Primary SIC and add'l.: 3679

CIK No: 0001020657

Subsidiaries: Biomoda Inc

Officers: Leslie S. Robins/Chmn., Exec. VP, Michael H. Pete/Dir., Pres., John J. Cousins/VP - Finance, Dir.

Directors: Leslie S. Robins/Chmn., Exec. VP, Michael H. Pete/Dir., Pres., John J. Cousins/VP - Finance, Dir., Linda C. Obenour/Dir.

Owners: Michael Pete, John Cousins, Insiders, Leslie Robins

Financial Data: Fiscal Year End:12/31   Latest Annual Data: 12/31/2006

Year	Sales	Net Income
2006	NA	-$2,242,000
2005	NA	-$2,056,000
2004	NA	-$5,048,000

Curr. Assets:	$180,000	Curr. Liab.:	$1,092,000	
Plant, Equip.:	$90,000	Total Liab.:	$1,092,000	Indic. Yr. Divd.: NA
Total Assets:	$531,000	Net Worth:	-$561,000	Debt/ Equity: NA

Advanced Oxygen Technologies Inc

133 W 13th St., New York, NY, 10011; PH: 1-212-727-7085; http:// www.aoxy-ca.com; Email: info@aoxy-ca.com

General - Incorporation............ DE	Stock- Price on:12/24/2007 ....$0.009
Employees 1	Stock Exchange.............................OTC
Auditor ......Bernstein Pinchuk & Kaminsky LLP	Ticker Symbol...................................AOXY
Stk Agt..... Computershare Investor Services LLC	Outstanding Shares.................45,850,000
Counsel.......................................NA	E.P.S...$0.00
DUNS No. 19-866-2124	Shareholders......................................NA

Business: The group's principle activity is to provide database management services, marketing and CD-ROM production/sales. The services offered by the group includes managing client databases, assisting clients in effective marketing with databases, providing database information to clients, list rentals, and utilizing and structuring databases for fax broadcasting. The group's quarterly revenue for September 2007 was 0.01 millions of USD.

Primary SIC and add'l.: 3572
CIK No: 0000352991
Subsidiaries: Mobile Group Inc
Owners: Hennistone Projects Ltd./25.65%, Eastern Star/5.91%, Robert E. Wolfe, Crossland Ltd./6.47%, Crossland Ltd. Belize/13.77%

Financial Data: Fiscal Year End:06/30 **Latest Annual Data:** 6/30/2007

Year	Sales	Net Income
2007	$72,000	$380,000
2006	$29,000	-$13,000
2005	NA	-$34,000

Curr. Assets:	$302,000	Curr. Liab.:	$686,000	P/E Ratio: 1.13
Plant, Equip.:	$650,000	Total Liab.:	$821,000	Indic. Yr. Divd.: NA
Total Assets:	$952,000	Net Worth:	$132,000	Debt/ Equity: NA

Advanced Photonix Inc

2925 Boardwalk, Ann Arbor, MI, 48104; PH: 1-734-864-5600; Fax: 1-734-998-3474; http:// www.advancedphotonix.com; Email: sales@picometrix.com

General - Incorporation............ DE	Stock- Price on:12/24/2007 ....$1.611
Employees 145	Stock Exchange.............................AMEX
Auditor .... Farber Hass Hurley & Mcewen LLP	Ticker Symbol......................................API
Stk Agt....... Continental Stock Transfer & Trust Co	Outstanding Shares.................19,110,000
Counsel.............. Dornbush Mensch Mandelstam	E.P.S...-$0.31
DUNS No. 61-780-4554	Shareholders......................................NA

Business: The group's principal activities are to develop and manufacture optoelectronic semiconductor based components, hybrid assemblies and other proprietary advanced solid state light and radiation detection devices. The group designs and manufactures silicon-based electro-optical components, assemblies and design solutions for a global original equipment manufacturers (OEMs) customer base. The products include customer specific assemblies for fiber optic data and telecommunications, pin photodetectors, photodetector hybrids, military and commercial aerospace products, custom optoelectronic assemblies and filtrode(r). The group also supplies detectors for high reliability (hi-rel) applications, including military and commercial aerospace and other applications requiring hi-rel specifications.

Primary SIC and add'l.: 3674
CIK No: 0000869986
Subsidiaries: Silicon Sensor, Inc, Texas Optoelectronics, Inc.
Officers: Richard D. Kurtz/Chmn., CEO/$275,846.00, Rob Risser/Dir., CFO/$256,532.00, Steven Williamson/CTO/$256,352.00
Directors: Richard D. Kurtz/Chmn., CEO, Rob Risser/Dir., CFO, Lance Brewer/Dir., Donald Pastor/Dir., Scott M. Farese/Dir., Stephen P. Soltwedel/Dir.
Owners: Paul Ludwig, Stephen P. Soltwedel/2.30%, Donald Pastor, Scott M. Farese/2.40%, Richard D. Kurtz/3.20%, Robin F. Risser/4.80%, Steven Williamson/9.20%, Insiders/23.00%

Financial Data: Fiscal Year End:03/31 **Latest Annual Data:** 03/31/2007

Year	Sales	Net Income
2007	$23,588,000	-$4,646,000
2006	$23,585,000	-$5,262,000
2005	$14,803,000	$5,078,000

Curr. Assets:	$14,465,000	Curr. Liab.:	$5,135,000	
Plant, Equip.:	$3,375,000	Total Liab.:	$12,538,000	Indic. Yr. Divd.: NA
Total Assets:	$38,001,000	Net Worth:	$25,431,000	Debt/ Equity: 0.1417

Advanced Plant Pharmaceuticals Inc

43 W 33rd St., New York, NY, 10001; PH: 1-212-695-3334; http:// www.advancedplantpharm.com; Email: info@advancedplantpharm.com

General - Incorporation............ DE	Stock- Price on:12/24/2007 ....NA
Employees ....NA	Stock Exchange.............................OTC
Auditor ....Meyler & Co. LLC	Ticker Symbol...................................APPIE
Stk Agt.............. Continental Stock Transfer & Trust Co	Outstanding Shares............................NA
Counsel.......................................NA	E.P.S...NA
DUNS No. ....NA	Shareholders......................................NA

Business: The group's principle activities include developing, producing and marketing natural dietary supplements. The company has a thirteen step process utilizing whole plants for the production of dietary supplements. The company's process utilizes the whole plant without the use of alcohol and allows the use of nearly the whole of the natural ingredients available from the plant. The company has also applied its process to manufacture garlic in the form of dietary supplement. The company has also developed two dietary supplements, lp-chol and perthon/abavca, which are comprised of several specific botanical components. The company has also developed an all natural dietary supplement called aca which it believes is an immune system enhancer. The company believes that aca has the ability to improve the quality of life of patients suffering from HIV-aids. The company also has a patent for its herbal composition, lo-chol. The group operates from United States.

Primary SIC and add'l.: 2834

CIK No: 0000943535
Subsidiaries: Amazing Nutritionals, Inc., Mazal Plant Pharmaceuticals, Inc.
Officers: David Lieberman/43/Dir., CFO, CEO, Pres.
Directors: David Lieberman/43/Dir., CFO, CEO, Pres.
Owners: David Lieberman/4.80%, C. J. Lieberman/50.00%, C. J. Lieberman/2.90%, David Lieberman/50.00%

Advanced Power Technology Inc

405 Sw Columbia St., Bend, OR, 97702; PH: 1-541-382-8028; http:// www.advancedpower.com

General - Incorporation .... DE	Stock- Price on:12/24/2007 ....$22.72
Employees 2,049	Stock Exchange.............................NDQ
Auditor ....KPMG LLP	Ticker Symbol.................................MSCS
Stk Agt..............Mellon Investor Services LLC	Outstanding Shares.................76,270,000
Counsel.......................................NA	E.P.S...$0.11
DUNS No. ....NA	Shareholders......................................NA

Business: The group's principal activities are to design, manufacture and market high-power semiconductors and modules for switching and radio frequency applications. The power semiconductors increase system efficiency, permit the design of more compact end products and improve features and functionality. The products are sold to original equipment manufacturers (OEM) and through distributors in North America, Europe and Asia. The major OEM customers of the group include advanced energy industries inc, mks instruments inc and fronius international gmbh.

Primary SIC and add'l.: 3674
CIK No: 0001114973
Subsidiaries: Advanced Power Technology Colorado, Inc., Advanced Power Technology Europe SAS, Advanced Power Technology RF Pennsylvania, Inc., Advanced Power Technology RF, Inc.

Financial Data: Fiscal Year End:12/31 **Latest Annual Data:** 10/1/2006

Year	Sales	Net Income
2006	$370,477,000	$35,665,000
2005	$297,440,000	$29,223,000
2004	$244,805,000	$5,636,000

Curr. Assets:	$152,361,000	Curr. Liab.:	$43,904,000	
Plant, Equip.:	$59,098,000	Total Liab.:	$48,121,000	Indic. Yr. Divd.: NA
Total Assets:	$232,998,000	Net Worth:	$184,877,000	Debt/ Equity: NA

Advanced Proteome Therapeutics Corp

Formerly: Thrilltime Entertainment Intl Inc
103 - 4585 Canada Way, Burnaby, BC, V5G 4L6; PH: 1-415-722-1209; http:// www.thrilltime.com

General - Incorporation ....Canada	Stock- Price on:12/24/2007 ....NA
Employees ....NA	Stock Exchange.................................NA
Auditor ....Davidson & Co LLP	Ticker Symbol...................................NA
Stk Agt.....................Computershare Trust Co	Outstanding Shares............................NA
Counsel.......................................NA	E.P.S...NA
DUNS No. ....NA	Shareholders......................................NA

Business: The group's principal activities are to develop, construct and market amusement rides. The group's products are skycoaster and top eliminator. The skycoaster includes part sky-diving and part hang-gliding. The top eliminator includes competition and skill with a thrilling race experience. The group also has its destination and regional amusement parks, thrill parks and family fun centers. The operations of the group are carried out in the United States of America.

Primary SIC and add'l.: 7999 3949
CIK No: 0001040368
Subsidiaries: Skycoaster, Inc., Superstar Dragsters, Inc., ThrillTime Entertainment (US), Inc.

Advanced Refractive Technologies Inc

1062 Calle Negocio Ste. D, San Clemente, CA, 92673; PH: 1-949-940-1300; http:// www.advancedrefractive.com; Email: admin@advancedrefractive.com

General - Incorporation .... DE	Stock- Price on:12/24/2007 ....NA
Employees ....NA	Stock Exchange.............................OTC
Auditor ....Peterson & Co., LLP	Ticker Symbol................................ARFRE
Stk Agt.......... Nevada Agency & Trust Company	Outstanding Shares............................NA
Counsel.......................................NA	E.P.S...NA
DUNS No. ....NA	Shareholders......................................NA

Business: The groups principal activity is to develop both medical devices as well as pharmaceutical agents to be used in important pathologies. In the year 2005 the group acquired OptiMetrix Technologies, Inc. The group operates from the United States. The groups net sale in the year 2005 was $ 1,087,136.

Primary SIC and add'l.: 3841
CIK No: 0001082249
Officers: Randal Bailey/CEO, Pres., Laurence Schreiber/COO, Corp. Sec., Treasurer, Larry Hood/Chief Engineer, Norman Schwartz/General Counsel - Public Relations, Richard Lindstrom/Chief Medical Advisor, Irving J. Bigio/Scientific Advisor, Eugene G. Levin/Scientific Advisor
Directors: Richard Keates/Chmn.

Advanced Semiconductor Engineering Inc

26 Chin Third Rd. , Nantze Export Processing Zone, Kaohsiung, 811; PH: 886-88673617131; http:// www.aseglobal.com

General - Incorporation ....China	Stock- Price on:12/24/2007 ....$6.89
Employees 29,039	Stock Exchange.............................NYSE
Auditor ....Deloitte & Touche LLP	Ticker Symbol....................................ASX
Stk Agt.................President Securities Corp	Outstanding Shares...............889,120,000
Counsel.......................................NA	E.P.S...$0.38
DUNS No. ....NA	Shareholders......................................NA

Business: The group's principal activities are provision of packaging and testing services for semiconductors companies. Other activities include the manufacture of electronic products, research and development of computers and related accessories and design and production of lead frames and substrates. It also provides investment services. Operations are carried out in Taiwan, Asia and North America.

Primary SIC and add'l.: 3679 3674

CIK No: 0001122411

Subsidiaries: ASE Capital Inc, ASE Investment Inc, ASE Japan, ASE Korea, ASE Shanghai, ASE Test, ASE Test Malaysia, ASE Test Taiwan, ISE Labs, J&R Holding Limited, PRC

Officers: Jason C.S. Chang/Chmn., CEO, Richard H.P. Chang/Vice Chmn., Pres., Tien Wu/Dir., COO, Joseph Tung/Dir., CFO, VP, Jeffrey Chen/Dir., VP, Mei-Jean Feng/Dir. - Supervisor, Samuel Liu/Dir. - Supervisor, Yen-Yi Tseng/Dir. - Supervisor, Freddie Liu/VP, Investor Relations Officer, Grace Teng/Contact - Finance Department, John Ho/Dir. - Supervisor, Tien-Szu Chen/Dir. - Supervisor

Directors: Jason C.S. Chang/Chmn., CEO, Richard H.P. Chang/Vice Chmn., Pres., Tien Wu/Dir., COO, Joseph Tung/Dir., CFO, VP, Jeffrey Chen/Dir., VP, Raymond Lo/Dir., Alan Cheng/Dir., Mei-Jean Feng/Dir. - Supervisor, Samuel Liu/Dir. - Supervisor, Yen-Yi Tseng/Dir. - Supervisor, John Ho/Dir. - Supervisor, Tien-Szu Chen/Dir. - Supervisor

Owners: Hung Ching/1.10%, ASE Test Taiwan/0.02%, Insiders/21.10%, ASE Enterprises/17.30%, J&R Holding Limited/2.00%

Financial Data: Fiscal Year End:12/31   Latest Annual Data: 12/31/2006

Year	Sales	Net Income
2006	$3,081,425,000	$433,345,000
2005	$2,562,067,000	-$168,614,000
2004	$2,574,437,000	$135,383,000

Curr. Assets:	$1,496,251,000	Curr. Liab.:	$910,300,000	P/E Ratio:	8.10
Plant, Equip.:	$2,173,762,000	Total Liab.:	$2,244,461,000	Indic. Yr. Divd.:	$0.140
Total Assets:	$4,103,438,000	Net Worth:	$1,858,977,000	Debt/ Equity:	NA

Advanced Technologies Group Ltd

921 Bergen Ave., Ste. 405, Jersey City, New Jersey , 07306; **PH:** 1-201-680-7142; **Fax:** 1-201-680-7179; **http://** www.atgworld.com; **Email:** Investors@ATGWORLD.COM

General - Incorporation	NV	Stock - Price on:12/24/2007	$0.21
Employees	NA	Stock Exchange	OTC
Auditor	Donahue Associates, LLC	Ticker Symbol	AVGG
Stk Agt	Interstate Transfer Company	Outstanding Shares	18,060,000
Counsel	NA	E.P.S.	NA
DUNS No.	NA	Shareholders	NA

Business: The groups principal activity is to develop an internet-based real time forex trading platform. The group operates from the United States.

Primary SIC and add'l.: 7372

CIK No: 0001119046

Officers: Alex J. Stelmak/59/Chmn., CEO, CFO, Alfred D. Morgan/Special Financial Advisor to The Dir., Alexander Gorlov/Chief Technology Advisor to The Dir., Mark Karpovsky/Special Technology Advisor to The Dir., Joseph Medved/Special Information Technology Advisor to The Dir., Theodore Jay/Patent Counsel to The Dir., Sholim Ginsburg/Strategic Technology Advisor to The Dir., Carl P. Ranno/Special Legal Advisor to The Dir., Ken R. Lew/Special Advisor to The Dir. Mergers, Acquisitions, Abel Raskas/67/Dir., Pres., Sr. Dir. - Marketing, Stan Mashov/Dir., CTO, Exec. VP, Dmitry Finkelstein/Dir. - Software Development

Directors: Alex J. Stelmak/59/Chmn., CEO, CFO, Abel Raskas/67/Dir., Pres., Sr. Dir. - Marketing, Stan Mashov/Dir., CTO, Exec. VP

Owners: Stan Mashov/4.58%, Alex Stelmak/24.31%, Insiders/53.20%, Abel Raskas/24.31%

Curr. Assets:	$262,000	Curr. Liab.:	$117,000
Plant, Equip.:	$51,000	Total Liab.:	$117,000	Indic. Yr. Divd.:	NA
Total Assets:	$367,000	Net Worth:	$250,000	Debt/ Equity:	NA

Advanced Technology Petroleum Corp

16660 N Dallas Pkwy, Dallas, TX, 75248;

General - Incorporation	DE	Stock - Price on:12/24/2007	NA
Employees	NA	Stock Exchange	NA
Auditor	Gately & Assoc. LLC	Ticker Symbol	NA
Stk Agt.	NA	Outstanding Shares	NA
Counsel	NA	E.P.S	NA
DUNS No.	NA	Shareholders	NA

Business: The groups principle activity is to provide a method for a foreign or domestic private company to become a reporting ("public") company whose securities are qualified for trading in the United States secondary market. The group operates from United States.

Primary SIC and add'l.: 6770

CIK No: 0001317836

Owners: Joseph Blimline/100.00%

Advanced Viral Research Corp

200 Corporate Blvd. S., Yonkers, NY, 10701; **PH:** 1-914-376-7383; **Fax:** 1-914-376-7368; **http://** www.adviral.com

General - Incorporation	DE	Stock - Price on:12/24/2007	$0.045
Employees	7	Stock Exchange	OTC
Auditor	Rachlin Cohen & Holtz LLP	Ticker Symbol	ADVR
Stk Agt	American Stock Transfer & Trust Co.	Outstanding Shares	799,610,000
Counsel	NA	E.P.S	-$0.006
DUNS No.	15-352-9284	Shareholders	NA

Business: The group's principal activity is to produce, market, promote and sell pharmaceutical drugs. The group is primarily into organizational activities, research and development activities and raising capital. The group operates under the trademark reticulose(R) that is currently known as avr118. This drug is used for the treatment of diseases such as cachexia, or body wasting, in patients with acquired immune deficiency syndrome (aids), and cancer; human immunodeficiency virus, or HIV, including aids as a combination therapy; human papilloma virus, or hpv, which causes genital warts and may lead to cervical cancer and rheumatoid arthritis. The group entered into distribution agreements with four separate entities granting rights to distribute reticulose in the countries of Canada, China, Japan, Hong Kong, macao, Taiwan, Mexico, Argentina, Bolivia, paraguay, uruguay, Brazil and Chile.

Primary SIC and add'l.: 2834 8731 2836

CIK No: 0000786623

Officers: Stephen M. Elliston/Dir., CEO, Pres./$162,061.00, Gayle Challinor/Contact - Investment Information

Directors: Stephen M. Elliston/Dir., CEO, Pres., Eli Wilner/51/Chmn., Nancy J. Van Sant/Dir., Roy S. Walzer/Dir., Angelo S. Botter/Dir.

Owners: Insiders/5.70%, Martin Bookman, James F. Dicke/10.60%, Roy S. Walzer/1.40%, Eli Wilner/4.30%, Shalom Z. Hirschman/5.30%, James F. Dicke/8.40%

Financial Data: Fiscal Year End:12/31   Latest Annual Data: 12/31/2006

Year	Sales	Net Income
2006	NA	-$3,847,000
2005	NA	-$5,200,000
2004	NA	-$6,213,000

Curr. Assets:	$1,102,000	Curr. Liab.:	$169,000		
Plant, Equip.:	$166,000	Total Liab.:	$169,000	Indic. Yr. Divd.:	NA
Total Assets:	$1,363,000	Net Worth:	$1,194,000	Debt/ Equity:	0.1596

Advanstar Inc

One Pk. Ave., New York, NY, 10016; **PH:** 1-212-956-0600; **http://** www.advanstar.com; **Email:** info@advanstar.com

General - Incorporation	DE	Stock - Price on:12/24/2007	NA
Employees	NA	Stock Exchange	NA
Auditor	PricewaterhouseCoopers LLP	Ticker Symbol	NA
Stk Agt	Bank of New York	Outstanding Shares	NA
Counsel	NA	E.P.S.	NA
DUNS No.	NA	Shareholders	NA

Business: The group's principal activity is to provide integrated business-to-business marketing communications products and services. The group is a wholly owned subsidiary of advanstar holdings corp. And operates through three operating segments: trade shows and conferences, trade publications and marketing services. The operations of group consist primarily of the management of trade shows and seminars held in convention and conference centers, creation and distribution of controlled circulation trade, business and professional magazines, sale of a variety of direct mail and database products, magazine editorial reprints, and classified advertising. During 2002, the group acquired ht — the magazine for healthcare travel professionals & aiim international exposition and conference. On 08-Mar-2004, the group acquired institute of validation technology.

Primary SIC and add'l.: 7389 7331

CIK No: 0001064243

Subsidiaries: Advanstar Communications Inc, Advanstar Holdings Corporation, Advanstar IH, Inc, Advanstar.com, Inc., The Thomson Corporation

Officers: Joseph Loggia/Dir., CEO, James M. Alic/Chmn., VP, Laura McConnell/38/Exec. VP - Fashion Group, Francis Heid/VP - Media Operations, Georgiann Decenzo/VP - Marketing, Communications, Ward Hewins/VP, General Counsel, Helen Gardner/MD - Europe, Mike Alic/VP, GM - License Group, Daniel Phillips/Exec. VP - Powersports, Automotive, Rick Treese/CTO, VP, Theodore S. Alpert/VP - Finance, Assist. Sec., CFO, Patricia Joseph/Chief Marketing Officer, Anthony Calanca/Exec. VP - Exhibitions, Nancy Nugent/VP - Human Resources, Adele D. Hartwick/VP, Treasurer, Controller (18 Officers included in Index)

Directors: Joseph Loggia/Dir., CEO, James M. Alic/Chmn., VP, Ohsang Kwon/Dir., Charles Pieper/Dir., Douglas B. Fox/Dir., James A. Finkelstein/Dir., Kamil Salame/Dir., Scott Marden/Dir.

Owners: Laura McConnell, Steven R. Morris, James M. Alic, Theodore S. Alpert, Joseph Loggia, DLJ Merchant Banking Partners III, L.P., Douglas B. Fox, Insiders, Eric I. Lisman, Rick Treese, Daniel M. Phillips

Advant-e Corp

2680 Indian Ripple Rd., Dayton, OH, 45440; **PH:** 1-937-429-4288; **Fax:** 1-937-429-4309; **http://** www.advant-e.com; **Email:** info@edictsystems.com

General - Incorporation	DE	Stock - Price on:12/24/2007	$1.65
Employees	50	Stock Exchange	OTC
Auditor	J. D. Cloud & Co. LLP	Ticker Symbol	AVEE
Stk Agt	Securities Transfer Corp	Outstanding Shares	6,480,000
Counsel	NA	E.P.S.	$0.14
DUNS No.	NA	Shareholders	NA

Business: The group's principal activity is to provide business-to-business (b2b) electronic commerce products and services. The group offers comprehensive, standards-based and proprietary solutions for businesses of all sizes. The group develops, markets and supports b2b e-commerce software products and provides Internet-based communication and e-commerce data processing services. These services helps businesses in processing reoccurring transactions required in the electronic procurement of goods and services and other b2b relationships. The group's software products enable businesses to engage in e-commerce with one another by allowing companies to fully integrate e-commerce data into their business infrastructure and operations.

Primary SIC and add'l.: 7375

CIK No: 0000925043

Subsidiaries: Edict Systems, Inc.

Officers: Jason K. Wadzinski/43/Chmn., CEO, Pres., James E. Lesch/62/Dir., CFO

Directors: Jason K. Wadzinski/43/Chmn., CEO, Pres., James E. Lesch/62/Dir., CFO

Owners: Insiders/56.50%, Jason Wadzinski/56.50%

Financial Data: Fiscal Year End:12/31   Latest Annual Data: 12/31/2006

Year	Sales	Net Income
2006	$5,404,000	$859,000
2005	$4,463,000	$600,000
2004	$3,601,000	$469,000

Curr. Assets:	$2,990,000	Curr. Liab.:	$500,000	P/E Ratio:	12.69
Plant, Equip.:	$387,000	Total Liab.:	$666,000	Indic. Yr. Divd.:	NA
Total Assets:	$3,625,000	Net Worth:	$2,958,000	Debt/ Equity:	NA

Advanta Corp

Welsh & McKean Rds, Spring House, PA, 19477; **PH:** 1-215-657-4000; **http://** www.advanta.com; **Email:** advantacommunications@advanta.com

General - Incorporation	DE
Employees	952
Auditor	KPMG LLP
Stk Agt.	Mellon Investor Services LLC
Counsel.	Wolf Block Schorr & Solis-Cohen LLP
DUNS No.	10-852-1469

Stock- Price on:12/24/2007	$33.63
Stock Exchange	NDQ
Ticker Symbol	ADVNB
Outstanding Shares	29,040,000
E.P.S.	NA
Shareholders	NA

Business: The group's principle activity is to provide innovative financial products and solutions. The group provides business credit cards, mortgage loans, insurance and deposit products. The group owns two depository institutions, which offer a variety of deposit products such as retail and large denomination certificates of deposit. The group's operations are carried out through three segments: business cards, venture capital and other. Business card offers business purpose credit cards, primarily to small businesses. Venture capital generally focused on early stage investment opportunities and growth capital financings and restructurings in the financial services and consumer and data information management services industries. The group operates from United States.

Primary SIC and add'l.: 6159 6153 6399 6021

CIK No: 0000096638

Subsidiaries: Advanta 101 GP Corp., Advanta Advertising, Inc., Advanta Auto Finance Corporation, Advanta Auto Receivables Corp. I, Advanta Bank Corp., Advanta Business Receivables Corp., Advanta Business Services Corp., Advanta Business Services Holding Corp., Advanta Capital LLC, Advanta Corp., Advanta Finance Corp., Advanta GCF GP Corp., Advanta GP Corp., Advanta GP II Corp., Advanta Growth Capital Fund LP 37 Subsidiaries included in the Index

Officers: Dennis Alter/Chmn., CEO/$2,828,446.00, Bill Rosoff/Vice Chmn., Pres., William A. Rosoff/Vice Chmn., Pres./$2,167,373.00, Amy B. Holderer/Investor Relations Officer, David M. Goodman/Contact - Media, Public Relations

Directors: Dennis Alter/Chmn., CEO, Bill Rosoff/Vice Chmn., Pres., William A. Rosoff/Vice Chmn., Pres., Thomas P. Costello/62/Dir.

Owners: Advanta Corp. Employee Stock Ownership Plan/9.69%, Robert S. Blank, Robert S. Blank, John F. Moore, Olaf Olafsson, Insiders/32.19%, Philip M. Browne/1.43%, John F. Moore, Dana Becker Dunn, William A. Rosoff/6.29%, Gisela Alter/100.00%, Dennis Alter/31.71%, William A. Rosoff, Dennis Alter/10.55%, Ronald Lubner *(24 Owners included in Index)*

Advantage Opportunity Corp

3450 Pk. Central Blvd., N. Pompano Beach, Pompano, FL, 33064; *PH:* 1-954-971-2383

General - Incorporation	Canada
Employees	NA
Auditor	NA
Stk Agt.	1st Pub Securities Transfer Corp.
Counsel	NA
DUNS No.	NA

Stock- Price on:12/24/2007	NA
Stock Exchange	NA
Ticker Symbol	NA
Outstanding Shares	NA
E.P.S.	NA
Shareholders	NA

Business: The group's principle activity is to provide property and casualty insurance services. The group operates from United States.

Primary SIC and add'l.: 9995

CIK No: 0001291992

Advantest Corp

3201 Scott Blvd., Santa Clara, CA, 95054; *PH:* 1-408-988-7700; *Fax:* 1-408-987-0691; *http://* www.advantest.co.jp

General - Incorporation	Japan
Employees	3,637
Auditor	KPMG Azsa & Co
Stk Agt.	Tokyo Securities Trnsfer Agent Co Ltd
Counsel	NA
DUNS No.	NA

Stock- Price on:12/24/2007	$42.41
Stock Exchange	NYSE
Ticker Symbol	ATE
Outstanding Shares	187,650,000
E.P.S.	$1.42
Shareholders	NA

Business: The group's principal activity is to design, manufacture and market automated test equipment and measuring instruments. The group operates in two segments: automated test equipment and measuring instruments. Automated test equipment are used in the manufacture of semiconductors. Measuring instruments are used in the design, production and maintenance of electronic hardware.

Primary SIC and add'l.: 3674 3829

CIK No: 0001158838

Subsidiaries: Advanmechatec Co., Ltd., Advantest (Europe) GmbH, Advantest (Singapore) Pte. Ltd., Advantest (Suzhou) Co., Ltd., Advantest America, Inc., Advantest Customer Support Corporation, Advantest DI Corporation, Advantest Finance Inc., Advantest Korea Co., Ltd., Advantest Laboratories Ltd., Advantest Manufacturing, Inc., Advantest Taiwan Inc., Japan Engineering Co., Ltd.

Officers: Toshio Maruyama/Dir., CEO, Pres., Yoshiaki Yoshida/Exec. Officer, Jiro Haneda/Corporate Auditor, Minoru Morishita/Exec. Officer, Megumi Yamamuro/Corporate Auditor, Yasuhiro Kawata/Exec. Officer, Takashi Sekino/Exec. Officer, Hiroshi Nakamura/Exec. Officer, Yuri Morita/Managing Exec. Officer, Hiroshi Tsukahara/Dir., Managing Exec. Officer, Junji Nishiura/Dir., Sr. Exec. Officer, Hitoshi Owada/Corporate Standing Auditor, Hideaki Imada/Exec. Officer, Shinichiro Kuroe/Exec. Officer, Akira Hatakeyama/Exec. Officer *(26 Officers included in Index)*

Directors: Toshio Maruyama/Dir., CEO, Pres., Shimpei Takeshita/Chmn., Naoyuki Akikusa/Dir., Yuichi Kurita/Dir., Managing Exec. Officer, Hiroshi Tsukahara/Dir., Managing Exec. Officer, Junji Nishiura/Dir., Sr. Exec. Officer, Hiroji Agata/Dir., Sr. Exec. Officer, Yasushige Hagio/Dir., Takashi Tokuno/Dir., Sr. Exec. Officer

Owners: Fujitsu Limited/10.09%, Hiroshi Oura, Yuichi Kurita, Yoshiaki Yoshida, Nomura Securities Co., Ltd. and its related entities/6.26%, Yasuhiro Kawata, Junji Nishiura, Shinichiro Kuroe, Hiroshi Tsukahara, Masao Shimizu, Naoyuki Akikusa, Hiroji Agata, Noboru Yamaguchi, Megumi Yamamuro, Yasushige Hagio *(34 Owners included in Index)*

Financial Data: Fiscal Year End:03/31   Latest Annual Data: 03/31/2007

Year	Sales	Net Income
2007	$1,990,784,000	$301,194,000
2006	$2,161,590,000	$352,209,000
2005	$2,229,621,000	$354,577,000

Curr. Assets:	$2,346,412,000	Curr. Liab.:	$653,316,000	P/E Ratio:	8.10
Plant, Equip.:	$432,391,000	Total Liab.:	$790,406,000	Indic. Yr. Divd.:	NA
Total Assets:	$2,986,090,000	Net Worth:	$2,195,684,000	Debt/ Equity:	NA

Advaxis Inc

The Technology Ctr. of New Jersey, Ste. 117, 675 U.S. Rte. 1, North Brunswick, NJ, 08902; *PH:* 1-732-545-1590; *Fax:* 1-732-545-1084; *http://* www.advaxis.com; *Email:* BD@advaxis.com

General - Incorporation	DE
Employees	9
Auditor	Goldstein Golub Kessler LLP
Stk Agt.	NA
Counsel	NA
DUNS No.	NA

Stock- Price on:12/24/2007	$0.287
Stock Exchange	OTC
Ticker Symbol	ADXS
Outstanding Shares	45,680,000
E.P.S.	-$0.15
Shareholders	NA

Business: The groups principle activity is to develop safe and effective cancer vaccines. The group products include Lovaxin C, Lovaxin P, Lovaxin B, and Lovaxin T. The group operates from the United States.

Primary SIC and add'l.: 2834

CIK No: 0001100397

Subsidiaries: Advaxis Inc

Officers: Thomas A. Moore/Chmn., CEO, Vafa Shahabi/Dir. - Research, Development, John Rothman/VP - Clinical Development, Fredrick D. Cobb/VP - Finance, Principal Financial Officer, Bennett Lorber/Member - Bennett Lorber, Michael Crawford/Contact - Investor Relations

Directors: Thomas A. Moore/Chmn., CEO, James Patton/Dir., Roni A. Appel/Dir., Thomas McKearn/Dir., Martin R. Wade/Dir., Richard Berman/Dir., Yvonne Paterson/Member - Scientific Advisory Board, Pramod K. Srivastava/Member - Scientific Advisory Board, Carl H. June/Member - Scientific Advisory Board, David B. Weiner/Member - Scientific Advisory Board

Owners: Emigrant Capital Corp./5.00%, Todd J. Derbin/5.20%, Amnon Mandelbaum/5.80%, Cornell Capital Partners LP/4.80%, Harvest Advaxis LLC/4.80%, John Rothman/1.80%, Richard Berman/1.20%, Roni Appel/14.60%, Nathan Low/6.80%, Insiders/41.00%, Martin R. Wade, Fredrick Cobb/0.90%, Estate of Scott Flamm/7.00%, James Patton/7.20%, Thomas McKearn/1.30% *(16 Owners included in Index)*

Financial Data: Fiscal Year End:10/31   Latest Annual Data: 10/31/2006

Year	Sales	Net Income
2006	$432,000	-$6,198,000
2005	$553,000	-$1,806,000

Curr. Assets:	$2,799,000	Curr. Liab.:	$1,545,000		
Plant, Equip.:	$65,000	Total Liab.:	$7,710,000	Indic. Yr. Divd.:	NA
Total Assets:	$4,003,000	Net Worth:	-$3,707,000	Debt/ Equity:	NA

Advent Software Inc

600 Townsend St., San Francisco, CA, 94103; *PH:* 1-415-543-7696; *Fax:* 1-415-556-0607; *http://* www.advent.com; *Email:* InvestorRelations@advent.com

General - Incorporation	DE
Employees	824
Auditor	PricewaterhouseCoopers LLP
Stk Agt.	Computershare Ltd.
Counsel	Wilson Sonsini Goodrich & Rosati
DUNS No.	11-271-3128

Stock- Price on:12/24/2007	$33.75
Stock Exchange	NDQ
Ticker Symbol	ADVS
Outstanding Shares	27,180,000
E.P.S.	$3.02
Shareholders	NA

Business: The group's principal activities are to provide enterprise investment management solutions by offering stand-alone and client/server software products, data and data integration services and professional services to the investment community. The products of the group automate, integrate and support certain mission-critical function of the front, middle and back office of investment management organization. The group provides professional services like consulting, implementation management, integration management, custom report writing and training. In may 2004 the group acquired advent Europe. The customers of the group include investment advisors, brokerage firms, banks, hedge funds, corporations, public funds, foundations, universities and non-profit organizations.

Primary SIC and add'l.: 7375 7372 7379 7376

CIK No: 0001002225

Subsidiaries: Advent Denmark AS, Advent Europe Limited, Advent Netherlands BV, Advent Norway AS, Advent Sweden AB, Advent Switzerland AG, Hub Data, Inc., Kinexus Corporation, MicroEdge, Inc., Second Street Securities, Inc., Techfi Corporation

Officers: Stephanie G. Dimarco/Founder, Dir., CEO, Pres./$1,307,735.00, Lily Chang/CTO, Exec. VP/$776,459.00, David P.F. Hess/37/Sr. VP/$902,970.00, Graham Smith/CFO/$1,133,719.00, James D. Kirsner/Dir., Independent Business Advisor, Heidi Flaherty/Sr. Dir.- Financial Planning, Investor Relations Officer, Peter Hess/Exec. VP, GM - Investment Management Group, John Brennan/VP - Human Resources, Will Clemens/VP - Straight, Through Processing, Todd Gottula/Co - Head - Global Accounting, VP - Product Development, Client Services, Support, Chris Momsen/Co - Head - Global Accounting, VP - Sales, Marketing, Anthony Sperling/Sr. VP - Services

Directors: Stephanie G. Dimarco/Founder, Dir., CEO, Pres., John H. Scully/Chmn., Wendell G. Van Auken/Dir., William F. Zuendt/Dir., James P. Roemer/Dir., James D. Kirsner/Dir., Independent Business Advisor, Terry H. Carlitz/Dir., George A. Battle/Dir., Robert A. Ettl/Dir.

Owners: Dan T. H. Nye, Lily S. Chang/2.00%, David P.F. Hess, William F. Zuendt, Terry H. Carlitz, Insiders/37.40%, James P. Roemer, James D. Kirsner, George A. Battle, Criterion Capital Management LLC/6.00%, Wendell G. Van Auken, John H. Scully/23.90%, Graham V. Smith, Clearbridge Advisors, LLC/17.00%, Stephanie G. DiMarco/8.60% *(16 Owners included in Index)*

Financial Data: Fiscal Year End:12/31   Latest Annual Data: 12/31/2006

Year	Sales	Net Income
2006	$184,093,000	$82,602,000
2005	$168,701,000	$14,135,000
2004	$149,990,000	-$16,244,000

Curr. Assets:	$117,039,000	Curr. Liab.:	$117,324,000		
Plant, Equip.:	$27,338,000	Total Liab.:	$130,020,000	Indic. Yr. Divd.:	NA
Total Assets:	$339,647,000	Net Worth:	$209,627,000	Debt/ Equity:	NA

Adventrx Pharmaceuticals Inc

6725 Mesa Ridge Rd., Ste. 100, San Diego, CA, 92121; *PH:* 1-858-552-0866; *Fax:* 1-858-552-0876; *http://* www.adventrx.com; *Email:* ir@adventrx.com

General - Incorporation	DE
Employees	24
Auditor	J. H. Cohn LLP
Stk Agt.	American Stock Transfer & Trust Co.
Counsel	Heller Ehrman LLP.
DUNS No.	96-439-8200

Stock- Price on:12/24/2007	$2.61
Stock Exchange	AMEX
Ticker Symbol	ANX
Outstanding Shares	89,710,000
E.P.S.	-$0.25
Shareholders	NA

Business: The group's principal activity is to conduct biomedical research and development focused on treatments for cancer and certain viral infections, including HIV. Its business is in the development stage. The products include cofactor, blockaide/cr in clinical trials and thiovir, eradicaide, blockaide/vp and selone in preclinical testing. Cofactor is a chemotherapy drug used with 5-fu for the treatment of cancer. Blockaide/cr is a drug that prevents viral entry and infection of immune system cells. Thiovir is an antiviral agent for HIV. Eradicaide is a therapeutic drug that stimulates disease-fighting cells against HIV infection. Blockaide/vp is an HIV viral entry inhibitor that changes the protein configuration to render the virus non-infectious. Selone is used for the treatment of drug-resistant cancers, leukemias and lymphomas. The trademarks include cofactor, blockaide, thiovir, eradicaide and selone.

Primary SIC and add'l.: 2834 8731

CIK No: 0001160308

Subsidiaries: Adventrx (europe) Ltd.

Officers: Evan M. Levine/Dir., CEO/$360,211.00, James A. Merritt/Pres., Chief Medical Officer/$501,686.00, Joachim P.H. Schupp/VP - Medical Affairs, Ioana C. Hone/Dir. - Investor Relations, Mark J. Cantwell/VP - Research, Development, Richard J. Galla/Member - Scientific Advisory Board, Joan M. Robbins/Chief Scientific Officer, Sr. VP/$400,995.00, Brian M. Culley/Chief Business Officer, Sr. VP - Business Development/$355,770.00, Patrick Keran/General Counsel, VP, Michele L. Yelmene/VP - Regulatory Affairs

Directors: Evan M. Levine/Dir., CEO, Jack Lief/Chmn., Douglas Richman/Member - Scientific Advisory Board, Jeffrey Weber/Member - Scientific Advisory Board, Bengt G. Gustavsson/Member - Scientific Advisory Board, Edward D. Ball/Member - Scientific Advisory Board, Edward Chu/Member - Scientific Advisory Board, Alexander J. Denner/Dir., Mark N.K. Bagnall/Dir., Michael M. Goldberg/Dir., Mark Pykett/Dir.

Owners: Evan M. Levine/5.00%, Ross M. Johnson/2.50%, Mark J. Pykett, Jack Lief, Mark N.K. Bagnall, James A. Merritt, Brian M. Culley, Joan M. Robbins, Robert A. Daniel, Alexander J. Denner/9.20%, Michael M. Goldberg, Funds affiliated with Carl C. Icahn/9.20%, Insiders/17.50%

Financial Data: ***Fiscal Year End:***12/31 ***Latest Annual Data:*** 12/31/2006

Year	Sales	Net Income
2006	NA	-$29,332,000
2005	$496,000	-$24,783,000
2004	$103,000	-$6,701,000

Curr. Assets:	$52,337,000	***Curr. Liab.:***	$32,805,000		
Plant, Equip.:	$403,000	***Total Liab.:***	$32,841,000	***Indic. Yr. Divd.:***	NA
Total Assets:	$52,798,000	***Net Worth:***	$19,958,000	***Debt/ Equity:***	NA

Advisory Board Co (The)

2445 M St., NW, Washington, DC, 20037; ***PH:*** 1-202-266-5600; ***Fax:*** 1-202-266-5700; ***http://*** www.advisoryboardcompany.com

General - Incorporation	DE	**Stock**- Price on:12/24/2007	$53.46
Employees	855	Stock Exchange	NDQ
Auditor	Ernst & Young LLP	Ticker Symbol	ABCO
Stk Agt	Wachovia Bank N.A	Outstanding Shares	18,060,000
Counsel	NA	E.P.S.	$1.54
DUNS No.	NA	Shareholders	NA

Business: The group's principal activities are to provide best practices research and analysis to hospitals, health systems, pharmaceutical and biotech companies, health care insurers and medical device companies in the United States. Research and analysis undertaken by the group identifies, analyzes and describes specific management initiatives, processes and strategies that solve common business problems. The group provides its products through discrete annual programs to the members in the United States. It offers 15 distinct membership programs focused on identifying best-demonstrated management practices, critiquing widely followed ineffective practices, analyzing emerging trends and supporting institutions' efforts to adopt best practices.

Primary SIC and add'l.: 8748 7389 8741

CIK No: 0001157377

Subsidiaries: Advisory Board Investments, Inc., Quality Team Associates, Inc

Officers: Frank J. Williams/Chmn., CEO, Member - Advisory Board, Leanne M. Zumwalt/Dir. - Financial Expert, Scott M. Fassbach/Chief Research Officer, David L. Felsenthal/COO, Michael T. Kirshbaum/CFO, Robert W. Musslewhite/Exec. VP, Scott A. Schirmeier/39/Chief Research Officer, Richard A. Schwartz/Exec. VP, Mary D. Van Hoose/Executive Dir. - Career Management, Chris Denby/Executive Dir., Chas Roades/Executive Dir., Michael Koppenheffer/MD, Julie Lane/MD, Ford Koles/Executive Dir., David Katz/Executive Dir. *(40 Officers included in Index)*

Directors: Frank J. Williams/Chmn., CEO, Member - Advisory Board, Kelt Kindick/Dir., Mark R. Neaman/Dir., Leon D. Shapiro/Dir., Leanne M. Zumwalt/Dir. - Financial Expert, Chris Denby/Executive Dir., Chas Roades/Executive Dir., Ford Koles/Executive Dir., David Katz/Executive Dir., Jim Field/Executive Dir., Steven Berkow/Executive Dir., Stephen Kett/Executive Dir., Tom Peterson/Executive Dir., Peter J. Grua/Dir., Marc N. Casper/Dir.

Owners: David L. Felsenthal, Mark R. Neaman, Marc N. Casper, Delaware Management Holdings Co, Inc./5.80%, Peter J. Grua, Michael T. Kirshbaum, Frank J. Williams/1.20%, TimesSquare Capital Management, LLC/6.90%, Morgan Stanley & Co./11.10%, LeAnne M. Zumwalt, Leon D. Shapiro, Kelt Kindick, Insiders/4.20%, T. Rowe Price Associates, Inc./9.00%, Richard A. Schwartz *(16 Owners included in Index)*

Financial Data: ***Fiscal Year End:***03/31 ***Latest Annual Data:*** 3/31/2007

Year	Sales	Net Income
2007	$189,843,000	$27,395,000
2006	$165,049,000	$25,642,000
2005	$141,649,000	$23,347,000

Curr. Assets:	$108,380,000	***Curr. Liab.:***	$146,323,000	***P/E Ratio:***	36.62
Plant, Equip.:	$17,421,000	***Total Liab.:***	$147,710,000	***Indic. Yr. Divd.:***	NA
Total Assets:	$286,174,000	***Net Worth:***	$138,464,000	***Debt/ Equity:***	NA

Advo Inc

One Targeting Ctr., Windsor, CT, 06095; ***PH:*** 1-860-285-6100; ***http://*** www.advo.com

General - Incorporation	DE	**Stock**- Price on:12/24/2007	NA
Employees	3,800	Stock Exchange	NYSE
Auditor	Ernst & Young LLP	Ticker Symbol	AD
Stk Agt	Mellon Investor Services LLC	Outstanding Shares	NA
Counsel	NA	E.P.S.	NA
DUNS No.	06-220-0878	Shareholders	NA

Business: The group's principal activity is soliciting and processing printed advertising from retailers, manufacturers and service companies for targeted distribution to consumer households. The group's mail products and services include both shared and solo mails, distributed in the United States and Canada on a national, regional and local basis. It provides ancillary services in conjunction with its direct mail marketing programs and also provides private carrier delivery in certain markets. The group is the largest commercial user of standard mail in the United States. Shopwise(tm) is the largest covering weekly distribution of the group. In Jun 2002, the group acquired facc corporation.

Primary SIC and add'l.: 7331

CIK No: 0000801622

Subsidiaries: ADVO Canada, Inc., ADVO Investment Company, Inc., Breezeway Communications LTD, Coupon Distributors, Inc., Detroit Weekend Direct, Mail Marketing Systems, Inc., MailCoups, Inc., MBV, Inc., New England Direct, LLC, ShopWise.com, Inc., Stighen, Inc., Value Fair, Inc.

Officers: Scott S. Harding/Dir., CEO

Directors: Scott S. Harding/Dir., CEO, David Dyer/Dir., Bobbie Gaunt/Dir., Todd C. Brown/Dir., Charles M. Herington/Dir., Karen Kaplan/Dir., John Mahoney/Dir., Howard Newman/Dir.

Owners: Howard H. Newman/3.00%, Jeffrey E. Epstein/0.20%, Donald E. McCombs/1.00%, Scott S. Harding, Bobbie Gaunt/0.10%, John J. Mahoney/0.10%, Noonday Asset Management, LP/9.20%, Insiders/4.00%, Charles M. Herington/0.10%, Karen Kaplan/0.10%, Donald S. Schneider/0.10%, UBS AG/7.10%, Stephanie Molnar/0.60%, David F. Dyer/2.00%, Todd C. Brown/0.10%

Advocat Inc

1621 Galleria Blvd., Brentwood, TN, 37027; ***PH:*** 1-615-771-7575; ***Fax:*** 1-615-771-7409; ***http://*** www.irinfo.com

General - Incorporation	DE	**Stock**- Price on:12/24/2007	$12.27
Employees	4,716	Stock Exchange	NDQ
Auditor	BDO Seidman LLP	Ticker Symbol	AVCA
Stk Agt	Computershare Investor Services LLC	Outstanding Shares	5,870,000
Counsel	NA	E.P.S.	$1.59
DUNS No.	93-138-8383	Shareholders	NA

Business: The group's principal activity is to provide long-term care services to nursing home patients and residents of assisted living facilities in 9 states, primarily in the southeast and three Canadian provinces. These facilities provide skilled nursing health care services, including room and board, nutrition services, recreational therapy, social services and housekeeping and laundry services. The group also provides delivery of ancillary medical services at the nursing homes. These specialty services include rehabilitation therapy services, such as speech therapy, audiology and occupational, hospital-based respiratory and physical therapies and the provision of medical supplies, nutritional support and infusion therapies. At 31-Dec-2003, the group had 62 nursing homes containing 7,080 licensed beds and 38 assisted living facilities containing 3,965 units. The group discontinued its Canadian operations in 2003.

Primary SIC and add'l.: 8741 8052 8051

CIK No: 0000919956

Subsidiaries: Advocat Ancillary Services, Inc., Advocat Distribution Services, Inc., Advocat Finance, Inc., Diversicare Afton Oaks, LLC, Diversicare Assisted Living Services , Inc., Diversicare Assisted Living Services NC I, LLC, Diversicare Assisted Living Services NC II, LLC, Diversicare Assisted Living Services NC, LLC, Diversicare Briarcliff, LLC, Diversicare General Partner, Inc., Diversicare Good Samaritan, LLC, Diversicare Hartford, LLC, Diversicare Leasing Corp., Diversicare Leasing Corp. of Alabama, Diversicare Management Services Co. 24 Subsidiaries included in the Index

Officers: William R. Council/Dir., CEO, Pres./$1,876,694.00, William C. O'Neil/Dir. - Private Investor, Robert Z. Hensley/Dir., Consultant, Glynn L. Riddle/CFO/$1,123,980.00, Ray Tyler/COO, Exec. VP/$858,267.00

Directors: William R. Council/Dir., CEO, Pres., Wallace E. Olson/Chmn., William C. O'Neil/Dir. - Private Investor, Richard M. Brame/Dir., Robert Z. Hensley/Dir., Consultant

Owners: Raymond L. Tyler, Altrinsic Global Advisors, LLC/6.80%, Richard M. Brame, Wallace E. Olson/10.90%, Glynn L. Riddle, Robert Z. Hensley, Insiders/15.10%, William C. ONeil, William R. Council/2.20%

Financial Data: ***Fiscal Year End:***12/31 ***Latest Annual Data:*** 12/31/2006

Year	Sales	Net Income
2006	$216,763,000	$21,944,000
2005	$203,658,000	$25,302,000
2004	$202,819,000	$2,781,000

Curr. Assets:	$37,795,000	***Curr. Liab.:***	$29,616,000	***P/E Ratio:***	4.48
Plant, Equip.:	$28,768,000	***Total Liab.:***	$81,775,000	***Indic. Yr. Divd.:***	NA
Total Assets:	$96,901,000	***Net Worth:***	$3,837,000	***Debt/ Equity:***	4.6013

Adzone Research Inc

4062-80 Grumman Blvd, Calverton, NY, 11933; ***PH:*** 1-631-369-1100; ***http://*** www.adzoneresearch.com

General - Incorporation	DE	**Stock**- Price on:12/24/2007	$0.07
Employees	NA	Stock Exchange	OTC
Auditor	Holtz Rubenstein Reminick LLP	Ticker Symbol	ADZR
Stk Agt	Island Stock Transfer	Outstanding Shares	NA
Counsel	Adzone Research	E.P.S.	NA
DUNS No.	NA	Shareholders	NA

Business: The group's principal activity is to provides Internet advertising research for the firm that extract data through the monitoring of Internet websites. The extracted data are then used to provide various market research statistics and other focused information as requested by the clients. The group directly and through its worldwide network of subsidiaries and affiliates, researches raw advertising and marketing data, consumer behavior, marketing strategies and market trends. The group has developed a subscription based online application for accessing data from websites that are hosted within the United States, the United Kingdom, Europe and Asia.

Primary SIC and add'l.: 7389 7375

CIK No: 0001102013

Officers: Charles Cardona/44/Chmn., CEO, John Cardona/41/Vice Chmn., COO

Directors: Charles Cardona/44/Chmn., CEO, John Cardona/41/Vice Chmn., COO, Warren Hamburger/55/Dir., Russell Stover Ivy/42/Dir.

Owners: Warren Hamburger/1.23%, Charles Cardona/16.95%, Russell Ivy, Insiders/34.29%, John Cardona/15.17%

AEC1 Inc

105-3325 N Service Rd., Burlington, ON, L7N 3G2; ***PH:*** 1-905-332-3110;
http:// www.cleanwatts.com

General - Incorporation	NV	**Stock**- Price on:12/24/2007	NA
Employees	NA	Stock Exchange	NA
Auditor	NA	Ticker Symbol	NA
Stk Agt	Computershare Trust Co	Outstanding Shares	NA
Counsel	NA	E.P.S	NA
DUNS No.	NA	Shareholders	NA

Business: The group's principle activity is to provide alternative methods of fuel and power production. It is involved primarily in hydrogen production and fuel cell development. The company focuses on production of on-demand hydrogen, which uses the company's own chemical process to yield fuel cell-quality hydrogen from fresh water or salt water without harmful by-products. The group targets commercial back-up power, on-site power and micro-technology power market segments along with technology backup, emergency power, marine power, bulk hydrogen gas sales and vehicle electric power/hybrid. It hopes to commercialize its hydrogen technology for customers wanting to be free from using exisitng electricity grids. Astris Energi Inc., world leader in alkaline fuel cell technology, has signed a Letter of Intent with Alternate Energy Corp., which has acquired the rights to a unique low-cost technology for the production of hydrogen gas required for fuel cell operation.

Primary SIC and add'l.: 2810

CIK No: 0001274893

Officers: Blaine Froats/Chmn., CEO, Sean Froats/Dir., Sec., VP - Operations, Jack Wasserman/Dir., Treasurer, Michael Mulshine/Investor Relations Officer, Jason Froats/Contact - Media, Public Communications, Corbee Dutchburn/Consultant - Management, Marketing, Product Development, Bill Varian/Consultant - Business Development, Government, Special Markets, Mike Hewitt/Consultant - Technical Team, James Lin/Consultant - Technical Team, Roman Eidenzon/Consultant - Technical Team

Directors: Blaine Froats/Chmn., CEO, Sean Froats/Dir., Sec., VP - Operations, Jack Wasserman/Dir., Treasurer, Ray Legge/Member - Advisory Board, David I. Gordon/Member - Advisory Board, John Tevlin/Member - Advisory Board

Financial Data: ***Fiscal Year End:***12/31 ***Latest Annual Data:*** 12/31/2006

Year	Sales	Net Income
2006	NA	-$2,671,000
2005	NA	-$4,017,000
2004	NA	-$5,348,000

Curr. Assets:	$275,000	***Curr. Liab.:***	$743,000		
Plant, Equip.:	$210,000	***Total Liab.:***	$743,000	***Indic. Yr. Divd.:***	NA
Total Assets:	$485,000	***Net Worth:***	-$258,000	***Debt/ Equity:***	NA

Aegean Marine Petroleum Network Inc

42 Hatzikyriakou Ave., Piraeus, Athens; ; ***http://*** www.ampni.com

General - Incorporation	Marshall Islands	**Stock**- Price on:12/24/2007	$19.44
Employees	344	Stock Exchange	NYSE
Auditor	NA	Ticker Symbol	ANW
Stk Agt	Computershare	Outstanding Shares	42,410,000
Counsel	NA	E.P.S	$0.69
DUNS No.	NA	Shareholders	NA

Business: The groups principle activities include supplying and marketing refined marine fuel and lubricants. The group operates from the United States. The group's quarterly revenue for September 2007 was 355.88 millions of USD.

Primary SIC and add'l.: 4412

CIK No: 0001344376

Subsidiaries: Aegean Breezer Shipping Pte. Ltd., Aegean Bunkering (Singapore) Pte. Ltd., Aegean Bunkering Gibraltar Ltd., Aegean Bunkering Jamaica Ltd., Aegean Bunkering Services Inc., Aegean Holdings S.A., Aegean Investments S.A., Aegean Marine Petroleum LLC, Aegean Marine Petroleum S.A., Aegean Oil (USA), LLC, Aegean Shipholdings Inc., Aegean Tanking S.A., Aegean VII Shipping Ltd., Aegean X Maritime Inc., Amorgos Maritime Inc. 48 Subsidiaries included in the Index

Officers: Nikolas E. Tavlarios/Pres., Principal Executive Officer, Dimitris Melisanidis/Founder, Head - Corporate Development, Spyros Fokas/General Counsel, Corp. Sec., Ziad Nakhleh/CFO, Gregory Robolakis/GM, Nick Hondos/GM

Directors: Peter C. Georgiopoulos/Chmn., Dimitris Melisanidis/Founder, Head - Corporate Development, Yiannis N. Papanicolaou/56/Dir., Abel L. Rasterhoff/68/Dir., John O. Hatab/Dir., Apostolis Tsitsirakis/38/Dir.

Owners: Dimitris Melisanidis, AMPNInvest LLC, Leveret International Inc., John P. Tavlarios, Peter C. Georgiopoulos

Financial Data: ***Fiscal Year End:***12/31 ***Latest Annual Data:*** 12/31/2006

Year	Sales	Net Income
2006	$803,812,000	$24,225,000
2005	$517,330,000	$21,475,000
2004	$263,012,000	$17,617,000

Curr. Assets:	$183,742,000	***Curr. Liab.:***	$68,019,000	***P/E Ratio:***	20.06
Plant, Equip.:	$109,266,000	***Total Liab.:***	$100,878,000	***Indic. Yr. Divd.:***	$0.040
Total Assets:	$315,877,000	***Net Worth:***	$214,999,000	***Debt/ Equity:***	NA

AEGON

1111 N Charles St., Baltimore, MD, 21201; ***PH:*** 1-410-576-4571; ***Fax:*** 1-410-347-8685;
http:// www.aegon.com; ***Email:*** gca-ir@aegon.com

General - Incorporation	Netherlands	**Stock**- Price on:12/24/2007	$20.17
Employees	27,159	Stock Exchange	NYSE
Auditor	Ernst & Young LLP	Ticker Symbol	AEG
Stk Agt	Citibank N.A	Outstanding Shares	NA
Counsel	Nw Van Vliet	E.P.S	NA
DUNS No.	40-584-1347	Shareholders	NA

Business: The group's principal activity is that of a leading international insurance company offering a full range of life insurance and associated financial services. The company is also active in accident, health and general insurance. Its American subsidiary aegon usa is the largest foreign insurance company in the United States. Aegon also operates in the banking sector through subsidiaries such as aegon bank (formerly known as spaarbeleg bank). Aegon the Netherlands also supplies prestigious sponsorship to the national dutch speed skating team.

Primary SIC and add'l.: 6321 6311 6331 6029

CIK No: 0000769218

Subsidiaries: AEGON Capital Management Inc., AEGON Dealer Services Inc., AEGON Fund Management Inc., Life Investors Insurance Company of America, Money Concepts (Canada) Limited, Monumental Life Insurance Company, Peoples Benefit Life Insurance Company, Stonebridge Casualty Insurance Company, Stonebridge Life Insurance Company, Transamerica Financial Life Insurance Company, Transamerica Life Canada, Transamerica Life Insurance Company, Transamerica Occidental Life Insurance Company, Veterans Life Insurance Company, Western Reserve Life Assurance Co. of Ohio

Officers: Pat Baird/CEO - Aegon USA, Otto Thoresen/CEO - Aegon UK, Donald J. Shepard/62/Chmn., CEO, Marc A. Van Weede/Sr. VP - Group Business Development, Alexander Rijn Wynaendts/48/COO, Michiel C. Van Katwijk/Exec. VP - Group Corporate Affairs, Investor Relations, Erik Lagendijk/Exec. VP - Group Legal, Compliance, Joseph B.M. Streppel/59/CFO, Fred Romijnsen/Exec. VP - Aegon Global Strategic Initiatives, Peter Tuit/Company Sec., Tom M.P. Grondin/Sr. VP - Group Risk, Patricia Plas/Dir. - Regulatory Affairs, Ruurd A. Van Den Berg/Exec. VP - Group Finance, Information, Adri D.J. Verzijl/Sr. VP - Group Tax

Directors: Donald J. Shepard/62/Chmn., CEO, John Olcay/72/Vice Chmn. - Supervisory Board, O. John Olcay/72/Vice Chmn. - Supervisory Board, Dudley G. Eustace/72/Chmn. - Supervisory Board, Kees J. Storm/66/Member - Supervisory Board, Karla M.H. Peijs/64/Member - Supervisory Board, Antony Burgmans/61/Member - Supervisory Board, Toni Rembe/72/Member - Supervisory Board, Rene Dahan/67/Member - Supervisory Board, Shemaya Levy/61/Member - Supervisory Board, Willem F.C. Stevens/70/Member - Supervisory Board, Leo M. Van Wijk/62/Member - Supervisory Board, Irving W. Bailey/67/Member - Supervisory Board

Aehr Test Systems

400 Kato Ter., Fremont, CA, 94539; ***PH:*** 1-510-623-9400; ***Fax:*** 1-510-623-9450;
http:// www.aehr.com; ***Email:*** info@aehr.com

General - Incorporation	CA	**Stock**- Price on:12/24/2007	$5.83
Employees	90	Stock Exchange	NDQ
Auditor	Burr, Pilger & Mayer, LLP	Ticker Symbol	AEHR
Stk Agt	U.S. Stock Transfer Corp	Outstanding Shares	7,800,000
Counsel	Wilson Sonsini Goodrich & Rosati	E.P.S	NA
DUNS No.	08-584-5477	Shareholders	NA

Business: The group's principal activities are to design, develop and manufacture test and burn-in equipment used in the semiconductor industry. The group's principal products are the mtx massively parallel test system, the max and atx burn-in systems, the fox full wafer contact system, test fixtures and the diepak carrier. The mtx massively parallel test system is designed to reduce the cost of memory testing by performing both test and burn-in on thousands of devices simultaneously. The fox is a full wafer contact burn-in and parallel test system designed to make contact with all pads of a wafer simultaneously. The diepak carrier product line includes reusable temporary die carriers and associated sockets. The group markets and sells its products to semiconductor manufacturers, semiconductor contract assemblers, electronics manufacturers and burn-in and test service companies. The group has foreign operations in Asia and Europe.

Primary SIC and add'l.: 3825

CIK No: 0001040470

Officers: Rhea J. Posedel/Chmn., CEO/$369,093.00, Mario M. Rosati/Dir., Sec., David S. Hendrickson/VP - Engineering/$324,469.00, Gregory M. Perkins/VP - Worldwide Sales, Service/$313,056.00, Kunio Sano/VP, Carl N. Buck/VP - Contactor Business Group/$261,001.00, Gary L. Larson/VP - Finance, CFO/$300,842.00

Directors: Rhea J. Posedel/Chmn., CEO, Robert R. Anderson/Dir., Mario M. Rosati/Dir., Sec., William W.R. Elder/Dir., Mukesh Patel/Dir.

Owners: Robert R. Anderson/2,00%, Rhea J. Posedel/14.30%, Private Capital Management/15.70%, RGM Capital, LLC/8.60%, Gary L. Larson/1.90%, David S. Hendrickson, Gregory M. Perkins, Insiders/27.10%, Carl N. Buck/1.60%, State of Wisconsin Investment Board/12.70%, Mukesh Patel/1.00%, Mario M. Rosati/3.00%, William W. R. Elder/1.00%

Financial Data: ***Fiscal Year End:***05/31 ***Latest Annual Data:*** 05/31/2007

Year	Sales	Net Income
2007	$27,351,000	$2,428,000
2006	$23,801,000	$810,000
2005	$16,080,000	-$4,870,000

Curr. Assets:	$23,135,000	***Curr. Liab.:***	$5,812,000	***P/E Ratio:***	19.43
Plant, Equip.:	$959,000	***Total Liab.:***	$6,076,000	***Indic. Yr. Divd.:***	NA
Total Assets:	$24,893,000	***Net Worth:***	$18,817,000	***Debt/ Equity:***	NA

Aeolus Pharmaceuticals Inc

23811 Inverness Pl., Laguna Niguel, CA, 92677; ***PH:*** 1-949-481-9825; ***http://*** www.incara.com

General - Incorporation	DE	**Stock**- Price on:12/24/2007	$0.9
Employees	1	Stock Exchange	OTC
Auditor	Grant Thornton LLP, Pricewater	Ticker Symbol	AOLS
Stk Agt	American Stock Transfer & Trust Co.	Outstanding Shares	31,950,000
Counsel	Wyrick Robbins Yates & Ponton	E.P.S	-$0.1
DUNS No.	NA	Shareholders	NA

Business: The group's principal activities are to develop a series of catalytic antioxidant molecules which protect against the damaging effects of reactive oxygen derived molecules. The group's target application will be the use of catalytic antioxidants to limit the side effects from damage caused by free radicals occurring in cancer radiation therapy. Free radicals, such as superoxide and peroxynitrite, cause damage in a broad group of diseases and conditions. The group was also developing adult liver stem cell therapy for the treatment of liver failure, which was sold in Oct 2002. On Oct 31, 2002, the group sold substantially all the assets of its wholly owned subsidiary, incara cell technologies, inc.

Primary SIC and add'l.: NA

CIK No: 0001261734

Subsidiaries: Aeolus Sciences, Inc., a Delaware corporation.

Officers: Jhon L. McManus/CEO, Pres., Brian J. Day/Chife Scientific Officer, Michael McManus/CFO

Directors: David C. Cavalier/Chmn., Jhon M. Farah/Dir., Joseph J. Krivulka/Dir., Michael E. Lewis/Dir., Chirs A. Rallis/Dir., Peter D. Suzdak/Dir., Amit Kumar/Dir.

Owners: Elaine Alexander, BVF Partners, L.P. and its affiliates, Michael P. McManus, Brain Day, Peter D. Suzdak, John L. McManus, Great Point Partners, LLC, Insiders, Xmark Opportunity Partners, LLC and its affiliates, John M. Farah, Richard P. Burgoon, David C. Cavalier, Joseph J. Krivulka, Efficacy Biotech Master Fund Ltd, Chris A. Rallis (*18 Owners included in Index*)

Financial Data: *Fiscal Year End:* 09/30   *Latest Annual Data:* 9/30/2006

Year	Sales	Net Income
2006	$92,000	-$5,728,000
2005	$252,000	-$6,905,000
2004	$305,000	-$17,167,000

Curr. Assets:	$3,428,000	**Curr. Liab.:**	$1,847,000		
Plant, Equip.:	NA	**Total Liab.:**	$1,847,000	**Indic. Yr. Divd.:**	NA
Total Assets:	$3,554,000	**Net Worth:**	$1,707,000	**Debt/ Equity:**	0.7194

AEP Generating Co

1 Riverside Plz, Columbus, OH, 43215; *PH:* 1-614-223-1000; *http://* www.aep.com

General - Incorporation	OH	**Stock**- Price on:12/24/2007	NA
Employees	NA	Stock Exchange	NA
Auditor	Deloitte & Touche LLP	Ticker Symbol	NA
Stk Agt..... Computershare Investor Services LLC		Outstanding Shares	NA
Counsel	NA	E.P.S.	NA
DUNS No.	36-152-1883	Shareholders	NA

Business: The group's principle activity is to provide electric services. The group operates from United States.

Primary SIC and add'l.: 4911

CIK No: 0000857571

Subsidiaries: AEGCo, AEPSC, APCo, CSPCo, I&M, Kingsport Power Company, KPCo, OPCo, PSO, SWEPCo, TCC, TNC, WPCo

Officers: Michael G. Morris/61/Chmn., CEO, Pres., Nick Akins/47/Exec. VP - Generation, Venita McCellon-Allen/COO, Pres. - Southwestern Electric Power Company, Carl English/61/Pres. - AEP Utilities, AEP, Aepsc, Holly Koeppel/49/CFO, Exec. VP - AEP, Aepsc, Susan Tomasky/54/Exec. VP - AEP, Exec. VP - Shared Services, Aepsc, Thomas M. Hagan/63/Exec. VP - AEP Utilities, West, Kevin Walker/COO, Pres. - Cspco, Opco, Dana E. Waldo/COO, Pres. - Apco, Kingsport Power Company, John B. Keane/61/Sr. VP, General Counsel, Sec., Robert P. Powers/53/Exec. VP, Joseph M. Buonaiuto/Sr. VP, Controller, Chief Accounting Officer, Stephen P. Smith/46/Dir., Sr. VP, Treasurer, Dennis E. Welch/56/Sr. VP - AEP

Directors: Michael G. Morris/61/Chmn., CEO, Pres., Lester A. Hudson/69/Dir., Donald G. Smith/72/Dir., John P. Desbarres/69/Dir., E. R. Brooks/71/Dir., Donald M. Carlton/71/Dir., William R. Howell/72/Dir., Richard L. Sandor/67/Dir., Lionel L. Nowell/53/Dir., Linda A. Goodspeed/45/Dir., Ralph D. Crosby/61/Dir., Robert W. Fri/72/Dir., Kathryn D. Sullivan/56/Dir.

Owners: Holly K. Koeppel, Venita McCellon-Allen, Susan Tomasky, Dennis E. Welch, Michael G. Morris, Insiders, Carl L. English, Nicholas K. Akins, John B. Keane, Thomas M. Hagan, Stephen P. Smith

AEP Industries Inc

125 Phillips Ave., South Hackensack, NJ, 07606; *PH:* 1-201-641-6600; *Fax:* 1-201-807-2490; *http://* www.aepind.com; *Email:* info@aepinc.com

General - Incorporation	DE	**Stock**- Price on:12/24/2007	$45.2
Employees	1,800	Stock Exchange	NDQ
Auditor	KPMG LLP	Ticker Symbol	AEPI
Stk Agt...... American Stock Transfer & Trust Co.		Outstanding Shares	7,550,000
Counsel .... Bachner, Tally, Polevoy & Misher		E.P.S.	$7.45
DUNS No.	05-209-1683	Shareholders	NA

Business: The group's principal activity is to manufacture and market plastic packaging films. They include polyethylene, polyvinyl chloride and polypropylene flexible packaging products. These products are used in the packaging, transportation, beverage, food, automotive, pharmaceutical, chemical, electronics, construction, agricultural and textile industries. The group either sells the film or further processes it by metallizing, printing, laminating, slitting or converting it to create value-added products according to customers' specifications. They are manufactured in nine countries in North America, Europe and the Asia/pacific region. The group sells directly to customers and also through distributors.

Primary SIC and add'l.: 3089 3081 2821

CIK No: 0000785787

Subsidiaries: AEP Belgium SA, AEP Bordex BV, AEP Canada Inc., AEP Films& Laminates Pty. Limited, AEP Industries (Australia) Pty. Limited, AEP Industries (Netherlands) BV, AEP Industries (NZ) Limited, AEP Industries (UK) Ltd., AEP Industries Packaging (Espana) SA, AEP Industries Polska.Sp. zoo., AEP Italia SrL, AEP Rigid Packaging Beuningen BV, AEP Rigid Packaging Venlo BV, Duplas Pty. Ltd, Fiap Hellas SA 17 Subsidiaries included in the Index

Officers: Brendan J. Barba/Chmn., CEO, Pres., Edgar Reich/Exec. VP - International, James B. Rafferty/VP, Treasurer, Paul Ten Brink/Group MD - Flexibles, Europe, Asia, David J. Cron/Exec. VP - Manufacturing, Paul C. Vegliante/Exec. VP - Operations, John J. Powers/Exec. VP - Sales, Marketing, Lawrence R. Noll/Dir., VP, Controller, Sec., Paul M. Feeney/Dir., Exec. VP - Finance, CFO, Richard Boyette/VP - Manufacturing Polyvinyl Chloride Products, North America, Robert Cron/Exec. VP - National Accounting, North America, Glenn K. Cooper/VP - Stretch Film Products, North America, Robert Covella/VP - Custom Films Division, North America, Joe Webb/Division Mgr. - Resinite Products, North America, Michael O'Neill/VP - Logistics

Directors: Brendan J. Barba/Chmn., CEO, Pres., Lee C. Stewart/Dir., Paul E. Gelbard/Dir., Kenneth Avia/Dir., Lawrence R. Noll/Dir., VP, Controller, Sec., Frank P. Gallagher/Dir., Paul M. Feeney/Dir., Exec. VP - Finance, CFO, Richard E. Davis/Dir.

Owners: Paul C. Vegliante/10.60%, Lee C. Stewart, Frank P. Gallagher, Brendan J. Barba/14.60%, Richard E. Davis, Paul M. Feeney/10.50%, Lawrence R. Noll, Kenneth Avia, Paul E. Gelbard, Insiders/19.50%

Financial Data: *Fiscal Year End:* 10/31   *Latest Annual Data:* 10/31/2006

Year	Sales	Net Income
2006	$802,109,000	$62,929,000
2005	$732,724,000	-$50,622,000
2004	$810,982,000	-$17,533,000

Curr. Assets:	$170,800,000	**Curr. Liab.:**	$85,264,000	**P/E Ratio:**	6.07
Plant, Equip.:	$139,183,000	**Total Liab.:**	$278,487,000	**Indic. Yr. Divd.:**	NA
Total Assets:	$336,080,000	**Net Worth:**	$57,593,000	**Debt/ Equity:**	NA

AEP Texas Central Co

1 Riverside Plz., Columbus, OH, 43215; *PH:* 1-614-716-1000; *Fax:* 1-614-716-1823; *http://* www.aep.com

General - Incorporation	TX	**Stock**- Price on:12/24/2007	$45.37
Employees	20,442	Stock Exchange	NYSE
Auditor	Deloitte & Touche LLP	Ticker Symbol	AEP
Stk Agt .... Computershare Investor Services LLC		Outstanding Shares	398,770,000
Counsel	NA	E.P.S.	$2.60
DUNS No.	00-792-4772	Shareholders	NA

Business: The group's principle activities are to generate, purchase, sell, transmit and distribute electric power. The group provides electric power to approximately 689,000 retail customers in southern Texas and wholesales to municipalities, rural electric cooperatives and other utilities. The group operates in three territories namely corpus christi, laredo and mcallen. The main users of the services include manufacturing, mining, agriculture, transportation and public utility sectors. The group is a member of the ercot power grid operating in Texas.

Primary SIC and add'l.: 4911

CIK No: 0000018734

Officers: Michael G. Morris/Chmn., CEO, Holly K. Koeppel/49/Dir., CFO, Exec. VP, Joseph M. Buonaiuto/Chief Accounting Officer, Controller, Nicholas K. Akins/47/Dir., Exec. VP, Charles R. Patton/COO, Pres.

Directors: Michael G. Morris/Chmn., CEO, Nicholas K. Akins/47/Dir., Exec. VP, John B. Keane/61/Dir., Holly K. Koeppel/49/Dir., CFO, Exec. VP, Susan Tomasky/54/Dir., Dennis E. Welch/56/Dir., Carl L. English/61/Dir., Thomas M. Hagan/63/Dir.

Owners: Thomas M. Hagan, Susan Tomasky, Holly K. Koeppel, Carl L. English, John B. Keane, Dennis E. Welch, Nicholas K. Akins, Michael G. Morris, Stephen P. Smith, Venita McCellon-Allen, Insiders

Financial Data: *Fiscal Year End:* 12/31   *Latest Annual Data:* 12/31/2006

Year	Sales	Net Income
2006	$12,622,000,000	$1,002,000,000
2005	$12,111,000,000	$814,000,000
2004	$14,057,000,000	$1,089,000,000

Curr. Assets:	$3,588,000,000	**Curr. Liab.:**	$5,456,000,000	**P/E Ratio:**	20.16
Plant, Equip.:	$26,825,000,000	**Total Liab.:**	$28,514,000,000	**Indic. Yr. Divd.:**	$1.640
Total Assets:	$37,987,000,000	**Net Worth:**	$9,473,000,000	**Debt/ Equity:**	1.3045

AEP Texas North Co

1 Riverside Plz., Columbus, OH, 43215; *PH:* 1-614-716-1000; *http://* www.aep.com

General - Incorporation	TX	**Stock**- Price on:12/24/2007	$79.5
Employees	NA	Stock Exchange	OTC
Auditor	Deloitte & Touche LLP	Ticker Symbol	ATXAN
Stk Agt .... Computershare Investor Services LLC		Outstanding Shares	NA
Counsel	NA	E.P.S.	NA
DUNS No.	00-792-3311	Shareholders	NA

Business: The group's principle activities include generating, selling, purchase and distributing electric power. As of 31-Dec-2003, the company supplies 22,075 customers located in west and central Texas. The principal industry served by the company is agriculture, military installations and correctional facilities. It is a wholly owned subsidiary of America electric power company inc. The group operates from United States.

Primary SIC and add'l.: 4911

CIK No: 0000105860

Officers: Michael G. Morris/Chmn., CEO, Pres. - American Electric Power Co, Inc, Charles R. Patton/COO, Pres. - AEP Texas, Kevin Walker/Pres., COO - AEP Ohio, Dana Waldo/COO, Pres. - Appalachian Power, Pat D. Hemlepp/Dir. - Corporate Media Relations, Melissa McHenry/Corporate Media Relations, David Hagelin/Corporate Media Relations, Dennis E. Welch/Dir., Sr. VP - Environment, Safety, Diane Fitzgerald/MD - Environment, Safety, Julie Sloat/VP - Investor Relations, Strategic Initiatives, Bette Jo Rozsa/MD - Investor Relations, Kathleen Kozero/Contact - Individual Investors, April Dawson/Contact - Individual Investors, John B. Keane/61/Dir., Sr. VP, General Counsel, Chief Compliance Officer, Sec., Joseph M. Buonaiuto/Controller, Chief Accounting Officer (*21 Officers included in Index*)

Directors: Michael G. Morris/Chmn., CEO, Pres. - American Electric Power Co, Inc, Robert W. Fri/72/Dir., John P. Desbarres/69/Dir., Kathryn D. Sullivan/56/Dir., E. R. Brooks/71/Dir., Donald M. Carlton/71/Dir., William R. Howell/72/Dir., Richard L. Sandor/67/Dir., Lionel L. Nowell/53/Dir., Linda A. Goodspeed/45/Dir., Ralph D. Crosby/61/Dir., Dennis E. Welch/Dir., Sr. VP - Environment, Safety, John B. Keane/61/Dir., Sr. VP, General Counsel, Chief Compliance Officer, Sec., Stephen P. Smith/46/Dir., Carl L. English/Dir., Pres. - AEP Utilities (*19 Directors included in Index*)

Owners: Insiders, Dennis E. Welch, Nicholas K. Akins, Susan Tomasky, Thomas M. Hagan, Stephen P. Smith, Venita McCellon-Allen, Michael G. Morris, Holly K. Koeppel, John B. Keane, Carl L. English

Financial Data: *Fiscal Year End:* 12/31   *Latest Annual Data:* 12/31/2006

Year	Sales	Net Income
2006	$329,470,000	$14,943,000
2005	$458,888,000	$33,004,000
2004	$492,145,000	$47,659,000

Curr. Assets:	$71,708,000	**Curr. Liab.:**	$93,308,000		
Plant, Equip.:	$841,932,000	**Total Liab.:**	$658,809,000	**Indic. Yr. Divd.:**	NA
Total Assets:	$967,514,000	**Net Worth:**	$308,705,000	**Debt/ Equity:**	NA

Aercap Holdings N.V.

Avioport Bldg., Evert van de Beekstraat 312, Schiphol Airport, Amsterdam; *PH:* 31-206559655; *Fax:* 31-206559100; *http://* www.aercap.com

General - Incorporation	Netherlands	**Stock**- Price on:12/24/2007	$32.16
Employees	351	Stock Exchange	NYSE
Auditor	NA	Ticker Symbol	AER
Stk Agt	NA	Outstanding Shares	NA
Counsel	NA	E.P.S.	$1.61
DUNS No.	NA	Shareholders	NA

Business: The groups principle activities include leasing, financing, selling and managing commercial aircraft. In April 26, 2006, the group acquired AeroTurbine. The group products sold under the trade name AerCap. The group operates from the United States.

Primary SIC and add'l.: 7359
CIK No: 0001378789
Subsidiaries: Acorn Aviation Limited, AerCap 1041 Limited, AerCap 320 A Limited, AerCap 320 B Limited, AerCap 320 C Limited, AerCap 320 Limited, AerCap A Bordeaux Limited, AerCap Administrative Services Limited, AerCap Aircraft Finance V B.V., AerCap Aircraft Finance VII B.V., AerCap Aircraft Finance VIII B.V., AerCap Aircraft Finance X B.V., AerCap Aircraft Finance XI B.V., AerCap Aircraft Finance XII B.V., AerCap Aircraft Finance XIII B.V. 141 Subsidiaries included in the Index
Officers: Klaus W. Heinemann/Executive Dir., CEO, Nicolas Finazzo/CEO - Aeroturbine, Robert B. Nichols/COO - Aeroturbine, Cole Reese/Chief Tax, Accounting Officer, Reynoud K. Simonis/CTO, Erwin Den Dikken/Chief Legal Officer, Patrick Den Elzen/Head - Trading, Frauke Oberdieck/Contact - Corporate Communications, Peter Wortel/Investor Relations Contact, Keith A. Helming/CFO - Investor Relations, Heinrich H. Loechteken/Chief Investment Officer, Wouter M. Den Dikken/Chief Legal Officer, Patrick P. Den Elzen/Head - Trading, Soeren E. Ferre/Head - Europe, Middle East, Africa, Asia Pacific, Aengus Kelly/Group Treasurer *(16 Officers included in Index)*
Directors: Klaus W. Heinemann/Executive Dir., CEO, Pieter Korteweg/Non Exec. Chmn., Ronald J. Bolger/Non Exec. Dir., James N. Chapman/Non Exec. Dir., Brett W. Ingersoll/Non Exec. Dir., Marius J.L Jonkhart/Non Exec. Dir., Gerald P. Strong/Non Exec. Dir., David J. Teitelbaum/Non Exec. Dir., Robert G. Warden/Non Exec. Dir.
Owners: Nicolas Finazzo/2.20%, Klaus W. Heinemann/2.10%, Soeren E. Ferr, Robert B. Nichols/2.20%, Cole T. Reese, Aengus Kelly, Stephen Feinberg/56.80%, Heinrich H. Loechteken/2.10%, Patrick den Elzen, Anil Mehta, Wouter M. den Dikken, Reynoud K. Simonis, Insiders/12.20%

Financial Data: *Fiscal Year End:*12/31 *Latest Annual Data:* 12/31/2006

Year	Sales	Net Income
2006	$814,419,000	$87,996,000

Curr. Assets:	$351,347,000	**Curr. Liab.:**	$496,545,000	**P/E Ratio:**	20.06
Plant, Equip.:	$2,966,779,000	**Total Liab.:**	$3,193,081,000	**Indic. Yr. Divd.:**	NA
Total Assets:	$3,922,992,000	**Net Worth:**	$729,911,000	**Debt/ Equity:**	NA

Aerocentury Corp

1440 Chapin Ave., Ste. 310, Burlingame, CA, 94010; *PH:* 1-650-340-1888; *Fax:* 1-650-696-3929; *http://* www.aerocentury.com

General - Incorporation	DE	**Stock**- Price on:12/24/2007	$15.1099
Employees	NA	Stock Exchange	AMEX
Auditor	BDO Seidman, LLP	Ticker Symbol	ACY
Stk Agt	Continental Stock Transfer & Trust Co	Outstanding Shares	1,540,000
Counsel	Morrison & Foerster LLP	E.P.S.	$1.55
DUNS No.	NA	Shareholders	NA

Business: The group's principle activity is to invest in used regional aircraft equipment leased to foreign and domestic regional air carriers. It's objective is to increase stockholder value by acquiring additional aircraft assets that will provide a return on investment through lease revenue from creditworthy lessees, and eventually from the sale proceeds. The group acquires additional assets in three ways: asset selection, lessee selection and obtaining acquisition financing. The group's quarterly revenue for September 2007 was 6.39 millions of USD.
Primary SIC and add'l.: 7359
CIK No: 0001036848
Subsidiaries: AeroCentury Investments II LLC, AeroCentury Investments V LLC
Officers: Neal D. Crispin/Chmn., Principal Executive Officer, Pres., Steve Wallace/VP - Aircraft Remarketing, Christopher B. Tigno/General Counsel, Jack Humphreys/VP - Maintenance, Brian J. Ginna/VP - Corporate Development, John S. Myers/Sr. VP, Marc J. Anderson/Dir., COO, Sr. VP, Toni M. Perazzo/Dir., Sec., Sr. VP - Finance, Principal Financial, Accounting Officer, Glenn Roberts/VP, Controller, Harold M. Lyons/VP - Finance
Directors: Neal D. Crispin/Chmn., Principal Executive Officer, Pres., Thomas W. Orr/Dir., Evan M. Wallach/Dir., Marc J. Anderson/Dir., COO, Sr. VP, Thomas Hiniker/Dir., Toni M. Perazzo/Dir., Sec., Sr. VP - Finance, Principal Financial, Accounting Officer
Owners: Insiders/22.71%, JetFleet Holding Corp./12.83%, Marc J. Anderson/1.84%, Neal D. Crispin/21.80%, Evan M. Wallach, Toni M. Perazzo/21.80%, Thomas G. Hiniker, Thomas W. Orr

Financial Data: *Fiscal Year End:*12/31 *Latest Annual Data:* 12/31/2006

Year	Sales	Net Income
2006	$18,322,000	$817,000
2005	$13,499,000	$193,000
2004	$10,904,000	$266,000

Curr. Assets:	$4,248,000	**Curr. Liab.:**	$78,157,000	**P/E Ratio:**	9.75
Plant, Equip.:	$93,675,000	**Total Liab.:**	$78,157,000	**Indic. Yr. Divd.:**	NA
Total Assets:	$98,505,000	**Net Worth:**	$20,348,000	**Debt/ Equity:**	NA

Aeroflex Inc

35 S Service Rd. , Plainview, NY, 11803; *PH:* 1-516-694-6700; *http://* www.aeroflex.com

General - Incorporation	DE	**Stock**- Price on:12/24/2007	$14.09
Employees	2,675	Stock Exchange	NDQ
Auditor	KPMG LLP	Ticker Symbol	ARXX
Stk Agt	American Stock Transfer & Trust Co.	Outstanding Shares	74,540,000
Counsel	NA	E.P.S.	NA
DUNS No.	00-205-0532	Shareholders	NA

Business: The group's principal activity is to produce microelectronic and testing solutions. The products are used in the aerospace, defense, fiber optic, wireless and satellite communications markets. It designs and manufactures motion control systems and shock and vibration isolation systems which are used for commercial, industrial and defense applications. The group operates through three segments: microelectronic solutions, test solutions and isolator products. Microelectronic solutions designs custom and standard integrated circuits such as databuses, transceivers, microcontrollers, microprocessors and memories that are radiation tolerant and are used for satellite and space applications. Test solutions provides product enhancement to communications systems manufacturers. Isolator products designs, develops, manufactures and sells shock and vibration isolation system. On 03-Sep-2003, the group acquired mce technologies inc and on 31-Oct-2003, celerity systems inc.
Primary SIC and add'l.: 6719 3825 3674 3663 3679 3812 3672
CIK No: 0000002601

Subsidiaries: Aeroflex / Inmet, Inc., Aeroflex / KDI, Inc., Aeroflex / Metelics, Inc., Aeroflex / Weinschel, Inc., Aeroflex Cambridge, Ltd., Aeroflex Colorado Springs, Inc., Aeroflex International Ltd., Aeroflex Microelectronics Solutions, Inc., Aeroflex Plainview, Inc., Aeroflex Powell, Inc., Aeroflex Systems Corp., Aeroflex Wichita, Inc., Bank of America, N.A., Europtest, S.A., Fleet National Bank 18 Subsidiaries included in the Index
Officers: Leonard Borow/COO, Pres., Philip P. Trahanas/Co - Pres.
Owners: Barclays/6.85%, Carl Caruso, Leonard Borow/3.40%, John Adamovich, Ernest E. Courchene, Harvey R. Blau/4.20%, Joseph E. Pompeo, Michael A. Nelson, Insiders/10.70%, Paul Abecassis, Barton D. Strong, Milton Brenner, John F. Benedik, NWQ Investment Management Company/10.00%, John Buyko/1.10%

Financial Data: *Fiscal Year End:*06/30 *Latest Annual Data:* 6/30/2006

Year	Sales	Net Income
2006	$551,846,000	$26,959,000
2005	$463,371,000	$17,041,000
2004	$414,101,000	$12,147,000

Curr. Assets:	$328,354,000	**Curr. Liab.:**	$119,215,000	**P/E Ratio:**	37.08
Plant, Equip.:	$77,940,000	**Total Liab.:**	$150,352,000	**Indic. Yr. Divd.:**	NA
Total Assets:	$638,022,000	**Net Worth:**	$487,670,000	**Debt/ Equity:**	0.0065

Aeropostale Inc

112 W 34th St., 22nd Fl., New York, NY, 10120; *PH:* 1-646-485-5398; *Fax:* 1-646-485-5430; *http://* www.aeropostale.com

General - Incorporation	DE	**Stock**- Price on:12/24/2007	$42.11
Employees	2,696	Stock Exchange	NYSE
Auditor	Deloitte & Touche LLP	Ticker Symbol	ARO
Stk Agt	American Stock Transfer & Trust Co.	Outstanding Shares	51,700,000
Counsel	NA	E.P.S.	$1.57
DUNS No.	NA	Shareholders	NA

Business: The group's principle activity is to retail casual apparel and accessories that target both young women and young men aged eleven to twenty. The group offers a focused collection of fashion basic apparel, including graphic t-shirts, tops, bottoms, sweaters, jeans, outerwear and accessories. The group provides customers with a focused selection of active-oriented, fashion basic merchandise at compelling values. The group uses creative visual merchandising, colorful in-store signage, bright lighting, popular music and an enthusiastic, well-trained sales force for retailing. The group's total revenue for year 2007 was 1,413.21 millions of USD.
Primary SIC and add'l.: 5621 5611
CIK No: 0001168213
Subsidiaries: Aropostale West, Inc., JimmyZ Surf Co., Inc.
Officers: Julian R. Geiger/Chmn., CEO, Ann E. Joyce/CIO, Sr. VP, Michael J. Cunningham/CFO, Exec. VP, Mary Jo Pile/Sr. VP, Chief Store Officer, Thomas P. Johnson/COO, Exec. VP, Barbara Pindar/Sr. VP - Planning, Allocation, Edward M. Slezak/Sr. VP, General Counsel, Sec., Olivera Lazic - Zangas/Sr. VP, Dir. - Design, Mindy C. Meads/Pres., Chief Merchandising Officer, Marc A. Babins/Sr. VP - Production, Scott K. Birnbaum/Sr. VP, Dir. - Marketing, Mark A. Dorwart/Sr. VP - Logistics, Marc D. Miller/Sr. VP - New Business Development, Strategic Planning
Directors: Julian R. Geiger/Chmn., CEO, Karin Hirtler-Garvey/Dir., John D. Howard/Dir., John Haugh/Dir., Ronald R. Beegle/Dir., Robert B. Chavez/Dir., Bodil Arlander/Dir., David B. Vermylen/Dir.
Owners: Barbara Pindar, Thomas P. Johnson, Mary Elizabeth Burton, Bodil Arlander, Insiders/1.76%, John D. Howard, Olivera Lazic-Zangas, Barclays Global Investors Japan Trust and Banking Company Limited/5.18%, David B. Vermylen, Julian R. Geiger, David H. Edwab, Robert B. Chavez, Karin Hirtler-Garvey, Michael J. Cunningham, Ronald R. Beegle *(16 Owners included in Index)*

Financial Data: *Fiscal Year End:*01/28 *Latest Annual Data:* 2/3/2007

Year	Sales	Net Income
2007	$1,413,208,000	$106,647,000
2006	$1,204,347,000	$83,954,000
2005	$964,212,000	$84,112,000

Curr. Assets:	$398,793,000	**Curr. Liab.:**	$164,798,000	**P/E Ratio:**	19.96
Plant, Equip.:	$175,591,000	**Total Liab.:**	$269,048,000	**Indic. Yr. Divd.:**	NA
Total Assets:	$581,164,000	**Net Worth:**	$312,116,000	**Debt/ Equity:**	NA

Aerosonic Corp

1212 N Hercules Ave., Clearwater, FL, 33765; *PH:* 1-727-461-3000; *Fax:* 1-727-447-5926; *http://* www.aerosonic.com; *Email:* info@aerosonic.com

General - Incorporation	DE	**Stock**- Price on:12/24/2007	$7.8001
Employees	240	Stock Exchange	AMEX
Auditor	Tedder, James, Worden & Assoc. P.A	Ticker Symbol	AIM
Stk Agt	American Stock Transfer & Trust Co.	Outstanding Shares	3,570,000
Counsel	Ruden Et Al	E.P.S.	-$0.58
DUNS No.	00-409-1765	Shareholders	NA

Business: The group's principal activities are to manufacture and sell aircraft instruments through its subsidiaries. It operates through four divisions: clearwater instruments, aerosonic wichita, avionic specialties and precision component division. Clearwater instruments manufactures altimeters, rate-of-climb indicators and other flight instrumentation. Aerosonic wichita is the source inspection location for wichita customers and the primary location for clearwater instruments' repair business. Avionic specialties manufactures angle of attack /stall warning systems, integrated multifunction probes, and engine vibration monitoring systems. Precision components performs precision high volume machining of mechanical components. The products are sold to manufacturers of commercial and private aircraft, both domestic and foreign, and the U.S. Military services.
Primary SIC and add'l.: 3812 3728
CIK No: 0000109471
Subsidiaries: Avionics-Specialties, Inc
Officers: David A. Baldini/Chmn., CEO, Pres./$290,131.00, Mark Perkins/Dir., Exec. VP/$225,629.00, Carm Russo/Exec. VP/$220,544.00, Charles Pope/CFO
Directors: David A. Baldini/Chmn., CEO, Pres., Robert J. McGill/Dir., Mark Perkins/Dir., Exec. VP, Thomas E. Whytas/Dir., Donald Russell/Dir.
Owners: Hillson Partners LLP/7.71%, Athena Capital Management, Inc./9.14%, David A. Baldini, Robert J. McGill, Gary E. Colbert, Thomas E. Whytas, Mark P. Perkins, Carmelo Russo, Insiders/4.57%, Donald Russell/2.28%

Financial Data: *Fiscal Year End:*01/31 *Latest Annual Data:* 1/31/2007

Year	Sales	Net Income
2007	$31,253,000	$565,000
2006	$34,763,000	$2,550,000
2005	$30,721,000	$1,541,000

Curr. Assets:	$16,132,000	**Curr. Liab.:**	$4,523,000	**P/E Ratio:**	780.01
Plant, Equip.:	$3,617,000	**Total Liab.:**	$7,133,000	**Indic. Yr. Divd.:**	NA
Total Assets:	$20,212,000	**Net Worth:**	$13,079,000	**Debt/ Equity:**	NA

Aerotelesis Inc

1554 S Sepulveda Blvd, Ste 118, Los Angeles, CA, 90025; *PH:* 1-310-235-1727; *http://* www.aerotelesis.com; *Email:* ir@aeroTelesis.com

General - Incorporation ... DE
Employees ... 7
Auditor ..... Cooper, Moss, Resnick & Klein, LLP
Stk Agt ... Stock Transfer & Trust Co
Counsel ... Mr. Narayanans
DUNS No. ... NA

Stock - Price on:12/24/2007 ... $0.018
Stock Exchange ... OTC
Ticker Symbol ... AOTL
Outstanding Shares ... 98,620,000
E.P.S. ... -$0.082
Shareholders ... NA

Business: The group's principal activities are to provide wireless telecommunication. The group's technology platform is a licensed modulation method known as ultra spectral modulation, that increases spectral efficiency and avoids bottlenecks. The group's targeted application markets includes satellite communications, mobile communications, voice over Internet protocol and other broadband applications. As on 02-Oct-2003 the group acquired aerotelesis Philippines inc., through a reverse merger.

Primary SIC and add'l.: 3669

CIK No: 0000017544

Subsidiaries: Aerotelesis Philippines, Inc

Officers: Joseph Gutierrez/52/Dir., CFO, Pres.

Directors: Maral Ajemian/46/Dir., Joseph Gutierrez/52/Dir., CFO, Pres.

Owners: Joseph Gutierrez/1.33%, Maral Ajemian/0.12%, Insiders/1.45%, Nations Mobile Networks Ltd./50.74%

Financial Data: **Fiscal Year End:**03/31 **Latest Annual Data:** 03/31/2007

Year	Sales	Net Income
2007	NA	-$5,581,000
2006	$9,000	-$7,619,000
2005	$409,000	-$1,061,000

Curr. Assets:	$96,000	**Curr. Liab.:**	$346,000		
Plant, Equip.:	$104,000	**Total Liab.:**	$1,304,000	**Indic. Yr. Divd.:**	NA
Total Assets:	$2,926,000	**Net Worth:**	$1,622,000	**Debt/ Equity:**	NA

AES Corp

285 Newbury St., Peabody, MA, 01960; *PH:* 1-978-535-7310; *Fax:* 1-978-535-7313; *http://* www.aes-corp.com; *Email:* invest@aes.com

General - Incorporation ... DE
Employees ... 32,000
Auditor ... Deloitte & Touche LLP
Stk Agt ... EquiServe Trust Co N.A
Counsel ... NA
DUNS No. ... 04-385-7812

Stock - Price on:12/24/2007 ... $20.74
Stock Exchange ... NYSE
Ticker Symbol ... AES
Outstanding Shares ... 667,580,000
E.P.S. ... -$0.15
Shareholders ... NA

Business: The group's principal activity is to generate and distribute electric power. The group operates in four business segments: contract generation: supplies wholesale electricity under long-term contracts for more than 75% of the group's output. Competitive supply: supplies electricity, both wholesale and retail, pursuant to short-term contracts or spot electricity markets. Large utilities: utilities of significant size that maintain a monopoly franchise within a defined service area. Growth distribution: offers significant potential for growth and challenges related to operational difficulties with respect to outdated equipment, significant non-technical losses, cultural problems, emerging economies. The group has international operations in South America, Europe, Africa, Asia and the Caribbean countries.

Primary SIC and add'l.: 4911

CIK No: 0000874761

Subsidiaries: Administradora Serdeco, C.A., Aee2, LLC, AES (India) Private Limited, Aes (ni) Limited, AES Abigail S.a.r.l., AES Aggregate Services, Ltd., AES Alamitos Development, Inc., AES Alamitos, LLC, AES Alicura Holdings S.C.A, AES Alicura S.A., AES Americas International Holdings, Limited, AES Americas Participacoes Ltda., AES Americas, Inc., AES Andes Energy, Inc., AES Andes, Inc. 807 Subsidiaries included in the Index

Officers: Steve Walsh/Pres., CEO - AES Ukraine, Paul Hanrahan/Dir., CEO, Pres./$7,196,561.00, Jean-David Bile/CEO - AES Sonel, Ann Murtlow/Pres., CEO - Indianapolis Power, Light Company, Felipe Ceron/CEO - AES Gener, Latin America, Venu Nambiar/VP, Group Mgr. - Middle East, South Asia, Lakshman Charanjiva/CIO, VP, Prabu Natarajan/VP - Tax, Rich Bulger/VP - Internal Audit, Roger Naill/Sr. VP - Forecasting, Strategy, Risk Management, William Luraschi/Exec. VP - Business Development/$3,004,305.00, Jay Kloosterboer/Exec. VP - Business Excellence, Robert Hemphill/Exec. VP, Brian Miller/Exec. VP, General Counsel, Corp. Sec., Acting Chief Compliance Officer, Victoria Harker/CFO, Exec. VP/$1,106,429.00 *(58 Officers included in Index)*

Directors: Paul Hanrahan/Dir., CEO, Pres., Richard Darman/Chmn., Sven Sandstrom/Dir., Charles O. Rossotti/Dir., Philip A. Odeen/Dir., Kristina M. Johnson/Dir., Philip Lader/Dir., John A. Koskinen/Dir., John H. McArthur/Dir., Sandra O. Moose/Dir.

Owners: Legg Mason Funds Management, Inc/17.77%, Charles O. Rossotti, Paul Hanrahan, FMR Corporation/9.91%, William R. Luraschi, Andres R. Gluski, Kristina M. Johnson, Haresh Jaisinghani, John H. McArthur, Sven Sandstrom, Philip A. Odeen, John A. Koskinen, Insiders/0.91%, Richard Darman, Barry J. Sharp *(18 Owners included in Index)*

Financial Data: **Fiscal Year End:**12/31 **Latest Annual Data:** 12/31/2006

Year	Sales	Net Income
2006	$11,564,000,000	$204,000,000
2005	$11,086,000,000	$630,000,000
2004	$9,463,000,000	$292,000,000

Curr. Assets:	$6,565,000,000	**Curr. Liab.:**	$5,029,000,000		
Plant, Equip.:	$17,197,000,000	**Total Liab.:**	$25,288,000,000	**Indic. Yr. Divd.:**	NA
Total Assets:	$31,201,000,000	**Net Worth:**	$2,965,000,000	**Debt/ Equity:**	4.9051

AES Gener

Mariano Sanchez Fontecilla 310, 3rd Fl., Santiago; *PH:* 56-26868900; *http://* www.aesgener.cl

General - Incorporation ... Chile
Employees ... NA
Auditor ... Deloitte & Touche LLP
Stk Agt ... Deposito Central De Valores
Counsel ... NA
DUNS No. ... 98-029-0233

Stock - Price on:12/24/2007 ... NA
Stock Exchange ... NA
Ticker Symbol ... NA
Outstanding Shares ... NA
E.P.S. ... NA
Shareholders ... NA

Business: The group's principal activities are the generation of electric power; extraction and distribution of coal; exploration, extraction and transportation of natural gas; exploration and exploitation of oil; preparation and distribution of densified bio-combustible or biofuel; and the provision of shipping and port services, engineering and sanitary. It operates in Chile, Argentina, Colombia and the Dominican Republic.

Primary SIC and add'l.: 1241 4931 8711 4924

CIK No: 0000926075

Officers: Felipe Ceron/45/CEO, Enio Belmonte/59/Operations Mgr., Juan Carlos Olmedo/44/Commercial Mgr., Cristian Antunez/46/Chief Accounting Officer, Maria Teresa Bravo/38/Mgr. - Communications, Nicolas Cubillos/42/General Counsel, Juan Ricardo Inostroza/46/Development, Regulation Mgr.

Directors: Andres Gluski/49/Chmn., Fernando Gonzalez/Dir., Axel Christensen/39/Dir., Eduardo Dutrey/47/Dir., Javier Giorgio/37/Dir., John Ruggirello/57/Dir., Rene Cortazar/55/Dir., Patricio Testorelli/43/Dir.

Owners: A.F.P. Provida S.A. Fondo tipo A/0.73%, A.F.P. Bansander S.A. Fondo tipo A/0.24%, Fondo Mutuo Santander Acciones Retail & Consumo/0.25%, A.F.P. Provida S.A. Fondo tipo B/0.31%, Celfin Small Cap. Amrica Latina Fondo de Inversin/0.26%, A.F.P. Provida S.A. Fondo tipo D/0.31%, Larran Vial S.A. Corredora de Bolsa/0.28%, A.F.P. Habitat S.A. Fondo tipo A/0.27%, Inversiones Cachagua Limitada/91.19%, Celfin Capital S.A. Corredores de Bolsa/1.49%, A.F.P. Provida S.A. Fondo tipo C/0.42%, Inversiones HB S.A./0.30%

Aeterna Zentaris Inc

111 Eighth Ave., 13th Fl., New York, NY, 10011; *PH:* 1-212-894-8638; *http://* www.aeternazentaris.com

General - Incorporation ... Canada
Employees ... 500
Auditor ... PricewaterhouseCoopers LLP
Stk Agt ... Nationall Bank Trust Inc
Counsel ... Ogilvy Renault
DUNS No. ... NA

Stock - Price on:12/24/2007 ... $3.31
Stock Exchange ... NDQ
Ticker Symbol ... AEZS
Outstanding Shares ... 53,180,000
E.P.S. ... $0.37
Shareholders ... NA

Business: The group's principle activities are manufacturing and distribution of nutritional and cosmetic and biopharmaceutical products. The group operates in three segments: cosmetics and nutrition, distribution and biopharmaceutical. Cosmetics and nutrition segment develops active ingredients used for the manufacture and distribution of cosmetics and nutritional products. Distribution segment distributes cosmetics, nutritional products, pharmaceuticals and fine chemicals. Biopharmaceutical segment focuses on the development of novel therapeutic approaches for diseases characterized by unmet medical needs. The group's quarterly revenue for September 2007 was 11.59 millions of USD.

Primary SIC and add'l.: 5122 2844 2834

CIK No: 0001113423

Subsidiaries: Atrium Biotechnologies Inc, Echelon Biosciences, Inc., Zentaris GmbH

Officers: David J. Mazzo/Dir., CEO, Pres., Gilles R. Gagnon/CEO, Pres., Jurgen Engel/Dir., Exec. VP, Chief Scientific Officer, Sonia Girouard/Contact - Human Resources, Canada, USA, Dennis Turpin/Sr. VP, CFO, Ellen McDonald/Sr. VP - Business Operations, Chief Business Officer, Nicholas J. Pelliccione/Sr. VP - Regulatory Affairs, Quality Assurance, Paul Blake/Sr. VP, Chief Medical Officer, Mario Paradis/Sr. VP - Administrative, Legal Affairs, Corp. Sec., Gerald Batist/Member - Scientific Advisory Board, Frans M.J. Debruyne/Member - Scientific Advisory Board, Alan H. Decherney/Member - Scientific Advisory Board, Klaus H.R. Diedrich/Member - Scientific Advisory Board, Rene Frydman/Member - Scientific Advisory Board, Fernand Labrie/Member - Scientific Advisory Board *(24 Officers included in Index)*

Directors: David J. Mazzo/Dir., CEO, Pres., Jurgen Ernst/Dir., Pierre MacDonald/Dir., Gerald J. Martin/Corp. Dir., Pierre Laurin/Dir., Gerard Limoges/Corp. Dir., Stormy Byorum/Dir., Jose P. Dorais/Dir., Jurgen Engel/Dir., Exec. VP, Chief Scientific Officer, Marcel Aubut/Dir.

Financial Data: **Fiscal Year End:**12/31 **Latest Annual Data:** 12/31/2006

Year	Sales	Net Income
2006	$41,392,000	$34,262,000
2005	$247,389,000	$15,970,000
2004	$193,666,000	-$2,224,000

Curr. Assets:	$101,723,000	**Curr. Liab.:**	$16,310,000	**P/E Ratio:**	35.56
Plant, Equip.:	$13,432,000	**Total Liab.:**	$58,960,000	**Indic. Yr. Divd.:**	NA
Total Assets:	$228,664,000	**Net Worth:**	$169,704,000	**Debt/ Equity:**	NA

Aethlon Medical Inc

3030 Bunker Hill St., San Diego, CA, 92109; *PH:* 1-858-459-7800; *http://* www.aethlonmedical.com

General - Incorporation ... NV
Employees ... 5
Auditor ... Squar, Rrrhl & Williamson, LLP
Stk Agt ... Computershare Trust Co
Counsel ... NA
DUNS No. ... NA

Stock - Price on:12/24/2007 ... $0.67
Stock Exchange ... OTC
Ticker Symbol ... AEMD
Outstanding Shares ... 32,660,000
E.P.S. ... -$0.18
Shareholders ... NA

Business: The groups principal activity is to develop a medical device to treat infectious disease. The group product includes Hemopurifier (TM). The group operates from the United States.

Primary SIC and add'l.: 3826

CIK No: 0000882291

Subsidiaries: Aethlon, Inc., Cell Activation, Inc., Hemex, Inc., Syngen Research, Inc.

Officers: James A. Joyce/Chmn., CEO/$240,000.00, Richard H. Tullis/VP, Chief Science Officer/$180,000.00, Kenneth R. Michael/Regulatory, Clinical Affairs Advisor, Harold H. Handley/Pres., James W. Dorst/CFO/$150,000.00, Jeff Richardson/Sr. Dir. - Communications

Directors: James A. Joyce/Chmn., CEO, Franklyn S. Barry/Dir., Edward G. Broenniman/Dir., Richard H. Tullis/VP, Chief Science Officer, Ken Alibek/Member - Scientific Advisory Board, Charles Bailey/Member - Scientific Advisory Board, Larry Cowgill/Member - Scientific Advisory Board, Pedro Cuatrecasas/Member - Scientific Advisory Board, Nathan W. Levin/Member - Scientific Advisory Board, Raveendran Pottathil/Member - Scientific Advisory Board, Claudio Ronco/Member - Scientific Advisory Board, Joseph A. Bellanti/Member - Scientific Advisory Board

Owners: Harold H. Handley, Franklyn S. Barry/1.61%, Edward G. Broenniman/2.02%, Insiders/24.56%, Richard H. Tullis/6.08%, James W. Dorst/1.03%, Allan S. Bird/9.90%, Calvin M. Leung/6.19%, Ellen R. Weiner Family Revocable Trust/9.90%, James A. Joyce/17.53%, Phillip A. Ward/9.62%

Financial Data: *Fiscal Year End:*03/31 *Latest Annual Data:* 03/31/2006

Year	Sales	Net Income
2006	NA	-$2,920,000
2005	NA	-$2,097,000
2004	NA	-$1,519,000

Curr. Assets:	$445,000	**Curr. Liab.:**	$7,705,000		
Plant, Equip.:	$14,000	**Total Liab.:**	$7,705,000	**Indic. Yr. Divd.:**	NA
Total Assets:	$613,000	**Net Worth:**	-$7,092,000	**Debt/ Equity:**	NA

Aetna Inc

151 Farmington Ave., Hartford, CT, 06156; ***PH:*** 1-860-273-0123; ***Fax:*** 1-860-273-3971; ***http://*** www.aetna.com

General - Incorporation	PA	**Stock**- Price on:12/24/2007	$49.48
Employees	30,000	Stock Exchange	NYSE
Auditor	KPMG LLP	Ticker Symbol	AET
Stk Agt	Computershare Trust Co	Outstanding Shares	512,300,000
Counsel	NA	E.P.S	$3.41
DUNS No.	NA	Shareholders	NA

Business: The group's principle activity is to provide information and resources to help the people better informed decision about their health care. The group operates from United States.

Primary SIC and add'l.: 6321 6371 6331 6324 6311

CIK No: 0001122304

Subsidiaries: Active Health Management, Inc., AE Fourteen, Incorporated, Aelan Inc., AET Health Care Plan of California, Inc., AET Health Care Plan, Inc., Aetna Affordable Housing, Inc., Aetna Behavioral Health of Delaware, LLC, Aetna Behavioral Health, LLC, Aetna Capital Management, LLC, Aetna Criterion Communications, Inc., Aetna Dental Inc., Aetna Dental Maintenance Organization, Inc., Aetna Dental of California Inc., Aetna Family Plans of Georgia Inc., Aetna Family Plans of Ohio Inc. 80 Subsidiaries included in the Index

Officers: Ronald A. Williams/Chmn., CEO/$19,802,480.00, Meg McCarthy/Sr. VP - Performance Improvement, CIO, Jeff Chaffkin/VP, Head - Investor Relations, William J. Casazza/Sr. VP, General Counsel, Timothy A. Holt/Chief Investment Officer, Sr. VP, Chief Enterprise Risk Officer/$3,896,224.00, Fred Laberge/Assist. VP, Christopher M. Todoroff/VP, Corp. Sec., Robert M. Mead/Sr. VP - Strategic Marketing, Communications, Elease E. Wright/Sr. VP - Human Resources, Craig R. Callen/Sr. VP - Strategic Planning, Business Development/$4,095,043.00, Mark T. Bertolini/Pres./$3,410,341.00, James K. Foreman/Exec. VP - National Businesses, Ronald M. Olejniczak/VP, Controller, Troyen A. Brennan/Sr. VP, Chief Medical Officer, Alan M. Bennett/CFO, Sr. VP/$4,561,374.00

Directors: Ronald A. Williams/Chmn., CEO, Joseph P. Newhouse/Dir., Roger N. Farah/Dir., Edward J. Ludwig/Dir., Earl G. Graves/Dir., Gerald Greenwald/Dir., Ellen M. Hancock/Dir., Michael H. Jordan/Dir., Frank M. Clark/Dir., Betsy Z. Cohen/Dir., Molly J. Coye/Dir., Barbara Hackman Franklin/Dir., Jeffrey E. Garten/Dir.

Owners: Craig R. Callen, Alan M. Bennett, Barbara Hackman Franklin, Joseph P. Newhouse, Michael H. Jordan, Gerald Greenwald, Capital Research and Management Company/7.49%, Mark Bertolini/5.00%, Timothy A. Holt, Molly J. Coye, Insiders/2.89%, Earl G. Graves, Insiders/2.89%, Legg Mason Capital Management, Inc./8.58%, Betsy Z. Cohen *(22 Owners included in Index)*

Financial Data: *Fiscal Year End:*12/31 *Latest Annual Data:* 12/31/2006

Year	Sales	Net Income
2006	$25,145,700,000	$1,701,700,000
2005	$22,491,900,000	$1,634,500,000
2004	$19,904,100,000	$2,245,100,000

Curr. Assets:	$18,303,800,000	**Curr. Liab.:**	$7,103,000,000	**P/E Ratio:**	15.81
Plant, Equip.:	$283,600,000	**Total Liab.:**	$38,481,300,000	**Indic. Yr. Divd.:**	$0.040
Total Assets:	$47,626,400,000	**Net Worth:**	$9,145,100,000	**Debt/ Equity:**	0.2738

Aetrium Inc

2350 Helen St., North St. Paul, MN, 55109; ***PH:*** 1-651-770-2000; ***Fax:*** 1-651-770-7975; ***http://*** www.aetrium.com; ***Email:*** humanresources@aetrium.com

General - Incorporation	MN	**Stock**- Price on:12/24/2007	$4.43
Employees	74	Stock Exchange	NDQ
Auditor	KPMG LLP	Ticker Symbol	ATRM
Stk Agt	Computershare Investor Services LLC	Outstanding Shares	10,340,000
Counsel	Oppenheimer Wolff & Donnelly	E.P.S	-$0.1
DUNS No.	07-271-0536	Shareholders	NA

Business: The group's principal activities are to design, manufacture and market a variety of electromechanical equipment. The group's products are used in handling and testing of semiconductor and passive electronic devices, such as integrated circuits and discrete electronic components. The group's operations are conducted through three business segments: test handler products, reliability test equipment and semiconductor automation products. Test handler products facilitates automated handling of ics and discrete electronic components during production test cycles. This segment also offers change kits that enhance performance of installed equipment. Reliability test equipment segment provides structural performance data in evaluation and improvement of ic designs and manufacturing process. Semiconductor automation segment sells automation products to OEMs.

Primary SIC and add'l.: 3825 3679 3674

CIK No: 0000908598

Officers: Joseph C. Levesque/Chmn., CEO, Pres./$327,220.00, Douglas L. Hemer/Dir., Chief Administrative Officer, Sec./$236,951.00, Paul H. Askegaard/Treasurer/$176,422.00, Daniel M. Koch/VP - Worldwide Sales/$212,545.00, John J. Pollock/VP, GM/$215,192.00, Timothy G. Foley/VP - Manufacturing, Dean K. Hedstrom/VP - Engineering

Directors: Joseph C. Levesque/Chmn., CEO, Pres., Darnell L. Boehm/Dir., Douglas L. Hemer/Dir., Chief Administrative Officer, Sec., Terrence W. Glarner/Dir., Andrew J. Greenshields/Dir.

Owners: Douglas L. Hemer/1.50%, John J. Pollock, Paul H. Askegaard, Andrew J. Greenshields, Joseph C. Levesque/3.10%, Daniel M. Koch/1.50%, Insiders/13.20%, Keith E. Williams/2.60%, Terrence W. Glarner, Darnell L. Boehm/1.10%

Financial Data: *Fiscal Year End:*12/31 *Latest Annual Data:* 12/31/2006

Year	Sales	Net Income
2006	$28,184,000	-$551,000
2005	$16,407,000	-$1,922,000
2004	$27,789,000	$3,403,000

Curr. Assets:	$18,258,000	**Curr. Liab.:**	$2,357,000		
Plant, Equip.:	$194,000	**Total Liab.:**	$2,414,000	**Indic. Yr. Divd.:**	NA
Total Assets:	$18,867,000	**Net Worth:**	$16,454,000	**Debt/ Equity:**	0.0034

AF Financial Group

21 E Ashe St., West Jefferson, NC, 28694; ***PH:*** 1-336-246-4344; ***Fax:*** 1-336-246-3966; ***http://*** www.ashefederal.com; ***Email:*** info@afgrp.com

General - Incorporation	Federally Chartered	**Stock**- Price on:12/24/2007	$17.05
Employees	111	Stock Exchange	OTC
Auditor	Dixon Hughes PLLC	Ticker Symbol	ASFE
Stk Agt	American Stock Transfer & Trust CO.	Outstanding Shares	1,050,000
Counsel	Vannoy & Reeves	E.P.S	$1.76
DUNS No.	NA	Shareholders	NA

Business: The group's principal activity is to provide banking and related services through its wholly owned subsidiaries. The subsidiaries include af bank, af insurance services, inc. And af brokerage, inc. The group accepts deposits such as savings accounts, checking accounts, money market deposit accounts, statement savings accounts, individual retirement accounts and certificates of deposit. The loan portfolio consists of mortgage loans, consumer loans and commercial loans. The group provides property and casualty, life and health insurance products and non-insured investment products. Its branch offices are located in boone, jefferson, sparta, warrensville and west jefferson in North Carolina.

Primary SIC and add'l.: 6712 6035

CIK No: 0001064025

Subsidiaries: AF Insurance Services, Inc

Officers: Robert E. Washburn/Dir., CEO, Pres., Melanie Paisley Miller/36/CFO, Exec. VP, Sec., Treasurer, Pam Barker/Dir. - Human Resources

Directors: Robert E. Washburn/Dir., CEO, Pres., Jan R. Caddell/Vice Chmn., Jimmy D. Reeves/Chmn., Jerry L. Roten/Dir., Wayne R. Burgess/Dir., Claudia L. Kelley/Dir., Donald R. Moore/Dir., Michael M. Sherman/Dir., Kenneth R. Greene/Dir.

Owners: AsheCo, MHC/51.20%, Jimmy D. Reeves, Joseph E. Eller, Robert E. Washburn, Insiders/10.00%, Claudia L. Kelley, Jerry L. Roten, Donald R. Moore, Wayne R. Burgess, Michael M. Sherman, Jan R. Caddell, Karen P. Powell, Martin G. Little/1.90%, Kenneth R. Greene, Melanie P. Miller/1.70%

Financial Data: *Fiscal Year End:*06/30 *Latest Annual Data:* 06/30/2007

Year	Sales	Net Income
2007	$20,588,000	$1,471,000
2006	$18,098,000	$1,021,000
2005	$15,961,000	$649,000

Curr. Assets:	$12,089,000	**Curr. Liab.:**	$184,891,000	**P/E Ratio:**	14.57
Plant, Equip.:	$14,014,000	**Total Liab.:**	$214,749,000	**Indic. Yr. Divd.:**	$0.200
Total Assets:	$229,355,000	**Net Worth:**	$14,002,000	**Debt/ Equity:**	1.8091

AFC Enterprises Inc

5555 Glendridge Connector NE, Ste. 300, Atlanta, GA, 30342; ***PH:*** 1-404-459-4450; ***http://*** www.afce.com; ***Email:*** investor.relations@afce.com

General - Incorporation	MN	**Stock**- Price on:12/24/2007	$18.07
Employees	1,751	Stock Exchange	NDQ
Auditor	Grant Thornton LLP	Ticker Symbol	AFCE
Stk Agt	U.S. Stock Transfer Corp	Outstanding Shares	29,350,000
Counsel	NA	E.P.S	$0.78
DUNS No.	NA	Shareholders	NA

Business: The group's principal activity is to operate, develop and franchise quick service restaurants, bakeries and cafes. The group primarily trades under the trade names popeyes chicken and biscuits, church's chicken, cinnabon, seattle's best coffee and torrefazione italia coffee. At 28-12-2003, the group operated and franchised 4,091 restaurants, bakeries and cafes. The group's international franchisees operate primarily in Canada, Mexico, Puerto Rico and Asia.

Primary SIC and add'l.: 2095 3556 2015 5812 6519

CIK No: 0001041379

Subsidiaries: Focus Brands Inc, Starbucks Corporation

Officers: Kenneth L. Keymer/59/CEO, Pres./$1,812,948.00, Frederick B. Beilstein/Interim CEO, Stan Stout/Chief People Officer - Popeyes Chicken, Biscuits, Mel H. Hope/CFO/$613,915.00, Harold M. Cohen/Sr. VP, General Counsel, Corp. Sec. AFC Enterprises - Inc/$535,011.00, Cheryl Fletcher/Dir. - Investor Relations, Finance, James W. Lyons/COO/$537,564.00, Robert Calderin/50/Chief Marketing Officer/$476,922.00

Directors: Frank J. Belatti/Chmn., Kelvin J. Pennington/Dir., Victor Arias/Dir., John M. Roth/Dir., Carolyn Hogan Byrd/Dir., William R. Ide/Dir., John M. Cranor/Dir., John F. Hoffner/60/Dir.

Owners: Carolyn Hogan Byrd, Chilton Investment Company, LLC/13.40%, Kenneth L. Keymer, Insiders/2.00%, Robert Calderin, Cardinal Capital Management, LLC/6.60%, William R. Ide, James W. Lyons, Morgan Stanley Investment Management, Inc./13.10%, Delta Partners LLC/13.20%, John M. Cranor, Baron Capital Group, Inc./7.60%, Morgan Stanley/18.50%, Cheryl A. Bachelder, John F. Hoffner *(21 Owners included in Index)*

Financial Data: *Fiscal Year End:*12/25 *Latest Annual Data:* 12/31/2006

Year	Sales	Net Income
2006	$153,000,000	$22,400,000
2005	$143,400,000	$149,600,000
2004	$163,900,000	$24,600,000

Curr. Assets:	$42,600,000	**Curr. Liab.:**	$36,100,000	**P/E Ratio:**	23.17
Plant, Equip.:	$39,900,000	**Total Liab.:**	$194,300,000	**Indic. Yr. Divd.:**	NA
Total Assets:	$163,100,000	**Net Worth:**	-$31,200,000	**Debt/ Equity:**	NA

Affiliated Computer Services Inc

2828 N Haskell, Dallas, TX, 75204; ***PH:*** 1-214-841-6111; ***Fax:*** 1-214-821-8315; ***http://*** www.acs-inc.com; ***Email:*** info@acs-inc.com

General - Incorporation .... DE
Employees 58,000
Auditor .... PricewaterhouseCoopers LLP
Stk Agt..... American Stock Transfer & Trust Co.
Counsel.. NA
DUNS No. 19-419-0609

Stock- Price on:12/24/2007 .... $58.76
Stock Exchange.. NYSE
Ticker Symbol.. ACS
Outstanding Shares 99,170,000
E.P.S. $2.56
Shareholders.. NA

Business: The group's principle activity is to provide business process outsourcing, information technology outsourcing solutions and system integration services. The group provides BPO services including administration, finance and accounting, human resources, payment services, sales, marketing, and customer care, and supply chain management. The information technology outsourcing solutions services include mainframe, mid-range, desktop, network and Web-hosting solutions. System integration services include application development and implementation, applications outsourcing, technical support and training, network designing and installation services. The group operates from United States.

Primary SIC and add'l.: 8748 7375 7379 8742 7374

CIK No: 0000002135

Subsidiaries: 1338738 Ontario Inc., ACS Application Management Services, Inc., ACS BPS de Guatemala S.A., ACS BPS de Guatemala Sociedad Anonima, ACS BRC Holdings, Inc., ACS Business Process Solutions (Dominican Republic), S.A., ACS Business Process Solutions (Jamaica) Ltd, ACS Business Process Solutions de Mexico S.A. de C.V., ACS Business Process Solutions Limited, ACS Business Resources Corporation, ACS Business Services, LLC, ACS Commercial Solutions, Inc., ACS Consultant Company, Inc., ACS Consultant Holdings Corporation, ACS Defense, LLC 100 Subsidiaries included in the Index

Officers: Lynn Blodgett/Dir., CEO, Pres., Bill Deckelman/Exec. VP, General Counsel, Daisy Fernandez Seebach/VP, Chief Ethics Officer, John Rexford/Dir., CFO, Exec. VP, Tom Burlin/COO, Exec. VP, Andy Wilson/Communications Dir., Tom Blodgett/Exec. VP, Group Pres. - Business Process Solutions, Chris Leach/Sr. VP, Chief Information Security Officer, Ann Vezina/Exec. VP, Group Pres. - Commercial, Lora Villarreal/Sr. VP, Chief People Officer, Kevin Kyser/Exec. VP - Finance, Accounting, Kevin Lightfoot/VP - Corporate Communications, Tom Clary/Communications Dir.

Directors: Lynn Blodgett/Dir., CEO, Pres., Darwin Deason/Chmn., Robert B. Holland/Dir., John Rexford/Dir., CFO, Exec. VP, Joseph P. O'Neill/Dir., Frank A. Rossi/Dir., Livingston J. Kosberg/Dir., Dennis McCuistion/Dir.

Owners: Insiders/100.00%, Mark A. King, Darwin Deason/100.00%, Capital Group Companies/10.85%, Warren D. Edwards, Pzena Investment Mgmt./5.24%, Tom Burlin, Lynn Blodgett, Insiders/5.08%, Darwin Deason/2.81%, Livingston J. Kosberg, Frank A. Rossi, Capital Research and Management Company/5.75%, Dennis McCuistion, Joseph P. ONeill

Financial Data: Fiscal Year End:06/30   Latest Annual Data: 6/30/2006

Year	Sales	Net Income
2006	$5,353,661,000	$358,806,000
2005	$4,351,159,000	$415,945,000
2004	$4,106,393,000	$529,843,000

Curr. Assets:	$1,529,263,000	Curr. Liab.:	$825,105,000	P/E Ratio:	20.69
Plant, Equip.:	$870,020,000	Total Liab.:	$3,046,219,000	Indic. Yr. Divd.:	NA
Total Assets:	$5,502,437,000	Net Worth:	$2,456,218,000	Debt/ Equity:	1.1707

Affiliated Managers Group Inc

600 Hale St., Prides Crossing, MA, 01965; *PH:* 1-617-747-3300; *Fax:* 1-617-747-3380; *http://* www.amg.com; *Email:* info@amg.com

General - Incorporation .... DE
Employees 75
Auditor .... PricewaterhouseCoopers LLP
Stk Agt.................................... LaSalle Bank N.A
Counsel...................... Goodwin, Procter & Hoar
DUNS No. 83-619-5925

Stock - Price on:12/24/2007 .... $127.84
Stock Exchange.. NYSE
Ticker Symbol.. AMG
Outstanding Shares 29,790,000
E.P.S. $4.25
Shareholders.. NA

Business: The group's principal activity is to provide asset management services. The group has equity investments in a diverse group of mid-sized investment management firms. The group operates through three segments namely institutional, high net worth and mutual fund. Institutional segment offers investment products across 25 different investment styles and manages assets for foundations and endowments, defined benefit and defined contribution plans for corporations and municipalities and taft-hartley plans. High net worth segment provides customized investment management services for high net worth individuals and families through direct relationships, as well as through managed account programs. Mutual fund segment of the group provides advisory or sub-advisory services to mutual funds.

Primary SIC and add'l.: 6722 6282 6719

CIK No: 0001004434

Subsidiaries: AMG Canada Corp., a Nova Scotia corporation, AMG Capital Corp., a Delaware corporation, Amg/fami Investment Corp., A Nova Scotia Corporation

Officers: Sean M. Healey/Dir., CEO, Pres./$8,117,557.00, Seth W. Brennan/Exec. VP/$2,329,183.00, Nathaniel Dalton/COO, Exec. VP/$4,163,009.00, Stephen H. Belgrad/VP, Lewis Collins/VP, Brett S. Perryman/VP, Darrell W. Crate/CFO, Exec. VP/$4,169,168.00, Peter Ferry/VP, Benjamin M. Scott/VP, Jay Horgen/Exec. VP - New Investments, Robert D. Goldbaum/Sr. VP, Riz Jamal/VP, Aaron M. Galis/VP, Claire Manning/VP, Jeffrey S. Murphy/Sr. VP (21 Officers included in Index)

Directors: Sean M. Healey/Dir., CEO, Pres., William J. Nutt/Chmn., Harold J. Meyerman/Dir., Patrick T. Ryan/Dir., Richard E. Floor/Dir., Rita M. Rodriguez/Dir., Jide J. Zeitlin/Dir.

Owners: Jide J. Zeitlin, Sean M. Healey/3.80%, Nathaniel Dalton/3.00%, William J. Nutt/5.30%, John Kingston/1.10%, Richard E. Floor, Harold J. Meyerman, Insiders/15.10%, Patrick T. Ryan, Rita M. Rodriguez, T. Rowe Price Associates, Inc./7.30%, Darrell W. Crate/3.00%

Financial Data: Fiscal Year End:12/31   Latest Annual Data: 12/31/2006

Year	Sales	Net Income
2006	$1,170,353,000	$151,277,000
2005	$916,492,000	$119,069,000
2004	$659,997,000	$77,147,000

Curr. Assets:	$554,279,000	Curr. Liab.:	$287,813,000	P/E Ratio:	31.57
Plant, Equip.:	$63,984,000	Total Liab.:	$1,896,464,000	Indic. Yr. Divd.:	NA
Total Assets:	$2,665,920,000	Net Worth:	$499,222,000	Debt/ Equity:	2.2137

Affinity Media International Corp

1850 Sawtelle Blvd., Ste. 470, Los Angeles, CA, 90025; *PH:* 1-310-479-1555; *Fax:* 1-310-479-1561; *http://* www.affinitymedia.net; *Email:* hcohl@mindspring.com

General - Incorporation ....
Employees .... NA
Auditor .... NA
Stk Agt .... American Stock Transfer & Trust Co.
Counsel.. NA
DUNS No. .... NA

Stock- Price on:12/24/2007 .... $5.71
Stock Exchange... OTC
Ticker Symbol.. AFMI
Outstanding Shares .... NA
E.P.S. $0.02
Shareholders.. NA

Business: The groups principle activity is to provide recruiting services. The groups service area includes the research and development, engineering, marketing, sales, information technology and manufacturing industries. The group operates from United States.

Primary SIC and add'l.: 6221

CIK No:

Officers: Peter H. Engel/Chmn., CEO, Howard Cohl/Dir., Pres., Peter Dombrowski/Dir., COO

Directors: Peter H. Engel/Chmn., CEO, Howard Cohl/Dir., Pres., Peter Dombrowski/Dir., COO, Michael Arthur/Dir., Marc E. Jaffe/Dir.

Financial Data: Fiscal Year End:NA   Latest Annual Data: 12/31/2006

Year	Sales	Net Income
2006	NA	$94,000

Curr. Assets:	$19,284,000	Curr. Liab.:	$890,000	P/E Ratio:	114.20
Plant, Equip.:	NA	Total Liab.:	$5,849,000	Indic. Yr. Divd.:	NA
Total Assets:	$19,284,000	Net Worth:	$13,435,000	Debt/ Equity:	NA

Affinity Technology Group Inc

1310 Lady St., Ste. 601, Columbia, SC, 29201; *PH:* 1-803-758-2511; *Fax:* 1-803-758-2560; *http://* www.affi.net

General - Incorporation .... DE
Employees 2
Auditor .... Scott McElveen LLP
Stk Agt .... Chase Mellon Shareholder Services LLC
Counsel....Robinson, Bradshaw & Hinson P.A.
DUNS No. 86-949-8535

Stock- Price on:12/24/2007 .... $0.075
Stock Exchange... OTC
Ticker Symbol.. AFFI
Outstanding Shares 45,270,000
E.P.S. .... -$0.04
Shareholders.. NA

Business: The group's principle activities are to develop and market technologies that enable financial institutions and other businesses to provide consumer financial services electronically. The group owns certain patents covering the automated establishment of loans and other financial accounts. Due to capital constraints, the group has suspended all efforts to further develop, market and operate these products and services. The company has no plans in the near term to engage in further sales or other activities related to its products or services, other than to license the patents that it owns. The group's quarterly revenue for September 2007 was 0.01 millions of USD.

Primary SIC and add'l.: 7372

CIK No: 0001007508

Subsidiaries: Affinity Bank Technology Corporation, Affinity Clearinghouse Corporation, Affinity Credit Corporation, Affinity Mortgage Technology Corporation, Affinity Processing Corporation, decisioning.com, Inc., Multi Financial Services, Inc.

Officers: Joseph A. Boyle/53/Chmn., CEO, CFO, Pres., Sean S. Douglas/39/COO, Exec. VP

Directors: Joseph A. Boyle/53/Chmn., CEO, CFO, Pres., Peter R. Wilson/55/Dir., Robert M. Price/77/Dir.

Owners: Joseph A. Boyle/7.01%, Robert M. Price/1.50%, The South Financial Group/11.04%, Insiders/10.54%, Sean S. Douglas/1.11%, Peter R. Wilson/1.38%

Financial Data: Fiscal Year End:12/31   Latest Annual Data: 12/31/2006

Year	Sales	Net Income
2006	$33,000	-$2,700,000
2005	$20,000	-$566,000
2004	$287,000	-$217,000

Curr. Assets:	$1,105,000	Curr. Liab.:	$1,139,000		
Plant, Equip.:	$8,000	Total Liab.:	$4,392,000	Indic. Yr. Divd.:	NA
Total Assets:	$1,112,000	Net Worth:	-$3,280,000	Debt/ Equity:	NA

Affirmative Insurance Holdings Inc

4450 Sojourn Dr., Ste. 500, Addison, TX, 75001; *PH:* 1-972-728-6300; *Fax:* 1-972-991-0882; *http://* www.affirmativeholdings.com

General - Incorporation .... DE
Employees 942
Auditor .... KPMG LLP
Stk Agt .... EquiServe Trust Co N.A
Counsel.. NA
DUNS No. .... NA

Stock- Price on:12/24/2007 .... $15.04
Stock Exchange... NDQ
Ticker Symbol....................................... AFFM
Outstanding Shares 15,360,000
E.P.S. $0.38
Shareholders.. NA

Business: The group's principal activity is to underwrite, service and distribute non-standard automobile insurance policies and related products and services. It offers products and services to individual consumers in 11 states, including Texas, Illinois, California and Florida. It operates in two segments, namely, agency segment and insurance segment. The agency segment comprises of underwriting agencies and retail agencies, which primarily design, distribute and service policies issued or reissued by insurance companies. The insurance segment issues non-standard personal automobile insurance policies through two Illinois-domiciled insurance company subsidiaries. On 7-May-2003, it acquired the remaining 20% interest in insureone independent agency, llc and on 31-Dec-2003, it acquired 100% of the stock of affirmative insurance company and insura property and casualty insurance company. The group became publicly held in Jul 2004.

Primary SIC and add'l.: 6411

CIK No: 0001282543

Subsidiaries: A-Affordable Insurance Agency, Inc., A-Affordable Managing General Agency, Inc., Affirmative Alternative Distribution, Inc., Affirmative Franchises, Inc., Affirmative Franchising Group, Inc., Affirmative Insurance Company, Affirmative Insurance Group, Inc., Affirmative Insurance Holdings Statutory Trust I, Affirmative Insurance Holdings Statutory Trust II, Affirmative Insurance Holdings, Inc., Affirmative Insurance Services of South Carolina, Inc., Affirmative Insurance Services, Inc., Affirmative Management Services, Inc., Affirmative Property Holdings, Inc., Affirmative Retail, Inc. 35 Subsidiaries included in the Index

Officers: Kevin R. Callahan/Chmn., CEO, Pres. - Retail, Robert Bondi/COO, Exec. VP, Mark Pape/Exec. VP, Cheif Financial Officer, Sean M. McPadden/Exec. VP, Chief Underwriting Officer, Joe Fisher/Sr. VP, Chief Legal Counsel, Jerome Zingg/CIO, Sr. VP, Charlene Barnard/Sr. VP, Chief Marketing Officer

Directors: Kevin R. Callahan/Chmn., CEO, Pres. - Retail, David I. Schamis/34/Dir.

Owners: Van V. Vaughan, Suzanne T. Porter, New Affirmative LLC/51.20%, FMR Corp./7.80%, Robert A. Bondi, Mark E. Pape, Kevin R. Callahan/1.70%, Paul J. Zucconi, Sean M. McPadden/1.10%, Thomas C. Davis, Insiders/3.80%

Financial Data: Fiscal Year End:12/31 Latest Annual Data: 12/31/2006

Year	Sales	Net Income
2006	$357,112,000	$9,744,000
2005	$381,479,000	$18,305,000
2004	$288,674,000	$24,433,000

Curr. Assets:	$201,040,000	Curr. Liab.:	$5,089,000	P/E Ratio:	39.58
Plant, Equip.:	$10,289,000	Total Liab.:	$350,874,000	Indic. Yr. Divd.:	$0.080
Total Assets:	$557,267,000	Net Worth:	$206,393,000	Debt/ Equity:	1.3251

Affymetrix Inc

3420 Central Expwy., Santa Clara, CA, 95051; *PH:* 1-408-731-5000; *Fax:* 1-408-731-5380; *http://* www.affymetrix.com; *Email:* support@affymetrix.com

General - Incorporation	DE	Stock- Price on:12/24/2007	$26.85
Employees	1,128	Stock Exchange	NDQ
Auditor	Ernst & Young LLP	Ticker Symbol	AFFX
Stk Agt.	American Stock Transfer & Trust Co.	Outstanding Shares	68,610,000
Counsel	Robert H. Ellis	E.P.S.	-$0.12
DUNS No.	80-668-2573	Shareholders	NA

Business: The group's principal activity is to create tools that drive the genomic revolution. The group has developed genechip-tm system for analyzing and managing genetic information. The genechip(R) platform consists of disposable dna probe arrays containing gene sequence, certain reagents for use with the probe arrays, a scanner and other instruments. The products are sold to pharmaceutical, biotechnology, agrochemical, diagnostics and consumer products companies and also to academic research centers, private foundations and clinical laboratories in the United States, Europe and Japan.

Primary SIC and add'l.: 5047 3829 8731 3826

CIK No: 0000913077

Subsidiaries: Affymetrix France S.A.S, Affymetrix GmbH, Affymetrix Japan K.K, Affymetrix Pte Ltd, Affymetrix Technology, Ltd, Affymetrix, UK Ltd, Genetic MicroSystems, Inc, Neomorphic, Inc, ParAllele BioScience, Inc

Officers: Stephen P.A Fodor/Chmn., CEO/$961,132.00, Barbara A. Caulfield/Exec. VP, General Counsel/$613,938.00, Thane Kreiner/Sr. VP - Corporate Affairs, Advanced Development/$529,865.00, John C. Batty/CFO, Exec. VP - Finance, Kevin M. King/Pres. - Life Sciences Business, Exec. VP, Doug Farrell/VP - Investor Relations

Directors: Stephen P.A Fodor/Chmn., CEO, John D. Diekman/Dir., Paul Berg/Dir., Susan Desmond-Hellmann/Dir., Vernon R. Loucks/Dir., David B. Singer/Dir., Robert H. Trice/Dir., John A. Young/Dir., Robert P. Wayman/Dir.

Owners: Susan E. Siegel, John A. Young, Thane Kreiner, PrimeCap Management Company/8.95%, Barbara A. Caulfield, Manning& Napier Advisors,Inc./5.67%, FMR Corp./14.43%, James R. Gibson, Legg Mason Capital Management,Inc./5.35%, Robert H. Trice, Paul Berg, David B. Singer, Stephen P.A. Fodor/1.09%, Barclays Global Investors, NA/5.13%, AXA Financial,Inc./12.05% (20 Owners included in Index)

Financial Data: Fiscal Year End:12/31 Latest Annual Data: 12/31/2006

Year	Sales	Net Income
2006	$355,317,000	-$13,704,000
2005	$367,602,000	$65,787,000
2004	$345,962,000	$47,608,000

Curr. Assets:	$383,892,000	Curr. Liab.:	$93,590,000		
Plant, Equip.:	$141,322,000	Total Liab.:	$228,252,000	Indic. Yr. Divd.:	NA
Total Assets:	$781,215,000	Net Worth:	$552,963,000	Debt/ Equity:	0.2139

Aflac Inc

1932 Wynnton Rd., Columbus, GA, 31999; *PH:* 1-706-323-3431; *Fax:* 1-706-324-6330; *http://* www.aflac.com; *Email:* webideas@aflac.com

General - Incorporation	GA	Stock- Price on:12/24/2007	$52.7
Employees	6,970	Stock Exchange	NYSE
Auditor	KPMG LLP	Ticker Symbol	AFL
Stk Agt.	NA	Outstanding Shares	489,140,000
Counsel	Skadden, Meagher & Flom LLP	E.P.S.	$3.20
DUNS No.	04-209-9168	Shareholders	NA

Business: The group's principle activity is to provide insurance services. The groups products include care plans, general medical expense plans, medical and sickness riders. The group operates through two segments namely flac Japan and Aflac U.S. The group operates from United States.

Primary SIC and add'l.: 6719 6324

CIK No: 0000004977

Subsidiaries: Aflac Counsel, Ltd., Aflac Information Technology, Incorporated, Aflac Insurance Service Company, Ltd., Aflac International, Incorporated, Aflac Payment Service Company, Ltd., aflacdirect.com, Ltd., American Family Life Assurance Company of Columbus, American Family Life Assurance Company of New York, Communicorp, Incorporated

Officers: Daniel P. Amos/Chmn., CEO/$14,123,260.00, James C. Woodall/CEO, Pres. - Communicorp, Inc, Hidefumi Matsui/63/Chmn., Pres. - Aflac Japan, Akitoshi Kan/Chmn. - Aflac Japan, Aflac International/$3,513,053.00, Hisayuki Shinkai/57/First Sr. VP - Financial Institutions, Bank Sales Project, Public Relations, Investor Relations, Hiroshi Yamauchi/56/First Sr. VP, Chief Administrative Officer - Japan, Shigehiko Akimoto/52/Sr. VP - Alliance Management, Japan, Yuji Arai/45/Sr. VP - Investments, Investment Analysis, Principal Financial Officer - Japan, Andrew J. Conrad/44/Sr. VP - Counsel, Dir. - Governmental, Legal Affairs, Aflac International Incorporated, Tomomichi Ito/58/Sr. VP - Government Affairs, Research, General Affairs, Public Relations, Japan, Takaaki Matsumoto/59/First Sr. VP, Dir. - Marketing, Sales, Japan, Audrey Boone Tillman/Sr. VP, Dir. - Corporate Services, William Jeremy Jeffery/Sr. VP - Investments, Chief Investment Officer, Bob Ottman/Sr. VP - Accounting Implementation, Management, David Pringle/Sr. VP - Federal Relations (34 Officers included in Index)

Directors: Daniel P. Amos/Chmn., CEO, Charles D. Lake/Vice Chmn. - Aflac Japan, Hidefumi Matsui/63/Chmn., Pres. - Aflac Japan, Robert B. Johnson/Dir., Paul Shelby Amos/Dir., Pres. - Aflac, COO - Aflac US, Barbara K. Rimer/Dir., Yoshiro Aoki/Dir., Shelby J. Amos/Dir., John Shelby Amos/Dir., Michael H. Armacost/Dir., Joe Frank Harris/Dir., Elizabeth J. Hudson/Dir., Kenneth S. Janke/Dir., Douglas W. Johnson/Dir., Charles B. Knapp/Dir. (19 Directors included in Index)

Owners: Charles B. Knapp, FMR Corp/5.30%, Kriss Cloninger, Paul S. Amos, Robert B. Johnson, Robert L. Wright, Michael H. Armacost, E. Stephen Purdom, Douglas W. Johnson, Barbara K. Rimer, John Shelby Amos, Yoshiro Aoki/0.70%, Daniel P. Amos/2.40%, Elizabeth J. Hudson, David Gary Thompson (18 Owners included in Index)

Financial Data: Fiscal Year End:12/31 Latest Annual Data: 12/31/2006

Year	Sales	Net Income
2006	$14,616,000,000	$1,483,000,000
2005	$14,363,000,000	$1,483,000,000
2004	$13,281,000,000	$1,299,000,000

Curr. Assets:	$1,738,000,000	Curr. Liab.:	$807,000,000		
Plant, Equip.:	$458,000,000	Total Liab.:	$51,464,000,000	Indic. Yr. Divd.:	$0.820
Total Assets:	$59,805,000,000	Net Worth:	$8,341,000,000	Debt/ Equity:	0.2854

AFP Imaging Corp

250 Clearbrook Rd., Elmsford, NY, 10523; *PH:* 1-914-592-6100; *Fax:* 1-914-592-6148; *http://* www.afpimaging.com

General - Incorporation	NY	Stock- Price on:12/24/2007	$1.8
Employees	83	Stock Exchange	OTC
Auditor	Goldstein Golub Kessler LLP	Ticker Symbol	AFPC
Stk Agt.	American Stock Transfer & Trust Co.	Outstanding Shares	17,930,000
Counsel	Snow Becker Kroll Klaris & Krauss	E.P.S.	$0.00
DUNS No.	09-383-5783	Shareholders	NA

Business: The group's principal activity is to design, develop, manufacture and distribute equipment for producing medical and dental X-ray images through digital technology as well as the chemical processing of photosensitive materials. The group also manufactures and distributes other closely related electro and optical imaging equipment. This includes filmless digital dental radiography system and intraoral video dental cameras. It also includes related image management software and a line of equipment designed for the veterinary marketplace. The customers include medical, dental, veterinary and industrial professionals. The trademarks of the group include afp imaging, dent-x, excel and eva.

Primary SIC and add'l.: 3841

CIK No: 0000319126

Subsidiaries: Dent-X International Inc., QR Imaging USA, Inc., Visiplex Instruments Corporation

Officers: Daniel Fields/Exec. VP - Sales, Susan Jablonski/Part Number Requests - Polski, Miguel Abud/Technical Support, Espanol, Roderick Brathwaite/Technical Support, Ion Mateescu/Technical Support, Romana, Liviu Banuta/Technical Support, Mgr. - Romana, Annemieke Woudstra/Contact - European Sales, Marketing (Nederland), Henk Peusken/Contact - European Sales, Marketing (Nederland), Marcel Hartsfield/International Customer Service, Joselin Jimenez/Customer Service - Espanol, Roberto Molteni/Exec. VP - Technology, Aida McKinney/VP - Administration, Adam Rabinovitch/VP - International Sales, Business Development, Eric Vozick/VP - Veterinary Business Development, Donald Rabinovitch/62/Principal Executive Officer, Pres. (25 Officers included in Index)

Directors: David Vozick/68/Chmn., Robert A. Blatt/68/Dir., Jack Becker/73/Dir.

Owners: Donald Rabinovitch/7.70%, David Vozick/8.40%, Roberto Molteni, Daniel Fields, Elise Nissen, Handelsbanken Fonder AB/6.40%, Jack Becker, Aida McKinney, ComVest Capital LLC/14.00%, Robert A. Blatt/4.60%, HealthInvest Global Long/Short Fund/19.70%, Insiders/22.30%

Financial Data: Fiscal Year End:06/30 Latest Annual Data: 6/30/2006

Year	Sales	Net Income
2006	$24,998,000	$1,005,000
2005	$23,135,000	$1,900,000
2004	$19,833,000	$1,345,000

Curr. Assets:	$13,582,000	Curr. Liab.:	$3,600,000		
Plant, Equip.:	$378,000	Total Liab.:	$8,416,000	Indic. Yr. Divd.:	NA
Total Assets:	$14,341,000	Net Worth:	$5,925,000	Debt/ Equity:	NA

African Platinum Plc

Formerly: Southern African Resources Plc
27 St. . James St. , London, E17 7PJ; *PH:* 44-2073890500; *http://* www.afplats.com; *Email:* info@afplats.com

General - Incorporation	UK	Stock- Price on:12/24/2007	NA
Employees	NA	Stock Exchange	NA
Auditor	Baker Tilly	Ticker Symbol	NA
Stk Agt.	NA	Outstanding Shares	NA
Counsel	NA	E.P.S.	NA
DUNS No.	NA	Shareholders	NA

Business: The group's principle activities include acquiring, developing and exploring for minerals. The company is in the process of exploring its resource properties to determine the economic feasibility of recovering ore reserves. The company intends to initiate and undertake its own mining operations. The company will produce a concentrate containing precious and base metals after the recovery of the minerals. The mining and processing method to concentrate the ore are not subject to any patent or proprietary processes. The design of the milling and flotation process to produce the concentrate will be provided by the consultants retained for such purposes. The group plans to sell the ore concentrate to a major PGM producer via an off-take agreement. The group is now known as African Platinum to identify and acquire quality PGM exploration and mining projects in Africa. The group operates from United States.

Primary SIC and add'l.: 1400

CIK No: 0001318953

Aftermarket Technology Corp

1400 Opus Pl., Ste. 600, Downers Grove, IL, 60515; *PH:* 1-630-271-8100; *Fax:* 1-630-663-8210; *http://* www.goatc.com; *Email:* info@corpatc.com

General - Incorporation	DE	Stock- Price on:12/24/2007	$30.24
Employees	4,000	Stock Exchange	NDQ
Auditor	Ernst & Young LLP	Ticker Symbol	ATAC
Stk Agt.	Mellon Investor Services LLC	Outstanding Shares	21,850,000
Counsel	Gibson, Dunn & Crutcher LLP	E.P.S.	$1.80
DUNS No.	87-743-7343	Shareholders	NA

Business: The group's principal activities are to remanufacture and distribute automobile drivetrain products. These products are used in the repair of automobiles and light trucks in the automotive aftermarket. The group operates through two segments: drivetrain remanufacturing and the logistics. The

drivetrain remanufacturing segment sells factory remanufactured drivetrain products directly to automobile manufacturers. The products include remanufactured transmissions, remanufactured torque converters, valve bodies and engines. The logistics segment provides value-added warehouse and distribution services, material reclamation and disposition services. This segment also remanufactures and distributes electronic components. The customers for remanufactured transmissions are daimlerchrysler corporation, ford motor company and general motors corporation.

Primary SIC and add'l.: 3714 7389

CIK No: 0000933405

Subsidiaries: Aarons Automotive Products, Inc., ACI Electronics Holding Corp., ACI Electronics Investment Corp., Aftermarket Technology (U.K.) Holding Limited, ATC Information Services, Inc., ATC Logistics & Electronics, L.P., ATS Remanufacturing Corp., Autocraft Industries, Inc., Autocraft Remanufacturing Corp., Automotive Development Limited, Component Remanufacturing Specialists, Inc., Elbar Industrial Limited, PROFormance Powertrain Products, Inc.

Officers: Donald T. Johnson/Chmn., CEO, Pres./$1,213,156.00, Joseph Salamunovich/VP, General Counsel, Sec./$362,246.00, Brett O. Dickson/VP - North American Remanufacturing Operations/$399,045.00, Mary Ryan/VP - Communications, Investor Relations, John J. MacHota/VP - Human Resources, William L. Conley/Pres. - ATC Logistics, Electronics/$541,912.00, Todd R. Peters/CFO, VP/$618,799.00, John Pinkerton/VP, Controller, Rick Stanley/Pres. - ATC Drivetrain

Directors: Donald T. Johnson/Chmn., CEO, Pres., Michael J. Hartnett/Dir., Edward D. Stewart/Dir., Robert L. Evans/Dir., Curtland E. Fields/Dir., Michael D. Jordan/Dir., Lawrence S. Prendergast/Dir.

Owners: FMR Corp./6.30%, Brett O. Dickson, Donald T. Johnson/1.50%, S. Lawrence Prendergast, Insiders/4.30%, Wells Fargo & Company/8.90%, Pzena Investment Management, LLC/7.50%, Daruma Asset Management, Inc./7.80%, Curtland E. Fields, William L. Conley, Edward Stewart, Robert L. Evans, Joseph Salamunovich, Michael J. Hartnett, Todd R. Peters (16 Owners included in Index)

Financial Data: Fiscal Year End:12/31   Latest Annual Data: 12/31/2006

Year	Sales	Net Income
2006	$497,974,000	$8,023,000
2005	$441,963,000	$31,008,000
2004	$395,577,000	$5,776,000

Curr. Assets:	$156,166,000	Curr. Liab.:	$67,153,000	P/E Ratio:	27.49
Plant, Equip.:	$53,008,000	Total Liab.:	$113,347,000	Indic. Yr. Divd.:	NA
Total Assets:	$345,677,000	Net Worth:	$232,330,000	Debt/ Equity:	0.0370

Aftersoft Group Inc

34052 La Plz. Dr., Ste. 201, Dana Point, CA, 92629; **PH:** 1-949-488-8860; **http://** www.aftersoftgroup.com; **Email:** info@aftersoftgroup.com

General - Incorporation	DE	Stock - Price on:12/24/2007	$0.47
Employees	NA	Stock Exchange	OTC
Auditor	KMJ Corbin & Co. LLP	Ticker Symbol	ASFG
Stk Agt	Corporate Stock Transfer, Inc.	Outstanding Shares	NA
Counsel	NA	E.P.S.	NA
DUNS No.	NA	Shareholders	NA

Business: The groups principle activities include providing software information and services to the automotive after markets. The groups services include business management systems comprised of after soft's proprietary software applications, implementation, training and third-party hardware and peripherals. Catalogue products related to parts, pricing and fitment information. Online services and products that provide online connectivity between manufacturers,warehouse distributors, retailers and automotive service providers. The customers of the group include wholesale parts and tire distributors, retailers, franchisees, cooperatives, auto service chains and single location auto service. In the year 2006, the group acquired Euro Software Services Limited. The group operates from the United States, the United Kingdom and Canada.

Primary SIC and add'l.: 6770

CIK No: 0000832488

Subsidiaries: AFS Autoservice, Inc., AFS Tire Management, Inc., AFS Warehouse Distribution Management, Inc., Aftersoft Dealer Software Limited, Aftersoft Network N.A., Inc., ANKA Design Limited, Distal Enterprises Limited, EXP Software Limited, MAM AutoCat Limited, MAM Autopart Limited, MAM Autowork Limited, MAM Software Limited, MMI Automotive Limited

Officers: Ian Warwick/46/Chmn., CEO, Joseph M. Zappulla/Investor Relations Officer, Michael O'Driscoll/55/CFO, Simon Chadwick/39/Dir., COO

Directors: Ian Warwick/46/Chmn., CEO, Simon Chadwick/39/Dir., COO, Dwight Mananteo/38/Dir., Marcus Wohlrab/45/Dir., Rick Wasserman/57/Dir.

Owners: Auto Data Network, Inc./81.85%

Financial Data: Fiscal Year End:12/31   Latest Annual Data: 6/30/2006

Year	Sales	Net Income
2006	$19,261,000	-$972,000
2004	NA	-$47,000
2003	NA	-$8,000

Curr. Assets:	$5,259,000	Curr. Liab.:	$9,213,000		
Plant, Equip.:	$155,000	Total Liab.:	$11,663,000	Indic. Yr. Divd.:	NA
Total Assets:	$34,421,000	Net Worth:	$22,758,000	Debt/ Equity:	0.0045

AFV Solutions Inc

9710 Research Dr., Irvine, CA, 92618; **PH:** 1-949-748-6600; **Fax:** 1-949-784-6611; **http://** www.afvsolutions.com

General - Incorporation	NV	Stock - Price on:12/24/2007	NA
Employees	NA	Stock Exchange	OTC
Auditor	Weaver & Martin, LLC	Ticker Symbol	AFVS
Stk Agt	Pacific Stock Transfer Company	Outstanding Shares	NA
Counsel	NA	E.P.S.	-$0.13
DUNS No.	NA	Shareholders	NA

Business: The group's principal activity is to focus on building or acquiring a chain of upscale pet care facilities under the name 'bed & biscuit inn'. The group's first bed & biscuit inn facility in flagler beach, Florida houses indoor/outdoor pet suites, an onsite pet bakery and groomingdale's, which provides full service grooming to guests. Services include indoor pet suites for overnight or prolonged boarding, 24/7 supervision by a professionally trained staff, off-leash playgrounds and training facilities, pick up and delivery services and pet related products and supplies. In addition, the group offers travel related services, through its agreement with global travel international.

Primary SIC and add'l.: 0752 4724

CIK No: 0001167868

Subsidiaries: AFV Research, Inc., Bed and Biscuit Inns of America, Inc

Officers: Carlos Zalduondo/63/Dir., CEO, COO, Pres., Suzanne Herring/43/CFO

Directors: Carlos Zalduondo/63/Dir., CEO, COO, Pres., Richard Steele/Chmn., Alexander Leon/46/Dir.

Owners: Caledonia Asset Holdings, Ltd./0.33%, Insiders/0.10%, Alex Leon, Carlos Zalduondo/0.01%, Elite Capital Management/0.09%, Richard Steele/0.09%

Financial Data: Fiscal Year End:12/31   Latest Annual Data: 06/30/2007

Year	Sales	Net Income
2007	$112,000	-$3,621,000
2006	$63,000	-$2,084,000
2005	$186,000	-$2,644,000

Curr. Assets:	$167,000	Curr. Liab.:	$53,000		
Plant, Equip.:	$668,000	Total Liab.:	$481,000	Indic. Yr. Divd.:	NA
Total Assets:	$854,000	Net Worth:	$373,000	Debt/ Equity:	NA

AGCO Corp

4205 River Green Pkwy., Duluth, GA, 30096; **PH:** 1-770-813-9200; **Fax:** 1-770-813-6118; **http://** www.agcocorp.com; **Email:** corporate.relations@agcocorp.com

General - Incorporation	DE	Stock - Price on:12/24/2007	$44.45
Employees	12,800	Stock Exchange	NYSE
Auditor	KPMG LLP	Ticker Symbol	AG
Stk Agt	Computershare Investor Services LLC	Outstanding Shares	91,480,000
Counsel	Stephen Lupton	E.P.S.	-$0.63
DUNS No.	61-893-8260	Shareholders	NA

Business: The group's principle activities include manufacturing and distributing agricultural equipment and related replacement parts. The groups selling products include agricultural equipment, including tractors, combines, self-propelled sprayers, hay tools, forage equipment and implements, and diesel engines. The groups products sold under the brand names AGCO, Challenger, Fendt, Gleaner, Hesston, Massey Ferguson, New Idea, RoGator, Spra-Coupe, Sunflower, Terra-Gator, Valtra and White Planters. The group operates from United States, Brazil, Germany, France, Australia and Ireland.

Primary SIC and add'l.: 6159 3523

CIK No: 0000880266

Subsidiaries: Ag-Chem (UK) Limited, Ag-Chem Danmark A/S, Ag-Chem Deutschland GmbH, Ag-Chem Europe B.V., Ag-Chem Europe Fertilizer Equipment BV, Ag-Chem Europe Industrial Equipment BV, AGCO A/S, AGCO AB, AGCO Argentina SA, AGCO Australia, Ltd., AGCO Canada Ltd., AGCO Danmark A/S, AGCO Deutschland Holding Limited & Co. KG, AGCO do Brazil Commercio e Industria Ltda., AGCO Equipment Company 70 Subsidiaries included in the Index

Officers: Martin Richenhagen/Chmn., CEO, Pres./$3,250,291.00, Gary Collar/Sr. VP, GM - Eame/$920,079.00, David L. Caplan/Sr. VP - Materials Management, Worldwide, Andrew H. Beck/CFO, Sr. VP/$833,859.00, Frank C. Lukacs/49/Sr. VP - Manufacturing, Quality, Norman L. Boyd/Sr. VP - Human Resources, Randall G. Hoffman/56/Sr. VP - Global Sales, Marketing, Garry L. Ball/Sr. VP - Engineering, Robert B. Crain/Sr. VP, GM - North America, Stephen D. Lupton/Sr. VP - Corporate Development, General Counsel, Corp. Sec./$1,162,213.00, Hubertus Muehlhaeuser/Sr. VP - Strategy, Integration, Information Technology, GM Engines/$854,792.00, Andre M. Carioba/Sr. VP, GM - South America

Directors: Martin Richenhagen/Chmn., CEO, Pres., Wayne W. Booker/73/Dir., Francisco R. Gros/65/Dir., George P. Benson/Dir., Herman Cain/Dir., Wolfgang Deml/Dir., Gerald B. Johanneson/Dir., Curtis E. Moll/Dir., David E. Momot/Dir., Gerald L. Shaheen/Dir., Hendrikus Visser/Dir.

Owners: Gerald B. Johanneson, Stephen D. Lupton, Martin Richenhagen, Curtis E. Moll, Hendrikus Visser, George P. Benson, David E. Momot, Gerald L. Shaheen, Wolfgang Deml, FMR Corp./12.95%, Andrew H. Beck, Insiders, Goldman Sachs Asset Management, L.P./11.79%, Herman Cain, NWQ Investment Management Company, LLC/11.31% (18 Owners included in Index)

Financial Data: Fiscal Year End:12/31   Latest Annual Data: 12/31/2006

Year	Sales	Net Income
2006	$5,435,000,000	-$64,900,000
2005	$5,449,700,000	$31,600,000
2004	$5,273,300,000	$158,800,000

Curr. Assets:	$2,309,000,000	Curr. Liab.:	$1,623,600,000		
Plant, Equip.:	$643,900,000	Total Liab.:	$2,620,900,000	Indic. Yr. Divd.:	NA
Total Assets:	$4,114,500,000	Net Worth:	$1,493,600,000	Debt/ Equity:	0.3762

AgFeed Industries Inc

Rm. 1602&1603, Nanchang National Economic & Technological Development Zone, Nanchang, Jiangxi, 330006; **PH:** 86-6622629347; **Fax:** 86-2145946128; **http://** www.agfeedinc.com; **Email:** info@agfeedinc.com

General - Incorporation	NV	Stock - Price on:12/24/2007	$5.6
Employees	NA	Stock Exchange	NDQ
Auditor	Goldman & Parks LLP	Ticker Symbol	FEED
Stk Agt	Holladay Stock Transfer, Inc.	Outstanding Shares	NA
Counsel	Beckman, Lieberman, & Barandes, LLP	E.P.S.	$0.17
DUNS No.	NA	Shareholders	NA

Business: The groups principle activities include manufacturing and marketing animal nutritional product. The group products include pre-mix and piglet blends The groups services include sampling of accompanying blend components such as grain content and proteins for those farmers blending their own feed as well as the distribution of sample products. In the year 2006, the group acquired Guangxi Huijie and Nanchang Best. The groups quarterly revenue for September 2007 was 11.89 millions of USD.

Primary SIC and add'l.: 2040

CIK No: 0001331427

Subsidiaries: Guangxi Huijie Sci. & Tech. Feed Co. , Ltd, Nanchang Best Animal Husbandry Co. , Ltd, Shanghai Best Animal Husbandry Co., Ltd.

Officers: Junhong Xiong/Vice Chmn., CEO, Liangfan Yan/CFO, Feng Zhou/VP, Financial Controller, Corp. Sec., Zhengru Xiong/VP - Technical Operation, Nicholas Giordano/Strategic Advisor, Bud Harmon/Technical Advisor, Sam Sheng/Corporate Advisor, Business Development, Yan Liang Fan/54/CFO

Directors: Junhong Xiong/Vice Chmn., CEO, Songyan Li/Chmn., John Egan/Dir., Robert Masucci/Dir., Lixiang Zhang/Dir.

Owners: Xiong Junhong/16.14%, Li Songyan/7.07%, Zhou Feng/7.54%, Xiong Zhengru/7.54%, Zheng Yunlin/7.54%, Insiders/30.75%, Leader Industrial Development, Ltd./8.91%

Financial Data: **Fiscal Year End:**12/31 **Latest Annual Data:** 12/31/2006

Year	Sales	Net Income
2006	$8,595,000	$1,175,000

Curr. Assets:	$5,336,000	**Curr. Liab.:**	$3,890,000	**P/E Ratio:**	114.20
Plant, Equip.:	$1,391,000	**Total Liab.:**	$3,890,000	**Indic. Yr. Divd.:**	NA
Total Assets:	$7,266,000	**Net Worth:**	$3,376,000	**Debt/ Equity:**	NA

Agile Software Corp

6373 San Ignacio Ave., San Jose, CA, 95119; ***PH:*** 1-408-284-4000; ***http://*** www.agile.com

General - Incorporation	DE	**Stock**- Price on:12/24/2007	$8.05
Employees	689	Stock Exchange	NDQ
Auditor	PricewaterhouseCoopers LLP	Ticker Symbol	AGIL
Stk Agt	Bank of Boston	Outstanding Shares	57,240,000
Counsel	Fenwick & West LLP	E.P.S	-$0.14
DUNS No.	NA	Shareholders	NA

Business: The group's principal activity is to develop and market collaborative manufacturing solutions that speed up the build and buy process across the manufacturing network. The solutions manage product content and critical communication, collaboration and commerce transactions among original equipment manufacturers, electronic manufacturing services providers, customers and suppliers. The products are licensed to customers in the following sectors: computers and peripherals, components, consumer electronics, data networking and telecommunications equipment, electronics manufacturing services, medical devices and equipment and others. Customers of the group include b/e aerospace, dell computer flextronics international, gateway, ge medical, hitachi, infocus, international paper, juniper networks, lucent, metaldyne, nvidia, playtex, philips and precor. The group acquired onerev inc and productfactory inc in fiscal 2003 and eigner and tradec inc in fiscal 2004.

Primary SIC and add'l.: 7378 7372

CIK No: 0001088653

Subsidiaries: Agile Canadian Holdings, Inc., Agile International Holdings, LLC, Agile Software (Suzhou) Co., Ltd., Agile Software AG, Agile Software Enterprise Pvt. Ltd., Agile Software GmbH, Agile Software International Corporation, Agile Software KK, Agile Software Limited, Cimmetry Systems Corporation

Owners: Paul Wahl, Insiders/9.23%, Bryan D. Stolle/2.97%, Dimensional Fund Advisors LP/8.15%, Perry Corp./5.84%, Carolyn V. Aver/1.15%, Nancy J. Schoendorf, Christopher Wong/1.03%, Jeff G. Johnson, BlackRock, Inc./8.52%, Kevin Kennedy, Jay B. Fulcher/2.10%, Gareth C. C. Chang, Ronald E. F. Codd, Columbia Wanger Asset Management, LP/6.85% *(16 Owners included in Index)*

Financial Data: **Fiscal Year End:**04/30 **Latest Annual Data:** 4/30/2006

Year	Sales	Net Income
2006	$132,069,000	-$8,388,000
2005	$116,987,000	-$7,194,000
2004	$96,305,000	-$24,095,000

Curr. Assets:	$205,516,000	**Curr. Liab.:**	$54,265,000		
Plant, Equip.:	$8,697,000	**Total Liab.:**	$60,018,000	**Indic. Yr. Divd.:**	NA
Total Assets:	$318,307,000	**Net Worth:**	$258,289,000	**Debt/ Equity:**	NA

Agilent Technologies Inc

5301 Stevens Creek Blvd., Santa Clara, CA, 95051; ***PH:*** 1-408-345-8886; ***Fax:*** 1-408-345-8474; ***http://*** www.agilent.com; ***Email:*** contact_us@agilent.com

General - Incorporation	DE	**Stock**- Price on:12/24/2007	$38.61
Employees	18,700	Stock Exchange	NYSE
Auditor	PricewaterhouseCoopers LLP	Ticker Symbol	A
Stk Agt	Computershare Investor Services LLC	Outstanding Shares	395,960,000
Counsel	Shearman & Sterling LLP	E.P.S	$1.57
DUNS No.	NA	Shareholders	NA

Business: The group's principle activity is to provide core bio-analytical and electronic measurement solutions to the communications, electronics, life sciences and chemical analysis industries. The group's services include life science and chemical analysis solutions. The group's products include test system and software, test accessories and cables. In the year 2007, the group acquired NetworkFab Corp. The group operates from United States.

Primary SIC and add'l.: 3826 3825 3845 3674

CIK No: 0001090872

Subsidiaries: Agilent Finance Limited, Agilent Technologies (Malaysia) Sdn. Bhd., Agilent Technologies Australia Pty Ltd, Agilent Technologies Canada Inc., Agilent Technologies Cayman Islands Inc., Agilent Technologies Company Limited, Agilent Technologies Coordination Center S.C./C.V., Agilent Technologies Deutschland Alpha GmbH, Agilent Technologies Deutschland GmbH, Agilent Technologies Deutschland GmbH & Co. Immobilien KG, Agilent Technologies Deutschland Holding GmbH, Agilent Technologies Europe B.V. (Holding), Agilent Technologies Europe B.V. Meyrin Branch, Agilent Technologies France S.A.S., Agilent Technologies Hong Kong Limited 46 Subsidiaries included in the Index

Officers: William P. Sullivan/Dir., CEO, Pres., Adrian T. Dillon/Exec. VP - Finance, Administration, CFO, Saleem Odeh/VP, GM - Sales, Service, Support Electronic Measurements Group, Lon Justice/VP, GM - Sales, Service, Support Life Sciences, Chemical Analysis, Michael C. Gasparian/VP, GM - Customer, Quality, Darlene J.S. Solomon/CTO, VP - Agilent Laboratories, Jean M. Halloran/Sr. VP - Human Resources, Craig D. Nordlund/Sr. VP, General Counsel, Sec., David Churchill/VP, GM - Network, Digital Solutions Business Unit Electronic Measurements Group, Mike Gasparian/VP, GM - Materials Science Solutions Unit, Life Sciences, Chemical Analysis, Gooi Soon Chai/VP, GM - Electronic Instruments Business Unit Electronic Measurements Group, Mike McMullen/VP, GM - Chemical Analysis Solutions Unit Life Sciences, Chemical Analysis, Ron Nersesian/VP, GM - Wireless Business Unit Electronic Measurements Group, Nick Roelofs/VP, GM - Life Sciences Solutions Unit Life Sciences, Chemical Analysis

Directors: William P. Sullivan/Dir., CEO, Pres., James G. Cullen/Non - Exec. Chmn., Barry A. Rand/Dir., Heidi Kunz/Dir., Paul N. Clark/Dir., Robert J. Herbold/Dir., Koh Boon Hwee/Dir., Robert L. Joss/Dir., David M. Lawrence/Dir.

Owners: William P. Sullivan, James G. Cullen, Koh Boon Hwee, Robert L. Joss, David M. Lawrence, Insiders/1.00%, Paul N. Clark, Robert J. Herbold, Barry A. Rand, Patrick J. Byrne, Craig D. Nordlund, Adrian T. Dillon, Christopher van Ingen, Heidi Kunz

Financial Data: **Fiscal Year End:**10/31 **Latest Annual Data:** 10/31/2006

Year	Sales	Net Income
2006	$4,973,000,000	$3,307,000,000
2005	$5,139,000,000	$327,000,000
2004	$7,181,000,000	$349,000,000

Curr. Assets:	$3,671,000,000	**Curr. Liab.:**	$1,663,000,000	**P/E Ratio:**	26.27
Plant, Equip.:	$801,000,000	**Total Liab.:**	$4,320,000,000	**Indic. Yr. Divd.:**	NA
Total Assets:	$7,554,000,000	**Net Worth:**	$3,234,000,000	**Debt/ Equity:**	0.4219

Agilysys Inc

2255 Glades Rd., Ste. 301E, Boca Raton, FL, 33431; ***PH:*** 1-561-999-8700; ***Fax:*** 1-561-999-8765; ***http://*** www.agilysys.com; ***Email:*** investors@agilysys.com

General - Incorporation	OH	**Stock**- Price on:12/24/2007	$23
Employees	996	Stock Exchange	NDQ
Auditor	Ernst & Young LLP	Ticker Symbol	AGYS
Stk Agt	National City Bank	Outstanding Shares	31,400,000
Counsel	NA	E.P.S	$7.59
DUNS No.	00-445-4211	Shareholders	NA

Business: The groups principle activity is to provide IT solutions for the retail and hospitality industries. The group also provides designing and implementing hardware, software and service solutions for the supermarket, chain drug and general retail marketplace. The group operates from United States.

Primary SIC and add'l.: 5065 5045

CIK No: 0000078749

Subsidiaries: Agilysys Canada Inc., Agilysys CH Limited, Agilysys Hong Kong Limited, Agilysys Information Services Limited, Agilysys MC Limited, Agilysys NV, LLC, Aprisa Holdings, LLC, Aprisa, Inc., The Dickens Services Group, A Pioneer-Standard company, LLC

Officers: Arthur Rhein/Chmn., CEO, Pres./$4,830,822.00, Richard A. Sayers/Chief Human Resources Officer, Exec. VP/$1,244,699.00, Peter J. Coleman/Exec. VP/$1,179,277.00, Robert J. Bailey/Exec. VP/$1,157,642.00, Martin F. Ellis/CFO, Exec. VP, Treasurer/$1,312,502.00, Kenneth J. Kossin/VP, Controller, Lawrence N. Schultz/Sec., Rita A. Thomas/VP, Corporate Counsel, Assist. Sec.

Directors: Charles F. Christ/Dir., Howard V. Knicely/Dir., Thomas C. Sullivan/70/Dir., Keith M. Kolerus/Dir., Robert A. Lauer/Dir., Robert G. McCreary/Dir., Curtis J. Crawford/Dir., Thomas A. Commes/Dir., Eileen Rudden/Dir.

Owners: Thomas C. Sullivan/0.20%, Keith M. Kolerus/0.10%, Thomas A. Commes/0.30%, Dimensional Fund Advisors, Inc./8.50%, Richard A. Sayers/1.40%, Robert G. McCreary, Curtis J. Crawford, Peter J. Coleman/1.40%, Howard V. Knicely/0.10%, Robert J. Bailey/1.20%, Martin F. Ellis/0.80%, Arthur Rhein/4.70%, Robert A. Lauer/0.20%, Insiders/10.10%, Barclays Global Investors, NA/7.50% *(16 Owners included in Index)*

Financial Data: **Fiscal Year End:**03/31 **Latest Annual Data:** 3/31/2007

Year	Sales	Net Income
2007	$474,570,000	$232,855,000
2006	$1,742,460,000	$28,114,000
2005	$1,622,925,000	$19,485,000

Curr. Assets:	$738,116,000	**Curr. Liab.:**	$251,360,000	**P/E Ratio:**	3.13
Plant, Equip.:	$17,279,000	**Total Liab.:**	$272,396,000	**Indic. Yr. Divd.:**	$0.120
Total Assets:	$899,240,000	**Net Worth:**	$626,844,000	**Debt/ Equity:**	NA

AGL Resources Inc

10 Peachtree Pl. NE, Atlanta, GA, 30309; ***PH:*** 1-404-584-4000; ***Fax:*** 1-404-584-3714; ***http://*** www.aglresources.com; ***Email:*** corpcomm@aglresources.com

General - Incorporation	GA	**Stock**- Price on:12/24/2007	$40.57
Employees	2,369	Stock Exchange	NYSE
Auditor	PricewaterhouseCoopers LLP	Ticker Symbol	ATG
Stk Agt	Wells Fargo Bank	Outstanding Shares	77,790,000
Counsel	NA	E.P.S	$2.47
DUNS No.	93-365-6211	Shareholders	NA

Business: The groups principle activity is to distribute natural gas. The group operates through four business segments namely distribution operations, retail energy operations, wholesale services and energy investments, and a non-operating corporate segment. In the year 2007, the group acquired Compass Energy Services, Inc. The group operates from United States.

Primary SIC and add'l.: 4924 4932 6719

CIK No: 0001004155

Subsidiaries: AGL Capital Corporation, AGL Networks, LLC, AGL Services Company, Atlanta Gas Light Company, Chattanooga Gas Company, Georgia Natural Gas Company, Jefferson Island Storage & Hub, LLC, NUI Utilities, Inc., Pivotal Jefferson Island Storage & Hub, LLC, Sequent Energy Management, LP, SouthStar Energy Services LLC, Virginia Natural Gas, Inc.

Officers: John W. Somerhalder/Chmn., CEO, Pres./$2,466,177.00, Bryan Batson/Sr. VP - External Affairs, Eric R. Martinez/Exec. VP - Utility Operations/$1,217,684.00, Bryan E. Seas/VP, Controller, Chief Accounting Officer, Ronald L. Lepionka/Chief Auditor, Eugene V. Rozgonyi/VP, Chief Risk Officer, Brett A. Stovern/VP, Treasurer, Kristin R. Kirkconnell/Sr. VP - Information Services, Technology, Ira G. Pearl/VP - Engineering Services, Supply Chain, Jodi Gidley/Pres. - Elizabethtown Gas, Elkton Gas, Virginia Natural Gas, Elizabeth W. Reese/VP - Finance, Peter Tumminello/Exec. VP - Business Development, Support, Sequent Energy Management, Henry P. Linginfelter/Exec. VP - Utility Operations, Suzanne Sitherwood/Sr. VP - Southern Operations, Douglas N. Schantz/Pres. - Sequent Energy Management/$1,729,673.00 *(45 Officers included in Index)*

Directors: John W. Somerhalder/Chmn., CEO, Pres., Raymond D. Riddle/Dir., Thomas D. Bell/Dir., Charles R. Crisp/Dir., James A. Rubright/Dir., Michael J. Durham/Dir., Wyck A. Knox/Dir., Bettina M. Whyte/Dir., Arthur E. Johnson/Dir., Dennis M. Love/Dir., Dean R. OHare/Dir., Felker W. Ward/Dir., Henry C. Wolf/Dir., Charles H. McTier/68/Dir.

Owners: Douglas N. Schantz, Dennis M. Love, John W. Somerhalder, Bettina M. Whyte, Kevin P. Madden, Michael J. Durham, James A. Rubright, Charles R. Crisp, Insiders, Raymond D. Riddle, Henry C. Wolf, Dean R. OHare, Wyck A. Knox, Thomas D. Bell, Felker W. Ward *(20 Owners included in Index)*

Financial Data: **Fiscal Year End:**12/31 **Latest Annual Data:** 12/31/2006

Year	Sales	Net Income
2006	$2,621,000,000	$212,000,000
2005	$2,718,000,000	$193,000,000
2004	$1,832,000,000	$153,000,000

Curr. Assets:	$1,822,000,000	**Curr. Liab.:**	$1,627,000,000		
Plant, Equip.:	$3,436,000,000	**Total Liab.:**	$4,496,000,000	**Indic. Yr. Divd.:**	$1.640
Total Assets:	$6,147,000,000	**Net Worth:**	$1,609,000,000	**Debt/ Equity:**	0.9672

Agnico-Eagle Mines Ltd

145 King St. E, Ste. 500, Toronto, ON, M5C 2Y7; *PH:* 1-416-947-1212; *Fax:* 1-416-367-4681; *http://* www.agnico-eagle.com; *Email:* info@agnico-eagle.com

General - Incorporation	Canada	Stock - Price on:12/24/2007	$37.09
Employees	933	Stock Exchange	NYSE
Auditor	Ernst & Young LLP	Ticker Symbol	AEM
Stk Agt	Computershare Trust Co	Outstanding Shares	121,210,000
Counsel	McGuire Woods Battle & Boothe	E.P.S.	$0.88
DUNS No.	20-706-5152	Shareholders	NA

Business: The group's principal activities are the exploration, development and mining of gold. Laronde, the group's gold deposit in Canada has a reserve and resource totaling 8.5 million ounces. The group operates in Canada. On 08-Jul-2002, the group acquired golden goliath resources ltd.

Primary SIC and add'l.: 1041

CIK No: 0000002809

Subsidiaries: Agnico-Eagle Sweden AB, Goldex Mines Limited

Officers: Sean Boyd/Vice Chmn., CEO, Donald G. Allan/Sr. VP - Corporate Development, Tim Haldane/VP - Latin America, Gregory R. Laing/VP - Legal, General Counsel, Corp. Sec., David Garofalo/Sr. VP - Finance, CFO, Eberhard Scherkus/Dir., COO, Pres., Alain Blackburn/Sr. VP - Exploration, Howard Stockford/Dir., Exec. VP, Jean Robitaille/VP - Metallurgy, Marketing, David Smith/VP - Investor Relations, Patrice Gilbert/VP - Human Resources, Louise Grondin/VP - Environment, Ingmar E. Haga/VP - Europe, Marc Legault/VP - Project Development, Daniel Racine/VP - Operations *(16 Officers included in Index)*

Directors: Sean Boyd/Vice Chmn., CEO, James D. Nasso/Chmn., Pertti Voutilainen/Chmn., Douglas R. Beaumont/Dir., Leanne M. Baker/Dir., Bernard Kraft/Dir., Mel Leiderman/Dir., Eberhard Scherkus/Dir., COO, Pres., Howard Stockford/Dir., Exec. VP

Financial Data: *Fiscal Year End:*12/31 *Latest Annual Data:* 12/31/2006

Year		Sales		Net Income
2006		$510,547,000		$161,337,000
2005		$246,334,000		$36,994,000
2004		$188,704,000		$47,879,000
Curr. Assets:	$622,833,000	Curr. Liab.:	$71,935,000	
Plant, Equip.:	$859,859,000	Total Liab.:	$269,083,000	Indic. Yr. Divd.: $0.120
Total Assets:	$1,521,488,000	Net Worth:	$1,252,405,000	Debt/ Equity: NA

Agree Realty Corp

31850 Nwestern Hwy., Farmington Hills, MI, 48334; *PH:* 1-248-737-4190; *Fax:* 1-248-737-9110; *http://* www.agreerealty.com

General - Incorporation	MD	Stock - Price on:12/24/2007	$32.98
Employees	8	Stock Exchange	NYSE
Auditor	BDO Seidman, LLP	Ticker Symbol	ADC
Stk Agt	Computershare Trust Co	Outstanding Shares	7,750,000
Counsel	NA	E.P.S.	$1.90
DUNS No.	NA	Shareholders	NA

Business: The groups principle activities include developing , acquiring and managing retail properties. The group operates from Midwestern United States and Florida. The group's quarterly revenue for September 2007 was 8.45 millions of USD.

Primary SIC and add'l.: 6798

CIK No: 0000917251

Subsidiaries: AC Realty Company, LLC, ACCP Maryland, LLC, Agree - Columbia Crossing Project, L.L.C., Agree - Milestone Center Project, L.L.C., Agree Bristol & Fenton Project, LLC, Agree Facility No. 1, L.L.C., Agree Realty South-East, LLC, ALPSC Associates, LLC, AMCP Germantown, LLC, Ann Arbor Store No 1, LLC, Boynton Beach Store No. 150, LLC, Indianapolis Store No. 16, LLC, Mt Pleasant Shopping Center L.L.C., Oklahoma City Store No. 151, L.L.C., Omaha Store No. 166, L.L.C. 18 Subsidiaries included in the Index

Officers: Richard Agree/Chmn., CEO, Pres./$573,570.00, Joey Agree/Exec. VP/$146,272.00, Kenneth R. Howe/VP - Finance, CFO/$294,685.00, David J. Prueter/Sr. VP/$294,792.00, Vicky Whalen-Umphryes/VP - Development/$269,253.00, Robert E. Zschering/VP - Construction

Directors: Richard Agree/Chmn., CEO, Pres., Farris G. Kalil/67/Dir., Eugene Silverman/72/Dir., Michael Rotchford/47/Dir., Ellis G. Wachs/76/Dir., Leon M. Schurgin/64/Dir.

Owners: Richard Agree/6.23%, Leon M. Schurgin/8.34%, Insiders/8.34%, Vicky Whalen-Umphryes, Wells Fargo and Company/5.30%, Michael Rotchford, Ellis G. Wachs, David J. Prueter, Gene Silverman, Joey Agree, Kenneth R. Howe, Farris G. Kalil

Financial Data: *Fiscal Year End:*12/31 *Latest Annual Data:* 12/31/2006

Year		Sales		Net Income
2006		$32,908,000		$13,974,000
2005		$31,579,000		$16,048,000
2004		$29,929,000		$13,123,000
Curr. Assets:	$1,196,000	Curr. Liab.:	$6,322,000	
Plant, Equip.:	$219,895,000	Total Liab.:	$93,096,000	Indic. Yr. Divd.: $1.960
Total Assets:	$223,515,000	Net Worth:	$130,419,000	Debt/ Equity: 0.5426

Agrium Inc

4582 S Ulster St., Ste. 1700, Denver, CO, 80237; *PH:* 1-303-804-4400; *Fax:* 1-303-804-4482; *http://* www.agrium.com

General - Incorporation	Canada	Stock - Price on:12/24/2007	$44.95
Employees	6,554	Stock Exchange	NYSE
Auditor	KPMG LLP	Ticker Symbol	AGU
Stk Agt	Mellon Trust Co	Outstanding Shares	134,000,000
Counsel	NA	E.P.S.	$1.55
DUNS No.	24-956-8056	Shareholders	NA

Business: The group's principal activities are carried out in two operating segments: wholesale and retail. The wholesale segment includes production and sale of four primary nutrients: nitrogen, phosphate, potash and sulphur. The retail segment includes sale of fertilizers, chemicals, seed, custom application services and agronomic consulting. The activities of the group are carried out in the United States, Argentina and other countries.

Primary SIC and add'l.: 2819 2874 2873

CIK No: 0000943003

Subsidiaries: Agrium Nitrogen Company, Agrium U.S. Inc., AGRIUM, a general partnership, Agroservicios Pampeanos S.A., Crop Production Services, Inc., Nu-West Industries, Inc., Profertil S.A., Royster-Clark Holdings, Inc., Royster-Clark Ltd., Royster-Clark ULC, Royster-Clark, Inc., Viridian Fertilizers Limited, Western Farm Service, Inc.

Officers: Michael M. Wilson/CEO, Pres., Bruce G. Waterman/Sr. VP - Finance, CFO, Leslie A. O'Donoghue/Sr. VP, General Counsel, Corp. Sec., Christopher W. Tworek/VP - Supply Management, Ron A. Wilkinson/Sr. VP - Agrium, Pres. - Wholesael, Richard L. Gearheard/Sr. VP - Agrium, Pres. - Retail, James M. Grossett/Sr. VP - Human Resources, Andrew K. Mittag/Sr. VP - Corporate Development, Strategy, Patrick J. Freeman/VP, Treasurer, Angela Lekatsas/VP, Corporate Controller, Kevin Helash/VP - Marketing, Distribution, Stephen Dyer/VP - Manufacturing, William Boycott/VP - Agrium, Pres. - Agrium Advanced Technologies

Directors: Frank W. Proto/64/Chmn., Grant D. Devine/62/Dir., Russell J. Horner/57/Dir., Frank W. King/Dir., Neil Carragher/68/Dir., Victor J. Zaleschuk/63/Dir., Susan A. Henry/60/Dir., Harry G. Schaefer/Dir., Ralph S. Cunningham/66/Dir., Germaine Gibara/62/Dir., Russell Girling/45/Dir., Anne McLellan/57/Dir.

Financial Data: *Fiscal Year End:*12/31 *Latest Annual Data:* 12/31/2006

Year		Sales		Net Income
2006		$4,193,000,000		$42,000,000
2005		$3,294,000,000		$270,000,000
2004		$3,001,000,000		$263,000,000
Curr. Assets:	$1,559,000,000	Curr. Liab.:	$960,000,000	
Plant, Equip.:	$1,332,000,000	Total Liab.:	$2,032,000,000	Indic. Yr. Divd.: $0.110
Total Assets:	$3,212,000,000	Net Worth:	$1,180,000,000	Debt/ Equity: NA

AHPC Holdings Inc

80 Internationale Blvd., Unit A, Glendale Heights, IL, 60139; *PH:* 1-630-407-0242; *Fax:* 1-630-407-0238; *http://* www.ahpc.com

General - Incorporation	MD	Stock - Price on:12/24/2007	NA
Employees	NA	Stock Exchange	OTC
Auditor	Grant Thornton LLP	Ticker Symbol	GLOV
Stk Agt	Illinois Stock Transfer Co	Outstanding Shares	NA
Counsel	NA	E.P.S.	-$5.19
DUNS No.	NA	Shareholders	NA

Business: The group's principal activities are to market medical examination, surgical and foodservice gloves through its wholly owned subsidiary, American health products corporation. The group also manufactures disposable gloves including latex, vinyl, synthetic and nitrile examination and surgical gloves. These products are primarily used in the food service, non-acute medical, dental and retail industries. The gloves are marketed under the brand names dermasafe, glovetex, profeel and safeprep.

Primary SIC and add'l.: 5169 3069

CIK No: 0000837038

Subsidiaries: American Health Products Corporation

Officers: Alan Zeffer/Dir., CEO, Pres., Deborah Bills/Officers

Directors: Alan Zeffer/Dir., CEO, Pres., Richard Swanson/Dir., Don L. Arnwine/Dir., Robert J. Simmons/Dir., Anthony F. Alibrio/Dir., Jeff G. Mennen/Dir.

Owners: Robert J. Simmons/2.30%, Don L. Arnwine/2.30%, Insiders/15.50%, George Jeff Mennen/2.50%, Anthony L. Alibrio/1.60%, Deborah J. Bills/0.50%, Richard J. Swanson/2.30%, M.A.G. Capital LLC/9.99%, Alan E. Zeffer/4.00%

Financial Data: *Fiscal Year End:*06/30 *Latest Annual Data:* 06/30/2006

Year		Sales		Net Income
2006		$25,297,000		-$3,314,000
2005		$26,553,000		-$1,152,000
2004		$36,560,000		-$2,850,000
Curr. Assets:	$8,866,000	Curr. Liab.:	$6,113,000	
Plant, Equip.:	$125,000	Total Liab.:	$6,200,000	Indic. Yr. Divd.: NA
Total Assets:	$8,992,000	Net Worth:	$2,792,000	Debt/ Equity: NA

AIDA Pharmaceuticals Inc

31 Dingjiang Rd., Jianggan District, Hangzhou, Zhejiang, 310016; *PH:* 617-723-1465; *http://* aidapharma.server286.com

General - Incorporation	NV	Stock - Price on:12/24/2007	$1.18
Employees	NA	Stock Exchange	OTC
Auditor	Weinberg & Company, P.A.	Ticker Symbol	AIDA
Stk Agt	OTC Stock Transfer, Inc.	Outstanding Shares	NA
Counsel	Cletha Walstrand	E.P.S.	NA
DUNS No.	NA	Shareholders	NA

Business: The groups principle activities include discovering, developing and marketing new therapies. The group products include Etimicin Sulfate, 5-Deoxy-Fluorordine, Vasostatin Apo2L, Apoptotic Factor rh-Apo2l, and Anti-CD86. The group marketed its products under the trade names Aida, AiYi, ChuangCheng, and PanRou. The group operates from China and the United States.

Primary SIC and add'l.: 2834

CIK No: 0001220286

Subsidiaries: Changzhou Fangyuan Pharmaceutical Co., Ltd. (Fangyuan), Earjoy Group Limited, (Earjoy), Hainan Aike Pharmaceutical Co., Ltd. (Aike), Hangzhou Aida Pharmaceutical Co., Ltd (Hangzhou Aida), Hangzhou Boda Medical Research and Development Co., Ltd. (Boda), Shanghai Qiaer Bio-technology Co., Ltd (Qiaer)

Officers: Jin Biao/Chmn., CEO - Aida Pharmaceuticals, Biao Jin/Dir., CEO, Bethany Tomich/Investor Relations Officer, Hui Lin/42/CFO, Yuejun Jiang/33/Sec., Lin Hui/CFO, Huang Daofei/CTO, Cletha Walstrand/Legal Counsel

Directors: Jin Biao/Chmn., CEO - Aida Pharmaceuticals, Biao Jin/Dir., CEO, Zhang Qiong/Dir., Qiu Jiajun/Dir., Qiong Zhang/41/Dir.

Owners: Cede & Co, Panasia Strategy Investment Co. Ltd, Insiders, Liming Wen, Qiong Zhang, Yuejun Jiang, Biao Jin, Union Zone Management Ltd, Winsummit China Growing Holdings, Ltd, Hui Lin, Jiajun Qiu

Financial Data: *Fiscal Year End:*12/31 *Latest Annual Data:* 12/31/2006

Year		Sales		Net Income
2006		$29,643,000		$1,454,000
2005		$24,527,000		$1,468,000

Curr. Assets:	$28,628,000	**Curr. Liab.:**	$34,377,000		
Plant, Equip.:	$14,006,000	**Total Liab.:**	$43,458,000	**Indic. Yr. Divd.:**	NA
Total Assets:	$53,810,000	**Net Worth:**	$10,352,000	**Debt/ Equity:**	NA

Aig Sunamerica Life Assurance Co

1 Sunamerica Ctr., Los Angeles, CA, 90067; *PH:* 1-800-445-7862; *http://* www.sunamerica.com; *Email:* mutualfundinquiry@sunamerica.com

General - Incorporation	AZ	**Stock**- Price on:12/24/2007	NA
Employees	NA	Stock Exchange	NA
Auditor	PricewaterhouseCoopers LLP	Ticker Symbol	NA
Stk Agt	NA	Outstanding Shares	NA
Counsel	NA	E.P.S	NA
DUNS No.	NA	Shareholders	NA

Business: The group's principal activities are to provide financial services including variable and fixed annuities. The operations are carried on through annuity operations which focuses on marketing, selling and administration of fixed and variable annuity products, the universal life business and guaranteed investment contracts. The group is a wholly owned subsidiary of sunamerica inc. Until Feb 2003, the group did business as anchor national life insurance company.

Primary SIC and add'l.: 6311 6159

CIK No: 0000006342

Subsidiaries: AIG SunAmerica Asset Management Corp, AIG SunAmerica Capital Services, Inc, AIG SunAmerica Fund Services, Inc.

Aims Worldwide Inc

10400 Eaton Pl., Ste. 450, Fairfax, VA, 22030; *PH:* 1-703-621-3875; *Fax:* 1-703-621-3865; *http://* www.aimsworldwide.com; *Email:* aatoole@aimsworldwide.com

General - Incorporation	NV	**Stock**- Price on:12/24/2007	$0.58
Employees	15	Stock Exchange	OTC
Auditor	Cordovano & Honeck LLP	Ticker Symbol	AMWW
Stk Agt	Interwest Transfer Company, Inc.	Outstanding Shares	42,850,000
Counsel	NA	E.P.S	-$0.18
DUNS No.	NA	Shareholders	NA

Business: The group's principle activity is to provide integrated marketing and media services to businesses. The company's trademarks include aimst82 and romit82. Aimst82 is an audio-logical-acronym for accurate integrated marketing solutions. Aimst82 is a proprietary marketing service and delivery system designed to improve the aim, reduce the cost and lessen the reach to target a market on a "One-To-One" basis. In the aims82 paradigm marketing efforts are judged on a standard based on return on marketing investment (romit82), which is a solution to the paradox of declining mass market audiences coupled with increasing advertising costs that integrates emerging technologies. On 25-Sep-2003, the company acquired atb media inc. The group operates from United States.

Primary SIC and add'l.: 3949

CIK No: 0001094363

Subsidiaries: AIMS Interactive, Inc., AIMS Worldwide, Inc., ATB, Bill Main & Associates, Inc., Enjoy the Game, Inc., Harrell Woodcock Linkletter and strategic partners Street Fighter Marketing, Inc, Prime Time Broadband, Inc

Officers: Gerald Garcia/CEO, Pres., Patrick J. Summers/CFO, Controller, Aliceann Toole/VP - Marketing Communications

Directors: Michael Foudy/56/Chmn., Joseph B. Vincent/Vice Chmn., Thomas W. Cady/Chmn. - Aims Interactive Group, Anthony Mikes/Chmn. - Aims Advertising Services Group, Arthur Stevens/Chmn. - Aims Public Relations Group, David Woodcock/Chmn. - Aims Strategy, Planning Group

Owners: Patrick Summers, Max Miller/5.38%, Joseph B. Vincent/6.78%, Charles H. Brunie/9.68%, Michael Foudy/10.67%, Gerald Garcia/5.28%, Insiders/12.40%

Financial Data: *Fiscal Year End:*12/31 *Latest Annual Data:* 12/31/2006

Year	Sales	Net Income
2006	$1,742,000	-$3,203,000
2005	$1,161,000	-$1,927,000
2004	$652,000	-$3,117,000

Curr. Assets:	$306,000	**Curr. Liab.:**	$4,479,000		
Plant, Equip.:	$245,000	**Total Liab.:**	$4,641,000	**Indic. Yr. Divd.:**	NA
Total Assets:	$2,826,000	**Net Worth:**	-$1,815,000	**Debt/ Equity:**	NA

Air France-KLM

Formerly: Air France
2, Rue Robert Esnault-pelterie 75007 Paris, Paris, 95747; *PH:* 33-1415-67800; *http://* www.airfrance.com

General - Incorporation	France	**Stock**- Price on:12/24/2007	$46.6
Employees	NA	Stock Exchange	NYSE
Auditor	Deloitte & Assoc.	Ticker Symbol	AKH
Stk Agt	Citibank N.A	Outstanding Shares	277,300,000
Counsel	NA	E.P.S	$6.89
DUNS No.	NA	Shareholders	NA

Business: The groups principle activity is to provide airline services. The group also provides cargo, aeronautics maintenance and other air-transport related activities. The group operates through three segments namely passenger, cargo and aircraft maintenance. The group operates from United States.

Primary SIC and add'l.: NA

CIK No: 0001110452

Subsidiaries: Air France Finance, Air Ivoire, Brit Air, CityJet, KLM, Rgional Compagnie Arienne Europenne, Servair, socit Air France

Officers: Jean-Cyril Spinetta/65/Chmn., CEO, Leo M. Van Wijk/Vice Chmn., CEO, Pres., Pascal Zadikian/Administrator - Representing Employees, Claude Gressier/Dir., Pres. - Department, Economic Affairs, Counsel General Public Works, Peter Hartman/Dir., MD, COO - KLM, Michael Wisbrun/Exec. VP - KLM Cargo, Marie-Jospeh Male/VP - Corporate Control, Pierre-Henri Gourgeon/62/Dir., COO, Pres., Philippe Calavia/60/Dir., CFO, Gilbert Rovetto/61/Exec. VP - Flight Operations, Cees Van Woudenberg/Dir. - Control, Internal Audit, Air France, KLM, Philippe Cadorel/Administrator - Representing Cabin Crews, Michel Faure/Administrator - Representing Employees, Daniel MacKay/Administrator - Representing Employees, Pascal Mathieu/Administrator - Representing Mgr. *(26 Officers included in Index)*

Directors: Jean-Cyril Spinetta/65/Chmn., CEO, Leo M. Van Wijk/Vice Chmn., CEO, Pres., Jean-Francois Dehecq/Dir., Jean-Marc Espalioux/Dir., Claude Gressier/Dir., Pres. - Department, Economic Affairs, Counsel General Public Works, Cornelis J.A. Van Lede/66/Dir., Didier Le Chaton/Dir., Christian Magne/Dir., Pierre Richard/Dir., Patricia Barbizet/Dir., Jean-Pierre Aubert/Dir., Dominique-Jean Chertier/Dir., Jean-Louis Chambon/Dir., Rose-Marie Van Lerbergh/Dir., Jean Peyrot/Dir. *(26 Directors included in Index)*

Owners: Didier Le Chaton, Patricia Barbizet, Leo van Wijk, Jean-Franois Dehecq, Frits Bolkestein, Pierre-Henri Gourgeon, Jean-Cyril Spinetta, Cornelis J. A. van Lede, Jean-Marc Espalioux, Pierre Richard, Christian Magne, Floris Maljers

Financial Data: *Fiscal Year End:*03/31 *Latest Annual Data:* 03/31/2007

Year	Sales	Net Income
2007	$30,773,180,000	$1,089,470,000
2006	$25,892,152,000	$1,212,430,000
2005	$24,727,600,000	$978,900,000

Curr. Assets:	$10,229,580,000	**Curr. Liab.:**	$9,761,031,000	**P/E Ratio:**	8.10
Plant, Equip.:	$14,225,528,000	**Total Liab.:**	$21,882,920,000	**Indic. Yr. Divd.:**	$0.380
Total Assets:	$30,343,365,000	**Net Worth:**	$8,460,446,000	**Debt/ Equity:**	NA

Air Industries Group Inc

Formerly: Gales Industries Inc
1479 N Clinton Ave., Bay Shore, NY, 11706; *PH:* 1-631-968-5000; *http://* www.airindmc.com

General - Incorporation	DE	**Stock**- Price on:12/24/2007	$0.29
Employees	NA	Stock Exchange	NA
Auditor	Goldstein Golub Kessler LLP	Ticker Symbol	NA
Stk Agt	Interwest Transfer Co.	Outstanding Shares	59,580,000
Counsel	NA	E.P.S	-$0.012
DUNS No.	NA	Shareholders	NA

Business: The groups principle activity is to manufacture aircraft structural parts and assemblies. Specific customers of the group include Sikorsky, Lockheed Martin, Boeing and Northrop Grumman. In November 2005, the group acquired Original Gales (Delaware corporation). The group operates from the United States.

Primary SIC and add'l.: 3728

CIK No: 0001009891

Subsidiaries: Air Industries Machining, Corp.

Officers: Dario Peragallo/Exec. VP/$261,733.00, Paula Castellano/Dir. - Contracts, James Pfister/Dir. - Engineering, Greg Warren/Dir. - Machining Operations, Wilson Zuluaga/Dir. - Production Planning, Control, Anthony Schiappa/Dir. - Integration, Anthony Landisi/Dir. - Integration

Owners: Dario Peragallo/2.12%, Louis A. Giusto/5.92%, David J. Buonanno, Louis A. Giusto, Peter D. Rettaliata/2.12%, George Elkins/5.23%, James A. Brown, Insiders, David J. Buonanno, Seymour G. Siegel, Hillson Partners LP/6.25%, Hillson Partners LP/16.21%, James A. Brown/1.33%, Ira A. Hunt/1.22%, Michael A. Gales/5.83% *(20 Owners included in Index)*

Financial Data: *Fiscal Year End:*12/31 *Latest Annual Data:* 12/31/2006

Year	Sales	Net Income
2006	$33,045,000	-$337,000
2005	$2,777,000	-$750,000
2004	$6,343,000	-$1,215,000

Curr. Assets:	$19,180,000	**Curr. Liab.:**	$14,268,000		
Plant, Equip.:	$3,565,000	**Total Liab.:**	$18,022,000	**Indic. Yr. Divd.:**	NA
Total Assets:	$24,892,000	**Net Worth:**	$6,870,000	**Debt/ Equity:**	0.3622

Air Methods Corp

7301 S Peoria, Englewood, CO, 80112; *PH:* 1-303-792-7400; *Fax:* 1-303-790-0499; *http://* www.airmethods.com

General - Incorporation	DE	**Stock**- Price on:12/24/2007	$35.72
Employees	1,837	Stock Exchange	NDQ
Auditor	KPMG LLP	Ticker Symbol	AIRM
Stk Agt	American Stock Transfer & Trust CO.	Outstanding Shares	11,890,000
Counsel	Davis, Graham & Stubbs	E.P.S	$1.81
DUNS No.	10-849-3503	Shareholders	NA

Business: The group's principal activity is to provide air medical transport services and systems. The group operates through three business segments: the community-based services segment provides medical care, aircraft operation and maintenance, 24-hour communications and dispatch and medical billing and collections. The division operates 72 helicopters and three fixed wing aircraft under both instrument flight rules and visual flight rules in 15 states, concentrations in California, Arizona, the midwest, the southeast and the metropolitan areas. The hospital-based services segment provides air medical transportation services to hospitals located in 16 states. The group's products division designs, manufactures and installs aircraft medical interiors and other aerospace products for domestic and international customers.

Primary SIC and add'l.: 4522

CIK No: 0000816159

Subsidiaries: LifeNet, Inc., Mercy Air Service, Inc., Rocky Mountain Holdings

Officers: Aaron D. Todd/Dir., CEO/$586,859.00, Sharon J. Keck/Chief Accounting Officer, Controller/$305,813.00, David L. Dolstein/Sr. VP - Community Based Services/$441,792.00, Trent J. Carman/CFO, Sec., Treasurer/$323,657.00, Michael Allen/Sr. VP - Air Medical Services/$486,434.00, Arthur Torwirt/VP, James Bryant/Customer Service Advisory Boards, Kathy Mayer/Member - Customer Service Advisory Board, Robert Broome/Information Technology Mgr., Kerin Zuger/Call Transfer Centersm Mgr., Andy Litteral/Mgr. - EMS Marketing Segment, Jim Wingate/Military Marketing Segment Mgr., David A. Gregory/International Sales Representative - Canada, Scott Yamazaki/International Sales Representative - Japan, Geoff Dinsdale/International Sales Representative - United Kingdom *(33 Officers included in Index)*

Directors: Aaron D. Todd/Dir., CEO, George W. Belsey/Chmn., Mg Carl H. McNair/Dir., Paul H. Tate/Dir., Morad Tahbaz/Dir., Lowell D. Miller/Dir., Samuel H. Gray/Dir., Ralph J. Bernstein/Dir., David C. Kikumoto/Dir., Clinton Burley/Member - Customer Service Advisory Board, Evelyn Jackson/Member - Customer Service Advisory Board

Owners: Morad Tahbaz/1.30%, Michael D. Allen, Insiders/14.70%, Paul H. Tate, Sharon J. Keck, David Kikumoto, Lowell D. Miller, Ralph J. Bernstein/10.80%, William Blair & Co., LLC/10.90%, David L. Dolstein, Independence Investments, LLC./7.00%, MG Carl H. McNair, Aaron D. Todd, Trent J. Carman, FMR Corp./5.40% *(17 Owners included in Index)*

Financial Data: *Fiscal Year End:*12/31 *Latest Annual Data:* 12/31/2006

Year	Sales	Net Income
2006	$319,504,000	$17,200,000
2005	$336,970,000	$11,832,000
2004	$273,103,000	$11,838,000

Curr. Assets:	$139,861,000	**Curr. Liab.:**	$47,829,000	**P/E Ratio:**	19.73
Plant, Equip.:	$95,575,000	**Total Liab.:**	$142,843,000	**Indic. Yr. Divd.:**	NA
Total Assets:	$250,157,000	**Net Worth:**	$107,314,000	**Debt/ Equity:**	0.5254

Air Products & Chemicals Inc

7201 Hamilton Blvd., Allentown, PA, 18195; ***PH:*** 1-610-481-4911; ***Fax:*** 1-610-481-5900; ***http://*** www.airproducts.com; ***Email:*** info@airproducts.com

General - Incorporation .... DE
Employees 20,000
Auditor .... KPMG LLP
Stk Agt...... American Stock Transfer & Trust Co.
Counsel .... NA
DUNS No. 00-300-1070

Stock- Price on:12/24/2007 .... $81.66
Stock Exchange .... NYSE
Ticker Symbol .... APD
Outstanding Shares 216,610,000
E.P.S. $4.64
Shareholders .... NA

Business: The groups principle activity is to provide industrial gas and related process equipments. The groups products include oxygen, nitrogen, argon, hydrogen and medical and specialty gases. The group operates from United States.

Primary SIC and add'l.: 2813 2891 2819 3569 2865 2869 2821

CIK No: 0000002969

Subsidiaries: Air Prod 99 S.A.S., Air Products (BR)Limited, Air Products (Chemicals) Public Limited Company, Air Products (Chemicals) Teesside Limited, Air Products (GB)Limited, Air Products (Shanghai) Co., Ltd., Air Products (UK)Limited, Air Products A/S, Air Products ACT Korea Limited, Air Products Amsterdam B.V., Air Products and Chemicals (Shanghai) Systems Co. Ltd., Air Products and Chemicals (Tongxiang) Co., Ltd., Air Products and Chemicals (Zhangjiagang) Co., Ltd., Air Products and Chemicals Co. Ltd., Air Products and Chemicals Co., Ltd. 161 Subsidiaries included in the Index

Officers: John E. McGlade/54/Dir., CEO, Pres., Paul E. Huck/CFO, VP, Santiago Zaldumbide/European Advisory Counsel, Pres.e, Asturiana de Zinc SA, Madrid, Spain, Nelson Squires/Dir. - Investor Relations, Patrick Faure/European Advisory Counsel, Paris, France, Jurgen Krumnow/European Advisory Counsel, Frankfurt, Germany, Adrian W. Loader/European Advisory Counsel, Pres. - Shell Canada Limited, Calgary, Alberta, Canada, Andrew Wood/European Advisory Counsel, London, England, Lynn C. Minella/49/Sr. VP - Human Resources, Communications, Robert D. Dixon/VP, GM - Merchant Gases, Michael F. Hilton/VP, GM - Electronics, Performance Materials, Stephen J. Jones/VP, General Counsel, Sec., John W. Marsland/VP, GM - Healthcare, Scott A. Sherman/VP, GM - Tonnage Gases, Equipment, Energy, Montgomery Alger/CTO, VP *(53 Officers included in Index)*

Directors: John E. McGlade/54/Dir., CEO, Pres., John P. Jones/57/Chmn., Evert Henkes/64/Dir., Ursula O. Fairbairn/64/Dir., Edward E. Hagenlocker/68/Dir., Mario L. Baeza/56/Dir., Michael J. Donahue/49/Dir., William L. Davis/64/Dir., W. Douglas Ford/63/Dir., Margaret G. McGlynn/48/Dir., Charles H. Noski/55/Dir., Lawrence S. Smith/60/Dir., Douglas W. Ford/63/Dir.

Owners: Paul E. Huck, John P. Jones, Mario L. Baeza, John E. McGlade, William L. Davis, Michael J. Donahue, Scott A. Sherman, Edward E. Hagenlocker, Insiders, Charles H. Noski, Lawrence S. Smith, Ursula O. Fairbairn, Douglas W. Ford, Douglas W. Brown

Financial Data: ***Fiscal Year End:***09/30 ***Latest Annual Data:*** 9/30/2006

Year	Sales	Net Income
2006	$8,850,400,000	$723,400,000
2005	$8,143,500,000	$711,700,000
2004	$7,411,400,000	$604,100,000

Curr. Assets:	$2,612,600,000	**Curr. Liab.:**	$2,323,400,000		
Plant, Equip.:	$6,162,000,000	**Total Liab.:**	$6,078,700,000	**Indic. Yr. Divd.:**	$1.520
Total Assets:	$11,180,700,000	**Net Worth:**	$4,924,000,000	**Debt/ Equity:**	0.5125

Air T Inc

3524 Airport Rd., Maiden, NC, 28650; ***PH:*** 1-828-464-8741; ***Fax:*** 1-828-465-5281; ***http://*** www.airt.net/home.html

General - Incorporation .... DE
Employees 390
Auditor .... Dixon Hughes PLLC
Stk Agt...... American Stock Transfer & Trust Co.
Counsel........ Robinson, Bradshaw & Hinson P.A.
DUNS No. 02-412-4661

Stock- Price on:12/24/2007 .... $10.45
Stock Exchange .... NDQ
Ticker Symbol .... AIRT
Outstanding Shares 2,660,000
E.P.S. $1.005
Shareholders .... NA

Business: The group's principal activities are to provide overnight air cargo services, aircraft parts, engine overhaul management and component repair services and aviation ground support equipment products. The group operates in two segments. Overnight air cargo segment provides small package airfreight delivery services on a contract basis throughout the eastern half of the United States, Canada, Puerto Rico and the U.S. Virgin Islands. Ground equipment segment manufactures, sells and provides services and supports aircraft devices including model aircraft deicers and scissor-lift ground support equipment. Aircraft maintenance and parts and other related services are provided to the commercial and military aviation industries. The group's air cargo service is provided exclusively to Federal Express Corporation.

Primary SIC and add'l.: 4731 4581 4513

CIK No: 0000353184

Subsidiaries: Global Ground Support, LLC, Mountain Air Cargo, Inc, Mountain Aircraft Services, LLC

Officers: Walter Clark/51/Chmn., CEO/$370,902.00, John J. Gioffre/64/Dir., VP - Finance, Sec., Treasurer/$324,148.00, William H. Simpson/60/Dir., Exec. VP/$316,053.00, John Parry/CFO

Directors: Walter Clark/51/Chmn., CEO, John J. Gioffre/64/Dir., VP - Finance, Sec., Treasurer, William H. Simpson/60/Dir., Exec. VP, Claude S. Abernethy/81/Dir., Sam Chesnutt/73/Dir., Allison T. Clark/52/Dir., George C. Prill/85/Dir., Dennis A. Wicker/55/Dir., Bradley J. Wilson/55/Dir.

Owners: Walter Clark/5.80%, William H. Simpson, George C. Prill, Insiders/6.80%, Claude S. Abernethy, Sam Chesnutt, Bradley J. Wilson, Dennis A. Wicker, Allison T. Clark, John J. Gioffre

Financial Data: ***Fiscal Year End:***03/31 ***Latest Annual Data:*** 3/31/2007

Year	Sales	Net Income
2007	$67,303,000	$2,486,000
2006	$79,529,000	$2,055,000
2005	$69,999,000	$2,106,000

Curr. Assets:	$20,604,000	**Curr. Liab.:**	$7,880,000	**P/E Ratio:**	11.38
Plant, Equip.:	$2,293,000	**Total Liab.:**	$9,167,000	**Indic. Yr. Divd.:**	$0.250
Total Assets:	$24,615,000	**Net Worth:**	$15,449,000	**Debt/ Equity:**	NA

Air Water International Corp

Formerly: Universal Communication Systems Inc

407 Lincoln Rd., Ste 12f, Miami Beach, FL, 33139; ***PH:*** 1-305-672-6344; ***http://*** www.ucsy.com

General - Incorporation .... NV
Employees 4
Auditor .... Reuben E. Price & Co
Stk Agt .... Nevada Agency & Trust Company
Counsel .... NA
DUNS No. .... NA

Stock- Price on:12/24/2007 .... NA
Stock Exchange .... NA
Ticker Symbol .... NA
Outstanding Shares .... NA
E.P.S. .... -$0.003
Shareholders .... NA

Business: The group's principal activity is to provide wireless communication services, including the acquisition of radio-frequency spectrum internationally. The group operates in the United States, Argentina and Peru. The group has purchased and has acquired an interest in high-speed wireless Internet frequencies in the United States, Peru, Thailand, India and El Salvador. The group is in the process of revising its business plan, de-emphasizing participation in the wireless Internet market, and seeking new business activities. On 30-Apr-2004, the group acquired remaining 50% equity of solar style limited.

Primary SIC and add'l.: 4899

CIK No: 0001098207

Subsidiaries: Air Water Fridges and Freezers, Inc., AirWater Corporation, AirWater Patents Corp, Atmospheric Water Technologies, Digital Way S. A., Millennium Electric TOU, Ltd., Misa Water Products, Ltd., Solar One, Inc., Solar Style (USA, I)nc., Solar Style, Ltd.

Financial Data: ***Fiscal Year End:***09/30 ***Latest Annual Data:*** 09/30/2005

Year	Sales	Net Income
2005	$1,295,000	-$3,776,000
2004	$375,000	-$3,532,000
2003	NA	-$1,905,000

Curr. Assets:	$934,000	**Curr. Liab.:**	$2,414,000		
Plant, Equip.:	$41,000	**Total Liab.:**	$3,964,000	**Indic. Yr. Divd.:**	NA
Total Assets:	$1,512,000	**Net Worth:**	-$2,453,000	**Debt/ Equity:**	NA

Airbee Wireless Inc

9400 Key W Ave., Rockville, MD, 20850; ***PH:*** 1-301-517-1860; ***http://*** www.airbeewireless.com; ***Email:*** investors@airbeewireless.com

General - Incorporation .... DE
Employees 35
Auditor .... Bagell, Josephs, Levine & Co. LLC
Stk Agt .... Holladay Stock Transfer, Inc.
Counsel .... NA
DUNS No. .... NA

Stock- Price on:12/24/2007 .... NA
Stock Exchange .... OTC
Ticker Symbol .... ABEW
Outstanding Shares .... NA
E.P.S. .... -$0.075
Shareholders .... NA

Business: The group's principal activity is developing intelligent connectivity software for wireless voice, data and video communications. The software, when embedded on microchips or in various devices, will enable consumer and business devices to connect to each other over short distances without requiring the use of cables or wires. The company intends to license this software, which has been designed and engineered to comply with the recently released ZigBee standard for short-range, low-energy consumption, voice and data wireless communications to manufacturers of microprocessors and OEM manufacturers, thereby enabling them to develop an increasing number of wireless communications applications using the software, including consumer electronics, medical equipment, sensor and metering equipment, and industrial automation equipment.

Primary SIC and add'l.: 7372

CIK No: 0001297533

Subsidiaries: Airbee Automotive, Airbee Wireless (India) Pvt. Ltd., Connexus Technologies (India) Pvt. Ltd

Officers: Raja Sundaresan/45/Chmn., CEO, Eugene E. Sharer/74/Dir., Pres., Ramanujam Satagopan/43/CTO, Srinivasan Krishnamurthy/49/VP - Business Development, David L. McCartney/52/VP - Sales, Marketing, V. V. Sundaram/67/Pres., MD, Thomas Hou/Member - Technical Board, Satagopan Kanthadai/Head - Engineering

Directors: Raja Sundaresan/45/Chmn., CEO, Jeffrey H. Reed/Chmn. - Technical Board, Mal Gurian/80/Dir., Eugene E. Sharer/74/Dir., Pres., Wayne Manges/Member - Technical Board, Ivan Howitt/Member - Technical Board

Owners: Insiders/57.07%, Eugene E. Sharer/14.88%, Ramanujam Satagopan/5.56%, V.V. Sundaram/1.55%, Srinivasan Krishnamurthy/4.83%, Mal Gurian, Montgomery Equity Partners/6.56%, Sundaresan Raja/27.98%, David McCartney/1.92%

Financial Data: ***Fiscal Year End:***12/31 ***Latest Annual Data:*** 12/31/2006

Year	Sales	Net Income
2006	$129,000	-$4,796,000
2005	$13,000	-$3,782,000
2004	NA	-$1,137,000

Curr. Assets:	$84,000	**Curr. Liab.:**	$4,395,000		
Plant, Equip.:	$184,000	**Total Liab.:**	$4,395,000	**Indic. Yr. Divd.:**	NA
Total Assets:	$771,000	**Net Worth:**	-$3,623,000	**Debt/ Equity:**	NA

Aircastle Ltd

300 First Stamford Pl., 5th Fl., Stamford, CT, 06902; ***PH:*** 1-203-504-1020; ***Fax:*** 1-203-504-1021; ***http://*** www.aircastle.com; ***Email:*** info@aircastle.com

General - Incorporation .... Bermuda
Employees 45
Auditor .... Ernst & Young, LLP
Stk Agt ..... American Stock Transfer & Trust Co.
Counsel .... NA
DUNS No. .... NA

Stock- Price on:12/24/2007 .... $39.9
Stock Exchange .... NYSE
Ticker Symbol .... AYR
Outstanding Shares 67,270,000
E.P.S. $1.84
Shareholders .... NA

Business: The groups principle activities include acquiring and leaseing commercial jet aircraft. Customers served by the group include passenger and cargo airlines. The groups operates through two segments namely aircraft leasing and debt investments. The group operates from Europe, Asia, Latin America and Africa. The group's quarterly revenue for September 2007 was 105.26 millions of USD.

Primary SIC and add'l.: 3721

CIK No: 0001362988

Subsidiaries: ABH 10 Limited, ABH 11 Limited, ABH 12 Limited, ACS Aircraft Finance Bermuda Limited, ACS Aircraft Finance Ireland PLC, ACS Aircraft Leasing (Ireland) Limited, Aircastle Advisor (International) Limited, Aircastle Advisor (Ireland) Limited, Aircastle Advisor LLC, Aircastle Bermuda Holding II Limited, Aircastle Bermuda Holding III Limited, Aircastle Bermuda Holding IV Limited, Aircastle Bermuda Holding IX Limited, Aircastle Bermuda Holding Limited, Aircastle Bermuda Holding V Limited 48 Subsidiaries included in the Index

Officers: Ron Wainshal/CEO, Mark J. Zeidman/Principal Financial Officer, David Walton/COO, General Counsel, Sec., Joseph Schreiner/Exec. VP - Technical, Jonathan Lang/CTO, Aaron Dahlke/Chief Accounting Officer, Julia Hallisey/Investor Relations Officer, Kevin Fackrell/52/Chief Risk Officer, Michael D. Platt/Chief Investment Officer

Directors: Wesley R. Edens/Chmn., Joseph P. Adams/Dep. Chmn., Peter V. Ueberroth/Dir., Ronald L. Merriman/Dir., Ronald W. Allen/Dir., Douglas A. Hacker/Dir., John Z. Kukral/Dir.

Owners: Insiders, John Z. Kukral, David Walton, Mark Zeidman, Ronald W. Allen, Ron Wainshal, Wesley R. Edens, Kevin Fackrell, Joseph P. Adams, Fortress Investment Group Holdings LLC, Ronald L. Merriman, Douglas A. Hacker, Joseph Schreiner, Peter V. Ueberroth

Financial Data: ***Fiscal Year End:***12/31 ***Latest Annual Data:*** 12/31/2006

Year	Sales	Net Income
2006	$189,327,000	$51,206,000
2005	$36,026,000	$228,000

Curr. Assets:	$171,883,000	**Curr. Liab.:**	$188,497,000	**P/E Ratio:**	32.73
Plant, Equip.:	$1,591,861,000	**Total Liab.:**	$1,281,506,000	**Indic. Yr. Divd.:**	$2.600
Total Assets:	$1,918,703,000	**Net Worth:**	$637,197,000	**Debt/ Equity:**	0.8577

Airgas Inc

259 N Radnor-Chester Rd., Ste. 100, Radnor, PA, 19087; ***PH:*** 1-610-687-5253; ***Fax:*** 1-610-225-3271; ***http://*** www.airgas.com

General - Incorporation	DE	**Stock**- Price on:12/24/2007	$47.76
Employees	11,000	Stock Exchange	NYSE
Auditor	KPMG LLP	Ticker Symbol	ARG
Stk Agt	Bank of New York	Outstanding Shares	79,050,000
Counsel	NA	E.P.S	$1.92
DUNS No.	02-449-2860	Shareholders	NA

Business: The groups principle activity is to distribute industrial, medical, and specialty gases and related equipment, safety supplies and MRO products and services to industrial and commercial markets. In the year 2007 the group acquired Gartech Refrigerant Reclamation Center, Inc. The group operates from United States.

Primary SIC and add'l.: 7359 2819 2813 5084 9999 5169

CIK No: 0000804212

Subsidiaries: Airgas Canada Inc., Airgas Carbonic Inc., Airgas Data LLC, Airgas East Inc., Airgas Gaspro Inc., Airgas Great Lakes Inc., Airgas Gulf States Inc., Airgas Intermountain Inc., Airgas Investments Inc., Airgas Mid America Inc., Airgas Mid South Inc., Airgas Nor Pac Inc., Airgas North Central Inc., Airgas Northern California & Nevada Inc., Airgas S.A. de C.V. 29 Subsidiaries included in the Index

Officers: Peter McCausland/Chmn., CEO/$3,153,470.00, Dwight T. Wilson/Sr. VP - Human Resources, Fred Manley/Regional Pres. - East, Michael L. Molinini/COO, Exec. VP/$877,769.00, Dean A. Bertolino/VP, General Counsel, Sec., David E. Coyne/Dir. - Internal Audit, Kevin McBride/Regional Pres. - Great Lakes, Terry Lodge/Regional Pres. - Mid South, Robert M. McLaughlin/CFO, Sr. VP/$523,962.00, Leslie J. Graff/VP - Corporate Development, Robert A. Dougherty/CIO, Sr. VP, Jay Worley/Dir. - Investor Relations, James S. Ely/VP - Communications, Chuck Broadus/Business Unit Pres. - Airgas Specialty Products, Phil Filer/Business Unit Pres. - Airgas Dry Ice, Carbonic *(40 Officers included in Index)*

Directors: Peter McCausland/Chmn., CEO, Richard C. /65/Dir., William Albertini/65/Dir., John C. Van Roden/59/Dir., James W. Hovey/62/Dir., David M. Stout/54/Dir., Paula A. Sneed/60/Dir., Lee M. Thomas/64/Dir., Thacher W. Brown/60/Dir.

Owners: Lee M. Thomas, Peter McCausland/10.30%, Robert McLaughlin, Michael L. Molinini, FMR Corp./7.30%, Ted R. Schulte, Richard C., Paula A. Sneed, Insiders/11.90%, Bonnie F. McCausland/9.10%, Thacher W. Brown, James W. Hovey, John C. van Roden, David M. Stout, B. Shaun Powers *(17 Owners included in Index)*

Financial Data: ***Fiscal Year End:***03/31 ***Latest Annual Data:*** 3/31/2007

Year	Sales	Net Income
2007	$3,205,051,000	$154,416,000
2006	$2,829,610,000	$123,551,000
2005	$2,411,409,000	$92,022,000

Curr. Assets:	$549,499,000	**Curr. Liab.:**	$427,956,000	**P/E Ratio:**	23.07
Plant, Equip.:	$1,865,418,000	**Total Liab.:**	$2,150,884,000	**Indic. Yr. Divd.:**	$0.360
Total Assets:	$3,333,457,000	**Net Worth:**	$1,125,382,000	**Debt/ Equity:**	NA

Airnet Systems Inc

7250 Star Check Dr., Columbus, OH, 43217; ***PH:*** 1-614-409-4900; ***Fax:*** 1-614-409-7852; ***http://*** www.airnet.com

General - Incorporation	OH	**Stock**- Price on:12/24/2007	$3.37
Employees	670	Stock Exchange	AMEX
Auditor	Deloitte & Touche, LLP	Ticker Symbol	ANS
Stk Agt	EquiServe Trust Co N.A	Outstanding Shares	10,170,000
Counsel	Vorys, Sater, Seymour & Pease	E.P.S	$0.50
DUNS No.	11-825-7484	Shareholders	NA

Business: The group's principal activity is to provide air carrier for time-sensitive deliveries operating between 100 us cities and delivering over 20,000 time-critical shipments each working day. The group has three product lines: bank services consist of cancelled check delivery. It aslo includes delivery reports, interoffice mail and related information for the U.S. Banking industry. Express services offers products that include medical services offered to customers requiring specialized handling, the transportation of which is often highly regulated by varying governmental authorities. Air courier services provide transportation solutions to forwarders, integrators and courier companies. Retail services are provided to end consumers whose shipment needs are highly time sensitive. Mercury business services provides nationwide overnight delivery. Aviation services product line offers passenger charter services such as on-demand cargo charters.

Primary SIC and add'l.: 4522

CIK No: 0001011696

Subsidiaries: AirNet Management, Inc., AirNet Systems Inc., Fast Forward Solutions, LLC, Float Control, Inc., Jetride, Inc., time express.com, inc.

Officers: Bruce D. Parker/Chmn., CEO/$395,342.00, Larry M. Glasscock/Sr. VP - Express Services/$443,217.00, Craig A. Leach/VP - Information Systems/$236,114.00, Jeffery B. Harris/Sr. VP/$403,319.00, Gary W. Qualmann/CFO, Treasurer, Sec./$373,027.00, Ray L. Druseikis/56/VP - Finance, Controller, Principal Accounting Officer

Directors: Bruce D. Parker/Chmn., CEO, James E. Riddle/Dir., Russell M. Gertmenian/Dir., James M. Chadwick/Dir., Gerald Hellerman/Dir.

Owners: FMR Corp./5.80%, BCB Consultants, LLC/2.20%, Gary W. Qualmann, Hummingbird Management, LLC/5.10%, Gerald Hellerman, Heartland Advisors, Inc./14.00%, Bruce D. Parker, Joel E. Biggerstaff, Larry M. Glasscock, Craig A. Leach, Dimensional Fund Advisors LP/8.80%, Phillip Goldstein/13.10%, Russell M. Gertmenian, James M. Chadwick/5.20%, Clam Partners, LLC/4.20% *(18 Owners included in Index)*

Financial Data: ***Fiscal Year End:***12/31 ***Latest Annual Data:*** 03/31/2007

Year	Sales	Net Income
2007	NA	NA
2006	$172,807,000	-$13,292,000
2005	$196,413,000	-$4,246,000

Curr. Assets:	$28,797,000	**Curr. Liab.:**	$16,521,000		
Plant, Equip.:	$27,690,000	**Total Liab.:**	$22,532,000	**Indic. Yr. Divd.:**	NA
Total Assets:	$56,547,000	**Net Worth:**	$34,015,000	**Debt/ Equity:**	0.1530

Airspan Networks Inc

777 Yamato Rd., Ste. 310, Boca Raton, FL, 33431; ***PH:*** 1-561-893-8670; ***Fax:*** 1-561-893-8671; ***http://*** www.airspan.com; ***Email:*** sales@airspan.com

General - Incorporation	WA	**Stock**- Price on:12/24/2007	$3.43
Employees	292	Stock Exchange	NDQ
Auditor	Grant Thornton LLP	Ticker Symbol	AIRN
Stk Agt	Mellon Investor Services	Outstanding Shares	40,780,000
Counsel	Davis Polk & Wardwell	E.P.S	-$0.75
DUNS No.	NA	Shareholders	NA

Business: The group's principal activity is to supply broadband wireless access equipment to service providers such as Internet service providers and other telecommunications users. These systems enable communication service providers to deliver integrated high-speed data and voice services. The systems are based on the direct sequence code division multiple access technology which provides wide area coverage, security and resistance to fading. The integrated solutions include software tools that provide coverage and spectrum optimization and ongoing network management. The group also offers network installation, integration, training and support services. The group has international operations in Asia-Pacific, Europe, Africa and the Middle East. On 23rd dec 2003,the group acquired proximity business from nortel networks.

Primary SIC and add'l.: 3669

CIK No: 0001105542

Subsidiaries: Airspan Communications Co. Ltd., Airspan Communications Holdings, Airspan Communications Ltd., Airspan Japan Kabushiki Kaisha, Airspan Networks Eastern Europe Ltd, Airspan Networks Ltd, Airspan Networks PTY Ltd, Airspan Networks South Africa Pty Limited, ArelNet Ltd, Radionet Nordic Ab, Radionet Oy, Limited, Radionet Works Oy, Limited, WW Broadband Limited

Officers: Eric D. Stonestrom/Dir., CEO, Pres./$776,537.00, David Brant/Sr. VP, CFO/$373,788.00, Arthur Levine/VP - Finance, Controller, Henrik Smith-Peterson/Pres. - Asia Pacific/$554,543.00, Niall Porter/VP - Operations, Jeremy Rowe/VP - Engineering, Uzi Shalev/VP, GM - Airspan Israel, Airspan Finland, Joe Yeung/VP - Global Product Implementation, Paul Senior/CTO, Anders Rendahl/VP, GM EMEA, Amit Ancikovsky/VP, GM Americas

Directors: Eric D. Stonestrom/Dir., CEO, Pres., Matthew J. Desch/Chmn., David A. Twyver/Dir., Thomas S. Huseby/Dir., Guillermo Heredia/Dir., Julianne M. Biagini/Dir., Michael T. Flynn/Dir., Frederick R. Fromm/Dir., Bandel L. Carano/Dir.

Owners: Matthew Desch/1.00%, Michael T. Flynn, Julianne M. Biagini, Peter Aronstam/1.00%, Henrik Smith-Petersen/1.10%, David Brant, Alastair Westgarth, Stephens Investment Management, LLC/9.20%, Bandel L. Carano/33.30%, Merrill Lynch & Co., Inc./5.60%, Thomas Huseby, Guillermo Heredia, Kern Capital Management, LLC/7.30%, Oak Investment Partners XI, Limited Partnership/33.30%, Eric D. Stonestrom/2.60% *(18 Owners included in Index)*

Financial Data: ***Fiscal Year End:***12/31 ***Latest Annual Data:*** 07/01/2007

Year	Sales	Net Income
2007	NA	NA
2006	$127,812,000	-$29,202,000
2005	$110,966,000	-$15,077,000

Curr. Assets:	$88,567,000	**Curr. Liab.:**	$41,145,000		
Plant, Equip.:	$5,705,000	**Total Liab.:**	$42,852,000	**Indic. Yr. Divd.:**	NA
Total Assets:	$110,554,000	**Net Worth:**	$67,702,000	**Debt/ Equity:**	0.0251

Airtran Holdings Inc

9955 AirTran Blvd., Orlando, FL, 32827; ***PH:*** 1-407-318-5600; ***Fax:*** 1-407-318-5900; ***http://*** www.airtran.com; ***Email:*** info@airtranweb.com

General - Incorporation	NV	**Stock**- Price on:12/24/2007	$11.28
Employees	7,400	Stock Exchange	NYSE
Auditor	Ernst & Young LLP	Ticker Symbol	AAI
Stk Agt	American Stock Transfer & Trust Co.	Outstanding Shares	91,490,000
Counsel	Richard Magurno	E.P.S	$0.55
DUNS No.	80-786-0648	Shareholders	NA

Business: The group's principle activity is to operate scheduled airline services in short-haul markets. The group provides services to the leisure and business traveler. The group operates from United States.

Primary SIC and add'l.: 4512

CIK No: 0000948846

Subsidiaries: AirTran Airways, Inc

Officers: Robert Fornaro/Dir., CEO, Pres. - Airtran Holdings, Inc/$2,712,833.00, Joseph B. Leonard/Chmn., CEO/$956,250.00, Stephen Kolski/Sr. VP - Operations, Airtran Airways/$731,660.00, Tad Hutcheson/VP - Marketing, Sales, Airtran Airways, Stan Gadek/CFO, Sr. VP - Finance - Airtran Airways/$705,281.00, Jim Tabor/VP - Operations, Airtran Airways, Loral Blinde/VP - Human Resources, Richard Magurno/Sr. VP, General Counsel, Sec. - Airtran Airways/$692,810.00, Rocky Wiggins/CIO, VP - Airtran Airways, Alfred J. Smith/Sr. VP - Customer Service, Airtran Airways, Mark W. Osterberg/VP, Chief Accounting Officer - Airtran Airways, Kirk Thornburg/VP - Maintenance, Engineering, Airtran Airways, Klaus Goersch/VP - Flight Operations, Jean-Pierre Dagon/Dir. - Corporate Safety, Airtran Airways, Kevin P. Healy/VP - Planning, Airtran Airways *(16 Officers included in Index)*

Directors: Robert Fornaro/Dir., CEO, Pres. - Airtran Holdings, Inc, Joseph B. Leonard/Chmn., CEO, Veronica J. Biggins/Dir., Don L. Chapman/Dir., Jere Drummond/Dir., William J. Usery/84/Dir., Lewis H. Jordan/Dir., John F. Fiedler/Dir., Robert L. Priddy/Dir., Peter G. D'Aloia/Dir., Alexis P. Michas/Dir.

Owners: Litespeed Management LLC/5.90%, David H. Treitel, John F. Bergstrom, Elizabeth T. Solberg, James R. Boris, David C. Reeve, Samuel K. Skinner, Octavian Master Fund, L.P./6.00%, T. Rowe Price Associates, Inc./5.10%, Insiders/7.30%, Curtis E. Sawyer, Carol N. Skornicka, Ulice Payne, Timothy E. Hoeksema/3.50%, Richard H. Sonnentag *(17 Owners included in Index)*

Financial Data: Fiscal Year End:12/31 Latest Annual Data: 12/31/2006

Year	Sales	Net Income
2006	$1,892,083,000	$14,714,000
2005	$1,450,544,000	$8,076,000
2004	$1,041,422,000	$12,255,000

Curr. Assets:	$416,957,000	*Curr. Liab.:*	$398,087,000		
Plant, Equip.:	$1,015,229,000	*Total Liab.:*	$1,224,299,000	*Indic. Yr. Divd.:*	NA
Total Assets:	$1,603,582,000	*Net Worth:*	$379,283,000	*Debt/ Equity:*	2.1449

Airtrax Inc

200 Fwy. Dr., Unit 1, Blackwood, NJ, 08012; *PH:* 1-856-232-3000; *Fax:* 1-856-227-9168; *http://* www.airtrax.com; *Email:* info@airtrax.com

General - Incorporation	NJ	Stock - Price on:12/24/2007	$0.51
Employees	13	Stock Exchange	OTC
Auditor	Robert G. Jeffrey, CPA	Ticker Symbol	AITX
Stk Agt	Signature Stock Transfer, Inc.	Outstanding Shares	24,820,000
Counsel	NA	E.P.S.	-$0.43
DUNS No.	NA	Shareholders	NA

Business: The group's principal activity is to design forklift vehicle using omni-directional technology. The products include omni-directional forklift, omni-directional wheel chair, military and others. Omni-directional forklift is available under atx and atx-e series. It was provided with research contracts under the department of defense's small business innovation research program ('sbir') and supervised by naval air warfare center aircraft to develop an omni-directional multiple purpose mobility platform (mp2) for military. It has also developed a helicopter ground-handling machine.

Primary SIC and add'l.: 3537

CIK No: 0001081372

Officers: Robert M. Watson/Dir., CEO, Acting CFO, Pres., Jason Bogutski/Investor Relations Officer, Robert Mullowney/VP - Engineering, Gary Geraci/Investor Relations Officer, Frank Cooper/Mgr. - Production, Raymond Rebholz/VP - Electrical Systems, Nicholas E. Fenelli/COO, Peter Greenwood/VP - Sales, Theodore G. Harrison/Controller

Directors: Robert M. Watson/Dir., CEO, Acting CFO, Pres., Andrew Guzzetti/Chmn., Donald B. Harris/Dir., James Hudson/Dir., Robert Borski/59/Dir., William Hungerville/Dir., Barney D. Harris/47/Dir., Peter Amico/Dir., Fil Filipov/Dir.

Owners: Fil Filipov, Barney D. Harris, Nicholas Fenelli, Peter Amico, William Hungerville, Crescent International, Ltd./5.50%, Robert M. Watson/1.23%, Robert Borski, Andrew Guzzetti, James Hudson, Insiders/5.40%

Financial Data: Fiscal Year End:12/31 Latest Annual Data: 12/31/2006

Year	Sales	Net Income
2006	$1,347,000	-$4,325,000
2005	$719,000	-$14,935,000
2004	NA	-$2,272,000

Curr. Assets:	$2,451,000	*Curr. Liab.:*	$5,489,000		
Plant, Equip.:	$284,000	*Total Liab.:*	$6,047,000	*Indic. Yr. Divd.:*	NA
Total Assets:	$2,884,000	*Net Worth:*	-$3,163,000	*Debt/ Equity:*	NA

Airxcel Inc

3050 N St. Francis, Wichita, KS, 67204; *PH:* 1-316-832-3400; *http://* www.airxcel.com; *Email:* rvpsales@airxcel.com

General - Incorporation	DE	Stock - Price on:12/24/2007	NA
Employees	NA	Stock Exchange	NA
Auditor	Ernst & Young LLP	Ticker Symbol	NA
Stk Agt	NA	Outstanding Shares	NA
Counsel	NA	E.P.S.	NA
DUNS No.	NA	Shareholders	NA

Business: The group's principle activities include designing, manufacturing and marketing recreational vehicle air conditioners and specialty wall mount air conditioners, environmental control units and heat pumps for various applications. New registrant. The group operates from United States.

Primary SIC and add'l.: 3585

CIK No: 0001050096

Subsidiaries: Airxcel Holdings Corporation

Officers: Mel Adams/Dir., CEO, Pres., Larry E. Sanford/General Counsel, VP, Richard L. Schreck/CFO, Sec., Treasurer, Gregory G. Guinn/VP

Directors: Mel Adams/Dir., CEO, Pres., Tad Donnelly/Dir., Larry Jones/Dir., Nick Sheppard/Dir., Steve Sherrill/Dir.

Aixtron Aktiengesellschaft

Kackertstr. 15-17, Aachen, CA, 52072; *PH:* 1-408-747-7140; *Fax:* 1-408-747-7198; *http://* www.aixtron.com

General - Incorporated Federal Republic of Germany	$8.48	Stock - Price on:12/24/2007	$8.48
Employees	NA	Stock Exchange	NDQ
Auditor	Deloitte & Touche Gmbh	Ticker Symbol	AIXG
Stk Agt	JP Morgan Chase Bank, N.A.	Outstanding Shares	NA
Counsel	NA	E.P.S.	$0.38
DUNS No.	NA	Shareholders	NA

Business: The groups principle activity is to provide deposition equipment. The products of the group include Optoelectronic devices, Silicon Carbide, Metal and oxide films and solar cells. The group products sold under the trade names OVPD(R), Tricent(R) and AVD(R), Customers served by the group include compound, organic, silicon semiconductors. The group operates from three geographical segments namely Asia, Europe and the United States. In the year 2005, the group acquired Genus, Inc. The group operates from the United Kingdom, Japan, South Korea, Sweden, Taiwan and the United States. The quarterly revenue of the group for September 2007 was 51.74 millions of EURO.

Primary SIC and add'l.: 3559

CIK No: 0001089496

Subsidiaries: AIXTRON Chu-sik-hoe-sa (AIXTRON Cshs), AIXTRON Inc., AIXTRON Kabushiki Kaisha, (AIXTRON KK), AIXTRON Taiwan Co., Ltd. (AIXTRON Taiwan), Dotron GmbH, Epigress AB, Thomas Swan Scientific Equipment Ltd. (TSSE Ltd.)

Officers: Paul Hyland/55/CEO, Pres., Wolfgang Breme/48/CFO, Exec. VP, Bernd Schulte/46/COO, Exec. VP, William W.R. Elder/70/Exec. VP, Guido Pickert/Investor Relations Officer

Directors: Paul Hyland/55/CEO, Pres., Kim Schindelhauer/Chmn. - Supervisory Board, Holger Jurgensen/Dep. Chmn., Rudiger Von Rosen/Member - Supervisory Board, Joachim Simmross/Member - Supervisory Board, Karl-Hermann Kuklies/Member - Supervisory Board, Wolfgang Blattchen/Member - Supervisory Board

Owners: Holger Jrgensen/11.18%, Rudiger von Rosen, Karl-Hermann Kuklies, Joachim Simmro, Wolfgang Blttchen, Kim Schindelhauer/1.16%, Insiders/12.52%, Approximate% held by U.S. holders/11.74%, William W.R. Elder

Financial Data: Fiscal Year End:12/31 Latest Annual Data: 12/31/2006

Year	Sales	Net Income
2006	$226,676,000	$6,839,000
2005	$165,108,000	-$113,666,000
2004	$191,021,000	$9,750,000

Curr. Assets:	$176,009,000	*Curr. Liab.:*	$100,938,000		
Plant, Equip.:	$54,511,000	*Total Liab.:*	$105,017,000	*Indic. Yr. Divd.:*	NA
Total Assets:	$345,682,000	*Net Worth:*	$240,666,000	*Debt/ Equity:*	NA

AK Steel Holding Corp

9227 Ctr. Pointe Dr., West Chester, OH, 45069; *PH:* 1-513-425-5000; *Fax:* 1-513-425-2676; *http://* www.aksteel.com

General - Incorporation	DE	Stock - Price on:12/24/2007	$35.67
Employees	7,000	Stock Exchange	NYSE
Auditor	Deloitte & Touche LLP	Ticker Symbol	AKS
Stk Agt	Computershare Investor Services LLC	Outstanding Shares	111,320,000
Counsel	NA	E.P.S.	$2.08
DUNS No.	60-607-2130	Shareholders	NA

Business: The group's principle activity is to provide flat rolled carbon, stainless and electrical steel products. Customers served by the group include automotive manufacturers, industrial machinery and equipment, and construction markets, and manufacturers of food handling. The group operates from United States.

Primary SIC and add'l.: 3316 3312 3479

CIK No: 0000918160

Subsidiaries: Advanced Materials Processing Inc., AFSG Holdings, Inc., AH (UK) Inc., AH Management, Inc., AK ISG Coatings, AK Asset Management Company, AK Coatings Inc., AK Electric Supply LLC, AK Electrogalvanizing LLC, AK Steel BV Holland, AK Steel Corporation, AK Steel Europe Limited, AK Steel GMBH, AK Steel Limited, AK Steel Properties, Inc. 49 Subsidiaries included in the Index

Officers: James L. Wainscott/Chmn., CEO, Pres./$5,261,286.00, Roger K. Newport/Controller, Chief Accounting Officer, David C. Horn/56/Sr. VP, General Counsel, Sec./$1,888,420.00, Alan H. McCoy/VP - Government, Public Relations, Albert E. Ferrara/CFO, VP - Finance/$1,407,248.00, John F. Kaloski/58/Sr. VP - Operations/$1,862,811.00, Douglas W. Gant/49/VP - Sales, Customer Service/$1,221,198.00, Doug Mitterholzer/Corporate Mgr. - Investor Relations, Investment Administration, Thomas F. McKenna/62/VP - Labor Relations, Lawrence F. Zizzo/59/VP - Human Resources

Directors: James L. Wainscott/Chmn., CEO, Pres., Richard A. Abdoo/Dir., Bonnie G. Hill/Dir., Robert H. Jenkins/Dir., Lawrence A. Leser/Dir., Daniel J. Meyer/Dir., Shirley D. Peterson/Dir., James A. Thomson/Dir., John S. Brinzo/Dir., William K. Gerber/Dir.

Owners: JGD Management Corp./10.12%, James A. Thomson, The Goldman Sachs Group, Inc/5.23%, Lawrence A. Leser, Donald Smith& Co./9.93%, Insiders/1.63%, Daniel J. Meyer, Douglas W. Gant, LMM LLC/7.65%, Richard A. Abdoo, John S. Brinzo, James L. Wainscott, Albert E. Ferrara, Shirley D. Peterson, William K. Gerber *(20 Owners included in Index)*

Financial Data: Fiscal Year End:12/31 Latest Annual Data: 12/31/2006

Year	Sales	Net Income
2006	$6,069,000,000	$12,000,000
2005	$5,647,400,000	-$2,300,000
2004	$5,217,300,000	$238,400,000

Curr. Assets:	$2,547,500,000	*Curr. Liab.:*	$931,500,000	*P/E Ratio:*	57.53
Plant, Equip.:	$2,133,400,000	*Total Liab.:*	$5,100,600,000	*Indic. Yr. Divd.:*	NA
Total Assets:	$5,517,600,000	*Net Worth:*	$417,000,000	*Debt/ Equity:*	1.8588

Akamai Technologies Inc

8 Cambridge Ctr., Cambridge, MA, 02142; *PH:* 1-617-444-3000; *Fax:* 1-617-444-3001; *http://* www.akamai.com

General - Incorporation	DE	Stock - Price on:12/24/2007	$47.72
Employees	1,058	Stock Exchange	NDQ
Auditor	PricewaterhouseCoopers LLP	Ticker Symbol	AKAM
Stk Agt	BankBoston, N.A.	Outstanding Shares	164,920,000
Counsel	Hale & Dorr LLP	E.P.S.	$0.49
DUNS No.	NA	Shareholders	NA

Business: The group's principal activity is to provide a broad range of secure e-business infrastructure solutions and software. The group's products and services enable customers to reduce the complexity, cost of deploying and operating a uniform ip infrastructure while ensuring superior performance, reliability, scalability and manageability. The group provides its services and software to enterprises and government agencies. The group's major customers include American suzuki motor corporation, apple computer, inc, barnes & noble, best buy.com inc, canon Japan, fedex corporation, general motors corporation ll bean, inc, microsoft corporation, molex incorporated, Nasdaq, sony music entertainment Japan, staples inc, verisign inc and veritas software corporation.

Primary SIC and add'l.: 4899 7375 7373 9651

CIK No: 0001086222

CIK No: 0001086222

Subsidiaries: Akamai International Bv, Akamai Japan K.k., Akamai Sales LLC, Akamai Technologies Gmbh, Akamai Technologies India Private Ltd., Akamai Technologies Ltd., Akamai Technologies Netherlands Bv, Akamai Technologies Sarl, Akamai Technologies Securities Corporation, K Streaming LLC, Kahua Hk Limited

Officers: Paul Sagan/Dir., CEO, Pres./$4,031,360.00, George Conrades/Exec. Chmn., Chris Schoettle/Exec. VP - Technology, Networks/$1,569,894.00, Robert W. Hughes/Exec. VP - Global Sales, Services, Marketing/$2,294,607.00, Melanie Haratunian/VP, General Counsel/$1,018,693.00, Tom Leighton/Dir., Co - Founder, Chief Scientist, J. D. Sherman/CFO/$1,705,515.00, Michael M. Afergan/CTO, Robert Wood/VP - Business Development, Sandra Smith/Dir. - Investor Relations, Jennifer C. Heizer/Sr. Investor Relations Analyst

Directors: Paul Sagan/Dir., CEO, Pres., George Conrades/Exec. Chmn., Frederic V. Salerno/Dir., Naomi O. Seligman/Dir., Martin M. Coyne/Dir., Tom Leighton/Dir., Co - Founder, Chief Scientist, Ronald Graham/Dir., Pete Kight/Dir., Geoffrey Moore/Dir.

Owners: FMR Corp./14.20%, Melanie Haratunian, Robert Cobuzzi, AXA Financial, Inc./6.60%, Naomi O. Seligman, Ronald L. Graham, Peter J. Kight, Robert Hughes, Paul Sagan, Insiders/4.60%, Frederic V. Salerno, Geoffrey A. Moore, George H. Conrades, Donald J. Sherman, Chris Schoettle *(17 Owners included in Index)*

Financial Data: ***Fiscal Year End:***12/31 ***Latest Annual Data:*** 12/31/2006

Year	Sales	Net Income
2006	$428,672,000	$57,401,000
2005	$283,115,000	$327,998,000
2004	$210,015,000	$34,364,000

Curr. Assets:	$374,673,000	***Curr. Liab.:***	$89,264,000	***P/E Ratio:***	125.58
Plant, Equip.:	$86,623,000	***Total Liab.:***	$293,239,000	***Indic. Yr. Divd.:***	NA
Total Assets:	$1,247,932,000	***Net Worth:***	$954,693,000	***Debt/ Equity:***	0.1721

Akeena Solar Inc

16005 Los Gatos Blvd, Los Gatos, CA, 95032; ***PH:*** 1-408-359-7979; ***http://*** www.akeena.net; ***Email:*** info@akeena.net

General - Incorporation	DE	***Stock***- Price on:12/24/2007	$3.83
Employees	106	Stock Exchange	NDQ
Auditor	Burr, Pilger & Mayer, LLP	Ticker Symbol	AKNS
Stk Agt	Empire Stock Transfer Inc.	Outstanding Shares	18,560,000
Counsel	DLA Piper US LLP	E.P.S	-$0.28
DUNS No.	NA	Shareholders	NA

Business: The groups principal activity is to design and integrate solar power systems. The groups services include Silicon Refiners, Wafer and Cell Manufacturers, Module Manufacturers, Distributors and Designer. The group operates from the United States. Of the total sale in the year 2006 was $13,390,139.

Primary SIC and add'l.: 5074

CIK No: 0001347452

Subsidiaries: Akeena Corp.

Officers: Barry Cinnamon/50/Chmn., CEO, Pres., Sec., Treasurer, Principal Executive Officer/$143,392.00, Bill Scott/Exec. VP, Steve Daniel/VP - Sales, Jeff Brown/Dir. - Installation, Development, Gary Effren/CFO, Jim Curran/COO, Gary Mull/VP - Marketing, Kirsten Berry/Contact - Media Relations

Directors: Barry Cinnamon/50/Chmn., CEO, Pres., Sec., Treasurer, Principal Executive Officer, Edward Roffman/58/Dir., Steve Westly/Member - Board Of Advisor, Joe Abrams/Member - Advisory Board, George L. Lauro/49/Dir., Jon Mathew Witkin/54/Dir., Ed Roffman/57/Dir.

Owners: George Lauro, Insiders/34.50%, Barry Cinnamon/33.90%, BB Trust/5.70%, Ed Roffman, Angeleno Investors II L.P./5.40%, David Wallace, Jon Witkin

Financial Data: ***Fiscal Year End:***12/31 ***Latest Annual Data:*** 12/31/2006

Year	Sales	Net Income
2006	$13,390,000	-$1,809,000

Curr. Assets:	$7,057,000	***Curr. Liab.:***	$6,067,000		
Plant, Equip.:	$195,000	***Total Liab.:***	$6,138,000	***Indic. Yr. Divd.:***	NA
Total Assets:	$7,529,000	***Net Worth:***	$1,391,000	***Debt/ Equity:***	0.0264

Akorn Inc

2500 Millbrook Dr., Buffalo Grove, IL, 60089; ***PH:*** 1-847-279-6100; ***http://*** www.akorn.com; ***Email:*** investor.relations@akorn.com

General - Incorporation	LA	***Stock***- Price on:12/24/2007	NA
Employees	327	Stock Exchange	NDQ
Auditor	BDO Seidman LLP	Ticker Symbol	AKRX
Stk Agt	Computershare Investor Services LLC	Outstanding Shares	NA
Counsel	Luce Forward Hamilton & Scripps LLP	E.P.S	-$0.24
DUNS No.	06-264-9876	Shareholders	NA

Business: The group's principal activities are to manufacture and market diagnostic and therapeutic pharmaceuticals in specialty areas such as ophthalmology, rheumatology, anesthesia and antidotes. The activities are carried out through three business segments: ophthalmic, injectable and contract services. The ophthalmic segment manufactures, markets and distributes diagnostic and therapeutic pharmaceuticals and surgical instruments and related supplies. The injectable segment manufactures, markets and distributes injectable pharmaceuticals, primarily in niche markets. The contract services segment provides contract-manufacturing services as well as product research and development services to pharmaceutical and biotechnology companies.

Primary SIC and add'l.: 3841 8731 2834

CIK No: 0000003116

Subsidiaries: Akorn (New Jersey) Inc.

Officers: Arthur S. Przybyl/Dir., CEO, Pres./$1,596,404.00, Neill Shanahan/VP - Human Resources, Jay W. Stern/VP - Contract Manufacturing, Michael P. Stehn/VP - Operations, GM - Somerset, Abu Alam/Sr. VP - New Business Development/$307,345.00, Mark M. Silverberg/Sr. VP - Global Quality Assurance, Decatur Operations/$307,848.00, John R. Sabat/Sr. VP - National Accounting, Trade Relations/$326,611.00, Jeffrey A. Whitnell/Sr. VP - Finance, CFO, Sec., Treasurer/$740,292.00, Sam Boddapati/VP - Regulatory Affairs, Douglas R. Pinnell/VP - Vaccine Sales, Shawn Silvestri/VP - New Product Development

Directors: Arthur S. Przybyl/Dir., CEO, Pres., John N. Kapoor/Chmn., Subhash V. Kapre/Dir., Randall J. Wall/Dir., Jerry I. Treppel/Dir., Jerry N. Ellis/Dir., Ronald M. Johnson/Dir.

Owners: Jeffrey A. Whitnell/0.37%, Pequot Capital Management Inc./23.01%, John R. Sabat/0.28%, Abu S. Alam, Arthur S. Przybyl/1.89%, Arjun C. Waney/5.96%, John N. Kapoor/33.09%, Ronald M. Johnson/0.08%, Mark Silverberg/0.09%, Insiders/35.83%, Jerry I. Treppel/0.57%, Jerry N. Ellis/0.12%

Financial Data: ***Fiscal Year End:***12/31 ***Latest Annual Data:*** 12/31/2006

Year	Sales	Net Income
2006	$71,250,000	-$5,963,000
2005	$44,484,000	-$8,609,000
2004	$50,708,000	-$3,026,000

Curr. Assets:	$39,654,000	***Curr. Liab.:***	$10,253,000		
Plant, Equip.:	$33,486,000	***Total Liab.:***	$11,769,000	***Indic. Yr. Divd.:***	NA
Total Assets:	$82,083,000	***Net Worth:***	$70,314,000	***Debt/ Equity:***	NA

Aksys Ltd

Two Marriott Dr., Libertyville, IL, 60069; ***PH:*** 1-847-229-2020; ***http://*** www.aksys.com; ***Email:*** productinfo@aksys.com

General - Incorporation	DE	***Stock***- Price on:12/24/2007	$0.03
Employees	87	Stock Exchange	OTC
Auditor	KPMG LLP	Ticker Symbol	AKSY
Stk Agt	EquiServe Trust Co N.A	Outstanding Shares	32,450,000
Counsel	Kirkland & Ellis LLP	E.P.S	-$1.733
DUNS No.	80-868-0730	Shareholders	NA

Business: The group's principal activity is to provide hemodialysis products and services for patients suffering from end-stage renal diseases, commonly known as chronic kidney failure. Currently in the development stage, it has developed an automated personal hemodialysis system, known as the aksys phd personal hemodialysis system. This system is designed to enable patients to perform frequent hemodialysis at alternate sites, such as the patient's home. The group plans to market this system in several foreign markets, including Japan and Europe.

Primary SIC and add'l.: 3841

CIK No: 0000902600

Subsidiaries: Aksys Healthcare, Ltd., Aksys International Inc, Aksys Japan, K.K.

Financial Data: ***Fiscal Year End:***12/31 ***Latest Annual Data:*** 12/31/2005

Year	Sales	Net Income
2005	$2,669,000	-$34,198,000
2004	$2,416,000	-$27,683,000
2003	$1,491,000	-$22,282,000

Curr. Assets:	$13,154,000	***Curr. Liab.:***	$7,123,000		
Plant, Equip.:	$5,186,000	***Total Liab.:***	$22,461,000	***Indic. Yr. Divd.:***	NA
Total Assets:	$19,156,000	***Net Worth:***	-$3,305,000	***Debt/ Equity:***	NA

Aktiebolaget Electrolux

St. Goransgatan 143, Se-105 45, Stockholm; ***PH:*** 46-87386000; ***http://*** www.electrolux.com; ***Email:*** press@electrolux.com

General - Incorporation	Sweden	***Stock***- Price on:12/24/2007	NA
Employees	NA	Stock Exchange	NA
Auditor	PricewaterhouseCoopers LLP	Ticker Symbol	NA
Stk Agt	NA	Outstanding Shares	NA
Counsel	NA	E.P.S	NA
DUNS No.	35-394-8151	Shareholders	NA

Business: The group's principal activities are the design, manufacture, development and distribution of consumer durables and professional products. The group operates through three divisions: consumer durables, professional indoor products and outdoor products. Consumer durables include refrigerators, freezers, cookers, washing machines, dishwashers, room air conditioners, microwave ovens, floor care products, garden equipment and light duty chainsaws. Indoor products include food service equipment for hotels, laundry equipment for apartment-house laundry rooms, launderettes, hotels and other professional users, compressor and motors, absorption refrigerators and other equipment for recreational vehicles. Outdoor products include high-performance chainsaws, clearing saws and turf-care equipment, power cutters, diamond tools and related cutting equipment.

Primary SIC and add'l.: 3639 3556 3524 5099 3589

CIK No: 0000813810

Officers: Hans Straberg/51/Dir., CEO, Pres., Keith R. McLoughlin/52/Head - Major Appliances North, Latin America, Cecilia Vieweg/53/Sec., Harry De Vos/52/Head - Group Staff Human Resources, Organizational Development, Fredrik Rystedt/45/CFO, Lars Goran Johansson/54/Head - Group Staff Communications, Branding, Magnus Yngen/50/Head - Major Appliances Europe, Detlef Munchow/56/Head - Professional Indoor Products, Susanne Fastesson/Assist. - Investor Relations, Financial Information, Peter Nyquist/VP - Investor Relations, Financial Information, Anders Edholm/VP - Media Relations - Issues Management, Ulrich Gartner/VP - Public Relations Europe, Maria Norin/Mgr. - Financial Information, Gunilla Nordstrom/49/Head - Major Appliances Asia Pacific, Morten Falkenberg/50/Head - Floor Care, Small Appliances *(21 Officers included in Index)*

Directors: Hans Straberg/51/Dir., CEO, Pres., Peggy Bruzelius/59/Dep. Chmn., Marcus Wallenberg/52/Chmn., Bengt Liwang/63/Dir., Peter Karlsson/43/Dir., Torben Ballegaard Sorensen/57/Dir., John Lupo/62/Dir., Johan Molin/49/Dir., Gerd Almlof/49/Dir., Ulf Carlsson/50/Dir., Louis R. Hughes/59/Dir., Caroline Sundewall/50/Dir., Barbara Milian Thoralfsson/49/Dir., Gunilla Brandt/55/Dir., Ola Bertilsson/53/Dir.

Akzo Nobel

Strawinskylaan 2555, Amsterdam, 1077 ZZ; ; ***http://*** www.akzonobel.com; ***Email:*** investor.relations@akzonobel.com

General - Incorporation	Netherlands	***Stock***- Price on:12/24/2007	NA
Employees	61,900	Stock Exchange	OTC
Auditor	KPMG LLP	Ticker Symbol	AKZOY
Stk Agt	Algemene Bank Nederland	Outstanding Shares	NA
Counsel	NA	E.P.S	$4.37
DUNS No.	40-237-1223	Shareholders	NA

Business: The group's principal activity is to manufacture diversified chemical products with activities in over 75 countries. The group's activities are carried out through four divisions: chemicals, coatings, pharmaceuticals and other. The chemicals division manufactures among others: polymer and rubber chemicals, fluid cracking and hydro processing catalysts, detergents, deicing and evaporated salt. The coating division produces paints, stains and synthetic resins for the industrial, professional and

consumer markets. The pharmaceuticals division is engaged in oral contraceptives (desogen, mercilon), psychiatric drugs (remeron, risperdal) and non-prescription products such as pregnancy tests, analgesic creams, hay fever preparations and vitamins. The group acquired the specialty coatings business of techni-coat international n.v. Of Belgium and the remaining 50% of interpon powder coatings (Korea) co. Ltd. Of South Korea in 2003.

Primary SIC and add'l.: 2823 2812 2819 2822 2851 2834 2821

CIK No: 0000003124

Subsidiaries: A.B.S. Italia S.r.l., A.O. Ankorit, Aacifar - Produtos Quimicos e Farmaceuticos, Lda, Acordis B.V., AgVax Developments Limited, Akcros Chemicals B.V., Akcros Chemicals Ltd, Akzo Nobel (C) Holdings B.V., Akzo Nobel (Malaysia) Sdn Bhd, Akzo Nobel (Netherlands Antilles) NV, Akzo Nobel (Shanghai) Co. Ltd., Akzo Nobel A/S (Denmark), Akzo Nobel AB, Akzo Nobel Aerospace Coatings B.V., Akzo Nobel Aerospace Coatings Ltd 599 Subsidiaries included in the Index

Officers: Hans G.J. Wijers/57/CEO, Rob R. Frohn/57/CFO, Toon Wilderbeek/GM, Th. J.A. Luijckx/Investor Relations Officer, Andre Veneman/Dir. - Corporate Social Responsibility, John De Munnik/Head - Corporate Public Affairs

Directors: Maarten Van Den Bergh/66/Chmn., Karel Vuursteen/67/Dep. Chmn., Peggy Bruzelius/59/Member - Supervisory Board, Antony Burgmans/61/Member - Supervisory Board, Abraham Cohen/72/Member - Supervisory Board, American, Virginia Bottomley/60/Member - Supervisory Board, Leif L. Darner/56/Dir., Dolf Van Den Brink/60/Member - Supervisory Board, Uwe-Ernst Bufe/64/Member - Supervisory Board, Cees Van Lede/66/Member - Supervisory Board, Alain Merieux/70/Member - Supervisory Board, French, Louis Hughes/59/Member - Supervisory Board

Owners: Leif Darner, Hans Wijers, Virginia Bottomley, Karel Vuursteen, Rob Frohn

Financial Data: ***Fiscal Year End:***12/31 ***Latest Annual Data:*** 12/31/2006

Year	Sales	Net Income
2006	$18,136,961,000	$1,320,300,000
2005	$15,397,200,000	$840,924,000
2004	$17,311,507,000	$1,135,181,000

Curr. Assets:	$9,309,435,000	***Curr. Liab.:***	$4,829,657,000	***P/E Ratio:***	8.10
Plant, Equip.:	$4,395,279,000	***Total Liab.:***	$11,316,291,000	***Indic. Yr. Divd.:***	NA
Total Assets:	$20,772,280,000	***Net Worth:***	$9,455,989,000	***Debt/ Equity:***	NA

Alabama Gas Corp

605 Richard Arrington Jr. Blvd. N, Birmingham, AL, 35203; ***PH:*** 1-205-326-8100; ***Fax:*** 1-205-326-2590; ***http://*** www.alagasco.com

General - Incorporation	AL	***Stock***- Price on:12/24/2007	NA
Employees	1,530	Stock Exchange	NYSE
Auditor	PricewaterhouseCoopers LLP	Ticker Symbol	NA
Stk Agt	Bank of New York	Outstanding Shares	71,730,000
Counsel	NA	E.P.S.	NA
DUNS No.	00-690-0104	Shareholders	NA

Business: The group's principle activities include distributing and transporting natural gas in the state of Alabama. The company purchases natural gas through interstate suppliers and marketers and distributes it to residential, commercial, industrial and other end-users. There are two main service categories under which gas is supplied to customers namely, interruptible and firm. The company serves approximately 188 cities and communities in 27 counties in central and north Alabama. The company served an average of 427,413 residential customers and 35,463 commercial, industrial and transportation customers in 2003. The distribution system of the company includes 9,810 miles of main and more than 11,494 miles of service lines, odorization and regulation facilities and customer meters. The company also operates two liquified natural gas facilities. The group operates from United States.

Primary SIC and add'l.: 4924 4922

CIK No: 0000003146

Subsidiaries: Alabama Gas Corporation, Energen Resources Corporation, Energen Resources TEAM, Inc

Officers: James T. McManus/CEO - Energen, Michael Wm. Warren/Chmn., CEO, Joseph G. Wheeler/VP - State Operations, Kenneth A. Smith/VP - Birmingham Operations, Amy Watson Stewart/VP - Rates, Regulations, Steve Murphy/Dir. - Commercial, Industrial Marketing, Judy Tramble/Mgr. - Business Development, Dan Javorka/Contact - Anniston, Birmingham Metro, Warren McCullars/Contact - Birmingham Metro, Gadsden, Jasper, Tuscaloosa, Steven R. Chapman/VP - Administration, External Affairs, Grace B. Carr/52/VP, Controller, David J. Woodruff/General Counsel, Sec. - Energen, Roger A. Putnam/VP - Technical Services, Sidney W. Quick/VP - Gas Supply, Dudley C. Reynolds/COO, Pres. *(32 Officers included in Index)*

Directors: Michael Wm. Warren/Chmn., CEO, James S.M. French/Dir., Michael T. Goodrich/Dir., David W. Wilson/Dir., Judy M. Merritt/Dir., Julian W. Banton/Dir.

Curr. Assets:	$489,579,000	***Curr. Liab.:***	$570,642,000		
Plant, Equip.:	$2,252,414,000	***Total Liab.:***	$1,634,818,000	***Indic. Yr. Divd.:***	NA
Total Assets:	$2,836,887,000	***Net Worth:***	$1,202,069,000	***Debt/ Equity:***	0.4845

Alabama National Bancorp

1927 1st Ave. N, Birmingham, AL, 35203; ***PH:*** 1-205-583-3600; ***Fax:*** 1-205-421-2255; ***http://*** www.alabamanational.com

General - Incorporation	DE	***Stock***- Price on:12/24/2007	$62.5
Employees	1,789	Stock Exchange	NDQ
Auditor	PricewaterhouseCoopers LLP	Ticker Symbol	ALAB
Stk Agt	Computershare Investor Services LLC	Outstanding Shares	20,600,000
Counsel	NA	E.P.S.	$4.03
DUNS No.	19-569-3734	Shareholders	NA

Business: The group's principal activity is to provide banking and bank-related services to individual and corporate customers. The group offers consumer, residential mortgage, commercial and real estate construction lending and accepts deposits from individuals, small businesses and other organizations. Other services provided by the group include trust services, investment services, securities brokerage services, insurance services, safe deposit and night depository facilities, sale of traveler's checks, money orders and cashier's checks. The group operates through 78 banking offices and four insurance offices in the states of Alabama, Georgia and Florida. On 19-Jun-2003, the group acquired millennium bank and on 27-Feb-2004, cypress bankshares, inc. And Indian river banking company.

Primary SIC and add'l.: 6712 6331 6021 6311

CIK No: 0000926966

Subsidiaries: AEB Investments, Inc., Alabama Exchange Bank, Alabama National Statutory Trust I, Alabama National Statutory Trust II, Alabama National Statutory Trust III, ANB Insurance Services, Inc., Ashland Insurance, Inc., Bank of Dadeville, Bill Eyerly Insurance, Inc., CBN Investments, Inc., Clay County Finance Company, Inc., Community Bank of Naples, National Association, Corporate Billing, Inc., CypressCoquina Bank, FAB Investments, Inc. 30 Subsidiaries included in the Index

Officers: John H. Holcomb/55/Chmn., CEO/$1,061,434.00, Richard Murray/44/Dir., COO, Pres./$649,408.00, Kimberly Moore/Corp. Sec., William R. Ireland/49/Exec. VP, Chief Risk Management Officer, Lucian F. Bloodworth/Dir. - First American Bank, Guy S. Clifton/Dir. - First American Bank, R. W. Orr/Dir. - First American Bank, William Jackson Fite/Dir. - First American Bank, Alan J. Swindall/Dir. - Bank, Dadeville, Jimmy R. McIntosh/Dir. - Bank, Dadeville, Phillip Earnest/Contact, Stacey Dunn/Contact, Stephen P. Thompson/Dir. - Georgia State Bank, Jayson Stringfellow/Dir. - Florida Choice Bank, William E. Matthews/42/CFO, Exec. VP/$614,716.00 *(100 Officers included in Index)*

Directors: John H. Holcomb/55/Chmn., CEO, Dan M. David/61/Vice Chmn., Stancil W. Starnes/Dir., Richard Murray/44/Dir., COO, Pres., Phillip C. McWane/Dir., Douglas W. Montgomery/Dir., Ruffner G. Page/Dir., John D. Johns/Dir., Edgar W. Welden/Dir., John M. Plunk/Dir., Ray W. Barnes/Dir., John V. Denson/Dir., Bobby Bradley/Dir., William D. Montgomery/59/Dir., Griffin A. Greene/Dir. *(17 Directors included in Index)*

Owners: Insiders/17.30%, Dan M. David, William E. Matthews, Drayton Nabers, W. Edgar Welden, W. Stancil Starnes, John J. McMahon/3.30%, Ray W. Barnes, Phillip C. McWane/6.20%, Richard Murray, William Britt Sexton/1.00%, William D. Montgomery, James R. Thompson, Ruffner G. Page/3.40%, John D. Johns *(19 Owners included in Index)*

Financial Data: ***Fiscal Year End:***12/31 ***Latest Annual Data:*** 12/31/2006

Year	Sales	Net Income
2006	$513,207,000	$79,816,000
2005	$380,983,000	$66,673,000
2004	$301,971,000	$54,644,000

Curr. Assets:	$308,070,000	***Curr. Liab.:***	$6,415,252,000	***P/E Ratio:***	15.13
Plant, Equip.:	$155,176,000	***Total Liab.:***	$6,817,651,000	***Indic. Yr. Divd.:***	$1.640
Total Assets:	$7,671,274,000	***Net Worth:***	$853,623,000	***Debt/ Equity:***	0.4602

Alabama Power Co

600 N 18th St., Birmingham, AL, 35291; ***PH:*** 1-205-257-1000; ***http://*** www.alapower.com

General - Incorporation	AL	***Stock***- Price on:12/24/2007	NA
Employees	NA	Stock Exchange	NYSE
Auditor	Deloitte & Touche LLP	Ticker Symbol	NA
Stk Agt	NA	Outstanding Shares	NA
Counsel	Balch & Bingham	E.P.S.	NA
DUNS No.	00-690-0120	Shareholders	NA

Business: The group's principle activity is to provide electric services in the state of Alabama. The company generates, purchases and distributes electricity at retail in over 1000 communities and at wholesale to 15 municipally-owned electric distribution systems. Electricity is supplied for residential, commercial, industrial and other purposes. The company also provides steam service in downtown birmingham and cooperates with dealers in selling and promoting the sale of electric appliances. The company has entered into cogeneration contracts with twelve industrial customers. Under the terms of these contracts, it purchases the excess generation of such companies. The company is a wholly owned subsidiary of the southern company. The group operates from United States.

Primary SIC and add'l.: 4911

CIK No: 0000003153

Subsidiaries: Alabama Power Capital Trust IV, Alabama Power Capital Trust V, Alabama Power Capital Trust VI, Alabama Power Capital Trust VII, Alabama Power Capital Trust VIII, Alabama Power Company, Alabama Property Company, Georgia Power Capital Trust IV, Georgia Power Capital Trust IX, Georgia Power Capital Trust V, Georgia Power Capital Trust VI, Georgia Power Capital Trust VII, Georgia Power Capital Trust VIII, Georgia Power Capital Trust X, Georgia Power Capital Trust XI 38 Subsidiaries included in the Index

Officers: Charles D. McCrary/Dir., CEO, Pres./$2,181,010.00, Alan C. Martin/59/Exec. VP/$1,089,856.00, Steven R. Spencer/Exec. VP/$859,547.00, Arthur P. Beattie/53/Exec. VP, CFO, Treasurer/$746,373.00, Jerry L. Stewart/Sr. VP/$1,084,968.00

Directors: Charles D. McCrary/Dir., CEO, Pres., John Cox Webb/Dir., David J. Cooper/Dir., James W. Wright/Dir., Whit Armstrong/Dir., David M. Ratcliffe/Dir., Patricia M. King/Dir., Malcolm Portera/Dir., Dowd C. Ritter/Dir., James K. Lowder/Dir., Robert D. Powers/Dir., James H. Sanford/Dir., John D. Johns/Dir.

Owners: Malcolm Portera, Alan C. Martin, Patricia M. King, David M. Ratcliffe, John D. Johns, Charles D. McCrary, Steve R. Spencer, Art P. Beattie, Dowd C. Ritter, James K. Lowder, David J. Cooper, James W. Wright, Insiders, John C. Webb, Whit Armstrong *(18 Owners included in Index)*

Aladdin Knowledge Systems Ltd

601 Campus Dr., Ste. C1, Arlington Heights, IL, 60004; ***PH:*** 1-847-818-3800; ***Fax:*** 1-847-818-3810; ***http://*** www.aks.com

General - Incorporation	Israel	***Stock***- Price on:12/24/2007	$20.58
Employees	400	Stock Exchange	NDQ
Auditor	Ernst & Young LLP	Ticker Symbol	ALDN
Stk Agt	American Stock Transfer & Trust Co.	Outstanding Shares	14,690,000
Counsel	Berkman, Wechsler, Sahar, Bloom & Co	E.P.S.	$1.06
DUNS No.	60-004-2543	Shareholders	NA

Business: The group's principle activities include designing, developing, manufacturing and marketing family of proprietary software security products which combine hardware and software to prevent unauthorized use of computer programs; and offers smart card application development tools, systems and products which designed to facilitate the integration of smart cards and personal computers. The group operates from United States.

Primary SIC and add'l.: 7372

CIK No: 0000911364

Subsidiaries: Aladdin Asia Limited, Aladdin ITALY SRL, Aladdin Japan & Co. Inc., Aladdin Knowledge Espana S.L., Aladdin Knowledge Systems Deutschland GmbH, Aladdin Knowledge Systems Inc., Aladdin Western Europe BV, Aladdin Western Europe Ltd., Aladdin Western Europe S.A.R.L., Hafalad BV

Officers: Jacob Margalit/Chmn., CEO, Ludger Wilmer/GM - Aladdin Europe, Elinor Nissensohn/Global VP - Sales, Marketing, Masaru Kosaka/Pres. - Aladdin Japan, Aviram Shemer/CFO, Dany Margalit/Founder, Dir. - Research, Development Mgr., Shimon Gruper/VP - Esafe Technologies, Avi Barir/VP - Software DRM, Shlomi Yanai/VP - Etoken, Tsion Gonen/VP - Esafe, John Gunn/GM - Aladdin USA, VP - Global Marketing, Matthew Zintel/Contact - Press, Mark Jones/Investor Relations Officer

Directors: Jacob Margalit/Chmn., CEO, David Assia/Dir., Menahem Gutterman/Dir., Dany Margalit/Founder, Dir. - Research, Development Mgr., Orna Berry/Dir.

Owners: Dany Margalit/6.48%, Tracer Capital Management L.P./7.85%, Insiders/20.50%, BlackRock, Inc./9.81%, Diker Management, L.L.C./6.85%, FMR Corp./8.92%, Galleon Advisors, L.L.C./11.50%, Juniper Trading Services, Inc./14.75%, Jacob Margalit/13.02%

Financial Data: Fiscal Year End:12/31 Latest Annual Data: 12/31/2006

Year	Sales	Net Income
2006	$89,038,000	$14,031,000
2005	$81,773,000	$12,356,000
2004	$69,121,000	$8,788,000

Curr. Assets:	$120,386,000	Curr. Liab.:	$20,585,000	P/E Ratio:	8.10
Plant, Equip.:	$5,695,000	Total Liab.:	$25,395,000	Indic. Yr. Divd.:	NA
Total Assets:	$148,044,000	Net Worth:	$122,649,000	Debt/ Equity:	NA

Alamo Group Inc

1502 E Walnut, Seguin, TX, 78155; **PH:** 1-830-379-1480; **Fax:** 1-830-372-9683; **http://** www.alamo-group.com; **Email:** info@alamo-group.com

General - Incorporation	DE	**Stock**- Price on:12/24/2007	$25.45
Employees	2,215	Stock Exchange	NYSE
Auditor	Ernst & Young LLP	Ticker Symbol	ALG
Stk Agt.	Mellon Investor Services LLC	Outstanding Shares	9,770,000
Counsel.	Oppenheimer Blend Harrison & Tate	E.P.S.	$1.03
DUNS No.	00-519-0632	Shareholders	NA

Business: The group's principal activity is to manufacture, distribute and service equipment for right-of-way maintenance and agriculture. The products include tractor-mounted mowing and other vegetation maintenance equipment, street sweepers, agricultural implements and related after-Market parts and services. Its products are sold under the alamo industrial, tiger, schwarz e, rhino, m&w, herschel-adams, schulte, mcconnel, bomford, sma, twose trade names. They are sold to governmental end-users, farmers, ranchers, farm equipment dealers, fleet stores, wholesale distributors, original equipment manufacturers and construction equipment dealers. The group has manufacturing and marketing bases in the United States, the United Kingdom, France and Canada. It also sells in Germany, scandinavia, Australia and the Far East.

Primary SIC and add'l.: 3523

CIK No: 0000897077

Subsidiaries: Adams Hard-Facing Company, Inc., Alamo Capital Inc., Alamo Group (Canada) Inc. , Alamo Group (EUR) Limited , Alamo Group (FR) S.A., Alamo Group (IA) Inc., Alamo Group (IL) Inc. , Alamo Group (KS) Inc., Alamo Group (OH) Inc. , Alamo Group (SMC) Inc. , Alamo Group (TX) L.P. , Alamo Group (USA) Inc., Alamo Group (WA) Inc. , Alamo Group Holdings, LLC , Alamo Group Management, L.P. 41 Subsidiaries included in the Index

Officers: Ronald A. Robinson/Dir., CEO, Pres./$494,158.00, Donald C. Duncan/VP, General Counsel/$155,935.00, Ian Burden/Exec. VP - North American Industrial Division, Robert H. George/VP, Sec., Treasurer/$154,547.00, Geoffrey Davies/VP/$309,187.00, Richard J. Wehrle/VP, Corporate Controller/$147,393.00, Richard D. Pummell/Exec. VP - North American Agricultural Division, Dan E. Malone/CFO, Exec. VP, Dennis M. Stevens/Dir. - Internal Audit

Directors: Ronald A. Robinson/Dir., CEO, Pres., Donald J. Douglass/Chmn., David H. Morris/Dir., James B. Skaggs/Dir., Jerry E. Goldress/Dir., David W. Grzelak/Dir., Gary L. Martin/Dir.

Owners: David H. Morris, Dimensional Fund Advisors Inc./7.87%, Capital Southwest Venture Corporation/28.98%, Donald C. Duncan, Donald J. Douglass/3.50%, Third Avenue Management LLC/30.98%, James B. Skaggs, William R. Thomas, Richard J. Wehrle, Robert H. George, Geoffrey Davies, Ronald A. Robinson, Insiders/36.60%, Jerry E. Goldress

Financial Data: Fiscal Year End:12/31 Latest Annual Data: 06/30/2007

Year	Sales	Net Income
2007	$131,986,000	$4,035,000
2006	$111,920,000	$1,141,000
2005	$368,110,000	$11,291,000

Curr. Assets:	$220,771,000	Curr. Liab.:	$59,803,000	P/E Ratio:	27.97
Plant, Equip.:	$57,712,000	Total Liab.:	$144,900,000	Indic. Yr. Divd.:	$0.240
Total Assets:	$326,634,000	Net Worth:	$181,734,000	Debt/ Equity:	0.5951

Alamogordo Financial Corp

500 E 10th St., Alamogordo, NM, 88310; **PH:** 1-505-437-9334; **Fax:** 1-505-437-7020; **http://** www.alamofed.com

General - Incorporation	Federal	**Stock**- Price on:12/24/2007	$29.5
Employees	NA	Stock Exchange	OTC
Auditor	Neff & Ricci LLP	Ticker Symbol	ALMG
Stk Agt.	Computershare Investor Services LLC	Outstanding Shares	NA
Counsel	NA	E.P.S.	NA
DUNS No.	NA	Shareholders	NA

Business: The groups principal activity is to provide banking business. The group financial products include savings and fixed deposits, on line, personal and business banking. The group operates from the United States.

Primary SIC and add'l.: 6035

CIK No: 0001100542

Officers: Miles R. Ledgerwood/Dir., Pres., CEO - Contact - Investor Relations, Norma J. Clute/VP, Treasurer, Kemmie Jeter/VP, Steven C. Cox/VP, COO, Susan L. White/VP, Norma Esquero/Assist. VP, Melissa Sturgess/Assist. VP, Marion Phillips/Assist. VP

Directors: Miles R. Ledgerwood/Dir., Pres., CEO - Contact - Investor Relations, Robert W. Hamilton/Chmn., Thomas S. Overstreet/Vice Chmn. - Overstreet, Associates, PC, Jimmie D. Randall/Dir., Earl E. Wallin/Dir., William F. Burt/Member - Advisory Board, Burt Broadcasting Inc, Randal L. Rabon/Member - Advisory Board, Mesa Verde Inc, Malcolmn M. Ramsey/Member - Advisory Board

Financial Data: Fiscal Year End:06/30 Latest Annual Data: 6/30/2003

Year	Sales	Net Income
2003	$9,644,000	$656,000
2002	$10,163,000	$554,000
2001	$10,622,000	$776,000

Curr. Assets:	$13,546,000	Curr. Liab.:	$127,827,000		
Plant, Equip.:	$8,155,000	Total Liab.:	$128,921,000	Indic. Yr. Divd.:	NA
Total Assets:	$156,999,000	Net Worth:	$28,077,000	Debt/ Equity:	0.0196

Alamosa Holdings Inc

5225 S Loop 289, Lubbock, TX, 79424; **PH:** 1-806-722-1100; **http://** www.sprint.com

General - Incorporation	DE	**Stock**- Price on:12/24/2007	$22.0928
Employees	64,600	Stock Exchange	NA
Auditor	PricewaterhouseCoopers LLP	Ticker Symbol	NA
Stk Agt.	UMB Bank, N.A.	Outstanding Shares	2,890,000,000
Counsel.	Skadden, Arps, Meagher & Flom LLP	E.P.S.	$0.12
DUNS No.	10-192-6165	Shareholders	NA

Business: The group's principal activity is to provide wireless personal communication services. The services are provided in the southwestern and midwestern United States. As a network partner of sprint pcs, the group has the exclusive right to provide digital wireless personal communication services under the sprint and sprint pcs brand names. As part of the affiliation agreements with sprint pcs, the group has the option of contracting with sprint pcs to provide back office services like customer activation, customer service, handset logistics and network monitoring services.

Primary SIC and add'l.: 4812 4813

CIK No: 0001120102

Subsidiaries: AirGate PCS, Inc., Alamosa (Delaware), Inc., Alamosa Delaware GP, LLC, Alamosa Holdings, Inc., Alamosa Holdings, LLC, Alamosa Limited, LLC, Alamosa Missouri, LLC, Alamosa PCS Holdings, Inc., Alamosa PCS, Inc., Alamosa Wisconsin GP, LLC, Alamosa Wisconsin Limited Partnership, Southwest PCS, L.P., Swgp, LLC, Swlp, LLC, Texas Telecommunications, LP 16 Subsidiaries included in the Index

Financial Data: Fiscal Year End:12/31 Latest Annual Data: 12/31/2006

Year	Sales	Net Income
2006	$41,028,000,000	$1,329,000,000
2005	$34,680,000,000	$1,785,000,000
2004	$27,428,000,000	-$1,012,000,000

Curr. Assets:	$10,304,000,000	Curr. Liab.:	$9,798,000,000	P/E Ratio:	93.22
Plant, Equip.:	$25,868,000,000	Total Liab.:	$44,030,000,000	Indic. Yr. Divd.:	$0.100
Total Assets:	$97,161,000,000	Net Worth:	$53,131,000,000	Debt/ Equity:	0.4145

Alanco Technologies Inc

15575 N 83rd Way, Ste. 3, Scottsdale, AZ, 85260; **PH:** 1-480-607-1010; **Fax:** 1-480-607-1515; **http://** www.alanco.com; **Email:** alanco@alanco.com

General - Incorporation	AZ	**Stock**- Price on:12/24/2007	$2.304
Employees	78	Stock Exchange	NDQ
Auditor	Semple & Cooper LLP	Ticker Symbol	ALAN
Stk Agt.	Computershare Trust Co	Outstanding Shares	20,160,000
Counsel	NA	E.P.S.	-$0.3
DUNS No.	01-842-7658	Shareholders	NA

Business: The group's principle activity is to provide advanced information technology solutions. The group operates under two segments: radio frequency identification (rfid) and data storage products. Rfid designs, produces, markets and distributes tracking technology. Data storage products manufacture, market and distribute data storage products. The group designs and manufactures proprietary data storage subsystems called emulators that serve as translators between computers and state-of-the-art storage devices and provide unique, cost-effective storage system solutions. It also manufacturers and integrates data storage networking products and services and provides optical storage devices, such as CD/DVD-rom servers. The products are sold in the United States and internationally through telemarketing, independent sales representatives and independent distributors. The group's quarterly revenue for September 2007 was 4.55 millions of USD.

Primary SIC and add'l.: 3572

CIK No: 0000098618

Subsidiaries: Alanco Technologies, Inc

Officers: Robert R. Kauffman/Chmn., CEO, Timothy P. Slifkin/Dir., Pres., CEO - Startrak Systems, John A. Carlson/Dir., CFO, Exec. VP, Richard Vanek/Pres. - Excel, Meridian Data, Thomas A. Robinson/47/Exec. VP - Startrak Systems, LLC, Greg M. Oester/Pres. - Alanco, TSI Prism

Directors: Robert R. Kauffman/Chmn., CEO, Timothy P. Slifkin/Dir., Pres., CEO - Startrak Systems, John A. Carlson/Dir., CFO, Exec. VP, James T. Hecker/Dir., Donald E. Anderson/Dir., Harold S. Carpenter/Dir., Thomas C. Lavoy/Dir.

Owners: Thomas C. LaVoy/0.04%, Robert R. Kauffman/1.02%, Robert R. Kauffman/1.02%, Technology Systems International, Inc./7.95%, Thomas C. LaVoy/1.40%, Harold S. Carpenter, Insiders/24.98%, James T. Hecker/0.12%, Harold S. Carpenter/8.64%, James T. Hecker/0.81%, Timothy P. Slifkin/10.57%, Donald E. Anderson/33.71%, Greg M. Oester/0.10%, Thomas A. Robinson/6.79%, Timothy P. Slifkin/10.57% *(31 Owners included in Index)*

Financial Data: Fiscal Year End:06/30 Latest Annual Data: 6/30/2006

Year	Sales	Net Income
2006	$6,660,000	-$4,009,000
2005	$7,184,000	-$3,791,000
2004	$4,911,000	-$3,176,000

Curr. Assets:	$6,648,000	Curr. Liab.:	$13,828,000		
Plant, Equip.:	$231,000	Total Liab.:	$17,244,000	Indic. Yr. Divd.:	NA
Total Assets:	$27,685,000	Net Worth:	$10,440,000	Debt/ Equity:	NA

Alaska Air Group Inc

19300 International Blvd., Seattle, WA, 98188; **PH:** 1-206-392-5040; **Fax:** 1-206-392-2804; **http://** www.alaskaair.com; **Email:** newsroom@alaskaair.com

General - Incorporation	DE	**Stock**- Price on:12/24/2007	NA
Employees	14,485	Stock Exchange	NYSE
Auditor	KPMG LLP	Ticker Symbol	ALK
Stk Agt.	Computershare Investor Services LLC	Outstanding Shares	40,440,000
Counsel	NA	E.P.S.	NA
DUNS No.	14-844-1256	Shareholders	NA

Business: The groups principle activity is to operate airlines. The group operates through two subsidiaries namely Alaska Airlines, Inc. (Alaska) and Horizon Air Industries, Inc. (Horizon). The group operates from United States.

Primary SIC and add'l.: 4512 4581 6719 4513 4522

CIK No: 0000766421

Subsidiaries: AAG Fueling Services, Inc., AAG Leasing, Inc, AAGL-I, Air Group Leasing Equity, Inc., Air Group Leasing, Inc., Alaska Airlines, Inc., Horizon Air Industries, Inc.

Officers: William S. Ayer/Chmn., CEO, Pres., Jeffrey D. Pinneo/CEO, Pres. - Horizon AIR Industries, INC, Karen Gruen/MD - Corporate Affairs, Assoc. General Counsel, Assist. Corp. Sec., Thomas M. Gerharter/Sr. VP - Operations, Horizon AIR Industries, INC, Andrea L. Schneider/Sr. VP - Customer Services, Horizon AIR Industries, INC, Brandon S. Pedersen/VP - Finance, Controller, John F. Schaefer/Sr. VP - Finance, Treasurer - Alaska Airlines, INC, Joseph A. Sprague/Sr. VP - In, Flight Services, Alaska Airlines, INC, Shannon K. Alberts/MD - Investor Relations, Assist. Corp. Sec., Eugene C. Hahn/VP - Flight Operations, Horizon AIR Industries, INC, Marne K. McCluskey/VP - Employee Resources, Horizon AIR Industries, INC, Rudi H. Schmidt/VP - Finance, Treasurer - Horizon AIR Industries, INC, Celia M. Sherbeck/VP - Maintenance, Engineering, Horizon AIR Industries, INC, Arthur E. Thomas/VP - Legal, Administration, Corp. Sec. - Horizon AIR Industries, INC, Gregg A. Saretsky/Exec. VP - Flight, Marketing, Alaska Airlines, INC *(31 Officers included in Index)*

Directors: William S. Ayer/Chmn., CEO, Pres., Phyllis J. Campbell/Dir., Richard A. Wien/Dir., Mark R. Hamilton/Dir., Patricia M. Bedient/Dir., Jessie J. Knight/Dir., Marc R. Langland/Dir., Dennis Madsen/Dir., Byron I. Mallott/Dir., John V. Rindlaub/Dir., Kenneth J. Thompson/Dir., Bruce R. Kennedy/Dir.

Owners: Patricia M. Bedient, Kevin P. Finan, Dennis F. Madsen, Jeffrey D. Pinneo, Jessie J. Knight, Insiders/2.40%, Mark R. Hamilton, Bruce R. Kennedy, Byron I. Mallott, PRIMECAP Management Company/6.20%, Kenneth J. Thompson, Brandon S. Pedersen, John F. Schaefer, R. Marc Langland, Barclays Global Investors, NA/5.70% *(26 Owners included in Index)*

Financial Data: Fiscal Year End:12/31   Latest Annual Data: 12/31/2006

Year	Sales	Net Income
2006	$3,334,400,000	-$52,600,000
2005	$2,975,300,000	-$5,900,000
2004	$2,723,800,000	-$15,300,000

Curr. Assets:	$1,572,300,000	**Curr. Liab.:**	$1,236,700,000		
Plant, Equip.:	$2,359,000,000	**Total Liab.:**	$3,191,600,000	**Indic. Yr. Divd.:**	NA
Total Assets:	$4,077,100,000	**Net Worth:**	$885,500,000	**Debt/ Equity:**	1.3215

Alaska Airlines Inc

19300 International Blvd. S, Seattle, WA, 98188; *PH:* 1-206-392-5040; *http://* www.alaska-air.com; *Email:* reservations@alaskaair.com

General - Incorporation	AK	Stock- Price on:12/24/2007	NA
Employees	NA	Stock Exchange	NA
Auditor	KPMG LLP	Ticker Symbol	NA
Stk Agt	Computershare Investor Services LLC	Outstanding Shares	NA
Counsel	NA	E.P.S.	NA
DUNS No.	00-794-2493	Shareholders	NA

Business: The group's principal activity is to provide airline service to the customers. It provides advance seat assignments, food and beverage service and other amenities required by the customers. It is a wholly owned subsidiary of Alaska air group, inc. The group serves 39 cities in six western states, Canada and seven cities in Mexico. The group also provides non-stop service between anchorage and Chicago, seattle and four eastern cities and seattle and Washington D.C.

Primary SIC and add'l.: 4512

CIK No: 0000003202

Officers: William S. Ayer/Chmn., CEO, Pres., Kevin P. Finan/Exec. VP - Strategic Projects, Gregg A. Saretsky/Exec. VP - Flight, Marketing, Bradley D. Tilden/CFO, Exec. VP - Finance, Shannon K. Alberts/MD - Investor Relations, Assist. Corp. Sec., Irving Bertram/Assoc. General Counsel, Assist. Sec., Karen Gruen/MD - Corporate Affairs, Assoc. General Counsel, Assist. Corp. Sec., John F. Schaefer/Sr. VP - Finance, Treasurer, Keith Loveless/VP - Legal, Corporate Affairs, General Counsel, Corp. Sec., Frederick L. Mohr/VP - Maintenance, Engineering, Edward White/VP - Corporate Real Estate, Kelley J. Dobbs/VP - Human Resources, Strategy, Culture, Inclusion, Benito Minicucci/Sr. VP - Maintenance, Thomas R. O'Grady/Sr. VP - Commercial, Regulatory Law, Deputy General Counsel, Brandon S. Pedersen/VP - Finance, Controller *(23 Officers included in Index)*

Directors: William S. Ayer/Chmn., CEO, Pres., Kenneth J. Thompson/Dir., Dennis Madsen/Dir., Phyllis J. Campbell/Dir., Jessie J. Knight/Dir., Richard A. Wien/Dir., Mark R. Hamilton/Dir., Marc R. Langland/Dir., Byron I. Mallott/Dir., Patricia M. Bedient/Dir.

Alaska Communications Systems Group Inc

600 Telephone Ave., Anchorage, AK, 99503; *PH:* 1-907-297-3000; *Fax:* 1-907-297-3100; *http://* www.acsalaska.com; *Email:* investors@acsalaska.com

General - Incorporation	DE	Stock- Price on:12/24/2007	$15.52
Employees	986	Stock Exchange	NDQ
Auditor	Deloitte & Touche LLP	Ticker Symbol	ALSK
Stk Agt	Mellon Investor Services LLC	Outstanding Shares	42,720,000
Counsel	Latham & Watkins	E.P.S.	$0.71
DUNS No.	NA	Shareholders	NA

Business: The group's principal activity is to provide facilities based telecommunications in Alaska. It also provides local telephone, cellular, long distance, data and Internet services to business and residential customers. The group operates in five segments namely, local telephones, cellular services, directory, Internet and interexchange businesses. The group also provides wireless cable television services in the fairbanks and anchorage service areas.

Primary SIC and add'l.: 2759 4813 4841 4812

CIK No: 0001089511

Subsidiaries: ACS InfoSource, Inc., ACS Internet, Inc., ACS Long Distance License Sub, Inc., ACS Long Distance, Inc., ACS Messaging, Inc., ACS of Alaska License Sub, Inc., ACS of Alaska, Inc., ACS of Anchorage License Sub, Inc., ACS of Anchorage, Inc., ACS of Fairbanks License Sub, Inc., ACS of Fairbanks, Inc., ACS of the Northland License Sub, Inc., ACS of the Northland, Inc., ACS Service, Inc., ACS Wireless License Sub, Inc. 17 Subsidiaries included in the Index

Officers: Liane Pelletier/Chairwoman, CEO, Pres./$3,034,620.00, David C. Eisenberg/Sr. VP - Corporate Strategy, Development, Marketing/$1,254,628.00, Leonard Steinberg/VP, General Counsel, Corp. Sec./$962,882.00, Sheldon Fisher/Pres. - Sales, Service/$1,117,990.00, Anand Vadapalli/Sr. VP - Network, Information Technology, David Wilson/CFO, Sr. VP, Treasurer/$1,264,937.00, Lynn S. Erwin/VP - Human Resources, Kirsten Chapman/Investor Relations Contact, Thomas L. Cooper/Transfer Agent, Michael Pitfick/Transfer Agent, Michael Gewirtz/Transfer Agent

Directors: Liane Pelletier/Chairwoman, CEO, Pres., Gary R. Donahee/Dir., John M. Egan/Dir., Patrick Pichette/Dir., Brian Rogers/Dir., Edward J. Hayes/Dir., Annette Jacobs/Dir., David Southwell/Dir.

Owners: Barclays Global Investors, N.A./5.00%, Leonard Steinberg, Insiders/1.30%, David C. Eisenberg, Prudential Financial, Inc./6.90%, John M. Egan, Kenneth L. Sprain, David Wilson, Jennison Associates LLC/6.90%, Sheldon Fisher, David Southwell, Annette Jacobs, Gary R. Donahee, Liane Pelletier, Brian Rogers *(17 Owners included in Index)*

Financial Data: Fiscal Year End:12/31   Latest Annual Data: 12/31/2006

Year	Sales	Net Income
2006	$349,817,000	$19,994,000
2005	$326,809,000	-$41,635,000
2004	$302,707,000	-$39,294,000

Curr. Assets:	$89,852,000	**Curr. Liab.:**	$76,941,000	**P/E Ratio:**	18.93
Plant, Equip.:	$396,543,000	**Total Liab.:**	$587,010,000	**Indic. Yr. Divd.:**	$0.860
Total Assets:	$562,321,000	**Net Worth:**	-$24,689,000	**Debt/ Equity:**	NA

Alaska Pacific Bancshares Inc

2094 Jordan Ave., Juneau, AK, 99801; *PH:* 1-907-789-4844; *Fax:* 1-907-790-5110; *http://* www.alaskapacificbank.com

General - Incorporation	AK	Stock- Price on:12/24/2007	$25.65
Employees	64	Stock Exchange	OTC
Auditor	Moss Adams LLP	Ticker Symbol	AKPB
Stk Agt	Computershare Investor Services LLC	Outstanding Shares	NA
Counsel	NA	E.P.S.	$1.74
DUNS No.	NA	Shareholders	NA

Business: The group operates through its subsidiary Alaska Pacific Bank, whose principal activity is banking business. The group products include deposits, loans on mortgage, real estate, loans on automobiles. The group operates from the United States.

Primary SIC and add'l.: 6712 6035

CIK No: 0001081860

Subsidiaries: Alaska Pacific Bank

Officers: Craig E. Dahl/Dir., CEO, Pres./$241,070.00, Roger K. White/CFO, Sr. VP, Sec./$169,694.00, Gillian Hays/Administrative Officer, Virginia Gibson/Assist. VP, Central Services Mgr., Bill Abbott/Human Resources Officer, Scott Manchee/VP, Information Technology Mgr., Lori Philo-Cook/VP, Marketing Dir., Cheryl Fellman/Assist. VP, Retail Operations Mgr., Nancy Christian/Assist. VP, Ketchikan Area Mgr., Commercial Loan Officer, Linda Brandt/Assist. VP, Sitka Office Mgr., Tom Sullivan/VP, Commercial Loan Officer, Heather Mitchell/Assist. VP, Commercial Loan Officer, George Pardee/VP, Commercial Loan Officer, Nicchia Leamer/Assist. VP, Commercial Loan Officer, Kristy Lundstrom/Consumer Loan Officer *(29 Officers included in Index)*

Directors: Craig E. Dahl/Dir., CEO, Pres., Roger Grummett/Chmn., Hugh N. Grant/Vice Chmn., Marta Ryman/71/Dir., Robert E. Allen/Dir., Eric McDowell/Dir., William J. Schmitz/Dir., Scott C. Milner/Dir., Bethann Boudah Chapman/Dir., Deborah Marshall/Dir.

Owners: Lance S. Gad/5.80%, Marta Ryman, Scott C. Milner, Deborah R. Marshall/1.10%, Roger Grummett/2.10%, Advisory Research, Inc./6.40%, Alaska Pacific Bancshares, Inc./8.10%, Hugh N. Grant/2.90%, Craig E. Dahl/4.90%, William J. Schmitz/2.10%, Roger K. White/3.10%, John E. Robertson, Eric McDowell/1.90%, David G. MacDonald/6.30%

Financial Data: Fiscal Year End:12/31   Latest Annual Data: 12/31/2006

Year	Sales	Net Income
2006	$13,215,000	$1,061,000
2005	$11,313,000	$731,000
2004	$10,587,000	$708,000

Curr. Assets:	$9,506,000	**Curr. Liab.:**	$160,390,000		
Plant, Equip.:	$3,537,000	**Total Liab.:**	$161,218,000	**Indic. Yr. Divd.:**	$0.400
Total Assets:	$178,923,000	**Net Worth:**	$17,705,000	**Debt/ Equity:**	NA

Albany International Corp

1373 Broadway, Albany, NY, 12204; *PH:* 1-518-445-2200; *Fax:* 1-518-445-2265; *http://* www.albint.com

General - Incorporation	DE	Stock- Price on:12/24/2007	$42.16
Employees	6,150	Stock Exchange	NYSE
Auditor	PricewaterhouseCoopers LLP	Ticker Symbol	AIN
Stk Agt	Computershare Investor Services LLC	Outstanding Shares	29,330,000
Counsel	NA	E.P.S.	$1.63
DUNS No.	00-207-5414	Shareholders	NA

Business: The group's principal activity is to design, manufacture and market paper machine clothing. The group operates in three segments: engineered fabrics, albany door systems and applied technologies. The engineered fabrics segment develops, manufactures, markets and services custom designed engineered fabrics used in the manufacture of paper, paperboard and products in other process industries. The albany door systems segment is an aggregation of the group's operations that manufacture, market and service high performance doors. The applied technologies segment manufactures products with applications outside of the core businesses of the group. The group has manufacturing facilities in Australia, Brazil, Canada, China, Finland, France, Germany, great Britain, Italy, Mexico, the Netherlands, South Korea, Sweden and the United States.

Primary SIC and add'l.: 3442 2297

CIK No: 0000819793

Subsidiaries: Brandon Drying Fabrics, Inc, Brandon Sales, Inc.

Officers: Joseph G. Morone/Dir., CEO, Pres./$1,430,289.00, Christoper J. Connally/56/Corporate Treasurer, Daniel A. Halftermeyer/47/Group VP - PMC Europe, John Cozzolino/VP - Strategic Planning, Sally Racicot/Executive Assist., Michael J. Joyce/45/Group VP - PMC Americas, John C. Standish/Dir., Sr. VP - Manufacturing, Americas Business Corridor, Richard A. Carlstrom/65/VP, Controller, Charles J. Silva/49/VP, General Counsel, Sec., Michael C. Nahl/66/CFO, Exec. VP/$1,316,012.00, David B. Madden/52/Group VP - PMC Asia, Pacific, Ralph M. Polumbo/57/Sr. VP - Human Resources, Robert A. Hansen/51/VP - Corporate R & D, Dawne H. Wimbrow/51/VP - Global Information Services, CIO, Joseph M. Gaug/45/Assoc. General Counsel, Assist. Sec.

Directors: Joseph G. Morone/Dir., CEO, Pres., Frank R. Schmeler/Chmn., Christine L. Standish/Dir., Paula H. Cholmondeley/Dir., Thomas R. Beecher/Dir., John C. Standish/Dir., Sr. VP - Manufacturing, Americas Business Corridor, Erland E. Kailbourne/Dir., Juhani Pakkala/Dir., John F. Cassidy/65/Dir., Edgar G. Hotard/Dir.

Owners: Artisan Partners/5.88%, Edgar G. Hotard, Spencer J. Standish/9.03%, Insiders/20.09%, John C. Standish/4.73%, Michael C. Nahl, William M. McCarthy, Thomas R. Beecher/19.95%, Barclays Global Investors, NA/5.22%, Dieter Polt, Frank R. Schmeler, J. S. Standish Company/26.82%, Erland E. Kailbourne, Christine L. Standish, LSV Asset Management/6.24% (26 Owners included in Index)

Financial Data: Fiscal Year End:12/31 Latest Annual Data: 12/31/2006

Year	Sales	Net Income
2006	$1,011,458,000	$58,039,000
2005	$978,710,000	$71,852,000
2004	$919,802,000	$10,385,000

Curr. Assets:	$529,196,000	Curr. Liab.:	$195,985,000	P/E Ratio:	25.87
Plant, Equip.:	$397,521,000	Total Liab.:	$807,422,000	Indic. Yr. Divd.:	$0.440
Total Assets:	$1,306,547,000	Net Worth:	$499,125,000	Debt/ Equity:	0.6769

Albany Molecular Research Inc

21 Corporate Cir., Albany, NY, 12212; *PH:* 1-518-464-0279; *Fax:* 1-518-464-0289; *http://* www.albmolecular.com; *Email:* info@albmolecular.com

General - Incorporation	DE	**Stock**- Price on:12/24/2007	$15.13
Employees	1,015	Stock Exchange	NDQ
Auditor	KPMG LLP	Ticker Symbol	AMRI
Stk Agt.	Mellon Investor Services LLC	Outstanding Shares	34,930,000
Counsel	Goodwin Procter LLP	E.P.S.	$0.28
DUNS No.	78-779-3900	Shareholders	NA

Business: The group's principal activities are to conduct chemistry research, drug discovery and development, focused on applications for the pharmaceutical and biotechnology industries. It conducts research and development projects and collaborates with many leading pharmaceutical, biotechnology and genomics companies and develops new chemistry technology for potential pharmaceutical products. The group's services are designed to permit customers to reduce overall drug development time and cost and to pursue greater number of drug discovery and development opportunities. It also conducts proprietary research and development to discover new lead compounds with commercial potential.

Primary SIC and add'l.: 8731

CIK No: 0001065087

Subsidiaries: Albany Molecular Research Export Corp., Albany Molecular Research Hyderabad Research Centre, PTE. LTD., Albany Molecular Research Singapore Research Centre, PTE. LTD., AMR Mauritius Pvt. Ltd., AMR Technology Inc., AMRI Bothell Research Center Inc., Organichem Corporation

Officers: Thomas E. D'Ambra/Chmn., CEO, Pres./$3,179,453.00, Patricia Ellis/VP - QA, RA, Michael D. Ironside/VP - Chemical Development, Small Scale Cgmp Manufacturing, Michael P. Trova/Sr. VP - Chemistry/$242,786.20, Bruce J. Sargent/VP - Discovery R & D, Mark T. Frost/CFO/$512,894.60, Brian D. Russell/VP - Human Resources, Kenton Shultis/VP, GM - Organichem/$8,184.00, Eric W. Smart/VP - Business Development, Harold Meckler/VP - Science, Technology, Jonathan Evans/VP - Pharmaceutical Development, Manufacturing, Steven R. Hagen/VP - Quality, Analytical Chemistry

Directors: Thomas E. D'Ambra/Chmn., CEO, Pres., Kevin O'Connor/Dir., Donald E. Kuhla/Dir., Arthur J. Roth/Dir., Paul S. Anderson/Dir., Anthony P. Tartaglia/Dir., Una S. Ryan/Dir., Veronica G.H. Jordan/Dir.

Owners: Mark T. Frost, Paul S. Anderson, Veronica G.H. Jordan, Thomas E. DAmbra/14.10%, Donald E. Kuhla, Insiders/16.00%, Kevin OConnor, Thomas E. DAmbra Family Trust/9.30%, Kenton L. Shultis, Advisory Research, Inc./5.50%, Michael P. Trova, Constance M. DAmbra/14.10%, Dimensional Fund Advisors LP/8.90%, Anthony P. Tartaglia, Una S. Ryan (17 Owners included in Index)

Financial Data: Fiscal Year End:12/31 Latest Annual Data: 12/31/2006

Year	Sales	Net Income
2006	$179,807,000	$2,183,000
2005	$183,906,000	$16,321,000
2004	$169,527,000	-$11,691,000

Curr. Assets:	$182,620,000	Curr. Liab.:	$32,688,000	P/E Ratio:	137.55
Plant, Equip.:	$153,202,000	Total Liab.:	$57,038,000	Indic. Yr. Divd.:	NA
Total Assets:	$375,493,000	Net Worth:	$318,455,000	Debt/ Equity:	0.0400

Albemarle Corp

330 S Fourth St., Richmond, VA, 23219; *PH:* 1-804-788-6000; *Fax:* 1-804-788-6020; *http://* www.albemarle.com

General - Incorporation	VA	**Stock**- Price on:12/24/2007	$37.69
Employees	3,560	Stock Exchange	NYSE
Auditor	PricewaterhouseCoopers LLP	Ticker Symbol	ALB
Stk Agt.	National City Bank	Outstanding Shares	95,810,000
Counsel	Hunton & Williams LLP	E.P.S.	$2.40
DUNS No.	82-677-4630	Shareholders	NA

Business: The groups principle activities include developing, manufacturing and marketing engineered specialty chemicals. The group operates through three business segments namely polymer additives, catalysts and fine chemicals. The group operates from United States.

Primary SIC and add'l.: 2869 2865 2819 2899 2833

CIK No: 0000915913

Subsidiaries: ACI Delaware Corporation, Albemarle Catalysts Company BV, Albemarle Catalysts Company LP, Albemarle Catalysts International, LLC, Albemarle Catalysts U.S., LLC, Albemarle Delaware One, LLC, Albemarle International Corporation, Albemarle Netherlands BV

Officers: Mark C. Rohr/Dir., CEO, Pres./$5,381,985.00, George A. Newbill/Exec. VP - Manufacturing Operations, John J. Nicols/43/VP - Catalysts, John M. Steitz/COO, Exec. VP/$2,334,064.00, Anthony S. Parnell/48/VP - Global Sales, Service, Operations Planning, Jack P. Harsh/VP - Human Resources, John G. Dabkowski/59/VP - Polymer Additives, Raymond Hurley/55/VP - Alternative Fuel Technologies, Ronald C. Zumstein/VP - Health, Safety, Environment, Luther C. Kissam/VP, General Counsel, Sec./$2,015,053.00, Kevin C. Wilson/46/Treasurer, Richard J. Diemer/CFO, Sr. VP/$2,096,263.00, Sandra B. Rodriguez/Investor Relations Officer, Ronald R. Gardner/56/VP - Fine Chemicals

Directors: Mark C. Rohr/Dir., CEO, Pres., William M. Gottwald/Chmn., Charles E. Stewart/Dir., Alfred J. Broaddus/Dir., John D. Gottwald/Dir., William R. Ide/Dir., Seymour S. Preston/Dir., John Sherman/Dir., Harriett Tee Taggart/Dir., Anne M. Whittemore/Dir., Richard L. Morrill/Dir.

Owners: John Sherman, Floyd D. Gottwald/1.92%, William R. Ide, Alfred J. Broaddus, Richard J. Diemer, Luther C. Kissam, Anne Marie Whittemore, JPMorgan Chase & Co./6.81%, Insiders/12.96%, William M. Gottwald/6.30%, John M. Steitz, Richard L. Morrill, John D. Gottwald/4.74%, Mark C. Rohr, Floyd D. Gottwald/16.67% (17 Owners included in Index)

Financial Data: Fiscal Year End:12/31 Latest Annual Data: 06/30/2007

Year	Sales	Net Income
2007	$563,812,000	$53,863,000
2006	$2,368,506,000	$142,969,000
2005	$2,107,499,000	$114,867,000

Curr. Assets:	$960,854,000	Curr. Liab.:	$482,949,000	P/E Ratio:	22.04
Plant, Equip.:	$980,575,000	Total Liab.:	$1,502,270,000	Indic. Yr. Divd.:	$0.420
Total Assets:	$2,530,368,000	Net Worth:	$1,028,098,000	Debt/ Equity:	0.6773

Alberta Star Development Corp

675 Hastings St. W , Unit 200, Vancouver, BC, V6B 1N2; *PH:* 1-604-681-3131; *Fax:* 1-604-801-5499; *http://* www.alberta-star.com; *Email:* astar@telus.net

General - Incorporation	AB	**Stock**- Price on:12/24/2007	$1.04
Employees	NA	Stock Exchange	OTC
Auditor	James Stafford	Ticker Symbol	ASXSF
Stk Agt	Computershare Trust Co	Outstanding Shares	NA
Counsel	Borden, Ladner, Gervais LLP	E.P.S.	NA
DUNS No.	NA	Shareholders	NA

Business: The groups principal activity is to explore minerals and natural gas. The group operates from the United States and Canada.

Primary SIC and add'l.: 1499

CIK No: 0001142462

Officers: Tim Coupland/Dir., CEO, Pres., Robert T. Hall/Dir., Dir. - Field Operations, Michael Bogin/Dir., CFO, Allan Feldman/Investor Relations Officer, Hamid Mumin/Sr. Geologist, Roger Watson/Sr. Geophysicist, Ann-marie Cederholm/Corp. Sec., Gary Vivian/Advisor, Lou Covello/Advisor, James Stafford/Auditor

Directors: Tim Coupland/Dir., CEO, Pres., Tracy Moore/Dir., Robert T. Hall/Dir., Dir. - Field Operations, Stuart Rogers/Dir., Michael Bogin/Dir., CFO

Owners: Goodman & Company, Investment Counsel Ltd./9.46%

Financial Data: Fiscal Year End:11/30 Latest Annual Data: 11/30/2006

Year	Sales	Net Income
2006	NA	-$11,518,000
2005	NA	-$2,424,000
2004	NA	-$1,593,000

Curr. Assets:	$27,066,000	Curr. Liab.:	$411,000		
Plant, Equip.:	$95,000	Total Liab.:	$411,000	Indic. Yr. Divd.:	NA
Total Assets:	$27,194,000	Net Worth:	$26,783,000	Debt/ Equity:	NA

Alberto Culver Co

2525 Armitage Ave, Melrose Park, IL, 60160; *PH:* 1-708-450-3039; *http://* www.alberto.com

General - Incorporation	DE	**Stock**- Price on:12/24/2007	$25.94
Employees	NA	Stock Exchange	NYSE
Auditor	KPMG LLP	Ticker Symbol	ACV
Stk Agt	Computershare Investor Services LLC	Outstanding Shares	97,410,000
Counsel	NA	E.P.S.	$0.80
DUNS No.	00-507-1378	Shareholders	NA

Business: The groups principle activities include developing, manufacturing, distributing and marketing beauty care, food and household products. The groups products are sold under the brand names Consort, Motions and Static Guard. The group operates from United States.

Primary SIC and add'l.: 5122 2844 7231

CIK No: 0000003327

Subsidiaries: Alberto-Culver (N.Z.) Ltd., Alberto-Culver (P.R.), Inc., Alberto-Culver AB, Alberto-Culver Canada, Inc., Alberto-Culver Company (U.K.), Limited, Alberto-Culver de Mexico, S.A. de C.V., Alberto-Culver Group Ltd., Alberto-Culver Holdings Australia Pty. Ltd., Alberto-Culver Holdings, Ltd., Alberto-Culver Holland B.V., Alberto-Culver International, Inc., Alberto-Culver USA, Inc., Armstrong-McCall Holdings, Inc., Armstrong-McCall Holdings, LLC, Armstrong-McCall L.P. 36 Subsidiaries included in the Index

Officers: James V. Marino/Dir., CEO, Pres., Ralph J. Nicoletti/CFO, Sr. VP, John R. Berschied/Group VP - Worldwide Research, Development, Gary P. Schmidt/Sr. VP, General Counsel, Sec., Richard J. Hynes/Sr. VP, Richard Mewborn/VP - Worldwide Operations, Doug Craney/Dir. - Corporate Development, Investor Relations

Directors: James V. Marino/Dir., CEO, Pres., Carol L. Bernick/Chmn., King Harris/Dir., Leonard H. Lavin/Dir., Robert H. Rock/Dir., Jim Edgar/Dir., James G. Brocksmith/Dir., Sam J. Susser/Dir., Thomas A. Dattilo/Dir., George L. Fotiades/Dir., Katherine S. Napier/Dir.

Financial Data: Fiscal Year End:09/30 Latest Annual Data: 09/30/2007

Year	Sales	Net Income
2007	$1,541,581,000	$78,264,000

Curr. Assets:	$857,538,000	Curr. Liab.:	$416,050,000	P/E Ratio:	22.04
Plant, Equip.:	$224,494,000	Total Liab.:	$514,196,000	Indic. Yr. Divd.:	NA
Total Assets:	$1,487,560,000	Net Worth:	$973,364,000	Debt/ Equity:	NA

Albina Community Bancorp OR

2002 Ne Martin Luther Kin, Portland, OR, 97212; *PH:* 1-503-287-7537; *http://* www.albinabank.com

General - Incorporation	OR	**Stock**- Price on:12/24/2007	$10.7
Employees	NA	Stock Exchange	OTC
Auditor	NA	Ticker Symbol	ACBC
Stk Agt	OTR Transfer Agency	Outstanding Shares	NA
Counsel	NA	E.P.S.	NA
DUNS No.	NA	Shareholders	NA

Business: The group operates through its subsidiary Shore bank Advisory Services, whose principle activity is to promote investment and development. The group financial products include loans, mortgage and deposits. The group operates from the United States.

Primary SIC and add'l.: 6712

CIK No: 0001009908

Officers: Robert L. McKean/Dir., CEO, Pres., Jim Schlotfeldt/Sr. VP, CFO

Directors: Robert L. McKean/Dir., CEO, Pres., Howard M. Shapiro/Vice Chmn., Michael C. Henderson/Chmn., Sheila D. Holden/Dir., Bernard V. Foster/Dir., Ted K. Gilbert/Dir., Jeana M. Woolley/Dir., James R. Bradshaw/Dir. - Albina Cmnty Bank, Graham C. Bryce/Dir. - Albina Cmnty Bank

Financial Data: Fiscal Year End:12/31   Latest Annual Data: 12/31/2002

Year	Sales	Net Income
2002	$6,567,000	$1,252,000
2001	$5,568,000	$1,092,000
2000	$4,051,000	$642,000

Curr. Assets:	$7,738,000	**Curr. Liab.:**	$70,843,000		
Plant, Equip.:	$1,172,000	**Total Liab.:**	$73,297,000	**Indic. Yr. Divd.:**	NA
Total Assets:	$80,033,000	**Net Worth:**	$6,736,000	**Debt/ Equity:**	0.1883

Alcan Inc

1188 Sherbrooke St. W, Montreal, QC, H3A 3G2; **PH:** 1-514-848-8000; **http://** www.alcan.com; **Email:** investor.relations@alcan.com

General - Incorporation ....Canada	**Stock**- Price on:12/24/2007 ....$82.32
Employees...64,700	Stock Exchange.. NYSE
Auditor ....PricewaterhouseCoopers LLP	Ticker Symbol.. AL
Stk Agt.............................. Mellon Trust Co	Outstanding Shares 367,870,000
Counsel...NA	E.P.S...$0.88
DUNS No...20-209-7614	Shareholders..NA

Business: The group's principle activities include bauxite mining, alumina refining, specialty chemicals, power generation, aluminum smelting, manufacturing, recycling and packaging. The group also produces and converts specialty packaging and packaging products for many industries including the food, pharmaceutical, cosmetic and health sectors. It distributes and markets aluminum, non-aluminum and packaging products and also produces and sells industrial chemicals. The group operates in over 38 countries including Canada, the United States, Germany, the United Kingdom, Switzerland, Australia and other.

Primary SIC and add'l.: 3355 1099 3341 3354 7389 3353

CIK No: 0000004285

Subsidiaries: 3712001 Canada Inc., 9121-5988 Qubec Inc., 9121-5996 Qubec Inc., A-l Financial Products Ltd., AFFIMET, Al Holding Usa LLC, Al Wifaq 5, Ala (nevada) Inc., Alcan (bermuda) Limited, Alcan Adminco (2000) Inc., Alcan Airex Ag, Alcan Alesa Engineering Ag, Alcan Alesa Technologies Ltd., Alcan Allega Ag, Alcan Alpe Adria D.o.o. 465 Subsidiaries included in the Index

Officers: Richard B. Evans/60/CEO, Pres., Jacynthe Cote/Sr. VP, Michel Jacques/Sr. VP, Roy Millington/Corp. Sec., David L. McAusland/Exec. VP - Corporate Development, Chief Legal Officer, Christel Bories/Sr. VP, Gaston Ouellet/65/Sr. VP, Rhodri J. Harries/VP, Treasurer, Daniel Gagnier/61/Sr. VP - Corporate, External Affairs, Michael Hanley/CFO, Exec. VP, Jean-Christophe Deslarzes/44/Sr. VP - Human Resources, Cesidio Ricci/VP, Controller, Pierre Chenard/VP, General Counsel - Operations, Corey Copeland/Sr. VP - Investor - Corporate Relations, Ilene Gordon/Sr. VP (23 Officers included in Index)

Directors: Jean-Paul Jacamon/60/Dir., Christine Morin-Postel/61/Dir., Gerhard Schulmeyer/69/Dir., Gwyn Morgan/Dir., Heather Munroe-Blum/57/Dir., Jeffrey E. Garten/Dir., Denis L. Desautels/64/Dir., Paul M. Tellier/68/Dir., Yves L. Fortier/72/Dir., Milton K. Wong/69/Dir., Roland Berger/70/Dir., Onno H. Ruding/68/Dir., Guy Saint-Pierre/Dir., Yves Mansion/57/Dir.

Financial Data: Fiscal Year End:12/31   Latest Annual Data: 3/1/2007

Year	Sales	Net Income
2007	$23,641,000,000	$1,786,000,000
2006	$23,641,000,000	$1,786,000,000
2005	$20,320,000,000	$129,000,000

Curr. Assets:	$7,677,000,000	**Curr. Liab.:**	$5,979,000,000	**P/E Ratio:**	16.08
Plant, Equip.:	$12,402,000,000	**Total Liab.:**	$17,774,000,000	**Indic. Yr. Divd.:**	$0.800
Total Assets:	$28,939,000,000	**Net Worth:**	$11,094,000,000	**Debt/ Equity:**	0.4469

Alcoa Inc

201 Isabella St., Pittsburgh, PA, 15212; **PH:** 1-412-553-4545; **Fax:** 1-412-553-4498; **http://** www.alcoa.com

General - Incorporation ....PA	**Stock**- Price on:12/24/2007 ....$42.57
Employees..123,000	Stock Exchange.. NYSE
Auditor ....PricewaterhouseCoopers LLP	Ticker Symbol.. AA
Stk Agt.......................... Computershare Trust Co	Outstanding Shares 869,520,000
Counsel...NA	E.P.S...$2.63
DUNS No...00-133-9472	Shareholders..NA

Business: The group's principle activities include production and management of primary aluminum, fabricated aluminum and alumina facilities. Customers served by the group include aerospace, automotive, packaging, building and construction, commercial transportation, and industrial markets, bringing design and engineering. The group operates from United States.

Primary SIC and add'l.: 3355 3497 3365 3353 3354 3399 4931

CIK No: 0000004281

Subsidiaries: AAC Holdings Company, Alcoa A Islandi ehf, Alcoa Aluminio S.A., Alcoa Canada Ltd., Alcoa Domestic LLC, Alcoa Europe Holding B.V., Alcoa Europe S.A., Alcoa Extruded Products (UK) Limited, Alcoa Extrusions, Inc., Alcoa Fujikura De Mexico, S. DE R. L. RE C. V., Alcoa Fujikura Holding, LLC, Alcoa Fujikura Ltd., Alcoa Global Fasteners, Inc., Alcoa Global Treasury Services S.r.l., Alcoa Inespal, S.A. 58 Subsidiaries included in the Index

Officers: Alain J.P. Belda/63/Chmn., CEO, Russell C. Wisor/VP - Government Affairs, Kevin J. Anton/VP - Alcoa, Pres. - Alcoa Materials Management, Peter Hong/VP, Treasurer, Olivier M. Jarrault/VP - Alcoa, Pres. - Alcoa Fastening Systems, Joseph R. Lucot/VP, Controller, Raymond B. Mitchell/VP, Alcoa Pres. - Alcoa Power, Propulsion, Wayne G. Osborn/VP - Alcoa, MD - Alcoa World Alumina Australia, Charles D. McLane/CFO, Exec. VP, Donna C. Dabney/Sec. - Corporate Governance Counsel, William F. Christopher/Exec. VP - Alcoa, Group Pres. - Engineered Products, Solutions/$3,722,435.00, Paul D. Thomas/Exec. VP, Group Pres. - Packaging, Consumer

Products/$2,968,499.00, Lawrence R. Purtell/Chief Compliance Officer, Exec. VP, General Counsel, Helmut Wieser/Exec. VP, Group Pres., Exec. VP, Group Pres. - Global Rolled Products, Hard, Alloy Extrusions, Asia/$3,795,237.00, Bernt Reitan/Exec. VP - Alcoa, Group Pres. - Global Primary Products/$2,342,810.00 (39 Officers included in Index)

Directors: Alain J.P. Belda/63/Chmn., CEO, Ratan N. Tata/70/Dir., Kathryn Fuller/61/Dir., James Owens/62/Dir., Carlos Ghosn/53/Dir., Henry B. Schacht/73/Dir., Joseph T. Gorman/70/Dir., Judith M. Gueron/66/Dir., Ernesto Zedillo/56/Dir., Franklin A. Thomas/73/Dir., Klaus Kleinfeld/50/Dir.

Owners: Capital Research and Management Company/9.40%, Wellington Management Company, LLP/9.00%

Financial Data: Fiscal Year End:12/31   Latest Annual Data: 12/31/2006

Year	Sales	Net Income
2006	$30,379,000,000	$2,248,000,000
2005	$26,159,000,000	$1,233,000,000
2004	$23,478,000,000	$1,310,000,000

Curr. Assets:	$9,157,000,000	**Curr. Liab.:**	$7,281,000,000	**P/E Ratio:**	16.19
Plant, Equip.:	$15,792,000,000	**Total Liab.:**	$20,752,000,000	**Indic. Yr. Divd.:**	$0.680
Total Assets:	$37,183,000,000	**Net Worth:**	$14,631,000,000	**Debt/ Equity:**	0.4092

Alcon Inc

6201 S Fwy., Fort Worth, TX, 76134; **PH:** 1-817-293-0450; **Fax:** 1-817-568-7201; **http://** www.alconlabs.com; **Email:** investor.relations@alconlabs.com

General - Incorporation ....Switzerland	**Stock**- Price on:12/24/2007 ....$135.08
Employees...13,500	Stock Exchange.. NYSE
Auditor .... KPMG LLP	Ticker Symbol.. ACL
Stk Agt................................ Bank of New York	Outstanding Shares 299,150,000
Counsel................Shearman & Sterling LLP	E.P.S...$5.16
DUNS No...NA	Shareholders..NA

Business: The group's principle activities of the company is to develop & manufacture surgical equipment, pharmaceuticals & contact lens care as well as other vision care products. All the company's medical products focus on the ophthalmic medicine segment. Although alcon is based in Switzerland and is a daughter company of nestle sa, the company's main operations are based in usa, while its shares are listed on the New York stock exchange. The group's quarterly revenue for September 2007 was 1,335.70 millions of USD.

Primary SIC and add'l.: 3851 2834 3841

CIK No: 0001167379

Subsidiaries: Alcon Capital and Investment Panama, S.A., Alcon Credit Corporation, Alcon Holdings Inc., Alcon Laboratories, Inc., Alcon Pharmaceuticals Ltd., Alcon Pharmaceuticals, Inc., Alcon RefractiveHorizons, Inc., N.V. Alcon Coordination Center

Officers: Cary Rayment/Chmn., CEO, Pres., Kevin J. Buehler/Sr. VP - United States, Chief Marketing Officer, Andre Bens/Sr. VP - Global Manufacturing, Technical Operations, Gerald D. Cagle/Sr. VP - Research, Development, Chief Scientific Officer, Jacqualyn Fouse/Sr. VP - Finance, Doug MacHatton/VP - Investor Relations, Strategic Corporate Communications, Matthew Head/Mgr. - Investor Relations, Joanne Beck/50/GM, Dir., Richard J. Croarkin/Sr. VP, CFO, Elaine E. Whitbeck/Sr. VP, Chief Legal Officer, General Counsel, Corp. Sec.

Directors: Cary Rayment/Chmn., CEO, Pres., Paul Polman/Dir., Joe Weller/Dir., Philip H. Geier/Dir., Werner J. Bauer/Dir., Francisco Castaner/Dir., Martin Schneider/48/Dir., Stefan Basler/53/Dir., Thomas G. Plaskett/Dir., Lodewijk J.R. De Vink/Dir., Joanne Beck/50/GM, Dir., Gerhard N. Mayr/Dir.

Financial Data: Fiscal Year End:12/31   Latest Annual Data: 12/31/2006

Year	Sales	Net Income
2006	$4,896,600,000	$1,348,100,000
2005	$4,368,500,000	$931,000,000
2004	$3,913,600,000	$871,800,000

Curr. Assets:	$3,462,100,000	**Curr. Liab.:**	$2,001,100,000	**P/E Ratio:**	8.10
Plant, Equip.:	$920,700,000	**Total Liab.:**	$2,513,700,000	**Indic. Yr. Divd.:**	$1.320
Total Assets:	$5,427,300,000	**Net Worth:**	$2,913,600,000	**Debt/ Equity:**	NA

Aldila Inc

13450 Stowe Dr., Poway, CA, 92064; **PH:** 1-858-513-1801; **Fax:** 1-858-513-1870; **http://** www.aldila.com; **Email:** sales@aldila.com

General - Incorporation ....DE	**Stock**- Price on:12/24/2007 ....$15.35
Employees...1,366	Stock Exchange.. NDQ
Auditor .... Peterson & Co. LLP	Ticker Symbol..ALDA
Stk Agt ..... American Stock Transfer & Trust Co.	Outstanding Shares 5,530,000
Counsel...............Fried Frank Harris Shriver & Jacobson	E.P.S...$1.14
DUNS No...06-310-7106	Shareholders..NA

Business: The group's principal activities are to design and manufacture graphite golf shafts. The group's product line consists of aldila branded products designed for custom club makers, as well as custom shafts developed in conjunction with its major customers. The product line is designed to improve the performance of any level of golfer from novice to tour professional. The group also helps develop cosmetic designs to give the customer's golf clubs a distinctive look. The major customers of the group include callaway, taylormade-addidas golf, acushnet and ping.

Primary SIC and add'l.: 3949

CIK No: 0000902272

Subsidiaries: Aldila Carbon Fibers Products (Zhuhai) Company Limited, Aldila de Mexico, S.A. de C.V., Aldila Golf Corp., Aldila Materials Technology Corp.

Officers: Peter R. Mathewson/Chmn., CEO/$343,190.00, Robert J. Cierzan/Dir., VP - Finance, Sec., Treasurer/$255,407.00, John E. Oldenburg/VP - Engineering - Aldila Golf Corp, David B. Lopez/VP - Manufacturing - Aldila Golf Corp, Scott Bier/VP - Controller - Aldila Golf Corp, Michael Rossi/VP - Sales, Marketing, Aldila Golf Corp

Directors: Peter R. Mathewson/Chmn., CEO, Thomas A. Brand/Dir., Robert J. Cierzan/Dir., VP - Finance, Sec., Treasurer, Andrew Leitch/Dir., Bryant R. Riley/Dir., Michael J. Sheldon/Dir.

Owners: Peter R. Mathewson/1.47%, Robert J. Cierzan, Insiders/8.44%, Andrew M. Leitch, Citigroup Global MarketsInc./6.77%, Thomas A. Brand, Bryant R. Riley/3.28%, Michael J. Rossi, Pike Capital Partners, LP/5.10%, Lloyd I. Miller/2.79%

Financial Data: Fiscal Year End:12/31   Latest Annual Data: 12/31/2006

Year	Sales	Net Income
2006	$72,370,000	$11,236,000
2005	$76,978,000	$13,404,000
2004	$52,762,000	$9,320,000

Curr. Assets:	$42,571,000	**Curr. Liab.:**	$6,521,000	**P/E Ratio:**	10.03
Plant, Equip.:	$8,794,000	**Total Liab.:**	$6,570,000	**Indic. Yr. Divd.:**	$0.600
Total Assets:	$55,896,000	**Net Worth:**	$49,326,000	**Debt/ Equity:**	NA

Aleris International Inc

Formerly: IMCO Recycling Inc
25825 Science Pk. Dr., Ste. 400, Beachwood, OH, 44122; ***PH:*** 1-216-910-3400;
http:// www.imcorecycling.com

General - Incorporation .... DE
Employees 4,200
Auditor .... Ernst & Young LLP
Stk Agt .... Mellon Investor Services LLC
Counsel .... Fulbright & Jaworski LLP
DUNS No. 00-737-2527

Stock- Price on:12/24/2007 .... NA
Stock Exchange .... NA
Ticker Symbol .... NA
Outstanding Shares .... NA
E.P.S .... NA
Shareholders .... NA

Business: The group's principal activity is to own and operate aluminum recycling and alloying facilities and zinc manufacturing facilities. The group operates in three segments: domestic aluminum, international aluminum and zinc. The aluminum segment includes processes such as aluminum melting, processing, alloying, brokering and salt cake activities. Aluminum beverage cans, aluminum scrap and dross are converted into molten metal to prepare precise aluminum alloy mixture. The processed aluminum is delivered in molten form or ingots. The zinc segment processing includes zinc melting, processing and brokering activities. Zinc scrap and dross are converted to various products such as zinc oxides, dust and metal. The customers of the group are aluminum producers and aluminum fabricators, diecasters, extruders, automotive, tire and rubber producers and galvanizers, steel companies and other processors.

Primary SIC and add'l.: 3341 5093

CIK No: 0000202890

Subsidiaries: Alchem Aluminum Shelbyville Inc., Alchem Aluminum, Inc, Aleris Asia Pacific Ltd., Aleris Blanking and Rim Products, Inc., Aleris do Brasil Holding Ltda., Aleris Mexico, S. de R.L. de C.V., Aleris Nuevo Leon, S. de R.L. de C.V., Aleris Ohio Management, Inc., Aleris Reciclagem Ltda., Aleris Reciclaje Servicios Administrativos, S. de R.L. de C.V., Aleris Reciclaje Servicios de Manufactura, S. de R.L. de C.V., ALSCO Holdings, Inc., ALSCO Metals Corporation, Alumitech of Cleveland, Inc., Alumitech of Wabash, Inc. 59 Subsidiaries included in the Index

Officers: Steven J. Demetriou/Chmn., CEO - Aleris International, Inc, Christopher R. Clegg/Exec. VP, General Counsel, Sec. - Aleris International, Inc, Sean M. Stack/Exec. VP, Pres. - Europe, Aleris International, Inc, Alfred Haszler/Sr. VP, Pres. - Rolled, Extruded Products, Europe, Aleris International, Inc, Paul E. Lego/Dir. - Aleris International, Inc, John J. Wasz/Exec. VP, Pres. - Aleris Rolled Products, North America, Aleris International, Inc, Dale V. Kesler/Dir. - Aleris International, Inc, Michael D. Friday/Exec. VP, CFO - Aleris International, Inc, Kelvin Davis/Dir. - Aleris International, Inc, Jonathan Garfinkel/Dir. - Aleris International, Inc, Michael MacDougall/Dir. - Aleris International, Inc, Alan K. Dick/Sr. VP - Metals Purchasing, Aleris International, Inc, Joseph M. Mallack/Sr. VP, Chief Accounting Officer - Aleris International, Inc, Scott A. McKinley/Sr. VP, Treasurer - Aleris International, Inc

Owners: Christopher R. Clegg, Scott McKinley, Michael MacDougall, Sean M. Stack, Steven J. Demetriou, Dale V. Kesler, Alan K. Dick, Alfred Haszler, John J. Wasz, Affiliates of TPG, Michael D. Friday, Insiders, Paul E. Lego, Aurora Acquisition Holdings, LLC, Kelvin Davis

Alesco Financial Inc

2929 Arch St., 17th Fl., Philadelphia, PA, 19104; ***PH:*** 1-215-701-9555; ***Fax:*** 1-215-701-8281;
http:// www.alescofinancial.com

General - Incorporation .... MD
Employees .... NA
Auditor .... Ernst & Young, LLP
Stk Agt .... Mellon Investor Services LLC
Counsel .... NA
DUNS No. .... NA

Stock- Price on:12/24/2007 .... $8.98
Stock Exchange .... NYSE
Ticker Symbol .... AFN
Outstanding Shares 55,460,000
E.P.S $1.21
Shareholders .... NA

Business: The groups principal activity is to provide financial services. The products of the group include debt securities, mortgage loans and leveraged loans. In October 6, 2006, Alesco Financial Trust, merger with Alesco Financial Inc. The group operates from the United States. The assets of the group for the year 2006 were $10,602,350 (thousands).

Primary SIC and add'l.: 6798

CIK No: 0001270436

Subsidiaries: Alesco Financial Holdings, LLC, Alesco Funding Inc., Alesco Holdings, Ltd., Alesco Loan Holdings Trust, Alesco Preferred Funding X, Ltd., Alesco Preferred Funding XI, Ltd., Alesco Preferred Funding XII, Ltd., Alesco Preferred Funding XIII, Ltd., Alesco Preferred Funding XIV, Ltd., Alesco Real Estate Holdings, LLC, Alesco TPS Holdings, LLC, Alesco Warehouse Conduit, LLC, Emporia Preferred Funding II, Ltd., Jaguar Acquisition, Inc., Kleros Real Estate CDO I, Ltd. 31 Subsidiaries included in the Index

Officers: James J. McEntee/CEO, Pres., Shami J. Patel/COO, Chief Investment Officer, John J. Longino/CFO, Treasurer

Directors: Daniel G. Cohen/Chmn., Charles W. Wolcott/54/Dir., Jack Haraburda/68/Dir., Lance Ullom/38/Dir., Rodney E. Bennett/66/Dir., Marc Chayette/57/Dir., Thomas P. Costello/62/Dir., Steven G. Dawson/49/Dir.

Owners: Rodney E. Bennett, Marc Chayette, Leon Cooperman/6.82%, Christian M. Carr, Jack Haraburda, Steven G. Dawson, Charles W. Wolcott, Osterweis Capital Management, LLC/6.27%, Thomas P. Costello, John J. Longino, Insiders/3.04%, Hunter Global Associates, L.L.C./6.75%, Shami J. Patel, James J. McEntee, Daniel G. Cohen/1.94% *(17 Owners included in Index)*

Financial Data: ***Fiscal Year End:***12/31 ***Latest Annual Data:*** 12/31/2006

Year	Sales	Net Income
2006	$217,740,000	$22,031,000
2005	$46,365,000	-$4,737,000
2004	$18,233,000	$644,000

Curr. Assets:	$447,588,000	**Curr. Liab.:**	$3,067,311,000		
Plant, Equip.:	NA	**Total Liab.:**	$10,173,548,000	**Indic. Yr. Divd.:**	$1.240
Total Assets:	$10,602,350,000	**Net Worth:**	$428,802,000	**Debt/ Equity:**	21.6779

Alexander & Baldwin Inc

822 Bishop St., Honolulu, HI, 96813; ***PH:*** 1-808-525-6611; ***Fax:*** 1-808-525-6652;
http:// www.alexanderbaldwin.com

General - Incorporation .... HI
Employees 2,197
Auditor .... Deloitte & Touche LLP
Stk Agt .... Mellon Investor Services LLC
Counsel .... NA
DUNS No. 00-913-1228

Stock- Price on:12/24/2007 .... NA
Stock Exchange .... NDQ
Ticker Symbol .... ALEX
Outstanding Shares 42,910,000
E.P.S $3.08
Shareholders .... NA

Business: The groups principle activities include property development and management, ocean transportation and agribusiness. The group also provides domestic intermodal transportation services. The group operates from United States.

Primary SIC and add'l.: 6552 6512 2061 4492 4491 4481 4424

CIK No: 0000003453

Subsidiaries: A & B Properties, Inc., A&B Development Company, ABHI-Crockett, Inc., East Maui Irrigation Company, Limited, Kahului Trucking & Storage, Inc., Kauai Coffee Company, Inc., Kauai Commercial Company, Incorporated, Kukuiula Development Company, Inc., Matson Integrated Logistics, Inc., Matson Navigation Company, Inc., Matson Terminals, Inc., McBryde Sugar Company, Limited, WDCI, Inc.

Officers: James S. Andrasick/CEO, Pres. - Matson Navigation Company, Inc, Stanley M. Kuriyama/Vice Chmn., CEO, Pres. - Land Group, CEO - A-B Properties, Inc, Allen Doane/Chmn., CEO/$7,614,177.00, Christopher J. Benjamin/CFO, Sr. VP, Treasurer/$1,402,698.00, Kevin C. O'Rourke/Sr. VP, General Counsel - Matson Navigation Company, Inc, Alyson J. Nakamura/Sec., Assist. General Counsel, Kevin L. Halloran/VP - Corporate Development, Investor Relations, Norbert M. Buelsing/Exec. VP - Property Management, A, B Properties, Inc, Nelson N.S. Chun/Sr. VP, Chief Legal Officer, Ronald J. Forest/Sr. VP - Operations, Matson Navigation Company, Inc, Matthew J. Cox/COO, Exec. VP - Matson Navigation Company, Inc, Son-Jai Paik/VP - Human Resources, Robert K. Sasaki/Pres. - Properties, A, B Properties, Inc, Gary J. North/Sr. VP - Pacific, Matson Navigation Company, Inc, Stephen G. Holaday/Pres. - Agribusiness *(18 Officers included in Index)*

Directors: Allen Doane/Chmn., CEO, Blake W. Baird/Dir., Michael J. Chun/Dir., Walter A. Dods/Dir., Constance H. Lau/Dir., Douglas M. Pasquale/Dir., Maryanna G. Shaw/Dir., Jeffrey N. Watanabe/Dir., Charles G. King/Dir.

Owners: FMR Corp./8.50%, Maryanna G. Shaw/0.70%, Insiders/4.20%, Charles G. King/0.10%, Blake W. Baird, Third Avenue Management LLC/6.20%, Michael J. Chun, James S. Andrasick/0.40%, Douglas M. Pasquale, Stanley M. Kuriyama/0.50%, Matthew J. Cox, Constance H. Lau, Hotchkis and Wiley Capital/5.00%, Allen W. Doane/1.50%, Jeffrey N. Watanabe *(17 Owners included in Index)*

Financial Data: ***Fiscal Year End:***12/31 ***Latest Annual Data:*** 3/31/2007

Year	Sales	Net Income
2007	NA	NA
2006	NA	NA
2005	$1,607,000,000	$126,000,000

Curr. Assets:	$285,000,000	**Curr. Liab.:**	$257,000,000		
Plant, Equip.:	$1,646,000,000	**Total Liab.:**	$1,224,000,000	**Indic. Yr. Divd.:**	$1.160
Total Assets:	$2,251,000,000	**Net Worth:**	$1,027,000,000	**Debt/ Equity:**	NA

Alexandria Real Estate Equities Inc

385 E Colorado Blvd., Ste. 299, Pasadena, CA, 91101; ***PH:*** 1-626-578-0777; ***Fax:*** 1-626-578-0896;
http:// www.labspace.com; ***Email:*** corporateinformation@labspace.com

General - Incorporation .... MD
Employees 105
Auditor .... Ernst & Young LLP
Stk Agt...... American Stock Transfer & Trust Co.
Counsel .... NA
DUNS No. .... NA

Stock- Price on:12/24/2007 .... $100.38
Stock Exchange .... NYSE
Ticker Symbol .... ARE
Outstanding Shares 29,470,000
E.P.S $2.49
Shareholders .... NA

Business: The groups principle activities include ownershiping, operationing, manageing, selective redeveloping , developing and acquiring properties. Customers served by the group include life sciences industry. The group operates from the United States. The group's quarterly revenue for September 2007 was 104.13 millions of USD.

Primary SIC and add'l.: 6798

CIK No: 0001035443

Subsidiaries: Alexandria Real Estate Equities, L.P., ARE - MA Region No. 31, LLC, ARE - Tech Square, LLC, ARE-QRS Corp.

Officers: Joel S. Marcus/60/Dir., CEO/$6,966,086.00, James H. Richardson/48/Dir., Pres./$3,919,223.00, Dean A. Shigenaga/41/CFO/$574,316.00, Peter J. Nelson/Sec.

Directors: Jerry M. Sudarsky/89/Chmn., James H. Richardson/48/Dir., Pres., Richard B. Jennings/64/Dir., Richard H. Klein/52/Dir., Martin A. Simonetti/50/Dir., Alan G. Walton/71/Dir., Richmond A. Wolf/37/Dir., John L. Atkins/64/Dir.

Owners: Dean A. Shigenaga, Jerry M. Sudarsky, Richmond A. Wolf, Martin A. Simonetti, Davis Selected Advisers, L.P./5.30%, Barclays Global Investors, N.A./5.48%, FMR Corp./8.96%, James H. Richardson, Stichting Pensioenfonds ABP/5.57%, The Vanguard Group, Inc./5.71%, Richard B. Jennings, Alan G. Walton, Cohen & Steers, Inc./6.87%, John L. Atkins, Joel S. Marcus/1.41% *(17 Owners included in Index)*

Financial Data: ***Fiscal Year End:***12/31 ***Latest Annual Data:*** 12/31/2006

Year	Sales	Net Income
2006	$316,821,000	$73,416,000
2005	$244,084,000	$63,433,000
2004	$183,284,000	$60,195,000

Curr. Assets:	$9,278,000	**Curr. Liab.:**	$1,099,917,000	**P/E Ratio:**	45.63
Plant, Equip.:	$0	**Total Liab.:**	-$3,877,000	**Indic. Yr. Divd.:**	$3.040
Total Assets:	$294,895,000	**Net Worth:**	$34,520,000	**Debt/ Equity:**	1.6851

Alexion Pharmaceuticals Inc

352 Knotter Dr., Cheshire, CT, 06410; ***PH:*** 1-203-272-2596; ***Fax:*** 1-203-271-8190;
http:// www.alexionpharmaceuticals.com

General - Incorporation .... DE
Employees 296
Auditor .... PricewaterhouseCoopers LLP
Stk Agt .... Continental Stock Transfer & Trust Co
Counsel .... Fulbright & Jaworski LLP
DUNS No. 78-935-9510

Stock- Price on:12/24/2007 .... $47.2
Stock Exchange .... NDQ
Ticker Symbol .... ALXN
Outstanding Shares 36,420,000
E.P.S .... -$3.37
Shareholders .... NA

Business: The group's principal activity is to develop therapeutic products for the treatment of severe diseases including cardiovascular and autoimmune disorders and cancer. The products include pexelizumab, eculizumab, unigraft-sci and unigraft-pd. Pexelizumab, is an antibody fragment being developed in collaboration with procter & gamble pharmaceuticals. Through its subsidiaries, the group is engaged in the discovery and development of a portfolio of additional antibody therapeutics targeting severe unmet medical needs. The columbus farming corporation was discontinued in Jan, 2004.

Primary SIC and add'l.: 8731 2834

CIK No: 0000899866

Subsidiaries: Alexion Antibody Technologies, Inc

Officers: Leonard Bell/Dir., Founder, CEO, Sec., Treasurer/$1,852,655.00, Thomas I.H. Dubin/Sr. VP, General Counsel, Paul W. Finnegan/VP - Commercial Operations, Development, Stephen P. Squinto/Founder, Exec. VP, Head - Research/$792,095.00, Barry P. Luke/VP - Finance, David W. Keiser/Dir., COO, Pres./$919,460.00, Stacey M. Hooks/Executive Dir. - Manufacturing, Technical Services, VP - Manufacturing - Technical Services, Christopher F. Mojcik/Sr. VP - Clinical Development/$775,418.00, Russell P. Rother/Sr. VP - Research, Scott A. Rollins/Sr. VP - Drug Development, Project Management, Katherine S. Bowdish/Sr. VP - Antibody Discovery, Pres. - Alexion Antibody Technologies, Nancy Motola/Sr. VP - Regulatory Affairs, Quality, Daniel N. Caron/Executive Dir. - Operations, Engineering, Vikas Sinha/Sr. VP, CFO/$1,053,492.00, Patrice Coissac/GM, Pres. - Alexion Europe SAS *(16 Officers included in Index)*

Directors: Leonard Bell/Dir., Founder, CEO, Sec., Treasurer, Max Link/Chmn., Joseph A. Madri/Dir., Stephen P. Squinto/Founder, Exec. VP, Head - Research, Douglas R. Norby/Dir., David W. Keiser/Dir., COO, Pres., Larry Mathis/Dir., Alvin S. Parven/Dir., Ruedi E. Waeger/Dir.

Owners: Thomas I.H. Dubin, Alvin S. Parven, Stephen P. Squinto, Larry L. Mathis, Fidelity Management& Research Company/14.55%, Christopher F. Mojcik, David W. Keiser, Max Link, Douglas R. Norby, Insiders/5.98%, T. Rowe Price Associates, Inc./8.11%, Ruedi E. Waeger, Vikas Sinha, Joseph A. Madri, Sectoral Asset Management, Inc./7.46% *(18 Owners included in Index)*

Financial Data: **Fiscal Year End:**07/31 **Latest Annual Data:** 12/31/2006

Year	Sales	Net Income
2006	$1,558,000	-$131,514,000
2005	$1,064,000	-$108,750,000

Curr. Assets:	$201,162,000	**Curr. Liab.:**	$24,714,000		
Plant, Equip.:	$11,546,000	**Total Liab.:**	$180,451,000	**Indic. Yr. Divd.:**	NA
Total Assets:	$248,122,000	**Net Worth:**	$67,671,000	**Debt/ Equity:**	1.6180

Alfa Corp

2108 E S Blvd., Montgomery, AL, 36116; ***PH:*** 1-334-288-3900; ***Fax:*** 1-334-613-4709; ***http://*** www.alfains.com

General		**Stock**	
Incorporation	DE	Price on:12/24/2007	$16.75
Employees	NA	Stock Exchange	NDQ
Auditor	KPMG LLP	Ticker Symbol	ALFA
Stk Agt	American Stock Transfer & Trust CO.	Outstanding Shares	80,520,000
Counsel	NA	E.P.S.	$1.35
DUNS No.	00-402-7900	Shareholders	NA

Business: The group's principle activity is to provide property, casualty and life insurance products. The group through the subsidiaries also provides consumer financing, commercial leasing, real estate investments, residential and commercial construction, real estate sales and benefit services. The group directly writes both traditional and universal life products. The traditional life policy includes whole life insurance, term life insurance policies and certain annuities with life contingencies. Universal life products include universal life insurance and other interest-sensitive life insurance policies. The group's quarterly revenue for September 2007 was 207.74 millions of USD.

Primary SIC and add'l.: 6311 6159 1531 6531 6331

CIK No: 0000743532

Subsidiaries: Alfa Agency Georgia, Inc, Alfa Agency Mississippi, Inc., Alfa Benefits Corporation, Alfa Financial Corporation, Alfa General Insurance Corporation, Alfa Insurance Corporation, Alfa Life Insurance Corporation, Alfa Vision Insurance Corporation, The Vision Insurance Group, LLC

Officers: Dionisio Garza Medina/54/CEO - Alfa, Jerry A. Newby/60/Chmn., Pres./$1,328,102.00, Lee C. Ellis/56/Exec. VP - Operations, Treasurer/$1,150,990.00, John T. Jung/61/CIO, Sr. VP, Jerry Johnson/52/Mgr. - Regional Claims, Alejandro M. Elizondo Barragan/Alternate Sec., Angel Casan/Sr. VP - Human Resources, Corporate Affairs, Enrique Flores Rodriguez/VP - Corporate Communications, Raul Gonzalez Casas/Mgr. - Investor Relations, Armando Garza Sada/Dir., Sr. VP - Development, Wyman Cabaniss/56/Sr. VP - Underwriting, Ralph Forsythe/53/VP - Finance, Assist. CFO, Chief Accounting Officer, Carlos Jimenez Barrera/Sec., Manuel Rivera/Pres. - Nemak, Mario H. Paez/Pres. - Sigma *(23 Officers included in Index)*

Directors: Jerry A. Newby/60/Chmn., Pres., Lorenzo H. Zambrano Trevino/Dir., John R. Thomas/Dir., Jose Calderon Rojas/Dir., Valentin Diez Morodo/Dir., Alvaro Fernandez Garza/Dir., Armando Garza Sada/Dir., Sr. VP - Development, Claudio X. Gonzalez Laporte/Dir., Ricardo Guajardo Touche/Dir., Antonio Madero Bracho/Dir., Rogelio M. Rebolledo Rojas/Dir., Adrian Sada Gonzalez/Dir., Fernando Senderos Mestre/Dir.

Owners: Dean Wysner, Steve Dunn, Jerry A. Newby/0.91%, Hal F. Lee/0.02%, C. Lee Ellis/0.70%, Russell R. Wiggins/0.02%, William B. Harper/0.39%, John R. Thomas/0.02%, B. Phil Richardson/0.32%, Boyd E. Christenberry/0.73%, Jacob C. Harper/0.02%, Insiders/59.28%, Stephen G. Rutledge/0.32%, Herman A. Watts/0.08%, Larry E. Newman/0.01%

Financial Data: **Fiscal Year End:**12/31 **Latest Annual Data:** 12/31/2006

Year	Sales	Net Income
2006	$812,138,000	$105,888,000
2005	$756,905,000	$99,034,000
2004	$660,368,000	$89,445,000

Curr. Assets:	$295,017,000	**Curr. Liab.:**	$68,677,000	**P/E Ratio:**	13.62
Plant, Equip.:	NA	**Total Liab.:**	$1,707,320,000	**Indic. Yr. Divd.:**	$0.470
Total Assets:	$2,534,239,000	**Net Worth:**	$826,919,000	**Debt/ Equity:**	NA

Alfacell Corp

225 Belleville Ave., Bloomfield, NJ, 07003; ***PH:*** 1-973-748-8082; ***Fax:*** 1-973-748-1355; ***http://*** www.alfacell.com; ***Email:*** info@alfacell.com

General		**Stock**	
Incorporation	DE	Price on:12/24/2007	NA
Employees	14	Stock Exchange	NDQ
Auditor	J. H. Cohn LLP	Ticker Symbol	ACEL
Stk Agt	American Stock Transfer & Trust Co.	Outstanding Shares	45,380,000
Counsel	NA	E.P.S.	-$0.2
DUNS No.	06-154-3591	Shareholders	NA

Business: The group's principle activities include discovering, investigating and developing a new class of drugs for the treatment of cancer and other pathological conditions. The company's research and development programs relate to the development of drugs to treat unresectable malignant mesothelioma, renal cell carcinoma, other cancers (epithelial malignancies), non-hodgkin's lymphoma, primary brain tumors, viral diseases, anti-inflammatory diseases, other pathological conditions such as organ transplantation and other diseases. The therapeutics is developed primarily from amphibian ribonuclei. The company is currently in discussions with several potential strategic alliance partners including major international biopharmaceutical companies to further the development and marketing of onconase (R), its principal product and other related products. The company is in its development stage. The group operates from United States.

Primary SIC and add'l.: 2834 8731

CIK No: 0000708717

Officers: Kuslima Shogen/Chmn., CEO, Diane Scudiery/Dir. - Clinical, Regulatory Operations, Paul M. Weiss/Dir., Pres. - Gala Design, Andrew P. Aromando/Sr. VP - Commercial Development, Operations, Lawrence A. Kenyon/43/Dir., Exec. VP, CFO, COO, Corp. Sec.

Directors: Kuslima Shogen/Chmn., CEO, David Sidransky/Dir., Member - Scientific Advisory Board, Stephen K. Carter/Dir., Member - Scientific Advisory Board, James J. Loughlin/Dir., Lawrence A. Kenyon/43/Dir., Exec. VP, CFO, COO, Corp. Sec., Ravi K. Acharya/Member - Scientific Advisory Board, Susanna Rybak/Member - Scientific Advisory Board, Paul M. Weiss/Dir., Pres. - Gala Design, Donald R. Conklin/Dir., John P. Brancaccio/Dir., Jacob V. Maizel/Member - Scientific Advisory Board, Zbigniew Darzynkiewicz/Member - Scientific Advisory Board, John J. Costanzi/Member - Scientific Advisory Board

Owners: Paul M. Weiss, the James O. McCash Trust/6.20%, McCash Family Limited Partnership/16.70%, Robert D. Love, Donald R. Conklin/1.00%, Insiders/5.80%, Knoll Capital Management LP, Fred Knoll and Europa International, Inc./10.70%, John P. Brancaccio, Kuslima Shogen/3.20%, James O. McCash/6.20%, Stephen K. Carter, James J. Loughlin, David Sidransky, Lawrence A. Kenyon

Financial Data: **Fiscal Year End:**07/31 **Latest Annual Data:** 7/31/2006

Year	Sales	Net Income
2006	$107,000	-$7,810,000
2005	$152,000	-$6,462,000
2004	$42,000	-$5,070,000

Curr. Assets:	$7,118,000	**Curr. Liab.:**	$1,830,000		
Plant, Equip.:	$137,000	**Total Liab.:**	$2,042,000	**Indic. Yr. Divd.:**	NA
Total Assets:	$7,820,000	**Net Worth:**	$5,778,000	**Debt/ Equity:**	NA

AlgoDyne Ethanol Energy Corp

301 W Holly St. Ste. D15, Bellingham, WA, 98225; ***PH:*** 1-360-820-2620; ***http://*** www.algodynecorp.com; ***Email:*** contact@algodynecorp.com

General		**Stock**	
Incorporation	NV	Price on:12/24/2007	$0.9
Employees	NA	Stock Exchange	OTC
Auditor	Amisano Hanson	Ticker Symbol	ADYN
Stk Agt	NA	Outstanding Shares	55,800,000
Counsel	NA	E.P.S.	NA
DUNS No.	NA	Shareholders	NA

Business: The groups principle activity is to buy and sell reclaimed textiles. The group operates from the United States and Canada.

Primary SIC and add'l.: 7389

CIK No: 0001346848

Subsidiaries: Algodyne Energy Operating Corp, Freshly Pressed Enterprises Inc.

Officers: Richard Ritter V. Raffay/Dir., CEO, CFO, Pres., Sec., Treasurer, Hans-Jurgen Franke/Dir., CTO, Troy K. Metz/Exec. VP - Business Development, Corporate Affairs

Directors: Richard Ritter V. Raffay/Dir., CEO, CFO, Pres., Sec., Treasurer, Vladislav Iaroukov/Dir., Hans-Jurgen Franke/Dir., CTO

Owners: Insiders/50.00%, Vladislav Iaroukov/50.00%

Financial Data: **Fiscal Year End:**08/31 **Latest Annual Data:** 08/31/2007

Year	Sales	Net Income
2007	NA	-$1,521,000
2006	$238,000	-$73,000

Curr. Assets:	$57,000	**Curr. Liab.:**	$72,000		
Plant, Equip.:	NA	**Total Liab.:**	$72,000	**Indic. Yr. Divd.:**	NA
Total Assets:	$57,000	**Net Worth:**	-$15,000	**Debt/ Equity:**	NA

Algoma Steel Inc

111 Eighth Ave. - Team 1, New York, NY, 10011; ***PH:*** 1-212-590-9100; ***http://*** www.algoma.com

General		**Stock**	
Incorporation	ON	Price on:12/24/2007	NA
Employees	NA	Stock Exchange	NA
Auditor	Ernst & Young LLP	Ticker Symbol	NA
Stk Agt	Computershare Investor Services LLC	Outstanding Shares	NA
Counsel	McCarthy Tetrault LLP	E.P.S.	NA
DUNS No.	20-149-5124	Shareholders	NA

Business: The group's principle activities are to manufacture and market steel plates. The products of the group include sheets and strips, plates and seamless tubular steels.

Primary SIC and add'l.: 5051 3441 3317 3312

CIK No: 0000943945

Officers: Denis Turcotte/Dir., CEO, Pres., Stephen Boniferro/VP - Human Resources, Tym Barker/Business Unit Mgr. - Welded Shapes, Profiles Division, Rick Biemann/Sales Representative - Welded Shapes, Profiles Division, Paul Royal/VP - Commercial, Armando Plastino/VP - Operations, Paul C. Finley/VP - Business Planning, Corp. Sec., Daniel J. Ardila/VP - Finance, CFO, Ray Bone/Technical Service Representative, Technical Service, Dave Rich/Sales Representative - Calgary Sales Office, Western Canada Sales, Brady Dunne/Sales Representative - Calgary Sales Office, Western Canada Sales, Lisa Tomie/Mgr. - Customer Service, Order Fulfillment, Service, James Albidone/Customer Service Specialist - Construction, Heavy Fabrication, Customer Service Specialist - Construction, Heavy Fabrication, Rob Wildman/Customer Service Specialist - Construction, Heavy Fabrication, Order Fulfillment, Service, Craig Coletti/Customer Service Specialist - Service Centers, Order Fulfillment, Service *(72 Officers included in Index)*

Directors: Denis Turcotte/Dir., CEO, Pres., Benjamin C. Duster/Chmn., Charles Masson/Dir., James J. Lawson/Dir., Alex Davidson/Dir., Marie Kelly/Dir., John Kallio/Dir., Murray Nott/Dir., Patrick J. Lavelle/Dir., Francis Petro/Dir., Nicholas Tolerico/Dir.

Alico Inc

640 S Main St., La Belle, FL, 33935; *PH:* 1-863-675-2966; *Fax:* 1-863-675-6928;
http:// www.alicoinc.com

General - Incorporation.....FL
Employees.....215
Auditor.....Mcgladrey & Pullen, LLP
Stk Agt.....Computershare Investor Services LLC
Counsel.....NA
DUNS No.....00-692-1951

Stock- Price on:12/24/2007.....$59.91
Stock Exchange.....NDQ
Ticker Symbol.....ALCO
Outstanding Shares.....NA
E.P.S.....-$1.88
Shareholders.....NA

Business: The group's principal activities are citrus fruit production, cattle ranching, sugarcane and sod production and forestry. The group also leases land for farming, cattle grazing, recreation and oil exploration. The citrus segment produces fruit for both fresh fruit and processed juice markets. The sugarcane segment produces sugarcane for processing. The ranch segment raises beef cattle to be sold in the wholesale market. The group sells forest products like sabal palms and other horticultural commodities to various landscaping companies. The group's land is managed for multiple use wherever possible. Saddlebag lake resorts inc, a subsidiary of the group develops and sells real estate while another, agri-insurance company ltd, writes crop insurance against catastrophic losses due to weather and disease.

Primary SIC and add'l.: 0133 1422 0174 0811 6510 0291

CIK No: 0000003545

Subsidiaries: Agri-Insurance Company, Ltd, Alico Plant World, LLC, Alico-Agri, Ltd., Saddlebag Lake Resorts, Inc

Officers: John R. Alexander/Chmn., CEO, Dan L. Gunter/COO, Pres., Denise Plair/Corp. Sec., Steven M. Smith/Sr. VP - Agricultural Operations, Michael R. Talaga/Sr. VP - Human Resources, Information Technology, Patrick Murphy/CFO, VP, Robert Bogart/Sr. VP - Non - Agricultural Operations

Directors: John R. Alexander/Chmn., CEO, Gregory T. Mutz/Dir., Baxter G. Troutman/Dir., Lee Caswell/Dir., Evelyn D'An/Dir., Charles L. Palmer/Dir., Gordon Walker/Dir., Phillip S. Dingle/Dir., Robert J. Viguet/Dir.

Owners: Phillip S. Dingle, Dan Gunter, Steven Smith, Insiders/0.85%, John R. Alexander/50.84%, Patrick W. Murphy, Charles L. Palmer, Evelyn DAn, Gregory T. Mutz, Robert E. Lee Caswell, Robert J. Viguet, GMT Capital Corp./8.17%, Gordon Walker, Third Avenue Management LLC/5.68%

Financial Data: *Fiscal Year End:*08/31 *Latest Annual Data:* 08/31/2007

Year	Sales	Net Income
2007	$134,837,000	-$13,844,000
2006	$77,434,000	$6,469,000
2005	$70,941,000	$6,090,000

Curr. Assets:	$110,913,000	Curr. Liab.:	$18,078,000		
Plant, Equip.:	$131,351,000	Total Liab.:	$121,650,000	Indic. Yr. Divd.:	NA
Total Assets:	$262,753,000	Net Worth:	$141,103,000	Debt/ Equity:	NA

Align Technology Inc

881 Martin Ave., Santa Clara, CA, 95050; *PH:* 1-408-470-1000; *Fax:* 1-408-470-1010;
http:// www.aligntech.com

General - Incorporation.....DE
Employees.....1,253
Auditor.....PricewaterhouseCoopers LLP
Stk Agt.....Computershare Investor Services LLC
Counsel.....Wilson Sonsini Goodrich & Rosati
DUNS No.....NA

Stock- Price on:12/24/2007.....$24.5
Stock Exchange.....NDQ
Ticker Symbol.....ALGN
Outstanding Shares.....66,500,000
E.P.S.....$0.18
Shareholders.....NA

Business: The group's principal activities are to design, develop and market a proprietary system for treating malocclusion or the misalignment of teeth. The system branded as invisalin (R), corrects malocclusion using a series of clear, removable appliances that gently move teeth to a desired final position. The invisalign system has two components: clincheck and aligners. Clincheck is an Internet-based application that allows orthodontists to simulate treatment in three dimensions by modeling two-week stages of tooth movement. Aligners are thin, clear plastic, removable dental appliances that correspond to each stage of the clincheck simulation. The products are sold in the United States, Europe, Canada, the United Kingdom, Mexico, Brazil, Australia and Hong Kong.

Primary SIC and add'l.: 3843

CIK No: 0001097149

Subsidiaries: Align Technology B.V., Align Technology De Costa Rica SRL, Align Technology GmbH

Officers: Thomas M. Prescott/Dir., CEO, Pres./$1,550,043.00, Len Hedge/VP - Operations, Roger E. George/VP - Legal Affairs, General Counsel, Eldon M. Bullington/VP - Finance, CFO/$686,562.00, Hossein Arjomand/VP - Research, Development/$863,311.00, Dan S. Ellis/VP - North American Sales, Gil Laks/VP - International, Darrell Zoromski/VP - Global Marketing, Chief Marketing Officer/$866,019.00, Shannon Mangum Henderson/Contact - Public Relations, Sonia Clark/VP - Human Resources

Directors: Thomas M. Prescott/Dir., CEO, Pres., Raymond C. Larkin/Chmn., David E. Collins/Dir., Gregory J. Santora/Dir., George J. Morrow/Dir., Kent H. Bowen/Dir., Warren S. Thaler/Dir., Joseph Lacob/Dir.

Owners: Greg J. Santora, Janus Capital Management LLC/5.14%, Warren S. Thaler, OrbiMed Advisors/6.75%, Kent H. Bowen, Fidelity Management& Research/9.96%, Joseph Lacob/4.49%, Gordon Gund and affiliated entities/11.04%, George J. Morrow, Hossein Arjomand, Michael Henry, Eldon M. Bullington, Kornitzer Capital Management Inc./6.11%, David Collins, Raymond C. Larkin
(19 Owners included in Index)

Financial Data: *Fiscal Year End:*12/31 *Latest Annual Data:* 12/31/2006

Year	Sales	Net Income
2006	$206,354,000	-$34,963,000
2005	$207,125,000	$1,413,000
2004	$172,830,000	$8,768,000

Curr. Assets:	$108,089,000	Curr. Liab.:	$67,783,000		
Plant, Equip.:	$26,904,000	Total Liab.:	$68,002,000	Indic. Yr. Divd.:	NA
Total Assets:	$151,558,000	Net Worth:	$83,556,000	Debt/ Equity:	NA

Alkermes Inc

88 Sidney St., Cambridge, MA, 02139; *PH:* 1-617-494-0171; *Fax:* 1-617-494-9263;
http:// www.alkermes.com; *Email:* financial@alkermes.com

General - Incorporation.....PA
Employees.....830
Auditor.....Deloitte & Touche LLP
Stk Agt.....Computershare Investor Services LLC
Counsel.....NA
DUNS No.....18-548-1132

Stock- Price on:12/24/2007.....$15.112
Stock Exchange.....NDQ
Ticker Symbol.....ALKS
Outstanding Shares.....101,380,000
E.P.S.....$0.091
Shareholders.....NA

Business: The group's principal activity is to develop and commercialize therapeutic products based on drug delivery technologies. The group has several areas of focus including controlled, extended-release of injectable drugs using prolease(R) and medisorb(R) delivery systems, and the development of pharmaceutical products based on its proprietary advanced inhalation research (air) pulmonary technology. Medisorb(R) is used for encapsulating traditional small molecule pharmaceuticals in microspheres made of common medical polymers. Air (TM) technology system enables the delivery of both small molecules and macromolecules to the lungs. Cereport(R) drug delivery system increases transiently the permeability of the blood-brain barrier.

Primary SIC and add'l.: 2834 8731

CIK No: 0000874663

Subsidiaries: Advanced Inhalation Research, Inc., Alkermes Controlled Therapeutics Inc.II, Alkermes Controlled Therapeutics, Inc., Alkermes Development CorporationII, Alkermes Europe, Ltd., Alkermes Investments, Inc., RC Royalty Sub LLC

Officers: David A. Broecker/CEO, Pres./$2,809,659.00, Madeline D. Coffin/VP - Human Resources, Ken F. Andrews/VP - Sales, Marketing, Chief Commercial Officer, Kathryn L. Biberstein/Sr. VP, General Counsel, Sec., Chief Compliance Officer/$1,182,840.00, Elliot W. Ehrich/Sr. VP - Research, Development, Chief Medical Officer, James M. Frates/Sr. VP, CFO, Treasurer/$1,605,610.00, Michael J. Landine/Sr. VP - Corporate Development/$1,443,347.00, Gordon G. Pugh/COO, Sr. VP

Directors: Michael A. Wall/Chmn. Emeritus, Robert A. Breyer/Dir., Floyd E. Bloom/Dir., Alexander Rich/Dir., Richard F. Pops/Dir., Mark B. Skaletsky/Dir., Paul J. Mitchell/Dir., Paul Schimmel/Dir., Gerri Henwood/Dir.

Owners: FMR Corp./14.92%, Geraldine Henwood, Mazama Capital Management, Inc./8.01%, Barclays Global Investors, NA./4.52%, Mark B. Skaletsky, Robert A. Breyer, Insiders/9.29%, Alexander Rich, David A. Broecker/1.37%, ClearBridge Advisors/6.68%, Elliot W. Ehrich, Wellington Management Company, LLP/11.55%, James M. Frates, Paul J. Mitchell, Michael A. Wall
(22 Owners included in Index)

Financial Data: *Fiscal Year End:*03/31 *Latest Annual Data:* 3/31/2007

Year	Sales	Net Income
2007	$239,965,000	$9,445,000
2006	$166,601,000	$3,818,000
2005	$76,126,000	-$73,916,000

Curr. Assets:	$432,875,000	Curr. Liab.:	$62,060,000	P/E Ratio:	83.96
Plant, Equip.:	$123,595,000	Total Liab.:	$365,160,000	Indic. Yr. Divd.:	NA
Total Assets:	$568,621,000	Net Worth:	$203,461,000	Debt/ Equity:	0.7711

All American Sportpark Inc

6730 South Las Vegas Blvd., Las Vegas, NV, 89119; *PH:* 1-702-798-7777; *http://* www.cellegy.com

General - Incorporation.....NV
Employees.....6
Auditor.....Piercy, Bowler, Taylor & Kern
Stk Agt.....American Stock Transfer & Trust Co.
Counsel.....NA
DUNS No.....12-204-5719

Stock- Price on:12/24/2007.....$0.29
Stock Exchange.....OTC
Ticker Symbol.....AASP
Outstanding Shares.....3,500,000
E.P.S.....-$0.19
Shareholders.....NA

Business: The group's principal activity is to manage and operate golf course and driving range property. The group developed family-oriented sports themed amusement parks: all- American sportspark (assp). Assp comprises of 2 centers: the callaway golf center ('cgc') and the all-american sportpark ('sportpark') amusement center. The group includes a 110-tee two-tiered driving range which is designed to have the appearance of an actual golf course with ten impact greens and a 1-1/2 acre lake with cascading waterfalls and an island green. The group has a 20,000 square foot clubhouse which includes an advanced state of the art golf swing analyzing system, the latest equipment and accessories, a restaurant and bar and an outdoor patio overlooking the golf course and driving range with the las vegas 'strip' in the background.

Primary SIC and add'l.: 7997

CIK No: 0000930245

Subsidiaries: All-American Golf Center, Inc.

Officers: Ronald S. Boreta/45/Dir., CEO, Pres., Treasurer, Sec.

Directors: Ronald S. Boreta/45/Dir., CEO, Pres., Treasurer, Sec., Vaso Boreta/73/Chmn., Robert R. Rosburg/80/Dir., William Kilmer/67/Dir.

Owners: Boreta Enterprises, Ltd./10.30%, John Boreta/14.30%, Robert R. Rosburg, Vaso Boreta/0.10%, William Kilmer, Ronald S. Boreta/18.60%, Insiders/20.70%, ASI Group LLC/18.20%

Financial Data: *Fiscal Year End:*12/31 *Latest Annual Data:* 12/31/2006

Year	Sales	Net Income
2006	$2,208,000	-$839,000
2005	$2,153,000	-$1,654,000
2004	$2,169,000	-$593,000

Curr. Assets:	$55,000	Curr. Liab.:	$2,929,000		
Plant, Equip.:	$938,000	Total Liab.:	$9,216,000	Indic. Yr. Divd.:	NA
Total Assets:	$992,000	Net Worth:	-$8,224,000	Debt/ Equity:	NA

All State Properties LP UT

360 Main St., Washington, VA, 22747; *PH:* 1-540-675-3149

General - Incorporation.....DE
Employees.....NA
Auditor.....Morrison, Brown, Angiz & Farra, LLP
Stk Agt.....American Stock Transfer & Trust Co.
Counsel.....NA
DUNS No.....NA

Stock- Price on:12/24/2007.....$0.11
Stock Exchange.....OTC
Ticker Symbol.....ATPTZ
Outstanding Shares.....3,120,000
E.P.S.....$0.05
Shareholders.....NA

Business: The groups principle activities include land development, construction and sale of residential housing. The group operates from the United States.

Primary SIC and add'l.: 1531

CIK No: 0000745543

Officers: Stanley R. Rosenthal/79/CEO, Pres.

Owners: Stanley R. Rosen/5.00%, J.W. Sopher/5.30%

Financial Data: *Fiscal Year End:*06/30 **Latest Annual Data:** 6/30/2006

Year	Sales	Net Income
2006	NA	-$78,000
2005	NA	-$72,000
2004	NA	-$69,000

Curr. Assets:	$1,000	**Curr. Liab.:**	$278,000	**P/E Ratio:**	1.83
Plant, Equip.:	NA	**Total Liab.:**	$278,000	**Indic. Yr. Divd.:**	$0.050
Total Assets:	$238,000	**Net Worth:**	-$40,000	**Debt/ Equity:**	1.1361

Allbritton Communications Co

800 Seventheen St. NW, Ste 300, Washington, DC, 20006; ***PH:*** 1-202-789-2130;
http:// www.allbritton.com

General - Incorporation	DE	**Stock**- Price on:12/24/2007	NA
Employees	NA	Stock Exchange	NA
Auditor	PricewaterhouseCoopers LLP	Ticker Symbol	NA
Stk Agt	NA	Outstanding Shares	NA
Counsel	NA	E.P.S	NA
DUNS No.	05-861-0890	Shareholders	NA

Business: The group's principal activities are to own and operate network-affiliated television stations serving seven markets in the United States. The stations operated by the group are wcft in tuscaloosa, Alabama; whtm in harrisburg, Pennsylvania; katv in little rock, Arkansas; ktul in tulsa, oklahama; wset in lynchburg, Virginia; wctv in charleston, South Carolina and wjla in Washington. The services offered by the group include public broadcasting, television broadcasting, cable television systems, direct broadcast satellite ('dbs') and local news.

Primary SIC and add'l.: 4833 7922

CIK No: 0000889156

Subsidiaries: ACC Licensee, Inc., Allbritton Television Productions, Inc., Allfinco, Inc., Harrisburg Television, Inc., KATV, LLC, KTUL, LLC, TV Alabama, Inc., WCIV, LLC, WSET, Incorporated

Officers: Robert L. Allbritton/39/Chmn., CEO, Frederick J. Ryan/53/Vice Chmn., COO, Pres., Jerald N. Fritz/57/Sr. VP - Legal, Strategic Affairs, General Counsel, Elizabeth A. Haley/VP, Controller, James C. Killen/46/VP - Sales, Barbara B. Allbritton/71/Dir., Exec. VP, Stephen P. Gibson/42/CFO, Sr. VP

Directors: Robert L. Allbritton/39/Chmn., CEO, Frederick J. Ryan/53/Vice Chmn., COO, Pres., Barbara B. Allbritton/71/Dir., Exec. VP

Alleghany Corp

7 Times Sq. Tower, New York, NY, 10036; ***PH:*** 1-212-752-1356; ***Fax:*** 1-212-759-8149;
http:// www.alleghany.com

General - Incorporation	DE	**Stock**- Price on:12/24/2007	$416.71
Employees	694	Stock Exchange	NYSE
Auditor	KPMG LLP	Ticker Symbol	Y
Stk Agt	Computershare Investor Services LLC	Outstanding Shares	8,150,000
Counsel	NA	E.P.S	$32.68
DUNS No.	00-697-9652	Shareholders	NA

Business: The group's principal activity is to provide property and casualty insurance and reinsurance businesses at lloyd's of london. It is also engaged in the industrial minerals business and steel fastener importing and distribution business through its subsidiaries. The subsidiaries of the group include world minerals inc, celite corporation, harborlite corporation, heads & threads international llc . During the year 2003, the group acquired resurgens specialty underwriting inc and rsui indemnity company.

Primary SIC and add'l.: 6541 3295 6719 3965 5051 6331

CIK No: 0000775368

Subsidiaries: Alleghany Capital Corporation, Alleghany Consulting, Inc., Alleghany Funding Corporation, Alleghany Insurance Holdings LLC, Alleghany Properties Holdings LLC, Alleghany Properties LLC, Bibb Steel and Supply Company, Capitol Facilities Corporation, Capitol Indemnity Corporation, Capitol Specialty Insurance Corporation, Capitol Transamerica Corporation, Darwin Group, Inc., Darwin National Assurance Company, Darwin Professional Underwriters, Inc., Darwin Select Insurance Company 24 Subsidiaries included in the Index

Officers: Weston M. Hicks/Dir., CEO, Pres./$9,534,618.00, Nicholas J. Spencer/CEO, Pres. - Alleghany Capital Partners LLC, James Little/CEO, Pres. - Employers Direct Corporation, James A. Dixon/Chmn., CEO - Rsui Group, Inc, David F. Pauly/CEO - Capitol Transamerica Corporation, Stephen J. Sills/Chmn., CEO, Pres. - Darwin Professional Underwriters, Inc, David J. Bugatto/CEO, Pres. - Alleghany Properties LLC, E. G. Lassiter/Pres. - Rsui Group, Inc, Roger B. Gorham/Sr. VP - Finance, Investments, CFO/$1,979,672.00, Jerry G. Borrelli/VP - Finance, Chief Accounting Officer/$888,425.00, Christopher K. Dalrymple/VP, Assoc. General Counsel, Assist. Sec., Susan E. Giarrusso/VP, General Auditor, Robert M. Hart/Sr. VP, General Counsel/$3,132,517.00, Peter R. Sismondo/VP, Controller, Assist. Sec., James P. Slattery/Sr. VP - Insurance/$2,261,851.00 *(17 Officers included in Index)*

Directors: Weston M. Hicks/Dir., CEO, Pres., James A. Dixon/Chmn., CEO - Rsui Group, Inc, Stephen J. Sills/Chmn., CEO, Pres. - Darwin Professional Underwriters, Inc, John J. Burns/Chmn., James F. Will/Dir., Raymond L.M. Wong/Dir., William K. Lavin/Dir. - Financial Consultant, Jefferson W. Kirby/Dir., Allan P. Kirby/Dir., Thomas S. Johnson/Dir., Dan R. Carmichael/Dir., Rex D. Adams/Dir.

Owners: Weston M. Hicks/0.78%, James P. Slattery/0.08%, John J. Burns/1.10%, Rex D. Adams/0.12%, William K. Lavin/0.17%, Allan P. Kirby/6.80%, Raymond L.M. Wong/0.01%, Jerry G. Borrelli, Insiders/12.31%, James F. Will/0.33%, Roger B. Gorham/0.06%, Thomas S. Johnson/0.18%, Robert M. Hart/0.28%, Dan R. Carmichael/0.24%, Jefferson W. Kirby/2.30%

Financial Data: *Fiscal Year End:*12/31 **Latest Annual Data:** 12/31/2006

Year	Sales	Net Income
2006	$1,209,165,000	$251,244,000
2005	$1,095,956,000	$52,334,000
2004	$1,240,927,000	$117,696,000

Curr. Assets:	$2,163,127,000	**Curr. Liab.:**	$157,957,000	**P/E Ratio:**	12.75
Plant, Equip.:	$40,991,000	**Total Liab.:**	$3,677,619,000	**Indic. Yr. Divd.:**	NA
Total Assets:	$6,178,740,000	**Net Worth:**	$2,423,246,000	**Debt/ Equity:**	NA

Allegheny Energy Inc

800 Cabin Hill Dr., Greensburg, PA, 15601; ***PH:*** 1-724-837-3000; ***Fax:*** 1-724-830-5284;
http:// www.alleghenyenergy.com

General - Incorporation	MD	**Stock**- Price on:12/24/2007	$50.62
Employees	4,362	Stock Exchange	NYSE
Auditor	PricewaterhouseCoopers LLP	Ticker Symbol	AYE
Stk Agt	Mellon Investor Services LLC	Outstanding Shares	NA
Counsel	NA	E.P.S	$2.16
DUNS No.	00-172-1273	Shareholders	NA

Business: The groups principle activities include operating electric generation facilities and delivering electric services. The group operates through two business segments namely delivery and services segment. The group operates from United States.

Primary SIC and add'l.: 4899 4931

CIK No: 0000003673

Subsidiaries: Allegheny Communications Connect, Inc., Allegheny Energy Service Corporation, Allegheny Energy Solutions, Inc, Allegheny Energy Supply Company, LLC, Allegheny Energy Supply Gleason Generating Facility, LLC, Allegheny Generating Company, Allegheny Ventures, Inc., American Electric Powers, Buchanan Energy Company of Virginia, LLC, Green Valley Hydro, Green Valley Hydro, LLC, Monongahela Power Company, The Potomac Edison Company, West Penn Power Company

Officers: Paul J. Evanson/Chmn., CEO, Pres./$9,329,832.00, Philip L. Goulding/CFO, Sr. VP/$2,310,695.00, David M. Feinberg/VP, General Counsel, Sec., Barry E. Pakenham/VP, Treasurer, Edward Dudzinski/VP - Human Resources/$891,323.00, Aldie Warnock/VP - External Affairs, Max Kuniansky/Exec. Dir. - Investor Relations, Corporate Communications, William F. Wahl/VP, Controller, Chief Accounting Officer, Joseph H. Richardson/COO - Generation/$1,338,832.00, David E. Flitman/Pres. - Allegheny Power, Michael Adams/VP - Quality, David C. Cannon/VP - Environment, Health, Safety, Thomas R. Gardner/CIO, VP/$902,951.00

Directors: Paul J. Evanson/Chmn., CEO, Pres., Eleanor Baum/Dir., Cyrus F. Freidheim/Dir., Ted J. Kleisner/Dir., Steven H. Rice/Dir., Gunnar E. Sarsten/Dir., Julia L. Johnson/Dir., Furlong H. Baldwin/Dir., Michael H. Sutton/Dir.

Owners: Gunnar E. Sarsten, Steven H. Rice, Furlong H. Baldwin, Eleanor Baum, Philip L. Goulding, Paul J. Evanson/1.05%, Ted J. Kleisner, Michael H. Sutton, Joseph H. Richardson, Edward Dudzinski, Thomas R. Gardner, Insiders/1.71%, Cyrus F. Freidheim, Julia L. Johnson

Financial Data: *Fiscal Year End:*12/31 **Latest Annual Data:** 12/31/2006

Year	Sales	Net Income
2006	$3,121,489,000	$319,321,000
2005	$3,037,887,000	$63,065,000
2004	$2,756,121,000	-$310,598,000

Curr. Assets:	$909,422,000	**Curr. Liab.:**	$820,779,000		
Plant, Equip.:	$6,512,893,000	**Total Liab.:**	$6,437,338,000	**Indic. Yr. Divd.:**	$0.600
Total Assets:	$8,552,446,000	**Net Worth:**	$2,080,395,000	**Debt/ Equity:**	1.6391

Allegheny Generating Co

800 Cabin Hill Dr., Greensburg, PA, 15601; ***PH:*** 1-724-837-3000; ***http://*** www.alleghenyenergy.com

General - Incorporation	VA	**Stock**- Price on:12/24/2007	$50.87
Employees	4,362	Stock Exchange	NA
Auditor	PricewaterhouseCoopers LLP	Ticker Symbol	NA
Stk Agt	Mellon Investor Services LLC	Outstanding Shares	165,710,000
Counsel	NA	E.P.S	$2.14
DUNS No.	88-472-8536	Shareholders	NA

Business: The group's principle activities include producing and supplying electricity to its three parent companies. The company is jointly owned by monongahela power company, 23% and allegheny energy supply company llc, 77%. Monongahela power company and allegheny energy supply company llc are wholly-owned subsidiaries of allegheny energy, inc. Allegheny generating company, an unregulated unit of allegheny energy supply company llc sells its generating capacity to its parents and operates under single business segment, generation and marketing. The group operates from United States.

Primary SIC and add'l.: 4911

CIK No: 0000774459

Officers: Paul J. Evanson/Chmn., CEO, Thomas R. Gardner/CIO, VP - Allegheny Energy, Inc, William F. Wahl/VP, Controller, Chief Accounting Officer, David M. Feinberg/VP, General Counsel, Sec. - Allegheny Energy, Inc, Philip L. Goulding/Sr. VP, CFO - Allegheny Energy, Inc, Michael Adams/VP - Allegheny Energy, Inc, Loyd Warnock/VP, Barry E. Pakenham/VP, Treasurer - Allegheny Energy, Inc, Edward Dudzinski/VP - Allegheny Energy, Inc, David C. Cannon/VP - Allegheny Energy, Inc, David E. Flitman/Pres. - Allegheny Power

Directors: Paul J. Evanson/Chmn., CEO, Eleanor Baum/Dir., Michael H. Sutton/Dir., Cyrus F. Friedheim/Dir., Julia L. Johnson/Dir., Ted J. Kleisner/Dir., Steven H. Rice/Dir., Gunnar E. Sarsten/Dir.

Financial Data: *Fiscal Year End:*12/31 **Latest Annual Data:** 12/31/2006

Year	Sales	Net Income
2006	$3,121,489,000	$319,321,000
2005	$3,037,887,000	$63,065,000
2004	$2,756,121,000	-$310,598,000

Curr. Assets:	$909,422,000	**Curr. Liab.:**	$820,779,000	**P/E Ratio:**	23.77
Plant, Equip.:	$6,512,893,000	**Total Liab.:**	$6,437,338,000	**Indic. Yr. Divd.:**	NA
Total Assets:	$8,552,446,000	**Net Worth:**	$2,080,395,000	**Debt/ Equity:**	1.5574

Allegheny Technologies Inc

1000 Six PPG Pl., Pittsburgh, PA, 15222; ***PH:*** 1-412-394-2800; ***Fax:*** 1-412-394-3034;
http:// www.alleghenytechnologies.com

General - Incorporation	DE	**Stock**- Price on:12/24/2007	$109.735
Employees	9,500	Stock Exchange	NYSE
Auditor	Ernst & Young LLP	Ticker Symbol	ATI
Stk Agt	Mellon Investor Services LLC	Outstanding Shares	102,150,000
Counsel	NA	E.P.S	$7.38
DUNS No.	94-926-2737	Shareholders	NA

Business: The group's principle activity is to manufacture specialty materials. The engineered products include the production of tungsten powder, tungsten heavy alloys, tungsten carbide materials and carbide cutting tools. The group also produces carbon alloy steel impression die forgings, large grey and ductile iron castings. The group provides precision metals processing services. The group operates in United States, United Kingdom, Germany, France, Canada, Japan and China.

Primary SIC and add'l.: 3497 3321 3325 3312 3356

CIK No: 0001018963

Subsidiaries: ALC Funding Corporation, Allegheny Ludlum Corporation, ATI Funding Corporation, ATI Properties, Inc., Oregon Metallurgical Corporation, TDY Holdings LLC, TDY Industries, Inc.

Officers: Patrick L. Hassey/Chmn., CEO, Pres./$15,378,990.00, Jon D. Walton/Exec. VP - Human Resources, Chief Legal, Compliance Officer, General Counsel, Corp. Sec./$6,181,489.00, Dale G. Reid/VP, Controller, Chief Accounting Officer, Treasurer, Douglas A. Kittenbrink/Exec. VP - Corporate Planning, International Business Development/$6,016,880.00, Richard J. Harshman/CFO, Exec. VP - Finance/$6,187,550.00

Directors: Patrick L. Hassey/Chmn., CEO, Pres., Craig W. McClelland/Dir., Kent H. Bowen/Dir., James C. Diggs/Dir., Louis J. Thomas/Dir., Robert P. Bozzone/Dir., John D. Turner/Dir., Diane C. Creel/Dir., Michael J. Joyce/Dir., James E. Rohr/Dir.

Owners: Douglas A. Kittenbrink, Diane C. Creel, John D. Turner, Richard J. Harshman, Michael J. Joyce, Insiders/2.30%, Jon D. Walton, Craig W. McClelland, Robert P. Bozzone/1.60%, Louis J. Thomas, Kent H. Bowen, FMR Corp./9.70%, James C. Diggs, James E. Rohr, The Singleton Group, LLC/5.70% *(17 Owners included in Index)*

Financial Data: *Fiscal Year End:*12/31 *Latest Annual Data:* 06/30/2007

Year	Sales	Net Income
2007	NA	NA
2006	$4,936,600,000	$571,900,000
2005	$3,539,900,000	$359,800,000
Curr. Assets: $1,987,900,000	*Curr. Liab.:* $645,500,000	
Plant, Equip.: $867,600,000	*Total Liab.:* $1,789,600,000	*Indic. Yr. Divd.:* $0.720
Total Assets: $3,282,200,000	*Net Worth:* $1,492,600,000	*Debt/ Equity:* 0.3085

Allegheny Valley Bancorp Inc PA

5137 Butler St., Pittsburgh, PA, 15201; *PH:* 1-412-781-0318; *Fax:* 1-412-781-6474; *http://* www.avbpgh.com; *Email:* custsrv@avbpgh.com

General - Incorporation	NA	Stock - Price on:12/24/2007	$70.25
Employees	NA	Stock Exchange	OTC
Auditor	NA	Ticker Symbol	AVLY
Stk Agt	NA	Outstanding Shares	NA
Counsel	NA	E.P.S.	$3.10
DUNS No.	NA	Shareholders	NA

Business: The groups principal activity is to provide banking business. The group financial products include savings and fixed deposits, on line, personal, commercial lending and business banking. The group operates from the United States.

Primary SIC and add'l.: 6022 6712

CIK No:

Officers: Nelson L. Person/CFO, Andrew W. Hasley/Pres. - Allegheny Valley Bank, Pittsburgh

Financial Data: *Fiscal Year End:*NA *Latest Annual Data:* 12/31/2002

Year	Sales	Net Income
2002	$18,642,000	$4,067,000
2001	$18,595,000	$3,502,000
2000	$19,191,000	$4,011,000
Curr. Assets: $6,708,000	*Curr. Liab.:* $241,381,000	
Plant, Equip.: $3,429,000	*Total Liab.:* $249,431,000	*Indic. Yr. Divd.:* NA
Total Assets: $288,908,000	*Net Worth:* $39,477,000	*Debt/ Equity:* NA

Allegiance Bank PA

70 E Lancaster Ave., Malvern, PA, 19355; *PH:* 1-610-889-0261; *http://* www.allegbank.com; *Email:* GreatService@AllegBank.com

General - Incorporation	NA	Stock - Price on:12/24/2007	$4.43
Employees	NA	Stock Exchange	OTC
Auditor	NA	Ticker Symbol	ABPA
Stk Agt	NA	Outstanding Shares	4,430,000
Counsel	NA	E.P.S.	NA
DUNS No.	NA	Shareholders	NA

Business: The groups principle activity is to provide personal, business and Internet banking services. The groups personal services include personal checking, personal savings and consumer loans. The groups business services include business interest checking, business money market, merchant deposit accounts, and Master Money(TM) Debit Card. The groups additional services include IOLTA accounts, sweep accounts, federal tax depository service, night depositor, safe deposit boxes, telephone transfers, remote deposit capture. The group operates from United States.

Primary SIC and add'l.: 6099

CIK No:

Officers: Andrew C. Cook/Dir., CEO, Pres., Smiley E. Dugan/Sr. VP, Chief Retail Officer, Kevin J. Gallagher/Sr. VP, Chief Lending Office, Debora A. Micka/Sr. VP, Chief Credit Officer, John Carrozza/Sr. VP, CFO, Chief Administrative Officer

Directors: Andrew C. Cook/Dir., CEO, Pres., Edgar D. Landis/Chmn., Robert S. Kramer/Vice Chmn., Lynne C. Davis/Dir., Stanley H. Engle/Dir., Steven P. Lerman/Dir., Amos B. Smith/Dir.

Allegiant Travel Company

3301 N Buffalo Dr., Ste. B-9, Las Vegas, NV, 89129; *PH:* 1-702-851-7300; *Fax:* 1-702-256-7209; *http://* www.allegiantair.com

General - Incorporation	NV	Stock - Price on:12/24/2007	$32.35
Employees	767	Stock Exchange	NDQ
Auditor	Ernst & Young LLP	Ticker Symbol	ALGT
Stk Agt	American Stock Transfer & Trust Co.	Outstanding Shares	20,080,000
Counsel	NA	E.P.S.	$1.27
DUNS No.	NA	Shareholders	NA

Business: The groups principle activity is to provide leisure travel services. The groups services include business traveler, flight connections, hotel rooms and rental cars. The group operates from Las Vegas, Nevada, Orlando, Florida in the United States. The quarterly revenue of the group for September 2007 was 86.33 millions of USD.

Primary SIC and add'l.: 4724 4522 4512

CIK No: 0001362468

Subsidiaries: AFH, Inc.,

Officers: Maurice J. Gallagher/Dir., CEO, Pres. - Allegiant Air, Ponder M. Harrison/MD - Marketing, Sales, Allegiant Air, Andrew C. Levy/CFO, MD - Planning, Allegiant Air, Linda A. Marvin/46/MD, CFO, Michael P. Baxter/Sr. VP - Operations, Allegiant Air

Directors: Maurice J. Gallagher/Dir., CEO, Pres. - Allegiant Air, Michael S. Falk/Dir. - Allegiant Air, Timothy P. Flynn/Dir. - Allegiant Air, Maurice A. Mason/Dir. - Allegiant Air, Robert L. Priddy/Dir. - Allegiant Air, Declan F. Ryan/44/Dir.

Owners: Maurice J. Gallagher, Andrew C. Levy, Timothy P. Flynn, Michael P. Baxter, Linda A. Marvin, Michael S. Falk, Robert L. Priddy, PAR Investment Partners, L.P., Insiders, Gilder, Gagnon, Howe & Co., Inc., Maurice A. Mason, ComVest Allegiant Holdings, LLC, Ponder M. Harrison, Declan F. Ryan

Financial Data: *Fiscal Year End:*12/31 *Latest Annual Data:* 12/31/2006

Year	Sales	Net Income
2006	$243,350,000	$8,740,000
2005	$132,500,000	$7,292,000
2004	$90,365,000	$9,135,000
Curr. Assets: $168,656,000	*Curr. Liab.:* $87,822,000	
Plant, Equip.: $131,214,000	*Total Liab.:* $152,255,000	*Indic. Yr. Divd.:* NA
Total Assets: $305,726,000	*Net Worth:* $153,471,000	*Debt/ Equity:* 0.3315

Allergan Inc

2525 Dupont Dr., Irvine, CA, 92612; *PH:* 1-714-246-4500; *Fax:* 1-714-246-4971; *http://* www.allergan.com

General - Incorporation	DE	Stock - Price on:12/24/2007	$117.75
Employees	6,772	Stock Exchange	NYSE
Auditor	KPMG LLP	Ticker Symbol	AGN
Stk Agt	Wells Fargo Bank, N.A.	Outstanding Shares	152,540,000
Counsel	NA	E.P.S.	$1.392
DUNS No.	14-479-6497	Shareholders	NA

Business: The groups principle activities include discovering and developing specialty pharmaceutical and medical device products. Customers served by the group include ophthalmic, neurological, medical aesthetics, medical dermatological, breast aesthetics, obesity intervention and other specialty markets. In February 2007, the group acquired Swiss medical technology developer, EndoArt SA. The group operates from United States.

Primary SIC and add'l.: 2834 8733

CIK No: 0000850693

Subsidiaries: Allergan (Thailand) Ltd., Allergan A/S, Allergan AG, Allergan America, LLC, Allergan AS, Allergan Asia Limited, Allergan Australia Pty Limited, Allergan B.V., Allergan Botox Limited, Allergan de Colombia S.A., Allergan de Venezuela, S.A., Allergan France S.A.S., Allergan Holdings B, Ltd., Allergan Holdings BV, Allergan Holdings C, Ltd. 55 Subsidiaries included in the Index

Officers: David E.I. Pyott/Chmn., CEO/$10,354,140.00, James F. Barlow/49/Sr. VP, Corporate Controller, Crystal Cienfuegos/Contact - Media, Cathy Diramio/Contact - Media, Michael F. Ball/Pres./$3,036,813.00, Jeffrey L. Edwards/Exec. VP - Finance, Business Development, CFO/$1,698,326.00, Douglas S. Ingram/Exec. VP, General Counsel, Sec./$2,096,622.00, Scott M. Whitcup/Exec. VP - Research, Development/$1,990,545.00, Raymond H. Diradoorian/Exec. VP - Global Technical Operations, Jim Hindman/Investor Relations Officer, Joann Bradley/Investor Relations Officer, Emil Schultz/Investor Relations Officer, Caroline Vanhove/Contact - Media, Heather Katt/Contact - Media

Directors: David E.I. Pyott/Chmn., CEO, Herbert W. Boyer/Vice Chmn., Michael R. Gallagher/Dir., Deborah Dunsire/Dir., Gavin S. Herbert/Dir., Robert A. Ingram/Dir., Trevor M. Jones/Dir., Louis J. Lavigne/Dir., Russell T. Ray/Dir., Stephen J. Ryan/Dir., Leonard D. Schaeffer/Dir.

Owners: Gavin S. Herbert, David E.I. Pyott/1.09%, Stephen J. Ryan, Trevor M. Jones, Handel E. Evans, Michael F. Ball, Russell T. Ray, Michael R. Gallagher, Insiders/1.84%, Herbert W. Boyer, Louis J. Lavigne, Leonard D. Schaeffer, Deborah Dunsire, Scott M. Whitcup, Jeffrey L. Edwards *(18 Owners included in Index)*

Financial Data: *Fiscal Year End:*12/31 *Latest Annual Data:* 12/31/2006

Year	Sales	Net Income
2006	$3,063,300,000	-$127,400,000
2005	$2,319,200,000	$403,900,000
2004	$2,045,600,000	$377,100,000
Curr. Assets: $2,130,300,000	*Curr. Liab.:* $658,100,000	*P/E Ratio:* 84.59
Plant, Equip.: $611,400,000	*Total Liab.:* $2,622,500,000	*Indic. Yr. Divd.:* $0.200
Total Assets: $5,767,100,000	*Net Worth:* $3,143,100,000	*Debt/ Equity:* 0.5088

Allergy Research Group Inc

2300 N Loop Rd., Alameda, CA, 94502; *PH:* 1-510-263-2000; *Fax:* 1-510-263-2100; *http://* www.allergyresearchgroup.com; *Email:* info@allergyresearchgroup.com

General - Incorporation	FL	Stock - Price on:12/24/2007	$0.806
Employees	31	Stock Exchange	OTC
Auditor	Clancy & Co. PLLC	Ticker Symbol	ALRG
Stk Agt	Holladay Stock Transfer, Inc.	Outstanding Shares	14,560,000
Counsel	NA	E.P.S.	$0.07
DUNS No.	NA	Shareholders	NA

Business: The group's principal activity is to develop, market and distribute natural nutritional supplements primarily to distributors and health care professionals throughout the United States. The group operates through its wholly owned subsidiary nutricology, inc. The group offers a line of approximately 200 products, including vitamins in multivitamin and single-entity formulas, minerals and herbals. The products are manufactured in various forms, including capsules, tablets, soft gels, powers and liquids. The trademarks of the group include complete immune (TM), complete heart (TM), complete heart ii (TM), complete nerve (TM), wholly immune (TM), take heart (TM) and steady on (TM).

Primary SIC and add'l.: 5122

CIK No: 0001044119

Subsidiaries: Nutricology, Inc.

Officers: Stephen Levine/Chmn., CEO, CFO, Daniel Rubin/Member - Medical Advisory Board, Technical Consultant, Luba Voloshko/Staff in Charge, Quality Control, Susan Levine/Dir., Sec., Chief Promotions Officer, Manfred Salomon/Pres., Dir. - Operations, Robert Jay Rowen/Editor in Chief - Second Opinion, Fred Salomon/69/Pres.

Directors: Stephen Levine/Chmn., CEO, CFO, Jeffery Anderson/Co - Chmn. - Medical Advisory Board, Ed Kane/Dir., Fouad I. Ghaly/Member - Medical Advisory Board, Ba Hoang/Member - Medical Advisory Board, Michael Rosenbaum/Member - Medical Advisory Board, Susan Levine/Dir., Sec., Chief Promotions Officer, Daniel Rubin/Member - Medical Advisory Board, Technical Consultant

Owners: Manfred Salomon/0.70%, Insiders/70.00%, Stephen Levine/70.00%

Financial Data: *Fiscal Year End:* 12/31 *Latest Annual Data:* 12/31/2006

Year	Sales	Net Income
2006	$16,273,000	$1,096,000
2005	$15,911,000	$1,209,000
2004	$15,137,000	$1,283,000

Curr. Assets:	$7,351,000	Curr. Liab.:	$438,000	P/E Ratio:	11.51
Plant, Equip.:	$504,000	Total Liab.:	$438,000	Indic. Yr. Divd.:	NA
Total Assets:	$7,868,000	Net Worth:	$7,430,000	Debt/ Equity:	NA

Allete Inc

30 W Superior St., Duluth, MN, 55802; *PH:* 1-218-279-5000; *Fax:* 1-218-720-2502; *http://* www.allete.com

General - Incorporation	MN	Stock- Price on: 12/24/2007	$46.71
Employees	1,400	Stock Exchange	NYSE
Auditor	PricewaterhouseCoopers LLP	Ticker Symbol	ALE
Stk Agt	Wells Fargo Bank, N.A.	Outstanding Shares	30,530,000
Counsel	NA	E.P.S.	NA
DUNS No.	00-696-1296	Shareholders	NA

Business: The group's principal activities are to provide automotive and energy services. Automotive services includes wholesale vehicle auctions and related vehicle redistribution services and dealer financing. Energy services include electric and gas services, coal mining and telecommunications. The group also has real estate operations, investments in emerging technologies related to the electric utility industry, a securities portfolio and corporate charges. The group operates in 42 states, 9 Canadian provinces and Mexico.

Primary SIC and add'l.: 4931 7549 6411 6531

CIK No: 0000066756

Subsidiaries: ALLETE Automotive Services, LLC, ALLETE Capital II, ALLETE Capital III, ALLETE Commercial, LLC, ALLETE Properties, LLC, ALLETE Water Services, Inc, ALLETE, Inc, Auto Replacement Property, LLC, BNI Coal, Ltd, Cape Coral Holdings, Inc, Cape Properties, Inc, Cliffside Properties, Inc, Energy Land, Incorporated, Energy Replacement Property, LLC, Enterprise Lehigh, Inc 46 Subsidiaries included in the Index

Officers: Donald J. Shippar/58/Chmn., CEO, Pres./$2,027,419.00, Alan R. Hodnik/COO - Minnesota P, Eric Norberg/Sr. VP - Strategy, Planning, Mary Hunter/Investor Relations Specialist, Vincent J. Meyer/Sr. Investor Relations Analyst, Mark A. Schober/Sr. VP, CFO/$553,693.00, Claudia Scott Welty/Chief Administrative Officer, Sr. VP - Business Support/$575,658.00, Laura A. Holquist/Pres. - Allete Properties/$755,682.00, Timothy J. Thorp/VP - Investor Relations, David J. McMillan/Sr. VP - Marketing, Regulatory, Public Affairs, Donald W. Stellmaker/Treasurer, Deborah A. Amberg/Sr. VP, General Counsel, Sec./$465,530.00, Steven Q. Devinck/Controller

Directors: Donald J. Shippar/58/Chmn., CEO, Pres., Madeleine W. Ludlow/52/Dir., Bruce W. Stender/65/Dir., Jack I. Rajala/67/Dir., Kathleen Brekken/59/Dir., Heidi J. Eddins/49/Dir., James J. Hoolihan/54/Dir., George L. Mayer/62/Dir., Roger D. Peirce/69/Dir., Douglas C. Neve/52/Dir., Sidney W. Emery/61/Dir.

Owners: Jack I. Rajala, Claudia Scott Welty, James K. Vizanko, Donald J. Shippar, Kathleen A. Brekken, Mark A. Schober, Sidney W. Emery, Nick Smith, Heidi J. Eddins, Deborah A. Amberg, James J. Hoolihan, George L. Mayer, Bruce W. Stender, Laura A. Holquist, Roger D. Peirce (18 Owners included in Index)

Financial Data: *Fiscal Year End:* 12/31 *Latest Annual Data:* 12/31/2006

Year	Sales	Net Income
2006	$767,100,000	$76,400,000
2005	$737,400,000	$13,300,000
2004	$751,400,000	$104,400,000

Curr. Assets:	$287,700,000	Curr. Liab.:	$143,500,000	P/E Ratio:	15.57
Plant, Equip.:	$921,600,000	Total Liab.:	$860,200,000	Indic. Yr. Divd.:	$1.640
Total Assets:	$1,533,400,000	Net Worth:	$665,800,000	Debt/ Equity:	0.5224

Alliance Atlantis Communications Inc

121 Bloor St. E., Ste 1500, Toronto, ON, M4W 3M3; *PH:* 1-416-966-7506; *http://* www.allianceatlantis.com; *Email:* info@allianceatlantis.com

General - Incorporation	Canada	Stock- Price on: 12/24/2007	$48.35
Employees	NA	Stock Exchange	OTC
Auditor	PricewaterhouseCoopers LLP	Ticker Symbol	AACB
Stk Agt	Computershare Investor Services LLC	Outstanding Shares	NA
Counsel	NA	E.P.S.	NA
DUNS No.	24-626-7207	Shareholders	NA

Business: The group's principle activities are carried out through three reportable segments: broadcast, motion picture distribution and entertainment. The broadcast group consists of the group's specialty television channels, which include lifestyle, drama and documentary programming. The motion picture distribution group includes the acquisition, distribution and financing of motion pictures. The entertainment group is involved in the development, production, acquisition and distribution of in-house motion pictures, primetime television drama, children's and documentary programming. Other activities are primarily comprised of the structured-filmed entertainment financing business and corporate functions.

Primary SIC and add'l.: 7812 4833 7822

CIK No: 0001005887

Subsidiaries: Alliance Atlantis BroadcastingInc., Alliance Atlantis Entertainment,Inc., Alliance Atlantis International Distribution Limited, Alliance Atlantis ProductionsLtd., Motion Picture DistributionLP

Officers: Phyllis N. Yaffe/Dir., CEO, Michael I.M. MacMillan/Executive Chmn., Jacquelyn Saad/Sr. VP - Human Resources, Heather Conway/Exec. VP - Marketing, Public Affairs, Norm Bolen/Exec. VP - Content Group, Errol Da-Re/Exec. VP - Sales, Andrew Akman/VP - Corporate Development, Investor Relations, Ted Riley/Exec. MD - International Distribution, Bryan Press/VP - English Broadcast Sales, Andrea Wood/Exec. VP, General Counsel, Andrew Callum/Sr. VP - Strategy, David Lazzarato/Exec. VP, CFO - Investor Contact

Directors: Phyllis N. Yaffe/Dir., CEO, Michael I.M. MacMillan/Executive Chmn., Donald R. Sobey/Dir., Barry J. Reiter/Dir., Margot Northey/Dir., Anthony F. Griffiths/Dir., Rupert Duchesne/Dir., Harold Gordon/Dir., Ellis Jacob/Dir., David J. Kassie/Dir., Allen Karp/Dir., Robert J. Steacy/Dir.

Financial Data: *Fiscal Year End:* 12/31 *Latest Annual Data:* 12/31/2005

Year	Sales	Net Income
2005	$895,237,000	$45,731,000
2004	$844,830,000	$38,858,000
2003	$494,683,000	-$135,068,000

Curr. Assets:	$464,264,000	Curr. Liab.:	$465,551,000		
Plant, Equip.:	$34,063,000	Total Liab.:	$955,555,000	Indic. Yr. Divd.:	NA
Total Assets:	$1,349,548,000	Net Worth:	$342,599,000	Debt/ Equity:	NA

Alliance Bank & Trust NC

412 S.Decalb St., Shelby, NC, 28150; *PH:* 1-704-471-1500; *Fax:* 1-704-471-0208; *http://* www.alliancebankandtrust.com

General - Incorporation		Stock- Price on: 12/24/2007	$10.95
Employees	NA	Stock Exchange	OTC
Auditor	NA	Ticker Symbol	ABTN
Stk Agt	NA	Outstanding Shares	NA
Counsel	NA	E.P.S.	NA
DUNS No.	NA	Shareholders	NA

Business: The groups principle activity is to provide banking services. The groups services include personal banking, business banking and online services. The groups personal banking services include alliance checking, alliance gold checking, alliance silver checking, money market account, regular savings, and super now. The group operates from United States.

Primary SIC and add'l.: 6733

CIK No:

Officers: William G. Sudyk/Dir., CEO, Pres., Jennifer Cook/Teller Associate, Pamela Martin/Administrative Assist., Brandy Nichols/Administrative Loan Assist., Chris Reynolds/Portfolio Mgr., Hope Stout/VP, Deposit Acquisition Officer, Dan Ayscue/Exec. VP, Chief Credit Officer, Matt Triplett/Sr. VP, Chief Credit Officer, Eric Dixon Dixon/Chief Development Officer, Sr. VP, Betsy Martin/VP, Controller, Leah Berry/VP, Branch Administrator, Shelby Mgr., Mary G. Butts/VP - Loan Operation, Joe Suttle/Assist. VP, Commercial Lending Officer, Jennifer Long/BSA, Compliance Officer, Tammy Darnell/Branch Mgr. - Shelby (22 Officers included in Index)

Directors: William G. Sudyk/Dir., CEO, Pres., Wayne F. Shovelin/Dir., Gene H. Washburn/Dir., John H. Whaley/Dir., David W. White/Dir., Jack R. Williams/Dir., Kelvin C. Harris/Dir., Susan J. Joyner/Dir., Jerry L. Kellar/Dir., William J. McLean/Dir., Gerald F. McSwain/Dir., Joseph H. Morgan/Dir., Lawrence H. Pearson/Dir., Carl J. Stewart/Dir.

Alliance Bankshares Corp

14200 Pk. Meadow Dr., Ste. 200 South, Chantilly, VA, 20151; *PH:* 1-703-814-7200; *Fax:* 1-703-378-7210; *http://* www.alliancebankva.com

General - Incorporation	VA	Stock- Price on: 12/24/2007	$13.25
Employees	113	Stock Exchange	NDQ
Auditor	Yount, Hyde & Barbour, P.C	Ticker Symbol	ABVA
Stk Agt	Registrar & Transfer Co	Outstanding Shares	5,560,000
Counsel	NA	E.P.S.	$0.34
DUNS No.	NA	Shareholders	NA

Business: The group's principal activities are to provide financial services to individuals, small to medium sized businesses, entrepreneurs, professionals and consumers. The lending service provided by the group consists of commercial business lending, commercial real estate lending, real estate construction lending, residential real estate lending, mortgage lending and consumer installment lending. The deposit services include demand, now, money market and savings accounts. The group operates through a wholly-owned subsidiary: alliance home funding llc, which provides mortgage banking services. It conducts its operations through the main office located in fairfax, Virginia and three branch offices located in city of manassas park, old town manassas and plaza America in reston, Virginia.

Primary SIC and add'l.: 6022 6712

CIK No: 0001181001

Subsidiaries: Alliance Bank Corporation, Alliance Home Funding, LLC, Alliance Insurance Agency Inc., Alliance Virginia Capital Trust I

Officers: Thomas A. Young/Dir., Pres., CEO - Alliance Bank, Paul M. Harbolick/Exec. VP, CFO - Alliance Bank, Craig W. Sacknoff/Sr. VP - Lender, Alliance Bank, Frank H. Grace/Sr. VP - Alliance Bank, John B. McKenny/Sr. VP, Chief Credit Officer - Alliance Bank, Michael C. O'Grady/Dir., Sr. VP - Alliance Bank

Directors: Thomas A. Young/Dir., Pres., CEO - Alliance Bank, Robert G. Weyers/Vice Chmn. - Alliance Bank, Harvey E. Johnson/Chmn. - Alliance Bank, George S. Webb/Vice Chmn. - Alliance Bank, Lawrence N. Grant/Dir. - Alliance Bank, William M. Drohan/Dir. - Alliance Bank, Thomas P. Danaher/Dir. - Alliance Bank, Serina Moy/Dir. - Alliance Bank, Michael C. O'Grady/Dir., Sr. VP - Alliance Bank, Oliver T. Carr/Dir. - Alliance Bank

Owners: Banc Fund V L.P./6.10%, Goldman Sachs Asset Management, L.P./5.70%, Insiders/18.99%, Frank H. Grace/1.33%, Robert G. Weyers/1.94%, Harvey E. Johnson/1.50%, Paul M. Harbolick/1.44%, Lawrence N. Grant/1.58%, Wellington Management Company, LLC/6.78%, John B. McKenney, Serina Moy/1.54%, Craig W. Sacknoff/1.75%, George S. Webb/4.77%, Thomas Patrick Danaher/1.33%, William M. Drohan/0.89% (16 Owners included in Index)

Financial Data: *Fiscal Year End:* 12/31 *Latest Annual Data:* 12/31/2006

Year	Sales	Net Income
2006	$45,742,000	$4,479,000
2005	$32,464,000	$4,058,000
2004	$25,332,000	$2,767,000

Curr. Assets:	$48,325,000	Curr. Liab.:	$574,530,000	P/E Ratio:	17.43
Plant, Equip.:	$2,394,000	Total Liab.:	$589,734,000	Indic. Yr. Divd.:	NA
Total Assets:	$644,371,000	Net Worth:	$54,637,000	Debt/ Equity:	0.1845

Alliance Data Systems Corp

17655 Waterview Pkwy., Dallas, TX, 75252; *PH:* 1-972-348-5100; *Fax:* 1-972-348-5335; *http://* www.alliancedata.com; *Email:* ir@alliancedatasystems.com

General - Incorporation: DE	**Stock**- Price on:12/24/2007: $77.7
Employees: 9,300	Stock Exchange: NYSE
Auditor: Deloitte & Touche LLP	Ticker Symbol: ADS
Stk Agt: EquiServe Trust Co N.A	Outstanding Shares: 78,700,000
Counsel: Akin, Gump, Strauss, Hauer & Feld LLP	E.P.S: $2.10
DUNS No.: NA	Shareholders: NA

Business: The groups principle activity is to provide transaction, credit and marketing services for the retail, petroleum, utility, financial services and hospitality markets. The groups services include business process outsourcing, loyalty marketing, and customer insight and database marketing services. The group operates from United States.

Primary SIC and add'l.: 9651 6159

CIK No: 0001101215

Subsidiaries: ADS Alliance Data Systems, Inc., ADS Commercial Services, Inc., ADS MB Corporation, ADS Reinsurance Ltd., Alliance Data FHC, Inc., Alliance Travel Services, Inc., Loyalty Management Group Canada, Inc., National Bank, World Financial Capital Bank, World Financial Network

Officers: Michael J. Parks/Chmn., CEO/$6,634,413.00, Dwayne H. Tucker/Exec. VP, Pres. - Human Resources, Transaction Services/$2,539,459.00, Transient C. Taylor/Exec. VP - Human Resources, Alan M. Utay/Exec. VP, Chief Administrative Officer, General Counsel, Sec., Ivan M. Szeftel/Exec. VP, Pres. - Retail Credit Services/$3,526,464.00, John W. Scullion/COO, Pres./$3,493,476.00, Edward J. Heffernan/CFO, Exec. VP/$2,714,479.00, Daniel P. Finkelman/Exec. VP - Corporate Development, Innovation, Robert P. Armiak/46/Sr. VP, Treasurer, Barry R. Carter/45/Sr. VP, Information Technology Officer, Michael D. Kubic/52/Sr. VP, Corporate Controller, Chief Accounting Officer, Richard E. Schumacher/41/Sr. VP - Tax, Michael L. Iaccarino/Exec. VP, Pres. - Marketing Services, Bryan A. Pearson/Exec. VP, Pres. - Loyalty Services, Jill Z. McBride/Contact - Public Relations

Directors: Michael J. Parks/Chmn., CEO, Bruce K. Anderson/68/Dir., Roger H. Ballou/57/Dir., Lawrence M. Benveniste/57/Dir., Keith D. Cobb/67/Dir., Linn E. Draper/66/Dir., Kenneth R. Jensen/64/Dir., Robert A. Minicucci/55/Dir.

Owners: Bruce K. Anderson/1.10%, Lawrence M. Benveniste, TimesSquare Capital Management, LLC/5.20%, John W. Scullion, Ivan M. Szeftel, Linn E. Draper, Keith D. Cobb, Dwayne H. Tucker, Roger H. Ballou, Robert A. Minicucci, Kenneth R. Jensen, Edward J. Heffernan, Insiders/3.80%, Michael J. Parks/1.00%

Financial Data: *Fiscal Year End:*12/31 *Latest Annual Data:* 12/31/2006

Year	Sales	Net Income
2006	$1,998,742,000	$189,605,000
2005	$1,552,437,000	$138,745,000
2004	$1,257,438,000	$102,371,000

Curr. Assets:	$1,309,975,000	**Curr. Liab.:**	$877,720,000	**P/E Ratio:**	33.35
Plant, Equip.:	$208,327,000	**Total Liab.:**	$2,332,482,000	**Indic. Yr. Divd.:**	NA
Total Assets:	$3,404,015,000	**Net Worth:**	$1,071,533,000	**Debt/ Equity:**	NA

Alliance Distributors Holding Inc

15-15 132nd St., College Point, NY, 11356; *PH:* 1-718-747-1500; *Fax:* 1-718-539-2528; *http://* www.alliancedistributors.com

General - Incorporation: DE	**Stock**- Price on:12/24/2007: $0.15
Employees: 40	Stock Exchange: OTC
Auditor: Mahoney Cohen & Co. CPA, P.C	Ticker Symbol: ADTR
Stk Agt: Pacific Stock Transfer Company	Outstanding Shares: 49,000,000
Counsel: NA	E.P.S: -$0.03
DUNS No.: NA	Shareholders: NA

Business: The group's principal activities are to design and develop real time tracking and sensory technologies. The real time tracking and sensory technologies can be used to provide the ultimate interface between man and machine. The group's products include p5(TM) which is engineered to capture five-finger bend sensitivity enabling gesture recognition. The p5(TM) is combined with an optical tracking technology that captures the movement of the hand in 3D space without the use of a mouse, joystick, keyboard or the like

Primary SIC and add'l.: 7372 7375 3577

CIK No: 0001115463

Officers: Jay Gelman/Chmn., CEO, Robert Becker/VP - Purchasing, Steve Gelman/VP - Marketing, Communications, Stephen Agress/CFO, Philip Devor/VP - Operations

Directors: Jay Gelman/Chmn., CEO, Humbert B. Powell/Dir., Steven H. Nathan/Dir., Thomas Vitiello/Dir.

Owners: Jay Gelman/32.50%, Theseus Fund, L.P./9.50%, Insiders/49.00%, Steven H. Nathan, Stephen Agress, f/k/a Minotaur Fund LLP/9.50%, Humbert B. Powell, Jim Corfman/10.40%, Nathan A. Low/11.30%, Thomas Vitiello, Francis Vegliante/9.40%, Andre Muller/16.90%

Financial Data: *Fiscal Year End:*12/31 *Latest Annual Data:* 12/31/2006

Year	Sales	Net Income
2006	$70,318,000	-$214,000
2005	$58,670,000	$186,000
2004	$35,037,000	-$242,000

Curr. Assets:	$18,221,000	**Curr. Liab.:**	$15,843,000		
Plant, Equip.:	$752,000	**Total Liab.:**	$15,887,000	**Indic. Yr. Divd.:**	NA
Total Assets:	$19,117,000	**Net Worth:**	$3,230,000	**Debt/ Equity:**	0.0011

Alliance Fiber Optic Products Inc

275 Gibraltar Dr., Sunnyvale, CA, 94089; *PH:* 1-408-736-6900; *Fax:* 1-408-736-4882; *http://* www.afop.com; *Email:* sales@afop.com

General - Incorporation: DE	**Stock**- Price on:12/24/2007: $1.77
Employees: 684	Stock Exchange: NDQ
Auditor: PricewaterhouseCoopers LLP	Ticker Symbol: AFOP
Stk Agt: American Stock Transfer & Trust Co.	Outstanding Shares: 40,640,000
Counsel: NA	E.P.S: $0.07
DUNS No.: NA	Shareholders: NA

Business: The group's principal activities are to design, manufacture and market fiber optic components for communication equipment manufacturers. The products include devices that are used to connect optical fibers and components. These products are used to divide and combine optical power and dense wavelength division multiplexing or dwdm, devices that separate and combine multiple specific wavelengths. Fiber optic components are used within optical networks to create, combine, isolate, amplify, split, direct and perform various other functions on the optical signals. The group operates in the United States and Taiwan. It also has established a subsidiary in the peoples republic of China to manufacture its products there. On 16-Jan-2004, the group acquired ritek corporation's photonics business.

Primary SIC and add'l.: 3357

CIK No: 0001122342

Subsidiaries: Alliance Fiber Optic Products

Officers: Peter C. Chang/Chmn., CEO, Pres./$201,450.00, Wei-Shin Tsay/VP - Product, Business Development/$152,290.00, David A. Hubbard/VP - Sales, Marketing/$151,450.00, Helen Chan/Mgr. - Investor Relations, Angeline Yu/Asia Sales Mgr. - Australia, India, Korea, Taiwan, Anita K. Ho/Acting CFO, Corporate Controller/$132,663.00

Directors: Peter C. Chang/Chmn., CEO, Pres., Richard B. Black/Dir., James C. Yeh/Dir., Gwong-Yih Lee/Dir., Ray Sun/Dir.

Owners: Wei-shin Tsay/2.10%, James C. Yeh/2.10%, Anita K. Ho, Foxconn Holding Limited/19.70%, Lloyd I. Miller/5.20%, Gwong-Yih Lee, Richard Black, Insiders/21.80%, David A. Hubbard/2.00%, Peter C. Chang/15.60%, Ray Sun

Financial Data: *Fiscal Year End:*12/31 *Latest Annual Data:* 12/31/2006

Year	Sales	Net Income
2006	$26,792,000	$657,000
2005	$20,963,000	-$2,617,000
2004	$14,558,000	-$9,343,000

Curr. Assets:	$40,253,000	**Curr. Liab.:**	$5,859,000	**P/E Ratio:**	59.00
Plant, Equip.:	$4,264,000	**Total Liab.:**	$6,789,000	**Indic. Yr. Divd.:**	NA
Total Assets:	$44,693,000	**Net Worth:**	$37,904,000	**Debt/ Equity:**	0.0133

Alliance Financial Corp NY

120 Madison St., Tower 2, 18th Fl., Syracuse, NY, 13202; *PH:* 1-315-475-4478; *Fax:* 1-315-475-4421; *http://* www.alliancebankna.com; *Email:* info@alliancefinancialcorp.com

General - Incorporation: NY	**Stock**- Price on:12/24/2007: $26.86
Employees: 324	Stock Exchange: NDQ
Auditor: PricewaterhouseCoopers LLP	Ticker Symbol: ALNC
Stk Agt: American Stock Transfer & Trust Co.	Outstanding Shares: 4,780,000
Counsel: NA	E.P.S: $1.92
DUNS No.: 15-650-7360	Shareholders: NA

Business: The group's principle activity is to provide commercial banking services to commercial, retail, government, and trust customers. It accepts deposits, which include interest and non-interest bearing checking accounts, money market accounts, savings accounts, time deposit accounts and individual retirement accounts. Its lending activities comprise of residential and commercial mortgage loans, business lines of credit, working capital facilities, business term loans, installment loans, home equity loans, student loans and personal lines of credit to individuals. Trust and investment department services include personal trust, employee benefit trust, investment management, custodial and financial planning. The services are rendered through two head offices located at cortland and oneida and 18 customer service facilities located in cortland, madison, onondaga and western oneida counties.

Primary SIC and add'l.: 6712 6021

CIK No: 0000796317

Subsidiaries: Alliance Bank, Alliance Financial Capital Trust I, Alliance Leasing, Inc., Alliance Preferred Funding Corp.

Officers: Jack H. Webb/Chmn., CEO, Pres./$474,228.00, Joseph M. Russo/Sr. VP - Marketing, Investor Relations, John H. Watt/Dir., Exec. VP - Commercial Banking Sales, Service, Leasing Businesses, Trust, Investments/$286,929.00, Daniel J. Mohr/CFO, Exec. VP/$148,222.00, Steven G. Cacchio/Sr. VP - Retail Banking Sales, Service, Claudia Tavernese/Sr. VP - Risk Management, James W. Getman/Exec. VP, Sr. Loan Officer - Credit Management, Administration, Judy A. Schultz/Sec. - Corporation, James A. Doolittle/VP, Trust Officer, Barry E. Shay/VP, Trust Officer, Donna Harlander/VP - Trust Operations, Bernard E. O'Donnell/Regional Mgr., Dean Murphy/VP, Trust Officer, Janet T. Boddie/Assist. VP, Trust Officer, Wayne Dziewa/Assist. VP, Trust Officer *(24 Officers included in Index)*

Directors: Jack H. Webb/Chmn., CEO, Pres., Charles H. Spaulding/Dir., Donald S. Ames/Dir., Samuel J. Lanzafame/Dir., Paul M. Solomon/Dir., Deborah F. Stanley/58/Dir., Donald H. Dew/Dir., Mary Pat Adams/Dir., Charles E. Shafer/Dir., Margaret Ogden/Dir., John H. Watt/Dir., Exec. VP - Commercial Banking Sales, Service, Leasing Businesses, Trust, Investments, John M. Endries/Dir., Lowell A. Seifter/55/Dir.

Owners: Lowell A. Seifter, Charles E. Shafer, Insiders/6.40%, Donald H. Dew, John M. Endries, Charles H. Spaulding, Paul M. Solomon, Samuel J. Lanzafame, Mary Pat Adams, John H. Watt, David P. Kershaw, Margaret G. Ogden, Deborah F. Stanley, Jack H. Webb/2.10%, Daniel j. Mohr *(16 Owners included in Index)*

Financial Data: *Fiscal Year End:*12/31 *Latest Annual Data:* 12/31/2006

Year	Sales	Net Income
2006	$75,493,000	$7,311,000
2005	$60,724,000	$7,507,000
2004	$49,142,000	$7,255,000

Curr. Assets:	$32,003,000	**Curr. Liab.:**	$938,247,000	**P/E Ratio:**	13.99
Plant, Equip.:	$22,492,000	**Total Liab.:**	$1,163,461,000	**Indic. Yr. Divd.:**	$0.880
Total Assets:	$1,272,967,000	**Net Worth:**	$109,506,000	**Debt/ Equity:**	1.9634

Alliance Health Inc

421 E Airport Fwy., Irving, TX, 75062; *PH:* 1-972-255-5533

General - Incorporation: DE	**Stock**- Price on:12/24/2007: $0.01
Employees: NA	Stock Exchange: OTC
Auditor: Whitley Penn	Ticker Symbol: ALNH
Stk Agt: NA	Outstanding Shares: NA
Counsel: NA	E.P.S: NA
DUNS No.: NA	Shareholders: NA

Business: The group's principal activity was to provide advertising and management services to medical clinics. The group was leasing equipment to medical clinics of affiliated companies. The group, through the marketing division of k clinics was performing advertising and marketing services for metroplex specialties, p.a., aldine medical associates, metroplex specialities, p.a. And metro pharmacy, inc. The group was leasing mri units and tractors to move these units to metroplex specialities, p.a. And a ct scanner to aldine medical associates. The group currently does not perform management services. The group has no business operations.

Primary SIC and add'l.: 9999

CIK No: 0000822434

Officers: Sarkis J. Kechejian/70/CEO, CFO, Sharilyn J. Bruntz/57/VP, Sec.

Owners: Sarkis J. Kechejian/51.89%, Nishan J. Kechejian/6.67%, Insiders/52.56%, Carl Generes/8.08%, Sharilyn J. Bruntz Wilson

Alliance Holdings GP LP

1717 S Boulder Ave., Tulsa, OK, 74119; **PH:** 1-918-295-1415; **Fax:** 1-918-295-7361; http:// www.arlp.com; **Email:** investorrelations@ahgp.com

General - Incorporation .... DE	Stock - Price on:12/24/2007 .... $29.88
Employees .... NA	Stock Exchange .... NDQ
Auditor ....Deloitte& Touche LLP	Ticker Symbol .... AHGP
Stk Agt...... American Stock Transfer & Trust Co.	Outstanding Shares 59,860,000
Counsel .... NA	E.P.S. $1.51
DUNS No. .... NA	Shareholders .... NA

Business: The group operates through its subsidiaries whose principle activities include producing and marketing coal. The group operates through four segments namely Illinois basin, central Appalachia, northern Appalachia and, other and corporate. Specific customers of the group include Tennessee Valley Authority, Northern Indiana Public Service Company and Seminole Electric Cooperative, Inc. The group operates from West Virginia, Illinois, and Kentucky in the United States. The group's quarterly revenue for September 2007 was 260.43 millions of USD.

Primary SIC and add'l.: 1222 1221

CIK No: 0001344980

Subsidiaries: Alliance Coal, LLC, Alliance Design Group, LLC, Alliance Land, LLC, Alliance Properties, LLC, Alliance Resource Management GP, LLC, Alliance Resource Operating Partners, L.P., Alliance Resource Partners, L.P., Alliance Service, Inc., ARMGPHoldings,Inc., Backbone Mountain, LLC, Excel Mining, LLC, Gibson County Coal, LLC, Hopkins County Coal, LLC, Matrix Design Group, LLC, MC Mining, LLC 25 Subsidiaries included in the Index

Officers: Joseph W. Craft/Dir., CEO, Pres., Eberley R. Davis/Sr. VP, General Counsel, Sec., Brian L. Cantrell/CFO, Sr. VP, Thomas L. Pearson/54/Sr. VP - Law, Administration, General Counsel, Sec.

Directors: Joseph W. Craft/Dir., CEO, Pres., Michael J. Hall/Dir., Thomas M. Davidson/Dir., Robert J. Druten/Dir.

Owners: Insiders, Management Group, Robert J. Druten, Thomas L. Pearson, Joseph W. Craft, Brian L. Cantrell

Financial Data: Fiscal Year End:12/31   Latest Annual Data: 12/31/2006

Year	Sales		Net Income
2006	$967,242,000		$85,709,000
Curr. Assets:	$170,562,000	Curr. Liab.:	$133,389,000	P/E Ratio:	20.33
Plant, Equip.:	$436,707,000	Total Liab.:	$408,130,000	Indic. Yr. Divd.:	$1.060
Total Assets:	$635,495,000	Net Worth:	$227,365,000	Debt/ Equity:	0.5411

Alliance Imaging Inc

1900 S State College Blvd., Ste. 600, Anaheim, CA, 92806; **PH:** 1-714-688-7100; **Fax:** 1-714-688-3333; http:// www.allianceimaging.com; **Email:** info@allianceimaging.com

General - Incorporation .... DE	Stock - Price on:12/24/2007 .... $9.01
Employees 1,955	Stock Exchange .... NYSE
Auditor ....Deloitte & Touche LLP	Ticker Symbol .... AIQ
Stk Agt...... American Stock Transfer & Trust Co.	Outstanding Shares 50,220,000
Counsel .... NA	E.P.S. $0.37
DUNS No. 10-922-0046	Shareholders .... NA

Business: The group's principal activities are to provide imaging and therapeutic services primarily to hospitals and other healthcare providers on a mobile, shared-service basis and on a full-time basis to single customers. The services offered include equipment maintenance and upgrades, management of day-to-day operations, the use of imaging or therapeutic systems and to provide technologists to operate the systems. The group also offers ancillary services including marketing support, education, training and billing assistance. As of 31-Dec-2003, the group had 472 diagnostic imaging systems including 363 mri systems and 1,344 clients in 44 states. The group operates mainly in the United States.

Primary SIC and add'l.: 3695 3845 8071

CIK No: 0000817135

Subsidiaries: Alliance Imaging NC, Inc. , Medical Diagnostics, Inc., SMT Health Services, Inc.

Officers: Paul S. Viviano/Chmn., CEO/$2,021,867.00, Howard K. Aihara/CFO, Exec. VP/$566,388.00, Michael F. Frisch/COO, Exec. VP, Eli H. Glovinsky/Exec. VP, General Counsel, Corp. Sec.

Directors: Paul S. Viviano/Chmn., CEO, Michael W. Michelson/Dir., Stephen A. Kaplan/49/Dir., Curtis S. Lane/50/Dir., Michael P. Harmon/39/Dir.

Owners: OCM Principal Opportunities Fund IV, L.P., Paul S. Viviano, Stephen A. Kaplan, Nicholas A. Poan, Christopher J. Joyce, Andrew P. Hayek, Insiders, MTS Health Investors II, L.P., Michael F. Frisch, Curtis S. Lane, Howard K. Aihara

Financial Data: Fiscal Year End:12/31   Latest Annual Data: 12/31/2006

Year	Sales		Net Income
2006	$455,775,000		$19,288,000
2005	$430,788,000		$19,849,000
2004	$432,080,000		-$486,000
Curr. Assets:	$100,515,000	Curr. Liab.:	$71,664,000	P/E Ratio:	24.35
Plant, Equip.:	$344,177,000	Total Liab.:	$677,124,000	Indic. Yr. Divd.:	NA
Total Assets:	$664,526,000	Net Worth:	-$16,974,000	Debt/ Equity:	NA

Alliance One International Inc

8001 Aerial Ctr. Pkwy., Morrisville, NC, 27560; **PH:** 1-919-379-4300; **Fax:** 1-919-379-4346; http:// www.aointl.com; **Email:** info@amstock.com

General - Incorporation .... VA	Stock - Price on:12/24/2007 .... $9.9
Employees 5,400	Stock Exchange .... NYSE
Auditor ....Deloitte & Touche LLP	Ticker Symbol .... AOI
Stk Agt...... American Stock Transfer & Trust Co.	Outstanding Shares 95,670,000
Counsel ....Hunton & Williams LLP	E.P.S. .... -$0.12
DUNS No. 00-794-0091	Shareholders .... NA

Business: The groups principle activity is to process tobacco for the cigarette industry. The group also provides agronomy expertise for growing leaf tobacco. The group operates from United States.

Primary SIC and add'l.: 5993 5194

CIK No: 0000939930

Subsidiaries: Agroexpansion S.A., Alliance One Congo S.p.r.l., Alliance One Exportadora de Tabacos Ltda., Alliance One International, Alliance One International A.G., Alliance One International ESS Processing, Alliance One International Services Limited, Alliance One International Singapore Pte Ltd., Alliance One International Tabak B.V., Alliance One International, Inc., Alliance One Macedonia AD, Alliance One Rotag AG, Alliance One Tabaco Mexico, S. A. de C.V., Alliance One Tobacco (Kenya) Limited, Alliance One Tobacco (Malawi) Limited 62 Subsidiaries included in the Index

Officers: Robert E. Harrison/Chmn., CEO, Pres./$2,135,561.00, Thomas G. Reynolds/VP, Controller, Hilton Kappaun/Exec. VP - Global Operations, Pieter J. Sikkel/Exec. VP - Business Strategy, Relationship Management, Michael K. McDaniel/Sr. VP - Human Resources/$548,278.00, James A. Cooley/CFO, Exec. VP/$1,118,815.00, William D. Pappas/CIO, Sr. VP, Henry C. Babb/Sr. VP, Chief Legal Officer, Sec./$643,980.00, Joel L. Thomas/VP, Treasurer

Directors: Robert E. Harrison/Chmn., CEO, Pres., Brian J. Harker/58/Chmn., William S. Sheridan/Dir., Albert C. Monk/68/Dir., Nigel G. Howard/Dir., Clyde B. Preslar/Dir., Mark W. Kehaya/Dir., John M. Hines/Dir., Richard C. Green/Dir., Gilbert L. Klemann/Dir., Joseph L. Lanier/Dir., Norman A. Scher/Dir., Martin R. Wade/Dir.

Owners: William D. Pappas, Joseph L. Lanier, Norman A. Scher, Barclays Global Investors, NA/6.66%, Pieter J. Sikkel, John M. Hines, Henry C. Babb, Steven B. Daniels, William S. Sheridan, Brian J. Harker, Insiders/7.44%, Robert E. Harrison, Franklin Resources, Inc./5.39%, Dimensional Fund Advisors LP/8.53%, Mark W. Kehaya/4.38% (26 Owners included in Index)

Financial Data: Fiscal Year End:03/31   Latest Annual Data: 03/31/2007

Year	Sales		Net Income
2007	$1,979,078,000		-$21,597,000
2006	$2,112,685,000		-$447,446,000
2005	$1,311,388,000		$13,288,000
Curr. Assets:	$1,368,197,000	Curr. Liab.:	$829,284,000		
Plant, Equip.:	$287,135,000	Total Liab.:	$1,687,174,000	Indic. Yr. Divd.:	NA
Total Assets:	$1,904,124,000	Net Worth:	$214,187,000	Debt/ Equity:	2.8348

Alliance Pharmaceutical Corp

4660 La Jolla Village Dr., Ste. 825, San Diego, CA, 92122; **PH:** 1-858-410-5200; **Fax:** 1-858-410-5201; http:// www.allp.com; **Email:** corpcom@allp.com

General - Incorporation .... NY	Stock - Price on:12/24/2007 .... $0.1
Employees 2	Stock Exchange .... OTC
Auditor ....KMJ Corbin & Co. LLP	Ticker Symbol .... ALLP
Stk Agt ..... American Stock Transfer & Trust Co.	Outstanding Shares 43,970,000
Counsel ....Stroock & Stroock & Lavan	E.P.S. .... -$0.087
DUNS No. 10-112-5995	Shareholders .... NA

Business: The group's principal activity is to identify, design and develop novel medical products. The group develops scientific discoveries into medical products for human health applications and licenses these products to multinational pharmaceutical companies. The product oxygent-tm is an intravascular oxygen carrier being developed to augment oxygen delivery in surgical and other patients at risk of acute tissue oxygen deficit. The group's primary drug substance is perflubron, a brominated perfluorochemical that has a high solubility for respiratory gases and when formulated into an emulsion, can be used to transport these gases throughout the body.

Primary SIC and add'l.: 8731 2834 5122

CIK No: 0000736994

Subsidiaries: Astral, Inc., Molecular Biosystems, Inc., Pfc Therapeutics, LLC, Talco Pharmaceutical, Inc.

Owners: SB Venture Capital III, LLC, Jean G. Riess, Special Situations Private Equity, Duane J. Roth, Carroll O. Johnson, Jan Dekker, Osiris Investment Partners LP, Technology Gateway Partnership,L.P., Pedro Cuatrecasas, MicroCapital Fund Ltd., MedCap Partners, L.P., Xmark Opportunity Fund, Ltd., MicroCapital Fund LP, Biomedical Value Fund, L.P., Biomedical Offshore Value Fund,Ltd. (20 Owners included in Index)

Financial Data: Fiscal Year End:06/30   Latest Annual Data: 6/30/2007

Year	Sales		Net Income
2007	$573,000		-$4,093,000
2006	$129,000		-$9,575,000
2005	$1,477,000		-$5,743,000
Curr. Assets:	$933,000	Curr. Liab.:	$13,015,000		
Plant, Equip.:	$126,000	Total Liab.:	$13,765,000	Indic. Yr. Divd.:	NA
Total Assets:	$1,069,000	Net Worth:	-$12,696,000	Debt/ Equity:	NA

Alliance Resource Partners LP

1717 S Boulder Ave., Ste. 600, Tulsa, OK, 74119; **PH:** 1-918-295-7600; **Fax:** 1-918-295-7358; http:// www.arlp.com; **Email:** investorrelations@arlp.com

General - Incorporation .... DE	Stock - Price on:12/24/2007 .... $43.8
Employees 2,500	Stock Exchange .... NYSE
Auditor ....Deloitte & Touche LLP	Ticker Symbol .... ARLP
Stk Agt ..... American Stock Transfer & Trust Co.	Outstanding Shares 36,550,000
Counsel .... NA	E.P.S. $3.07
DUNS No. .... NA	Shareholders .... NA

Business: The groups principle activities include producing and marketing coal. The group operates through four segments namely Illinois basin, central Appalachia, northern Appalachia and, other and corporate. Specific customers of the group include Tennessee Valley Authority, Northern Indiana Public Service Company and Seminole Electric Cooperative, Inc. The group operates from West Virginia, Illinois, and Kentucky in the United States. The group's quarterly revenue for September 2007 was 260.53 millions of USD.

Primary SIC and add'l.: 1241 1221 5052 1222

CIK No: 0001086600

Subsidiaries: Alliance Coal, LLC, Alliance Design Group, LLC, Alliance Land, LLC, Alliance Properties, LLC, Alliance Resource Operating Partners, L.P., Alliance Service, Inc., Backbone Mountain, LLC, Excel Mining, LLC, Gibson County Coal, LLC, Hopkins County Coal, LLC, Matrix Design Group, LLC, MC Mining, LLC, Mettiki Coal (WV), LLC, Mettiki Coal, LLC, Mt. Vernon Transfer Terminal, LLC 22 Subsidiaries included in the Index

Officers: Joseph W. Craft/Dir., CEO, Pres., Robert G. Sachse/Exec. VP - Marketing, Charles R. Wesley/Sr. VP - Operations, Brian L. Cantrell/Sr. VP, CFO, Eberley R. Davis/Sr. VP, General Counsel, Sec.

Directors: Joseph W. Craft/Dir., CEO, Pres., John P. Neafsey/Chmn., John H. Robinson/Dir., Michael J. Hall/Dir., Merribel S. Ayres/Dir., Wilson M. Torrence/Dir.

Owners: Michael J. Hall, Brian L. Cantrell, Insiders/44.46%, John P. Neafsey, Alliance Holdings GP, L.P./42.53%, Joseph W. Craft/43.58%, M&G Investment Funds 1/5.03%, John H. Robinson, Gary J. Rathburn, Charles R. Wesley, Thomas L. Pearson, Wilson M. Torrence, Robert G. Sachse

Financial Data: *Fiscal Year End:*12/31 *Latest Annual Data:* 12/31/2006

Year	Sales	Net Income
2006	$967,557,000	$172,927,000
2005	$838,718,000	$160,010,000
2004	$653,289,000	$76,621,000

Curr. Assets:	$170,088,000	**Curr. Liab.:**	$132,702,000	**P/E Ratio:**	14.65
Plant, Equip.:	$436,707,000	**Total Liab.:**	$386,482,000	**Indic. Yr. Divd.:**	$2.240
Total Assets:	$634,962,000	**Net Worth:**	$248,480,000	**Debt/ Equity:**	0.4800

Alliance Semiconductor Corp

2575 Augustine Dr., Santa Clara, CA, 95054; *PH:* 1-408-855-4900; *Fax:* 1-408-855-4999; *http://* www.alsc.com; *Email:* info@alsc.com

General - Incorporation	DE	**Stock**- Price on:12/24/2007	$4.94
Employees	197	Stock Exchange	OTC
Auditor	PricewaterhouseCoopers LLP	Ticker Symbol	ALSC
Stk Agt	Chase Mellon Shareholder Services	Outstanding Shares	32,610,000
Counsel	NA	E.P.S	$3.48
DUNS No.	13-160-8663	Shareholders	NA

Business: The group's principal activity is to design, develop and market high-performance memory, mixed signal and system solutions products used in the networking, wireless, consumer and computing markets. The group markets its products to domestic and international manufacturers of personal computer and computer peripherals, consumer networking, telecommunications and wireless products. The group's major customers include takebishi, mitronics, celestica, 3com, mecnet, kanematsu, benq technologies, teksel, general instruments, solectron, samsung, eastele, linpo sabre, republic electronics, sci systems and rockwell. The group markets its products in the United States, Europe, Japan and Asia. In jan 2003, the group acquired chip engines inc.

Primary SIC and add'l.: 3674

CIK No: 0000913293

Subsidiaries: Alliance Semiconductor (India) Private Limited, Alliance Semiconductor (S.A.) (Pty) Ltd., Alliance Semiconductor Holding Company, LLC, Alliance Semiconductor International Corporation, Alliance Semiconductor, South Africa, LLC, Alliance Venture Management, LLC, Alliance Ventures I, LP, Alliance Ventures II, LP, Alliance Ventures III, LP, Alliance Ventures IV, LP, Alliance Ventures V, LP, Chip Engines, Inc., Dioptech, Inc., Nimbus Technology, Inc., SiPackets, Inc. 16 Subsidiaries included in the Index

Officers: Melvin L. Keating/CEO, Pres., C. N. Reddy/Exec. VP - Investments, Dir., Alan B. Howe/VP - Business Development Covad Communications, Karl H. Moeller/Interim CFO

Directors: Bryant R. Riley/Chmn., Michael J. Gullard/Dir., C. N. Reddy/Exec. VP - Investments, Dir., Bob D'Agostino/Dir.

Owners: Alan B. Howe, Lloyd Miller/11.00%, Bob DAgostino, Dimensional Fund Advisors/4.60%, C.N. Reddy/11.80%, Harvey Partners, LLC/5.00%, David J. Greene & Co. LLC/6.40%, Damodar N. Reddy/11.50%, Francis Capital Management, LLC/5.00%, Schneider Capital Management Corporation/10.90%, Karl H. Moeller, Bryant R. Riley/9.10%, Michael J. Gullard, Melvin L. Keating

Financial Data: *Fiscal Year End:*03/31 *Latest Annual Data:* 03/31/2007

Year	Sales	Net Income
2007	NA	$105,396,000
2006	$7,556,000	-$26,574,000
2005	$23,599,000	-$49,811,000

Curr. Assets:	$76,467,000	**Curr. Liab.:**	$45,316,000	**P/E Ratio:**	1.61
Plant, Equip.:	$33,000	**Total Liab.:**	$47,482,000	**Indic. Yr. Divd.:**	NA
Total Assets:	$109,661,000	**Net Worth:**	$61,884,000	**Debt/ Equity:**	NA

Alliant Energy Corp

4902 N Biltmore Ln., Madison, WI, 53718; *PH:* 1-608-458-3311; *Fax:* 1-608-458-4824; *http://* www.alliantenergy.com; *Email:* customercare@alliantenergy.com

General - Incorporation	WI	**Stock**- Price on:12/24/2007	$39.7
Employees	5,151	Stock Exchange	NYSE
Auditor	Deloitte & Touche LLP	Ticker Symbol	LNT
Stk Agt	Alliant Energy Corp	Outstanding Shares	113,740,000
Counsel	NA	E.P.S	$3.32
DUNS No.	18-717-3612	Shareholders	NA

Business: The groups principle activities include generation, transmission, distribution and sale of electric energy. The group operates from United States.

Primary SIC and add'l.: 4931 4923 4911 8731 4941 6552

CIK No: 0000352541

Subsidiaries: Alliant Energy Holdings do Brasil Limitada, Alliant Energy International, Inc., Alliant Energy Resources, Inc., Interstate Power and Light Company, Wisconsin Power and Light Company, WPL Transco LLC

Officers: William D. Harvey/59/Chmn., CEO, Pres./$5,040,415.00, Hollis Dale Withers/VP - Construction, Becky Johnson/Mgr. - Investor Relations, Joni Aeschbach/Mgr. - Shareowner Services, Thomas L. Aller/Sr. VP - Energy Delivery/$1,091,767.00, Eliot G. Protsch/CFO, Sr. Exec. VP/$2,472,666.00, Barbara J. Swan/Exec. VP, General Counsel/$1,604,177.00, Timothy R. Bennington/VP - Generation, Dundeana K. Doyle/VP - Strategy, Regulatory Affairs/$741,659.00, Vern A. Gebhart/VP - Customer Service Operations, West, Thomas L. Hanson/VP, Controller, Chief Accounting Officer, Peggy Howard Moore/VP - Finance, Patricia L. Kampling/VP, Treasurer, John E. Kratchmer/VP - Customer Service Operations, East, John O. Larsen/VP - Technical, Integrated *(21 Officers included in Index)*

Directors: William D. Harvey/59/Chmn., CEO, Pres., David A. Perdue/58/Dir., James A. Leach/66/Dir., Dean C. Oestreich/56/Dir., Singleton B. McAllister/56/Dir., Michael L. Bennett/54/Dir., Ann K. Newhall/57/Dir., Judith D. Pyle/65/Dir., Carol P. Sanders/41/Dir., Darryl B. Hazel/60/Dir.

Owners: Thomas L. Aller, Michael L. Bennett, Singleton B. McAllister, Barclays Global Investors, N. A./10.44%, William D. Harvey, Dean C. Oestreich, Dundeana K. Doyle, Barbara J. Swan, Darryl B. Hazel, David A. Perdue, Carol P. Sanders, Erroll B. Davis, Anthony R. Weiler, Eliot G. Protsch, Judith D. Pyle *(17 Owners included in Index)*

Financial Data: *Fiscal Year End:*12/31 *Latest Annual Data:* 12/31/2006

Year	Sales	Net Income
2006	$3,359,400,000	$315,700,000
2005	$3,279,600,000	-$7,700,000
2004	$2,958,700,000	$145,500,000

Curr. Assets:	$1,173,800,000	**Curr. Liab.:**	$1,102,100,000	**P/E Ratio:**	11.96
Plant, Equip.:	$4,944,900,000	**Total Liab.:**	$4,184,100,000	**Indic. Yr. Divd.:**	$1.270
Total Assets:	$7,084,100,000	**Net Worth:**	$2,895,100,000	**Debt/ Equity:**	NA

Alliant Techsystems Inc

5050 Lincoln Dr., Edina, MN, 55436; *PH:* 1-952-351-3000; *Fax:* 1-952-351-3009; *http://* www.atk.com; *Email:* atk.corporate@atk.com

General - Incorporation	DE	**Stock**- Price on:12/24/2007	$100
Employees	16,000	Stock Exchange	NYSE
Auditor	Deloitte & Touche LLP	Ticker Symbol	ATK
Stk Agt	Mellon Investor Services LLC	Outstanding Shares	33,120,000
Counsel	NA	E.P.S	$6.04
DUNS No.	61-870-5925	Shareholders	NA

Business: The groups principle activity is to supply aerospace and defense products. The groups products include rocket motor systems, cargo launch vehicles, conventional and strategic missiles. The group operates through three segments namely Mission Systems Group, Ammunition Systems Group and Launch Systems Group. The group operates from United States.

Primary SIC and add'l.: 3764 3483 3812 3489 8711

CIK No: 0000866121

Subsidiaries: Alliant Ammunition and Powder Company LLC, Alliant Ammunition Systems Company LLC, Alliant Lake City Small Caliber Ammunition Company LLC, Alliant Southern Composites Company LLC, Ammunition Accessories Inc., ATK Commercial Ammunition Company Inc., ATK Commercial Ammunition Holdings Company Inc., ATK Insurance Company, ATK Missile Systems Company LLC, ATK Ordnance and Ground Systems LLC, ATK Space Systems Inc., ATK Tactical Systems Company LLC, ATK Thiokol Inc., COI Ceramics,Inc. (59% ownership), Composite Optics, Incorporated 20 Subsidiaries included in the Index

Officers: Daniel J. Murphy/Chmn., CEO/$10,702,510.00, Steven J. Cortese/Sr. VP - Washington Operations, John J. Cronin/Sr. VP, Pres. - Mission Systems Group, Mark W. Deyoung/Sr. VP/$2,447,704.00, Ronald D. Dittemore/Sr. VP/$2,153,160.00, Blake E. Larson/VP, GM/$1,777,616.00, John L. Shroyer/CFO, Sr. VP/$1,518,346.00, Steve Wold/VP - Investor Relations, Dianne Deering Anton/Sr. VP - Contracts, Supply Chain Management, Keith D. Ross/Sr. VP, General Counsel, Sec./$1,543,661.00, Mark L. Mele/Sr. VP - Corporate Strategy, Paula J. Patineau/Sr. VP - Human Resources, Administrative Services, Michael B. Dolby/Vice Presidenrt, Corporate Development

Directors: Daniel J. Murphy/Chmn., CEO, Ronald R. Fogleman/Dir., Cynthia L. Lesher/Dir., Douglas L. Maine/Dir., Roman Martinez/Dir., Michael T. Smith/Dir., William G. Van Dyke/Dir., Martin C. Faga/Dir., Mark H. Ronald/Dir., Frances D. Cook/Dir.

Owners: Daniel J. Murphy, Neuberger Berman Inc./7.50%, William G. Van Dyke, Roman Martinez, Douglas L. Maine, John L. Shroyer, Thomas R. Wilson, T. Rowe Price Associates, Inc./5.80%, Cynthia L. Lesher, Blake E. Larson, Keith D. Ross, Ronald D. Dittemore, Frances D. Cook, FMR Corp./9.30%, Martin C. Faga *(22 Owners included in Index)*

Financial Data: *Fiscal Year End:*03/31 *Latest Annual Data:* 3/31/2007

Year	Sales	Net Income
2007	$3,564,940,000	$184,128,000
2006	$3,216,807,000	$153,882,000
2005	$2,801,129,000	$153,540,000

Curr. Assets:	$1,029,018,000	**Curr. Liab.:**	$503,272,000	**P/E Ratio:**	17.39
Plant, Equip.:	$454,748,000	**Total Liab.:**	$2,308,766,000	**Indic. Yr. Divd.:**	NA
Total Assets:	$2,874,682,000	**Net Worth:**	$557,881,000	**Debt/ Equity:**	2.6080

Allianz

Kniginstrasse 28, Munich, 80802; *PH:* 49-89-380-03-899; *http://* www.allianz.com

General - Incorporation	Germany	**Stock**- Price on:12/24/2007	$23.66
Employees	166,505	Stock Exchange	NYSE
Auditor	KPMG Deutsche Treuhand Gesellschaft	Ticker Symbol	AZ
Stk Agt	NA	Outstanding Shares	4,310,000,000
Counsel	Sebastian Ippisch	E.P.S	$2.89
DUNS No.	NA	Shareholders	NA

Business: The group's principle activities are carried out through four divisions: life/health: provides any of life and heath insurances; property/casualty: provides property and casualty insurance, travel insurance and credit insurance; banking: provides a range of banking services, including lending, deposit taking, investment banking; asset management: asset management for third party investor and asset under management which cover the own investments.

Primary SIC and add'l.: 6321 6331 6311 6351 6411 6021 6324

CIK No: 0001127508

Subsidiaries: 4212657 Canada Inc., 5557 Greens Farm LLC, 75 Wall Street Advisers, A. Diffusion, AAAM S.A., ACMAR, ACP Vermgensverwaltung GmbH& Co. KG Nr. 4, ADAM Hellas S.A., Adam U.s. Partners Gp, ADEUS Aktienregister-Service-GmbH, Adritica de Seguros C.A., Advisa Zrich AG, Aero-Fonte S.r.l, AFA, AFC Assecuranz und Finanzvermittlungs-Contor GmbH 1629 Subsidiaries included in the Index

Officers: Michael Diekmann/Chmn., Board Of Management, CEO, Werner Zedelius/Management, Insurance Growth Markets, Paul Achleitner/Finance, Helmut Perlet/Dir., CFO, Gerhard Rupprecht/Management, Insurance Germany, Jean-Philippe Thierry/Management, Insurance Europe 2, Herbert Walter/Management, Banking Worldwide

Directors: Michael Diekmann/Chmn., Board Of Management, CEO, Norbert Blix/Dep. Chmn. - Supervisory Board, Wulf H. Bernotat/Chmn. - Supervisory Board, Franz Fehrenbach/Member - Supervisory Board, Enrico Tomaso Cucchiani/Dir., Henning Schulte-Noelle/Member - Supervisory Board, Franz B. Humer/Member - Supervisory Board, Max Link/Member - Supervisory Board, Iris Mischlau-Meyrahn/Member - Supervisory Board, Manfred Schneider/Member - Supervisory Board, Igor Landau/64/Member - Supervisory Board, Diethart Breipohl/Member - Supervisory Board, Karl Neumeier/Member - Supervisory Board, Peter Haimerl/Member - Supervisory Board, Margit Schoffer/Member - Supervisory Board *(25 Directors included in Index)*

Financial Data: *Fiscal Year End:*12/31 *Latest Annual Data:* 12/31/2006

Year	Sales	Net Income
2006	$126,788,409,000	$8,604,395,000
2005	$115,722,986,000	$4,373,989,000
2004	$130,473,479,000	$3,930,836,000

Curr. Assets: $314,957,565,000 **Curr. Liab.:** $656,686,853,000 **P/E Ratio:** 8.10
Plant, Equip.: NA **Total Liab.:** $1,334,399,484,000 **Indic. Yr. Divd.:** $0.410
Total Assets: $1,404,374,063,000 **Net Worth:** $69,974,580,000 **Debt/ Equity:** NA

Allied Capital Corp

1919 Pennsylvania Ave. NW, Washington, DC, 20006; ***PH:*** 1-202-721-6100; ***Fax:*** 1-202-721-6101; ***http://*** www.alliedcapital.com

General - Incorporation	MD	**Stock**- Price on:12/24/2007	$31.84
Employees	170	Stock Exchange	NYSE
Auditor	KPMG LLP	Ticker Symbol	ALD
Stk Agt	American Stock Transfer & Trust Co.	Outstanding Shares	152,280,000
Counsel	NA	E.P.S.	$1.88
DUNS No.	NA	Shareholders	NA

Business: The groups principal activity is to provide financial services. The groups services include long term debt and equity capital. The group operates from the United States. The assets of the group for the year 2006 were $4,887,505 (thousands)

Primary SIC and add'l.: 6726

CIK No: 0000003906

Subsidiaries: A.C. Corporation

Officers: William L. Walton/Chmn., CEO, Pres./$7,450,763.00, Joan M. Sweeney/Dir., COO/$4,134,418.00, Penni F. Roll/CFO/$2,144,139.00, Scott S. Binder/Chief Valuation Officer, Christina L. Deldonna/MD - Washington Office, John D. Shulman/MD - Washington/$5,692,022.00, John M. Fruehwirth/MD - Washington Office, Michael J. Grisius/MD - Washington Office/$3,138,483.00, Jeri J. Harman/MD - Los Angeles, Frederick W. Hill/MD - New York, Bruce M. Kelleher/MD - Washington Office, Thomas C. Lauer/MD - Chicago Office, Robert D. Long/MD - New York, Justin S. MacCarone/MD - New York, Paul R. Tanen/MD - Washington *(33 Officers included in Index)*

Directors: William L. Walton/Chmn., CEO, Pres., Joan M. Sweeney/Dir., COO, Ann Torre Bates/Dir., Brooks H. Browne/Dir., John D. Firestone/Dir., Anthony T. Garcia/Dir., Edwin L. Harper/Dir., Lawrence I. Hebert/Dir., John I. Leahy/Dir., Robert E. Long/Dir., Alex J. Pollock/Dir., Marc F. Racicot/Dir., Guy T. Steuart/Dir., Laura W. Van Roijen/Dir.

Owners: William L. Walton/2.40%, Brooks H. Browne, Anthony T. Garcia, Michael J. Grisius, Robert E. Long, Capital Research and Management Company/5.00%, Ann Torre Bates, Lawrence I. Hebert, Insiders/9.00%, Penni F. Roll, Guy T. Steuart, Alex J. Pollock, Marc F. Racicot, Joan M. Sweeney/1.30%, Laura W. van Roijen *(19 Owners included in Index)*

Financial Data: ***Fiscal Year End:***12/31 ***Latest Annual Data:*** 12/31/2006

Year	Sales	Net Income
2006	$452,558,000	$245,123,000
2005	$374,152,000	$872,814,000
2004	$367,090,000	$249,486,000

Curr. Assets: $268,463,000 **Curr. Liab.:** $147,117,000 **P/E Ratio:** 16.94
Plant, Equip.: NA **Total Liab.:** $2,046,261,000 **Indic. Yr. Divd.:** $2.560
Total Assets: $4,887,505,000 **Net Worth:** $2,841,244,000 **Debt/ Equity:** 0.6351

Allied Defense Group Inc

8000 Towers Crescent Dr., Ste. 260, Vienna, VA, 22182; ***PH:*** 1-703-847-5268; ***Fax:*** 1-703-847-5334; ***http://*** www.allieddefensegroup.com; ***Email:*** headquarters@allieddefensegroup.com

General - Incorporation	DE	**Stock**- Price on:12/24/2007	$9.25
Employees	679	Stock Exchange	AMEX
Auditor	BDO Seidman, LLP	Ticker Symbol	ADG
Stk Agt	Mellon Investor Services LLC	Outstanding Shares	6,470,000
Counsel	Baxter, Baker, Conn & Jones P.A.	E.P.S.	-$7.758
DUNS No.	10-147-8568	Shareholders	NA

Business: The group's principal activities are to manufacture ammunition and security systems. The operations conducted by its two subsidiaries, mecar sa and the vsk group. Mecar manufactures and sells ammunition and light weapons for infantry use. They include grenades and ammunition for medium caliber, artillery, anti-tank and anti-personnel categories. The vsk group manufactures and sells security systems for government and private industry. The ammunitions are sold to governments and their agencies and prime contractors. The security systems are sold to banks, hospitals, commercial businesses and independent distributors. On 12-Aug-2004, the group acquired control monitor systems.

Primary SIC and add'l.: 7372 7382 3483

CIK No: 0000003952

Subsidiaries: Allied Research Corporation Limited, a U.K. Corporation, Allied Technology, LLC, ARC Europe, S.A., a Belgian Corporation, Belgian Automation Units, N.V, CMS Security Systems, Inc., Energa Corporation, Global Microwave Systems, Inc, Hendrickx N.V., Intelligent Data Capturing Systems, N.V., Mecar S.a., Mecar Usa, Inc., News/Sports Microwave Rental, Inc., SeaSpace Corporation, Sedachim S.I., S.A., Tele Technique Generale, S.A. 18 Subsidiaries included in the Index

Officers: John J. Marcello/Dir., CEO, Pres., Robert P. Dowski/53/Treasurer, Wayne F.C. Hosking/VP - Corporate Strategic Development, Monte L. Pickens/COO, Exec. VP, Simon Haye/MD - Mecar SA, Steve Dart/Pres. - Mecar USA, Roger E. Paul/MD - VSK Group, Andrew R. Berdy/Pres. - NS Microwave, Sam Nasiri/Pres. - Global Microwave Systems, David Collins/Pres. - Seaspace Corporation, Crystal B. Leiderman/Dir. - Investor Relations, Jim Drewitz/Investor Relations, Deborah F. Ricci/CFO, Luis M. Palacio/VP - Business Development

Directors: John J. Marcello/Dir., CEO, Pres., Binford J.H. Peay/Chmn., Ronald H. Griffith/Dir., John G. Meyer/Dir., Frederick G. Wasserman/Dir., Thomas R. Hudson/Dir., Gilbert F. Decker/Dir., Charles S. Ream/Dir.

Owners: Wayne F. Hosking, Ronald H. Griffith, FMR Corp/5.40%, Insiders/21.90%, Gilbert F. Decker, Deborah F. Ricci, Frederick G. Wasserman, Binford J. H. Peay/3.60%, John J. Marcello, Luis Palacio, Monte L. Pickens, Wynnefield Capital Management, LLC/7.30%, John G. Meyer, Thomas R. Hudson/14.70%, Charles S. Ream *(18 Owners included in Index)*

Financial Data: ***Fiscal Year End:***12/31 ***Latest Annual Data:*** 12/31/2006

Year	Sales	Net Income
2006	$128,685,000	-$41,097,000
2005	$112,222,000	-$38,920,000
2004	$150,131,000	$3,934,000

Curr. Assets: $102,904,000 **Curr. Liab.:** $106,068,000
Plant, Equip.: $33,331,000 **Total Liab.:** $112,698,000 **Indic. Yr. Divd.:** NA
Total Assets: $168,045,000 **Net Worth:** $55,347,000 **Debt/ Equity:** 0.0978

Allied First Bancorp Inc MD

3201 Orchard Rd., Oswego, IL, 60543; ***PH:*** 1-630-554-8899; ***Fax:*** 1-630-554-3311; ***http://*** www.alliedfirst.com

General - Incorporation		**Stock**- Price on:12/24/2007	$16.1
Employees	NA	Stock Exchange	OTC
Auditor	NA	Ticker Symbol	AFBA
Stk Agt	Registrar & Transfer Co	Outstanding Shares	NA
Counsel	NA	E.P.S.	NA
DUNS No.	NA	Shareholders	NA

Business: The groups principle activity is to provide banking products and services. The group provides deposit products, mortgage loans, consumer loans, and commercial services. The group operates from United States.

Primary SIC and add'l.: 6035 6712

CIK No: 0001158865

Financial Data: ***Fiscal Year End:***NA ***Latest Annual Data:*** 6/30/2004

Year	Sales	Net Income
2004	$7,689,000	$1,121,000
2003	$6,127,000	$387,000
2002	$6,246,000	$531,000

Curr. Assets: $9,067,000 **Curr. Liab.:** $84,663,000
Plant, Equip.: $340,000 **Total Liab.:** $121,945,000 **Indic. Yr. Divd.:** NA
Total Assets: $132,808,000 **Net Worth:** $10,864,000 **Debt/ Equity:** 3.5842

Allied Healthcare International Inc

555 Madison Ave., New York, NY, 10022; ***PH:*** 1-212-750-0064; ***Fax:*** 1-212-750-7221; ***http://*** www.alliedhealthcare.com

General - Incorporation	NY	**Stock**- Price on:12/24/2007	$2.79
Employees	960	Stock Exchange	NDQ
Auditor	Eisner LLP	Ticker Symbol	AHCI
Stk Agt	American Stock Transfer & Trust Co.	Outstanding Shares	44,960,000
Counsel	NA	E.P.S.	$1.47
DUNS No.	10-113-1217	Shareholders	NA

Business: The group's principal activities are to provide healthcare staffing and ancillary services. The staff includes nurses, carers and specialized medical personnel primarily in the United Kingdom. The staff is deputed to hospitals, local governmental authorities, nursing homes and private patients. The group also supplies medical grade oxygen for respiratory therapies in the United Kingdom and northern Ireland. The group's American operations include supply of infusion therapy, respiratory therapy and home medical equipment in New York and New Jersey. The group operated 115 community-based branches all over the United Kingdom. The group acquired cynon health agency on 08-Jul-2003, carewise nursing agency on 27-Jun-2003, first force medical recruitments limited 11-Apr-2003, ablecare oxfordshire and ablecare northamptonshire 17-Mar-2003, yorkshire careline 13-Jan-2003, medic-one 28-Nov-2002 and dalesway nursing services 18-Nov-2002.

Primary SIC and add'l.: 8082 7352

CIK No: 0000890634

Subsidiaries: Allied Healthcare Group Holdings Limited, Allied Healthcare Group Limited, Allied Healthcare Holdings Limited, Allied Respiratory Limited, Allied Staffing Professionals Limited, Limited and as Transworld Holdings (UK) Limited), Medigas Limited, Omnicare Limited

Officers: Timothy M. Aitken/63/Chmn., CEO, Sarah L. Eames/49/Dir., Exec. VP, David Moffatt/CFO, Leslie J. Levinson/53/Sec.

Directors: Timothy M. Aitken/63/Chmn., CEO, Wayne Palladino/Dir., Jeffrey S. Peris/Dir., Scott A. Shay/50/Dir., Richard G. Green/Dir., Mark Tompkins/Dir., Sophia Corona/Dir., Ann Thornburg/Dir.

Owners: Insiders/3.30%, Jeffrey S. Peris, Dimensional Fund Advisors LP/7.40%, Richard G. Green, Wayne Palladino, Washington & Congress Capital Partners, L.P./17.10%, Sarah L. Eames/2.60%, Rutabaga Capital Management LLC/8.90%, David Moffatt, Ann Thornburg, Mark Tompkins, Sophia Corona

Financial Data: ***Fiscal Year End:***09/30 ***Latest Annual Data:*** 9/30/2006

Year	Sales	Net Income
2006	$294,607,000	-$123,771,000
2005	$351,189,000	$18,736,000
2004	$325,298,000	$9,869,000

Curr. Assets: $47,871,000 **Curr. Liab.:** $49,036,000
Plant, Equip.: $27,076,000 **Total Liab.:** $108,959,000 **Indic. Yr. Divd.:** NA
Total Assets: $195,342,000 **Net Worth:** $86,383,000 **Debt/ Equity:** 0.5417

Allied Healthcare Products Inc

1720 Sublette Ave., St. Louis, MO, 63110; ***PH:*** 1-314-771-2400; ***Fax:*** 1-314-771-0650; ***http://*** www.alliedhpi.com

General - Incorporation	DE	**Stock**- Price on:12/24/2007	$6.45
Employees	417	Stock Exchange	NDQ
Auditor	Rubin Brown LLP	Ticker Symbol	AHPI
Stk Agt	American Stock Transfer & Trust Co.	Outstanding Shares	7,880,000
Counsel	NA	E.P.S.	$0.17
DUNS No.	09-967-4145	Shareholders	NA

Business: The group's principal activity is to manufacture, market and distribute a range of respiratory products used in the health care industry. The products offered by the group include respiratory care products, medical gas equipment and emergency medical products. Respiratory care products are used in the treatment of respiratory disorders like asthma, emphysema, bronchitis and pneumonia. Medical gas equipment consists of in-wall medical gas components, central suction pumps, compressors and headwalls. Emergency medical products are used in the treatment of trauma-induced injuries which provide ventilation during respiratory distress, immobilization and in the treatment of burns. These products are marketed and distributed to hospitals, hospital equipment dealers, hospital construction contractors, home health care dealers and emergency medical product dealers. The group's products are mainly exported to Europe, Canada, Latin America, Middle East and the Far East.

Primary SIC and add'l.: 3841

CIK No: 0000874710

Subsidiaries: B&F Medical Products, Inc, Life Support Products, Inc., Omni-Tech Medical, Inc.

Officers: Robert B. Harris/51/VP - Operations

Directors: Joseph E. Root/63/Dir.

Owners: Eldon P. Rosentrater, John D. Weil/39.20%, Robert B. Harris, Dimensional Fund Advisors Inc./6.30%, Earl R. Refsland/8.60%, Judith T. Graves, Joseph E. Root, Daniel C. Dunn, Royce & Associates, LLC/6.10%, Richard A. Setzer, Wells Fargo & Company/15.00%, Insiders/46.00%, William A. Peck

Financial Data: Fiscal Year End:06/30　**Latest Annual Data:** 6/30/2006

Year	Sales	Net Income
2006	$57,546,000	$1,649,000
2005	$56,120,000	$2,341,000
2004	$59,103,000	$1,875,000

Curr. Assets:	$21,842,000	*Curr. Liab.:*	$7,198,000		
Plant, Equip.:	$11,253,000	*Total Liab.:*	$8,671,000	*Indic. Yr. Divd.:*	NA
Total Assets:	$49,330,000	*Net Worth:*	$40,660,000	*Debt/ Equity:*	NA

Allied Irish Banks Plc

405 Pk. Ave., 4th Fl., New York, NY, 10022; *PH:* 1-212-515-6788; *http://* www.aib.ie; *Email:* investor.relations@aib.ie

General - Incorporation	Ireland	**Stock** - Price on:12/24/2007	$58.62
Employees	24,085	Stock Exchange	NYSE
Auditor	KPMG	Ticker Symbol	AIB
Stk Agt	Bank of New York	Outstanding Shares	437,830,000
Counsel	NA	E.P.S.	$6.42
DUNS No.	98-852-4518	Shareholders	NA

Business: The group's principal activities are the provision of banking and financial services. It operates principally in Ireland, Britain, Poland and the USA. The group operates through five divisions. AIB Bank ROI which consists of the retail and commercial activities in the Republic of Ireland. AIB Bank GB & NI which provides retail and commercial banking services in Great Britain and Northern Ireland. USA includes Allfirst and Allied Irish America. AIB capital markets comprise treasury and international, investment and corporate banking. Poland refers to the group's majority shareholding in Bank Zachodni WBK and Wroclaw-based Bank Zachodni.

Primary SIC and add'l.: 6726 6311 6021 6211

CIK No: 0000850364

Subsidiaries: AIB Asset Management Holdings Ltd., AIB Bank (CI) Ltd., AIB Capital Markets plc, AIB Corporate Finance Ltd., AIB Finance Ltd., AIB Fund Services Ltd., AIB Group p.l.c., AIB Insurance Services Ltd., AIB International Financial Services Ltd., AIB Leasing Ltd., Ark Life Assurance Company Ltd, Bank Zachodni WBK S.A., Goodbody Holdings Ltd.

Officers: Eugene Sheehy/53/Dir., CEO, Shom Bhattacharya/57/Group Chief Risk Officer, Pat Clarke/Mgr. - Group Investor Relations, Alma Pearson/Admin Assist. - Group Investor Relations, Gerry Byrne/52/MD, Robbie Henneberry/44/MD - AIB Group, UK plc, Alan Kelly/GM, Rose O'Donovan/Group Mgr. - Investor Relations, John O'Donnell/53/Dir., Group Dir. - Finance, Mary Toomey/59/Head - Group Strategic, Human Resources, Steven Meadows/54/Group Dir. - Operations, Technology

Directors: Eugene Sheehy/53/Dir., CEO, Dermot Gleeson/58/Chmn., Robert G. Wilmers/73/Dir., John O'Donnell/53/Dir., Group Dir. - Finance, Sean O'Driscoll/51/Dir., Bernard Somers/59/Dir., Anne Maher/Dir., Daniel O'Connor/48/Dir., David Pritchard/64/Dir., Stephen Kingon/Dir., Kieran Crowley/56/Dir., Jennifer Winter/48/Dir., Donal Forde/47/Dir., Don Godson/68/Dir., Colm Doherty/49/Dir. *(19 Directors included in Index)*

Owners: Robert G. Wilmers, Don Godson, Michael J. Sullivan, Padraic M. Fallon, Insiders, Dermot Gleeson, Jennifer Winter, Kieran Crowley, Sean ODriscoll, John ODonnell, John B. McGuckian, Adrian Burke, W. M. Kinsella, Colm Doherty, Jim OLeary *(16 Owners included in Index)*

Financial Data: Fiscal Year End:12/31　**Latest Annual Data:** 12/31/2005

Year	Sales	Net Income
2005	$7,595,557,000	$1,697,245,000
2004	$7,352,752,000	$1,604,534,000
2003	$6,219,482,000	$1,886,061,000

Curr. Assets:	$15,773,625,000	*Curr. Liab.:*	$145,008,550,000	*P/E Ratio:*	8.10
Plant, Equip.:	$782,938,000	*Total Liab.:*	$199,782,515,000	*Indic. Yr. Divd.:*	$2.020
Total Assets:	$209,943,544,000	*Net Worth:*	$10,161,029,000	*Debt/ Equity:*	NA

Allied Motion Technologies Inc

23 Inverness Way E., Ste. 150, Englewood, CO, 80112; *PH:* 1-303-799-8520; *Fax:* 1-303-799-8521; *http://* www.alliedmotion.com; *Email:* corpinfo@alliedmotion.com

General - Incorporation	CO	**Stock** - Price on:12/24/2007	$6.88
Employees	517	Stock Exchange	NDQ
Auditor	Ehrhardt Keefe Steiner & Hottman P.C	Ticker Symbol	AMOT
Stk Agt	American Stock Transfer & Trust Co.	Outstanding Shares	6,650,000
Counsel	NA	E.P.S.	$0.30
DUNS No.	00-706-7713	Shareholders	NA

Business: The group's principal activities are to design, manufacture and sell motor and servo motion products. The group is organized into three subsidiaries: emoteq corporation (emoteq), computer optical products inc (copi) and motor products corporation (motor products). Emoteq designs, manufactures and markets direct current brushless motors, related components, and drive and control electronics as well as a family of static frequency converters. Copi manufactures optical encoders, which are used to measure rotational and linear movements of parts in diverse applications such as printers, sorting machinery, machine tools, robots, medical equipment, tunable lasers and spectrum analysers. Motor products is a vertically integrated manufacturer of customized, highly engineered sub-fractional horsepower permanent magnet dc and brushless dc motors serving a wide range of original equipment applications. The group acquired precision motor technology b v (premotec) in 2004.

Primary SIC and add'l.: 3679 7372 3625

CIK No: 0000046129

Subsidiaries: Computer Optical Products, Inc, Emoteq Corporation, Motor Products Corporation, Precision Motor Technology B.V., Stature Electric, Inc.

Officers: Richard D. Smith/Dir., CEO, CFO/$506,419.00, Richard S. Warzala/Dir., COO, Pres./$481,324.00, Kenneth R. Wyman/VP - Marketing, CTO/$192,011.00, Susan M. Chiarmonte/Sec., Treasurer

Directors: Richard D. Smith/Dir., CEO, CFO, Delwin D. Hock/Chmn., Graydon D. Hubbard/Dir., George J. Pilmanis/Dir., Michel M. Robert/Dir., Richard S. Warzala/Dir., COO, Pres., S. R. Heath/Dir.

Owners: George J. Pilmanis, Richard S. Warzala/7.90%, Graydon D. Hubbard/1.00%, Delwin D. Hock, Insiders/33.90%, Kenneth R. Wyman, Peter H. Kamin/8.70%, Michel M. Robert/3.80%, Eugene E. Prince/12.30%, Richard D. Smith/10.60%

Financial Data: Fiscal Year End:12/31　**Latest Annual Data:** 03/31/2007

Year	Sales	Net Income
2007	NA	NA
2006	$82,768,000	$1,931,000
2005	$74,302,000	$923,000

Curr. Assets:	$23,098,000	*Curr. Liab.:*	$19,297,000	*P/E Ratio:*	20.85
Plant, Equip.:	$12,173,000	*Total Liab.:*	$24,102,000	*Indic. Yr. Divd.:*	NA
Total Assets:	$53,624,000	*Net Worth:*	$29,522,000	*Debt/ Equity:*	NA

Allied Resources Inc

400 Imperial Blvd., Cape Canaveral, FL, 32920; *Fax:* 1-321-799-9222; *http://* www.calloneonline.com; *Email:* info@alliedresources.com

General - Incorporation	NV	**Stock** - Price on:12/24/2007	$0.85
Employees	NA	Stock Exchange	OTC
Auditor	Jones Simkins, P.C.	Ticker Symbol	ALOD
Stk Agt.	NA	Outstanding Shares	5,650,000
Counsel	NA	E.P.S.	$0.03
DUNS No.	NA	Shareholders	NA

Business: The groups principle activity is to explore minerals and natural gas. The group operates from the United States. The groups quarterly revenue for September 2007 was 52.43 millions of USD.

Primary SIC and add'l.: 1321 1311 1321 1311

CIK No: 0001211524

Officers: Ruairidh Campbell/44/CEO, CFO, Principal Accounting Officer, Dir., Paul Crow/61/Dir., Sec., Krista Mattson/Accounting Exec. - Northern California, Jim Schwarz/Contact - Sales, Berchet O'Daniel/Pres., William Mays/VP, Sharon Brightman/Customer Service - Northern California, Rick Blythe/Accounting Exec. - Southern California, Brad Gombold/Branch Mgr. - Minneapolis, Bill Kennedy/Branch Executive, Nahsua, Emmett Carr/Branch Mgr. - Chicago, Patricia Taylor/Contact - Customer Service, Washington, DC, Bob MacKinnon/Branch Mgr. - Washington, Dave Heagy/Branch Mgr. - Atlanta, Sandra Prater/Contact - Customer Service, Atlanta *(17 Officers included in Index)*

Directors: Ruairidh Campbell/44/CEO, CFO, Principal Accounting Officer, Dir., Ed Haidenthaller/44/Dir., Paul Crow/61/Dir., Sec.

Owners: Ruairidh Campbell/27.10%, Ed Haidenthaller, Insiders/27.40%, Paul Crow

Financial Data: Fiscal Year End:12/31　**Latest Annual Data:** 12/31/2006

Year	Sales	Net Income
2006	NA	NA
2005	NA	NA

Curr. Assets:	$1,189,000	*Curr. Liab.:*	NA		
Plant, Equip.:	$564,000	*Total Liab.:*	$149,000	*Indic. Yr. Divd.:*	NA
Total Assets:	$3,424,000	*Net Worth:*	$3,274,000	*Debt/ Equity:*	NA

Allied Security Innovations Inc

Formerly: Digital Descriptor Systems Inc
1709 Rte. 34, Farmingdale, NY, 07727; *PH:* 1-732-359-0260; *http://* www.ddsi-cpc.com

General - Incorporation	DE	**Stock** - Price on:12/24/2007	NA
Employees	20	Stock Exchange	NA
Auditor	Bagell, Josephs, Levine & Co. LLC	Ticker Symbol	NA
Stk Agt.	Continental Stock Transfer & Trust Co	Outstanding Shares	NA
Counsel	NA	E.P.S.	NA
DUNS No.	86-945-2383	Shareholders	NA

Business: The group's principle activities include developing, assembling, marketing and installing computer systems. The computer systems capture video, digitally captured images and scanned images, digitize the image, link the digitized images to text or data and store the image and text on a computer database. This allows for transmitting the image and text by computer or over telephone transmission lines to remote locations. The principal product of the company is the compu-capture law enforcement program, which is marketed to law enforcement agencies and jail facilities. The company has one patent application, number 09/08/800, for a device and method for scanning and mapping a surface and it owns the proprietary rights to the software used in the compu-capture(R) programs. In addition, ddsi owns the rights to the trademarks compu-capture(R), compu-color(R) and compu-scan(R) both trademarks have been registered with the United States patent and trademark office.

Primary SIC and add'l.: 7379 3572 7378 7372

CIK No: 0000927454

Subsidiaries: Cgm Applied Security Technologies, Inc.

Officers: Anthony Shupin/Chmn., CEO, Pres., Gary Bouchard/Dir. - Development, Technical Services, Michael Pellegrino/Dir., CFO, Sr. VP, Erik Hoffer/60/Dir., Exec. VP, Margie Caputo/Dir. - Sales, Carolyn McDaniel/Accounting Department

Directors: Anthony Shupin/Chmn., CEO, Pres., Bob Gowell/Co - Chmn., Vince Moreno/Dir., Michael Pellegrino/Dir., CFO, Sr. VP, Erik Hoffer/60/Dir., Exec. VP, Robert Gowell/39/Dir.

Owners: Anthony R. Shupin/0.00%, Michael Pellegrino/0.00%, Insiders/0.00%, Robert Gowell

Financial Data: Fiscal Year End:12/31　**Latest Annual Data:** 12/31/2006

Year	Sales	Net Income
2006	$4,529,000	-$4,350,000
2005	$3,336,000	-$3,949,000
2004	$412,000	-$2,022,000

Curr. Assets:	$1,490,000	*Curr. Liab.:*	$13,345,000		
Plant, Equip.:	$318,000	*Total Liab.:*	$18,812,000	*Indic. Yr. Divd.:*	NA
Total Assets:	$6,033,000	*Net Worth:*	-$12,779,000	*Debt/ Equity:*	NA

Allied Systems Holdings Inc

Formerly: Allied Holdings Inc
160 Clairemont Ave, Ste. 200, Decatur, GA, 30030; *PH:* 1-404-373-4285; *http://* www.alliedholdings.com

General - Incorporation	GA	**Stock** - Price on:12/24/2007	$0.62
Employees	NA	Stock Exchange	AMEX
Auditor	KPMG LLP	Ticker Symbol	AHI
Stk Agt.	EquiServe Trust Co N.A	Outstanding Shares	NA
Counsel	Troutman Saunders LLP	E.P.S.	NA
DUNS No.	80-981-0179	Shareholders	NA

Business: The group's principal activities are carried through two business segments: allied automotive group and axis group. Allied automotive group provides a range of automotive delivery services including transporting new, used and off-lease vehicles to dealers from plants, rail ramps, ports and auctions and providing vehicle rail-car loading and unloading services. Axis group provides distribution, automotive inspection services and logistics support services for the automotive industry. It also provides carrier management services for various automotive clients, leases equipment for containerized international shipment of vehicles and provides vehicle processing services at ports and inland distribution centers. It operates in the United States and Canada.

Primary SIC and add'l.: 6719 4213

CIK No: 0000909950

Subsidiaries: ACE Operations, LLC, AH Industries, Inc., Allied Automotive Group, Inc., Allied Freight Broker, LLC, Allied Systems (Canada) Company, Allied Systems, Ltd., LP, Arrendadora de Equipo para el, Axis Areta, LLC, Axis Canada Company, Axis Group, Inc., Axis Logistica, S. de R.L. de C.V., Axis Netherlands, LLC, Axis Operadora Hermosillo, Commercial Carriers, Inc., Cordin Transport, LLC 27 Subsidiaries included in the Index

Officers: Thomas H. King/CFO, Exec. VP - Finance

Owners: Guy W. Rutland/9.50%, Thomas E. Boland, Robotti & Company, LLC,/6.60%, Robert J. Rutland/12.50%, Leland J. Strange, Armory Master Fund Ltd/7.20%, David G. Bannister, Berner F. Wilson/1.20%, Nikon Hecht Aspen Advisors LLC/9.90%, Guy W. Rutland/7.30%, Thomas H. King, Robert R. Woodson, Thomas M. Duffy/1.20%, Hugh E. Sawyer/6.50%, Insiders/37.00% (16 Owners included in Index)

Allied Waste Industries Inc

18500 N Allied Way, Phoenix, AZ, 85054; **PH:** 1-480-627-2700; **Fax:** 1-480-627-2701; http:// www.alliedwaste.com

General - Incorporation	DE	**Stock** - Price on:12/24/2007	$13.98
Employees	25,000	Stock Exchange	NYSE
Auditor	PricewaterhouseCoopers LLP	Ticker Symbol	AW
Stk Agt	American Stock Transfer & Trust Co.	Outstanding Shares	369,980,000
Counsel	NA	E.P.S.	$0.48
DUNS No.	18-061-5429	Shareholders	NA

Business: The groups principle activities include collecting, transferring, disposing and recycling of non-hazardous solid waste. In the year 2007, the group acquired Waste Services, Inc. The group operates from United States.

Primary SIC and add'l.: 4953 4959

CIK No: 0000848865

Subsidiaries: 3003304 Nova Scotia Company, 572060 B.c. Ltd., Abilene Landfill TX, LP, Action Disposal, Inc., Ada County Development Company, Inc., Adrian Landfill, Inc., ADS of Illinois, Inc., ADS, Inc., Agri-Tech, Inc. of Oregon, Alabama Recycling Services, Inc., Albany-Lebanon Sanitation, Inc., Allied Acquisition Pennsylvania, Inc., Allied Acquisition Two, Inc., Allied Enviroengineering, Inc., Allied Gas Recovery Systems, LLC 452 Subsidiaries included in the Index

Officers: John J. Zillmer/Chmn., CEO/$4,889,555.00, Edward A. Evans/Exec. VP, Chief Personnel Officer/$1,595,094.00, Donald W. Slager/COO, Pres./$3,091,712.00, Peter S. Hathaway/CFO, Exec. VP/$2,557,860.00, Timothy R. Donovan/Exec. VP, General Counsel, Corp. Sec.

Directors: John J. Zillmer/Chmn., CEO, James A. Quella/Dir., Stephanie Drescher/35/Dir., David I. Foley/Dir., Nolan Lehmann/Dir., Charles H. Cotros/Dir., James W. Crownover/Dir., Robert M. Agate/Dir., Steven Martinez/39/Dir., Leon J. Level/Dir., William J. Flynn/Dir., John M. Trani/Dir.

Owners: Apollo Investment Fund III, L.P./8.90%, EARNEST Partners, LLC,/6.10%, Robert M. Agate, Charles H. Cotros, Peter S. Hathaway, David I. Foley/13.00%, John J. Zillmer, Goldman Sachs Asset Mgmt., L.P./5.50%, James A. Quella/13.00%, Edward A. Evans, Stephanie Drescher/8.90%, John M. Trani, Donald W. Slager, Capital Research and Management Company/7.90%, Dennis R. Hendrix (22 Owners included in Index)

Financial Data: Fiscal Year End:12/31 **Latest Annual Data:** 12/31/2006

Year	Sales	Net Income
2006	$6,028,800,000	$160,900,000
2005	$5,734,800,000	$203,800,000
2004	$5,362,000,000	$49,300,000

Curr. Assets:	$1,047,700,000	Curr. Liab.:	$1,532,700,000	P/E Ratio:	42.36
Plant, Equip.:	$4,354,000,000	Total Liab.:	$10,212,100,000	Indic. Yr. Divd.:	NA
Total Assets:	$13,811,000,000	Net Worth:	$3,598,900,000	Debt/ Equity:	2.0456

Allied World Assurance Company Holdings Ltd

225 Franklin, 27th Fl., Boston, MA, 02110; **PH:** 1-857-288-6000; **Fax:** 1-617-556-8060; http:// www.awac.com; **Email:** info@awac.com

General - Incorporation	Bermuda	**Stock** - Price on:12/24/2007	$51.53
Employees	279	Stock Exchange	NYSE
Auditor	Gordon & Reindel LLP	Ticker Symbol	AWH
Stk Agt	Stock Transfer & Trust Co	Outstanding Shares	60,390,000
Counsel	NA	E.P.S.	$7.50
DUNS No.	NA	Shareholders	NA

Business: The groups principle activity is to provide property and casualty insurance and reinsurance. The groups product is property underwriting. The groups services include general casualty, professional liability, specialty lines and property catastrophe coverages. The groups operates through three segments namely property insurance, casualty insurance and reinsurance. The group operates from Bermuda, the United States, Ireland and the United Kingdom. The group's quarterly revenue for September 2007 was 355.80 millions of USD.

Primary SIC and add'l.: 6331

CIK No: 0001163348

Subsidiaries: Allied World Assurance Company (Europe) Limited, Allied World Assurance Company (Reinsurance) Limited, Allied World Assurance Company (U.S.) Inc., Allied World Assurance Company, Ltd., Allied World Assurance Holdings (Ireland) Ltd, Newmarket Administrative Services, Inc., Newmarket Underwriters Insurance Company

Officers: Scott A. Carmilani/Dir., CEO, Pres./$3,534,858.00, William G. Davis/63/Exec. VP - Worldwide Treaty, Facultative Reinsurance/$1,589,312.00, Richard E. Jodoin/Pres. - Allied World Assurance Company, US Inc/$942,941.00, John T. Redmond/Pres. - Allied World Assurance Company, Europe Limited, Allied World Assurance Company, Reinsurance Limited, Joan H.

Dillard/CFO, Sr. VP/$1,294,039.00, Wesley D. Dupont/Sr. VP, General Counsel, Sec./$1,078,662.00, Marshall J. Grossack/Sr. VP, Chief Corporate Actuar, Dick Jodoin/Pres. - Allied World Assurance Company, US Inc, Faye Cook/Assist. VP - Marketing, Communications/$1,452,578.00, Michael J. Baldwin/66/MD

Directors: Scott A. Carmilani/Dir., CEO, Pres., Michael I.D. Morrison/Chmn., Bart Friedman/Dep. Chmn., James F. Duffy/Dir., Scott Hunter/Dir., Mark R. Patterson/Dir., Samuel J. Weinhoff/Dir., Philip D. Defeo/Dir., Hugh Governey/65/Non - Exec. Dir.

Owners: William G. Davis, Insiders, The Chubb Corporation, Wesley D. Dupont, Philip D. DeFeo, American International Group, Inc., Scott A. Carmilani, Mark R. Patterson, Joan H. Dillard, Samuel J. Weinhoff, Scott Hunter, Bart Friedman, James F. Duffy, Michael I.D. Morrison, Richard E. Jodoin

Financial Data: Fiscal Year End:NA **Latest Annual Data:** 12/31/2006

Year	Sales	Net Income
2006	$1,467,692,000	$442,838,000
2005	$1,439,848,000	-$159,776,000
2004	$1,465,233,000	$197,173,000

Curr. Assets:	$1,674,670,000	Curr. Liab.:	$427,211,000	P/E Ratio:	6.65
Plant, Equip.:	NA	Total Liab.:	$5,400,496,000	Indic. Yr. Divd.:	$0.720
Total Assets:	$7,620,580,000	Net Worth:	$2,220,084,000	Debt/ Equity:	0.4583

Allin Corp

381 Mansfield Ave., Ste. 400, Pittsburgh, PA, 15220; **PH:** 1-412-928-8800; **Fax:** 1-412-928-0887; http:// www.allin.com; **Email:** webcorporate@allin.com

General - Incorporation	DE	**Stock** - Price on:12/24/2007	$0.85
Employees	139	Stock Exchange	OTC
Auditor	Malin, Bergquist & Co LLP	Ticker Symbol	ALLN
Stk Agt	National City Bank	Outstanding Shares	7,830,000
Counsel	NA	E.P.S.	$0.15
DUNS No.	95-828-1420	Shareholders	NA

Business: The group's principle activity is to provide technology consulting and systems integration services. The group operates through seven segments: e-business consulting, technology infrastructure consulting, interactive media consulting, interactive media systems integration, outsourced services, information system product sales and other services. The trade names used are allin interactive, allin consulting and allin corporation. The major customers of the group include royal Caribbean, carnival and costa. The group offers services through its subsidiaries: allin consulting-California, allin consulting-Pennsylvania, allin interactive, allin digital allin interactive, allin digital and allin network. The group's quarterly revenue for September 2007 was 5.68 millions of USD.

Primary SIC and add'l.: 7389 4841 6719 7379 7373

CIK No: 0001020391

Subsidiaries: Allin Consulting of Pennsylvania, Inc., Allin Corporation of California, Allin Holdings Corporation, Allin Interactive Corporation, Allin Network Products, Inc., CodeLab Technology Group, Inc.

Officers: Richard W. Talarico/52/Chmn., CEO, Pres./$209,000.00, Dean C. Praskach/VP - Finance, CFO, Treasurer, Sec./$156,250.00

Directors: Richard W. Talarico/52/Chmn., CEO, Pres., William C. Kavan/57/Dir., Anthony L. Bucci/59/Dir., Brian K. Blair/45/Dir., James S. Kelly/57/Dir., Anthony C. Vickers/58/Dir.

Owners: Insiders, Dean C. Praskach, Anthony C. Vickers, Henry Posner/75.30%, David S. Ritchie, Thomas D. Wright/6.70%, William C. Kavan/6.70%, Dean C. Praskach/1.30%, Anthony L. Bucci, William C. Kavan, Brian K. Blair, Richard W. Talarico, Henry Posner, Richard W. Talarico/6.70%, Insiders/14.70% (17 Owners included in Index)

Financial Data: Fiscal Year End:12/31 **Latest Annual Data:** 12/31/2006

Year	Sales	Net Income
2006	$19,048,000	$1,860,000
2005	$14,303,000	-$954,000
2004	$12,566,000	$284,000

Curr. Assets:	$5,949,000	Curr. Liab.:	$4,848,000	P/E Ratio:	17.00
Plant, Equip.:	$189,000	Total Liab.:	$8,192,000	Indic. Yr. Divd.:	NA
Total Assets:	$13,235,000	Net Worth:	$5,043,000	Debt/ Equity:	NA

Allion Healthcare Inc

1660 Walt Whitman Rd., Ste. 105, Melville, NY, 11747; **PH:** 1-631-547-6520; **Fax:** 1-631-249-5863; http:// www.allionhealthcare.com

General - Incorporation	DE	**Stock** - Price on:12/24/2007	$6
Employees	180	Stock Exchange	NDQ
Auditor	BDO Seidman, LLP	Ticker Symbol	ALLI
Stk Agt	NA	Outstanding Shares	16,200,000
Counsel	NA	E.P.S.	$0.13
DUNS No.	NA	Shareholders	NA

Business: The groups principle activity is to provide pharmacy and disease management services. The groups services include MOMSPak prescription packaging and Information systems, ancillary drugs, nutritional supplies, and prescription automation solutions. The group products sold under the trade name MOMS. Customers served by the group include clinics and physician. In the year 2005, the group acquired Oris Medical Systems, Inc, North American Home Health Supply, Inc and Specialty Pharmacies, Inc. The group operates from California, New York and Florida. The group's quarterly revenue for September 2007 was 61.82 millions of USD.

Primary SIC and add'l.: 5122 5912

CIK No: 0000847935

Subsidiaries: Allion Healthcare, Inc., Medicine Made Easy, Moms Pharmacy of Brooklyn, Inc., Moms Pharmacy, Inc., Moms Pharmacy, LLC, North American Home Health Supply, Inc., Oris Health, Inc., Specialty Pharmacies, Inc.

Officers: Michael P. Moran/Chmn., CEO, Pres., James G. Spencer/39/CFO, Sec., Treasurer, Robert E. Fleckenstein/VP - Pharmacy Operations, Corporate Compliance Officer, Anthony D. Luna/VP - HIV Sales, Oris Health, Inc.

Directors: Michael P. Moran/Chmn., CEO, Pres., Russell J. Fichera/Dir., John Pappajohn/Dir., Derace Schaffer/Dir., Harvey Z. Werblowsky/Dir., Gary P. Carpenter/Dir.

Owners: Cortina Asset Management, LLC/5.30%, Discovery Group/6.60%, James G. Spencer, Harvey Z. Werblowsky, Stephen A. Maggio, Royce & Associates, LLC/8.10%, Kennedy Capital Management, Inc./7.00%, HealthInvest Partners AB et al./8.50%, Derace Schaffer, WS Capital, L.L.C./5.00%, Insiders/9.40%, Michael P. Moran/2.80%, John Pappajohn/5.20%, Anthony D. Luna, Robert E. Fleckenstein (17 Owners included in Index)

Financial Data: **Fiscal Year End:**12/31 **Latest Annual Data:** 12/31/2006

Year	Sales	Net Income
2006	$209,503,000	$3,190,000
2005	$123,108,000	-$1,045,000
2004	$60,080,000	-$2,680,000

Curr. Assets:	$47,882,000	**Curr. Liab.:**	$18,347,000	**P/E Ratio:**	40.00
Plant, Equip.:	$890,000	**Total Liab.:**	$19,796,000	**Indic. Yr. Divd.:**	NA
Total Assets:	$121,603,000	**Net Worth:**	$101,807,000	**Debt/ Equity:**	0.0003

Allis-Chalmers Energy Inc

5075 Westheimer, Ste. 890, Houston, TX, 77056; ***PH:*** 1-713-369-0550; ***http://*** www.alchenergy.com

General - Incorporation.......DE
Employees.......2,567
Auditor .UHY Mann Frankfort Stein & Lipp LLP
Stk Agt....... Continental Stock Transfer & Trust Co
Counsel.......NA
DUNS No. 00-607-5816

Stock- Price on:12/24/2007.......$23.1799
Stock Exchange.......NYSE
Ticker Symbol.......ALY
Outstanding Shares.......34,640,000
E.P.S.......$1.71
Shareholders.......NA

Business: The group's principal activities are to provide oilfield services and equipment. The group's operations are carried through three business segments: casing services, directional drilling services and compressed air drilling services. The casing services are used during drilling and the completion phase of well. Air compression equipment provides cost-effective alternative to traditional drilling methods for certain types of reservoirs. Drilling operations are found in the Middle East, Latin America, western Canada and other areas. The group's major customers are el paso production oil & gas, materiales y equipos petroleros, anadarko petroleum corporation, burlington resources oil & gas co lp and calpine corporation. On 23-Sep-2004, the group acquired safco-oil field products inc.

Primary SIC and add'l.: 7699 1381

CIK No: 0000003982

Subsidiaries: AirComp LLC, Allis-Chalmers GP, LLC, Allis-Chalmers LP, LLC, Allis-Chalmers Management LP, Allis-Chalmers Production Services, Inc., Allis-Chalmers Rental Tools, Inc., Allis-Chalmers Tubular Services, Inc., Mountain Compressed Air Inc., OilQuip Rentals, Inc., Strata Directional Technology, Inc., Target Energy Inc.

Officers: Munawar H. Hidayatallah/Chmn., CEO/$1,733,934.00, Burt A. Adams/Vice Chmn., COO, Pres., Steven L. Collins/Pres. - Allis, Chalmers Production Services, Inc, David K. Bryan/Pres. - Directional Drilling Services/$407,975.00, Gary Edwards/Pres. - Casting, Tubing Services, Jeffrey R. Freedman/VP - Investor Relations, Terrence P. Keane/Pres. - Underbalanced Drilling Services, Martin Zoldi/Pres. - International Drilling, Victor M. Perez/CFO/$603,185.00, Theodore F. Pound/General Counsel, Sec./$541,565.00, Bruce Sauers/VP, Corporate Controller, Luke Prestridge/VP - Sales, Marketing

Directors: Munawar H. Hidayatallah/Chmn., CEO, Burt A. Adams/Vice Chmn., COO, Pres., Carlos A. Bulgheroni/Dir., Ali H.M. Afdhal/Dir., Victor F. Germack/Dir., James M. Hennessy/Dir., Zane Tankel/Dir., John E. McConnaughy/Dir., Robert E. Nederlander/Dir., Leonard Toboroff/Dir., Alejandro P. Bulgheroni/Dir.

Owners: Robert E. Nederlander/2.10%, Oil& Gas Rental Services, Inc./9.20%, Leonard Toboroff/2.00%, Palo Alto Investors/9.50%, Burt A. Adams, Victor M. Perez, Ali H. M. Afdhal, Munawar H. Hidayatallah/5.50%, Grupo Carso, S.A.B. de C.V./7.20%, John E. McConnaughy, Insiders/27.00%, David Bryan, Alejandro P. Bulgheroni/4.30%, Carlos A. Bulgheroni/2.90%, Theodore F. Pound *(17 Owners included in Index)*

Financial Data: **Fiscal Year End:**12/31 **Latest Annual Data:** 12/31/2006

Year	Sales	Net Income
2006	$307,304,000	$35,626,000
2005	$105,344,000	$7,175,000
2004	$47,726,000	$888,000

Curr. Assets:	$180,762,000	**Curr. Liab.:**	$72,371,000	**P/E Ratio:**	13.32
Plant, Equip.:	$554,258,000	**Total Liab.:**	$654,393,000	**Indic. Yr. Divd.:**	NA
Total Assets:	$908,326,000	**Net Worth:**	$253,933,000	**Debt/ Equity:**	1.3910

Allos Therapeutics Inc

11080 Cir.Point Rd., Ste. 200, Westminster, CO, 80020; ***PH:*** 1-303-426-6262; ***Fax:*** 1-303-426-4731; ***http://*** www.allos.com; ***Email:*** investorrelations@allos.com

General - Incorporation.......DE
Employees.......59
Auditor.......PricewaterhouseCoopers LLP
Stk Agt.......Mellon Investor Services LLC
Counsel.......Cooley Godward LLP
DUNS No.......NA

Stock- Price on:12/24/2007.......$5.6
Stock Exchange.......NDQ
Ticker Symbol.......ALTH
Outstanding Shares.......66,100,000
E.P.S.......-$0.58
Shareholders.......NA

Business: The group's principal activity is to develop and commercialize innovative small molecule drugs for improving cancer treatments. Small molecule drugs are non-protein products produced by chemical synthesis. The group's two product candidates that are currently under development: rsr13 (efaproxiral) and pdx (10-propargyl-10-deazaaminopterin). Rsr13 is a synthetic small molecule that has the potential to sensitize hypoxic (oxygen deprived) tumor tissues and enhance the efficacy of standard radiation therapy. Pdx is an injectable small molecule chemotherapeutic agent that has a superior potency and toxicity profile relative to methotrexate and other related dihydrofolate reductase inhibitors.

Primary SIC and add'l.: 2834

CIK No: 0001097264

Officers: Paul L. Berns/Dir., CEO, Pres./$1,717,700.00, James V. Caruso/Exec. VP, Chief Commercial Officer/$709,500.00, David C. Clark/Principal Financial Officer/$278,000.00, Vicki Baca/Contact - Human Resources, Jeremy Bender/Contact - Strategic Alliances, Business Development, Derek Cole/Investor Relations Officer, Marc H. Graboyes/VP, General Counsel/$435,600.00, Douglas G. Johnson/VP - Manufacturing, Jennifer Neiman/Investor Relations Officer, Pablo J. Cagnoni/Sr. VP, Chief Medical Officer, Sunil Patel/Contact - Strategic Alliances, Business Development

Directors: Paul L. Berns/Dir., CEO, Pres., Stephen J. Hoffman/Chmn., Mark G. Edwards/Dir., Stewart Hen/41/Dir., Jonathan S. Leff/Dir., Michael D. Casey/62/Dir., Timothy P. Lynch/Dir., Jeffrey R. Latts/Dir., William R. Ringo/Dir.

Owners: James V. Caruso, Warburg Pincus Private Equity VIII, L.P., Jonathan S. Leff, Stewart Hen, William R. Ringo, Timothy P. Lynch, Insiders, Stephen J. Hoffman, Marc H. Graboyes, Entities affiliated with Felix J. Baker and Julian C. Baker, Mark G. Edwards, Michael E. Saunders, David A. DeLong, Michael D. Casey, Paul L. Berns *(17 Owners included in Index)*

Financial Data: **Fiscal Year End:**12/31 **Latest Annual Data:** 12/31/2006

Year	Sales	Net Income
2006	NA	-$30,212,000
2005	NA	-$20,137,000
2004	NA	-$21,837,000

Curr. Assets:	$35,729,000	**Curr. Liab.:**	$6,832,000		
Plant, Equip.:	$604,000	**Total Liab.:**	$6,832,000	**Indic. Yr. Divd.:**	NA
Total Assets:	$36,382,000	**Net Worth:**	$29,550,000	**Debt/ Equity:**	NA

Allot Communications Ltd

7664 Golden Triangle Dr., Eden Prairie, MN, 55344; ***PH:*** 1-952-944-3100; ***Fax:*** 1-952-944-3555; ***http://*** www.allot.com; ***Email:*** sales-usa@allot.com

General - Incorporation.......Israel
Employees.......NA
Auditor.......Kost Forer Gabbay & Kasierer
Stk Agt......American Stock Transfer & Trust Co.
Counsel.......NA
DUNS No.......NA

Stock- Price on:12/24/2007.......$6.93
Stock Exchange.......NDQ
Ticker Symbol.......ALLT
Outstanding Shares.......21,010,000
E.P.S.......-$0.15
Shareholders.......NA

Business: The group's principle activities include designing and developing broadband products and services. The groups products include NetEnforcer AC-400, NetEnforcer AC-800 and NetEnforcer AC-1000. The group operates from United States.

Primary SIC and add'l.: 3577 3669

CIK No: 0001365767

Subsidiaries: Allot Communication Europe SARL, Allot Communications (Asia Pacific) Pte. Ltd., Allot Communications (UK) Limited, Allot Communications Japan K.K., Allot Communications, Inc.

Officers: Rami Hadar/Dir., CEO, Pres., Azi Ronen/Exec. VP - Corporate Development, Amir Weinstein/Exec. VP - Products, Technology, Jay Klein/CTO, VP, Vin Costello/VP - Americas, Memashe Mukhtar/VP - International Sales, Sharon Hess/VP - Marketing, Ramy Moriah/VP - Customer Care, Information Technology, Pini Gvili/VP - Operations, Anant Shenig/VP - Human Resources, Elazar Ronen/46/Exec. VP - Corporate Development, Doron Arazi/CFO, Andrei Elefant/VP - Products, Strategic Projects, Jay Kalish/Exec. Dir. - Investor Relations

Directors: Rami Hadar/Dir., CEO, Pres., Yigal Jacoby/Chmn., Yossi Sela/Dir., Eyal Kishon/Dir., Shai Saul/Dir., Nurit Benjamini/Dir., Hezi Lapid/60/Dir., Steven D. Levy/Dir.

Owners: Brookside Capital Fund/10.40%, Jerusalem Venture Partners/5.00%, Shai Saul/11.00%, Genesis Partners/9.60%, Eyal Kishon/9.60%, Partech International Group/6.00%, Insiders/42.30%, Yigal Jacoby/8.60%, Yossi Sela/10.40%, Tamir Fishman Ventures/11.00%, Gemini Group/10.40%

Financial Data: **Fiscal Year End:**12/31 **Latest Annual Data:** 12/31/2006

Year	Sales	Net Income
2006	$34,144,000	$616,000
2005	$22,972,000	-$2,376,000
2004	$18,085,000	-$3,288,000

Curr. Assets:	$88,694,000	**Curr. Liab.:**	$13,042,000	**P/E Ratio:**	40.00
Plant, Equip.:	$2,939,000	**Total Liab.:**	$16,997,000	**Indic. Yr. Divd.:**	NA
Total Assets:	$101,184,000	**Net Worth:**	$84,187,000	**Debt/ Equity:**	NA

Alloy Inc

151 W 26th St., 11th Fl., New York, NY, 10001; ***PH:*** 1-212-244-4307; ***Fax:*** 1-212-244-4311; ***http://*** www.alloy.com

General - Incorporation.......DE
Employees.......601
Auditor.......BDO Seidman LLP
Stk Agt......American Stock Transfer & Trust Co.
Counsel.......NA
DUNS No.......NA

Stock- Price on:12/24/2007.......$9.9
Stock Exchange.......NDQ
Ticker Symbol.......ALOY
Outstanding Shares.......14,040,000
E.P.S.......$0.62
Shareholders.......NA

Business: The group's principal activities are to provide media, marketing services and direct marketing. The group operates through three segments: direct marketing, retail stores and sponsorship and advertising. Direct marketing segment provides marketing services through catalogs and websites. Retail stores include outlet stores of apparel and accessories. The sponsorship and advertising segment helps advertisers to reach customers through magazines, books, websites and display media boards. The group also provides services through promotional events, product sampling, college and high school newspaper advertising and customer acquisition programs. The group uses its catalogs and websites to sell third party branded products such as apparel, action sports equipment and accessories. The group acquired delias corp and substantially all of the assets and liabilities of ocm direct inc., collegiate carpets, inc. And carepackages inc in 2003

Primary SIC and add'l.: 7331 7375

CIK No: 0001080359

Subsidiaries: 360 Youth, LLC, Alloy Edward Acquisition Sub, Inc., Alloy Mall Marketing Services, LLC, Alloy Marketing and Promotions, LLC, Armed Forces Communications, Inc, Canal Park, LLC, Care Packages, LLC, Collegiate Carpets, LLC, DX Company, Inc., InSite Advertising, Inc., MPM Holdings, Inc., On Campus Marketing, LLC, Sconex, LLC, The Staffing Authority, LLC, Triple Rewards LLC

Officers: Matthew C. Diamond/Chmn., CEO, Treasurer/$1,009,821.00, Gary Yusko/53/CFO/$418,950.00, James K. Johnson/Dir., COO, Pres./$1,009,821.00, Robert L. Bell/58/CTO/$448,433.00, Gina Digioia/37/Chief Legal Officer, Corp. Sec./$254,508.00, Joseph D. Frehe/CFO

Directors: Matthew C. Diamond/Chmn., CEO, Treasurer, Peter M. Graham/53/Dir., Samuel A. Gradess/42/Dir., James K. Johnson/Dir., COO, Pres., Edward A. Monnier/44/Dir., Anthony N. Fiore/66/Dir., Jeffrey Hollender/53/Dir., Richard E. Perlman/Dir.

Owners: Gilder, Gagnon, Howe& Co. LLC/7.20%, Gary J. Yusko, Edward A. Monnier, Gina R. DiGioia, Loomis Sayles& Co., L.P./6.60%, Matthew C. Diamond/3.30%, Insiders/10.30%, Jeffrey Hollender, Richard E. Perlman, Brightpoint Capital Advisors, LLC/5.00%, Robert L. Bell, Peter M. Graham, Samuel A. Gradess/2.00%, RGM Capital, LLC/5.80%, James K. Johnson/3.20% *(18 Owners included in Index)*

Financial Data: **Fiscal Year End:**01/31 **Latest Annual Data:** 1/31/2007

Year	Sales	Net Income
2007	$196,104,000	-$7,233,000
2006	$195,324,000	-$35,508,000
2005	$402,493,000	-$91,766,000

Curr. Assets:	$65,132,000	**Curr. Liab.:**	$31,675,000		
Plant, Equip.:	$4,403,000	**Total Liab.:**	$33,895,000	**Indic. Yr. Divd.:**	NA
Total Assets:	$196,566,000	**Net Worth:**	$162,671,000	**Debt/ Equity:**	0.0085

Alloy Steel International Inc

42 Mercantile Way, Malaga D C, Western Australia, 6945; ; ***http://*** www.alloysteel.net

General - Incorporation	DE	***Stock***- Price on:12/24/2007	$0.5
Employees	25	Stock Exchange	OTC
Auditor	Rothstein, Kass & Co, P.C	Ticker Symbol	AYSI
Stk Agt	Continental Stock Transfer & Trust Co	Outstanding Shares	16,950,000
Counsel	NA	E.P.S	$0.02
DUNS No.	NA	Shareholders	NA

Business: The group's principal activity is to manufacture and distribute arcoplate, a wear-resistant fused-alloy-clad steel wear plate, through a patented production process. The arcoplate process enables an alloy overlay to be smoothly and evenly applied to a sheet of steel, which creates a metallurgical bond between the alloy and the steel. This bond is resistant to wear caused by impact, abrasion and erosion. This product is used in machinery, which is used for iron, gold, nickel, copper mining, bulldozer arms and blades, truck box liners and bucket loader liners. The group markets its product in the United States, Australia, Asia and South America.

Primary SIC and add'l.: 3325

CIK No: 0001127454

Subsidiaries: Alloy Steel Australia (Int.) Pty Ltd.

Officers: Daniel Byrne/Investor Relation Officer

Owners: Alan C. Winduss/11.20%, Gene Kostecki/62.53%

Financial Data: Fiscal Year End:09/30 ***Latest Annual Data:*** 9/30/2006

Year	***Sales***	***Net Income***
2006	$3,386,000	-$274,000
2005	$3,620,000	$239,000
2004	$2,987,000	-$4,000

Curr. Assets:	$1,140,000	***Curr. Liab.:***	$1,294,000	***P/E Ratio:***	25.00
Plant, Equip.:	$1,888,000	***Total Liab.:***	$1,762,000	***Indic. Yr. Divd.:***	NA
Total Assets:	$3,264,000	***Net Worth:***	$1,503,000	***Debt/ Equity:***	0.2107

Allscripts Healthcare Solutions Inc

222 Merchandise Mart Plz., Ste. 2024, Chicago, IL, 60654; ***PH:*** 1-312-506-1200; ***Fax:*** 1-312-506-1201; ***http://*** www.allscripts.com

General - Incorporation	DE	***Stock***- Price on:12/24/2007	$25.31
Employees	914	Stock Exchange	NDQ
Auditor	Grant Thornton, LLP	Ticker Symbol	MDRX
Stk Agt	LaSalle Bank N.A	Outstanding Shares	55,360,000
Counsel	Sonnenschein Nath & Rosenthal LLP	E.P.S	$0.33
DUNS No.	NA	Shareholders	NA

Business: The group's principle activity is to provide clinical software and information solutions for physicians. It offers decision support solutions that are designed to improve the quality and reduce the cost of healthcare. The group's operations are conducted through three business segments: prepackaged medications, software and related services and information services. The prepackaged medications segment provides repackaging, sale, and distribution of medications and medical supplies. Software and related services segment derives its revenue from the sale and installation of software that provides point-of-care decision support solutions and the resale of related hardware. Information services segment provides interactive physician education sessions. The group's quarterly revenue for September 2007 was 73.44 millions of USD.

Primary SIC and add'l.: 7375 5122 7372

CIK No: 0001124804

Subsidiaries: A4 Health Systems, Inc, A4 Realty, LLC, Allscripts LLC

Officers: Glen E. Tullman/Chmn., CEO/$697,101.00, John G. Cull/Pres. - Medication Services, Joseph E. Carey/50/COO/$505,785.00, John Nebergall/VP - Client Support, Dan Michelson/Chief Marketing Officer, Steven P. Schwartz/Sr. VP - Business Development, Laurie McGraw/Pres. - Clinical Solutions, Lee Shapiro/Pres./$580,693.00, Douglas A. Gentile/Chief Medical Officer, Benjamin Bulkley/COO, Troy Moritz/Chief Security Officer, Brian Vandenberg/VP, General Counsel, Mike Gluth/Sr. VP - Product Mannagement, Greg Moyer/VP - Client Services, Acute Care Division, Donato J. Tramuto/Pres. - Physicians Interactive *(19 Officers included in Index)*

Directors: Glen E. Tullman/Chmn., CEO, Marcel L. Gamache/65/Dir., Bernard Goldstein/77/Dir., Philip D. Green/57/Dir., Robert A. Compton/52/Dir., Michael J. Kluger/51/Dir., John P. McConnell/57/Dir., Fazle M. Husain/44/Dir.

Owners: Glen E. Tullman/1.80%, John P. McConnell, Lee A. Shapiro, Robert A. Compton, David A. Bond, Franklin Resources, Inc./11.20%, Fazle M. Husain, Insiders/5.70%, Michael J. Kluger, Philip D. Green, Lone Pine Capital, LLC/6.70%, Marcel L. Gamache, Joseph E. Carey, William J. Davis, Bernard Goldstein *(18 Owners included in Index)*

Financial Data: Fiscal Year End:12/31 ***Latest Annual Data:*** 12/31/2006

Year	***Sales***	***Net Income***
2006	$227,969,000	$11,895,000
2005	$120,564,000	$9,710,000
2004	$100,770,000	$3,108,000

Curr. Assets:	$153,897,000	***Curr. Liab.:***	$71,647,000	***P/E Ratio:***	93.74
Plant, Equip.:	$14,094,000	***Total Liab.:***	$161,360,000	***Indic. Yr. Divd.:***	NA
Total Assets:	$477,610,000	***Net Worth:***	$316,250,000	***Debt/ Equity:***	0.2635

Allstate Corp

2775 Sanders Rd., Northbrook, IL, 60062; ***PH:*** 1-847-402-5000; ***Fax:*** 1-847-326-7519; ***http://*** www.allstate.com; ***Email:*** invrel@allstate.com

General - Incorporation	DE	***Stock***- Price on:12/24/2007	$61.81
Employees	36,800	Stock Exchange	NYSE
Auditor	Deloitte & Touche LLP	Ticker Symbol	ALL
Stk Agt	Wells Fargo Shareowner Services	Outstanding Shares	607,410,000
Counsel	NA	E.P.S	$8.33
DUNS No.	00-693-5886	Shareholders	NA

Business: The group's principle activity is to provide auto, property, life and commercial insurance services including retirement and investment products and banking services. The group operates from United States.

Primary SIC and add'l.: 6311 6331

CIK No: 0000899051

Subsidiaries: ALFS, Inc., ALIC Reinsurance Company, Allstate Assignment Company, Allstate Assurance Company, Allstate Bank, Allstate County Mutual Insurance, Allstate Distributors, LLC, Allstate Financial Advisors, LLC, Allstate Financial Corporation, Allstate Financial Services, LLC, Allstate Financial, LLC, Allstate Fire and Casualty Insurance, Allstate Floridian Indemnity Company, Allstate Floridian Insurance Company, Allstate Holdings, LLC 75 Subsidiaries included in the Index

Officers: Edward M. Liddy/62/Chmn., CEO/$23,983,780.00, James E. Hohmann/CEO, Pres. - Allstate Financial, Steven P. Sorenson/Sr. VP - Protection Distribution, Allstate Insurance Company, Casey J. Sylla/64/Sr. VP - AIC, Frederick F. Cripe/Sr. VP - Product Operations, Allstate Insurance Company, Nicole Alley/National Media Relations Team, Karen Doyle/National Media Relations Team, Raleigh Floyd/National Media Relations Team, Brad Keena/National Media Relations Team, Thomas J. Wilson/50/Dir., COO, Pres./$7,831,055.00, Samuel H. Pilch/61/Controller - Allstate Corporation, Group VP, Controller - AIC, Eric A. Simonson/Chief Investment Officer, Sr. VP-Allstate Insurance Company/$4,920,477.00, Catherine S. Brune/CIO, Sr. VP - Allstate Insurance Company, George E. Ruebenson/Pres. - Allstate Protection, Allstate Insurance Company, Michael J. Roche/56/Sr. VP - AIC *(24 Officers included in Index)*

Directors: Edward M. Liddy/62/Chmn., CEO, Judith A. Sprieser/53/Dir., Mary Alice Taylor/57/Dir., Christopher J. Reyes/54/Dir., Jack M. Greenberg/65/Dir., James G. Andress/69/Dir., Thomas J. Wilson/50/Dir., COO, Pres., Joshua I. Smith/67/Dir., Duane F. Ackerman/65/Dir., Robert D. Beyer/48/Dir., John H. Riley/67/Dir., James W. Farrell/65/Dir., Ronald T. Lemay/62/Dir.

Owners: Eric A. Simonson, Jack M. Greenberg, James W. Farrell, Insiders, Casey J. Sylla, Christopher J. Reyes, Danny L. Hale, Robert D. Beyer, Mary Alice Taylor, Ronald T. LeMay, Joshua I. Smith, John H. Riley, James G. Andress, Judith A. Spriesеr, Northern Trust Corporation/5.23% *(18 Owners included in Index)*

Financial Data: Fiscal Year End:12/31 ***Latest Annual Data:*** 12/31/2006

Year	***Sales***	***Net Income***
2006	$35,796,000,000	$4,993,000,000
2005	$35,383,000,000	$1,765,000,000
2004	$33,936,000,000	$3,181,000,000

Curr. Assets:	$13,489,000,000	***Curr. Liab.:***	$729,000,000		
Plant, Equip.:	$1,010,000,000	***Total Liab.:***	$135,708,000,000	***Indic. Yr. Divd.:***	$1.520
Total Assets:	$157,554,000,000	***Net Worth:***	$21,846,000,000	***Debt/ Equity:***	0.2063

Allstate Insurance Company

100 Motor Pkwy., Ste. 132, Happauge, NY, 11788; ***PH:*** 1-800-574-3553; ***http://*** www.allstate.com; ***Email:*** invrel@allstate.com

General - Incorporation	NY	***Stock***- Price on:12/24/2007	NA
Employees	NA	Stock Exchange	NA
Auditor	Deloitte & Touche LLP	Ticker Symbol	NA
Stk Agt	Wells Fargo Shareowner Services	Outstanding Shares	NA
Counsel	NA	E.P.S	NA
DUNS No.	80-744-6190	Shareholders	NA

Business: The group's principle activities include marketing and selling life insurance products in the state of New York. The products are sold through a combination of exclusive and independent agencies, securities firms, banks, specialized brokers and direct response marketing. The company currently offers single premium variable life insurance. The products include traditional products, including term and whole life, interest-sensitive life, and immediate annuities with life contingencies. Investment products include deferred annuities and immediate annuities without life contingencies. Deferred annuities include fixed rate, market value adjusted and variable annuities. The company is a wholly owned subsidiary of allstate life insurance company. The group operates from United States.

Primary SIC and add'l.: 6311 6321

CIK No: 0000839759

Subsidiaries: The Prudential Insurance Company

Officers: James E. Hohmann/CEO, Pres., Casey J. Sylla/Chmn., Pres., Principal Executive Officer, Sr. VP, Rusty Johnson/Contact - Marianna, FL, Richard Younger/Contact - Younger Agency Inc, Palm Bay, FL, Larry Silverman/Contact - Pompano Beach, FL, Michael J. Roche/Sr. VP - Protection Technology - Administration, Al Karim/Contact - Mt. Dora, FL, Charles Onoko/Contact - Margate, FL, Jeff Paglialonga/Contact - Altamonte Springs, FL, Catherine S. Brune/CIO, Sr. VP, Joan M. Crockett/Sr. VP - Human Resources, Jerome Barbieri/Contact - St. Lucie West, FL, Renay Proenza/Contact - Debary, FL, Dominick Scarangella/Contact - Oviedo, FL, Richard Snyder/Contact - Naples, FL *(31 Officers included in Index)*

Directors: Casey J. Sylla/Chmn., Pres., Principal Executive Officer, Sr. VP, Cleveland Johnson/Dir., Duane F. Ackerman/65/Dir., James G. Andress/69/Dir., Robert D. Beyer/48/Dir., James W. Farrell/65/Dir., Jack M. Greenberg/65/Dir., Ronald T. Lemay/62/Dir., Vincent A. Fusco/Dir., Kenneth R. O'Brien/Dir., John R. Raben/Dir., Marcia D. Alazraki/Dir., Patricia W. Wilson/Dir., Phyllis Hill Slater/Dir., Kevin R. Slawin/Dir. *(26 Directors included in Index)*

Allstates Worldcargo Inc

4 Lakeside Dr. S, Forked River, NJ, 08731; ***PH:*** 1-609-693-5950; ***http://*** www.allstatesair.com

General - Incorporation	NJ	***Stock***- Price on:12/24/2007	NA
Employees	NA	Stock Exchange	NA
Auditor	Toms River	Ticker Symbol	NA
Stk Agt	NA	Outstanding Shares	NA
Counsel	NA	E.P.S	NA
DUNS No.	00-839-4447	Shareholders	NA

Business: The group's principle activity is freight forwarding, marketing and distribution of safety equipment, development of audio-visual products including safety training program. It is also into sales and marketing presentations, development of a device to treat tinnitus and development of an echolocation device to assist sighted persons in conditions of low visibility and the blind. It provides domestic and international freight forwarding services to over 1,700 customers utilizing ground transportation, commercial air carriers and ocean vessels. The major customers of the group are j.b. Williams, raytheon, giorgio perfume, cosmair, ashton tate, merisel corporation, budd corporation, home box office, sensormatic, at&t, and polaris. It maintains operating facilities throughout the United States and has agents in Europe and South America.

Primary SIC and add'l.: 4522 3651 5999 4499 4789

CIK No: 0001072293

Subsidiaries: Allstates Air Cargo, Inc., Allstates Logistics, Audiogenesis Systems, B&G Plastics, Inc., Biowaste Technologies Systems, T.H. Weiss, Inc.

Officers: Sam Digiralomo/64/Dir., CEO, Pres., Barton C. Theile/61/Dir., Exec. VP, COO, Craig D. Stratton/56/Dir., Sec., CFO, Treasurer

Directors: Sam Digiralomo/64/Dir., CEO, Pres., Joseph M. Guido/73/Chmn. Emeritus, Barton C. Theile/61/Dir., Exec. VP, COO, Craig D. Stratton/56/Dir., Sec., CFO, Treasurer

Owners: Barton C. Theile/1.54%, Insiders/72.46%, Craig D. Stratton/0.61%, Joseph M. Guido/58.47%, Sam DiGiralomo/11.84%

Alltel Corp

1 Allied Dr., Little Rock, AR, 72202; *PH:* 1-501-905-8000; *Fax:* 1-501-905-5444; *http://* www.alltel.com

General - Incorporation............................ DE	Stock- Price on:12/24/2007 ....$67.55
Employees 14,899	Stock Exchange...NA
Auditor ....PricewaterhouseCoopers LLP	Ticker Symbol..NA
Stk Agt..... Computershare Investor Services LLC	Outstanding Shares 345,480,000
Counsel..NA	E.P.S...$2.26
DUNS No. 00-790-2802	Shareholders...NA

Business: The groups principle activity is to provide communication services. The group operates through three segments namely wireless, wire line and communication services. The group operates from United States.

Primary SIC and add'l.: 7375 4813 4812 4899 5063

CIK No: 0000065873

Subsidiaries: Accucomm Networks, Inc., Accucomm Telecommunications, Inc., Allied Information Services of the Philippines, Inc., Alltel Alabama, Inc., Alltel Arkansas, Inc., Alltel Carolina, Inc., ALLTEL Cellular Associates of Arkansas Limited Partnership, ALLTEL Central Arkansas Cellular Limited Partnership, Alltel Communications Holdings of the Midwest, Inc., Alltel Communications Investments, Inc., ALLTEL Communications of Arkansas RSA #12 Cellular Limited Partnership, ALLTEL Communications of LaCrosse Limited Partnership, Alltel Communications of Michigan RSA #4, Inc., ALLTEL Communications of Michigan RSA #6 Cellular Limited Partnership, Alltel Communications of Michigan RSAs, Inc. 241 Subsidiaries included in the Index

Officers: Scott T. Ford/Dir., CEO, Pres./$14,115,770.00, Kevin L. Beebe/Pres. - Operations/$8,743,173.00, Jeffrey H. Fox/Pres. - Operations/$9,054,918.00, Richard Massey/Exec. VP, Corp. Sec., General Counsel/$3,099,673.00, John Ebner/Treasure, Sr. VP - Investor Relations, Tim Hicks/Dir. - Investor Relations, Treasury Services, Andrew Moreau/VP - Corporate Communications, Dale Ingram/VP - Public Relations, Sharilyn Gasaway/CFO, Exec. VP/$2,872,900.00, Keith A. Kostuch/Sr. VP - Strategic Planning, C. J. Duvall/Sr. VP - Human Resources, Sue Mosley/Controller

Directors: Scott T. Ford/Dir., CEO, Pres., Joe Ford/69/Chmn., John R. Belk/48/Dir., Peter A. Bridgman/54/Dir., William H. Crown/43/Dir., Josie C. Natori/59/Dir., Warren Stephens/50/Dir., Ronald Townsend/65/Dir., John W. Stanton/52/Dir., Lawrence L. Gellerstedt/51/Dir., Emon A. Mahony/65/Dir., John P. McConnell/53/Dir.

Financial Data: Fiscal Year End:12/31   Latest Annual Data: 12/31/2006

Year	Sales	Net Income
2006	$7,884,000,000	$1,129,400,000
2005	$9,487,000,000	$1,331,400,000
2004	$8,246,100,000	$1,046,200,000
Curr. Assets:	$2,032,100,000	Curr. Liab.:	$1,197,300,000	P/E Ratio:	24.04
Plant, Equip.:	$5,231,400,000	Total Liab.:	$5,681,800,000	Indic. Yr. Divd.:	NA
Total Assets:	$18,343,700,000	Net Worth:	$12,661,900,000	Debt/ Equity:	0.2229

Almaden Minerals Ltd

750 W Pender St., Ste. 1103, Vancouver, BC, V6T 2T8; *PH:* 1-604-689-7644; *Fax:* 1-604-689-7645; *http://* www.almadenminerals.com; *Email:* info@almadenminerals.com

General - Incorporation............................ BC	Stock- Price on:12/24/2007 ....$2.3299
Employees 6	Stock Exchange......................................AMEX
Auditor ....Deloitte& Touche LLP	Ticker Symbol..AAU
Stk Agt.................... Pacific Corporate Trust Co	Outstanding Shares 44,070,000
Counsel.................. William J. Worral, Q.C.	E.P.S...-$0.03
DUNS No. ....NA	Shareholders...NA

Business: The groups principle activities include acquiring, exploring and developing mineral properties. The group operates from the Canada, Japan and Mexico. The groups quarterly revenue for September 2007 was 0.16 millions of CAD.

Primary SIC and add'l.: 1499 1041 1021 1044

CIK No: 0001015647

Subsidiaries: Almaden America Inc., Almaden de Mexico, S.A. de C.V., Compania Minera Zapata, S.A. de C.V., Minera Gavilan, S.A. de C.V., Republic Resources Ltd.

Officers: Morgan Poliquin/Dir., COO, Pres., Dione Bitzer/CFO

Directors: Duane Poliquin/Chmn., Morgan Poliquin/Dir., COO, Pres., Jack McLeary/Dir., Gerald Carlson/Dir., James E. McInnes/Dir., Donald M. Lorimer/Dir., Barry Smee/Dir., Joe Montgomery/Dir.

Owners: Joseph Montgomery/0.17%, Dione Bitzer/0.44%, James E. McInnes/1.68%, Gerald G. Carlson/0.35%, Insiders/15.34%, Morgan Poliquin/4.03%, Jack McCleary/0.85%, Duane Poliquin/7.10%, Barry Smee/0.33%, Donald Lorimer/0.39%

Financial Data: Fiscal Year End:12/31   Latest Annual Data: 12/31/2006

Year	Sales	Net Income
2006	$718,000	-$5,176,000
2005	$211,000	-$1,330,000
2004	$202,000	-$3,138,000
Curr. Assets:	$18,013,000	Curr. Liab.:	$643,000		
Plant, Equip.:	$2,806,000	Total Liab.:	$643,000	Indic. Yr. Divd.:	NA
Total Assets:	$21,211,000	Net Worth:	$20,568,000	Debt/ Equity:	NA

Almost Family Inc

9510 Ormsby Sta. Rd., Ste. 300, Louisville, KY, 40223; *PH:* 1-502-891-1000; *Fax:* 1-502-891-8067; *http://* www.almost-family.com; *Email:* info@afam-inc.com

General - Incorporation............................ DE	Stock- Price on:12/24/2007 ....$18.72
Employees 4,000	Stock Exchange...NDQ
Auditor ....Ernst & Young LLP	Ticker Symbol...AFAM
Stk Agt.....................Registrar & Transfer Co	Outstanding Shares 5,420,000
Counsel..NA	E.P.S...$1.12
DUNS No. 15-360-0796	Shareholders...NA

Business: The group's principal activity is to provide integrated adult day health services and visiting nurse services. The group's adult day health centers provide professional, high quality adult day health services for disabled or frail adults. The adult day health centers provide a range of therapeutic and medical services designed to promote the independence of participants. The group also provides services like meals, family counseling, individualized and creative activities program. The visiting nurses segment provides skilled medical services in patients' homes largely to enable recipients to reduce or avoid periods of hospitalization and nursing home care. The group has operations in Alabama, Connecticut, Florida, Indiana, Kentucky, Maryland, Massachusetts and Ohio.

Primary SIC and add'l.: 8082 8099

CIK No: 0000799231

Subsidiaries: Adult Day Care of America, Inc., Adult Day Care of Louisville, Inc., Adult Day Care of Maryland, Inc., Adult Day Clubs of America Joint Venture, Ltd., Caretender Visiting Services of Dist 6, LLC, Caretenders Homecare, Inc., Caretenders Infusion Corp., Caretenders Infusion of Birmingham, Inc., Caretenders of Birmingham, Inc., Caretenders of Boston, Inc., Caretenders of Charlotte, Inc., Caretenders of Cincinnati, Inc., Caretenders of Cleveland, Inc., Caretenders of Columbus, Inc., Caretenders of Elizabethtown, Inc. 52 Subsidiaries included in the Index

Officers: William B. Yarmuth/Chmn., CEO, Pres./$766,419.00, Mark Sutton/VP - Human Resources, Anne T. Liechty/Sr. VP - Visiting Operations/$307,395.00, David M. Pruitt/VP - In, Home Program/$128,907.00, Patrick Todd Lyles/Sr. VP - Administration/$333,412.00, Steven C. Guenthner/Sr. VP, CFO/$389,421.00, Phyllis D. Montville/Sr. VP - Visiting Operations, Vicki Suplizio/VP - Operations, Susan Long/VP - Operations, Cathy Newhouse/VP - Clinical Operations, Business Management, Mark Hunt/VP - Human Resources, John Walker/VP, Chief Accounting Officer

Directors: William B. Yarmuth/Chmn., CEO, Pres., Earl W. Reed/Dir., Donald G. McClinton/Dir., Jonathan D. Goldberg/Dir., Steven B. Bing/Dir., Henry M. Altman/Dir., Tyree G. Wilburn/Dir.

Owners: Patrick T. Lyles/1.40%, Steven B. Bing, Earl W. Reed/2.60%, Henry M. Altman, Insiders/25.10%, Anne T. Liechty/0.40%, Healthinvest Partners AB/7.60%, Donald G. McClinton/1.70%, Steven C. Guenthner/3.20%, Banque Carnegie Luxembourg S.A./8.20%, Jonathan D. Goldberg/1.50%, William B. Yarmuth/11.00%, David T. Russell/6.60%, Yarmuth Family Limited Partnership/5.80%, Tyree G. Wilburn/0.90%

Financial Data: Fiscal Year End:12/31   Latest Annual Data: 12/31/2006

Year	Sales	Net Income
2006	$91,812,000	$4,239,000
2005	$75,620,000	$7,868,000
2004	$86,827,000	$1,257,000
Curr. Assets:	$19,298,000	Curr. Liab.:	$12,135,000	P/E Ratio:	16.71
Plant, Equip.:	$1,517,000	Total Liab.:	$25,655,000	Indic. Yr. Divd.:	NA
Total Assets:	$53,395,000	Net Worth:	$27,740,000	Debt/ Equity:	0.4780

Alnylam Pharmaceuticals Inc

300 3rd St., 3rd Fl., Cambridge, MA, 02142; *PH:* 1-617-551-8200; *Fax:* 1-617-551-8101; *http://* www.alnylam.com; *Email:* investors@alnylam.com

General - Incorporation .... DE	Stock- Price on:12/24/2007 ....$15.62
Employees 122	Stock Exchange...NDQ
Auditor ....PricewaterhouseCoopers LLP	Ticker Symbol...ALNY
Stk Agt........................ EquiServe Trust Co N.A	Outstanding Shares 37,540,000
Counsel..NA	E.P.S...-$1.41
DUNS No. ....NA	Shareholders...NA

Business: The group's principle activity is to develop novel therapeutics based on ribonucleic acid interference. The group also develops an RNAi therapeutic for the treatment of hypercholesterolemia. The group provides treatments for diseases including Parkinsons disease (PD), Huntingtons disease (HD), neuropathic pain, progressive multifocal leukoencephalopathy (PML), Ebola virus infection and cystic fibrosis (CF). The group operates from United States.

Primary SIC and add'l.: NA

CIK No: 0001178670

Subsidiaries: Alnylam Europe AG, Alnylam U.S., Inc.

Officers: John M. Maraganore/CEO, Pres., Muthiah Manoharan/VP - Drug Discovery, Barry Greene/COO, David Konys/VP - Corporate Development, Operations, Patricia Allen/VP - Finance, Vincent Miles/Sr. VP - Business Development, Roland Kreutzer/MD - Alnylam Europe AG, Saraswathy Nochur/VP - Regulatory Affairs, Victor Kotelianski/VP - Research, Akshay Vaishnaw/VP - Clinical Research, Eric Raichle/VP - Human Resources, David Bartel/Scientific Advisor, Founder, Fritz Eckstein/Scientific Advisor, Founder, Edward Harlow/Scientific Advisor, Founder, Jason Rhodes/VP - Business Development *(16 Officers included in Index)*

Directors: Kevin Starr/Dir., Victor Dzau/Dir., David Bartel/Scientific Advisor, Founder, Fritz Eckstein/Scientific Advisor, Founder, Edward Harlow/Scientific Advisor, Founder, Robert Langer/Founder, Member - Scientific Advisory Board, Judy Lieberman/Founder, Member - Scientific Advisory Board, Stephen N. Oesterle/Founder, Member - Scientific Advisory Board, Markus Stoffel/Founder, Member - Scientific Advisory Board, Thomas Tuschl/Founder, Member - Scientific Advisory Board, Phillip D. Zamore/Founder, Member - Scientific Advisory Board, John Clarke/Dir., James L. Vincent/Dir., Phillip Sharp/Dir., Peter Barrett/55/Dir. *(17 Directors included in Index)*

Owners: John M. Maraganore/2.50%, Paul R. Schimmel, Phillip A. Sharp, Novartis Pharma AG/14.10%, Abingworth BioVentures/5.50%, Vincent J. Miles, Barry E. Greene, John K. Clarke, FMR Corp./14.80%, Peter Barrett, Insiders/5.40%, Patricia L. Allen, James L. Vincent

Financial Data: Fiscal Year End:12/31   Latest Annual Data: 12/31/2006

Year	Sales	Net Income
2006	$26,930,000	-$34,608,000
2005	$5,716,000	-$42,914,000
2004	$4,278,000	-$32,654,000
Curr. Assets:	$222,784,000	Curr. Liab.:	$22,925,000		
Plant, Equip.:	$12,173,000	Total Liab.:	$38,832,000	Indic. Yr. Divd.:	NA
Total Assets:	$240,006,000	Net Worth:	$201,174,000	Debt/ Equity:	0.0266

Alon USA Energy Inc

7616 LBJ Fwy., Ste. 300, Dallas, TX, 75251; *PH:* 1-972-367-3600; *Fax:* 1-972-367-3728; *http://* www.alonusa.com; *Email:* customerservice@alonusa.com

General - Incorporation .... DE
Employees .... NA
Auditor .... KPMG LLP
Stk Agt........ Mellon Investor Services LLC
Counsel .... NA
DUNS No. .... NA

Stock- Price on:12/24/2007 .... $43.764
Stock Exchange .... NYSE
Ticker Symbol .... ALJ
Outstanding Shares 46,810,000
E.P.S. $3.49
Shareholders .... NA

Business: The groups principal activities include refining and marketing petroleum products. The products of the group include gasoline, diesel fuel, jet fuel, petrochemicals, petrochemical feedstocks and asphalt. The groups operates through three segments namely refining and marketing, asphalt and retail. In the year 2006, the group acquired Paramount Petroleum Corporation and Edgington Oil Company. The group operates from the United States. Of the net sale in the year 2006, refining and marketing accounted for $2,849,137, asphalt $389,634 and retail $351,493 (thousands).

Primary SIC and add'l.: 5541 2911

CIK No: 0001325955

Subsidiaries: Alon Asphalt Bakersfield, Inc., Alon Assets, Inc., Alon Petroleum Pipe Line LP, Alon Pipeline Logistics, LLC, Alon Texas Star GP, LLC, Alon USA Asphalt, Inc, Alon USA Capital, Inc., Alon USA Delaware, LLC, Alon USA GP, LLC, Alon USA Interests, LLC, Alon USA Operating, Inc, Alon USA Operating, Inc., Alon USA Pipeline, Inc, Alon USA Refining, Inc, Alon USA, Inc. 29 Subsidiaries included in the Index

Officers: Jeff D. Morris/CEO, Pres./$1,092,250.00, Yossi Lipman/Pres., CEO - Southwest Convenience Stores, Joseph Lipman/62/Pres., CEO - SCS, Alan Moret/53/Sr. VP - Asphalt Operations, Jimmy C. Crosby/VP - Supply, Planning, Joseph A. Concienne/Sr. VP - Refining, Transportation/$2,037,463.00, Joseph Israel/VP - Mergers, Acquisitions, Business Development/$635,987.00, Claire A. Hart/Sr. VP, Shai Even/CFO, VP, Treasurer/$548,940.00, Harlin R. Dean/VP - Legal, General Counsel, Sec./$1,261,562.00

Directors: David Wiessman/Chmn., Zalman Segal/71/Dir., Itzhak Bader/62/Dir., Boaz Biran/44/Dir., Shaul Gliksberg/46/Dir., Yeshayahu Pery/74/Dir., Ron W. Haddock/67/Dir., Avraham Shochat/71/Dir., Erez Meltzer/50/Dir.

Owners: Alon Israel Oil Company, Ltd./72.28%, Harlin R. Dean, David Wiessman/4.50%, Zalman Segal, Insiders/4.63%, Ron W. Haddock, Joseph A. Concienne, Joseph Israel, Shai Even, Jeff D. Morris, Avraham Shochat

Financial Data: ***Fiscal Year End:***12/31 ***Latest Annual Data:*** 12/31/2006

Year	Sales	Net Income
2006	$3,198,084,000	$157,368,000
2005	$2,328,507,000	$103,988,000
2004	$1,707,564,000	$25,132,000

Curr. Assets:	$515,173,000	***Curr. Liab.:***	$286,394,000		
Plant, Equip.:	$775,836,000	***Total Liab.:***	$1,118,455,000	***Indic. Yr. Divd.:***	$0.160
Total Assets:	$1,408,785,000	***Net Worth:***	$290,330,000	***Debt/ Equity:***	1.6943

Alpha Innotech Corp

2401 Merced St., San Leandro, CA, 94577; ***PH:*** 1-510-483-9620; ***Fax:*** 1-510-483-3227; ***http://*** alphainnotech.com; ***Email:*** info@aicemail.com

General - Incorporation .... DE
Employees 44
Auditor .... Rowbotham And Co LLP
Stk Agt...... American Stock Transfer & Trust Co.
Counsel .... NA
DUNS No. 61-276-4480

Stock- Price on:12/24/2007 .... $1.2
Stock Exchange .... OTC
Ticker Symbol .... APNO
Outstanding Shares 10,420,000
E.P.S. .... -$0.06
Shareholders .... NA

Business: The group's principle activities include developing and commercializing technologies to simplify the analysis of dna /rna testing kits.these technologies are designed to be easy to use outside of a traditional molecular biology laboratory. These diagnostic tests are intended for use in drug discovery, detection of environmental and food contaminants, forensics and identity testing, human and animal diseases, genetic predisposition to disease, and other applications. The trademarks of the company include xtrana, xtra amp, xtra bind and scip. The group operates solely in the domestic country. The group operates from United States.

Primary SIC and add'l.: 3841 2834 2835

CIK No: 0000830736

Subsidiaries: Alpha Innotech Corporation

Officers: Ron Bissinger/Dir., CEO, CFO/$234,794.00, Diping Che/VP - Research, Development, Siavash Ghazvini/VP - Marketing, Business Development, Ernie Marquez/VP - Quality Engineering, Mark Allen/VP - Operations, Jeff Whitmore/VP - Global Sales

Directors: Ron Bissinger/Dir., CEO, CFO, Haseeb Chaudhry/Co - Founder, Vice Chmn., Michael D. Bick/Dir., James H. Chamberlain/Dir., Gus E. Davis/Dir., Joseph Keegan/Dir.

Owners: William Snider/1.04%, Haseeb Chaudhry/11.44%, Nagesh Mhatre/1.13%, Michael D. Bick, ETP/FBR Venture Capital, LLC/12.48%, Darryl Ray/2.23%, Insiders/28.89%, E-Health Holdings Limited/7.62%, Kowloon, Hong Kong/11.44%, Biotechnology Development Fund II/16.64%, Ronald H. Bissinger/1.32%

Financial Data: ***Fiscal Year End:***12/31 ***Latest Annual Data:*** 12/31/2006

Year	Sales	Net Income
2006	$13,254,000	-$998,000
2005	$12,051,000	-$2,495,000
2004	$102,000	$1,258,000

Curr. Assets:	$3,458,000	***Curr. Liab.:***	$5,284,000		
Plant, Equip.:	$1,049,000	***Total Liab.:***	$5,773,000	***Indic. Yr. Divd.:***	NA
Total Assets:	$4,598,000	***Net Worth:***	-$1,175,000	***Debt/ Equity:***	NA

Alpha Natural Resources Inc

1 Alpha Pl., Abingdon, VA, 24212; ***PH:*** 1-276-619-4410; ***http://*** www.alphanr.com; ***Email:*** ir@alphanr.com

General - Incorporation .... DE
Employees 3,546
Auditor .... KPMG LLP
Stk Agt........ Computershare Trust Co
Counsel .... NA
DUNS No. .... NA

Stock- Price on:12/24/2007 .... $19.32
Stock Exchange .... NYSE
Ticker Symbol .... ANR
Outstanding Shares 65,540,000
E.P.S. $1.32
Shareholders .... NA

Business: The groups principle activities include producing, processing and selling steam and metallurgical coal. The group operates from the United States, Canada, Italy, France, India, Brazil, and Turkey. The group's quarterly revenue for September 2007 was 507.14 millions of USD.

Primary SIC and add'l.: 1221 1222

CIK No: 0001310243

Subsidiaries: Alpha Coal Sales Co., LLC, Alpha Land and Reserves, LLC, Alpha Natural Resources Capital Corp., Alpha Natural Resources Services, LLC, Alpha Natural Resources, Inc., Alpha Natural Resources, LLC, Alpha NR Holding, Inc., Alpha Terminal Company, LLC, AMFIRE Holdings, Inc., AMFIRE Mining Company, LLC, AMFIRE WV, L.P., AMFIRE, LLC, Black Dog Coal Corp., Brooks Run Mining Company, LLC, Buchanan Energy Company, LLC 43 Subsidiaries included in the Index

Officers: Michael J. Quillen/Chmn., CEO, Pres., Kevin S. Crutchfield/Pres., Jack Porco/VP, David C. Stuebe/CFO, VP, Vaughn R. Groves/VP, General Counsel, Eddie W. Neely/VP, Controller, Randy L. McMillion/VP - Operations, Joachim V. Porco/53/VP

Directors: Michael J. Quillen/Chmn., CEO, Pres., Ted G. Wood/Dir., Mary Ellen Bowers/Dir., John S. Brinzo/Dir., Linn E. Draper/Dir., Glenn A. Eisenberg/Dir., John W. Fox/Dir.

Owners: Scott D. Kroh, Linn E. Draper, Prudential Financial, Inc./6.69%, John W. Fox, FMR Corp/14.87%, John S. Brinzo, Insiders/2.09%, Kevin S. Crutchfield, David C. Stuebe, Michael J. Quillen/1.15%, Michael D. Brown, Ted G. Wood, Vaughn R. Groves, Glenn A. Eisenberg, Snyder Capital Management, L.P./8.70%

Financial Data: ***Fiscal Year End:***12/31 ***Latest Annual Data:*** 12/31/2006

Year	Sales	Net Income
2006	$233,265,000	$128,168,000
2005	$1,554,400,000	$21,213,000
2004	- $2,017,000	$20,015,000

Curr. Assets:	$338,654,000	***Curr. Liab.:***	$222,190,000	***P/E Ratio:***	11.36
Plant, Equip.:	$637,136,000	***Total Liab.:***	$801,744,000	***Indic. Yr. Divd.:***	NA
Total Assets:	$1,145,793,000	***Net Worth:***	$344,049,000	***Debt/ Equity:***	1.1860

Alpha Pro Tech Ltd

60 Centurian Dr., Ste. 112, Markham, ON, L3R 9R2; ***PH:*** 1-905-479-0654; ***http://*** www.alphaprotech.com; ***Email:*** sales@alphaprotech.com

General - Incorporation .... DE
Employees 152
Auditor .... PricewaterhouseCoopers LLP
Stk Agt ..... American Stock Transfer & Trust Co.
Counsel........ Foreht Last Landau & Katz
DUNS No. 24-817-1977

Stock- Price on:12/24/2007 .... $2.5
Stock Exchange .... AMEX
Ticker Symbol .... APT
Outstanding Shares 25,020,000
E.P.S. $0.12
Shareholders .... NA

Business: The group's principle activities include developing, manufacturing and marketing disposable protective apparel, food industry, infection control, wound care and consumer products for cleanroom, food services, industrial, medical, dental and consumer markets. The group operates from United States.

Primary SIC and add'l.: 3841

CIK No: 0000884269

Subsidiaries: Alpha Pro Tech Engineered Products, Inc

Officers: Sheldon Hoffman/Dir., CEO, Lloyd Hoffman/CFO, Sr. VP, Michael Scheerer/Sr. VP - Sales, Marketing, Alexander W. Millar/Dir., Pres., Danny Montgomery/Sr. VP - Engineered Products, Bill Steinke/Plant Mgr., Lisa Millar/Medical, Area Mgr., Donna Millar/Contact - Investor Relations, John MacRonald/Southeast US Area Mgr., Judy Hill/Pet, Area Mgr., Jeff Bordin/Northwest US Area Mgr., Mark Freeman/Northcentral US Area Mgr., Richard Pepi/Northeast US Area Mgr., Rafael Figueroa/Plant Mgr. - Apparel, Shields, Gary Huckabaa/Plant Mgr. - Mask *(17 Officers included in Index)*

Directors: Sheldon Hoffman/Dir., CEO, Robert H. Isaly/Dir., John Ritota/Dir., Russell Manock/Dir., Donald E. Bennett/Dir., Alexander W. Millar/Dir., Pres., David B. Anderson/Dir.

Owners: David B. Anderson, Lloyd Hoffman/1.10%, Al Millar/6.80%, John Ritota, Michael Scheerer/1.80%, Danny Montgomery, Russell Manock, Robert H. Isaly/2.20%, William R. Lykken/6.00%, Insiders/19.70%, Sheldon Hoffman/5.30%

Financial Data: ***Fiscal Year End:***12/31 ***Latest Annual Data:*** 12/31/2006

Year	Sales	Net Income
2006	$37,338,000	$3,739,000
2005	$31,095,000	$2,450,000
2004	$24,841,000	$1,847,000

Curr. Assets:	$22,297,000	***Curr. Liab.:***	$2,679,000	***P/E Ratio:***	20.83
Plant, Equip.:	$3,355,000	***Total Liab.:***	$3,372,000	***Indic. Yr. Divd.:***	NA
Total Assets:	$26,852,000	***Net Worth:***	$23,480,000	***Debt/ Equity:***	NA

Alpharma Inc

440 Rte., 22 E, Bridgewater, NJ, 08807; ***PH:*** 1-908-566-3800; ***Fax:*** 1-908-566-4137; ***http://*** www.alpharma.com; ***Email:*** investorrelations@alpharma.com

General - Incorporation .... DE
Employees 1,400
Auditor .... PricewaterhouseCoopers LLP
Stk Agt .... Computershare Investor Services LLC
Counsel .... NA
DUNS No. 07-095-4094

Stock- Price on:12/24/2007 .... $26.02
Stock Exchange .... NYSE
Ticker Symbol .... ALO
Outstanding Shares 43,360,000
E.P.S. $1.19
Shareholders .... NA

Business: The group's principal activities are to develop, manufacture and market human pharmaceutical and animal health products. The group operates in two business segments namely human pharmaceuticals and animal pharmaceuticals. The human pharmaceutical segment operates through international pharmaceutical division, u s pharmaceuticals division and fine chemicals division. The animal pharmaceuticals segment operates through animal health division and aquatic animal health division. The group is a manufacturer of generic liquid and topical pharmaceutical, specialty antibiotics, animal health feed additives for poultry and livestock, and vaccines for farmed fish. The group manufactures and markets approximately 800 pharmaceutical products for human use and 100 animal health products. On 30-Sep-2003, the group discontinued its French subsidiary operations.

Primary SIC and add'l.: 2834 9999

CIK No: 0000730469

Subsidiaries: Allabinc de Mexico, S.A. de C.V., Alpharma (Belgium) B.V.B.A., Alpharma (Luxembourg) Sarl, Alpharma Animal Health Pty Ltd., Alpharma ApS, Alpharma AS, Alpharma Bermuda G.P., Alpharma do Brazil Ltda, Alpharma Fine Chemicals, Kft., Alpharma International AS, Alpharma Operating Corporation, Alpharma SARL, Alpharma U.S. Inc., Empresa Laboratories de Mexico S.A. de C.V., ParMed Pharmaceuticals, Inc. 16 Subsidiaries included in the Index

Officers: Dean J. Mitchell/Dir., CEO, Pres./$1,412,244.00, Jeffrey S. Campbell/CFO/$921,962.00, Thomas J. Spellman/Exec. VP - CLO, Sec., Stefan Aigner/Exec. VP - Corporate Development, Peter Watts/Exec. VP - Human Resources, Communications, Carl-Ake Carlsson/Pres. - API Active Pharmaceutical Ingredients, Ronald N. Warner/Pres. - Pharmaceuticals/$1,690,499.00, Carol A. Wrenn/Pres. - Animal Health

Directors: Dean J. Mitchell/Dir., CEO, Pres., Peter G. Tombros/Chmn., Ramon M. Perez/Dir., Peter W. Ladell/Dir., David C. U'Prichard/Dir., Finn-Berg Jacobsen/Dir.

Owners: Glen E. Hess, Ingrid Wiik, Ronald N. Warner, Matthew T. Farrell, George Rose, Insiders/1.40%, LSV Asset Management/6.55%, Robert F. Wrobel, Jeffrey S. Campbell, Barclays Global Investors NA./6.40%, Dean Mitchell, Peter G. Tombros, Dimensional Fund Advisors LP/7.85%

Financial Data: Fiscal Year End:12/31   Latest Annual Data: 06/30/2007

Year	Sales	Net Income
2007	NA	NA
2006	NA	NA
2005	$553,617,000	$133,769,000

Curr. Assets:	$353,541,000	Curr. Liab.:	$155,573,000	P/E Ratio:	21.87
Plant, Equip.:	$233,447,000	Total Liab.:	$203,240,000	Indic. Yr. Divd.:	$0.180
Total Assets:	$927,239,000	Net Worth:	$723,999,000	Debt/ Equity:	NA

AlphaRx Inc

168 Konrad Crescent, Ste. 200, Markham, ON, L3R 9T9; *PH:* 1-905-479-3245; *http://* www.alpharx.com; *Email:* info@alpharx.com

General - Incorporation	DE	Stock - Price on:12/24/2007	$0.055
Employees	NA	Stock Exchange	OTC
Auditor	Schwartz Levitsky Feldman LLP	Ticker Symbol	ALRX
Stk Agt	Signature Stock Transfer, Inc.	Outstanding Shares	NA
Counsel	NA	E.P.S.	NA
DUNS No.	NA	Shareholders	NA

Business: The group's principle activity is to develop novel formulations of existing drugs that are insoluble or poorly soluble in water, utilizing its proprietary bioadhesive colloidaldispersion (bcd) drug delivery systems. The group operates from United States.

Primary SIC and add'l.: 2834

CIK No: 0001114936

Subsidiaries: AlphaRx Canada Limited, AlphaRx International Holdings Limited, British Virgin Island company

Officers: Michael M. Lee/45/Founder, Chmn., CEO, Marcel Urbanc/CFO, Joseph Schwarz/Chief Scientist, Michael Weisspapir/Chief Medical Scientist, Douglas Dicconson/Dir. - Marketing, Business Development

Directors: Michael M. Lee/45/Founder, Chmn., CEO, Peter Carlen/Member - Scientific Advisory Board, David Milroy/56/Dir., Ford Moore/56/Dir., Michael S. Berlin/Member - Scientific Advisory Board

Owners: Marcel Urbanc/0.14%, Michael Weisspapir/0.53%, Michael Lee/13.14%, Ford Moore/3.94%, Joseph Schwarz/0.74%, David Milroy/2.04%, Insiders/20.55%, Sandro Persia/0.02%

Financial Data: Fiscal Year End:09/30   Latest Annual Data: 9/30/2006

Year	Sales	Net Income
2006	$1,025,000	-$2,522,000
2005	$69,000	-$4,852,000
2004	$384,000	-$2,934,000

Curr. Assets:	$1,189,000	Curr. Liab.:	$1,365,000		
Plant, Equip.:	$283,000	Total Liab.:	$1,526,000	Indic. Yr. Divd.:	NA
Total Assets:	$1,472,000	Net Worth:	-$55,000	Debt/ Equity:	NA

Alphatec Holdings Inc

2051 Palomar Airport Rd., Ste. 100, Carlsbad, CA, 92011; *PH:* 1-760-431-9286; *Fax:* 1-760-431-9823; *http://* www.alphatecspine.com

General - Incorporation	DE	Stock - Price on:12/24/2007	$4
Employees	295	Stock Exchange	NDQ
Auditor	Ernst & Young, LLP	Ticker Symbol	ATEC
Stk Agt	Mellon Investor Services LLC	Outstanding Shares	35,040,000
Counsel	NA	E.P.S.	-$1.07
DUNS No.	NA	Shareholders	NA

Business: The groups principle activities include designing, developing, manufacturing and marketing products for spine fusion surgery. The products of the group include lumbar fusion systems, zodiac lumbar fixation, mirage spinal fixation, roc lumbar plating and zodiac deformity. The group products sold under the trade names Alphatec, Cortek, C, Corlok, Osteocor, Biocarpentry, Dovetome, Deltaloc, Duet, Connect and Venta. In March 2005, the group acquired Alphatec Manufacturing, Inc. The group operates from the United States and Asia.

Primary SIC and add'l.: 3841 3841

CIK No: 0001350653

Subsidiaries: Alphatec Pacific, Inc., Alphatec Spine, Inc

Officers: Dirk Kuyper/CEO, Pres., Michael M. Soloway/VP - Medical Education, Alphatec Spine, Gordon C. Bigler/VP - Finance, Investor Relations Officer - Corp Communications, Alphatec Spine, Glen Paul Freiberg/VP - Regulatory Affairs, Quality Assurance, Alphatec Spine, Kathryn Liljestrand/VP - Marketing, Alphatec Spine, Kermit P. Stott/VP - Operations, Alphatec Spine, Ross M. Simmonds/52/COO, Sr. VP, Steven M. Yasbek/CFO, VP, Treasurer/$212,322.00, Steven M. Reinecke/CTO, VP/$446,185.00, Herbert J. Bellucci/58/VP - Manufacturing, International, Charles O. Boyles/VP - Finance, Corporate Controller - Alphatec Spine, Ebun S. Garner/General Counsel, VP - Compliance, Sec., Susan L. Johnson/VP - Human Resources, Alphatec Spine, Stephen A. Lubischer/VP - Sales/$413,924.00

Directors: Mortimer Berkowitz/Chmn., James R. Glynn/Dir., Richard Ravitch/Dir., John H. Foster/Dir., Ian R. Molson/Dir., Stephen E. O'Neil/Dir., Stephen J. Hochschuler/Dir.

Owners: Ian R. Molson, John H. Foster, Insiders, HealthpointCapital Partners, LP, Steven Reinecke, Mortimer Berkowitz, Shunshiro Yoshimi, Ebun S. Garner, Federal Insurance Company, Stephen Lubischer, Steven M. Yasbek, Herbert J. Bellucci, Stephen H. Hochschuler

Financial Data: Fiscal Year End:12/31   Latest Annual Data: 12/31/2006

Year	Sales	Net Income
2006	$74,005,000	-$25,816,000

Curr. Assets:	$45,498,000	Curr. Liab.:	$21,390,000	P/E Ratio:	40.00
Plant, Equip.:	$12,583,000	Total Liab.:	$30,578,000	Indic. Yr. Divd.:	NA
Total Assets:	$129,277,000	Net Worth:	$74,996,000	Debt/ Equity:	NA

AlphaTrade.com

930 W 1st St., Ste. 116C, Vancouver, BC, V7P 3N4; *PH:* 1-604-986-9866; *Fax:* 1-604-987-9865; *http://* www.alphatrade.com; *Email:* sales@alphatrade.com

General - Incorporation	NV	Stock - Price on:12/24/2007	$0.22
Employees	NA	Stock Exchange	OTC
Auditor	Chisholm, Bierwolf & Nilson, LLC	Ticker Symbol	APTD
Stk Agt	Signature Stock Transfer, Inc.	Outstanding Shares	NA
Counsel	NA	E.P.S.	NA
DUNS No.	NA	Shareholders	NA

Business: The group's principal activity is to provide stock market data for investors, day traders, professionals and other financial parties via a product called e-gate. They also provides a cost-effective solution for streaming, multi-lingual market data to companies and individuals, interested in real time stock market information. These services are provided through five principal market segments: banking, financial, public and investor relations, Web sites, and related companies. The group's customers include brokerage firms, financial oriented websites, other websites that are seeking new products to offer their visitors, day traders, individual investors, public and investor relations companies.

Primary SIC and add'l.: 7375

CIK No: 0001076462

Officers: Penny Perfect/Chmn., CEO/$1,963,977.00, Gordon Muir/Founder, CCO/$1,963,977.00, Kerry Johnston/VP, Corporate Growth Dir., Mike Jackson/Mgr. - Business Development, Mark Sommer/Sales, Marketing, Kaelan Phipps/Sales, Marketing, Kevan King/Sales, Marketing, Rob Harrison/Fulfillment Mgr., Nolan Giesbrecht/Sr. System Support, Teunis Peters/Network Administrator, Dmitry Feld/Chief Software Architect, Chris Jia/Accountant, Oxana Diatchenko/Administrative Assist., Ambrose Oba-Underwood/Software Developer, Anton Parygin/Software Developer *(20 Officers included in Index)*

Directors: Penny Perfect/Chmn., CEO, Gordon Muir/Founder, CCO, Kerry Johnston/VP, Corporate Growth Dir.

Owners: Insiders/72.77%, Gordon Muir/36.12%, Penny Perfect/36.65%

Financial Data: Fiscal Year End:12/31   Latest Annual Data: 12/31/2006

Year	Sales	Net Income
2006	$4,396,000	-$4,737,000
2005	$3,020,000	-$527,000
2004	$1,919,000	-$2,061,000

Curr. Assets:	$219,000	Curr. Liab.:	$1,503,000		
Plant, Equip.:	$38,000	Total Liab.:	$1,503,000	Indic. Yr. Divd.:	NA
Total Assets:	$541,000	Net Worth:	-$962,000	Debt/ Equity:	NA

Alpine Air Express Inc

1177 Alpine Air Way, Provo, UT, 84601; *PH:* 1-801-373-1508; *Fax:* 1-801-377-3781; *http://* www.alpine-air.com; *Email:* info@alpine-air.com

General - Incorporation	DE	Stock - Price on:12/24/2007	$0.41
Employees	56	Stock Exchange	OTC
Auditor	Pritchett Siler & Hardy P.C	Ticker Symbol	APNX
Stk Agt	Colonial Stock Transfer Co Inc	Outstanding Shares	36,270,000
Counsel	Max A. Hansen & Associates PC	E.P.S.	$0.02
DUNS No.	NA	Shareholders	NA

Business: The group's principal activity is to transport mail packages and other time-sensitive cargo between 16 cities in the western portion of the United States. The cargo operations of the group are carried out through its wholly subsidiary alpine aviation, inc. The group's focus is on hauling mail for the United States postal service because of their favorable contracts, routes and payment practices. The group currently has 12 routes covering 16 western cities in 4 states. The group operates in the United States and Chile.

Primary SIC and add'l.: 4513 4581

CIK No: 0001092807

Subsidiaries: Alpine Air Chile S.A., Alpine Aviation, Inc.

Officers: Eugene R. Mallette/Chmn., CEO, Bill Distefano/Pres., Dir. - Alpine Air Chile SA, GM - Alpine Aviation Inc, Max Hansen/Dir. - General Counsel, Sec., Treasurer, Linda Anderson/Dir. - Operations, Don Squire/CFO

Directors: Eugene R. Mallette/Chmn., CEO, Ken Holliday/Dir., Paul Moxley/Dir., Max Hansen/Dir. - General Counsel, Sec., Treasurer, Joe Etchart/Dir., Michael Brown/66/Dir., Ronald L. Pattison/50/Dir.

Owners: SCS Inc./6.70%, Eugene R. Mallette/76.40%, Max Hansen, Ronald Pattison, Insiders/76.80%, Joseph O. Etchart, Don T. Squire

Financial Data: Fiscal Year End:06/30   Latest Annual Data: 10/31/2006

Year	Sales	Net Income
2006	$20,157,000	$401,000
2005	$22,630,000	-$1,438,000
2004	$14,958,000	-$1,380,000

Curr. Assets:	$4,497,000	Curr. Liab.:	$3,789,000	P/E Ratio:	20.50
Plant, Equip.:	$16,480,000	Total Liab.:	$11,300,000	Indic. Yr. Divd.:	NA
Total Assets:	$22,837,000	Net Worth:	$3,959,000	Debt/ Equity:	NA

Alpine Group Inc

660 Pennsylvania, SE, Ste. 201, Washington, DC, 20003; *PH:* 1-202-547-1831; *http://* www.alpinegroup.com

General - Incorporation	DE	Stock - Price on:12/24/2007	NA
Employees	410	Stock Exchange	OTC
Auditor	Deloitte & Touche LLP	Ticker Symbol	APNI
Stk Agt	American Stock Transfer & Trust Co.	Outstanding Shares	NA
Counsel	NA	E.P.S.	$0.88
DUNS No.	00-194-5435	Shareholders	NA

Business: The group's principal activity is to manufacture and market electric wire and cable products. The group operates through four segments: communications, OEM, electrical and dne. Communications segment includes outside plant wire and cable for voice and data transmission in telecommunications networks, copper and fiber optic datacom or premise wire and cable and Internet

connectivity. Oem segment includes magnet wire and related products. Electrical segment includes building and industrial wire and cable. Dne segment manufactures multiplexers and other communications and electronic products. The group manufactures and markets products for the communications, original equipment manufacturer and electrical markets.

Primary SIC and add'l.: 3357 3351 6719

CIK No: 0000004164

Subsidiaries: Alpine Holdco Inc., Essex Electric Inc., Mastin Limited, Sartin Investments Limited, Superior Cable Holdings (1997) Ltd., Texas SUT Inc.

Officers: Stephen Waguespack/Government Relations Consultant, James W. Hawkins/Government Relations Consultant, Elizabeth Hill/Government Relations Consultant, Les Spivey/Government Relations Consultant, Charles A. Barnett/VP, Michael K. Henry/Government Relations Consultant, Courtney Johnson/Government Relations Consultant, Bob Brooks/Government Relations Consultant, Ansley Davis/Government Relations Consultant, Alicia Fitzpatrick/Government Relations Consultant

Directors: James D. Massie/Partner, Greg Means/Partner, Rhod Shaw/Partner, Richard C. White/Partner

Financial Data: Fiscal Year End:12/31 **Latest Annual Data:** 12/31/2005

Year	Sales	Net Income
2005	$447,815,000	$4,573,000
2004	$315,894,000	$13,440,000
2003	$330,484,000	$834,776,000

Curr. Assets:	$119,634,000	Curr. Liab.:	$78,184,000		
Plant, Equip.:	$17,728,000	Total Liab.:	$100,481,000	Indic. Yr. Divd.:	NA
Total Assets:	$140,527,000	Net Worth:	$29,255,000	Debt/ Equity:	NA

ALR Technologies Inc

114M Reynolda Village, Winston-Salem, NC, 27106; **PH:** 1-336-722-2254; **Fax:** 1-336-722-2775; **http://** www.alrt.com; **Email:** info@alrt.com

General - Incorporation	NV	**Stock**- Price on:12/24/2007	$0.13
Employees	9	Stock Exchange	OTC
Auditor	Telford Sadovnick, PLLC	Ticker Symbol	ALRT
Stk Agt.	Pacific Stock Transfer Company	Outstanding Shares	76,080,000
Counsel	NA	E.P.S.	-$0.03
DUNS No.	NA	Shareholders	NA

Business: The groups principle activity is to provide new solutions for Disease and Health Management with Compliance and Intervention. The group products include ALRT Med Reminder, ALRT Once- A-Day, ALRT Weekly, ALRT Contact Lens Replacement, ALRT PC100, and ALRT PC200. The group operates from the United States.

Primary SIC and add'l.: 3873 3829 3842 3845

CIK No: 0001087022

Subsidiaries: Timely Devices, Inc.

Officers: Sidney S. Chan/Chmn., CEO, Stan Cruitt/Pres., Jaroslav V. Tichy/VP - Technology

Directors: Sidney S. Chan/Chmn., CEO, Michael Baumgardner/Member - Advisory Board, Arnold Da Silva/Member - Advisory Board, William Lorentz/Member - Advisory Board, Betsy Pearce/Member - Advisory Board, Ronald H. Small/Member - Advisory Board

Owners: Jaroslav Tichy, Stanley Cruitt/17.61%, Insiders/54.42%, Sidney Chan/36.15%

Financial Data: Fiscal Year End:12/31 **Latest Annual Data:** 12/31/2006

Year	Sales	Net Income
2006	$243,000	-$2,611,000
2005	$319,000	-$1,793,000
2004	$364,000	-$4,339,000

Curr. Assets:	$89,000	Curr. Liab.:	$9,347,000		
Plant, Equip.:	$6,000	Total Liab.:	$9,347,000	Indic. Yr. Divd.:	NA
Total Assets:	$95,000	Net Worth:	-$9,252,000	Debt/ Equity:	NA

Altair Nanotechnologies Inc

204 Edison Way, Reno, NV, 89502; **PH:** 1-775-856-2500; **Fax:** 1-775-856-1619; **http://** www.altairinc.com

General - Incorporation	Canada	**Stock** - Price on:12/24/2007	$3.311
Employees	80	Stock Exchange	NDQ
Auditor	Perry-Smith LLP	Ticker Symbol	ALTI
Stk Agt.	Equity Transfer Services Inc	Outstanding Shares	70,020,000
Counsel	Goodman & Carr LLP	E.P.S.	-$0.32
DUNS No.	96-898-8287	Shareholders	NA

Business: The group's principal activities are to develop, produce and market metal oxide nanoparticles. The other activities include exploring and developing mineral properties in the United States. It also develops mineral processing equipment for use in the recovery of fine and heavy mineral particles. The products include titanium dioxide, lithium titanate spinel and stabilized zirconia nanomaterials. The nanomaterials and titanium dioxide pigment technology enables the production of customized products for catalyst support structures and porous titanium oxide electrode structures for titanium metal production. The group is in the development stage.

Primary SIC and add'l.: 1099 3532 1041

CIK No: 0001016546

Subsidiaries: Altair US Holdings, Inc

Officers: Alan J. Gotcher/57/Dir., CEO, Pres./$802,531.00, Bruce Sabacky/CTO, VP/$254,584.00, Edward Dickinson/CFO/$294,379.00, Doug Ellsworth/VP - Performance Materials Division/$185,763.00, Robert C. Pedraza/VP - Strategy, Business Development, Stephen A. Balogh/VP - Human Resources/$157,272.00, Evan V. House/VP - Research - Engineering, Design, Toni Bondi/Dir. - Administration, Accounting, Bob Goebel/VP - Sales, Marketing, Jeffrey A. McKinney/VP, Chief Patent Counsel, Fayth Ross/Marketing Mgr.

Directors: Alan J. Gotcher/57/Dir., CEO, Pres., Jon N. Bengtson/62/Dir., George E. Hartman/58/Dir., Christopher E. Jones/61/Dir., Michel Bazinet/51/Dir., Pierre Lortie/61/Dir., Robert F. Hemphill/65/Dir.

Owners: Stephen Balogh, Pierre Lortie, Alan J. Gotcher/1.00%, Insiders/4.10%, George Hartman, Christopher Jones, Robert F. Hemphill/1.30%, James I. Golla, Jon N. Bengtson, Edward H. Dickinson, Bruce J. Sabacky, Douglas K. Ellsworth, Michel Bazinet

Financial Data: Fiscal Year End:12/31 **Latest Annual Data:** 12/31/2006

Year	Sales	Net Income
2006	$4,324,000	-$17,200,000
2005	$2,807,000	-$9,937,000
2004	$1,152,000	-$7,002,000

Curr. Assets:	$29,428,000	Curr. Liab.:	$3,500,000		
Plant, Equip.:	$11,229,000	Total Liab.:	$5,300,000	Indic. Yr. Divd.:	NA
Total Assets:	$43,121,000	Net Worth:	$37,821,000	Debt/ Equity:	0.0325

Altana AG

712 5th Ave., 39th Fl., New York, NY, 10022; **PH:** 1-212-974-9800; **Fax:** 1-212-974-6190; **http://** www.altana.de; **Email:** pr@altana.de

General - Incorporation	Germany	**Stock**- Price on:12/24/2007	$24.5
Employees	NA	Stock Exchange	OTC
Auditor	PricewaterhouseCoopers LLP	Ticker Symbol	AANAF
Stk Agt	Bank of New York	Outstanding Shares	NA
Counsel	NA	E.P.S.	NA
DUNS No.	NA	Shareholders	NA

Business: The group's principal activities are to research, manufacture and market innovative prescription drugs and chemical products. The group operates under two operating segments: pharmaceuticals and chemicals. Pharmaceuticals segment develops, manufactures and markets pharmaceutical products. Pharmaceuticals product range comprises therapeutics, which includes prescription drugs for a variety of indications, diagnostics, which includes laboratory diagnostic devices and reagents as well as imaging. The chemicals segment offers a wide range of specialty chemicals, including additives and instruments, coatings and sealant and electrical insulation. The group has operations in Europe, North America, Latin America and Asia.

Primary SIC and add'l.: 3841 2835 5122 5047 2819 2816 2834

CIK No: 0001182802

Subsidiaries: ALTANA Chemie AG, ALTANA Inc., ALTANA Madaus (Pty.), ALTANA Pharma AG, ALTANA Pharma B.V., ALTANA Pharma Deutschland GmbH, ALTANA Pharma GmbH, ALTANA Pharma Inc., ALTANA Pharma Ltd., ALTANA Pharma Ltda., ALTANA Pharma N.V. /S.A., ALTANA Pharma Oranienburg GmbH, ALTANA Pharma S.A., ALTANA Pharma S.A. de C.V., ALTANA Pharma S.A.S. 33 Subsidiaries included in the Index

Officers: Nikolaus Schweickart/CEO, Pres., Matthias L. Wolfgruber/54/Pres., CEO - Altana AG, Wesel, Christoph Schlunken/46/Pres. - Division Effect Pigments, Chmn. - Management Board, Wolfgang Schutt/44/Pres. - Division Electrical Insulation, Martin Babilas/37/Member - Management Board, CFO, Roland Peter/51/Pres. - Division Additives, Instruments, Guido Forstbach/49/Pres. - Division Coatings, Sealants

Directors: Fritz Frohlich/Chmn. - Supervisory Board, Ulrich Gajewiak/Dep. Chmn. - Supervisory Board, Susanne Klatten/Dep. Chmn. - Supervisory Board, Klaus-Jurgen Schmieder/Member - Supervisory Board, Thomas J. Martin/Member - Supervisory Board, Ralf Giesen/Member - Supervisory Board, Martin Babilas/37/Member - Management Board, CFO, Roland Peter/51/Pres. - Division Additives, Instruments, Gotz Kruger/Member - Supervisory Board, Armin Glashauser/Member - Supervisory Board, Olaf Jung/Member - Supervisory Board, Helmut Eschwey/Member - Supervisory Board, Werner Spinner/Member - Supervisory Board, Carl Voigt/Member - Supervisory Board

Altera Corp

101 Innovation Dr., San Jose, CA, 95134; **PH:** 1-408-544-7000; **Fax:** 1-408-544-6408; **http://** www.altera.com

General - Incorporation	DE	**Stock**- Price on:12/24/2007	$22.84
Employees	2,654	Stock Exchange	NDQ
Auditor	PricewaterhouseCoopers LLP	Ticker Symbol	ALTR
Stk Agt	Computershare Trust Co	Outstanding Shares	355,060,000
Counsel	NA	E.P.S.	$0.94
DUNS No.	11-817-1834	Shareholders	NA

Business: The group's principle activities include designing, manufacturing and marketing high-performance, high-density programmable logic devices, intellectual property cores and associated development tools. The programmable logic devices are semiconductor integrated circuits operating on personal computers and engineering workstations that can be programmed by the customers. Intellectual property cores are proprietary pre-verified hardware description languages or design files used in system level logic functions. These products serve various markets such as telecommunication, data communication, electronic data processing, computer peripheral, and industrial applications. The group operates from United States.

Primary SIC and add'l.: 3674 7371

CIK No: 0000768251

Subsidiaries: Altera International Limited, Altera International, Inc

Officers: John P. Daane/Chmn., CEO, Pres./$3,887,307.00, Lance M. Lissner/Sr. VP - Business Development, George A. Papa/Sr. VP - Worldwide Sales/$1,529,519.00, Scott Wylie/VP - Investor Relations, Jordan S. Plofsky/Sr. VP - Marketing/$1,500,821.00, Denis M. Berlan/COO, Exec. VP/$2,020,231.00, Katherine E. Schuelke/VP, General Counsel, Sec., James W. Callas/Principal Financial, Accounting Officer, Acting CFO/$660,236.00, Misha Burich/Sr. VP - Research, Development, William Y. Hata/VP - Worldwide Operations, Engineering, Timothy R. Morse/Sr. VP, CFO

Directors: John P. Daane/Chmn., CEO, Pres., Robert W. Reed/Vice Chmn., Robert J. Finocchio/Dir., Kevin McGarity/Dir., Susan Wang/Dir., John Shoemaker/Dir., Greg Myers/Dir.

Owners: Insiders/3.15%, Denis M. Berlan, Kevin McGarity, Robert J. Finocchio, John P. Daane, Charles M. Clough, Capital Research and Management Company/13.09%, Paul Newhagen, Nathan M. Sarkisian, Robert W. Reed, Jordan S. Plofsky, Susan Wang, James W. Callas, Capital Group International, Inc./10.68%, William E. Terry *(17 Owners included in Index)*

Financial Data: Fiscal Year End:12/30 **Latest Annual Data:** 12/29/2006

Year	Sales	Net Income
2006	$1,285,535,000	$323,236,000
2005	$1,123,739,000	$278,829,000
2004	$1,016,364,000	$275,111,000

Curr. Assets:	$1,537,097,000	Curr. Liab.:	$468,042,000	P/E Ratio:	24.30
Plant, Equip.:	$159,587,000	Total Liab.:	$468,042,000	Indic. Yr. Divd.:	$0.080
Total Assets:	$1,746,666,000	Net Worth:	$1,278,624,000	Debt/ Equity:	0.0852

Alternate Energy Corp

105-3325 N Service Rd., Burlington, ON, L7N 3G2; *PH:* 1-905-332-3110; *Fax:* 1-905-332-2068;
http:// www.cleanwatts.com; *Email:* info@cleanwatts.com

General - Incorporation	NV	*Stock*- Price on:12/24/2007	$0.06
Employees	NA	Stock Exchange	OTC
Auditor	Danziger & Hochman	Ticker Symbol	ARGY
Stk Agt	Computershare Trust Co	Outstanding Shares	NA
Counsel	NA	E.P.S.	NA
DUNS No.	NA	Shareholders	NA

Business: The groups principal activity is to produce small-scale electricity, bulk production of hydrogen and a saleable by-product. The group product is Energys model E8 2.4 kW. The group operates from Canada and the United State.

Primary SIC and add'l.: 3692 3674 3629 3691 4911

CIK No: 0001075773

Subsidiaries: 2040412 Ontario Inc

Officers: Blaine Froats/Chmn., CEO, Sean C. Froats/Dir., VP - Operations, Sec., Jack Wasserman/Dir., Treasurer, Michael Mulshine/Investor Relations Officer, Amy Trombly/Contact - Legal, David Danziger/Corporate Accountant, Mike Cunniff/Investor Relation - Osprey Partner, Mike Mulshine/Investor Relation - Osprey Partner

Directors: Blaine Froats/Chmn., CEO, Sean C. Froats/Dir., VP - Operations, Sec., Jack Wasserman/Dir., Treasurer

Owners: Sean Froats/5.79%, Jason Froats/5.00%, Insiders/27.75%, Jack Wasserman, Blaine Froats/22.64%

*Financial Data: Fiscal Year End:*12/31 *Latest Annual Data:* 12/31/2006

Year	Sales	Net Income
2006	NA	-$2,671,000
2005	NA	-$4,017,000
2004	NA	-$5,348,000

Curr. Assets:	$275,000	*Curr. Liab.:*	$743,000	*P/E Ratio:*	111.14
Plant, Equip.:	$210,000	*Total Liab.:*	$743,000	*Indic. Yr. Divd.:*	NA
Total Assets:	$485,000	*Net Worth:*	-$258,000	*Debt/ Equity:*	NA

Alternative Energy Sources Inc

310 W 20th St., 2nd Fl., Kansas City, MO, 64108; *PH:* 1-816-842-3835; *Fax:* 1-816-842-3836;
http:// www.aensi.com

General - Incorporation	DE	*Stock*- Price on:12/24/2007	$0.93
Employees	7	Stock Exchange	OTC
Auditor	Bagell, Josephs, Levine & Co., L.Lc.	Ticker Symbol	AENS
Stk Agt	NA	Outstanding Shares	40,500,000
Counsel	NA	E.P.S.	-$0.14
DUNS No.	NA	Shareholders	NA

Business: The groups principal activities include constructing, owning and operating fuel grade ethanol plants in the Midwest cornbelt. The group products include Ethanol and Dried Distillers Grains. The group operates from the United States.

Primary SIC and add'l.: 2860

CIK No: 0001175867

Subsidiaries: Beemer Energy, Inc

Officers: Mark A. Beemer/Chmn., CEO, Lee L. Blank/Dir., COO, Pres., John J. Holland/CFO, Exec. VP/$116,707.00, John A. Ward/Exec. VP, Dir. - Operations, Kathy Newton/Executive Assist., J. B. Voss/VP - Business Developement, Verlin Friendly/Dir. - Engineering, Grain, Logistics

Directors: Mark A. Beemer/Chmn., CEO, Lee L. Blank/Dir., COO, Pres., Mike Espy/Dir., John D. McNamara/Dir., Gordon W. Snyder/Dir., James L. Spigarelli/Dir., Douglas D. Wilner/Dir.

Owners: Insiders/33.13%, Mark A. Beemer/19.74%, Gordon W. Snyder, John A. Ward, Lee L. Blank/12.78%

*Financial Data: Fiscal Year End:*12/31 *Latest Annual Data:* 12/31/2006

Year	Sales	Net Income
2006	NA	-$2,349,000
2005	NA	-$218,000
2004	NA	-$14,000

Curr. Assets:	$8,445,000	*Curr. Liab.:*	$203,000		
Plant, Equip.:	$34,000	*Total Liab.:*	$203,000	*Indic. Yr. Divd.:*	NA
Total Assets:	$9,072,000	*Net Worth:*	$8,868,000	*Debt/ Equity:*	NA

Alternet Systems Inc

815 W Hastings St., Ste. 610, Vancouver, BC, V6C 1B4; *PH:* 1-604-608-2540;
Fax: 1-604-608-8775; *http://* www.alternetsystems.com; *Email:* info@alternetsystems.com

General - Incorporation	NV	*Stock*- Price on:12/24/2007	$0.065
Employees	NA	Stock Exchange	OTC
Auditor	Dale Matheson Carr-Hilton Labonte	Ticker Symbol	ASYI
Stk Agt	Transfer Online, Inc.	Outstanding Shares	NA
Counsel	NA	E.P.S.	NA
DUNS No.	NA	Shareholders	NA

Business: The group's principal activities are to distribute, market and sell Internet access systems and software. The group's products are marketed under the names 'schoolweb systems', 'interlink', 'community link' and 'healthweb'. The schoolweb software is an Internet access system developed specifically for schools. The schoolweb system delivers up to ten times more user capacity than a telecom line system of equivalent cost and provides students with e-mail and Website hosting capabilities.

Primary SIC and add'l.: 7373 7372 7375

CIK No: 0001126003

Subsidiaries: AI Systems Group, Inc.

Officers: Patrick Fitzsimmons/Dir., CEO, Pres., Robin Bjorklund/43/Dir., Sec., Treasurer, Griffin Jones/Dir., CFO, Sec., Treasurer, Ken Kiewitz/Mgr. - Information Technology Services

Directors: Patrick Fitzsimmons/Dir., CEO, Pres., Michael Dearden/Dir., Griffin Jones/Dir., CFO, Sec., Treasurer, Marc Boileau/Member - Advisory Board, Trevor Schofield/Member - Advisory Board, Robin Bjorklund/43/Dir., Sec., Treasurer, Henryk Dabrowski/Dir.

Owners: Patrick Fitzsimmons/4.00%, Robin Bjorklund/2.00%, Insiders/5.40%

*Financial Data: Fiscal Year End:*12/31 *Latest Annual Data:* 03/31/2007

Year	Sales	Net Income
2007	NA	NA
2006	$4,000	-$1,001,000
2005	$15,000	-$264,000

Curr. Assets:	$4,000	*Curr. Liab.:*	$226,000		
Plant, Equip.:	$11,000	*Total Liab.:*	$226,000	*Indic. Yr. Divd.:*	NA
Total Assets:	$15,000	*Net Worth:*	-$211,000	*Debt/ Equity:*	NA

Altex Industries Inc

6831 - 42nd St., Edmonton, AB, T6B 2X1; *PH:* 1-780-468-6862; *http://* www.altexindustriesinc.com;
Email: info@altexindustriesinc.com

General - Incorporation	DE	*Stock*- Price on:12/24/2007	$0.24
Employees	1	Stock Exchange	OTC
Auditor	Comiskey & Co. P.C	Ticker Symbol	ALTX
Stk Agt	American Stock Transfer & Trust Co.	Outstanding Shares	14,350,000
Counsel	NA	E.P.S.	-$0.014
DUNS No.	14-857-1177	Shareholders	NA

Business: The group's principal activity is that of a holding company. The group currently owns interests, including working interests, in productive onshore oil and gas properties. In addition, the group also buys and sells producing oil and gas properties and to a lesser extent, participates in the drilling of exploratory and development wells and in recompletions of existing wells.

Primary SIC and add'l.: 1311 6719

CIK No: 0000775057

Officers: Steven H. Cardin/Dir., Principal Executive Officer, Principal Financial Officer, Principal Accounting Officer

Directors: Steven H. Cardin/Dir., Principal Executive Officer, Principal Financial Officer, Principal Accounting Officer, Stephen F. Fante/Dir.

Owners: Steven H. Cardin/50.63%, Insiders/50.63%

*Financial Data: Fiscal Year End:*09/30 *Latest Annual Data:* 09/30/2006

Year	Sales	Net Income
2006	$3,124,000	$2,260,000
2005	$1,029,000	$156,000
2004	$853,000	$38,000

Curr. Assets:	$5,211,000	*Curr. Liab.:*	$376,000		
Plant, Equip.:	$3,000	*Total Liab.:*	$376,000	*Indic. Yr. Divd.:*	NA
Total Assets:	$5,224,000	*Net Worth:*	$4,848,000	*Debt/ Equity:*	NA

Altigen Communications Inc

4555 Cushing Pkwy., Fremont, CA, 94538; *PH:* 1-510-252-9712; *Fax:* 1-510-252-9738;
http:// www.altigen.com; *Email:* info@altigen.com

General - Incorporation	DE	*Stock*- Price on:12/24/2007	$1.66
Employees	88	Stock Exchange	NDQ
Auditor	Moss Adams LLP	Ticker Symbol	ATGN
Stk Agt	EquiServe Trust Co N.A	Outstanding Shares	15,590,000
Counsel	Pillsbury, Madison & Sutro	E.P.S.	-$0.06
DUNS No.	NA	Shareholders	NA

Business: The group's principal activities are to design, manufacture and market time-tested Internet protocol phone systems and contact centers. The products enable businesses to use data networks, such as the Internet and public telephone network to take advantage of the convergence of voice and data communications. The products include altiware ip, altiview, altiware oe, triton board, triton t1/ pri board, quantum board and server chassis. The group's altiserv system is a complete communication system capable of coordinating different types of communication, including e-mail and voicemail. The altiserv system answers incoming phone calls, transfers calls to individual extensions or to groups of company representatives and tracks the call activity for future performance improvements. The customers of the group are primarily distributors and dealers who sell and resell the products to end-users.

Primary SIC and add'l.: 7373 4813

CIK No: 0001003607

Officers: Gilbert Hu/Chmn., CEO, Simon Chouldjian/VP - Hardware Engineering, Philip M. McDermott/CFO, Shirley Sun/VP - Research, Development, Mike Plumer/VP - Sales, Jeremiah Fleming/COO, Pres.

Directors: Gilbert Hu/Chmn., CEO, Tacheng Chester Wang/60/Dir., Richard B. Black/74/Dir., Mike Mon Yen Tsai/57/Dir., Eric Wanger/45/Dir.

Owners: Gilbert Hu/9.20%, Philip McDermott, Shirley Tsyr-Yi Sun, Richard B. Black, Insiders/14.30%, Simon Chouldjian, Eric Wanger/5.10%, Michael Plumer

*Financial Data: Fiscal Year End:*09/30 *Latest Annual Data:* 9/30/2006

Year	Sales	Net Income
2006	$17,896,000	-$12,000
2005	$15,441,000	-$311,000
2004	$14,842,000	$28,000

Curr. Assets:	$13,657,000	*Curr. Liab.:*	$2,630,000		
Plant, Equip.:	$681,000	*Total Liab.:*	$2,807,000	*Indic. Yr. Divd.:*	NA
Total Assets:	$14,644,000	*Net Worth:*	$11,837,000	*Debt/ Equity:*	NA

Altiris Inc

588 W 400 S, Lindon, UT, 84042; *PH:* 1-801-805-2400; *http://* www.altiris.com

General - Incorporation	DE	*Stock*- Price on:12/24/2007	NA
Employees	878	Stock Exchange	NDQ
Auditor	KPMG LLP	Ticker Symbol	ATRS
Stk Agt	Computershare Investor Services LLC	Outstanding Shares	NA
Counsel	NA	E.P.S.	NA
DUNS No.	NA	Shareholders	NA

Business: The group's principal activity is to develop, market and support integrated Web-enabled software solutions that enable organizations to manage it assets throughout their lifecycles. The solutions address deployment and migration, software and operations management, inventory and asset management, and help desk and problem resolution, which are the critical aspects of it lifecycle management. The products are licensed to customers as integrated suites or as separate modules, depending on the customer requirements. In addition, the group provides services such as on-site services, training and education and priority support. In 2003, the group acquired wise solutions incorporated and in 2004 it acquired fslogic inc and bridgewater technologies inc.

Primary SIC and add'l.: 7371 7372

CIK No: 0001139650

Subsidiaries: Altiris AB, Altiris Australia Pty Ltd., Altiris B.V., Altiris Computing Edge, Inc., Altiris Estonia O, Altiris GmbH, Altiris Japan K.K., Altiris Ltd., Altiris Mexico S.A de C.V., Altiris S.A.R.L., Altiris Services GmbH, Altiris Singapore Pte Ltd., FSL, LLC, Pedestal Software International, Inc., Pedestal Software, Inc. 18 Subsidiaries included in the Index

Officers: Gregory S. Butterfield/48/Chmn., CEO, Pres., Group Pres. - Altiris Business Unit, Stephen C. Erickson/VP - Operations, Michael R. Samuelian/VP - Sales, Ed Reilly/VP - Sales EMEA, Carine Clark/VP - Marketing, Dwain Kinghorn/VP - Engineering, Chad Latimer/VP - Global Services, Craig Christensen/General Counsel, Steve Erickson/VP - Operations, Rhett Glauser/Press Contact, Clayton Blackham/Agency Contact, Bradley Gittings/Investor Contact, Helyn Corcos/VP - Investor Relations, David Gennarelli/Dir. - Investor Relations, Sailesh Munagala/Mgr. - Investor Relations

Directors: Gregory S. Butterfield/48/Chmn., CEO, Pres., Group Pres. - Altiris Business Unit

Owners: Gregory S. Butterfield, Michael R. Samuelian, Craig H. Christensen, Stephen C. Erickson, Dwain A. Kinghorn, Michael J. Levinthal, Jay C. Hoag/10.50%, Insiders/13.50%, Mark E. Sunday, Eric V. Roach, Gary B. Filler, Technology Crossover Ventures/10.40%

Alto Palermo

Moreno 877, Piso 22, Buenos Aires; **PH:** 54-1143444600; **http://** www.altopalermo.com.ar

General - Incorporation	AR	Stock - Price on:12/24/2007	$21.75
Employees	NA	Stock Exchange	NDQ
Auditor	PricewaterhouseCoopers LLP	Ticker Symbol	APSA
Stk Agt.	Caja de Valores S.A.	Outstanding Shares	19,550,000
Counsel	NA	E.P.S.	$0.44
DUNS No.	NA	Shareholders	NA

Business: The group's principal activities are developing, administering, acquiring and locating productive commercial centers and residential complexes. Invest in properties and furnitures, industrializes and raw materials, exports and imports raw materials and other materials. Functions as a developer of bound/joint residential complexes at the commercial centers that they operate or develop. It also participates in the credit card business through its subsidiary and also develops Internet sites to stimulate e-commerce through e-commerce latina sa.

Primary SIC and add'l.: 6531 6510 6519

CIK No: 0001128173

Subsidiaries: AltoCity.Com S.A., E-Commerce Latina S.A., Emprendimiento Recoleta S.A., Fibesa S.A., Inversora del Puerto S.A., Mendoza Plaza Shopping S.A., Shopping Alto Palermo S.A., Shopping Neuqun S.A., Tarshop S.A.

Officers: Alejandro G. Elsztain/42/Executive Vice Chmn., CEO, David A. Perednik/51/Alternate Dir., Chief Administrative Officer, Daniel R. Elsztain/36/Dir., Chief Commercial Officer, Gabriel Blasi/48/CFO

Directors: Alejandro G. Elsztain/42/Executive Vice Chmn., CEO, Eduardo S. Elsztain/48/Chmn., Saul Zang/63/Vice Chmn., Gabriel A.G. Reznik/50/Dir., David A. Perednik/51/Alternate Dir., Chief Administrative Officer, Jose D. Eluchans Urenda/55/Alternate Dir., Fernando A. Elsztain/47/Dir., Jose Said Saffie/78/Dir., Leonardo Fernandez/41/Alternate Dir., Abraham Perelman/67/Dir., Daniel R. Elsztain/36/Dir., Chief Commercial Officer, Hernan Buchi Buc/59/Alternate Dir., Andres Olivos/50/Dir., Juan M. Quintana/42/Alternate Dir., Ira Chaplik/47/Dir. *(20 Directors included in Index)*

Owners: Parque Arauco, Angel D. Vergara del Carril, IRSA, Eduardo S. Elsztain, Alejandro G. Elsztain

Financial Data: Fiscal Year End:06/30   Latest Annual Data: 6/30/2006

Year	Sales		Net Income
2006	$117,188,000		$15,245,000
2005	$79,565,000		$12,504,000
2004	$48,390,000		$2,449,000
Curr. Assets:	$69,304,000	Curr. Liab.:	$95,200,000
Plant, Equip.:	$294,738,000	Total Liab.:	$176,234,000	Indic. Yr. Divd.: $0.890
Total Assets:	$385,033,000	Net Worth:	$208,800,000	Debt/ Equity: 0.3152

Altria Group Inc

120 Pk. Ave, Newyork, NY, 10017; **PH:** 1-917-663-4000; **http://** www.altria.com

General - Incorporation	VA	Stock - Price on:12/24/2007	$68.27
Employees	175,000	Stock Exchange	NYSE
Auditor	PricewaterhouseCoopers LLP	Ticker Symbol	NA
Stk Agt.	Computershare Investor Services LLC	Outstanding Shares	2,100,000,000
Counsel	NA	E.P.S.	$5.12
DUNS No.	00-130-6497	Shareholders	NA

Business: The group's principle activities include manufacturing and selling of cigarettes and various tobacco products. The group products are sold under the brand names Marlboro, L&M, Philip Morris, Lark, Bond Street Parliament, Basic, Chesterfield, Lark, L and M, and Virginia Slims. The group operates from United States.

Primary SIC and add'l.: 2082 6159 2022 2095 2111 2011 2099

CIK No: 0000764180

Subsidiaries: 152999 Canada Inc., 3072440 Nova Scotia Company, AB Kraft Foods Lietuva, Abal Hermanos S.A., Aberdare Developments Ltd., Aberdare Two Developments Ltd., AGF Pack, Inc., AGF SP, Inc., Agrotab Empreendimentos Agro-Industriais, S.A., Airco IHC, Inc., Ajinomoto General Foods, Inc., Alimentos Especiales, Sociedad Anonima, Altria Corporate Services International, Inc., Altria Corporate Services, Inc., Altria Finance (Cayman Islands) Ltd. 363 Subsidiaries included in the Index

Officers: Andre Calantzopoulos/CEO, Pres. - Philip Morris International Inc, John J. Mulligan/CEO, Pres. - Philip Morris Capital Corporation, Michael E. Szymanczyk/Chmn., CEO - Philip Morris USA Inc/$21,030,880.00, Louis C. Camilleri/Chmn., CEO/$33,992,340.00, Charles R. Wall/Sr. VP, General Counsel/$17,117,560.00, Greg Prager/Contact - External Communications, Philip Morris International, Carol Springstun/Contact - External Communications, Lisa Gonzalez/Contact - External Communications, Dawn Schneider/Contact - External Communications, John Sorrells/Contact - External Communications, Steven C. Parrish/Sr. VP - Corporate Affairs/$12,047,730.00, Walter V. Smith/VP - Taxes, Amy J. Engel/VP, Treasurer, Penn G. Holsenbeck/VP, Assoc. General Counsel, Corp. Sec., Joseph A. Tiesi/VP, Controller *(18 Officers included in Index)*

Directors: Michael E. Szymanczyk/Chmn., CEO - Philip Morris USA Inc, Louis C. Camilleri/Chmn., CEO, Thomas W. Jones/Dir., Mathis Cabiallavetta/63/Dir., Harold Brown/81/Dir., Stephen M. Wolf/Dir., Dudley J. Fishburn/62/Dir., Robert E.R. Huntley/Dir., Elizabeth E. Bailey/70/Dir., George Munoz/Dir., Lucio A. Noto/Dir., John Reed/Dir.

Owners: Insiders, Elizabeth E. Bailey, Stephen M. Wolf, George Munoz, Louis C. Camilleri, Michael E. Szymanczyk, Capital Research and Management Company, Dinyar S. Devitre, Steven C. Parrish, Charles R. Wall, Lucio A. Noto, John S. Reed, Harold Brown, J. Dudley Fishburn, Thomas W. Jones *(17 Owners included in Index)*

Financial Data: Fiscal Year End:12/31   Latest Annual Data: 12/31/2006

Year	Sales		Net Income
2006	$101,407,000,000		$12,022,000,000
2005	$97,854,000,000		$10,435,000,000
2004	$89,610,000,000		$9,416,000,000
Curr. Assets:	$26,152,000,000	Curr. Liab.:	$25,427,000,000	P/E Ratio: 13.33
Plant, Equip.:	$17,274,000,000	Total Liab.:	$61,123,000,000	Indic. Yr. Divd.: $2.760
Total Assets:	$104,270,000,000	Net Worth:	$39,619,000,000	Debt/ Equity: 0.5480

Altrust Financial Services Inc

811 2nd Ave. S.w., Cullman, AL, 35055; **PH:** 1-256-737-7000

General - Incorporation	AL	Stock - Price on:12/24/2007	$11.85
Employees	165	Stock Exchange	OTC
Auditor	Dixon Hughes PLLC	Ticker Symbol	ATFS
Stk Agt	Registrar & Transfer Co	Outstanding Shares	5,490,000
Counsel	NA	E.P.S.	$1.04
DUNS No.	NA	Shareholders	NA

Business: The group's principal activity is to provide retail and commercial banking in Blount, Cullman, Marshall and Morgan Counties, Alabama, as well as the northern portion of Jefferson County, Alabama. The group provides mostly traditional banking services, principally the taking of demand and time deposits and the making of secured and unsecured consumer loans and commercial loans to its business customers.

Primary SIC and add'l.: 6022

CIK No: 0001174771

Subsidiaries: Peoples Bank of North Alabama, Southern Appraisal Services, Inc., Southern Insurance of Cullman

Officers: James Robin Cummings/61/Dir., CEO, Pres., Debra Brown Goble/46/Exec. VP, Raymond Oneal Lindsey/71/Exec. VP, Candace Nail Hooten/54/Exec. VP - Bank, John Edwin Whitley/50/Exec. VP, Kenneth Howard Weldon/56/Exec. VP, Morris Steven Stanford/45/Exec. VP - Commercial Lending, Lionel James Powell/55/CFO, Treasurer

Directors: James Robin Cummings/61/Dir., CEO, Pres., Timothy Dudley Walker/47/Dir., Brian C. Witcher/44/Dir., Whit Drake/43/Dir., Jasper N. Estes/72/Dir., Cecil Alan Walker/51/Dir., Terry Neal Walker/43/Dir.

Owners: Terry Neal Walker/6.49%, Lionel James Powell, Debra Brown Goble/0.03%, Cecil Alan Walker/6.59%, Morris Steven Stanford/0.02%, Timothy Dudley Walker/5.06%, Candace Nail Hooten/0.50%, George Whit Drake/0.44%, Insiders/26.35%, James Robin Cummings/4.98%, Altrust Financial Services, Inc./19.26%, Brian Clark Witcher/0.60%, John Edwin Whitley/0.38%, Kenneth Howard Weldon/0.12%, Raymond ONeal Lindsey/0.23% *(16 Owners included in Index)*

Financial Data: Fiscal Year End:12/31   Latest Annual Data: 12/31/2006

Year	Sales		Net Income
2006	$33,138,000		$6,051,000
Curr. Assets:	$21,160,000	Curr. Liab.:	$373,297,000	P/E Ratio: 10.68
Plant, Equip.:	$16,465,000	Total Liab.:	$378,151,000	Indic. Yr. Divd.: NA
Total Assets:	$426,043,000	Net Worth:	$35,056,000	Debt/ Equity: 0.0754

Altus Exploration Inc

5868, Ste. 308, Westheimer Rd., Houston, TX, 77057;

General - Incorporation	NV	Stock - Price on:12/24/2007	NA
Employees	NA	Stock Exchange	OTC
Auditor	Malone & Bailey, P.C	Ticker Symbol	ALXP
Stk Agt	Nevada Agency & Trust Company	Outstanding Shares	NA
Counsel	NA	E.P.S.	NA
DUNS No.	NA	Shareholders	NA

Business: The groups principle activity is to explore minerals and natural gas. The group operates from the United States.

Primary SIC and add'l.: 1040

CIK No: 0001165639

Officers: Greg A. Thompson/53/Dir., Pres., Sec., Principal Exec. Officer, Yazmin Leyva/30/Treasurer, Principal Financial Officer, Principal Accounting Officer

Directors: Greg A. Thompson/53/Dir., Pres., Sec., Principal Exec. Officer, Dion Burkard/59/Dir.

Owners: Milton Cox/14.02%, Sterling Management of Belize/8.59%, Greg A. Thompson/1.29%, Bassam Nastat/9.68%, Insiders/1.29%

Curr. Assets:	$5,000	Curr. Liab.:	$130,000	
Plant, Equip.:	$0	Total Liab.:	$130,000	Indic. Yr. Divd.: NA
Total Assets:	$6,000	Net Worth:	-$125,000	Debt/ Equity: NA

Altus Pharmaceuticals Inc

125 Sidney St., Cambridge, MA, 02139; **PH:** 1-617-299-2900; **Fax:** 1-617-299-2999; **http://** www.altus.com; **Email:** ir@altus.com

General - Incorporation	DE	Stock - Price on:12/24/2007	$12.36
Employees	144	Stock Exchange	NDQ
Auditor	Deloitte & Touche LLP	Ticker Symbol	ALTU
Stk Agt	Computershare Shareholder Ser Inc	Outstanding Shares	30,580,000
Counsel	NA	E.P.S.	-$3.14
DUNS No.	NA	Shareholders	NA

Business: The groups principle activities include developing and commercializing oral and injectable protein therapeutics. The products of the group include ALTU-135, ALTU-238, ALTU-237 and ALTU-236. The group operates from United States.

Primary SIC and add'l.: 2836 2834

CIK No: 0001340744

Subsidiaries: Altus Pharmaceuticals Securities Corp.

Officers: Sheldon Berkle/Dir., CEO, Pres., Burkhard Blank/Sr. VP - Medicine, Regulatory Affairs, Project Management, Bruce Leicher/Sr. VP, General Counsel, Sec., Alexey L. Margolin/Sr. VP - Research, Pre, Clinical Development, Chief Scientific Officer, Robert Gallotto/VP - Strategic Planning, Alliance Management, Jonathan I. Lieber/CFO, VP, Treasurer, Lauren Sabella/VP - Commercial Development, John M. Sorvillo/VP - Business Development, John A. Jordan/Sr. Dir. - Corporate Communications

Directors: Sheldon Berkle/Dir., CEO, Pres., John P. Richard/Chmn., Stewart J. Hen/Dir., Jonathan S. Leff/Dir., Manuel A. Navia/Dir., David D. Pendergast/Dir., Harry H. Penner/Dir., Jonathan D. Root/Dir., Michael S. Wyzga/Dir.

Owners: Entities affiliated with U.S. Venture Partners, Entities affiliated with Nomura International plc, Lauren M. Sabella, Adage Capital Partners, Manuel A. Navia, Burkhard Blank, Warburg Pincus Private Equity VIII, David D. Pendergast, Jonathan I. Lieber, Alexey L. Margolin, Michael S. Wyzga, Jonathan S. Leff, Sheldon Berkle, Harry H. Penner, Jonathan D. Root *(19 Owners included in Index)*

Financial Data: ***Fiscal Year End:***12/31 ***Latest Annual Data:*** 12/31/2006

Year	Sales	Net Income
2006	$5,107,000	-$55,680,000
2005	$8,288,000	-$27,124,000
2004	$4,230,000	-$20,957,000

Curr. Assets:	$88,490,000	**Curr. Liab.:**	$17,183,000		
Plant, Equip.:	$6,717,000	**Total Liab.:**	$20,758,000	**Indic. Yr. Divd.:**	NA
Total Assets:	$96,461,000	**Net Worth:**	$69,422,000	**Debt/ Equity:**	0.0330

Alumina Ltd

GPO Box 5411, Melbourne, Victoria, 3001; ; ***http://*** www.aluminalimited.com

General - Incorporation	Australia	**Stock**- Price on:12/24/2007	$26.5801
Employees	10	Stock Exchange	NYSE
Auditor	PricewaterhouseCoopers LLP	Ticker Symbol	AWC
Stk Agt	Bank of New York	Outstanding Shares	291,900,000
Counsel	NA	E.P.S.	$1.62
DUNS No.	75-400-9876	Shareholders	NA

Business: The group's principal activity focuses on mining and refining of bauxite ores to produce alumina for the aluminium and alumina chemicals industries. It owns 40% of alcoa world alumina & chemicals (awac), a partnership with alcoa. Awac has interests in bauxite mining, alumina refining, alumina-based chemicals and two operating aluminium smelters. Awac has a global network of mines, refineries and smelters in Australia, guinea, suriname, jamaica, Brazil, Spain and the United States.

Primary SIC and add'l.: 1061 3334 1479 1099 1021 1041

CIK No: 0000857071

Subsidiaries: Alcoa Inc., Alumina (U.S.A.) Inc., Alumina Group consists, Alumina Holdings (USA) Inc., Alumina International Holdings Pty. Ltd., Awac, Wmc Resources Ltd, Butia Participaoes SA, Westminer (Investments) B.V., Westminer Acquisition (U.K.) Limited, Westminer International (U.K.) Limited

Officers: John Marlay/Dir., CEO, Camille Dixon/Assist., Stephen Foster/General Counsel, Company Sec., Ken Dean/Alternate Dir., CFO

Directors: John Marlay/Dir., CEO, Donald M. Morley/Chmn., Mark R. Rayner/Dir., Ronald J. McNeilly/Dir., Ken Dean/Alternate Dir., CFO, Peter A.F. Hay/Dir., John G. Pizzey/Dir., George J. Pizzey/Dir.

Owners: Merrill Lynch& Co. Inc./6.00%, Commonwealth Bank of Australia/9.34%, NWQ Investment Management Company LLC/8.70%

Financial Data: ***Fiscal Year End:***12/31 ***Latest Annual Data:*** 12/31/2006

Year	Sales	Net Income
2006	$1,105,000	$441,850,000
2005	$2,920,000	$239,838,000
2004	NA	$258,759,000

Curr. Assets:	$135,128,000	**Curr. Liab.:**	$311,616,000		
Plant, Equip.:	$158,000	**Total Liab.:**	$475,948,000	**Indic. Yr. Divd.:**	$0.790
Total Assets:	$2,005,217,000	**Net Worth:**	$1,529,269,000	**Debt/ Equity:**	NA

Aluminum Corp of China Ltd

No. B12 Fuxing Rd. , People's Republic of China, Haidian District, Beijing, 100814; ***PH:*** 86-1063971767; ***http://*** www.chalco.com.cn

General - Incorporation	China	**Stock**- Price on:12/24/2007	$40.8601
Employees	88,000	Stock Exchange	NYSE
Auditor	PricewaterhouseCoopers LLP	Ticker Symbol	ACH
Stk Agt	U.S. Bancorp	Outstanding Shares	116,620,000
Counsel	NA	E.P.S.	$12.20
DUNS No.	NA	Shareholders	NA

Business: The group's principal activities are the production and distribution of alumina and primary aluminum. It also manufactures and sells mechanical equipment, ceramic products, automated system, electrode system and electronic products. Other activities include provision of repair and maintenance services for electrical plant and machinery and design of production process and provision of technical services.

Primary SIC and add'l.: 2819 3334

CIK No: 0001161611

Subsidiaries: China Aluminum Development Company Limited, Shandong Aluminum, Shandong Aluminum Industry Co., Ltd, Shanxi Huaze

Officers: Xiao Yaqing/49/Chmn., CEO, Xiong Weiping/Executive Dir., Yuan Li/50/Supervisor, Liu Xiangmin/46/Dir., VP, Liu Qiang/44/Sec., Chen Jihua/40/Dir., VP, CFO, Zhang Chengzhong/48/Dir., VP, Luo Jianchuan/45/Dir., Sr. VP

Directors: Xiao Yaqing/49/Chmn., CEO, Xiong Weiping/Executive Dir., Liu Xiangmin/46/Dir., VP, Chen Jihua/40/Dir., VP, CFO, Zhang Chengzhong/48/Dir., VP, Wang Dianzuo/74/Dir., Kang Yi/67/Dir., Luo Jianchuan/45/Dir., Sr. VP, Joseph C. Muscari/61/Dir., Shi Chungui/68/Dir., Poon Yiu Kin Samuel/48/Dir., Helmet Wieser/54/Dir.

Owners: Guizhou Development/1.00%, Guangxi Investment/1.53%, China Development Bank/4.31%, Chinalco/40.46%, Lanzhou Economy and Information Consulting Company, China Construction Bank/5.51%, Alcoa/6.86%, Public investors of A Shares/8.91%, China Cinda/6.99%, Other public investors/23.74%, Lanzhou Aluminum

Financial Data: ***Fiscal Year End:***12/31 ***Latest Annual Data:*** 12/31/2006

Year	Sales	Net Income
2006	$7,931,250,000	$1,502,604,000
2005	$4,598,439,000	$895,785,000
2004	$3,995,569,000	$801,373,000

Curr. Assets:	$3,296,717,000	**Curr. Liab.:**	$2,762,725,000		
Plant, Equip.:	$5,934,806,000	**Total Liab.:**	$4,357,265,000	**Indic. Yr. Divd.:**	$0.830
Total Assets:	$9,775,324,000	**Net Worth:**	$5,418,059,000	**Debt/ Equity:**	NA

Alvarion Ltd

2495 Leghorn St., Mountain View, CA, 94043; ***PH:*** 1-650-314-2500; ***Fax:*** 1-650-967-3966; ***http://*** www.alvarion.com; ***Email:*** corporate-sales@alvarion.com

General - Incorporation	Israel	**Stock**- Price on:12/24/2007	$8.98
Employees	941	Stock Exchange	NDQ
Auditor	Kost Forer Gabbay & Kasierer	Ticker Symbol	ALVR
Stk Agt	American Stock Transfer & Trust Co.	Outstanding Shares	61,630,000
Counsel	Weil, Gotshal & Manges LLP	E.P.S.	-$0.1
DUNS No.	NA	Shareholders	NA

Business: The group's principle activity is to provide broadband wireless access systems used by service providers and enterprises. The products provide a wireless alternative to wired access solutions, such as digital subscriber lines and DSL and cable modems. It also offers products that enable indoor, outdoor, fixed and mobile wireless connectivity to a local computer network or LAN. The group operates from United States.

Primary SIC and add'l.: 5045

CIK No: 0001108332

Subsidiaries: Alvarion Asia Pacific Ltd., Alvarion De Mexico SA, Alvarion Do Brasil LTDA, Alvarion Inc, Alvarion Israel (2003) Ltd., Alvarion Japan KK, Alvarion Mobile Inc., Alvarion PTE LTD, Alvarion SARL, Alvarion Spain SL, Alvarion Srl, Alvarion Telsiz Sistemleri A.S., Alvarion UK Ltd, Alvarion Uruguay SA, International Wave Communications Netowrks Inc. 20 Subsidiaries included in the Index

Officers: Tzvika Friedman/CEO, Pres., Avi Wellingstein/Pres. - Customer Business Division, Avinoam Barak/Pres. - Broadband Wireless Access Division, Efrat Makov/CFO, Amir Tirosh/Corporate VP - Corporate Development, Greg Daily/Pres., Rudy Leser/Corporate VP - Strategy, Marketing, Avi Mazaltov/Pres. - Operations, Infrastructure Division, Haim Srur/Corporate VP - Human Resources, Uzi Breier/Pres. - Broadband Mobile Unit

Directors: Anthony Maher/Chmn., Raphael Amit/Dir., David Kettler/Dir., Meir Barel/Dir., Amnon Yacoby/Dir., Zvi Slonimsky/Dir., Robin Hacke/External Dir., Oded Eran/Dir., Benny Hanigal/Dir.

Owners: Tzvika Friedman/1.14%, Insiders/5.73%, Amnon Yacoby/1.35%

Financial Data: ***Fiscal Year End:***12/31 ***Latest Annual Data:*** 12/31/2006

Year	Sales	Net Income
2006	$181,594,000	-$40,751,000
2005	$195,715,000	-$12,618,000
2004	$201,507,000	$851,000

Curr. Assets:	$169,237,000	**Curr. Liab.:**	$72,068,000		
Plant, Equip.:	$10,379,000	**Total Liab.:**	$84,762,000	**Indic. Yr. Divd.:**	NA
Total Assets:	$280,063,000	**Net Worth:**	$195,301,000	**Debt/ Equity:**	NA

Amacore Group Inc

1511 N Westshore Blvd., Ste. 925, Tampa, FL, 33607; ***PH:*** 1-813-289-5552; ***Fax:*** 1-813-289-5553; ***http://*** www.ecivisionplan.com; ***Email:*** support@ecivisionplan.com

General - Incorporation	DE	**Stock**- Price on:12/24/2007	$0.29
Employees	7	Stock Exchange	OTC
Auditor	Brimmer, Burek & Keelan LLP	Ticker Symbol	ACGI
Stk Agt	American Stock Transfer & Trust Co.	Outstanding Shares	121,340,000
Counsel	NA	E.P.S.	-$0.08
DUNS No.	NA	Shareholders	NA

Business: The group's principle activity is to market memberships in a comprehensive, national, non-insurance based, eye care and eyewear plan. This plan entitles members and subscribers to obtain eye care service and products from a network of ophthalmic physicians. The company's vision network combines ophthalmology services provided by medical doctors with optometrical products and services provided by optometrists, opticians and optical locations. The network has providers at nearly 14,000 locations, and is comprised of over 1,600 ophthalmologic practices and over 12,000 optometric, optician and optical locations in the United States. The customers of the company are corporations, large sales organizations such as insurance companies, and sellers of multi-discount programs and affinity groups. The group's quarterly revenue for Sep'07 was 0.21 millions of USD.

Primary SIC and add'l.: 6324

CIK No: 0000949394

Subsidiaries: LBI, Inc

Officers: Clark A. Marcus/Chmn., CEO, Pres., James L. Koenig/61/Dir., Sec., Bill Heneghan/Dir. - Operations, Jay Shafer/Dir., Pres., Guy Norberg/Sr. VP, Joe Crisafi/CFO, Jerry Katzman/Dir., Chief Medical Officer

Directors: Clark A. Marcus/Chmn., CEO, Pres., William H. Koch/69/Dir., Arthur Yeap/52/Dir., Arnold Finestone/77/Dir., Sharon K. Ray/50/Dir., James L. Koenig/61/Dir., Sec., Jay Shafer/Dir., Pres., Jerry Katzman/Dir., Chief Medical Officer

Owners: Sharon Kay Ray, Insiders/5.60%, Clark Marcus/52.30%, Arnold Finestone, Arnold Finestone, Jay Shafer/2.50%, Insiders/100.00%, Arthur Yeap, William Koch, Jerry Katzman, Arthur Yeap, Jerry Katzman/37.00%, William Koch, Clark Marcus/1.40%, Sharon Kay Ray *(16 Owners included in Index)*

Financial Data: ***Fiscal Year End:***12/31 ***Latest Annual Data:*** 12/31/2006

Year	Sales	Net Income
2006	$365,000	-$1,736,000
2005	$461,000	-$4,354,000
2004	$163,000	-$38,361,000

Curr. Assets:	$268,000	**Curr. Liab.:**	$4,092,000		
Plant, Equip.:	$21,000	**Total Liab.:**	$4,125,000	**Indic. Yr. Divd.:**	NA
Total Assets:	$289,000	**Net Worth:**	-$3,837,000	**Debt/ Equity:**	NA

Amador Gold Corp

711-675 W. Hastings St., Vancouver, BC, V6B 1N2; *PH:* 1-604-685-2222; *Fax:* 1-604-685-3764; *http://* www.amadorgoldcorp.com; *Email:* info@amadorgoldcorp.com

General - Incorporation .... BC	Stock- Price on:12/24/2007 ....$0.2671
Employees ....NA	Stock Exchange...OTC
Auditor .... Morgan & Co	Ticker Symbol...................................... ADRGF
Stk Agt........Computershare Trust Co. of Canada	Outstanding Shares ....NA
Counsel...NA	E.P.S..NA
DUNS No. ....NA	Shareholders...NA

Business: The groups principle activity is to engaged in the acquisition, exploration of mineral resource properties, principally for copper and gold. The group operates from United States. The group was incorporated on October 24, 1980. On May 16, 2003, the group changed its name to Amador Gold Corp.

Primary SIC and add'l.: 1040

CIK No: 0001266833

Officers: Richard W. Hughes/74/Dir., CEO, Pres., Beverly J. Bullock/Corp. Sec., Alan Campbell/Dir., CFO

Directors: Richard W. Hughes/74/Dir., CEO, Pres., Lynn W. Evoy/Dir., Alan Campbell/Dir., CFO, John Keating/Dir., James M. McDonald/Dir., Joe Montgomery/Dir.

Owners: Maxwell Munday/9.50%, Munday Home Sales Ltd./9.50%, CDS & Co./69.80%, Richard W. Hughes/8.90%

AMAG Pharmaceuticals Inc

Formerly: Advanced Magnetics Inc
125 Cambridge Pk. Dr., 6th Fl., Cambridge, MA, 02140; *PH:* 1-617-498-3300; *http://* www.advancedmagnetics.com

General - Incorporation .... DE	Stock- Price on:12/24/2007 ....$60.79
Employees 42	Stock Exchange..NDQ
Auditor .... PricewaterhouseCoopers LLP	Ticker Symbol.. AMAG
Stk Agt.................. PricewaterhouseCoopers LLP	Outstanding Shares 14,240,000
Counsel....................Testa, Hurwitz & Thibeault	E.P.S...-$2.68
DUNS No. 55-721-2974	Shareholders...NA

Business: The group's principal activities are to develop and manufacture iron replacement therapeutics and magnetic resonance imaging (mri) contrast agents. The products of the group are used in the treatment of chronic anemia and diagnostic imaging agents. Mri is the diagnostic imaging technique of choice for the central nervous system and is widely used for the imaging of ligaments and tendons. The therapeutic agents are used in conjunction with magnetic resonance imaging (mri) in the diagnosis of cancer and other diseases. The contrast agents developed by the group improve the quality of diagnostic images by increasing the contrast between different internal structures. The principal brand names of the group include feridex i.v. And combidex. The products of the group are marketed in the United States, Europe, Argentina, Japan, South Korea, China and Israel.

Primary SIC and add'l.: 2834 2835 8731

CIK No: 0000792977

Officers: Brian J.G. Pereira/CEO, Pres., Jerome Goldstein/Executive Chmn., Louis Brenner/Sr. VP, Terri Clark/VP - Clinical Affairs, Mohammed A. Salem/VP - Regulatory Affairs, Joseph L. Farmer/General Counsel VP - Legal Affairs, Dennis R. Lawler/VP - Quality Control, Jerome M. Lewis/VP - Scientific Operations, David A. Arkowitz/CFO, Chief Business Officer, Timothy G. Healey/Sr. VP - Commercial Operations

Directors: Brian J.G. Pereira/CEO, Pres., Jerome Goldstein/Executive Chmn., Michael D. Loberg/Dir., Mark Skaletsky/Dir., Davey S. Scoon/Dir., Michael Narachi/Dir., Ron Zwanziger/Dir.

Owners: Insiders/2.30%, Capital Research and Management Company/5.20%, Joseph L. Farmer, Louis Brenner, Michael D. Loberg, Jerome Goldstein, Brian J.G. Pereira/1.60%, FMR Corp./8.50%, Michael Narachi, Mark Skaletsky, Ron Zwanziger

*Financial Data: Fiscal Year End:*09/30   *Latest Annual Data:* 9/30/2006

Year	Sales	Net Income
2006	$2,673,000	-$25,365,000
2005	$2,445,000	-$12,715,000
2004	$3,756,000	-$4,495,000

Curr. Assets:	$43,123,000	Curr. Liab.:	$9,501,000		
Plant, Equip.:	$4,232,000	Total Liab.:	$11,296,000	Indic. Yr. Divd.:	$0.050
Total Assets:	$47,371,000	Net Worth:	$36,075,000	Debt/ Equity:	NA

Amanasu Environment Corp

115 E 57th St., 11th Fl., New York, NY, 10022; *PH:* 1-646-274-1274; *http://* www.casefinancial.com

General - Incorporation .... NV	Stock- Price on:12/24/2007 ....$0.12
Employees 2	Stock Exchange...OTC
Auditor .... Robert G. Jeffrey, CPA	Ticker Symbol.. AMSU
Stk Agt......................Jersey Transfer & Trust Co	Outstanding Shares 44,000,000
Counsel...NA	E.P.S...-$0.03
DUNS No. ....NA	Shareholders...NA

Business: The group's principle activities include manufacturing and selling toxic waste disposal systems and hot water boiler systems. It has obtained a worldwide license to a technology that disposes of toxic and hazardous wastes through a proprietary, high temperature combustion system known as the amanasu furnace. The company is in the development stage and has not commenced its planned operations of manufacturing and selling the hazardous waste disposal systems and hot water boiler. The company's hot water boiler system will be marketed throughout North America. The group operates from United States.

Primary SIC and add'l.: 5084

CIK No: 0001142801

Subsidiaries: Amanasu Holdings Corporation, Amanasu Holdings, Inc, Amanasu Shinwa Corporation

Officers: Atsushi Maki/60/Chmn., Treasurer, Pres., Principal Financial Officer, CEO, CFO, Chief Accounting Officer, Lina Lei/47/Sec.

Directors: Atsushi Maki/60/Chmn., Treasurer, Pres., Principal Financial Officer, CEO, CFO, Chief Accounting Officer

Owners: Lina Lei, Insiders, Amanasu Corporation, Atsushi Maki

*Financial Data: Fiscal Year End:*12/31   *Latest Annual Data:* 12/31/2006

Year	Sales	Net Income
2006	$472,000	-$1,119,000
2005	$478,000	-$568,000
2004	NA	-$107,000

Curr. Assets:	$1,723,000	Curr. Liab.:	$55,000		
Plant, Equip.:	$242,000	Total Liab.:	$55,000	Indic. Yr. Divd.:	NA
Total Assets:	$2,495,000	Net Worth:	$2,015,000	Debt/ Equity:	NA

Amanasu Technologies Corp

115 East 57th St., 11th Fl., Newyork, NY, 10022; *PH:* 1-212-939-7278

General - Incorporation .... NV	Stock- Price on:12/24/2007 ....$0.05
Employees ....NA	Stock Exchange...OTC
Auditor ....Robert G. Jeffrey	Ticker Symbol....................................... ANSUE
Stk Agt ....NA	Outstanding Shares 46,510,000
Counsel...NA	E.P.S...$0.00
DUNS No. ....NA	Shareholders...NA

Business: The groups principal activities include designing, manufacturing, and selling motor scooters. The group products include lightweight motor scooter, electric motor scooters, and gas powered scooters. The group operates from the United States.

Primary SIC and add'l.: 3751

CIK No: 0001168663

Subsidiaries: Amanasu Techno Holdings Corporation

Officers: Yukinori Yoshino/CEO, Hideyuki Shiraishi/49/Chmn., CFO, Pres., Lina Lei/47/Sec.

Directors: Hideyuki Shiraishi/49/Chmn., CFO, Pres., Atsushi Maki/60/Dir.

Owners: Atsushi Maki, Lina Lei, Amanasu Corporation, Insiders, Hideyuki Shiraishi

*Financial Data: Fiscal Year End:*12/31   *Latest Annual Data:* 12/31/2006

Year	Sales	Net Income
2006	NA	-$144,000
2005	NA	-$87,000

Curr. Assets:	$1,000	Curr. Liab.:	$226,000		
Plant, Equip.:	$0	Total Liab.:	$226,000	Indic. Yr. Divd.:	NA
Total Assets:	$2,000	Net Worth:	-$225,000	Debt/ Equity:	NA

Amarc Resources Ltd

800 Pender St. W , Ste. 1020, Vancouver, BC, V6C 2V6; *PH:* 1-604-684-6365; *Fax:* 1-604-681-2741; *http://* www.amarcresources.com

General - Incorporation .... BC	Stock- Price on:12/24/2007 ....$0.605
Employees ....NA	Stock Exchange...OTC
Auditor ....De Visser Gray LLP	Ticker Symbol...................................... AXREF
Stk Agt .... Computershare Trust Co	Outstanding Shares ....NA
Counsel...NA	E.P.S..NA
DUNS No. ....NA	Shareholders...NA

Business: The groups principal activity is to explore minerals and natural gas. The group operates from the United States and Canada.

Primary SIC and add'l.: 1081

CIK No: 0001175596

Officers: Ronald Thiessen/Dir., CEO, Pres., Jeffery Mason/Dir., Sec., CFO, Scott D. Cousens/Dir. - Capital Finance

Directors: Ronald Thiessen/Dir., CEO, Pres., Robert Dickinson/Chmn., Jeffery Mason/Dir., Sec., CFO

Owners: Jeffrey R. Mason/4.40%, Robert A. Dickinson/10.00%, Scott D. Cousens, David J. Copeland/1.40%, Ronald W. Thiessen/2.40%

*Financial Data: Fiscal Year End:*03/31   *Latest Annual Data:* 3/31/2006

Year	Sales	Net Income
2006	NA	-$3,291,000
2005	NA	-$7,085,000
2004	NA	$636,000

Curr. Assets:	$4,174,000	Curr. Liab.:	$33,000		
Plant, Equip.:	$32,000	Total Liab.:	$33,000	Indic. Yr. Divd.:	NA
Total Assets:	$4,290,000	Net Worth:	$4,258,000	Debt/ Equity:	NA

Amarillo Biosciences Inc

4134 Business Pk. Dr., Amarillo, TX, 79110; *PH:* 1-806-376-1741; *Fax:* 1-806-376-9301; *http://* www.amarbio.com; *Email:* abi@amarbio.com

General - Incorporation .... TX	Stock- Price on:12/24/2007 ....$0.63
Employees 6	Stock Exchange...OTC
Auditor ....Lopez, Blevins, Bork & Assoc. LLP	Ticker Symbol.. AMAR
Stk Agt ..... American Stock Transfer & Trust Co.	Outstanding Shares 25,600,000
Counsel.............................SandersBaker PC	E.P.S...-$0.1
DUNS No. 14-817-0533	Shareholders...NA

Business: The group's principal activity is to develop biologics for the treatment of human and animal diseases. The group is currently focusing its research on human health indications for the use of low-dose orally administered natural human interferon alpha. This is particularly for the treatment of sjogren's syndrome, behcet's disease, fibromyalgia, idiopathic pulmonary fibrosis and oral warts in HIV+ patients. The group owns 18 patents relating to low-dose oral natural interferon alpha.

Primary SIC and add'l.: 2836 8731

CIK No: 0001014763

Subsidiaries: ABI Taiwan, Inc, Amarillo Cell of Canada, Inc., Vanguard Biosciences, Inc, Veldona Africa, Inc., Veldona Poland, Inc

Officers: Joseph M. Cummins/Chmn., CEO, Pres., Martin J. Cummins/40/VP - Clinical, Regulatory Affairs, Gary W. Coy/63/CFO, VP

Directors: Joseph M. Cummins/Chmn., CEO, Pres., Masashi Kurimoto/Member - Scientific Advisory Board, James A. Page/Dir., Member - Scientific Advisory Board, Stephen Chen/Dir., Manfred W. Beilharz/Member - Scientific Advisory Board, Jun Minowada/Member - Scientific Advisory Board, Michael Lange/Member - Scientific Advisory Board, Kunihiro Ohashi/Member -

Scientific Advisory Board, Kouichi Noda/Member - Scientific Advisory Board, Doug Testa/Member - Scientific Advisory Board, Bryan R.G. Williams/Member - Scientific Advisory Board, Wayne A.F. Tomkins/Member - Scientific Advisory Board, Dennis Moore/Dir., Thomas Ulie/59/Dir., Thomas D'Alonzo/Dir.

Owners: Hayashibara Biochemical Laboratories, Inc./12.24%, Dennis Moore/2.80%, James Page/2.60%, Martin J. Cummins/2.60%, Stephen Chen/2.50%, Insiders/20.30%, Joseph M. Cummins/6.80%, Thomas DAlonzo, Thomas Ulie/2.00%, Gary W. Coy

Financial Data: *Fiscal Year End:* 12/31 *Latest Annual Data:* 12/31/2006

Year	Sales	Net Income
2006	$134,000	-$2,778,000
2005	$155,000	-$669,000
2004	$52,000	-$595,000

Curr. Assets:	$248,000	**Curr. Liab.:**	$2,754,000		
Plant, Equip.:	$16,000	**Total Liab.:**	$2,754,000	**Indic. Yr. Divd.:**	NA
Total Assets:	$390,000	**Net Worth:**	-$2,364,000	**Debt/ Equity:**	NA

Amarin Corp Plc

7 Curzon St., London, W1J 5HE; *PH:* 44-2074999009; *http://* www.amarincorp.com; *Email:* investor.relations@amarincorp.com

General - Incorporation	England And Wales	**Stock** - Price on:12/24/2007	$0.5499
Employees	18	Stock Exchange	NDQ
Auditor	PricewaterhouseCoopers LLP	Ticker Symbol	AMRN
Stk Agt	Lloyds TSB Registrars	Outstanding Shares	90,700,000
Counsel	NA	E.P.S	-$0.38
DUNS No.	50-329-2773	Shareholders	NA

Business: The group's principal activities are marketing, selling and developing pharmaceutical products utilising its proprietary drug delivery technologies. Some of its products are permax a treatment for Parkinson's disease, zelapar an oral tablet uses a selective mao-b inhibitor and lax-101 which is to treat huntington's disease. It focuses on neurology and pain management, pharmaceutical development and marketing business, and drug delivery business in the United Kingdom, United States and Sweden.

Primary SIC and add'l.: 5122 2834

CIK No: 0000897448

Subsidiaries: Amarin Neuroscience Limited, Amarin Pharmaceuticals Company Limited, Amarin Pharmaceuticals Ireland Limited

Officers: Rick Stewart/Dir., CEO, Alan Cooke/37/Dir., CFO, Mehar Manku/VP - Research - Development, Member - Scientific Advisor, Darren Cunningham/Exec. VP - Strategic Development, Anthony Clarke/VP - Clinical Development, David Boal/VP - Business Development, Tom Maher/General Counsel, Company Sec., Declan Doogan/Pres. - Research, Development, Paul F. Duffy/Pres. - US Commercial Operations, Conor Dalton/VP - Finance, Tony Clarke/52/VP - Clinical Development

Directors: Rick Stewart/Dir., CEO, Thomas Lynch/51/Chmn., John Groom/Non Exec. Dir., Anthony Russell-Roberts/Non Exec. Dir., William Mason/Non Exec. Dir., Michael Walsh/Dir., Prem Lachman/Dir., William Hall/Non Exec. Dir., Simon Kukes/Dir., Alan Cooke/37/Dir., CFO, Mehar Manku/VP - Research - Development, Member - Scientific Advisor, John Climax/Dir., Member - Scientific Advisory Board, Jan Wallace/Member - Scientific Advisory Board, Reid Patterson/Member - Scientific Advisory Board, Mark W. Pierce/Member - Scientific Advisory Board

Owners: Southpoint/10.60%, S. Kukes/8.30%, R. A. B. Stewart, J. Groom, A. Russell-Roberts, Simon G. Kukes/7.30%, T. Maher, J. Climax/7.00%, M. Walsh, T. G. Lynch/11.00%, Amarin Investment Holding Limited/9.80%, A. Cooke, D. Cunningham

Financial Data: *Fiscal Year End:* 12/31 *Latest Annual Data:* 12/31/2006

Year	Sales	Net Income
2006	$111,000	-$23,707,000
2005	$500,000	-$19,630,000
2004	$1,017,000	-$67,202,000

Curr. Assets:	$39,591,000	**Curr. Liab.:**	$10,756,000		
Plant, Equip.:	$282,000	**Total Liab.:**	$53,115,000	**Indic. Yr. Divd.:**	NA
Total Assets:	$39,923,000	**Net Worth:**	-$13,192,000	**Debt/ Equity:**	NA

Amazing Nutritionals Inc

43 W 33Rd St., Ste. 405, New York, NY, 10001; *PH:* 1-212-695-3334; *http://* www.amazingnutritional.com

General - Incorporation	DE	**Stock** - Price on:12/24/2007	NA
Employees	NA	Stock Exchange	NA
Auditor	NA	Ticker Symbol	NA
Stk Agt	Stock Transfer & Trust Co	Outstanding Shares	NA
Counsel	NA	E.P.S	NA
DUNS No.	NA	Shareholders	NA

Business: The groups principle activity is to manufacture, market and distribute dietary supplements. The group operates from United States.

Primary SIC and add'l.: 2834

CIK No: 0001276050

Amazing Technologies Corp

23 Corporate Plz. Dr., Ste 200, Newport Beach, CA, 92660; *PH:* 1-949-706-7845; *http://* www.amazingca.com

General - Incorporation	NV	**Stock** - Price on:12/24/2007	$9.5
Employees	NA	Stock Exchange	OTC
Auditor	Corbin & Co LLP	Ticker Symbol	MVIV
Stk Agt	Empire Stock Transfer Inc.	Outstanding Shares	NA
Counsel	NA	E.P.S	NA
DUNS No.	NA	Shareholders	NA

Business: The group's principal activity is to acquire venture backed 'vertical silo' software publishers that have fully developed, customer-validated products. The company also acquires successful regional software companies that can be positioned as complementary 'plug and play' add-ons to existing customer sites. The group is acquiring established distribution in the largely regional, disparate JD Edwards (JDE) reseller channel. JDE, now owned by Oracle, was the leading supplier of an Enterprise Resource Planning (ERP) platform that automates workflows in the Server Message Block space.

Primary SIC and add'l.: 4899

CIK No: 0001323595

Officers: Bradley J. Hall/Chmn., CEO, Simon Arkell/Pres., Peter Griffith-Jones/CFO, John Gainor/VP - Business Development, Marcelo Di Rosa/Mananing Dir. - Europe, Dario Hernandez/Inancial Dir. - Latin America

Directors: Bradley J. Hall/Chmn., CEO

Amazon Biotech Inc

43 W 33rd St. Rm 405, New York, NY, 10001; *PH:* 1-212-695-3003; *http://* www.amazonbiotech.com; *Email:* info@amazonbiotech.com

General - Incorporation	UT	**Stock** - Price on:12/24/2007	NA
Employees	NA	Stock Exchange	OTC
Auditor	Meyler & Company, LLC	Ticker Symbol	AMZO
Stk Agt	Interwest Transfer Company, Inc.	Outstanding Shares	NA
Counsel	NA	E.P.S	NA
DUNS No.	NA	Shareholders	NA

Business: The groups principal activity is to research and development of novel all-natural drugs. The group products include AMZ0026-H, AMZHG001 and AZC0027. The group operates from the United States

Primary SIC and add'l.: 8732

CIK No: 0001088781

Subsidiaries: ASYST Corporation

Officers: Arthur Englard/Member - Scientific Advisory Board, Scientific Dir., Mechael Kanovsky/Dir., Pres., Simcha Edell/Dir., CFO, Avraham Harris/Dir - Clinical, Regulatory Operations., Rick Lutz/Investor Relations Officer

Directors: Arthur Englard/Member - Scientific Advisory Board, Scientific Dir., Mechael Kanovsky/Dir., Pres., Simcha Edell/Dir., CFO, Kathleen K. Casey/Member - Scientific Advisory Board, Anthony J. Mangia/Member - Scientific Advisory Board, Jeffrey L. Gilbert/Member - Scientific Advisory Board, Angelo Chinnici/Member - Scientific Advisory Board

Owners: Simcha Edell, Chaim Lieberman/13.10%, Insiders/1.30%, Mechael Kanovsky

Curr. Assets:	$582,000	**Curr. Liab.:**	$702,000		
Plant, Equip.:	$3,000	**Total Liab.:**	$702,000	**Indic. Yr. Divd.:**	NA
Total Assets:	$769,000	**Net Worth:**	$67,000	**Debt/ Equity:**	NA

Amazon.com Inc

1200 12th Ave. S, Ste. 1200, Seattle, WA, 98144; *PH:* 1-206-266-1000; *http://* www.amazon.com; *Email:* ir@amazon.com

General - Incorporation	DE	**Stock** - Price on:12/24/2007	$72.2
Employees	13,900	Stock Exchange	NDQ
Auditor	Ernst& Young LLP	Ticker Symbol	AMZN
Stk Agt	Mellon Investor Services LLC	Outstanding Shares	409,700,000
Counsel	NA	E.P.S	$0.87
DUNS No.	NA	Shareholders	NA

Business: The groups principal activity is to operate retail websites. The groups services include amazon enterprise solutions, co-branded credit cards, web services, fulfillment and miscellaneous marketing. The web site of the group includes www.amazon.com, www.amazon.ca, www.amazon.de, www.amazon.fr and www.joyo.com. The group operates through segment namely North America and International. The group operates from the United States. Of the net sale in the year 2006, North America accounted for $5,869 and International $4,842 (millions).

Primary SIC and add'l.: 5099 5961 5499 5045 5072 7372 5192 5912 5719 5712 3632 3429 3942 2844 3633 3635 2392 2519 3861 3639 5043 3634 3661 3651 3944 5021 3631 3652 5023

CIK No: 0001018724

Subsidiaries: Amazon EU Sarl, Amazon Europe Holding Technologies SCS, Amazon Global Resources, Inc., Amazon Services Europe S.a.r.l., Amazon Services LLC, Amazon Technologies, Inc., Amazon.com Holdings LLC, Amazon.com Intl Sales, Inc., Amazon.com LLC, Amazon.com NV Investment Holdings, Inc., Amazon.com.dedc, LLC, Amazon.com.kydc, Inc., NV Services, Inc.

Officers: Jeffrey P. Bezos/Chmn., CEO, Pres./$1,281,840.00, Jeffrey Blackburn/Sr. VP - Business Development, Richard L. Dalzell/CIO, Sr. VP/$3,469,834.00, Sebastian J. Gunningham/Sr. VP - Merchant Services, Andrew Jassy/Sr. VP - Web Services, Steven Kessel/Sr. VP - Worldwide Digital Media, Marc Onetto/Sr. VP - Worldwide Operations, Diego Piacentini/Sr. VP - International Retail/$2,148,546.00, Tom Szkutak/CFO, Sr. VP/$1,858,693.00, Brian Valentine/Sr. VP - eCommerce Platform, Jeff Wilke/Sr. VP - North America Retail/$2,380,915.00, Michelle Wilson/Sr. VP, General Counsel, Sec., Shelley Reynolds/VP - Finance, Controller, Principal Accounting Officer

Directors: Jeffrey P. Bezos/Chmn., CEO, Pres., Tom A. Alberg/67/Dir., John Seely Brown/66/Dir., John L. Doerr/56/Dir., William B. Gordon/57/Dir., Myrtle S. Potter/48/Dir., Thomas O. Ryder/62/Dir., Patricia Q. Stonesifer/50/Dir.

Owners: Thomas J. Szkutak, Myrtle S. Potter, Richard L. Dalzell, Insiders/25.85%, Thomas O. Ryder, The TCW Group, Inc. on behalf of the TCW Business Unit/5.22%, ClearBridge Advisors, LLC/5.60%, Diego Piacentini, Tom A. Alberg, Jeffrey A. Wilke, Legg Mason Capital Management, Inc./19.99%, John L. Doerr, William B. Gordon, Patricia Q. Stonesifer, Jeffrey P. Bezos/24.74% *(17 Owners included in Index)*

Financial Data: *Fiscal Year End:* 12/31 *Latest Annual Data:* 12/31/2006

Year	Sales	Net Income
2006	$10,711,000,000	$190,000,000
2005	$8,490,000,000	$359,000,000
2004	$6,921,124,000	$588,451,000

Curr. Assets:	$3,373,000,000	**Curr. Liab.:**	$2,532,000,000		
Plant, Equip.:	$457,000,000	**Total Liab.:**	$3,932,000,000	**Indic. Yr. Divd.:**	NA
Total Assets:	$4,363,000,000	**Net Worth:**	$431,000,000	**Debt/ Equity:**	NA

AMB Financial Corp

8230 Hohman Ave., Munster, IN, 46321; *PH:* 1-219-836-5870; *Fax:* 1-219-836-5883; *http://* www.ambfinancial.com

General - Incorporation	DE	**Stock** - Price on:12/24/2007	$15.4
Employees	31	Stock Exchange	OTC
Auditor	Cobitz, Vandenberg & Fennessy	Ticker Symbol	AMFC
Stk Agt	Registrar & Transfer Co	Outstanding Shares	1,040,000
Counsel	Abrahamson, Reed & Adley	E.P.S	$0.13
DUNS No.	07-440-6596	Shareholders	NA

Business: The group's principal activities are to attract deposits from general public and originate consumer, mortgage and real estate loans. The group is a savings and loan holding company. The group also invests in mortgage-backed securities, investment securities consisting primarily of United States government obligations and various types of short-term liquid assets. The services provided include commercial lending, real estate lending, personal loans and other financial services. The activities of the group are conducted through three offices located in munster, dyer and hammond, Indiana.

Primary SIC and add'l.: 6712 6035

CIK No: 0000915393

Subsidiaries: AMB Financial Statutory Trust I, American Savings, FSB, NIFCO, Inc., Ridge Management, Inc.

Officers: Clement Knapp/CEO, Pres./$232,025.00, Michael Mellon/Exec. VP - American Savings, FSB/$225,161.00, Louis Green/Sr. VP - Lending, American Savings, FSB/$144,198.00, Todd C. Williams/VP - Lending, American Savings, FSB, Denise Knapp/Branch Mgr. - Dyer, American Savings, FSB, Ginger Watts/Branch Mgr., Assist. VP, Compliance Officer - American Savings, FSB, Christine Bryant/Branch Mgr. - Hammond, American Savings, FSB, Mohammad Saleem/Assist. VP - Operations Merchant Services, American Savings, FSB, Bryan Pawola/Registered Financial Consultant, Investments, American Savings, FSB, Scott Gyure/53/VP, Chief Financial/$82,869.00, Robert Rossa/VP - Lending, American Savings, FSB, Steven A. Bohn/CFO, VP

Directors: Donald L. Harle/69/Dir., Robert E. Tolley/70/Dir., John G. Pastrick/76/Dir.

Owners: Insiders/25.17%, Ronald W. Borto/4.18%, AMB Financial Corp. Employee Stock Ownership Plan/10.50%, John G. Pastrick/1.36%, Tontine Financial Partners L.P., Tontine Management L.L.C./6.08%, Clement B. Knapp/12.37%, Donald L. Harle/3.09%, Robert E. Tolley/1.56%, Michael Mellon/3.65%

Financial Data: Fiscal Year End:12/31   Latest Annual Data: 12/31/2006

Year	Sales	Net Income
2006	$11,551,000	$648,000
2005	$10,406,000	$860,000
2004	$9,209,000	$881,000

Curr. Assets:	$13,823,000	**Curr. Liab.:**	$126,624,000	**P/E Ratio:**	51.33
Plant, Equip.:	$5,819,000	**Total Liab.:**	$167,621,000	**Indic. Yr. Divd.:**	$0.360
Total Assets:	$182,282,000	**Net Worth:**	$14,661,000	**Debt/ Equity:**	2.5943

AMB Property Corp

Pier 1, Bay 1, San Francisco, CA, 94111; **PH:** 1-415-394-9000; **Fax:** 1-415-394-9001; **http://** www.amb.com

General - Incorporation	MD	**Stock** - Price on:12/24/2007	$53.96
Employees	416	Stock Exchange	NYSE
Auditor	PricewaterhouseCoopers LLP	Ticker Symbol	AMB
Stk Agt	EquiServe Trust Co N.A	Outstanding Shares	99,630,000
Counsel	NA	E.P.S.	$2.25
DUNS No.	NA	Shareholders	NA

Business: The groups principle activities include acquiring, developing and operating industrial properties. Specific customers of the group include Harmonic Inc, Panalpina, Inc, Nippon Express and UTi United States Inc. The group operates from North America, Europe and Asia. The group's quarterly revenue for September 2007 was 166.30 millions of USD.

Primary SIC and add'l.: 4225 6798

CIK No: 0001045609

Subsidiaries: AMB Property II, L.P., AMB Property, L.P.

Officers: Hamid R. Moghadam/Chmn., CEO/$5,074,168.00, Thomas S. Olinger/CFO, Michael A. Coke/40/Exec. VP/$2,771,704.00, Guy F. Jaquier/Pres. - Europe, Asia/$1,927,532.00, Eugene F. Reilly/Pres. - North America/$1,416,900.00, John T. Roberts/Sr. VP - Capital Markets/$1,951,709.00, Tamra D. Browne/Sr. VP, General Counsel, Sec.

Directors: Hamid R. Moghadam/Chmn., CEO, Afsaneh M. Beschloss/52/Dir., Robert T. Burke/Co - Founder, David A. Cole/Dir., Lydia H. Kennard/Dir., Frederick W. Reid/Dir., Jeffrey L. Skelton/Dir., Michael J. Losh/Dir., Thomas W. Tusher/Dir., Carl B. Webb/Dir.

Owners: Eugene F. Reilly, The Vanguard Group, Inc./4.90%, Frederick W. Reid, John T. Roberts, Michael J. Losh, Afsaneh M. Beschloss, Barclays Global Investors, NA./5.00%, Jeffrey L. Skelton, Thomas W. Tusher, Lydia H. Kennard, Robert T. Burke, Insiders/7.70%, Michael A. Coke, Hamid R. Moghadam/5.20%, David A. Cole (18 Owners included in Index)

Financial Data: Fiscal Year End:12/31   Latest Annual Data: 12/31/2006

Year	Sales	Net Income
2006	$729,896,000	$224,072,000
2005	$676,149,000	$257,807,000
2004	$665,689,000	$125,471,000

Curr. Assets:	$329,876,000	**Curr. Liab.:**	$271,880,000	**P/E Ratio:**	23.98
Plant, Equip.:	$5,960,992,000	**Total Liab.:**	$3,709,295,000	**Indic. Yr. Divd.:**	$2.000
Total Assets:	$6,713,512,000	**Net Worth:**	$2,166,657,000	**Debt/ Equity:**	1.2451

Ambac Financial Group Inc

1 State St. Plz., New York, NY, 10004; **PH:** 1-212-668-0340; **Fax:** 1-212-509-9190; **http://** www.ambac.com

General - Incorporation	DE	**Stock** - Price on:12/24/2007	$87.64
Employees	359	Stock Exchange	NYSE
Auditor	KPMG LLP	Ticker Symbol	ABK
Stk Agt	Citibank N.A	Outstanding Shares	101,930,000
Counsel	NA	E.P.S.	$7.56
DUNS No.	13-135-5612	Shareholders	NA

Business: The groups principle activity is to provide financial guarantee products and other financial services to clients in both the public and private sector industries. The group operates from United States.

Primary SIC and add'l.: 6351 6719 6289 6282

CIK No: 0000874501

Subsidiaries: Ambac Assurance Corporation, Ambac Assurance UK Limited, Ambac Capital Corporation, Ambac Capital Funding, Inc., Ambac Capital Services, LLC, Ambac Credit Products, LLC, Ambac Financial Services, LLC, Ambac Investments, Inc.

Officers: Robert J. Genader/61/Chmn., CEO, Pres./$11,235,530.00, Bruce Mattaway/First VP - Public Finance East Region, New York, Mark Spinelli/MD - Project Finance North America, New York, Ted Molin/First VP - Public Finance West Region, New York, Debra Saunders/MD - Public Finance West Region, New York, Hideshi Amemiya/First VP - Asia Pacific, Tokyo, Anne Gill Kelly/MD, Corp. Sec., Assist. General Counsel, Thomas J. Gandolfo/Sr. MD - Capital Markets, Structured Credit, Gregg L. Bienstock/Sr. VP - CAO, Employment Counsel, Kevin J. Doyle/Sr. VP,

General Counsel - Internal Audit, Robert G. Shoback/Sr. MD - Public Finance, Sean T. Leonard/CFO, Sr. VP/$1,301,558.00, William T. McKinnon/Sr. MD - Credit Risk Management/$2,369,382.00, John W. Uhlein/Exec. VP - ABS, MBS, Conduits, Global Utilities/$2,484,085.00, David W. Wallis/Sr. MD - Portfolio, Marketing Risk Management (47 Officers included in Index)

Directors: Robert J. Genader/61/Chmn., CEO, Pres., Michael A. Callen/67/Dir., Philip N. Duff/50/Dir., Henry D.G. Wallace/62/Dir., Jill M. Considine/63/Dir., Grant W. Gregory/67/Dir., Thomas C. Theobald/70/Dir., Laura S. Unger/47/Dir.

Owners: Robert J. Genader, John W. Uhlein, Douglas C. Renfield-Miller, Insiders/1.56%, William T. McKinnon, J.P. Morgan Chase& Co./5.40%, Henry D.G. Wallace, Laura S. Unger, Phillip B. Lassiter, Thomas C. Theobald, W. Grant Gregory, Michael A. Callen, Goldman, Sachs Asset Management, L.P./7.80%, Jill M. Considine

Financial Data: Fiscal Year End:12/31   Latest Annual Data: 12/31/2006

Year	Sales	Net Income
2006	$1,833,518,000	$875,911,000
2005	$1,661,707,000	$751,010,000
2004	$1,406,708,000	$724,551,000

Curr. Assets:	$948,903,000	**Curr. Liab.:**	$8,627,983,000	**P/E Ratio:**	11.59
Plant, Equip.:	NA	**Total Liab.:**	$14,083,624,000	**Indic. Yr. Divd.:**	NA
Total Assets:	$20,267,813,000	**Net Worth:**	$6,184,189,000	**Debt/ Equity:**	1.6347

Ambase Corp

100 Putnam Green, 3rd Fl., Greenwich, CT, 06830; **PH:** 1-203-532-2000

General - Incorporation	DE	**Stock** - Price on:12/24/2007	$0.47
Employees	6	Stock Exchange	OTC
Auditor	PricewaterhouseCoopers LLP	Ticker Symbol	ABCP
Stk Agt	American Stock Transfer & Trust Co.	Outstanding Shares	44,970,000
Counsel	NA	E.P.S.	-$0.07
DUNS No.	09-506-7278	Shareholders	NA

Business: The group is a holding company which, through its wholly owned subsidiary sdg financial corp owns a 6.3% ownership interest in sdg, inc. The group continues to evaluate a number of possible acquisitions and is engaged in the management of its remaining assets and liabilities.

Primary SIC and add'l.: 6282 9999 6531

CIK No: 0000020639

Subsidiaries: Carteret Bancorp, Inc, Home Capital Services, Inc., Maiden Lane Associates, Ltd., SDG Financial Corp.

Owners: Robert E. Long, Richard A. Bianco/37.04%, John P. Ferrara, Insiders/37.55%

Financial Data: Fiscal Year End:12/31   Latest Annual Data: 12/31/2006

Year	Sales	Net Income
2006	$92,000	-$5,463,000
2005	$170,000	$5,128,000
2004	$2,229,000	-$3,351,000

Curr. Assets:	$3,802,000	**Curr. Liab.:**	$1,171,000		
Plant, Equip.:	$2,171,000	**Total Liab.:**	$17,481,000	**Indic. Yr. Divd.:**	NA
Total Assets:	$42,148,000	**Net Worth:**	$24,667,000	**Debt/ Equity:**	NA

Ambassadors Group Inc

Dwight D. Eisenhower Bldg., 110 S. Ferrall St., Spokane, WA, 99202; **PH:** 1-509-534-6200; **Fax:** 1-509-534-5245; **http://** www.ambassadorsgroup.com; **Email:** web_administrator@studentambassadors.org

General - Incorporation	DE	**Stock** - Price on:12/24/2007	$34.06
Employees	249	Stock Exchange	NDQ
Auditor	BDO Seidman LLP	Ticker Symbol	EPAX
Stk Agt	Mellon Investor Services LLC	Outstanding Shares	19,380,000
Counsel	NA	E.P.S.	$1.33
DUNS No.	NA	Shareholders	NA

Business: The group's principal activities are to organize and promote international educational travel and sports programs for students, athletes and professionals. It provides specialized private-label travel programs, which include people to people student ambassador programs, people to people sports ambassador programs and people to people ambassador programs. People to people student ambassador programs provide opportunities for grade school, junior and senior high students to visit domestic and foreign destinations to learn about history, government, economy and culture of such countries. People to people sports ambassadors programs provide opportunities for junior and senior high school athletes to participate in domestic and international sports travel programs. People to people ambassador programs provide foreign travel experiences for professionals, with emphasis on meetings and seminars between participants and persons in similar professions abroad.

Primary SIC and add'l.: 4725

CIK No: 0001162315

Subsidiaries: Ambassador Programs, Inc., Ambassadors Specialty Group, Inc., Ambassadors Unlimited, LLC.

Officers: Jeffrey D. Thomas/41/Dir., CEO, Pres./$2,502,203.00, Chadwick J. Byrd/CFO/$286,900.00, Julie Strugar/Contact - Investor Relations, Margaret M. Thomas/Exec. VP/$746,919.00

Directors: Jeffrey D. Thomas/41/Dir., CEO, Pres., John A. Ueberroth/64/Chmn., Joseph J. Ueberroth/39/Dir., James M. Kalustian/47/Dir., Rafer L. Johnson/73/Dir., Richard D.C. Whilden/Dir., Ricardo Lopez Valencia/42/Dir., Brigitte M. Bren/42/Dir., Daniel G. Byrne/Dir.

Owners: Dale F. Frey, Peter V. Ueberroth/7.30%, John A. Ueberroth/4.40%, James M. Kalustian, Insiders/14.10%, Richard D. C. Whilden, Jeffrey D. Thomas/4.20%, Joseph J. Ueberroth, Barclays Global Investors NA/5.10%, Chadwick J. Byrd, Morgan Stanley/10.70%, Margaret M. Thomas/4.20%, Daniel G. Byrne, Punch Card Capital, LLC./5.90%, Brigitte M. Bren (17 Owners included in Index)

Financial Data: Fiscal Year End:12/31   Latest Annual Data: 12/31/2006

Year	Sales	Net Income
2006	$88,955,000	$26,692,000
2005	$69,290,000	$22,410,000
2004	$51,824,000	$15,647,000

Curr. Assets:	$140,166,000	**Curr. Liab.:**	$69,710,000	**P/E Ratio:**	28.62
Plant, Equip.:	$12,267,000	**Total Liab.:**	$69,906,000	**Indic. Yr. Divd.:**	$0.460
Total Assets:	$153,953,000	**Net Worth:**	$84,047,000	**Debt/ Equity:**	0.0033

Ambassadors International Inc

1071 Camelback St., Newport Beach, CA, 92660; *PH:* 1-949-759-5900; *Fax:* 1-949-759-5901;
http:// www.ambassadors.com; *Email:* info@ambassadors.com

General - Incorporation.............................. DE	Stock- Price on:12/24/2007 ....$31.57
Employees 765	Stock Exchange...NDQ
Auditor ....Ernst & Young LLP	Ticker Symbol...AMIE
Stk Agt........ Chase Mellon Shareholder Services	Outstanding Shares 11,090,000
Counsel...........................Latham & Watkins LLP	E.P.S...-$0.39
DUNS No. 15-152-5177	Shareholders..NA

Business: The group's principal activities are to develop, market and manage performance improvement programs, provide comprehensive hotel reservation, registration and travel services for meetings, conventions, expositions and trade shows and to provide event portfolio management software solutions. The group operates through three segments: the performance group, the services group and the technology group. The technology group was formed in Dec 2002. It caters to a nationwide roster of corporate clients utilizing incentive travel, merchandise award programs and corporate meeting management services.

Primary SIC and add'l.: 8999 7372

CIK No: 0000946842

Subsidiaries: Ambassadors Cruise Group, LLC, Ambassadors, LLC, BellPort Group, Inc., Cypress Reinsurance, Ltd

Officers: Joseph J. Ueberroth/Chmn., CEO, Pres., Joseph G. McCarthy/VP - Corporate Development, General Counsel, Sean Walsh/Dir. - Development, Bellport, Marine Management, Mathieu Guilmineau/Exec. VP - Operations, Travel, Events Management, Tim Whorton/Exec. VP, GM - Travel, Events Management, Molly Risak/VP - Marketing, Travel, Events Management, Laura L. Tuthill/Interim CFO, Treasurer, Sec., Jerry McGee/Pres. - Travel, Events Management, Brian R. Schaefgen/38/Corp. Sec., Brandi Bowman/Investor Relations Officer, Brett Jones/VP - Information Technology, David Giersdorf/Pres. - Cruise Management/$1,295,971.00, Kerry Jewett/VP - Guest Services, Cruise Management, David Simmons/VP - Hotel Operations, Cruise Management, Jevonne Glaser/Controller - Travel, Events Management

Directors: Joseph J. Ueberroth/Chmn., CEO, Pres., Fife J. Symington/Dir., Peter V. Ueberroth/Dir., John C. Spence/Dir., James L. Easton/Dir., Kevin M. Luebbers/Dir., Brigitte M. Bren/Dir., Richard D.C. Whilden/Dir., Rafer L. Johnson/Dir.

Owners: Brigitte M. Bren, David A. Giersdorf, Fife J. Symington, John C. Spence, Kevin M. Luebbers, Dimensional Fund Advisors Inc./5.39%, James L. Easton, Ashford Capital Management/12.82%, MLF Investments/19.91%, Joseph G. McCarthy, Jerry G. McGee/1.05%, Joseph J. Ueberroth/7.83%, Richard D.C. Whilden, Brian R. Schaefgen, Insiders/23.05% *(17 Owners included in Index)*

Financial Data: Fiscal Year End:12/31   Latest Annual Data: 12/31/2006

Year	Sales		Net Income
2006	$144,419,000		$5,627,000
2005	$26,940,000		$3,142,000
2004	$18,736,000		-$1,937,000
Curr. Assets:	$120,608,000	Curr. Liab.:	$68,364,000
Plant, Equip.:	$118,630,000	Total Liab.:	$140,183,000	Indic. Yr. Divd.: $0.400
Total Assets:	$255,920,000	Net Worth:	$115,737,000	Debt/ Equity: 0.6512

Amber Resources Co of Colorado

370 17th St., Ste. 4300, Denver, CO, 80202; *PH:* 1-303-293-9133

General - Incorporation.............................. DE	Stock- Price on:12/24/2007 ....$0.0001
Employees ....NA	Stock Exchange...OTC
Auditor ....KPMG LLP	Ticker Symbol..AMBE
Stk Agt..NA	Outstanding Shares ....NA
Counsel..NA	E.P.S..NA
DUNS No. 09-416-2773	Shareholders..NA

Business: The group's principal activities are to acquire, explore, develop and produce oil and gas properties. The operations are carried out onshore in the continental United States and in the U.S. Coastal waters offshore, California. The group's principal operations are comprised solely of the development of off shore interests in undeveloped offshore federal leases and units near sanata barbara and California.

Primary SIC and add'l.: 1311

CIK No: 0000276750

Subsidiaries: Delta Petroleum Corporation

Owners: Insiders, Jerrie F. Eckelberger, Stanley F. Freedman, Roger A. Parker, Kevin K. Nanke, Delta Petroleum Corporation

Ambient Corp

79 Chapel St., Newton, MA, 02458; *PH:* 1-617-332-0004; *Fax:* 1-617-332-7260;
http:// www.ambientcorp.com; *Email:* info@ambientcorp.com

General - Incorporation.............................. DE	Stock- Price on:12/24/2007 ....$0.041
Employees 34	Stock Exchange...OTC
Auditor ....Rotenberg Meril Solomon	Ticker Symbol..ABTG
Stk Agt..... American Stock Transfer & Trust Co.	Outstanding Shares 241,690,000
Counsel..NA	E.P.S...-$0.067
DUNS No. 17-901-2703	Shareholders..NA

Business: The group's principal activities are to design, develop and implement a proposed comprehensive high-speed communication infrastructure. This is designed to utilize existing electrical power distribution lines as a high-speed communication medium, thereby enabling existing electrical distribution systems to function as broadband pipelines. The group's proposed powerline telecommunication solution is based on establishing and maintaining partnership relationships with utilities and electrical power distribution companies, as well as developing and maintaining business relations with telecommunication service and technology companies. The four primary sectors for the proposed powerline communications related products and services are urban, rural, suburban and underserved/underdeveloped.

Primary SIC and add'l.: 4813

CIK No: 0001047919

Officers: John J. Joyce/CEO, Pres./$326,057.00, Senator Bennett Johnston/Chmn., Ambient's Advisory Board, Ramdas Rao/CTO/$225,582.00, Dave Goldblatt/VP - Engineering, Mike Quarella/VP, Head - Operations, John Burruss/VP - Services, Anna E. Croop/Dir. - Corporate Communications, Aron Viner/Dir. - Compliance, Standardization, Jamie Dryer/Flagler Communications

Directors: Howard Pierce/Dir., Robert Abrams/Member - Advisory Board, Michael Widland/Dir., Stephen Howe/Member - Advisory Board, George Jee/Member - Advisory Board, Thomas Higgins/Dir.

Owners: Michael Widland, Ramdas Rao/1.56%, John J. Joyce/1.72%, Howard D. Pierce, Consolidated Edison, Inc./13.82%, Thomas Higgins, Insiders/5.27%

Financial Data: Fiscal Year End:12/31   Latest Annual Data: 12/31/2006

Year	Sales		Net Income
2006	$2,337,000		-$12,739,000
2005	$237,000		-$11,227,000
2004	NA		-$7,514,000
Curr. Assets:	$3,668,000	Curr. Liab.:	$2,369,000
Plant, Equip.:	$712,000	Total Liab.:	$2,634,000	Indic. Yr. Divd.: NA
Total Assets:	$5,429,000	Net Worth:	$2,795,000	Debt/ Equity: 0.0948

Amcol International Corp

1 N Arlington, 1500 W Shure Dr., Ste. 500, Arlington Heights, IL, 60004; *PH:* 1-847-394-8730;
Fax: 1-847-506-6199; *http://* www.amcol.com

General - Incorporation .... DE	Stock- Price on:12/24/2007 ....$25.37
Employees 1,759	Stock Exchange..NYSE
Auditor ....Ernst & Young, LLP	Ticker Symbol...ACO
Stk Agt..... American Stock Transfer & Trust Co.	Outstanding Shares 30,110,000
Counsel..............................Lord, Bissell & Brook	E.P.S..$1.76
DUNS No. 00-509-2556	Shareholders..NA

Business: The group's principal activities are divided into three industry segments: minerals, environmental and transportation. The minerals segment mines, processes and distributes clays and products with similar applications to various industrial and consumer markets. The environmental segment processes and distributes clays and products with similar applications for use as a moisture barrier in commercial construction, landfill liners and in a variety of other industrial and commercial applications. The transportation segment includes a long haul trucking business and a freight brokerage business, which provide services to both the group's plants and outside customers.

Primary SIC and add'l.: 4213 3295 2821 9999

CIK No: 0000813621

Subsidiaries: AMCOL (Holdings) Ltd., AMCOL Egypt SAE, AMCOL Europe Limited, AMCOL Health & Beauty Solutions, Incorporated, AMCOL Holdings Canada Ltd., AMCOL International B.V., AMCOL Specialties Holdings, Inc., Ameri-Co Carriers, Inc., Ameri-Co Logistics, Inc., American Colloid Company, Ashapura Minechem Ltd., Ashapura Volclay Limited, CETCO (Europe) Limited, CETCO China Ltd., CETCO Contracting Services Company 45 Subsidiaries included in the Index

Officers: Larry Washow/52/Dir., CEO, Pres./$1,885,646.00, Gary Morrison/VP - Amcol, Pres. - American Colloid Company/$539,921.00, Gary L. Castagna/Sr. VP, CFO/$774,174.00, Ryan F. McKendrick/VP - Amcol, Pres. - Cetco/$900,131.00

Directors: Larry Washow/52/Dir., CEO, Pres., John Hughes/63/Chmn., Audrey L. Weaver/52/Dir., Paul C. Weaver/Dir., Robert E. Driscoll/68/Dir., Dale E. Stahl/59/Dir., Jay D. Proops/65/Dir., Clarence O. Redman/64/Dir., Arthur Brown/65/Dir., Daniel P. Casey/64/Dir.

Owners: Lord, Abbett & Co. LLC/8.05%, Ryan F. McKendrick, Annamarie Weaver/11.60%, Clarence O. Redman, Lawrence E. Washow/2.30%, Harris Financial Corp./11.26%, Arthur Brown, Insiders/11.60%, Dale E. Stahl, Paul C. Weaver/1.30%, Leslie Weaver/14.90%, Gary L. Castagna, Jay D. Proops, Audrey L. Weaver/3.90%, Daniel P. Casey *(17 Owners included in Index)*

Financial Data: Fiscal Year End:12/31   Latest Annual Data: 12/31/2006

Year	Sales		Net Income
2006	$611,556,000		$50,248,000
2005	$535,924,000		$41,045,000
2004	$459,105,000		$31,565,000
Curr. Assets:	$251,684,000	Curr. Liab.:	$78,383,000	P/E Ratio: 14.41
Plant, Equip.:	$140,772,000	Total Liab.:	$216,130,000	Indic. Yr. Divd.: $0.640
Total Assets:	$511,224,000	Net Worth:	$294,818,000	Debt/ Equity: 0.5095

AmCOMP Inc

701 U.S. Hwy. One, North Palm Beach, FL, 33408; *PH:* 1-561-840-7171

General - Incorporation .... DE	Stock- Price on:12/24/2007 ....$10.01
Employees 498	Stock Exchange...NDQ
Auditor ....Deloitte& Touche LLP	Ticker Symbol...AMCP
Stk Agt..............Continental Stock Transfer & Trust Co	Outstanding Shares 15,770,000
Counsel..NA	E.P.S..$0.93
DUNS No. ....NA	Shareholders..NA

Business: The group operates through its subsidiaries whose principle activity is to provide workers' compensation insurance business. The groups services include insurance coverage and medical care. The groups product is guaranteed cost policy. The group operates from Florida, Wisconsin, Texas, Indiana, Tennessee, Georgia, Kentucky, Virginia and South Carolina. The quarterly revenue of the group for September 2007 was 62.96 millions of USD.

Primary SIC and add'l.: 6331

CIK No: 0001009667

Subsidiaries: AmComp Assurance Corporation, Amcomp Preferred Insurance Company, Amserv, Inc., Pinnacle Administrative Company, Pinnacle Benefits, Inc.

Officers: Lisa Perrizo/Pres. - Midwest Region/$172,938.00

Owners: Insiders/17.80%, Entities affiliated with Credit Suisse/10.70%, Entities affiliated with Diaco Investments, L.P./9.80%, Donald C. Stewart, Entities affiliated with TCW Group, Inc./5.30%, Spencer L. Cullen, Entities affiliated with Welsh Carson/8.70%, Paul B. Queally/8.70%, Timothy J. Spear, Frank Pinson, Entities affiliated with Wells Fargo & Company/9.90%, Debra Cerre-Ruedisili, Fred R. Lowe/1.70%, Lisa Perrizo, Colin Williams *(18 Owners included in Index)*

Financial Data: Fiscal Year End:12/31   Latest Annual Data: 12/31/2006

Year	Sales		Net Income
2006	$283,943,000		$16,562,000
2005	$267,301,000		$16,785,000
2004	$188,577,000		$5,030,000
Curr. Assets:	$205,139,000	Curr. Liab.:	$51,694,000	P/E Ratio: 10.76
Plant, Equip.:	$2,705,000	Total Liab.:	$545,209,000	Indic. Yr. Divd.: NA
Total Assets:	$684,497,000	Net Worth:	$139,288,000	Debt/ Equity: 0.2619

Amcon Distributing Co

7405 Irvington Rd., Omaha, NE, 68122; ***PH:*** 1-402-331-3727; ***Fax:*** 1-402-331-4834;
http:// www.amcon-dist.com; ***Email:*** corporate@amcon.com

General - Incorporation	DE	**Stock**- Price on:12/24/2007	$24.3
Employees	901	Stock Exchange	AMEX
Auditor	Mcgladrey & Pullen, LLP	Ticker Symbol	DIT
Stk Agt	Deloitte & Touche LLP	Outstanding Shares	NA
Counsel	NA	E.P.S	$1.72
DUNS No.	03-792-8660	Shareholders	NA

Business: The group's principal activities are the wholesale distribution of consumer products including tobacco, candy, groceries, natural food, beverages, health and beauty care products, confectionery and institutional food service products. The group distributes over 13,000 different consumer products to around 7,500 retail outlets. The products of the group are distributed primarily to retailers such as convenience stores, discount and general merchandise stores, grocery stores and supermarkets, health food stores, natural food stores, drug stores and gas stations. The group operates six distribution centers and thirteen retail health food stores in the great plains, rocky mountain, and southern regions of the United States. In 2003, the group acquired bahia company.

Primary SIC and add'l.: 5182 5087 5194 5149 5499 5145 2086

CIK No: 0000928465

Officers: Kathleen Evans/Pres., Andy Plummer/CFO, VP, Clem O'Donnell/VP - Sales, Dennis Herweyer/Regional VP - Sales, Rick Vance/VP - Marketing, Mark O'Brien/VP - Information Technology, John Job/Division Mgr. - Bismarck, Bill MacKinnon/District Sales Mgr. - Bismarck, Dan Johnson/Division Mgr. - Omaha, Wally Smolinski/Division Sales Mgr. - Omaha, Chuck Fosnaugh/Division Mgr. - Quincy, Doug Sperry/Division Sales Mgr. - Quincy, Bill Bailey/GM - Rapid City, Tim Nold/Division Sales Mgr. - Rapid City, Dave Clem/Regional VP - Springfield *(16 Officers included in Index)*

Owners: Timothy R. Pestotnik, Insiders, Kathleen M. Evans, Allen D. Petersen, Raymond F. Bentele, William F. Wright, Jeremy W. Hobbs, Stanley Mayer, Draupnir, LLC/ Draupnir Capital, LLC, Alexander Dawson Foundation, Eric J. Hinkefent, Insiders, Draupnir, LLC/ Draupnir Capital, LLC, Ane Patterson Shields, Christopher H. Atayan *(18 Owners included in Index)*

Financial Data: ***Fiscal Year End:***09/24 ***Latest Annual Data:*** 9/30/2006

Year	Sales	Net Income
2006	$839,540,000	-$1,111,000
2005	$845,923,000	-$12,742,000
2004	$821,766,000	-$4,139,000

Curr. Assets:	$61,255,000	***Curr. Liab.:***	$33,251,000	***P/E Ratio:***	9.27
Plant, Equip.:	$12,529,000	***Total Liab.:***	$96,614,000	***Indic. Yr. Divd.:***	NA
Total Assets:	$94,867,000	***Net Worth:***	-$1,747,000	***Debt/ Equity:***	NA

Amcor Ltd

6600 Valley View St., Buena Park, CA, 90620; ***PH:*** 1-714-562-6000; ***Fax:*** 1-714-562-6059;
http:// www.amcor.com.au

General - Incorporation	Australia	**Stock**- Price on:12/24/2007	NA
Employees	NA	Stock Exchange	OTC
Auditor	KPMG LLP	Ticker Symbol	AMCRY
Stk Agt	Morgan ADR Service Center	Outstanding Shares	NA
Counsel	NA	E.P.S	$0.51
DUNS No.	75-319-8399	Shareholders	NA

Business: The group' s principal activities are carried out through the following business segments: plastic, metal and fiber involves the manufacture of plastic, fibre and metal packaging. Pet (polyethylene terephthalate) is focused on providing packaging solutions to the consumer products industry. Distribution involves the manufacture and distribution of corrugated boxes, an assortment of packaging materials, shipping supplies and janitorial products, as well as custom corrugated with up to 5 color printing capabilities. Flexible packaging manufactures flexible packaging supplying the pharmaceutical and food and beverage markets and the distribution of corrugated and tobacco packaging such as closures, flexible packaging and paper sacks. Rentsch/closures produces metal lug closure for glass jars and bottles and metal and plastic vacuum seal closures. The group is also involved in the management of recycling of packaging paper mills.

Primary SIC and add'l.: 6726 7389 2673 3565 3411 3081 3497

CIK No: 0000869428

Subsidiaries: Amcor Europe, Amcor European Consolidated Holdings Limited, Amcor European Holdings Pty. Ltd., Amcor Flexibles A/S, Amcor Holding, Amcor Investments Pty. Ltd., Amcor Packaging (Australia) Pty. Ltd., Amcor Packaging (New Zealand) Ltd., Amcor Packaging (U.S.A.),Inc., Amcor Packaging Asia Pty. Ltd., Amcor Sunclipse North America,Inc.

Officers: Ken N. MacKenzie/44/Dir., MD, CEO, Eric Bloom/58/CEO - Amcor Sunclipse North America, Bill Long/51/CEO, Pres. - Amcor PET Packaging, John Murray/49/Exec. GM - Corporate Affairs, Steve Keogh/47/Exec. General Manage Human Resources, Ian Wilson/49/Strategic Development Dir., W. P. Day/57/Exec. GM - Finance, Ron Delia/36/Exec. GM - Operations Development, L. J. Lachal/MD - Amcor Australasia, Julie McPherson/Dir., Company Sec., Group General Counsel, Bill Chan/57/MD - Amcor Asia, Jerzy Czubak/48/MD - Amcor Rentsch, Amcor Flexibles Eastern Europe, Leslie Desjardins/Exec. GM - Finance, Greg Beatty/MD - Amcor Australasia, Chan Chew Keak/MD - Amcor Asia *(17 Officers included in Index)*

Directors: Ken N. MacKenzie/44/Dir., MD, CEO, Chris Roberts/Chmn., Julie McPherson/Dir., Company Sec., Group General Counsel, Ern Pope/Dir., John Pizzey/Dir., John Thorn/Dir., Geoff Tomlinson/Dir., Keith Barton/Dir.

Owners: I. G. Wilson, J. V. Murray, G. A. Tomlinson, W. P. Day, R. K. Barton, W. J. Long, C. K. Chan, E. J.J. Pope, G. S. James, D. C. K. Allen, E. E. Bloom, E. A. Alexander, C. I. Roberts, J. G. Thorn, G. J. Pizzey *(17 Owners included in Index)*

Financial Data: ***Fiscal Year End:***06/30 ***Latest Annual Data:*** 06/30/2006

Year	Sales	Net Income
2006	$8,061,691,000	$112,873,000
2005	$8,591,017,000	$156,743,000
2004	$7,303,995,000	$264,178,000

Curr. Assets:	$2,334,057,000	***Curr. Liab.:***	$2,613,101,000		
Plant, Equip.:	$3,029,185,000	***Total Liab.:***	$4,844,287,000	***Indic. Yr. Divd.:***	NA
Total Assets:	$7,802,725,000	***Net Worth:***	$2,958,438,000	***Debt/ Equity:***	NA

Amcore Financial Inc

501 7th St., Rockford, IL, 61104; ***PH:*** 1-815-968-2241; ***Fax:*** 1-815-961-7544;
http:// www.amcore.com

General - Incorporation	NV	**Stock**- Price on:12/24/2007	$29.53
Employees	1,545	Stock Exchange	NDQ
Auditor	KPMG LLP	Ticker Symbol	AMFI
Stk Agt	Wells Fargo Bank, N.A.	Outstanding Shares	23,090,000
Counsel	NA	E.P.S	$1.86
DUNS No.	10-237-1937	Shareholders	NA

Business: The group's principal activity is to provide personal banking, commercial banking and related financial services. Retail banking services to individuals include, demand, savings and time deposit accounts. Loan services include installment loans, mortgage loans, overdraft protection, personal credit lines and credit card programs. Financial services are provided to commercial, small business and governmental organizations. These services include lending, deposits, letters of credit and cash management services. As on 30-Sep-2003, the group operated 64 branches.

Primary SIC and add'l.: 6712 6021

CIK No: 0000714756

Subsidiaries: AFI Nevada, Inc, AMCORE Bank, N.A, AMCORE Capital Trust I, AMCORE Consumer Finance Company, Inc., AMCORE Investment Group, N.A, AMCORE Investment Services, Inc, AMCORE Real Properties, LLC, ARP Holdings, LLC, Property Exchange Company

Officers: Kenneth E. Edge/Chmn., CEO/$1,927,254.00, Eleanor F. Doar/Exec. VP, Chief Marketing Officer, Donald H. Wilson/COO, Pres./$600,416.00, Kay Rouzan/Contact - Shareholder Services, Patricia M. Bonavia/Exec. VP/$455,917.00, James S. Waddell/Exec. VP, Chief Administrative Officer, Sec./$655,034.00, Thomas R. Szmanda/Exec. VP, Chief Retail Officer, John R. Hecht/Exec. VP, Chief Commercial Officer/$554,259.00, Katherine Taylor/Investor Relations Contact, Russell Campbell/Exec. VP - Amcore Investment Group, Richard Stiles/Exec. VP - Commercial Banking Group, Nancy Moore/Sr. VP, Residential Production Mgr.

Directors: Kenneth E. Edge/Chmn., CEO, Paula A. Bauer/Dir., Gary L. Watson/Dir., John W. Gleeson/Dir., Steven S. Rogers/Dir., Frederick D. Hay/Dir., Jack D. Ward/Dir., William R. McManaman/Dir., Paul Donovan/Dir., John A. Halbrook/Dir., Teresa Iglesias-Solomon/Dir.

Owners: Teresa Iglesias-Solomon, Steven S. Rogers, Gary L. Watson, John R. Hecht/0.64%, Donald H. Wilson, Paula A. Bauer, Frederick D. Hay, William R. McManaman, James S. Waddell/0.73%, John W. Gleeson, Kenneth E. Edge/1.26%, John A. Halbrook, Patricia M. Bonavia, Paul Donovan, Jack D. Ward *(18 Owners included in Index)*

Financial Data: ***Fiscal Year End:***12/31 ***Latest Annual Data:*** 12/31/2006

Year	Sales	Net Income
2006	$414,765,000	$47,275,000
2005	$347,778,000	$44,941,000
2004	$304,364,000	$45,696,000

Curr. Assets:	$149,536,000	***Curr. Liab.:***	$4,482,929,000	***P/E Ratio:***	15.88
Plant, Equip.:	$92,808,000	***Total Liab.:***	$4,892,337,000	***Indic. Yr. Divd.:***	$0.740
Total Assets:	$5,292,383,000	***Net Worth:***	$400,046,000	***Debt/ Equity:***	NA

AMDL Inc

2492 Walnut Ave., Ste. 100, Tustin, CA, 92780; ***PH:*** 1-714-505-4460; ***Fax:*** 1-714-505-4464;
http:// www.amdl.com; ***Email:*** info@amdl.com

General - Incorporation	DE	**Stock**- Price on:12/24/2007	$3.77
Employees	305	Stock Exchange	AMEX
Auditor	Corbin & Co LLP	Ticker Symbol	ADL
Stk Agt	Corporate Stock Transfer, Inc.	Outstanding Shares	11,880,000
Counsel	NA	E.P.S	-$0.77
DUNS No.	60-367-9697	Shareholders	NA

Business: The group's principle activities include developing, manufacturing and marketing various immunodiagnostic kits for the detection of cancer and other diseases. The products of the company are used by hospital, clinical, research and forensic laboratories and doctors' offices to obtain precise and rapid identification of certain types of cancer and other diseases. The company has two primary kits: dr-70(R) and pylori-probe. Dr-70(R) testing kit is used for the detection of 13 different types of cancers including cancer of lung, stomach, breast, rectal, colon and liver. Pylori-probe is an in vitro diagnostic testing kit, which is used for the detection of helicobacter pylori, a bacterium that colonizes the mucus lining associated with gastric and peptic ulcers. The products are primarily marketed in Europe and Asia. The group operates from United States.

Primary SIC and add'l.: 8731 2835

CIK No: 0000838879

Officers: Gary L. Dreher/Dir., CEO, Pres./$1,170,786.00, Akio Ariura/CFO/$188,771.00, Andrea Small-Howard/Mgr. - Research, Development

Directors: Gary L. Dreher/Dir., CEO, Pres., William M. Thompson/Chmn., Douglas C. MacLellan/Dir., Edward R. Arquilla/Dir., Minghui Jia/Dir., Frank Zheng/Dir., Yuanda Xia/Dir.

Owners: William M. Thompson/1.60%, Fang Zheng/16.50%, Douglas C. MacLellan/2.20%, Edward R. Arquilla, Minghui Jia/16.50%, Insiders/25.60%, Akio Ariura, Jade Capital Group/9.90%, Gary L. Dreher/9.00%

Financial Data: ***Fiscal Year End:***12/31 ***Latest Annual Data:*** 12/31/2006

Year	Sales	Net Income
2006	$2,104,000	-$5,867,000
2005	$68,000	-$2,507,000
2004	$186,000	-$2,629,000

Curr. Assets:	$4,577,000	***Curr. Liab.:***	$4,971,000		
Plant, Equip.:	$9,130,000	***Total Liab.:***	$6,578,000	***Indic. Yr. Divd.:***	NA
Total Assets:	$19,241,000	***Net Worth:***	$12,663,000	***Debt/ Equity:***	0.1269

Amdocs Ltd

1390 Timberlake Manor Pkwy., Chesterfield, MO, 63017; ***PH:*** 1-314-212-7000;
Fax: 1-314-212-7500; ***http://*** www.amdocs.com; ***Email:*** learning@amdocs.com

General - Incorporation	UK	**Stock**- Price on:12/24/2007	$39.23
Employees	16,234	Stock Exchange	NYSE
Auditor	Ernst & Young LLP	Ticker Symbol	DOX
Stk Agt	American Stock Transfer & Trust Co.	Outstanding Shares	207,290,000
Counsel	Hale & Dorr LLP	E.P.S	$1.56
DUNS No.	23-091-1229	Shareholders	NA

Business: The group's principle activity is to provide information solutions to the communications and the Internet protocol industry worldwide. The group offers customer relationship management, order management, call rating, invoice calculation and preparation, bill formatting, fraud management, partner relationship management and directory publishing services to its customers. In addition, the group also provides directory sales and publishing systems to publishers of traditional printed yellow page and white page directories and electronic Internet directories. In addition, it supports companies that offer bundled

or convergent services and offers managed services, including system modernization and consolidation, management and operation of data centers and application support. The group operates in North America, Europe, the Middle East, Africa and the Asia-pacific region. The group's quarterly revenue for September 2007 was 726.69 millions of USD.

Primary SIC and add'l.: 7372 7373 7379
CIK No: 0001062579
Subsidiaries: carry forward operating losses
Officers: Thomas G. O'Brien/Treasurer, VP - Investor Relations, Darcy Hansen/Global Public Relations Mgr., Holly Rossetti/Global Public Relations Mgr., Susan MacCall/Analyst Relations Mgr., Philippa Tozer/Analyst Relations, Brian McManus/Analyst Relations Mgr., Dusya Broytman/Dir. - Corporate Communications, Anthony Piniella/Dir. - Communications, Analyst Relations Programs, Laliv Amrami/Global Public Relations Mgr., Normalinda Gonzalez/Global Public Relations Mgr.
Directors: Joseph Vardi/66/Dir., Adrian Gardner/46/Dir.
Owners: Insiders/2.80%, AT&T Inc./5.10%, Massachusetts Financial Services Company/5.50%, Thornburg Investment Management, Inc./5.30%, T. Rowe Price Associates, Inc./5.40%
Financial Data: Fiscal Year End:09/30 Latest Annual Data: 9/30/2006

Year	Sales	Net Income
2006	$2,480,050,000	$318,636,000
2005	$2,038,621,000	$288,636,000
2004	$1,773,732,000	$234,860,000

Curr. Assets:	$1,638,706,000	**Curr. Liab.:**	$1,031,687,000		
Plant, Equip.:	$220,290,000	**Total Liab.:**	$1,808,663,000	**Indic. Yr. Divd.:**	NA
Total Assets:	$3,962,828,000	**Net Worth:**	$2,154,165,000	**Debt/ Equity:**	NA

Amecs Inc

1 Yonge St., Ste. 1801, Toranto, ON, M5E1W7; **PH:** 1-416-879-4337

General - Incorporation	NV	Stock - Price on:12/24/2007	$2.25
Employees	NA	Stock Exchange	OTC
Auditor	Manning Elliott LLP	Ticker Symbol	AMEC
Stk Agt	Pacific Stock Transfer Company	Outstanding Shares	NA
Counsel	NA	E.P.S.	NA
DUNS No.	NA	Shareholders	NA

Business: The groups principal activity is to develop website, that will serve as an electronic market place for automotive dealerships. The groups services include supporting the market place and facilitating the trades, admission services and maintenance, complimentary services, data collection and data analyses. The group operates from the United States.

Primary SIC and add'l.: 5521
CIK No: 0001318820
Officers: Alexei Gavriline/44/Dir., CEO, Pres., Sec., Treasurer, CFO, Chief Accounting Officer
Directors: Alexei Gavriline/44/Dir., CEO, Pres., Sec., Treasurer, CFO, Chief Accounting Officer
Owners: Alexei Gavriline/83.20%
Financial Data: Fiscal Year End:12/31 Latest Annual Data: 12/31/2006

Year	Sales	Net Income
2006	NA	-$43,000

Curr. Assets:	$27,000	**Curr. Liab.:**	$1,000		
Plant, Equip.:	NA	**Total Liab.:**	$1,000	**Indic. Yr. Divd.:**	NA
Total Assets:	$27,000	**Net Worth:**	$26,000	**Debt/ Equity:**	NA

Amedia Networks Inc

2 Corbett Way, Eatontown, NJ, 07724; **PH:** 1-732-440-1992; **Fax:** 1-732-389-7541;
http:// www.amedianetworks.com; **Email:** info@amedia.com

General - Incorporation	DE	Stock - Price on:12/24/2007	NA
Employees	34	Stock Exchange	OTC
Auditor	Marcum & Kliegman LLP	Ticker Symbol	AANI
Stk Agt	American Stock Transfer & Trust Co.	Outstanding Shares	NA
Counsel	NA	E.P.S.	-$0.056
DUNS No.	01-439-3552	Shareholders	NA

Business: The group's principal activity is to seek new business alternatives through acquisition, development or investment in new lines of business. Effective 16-Jan-2004, the group entered into the development and licensing agreement. Pursuant to this agreement, lucent has agreed to develop for and license to the group, next-generation management and routing technologies and equipment. These are designed to provide fiber-to-the-premises capabilities for voice, video, data, and voice-over-Internet protocol services. On 28-May-2003, the group sold the existing copy protection business and ceased all its activities.

Primary SIC and add'l.: 7379 7372
CIK No: 0000933955
Subsidiaries: TTR Technologies, Ltd
Officers: Frank Galuppo/Dir., CEO, Pres./$351,998.00, James O'Connor/Officer - Product Management, Stuart Waldman/Officer - International Business Development, Alan Sheinwald/Contact - Investor Relations, Raj Varadarajan/Officer - Business Operations, J. D. Gardner/CFO - Principal Financial, Accounting Officer/$231,965.00, David Militello/VP - Sales, Contact - Product Inquires, John Colton/CTO/$215,731.00
Directors: Frank Galuppo/Dir., CEO, Pres., Juan Mendez/Chmn., Gerald Butters/Dir., Richard Rosenblum/Dir., Bob Martin/Dir., Duane Elmquist/Member - Advisory Board, William F. Lenahan/Member - Advisory Board, Terence Seese/Member - Advisory Board, Thomas M. Super/Member - Advisory Board, Sammy J. Thomas/Member - Advisory Board
Owners: James D. Gardner, Juan Mendez/6.47%, John R. Colton, Insiders/14.82%, Richard Rosenblum/1.21%, Gerald Butters, Bob Martin, Frank Galuppo/4.45%
Financial Data: Fiscal Year End:12/31 Latest Annual Data: 12/31/2006

Year	Sales	Net Income
2006	$33,000	-$18,655,000
2005	$6,000	-$9,215,000
2004	NA	-$5,682,000

Curr. Assets:	$878,000	**Curr. Liab.:**	$489,000		
Plant, Equip.:	$1,312,000	**Total Liab.:**	$6,006,600,000	**Indic. Yr. Divd.:**	NA
Total Assets:	$199,000	**Net Worth:**	$20,464,550,000	**Debt/ Equity:**	NA

Amedisys Inc

5959 S Sherwood Forest Blvd., Baton Rouge, LA, 70816; **PH:** 1-225-292-2031;
Fax: 1-225-292-8163; http:// www.amedisys.com; **Email:** info@amedisys.com

General - Incorporation	DE	Stock - Price on:12/24/2007	$35.98
Employees	5,232	Stock Exchange	NDQ
Auditor	KPMG LLP	Ticker Symbol	AMED
Stk Agt	American Stk Trnsfer Shareholder Srvs	Outstanding Shares	25,960,000
Counsel	Michael D. Lutgring	E.P.S.	$2.33
DUNS No.	80-850-6331	Shareholders	NA

Business: The group's principal activity is to provide home health care nursing services. The group operates 79 home care nursing offices and 2 corporate offices in the southern and southeastern United States. The group operates in 11 states including Louisiana, Tennessee, North Carolina, Georgia, Oklahoma, Alabama, Florida, Virginia, South Carolina, Arkansas and Texas.

Primary SIC and add'l.: 8051 8099
CIK No: 0000896262
Subsidiaries: Adventa Hospice of Louisiana, Adventa Hospice, Inc., A Florida Corporation, All Saints Home Care, an Amedisys Company, Alliance Home Health, Inc., An Oklahoma Corporation, Amedisys, Amedisys Arkansas, LLC, An Arkansas Limited Liability Company, Amedisys Customer Service Center, Amedisys Diabetic Supply, LLC, A Louisiana Limited Liability Company, Amedisys Equity Group, LLC, A Louisiana Limited Liability Company, Amedisys Georgia, LLC, A Georgia Limited Liability Company, Amedisys Gulf Coast, Amedisys Health Management, LLC, A Texas Limited Liability Company, Amedisys Holding, LLC, A Louisiana Limited Liability Company, Amedisys Home Care, Amedisys Home Health 156 Subsidiaries included in the Index
Officers: William Borne/Chmn., CEO, Dale E. Redman/CFO, Janet A. Britt/Sr. VP - Billing, Collections, Tom Dolan/Sr. VP - Finance, Edna Fannin/VP - Operations, Scott Ginn/Sr. VP - Accounting, Kevin Gunter/Sr. VP - Business Development, Arthur Hulbert/VP - Arnica Therapy Services, Judy T. Postle/VP - Arete Medical Services LLC, Alice Ann Schwartz/CIO/$392,381.00, Larry R. Graham/COO, Pres./$1,116,087.00, Jeffrey D. Jeter/Chief Compliance Officer, Corporate Counsel/$219,950.00, Patti Waller/Sr. VP - Operations, Alabama, Florida, Georgia, Cindy Phillips/Sr. VP - Human Resources, John R. Nugent/Chief Development Officer (21 Officers included in Index)
Directors: William Borne/Chmn., CEO, Jake L. Netterville/Dir., David R. Pitts/68/Dir., Ronald Laborde/Dir., Peter Ricchiuti/Dir., Donald A. Washburn/Dir.
Owners: Donald Loverich, Larry R. Graham, Peter F. Ricchiuti, Jeffrey D. Jeter, Gregory H. Browne, Ronald A. LaBorde, Dale E. Redman, Alice A. Schwartz, William F. Borne, Insiders/4.40%, Jake L. Netterville, Lord, Abbett & Co., LLC/13.40%, John F. Giblin, David R. Pitts, Donald A. Washburn
Financial Data: Fiscal Year End:12/31 Latest Annual Data: 12/31/2006

Year	Sales	Net Income
2006	$541,148,000	$38,255,000
2005	$381,558,000	$30,102,000
2004	$227,089,000	$20,504,000

Curr. Assets:	$179,205,000	**Curr. Liab.:**	$81,918,000	**P/E Ratio:**	17.55
Plant, Equip.:	$52,960,000	**Total Liab.:**	$99,749,000	**Indic. Yr. Divd.:**	NA
Total Assets:	$463,756,000	**Net Worth:**	$364,007,000	**Debt/ Equity:**	0.0219

Amegy Bank

4400 Post Oak Pk.way, Houston, TX, 77027; **PH:** 1-713-235-8800; http:// www.swbanktx.com

General - Incorporation	TX	Stock - Price on:12/24/2007	NA
Employees	NA	Stock Exchange	NDQ
Auditor	PricewaterhouseCoopers LLP	Ticker Symbol	ABNK
Stk Agt	Computershare Trust Co	Outstanding Shares	NA
Counsel	NA	E.P.S.	NA
DUNS No.	96-383-1599	Shareholders	NA

Business: The group's principal activities are to provide commercial and private banking services to small and middle market businesses and individuals. These services are provided through 44 full service banking facilities. The group provides commercial, industrial, real estate construction, land development and consumer loans. It also accepts demand, money market accounts, savings and time deposits. The group is a bank holding company operating through its subsidiaries, southwest bank of Texas national association and mitchell mortgage company. On 01-Jul-2003 the group acquired maxim financial holdings, inc and on 02-Feb-2004, acquired reunion bancshares, inc.

Primary SIC and add'l.: 6021 6712
CIK No: 0001027258
Subsidiaries: Amegy Bank National Association, Amegy Holding Delaware, Inc., Amegy Insurance Agency, Inc., Amegy Investments, Inc., Amegy Mortgage Company, LLC, Southwest/Catalyst Capital, Ltd., SWBT Statutory Trust I, SWBT Statutory Trust II, SWBT Statutory Trust III
Officers: Paul B. Murphy/Dir., CEO, Scott J. McLean/Dir., Pres. Amegy Bank NA
Directors: Paul B. Murphy/Dir., CEO, Walter E. Johnson/Chmn. - Bank, Dir. - Amegy Bank NA, Wilhelmina E. Robertson/Dir., Kirbyjon H. Caldwell/Dir., David J. Heaney/Dir., John W. Johnson/Dir., Manuel Urquidi/Dir., Timothy R. Brown/Dir., Carin M. Barth/Dir., Andres Palandjoglou/Dir., John B. Brock/Dir., Fred R. Lummis/Dir., Stanley D. Stearns/Dir., Mark A. Wallace/Dir., Christopher J. Pappas/Dir. (21 Directors included in Index)

Amen Properties Inc

303 W Wall St., Ste. 2300, Midland, TX, 79701; **PH:** 1-432-684-3821; **Fax:** 1-432-685-3143;
http:// amenproperties.com; **Email:** info@amenproperties.com

General - Incorporation	DE	Stock - Price on:12/24/2007	$6.13
Employees	1	Stock Exchange	NDQ
Auditor	Johnson Miller & Co	Ticker Symbol	AMEN
Stk Agt	American Stock Transfer & Trust Co.	Outstanding Shares	2,290,000
Counsel	NA	E.P.S.	$0.41
DUNS No.	88-335-9200	Shareholders	NA

Business: The group's principal activity was developing and operating webster for online christian community with comprehensive array of christian content assembled on the Internet. The content provided by the group was presented in the form of different online topical areas or channels. The group focused on entertainment, money, home schooling, news and culture, family living, women, travel, bible study,

book reviews and spiritual life. Currently the group provides leases to prospective tenants and in re-letting space to current tenants upon expiration of their respective leases. On 01-Jan-2004, the group acquired 6.5% of additional limited partnership interest in tctb and during the quarter ended 30-Jun-2004, the group acquired two separate royalty interests, one in the state of Texas and one in the state of Oklahoma.

Primary SIC and add'l.: 6519

CIK No: 0001037599

Subsidiaries: Amen Delaware, L.P., Amen Minerals, L.P., NEMA Properties, LLC, W Power and Light, L.P.

Officers: Jon M. Morgan/49/Dir., CEO, COO, Kevin Yung/45/COO, Pres. - W Power, Light/$218,589.00, Padraig Ennis/48/VP - Priority Power/$183,333.00, John Bick/41/Managing Principal - Priority Power/$141,495.00, Kris Oliver/42/CFO

Directors: Jon M. Morgan/49/Dir., CEO, COO, Eric L. Oliver/49/Chmn., Bruce E. Edgington/50/Dir., Donald M. Blake/52/Dir., Earl E. Gjelde/63/Dir., Randy G. Nicholson/70/Dir.

Owners: Steve Wike/5.29%, Frosty Gilliam, John Norwood/7.95%, Moriah Investment Partners/6.15%, Dodge Jones Foundation/9.14%, Frosty Gilliam/6.73%, McGraw Brothers Investments/6.15%, Dodge Jones Foundation, Jon Morgan/12.25%, Insiders/42.47%, Donald M. Blake/3.02%, Bruce Edgington/9.24%, Earl E. Gjelde/2.56%, Eric Oliver/14.68%, Moriah Investment Partners *(20 Owners included in Index)*

Financial Data: **Fiscal Year End:**12/04 **Latest Annual Data:** 12/31/2006

Year	Sales	Net Income
2006	$15,057,000	$2,161,000
2005	$10,181,000	-$705,000
2004	$2,462,000	$801,000

Curr. Assets:	$5,856,000	**Curr. Liab.:**	$1,717,000	**P/E Ratio:**	9.58
Plant, Equip.:	$146,000	**Total Liab.:**	$4,441,000	**Indic. Yr. Divd.:**	NA
Total Assets:	$13,099,000	**Net Worth:**	$8,635,000	**Debt/ Equity:**	0.2883

Amera Resources Corp

837 W Hastings St., Ste. 709, Vancouver, BC, V6C 3N6; ***PH:*** 1-604-687-1828; ***Fax:*** 1-604-687-1858; ***http://*** www.amerarescources.com; ***Email:*** info@amerarescources.com

General - Incorporation	BC	**Stock**- Price on:12/24/2007	$0.345
Employees	NA	Stock Exchange	OTC
Auditor	Ernst & Young LLP	Ticker Symbol	AJRSF
Stk Agt	Computershare Trust Co of Canada	Outstanding Shares	NA
Counsel	Salley Bowes Harwardt LLP	E.P.S	NA
DUNS No.	NA	Shareholders	NA

Business: The group's principal activity is gold exploration in the America's. The group is committed to growth and added shareholder value through gold and precious metal discoveries. The Company has key projects in Argentina, Peru, and Nevada and through the management's network of contacts in the resources sector new opportunities are constantly being evaluated. The group trades under the symbol AMS on the TSX Venture Exchange (TSX-V) in Canada and is managed by The Grosso Group.

Primary SIC and add'l.: 1400

CIK No: 0001303180

Subsidiaries: Amera Resources (US) Inc., Amera-Chile Sociedad Contractual Minera, Recursos de los Andes S.A.C.

Officers: Nikolaos Cacos/Dir., CEO, Pres., David A. Terry/VP - Exploration, Arthur Lang/CFO

Directors: Nikolaos Cacos/Dir., CEO, Pres., Joseph Grosso/Chmn., Jerry Minni/Dir., Robert Coltura/Dir., Gerald Carlson/Dir.

Owners: Robert Coltura, Jerry Minni, Insiders/15.80%, Nikolaos Cacos/6.40%, Arthur Lang, David A. Terry, Joseph Grosso/6.20%, Gerald Carlson

Financial Data: **Fiscal Year End:**12/31 **Latest Annual Data:** 12/31/2006

Year	Sales	Net Income
2006	NA	-$1,875,000

Curr. Assets:	$848,000	**Curr. Liab.:**	$100,000	**P/E Ratio:**	10.68
Plant, Equip.:	NA	**Total Liab.:**	$100,000	**Indic. Yr. Divd.:**	NA
Total Assets:	$854,000	**Net Worth:**	$753,000	**Debt/ Equity:**	NA

Ameralia Inc

20971 E Smoky Hill Rd., Centennial, CO, 80015; ***PH:*** 1-720-876-2373; ***http://*** www.naturalsoda.com

General - Incorporation	UT	**Stock**- Price on:12/24/2007	$0.33
Employees	NA	Stock Exchange	OTC
Auditor	HJ Assoc. & Consultants LLP	Ticker Symbol	AALA
Stk Agt	NA	Outstanding Shares	NA
Counsel	NA	E.P.S	NA
DUNS No.	NA	Shareholders	NA

Business: The group's principal activity is to establish chemical business for the manufacture of sodium bicarbonate and related products. The group is in its development stage. The products of the group are used in animal feed, industrial pharmaceutical and food grade markets. The production of sodium bicarbonate also enables the production of soda ash, caustic soda and other sodium chemicals commonly used in the manufacture of glass, detergents and a variety of inorganic and organic chemicals. Sodium bicarbonate is also used as an agent for flue gas desulfurization.

Primary SIC and add'l.: 1474

CIK No: 0000811419

Subsidiaries: Natural Soda, Inc.

Officers: Bill H. Gunn/65/Chmn., CEO, Pres., Robert C.J. Van/54/Dir., CFO, Exec. VP, Sec., Treasurer, Geoffrey C. Murphy/66/General Business Consultant

Directors: Bill H. Gunn/65/Chmn., CEO, Pres., Robert C.J. Van/54/Dir., CFO, Exec. VP, Sec., Treasurer, Neil E. Summerson/59/Dir., James V. Riley/Dir., Robert C. Woolard/71/Dir., Jeffrey J. Geldermann/57/Dir.

Owners: Robert van Mourik, Insiders, Geoffrey C. Murphy, James V. Riley, Jacqueline Badger Mars, as trustee, Sentient Global Resource Trust No. 1, Neil E. Summerson, Karen O. Woolard, Bill H. Gunn, Jeffrey J. Geldermann, Charles D. OKieffe, Robert C. Woolard

Financial Data: **Fiscal Year End:**06/30 **Latest Annual Data:** 6/30/2005

Year	Sales	Net Income
2005	$14,142,000	-$6,650,000
2004	$12,609,000	-$7,306,000
2002	NA	-$2,765,000

Curr. Assets:	$4,087,000	**Curr. Liab.:**	$27,504,000		
Plant, Equip.:	$20,761,000	**Total Liab.:**	$51,494,000	**Indic. Yr. Divd.:**	NA
Total Assets:	$35,949,000	**Net Worth:**	-$15,545,000	**Debt/ Equity:**	NA

Amerco

1325 Airmotive Way, Ste. 100, Reno, NV, 89502; ***PH:*** 1-775-688-6300; ***Fax:*** 1-775-688-6338; ***http://*** www.amerco.com; ***Email:*** investor_relations@amerco.com

General - Incorporation	NV	**Stock**- Price on:12/24/2007	$79.99
Employees	18,000	Stock Exchange	NDQ
Auditor	BDO Seidman, Semple & Cooper	Ticker Symbol	UHAL
Stk Agt	Mellon Investor Services LLC	Outstanding Shares	20,130,000
Counsel	NA	E.P.S	$2.65
DUNS No.	05-440-8745	Shareholders	NA

Business: The group's principle actiivty is to provide moving and storage and supplies products and services to help people move and stoe household and commercial goods. The group's products include U-Haul brand boxes, tape and other moving and self-storage products. The group operates from United States.

Primary SIC and add'l.: 7513 6531 6331 6311

CIK No: 0000004457

Subsidiaries: A&M Associates, Inc., Amerco Real Estate Company, Amerco Real Estate Company of Alabama, Inc., Amerco Real Estate Company of Texas, Inc, Amerco Real Estate Services, Inc., Arec 1, LLC, Arec 10, LLC, Arec 11, LLC, Arec 12, LLC, Arec 13, LLC, Arec 2, LLC, Arec 3, LLC, Arec 4, LLC, Arec 5, LLC, Arec 6, LLC 108 Subsidiaries included in the Index

Officers: Edward J. Shoen/59/Chmn., Pres., Principal Executive Officer, Ronald C. Frank/67/Exec. VP - U, Haul Field Operations, Mark V. Shoen/57/VP - U, Haul Business Consultants, Richard M. Amoroso/49/Resident, Republic Western Insurance Company, Jason A. Berg/35/Chief Accounting Officer, Principal Accounting Officer, Robert T. Peterson/57/Controller - U, Haul, Laurence J. Derespino/47/General Counsel, Gary B. Horton/64/Treasurer - Amerco, U, Haul, James P. Shoen/48/Dir., VP - U, Haul Business Consultants, Jennifer M. Settles/Sec., Robert R. Willson/57/Exec. VP - U, Haul Field Operations, John C. Taylor/50/Pres., Dir. - U, Haul, Rocky D. Wardrip/50/Assist. Treasurer - Amerco, U, Haul, Mark A. Haydukovich/51/Pres. - Oxford Life Insurance Company, Carlos Vizcarra/61/Pres. - Amerco Real Estate Company

Directors: Edward J. Shoen/59/Chmn., Pres., Principal Executive Officer, Charles J. Bayer/68/Dir., Frank M. Lyons/72/Dir., Daniel R. Mullen/67/Dir., John M. Dodds/71/Dir., Michael L. Gallagher/64/Dir., Samuel J. Shoen/Dir., Robert A. Dolan/Dir., John P. Brogan/64/Dir., James P. Shoen/48/Dir., VP - U, Haul Business Consultants

Owners: Adagio Trust Company, Rosemarie T. Donovan, Sophia M. Shoen, Atticus Capital, L.L.C., John C. Taylor, Jason A. Berg, Mark V. Shoen, Frank M. Lyons, Daniel R. Mullen, James P. Shoen, Insiders, The AMERCO Employee Stock Ownership Plan, Charles J. Bayer, Edward J. Shoen, John P. Brogan

Financial Data: **Fiscal Year End:**03/31 **Latest Annual Data:** 3/31/2006

Year	Sales	Net Income
2006	$2,106,626,000	$121,154,000
2005	$2,008,121,000	$89,424,000
2004	$2,167,495,000	-$2,852,000

Curr. Assets:	$506,351,000	**Curr. Liab.:**	$235,878,000		
Plant, Equip.:	$1,535,165,000	**Total Liab.:**	$2,671,614,000	**Indic. Yr. Divd.:**	NA
Total Assets:	$3,367,218,000	**Net Worth:**	$695,604,000	**Debt/ Equity:**	1.6469

Ameren Corp

1901 Chouteau Ave., St. Louis, MO, 63103; ***PH:*** 1-314-621-3222; ***Fax:*** 1-314-554-3801; ***http://*** www.ameren.com

General - Incorporation	MO	**Stock**- Price on:12/24/2007	$49.77
Employees	8,988	Stock Exchange	NYSE
Auditor	PricewaterhouseCoopers LLP	Ticker Symbol	AEE
Stk Agt	Ameren Common Stk & Union Electric Co	Outstanding Shares	207,020,000
Counsel	NA	E.P.S	$2.76
DUNS No.	36-413-8990	Shareholders	NA

Business: The groups principle activities include generating, transmitting and distributing of electricity and natural gas. The group operates from United States.

Primary SIC and add'l.: 4911 4923 6719

CIK No: 0001002910

Subsidiaries: AFS Development Company, LLC, Agricultural Research& Development Corp., Ameren Corporation, Ameren Development Company, Ameren Energy Communications, Inc., Ameren Energy Development Company, Ameren Energy Fuels and Services Company, Ameren Energy Generating Company, Ameren Energy Marketing Company, Ameren Energy Resources Company, Ameren Energy, Inc., Ameren ERC, Inc., Ameren Services Company, AmerenEnergy Medina Valley Cogen (No. 2) LLC, AmerenEnergy Medina Valley Cogen, (No. 4) LLC 72 Subsidiaries included in the Index

Officers: Gary L. Rainwater/62/Chmn., CEO, Pres./$3,244,392.00, Steven R. Sullivan/48/Sr. VP, General Counsel, Sec./$950,555.00, Jerre E. Birdsong/54/VP, Treasurer, Martin J. Lyons/42/VP, Controller, Warner L. Baxter/47/CFO, Exec. VP/$1,270,000.00, Thomas R. Voss/61/COO, Exec. VP/$1,196,690.00

Directors: Gary L. Rainwater/62/Chmn., CEO, Pres., Harvey Saligman/69/Dir., Gordon R. Lohman/73/Dir., Douglas R. Oberhelman/54/Dir., Susan S. Elliott/70/Dir., Gayle P.W. Jackson/61/Dir., James C. Johnson/55/Dir., Richard A. Liddy/72/Dir., Patrick T. Stokes/65/Dir., Stephen F. Brauer/62/Dir.

Owners: Douglas R. Oberhelman, Richard A. Lumpkin, Charles D. Naslund, Lord, Abbett & Co. LLC/5.40%, Insiders, Harvey Saligman, Warner L. Baxter, Richard A. Liddy, Capital Research and Management Company/5.90%, Susan S. Elliott, Jack D. Woodard, Franklin Resources, Inc./7.10%, Gary L. Rainwater, James C. Johnson, Steven R. Sullivan *(21 Owners included in Index)*

Financial Data: **Fiscal Year End:**12/31 **Latest Annual Data:** 06/30/2007

Year	Sales	Net Income
2007	NA	NA
2006	$6,880,000,000	$547,000,000
2005	$6,780,000,000	$606,000,000

Curr. Assets:	$1,874,000,000	**Curr. Liab.:**	$2,202,000,000	**P/E Ratio:**	17.10
Plant, Equip.:	$14,299,000,000	**Total Liab.:**	$12,766,000,000	**Indic. Yr. Divd.:**	$2.540
Total Assets:	$19,578,000,000	**Net Worth:**	$6,778,000,000	**Debt/ Equity:**	0.8168

Ameriana Bancorp

2118 Bundy Ave., New Castle, IN, 47362; *PH:* 1-765-529-2230; *Fax:* 1-765-529-2232; *http://* www.ameriana.com

General - Incorporation	IN	**Stock**- Price on:12/24/2007	$9.91
Employees	NA	Stock Exchange	NDQ
Auditor	BKD LLP	Ticker Symbol	ASBI
Stk Agt	Registrar & Transfer Co	Outstanding Shares	2,990,000
Counsel	Hayes, Copenhaver, Crider	E.P.S	-$0.4
DUNS No.	07-206-0569	Shareholders	NA

Business: The group's principal activities are to provide banking services and loan services through its subsidiaries. The group's banking services consist of attracting deposits from the general public and originating mortgage loans on single-family residences, and to a lesser extent on multi-family housing and commercial property. The loan services include home improvement loans and consumer loans and insurance and brokerage activities. The group also operates a trust department that provides trust, investment and estate planning services. The activities of the group are conducted through ten branch offices located in Indiana and Ohio. The subsidiaries of the group include ameriana bank and trust, sb, ameriana insurance agency, inc., ameriana financial services, inc., deer park service corporation, family financial life insurance company and Indiana title insurance company, llc.

Primary SIC and add'l.: 6712 6035

CIK No: 0000855574

Subsidiaries: Ameriana Bank and Trust, SB, Ameriana Financial Services, Inc., Ameriana Insurance Agency, Inc., Ameriana Investment Management, Inc, Family Financial Life Insurance Company, Indiana Title Insurance Company, LLC, Midwest Corporate Tax Credit Fund

Officers: Jerome J. Gassen/Dir., CEO, Pres./$286,933.00, Bradley L. Smith/CFO, Sr. VP, Treasurer/$135,031.00, Timothy G. Clark/COO, Exec. VP/$220,478.00, Nancy A. Rogers/Sr. VP - Marketing Services, Corp. Sec., James A. Freeman/Chief Lending Officer, Sr. VP/$117,842.00

Directors: Jerome J. Gassen/Dir., CEO, Pres., Michael E. Kent/Chmn., Ronald R. Pritzke/Vice Chmn., Charles M. Drackett/Dir., Scott R. Hayes/Dir., Donald Carroll Danielson/Dir., Richard E. Hennessey/Dir.

Owners: Insiders/10.54%, Scott R. Hayes/1.43%, Donald C. Danielson/3.23%, Timothy G. Clark/1.38%, Ronald R. Pritzke/1.28%, Charles M. Drackett/1.16%, Jerome J. Gassen, Michael E. Kent/1.39%, Jeffrey L. Gendell/8.23%

Financial Data: ***Fiscal Year End:***12/31 ***Latest Annual Data:*** 12/31/2006

Year	Sales	Net Income
2006	$26,401,000	-$970,000
2005	$23,897,000	$2,058,000
2004	$22,292,000	$1,426,000

Curr. Assets:	$12,070,000	**Curr. Liab.:**	$324,531,000		
Plant, Equip.:	$7,346,000	**Total Liab.:**	$404,122,000	**Indic. Yr. Divd.:**	NA
Total Assets:	$437,246,000	**Net Worth:**	$33,124,000	**Debt/ Equity:**	2.3655

America California Bank

2390 El Camino Real, Palo Alto, CA, 94306; *PH:* 1-650-858-1400; *Fax:* 1-650-424-8157; *http://* www.acbank.com

General - Incorporation		**Stock**- Price on:12/24/2007	$19.25
Employees	NA	Stock Exchange	OTC
Auditor	NA	Ticker Symbol	ACAL
Stk Agt	NA	Outstanding Shares	NA
Counsel	NA	E.P.S	NA
DUNS No.	NA	Shareholders	NA

Business: The groups principle activity is to provide lending services. The group also provides merchant card processing services. The groups services include capital lines, asset based lending, equipment loans, commercial and multi-family residential real estate lending. The group operates from United States.

Primary SIC and add'l.: 6022

CIK No:

Officers: Stuart O. Keirle/Dir., CEO, Pres.

Directors: Stuart O. Keirle/Dir., CEO, Pres., Charles Wang/Chmn., Elton See Tan/Chmn. Emeritus, Mostyn T. Lloyd/Dir., Victor J. Reizman/Dir., Shao-Yu Wang/Dir., Gerry Sy/Dir.

America First Apartment Investors Inc

1004 Farnam St., Ste. 100, Omaha, NE, 68102; *PH:* 1-402-557-6360; *http://* www.am1st.com

General - Incorporation	MD	**Stock**- Price on:12/24/2007	$22.12
Employees	NA	Stock Exchange	NDQ
Auditor	Deloitte & Touche LLP, KPMG LLP	Ticker Symbol	APRO
Stk Agt	Bank of New York	Outstanding Shares	11,050,000
Counsel	NA	E.P.S	-$0.07
DUNS No.	NA	Shareholders	NA

Business: The group's principal activities are carried on through following segments: multifamily apartment properties, commercial property and investment in agency securities. Through multifamily apartment properties and commercial property the group acquires, holds, operates and sells multifamily apartments and commercial properties. Through investment in agency securities, the group invests in mortgage-backed securities. The group merged with America first apartment investors, l.p. On 01-Jan-2003 and with America first real estate investment partners, l.p on 03-Jun-2004. The group is a real estate investment trust. As of 30-Jun-2004, the group owned 29 multifamily apartment complexes containing a total of 6,118 rental units and one commercial property.

Primary SIC and add'l.: 6798

CIK No: 0001175167

Subsidiaries: America First Fresno Apartment Investors, L.P. and Operating Company, America First PM Group, Inc., Apollo Associates GP, LLC, Apollo Associates, Ltd., Arbor Hills Investor LLC, Arbor Knoll-Crest, LLC, Arizona Coral Point Apartments Limited Partnership, Belvedere Apartments Limited Partnership, Belvedere GP, LLC, Bluff Ridge Associates Limited Partnership, Brentwood Oaks Apartments L.P., Brentwood Oaks Operating Company, Capital Source GP, LLC, Centrum Monticello Limited Partnership, Coral Point Apartments Operating Company 49 Subsidiaries included in the Index

Owners: Paul Beldin, Michael B. Yanney/4.70%, Steven W. Seline, Gregor Medinger, George Behringer, John H. Cassidy, George H. Krauss, George V. Janzen, James Egan, Insiders/7.10%, Lisa Y. Roskens/4.70%, John Schlegel

Financial Data: ***Fiscal Year End:***12/31 ***Latest Annual Data:*** 12/31/2006

Year	Sales	Net Income
2006	$49,357,000	$19,557,000
2005	$45,300,000	$10,952,000
2004	$36,301,000	-$2,765,000

Curr. Assets:	$15,115,000	**Curr. Liab.:**	$14,204,000		
Plant, Equip.:	$341,732,000	**Total Liab.:**	$279,093,000	**Indic. Yr. Divd.:**	$1.080
Total Assets:	$385,764,000	**Net Worth:**	$106,671,000	**Debt/ Equity:**	2.4440

America First Assoc Corp

160 E 56Th St., 6Th Fl., New York, NY, 10022; *PH:* 1-212-644-8520; *http://* www.aftrader.com

General - Incorporation	DE	**Stock**- Price on:12/24/2007	NA
Employees	NA	Stock Exchange	NA
Auditor	NA	Ticker Symbol	NA
Stk Agt	Stock Transfer & Trust Co	Outstanding Shares	NA
Counsel	NA	E.P.S	NA
DUNS No.	NA	Shareholders	NA

Business: The group's principal activity is to provide online brokerage services which targets savvy investors and small to mid-sized institutions such as money managers, mutual funds, and pensions. The company was founded as a traditional brokerage which now moved to online brokerage. In addition to stock trading, the full-service financial services company offers various IRAs, asset management, and investment banking services. Transactions are completed via phone or the company's web site, which allows clients access make trades, check accounts, review portfolios, conduct research, and even contact an advisor.

Primary SIC and add'l.: 6211

CIK No: 0001084203

America Movil

Lago Alberto 366, Edificio Telcel 2, Colonia Anahuac, 11320; *PH:* 52-57033990; *http://* www.americamovil.com

General - Incorporation	Mexico	**Stock**- Price on:12/24/2007	$62.85
Employees	34,650	Stock Exchange	NYSE
Auditor	Mancera, S.C	Ticker Symbol	AMX
Stk Agt	JP Morgan Chase Bank, N.A.	Outstanding Shares	1,800,000,000
Counsel	NA	E.P.S	$2.72
DUNS No.	NA	Shareholders	NA

Business: The group's principal activity is the provision of wireless communications services in Mexico through its subsidiary radiomovil dipsa sa de cv, which operates under the trademark 'telcel'. It has international telecommunications operations in Mexico, Guatemala, Ecuador, Brazil, Argentina, Colombia and United States.

Primary SIC and add'l.: 4899 4813

CIK No: 0001129137

Subsidiaries: AM Wireless Uruguay, S.A., Amrica Mvil Per, S.A.C., Americel S.A., AMX Paraguay, S.A., AMX Tenedora, S.A de C.V. ., BCP S.A., Compaa de Telecomunicaciones de El Salvador (CTE), Comunicacin Celular S.A. (Comcel)., Consorcio Ecuatoriano de Telecomunicaciones, S.A. (CONECEL)., CTI Compaa de Telfonos del Interior, S.A, CTI Holdings, S.A., Cti Pcs, S.a., Empresa Nicaragense de Telecomunicaciones, S.A., Radiomvil Dipsa, S.A. de C.V., Sercotel, S.A. de C.V. 23 Subsidiaries included in the Index

Officers: Daniel Hajj Aboumrad/42/Dir., CEO, Alejandro Cantu Jimenez/General Counsel, Rafael Robles Miaja/Corporate Pro Sec., Santiago De Olano/Investor Relations Officer, Carlos Cardenas Blasquez/Latin American Operations, Jose Elias Briones Capetillo/Administration, Finance, Daniela Lecuona Torras/Investor Relations Officer, Patricia Ramirez Valdivia/Mgr. - Corporate Communications, Public Relations, Adriana Arenas Vega/Investor Relations Officer, Carlos Jose Garcia Moreno Elizondo/CFO

Directors: Daniel Hajj Aboumrad/42/Dir., CEO, Patrick Slim Domit/39/Chmn., Carlos Bremer Gutierrez/48/Dir., Alejandro Soberon Kuri/48/Dir., Rayford Wilkins/57/Dir., David Ibarra Munoz/78/Dir., John Stephens/49/Dir., Jaime Chico Pardo/58/Dir., Maria Asuncion Aramburuzababa Larregui/45/Dir.

Owners: Inmobiliaria Carso/5.90%, Inmobiliaria Carso/5.90%, AT&T Inc./24.50%, Control Trust/46.50%

Financial Data: ***Fiscal Year End:***12/31 ***Latest Annual Data:*** 12/31/2006

Year	Sales	Net Income
2006	$21,735,760,000	$3,634,960,000
2005	$16,940,248,000	$2,940,489,000
2004	$11,962,000,000	$1,466,000,000

Curr. Assets:	$10,089,310,000	**Curr. Liab.:**	$11,293,096,000		
Plant, Equip.:	$13,993,717,000	**Total Liab.:**	$20,084,217,000	**Indic. Yr. Divd.:**	$2.230
Total Assets:	$31,256,767,000	**Net Worth:**	$11,172,550,000	**Debt/ Equity:**	NA

America Service Group Inc

105 W Pk. Dr., Ste. 200, Brentwood, TN, 37027; *PH:* 1-615-373-3100; *Fax:* 1-615-376-1350; *http://* www.asgr.com; *Email:* info@asgr.com

General - Incorporation	DE	**Stock**- Price on:12/24/2007	$16.76
Employees	5,030	Stock Exchange	NDQ
Auditor	Ernst & Young LLP	Ticker Symbol	ASGR
Stk Agt	Mellon Investor Services LLC	Outstanding Shares	9,550,000
Counsel	Bass, Berry & Sims PLC	E.P.S	NA
DUNS No.	62-487-7056	Shareholders	NA

Business: The group's principal activity is to provide managed healthcare services to correctional facilities and to military personnel. It makes contracts with state, county and local governmental agencies to provide comprehensive healthcare services to the inmates of prisons, county/municipal jails and detention centers. These services include the distribution of pharmaceuticals and certain medical supplies. The hospitalization and specialty outpatient care is performed through subcontract arrangements with independent doctors and local hospitals. The group also provides emergency medicine and primary healthcare services to active and retired military personnel and their dependents. These are offered in the medical facilities operated by the United States department of defense and the United States veterans administration. The correction department of riker's island in New York and the state of Pennsylvania are the major customers of the group.

Primary SIC and add'l.: 8099 8059

CIK No: 0000877476

Subsidiaries: America Service Group Inc., Correctional Health Services, LLC, EMSA Limited Partnership, Prison Health Services of Indiana, LLC, Prison Health Services, Inc., Secure Pharmacy Plus, LLC

Officers: Michael Catalano/Chmn., CEO, Pres./$1,520,321.00, Lawrence H. Pomeroy/Chief Development Officer, Sr. VP/$568,992.00, Scott T. Hoffman/Sr. VP, Chief Administrative Officer, Carl J. Keldie/Chief Medical Officer - Prison Health Services/$469,700.00, Michael W. Taylor/Sr. VP, CFO/$609,805.00, Richard Hallworth/COO/$374,693.00, Sam B. Devane/Accountant

Directors: Michael Catalano/Chmn., CEO, Pres., Richard D. Wright/Dir., William D. Eberle/Dir., Burton C. Einspruch/Dir., William M. Fenimore/Dir., John W. Gildea/Dir., William E. Hale/Dir., John C. McCauley/Dir.

Owners: Southern Sun Asset Management/18.80%, Carl J. Keldie, Healthinvest Partners AB/5.90%, William E. Hale, Epoch Investment Partners, Inc./6.80%, Lawrence H. Pomeroy/1.52%, Burton C. Einspruch, John C. McCauley, William D. Eberle/1.05%, Richard Hallworth, A group comprised of Wells Fargo & Company and Wells Fargo Capital Management, Inc/5.80%, William M. Fenimore, John W. Gildea, Richard D. Wright, A group comprised of Artisan Partners Limited Partnership,/11.50% (18 Owners included in Index)

Financial Data: Fiscal Year End:12/31 Latest Annual Data: 06/30/2007

Year	Sales	Net Income
2007	NA	NA
2006	NA	NA
2005	$562,676,000	$4,365,000

Curr. Assets:	$123,466,000	Curr. Liab.:	$117,095,000		
Plant, Equip.:	$6,800,000	Total Liab.:	$138,277,000	Indic. Yr. Divd.:	NA
Total Assets:	$184,731,000	Net Worth:	$46,454,000	Debt/ Equity:	NA

America West Holdings Corp

111 W Rio Salado Pk.way, Tempe, AZ, 85281; **PH:** 1-480-693-0800

General - Incorporation	DE	Stock - Price on:12/24/2007	NA
Employees	NA	Stock Exchange	NA
Auditor	PricewaterhouseCoopers LLP	Ticker Symbol	NA
Stk Agt	Computershare Investor Services LLC	Outstanding Shares	NA
Counsel	NA	E.P.S.	NA
DUNS No.	62-308-4696	Shareholders	NA

Business: The group's principal activity is to operate as a commercial airline carrier. The operations of the group are conducted through its principal hubs located in phoenix, Arizona, las vegas and columbus. The group operates and serves 62 destinations including 8 in Mexico, 3 in Canada and 1 in Costa Rica, with a fleet of 139 aircraft. The group also has a connecting service to additional 52 destinations through alliances with other airlines. The group sells the travel products directly to consumers and through retail travel agencies in the United States, Canada and Mexico.

Primary SIC and add'l.: 4512 4724 4522

CIK No: 0001029863

Subsidiaries: America West Airlines, Inc., AWHQ LLC, FTCHP LLC

America's Car- Mart Inc

802 SE Plz. Ave., Ste. 200, Bentonville, AR, 72712; **PH:** 1-479-464-9944; **Fax:** 1-479-273-7556; **http://** www.car-mart.com

General - Incorporation	TX	Stock - Price on:12/24/2007	$12.905
Employees	779	Stock Exchange	NDQ
Auditor	Grant Thornton LLP	Ticker Symbol	CRMT
Stk Agt.	Securities Transfer Corp	Outstanding Shares	11,850,000
Counsel	Smith, Gambrell & Russell	E.P.S.	NA
DUNS No.	13-117-0987	Shareholders	NA

Business: The group's principal activities are to sell and finance older model used vehicles to customers with limited credit histories. The subsidiaries of the group include America's car-Mart inc and colonial auto finance inc. At 30-Apr-2004, the group operated 70 stores located primarily in small cities throughout the south-central United States. The group provides financing for substantially all of its customers, many of whom may not qualify for conventional financing as a result of limited credit histories or past credit problems.

Primary SIC and add'l.: 6162 5521 7359 6719

CIK No: 0000799850

Subsidiaries: Americas Car-Mart, Inc., Auto Finance Investors, Inc., Colonial Auto Finance, Inc., Colonial Underwriting, Inc., Crown Delaware Investments Corp., Crown Group of Nevada, Inc., Texas Car-Mart, Inc.

Officers: Tilman J. Falgout/Chmn., CEO, General Counsel/$476,227.00, William H. Henderson/Vice Chmn., Pres./$408,032.00, Eddie L. Hight/COO/$267,611.00, Carl E. Baggett/Advisory Dir., Jeffrey A. Williams/CFO/$280,487.00

Directors: Tilman J. Falgout/Chmn., CEO, General Counsel, William H. Henderson/Vice Chmn., Pres., William M. Sams/Dir., John David Simmons/Dir., William A. Swanston/Dir., Daniel Englander/Dir.

Owners: Jeffrey A. Williams, Eddie L. Hight, John David Simmons, F&C Asset Management plc/5.60%, William M. Sams/4.90%, Royce & Associates, LLC/6.00%, William H. Henderson/1.00%, William A. Swanston, Skystone Advisors LLC/5.80%, Insiders/16.80%, Tilman J. Falgout/8.50%, Daniel J. Englander/1.50%, Wasatch Advisors, Inc./10.00%

Financial Data: Fiscal Year End:04/30 Latest Annual Data: 04/30/2007

Year	Sales	Net Income
2007	$240,334,000	$4,232,000
2006	$234,207,000	$16,705,000
2005	$204,788,000	$17,976,000

Curr. Assets:	$11,996,000	Curr. Liab.:	$13,685,000		
Plant, Equip.:	$15,436,000	Total Liab.:	$58,362,000	Indic. Yr. Divd.:	NA
Total Assets:	$177,613,000	Net Worth:	$119,251,000	Debt/ Equity:	NA

American Access Technologies Inc

6670 Spring Lake Rd., Keystone Heights, FL, 32656; **PH:** 1-352-473-6673; **http://** www.aatk.com

General - Incorporation	FL	Stock - Price on:12/24/2007	NA
Employees	100	Stock Exchange	NDQ
Auditor	Tedder, James, Worden & Assoc. P.A	Ticker Symbol	AATK
Stk Agt	Florida Atlantic Stock Transfer, Inc.	Outstanding Shares	NA
Counsel	NA	E.P.S.	NA
DUNS No.	NA	Shareholders	NA

Business: The group's principal activities are to develop, manufacture and market zone cabling enclosures for the telecommunication industry. The group's operations are conducted through two business segments: formed metal products and zone cabling products. The group's products enable businesses and government entities to move, add to, and change copper and fiber optic cabling to keep pace with changes in high-speed communications networks. The group provides its solutions to open office architecture, routing high speed cabling, copper wiring and wireless solutions into and through office buildings, hospitals, convention centers, schools, hotels, entertainment and theme parks, government buildings, and industrial complexes.

Primary SIC and add'l.: 3661

CIK No: 0001043186

Subsidiaries: Zonecabling.com, Inc

Officers: Arthur G. Dauber/CEO, Pres., Jason Beasley/VP - Sheet Metal Sales, John H. Untereker/Sr. VP, CFO, Sec., Principal Financial Officer, Erik W. Wiisanen/63/VP - Sales, Omega Metals Division/$140,000.00, Tim Adams/56/COO, Sr. VP/$115,601.00, Bill Wiisanen/GM, Chief Engineer, Renee Perrotta/Materials Mgr.

Directors: Howard W. Kelley/65/Chmn., Ken Cornell/39/Dir., Clark Schaffer/50/Dir., Lamar Nash/61/Dir.

Owners: James J. Steffek/11.70%, Paul N. Katz, Howard W. Kelley, Stuart Schube/4.20%, Erik Wiisanen/2.10%, Timothy C. Adams, Insiders/67.50%, Arthur G. Dauber/31.10%, Lamar Nash, Joseph F. McGuire/2.10%, Hoke J. Peacock/5.60%

American Airlines Inc

4333 Amon Carter Blvd, Ft Worth, TX, 76155; **PH:** 1-817-963-1234; **http://** www.americanair.com

General - Incorporation	DE	Stock - Price on:12/24/2007	NA
Employees	NA	Stock Exchange	NA
Auditor	Ernst & Young LLP	Ticker Symbol	NA
Stk Agt	American Stock Transfer & Trust Co.	Outstanding Shares	NA
Counsel	NA	E.P.S.	NA
DUNS No.	00-697-9801	Shareholders	NA

Business: The group's principle activity is to provide scheduled passenger, freight and mail services. The company is a wholly owned subsidiary of amr corporation. The company operates five hubs namely, Dallas/fort worth, Chicago o'hare, miami, st. Louis and san juan, Puerto Rico. The company provides transportation services across 150 destinations throughout North America, the Caribbean, Latin America, Europe and the pacific. The group operates from United States.

Primary SIC and add'l.: 4512 4513

CIK No: 0000004515

Subsidiaries: AMR Corporation, AMR, American Eagle Airlines, Inc., Executive Airlines, Inc, Trans World Airlines, Inc.

Officers: Gerard J. Arpey/Chmn., CEO, Pres. - American Airlines, Daniel P. Garton/Exec. VP - Marketing, American Airlines, David C. Cush/Sr. VP - Global Sales, American Airlines, Thomas W. Horton/CFO, Exec. VP - Finance - American Airlines, Monte E. Ford/Sr. VP - Information Technology, CIO - American Airlines, Jeffrey J. Brundage/Sr. VP - Human Resources, American Airlines, Kenji Hashimoto/MD - Investor Relations, Janice Feltus/Assist. - Investor Relations, Kurt Stache/Pres. - Aadvantage Marketing Programs, Carolyn E. Wright/VP - Corporate Human Resources, David R. Brooks/Pres. - American Airlines Cargo Division, Tom R. Del Valle/Sr. VP - Airport Services, Timothy J. Ahern/VP - Airport Services, Mark Burdette/VP - Employee Relations, Robert C. Cordes/VP - Operations Planning, Performance (41 Officers included in Index)

Directors: Gerard J. Arpey/Chmn., CEO, Pres. - American Airlines, Armando M. Codina/Dir., Ann M. Korologos/Dir., Philip J. Purcell/Dir., Matthew K. Rose/Dir., John W. Bachmann/Dir., David L. Boren/Dir., Roger T. Staubach/Dir., Earl G. Graves/Dir., Michael A. Miles/Dir., Ray M. Robinson/Dir., Judith Rodin/Dir.

American Ammunition Inc FL

Formerly: American Ammunition Inc CA
3545 Nw 71st St., Miami, FL, 33147; **PH:** 1-305-835-7400; **http://** www.a-merc.com

General - Incorporation	CA	Stock - Price on:12/24/2007	$0.23
Employees	45	Stock Exchange	OTC
Auditor	S. W. Hatfield, CPA	Ticker Symbol	AAMU
Stk Agt	Atlas Stock Transfer Corp	Outstanding Shares	23,290,000
Counsel	NA	E.P.S.	-$0.58
DUNS No.	NA	Shareholders	NA

Business: The group's principle activities are to manufacture and sell small arms ammunition for retail and wholesale. The products manufactured include 9mm, .45auto, .380auto, .32auto, .40s&w, 38spl, 30carbine and .223 rem. The group is an approved department of defence contractor.the group's international sales is solely to foreign governments, principley for military use.

Primary SIC and add'l.: 3482

CIK No: 0001123648

Subsidiaries: F&F Equipment, Inc, Industrial Plating Enterprise Co.

Owners: Maria A. Fernandez/0.00%, Insiders/0.04%, J. A. Fernandez, Emilio D. Jara, National Business Investors/8.40%, Capital Investment Services/76.80%, Andres F. Fernandez/0.01%

Financial Data: Fiscal Year End:12/31 Latest Annual Data: 12/31/2006

Year	Sales	Net Income
2006	$2,241,000	-$8,100,000
2005	$3,244,000	-$5,942,000
2004	$3,247,000	-$3,318,000

Curr. Assets:	$2,175,000	Curr. Liab.:	$1,490,000		
Plant, Equip.:	NA	Total Liab.:	$2,838,000	Indic. Yr. Divd.:	NA
Total Assets:	$2,415,000	Net Worth:	-$424,000	Debt/ Equity:	NA

American Asset Mgmt Corp

1280 Rte. 46 W, Parsippany, NJ, 07054; **PH:** 1-973-299-8713; **http://** www.hsh.com

General - Incorporation	NJ	**Stock**- Price on:12/24/2007	$0.12
Employees	NA	Stock Exchange	OTC
Auditor	WithumSmith & Brown, P.C	Ticker Symbol	AAMC
Stk Agt	Continental Stock Transfer & Trust Co	Outstanding Shares	NA
Counsel	NA	E.P.S	NA
DUNS No.	60-517-9605	Shareholders	NA

Business: The group's principal activity is to provide mortgage-banking activities. The mortgage banking activities of the group includes origination and sale of residential first mortgage loans collateralized by one to four family homes. The group's other activities include obtaining final subdivision approval, complete physical improvements to the property and sell the subdivided lots. The group solely operates in the United States of America.

Primary SIC and add'l.: 6162 6719 6552

CIK No: 0000852015

Subsidiaries: Capital Financial Corp.

Financial Data: *Fiscal Year End:*12/31 *Latest Annual Data:* 12/31/2004

Year	Sales	Net Income
2004	$359,000	-$423,000
2003	$2,350,000	-$75,000
2002	$1,665,000	-$103,000

Curr. Assets:	$677,000	**Curr. Liab.:**	$940,000		
Plant, Equip.:	$5,000	**Total Liab.:**	$940,000	**Indic. Yr. Divd.:**	NA
Total Assets:	$739,000	**Net Worth:**	-$200,000	**Debt/ Equity:**	NA

American Axle & Manufacturing Hldgs Inc

1 Dauch Dr., Detroit, MI, 48211; *PH:* 1-313-758-2000; *Fax:* 1-313-758-4257; *http://* www.aam.com; *Email:* salesmarketing@aam.com

General - Incorporation	DE	**Stock**- Price on:12/24/2007	$29.79
Employees	10,000	Stock Exchange	NYSE
Auditor	Deloitte & Touche LLP	Ticker Symbol	AXL
Stk Agt	Computershare Investor Services LLC	Outstanding Shares	53,010,000
Counsel	Simpson Thacher & Bartlett LLP	E.P.S	-$2.48
DUNS No.	NA	Shareholders	NA

Business: The groups principle activities include manufacturing, engineering, design and validation of driveline and drive train systems and related components and chassis modules for light trucks, sport utility vehicles (SUVs), passenger cars and crossover vehicles. The group operates from United States.

Primary SIC and add'l.: 3714

CIK No: 0001062231

Subsidiaries: AAM Comrcio e Participaes Ltda., AAM do Brasil Ltda., AAM Europe GmbH, AAM International Holdings, Inc., AAM Poland sp z.o.o., AAM Services India Private Limited, Albion Automotive (Holdings) Limited, Albion Automotive Limited, American Axle & Manufacturing de Mexico Holdings S. de R.L. de C.V., American Axle & Manufacturing de Mexico S.A. de C.V., American Axle & Manufacturing Holdings, Inc., American Axle & Manufacturing Korea, Inc., American Axle & Manufacturing, Inc., Colfor Manufacturing Inc., Guanajuato Gear & Axle de Mexico S. de R.L. de C.V. 17 Subsidiaries included in the Index

Officers: Richard E. Dauch/Chmn., CEO, Co - Founder/$9,329,628.00, Steven J. Proctor/VP - Sales, Marketing, Patrick J. Spohn/48/VP, Controller, Renee Rogers/Mgr. - Corporate Communications, Media Relations, John E. Jerge/VP - Human Resources, Michael C. Flynn/VP - Procurement, Abdallah F. Shanti/VP - Information Technology, Electronic Product Integration, CIO, Michael K. Simonte/CFO, VP - Finance/$478,982.00, David C. Dauch/43/Exec. VP - Commercial, Strategic Development/$594,977.00, John S. Sofia/VP - Engineering, Product Development, Alberto L. Satine/VP - Strategic, Business Development, John J. Bellanti/53/VP - Manufacturing Services, Capital Planning, Cost Estimating, Patrick S. Lancaster/VP, Chief Administrative Officer, Sec., Thomas O. Delanoy/VP - Special Projects, Marion A. Cumo/65/VP - Special Projects/$711,086.00 *(17 Officers included in Index)*

Directors: Richard E. Dauch/Chmn., CEO, Co - Founder, John A. Casesa/Dir., Larry K. Switzer/Dir., Beth A. Chappell/Dir., Forest J. Farmer/67/Dir., Richard C. Lappin/Dir., William P. Miller/Dir., Thomas K. Walker/67/Dir., Henry T. Yang/Dir., Elizabeth A. Chappell/50/Dir.

Owners: Capital Research and Management Company/5.50%, FMR Corp./14.30%, Richard E. Dauch/8.70%, Wellington Management Company, LLP/10.18%, B.G. Mathis, Henry T. Yang, Larry K. Switzer, Forest J. Farmer, Richard C. Lappin, Barrow, Hanley, Mewhinney& Strauss, Inc/5.46%, Michael K. Simonte, Insiders/12.50%, Yogendra N. Rahangdale, Thomas K. Walker, Elizabeth A. Chappell *(21 Owners included in Index)*

Financial Data: *Fiscal Year End:*12/31 *Latest Annual Data:* 12/31/2006

Year	Sales	Net Income
2006	$3,191,700,000	-$222,500,000
2005	$3,387,300,000	$56,000,000
2004	$3,599,600,000	$159,500,000

Curr. Assets:	$639,400,000	**Curr. Liab.:**	$541,300,000		
Plant, Equip.:	$1,731,700,000	**Total Liab.:**	$1,783,800,000	**Indic. Yr. Divd.:**	$0.600
Total Assets:	$2,597,500,000	**Net Worth:**	$813,700,000	**Debt/ Equity:**	1.0268

American Bancorp of New Jersey Inc

365 Broad St., Bloomfield, NJ, 07003; *PH:* 1-973-748-3600; *Fax:* 1-973-748-2047; *http://* www.americansavingsnj.com

General - Incorporation	NJ	**Stock**- Price on:12/24/2007	$10.4
Employees	64	Stock Exchange	NDQ
Auditor	Crowe, Chizek and Company LLC	Ticker Symbol	ABNJ
Stk Agt	Registrar & Transfer Co	Outstanding Shares	12,750,000
Counsel	NA	E.P.S	$0.10
DUNS No.	NA	Shareholders	NA

Business: The groups principal activity is to provide banking services. The groups services include retail banking services, residential mortgage loans, home equity loans and lines of credit and business and consumer loans. The group operates from Bloomfield, Cedar Grove and Verona.

Primary SIC and add'l.: 6712 6035

CIK No: 0001330039

Subsidiaries: American Savings Investment Corp., ASB Investment Corp

Officers: Joseph Kliminski/Dir., CEO, Richard M. Bzdek/Sr. VP, Sec., Fred G. Kowal/Dir., COO, Pres., Eric B. Heyer/Sr. VP, CFO

Directors: Joseph Kliminski/Dir., CEO, George W. Parker/Chmn., James H. Ward/Vice Chmn., Joseph H. North/Dir., Vincent S. Rospond/Dir., Robert A. Gaccione/Dir., Fred G. Kowal/Dir., COO, Pres.

Owners: James W. Ward/1.89%, Vincent S. Rospond/1.46%, Richard M. Bzdek/1.51%, Fred G. Kowal/0.94%, Joseph Kliminski/2.71%, Catherine M. Bringuier/0.90%, Stanley Obal/0.56%, Insiders/13.74%, W. George Parker/1.87%, Eric B. Heyer/1.00%, Wellington Management Company, LLP/6.33%, American Bank of New Jersey Bank Employee Stock/8.64%, H. Joseph North/0.39%

Financial Data: *Fiscal Year End:*09/30 *Latest Annual Data:* 9/30/2006

Year	Sales	Net Income
2006	$26,636,000	$2,133,000
2005	$21,813,000	$2,043,000
2004	$19,502,000	$2,162,000

Curr. Assets:	$9,144,000	**Curr. Liab.:**	$330,917,000	**P/E Ratio:**	104.00
Plant, Equip.:	$6,523,000	**Total Liab.:**	$389,458,000	**Indic. Yr. Divd.:**	$0.160
Total Assets:	$514,319,000	**Net Worth:**	$124,861,000	**Debt/ Equity:**	NA

American Bank Inc

5120 S Padre Island Dr., Corpus Christi, TX, 78411; *PH:* 1-361-992-9905; *Fax:* 1-361-985-6528; *http://* www.americanbank.com

General - Incorporation	PA	**Stock**- Price on:12/24/2007	$8.27
Employees	46	Stock Exchange	OTC
Auditor	S. R. Snodgrass, A.C.	Ticker Symbol	AMBK
Stk Agt	StockTrans, Inc.	Outstanding Shares	6,000,000
Counsel	NA	E.P.S	$0.63
DUNS No.	NA	Shareholders	NA

Business: The group's principal activities are to accept deposits from the general public and to originate loans. The group offers deposit and loan products for consumer, business, institutional and governmental customers, including interest-bearing checking and money market accounts, savings accounts, certificates of deposit and individual retirement accounts. The group's lending activities include commercial mortgage loans, commercial business loans, commercial construction loans and consumer loans, including home equity, home equity lines of credit and conventional first mortgage loans secured by one- to four-family properties. On 29-Jul-2004, the group acquired Americana national bank.

Primary SIC and add'l.: 6712 6021

CIK No: 0001163747

Subsidiaries: state-chartered bank

Officers: Al Jones/Chmn., CEO, Pres. - American Bank, Mark W. Jaindl/48/Chmn., CEO, Pres., Sandra A. Berg/51/Sec., COO, Sr. VP, Chris J. Persichetti/45/Chief Lending Officer, Sr. VP, Robert W. Turner/46/CIO, Sr. VP, Peggy Spooner/Sr. Mortgage Lending Officer - Rockport, Pat Brandenburg/Austin Area Pres. - Austin Westlake, Branch, Lisa Killough/Sr. Lending Officer - Austin Westlake, Branch, Jeff Brinkley/Sr. Lending Officer - Lakeway, Branch, Harry C. Birkhimer/59/Treasurer, Sr. VP, CFO, Jim Pickett/Sr. Lending Officer - South, James Bain/Investment Representative - American Investment Services, Mack Ray/Branch Executive Officer, Sr. Lending Officer - Uptown, Corpus Christi, Branch, Charles Brett/Sr. Lending Officer - Uptown, Corpus Christi, Branch, Kim Czajkowski/Branch Operations Officer - Rockport *(65 Officers included in Index)*

Directors: Al Jones/Chmn., CEO, Pres. - American Bank, Mark W. Jaindl/48/Chmn., CEO, Pres., George Hawn/Chmn. Emeritus, Ben Wallace/Vice Chmn., Frank Adams/Member - Advisory Board, Kathleen White/Member - Advisory Board, C. C. Winn/Member - Advisory Board, Christina Hawn/Dir., Phillip S. Schwartz/62/Dir., Martin F. Spiro/74/Dir., Donald J. Whiting/48/Dir., John F. Eureyecko/53/Dir., John W. Galuchie/55/Dir., Karen O'Connor Urban/Member - Advisory Board, Michael S. Pedrotti/Member - Advisory Board *(52 Directors included in Index)*

Owners: Mark W. Jaindl/57.86%, Robert W. Turner/0.01%, Phillip S. Schwartz/4.63%, Chris J. Persichetti/0.04%, Insiders/71.73%, John F. Eureyecko/0.36%, John W. Galuchie/0.21%, Martin F. Spiro/7.41%, Michael D. Molewski/0.20%, Harry C. Birkhimer/0.14%, Sandra A. Berg/0.02%, Donald J. Whiting/0.86%

Financial Data: *Fiscal Year End:*12/31 *Latest Annual Data:* 03/31/2007

Year	Sales	Net Income
2007	NA	NA
2006	NA	NA
2005	$25,836,000	$3,532,000

Curr. Assets:	$6,053,000	**Curr. Liab.:**	$397,482,000	**P/E Ratio:**	18.38
Plant, Equip.:	$893,000	**Total Liab.:**	$470,376,000	**Indic. Yr. Divd.:**	$0.200
Total Assets:	$504,595,000	**Net Worth:**	$34,219,000	**Debt/ Equity:**	2.0879

American Bank Note Holographics Inc

2 Applegate Dr., Robbinsville, NJ, 08691; *PH:* 1-609-632-0800; *Fax:* 1-609-632-0850; *http://* www.abnh.com; *Email:* abnh@abnh.com

General - Incorporation	DE	**Stock**- Price on:12/24/2007	$3.55
Employees	111	Stock Exchange	OTC
Auditor	PricewaterhouseCoopers LLP	Ticker Symbol	ABHH
Stk Agt	American Stock Transfer & Trust Co.	Outstanding Shares	19,110,000
Counsel	Fulbright & Jaworski LLP	E.P.S	$0.26
DUNS No.	02-468-2635	Shareholders	NA

Business: The group's principle activities include originating, producing and marketing holograms. The holograms produced by the company are used primarily for security applications such as counterfeiting protection for credit and authentication of transaction cards, identification cards and documents of value and consumer products. The company also produces non-secure holograms for packaging and promotional applications. The products are used by over 150 companies worldwide including master card, visa, American express, discover, diners club, quaker state and eli lilly as well as agencies of the United States government and certain foreign governments. The group operates from United States.

Primary SIC and add'l.: 2759

CIK No: 0001052489

Officers: Kenneth H. Traub/CEO, Pres./$806,386.00, Mark J. Bonney/CFO, Exec. VP/$635,578.00, William C. Morwald/VP - Quality, Product Management, Michael T. Banahan/VP - Sales, George Condos/VP, Controller, Adam L.A. Scheer/VP - Corporate Development, Marketing, Ron G. McClenny/VP - Operations, John Hynes/CTO, VP

Directors: Salvatore F. D'Amato/Chmn.

Owners: Crane & Co., Inc./17.90%, VN Capital Fund I, L.P./6.10%, Fred J. Levin, Libra Advisors, LLC/11.40%, SEP IRA F/B/O Norman H. Pessin/7.20%, Jordan S. Davis, Michael J. Harkins/9.00%, Kenneth H. Traub/5.40%, Salvatore F. DAmato/2.00%, Insiders/9.00%, Mark J. Bonney/1.10%, Eric Haskell, Randall C. Bassett, Richard L. Robbins

Financial Data: Fiscal Year End: 12/31   **Latest Annual Data:** 06/30/2007

Year	Sales	Net Income
2007	$7,936,000	$1,207,000
2006	$32,532,000	$3,595,000
2005	$32,319,000	-$581,000

Curr. Assets:	$24,809,000	**Curr. Liab.:**	$5,687,000	**P/E Ratio:**	19.72
Plant, Equip.:	$6,098,000	**Total Liab.:**	$6,839,000	**Indic. Yr. Divd.:**	NA
Total Assets	$30,968,000	**Net Worth:**	$24,129,000	**Debt/ Equity:**	NA

American Basketball Association Inc

Formerly: Souvallpage & Co Inc
9421 Holliday Dr., Inidanapolis, IN, 46260; **PH:** 1-407-540-0452

General	- Incorporation	UT	Stock	- Price on:12/24/2007	NA
Employees		NA	Stock Exchange		NA
Auditor	Child, Van Wagoner & Bradshaw, PLLC		Ticker Symbol		NA
Stk Agt		NA	Outstanding Shares		NA
Counsel		NA	E.P.S.		NA
DUNS No.		NA	Shareholders		NA

Business: The group's principal activity is of manufacturing, selling and distributing wood burning stoves, and any related business.

Primary SIC and add'l.: 6770

CIK No: 0001332044

Officers: Joseph F. Newman/71/Chmn., CEO/$250,000.00, Darren Cioffi/42/CFO, Controller, Richard Tinkham/75/Dir., Sec., Special Counsel/$250,000.00, Brad Hester/41/VP - Team Operations/$60,000.00

Directors: Joseph F. Newman/71/Chmn., CEO, Richard Tinkham/75/Dir., Sec., Special Counsel

Owners: Joseph F. Newman/24.08%, Richard P. Tinkham/24.08%, Millennium Partners, L.P./7.05%, Insiders/67.30%, Darren J. Cioffi/2.07%, Brax Capital Group LLC/9.10%, Brad Hester/1.03%

American Beverage Co

Rua Dr. Renato Paes De Barros, 1017 - 4 Andar, So Paulo; **PH:** 55-1121221200;
http:// www.ambev.com.br; **Email:** ir@ambev.com.br

General	- Incorporation	Brazil	Stock	- Price on:12/24/2007	$71.15
Employees		NA	Stock Exchange		NA
Auditor	Deloitte Touche Tohmatsu		Ticker Symbol		NA
Stk Agt	Bank of New York		Outstanding Shares		NA
Counsel	Cravath, Swaine & Moore LLP		E.P.S.		NA
DUNS No.		NA	Shareholders		NA

Business: The group's principle activity is the production, sale and distribution of a wide range of beverages in both the domestic and the international market such as; beer, soft drinks, mineral waters, isotonic beverages and fruit juices. The group has the license to bottle, sale and distribute pepsi, calsberg and miller products in Brazil.

Primary SIC and add'l.: 2086 2082

CIK No: 0001113172

Subsidiaries: Labatt Brewing Canada Holding Ltd, Labatt Brewing Company Ltd., Labatt USA, LLC), Quilmes International (Bermuda) Ltd

Officers: Luiz Fernando Ziegler De St. Edmond/42/CEO - Latin America, Miguel Nuno Da Mata Patricio/42/CEO - North America, Jorge Luiz Gualberti Martins Da Rocha/42/Executive Officer, Joao Mauricio Giffoni De Castro Neves/41/CFO, Investor Relations Officer, Bernardo Pinto Paiva/39/Sales Executive, Officer, Carlos Eduardo Klutzenschell Lisboa/38/Marketing Executive Officer, Claudio Braz Ferro/53/Industrial Executive Officer, Francisco De Sa Neto/42/Soft Drinks Executive Officer, Milton Seligman/56/Corporate Affairs Executive Officer, Pedro De Abreu-Mariani/41/Legal Officer, Graham David Staley/52/CFO, Investor Relations Officer, Nicolas Ernesto Bamberg/51/Industrial Executive Officer

Directors: Victorio Carlos De Marchi/69/Co - Chmn., Carlos Alves De Brito/48/Co - Chmn., Marcel Herrmann Telles/58/Dir., Carlos Alberto Da Veiga Sicupira/60/Dir., Jose Heitor Attilio Gracioso/75/Dir., Roberto Herbster Gusmao/85/Dir., Vicente Falconi Campos/66/Dir., Luis Felipe Pedreira Dutra Leite/42/Dir., Johan M.J.J. Van Biesbroeck/51/Dir., Jorge Paulo Lemann/68/Alternate Dir., Roberto Moses Thompson Motta/50/Alternate Dir., Carlos Alberto Da Veiga Sicupira/60/Dir.

Owners: The Bank of New York - ADR Department/1.31%, Caixa da Previdncia dos Funcionrios do Banco Central do Brasil - PREVI/9.09%, FAHZ/16.04%, Interbrew International B.V./65.05%, AmBrew S.A./5.70%, AmBrew S.A./8.49%, The Bank of New York - ADR Department/21.18%, Caixa da Previdncia dos Funcionrios do Banco Central do Brasil - PREVI/1.56%, FAHZ, Interbrew International B.V./35.95%

American Biltrite Inc

57 River St., Wellesley Hills, MA, 02481; **PH:** 1-781-237-6655; **Fax:** 1-781-237-6880;
http:// www.americanbiltriteinc.com; **Email:** info@ambilt.com

General	- Incorporation	DE	Stock	- Price on:12/24/2007	$8.25
Employees		1,590	Stock Exchange		AMEX
Auditor	Ernst & Young LLP		Ticker Symbol		ABL
Stk Agt	Registrar & Transfer Co		Outstanding Shares		3,440,000
Counsel	Henry W. Winkleman		E.P.S.		$0.32
DUNS No.		00-103-0493	Shareholders		NA

Business: The group's principal activities are organized into four segments: flooring products, tape products, jewelry and the Canadian division. The flooring products segment manufactures vinyl and vinyl composition floor coverings. The tape products segment manufactures adhesive-coated, pressure-sensitive papers and films to protect material during handling or storage and for use in the footwear, automotive and electrical and electronic industries. The jewelry segment supplies fashion jewelry and related accessories to merchandisers and department stores. The Canadian division produces flooring, rubber products, including materials used by footwear manufacturers and other industrial products. Some of the trademarks of the group are transferrite(R), amtico(R) and anne klein(r). During the year 2003, the group discontinued janus flooring corporation, its hardwood flooring manufacturing subsidiary in Canada.

Primary SIC and add'l.: 2672 3021 3069 5094 3052 1752

CIK No: 0000004611

Subsidiaries: ABIcan, Ltd., Abimex, LLC., ABItalia, Inc., ABTRE, Inc., Aimpar, Inc., American Biltrite (Canada) Ltd, American Biltrite Far East, Inc., American Biltrite Intellectual Properties, Inc., Congoleum Corporation, Ideal Tape Co., Inc., Janus Flooring Corporation, K & M Trading (H.K.) Limited, K&M Associates L.P., K&M Legendary Services, Inc., Majestic Jewelry, Inc. 16 Subsidiaries included in the Index

Officers: Roger S. Marcus/63/Chmn., CEO/$742,024.00, William M. Marcus/70/Exec. VP, Treasurer/$559,570.00, Diana Lew/43/Corporate Controller, Edward J. Lapointe/66/Dir. - Internal Audit, Jean Richard/VP, GM, Howard N. Feist/52/CFO, VP - Finance/$326,633.00, Henry W. Winkleman/63/VP, Richard G. Marcus/61/COO, Pres./$754,976.00, Dennis J. Burns/68/GM - Tape Division/$30,885.00

Directors: Roger S. Marcus/63/Chmn., CEO

Owners: Kenneth I. Watchmaker, John C. Garrels, Natalie S. Marcus/24.70%, James S. Marcus, Frederick H. Joseph, Wilen Management Company, Inc./5.60%, Gilbert K. Gailius, Mark N. Kaplan, Leo R. Breitman, Dennis J. Burns, Dimensional Fund Advisors, Inc./6.40%, William M. Marcus/11.00%, Howard N. Feist, Roger S. Marcus/15.40%, Richard G. Marcus/15.80% (16 Owners included in Index)

Financial Data: Fiscal Year End: 12/31   **Latest Annual Data:** 12/31/2006

Year	Sales	Net Income
2006	$435,537,000	$685,000
2005	$445,172,000	-$17,633,000
2004	$433,869,000	$1,953,000

Curr. Assets:	$182,322,000	**Curr. Liab.:**	$141,440,000		
Plant, Equip.:	$106,380,000	**Total Liab.:**	$312,550,000	**Indic. Yr. Divd.:**	NA
Total Assets:	$331,672,000	**Net Worth:**	$18,035,000	**Debt/ Equity:**	0.4791

American Bio Medica Corp

122 Smith Rd., Kinderhook, NY, 12106; **PH:** 1-518-758-8158; **Fax:** 1-518-758-8171;
http:// www.americanbiomedica.com; **Email:** info@abmc.com

General	- Incorporation	NY	Stock	- Price on:12/24/2007	$1.15
Employees		120	Stock Exchange		NDQ
Auditor	UHY LLP		Ticker Symbol		ABMC
Stk Agt	Registrar & Transfer Co		Outstanding Shares		21,720,000
Counsel		NA	E.P.S.		-$0.029
DUNS No.		96-666-5036	Shareholders		NA

Business: The group's principal activity is to develop, manufacture and market immunoassay diagnostic test kits. The group owns two technologies for screening drugs of abuse, a workplace screening test and a preliminary test for use by laboratories. The group's drugs of abuse screening products offer health care, law enforcement, government, industrial safety and educational professionals, self-contained, one-step screening devices capable of identifying illicit drug use. The products of the group include rapid drug screen(R), rapid one(R), rapid tec(R), oralstat(R), drug detector(tm), rapid drug screen scan-r(tm) and rapid tec cup(tm). As of Feb 2004, the group had 18 distributors representing 30 countries outside the United States.

Primary SIC and add'l.: 5192 2835 7372

CIK No: 0000896747

Officers: Stan Cipkowski/Dir., CEO/$221,000.00, Edmund Jaskiewicz/Chmn., Pres., Todd Bailey/VP - Sales, Marketing, Melissa Waterhouse/Corp. Sec. - Corporate Compliance, Stefan Parker/CFO, Exec. VP, Martin Gould/Chief Scientific Officer, Exec. VP/$141,500.00, Henry Wells/VP - Product Development, Keith Palmer/47/Exec VP - Finance, Treasurer/$224,600.00

Directors: Stan Cipkowski/Dir., CEO, Edmund Jaskiewicz/Chmn., Pres., Carl Florio/Dir., Daniel Kollin/Dir., Richard Koskey/Dir., Anthony Costantino/Dir.

Owners: Martin R. Gould/1.70%, Carl A. Florio, Edmund M. Jaskiewicz/9.50%, Marathon Capital Management/7.70%, Daniel W. Kollin, Richard P. Koskey, Stan Cipkowski/10.30%, Anthony G. Costantino, Keith E. Palmer/1.00%, Insiders/22.50%

Financial Data: Fiscal Year End: 12/31   **Latest Annual Data:** 12/31/2006

Year	Sales	Net Income
2006	$13,838,000	$196,000
2005	$13,015,000	-$376,000
2004	$12,241,000	$266,000

Curr. Assets:	$6,978,000	**Curr. Liab.:**	$2,122,000		
Plant, Equip.:	$1,982,000	**Total Liab.:**	$2,980,000	**Indic. Yr. Divd.:**	NA
Total Assets:	$9,017,000	**Net Worth:**	$6,037,000	**Debt/ Equity:**	0.2055

American Bonanza Resources Corp

455 Granville St., Ste. 206, Vancouver, BC, V6C1T1; **PH:** 1-604-681-8123

General	- Incorporation	NV	Stock	- Price on:12/24/2007	NA
Employees		NA	Stock Exchange		OTC
Auditor	Chang G. Park, CPA		Ticker Symbol		ABOZ
Stk Agt	Holladay Stock Transfer, Inc.		Outstanding Shares		NA
Counsel		NA	E.P.S.		NA
DUNS No.		NA	Shareholders		NA

Business: The groups principal activity is to explore minerals. The group operates from Canada and the United States.

Primary SIC and add'l.: 1000

CIK No: 0001342916

Officers: Thomas Gelfand/76/Dir., CEO, CFO, Pres., Sec.

Directors: Thomas Gelfand/76/Dir., CEO, CFO, Pres., Sec.

Owners: Thomas Gelfand/33.00%, Insiders/33.00%

American Business Corp

11921 Brinley Ave., Louisville, KY, 40243; **PH:** 1-502-410-6900

General	- Incorporation	CO	Stock	- Price on:12/24/2007	$0.008
Employees		NA	Stock Exchange		OTC
Auditor	Mountjoy & Bressler, LLP		Ticker Symbol		AMBCE
Stk Agt	Corporate Stock Transfer, Inc.		Outstanding Shares		NA
Counsel		NA	E.P.S.		NA
DUNS No.		NA	Shareholders		NA

Business: The group's principle activity is to provide seeking a business combination with a profitable privately owned company. The company's principal activity was to provide freight transportation services to large corporations and the operation of a regional truckload carrier specializing in the short to medium market segments.The group operates from United States.

Primary SIC and add'l.: 9999
CIK No: 0000820408
Subsidiaries: U.S. Trucking, Inc
Officers: Anthony R. Russo/Dir., CEO, CFO, Pres.
Directors: Anthony R. Russo/Dir., CEO, CFO, Pres.
Owners: Midwest Merger Management, LLC/49.70%

American Business Financial Services Inc

100 Penn Sq. E, Philadelphia, PA, 19107; *PH:* 1-877-613-3131; *http://* www.abfsonline.com; *Email:* cco@parafincorp.com

General - Incorporation	DE	Stock- Price on:12/24/2007	$0.025
Employees	931	Stock Exchange	OTC
Auditor	BDO Seidman LLP	Ticker Symbol	ABFIQ
Stk Agt.	NA	Outstanding Shares	3,600,000
Counsel	Stephen M. Giroux	E.P.S.	-$34.708
DUNS No.	NA	Shareholders	NA

Business: The group's principal activities are to originate, sell and service loans to businesses secured by real estate and other business assets. The group operates through three segments: loan origination, servicing and treasury and funding. The loan origination segment originates business purpose loans secured by real estate and other business assets, home equity loans and loans secured by one-to-four family residential real estate. The servicing segment services the loans and leases originated by the group. This segment includes billing and collecting payments from borrowers, transmitting payments to trust investors, accounting for principal and interest, collections and foreclosure activities. The treasury and funding segment offers subordinated debt securities to obtain funds for the group's operating and lending activities.

Primary SIC and add'l.: 6159
CIK No: 0000772349
Officers: Mark Herman/Contact - Servicers Securitized Loans, Paul Graff/Contact - Servicers Securitized Loans

Financial Data: Fiscal Year End:12/31 Latest Annual Data: 6/30/2004

Year	Sales	Net Income
2004	$98,391,000	-$111,428,000
2003	$241,406,000	-$29,902,000
2002	$247,901,000	$7,859,000

Curr. Assets:	$38,555,000	Curr. Liab.:	$65,771,000		
Plant, Equip.:	$27,967,000	Total Liab.:	$1,030,955,000	Indic. Yr. Divd.:	NA
Total Assets:	$1,042,870,000	Net Worth:	$11,915,000	Debt/ Equity:	77.3148

American Campus Communities Inc

805 Las Cimas Pkwy., Ste. 400, Austin, TX, 78746; *PH:* 1-512-732-1000; *Fax:* 1-512-732-2450; *http://* www.studenthousing.com; *Email:* info@studenthousing.com

General - Incorporation	MD	Stock- Price on:12/24/2007	$28.62
Employees	897	Stock Exchange	NYSE
Auditor	Ernst& Young LLP	Ticker Symbol	ACC
Stk Agt	Bank of New York	Outstanding Shares	23,170,000
Counsel	NA	E.P.S	$0.65
DUNS No.	NA	Shareholders	NA

Business: The groups principle activities include developing, redeveloping, acquiring and operating student housing communities. The groups operates through four segments namely Owned off campus properties, on campus participating properties, development services and property management services. The group operates from the United States. The group's quarterly revenue for September 2007 was 36.52 millios of USD.

Primary SIC and add'l.: 6798
CIK No: 0001283630
Subsidiaries: 1772 Sweet Home Road, LLC, ACC (Outpost San Marcos) LP, ACC (Raiders Crossing) LP, ACC (Raiders Pass) LP, ACC (Woods at Greenland) LP, ACC OP (Callaway Villas) LP, ACC OP (Village at Gainesville) LLC, ACC OP UC I - Tallahassee LLC, ACC OP UC II - Tallahassee LLC, ACT-Village at Fresno State, LLC, American Campus Communities Operating Partnership, LP, American Campus Communities Services, Inc., American Campus Communities, Inc., RAP Student Housing Properties, LLC, Royal Orlando Limited Partnership 24 Subsidiaries included in the Index
Officers: William C. Bayless/Dir., CEO, Pres./$526,954.00, Brian Nickel/Dir., Exec. VP, CFO/$399,829.00, Greg A. Dowell/COO, Exec. VP/$247,448.00, James C. Hopke/CIO, Exec. VP/$210,923.00, Clint Braun/Sr. VP - Construction Management, Steve Crawford/Sr. VP - Management Services, Jorge De Cardenas/Sr. VP - Information Technology, Jonathan A. Graf/Sr. VP - CAO, Treasurer, James Sholders/Sr. VP - Management Services, William Talbot/Sr. VP - Investments, Brian Winger/Sr. VP - Transactions, Jason R. Wills/Sr. VP - On - Campus Development, Gina Cowart/Contact - Media Inquiry
Directors: William C. Bayless/Dir., CEO, Pres., R. D. Burck/Chmn., Brian Nickel/Dir., Exec. VP, CFO, Cydney C. Donnell/Dir., Winston W. Walker/Dir., Steven G. Dawson/Dir., Edward Lowenthal/Dir., Scott H. Rechler/Dir., Michael J. Henneman/Dir.
Owners: R. D. Burck, Insiders/3.40%, Cohen & Steers, Inc./11.80%, James C. Hopke, Cydney C. Donnell, Greg A. Dowell, Steven G. Dawson, Edward Lowenthal, Michael J. Henneman/2.30%, The Vanguard Group, Inc./5.40%, Deutsche Bank AG/8.00%, Winston W. Walker, Scott H. Rechler, Morgan Stanley/7.10%, Brian B. Nickel (16 Owners included in Index)

Financial Data: Fiscal Year End:12/31 Latest Annual Data: 12/31/2006

Year	Sales	Net Income
2006	$118,953,000	$22,597,000
2005	$87,474,000	$9,662,000
2004	$60,823,000	-$1,339,000

Curr. Assets:	$93,496,000	Curr. Liab.:	$13,616,000	P/E Ratio:	42.72
Plant, Equip.:	$770,885,000	Total Liab.:	$514,907,000	Indic. Yr. Divd.:	$1.350
Total Assets:	$884,381,000	Net Worth:	$369,474,000	Debt/ Equity:	1.4680

American Capital Holdings Inc

1016 Clemmons St., Ste 302, Palm Beach Gardens, FL, 33477; *PH:* 1-561-880-0004; *Fax:* 1-561-337-9356; *http://* www.americancapitalholdings.com

General - Incorporation	FL	Stock- Price on:12/24/2007	NA
Employees	NA	Stock Exchange	NA
Auditor	Wieseneck, Andres & Co P.A	Ticker Symbol	NA
Stk Agt.	Florida Atlantic Stock Transfer, Inc.	Outstanding Shares	NA
Counsel	NA	E.P.S.	NA
DUNS No.	NA	Shareholders	NA

Business: The group principal activity is originated through a series of transactions and restructurings from US Amateur Sports Company, one of ten wholly-owned subsidiaries of eCom eCom.com ("eCom"), an internet-based e-commerce company with businesses ranging from sports memorabilia and equipment to data compression technology. The Company changed its name to USA SportsNet, Inc., and recently changed its name to American Capital Holdings, Inc. in connection with its spin-off by eCom and its acquisition of certain assets of a company formerly known as American Capital Holdings, Inc. (now known as ACHI, Inc.) The group's gross profit for the year ended 31 Dec,2005 $10,716.

Primary SIC and add'l.: 6770
CIK No: 0001288012
Subsidiaries: IS Direct Agency, Inc., Universe Life
Officers: Barney A. Richmond/Chmn., CEO, Pres., Richard C. Turner/Dir., CFO
Directors: Barney A. Richmond/Chmn., CEO, Pres., Richard C. Turner/Dir., CFO, Douglas Sizemore/75/Dir.
Owners: Barney A. Richmond/29.50%, Insiders/32.40%, Richard C. Turner/2.90%, David W. Pong/12.40%

Curr. Assets:	$67,000	Curr. Liab.:	$155,000		
Plant, Equip.:	$0	Total Liab.:	$876,000	Indic. Yr. Divd.:	NA
Total Assets:	$67,000	Net Worth:	-$809,000	Debt/ Equity:	NA

American Capital Partners Ltd Inc

319 Clematis St., Ste 203, West Palm Beach, FL, 33401; ; *http://* www.acpbdc.com; *Email:* info@americancapitalpartners.com

General - Incorporation	NV	Stock- Price on:12/24/2007	$0.11
Employees	31	Stock Exchange	OTC
Auditor	Jewett, Schwartz, & Assoc.	Ticker Symbol	APRJ
Stk Agt.	International Stock Transfer & Trust	Outstanding Shares	NA
Counsel	Joseph.I Emas Esq	E.P.S.	NA
DUNS No.	NA	Shareholders	NA

Business: The group's principle activities include designing, manufacturing and marketing consumer electronic products that target the home health and safety and the quality of life and leisure markets.The group operates from United States.

Primary SIC and add'l.: 3629
CIK No: 0001114098
Subsidiaries: the business development company
Officers: Joseph I. Emas/Legal Counsel

Financial Data: Fiscal Year End:12/31 Latest Annual Data: 12/31/2004

Year	Sales	Net Income
2004	$891,000	-$15,000
2000	$6,000	-$397,000

Curr. Assets:	$89,000	Curr. Liab.:	$290,000		
Plant, Equip.:	$8,000	Total Liab.:	$311,000	Indic. Yr. Divd.:	NA
Total Assets:	$390,000	Net Worth:	$80,000	Debt/ Equity:	NA

American Capital Strategies Ltd

2 Bethesda Metro Ctr., 14th Fl., Bethesda, MD, 20814; *PH:* 1-301-951-6122; *Fax:* 1-301-654-6714; *http://* www.american-capital.com; *Email:* info@americancapital.com

General - Incorporation	DE	Stock- Price on:12/24/2007	$44.75
Employees	484	Stock Exchange	NDQ
Auditor	Ernst & Young LLP	Ticker Symbol	ACAS
Stk Agt.	Computershare Investor Services LLC	Outstanding Shares	161,550,000
Counsel	Arnold & Porter LLP	E.P.S.	NA
DUNS No.	NA	Shareholders	NA

Business: The group's principle activity of the company is the provision of financial advisory services to and invest in middle market companies which includes provision of senior debt, subordinated debt and equity to middle market companies in need of capital for management buyouts including employee stock option plan buyouts, growth, acquisitions, liquidity and restructuring. The group's quarterly revenue for September 2007 was 310.00 millions of USD.

Primary SIC and add'l.: 6159
CIK No: 0000817473
Subsidiaries: European Capital Financial Services Guernsey) Limited, European Capital S.A. SICAR
Officers: Malon Wilkus/Chmn., CEO, Pres./$7,579,944.00, Brian S. Graff/Principal, Regional MD - New York, Simon Henderson/MD - London, Sean Eagle/Principal, Bethesda, Kimberly Reed/Principal - Los Angeles, Attila Freska/Dir. - Emerging Markets, Bethesda, Douglas Cooper/MD - Bethesda, John Drennan/VP - Dallas, Joshua Lefkowitz/Assist. General Counsel - Bethesda, Michael Messersmith/VP, Assoc. General Counsel - Bethesda, Sean Reid/Assist. General Counsel - Bethesda, Julie Southfield/Assist. General Counsel - Bethesda, Robert J. Bogart/VP - Human Resources, Bethesda, Frank Burdine/VP - Human Resources, Bethesda, Robin Lachapelle/VP - Human Resources, Bethesda (153 Officers included in Index)
Directors: Malon Wilkus/Chmn., CEO, Pres., Alvin Puryear/Dir., Mary C. Baskin/Dir., Philip R. Harper/Dir., Jacques Pancrazi/Dir. - Paris, Neil Hahl/Dir., Stan Lundine/Dir., Jerry Tebbutt/Dir., Matthew Gordon Clark/Dir., Kenneth Peterson/Dir., Giles Cheek/Dir., John Koskinen/Dir.
Owners: Stan Lundine, Malon Wilkus/1.40%, Kenneth D. Peterson, John R. Erickson, Alvin N. Puryear, Ira J. Wagner, Philip R. Harper, Gordon J. OBrien, Mary C. Baskin, Insiders/2.40%, Darin R. Winn, Neil M. Hahl

Financial Data: Fiscal Year End:12/31 Latest Annual Data: 12/31/2006

Year	Sales	Net Income
2006	$1,330,000,000	$896,000,000
2005	$554,500,000	$364,909,000
2004	$435,296,000	$281,445,000

Curr. Assets:	$354,000,000	**Curr. Liab.:**	$130,000,000		
Plant, Equip.:	NA	**Total Liab.:**	$4,267,000,000	**Indic. Yr. Divd.:**	$3.640
Total Assets:	$8,609,000,000	**Net Worth:**	$4,342,000,000	**Debt/ Equity:**	0.0031

American Caresource Holdings Inc

5429 Lyndon B. Johnson Fwy., Ste. 700, Dallas, TX, 75240; ***PH:*** 1-214-596-2400; ***Fax:*** 1-972-980-2560; ***http://*** www.anci-care.com; ***Email:*** investorrelations@anci-care.com

General - Incorporation	DE	**Stock**- Price on:12/24/2007	$1.83
Employees	33	Stock Exchange	AMEX
Auditor	McGladrey & Pullen, LLP	Ticker Symbol	XSI
Stk Agt	Continental Stock Transfer & Trust Co	Outstanding Shares	14,490,000
Counsel	NA	E.P.S	-$0.125
DUNS No.	NA	Shareholders	NA

Business: The groups principle activity is to provide ancillary care services. The group operates from the United States. The groups quarterly revenue for September 2007 was 7.09 millions of USD.

Primary SIC and add'l.: 8741

CIK No: 0001316645

Subsidiaries: Ancillary Care Services, Inc.

Officers: Wayne A. Schellhammer/55/Dir., CEO, Pres., David S. Boone/CEO, Pres., Edward B. Berger/Executive Chmn., Kurt M. Fullmer/VP - Operations, Information Technology, Steven M. Phillips/41/Principal Accounting Officer, Controller, Steven J. Armond/CFO, Maria L. Baker/VP - Marketing, Jennifer Boone/VP - Network Development

Directors: Wayne A. Schellhammer/55/Dir., CEO, Pres., Edward B. Berger/Executive Chmn., John W. Colloton/Dir., David A. George/52/Dir., John N. Hatsopoulos/Dir., Derace L. Schaffer/Dir., John Pappajohn/Dir., Kenneth S. George/Dir.

Owners: David S. Boone/1.00%, Derace L. Schaffer/6.40%, Kenneth George/0.30%, John N. Hatsopoulos, Insiders/41.70%, Wayne A. Schellhammer/3.50%, John Pappajohn/33.40%, David A. George/0.40%, Edward B. Berger/0.70%, Steven M. Phillips, Principal Life Insurance Company/13.00%, John W. Colloton/0.20%

Financial Data: ***Fiscal Year End:***12/31 ***Latest Annual Data:*** 12/31/2006

Year	Sales	Net Income
2006	$11,419,000	-$1,314,000
2005	$4,417,000	-$2,407,000

Curr. Assets:	$6,394,000	**Curr. Liab.:**	$2,192,000		
Plant, Equip.:	$267,000	**Total Liab.:**	$2,293,000	**Indic. Yr. Divd.:**	NA
Total Assets:	$12,875,000	**Net Worth:**	$10,581,000	**Debt/ Equity:**	NA

American Claims Evaluation Inc

One Jericho Plz., Jericho, NY, 11753; ***PH:*** 1-516-938-8000; ***http://*** www.sportparkvegas.com

General - Incorporation	NY	**Stock**- Price on:12/24/2007	$1.97
Employees	15	Stock Exchange	NDQ
Auditor	J. H. Cohn LLP, KPMG LLP	Ticker Symbol	AMCE
Stk Agt	Continental Stock Transfer & Trust Co	Outstanding Shares	4,760,000
Counsel	Hartman & Craven LLP	E.P.S	-$0.06
DUNS No.	01-786-7417	Shareholders	NA

Business: The group's principal activity is to provide vocational rehabilitation and disability management services. These services are designed to maximize injured workers' abilities in order to reintegrate them into their respective communities. The group provides services through its wholly-owned subsidiary, rpm rehabilitation and associates, inc. In-house vocational evaluations are utilized to assess aptitudes, interests, values and abilities of workers. Issues of medical restrictions, functional overlays, illiteracy and occupational diseases are assessed and factored into the development of a rehabilitation strategy. The major customer of the group is Washington state department of labor and industries.

Primary SIC and add'l.: 8331

CIK No: 0000774517

Subsidiaries: RPM Rehabilitation and Associates, Inc.

Owners: Insiders/69.60%, Peter Gutmann/2.50%, Edward M.Elkin/1.70%, Gary J. Knauer/5.00%, Joseph Looney, Kinder Investments/6.10%, Morton J. Davis/8.10%, Gary Gelman/66.50%

Financial Data: ***Fiscal Year End:***03/31 ***Latest Annual Data:*** 3/31/2006

Year	Sales	Net Income
2006	$1,142,000	-$327,000
2005	$1,140,000	-$481,000
2004	$1,191,000	-$475,000

Curr. Assets:	$6,753,000	**Curr. Liab.:**	$124,000		
Plant, Equip.:	$84,000	**Total Liab.:**	$124,000	**Indic. Yr. Divd.:**	NA
Total Assets:	$6,837,000	**Net Worth:**	$6,713,000	**Debt/ Equity:**	NA

American Commerce Solutions Inc

1400 Chamber Dr., Bartow, FL, 33830; ***PH:*** 1-863-533-0326; ***Fax:*** 1-863-533-0327; ***http://*** www.aacssymbol.com; ***Email:*** aacs@4lfs.com

General - Incorporation	DE	**Stock**- Price on:12/24/2007	$0.01
Employees	31	Stock Exchange	OTC
Auditor	Pender Newkirk & Co	Ticker Symbol	AACS
Stk Agt	Jersey Transfer & Trust Co	Outstanding Shares	239,020,000
Counsel	NA	E.P.S	-$0.005
DUNS No.	79-549-1448	Shareholders	NA

Business: The group's principal activities are to market OEM and after-Market repair parts and provide specialized machining services for heavy equipment industry. The operations of the group are carried out through its wholly owned subsidiary, international machine and welding, inc. The customers of the group include mining, agricultural processing, maritime, power generation and industrial machinery, construction, forestry and waste and scrap industries. The group's through its subsidiary also manufactures motorcycle trailers with fiberglass bodies. These trailers are used in transportation of motorcycles, atvs, personal watercraft, small vehicles, vending, mobile fiber optic workstations, utility and other specialized applications. The group also provides non warranty repairs, modification of existing chariot trailers. On 14-Oct-2003, the group acquired chariot manufacturing company inc and on 07-Jun-2004, it acquired crystal clear entertainment inc.

Primary SIC and add'l.: 7699 8741

CIK No: 0000949982

Subsidiaries: Chariot Manufacturing Company, Inc, International Machine and Welding, Inc

Officers: Daniel L. Hefner/57/CEO, Pres., Frank D. Puissegur/49/Dir., CFO

Directors: Robert Maxwell/73/Chmn., Frank D. Puissegur/49/Dir., CFO, Andrew Mueller/62/Dir.

Owners: Insiders/34.31%, Andrew Mueller, Daniel L. Hefner/3.89%, Frank D. Puissegur, Robert E. Maxwell/29.58%

Financial Data: ***Fiscal Year End:***02/28 ***Latest Annual Data:*** 2/28/2007

Year	Sales	Net Income
2007	$2,351,000	-$1,450,000
2006	$2,302,000	-$922,000
2005	$2,754,000	-$1,279,000

Curr. Assets:	$458,000	**Curr. Liab.:**	$1,898,000		
Plant, Equip.:	$4,914,000	**Total Liab.:**	$3,489,000	**Indic. Yr. Divd.:**	NA
Total Assets:	$5,433,000	**Net Worth:**	$1,945,000	**Debt/ Equity:**	0.3845

American Commercial Lines Inc

1701 E Market St., Jeffersonville, IN, 47130; ***PH:*** 1-812-288-0100; ***Fax:*** 1-812-288-1664; ***http://*** www.aclines.com

General - Incorporation	DE	**Stock**- Price on:12/24/2007	$23.16
Employees	2,795	Stock Exchange	NDQ
Auditor	Ernst& Young LLP	Ticker Symbol	ACLI
Stk Agt	American Stock Transfer & Trust Co.	Outstanding Shares	62,460,000
Counsel	NA	E.P.S	$0.92
DUNS No.	NA	Shareholders	NA

Business: The groups principle activity is to provide marine transportation and service. The groups services include transportation, port, terminal and logistics. The products of the group include barges, towboats and other vessels and ocean going liquid tank barges. The groups operates through two segments namely transportation and manufacturing. Customers served by the group include industrial and agricultural companies. Specific customers of the group include Cargill, Inc, Alcoa, Inc, BASF Corporation, Bunge North America, Inc, the David J. Joseph Company and Lyondell Chemical Company. The group own 50% of BargeLink LLC. The group operates from the United States and South America. The group's quarterly revenue for September 2007 was 258.37 millions of USD.

Primary SIC and add'l.: 4492 4449 4491 3731

CIK No: 0001324479

Subsidiaries: ACBL Dominicana S.A., ACL Finance Corp., ACL Transportation Services LLC, American Barge Line Company, American Commercial Barge Line LLC, American Commercial Lines International LLC, American Commercial Lines LLC, Commercial Barge Line Company, Jeffboat LLC

Officers: Mark R. Holden/Dir., CEO, Pres., Jacques J. Vanier/46/VP - Manufacturing, Robert P. Murgatroyd/Mgr. - Connection Services, W. N. Whitlock/Exec. VP - Governmental Affairs, Jerry R. Linzey/COO, Sr. VP, Christopher A. Black/Sr. VP, CFO, Richard A. Mitchell/Sr. VP - Corporate Strategy, Michael P. Ryan/Sr. VP - Sales, Marketing, Nick C. Fletcher/Sr. VP - Human Resources, Tamra L. Koshewa/VP - Finance, Corporate Controller, Larry M. Cuculic/VP - Legal, Corp. Sec., Michael J. Monahan/Sr. VP - Transportation Services, Kevin S. Boyle/VP, Treasurer

Directors: Mark R. Holden/Dir., CEO, Pres., Clayton K. Yeutter/Chmn., Emanuel L. Rouvelas/Dir., Christopher R. Weber/Dir., Eugene I. Davis/Dir., Richard L. Huber/Dir., Nils E. Larsen/Dir.

Owners: Insiders/2.40%, Wellington Management Company, LLP/13.80%, Nils E. Larsen, Eugene I. Davis, Christopher R. Weber, Richard L. Huber/1.10%, Tremblant Capital Group/5.60%, Emanuel L. Rouvelas, W. Norbert Whitlock, Jerry R. Linzey, GVI Holdings, Inc./18.50%, Clayton K. Yeutter, FMR Corp./14.80%, Christopher A. Black, Mark R. Holden

Financial Data: ***Fiscal Year End:***12/31 ***Latest Annual Data:*** 12/31/2006

Year	Sales	Net Income
2006	$942,552,000	$92,252,000
2005	$741,370,000	$11,813,000

Curr. Assets:	$197,003,000	**Curr. Liab.:**	$152,752,000		
Plant, Equip.:	$455,710,000	**Total Liab.:**	$312,168,000	**Indic. Yr. Divd.:**	NA
Total Assets:	$670,821,000	**Net Worth:**	$358,653,000	**Debt/ Equity:**	0.4517

American Community Bancshares Inc

4500 Cameron Valley Pkwy., Ste. 150, Charlotte, NC, 28211; ***PH:*** 1-704-225-8444; ***Fax:*** 1-704-225-8445; ***http://*** www.americancommunitybank.com

General - Incorporation	NC	**Stock**- Price on:12/24/2007	$11.56
Employees	105	Stock Exchange	NDQ
Auditor	Dixon Hughes PLLC	Ticker Symbol	ACBA
Stk Agt	Registrar & Transfer Co	Outstanding Shares	7,020,000
Counsel	Gaeta & Glesener	E.P.S	$0.75
DUNS No.	NA	Shareholders	NA

Business: The group's principal activity is to provide general commercial and retail banking services to individuals and small to medium-sized businesses. These services include checking, certificate of deposit and savings accounts. It also includes commercial, consumer and personal loans, mortgage, factoring and leasing services and other associated financial services. The group's activities are carried out through seven branch offices in North Carolina. The group's wholly owned subsidiaries are American community bank and American community capital trust i.

Primary SIC and add'l.: 6712 6022

CIK No: 0001106980

Subsidiaries: American Community Bank

Officers: Randy P. Helton/Chmn., CEO, Pres./$343,644.00, Richard M. Cochrane/Sr. VP - City Exec., Mint Hill, Jeff Coley/Sr. VP - City Exec., Marshville, Randy W. Adcock/Sr. VP - City Exec., Monroe, Michael E. Gudely/COO, Sr. VP/$152,445.00, Steve Barnes/Sr. VP - City Exec., Indian Trail, Dan R. Ellis/CFO, Sr. VP, Investor Relations Officer/$143,029.00, Douglas F. Sutherland/City Exec., Charlotte, Stephanie D. Helms/Sr. VP, Chief Administrative Officer

Directors: Randy P. Helton/Chmn., CEO, Pres., Robert G. Dinsmore/Dir., Peter A. Pappas/Dir., Gregory N. Wylie/Dir., Steven L. Phillips/Dir., Thomas J. Hall/Dir., David J. Guilford/Dir., Frank L. Gentry/Dir., Alison J. Smith/Dir., Philip R. Gilboy/Dir., Larry S. Helms/Dir., Zebulon Morris/Dir. Emeritus, Stephen V. Moss/Dir., Carlton L. Tyson/Dir. Emeritus, Carroll Edwards/Dir. Emeritus *(16 Directors included in Index)*

Owners: Insiders/8.71%, Randy P. Helton/2.04%, Steven L. Phillips/1.07%, Larry S. Helms, Dan R. Ellis, Peter A. Pappas, David J. Guilford, Robert G. Dinsmore, Frank L. Gentry, Harry C. Parlier, Marla Braun/6.81%, Thomas J. Hall, Stephen V. Moss, Michael E. Gudely, David D. Whitley *(18 Owners included in Index)*

Financial Data: Fiscal Year End:12/31   **Latest Annual Data:** 12/31/2006

Year	Sales	Net Income
2006	$35,687,000	$4,276,000
2005	$28,878,000	$4,508,000
2004	$21,554,000	$2,743,000

Curr. Assets:	$40,183,000	Curr. Liab.:	$417,978,000	P/E Ratio:	19.59
Plant, Equip.:	$9,300,000	Total Liab.:	$439,590,000	Indic. Yr. Divd.:	$0.200
Total Assets:	$494,658,000	Net Worth:	$55,068,000	Debt/ Equity:	0.3924

American Community Newspapers Inc

Formerly: Courtside Acquisition Corp
1700 Brd.way, 17th Fl., New York, NY, 10019; *PH:* 1-212-641-5000

General - Incorporation	DE	Stock- Price on:12/24/2007	$5.6
Employees	NA	Stock Exchange	AMEX
Auditor	Goldstein Golub Kessler LLP	Ticker Symbol	CRB
Stk Agt.	NA	Outstanding Shares	16,800,000
Counsel	NA	E.P.S.	$0.067
DUNS No.	NA	Shareholders	NA

Business: The groups principle activities include acquiring, developing and operating real estate properties. The group operates from the United States.

Primary SIC and add'l.: 2711

CIK No: 0001321544

Officers: Eugene M. Carr/Chmn., CEO, Oded Aboodi/Special Advisor, Carl D. Harnick/73/VP, Gregg H. Mayer/33/VP, Controller, Sec., Daniel J. Wilson/CFO, Roy D. Biondi/VP - Group Publisher, American Community Newspapers Columbus, Bill Weaver/Group Publisher, Star Community Newspapers, Donna M. Talla/Group Publisher, Sun Gazette Newspapers, Norman K. Styer/Publisher, Editor - in - Chief - Leesburg Today - Executive Editor, Loudoun Magazine, Loudoun Business, Roger A. Will/Interim Group Publisher, Minnesota Sun Newspapers, Dir. - New Media, Business Development, American Community Newspapers, Richard D. Hendrickson/Corporate Controller - American Community Newspapers LLC, CFO, VP - Operations, Minnesota Sun Publications

Directors: Eugene M. Carr/Chmn., CEO, John A. Erickson/Dir., Darren M. Sardoff/41/Dir., Robert H. Bloom/Dir., Richard D. Goldstein/Dir., Bruce M. Greenwald/Dir., Dennis H. Leibowitz/Dir., Peter R. Haje/Dir.

Owners: Richard D. Goldstein/6.50%, Bruce M. Greenwald/4.30%, Insiders/13.90%, Fir Tree, Inc./9.90%, Darren Sardoff, Peter R. Haje, Gregg H. Mayer, Dennis H. Leibowitz, The Baupost Group, L.L.C./8.90%, Carl D. Harnick

Financial Data: Fiscal Year End:12/31   **Latest Annual Data:** 12/31/2006

Year	Sales	Net Income
2006	$1,997,000	$1,046,000
2005	$711,000	$411,000

Curr. Assets:	$78,267,000	Curr. Liab.:	$1,181,000	P/E Ratio:	83.58
Plant, Equip.:	NA	Total Liab.:	$15,927,000	Indic. Yr. Divd.:	NA
Total Assets:	$78,354,000	Net Worth:	$62,427,000	Debt/ Equity:	NA

American Community Properties Trust

222 Smallwood Village Ctr., St. Charles, MD, 20602; *PH:* 1-301-843-8600; *Fax:* 1-301-870-8481; *http://* www.acptrust.com; *Email:* info@acptrust.com

General - Incorporation	MD	Stock- Price on:12/24/2007	$19.75
Employees	274	Stock Exchange	AMEX
Auditor	Ernst & Young LLP	Ticker Symbol	APO
Stk Agt.	Registrar & Transfer Co	Outstanding Shares	5,160,000
Counsel	NA	E.P.S.	$0.79
DUNS No.	NA	Shareholders	NA

Business: The groups principle activities include acquiring and operating real estate properties. The group operates from the United States. The groups quarterly revenue for September 207 is 19.04 millions of USD.

Primary SIC and add'l.: 6552 6519 6798 1521

CIK No: 0001065645

Subsidiaries: Alturas del Senorial Associates Limited Partnership, American Community Properties Trust, American Housing Management Company, American Housing Properties L.P., American Land Development U.S. Inc., American Rental Management Company, American Rental Properties Trust, Bannister Associates Limited Partnership, Bayamon Garden Associates Limited Partnership, Brookside Gardens Limited Partnership, Carolina Associates Limited Partnership, Coachman's LLC, Colinas de San Juan Associates Limited Partnership, Crossland Associates Limited Partnership, ELI GP Inc. 47 Subsidiaries included in the Index

Officers: Michael J. Wilson/42/Chmn., CEO/$470,000.00, Edwin L. Kelly/66/Trustee, COO, Pres./$529,524.00, Carlos R. Rodriguez/62/Exec. VP/$374,582.00, Cynthia L. Hedrick/55/CFO, Exec. VP, Sec., Treasurer/$308,046.00, Jorge Garcia Massuet/69/VP/$267,957.00, Matthew M. Martin/32/VP, Chief Accounting Officer, Paul A. Resnik/60/Sr. VP, Assist. Sec., Eduardo Cruz Ocasio/61/Sr. VP, Assist. Sec., Harry Chalstrom/47/VP, Mark L. MacFarland/38/VP, Rafael Velez/51/VP

Directors: Michael J. Wilson/42/Chmn., CEO, Edwin L. Kelly/66/Trustee, COO, Pres., Michael T. Scott/49/Trustee, Thomas S. Condit/66/Trustee, Antonio Ginorio/65/Trustee, Thomas Shafer/78/Trustee

Owners: Insiders/4.11%, The Wilson Group/50.68%, Antonio Ginorio, Interstate Business Corporation/29.64%, Michael T. Scott, Edwin L. Kelly/1.04%, Thomas J. Shafer, Robert Chapman/9.23%, Thomas S. Condit, Paul J. Isaac/9.77%, Michael J. Wilson/2.06%, Wilson Securities Corporation/10.43%

Financial Data: Fiscal Year End:12/31   **Latest Annual Data:** 12/31/2006

Year	Sales	Net Income
2006	$98,163,000	$4,591,000
2005	$62,313,000	$7,545,000
2004	$49,011,000	$2,831,000

Curr. Assets:	$65,166,000	Curr. Liab.:	$27,183,000		
Plant, Equip.:	$244,604,000	Total Liab.:	$330,845,000	Indic. Yr. Divd.:	NA
Total Assets:	$346,699,000	Net Worth:	$15,854,000	Debt/ Equity:	22.1625

American Consumers Inc

55 Hannah Way, Rossville, GA, 30742; *PH:* 1-706-861-3347

General - Incorporation	GA	Stock- Price on:12/24/2007	$1.25
Employees	90	Stock Exchange	OTC
Auditor	Hazlett, Lewis & Bister PLLC	Ticker Symbol	ANCS
Stk Agt.	NA	Outstanding Shares	NA
Counsel	Gaither & Whitaker	E.P.S.	$0.16
DUNS No.	04-592-8140	Shareholders	NA

Business: The group's principle activity is to operate seven supermarkets within the geographical area that comprises northwest Georgia, northeast Alabama and southeast Tennessee. The supermarkets are operated under the name "Shop-Rite" which is self-service and involves in the retail selling of groceries including meat, fresh produce, tobacco products, dairy products, frozen foods, bakery products and various other non-food items. All the supermarkets are operated under the name shop-rite. The company's supermarkets also offer milk and certain dairy products, as well as frozen vegetables and jellies, under the controlled-labels foodland, ultimate choice, freshland, price saver and select. Bread and related bakery items are also offered as controlled-label groceries. The group operates from United States.

Primary SIC and add'l.: 5431 5411 5461 5451 5421

CIK No: 0000004811

Officers: Michael A. Richardson/62/Chmn., CEO, Pres./$101,592.00, Paul R. Cook/58/Dir., Exec. VP, CFO, Treasurer/$77,064.00

Directors: Michael A. Richardson/62/Chmn., CEO, Pres., Virgil E. Bishop/69/Dir., Paul R. Cook/58/Dir., Exec. VP, CFO, Treasurer, Danny R. Skates/55/Dir., Thomas L. Richardson/78/Dir., Andrew V. Douglas/79/Dir.

Owners: ZBR, Inc, Michael A. Richardson, Diana K. Richardson, Insiders

Financial Data: Fiscal Year End:05/29   **Latest Annual Data:** 6/3/2006

Year	Sales	Net Income
2006	$33,280,000	-$167,000
2005	$32,101,000	-$331,000

Curr. Assets:	$3,068,000	Curr. Liab.:	$1,847,000		
Plant, Equip.:	$444,000	Total Liab.:	$1,991,000	Indic. Yr. Divd.:	NA
Total Assets:	$3,512,000	Net Worth:	$1,520,000	Debt/ Equity:	0.0624

American Crystal Sugar Co

101 N 3rd St., Moorhead, MN, 56560; *PH:* 1-218-236-4400; *http://* www.crystalsugar.com

General - Incorporation	MN	Stock- Price on:12/24/2007	NA
Employees	NA	Stock Exchange	NA
Auditor	Eide Bailly LLP	Ticker Symbol	NA
Stk Agt.	NA	Outstanding Shares	NA
Counsel	Oppenheimer Wolff & Donnelly	E.P.S.	NA
DUNS No.	06-479-2773	Shareholders	NA

Business: The group's principal activity is to process and market sugar, sugarbeet pulp, molasses and seed. The group processes sugarbeets grown by its members in five factories located in the red river valley area of Minnesota and North Dakota. The group operates through two segments namely sugar and leasing. The sugar segment is primarily engaged in the production and marketing of sugar from sugarbeets. It also sells agri-products and sugarbeet seed. The leasing segment is engaged in the leasing of a corn wet milling plant used in the production of high-fructose corn syrup sweetener.

Primary SIC and add'l.: 2046 2062 2061 2063

CIK No: 0000004828

Subsidiaries: Crab Creek Sugar Company, Crystech, LLC, Midwest Agri-Commodities Company, ProGold Limited Liability Company, Sidney Sugars Incorporated, United Sugars Corporation

American Dental Partners Inc

201 Edgewater Dr., Ste. 285, Wakefield, MA, 01880; *PH:* 1-781-224-0880; *Fax:* 1-781-224-4216; *http://* www.amdpi.com; *Email:* geninfo@amdpi.com

General - Incorporation	DE	Stock- Price on:12/24/2007	$26.38
Employees	2,347	Stock Exchange	NDQ
Auditor	PricewaterhouseCoopers LLP	Ticker Symbol	ADPI
Stk Agt.	Registrar & Transfer Co	Outstanding Shares	12,550,000
Counsel	Baker & Hostetler	E.P.S.	$1.05
DUNS No.	95-688-0587	Shareholders	NA

Business: The group's principle activity is to provide business services to multi-disciplinary dental groups. It provides all services necessary for the administration of the non-clinical aspects of dental operations. They include providing assistance with organizational planning and development, recruiting, retention and training programs, quality assurance initiatives, facilities development and management. The services also include employees benefits administration, procurement, information systems, marketing and payer relations and financial planning, reporting and analysis. The group operates by affiliating with dental groups throughout the United States. The group's quarterly revenue for September 2007 was 67.16 millions of USD.

Primary SIC and add'l.: 7389 8099

CIK No: 0001028087

Subsidiaries: ADP of New York LLC, American Dental Partners of Alabama LLC, American Dental Partners of California Inc., American Dental Partners of Louisiana LLC, American Dental Partners of Maryland LLC, American Dental Partners of Michigan LLC, American Dental Partners of Missouri LLC, American Dental Partners of North Carolina LLC, American Dental Partners of Ohio Inc., American Dental Partners of Oklahoma LLC, American Dental Partners of Pennsylvania LLC, American Dental Partners of Tennessee LLC, American Dental Partners of Virginia LLC, American Dental Partners of Wisconsin LLC, American Dental Professional Services LLC 21 Subsidiaries included in the Index

Officers: Gregory A. Serrao/Chmn., CEO, Pres./$979,226.00, George R. Sullivan/VP - Human Resources, Mark W. Vargo/VP, Chief Accounting Officer/$217,200.00, Ian H. Brock/VP - Planning, Investment, Robert A. Duncan/VP - Information Systems, Breht T. Feigh/Exec. VP, CFO, Treasurer/$659,799.00, Jesley C. Ruff/Sr. VP, Chief Professional Officer, Michael J. Kenneally/Sr. VP - Regional Operations, Paul F. Gill/Sr. VP - Regional Operations, Michael J. Vaughan/COO, Exec. VP/$710,200.00, William P. Koffler/VP - Corporate Development

Directors: Gregory A. Serrao/Chmn., CEO, Pres., Derril W. Reeves/Dir., Martin J. Mannion/Dir., Robert E. Hunter/Dir., Gerard M. Moufflet/Dir., James T. Kelly/Dir.

Owners: Insiders/12.53%, Skystone Advisors LLC/7.41%, Robert E. Hunter, TimesSquare Capital Management, LLC/7.26%, James T. Kelly, Gerard M. Moufflet, Gregory A. Serrao/7.14%, Michael J. Vaughan/1.98%, Brown Brothers Harriman& Co./8.63%, Stadium Capital Management, LLC/16.91%, Martin J. Mannion, Derril W. Reeves, Bares Capital Management, Inc./6.16%, Mark W. Vargo, Breht T. Feigh/2.37%

Financial Data: Fiscal Year End:12/31   Latest Annual Data: 12/31/2006

Year	Sales	Net Income
2006	$217,917,000	$11,134,000
2005	$196,928,000	$10,291,000
2004	$178,554,000	$8,519,000

Curr. Assets:	$24,619,000	Curr. Liab.:	$29,432,000	P/E Ratio:	25.37
Plant, Equip.:	$46,460,000	Total Liab.:	$79,455,000	Indic. Yr. Divd.:	NA
Total Assets:	$195,820,000	Net Worth:	$116,311,000	Debt/ Equity:	0.3024

American Eagle Outfitters Inc

77 Hot Metal St., Pittsburgh, PA, 15203; *PH:* 1-412-432-3300; *Fax:* 1-412-432-3955; *http://* www.ae.com

General - Incorporation .... DE	Stock - Price on:12/24/2007 ....NA
Employees..5,000	Stock Exchange.............................NYSE
Auditor ....Ernst & Young LLP	Ticker Symbol..................................AEO
Stk Agt.............................National City Bank	Outstanding Shares ....NA
Counsel........Porter Wright Morris & Arthur LLP	E.P.S...$1.83
DUNS No. 05-666-7231	Shareholders....................................NA

Business: The groups principle activity is to operate retail stores. The groups products include accessories, outerwear, footwear, basics and swimwear. The groups products are sold under the band names American Eagle Outfitters, American Eagle and AE brand names. The group operates from United States.

Primary SIC and add'l.: 5699 5611 5651 5632 5621 5661

CIK No: 0000919012

Subsidiaries: 3049462 Nova Scotia ULC, 3049463 Nova Scotia ULC, AE Admin Services Co LLC, AE Corporate Services Co., AE Direct Co. LLC, AE Distribution Co., AE FinCanada LP, AE First Co., AE Holdings Co., AE Limited Partnership, AE Outfitters Retail Co., AE Retail West LLC, AEH Holding Company, AEO International Corp., AEO Management Co. 35 Subsidiaries included in the Index

Officers: James V. O'Donnell/Dir., CEO/$15,280,340.00, Susan P. McGalla/Pres., Chief Merchandising Officer/$5,286,651.00, Thomas Didonato/Exec. VP - Human Resources, Joan Holstein Hilson/CFO, Exec. VP - AE Brand/$2,001,225.00, Joseph E. Kerin/Exec. VP, Dir. - Store Operations, Leann Nealz/Exec. VP, Chief Design Officer, Dennis R. Parodi/COO, Exec. VP - NY Design Center, Katherine J. Savitt/Exec. VP, Chief Marketing Officer/$4,095,506.00, Guy Bradford/VP - Corporate Responsibility, Customs Compliance Officer

Directors: James V. O'Donnell/Dir., CEO, Jay L. Schottenstein/Chmn., Roger S. Markfield/Vice Chmn., Jon P. Diamond/Dir., Michael G. Jesselson/Dir., Janice E. Page/Dir., Thomas J. Presby/Dir., Gerald E. Wedren/Dir., Larry M. Wolf/Dir., Alan T. Kane/Dir., Cary D. /Dir., Cary D. McMillan/50/Dir.

Owners: Joan Holstein Hilson, Thomas J. Presby, James V. ODonnell/1.20%, Larry M. Wolf, Jon P. Diamond/2.10%, Janice E. Page, Gerald E. Wedren, Jay L. Schottenstein/6.30%, Barclays Global Investors, N.A./10.50%, Roger S. Markfield/1.30%, Michael G. Jesselson, Insiders/11.20%, Susan P. McGalla, Alan T. Kane, Katherine J. Savitt

Financial Data: Fiscal Year End:01/28   Latest Annual Data: 2/3/2007

Year	Sales	Net Income
2007	$2,794,409,000	$387,359,000
2006	$2,309,371,000	$294,153,000
2005	$1,881,241,000	$213,343,000

Curr. Assets:	$1,198,254,000	Curr. Liab.:	$460,464,000		
Plant, Equip.:	$481,645,000	Total Liab.:	$570,172,000	Indic. Yr. Divd.:	$0.400
Total Assets:	$1,987,484,000	Net Worth:	$1,417,312,000	Debt/ Equity:	NA

American Ecology Corp

300 E Mallard Dr., Ste. 300, Boise, ID, 83706; *PH:* 1-208-331-8400; *Fax:* 1-208-331-7900; *http://* www.americanecology.com; *Email:* info@americanecology.com

General - Incorporation .... DE	Stock - Price on:12/24/2007 ....$21.68
Employees..226	Stock Exchange.................................NDQ
Auditor ....Moss Adams LLP	Ticker Symbol..................................ECOL
Stk Agt..... American Stock Transfer & Trust Co.	Outstanding Shares 18,220,000
Counsel..NA	E.P.S...$0.92
DUNS No. 11-880-6587	Shareholders....................................NA

Business: The group's principal activities are to provide radioactive, hazardous and industrial waste management services. The group operates through two segments: operating disposal facilities and non-operating disposal facilities. Operating disposal facilities accepts hazardous and radioactive waste and includes the group's hazardous waste treatment and disposal facilities. Non-operating disposal facilities segment includes the closed hazardous waste disposal, processing, and deep-well injection facilities. The services are provided to commercial and government entities, such as nuclear power plants, medical and academic institutions, steel mills and petro-chemical facilities. The customers of the group include the United States army corps of engineers, nucor steel company and shaw environmental & infrastructure, inc.

Primary SIC and add'l.: 4953

CIK No: 0000742126

Subsidiaries: American Ecology Environmental Services Corporation, American Ecology Holdings Corporation, American Ecology Recycle Center, Inc., American Ecology Services Corporation, Texas Ecologists, Inc., US Ecology Idaho, Inc., US Ecology Nevada, Inc., US Ecology Texas, L.P., US Ecology Washington, Inc., US Ecology, Inc.

Officers: Stephen A. Romano/53/Dir., CEO, Pres., COO/$821,860.00, Jeffrey R. Feeler/VP, Controller, CFO/$103,349.00, Robert Marchand/US Ecology Nevada GM, John M. Cooper/CIO, VP/$212,354.00, Richard OHara/Environmental Health, Safety Dir., Ken Knibbs/US Ecology Texas Facility Mgr., Chuck Overman/Transportation Dir., Betsy Sterk/Dir. - Human Resources, Mike Ault/US Ecology Washington Facility Mgr., Kevin Trader/US Ecology Idaho GM, Terry Andrew Geis/Dir. - Occupational Health, Safety, VPP, Simon Bell/VP - Hazardous Waste Operations/$213,508.00, Steven D. Welling/VP - Sales, Marketing/$382,811.00, Chad Hyslop/Marketing, External Affairs Dir.

Directors: Stephen A. Romano/53/Dir., CEO, Pres., COO, John W. Poling/Dir., Kenneth C. Leung/Dir., Richard Riazzi/Dir., Jimmy D. Ross/Dir., Roy C. Eliff/Dir., Richard T. Swope/Dir., Edward F. Heil/Dir.

Owners: Richard Riazzi, Stephen A. Romano/1.40%, Jimmy D. Ross, Simon G. Bell, Edward F. Heil/9.40%, Quaker Investment Trust/5.00%, Jeffrey R. Feeler, John M. Cooper, Insiders/11.10%, Richard T. Swope, Roy C. Eliff, Steven D. Welling, Kenneth C. Leung, John W. Poling, DG Capital Management, Inc./9.60%

Financial Data: Fiscal Year End:12/31   Latest Annual Data: 12/31/2006

Year	Sales	Net Income
2006	$116,838,000	$15,889,000
2005	$79,387,000	$15,438,000
2004	$54,167,000	$23,410,000

Curr. Assets:	$43,042,000	Curr. Liab.:	$18,493,000	P/E Ratio:	23.57
Plant, Equip.:	$55,460,000	Total Liab.:	$30,686,000	Indic. Yr. Divd.:	$0.600
Total Assets:	$104,041,000	Net Worth:	$73,355,000	Debt/ Equity:	0.0002

American Energy Production Inc

6073 Hwy 281 S, Mineral Wells, TX, 76067; *PH:* 1-210-410-8158; *http://* www.americanenergyproduction.com

General - Incorporation .... DE	Stock - Price on:12/24/2007 ....$0.0371
Employees..1	Stock Exchange.................................OTC
Auditor ....Salberg & Co P.A	Ticker Symbol..................................AENP
Stk Agt ....Transfer Online, Inc.	Outstanding Shares 494,170,000
Counsel..NA	E.P.S...$0.00
DUNS No. ....NA	Shareholders....................................NA

Business: The group's principle activities include acquiring, developing, producing, exploring and selling oil and gas in the United States. On 20-Feb-2003, the company acquired proco operating co inc and on 05-Jan-2004, it acquired production resources inc. The group operates from United States.

Primary SIC and add'l.: 1381

CIK No: 0001111391

Officers: Charles Bitters/Dir., CEO, Pres./$120,000.00

Directors: Charles Bitters/Dir., CEO, Pres., Larry P. Horner/Dir., John Powell/Dir.

Owners: Insiders, Charles Bitters

Financial Data: Fiscal Year End:12/31   Latest Annual Data: 12/31/2006

Year	Sales	Net Income
2006	NA	$34,000
2005	NA	$13,920,000
2004	$40,000	-$5,050,000

Curr. Assets:	$2,000	Curr. Liab.:	$707,000		
Plant, Equip.:	$19,000	Total Liab.:	$707,000	Indic. Yr. Divd.:	NA
Total Assets:	$21,687,000	Net Worth:	$20,980,000	Debt/ Equity:	NA

American Enterprise Development Corp

2544 Tarpley, Ste. 104, Carrollton, TX, 75006; *PH:* 1-972-418-0225

General - Incorporation .... TX	Stock - Price on:12/24/2007 ....$0.28
Employees..6	Stock Exchange.................................OTC
Auditor ....James Carroll	Ticker Symbol..................................AEND
Stk Agt ....Transfer Online, Inc.	Outstanding Shares 47,910,000
Counsel..NA	E.P.S..-$0.15
DUNS No. ....NA	Shareholders....................................NA

Business: The group's principal activity was to develop and deliver online e-learning products to the consumer education market. On 29-Aug-2003, the group opted to abandon the existing business plan and elected to become a business development company under the investment company act of 1940.

Primary SIC and add'l.: 7389

CIK No: 0001136725

Subsidiaries: American Development Fund, Inc.

Owners: Carey Kent Williams/22.10%, William Carmichael, Wendell Eugene Ormiston/16.70%, Jonathan Gilchrist/6.70%, Miles Lim, Marco Arce/5.40%, William G. Martin/3.90%, Robert Wilson, Bob Hamlin, Andre Niclolson/5.40%, William Samuel Davis/16.60%, Insiders/43.70%

Financial Data: Fiscal Year End:12/31   Latest Annual Data: 03/31/2007

Year	Sales	Net Income
2007	NA	NA
2006	$19,000	-$2,267,000
2005	$218,000	-$292,000

Curr. Assets:	$1,100,000	Curr. Liab.:	$1,323,000		
Plant, Equip.:	$35,000	Total Liab.:	$4,087,000	Indic. Yr. Divd.:	NA
Total Assets:	$1,467,000	Net Worth:	-$2,620,000	Debt/ Equity:	1.4893

American Equity Investment Life Hldg Co

5000 Westown Pkwy., Ste. 440, West Des Moines, IA, 50266; *PH:* 1-515-221-0002; *Fax:* 1-515-221-9947; *http://* www.american-equity.com

General - Incorporation .... IA	Stock - Price on:12/24/2007 ....$12.2
Employees..280	Stock Exchange.................................NDQ
Auditor ....KPMG	Ticker Symbol..................................AEL
Stk Agt ....Computershare Ltd.	Outstanding Shares 56,840,000
Counsel..NA	E.P.S...$1.03
DUNS No. ....NA	Shareholders....................................NA

Business: The group's principal activities are to provide financial products and services primarily of the sale of fixed rate and index annuities. It's products include fixed rate annuities, index annuities, a variable annuity and life insurance. Fixed rate annuities includes single premium deferred annuities, flexible premium deferred annuities and single premium immediate annuities. Index annuities allow policyholders to link returns to the performance of a particular index without the risk of loss of their principal. Life insurance include traditional ordinary and term, universal life and other interest-sensitive life insurance products. The group markets its products through a variable cost brokerage distribution network. As of 31st dec 2003, it had approximately 60 national marketing organizations and 42,000 independent agents .

Primary SIC and add'l.: 6311
CIK No: 0001039828
Subsidiaries: American Equity Investment Life Holding Company, American Equity Investment Life Insurance Company, American Equity Investment Life Insurance Company of New York, EquiTrust Life Insurance Company, FBL Financial Group, Inc, Swiss Reinsurance Company
Officers: David J. Noble/Chmn., CEO, Pres./$120,000.00, James M. Gerlach/Vice Chmn., Exec. VP, Wendy L. Carlson/CFO, General Counsel/$320,867.00, Terry A. Reimer/Exec. VP, Debra J. Richardson/Sr. VP, Corp. Sec./$320,834.00
Directors: David J. Noble/Chmn., CEO, Pres., James M. Gerlach/Vice Chmn., Exec. VP, John C. Anderson/Dir., Kevin R. Wingert/Dir., Harley A. Whitfield/Dir., Robert L. Hilton/Dir., Robert L. Howe/63/Dir., John M. Matovina/Dir., A. J. Strickland/Dir., Alex M. Clark/Dir.
Owners: FMR Corp./5.15%, David J. Noble/5.28%, Insiders/7.78%, Farm Bureau Life Insurance Company/5.38%, Robert L. Hilton, A. J. Strickland, Cramer Rosenthal McGlynn, LLC/6.65%, Kevin R. Wingert, Robert L. Howe, Harley A. Whitfield, Debra J. Richardson, Dimensional Fund Advisors LP/8.31%, James M. Gerlach, John C. Anderson, John M. Matovina *(17 Owners included in Index)*
Financial Data: ***Fiscal Year End:***12/31 ***Latest Annual Data:*** 12/31/2006

Year	Sales	Net Income
2006	$915,860,000	$75,485,000
2005	$567,718,000	$42,992,000
2004	$495,601,000	$29,323,000

Curr. Assets:	$34,475,000	**Curr. Liab.:**	$385,973,000	**P/E Ratio:**	11.40
Plant, Equip.:	NA	**Total Liab.:**	$14,395,057,000	**Indic. Yr. Divd.:**	$0.060
Total Assets:	$14,990,123,000	**Net Worth:**	$595,066,000	**Debt/ Equity:**	0.8801

American Express Co

World Financial Ctr., 200 Vesey St., New York, NY, 10285; ***PH:*** 1-212-640-2000; ***Fax:*** 1-212-640-2458; ***http://*** www.americanexpress.com

General		***Stock***	
Incorporation	NY	Price on:12/24/2007	$63.06
Employees	65,400	Stock Exchange	NYSE
Auditor	PricewaterhouseCoopers LLP	Ticker Symbol	AXP
Stk Agt	Mellon Investor Services LLC	Outstanding Shares	1,190,000,000
Counsel	NA	E.P.S	$3.40
DUNS No.	00-697-9900	Shareholders	NA

Business: The groups principle activity is to provide global payments, network and travel services. The groups products include charge card, credit cards for consumers and business, consumer and small business lending products, travelers cheques and gift cards. The group operates from United States.
Primary SIC and add'l.: 6099 4724 6712 6282 6211 6141
CIK No: 0000004962
Subsidiaries: 1001674 Ontario Inc., 1001675 Ontario Inc., 56th Street AXP Campus LLC(AZ), Acamex Holdings, Inc., ACS AllCard Service GmbH, AE Exposure Management Limited, AEB - International Portfolios Management Company, AEB Global Trading Investments, Ltd., AEBL Uruguay Limited, AEOCC Management Company, Ltd., Ainwick Corporation, AITG Corporate Secretaries Li mited, Alpha Card Merchant Services SCRL (12.5% owned), Alpha Card SCRL (50% owned), American Express (China) Ltd. 240 Subsidiaries included in the Index
Officers: Edward P. Gilligan/Vice Chmn. - American Express Company, Group CEO - Business, to, Business/$10,346,530.00, Kenneth I. Chenault/Chmn., CEO/$29,137,010.00, Judson C. Linville/CEO, Pres. - Consumer Services, Douglas E. Buckminster/Pres. - International Consumer, Ashwini Gupta/Chief Risk Officer, Dan Henry/Exec. VP, Acting CFO, Steve Squeri/CIO, Exec. VP, Stephen P. Norman/Sec., Corporate Governance Officer, Alfred F. Kelly/Pres./$7,504,969.00, John D. Hayes/Exec. VP - Global Advertising, Brand Management, Chief Marketing Officer, Thomas Sclafani/Dir. - Public Affairs, Communications, Europe, Kevin L. Cox/Exec. VP - Human Resources - Quality, William H. Glenn/Pres. - Global Establishment Services, Global Merchant Group, Judy Tenzer/VP - Public Affairs, Communications, Louise M. Parent/Exec. VP, General Counsel/$6,026,735.00 *(39 Officers included in Index)*
Directors: Edward P. Gilligan/Vice Chmn. - American Express Company, Group CEO - Business, to, Business, Kenneth I. Chenault/Chmn., CEO, Peter Chernin/Dir., Charlene Barshefsky/Dir., Ursula M. Burns/Dir., Richard A. McGinn/Dir., Daniel F. Akerson/Dir., Edward D. Miller/Dir., Vernon E. Jordan/Dir., Jan Leschly/Dir., Frank P. Popoff/Dir., Robert D. Walter/Dir., Richard C. Levin/Dir., Steven S. Reinemund/Dir., Ronald A. Williams/Dir.
Owners: Davis Selected Advisers, LP/6.50%, Edward P. Gilligan, Peter Chernin, Ursula M. Burns, Edward D. Miller, Robert D. Walter, Kenneth I. Chenault, Richard A. McGinn, Jan Leschly, Frank P. Popoff, Gary L. Crittenden, Louise M. Parent, Charlene Barshefsky, Ronald A. Williams, Insiders/1.11% *(20 Owners included in Index)*
Financial Data: ***Fiscal Year End:***12/31 ***Latest Annual Data:*** 12/31/2006

Year	Sales	Net Income
2006	$27,136,000,000	$3,707,000,000
2005	$24,267,000,000	$3,734,000,000
2004	$29,115,000,000	$3,445,000,000

Curr. Assets:	$46,807,000,000	**Curr. Liab.:**	$55,797,000,000		
Plant, Equip.:	$2,448,000,000	**Total Liab.:**	$117,342,000,000	**Indic. Yr. Divd.:**	$0.720
Total Assets:	$127,853,000,000	**Net Worth:**	$10,511,000,000	**Debt/ Equity:**	4.1666

American Express Credit Corp

One Christina Ctr. 301 N Walnut St., Ste 1002, Wilmington, DE, 19801; ***PH:*** 1-302-594-3350; ***http://*** www.axpcp.com

General		***Stock***	
Incorporation	DE	Price on:12/24/2007	NA
Employees	NA	Stock Exchange	NA
Auditor	PricewaterhouseCoopers LLP	Ticker Symbol	NA
Stk Agt	NA	Outstanding Shares	NA
Counsel	NA	E.P.S	NA
DUNS No.	04-766-0337	Shareholders	NA

Business: The group's principal activity is to finance most non-interest-bearing charge cardmember receivables arising from the use of the American express(R) card. The cards include the American express(R) gold card, platinum card(R) and corporate card issued in the United States. The group also purchases certain revolving credit receivables arising from the use of American express credit cards, interest-bearing receivables from extended payment plans and interest-bearing equipment financing installment loans and leases.
Primary SIC and add'l.: 6153
CIK No: 0000004969
Subsidiaries: American Express Company, American Express International, Inc., American Express Travel Related Services Company, Inc.
Officers: Christopher S. Forno/Dir., CEO, Pres., David L. Yowan/Dir., CFO, Kevin M. Gould/VP, Chief Accounting Officer
Directors: Christopher S. Forno/Dir., CEO, Pres., David L. Yowan/Dir., CFO

American Express Financial Corp

55 Ameriprise Financial Ctr., Minneapolis, MN, 55474; ***PH:*** 1-612-671-3131; ***http://*** www.americanexpress.com

General		***Stock***	
Incorporation	DE	Price on:12/24/2007	$67.2
Employees	11,858	Stock Exchange	NYSE
Auditor	Ernst & Young LLP	Ticker Symbol	AMP
Stk Agt	Computershare Trust Co., N.A.	Outstanding Shares	235,250,000
Counsel	NA	E.P.S	$2.889
DUNS No.	NA	Shareholders	NA

Business: The groups principle activity is to provide financial services. The group operates from United States.
Primary SIC and add'l.: 6282
CIK No: 0000820027
Subsidiaries: ADT Nominees Ltd., Advisory Capital Partners LLC, Advisory Capital Strategies Group, Inc., Advisory Convertible Arbitrage LLC, Advisory Credit Opportunities GP LLC, Advisory European (General Partners) Inc., Advisory Quantitative Equity (General Partner) LLC, Advisory Select LLC, AEXP Affordable Housing LLC, American Centurion Life Assurance Company, American Enterprise Investment Services Inc., American Enterprise Life Insurance Company, American Enterprise REO 1, LLC, American Express Asset Management International (Japan) Ltd., American Express Asset Management International Inc. 94 Subsidiaries included in the Index
Officers: James M. Cracchiolo/49/Chmn., CEO/$18,307,530.00, Judson C. Linville/CEO, Pres. - Consumer Services, Douglas E. Buckminster/Pres. - International Consumer, William H. Glenn/Pres. - Global Establishment Services, Global Merchant Group, Thomas Schick/Exec. VP - Corporate Affairs - Communications, Thomas R. Moore/VP, Corp. Sec., Chief Governance Officer, Alfred F. Kelly/Pres. - American Express Company, Louise M. Parent/Exec. VP, General Counsel, Steve Squeri/CIO, Exec. VP, Mark Schwarzmann/46/Pres. - Insurance, Annuities, Product Distribution, William F. Truscott/47/Pres. - US Asset Management, Chief Investment Officer/$7,122,315.00, Walter S. Berman/65/CFO, Exec. VP/$6,998,583.00, Kim M. Sharan/50/Exec. VP, Chief Marketing Officer , Kelli A. Hunter/46/Exec. VP - Human Resources, John Junek/58/Exec. VP, General Counsel *(22 Officers included in Index)*
Directors: James M. Cracchiolo/49/Chmn., CEO, Edward P. Gilligan/Vice Chmn. - American Express Company, Ronald A. Williams/Dir., Richard C. Levin/Dir., Steven S. Reinemund/Dir., Jay H. Sarles/63/Dir., Robert F. Sharpe/56/Dir., Walker W. Lewis/63/Dir., Siri S. Marshall/59/Dir., Warren D. Knowlton/61/Dir., Daniel F. Akerson/Dir., Charlene Barshefsky/Dir., Kenneth I. Chenault/Dir., Peter Chernin/Dir., Vernon E. Jordan/Dir. *(24 Directors included in Index)*
Owners: Davis Selected Advisers, L.P./9.20%, Walker w. Lewis, Robert F. Sharpe, Jeffrey Noddle, Walter S. Berman, Siri S. Marshall, Brian M. Heath, James M. Cracchiolo, Glen Salow, Richard F. Powers, Jay H. Sarles, William H. Turner, Ira D. Hall, William F. Truscott, Insiders/1.10% *(17 Owners included in Index)*
Financial Data: ***Fiscal Year End:***12/31 ***Latest Annual Data:*** 12/31/2006

Year	Sales	Net Income
2006	$8,140,000,000	$631,000,000
2005	$7,484,000,000	$574,000,000

Curr. Assets:	$6,913,000,000	**Curr. Liab.:**	$8,509,000,000	**P/E Ratio:**	23.26
Plant, Equip.:	NA	**Total Liab.:**	$96,247,000,000	**Indic. Yr. Divd.:**	$0.600
Total Assets:	$104,172,000,000	**Net Worth:**	$7,925,000,000	**Debt/ Equity:**	0.2878

American Financial Group Inc

1 E 4th St., Cincinnati, OH, 45202; ***PH:*** 1-513-579-2121; ***Fax:*** 1-513-579-2113; ***http://*** www.amfnl.com; ***Email:*** afginvestorrelations@gaic.com

General		***Stock***	
Incorporation	OH	Price on:12/24/2007	$35.07
Employees	5,200	Stock Exchange	NYSE
Auditor	Ernst & Young LLP	Ticker Symbol	AFG
Stk Agt	American Stock Transfer & Trust Co.	Outstanding Shares	119,550,000
Counsel	NA	E.P.S	$3.51
DUNS No.	79-993-9913	Shareholders	NA

Business: The group's principle activity is to provide property and casualty insurance services. The group also provides sale of retirement annuities, life and supplemental health insurance products. The group operates from United States, Mexico, Canada, Puerto Rico, Europe and Asia.
Primary SIC and add'l.: 6331 6719
CIK No: 0001042046
Subsidiaries: AAG Holding Company, Inc., AFC Coal Properties, Inc., American Annuity Group Capital Trust II, American Empire Insurance Company, American Empire Surplus Lines Insurance Company, American Money Management Corporation, American Premier Underwriters, Inc., Annuity Investors Life Insurance Company, APU Holding Company, Brothers Property Corporation, Farmers Crop Insurance Alliance, Inc., GAI Warranty Company, GAI Warranty Company of Florida, Great American Alliance Insurance Company, Great American Assurance Company 46 Subsidiaries included in the Index
Officers: Carl H. Lindner/Chmn., CEO, Craig S. Lindner/Dir., Co - CEO, Pres./$6,731,919.00, Carl H. Lindner/Dir., Co - Pres./$7,006,703.00, Kathleen J. Brown/VP - Taxation, Robert E. Dobbs/VP - Internal Audit, James E. Evans/Dir., Sr. VP, General Counsel/$3,499,815.00, Keith A. Jensen/CFO, Sr. VP/$1,739,877.00, Thomas E. Mischell/Sr. VP - Taxes/$2,281,552.00, Karl J. Grafe/VP, Assist. General Counsel, Sandra W. Heimann/VP, James C. Kennedy/VP, Deputy General Counsel, Sec., Piyush K. Singh/CIO, VP, Robert H. Ruffing/VP, Controller, Anne N. Watson/VP - Investor Relations, David J. Witzgall/VP, Treasurer
Directors: Carl H. Lindner/Chmn., CEO, Craig S. Lindner/Dir., Co - CEO, Pres., Kenneth C. Ambrecht/Dir., Theodore H. Emmerich/Dir., Carl H. Lindner/Dir., Co - Pres., Terry S. Jacobs/Dir., James E. Evans/Dir., Sr. VP, General Counsel, William R. Martin/Dir., William W. Verity/Dir.
Owners: Carl H. Lindner/7.70%, The American Financial Group, Inc./5.80%, Keith E. Lindner/5.00%, Craig S. Lindner/7.80%, Carl H. Lindner/11.10%
Financial Data: ***Fiscal Year End:***12/31 ***Latest Annual Data:*** 12/31/2006

Year	Sales	Net Income
2006	$4,250,100,000	$453,400,000
2005	$4,038,283,000	$206,580,000
2004	$3,906,265,000	$359,860,000

Curr. Assets:	$5,978,600,000	Curr. Liab.:	$1,713,800,000	P/E Ratio:	10.47
Plant, Equip.:	NA	Total Liab.:	$21,888,300,000	Indic. Yr. Divd.:	$0.500
Total Assets:	$25,101,100,000	Net Worth:	$2,928,900,000	Debt/ Equity:	0.3039

American Financial Realty Trust

610 Old York Rd., Jenkintown, PA, 19046; *PH:* 1-215-887-2280; *Fax:* 1-215-884-9681; *http://* www.afrt.com; *Email:* ir@afrt.com

General - Incorporation	MD	**Stock**- Price on:12/24/2007	$10.55
Employees	175	Stock Exchange	NYSE
Auditor	KPMG LLP	Ticker Symbol	AFR
Stk Agt	American Stock Transfer & Trust Co.	Outstanding Shares	130,270,000
Counsel	NA	E.P.S.	$0.14
DUNS No.	NA	Shareholders	NA

Business: The groups principal activities include acquiring and operating properties leased to regulated financial institutions. In the year 2006, the group acquired 239 bank branches from National City Corporation, Sterling Bank, Citizens Bank, Charter One Bank and two bank subsidiaries of Citizens Financial Group, Inc. The group operates from 37 states in the United States

Primary SIC and add'l.: 6798 6798

CIK No: 0001193558

Subsidiaries: American Financial Realty Abstract, LLC, American Financial TRS, Inc., Chester Court Realty LP, Dresher Court Realty LP, First States Charleston, L.P., First States Charleston, LLC, First States Chester, LLC, First States Dresher, LLC, First States Group, LLC, First States Group, LP, First States Holdings, LLC, First States Holdings, LP, First States Investors 104, L.P., First States Investors 2001, LLC, First States Investors 2004, LLC 170 Subsidiaries included in the Index

Officers: Harold W. Pote/CEO, Pres., Glenn Blumenthal/COO, Co - Pres., David J. Nettina/CFO, Co - Pres., Chief Real Estate Officer, Edward J. Matey/Co - Pres., General Counsel, Sonya A. Huffman/Sr. VP - Operations, Muriel Lange/Dir. - Investor Relations, Anthony Defazio/Dir. - Public Relations, Christopher J. Barone/VP, Chief Accounting Officer, Jeffrey P. Foster/Sr. VP - Real Estate Transactions, Assoc. General Counsel, Fred Arena/Sr. VP - Asset Management

Directors: Lewis S. Ranieri/Chmn. - Board of Trust, Richard A. Kraemer/Trustee, Vice Chmn., John P. Hollihan/Trustee, Raymond Garea/Trustee, Alan E. Master/Trustee, Richard J. Berry/Trustee, John R. Biggar/Trustee

Owners: David J. Nettina, Glenn Blumenthal, Alan E. Master, Neuberger Berman Inc./9.50%, The Vanguard Group, Inc./6.00%, Insiders/4.10%, Barclays Global Investors, NA/6.40%, Hunter Global Investors L.P./5.40%, Barrow, Hanley, Mewhinney & Strauss, Inc./6.10%, John P. Hollihan, Richard A. Kraemer, John R. Biggar, Robert M. Patterson, Lewis S. Ranieri, Michael J. Hagan (*20 Owners included in Index*)

Financial Data: *Fiscal Year End:*12/31 *Latest Annual Data:* 12/31/2006

Year	Sales	Net Income
2006	$426,622,000	-$20,598,000
2005	$520,349,000	-$93,615,000
2004	$337,352,000	-$22,245,000

Curr. Assets:	$245,400,000	Curr. Liab.:	$107,115,000		
Plant, Equip.:	$2,893,478,000	Total Liab.:	$2,820,200,000	Indic. Yr. Divd.:	$0.760
Total Assets:	$3,606,164,000	Net Worth:	$785,964,000	Debt/ Equity:	2.9965

American General Finance Corp

601 N.W. Second St., Evansville, IN, 47708; *PH:* 1-812-424-8031; *http://* www.amanasugroup.com

General - Incorporation	IN	**Stock**- Price on:12/24/2007	NA
Employees	NA	Stock Exchange	NA
Auditor	PricewaterhouseCoopers LLP	Ticker Symbol	NA
Stk Agt	NA	Outstanding Shares	NA
Counsel	NA	E.P.S.	NA
DUNS No.	00-693-6918	Shareholders	NA

Business: The group's principle activities are to provide consumer finance and insurance services. The group operates in two business segments: consumer finance and insurance. The consumer finance segment makes home equity loans, originates secured and unsecured consumer loans, extends lines of credit, and purchases retail sales contracts from, and provides revolving retail services for, retail merchants. The insurance segment, writes and assumes credit and non-credit insurance through products that are sold through consumer branches.

Primary SIC and add'l.: 6311 6141 6321 6719 6331

CIK No: 0000025598

Subsidiaries: American General Finance, Inc., American International Group, Inc

American General Finance Inc

PO Box 3662, Evansville, IN, 47735; *PH:* 1-812-424-8031; *http://* loansfast.com

General - Incorporation	IN	**Stock**- Price on:12/24/2007	NA
Employees	NA	Stock Exchange	NA
Auditor	PricewaterhouseCoopers LLP	Ticker Symbol	NA
Stk Agt	NA	Outstanding Shares	NA
Counsel	NA	E.P.S.	NA
DUNS No.	00-693-6918	Shareholders	NA

Business: The group's principle activities are to provide consumer finance, life and health insurance services and real estate properties through 1,403 offices in Puerto Rico and U.S. Virgin islands. The group operates in two segments: consumer finance and insurance. The consumer finance segment provides home equity loans, originates secured and unsecured consumer loans and extends lines of credit, purchases retail sales contracts from retail merchants and other services. The services also include credit and non-credit insurance to consumer finance customers. The insurance segment writes and assumes credit and non-credit insurance.

Primary SIC and add'l.: 6321 6162 6311 6331 6141

CIK No: 0000025600

Subsidiaries: AGFC, Merit Life Insurance Co

Officers: Frederick W. Geissinger/Chmn., CEO, Pres., George W. Schmidt/VP, Controller, Assist. Sec., Principal Accounting Officer, Donald R. Breivogel/Dir., CFO, Sr. VP

Directors: Frederick W. Geissinger/Chmn., CEO, Pres., Donald R. Breivogel/Dir., CFO, Sr. VP, Stephen L. Blake/Dir., Robert A. Cole/Dir., William N. Dooley/Dir., Jerry L. Gilpin/Dir., Stephen H. Loewenkamp/Dir., George D. Roach/Dir.

American Golden Century Investments Inc

601 W Brd.way, Ste. 400, Vancouver, BC, V5Z 4C2; *PH:* 1-604-675-6930

General - Incorporation	NV	**Stock**- Price on:12/24/2007	NA
Employees	NA	Stock Exchange	NA
Auditor	Hansen, Barnett & Maxwell	Ticker Symbol	NA
Stk Agt	NA	Outstanding Shares	NA
Counsel	NA	E.P.S.	NA
DUNS No.	NA	Shareholders	NA

Business: The group's principle activity is to market and sell vitamins, minerals, nutritional supplements and other health and fitness products. The products can be sold to medical professionals, alternative health professionals, martial arts studios and instructors, sports and fitness trainers and other customers. The company intends to market its products through its Website vitamineralherb.com. Currently, the company has no operations and is in the process of acquiring assets and raising capital to develop a business plan. The group operates from United States.

Primary SIC and add'l.: 7375 5122

CIK No: 0001094656

Subsidiaries: Sichuan Golden Ant Biotechnology Development Limited Company

American Goldfields Inc

4170 Still Creek Dr., Ste. 200, Vancouver, BC, V5C 6C6; *PH:* 1-604-299-6600; *http://* www.americangoldfields.com; *Email:* info@americangoldfields.com

General - Incorporation	NV	**Stock**- Price on:12/24/2007	$0.75
Employees	NA	Stock Exchange	OTC
Auditor	Morgan & Company	Ticker Symbol	AGFL
Stk Agt	Pacific Stock Transfer Company	Outstanding Shares	NA
Counsel	David Lubin and Associates	E.P.S.	NA
DUNS No.	NA	Shareholders	NA

Business: The groups principal activity is to explore minerals. The group operates from Canada and the United States.

Primary SIC and add'l.: 1382

CIK No: 0001167886

Subsidiaries: Baymont Explorations Inc

Officers: Donald Neal/Dir., CEO, COO, Pres., Sec., Treasurer

Directors: Donald Neal/Dir., CEO, COO, Pres., Sec., Treasurer, David Gladwell/Dir., Richard Kern/Dir., Jared Beebe/Dir.

Owners: Insiders/1.00%, Donald Neal/1.00%, Donald Neal/1.00%, Insiders/1.00%

Financial Data: *Fiscal Year End:*01/31 *Latest Annual Data:* 01/31/2007

Year	Sales	Net Income
2007	NA	-$692,000
2006	NA	-$1,820,000
2005	NA	-$325,000

Curr. Assets:	$387,000	Curr. Liab.:	$170,000		
Plant, Equip.:	NA	Total Liab.:	$170,000	Indic. Yr. Divd.:	NA
Total Assets:	$421,000	Net Worth:	$252,000	Debt/ Equity:	NA

American Greetings Corp

1 American Rd., Cleveland, OH, 44144; *PH:* 1-216-252-7300; *Fax:* 1-216-252-6778; *http://* corporate.americangreetings.com

General - Incorporation	OH	**Stock**- Price on:12/24/2007	$24.98
Employees	9,400	Stock Exchange	NYSE
Auditor	Ernst & Young LLP	Ticker Symbol	AM
Stk Agt	National City Bank	Outstanding Shares	55,160,000
Counsel	Jones, Day, Reavis & Pogue	E.P.S.	$1.02
DUNS No.	00-418-0022	Shareholders	NA

Business: The groups principle activity is designing, manufacturing and selling seasonal greeting cards. The group distributes social expression products, including e-mail greetings, personalized printable greeting cards and a range of graphics, through a variety of digital and other electronic channels, including websites, Internet portals and electronic mobile devices. In 2007 the group acquired webshots brand from CNET Networks, Inc. The group operates from United States.

Primary SIC and add'l.: 2678 2679 2771 7379 3999 3069

CIK No: 0000005133

Subsidiaries: A.g. (UK), Inc., A.G.C. Investments, Inc., AG Interactive, Inc., AGC Funding Corporation, AGC Holdings, Inc., Carlton Cards Limited, Carlton Cards Retail, Inc., Gibson Greetings, Inc., Gibson Hanson Graphics Ltd., John Sands (N.Z.) Ltd., Plus Mark, Inc., Those Characters From Cleveland, Inc.

Officers: Zev Weiss/Dir., CEO/$2,828,283.00, Josef Mandelbaum/CEO - AG Intellectual Properties, Jeffrey Weiss/Dir., COO, Pres./$2,171,468.00, William R. Mason/Sr. VP - Wal, Mart Team, John S.N. Charlton/Sr. VP - International, Brian T. McGrath/Sr. VP - Human Resources, Douglas W. Rommel/VP - Information Services Division, Stephen J. Smith/CFO, Sr. VP/$549,863.00, Thomas H. Johnston/Sr. VP - Creative, Merchandising, Michael L. Goulder/Sr. VP, Exec. Supply Chain Officer/$1,317,609.00, Joseph B. Cipollone/VP, Corporate Controller, Steven S. Willensky/Sr. VP - Exec. Sales, Marketing Officer/$1,232,941.00, Catherine M. Kilbane/Sr. VP - General Counsel, Sec., Gregory M. Steinberg/Treasurer & Dir. - Investor Relations, Erwin Weiss/Sr. VP - Enterprise Resource Planning

Directors: Zev Weiss/Dir., CEO, Morry Weiss/Chmn., Jeffrey Weiss/Dir., COO, Pres., Scott S. Cowen/Dir., Michael J. Merriman/Dir., Jerry Sue Thornton/Dir., Jeffrey D. Dunn/Dir., William E. MacDonald/Dir., Joseph S. Hardin/Dir., Stephen R. Hardis/Dir., Charles A. Ratner/Dir.

Owners: Stephen J. Smith, Michael L. Goulder, Stephen R. Hardis, Insiders/27.92%, Stephen R. Hardis, Joseph S. Hardin, Steven S. Willensky, Charles A. Ratner, Morry Weiss/19.05%, Insiders/2.18%, TowerView LLC/5.76%, Zev Weiss/6.07%, Dimensional Fund Advisors, LP/8.73%, Jerry Sue Thornton, Vanguard Fiduciary Trust Company, as Trustee for American Greetings Corporation/20.74% (*31 Owners included in Index*)

Financial Data: *Fiscal Year End:*02/28 *Latest Annual Data:* 2/28/2007

Year	Sales	Net Income
2007	$1,744,603,000	$42,378,000
2006	$1,885,701,000	$84,376,000
2005	$1,902,727,000	$95,279,000

Curr. Assets:	$799,281,000	Curr. Liab.:	$373,000,000	P/E Ratio: 35.18
Plant, Equip.:	$285,072,000	Total Liab.:	$765,640,000	Indic. Yr. Divd.: $0.400
Total Assets:	$1,778,214,000	Net Worth:	$1,012,574,000	Debt/ Equity: 0.2211

American Healthchoice Inc

2221 Justin Rd., No. 119-154, Flower Mound, TX, 75028; PH: 1-972-751-1900;
Fax: 1-972-538-0131; http:// www.americanhealthchoice.com

General - Incorporation............NY	Stock- Price on:12/24/2007 ....NA
Employees.............................65	Stock Exchange.........................OTC
Auditor .... Lane Gorman Trubitt LLP	Ticker Symbol.........................AMHI
Stk Agt.........Corporate Stock Transfer, Inc.	Outstanding Shares ....NA
Counsel.................................NA	E.P.S..............................$0.001
DUNS No. 83-547-9163	Shareholders............................NA

Business: The group's principal activities are to provide medical, physical therapy and chiropractic services through primary care medical clinics and chiropractic clinics. The services offered include chiropractic, neuro-muscular diagnostic, physical therapy and rehabilitative services. Other services of the group include urgent care and diagnostic testing. As on 31-Sep-2003 the group owned and operated 13 clinics. Of these, twelve are primary care clinics, of which two are medical clinics and ten are chiropractic clinics. The clinics are located in Texas and Louisiana. The chiropractic services are based on preventative treatment and treatment of the nerve system and body structure, such as the spinal column. The group depends upon third party payers for reimbursement of approximately 98% of patient services.

Primary SIC and add'l.: 8011 8049
CIK No: 0000854862
Subsidiaries: American HealthChoice, Inc., Texas corporation, RehabCo, Inc., Texas corporation, Texas corporation, Texas corporation.
Officers: J. W. Stucki/Chmn., CEO, Pres., John C. Stuecheli/CFO, GM, Jeff Jones/Contact - American Healthchoice Clinics, New Orleans Clinic, Knotts /Contact - American Healthchoice Clinics, Antioch, Doug Stucki/Contact - American Healthchoice Clinics, Franklin, Mccoy /Contact - American Healthchoice Clinics, Nashville, Totty /Contact - American Healthchoice Clinics, Nashville, Benedict /Contact - American Healthchoice Clinics, Nashville, Farmer /Contact - American Healthchoice Clinics, Nashville, Jeff Echols/Contact - American Healthchoice Clinics, Austin, Joe Hood/Contact - American Healthchoice Clinics, Austin, Lones /Contact - American Healthchoice Clinics, Austin, North Lamar/Contact - American Healthchoice Clinics, Austin, Robert R. Dorn/Contact - American Healthchoice Clinics, Killeen, Hal Lewis/Contact - American Healthchoice Clinics, Abilene (47 Officers included in Index)
Directors: J. W. Stucki/Chmn., CEO, Pres.
Owners: Michael R. Smith, Joseph W. Stucki/39.00%, Jeffrey Jones/8.50%, Insiders/48.60%, John C. Stuecheli, James Roberts, David P. Voracek/13.20%

Financial Data: Fiscal Year End:09/30   Latest Annual Data: 09/30/2005

Year	Sales	Net Income
2005	$6,623,000	$475,000
2004	$5,263,000	-$1,498,000
2003	$4,523,000	-$1,791,000

Curr. Assets:	$6,240,000	Curr. Liab.:	$4,642,000	
Plant, Equip.:	$469,000	Total Liab.:	$4,642,000	Indic. Yr. Divd.: NA
Total Assets:	$8,057,000	Net Worth:	$3,416,000	Debt/ Equity: NA

American Home Food Products Inc

67 Wall St., Ste. 2001, New York, NY, 10005; PH: 1-212-825-1400

General - Incorporation.............Fny	Stock- Price on:12/24/2007 ....$0.25
Employees.................................1	Stock Exchange.........................OTC
Auditor ....Sherb & Co. LLP	Ticker Symbol.........................AHFP
Stk Agt............Signature Stock Transfer, Inc.	Outstanding Shares 4,470,000
Counsel.................................NA	E.P.S.............................$0.01
DUNS No. 25-333-0781	Shareholders............................NA

Business: The group's principal activity is to manufacture and market premium building products. The first line of products are pre-packaged concrete repair and floor resurfacing products. The second line of products are masonry waterproofing products. The third line of product is a line of polypropylene concrete reinforcing fibers. The customers of the group include retailers, construction professionals and distributors located throughout the United States and some parts of Canada. The operations are conducted at its 25,000 square feet facility and two 10,000 square feet warehouses located in clifton, New Jersey. The overall facility consists of three buildings located on a 1.6 acre tract of commercially-zoned land.

Primary SIC and add'l.: 3241 5211 3271 3273 5032 3272 2452
CIK No: 0000945634
Subsidiaries: Novex Systems International, Ltd.
Owners: Edward J. Malloy/0.20%, Daniel W. Dowe/9.00%, William K. Lavin/0.30%, Kevin DeMatties/0.60%, Insiders/10.10%

Financial Data: Fiscal Year End:05/31   Latest Annual Data: 05/31/2007

Year	Sales	Net Income
2007	$246,000	-$364,000
2006	$224,000	-$307,000
2005	$209,000	-$382,000

Curr. Assets:	$17,000	Curr. Liab.:	$3,541,000	
Plant, Equip.:	NA	Total Liab.:	$3,541,000	Indic. Yr. Divd.: NA
Total Assets:	$458,000	Net Worth:	-$3,083,000	Debt/ Equity: NA

American Home Mortgage Investment Corp

538 Broadhollow Rd., Melville, NY, 11747; PH: 1-516-396-7700; http:// www.americanhm.com

General - Incorporation ....MD	Stock- Price on:12/24/2007 ....$22.46
Employees.........................7,409	Stock Exchange.........................NYSE
Auditor ....Deloitte & Touche LLP	Ticker Symbol.........................AHM
Stk Agt..... American Stock Transfer & Trust Co.	Outstanding Shares 54,280,000
Counsel.................................NA	E.P.S..................................NA
DUNS No..................................NA	Shareholders............................NA

Business: The group operates through its subsidiaries whose principle activity is to provide mortgage loans. The group operates through four segments namely, mortgage holdings, loan origination, loan servicing and banking. The group operates from the United States. The group's quarterly revenue for September 2007 was 197.24 millions of USD.

Primary SIC and add'l.: 6798
CIK No: 0001256536
Subsidiaries: AHM Acceptance, AHM Financial, AHM Mortgage, AHM Servicing Inc., American Brokers Conduit, American Home Mortgage, American Home Mortgage Acceptance, Inc., American Home Mortgage Corp of New York, American Home Mortgage Corp., American Home Mortgage Holdings, Inc., American Home Mortgage of NewYork, American Home Mortgage Servicing, Inc., American Home Mtg Servicing, American Mortgage, CNI 37 Subsidiaries included in the Index
Officers: Michael Strauss/49/Chmn., CEO, Pres., John A. Johnston/54/Dir., Pres. - Western Division, Ronald L. Bergum/46/Exec. VP - Western Division, Robert Bernstein/42/Exec. VP, Controller, Christopher J. Cavaco/39/CIO, Exec. VP, Al Crisanty/46/Exec. VP - Wholesale, Doug Douglas/60/Exec. VP - Business Processes, Thomas J. Fiddler/42/Exec. VP - Eastern Division, David M. Friedman/56/Dir. - Servicing, Exec. VP, Kathleen R. Heck/53/Exec. VP - Eastern Division, Donald Henig/49/Pres. - Wholesale and Direct-to-Consumer Division, Alan B. Horn/56/Exec. VP, General Counsel, Sec., Stephen A. Hozie/49/CFO, Exec. VP, Robert F. Johnson/35/Exec. VP - Capital Markets, Dena L. Kwaschyn/47/Exec. VP - Operations (22 Officers included in Index)
Directors: Michael Strauss/49/Chmn., CEO, Pres., Nicholas R. Marfino/52/Dir., Michael A. McManus/65/Dir., Cathleen C. Raffaeli/51/Dir., John A. Johnston/54/Dir., Pres. - Western Division, Irving J. Thau/68/Dir., Kristian R. Salovaara/47/Dir.
Owners: Nicholas R. Marfino, Robert F. Johnson, Goldman Sachs Asset Management, L.P./7.20%, Cathleen C. Raffaeli, Michael A. McManus, Insiders/10.13%, Kristian R. Salovaara, Thomas M. McDonagh, Stephen A. Hozie, Munder Capital Management/6.80%, John A. Johnston, Irving J. Thau, Richard S. Loeffler, Michael Strauss/9.47%, NWQ Investment Management Company, LLC/5.80%

Financial Data: Fiscal Year End:12/31   Latest Annual Data: 12/31/2006

Year	Sales	Net Income
2006	$2,196,891,000	$263,527,000
2005	$1,391,813,000	$260,786,000
2004	$566,614,000	$74,912,000

Curr. Assets:	$830,584,000	Curr. Liab.:	$9,359,203,000	
Plant, Equip.:	$86,211,000	Total Liab.:	$17,558,699,000	Indic. Yr. Divd.: $4.480
Total Assets:	$18,828,985,000	Net Worth:	$1,270,286,000	Debt/ Equity: 9.7480

American Homepatient Inc

5200 Maryland Way, Ste. 400, Brentwood, TN, 37027; PH: 1-615-221-8884; Fax: 1-615-373-9932; http:// www.ahom.com

General - Incorporation ....DE	Stock- Price on:12/24/2007 ....$2.37
Employees.........................2,454	Stock Exchange.........................OTC
Auditor ....KPMG LLP	Ticker Symbol.........................AHOM
Stk Agt...........................SunTrust Bank	Outstanding Shares 17,570,000
Counsel.................................NA	E.P.S.................................-$0.22
DUNS No. 55-628-0899	Shareholders............................NA

Business: The group's principal activity is to provide home health care services and products. The group operates in three segments: respiratory therapy services, medical equipment and medical supplies and infusion therapy services. The respiratory therapy service segment provides services primarily to patients with severe and chronic pulmonary diseases. Medical equipment and supplies segment provides a comprehensive line of equipment to serve the needs of home care patients. The infusion therapy segment provides infusion therapy services. At 31-Dec-2003, the group provided its services in 286 centers in 35 states. The trademarks of the group are homepatient(R) , aermeds (R), redism, entercare sm, resource sm, enspire sm, opus sm, sleep sm, go paperless sm and personal caring service sm.

Primary SIC and add'l.: 8082 7352 8099
CIK No: 0000879181
Subsidiaries: AHP Alliance of Columbia, AHP Delmarva, LLP, AHP Finance, Inc., AHP Home Care Alliance of Gainesville, AHP Home Care Alliance of Tennessee, AHP Home Care Alliance of Virginia, AHP Home Medical Equipment, AHP Knoxville Partnership, AHP, L.P., AHP-MHR Home Care, LLP, American HomePatient Arkansas Ventures, Inc., American HomePatient Delaware Ventures, Inc., American HomePatient of Illinois, Inc., American HomePatient of New York, Inc., American HomePatient of Sanford, LLC 40 Subsidiaries included in the Index
Officers: Joseph F. Furlong/CEO/$1,247,183.00, Stephen L. Clanton/CFO, Exec. VP/$581,521.00, Frank Powers/COO, Exec. VP/$647,208.00
Directors: Henry T. Blackstock/65/Dir., Donald R. Millard/60/Dir., William C. Oneil/73/Dir., Wayne W. Woody/66/Dir.
Owners: Joseph F. Furlong/7.40%, Highland Capital Management, L.P./48.00%, Fidelity Management and Research Company/9.90%, Insiders/10.50%, Henry T. Blackstock, William C. ONeil, Donald R. Millard, Wayne W. Woody, Stephen L. Clanton, Frank D. Powers, John D. Gouy

Financial Data: Fiscal Year End:12/31   Latest Annual Data: 12/31/2006

Year	Sales	Net Income
2006	$328,080,000	-$2,587,000
2005	$328,418,000	$7,744,000
2004	$335,823,000	$13,231,000

Curr. Assets:	$78,468,000	Curr. Liab.:	$47,128,000	
Plant, Equip.:	$51,411,000	Total Liab.:	$297,369,000	Indic. Yr. Divd.: NA
Total Assets:	$276,671,000	Net Worth:	-$21,316,000	Debt/ Equity: NA

American Independence Corp

485 Madison Ave., New York, NY, 10022; PH: 1-212-355-4141; Fax: 1-212-644-7450; http:// www.americanindependencecorp.com

General - Incorporation: DE
Employees: 59
Auditor: KPMG LLP
Stk Agt: Registrar & Transfer Co
Counsel: NA
DUNS No.: 00-181-0803

Stock- Price on:12/24/2007: $10.73
Stock Exchange: NDQ
Ticker Symbol: AMIC
Outstanding Shares: 8,460,000
E.P.S.: $0.35
Shareholders: NA

Business: The group's principal activity is to provide health insurance and reinsurance services. These services are provided through its wholly owned subsidiaries: independence American insurance company, independencecare, risk assessment strategies and voorhees risk management llc. Prior to acquiring the insurance operations on Nov 14, 2002, it was a holding company engaged in providing Internet services through its subsidiary companies. In Feb 2003, the group acquired 80% interest in voorhees risk management llc.

Primary SIC and add'l.: 6311

CIK No: 0000097196

Subsidiaries: Independence American Holdings Corp, Independence American Insurance Company, IndependenceCare Holdings LLC, IndependenceCare Management Corp, IndependenceCare Underwriting Administrators, LLC, IndependenceCare Underwriting Services, IndependenceCare Underwriting Services - Minneapolis, LLC, IndependenceCare Underwriting Services - Tennessee, LLC, IndependenceCare Underwriting Services, LLC, Risk Assessment Strategies, Inc., Voorhees Risk Management LLC

Officers: Roy T.K. Thung/Dir., CEO, Pres., David T. Kettig/Dir., Sr. VP, Co - COO, Teresa A. Herbert/CFO, VP, Brian R. Schlier/VP - Taxation, Henry B. Spencer/VP - Investments, Ronald I. Simon/Dir., Independent Financial Consultant, Gary J. Balzofiore/VP - Finance, Myron M. Picoult/Dir., Independent Insurance Consultant, Bill Murphy/Pres. - Majestic Underwriters LLC, Frank Dalicandro/Pres. - Marlton Risk Group, Bob Shea/Pres. - Risk Assesment Strategies, Scott Wood/Sr. VP, Co - COO, Jeff Smedsrud/Sr. VP, Chief Strategic Development Officer, Adam C. Vandervoort/33/VP, General Counsel, Sec.

Directors: Roy T.K. Thung/Dir., CEO, Pres., David T. Kettig/Dir., Sr. VP, Co - COO, Edward Netter/Dir., Martin E. Winter/Dir., Ronald I. Simon/Dir., Independent Financial Consultant, Myron M. Picoult/Dir., Independent Insurance Consultant, Edward A. Bennett/Dir.

Owners: Myron M. Picoult, Martin E. Winter, Edward A. Bennett/1.19%, Insiders/3.73%, Teresa A. Herbert, Ronald I. Simon, Independence Holding Company

Financial Data: *Fiscal Year End:*12/31 *Latest Annual Data:* 12/31/2006

Year	Sales	Net Income
2006	$81,485,000	$1,454,000
2005	$83,130,000	$5,460,000
2004	$80,378,000	$5,904,000

Curr. Assets:	$46,312,000	**Curr. Liab.:**	$42,993,000	**P/E Ratio:**	30.66
Plant, Equip.:	$150,000	**Total Liab.:**	$47,650,000	**Indic. Yr. Divd.:**	NA
Total Assets:	$134,760,000	**Net Worth:**	$83,084,000	**Debt/ Equity:**	0.0103

American International Group Inc

70 Pine St., New York, NY, 10270; ***PH:*** 1-212-770-7000; ***Fax:*** 1-212-509-9705; ***http://*** www.aigcorporate.com; ***Email:*** aigcs@aig.com

General - Incorporation: DE
Employees: 106,000
Auditor: PricewaterhouseCoopers LLP
Stk Agt: Wells Fargo Shareowner Services
Counsel: NA
DUNS No.: NA

Stock- Price on:12/24/2007: $72.02
Stock Exchange: NYSE
Ticker Symbol: AIG
Outstanding Shares: 2,590,000,000
E.P.S.: $5.73
Shareholders: NA

Business: The group operates through its subsidiaries whose principle activity is to provide insurance and insurance related services. The groups services include general insurance, financial services, and life insurance and retirement services. The group operates through four segments namely, general insurance, life insurance and retirement services, financial services and asset management. The group acquired Travel Guard international and Central Insurance Co., Ltd. in the year 2006 and 21st Century in the year 2007. The group operates from the United States, Poerto Rico and U.S. Virgin Islands. The group's quarterly revenue for September 2007 was 29,836.00 millions of USD.

Primary SIC and add'l.: 6351 6311 6331 6722 6371 6799 6282

CIK No: 0000005272

Subsidiaries: 21stCentury Casualty Company, 21stCentury Insurance Company, 21stCentury Insurance Company of the Southwest, 21stCentury Insurance Group, A.I. Credit Consumer Discount Corp., A.I. Credit Corp., A.I.G. Colombia Seguros Generales S.A., A.I.G. Mortgage Holdings Israel, Ltd., Advantage Capital Corporation, AGC Life Insurance Company, Agency Management Corporation, AI Network Corporation, AICCO, Inc., AIG Advantage Insurance Company, AIG Advisor Group, Inc. 233 Subsidiaries included in the Index

Officers: Martin J. Sullivan/Dir., CEO, Pres./$21,229,680.00, Win J. Neuger/Exec. VP, Chief Investment Officer/$8,788,744.00, Hans K. Danielsson/Sr. VP - Investments/$9,960,886.00, Kevin P. Fitzpatrick/VP - Real Estate Investments, Steven Guterman/VP, David L. Herzog/Sr. VP, Controller, Steven J. Bensinger/CFO, Exec. VP/$7,594,592.00, Richard W. Scott/Sr. VP - Investments

Directors: Martin J. Sullivan/Dir., CEO, Pres., Robert B. Willumstad/Chmn., Edmund S.W. Tse/Dir., Frank G. Zarb/Dir., Pei-Yuan Chia/Dir., Michael H. Sutton/Dir., James F. Orr/Dir., Virginia M. Rometty/Dir., Marshall A. Cohen/Dir., Martin S. Feldstein/Dir., Ellen V. Futter/Dir., Stephen L. Hammerman/Dir., Richard C. Holbrooke/Dir., Fred H. Langhammer/Dir., George L. Miles/Dir. *(16 Directors included in Index)*

Owners: Martin S. Feldstein, Robert M. Sandler, Win J. Neuger, Michael H. Sutton, Morris W. Offit, Martin J. Sullivan, Fred H. Langhammer, Robert B. Willumstad, Richard C. Holbrooke, C.V. Starr & Co., Inc./13.60%, FMR Corp. and Edward C. Johnson 3d/5.99%, James F. Orr, Edmund S.W. Tse, Marshall A. Cohen, Stephen L. Hammerman *(21 Owners included in Index)*

Financial Data: *Fiscal Year End:*12/31 *Latest Annual Data:* 12/31/2006

Year	Sales	Net Income
2006	$113,194,000,000	$14,048,000,000
2005	$108,905,000,000	$10,477,000,000
2004	$97,666,000,000	$9,839,000,000

Curr. Assets:	$67,983,000,000	**Curr. Liab.:**	$133,902,000,000	**P/E Ratio:**	12.57
Plant, Equip.:	$4,381,000,000	**Total Liab.:**	$877,737,000,000	**Indic. Yr. Divd.:**	$0.660
Total Assets:	$979,414,000,000	**Net Worth:**	$101,677,000,000	**Debt/ Equity:**	2.0362

American International Industries Inc

601 Cien St., Ste. 235, Kemah, TX, 77565; ***PH:*** 1-281-334-9479; ***Fax:*** 1-281-334-9508; ***http://*** www.americanii.com; ***Email:*** amin@americanii.com

General - Incorporation: NV
Employees: 109
Auditor: Glo Cpas, LLP
Stk Agt: SunTrust Bank
Counsel: Thomas J. Craft Jr. P.A
DUNS No.: NA

Stock- Price on:12/24/2007: $4.65
Stock Exchange: NDQ
Ticker Symbol: AMIN
Outstanding Shares: 5,450,000
E.P.S.: -$0.35
Shareholders: NA

Business: The group's principal activities are to manufacture, distribute and supply barbecue pits, custom sheet metal products, specialty chemicals and automotive after-Market products. The group has interests in oil and gas and real estate. The group is a holding company operating through its subsidiaries, which include brenham oil & gas, inc. (brenham), Texas real estate enterprises, inc. (tree), acqueren, inc., marald, inc. And unlimited coatings corporation. Brenham has a non-operating royalty interest in a producing gas well. Tree acquires and holds real estate, which is available for resale. Northern plastics, inc., a wholly owned subsidiary of acqueren, inc., is a supplier of automotive after-Market products and consumer durable goods. On 19-Nov-2003, the group acquired delta seaboard well services inc.

Primary SIC and add'l.: 5063 6792 6552 3444 5013 5084 3631

CIK No: 0001073146

Subsidiaries: Brenham Oil & Gas, Inc., Delta Seaboard Well Service, Inc., Hammonds Technical Services, Inc, International American Technologies, Inc, Northeastern Plastics, Inc, T.R.E. Enterprises, Inc

Officers: Daniel Dror/Chmn., CEO, Pres., Rebekah Laird-Ruthstrom/Sec., Treasurer, Sherry L. Couturier/CFO, VP, John A. Braden/Auditor

Directors: Daniel Dror/Chmn., CEO, Pres., Charles R. Zeller/Dir., Robert W. Derrick/Dir., Thomas J. Craft/Dir., John W. Stump/Dir.

Owners: Insiders/4.43%, Thomas J. Craft, Charles R. Zeller, Insiders/4.43%, Gary D. Woerz, Daniel Dror/6.60%, Robert W. Derrick, International Diversified Corporation, Ltd./27.72%, John W. Stump

Financial Data: *Fiscal Year End:*12/31 *Latest Annual Data:* 12/31/2006

Year	Sales	Net Income
2006	$33,409,000	$1,570,000
2005	$25,476,000	-$4,524,000
2004	$16,687,000	$1,029,000

Curr. Assets:	$22,653,000	**Curr. Liab.:**	$5,028,000	**P/E Ratio:**	27.35
Plant, Equip.:	$3,142,000	**Total Liab.:**	$12,476,000	**Indic. Yr. Divd.:**	NA
Total Assets:	$36,597,000	**Net Worth:**	$22,562,000	**Debt/ Equity:**	0.3313

American International Ventures Inc

260 Garibaldi Ave., Lodi, NJ, 07644; ***PH:*** 1-973-335-4400; ***http://*** www.aivnotc.com

General - Incorporation: DE
Employees: NA
Auditor: Robert G. Jeffrey
Stk Agt: Interwest Transfer Company, Inc.
Counsel: NA
DUNS No.: NA

Stock- Price on:12/24/2007: $0.07
Stock Exchange: OTC
Ticker Symbol: AIVN
Outstanding Shares: 19,350,000
E.P.S.: -$0.01
Shareholders: NA

Business: The groups principal activity is to explore minerals. In the year 2005, the group acquired by Electrum. The group operates from Canada and the United States.

Primary SIC and add'l.: 8742

CIK No: 0000005656

Officers: Steven R. Davis/CEO, Pres., Myron A. Goldstein/Chmn., CFO

Directors: Myron A. Goldstein/Chmn., CFO, James K. Duff/Dir., Brian G. Russell/Dir., Walter J. Salvadore/Dir., Arthur Dewitt Ackerman/Dir., Jack Wagenti/Dir.

Owners: Insiders/20.50%, Walter Salvadore/2.60%, Myron Goldstein/4.40%, Steven Davis/1.50%, Electrum Resources, LLC./10.30%, Emanuel Ploumis/7.80%, James Duff/2.80%, Jonathan Downs/7.20%, Jack Wagenti/9.20%, Arthur DeWitt Ackerman/5.50%, Brian G. Russell/1.70%

Financial Data: *Fiscal Year End:*05/31 *Latest Annual Data:* 5/31/2006

Year	Sales	Net Income
2006	$15,000	-$163,000
2005	NA	-$218,000
2004	NA	-$118,000

Curr. Assets:	$89,000	**Curr. Liab.:**	$39,000		
Plant, Equip.:	NA	**Total Liab.:**	$39,000	**Indic. Yr. Divd.:**	NA
Total Assets:	$123,000	**Net Worth:**	$84,000	**Debt/ Equity:**	NA

American Israeli Paper Mills Ltd

PO Box 142, Hadera, 38101; ***PH:*** 212-697-2310; ***http://*** www.aipm.co.il

General - Incorporation: Israel
Employees: 3,453
Auditor: Brightman Almagor & Co
Stk Agt: American Stock Transfer & Trust Co.
Counsel: Becker, Ross, Stone Et Al
DUNS No.: 60-000-1432

Stock- Price on:12/24/2007: $58
Stock Exchange: AMEX
Ticker Symbol: AIP
Outstanding Shares: 4,030,000
E.P.S.: $1.78
Shareholders: NA

Business: The group's principle activities are production and distribution of different paper types, household paper products, hygienic products, disposable baby diapers, absorbent products for the incontinent, office supplies, corrugated board and consumer packaging. The group is also involved in recycling operations in the fields of paper and plastics as well as in the treatment of solid waste. The company's shares are traded on both the Tel Aviv stock exchange and the New York stock exchange. The group's quarterly revenue for September 2007 was 150.96 millions of ILS.

Primary SIC and add'l.: 2679 4783

CIK No: 0000005337

Subsidiaries: American Israeli Paper Mills Paper Industry (1995) Ltd., Amnir Recycling Industries Ltd., Attar Marketing Office Supplies Ltd., Graffiti Office Supplies & Paper Marketing Ltd.

Officers: Gur Ben David/56/GM - Packaging Paper, Recycling Division, Amir Moshe/42/GM - Graffiti Office Supplies, Paper Marketing Ltd, Uzi Carmi/GM - Amnir Recycling Industries Ltd, Simcha Kenigsbuch/50/CIO

Owners: Discount Investments Corporation Ltd./21.37%, Clal Industries Ltd./37.83%

Financial Data: *Fiscal Year End:*12/31 *Latest Annual Data:* 12/31/2006

Year	Sales	Net Income
2006	$125,848,000	$5,676,000
2005	$105,514,000	$9,155,000
2004	$111,684,000	$13,582,000

Curr. Assets:	$92,696,000	**Curr. Liab.:**	$105,534,000		
Plant, Equip.:	$95,014,000	**Total Liab.:**	$176,256,000	**Indic. Yr. Divd.:**	NA
Total Assets:	$265,226,000	**Net Worth:**	$88,970,000	**Debt/ Equity:**	NA

American Italian Pasta Co

Briarcliff One, 4100 N Mulberry Dr., Ste. 200, Kansas City, MO, 64116; ***PH:*** 1-816-584-5000; ***http://*** www.pastalabella.com; ***Email:*** consumeraffairs@aipc.com

General		**Stock**	
Incorporation	DE	Price on:12/24/2007	NA
Employees	NA	Stock Exchange	NA
Auditor	Ernst & Young LLP	Ticker Symbol	NA
Stk Agt	UMB Bank, N.A.	Outstanding Shares	NA
Counsel	Blackwell Sanders Peper Martin LLP	E.P.S	NA
DUNS No.	NA	Shareholders	NA

Business: The group's principal activity is to produce, manufacture, market and distribute dry pasta products in the United States and continental Europe. The group produces more than 175 dry pasta shapes. Its production and distribution centers in North America are located in South Carolina, Wisconsin, Missouri and southern California. Major customers include sysco, sam's wholesale club and wal-Mart, inc. The group products include long goods like spaghetti, linguine, fettuccine, angle hair and lasagna and short goods such as macaroni, mostaccioli, rigatoni, ziti and egg noodles. The products are sold and marketed through 45 food brokers and distributors throughout the United States, Canada and Mexico. The group has registered aipc, American Italian pasta company, pasta labella, montalcino, calabria, heartland, mueller's, anthony's, globe/a-1, luxury, mrs. Grass, Pennsylvania dutch, r and f and roncoand law trademarks.

Primary SIC and add'l.: 2099 2098

CIK No: 0000849667

Subsidiaries: AIPC Arizona, LLC, AIPC Finance, Inc., AIPC Missouri, LLC, AIPC Sales Co., AIPC South Carolina, Inc., AIPC Wisconsin, Limited Partnership, IAPC BV, IAPC CV, IAPC Holding UK Limited, IAPC Italia Leasing s.r.l., IAPC UK Limited, Pasta Lensi, S.r.l.

Officers: Jim Fogarty/CEO, Pres., Robert Schuller/Exec. VP, General Counsel, Drew Lericos/VP - Marketing, Tim Lethcoe/VP, GM - Excelsior Springs, MO Facility, Jerry H. Dear/Exec. VP - Ingredient - Food Service, Club Channels, Patrick D. Regan/Sr. VP - National Accounting, G. M. Willhoite/VP, GM - Columbia, SC Facility, Walter N. George/Exec. VP - Operations, Supply Chain, Francesco Bonfanti/Pres., Brian Fox/VP - Food Service, Hannah Arnold/Contact - Media, Jayne Hoover/VP - Quality, Research & Development, Thomas Branich/Sr. VP - West Region, Chrystal L. Johnson/VP - Information Systems, Michael J. Kaczynski/Sr. VP - East Region *(18 Officers included in Index)*

Directors: Mark C. Demetree/Dir., William R. Patterson/Dir., David Allen/Dir., Ronald Kesselman/Dir., Terence C. Obrien/Dir., Tim M. Pollak/Dir., Jonathan E. Baum/Dir., James A. Heeter/Dir., Robert H. Niehaus/Dir.

Financial Data: ***Fiscal Year End:***09/30 ***Latest Annual Data:*** 10/01/2004

Year	Sales	Net Income
2004	$417,354,000	$2,989,000
2003	$438,844,000	$42,633,000
2002	$380,799,000	$41,299,000

Curr. Assets:	$152,082,000	**Curr. Liab.:**	$64,546,000		
Plant, Equip.:	$424,120,000	**Total Liab.:**	$426,990,000	**Indic. Yr. Divd.:**	NA
Total Assets:	$770,495,000	**Net Worth:**	$343,505,000	**Debt/ Equity:**	0.7690

American Land Lease Inc

29399 US Hwy. 19 N, Ste. 320, Clearwater, FL, 33761; ***PH:*** 1-727-726-8868; ***Fax:*** 1-727-725-4391; ***http://*** www.americanlandlease.com

General		**Stock**	
Incorporation	DE	Price on:12/24/2007	$24.4
Employees	219	Stock Exchange	NYSE
Auditor	Ernst & Young LLP	Ticker Symbol	ANL
Stk Agt	Wells Fargo Bank Minnesota N.A	Outstanding Shares	8,020,000
Counsel	NA	E.P.S	NA
DUNS No.	NA	Shareholders	NA

Business: The group's principle activities include ownership, development, expansion, management, and acquisition of residential land lease communities. In the year 2006, the group acquired 465 home sites in Sebastian, Florida, 425 home sites in Foley, Alabama, and 314 home sites in Bullhead City. The group operates through two segments namely, real estate and home sales. The group operates from Florida, Arizona and Alabama in the United States. The group's quarterly revenue for September 2007 was 16.78 millions of USD.

Primary SIC and add'l.: 5271 6798

CIK No: 0000804138

Subsidiaries: AIOP Brentwood West, LLC, AIOP Florida Properties I, LLC, AIOP Florida Properties II, LLC, AIOP Gulfstream Harbor, LLC, AIOP Gulfstream Outlots, LLC, AIOP Lost Dutchman Notes, LLC, AIOP Mullica, LLC, AIOP Serendipity, LLC, ALL Homes Corp., ALL Management, L.L.C., ALL Services, L.L.C., ALL TRS Holding Company, Inc., Asset Investors Finance Corp., Asset Investors Operating Partnership, L.P., Asset Investors Secured Financing Corp. 49 Subsidiaries included in the Index

Officers: Terry Considine/Chmn., CEO/$305,132.00, Robert G. Blatz/COO, Pres./$862,298.00, Shannon E. Smith/CFO, Treasurer, Sec./$568,327.00

Directors: Terry Considine/Chmn., CEO, Thomas L. Rhodes/Vice Chmn., Bruce E. Moore/Dir., Bruce D. Benson/Dir., Todd W. Sheets/Dir., Thomas Harvey/Dir.

Owners: Cliffwood Partners/7.00%, Bruce E. Moore/3.00%, Todd W. Sheets/1.00%, Thomas Harvey, Shannon E. Smith/2.70%, Terry Considine/14.00%, The Wilder Corporation of Delaware/7.40%, Third Avenue Management, LLC/8.00%, Bruce D. Benson/3.30%, Insiders/29.80%, Thomas L. Rhodes/4.70%, Robert G. Blatz/3.90%

Financial Data: ***Fiscal Year End:***12/31 ***Latest Annual Data:*** 03/31/2007

Year	Sales	Net Income
2007	$17,891,000	$1,735,000
2006	$19,175,000	$3,126,000
2005	$84,017,000	$11,950,000

Curr. Assets:	$253,000	**Curr. Liab.:**	$33,275,000	**P/E Ratio:**	23.69
Plant, Equip.:	$405,833,000	**Total Liab.:**	$268,842,000	**Indic. Yr. Divd.:**	$1.000
Total Assets:	$422,055,000	**Net Worth:**	$136,711,000	**Debt/ Equity:**	1.7231

American Leisure Holdings Inc

2460 Sand Lake Rd., Orlando, FL, 32809; ***PH:*** 1-407-251-2240; ***Fax:*** 1-407-251-8455; ***http://*** www.americanleisureholdings.com; ***Email:*** contact@americanleisureholdings.com

General		**Stock**	
Incorporation	NV	Price on:12/24/2007	$0.81
Employees	295	Stock Exchange	OTC
Auditor	Lopez, Blevins, Bork & Assoc. LLP	Ticker Symbol	AMLH
Stk Agt	Signature Stock Transfer, Inc.	Outstanding Shares	10,880,000
Counsel	NA	E.P.S	-$1.55
DUNS No.	NA	Shareholders	NA

Business: The group's principal activity is to own and operate vacation hotel or resort properties. On Jun 14, 2002, the group acquired American leisure holdings, inc and its subsidiaries. The group has been re-designed and structured to own, control and direct a series of companies in the travel and tourism industries. Previously the group activities consisted of marketing computer and computer peripheral products over the Internet. On 02-Oct-2003, the group acquired hts holdings inc and on 09-10-2003, oak holding antigua ltd.

Primary SIC and add'l.: 4724 7011 4725

CIK No: 0001124197

Subsidiaries: AAH Kissimmee LLC, Advantage Professional Management Group, Inc. (APMG), Affinity Travel Club, Inc., Affinity Travel, Inc., American Access Telecommunications Corporation, American Leisure Corporation, Inc. (ALC) and Subsidiaries, American Leisure Equities Corporation, American Leisure Homes, Inc. (ALH), American Leisure Marketing and Technology, Inc., American Leisure Reedy Creek, Inc., American Leisure Travel Group, Inc., American Leisure, Inc. (ALI), American Sterling Corp., American Sterling Motorcoaches, Inc., American Switching Technologies, Inc. 38 Subsidiaries included in the Index

Officers: Omar Jimenez/46/CFO

Owners: Frederick Pauzar, Insiders, Malcolm J. Wright, James Leaderer, Michael Crosbie, Stanford Venture Capital Holdings, Inc., William L. Chiles, Roger Maddock, Omar Jimenez, StanfordInternational Bank Limited

Financial Data: ***Fiscal Year End:***12/31 ***Latest Annual Data:*** 12/31/2006

Year	Sales	Net Income
2006	$38,873,000	-$8,149,000
2005	$38,556,000	-$4,127,000
2004	$6,419,000	-$6,634,000

Curr. Assets:	$7,282,000	**Curr. Liab.:**	$56,632,000		
Plant, Equip.:	$81,101,000	**Total Liab.:**	$120,019,000	**Indic. Yr. Divd.:**	NA
Total Assets:	$120,143,000	**Net Worth:**	$125,000	**Debt/ Equity:**	NA

American Life Holding Co Inc

4823 Old Kingston Pike, Ste. 140, Knoxville, TN, 37919; ***PH:*** 1-865-588-8228

General		**Stock**	
Incorporation	FL	Price on:12/24/2007	$1.5
Employees	NA	Stock Exchange	OTC
Auditor	Henderson, Hutcherson & Mccullough	Ticker Symbol	ALFE
Stk Agt	Atlantic Stock Transfer	Outstanding Shares	NA
Counsel	NA	E.P.S	-$0.45
DUNS No.	NA	Shareholders	NA

Business: The group's principal activity is to reinsure single premium deferred annuity and flexible premium deferred annuity contracts for tax qualified and non-qualified investments. The annuity contracts are subject to discretionary surrender or withdrawal by the customers. These policies and contracts represent assumed reinsurance with allianz life insurance company of North America and hannover life reassurance company of America.

Primary SIC and add'l.: 6799

CIK No: 0001187449

Subsidiaries: American Life, American Life and Annuity Company, Inc

Officers: Lila K. Pfleger/47/Pres., Treasurer, Dir., Pres. - American Life, Principal Executive Officer, Principal Accounting and Financial Officer

Directors: Archer W. Bishop/64/Chmn., Lila K. Pfleger/47/Pres., Treasurer, Dir., Pres. - American Life, Principal Executive Officer, Principal Accounting and Financial Officer, John H. Bell/73/Dir.

Owners: Lila K. Pfleger/2.00%, Archer W. Bishop/59.30%, John H. Bell/10.60%, Insiders/71.60%, RM Consulting LLC/6.40%

Financial Data: ***Fiscal Year End:***12/31 ***Latest Annual Data:*** 12/31/2006

Year	Sales	Net Income
2006	$266,000	-$192,000
2005	$365,000	-$109,000
2004	$463,000	-$354,000

Curr. Assets:	$754,000	**Curr. Liab.:**	$6,511,000		
Plant, Equip.:	NA	**Total Liab.:**	$6,837,000	**Indic. Yr. Divd.:**	NA
Total Assets:	$7,438,000	**Net Worth:**	$602,000	**Debt/ Equity:**	0.5591

American Locker Group Inc

815 S Main St., Grapevine, TX, 76051; ***PH:*** 1-817-329-1600; ***Fax:*** 1-817-329-1600; ***http://*** www.americanlocker.com

General		**Stock**	
Incorporation	DE	Price on:12/24/2007	$4.2
Employees	149	Stock Exchange	OTC
Auditor	Travis, Wolff & Co., LLP	Ticker Symbol	ALGI
Stk Agt	Mellon Investor Services LLC	Outstanding Shares	1,550,000
Counsel	Kirkpatrick & Lockhart	E.P.S	$0.41
DUNS No.	00-212-7454	Shareholders	NA

Business: The group's principal activity is the sale of lockers. The group markets and rent coin, key and electronically controlled checking lockers, plastic centralized mail and parcel distribution lockers. The key controlled checking lockers are sold to the recreational and transportation industries, bookstores, military posts, law enforcement agencies and libraries and for export. The electronically controlled lockers are sold for use as secure storage in the business environment and the electronically controlled, coin operated lockers are sold for use in transportation industry and other uses. The plastic centralized mail and parcel distribution lockers are sold to the United States postal service (usps) for use in centralized mail and parcel delivery in new housing and industrial developments. The group operates in the United States and Canada.

Primary SIC and add'l.: 3499 3429 3581

CIK No: 0000008855

Subsidiaries: Altreco, Inc, American Locker Company, Inc. and American Locker Security Systems, Inc., American Locker Security Systems, Inc, American Locker Security Systems, Inc., Canadian Locker Company, Ltd.

Officers: Edward Ruttenberg/Chmn., CEO - American Locker Security Systems, Inc, John Kormanik/National Sales Mgr. - American Locker Security Systems, Inc, Jonathan Ruttenberg/Dir. - Marketing, American Locker Security Systems, Inc, Chris Beck/Alss Sales Reps, Western Territory, American Locker Security Systems, Inc, Dale Granger/Alss Sales Reps, Midwest, Southwest, Kevin Paris/Alss Sales Reps, Mid, Atlantic, Jim Lange/Supervisor, International Sales, Service, Tom Davidson/Contact - Canadian Locker, Paul M. Zaidins/40/CFO

Directors: Edward Ruttenberg/Chmn., CEO - American Locker Security Systems, Inc, John E. Harris/47/Dir., Mary A. Stanford/48/Dir., James T. Vanasek/38/Dir., Craig R. Frank/48/Dir., Anthony B. Johnson/48/Dir.

Owners: James T. Vanasek/7.90%, Craig R. Frank, Paul M. Zaidins, Edward F. Ruttenberg/5.70%, Santa Monica Partners, L.P./8.80%, Insiders/14.40%, Mary A. Stanford, VN Capital Fund I, L.P./7.80%, John E. Harris

Financial Data: *Fiscal Year End:* 12/31   *Latest Annual Data:* 12/31/2006

Year	Sales	Net Income
2006	$25,065,000	$639,000
2005	$32,304,000	-$8,092,000
2004	$49,023,000	$2,703,000

Curr. Assets:	$10,315,000	Curr. Liab.:	$2,408,000			
Plant, Equip.:	$4,078,000	Total Liab.:	$5,216,000	Indic. Yr. Divd.:	NA	
Total Assets:	$14,470,000	Net Worth:	$9,255,000	Debt/ Equity:	NA	

American Lorain Corp

Formerly: Millennium Quest Inc
4089 Mount Olympus Way, Salt Lake City, UT, 84124; *PH:* 1-801-278-6990

General - Incorporation	DE	**Stock**- Price on:12/24/2007	$0.32
Employees	NA	Stock Exchange	OTC
Auditor	Michael J. Larsen LLC	Ticker Symbol	ALRC
Stk Agt	Interwest Transfer Company, Inc.	Outstanding Shares	NA
Counsel	NA	E.P.S.	NA
DUNS No.	NA	Shareholders	NA

Business: The group's principle activity is to seek business enterprise for acquisition, reorganization or merger, or participation by the Company. It is engaged in the search for potential business opportunities for acquisition or involvement with the Company, which activities are severely limited by the Company's lack of resources. Its in development stage. The group operates from United States.

Primary SIC and add'l.: 2060

CIK No: 0001117057

Subsidiaries: Dix Hills Equities Group, Inc.

Officers: Dimitri Cocorinis/53/Dir., CEO, Pres./$1,500.00, Terry Cononelos/54/Dir., Sec., Treasurer, CFO/$1,500.00

Directors: Dimitri Cocorinis/53/Dir., CEO, Pres., Terry Cononelos/54/Dir., Sec., Treasurer, CFO

Owners: Jayhawk Private Equity Co-Invest Fund, L.P., Gary C. Evans, Yali Lin, Civilian Capital, Inc., Clifton O. Gooding, Silver Rock I, Ltd., Jack Thompson, Richard D. Squires, Excalibur Limited Partnership, Zhenwei Ji, Professional Traders Fund, LLC, Yuexing Zhu, Halter Financial Group, L.P., Hua-Mei 21st Century Partners, LP, Peter Orthwein *(61 Owners included in Index)*

Financial Data: *Fiscal Year End:* 12/31   *Latest Annual Data:* 12/31/2006

Year	Sales	Net Income
2006	NA	-$32,000
2005	NA	-$11,000

Curr. Assets:	$1,000	Curr. Liab.:	$44,000			
Plant, Equip.:	NA	Total Liab.:	$44,000	Indic. Yr. Divd.:	NA	
Total Assets:	$1,000	Net Worth:	-$43,000	Debt/ Equity:	NA	

American Media Operations Inc

1000 American Media Way, Boca Raton, FL, 33464; *PH:* 1-569-697-7733;
http:// www.nationalenquirer.com

General - Incorporation	DE	**Stock**- Price on:12/24/2007	NA
Employees	NA	Stock Exchange	NA
Auditor	Deloitte & Touche LLP	Ticker Symbol	NA
Stk Agt	NA	Outstanding Shares	NA
Counsel	NA	E.P.S.	NA
DUNS No.	55-593-4389	Shareholders	NA

Business: The group's principal activity is to publish general interest magazines. The group is a wholly owned subsidiary of American media, inc and publishes national enquirer, globe, star, national examiner, weekly world news, sun, country weekly, country music magazine, mira, auto world magazine, muscle & fitness, shape, men's fitness, muscle & fitness hers, flex, fit pregnancy, natural health and other monthly magazines. Distribution services, inc arranges for the placement and merchandising of the group's publications and third-party publications at approximately 150,000 retail outlets throughout the United States and Canada. Country music magazine is a bi-monthly magazine presenting various aspects of country music, lifestyles, events and personalities. On 23-Jan-2003, the group acquired weider publications, llc.

Primary SIC and add'l.: 2721

CIK No: 0000853927

Subsidiaries: American Media, Inc, Distribution Services, Inc, EMP Acquisition Corp., EMP Group LLC

Officers: David J. Pecker/Chmn., CEO, Michael J. Porche/51/CEO, Pres. - Distribution Services, Inc, Michael B. Kahane/46/Exec. VP, Corp. Sec., General Counsel, Kate Piasecki/Contact - New York, Country Weekly, Molly Mackenzie Price/Contact - Country Weekly, Chicago, John M. Hughes/Sr. VP - Special Projects - Business Affairs, Gary Berger/VP - Corporate Sales, Aaron Wolof/Ad Sales Dir. - Interactive, David Hurley/Contact - New York, Country Weekly, Bonnie Fuller/Exec. VP, Chief Editorial Dir., Kevin Hyson/Exec. VP, Chief Marketing Officer, John J. Miller/COO, Pres., Jack Craven/CFO, Exec. VP, Dave Leckey/Exec. VP - Consumer Marketing, Daniel Rotstein/Sr. VP - Human Resources, Administration *(28 Officers included in Index)*

Directors: David J. Pecker/Chmn., CEO, Jeffrey Sagansky/56/Dir., Anthony J. Dinovi/45/Dir., Michael Garin/62/Dir., Richard J. Bressler/50/Dir., Daniel G. Ross/32/Dir., Kathleen Reiland/43/Dir., Soren L. Oberg/37/Dir.

Owners: David J. Pecker/65.40%, John F. Craven/0.30%, Bonnie Fuller/2.50%, Evercore Partners L.L.C./2.40%, Thomas H. Lee Equity Fund V, L.P./59.00%, John J. Miller/1.90%, Insiders/85.80%, Evercore Partners II L.L.C./19.40%, David J. Pecker/4.90%, Insiders/73.40%

American Media Systems Company

5190 Neil Rd. Ste. 430, Reno, NV, 89502; *PH:* 1-866-651-2219; *http://* www.american-media.com; *Email:* info@american-media.com

General - Incorporation	NV	**Stock**- Price on:12/24/2007	$0.4
Employees	NA	Stock Exchange	OTC
Auditor	Vellmer & Chang	Ticker Symbol	AMMS
Stk Agt	NA	Outstanding Shares	2,000,000
Counsel	NA	E.P.S.	-$0.03
DUNS No.	NA	Shareholders	NA

Business: The groups principle activity is to operate media industry. The groups services include DVD shows out-takes from TV, feature films, and corporate commercials and showcases. The group operates from the United States.

Primary SIC and add'l.: 3577

CIK No: 0001318060

Subsidiaries: American Media Systems Canada Ltd.

Officers: Alexander Vesak/51/Dir., CEO, CFO, Pres.

Directors: Alexander Vesak/51/Dir., CEO, CFO, Pres., Patricia Castillo/Dir.

Owners: Alexander Vesak/50.10%, Insiders/50.10%

Financial Data: *Fiscal Year End:* 12/31   *Latest Annual Data:* 03/31/2007

Year	Sales	Net Income
2007	$2,000	-$13,000
2006	$25,000	-$75,000
2005	$107,000	-$36,000

Curr. Assets:	$67,000	Curr. Liab.:	$51,000			
Plant, Equip.:	$27,000	Total Liab.:	$51,000	Indic. Yr. Divd.:	NA	
Total Assets:	$94,000	Net Worth:	$43,000	Debt/ Equity:	NA	

American Medical Alert Corp

3265 Lawson Blvd., Oceanside, NY, 11572; *PH:* 1-516-536-5850; *Fax:* 1-516-536-5276; *http://* www.amacalert.com

General - Incorporation	NY	**Stock**- Price on:12/24/2007	$7.53
Employees	531	Stock Exchange	NDQ
Auditor	Margolin, Winer & Evens LLP	Ticker Symbol	AMAC
Stk Agt	Continental Stock Transfer & Trust Co	Outstanding Shares	9,300,000
Counsel	Jenkens & Gilchrist	E.P.S.	$0.16
DUNS No.	01-780-6340	Shareholders	NA

Business: The group's principal activities are to design, engineer, market, install and monitor computerized personal emergency response systems. These systems carry personal security and smoke/fire detection capabilities, which are linked to an emergency response-monitoring center. It also provides medical response and 24-hour on-call-monitoring services. The services of the group include message desk services, appointment making, referral services, voice-mail, paging and wireless communication services to the healthcare community. The customers of the group include hospitals, home care providers, physicians, medical transportation companies, social service agencies and health maintenance organizations. It also provides after-hours telephone answering services through its subsidiary, hci acquisition corp. The group acquired alphaconnect, inc on 12-Apr-2004.

Primary SIC and add'l.: 7389 3669 8099 7352

CIK No: 0000700721

Subsidiaries: Answer Connecticut Acquisition Corp., HCI Acquisition Corp., Live Message America Acquisition Corp., MD OnCall Acquisition Corp., North Shore Answering Service, Inc., Safe Com Inc.

Officers: Jack Rhian/Dir., CEO, Pres./$421,463.00, Howard M. Siegel/Chmn. - Sr. Advisor/$348,729.00, John Rogers/VP - Field Operations, Sec., Richard Rallo/CFO/$205,686.00, Frederic S. Siegel/Dir., Exec. VP/$212,000.00, Randi M. Baldwin/Sr. VP - Marketing, Program Development

Directors: Jack Rhian/Dir., CEO, Pres., Howard M. Siegel/Chmn. - Sr. Advisor, Frederic S. Siegel/Dir., Exec. VP, Yacov Shamash/Dir., James F. Lapolla/Dir., John Gallagher/Dir., Ronald Levin/Dir., Gregory Fortunoff/Dir.

Owners: Insiders/30.90%, Frederic S. Siegel/3.80%, Jack Rhian/3.50%, Ron Levin/1.90%, Howard M. Siegel/12.30%, Randi Baldwin, Richard Rallo/1.30%, Yacov Shamash, John Gallagher, Gregory Fortunoff/8.20%

Financial Data: *Fiscal Year End:* 12/31   *Latest Annual Data:* 12/31/2006

Year	Sales	Net Income
2006	$30,794,000	$1,263,000
2005	$22,448,000	$932,000
2004	$19,128,000	$411,000

Curr. Assets:	$7,217,000	Curr. Liab.:	$4,029,000	P/E Ratio:	53.79
Plant, Equip.:	$9,308,000	Total Liab.:	$11,263,000	Indic. Yr. Divd.:	NA
Total Assets:	$32,608,000	Net Worth:	$21,345,000	Debt/ Equity:	NA

American Medical Systems Holdings Inc

10700 Bren Rd. W, Minnetonka, MN, 55343; *PH:* 1-952-930-6000; *Fax:* 1-952-930-6373; *http://* www.visitAMS.com; *Email:* info@americanmedicalsystems.com

General - Incorporation	DE	**Stock**- Price on:12/24/2007	$17.98
Employees	1,095	Stock Exchange	NDQ
Auditor	Ernst & Young LLP	Ticker Symbol	AMMD
Stk Agt	Wells Fargo Shareowner Services	Outstanding Shares	72,060,000
Counsel	Oppenheimer Wolff & Donnelly	E.P.S.	$0.33
DUNS No.	NA	Shareholders	NA

Business: The group's principal activity is to manufacture and market medical devices to physicians for the treatment of urological disorders. It offers products for erectile restoration, incontinence, stricture and prostate disease. It also offers products for products for women for incontinence, menorrhagia,

prolapse and other pelvic floor disorders. The products include artificial urinary sphincters; sling systems, inflatable and malleable prostheses. The group operates in the United States, western Europe, Australia and Canada. In 2003, the group acquired cryogen inc and dura ii line of erectile restoration products from endocare inc and on 15-Jun-2004, the group acquired thermax inc

Primary SIC and add'l.: 3841 6719 3842

CIK No: 0001114200

Subsidiaries: American Medical Systems Australia Pty. Ltd., American Medical Systems Benelux B.V.B.A., American Medical Systems Canada Inc., American Medical Systems Deutschland GmbH, American Medical Systems Europe B.V., American Medical Systems France S.A.S., American Medical Systems Gynecology Inc., American Medical Systems Iberica S.L., American Medical Systems UK Limited, American Medical Systems, Inc., AMS American Medical Systems do Brasil Produtos Urolgicos e Ginecolgicos Ltda., AMS Research Corporation, AMS Sales Corporation, CryoGen Europe S.A.S., Influence Medical Technologies, Ltd. 17 Subsidiaries included in the Index

Officers: Martin J. Emerson/44/Dir., CEO, Pres./$1,348,245.00, Kathie J. Lenzen/Corporate Controller, John F. Nealon/45/Sr. VP - Business Development/$646,815.00, Lawrence W. Getlin/61/Sr. VP - Compliance, Quality Systems, Legal, Janet L. Dick/51/Sr. VP - Human Resources, Stephen J. McGill/VP - Global Sales/$979,734.00, Michael J. Casey/Dir. - Information Technology, Ross A. Longhini/COO, Exec. VP/$1,311,674.00, Scott R. Etlinger/Sr. VP - Global Operations, Andrew E. Joiner/VP, GM - Women's Health, Mark A. Heggestad/CFO, Exec. VP/$21,418.00, Whitney Erickson/VP, GM Mens Health, Daniel R. Mans/VP - Clinical, Regulatory Affairs, Thomas A. Letscher/Sec.

Directors: Martin J. Emerson/44/Dir., CEO, Pres., Thomas E. Timbie/50/Dir., Elizabeth H. Weatherman/48/Dir., Albert Jay Graf/60/Dir., Richard B. Emmitt/63/Dir., Christopher H. Porter/64/Dir., Robert McLellan/53/Dir., Verne D. Sharma/57/Dir., Jane E. Kiernan/46/Dir.

Owners: Ross A. Longhini, Neuberger Berman, Inc./7.94%, Thomas E. Timbie, Christopher H. Porter, John F. Nealon, Carmen L. Diersen, Martin J. Emerson, Stephen J. McGill, Richard B. Emmitt/1.80%, Franklin Resources, Inc./7.34%, Elizabeth H. Weatherman, Wells Fargo & Company/5.92%, Insiders/5.63%, Albert Jay Graf

Financial Data: Fiscal Year End:12/31 Latest Annual Data: 12/30/2006

Year	Sales	Net Income
2006	$358,318,000	-$49,317,000
2005	$262,591,000	$39,275,000

Curr. Assets:	$122,908,000	Curr. Liab.:	$53,375,000	
Plant, Equip.:	$21,371,000	Total Liab.:	$56,447,000	Indic. Yr. Divd.: NA
Total Assets:	$359,326,000	Net Worth:	$302,879,000	Debt/ Equity: 2.2915

American Medical Technologies Inc

5655 Bear Ln., Corpus Christi, TX, 78405; *PH:* 1-361-289-1145; *Fax:* 1-361-289-5554; *http://* www.americanmedicaltech.com; *Email:* investor@americanmedicaltech.com

General - Incorporation	DE	Stock- Price on:12/24/2007	$0.34
Employees	17	Stock Exchange	OTC
Auditor	Hein & Assoc. LLP	Ticker Symbol	ADLI
Stk Agt	NY Drop-SS Bank & Trust Co	Outstanding Shares	8,190,000
Counsel	NA	E.P.S.	-$0.11
DUNS No.	19-982-4285	Shareholders	NA

Business: The group's principle activities include developing, manufacturing and marketing technology products designed for general dentistry. The products include pulsed dental lasers, the anthos system line of dental chairs and units, high speed curing lights, air abrasive kinetic cavity preparation systems, and intra oral cameras. Group also develops, manufactures and markets precision air abrasive jet machining (ajm) systems for industrial applications. The products of group are marketed through independent distributors to general practitioners and other dental specialists. It operates in the North America, Europe, Japan and other countries. Group also markets some industrial products directly to customers through advertisements or customer referrals and through original equipment manufacturers of grinding equipment.The group operates from United States.

Primary SIC and add'l.: 3843 3845

CIK No: 0000874388

Subsidiaries: Texas Airsonics, Inc.

Officers: Judd D. Hoffman/CEO, Pres., Barbara D. Woody/46/Controller, VP - Administration, Finance, Principal Accounting Officer, Rolf Humm/Independent Equipment Representative - SC, NC, GA, Eastern TN, Annemarie Humm/Independent Equipment Representative - SC, NC, GA, Eastern TN, Bob Doling/Independent Equipment Representative - Southern CA, Judy Doling/Independent Equipment Representative - Southern CA, Pat O Driscoll/Independent Equipment Representative - IL, WI, Paul Rouillard/Independent Equipment Representative - ME, NH, VT, MA, CT, RI, Eastern NY, Ralph Toland/Independent Equipment Representative - TX, OK, Mark Sernatinger/VP - Operations, Sales, The Americas, Scott G. Juhl/Dir. - Sales, Europe, The Middle East, Africa, Asia, Michel Van Rossom/Contact - Europe, Diaa Khreish/Contact - Middle East, Chuck Mertz/Independent Equipment Representative - MD - VA DC

Directors: Roger Dartt/Dir., Gary A. Chatham/63/Dir., William D. Maroney/70/Dir., Charles A. Nichols/83/Dir., Bertrand R. Williams/79/Dir.

Owners: Michael F. Radner/6.50%, Insiders/29.20%, Judd D. Hoffman/2.40%, Gary Chatham, Roger W. Dartt/3.20%, Robert Hayman/10.90%, Charles A. Nichols/9.20%, Charles A. Nichols/25.00%, William D. Maroney/50.00%, William D. Maroney/11.10%, Bertrand R. Williams/25.00%, Insiders/100.00%, Bertrand R. Williams/3.20%, Irene M. Myers/11.50%

Financial Data: Fiscal Year End:12/31 Latest Annual Data: 12/31/2006

Year	Sales	Net Income
2006	$2,763,000	-$1,382,000
2005	$2,161,000	-$1,545,000
2004	$2,256,000	$29,000

Curr. Assets:	$1,480,000	Curr. Liab.:	$2,262,000	
Plant, Equip.:	$110,000	Total Liab.:	$2,918,000	Indic. Yr. Divd.: NA
Total Assets:	$2,063,000	Net Worth:	-$855,000	Debt/ Equity: NA

American Metal & Technology Inc

Formerly: Murray United Development Corp
PO Box 669, Huntington, NY, 11743; *PH:* 1-908-979-3025

General - Incorporation	DE	Stock- Price on:12/24/2007	NA
Employees	NA	Stock Exchange	NA
Auditor	Blanchfield, Kober & Company, P.C.	Ticker Symbol	NA
Stk Agt	American Stock Transfer & Trust Co.	Outstanding Shares	NA
Counsel	NA	E.P.S.	$0.027
DUNS No.	NA	Shareholders	NA

Business: The groups principle activity is to provide recruiting services. The groups service area includes the research and development, engineering, marketing, sales, information technology and manufacturing industries. The group operates from United States.

Primary SIC and add'l.: 3320

CIK No: 0000826444

Owners: Chen Gao/14.73%, Xin Yan Yuan/11.15%

Financial Data: Fiscal Year End:07/31 Latest Annual Data: 7/31/2006

Year	Sales	Net Income
2006	NA	$438,000
2005	NA	-$267,000
2004	NA	-$253,000

Curr. Assets:	$4,000	Curr. Liab.:	$26,000	
Plant, Equip.:	NA	Total Liab.:	$1,144,000	Indic. Yr. Divd.: NA
Total Assets:	$4,000	Net Worth:	-$1,140,000	Debt/ Equity: NA

American Mold Guard Inc

30200 Rancho Viejo Rd., Ste. G, San Juan Capistrano, CA, 92675; *PH:* 1-949-240-5144; *Fax:* 1-949-240-6144; *http://* www.americanmoldguard.com; *Email:* info@americanmoldguard.com

General - Incorporation	CA	Stock- Price on:12/24/2007	$2.02
Employees	106	Stock Exchange	NDQ
Auditor	Haskell and White LLP	Ticker Symbol	AMGI
Stk Agt	U.S. Stock Transfer Corp	Outstanding Shares	4,630,000
Counsel	NA	E.P.S.	-$1.84
DUNS No.	NA	Shareholders	NA

Business: The groups principle activity is to provide antimicrobial surface protection services. The groups services include mold prevention and infection control. Customers served by the group include construction industry and health care facilities. In February 2005, the group acquired Trust One Termite, Inc. Specific customers of the group include Lennar Corporation, DR Horton, Inc. and Centex, Inc, Issa Homes, Inc. and Lenox Homes. The group operates from California, Florida, Gulf, Midwest and other. The group's quarterly revenue for September 2007 was 1.76 millions of USD.

Primary SIC and add'l.: 4959 1799 4955 8999

CIK No: 0001344708

Subsidiaries: American Mold Guard Franchise, Inc, AMG Scientific, LLC, Trust One Termite, Inc

Officers: Thomas Blakeley/49/Chmn., CEO, Mark Davidson/CEO, Paul Bowman/CFO

Directors: Thomas Blakeley/49/Chmn., CEO, John W. Martin/Dir., Frank Brandenberg/Dir., James Crofton/Dir., Dario Bianchi/66/Dir., Robert Simplot/Dir.

Owners: John W. Martin/1.60%, Frank Brandenberg, Austin W. Marxe/12.00%, Jacqueline M. Paulson/12.80%, James Crofton, Robert Simplot, Thomas Blakeley/5.00%, Insiders/10.00%, Dario Bianchi, Paul Bowman, Mark Davidson/2.10%

Financial Data: Fiscal Year End:12/31 Latest Annual Data: 12/31/2006

Year	Sales	Net Income
2006	$9,425,000	-$7,572,000
2005	$5,829,000	-$5,932,000
2004	$1,553,000	-$3,290,000

Curr. Assets:	$6,339,000	Curr. Liab.:	$1,960,000	
Plant, Equip.:	$875,000	Total Liab.:	$2,421,000	Indic. Yr. Divd.: NA
Total Assets:	$7,969,000	Net Worth:	$5,549,000	Debt/ Equity: 0.0972

American Mortgage Acceptance Company

625 Madison Ave., New York, NY, 10022; *PH:* 1-800-831-4826; *Fax:* 1-212-751-3550; *http://* www.americanmortgageco.com

General - Incorporation	MA	Stock- Price on:12/24/2007	$10.201
Employees	NA	Stock Exchange	AMEX
Auditor	Janofsky & Walker LLP	Ticker Symbol	AMC
Stk Agt	Computershare Trust Co	Outstanding Shares	8,400,000
Counsel	NA	E.P.S.	$0.29
DUNS No.	NA	Shareholders	NA

Business: The groups principle activities include originating and acquiring mortgage loans and other debt instruments. The group also invests in mezzanine loans, construction loans, first mortgage loans, subordinated interests in first mortgage loans and bridge loans. The group operates from the United States. The groups quarterly revenue for September 2007 was 16.95 millions of USD.

Primary SIC and add'l.: 6798

CIK No: 0000878774

Officers: Larry J. Duggins/Managing Trustee, CEO, Daryl J. Carter/52/Pres., Robert L. Levy/CFO, Donald J. Meyer/Chief Investment Officer, Brenda Abuaf/Dir. - Corporate Communications, John J. Kelly/43/Chief Accounting Officer

Directors: Larry J. Duggins/Managing Trustee, CEO, Marc D. Schnitzer/Chmn., Jeff T. Blau/Managing Trustee, George P. Jahn/Managing Trustee, Harry Levine/Managing Trustee, Scott M. Mannes/Managing Trustee, Stanley R. Perla/Managing Trustee, Richard M. Rosan/66/Trustee

Owners: Harry Levine, Richard M. Rosan, Stanley R. Perla, Marc D. Schnitzer, Insiders, George P. Jahn, Scott M. Mannes, Jeff T. Blau

Financial Data: Fiscal Year End:12/31 Latest Annual Data: 12/31/2006

Year	Sales	Net Income
2006	$38,628,000	$2,687,000
2005	$39,163,000	$15,235,000
2004	$15,909,000	$11,273,000

Curr. Assets:	$30,174,000	Curr. Liab.:	$30,456,000	
Plant, Equip.:	$48,692,000	Total Liab.:	$635,976,000	Indic. Yr. Divd.: $0.900
Total Assets:	$720,984,000	Net Worth:	$85,008,000	Debt/ Equity: NA

American Mortgage Network Inc

10421 Wateridge Cir., Ste. 250, San Diego, CA, 92121; *PH:* 1-858-909-1200; *Fax:* 1-858-909-1259; *http://* www.amnetmortgage.com; *Email:* custserv@amnetmortgage.com

General - Incorporation .... MD	Stock - Price on:12/24/2007 .... NA
Employees .... NA	Stock Exchange..OTC
Auditor ....PricewaterhouseCoopers LLP	Ticker Symbol..AMNT
Stk Agt........................ Mellon Trust Co	Outstanding Shares ....NA
Counsel .... NA	E.P.S. ....NA
DUNS No. .... NA	Shareholders...NA

Business: The group's principal activity is to provide wholesale mortgage banking services. The group's operating subsidiary, American mortgage network inc (amnet) provides mortgage banking services. Amnet originates loans through mortgage brokers and then sells them to institutional purchasers through a network of regional offices in the United States. All servicing rights are also sold along with the mortgage loans. The group elected to terminate its status as a real estate investment trust in 2003.

Primary SIC and add'l.: 6162

CIK No: 0001035744

Subsidiaries: American Mortgage Network, Inc., American Residential Eagle 2, Inc., American Residential Eagle, Inc.

Officers: Danielle Royal/Regional Mgr. - San Diego, California, Georgeann Gunn/Operations Mgr. - Concord, CA, Cathy Previte/Regional Operations Mgr. - Colorado Springs, Colorado, Christine Meyers/Regional Operations Mgr. - New Haven, Connecticut, Monte Preece/Sales Mgr. - Denver, CO, Michelle Myhrvold-Roy/Regional Mgr. - Portland, Oregon, Rhonda Elzie/Operations Mgr. - Portland, Oregon, Wayne Goodwin/Regional Mgr. - Boston, Massachusetts, Jerry Hassler/Regional Mgr., Jeanne Trimmer/Operations Mgr., Rick Rice/Sales Mgr. - Concord, CA, Thomas Michel/Sales Mgr. - Ontario, CA, Jason Wood/Sales Mgr. - Orange, CA, Mary Rodgers/Operations Mgr. - Orange, CA, Robin Ylitalo/Sales Mgr. - Sacramento, CA (69 Officers included in Index)

Curr. Assets:	$1,000	Curr. Liab.:	$8,000		
Plant, Equip.:	NA	Total Liab.:	$8,000	Indic. Yr. Divd.:	NA
Total Assets:	$1,000	Net Worth:	-$8,000	Debt/ Equity:	NA

American Municipal Income Portfolio Inc

U.s. Bancorp Ctr., 800 Nicollet Mall, Minneapolis, MN, 55402;

General - Incorporation .... MN	Stock - Price on:12/24/2007 ....$15.48
Employees .... NA	Stock Exchange..NYSE
Auditor .... Ernst & Young, LLP	Ticker Symbol..XAA
Stk Agt................State Street Bank & Trust Co	Outstanding Shares 5,760,000
Counsel .... NA	E.P.S. $0.911
DUNS No. .... NA	Shareholders...NA

Business: The groups principal activity is to invest in real estate properties. The group operates from the United States

Primary SIC and add'l.: 6199

CIK No: 0000902750

Officers: Thomas S. Schreier/46/CEO, Chief Investment Officer - Adviser, Kathleen L. Prudhomme/Sec., Jeffery M. Wilson/52/Sr. VP - Adviser, David H. Lui/48/Chief Compliance Officer, Jason K. Mitchell/32/Anti-Money Laundering Officer, Charles D. Garibaldi/Treasurer, Jill M. Stevenson/43/Assist. Treasurer, Brett L. Agnew/37/Assist. Sec., Richard J. Ertel/41/Assist. Sec., James D. Alt/57/Assist. Sec.

Directors: Virginia L. Stringer/64/Chmn., Joseph D. Strauss/68/Dir., Leonard W. Kedrowski/67/Dir., Richard K. Riederer/64/Dir., Benjamin R. Field/70/Dir., Roger A. Gibson/62/Dir., Victoria J. Herget/57/Dir., John P. Kayser/59/Dir., James M. Wade/65/Dir.

Owners: Sit Investment Associates, Inc./21.92%, Karpus Management, Inc./5.02%

Financial Data: Fiscal Year End:08/31 Latest Annual Data: 8/31/2006

Year	Sales	Net Income
2006	$7,821,000	$4,471,000
2005	$5,081,000	$4,482,000

Curr. Assets:	$1,825,000	Curr. Liab.:	$115,000	P/E Ratio:	23.69
Plant, Equip.:	NA	Total Liab.:	$115,000	Indic. Yr. Divd.:	$0.860
Total Assets:	$132,616,000	Net Worth:	$132,501,000	Debt/ Equity:	NA

American National Bankshares Inc

628 Main St., Danville, VA, 24541; **PH:** 1-434-792-5111; **Fax:** 1-434-792-1582;
http:// www.amnb.com

General - Incorporation .... VA	Stock - Price on:12/24/2007 ....$22.27
Employees 253	Stock Exchange..NDQ
Auditor .... Yount, Hyde & Barbour, P.C	Ticker Symbol..AMNB
Stk Agt........................ Carolyn Compton	Outstanding Shares 6,150,000
Counsel .... NA	E.P.S. $1.90
DUNS No. 00-794-0075	Shareholders...NA

Business: The group's principal activity is to provide retail, commercial and trust banking services. The services include commercial, individual, demand and time deposit accounts, loans and trust services. The group operates through the American national bank and trust company and two of its wholly owned subsidiaries. The group operates through fourteen full service offices and twenty automated teller machines. These are located in the cities of danville and martinsville, south Boston, and the counties of pittsylvania, henry and halifax in Virginia and the county of caswell in North Carolina. The wholly owned subsidiaries make and sell mortgage loans and to offer non-deposit investment products such as mutual funds and insurance.

Primary SIC and add'l.: 6021 9999 6712

CIK No: 0000741516

Subsidiaries: American National Bank and Trust Company

Officers: Charles H. Majors/Dir., CEO, Pres./$435,438.00, Jeffrey V. Haley/Sr. VP, Exec. VP, COO - American National Bank/$184,367.00, Tommy Freeze/Contact - Investment Consultant, Lorrie Teegen/Contact - Trust Officer - Martinsville Office, Mark Lewis/Contact - Investment Consultant, Joanne Mann/Contact - Business Development, Associate, Neal A. Petrovich/CFO, Sr. Exec. VP/$165,949.00, Helm R. Dobbins/Sr. VP, Exec. VP, Chief Credit Officer - American National Bank/$167,362.00, Karen P. Kinnier/Sr. VP - Regional Executive, Michael L. Dance/Sr. VP - Regional Executive, E. C. Jordan/Sr. VP - Regional Executive, Danny K. Wrenn/Sr. VP, Sr. Trust Officer, Jhon B. Hall/Trust Officer, Loretta B. Aron/Contact - Trust Officer, Joan Butler/Contact - Trust Officer - Lynchburg Office

Directors: Charles H. Majors/Dir., CEO, Pres., Ben J. Davenport/Dir., Lester A. Hudson/Dir., Willie G. Barker/Dir. Emeritus, Franklin W. Maddux/Dir., Claude B. Owen/Dir., Dan H. Davis/Dir., Fred B. Leggett/Dir., Michael P. Haley/Dir., Budge E. Kent/Dir., Fred A. Blair/Dir., Frank C. Crist/Dir.

Owners: Fred A. Blair, Charles H. Majors/1.70%, Insiders/7.89%, Ben J. Davenport, Fred B. Leggett, Helm R. Dobbins, Michael P. Haley, Claude B. Owen, Jeffrey V. Haley, Budge E. Kent, Lester A. Hudson, Dan H. Davis/2.10%, Frank C. Crist/1.17%, Neal A. Petrovich, Franklin W. Maddux

Financial Data: Fiscal Year End:12/31 Latest Annual Data: 12/31/2006

Year	Sales	Net Income
2006	$53,528,000	$11,426,000
2005	$40,375,000	$9,994,000
2004	$37,615,000	$8,013,000

Curr. Assets:	$40,738,000	Curr. Liab.:	$662,109,000	P/E Ratio:	11.78
Plant, Equip.:	$12,438,000	Total Liab.:	$682,728,000	Indic. Yr. Divd.:	$0.920
Total Assets:	$777,720,000	Net Worth:	$94,992,000	Debt/ Equity:	NA

American National Insurance Company

1 Moody Plz., Galveston, TX, 77550; **PH:** 1-409-763-4661; **Fax:** 1-409-766-6663;
http:// www.anico.com

General - Incorporation .... TX	Stock - Price on:12/24/2007 ....$154.66
Employees .... NA	Stock Exchange..NDQ
Auditor .... KPMG LLP	Ticker Symbol..ANAT
Stk Agt .... Mellon Investor Services LLC	Outstanding Shares 26,480,000
Counsel.................... Greer, Herz & Adams LLP	E.P.S. $11.21
DUNS No. .... NA	Shareholders...NA

Business: The groups principal activity is to provide insurance services. The products of the group include mutual fund, credit insurance, health insurance and life insurance. The group operates from the United States.

Primary SIC and add'l.: 6211 6311 6331 6282 6321

CIK No: 0000904163

Officers: Robert L. Moody/Chmn., CEO, Richard G. Ferdinandtsen/COO, Pres.

Directors: Robert L. Moody/Chmn., CEO

Financial Data: Fiscal Year End:12/31 Latest Annual Data: 12/31/2002

Year	Sales	Net Income
2002	$2,241,343,000	$16,855,000
2001	$2,134,381,000	$64,931,000
2000	$1,834,481,000	$140,174,000

Curr. Assets:	$1,738,251,000	Curr. Liab.:	-$47,346,000		
Plant, Equip.:	$79,422,000	Total Liab.:	$9,265,443,000	Indic. Yr. Divd.:	$3.080
Total Assets:	$12,139,172,000	Net Worth:	$2,873,729,000	Debt/ Equity:	NA

American Oil & Gas Inc

1050 17th St., Ste. 1850, Denver, CO, 80265; **PH:** 1-303-991-0173; **Fax:** 1-303-595-0709;
http:// www.americanoilandgasinc.com

General - Incorporation .... NV	Stock - Price on:12/24/2007 ....$6.56
Employees 13	Stock Exchange..AMEX
Auditor .... Ryder Scott Co	Ticker Symbol..AEZ
Stk Agt .... Corporate Stock Transfer, Inc.	Outstanding Shares 46,030,000
Counsel.............................. Patton Boggs LLP	E.P.S. ....-$0.11
DUNS No. .... NA	Shareholders...NA

Business: The group's principle activities include acquiring, developing and managing oil and gas properties. On 17-Jan-2003, the company executed a purchase and sale agreement with tower Colombia corporation and north finn llc, whereby it acquired an undivided 50% working interest in four prospects located in the powder river basin of Wyoming and the northern bighorn basin of Montana. These interests include a coalbed methane prospect in carbon county, Montana, a multi-zone oil and gas prospect in niobrara county, Wyoming and certain coal bed methane leases in powder river basin in north eastern Wyoming. Previously, the company operated drgoodteeth.com, an online dental resource Website. The company is in development stage. The group operates from United States.

Primary SIC and add'l.: 1382

CIK No: 0001120916

Subsidiaries: Brigham Oil & Gas, L.P., Turnkey E&P Corporation

Officers: Patrick D. O'Brien/Chmn., CEO/$110,158.00, Andrew P. Calerich/Dir., Pres./$384,556.00, Kendell V. Tholstrom/VP - Oil, Gas Operations/$123,186.00, Bob Solomon/VP - Oil, Gas Economics/$117,712.00, Joseph B. Feiten/CFO/$201,210.00, Peter Loeffler/VP - Exploration, Production, Don Schroeder/VP - Land

Directors: Patrick D. O'Brien/Chmn., CEO, Nick Demare/Dir., M. S. Minhas/Dir., Jon R. Whitney/Dir., Andrew P. Calerich/Dir., Pres.

Owners: GLG Partners LP/5.76%, Joseph B. Feiten, Nick DeMare, Wellington Management Company, LLP/6.01%, Jon R. Whitney, Bob Solomon/5.52%, Insiders/20.39%, Kendell Tholstrom/5.31%, Patrick D. OBrien/6.03%, M. S. Minhas, Andrew P. Calerich/2.59%

Financial Data: Fiscal Year End:12/31 Latest Annual Data: 12/31/2006

Year	Sales	Net Income
2006	$3,787,000	$1,211,000
2005	$4,691,000	$1,033,000
2004	$746,000	-$438,000

Curr. Assets:	$17,502,000	Curr. Liab.:	$4,656,000		
Plant, Equip.:	$39,121,000	Total Liab.:	$7,048,000	Indic. Yr. Divd.:	NA
Total Assets:	$69,136,000	Net Worth:	$62,088,000	Debt/ Equity:	NA

American Oriental Bioengineering Inc

90 Pk. Ave., 17th Fl., New York, NY, 10016; **PH:** 1-212-786-7568; **Fax:** 1-212-509-9190;
http:// www.bioaobo.com; **Email:** aobo@bioaobo.com

General - Incorporation	NV	**Stock**- Price on:12/24/2007	$9.52
Employees	1,981	Stock Exchange	NYSE
Auditor	Weinberg & Co. P.A	Ticker Symbol	AOB
Stk Agt	Computershare Ltd.	Outstanding Shares	64,790,000
Counsel	NA	E.P.S	$0.57
DUNS No.	NA	Shareholders	NA

Business: The group's principal activities are to manufacture and formulate supplemental and medicinal products using proprietary processes. The group focuses on new product research to combine biotechnology and Chinese medical technology to capture the increasing demand for traditional Chinese medicines and health supplements. The group owns and operates several plants in addition to a large capacity soybean peptide manufacturing plant. Soybean peptides are used widely in general food and health food products, sports foods, medicines, the fermentation industry and environmental protection applications. These are easily absorbed by the body and can lower blood pressure and blood fat levels, enhance immunity, lower cholesterol, prevent cardiac and brain blood vessel diseases and inhibit the growth of tumors. During the year the group acquired bestkey international ltd & harbin three bioengineering limited.

Primary SIC and add'l.: 2834

CIK No: 0001090514

Subsidiaries: Harbin Bioengineering, HSPL

Officers: Shujun Liu/Chmn., CEO, Yanchun Li/Dir., Acting CFO, COO, Sec., Jun Min/Dir., VP, Binsheng Li/Dir., Chief Accounting and Finance Officer

Directors: Shujun Liu/Chmn., CEO, Eileen Bridget Brody/Dir., Jun Min/Dir., VP, Binsheng Li/Dir., Chief Accounting and Finance Officer, Xianmin Wang/Dir., Cosimo J. Patti/Dir., Lawrence S. Wizel/Dir., Yanchun Li/Dir., Acting CFO, COO, Sec., Baiqing Zhang/55/Dir.

Owners: Yanchun Li/1.00%, Tony Liu/100.00%, Xianmin Wang, Tony Liu/19.70%, Cosimo J. Patti, Lawrence S. Wizel, Binsheng Li, Jun Min/1.20%, Insiders/22.50%, Eileen Bridget Brody

Financial Data: *Fiscal Year End:*12/31 *Latest Annual Data:* 12/31/2006

Year	Sales	Net Income
2006	$110,182,000	$29,201,000
2005	$54,733,000	$13,426,000
2004	$31,967,000	$7,771,000

Curr. Assets:	$115,587,000	**Curr. Liab.:**	$23,335,000	**P/E Ratio:**	19.83
Plant, Equip.:	$32,521,000	**Total Liab.:**	$29,097,000	**Indic. Yr. Divd.:**	NA
Total Assets:	$185,274,000	**Net Worth:**	$156,177,000	**Debt/ Equity:**	0.0070

American Pacific Corp

3770 Howard Hughes Pkwy., Ste. 300, Las Vegas, NV, 89169; *PH:* 1-702-735-2200; *Fax:* 1-702-735-4876; *http://* www.apfc.com

General - Incorporation	DE	**Stock**- Price on:12/24/2007	$15.49
Employees	485	Stock Exchange	NDQ
Auditor	Deloitte & Touche LLP	Ticker Symbol	APFC
Stk Agt	American Stock Transfer & Trust Co.	Outstanding Shares	7,360,000
Counsel	NA	E.P.S	$0.07
DUNS No.	07-758-5024	Shareholders	NA

Business: The group's principal activity is to produce specialty chemicals and environmental protection products. The group also has interests in two real estate assets in the las vegas, Nevada area. The group produces ammonium perchlorate (ap), a specialty chemical product used as an oxidizing agent in composite solid propellants for rockets, booster motors and missiles. Ap is used in the space shuttle, the minuteman missile, the titan space launch vehicle, the delta and atlas families of commercial space launch vehicles, a number of defense related missiles and rockets and most other solid fuel rocket motors. The group also produces sodium azide used in the inflation of automotive airbags, water treatment equipment used for disinfection of wastewater streams and treatment of seawater and halotron (TM) products, used to extinguish fires.

Primary SIC and add'l.: 6552 3589 5169

CIK No: 0000350832

Subsidiaries: American Azide Corporation, Ampac Farms, Inc., Ampac Fine Chemicals, LLC, Ampac-ISP (UK)Limited, Ampac-ISP Corp., LLC, Energetic Additives Inc., LLC

Officers: John R. Gibson/Chmn., CEO, Pres., Robert Huebner/VP - Ampac ISP, Linda G. Ferguson/VP - Administration, Corp. Sec., Joseph Carleone/Dir., COO, Pres., Dana Kelley/CFO, VP, Treasurer, Kent Richmond/VP - Research, Product Development, Dave A. Thayer/VP, GM - Utah Operations, Aslam Malik/Pres. - Ampac Fine Chemicals, Jeffrey M. Gibson/CTO, VP, Dirk Venderink/VP - Engineering

Directors: John R. Gibson/Chmn., CEO, Pres., Dean M. Willard/Dir., Berlyn D. Miller/Dir., Fred D. Gibson/Dir., Norval F. Pohl/Dir., Jan H. Loeb/Dir., Jane L. Williams/Dir., Joseph Carleone/Dir., COO, Pres., Keith C. Rooker/Dir.

Owners: Aegis Financial Corporation/11.50%, John R. Gibson/2.40%, Norval F. Pohl, Joseph Carleone, Franklin Resources, Inc./9.00%, Dean M. Willard, Dana M. Kelley, Evergreen Investment Management/5.20%, Keith C. Rooker, Seth L. VanVoorhees, Jan H. Loeb, Fred D. Gibson/6.50%, Dimensional FundAdvisors, Inc./6.20%, Berlyn D. Miller, Donald Smith& Co., Inc./8.30% *(20 Owners included in Index)*

Financial Data: *Fiscal Year End:*09/30 *Latest Annual Data:* 9/30/2006

Year	Sales	Net Income
2006	$141,904,000	-$3,894,000
2005	$83,347,000	-$9,691,000
2004	$59,489,000	-$397,000

Curr. Assets:	$98,044,000	**Curr. Liab.:**	$36,337,000	**P/E Ratio:**	221.29
Plant, Equip.:	$116,965,000	**Total Liab.:**	$173,718,000	**Indic. Yr. Divd.:**	NA
Total Assets:	$249,407,000	**Net Worth:**	$75,689,000	**Debt/ Equity:**	NA

American Petro-Hunter Inc

700 W Georgia St., Pacific Ctr., Ste. 3000, Vancouver, BC, V7Y 1A1; *PH:* 1-604-689-8336

General - Incorporation	NV	**Stock**- Price on:12/24/2007	$0.125
Employees	NA	Stock Exchange	OTC
Auditor	Moore Stephens Ellis Foster Ltd	Ticker Symbol	AAPH
Stk Agt	Pacific Stock Transfer Company	Outstanding Shares	NA
Counsel	NA	E.P.S	NA
DUNS No.	25-506-0014	Shareholders	NA

Business: The group's principle activity is to seek privately held business, to reorganize and take advantage of the company's status as a publicly held corporation. At 31-Dec-2002, the company has not proceeded with any reorganization and has no agreement for such reorganization. The company also investigates the acquisition and development of natural resource projects without reorganizing with another party. The group operates from United States.

Primary SIC and add'l.: 9999

CIK No: 0001040482

Owners: Peter G. Rook-Green/0.87%, Patrick A. McGowan/2.73%, Insiders/3.60%

Financial Data: *Fiscal Year End:*12/31 *Latest Annual Data:* 12/31/2006

Year	Sales	Net Income
2006	NA	-$72,000
2005	NA	-$71,000
2004	NA	-$144,000

Curr. Assets:	$23,000	**Curr. Liab.:**	$407,000		
Plant, Equip.:	NA	**Total Liab.:**	$407,000	**Indic. Yr. Divd.:**	NA
Total Assets:	$23,000	**Net Worth:**	-$385,000	**Debt/ Equity:**	NA

American Physicians Capital Inc

1301 N Hagadorn Rd., East Lansing, MI, 48823; *PH:* 1-517-351-1150; *Fax:* 1-517-351-7866; *http://* www.apcapital.com; *Email:* investorrelations@apcapital.com

General - Incorporation	MI	**Stock**- Price on:12/24/2007	$40.48
Employees	164	Stock Exchange	NDQ
Auditor	BDO Seidman LLP	Ticker Symbol	ACAP
Stk Agt	Illinois Stock Transfer Co	Outstanding Shares	11,200,000
Counsel	NA	E.P.S	$4.59
DUNS No.	NA	Shareholders	NA

Business: The group's principle activity is to write medical professional liability and workers' compensation insurance. The activities are carried out through five segments: medical professional liability, workers' compensation, health, personal and commercial and corporate and other. The medical professional liability segment underwrites policy coverage for physicians and physician medical groups, clinics and other providers in the health care industry. The workers' compensation segment provides coverage to smaller accounts, having less than $75,000 in annual premiums and mid-level accounts, having $75,000 to $750,000 in annual premiums. The health insurance segment writes employee health insurance through a single preferred provider organization. The group also provides limited amount of personal and commercial coverage. The group's quarterly revenue for September 2007 was 46.37 millions of USD.

Primary SIC and add'l.: 6321 6351

CIK No: 0001118148

Subsidiaries: Alpha Advisors, Inc., American Physicians Assurance Corporation, American Physicians Capital Statutory Trust I, APCapital Trust II, APCpnsulting, LLC, APDirect Sales, LLC, APIndemnity Ltd., APManagement Ltd., APSpecialty Insurance Corporation, Insurance Corporation of America, Physicians Insurance Company

Officers: Kevin R. Clinton/Dir., CEO, Pres./$2,150,834.00, Frank H. Freund/Exec. VP, Treasurer, CFO/$1,005,171.00, Ann Storberg/VP - Investor Relations, Nancy Axtell/VP - Human Resources, Kevin M. Dyke/VP, Chief Actuary, Dawn E. Springer/Dir. - American Physicians Assurance Corporation, Thomas E. Stone/Dir. - American Physicians Assurance Corporation, Laura A. Kline/VP - Marketing, American Physicians, Annette E. Flood/Exec. VP - Apcapital, COO - Apcapital, American Physicians/$1,089,544.00

Directors: Kevin R. Clinton/Dir., CEO, Pres., Thomas R. Berglund/Chmn., Spencer L. Schneider/Dir., Apparao Mukkamala/Dir., Larry W. Thomas/Dir., Stephen H. Haynes/Dir., Mitchell A. Rinek/Dir., Joseph D. Stilwell/Dir., Billy B. Baumann/Dir.

Owners: Dimensional FundAdvisors Inc./9.80%, Daniel L. Gorman/2.10%, Thomas R. Berglund, AppaRao Mukkamala, Mitchell A. Rinek, JPMorgan Chase& Co./6.00%, AXA Assurances I.A.R.D. Mutuelle/5.30%, Joseph D. Olson, Stephen H. Haynes, Stilwell Value PartnersV, L.P./9.30%, Insiders/17.30%, Annette E. Flood, Billy B. Baumann, Spencer L. Schneider, Joseph D. Stilwell/9.30% *(18 Owners included in Index)*

Financial Data: *Fiscal Year End:*12/31 *Latest Annual Data:* 12/31/2006

Year	Sales	Net Income
2006	$199,282,000	$43,187,000
2005	$212,866,000	$72,366,000
2004	$250,680,000	$20,030,000

Curr. Assets:	$260,308,000	**Curr. Liab.:**	$37,302,000	**P/E Ratio:**	10.85
Plant, Equip.:	$9,775,000	**Total Liab.:**	$827,005,000	**Indic. Yr. Divd.:**	$0.400
Total Assets:	$1,095,815,000	**Net Worth:**	$268,810,000	**Debt/ Equity:**	0.1163

American Physicians Service Group Inc

1301 Capital of Texas Hwy., Ste. C300, Austin, TX, 78746; *PH:* 1-512-328-0888; *Fax:* 1-512-314-4398; *http://* www.amph.com; *Email:* amphinfo@amph.com

General - Incorporation	TX	**Stock**- Price on:12/24/2007	$18.82
Employees	107	Stock Exchange	NDQ
Auditor	BDO Seidman LLP	Ticker Symbol	AMPH
Stk Agt	American Stock Transfer & Trust Co.	Outstanding Shares	4,830,000
Counsel	Akin, Gump, Strauss, Hauer & Feld LLP	E.P.S	$0.87
DUNS No.	08-073-9857	Shareholders	NA

Business: The group's principal activity is to provide management services to insurance companies and brokerage and investment services to individuals and institutions. The financial services segment provides investment and investment advisory services to institutions and individuals. The insurance services segment provides management and agency services to medical malpractice insurance companies. The real estate segment owns and leases condominium space located in austin.

Primary SIC and add'l.: 6282 6519 6411

CIK No: 0000724024

Subsidiaries: American Physicians Insurance Agency, Inc., American Physicians Management Consulting, Inc., APMC Financial Services, Inc., APS Asset Management. Inc., APS Clearing, Inc., APS Facilities Management, Inc., APS Financial, Inc., APS Insurance Services, Inc., APS Investment Services, Inc., APS Professional Liability Insurance Agency, Inc., APSC, Inc., APSFM, Inc., FMI Partners, Ltd.

Officers: Kenneth S. Shifrin/Chariman, Sr. VP - Finance, Treasurer, CEO/$910,261.00, William H. Hayes/Sec., Treasurer, Previously Served as Sr. VP - Finance, CFO/$314,958.00, Thomas R. Solimine/Controller/$179,262.00, Maury L. Magids/Sr. VP - Insurance Services/$655,927.00, Bill Hayes/Investor Relations, Timothy L. Lafrey/Dir., COO, Pres.

Directors: Kenneth S. Shifrin/Chariman, Sr. VP - Finance, Treasurer, CEO, Cheryl Williams/Dir., Lew N. Little/51/Dir., Jackie Majors/74/Dir., Norris C. Knight/Dir., Timothy L. Lafrey/Dir., COO, Pres., William J. Peche/Dir., William A. Searles/Dir.

Owners: Cheryl Williams, William H. Hayes/1.00%, Norris C. Knight, Thomas R. Solimine, Lew N. Little, William J. Peche, William A. Searles, Jackie Majors, Kenneth S. Shifrin/8.10%, Insiders/13.50%, Maury L. Magids/1.40%

Financial Data: *Fiscal Year End:*12/31 *Latest Annual Data:* 12/31/2006

Year	Sales	Net Income
2006	$32,360,000	$3,194,000
2005	$33,973,000	$5,460,000
2004	$32,021,000	$2,152,000

Curr. Assets:	$25,934,000	*Curr. Liab.:*	$6,687,000	*P/E Ratio:*	17.27
Plant, Equip.:	$556,000	*Total Liab.:*	$6,687,000	*Indic. Yr. Divd.:*	NA
Total Assets:	$36,276,000	*Net Worth:*	$29,568,000	*Debt/ Equity:*	NA

American Power Conversion Corp

132 Fairgrounds Rd. , West Kingston, RI, 02892; *PH:* 1-401-789-5735; *http://* www.apcc.com

General - Incorporation	MA	**Stock**- Price on:12/24/2007	NA
Employees	7,580	Stock Exchange	NDQ
Auditor	KPMG LLP	Ticker Symbol	APCC
Stk Agt	Computershare Trust Co	Outstanding Shares	NA
Counsel	Testa, Hurwitz & Thibeault	E.P.S.	NA
DUNS No.	00-520-7816	Shareholders	NA

Business: The group's principal activities are to design, develop, manufacture and market power protection and management solutions for computer, communication and electronic applications. It operates in three segments namely small systems, large systems and other. It's solutions include uninterruptible power supply products, dc- power solutions, electrical surge protection devices, power conditioning products, precision cooling equipment and associated software, services and accessories. The group markets its products to businesses, small offices/home offices and home users around the world through computer distributors and dealers, value-added resellers, mass merchandisers, catalog merchandisers and e-commerce vendors. The group operates in North America, Europe, Asia, Africa and Middle East.

Primary SIC and add'l.: 7372 3629 3679

CIK No: 0000835910

Subsidiaries: A.B.L. Electronics Corporation, American Power Conversion (India) Private Limited, American Power Conversion (Phils.),Inc., American Power Conversion Brasil Ltda., American Power Conversion Corporation (A.P.C.) B.V., American Power Conversion Denmark ApS, American Power Conversion Dublin Limited, American Power Conversion Europe S.A.R.L., American Power Conversion France SARL, American Power Conversion Holdings (UK) Limited, American Power Conversion Holdings Inc., American Power Conversion Hong Kong Limited, American Power Conversion Italia S.R.L., American Power Conversion Land Holdings Inc. (40%; 60% Filipino nationals), American Power Conversion Mexico, S.A. de C.V. 43 Subsidiaries included in the Index

Officers: Robert J. Johnson/CEO, Interim Pres., Neil E. Rasmussen/CTO, Sr. VP

Directors: Neil E. Rasmussen/CTO, Sr. VP

American Railcar Industries Inc

100 Clark St., St. Charles, MO, 63301; *PH:* 1-636-940-6000; *Fax:* 1-636-940-6030; *http://* www.americanrailcar.com; *Email:* sales@americanrailcar.com

General - Incorporation	DE	**Stock**- Price on:12/24/2007	$42.2
Employees	2,575	Stock Exchange	NDQ
Auditor	Grant Thornton LLP	Ticker Symbol	ARII
Stk Agt	American Stock Transfer & Trust Co.	Outstanding Shares	21,240,000
Counsel	NA	E.P.S.	$1.66
DUNS No.	NA	Shareholders	NA

Business: The groups principle activities include designing, manufacturing and marketing covered hopper and tank railcars. The groups services include repair, maintenance, consulting, engineering and refurbish railcars and fleet management. The products of the group include Grain, Plastic Pellet, Cement and Pressureaide(R) Railcars. The groups operates through two segments namely manufacturing and railcar services. The group acquired stock of Custom Steel, Inc in the year 2006 and ACF Industries Holding Corp. in the year 2005. Specific customers of the group include CIT, Dow Chemical Company, GE The group operates from the United States. Capital Corporation and Solvay America, Inc. The group's quarterly revenue for September 2007 was 139.89 millions of USD.

Primary SIC and add'l.: 3743

CIK No: 0001344596

Subsidiaries: American Railcar Marmaduke I LLC, American Railcar Marmaduke II LLC, American Railcar Paragould I LLC, American Railcar Paragould II LLC, ARI Acquisition Sub, LLC, ARI Fleet Services of Canada, Inc, Castings LLC,, Custom Steel, Inc, Southwest Steel I, LLC, Southwest Steel II, LLC, Southwest Steel III, LLC

Officers: James J. Unger/Dir., CEO, Pres., James A. Cowan/COO, Exec. VP, William P. Benac/Sr. VP, CFO, Treasurer, Alan C. Lullman/Sr. VP - Sales - Marketing, Services, Jeff Harrison/Sr. Accounting Executive, Railcar Repair Services, Vickie Bruening/Sr. Accounting Executive, Railcar Repair Services, Diane Weaver/Sr. Mgr. - Fleet Management Services, Steve Johnson/VP - Sales, Lisa Hollinshed/Supervisor, Sales

Directors: James J. Unger/Dir., CEO, Pres., Carl C. Icahn/Chmn., Harold First/Dir., Peter Shea/Dir., Keith Meister/Dir., James C. Pontious/Dir., James M. Laisure/Dir., Brett Icahn/Dir., Vincent J. Intrieri/Dir.

Owners: Keeley Asset Management Corp./7.70%, Carl C. Icahn/52.60%, James C. Pontious, James A. Cowan, Harold First, Insiders/53.90%, Alan C. Lullman, James J. Unger, Marsico Capital Management, LL/12.60%

Financial Data: *Fiscal Year End:*12/31 *Latest Annual Data:* 12/31/2006

Year	Sales	Net Income
2006	$646,052,000	$35,204,000
2005	$608,160,000	$14,768,000
2004	$355,056,000	$1,921,000

Curr. Assets:	$196,874,000	*Curr. Liab.:*	$70,788,000	*P/E Ratio:*	21.64
Plant, Equip.:	$130,293,000	*Total Liab.:*	$88,746,000	*Indic. Yr. Divd.:*	$0.120
Total Assets:	$338,926,000	*Net Worth:*	$250,180,000	*Debt/ Equity:*	1.0407

American Realty Investors Inc

1800 Valley View Ln., Ste. 300, Dallas, TX, 75234; *PH:* 1-469-522-4233; *Fax:* 1-469-522-4299; *http://* www.amrealtytrust.com; *Email:* investor.relations@primeasset.com

General - Incorporation	NV	**Stock**- Price on:12/24/2007	$8.35
Employees	NA	Stock Exchange	NYSE
Auditor	BDO Seidman, LLP	Ticker Symbol	ARL
Stk Agt	American Stock Transfer & Trust Co.	Outstanding Shares	10,140,000
Counsel	NA	E.P.S.	-$1.28
DUNS No.	NA	Shareholders	NA

Business: The groups principle activity is to provide real estate loans and mortgage loans. The group operates through six segments namely, apartments, commercial properties, hotels, land ownership, quick-service restaurants, and notes receivable. The group operates from the United States. The group's quarterly revenue for September 2007 was 50.73 millions of USD.

Primary SIC and add'l.: 6519 1522 6513 1541 6552

CIK No: 0001102238

Subsidiaries: A Williamsburg, Inc., A Williamsburg, LLC, American Mart Hotel Corporation, American Realty Trust, Inc., ARI Enterprise, Inc., ART Blessin, Inc., ART Carriage Park Associates, LTD, ART Chateau Corporation, ART Collection I, LLC, ART Collection, Inc., ART Edina, Inc., ART Elm Fork Ranch, Inc., ART Florentina, Inc., ART Florida Partners I, Inc., ART Florida Partners II, Inc. 97 Subsidiaries included in the Index

Officers: Louis J. Corna/Exec. VP - Tax, General Counsel, Sec., Steven A. Abney/CFO, Exec. VP, Mickey N. Phillips/Mgr., Ryan T. Phillips/Mgr., Daniel J. Moos/56/COO, Pres., Alfred Crozier/55/Exec. VP - Residential Construction, Reagan K. Vidal/47/Exec. VP, MD - Capital Markets

Directors: Ted P. Stokely/74/Chmn., Reagan K. Vidal/47/Exec. VP, MD - Capital Markets, Henry A. Butler/57/Dir., Sharon Hunt/65/Dir., Robert A. Jakuszewski/45/Dir., Ted R. Munselle/51/Dir.

Owners: Daniel J. Moos, Transcontinental Realty Investors, Inc., Insiders, Prime Income Asset Management, Inc., Henry A. Butler, Ted R. Munselle, Reagan K. Vidal, Louis J. Corna, Sharon Hunt, Alfred Crozier, Ryan T. Phillips, Steven A. Abney, Ted P. Stokely, Robert A. Jakuszewski, Realty Advisors, Inc. *(16 Owners included in Index)*

Financial Data: *Fiscal Year End:*12/31 *Latest Annual Data:* 03/31/2007

Year	Sales	Net Income
2007	$51,107,000	-$8,458,000
2006	$18,013,000	$25,207,000
2005	$202,639,000	$47,417,000

Curr. Assets:	$13,035,000	*Curr. Liab.:*	$107,771,000		
Plant, Equip.:	$1,272,424,000	*Total Liab.:*	$1,333,182,000	*Indic. Yr. Divd.:*	NA
Total Assets:	$1,493,671,000	*Net Worth:*	$160,489,000	*Debt/ Equity:*	6.5102

American Reprographics Company

700 N Central Ave., Ste. 550, Glendale, CA, 91203; *PH:* 1-818-500-0225; *Fax:* 1-818-500-0195; *http://* www.e-arc.com

General - Incorporation	DE	**Stock**- Price on:12/24/2007	$30.79
Employees	4,400	Stock Exchange	NYSE
Auditor	PricewaterhouseCoopers LLP	Ticker Symbol	ARP
Stk Agt	Mellon Investor Services LLC	Outstanding Shares	45,490,000
Counsel	NA	E.P.S.	$1.18
DUNS No.	NA	Shareholders	NA

Business: The groups principle activity is to provide services include document management, distribution and logistics, print on demand and on site services. The group services marketed under the trademarks include BidCasterSM, PlanWell(R), MetalPrint(TM) and Abacus PCR(TM). The group acquired 14 reprographics companies in the year 2005 and 16 reprographics companies in the year 2006. The group operates from the United States, Columbia, Canada and Mexico City. The group's quarterly revenue for September 2007 was 176.21 millions of USD.

Primary SIC and add'l.: 3861 7372 5045 3555 7334

CIK No: 0001305168

Subsidiaries: A-C Reproduction Company, American Reprographics Company India Private Limited, American Reprographics Company, L.L.C, American Reprographics Servicios,S.A. de D.V., ARC Acquisition Corporation, ARC Reprographics Canada Corp., Arcprint and Imaging Ltd., Argo-ICC Reprographics Ltd., Blue Print Service Company, Inc., BPI Repro, LLC, Dunn Blue Print Company, E.Pavilion, L.L.C. (owns a 60% interest), Engineering Repro Systems, Inc., Franklin Graphics Corporation, Georgia Blue Print Company, L.L.C. 38 Subsidiaries included in the Index

Officers: K. Suriyakumar/Dir., CEO, Pres., Jonathan F. Styrlund/Dir. - Integration, Kumar Wiratunga/Dir. - Digital Operations, Jonathan Mather/CFO, Rahul Roy/CTO, Theodore J. Carlson/VP - Mergers, Acquisitions, Ken Gini/VP - Integration, Joe Abeyesinhe/VP - Purchasing, David Stickney/VP - Corporate Communications, Ted Buscaglia/VP - Premier Accounting, Janine Brandel/Dir. - Integration

Directors: K. Suriyakumar/Dir., CEO, Pres., S. Chandramohan/Chmn., Thomas J. Formolo/Dir., Manuel J. Perez De La Mesa/Dir., Eriberto R. Scocimara/Dir., Mark W. Mealy/Dir., Dewitt Kerry McCluggage/Dir.

Owners: Dewitt Kerry McCluggage, Kumarakulasingam Suriyakumar/17.00%, Micro Device, Inc./12.50%, Wellington Management Company, LLP/6.50%, Manuel Perez de la Mesa, FMR Corp./6.00%, Eriberto R. Scocimara, Sathiyamurthy Chandramohan/15.50%, Rahul K. Roy/1.00%, Thomas J. Formolo/1.70%, Eagle Asset Management, Inc./5.30%, Insiders/21.90%, Mark W. Mealy, Mark W. Legg, Times Square Capital Management, LLC/6.40%

Financial Data: *Fiscal Year End:*12/31 *Latest Annual Data:* 12/31/2006

Year	Sales	Net Income
2006	$591,838,000	$51,394,000
2005	$494,204,000	$60,476,000
2004	$443,864,000	$29,548,000

Curr. Assets:	$131,068,000	*Curr. Liab.:*	$111,240,000	*P/E Ratio:*	26.09
Plant, Equip.:	$60,138,000	*Total Liab.:*	$363,337,000	*Indic. Yr. Divd.:*	NA
Total Assets:	$547,581,000	*Net Worth:*	$184,244,000	*Debt/ Equity:*	1.2413

American Retirement Corp

111 Wwood Pl., Ste. 200, Brentwood, TN, 37027; *PH:* 1-615-221-2250; *http://* www.arclp.com

General - Incorporation	TN	Stock - Price on:12/24/2007	NA
Employees	NA	Stock Exchange	NYSE
Auditor	KPMG LLP	Ticker Symbol	ACR
Stk Agt..... American Stock Transfer & Trust Co.		Outstanding Shares	NA
Counsel	Bass, Berry & Sims PLC	E.P.S.	NA
DUNS No.	08-954-9737	Shareholders	NA

Business: The group's principal activities are to own, operate and manage various senior living communities throughout the United States. These communities provide independent living, assisted living and skilled nursing services. They also provide specialized care programs for residents with alzheimer's disease and other forms of dementia. The group currently operates 65 senior living communities in 14 states with an aggregate capacity for approximately 14,500 residents. It currently owns 19 communities, leases 41 communities, and manages 5 communities.

Primary SIC and add'l.: 8051 8748 8361

CIK No: 0000787784

Subsidiaries: A.R.C. Management Corporation, Alabama Somerby, LLC, ARC Air Force Village, L.P., ARC Aurora, LLC., ARC Bahia Oaks, Inc., ARC Bay Pines, Inc., ARC Boca Raton, Inc., ARC Boynton Beach, LLC, ARC Bradenton HC, Inc., ARC Bradenton Management, Inc., ARC Bradenton RC, Inc., ARC Brandywine GP, LLC, ARC Brandywine, L.P., ARC Brookmont Terrace, Inc., ARC Carriage Club of Jacksonville, Inc. 135 Subsidiaries included in the Index

Officers: W. E. Sheriff/Chmn., CEO, Pres., Sheila Garner/Regional VP - Operations, Bryan Richardson/CFO, Exec. VP, Lee Anne Fein/Sr. VP - Innovative Sr. Care, Nadine Smith/Dir., Consultant, Lawrence J. Stuesser/Dir., Consultant, Jim Seward/Dir. - Private Investor, Greg Richard/COO, Exec. VP, Ross Roadman/Sr. VP - Strategic Planning, Investor Relations, Lee A. McKnight/Sr. VP - Retirement Community Marketing, Kimberley P. Myers/VP, Corporate Controller, Ron Aylor/Sr. VP - Sales, Jack Leebron/Sr. VP - Legal Services, Eddie Fenoglio/Regional VP - Operations, George T. Hicks/Exec. VP - Finance, Internal Audit, Sec., Treasurer (26 Officers included in Index)

Directors: W. E. Sheriff/Chmn., CEO, Pres., John McCauley/Dir., John A. Morris/Dir., Daniel K. Oconnell/Dir., Edward J. Pearson/Dir., Nadine Smith/Dir., Consultant, Lawrence J. Stuesser/Dir., Consultant, Donald D. Davis/Dir., Jim Seward/Dir. - Private Investor, Frank M. Bumstead/Dir.

American River Bankshares

3100 Zinfandel Dr., Ste. 450, Rancho Cordova, CA, 95670; **PH:** 1-916-851-0123; **Fax:** 1-916-641-1262; **http://** www.amrb.com; **Email:** investor.relations@amrb.com

General - Incorporation	CA	Stock - Price on:12/24/2007	$23.83
Employees	129	Stock Exchange	NDQ
Auditor	Perry-Smith LLP	Ticker Symbol	AMRB
Stk Agt	U.S. Stock Transfer Corp	Outstanding Shares	5,520,000
Counsel	NA	E.P.S.	$1.48
DUNS No.	NA	Shareholders	NA

Business: The group's principal activity is to provide commercial banking services to individuals and businesses. The group accepts checking and savings deposits, originates secured and unsecured commercial, secured real estate and other installment and term loans and offers money market deposit accounts, certificates of deposit and other customary banking services. The subsidiaries include American river bank, first source capital and north coast bank. The group operates four banking offices in sacramento, placer, el dorado and yolo counties. The principal communities served by the group are located in sacramento, placer, yolo, el dorado, sonoma, napa, marin and mendocino counties.

Primary SIC and add'l.: 6022 6712

CIK No: 0001108236

Subsidiaries: American River Bank

Officers: David T. Taber/Dir., CEO/$434,178.00, Mitchell A. Derenzo/46/CFO, Exec. VP/$205,346.00, Kevin B. Bender/44/CIO, Exec. VP/$164,601.00, Douglas E. Tow/54/Exec. VP, Chief Credit Officer/$214,819.00

Directors: David T. Taber/Dir., CEO, Charles D. Fite/Chmn., Robert J. Fox/Dir., Michael A. Ziegler/Dir., Roger J. Taylor/Dir., Stephen H. Waks/Dir., Amador Bustos/Dir., William Robotham/Dir., Dorene Dominguez/Dir.

Owners: Larry D. Standing/0.50%, Mitchell A. Derenzo/0.70%, Richard P. Vinson/0.30%, Douglas E. Tow/0.40%, Robert J. Fox/0.20%, Raymond F. Byrne/0.10%, Insiders/12.10%, Gregory N. Patton/0.30%, Philip A. Wright/1.00%, Charles D. Fite/2.30%, Kevin B. Bender/0.40%, Stephen H. Waks/1.10%, David T. Taber/2.30%, Amador S. Bustos/0.20%, Michael A. Ziegler/0.20% (17 Owners included in Index)

Financial Data: Fiscal Year End:12/31   Latest Annual Data: 12/31/2006

Year	Sales		Net Income
2006	$40,397,000		$9,062,000
2005	$35,542,000		$9,184,000
2004	$25,031,000		$5,827,000
Curr. Assets:	$50,031,000	Curr. Liab.:	$536,632,000	P/E Ratio:	15.58
Plant, Equip.:	$1,846,000	Total Liab.:	$541,632,000	Indic. Yr. Divd.:	$0.600
Total Assets:	$604,003,000	Net Worth:	$62,371,000	Debt/ Equity:	NA

American Riviera Bank

1033 Anacapa St., Santa Barbara, CA, 93101; **PH:** 1-805-965-5942; **http://** www.americanrivierabank.com; **Email:** info@americanrivierabank.com

General - Incorporation		Stock - Price on:12/24/2007	NA
Employees	NA	Stock Exchange	OTC
Auditor	Perry-smith LLP	Ticker Symbol	ARBV
Stk Agt	U.S. Stock Transfer Corp	Outstanding Shares	NA
Counsel	NA	E.P.S.	NA
DUNS No.	NA	Shareholders	NA

Business: The groups principal activity is to provide banking business. The group financial products include savings and fixed deposits, on line, personal and business banking. The group operates from the United States.

Primary SIC and add'l.: 6022

CIK No:

Officers: Michael Salsbury/Dir., CEO, Pres., David A. Duarte/Dir., Exec. VP, COO, Chief Credit Officer, Michelle Martinich/Sr. VP, CFO, Laurie Leighty/Sr. VP, Head - Operations, Human Resources, Dennis Baker/Founding Organizer, Barbara Donnelly/Founding Organizer, Julie Friedman/Founding Organizer, Morrie Jurkowitz/Founding Organizer

Directors: Michael Salsbury/Dir., CEO, Pres., Lawrence Koppelman/Chmn., Bruce N. Anticouni/Dir., David A. Duarte/Dir., Exec. VP, COO, Chief Credit Officer, Tad Buchanan/Dir., Frank Burgess/Dir., Darren D. Caesar/Dir., Joe Campanelli/Dir., Michael Giles/Dir., Jeffrey M. Giller/Dir., Palmer G. Jackson/Dir., Douglas Margerum/Dir., Alixe Mattingly/Dir., Gordon Mckay/Dir., Guy Taylor/Dir.

American Safety Insurance Holdings Ltd

100 Galleria Pkwy. SE, Ste. 700, Atlanta, GA, 30339; **PH:** 1-770-916-1908; **Fax:** 1-770-916-0618; **http://** www.americansafetygroup.com; **Email:** info@americansafetyinsurance.com

General - Incorporation	Bermuda	Stock - Price on:12/24/2007	$22.95
Employees	138	Stock Exchange	NYSE
Auditor	BDO Seidman LLP	Ticker Symbol	ASI
Stk Agt..... Computershare Investor Services LLC		Outstanding Shares	10,560,000
Counsel	Appleby Spurling Hunter	E.P.S.	$2.40
DUNS No.	87-565-1325	Shareholders	NA

Business: The group's principal activities are to develop, underwrite, manage and market primary casualty insurance and reinsurance programs. The specialty insurance programs include coverage for general liability, pollution liability, professional liability and workers' compensation. The group also offers custom designed risk management programs for contractors, consultants and other businesses and property owners who are involved with environmental remediation, contracting and other specialty risks. The group has operations in the United States and Bermuda.

Primary SIC and add'l.: 6331 6719

CIK No: 0000783603

Subsidiaries: American Safety Assurance, Ltd, American Safety Capital Trust, American Safety Capital Trust II, American Safety Capital Trust III, American Safety Casualty Insurance Company, American Safety Financial Corp, American Safety Holdings Corp, American Safety Indemnity Company, American Safety Insurance Services, Inc., American Safety Purchasing Group, Inc, American Safety Reinsurance Ltd, Environmental Claims Service, Inc, Ponce Lighthouse Properties Inc, RiverMar Contracting Company, Sureco Bond Services, Inc

Officers: Stephen R. Crim/Dir., CEO, Pres./$662,742.00, William C. Tepe/CFO - Contact - Investor Relations/$437,966.00, Ambuj Jain/VP - Planning, Operations Support, Joseph D. Scollo/COO, Exec. VP/$556,527.00, Steven B. Mathis/40/VP - Planning, Treasurer/$259,833.00, Randolph Hutto/59/General Counsel, Sec./$228,080.00, Geoff Gregory/Chief Underwriting Officer, Thomas M. Callahan/44/Sr. VP

Directors: Stephen R. Crim/Dir., CEO, Pres., Cody W. Birdwell/55/Chmn., Thomas W. Mueller/54/Dep. Chmn., William A. Robbie/57/Dir., Jerome D. Weaver/53/Dir., David V. Brueggen/61/Dir., Steven L. Groot/58/Dir., Frank D. Lackner/39/Dir., Lawrence I. Geneen/64/Dir.

Owners: Cody W. Birdwell/1.95%, Insiders/11.20%, David V. Brueggen/2.81%, Steven L. Groot, Lawrence I. Geneen, HCC Insurance Holdings, Inc./12.54%, Frank L. Lackner, Wells Fargo & Co./7.88%, William C. Tepe, Joseph D. Scollo, Thomas W. Mueller/3.14%, William A. Robbie, Stephen R. Crim/2.04%, Eagle Asset Management/5.43%, Steven B. Mathis (17 Owners included in Index)

Financial Data: Fiscal Year End:12/31   Latest Annual Data: 12/31/2006

Year	Sales		Net Income
2006	$171,440,000		$20,532,000
2005	$155,874,000		$14,656,000
2004	$214,656,000		$14,757,000
Curr. Assets:	$216,917,000	Curr. Liab.:	$35,702,000	P/E Ratio:	9.56
Plant, Equip.:	$3,900,000	Total Liab.:	$470,629,000	Indic. Yr. Divd.:	NA
Total Assets:	$584,160,000	Net Worth:	$108,780,000	Debt/ Equity:	0.1871

American Science & Engineering Inc

829 Middlesex Tpke., Billerica, MA, 01821; **PH:** 1-978-262-8700; **Fax:** 1-978-262-8804; **http://** www.as-e.com; **Email:** intlsales@as-e.com

General - Incorporation	MA	Stock - Price on:12/24/2007	$56.01
Employees	299	Stock Exchange	NDQ
Auditor	Vitale, Caturano & Co., Ltd.	Ticker Symbol	ASEI
Stk Agt..... American Stock Transfer & Trust Co.		Outstanding Shares	9,190,000
Counsel	Ken Galaznik	E.P.S.	$2.62
DUNS No.	00-176-7763	Shareholders	NA

Business: The group's principal activities are to develop, produce, market, maintain and provide research, engineering and training services with respect to X-ray inspection systems. The products of the group are used for critical detection and security applications. These security applications include X-ray inspection and screening systems for combating terrorism, drug and weapon smuggling, trade fraud and illegal immigration. These applications are used by seaport and border authorities, federal facilities and military bases, airports and corporation in the United States and around the globe. The group's patented z(R) backscatter and shaped energy technologies detect plastic explosives, plastic weapons, illegal drugs and other contrabands.

Primary SIC and add'l.: 3844 3829

CIK No: 0000005768

Officers: Anthony R. Fabiano/Dir., CEO, Pres., Kenneth J. Galaznik/CFO, Treasurer, Joseph Callerame/VP - Science, Technology, Paul Grazewski/VP - Product Management, Andrey V. Mishin/VP, Sr. Technology Fellow, Kenneth Breur/VP - Operations, Robert Postle/VP - Worldwide Marketing, Sales, George M. Peterman/VP - Human Resources, William F. Grieco/VP, General Counsel

Directors: Anthony R. Fabiano/Dir., CEO, Pres., William E. Odom/Dir., Carl W. Vogt/Dir., Mark Thompson/Dir., Ernest Moniz/Dir., Denis R. Brown/Dir., Hamilton W. Helmer/Dir., Roger P. Heinisch/Dir.

Owners: William E. Odom, Joseph Callerame, Hamilton W. Helmer, Robert G. Postle, Roger P. Heinisch, Kenneth J. Galaznik, Ernest J. Moniz, Mark Thompson, Insiders/4.78%, Denis R. Brown, Carl W. Vogt, Anthony R. Fabiano, William F. Grieco

Financial Data: Fiscal Year End:03/31   Latest Annual Data: 3/31/2006

Year	Sales		Net Income
2006	$163,604,000		$29,786,000
2005	$88,314,000		$11,185,000
2004	$76,342,000		$1,911,000
Curr. Assets:	$153,924,000	Curr. Liab.:	$28,893,000		
Plant, Equip.:	$18,717,000	Total Liab.:	$43,191,000	Indic. Yr. Divd.:	$0.800
Total Assets:	$173,389,000	Net Worth:	$130,198,000	Debt/ Equity:	0.0566

American Security Resources Corp

9601 Katy Fwy., Ste 220, Houston, TX, 77024; *PH:* 1-713-465-1001;
http:// www.americansecurityresources.com; *Email:* info@amsrcorp.com

General - Incorporation	NV	**Stock**- Price on:12/24/2007	$0.044
Employees	2	Stock Exchange	OTC
Auditor	Malone & Bailey, P.C	Ticker Symbol	ARSC
Stk Agt	Atlas Stock Transfer Corp	Outstanding Shares	134,310,000
Counsel	NA	E.P.S.	-$0.075
DUNS No.	NA	Shareholders	NA

Business: The group's principal activity is to provide network security solutions and network security hardware. It operates in three segments, consulting services: offers network security consulting services, network security compliance, network intrusion analysis and review. Network security software and appliance solutions: offers security solutions such as fortigate series of asic- accelerated antivirus firewalls from fortinet. Managed security services provider: provides installation and 24*7 monitoring of its clients' network systems. The services are offered to companies seeking to increase productivity, maintain regulatory compliance for securing confidential data and to reduce downtime costs by investing in secured network technology. On 23-Feb-2004, the group acquired simple network solutions, inc.

Primary SIC and add'l.: 7371 3577 7372 7373 7379

CIK No: 0001085069

Subsidiaries: Kahuna Network Security, Inc

Officers: Frank Neukomm/Chmn., CEO, Robert C. Farr/Dir., COO, Pres., Marlin Williford/CFO, Michael E. Cherry/VP - Marketing, Nancy Finney/Controller

Directors: Frank Neukomm/Chmn., CEO, Robert C. Farr/Dir., COO, Pres., Robert J. Wilson/Dir., James R. Twedt/Dir., Alvie T. Merrill/Dir.

Owners: Frank Neukomm/6.80%, Edward L. Davis/7.20%

Financial Data: *Fiscal Year End:*12/31 *Latest Annual Data:* 12/31/2006

Year	Sales	Net Income
2006	NA	-$8,600,000
2005	NA	-$5,385,000
2004	NA	-$28,088,000

Curr. Assets:	$13,000	**Curr. Liab.:**	$419,000		
Plant, Equip.:	$133,000	**Total Liab.:**	$419,000	**Indic. Yr. Divd.:**	NA
Total Assets:	$146,000	**Net Worth:**	-$273,000	**Debt/ Equity:**	NA

American Shared Hospital Services

4 Embarcadero Ctr., Ste. 3700, San Francisco, CA, 94111; *PH:* 1-415-788-5300;
Fax: 1-415-788-5660; *http://* www.ashs.com; *Email:* e.bates@ashs.com

General - Incorporation	CA	**Stock**- Price on:12/24/2007	$5.95
Employees	12	Stock Exchange	AMEX
Auditor	Moss Adams LLP	Ticker Symbol	AMS
Stk Agt	American Stock Transfer & Trust Co.	Outstanding Shares	5,020,000
Counsel	Davis Polk & Wardwell	E.P.S.	$0.25
DUNS No.	05-866-9235	Shareholders	NA

Business: The group's principal activity is to provide gamma knife stereotactic radiosurgery services to seventeen medical centers in fifteen states. The group provides gamma knife equipment as well as planning, installation, reimbursements and marketing support services to major urban medical centers. Gamma knife stereotactic radiosurgery, a non-invasive procedure, is an alternative to conventional brain surgery or can be an adjunct to conventional brain surgery. The gamma knife treats selected benign brain tumors, malignant tumors, arteriovenous malformations and trigeminal neuralgia. The group is conducting research for treatment of Parkinson's disease, epilepsy and other functional disorders.

Primary SIC and add'l.: 8099 8071

CIK No: 0000744825

Subsidiaries: American Shared Radiosurgery Services, GK Financing, LLC, MedLeader.com, Inc., OR21, Inc.

Officers: Ernest A. Bates/Chmn., CEO - Investor Relations/$653,302.00, Craig K. Tagawa/CFO, COO, Sr. VP/$376,576.00, Ernest R. Bates/VP - Sales, Business Development, Willie R. Barnes/Corp. Sec., Norman A. Houck/VP, Controller

Directors: Ernest A. Bates/Chmn., CEO - Investor Relations, Olin C. Robison/Dir., John F. Ruffle/Dir., Stanley S. Trotman/Dir., Ernest R. Bates/VP - Sales, Business Development

Owners: John F. Ruffle/4.00%, Stanley S. Trotman/2.90%, Ernest A. Bates/16.90%, Olin C. Robison, Ernest R. Bates, Insiders/26.00%, Craig K. Tagawa/1.70%, Banque Carnegie Luxembourg S.A./6.20%

Financial Data: *Fiscal Year End:*12/31 *Latest Annual Data:* 12/31/2006

Year	Sales	Net Income
2006	$20,385,000	$1,656,000
2005	$18,231,000	$1,767,000
2004	$16,389,000	$1,985,000

Curr. Assets:	$11,125,000	**Curr. Liab.:**	$11,666,000	**P/E Ratio:**	23.80
Plant, Equip.:	$34,166,000	**Total Liab.:**	$28,851,000	**Indic. Yr. Divd.:**	$0.190
Total Assets:	$50,905,000	**Net Worth:**	$19,009,000	**Debt/ Equity:**	0.7990

American Skandia Life Assurance Corp

1 Corporate Dr., Shelton, CT, 06484; *PH:* 1-203-926-1888;
http:// www.americanskandia.prudential.com

General - Incorporation	CT	**Stock**- Price on:12/24/2007	$99.22
Employees	39,814	Stock Exchange	NA
Auditor	PricewaterhouseCoopers LLP	Ticker Symbol	NA
Stk Agt	American Skandia Advisor Funds, Inc	Outstanding Shares	465,000,000
Counsel	NA	E.P.S.	$8.25
DUNS No.	17-435-2377	Shareholders	NA

Business: The group's principal activity is to develop long-term savings and retirement products distributed through its affiliated broker/dealer company, American skandia marketing incorporated. The group currently issues variable and term life insurance and variable, fixed, market value adjusted deferred and immediate annuities for individuals, groups and qualified pension plans. The group's products are sold to individuals for long-term savings and retirement purposes and to address the economic impact of premature death, estate and business planning concerns and supplemental retirement needs. The group was a wholly owned subsidiary of American skandia inc. On 01-May-2003, prudential financial inc acquired the parent company along with the subsidiaries. The group is an indirect majority-owned subsidiary of prudential financial inc from 01-May-2003.

Primary SIC and add'l.: 6311

CIK No: 0000881453

Subsidiaries: American Skandia, Inc., Prudential Financial, Inc.

Officers: David R. Odenath/Dir., CEO, Pres., Michael A. Bohm/CFO, Exec. VP

Directors: David R. Odenath/Dir., CEO, Pres., Helen M. Galt/Dir., Ronald Paul Joelson/Dir., James J. Avery/Dir., Bernard J. Jacob/Dir., Kenneth Y. Tanji/Dir.

Financial Data: *Fiscal Year End:*12/31 *Latest Annual Data:* 12/31/2006

Year	Sales	Net Income
2006	$32,488,000,000	$3,428,000,000
2005	$31,708,000,000	$3,540,000,000
2004	$28,348,000,000	$2,256,000,000

Curr. Assets:	$15,581,000,000	**Curr. Liab.:**	$28,860,000,000	**P/E Ratio:**	12.03
Plant, Equip.:	NA	**Total Liab.:**	$431,374,000,000	**Indic. Yr. Divd.:**	$0.950
Total Assets:	$454,266,000,000	**Net Worth:**	$22,892,000,000	**Debt/ Equity:**	0.7675

American Skllng Co

136 Heber Ave., No. 303, Park City, UT, 84060; *PH:* 1-435-615-0340; *http://* www.peaks.com

General - Incorporation	DE	**Stock**- Price on:12/24/2007	$0.145
Employees	1,300	Stock Exchange	OTC
Auditor	KPMG LLP	Ticker Symbol	AESKE
Stk Agt	American Stock Transfer & Trust Co.	Outstanding Shares	31,760,000
Counsel	Pierce Atwood	E.P.S.	-$2.28
DUNS No.	96-987-0716	Shareholders	NA

Business: The group's principal activity is to market and operate alpine ski resorts. The operations are carried out through two business segments: resort and real estate. Resort operations consist of nine ski resorts in Vermont, Maine, Colorado, Utah, California, Nevada and New Hampshire. The ski resorts provide resort facilities, golf courses, ski and golf schools, retail shops and other activities on lands leased out for a long-term period. The real estate segment develops the mountainside of the ski resorts and sells and leases out interests in such developments. The group also develops whole ownership and time-share condominiums, townhouses and retail space.

Primary SIC and add'l.: 7011 7999 6552

CIK No: 0001043432

Subsidiaries: American Skiing Company Resort PropertiesInc., ASC Leasing Inc., ASC Utah, Blunder Bay Development Inc., Community Water Company, Dover RestaurantsInc., Grand Summit Resort Hotel Sales Inc., Grand Summit Resort PropertiesInc., Killington Ltd., Killington RestaurantsInc., L.B.O. Holding Inc., Mount Snow Ltd, Mountainside, Pico Ski Area Management Company, S-K-I Ltd. 28 Subsidiaries included in the Index

Officers: William J. Fair/45/Dir., CEO, Pres., Franklin Carey/60/Sr. VP - Marketing, Sales, John W. Diller/60/Pres., MD - Sugarloaf Resort, Scott F. Pierpont/54/Pres., MD - Canyons Resort, Stan Hansen/65/Sr. VP - Real Estate, Allen W. Wilson/55/Pres., MD - Killington, Pico Resort, Foster A. Stewart/40/Sr. VP, General Counsel, Sec., Christopher S. Diamond/61/Pres., MD - Steamboat Resort, Helen E. Wallace/54/Sr. VP, CFO, Treasurer, Dana A. Bullen/42/Pres., MD - Sunday River Resort, John D. Lowell/54/MD - Attitash Resort, Kelly Pawlak/42/MD - Mount Snow Resort

Directors: William J. Fair/45/Dir., CEO, Pres., Steven B. Gruber/50/Chmn., Paul Wachter/51/Dir., Leslie B. Otten/58/Dir., Edward V. Dardani/45/Dir., Gordon M. Gillies/63/Dir., John W. Diller/60/Pres., MD - Sugarloaf Resort, Taylor J. Crandall/53/Dir., Robert J. Branson/59/Dir., William S. Janes/54/Dir., David B. Hawkes/63/Dir.

Owners: Stan Hansen, Foster A. Stewart, Insiders/3.40%, OHCP Ski, L.P., Oak Hill Capital Partners, L.P., Oak Hill Capital Partners, L.P., OHCP Ski, L.P., Oak Hill Capital Partners, L.P./5.53%, Paul Wachter, Robert J. Branson, Oak Hill Securities Fund, L.P., Gordon M. Gillies, Leslie B. Otten/100.00%, Oak Hill Securities FundLiquidating Trust, Leslie B. Otten/3.85% *(27 Owners included in Index)*

Financial Data: *Fiscal Year End:*07/30 *Latest Annual Data:* 7/30/2006

Year	Sales	Net Income
2006	$307,810,000	-$65,653,000
2005	$276,477,000	-$73,315,000
2004	$284,111,000	-$28,502,000

Curr. Assets:	$29,341,000	**Curr. Liab.:**	$96,581,000	**P/E Ratio:**	1.36
Plant, Equip.:	$370,923,000	**Total Liab.:**	$427,084,000	**Indic. Yr. Divd.:**	NA
Total Assets:	$422,934,000	**Net Worth:**	-$314,277,000	**Debt/ Equity:**	NA

American Software Inc

470 E Paces Ferry Rd., Atlanta, GA, 30305; *PH:* 1-404-264-5296; *Fax:* 1-404-264-5206;
http:// www.amsoftware.com; *Email:* askasi@amsoftware.com

General - Incorporation	GA	**Stock**- Price on:12/24/2007	$10.6319
Employees	321	Stock Exchange	NDQ
Auditor	KPMG LLP	Ticker Symbol	AMSWA
Stk Agt	American Stock Transfer & Trust Co.	Outstanding Shares	24,740,000
Counsel	NA	E.P.S.	$0.37
DUNS No.	03-005-4860	Shareholders	NA

Business: The group's principal activities are to develop, market and support a portfolio of software and services that deliver e-business and enterprise management solutions. These software and services are designed to bring business value to enterprises by supporting their operations over intranets, extranets, client/servers or the Internet. The group operates through three segments: the enterprise resource planning segment automates customers' internal financing, human resources, and manufacturing functions. The collaborative supply chain management segment provides collaborative supply chain solutions to streamline and optimize the production and distribution of products between trading partners. The it consulting segment specializes in assisting a diverse customer base to solve business issues with custom-developed technology solutions.

Primary SIC and add'l.: 7371

CIK No: 0000713425

Subsidiaries: American Software France S.A., American Software Research and Development Corporation, American Software U.K., Ltd., American Software USA, Inc., ASI Properties, Inc., Demand Management, Inc., Logility, Inc., New Generation Computing, Inc., The Proven Method, Inc.

Officers: James C. Edenfield/CEO, Pres., Treasurer/$964,343.00, Jeffrey W. Coombs/COO, Exec. VP/$227,052.00, Vincent C. Klinges/CFO/$301,526.00, Michael J. Edenfield/Dir., Exec. VP/$819,556.00, James R. McGuone/Sec.

Directors: Thomas L. Newberry/Chmn., David H. Gambrell/Dir., Michael J. Edenfield/Dir., Exec. VP, Dennis Hogue/Dir., John J. Jarvis/Dir., James B. Miller/Dir.

Owners: Thomas L. Newberry/100.00%, John J. Jarvis/0.30%, Insiders/5.80%, Insiders/100.00%, Michael J. Edenfield/2.80%, Thomas L. Newberry/1.10%, Wellington Management Company, LLC/7.40%, Dennis W. Hogue, Jeffrey W. Coombs/0.50%, Vincent C. Klinges/0.60%, Thomas L. Newberry, James C. Edenfield/1.10%, James B. Miller, James C. Edenfield/100.00%, AXA Assurances I.A.R.D. Mutuelle/5.30%

Financial Data: Fiscal Year End:04/30 Latest Annual Data: 04/30/2007

Year	Sales	Net Income
2007	$84,367,000	$8,433,000
2006	$76,630,000	$5,019,000
2005	$64,544,000	$3,284,000

Curr. Assets:	$80,536,000	Curr. Liab.:	$25,488,000	P/E Ratio: 39.97
Plant, Equip.:	$7,669,000	Total Liab.:	$26,358,000	Indic. Yr. Divd: $0.320
Total Assets:	$109,889,000	Net Worth:	$79,372,000	Debt/ Equity: NA

American Soil Technologies Inc

12224 Montague St., Pacoima, CA, 91331; **PH:** 1-818-899-4686; **Fax:** 1-818-899-4670; **http://** www.americansoiltech.com; **Email:** info@americansoiltech.com

General - Incorporation	NV	**Stock** - Price on:12/24/2007	$0.24
Employees	17	Stock Exchange	OTC
Auditor	Epstein Weber & Conover, PLC	Ticker Symbol	SOYL
Stk Agt	Atlas Stock Transfer Corp	Outstanding Shares	47,270,000
Counsel	Oswald & Yap	E.P.S	-$0.07
DUNS No.	60-835-8446	Shareholders	NA

Business: The group's principal activity is to develop, manufacture and market soil enhancement products for the agricultural community. The group offers technology that decreases the need for water in dry land farming, irrigated farming and other plant growing environments and increases crop yield. The two primary products of the group are agriblend(R), a patented soil amendment developed for agriculture and nutrimoist(tm), developed for homes, parks, golf courses and other turf related applications. The products are marketed primarily in the United States and Mexico.

Primary SIC and add'l.: 0782 2899 2879 0711

CIK No: 0001031896

Officers: Carl P. Ranno/Dir., CEO, Pres., Acting CFO, Treasurer, Johnny Dickinson/VP - Marketing, Diana Visco/Sec., Neil C. Kitchen/Dir., VP, Donette Lamson/VP - Turf, Horticulture, Landscape, Forrest Thorpe/Dir. - Business Development

Directors: Carl P. Ranno/Dir., CEO, Pres., Acting CFO, Treasurer, Louie Visco/Chmn., Scott Baker/Dir., Neil C. Kitchen/Dir., VP

Owners: Carl P. Ranno, Insiders/47.00%, Johnny Dickinson, The Benz Group/6.50%, Scott Baker, Donette Lamson, Diana Visco, Neil C. Kitchen, UTEK Corporation/16.00%, Louie Visco/36.30%, FLD Corporation/29.80%

Financial Data: Fiscal Year End:12/30 Latest Annual Data: 12/31/2006

Year	Sales	Net Income
2006	$586,000	-$2,312,000
2005	$644,000	-$2,075,000
2004	$598,000	-$1,655,000

Curr. Assets:	$593,000	Curr. Liab.:	$1,159,000	
Plant, Equip.:	$402,000	Total Liab.:	$4,123,000	Indic. Yr. Divd: NA
Total Assets:	$5,649,000	Net Worth:	$1,526,000	Debt/ Equity: 0.4962

American Southwest Music Distribution Inc

8721 Sunset Blvd. Penthhouse, West Hollywood, City Of Industry, CA, 90069; **PH:** 1-310-659-8770; **Fax:** 1-310-659-2499; **http://** www.aswmd.com

General - Incorporation	DE	**Stock** - Price on:12/24/2007	$0.04
Employees	6	Stock Exchange	OTC
Auditor	KBL, LLP	Ticker Symbol	ASWD
Stk Agt	Holladay Stock Transfer, Inc.	Outstanding Shares	10,370,000
Counsel	NA	E.P.S	-$0.489
DUNS No.	NA	Shareholders	NA

Business: The groups principal activity is to explore minerals. The group operates from the United States.

Primary SIC and add'l.: 5736

CIK No: 0001122771

Subsidiaries: American Southwest Music Distribution, Inc

Officers: David Michery/Dir., CEO, Pres., Juan Garcia/Production Mgr., Ron Urban/Pres., Michael Green/Contact - A/R, Evelyn Lander/Contact - Human Resources, Robert Guillerman/GM, Alex Jarmisian/Finance Mgr., Marcus Sanders/COO, Robert Cardenas/Head - Creative Services, Bryan Gonzales/Sr. Exec. VP, Darlene Guevara/Web Development, Admin, Kent Puckett/42/Dir., CFO, Sec., Treasurer, Garland Scyrus/Contact - A/R

Directors: David Michery/Dir., CEO, Pres., Kent Puckett/42/Dir., CFO, Sec., Treasurer

Owners: Insiders/72.80%, Kent Puckett/7.10%, Donald Byers/1.90%, David Michery/65.70%

Financial Data: Fiscal Year End:04/30 Latest Annual Data: 4/30/2006

Year	Sales	Net Income
2006	NA	-$1,954,000
2005	NA	-$97,000
2004	NA	-$692,000

Curr. Assets:	NA	Curr. Liab.:	$2,301,000	
Plant, Equip.:	$61,000	Total Liab.:	$2,301,000	Indic. Yr. Divd: NA
Total Assets:	$4,281,000	Net Worth:	$1,980,000	Debt/ Equity: NA

American Spectrum Realty Inc

5850 San Felipe, Ste. 450, Houston, TX, 77057; **PH:** 1-713-706-6200; **Fax:** 1-713-706-6201; **http://** www.americanspectrum.com

General - Incorporation	MD	**Stock** - Price on:12/24/2007	$21.7502
Employees	34	Stock Exchange	AMEX
Auditor	Hein & Assoc., LLP	Ticker Symbol	AQQ
Stk Agt	Mellon Investor Services LLC	Outstanding Shares	1,380,000
Counsel	NA	E.P.S	$4.71
DUNS No.	NA	Shareholders	NA

Business: The groups principle activities include owning, acquiring, managing and operating income-producing properties. In the year 2005, the group acquired two office buildings in Houston. The group operates from the United States. The groups quarterly revenue for September 2007 was 7.55 millions of USD.

Primary SIC and add'l.: 6519 6512

CIK No: 0001121783

Subsidiaries: American Spectrum Holdings (Lindbergh). LLC, American Spectrum Holdings (Pasadena), LLC, American Spectrum Holdings (SPIP-V), LLC, American Spectrum Holdings (Washington), LLC, American Spectrum Holdings (Westheimer), LLC, American Spectrum Holdings-Hazelwood, L.P., American Spectrum Realty Management, Inc., American Spectrum Realty Operating Partnership, L.P., American Spectrum Realty Properties, Inc., American Spectrum Realty-1501 Mockingbird, LLC, American Spectrum Realty-2855 Mangum, LLC, American Spectrum Realty-6420 Richmond Atrium, LLC, American Spectrum Realty-6430 Richmond Atrium, LLC, American Spectrum Realty-Gray Falls, LLC, ASR 11500 NW, L.P. 76 Subsidiaries included in the Index

Officers: William J. Carden/Chmn., CEO, Pres., Acting CFO/$482,000.00, Anthony G. Eppolito/VP, Treasurer, Sec. - Investor Relations/$137,171.00, Richard M. Holland/VP - Investments/$189,036.00, Jay Carden/Acquisition, Dispositions Information Contact, Ed Tiemann/Management Issues Contact - Texas, Kimberlee Scheibly/Management Issues, California, Arizona, Tim Dempsey/Management Issues, South Carolina, Ric Holland/Contact - Leasing Information/$185,065.00, Bill McGrath/Contact - Leasing Information, Megan McKenzie/Contact - Management Issues

Directors: William J. Carden/Chmn., CEO, Pres., Acting CFO, Timothy R. Brown/Dir., William W. Geary/Dir., John N. Galardi/Dir., John F. Itzel/Dir., Presley E. Werlein/Dir.

Owners: William W. Geary, Timothy R. Brown/1.40%, John V. Winfield/13.20%, John F. Itzel/, Presley E. Werlein, William J. Carden/33.70%, Insiders/48.70%, John N. Galardi/31.90%

Financial Data: Fiscal Year End:12/31 Latest Annual Data: 12/31/2006

Year	Sales	Net Income
2006	$26,047,000	$6,534,000
2005	$20,269,000	-$2,266,000
2004	$27,158,000	-$9,107,000

Curr. Assets:	$1,636,000	Curr. Liab.:	$8,010,000	
Plant, Equip.:	$172,813,000	Total Liab.:	$174,843,000	Indic. Yr. Divd.: NA
Total Assets:	$190,182,000	Net Worth:	$15,339,000	Debt/ Equity:10.9740

American Sports Development Group Inc

155 Verdin Rd. , Greenville, SC, 29607; **PH:** 1-864-297-0507; **http://** www.asdg.com

General - Incorporation	DE	**Stock** - Price on:12/24/2007	$0.0021
Employees	NA	Stock Exchange	OTC
Auditor	Tatum CFO Partners LLP	Ticker Symbol	ASDP
Stk Agt	Computershare Trust Co	Outstanding Shares	NA
Counsel	NA	E.P.S	NA
DUNS No.	NA	Shareholders	NA

Business: The group's principal activities are to manufacture and distribute paintballs mainly used in shooting competition. Paintball products include paintball guns, paintballs and safety equipment such as goggles. The group also sells accessories like goggles, soft goods, barrels and clothing. The group also designs and manufactures hot air and cold air inflatables. Inflatable products range from custom inflatable designs and product replicas to standard designs such as cold air and helium filled advertising balloons, airships, 'hot air balloon' rooftop displays, airborne helium balls and large flying signs. The brands of paintball include proball and power ball. The primary customers include paintball fields and stores worldwide. On 17-May-2002, the group acquired American inflatables, inc.

Primary SIC and add'l.: 3949

CIK No: 0001073874

Subsidiaries: American Inflatables, Inc., ILM, Inc., National Paintball Supply Company, Inc, Paintball Incorporated and ILM, Inc., Paintball, Inc.

Officers: William R. Fairbanks/Pres., Douglas L. Brown/VP, William B. Kearney/CFO

Financial Data: Fiscal Year End:12/31 Latest Annual Data: 12/31/2002

Year	Sales	Net Income
2002	$19,300,000	-$1,964,000
2001	$1,181,000	-$794,000
2000	$1,478,000	-$2,616,000

Curr. Assets:	$3,919,000	Curr. Liab.:	$5,362,000	
Plant, Equip.:	$470,000	Total Liab.:	$5,380,000	Indic. Yr. Divd.: NA
Total Assets:	$6,534,000	Net Worth:	$1,153,000	Debt/ Equity: NA

American Standard Companies Inc

6200 Troup Hwy., Tyler, TX, 75711; ; **http://** www.americanstandardair.com

General - Incorporation	DE	**Stock** - Price on:12/24/2007	$60.15
Employees	62,200	Stock Exchange	NYSE
Auditor	Ernst & Young LLP	Ticker Symbol	TT
Stk Agt	Bank of New York	Outstanding Shares	202,130,000
Counsel	NA	E.P.S	$2.99
DUNS No.	00-134-4621	Shareholders	NA

Business: The groups principle activity is to provide air conditioning systems. The group operates through three segments namely air conditioning systems and services, bath and kitchen, and vehicle control systems. The group operates from United States.

Primary SIC and add'l.: 3714 3585 3432 3261

CIK No: 0000836102

Subsidiaries: A-S (Beijing) Enamel Steel Sanitaryware Co., Ltd., A-S (China) Co., Limited, A-S (Guangzhou) Enamel Ware Company Limited, A-S (Jiangmen) Fittings Co. Ltd., A-S (Shanghai) Pottery Co., Ltd., A-S (Tianjin) Consulting Co., Ltd., A-S (Tianjin) Pottery Co., Ltd., A-S Air

Conditioning Products Limited, A-S Air Conditioning System (Tianjin) Co. Ltd., A-S Air-Conditioning System (Shanghai) Co., Ltd., A-S China Plumbing Products Limited, A-S China Plumbing Products Servco Limited, A-S Energy, Inc., A-S Thai Holdings Ltd., Air Conditioning Service (Midlands) Limited 304 Subsidiaries included in the Index

Officers: Frederic M. Poses/Chmn., CEO/$10,675,810.00, Peter G. D'Aloia/CFO, Sr. VP/$3,825,155.00, Jacques Esculier/Pres. - Vehicle Control Systems/$2,313,346.00, Lawrence B. Costello/Sr. VP - Human Resources/$2,307,285.00, Paul J. McGrath/Sr. VP, General Counsel, Sec., David R. Pannier/Pres. - Residential Systems, Richard S. Paradise/46/VP, Controller, Mary Beth Gustafsson/Sr. VP, General Counsel, Sec., Scott R. Massengill/45/VP, Treasurer, Nicholas A. Anthony/VP - General Tax Counsel, Brad Cerepak/VP, Controller, Dale F. Elliott/Pres. - Global Bath, Kitchen, Bruce R. Fisher/VP - Strategic Planning, Investor Relations, Craig W. Kissel/Pres. - Trane Commercial Systems/$3,502,896.00, David Kuhl/VP, Treasurer *(25 Officers included in Index)*

Directors: Frederic M. Poses/Chmn., CEO, Paul J. Curlander/Dir., Ruth Ann Marshall/Dir., Steven E. Anderson/Dir., Steven F. Goldstone/Dir., Kirk S. Hachigian/Dir., Jared L. Cohon/Dir., James F. Hardymon/Dir., Edward E. Hagenlocker/Dir., Dale F. Morrison/Dir.

Owners: Kirk S. Hachigian, Peter G. DAloia, Jared L. Cohon, Steven F. Goldstone, Lawrence B. Costello, Paul J. Curlander, Jacques Esculier, Craig W. Kissel, Ruth Ann Marshall, Insiders/3.49%, Frederic M. Poses/1.99%, Edward E. Hagenlocker, Steven E. Anderson, Dale F. Morrison

Financial Data: *Fiscal Year End:*12/31 *Latest Annual Data:* 12/31/2006

Year	Sales	Net Income
2006	$11,208,200,000	$541,000,000
2005	$10,264,400,000	$556,300,000
2004	$9,508,800,000	$313,400,000

Curr. Assets:	$3,436,700,000	**Curr. Liab.:**	$2,568,100,000		
Plant, Equip.:	$1,725,800,000	**Total Liab.:**	$6,489,600,000	**Indic. Yr. Divd.:**	$0.640
Total Assets:	$7,413,100,000	**Net Worth:**	$923,500,000	**Debt/ Equity:**	1.4119

American States Water Co

630 E Foothill Blvd., San Dimas, CA, 91773; ***PH:*** 1-909-394-3600; ***Fax:*** 1-909-394-1382; ***http://*** www.aswater.com; ***Email:*** investorinfo@aswater.com

General		**Stock**	
Incorporation	CA	Price on:12/24/2007	$34.74
Employees	557	Stock Exchange	NYSE
Auditor	PricewaterhouseCoopers LLP	Ticker Symbol	AWR
Stk Agt	Mellon Investor Services LLC	Outstanding Shares	17,060,000
Counsel	NA	E.P.S.	$1.44
DUNS No.	02-364-0589	Shareholders	NA

Business: The group's principal activity is to purchase, produce, distribute and sell water and electricity. It operates through three business segments: water, electric and non-regulated. The water segment purchases and distributes water in the state of California. The electric segment provides electric service to the city of big bear lake in san bernardino county. The non-regulated segment performs water related services such as wastewater treatment, customer billing, meter reading and operation of water utility related systems. It operates within 75 communities in 10 counties in California. As of 31-Dec-2003, it served 250,082 water customers and 22,276 electric customers and operated 29 miles of overhead 34.5 kv transmission lines, 1 mile of underground 34.5 kv transmission lines, 174 miles of 4.16 kv or 2.4 kv distribution lines, 42 miles of underground cable and 14 sub-stations.

Primary SIC and add'l.: 4911 4941 6719

CIK No: 0001056903

Subsidiaries: American States Utility Services, Inc., California Cities Water Company, Inc., Chaparral City Water Company, Fort Bliss Water Services Company, Golden State Water Company, Old Dominion Utility Services, Inc., Terrapin Utility Services, Inc.

Officers: Diane Rentfrow/Contact - Dean, Employee Development University, Kris Oconnor/Mgr. - Human Resources, Michael Patrick George/Exec. VP, Dee Shea/Computer Operations Supervisor, Information Technology, Roland S. Tanner/VP - Customer Service Region I, Lori Simperman/Administrative Sec. - Region I Headquarters, Kenneth Baird/Regional Administration Mgr. - Region I Headquarters, Skip Faria/Coastal District Mgr. - Region I Headquarters, Paul Schubert/Northern District Manger, Region I Headquarters, Ernest Gisler/Engineering, Planning Mgr. - Region I Headquarters, Dawn White/Water Quality Mgr. - Region I Headquarters, Patrick R. Scanlon/VP - Customer Service Region II, Lisa Ring/Administrative Sec. - Region II Headquarters, Toby Moore/Central District Mgr. - Region II Headquarters, David Chang/Engineering, Planning Mgr. - Region II Headquarters *(67 Officers included in Index)*

Directors: Lloyd E. Ross/Chmn., James L. Anderson/Dir., Gary F. King/Dir., Anne M. Holloway/Dir., Floyd E. Wicks/Dir., Robert F. Kathol/Dir., N. P. Dodge/Dir., Diane Rentfrow/Contact - Dean, Employee Development University, Diana M. Bonta'/Dir.

Owners: Gary F. King, N. P. Dodge, Insiders/3.05%, Anne M. Holloway, Harris McClellan, Robert F. Kathol, AMVESCAP PLC/5.51%, Robert J. Sprowls, Floyd E. Wicks, Denise L. Kruger, Lloyd E. Ross, James L. Anderson, Diana M. Bont, Joel A. Dickson, Barclays Global Investors, NA/5.08%

Financial Data: *Fiscal Year End:*12/31 *Latest Annual Data:* 12/31/2006

Year	Sales	Net Income
2006	$268,629,000	$23,081,000
2005	$236,197,000	$26,766,000
2004	$228,005,000	$18,541,000

Curr. Assets:	NA	**Curr. Liab.:**	NA	**P/E Ratio:**	25.17
Plant, Equip.:	NA	**Total Liab.:**	NA	**Indic. Yr. Divd.:**	$0.940
Total Assets:	NA	**Net Worth:**	NA	**Debt/ Equity:**	0.9439

American Superconductor Corp

2 Technology Dr., Westborough, MA, 01581; ***PH:*** 1-508-836-4200; ***Fax:*** 1-508-836-4248; ***http://*** www.amsuper.com; ***Email:*** investor@amsuper.com

General		**Stock**	
Incorporation	DE	Price on:12/24/2007	$17.59
Employees	263	Stock Exchange	NDQ
Auditor	PricewaterhouseCoopers LLP	Ticker Symbol	AMSC
Stk Agt	American Stock Transfer & Trust Co.	Outstanding Shares	35,670,000
Counsel	WilmerHale	E.P.S.	-$1.04
DUNS No.	18-590-4497	Shareholders	NA

Business: The group's principal activities are to design, develop, manufacture and market high temperature superconductor (hts) wires and power electronic converters. The group operates through three segments namely: amsc , supermachines and power electronic systems. The amsc wire segment develops and markets hts wires. The supermachines division develops and markets electric motors and generators based on hts wires. The power electronic systems division designs, develops and markets power electronic converters and integrated systems. The product offerings are sold to electrical equipment manufacturers, industrial power users, builders of ships that utilize electric drives and businesses that produce and deliver electric power. The group has operations in the United States and Germany.

Primary SIC and add'l.: 3357 3674

CIK No: 0000880807

Subsidiaries: American Superconductor Europe GmbH, ASC Devens LLC, ASC Securities Corp., NST Asset Holding Corporation, Superconductivity, Inc.

Officers: Gregory J. Yurek/Founder, Chmn., CEO, Pres./$1,342,549.00, Charles W. Stankiewicz/Exec. VP - Amsc Power Systems/$504,171.00, Susan Dicecco/VP - Human Resources, Gerald Hehenberger/VP, GM - Windtec, Kerry Diehl/Contact - Power Quality, Juergen Jesenko/Contact - Sales, Angelo Santamaria/VP, GM - Amsc Superconductors, Alexis P. Malozemoff/CTO, Exec. VP/$473,693.00, Hiroshi Ohkubo/Contact - Sales, Japan, Jeong Min Han/Contact - Sales, Korea, David Henry/Sr. VP, CFO, Treasurer, Dan McGahn/VP - Strategic Planning, Development, Jasper Lim/Contact - Sales, Power Electronic Systems, Asia Pacific, Werner Zoske/Contact - Sales, Power Electronic Systems, Europe, Tim Poor/VP, Deputy GM - Amsc Power Systems *(22 Officers included in Index)*

Directors: Gregory J. Yurek/Founder, Chmn., CEO, Pres., Peter O. Crisp/74/Dir., John B. Vander Sande/64/Dir., David R. Oliver/66/Dir., John W. Wood/64/Dir., Richard Drouin/75/Dir., Vikram S. Budhraja/59/Dir.

Owners: Terry M. Winter, Vikram S. Budhraja, Thomas M. Rosa, Alexis P. Malozemoff, Peter O. Crisp, Richard Drouin, Gregory J. Yurek/5.20%, Albert J. Baciocco, AMVESCAP PLC/6.00%, John B. Vander Sande, Insiders/8.40%, Andrew G.C. Sage, David R. Oliver, Kevin Douglas/8.90%, BlackRock, Inc./13.00% *(16 Owners included in Index)*

Financial Data: *Fiscal Year End:*03/31 *Latest Annual Data:* 3/31/2007

Year	Sales	Net Income
2007	$52,183,000	-$34,675,000
2006	$50,872,000	-$30,876,000
2005	$58,283,000	-$19,660,000

Curr. Assets:	$62,249,000	**Curr. Liab.:**	$27,307,000		
Plant, Equip.:	$52,099,000	**Total Liab.:**	$30,812,000	**Indic. Yr. Divd.:**	NA
Total Assets:	$132,433,000	**Net Worth:**	$101,621,000	**Debt/ Equity:**	NA

American Technical Ceramics Corp

1 Norden Ln., Huntington Station, NY, 11746; ***PH:*** 1-631-622-4700; ***http://*** www.atceramics.com

General		**Stock**	
Incorporation	DE	Price on:12/24/2007	$23.9401
Employees	769	Stock Exchange	AMEX
Auditor	KPMG LLP	Ticker Symbol	AMK
Stk Agt	American Stock Transfer & Trust Co.	Outstanding Shares	9,010,000
Counsel	Mintz Levin Cohn Ferris Et Al	E.P.S.	$0.979
DUNS No.	00-990-1059	Shareholders	NA

Business: The group's principal activities are to design, develop, manufacture and sell ceramic multilayer capacitors and thin film products for commercial and military purposes. The group's products are focused on ultra-high frequency and microwave applications, including wireless electronics, fiber optics, medical electronics, semiconductor equipment and satellite equipment. It is developing new capacitor products. The group exports its products primarily to western Europe, Canada and the Far East. Major customer of the group includes general electric company.

Primary SIC and add'l.: 3674 3675

CIK No: 0000766430

Subsidiaries: American Technical Ceramics (China), Ltd., American Technical Ceramics (Florida), Inc., American Technical Ceramics Europe, Aktiebolag, American Technical Components Costa Rica, S.A., Phase Components, Ltd.

Officers: Andrew R. Perz/VP - Finance, Principal Accounting Officer, Victor Insetta/Dir., Pres., Principal Executive Officer

Directors: Victor Insetta/Dir., Pres., Principal Executive Officer, Stuart P. Litt/Dir., Thomas J. Volpe/Dir., Dov S. Bacharach/Dir.

Owners: Andrew R. Perz, Joseph Colandrea/2.20%, Dov S. Bacharach, Royce & Associates, LLC/5.20%, David Ott, Robert Grossbach, Harrison Tarver, William Johnson, Insiders/51.10%, Stuart P. Litt, Victor Insetta/46.20%, Thomas J. Volpe, Richard Monsorno/1.60%, Kathleen M.Kelly, Chester E. Spence *(16 Owners included in Index)*

Financial Data: *Fiscal Year End:*06/30 *Latest Annual Data:* 6/30/2006

Year	Sales	Net Income
2006	$84,131,000	$5,988,000
2005	$72,965,000	$4,268,000
2004	$61,183,000	$2,176,000

Curr. Assets:	$58,805,000	**Curr. Liab.:**	$12,156,000	**P/E Ratio:**	24.43
Plant, Equip.:	$31,375,000	**Total Liab.:**	$22,476,000	**Indic. Yr. Divd.:**	NA
Total Assets:	$90,543,000	**Net Worth:**	$68,067,000	**Debt/ Equity:**	0.0724

American Technologies Group Inc

412 W Bolt St., Ft. Worth, TX , 76113; ***PH:*** 1-817-927-5333; ***http://*** www.icongrouponline.com

General		**Stock**	
Incorporation	NV	Price on:12/24/2007	NA
Employees	NA	Stock Exchange	OTC
Auditor	Russell Bedford Stefanou Mirchandani	Ticker Symbol	ATGR
Stk Agt	Online Transfer, Inc	Outstanding Shares	NA
Counsel	NA	E.P.S.	-$0.213
DUNS No.	79-738-9236	Shareholders	NA

Business: The group's principal activity is to develop, commercialize and sell patented and proprietary technology products. The group focuses its technology discovery and development processes in two core technology areas: catalyst technology and water purification. Catalyst technology is offers cost effective solutions to reduce and eliminate hazardous chemical by-products or emissions resulting from industrial and combustion processes. It also includes detergents and cosmetics. Water purification technology is currently being developed into a consumer distiller.

Primary SIC and add'l.: 3559

CIK No: 0000878547

Subsidiaries: Omaha Holdings Corp.

Officers: William N. Plamondon/Chmn., CEO, Thomas E. Durkin/55/Dir., Pres., Barry Ennis/62/Pres. - North Texas, Dir.

Directors: William N. Plamondon/Chmn., CEO, Barry Ennis/62/Pres. - North Texas, Dir., Thomas E. Durkin/55/Dir., Pres., Gary Fromm/Dir., Michael S. Luther/50/Dir.

Owners: The Keshet Fund LP/11.15%, Charles Matteson/28.65%, Gary Fromm/16.80%, Luther Capital Management, LLC/11.01%, Thomas E. Durkin/7.60%, Insiders/18.63%, Barbara Dritz Trust/7.00%

Financial Data: Fiscal Year End:07/31 Latest Annual Data: 07/31/2007

Year	Sales	Net Income
2007	$32,331,000	-$3,867,000
2006	$21,951,000	-$16,893,000
2005	$12,000	-$503,000

Curr. Assets:	$12,823,000	Curr. Liab.:	$19,185,000		
Plant, Equip.:	$2,446,000	Total Liab.:	$19,185,000	Indic. Yr. Divd.:	NA
Total Assets:	$18,761,000	Net Worth:	-$425,000	Debt/ Equity:	NA

American Technology Corp

15378 Ave. of Science, Ste. 100, San Diego, CA, 92128; *PH:* 1-858-676-1112; *Fax:* 1-858-676-1120; *http://* www.atcsd.com; *Email:* info@atcsd.com

General - Incorporation	DE	Stock- Price on:12/24/2007	$3.74
Employees	41	Stock Exchange	NDQ
Auditor	BDO Seidman LLP, Swenson Advisors LLP	Ticker Symbol	ATCO
Stk Agt	Interwest Transfer Company, Inc.	Outstanding Shares	30,540,000
Counsel	NA	E.P.S.	-$0.204
DUNS No.	01-449-3803	Shareholders	NA

Business: The group's principle activities include developing, manufacturing and marketing consumer acoustical and audio products. The proprietary technologies of the company include hypersonic sound technology (hss), neoplanar technology, purebass woofer technology and high intensity directional acoustics (hidt). Hss technology employs a laser-like beam to project sound to any listening environment; neoplanar technology is a thin film magnetic speaker that uses unique films and materials; purebass is an extended range woofer designed to complement hss, neoplanar technologies and other high performance satellite systems; hida technology employs proprietary techniques and components to produce variable intensity directional acoustical sound. The group operates from United States.

Primary SIC and add'l.: 3651

CIK No: 0000924383

Officers: Thomas R. Brown/57/Dir., CEO, Pres., Sec., Interim CFO, James Croft/CTO, Charles W. Peacock/VP - Sales, Karen Jordan/Chief Accounting Officer, Katherine H. McDermott/Controller - CAO

Directors: Thomas R. Brown/57/Dir., CEO, Pres., Sec., Interim CFO, Elwood G. Norris/Chmn., David J. Carter/59/Dir., Daniel Hunter/56/Dir., John Zavoli/48/Dir., Admiral Ray Smith/Dir., Raymond C. Smith/64/Dir., Laura M. Clague/Dir.

Owners: Raymond C. Smith, Karen Jordan, Daniel Hunter, Thomas R. Brown, Elwood G. Norris/13.30%, James Croft, Austin W. Marxe/15.40%, Insiders/14.70%

Financial Data: Fiscal Year End:09/30 Latest Annual Data: 9/30/2006

Year	Sales	Net Income
2006	$8,923,000	-$7,708,000
2005	$10,196,000	-$9,087,000
2004	$5,753,000	-$5,960,000

Curr. Assets:	$16,540,000	Curr. Liab.:	$3,882,000		
Plant, Equip.:	$694,000	Total Liab.:	$5,105,000	Indic. Yr. Divd.:	NA
Total Assets:	$18,708,000	Net Worth:	$13,603,000	Debt/ Equity:	NA

American Telecom Services Inc

2466 Peck Rd., City of Industry, CA, 90601; *PH:* 1-562-908-1287; *Fax:* 1-562-205-1088; *http://* www.atsphone.com; *Email:* info@atsphone.com

General - Incorporation	DE	Stock- Price on:12/24/2007	$2.09
Employees	12	Stock Exchange	AMEX
Auditor	BDO Seidman, LLP	Ticker Symbol	TES
Stk Agt	Continental Stock Transfer & Trust Co	Outstanding Shares	6,500,000
Counsel	NA	E.P.S.	NA
DUNS No.	NA	Shareholders	NA

Business: The groups principle activities include marketing and selling internet phone communications. The group operates from the United States.

Primary SIC and add'l.: 3661 4813

CIK No: 0001336467

Subsidiaries: American Telecom Services (Hong Kong) Limited

Officers: Bruce Hahn/CEO, Dir., Bruce Layman/COO, Edward R. James/CFO, Adam Somer/Pres. - Communications Services, Sec., Yu Wen Ching/Pres. - Manufacturing, Sourcing

Directors: Bruce Hahn/CEO, Dir., Lawrence Burstein/Chmn., Robert Doherty/Dir., Elliott Kerbis/Dir., Donald Norris/Dir., Robert Picow/Dir.

Owners: Adam Somer/3.40%, Yu Wen Ching/10.40%, I NET Financial Management, Ltd./10.40%, Donald G. Norris, Jack Silver/8.50%, The Future, LLC/5.60%, Bruce Hahn/12.30%, Elliott J. Kerbis, Credit Suisse/20.20%, Robert S. Picow, Lawrence Burstein/3.30%, Robert F. Doherty, Insiders/19.10%

Financial Data: Fiscal Year End:06/30 Latest Annual Data: 03/31/2007

Year	Sales	Net Income
2007	NA	NA
2006	$3,100,000	-$5,738,000
2005	NA	-$170,000

Curr. Assets:	$16,423,000	Curr. Liab.:	$1,361,000		
Plant, Equip.:	$175,000	Total Liab.:	$1,361,000	Indic. Yr. Divd.:	NA
Total Assets:	$16,674,000	Net Worth:	$15,313,000	Debt/ Equity:	NA

American TonerServ Corp

420 Aviation Blvd., Ste. 103, Santa Rosa, CA, 95403; *PH:* 1-800-736-3515; *Fax:* 1-707-578-7304; *http://* www.americantonerserv.com; *Email:* info@americantonerserv.com

General - Incorporation	DE	Stock- Price on:12/24/2007	$0.595
Employees	9	Stock Exchange	OTC
Auditor	Perry-smith LLP	Ticker Symbol	ASVP
Stk Agt	Island Stock Transfer	Outstanding Shares	NA
Counsel	NA	E.P.S.	-$0.18
DUNS No.	NA	Shareholders	NA

Business: The groups principle activity is to remanufactured tuner products. The groups services include full time service maintenance agreement, material programming and print management solution. In the year 2006, the group acquired Brody Enterprises. Customers of the group include Hewlett-Packard, Lexmark, Canon and Epson. The group operates from the United States. The groups revenue for September 2007 was 1.09 millions of USD.

Primary SIC and add'l.: 7378

CIK No: 0001009479

Officers: Daniel J. Brinker/50/Chmn., CEO, Pres., Andrew Beaurline/Sr. VP - Corporate Development, Strategy, Aaron Brinker/COO, Ryan Vice/CFO, Dave Ferrari/Strategic Advisor, Gene Klein/Strategic Advisor, Finance, Bryan Thomas/Strategic Advisor, Mergers, Acquisitions, Pamela A. Solly/Contact - Investor Relations, Henry Manayan/Strategic Advistrategic Advisor, Chuck Mache/Strategic Advisor, Sales, Marketing, Jon Myers/Dir. - Business Development, Tom Hakel/Dir., Sec., Michael V. Ducey/Sr. VP - Sales, Marketing, Rick Bosworth/Strategic Advisor, Mergers, Acquisitions

Directors: Daniel J. Brinker/50/Chmn., CEO, Pres., William Robotham/Dir., Tom Hakel/Dir., Sec.

Owners: Ryan Vice, Lynn J. Brinker, Insiders, Aaron L. Brinker, William A. Robotham, Fort Holdings Ltd., Basilio Chen, Daniel J. Brinker, Andrew Beaurline, BRAM Enterprises, James Laier, Thomas Hakel

Financial Data: Fiscal Year End:12/31 Latest Annual Data: 12/31/2006

Year	Sales	Net Income
2006	$456,000	-$1,934,000
2005	$440,000	-$444,000

Curr. Assets:	$512,000	Curr. Liab.:	$1,084,000		
Plant, Equip.:	$27,000	Total Liab.:	$2,313,000	Indic. Yr. Divd.:	NA
Total Assets:	$1,450,000	Net Worth:	-$863,000	Debt/ Equity:	3.1191

American Tower Corp

116 Huntington Ave., Boston, MA, 02116; *PH:* 1-617-375-7500; *Fax:* 1-617-375-7575; *http://* www.americantower.com; *Email:* ir@americantower.com

General - Incorporation	DE	Stock- Price on:12/24/2007	$42.57
Employees	995	Stock Exchange	NYSE
Auditor	Deloitte & Touche LLP	Ticker Symbol	AMT
Stk Agt	Bank of New York	Outstanding Shares	NA
Counsel	Edwards Angell Palmer & Dodge LLP	E.P.S.	$0.19
DUNS No.	92-639-6870	Shareholders	NA

Business: The group's principal activity is to lease antenna space on multi-tenant communication towers to wireless and broadcast companies. The group operates in two segments: rental and management segment and network development services segment. The rental and management segment provides leasing and subleasing of antenna sites on multi-tenant towers and other properties primarily for customers in the wireless communication and broadcast industries. The network development services segment offers antenna and line installation, maintenance, construction, site acquisition, zoning, radio frequency engineering, network design, tower monitoring, steel fabrication and other services.

Primary SIC and add'l.: 8742 4899 4813

CIK No: 0001053507

Subsidiaries: American Tower Corporation de Mexico, S. de R.L. de C.V. , American Tower Delaware Corporation, American Tower do Brasil, Ltda. , American Tower International, Inc., American Tower LLC, American Tower Management, LLC, American Tower, L.P. , American Towers, Inc., ATC GP, Inc., ATC International Holding Corp., ATC LP, Inc., ATC MexHold, Inc., ATC Mexico Holding Corp., ATC Midwest, LLC, ATC Presidential Way, Inc. 70 Subsidiaries included in the Index

Officers: James Taiclet/Chmn., CEO, Pres./$4,916,026.00, Steven J. Moskowitz/Pres. - US Tower Division/$3,852,979.00, William H. Hess/Exec. VP - International Operations, General Counsel/$1,864,219.00, Brad Singer/CFO, Treasurer/$4,031,361.00, Hal Hess/Exec. VP - International Operations, Pres. - Latin America, Michael Powell/Dir. - Investor Relations, Jean A. Bua/Exec. VP - Finance, Corporate Controller, Ed Disanto/Exec. VP, Chief Administrative Officer, General Counsel

Directors: James Taiclet/Chmn., CEO, Pres., Gustavo Lara Cantu/58/Dir., Raymond P. Dolan/50/Dir., Carolyn F. Katz/46/Dir., Fred R. Lummis/Dir., Pamela D.A. Reeve/58/Dir., Samme L. Thompson/62/Dir., David E. Sharbutt/58/Dir., Ronald M. Dykes/61/Dir.

Owners: Fred R. Lummis, Pamela D.A. Reeve, David E. Sharbutt, William H. Hess, Raymond P. Dolan, T. Rowe Price Associates, Inc./11.10%, Michael J. Gearon, Steven J. Moskowitz, Carolyn F. Katz, James D. Taiclet, Bradley E. Singer, Gustavo Lara Cantu, Samme L. Thompson, FMR Corp./8.40%, Insiders/1.20%

Financial Data: Fiscal Year End:12/31 Latest Annual Data: 12/31/2006

Year	Sales	Net Income
2006	$1,317,385,000	$27,484,000
2005	$944,786,000	-$181,359,000
2004	$706,660,000	-$247,587,000

Curr. Assets:	$486,022,000	Curr. Liab.:	$569,629,000	P/E Ratio:	709.50
Plant, Equip.:	$3,218,124,000	Total Liab.:	$4,224,712,000	Indic. Yr. Divd.:	NA
Total Assets:	$8,613,219,000	Net Worth:	$4,384,916,000	Debt/ Equity:	0.8940

American United Gold Corp

555 Burrard St., Ste 900, Vancouver, BC, V7X 1M8; *PH:* 1-604-692-2808; *http://* www.americanunitedgold.com

General - Incorporation	NV	Stock- Price on:12/24/2007	$0.058
Employees	NA	Stock Exchange	OTC
Auditor	Amisano Hanson	Ticker Symbol	AMUG
Stk Agt	Empire Stock Transfer Inc.	Outstanding Shares	NA
Counsel	NA	E.P.S.	NA
DUNS No.	NA	Shareholders	NA

Business: The groups principle activities include acquiring, exploring, and if warranted, developing natural resource properties. The group continues to run its operations with the use of contract operators. The group operates from United States.

Primary SIC and add'l.: NA

CIK No: 0001079222

Subsidiaries: Micron Milling and Packaging Company Ltd

Officers: David R. Uppal/45/Dir., Pres.

Directors: David R. Uppal/45/Dir., Pres.

Owners: Insiders/20.40%, B.D. G. Solvents Inc./6.80%, Paul Uppal/19.90%, David Uppal/20.40%

Financial Data: *Fiscal Year End:*09/30 *Latest Annual Data:* 9/30/2006

Year	Sales	Net Income
2006	NA	-$56,000
2005	NA	-$63,000
2004	NA	-$638,000

Curr. Assets:	$1,000	**Curr. Liab.:**	$442,000	
Plant, Equip.:	NA	**Total Liab.:**	$442,000	**Indic. Yr. Divd.:** NA
Total Assets:	$1,000	**Net Worth:**	-$441,000	**Debt/ Equity:** NA

American Unity Investments Inc

46 Fl. 140 Broadway, Ste. 315, New York City, NY, 10005; *PH:* 1-212-208-1495; *http://* www.ameriunity.com; *Email:* info@ameriunity.com

General - Incorporation .... FL	**Stock** - Price on:12/24/2007 .... NA
Employees .... NA	Stock Exchange .... OTC
Auditor .... Jimmy C.H. Cheung & Co	Ticker Symbol .... AUNI
Stk Agt .... X-clearing Corp	Outstanding Shares .... NA
Counsel .... NA	E.P.S .... -$0.01
DUNS No. .... NA	Shareholders .... NA

Business: The groups principle activity is to provide unique investment opportunities for all size companies. The group financial products include financial resources and solutions, merger, purchases, corporate investments, other enterprise consultations and analysis. In the year 2006, the group merged with Amerimine. The group operates from the United States and China.

Primary SIC and add'l.: 3911

CIK No: 0001075861

Officers: Christian Lillieroos/48/Dir., CEO, Pres., Guo Pingshan/53/Dir., Sr. VP - China Affairs

Directors: Christian Lillieroos/48/Dir., CEO, Pres., Zhenkai Jiang/44/Chmn., Rodger Spainhower/63/Dir., Guo Pingshan/53/Dir., Sr. VP - China Affairs

Owners: Insiders/37.60%, Guo Pingshan/1.40%, Sure Form Investments/35.20%, Christian Lillieroos/2.20%

Financial Data: *Fiscal Year End:*12/31 *Latest Annual Data:* 12/31/2006

Year	Sales	Net Income
2006	$3,034,000	-$1,790,000
2005	NA	-$364,000
2004	NA	-$481,000

Curr. Assets:	$3,245,000	**Curr. Liab.:**	$4,008,000	
Plant, Equip.:	$216,000	**Total Liab.:**	$4,360,000	**Indic. Yr. Divd.:** NA
Total Assets:	$3,461,000	**Net Worth:**	-$898,000	**Debt/ Equity:** NA

American Vanguard Corp

4695 MacArthur Ct., Newport Beach, CA, 92660; *PH:* 1-949-260-1200; *Fax:* 1-949-260-1201; *http://* www.american-vanguard.com

General - Incorporation .... DE	**Stock** - Price on:12/24/2007 .... $13.59
Employees 285	Stock Exchange .... NYSE
Auditor .... BDO Seidman LLP	Ticker Symbol .... AVD
Stk Agt ...... American Stock Transfer & Trust Co.	Outstanding Shares 26,220,000
Counsel .... NA	E.P.S $0.61
DUNS No. 04-934-3924	Shareholders .... NA

Business: The group's principal activities are to manufacture, develop and marketing of specialty chemicals for agricultural and commercial uses. The group manufactures and formulates chemicals for crops, human and animal health protection. Chemicals include insecticides, fungicides, molluscicides, growth regulators and soil fumigants. Products are marketed in the form of liquid, powder and granular forms. The group also distributor of various pharmaceutical and nutritional supplement products.

Primary SIC and add'l.: 6719 2879

CIK No: 0000005981

Subsidiaries: 2110 Davie Corporation, ABSCO Distributing, Agroservicios Amvac, SA de CV, American Vanguard Corporation of Imperial Valley, AMVAC Ag-Chem, AMVAC Chemical Corporation, AMVAC Chemical Corporation-Nevada, AMVAC Chemical GmbH, AMVAC Chemical UK Ltd., Calhart Corporation, Environmental Mediation, Inc., GemChem, Inc., Manufacturers Mirror& Glass Co., Inc., Quimica Amvac de Mexico SA de CV, Todagco

Officers: Eric G. Wintemute/52/Dir., CEO, Pres./$536,568.00, Richard M. Porter/Mgr. - Product Development, Midwest Region, Glen Johnson/Sr. VP, Dir. - Business Development/$296,664.00, Graciela Galvan/International Sales, Marketing Assist., Jon Wood/Dir. - Registrations, John A. Immaraju/Mgr. - International Product Development, Ann Taylor/Sr. Regulatory Affairs Mgr., Doug Ashmore/VP, Dir. - Manufacturing, James A. Barry/57/CFO, Sr. VP/$272,392.00, Ian Chart/Dir. - Regulatory Affairs, Alfredo Pelaez/Dir. - International Business, Timothy J. Donnelly/VP, General Counsel, Bill O'Neal/Technical Product Mgr. - Impact, Product Development Mgr. - Northeast Region, Robert F. Gilbane/57/Commercial Mgr./$272,438.00, Christopher K. Hildreth/Sr. VP, Dir. - Sales/$308,029.00 *(30 Officers included in Index)*

Directors: Eric G. Wintemute/52/Dir., CEO, Pres., Herbert A. Kraft/84/Co - Chmn., Glenn A. Wintemute/83/Co - Chmn., Lawrence S. Clark/49/Dir., John B. Miles/64/Dir., Carl R. Soderlind/74/Dir., Irving J. Thau/68/Dir.

Owners: Irving J. Thau, Bob Gilbane/1.40%, James A. Barry, Glenn A. Wintemute/6.90%, Lawrence S. Clark, Glen D. Johnson, John B. Miles, Insiders/27.50%, St. Denis J. Villere& Company/10.30%, Carl R. Soderlind, Herbert A. Kraft/11.50%, Jay R. Harris/7.80%, Eric G. Wintemute/5.20%, T. Rowe Price Associates, Inc./8.00%, Christopher K. Hildreth

Financial Data: *Fiscal Year End:*12/31 *Latest Annual Data:* 12/31/2006

Year	Sales	Net Income
2006	$193,771,000	$15,448,000
2005	$189,796,000	$19,002,000
2004	$150,855,000	$14,477,000

Curr. Assets:	$145,570,000	**Curr. Liab.:**	$46,337,000	**P/E Ratio:** 24.71
Plant, Equip.:	$36,863,000	**Total Liab.:**	$141,499,000	**Indic. Yr. Divd.:** $0.060
Total Assets:	$262,376,000	**Net Worth:**	$120,877,000	**Debt/ Equity:** 0.8329

American Vantage Cos

4735 S Durango Dr., Ste. 105, Las Vegas, NV, 89147; *PH:* 1-702-227-9800; *Fax:* 1-702-227-8525; *http://* www.americanvantage.com

General - Incorporation .... NV	**Stock** - Price on:12/24/2007 .... $2
Employees 2	Stock Exchange .... OTC
Auditor .... Piercy Bowler Taylor & Kern	Ticker Symbol .... AVCS
Stk Agt .... Int Registrar and Transfer Agency	Outstanding Shares 5,730,000
Counsel .... NA	E.P.S .... -$0.07
DUNS No. 10-571-5163	Shareholders .... NA

Business: The group's principle activity is to provide end-to-end interactive solutions and create advertiser-driven interactive games and marketing solutions. The group creates Internet games for its clients to be utilized in employee-training programs and for internal communications solutions. The group's quarterly revenue for June 2007 was 0.07 millions of USD.

Primary SIC and add'l.: 7372

CIK No: 0000315428

Subsidiaries: American Care Group, Inc., American Casino Enterprises, Inc., American Vantage/Hypnotic, Inc., Vantage Bay Group, Inc., YaYa Media, Inc.

Officers: Ronald J. Tassinari/65/Founder, Chmn., CEO, Pres., Anna M. Morrison/52/Chief Accounting Officer

Directors: Ronald J. Tassinari/65/Founder, Chmn., CEO, Pres., Jeanne Hood/80/Dir., Steven G. Barringer/52/Dir., Douglas R. Sanderson/63/Dir., Brian T. Seager/48/Dir.

Owners: 0792725 B.C. Ltd./10.80%, Jeanne Hood/1.40%, Viviendi Universal Entertainment LLLP/7.20%, Rosalind Davidowitz/6.70%, Michael C. Woloshin/14.80%, Steven G. Barringer, Engex, Inc./7.10%, L.P., Corriente Advisors, LLC/6.70%, Ronald J. Tassinari/11.50%, Jay H. Brown/5.10%, Anna M. Morrison/2.10%

Financial Data: *Fiscal Year End:*12/31 *Latest Annual Data:* 12/31/2006

Year	Sales	Net Income
2006	$2,045,000	-$402,000
2005	$313,000	-$4,791,000
2004	$17,766,000	-$4,017,000

Curr. Assets:	$3,878,000	**Curr. Liab.:**	$1,322,000	
Plant, Equip.:	NA	**Total Liab.:**	$1,322,000	**Indic. Yr. Divd.:** NA
Total Assets:	$14,045,000	**Net Worth:**	$12,723,000	**Debt/ Equity:** NA

American Wagering Inc

675 Grier Dr., Las Vegas, NV, 89119; *PH:* 1-702-735-5529; *Fax:* 1-702-735-0142; *http://* www.americanwagering.com; *Email:* info@americanwagering.com

General - Incorporation .... NV	**Stock** - Price on:12/24/2007 .... $0.93
Employees 190	Stock Exchange .... OTC
Auditor .... Piercy, Bowler, Taylor & Kern	Ticker Symbol .... BETM
Stk Agt .... American Stock Transfer & Trust Co.	Outstanding Shares 8,070,000
Counsel .... Schnader, Harrison, Segal & Lewis	E.P.S $0.08
DUNS No. 96-139-8013	Shareholders .... NA

Business: The group's principal activities are to own and operate race and sports wagering facilities throughout the state of Nevada. The group designs, sells, installs and maintains computerized race and sports book systems, including wagering by telephone and systems. The group operates in two business segments: wagering unit and systems unit. The wagering unit operates 49 race and sports books throughout Nevada. The systems unit designs, markets, installs and maintains sports and race book systems for the sports betting industry.

Primary SIC and add'l.: 7999 7371 7011

CIK No: 0001005214

Subsidiaries: AWI Gaming, Inc., AWI Manufacturing, Inc, Computerized Bookmaking Systems, Inc, Contest Sports Systems, Inc., Leroys Horse & Sports Place, Inc, Sturgeons, LLC

Officers: Victor J. Salerno/Dir., CEO, Pres., COO, Tim Lockinger/Dir., CFO, Sec., Treasurer, John Salerno/Sec.

Directors: Victor J. Salerno/Dir., CEO, Pres., COO, Tim Lockinger/Dir., CFO, Sec., Treasurer, Judith Zimbelmann/Dir., Larry W. Swecker/Dir., Bruce Dewing/Dir., Robert R. Barengo/Dir.

Owners: Insiders/49.10%, Bruce Dewing/1.72%, Larry W. Swecker, Victor J. Salerno/29.51%, Judy Zimbelmann/11.98%, Robert R. Barengo/6.34%

Financial Data: *Fiscal Year End:*01/31 *Latest Annual Data:* 1/31/2007

Year	Sales	Net Income
2007	$19,370,000	$1,831,000
2006	$12,524,000	$419,000
2005	$11,108,000	-$1,128,000

Curr. Assets:	$7,742,000	**Curr. Liab.:**	$6,537,000	**P/E Ratio:** 11.63
Plant, Equip.:	$4,462,000	**Total Liab.:**	$10,830,000	**Indic. Yr. Divd.:** NA
Total Assets:	$13,172,000	**Net Worth:**	$2,018,000	**Debt/ Equity:** 0.9324

American Water Star Inc

4560 S Decatur Blvd, Las Vegas, NV, 89103; *PH:* 1-702-740-7036; *http://* www.americanwaterstar.com; *Email:* sales@americanwaterstar.com

General - Incorporation .... NV	**Stock** - Price on:12/24/2007 .... $0.08
Employees .... NA	Stock Exchange .... AMEX
Auditor .... Weaver & Martin LLC	Ticker Symbol .... AMW
Stk Agt .... NA	Outstanding Shares .... NA
Counsel .... NA	E.P.S .... NA
DUNS No. .... NA	Shareholders .... NA

Business: The group's principal activities are to produce and sell nonalcoholic and un-carbonated beverages. The group's products line includes four branded beverages: geyser fruit, geyser sport, geyser fruta and hawaiian tropic. It also offers geyser sport in eight different fruit flavored waters: cherry, peach, wildberry, cranberry raspberry, strawberry kiwi, kiwi watermelon, cherry lime and lemonade. Geyser fruta label, we offer mango, jamaica, tamarindo and kiwi melon. The group sells its products through brokers to distributors and customers. The group customers include retail operations and governmental agencies. During first quarter of the year 2004, the group acquired sunset bottling co.

Primary SIC and add'l.: 2086

CIK No: 0001041580

Subsidiaries: All Star Beverages JAX, All Star Beverages Mississippi, All Star Beverages, Arizona, C.R.D. of Nevada, Hawaiian Tropicals, Tunlaw Capital Corporation

Officers: Roger Mohlman/59/Chmn., CEO, Pres.

Directors: Roger Mohlman/59/Chmn., CEO, Pres.

Owners: Insiders/45.00%, Roger Mohlman/45.00%

American Woodmark Corp

3102 Shawnee Dr., Winchester, VA, 22601; *PH:* 1-540-665-9100; *Fax:* 1-540-665-9176;
http:// www.americanwoodmark.com

General - Incorporation			
Incorporation	VA	**Stock**- Price on:12/24/2007	$34.53
Employees	6,360	Stock Exchange	NDQ
Auditor	KPMG LLP	Ticker Symbol	AMWD
Stk Agt...... American Stock Transfer & Trust Co.		Outstanding Shares	15,650,000
Counsel	NA	E.P.S	$1.06
DUNS No.	02-145-8534	Shareholders	NA

Business: The group's principal activity is to manufacture and distribute kitchen cabinets and vanities for the remodeling and new-home construction markets. It provides framed stock cabinets in approximately 230 different cabinet lines. The stock cabinets include approximately 80 door designs in nine colors. The group owns twelve manufacturing facilities located primarily in the eastern United States. The products are marketed through three primary market channels: home centers, major builders and independent dealers and distributors. They are primarily sold under the brand names of American woodmark, timberlake and shenandoah cabinetry.

Primary SIC and add'l.: 2434 2511

CIK No: 0000794619

Subsidiaries: Amende Cabinet Corporation

Officers: Jonathan H. Wolk/CFO, Sec., VP/$831,365.00, Kent B. Guichard/52/COO, Pres./$1,294,232.00, Cary S. Dunston/Exec. VP - Manufacturing/$513,797.00

Directors: James J. Gosa/61/Dir., Martha M. Dally/57/Dir., Kent J. Hussey/62/Dir., Carol B. Moerdyk/58/Dir., William F. Brandt/62/Dir., Daniel T. Carroll/82/Dir., James G. Davis/49/Dir., Thomas G. McKane/64/Dir., Daniel T. Hendrix/53/Dir.

Owners: Kent J. Hussey, Neil P. DeFeo, James J. Gosa/5.00%, Mary Jo Stout/9.00%, Kent B. Guichard, Jonathan H. Wolk, Carol B. Moerdyk, William F. Brandt/23.40%, Royce & Associates, LLC/5.20%, Wellington Management Company, LLP/6.20%, Cary S. Dunston, Thomas G. McKane, Daniel T. Carroll, Daniel T. Hendrix, Insiders/30.10% (20 Owners included in Index)

Financial Data: Fiscal Year End:04/30 Latest Annual Data: 04/30/2007

Year		Sales	Net Income
2007		$760,925,000	$32,561,000
2006		$837,671,000	$33,210,000
2005		$776,990,000	$35,591,000
Curr. Assets:	$183,599,000	**Curr. Liab.:** $83,073,000	
Plant, Equip.:	$175,384,000	**Total Liab.:** $135,882,000	**Indic. Yr. Divd.:** $0.240
Total Assets:	$377,543,000	**Net Worth:** $241,661,000	**Debt/ Equity:** NA

Americana Distribution Inc

18851 Ne 29th Ave., Ste. 306, Aventura, FL, 33180; *PH:* 1-973-726-5240;
http:// www.americanainc.com

General - Incorporation			
Incorporation	NA	**Stock**- Price on:12/24/2007	$0.0003
Employees	NA	Stock Exchange	OTC
Auditor	NA	Ticker Symbol	ADBN
Stk Agt	National Stock Transfer, Inc.	Outstanding Shares	1,350,000,000
Counsel	NA	E.P.S	$0.00
DUNS No.	NA	Shareholders	NA

Business: The groups principle activity is to distribute flowers. The group's customers include retail florists, interior decorators, event planners, and caterers. The group operates from United States.

Primary SIC and add'l.: 5192 5021

CIK No: 0001081751

Subsidiaries: Americana Imports and Trading Inc., Americana Licensing Holding Inc.

Officers: Donna Silverman/49/Dir., CEO, CFO, Pres.

Directors: Donna Silverman/49/Dir., CEO, CFO, Pres., Craig Press/61/Dir., Jeffrey Sternberg/58/Dir.

Owners: Alexy Resources LLC/1.10%, Advantage Capital Development Corp./1.50%, Donna Silverman/2.80%, Advantage Fund I Inc./1.50%, Craig Press/1.80%, Insiders/4.60%

Financial Data: Fiscal Year End:12/31 Latest Annual Data: 12/31/2006

Year		Sales	Net Income
2006		NA	-$865,000
2005		$335,000	-$2,363,000
2004		$1,230,000	-$820,000
Curr. Assets:	$1,000	**Curr. Liab.:** $2,190,000	
Plant, Equip.:	NA	**Total Liab.:** $2,190,000	**Indic. Yr. Divd.:** NA
Total Assets:	$1,000	**Net Worth:** -$2,189,000	**Debt/ Equity:** NA

Americanwest BanCorp

41 W Riverside Ave., Ste. 400, Spokane, WA, 99201; *PH:* 1-509-467-6993; *Fax:* 1-509-465-9681;
http:// www.awbank.net; *Email:* info@awbank.net

General - Incorporation			
Incorporation	WA	**Stock**- Price on:12/24/2007	$19.42
Employees	508	Stock Exchange	NDQ
Auditor	Moss Adams LLP	Ticker Symbol	AWBC
Stk Agt	Illinois Stock Transfer Co	Outstanding Shares	17,180,000
Counsel	NA	E.P.S	$0.77
DUNS No.	15-650-7121	Shareholders	NA

Business: The group's principal activity is to offer banking and other financial services to commercial and individual customers. The group provides short and medium term loans and revolving credit facilities. The services provided by the group include inventory and accounts receivable financing, equipment financing, residential and small commercial construction lending and agricultural lending. The group offers various saving programs, checking accounts, installment and personal loans and bank credit cards. The depository and lending services are provided mainly to commercial, industrial and agricultural enterprises and government entities. The group operates solely in the domestic market. The operations are conducted through thirty-four branches located in the communities throughout eastern Washington, including spokane and eight branches in north Idaho.

Primary SIC and add'l.: 6022 6712

CIK No: 0000726990

Subsidiaries: AmericanWest Bank (AWB or Bank), AmericanWest Statutory Trust I

Officers: Robert M. Daugherty/Dir., CEO, Pres./$944,336.00, Ed Allen/VP, Team Lead Private Banking Officer - Tri Cities, Gregory Hansen/Exec. VP, Dir. - Commercial Lending/$209,370.00, Nicole B. Sherman/Exec. VP, Dir. - Retail Banking, Blair R. Reynolds/Exec. VP, General Counsel, Diane L. Kelleher/CFO, Exec. VP/$237,967.00, Wade A. Griffith/CIO, Exec. VP, Rick E. Shamberger/Exec. VP, Chief Credit Officer/$202,612.00, Paul Ellyson/VP, Team Lead Private Banking Officer - Spokane, Robert M. Bowen/Exec. VP - Commercial Lending, Utah, Robert A. Harris/Exec. VP, Dir. - Commercial Lending WA, ID, Don H. Norton/Regional Dir. - Americanwest Bank, Utah

Directors: Robert M. Daugherty/Dir., CEO, Pres., Craig D. Eerkes/Chmn., Donald H. Livingstone/Dir., Donald H. Swartz/Dir., Frank J. Armijo/Dir., Kay C. Carnes/Dir., Mike P. Taylor/Dir., Ivan T. Call/Dir.

Owners: Donald H. Livingstone, Rick E. Shamberger, Diane L. Kelleher, Kay C. Carnes, Mike P. Taylor, Don H. Norton/6.17%, Insiders/10.09%, Robert M. Daugherty, Frank J. Armijo, Ivan T. Call/1.81%, Donald H. Swartz, Craig D. Eerkes

Financial Data: Fiscal Year End:12/31 Latest Annual Data: 12/31/2006

Year		Sales	Net Income
2006		$103,128,000	$7,630,000
2005		$80,703,000	$13,872,000
2004		$82,970,000	$9,505,000
Curr. Assets:	$64,040,000	**Curr. Liab.:** $1,233,968,000	**P/E Ratio:** 27.35
Plant, Equip.:	$31,128,000	**Total Liab.:** $1,264,491,000	**Indic. Yr. Divd.:** $0.160
Total Assets:	$1,416,528,000	**Net Worth:** $152,037,000	**Debt/ Equity:** NA

Americas Wind Energy Corp

24 Palace Arch Dr., Toronto, ON, M9A 2S1; *PH:* 1-416-233-5670; *Fax:* 1-416-233-6493;
http:// awe-wind.com

General - Incorporation			
Incorporation	NV	**Stock**- Price on:12/24/2007	$1.13
Employees	NA	Stock Exchange	OTC
Auditor	Sf Partnership, LLP	Ticker Symbol	AWNE
Stk Agt...... Pacific Stock Transfer Company		Outstanding Shares	NA
Counsel	NA	E.P.S	NA
DUNS No.	NA	Shareholders	NA

Business: The groups principal activities include manufacturing, marketing and licensing medium sized wind turbines. Customers of the group include small wind farms, developers, and wind power co-ops. In the year 2006, the group acquired Private Ontario Corporation. The group operates from the North America.

Primary SIC and add'l.: 3510

CIK No: 0001265840

Subsidiaries: 6544797 Canada Ltd, Americas Wind Energy Inc.

Officers: Harold C.F. Dickout/73/Chmn., CEO, Pres., Frank Pickersgill/Dir., Sec.

Directors: Harold C.F. Dickout/73/Chmn., CEO, Pres., Frank Pickersgill/Dir., Sec., Shashi Dewan/66/Dir.

Owners: Frank Pickersgill/15.90%, Roche Capital Group SA/8.71%, Harold C.F. Dickout/40.82%, Digital Predictive Systems Inc./9.09%, Insiders/52.13%

Financial Data: Fiscal Year End:06/30 Latest Annual Data: 06/30/2006

Year		Sales	Net Income
2006		NA	-$7,000
Curr. Assets:	$0	**Curr. Liab.:** $2,000	
Plant, Equip.:	NA	**Total Liab.:** $2,000	**Indic. Yr. Divd.:** NA
Total Assets:	$0	**Net Worth:** -$1,000	**Debt/ Equity:** NA

Americasbank Corp

500 York Rd. , Towson, MD, 21204; *PH:* 1-410-823-0500; *http://* www.americasbank.com

General - Incorporation			
Incorporation	MD	**Stock**- Price on:12/24/2007	$6.4
Employees	36	Stock Exchange	NDQ
Auditor	Rowles & Co. LLP	Ticker Symbol	AMAB
Stk Agt...... American Stock Transfer & Trust Co.		Outstanding Shares	2,650,000
Counsel	NA	E.P.S	$0.15
DUNS No.	NA	Shareholders	NA

Business: The group is a community-oriented financial institution providing general commercial banking business with particular emphasis on the needs of individuals and small to mid-sized businesses. The company is a bank holding company operating through its subsidiaries: Americasbank and Americasbank holdings corporation. The company attracts deposits like checking accounts, savings accounts, money market accounts and certificates of deposits and invests these along with funds generated from operations and borrowings in a full range of short-to-medium-term commercial, personal and mortgage loans. The bank's customers include individuals and commercial enterprises throughout central Maryland.

Primary SIC and add'l.: 6022 6712

CIK No: 0001040491

Subsidiaries: AmericasBank

Officers: Mark H. Anders/Dir., CEO, Pres./$208,888.00, Gary A. Rever/Dir., CFO, Exec. VP/$181,356.00, John D. Muncks/Exec. VP/$176,038.00, David Garman/Sr. Branch Administration Officer, Constance M. Hess/VP, Mortgage Loan Department Mgr., Nancy B. Bhar/VP, Mortgage Operations Mgr., Pat Riley/VP - Operations, Accounting, Lucas P. Flynn/VP, Portfolio Mgr.

Directors: Mark H. Anders/Dir., CEO, Pres., Lee W. Warner/Chmn., Mark D. Noar/Vice Chmn., William L. Wilcox/Dir., Allen S. Lloyd/Dir., Graylin E. Smith/Dir., Richard C. Faint/Dir., Gary A. Rever/Dir., CFO, Exec. VP, Nicholas J. Belitsos/Dir., Savas J. Karas/Dir., Kenneth D. Pezzulla/Dir., Ramon F. Roig/Dir., John C. Weiss/Dir.

Owners: William L. Wilcox, Allen S. Lloyd, First Manhattan Co., John D. Muncks, Insiders, Hot Creek Capital, LLC, John C. Weiss, TRF Partners, LLC, Resource America, Lee W. Warner, Richard C. Faint, Jeffrey A. Miller, L.L.C. and Acadia Master Fund I, Ltd., Mark H. Anders, Nicholas J. Belitsos, Mark D. Noar (21 Owners included in Index)

Financial Data: Fiscal Year End:12/31 Latest Annual Data: 12/31/2006

Year		Sales	Net Income
2006		$6,883,000	-$431,000
2005		$4,073,000	-$308,000
2004		$1,845,000	-$1,295,000
Curr. Assets:	$19,112,000	**Curr. Liab.:** $91,585,000	**P/E Ratio:** 640.00
Plant, Equip.:	$1,129,000	**Total Liab.:** $92,166,000	**Indic. Yr. Divd.:** NA
Total Assets:	$108,158,000	**Net Worth:** $15,992,000	**Debt/ Equity:** NA

AmeriChip International Inc

247000Capital Blvd, Clinton Township, MI, 48036; **PH:** 1-586-783-4598; **Fax:** 1-905-898-0820; **http://** www.americhiplacc.com; **Email:** info@americhiplacc.com

General - Incorporation	NV	Stock - Price on:12/24/2007	$0.0135
Employees	24	Stock Exchange	OTC
Auditor	Williams & Webster, P.S.	Ticker Symbol	ACII
Stk Agt	Pacific Stock Transfer Company	Outstanding Shares	637,810,000
Counsel	NA	E.P.S.	-$0.17
DUNS No.	NA	Shareholders	NA

Business: The groups principle activity is to design and testing of our patented laser assisted chip control technology. The group operates from the United States.

Primary SIC and add'l.: 3550

CIK No: 0001132487

Subsidiaries: AmeriChip Automotive, Inc., AmeriChip Canada, Inc., AmeriChip International Holdings, LLC, AmeriChip Pipe Technologies, Inc, AmeriChip Tool and Abrasives, LLC

Officers: Marc Walther/Co - Chmn., CEO, Pres., Edward Rutkowski/Founder, Co - Chmn., CTO, Richard H. Rossmann/62/Dir., Pres. - Americhip Automotive Inc., Thomas P. Schwanitz/Dir., CFO, Member - Advisory Board

Directors: Marc Walther/Co - Chmn., CEO, Pres., Edward Rutkowski/Founder, Co - Chmn., CTO, Thomas P. Schwanitz/Dir., CFO, Member - Advisory Board, Peter Wanner/Dir., Rhonda G. Windsor/Member - Advisory Board, Alvin Snaper/Member - Advisory Board, John Aguero/Member - Advisory Board

Owners: Richard H. Rossmann/5.55%, Thomas P. Schwanitz, Marc A. Walther/15.06%, Edward Rutkowski/15.06%, Insiders/36.52%

Financial Data: Fiscal Year End:11/30 Latest Annual Data: 08/31/2007

Year	Sales	Net Income
2007	NA	NA
2006	$133,000	-$10,987,000
2005	$126,000	-$5,102,000

Curr. Assets:	$273,000	Curr. Liab.:	$2,451,000		
Plant, Equip.:	$551,000	Total Liab.:	$2,642,000	Indic. Yr. Divd.:	NA
Total Assets:	$1,043,000	Net Worth:	-$1,599,000	Debt/ Equity:	NA

Americredit Corp

801 Cherry St., Ste. 3900, Fort Worth, TX, 76102; **PH:** 1-817-302-7000; **Fax:** 1-817-302-7101; **http://** www.americredit.com

General - Incorporation	TX	Stock - Price on:12/24/2007	$27.24
Employees	4,025	Stock Exchange	NYSE
Auditor	Deloitte & Touche, LLP	Ticker Symbol	ACF
Stk Agt	Chase Mellon Shareholder Services	Outstanding Shares	117,920,000
Counsel	NA	E.P.S.	$2.69
DUNS No.	17-778-1390	Shareholders	NA

Business: The groups principle activity is to provide financing solutions indirectly through auto dealers and directly to consumers. The group operates from United States.

Primary SIC and add'l.: 6141

CIK No: 0000804269

Subsidiaries: ACF Investment Corp., AFS Conduit Corp., AFS Funding Corp., AFS Funding Trust, AFS Management Corp., AFS SenSub Corp., AFS Warehouse Corp., AmeriCredit Canada 2002-A Corp., AmeriCredit Consumer Discount Company, AmeriCredit Consumer Loan Company, Inc., Americredit Corporation of California, AmeriCredit Finance Canada LP, AmeriCredit Financial Services of Canada Ltd., AmeriCredit Financial Services, Inc., AmeriCredit Flight Operations, LLC 33 Subsidiaries included in the Index

Officers: Daniel E. Berce/Dir., CEO, Pres./$4,023,302.00, Caitlin Deyoung/VP - Investor Relations, Steven P. Bowman/Exec. VP, Chief Credit Risk Officer, Chris A. Choate/CFO, Exec. VP, Treasurer/$1,673,130.00, Mark S. Floyd/COO - Customer Service, Collections/$1,760,927.00, Preston A. Miller/COO, Exec. VP - Originations/$1,759,982.00, Michael J. May/Sec.

Directors: Daniel E. Berce/Dir., CEO, Pres., Clifton H. Morris/Chmn., John R. Clay/Dir., A. R. Dike/Dir., James H. Greer/Dir., Douglas K. Higgins/Dir., Kenneth H. Jones/Dir.

Owners: Mark Floyd, John R. Clay, Chris A. Choate, Kenneth H. Jones, Goldman Sachs Asset Management./12.96%, Clifton H. Morris/1.63%, Capital Guardian Trust Company/7.15%, NWQ Investment Management, LLC/8.40%, Preston A. Miller, James H. Greer, Douglas K. Higgins, Barclays Global Investors, N.A./10.67%, A. R. Dike, Columbia Wanger Asset Management, L.P./8.32%, Daniel E. Berce (16 Owners included in Index)

Financial Data: Fiscal Year End:06/30 Latest Annual Data: 6/30/2006

Year	Sales	Net Income
2006	$1,811,338,000	$306,183,000
2005	$1,450,846,000	$285,909,000
2004	$1,215,836,000	$226,983,000

Curr. Assets:	$1,577,823,000	Curr. Liab.:	$155,799,000	P/E Ratio:	10.09
Plant, Equip.:	$57,225,000	Total Liab.:	$11,058,979,000	Indic. Yr. Divd.:	NA
Total Assets:	$13,067,865,000	Net Worth:	$2,008,886,000	Debt/ Equity:	NA

AmeriGas Partners LP

460 N Gulph Rd., King of Prussia, PA, 19406; **PH:** 1-610-337-7000; **Fax:** 1-610-992-3259; **http://** www.amerigas.com

General - Incorporation	DE	Stock - Price on:12/24/2007	$37.08
Employees	NA	Stock Exchange	NYSE
Auditor	PricewaterhouseCoopers LLP	Ticker Symbol	APU
Stk Agt	Computer share & Trust Co.	Outstanding Shares	56,820,000
Counsel	NA	E.P.S.	$3.26
DUNS No.	NA	Shareholders	NA

Business: The group operates through its subsidiaries whose principle activity is to distribute propane. The group operates from 600 district locations in 46 states in the United States. The group's quarterly revenue for September 2007 was 2,277.38 millions of USD.

Primary SIC and add'l.: 5984

CIK No: 0000932628

Subsidiaries: Active Propane of Wisconsin, LLC, AmerE Holdings, Inc., AmeriGas Eagle Finance Corp., AmeriGas Eagle Holdings, Inc.(3), AmeriGas Eagle Parts & Service, Inc., AmeriGas Eagle Propane, Inc., AmeriGas Eagle Propane, L.P., AmeriGas Finance Corp, AmeriGas Propane L.P., AmeriGas Propane Parts & Service, Inc., AP Eagle Finance Corp.

Officers: Robert Krick/Contact - Investor Relations, Media, Brenda Blake/Contact - Investor Relations, Media

Owners: James W. Stratton, Robert H. Knauss, Richard C. Gozon, Lon R. Greenberg, William J. Marrazzo, Petrolane Incorporated, Jerry E. Sheridan, AmeriGas Propane, Inc., AmeriGas, Inc., Eugene V. N. Bissell, UGI Corporation, Insiders

Financial Data: Fiscal Year End:09/30 Latest Annual Data: 09/30/2006

Year	Sales	Net Income
2006	$2,119,266,000	$91,158,000
2005	$1,963,256,000	$60,845,000
2004	$1,775,900,000	$91,854,000

Curr. Assets:	$368,209,000	Curr. Liab.:	$380,156,000		
Plant, Equip.:	$580,592,000	Total Liab.:	$1,390,264,000	Indic. Yr. Divd.:	$2.440
Total Assets:	$1,611,767,000	Net Worth:	$221,503,000	Debt/ Equity:	NA

Amerigon Inc

21680 Haggerty Rd., Ste. 101, Northville, MI, 48167; **PH:** 1-248-504-0500; **Fax:** 1-248-348-9735; **http://** www.amerigon.com

General - Incorporation	MI	Stock - Price on:12/24/2007	$16.58
Employees	59	Stock Exchange	NDQ
Auditor	PricewaterhouseCoopers LLP	Ticker Symbol	ARGN
Stk Agt	U.S. Stock Transfer Corp	Outstanding Shares	21,620,000
Counsel	Honigman Miller Schwartz & Cohn	E.P.S.	$0.30
DUNS No.	55-687-9252	Shareholders	NA

Business: The group's principal activities are to develop, manufacture and market high technology electronic components and systems for car and truck original equipment manufactures. The group's products include climate control seat that provides both heating and cooling to seat occupants to improve the temperature comfort of automobile passengers. The group's subsidiary, bsst llc conducts research and development to improve the efficiency of thermoelectric devices and develop products based on this new technology. The major customers of the group include johnson controls, inc, lear corporation and nhk spring company ltd.

Primary SIC and add'l.: 3714 3812

CIK No: 0000903129

Subsidiaries: Amerigon Asia Pacific Inc., BSST LLC

Officers: Lon E. Bell/Dir., CEO, Pres. - Bsst LLC/$545,252.00, Daniel R. Coker/Dir., CEO, Pres./$917,794.00, Barry G. Steele/37/CFO, VP - Finance, Sec., Treasurer/$414,567.00, Jill Bertotti/Investor Relations Officer, Jim Mertes/VP - Operations, James L. Mertes/VP - Quality, Operations/$369,942.00, Sandra L. Grouf/48/CIO, Daniel J. Pace/VP - Sales, Marketing/$359,499.00

Directors: Lon E. Bell/Dir., CEO, Pres. - Bsst LLC, Daniel R. Coker/Dir., CEO, Pres., Oscar B. Marx/Chmn., James J. Paulsen/Dir., François J. Castaing/Dir., John W. Clark/63/Dir., Robert T. Howard/Dir., Maurice E.P. Gunderson/Dir.

Owners: FMR Corp./12.50%, Oscar B. Marx/4.70%, Daniel J. Pace, Arbor Capital Management, LLC/8.20%, Insiders/9.30%, James L. Mertes, Lon E. Bell/1.30%, Barry G. Steele, Daniel R. Coker/1.30%, Gilder, Gagnon, Howe& Co. LLC/6.70%, Westar Capital II, LLC/10.40%, John W. Clark

Financial Data: Fiscal Year End:12/31 Latest Annual Data: 12/31/2006

Year	Sales	Net Income
2006	$50,609,000	$3,514,000
2005	$35,737,000	$16,549,000
2004	$32,710,000	$1,059,000

Curr. Assets:	$32,337,000	Curr. Liab.:	$8,572,000	P/E Ratio:	82.90
Plant, Equip.:	$1,986,000	Total Liab.:	$9,222,000	Indic. Yr. Divd.:	NA
Total Assets:	$42,396,000	Net Worth:	$33,174,000	Debt/ Equity:	NA

Amerigroup Corp

4425 Corporation Ln., Virginia Beach, VA, 23462; **PH:** 1-757-490-6900; **Fax:** 1-757-222-2330; **http://** www.amerigroupcorp.com; **Email:** ir@amerigroupcorp.com

General - Incorporation	DE	Stock - Price on:12/24/2007	$24.13
Employees	3,500	Stock Exchange	NYSE
Auditor	KPMG LLP	Ticker Symbol	AGP
Stk Agt	American Stock Transfer & Trust Co.	Outstanding Shares	52,760,000
Counsel	NA	E.P.S.	$2.15
DUNS No.	NA	Shareholders	NA

Business: The group's principle activity is to provide healthcare services. The group operates from United States.

Primary SIC and add'l.: 6324

CIK No: 0001064863

Subsidiaries: Amerigroup Florida, Inc., Amerigroup Illinois, Inc., Amerigroup Maryland, Inc., A Managed Care Orgnization, Amerigroup New Jersey, Inc., Amerigroup Ohio, Inc., Amerigroup Texas, Inc., Amerigroup Virginia, Inc., Amerivantage, Inc., AMGP Georgia Managed Care Company, AMGP Georgia, Inc., Careplus LLC, Intelli-dent IPA, Inc., PHP Holdings, Inc.

Officers: James G. Carlson/Dir., CEO, Pres./$2,600,811.00, James W. Truess/CFO, Exec. VP/$1,280,621.00, Stanley F. Baldwin/Exec. VP, General Counsel, Sec., Steven B. Larsen/48/Exec. VP - Health Plan Operations/$997,947.00, Catherine S. Callahan/Exec. VP - Assoc. Services, Nancy L. Grden/Exec. VP, Chief Marketing Officer, Leon A. Root/CIO, Exec. VP, John E. Littel/Exec. VP - Government Relations, Richard C. Zoretic/COO, Exec. VP/$1,419,202.00, Julie Loftus Trudell/Primary Investor Relations Officer, Margaret M. Roomsburg/Chief Accounting Officer, Sr. VP, William T. Keena/Exec. VP - Support Operations, Mary McCluskey/Chief Medical Officer, Exec. VP

Directors: James G. Carlson/Dir., CEO, Pres., Jeffrey L. McWaters/Chmn., Richard D. Shirk/Dir., Thomas E. Capps/Dir., Jeffrey B. Child/48/Dir., Kay Coles James/Dir., William J. McBride/Dir., Uwe E. Reinhardt/Dir.

Owners: EARNEST Partners, LLC/9.70%, Richard C. Zoretic, William J. McBride, American Century Investment Management, Inc./5.30%, James W. Truess, Insiders/5.90%, Goldman Sachs Asset Management, L.P./10.30%, James G. Carlson/1.60%, Barclays Global Investors, N.A./6.30%, Sherri E. Lee, Steven B. Larsen, Thomas E. Capps, Jeffrey B. Child, FMR Corp./5.20%, Uwe E. Reinhardt (19 Owners included in Index)

Financial Data: *Fiscal Year End:* 12/31 *Latest Annual Data:* 12/31/2006

Year	Sales	Net Income
2006	$2,835,089,000	$107,106,000
2005	$2,329,909,000	$53,651,000
2004	$1,823,731,000	$86,014,000

Curr. Assets:	$501,109,000	**Curr. Liab.:**	$562,922,000		
Plant, Equip.:	$46,983,000	**Total Liab.:**	$577,110,000	**Indic. Yr. Divd.:**	NA
Total Assets:	$1,345,695,000	**Net Worth:**	$768,585,000	**Debt/ Equity:**	0.4630

Amerinst Insurance Group Ltd

C/o Usa Risk Group (Bermuda) Ltd., Windsor Pl., 18 Queen St., Hamilton; ; *http://* www.amerinst.bm

General - Incorporation	Bermuda	**Stock** - Price on:12/24/2007	NA
Employees	NA	Stock Exchange	NA
Auditor	Deloitte & Touche LLP	Ticker Symbol	NA
Stk Agt	Butterfield Corporate Services Ltd	Outstanding Shares	NA
Counsel	NA	E.P.S	NA
DUNS No.	NA	Shareholders	NA

Business: The group's principal activity is to provide reinsurance of professional liability insurance policies. The professional liability insurance policies offer coverage to accounting firms. At 31-Dec-2003, the group had insured approximately 24,000 accounting firms under the plan. The group conducts casualty insurance underwriting and also investment business for their own accounts through investment advisors.

Primary SIC and add'l.: 6331

CIK No: 0001065201

Subsidiaries: AmerInst Insurance Company, Ltd, AmerInst Investment Company, Ltd.

Officers: Stuart H. Grayston/Dir., CEO, Pres.

Directors: Stuart H. Grayston/Dir., CEO, Pres., Ronald S. Katch/74/Chmn., Irvin F. Diamond/Dir., Jerrell A. Atkinson/Dir., Murray Nicol/Dir., Jeffry I. Gillman/Dir., John T. Schiffman/Dir., Jerome A. Harris/Dir., David N. Thompson/Dir., Thomas B. Lillie/55/Dir.

Owners: John T. Schiffman, Jerrell A. Atkinson, Jerome A. Harris, AmerInst Investment Company, Ltd/23.80%, David N. Thompson, Insiders/3.30%, Ronald S. Katch, Irvin F. Diamond/1.20%, Jeffry I. Gillman, Thomas B. Lillie

Ameripath Inc

7111 Fairway Dr., Ste. 400, Palm Beach Gardens, FL, 33418; *PH:* 1-561-712-6200; *Fax:* 1-561-845-0129; *http://* www.ameripath.com

General - Incorporation	DE	**Stock** - Price on:12/24/2007	NA
Employees	NA	Stock Exchange	NA
Auditor	Ernst & Young LLP	Ticker Symbol	NA
Stk Agt	NA	Outstanding Shares	NA
Counsel	Alston & Bird LLP	E.P.S	NA
DUNS No.	94-970-2468	Shareholders	NA

Business: The group's principle activities are to provide anatomic pathology, cancer diagnostic, genomics and health information services. The group operates in two operating segments, owned practices and managed practices. Owned practices segment provides anatomic pathology services to hospitals and referring physicians. Managed practices segment provides anatomic pathology services to affiliated physician groups. The group provides services to physicians, hospitals and outpatient surgery center administrators, national clinical laboratories and managed care organizations. It also manages and controls all of the non-medical functions of the practices.

Primary SIC and add'l.: 8099 6719 8093 8741 8071

CIK No: 0001027532

Subsidiaries: A. Bernard Ackerman, M.D., Dermatopathology, P.C., AmeriPath 5.01(a) Corporation, AmeriPath Associates, LLC, AmeriPath Cincinnati, Inc., AmeriPath Cleveland, Inc., AmeriPath Consolidated Labs, Inc., AmeriPath Consulting Pathology Services, P.A., AmeriPath Florida, LLC, AmeriPath Indemnity, Ltd., AmeriPath Indiana, LLC, AmeriPath Indianapolis, P.C., AmeriPath Institute of Urological Pathology, P.C., AmeriPath Kentucky, Inc., AmeriPath LLC, AmeriPath Lubbock 5.01(a) Corporation 76 Subsidiaries included in the Index

Officers: Steven E. Casper/Pres. - Dermatopathology Services, Russell L. Maiese/Medical, Scientific Staff, Steven L. Gersen/Medical, Scientific Staff, MD, Bradley D.O. Bakotic/Consultant, Carlos H. Nousari/Consultant, Philip A. Spencer/Pres. - Anatomic Pathology Services, David L. Redmond/Pres., Jeffrey A. Mossler/VP, Chief Anatomic Pathology Officer, Robert E. Petras/Consultant, Terry L. Gramlich/Consultant, Kirk J. Wojno/Dir. - Institute, Urological Pathology

Owners: Donald E. Steen, Sean M. Traynor, Jeffrey A. Mossler, Steven E. Casper, David L. Redmond, Paul B. Queally, Brett P. Brodnax, James B. Peter, Raymond A. Ranelli, Keith R. Laughman, Welsh, Carson, Anderson & Stowe, Clay J. Cockerell, Specialty Family Limited Partnership, Arnold C. Renschler, Insiders

Ameriresource Technologies Inc

3440 E Russell Rd., Ste. 217, Las Vegas, NV, 89120; *PH:* 1-702-214-4249; *Fax:* 1-702-214-4221; *http://* www.ameriresourcetechnologies.com

General - Incorporation	DE	**Stock** - Price on:12/24/2007	$0.0011
Employees	17	Stock Exchange	OTC
Auditor	De Joya Griffith & Co., LLC	Ticker Symbol	AMREE
Stk Agt	Interwest Transfer Company, Inc.	Outstanding Shares	512,070,000
Counsel	NA	E.P.S	-$0.008
DUNS No.	60-520-6820	Shareholders	NA

Business: The group's principal activities are to manufacture racing engines, research for the development of potential new product lines and analyze the viability of drilling additional oil and gas wells. The operations of the group are conducted through its wholly owned subsidiaries jim butler performance and west Texas real estate & resources, inc. The group seeks to obtain new contacts and additional financing to attain a profitable level of operations. The group acquired butler performance inc at 26-Sep-2003.

Primary SIC and add'l.: 9999

CIK No: 0000876490

Subsidiaries: Auction Soft Pro Corporation, AuctionWagon, Inc., Net2Auction Corporation, Net2Auction, Inc., RoboServer Systems Corp., Self-Serve Technologies, Inc., VoIPCom USA, Inc., West Texas Real Estate & Resources, Inc.

Officers: Delmar A. Janovec/Dir., CEO, Pres., Principal Financial Officer

Directors: Delmar A. Janovec/Dir., CEO, Pres., Principal Financial Officer

Owners: Delmar Janovec, Delmar Janovec/100.00%, Insiders/82.80%, Delmar Janovec/82.50%

Financial Data: *Fiscal Year End:* 12/31 *Latest Annual Data:* 12/31/2006

Year	Sales	Net Income
2006	$892,000	-$2,332,000
2005	$149,000	-$2,038,000
2004	$102,000	-$2,519,000

Curr. Assets:	NA	**Curr. Liab.:**	NA		
Plant, Equip.:	NA	**Total Liab.:**	NA	**Indic. Yr. Divd.:**	NA
Total Assets:	NA	**Net Worth:**	NA	**Debt/ Equity:**	NA

Ameris Bancorp

Formerly: ABC Bancorp

24 2/nd/ Ave., Moultrie, GA, 31768; *PH:* 1-912-890-1111; *http://* www.amerisbank.com

General - Incorporation	GA	**Stock** - Price on:12/24/2007	$22.73
Employees	600	Stock Exchange	NDQ
Auditor	Mauldin & Jenkins LLC	Ticker Symbol	ABCB
Stk Agt	Computershare, Inc.	Outstanding Shares	13,540,000
Counsel	Mauldin & Jenkins, LLC	E.P.S	$1.64
DUNS No.	17-813-5851	Shareholders	NA

Business: The group's principle activity is to provide banking services to individuals and businesses. It is a multi-bank holding company that operates in southern and southern Georgia, southeastern Alabama and northern Florida. The group accepts deposits and provides loans and other services. Deposits include checking, savings, now and money market accounts and time deposits of various type. Loans are provided for business, agriculture, real estate, personal uses and home improvement and on mortgages. The lending activity also includes revolving loans and loan participation. Other services provided by the group are personal trust and employee benefit services, credit cards, letters of credit, brokerage and fixed rate annuities. The group also provides safe deposit box rentals, electronic funds transfer and automated teller machines services. The group's quarterly income for Sep'07 was 3.57 millions of USD.

Primary SIC and add'l.: 6022 6021 6712

CIK No: 0000351569

Subsidiaries: ABC Bancorp Capital Trust I, American Banking Company, Bank of Thomas County, Cairo Banking Company, Cairo Holding Company, Inc., Cairo Real Estate Holdings, Inc., Citizens Bancshares, Inc., Citizens Bank Wakulla, Citizens Holding Company, Inc., Citizens Real Estate Holdings, Inc., Cordele Holding Company, Inc., Cordele Real Estate Holdings, Inc., First National Holding Company, Inc., First National Real Estate Holdings, Inc., M&F Holding Company, Inc. 26 Subsidiaries included in the Index

Officers: Edwin W. Hortman/Dir., CEO, Pres./$860,431.00, Gregory H. Walls/CIO, Sr. VP, Dennis J. Zember/CFO, Exec. VP/$386,449.00, Charles A. Robinson/Sr. VP, Dir. - Internal Audit, Thomas T. Dampier/Exec. VP - North Regional Executive/$288,772.00, Cindi H. Lewis/Exec. VP, Dir. - Human Resources, Corp. Sec., Michael F. McDonald/Sr. VP, Dir. - Retail Banking, John C. Hipp/Exec. VP, Group Pres. South Carolina, Johnny Myers/Exec. VP - South Regional Executive/$246,898.00, Jon S. Edwards/Exec. VP, Dir. - Credit Administration/$286,795.00

Directors: Edwin W. Hortman/Dir., CEO, Pres., Kenneth J. Hunnicutt/Chmn., Daniel B. Jeter/Dir., Johnny W. Floyd/Dir., Robert P. Lynch/Dir., Henry C. Wortman/Dir., Raymond J. Fulp/Dir., Glen Kirbo/Dir., Brooks Sheldon/Dir., Eugene M. Vereen/Dir.

Owners: Johnny W. Floyd, Kenneth J. Hunnicutt/1.53%, Jon S. Edwards, Johnson C. Hipp, Dennis J. Zember, Thomas T. Dampier, Cindi H. Lewis, Glenn A. Kirbo, Daniel B. Jeter, Eugene M. Vereen, Insiders/6.38%, Johnny R. Myers, Robert P. Lynch, Raymond J. Fulp, Edwin W. Hortman *(20 Owners included in Index)*

Financial Data: *Fiscal Year End:* 12/31 *Latest Annual Data:* 12/31/2006

Year	Sales	Net Income
2006	$143,681,000	$22,128,000
2005	$93,460,000	$13,728,000
2004	$77,388,000	$13,101,000

Curr. Assets:	$202,088,000	**Curr. Liab.:**	$1,726,096,000	**P/E Ratio:**	13.78
Plant, Equip.:	$46,604,000	**Total Liab.:**	$1,868,810,000	**Indic. Yr. Divd.:**	NA
Total Assets:	$2,047,542,000	**Net Worth:**	$178,732,000	**Debt/ Equity:**	0.6443

Amerisafe Inc

2301 Hwy. 190 W, DeRidder, LA, 70634; *PH:* 1-337-463-9052; *Fax:* 1-337-463-7298; *http://* www.amerisafe.com

General - Incorporation	TX	**Stock** - Price on:12/24/2007	$17.79
Employees	448	Stock Exchange	NDQ
Auditor	Ernst & Young LLP	Ticker Symbol	AMSF
Stk Agt	American Stock Transfer & Trust Co.	Outstanding Shares	18,800,000
Counsel	NA	E.P.S	$2.25
DUNS No.	NA	Shareholders	NA

Business: The group operates through its subsidiaries whose principle activity is to provide workers compensation insurance. The groups services include coverage, indemnity payments medical facility. The services provide to construction, trucking, logging, agriculture, oil and gas, maritime and sawmills employee. The group operates from Georgia, Louisiana, North Carolina, Florida, Virginia, Texas, Pennsylvania, Illinois, South Carolina, Alaska and Oklahoma. The group's quarterly revenue for September 2007 was 88.29 millions of USD.

Primary SIC and add'l.: 6331 6411

CIK No: 0001018979

Subsidiaries: American Interstate Insurance Company, Amerisafe General Agency, Inc, Amerisafe Risk Services, Inc, Silver Oak Casualty

Officers: Allen C. Bradley/Chmn., CEO, Pres./$969,980.00, Geoffrey R. Banta/CFO, Exec. VP/$597,927.00, Craig P. Leach/Exec. VP - Sales, Marketing/$534,948.00, David O. Narigon/Exec. VP/$132,010.00, Todd Walker/Exec. VP, General Counsel, Sec./$102,451.00, Allan E. Farr/Sr. VP - Enterprise Risk Management, Kelly R. Goins/Sr. VP - Underwriting Operations, Cynthia P. Harris/Sr. VP - Human Resources, Client Services, Leon J. Lagneaux/Sr. VP - Safety Operations, Henry O. Lestage/Sr. VP - Claims Operations, Edwin R. Longanacre/Sr. VP - Information Technology, Angela S. Lannen/VP, Treasurer, Janelle G. Frost/VP, Controller

Directors: Allen C. Bradley/Chmn., CEO, Pres., Thomas W. Hallagan/Dir., Jared Morris/Dir., Randy Roach/Dir., Sean M. Traynor/Dir., Austin P. Young/Dir., Millard E. Morris/63/Dir., Daniel Phillips/61/Dir.

Owners: Geoffrey R. Banta, Millard E. Morris, Insiders/1.30%, Craig P. Leach, Jared A. Morris, Sean M. Traynor, Thomas W. Hallagan, Randy Roach, Allen C. Bradley, Austin P. Young, David O. Narigon

Financial Data: *Fiscal Year End:* 12/31 *Latest Annual Data:* 12/31/2006

Year	Sales	Net Income
2006	$332,720,000	$37,358,000
2005	$276,283,000	$5,930,000
2004	$248,960,000	$10,557,000

Curr. Assets: $286,656,000 **Curr. Liab.:** $37,306,000 **P/E Ratio:** 9.22
Plant, Equip.: $5,687,000 **Total Liab.:** $810,362,000 **Indic. Yr. Divd.:** NA
Total Assets: $994,146,000 **Net Worth:** $158,784,000 **Debt/ Equity:** 0.2146

Ameriserv Financial Inc

216 Franklin St., Johnstown, PA, 15907; *PH:* 1-814-533-5300; *Fax:* 1-814-533-5427; *http://* www.ameriservfinancial.com

General - Incorporation .... PA
Employees 304
Auditor .... S. R. Snodgrass, A.C.
Stk Agt..... Computershare Investor Services LLC
Counsel .... NA
DUNS No. 05-797-6284

Stock- Price on:12/24/2007 .... $4.39
Stock Exchange .... NDQ
Ticker Symbol .... ASRV
Outstanding Shares 22,160,000
E.P.S. $0.11
Shareholders .... NA

Business: The group's principal activity is to provide retail-banking services. These services include accepting demand, savings and time deposits, money market accounts, originating secured and unsecured loans, mortgage loans, safe deposit boxes, holiday club accounts, collection services, money orders and traveler's checks. Lending and other financial services consist of real estate-mortgage loans, short and medium-term loans, revolving credit arrangements, lines of credit, inventory and accounts receivable financing, real estate-construction loans, business savings accounts, certificates of deposit, wire transfers, night depository and lock box services. The operations are conducted through 23 banking locations in 6 counties of Pennsylvania. The group also operates 27 automated bank teller machines through its 24-hour banking network.

Primary SIC and add'l.: 6712 6022

CIK No: 0000707605

Subsidiaries: AmeriServ Associates, Inc, AmeriServ Financial Bank, AmeriServ Life Insurance Company, AmeriServ Trust and Financial Services Company

Officers: Allan R. Dennison/61/Dir., CEO, Pres./$423,063.00, Ronald W. Virag/62/Pres., CEO - Ameriserv Trust, Financial Services Company/$219,020.00, Sharon M. Callihan/Corp. Sec., Dave Gilbert/Loan Officer - Servicing, Cambria, Somerset, Bedford Counties, Jeffrey A. Stopko/45/Sr. VP, CFO/$170,898.00, Dan L. Hummel/55/Sr. VP - Retail Banking - Marketing, Ameriserv Financial Bank/$169,570.00, Gary M. McKeown/63/Sr. VP, Chief Lending Officer - Ameriserv Financial Bank/$181,656.00, Dave Baird/Loan Officer - Servicing, Westmoreland County, Kym Jackson/Loan Officer - Servicing, Centre County, Jessica Genter/Loan Officer - Servicing, Blair County, Glenn St. Mars/Loan Officer - Servicing, South Allegheny, Washington, Fayette Counties, James Badzgon/Loan Officer - Servicing, North, East Allegheny County

Directors: Allan R. Dennison/61/Dir., CEO, Pres., Craig G. Ford/78/Chmn., Kim W. Kunkle/53/Dir., James C. Dewar/70/Dir., Bruce E. Duke/64/Dir., Michael J. Adams/46/Dir., Edward J. Cernic/75/Dir., Margaret A. Omalley/48/Dir., Mark E. Pasquerilla/48/Dir., Thomas C. Slater/65/Dir., James M. Edwards/68/Dir., Christian R. Oravec/70/Dir., Howard M. Picking/70/Dir., Sara A. Sargent/60/Dir., Robert L. Wise/64/Dir. *(16 Directors included in Index)*

Owners: Margaret A. OMalley/1.10%, Bruce E. Duke, Wellington Management Company, LLP/6.72%, Jeffrey A. Stopko, Dan L. Hummel, James C. Dewar, Very Christian R. Oravec, Howard M. Picking, Craig G. Ford, James M. Edwards, Sara A. Sargent, Dimensional FundAdvisors Inc./6.97%, Thomas C. Slater, Financial Stocks Capital PartnersIII L.P./9.78%, Edward J. Cernic *(26 Owners included in Index)*

Financial Data: **Fiscal Year End:**12/31 **Latest Annual Data:** 12/31/2006

Year	Sales	Net Income
2006	$59,406,000	$2,332,000
2005	$58,573,000	-$9,141,000
2004	$64,116,000	-$9,719,000

Curr. Assets: $28,069,000 **Curr. Liab.:** $791,792,000 **P/E Ratio:** 43.90
Plant, Equip.: $8,562,000 **Total Liab.:** $811,308,000 **Indic. Yr. Divd.:** NA
Total Assets: $895,992,000 **Net Worth:** $84,684,000 **Debt/ Equity:** NA

Amerisourcebergen Corp

1300 Morris Dr., Ste. 100, Chesterbrook, PA, 19087; *PH:* 1-610-727-7000; *Fax:* 1-610-727-3600; *http://* www.amerisourcebergen.com; *Email:* info@amerisourcebergen.com

General - Incorporation .... DE
Employees 13,200
Auditor .... Ernst & Young LLP
Stk Agt .... Bank of New York
Counsel .... NA
DUNS No. .... NA

Stock- Price on:12/24/2007 .... $50.22
Stock Exchange .... NYSE
Ticker Symbol .... ABC
Outstanding Shares 191,080,000
E.P.S. $2.50
Shareholders .... NA

Business: The group's principle activity is to distribute pharmaceutical and healthcare products and services. The group also provides contract packaging, business support and consulting services. The group operates from United States.

Primary SIC and add'l.: 5122

CIK No: 0001140859

Subsidiaries: Amerisource Health Services Corporation, Amerisource Heritage Corporation, AmerisourceReceivablesFinancialCorporation, AmerisourceBergen Drug Corporation, AmerisourceBergen Holding Corporation, PharMerica, Inc., PMSI, Inc.

Officers: David R. Yost/60/Dir., CEO, Kurt J. Hilzinger/47/Dir., COO, Pres., Michael D. Dicandilo/CFO, Exec. VP, Steven H. Collis/Exec. VP, Pres. - Amerisourcebergen Specialty Group, Terrance P. Haas/Exec. VP, Chief Integration Officer, Len Decandia/Sr. VP - Supply Chain Management, Jeanne Fisher/Sr. VP - Human Resources, David W. Neu/Sr. VP - Retail Sales, Marketing, John Palumbo/Sr. VP - Health Systems Solutions, Thomas H. Murphy/CIO, Sr. VP, John G. Chou/VP, Deputy General Counsel, Sec., Tim G. Guttman/VP, Corporate Controller, J. F. Quinn/VP, Corporate Treasurer, David M. Senior/Sr. VP - Strategy, Corporate Development, Michael Kilpatric/VP - Corporate, Investor Relations *(16 Officers included in Index)*

Directors: David R. Yost/60/Dir., CEO, Richard C. Gozon/69/Chmn., Kurt J. Hilzinger/47/Dir., COO, Pres., Henry W. McGee/55/Dir., Rodney H. Brady/75/Dir., Charles H. Cotros/70/Dir., Edward E. Hagenlocker/68/Dir., Jane E. Henney/60/Dir., Lawrence J. Wilson/71/Dir., Michael J. Long/49/Dir.

Owners: State Street Corp./6.00%, Insiders/2.60%, Michael J. Long, Charles H. Cotros, David R. Yost/1.00%, Steven H. Collis, Terrance P. Haas, Henry W. McGee, Edward E. Hagenlocker, Richard C. Gozon, Rodney H. Brady, Goldman Sachs Group Inc./11.70%, PzenaInvestmentManagement,LLC/5.10%, Kurt J. Hilzinger, Jane E. Henney *(17 Owners included in Index)*

Financial Data: **Fiscal Year End:**09/30 **Latest Annual Data:** 06/30/2007

Year	Sales	Net Income
2007	NA	NA
2006	$61,203,145,000	$467,714,000
2005	$54,577,321,000	$264,645,000

Curr. Assets: $9,210,407,000 **Curr. Liab.:** $7,459,188,000 **P/E Ratio:** 20.25
Plant, Equip.: $509,746,000 **Total Liab.:** $8,642,763,000 **Indic. Yr. Divd.:** $0.200
Total Assets: $12,783,920,000 **Net Worth:** $4,141,157,000 **Debt/ Equity:** 0.2928

Ameristar Casinos Inc

3773 Howard Hughes Pkwy., Ste. 490 South, Las Vegas, NV, 89109; *PH:* 1-702-567-7000; *Fax:* 1-702-369-8860; *http://* www.ameristarcasinos.com

General - Incorporation .... NV
Employees 7,200
Auditor .... Ernst & Young LLP
Stk Agt .... U.S. Stock Transfer Corp
Counsel........ Gibson, Dunn & Crutcher LLP
DUNS No. 82-745-2111

Stock- Price on:12/24/2007 .... $35.55
Stock Exchange .... NDQ
Ticker Symbol .... ASCA
Outstanding Shares 57,330,000
E.P.S. $1.36
Shareholders .... NA

Business: The group's principal activity is to develop, own and operate casinos and related hotel and entertainment facilities. The group owns six properties in five markets located in Missouri, Iowa, Mississippi and Nevada catering to customers primarily residing within a 100-mile radius of our properties. The group offers table games such as Blackjack, Craps, Roulette, Poker, Keno and sports book wagering. The group also provides dining, lodging and entertainment services.

Primary SIC and add'l.: 5399 5812 7993 7021 7011

CIK No: 0000912145

Subsidiaries: A.C. Food Services Inc., Ameristar Casino Black Hawk Inc., Ameristar Casino Council Bluffs inc, Ameristar Casino Kansas City Inc., Ameristar Casino Las Vegas Inc, Ameristar Casino St. Charles Inc., Ameristar Casino St. Louis Inc., Ameristar Casino Vicksburg Inc., Cactus Petes Inc., dba Cactus Petes Resort Casino, dba Mountain High Casino, Richmond Street Development Inc., The Horseshu Hotel & Casino

Officers: John M. Boushy/Dir., CEO, Pres./$2,190,812.00, Gordon R. Kanofsky/Co - Chmn., Exec. VP/$1,568,023.00, Ray H. Neilsen/Co - Chmn., Sr. VP, Kari Francisco/Contact, Peter C. Walsh/Sr. VP, General Counsel/$1,870,809.00, Thomas M. Steinbauer/Dir., CFO, Sr. VP - Finance/$901,849.00

Directors: John M. Boushy/Dir., CEO, Pres., Gordon R. Kanofsky/Co - Chmn., Exec. VP, Ray H. Neilsen/Co - Chmn., Sr. VP, Carl Brooks/Dir., Thomas M. Steinbauer/Dir., CFO, Sr. VP - Finance, Craig H. Neilsen/Founder, Larry A. Hodges/Dir., Leslie Nathanson Juris/Dir., William J. Richardson/Dir., Luther P. Cochrane/Dir.

Owners: Luther P. Cochrane, Private Capital Management, L.P./12.10%, Peter C. Walsh, J. William Richardson, Gordon R. Kanofsky/55.50%, Leslie Nathanson Juris, Estate of Craig H. Neilsen/55.40%, Thomas M. Steinbauer, John M. Boushy, Insiders/56.50%, Larry A. Hodges, Ray H. Neilsen/55.70%, Angela R. Frost

Financial Data: **Fiscal Year End:**12/31 **Latest Annual Data:** 12/31/2006

Year	Sales	Net Income
2006	$1,000,298,000	$59,565,000
2005	$961,358,000	$66,285,000
2004	$854,698,000	$61,979,000

Curr. Assets: $139,492,000 **Curr. Liab.:** $115,906,000 **P/E Ratio:** 25.76
Plant, Equip.: $1,285,694,000 **Total Liab.:** $1,107,311,000 **Indic. Yr. Divd.:** $0.410
Total Assets: $1,541,475,000 **Net Worth:** $434,164,000 **Debt/ Equity:** 1.9118

Ameritrade Holding Corp

4211 S 102nd St., Omaha, NE, 68127; *PH:* 1-402-331-7856; *http://* www.ameritradeholding.com

General - Incorporation .... DE
Employees 3,947
Auditor .... RNST & Young LLP
Stk Agt .... Bank of New York
Counsel .... NA
DUNS No. .... NA

Stock- Price on:12/24/2007 .... $20.48
Stock Exchange .... NDQ
Ticker Symbol .... NA
Outstanding Shares 596,920,000
E.P.S. $1.06
Shareholders .... NA

Business: The group's principle actiivty is to provide securities brokerage services and technology-based financial services to retail investors and business partners. The group operates from United States.

Primary SIC and add'l.: 6211

CIK No: 0001173431

Subsidiaries: AmeriFirst Capital Corp., Ameritrade Advisory Services, LLC, Ameritrade Canada, Inc., Ameritrade Institutional Services, Inc., Ameritrade International Company, Inc., Ameritrade IP Company, Inc., Ameritrade Northwest, Inc., Ameritrade Online Holdings Corp., Ameritrade Services Company, Inc., Ameritrade, Inc., Amerivest Investment Management, LLC, Datek Online Holdings Corp., Datek Online Management Corp., Financial Passport, Inc., Freetrade.com, Inc. 24 Subsidiaries included in the Index

Officers: Joseph H. Moglia/Dir., CEO, Christian T. Armstrong/Exec. VP - Client Group, Randy J. MacDonald/COO, Exec. VP, Michael D. Chochon/MD - Finance, Treasurer, Ellen L.S. Koplow/Exec. VP, General Counsel, Sec., Raymond J. Bartlett/47/CIO, Sr. VP, Laurine M. Garrity/Sr. VP, Chief Marketing Officer, William J. Gerber/CFO, Exec. VP, John R. MacDonald/52/COO, Exec. VP, Tom Bradley/Pres. - TD Ameritrade Institutional, John Bunch/Pres. - Retail Sales, Wayne Ferbert/VP - Business Development, Dave Kelley/Sr. VP - Retail Investor Group, Jerry R. Bartlett/CIO, Sr. VP, Bryce B. Engel/Sr. VP, Chief Brokerage Operation Officer *(16 Officers included in Index)*

Directors: Joseph H. Moglia/Dir., CEO, Joe J. Ricketts/Chmn., Founder, Edmund W. Clark/Vice Chmn., Daniel W. Cook/Dir., Marshall A. Cohen/Dir., Robert T. Slezak/Dir., Mark L. Mitchell/Dir., Peter J. Ricketts/Dir., Daniel A. Marinangeli/Dir., Fredric J. Tomczyk/Dir., Wilbur J. Prezzano/Dir., William H. Hatanaka/Dir., Thomas J. Mullin/Dir., Allan R. Tessler/Dir., Thomas S. Ricketts/Dir. *(17 Directors included in Index)*

Owners: W. Edmund Clark, Marshall A. Cohen, Fredric J. Tomczyk, Mark L. Mitchell, Wilbur J. Prezzano, Thomas S. Ricketts, Dan W. Cook, Joseph H. Moglia/1.50%, Ricketts Grandchildren Trust/3.20%, T. Rowe Price Associates, Inc./5.00%, Insiders/20.10%, The Toronto-Dominion Bank/40.10%, Joe J. Ricketts/18.00%, Allan R. Tessler, Robert T. Slezak *(17 Owners included in Index)*

Financial Data: **Fiscal Year End:**09/30 **Latest Annual Data:** 9/29/2006

Year	Sales	Net Income
2006	$1,803,531,000	$526,759,000
2005	$1,003,153,000	$339,753,000
2004	$921,974,000	$282,818,000

Curr. Assets:	$15,201,156,000	**Curr. Liab.:**	$14,742,815,000	**P/E Ratio:**	22.76
Plant, Equip.:	$33,259,000	**Total Liab.:**	$14,898,243,000	**Indic. Yr. Divd.:**	NA
Total Assets:	$16,417,110,000	**Net Worth:**	$1,518,867,000	**Debt/ Equity:**	0.9176

Ameritrans Capital Corp

747 3rd Ave., 4th Fl., New York, NY, 10017; ***PH:*** 1-212-355-2449; ***Fax:*** 1-212-759-3338; ***http://*** www.ameritranscapital.com; ***Email:*** smullens@elkassociates.com

General - Incorporation	DE	**Stock**- Price on:12/24/2007	$4.75
Employees	10	Stock Exchange	NDQ
Auditor	Rosen Seymour Shapss Martin & Co	Ticker Symbol	AMTC
Stk Agt	Continental Stock Transfer & Trust Co	Outstanding Shares	3,390,000
Counsel	NA	E.P.S	-$0.14
DUNS No.	NA	Shareholders	NA

Business: The group's principal activities are to provide loans to taxi owners, finance the acquisition and operation of the medallion taxi businesses and to other small businesses. The subsidiaries include Elk Associates Funding Corporation, EAF Holding Corporation and Elk Capital Corporation. The group has operations in the Chicago, New York City, Miami and Boston markets.

Primary SIC and add'l.: 6141

CIK No: 0001064015

Subsidiaries: EAF Leasing II, EAF Leasing III, EAF Leasing LLC, Elk Associates Funding Corporation, Elk Capital Corporation

Officers: Gary C. Granoff/60/Chmn., CEO, CFO, Pres., Silvia M. Mullens/56/VP, Ellen M. Walker/52/Dir., Exec. VP, Harvey Goldman/Sr. Loan Administrator, Margaret Chance/53/Sec., VP, Lee A. Forlenza/50/Dir., Sr. VP, Steven Etra/58/Dir., VP

Directors: Gary C. Granoff/60/Chmn., CEO, CFO, Pres., Paul Creditor/Dir., Wesley Finch/60/Dir., John R. Laird/65/Dir., Lee A. Forlenza/50/Dir., Sr. VP, Steven Etra/58/Dir., VP, Allen S. Kaplan/Dir., Ellen M. Walker/52/Dir., Exec. VP, Michael Feinsod/37/Dir., Murray A. Indick/49/Dir., Howard F. Sommer/67/Dir., Heidi J. Sorvino/Dir., Ivan J. Wolpert/42/Dir.

Owners: John R. Laird, Mitchell Partners L.P./8.50%, Lee A. Forlenza/1.41%, Wesley Finch/3.33%, Performance Capital, L.P./9.90%, Margaret Chance, Howard F. Sommer, Prides Capital Partners, LLC/31.40%, Gary C. Granoff/10.60%, Gary C. Granoff/2.35%, Lee A. Forlenza, Ellen M. Walker, Insiders/6.10%, Silvia Mullens, Ivan Wolpert *(23 Owners included in Index)*

Financial Data: ***Fiscal Year End:***06/30 ***Latest Annual Data:*** 6/30/2006

Year	Sales	Net Income
2006	$5,291,000	-$219,000
2005	$6,132,000	$113,000
2004	$5,634,000	-$367,000

Curr. Assets:	$1,992,000	**Curr. Liab.:**	$1,332,000		
Plant, Equip.:	$244,000	**Total Liab.:**	$34,260,000	**Indic. Yr. Divd.:**	NA
Total Assets:	$56,019,000	**Net Worth:**	$21,759,000	**Debt/ Equity:**	1.5753

Amerityre Corp

1501 Industrial Rd. , Boulder City, NV, 89005; ***PH:*** 1-800-808-1268; ***http://*** www.amerityre.com; ***Email:*** information@amerityre.com

General - Incorporation	NV	**Stock**- Price on:12/24/2007	$4.6
Employees	26	Stock Exchange	NDQ
Auditor	HJ & Assoc. LLC	Ticker Symbol	AMTY
Stk Agt	Interwest Transfer Company, Inc.	Outstanding Shares	23,230,000
Counsel	NA	E.P.S	-$0.22
DUNS No.	88-367-0242	Shareholders	NA

Business: The group's principle activities include manufacturing, marketing and distributing tires and tire-wheel assemblies. It has developed a technology relating to the manufacture of flat free tires at its facility in las vegas. Flat free tires differ from pneumatic tires as they do not require inflation. The products are designed for use in bicycles, wheelchairs, lawn and garden equipment, commercial and riding lawnmowers and also golf cars. In addition to manufacturing the flatfree products the company is also engaged in development of polyurethane elastomer tires for highway and agricultural use based on the proprietary technology and various methods and processes relating to the manufacturing of those tires from liquid elastomers. American (TM), flatfree(tm), amerityre (TM), amerithane (TM), elastothane (TM), urathon (TM) are the trademarks under which they are marketed. The group operates from United States.

Primary SIC and add'l.: 3011

CIK No: 0000945828

Officers: Richard A. Steinke/Chmn., CEO, Pres., Anders Suarez/CFO, Elliott N. Taylor/Exec. VP - Legal Counsel, James G. Moore/VP - Operations, Engineering, Gary N. Benninger/COO, David K. Griffiths/Sec., Treasurer, Sean Collins/Sr. Partner, CCG Investor Relations, Strategic Communications

Directors: Richard A. Steinke/Chmn., CEO, Pres., Louis M. Haynie/Dir., Kenneth C. Johnsen/Dir., Steve M. Hanni/Dir., Norman H. Tregenza/Dir., Henry D. Moyle/Dir.

Owners: Kenneth C. Johnsen/0.24%, Norman H. Tregenza/1.61%, Gary N. Benninger/0.47%, James G. Moore, Apex Capital, LLC/7.76%, Henry D. Moyle/3.10%, Joseph J. Grano/5.99%, Wesley G. Sprunk/0.68%, Anders A. Suarez/0.45%, Richard A. Steinke/7.02%, Steve Hanni/0.03%, Louis M. Haynie/1.92%, Insiders/8.82%

Financial Data: ***Fiscal Year End:***06/30 ***Latest Annual Data:*** 06/30/2007

Year	Sales	Net Income
2007	$3,427,000	-$5,008,000
2006	NA	NA
2005	$1,681,000	-$10,073,000

Curr. Assets:	$4,289,000	**Curr. Liab.:**	$357,000		
Plant, Equip.:	$1,352,000	**Total Liab.:**	$357,000	**Indic. Yr. Divd.:**	NA
Total Assets:	$6,140,000	**Net Worth:**	$5,784,000	**Debt/ Equity:**	NA

Ameriwest Energy Corp

Formerly: Henley Ventures Inc

3rd Fl. - 830, W Pender St., Vancouver, BC, V6B4N7; ***PH:*** 1-604-683-6991

General - Incorporation	NV	**Stock**- Price on:12/24/2007	NA
Employees	NA	Stock Exchange	NA
Auditor	Cordovano & Honeck LLP	Ticker Symbol	NA
Stk Agt	American Transfer Station	Outstanding Shares	NA
Counsel	NA	E.P.S	NA
DUNS No.	NA	Shareholders	NA

Business: The groups principle activity is to provide recruiting services. The groups service area includes the research and development, engineering, marketing, sales, information technology and manufacturing industries. The group operates from United States.

Primary SIC and add'l.: 1400

CIK No: 0001162200

Officers: Sam Hirji/59/Dir., Principal Exec. Officer, Pres., Herbert Moeller/58/Dir., Principal Financial Officer, Principal Accounting Officer, Sec., Treasurer

Directors: Sam Hirji/59/Dir., Principal Exec. Officer, Pres., Herbert Moeller/58/Dir., Principal Financial Officer, Principal Accounting Officer, Sec., Treasurer, Terry Heard/70/Dir.

Owners: Insiders/24.14%, Herbert Moeller/6.90%, Sam Hirji/10.34%, Terry Heard/6.90%

Ameron International Corp

245 S Los Robles Ave., Pasadena, CA, 91101; ***PH:*** 1-626-683-4000; ***Fax:*** 1-626-683-4060; ***http://*** www.ameron.com

General - Incorporation	DE	**Stock**- Price on:12/24/2007	$90.78
Employees	2,500	Stock Exchange	NYSE
Auditor	PricewaterhouseCoopers LLP	Ticker Symbol	AMN
Stk Agt	National City Bank	Outstanding Shares	9,110,000
Counsel	NA	E.P.S	$6.02
DUNS No.	14-767-3354	Shareholders	NA

Business: The group's principal activities are carried through four segments: the performance coatings and finishes group, the fiberglass-composite pipe group, the water transmission group and the infrastructure products group. The performance coatings group develops, manufactures and markets high-performance coatings and surfacer systems which are used for the preservation of structures. The fiberglass group manufactures and markets filament-wound and molded fiberglass pipes and fittings that are used by process industries. The water transmission group supplies products and services used in the construction of water pipelines. The infrastructure group supplies ready-mix concrete pipes, crushed and sized basaltic aggregates, dune sand, and concrete pipes and box culverts to the construction industry.

Primary SIC and add'l.: 3479 3272

CIK No: 0000790730

Subsidiaries: Amercoat Japan Company, Limited, American Pipe & Construction International, Ameron B.V., Ameron Composites Inc., Ameron Limited, Ameron Ltd., Ameron Malaysia Sdn. Bhd., Ameron Pty. Limited, Ameron Saudi Arabia, Ltd., Bondstrand, Ltd., Centron International, Inc., Island Ready-Mix Concrete, Inc., Oasis-Ameron, Ltd., TAMCO

Officers: James S. Marlen/Chmn., CEO, Pres., James R. McLaughlin/CFO, Sr. VP, Treasurer, Eric Yoshizawa/VP - Operations - Maui, Ameron Hawaii Division, Bill Smith/VP - Manufacturing, Water Transmission Group, Thomas P. Giese/VP, Group Pres. - Water Transmission Group, Gary Wagner/COO, Exec. VP, Terrence P. O'Shea/VP - Human Resources, Daniel J. Emmett/VP, Controller, Javier Solis/Sr. VP - Administration, Sec., General Counsel, Rocky S. Friedrich/VP - Research, Engineering, Long Beach, California, Christine Stanley/Group Executive, Corporate Research, Development, Wesley Olison/Operations Dir. - Concrete, Pole Products, Mark Nowak/Group Pres. - Houston, Texas, Fiberglass, Composite Pipe Group, Pres. - Fiberglass, Composite Pipe Americas Mineral Wells, TX, Allen Chiu/MD - Ameron, Pte Ltd Singapore, David B. Jones/VP - Operations, Fiberglass, Composite Pipe Group *(21 Officers included in Index)*

Directors: James S. Marlen/Chmn., CEO, Pres., John E. Peppercorn/Dir., Dennis C. Poulsen/Dir., William D. Horsfall/Dir., Peter K. Barker/Dir., David Davenport/Dir., Michael J. Hagan/Dir., Terry L. Haines/Dir.

Owners: Estate of Taro Iketani/6.75%, T. Rowe Price Associates, Inc./8.87%, David Davenport, Javier Solis, Thomas P. Giese, Tontine Overseas Associates, L.L.C./8.73%, James S. Marlen, Dennis C. Poulsen, Insiders/1.52%, Dimensional Fund Advisors LP/7.44%, John E. Peppercorn, Terry L. Haines, Gary Wagner, Michael J. Hagan

Financial Data: ***Fiscal Year End:***11/30 ***Latest Annual Data:*** 11/30/2006

Year	Sales	Net Income
2006	$549,180,000	$52,200,000
2005	$704,574,000	$32,610,000
2004	$605,853,000	$13,459,000

Curr. Assets:	$416,568,000	**Curr. Liab.:**	$136,101,000	**P/E Ratio:**	15.08
Plant, Equip.:	$149,207,000	**Total Liab.:**	$271,439,000	**Indic. Yr. Divd.:**	$1.000
Total Assets:	$634,664,000	**Net Worth:**	$363,225,000	**Debt/ Equity:**	0.1910

Amersin Life Sciences Corp

410 Pk. Ave., 15th Fl., New York, NY, 10022; ***PH:*** 1-604-882-2899; ***Fax:*** 1-604-882-2892; ***http://*** www.amersin.com; ***Email:*** reid@amersin.com

General - Incorporation	NV	**Stock**- Price on:12/24/2007	NA
Employees	NA	Stock Exchange	OTC
Auditor	Moen & Co LLP	Ticker Symbol	GTGR
Stk Agt	Pacific Stock Transfer Company	Outstanding Shares	NA
Counsel	NA	E.P.S	NA
DUNS No.	NA	Shareholders	NA

Business: The group's principal activity is to develop, produce and sell bulk pharmaceutical products. It has operated two pharmaceutical divisions: a bulk division, producing bulk pharmaceuticals and pharmaceutical ingredients; and a dosage division producing generic and patented medicines in dosage formats including injections, tablets, capsules, syrups and other forms for over-the-counter sale and use within the healthcare system through prescription by medical professionals. On 25-Jul-2003, the group acquired red dot capital inc's 57.14% joint venture interest in hubei pharmaceutical co ltd

Primary SIC and add'l.: 2834

CIK No: 0001009919

Subsidiaries: Hubei Tongji Benda Ebei Pharmaceutical Co. Ltd.

Financial Data: ***Fiscal Year End:***01/31 ***Latest Annual Data:*** 01/31/2006

Year	Sales	Net Income
2006	NA	-$2,425,000
2005	$6,611,000	$259,000
2004	NA	-$616,000

Curr. Assets:	$224,000	**Curr. Liab.:**	$91,000		
Plant, Equip.:	$4,000	**Total Liab.:**	$91,000	**Indic. Yr. Divd.:**	NA
Total Assets:	$228,000	**Net Worth:**	$137,000	**Debt/ Equity:**	NA

Amerus Group Co

699 Walnut St., Des Moines, IA, 50309; ***PH:*** 1-515-362-3600; ***http://*** www.amerus.com

General - Incorporation ....IA
Employees ....NA
Auditor .... Ernst & Young LLP
Stk Agt.... Mellon Investor Services LLC
Counsel ....NA
DUNS No. ....NA

Stock- Price on:12/24/2007 ....NA
Stock Exchange ....NYSE
Ticker Symbol ....AMH
Outstanding Shares ....NA
E.P.S ....NA
Shareholders ....NA

Business: The group's principal activity is to market, underwrite and distribute a range of individual life, annuity and insurance deposit products. The group operates in two segments: protection products and accumulation products. The protection products segment primarily offers interest-sensitive whole life, term life, universal life and equity-indexed life insurance policies. The accumulation products segment offers individual deferred fixed annuities, equity-indexed annuities and funding agreements. The group markets its products to individuals and businesses in 50 states in the district of columbia and the U.S. Virgin islands. The customers are individuals in the middle and upper income brackets and small businesses.

Primary SIC and add'l.: 6719 6311

CIK No: 0001051717

Subsidiaries: American Investors Life Insurance Company, Inc., AmerUs Annuity Group Co., AmerUs Capital Management Group, Inc., AmerUs Life Insurance Company, Bankers Life Insurance Company of New York, ILICO Holdings, Inc., Indianapolis Life Insurance Company

Ames National Corp

405 5th St., Ames, IA, 50010; ***PH:*** 1-515-232-6251; ***Fax:*** 1-515-663-3033; ***http://*** www.amesnational.com; ***Email:*** info@amesnational.com

General - Incorporation ....IA
Employees 184
Auditor ....Clifton Gunderson LLP
Stk Agt.... BNY Trust Company
Counsel ....NA
DUNS No. ....NA

Stock- Price on:12/24/2007 ....$21.5
Stock Exchange ....NYSE
Ticker Symbol ....ATLO
Outstanding Shares 9,430,000
E.P.S $1.17
Shareholders ....NA

Business: The group operates through its subsidiaries whose principle activity is to provide banking services. The groups services include loans, deposits and trust. The groups financial product include commercial and residential real estate loans, agricultural and business operating loans and lines of credit, equipment loans, vehicle loans, personal loans, home improvement loans and secondary mortgage loan origination. The group operates from the United States. The group's quarterly income for September 2007 was 2.94 millions of USD.

Primary SIC and add'l.: 6021 6022 6712

CIK No: 0001132651

Subsidiaries: Boone Bank and Trust Co., First National Bank, Randall-Story State Bank, State Bank & Trust Co., United Bank & Trust NA

Officers: Thomas H. Pohlman/CEO, Pres./$215,287.00, Daniel L. Krieger/Chmn., Pres./$281,198.00, Matthew R. Hackbart/Assist. Information Systems Mgr., Timothy J. Lupardus/Assist. VP, Information Systems Mgr., John P. Nelson/CFO, VP/$130,341.00, Lisa K. Robinson/Auditor, Jeffrey M. Vetter/Information Technology Technician, Jennifer J. Thompson/Assist. VP, Dir. - Human Resources, Charles D. Jons/Dir., Independent Medical Consultant, Kevin G. Deardorff/VP, Technology Dir., Tracy W. Laws/Assist. VP, Auditor, Lori J. Hill/Assist. Corp. Sec., Nicole J. Gebhart/Assist. VP, Marketing Dir.

Directors: Daniel L. Krieger/Chmn., Pres., Marvin J. Walter/Dir., Warren R. Madden/Dir., Charles D. Jons/Dir., Independent Medical Consultant, James R. Larson/Dir., Douglas C. Gustafson/Dir., Frederick C. Samuelson/Dir., Robert L. Cramer/Dir., Betty A. Baudler/Dir.

Owners: Suzanne Ammerman/5.34%, Insiders/14.76%, Charles D. Jons, John P. Nelson, Thomas H. Pohlman/7.91%, Terrill L. Wycoff/1.38%, Jeffrey K. Putzier, Steven D. Forth, Douglas C. Gustafson, Frederick C. Samuelson, Larry A. Raymon, George B. Coover/6.69%, Daniel L. Krieger/9.64%, Warren R. Madden, James R. Larson *(20 Owners included in Index)*

Financial Data: ***Fiscal Year End:***12/31 ***Latest Annual Data:*** 12/31/2006

Year	Sales	Net Income
2006	$50,970,000	$10,944,000
2005	$46,919,000	$11,609,000
2004	$42,623,000	$12,390,000

Curr. Assets:	$31,154,000	**Curr. Liab.:**	$724,741,000		
Plant, Equip.:	$12,618,000	**Total Liab.:**	$725,930,000	**Indic. Yr. Divd.:**	$1.080
Total Assets:	$838,853,000	**Net Worth:**	$112,923,000	**Debt/ Equity:**	NA

Ametek Inc

37 N Valley Rd., Bldg. 4, Paoli, PA, 19301; ***PH:*** 1-610-647-2121; ***Fax:*** 1-610-323-9337; ***http://*** www.ametek.com

General - Incorporation ....DE
Employees 10,400
Auditor ....Ernst & Young LLP
Stk Agt.... American Stock Transfer & Trust Co.
Counsel ....Stroock & Stroock & Lavan
DUNS No. 00-134-5149

Stock- Price on:12/24/2007 ....$38.51
Stock Exchange ....NYSE
Ticker Symbol ....AME
Outstanding Shares 106,730,000
E.P.S $2.00
Shareholders ....NA

Business: The groups principle activity is to manufacture electronic instruments and electromechanical devices. In the year 2007 the group acquired California Instruments Corporation and CAMECA SAS. The group operates from United States.

Primary SIC and add'l.: 3621 3823 3399

CIK No: 0001037868

Subsidiaries: Advanced Measurement Technology, Inc., Aircontrol Technologies Limited, Airscrew Limited, Airtechnology Group Limited, Airtechnology Holdings Limited, Airtechnology Pension Trustees Ltd., Amekai (BVI), Ltd., Amekai Meter (Xiamen) Co., Ltd., Amekai Singapore Private Ltd., AmeKai Taiwan Co., Ltd., AMELON, Inc., AMETEK (Bermuda), Ltd., AMETEK (Canada), Ltd., Ametek (fsc), Inc., AMETEK Denmark A/S 94 Subsidiaries included in the Index

Officers: Frank S. Hermance/Chmn., CEO/$7,229,094.00, John J. Molinelli/CFO, Exec. VP/$1,645,176.00, David A. Zapico/Pres. - Electronic Instruments/$1,140,398.00, Robert W. Chlebek/Pres. - Electronic Instruments/$1,321,906.00, Robert R. Mandos/49/Sr. VP, Controller, Timothy N. Jones/Pres. - Electromechanical Group/$851,152.00, Kathryn E. Sena/Corp. Sec.

Directors: Frank S. Hermance/Chmn., CEO, James R. Malone/65/Dir., David P. Steinmann/66/Dir., Elizabeth R. Varet/64/Dir., Steven W. Kohlhagen/60/Dir., Lewis G. Cole/Dir., Charles D. Klein/69/Dir., Sheldon S. Gordon/72/Dir., Dennis K. Williams/Dir.

Owners: David P. Steinmann, Sheldon S. Gordon, Frank S. Hermance/1.90%, Lewis G. Cole, Charles D. Klein, Insiders/4.10%, James R. Malone, Robert W. Chlebek, Steven W. Kohlhagen, John J. Molinelli, Elizabeth R. Varet, Timothy N. Jones, David A. Zapico

Financial Data: ***Fiscal Year End:***12/31 ***Latest Annual Data:*** 12/31/2006

Year	Sales	Net Income
2006	$1,819,290,000	$181,934,000
2005	$1,434,457,000	$140,643,000
2004	$1,232,318,000	$112,711,000

Curr. Assets:	$684,063,000	**Curr. Liab.:**	$480,900,000	**P/E Ratio:**	20.16
Plant, Equip.:	$258,008,000	**Total Liab.:**	$1,164,204,000	**Indic. Yr. Divd.:**	$0.240
Total Assets:	$2,130,876,000	**Net Worth:**	$966,672,000	**Debt/ Equity:**	0.5128

Amexdrug Corp

369 S Doheny Dr., Ste. 326, Beverly Hills, CA, 90211; ***PH:*** 1-310-855-0475; ***Fax:*** 1-310-855-0477; ***http://*** www.amexdrug.com

General - Incorporation ....NV
Employees 3
Auditor ....Hansen, Barnett & Maxwell
Stk Agt.... Mellon Investor Services LLC
Counsel ....NA
DUNS No. 00-830-8512

Stock- Price on:12/24/2007 ....$1.5
Stock Exchange ....OTC
Ticker Symbol ....AXRX
Outstanding Shares 8,470,000
E.P.S $0.01
Shareholders ....NA

Business: The group's principle activity is to provide potential business opportunity. The group operates from United States.

Primary SIC and add'l.: 3911 6799

CIK No: 0000045621

Subsidiaries: Allied Med, Inc., Biorx Pharmaceuticals, Inc., Dermagen, Inc., Royal Health Care, Inc.

Officers: Jack Amin/Chmn., CEO, CFO, Leon Hines/Dir., Advisor, Raymond Chow/Advisor, Que Phan/Advisor, Humberto Zardo/Advisor, John Kim/Advisor, Ike Alabata/Advisor, Erskine Cartwright/Advisor

Directors: Jack Amin/Chmn., CEO, CFO, Behrooz Meimand/59/Dir., Rodney S. Barron/Dir., Ben Meimand/Dir., Leon Hines/Dir., Advisor

Owners: Insiders/91.60%, Jack Amin/91.60%

Financial Data: ***Fiscal Year End:***12/31 ***Latest Annual Data:*** 12/31/2006

Year	Sales	Net Income
2006	$4,650,000	$21,000
2005	$4,951,000	$14,000
2004	$6,530,000	$10,000

Curr. Assets:	$421,000	**Curr. Liab.:**	$450,000	**P/E Ratio:**	75.00
Plant, Equip.:	$32,000	**Total Liab.:**	$464,000	**Indic. Yr. Divd.:**	NA
Total Assets:	$494,000	**Net Worth:**	$31,000	**Debt/ Equity:**	NA

AMF Bowling Centers Inc

7313 Bell Creek Rd. , Mechanicsville, VA, 23111; ***PH:*** 1-804-730-4000; ***http://*** www.amf.com

General - Incorporation ....DE
Employees ....NA
Auditor ....KPMG LLP
Stk Agt ....NA
Counsel ....NA
DUNS No. ....NA

Stock- Price on:12/24/2007 ....NA
Stock Exchange ....NA
Ticker Symbol ....NA
Outstanding Shares ....NA
E.P.S ....NA
Shareholders ....NA

Business: The group's principal activities are to operate bowling centers and to manufacture and market bowling equipment. The bowling equipment includes automatic pinspotters, automatic scoring equipment, bowling pins, lanes, ball returns, lane machines, bowling center supplies and the resale of other related products, including bowling balls, bags and shoes. As of 29-Jun-2002, the group operated 378 bowling centers in the United States and 97 bowling centers in Australia, the United Kingdom, Mexico, France and Japan. The group also manufactures and sells its playmaster, highland and renaissance brands of billiard tables.

Primary SIC and add'l.: 3949 7933

CIK No: 0001015535

Subsidiaries: 300, Inc., ABC Ventures LLC, American Recreation Centers, Inc., Amf Bch LLC, AMF Beverage Company of Oregon, Inc., AMF Bowling Centers Holdings Inc., AMF Bowling Centers International Inc., AMF Bowling Centers, Inc., AMF Bowling de Lyon La Part Dieu SNC, AMF Bowling Mexico Holding, Inc., AMF Bowling Products UK Limited, AMF Holdings, Inc., Amf Wbch LLC, AMF Worldwide Bowling Centers Holdings Inc., Boliches AMF y Compania 31 Subsidiaries included in the Index

Officers: Frederick R. Hipp/CEO, Pres., William A. McDonnell/CFO, VP, Thomas W. Didlake/VP, Corporate Controller, Principal Accounting Officer

Directors: Frederick R. Hipp/CEO, Pres.

Owners: Merrell Wreden, Fredrick R. Hipp/3.70%, John B. Walker, Anthony J. Ponsiglione, Insiders/4.20%, J. Simon Shearer

AMG Oil Ltd

600 17th St., Ste. 2800 S, Denver, CO, 80202; ***PH:*** 1-303-226-5889

General - Incorporation ....NV
Employees ....NA
Auditor .... Smythe Ratcliffe LLP
Stk Agt .... Computershare Trust Co
Counsel ....NA
DUNS No. ....NA

Stock- Price on:12/24/2007 ....$0.65
Stock Exchange ....OTC
Ticker Symbol ....AMGO
Outstanding Shares 23,200,000
E.P.S $0.00
Shareholders ....NA

Business: The groups principal activity is to explore minerals and natural gas. The group operates from the United States and Canada.

Primary SIC and add'l.: 1382
CIK No: 0001109504
Officers: Michael Hart/56/Dir., CEO, Pres., Sec., Treasurer, Garth Johnson/35/CFO
Directors: Michael Hart/56/Dir., CEO, Pres., Sec., Treasurer, John Campbell/75/Dir., Dan Brown/35/Dir.
Owners: Insiders/38.05%, Robert Pollock/37.07%, John Campbell/0.70%, Dan Brown/0.19%, Michael Hart/0.09%
Financial Data: Fiscal Year End:09/30   Latest Annual Data: 9/30/2006

Year	Sales	Net Income
2006	NA	-$36,000
2005	NA	-$19,000
2004	NA	-$64,000

Curr. Assets:	$1,348,000	Curr. Liab.:	$15,000		
Plant, Equip.:	NA	Total Liab.:	$15,000	Indic. Yr. Divd.:	NA
Total Assets:	$1,348,000	Net Worth:	$1,333,000	Debt/ Equity:	NA

Amgen Inc

1 Amgen Ctr. Dr., Thousand Oaks, CA, 91320; **PH:** 1-805-447-1000; **Fax:** 1-805-447-1010; http:// www.amgen.com; **Email:** investor.relations@amgen.com

General - Incorporation	DE	Stock- Price on:12/24/2007	$58.3
Employees	20,000	Stock Exchange	NDQ
Auditor	Ernst & Young LLP	Ticker Symbol	AMGN
Stk Agt	American Stock Transfer & Trust Co.	Outstanding Shares	1,160,000,000
Counsel	NA	E.P.S.	$2.59
DUNS No.	03-997-6196	Shareholders	NA

Business: The groups principle activities include discovering, developing, manufacturing and marketing human therapeutics based on advances in cellular and molecular biology. The groups products include epogen(R), aranesp(R), neulasta(R), neupogen(R), enbrel(r) and Epogen(R). In the year 2007, the group acquired Alantos and Ilypsa. The group operates from United States, Europe, Canada, Australia, and New Zealand.
Primary SIC and add'l.: 2834 2836
CIK No: 0000318154
Subsidiaries: Amgen Manufacturing, Limited, Immunex Corporation
Officers: Kevin W. Sharer/Chmn., CEO, Pres./$24,075,520.00, George Morrow/Exec. VP - Global Commercial Operations/$8,765,918.00, Roger M. Perlmutter/Exec. VP - Research, Development/$10,059,510.00, Dennis Fenton/Exec. VP/$8,267,541.00, David Scott/Sr. VP, General Counsel, Sec., Brian McNamee/Sr. VP - Human Resources, Tom Flanagan/CIO, Sr. VP, Fabrizio Bonanni/Exec. VP - Operations, Robert Bradway/CFO, Exec. VP
Directors: Kevin W. Sharer/Chmn., CEO, Pres., David Baltimore/Dir., Frank J. Biondi/Dir., Jerry D. Choate/Dir., Frederick W. Gluck/Dir., Frank C. Herringer/Dir., Gilbert S. Omenn/Dir., Judith C. Pelham/Dir., Paul J. Reason/Dir., Leonard D. Schaeffer/Dir., Vance D. Coffman/Dir.
Owners: Paul J. Reason, Insiders, Jerry D. Choate, Leonard D. Schaeffer, Gilbert S. Omenn, Frank C. Herringer, Frank J. Biondi, Dennis M. Fenton, Roger M. Perlmutter, David Baltimore, Frederick W. Gluck, George J. Morrow, Barclays Global Investors, NA./6.00%, Richard D. Nanula, Judith C. Pelham *(16 Owners included in Index)*
Financial Data: Fiscal Year End:12/31   Latest Annual Data: 12/31/2006

Year	Sales	Net Income
2006	$14,268,000,000	$2,950,000,000
2005	$12,430,000,000	$3,674,000,000
2004	$10,550,000,000	$2,363,000,000

Curr. Assets:	$11,712,000,000	Curr. Liab.:	$7,022,000,000	P/E Ratio:	22.51
Plant, Equip.:	$5,921,000,000	Total Liab.:	$14,824,000,000	Indic. Yr. Divd.:	NA
Total Assets:	$33,788,000,000	Net Worth:	$18,964,000,000	Debt/ Equity:	0.3659

AMICAS Inc

20 Guest St., Ste. 200, Boston, MA, 02135; **PH:** 1-617-779-7878; **Fax:** 1-617-779-7879; http:// www.amicas.com; **Email:** info@amicas.com

General - Incorporation	DE	Stock - Price on:12/24/2007	$3.3919
Employees	247	Stock Exchange	NDQ
Auditor	BDO Seidman LLP	Ticker Symbol	AMCS
Stk Agt	StockTrans, Inc.	Outstanding Shares	44,550,000
Counsel	NA	E.P.S.	-$0.03
DUNS No.	11-149-6121	Shareholders	NA

Business: The group's principal activity is to provide information management technology and services to healthcare practices and organizations throughout the United States. It provides it-based solutions for general medical practices and has specialty-specific products and services for practices such as radiology, anesthesiology, ophthalmology, emergency medicine, plastic surgery, and dermatology. It offers enterprise-level systems designed for large physician groups and networks. The group's range of software solutions automates the administrative, financial, and clinical information management functions for physicians and other healthcare providers. The group provides its clients with ongoing software support, implementation, training, electronic data interchange, or edi, services for patient billing and claims processing, and a variety of Web-based services. On 25-Nov-2003, the group acquired amicas inc.
Primary SIC and add'l.: 7372 7375 7376 6794
CIK No: 0001028584
Subsidiaries: PracticeWorks, Inc.
Officers: Stephen N. Kahane/Chmn., CEO/$702,853.00, Peter McClennen/COO, Pres./$731,236.00, Kang Wang/Sr. VP - Research & Development, CTO, Rodney Hawkins/VP - Product Management, Paul Merrild/VP - Marketing, John Esposito/VP - Sales, Hospital Strategy, Kurt Hammond/VP - Sales, Outpatient Strategy, Denise Mitchell/VP - Human Resources, Barry Gutwillig/VP - Strategic Partnerships, Initiatives, Kevin Burns/VP - Finance, Corporate Development, Lisa Gould/Dir. - Financial Planning, Analysis, Aine Cryts/Mgr. - Marketing Communications, Joseph Hill/Sr. VP, CFO/$560,996.00
Directors: Stephen N. Kahane/Chmn., CEO, Stephen J. Denelsky/Dir., Phillip M. Berman/Dir., David B. Shepherd/Dir., John J. Sviokla/Dir., Lisa W. Zappala/Dir.
Financial Data: Fiscal Year End:12/31   Latest Annual Data: 12/31/2006

Year	Sales	Net Income
2006	$49,437,000	-$1,024,000
2005	$52,811,000	$44,215,000
2004	$42,319,000	-$12,457,000

Curr. Assets:	$87,883,000	Curr. Liab.:	$18,919,000		
Plant, Equip.:	$1,369,000	Total Liab.:	$19,316,000	Indic. Yr. Divd.:	NA
Total Assets:	$126,871,000	Net Worth:	$107,555,000	Debt/ Equity:	NA

Amis Holdings Inc

2300 W Buckskin Rd., Pocatello, ID, 83201; **PH:** 1-208-233-4690; **Fax:** 1-208-234-6796; http:// www.amis.com

General - Incorporation	DE	Stock- Price on:12/24/2007	$12.73
Employees	2,924	Stock Exchange	NDQ
Auditor	Ernst & Young LLP	Ticker Symbol	AMIS
Stk Agt	Wells Fargo Shareowner Services	Outstanding Shares	88,640,000
Counsel	NA	E.P.S.	$0.35
DUNS No.	NA	Shareholders	NA

Business: The group's principal activities are to design, develop, manufacture and market custom and semi-custom integrated circuits of high complexity. They operate in the automotive, medical and industrial markets, which have many products with significant real world, or analog, interface requirements. The products are used in electronic system, interpreting and managing analog inputs such as light, heat, pressure, power and radio waves. They operate in three segments: integrated mixed signal products, mixed signal foundry services and structured digital products. The markets of the group are alcatel, delphi, general electric, guidant, hella, hewlett packard, johnson controls, siemens, stmicroelectronics and Texas instruments.
Primary SIC and add'l.: 3674
CIK No: 0001161963
Subsidiaries: AMI Acquisition LLC, AMI Semiconductor Asia Limited, AMI Semiconductor Belgium BVBA, AMI Semiconductor Bulgaria EEOD, AMI Semiconductor Canada Company, AMI Semiconductor Czech s.r.o., AMI Semiconductor GmbH, AMI Semiconductor Israel Ltd, AMI Semiconductor Japan Co. Ltd., AMI Semiconductor Leasing BVBA, AMI Semiconductor Netherlands BV, AMI Semiconductor Philippines, Inc., AMI Semiconductor Switzerland S.A., AMI Semiconductor U.K. Ltd, AMI Semiconductor, Inc. 17 Subsidiaries included in the Index
Officers: Christine King/Dir., CEO, Pres./$1,955,410.00, Michael O'Neill/Sr. VP - Mil, Aero, High Voltage Communications, Digital Group, Bob Klosterboer/Sr. VP - Automotive, Industrial Group, David A. Henry/46/Sr. VP/$564,105.00, Robert Tong/Sr. VP - Medical Group, Tim Forhan/Sr. VP - Quality, Darlene Gerry/Sr. VP, General Counsel, Charlie Lesko/Sr. VP - Worldwide Sales, Marketing/$608,233.00, Ted Tewksbury/COO, Pres./$712,699.00, John Kent/VP - Worldwide Technology Research & Development, Wade Olsen/Investor Relations Contact, Tamera Drake/Public, Media Relations, North America, Europe, Bruno Verbeiren/Procurement Engineer - Oudenaarde, Developmental Services, Patricia Lepez/Procurement Specialist - Oudenaarde, Developmental Services, Simon Flatt/Public, Media Relations, Europe Contact *(96 Officers included in Index)*
Directors: Christine King/Dir., CEO, Pres., Atiq S. Raza/Dir., William N. Starling/Dir., Dipanjan Deb/Dir., Paul C. Schorr/Dir., J. D. Sherman/Dir., Colin Slade/Dir., David Stanton/Dir., James A. Urry/Dir.
Owners: Insiders/27.00%, Charlie Lesko, James A. Urry/12.00%, David Stanton/12.00%, Christine King/1.00%, Colin Slade, Jon Stoner, David A. Henry, Theodore L. Tewksbury, William N. Starling, Atiq S. Raza, Dipanjan Deb/12.00%
Financial Data: Fiscal Year End:12/31   Latest Annual Data: 12/31/2006

Year	Sales	Net Income
2006	$605,600,000	$37,400,000
2005	$503,600,000	$21,700,000
2004	$517,283,000	$52,369,000

Curr. Assets:	$300,900,000	Curr. Liab.:	$121,700,000	P/E Ratio:	33.50
Plant, Equip.:	$215,900,000	Total Liab.:	$404,200,000	Indic. Yr. Divd.:	NA
Total Assets:	$786,900,000	Net Worth:	$382,700,000	Debt/ Equity:	0.7011

Amish Naturals Inc

8224 CR 245, Holmesville, OH, 44633; **PH:** 1-330-674-0998; http:// www.amishnaturals.com; **Email:** info@amishnaturals.com

General - Incorporation	NV	Stock- Price on:12/24/2007	$1.65
Employees	8	Stock Exchange	OTC
Auditor	Kelly & Co.	Ticker Symbol	AMNT
Stk Agt	NA	Outstanding Shares	NA
Counsel	NA	E.P.S.	NA
DUNS No.	NA	Shareholders	NA

Business: The groups principal activity is to provide online fashion services. The groups services include designer collections, designer biographies, interactive fashion consulting and communication, news and media, education and employment, newsletter. The group operates through five segments namely designers, manufacturers, distributors, retailers and consumers. The group operates from the United States.
Primary SIC and add'l.: 2090
CIK No: 0001179651
Officers: David Skinner/Dir., CEO, Pres., Troy Treangen/COO, Exec. VP, Carlo Varesco/Dir. - Technical, Business Advisor, Lisa Sherman/Marketing Team, Anna Kotler/Marketing Team, Stacey Dehass/Executive Chef, Dale P. Paisley/67/CFO
Directors: David Skinner/Dir., CEO, Pres., Marty Silver/Chmn., Alex Ngan/Dir., Carlo Varesco/Dir. - Technical, Business Advisor, Kenny Troyer/Dir.
Owners: Martin Silver/13.60%, Ronald Sparkman/9.28%, Dale Paisley, Troy Treangen, Shlomie Stein/8.60%, Insiders/36.70%, Carlo Varesco, David C. Skinner/20.90%, Kenneth Troyer/2.30%
Financial Data: Fiscal Year End:12/31   Latest Annual Data: 12/31/2005

Year	Sales	Net Income
2005	NA	-$10,000

Curr. Assets:	$1,000	Curr. Liab.:	$8,000		
Plant, Equip.:	NA	Total Liab.:	$8,000	Indic. Yr. Divd.:	NA
Total Assets:	$1,000	Net Worth:	-$8,000	Debt/ Equity:	NA

Amistar Corp

237 Via Vera Cruz, San Marcos, CA, 92069; **PH:** 1-760-471-1700; **Fax:** 1-760-471-9065; http:// www.amistar.com

General - Incorporation .... CA
Employees 42
Auditor .... BDO Seidman LLP
Stk Agt............ U.S. Stock Transfer Corp
Counsel............ Riordan & McKinzie
DUNS No. 06-207-4927

Stock- Price on:12/24/2007 .... NA
Stock Exchange............ OTC
Ticker Symbol............ AMTA
Outstanding Shares .... NA
E.P.S............ $0.16
Shareholders............ NA

Business: The group's principal activity is to provide industrial automation solutions primarily for electronic product manufacturers. The group designs, develops, manufactures, markets and services a variety of automatic equipment used to assemble electronic components and product identification media to printed circuit boards and other assemblies. It also provides contract-manufacturing services to companies that outsource the manufacturing of their electronic products. The products dataplace(R) 100lp and the dataplace(R) 1m can be customized, through mechanical or software modifications to meet the needs of a specific application. The group provides contract manufacturing services to original equipment manufacturers in the medical, computer peripherals, audio/video, industrial test and controls, data networking and telecommunications industries. The customers of the group include merit medical systems, inc, signet scientific, systech corp and chad therapeutics.

Primary SIC and add'l.: 5084

CIK No: 0000741559

Subsidiaries: Delivery Networks Corporation, Distributed Delivery Networks

Officers: William K. Holmes/CEO, Pres., Stuart C. Baker/Chmn., Pres., Daniel C. Finn/VP, GM, Harry A. Munn/VP - Sales, Marketing, William W. Holl/Dir., Sec., Treasurer, Gregory D. Leiser/VP - Finance, CFO

Directors: Stuart C. Baker/Chmn., Pres., Sanford B. Ehrlich/Dir., Mark D. Fowler/Dir., William W. Holl/Dir., Sec., Treasurer, Gordon S. Marshall/Dir., Howard C. White/Dir.

Financial Data: **Fiscal Year End:**12/31 **Latest Annual Data:** 12/31/2005

Year	Sales	Net Income
2005	$3,418,000	-$4,158,000
2004	$10,882,000	-$3,370,000
2003	$12,083,000	-$349,000

Curr. Assets:	$4,842,000	**Curr. Liab.:**	$2,462,000		
Plant, Equip.:	$98,000	**Total Liab.:**	$5,881,000	**Indic. Yr. Divd.:**	NA
Total Assets:	$5,397,000	**Net Worth:**	-$483,000	**Debt/ Equity:**	NA

Amkor Technology Inc

1900 S Price Rd., Chandler, AZ, 85248; **PH:** 1-480-821-5000; **Fax:** 1-480-821-8276; **http://** www.amkor.com

General - Incorporation .... DE
Employees 22,700
Auditor .... PricewaterhouseCoopers LLP
Stk Agt..... Computershare Investor Services LLC
Counsel............ Jerry Allison
DUNS No. 05-139-6653

Stock- Price on:12/24/2007 .... $14.26
Stock Exchange............ NDQ
Ticker Symbol............ AMKR
Outstanding Shares 179,730,000
E.P.S............ $0.95
Shareholders............ NA

Business: The groups principle activity is to provide sub-contract semiconductor packaging and test services. The groups products include PSvfBGA, TapeArray(R) (TABGA), Flip Chip CSP and SuperBGA(R). The groups services include die processing, wafer bumping and hermetic services. The group operates from United States.

Primary SIC and add'l.: 3674

CIK No: 0001047127

Subsidiaries: Amkor Assembly & Test (Shanghai) Co., Ltd., Amkor International Holdings, Amkor Iwate Company, Ltd., Amkor Technology Euroservices, S.A.R.L., Amkor Technology Greater China, Ltd., Amkor Technology Hong Kong Limited, Amkor Technology Japan, K.K., Amkor Technology Korea, Inc., Amkor Technology Limited, Amkor Technology Philippines, Amkor Technology Singapore Pte. Ltd., Amkor Technology Taiwan Ltd., Amkor Wafer Fabrication Services, S.A.R.L., Amkor Worldwide Services LLC, Guardian Assets, Inc. 21 Subsidiaries included in the Index

Officers: James Kim/Chmn., CEO/$2,304,690.00, Mike Lamble/Corporate VP - Worldwide Sales, Jerry Allison/VP, Assist. Corporate Counsel, Kyu-Hyun Kim/59/Pres. - Amkor Technology Korea/$868,366.00, Jim Fusaro/Corporate VP - Product Management, Oleg Khaykin/COO, Exec. VP/$921,742.00, Kenneth T. Joyce/Exec. VP - Administration, CFO, Jooho Kim/Corporate VP - ICS, James M. Fusaro/Corporate VP - Product Management/$759,121.00, Gil C. Tily/Corporate VP, General Counsel

Directors: James Kim/Chmn., CEO, Roger Carolin/Dir., John F. Osborne/Dir., John T. Kim/Dir., Constantine N. Papadakis/61/Dir., Winston J. Churchill/65/Dir., James W. Zug/Dir.

Owners: Kenneth T. Joyce, Oleg Khaykin, James M. Fusaro, Constantine N. Papadakis, Gregory K. Hinckley, KyuHyun Kim, Roger A. Carolin, James J. Kim Family Control Group/44.92%, John T. Kim/16.27%, Insiders/30.15%, Winston J. Churchill, James W. Zug, James J. Kim/14.52%, FMR Corp./14.42%

Financial Data: **Fiscal Year End:**12/31 **Latest Annual Data:** 12/31/2006

Year	Sales	Net Income
2006	$2,728,560,000	$170,084,000
2005	$2,099,949,000	-$137,235,000
2004	$1,901,279,000	-$37,536,000

Curr. Assets:	$837,857,000	**Curr. Liab.:**	$622,762,000	**P/E Ratio:**	15.67
Plant, Equip.:	$1,443,603,000	**Total Liab.:**	$2,642,741,000	**Indic. Yr. Divd.:**	NA
Total Assets:	$3,041,264,000	**Net Worth:**	$393,920,000	**Debt/ Equity:**	3.9265

AML Communications Inc

1000 Ave.nida Acaso, Camarillo, CA, 93012; **PH:** 1-805-388-1345; **Fax:** 1-805-484-2191; **http://** www.amlj.com; **Email:** sales@amlj.com

General - Incorporation .... DE
Employees 71
Auditor .... Kabani & Co, Inc
Stk Agt...... American Stock Transfer & Trust Co.
Counsel............ Guth Christopher
DUNS No. 16-139-3509

Stock- Price on:12/24/2007 .... $1.4
Stock Exchange............ OTC
Ticker Symbol............ AMLJ
Outstanding Shares 10,260,000
E.P.S............ $0.15
Shareholders............ NA

Business: The group's principal activity is to design, manufacture and market amplifiers for a variety of frequency ranges and transmission protocols. The group's defense industry products are used in communications equipment integrated into electronic systems for tactical aircraft, ships, ground systems and missile systems. Wireless products consist of a range of low noise and power amplifiers serving the wireless, pcs, two-way messaging market as well as cellular coverage enhancement amplifiers. The cellular and pcs products are low noise amplifiers used in the amplification of analog and digital communications formats. The products are sold to customers in the United States, South America, western Europe, Canada, Israel and Russia. The major customers include raytheon, boeing, lockheed sanders and rockwell, itt and l3-communications. On 18-Jun-2004, the group acquired microwave power, inc.

Primary SIC and add'l.: 3663

CIK No: 0001003640

Subsidiaries: Microwave Power, Inc.

Officers: Jacob Inbar/Chmn., CEO, Pres./$182,200.00, Tibby Mazilu/Dir., Exec. VP - Engineering/$147,400.00, Edwin J. McAvoy/Dir., Exec. VP - Sales, Marketing, Sec./$151,114.00, Heera Lee/Dir. - Finance, Principal Accounting Officer

Directors: Jacob Inbar/Chmn., CEO, Pres., David A. Derby/Dir., Richard W. Flatow/Dir., Gerald M. Starek/Dir., Tibby Mazilu/Dir., Exec. VP - Engineering, Edwin J. McAvoy/Dir., Exec. VP - Sales, Marketing, Sec.

Owners: Tiberiu Mazilu/10.09%, Gerald M. Starek/3.13%, Jacob Inbar/16.46%, Edwin J. McAvoy/6.80%, Richard W. Flatow/1.54%, Insiders/34.20%

Financial Data: **Fiscal Year End:**03/31 **Latest Annual Data:** 03/31/2007

Year	Sales	Net Income
2007	$8,854,000	$1,559,000
2006	$9,466,000	$2,245,000
2005	$8,650,000	$935,000

Curr. Assets:	$5,297,000	**Curr. Liab.:**	$1,001,000	**P/E Ratio:**	10.00
Plant, Equip.:	$1,681,000	**Total Liab.:**	$1,630,000	**Indic. Yr. Divd.:**	NA
Total Assets:	$9,924,000	**Net Worth:**	$8,294,000	**Debt/ Equity:**	0.0735

AmMex Gold Mining Corp

346 WAve.RLEY St., Ottawa, ON, K2P 0W5; **PH:** 1-613-226-7883; **Fax:** 1-613-226-5106; **http://** www.ammexgoldmining.com; **Email:** info@ammexgoldmining.com

General - Incorporation .... NV
Employees .... NA
Auditor .... Cinnamon Jang Willoughby & Co.
Stk Agt .... Corporate Stock Transfer, Inc.
Counsel............ NA
DUNS No. .... NA

Stock- Price on:12/24/2007 .... $0.4
Stock Exchange............ OTC
Ticker Symbol............ AMXG
Outstanding Shares .... NA
E.P.S............ NA
Shareholders............ NA

Business: The groups principal activity is to explore minerals and natural gas. In the year 2006, the group acquired Minera Jeronimo S.A. The group operates from the United States and Canada.

Primary SIC and add'l.: 1040

CIK No: 0001273507

Subsidiaries: Oasis Wireless Inc

Officers: Christopher Crupi/Dir., CEO, Pres., Bill Reed/VP - Exploration, North America, Charles William Reed/66/VP, Dir., Lucie Letellier/47/CFO, Treasurer

Directors: Christopher Crupi/Dir., CEO, Pres., Charles William Reed/66/VP, Dir.

Owners: Christopher Crupi/9.00%, Charles Reed/4.70%

Financial Data: **Fiscal Year End:**06/30 **Latest Annual Data:** 06/30/2007

Year	Sales	Net Income
2007	$3,000	-$2,035,000
2006	NA	-$60,000

Curr. Assets:	$0	**Curr. Liab.:**	$10,000		
Plant, Equip.:	NA	**Total Liab.:**	$10,000	**Indic. Yr. Divd.:**	NA
Total Assets:	$0	**Net Worth:**	-$9,000	**Debt/ Equity:**	NA

AMN Healthcare Inc

12400 High Bluff Dr., Ste. 100, San Diego, CA, 92130; **PH:** 1-866-871-8519; **Fax:** 1-800-282-0328; **http://** www.amnhealthcare.com; **Email:** staffing@amnhealthcare.com

General - Incorporation .... DE
Employees 2,000
Auditor .... KPMG LLP
Stk Agt ..... American Stock Transfer & Trust Co.
Counsel............ Paul, Wharton & Garrison LLP
DUNS No. .... NA

Stock- Price on:12/24/2007 .... $22.22
Stock Exchange............ NYSE
Ticker Symbol............ AHS
Outstanding Shares 34,690,000
E.P.S............ $1.07
Shareholders............ NA

Business: The group's principal activity is to provide temporary healthcare staffing and travel nurse staffing services. The group's services are marketed to 2 distinct customer bases namely: temporary healthcare professionals and hospital and healthcare facility clients. The group recruits healthcare professionals comprising of nurses, technicians and technologists. The healthcare professionals are placed at hospitals and healthcare facilities, on temporary assignments, throughout the United States. The group provides the temporary healthcare professionals with benefits package, including free or subsidized housing, travel reimbursement, professional development opportunities, a 401(k) plan and health insurance. The group has seven recruitment brands that include American mobile healthcare, medical express, nursesrx, preferred healthcare staffing, hrmc, thera tech staffing and o'grady-peyton international.

Primary SIC and add'l.: 8099 8059 7361

CIK No: 0001142750

Subsidiaries: AMN Healthcare, Inc., AMN Services, Inc., AMN Staffing Services, Inc., International Healthcare Recruiters, Inc., Med Travelers, Inc., Med Travelers, LLC, Merritt, Hawkins& Associates, MHA Allied Consulting, Inc., OGrady-Peyton International (Australia) (Pty), Inc., OGrady-Peyton International (Europe) Limited, OGrady-Peyton International (USA), Inc., OGrady-PeytonInternational(SA)(Proprietary)Limited, OGradyPeytonInternationalRecruitmentU.K.Limited, RN Demand, Inc., Staff Care, Inc. 16 Subsidiaries included in the Index

Officers: Susan R. Nowakowski/43/Dir., CEO, Pres./$2,329,466.00, Marcia R. Faller/Chief Nursing Officer, Exec. VP - Operations, Bruce R. Carothers/CTO, Sr. VP, Kenneth R. Gowen/Sr. VP - Human Resources, David C. Dreyer/CFO, Chief Accounting Officer, Treasurer/$1,173,457.00, Denise L. Jackson/General Counsel, Sr. VP, Sec./$802,648.00, Beth L. MacHado/Sr. VP - Recruitment, Travel Nurse Staffing, Stephen M. Wehn/Sr. VP - Corporate Development, Richard A. Cassidy/Sr. VP - Facility Client Services, Travel Nurse Staffing, Ralph S. Henderson/Pres. - Nurse Staffing

Directors: Susan R. Nowakowski/43/Dir., CEO, Pres., Steven C. Francis/53/Chmn., Co - Founder, Kenneth F. Yontz/Dir., Andrew M. Stern/59/Dir., Douglas D. Wheat/57/Dir., William F. Miller/58/Dir., Jeffrey R. Harris/53/Dir., Paul E. Weaver/62/Dir.

Owners: Jeffrey R. Harris, Steven C. Francis/1.20%, Eastbourne Capital Management L.L.C/10.60%, Douglas D. Wheat, Denise L. Jackson, FMR Corp./9.00%, Insiders/3.60%, David C. Dreyer, William F. Miller, Andrew M. Stern, Susan R. Nowakowski, Kenneth F. Yontz

Financial Data: Fiscal Year End:12/31 Latest Annual Data: 06/30/2007

Year	Sales	Net Income
2007	NA	NA
2006	$1,081,703,000	$35,091,000
2005	$705,843,000	$22,234,000

Curr. Assets:	$235,855,000	Curr. Liab.:	$120,967,000	P/E Ratio:	22.00
Plant, Equip.:	$23,236,000	Total Liab.:	$377,635,000	Indic. Yr. Divd.:	NA
Total Assets:	$622,181,000	Net Worth:	$244,546,000	Debt/ Equity:	0.6009

AMP Productions Inc

500 Wood Forest Ct, Marietta, GA, 30066; *PH:* 1-770-794-1412;
http:// americanmediaproductions.com; *Email:* info@americanmediaproductions.com

General - Incorporation		Stock - Price on:12/24/2007	$0.51
Employees	NA	Stock Exchange	OTC
Auditor	NA	Ticker Symbol	AMPC
Stk Agt	Pacific Stock Transfer Company	Outstanding Shares	NA
Counsel	NA	E.P.S	NA
DUNS No.	NA	Shareholders	NA

Business: The groups principal activity is to provide television news, videotape location production personnel and equipment. The group operates from the United States.

Primary SIC and add'l.: 8631

CIK No: 0001116479

Financial Data: Fiscal Year End:12/31 Latest Annual Data: 03/31/2007

Year	Sales	Net Income
2007	NA	-$17,000
2006	NA	-$27,000

Curr. Assets:	$84,000	Curr. Liab.:	$1,000		
Plant, Equip.:	$7,000	Total Liab.:	$1,000	Indic. Yr. Divd.:	NA
Total Assets:	$91,000	Net Worth:	$90,000	Debt/ Equity:	NA

Ampal American Israel Corp

111 Arlozorov St., Tel Aviv, 62098; *PH:* 972-8664478636; *http://* www.ampal.com;
Email: careers@ampal.com

General - Incorporation	NY	Stock - Price on:12/24/2007	$5.96
Employees	293	Stock Exchange	NDQ
Auditor	Kesselman & Kesselman	Ticker Symbol	AMPL
Stk Agt	Mellon Investor Services LLC	Outstanding Shares	49,360,000
Counsel	Kronish, Lieb, Weiner & Hellman	E.P.S	-$0.49
DUNS No.	04-436-4560	Shareholders	NA

Business: The group's principal activity is to acquire interests in businesses located in the state of Israel or that are Israel-related. The group invests in companies that are engaged in high technology and communications, leisure-time, real estate, capital markets, energy distribution and industry. The group operates through three segments namely: finance, real estate and leisure time.

Primary SIC and add'l.: 6029 6799 6159 7011 6552

CIK No: 0000731859

Subsidiaries: AD 120 Hod Hasharon Limited Partnership, AD 120 Managements - Hod Hasharon (1966) Ltd., AD 120 Ramat Hachayal (Management) Ltd., AD 120 Ramat Hachayal Limited Partnership, Am-Hal Ltd., Ampal (Israel) Ltd., Ampal Communication Holdings Ltd., Ampal Communication LP, Ampal Communications Inc., Ampal Development (Israel) Ltd., Ampal Energy Ltd., Ampal Enterprises Ltd., Ampal Financial Services Ltd., Ampal Holdings (1991) Ltd., Ampal Industries (Israel) Ltd. 25 Subsidiaries included in the Index

Officers: Yosef A. Maiman/Chmn., CEO, Pres./$1,716,323.00, Giora Bar-Nir/VP - Accounting, Controller/$269,882.00, Irit Eluz/CFO, VP - Finance, Treasurer/$1,243,133.00, Amit Mantsur/VP - Investments/$280,114.00, Yoram Firon/VP - Investments - Corporate Affairs/$567,897.00

Directors: Yosef A. Maiman/Chmn., CEO, Pres.

Owners: Yoav Maiman/49.40%, Ohad Maiman/49.40%, Leo Malamud, Yosef A. Maiman/57.40%, Noa Maiman/49.40%, Di-Rapallo Holdings Ltd/32.70%, Amit Mantsur, Nimrod Novik, Giora Bar-Nir, Irit Eluz, Yehuda Karni, Di-Rapallo Holdings Ltd./16.70%, Menahem Morag, Yoram Firon, Joseph Yerushalmi *(20 Owners included in Index)*

Financial Data: Fiscal Year End:12/31 Latest Annual Data: 12/31/2006

Year	Sales	Net Income
2006	$23,949,000	-$7,087,000
2005	$30,530,000	-$5,958,000
2004	$31,587,000	-$18,385,000

Curr. Assets:	$48,883,000	Curr. Liab.:	$54,979,000		
Plant, Equip.:	$71,881,000	Total Liab.:	$191,568,000	Indic. Yr. Divd.:	NA
Total Assets:	$401,683,000	Net Worth:	$208,813,000	Debt/ Equity:	0.6016

Ampco Pittsburgh Corp

600 Grant St., Ste. 4600, Pittsburgh, PA, 15219; *PH:* 1-412-456-4400; *Fax:* 1-412-456-4404;
http:// www.ampcopgh.com

General - Incorporation	PA	Stock - Price on:12/24/2007	$38.78
Employees	1,324	Stock Exchange	NYSE
Auditor	Deloitte & Touche LLP	Ticker Symbol	AP
Stk Agt	Mellon Investor Services LLC	Outstanding Shares	9,910,000
Counsel	NA	E.P.S	$2.67
DUNS No.	00-432-7862	Shareholders	NA

Business: The group's principal activities are carried out by two business segments: forged and cast rolls and air and liquid processing. Forged and cast rolls segment produces forged hardened steel rolls and cast rolls for the producers of steel, aluminium and other metals. Air and liquid processing segment produces plate finned heat exchange coils and air handling systems for the commercial and industrial construction, process and utility industries. It also manufactures refrigeration centrifugal pumps for the power generation and marine defence industries. Manufacturing plants are located in Pennsylvania, Virginia, New York, and the United Kingdom.

Primary SIC and add'l.: 3561 3312 5085

CIK No: 0000006176

Subsidiaries: Aerofin Corporation, Ampco UES Sub, Inc., Ampco-Pittsburgh Securities III Corporation, Ampco-Pittsburgh Securities V Corporation, Buffalo Air Handling Company, Buffalo Pumps, Inc., The Davy Roll Company Limited, Union Electric Steel (UK) Limited, Union Electric Steel B.V.B.A., Union Electric Steel Corporation

Officers: Robert A. Paul/Chmn., CEO/$835,080.00, Linda Sismondo/Dir. - Pension, Risk Management, Ernest G. Siddons/Pres./$809,257.00, Marliss D. Johnson/43/VP, Controller, Treasurer, Principal Financial Officer/$185,366.00, Terrence W. Kenny/Group VP/$290,155.00, Robert F. Schultz/VP - Industrial Relations, Sr. Counsel/$343,658.00, Dee Ann Johnson/VP, Controller, Treasurer, Rose Hoover/VP - Administration, Corp. Sec./$248,589.00

Directors: Robert A. Paul/Chmn., CEO, Louis Berkman/99/Chmn. Emeritus, Leonard M. Carroll/65/Dir., Robert J. Appel/76/Dir., William D. Eberle/83/Dir., Paul A. Gould/62/Dir., William K. Lieberman/60/Dir., Laurence E. Paul/43/Dir., Stephen E. Paul/40/Dir., Carl H. Pforzheimer/71/Dir.

Owners: Robert J. Appel, William D. Eberle, Terrence W. Kenny/0.13%, Dee Ann Johnson/0.13%, Leonard M. Carroll, Laurence E. Paul, Dimensional Fund Advisors LP/5.26%, Robert A. Paul/1.81%, Louis Berkman/27.46%, Carl H. Pforzheimer, Gabelli Funds, Inc./16.58%, Robert F. Schultz/0.15%, Paul A. Gould, Van Den Berg Management/8.24%, Insiders/30.46% *(20 Owners included in Index)*

Financial Data: Fiscal Year End:12/31 Latest Annual Data: 12/31/2006

Year	Sales	Net Income
2006	$301,780,000	$16,635,000
2005	$246,999,000	$15,036,000
2004	$202,861,000	-$2,599,000

Curr. Assets:	$186,980,000	Curr. Liab.:	$74,962,000		
Plant, Equip.:	$68,593,000	Total Liab.:	$241,007,000	Indic. Yr. Divd.:	$0.600
Total Assets:	$381,211,000	Net Worth:	$140,204,000	Debt/ Equity:	NA

Ampex Corp

1228 Douglas Ave., Redwood City, CA, 94063; *PH:* 1-650-367-2011; *Fax:* 1-650-367-4669;
http:// www.ampex.com; *Email:* info@ampex.com

General - Incorporation	DE	Stock - Price on:12/24/2007	$13.932
Employees	121	Stock Exchange	NDQ
Auditor	BDO Seidman LLP	Ticker Symbol	AMPX
Stk Agt	American Stock Transfer & Trust Co.	Outstanding Shares	3,870,000
Counsel	NA	E.P.S	$0.11
DUNS No.	79-348-5681	Shareholders	NA

Business: The group's principle activities are innovation and licensing of visual information technology. The group has developed substantial proprietary technology relating to the electronic storage, processing and retrieval of data, particularly images. The group currently holds 600 patents and patent applications covering digital image processing, data compression and recording technologies. Through its wholly-owned subsidiary, ampex data systems corporation (data systems), the group incorporates this technology in the design and manufacture of its products. The products are used in the digital recording, archiving and rapid restore/backup applications. The group also leverages its investment in research and development through its corporate licensing division that licenses ampex patents to manufacturers of consumer electronics products. The group operate a total of six sales offices, including four in the United States, one in Japan and one in the United Kingdom. The group's quarterly revenue for September 2007 was 9.39 millions of USD.

Primary SIC and add'l.: 9999 3572 7375 6794 3695 3663

CIK No: 0000887433

Subsidiaries: AFC Holdings Corporation, Ampex Cintas Magneticas, S.A., Ampex Data International Corporation, Ampex Data Systems Corporation, Ampex de Colombia, S.A., Ampex de Mexico, S.A de C.V. , Ampex do Brasil Electronica Ltd., Ampex Europa GmbH, Ampex Finance Corporation, Ampex Great Britain Limited, Ampex Holdings Corporation, Ampex International Sales Corporation, Ampex Japan Ltd., Ampex S.A.

Officers: Gordon D. Strickland/Chmn., CEO, Pres., Sharon M. Genberg/VP, Robert L. Atchison/VP/$694,218.00, Joel D. Talcott/VP, Sec./$337,829.00, Ramon C. Venema/VP, Assist. Treasurer, Assist. Sec./$239,299.00, Craig L. McKibben/57/Dir., CFO, VP, Treasurer/$354,214.00, Karen Dexter/Dir. - Investor Relations

Directors: Gordon D. Strickland/Chmn., CEO, Pres., Alain C. Briancon/Dir., Charles W. Dyke/Dir., Ned S. Goldstein/Dir., Douglas T. McClure/55/Dir., Peter Slusser/78/Dir., William A. Stoltzfus/Dir., Craig L. McKibben/57/Dir., CFO, VP, Treasurer

Owners: Peter Slusser, William A. Stoltzfus, Douglas T. McClure

Financial Data: Fiscal Year End:12/31 Latest Annual Data: 12/31/2006

Year	Sales	Net Income
2006	$35,921,000	-$3,948,000
2005	$53,154,000	$6,727,000
2004	$101,451,000	$46,362,000

Curr. Assets:	$25,622,000	Curr. Liab.:	$16,375,000	P/E Ratio:	137.94
Plant, Equip.:	$923,000	Total Liab.:	$131,320,000	Indic. Yr. Divd.:	NA
Total Assets:	$26,917,000	Net Worth:	-$104,403,000	Debt/ Equity:	NA

Amphenol Corp

358 Hall Ave., Wallingford, CT, 06492; *PH:* 1-203-265-8900; *Fax:* 1-203-265-8516;
http:// www.amphenol.com

General - Incorporation	DE	Stock - Price on:12/24/2007	$35.82
Employees	25,600	Stock Exchange	NYSE
Auditor	Deloitte & Touche LLP	Ticker Symbol	APH
Stk Agt	EquiServe Trust Co N.A	Outstanding Shares	178,920,000
Counsel	NA	E.P.S	$1.68
DUNS No.	17-722-0647	Shareholders	NA

Business: The groups principle activity is to manufacture interconnect products. The groups products include cable and pipe supports, backplane interconnect and flexible circuit interconnects. The group operates from United States.

Primary SIC and add'l.: 3678 3357

CIK No: 0000820313

Subsidiaries: Advanced Circuit Technology,Inc., Amphenol (Changzhou) Connector Systems Co. Ltd., Amphenol Aerospace France,Inc., Amphenol Air LB GmbH, Amphenol Air LB International Development S.A., Amphenol Air LB North America,Inc., Amphenol Air LB S.A. S., Amphenol Antel,Inc., Amphenol Assembletech (Xiamen) Co., Ltd., Amphenol Australia Pty Ltd., Amphenol Benelux B.V., Amphenol Borg Limited, Amphenol Borg Pension Trustees Ltd., Amphenol Canada Corp., Amphenol Commercial and Industrial UK, Limited 25 Subsidiaries included in the Index

Officers: Martin H. Loeffler/Chmn., CEO, Pres./$5,207,503.00, Gary A. Anderson/57/Sr. VP, Group GM - Aerospace, Industrial Operations Division/$1,340,000.00, Zachary W. Raley/39/VP, Group GM - Worldwide RF, Microwave Products Division, Stephan D. Memmen/38/VP - Mobile Consumer Products Division, Paul H. Jona/47/VP - Commercial Products Division, Craig A. Lampo/38/VP, Controller, Udo Naujoks/57/Sr. VP - Amphenol, Tuchel Electronics Division, Group GM - Amphenol, Tuchel Electronics Division, Luc Walter/49/Sr. VP, Group GM - European Military, Aerospace Operations Division/$995,298.00, Diana Reardon/CFO, Sr. VP/$1,429,037.00, Edward C. Wetmore/51/VP, Sec., General Counsel, Jamie A. Fraser/45/Sr. VP, Group GM - Interconnect Systems Division, Jerome F. Monteith/58/VP - Human Resources, Adam R. Norwitt/38/Pres., Chief Operating Office

Directors: Martin H. Loeffler/Chmn., CEO, Pres., Andrew E. Lietz/69/Dir., Ronald P. Badie/65/Dir., Dean H. Secord/72/Dir., Edward G. Jepsen/64/Dir., John R. Lord/64/Dir., Stanley L. Clark/64/Dir.

Owners: John R. Lord, Timothy F. Cohane, Andrew E. Lietz, Edward G. Jepsen, Dean H. Secord, Luc Walter, Diana G. Reardon, Ronald P. Badie, Insiders/3.44%, Stanley L. Clark, Gary A. Anderson, Martin H. Loeffler/1.85%

Financial Data: Fiscal Year End:12/31 Latest Annual Data: 12/31/2006

Year	Sales	Net Income
2006	$2,471,430,000	$255,691,000
2005	$1,808,147,000	$206,339,000
2004	$1,530,446,000	$163,311,000

Curr. Assets:	$934,605,000	Curr. Liab.:	$447,659,000	P/E Ratio:	21.32
Plant, Equip.:	$274,143,000	Total Liab.:	$1,292,403,000	Indic. Yr. Divd.:	$0.060
Total Assets:	$2,195,397,000	Net Worth:	$902,994,000	Debt/ Equity:	0.7033

AMR Corp

4333 Amon Carter Blvd., Fort Worth, TX, 76155; *PH:* 1-817-963-1234; *Fax:* 1-817-967-9641; *http://* www.aa.com; *Email:* info@amstock.com

General		Stock	
Incorporation	DE	Price on:12/24/2007	$24.6
Employees	NA	Stock Exchange	NYSE
Auditor	Ernst & Young LLP	Ticker Symbol	AMR
Stk Agt	American Stock Transfer & Trust Co.	Outstanding Shares	NA
Counsel	NA	E.P.S.	NA
DUNS No.	07-256-0154	Shareholders	NA

Business: The group operates through subsidiary whose principle activity is to provide airline services. The group's products include trip insurance,air line credit cards and luggage tags. The group operates from United States.

Primary SIC and add'l.: 4581 4512 4111 4513

CIK No: 0000006201

Subsidiaries: 50/50 Aa/rolls-royce, AA 2002 ClassC Certificate Corporation, AA 2002 ClassD Certificate Corporation, Aa 2003-1 Classe Certificate Corporation, Aa 2003-1 Classd Certificate Corporation, Aa 2004-1 Classb Note Corporation, Aa 2005-1 Classc Note Corporation, AA Real Estate Holding GP LLC, AA Real Estate Holding LP, AAV Tours LLC, Admirals Club, Inc. (Massachusetts only), Aero Perlas, Aerodespachos Colombia, S.A., AEROSAN Airport Services S.A., Aerosan S.a. 41 Subsidiaries included in the Index

Officers: Gerard J. Arpey/Chmn., CEO, Pres./$10,201,060.00, Peter M. Bowler/CEO, Pres. - American Eagle Airlines, Inc, William F. Quinn/Chmn., CEO - American Beacon Advisors, Inc, Thomas W. Horton/CFO, Exec. VP/$7,841,134.00, Robert W. Reding/Exec. VP/$4,525,192.00, Kenneth W. Wimberly/Corp. Sec., Jeffrey J. Brundage/Sr. VP - Human Resources, American Airlines, David C. Cush/Sr. VP - Global Sales, American Airlines, Peter J. Dolara/Sr. VP - Miami, Caribbean, Latin America, American Airlines, Monte E. Ford/Sr. VP - Information Technology, CIO - American Airlines, Isabella D. Goren/Sr. VP - Customer, Relationship Marketing, Reservations, American Airlines, Henry C. Joyner/Sr. VP - Planning, American Airlines, Carmine J. Romano/Sr. VP - Maintenance, Engineering, American Airlines, William K. Ris/Sr. VP - Government Affairs, American Airlines, Timothy J. Ahern/VP - Airport Services, American Airlines *(46 Officers included in Index)*

Directors: Gerard J. Arpey/Chmn., CEO, Pres., Matthew K. Rose/48/Dir., Edward A. Brennan/Dir., John W. Bachmann/Dir., David L. Boren/Dir., Armando M. Codina/Dir., Earl G. Graves/Dir., Ann M. Korologos/Dir., Michael A. Miles/Dir., Philip J. Purcell/Dir., Ray M. Robinson/Dir., Judith Rodin/Dir., Roger T. Staubach/Dir.

Owners: Michael A. Miles, Gary F. Kennedy, FL Group hf./5.35%, Jeffrey L. Gendell/7.45%, David L. Boren, Robert W. Reding, Matthew K. Rose, John W. Bachmann, Gerard J. Arpey, Philip J. Purcell, Edward A. Brennan, Ray M. Robinson, Thomas W. Horton, Roger T. Staubach, Daniel P. Garton *(20 Owners included in Index)*

AmREIT Inc

8 Greenway Plz., Ste. 1000, Houston, TX, 77046; *PH:* 1-713-850-1400; *Fax:* 1-713-850-0498; *http://* www.amreit.com

General		Stock	
Incorporation	TX	Price on:12/24/2007	$8.1
Employees	64	Stock Exchange	AMEX
Auditor	KPMG LLP	Ticker Symbol	AMY
Stk Agt	Wells Fargo Bank, N.A.	Outstanding Shares	6,410,000
Counsel	NA	E.P.S.	-$0.6
DUNS No.	NA	Shareholders	NA

Business: The groups principle activities include acquiring, developing and operating shopping centers and pipelines. The group operates through four segments namely, portfolio, real estate development, securities operations and merchant development funds. The group operates from the United States. The groups quarterly revenue for September 2007 was 12.79 millions of USD.

Primary SIC and add'l.: 6798

CIK No: 0000913957

Subsidiaries: AmREIT Plaza in the Park, LP, AmREIT Realty Investment Corporation, AmREIT Securities Company, AmREIT Uptown Park, LP, Mac Arthur Park, LP

Officers: Kerr H. Taylor/Chmn., CEO/$810,561.00, Jason Lax/VP - Construction Management, Max Shilstone/VP - Property Management, Kristen Barker/VP - Leasing, Horst Hendreks/VP - Brokerage, Phil P. Moss/VP - Leasing, Anne Newtown/General Counsel, Jeff Noblin/VP - Western Regional Sales, Rod Curtis/VP - Midwest Regional Sales, Gary Callahan/VP - Eastern Regional Sales, Kent W. Maxey/Sr. Property Mgr., Chris Nichols/Real Estate Construction Mgr., Craig Vance/Property Management Mgr., Michael Hale/VP - Real Estate Leasing, Trey Vick/Project Mgr. - Construction *(31 Officers included in Index)*

Directors: Kerr H. Taylor/Chmn., CEO, Robert S. Cartwright/Dir., Steven G. Dawson/Dir., H. L. Rush/Dir., Philip Taggart/Dir., Stephen Hefner/VP, MD - Dallas Region

Owners: Insiders/5.75%, Chad C. Braun, Steven G. Dawson, Kerr H. Taylor/4.97%, Robert S. Cartwright, Philip Taggart, H. L. Rush

Financial Data: Fiscal Year End:12/31 Latest Annual Data: 12/31/2006

Year	Sales	Net Income
2006	$59,342,000	$7,563,000
2005	$34,686,000	$10,126,000
2004	$21,759,000	$588,000

Curr. Assets:	$11,182,000	Curr. Liab.:	$9,830,000		
Plant, Equip.:	$263,906,000	Total Liab.:	$159,380,000	Indic. Yr. Divd.:	$0.500
Total Assets:	$328,430,000	Net Worth:	$169,050,000	Debt/ Equity:	0.9914

AMREP Corp

300 Alexander Pk., Ste. 204, Princeton, NJ, 08540; *PH:* 1-609-716-8200; *Fax:* 1-609-716-8255; *http://* amrepcorp.com

General		Stock	
Incorporation	OK	Price on:12/24/2007	$48.15
Employees	1,295	Stock Exchange	NYSE
Auditor	McGladrey & Pullen LLP	Ticker Symbol	AXR
Stk Agt	Bank of New York	Outstanding Shares	6,650,000
Counsel	McElroy Deutsch Mulaney & Crp LLP	E.P.S.	$3.50
DUNS No.	00-377-8412	Shareholders	NA

Business: The group's principal activities are to develop real estate, build single-family homes and provide fulfillment services and magazine distribution. The real estate business is operated thorough amrep southwest inc. And the fulfillment services and magazine distribution businesses are operated through kable news company, inc. And kable distribution services, inc. As on 30-Apr-2004, the group owned one residential property of 160 acres and one property of approximately 10 acres for commercial use. Fulfillment and magazine distribution business provides fulfillment and related services for publishers and other customers and distributes periodicals nationally and in Canada and other foreign countries. The fulfillment services include magazine subscription fulfillment services, list services and product fulfillment services. The group operates solely in domestic market.

Primary SIC and add'l.: 6552 5192

CIK No: 0000006207

Subsidiaries: AMREP Southwest Inc

Officers: Michael P. Duloc/Pres., CEO - Kable Media Services, Inc/$372,587.00, Peter M. Pizza/CFO, VP, Treasurer/$199,459.00, James Wall/Dir., Sr. VP/$391,315.00, Samuel N. Seidman/Dir., Pres., Irving Needleman/VP, General Counsel/$91,670.00, John F. Meneough/Exec. VP - Fulfillment Services, Kable/$98,648.00

Directors: Edward B. Cloues/Chmn., Nicholas G. Karabots/Vice Chmn., Albert V. Russo/Dir., Jonathan B. Weller/Dir., Lonnie A. Coombs/Dir., James Wall/Dir., Sr. VP, Samuel N. Seidman/Dir., Pres.

Owners: James Wall, Albert V. Russo/16.80%, Lonnie A. Coombs, Michael P. Duloc, Insiders/71.20%, Edward B. Cloues, Samuel N. Seidman, Goldman Sachs Asset Management, L.P./6.90%, Nicholas G. Karabots/54.00%

Financial Data: Fiscal Year End:04/30 Latest Annual Data: 4/30/2006

Year	Sales	Net Income
2006	$148,296,000	$26,050,000
2005	$134,506,000	$15,525,000
2004	$131,107,000	$11,677,000

Curr. Assets:	$98,614,000	Curr. Liab.:	$48,837,000		
Plant, Equip.:	$58,412,000	Total Liab.:	$70,071,000	Indic. Yr. Divd.:	NA
Total Assets:	$189,041,000	Net Worth:	$118,970,000	Debt/ Equity:	0.2746

AMS Health Sciences Inc

711 NE 39th St., Oklahoma City, OK, 73105; *PH:* 1-405-842-0131; *Fax:* 1-405-843-4935; *http://* www.amsonline.com; *Email:* info@amsmainline.com

General		Stock	
Incorporation	OK	Price on:12/24/2007	$0.45
Employees	25	Stock Exchange	OTC
Auditor	Cole & Reed P.C	Ticker Symbol	AMSI
Stk Agt	U.S. Stock Transfer Corp	Outstanding Shares	8,520,000
Counsel	NA	E.P.S.	-$0.291
DUNS No.	NA	Shareholders	NA

Business: The group's principal activity is to market a product line consisting of three categories: weight management, dietary supplement and personal care products. The group markets its products through a network of independent distributors. The weight management and dietary supplement products include specialized blend of herbs, vitamins, minerals and other natural ingredients. The personal care category includes skin-care system, cleansing lotion, skin freshener, oatmeal scrub, moisturizer, shampoo and all other regular cosmetic products. The group also sells supplies and materials to its independent associates.

Primary SIC and add'l.: 5122

CIK No: 0000841866

Subsidiaries: AMS Manufacturing, Inc., Heartland Cup, Inc.

Officers: Jerry W. Grizzle/Chmn., CEO, Pres./$166,369.00, Robin L. Jacob/VP, Sec., Treasurer, CFO/$119,969.00, Dennis P. Loney/VP - Operations/$120,390.00

Directors: Jerry W. Grizzle/Chmn., CEO, Pres., Ronald L. Smith/61/Dir., Richard C. Wiser/59/Dir., Lawrence R. Moreau/64/Dir.

Owners: Insiders/13.50%, Lawrence R. Moreau, Robin L. Jacob, Stephen E. Jones, James M. Lee, Ascendiant Capital Group, LLC/8.80%, John W. Hail/7.20%, Jerry W. Grizzle, Thomas M. Buxton/1.00%, Dennis P. Loney/3.00%

Financial Data: Fiscal Year End:12/31 Latest Annual Data: 12/31/2006

Year	Sales	Net Income
2006	$9,681,000	-$2,215,000
2005	$13,701,000	-$3,766,000
2004	$18,203,000	-$6,267,000

Curr. Assets:	$1,996,000	Curr. Liab.:	$2,248,000		
Plant, Equip.:	$2,794,000	Total Liab.:	$4,875,000	Indic. Yr. Divd.:	NA
Total Assets:	$6,933,000	Net Worth:	$2,057,000	Debt/ Equity:	0.3311

AMS Homecare Inc

1360 Cliveden Ave., Delta, BC, V3M 6K2; *PH:* 1-604-273-5173; *http://* www.amshomecare.com; *Email:* sales@amshomecare.com

General - Incorporation	Canada	*Stock*- Price on:12/24/2007	$0.01
Employees	NA	Stock Exchange	OTC
Auditor	STS Partners LLP	Ticker Symbol	AHCKF
Stk Agt	Computershare Trust Co	Outstanding Shares	NA
Counsel	NA	E.P.S	NA
DUNS No.	NA	Shareholders	NA

Business: The groups principle activity is to provide healthcare products including mobility and technology products. The groups products include powerchairs, scoters, rollators and wheelchairs. The group operates from Canada.

Primary SIC and add'l.: 9999

CIK No: 0001201784

Subsidiaries: AMS Homecare Canada Inc, AMS Homecare USA Inc.

Officers: Harj Gill/CEO, Daryl Hixt/Mgr., Rani Gill/Pres., Debbie Gorst/Mgr., Kelly Langlois/Mgr., Rav Banga/Project Mgr. - IER Systems, Fred Podzun/GM, Rahul Derodra/Accounting Executive

Directors: Amarjit Mann/Dir., Jan Karnik/Dir., Ranjodh Sahota/Dir.

Owners: Rani Gill, Insiders, Ranjodh Sahota, Amarjit Mann, Harj Gill, Jan Karnik

*Financial Data: Fiscal Year End:*02/28 **Latest Annual Data:** 2/28/2006

Year	Sales		Net Income
2006	$6,056,000		-$3,038,000
2005	$4,416,000		$16,000
2004	$3,294,000		$192,000
Curr. Assets:	$1,296,000	*Curr. Liab.:*	$737,000	
Plant, Equip.:	$37,000	*Total Liab.:*	$1,189,000	*Indic. Yr. Divd.:*	NA
Total Assets:	$1,379,000	*Net Worth:*	$189,000	*Debt/ Equity:*	NA

Amscan Holdings Inc

80 Grasslands Rd., Ste. 4, Elmsford, NY, 10523; *PH:* 1-914-345-2020; *Fax:* 1-914-345-3884; *http://* www.amscan.com

General - Incorporation	DE	*Stock*- Price on:12/24/2007	NA
Employees	NA	Stock Exchange	NA
Auditor	Ernst & Young LLP	Ticker Symbol	NA
Stk Agt	American Stock Transfer & Trust Co.	Outstanding Shares	NA
Counsel	NA	E.P.S	NA
DUNS No.	96-479-393	Shareholders	NA

Business: The group's principle activities include designing, manufacturing and distributing numerous articles and goods including paper and plastic party goods, accessories and novelties. The company is a holding company of amscan inc. And certain affiliates. The company acquired AM-source, inc. In 96. The company became publicly held in 96. The group operates from United States.

Primary SIC and add'l.: 2679

CIK No: 0001024729

Subsidiaries: AAH Holdings Corporation, Am-Source, LLC, Amscan (Asia-Pacific) Pty. Ltd., Amscan de Mexico, S.A. de C.V., Amscan Distributors (Canada) Ltd., Amscan Holdings Limited, Amscan Inc., Amscan Partyartikel GmbH, Anagram Espana, S.A., Anagram France S.C.S., Anagram International (Japan) Co., Ltd., Anagram International Holdings, Inc., Anagram International, Inc., Anagram International, LLC, JCS Hong Kong Ltd.

Owners: John R. Ranelli, GB Retail Funding LLC, Kevin M. Hayes, Jordan A. Kahn, Weston Presidio, James M. Harrison, Berkshire Partners LLC, Carol M. Meyrowitz, Insiders, Robert J. Small, Michael C. Ascione, Gerald C. Rittenberg, Richard K. Lubin, Michael F. Cronin, Michael A. Correale

AmSouth BanCorp

1900 Fifth Ave. N, Amsouthre Ctr., Birmingham, AL, 35203; *PH:* 1-205-320-7151; *http://* www.amsouth.com

General - Incorporation	DE	*Stock*- Price on:12/24/2007	NA
Employees	NA	Stock Exchange	NYSE
Auditor	Ernst & Young LLP	Ticker Symbol	ASO
Stk Agt	Bank of New York	Outstanding Shares	NA
Counsel	NA	E.P.S	NA
DUNS No.	06-366-6507	Shareholders	NA

Business: The group's principal activity is to provide banking services. The group provides the services under three segments: consumer banking, commercial banking and wealth management. Consumer banking provides financial services to individuals and small businesses like residential mortgages, equity lending, credit cards and loans for automobile and other personal financing needs and various products. Commercial banking provides specialty services such as real estate finance, asset based lending and commercial leasing. Wealth management is comprised of trust, institutional, retirement and broker-dealer services. The operations are conducted through 650 offices located in Alabama, Florida, Tennessee, Mississippi, Louisiana and Georgia. It also operates a network of 1,200 automated teller machines.

Primary SIC and add'l.: 6022 6712

CIK No: 0000003133

Subsidiaries: A-F Leasing, LLC, A-F Leasing, Ltd., AmSouth Asset Management, Inc., AmSouth Auto Receivables LLC, Amsouth Bank, AmSouth Capital Corporation, AmSouth Finance Corporation, AmSouth Investment Management Company LLC, AmSouth Investment Services, Inc., AmSouth Investment Services, Inc. of Louisiana, AmSouth Investment Services, Inc. of Mississippi, AmSouth Investment Services, Inc. of Virginia, AmSouth Leasing Corporation, AmSouth Leasing, Ltd., AmSouth Reinsurance Company, Ltd. 27 Subsidiaries included in the Index

Officers: Douglas G. Edwards/56/Pres., CEO - Morgan Keegan, Co, Inc, Dowd C. Ritter/60/Dir., CEO, Pres., Jackson W. Moore/Executive Chmn., Timothy G. Laney/48/Sr. Exec. VP - Business Services, Alton E. Yother/55/CFO, Exec. VP - Finance Group, William C. Wells/Chief Risk Officer, Sr. Exec. VP - Risk Management Group, David B. Edmonds/Sr. Exec. VP - Human Resources Group, Candice W. Bagby/Sr. Exec. VP - Consumer Services Group, O. B. Grayson Hall/Sr. Exec. VP - General Banking Group

Directors: Dowd C. Ritter/60/Dir., CEO, Pres., Jackson W. Moore/Executive Chmn., Martha R. Ingram/Dir., James R. Malone/Dir., Earnest W. Deavenport/Dir., Samuel W. Bartholomew/Dir., George W. Bryan/Dir., Susan W. Matlock/Dir., John E. Maupin/Dir., Allen B. Morgan/Dir., Jorge M. Perez/Dir., John R. Roberts/Dir., Lee J. Styslinger/Dir., Spence L. Wilson/Dir., Harry W. Witt/Dir. *(19 Directors included in Index)*

Amsurg Corp

20 Burton Hills Blvd., Nashville, TN, 37215; *PH:* 1-615-665-1283; *Fax:* 1-615-665-0755; *http://* www.amsurg.com; *Email:* info@amsurg.com

General - Incorporation	TN	*Stock*- Price on:12/24/2007	$24.33
Employees	1,300	Stock Exchange	NDQ
Auditor	Deloitte & Touche LLP	Ticker Symbol	AMSG
Stk Agt	SunTrust Bank Atlanta Corp Trust Dept	Outstanding Shares	30,550,000
Counsel	Bass, Berry & Sims PLC	E.P.S	$1.33
DUNS No.	78-605-6820	Shareholders	NA

Business: The group's principal activities are to develop, acquire and operate practice based ambulatory surgery centers in partnerships with physician practice groups. These surgery centers provide a narrow range of high volume, lower risk surgical procedures. These surgical centers are located in a close vicinity of the specialty medical practice of a physician group partner's office. The group's primary surgical specialties of interest are gastroenterology, ophthalmology, orthopedics, otolaryngology and urology. On 31-Mar-2004, the group acquired majority interests in two physician practice-based surgery centers.

Primary SIC and add'l.: 8062

CIK No: 0000895930

Subsidiaries: AmSurg Abilene Eye, Inc., AmSurg Abilene, Inc., AmSurg Burbank, Inc., AmSurg Crystal River, Inc., AmSurg EC Beaumont, Inc., AmSurg EC Centennial, Inc., AmSurg EC Santa Fe, Inc., AmSurg EC St. Thomas, Inc., AmSurg EC Topeka, Inc., AmSurg EC Washington, Inc., AmSurg El Paso, Inc., AmSurg Encino, Inc., AmSurg Escondido CA, Inc., AmSurg FL EyeCare Network, Inc., AmSurg Glendale, Inc. 196 Subsidiaries included in the Index

Officers: Christopher A. Holden/Dir., CEO, Pres., Ken P. McDonald/Dir., Immediate Past Pres./$1,639,050.00, Royce D. Harrell/Sr. VP - Corporate Services, Chief Compliance Officer/$535,745.00, Claire M. Gulmi/Dir., CFO, Exec. VP, Sec./$948,518.00, David L. Manning/Exec. VP, Chief Development Officer/$1,152,191.00

Directors: Christopher A. Holden/Dir., CEO, Pres., Thomas G. Cigarran/Chmn., Ken P. McDonald/Dir., Immediate Past Pres., Debora A. Guthrie/Dir., Henry D. Herr/Dir., James A. Deal/Dir., Kevin P. Lavender/Dir., Steven I. Geringer/Dir., Claire M. Gulmi/Dir., CFO, Exec. VP, Sec., Bergein F. Overholt/Dir.

Owners: Thomas G. Cigarran, Steven I. Geringer, James A. Deal, Wellington Management Company, LLP/11.40%, Debora A. Guthrie, Bergein F. Overholt, FMR Corp./13.10%, Insiders/7.30%, Barclays Global Investors, NA./6.50%, Neuberger Berman Inc./10.90%, Henry D. Herr, David L. Manning/1.70%, Claire M. Gulmi/1.10%, Wasatch Advisors, Inc./8.80%, Ken P. McDonald/2.50% *(16 Owners included in Index)*

*Financial Data: Fiscal Year End:*12/31 **Latest Annual Data:** 12/31/2006

Year	Sales		Net Income
2006	$464,592,000		$37,739,000
2005	$391,790,000		$35,151,000
2004	$334,304,000		$39,706,000
Curr. Assets:	$94,003,000	*Curr. Liab.:*	$27,412,000	*P/E Ratio:*	18.43
Plant, Equip.:	$89,175,000	*Total Liab.:*	$194,583,000	*Indic. Yr. Divd.:*	NA
Total Assets:	$590,032,000	*Net Worth:*	$343,108,000	*Debt/ Equity:*	0.4153

Amtech Systems Inc

131 S Clark Dr., Tempe, AZ, 85281; *PH:* 1-480-967-5146; *Fax:* 1-480-968-3763; *http://* www.amtechsystems.com; *Email:* corporate@amtechsystems.com

General - Incorporation	AZ	*Stock*- Price on:12/24/2007	NA
Employees	153	Stock Exchange	NDQ
Auditor	Mayer Hoffman Mccann, P.C	Ticker Symbol	ASYS
Stk Agt	Computershare Trust Co	Outstanding Shares	6,500,000
Counsel	Squire, Sanders & Dempsey LLP	E.P.S	$0.24
DUNS No.	03-575-3920	Shareholders	NA

Business: The group's principal activities are to design, assemble, market and install capital equipment and related consumables. The products are used in the manufacture of wafers of various materials, primarily silicon wafers for the semiconductor industry and in certain semiconductor fabrication processes. The group operates through two business segments: semiconductor equipment and polishing supplies. The semiconductor equipment segment designs, manufactures and markets semiconductor wafer processing and handling equipment used in the fabrication of integrated circuits. The polishing supplies segment designs, manufactures and markets carriers, templates and equipment used in the lapping and polishing of wafer thin materials. The products include diffusion furnaces, ibal automation, double-sided precision lapping and polishing machines and complementary products.

Primary SIC and add'l.: 3471 3559

CIK No: 0000720500

Subsidiaries: Bruce Technologies Europe Gmbh, Bruce Technologies, Inc., P.R. Hoffman Machine Products, Inc., Tempress Systems, Inc.

Officers: Jong S. Whang/62/Chmn., CEO, Pres., Robert T. Hass/Chief Accounting Officer, Bradley C. Anderson/VP - Finance, CFO, Treasurer, Sec.

Directors: Jong S. Whang/62/Chmn., CEO, Pres., Robert F. King/Dir., Alfred W. Giese/Dir., Michael Garnreiter/Dir., Brian L. Hoekstra/Dir.

Owners: David M. Greenhouse/14.00%, Robert F. King, Insiders/4.30%, Richard L. Scott/7.90%, Jong S. Whang/3.50%, Bradley C. Anderson, Michael A. Roth/6.50%, Austin W. Marxe/14.00%, Robert T. Hass, Brian J. Stark/6.50%

*Financial Data: Fiscal Year End:*09/30 **Latest Annual Data:** 9/30/2006

Year	Sales		Net Income
2006	$40,445,000		$1,318,000
2005	$27,899,000		-$259,000
2004	$19,299,000		-$3,165,000
Curr. Assets:	$19,220,000	*Curr. Liab.:*	$7,337,000	
Plant, Equip.:	$2,382,000	*Total Liab.:*	$7,954,000	*Indic. Yr. Divd.:*	NA
Total Assets:	$23,563,000	*Net Worth:*	$15,609,000	*Debt/ Equity:*	0.0556

Amtrol Inc

1400 Div. Rd. , West Warwick, RI, 02893; *PH:* 1-408-284-6300; *http://* www.amtrol.com; *Email:* info@amtrol.com

General		Stock	
Incorporation	RI	Price on:12/24/2007	NA
Employees	NA	Stock Exchange	NA
Auditor	Ernst & Young LLP	Ticker Symbol	NA
Stk Agt	NA	Outstanding Shares	NA
Counsel	NA	E.P.S.	NA
DUNS No.	00-119-2145	Shareholders	NA

Business: The group's principle activities include designing and manufacturing different range of water systems products, which include, well water tanks, hot water expansion tanks and non-returnable chemical containers. These products are based on technology originated and developed by the company. The company also manufactures and markets specialized residential and commercial water treatment equipment, including water softeners, filters, reverse oxmosis accumulators and other related systems which may be utilized to purify or treat municipal and well water. In the hvac market, the company provides residential and commercial systems and equipment for use in hot water and cilmate control applications ranging from single family homes to large commercial and industrial facilities. These products include expansion tanks, indirect-fired water heaters and other related prokucts and accessories. In Sept, 1995 the company ceased operations in its plano plant in Texas. The group operates from United States.

Primary SIC and add'l.: 3589 3443

CIK No: 0000853547

Subsidiaries: AMTROL Asia Pacific Ltd., AMTROL Canada Ltd., AMTROL Europe Ltd., AMTROL Holdings Netherlands B.V., AMTROL Holdings Portugal, SGPS, Unipessoal, Lda., AMTROL International Investments Inc., AMTROL Poland Sp z.o.o., Amtrol-alfa Metalomecanica, S.a., Water Soft Inc.

Officers: Larry T. Guillemette/Sales Representative - ID

Directors: Larry T. Guillemette/Sales Representative - ID

AmTrust Financial Services Inc

25800 Science Pk. Dr., Cleveland, OH, 44122; *PH:* 1-216-292-8730; *http://* www.amtrustgroup.com

General		Stock	
Incorporation	DE	Price on:12/24/2007	$16.7401
Employees	325	Stock Exchange	NDQ
Auditor	BDO Seidman, LLP	Ticker Symbol	AFSI
Stk Agt	American Stock Transfer & Trust Co.	Outstanding Shares	59,960,000
Counsel	NA	E.P.S.	$1.015
DUNS No.	NA	Shareholders	NA

Business: The groups principle activity is to provide property and casualty insurance. The groups service is insurance coverage. The groups operates through three segments namely small business workers compensation insurance, specialty risk and extended warranty and specialty middle-market property and casualty insurance. The group acquired Wesco Insurance Company, Muirfield Underwriters, Ltd in the year 2006 and Alea North America, Inc in the year 2005. The group operates from Florida, New Jersey, New York, Georgia, Pennsylvania, Illinois, Texas, South Carolina, Missouri and Tennessee. The group's quarterly revenue for September 2007 was 137.47 millions of USD.

Primary SIC and add'l.: 7389

CIK No: 0001365555

Subsidiaries: AFS Capital Corp., AII Insurance Management Limited, AII Reinsurance Brokers, Ltd, AMT Service Corp., AMT Service Corp. of Canada, AmTrust Capital Management, Inc., AmTrust International Insurance, Ltd, AmTrust International Underwriters, Ltd, AmTrust Management Services, Ltd, AmTrust Managers, Inc., AmTrust New Gulf Holdings, LLC, AmTrust Nordic, AB, AmTrust North America, Inc., AmTrust South, Inc., AmTrust Underwriters, Inc. 25 Subsidiaries included in the Index

Officers: Barry D. Zyskind/Dir., CEO, Pres., Max G. Caviet/Pres. - Amtrust International Insurance Ltd, Amtrust International Underwriters Ltd, Michael J. Saxon/COO, Ronald E. Pipoly/CFO, Christopher M. Longo/CIO, Stephen B. Ungar/General Counsel, Sec.

Directors: Barry D. Zyskind/Dir., CEO, Pres., Michael Karfunkel/Chmn., George Karfunkel/Dir., Donald T. Decarlo/Dir., Abraham Gulkowitz/Dir., Isaac M. Neuberger/Dir., Jay J. Miller/Dir.

Owners: Donald T. DeCarlo, Insiders, Barry D. Zyskind, Abraham Gulkowitz, Isaac M. Neuberger, Stephen Ungar, George Karfunkel, Michael J. Saxon, Jay J. Miller, Max G. Caviet, New Gulf Holdings, Inc., Christopher M. Longo, G/MK Acquisition Corp., Michael Karfunkel, Ronald E. Pipoly

Financial Data: ***Fiscal Year End:*** 12/31 ***Latest Annual Data:*** 12/31/2006

Year	Sales	Net Income
2006	$384,025,000	$48,856,000
2005	$240,635,000	$37,559,000
2004	$149,955,000	$14,110,000

Curr. Assets:	$526,539,000	**Curr. Liab.:**	$107,221,000		
Plant, Equip.:	$11,175,000	**Total Liab.:**	$844,913,000	**Indic. Yr. Divd.:**	$0.100
Total Assets:	$1,185,392,000	**Net Worth:**	$340,479,000	**Debt/ Equity:**	NA

Amylin Pharmaceuticals Inc

9360 Towne Ctr. Dr., San Diego, CA, 92121; *PH:* 1-858-552-2200; *Fax:* 1-858-552-2212; *http://* www.amylin.com; *Email:* ir@amylin.com

General		Stock	
Incorporation	DE	Price on:12/24/2007	$41.4
Employees	1,550	Stock Exchange	NDQ
Auditor	Ernst & Young LLP	Ticker Symbol	AMLN
Stk Agt	American Stock Transfer & Trust Co.	Outstanding Shares	131,550,000
Counsel	Cooley Godward LLP	E.P.S.	-$1.47
DUNS No.	19-687-7526	Shareholders	NA

Business: The group's principal activity is to discover, develop and markets potential drug candidates for the treatment of diabetes and other metabolic disorders. It has exclusive rights to two drug candidates, which are in late-stage development, for the treatment of diabetes, symlin(TM) (pramlintide acetate) and ac2993 (synthetic exendin-4). Symlin(TM) is a synthetic analog of the human hormone, amylin for the treatment of the people with diabetes who use insulin. Ac2993, a code name for synthetic exendin-4, is for the treatment of type 2 diabetes. The group also has a third drug candidate ac3056, which is in early stage clinical trials. It is used in the treatment of metabolic disorders relating to cardiovascular disease.

Primary SIC and add'l.: 2834 8731

CIK No: 0000881464

Subsidiaries: Alkermes Controlled Therapeutics II, Amylin Ohio LLC

Officers: Daniel M. Bradbury/Dir., CEO, Pres./$2,528,005.00, Roger Marchetti/Sr. VP - Human Resources, Corporate Services, Harold E. Lebovitz/Member - North American Advisory Board, Matthew C. Riddle/Member - North American Advisory Board, Mark G. Foletta/CFO, Sr. VP - Finance/$1,137,819.00, David Maggs/VP - Medical Affairs, Craig Eberhard/VP - Sales, Gregg Stetsko/VP - Operations, Bernard Zinman/Member - North American Advisory Board, Mark J. Gergen/Sr. VP - Corporate Development, Carol Wysham/Member - North American Advisory Board, Dawn Viveash/VP - Regulatory Affairs, Safety, Jonathan P. Mow/VP - Business Development, Paul Marshall/VP - Operations, Sarah L. Hanssen/VP - Strategic Relationship Management *(26 Officers included in Index)*

Directors: Daniel M. Bradbury/Dir., CEO, Pres., Joseph C. Cook/Chmn., Robert S. Sherwin/Chmn. - North American Advisory Board, Jeffrey M. Friedman/Chmn. - Scientific Advisory Board, Kenneth S. Polonsky/Member - North American Advisory Board, Robert R. Henry/Member - North American Advisory Board, Rury R. Holman/Member - North American Advisory Board, John B. Buse/Member - North American Advisory Board, Alan D. Cherrington/Member - North American Advisory Board, Stephen N. Davis/Member - North American Advisory Board, Ralph A. Defronzo/Member - North American Advisory Board, Timothy J. Rink/Member - Scientific Advisory Board, James N. Wilson/Dir., Joseph P. Sullivan/Dir., Thomas R. Testman/71/Dir. *(25 Directors included in Index)*

Owners: Wellington Management Company, LLP/10.53%, Vaughn D. Bryson, Eastbourne Capital Management, L.L.C./14.65%, Janus Capital Management LLC/8.13%, Steven R. Altman, Daniel M. Bradbury, Mark G. Foletta, Thomas R. Testman, James N. Wilson, Teresa Beck, Insiders/6.87%, Howard E. Greene/1.31%, James R. Gavi, Jay S. Skyler, Joseph P. Sullivan *(22 Owners included in Index)*

Financial Data: ***Fiscal Year End:*** 12/31 ***Latest Annual Data:*** 12/31/2006

Year	Sales	Net Income
2006	$510,875,000	-$218,856,000
2005	$140,474,000	-$206,832,000
2004	$34,268,000	-$157,157,000

Curr. Assets:	$906,817,000	**Curr. Liab.:**	$203,887,000		
Plant, Equip.:	$146,779,000	**Total Liab.:**	$425,095,000	**Indic. Yr. Divd.:**	NA
Total Assets:	$1,060,386,000	**Net Worth:**	$635,291,000	**Debt/ Equity:**	0.3494

Anadarko Petroleum Corp

1201 Lake Robbins Dr., The Woodlands, TX, 77380; *PH:* 1-832-636-1000; *Fax:* 1-832-636-8220; *http://* www.anadarko.com; *Email:* investor@anadarko.com

General		Stock	
Incorporation	DE	Price on:12/24/2007	$53.82
Employees	5,200	Stock Exchange	NYSE
Auditor	KPMG LLP	Ticker Symbol	APC
Stk Agt	Mellon Shareholder Services LLC	Outstanding Shares	463,930,000
Counsel	NA	E.P.S.	$8.89
DUNS No.	02-640-9797	Shareholders	NA

Business: The groups principle activities include exploring, developing and marketing oil and natural gas. In the year 2006, the group acquired Kerr-McGee Corporation and Western Gas Resources, Inc. The group operates from United States.

Primary SIC and add'l.: 1311 1321

CIK No: 0000773910

Subsidiaries: Anadarko Algeria Company LLC, Anadarko Canada Corporation, Anadarko E&P Company LP, Anadarko Energy Services Company, Anadarko Holding Company, Anadarko Land Corp., Headwater LLC, Howell Petroleum Corporation

Officers: James T. Hackett/Chmn., CEO, Pres./$13,434,470.00, Charles A. Meloy/Sr. VP - Worldwide Operations, John Colglazier/Dir. - Investor Relations, John Christiansen/Mgr. - External Communications, Paula Beasley/Sr. Public Affairs Representative, Mark Hanley/Public Affairs Mgr. - Alaska, Charlene A. Ripley/VP, Gregory M. Pensabene/VP - Government Relations, Mario M. Coll/CIO, VP, Albert L. Richey/VP - Corporate Development, Robert K. Reeves/Sr. VP, General Counsel, Chief Administrative Officer/$2,650,348.00, R. A. Walker/CFO, Sr. VP - Finance/$2,893,752.00, Bruce W. Busmire/VP, Chief Accounting Officer, Robert P. Daniels/Sr. VP - Worldwide Exploration, Robert G. Gwin/VP, Treasurer *(17 Officers included in Index)*

Directors: James T. Hackett/Chmn., CEO, Pres., Larry Barcus/Dir., Luke R. Corbett/Dir., Peter J. Fluor/Dir., Paula Rosput Reynolds/Dir., John R. Gordon/Dir., James L. Bryan/Dir., Robert J. Allison/Dir., Paulett H. Eberhart/Dir., John W. Poduska/Dir., John R. Butler/Dir.

Owners: John R. Butler, Robert K. Reeves, David R. Larson, R. A. Walker, John W. Poduska, Robert J. Allison, Insiders, ClearBridge Advisors, LLC/9.09%, John R. Gordon, Neuberger Berman Inc./6.24%, Luke R. Corbett, Karl F. Kurz, James L. Bryan, Barclays Global Investors, NA./7.19%, Diane L. Dickey *(19 Owners included in Index)*

Financial Data: ***Fiscal Year End:*** 12/31 ***Latest Annual Data:*** 12/31/2006

Year	Sales	Net Income
2006	$10,187,000,000	$4,854,000,000
2005	$7,100,000,000	$2,471,000,000
2004	$6,067,000,000	$1,606,000,000

Curr. Assets:	$4,614,000,000	**Curr. Liab.:**	$16,758,000,000	**P/E Ratio:**	6.05
Plant, Equip.:	$48,749,000,000	**Total Liab.:**	$43,931,000,000	**Indic. Yr. Divd.:**	$0.360
Total Assets:	$58,844,000,000	**Net Worth:**	$14,913,000,000	**Debt/ Equity:**	0.7629

Anadigics Inc

141 Mt. Bethel Rd., Warren, NJ, 07059; *PH:* 1-908-668-5000; *Fax:* 1-908-668-5068; *http://* www.anadigics.com

General		Stock	
Incorporation	DE	Price on:12/24/2007	$13.72
Employees	508	Stock Exchange	NDQ
Auditor	J.H. Cohn, LLP	Ticker Symbol	ANAD
Stk Agt	Mellon Financial Services LLC	Outstanding Shares	58,880,000
Counsel	NA	E.P.S.	$0.06
DUNS No.	13-967-8270	Shareholders	NA

Business: The group's principal activity is to design, develop and manufacture radio frequency integrated circuit solutions for the wireless and broadband communications markets. The group's operations are conducted through two business segments: wireless and broadband. The group's products enable manufactures of communication equipment to enhance overall system performance and reduce manufacturing cost and time to market. These products are used to send and receive signals in a variety of broadband and wireless communications applications. The group acquired certain assets and liabilities of the wireless LAN power amplifier business of rf solutions. The group has operations in the United States, Canada, Asia, Europe and Latin America.

Primary SIC and add'l.: 3674 5065

CIK No: 0000940332

Subsidiaries: Anadigics (u.k.) Limited, Anadigics Acquisition Corp, Anadigics Denmark Aps, Anadigics Holding Corp., Anadigics, Limited, Broadband & Wireless Investors, Incorporated, Integral Pathway, Inc., Telcom Devices Corp.

Officers: Bami Bastani/Dir., CEO, Pres./$1,394,421.00, Kristina Panek/Mgr. - Investor Relations, Stock Plan Administration, Charles Huang/CTO, Exec. VP/$549,544.00, Thomas C. Shields/CFO, Exec. VP/$657,689.00, Ali M. Khatibzadeh/Sr. VP, GM - Wireless Business, Ron Michels/Sr. VP, GM - Broadband Business, Jennifer Palella/Sr. Dir. Marketing - Worldwide Distribution

Directors: Bami Bastani/Dir., CEO, Pres.

Owners: Harry Rein, Lewis Solomon, Charles Huang/1.40%, Bami Bastani/2.30%, Paul Bachow, Garry McGuire, Lord, Abbett & Co. LLC/10.70%, Ronald Rosenzweig, Dennis Strigl, FMR Corp./10.50%, Chilton Investment Company LLC/7.10%, Thomas C. Shields, Insiders/6.20%

Financial Data: ***Fiscal Year End:*** 12/31 ***Latest Annual Data:*** 12/31/2006

Year	Sales	Net Income
2006	$169,885,000	-$8,850,000
2005	$45,716,000	-$20,540,000

Curr. Assets:	$110,454,000	**Curr. Liab.:**	$13,961,000		
Plant, Equip.:	$37,501,000	**Total Liab.:**	$101,750,000	**Indic. Yr. Divd.:**	NA
Total Assets:	$167,286,000	**Net Worth:**	$65,536,000	**Debt/ Equity:**	0.1786

Anadys Pharmaceuticals Inc

3115 Merryfield Row, San Diego, CA, 92121; ***PH:*** 1-858-530-3600; ***Fax:*** 1-858-527-1540; ***http://*** www.anadyspharma.com; ***Email:*** ir@anadyspharma.com

General - Incorporation	DE	**Stock** - Price on:12/24/2007	$4.13
Employees	86	Stock Exchange	NDQ
Auditor	Ernst & Young LLP	Ticker Symbol	ANDS
Stk Agt	Computershare Investor Services LLC	Outstanding Shares	28,630,000
Counsel	NA	E.P.S	-$0.31
DUNS No.	NA	Shareholders	NA

Business: The groups principle activities include discovering, developing and commercializing mall-molecule medicines for the treatment of hepatitis and cancer. The groups clinical development programs include ANA975, an oral prodrug of the Toll-like receptor-7 (TLR-7) agonist isatoribine, for the treatment of hepatitis C virus (HCV) and hepatitis B virus (HBV). The group operates from United States.

Primary SIC and add'l.: NA

CIK No: 0001128495

Subsidiaries: Anadys Pharmaceuticals Europe GmbH

Officers: Lawrence C. Fritz/55/Dir., CEO, Pres./$186,137.00, Stephen T. Worland/50/Pres. - Pharmaceuticals/$970,102.00, James T. Glover/58/Sr. VP - Operations, CFO/$162,640.00, Elizabeth E. Reed/37/VP - Legal Affairs, Corp. Sec./$353,559.00, Mary Yaroshevsky-Glanville/VP - Human Capital, James L. Freddo/Chief Medical Officer, Carol G. Gallagher/Sr. VP - Corporate Development, Commercial Affairs

Directors: George A. Scangos/Chmn., Mark G. Foletta/Dir., Steven H. Holtzman/Dir., Kleanthis G. Xanthopoulos/Dir., Devron R. Averett/Member - Advisory Board, Robert Schooley/Member - Advisory Board, Marios Fotiadis/Dir., Jason Fisherman/Member - Advisory Board, Stelios Papadopoulos/Dir., Douglas E. Williams/Dir., Douglas D. Richman/Member - Advisory Board, Spyros Artavanis-Tsakonas/Member - Advisory Board, Frank V. Chisari/Member - Advisory Board, David P. Clough/Member - Advisory Board, Anna Suk-fong Lok/Member - Advisory Boardanna Suk - Fong Lok *(17 Directors included in Index)*

Owners: Entities related to Federated Investors, Inc./7.10%, Entities related to Deerfield Management Co., L.P. and James E. Flynn/7.70%, Wellington Management Company, LLP/12.20%, Mark G. Foletta, Entities related to Biotechnology Value Fund II, L.P./5.50%, Marios Fotiadis, Stelios Papadopoulos/2.40%, Entities related to BB Biotech AG/7.00%, Insiders/7.90%, George A. Scangos, Xmark Opportunity Partners, LLC/5.40%, James T. Glover, Kleanthis G. Xanthopoulos/2.80%, Devron R. Averett, Douglas E. Williams *(18 Owners included in Index)*

Financial Data: ***Fiscal Year End:*** 12/31 ***Latest Annual Data:*** 12/31/2006

Year	Sales	Net Income
2006	$5,420,000	-$26,760,000
2005	$4,887,000	-$21,923,000
2004	$1,762,000	-$32,979,000

Curr. Assets:	$84,265,000	**Curr. Liab.:**	$9,211,000		
Plant, Equip.:	$3,749,000	**Total Liab.:**	$29,076,000	**Indic. Yr. Divd.:**	NA
Total Assets:	$89,401,000	**Net Worth:**	$60,325,000	**Debt/ Equity:**	NA

Analex Corp

2677 Prosperity Ave., Ste. 400, Fairfax, VA, 22031; ***PH:*** 1-703-852-4000; ***http://*** www.analex.com

General - Incorporation	DE	**Stock** - Price on:12/24/2007	NA
Employees	1,100	Stock Exchange	NDQ
Auditor	Ernst & Young LLP	Ticker Symbol	NMGC
Stk Agt	American Stock Transfer & Trust Co.	Outstanding Shares	NA
Counsel	Holland & Knight LLP	E.P.S	NA
DUNS No.	04-764-4638	Shareholders	NA

Business: The group's principal activity is to support homeland security through the design, implementation and support of innovative solutions. The group specializes in three facets of homeland security: intelligence systems, bio-defense and aerospace programs. The abs homeland segment operates in the bio-defense market. It provides training on the use of biological warfare agents, their effects and defensive strategies to improve preparedness. The homeland security group supports the United States intelligence community. This segment provides hardware and software engineering, systems integration, information technology solutions and independent quality assurance to support intelligence systems. The aerospace group supports nasa, department of defense and other major aerospace contractors. On 01-Jun-2004, the group acquired beta analytics inc.

Primary SIC and add'l.: 7373 8711 7371

CIK No: 0000044800

Subsidiaries: Beta Analytics, Incorporated, ComGlobal Systems, Incorporated, SyCom Services, Inc.

Officers: Sterling E. Phillips/Chmn., CEO, William Torpey/Sr. VP - Security, Intelligence, Michael G. Stolarik/Pres., Joseph V. Broadwater/Sr. VP - National Systems, Heinz Wimmer/VP - Central Division, Stephen Matthews/Sr. VP - Business Development, Elisa Rivera/VP - Human Resources, Charlie Floyd/VP, Elvis Program Mgr., Mike Bucchi/Sr. VP - Systems Engineering, Integration, Denis Clements/VP - Systems Development, Integration, Gifford Justice/VP - Engineering Services, Teresa Patterson/VP - C4I Division, Lew Thompson/VP

Directors: Sterling E. Phillips/Chmn., CEO, Lincoln D. Faurer/Dir., Thomas C. Faulders/Dir., Thomas L. Hewitt/Dir., Daniel March/Dir., Gerald Poch/Dir., Martin Hale/Dir., Peter C. Belford/Dir., Daniel R. Young/Dir.

Analog Devices Inc

1 Technology Way, Norwood, MA, 02062; ***PH:*** 1-781-329-4700; ***Fax:*** 1-781-461-4482; ***http://*** www.analog.com

General - Incorporation	MA	**Stock** - Price on:12/24/2007	$37.79
Employees	9,800	Stock Exchange	NYSE
Auditor	Ernst & Young LLP	Ticker Symbol	ADI
Stk Agt	Computershare Investor Services LLC	Outstanding Shares	327,100,000
Counsel	Hale & Dorr LLP	E.P.S	$1.50
DUNS No.	00-141-8417	Shareholders	NA

Business: The groups principle activity is to provide signal processing solutions. The groups products include audio amplifiers, A/D converters, touchscreen controllers and voltage to frequency converters. The groups solutions include audio, automotive and computer solutions. The group operates from United States.

Primary SIC and add'l.: 3674 3825

CIK No: 0000006281

Subsidiaries: ADI Micromachines, Inc., Analog Development (Israel) 1996 Ltd., Analog Devices (China) Co. Ltd., Analog Devices (Philippines), Inc., Analog Devices A.B., Analog Devices ApS, Analog Devices Asian Sales, Inc., Analog Devices Australia Pty. Ltd., Analog Devices Canada, Ltd., Analog Devices ChipLogic, Inc., Analog Devices Foundry Services, Inc., Analog Devices Gen. Trias, Inc., Analog Devices Holdings, B.V., Analog Devices Hong Kong, Ltd., Analog Devices IMI, Inc. 41 Subsidiaries included in the Index

Officers: Jerald G. Fishman/Dir., CEO, Pres., Gerry Dundon/VP - Planning, Supply Chain Logistics, Manufacturing Division, Dennis Dempsey/VP, GM - Limerick Manufacturing, Limerick Site Division, Joseph E. McDonough/CFO, VP - Finance, Robert Marshall/VP - Worldwide Manufacturing, Brian McAloon/Group VP - DSP, System Products Group Division, Dick Meaney/VP - Precision Conversion Products - Limerick Site Division, Mark Norton/VP, GM - Manufacturing, Wilmington Site Division, Vincent Roche/VP - Worldwide Sales, Corporate Division, Margaret K. Seif/VP, General Counsel, Sec., William N. Giudice/53/VP, GM - Micromachined Products Division, Howard Cheng/VP - China Sales, Mark Martin/GM - Micromachined Products Division, William Matson/VP - Human Resources, Osamu Mawatari/VP - Japan Sales *(24 Officers included in Index)*

Directors: Jerald G. Fishman/Dir., CEO, Pres., Ray Stata/Chmn., Paul J. Severino/61/Dir., Christine King/Dir., Lester C. Thurow/Dir., Grant F. Saviers/Dir., Kenton J. Sicchitano/Dir., John C. Hodgson/64/Dir., James Champy/Dir., John L. Doyle/Dir.

Owners: James A. Champy, T. Rowe Price Associates, Inc./8.80%, Grant F. Saviers, Joseph E. McDonough, John L. Doyle, Christine King, Ray Stata/1.60%, Capital Research and Management Company/10.50%, Robert R. Marshall, Paul J. Severino, Lester C. Thurow, Insiders/3.50%, Kenton J. Sicchitano, John C. Hodgson, Brian P. McAloon *(18 Owners included in Index)*

Financial Data: ***Fiscal Year End:*** 12/05 ***Latest Annual Data:*** 10/28/2006

Year	Sales	Net Income
2006	$2,573,176,000	$549,482,000
2005	$2,388,808,000	$414,787,000
2004	$2,633,800,000	$570,738,000

Curr. Assets:	$3,528,611,000	**Curr. Liab.:**	$567,002,000	**P/E Ratio:**	23.77
Plant, Equip.:	$667,779,000	**Total Liab.:**	$920,511,000	**Indic. Yr. Divd.:**	$0.720
Total Assets:	$4,720,083,000	**Net Worth:**	$3,799,572,000	**Debt/ Equity:**	NA

Analogic Corp

8 Centennial Dr., Peabody, MA, 01960; ***PH:*** 1-978-326-4000; ***Fax:*** 1-978-977-6810; ***http://*** www.analogic.com; ***Email:*** csd@analogic.com

General - Incorporation	MA	**Stock** - Price on:12/24/2007	$71.89
Employees	1,500	Stock Exchange	NDQ
Auditor	PricewaterhouseCoopers LLP	Ticker Symbol	ALOG
Stk Agt	Computershare Trust Co	Outstanding Shares	14,000,000
Counsel	NA	E.P.S	$1.97
DUNS No.	01-967-7418	Shareholders	NA

Business: The group's principal activities are to design, manufacture and sell data acquisition, signal and imaging processing based medical imaging and industrial systems and subsystems. The group operates through two business segments: imaging technology products and signal processing technology products. Imaging technology products consist primarily of electronic systems and subsystems for medical imaging equipment and advanced explosive detection systems. Signal processing technology products consist of analog to digital (a/d) converters and supporting modules, and high-speed digital signal processors. It also owns a hotel, which is located in the area of Boston's north shore.

Primary SIC and add'l.: 7011 3812 3825 3841

CIK No: 0000006284

Subsidiaries: Anadventure 3 Corporation, Anadventure Delaware, Inc., Anadventure Ii Corporation, Analogic Foreign Sales Corporation, Analogic Holding Luxembourg S.a.r.l., Analogic Limited, Analogic Securities Corporation, Anatel Communications Corporation, ANEXA Corporation, Anexa Financial Services, Inc., Anrad Corporation, B-K Medical (Asia) Pte. Ltd., B-K Medical (China) Limited, B-K Medical AB, B-K Medical ApS 25 Subsidiaries included in the Index

Officers: James W. Green/CEO, Pres., Edmund F. Becker/COO, Exec. VP, John J. Millerick/Sr. VP, CFO, Treasurer, Alex A. Van Adzin/VP, General Counsel, Corporation Sec.

Directors: Bernard M. Gordon/Chmn., John A. Tarello/Vice Chmn., Gerald L. Wilson/Dir., James J. Judge/Dir., Edward F. Voboril/Dir., Bruce W. Steinhauer/Dir., Ross M. Brown/Dir., Michael T. Modic/Dir., Fred B. Parks/Dir.

Owners: John J. Millerick, Bruce W. Steinhauer, James J. Judge, Donald B. Melson, Barclays Global Investors, N.A./5.16%, Advisory Research, Inc./5.23%, T. Rowe Price Associates, Inc./7.70%, Michael T. Modic, Gerald L. Wilson, Insiders, Edward F. Voboril, John J. Fry, Edmund F. Becker, Alex A. Van Adzin, James W. Green *(18 Owners included in Index)*

Financial Data: ***Fiscal Year End:*** 07/31 ***Latest Annual Data:*** 7/31/2006

Year	Sales	Net Income
2006	$351,445,000	$25,066,000
2005	$364,571,000	$28,862,000
2004	$355,557,000	$8,354,000

Curr. Assets:	$390,835,000	Curr. Liab.:	$55,880,000		
Plant, Equip.:	$81,853,000	Total Liab.:	$56,720,000	Indic. Yr. Divd.:	$0.400
Total Assets:	$488,645,000	Net Worth:	$431,925,000	Debt/ Equity:	NA

Analysts International Corp

3601 W 76th St., Minneapolis, MN, 55435; *PH:* 1-952-835-5900; *Fax:* 1-952-897-4555;
http:// www.analysts.com

General - Incorporation	MN	*Stock*- Price on:12/24/2007	$1.63
Employees	2,984	Stock Exchange	NDQ
Auditor	Deloitte & Touche LLP	Ticker Symbol	ANLY
Stk Agt	Computershare Investor Services LLC	Outstanding Shares	25,140,000
Counsel	NA	E.P.S.	-$0.14
DUNS No.	06-478-0281	Shareholders	NA

Business: The group's principal activities are to provide ebusiness services and information technology consulting and services. These services and solutions include custom software application development, network infrastructure services, ebusiness consulting, mobile and wireless computing. Services and solutions also include single source staffing (or vendor management services) of programmers and other software professionals through our managed services group (msg), applications development and legacy system maintenance. The group provides services to telecommunications, transportation, oil and chemical and health care industries. The customers of the group include Fortune 500(R) companies. The group operates in the United States, Canada and the United Kingdom.

Primary SIC and add'l.: 7379 7371

CIK No: 0000006292

Subsidiaries: AiC Analysts Limited, Analysts International Business Resources Services, LLC, Analysts International Business Solutions Services, LLC, Analysts International Management Services, LLC, Analysts International Strategic Sourcing Services, LLC, Medical Concepts Staffing, Inc.

Officers: Elmer N. Baldwin/CEO, Pres., Michael Souders/Sr. VP - Solutions/$246,096.00, David Jenkins/CIO, Colleen M. Davenport/General Counsel, Sec./$253,143.00, John D. Bamberger/Exec. VP, Sr. VP - Solutions/$473,514.00, Paulette M. Quist/Sr. VP - Business Development, Strategy, David J. Steichen/CFO/$247,779.00

Directors: Krzysztof K. Burhardt/Chmn., Willard W. Brittian/Dir., Michael B. Esstman/Dir., Michael J. Lavelle/Dir., Margaret A. Loftus/Dir., Robb L. Prince/Dir., Brigid A. Bonner/47/Dir.

Owners: Walter Michels, Heartland Advisors, Inc./6.37%, John D. Bamberger/2.20%, Dimensional Fund Advisors Inc./6.00%, Brigid A. Bonner, Insiders/6.79%, Bank of America Corporation/10.33%, Colleen M. Davenport, Michael B. Esstman, Michael J. LaVelle, Michael W. Souders, Jeffrey P. Baker/2.01%, Krzysztof K. Burhardt, Willard W. Brittain, Robb L. Prince *(17 Owners included in Index)*

Financial Data: Fiscal Year End:12/31   Latest Annual Data: 3/31/2007

Year	Sales	Net Income
2007	$89,107,000	-$2,027,000
2006	$85,480,000	-$522,000

Curr. Assets:	$69,415,000	Curr. Liab.:	$43,233,000		
Plant, Equip.:	$4,056,000	Total Liab.:	$45,692,000	Indic. Yr. Divd.:	NA
Total Assets:	$102,004,000	Net Worth:	$56,312,000	Debt/ Equity:	NA

Analytical Surveys Inc

9725 Datapoint Dr., Ste. 300B, San Antonio, TX, 78229; *PH:* 1-210-657-1500;
Fax: 1-210-599-3162; *http://* www.anlt.com; *Email:* info@anlt.com

General - Incorporation	CO	*Stock*- Price on:12/24/2007	NA
Employees	82	Stock Exchange	OTC
Auditor	Pannell Kerr Forster Of Texas, P.C	Ticker Symbol	ANLT
Stk Agt	Computershare Investor Services LLC	Outstanding Shares	NA
Counsel	Loeffler Tuggey Pauerstein Rosenthal	E.P.S.	-$0.711
DUNS No.	00-830-0394	Shareholders	NA

Business: The group's principal activity is to provide customized data conversion, digital mapping services, spatial data management and technical services for the geographic information systems market. A geographic information system ('gis') is an intelligent map that allows users to input, update, query, analyze and display detailed information about a geographic area. The group transforms raw, often confusing information from multiple sources into a high-resolution, large-scale richly detailed digital and visual representation that organizations can use for making better decisions. The products are used by state and local governments and utility companies to manage information relating to utilities, natural resources, streets, land use and property taxation.

Primary SIC and add'l.: 7374 7389

CIK No: 0000753048

Officers: Lori A. Jones/50/Dir., CEO, Bill Nantell/CEO - US Operations, Donald L. Fryhover/Sr. VP, Manish Sanwalka/Pres., Ashoo Vijeshwar/VP

Directors: Lori A. Jones/50/Dir., CEO, Thomas Roddy/67/Chmn., Edward P. Gistaro/72/Dir., Rad Weaver/32/Dir., Hank Cohn/39/Dir.

Owners: Insiders/11.06%, Louis Dorfman/1.31%, Alpha Capital, AG/12.55%, DKR Soundshore Oasis Holding Fund Ltd./17.31%, Thomas P. Roddy/1.43%, Rad Weaver/1.34%, Harborview Master Fund L.P./17.31%, Lori A. Jones/4.02%, Don Fryhover/2.57%, Edward P. Gistaro/1.43%, Longview Fund, LLP/12.99%, Monarch Capital Fund Ltd./17.31%

Financial Data: Fiscal Year End:09/30   Latest Annual Data: 09/30/2006

Year	Sales	Net Income
2006	$4,320,000	-$335,000
2005	$6,063,000	-$3,340,000
2004	$11,608,000	-$1,247,000

Curr. Assets:	$2,954,000	Curr. Liab.:	$2,488,000		
Plant, Equip.:	$2,083,000	Total Liab.:	$2,501,000	Indic. Yr. Divd.:	NA
Total Assets:	$5,037,000	Net Worth:	$2,536,000	Debt/ Equity:	NA

Anaren Inc

6635 Kirkville Rd., East Syracuse, NY, 13057; *PH:* 1-315-432-8909; *Fax:* 1-315-432-9121;
http:// www.anaren.com

General - Incorporation	NY	*Stock*- Price on:12/24/2007	$16.91
Employees	602	Stock Exchange	NDQ
Auditor	KPMG LLP	Ticker Symbol	ANEN
Stk Agt	American Stock Transfer & Trust Co.	Outstanding Shares	17,150,000
Counsel	NA	E.P.S.	NA
DUNS No.	04-235-2922	Shareholders	NA

Business: The group's principal activities are to provide microwave components and assemblies for the wireless and space and defense markets. The group operates through two segments: wireless segment and space and defense segment. The wireless segment designs, manufactures and markets products including xinger components, resistive components, ferrite components and printed wiring boards used by the wireless communications market. The space and defense segment manufactures and markets radar countermeasure subsystems and beamforming networks to the radar and satellite communications markets. The group operates in the United States, Asia-Pacific, Europe and Americas. The major customers include alcatel, avnet, bae optilas, celestica corp, eg components, lucent technologies, mks instruments, motorola, nokia, remec, richardson electronics inc, st jude, solectron, bae, boeing inc, corbett, harris, itt avionics, lg innotek co ltd, lockheed martin, northrup grumman and raytheon.

Primary SIC and add'l.: 3812 3663 3674 3679

CIK No: 0000006314

Subsidiaries: Anaren Ceramics, Inc., Anaren Communications Suzhou Company, Ltd., Anaren GP, Inc., Anaren Microwave, Inc., Anaren Properties LLC, RF Power Components, Inc.

Officers: Bill Barrett/Western US, Canada Regional Sales Mgr., Rob Orford/Northern European Regional Sales Mgr., Eddie Petch/Southern European Regional Sales Mgr., Yong Chen/Asia, Australia Regional Sales Mgr.

Directors: Carl W. Gerst/Founder, Hugh A. Hair/Founder

Owners: Insiders/10.78%, James G. Gould, Dale F. Eck, Gert R. Thygesen/1.01%, Dimensional Fund Advisors Inc/7.82%, Mark P. Burdick, David Wilemon, Lord, Abbett & Co. LLC/14.90%, Matthew S. Robison, Carl W. Gerst/3.02%, Lawrence A. Sala/3.58%, Timothy P. Ross, Robert U. Roberts, Herbert I. Corkin, Joseph E. Porcello

Financial Data: Fiscal Year End:06/30   Latest Annual Data: 6/30/2006

Year	Sales	Net Income
2006	$105,464,000	$11,099,000
2005	$94,461,000	$7,413,000
2004	$85,079,000	$7,957,000

Curr. Assets:	$124,171,000	Curr. Liab.:	$12,010,000	P/E Ratio:	19.44
Plant, Equip.:	$27,635,000	Total Liab.:	$16,908,000	Indic. Yr. Divd.:	NA
Total Assets:	$189,026,000	Net Worth:	$172,118,000	Debt/ Equity:	NA

Anchor Bancorp Wisconsin Inc

25 W Main St., Madison, WI, 53703; *PH:* 1-608-252-8700; *Fax:* 1-608-252-8976;
http:// www.anchorbank.com

General - Incorporation	WI	*Stock*- Price on:12/24/2007	$27.31
Employees	831	Stock Exchange	NDQ
Auditor	Mcgladrey & Pullen, LLP	Ticker Symbol	ABCW
Stk Agt	American Stock Transfer & Trust Co.	Outstanding Shares	21,620,000
Counsel	NA	E.P.S.	$1.80
DUNS No.	05-083-1106	Shareholders	NA

Business: The group's principal activity is to provide general banking business. The community banking segment of the group offers deposit products include passbook savings accounts, demand accounts, now accounts, money market deposit accounts and certificates of deposit. It originates mortgage loans, home equity and other consumer loans, student loans, credit cards, annuities and related consumer financial services, lines of credit, secured loans and commercial real estate loans. The real estate investments segment primarily invests in real estate developments. Such developments include recreational residential developments and industrial developments such as office parks. The group conducts its business from the headquarters located in madison, Wisconsin and from 56 other full-service offices located primarily in south-central and southwest Wisconsin and two loan origination offices.

Primary SIC and add'l.: 6531 6712 6035

CIK No: 0000885322

Subsidiaries: Investment Directions, Inc.

Officers: Douglas J. Timmerman/Chmn., CEO/$419,164.00, Anthony J. Cattelino/65/Exec. VP, Recording Sec./$182,475.00, Michael W. Helser/63/CFO, Exec. VP, Treasurer/$180,654.00

Directors: Douglas J. Timmerman/Chmn., CEO, Richard A. Bergstrom/Dir., Holly Cremer Berkenstadt/Dir., Donald D. Kropidlowski/Dir., Greg M. Larson/Dir., David L. Omachinski/Dir., Donald D. Parker/Dir., Pat Richter/Dir., James D. Smessaert/Dir., Mark Timmerman/Dir.

Owners: Anthony J. Cattelino, Donald D. Parker, Pat Richter, Greg M. Larson, James D. Smessaert, Anchor BanCorp Wisconsin Inc./6.06%, Daniel K. Nichols, Donald D. Kropidlowski, Barclays Global Investors, NA/5.23%, Douglas J. Timmerman/6.44%, David L. Omachinski, Columbia Wanger Asset Management, L.P./6.80%, Holly Cremer Berkenstadt, Michael W. Helser, Richard A. Bergstrom *(17 Owners included in Index)*

Financial Data: Fiscal Year End:03/31   Latest Annual Data: 3/31/2007

Year	Sales	Net Income
2007	$334,974,000	$38,972,000
2006	$305,526,000	$44,683,000
2005	$334,843,000	$48,335,000

Curr. Assets:	$178,513,000	Curr. Liab.:	$3,720,646,000	P/E Ratio:	15.43
Plant, Equip.:	$99,748,000	Total Liab.:	$4,195,333,000	Indic. Yr. Divd.:	$0.680
Total Assets:	$4,539,685,000	Net Worth:	$336,866,000	Debt/ Equity:	1.2707

Anchor Glass Container Corp

1 Anchor Plz., 4343 Anchor Plz. Pkwy., Tampa, FL, 33634; *PH:* 1-813-884-0000;
http:// www.anchorglass.com

General - Incorporation	DE	*Stock*- Price on:12/24/2007	NA
Employees	822	Stock Exchange	OTC
Auditor	PricewaterhouseCoopers LLP	Ticker Symbol	AGCC
Stk Agt	Continental Stock Transfer & Trust Co	Outstanding Shares	NA
Counsel	NA	E.P.S.	NA
DUNS No.	10-186-4668	Shareholders	NA

Business: The group's principle activity is to manufacture a line of clear, amber, green and other colored glass containers. These glasses are produced in different types, designs and sizes. The company markets its products to the producers of beer, liquor, food, tea and other beverages in the United States. The company's customers include anheuser-busch companies, inc., the stroh brewery company, the coca-cola trading company, specialty products company, jim beam brands and hunt-wesson. The group operates from United States.

Primary SIC and add'l.: 3221

CIK No: 0001052163

Anchor Lamina Inc

2590 Ouellette Ave., Windsor, ON, N8X 1L7; **PH:** 1-519-966-4431; *http://* www.anchorlamina.com

General - Incorporation......................Canada	Stock- Price on:12/24/2007 ....NA
Employees ....NA	Stock Exchange.......................................NA
Auditor ....Deloitte & Touche LLP	Ticker Symbol...NA
Stk Agt..Mellon Trust Co	Outstanding Shares ....NA
Counsel...NA	E.P.S...NA
DUNS No. 20-976-4984	Shareholders...NA

Business: The group's principle activities include producing and selling various mold bases and components to the metal-working and plastic mould industries; manufacture complete line of plain-bearing and ball-bearing die sets as well as custom die sets including weldments and bolster plates; and offer machining services including cutting, grinding and stress-relieving steel plates. The group operates from United States.

Primary SIC and add'l.: 6719 3544

CIK No: 0001001987

Subsidiaries: Anchor Lamina (Barbados) Inc, Anchor Lamina Die Sets GmbH, Anchor Lamina Holdings GmbH

Officers: Roy Verstraete/CEO, Pres., Jim Meloche/VP - Nads Operations, Harvey Van Huizen/VP - Sales, US Die Sets, Paul Brisebois/VP - Sales, Canadian Die Sets, Todd Castile/VP - Sales, Components, Wolfgang Neubert/MD - Anchor Lamina Gmbh, Steve Zerio/CFO, VP, Joe Lerman/VP - Component Operations

Ancor Resources Inc

Plz. Paseo, 110 - 4801 Lang Ave., Albuquerque, NM, 87109; **PH:** 52-505-842-5537

General - Incorporation............................NV	Stock- Price on:12/24/2007 ....NA
Employees ....NA	Stock Exchange.....................................OTC
Auditor ....James Stafford, Inc	Ticker Symbol....................................NUMX
Stk Agt..NA	Outstanding Shares ....NA
Counsel...NA	E.P.S...NA
DUNS No. ....NA	Shareholders...NA

Business: The groups principal activity is to explore minerals and natural gas. The group operates from the United States and Canada.

Primary SIC and add'l.: 1000

CIK No: 0001348788

Officers: Michael Sweeney/44/Dir., CEO, Pres., Jim Callaghan/50/Dir., Principal Accounting Officer, Principal Financial Officer, Sec., Treasurer

Directors: Michael Sweeney/44/Dir., CEO, Pres., Jim Callaghan/50/Dir., Principal Accounting Officer, Principal Financial Officer, Sec., Treasurer, Allan J. Beaton/57/Dir.

Owners: Michael Sweeney/16.30%, Insiders/32.70%, Jim Callaghan/16.30%

Financial Data: Fiscal Year End:02/28 Latest Annual Data: 2/28/2007

Year	Sales	Net Income
2007	NA	-$65,000

Curr. Assets:	$4,000	Curr. Liab.:	$35,000		
Plant, Equip.:	NA	Total Liab.:	$35,000	Indic. Yr. Divd.:	NA
Total Assets:	$4,000	Net Worth:	-$30,000	Debt/ Equity:	NA

Andain Inc

5190 Neil Rd., Ste. 430, Reno, NV, 89502; **PH:** 1-775-333-5997

General - Incorporation............................NV	Stock- Price on:12/24/2007 ....NA
Employees ....NA	Stock Exchange.......................................NA
Auditor Child, Van Wagoner & Bradshaw, PLLC	Ticker Symbol...NA
Stk Agt..NA	Outstanding Shares ....NA
Counsel...NA	E.P.S...NA
DUNS No. ....NA	Shareholders...NA

Business: The groups principle activity is to develop novel technologies and products in the biotechnology and medical fields. The group also provides nano-particle drug delivery system capable of carrying the designed drug for pulmonary applications into a lead compound to enter pre-clinical tests. The group operates from United States.

Primary SIC and add'l.: 6770

CIK No: 0001321502

Owners: Pangea Investments GmbH/99.50%

Andersons Inc

480 W Dussel Dr., Maumee, OH, 43537; **PH:** 1-419-893-5050; **Fax:** 1-419-891-2781; *http://* www.andersonsinc.com; **Email:** hostmaster@andersonsinc.com

General - Incorporation............................OH	Stock- Price on:12/24/2007 ....$41.17
Employees 1,277	Stock Exchange....................................NDQ
Auditor ....PricewaterhouseCoopers LLP	Ticker Symbol....................................ANDE
Stk Agt..... Computershare Investor Services LLC	Outstanding Shares 17,800,000
Counsel...NA	E.P.S..$3.19
DUNS No. 60-675-6716	Shareholders...NA

Business: The group's principal activities are carried out through four operating segments groups: agriculture group, processing group, rail group and retail group. The agriculture group purchases and merchandises grain, operates grain elevator facilities, manufactures and sells dry and liquid agricultural

nutrients, distributes agricultural inputs to dealers and farmers. The processing group manufactures turf and ornamental plant fertilizer and control products for lawn and garden use, professional golf and landscaping industries. The rail group sells, repairs, reconfigures, manages and leases railcars and locomotives. The retail group operates six retail stores and a distribution center in Ohio.

Primary SIC and add'l.: 5153 6517 3524 2874 5999

CIK No: 0000821026

Subsidiaries: Cap Acquire Canada ULC, Cap Acquire LLC, Cap Acquire Mexico S. de R.L. de C.V., Carcat Ulc, Crop & Soil Service, Inc., Metamora Commodity Company Incorporated, Narcat LLC, NARCAT Mexico S. de R.L. de C.V., NuRail Canada ULC, NuRail USA LLC, TAI Holdings, Inc., The Andersons Ag Software, Inc., The Andersons Agriculture Group, L.P., The Andersons Agriservices, Inc., The Andersons AgVantage Agency, LLC 21 Subsidiaries included in the Index

Officers: Michael J. Anderson/Dir., CEO, Pres./$1,369,531.00, Charles E. Gallagher/VP - Human Resources, Dennis J. Addis/Pres. - Plant Nutrient Group/$563,840.00, Daniel T. Anderson/Pres. - Retail Group, Philip C. Fox/VP - Corporate Planning, Naran U. Burchinow/VP, General Counsel, Corp. Sec., Richard R. George/VP, Corporate Controller, CIO/$427,017.00, Dale W. Fallat/VP - Corporate Services, Harold M. Reed/Pres. - Grain, Ethanol Group/$655,453.00, Rasesh H. Shah/Pres. - Rail Group/$787,339.00, Gary L. Smith/VP - Finance, Treasurer/$521,001.00, Thomas L. Waggoner/Pres. - Turf, Specialty Group

Directors: Michael J. Anderson/Dir., CEO, Pres., Richard P. Anderson/Chmn., Master /Dir., Robert J. King/Dir., Paul M. Kraus/Dir., Donald L. Mennel/Dir., David L. Nichols/Dir., Sidney A. Ribeau/Dir., Charles A. Sullivan/Dir., Jacqueline F. Woods/Dir.

Owners: Rasesh H. Shah, Richard R. George, David L. Nichols, Jacqueline F. Woods, Michael J. Anderson/2.80%, Dennis J. Addis, Robert J. King, Harold M. Reed, John F. Barrett, Donald L. Mennel, Charles A. Sullivan, Richard P. Anderson/3.60%, Paul M. Kraus, Sidney A. Ribeau, Insiders/12.60% *(16 Owners included in Index)*

Financial Data: Fiscal Year End:12/31 Latest Annual Data: 12/31/2006

Year	Sales	Net Income
2006	$1,458,053,000	$36,347,000
2005	$1,296,652,000	$26,087,000
2004	$1,275,273,000	$19,144,000

Curr. Assets:	$496,448,000	Curr. Liab.:	$340,040,000	P/E Ratio:	12.91
Plant, Equip.:	$240,561,000	Total Liab.:	$539,169,000	Indic. Yr. Divd.:	$0.190
Total Assets:	$809,344,000	Net Worth:	$270,175,000	Debt/ Equity:	0.5516

Andina Bottling Co Inc

Av. El Golf 40, Office 401, Santiago, Las Condes; **PH:** 56-23380500; *http://* www.koandina.com

General - Incorporation ....Chile	Stock- Price on:12/24/2007 ....$2.9041
Employees ....NA	Stock Exchange.......................................NA
Auditor ....PricewaterhouseCoopers LLP	Ticker Symbol...NA
Stk Agt..NA	Outstanding Shares ....NA
Counsel........... Simpson Thacher & Bartlett LLP	E.P.S...NA
DUNS No. ....NA	Shareholders...NA

Business: The group's principal activity is the production and distribution of all kinds of mineral water, juices, soft drinks and carbonated beverages. Its other activities are processing of fruits and manufacture of all types of containers and packaging. The company operates in Chile, Argentina and Brazil.

Primary SIC and add'l.: 2086 3085 2033

CIK No: 0000925261

Subsidiaries: Abisa Corp. S.A., Andina Bottling Investments Dos S.A., Andina Inversiones Societarias S.A., Embotelladora del Atlntico S.A., Envases Multipack S.A., Rio de Janeiro Refrescos Ltda., RJR Investments Corp., Servicios Multivending Ltda., Transportes Andina Refrescos Ltda., Vital Aguas S.A., Vital S.A.

Officers: Jaime R. Garcia/CEO, Pedro R. Pellegrini/Chief Legal, Communications Officer, Fernando Patrito/Logistics Mgr. - Embotelladora Del Atlantico SA, Renato F. Ramirez/56/GM - Embotelladora Andina SA, Chile, Cesar Vargas/GM - Vital SA, Vital Aguas SA, Fernando Calcagno/Finance, Administration Mgr. - Rio de Janeiro Refrescos Ltda, Brazil, Rodrigo Agliati/Sales Mgr. Key Accounting - Embotelladora Andina SA, Chile, Edson Bregolato/Marketing Mgr. - Rio de Janeiro Refrescos Ltda, Brazil, Luciano Moreira/Sales Mgr. - Rio de Janeiro Refrescos Ltda, Brazil, Alberto Marques/Industrial Mgr. - Rio de Janeiro Refrescos Ltda, Brazil, Adriane Chatkin/Finance, Administration Mgr. - Embotelladora Del Atlantico SA, Fernando Fragata/Legal Mgr. - Rio de Janeiro Refrescos Ltda, Brazil, Pablo Bardin/Industrial Mgr. - Embotelladora Del Atlantico SA, Osvaldo Garay/CFO, Michael Cooper/COO *(35 Officers included in Index)*

Directors: Juan Claro/58/Chmn., Ernesto Bertelsen/63/Alternate Dir., Patricio Parodi/45/Alternate Dir., Jose Domingo Eluchans/55/Alternate Dir., Jose Miguel Barros/44/Alternate Dir., Pedro Vicente/57/Alternate Dir., Jose Maria Eyzaguirre/46/Alternate Dir., Gonzalo Said/44/Dir., Jose Antonio Garces/42/Dir., Jorge G. Hurtado/62/Alternate Dir., Arturo Majlis/46/Dir., Heriberto Urzua/46/Dir., James Robert Quincey/43/Dir., Salvador Said/44/Dir.

Owners: Insiders, Freire, Principal foreign mutual funds as a group, The Bank of New York/12.42%, The Coca-Cola Company, directly or through subsidiaries/11.04%, Insiders/0.05%, Principal foreign mutual funds as a group/2.48%, Gonzalo Said Handal, Freire/42.42%, The Coca-Cola Company, directly or through subsidiaries, The Bank of New York, AFPs as a group, Gonzalo Said Handal/4.07%, AFPs as a group/7.34%

Andover Medical Inc

501 Tpke. St. 204, North Andover, MA, 01845; **PH:** 1-978-557-1001; *http://* www.andovermedical.com; **Email:** info@andovermedical.com

General - Incorporation ....DE	Stock- Price on:12/24/2007 ....$0.51
Employees 3	Stock Exchange....................................OTC
Auditor .... Mantyla McReynolds, LLC	Ticker Symbol....................................ADOV
Stk Agt..NA	Outstanding Shares ....NA
Counsel...NA	E.P.S...NA
DUNS No. ....NA	Shareholders...NA

Business: The groups principal activity is to modify infectious microorganism to activate the immune system. The group products include Lovaxin B, Lovaxin C, Lovaxin H, Lovaxin NY and Lovaxin P. The group operates from the United States.

Primary SIC and add'l.: 5047

CIK No: 0001339256

Subsidiaries: Andover Management Services, Inc.

Officers: Edwin A. Reilly/Chmn., CEO, James Shanahan/CFO

Directors: Edwin A. Reilly/Chmn., CEO, Robert G. Coffill/Dir., Marshall Sterman/Dir., Robert A. Baron/Dir.

Owners: Robert G. Coffill, Odett Holding Ltd, Meyers Associates, LP, Marshall Sterman, TriCounty Grain Corp, Bruce Meyers, Robert A. Baron, Michael Stone, James Shanahan, Edwin A. Reilly, James Muir Drummond, Vicis Capital Master Fund, Eusibio Mario Lopez Perez, Hjortur Eiriksson, Insiders *(19 Owners included in Index)*

Financial Data: *Fiscal Year End:*12/31 *Latest Annual Data:* 12/31/2006

Year	Sales	Net Income
2006	NA	-$730,000

Curr. Assets:	$2,512,000	**Curr. Liab.:**	$193,000		
Plant, Equip.:	$56,000	**Total Liab.:**	$193,000	**Indic. Yr. Divd.:**	NA
Total Assets:	$2,577,000	**Net Worth:**	$2,384,000	**Debt/ Equity:**	NA

Andrea Electronics Corp

65 Orville Dr., Ste. 1, Bohemia, NY, 11716; *PH:* 1-631-719-1800; *Fax:* 1-631-719-1998; *http://* www.andreaelectronics.com

General - Incorporation	NY	**Stock**- Price on:12/24/2007	$0.14
Employees	16	Stock Exchange	OTC
Auditor	Marcum & Kliegman LLP	Ticker Symbol	ANDR
Stk Agt	Continental Stock Transfer & Trust Co	Outstanding Shares	59,680,000
Counsel	Muldoon Murphy & Aguggia LLP	E.P.S.	-$0.01
DUNS No.	00-136-0692	Shareholders	NA

Business: The group's principal activity is to design, develop and manufacture communication products. The products are used in military and commercial aircraft communications systems and call centers. The group operates in three business segments: andrea anti-noise products, aircraft communication products and andrea dsp microphone and audio software products. The anti-noise products include noise cancellation and active noise cancellation computer headset products. The aircraft communication products include intercom systems, amplifiers and electronic control boxes for the industrial and military markets. The dsp microphone products include far-field microphone products used in videoconferencing systems and in-vehicle communications systems. The group operates in the United States, Europe, America and Asia. On 11-Apr-2003, the group completed the sale of andrea aircraft communications products division.

Primary SIC and add'l.: 3669 3661 3663

CIK No: 0000006494

Subsidiaries: Andrea ANC Manufacturing Inc., Andrea Digital Technologies, Inc., Andrea Direct Marketing Inc., Andrea Electronics Europe Inc., Andrea Marketing Inc., Lamar Signal Processing, Ltd.

Officers: Douglas J. Andrea/Chmn., CEO, Pres., Corp. Sec., Corisa L. Guiffre/VP, CFO, Assist. Corp. Sec.

Directors: Douglas J. Andrea/Chmn., CEO, Pres., Corp. Sec., Gary A. Jones/Dir., Louis Libin/Dir., Joseph J. Migliozzi/Dir., Jonathan D. Spaet/Dir.

Owners: Insiders/7.47%, Louis Libin, Douglas J. Andrea/4.96%, Gary A. Jones, Jonathan D. Spaet, Joseph J. Migliozzi, Corisa L. Guiffre

Financial Data: *Fiscal Year End:*12/31 *Latest Annual Data:* 12/31/2006

Year	Sales	Net Income
2006	$5,735,000	$19,000
2005	$4,230,000	-$628,000
2004	$5,623,000	-$1,679,000

Curr. Assets:	$2,599,000	**Curr. Liab.:**	$1,037,000		
Plant, Equip.:	$39,000	**Total Liab.:**	$1,037,000	**Indic. Yr. Divd.:**	NA
Total Assets:	$6,089,000	**Net Worth:**	$5,052,000	**Debt/ Equity:**	NA

Andrew Corp

3 Westbrook Corporate Ctr., Ste. 900, Westchester, IL, 60154; *PH:* 1-708-236-6600; *Fax:* 1-708-349-5444; *http://* www.andrew.com; *Email:* aopcustomersupportCtr.@andrew.com

General - Incorporation	DE	**Stock**- Price on:12/24/2007	$13.13
Employees	11,778	Stock Exchange	NDQ
Auditor	Ernst & Young LLP	Ticker Symbol	ANDW
Stk Agt	Computershare Investor Services LLC	Outstanding Shares	155,720,000
Counsel	NA	E.P.S.	-$1.04
DUNS No.	00-517-7084	Shareholders	NA

Business: The groups principle activities include designing, manufacturing, and supplying communications equipment, services, and systems for global communications infrastructure markets. The groups products include antennas, coverage and capacity products, and transmission line systems. The group operates from United States.

Primary SIC and add'l.: 3663 3357 4899 3812 3679

CIK No: 0000317093

Subsidiaries: Allen Telecom LLC, Allen Telecom Sweden, AB, Andrew AG, Andrew Amplifiers Inc., Andrew Australia Pty Ltd, Andrew Broadband Telecommunications (Yantai) Co. Ltd., Andrew Canada Inc., Andrew Corporation S.A. de C.V., Andrew Corporation Taiwan, Andrew do Brazil, Ltda., Andrew GmbH, Andrew Hong Kong Ltd., Andrew International Corporation, Andrew International Holding Corporation, Andrew Japan KK 25 Subsidiaries included in the Index

Officers: Ralph E. Faison/49/Dir., CEO, Pres., Justin C. Choi/Sr. VP, General Counsel, Corp. Sec., Daniel J. Hartnett/VP - tax, Treasury, Mark A. Olson/VP, Corporate Controller, Chief Accounting Officer, John E. Desana/Exec. VP, Group Pres. - Antenna, Cable Products, Marty R. Kittrell/CFO, Exec. VP, Asmadi Aziz/Area Sales Mgr. - Brunei Darussalam, Carleton Miller/Exec. VP, Group Pres. - Wireless Network Solutions, Peter Masih/Contact - Manufacturing, Sales, Canada, Roberto Mangullo/Regional Sales Mgr. - Brazil, Marcio Veronesi/System Engineer, Flavia Holtz/Contact - Customer Service, Samuel Buttarelli/Mgr. - Regional Sales South Eastern Europe, Italy, Vick Mamlouk/Contact - Sales, Pre Sales, Afganistan, Ulf Lofberg/System Engineer - Afganistan *(46 Officers included in Index)*

Directors: Ralph E. Faison/49/Dir., CEO, Pres., Gerald A. Poch/60/Chmn., Anne F. Pollack/51/Dir., Glen O. Toney/68/Dir., Jere D. Fluno/66/Dir., William O. Hunt/73/Dir., William L. Bax/63/Dir., Thomas A. Donahoe/72/Dir., Andrea L. Zopp/50/Dir.

Owners: Glen O. Toney, Ralph E. Faison, William L. Bax, Thomas A. Donahoe, John E. DeSana, Marty R. Kittrell, Jere D. Fluno, Gerald A. Poch, William O. Hunt, Roger J. Manka, Carleton M. Miller, Insiders/2.10%

Financial Data: *Fiscal Year End:*09/30 *Latest Annual Data:* 9/30/2006

Year	Sales	Net Income
2006	$2,146,093,000	-$34,290,000
2005	$1,961,234,000	$38,858,000
2004	$1,838,749,000	$32,985,000

Curr. Assets:	$1,153,021,000	**Curr. Liab.:**	$567,886,000		
Plant, Equip.:	$264,011,000	**Total Liab.:**	$901,646,000	**Indic. Yr. Divd.:**	NA
Total Assets:	$2,408,921,000	**Net Worth:**	$1,507,275,000	**Debt/ Equity:**	NA

Andrx Corp

4955 Orange Dr., Davie, FL, 33314; *PH:* 1-954-584-0300; *http://* www.andrx.com

General - Incorporation	DE	**Stock**- Price on:12/24/2007	$32.23
Employees	5,830	Stock Exchange	NA
Auditor	Ernst & Young LLP	Ticker Symbol	NA
Stk Agt	American Stock Transfer & Trust Co.	Outstanding Shares	102,530,000
Counsel	Broad & Cassel	E.P.S.	-$3.75
DUNS No.	NA	Shareholders	NA

Business: The group's principal activities are to develop and commercialize generic versions of controlled-release brand name pharmaceuticals using the proprietary controlled-release drug delivery technologies and generic versions of niche and immediate-release pharmaceutical products, including oral contraceptives. It distributes pharmaceuticals, primarily generics to independent pharmacies, pharmacy chains, pharmacy buying group's and physician's offices. The group also commercializes brand name pharmaceuticals. The controlled-release pharmaceuticals of the group provide consistent drug levels in the bloodstream than immediate-release dosage forms and may improve drug efficiency and reduce side effects, by releasing drug dosages at specific times and in specific locations in the body.

Primary SIC and add'l.: 2834 5122

CIK No: 0001123337

Subsidiaries: Anda Inc., Anda Marketing Inc., Anda Pharmaceuticals Inc., Anda Puerto Rico Inc., Anda Veterinary Supply Inc., Andrx EU Limited a UK company, Andrx Laboratories (NJ), Andrx Labs LLC, Andrx Management Corporation, Andrx Pharmaceuticals (MASS) Inc, Andrx Pharmaceuticals (NC) inc, Andrx Pharmaceuticals (NC)Equipment LLC, Andrx Pharmaceuticals Equipment #1 LLC, Andrx Pharmaceuticals inc, Andrx Pharmaceuticals LLC 25 Subsidiaries included in the Index

Financial Data: *Fiscal Year End:*12/31 *Latest Annual Data:* 12/31/2006

Year	Sales	Net Income
2006	$1,979,244,000	-$445,005,000
2005	$1,646,203,000	$138,233,000
2004	$1,640,551,000	$151,333,000

Curr. Assets:	$1,261,676,000	**Curr. Liab.:**	$689,929,000		
Plant, Equip.:	$697,415,000	**Total Liab.:**	$2,080,189,000	**Indic. Yr. Divd.:**	NA
Total Assets:	$3,760,577,000	**Net Worth:**	$1,680,388,000	**Debt/ Equity:**	0.6267

Anesiva Inc

650 Gateway Blvd., South San Francisco, CA, 94080; *PH:* 1-650-624-9600; *Fax:* 1-650-624-7540; *http://* www.anesiva.com; *Email:* investors@anesiva.com

General - Incorporation	DE	**Stock**- Price on:12/24/2007	$6.73
Employees	62	Stock Exchange	NDQ
Auditor	Ernst& Young LLP	Ticker Symbol	ANSV
Stk Agt	Mellon Investor Services LLC	Outstanding Shares	27,540,000
Counsel	NA	E.P.S.	-$2.15
DUNS No.	NA	Shareholders	NA

Business: The groups principle activities include developing and commercializing novel therapeutic treatments. The products of the group include Zingo(TM) and 4975. The group products sold under the trade names Avrina(TM) and Zingo(TM). In December 2005, the group merged with AlgoRx Pharmaceuticals, Inc. Specific customers of the group include Johnson & Johnson, Purdue Pharma and Genzyme. The group operates from the United States. The group's quarterly revenue for September 2007 was 0.05 millions of USD.

Primary SIC and add'l.: 2834

CIK No: 0001131517

Subsidiaries: AlgoRx Pharmaceuticals, Inc.

Officers: John P. McLaughlin/Dir., CEO, James Z. Huang/Pres., Patrick A. Broderick/VP, General Counsel, Corp. Sec., Nancy E. Donahue/Sr. VP - Sales, Marketing, Paul Goodson/Sr. Dir. - Investor Relations, Samantha R. Miller/VP - Business Development, Susan M. Kramer/VP - Preclinical Development, Melissa Morandi/VP - Quality Assurance, Richard P. Powers/CFO, VP, Jean-Frederic Viret/VP - Finance, Jennifer Cook Williams/VP - Investor Relations, Peony K. Yu/VP - Clinical Research, James R. Carr/VP - Marketing, Jack Regan/Sr. VP - Operations, Yvonne Richardson/VP - Manufacturing

Directors: John P. McLaughlin/Dir., CEO, Rodney Ferguson/Chmn., Carter H. Eckert/Dir., Arnold L. Oronsky/Dir., Michael F. Powell/Dir., James A. Harper/Dir., Charles M. Cohen/57/Dir., Thomas J. Colligan/Dir., Robert L. Zerbe/Dir., James N. Campbell/Dir.

Owners: Charles M. Cohen/4.20%, Robert L. Zerbe, Michael F. Powell/4.60%, Thomas J. Colligan, Arnold L. Oronsky/10.50%, Patrick A. Broderick, Richard P. Powers, Rodney A. Ferguson, Carter H. Eckert, Entities affiliated with J.P. Morgan Partners/12.50%, John P. McLaughlin/2.70%, Insiders/54.40%, James Z. Huang/1.40%, Entities affiliated with InterWest Partners/10.50%, Entities affiliated with Federated Investors Inc./5.10% *(16 Owners included in Index)*

Financial Data: *Fiscal Year End:*12/31 *Latest Annual Data:* 12/31/2006

Year	Sales	Net Income
2006	$89,000	-$55,567,000
2005	NA	-$33,518,000
2004	$36,382,000	-$39,848,000

Curr. Assets:	$86,208,000	**Curr. Liab.:**	$6,831,000		
Plant, Equip.:	$8,446,000	**Total Liab.:**	$7,048,000	**Indic. Yr. Divd.:**	NA
Total Assets:	$95,376,000	**Net Worth:**	$88,328,000	**Debt/ Equity:**	NA

Angeion Corp

350 Oak Grove Pkwy., St. Paul, MN, 55127; *PH:* 1-651-484-4874; *Fax:* 1-651-379-8227; *http://* www.angeion.com; *Email:* investor@angeion.com

General - Incorporation........MN
Employees........144
Auditor........KPMG LLP
Stk Agt........Wells Fargo Shareowner Services
Counsel........Oppenheimer Wolff & Donnelly
DUNS No........15-750-7237

Stock- Price on:12/24/2007........$8.444
Stock Exchange........NDQ
Ticker Symbol........ANGN
Outstanding Shares........4,080,000
E.P.S........$0.52
Shareholders........NA

Business: The group's principle activities are to develop, manufacture and market noninvasive cardio-respiratory diagnostic systems and related software used for the management and improvement of cardio-respiratory health. The group operates through its subsidiary medical graphics corp and the products of the group are sold under the trade name 'medgraphics'. The principal products of the group include pulmonary function and cardiopulmonary exercise testing systems. Pulmonary function applications include screening asthma patients, pre-operative and post-operative assessment of heart and lung surgery patients, evaluating lung damage from occupational exposures and documenting responses to therapy. Cardiopulmonary exercise (cpx) testing systems measure fitness or conditioning levels as well as help physicians diagnose heart and lung diseases. The group's quarterly revenue for September 2007 was 8.87 millions of USD.

Primary SIC and add'l.: 3841 8731

CIK No: 0000815093

Subsidiaries: Medical Graphics Corporation

Officers: Rodney A. Young/53/Dir., CEO, Pres., Dale Johnson/CFO, Tim Fitzgerald/VP - Operations, Sheryl Rapheal/VP - Human Resources, Administra, Jim Gaul/VP - Sales, Terry Kapsen/VP - Marketing, Business Development New Leaf Products, Michael G. Snow/VP - Research, Development, Marketing, Quality, Tim Quinn/VP - Sales New Leaf Products, Tom Sullivan/VP - Technical Services

Directors: Rodney A. Young/53/Dir., CEO, Pres., Arnold A. Angeloni/66/Chmn., James K. Ehlen/64/Dir., John C. Penn/68/Dir., John R. Baudhuin/Dir., Philip I. Smith/Dir.

Owners: Insiders/5.80%, Healthinvest Partners/7.90%, Arnold A. Angeloni/1.00%, James K. Ehlen, John R. Baudhuin, Rodney A. Young/2.80%, John C. Penn, Dale H. Johnson

Financial Data: *Fiscal Year End:*12/31 *Latest Annual Data:* 10/31/2006

Year	Sales	Net Income
2006	$33,651,000	$1,437,000
2005	$23,774,000	-$919,000
2004	$20,688,000	-$2,300,000

Curr. Assets:	$16,890,000	**Curr. Liab.:**	$6,686,000		
Plant, Equip.:	$1,096,000	**Total Liab.:**	$7,443,000	**Indic. Yr. Divd.:**	NA
Total Assets:	$21,753,000	**Net Worth:**	$14,310,000	**Debt/ Equity:**	NA

Angelciti Entertainment Inc

9000 Sheridan St., Ste. 7, Pembroke Pines, FL, 33024; *PH:* 1-800-908-9574

General - Incorporation........NV
Employees........9
Auditor........Salberg & Co P.A
Stk Agt........Holladay Stock Transfer, Inc.
Counsel........NA
DUNS No........NA

Stock- Price on:12/24/2007........$0.015
Stock Exchange........OTC
Ticker Symbol........AGCI
Outstanding Shares........9,610,000
E.P.S........$0.006
Shareholders........NA

Business: The group's principal activity is to administer the online gaming operations of equivest opportunity fund, which owns the online casino url known as shark casino.com. Other activities include sublicense of online gaming software. The group has license to use, exploit and sublicense the gaming software product owned by real time gaming (rtg). The group uses state-of-the-art casino gaming and sports book software under a license arrangement with a casino software development company. It operates principally in the United States. On 20-Jan-2003, the group acquired worldwide management sa.

Primary SIC and add'l.: 7999

CIK No: 0001084122

Subsidiaries: First National Consulting, Inc, Worldwide Management, SA

Officers: George Gutierrez/43/Dir., CEO, CFO, Pres., Treasurer, Sec., Dean Ward-Vice/Pres., Treasurer, Sec.

Directors: George Gutierrez/43/Dir., CEO, CFO, Pres., Treasurer, Sec., Grace Bustamente/32/Dir.

Owners: Insiders/0.33%, George Gutierrez/50.00%, George Gutierrez/0.33%, Dean Ward/50.00%

Financial Data: *Fiscal Year End:*12/31 *Latest Annual Data:* 12/31/2006

Year	Sales	Net Income
2006	$105,000	-$88,000
2005	$650,000	-$3,593,000
2004	$863,000	-$700,000

Curr. Assets:	$12,000	**Curr. Liab.:**	$4,000		
Plant, Equip.:	NA	**Total Liab.:**	$4,000	**Indic. Yr. Divd.:**	NA
Total Assets:	$177,000	**Net Worth:**	$173,000	**Debt/ Equity:**	NA

Angelica Corp

424 S Woods Mill Rd., Chesterfield, MO, 63017; *PH:* 1-314-854-3800; *Fax:* 1-314-854-3890; *http://* www.angelica.com

General - Incorporation........MO
Employees........6,400
Auditor........Deloitte & Touche LLP
Stk Agt........Computershare Trust Co., N.A.
Counsel........NA
DUNS No........00-629-1694

Stock- Price on:12/24/2007........$23.62
Stock Exchange........NYSE
Ticker Symbol........AGL
Outstanding Shares........9,590,000
E.P.S........$0.57
Shareholders........NA

Business: The group's principle activity is to provide textile rental and laundry services. The group provides products and services to health care institutions, hotels, motels and restaurants in or near major metropolitan areas. The group operates in two segments: textile services and life uniform. On 31-Jan-2004, the textile services segment had 28 laundry plants operating in the United States providing textile rental and laundry services for health care institutions. This segment also provides a limited amount of general linen services in selected areas, such as hotels, motels and restaurants. The retail sales segment consists of approximately 1,250 specialty retail stores and approximately 10 catalogue operations in the United States. The group's total revenue for year 2007 was 425.74 millions of USD.

Primary SIC and add'l.: 5661 7213 5699 2326 2339

CIK No: 0000006571

Subsidiaries: Angelica Realty Co., Angelica Textile Services, Inc., Royal Institutional Services, Inc., Southern Service Company, The Surgi-Pack Corporation

Officers: Stephen M. O'Hara/Dir., CEO, Pres., James W. Shaffer/VP, Treasurer, CFO, Steven L. Frey/VP, General Counsel, Sec., Steven J. Mosetti/Corporate Controller, John S. Olbrych/Sr. VP, Chief Administrative Officer, Richard M. Oliva/Sr. VP - Sales, Service, Russell W. Watson/Sr. VP - Strategy, Marketing, Sales Administration, Melton E. Davis/VP - Operations

Directors: Stephen M. O'Hara/Dir., CEO, Pres., Ronald J. Kruszewski/Non Exec. Chmn., John J. Quicke/Vice Chmn., James R. Henderson/Dir., Charles W. Mueller/Dir., Kelvin R. Westbrook/Dir., Don W. Hubble/Dir., Ronald N. Riner/Dir.

Owners: Steven L. Frey, T. Rowe Price Associates, Inc/9.31%, Stephen M. OHara, John S. Olbrych, Insiders, Don W. Hubble, Steel Partners II, L.P./18.70%, Ronald N. Riner, Dimensional Fund Advisors, Inc/7.95%, Ronald J. Kruszewski, Pirate Capital LLC/9.75%, Kelvin R. Westbrook, Charles W. Mueller

Financial Data: *Fiscal Year End:*01/28 *Latest Annual Data:* 1/27/2007

Year	Sales	Net Income
2007	$425,735,000	$3,633,000
2006	$418,357,000	$248,000
2005	$316,074,000	$6,361,000

Curr. Assets:	$93,429,000	**Curr. Liab.:**	$55,718,000	**P/E Ratio:**	54.93
Plant, Equip.:	$101,665,000	**Total Liab.:**	$137,597,000	**Indic. Yr. Divd.:**	$0.440
Total Assets:	$288,953,000	**Net Worth:**	$151,356,000	**Debt/ Equity:**	0.6000

Angiodynamics Inc

603 Queensbury Ave., Queensbury, NY, 12804; *PH:* 1-518-798-1215; *Fax:* 1-518-798-3625; *http://* www.angiodynamics.com; *Email:* info@angiodynamics.com

General - Incorporation........DE
Employees........305
Auditor........PricewaterhouseCoopers LLP
Stk Agt........Registrar & Transfer Co
Counsel........Davies, Ward, Phillips & Vineburg LLP
DUNS No........09-091-0639

Stock- Price on:12/24/2007........$17.19
Stock Exchange........NDQ
Ticker Symbol........ANGO
Outstanding Shares........23,930,000
E.P.S........-$0.42
Shareholders........NA

Business: The group's principle activities include designing, developing, manufacturing and marketing a broadline of therapeutic and diagnostic devices used by interventional radiologists and other physicians for the treatment of peripheral vascular disease (pvd). Pvd is a condition in which the arteries or veins that carry blood to or from the legs, arms and non-cardiac organs (kidney, intestines, brain) become narrowed, obstructed or ballooned. The products of the company include angiographic products and accessories, hemodialysis catheters, pta dilation catheters, thrombolytic products, image-guided vascular access products, endovascular laser venous system products, drainage products and other. The group operates from United States.

Primary SIC and add'l.: NA

CIK No: 0001275187

Subsidiaries: Leocor, Inc

Officers: Eamonn P. Hobbs/Dir., Co - Founder, CEO, Pres./$814,547.00, Joseph Gersuk/CFO, Exec. VP/$88,015.00, John Soto/VP - Global Sales/$352,243.00, Robert D. Mitchell/46/COO, Exec. VP, Joseph G. Gerardi/VP - Special Projects/$314,066.00, Harold C. Mapes/VP - Operations/$343,820.00, Robert M. Rossell/VP - Corporate Accounting/$350,708.00, William M. Appling/Sr. VP - Research, Development, Brian S. Kunst/VP - Regulatory Affairs, Quality Assurance, Daniel K. Recinella/VP - Product Development

Directors: Eamonn P. Hobbs/Dir., Co - Founder, CEO, Pres., Vincent Bucci/Chmn., Wesley E. Johnson/Dir., Robert E. Flaherty/Dir., Howard W. Donnelly/Dir., Steve Laporte/Dir., Dennis S. Meteny/Dir., Paul S. Echenberg/Dir., Jeffrey G. Gold/Dir.

Owners: Jeffery Gold, Dennis S. Meteny, Linda B. Stern/5.50%, Eamonn P. Hobbs, Joseph D. Gersuk, Robert M. Rossell, Paul S. Echenberg, Joseph G. Gerardi, Insiders/2.70%, Harold C. Mapes, Steve LaPorte, Robert E. Flaherty, Wellington Management Company, LLC/11.90%, Vincent Bucci, Howard W. Donnelly *(17 Owners included in Index)*

Financial Data: *Fiscal Year End:*06/03 *Latest Annual Data:* 06/02/2007

Year	Sales	Net Income
2007	$112,227,000	-$9,127,000
2006	$78,451,000	$6,866,000
2005	$60,289,000	$4,548,000

Curr. Assets:	$122,156,000	**Curr. Liab.:**	$10,807,000		
Plant, Equip.:	$10,802,000	**Total Liab.:**	$13,562,000	**Indic. Yr. Divd.:**	NA
Total Assets:	$137,000,000	**Net Worth:**	$123,438,000	**Debt/ Equity:**	0.0519

AngioGenex Inc

425 Madison Ave. 902, New York, NY, 10017; *PH:* 1-212-874-6608; *http://* www.angiogenex.com; *Email:* info@angiogenex.com

General - Incorporation........NV
Employees........NA
Auditor........Williams & Webster, P.S.
Stk Agt........Nevada Agency & Trust Company
Counsel........NA
DUNS No........NA

Stock- Price on:12/24/2007........$0.505
Stock Exchange........OTC
Ticker Symbol........AGGX
Outstanding Shares........20,430,000
E.P.S........-$0.02
Shareholders........NA

Business: The groups principal activities include discovering and developing id-based products for treatment and diagnosis of cancer. In the year 2005, the group merged with eClic Acquisition, Inc. The group operates from the United States.

Primary SIC and add'l.: 2836

CIK No: 0001085596

Subsidiaries: eClic, Inc

Officers: Richard A. Salvador/Dir., CEO, Pres., Michael M. Strage/Chmn., Head - Business Devlopment, Martin Murray/Dir., CFO, Sec., Treasurer, William Garland/61/COO, George Gould/68/Gerneral Counsel, Jiadeep Chaudhary/Principal Advisor, Neal Rosen/Member - Scientific Advisory Board

Directors: Richard A. Salvador/Dir., CEO, Pres., Michael M. Strage/Chmn., Head - Business Devlopment, Martin Murray/Dir., CFO, Sec., Treasurer, Shahin Rafii/Member - Scientific Advisory Board, Robert Benezra/Member - Scientific Advisory Board, Antonio Iavarone/Member - Scientific Advisory Board, Glenn Stoller/Member - Scientific Advisory Board, Patrica D'Amore/Member - Scientific Advisory Board, John Chen/Member - Scientific Advisory Board

Owners: William Garland/5.85%, George Gould/3.48%, Granadilla Holdings Ltd/19.28%, Atypical BioVentures Fund LLC/14.88%, Insiders/33.09%, Michael Strage/15.71%, Martin Murray, Richard Salvador/9.91%

Financial Data: *Fiscal Year End:*12/31 *Latest Annual Data:* 12/31/2006

Year	Sales	Net Income
2006	NA	-$343,000

Curr. Assets:	$20,000	**Curr. Liab.:**	$402,000		
Plant, Equip.:	$2,000	**Total Liab.:**	$402,000	**Indic. Yr. Divd.:**	NA
Total Assets:	$22,000	**Net Worth:**	-$380,000	**Debt/ Equity:**	NA

Angiotech Pharmaceuticals Inc

1618 Sta. St., Vancouver, BC, V6A 1B6; ***PH:*** 1-604-221-7676; ***http://*** www.angiotech.com; ***Email:*** info@angio.com

General - Incorporation	Canada	**Stock**- Price on:12/24/2007	$7.23
Employees	215	Stock Exchange	NDQ
Auditor	Ernst & Young LLP	Ticker Symbol	ANPI
Stk Agt	Computershare Trust Co of Canada	Outstanding Shares	85,010,000
Counsel	Irwin, White & Jennings	E.P.S.	-$0.59
DUNS No.	NA	Shareholders	NA

Business: The group's principal activities are to enhance the performance of medical devices and bio materials through the innovative use of therapeutics. The group operates through two segments: medical device coatings/implants and therapeutics. Medical device coatings/implants comprise the research and development of drug loaded coatings for medical devices and drug loaded medical implants. Therapeutics comprises the research and development of pharmaceuticals for the treatment of chronic inflammatory diseases such as rheumatoid arthritis and psoriasis. On 31-Jan-2003, it acquired cohesion technologies inc.

Primary SIC and add'l.: 3845 8731

CIK No: 0001096481

Subsidiaries: Angiotech BioCoatings Corp., Angiotech International Holdings Inc, Angiotech Investment Partnership, Angiotech Pharmaceuticals (US), Inc

Officers: William Hunter/Dir., CEO, Pres., Gary Ingenito/Chief Clinical, Regulatory Affairs Officer, David D. McMasters/Sr. VP - Legal, General Counsel, Tom Bailey/CFO, David M. Hall/Chief Compliance Officer, Sr. VP - Government, Community Relations, Rui Avelar/Chief Medical Officer, Jeffrey P. Walker/Sr. VP - Research, Development, Jodi Regts/Mgr. - Investor Relations, Corporate Communications, Deirdre Neary/Mgr. - Investor Relations

Directors: William Hunter/Dir., CEO, Pres., David T. Howard/Chmn., Hartley T. Richardson/Dir., Glen D. Nelson/Dir., Greg Peet/Dir., Ned Brown/Dir., Arthur H. Willms/Dir., Edward M. Brown/Dir., Laura A. Brege/Dir.

Financial Data: ***Fiscal Year End:***12/31 ***Latest Annual Data:*** 12/31/2006

Year	Sales	Net Income
2006	$315,075,000	$4,585,000
2005	$199,648,000	-$1,187,000
2004	$130,780,000	$51,792,000

Curr. Assets:	$181,507,000	**Curr. Liab.:**	$72,542,000		
Plant, Equip.:	$59,783,000	**Total Liab.:**	$723,041,000	**Indic. Yr. Divd.:**	NA
Total Assets:	$1,205,874,000	**Net Worth:**	$482,833,000	**Debt/ Equity:**	NA

Anglo American Plc

20 Carlton House Ter., London, SW1Y 5AG; ***PH:*** 44-02079688888; ***Fax:*** 44-2079688500; ***http://*** www.angloamerican.co.uk; ***Email:*** corporateaffairs@angloamerican.co.uk

General - Incorporation		**Stock**- Price on:12/24/2007	$30.52
Employees	NA	Stock Exchange	NDQ
Auditor	NA	Ticker Symbol	AAUK
Stk Agt	Mellon Investor Services LLC	Outstanding Shares	NA
Counsel	NA	E.P.S.	$11.56
DUNS No.	NA	Shareholders	NA

Business: The groups principal activity is to provide mining and natural resources. The products of the group include gold, diamond, platinum and coal. The group operates from the Africa, Europe, South and North America and Australia.

Primary SIC and add'l.: 1221 1061 0811 2611 1099 1041 3399 0831 1222 2671 1021 5052 1499

CIK No: 0001088370

Officers: Cynthia Carroll/51/Executive Dir., Rene Medori/50/Executive Dir., Nick Von Schirnding/Head - Investor, Corporate Affairs, Charles Gordon/Investor Relations Analyst, Anna Poulter/Investor Relations Analyst

Directors: Cynthia Carroll/51/Executive Dir., Rene Medori/50/Executive Dir., Fred Phaswana/63/Non Exec. Dir., Bobby Godsell/55/Non Exec. Dir., David Challen/64/Non Exec. Dir., Mark Moody-Stuart/67/Non Exec. Dir., Rob Margetts/61/Non Exec. Dir., Nicky Oppenheimer/62/Non Exec. Dir., Peter Woicke/65/Non Exec. Dir., Chris Fay/62/Non Exec. Dir., Mamphela Ramphele/60/Non Exec. Dir., Karel Van Miert/66/Non Exec. Dir.

Financial Data: ***Fiscal Year End:***NA ***Latest Annual Data:*** 12/31/2006

Year	Sales	Net Income
2006	$33,072,000,000	$6,922,000,000
2005	$29,434,000,000	$3,521,000,000
2004	$24,930,000,000	$2,913,000,000

Curr. Assets:	$11,844,000,000	**Curr. Liab.:**	$8,799,000,000	**P/E Ratio:**	53.58
Plant, Equip.:	$24,686,000,000	**Total Liab.:**	$19,356,000,000	**Indic. Yr. Divd.:**	NA
Total Assets:	$46,483,000,000	**Net Worth:**	$27,127,000,000	**Debt/ Equity:**	NA

Anglo Swiss Resources Inc

837 W Hastings St., Ste. 1904, Vancouver, BC, V6C 3N6; ***PH:*** 1-604-683-0484; ***http://*** www.anglo-swiss.com; ***Email:*** info@anglo-swiss.com

General - Incorporation	BC	**Stock**- Price on:12/24/2007	$0.1
Employees	NA	Stock Exchange	OTC
Auditor	PricewaterhouseCoopers LLP	Ticker Symbol	ASWRF
Stk Agt	Computershare Trust Co	Outstanding Shares	NA
Counsel	NA	E.P.S.	NA
DUNS No.	25-329-4607	Shareholders	NA

Business: The group's principal activities are to acquire, explore and purchase mineral properties. The group owns trapichillo and catamayo gold properties in southern equador.

Primary SIC and add'l.: 1041 1499

CIK No: 0000277910

Subsidiaries: Anglo Swiss International Holdings Inc, Blu Starr Germstone Property(2), Northwest Territories Diamond Proprities

Officers: Leonard Danard/Dir., CEO, Pres., Christopher C. Robbins/49/Dir., CFO, VP, Brian Canfield/Corp. Sec.

Directors: Leonard Danard/Dir., CEO, Pres., Glen C. MacDonald/Dir., Leroy Wolbaum/Dir., Christopher C. Robbins/49/Dir., CFO, VP, Greg Pendura/Dir.

Owners: Brian Canfield/0.70%, Len Danard/9.10%, Cede & Co./10.16%, Chris Robbins/6.20%, CDS & Co./65.73%, Leroy Wolbaum/3.60%

Financial Data: ***Fiscal Year End:***12/31 ***Latest Annual Data:*** 12/31/2006

Year	Sales	Net Income
2006	NA	-$1,028,000
2005	NA	-$1,316,000
2004	NA	-$316,000

Curr. Assets:	$83,000	**Curr. Liab.:**	$473,000		
Plant, Equip.:	$856,000	**Total Liab.:**	$473,000	**Indic. Yr. Divd.:**	NA
Total Assets:	$955,000	**Net Worth:**	$482,000	**Debt/ Equity:**	NA

AngloGold Ashanti Ltd

11 Diagonal St., Johannesburg, 2001; ***PH:*** 27-27116376000; ***http://*** www.anglogoldashanti.com; ***Email:*** investors@anglogoldashanti.com

General - Incorporation	South Africa	**Stock**- Price on:12/24/2007	$40.44
Employees	61,453	Stock Exchange	NYSE
Auditor	Ernst & Young LLP	Ticker Symbol	AU
Stk Agt	Capita Registrars	Outstanding Shares	280,840,000
Counsel	NA	E.P.S.	-$0.53
DUNS No.	NA	Shareholders	NA

Business: The group's principal activities are mining, extraction and production of gold. The group also engaged in marketing and selling of gold products. The group operates in Africa, North America, South America and Australia.

Primary SIC and add'l.: NA

CIK No: 0001067428

Subsidiaries: Aurum Health Research, DRDGolds North West, groups Guinea, ISS International Ltd

Officers: Mark Cutifani/50/Exec. Dir., CEO - Designate, Robert M. Godsell/55/Exec. Dir., CEO, R. M. Godsell/55/Exec. Dir., CEO, Steve J. Lenahan/52/Exec. Officer - Corporate Affairs, Dave H. Diering/56/Exec. Officer - Business Planning, Africa, Lynda Eatwell/Company Sec., Sunrise Dam/Business Unit Contact - Australia, Ladji Mangassy/Business Unit Contact - Mali, Leslie Louw/Business Unit Contact - Tanzania, Himesh Persotam/Investor Relations Officer, Michael F. O'Brien/50/Mgr. - Evaluation, Eric Roth/41/Head - Exploration, Greenfields, Mphedziseni Rollet Masakona/Sr. Metallurgist, Sunrise Dam, Australia, Tshepo Molale/SOX Mgr. - Corporate Office, Johannesbrg, South Africa, Wendall Naidoo/Human Resources Management Trainee, Tautona Mine, West Wits, South Africa *(64 Officers included in Index)*

Directors: Mark Cutifani/50/Exec. Dir., CEO - Designate, Robert M. Godsell/55/Exec. Dir., CEO, R. M. Godsell/55/Exec. Dir., CEO, Thokoana J. Motlatsi/56/Dep. Chmn., Russell P. Edey/65/Chmn., Colin B. Brayshaw/72/Dir., William A. Nairn/63/Dir., Reginald E. Bannerman/73/Non - Exec. Dir., Neville F. Nicolau/48/Exec. Dir., COO - Africa, Roberto Carvalho Silva/56/Exec. Dir., COO - International, Frank B. Arisman/63/Non - Exec. Dir., Elisabeth Le R. Bradley/69/Non - Exec. Dir., Arthur H. Calver/60/Alternate Dir., Rene Medori/50/Non - Exec. Dir., Simon R. Thompson/48/Non - Exec. Dir. *(21 Directors included in Index)*

Owners: S. Venkatakrishnan, R. M. Godsell, N. F. Nicolau

Financial Data: ***Fiscal Year End:***12/31 ***Latest Annual Data:*** 12/31/2006

Year	Sales	Net Income
2006	$2,715,000,000	-$142,000,000
2005	$2,485,000,000	-$292,000,000
2004	$2,238,000,000	$97,000,000

Curr. Assets:	$1,876,000,000	**Curr. Liab.:**	$2,467,000,000	**P/E Ratio:**	9.56
Plant, Equip.:	$6,483,000,000	**Total Liab.:**	$6,205,000,000	**Indic. Yr. Divd.:**	$0.250
Total Assets:	$9,513,000,000	**Net Worth:**	$3,308,000,000	**Debt/ Equity:**	NA

Anheuser-Busch Companies Inc

1 Busch Pl., St. Louis, MO, 63118; ***PH:*** 1-314-577-2000; ***Fax:*** 1-314-577-2900; ***http://*** www.anheuser-busch.com

General - Incorporation	DE	**Stock**- Price on:12/24/2007	$54.3
Employees	30,183	Stock Exchange	NYSE
Auditor	PricewaterhouseCoopers LLP	Ticker Symbol	BUD
Stk Agt	Mellon Investor Services LLC	Outstanding Shares	759,800,000
Counsel	NA	E.P.S.	$2.62
DUNS No.	00-628-8799	Shareholders	NA

Business: The group operates through its subsidiaries whose principle activities include producing and marketing beer and various alcoholic beverages. The group operates through four segments namely domestic, international beer, packaging and entertainment. The group operates from United States.

Primary SIC and add'l.: 7996 6719 2082 5181 3411

CIK No: 0000310569

Subsidiaries: A-B Jade Hong Kong Holding Company, Limited, Anheuser-Busch Asia, Inc., Anheuser-Busch Brasil Holdings Ltda., Anheuser-Busch Canada, Inc., Anheuser-Busch Distributors of New York, Inc., Anheuser-Busch Europe Limited, Anheuser-Busch Europe, Inc., Anheuser-Busch Hong Kong Investment Company, Limited, Anheuser-Busch Hong Kong Trading Company, Limited, Anheuser-Busch Import Investments, Inc., Anheuser-Busch International Holdings, Inc., Anheuser-Busch International Holdings, Inc. Chile I Limitada, Anheuser-Busch International, Inc., Anheuser-Busch Investments, S.L., Anheuser-Busch Latin American Development Corporation 107 Subsidiaries included in the Index

Officers: Stephen J. Burrows/CEO, Pres. - Asia Pacific Operations, Anheuser, Busch International, Inc, Thomas W. Santel/CEO, Pres. - Anheuser, Busch International, Inc, August A. Busch/Dir., CEO, Pres., Michael S. Harding/CEO, Pres. - Anheuser, Busch Packaging Group, Inc, Marlene V. Coulis/VP - Consumer Strategy, Innovation, W. R. Baker/CFO, VP/$3,522,038.00, Michael J. Owens/VP - Marketing, Anheuser, Busch, Incorporated/$2,527,137.00, Jobeth G. Brown/VP, Sec., Randolph W. Baker/CFO, VP, Mark T. Bobak/Group VP, Chief Legal Officer/$3,086,001.00, Robert C. Lachky/Exec. VP - Global Industry, Creative Development ,

Anheuser, Busch, Inc, John F. Kelly/VP, Controller, Joseph P. Sellinger/CIO, VP, Douglas J. Muhleman/Group VP - Brewing Operations, Technology, Anheuser, Busch, Inc/$2,863,109.00, Anthony T. Ponturo/VP - Global Media, Sports Marketing , Anheuser, Busch, Inc *(18 Officers included in Index)*

Directors: August A. Busch/Dir., CEO, Pres., Patrick T. Stokes/Chmn., Edward E. Whitacre/Dir., William Porter Payne/Dir., Vernon R. Loucks/Dir., Henry Hugh Shelton/Dir., Carlos G. Fernandez/Dir., Andrew C. Taylor/Dir., Douglas A. Warner/Dir., James R. Jones/Dir., James J. Forese/Dir., Vilma S. Martinez/Dir., John E. Jacob/Dir., August A. Busch/Dir., Charles F. Knight/Dir. *(16 Directors included in Index)*

Owners: August A. Busch, Mark T. Bobak, Douglas A. Warner, John E. Jacob, Andrew C. Taylor, Douglas J. Muhleman, Joyce M. Roch, Michael J. Owens, Vernon R. Loucks, William Porter Payne, Vilma S. Martinez, Randolph W. Baker, Insiders, James J. Forese, Carlos G. Fernandez *(22 Owners included in Index)*

Financial Data: Fiscal Year End:12/31 Latest Annual Data: 12/31/2006

Year	Sales	Net Income
2006	$15,717,100,000	$1,965,200,000
2005	$15,035,700,000	$1,839,200,000
2004	$14,934,200,000	$2,240,300,000

Curr. Assets:	$1,829,500,000	**Curr. Liab.:**	$2,246,100,000	**P/E Ratio:**	20.73
Plant, Equip.:	$8,916,100,000	**Total Liab.:**	$12,438,500,000	**Indic. Yr. Divd.:**	$1.320
Total Assets:	$16,377,200,000	**Net Worth:**	$3,938,700,000	**Debt/ Equity:**	2.1676

Anika Therapeutics Inc

160 New Boston St., Woburn, MA, 01801; *PH:* 1-781-932-6616; *Fax:* 1-781-935-7803; *http://* www.anikatherapeutics.com; *Email:* contact@anikatherapeutics.com

General - Incorporation	MA	**Stock** - Price on:12/24/2007	$15.46
Employees	64	Stock Exchange	NDQ
Auditor	PricewaterhouseCoopers LLP	Ticker Symbol	ANIK
Stk Agt	Continental Stock Transfer	Outstanding Shares	10,980,000
Counsel	Goodwin Procter LLP	E.P.S.	$0.47
DUNS No.	80-761-3393	Shareholders	NA

Business: The group's principal activities are to develop, manufacture and distribute therapeutic products and devices. The products promote the protection and healing of bone, cartilage and soft tissue. The group's products include orthovisc (R), which is based on hyaluronic acid (ha), used in the treatment of some forms of osteoarthritis in humans, and hyvisc (R), used in the treatment of equine osteoarthritis. Orthovisc(R) is currently marketed in Canada, parts of Europe, turkey and Israel. The group also manufactures amvisc(R) and amvisc(R) plus for bausch & lomb, which are used as viscoelastic supplements in ophthalmic surgery.

Primary SIC and add'l.: 2834 3844

CIK No: 0000898437

Subsidiaries: Anika Securities Corp.

Officers: Charles H. Sherwood/59/Dir., CEO, Pres./$927,681.00, Frank Luppino/37/VP - Operations/$406,721.00, Kevin W. Quinlan/56/CFO, Principal Financial Officer/$390,577.00, William J. Mrachek/VP - Human Resources

Directors: Charles H. Sherwood/59/Dir., CEO, Pres., Steven E. Wheeler/Dir., Eugene A. Davidson/Dir., Joseph L. Bower/Dir., Raymond J. Land/Dir., John C. Moran/Dir.

Owners: Joseph L. Bower, Raymond J. Land, John C. Moran, Steven E. Wheeler, Insiders/7.60%, Kevin Quinlan, Herbert H. Hastings and Euretta L. Hastings/7.53%, Frank Luppino, Charles H. Sherwood/4.25%, Ashford Capital Management,Inc./7.09%, Eugene A. Davidson, Royce& Associates, LLC/12.24%

Financial Data: Fiscal Year End:12/31 Latest Annual Data: 12/31/2006

Year	Sales	Net Income
2006	$26,841,000	$4,604,000
2005	$29,835,000	$5,893,000
2004	$26,466,000	$11,190,000

Curr. Assets:	$57,606,000	**Curr. Liab.:**	$5,461,000	**P/E Ratio:**	35.14
Plant, Equip.:	$3,018,000	**Total Liab.:**	$22,626,000	**Indic. Yr. Divd.:**	NA
Total Assets:	$68,114,000	**Net Worth:**	$45,488,000	**Debt/ Equity:**	NA

Animas Corp

200 Lawrence Dr., West Chester, PA, 19380; *PH:* 1-610-644-8990; *http://* www.animascorp.com

General - Incorporation	DE	**Stock** - Price on:12/24/2007	$24.49
Employees	NA	Stock Exchange	NDQ
Auditor	KPMG LLP	Ticker Symbol	PUMP
Stk Agt	Computershare Trust Co	Outstanding Shares	NA
Counsel	NA	E.P.S.	NA
DUNS No.	NA	Shareholders	NA

Business: The groups principle activities include designing, manufacturing and selling external insulin pumps for people with diabetes. The group also provides ancillary supplies on an ongoing basis for patients using its pumps, including insulin cartridges, infusion sets, batteries, and various accessories. The group operates from Australia, Austria, Canada, the Czech Republic, France, Finland, Greece, Germany, Hungary, the Republic of Ireland, Israel, Italy, New Zealand, Spain, Sweden and the United Kingdom.

Primary SIC and add'l.: NA

CIK No: 0001033660

Subsidiaries: Animas Diabetes Care, LLC, Animas Holdings, Inc., Animas Technologies LLC

Officers: Mindy Cooper/Managing Editor, Joe Solowiejczyk/Contributors, Sweettalk, Jamie Smith/Contributors, Sweettalk, Greg Hunt/Art Direction, Design, Sweettalk, Audrey Finkelstein/Exec. VP - WW Clinical, Government Affairs

Anixter International Inc

2301 Patriot Blvd., Glenview, IL, 60026; *PH:* 1-224-521-8000; *Fax:* 1-224-521-8100; *http://* www.anixter.com

General - Incorporation	DE	**Stock** - Price on:12/24/2007	NA
Employees	7,500	Stock Exchange	NYSE
Auditor	Ernst & Young LLP	Ticker Symbol	AXE
Stk Agt	National City Bank	Outstanding Shares	36,900,000
Counsel	NA	E.P.S.	$5.51
DUNS No.	04-651-6753	Shareholders	NA

Business: The group's principle activity is to distribute data, voice and video network communication products. The group also provides contractual supply chain management of installation and repair related materials for customers who install and maintain communication equipment. The group operates from United States, Canada, United Kingdom, Europe, Latin America, Australia and Asia.

Primary SIC and add'l.: 5063

CIK No: 0000052795

Subsidiaries: Accu-Tech Corporation, Accu-Tech Enterprises, Inc. , Adesco Limited, ALLNET Technologies Pty. Ltd., Anixter (CIS) LLC, Anixter AEH Holdings Inc., Anixter Argentina S.A., Anixter Australia Pty. Ltd., Anixter Austria GmbH, Anixter Belgium B.V.B.A., Anixter Cables y Manufacturas, S.A. de C.V., Anixter Canada Inc., Anixter Chile S.A., Anixter Colombia S.A., Anixter Communications (Malaysia) Sdn Bhd 124 Subsidiaries included in the Index

Officers: Robert W. Grubbs/52/Dir., CEO, Pres./$4,993,398.00, Dennis J. Letham/57/CFO, Exec. VP - Finance/$2,148,740.00, Terrance A. Faber/56/VP, Controller/$660,410.00, Rodney A. Shoemaker/50/VP, Treasurer/$455,987.00, Philip F. Meno/49/VP - Taxes, John A. Dul/47/VP, General Counsel, Sec./$695,653.00, Robert J. Eck/50/COO, Exec. VP, Rodney A. Smith/51/VP - Human Resources

Directors: Robert W. Grubbs/52/Dir., CEO, Pres., Samuel Zell/67/Chmn., Thomas C. Theobald/70/Dir., Matthew Zell/41/Dir., Robert L. Crandall/72/Dir., Lord James Blyth/67/Dir., Linda W. Bynoe/55/Dir., Philip F. Handy/63/Dir., Melvyn N. Klein/66/Dir., George Munoz/56/Dir., Stuart M. Sloan/64/Dir.

Owners: John A. Dul, Melvyn N. Klein, Lord James Blyth, Stuart Sloan, Matthew Zell, Thomas C. Theobald, George Munoz, Linda Walker Bynoe, Robert W. Grubbs/2.90%, Rodney A. Shoemaker, Samuel Zell/14.20%, Robert L. Crandall, Insiders/19.20%, Terrance A. Faber, Philip F. Handy *(16 Owners included in Index)*

Financial Data: Fiscal Year End:12/30 Latest Annual Data: 12/29/2006

Year	Sales	Net Income
2006	$4,938,600,000	$209,300,000
2005	$3,847,400,000	$90,000,000
2004	$3,275,200,000	$77,700,000

Curr. Assets.	$1,281,900,000	**Curr. Liab.**	$466,600,000		
Plant, Equip.:	$42,600,000	**Total Liab.:**	$943,600,000	**Indic. Yr. Divd.:**	NA
Total Assets:	$1,706,600,000	**Net Worth:**	$763,000,000	**Debt/ Equity:**	0.9969

Annaly Capital Management Inc

1211 Ave. of the Americas, Ste. 2902, New York, NY, 10036; *PH:* 1-212-696-0100; *Fax:* 1-212-696-9809; *http://* www.annaly.com

General - Incorporation	MD	**Stock** - Price on:12/24/2007	$14.08
Employees	34	Stock Exchange	NYSE
Auditor	Deloitte & Touche LLP	Ticker Symbol	NLY
Stk Agt	Mellon Investor Services LLC	Outstanding Shares	262,890,000
Counsel	NA	E.P.S.	NA
DUNS No.	NA	Shareholders	NA

Business: The groups principal activities include managing and financing investment securities, including mortgage pass-through certificates, collateralized mortgage obligations, agency callable debentures, and other securities representing mortgage loans. The group operates from the United States.

Primary SIC and add'l.: 6798

CIK No: 0001043219

Officers: Michael A.J. Farrell/Chmn., CEO, Pres./$7,549,025.00, Wellington J. Denahan-Norris/Vice Chmn., Chief Investment Officer, COO/$6,084,803.00, Kathryn F. Fagan/CFO, Treasurer/$3,000,461.00, Ronald D. Kazel/MD, Jeremy Diamond/MD, Nicholas R. Singh/Exec. VP, General Counsel, James P. Fortescue/Exec. VP, Head - Liabilities/$1,510,675.00, Kristopher R. Konrad/Exec. VP, Co - Head - Portfolio Management/$1,510,675.00, Rose-Marie Lyght/Exec. VP, Co - Head - Portfolio Management, Matthew Lambiase/Exec. VP - Structured Products, Dennis E. Malloy/Sr. VP - Marketing, Sales, Alexandra A. Denahan/Controller, Konstantin Pavlov/Sr. VP - Sr. Repo Trader, Eric Szabo/Sr. VP - Investment Strategist, Mohit Marria/VP, Portfolio Mgr. *(17 Officers included in Index)*

Directors: Michael A.J. Farrell/Chmn., CEO, Pres., Wellington J. Denahan-Norris/Vice Chmn., Chief Investment Officer, COO, Kevin P. Brady/Dir., Jonathan D. Green/Dir., John A. Lambiase/Dir., Wayne E. Nordberg/Dir., Donnell A. Segalas/Dir.

Owners: Donnell A. Segalas, Kathryn F. Fagan, Kevin P. Brady, Jonathan D. Green, Wellington J. Denahan-Norris, James P. Fortescue, Michael A.J. Farrell, Insiders/1.58%, John Lambiase, Wayne E. Nordberg, Kristopher R. Konrad

Financial Data: Fiscal Year End:12/31 Latest Annual Data: 12/31/2006

Year	Sales	Net Income
2006	$1,258,901,000	$93,816,000
2005	$740,671,000	-$9,247,000
2004	$550,055,000	$248,592,000

Curr. Assets.	$259,414,000	**Curr. Liab.:**	$27,697,798,000		
Plant, Equip.:	NA	**Total Liab.:**	$28,167,615,000	**Indic. Yr. Divd.:**	NA
Total Assets:	$30,715,980,000	**Net Worth:**	$2,543,041,000	**Debt/ Equity:**	NA

Annapolis Bancorp Inc

1000 Bestgate Rd., Ste. 400, Annapolis, MD, 21401; *PH:* 1-410-224-4455; *Fax:* 1-410-224-3132; *http://* www.bankannapolis.com

General - Incorporation	MD	**Stock** - Price on:12/24/2007	$9.5
Employees	81	Stock Exchange	NDQ
Auditor	Stegman & Co	Ticker Symbol	ANNB
Stk Agt	Registrar & Transfer Co	Outstanding Shares	4,100,000
Counsel	Patton Boggs LLP	E.P.S.	$0.66
DUNS No.	61-504-3916	Shareholders	NA

Business: The group's principal activities are to originate loans and accept deposits from the general public. The group operates through its subsidiary, bankannapolis. It provides commercial loans, commercial real estate loans, construction loans, one- to four-family real estate loans, home equity and consumer loans. It also invests in U.S. Treasury and U.S. Government agency securities and mortgage backed securities issued by the government. The deposit accounts consist of savings, now accounts, checking accounts, money market accounts and certificate of deposit accounts. The bank also offers individual retirement accounts. The group operates through its headquarters in annapolis, and its five branches located in anne arundel county, Maryland and one branch in queen anne's county, Maryland.

Primary SIC and add'l.: 6712 6022

CIK No: 0001041429

Officers: Richard M. Lerner/48/Chmn., CEO/$230,601.00, Margaret Theiss Faison/50/CFO, Treasurer/$165,245.00

Directors: Richard M. Lerner/48/Chmn., CEO, Stanley J. Klos/56/Vice Chmn., Clyde E. Culp/65/Dir., Lawrence E. Lerner/75/Dir., Clifford T. Solomon/46/Dir., Lawrence W. Schwartz/50/Dir., Nancy Lowell/53/Dir., Ermis Sfakiyanudis/39/Dir., Walter L. Bennett/51/Dir., Carter F. Heim/54/Dir.

Owners: Mitchell J. Krebs, Insiders/49.45%, Nancy Lowell/0.03%, Robert E. Kendrick, Ermis Sfakiyanudis/0.30%, Margaret Theiss Faison/0.85%, Kendel S. Ehrlich/0.03%, Walter L. Bennett, Lawrence W. Schwartz/1.07%, Richard M. Lerner/5.96%, Lawrence E. Lerner/38.53%, Stanley J. Klos/1.13%, Carter F. Heim, Clifford T. Solomon/0.08%, Clyde E. Culp

Financial Data: *Fiscal Year End:* 12/31 *Latest Annual Data:* 12/31/2006

Year	Sales	Net Income
2006	$21,719,000	$2,951,000
2005	$19,314,000	$2,981,000
2004	$15,294,000	$2,173,000

Curr. Assets:	$37,732,000	**Curr. Liab.:**	$292,740,000	**P/E Ratio:**	14.39
Plant, Equip.:	$9,173,000	**Total Liab.:**	$327,740,000	**Indic. Yr. Divd.:**	NA
Total Assets:	$351,861,000	**Net Worth:**	$24,121,000	**Debt/ Equity:**	1.4510

Anntaylor Stores Corp

PO Box 571650, Taylorsville, UT, 84157; ***Fax:*** 1-866-232-9266; ***http://*** www.anntaylor.com

General - Incorporation	DE	**Stock**- Price on:12/24/2007	$36.88
Employees	5,700	Stock Exchange	NYSE
Auditor	Deloitte & Touche LLP	Ticker Symbol	ANN
Stk Agt	Mellon Investor Services LLC	Outstanding Shares	64,680,000
Counsel	Skadden, Meagher & Flom LLP	E.P.S.	$1.90
DUNS No.	17-373-7628	Shareholders	NA

Business: The groups principle activity is to operate womens retail stores. The groups products include apparel, shoes, dresses, tops, weekend wear and accessories. The groups products are sold under the brand names Ann Taylor, Ann Taylor Loft and Ann Taylor Factory brands. The group operates from United States.

Primary SIC and add'l.: 5699 5621 5632 5661

CIK No: 0000874214

Subsidiaries: AnnTaylor Distribution Services, Inc., AnnTaylor, Inc.

Officers: Kay Krill/CEO, Pres./$11,678,690.00, James Smith/CFO, Exec. VP, Treasurer/$997,788.00, Barbara Eisenberg/Exec. VP, General Counsel, Corp. Sec., Anthony M. Romano/Exec. VP, Chief Supply Chain Officer/$1,466,704.00, Adrienne Lazarus/Pres. - Ann Taylor Stores/$1,894,059.00, Brian Lynch/Pres. - Ann Taylor Factory/$1,314,988.00, Linda Siluk/Sr. VP - Finance, Judith Pirro/Dir. - Investor Relations

Directors: Ronald W. Hovsepian/47/Non - Exec. Chmn., Dale W. Hilpert/65/Dir., Linda A. Huett/63/Dir., Wesley E. Cantrell/73/Dir., Robert C. Grayson/63/Dir., Michael W. Trapp/68/Dir., James J. Burke/56/Dir.

Owners: Highfields Capital Management LP/6.22%, Anthony M. Romano, Barclays Global Investors, N.A./8.78%, James J. Burke, Wesley E. Cantrell, Ronald W. Hovsepian, Dale W. Hilpert, Robert C. Grayson, Adrienne Lazarus, FMR Corp./8.11%, Laura A. Weil, Insiders/3.14%, James M. Smith, Linda A. Huett, Brian Lynch *(18 Owners included in Index)*

Financial Data: *Fiscal Year End:* 01/28 *Latest Annual Data:* 2/3/2007

Year	Sales	Net Income
2007	$2,342,907,000	$142,982,000
2006	$2,073,146,000	$81,872,000
2005	$1,853,583,000	$63,276,000

Curr. Assets:	$690,605,000	**Curr. Liab.:**	$299,418,000	**P/E Ratio:**	19.31
Plant, Equip.:	$564,108,000	**Total Liab.:**	$518,592,000	**Indic. Yr. Divd.:**	NA
Total Assets:	$1,568,503,000	**Net Worth:**	$1,049,911,000	**Debt/ Equity:**	NA

Annuity & Life Re Holdings Ltd

124 Palasido Ave., Windsor, CT, 06095; ***PH:*** 1-860-285-8252; ***Fax:*** 1-860-285-0233; ***http://*** www.annuityandlifere.com

General - Incorporation	Bermuda	**Stock**- Price on:12/24/2007	$0.6
Employees	NA	Stock Exchange	OTC
Auditor	Marcum & Kliegman LLP	Ticker Symbol	ANNRF
Stk Agt	Computershare Trust Company NY	Outstanding Shares	NA
Counsel	NA	E.P.S.	NA
DUNS No.	NA	Shareholders	NA

Business: The group's principle activity is to provide annuity and life reinsurance to select insurers and reinsurers. The group operates from United States.

Primary SIC and add'l.: 6719 6311

CIK No: 0001051628

Subsidiaries: Annuity and Life Re America, Inc, Annuity and Life Reassurance, Ltd.

Officers: Bill Mawdsley/Pres., CEO - Annuity, Life Reassurance, Ltd, John Lockwood/CFO - Annuity, Life Reassurance, Ltd

Financial Data: *Fiscal Year End:* 12/31 *Latest Annual Data:* 12/31/2004

Year	Sales	Net Income
2004	$77,092,000	-$68,326,000
2003	$226,411,000	-$132,156,000
2002	$456,296,000	-$128,887,000

Curr. Assets:	$199,550,000	**Curr. Liab.:**	$6,187,000		
Plant, Equip.:	NA	**Total Liab.:**	$222,988,000	**Indic. Yr. Divd.:**	NA
Total Assets:	$289,405,000	**Net Worth:**	$66,417,000	**Debt/ Equity:**	NA

Anooraq Resources Corp

800 W Pender St., Ste. 1020, Vancouver, BC, V6C 2V6; ***PH:*** 1-604-684-6365; ***http://*** www.anooraqresources.com

General - Incorporation	Canada	**Stock**- Price on:12/24/2007	$2.6999
Employees	NA	Stock Exchange	AMEX
Auditor	KPMG LLP	Ticker Symbol	ANO
Stk Agt	Computershare Trust Co of Canada	Outstanding Shares	148,310,000
Counsel	NA	E.P.S.	-$0.03
DUNS No.	NA	Shareholders	NA

Business: The groups principle activities include acquiring and exploring mineral properties. The group operates from Canada.

Primary SIC and add'l.: NA

CIK No: 0001028277

Subsidiaries: Plateau Resources (Proprietary) Limited.

Officers: Ronald W. Thiessen/55/Dir., CEO, Pres., Joel Kesler/Investor Relations Officer, Harold Motaungi/38/Exec. Dir., COO, Scott D. Cousens/42/Exec. Dir., Iemrahn Hassen/CFO, Sec.

Directors: Ronald W. Thiessen/55/Dir., CEO, Pres., Robert A. Dickinson/58/Co - Chmn., Tumelo Motsisi/45/Co - Chmn., Popo S. Molefe/55/Dir., David Elliot/62/Dir., Scott D. Cousens/42/Exec. Dir., Rizelle M. Sampson/32/Dir., Sipho Nkosi/53/Dir., Harold Motaungi/38/Exec. Dir., COO, Wayne Kirk/Dir.

Owners: The Canadian Depository for Securities Limited, Tumelo M. Motsisi, The Pelawan Trust, as Trustee

Financial Data: *Fiscal Year End:* 12/31 *Latest Annual Data:* 12/31/2006

Year	Sales	Net Income
2006	NA	-$3,866,000
2005	NA	-$10,557,000
2004	NA	-$10,817,000

Curr. Assets:	$11,307,000	**Curr. Liab.:**	$887,000		
Plant, Equip.:	$63,000	**Total Liab.:**	$11,029,000	**Indic. Yr. Divd.:**	NA
Total Assets:	$18,731,000	**Net Worth:**	$7,702,000	**Debt/ Equity:**	NA

Anpath Group Inc

Formerly: Telecomm Sales Network Inc
116 Morlake Dr., Ste. 201, Mooresville, NC, 28117; ***PH:*** 1-704-658-3350

General - Incorporation	DE	**Stock**- Price on:12/24/2007	NA
Employees	NA	Stock Exchange	NA
Auditor	Williams & Webster, P.S.	Ticker Symbol	NA
Stk Agt	Registrar & Transfer Co	Outstanding Shares	NA
Counsel	NA	E.P.S.	-$0.22
DUNS No.	NA	Shareholders	NA

Business: The groups principle activities include producing cleaning and disinfecting products that help prevent the spread of infectious micro organisms without harmful effects to people, equipment or the environment. The group markets its product under the tradename EcoTru(R). In January 2006, the group acquired EnviroSystems. The group operates from the United States.

Primary SIC and add'l.: 2842

CIK No: 0001310527

Subsidiaries: EnviroSystems Holdings, Inc., EnviroSystems, Inc.

Owners: Insiders/10.10%, Alma and Gabriel Elias/9.10%, The Singer Childrens Management Trust/5.10%, Stephen Hoelscher/2.10%, Charles Cottrell, Lloyd J. Breedlove/3.50%, Jeffrey Connally, MV Nanotech Corp./5.70%, The Ferguson Living Trust UDT 8/13/74/19.10%, Stephen A. Schneider/4.00%

Financial Data: *Fiscal Year End:* 03/31 *Latest Annual Data:* 3/31/2006

Year	Sales	Net Income
2006	$487,000	-$3,658,000
2005	NA	-$95,000

Curr. Assets:	$83,000	**Curr. Liab.:**	$85,000		
Plant, Equip.:	NA	**Total Liab.:**	$85,000	**Indic. Yr. Divd.:**	NA
Total Assets:	$83,000	**Net Worth:**	-$2,000	**Debt/ Equity:**	NA

ANR Pipeline Company

El Paso Bldg., 1001 Louisiana St., Houston, TX, 77002; ***PH:*** 1-713-420-2600; ***Fax:*** 1-713-420-6969; ***http://*** www.anrpl.com

General - Incorporation	DE	**Stock**- Price on:12/24/2007	NA
Employees	NA	Stock Exchange	NA
Auditor	Ernst & Young, LLP	Ticker Symbol	NA
Stk Agt	NA	Outstanding Shares	NA
Counsel	NA	E.P.S.	NA
DUNS No.	00-695-8581	Shareholders	NA

Business: The group's principle activities include transporting, storaging and gathering of natural gas and related services. The company is an indirect wholly owned subsidiary of el paso corporation. The company's two interconnected, large-diameter multiple pipeline systems transport natural gas from natural gas producing fields in Louisiana, Oklahoma, Texas, and the gulf of Mexico to markets in the midwestern and northeastern regions of the United States, including the metropolitan areas of Chicago, detroit and milwaukee. The system consists of 10,600 miles of pipeline with a design capacity of approximately 6,414 mmcf/d. The group operates from United States.

Primary SIC and add'l.: 4923

CIK No: 0000065695

Officers: Stephen C. Beasley/Dir., Pres., Principal Executive Officer, Joseph Pollard/Dir. - Transportation Services, Gary Charette/Dir., VP, Bob Gibb/Dir. - Supply Development, Brian Rhodes/Contact - ANR Marketing, John R. Sult/CFO, Sr. VP, Controller, Daniel B. Martin/Dir., Sr. VP, Dean Ferguson/VP - Business Development, Martin Wilde/Dir. - ANR Marketing, Larry Anderson/Contact - ANR Marketing, Joe Clements/Contact - ANR Marketing Department

Directors: James C. Yardley/Chmn., Daniel B. Martin/Dir., Sr. VP, Stephen C. Beasley/Dir., Pres., Principal Executive Officer, Gary Charette/Dir., VP

Ansell Ltd

678 Victoria St., Richmond, Victoria, 3121; ; ***http://*** www.ansell.com

General - Incorporation.....................Australia
Employees ....NA
Auditor ....KPMG LLP
Stk Agt.....................Morgan Guaranty Trust Co
Counsel..NA
DUNS No. 75-317-2428

Stock- Price on:12/24/2007 ....$9.95
Stock Exchange...OTC
Ticker Symbol...ANSLF
Outstanding Shares ....NA
E.P.S...NA
Shareholders...NA

Business: The group's principal activities are the development, manufacturing and sourcing, distribution and sale of gloves and protective products in the professional healthcare, occupational healthcare and personal healthcare markets. Brand names include ansell, ansell perry, gammex, conforme, encore, nutex, microptic, x-AM, synsation, dermaclean and nitratouch.

Primary SIC and add'l.: 3841 3069

CIK No: 0000791440

Subsidiaries: Accufix Research Institute Inc., Ansell (Kedah) Sdn. Bhd., Ansell (Kulim) Sdn. Bhd., Ansell (Thailand) Ltd., Ansell Ambi Sdn. Bhd., Ansell Brazil LTDA, Ansell Canada Inc., Ansell Edmont Industrial de Mexico S.A. de C.V., Ansell GmbH, Ansell Healthcare Europe N.V., Ansell Healthcare Japan Co. Ltd., Ansell Healthcare Products LLC., Ansell Italy Srl, Ansell Kemwell Ltd., Ansell Lanka (Pvt.) Ltd. 98 Subsidiaries included in the Index

Officers: Douglas D. Tough/Dir., MD, CEO, William G. Reilly/Sr. VP, General Counsel, Rainer Wolf/Head - Global Manufacturing, William Reed/Sr. VP, Regional Dir. - Americas, Mike Zedalis/Sr. VP - Science, Technology, David Graham/GM - Finance, Accounting, Werner Heintz/Sr. VP, Regional Dir. - Europe, Phil Corke/Sr. VP - Human Resources, Rustom Jilla/42/CFO, Scott Papier/VP - Global Supply, Logistics, Rob Bartlett/Company Sec., GM, Shawn Knox/CIO, Sr. VP, Scott R. Corriveau/Head - Global Business Development

Directors: Douglas D. Tough/Dir., MD, CEO, Peter L. Barnes/Chmn., Dale L. Crandall/Dir., Glenn L.L. Barnes/Dir., Ronald J.S. Bell/Dir., Marissa T. Peterson/Dir.

Owners: Perennial Group/6.68%, W. Heintz, Maple Brown Abbott/11.23%, Mr N. ODonnell, Mr W. Reed, Perpetual Investments/12.84%, Mr W. Reilly, Investors Mutual/5.50%, Mr R. Jilla, Mr P. Corke

Financial Data: Fiscal Year End:06/30   Latest Annual Data: 6/30/2006

Year	Sales	Net Income
2006	$841,294,000	$86,371,000
2005	$845,744,000	$99,136,000
2004	$780,798,000	$62,403,000

Curr. Assets:	$538,887,000	*Curr. Liab.:*	$232,099,000		
Plant, Equip.:	$142,808,000	*Total Liab.:*	$486,831,000	*Indic. Yr. Divd.:*	NA
Total Assets:	$1,094,274,000	*Net Worth:*	$597,222,000	*Debt/ Equity:*	NA

Ansoft Corp

225 W Sta. Sq. Dr., Ste. 200, Pittsburgh, PA, 15219; *PH:* 1-412-261-3200; *Fax:* 1-412-471-9427; *http://* www.ansoft.com; *Email:* info@ansoft.com

General - Incorporation...............................DE
Employees 298
Auditor ....KPMG LLP
Stk Agt......American Stock Transfer & Trust Co.
Counsel............................Buchanan Ingersoll P.C.
DUNS No. 11-911-2688

Stock- Price on:12/24/2007 ....$30.5
Stock Exchange...NDQ
Ticker Symbol..ANST
Outstanding Shares 23,990,000
E.P.S...$0.79
Shareholders...NA

Business: The group's principle activity is to design and develop electronic design automation software used in high technology products and industries. The software products allow electrical engineers to model component level and system level electromagnetic interactions thereby enabling the design of cellular telephones, satellite communications systems, radar systems, computer chips, circuit boards, electronic sensors and motors. The group maintains sales and support offices in Japan, Korea, Singapore, Taiwan, China, England, Germany, France, Italy and Sweden. Major customers include communications companies like motorola, ericsson and hughes, semiconductor manufacturers like intel, anam semiconductor and broadcom and other companies like abb, dupont, daimler-chrysler and delphi packard. The group's total revenue for year 2007 was 89.14 millions of USD.

Primary SIC and add'l.: 7379 7372

CIK No: 0000849433

Officers: Nicholas Csendes/CEO, Pres./$426,000.00, Zoltan J. Cendes/Chmn., CTO/$426,000.00, Thomas A.N. Miller/CFO/$281,000.00, Mark Ravenstahl/Investor Relations, Dan Martin/Contact - Eastern US, Cindy Hines/Contact - Central US, Meera Rao/Contact - Western US, Emi Martin/Contact - Western US

Directors: Zoltan J. Cendes/Chmn., CTO

Owners: Thomas A.N. Miller/6.30%, Nicholas Csendes/9.20%, Peter Robbins, Thomas Flynn, Insiders/24.70%, Paul Quast, John N. Whelihan, Zoltan J. Cendes/7.80%, Goldman Sachs Asset Management LP/6.70%, Ulrich L. Rohde/9.20%, Padmanabhan Premkumar

Financial Data: Fiscal Year End:04/30   Latest Annual Data: 4/30/2006

Year	Sales	Net Income
2006	$77,211,000	$17,797,000
2005	$67,670,000	$9,441,000
2004	$54,653,000	$2,556,000

Curr. Assets:	$78,357,000	*Curr. Liab.:*	$34,983,000	*P/E Ratio:*	36.31
Plant, Equip.:	$2,514,000	*Total Liab.:*	$36,387,000	*Indic. Yr. Divd.:*	NA
Total Assets:	$111,170,000	*Net Worth:*	$74,783,000	*Debt/ Equity:*	NA

Answers Corp

237 W 35th St., Ste. 1101, New York, NY, 10001; *PH:* 1-646-502-4777; *Fax:* 1-646-502-4778; *http://* www.answers.com

General - Incorporation...............................DE
Employees 53
Auditor ....KPMG
Stk Agt......American Stock Transfer & Trust Co.
Counsel..NA
DUNS No. ....NA

Stock- Price on:12/24/2007 ....$11.72
Stock Exchange...NDQ
Ticker Symbol...ANSW
Outstanding Shares 7,850,000
E.P.S..-$0.58
Shareholders...NA

Business: The groups principle activity is to provide online answer based information. The groups service is 1-Click Answers. In December 1, 2005, the group acquired Brainboost Technology, LLC. The group operates from the United Sates. The group's quarterly revenue for September 2007 was 2.21 millions of USD.

Primary SIC and add'l.: 7375 7379

CIK No: 0001283073

Subsidiaries: GuruNet Israel Ltd.

Officers: Robert S. Rosenschein/Chmn., CEO, Pres., Steven Steinberg/CFO, Jeff Schneiderman/CTO, Jeffrey S. Cutler/44/Chief Revenue Officer, Bruce D. Smith/Chief Strategic Officer

Directors: Robert S. Rosenschein/Chmn., CEO, Pres., Mark A. Tebbe/Vice Chmn., Edward G. Sim/Dir., Yehuda Sternlicht/Dir., Jerry Colonna/Dir., Mark B. Segall/Dir., Lawrence S. Kramer/Dir.

Owners: Edward G. Sim, Mark A. Tebbe, Bruce D. Smith, Yehuda Sternlicht, Robert S. Rosenschein/6.80%, Mark B. Segall, Lawrence S. Kramer, Jeffrey S. Cutler/1.52%, Insiders/12.92%, Jerry Colonna, Jeff Schneiderman, Steven Steinberg, Royce & Associates, LLC/12.38%, Trellus Management Company, LLC/5.60%

Financial Data: Fiscal Year End:12/31   Latest Annual Data: 12/31/2006

Year	Sales	Net Income
2006	$7,029,000	-$8,617,000
2005	$2,053,000	-$6,014,000
2004	$193,000	-$6,591,000

Curr. Assets:	$10,798,000	*Curr. Liab.:*	$2,259,000		
Plant, Equip.:	$998,000	*Total Liab.:*	$3,281,000	*Indic. Yr. Divd.:*	NA
Total Assets:	$19,630,000	*Net Worth:*	$16,349,000	*Debt/ Equity:*	NA

Answerthink Inc

1001 Brickell Bay Dr., Ste. 3000, Miami, FL, 33131; *PH:* 1-305-375-8005; *Fax:* 1-305-379-8810; *http://* www.answerthink.com

General - Incorporation ....FL
Employees 800
Auditor ....BDO Seidman LLP
Stk Agt.....................Computershare Trust CO.
Counsel..NA
DUNS No. 06-518-3097

Stock- Price on:12/24/2007 ....$3.5
Stock Exchange...NDQ
Ticker Symbol..ANSR
Outstanding Shares 44,990,000
E.P.S..-$0.04
Shareholders...NA

Business: The group's principle activity is to provide technology-enabled transformation solutions. The group provides multi-disciplinary expertise in benchmarking, business transformation, interactive direct marketing, business applications and technology integration. The group's solutions span all functional areas of a company, including finance, human resources, information technology, sales, marketing, customer service and supply chain, as well as across a variety of industry sectors. It has offices in 14 cities throughout the United States and Europe. The customers of the group are waste management, verizon, exelon (unicom/peco), cpa2biz, inc., fannie mae and the mcgraw hill companies.

Primary SIC and add'l.: 7372 7379

CIK No: 0001057379

Subsidiaries: Advis Acquisition Corporation, Answerthink Europe GmbH, AnswerThink Florida, Inc. f/k/a UbiComs, Inc., Answerthink Ltd., Answerthink Netherlands BV, Answerthink Switzerland AG, Beacon Analytics, Inc., CFT Consulting, Inc., Delphi Partners, Inc., Epic Acquisition Corporation, EZCommerce Global Solutions, EZCommerce India Limited, GCSB Acquisition Corporation, Group Cortex, Inc., Infinity Consulting Group, Inc. 46 Subsidiaries included in the Index

Owners: Insiders/5.20%, Ted A. Fernandez/1.60%, Columbia Wanger Asset Management, L.P./20.40%, John R. Harris, Edwin A. Huston, WAM Acquisition GP, Inc./18.60%, Alan T.G. Wix, Grant Fitzwilliam, Richard N. Hamlin, David N. Dungan/3.20%, Robert Ramirez

Financial Data: Fiscal Year End:12/30   Latest Annual Data: 12/29/2006

Year	Sales	Net Income
2006	$180,555,000	-$5,048,000
2005	$163,318,000	$604,000
2004	$143,547,000	-$148,000

Curr. Assets:	$71,232,000	*Curr. Liab.:*	$21,372,000		
Plant, Equip.:	$7,568,000	*Total Liab.:*	$28,879,000	*Indic. Yr. Divd.:*	NA
Total Assets:	$128,733,000	*Net Worth:*	$99,854,000	*Debt/ Equity:*	NA

ANSYS Inc

275 Technology Dr., Canonsburg, PA, 15317; *PH:* 1-724-746-3304; *Fax:* 1-724-514-9494; *http://* www.ansys.com; *Email:* ansysinfo@ansys.com

General - Incorporation ....DE
Employees 1,400
Auditor ....Deloitte & Touche LLP
Stk Agt.................Mellon Investor Services LLC
Counsel................................Goodwin Procter LLP
DUNS No. 06-374-7653

Stock- Price on:12/24/2007 ....$0.72
Stock Exchange...NDQ
Ticker Symbol..ANSS
Outstanding Shares 77,530,000
E.P.S...$0.81
Shareholders...NA

Business: The group's principal activities are to develop, market and support engineering simulation software products. The group give product designers and engineers the ability to conceptualize and design products by using 3-dimensional modeling and incorporating all necessary structural, thermal, electromagnetic and fluid-flow design properties. Its products are used by engineers in aerospace, automotive, manufacturing, nuclear, electronics and biomedical industries. The group's development and production facility is located at canonsburg, Pennsylvania. Major customers include compaq, hewlett-packard, sun microsystems, autodesk, ugs and intel. Its products, ansys(R), designspace(R), ai solutions(tm), icem cfd engineering and cadoe, are sold in 7 countries across the world. On 26-Feb-2003, the group acquired cfx.

Primary SIC and add'l.: 7379 7372

CIK No: 0001013462

Subsidiaries: 2011767 Ontario, Inc., ANSYS Canada Limited, ANSYS Europe Limited, ANSYS Germany GmbH, ANSYS KK, ANSYS Software Private Limited, CADOE S.A, Century Dynamics, Inc., Century Dynamics, Ltd, CFX Limited, SAS IP, Inc, Silver Nugget Ltd

Officers: James E. Cashman/Dir., CEO, Pres./$2,628,429.00, Sheila S. Dinardo/VP, General Counsel, Sec., Christopher J. Reid/VP - Marketing/$837,049.00, Michael J. Wheeler/VP, GM - Mechanical Business Unit/$769,163.00, Joseph C. Fairbanks/VP - Sales, Support/$865,005.00, Maria T. Shields/CFO, VP/$802,430.00, Hasan Ferit Boysan/VP, GM - Fluids Business Unit, Brian C. Drew/VP, GM - Central Business Unit, Elaine V. Keim/VP - Human Resources

Directors: James E. Cashman/Dir., CEO, Pres., Peter J. Smith/Chmn., Jacqueline C. Morby/Dir., John F. Smith/Dir., Bradford C. Morley/Dir., Patrick J. Zilvitis/Dir.

Owners: James E. Cashman/2.20%, Jacqueline C. Morby, Bradford C. Morley, Eagle Asset Management, Inc./9.50%, Michael J. Wheeler, Christopher J. Reid, Maria T. Shields, John F. Smith, Joseph C. Fairbanks, FMR Corp./11.70%, Insiders/4.30%, Patrick J. Zilvitis, Peter J. Smith, Roger J. Heinen

Financial Data: Fiscal Year End:12/31   Latest Annual Data: 12/31/2006

Year	Sales	Net Income
2006	$263,640,000	$14,156,000
2005	$158,036,000	$43,903,000
2004	$134,539,000	$34,567,000

Curr. Assets:	$215,156,000	**Curr. Liab.:**	$179,300,000	**P/E Ratio:**	1.07
Plant, Equip.:	$25,530,000	**Total Liab.:**	$343,250,000	**Indic. Yr. Divd.:**	NA
Total Assets:	$878,043,000	**Net Worth:**	$534,793,000	**Debt/ Equity:**	0.1832

Antares Pharma Inc

250 Phillips Blvd., Ste. 290, Ewing, NJ, 08618; *PH:* 1-609-359-3020; *Fax:* 1-609-359-3015; *http://* www.antarespharma.com; *Email:* info@antarespharma.com

General - Incorporation	DE	**Stock**- Price on:12/24/2007	$1.98
Employees	27	Stock Exchange	AMEX
Auditor	KPMG LLP	Ticker Symbol	AIS
Stk Agt	Wells Fargo Shareowner Services	Outstanding Shares	54,230,000
Counsel	Leonard, Street & Deinard	E.P.S.	-$0.119
DUNS No.	08-536-9585	Shareholders	NA

Business: The group's principal activity is to develop, produce and market pharmaceutical delivery solutions. Pharmaceutical delivery solutions includes needle-free and mini-needle injector systems, gel technologies and transdermal products. The group distributes its needle-free injector systems for the delivery of insulin and growth hormone in more than 20 countries. The group has several products and compound formulations under development and is conducting ongoing research to create new products and formulations that combine various elements of the company's technology portfolio. The group's major customers include ferring pharmaceutical nv and biosante pharmaceuticals, inc.

Primary SIC and add'l.: 8731 3842

CIK No: 0001016169

Subsidiaries: Antares Pharma AG, Antares Pharma IPL AG, Permatec NV

Officers: Jack E. Stover/Dir., CEO, Pres./$756,593.00, Robert F. Apple/Sr. VP, CFO/$564,056.00, Peter Sadowski/VP - Devices Group/$281,490.00, James E. Hattersley/VP - Corporate Business Development/$296,353.00, Dario N.R. Carrara/Sr. VP, MD/$515,535.00, Michael L. Kasprick/VP - Business Development, Devices Group, Stephanie M. Baldwin/Mgr. - Investor Relations

Directors: Jack E. Stover/Dir., CEO, Pres., Jacques Gonella/Chmn., Thomas J. Garrity/Dir., Anton Gueth/Dir., Rajesh Shrotriya/Dir., Paul K. Wotton/Dir., Leonard S. Jacob/Dir.

Owners: Rajesh C. Shrotriya, Insiders/26.40%, Leonard Jacob, Peter Sadowski, Jack E. Stover/1.20%, Anton G. Gueth, Paul K. Wotton, Robert F. Apple, Lawrence M. Christian, Dario Carrara, Jacques Gonella/23.00%, Thomas J. Garrity, James E. Hattersley

Financial Data: ***Fiscal Year End:***12/31 ***Latest Annual Data:*** 12/31/2006

Year	Sales	Net Income
2006	$4,268,000	-$8,100,000
2005	$2,225,000	-$8,498,000
2004	$2,746,000	-$8,349,000

Curr. Assets:	$8,878,000	**Curr. Liab.:**	$2,898,000		
Plant, Equip.:	$382,000	**Total Liab.:**	$6,454,000	**Indic. Yr. Divd.:**	NA
Total Assets:	$11,534,000	**Net Worth:**	$5,080,000	**Debt/ Equity:**	0.7238

Anteon International Corp

3211 Jermantowne Rd., Ste. 700, Fairfax, VA, 22030; *PH:* 1-703-246-0200; *http://* www.anteon.com

General - Incorporation	DE	**Stock**- Price on:12/24/2007	NA
Employees	NA	Stock Exchange	NA
Auditor	KPMG LLP	Ticker Symbol	NA
Stk Agt	American Stock Transfer & Trust Co.	Outstanding Shares	NA
Counsel	Cravath, Swaine & Moore LLP	E.P.S.	NA
DUNS No.	NA	Shareholders	NA

Business: The group's principal activities are to provide information technology solutions and systems engineering and integration services to government clients. It designs, integrates, maintains and upgrades state-of-the-art information systems for national defense, intelligence, emergency response and other high priority government missions. The group also provides systems analysis, integration and program management skills necessary to manage mission systems, including ships, aircraft, weapons and communications systems. It also provides mission area and threat analyses, research and development management, systems engineering and design acquisition management, systems integration and testing, operations concept planning. The group currently serves over eight hundred U.S. Federal government clients, as well as state and foreign governments. On 23-May-2003, the group acquired information spectrum, inc. On 27-Jul-2004, the group acquired simulation technologies inc.

Primary SIC and add'l.: 6719 7379 7371

CIK No: 0001163842

Subsidiaries: General Dynamics agreed

Anthony Clark International Insurance Brokers Ltd

10333 Sport Rd. SW, Ste. 355, Calgary, AB, T2W 3X6; *PH:* 1-403-278-8811; *Fax:* 1-403-259-4429; *http://* www.anthonyclk.com

General - Incorporation	AB	**Stock**- Price on:12/24/2007	$0.305
Employees	NA	Stock Exchange	OTC
Auditor	D&H Group LLP	Ticker Symbol	ACKBF
Stk Agt	KPMG LLP	Outstanding Shares	NA
Counsel	Joseph Giuffre	E.P.S.	NA
DUNS No.	NA	Shareholders	NA

Business: The group's principal activity is general insurance brokerage. At 31-03-2002, the group operated through seven offices, all located in the province of alberta, Canada. During the year 2002, the group acquired 100% of the voting shares of alberta ltd. The group has serviced more than 24,000 insurance policies to 18,000 customers and places its general insurance business with 66 insurance carriers.

Primary SIC and add'l.: 6411

CIK No: 0001098712

Officers: Primo Podorieszach/Dir., CEO, Pres., Mahesh Bhatia/CFO, Tony Consalvo/Dir., COO

Directors: Primo Podorieszach/Dir., CEO, Pres., Tony Consalvo/Dir., COO, Normand Cournoyer/Dir., Thomas Milley/Dir., Douglas O. Farmer/Dir., Robert Sadler/Dir.

Financial Data: ***Fiscal Year End:***03/31 ***Latest Annual Data:*** 3/31/2005

Year	Sales	Net Income
2005	$10,736,000	-$1,607,000
2004	$5,713,000	-$810,000
2003	$3,517,000	-$247,000

Curr. Assets:	$1,917,000	**Curr. Liab.:**	$14,540,000		
Plant, Equip.:	$328,000	**Total Liab.:**	$14,816,000	**Indic. Yr. Divd.:**	NA
Total Assets:	$18,851,000	**Net Worth:**	$4,035,000	**Debt/ Equity:**	NA

Anthracite Capital Inc

40 E 52nd St., New York City, NY, 10022; *PH:* 1-212-409-3333; *Fax:* 1-212-754-8760; *http://* www.anthracitecapital.com; *Email:* anthracitebod@blackrock.com

General - Incorporation	MD	**Stock**- Price on:12/24/2007	$12.7
Employees	NA	Stock Exchange	NYSE
Auditor	Deloitte & Touche LLP	Ticker Symbol	AHR
Stk Agt	Mellon Investor Services LLC	Outstanding Shares	58,370,000
Counsel	NA	E.P.S.	NA
DUNS No.	NA	Shareholders	NA

Business: The groups principal activity is to invest in commercial real estate debt and equity. The group operates from the Unites States.

Primary SIC and add'l.: 6798

CIK No: 0001050112

Subsidiaries: AHR Capital B of A Limited, AHR Capital DB Limited, AHR Capital Limited, AHR Capital MS Limited, Anthracite 2004-HY1 Corp., Anthracite 2004-HY1 Depositor, LLC, Anthracite 2004-HY1 Ltd., Anthracite 2005-HY2 Corp., Anthracite 2005-HY2 Depositor, LLC, Anthracite 2005-HY2 Ltd., Anthracite Capital Trust I, Anthracite Capital Trust II, Anthracite Capital Trust III, Anthracite CDO Depositor, LLC, Anthracite CDO I Corp. 26 Subsidiaries included in the Index

Owners: Insiders/1.90%, Richard M. Shea, Ralph L. Schlosstein, Daniel P. Sefcik, James J. Lillis, Deborah J. Lucas, Carl F. Geuther, Hugh R. Frater, NWQ Investment Management Company, LLC/5.80%, Mark S. Warner, Donald G. Drapkin, Jeffrey C. Keil, Chris A. Milner, Leon T. Kendall

Financial Data: ***Fiscal Year End:***12/31 ***Latest Annual Data:*** 12/31/2006

Year	Sales	Net Income
2006	$303,417,000	$80,471,000
2005	$260,457,000	$70,597,000
2004	$203,866,000	$43,192,000

Curr. Assets:	$66,388,000	**Curr. Liab.:**	$41,465,000		
Plant, Equip.:	NA	**Total Liab.:**	$4,562,154,000	**Indic. Yr. Divd.:**	NA
Total Assets:	$5,218,263,000	**Net Worth:**	$656,109,000	**Debt/ Equity:**	6.0212

Antigenics Inc

162 5th Ave., Ste. 900, New York, NY, 10111; *PH:* 1-212-994-8200; *Fax:* 1-212-994-8299; *http://* www.antigenics.com; *Email:* clinicalaffairs@antigenics.com

General - Incorporation	DE	**Stock**- Price on:12/24/2007	$2.95
Employees	100	Stock Exchange	NDQ
Auditor	KPMG LLP	Ticker Symbol	AGEN
Stk Agt	American Stock Transfer & Trust Co.	Outstanding Shares	45,890,000
Counsel	Garo Armen	E.P.S.	-$1.01
DUNS No.	NA	Shareholders	NA

Business: The group's principal activities are to develop treatments for cancers, serious infectious diseases, autoimmune disorders and degenerative disorders using proprietary technologies to program the immune system and to improve quality of life. The group primarily develops immunotherapeutics, including lead product and oncophage (r). Lead development programs include immunotherapeutics that are based on a specific class of proteins known as heat shock proteins (hsps) and an immune system adjuvant called qs-21. The products under development include oncophage (R), aroplatin, atra-iv, ag-702, qs-21 adjuvant, CD91 and CD1. The related business activities include product research and development activities, regulatory and clinical affairs, establishing manufacturing capabilities, production for clinical trials and administrative and corporate development activities.

Primary SIC and add'l.: 8731 2834

CIK No: 0001098972

Subsidiaries: Aronex Pharmaceuticals, Inc, igenics Therapeutics Limited

Officers: Garo H. Armen/Chmn., CEO/$1,420,269.00, Hyam I. Levitsky/Dir., Member - Medical Advisory Counsel, John Cerio/VP - Human Resources, Deanna M. Petersen/VP - Business Development, Shalini Sharp/CFO, VP/$324,380.00, Sunny Uberoi/VP - Corporate Communications, Kerry A. Wentworth/VP - Clinical Operations, Regulatory Affairs/$365,710.00, John M. Kirkwood/Member - Medical Advisory Counsel, Pramod K. Srivastava/Dir., Founding Scientis, Ronald M. Bukowski/Member - Medical Advisory Counsel, Andrew T. Parsa/Member - Medical Advisory Counsel, Mace L. Rothenberg/Member - Medical Advisory Counsel, Robert Anstey/Investor Relations Officer, Pierre Champagne/Head - Clinical, Medical Affairs, Karen Higgins Valentine/VP - Legal *(18 Officers included in Index)*

Directors: Garo H. Armen/Chmn., CEO, Hyam I. Levitsky/Dir., Member - Medical Advisory Counsel, Tom Dechaene/Dir., Margaret M. Eisen/Dir., Peter Thornton/Dir., Brian Corvese/Dir., Timothy R. Wright/Dir., John N. Hatsopoulos/Dir., Wadih Jordan/Dir., Pramod K. Srivastava/Dir., Founding Scientis

Owners: Insiders/5.20%, Renu Gupta, Noubar Afeyan, Kerry A. Wentworth, Antigenics Holdings L.L.C./24.30%, Frank V. AtLee, Garo H. Armen/2.80%, Wadih Jordan, Roman M. Chicz, Brad M. Kelley/12.10%, Brad M. Kelley/100.00%, Pramod K. Srivastava, Shalini Sharp, Peter Thornton, Margaret M. Eisen *(16 Owners included in Index)*

Financial Data: ***Fiscal Year End:***12/31 ***Latest Annual Data:*** 12/31/2006

Year	Sales	Net Income
2006	$692,000	-$51,881,000
2005	$630,000	-$74,104,000
2004	$707,000	-$56,162,000

Curr. Assets:	$42,298,000	**Curr. Liab.:**	$9,078,000		
Plant, Equip.:	$18,619,000	**Total Liab.:**	$90,345,000	**Indic. Yr. Divd.:**	NA
Total Assets:	$72,952,000	**Net Worth:**	-$17,393,000	**Debt/ Equity:**	NA

Ants Software Inc

700 Airport Blvd., Ste. 300, Burlingame, CA, 94010; *PH:* 1-650-931-0500; *Fax:* 1-650-931-0510; *http://* www.ants.com; *Email:* info@ants.com

General - Incorporation: DE
Employees: 49
Auditor: Burr, Pilger & Mayer LLP
Stk Agt: Wells Fargo Shareowner Services
Counsel: NA
DUNS No.: 15-426-3511

Stock- Price on:12/24/2007: $1.65
Stock Exchange: OTC
Ticker Symbol: ANTS
Outstanding Shares: 56,390,000
E.P.S: -$0.31
Shareholders: NA

Business: The group's principal activity is to develop and market proprietary software technology that improves the speed at which computers can process database transactions. The operations currently consist of research and development of proprietary software technology, marketing the technology to potential customers and raising capital for operations. The group's ace (ants concurrency engine) is comprised of a unique data processing engine coupled with lock-free data structures. The first implementation of ace is the ants data server (ads), a standards-compliant sql relational database server. Ace can be used as the engine for any application that manipulates data.

Primary SIC and add'l.: 7372 7374

CIK No: 0000796655

Subsidiaries: Intellectual Properties and Technologies, Inc.

Officers: Joseph Kozak/Chmn., CEO, Pres./$448,767.00, Clifford Hersh/Chief Scientist/$220,000.00, Jeffrey R. Spirn/VP - Research, Development/$266,355.00, Kenneth Ruotolo/47/Exec. VP - Finance, Administration, CFO/$230,479.00, Rao Yendluri/VP - Engineering, David Segleau/47/VP - Support Services

Directors: Joseph Kozak/Chmn., CEO, Pres., Don Haderle/Member - Technical Advisory Board, Barry J. Thompson/Member - Technical Advisory Board, Curt Miller/Member - Technical Advisory Board, John R. Gaulding/Dir., Francis K. Ruotolo/70/Dir., Thomas Holt/Dir., Robert H. Kite/Dir., Robert Peterson/Member - Technical Advisory Board, Craig Campbell/Dir., Robert Jett/Dir., Ari Kaplan/Dir.

Owners: Perry Logan/7.74%, Joseph Kozak/1.79%, Robert H. Kite/1.11%, Thomas Holt, Constantin Zdarsky/12.26%, Insiders/8.67%, Kenneth Ruotolo/1.01%, John R. Gaulding, Jeffrey Spirn, Clifford Hersh/1.10%, Lyle P. Campbell/10.06%, Donald R. Hutton/6.27%, Francis K. Ruotolo/1.87%

Financial Data: *Fiscal Year End:*12/31 *Latest Annual Data:* 12/31/2006

Year	Sales	Net Income
2006	$288,000	-$15,126,000
2005	$467,000	-$8,704,000
2004	NA	-$5,060,000

Curr. Assets:	$4,919,000	*Curr. Liab.:*	$1,037,000		
Plant, Equip.:	$736,000	*Total Liab.:*	$2,173,000	*Indic. Yr. Divd.:*	NA
Total Assets:	$5,996,000	*Net Worth:*	$3,823,000	*Debt/ Equity:*	1.4190

Anworth Mortgage Asset Corp

1299 Ocean Ave., Ste. 250, Santa Monica, CA, 90401; *PH:* 1-310-255-4493; *Fax:* 1-310-434-0070; *http://* www.anworth.com

General - Incorporation: MD
Employees: 11
Auditor: BDO Seidman, LLP
Stk Agt: American Stock Transfer & Trust Co.
Counsel: Manatt, Phelps & Phillips, LLP
DUNS No.: NA

Stock- Price on:12/24/2007: $9.11
Stock Exchange: NYSE
Ticker Symbol: ANH
Outstanding Shares: 45,620,000
E.P.S: -$0.4
Shareholders: NA

Business: The groups principal activity is to provide loans services. The groups services include residential mortgage loans and real estate loan. The group operates from the United States.

Primary SIC and add'l.: 6798

CIK No: 0001047884

Subsidiaries: BellaVista Finance Corporation, BellaVista Funding Corporation, Belvedere Trust Finance Corporation, Belvedere Trust Mortgage Corporation, Belvedere Trust Secured Assets Corporation, BT Management Company, L.L.C., BT Management Holding Corporation, BT Residential Funding Corporation

Officers: Lloyd McAdams/Chmn., CEO, Pres./$711,122.00, Claus H. Lund/Dir., Pres., CEO - Belvedere Trust Mortgage Corporation, John T. Hillman/Dir. - Investor Relations, Russell J. Thompson/Treasurer, Mark J. Kelson/Sec., Joseph E. McAdams/Dir., Exec. VP, Chief Investment Officer/$461,860.00, Thad M. Brown/CFO, Treasurer, Sec./$281,258.00, Heather U. Baines/Exec. VP, Charles J. Siegel/Sr. VP - Finance, Assist. Sec./$236,915.00, Evangelos Karagiannis/VP, Portfolio Mgr., Bistra Pashamova/VP, Portfolio Mgr./$160,633.00, Angelina Greve/VP, Controller

Directors: Lloyd McAdams/Chmn., CEO, Pres., Claus H. Lund/Dir., Pres., CEO - Belvedere Trust Mortgage Corporation, Lee A. Ault/Dir., Robert C. Davis/Dir., Joseph E. McAdams/Dir., Exec. VP, Chief Investment Officer, Charles H. Black/Dir., Joe E. Davis/Dir.

Owners: Evangelos Karagiannis, Thad M. Brown, Wells Capital Management Inc./7.26%, Insiders/6.35%, Heather U. Baines/1.81%, Claus H. Lund, Joseph E. McAdams, Bistra Pashamova, Lee A. Ault, Charles H. Black, Joe E. Davis, Robert C. Davis, Russell J. Thompson, Schneider Capital Management LP/6.97%, Lloyd McAdams/2.35% *(16 Owners included in Index)*

Financial Data: *Fiscal Year End:*12/31 *Latest Annual Data:* 12/31/2006

Year	Sales	Net Income
2006	$311,987,000	-$14,204,000
2005	$281,881,000	$28,885,000
2004	$163,622,000	$55,805,000

Curr. Assets:	$35,698,000	*Curr. Liab.:*	$4,680,318,000		
Plant, Equip.:	NA	*Total Liab.:*	$6,196,299,000	*Indic. Yr. Divd.:*	$0.200
Total Assets:	$6,687,389,000	*Net Worth:*	$491,002,000	*Debt/ Equity:*	3.0875

ANZA Capital Inc

Viking Investments, 65 Broadway, Ste. 888, New York, NY, 10006; *PH:* 1-212-430-6548; *http://* www.anzacapital.com

General - Incorporation: NV
Employees: NA
Auditor: Singer Lewak Greenbaum & Goldstein
Stk Agt: Securities Transfer Corp
Counsel: NA
DUNS No.: NA

Stock- Price on:12/24/2007: $2.55
Stock Exchange: OTC
Ticker Symbol: AZACE
Outstanding Shares: NA
E.P.S: NA
Shareholders: NA

Business: The group's principal activity is to provide mortgage banking and mortgage brokering services. It also provides real estate brokerage services. The group through the loan agents identifies prospective borrowers from real estate brokers, home developers and markets to the general public. It processes the loan package, including obtaining credit and appraisal reports. The group operates through its wholly owned subsidiaries, American residential funding, inc., a Nevada corporation (amres), expidoc.com, inc., a California corporation (expidoc), titus real estate llc, a California limited liability company (titus real estate), bravo realty.com, a Nevada corporation (bravorealty.com) and bravo real estate, inc. (bravo real estate network).

Primary SIC and add'l.: 6531 6162 6719 7375

CIK No: 0000926844

Subsidiaries: American Residential Funding, Inc., Renhuang Pharmaceuticals, Inc.

Officers: Shaoming Li/45/Chmn., CEO, Pres., Vincent Rinehart/Chmn., Pres., David Villarreal/Pres. - Bravorealty, Tom White/CFO - Bravorealty, Expidoccom, Christina Lee/Pres. - Expidoccom, Venerada Toledo/CFO - American Residential Funding, Inc, Zuoliang Wang/36/Interim CFO, Jiang He/36/Sec.

Directors: Shaoming Li/45/Chmn., CEO, Pres., Vincent Rinehart/Chmn., Pres., Scott Presta/Dir., Fanrong Meng/35/Dir., Andy Wu/39/Dir.

Owners: Viking Investments USA, Inc./74.07%

Financial Data: *Fiscal Year End:*04/30 *Latest Annual Data:* 04/30/2007

Year	Sales	Net Income
2007	NA	NA
2006	NA	$879,000
2005	$50,289,000	-$3,453,000

Curr. Assets:	NA	*Curr. Liab.:*	NA		
Plant, Equip.:	NA	*Total Liab.:*	NA	*Indic. Yr. Divd.:*	NA
Total Assets:	$0	*Net Worth:*	NA	*Debt/ Equity:*	NA

AOB Holdings Inc

Formerly: Asia Network Inc
4790 Irvine Blvd., No. 105-492, Irvine, CA, 92620;

General - Incorporation: DE
Employees: NA
Auditor Child, Van Wagoner & Bradshaw, PLLC
Stk Agt: NA
Counsel: NA
DUNS No.: NA

Stock- Price on:12/24/2007: NA
Stock Exchange: NA
Ticker Symbol: NA
Outstanding Shares: NA
E.P.S: NA
Shareholders: NA

Business: The group's principle activity is to provide liberal arts education to help prepare succeeding generations of undergraduates. The group operates from United States.

Primary SIC and add'l.: 9995

CIK No: 0001307715

Subsidiaries: AOBC

Officers: Teodora O. Amoloza/Executive Dir., Roger Ames/Counsel, Advisor, Vishaka Desai/Counsel, Advisor, Roberta H.I. Martin/Counsel, Advisor, Barbara D. Metcalf/Counsel, Advisor, Richard Smith/Counsel, Advisor, Patricia Stranahan/Counsel, Advisor, Lucien Ellington/Counsel, Advisor, James Huffman/Counsel, Advisor, Cathy Benton/Exec. Officio - Development, Paul Watt/Exec. Officio - Development, David Adams/Counsel, Advisor

Directors: Donald Clark/Chmn., Erin McCarthy/Vice Chmn., James Kodera/Dir., Mary-Ann Milford-Lutzker/Dir., Gary Decoker/Dir., Teodora O. Amoloza/Executive Dir., Robert Y. Eng/Dir., Zhenhu Jin/Dir., Ronnie Littlejohn/Dir., Lisa N. Trivedi/Dir.

Aon Corp

Aon Ctr., 200 East Randolph St., Chicago, IL, 60601; *PH:* 1-312-381-1000; *Fax:* 1-312-381-6032; *http://* www.aon.com; *Email:* investors@asc.aon.com

General - Incorporation: DE
Employees: 43,100
Auditor: Ernst & Young LLP
Stk Agt: Computershare Investor Services LLC
Counsel: NA
DUNS No.: 03-850-3546

Stock- Price on:12/24/2007: $42.69
Stock Exchange: NYSE
Ticker Symbol: AOC
Outstanding Shares: 293,610,000
E.P.S: $2.40
Shareholders: NA

Business: The group's principle activities are to provide insurance brokerage, consulting and insurance underwriting services through subsidiaries. The group's operates through three segments: risk and insurance brokerage services: that acts an advisor and insurance broker, helps clients manage their risks and negotiates and places insurance risk with insurance carriers through our global distribution network. Consulting: provides advice and services to clients for employee benefits, compensation, management consulting, communications and human resources outsourcing. Insurance underwriting: provides specialty insurance products including supplemental accident, health and life insurance; credit life, extended warranty products and select property and casualty insurance products and services. The group's quarterly revenue for year 2007 was 2,407.00 millions of USD.

Primary SIC and add'l.: 6331 6411 6321 6311

CIK No: 0000315293

Subsidiaries: 1c Katharinastrase 29 Vermogensverwaltungsges mbH, 2e Katharinastrase 29 Vermogensverwaltungsges mbH, A Morel & Cie Sa, A. J. Norcott & Company (Holdings) Limited, A. J. Norcott & Partners (Northern) Limited, A.g.y.c. Corretores De Seguros Lda., A.H. Laseur b.v., A.H.E. Alexander Howden de Espana S.A., A/S Assurance, ABS Insurance Agency Ltd., ACGMGA Corp., Acn 006 278 226, Acn 008 497 318, Acn 051 158 984, Acn 075 486 243 1394 Subsidiaries included in the Index

Officers: Dirk P.M. Verbeek/Chmn., CEO - Aon Risk Services International, Stephen P. McGill/CEO - Aon Risk Services Americas, Mark Boozell/CEO, Aon Underwriting Mgr., Richard Ravin/CEO, Pres. - Combined Insurance Company, Roelof Hendriks/CEO - Europe, Middle East, Africa, EMEA, Bernard Fung/CEO - Aon Asia Pacific, Apac, Peter Harmer/CEO - United Kingdom, Andrew M. Appel/CEO - Aon Consulting Worldwide, Inc, Gregory C. Case/Dir., CEO, Pres./$7,519,433.00, Kip Kelley/Chmn. - Global Practice Groups, Affinity, Patrick G. Ryan/Exec. Chmn./$7,330,451.00, Mike Rice/Chmn. - Aon Risk Services Americas/$5,381,863.00, Jim Eisenmann/Chmn. - Global Practice Groups, Dave Nugent/Contact - Property Risk Control, Aon Risk Consultants, Mimi E. Morgan/Contact - Aon Risk Services, Affinity Insurance Services *(98 Officers included in Index)*

Directors: Gregory C. Case/Dir., CEO, Pres., Dennis L. Mahoney/Chmn. - Aon Global, Aon Limited, Patrick G. Ryan/Exec. Chmn., Gloria Santona/Dir., Eden R. Martin/Dir., Jan Kalff/Dir., Lester B. Knight/Dir., Carolyn Y. Woo/Dir., Edgar D. Jannotta/Dir., Michael J. Losh/Dir., Andrew J. McKenna/Dir., Robert S. Morrison/Dir., Richard B. Myers/Dir., Richard C. Notebaert/Dir., John W. Rogers/Dir.

Owners: Patrick G. Ryan/7.23%, NWQ Investment Management Company,LLC/7.62%, State Street Bank and Trust Company/5.55%, Southeastern Asset Management,Inc./13.71%, Davis Selected Advisers,L.P./5.79%

Financial Data: **Fiscal Year End:**12/31 **Latest Annual Data:** 12/31/2006

Year	Sales	Net Income
2006	$8,954,000,000	$720,000,000
2005	$9,837,000,000	$737,000,000
2004	$10,172,000,000	$546,000,000

Curr. Assets:	$13,852,000,000	**Curr. Liab.:**	$9,746,000,000	**P/E Ratio:**	17.79
Plant, Equip.:	$504,000,000	**Total Liab.:**	$19,100,000,000	**Indic. Yr. Divd.:**	$0.600
Total Assets:	$24,318,000,000	**Net Worth:**	$5,218,000,000	**Debt/ Equity:**	0.3939

AP Henderson Group

600 Wilshire Blvd, Ste 1252, Los Angeles, CA, 90017; ***PH:*** 1-404-816-9220;
http:// www.aphenderson.com; ***Email:*** email@aphenderson.com

General - Incorporation	NV	**Stock**- Price on:12/24/2007	$0.011
Employees	NA	Stock Exchange	OTC
Auditor	Kyle L. Tingle, Cpa LLC	Ticker Symbol	APHG
Stk Agt	Pacific Stock Transfer Company	Outstanding Shares	NA
Counsel	NA	E.P.S	NA
DUNS No.	NA	Shareholders	NA

Business: The group's principle activity is to evaluate possible acquisition with private companies, which either possess marketable intellectual properties, such as patents or is currently in production but looking to lower production cost. The company intends to manufacture and market patented multi-screen slide view laptop notebook computer design, x-panel(tm). The company has generated no revenues and is in the development stage.

Primary SIC and add'l.: 7379

CIK No: 0001096653

Subsidiaries: Slideview Corporation

Financial Data: **Fiscal Year End:**12/31 **Latest Annual Data:** 12/31/2004

Year	Sales	Net Income
2004	NA	-$760,000
2003	NA	-$647,000
2002	$106,578,000	$6,610,000

Curr. Assets:	$9,180,000	**Curr. Liab.:**	$899,000		
Plant, Equip.:	NA	**Total Liab.:**	$913,000	**Indic. Yr. Divd.:**	NA
Total Assets:	$9,184,000	**Net Worth:**	$8,272,000	**Debt/ Equity:**	NA

APA Enterprises Inc

2950 NE 84th Ln., Blaine, MN, 55449; ***PH:*** 1-763-784-4995; ***Fax:*** 1-763-784-2038;
http:// www.apaenterprises.com; ***Email:*** info@apaenterprises.com

General - Incorporation	DE	**Stock**- Price on:12/24/2007	$1.25
Employees	128	Stock Exchange	NDQ
Auditor	Grant Thornton, LLP	Ticker Symbol	APAT
Stk Agt	Wells Fargo Shareowner Services	Outstanding Shares	11,870,000
Counsel	NA	E.P.S	-$0.29
DUNS No.	NA	Shareholders	NA

Business: The group's principal activities are to design, manufacture and market optical components. The group also develops fiber optic components for metro and access communications networks, gallium nitride (gan) and optoelectronics. The dwdm optical components enable fiber optic networks to transmit data simultaneously on several wavelengths of light within each optical fiber of cable. Other products include optical lens systems, optical thin film coatings, optical windows and flats, ultraviolet detectors etc. Currently, the group's research and development activities are focused in the areas of compound semiconductor electronic devices and components and modules for fiber optics networks. The group trade names are sun (uv) and truvmeter (TM).

Primary SIC and add'l.: 3357 3827

CIK No: 0000796505

Subsidiaries: APA Cables and Networks, Inc., APA Optronics (India) Private Limited.

Officers: Anil K. Jain/62/CEO, CFO, Pres./$228,577.00, Chris M. Goettl/Principal Accounting Officer, Cheryl Podzimek/Contact - Investor Relations Officer/$157,698.00, Janna R. Severance/Sec.

Directors: Anil K. Jain/62/CEO, CFO, Pres., Ronald G. Roth/63/Dir., Stephen L. Zuckerman/66/Dir., John G. Reddan/77/Dir., Janna R. Severance/Sec.

Owners: John G. Reddan, Ronald G. Roth/3.00%, Insiders/17.70%, Anil K. Jain/14.10%, Cheryl Beranek Podzimek, Herman Lee/6.40%, Stephen L. Zuckerman

Financial Data: **Fiscal Year End:**12/31 **Latest Annual Data:** 03/31/2007

Year	Sales	Net Income
2007	$18,560,000	-$2,147,000
2006	$15,718,000	-$3,349,000
2005	$13,886,000	-$3,420,000

Curr. Assets:	$12,977,000	**Curr. Liab.:**	$3,723,000		
Plant, Equip.:	$2,623,000	**Total Liab.:**	$4,013,000	**Indic. Yr. Divd.:**	NA
Total Assets:	$19,594,000	**Net Worth:**	$15,579,000	**Debt/ Equity:**	0.0004

Apac Customer Services Inc

6 Pkwy. N, Deerfield, IL, 60015; ***PH:*** 1-847-374-4980; ***Fax:*** 1-847-236-5453;
http:// www.apaccustomerservices.com

General - Incorporation	IL	**Stock**- Price on:12/24/2007	$2.99
Employees	7,900	Stock Exchange	NDQ
Auditor	Deloitte & Touche LLP	Ticker Symbol	APAC
Stk Agt	LaSalle Bank N.A	Outstanding Shares	50,090,000
Counsel	NA	E.P.S	-$0.34
DUNS No.	83-589-9501	Shareholders	NA

Business: The group's principle activities are to provide customer interaction solutions and electronic solutions. These services are provided to financial services, insurance, telecommunications, healthcare and logistics industries. The group develops and delivers end-to-end customer care, customer acquisition and Web-enabled programs. The group has two primary service offerings: customer acquisition and customer care. The customer acquisition services include sales support to consumers and businesses, market research, targeted marketing plan development and customer lead generation, acquisition and retention. The customer care services involve the receipt of a call from a client's customer, and the identification and routing of the call to the appropriate customer service representative. The group's quarterly revenue for September 2007 was 56.82 millions of USD.

Primary SIC and add'l.: 6411 7389 7363

CIK No: 0000949297

Subsidiaries: APAC Customer Services General Partner,Inc., APAC Customer Services of Illinois,Inc., APAC Customer Services of Iowa, LLC, APAC Customer Services of Texas, L.P., APAC Customer Services, LLC, APAC Customer Services,Inc., ITI Holdings, LLC

Officers: Robert J. Keller/Dir., CEO, Pres./$920,619.00, Mark McDermott/CIO, Sr. VP, Karen R. Tulloch/Sr. VP - Human Resources, George H. Hepburn/Sr. VP, CFO/$404,105.00, James M. McClenahan/Sr. VP - Sales, Marketing/$448,937.00, Pamela R. Schneider/Sr. VP, General Counsel, Sec./$364,497.00, David Labonte/Sr. VP - Operations/$400,428.00, James C. Gari/VP - Finance

Directors: Robert J. Keller/Dir., CEO, Pres., Theodore G. Schwartz/Chmn., Founder, Cindy K. Andreotti/Dir., John C. Kraft/Dir., John W. Gerdelman/54/Dir., John J. Park/Dir.

Owners: Cindy K. Andreotti, Pamela R. Schneider, George H. Hepburn, Trust Four Hundred Thirty U/A/D 4/2/94/4.10%, Trust 3081/1.00%, Trust 3080/1.00%, Sidus Investment Partners, L.P./5.90%, Wells Fargo & Company/8.60%, John C. Kraft, Thomas M. Collins, John J. Park, Trust Seven Hundred Thirty U/A/D 4/2/94/4.10%, John W. Gerdelman, Robert J. Keller/1.70%, Theodore G. Schwartz/37.90% *(18 Owners included in Index)*

Financial Data: **Fiscal Year End:**01/01 **Latest Annual Data:** 12/31/2006

Year	Sales	Net Income
2006	$224,297,000	-$30,539,000
2005	$273,239,000	-$6,499,000

Curr. Assets:	$45,880,000	**Curr. Liab.:**	$62,559,000		
Plant, Equip.:	$23,930,000	**Total Liab.:**	$68,748,000	**Indic. Yr. Divd.:**	NA
Total Assets:	$92,054,000	**Net Worth:**	$23,306,000	**Debt/ Equity:**	0.3405

Apache Corp

2000 Post Oak Blvd., Ste. 100, Houston, TX, 77056; ***PH:*** 1-713-296-6000; ***Fax:*** 1-713-296-6496;
http:// www.apachecorp.com

General - Incorporation	DE	**Stock**- Price on:12/24/2007	$87.36
Employees	3,150	Stock Exchange	NYSE
Auditor	Ernst & Young LLP	Ticker Symbol	APA
Stk Agt	Wells Fargo Bank, N.A.	Outstanding Shares	331,160,000
Counsel	NA	E.P.S	$7.15
DUNS No.	00-696-1551	Shareholders	NA

Business: The groups principle activities include exploring, developing and producing oil and natural gas. The group operates from United States.

Primary SIC and add'l.: 1311 1382 1321

CIK No: 0000006769

Subsidiaries: Apache Abu Gharadig Corporation LDC, Apache Argentina Corporation LDC, Apache Asyout Corporation LDC, Apache Australia Holdings Pty Limited, Apache Australia Management Pty Limited, Apache Aviation, Inc., Apache Bohai Corporation LDC, Apache Canada Argentina Holdings ULC, Apache Canada Argentina Investment ULC, Apache Canada Holdings Ltd, Apache Canada Ltd., Apache Canada Management II Ltd, Apache Canada Management Ltd, Apache Canada Properties Ltd., Apache China Corporation LDC 113 Subsidiaries included in the Index

Officers: Steven G. Farris/59/Dir., CEO, COO, Pres./$5,278,950.00, Jeffrey M. Bender/56/VP - Human Resources, James L. House/47/Regional VP, MD - Apache North Sea Ltd, Thomas P. Chambers/52/VP - Corporate Planning, Glenn Joyce/Regional Contact - Egypt, Mike Rose/Regional Contact - United Kingdom, Kim Crider/Regional Contact - United States, Michelle Markey/Contributor, Anthony P. Lannie/54/Sr. VP, General Counsel, Anne Hedrich/Mgr. - e, Communications, Scott Byrd/Mgr. - Global Sourcing, Special Projects, John Williams/Mgr. - Environmental, Mike McKenna/Mgr. - Safety, Obie O'Brien/Dir. - Governmental, Regulatory Affairs, Corporate Outreach, Carol Foster/Regional Contact - Australia *(43 Officers included in Index)*

Directors: Steven G. Farris/59/Dir., CEO, COO, Pres., Raymond Plank/Chmn., Founder, George D. Lawrence/57/Dir., Patricia Albjerg Graham/72/Dir., John A. Kocur/80/Dir., Eugene C. Fiedorek/76/Dir., Randolph M. Ferlic/71/Dir., Rodman D. Patton/64/Dir., A. D. Frazier/63/Dir., F. H. Merelli/71/Dir., Frederick M. Bohen/70/Dir., Charles J. Pitman/65/Dir., Jay A. Precourt/70/Dir.

Owners: John A. Crum, Insiders/1.26%, Charles J. Pitman, Roger B. Plank, George D. Lawrence, Jay A. Precourt, Randolph M. Ferlic, Raymond Plank, Patricia A. Graham, Frederick M. Bohen, Rodney J. Eichler, F. H. Merelli, Eugene C. Fiedorek, Rodman D. Patton, A. D. Frazier *(17 Owners included in Index)*

Financial Data: **Fiscal Year End:**12/31 **Latest Annual Data:** 12/31/2006

Year	Sales	Net Income
2006	$8,288,779,000	$2,552,451,000
2005	$7,584,244,000	$2,623,730,000
2004	$5,332,577,000	$1,668,754,000

Curr. Assets:	$2,490,271,000	**Curr. Liab.:**	$3,811,612,000		
Plant, Equip.:	$21,346,252,000	**Total Liab.:**	$11,117,122,000	**Indic. Yr. Divd.:**	$0.600
Total Assets:	$24,308,175,000	**Net Worth:**	$13,191,053,000	**Debt/ Equity:**	0.2647

Apartment Investment and Management Company

4582 S Ulster St. Pkwy., Ste. 1100, Denver, CO, 80237; ***PH:*** 1-303-757-8101; ***Fax:*** 1-303-759-3226;
http:// www.aimco.com; ***Email:*** investor@aimco.com

General - Incorporation	MD	**Stock**- Price on:12/24/2007	$51.01
Employees	6,000	Stock Exchange	NYSE
Auditor	Ernst & Young LLP	Ticker Symbol	AIV
Stk Agt	Computershare Trust Co	Outstanding Shares	97,150,000
Counsel	NA	E.P.S	$0.59
DUNS No.	NA	Shareholders	NA

Business: The groups principle activities include acquiring, owning, managing and redeveloping apartment properties. The group operates through two segments namely, real estate and investment management business. The group operates from the United States, Columbia and Puerto Rico. The group's quarterly revenue for September 2007 was 431.20 millions of USD.

Primary SIC and add'l.: 6798

CIK No: 0000922864

Subsidiaries: 1-36 Jaidee Drive Associates Limited Partnership, 107-145 West 135TH Street Associate Limited Partnership, 1133 15TH STREET TWO ASSOCIATES (A MARYLAND LIMITED PARTNERSHIP), 1133 FIFTEENTH STREET ASSOCIATES, 1133 FIFTEENTH STREET FOUR ASSOCIATES (A MARYLAND LIMITED PARTNERSHIP), 1212 SOUTH MICHIGAN LLC, 5 MILE LIMITED PARTNERSHIP, 62ND STREET JOINT VENTURE, 630

EAST LINCOLN AVENUE ASSOCIATES LIMITED PARTNERSHIP, 7400 ROOSEVELT CORP., 7400 ROOSEVELT INVESTORS, 76 HOUSING PARTNERSHIP INVESTMENTS LIMITED, A & G PROPERTIES, LLC, ABBOTT ASSOCIATES LIMITED PARTNERSHIP, ABINGTON CORPORATION 2247 Subsidiaries included in the Index

Officers: Terry Considine/Chmn., CEO, Pres./$4,568,831.00, David Robertson/Exec. VP, Pres., CEO - Aimco Capital/$5,633,104.00, Melanie G. French/Sr. VP - Learning, Organizational Development, Thomas M. Herzog/CFO, Exec. VP/$1,690,130.00, James G. Purvis/Exec. VP - Human Resources, Timothy J. Beaudin/Exec. VP, Chief Development Officer/$2,534,970.00, Miles Cortez/Exec. VP, General Counsel, Sec., Patti K. Fielding/Exec. VP - Securities, Debt, Treasurer, Lance J. Graber/Exec. VP - Aimco Capital, Transactions, East/$1,994,189.00, Terri C. Heredia/Sr. VP - Talent, Anthony Dalto/Division VP - Gulf, Eric L. Hilty/Sr. VP, Assist. General Counsel, Assist. Sec., Becky Holeman/Sr. VP, Controller, Sherlyn M. Keiling/Sr. VP - Performance Excellence, Martha L. Long/Sr. VP - Partnership Transactions *(82 Officers included in Index)*

Directors: Terry Considine/Chmn., CEO, Pres., James N. Bailey/Dir., Richard Ellwood/Dir., Landis J. Martin/Dir., Thomas L. Rhodes/Dir., Michael A. Stein/Dir., Robert A. Miller/Dir., Thomas L. Keltner/Dir.

Owners: Richard S. Ellwood, Thomas L. Rhodes, Timothy J. Beaudin, Landis J. Martin, Michael A. Stein, Cohen& Steers, Inc./8.62%, James N. Bailey, Lance J. Graber, The Vanguard Group/7.33%, Thomas M. Herzog, Deutsche Bank AG/7.02%, David Robertson, Terry Considine/7.36%, Insiders/9.40%

Financial Data: Fiscal Year End:12/31 **Latest Annual Data:** 03/31/2007

Year	Sales	Net Income
2007	NA	$370,477,000
2006	$1,690,994,000	$176,787,000
2005	$1,521,523,000	$70,982,000

Curr. Assets:	$683,865,000	**Curr. Liab.:**	$509,471,000		
Plant, Equip.:	$9,081,218,000	**Total Liab.:**	$7,949,883,000	**Indic. Yr. Divd.:**	$2.400
Total Assets:	$10,289,775,000	**Net Worth:**	$2,339,892,000	**Debt/ Equity:**	NA

APCO Argentina Inc

One Williams Ctr., Mail Drop 26-4, Tulsa, OK, 74172; **PH:** 1-918-573-2164; *http://* www.williams.com

General - Incorporation.......... Cayman Islands	**Stock**- Price on:12/24/2007 ....$87.87
Employees...13	Stock Exchange...NDQ
Auditor ....Ryder Scott Co., L.p.	Ticker Symbol...APAGF
Stk Agt.................................Bank of New York	Outstanding Shares..............................7,360,000
Counsel...NA	E.P.S...$5.00
DUNS No. 15-036-6243	Shareholders..NA

Business: The group's principle activities inclue exploring and producing oil and gas through joint ventures in Argentina. The group operates from United States.

Primary SIC and add'l.: 1311

CIK No: 0000311471

Subsidiaries: Apco Argentina S.A., Apco Austral S.A, Apco Properties Ltd., The Williams Companies, Inc, Williams Global Energy (Cayman) Limited

Officers: Ralph A. Hill/48/Chmn., CEO, Thomas Bueno/56/COO, Pres., Landy L. Fullmer/55/CFO, Chief Accounting Officer, Controller, VP

Directors: Ralph A. Hill/48/Chmn., CEO, Piero Ruffinengo/63/Dir., Keith E. Bailey/65/Dir., John H. Williams/89/Dir., Rodney J. Sailor/49/Dir., Bryan K. Guderian/48/Dir., Robert J. Lafortune/81/Dir.

Owners: Williams Global Energy (Cayman) Limited, Lehman Brothers Holdings Inc., Robert J. LaFortune, John H. Williams, Brown Advisory Holdings Incorporated, Thomas Bueno, Insiders, The Williams Companies, Inc.

Financial Data: Fiscal Year End:12/31 **Latest Annual Data:** 12/31/2006

Year	Sales	Net Income
2006	$57,952,000	$40,062,000
2005	$41,739,000	$29,846,000
2004	$41,562,000	$15,506,000

Curr. Assets:	$60,114,000	**Curr. Liab.:**	$12,337,000	**P/E Ratio:**	17.57
Plant, Equip.:	$45,697,000	**Total Liab.:**	$14,090,000	**Indic. Yr. Divd.:**	$1.400
Total Assets:	$164,244,000	**Net Worth:**	$150,003,000	**Debt/ Equity:**	NA

APD Antiquities Inc

1314 S Grand Blvd, Ste. 2 - 176, Spokane, WA, 99202; **PH:** 1-509-744-8590; *http://* www.apd-international.com; **Email:** apdintl@apd-international.com

General - Incorporation.............................NV	**Stock**- Price on:12/24/2007 ....NA
Employees...NA	Stock Exchange...OTC
Auditor ....Williams & Webster, P.S	Ticker Symbol...NA
Stk Agt..........Nevada Agency & Trust Company	Outstanding Shares.......................................NA
Counsel...NA	E.P.S..NA
DUNS No. ....NA	Shareholders..NA

Business: The group's principle activity being an e-Commerce based company is to acquire and market antiques including rare, high quality Asian antiques, Chinese art, and other collectibles ideal for discriminating collectors, buyers and interior decorators. In particular, we specialize in museum quality antique items such as pottery, statues, porcelain, gilt lacquer accessories and earthen sculptures. As of December 31, 2004 its inventory consists of two antiques, with an inventory cost of $350. Retail sales of antiques and collectibles are primarily facilitated through the group's website. Antique pieces are acquired through sources in Hong Kong and the Peoples Republic of China. The group guarantees the authenticity of each piece.

Primary SIC and add'l.: 6770

CIK No: 0001289046

Officers: Cindy K. Swank/54/Dir., CEO, CFO, Pres., Timothy J. Kuh/33/Dir., VP, Edward W. Wah On/57/Dir., Sec.

Directors: Cindy K. Swank/54/Dir., CEO, CFO, Pres., Timothy J. Kuh/33/Dir., VP, Edward W. Wah On/57/Dir., Sec.

Owners: Edward Wong/2.76%, Insiders/13.84%, Raymond Kuh/13.81%, Timothy Kuh, Cindy Swank/13.81%

Apex Minerals Corp

57 W 200 S, Ste. 310, Salt Lake City, UT, 84101; **PH:** 1-801-359-9300

General - Incorporation .... DE	**Stock**- Price on:12/24/2007 ....NA
Employees...NA	Stock Exchange...NA
Auditor ....Deloitte & Touche LLP	Ticker Symbol...NA
Stk Agt........... American Registrar & Transfer Co	Outstanding Shares.......................................NA
Counsel...NA	E.P.S..NA
DUNS No. 95-766-4253	Shareholders..NA

Business: The group currently has no operations and is currently seeking potential business acquisitions or opportunities.

Primary SIC and add'l.: 9999

CIK No: 0001019507

Apex Resources Group Inc

610 - 800 W Pender St., Vancouver, BC, V6C 256; **PH:** 1-604-669-2723; *http://* www.apexresourcesgroup.com; **Email:** contactus@apexresourcesgroup.com

General - Incorporation .... UT	**Stock**- Price on:12/24/2007 ....NA
Employees...NA	Stock Exchange...OTC
Auditor ....Madsen & Assoc. CPAs, Inc	Ticker Symbol...APXR
Stk Agt.......................Atlas Stock Transfer Corp	Outstanding Shares.......................................NA
Counsel...NA	E.P.S...$0.00
DUNS No. 13-768-6531	Shareholders..NA

Business: The group is in the development stage since inception and has been engaged in the business of the acquisition of mining and oil property interests and other business activities. On 26-Mar-2003 the group changed is name from ambra resources group, inc to apex resources group, inc.

Primary SIC and add'l.: 1311 1389

CIK No: 0000742248

Officers: John M. Hickey/66/Dir., Sec., Principal Financial Officer, John R. Rask/58/Dir., Pres., Principal Executive Officer

Directors: John R. Rask/58/Dir., Pres., Principal Executive Officer, John M. Hickey/66/Dir., Sec., Principal Financial Officer, Stephen Golde/60/Dir., Rafiq Chinoy/Dir.

Owners: Insiders/4.10%, John R. Rask, John M. Hickey/3.20%, Stephen Golde

Financial Data: Fiscal Year End:06/30 **Latest Annual Data:** 06/30/2006

Year	Sales	Net Income
2006	$5,000	-$643,000
2005	$12,000	-$739,000
2004	$27,000	-$748,000

Curr. Assets:	$7,000	**Curr. Liab.:**	$882,000		
Plant, Equip.:	$260,000	**Total Liab.:**	$882,000	**Indic. Yr. Divd.:**	NA
Total Assets:	$407,000	**Net Worth:**	-$475,000	**Debt/ Equity:**	NA

Apex Silver Mines Ltd

1700 Lincoln St., Ste. 3050, Denver, CO, 80203; **PH:** 1-303-839-5060; **Fax:** 1-303-839-5907 ; *http://* www.apexsilver.com; **Email:** information@apexsilver.com

General - Incorporation .... Cayman Islands	**Stock**- Price on:12/24/2007 ....$20.58
Employees...830	Stock Exchange..AMEX
Auditor ....PricewaterhouseCoopers LLP	Ticker Symbol...SIL
Stk Agt..... American Stock Transfer & Trust Co.	Outstanding Shares..............................58,640,000
Counsel...NA	E.P.S...-$8.7
DUNS No. ....NA	Shareholders..NA

Business: The group's principal activities are to explore and develop silver properties in South America, Mexico and Central America. It has control over 100 silver and other mineral exploration holdings, divided into 34 property groups, located in or near the traditional silver producing regions of Bolivia, Mexico, Peru, El Salvador and Kyrgystan.

Primary SIC and add'l.: 1081 1044

CIK No: 0001011509

Subsidiaries: Apex Luxembourg S.a.r.l., Apex Metals GmbH, Apex Silver Mines Corporation, Apex Silver Mines Sweden AB, Minera San Cristobal S.A.

Officers: Jeffrey G. Clevenger/Dir., CEO, Pres./$1,852,465.00, Gerald J. Malys/Sr. VP, CFO/$536,903.00, Robert B. Blakestad/VP - Exploration, Mark Lettes/Contact - Person/$782,305.00, Jerry W. Danni/Sr. VP - Corporate Affairs, Donald Ratcliff/VP - Marketing, Commodity Risk Management, Gerardo Garrett/VP - Minera San Cristobal Corporate, Terry L. Owen/Sr. VP - Project Development, Bob Vogels/VP, Controller, Deborah Friedman/Sr. VP - General Councel, Sec.

Directors: Jeffrey G. Clevenger/Dir., CEO, Pres., Keith R. Hulley/Chmn., Paul Soros/Dir., Rodman L. Drake/Dir., Ian Masterson-Hume/Dir., Charles B. Smith/Dir., Kevin R. Morano/Dir., Harry M. Conger/Dir., Ove Hoegh/Dir., Terry M. Palmer/Dir.

Owners: Terry M. Palmer, NWQ Investment Management Company, LLC/29.10%, Insiders/2.00%, Moore Macro Fund/Moore Emerging Markets Fund/9.80%, Jeffrey G. Clevenger, Gerald J. Malys, Wells Fargo & Co./12.90%, Harry M. Conger, Keith R. Hulley, Kevin R. Morano, Alan R. Edwards, Paul Soros, Ove Hoegh, Robert P. Vogels, Charles B. Smith

Financial Data: Fiscal Year End:12/31 **Latest Annual Data:** 12/31/2006

Year	Sales	Net Income
2006	NA	-$513,545,000
2005	NA	-$67,038,000
2004	NA	-$18,845,000

Curr. Assets:	$488,977,000	**Curr. Liab.:**	$94,872,000		
Plant, Equip.:	$663,099,000	**Total Liab.:**	$1,373,346,000	**Indic. Yr. Divd.:**	NA
Total Assets:	$1,270,096,000	**Net Worth:**	-$103,290,000	**Debt/ Equity**	117.9120

Aphton Corp

8 Penn Ctr, 1628 Jfk Blvd., Ste 2300, Philadelphia, PA, 19103; **PH:** 1-215-218-4340; *http://* www.aphton.com; **Email:** ir@aphton.com

General - Incorporation .... DE	**Stock**- Price on:12/24/2007 ....$0.0022
Employees...66	Stock Exchange...OTC
Auditor ....Ernst & Young LLP	Ticker Symbol...APHTQ
Stk Agt.....................U.S. Stock Transfer Corp	Outstanding Shares..............................67,060,000
Counsel...NA	E.P.S...-$1.174
DUNS No. 10-284-6003	Shareholders..NA

Business: The group's principle activity is to develop biopharmaceutical products using its innovative vaccine-like technology for neutralizing hormones that participate in gastrointestinal system and reproductive system cancer and non-cancer diseases. These products are also used in the prevention of pregnancy. The company has strategic alliances with aventis pasteur, glaxosmithkline, schering plough animal health and the world health organization. The company's anti-gastrin immunogen product treats several human gastrointestinal system adenocarcinomas, including those of the esophagus, stomach, pancreas, liver, colon and rectum. The group operates from United States.

Primary SIC and add'l.: 2836

CIK No: 0000840319

Financial Data: Fiscal Year End: 12/31 **Latest Annual Data:** 12/31/2005

Year	Sales	Net Income
2005	NA	-$65,486,000
2004	NA	-$28,762,000
2003	NA	-$26,300,000

Curr. Assets:	$6,056,000	**Curr. Liab.:**	$8,695,000		
Plant, Equip.:	$706,000	**Total Liab.:**	$11,642,000	**Indic. Yr. Divd.:**	NA
Total Assets:	$6,776,000	**Net Worth:**	-$4,865,000	**Debt/ Equity:**	NA

API Electronics Group Inc

505 University Ave., Ste. 1400, Toronto, ON, M5G 1X3; ; *http://* www.apielectronics.com

General - Incorporation	Canada	**Stock**- Price on:12/24/2007	NA
Employees	NA	Stock Exchange	NA
Auditor	BDO Dunwoody LLP	Ticker Symbol	NA
Stk Agt	Equity Transfer Services Inc	Outstanding Shares	NA
Counsel	Canadian Legal Counsel	E.P.S.	NA
DUNS No.	20-120-0008	Shareholders	NA

Business: The group's principle activity is to manufacture and supply semiconductors and microelectronic circuits for military, aerospace and commercial applications. On 11-Feb-2003, the company acquired(TM) systems inc. The group operates from United States.

Primary SIC and add'l.: 1499 1481

CIK No: 0001022282

Subsidiaries: API Electronics, Inc., Filtran Inc., Filtran Limited, TM Systems II, Inc.

Officers: Phillip Dezwirek/Chmn., CEO, Martin Moskovits/CTO, Claudio Mannarino/37/CFO, Thomas Mills/Dir., COO, Pres., Arnold Markowitz/VP - Sales, Robert Alini/Dir. - Operations

Directors: Phillip Dezwirek/Chmn., CEO, Donald Wright/Dir., Jason Dezwirek/Dir., Thomas Mills/Dir., COO, Pres., Arthur Cape/Dir., Jonathan Pollack/Dir.

API Nanotronics Corp

375 Rabro Dr., Hauppauge, NY, 11788; *PH:* 1-631-582-6767; *Fax:* 1-631-582-6771; *http://* www.apinanotronics.com; *Email:* investors@apinanotronics.com

General - Incorporation	DE	**Stock**- Price on:12/24/2007	$1.61
Employees	244	Stock Exchange	OTC
Auditor	Withumsmith+brown, P.C	Ticker Symbol	APIO
Stk Agt	Equity Transfer Services Inc	Outstanding Shares	55,970,000
Counsel	Sugar, Friedberg & Felsenthal LLP	E.P.S.	NA
DUNS No.	NA	Shareholders	NA

Business: The groups principal activity is to provide custom microelectronic and semiconductor replacement parts for the defense, automotive and medical sectors. The group products include power transformers, reactors, magnetic amplifiers, power supplies and converters. The group operates from the United States.

Primary SIC and add'l.: 3674

CIK No: 0001081078

Officers: Phillip Dezwirek/Chmn., CEO, Treasurer/$449,490.00, Thomas Mills/Dir., COO, Pres./$176,232.00, Martin Moskovits/CTO/$535,188.00, Claudio Mannarino/37/CFO, Arnold Markowitz/VP - Sales, Robert Alini/Dir. - Operations

Directors: Phillip Dezwirek/Chmn., CEO, Treasurer, Thomas Mills/Dir., COO, Pres., Jason Dezwirek/Dir., Donald Wright/Dir., Arthur Cape/Dir., Jonathan Pollack/Dir.

Owners: Insiders/23.75%, Jason DeZwirek/13.28%, Jonathan Pollack, Phillip DeZwirek/14.44%, Can-Med Technology, Inc./5.07%, Martin Moskovits, Thomas Mills, Donald A. Wright

Curr. Assets:	$18,268,000	**Curr. Liab.:**	$4,471,000		
Plant, Equip.:	$6,522,000	**Total Liab.:**	$5,367,000	**Indic. Yr. Divd.:**	NA
Total Assets:	$27,347,000	**Net Worth:**	$21,979,000	**Debt/ Equity:**	NA

Apiva Ventures Ltd

1455-409 Granville St., Vancouver, BC, V6C1T2;

General - Incorporation	BC	**Stock**- Price on:12/24/2007	$0.008
Employees	NA	Stock Exchange	OTC
Auditor	Madsen & Associates, CPA's Inc.	Ticker Symbol	APVL
Stk Agt	Computershare Investor Services LLC	Outstanding Shares	NA
Counsel	NA	E.P.S.	NA
DUNS No.	NA	Shareholders	NA

Business: The groups principal activity is to explore minerals and natural gas. The group operates from the United States and Canada.

Primary SIC and add'l.: 6712

CIK No: 0001000791

Officers: Christopher Dean/44/Dir., Pres., Nicholas Alexander/23/Dir., Sec.

Directors: Christopher Dean/44/Dir., Pres., Nicholas Alexander/23/Dir., Sec.

Owners: Christopher Dean/73.64%, Nicholas Alexander/6.35%, CDS Canadian Depository/15.28%

Financial Data: Fiscal Year End: 12/31 **Latest Annual Data:** 12/31/2006

Year	Sales	Net Income
2006	NA	-$47,000
2005	NA	-$45,000
2004	NA	-$82,000

Curr. Assets:	$2,000	**Curr. Liab.:**	$145,000		
Plant, Equip.:	NA	**Total Liab.:**	$145,000	**Indic. Yr. Divd.:**	NA
Total Assets:	$2,000	**Net Worth:**	-$143,000	**Debt/ Equity:**	NA

Apogee Enterprises Inc

7900 Xerxes Ave. S, Ste. 1800, Minneapolis, MN, 55431; *PH:* 1-952-835-1874; *Fax:* 1-952-487-7565; *http://* www.apog.com; *Email:* ir@apog.com

General - Incorporation	MN	**Stock**- Price on:12/24/2007	$26.1
Employees	4,645	Stock Exchange	NDQ
Auditor	Deloitte & Touche LLP	Ticker Symbol	APOG
Stk Agt	Bank of New York	Outstanding Shares	NA
Counsel	Dorsey & Whitney LLP	E.P.S.	NA
DUNS No.	00-196-2042	Shareholders	NA

Business: The group's principal activities are carried out by the three segments: the architectural products and service (aps) segment, the large-scale optical technologies (lso) segment and the automotive replacement glass services (auto glass) segment. Aps designs, fabricates and installs the walls of glass and windows that form the outer shell of commercial and institutional buildings. The lso segment develops and produces picture framing glass products and optical coatings on glass and acrylic for the display and imaging markets. Auto glass fabricates, repairs and replaces automobile windshields and windows. Viratec (R), tru vue(R), ppg auto glass etc. Are some of the trademarks of the group. During fiscal 2004, the group sold its subsidiary harmon autoglass.

Primary SIC and add'l.: 3211 1793 7533 7536 3443

CIK No: 0000006845

Subsidiaries: Apogee Wausau Group, Inc., Balangier Designs, Inc., Harmon Contract Asia Sdn Bhd, Harmon Contract Asia, Ltd., Harmon Contract U.K., Limited, Harmon Contract, Inc., Harmon, Inc., Prism Assurance, Ltd., Tru Vue, Inc., Viracon Asia, Inc., Viracon Georgia, Inc., Viracon, Inc., Viracon/Curvlite, Inc.

Officers: Russell Huffer/Chmn., CEO/$2,964,768.00, Mary Ann Jackson/Dir. - Investor Relations, Patricia A. Beithon/General Counsel, Sec., Ethics Officer/$860,949.00, James S. Porter/CFO/$827,838.00, Gary R. Johnson/VP, Treasurer/$381,359.00, Sara L. Hays/Dir., Member - Finance

Directors: Russell Huffer/Chmn., CEO, Terry T. Manning/Dir., Richard V. Reynolds/Dir., Bernard P. Aldrich/Dir., Michael E. Shannon/Dir., Stephen C. Mitchell/Dir., David E. Weiss/Dir., Robert J. Marzec/Dir., James L. Martineau/Dir., Jerome L. Davis/Dir., Sara L. Hays/Dir., Member - Finance

Owners: James S. Porter, Jerome L. Davis, Patricia A. Beithon, Gary R. Johnson, James L. Martineau, Stephen C. Mitchell, Robert J. Marzec, Franklin Resources, Inc./7.60%, Barclays Global Investors, NA. and related companies/5.00%, David E. Weiss, Michael B. Clauer, Bernard P. Aldrich, Daruma Asset Management, Inc./5.50%, Richard V. Reynolds, John T. Manning (19 Owners included in Index)

Curr. Assets	$222,484,000	**Curr. Liab.:**	$145,859,000		
Plant, Equip.:	$134,256,000	**Total Liab.:**	$213,493,000	**Indic. Yr. Divd.:**	NA
Total Assets	$449,161,000	**Net Worth:**	$235,668,000	**Debt/ Equity:**	0.1502

Apogee Technology Inc

129 Morgan Dr., Norwood, MA, 02062; *PH:* 1-781-551-9450; *Fax:* 1-781-440-9528; *http://* www.apogeemems.com; *Email:* info@apogeetechinc.com

General - Incorporation	DE	**Stock**- Price on:12/24/2007	$0.73
Employees	11	Stock Exchange	AMEX
Auditor	Miller Wachman LLP	Ticker Symbol	ATA
Stk Agt	American Stock Transfer & Trust Co.	Outstanding Shares	11,970,000
Counsel	Mintz Levin Cohn Ferris Et Al	E.P.S.	-$0.25
DUNS No.	NA	Shareholders	NA

Business: The group's principle activity is to develop and design digital amplifier technology to be used in audio and entertainment media applications. It has patented a technology, the direct digital amplification or ddx(R) that eliminates the digital-to-analog converter for amplification of signals in audio systems. The technology has applications in home theater systems, powered speakers, car audio, commercial audio, and PC multi-media. The group has signed an agreement with stmicroelectronics, nv to jointly develop new semiconductor products and intellectual properties that use the ddx technology. It also sells circuit boards to support the marketing and sales of ddx semiconductor products. Korea, China, Japan, Taiwan, Hong Kong and the Asia-Pacific are the major markets for the group. Oki semiconductor supplies the ddx devices and stmicroelectronics, the ddx integrated circuits. The group's quarterly revenue for September 2007 was 0.01 millions of USD.

Primary SIC and add'l.: 7389 3674

CIK No: 0000823876

Subsidiaries: Apogee Acoustics, Incorporated

Officers: Herbert M. Stein/79/Chmn., CEO, Pres./$801,779.00, Paul J. Murphy/60/CFO, VP - Finance/$175,403.00, David B. Meyers/49/COO/$173,228.00, Alexander K. Andrianov/50/VP - Research, Development/$43,661.00

Directors: Herbert M. Stein/79/Chmn., CEO, Pres., Craig A. Dubitsky/42/Dir., Arthur S. Reynolds/64/Dir., Sheryl B. Stein/53/Dir., Alan W. Tuck/59/Dir.

Owners: Leo Spiegel/6.55%, H.M. Stein Associates/12.25%, Herbert M. Stein/28.57%, Alan W. Tuck/2.52%, David B. Meyers/2.75%, Paul J. Murphy, Insiders/35.05%, Arthur S. Reynolds, Sheryl B. Stein/7.36%, Craig A. Dubitsky, David Spiegel/15.16%

Financial Data: Fiscal Year End: 12/31 **Latest Annual Data:** 12/31/2006

Year	Sales	Net Income
2006	$1,885,000	-$2,971,000
2005	$5,173,000	$2,952,000
2004	$6,158,000	-$3,385,000

Curr. Assets:	$3,132,000	**Curr. Liab.:**	$710,000		
Plant, Equip.:	$208,000	**Total Liab.:**	$710,000	**Indic. Yr. Divd.:**	NA
Total Assets:	$3,571,000	**Net Worth:**	$2,861,000	**Debt/ Equity:**	NA

Apollo Capital Group

506 Eleventh St., New Westminster, BC, V3M 4G3; *PH:* 1-604-517-1670; *http://* www.apollocapital.com

General - Incorporation	NV	**Stock**- Price on:12/24/2007	NA
Employees	NA	Stock Exchange	NA
Auditor	NA	Ticker Symbol	NA
Stk Agt	NA	Outstanding Shares	NA
Counsel	NA	E.P.S.	NA
DUNS No.	NA	Shareholders	NA

Business: The group is in the business of computer software, technology, processes and equipment known as "MAXX-NET". The group operates from United States.
Primary SIC and add'l.: 7381
CIK No: 0001289817

Apollo Drilling Inc

Apollo Drilling, 3001 Knox St., Ste. 403, Dallas, TX, 75205; **PH:** 1-214-389-9800;
Fax: 1-214-389-9806; **http://** www.apollodrillinginc.com; **Email:** contact@apollodrillinginc.com

General - Incorporation	NV	Stock- Price on:12/24/2007	NA
Employees	NA	Stock Exchange	OTC
Auditor	Franklin Griffith & Associates	Ticker Symbol	APDR
Stk Agt	Signature Stock Transfer, Inc.	Outstanding Shares	NA
Counsel	NA	E.P.S	-$0.016
DUNS No.	NA	Shareholders	NA

Business: The groups principal activities include import and distribute various Southeast Asian gifts, skin products, house wares, furniture and decorative items. The group products include handmade stainless steel cutlery, Thai silk products, products made with mango wood, ornamental wall hangings and all natural skin care and beauty products. The group operates from the United States.
Primary SIC and add'l.: 1781
CIK No: 0001295923
Officers: Dennis McLaughlin/41/Chmn., CEO, Robert H. Nelson/62/Dir., CFO
Directors: Dennis McLaughlin/41/Chmn., CEO, Robert H. Nelson/62/Dir., CFO, William Pritchard/56/Dir.
Owners: Robert Nelson/4.70%, Jeff F. Raley/2.30%, Insiders/11.80%, Apollo Resources International, Inc/63.10%, Dennis McLaughlin/4.80%

Financial Data: Fiscal Year End:12/31   **Latest Annual Data:** 12/31/2005

Year	Sales		Net Income
2005	NA		-$48,000
2004	NA		-$21,000
Curr. Assets:	$1,139,000	Curr. Liab.:	$1,506,000
Plant, Equip.:	$1,765,000	Total Liab.:	$1,506,000 Indic. Yr. Divd.: NA
Total Assets:	$2,904,000	Net Worth:	$1,399,000 Debt/ Equity: NA

Apollo Gold Corp

5655 S Yosemite St., Ste. 200, Greenwood Village, CO, 80111; **PH:** 1-720-886-9656;
Fax: 1-720-482-0957; **http://** www.apollogold.com; **Email:** info@apollogold.com

General - Incorporation	Canada	Stock- Price on:12/24/2007	$0.4319
Employees	160	Stock Exchange	AMEX
Auditor	Deloitte & Touche LLP	Ticker Symbol	AGT
Stk Agt	Mellon Trust Co	Outstanding Shares	143,470,000
Counsel	Donald W. Vagstad	E.P.S	NA
DUNS No.	NA	Shareholders	NA

Business: The groups principle activities include acquiring and developing gold and precious metal properties. The group operates from United States.
Primary SIC and add'l.: 9999
CIK No: 0000938113
Subsidiaries: Apollo Gold, Inc., Minas de Argonautas, S. de R.L. de C.V., Mine Development Finance, Inc., Minera Sol de Oro S.A. de C.V, Montana Tunnels Mining, Inc.
Officers: David R. Russell/Dir., CEO, Pres./$707,541.00, Michael G. Hobart/Dir., Assist. Sec., Timothy G. Smith/GM - Montana Tunnels Mine/$146,548.00, Richard F. Nanna/Sr. VP - Exploration/$358,467.00, Melvyn Williams/CFO, Sr. VP - Finance, Corporate Development/$419,654.00
Directors: David R. Russell/Dir., CEO, Pres., Marvin K. Kaiser/Dir., David W. Peat/55/Dir., W. S. Vaughan/Dir., Robert W. Babensee/Dir., Charles E. Stott/Dir., Michael G. Hobart/Dir., Assist. Sec.
Owners: Michael G. Hobart, Insiders/5.04%, Robert W. Babensee, Charles E. Stott, Jipangu Inc./16.48%, Timothy G. Smith, St. Andrew Goldfields Ltd./12.55%, David W. Peat, Donald O. Miller, RAB Special Situations/19.37%, Richard F. Nanna/1.34%, David R. Russell/2.19%, Melvyn Williams, Marvin K. Kaiser, W. S. Vaughan (16 Owners included in Index)

Financial Data: Fiscal Year End:12/31   **Latest Annual Data:** 12/31/2006

Year	Sales		Net Income
2006	$10,177,000		-$12,163,000
2005	$43,254,000		-$22,208,000
2004	$64,741,000		-$25,125,000
Curr. Assets:	$8,066,000	Curr. Liab.:	$11,737,000
Plant, Equip.:	$14,476,000	Total Liab.:	$20,575,000 Indic. Yr. Divd.: NA
Total Assets:	$27,515,000	Net Worth:	$6,940,000 Debt/ Equity: NA

Apollo Resources International Inc

Apollo Resources, 3001 Knox St., Ste. 403, Dallas, TX, 75205; **PH:** 1-866-765-4939;
Fax: 1-214-389-9805; **http://** www.apolloresources.com; **Email:** press@apolloresources.com

General - Incorporation	UT	Stock- Price on:12/24/2007	NA
Employees	NA	Stock Exchange	OTC
Auditor	Chisholm, Bierwolf & Nilson, LLC	Ticker Symbol	AOORE
Stk Agt	Colonial Stock Transfer Co Inc	Outstanding Shares	NA
Counsel	NA	E.P.S	NA
DUNS No.	NA	Shareholders	NA

Business: The groups principle activity is to explore minerals and natural gas. The group operates through three segments namely production and operating, Alternative fuels and LNG. The group acquired Mountain States and TxHLDM, Inc and Earth Biofuels in ., in Dec 7,2005. The group operates from the United States and Canada.
Primary SIC and add'l.: 1781
CIK No: 0000048237
Subsidiaries: Apollo LNG, Inc., Earth Biofuels
Officers: Dennis G. McLaughlin/Chmn., CEO, Kit Chambers/Dir., Corp. Sec., Darren L. Miles/Member - Executive Board, Christopher P. Chambers/Dir., Corp. Sec.
Directors: Dennis G. McLaughlin/Chmn., CEO, Kit Chambers/Dir., Corp. Sec., Billy A. Mickle/Dir., Glenn E. Floyd/Dir., Christopher P. Chambers/Dir., Corp. Sec.

Owners: Dennis McLaughlin/42.90%, Insiders/43.20%, Christopher P. Chambers

Apolo Gold & Energy Inc

409 Granville St., Ste. 1209, Vancouver, BC, V6C 1T2; **PH:** 1-604-687-4150; **Fax:** 1-604-687-4155;
http:// www.apologoldandenergy.com; **Email:** info@apologoldandenergy.com

General - Incorporation	NV	Stock- Price on:12/24/2007	$0.05
Employees	NA	Stock Exchange	OTC
Auditor	Williams & Webster, P.S.	Ticker Symbol	APLL
Stk Agt	Pacific Stock Transfer Company	Outstanding Shares	NA
Counsel	NA	E.P.S	NA
DUNS No.	NA	Shareholders	NA

Business: The groups principal activity is to explore minerals and natural gas. The group operates from the United States and Canada.
Primary SIC and add'l.: 1000
CIK No: 0001040721
Subsidiaries: Compania Minera Apologold, C.A
Officers: Peter Bojtos/Chmn., CEO, Pres., Robert G. Dinning/Dir., CFO, Sec., Brant Little/Advisor to The Board
Directors: Peter Bojtos/Chmn., CEO, Pres., Robert G. Dinning/Dir., CFO, Sec., David Yu/Dir., Robert Lee/Dir., Glen Kelleway/Dir.
Owners: Robert Dinning/8.57%, Brant Little/4.15%, Insiders/26.12%, Peter Bojtos/1.92%, Glen Kelleway/0.38%, David Yu/7.80%, Robert Lee/3.30%

Financial Data: Fiscal Year End:06/30   **Latest Annual Data:** 06/30/2007

Year	Sales		Net Income
2007	NA		-$872,000
2006	NA		-$1,404,000
2005	NA		-$1,018,000
Curr. Assets:	$231,000	Curr. Liab.:	$47,000
Plant, Equip.:	$65,000	Total Liab.:	$47,000 Indic. Yr. Divd.: NA
Total Assets:	$296,000	Net Worth:	$248,000 Debt/ Equity: NA

Appalachian Bancshares Inc

PO Box G, 829 Industrial Blvd., Ellijay, GA, 30540; **PH:** 1-706-276-8000; **Fax:** 1-706-276-8010;
http:// www.appalachianbank.com

General - Incorporation	GA	Stock- Price on:12/24/2007	$17.8
Employees	262	Stock Exchange	NDQ
Auditor	Mauldin & Jenkins LLC	Ticker Symbol	APAB
Stk Agt	Registrar & Transfer Co	Outstanding Shares	5,210,000
Counsel	Troutman Saunders LLP	E.P.S	$1.16
DUNS No.	17-449-3114	Shareholders	NA

Business: The group's principal activity is to provide a full range of commercial banking services to individuals, small to medium-sized businesses and farmers. It is a holding group for the appalachian community bank that was merged with the gilmer county bank. The group's lending activity consists of providing secured real estate loans, primarily residential and commercial construction loans, and primary and secondary mortgage loans for the acquisition of personal residences. Other loans include consumer loans to individuals and commercial loans to small and medium-sized businesses and professional concerns. A major area of lending is the poultry industry. Loans are also made to apple farmers. The group accepts demand and time deposits that are insured by the federal deposit insurance corporation. Areas of business consist of gilmer county, fannin county, union county, towns county, northern pickens county, western dawson county and southeastern murray county, Georgia.
Primary SIC and add'l.: 6712 6022
CIK No: 0001019883
Subsidiaries: Appalachian Capital Trust I, Appalachian Community Bank, Appalachian Information Management, Inc.
Officers: Tracy R. Newton/Dir., CEO/$496,961.00, Virginia C. Cochran/Exec. VP, Chief Credit Officer, Joseph T. Moss/COO, Pres./$573,945.00, Keith J. Hales/CFO, Exec. VP
Directors: Tracy R. Newton/Dir., CEO, Ronald J. Knight/64/Chmn., Charles A. Edmondson/59/Vice Chmn., Roger E. Futch/61/Dir., Frank E. Jones/54/Dir., Kenneth D. Warren/56/Dir., Alan S. Dover/50/Dir., Joseph C. Hensley/49/Dir.
Owners: Insiders/19.42%, Joseph C. Hensley/2.09%, Roger E. Futch/2.29%, Joseph T. Moss, Keith J. Hales, Kenneth D. Warren/2.55%, Alan S. Dover/2.12%, Frank E. Jones/1.51%, Tracy R. Newton/3.78%, Appalachian Bancshares, Inc/7.55%, Charles A. Edmondson/2.40%, Ronald J. Knight/2.99%

Financial Data: Fiscal Year End:12/31   **Latest Annual Data:** 12/31/2006

Year	Sales		Net Income
2006	$57,164,000		$6,004,000
2005	$38,052,000		$5,122,000
2004	$28,588,000		$4,047,000
Curr. Assets:	$19,745,000	Curr. Liab.:	$682,376,000
Plant, Equip.:	$23,412,000	Total Liab.:	$691,451,000 Indic. Yr. Divd.: NA
Total Assets:	$758,214,000	Net Worth:	$66,763,000 Debt/ Equity: 0.0903

Appalachian Power Co

40 Franklin Rd. SW, Roanoke, VA, 24011; **PH:** 1-703-985-2300;
http:// www.appalachianpower.com; **Email:** customer_service@aep.com

General - Incorporation	VA	Stock- Price on:12/24/2007	NA
Employees	NA	Stock Exchange	NA
Auditor	Deloitte & Touche LLP	Ticker Symbol	NA
Stk Agt	NA	Outstanding Shares	NA
Counsel	NA	E.P.S	NA
DUNS No.	00-794-1537	Shareholders	NA

Business: The group's principal activities are to generate, purchase, market, transmit and distribute electric power to about 929,000 retail customers in southwestern Virginia and southern west Virginia. The group is a wholly owned subsidiary of American electric power company, inc. The customers of the group include retailers, other electric utility companies and municipalities. The industries served by the group are coal mining, primary metals, chemicals and textile mill products. The subsidiaries of the group are cedar coal co., central appalachian coal company and southern appalachian coal company.
Primary SIC and add'l.: 4911

CIK No: 0000006879

Officers: Michael G. Morris/61/Chmn., CEO/$14,222,010.00, Robert P. Powers/54/Dir., VP, Vice Chmn./$2,938,804.00, Susan Tomasky/54/Dir., VP/$3,480,398.00, Heather L. Geiger/Sec., Nicholas K. Akins/47/Dir., VP, Carl L. English/61/Dir., VP/$2,789,102.00, John B. Keane/61/Dir., VP/$1,743,708.00, Holly K. Koeppel/49/Dir., VP/$2,569,754.00, Dana Waldo/Pres., COO - Appalachian Power, Todd Burns/Contact - Power Outages, Local Service Issues, Public Safety Issues, John Shepelwich/Contact - Virginia, Tennessee Hydro, Power Plants, Public Policy, Regulatory, Environmental, Other Statewide Issues, Phil Moye/Contact - Power Outages, Local Service Issues, Power Plants, Public Safety Issues, Charleston, Carmen Prati-Miller/Contact - Power Outages, Local Service Issues, Power Plants, Public Safety Issues, West Virginia, Jeri Matheney/Contact - West Virginia Public Policy, Regulatory, Environmental, Other Statewide Issues, Stephen P. Smith/47/Dir., VP, Treasurer *(16 Officers included in Index)*

Directors: Michael G. Morris/61/Chmn., CEO, Robert P. Powers/54/Dir., VP, Vice Chmn., Susan Tomasky/54/Dir., VP, John B. Keane/61/Dir., VP, Holly K. Koeppel/49/Dir., VP, Carl L. English/61/Dir., VP, Stephen P. Smith/47/Dir., VP, Treasurer, Dennis E. Welch/56/Dir., VP

Owners: D. E. Waldo, C. L. English, D. E. Welch, N. K. Akins, M. G. Morris, R. P. Powers, S. Tomasky, S. P. Smith, Insiders, J. B. Keane, H. K. Koeppel

Apple Computer Inc

1 Infinite Loop, Cupertino, CA, 95014; ***PH:*** 1-408-996-1010; ***http://*** www.apple.com

General - Incorporation	CA	**Stock**- Price on:12/24/2007	$125.09
Employees	17,787	Stock Exchange	NDQ
Auditor	KPMG LLP	Ticker Symbol	AAPL
Stk Agt	Computershare Investor Services LLC	Outstanding Shares	864,950,000
Counsel	NA	E.P.S.	$3.93
DUNS No.	06-070-4780	Shareholders	NA

Business: The group's principle activities include designing, manufacturing and marketing personal computers and related software products. The groups products line include portable digital music players and mobile communication devices. The group operates from United States.

Primary SIC and add'l.: 5045 3575 3572 3577 3571 7372

CIK No: 0000320193

Subsidiaries: Apple Computer Inc. Limited, Apple Computer International, Apple Computer Limited

Officers: Steve Jobs/Dir., CEO, Tony Fadell/Sr. VP - Ipod Division Apple, Jonathan Ive/Sr. VP - Industrial Design Apple, Ron Johnson/Sr. VP - Retail Apple, Timothy D. Cook/COO, Philip W. Schiller/Sr. VP - Worldwide Product Marketing Apple, Sina Tamaddon/Sr. VP - Applications, Bertrand Serlet/Sr. VP - Software Engineering Apple, Peter Oppenheimer/CFO, Sr. VP, Daniel Cooperman/Sr. VP, General Counsel, Sec.

Directors: Steve Jobs/Dir., CEO, Albert Gore/Dir., Bill Campbell/Dir., Millard Drexler/Dir., Arthur D. Levinson/Dir., Eric Schmidt/Dir., Jerry York/Dir., William V. Campbell/68/Dir., Jerome B. York/Dir.

Owners: Peter Oppenheimer, Jerome B. York, Albert A. Gore, Millard S. Drexler, Fidelity Investments/6.55%, Eric E. Schmidt, William V. Campbell, Steven P. Jobs, Insiders/1.00%, Timothy D. Cook, Arthur D. Levinson, Philip W. Schiller, Ronald B. Johnson

Financial Data: ***Fiscal Year End:***09/24 ***Latest Annual Data:*** 9/30/2006

Year	Sales	Net Income
2006	$19,315,000,000	$1,989,000,000
2005	$13,931,000,000	$1,335,000,000
2004	$8,279,000,000	$276,000,000

Curr. Assets:	$14,509,000,000	***Curr. Liab.:***	$6,471,000,000	***P/E Ratio:***	35.34
Plant, Equip.:	$1,281,000,000	***Total Liab.:***	$7,221,000,000	***Indic. Yr. Divd.:***	NA
Total Assets:	$17,205,000,000	***Net Worth:***	$9,984,000,000	***Debt/ Equity:***	NA

Apple Valley Bank & Trust Company

286 Maple Ave., Cheshire, CT, 06410; ***PH:*** 1-203-271-1268; ***http://*** www.applevalleybank.com; ***Email:*** info@applevalleybank.com

General - Incorporation		**Stock**- Price on:12/24/2007	$8.25
Employees	NA	Stock Exchange	OTC
Auditor	NA	Ticker Symbol	AVBK
Stk Agt	Registrar & Transfer Co	Outstanding Shares	NA
Counsel	NA	E.P.S.	NA
DUNS No.	NA	Shareholders	NA

Business: The groups principal activity is to provide banking business. The group financial products include savings and fixed deposits, on line, personal, commercial lending and business banking. The group operates from the United States.

Primary SIC and add'l.: 6029

CIK No:

Officers: Maureen A. Frank/CEO, Pres., Kathryn C. Reinhard/Vice Chmn., Sec., Trudy Mason/Cheshire Branch Mgr., Robert Thornton/Branch Mgr. - Wallingford, Robert N. Young/Sr. Lending Officer, Sr. VP, Vincent Ruggiero/Commercial Loan Officer, VP, Randall J. Gage/Consumer Lending, VP, Scott Otis/Business Development Officer - Financial Advisor, Janet Poveromo/Regional Branch Mgr., Assist. VP, Susan Vishe/Compliance Officer, VP, Jonathan P. Rappi/CFO, Sr. VP, Darlene Levasseur/Operations Officer, Assist. VP, Lisa A. Godbout/Corp. Sec., Human Resources Specialist - Marketing

Directors: Robert S. Stanek/Chmn., Kathryn C. Reinhard/Vice Chmn., Sec., Donald A. Sirois/Dir., Thomas Stanton/Dir., Donald G. Jacobson/Dir., Allen J. Lamb/Dir., Raymond E. Koontz/Dir., Michael J. Alfieri/Dir., John Wolfe/Dir.

Applebee's International Inc

11201 Renner Blvd., Ste. 100, Lenexa, KS, 66219; ***PH:*** 1-913-967-4000; ***Fax:*** 1-913-341-1694; ***http://*** www.applebees.com

General - Incorporation	DE	**Stock**- Price on:12/24/2007	$24.52
Employees	32,600	Stock Exchange	NDQ
Auditor	Deloitte& Touche LLP	Ticker Symbol	APPB
Stk Agt	Wells Fargo Bank, N.A.	Outstanding Shares	74,650,000
Counsel	NA	E.P.S.	$0.84
DUNS No.	NA	Shareholders	NA

Business: The groups principle activities include developing, franchising and operating restaurants. The groups services include food and beverage items and table service. The products of the group include cuisines, appetizers, salads, sandwiches, beer, wine and desserts. The group products sold under the trade name Weight Watchers(R). Customers served by the group include young adults, senior citizens and families with children. The group operates from the United States.

Primary SIC and add'l.: 5812 5812

CIK No: 0000853665

Subsidiaries: ACME, Inc., AFSS, INC., AII Euro Services (Holland) B.V., AII Services - Europe, Limited, AII Services, Inc., Anne Arundel Apple Holding, Apple American Limited, Apple Vermont Restaurants, Inc., Applebees Beverage, Inc., Applebees Brazil, LLC, Applebees Canada Corp., Applebees Investments, LLC, Applebees Michigan Services, LLC, Applebees Neighborhood Grill & Bar of Georgia, Inc., Applebees Northeast, Inc. 52 Subsidiaries included in the Index

Officers: David L. Goebel/Dir., CEO, Pres., Steven K. Lumpkin/Dir., Chief Financial, Strategy Officer, Exec. VP, Stanley M. Sword/Chief People Officer, Exec. VP, Carin L. Stutz/Exec. VP - Operations, George Williams/Chief Marketing Officer, Exec. VP, Rohan St. George/Pres. - International Division, Philip R. Crimmins/Sr. VP - Development, Larry C. Miller/VP - Finance, Samuel M. Rothschild/VP - Franchise, Beverage Operations, Rebecca R. Tilden/VP, General Counsel, Sec., Matthew Drennan/Regional VP - Operations, John Mallon/Regional VP - Operations, Mark Killeen/Regional VP - Operations, Scott W. White/VP - Human Resources, Design, Services, Michael Czinege/CIO, Sr. VP *(21 Officers included in Index)*

Directors: David L. Goebel/Dir., CEO, Pres., Lloyd L. Hill/Chmn., Erline Belton/Dir., Richard C. Breeden/Dir., Laurence E. Harris/Dir., Patrick D. Curran/Dir., Gina R. Boswell/Dir., Douglas R. Conant/Dir., Eric L. Hansen/Dir., Jack P. Helms/Dir., Steven K. Lumpkin/Dir., Chief Financial, Strategy Officer, Exec. VP, Rogelio Rebolledo/Dir., Burton M. Sack/Dir., Michael A. Volkema/Dir.

Owners: Breeden Capital Management LLC/5.20%, Rogelio Rebolledo, Douglas R. Conant/0.20%, Rohan St. George/0.10%, Patrick D. Curran, Burton M. Sack/3.40%, David L. Goebel/0.50%, Eric L. Hansen/0.10%, Lloyd L. Hill/0.60%, Michael A. Volkema/0.10%, Stanley M. Sword/0.10%, FMR Corp./14.30%, Jack P. Helms/0.40%, Richard C. Breeden/5.20%, Steven K. Lumpkin/0.40% *(21 Owners included in Index)*

Financial Data: ***Fiscal Year End:***12/31 ***Latest Annual Data:*** 12/31/2006

Year	Sales	Net Income
2006	$1,337,921,000	$80,906,000
2005	$1,216,650,000	$101,802,000
2004	$1,111,634,000	$110,865,000

Curr. Assets:	$105,293,000	***Curr. Liab.:***	$186,919,000	***P/E Ratio:***	29.19
Plant, Equip.:	$636,031,000	***Total Liab.:***	$448,802,000	***Indic. Yr. Divd.:***	$0.220
Total Assets:	$935,456,000	***Net Worth:***	$486,654,000	***Debt/ Equity:***	0.3092

Applera Corp

301 Merritt 7, Norwalk, CT, 06856; ***PH:*** 1-203-840-2000; ***Fax:*** 1-203-840-2312; ***http://*** www.applera.com

General - Incorporation	DE	**Stock**- Price on:12/24/2007	$29.74
Employees	5,090	Stock Exchange	NYSE
Auditor	PricewaterhouseCoopers LLP	Ticker Symbol	ABI
Stk Agt	EquiServe Trust Co N.A	Outstanding Shares	184,950,000
Counsel	NA	E.P.S.	$1.56
DUNS No.	00-118-4480	Shareholders	NA

Business: The groups principle activity is to develop breakthrough research technologies and diagnostic products for the healthcare industry. The group operates through two business segments namely Applied Biosystems unit and Celera unit. The group operates from United States.

Primary SIC and add'l.: 3845 9999 3826

CIK No: 0000077551

Subsidiaries: AB Advanced Genetic Analysis Corporation, Ambion (UK) Limited, Ambion Europe, Limited, Ambion K.K., Ambion, Inc., Applera Austria Handels GmbH, Applera Ceska Republica s.r.o., Applera Charitable Foundation, Applera Deutschland GmbH, Applera Europe BV, Applera Finance BV, Applera France S.A., Applera Hispania SA, Applera Holding BV, Applera Holding GmbH 64 Subsidiaries included in the Index

Officers: Tony L. White/62/Chmn., CEO, Pres./$10,947,970.00, Donald Lemma/CIO, VP - Global Information Technology, Dennis L. Winger/CFO, Sr. VP/$3,502,695.00, John S. Ostaszewski/VP, Treasurer, Jay Sheldon Wesley/Corporate Supplier Diversity Mgr., Kathy Ordonez/Sr. VP/$2,215,840.00, William B. Sawch/Sr. VP, General Counsel/$2,542,796.00, Barbara J. Kerr/VP - Human Resources/$1,799,988.00, Sandeep Nayyar/48/Assist. Controller, Ugo Deblasi/46/VP, Corporate Controller, Thomas P. Livingston/VP, Sec., Joel R. Jung/50/Assist. Controller, Mark P. Stevenson/Exec. VP - Applied Biosystems

Directors: Tony L. White/62/Chmn., CEO, Pres., Theodore E. Martin/68/Dir., James R. Tobin/64/Dir., Arnold J. Levine/69/Dir., Elaine R. Mardis/45/Dir., Orin R. Smith/72/Dir., Richard H. Ayers/64/Dir., Carolyn W. Slayman/71/Dir., William H. Longfield/70/Dir., Jean-Luc Belingard/60/Dir., Robert H. Hayes/72/Dir.

Owners: Capital Research and Management Company/5.60%, AXA/AllianceBernstein L.P./4.30%, Goldman Sachs Asset Management, L.P./9.10%, FMR Corp./13.40%, Wellington Management Company, LLP/7.90%, Primecap Management Company/12.10%, AXA/AllianceBernstein L.P./9.90%

Financial Data: ***Fiscal Year End:***06/30 ***Latest Annual Data:*** 6/30/2006

Year	Sales	Net Income
2006	$1,949,390,000	$212,492,000
2005	$1,845,140,000	$159,795,000
2004	$1,825,193,000	$125,581,000

Curr. Assets:	$1,626,965,000	***Curr. Liab.:***	$608,290,000	***P/E Ratio:***	33.42
Plant, Equip.:	$396,436,000	***Total Liab.:***	$808,641,000	***Indic. Yr. Divd.:***	$0.170
Total Assets:	$3,012,975,000	***Net Worth:***	$2,204,334,000	***Debt/ Equity:***	NA

Appliance Recycling Centers of America Inc

7400 Excelsior Blvd., Minneapolis, MN, 55426; ***PH:*** 1-952-930-9000; ***Fax:*** 1-952-930-1800; ***http://*** www.arcainc.com; ***Email:*** investor@arcainc.com

General		Stock	
Incorporation	MN	Price on:12/24/2007	$4.3247
Employees	301	Stock Exchange	NDQ
Auditor	Virchow, Krause & Co. LLP	Ticker Symbol	ARCI
Stk Agt	Wells Fargo Shareowner Services	Outstanding Shares	4,340,000
Counsel	Mackall Crounse & Moore PLC	E.P.S	$0.022
DUNS No.	10-225-8696	Shareholders	NA

Business: The group's principal activity is the provision of reverse logistics, energy efficiency and appliance recycling services. Appliances are acquired from a wide range of sources, including appliance manufacturers and retailers, utility companies, waste management businesses, vending machine companies, property managers, local governments and the general public. Appliances deemed suitable for sale are repaired and distributed to the group's appliancesmart retail outlets. As on 31-Dec-2003, the group operated nine retail stores. Appliances that do not meet quality standards for the group's retail operations and appliances collected through utility customers' energy conservation programs are processed and recycled in an environmentally sound manner. The group operates in the United States.

Primary SIC and add'l.: 5093 4959 5722

CIK No: 0000862861

Subsidiaries: Appliance Recycling Centers of America-California, Inc., ARCA of St. Louis, Inc., North America Appliance Company, LLC

Officers: Edward R. Cameron/Chmn., CEO, Pres./$229,615.00, Denis E. Grande/Sec., Bruce J. Wall/VP - Resource Efficiency Programs, Thomas B. Owen/GM - Arca Ohio, Morgan Wolf/GM - Arca Minnesota, William W. Bednarczyk/63/Dir. - Management Consultant, Bradley S. Bremer/VP - Retail Operations, Patrick Winters/Controller, Rachel Holmes/Contact - Investor Relations

Directors: Edward R. Cameron/Chmn.; CEO, Pres., Harry W. Spell/Dir., Duane S. Carlson/Dir., George B. Bonniwell/Dir., Marvin Goldstein/Dir., William W. Bednarczyk/63/Dir. - Management Consultant, Albin S. Dubiak/67/Dir.

Owners: William W. Bednarczyk/6.40%, Perkins Capital Mgmt. Inc./18.30%, Edward R. Cameron/8.60%, Insiders/16.30%, White Pine Capital, LLC/10.80%, Duane S. Carlson/1.40%, Medallion Capital, Inc./11.90%, Albin S. Dubiak

Financial Data: ***Fiscal Year End:*** 12/31 ***Latest Annual Data:*** 12/30/2006

Year	Sales	Net Income
2006	$77,790,000	-$1,409,000
2005	$74,893,000	-$933,000

Curr. Assets:	$17,733,000	**Curr. Liab.:**	$13,854,000		
Plant, Equip.:	$6,052,000	**Total Liab.:**	$19,070,000	**Indic. Yr. Divd.:**	NA
Total Assets:	$24,491,000	**Net Worth:**	$5,421,000	**Debt/ Equity:**	1.2781

Applica Inc

3633 Flamingo Rd., Miramar Lakes, FL, 33027; ***PH:*** 1-954-883-1000; ***http://*** www.applicainc.com

General		Stock	
Incorporation	FL	Price on:12/24/2007	NA
Employees	NA	Stock Exchange	NYSE
Auditor	Grant Thornton LLP	Ticker Symbol	APN
Stk Agt	American Stock Transfer & Trust Co.	Outstanding Shares	NA
Counsel	NA	E.P.S	NA
DUNS No.	NA	Shareholders	NA

Business: The groups principal activities include marketing and distributing small appliances and personal care products. The groups products include coffee makers, toaster ovens, irons, hair dryers and curling irons. In the year 2007, the group is acquired by Harbinger Capital Partners. The group operates from the United States

Primary SIC and add'l.: 3634

CIK No: 0000217084

Subsidiaries: Applica Americas, Inc., Applica Asia Limited, Applica Canada Corporation, Applica Consumer Products, Inc., Applica de Colombia Limitada, Applica de Mexico, S. de R.L. de C.V., Applica de Venezuela, C.A., Applica Manufacturing, S. de R.L. de C.V., Applica Mexico Holdings, Inc., Applica Servicios de Mexico, S. de R.L. de C.V., Corporacion Applica de Centro America, Ltda., Household Products Chile Comercial Limitada, HP (BVI)Limited, HP Delaware, Inc., HPG LLC 22 Subsidiaries included in the Index

Applied Digital Solutions Inc

1690 S Congress Ave., Ste. 200, Delray Beach, FL, 33445; ***PH:*** 1-561-805-8000; ***Fax:*** 1-561-805-8001; ***http://*** www.adsx.com; ***Email:*** info@adsx.com

General		Stock	
Incorporation	MO	Price on:12/24/2007	NA
Employees	582	Stock Exchange	NDQ
Auditor	Eisner LLP	Ticker Symbol	ADSX
Stk Agt	Registrar & Transfer Co	Outstanding Shares	NA
Counsel	Akin, Gump, Strauss, Hauer & Feld LLP	E.P.S	-$0.54
DUNS No.	18-984-1349	Shareholders	NA

Business: The group's principal activity is to develop life-enhancing technology products and services. The group operates in three business segments: advanced technology, digital angel corporation and infotech United States inc. Advanced technology specializes in security-related data collection, value-added data intelligence and complex data delivery systems. Digital angel delivery system develops and markets proprietary technologies used to identify, locate and monitor people, animals and objects. Infotech United States inc provides it consulting, networking, procurement, deployment, integration, migration and security services and solutions. The products of the group include digital angel, thermo life, verichip and bio-thermo. The group has operations in the United States, Canada and the United Kingdom.

Primary SIC and add'l.: 7377 6719 4812 7372 4813

CIK No: 0000924642

Subsidiaries: ACT Communications Inc., ACT-GFX Canada, Inc., ADS Bay Area, Inc., ADSI Telecomm Services, Inc., Advanced Telecomm of Maryland, Inc., Advanced Telecomm of Pittsburgh, Advanced Telecommunications, Inc., Applied Digital Oracle Practice, Inc., Applied Digital Retail Limited, Applied Digital Solutions Financial Corp., Applied Digital Solutions International Limited, Arjang, Inc. f/k/a Applied Digital Retail, Inc., Blue Star Electronics, Inc., Bostek, Inc., Caledonian Venture Holdings Limited 54 Subsidiaries included in the Index

Officers: Michael Krawitz/Dir., CEO, Pres./$707,613.00, Lorraine Breece/Sr. VP, Acting CFO, Chief Accounting Officer, Treasurer, Assist. Sec./$211,490.00, Kay E. Langsford/VP - Administration, Sec., Ronald D. Landers/VP - Internal Audit, Allison Tomek/VP - Investor Relations, Corporate Communications

Directors: Michael Krawitz/Dir., CEO, Pres., Dennis G. Rawan/Dir., Constance K. Weaver/Dir., Michael J. Norris/Dir., Daniel E. Penni/Dir.

Owners: John R. Block/1.00%, Lorraine M. Breece, David Cairnie, Kevin N. McGrath/5.10%, Howard S. Weintraub/1.20%, Lasse Nordfjeld, Barry M. Edelstein, Scott R. Silverman/3.30%, Michael S. Zarriello/1.20%, Insiders/7.90%, James P. Santelli, Applied Digital Solutions, Inc./55.60%

Financial Data: ***Fiscal Year End:*** 12/31 ***Latest Annual Data:*** 12/31/2006

Year	Sales	Net Income
2006	$122,688,000	-$27,209,000
2005	$113,737,000	-$10,165,000
2004	$111,999,000	-$17,299,000

Curr. Assets:	$50,160,000	**Curr. Liab.:**	$54,951,000		
Plant, Equip.:	$12,131,000	**Total Liab.:**	$78,412,000	**Indic. Yr. Divd.:**	NA
Total Assets:	$171,350,000	**Net Worth:**	$43,864,000	**Debt/ Equity:**	NA

Applied DNA Sciences Inc

25 Health Sciences Dr., Ste. 113, Stony Brook, NY, 11790; ***PH:*** 1-631-444-6862; ***Fax:*** 1-631-444-8848; ***http://*** www.adnas.com; ***Email:*** info@adnas.com

General		Stock	
Incorporation	NV	Price on:12/24/2007	$0.115
Employees	7	Stock Exchange	OTC
Auditor	Russell Bedford Stefanou Mirchandani	Ticker Symbol	APDN
Stk Agt	American Stock Transfer & Trust Co.	Outstanding Shares	130,810,000
Counsel	Fulbright & Jaworski, LLP	E.P.S	NA
DUNS No.	NA	Shareholders	NA

Business: The groups principle activities include botanical DNA encryption, embedment and authentication solutions. In the year 2005, the group acquired Bowell Technology, Inc. The group operates from the United States.

Primary SIC and add'l.: 2836

CIK No: 0000744452

Officers: James A. Hayward/CEO, Ming-Hwa Benjamin Liang/Corp. Sec.

Directors: Jun-Jei Sheu/Chmn., Yacov Shamash/Dir., Sanford R. Simon/Dir.

Owners: Jun-Jei Sheu/2.57%, Yacov Shamash, James A. Hayward/6.40%, Sanford R. Simon, Insiders/9.39%

Curr. Assets:	$1,350,000	**Curr. Liab.:**	$9,732,000		
Plant, Equip.:	$156,000	**Total Liab.:**	$14,263,000	**Indic. Yr. Divd.:**	NA
Total Assets:	$4,677,000	**Net Worth:**	-$9,586,000	**Debt/ Equity:**	NA

Applied Imaging Corp

120 Baytech Dr., San Jose, CA, 95134; ***PH:*** 1-408-719-6400; ***http://*** www.aicorp.com

General		Stock	
Incorporation	DE	Price on:12/24/2007	NA
Employees	NA	Stock Exchange	NA
Auditor	Burr, Pilger & Mayer LLP	Ticker Symbol	NA
Stk Agt	Wells Fargo Shareowner Services	Outstanding Shares	NA
Counsel	Wilson Sonsini Goodrich & Rosati	E.P.S	NA
DUNS No.	17-547-9161	Shareholders	NA

Business: The group's principal activities are to develop, manufacture and market automated genetic imaging systems for use in cytogenetic laboratories. These systems are used for cancer testing, prenatal testing and other genetic testing applications. The group's systems are sold to government and private clinical laboratories, research institutions, universities and pharmaceutical companies in the United States, Canada, Europe, Japan and other countries. The group also markets imaging systems, which are designed for use in plant and animal genetic research programs. In addition, the group introduced a clinical system to detect micrometastatic cancer cells in bone marrow from cancer patients. This system and its research capabilities assist physicians in determining the initial stages of cancer cases, in detecting disease recurrence and in genetically characterizing cancer cells. The customers include public and private clinical laboratories and research organizations.

Primary SIC and add'l.: 7379 3826

CIK No: 0000816066

Officers: Robin Stracey/CEO, Pres., Terence J. Griffin/CFO

Applied Industrial Technologies Inc

1 Applied Plz., Cleveland, OH, 44115; ***PH:*** 1-216-426-4000; ***Fax:*** 1-216-426-4845; ***http://*** www.appliedindustrial.com; ***Email:*** appliedindustrial@applied.com

General		Stock	
Incorporation	OH	Price on:12/24/2007	$28.95
Employees	4,683	Stock Exchange	NYSE
Auditor	Deloitte & Touche LLP	Ticker Symbol	AIT
Stk Agt	Computershare Investor Services LLC	Outstanding Shares	43,070,000
Counsel	NA	E.P.S	$2.02
DUNS No.	94-800-5970	Shareholders	NA

Business: The groups principle activity is to distribute industrial products and services. The groups products include bearings, power transmission components, fluid power components and systems, industrial rubber products, safety products, and a variety of mill supply products. The group services include repair services to hazardous material handling and technical training solutions. In the year 2007 the group acquired VYCMEX S.A. de C.V. and its group of companies. The group operates from United States.

Primary SIC and add'l.: 7539 5084 5085

CIK No: 0000109563

Subsidiaries: Air and Hydraulics Engineering, Incorporated, Air Draulics Engineering Co., Air-Hydraulic Systems, Inc., AIT Limited Partnership, Applied - Michigan, Ltd., Applied Industrial Technologies - MBC, Inc., Applied Industrial Technologies — CA LLC, Applied Industrial Technologies — CAPITAL LLC, Applied Industrial Technologies — DBB, Inc., Applied Industrial Technologies — Dixie, Inc., Applied Industrial Technologies — Indiana LLC, Applied Industrial Technologies — Mainline, Inc., Applied Industrial Technologies — PA LLC, Applied Industrial Technologies — PACIFIC LLC, Applied Industrial Technologies — TX LP 31 Subsidiaries included in the Index

Officers: David L. Pugh/59/Chmn., CEO/$5,291,254.00, Michael L. Coticchia/46/VP, Chief Administrative Officer - Government Business, Mark O. Eisele/51/CFO, VP, Treasurer/$1,792,874.00, James T. Hopper/65/CIO, VP, Benjamin J. Mondics/50/COO, Exec. VP, Richard C. Shaw/60/VP - Communications, Learning, Todd A. Barlett/53/VP - Acquisitions, Global Business Development, Jeffrey A. Ramras/53/VP - Marketing, Supply Chain Management/$1,265,610.00, Daniel T. Brezovec/47/Corporate Controller, Bill L. Purser/65/Pres./$2,950,372.00, Alan M. Krupa/52/Assist. Treasurer, Jody A. Chabowski/Assist. Controller, Fred D. Bauer/43/VP, General Counsel, Sec./$1,099,629.00

Directors: David L. Pugh/59/Chmn., CEO, Thomas A. Commes/66/Dir., William G. Bares/67/Dir., Edith Kelly-Green/55/Dir., Peter C. Wallace/54/Dir., Peter A. Dorsman/53/Dir., Stephen E. Yates/60/Dir., Jerry Sue Thornton/61/Dir., John F. Meier/61/Dir., Thomas L. Hiltz/63/Dir., Michael J. Moore/65/Dir.

Owners: Barclays Global Investors, NA/8.10%, Thomas A. Commes, Fred D. Bauer, Peter A. Dorsman, Stephen E. Yates, William G. Bares, David L. Pugh/2.90%, Bill L. Purser, Dimensional Fund Advisors Inc./8.70%, J. Michael Moore, John F. Meier, Jerry Sue Thornton, Royce & Associates, LLC/5.10%, T. Rowe Price Associates, Inc./6.20%, Edith Kelly-Green *(21 Owners included in Index)*

Financial Data: Fiscal Year End:06/30   Latest Annual Data: 6/30/2006

Year	Sales	Net Income
2006	$1,900,780,000	$72,299,000
2005	$1,717,055,000	$55,339,000
2004	$1,517,004,000	$31,471,000

Curr. Assets:	$558,444,000	**Curr. Liab.:**	$188,431,000	**P/E Ratio:** 15.00
Plant, Equip.:	$70,794,000	**Total Liab.:**	$315,849,000	**Indic. Yr. Divd.:** $0.600
Total Assets:	$730,671,000	**Net Worth:**	$414,822,000	**Debt/ Equity:** NA

Applied Innovation Inc

5800 Innovation Dr., Dublin, OH, 43017; *PH:* 1-614-798-2000; *http://* www.aiinet.com

General - Incorporation .... DE	**Stock**- Price on:12/24/2007 .... NA
Employees 108	Stock Exchange .... NDQ
Auditor .... KPMG LLP	Ticker Symbol .... AINN
Stk Agt .... National City Bank Corp Trust Ops	Outstanding Shares .... NA
Counsel .... Porter Wright Morris & Arthur LLP	E.P.S. .... NA
DUNS No. 10-162-9988	Shareholders .... NA

Business: The group's principal activity is to provide network management solutions. These solutions are used to simplify and enhance the operation of complex, distributed voice and data networks. The products of the group are used to mediate, monitor and manage large-scale, complex telecommunications and wireless networks and increases the speed and delivery of broadband services. Services include network security solutions, operational support system services, installation services and extended maintenance agreements. All the hardware is manufactured at the group's facility in dublin, Ohio. The products include aiswitch(tm), aiscout(tm), aibadger(tm), and aiflex(tm) etc. The customers of the group consist of regional bell operating companies, long distance carriers, wireless and cable companies and local exchange carriers. The group's international markets include Australia, Brazil, Mexico, South Africa and Canada.

Primary SIC and add'l.: 3661

CIK No: 0000798399

Officers: William H. Largent/Dir., CEO, Julia A. Fratianne/CFO, VP, Treasurer

Directors: William H. Largent/Dir., CEO, Gerard B. Moersdorf/Chmn., Kenneth E. Jones/Dir., Thomas W. Huseby/Dir., Curtis A. Loveland/Dir., Alexander B. Trevor/Dir.

Owners: Insiders, Linda S. Moersdorf, Thomas W. Huseby, William H. Largent, Systematic Financial Management, L.P., FMR Corp., Kenneth E. Jones, Gerard B. Moersdorf, Julia A. Fratianne, KEG Holdings, Inc., Eric W. Langille, Curtis A. Loveland, Thomas G. Berlin, Alexander B. Trevor

Applied Materials Inc

3050 Bowers Ave., Santa Clara, CA, 95054; *PH:* 1-408-727-5555; *Fax:* 1-408-748-9943; *http://* www.appliedmaterials.com; *Email:* investor_relations@appliedmaterials.com

General - Incorporation .... DE	**Stock**- Price on:12/24/2007 .... NA
Employees 14,072	Stock Exchange .... NDQ
Auditor .... KPMG LLP	Ticker Symbol .... AMAT
Stk Agt ..... Computershare Investor Services LLC	Outstanding Shares 1,380,000,000
Counsel .... Orrick, Herrington & Sutcliffe LLP	E.P.S. $1.20
DUNS No. 04-272-8840	Shareholders .... NA

Business: The groups principle activities include developing, manufacturing, marketing and servicing semiconductor wafers fabrication equipment and related spare parts for the semiconductor industry. Customers of the group include semiconductor wafer manufacturers and semiconductor integrated circuit manufacturers. The group operates from United States, Europe and Japan.

Primary SIC and add'l.: 3674 3559

CIK No: 0000006951

Subsidiaries: AKT America, Inc., AKT Japan, LLC, AKT, Inc., AMAT (Thailand) Limited, Applied Materials (AMSEA)Sdn Bhd, Applied Materials (China), Inc., Applied Materials (Holdings), Applied Materials (Shanghai) Co., Ltd., Applied Materials Asia-Pacific, Ltd., Applied Materials Belgium N.V., Applied Materials China (Holdings), Ltd., Applied Materials China (Tianjin) Co., Ltd., Applied Materials China, Ltd., Applied Materials Europe BV, Applied Materials France SARL 66 Subsidiaries included in the Index

Officers: Michael R. Splinter/Dir., CEO, Pres./$11,385,040.00, Farhad Moghadam/Sr. VP, GM - Thin Films Product Business Group, Foundation Engineering/$2,753,904.00, In Doo Kang/VP, GM Display Industry Product Groups - AKT, Avi Tepman/VP - New Disruptive Products, Werner Finsterbusch/VP, GM Business Management - Applied Global Services, Charlie Gay/VP, GM Solar Business Group, Erix Yu/VP, GM UMC - Taiwan Regional Accounting, Thomas T. Edman/VP, GM Emerging Business Group, William H. McClintock/VP - Strategy, Marketing Silicon Systems Group, Joseph J. Sweeney/Sr. VP, General Counsel, Corp. Sec. - Applied Materials, Inc, Charlie Pappis/VP, GM Core Services - Applied Global Services, Hichem M'Saad/VP, GM Blanket DSM - Thin Films Product Business Group, Mike Rice/VP, Mgr. Platform Product Engineering - Foundation Engineering, Norm Armour/VP, Mgr. Corporate Asset Services, Liang Chen/VP, GM Alternative Energy Products Business Group *(31 Officers included in Index)*

Directors: Michael R. Splinter/Dir., CEO, Pres., James C. Morgan/Chmn., Charles Y.S. Liu/Dir., Robert H. Brust/Dir., Gerhard H. Parker/Dir., Willem P. Roelandts/Dir., Deborah A. Coleman/Dir., Thomas J. Iannotti/Dir., Aart J. De Geus/Dir., Dennis D. Powell/Dir., Philip V. Gerdine/Dir., Michael H. Armacost/Dir.

Owners: Michael H. Armacost, Capital Research and Management Company/11.80%, Charles Y.S. Liu, Thomas St. Dennis, Capital Group International, Inc./6.94%, James C. Morgan, Franz Janker, Insiders/1.07%, Philip V. Gerdine, George S. Davis, Farhad Moghadam, Deborah A. Coleman, Willem P. Roelandts, Gerhard H. Parker, Thomas J. Iannotti *(17 Owners included in Index)*

Financial Data: Fiscal Year End:10/30   Latest Annual Data: 10/29/2006

Year	Sales	Net Income
2006	$9,167,014,000	$1,516,663,000
2005	$6,991,823,000	$1,209,900,000
2004	$8,013,053,000	$1,351,303,000

Curr. Assets:	$10,281,519,000	**Curr. Liab.:**	$2,287,981,000	
Plant, Equip.:	$1,345,528,000	**Total Liab.:**	$2,831,418,000	**Indic. Yr. Divd.:** $0.240
Total Assets:	$12,093,445,000	**Net Worth:**	$9,262,027,000	**Debt/ Equity:** 0.0290

Applied Medical Devices Inc

5528 Wcott Cir., Frederick, MD, 21703; *PH:* 1-310-396-1691

General - Incorporation .... CO	**Stock**- Price on:12/24/2007 .... NA
Employees .... NA	Stock Exchange .... OTC
Auditor .... A.J. Robbins P.C.	Ticker Symbol .... APMD
Stk Agt .... Corporate Stock Transfer, Inc.	Outstanding Shares .... NA
Counsel .... NA	E.P.S. .... -$0.8
DUNS No. .... NA	Shareholders .... NA

Business: The groups principal activity is to develop and sale of medical devices and medical technology. The group operates from the United States.

Primary SIC and add'l.: 9995

CIK No: 0000312258

Officers: Thomas W. Colligan/37/Dir., CEO, Pres., Treasurer, Sec.

Directors: Thomas W. Colligan/37/Dir., CEO, Pres., Treasurer, Sec.

Owners: Fountainhead Capital Partners Limited/56.43%

Financial Data: Fiscal Year End:04/30   Latest Annual Data: 04/30/2006

Year	Sales	Net Income
2006	NA	-$22,000
2005	NA	-$66,000
2004	NA	-$35,000

Curr. Assets:	$121,000	**Curr. Liab.:**	NA	
Plant, Equip.:	NA	**Total Liab.:**	NA	**Indic. Yr. Divd.:** NA
Total Assets:	$121,000	**Net Worth:**	$121,000	**Debt/ Equity:** NA

Applied Micro Circuits Corp

215 Moffett Dr., Sunnyvale, CA, 94089; *PH:* 1-408-542-8600; *Fax:* 1-858-450-9885; *http://* www.amcc.com

General - Incorporation .... DE	**Stock**- Price on:12/24/2007 .... $2.7
Employees 619	Stock Exchange .... NDQ
Auditor .... Ernst & Young LLP	Ticker Symbol .... AMCC
Stk Agt .... Computershare Investor Services LLC	Outstanding Shares 283,210,000
Counsel .... Cooley Godward LLP	E.P.S. .... -$0.12
DUNS No. 09-853-8341	Shareholders .... NA

Business: The group's principal activities are to design, develop, manufacture and market high-performance, high-bandwidth silicon integrated circuits (ic). The group provides integrated circuit products that enable the transport of voice and data over wide area network. The group utilizes a combination of high-frequency analog, mixed signal and digital design expertise coupled with system-level knowledge and multiple silicon process technologies. The group operates in the United States, Europe, Israel and Asia. Major customers of the group include communications equipment manufacturers (OEMs) such as alcatel, ciena, cisco, fujitsu, huawei, jds uniphase, juniper, lucent, marconi, nec, nortel, oni, opnext, redback, siemens-unisphere, sycamore and tellabs. On 01-Apr-2004, the group acquired 3ware inc and

Primary SIC and add'l.: 3674

CIK No: 0000711065

Subsidiaries: Amcc (UK) Limited, AMCC China, Inc., AMCC Deutschland GmbH, AMCC Enterprise Corporation, AMCC France s.a.r.l., AMCC Japan Co., Ltd., AMCC Sales Corporation, AMCC Technology Solutions India Pvt. Ltd., Applied Micro Circuits Corporation Canada, Law 1111 Limited

Officers: Kambiz Hooshmand/Dir., CEO, Pres./$2,463,757.00, Arthur B. Stabenow/Dir., Financial Expert, Daryn Lau/Sr. VP, GM - Integrated Communications Products, Cynthia J. Moreland/VP, General Counsel, Sec., Robert G. Gargus/Sr. VP, CFO/$699,638.00, Barbara Murphy/VP, GM - Storage/$683,482.00, Robert H. Bagheri/Sr. VP - Operations, Quality/$627,547.00, Roger Wendelken/VP - World Wide Sales, Scott Dawson/Primary Investor Relations Officer

Directors: Kambiz Hooshmand/Dir., CEO, Pres., Cesar Cesaratto/Chmn., Julie H. Sullivan/Dir., Arthur B. Stabenow/Dir., Financial Expert, Niel Ransom/Dir., Fred Shlapak/Dir., Donald Colvin/Dir.

Owners: S.A.C. Capital Advisors, LLC and its affiliates/5.40%, Julie H. Sullivan, Kambiz Y. Hooshmand, Cesar Cesaratto, Dimensional Fund Advisors LP/8.00%, Insiders/1.55%, Donald Colvin, Robert H. Bagheri, Niel Ransom, Fred Shlapak, Robert G. Gargus, Barbara Murphy, Arthur B. Stabenow, FMR Corp. and its affiliates/7.60%, Onchuen Daryn Lau

Financial Data: Fiscal Year End:03/31   Latest Annual Data: 3/31/2007

Year	Sales	Net Income
2007	$292,852,000	-$24,208,000
2006	$261,844,000	-$148,372,000
2005	$253,756,000	-$127,373,000

Curr. Assets:	$362,752,000	**Curr. Liab.:**	$55,690,000	
Plant, Equip.:	$27,150,000	**Total Liab.:**	$55,690,000	**Indic. Yr. Divd.:** NA
Total Assets:	$816,512,000	**Net Worth:**	$760,822,000	**Debt/ Equity:** NA

Applied Neurosolutions Inc

50 Lakeview Pkwy S, Ste. 111, Vernon Hills, IL, 60061; *PH:* 1-847-573-8000; *http://* www.appliedneurosolutions.com; *Email:* ellison@appns.com

General - Incorporation .... DE	**Stock**- Price on:12/24/2007 .... $0.285
Employees 8	Stock Exchange .... OTC
Auditor .... Virchow, Krause & Co. LLP	Ticker Symbol .... APNS
Stk Agt ..... American Stock Transfer & Trust Co.	Outstanding Shares 108,480,000
Counsel .... NA	E.P.S. .... -$0.03
DUNS No. 61-865-1277	Shareholders .... NA

Business: The group's principal activity is to conduct research and development aimed at improving tissue oxygenation by increasing oxygen release from hemoglobin to provide therapeutic value to patients with serious, although unmet or underserved, medical needs. The group is a development stage company.

Primary SIC and add'l.: 2834

CIK No: 0000872947

Subsidiaries: Molecular Geriatrics Acquisition, Inc., Ophidian Holdings, Inc

Officers: Ellen R. Hoffing/Dir., CEO, Pres., Ryan Rauch/Investor Relations Officer, David Ellison/CFO, Corp. Sec., John F. Debernardis/Chief Scientific Officer, Daniel J. Kerkman/56/VP - Research, Development, Peter Davies/Founding Scientist

Directors: Ellen R. Hoffing/Dir., CEO, Pres., Robert S. Vaters/Chmn., Jay B. Langner/Dir., Michael Sorell/Dir., Bruce N. Barron/Dir., Alan L. Heller/Dir., David C. Tiemeier/Dir.

Owners: Insiders/7.80%, SF Capital Partners Ltd./19.80%, Benjamin Family Trusts/6.40%, Ellen R. Hoffing/2.20%, Alan L. Heller, Jay B. Langner, David Ellison, Bruce N. Barron/2.80%, Robert S. Vaters/2.00%

Financial Data: Fiscal Year End:12/31 **Latest Annual Data:** 12/31/2006

Year	Sales	Net Income
2006	$252,000	-$4,289,000
2005	$480,000	-$2,621,000
2004	$253,000	-$2,801,000

Curr. Assets:	$1,778,000	Curr. Liab.:	$1,710,000			
Plant, Equip.:	$38,000	Total Liab.:	$2,345,000	Indic. Yr. Divd.:	NA	
Total Assets:	$1,874,000	Net Worth:	-$471,000	Debt/ Equity:	NA	

Applied Signal Technology Inc

400 W California Ave., Sunnyvale, CA, 94086; *PH:* 1-408-749-1888; *Fax:* 1-408-738-1928; *http://* www.appsig.com; *Email:* customer@appsig.com

General - Incorporation	CA	Stock - Price on:12/24/2007	$15.55
Employees	647	Stock Exchange	NDQ
Auditor	Ernst & Young LLP	Ticker Symbol	APSG
Stk Agt.	Mellon Investor Services LLC	Outstanding Shares	12,170,000
Counsel	Gray Cary Ware & Freidenrich	E.P.S.	$0.41
DUNS No.	13-163-3125	Shareholders	NA

Business: The group's principal activities are to design, develop and manufacture signal processing equipment to collect and process telecommunication signals. The equipment is used for the reconnaissance, gathering and analysis of foreign telecommunications, predominantly by the United States government and its foreign allies. It scans thousands of cellular telephone, microwave, ship-to-shore and military transmissions in the radio frequency, evaluates them and selects the ones that contain relevant information. The group's subsidiary, enetsecure, inc offers market intrusion detection technology with its product, icemon, to detect unauthorized system entry for the purpose of altering or pirating data on networks. Transcendent technologies, inc, another subsidiary constructs monitoring products to improve the quality of satellite telecommunications. The major customer is the United States government with its six military and intelligence agencies.

Primary SIC and add'l.: 3663

CIK No: 0000741696

Subsidiaries: eNetSecure, Inc., Transcendent Technologies, Inc

Officers: Gary L. Yancey/Chmn., CEO, Pres., Founder, Alice Delgado/Investor Relations, James E. Doyle/CFO - Investor Relations, John R. Treichler/Dir., Founder, CTO, Al Rojas/Marketing, Sales, US

Directors: Gary L. Yancey/Chmn., CEO, Pres., Founder, John P. Devine/Dir., Stuart G. Whittelsey/Dir., John R. Treichler/Dir., Founder, CTO, Milton E. Cooper/Dir., David Elliman/Dir., Robert J. Richardson/Dir.

Owners: Robert Blanchard, Michael Ready, Stuart G. Whittelsey, William B. Van Vleet, Milton E. Cooper, Gary L. Yancey/2.42%, Renato F. Roscher, Insiders/8.46%, Bani M. Scribner, Lazard Asset Management LLC/10.09%, Heartland Advisors, Inc./7.00%, Robert T. Teague, David Elliman, Kennedy Capital Management, Inc./7.58%, James E. Doyle (23 Owners included in Index)

Financial Data: Fiscal Year End:10/31 **Latest Annual Data:** 05/04/2007

Year	Sales	Net Income
2007	NA	NA
2006	NA	NA
2005	$156,061,000	$9,244,000

Curr. Assets:	$89,455,000	Curr. Liab.:	$22,267,000	P/E Ratio:	37.93
Plant, Equip.:	$16,815,000	Total Liab.:	$30,902,000	Indic. Yr. Divd.:	$0.500
Total Assets:	$136,532,000	Net Worth:	$105,630,000	Debt/ Equity:	0.0537

Applix Inc

289 Tpke. Rd., Westborough, MA, 01581; *PH:* 1-508-870-0300; *Fax:* 1-508-366-2278; *http://* www.applix.com; *Email:* invest@applix.com

General - Incorporation	MA	Stock - Price on:12/24/2007	$16.04
Employees	210	Stock Exchange	NDQ
Auditor	Deloitte & Touche LLP	Ticker Symbol	APLX
Stk Agt.	American Stock Transfer & Trust CO.	Outstanding Shares	15,910,000
Counsel	Wilmer Cutler Pickering H & D LLP	E.P.S.	$0.55
DUNS No.	10-583-8627	Shareholders	NA

Business: The group's principal activities are to develop, provide and market business intelligence and business performance management software solutions. These solutions enable the continuous management and monitoring of performance across the financial, operational, customer and organizational functions within the enterprise. The trademarks of the group are applix tm1, applix integra, applix interactive planning and applix service analytics. The group operates in the United States, Germany, Europe, North America and the Pacific Rim. In Jan 2003, the group sold its customer relationship management business

Primary SIC and add'l.: 7372

CIK No: 0000932112

Subsidiaries: Applix (UK) Limited, Applix AG, Applix Asia Pacific Pty. Ltd., Applix Canada, Inc., Applix GmbH, Applix Securities Corp., Applix Singapore, Inc., Dynamic Decisions Pty. Ltd., Sinper Corporation, Target Systems Corporation, Veriteam France, Veriteam GmbH, Veriteam Limited, Veriteam, Inc.

Officers: David C. Mahoney/Dir., CEO, Pres./$903,613.00, Manny Perez/CTO, Milton Alpern/CFO, Sr. VP - Finance, Corporate Development/$602,070.00, Michael A. Morrison/COO/$745,264.00, Edward G. Gromann/VP - Services, Support, Martin Richmond-Coggan/VP - EMEA Operations, Chanchal Samanta/Sr. VP - Research, Development/$470,345.00, Jay Howald/VP - Asia Pacific, Hubert H.M. Heijkers/VP, Chief Architect, Mary Murphy/VP - Human Resources, Ben Plummer/VP - Worldwide Marketing, Strategic Alliances

Directors: David C. Mahoney/Dir., CEO, Pres., John D. Loewenberg/66/Chmn., Bradley D. Fire/37/Dir., Alain J. Hanover/58/Dir., Peter Gyenes/61/Dir., Charles F. Kane/50/Dir.

Owners: Bradley D. Fire/12.10%, Insiders/23.36%, Arbor Capital Management, LLC/10.18%, Michael Morrison/1.76%, Alain J. Hanover, Milton A. Alpern/1.19%, David C. Mahoney/6.02%, Chanchal Samanta, Charles F. Kane, John D. Loewenberg, Peter Gyenes

Financial Data: Fiscal Year End:12/31 **Latest Annual Data:** 12/31/2006

Year	Sales	Net Income
2006	$52,173,000	$9,331,000
2005	$36,978,000	$6,738,000
2004	$30,915,000	$4,702,000

Curr. Assets:	$42,996,000	Curr. Liab.:	$24,662,000	P/E Ratio:	29.16
Plant, Equip.:	$1,313,000	Total Liab.:	$28,737,000	Indic. Yr. Divd.:	NA
Total Assets:	$66,087,000	Net Worth:	$37,350,000	Debt/ Equity:	0.0815

Apria Healthcare Group Inc

26220 Enterprise Ct., Lake Forest, CA, 92630; *PH:* 1-949-639-2000; *Fax:* 1-949-587-9363; *http://* www.apria.com; *Email:* investor_relations@apria.com

General - Incorporation	DE	Stock - Price on:12/24/2007	$28.78
Employees	10,657	Stock Exchange	NYSE
Auditor	Deloitte & Touche LLP	Ticker Symbol	AHG
Stk Agt.	American Stock Transfer & Trust Co.	Outstanding Shares	43,650,000
Counsel	NA	E.P.S.	$1.85
DUNS No.	10-404-2361	Shareholders	NA

Business: The group's principal activities are to provide a variety of clinical services and related products and supplies as prescribed by a physician or authorized by a case manager as part of a care plan. The products and services offered by the group are provided through the group's network of approximately 425 branch facilities, which are located throughout the United States and are organized into 16 geographic regions. The group has three major service lines namely home respiratory therapy, home infusion therapy and home medical equipment. The products and services are marketed primarily to manage care organizations, physicians, hospitals, medical groups, home health agencies and case managers.

Primary SIC and add'l.: 8082

CIK No: 0000882289

Subsidiaries: Apria Healthcare of New York State, Inc, Apria Healthcare, Inc., Apria Number Two, Inc., ApriaCare Management Systems, Inc., Biomedical Home Care, Inc.

Officers: Lawrence M. Higby/Dir., CEO/$3,364,743.00, David L. Goldsmith/Chmn. - Private Investor, Chris A. Karkenny/CFO, Exec. VP/$170,511.00, Robin Barton/Exec. VP - Revenue Management, Cameron Thompson/Exec. VP - Logistics, Jeffrey W. Ingram/Exec. VP - Sales/$702,130.00, Robert S. Holcombe/Exec. VP, General Counsel, Sec., Lawrence A. Mastrovich/COO, Pres./$1,821,893.00, Anthony F. Giambone/Sr. VP - Enterprise Business Systems, Jeri L. Lose/CIO, Exec. VP, Daniel J. Starck/Exec. VP - Customer Services/$473,381.00, Amin I. Khalifa/Exec. VP/$775,142.00, Frank C. Bianchi/Sr. VP - Human Resources, Lisa M. Getson/Exec. VP - Government Relations, Investor Services, Compliance, Vanessa Pfeiffer/Sr. VP - Marketing, Sales Planning (17 Officers included in Index)

Directors: Lawrence M. Higby/Dir., CEO, David L. Goldsmith/Chmn. - Private Investor, Philip R. Lochner/Dir., Terry P. Bayer/Dir., I. T. Corley/Dir., Richard Koppes/Dir., Norman C. Payson/Dir., Vicente Anido/Dir., Mahvash Yazdi/Dir.

Owners: FMR Corp./10.30%, Capital Research and Management Company/9.95%, Lawrence A. Mastrovich, Norman C. Payson, Jeffrey W. Ingram, Vicente Anido, Morgan Stanley/5.61%, David L. Goldsmith/1.02%, The New Economy Fund/5.06%, Philip R. Lochner, Lawrence M. Higby/2.03%, I. T. Corley, Terry P. Bayer, Barclays Global Investors, N.A./14.13%, Insiders/4.97% (17 Owners included in Index)

Financial Data: Fiscal Year End:12/31 **Latest Annual Data:** 12/31/2006

Year	Sales	Net Income
2006	$1,517,307,000	$74,980,000
2005	$1,474,101,000	$66,941,000
2004	$1,451,449,000	$114,008,000

Curr. Assets:	$344,937,000	Curr. Liab.:	$203,523,000	P/E Ratio:	15.56
Plant, Equip.:	$265,043,000	Total Liab.:	$758,065,000	Indic. Yr. Divd.:	NA
Total Assets:	$1,168,496,000	Net Worth:	$410,431,000	Debt/ Equity:	1.0988

APT Satellite Holdings Ltd

22 Dai Kwai St., Tai Po Industrial Estate, New Territories, Tai Po; *PH:* 852-26002100; *http://* www.apstar.com; *Email:* investors@apstar.com

General - Incorporation	Bermuda	Stock - Price on:12/24/2007	$1.97
Employees	161	Stock Exchange	NYSE
Auditor	KPMG	Ticker Symbol	ATS
Stk Agt.	Bank of New York	Outstanding Shares	51,660,000
Counsel	NA	E.P.S.	-$0.14
DUNS No.	66-304-2265	Shareholders	NA

Business: The group's principal activity is the provision of services in satellite transponder leasing, broadcasting and telecommunication for broadcasting and telecommunication sectors. It operates three in-orbit geostationary satellites namely apstar i, apstar ia and apstar iir. The group has procured two high power satellite, apstar v and apstar ia respectively, which will be lunched in Sept 2003 and 2005 respectively as replacement satellites of apstar i and apstar ia respectively.

Primary SIC and add'l.: 6719 4899

CIK No: 0001027229

Subsidiaries: APT Satellite Telecommunications Limited, APT Telecom Services Limited

Officers: Tong Xudong/44/Dir., VP, Chen Xun/37/VP, Ni Yifeng/60/Dir., Pres., Yang Qing/44/VP, Dong Gang/54/VP, Brian Lo Kin Hang/VP, Company Sec.

Directors: Rui Xiaowu/49/Chmn., Lim Toon/65/Dir., Zhao Liqiang/47/Dir., Yong Foo Chong/41/Dir., Lam Sek Kong/48/Dir., Cui Liguo/38/Dir., Tong Xudong/44/Dir., VP, Huan Guocang/58/Dir., Tseng Ta-Mon/50/Alternate Dir., Ni Yifeng/60/Dir., Pres., Lui King Man/53/Dir., Yin Yen-Liang/57/Dir., Yuen Pak Yiu Philip/70/Dir., Wu Zhen Mu/62/Dir.

Owners: SingaSat PTE Ltd., China Aerospace Science & Technology Corporation, China Telecommunications Broadcast Satellite Corporation, Sinolike Investments Limited, CASIL Satellite Holdings Limited, APT Satellite International Company Limited, Insiders, Kwang Hua Development and Investment Limited

Financial Data: Fiscal Year End:12/31 **Latest Annual Data:** 12/31/2006

Year	Sales	Net Income
2006	$54,911,000	-$10,477,000
2005	$43,143,000	-$16,698,000
2004	$35,656,000	-$7,535,000

Curr. Assets:	$70,998,000	**Curr. Liab.:**	$44,408,000		
Plant, Equip.:	$349,724,000	**Total Liab.:**	$183,528,000	**Indic. Yr. Divd.:**	NA
Total Assets:	$437,759,000	**Net Worth:**	$254,232,000	**Debt/ Equity:**	NA

Aptargroup Inc

475 W Terra Cotta Ave., Ste. E, Crystal Lake, IL, 60014; ***PH:*** 1-815-477-0424; ***Fax:*** 1-815-477-0481; ***http://*** www.aptar.com; ***Email:*** info@aptargroup.com

General - Incorporation .... DE
Employees 8,200
Auditor .... PricewaterhouseCoopers LLP
Stk Agt .... National City Bank
Counsel .... Sidley, Austin, Brown & Wood
DUNS No. 80-561-9681

Stock- Price on:12/24/2007 .... $36.83
Stock Exchange .... NYSE
Ticker Symbol .... ATR
Outstanding Shares 69,220,000
E.P.S $1.86
Shareholders .... NA

Business: The groups principle activity is to provide dispensing systems for the personal care, cosmetic, pharmaceutical, and household and food markets. The group operates from United States.

Primary SIC and add'l.: 3499 3089

CIK No: 0000896622

Subsidiaries: Airlessystems S.A.S., Aptar GmbH, Aptar India Private Ltd., Aptar South Europe SARL, Aptar Suzhou Dispensing Systems Co., Ltd., Aptar U.K. Ltd., AptarGroup Holding S.A.S., AptarGroup International Holding B.V., AptarGroup International LLC, AptarGroup S.A.S., AptarGroup SAR Finance Unlimited, Asia Pacific Inspection Center (Suzhou) Co., Ltd., Caideil M.P. Teoranta, EMSAR Brasil Ltda., EMSAR France SCA 56 Subsidiaries included in the Index

Officers: Carl A. Siebel/Dir., CEO, Pres./$3,912,050.00, Stephen J. Hagge/Dir., CFO, Exec. VP, Sec./$1,854,537.00, Patrick F. Doherty/52/Pres. - Seaquistperfect Dispensing Group, Jacques Blanie/61/Exec. VP - Seaquistperfect Dispensing Group, Francois Boutan Boutan/VP - Finance - Europe, Matthew J. Dellamaria/VP - Corporate Communications, Robert Kuhn/VP - Financial Reporting, Lawrence Lowrimore/VP - Human Resources, Emil D. Meshberg/VP/$1,112,323.00, Ralph Poltermann/VP, Treasurer, Eric S. Ruskoski/60/Pres. - Seaquist Closures Group/$1,013,491.00, Olivier Fourment/50/Co - Pres. - Valois Group, Lothar Graf/58/Pres. - Pfeiffer Group

Directors: Carl A. Siebel/Dir., CEO, Pres., Peter H. Pfeiffer/Vice Chmn., King W. Harris/64/Chmn., Leo Guthart/Dir., Stephan A. Baustert/Dir., Ralph Gruska/Dir., Stephen J. Hagge/Dir., CFO, Exec. VP, Sec., Alain Chevassus/Dir., Joanne C. Smith/Dir., Rodney Goldstein/56/Dir.

Owners: Carl A. Siebel/1.50%, Alain Chevassus, State Farm Mutual Automobile Insurance Company/8.10%, Rodney L. Goldstein, Leo A. Guthart, Barclays Global Investors, N.A./5.00%, Insiders/7.90%, Ralph Gruska, Peter H. Pfeiffer/2.50%, King W. Harris, Stefan A. Baustert, Emil D. Meshberg, Eric S. Ruskoski, Joanne C. Smith, Stephen J. Hagge *(16 Owners included in Index)*

Financial Data: ***Fiscal Year End:***12/31 ***Latest Annual Data:*** 12/31/2006

Year	Sales	Net Income
2006	$1,601,385,000	$102,896,000
2005	$1,380,009,000	$100,034,000
2004	$1,296,608,000	$93,287,000

Curr. Assets:	$762,820,000	**Curr. Liab.:**	$400,185,000	**P/E Ratio:**	21.54
Plant, Equip.:	$591,077,000	**Total Liab.:**	$645,049,000	**Indic. Yr. Divd.:**	$0.520
Total Assets:	$1,592,012,000	**Net Worth:**	$946,400,000	**Debt/ Equity:**	0.1716

Aptimus Inc

199 Fremont St., Ste. 1800, San Francisco, CA, 94105; ***PH:*** 1-415-896-2123; ***Fax:*** 1-415-896-2561; ***http://*** www.aptimus.com

General - Incorporation .... WA
Employees 58
Auditor .... Moss Adams LLP
Stk Agt .... Chase Mellon Shareholder Services
Counsel .... Dorsey & Whitney LLP
DUNS No. .... NA

Stock- Price on:12/24/2007 .... $5.56
Stock Exchange .... NDQ
Ticker Symbol .... APTM
Outstanding Shares 6,590,000
E.P.S .... -$0.69
Shareholders .... NA

Business: The group's principle activity is to provide single-source online marketing solution that enables marketers to reach targeted audiences with specific promotional offers throughout the Internet. The company operates a powerful online direct marketing network known as the aptimus network. This network presents consumers with relevant offers geared to their immediate interests, allowing marketers to reach consumers with the right offers when they are most likely to respond. This network can support millions of users and hundreds of marketers and Web site partners. Through this network, the company generates sales leads, creates product awareness and initiates consumer purchases through multiple online marketing vehicles, including free and trial offers, banner advertising, e-mail newsletter sponsorship and others. The company operates in the United States.

Primary SIC and add'l.: 7319 7311

CIK No: 0001087277

Subsidiaries: FreeShop International, Inc., Neighbornet LLC

Officers: Robert W. Wrubel/Dir., CEO, Pres./$338,197.00, Michael Mayor/Sr. VP - Strategic Business Development, East Coast/$276,815.00, Brad Benz/Sr. VP/$293,287.00, Lance Nelson/VP - Technology/$195,509.00, John A. Wade/CFO/$175,000.00, David H. Davis/General Counsel, Sec./$182,000.00, Moss Adams/Independent Auditor, Michael Sullivan/Sr. VP - Media Services, Marketing

Directors: Robert W. Wrubel/Dir., CEO, Pres., Timothy C. Choate/Chmn., Eric Helgeland/Dir., Bob Bejan/Dir., John B. Balousek/Dir.

Owners: Eric Helgeland, Robert Wrubel/5.50%, David Davis/3.50%, Michael Mayor, Munder Capital Management/5.30%, John Balousek/1.50%, Brad Benz, Loeb Arbitrage Fund/7.60%, John Wade/2.60%, Timothy Choate/25.30%, Bob Bejan, Stiassni Capital Partners, LP/5.90%, Lance Nelson/2.40%, Insiders/44.00%

Financial Data: ***Fiscal Year End:***12/31 ***Latest Annual Data:*** 12/31/2006

Year	Sales	Net Income
2006	$15,198,000	-$3,800,000
2005	$15,894,000	$1,352,000
2004	$13,993,000	$2,126,000

Curr. Assets:	$8,469,000	**Curr. Liab.:**	$5,101,000		
Plant, Equip.:	$901,000	**Total Liab.:**	$5,101,000	**Indic. Yr. Divd.:**	NA
Total Assets:	$14,720,000	**Net Worth:**	$9,619,000	**Debt/ Equity:**	NA

Aqua America Inc

762 W Lancaster Ave., Bryn Mawr, PA, 19010; ***PH:*** 1-610-527-8000; ***Fax:*** 1-610-525-7658; ***http://*** www.aquaamerica.com

General - Incorporation .... PA
Employees 1,540
Auditor .... PricewaterhouseCoopers LLP
Stk Agt .... Computershare Ltd.
Counsel .... NA
DUNS No. 04-834-1648

Stock- Price on:12/24/2007 .... $22.19
Stock Exchange .... NYSE
Ticker Symbol .... WTR
Outstanding Shares 132,590,000
E.P.S $0.72
Shareholders .... NA

Business: The group's principal activities are to provide water or wastewater services to residential, commercial and industrial customers. The group is a water utility serving 2.5 million residents in Pennsylvania, Ohio, Illinois, Texas, New Jersey, Indiana, Virginia, Florida, North Carolina, Maine, Missouri, New York, South Carolina and Kentucky. It also preserves and improves the environment. On 31-Jul-2003, the group acquired aquasource inc, on 26-Dec-2003, it acquired forest pines water system and heater utilities inc on 01-Jun-2004.

Primary SIC and add'l.: 4952 6719 4941

CIK No: 0000078128

Subsidiaries: Aqua Illinois, Inc., Aqua Indiana, Inc., Aqua Maine, Inc., Aqua Missouri, Inc., Aqua New Jersey, Inc., Aqua New York, Inc., Aqua North Carolina, Inc., Aqua Ohio, Inc., Aqua Pennsylvania, Inc., Aqua Resources, Inc., Aqua Services, Inc., Aqua South Carolina, Inc., Aqua Texas, Inc., Aqua Utilities Florida, Inc., Aqua Utilities, Inc. 17 Subsidiaries included in the Index

Officers: Nicholas Debenedictis/Chmn., CEO, Pres./$1,984,360.00, Christopher Franklin/Regional Pres. - Southern Operations, Sr. VP - Public Affairs, Customer Operations, Robert Liptak/Pres. - Aqua America, North, Robert A. Rubin/VP, Chief Accounting Officer, Controller, Roy H. Stahl/Chief Administrative Officer, General Counsel, Sec./$776,347.00, Richard R. Riegler/Sr. VP - Engineering, Environmental Affairs/$385,413.00, Karl M. Kyriss/Regional Pres. - Aqua America Mid, Atlantic Operations/$425,594.00, David P. Smeltzer/CFO/$596,004.00, Mark J. Kropilak/Sr. VP - Corporate Development, Corporate Counsel

Directors: Nicholas Debenedictis/Chmn., CEO, Pres., Mary Carroll/Dir., Richard L. Smoot/Dir., Richard Glanton/Dir., Lon R. Greenberg/Dir., William Hankowsky/Dir., Constantine Papadakis/Dir., Ellen T. Ruff/Dir., Andrew J. Sorodini/64/Dir.

Owners: Andrew J. Sordoni, William P. Hankowsky, Insiders, Richard L. Smoot, Mary C. Carroll, Karl M. Kyriss, Lon R. Greenberg, Roy H. Stahl, David P. Smeltzer, Richard H. Glanton, Richard R. Riegler, Nicholas Debenedictis, Constantine Papadakis

Financial Data: ***Fiscal Year End:***12/31 ***Latest Annual Data:*** 12/31/2006

Year	Sales	Net Income
2006	$533,491,000	$92,004,000
2005	$496,779,000	$91,156,000
2004	$442,039,000	$80,007,000

Curr. Assets:	$134,700,000	**Curr. Liab.:**	$255,611,000	**P/E Ratio:**	31.70
Plant, Equip.:	$2,505,995,000	**Total Liab.:**	$1,954,459,000	**Indic. Yr. Divd.:**	$0.500
Total Assets:	$2,877,903,000	**Net Worth:**	$921,630,000	**Debt/ Equity:**	NA

Aqua Society Inc

6138 Sub Blvd, Vancouver, BC, V6T 2A5; ***PH:*** 1-604-822-3329; ***Fax:*** 1-604-822-9019; ***http://*** www.aqua-society.com; ***Email:*** info@aqua-society.com

General - Incorporation .... NV
Employees .... NA
Auditor .... Amisano Hanson
Stk Agt .... NA
Counsel .... NA
DUNS No. .... NA

Stock- Price on:12/24/2007 .... $0.29
Stock Exchange .... OTC
Ticker Symbol .... AQAS
Outstanding Shares .... NA
E.P.S .... NA
Shareholders .... NA

Business: The groups principle activities include designing and developing applied technologies, and providing consulting services. The group product is Yellow Box. In the year 2006, the group acquired TMR GmbH. The group operates from the United States and Germany. The group's quarterly revenue for September 2007 was 0.03 millions of USD.

Primary SIC and add'l.: 7999

CIK No: 0001213111

Subsidiaries: Aqua Society GmbH

Owners: Erwin Oser, Hubert Hamm, Achim Stamm, Insiders, Water-Capital-Holding Ltd., Robert Terberg

Financial Data: ***Fiscal Year End:***09/30 ***Latest Annual Data:*** 9/30/2006

Year	Sales	Net Income
2006	$2,204,000	-$4,328,000
2005	$897,000	-$25,788,000
2004	NA	-$67,000

Curr. Assets:	$855,000	**Curr. Liab.:**	$2,914,000		
Plant, Equip.:	$65,000	**Total Liab.:**	$2,914,000	**Indic. Yr. Divd.:**	NA
Total Assets:	$1,114,000	**Net Worth:**	-$1,801,000	**Debt/ Equity:**	NA

Aquacell Technologies Inc

10410 Trademark St., Rancho Cucamonga, CA, 91730; ***PH:*** 1-909-987-0456; ***Fax:*** 1-909-987-6306; ***http://*** www.aquacell.com; ***Email:*** investorrelations@aquacell.com

General - Incorporation .... DE
Employees 20
Auditor .... Wolinetz, Lafazan & Co. P.C
Stk Agt .... U.S. Stock Transfer Corp
Counsel .... Harold Paul
DUNS No. .... NA

Stock- Price on:12/24/2007 .... $0.4975
Stock Exchange .... OTC
Ticker Symbol .... AQUA
Outstanding Shares 27,910,000
E.P.S .... -$0.238
Shareholders .... NA

Business: The group's principal activity is to manufacture and market water filtration and purification products in the United States. These products address various water treatment applications for industrial, commercial, institutional and residential purposes. These applications include providing purified drinking water through point-of- use patented self-filling purific (registered) water cooler and production of water bottling plant equipment. The primary product of the group is the five-gallon self-refilling bottle purific water cooler. The group also offers replacement filters for the purific water coolers.

Primary SIC and add'l.: 6794 3589

CIK No: 0001114655

Subsidiaries: AquaCell Media, Inc.

Officers: James C. Witham/Chmn., CEO, Gary S. Wolff/69/Dir., CFO, Treasurer
Directors: James C. Witham/Chmn., CEO, Gary S. Wolff/69/Dir., CFO, Treasurer
Financial Data: Fiscal Year End:06/30 **Latest Annual Data:** 6/30/2005

Year	Sales	Net Income
2005	$837,000	-$3,888,000
2004	$729,000	-$4,512,000
2003	$1,588,000	-$2,574,000

Curr. Assets:	$352,000	**Curr. Liab.:**	$2,023,000		
Plant, Equip.:	$1,211,000	**Total Liab.:**	$2,474,000	**Indic. Yr. Divd.:**	NA
Total Assets:	$2,383,000	**Net Worth:**	-$91,000	**Debt/ Equity:**	NA

Aquamatrix Inc

Formerly: Nesco Industries Inc
305 Madison Ave., Ste. 4510, New York, NY, 10165; **PH:** 1-212-986-0886

General - Incorporation	NV	Stock- Price on:12/24/2007	NA
Employees	9	Stock Exchange	NA
Auditor	Rothstein, Kass & Co, P.C	Ticker Symbol	NA
Stk Agt	Interwest Transfer Company, Inc.	Outstanding Shares	NA
Counsel	NA	E.P.S.	NA
DUNS No.	NA	Shareholders	NA

Business: The group's principal activity is to provide asbestos abatement and indoor air quality testing monitoring, remediation services. The group has expertise in all types of asbestos abatement including removal and disposal, enclosure and encapsulation in commercial buildings, hospitals, government and institutional buildings, universities and industrial facilities. The group provides an integrated approach to indoor air quality issues by offering facility investigation and diagnosis, remediation and preventative monitoring and maintenance services. The group also used to provide a variety of environmental services including remediation, underground storage tank removals in the past. The group discontinued this line of services in fiscal 2003 and relocated resources in favor of indoor air quality services. In may 2003, the group ceased operations and became inactive.on 25-May-2004, the group acqired hydrogel design systems, inc.
Primary SIC and add'l.: 7389 6719
CIK No: 0001099609
Subsidiaries: NAC Environmental Services, Inc., NAC/Indoor Air Professionals, Inc., National Abatement Corporation
Owners: Santo Petrocelli, Richard Harriton, Alvin Block, CIBC Trust Company Bahamas) Limited as Trustee, Gottbetter Capital Master, Ltd, Arlen Reynolds, BridgePoint Master Fund, Ltd., Insiders, Matthew Harriton, Harborview Master Fund, Ltd., Lynn November, Kanter Family Foundation, Gene E. Burleson, Chicago Investments, Inc.

Aquantive Inc

821 Second Ave., Ste. 1800, Seattle, WA, 98101; **PH:** 1-206-816-8700; **http://** www.aquantive.com

General - Incorporation	WA	Stock- Price on:12/24/2007	$63.23
Employees	2,106	Stock Exchange	NDQ
Auditor	KPMG LLP	Ticker Symbol	AQNT
Stk Agt	Mellon Investor Services LLC	Outstanding Shares	78,920,000
Counsel	Perkins Coie LLP	E.P.S.	$0.703
DUNS No.	NA	Shareholders	NA

Business: The group's principal activities are to provide digital marketing services and Internet advertising based technology to businesses. The group is organized into two operating units: atlas dmt and avenue a. Atlas dmt is an advertising technology provider that created the atlas digital marketing suite, a digital marketing management system. Avenue a is an interactive advertising agency that offers a suite of services including Web advertising, affiliate programs, search engine optimization, strategic portal relationships, e-mail prospecting, list management, customer targeting, profiling and advanced analytical services to help advertisers increase the effectiveness and return on investment of their Internet advertising campaigns. The group operates only in domestic market. On 15-Dec-2003, the group acquired go toast llc, on 11-Feb-2004, acquired netconversions, inc and on 27-Jul-2004, acquired sbi.razorfish.
Primary SIC and add'l.: 7311 7319
CIK No: 0001071806
Subsidiaries: aQuantive Australia Pty Ltd., aQuantive Paymaster, LLC, Atlas DMT LLC, Atlas Europe Ltd. (formerly TechnologyBrokers Ltd.), Atlas OnePoint, LLC(formerly Go Toast, LLC), Avenue A LLC, Avenue A/Razorfish Philadelphia LLC., Avenue A/Razorfish Search, LLC(formerly eonMedia, LLC), Avenue A/Razorfish, Inc. (formerly SBI Group, Inc.), DNA Consulting Ltd., Drive Performance Media LLC, MediaBrokers Ltd., NetConversions, Inc.
Officers: Clark M. Kokich/CEO - Avenue A | Razorfish/$1,487,238.00, Brian P. McAndrews/49/CEO, Pres., Sr. VP - Advertiser · Publisher Solutions, APS Group/$3,091,804.00, Brad Aronson/Exec. VP - Product Development, David Friedman/Pres. - Avenue A, Razorfish, Central Region, Ona Karasa/Pres. - Atlas, Michael T. Galgon/Co - Founder, Chief Advertising Strategist - Microsoft/$1,300,802.00, Linda A. Schoemaker/Sr. VP, General Counsel/$1,017,213.00, Bob Lord/Pres. - Avenue A, Razorfish, East Region, Wayne M. Wisehart/CFO/$695,888.00, Karl Siebrecht/Pres. - Atlas, Scott Howe/Pres. - Drivepm, Mediabrokers, Atlas International, Jamie Leady/Media Relations Mgr.
Directors: Nicolas J. Hanauer/48/Chmn., Co - Founder, Jaynie Miller Studenmund/53/Dir., Linda J. Srere/52/Dir., Michael B. Slade/50/Dir., Jack Sansolo/64/Dir., Richard P. Fox/60/Dir.
Owners: Nicolas J. Hanauer/5.30%, Clark M. Kokich, Jaynie M. Studenmund, M. Wayne Wisehart, Insiders/9.80%, Linda A. Schoemaker, Scott E. Howe, Jack Sansolo, Mazama Capital Management, Inc/7.30%, Michael T. Galgon/1.20%, Brian P. McAndrews/2.60%, Richard P. Fox, T. Rowe Price Associates, Inc/9.90%, Karl F. Siebrecht, Linda J. Srere (**16 Owners included in Index**)
Financial Data: Fiscal Year End:12/31 **Latest Annual Data:** 12/31/2006

Year	Sales	Net Income
2006	$442,211,000	$53,954,000
2005	$308,405,000	$35,181,000
2004	$157,937,000	$42,883,000

Curr. Assets:	$563,227,000	**Curr. Liab.:**	$296,561,000	**P/E Ratio:**	89.94
Plant, Equip.:	$34,343,000	**Total Liab.:**	$384,502,000	**Indic. Yr. Divd.:**	NA
Total Assets:	$952,328,000	**Net Worth:**	$567,826,000	**Debt/ Equity:**	0.1335

Aquasol Envirotech Ltd

1055 W Hastings St., Ste. 1980, Vancouver, BC, V6E 2E9; **PH:** 1-604-688-8002;
Fax: 1-604-688-8030; **http://** www.aquasoltech.com; **Email:** info@aquasoltech.com

General - Incorporation	Cayman Islands	Stock- Price on:12/24/2007	NA
Employees	NA	Stock Exchange	OTC
Auditor Child, Van Wagoner & Bradshaw, PLLC		Ticker Symbol	NA
Stk Agt	NA	Outstanding Shares	NA
Counsel	NA	E.P.S.	NA
DUNS No.	NA	Shareholders	NA

Business: The groups principle activities include development, acquiring, and marketing of water and wastewater technology solutions. The group also provides stand-alone aeration equipment, digestion technology, and complete wastewater treatment systems. The group operates from United States.
Primary SIC and add'l.: 4950
CIK No: 0001336655
Subsidiaries: Aquasol EnviroTech (Canada) Ltd.
Officers: Ken Z. Cai/Chmn., CEO, Jeff Yenyou Zheng/Dir., CFO, Pres., Brigitte M. McArthur/Corp. Sec.
Directors: Ken Z. Cai/Chmn., CEO, Jeff Yenyou Zheng/Dir., CFO, Pres., Troy Vassos/Dir.
Owners: Tianying Zheng/9.64%, Jeff Yenyou Zheng/9.60%, Zhibin Cai/7.23%, Thomas Wayne Spilsbury/7.23%, Ken Z. Cai/13.72%, Hans Wick/12.05%, Zhiquan Cai/6.65%, Chuan Mei Deng/7.23%, Insiders/23.32%, Affaires Financiers SA/10.46%, Bunnaton Ltd./5.54%

Aquatic Cellulose International Corp

2504 - 43rd St., Ste. 5, Vernon, BC, V1T 6K9; **PH:** 1-250-558-4216;
http:// www.aquaticcellulose.com

General - Incorporation	NV	Stock- Price on:12/24/2007	$0.024
Employees	NA	Stock Exchange	OTC
Auditor	KPMG LLP	Ticker Symbol	AQCI
Stk Agt	Computershare Trust CO.	Outstanding Shares	NA
Counsel	NA	E.P.S.	-$0.086
DUNS No.	NA	Shareholders	NA

Business: The group's principal activity is the underwater harvesting and salvaging of submerged timber, and the sale of lumber produced from such timber. The group harvests trees with a surface mounted robotic arm, called the ath-60, has the ability to reach under water, extract a targeted submerged tree and bring it to the surface. The submerged timber is preserved by the water and is used for plywood, sawn lumber, special cuts for fine furniture building plus a wide variety of other wood fiber processes. The products are used to create osb plywood (chip board) or processed for the pulp and paper industry. The group operates primarily in the United States, Canada and Brazil.
Primary SIC and add'l.: 2411 0811 1629
CIK No: 0001081242
Subsidiaries: Aquatic Cellulose Ltd
Officers: Sheridan B. Westgarde/39/Chmn., CEO, CFO, Pres., Lonnie Hayward/39/Dir., VP
Directors: Sheridan B. Westgarde/39/Chmn., CEO, CFO, Pres., Lonnie Hayward/39/Dir., VP
Owners: Lonnie Hayward/46.95%, Insiders/100.00%, Insiders/1.50%, Sheridan Westgarde/53.05%, Lonnie Hayward, Sheridan Westgarde/1.00%
Financial Data: Fiscal Year End:05/31 **Latest Annual Data:** 5/31/2006

Year	Sales	Net Income
2006	NA	-$5,107,000
2005	$92,000	-$1,425,000
2002	$33,000	-$1,456,000

Curr. Assets:	$84,000	**Curr. Liab.:**	$11,089,000		
Plant, Equip.:	$2,000	**Total Liab.:**	$11,089,000	**Indic. Yr. Divd.:**	NA
Total Assets:	$1,471,000	**Net Worth:**	-$9,618,000	**Debt/ Equity:**	NA

Aquila Inc

20 W Ninth St., Kansas City, MO, 64105; **PH:** 1-816-421-6600; **http://** www.aquila.com

General - Incorporation	DE	Stock- Price on:12/24/2007	$4.12
Employees	2,456	Stock Exchange	NYSE
Auditor	KPMG LLP	Ticker Symbol	ILA
Stk Agt	UMB Bank, N.A.	Outstanding Shares	374,680,000
Counsel	Blackwell Sanders Peper Martin LLP	E.P.S.	$0.18
DUNS No.	00-696-6055	Shareholders	NA

Business: The groups principle activity is to distribute electric and natural gas. The group operates through three business segments namely electric utilities, gas utilities and merchant services. The group operates from United States.
Primary SIC and add'l.: 4922 4931 4939
CIK No: 0000066960
Subsidiaries: Aquila Merchant Services, Inc.
Officers: Richard C. Green/Chmn., CEO, Pres./$1,324,847.00, Leo E. Morton/Sr. VP, Chief Administrative Officer/$508,561.00, Keith G. Stamm/COO, Sr. VP/$578,147.00, Christopher M. Reitz/Sr. VP, General Counsel, Corp. Sec./$420,434.00, Jim Anderson/Contact - Media, Iowa, Western Natural Gas, Alan Hersch/Contact - Media, Lincoln, Nebraska, Lynnette Wilson/VP - Communications, Investor Relations, Roger Kort/Contact - Media, Colorado, Beth A. Armstrong/VP, Chief Accounting Officer/$386,581.00, Lynn Fountain/VP - Risk Assessment, Audit Services, Tricia Harrod/VP - Strategic Sourcing, Al Butkus/VP - Media Relations, Curt Floerchinger/Contact - Media, Lawrence, Kansas, Bob McKeon/Contact - Media, Raytown, Missouri, Jon R. Empson/Sr. VP - Regulated Operations/$518,525.00 (**18 Officers included in Index**)
Directors: Richard C. Green/Chmn., CEO, Pres., Patrick J. Lynch/Dir., Michael M. Crow/Dir., Herman Cain/Dir., Heidi E. Hutter/Dir., Irvine O. Hockaday/Dir., Nicholas J. Singer/Dir., Stanley O. Ikenberry/Dir.
Owners: Patrick J. Lynch, Irvine O. Hockaday, Stanley O. Ikenberry, Christopher M. Reitz, Insiders, Richard C. Green, Beth A. Armstrong, Horizon Asset Management, Inc./19.50%, GAMCO Investors, Inc./6.30%, Herman Cain, Michael M. Crow, Nicholas J. Singer, Heidi E. Hutter, Advisory Research, Inc./5.60%, Leo E. Morton (**16 Owners included in Index**)
Financial Data: Fiscal Year End:12/31 **Latest Annual Data:** 12/31/2006

Year	Sales	Net Income
2006	$1,369,600,000	$23,900,000
2005	$1,314,200,000	-$230,000,000
2004	$1,711,000,000	-$292,500,000

Curr. Assets:	$874,000,000	**Curr. Liab.:**	$501,700,000		
Plant, Equip.:	$1,955,300,000	**Total Liab.:**	$2,166,300,000	**Indic. Yr. Divd.:**	NA
Total Assets:	$3,472,400,000	**Net Worth:**	$1,306,100,000	**Debt/ Equity:**	NA

Arabian American Development Co

10830 N Central Expwy., Ste. 175, Dallas, TX, 75231; *PH:* 1-214-692-7872; *Fax:* 1-214-692-7874; *http://* www.jm.se

General - Incorporation	DE	**Stock**- Price on:12/24/2007	$6.01
Employees	130	Stock Exchange	OTC
Auditor	Moore Stephens Travis Wolff LLP	Ticker Symbol	ARSD
Stk Agt	NA	Outstanding Shares	22,900,000
Counsel	NA	E.P.S.	$0.40
DUNS No.	04-667-0634	Shareholders	NA

Business: The group's principal activities are to refine specialty petrochemical products and develop mineral properties in the United States, saudi arabia and Mexico. The group operates in two business segments: specialty petrochemicals and mining. The specialty petrochemicals segment activities are mainly conducted through its wholly owned subsidiary, American shield refining company, which owns and operates specialty petrochemical products refinery near silsbee, Texas, which manufactures pentanes. The specialty petrochemical refinery in Mexico produces high purity solvents that are used in the expandable polystyrene and polystyrene foam industries. The refining segment sells its products and services to companies in the chemical and plastics industries. Mining segment includes exploration and development works in the al masane area in saudi arabia.

Primary SIC and add'l.: 2911 1081

CIK No: 0000007039

Subsidiaries: American Shield Refining Company

Officers: Johan Skoglund/Dir., CEO, Pres., Hatem El-Khalidi/83/Dir., CEO, Pres./$80,000.00, Urban Lilja/Head - Legal Affairs, Development, Claes Magnus Akesson/CFO, Group Staff Finance, Treasury, Karin Ljuden/Head - Corporate Communications, Jonatan Sundelin/Dir., Employee Representative, Peter Skogert/Dir., Employee Representative, Johan Wegin/Dir., Employee Representative, Nicholas N. Carter/61/Dir., Sec., Treasurer/$291,038.00, Lennart Henriz/Head - Operations Development, Quality, Environment, Information Technology, Zdravko Markovski/Head - JM Residential Stockholm, JM Production, Sten Hamberg/Head - JM Residential Stockholm, JM Production, Soren Bergstrom/Head - JM Residential Sweden, Head - Purchasing, Thor Olaf Askjer/Head - JM Residential Norway, Anders Wahrer/Head - JM Residential oresund (*17 Officers included in Index*)

Directors: Johan Skoglund/Dir., CEO, Pres., Hatem El-Khalidi/83/Dir., CEO, Pres., John A. Crichton/91/Chmn., Nicholas N. Carter/61/Dir., Sec., Treasurer, Elisabet Annell/Dir., Berthold Lindqvist/Dir., Torbjorn Torell/Dir., Bengt Larsson/Dir., Eva-Britt Gustafsson/Dir., Johan Wegin/Dir., Employee Representative, Jonatan Sundelin/Dir., Employee Representative, Peter Skogert/Dir., Employee Representative, Stefan Broden/Dir., Employee Representative, Asa Soderstrom Jerring/Dir., Robert E. Kennedy/64/Dir. (*17 Directors included in Index*)

Owners: Mohammad Salem ben Mahfouz c/o National Commercial Bank/6.44%, Hatem El-Khalidi/2.04%, Insiders/3.30%, Ghazi Sultan, Harb S. Al Zuhair/6.12%, Nicholas N. Carter/0.29%, Prince Talal Bin Abdul Aziz/5.47%, John A. Crichton/0.01%, Fahad Mohammed Saleh Al-Athel c/o Saudi Fal/15.52%

Financial Data: *Fiscal Year End:*12/31 **Latest Annual Data:** 12/31/2006

Year	Sales		Net Income
2006	$98,502,000		$7,875,000
2005	$80,374,000		$16,636,000
2004	$59,793,000		-$2,551,000
Curr. Assets:	$18,538,000	**Curr. Liab.:** $18,756,000	**P/E Ratio:** 13.98
Plant, Equip.:	$11,711,000	**Total Liab.:** $26,025,000	**Indic. Yr. Divd.:** NA
Total Assets:	$71,590,000	**Net Worth:** $44,747,000	**Debt/ Equity:** 0.0626

Aracruz Celulose

16300 NE 19th Ave., Ste. 210, North Miami Beach, FL, 33162; *PH:* 1-305-940-9762; *Fax:* 1-305-940-9763; *http://* www.aracruz.com.br; *Email:* aracruz@aracruz.com.br

General - Incorporation	Brazil	**Stock**- Price on:12/24/2007	$66.1
Employees	2,361	Stock Exchange	NYSE
Auditor	PricewaterhouseCoopers LLP	Ticker Symbol	ARA
Stk Agt	Bank of New York	Outstanding Shares	103,060,000
Counsel	Citigate Dewe Rogerson	E.P.S.	$6.39
DUNS No.	90-063-6572	Shareholders	NA

Business: The group's principal activities are the production, distribution and export of bleached eucalyptus, high-grade hardwood and eucalyptus pulp and other related activities. The group's products are mainly used in the manufacture of products such as tissue and high-quality printing, writing and specialty papers.the group has distributors in Italy, Spain, Belgium, Holland, luxembourg, scandinavia and France.

Primary SIC and add'l.: 0851 2611 2449 2631 2499 2621

CIK No: 0000883952

Subsidiaries: Aracruz Produtos de Madeira S.A

Officers: Carlos Augusto Lira/62/CEO, Carlos Augusto Lira Aguiar/63/CEO, Denys Ferrez/Mgr. - Investor Relations, Andre Goncalves/Investor Relations Specialist, Carmela Marcia Goncalves/Investor Relations Assist., Walter Lidio Nunes/59/Executive Officer, Isac Roffe Zagury/57/Officer, Joao Felipe Carsalade/54/Officer

Directors: Isaac Selim Sutton/Alternate Member to The Chmn., Carlos Alberto Vieira/74/Chmn., Ernane Galveas/86/Dir., Jorge Eduardo Martins Moraes/Dir., Nelson Koichi Shimada/54/Dir., Sandra Meira Starling/63/Dir., Mauro Agonilha/Dir., Alexandre S. D'Ambrosio/46/Dir., Joao Carlos Chede/74/Dir., Luiz Aranha Correa Do Lago/58/Dir., Eliezer Batista Da Silva/84/Dir., Haakon Lorentzen/54/Dir., Raul Calfat/56/Dir., alvaro Luis Veloso/44/Dir.

Owners: Arainvest Participaes S/A, BNDES Participaes S.A, Newark Finance Inc., Treasure Hold Investments/10.80%, BNDES Participaes S.A/26.30%, BNDES Participaes S.A/5.60%, Arapar S.A., Arainvest Participaes S/A/72.90%

Financial Data: *Fiscal Year End:*12/31 **Latest Annual Data:** 12/31/2006

Year	Sales		Net Income
2006	$1,680,833,000		$455,317,000
2005	$1,345,233,000		$341,098,000
2004	$1,167,113,000		$227,237,000
Curr. Assets:	$1,200,924,000	**Curr. Liab.:** $286,819,000	
Plant, Equip.:	$2,151,212,000	**Total Liab.:** $1,793,505,000	**Indic. Yr. Divd.:** $1.770
Total Assets:	$3,995,928,000	**Net Worth:** $2,202,423,000	**Debt/ Equity:** NA

Aradigm Corp

3929 Point Eden Way, Hayward, CA, 94545; *PH:* 1-510-265-9000; *Fax:* 1-510-265-0277; *http://* www.aradigm.com; *Email:* investor@aradigm.com

General - Incorporation	CA	**Stock**- Price on:12/24/2007	$1
Employees	NA	Stock Exchange	OTC
Auditor	Ernst & Young LLP	Ticker Symbol	ARDM
Stk Agt	Aradigm Corp	Outstanding Shares	NA
Counsel	Cooley Godward LLP	E.P.S.	NA
DUNS No.	79-299-8783	Shareholders	NA

Business: The group's principal activity is to develop advanced needle-free drug delivery systems for the treatment of lung and systemic diseases. The group's hand-held aerx platform is being designed for reproducible delivery of pharmaceutical drugs and biotech compounds via pulmonary delivery or through the lung. The pen-sized needle-free subcutaneous intraject system is designed to deliver drugs to the subcutaneous region of the skin where it can gain access to the bloodstream. Aerx and intraject systems perform equivalent to injection will be alternative to injection-based drug delivery. During the year 2003, the group acquired selected assets of weston medical.

Primary SIC and add'l.: 2834 3842

CIK No: 0001013238

Officers: Igor Gonda/Dir., CEO, Pres./$375,841.00, Babatunde A. Otulana/Dir., Sr. VP - Development/$538,689.00

Directors: Igor Gonda/Dir., CEO, Pres., Virgil D. Thompson/Chmn., Stephen O. Jaeger/Dir., Peter R. Byron/Member - Scientific Advisory Board, Peter S. Creticos/Member - Scientific Advisory Board, Stephen J. Farr/Member - Scientific Advisory Board, Babatunde A. Otulana/Dir., Sr. VP - Development, Frank H. Barker/Dir., John M. Siebert/Dir., Phyllis Gardner/Member - Scientific Advisory Board, Michael Konstan/Member - Scientific Advisory Board, Michael Powell/Member - Scientific Advisory Board, Adam Wanner/Member - Scientific Advisory Board, Martin Wasserman/Member - Scientific Advisory Board

Owners: V. Bryan Lawlis, Insiders/1.20%, Stephen J. Farr, Igor Gonda, Thomas C. Chesterman, Frank H. Barker, Stephen O. Jaeger, Kevin C. Tang/11.60%, Virgil D. Thompson, Deerfield Capital, L.P./6.10%, RA Capital Management, LLC/11.90%, Wellington Management Company LLP/11.90%, John M. Siebert, Babatunde A. Otulana, Highbridge International LLC/8.00%

Aradyme Corp

677 E 700 S, Ste 201, American Fork, UT, 84003; *PH:* 1-801-705-5000; *http://* www.aradyme.com; *Email:* info@aradyme.com

General - Incorporation	DE	**Stock**- Price on:12/24/2007	NA
Employees	33	Stock Exchange	OTC
Auditor	HJ & Assoc. LLC	Ticker Symbol	ADYE
Stk Agt	Colonial Stock Transfer Co Inc	Outstanding Shares	NA
Counsel	NA	E.P.S.	-$0.039
DUNS No.	NA	Shareholders	NA

Business: The group's principal activities are to develop, manufacture, market and distribute computer database management software, based on a proprietary technology that is being acquired. On 31-Mar-2003, the group completed reorganization with aradyme development corporation which is accounted as a reverse acquisition. Prior to Mar 2003, the group was a holding company for svetlana aviation, inc., through which it operated a charter airline business. As a result of the reorganization, the group discontinued the operations of its wholly-owned subsidiary, svetlana aviation, inc. The group is in development stage.

Primary SIC and add'l.: 7372 7373

CIK No: 0001123580

Subsidiaries: Aradyme Development Corporation

Officers: James R. Spencer/Chmn., CEO, Merwin D. Rasmussen/Vice Chmn., Corp. Sec., Rick Louder/COO, VP - Sales, Marketing

Directors: James R. Spencer/Chmn., CEO, Merwin D. Rasmussen/Vice Chmn., Corp. Sec.

Owners: Merwin D . Rasmussen/31.30%, James R . Spencer/4.00%, A. Mayfield, Lynn Rob Ledbetter/11.80%, Kirk L . Tanner/4.00%, Insiders/35.70%

Financial Data: *Fiscal Year End:*09/30 **Latest Annual Data:** 09/30/2006

Year	Sales		Net Income
2006	$816,000		-$2,748,000
2005	$1,130,000		-$2,333,000
2004	$57,000		-$1,801,000
Curr. Assets:	$204,000	**Curr. Liab.:** $1,596,000	
Plant, Equip.:	$127,000	**Total Liab.:** $1,596,000	**Indic. Yr. Divd.:** NA
Total Assets:	$442,000	**Net Worth:** -$1,154,000	**Debt/ Equity:** NA

Aramark Corp

Aramark Tower, 1101 Market St., Philadelphia, PA, 19107; *PH:* 1-215-238-3000; *http://* www.aramark.com

General - Incorporation	DE	**Stock**- Price on:12/24/2007	NA
Employees	160,000	Stock Exchange	NA
Auditor	KPMG LLP	Ticker Symbol	NA
Stk Agt	Mellon Investor Services LLC	Outstanding Shares	NA
Counsel	Simpson Thacher & Bartlett LLP	E.P.S.	NA
DUNS No.	00-791-3098	Shareholders	NA

Business: The groups principle activity is to provide award-winning food, hospitality, and facility management services. Customers served by the group include health care, sports and entertainment, and park and resorts. The group operates from United States.

Primary SIC and add'l.: 5812 2389 8351

CIK No: 0001144528

Subsidiaries: 933291 N.w.t. Ltd., AAMARK India Holdings LLC, Addison Concessions, Inc., AIM Services Co. Ltd., American Snack& Beverage, Inc., ARA Catering and Vending Services Limited, ARA Coffee Club Limited, ARA Coffee System Limited, ARA Food Services Limited, ARA Marketing Services Limited, ARA Offshore Service Limited, ARAKOR Co. Ltd., Aramark (asia) Pte Limited, Aramark (bvi) Limited, ARAMARK Airport Services Limited 242 Subsidiaries included in the Index

Officers: Joseph L. Neubauer/Chmn., CEO, Lynn B. McKee/Exec. VP - Human Resources, Timothy P. Cost/Exec. VP - Corporate Affairs, Bart J. Colli/Exec. VP, General Counsel, Sec., Debbie Albert/Corporate, General Media Inquiries, Kristine Grow/Contact - Refreshment Services, Greg

Healy/Contact - Sports, Entertainment, David Gargione/Contact - Corporate, General Media, Doug Warner/Contact - Culinary, Chris Collom/Contact - Healthcare, Ravi K. Saligram/Exec. VP, Andrew C. Kerin/Exec. VP, Frederick L. Sutherland/CFO, Exec. VP, Karen Cutler/Contact - Education, Leanne Scott Brown/Contact - Education *(18 Officers included in Index)*

Directors: Joseph L. Neubauer/Chmn., CEO, James E. Preston/Dir., Ronald L. Sargent/Dir., Karl M. Von Der Heyden/Dir., Ronald R. Davenport/Dir., James E. Ksansnak/Dir., Thomas H. Kean/Dir., Lawrence T. Babbio/Dir., Patricia C. Barron/Dir., Leonard S. Coleman/Dir.

Owners: Frederick L. Sutherland/1.60%, Joseph Neubauer/42.90%, Karl M. von der Heyden, Bruce C. Lindsay/3.40%, Joseph Neubauer/16.20%, Ravi K. Saligram, Thomas J. Vozzo, Ronald L. Sargent, Insiders/20.70%, Thomas H. Kean, Bart J. Colli, Karl M. von der Heyden, Wachovia Corporation/6.40%, Lawrence T. Babbio, Thomas J. Vozzo *(44 Owners included in Index)*

Arauco & Constitution Pulp Inc

Avenida El Golf 150, 14th Fl., Las Condes, Santiago; ***PH:*** 56-24617200; ***http://*** www.arauco.cl; ***Email:*** investor_relations@arauco.cl

General		Stock	
Incorporation	Chile	Price on:12/24/2007	NA
Employees	NA	Stock Exchange	NA
Auditor	PricewaterhouseCoopers LLP	Ticker Symbol	NA
Stk Agt	NA	Outstanding Shares	NA
Counsel	NA	E.P.S	NA
DUNS No.	NA	Shareholders	NA

Business: The group's principle activity is to own forest plantations, exports forestry and wood products; and produce bleached and unbleached softwood kraft pulp in Chile. The group operates from United States.

Primary SIC and add'l.: 2611 0811

CIK No: 0001004156

Subsidiaries: Agenciamiento y Servicios Profesionales S.A., Alto Paran S.A., Arauco Denmark ApS, Arauco Distribucin S.A., Arauco Ecuador S.A., Arauco Europe S.A., Arauco Forest Brasil S.A., Arauco Forest Products B.V., Arauco Generacin S.A., Arauco Honduras S. De R.L. de C.V., Arauco Internacional S.A., Arauco Per S.A., Arauco Wood Products, Inc., Araucomex S.A. de C.V., Aserraderos Arauco S.A. 42 Subsidiaries included in the Index

Officers: Matias Domeyko/CEO, Pres., Charles Kimber/Corporate Affairs, Marketing Dir., Gianfranco Truffello/CFO, Mario Urrutia/Dir. - Nueva Aldea Project, Robinson Tajmuch/Dir., Controller, Hernan Arriagada/Dir. - Engineering, Construction, Alvaro Saavedra/Dir. - Forestry Area Managing, Antonio Luque/Dir. - Sawntimber Area Managing, Pablo Mainardi/Dir. - Brazil Managing, Juan Pablo Guzman/Dir. - Administration, Mauricio Pinto/Dir. - Human Resources

Directors: Roberto Angelini/Vice Chmn., Jose Tomas Guzman/79/Chmn., Timothy C. Purcell/Dir., Anacleto Angelini/Dir., Jorge Garnham/Dir. - Woodpulp Area Managing, Cristian Infante/Dir. - Argentina Managing, Alberto Etchegaray/Dir., Manuel Enrique Bezanilla/Dir., Carlos Croxatto/Dir., Jorge Bunster/Dir., Jorge Andueza/Dir.

Owners: Empresas Copec/99.98%

Arbinet-thexchange Inc

120 Albany St., Tower II, Ste. 450, New Brunswick, NJ, 08901; ***PH:*** 1-732-509-9100; ***Fax:*** 1-732-509-9101; ***http://*** www.arbinet.com; ***Email:*** ir@arbinet.com

General		Stock	
Incorporation	DE	Price on:12/24/2007	$5.67
Employees	137	Stock Exchange	NDQ
Auditor	Ernst & Young LLP	Ticker Symbol	ARBX
Stk Agt	Registrar & Transfer Co	Outstanding Shares	25,740,000
Counsel	NA	E.P.S	-$0.02
DUNS No.	NA	Shareholders	NA

Business: The groups principle activity is to provide electronic market for trading, routing and settling communications capacity. The groups services include Voice, Internet Exchange and Music and Video Rights, Licensing and Distribution. The group products sold under the trade names PrimeVoice(SM), SelectVoice(SM), rightsrouter(R), PrimeIP(SM), RapidClear(SM) and Optimize dip(SM). The group operates from the United States. The group's quarterly revenue for September 2007 was 129.24 millions of USD.

Primary SIC and add'l.: 6231 4899 7389 6289

CIK No: 0001136655

Subsidiaries: ANIP, Inc., Arbinet Communications, Inc., Arbinet Digital Media Corporation, Arbinet ETE Corporation, Arbinet Services, Inc., Arbinet-thexchange HK Limited, Arbinet-thexchange LTD, Bell Fax, Inc., Broad Street Digital Limited

Officers: Roger H. Moore/CEO, John H. Chapel/Sr. VP - Trading, Steven Heap/CTO, John Wynne/CFO/$202,788.00, William Terrell Wingfield/General Counsel/$148,206.00, Peter P. Sach/CIO, Sr. VP - Operations/$444,586.00, Robert A. Barbiere/Sr. VP - Product Marketing, COO Digital Media

Directors: Robert C. Atkinson/Chmn., Michael J. Donahue/Dir., Alex Mashinsky/Dir., John B. Penney/Dir., Michael J. Ruane/Dir., Stanley Kreitman/Dir., Shawn F. ODonnell/Dir.

Owners: Chi K. Eng, John B. Penney, Michael J. Ruane, Peter F. Pastorelle, AMVESCAP PLC and related entities/13.61%, Peter P. Sach, Roger H. Moore, Curt J. Hockemeier/4.80%, Terrell W. Wingfield, Lampe, Conway& Co., LLC and related entities/5.10%, Jill Thoerle, J.P. Morgan SBIC LLC/1.28%, Robert C. Atkinson, Insiders/7.83%, Sixty Wall Street SBIC Fund L.P./0.33% *(22 Owners included in Index)*

Financial Data: *Fiscal Year End:*12/31 *Latest Annual Data:* 12/31/2006

Year	Sales	Net Income
2006	$542,979,000	-$388,000
2005	$530,455,000	$9,675,000
2004	$519,966,000	$7,865,000

Curr. Assets:	$99,812,000	**Curr. Liab.:**	$42,331,000	**P/E Ratio:**	29.19
Plant, Equip.:	$23,828,000	**Total Liab.:**	$45,591,000	**Indic. Yr. Divd.:**	NA
Total Assets:	$132,522,000	**Net Worth:**	$86,931,000	**Debt/ Equity:**	NA

Arbios Systems Inc

1050 Winter St. Ste. 1000, Waltham, MA, 02154; ***PH:*** 1-781-839-7292; ***Fax:*** 1-781-839-7295; ***http://*** www.arbios.com

General		Stock	
Incorporation	NV	Price on:12/24/2007	$0.88
Employees	6	Stock Exchange	OTC
Auditor	KPMG LLP	Ticker Symbol	ABOS
Stk Agt	Nevada Agency & Trust Company	Outstanding Shares	25,140,000
Counsel	NA	E.P.S	-$0.3
DUNS No.	NA	Shareholders	NA

Business: The groups principle activity is to provide medical devices and cell based therapies. The groups products include SEPET Liver Assist Device, and the HepatAssist(TM) Cell-Based Liver Support System. The group operates from United States.

Primary SIC and add'l.: NA

CIK No: 0001138862

Officers: Shawn P. Cain/CEO, Pres./$209,435.00, Walter C. Ogier/51/Dir., CEO, Pres./$307,980.00, Santiago J. Munoz/Member - Scientific Advisory Board, Scott L. Hayashi/CFO/$116,598.00, Jacek Rozga/Co - Founder, Chief Scientific Officer/$189,553.00, David J. Zeffren/51/VP - Product Development/$146,130.00

Directors: Walter C. Ogier/51/Dir., CEO, Pres., Dennis Kogod/Dir., Jack E. Stover/55/Dir., Amy Factor/Dir., Thomas C. Seoh/Dir., John M. Vierling/Dir., Thomas M. Tully/Dir., Jacek Rozga/Co - Founder, Chief Scientific Officer, Achilles A. Demetriou/Member - Scientific Advisory Board, Paul Martin/Member - Scientific Advisory Board, Hector J. Rodriguez/Member - Scientific Advisory Board, Philip Rosenthal/Member - Scientific Advisory Board, Robert S. Brown/Member - Scientific Advisory Board

Owners: Dennis Kogod, LibertyView Funds, LP/6.60%, Scott L. Hayashi, Walter C. Ogier/1.60%, Achilles A. Demetriou/9.90%, Thomas C. Seoh, Insiders/14.00%, David Zeffren, Thomas Tully, Gary Ballen/4.40%, Jack E. Stover, LibertyView Special Opportunities Fund, LP/9.60%, Neuberger Berman LLC/18.10%, Jacek Rozga/8.80%, Shawn Cain *(16 Owners included in Index)*

Financial Data: *Fiscal Year End:*12/31 *Latest Annual Data:* 12/31/2006

Year	Sales	Net Income
2006	NA	-$4,462,000
2005	NA	-$3,824,000
2004	$72,000	-$3,328,000

Curr. Assets:	$2,201,000	**Curr. Liab.:**	$442,000		
Plant, Equip.:	$73,000	**Total Liab.:**	$1,206,000	**Indic. Yr. Divd.:**	NA
Total Assets:	$2,490,000	**Net Worth:**	$1,284,000	**Debt/ Equity:**	NA

Arbitron Inc

142 W 57th St., New York, NY, 10019; ***PH:*** 1-212-887-1300; ***Fax:*** 1-212-887-1390; ***http://*** www.arbitron.com

General		Stock	
Incorporation	DE	Price on:12/24/2007	$49.72
Employees	1,045	Stock Exchange	NYSE
Auditor	KPMG LLP	Ticker Symbol	ARB
Stk Agt	Bank of New York	Outstanding Shares	29,930,000
Counsel	Hogan & Hartson LLP	E.P.S	$1.49
DUNS No.	00-625-5996	Shareholders	NA

Business: The group's principle activities are to provide media and market research information to radio, broadcast television, cable companies, advertising agencies and advertisers in the United States, Mexico and Europe. In addition, the group provides radio audience measurement and related services in the United States to approximately 4,400 radio stations and 2,500 advertising agencies and advertisers. The group also provides software applications, which provides its customers to access to the group's proprietary database. This enables customers to understand the information for sales, management and programming purposes. Further, the group also provides qualitative measurements of consumer demographics, retail behavior and media usage in approximately 177 local markets throughout the United States. The group's quarterly revenue for September 2007 was 96.52 millions of USD.

Primary SIC and add'l.: 7372 8732 7375

CIK No: 0000109758

Subsidiaries: Arbitron Holdings Inc., Arbitron International, LLC, Audience Research Bureau S.A. de C.V., Ceridian Infotech (India) Private Limited, CSW Research Limited, Euro Fieldwork Limited

Officers: Stephen B. Morris/Dir., CEO, Pres./$3,087,168.00, Dave Chilvers/Chmn. - Continental Research, UK, International, Brad Bedford/VP - International Sales, International, Clara P. Carneiro/VP - Sales, Marketing, Latin American Marketing, International, Scott Musgrave/Sr. VP - Client Software Business, US Media Services, Bill Rose/Sr. VP - Marketing, US Media Services, Jim Tobolski/VP - Sales, Advertiser, Agency Services, Carol Edwards/VP - Cable, Outdoor Services, Cable, Owen Charlebois/Pres. - Operations, Technology, Research, Development/$1,405,654.00, Kathleen T. Ross/Exec. VP, Chief Administrative Officer, Sean Creamer/Exec. VP - Finance, Planning, CFO/$845,427.00, Jay Guyther/Sr. VP - Ratings Services, Portable People Meter, PPM, Tom OSullivan/VP - Local Radio Sales, Radio Broadcasters, Bruce Supovitz/VP - National Radio Services, Radio Broadcasters, Brad Kelly/VP - Group Sales, Radio Broadcasters *(23 Officers included in Index)*

Directors: Stephen B. Morris/Dir., CEO, Pres., Lawrence Perlman/Chmn., Alan Aldworth/Dir., Shellye Archambeau/Dir., Larry E. Kittelberge/Dir., Philip Guarascio/Dir., Richard A. Post/Dir., Luis G. Nogales/Dir., David W. Devonshire/Dir., William T. Kerr/Dir.

Owners: Lawrence Perlman, Vaughan Scott Henry, Shellye L. Archambeau, Alan Aldworth, Insiders/3.81%, Stephen B. Morris/1.15%, Larry E. Kittelberger, Richard A. Post, Owen Charlebois, Sean R. Creamer, Luis G. Nogales, Pierre C. Bouvard, Erica Farber, Philip Guarascio

Financial Data: *Fiscal Year End:*12/31 *Latest Annual Data:* 12/31/2006

Year	Sales	Net Income
2006	$329,250,000	$50,658,000
2005	$309,955,000	$67,308,000
2004	$296,553,000	$60,565,000

Curr. Assets:	$105,545,000	**Curr. Liab.:**	$110,105,000	**P/E Ratio:**	33.37
Plant, Equip.:	$41,470,000	**Total Liab.:**	$121,064,000	**Indic. Yr. Divd.:**	$0.400
Total Assets:	$210,320,000	**Net Worth:**	$89,256,000	**Debt/ Equity:**	NA

Arbor EnTech Corp

PO Box 656, Tuxedo Pk., New York, PA, 10987; ***PH:*** 1-201-782-9237

General		Stock	
Incorporation	DE	Price on:12/24/2007	$2.05
Employees	NA	Stock Exchange	OTC
Auditor	Wolinetz, Lafazan & Company, P.C.	Ticker Symbol	ARBE
Stk Agt	Affiliated Stock Transfer Co.	Outstanding Shares	7,050,000
Counsel	NA	E.P.S	NA
DUNS No.	NA	Shareholders	NA

Business: The groups principal activities include production, wholesale and distribution of wood products. The group products include fireplace wood and garden stakes. The group operates from the United States.

Primary SIC and add'l.: 7389

CIK No: 0000710782

Owners: Rushmore Financial Services, Inc., Insiders, Mark Shefts

Curr. Assets:	$442,000	***Curr. Liab.:***	$9,000		
Plant, Equip.:	NA	***Total Liab.:***	$9,000	***Indic. Yr. Divd.:***	NA
Total Assets:	$442,000	***Net Worth:***	$433,000	***Debt/ Equity:***	NA

Arbor Realty Trust Inc

Formerly: Arbor Realty Trust

333 Earle Ovington Blvd., Ste. 900, Uniondale, NY, 11553; ***PH:*** 1-516-832-8002; *http://* www.arborrealtytrust.com

General - Incorporation .... MD	***Stock***- Price on:12/24/2007 ....$26.84
Employees 30	Stock Exchange............................. NYSE
Auditor .... Ernst & Young LLP	Ticker Symbol.................................. ABR
Stk Agt..... American Stock Transfer & Trust Co.	Outstanding Shares 17,350,000
Counsel...NA	E.P.S..$3.01
DUNS No. ....NA	Shareholders...NA

Business: The groups principle activity is to provide loans services. The groups services include residential mortgage loans and real estate loan. The group operates from the United States. The group's quarterly revenue for September 2007 was 70.47 millions of USD.

Primary SIC and add'l.: 6798

CIK No: 0001253986

Subsidiaries: 420 5thInvestor, LLC, AC Flushing, LLC, ACM Gateway LLC, ACM Lakeview, LLC, ANMB Holdings LLC, AR Prime Holdings LLC, Arbor Capital TrustI, Arbor Capital TrustII, Arbor Capital TrustIII, Arbor Capital TrustIV, Arbor Capital TrustV, Arbor Capital TrustVI, Arbor Capital TrustVII, Arbor Realty Collateral Management, LLC, Arbor Realty Funding, LLC 45 Subsidiaries included in the Index

Officers: Ivan Kaufman/Chmn., CEO, Pres., Walter K. Horn/Dir., Sec., Compliance Officer, General Counsel, Paul Elenio/CFO, Fred Weber/Exec. VP - Structured Finance, Gene Kilgore/Exec. VP - Structured Securitization, John Kovarik/Chief Credit Officer, Mark Fogel/Sr. VP - Asset Management, Ronald D. Gaither/Exec. VP

Directors: Ivan Kaufman/Chmn., CEO, Pres., Walter K. Horn/Dir., Sec., Compliance Officer, General Counsel, Joseph Martello/Dir., William Helmreich/Dir., Michael C. Kojaian/Dir., Melvin F. Lazar/Dir., Karen Edwards/Dir., Kyle Permut/Dir., Archie R. Dykes/Dir., John J. Bishar/58/Dir.

Owners: John J. Bishar, Walter K. Horn, Archie R. Dykes, Arbor Commercial Mortgage, LLC/20.60%, William Helmreich, Putnam LLC d/b/a Putnam Investments/5.50%, Kensington Investment Group, Inc/6.90%, Fred Weber, Gene Kilgore, Ivan Kaufman/20.70%, Karen K. Edwards, Michael C. Kojaian/5.80%, Kyle A. Permut, Paul Elenio, Melvin F. Lazar *(18 Owners included in Index)*

Financial Data: *Fiscal Year End:*12/31 ***Latest Annual Data:*** 12/31/2006

Year	Sales	Net Income
2006	$173,701,000	$50,414,000
2005	$121,607,000	$50,387,000
2004	$57,969,000	$25,073,000

Curr. Assets:	$92,529,000	***Curr. Liab.:***	$415,898,000	***P/E Ratio:***	8.92
Plant, Equip.:	NA	***Total Liab.:***	$1,908,234,000	***Indic. Yr. Divd.:***	$2.480
Total Assets:	$2,204,345,000	***Net Worth:***	$296,111,000	***Debt/ Equity:***	4.9517

ARC Corporate Realty Trust Inc

1401 Broad St., Clifton, NJ, 07013; ***PH:*** 1-973-249-1000; ***Fax:*** 1-973-249-1001; *http://* www2.arcproperties.com

General - Incorporation .... MD	***Stock***- Price on:12/24/2007 ....NA
Employees ....NA	Stock Exchange.....................................NA
Auditor .... KPMG LLP	Ticker Symbol......................................NA
Stk Agt..NA	Outstanding Shares ....NA
Counsel...NA	E.P.S...NA
DUNS No. ....NA	Shareholders...NA

Business: The group's principal activity is the acquisition of credit lease properties throughout the United States. Credit lease properties are general-purpose retail, office and industrial properties, each of which are 100% leased to one or more creditworthy tenants under a long-term lease that generally requires tenants to pay most or all of the operating costs of the property, including real estate taxes and insurance. As of December 31, 2004, the company had 29 leases with credit tenants in 22 properties encompassing 1,071,266 rentable square feet. The properties are 75% leased to retail tenants, 13% to office tenants and the remaining 12% to industrial or warehouse tenants. During 2004, it purchased two retail properties, including unconsolidated investments, totaling approximately 93,000 rent able square feet for $8,300,000.

Primary SIC and add'l.: 6798

CIK No: 0001230358

Subsidiaries: ACRT

Officers: Robert J. Ambrosi/57/Chmn., CEO, Pres., Marc Perel/Exec. VP, Claudia L. Graff/VP - Capital Markets, Joseph Morena/Exec. VP - Site Acquisitions, Gil Rivera/VP - Development, Bruse Nelson/CFO, Gary S. Baumann/Dir. - Construction, Michael R. Ambrosi/Real Estate Analyst

Directors: Robert J. Ambrosi/57/Chmn., CEO, Pres., James Steuterman/51/Dir., Richard G. Kelley/76/Dir., Garrett E. Sheehan/59/Dir., Dietmar Georg/53/Dir.

Owners: Mervin H. Goldman, Robert J. Ambrosi/1.00%, Claudia Graff, Joseph Morena, Bruce Nelson, Richard G. Kelley, Insiders/1.60%, Marc Perel

ARC Wireless Solutions Inc

10601 W 48th Ave., Wheat Ridge, CO, 80033; ***PH:*** 1-303-421-4063; ***Fax:*** 1-303-424-5085; *http://* www.arcwireless.net

General - Incorporation .... UT	***Stock***- Price on:12/24/2007 ....NA
Employees 111	Stock Exchange.................................NDQ
Auditor .... Hein & Assoc. LLP	Ticker Symbol.................................ARCW
Stk Agt...................... Computershare Trust Co	Outstanding Shares ....NA
Counsel...NA	E.P.S..-$0.32
DUNS No. 60-241-6869	Shareholders...NA

Business: The group's principal activities are to design, develop, manufacture and market diversified line of antennas and related wireless communication systems. The products include mobile antennas, cellular base station antennas, flat panel antennas, conformal antennas and multi-channel, multipoint distribution systems (mmds) antennas. These products are an alternative to the conventional wire type antenna and are used for numerous mobile applications. The group operates in three segments: wireless communication products, antenna manufacturing and cable products. The group markets its products directly to the distributors, installers and retailers of antenna accessories.

Primary SIC and add'l.: 3679 3663

CIK No: 0000826326

Subsidiaries: Starworks Wireless Inc., Winncom Technologies Corp

Officers: Randall P. Marx/55/CEO, Sec., Dir./$245,000.00, Monty R. Lamirato/52/CFO, Treasurer/$155,000.00, Steve C. Olson/51/CTO/$175,000.00

Directors: Randall P. Marx/55/CEO, Sec., Dir., Donald A. Huebner/62/Dir., Robert E. Wade/61/Dir., Sigmund A. Balaban/66/Dir.

Owners: Sigmund A. Balaban/1.10%, Randall P. Marx/5.40%, Insiders/9.80%, Donald A. Huebner, Paul J. Rini/9.60%, Steve C. Olson, Robert E. Wade/2.80%, Monty R. Lamirato, Evansville Limited/8.40%, Hudson River Investments, Inc./7.80%

Financial Data: *Fiscal Year End:*12/31 ***Latest Annual Data:*** 12/31/2006

Year	Sales	Net Income
2006	$6,470,000	-$742,000
2005	$39,657,000	$1,292,000
2004	$37,365,000	$688,000

Curr. Assets:	$17,544,000	***Curr. Liab.:***	$1,865,000		
Plant, Equip.:	$297,000	***Total Liab.:***	$1,888,000	***Indic. Yr. Divd.:***	NA
Total Assets:	$17,975,000	***Net Worth:***	$16,087,000	***Debt/ Equity:***	NA

Arcadia Resources Inc

26777 Central Pk. Blvd., Ste. 200, Southfield, MI, 48076; ***PH:*** 1-248-352-7530; ***Fax:*** 1-248-352-7534; *http://* www.arcadiaresourcesinc.com; ***Email:*** info@arcadiaservices.com

General - Incorporation .... NV	***Stock***- Price on:12/24/2007 ....NA
Employees ....NA	Stock Exchange...............................AMEX
Auditor .... BDO Seidman, LLP	Ticker Symbol..................................KAD
Stk Agt ....National City Bank	Outstanding Shares 110,630,000
Counsel............................ Kerr Russell & Weber	E.P.S..-$0.556
DUNS No. ....NA	Shareholders...NA

Business: The group operates through its subsidiaries whose principle activity is to provide home health care services and products. The group operates through three segments namely, services, products and retail. The group operates from the United States. The group's quarterly revenue for September 2007 was 38.72 millions of USD.

Primary SIC and add'l.: 3841 7363 3842 3845 3821 5047 8082 7361

CIK No: 1001071941

Subsidiaries: American Oxygen and Medical Equipment, Inc, Arcadia Employee Services, Inc., Arcadia Health Services of Michigan, Inc., Arcadia Health Services, Inc., Arcadia Healthcare Solutions, inc., Arcadia Home Health Care Services, Inc, Arcadia Home Health Products, Inc., Arcadia Home Oxygen & Medical Equipment, Inc., Arcadia Products, Inc., Arcadia Services, Inc., ASR Staffing, Inc., Beacon Respiratory Services of Alabama, Inc, Beacon Respiratory Services of Colorado, Inc., Beacon Respiratory Services of Georgia, Inc., Beacon Respiratory Services, Inc 25 Subsidiaries included in the Index

Officers: Tres Lund/47/Chmn., CEO, Marvin R. Richardson/CEO, Principal Executive Officer, Dir., Cathy Sparling/52/VP - Administration, Sharon Boughter/Transfer Agent, Krista Finkbeiner/Investor Relations, Peter Anthony Brusca/Physician, James E. Haifley/50/Exec. VP

Directors: John T. Thornton/Dir.

Owners: Timothy J. Araiza, Marjorie J. Hess, Roger Malkin, Edwin R. Bindseil, Health Care Partners, Inc, Edwin R. Bindseil, David Lerner, Jane E. Cosand, John E. Elliott, Lawrence R. Kuhnert, Sandgrain Securities, Inc, Stephen J. Garchick, John Thornton, Shajan Kiriyan Ninan, Hess J. Marjorie *(17 Owners included in Index)*

Financial Data: *Fiscal Year End:*03/31 ***Latest Annual Data:*** 03/31/2007

Year	Sales	Net Income
2007	$158,411,000	-$43,772,000
2005	$105,341,000	-$7,434,000
2003	$5,446,000	-$4,012,000

Curr. Assets:	$48,000	***Curr. Liab.:***	$188,000		
Plant, Equip.:	$7,000	***Total Liab.:***	$188,000	***Indic. Yr. Divd.:***	NA
Total Assets:	$166,000	***Net Worth:***	-$22,000	***Debt/ Equity:***	0.2011

Arcadis

Nieuwe Sta.sstraat 10, Arnhem; ; *http://* www.arcadis.nl; ***Email:*** info@arcadis.nl

General - Incorporation .... Netherlands	***Stock***- Price on:12/24/2007 ....NA
Employees 9,143	Stock Exchange.....................................NA
Auditor .... KPMG Accountants N.V	Ticker Symbol......................................NA
Stk Agt .... Bank of New York	Outstanding Shares ....NA
Counsel........... Schut & Grosheide, Alston & Bird	E.P.S...NA
DUNS No. 40-389-6368	Shareholders...NA

Business: The group's principal activities are to provide engineering and consulting services. The group operates through four sectors: infrastructure, environment building and communications. Infrastructure segment develops new residential area and business parks, redevelopment of inner-city locations, railways, roads, ports and airports. Environment segment, helps clients turn polluted sites into property with development opportunity. Buildings segment builds offices, manufacturing facilities, government buildings and new living spaces. Communications segment helps in the construction of telecommunication networks, including wireless telecommunication and e-business services. The group has its operates in the Netherlands, rest of Europe, north and South America.

Primary SIC and add'l.: 8741 8742 8711 8713

CIK No: 0000913596

Subsidiaries: ACD Vermessung GmbH, Adviseurs Bouwplan Ontwikkeling BGN Partners B.V., Afid Consultants Sarl, ARCADIS ENERGY Y Associados, SA (Consortium), Arcadis Aqumen Facility Management B.v., ARCADIS Asia B.V., ARCADIS Bauconsult GmbH, ARCADIS Belgium N.V., Arcadis Bmb Management Consultants B.v., ARCADIS Bonaire N.V., ARCADIS Bouw en Vastgoed B.V., ARCADIS Brasil Ltda, ARCADIS Capital,Inc., ARCADIS Caribbean N.V., ARCADIS Cert GmbH 229 Subsidiaries included in the Index

Officers: Uli Behr/56/CEO - Arcadis Germany, Steven B. Blake/52/CEO - Arcadis US, Robert K. Goldman/51/CEO - Arcadis Deutschland Gmbh, Marek Adamek/48/CEO - Arcadis Polska, Yann Leblais/56/CEO - Arcadis FCI, Antonio Rocha/67/CEO - Arcadis Logos, Leo Van Der Kemp/52/MD - PRC BV, Peter Vince/50/MD - AYH, Anja M. Van Bergen/47/Company Sec., Friedrich M.T. Schneider/46/Member - Exec. Board, Michiel C. Jaski/49/Member - Exec. Board, Ben A. Van Der Klift/49/CFO, Hans Van Dord/64/Dir. - Business Development, Craig E. Eisen/57/Dir. - Mergers, Acquisitions, Ludo Smans/61/MD - Arcadis Belgium *(19 Officers included in Index)*

Directors: Harrie L.J. Noy/57/Chmn., Gerrit Ybema/63/Member - Supervisory Board, Jan Peelen/68/Member - Supervisory Board, Thomas M. Cohn/66/Member - Supervisory Board, Carlos Espinosa De Los Monteros/64/Member - Supervisory Board, George R. Nethercutt/64/Member - Supervisory Board, Rijnhard W.F. Van Tets/61/Member - Supervisory Board

Owners: Harrie L.J. Noy, Ross A. Webber, Michiel C. Jaski, Ben A. van der Klift

Financial Data: ***Fiscal Year End:***12/31 ***Latest Annual Data:*** 12/31/2006

Year	Sales	Net Income
2006	$1,105,698,000	$61,269,000
2005	$832,929,000	$33,298,000
2004	$1,229,026,000	$20,522,000

Curr. Assets:	$662,479,000	***Curr. Liab.:***	$488,842,000		
Plant, Equip.:	$72,624,000	***Total Liab.:***	$722,982,000	***Indic. Yr. Divd.:***	NA
Total Assets:	$972,361,000	***Net Worth:***	$249,380,000	***Debt/ Equity:***	NA

Arch Capital Group Ltd

Arch Reinsurance Company, 360 Mt. Kemble Ave., Morristown, NJ, 07962; ***PH:*** 1-973-898-9575; ***Fax:*** 1-973-898-9570; ***http://*** www.archcapgroup.com

General - Incorporation	Bermuda	***Stock***- Price on:12/24/2007	$69.4
Employees	1,100	Stock Exchange	NDQ
Auditor	PricewaterhouseCoopers LLP	Ticker Symbol	NA
Stk Agt	American Stock Transfer & Trust Co.	Outstanding Shares	73,640,000
Counsel	Conyers Dill & Pearman	E.P.S	$11.13
DUNS No.	NA	Shareholders	NA

Business: The group's principal activity is the provision of property and casualty insurance and reinsurance. The group also conducts insurance advisory and other businesses through there subsidiaries. The group operates under two segments: reinsurance and insurance. The reinsurance segment primary focus is to write significant portions of business on a select number of specialty property and casualty treaties. This includes property catastrophe reinsurance, other property business, casualty, other specialty business, marine, aviation and space, casualty clash and non-traditional business the insurance segment consists of the group's insurance underwriting subsidiaries, which primarily write on a direct basis. The insurance segment consists of six profit centers, including property, casualty, executive assurance, healthcare, professional liability insurance and program business. On 23-Jun-2003, the group acquired western diversified.

Primary SIC and add'l.: 6331 6719

CIK No: 0000947484

Subsidiaries: Alternative Insurance Company Limited, Alternative Re Holdings Ltd., Alternative Re, Ltd., Arch Capital Group (U.S.) Inc., Arch Capital Services Inc., Arch Excess& Surplus Insurance Company, Arch Insurance Company, Arch Insurance Company (Europe) Limited, Arch Insurance Group Inc., Arch Reinsurance Company, Arch Reinsurance Ltd., Arch Risk Transfer Services Ltd., Arch Specialty Insurance Company, Western Diversified Casualty Insurance Company

Officers: Constantine Iordanou/Dir., CEO, Pres./$10,084,820.00, Marc Grandisson/Chmn., CEO - Arch Worldwide Reinsurance Group/$3,940,179.00, Ralph E. Jones/51/Chmn., CEO - Arch Worldwide Insurance Group/$2,022,636.00, Nicolas Papadopoulo/45/CEO, Pres. - Arch Re, Bermuda, Preston W. Hutchings/Chief Investment Officer, Sr. VP/$1,623,989.00, Mark C. Gillen/Dir. - Information Technology, Reinsurance, Arch Capital Services Inc, Louis T. Petrillo/Pres., General Counsel - Arch Capital Services Inc, John D. Vollaro/CFO, Exec. VP/$2,217,291.00, William Hitter/Sr. VP, Dir. - Internal Audit Services, Arch Capital Services, Jennifer Mangino/Sr. VP - Arch Capital Services Inc, Debra M. O'Connor/CFO, VP - Arch Capital Services Inc, Donald Watson/Exec. VP - Financial Services, Arch Capital Services, Dawna Ferguson/Sec.

Directors: Ralph E. Jones/51/Chmn., CEO - Arch Worldwide Insurance Group, Constantine Iordanou/Dir., CEO, Pres., Marc Grandisson/Chmn., CEO - Arch Worldwide Reinsurance Group, Paul B. Ingrey/Chmn., John M. Pasquesi/Vice Chmn., James J. Meenaghan/Dir., Robert F. Works/Dir., Wolfe H. Bragin/Dir., John L. Bunce/Dir., Kewsong Lee/Dir., Sean Carney/Dir., Jeffrey A. Goldstein/52/Dir.

Owners: Robert F. Works, Constantine Iordanou/1.10%, James J. Meenaghan, Sean D. Carney/25.60%, Kewsong Lee/25.60%, Paul B. Ingrey, Jeffrey A. Goldstein, Warburg Pincus/25.60%, Baron Capital Group,Inc./5.50%, John D. Vollaro, John L. Bunce, John M. Pasquesi/2.10%, Insiders/29.70%, H&F Corporate Investors IV (Bermuda), Ltd./6.30%, Wolfe H. Bragin *(18 Owners included in Index)*

Financial Data: ***Fiscal Year End:***12/31 ***Latest Annual Data:*** 12/31/2006

Year	Sales	Net Income
2006	$3,452,678,000	$713,214,000
2005	$3,167,529,000	$256,486,000
2004	$3,104,050,000	$316,899,000

Curr. Assets:	$5,333,049,000	***Curr. Liab.:***	$764,895,000		
Plant, Equip.:	NA	***Total Liab.:***	$10,721,848,000	***Indic. Yr. Divd.:***	NA
Total Assets:	$14,312,467,000	***Net Worth:***	$3,590,619,000	***Debt/ Equity:***	0.3859

Arch Chemicals Inc

501 Merritt 7, Norwalk, CT, 06851; ***PH:*** 1-203-229-2900; ***Fax:*** 1-203-229-3652; ***http://*** www.archchemicals.com

General - Incorporation	VA	***Stock***- Price on:12/24/2007	$35.36
Employees	2,640	Stock Exchange	NYSE
Auditor	KPMG LLP	Ticker Symbol	ARJ
Stk Agt	Bank of New York	Outstanding Shares	24,310,000
Counsel	NA	E.P.S	-$0.14
DUNS No.	NA	Shareholders	NA

Business: The group's principal activities are to manufacture specialty chemicals and to supply value added products and services. These products and services are provided to several industries on a worldwide basis, including the consumer products and the semiconductor industries. The group's principal business segments are microelectronic materials, treatment products, performance products and other specialty products. The group's major customers include semiconductor manufacturers, flat panel display manufacturers, world-renowned consumer product companies, furniture manufacturers, national and regional chemical and equipment distributors, treaters of softwood, sawmills, other chemical manufacturers and the United States government. The group's major brands are wolman(R), dricon(R), tanalith(R), vacsol(R), and resistol(r). On Apr 2, 2004 the group acquired avecia's pool & spa and protection & hygiene businesses.

Primary SIC and add'l.: 2869 2899 2819

CIK No: 0001072343

Subsidiaries: Arch Acquisition, LLC, Arch Asia Holdings, Ltd., Arch Chemicals (Hong Kong) Limited, Arch Chemicals (Suzhou) Co., Ltd., Arch Chemicals B.V., Arch Chemicals California Holdings, Inc., Arch Chemicals Canada, Inc., Arch Chemicals Coatings Singapore Pte Ltd, Arch Chemicals Far East, Limited, Arch Chemicals GmbH, Arch Chemicals Holdings, Inc., Arch Chemicals Japan, Inc., Arch Chemicals Limited, Arch Chemicals Receivables Corp., Arch Chemicals S.A. 54 Subsidiaries included in the Index

Officers: Michael E. Campbell/60/Chmn., CEO, Pres./$3,993,093.00, Steven C. Giuliano/CFO, VP, Sarah A. O'Connor/VP, General Counsel, Corp. Sec./$945,135.00, Louis S. Massimo/COO, Exec. VP/$1,566,539.00, Hayes Anderson/VP - Human Resources/$928,749.00, Mark E. Faford/Dir. - Investor Relations, Communications, Peggy N. Geimer/Corporate Medical Dir., Ross A. Barnes/Corporate Security Officer

Directors: Michael E. Campbell/60/Chmn., CEO, Pres., John P. Schaefer/72/Dir., Daniel S. Sanders/68/Dir., Richard E. Cavanagh/61/Dir., Janice J. Teal/55/Dir., Michael O. Magdol/70/Dir., David Lilley/Dir., William H. Powell/Dir., Douglas J. Wetmore/Dir.

Owners: Hayes Anderson, Snyder Capital Management, L.P./6.90%, Michael E. Campbell/1.40%, Dimensional Fund Advisors LP/5.60%, Daniel S. Sanders, William H. Lichtenberger, Sarah A. OConnor, Barclays Global Investors, NA/5.00%, Louis S. Massimo, Insiders/2.90%, T. Rowe Price Associates, Inc./11.60%, Janice J. Teal, Michael O. Magdol, John P. Schaefer, Richard E. Cavanagh *(16 Owners included in Index)*

Financial Data: ***Fiscal Year End:***12/31 ***Latest Annual Data:*** 12/31/2006

Year	Sales	Net Income
2006	$1,434,700,000	$14,200,000
2005	$1,305,100,000	$40,500,000
2004	$1,120,900,000	$19,900,000

Curr. Assets:	$511,100,000	***Curr. Liab.:***	$430,600,000	***P/E Ratio:***	52.78
Plant, Equip.:	$193,200,000	***Total Liab.:***	$783,400,000	***Indic. Yr. Divd.:***	$0.800
Total Assets:	$1,149,600,000	***Net Worth:***	$366,200,000	***Debt/ Equity:***	0.5546

Arch Coal Inc

1 City Pl. Dr., Ste. 300, St. Louis, MO, 63141; ***PH:*** 1-314-994-2700; ***Fax:*** 1-314-994-2878; ***http://*** www.archcoal.com; ***Email:*** careers@archcoal.com

General - Incorporation	DE	***Stock***- Price on:12/24/2007	$36.94
Employees	4,050	Stock Exchange	NYSE
Auditor	Ernst & Young LLP	Ticker Symbol	ACI
Stk Agt	American Stock Transfer & Trust Co.	Outstanding Shares	142,620,000
Counsel	NA	E.P.S	$1.20
DUNS No.	05-262-4962	Shareholders	NA

Business: The groups principle activity is to produce coal. The group also produces steam and metallurgical coal from surface and underground mines for sale to utility, industrial and export markets. The group operates from United States.

Primary SIC and add'l.: 1222 1221 9999

CIK No: 0001037676

Subsidiaries: Allegheny Land Company, Apogee Holdco, Inc., Arch Coal Sales Company, Inc., Arch Coal Terminal, Inc., Arch Energy Resources, Inc., Arch of Wyoming, LLC, Arch Receivable Company, LLC, Arch Reclamation Services, Inc., Arch Western Acquisition Corporation, Arch Western Bituminous Group LLC, Arch Western Finance LLC, Arch Western Resources, LLC, Ark Land Company, Ark Land LT, Inc., Ark Land WR, Inc. 36 Subsidiaries included in the Index

Officers: Steven F. Leer/Chmn., CEO/$5,615,472.00, Robert W. Shanks/Pres. - Eastern Operations, Allen R. Kelley/Dir. - Internal Audit, Michael T. Abbene/CIO, VP, Sheila B. Feldman/VP - Human Resources, David B. Peugh/VP - Business Development, Deck S. Slone/VP - Investor Relations, Public Affairs, Robert J. Messey/CFO, Sr. VP/$2,502,276.00, John W. Eaves/Dir., COO, Pres./$3,670,987.00, Henry C. Besten/Sr. VP - Strategic Development/$1,433,309.00, Robert G. Jones/VP - Law, General Counsel, Sec./$1,588,958.00, John W. Lorson/Controller, James E. Florczak/Treasurer, Anthony S. Bumbico/VP - Safety, David C. Steele/VP - Tax *(17 Officers included in Index)*

Directors: Steven F. Leer/Chmn., CEO, Michael A. Perry/Dir., Frank M. Burke/Dir., Brian J. Jennings/Dir., Thomas A. Lockhart/Dir., Robert G. Potter/Dir., Theodore D. Sands/Dir., James R. Boyd/Dir., Wesley M. Taylor/Dir., Patricia Fry Godley/Dir., John W. Eaves/Dir., COO, Pres., Douglas H. Hunt/Dir.

Owners: A. Michael Perry, James R. Boyd, Frank M. Burke, Steven F. Leer, Insiders, Theodore D. Sands, C. Henry Besten, Robert G. Potter, Brian J. Jennings, Robert J. Messey, Robert G. Jones, Douglas H. Hunt, John W. Eaves, Patricia F. Godley, Wesley M. Taylor *(16 Owners included in Index)*

Financial Data: ***Fiscal Year End:***12/31 ***Latest Annual Data:*** 12/31/2006

Year	Sales	Net Income
2006	$2,500,431,000	$260,931,000
2005	$2,508,773,000	$38,123,000
2004	$1,907,168,000	$113,706,000

Curr. Assets:	$487,277,000	***Curr. Liab.:***	$440,806,000	***P/E Ratio:***	26.96
Plant, Equip.:	$2,243,068,000	***Total Liab.:***	$1,955,220,000	***Indic. Yr. Divd.:***	$0.280
Total Assets:	$3,320,814,000	***Net Worth:***	$1,365,594,000	***Debt/ Equity:***	0.7985

Archer-Daniels-Midland Co

4666 Faries Pkwy., Decatur, IL, 62526; ***PH:*** 1-217-424-5200; ***Fax:*** 1-217-424-6196; ***http://*** www.admworld.com

General - Incorporation	DE	***Stock***- Price on:12/24/2007	$34.73
Employees	26,821	Stock Exchange	NYSE
Auditor	Ernst & Young LLP	Ticker Symbol	ADM
Stk Agt	Hickory Point Bank & Trust	Outstanding Shares	653,180,000
Counsel	NA	E.P.S	$3.37
DUNS No.	00-130-7586	Shareholders	NA

Business: The group's principle activities include procuring, transporting, storing, processing, and merchandising agricultural commodities and products. The group's products include baking and cereals, beverages, candy and confectionary, meat products and snack foods. The group also provides AG services including grain trading, transportation and terminal services. The group operates from United States.

Primary SIC and add'l.: 5153 2046 2074 2079 2041 2075

CIK No: 0000007084

Subsidiaries: ADM Agri-Industries Company, ADM Canadian Holdings BV, ADM Europe BV, ADM International Ltd., ADM Ireland Holdings Ltd., ADM Worldwide Holdings LP

Officers: Patricia A. Woertz/Chmn., CEO, Pres./$7,637,295.00, Lewis W. Batchelder/Sr. VP - Toepfer, ADM Value Creation Team/$3,913,201.00, Ismael Roig/VP - Planning, Business Development, Scott A. Roberts/Assist. General Counsel, Assist. Sec., Douglas J. Schmalz/CFO, Sr. VP/$3,705,928.00, Edward A. Harjehausen/Sr. VP - Food, Feed Ingredients, Ronald S. Bandler/Assist. Treasurer, Matthew J. Jansen/VP - Grain Group, Michael Lusk/VP - Insurance, Risk Management, John P. Stott/41/VP, Controller, David J. Smith/Exec. VP, Sec., General Counsel/$3,353,006.00, William H. Camp/Exec. VP - Global Processing/$4,377,227.00, John D. Rice/Exec. VP - Commercial, Production/$3,297,597.00, Dennis Riddle/VP - Corn Processing, Michael Dambrose/Sr. VP - Human Resources *(25 Officers included in Index)*

Directors: Patricia A. Woertz/Chmn., CEO, Pres., Dwayne O. Andreas/Chmn. Emeritus, Glenn O. Webb/Dir., Antonio Maciel Neto/Dir., Brian M. Mulroney/Dir., Roger S. Joslin/Dir., A. Maclel/Dir., Alan L. Boeckmann/Dir., Mollie Hale Carter/Dir., Kelvin R. Westbrook/Dir., Patrick J. Moore/Dir., Thomas F. O'Neill/Dir.

Owners: Brian M. Mulroney, Barclays Global Investors, NA/10.65%, Alan L. Boeckmann, Patrick J. Moore, Mollie Hale Carter/1.81%, State Farm Mutual Automobile Insurance Company/8.78%, Kelvin R. Westbrook, Thomas F. ONeill, Antonio Maciel Neto, Patricia A. Woertz

Financial Data: *Fiscal Year End:*06/30 *Latest Annual Data:* 6/30/2006

Year	Sales	Net Income
2006	$36,596,111,000	$1,312,070,000
2005	$35,943,810,000	$1,044,385,000
2004	$36,151,394,000	$494,710,000

Curr. Assets:	$11,826,277,000	**Curr. Liab.:**	$6,164,767,000	**P/E Ratio:**	26.96
Plant, Equip.:	$5,293,032,000	**Total Liab.:**	$11,462,150,000	**Indic. Yr. Divd.:**	$0.460
Total Assets:	$21,269,030,000	**Net Worth:**	$9,806,880,000	**Debt/ Equity:**	0.4829

Archipelago Holdings Inc

100 S Wacker Dr., Ste. 1800, Chicago, IL, 60606; *PH:* 1-312-960-1696; *http://* www.archipelago.com

General - Incorporation	DE	**Stock**- Price on:12/24/2007	$76.64
Employees	2,578	Stock Exchange	NA
Auditor	Ernst & Young LLP	Ticker Symbol	NA
Stk Agt	Wells Fargo Shareowner Services	Outstanding Shares	263,900,000
Counsel	NA	E.P.S.	$1.87
DUNS No.	NA	Shareholders	NA

Business: The group's principal activity is to operate an open all-electronic stock market in the United States for trading in nyse, Nasdaq, amex and pcx listed equity securities, exchange-traded funds and other exchange-listed securities. The group operates in two segments: transaction execution services and agency brokerage services. Transaction execution services consists primarily of transaction execution services, market data services on a real-time or summary basis and through our alliance with pcx equities, a trading venue for issuers of equity securities, exchange funds and structured products listed on pcx. The agency brokerage services are provided through the wave broker-dealer subsidiary. It provides order execution services, on an agency basis, for orders received exclusively from institutions involving Nasdaq and listed securities.

Primary SIC and add'l.: 6289 6211

CIK No: 0001107389

Subsidiaries: Archipelago Exchange, LLC, Wave Securities, LLC

Financial Data: *Fiscal Year End:*12/31 *Latest Annual Data:* 12/31/2006

Year	Sales	Net Income
2006	$2,375,950,000	$204,977,000

Curr. Assets:	$1,443,068,000	**Curr. Liab.:**	$832,193,000	**P/E Ratio:**	49.96
Plant, Equip.:	$378,128,000	**Total Liab.:**	$1,796,523,000	**Indic. Yr. Divd.:**	$1.000
Total Assets:	$3,465,542,000	**Net Worth:**	$1,669,019,000	**Debt/ Equity:**	NA

Archon Corp

4336 Losee Rd., Ste. 5, North Las Vegas, NV, 89030; *PH:* 1-702-732-9120; *http://* www.ateg.com

General - Incorporation	NV	**Stock**- Price on:12/24/2007	$51.5
Employees	512	Stock Exchange	OTC
Auditor	Ernst & Young, LLP	Ticker Symbol	ARHN
Stk Agt	American Stock Transfer & Trust Co.	Outstanding Shares	6,280,000
Counsel	NA	E.P.S.	-$0.66
DUNS No.	06-896-9971	Shareholders	NA

Business: The group's principal activities are carried out through its wholly owned subsidiary, pioneer hotel inc. It operates the pioneer hotel & gambling hall in laughlin, Nevada under long-term lease and license arrangements. In addition, the group owns real estate on las vegas boulevard south and at the corner of rainbow and lone mountain road, both in las vegas, Nevada, and also owns investment properties in dorchester, Massachusetts and gaithersburg, Maryland.

Primary SIC and add'l.: 7993 7999 7011 6798

CIK No: 0000812482

Subsidiaries: Archon Sparks Management Company, Archon Sparks Management Corporation, Casino Properties, Inc., Ever-Ski Properties, Inc., Hacienda Hawaiian Properties, Hacienda Hotel Inc., Pioneer Finance Corp., Pioneer Hotel & Gambling Hall, Pioneer Hotel Inc, Pioneer Hotel Inc., SAHAC Corp., Sahara Las Vegas Corp, Sahara Las Vegas Corp., Sahara Nevada Corp., Sahara Resorts 19 Subsidiaries included in the Index

Officers: Paul W. Lowden/64/Chmn., CEO, Pres./$787,203.00, John M. Garner/48/CFO, Sr. VP, Sec., Treasurer/$122,784.00, Suzanne Lowden/55/Dir., Exec. VP, Assist. Sec.

Directors: Paul W. Lowden/64/Chmn., CEO, Pres., Richard Taggart/65/Dir., John W. Delaney/59/Dir., Suzanne Lowden/55/Dir., Exec. VP, Assist. Sec., William J. Raggio/81/Dir., Howard E. Foster/63/Dir.

Owners: Paul W. Lowden/74.70%, Suzanne Lowden, John W. Delaney, William J. Raggio, Paul W. Lowden/18.40%, Suzanne Lowden, Magten Asset Management Corp/8.40%, Howard Foster, William J. Raggio, David E. Shaw/8.20%, Richard H. Taggart, Plainfield Special Situations Master Fund/5.80%, Howard Foster, Insiders/75.40%, Insiders/18.90%

Financial Data: *Fiscal Year End:*09/30 *Latest Annual Data:* 9/30/2006

Year	Sales	Net Income
2006	$45,154,000	-$3,356,000
2005	$43,688,000	-$4,912,000
2004	$53,546,000	-$1,882,000

Curr. Assets:	$14,755,000	**Curr. Liab.:**	$26,979,000		
Plant, Equip.:	$175,647,000	**Total Liab.:**	$176,318,000	**Indic. Yr. Divd.:**	NA
Total Assets:	$198,050,000	**Net Worth:**	$21,733,000	**Debt/ Equity:**	3.2100

Arctic Cat Inc

601 Brooks Ave. S, Thief River Falls, MN, 56701; *PH:* 1-218-681-8558; *Fax:* 1-218-681-3162; *http://* www.arctic-cat.com

General - Incorporation	MN	**Stock**- Price on:12/24/2007	$20.5
Employees	1,840	Stock Exchange	NDQ
Auditor	Grant Thornton LLP	Ticker Symbol	ACAT
Stk Agt	Wells Fargo Shareowner Services	Outstanding Shares	18,360,000
Counsel	Robins, Kaplan, Miller & Ciresi LLP	E.P.S.	$0.72
DUNS No.	07-242-9947	Shareholders	NA

Business: The group's principal activities are to design, engineer, manufacture and market snowmobiles and all-terrain vehicles (atvs) under the arctic cat brand name. The group also manufactures related parts, garments and accessories. The group produces a full line of snowmobiles, consisting of 52 models, sold in the United States, Canada, scandinavia and other international markets. The features of snowmobile include hydraulic disc brakes and a technologically advanced front and rear suspension. The all-terrain vehicles are generally one person vehicles used for a variety of off-road uses. The most popular atv is used for recreation. The products are marketed through a network of independent dealers located throughout the United States and Canada and through distributors representing dealers in Alaska, Europe, the Middle East, Asia and other international markets.

Primary SIC and add'l.: 5699 2385 5048 5131 3799 2311

CIK No: 0000719866

Subsidiaries: Arctic Cat AG, Arctic Cat Production LLC, Arctic Cat Production Support LLC, Arctic Cat Sales Inc., Arctic Cat Shared Services LLC

Officers: Christopher A. Twomey/Chmn., CEO/$1,542,698.00, Ole E. Tweet/VP - New Product Development/$522,649.00, Timothy C. Delmore/CFO, Sec./$681,621.00, Terry J. Blount/VP - Human Resources, Ronald G. Ray/VP - Operations/$562,977.00, Roger H. Skime/VP - Research, Development/$413,768.00

Directors: Christopher A. Twomey/Chmn., CEO, William G. Ness/Vice Chmn., Kenneth J. Roering/Dir., Susan E. Lester/Dir., Robert J. Dondelinger/Dir., Gregg A. Ostrander/Dir., Masayoshi Ito/Dir., David Roberts/Dir.

Owners: Barclays Global Investors, NA/7.50%, Roger H. Skime/1.20%, Rutabaga Capital Management/12.50%, Robert J. Dondelinger/1.10%, Kenneth J. Roering, Ronald G. Ray, Putnam, LLC d/b/a Putnam Investments/6.70%, Royce & Associates, LLC/12.30%, Ole E. Tweet, David A. Roberts, William G. Ness, Insiders/12.70%, Timothy C. Delmore/1.40%, Gregg A. Ostrander, Suzuki Motor Corporation *(17 Owners included in Index)*

Financial Data: *Fiscal Year End:*03/31 *Latest Annual Data:* 03/31/2007

Year	Sales	Net Income
2007	$782,431,000	$22,070,000
2006	$732,794,000	$23,746,000
2005	$689,145,000	$28,299,000

Curr. Assets:	$218,750,000	**Curr. Liab.:**	$110,402,000	**P/E Ratio:**	19.90
Plant, Equip.:	$88,947,000	**Total Liab.:**	$121,871,000	**Indic. Yr. Divd.:**	$0.280
Total Assets:	$311,236,000	**Net Worth:**	$189,365,000	**Debt/ Equity:**	NA

Ardea Biosciences Inc

Formerly: IntraBiotics Pharmaceuticals Inc
2131 Palomar Rd., Ste. 300, Carlsbad, CA, 92011; *PH:* 1-760-602-8422; *http://* www.intrabiotics.com

General - Incorporation	DE	**Stock**- Price on:12/24/2007	NA
Employees	NA	Stock Exchange	NA
Auditor	Stonefield Josephson, Inc	Ticker Symbol	NA
Stk Agt	Computershare Trust Co	Outstanding Shares	NA
Counsel	Cooley Godward LLP	E.P.S.	-$0.98
DUNS No.	NA	Shareholders	NA

Business: The group's principal activities are to develop novel biopharmaceutical products for the management of serious infections and multi-drug-resistant organisms. The group is currently developing an antimicrobial drug, for the prevention of ventilator-associated pneumonia (vap). Vap is a bacterial pneumonia that can develop in patients receiving mechanical ventilation and is the most common infection occurring in patients in the intensive care unit.

Primary SIC and add'l.: 8731 2834

CIK No: 0001103390

Officers: Barry D. Quart/Dir., CEO, Pres./$1,059,400.00, Denis Hickey/CFO/$96,000.00, Kimberly J. Manhard/Sr. VP - Regulatory Affairs, Operations/$380,237.00, Christopher W. Krueger/Sr. VP, Chief Business Officer, Colin E. Rowlings/Sr. VP - Pharmaceutical Sciences, Patrick M. Oconnor/Sr. Scientific Consultant

Directors: Barry D. Quart/Dir., CEO, Pres., Jack S. Remington/Dir., Henry J. Fuchs/Dir., Kevin C. Tang/Dir., John W. Beck/Dir., John Poyhonen/Dir.

Owners: Jack S. Remington, Denis Hickey, Kevin C. Tang, Insiders, Henry J. Fuchs, Entities affiliated with Andreeff Equity Advisors, L.L.C., Deutsche Bank AG, Tang Capital Partners, L.P., Entities affiliated with Baker Biotech Funds

Financial Data: *Fiscal Year End:*12/31 *Latest Annual Data:* 12/31/2006

Year	Sales	Net Income
2006	NA	-$367,000
2005	NA	-$3,171,000
2004	NA	-$16,700,000

Curr. Assets:	$49,514,000	**Curr. Liab.:**	$1,176,000		
Plant, Equip.:	$726,000	**Total Liab.:**	$1,176,000	**Indic. Yr. Divd.:**	NA
Total Assets:	$50,240,000	**Net Worth:**	$49,064,000	**Debt/ Equity:**	NA

Arden Group Inc

2020 S Central Ave., Compton, CA, 90220; *PH:* 1-310-638-2842; *Fax:* 1-310-631-0950; *http://* www.gelsons.com

General - Incorporation: DE
Employees: 1,394
Auditor: PricewaterhouseCoopers LLP
Stk Agt: Continental Stock Transfer & Trust Co
Counsel: NA
DUNS No.: 03-086-6602

Stock- Price on:12/24/2007: $130.4
Stock Exchange: NDQ
Ticker Symbol: ARDNA
Outstanding Shares: 3,160,000
E.P.S: $8.24
Shareholders: NA

Business: The group's principal activities is to operate 18 supermarkets in the southern California. Out of them 17 are under the name gelson's and 1 under the name mayfair. The supermarkets are self-service cash-and-carry markets that offer a broad selection of local and national brands as well as a limited number of private label items. The products sold in the supermarkets include all of the traditional grocery categories such as dry groceries, produce, meat, seafood, bakery, dairy, wine and liquor, floral, sushi, vitamins, health and natural food products and health and beauty aids. The gelson's supermarkets target the consumer who values superior customer service, merchandise presentation, selection and quality products. The mayfair stores offer a merchandise selection equal in quality to a gelson's but generally less broad. The group also offers other support services like on-site stockroom. The group's subsidiary is arden mayfair inc and its subsidiaries.

Primary SIC and add'l.: 5411

CIK No: 0000225051

Subsidiaries: Arden-Mayfair, Inc, Gelsons Markets

Officers: Bernard Briskin/83/Chmn., CEO/$2,082,516.00

Directors: Bernard Briskin/83/Chmn., CEO, Steven Romick/44/Dir., John G. Danhakl/51/Dir., Robert A. Davidow/65/Dir., Kenneth A. Goldman/65/Dir., Mark M. Albert/45/Dir.

Owners: Bernard Briskin/60.00%, Kenneth A. Goldman/4.10%, Insiders/64.10%, Royce& Associates, LLC/6.20%

Financial Data: **Fiscal Year End:**12/31 **Latest Annual Data:** 12/30/2006

Year	Sales	Net Income
2006	$482,737,000	$23,224,000
2005	$470,354,000	$19,851,000

Curr. Assets:	$88,764,000	**Curr. Liab.:**	$47,460,000	**P/E Ratio:**	15.83
Plant, Equip.:	$50,025,000	**Total Liab.:**	$64,707,000	**Indic. Yr. Divd.:**	$1.000
Total Assets:	$147,027,000	**Net Worth:**	$82,320,000	**Debt/ Equity:**	0.0139

Ardnet Mines Ltd

110 Jardine Dr., Ste.13, Concord, ON, L4K2T7; *PH:* 1-905-761-1096

General - Incorporation:
Employees: NA
Auditor: Malone & Bailey, P.C
Stk Agt: Pacific Stock Transfer Company
Counsel: Conrad C. Lysiak
DUNS No.: NA

Stock- Price on:12/24/2007: $0.24
Stock Exchange: OTC
Ticker Symbol: ADNT
Outstanding Shares: NA
E.P.S: NA
Shareholders: NA

Business: The groups principle activity is to provide recruiting services. The groups service area includes the research and development, engineering, marketing, sales, information technology and manufacturing industries. The group operates from United States.

Primary SIC and add'l.: 1040

CIK No: 0001129018

Officers: Taras Chebountchak/36/Dir., Pres., Sec., Treasurer, CFO, Principal Exec. Officer

Directors: Taras Chebountchak/36/Dir., Pres., Sec., Treasurer, CFO, Principal Exec. Officer

Owners: Corporate Resource Group, Inc./6.97%, Taras Chebountchak/35.07%, Insiders/35.07%

Financial Data: **Fiscal Year End:**06/30 **Latest Annual Data:** 06/30/2007

Year	Sales	Net Income
2007	NA	-$40,000
2006	NA	-$12,000
2005	NA	-$17,000

Curr. Assets:	$48,000	**Curr. Liab.:**	$102,000		
Plant, Equip.:	NA	**Total Liab.:**	$102,000	**Indic. Yr. Divd.:**	NA
Total Assets:	$48,000	**Net Worth:**	-$55,000	**Debt/ Equity:**	NA

Arena Pharmaceuticals Inc

6166 Nancy Ridge Dr., San Diego, CA, 92121; *PH:* 1-858-453-7200; *Fax:* 1-858-453-7210; *http://* www.arenapharm.com; *Email:* businessdevelopment@arenapharm.com

General - Incorporation: DE
Employees: 371
Auditor: Ernst & Young LLP
Stk Agt: Computershare Investor Services
Counsel: NA
DUNS No.: NA

Stock- Price on:12/24/2007: $11.2
Stock Exchange: NDQ
Ticker Symbol: ARNA
Outstanding Shares: 60,950,000
E.P.S: -$2.1
Shareholders: NA

Business: The group's principal activities are to discover, develop and commercialize novel and improve orally available drugs. It focuses drug discovery efforts across g protein-coupled receptors and compounds within four therapeutic areas: metabolic diseases, central nervous system disorders, cardiovascular diseases and inflammatory disorders. It uses carttm which is its constitutively activated receptor technology, melanophore technology and other proprietary technologies to better understand gpcrs and to identify compounds that may lead to new drugs. The group intends to commercialize drugs independently and through collaborations with pharmaceutical partners.

Primary SIC and add'l.: 2834 8731

CIK No: 0001080709

Subsidiaries: BRL Screening, Inc

Officers: Jack Lief/Co - Founder, Dir., CEO, Pres./$1,697,205.00, Robert E. Hoffman/VP - Finance, CFO/$609,535.00, Dominic P. Behan/Co - Founder, Dir., Sr. VP, Chief Scientific Officer/$843,738.00, William R. Shanahan/Chief Medical Officer, VP/$558,998.00, K. A. Ajit-Simh/VP - Quality Systems, Louis J. Scotti/VP - Marketing, Business Development, Steven W. Spector/Sr. VP, General Counsel, Sec./$707,065.00

Directors: Jack Lief/Co - Founder, Dir., CEO, Pres., Donald D. Belcher/Dir., Clayburn J. La Force/Dir., Harry F. Hixson/Dir., Scott H. Bice/Dir., Dominic P. Behan/Co - Founder, Dir., Sr. VP, Chief Scientific Officer, Tina S. Nova/Dir., Christine A. White/Dir.

Owners: FMR Corp./8.40%, William R. Shanahan, Robert E. Hoffman, Wellington Management Company/10.10%, Insiders/4.60%, Smithfield Fiduciary LLC/6.00%, Jack Lief/1.80%, Entities affiliated with Deerfield Capital, L.P./5.70%, Mainfield Enterprises,Inc./7.90%, Donald D. Belcher, TCW Business Unit/6.80%, Christine A. White, OppenheimerFunds,Inc./8.80%, Scott H. Bice, Harry F. Hixson *(19 Owners included in Index)*

Financial Data: **Fiscal Year End:**12/31 **Latest Annual Data:** 12/31/2006

Year	Sales	Net Income
2006	$30,569,000	-$86,248,000
2005	$23,233,000	-$67,901,000
2004	$13,686,000	-$57,992,000

Curr. Assets:	$399,686,000	**Curr. Liab.:**	$36,001,000		
Plant, Equip.:	$56,500,000	**Total Liab.:**	$50,542,000	**Indic. Yr. Divd.:**	NA
Total Assets:	$468,465,000	**Net Worth:**	$366,115,000	**Debt/ Equity:**	0.0407

Arena Resources Inc

4290 S Lewis Ave., Ste. 107, Tulsa, OK, 74105; *PH:* 1-918-747-6060; *Fax:* 1-918-747-7620; *http://* www.arenaresourcesinc.com; *Email:* arenaresourcesok@aol.com

General - Incorporation: NV
Employees: 52
Auditor: Lee Keeling & Assoc., Inc.
Stk Agt: Atlas Stock Transfer Corp
Counsel: NA
DUNS No.: NA

Stock- Price on:12/24/2007: $55.7
Stock Exchange: NYSE
Ticker Symbol: ARD
Outstanding Shares: 14,900,000
E.P.S: $1.70
Shareholders: NA

Business: The group's principal activities are to acquire, explore and develop oil and gas properties. The group also produces and sells oil and gas. The group owns interests in oil and gas properties located in Oklahoma, Texas and Kansas. The major customers of the company are plains marketing l.p, sun oil company and navajo refining company.

Primary SIC and add'l.: 1382

CIK No: 0001123871

Officers: Lloyd T. Rochford/CEO/$36,000.00, William Randall Broaddrick/CFO, VP/$65,666.00, Phillip W. Terry/COO, Pres./$130,583.00, Bill Parsons/VP - Investor Relations

Directors: Stanley McCabe/Chmn.

Owners: Lloyd T. Rochford/4.70%, William R. Broaddrick, Stanley M. McCabe/3.50%, Neuberger Berman Inc./10.70%, Insiders/10.10%, Anthony B. Petrelli, Clayton E. Woodrum, QVT Financial LP/5.20%, Vaughan Nelson Investment Management, L.P./6.00%, Phillip W. Terry, Rainier Investment Management, Inc./6.50%, Carl H. Fiddner

Financial Data: **Fiscal Year End:**12/31 **Latest Annual Data:** 12/31/2006

Year	Sales	Net Income
2006	$59,760,000	$23,268,000
2005	$25,843,000	$9,461,000
2004	$8,482,000	$2,452,000

Curr. Assets:	$14,674,000	**Curr. Liab.:**	$14,996,000	**P/E Ratio:**	35.94
Plant, Equip.:	$161,639,000	**Total Liab.:**	$56,269,000	**Indic. Yr. Divd.:**	NA
Total Assets:	$176,313,000	**Net Worth:**	$120,044,000	**Debt/ Equity:**	0.1641

Arete Industries Inc

7102 La Vista Pl, Ste 100, Niwot, CO, 80503; *PH:* 1-303-652-3113; *Fax:* 1-303-429-9664; *http://* www.areteindustries.com; *Email:* ceo@areteindustries.com

General - Incorporation: CO
Employees: NA
Auditor: Ronald R. Chadwick, P.C
Stk Agt: Computershare Trust Co
Counsel: NA
DUNS No.: NA

Stock- Price on:12/24/2007: $0.0045
Stock Exchange: OTC
Ticker Symbol: ARET
Outstanding Shares: 307,150,000
E.P.S: -$0.001
Shareholders: NA

Business: The group's principal activities are to create, design, develop, produce and market highly innovative outdoor adventure sports products and adventure travel services. The group is engaged in the development of a patented neural-networking, intelligent agent software engine and its unique applications for language learning, voice recognition, speech interpretation, vision recognition and intelligent robotics. During 2002, the group changed its focus to a program to attract new acquisition opportunities for funding and development through its dividend/spin-off program, and to create an affiliated funding entity that would generate capital for these prospects through corporate debt investment vehicles. During 2003, the group changed its business model based on pursuing projects in traditional oil and gas ventures and develops alternative and renewable energy projects.

Primary SIC and add'l.: 7389

CIK No: 0000820901

Subsidiaries: Aggression Sports, Inc., Colorado Oil & Gas, Inc., Global Direct Marketing Services, Inc., Le Mail, Inc.

Officers: Charles L. Gamber/54/Dir., CEO, Pres., William W. Stewart/43/Dir., Company Sec., John R. Herzog/61/Dir., Interim CFO

Directors: Charles L. Gamber/54/Dir., CEO, Pres., William W. Stewart/43/Dir., Company Sec., John R. Herzog/61/Dir., Interim CFO, Donald W. Prosser/54/Dir.

Financial Data: **Fiscal Year End:**12/31 **Latest Annual Data:** 12/31/2005

Year	Sales	Net Income
2005	$1,000	-$603,000
2004	NA	-$923,000
2003	NA	-$723,000

Curr. Assets:	$3,000	**Curr. Liab.:**	$891,000		
Plant, Equip.:	$2,000	**Total Liab.:**	$891,000	**Indic. Yr. Divd.:**	NA
Total Assets:	$5,000	**Net Worth:**	-$886,000	**Debt/ Equity:**	NA

Argan Inc

1 Church St., Ste. 401, Rockville, MD, 20850; *PH:* 1-301-315-0027; *Fax:* 1-301-315-0064; *http://* www.arganinc.com; *Email:* info@arganinc.com

General - Incorporation: DE
Employees: 525
Auditor: Grant Thornton, LLP
Stk Agt: Continental Stock Transfer & Trust Co
Counsel: NA
DUNS No.: 00-132-5877

Stock- Price on:12/24/2007: $6.4
Stock Exchange: AMEX
Ticker Symbol: AGX
Outstanding Shares: 11,090,000
E.P.S: -$0.22
Shareholders: NA

Business: The group's principal activity is to provide telecommunications infrastructure services. These services include project management, construction and maintenance services. The group provides inside plant, premise wiring services to the federal government and maintenance and upgrade services to

the telecommunication providers. It also provides services to broadband service providers and electric utilities. The group operates only in United States. On 31-Oct-2003, the group disposed Puroflow Incorporated. The group acquired Southern Maryland Cable, Inc on 17-Jul-2003 and Vitarich Laboratories, Inc on 31-Aug-2004.

Primary SIC and add'l.: 7389

CIK No: 0000100591

Subsidiaries: Southern Maryland Cable, Inc, Vitarich Laboratories, Inc

Owners: Kevin Thomas/4.50%, Champion W.G. Mitchell, Richard L. Scott/8.70%, Arthur F. Trudel/1.10%, MSR Advisors, Inc./12.00%, Joel M. Canino/14.40%, DeSoto S. Jordan, James W. Quinn, Daniel A. Levinson/12.10%, William F. Griffin/14.40%, Kent T. Pugmire, Rainer H. Bosselmann/3.30%, Peter L. Winslow

Financial Data: Fiscal Year End:01/31 **Latest Annual Data:** 1/31/2007

Year	Sales	Net Income
2007	$68,867,000	-$113,000
2006	$28,452,000	-$9,508,000
2005	$14,518,000	-$3,193,000

Curr. Assets:	$80,925,000	**Curr. Liab.:**	$68,419,000		
Plant, Equip.:	$3,250,000	**Total Liab.:**	$76,619,000	**Indic. Yr. Divd.:**	NA
Total Assets:	$121,130,000	**Net Worth:**	$44,511,000	**Debt/ Equity:**	NA

Argentex Mining Corp

1066 W Hastings St. , Ste. 23, Vancouver, BC, V6E 3X2; **PH:** 1-604-601-8366; **http://** www.argentexmining.com; **Email:** info@argentexmining.com

General - Incorporation	NV	**Stock** - Price on:12/24/2007	$1.43
Employees	NA	Stock Exchange	OTC
Auditor	Morgan & Company	Ticker Symbol	AGXM
Stk Agt	Nevada Agency & Trust Company	Outstanding Shares	NA
Counsel	NA	E.P.S.	NA
DUNS No.	NA	Shareholders	NA

Business: The groups principal activity is to explore minerals. The group operates from Canada and the United States.

Primary SIC and add'l.: 1499

CIK No: 0001167887

Subsidiaries: Delbrook Mining Corp., SCRN Properties Ltd

Officers: Kenneth E. Hicks/Chmn., Pres., Principal Exec. Officer/$215,883.00, Hamish Malkin/CFO, Diego Guido/Sr. Technical Advisor, Sebastian Jovic/Technical Advisor, Orlando Rionda/42/Legal Representative

Directors: Kenneth E. Hicks/Chmn., Pres., Principal Exec. Officer, Colin Godwin/Dir., Jenna Hardy/Dir., Rick Thibault/Dir.

Owners: Colin Godwin, Hamish Malkin, Insiders/7.09%, Passport Materials Master Fund LP/9.54%, Jenna Hardy, Rick Thibault, Kenneth E. Hicks/3.92%, Orlando Rionda

Financial Data: Fiscal Year End:01/31 **Latest Annual Data:** 01/31/2007

Year	Sales	Net Income
2007	NA	-$2,332,000
2006	NA	-$1,478,000
2005	NA	-$2,293,000

Curr. Assets:	$902,000	**Curr. Liab.:**	$2,027,000		
Plant, Equip.:	$3,000	**Total Liab.:**	$2,027,000	**Indic. Yr. Divd.:**	NA
Total Assets:	$905,000	**Net Worth:**	-$1,123,000	**Debt/ Equity:**	NA

Argo Tech Corp

23555 Euclid Ave., Cleveland, OH, 44117; **PH:** 1-216-692-6000; **Fax:** 1-216-692-5293; **http://** www.argo-tech.com

General - Incorporation	DE	**Stock** - Price on:12/24/2007	NA
Employees	NA	Stock Exchange	NA
Auditor	Deloitte & Touche LLP	Ticker Symbol	NA
Stk Agt	NA	Outstanding Shares	NA
Counsel	NA	E.P.S.	NA
DUNS No.	15-736-7301	Shareholders	NA

Business: The group's principal activities are to design, manufacture and sell high performance fuel flow devices and systems for both aerospace and general industrial applications. It operates in two business segments, aerospace and industrial. The aerospace segment includes the manufacture of aviation products consisting of aircraft engine fuel pumps, fuel flow related products and systems found on a plane's airframe and aerial refueling pumps and related equipment. The industrial segment includes the manufacture of industrial pumps, ground fueling valves and related components, cryogenic pumps and nozzles for transferring liquefied natural gas and operation of a business park in cleveland, Ohio. The customers of the group include general electric, honeywell, pratt and whitney, rolls-royce, snecma, williams international corp, airbus, boeing, cessna, gulfstream, lockheed martin, raytheon, rolls royce power engineering, rolls royce energy systems.

Primary SIC and add'l.: 3561 3586 3728 3594 3724

CIK No: 0001047837

Subsidiaries: Argo Tracker Corporation

Officers: Barb Bambrick/Contact - Cleveland, Ohio, Sharon Iafelice/Human Resources, Linda Kaufman/Contact - Argo, Tech Repair, Cleveland, John Muhvic/Argo, Tech Repair Contact - Cleveland, Sharky Ikeda/Contact - Argo, Tech Repair, Inglewood, John Vyn/Contact - Argo, Tech Repair, Costa Mesa, Joe Brown/Contact - Argo, Tech Repair, Costa Mesa, Rita A. Koroluk/Corporate Controller, Principal Accounting Officer

Owners: Vestar Capital Partners IV, L.P., Paul R. Keen, John Daileader, Michael S. Lipscomb, Insiders, Insiders/32.50%, Paul R. Keen/5.00%, Reginald L. Jones, John S. Glover/5.00%, Kathleen Moran, Jeffrey W. Long, Michael S. Lipscomb/22.50%, Daniel S. OConnell, Greenbriar Equity Group LLC, John S. Glover

Argon St Inc

12701 Fair Lakes Cir., Ste. 800, Fairfax, VA, 22033; **PH:** 1-703-322-0881; **Fax:** 1-703-322-0885; **http://** www.argonst.com

General - Incorporation	DE	**Stock** - Price on:12/24/2007	$23.08
Employees	840	Stock Exchange	NDQ
Auditor	Grant Thornton LLP	Ticker Symbol	STST
Stk Agt	American Stock Transfer & Trust Co.	Outstanding Shares	22,400,000
Counsel	Holland & Knight LLP	E.P.S.	$0.65
DUNS No.	NA	Shareholders	NA

Business: The group's principal activities are to design, develop and manufacture systems and equipment for integrated passive surveillance systems, electronic countermeasures and simulators for military and commercial customers. The defense systems segment designs and develops products that intercept, analyze, classify, identify, localize and track microwave signals from radars and weapons. The communication segment designs and develops products that intercept signals, analyze the on-line communication and identify and localize the involved parties. The imaging segment designs and develops products for multispectral, infrared and light imaging systems. On 14-Apr-2004, the group acquired imaging sensors and systems inc.

Primary SIC and add'l.: 3812 3829

CIK No: 0000026537

Subsidiaries: Radix Technologies, Inc., Sensytech Financial Services, Inc., ST Production Systems, Inc.

Officers: Terry L. Collins/Chmn., CEO, Pres., Kent S. Rockwell/Vice Chmn., VP - Corporate Development, Victor F. Sellier/Dir., VP, CFO, Treasurer, Sec., Robert S. Tamaru/VP - Technology, Strategic Development, Joseph W. Carlin/VP - Information Dominance, Grant Thornton/Accountant, Jay R. Grove/VP - Network Systems, Stanford K. Harmon/VP - Operations Support, Lindsey McClure/VP, James Ross/VP - National Programs, Sarah Fram/Primary Investor Relations Officer, Kerry M. Rowe/VP, COO

Directors: Terry L. Collins/Chmn., CEO, Pres., Kent S. Rockwell/Vice Chmn., VP - Corporate Development, Maureen Baginski/Dir., David C. Karlgaard/Dir., Victor F. Sellier/Dir., VP, CFO, Treasurer, Sec., John Irvin/Dir., Lloyd A. Semple/Dir., Thomas E. Murdock/Dir., Peter A. Marino/Dir., Robert McCashin/Dir.

Owners: Victor F. Sellier/11.90%, Robert McCashin, FMR Corp./10.30%, Lloyd A. Semple, Insiders/41.90%, Peter A. Marino, Terry L. Collins/12.20%, Joseph W. Carlin/1.10%, John Irvin, Thomas E. Murdock/10.90%, David C. Karlgaard, Robert S. Tamaru/2.40%, Kent S. Rockwell/2.70%, Kerry M. Rowe

Financial Data: Fiscal Year End:09/30 **Latest Annual Data:** 09/30/2007

Year	Sales	Net Income
2007	$282,209,000	$14,702,000
2006	$258,835,000	$19,395,000
2005	$271,754,000	$21,781,000

Curr. Assets:	$133,478,000	**Curr. Liab.:**	$43,307,000	**P/E Ratio:**	28.15
Plant, Equip.:	$16,726,000	**Total Liab.:**	$47,835,000	**Indic. Yr. Divd.:**	NA
Total Assets:	$313,531,000	**Net Worth:**	$265,696,000	**Debt/ Equity:**	NA

Argonaut Group Inc

10101 Reunion Pl., Ste. 500, San Antonio, TX, 78216; **PH:** 1-210-321-8500; **http://** www.argonautgroup.com

General - Incorporation	DE	**Stock** - Price on:12/24/2007	$32.29
Employees	1,122	Stock Exchange	NDQ
Auditor	Ernst & Young LLP	Ticker Symbol	AGII
Stk Agt	Computershare Investor Services LLC	Outstanding Shares	33,640,000
Counsel	NA	E.P.S.	$3.25
DUNS No.	10-297-1728	Shareholders	NA

Business: The group's principle activity is to provide specialty insurance products for specific niches of the property and casualty market. The group provides excess and surplus insurance to businesses where insurance through standard markets is unavailable due to unique characteristics of the insured caused by physical perils, nature of the business and history of claims. It also provides risk management solutions and services to protect companies and their employees. The group's specialty commercial products include standard market insurance for commercial entities to cover property and casualty risks incurred in the general course of operating a business. Other services include integrated underwriting, safety and claims management. In addition, the group's public entity segment, trident insurance services, markets risk management, risk financing and risk control products and services to serve the insurance needs of preferred governmental entities.

Primary SIC and add'l.: 6331 6719

CIK No: 0000800082

Subsidiaries: AGI Limited Risks, AGI Properties, Inc., Alpha Credit Corporation, Argonaut Claims Management, LLC, Argonaut Claims Services, Ltd., Argonaut Fund to Secure the Future, Argonaut Group Statutory Trust, Argonaut Group Statutory Trust III, Argonaut Group Statutory Trust IV, Argonaut Group Statutory Trust IX, Argonaut Group Statutory Trust V, Argonaut Group Statutory Trust VI, Argonaut Group Statutory Trust VII, Argonaut Group Statutory Trust VIII, Argonaut Group Statutory Trust X 42 Subsidiaries included in the Index

Officers: Mark E. Watson/CEO, Pres./$3,946,405.00, Byron L. Leflore/Sr. VP, General Counsel/$785,140.00, Mark W. Haushill/Sr. VP, CFO/$725,868.00, Craig S. Comeaux/VP, Sec., Deputy General Counsel, Barbara C. Bufkin/Sr. VP - Corporate Business Development/$774,082.00, Steven E. Math/VP, Chief Actuary, Karen C. Meriwether/VP - Internal Audit, Jack F. Reddy/Sr. VP - Human Resources, Dan G. Platt/VP, Controller, Charles W. Weaver/Sr. VP - Claims/$621,249.00, Robert C. Ingram/CIO, Sr. VP, Lynn K. Geurin/VP, Treasurer, Gregory M. Vezzosi/COO, Exec. VP, Ronald B. Given/Sr. VP, General Counsel

Directors: Gary V. Woods/Chmn., John R. Power/Dir., Berry H. Cash/Dir., Allan W. Fulkerson/Dir., Hector De Leon/Dir., David Hartoch/Dir., Frank Maresh/Dir., Fayez F. Sarofim/Dir.

Owners: Gary V. Woods, Frank W. Maresh, Mark E. Watson/2.20%, John R. Power, Singleton Group LLC/13.90%, Mellon Financial Corp/5.84%, Insiders/6.50%, Hector De Leon, David Hartoch, Fayez S. Sarofim/3.30%, Charles W. Weaver, Mark W. Haushill/0.20%, Berry H. Cash, Allan W. Fulkerson, Byron L. LeFlore (17 Owners included in Index)

Financial Data: Fiscal Year End:12/31 **Latest Annual Data:** 12/31/2006

Year	Sales	Net Income
2006	$938,700,000	$106,000,000
2005	$786,200,000	$80,500,000
2004	$704,200,000	$71,800,000

Curr. Assets:	$822,745,000	**Curr. Liab.:**	$89,671,000	**P/E Ratio:**	9.94
Plant, Equip.:	NA	**Total Liab.:**	$904,576,000	**Indic. Yr. Divd.:**	NA
Total Assets:	$1,401,343,000	**Net Worth:**	$496,767,000	**Debt/ Equity:**	0.1635

Argosy Minerals Inc

57 Labouchere Road, Ste. 10, South Perth, WA, 6151; *PH:* 618-947-44178; *Fax:* 618-947-44236;
http:// www.argosyminerals.com

General - Incorporation......................Canada	Stock- Price on:12/24/2007 ....NA
Employees ....NA	Stock Exchange.....................................NA
Auditor ....Horwath Orenstein LLP	Ticker Symbol.......................................NA
Stk Agt.......................Computershare Trust Co	Outstanding Shares ....NA
Counsel.........................Dorsey & Whitney LLP	E.P.S..NA
DUNS No. 75-264-3197	Shareholders...NA

Business: The group's principal activities are the exploration of precious metals, base metals and diamonds. The group is involved in studies for the development of nickel/cobalt processing facilities at nakety in new caledonia and musongati in the republic of burundi and gold exploration in the slovak republic. In Jul 2001, the group entered into a joint venture with mmc norilsk nickel to form new caledonian nickel project.

Primary SIC and add'l.: 1061 1099 1041
CIK No: 0001047363
Subsidiaries: Andover resources N.L., Argosy mining Corporation pty Ltd.
Officers: Peter Lloyd/Dir., CEO
Directors: Peter Lloyd/Dir., CEO, John Maloney/Chmn., Cecil R. Bond/Dir., Malcolm Smartt/Dir.
Owners: PETER H. LLOYD/8.90%, Cecil R. Bond/2.00%, JOHN MALONEY/1.00%, MALCOLM SMARTT/1.00%

Argyle Security Acquisition Corp

200 Concord Plz., Ste.700, San Antanio, TX, 78216;

General - Incorporation............................DE	Stock- Price on:12/24/2007 ....$7.78
Employees ....NA	Stock Exchange.....................................OTC
Auditor ....Ernst & Young, LLP	Ticker Symbol....................................ARGL
Stk Agt......American Stock Transfer & Trust Co.	Outstanding Shares 4,780,000
Counsel...NA	E.P.S..$0.07
DUNS No. ....NA	Shareholders...NA

Business: The groups principal activity is to provide security services. The group products include video surveillance, motion analytics systems and video monitoring services, access control systems, intrusion systems and threat analysis. The group operates from the United States.

Primary SIC and add'l.: 7382
CIK No: 0001332585
Subsidiaries: ISI Security Group, Inc.
Officers: Bob Marbut/72/Chmn., Co - CEO, Ron Chaimovski/48/Vice Chmn., Co - CEO
Directors: Bob Marbut/72/Chmn., Co - CEO, Ron Chaimovski/48/Vice Chmn., Co - CEO, John J. Smith/59/Dir., Wesley Clark/62/Dir.
Owners: Sapling, LLC/6.10%, Ron Chaimovski/6.50%, Insiders/22.61%, John J. Smith/1.00%, Bob Marbut/13.60%, Argyle Joint Venture/5.80%, Wesley Clark/1.50%, Jonathan M. Glaser/5.20%

Financial Data: *Fiscal Year End:*12/31 *Latest Annual Data:* 12/31/2006

Year	Sales	Net Income
2006	NA	$173,000
2005	NA	-$8,000

Curr. Assets:	$30,155,000	Curr. Liab.:	$1,905,000	P/E Ratio:	111.14
Plant, Equip.:	$5,000	Total Liab.:	$7,819,000	Indic. Yr. Divd.:	NA
Total Assets:	$30,681,000	Net Worth:	$22,862,000	Debt/ Equity:	NA

Ari Network Services Inc

11425 W Lake Pk. Dr., Ste. 900, Milwaukee, WI, 53224; *PH:* 1-414-973-4300;
Fax: 1-414-973-4618; *http://* www.arinet.com; *Email:* info@arinet.com

General - Incorporation..............................WI	Stock- Price on:12/24/2007 ....$1.65
Employees 91	Stock Exchange.....................................OTC
Auditor ....Wipfli LLP	Ticker Symbol......................................ARIS
Stk Agt......American Stock Transfer & Trust CO.	Outstanding Shares 6,620,000
Counsel.......................................Godfrey & Kahn	E.P.S..$0.15
DUNS No. 05-755-9338	Shareholders...NA

Business: The group's principle activity is to provide technology enabled business solutions that connect manufacturers in selected industries with their service and distribution networks. The company provides both electronic catalog and transaction services, enabling partners in a service and distribution network to exchange electronic business documents such as purchase orders, invoices, warranty claims and status inquiries. The company also provides transaction management services and data management services. The electronic catalogue products and services include empartweb(tm), partsmart(tm), empartviewer(tm), empartpublisher(tm) and electronic publishing services. The company's customers are located primarily in the United States, Europe and Canada. The group operates from United States.

Primary SIC and add'l.: 7379 7375 7372
CIK No: 0000879796
Subsidiaries: ARI Europe B.V.
Officers: Brian E. Dearing/Chmn., CEO, Pres., Acting CFO, John C. Bray/VP - Business Development, Strategy, Roy W. Olivier/49/VP - Global Sales, Marketing
Directors: Brian E. Dearing/Chmn., CEO, Pres., Acting CFO, Ted Feierstein/Dir., Richard W. Weening/Dir., Gordon J. Bridge/Dir., William C. Mortimore/Dir.
Owners: Gordon J. Bridge/2.60%, Ted C. Feierstein/1.20%, Richard W. Weening/3.80%, Peter H. Kamin/8.90%, John C. Bray/2.40%, Timothy Sherlock/1.20%, Insiders/19.60%, Roy W. Olivier, Briggs & Stratton Corporation/12.60%, William C. Mortimore, Brian E. Dearing/9.60%

Financial Data: *Fiscal Year End:*07/31 *Latest Annual Data:* 7/31/2006

Year	Sales	Net Income
2006	$14,002,000	$3,210,000
2005	$13,661,000	$2,815,000
2004	$13,439,000	$1,055,000

Curr. Assets:	$5,561,000	Curr. Liab.:	$8,918,000	P/E Ratio:	11.00
Plant, Equip.:	$982,000	Total Liab.:	$9,748,000	Indic. Yr. Divd.:	NA
Total Assets:	$9,436,000	Net Worth:	-$312,000	Debt/ Equity:	0.6220

Ariad Pharmaceuticals Inc

26 Landsdowne St., Cambridge, MA, 02139; *PH:* 1-617-494-0400; *Fax:* 1-617-494-8144;
http:// www.ariad.com; *Email:* investor@ariad.com

General - Incorporation ....DE	Stock- Price on:12/24/2007 ....$5.5
Employees 103	Stock Exchange.....................................NDQ
Auditor ....Deloitte & Touche LLP	Ticker Symbol.....................................ARIA
Stk Agt.......................Computershare Trust Co	Outstanding Shares 68,680,000
Counsel........ Mintz, Levin, Glovsky & Popeo PC	E.P.S..-$0.94
DUNS No. 78-622-7231	Shareholders...NA

Business: The group's principal activities are the discovery and development of medicines that treat cancer by regulating cell signaling with small molecules. The group's lead product candidate, ap23573, is in phase 1 clinical trials and is used for the treatment of solid tumors and other malignancies. Other product candidates include ap23464, to block the spread of cancer and treat certain forms of leukemia and ap23841, to treat primary bone cancers, such as osteogenic sarcomas and cancer that has spread to bone. In addition, the group has an exclusive license to pioneering technology and patents related to the discovery, development and use of drugs to regulate nf-kb cell-signaling activity, which can be used to treat disorders such as inflammation, cancer and osteoporosis.

Primary SIC and add'l.: 8731 2834
CIK No: 0000884731
Subsidiaries: ARIAD Corporation, ARIAD Gene Therapeutics, Inc., ARIAD Pharma S.A.
Officers: Harvey J. Berger/Chmn., CEO/$1,168,572.00, Edward M. Fitzgerald/Sr. VP - Finance, Corporate Operations, CFO, Treasurer/$660,149.00, David C. Dalgarno/VP - Research Technologies, Timothy P. Clackson/Chief Scientific Officer, Sr. VP/$697,275.00, Joseph Bratica/VP - Finance, Controller, David L. Berstein/Sr. VP, Chief Patent Counsel/$664,404.00, John D. Iuliucci/Chief Development Officer, Sr. VP/$673,224.00, Laurie A. Allen/Sr. VP - Legal, Business Development, Chief Legal Officer, Sec., Camille L. Bedrosian/Chief Medical Officer, VP, Shirish Hirani/VP - Development Operations, Planning, John W. Loewy/VP - Biostatistics, Outcomes Research, Richard W. Pascoe/Sr. VP, Chief Commercial Officer, Kathy Lawton/Mgr. - Human Resources, Pierre F. Dodion/Sr. VP - Oncology, Ross D. Pettit/VP - Clinical Operations
Directors: Harvey J. Berger/Chmn., CEO, Sandford D. Smith/Vice Chmn., Peter J. Nelson/Dir., Elizabeth H.S. Wyatt/Dir., Burton E. Sobel/Dir., Athanase Lavidas/Dir., Michael D. Kishbauch/Dir., Jay R. Lamarche/Dir.
Owners: Sandford D. Smith, Harvey J. Berger/1.50%, OrbiMed Advisors LLC/9.00%, Athanase Lavidas, Timothy P. Clackson, Elizabeth H.S. Wyatt, Jay R. LaMarche, John D. Iuliucci, Peter J. Nelson, Edward M. Fitzgerald, Michael D. Kishbauch, Insiders/5.30%, Burton E. Sobel, David L. Berstein

Financial Data: *Fiscal Year End:*12/31 *Latest Annual Data:* 12/31/2006

Year	Sales	Net Income
2006	$896,000	-$61,928,000
2005	$1,217,000	-$55,482,000
2004	$742,000	-$35,573,000

Curr. Assets:	$41,643,000	Curr. Liab.:	$15,784,000		
Plant, Equip.:	$5,082,000	Total Liab.:	$20,781,000	Indic. Yr. Divd.:	NA
Total Assets:	$51,043,000	Net Worth:	$30,262,000	Debt/ Equity:	NA

Ariba Inc

807 11th Ave., Sunnyvale, CA, 94089; *PH:* 1-650-390-1000; *Fax:* 1-650-390-1100;
http:// www.ariba.com

General - Incorporation ....DE	Stock- Price on:12/24/2007 ....$9.85
Employees 1,676	Stock Exchange.....................................NDQ
Auditor ....KPMG LLP	Ticker Symbol....................................ARBA
Stk Agt.....Computershare Investor Services LLC	Outstanding Shares 78,370,000
Counsel..............................Fenwick & West LLP	E.P.S..-$0.21
DUNS No. ....NA	Shareholders...NA

Business: The group's principal activity is to provide enterprise spend management solutions. Its spend management applications comprises of three solution sets: ariba analysis solution: provides strategic planning and analysis capabilities that leverage historical spending patterns. Ariba sourcing solution enables the sourcing, negotiation and creation of contracts for products and services. Ariba procurement solution enables contract compliance for the purchase of goods and services and manages purchasing workflow on an ongoing basis. The ariba supplier network connects buyers and suppliers via the Internet and offers electronic payment, catalog and content management, business document routing and multi-protocol translation for standard business documents. It operates in North America, Europe, Asia, Australia and Latin America. During the year 2003, the group acquired goodex ag. On 13-Jan-2004, it acquired alliente inc and freemakets inc on 01-Jul-2004.

Primary SIC and add'l.: 7372 7373 7379 7371
CIK No: 0001084755
Subsidiaries: Alliente Ireland Limited, Alliente Limited, Alliente, Inc., Ariba (China) Limited, Ariba Argentina S.R.L., Ariba Australia Pty Ltd., Ariba Belgium N.V., Ariba Czech s.r.o., Ariba Deutschland GmbH, Ariba France, SAS, Ariba Holdings, Inc., Ariba Iberia, S.L., Ariba India Pvt. Ltd., Ariba International Inc., Ariba International Singapore Pte. Ltd. 40 Subsidiaries included in the Index
Officers: Robert M. Calderoni/Chmn., CEO, Kent Parker/Exec. VP, GM - Ariba Global Services Organization, Daryl T. Rolley/Sr. VP, GM - Ariba International Operations, H. Tayloe/Exec. VP, Jim Frankola/CFO, Kevin Costello/Chief Commercial Officer, Tayloe H. Stansbury/Exec. VP - Products, Operations, Karen Master/Public Relations Representative, Corporate, North America, Europe, Gerard Dahan/Public Relations Representative, Europe, Sonal Bansal/Public Relations Representative, India, Alyssa Mack/Public Relations Representative, Industry Analyst Relations, Bhaskar Himatsingka/CTO
Directors: Robert M. Calderoni/Chmn., CEO, Robert D. Johnson/Dir., Thomas F. Monahan/Dir., Karl E. Newkirk/Dir., Richard A. Kashnow/Dir., Robert E. Knowling/Dir., Richard F. Wallman/Dir.
Owners: Insiders/4.20%, Robert D. Johnson, Robert M. Calderon/1.70%, Kent L. Parker, Tayloe H. Stansbury, Robert E. Knowling, Richard A. Kashnow, Karl E. Newkirk, Richard F. Wallman, Thomas F. Monahan, Kevin S. Costello, James W. Frankola

Financial Data: *Fiscal Year End:*09/30 *Latest Annual Data:* 09/30/2007

Year	Sales	Net Income
2007	$301,667,000	-$14,977,000
2006	$296,016,000	-$47,801,000
2005	$323,043,000	-$349,628,000

Curr. Assets:	$183,137,000	Curr. Liab.:	$124,641,000		
Plant, Equip.:	$19,830,000	Total Liab.:	$253,921,000	Indic. Yr. Divd.:	NA
Total Assets:	$586,944,000	Net Worth:	$333,023,000	Debt/ Equity:	NA

Ariel Way Inc

8000 Towers Crescent Dr., Ste. 1220, Vienna, VA, 22182; *PH:* 1-703-918-2420; *Fax:* 1-703-991-0841; *http://* www.arielway.com; *Email:* investorrelations@arielway.com

General - Incorporation	FL	Stock - Price on:12/24/2007	$0.001
Employees	2	Stock Exchange	OTC
Auditor	Bagell, Josephs, Levine & Co. LLC	Ticker Symbol	AWYI
Stk Agt	Interwest Transfer Company, Inc.	Outstanding Shares	66,140,000
Counsel	NA	E.P.S.	$0.002
DUNS No.	NA	Shareholders	NA

Business: The group's principle activities include designing, hosting and related services. It franchises Internet Web site design, hosting, updating, maintenance, administration, e-mail publishing and consulting services, marketing and advertising services and related services under its servicemark "Netspace". The franchisees sell Internet solutions developed and provided by the company. Their services include Web site design and development, Web site hosting, Web site promotion, Web-based advertising, e-mail publishing and advanced solutions such as e-commerce. The company has a total of 68 franchises in the United States and 18 in the United Kingdom as of 24-Mar-2004. The group operates from United States.

Primary SIC and add'l.: 7375 6794

CIK No: 0001145254

Subsidiaries: dbsXmedia, Inc., dbsXmedia, Ltd., Enfotec, Inc.

Officers: Arne Dunhem/57/Chmn., CEO, Pres., Acting CFO, Acting Chief Accounting Officer, Magdy Battikha/Sr. VP - Engineering Development

Directors: Arne Dunhem/57/Chmn., CEO, Pres., Acting CFO, Acting Chief Accounting Officer, Leif Carlsson/Dir.

Owners: Market Central, Inc./7.70%, Loral Skynet Network Services, Inc./7.60%, Leif T. Carlsson/3.40%, Aziz Bennani/5.30%, Insiders/28.40%, Arne Dunhem/26.50%, Elliot Krasnow/3.10%, Anand Kumar/11.70%, Voula Kanellias/5.30%, Magdy Battikha/8.20%

Financial Data: **Fiscal Year End:**09/30 **Latest Annual Data:** 9/30/2006

Year		Sales		Net Income
2006		$2,459,000		-$3,623,000
2005		$1,053,000		-$2,594,000
2004		$275,000		-$509,000
Curr. Assets:	$97,000	Curr. Liab.:	$3,288,000	
Plant, Equip.:	$41,000	Total Liab.:	$3,288,000	Indic. Yr. Divd.: NA
Total Assets:	$138,000	Net Worth:	-$3,150,000	Debt/ Equity: NA

Aries Maritime Transport Ltd

18, Zerva Nap. Str., Glyfada, Athens; *PH:* 30-2108983787; *http://* www.ariesmaritime.com; *Email:* info@ariesmaritime.com

General - Incorporation	Bermuda	Stock - Price on:12/24/2007	$9.39
Employees	3	Stock Exchange	NDQ
Auditor	PricewaterhouseCoopers LLP	Ticker Symbol	RAMS
Stk Agt	Computershare Trust Co	Outstanding Shares	28,400,000
Counsel	NA	E.P.S.	-$0.05
DUNS No.	NA	Shareholders	NA

Business: The groups principle activity is to provide shipping services. The group operates from Europe, Asia, Africa and South America. The groups quarterly revenue for September 2007 was 23.22 millions of USD.

Primary SIC and add'l.: 4412

CIK No: 0001322587

Subsidiaries: AMT Management Ltd., Bora Limited, Dynamic Maritime Co., Ermina Marine Ltd., Jubilee Shipholding S.A., Mote Shipping Ltd., Ocean Hope Shipping Company Ltd., Olympic Galaxy Shipping Ltd., Statesman Shipping Ltd., Trans Continent Navigation Ltd., Trans State Navigation Ltd., Vintage Marine S.A.

Officers: Mons Staffan Bolin/Dir., CEO, Pres., Richard J.H. Coxall/Dir., CFO

Directors: Mons Staffan Bolin/Dir., CEO, Pres., Per Olav Karlsen/Chmn., Panagiotis Skiadas/Dep. Chmn., Henry S. Marcus/Dir., Richard J.H. Coxall/Dir., CFO

Owners: Captain Gabriel Petridis, Transamerica Investment, Mons Bolin, Rocket Marine Inc., Wellington Management, Insiders

Financial Data: **Fiscal Year End:**12/31 **Latest Annual Data:** 12/31/2006

Year		Sales		Net Income
2006		$94,199,000		$2,199,000
2005		$75,905,000		$14,771,000
Curr. Assets:	$22,430,000	Curr. Liab.:	$29,622,000	P/E Ratio: 29.19
Plant, Equip.:	$431,396,000	Total Liab.:	$325,452,000	Indic. Yr. Divd.: $0.560
Total Assets:	$458,040,000	Net Worth:	$132,588,000	Debt/ Equity: NA

Aristotle Corp (The)

96 Cummings Point Rd. , Stamford, CT, 06902; *PH:* 1-203-358-8000; *http://* www.aristotlecorp.net

General - Incorporation	DE	Stock - Price on:12/24/2007	$11.35
Employees	850	Stock Exchange	NDQ
Auditor	Ernst & Young, LLP	Ticker Symbol	ARTL
Stk Agt	American Stock Transfer & Trust Co.	Outstanding Shares	17,300,000
Counsel	NA	E.P.S.	$0.94
DUNS No.	15-117-9603	Shareholders	NA

Business: The group's principal activities are to manufacture educational, health and agricultural products. The group operates in two segments: educational: provides instructional teaching aids and materials, which are distributed to educational institutions for kindergarten through grade 12 classes, and for nursing school and emergency medical instructors. Commercial: provides agricultural products, sterile sampling containers and systems, materials for nursing home activities, and novelty and gift products. These products are marketed in the United States and internationally to end users such as fire and emergency medical departments and nursing and medical schools. The group's brands include nasco, triarco, summit learning, hubbard scientific, scott resources and spectrum educational supplies. On 17-Jun-2002, it acquired nasco international inc and on 04-Jun-2003, haan crafts corporation.

Primary SIC and add'l.: 6719 3523 8099

CIK No: 0000790071

Subsidiaries: American Educational Products LLC, ARTL, LLC, Haan Crafts Real Estate Holdings LLC, Haan Crafts, LLC, Hubbard Scientific LLC, Nasco Exports, Inc., NHI, LLC, S-A Subsidiary, Inc., Scott Resources LLC, Simulaids, Inc. , Spectrum Educational Supplies, Ltd., SREH, Inc., Triarco Arts & Crafts LLC

Officers: Phillip W. Niemeyer/Pres. - Nasco Division, VP - Production Coordination/$404,238.00, Dean T. Johnson/CFO, VP/$247,070.00, Steven B. Lapin/Dir., COO, Pres., Principal Executive Officer/$336,600.00, Brian R. Schlier/VP - Taxation, William H. Smith/VP, General Counsel, Sec./$201,600.00

Directors: John L. Lahey/Dir., Roy T.K. Thung/Dir., John A. Whritner/Dir., Ira R. Harkavy/Dir., Donald T. Netter/Dir., Steven B. Lapin/Dir., COO, Pres., Principal Executive Officer, Edward Netter/Dir., James G. Tatum/Dir.

Owners: Steven B. Lapin, John L. Lahey, Geneve Corporation, Donald T. Netter, Phillip W. Niemeyer, James G. Tatum, Brian R. Schlier, Dean T. Johnson, Insiders, John A. Whritner, Ira R. Harkavy, William H. Smith, Edward Netter

Financial Data: **Fiscal Year End:**12/31 **Latest Annual Data:** 12/31/2006

Year		Sales		Net Income
2006		$202,978,000		$23,801,000
2005		$188,769,000		$17,857,000
2004		$175,077,000		$17,564,000
Curr. Assets:	$85,519,000	Curr. Liab.:	$20,093,000	P/E Ratio: 12.07
Plant, Equip.:	$25,426,000	Total Liab.:	$38,930,000	Indic. Yr. Divd.: NA
Total Assets:	$133,321,000	Net Worth:	$94,391,000	Debt/ Equity: 0.1536

Arizona Land Income Corp

2999 N 44th St., Ste. 100, Phoenix, AZ, 85018; *PH:* 1-602-952-6800; *Fax:* 1-602-952-0924; *http://* www.peacockhislop.com

General - Incorporation	AZ	Stock - Price on:12/24/2007	$8.45
Employees	NA	Stock Exchange	AMEX
Auditor	Epstein, Weber & Conover, PLC	Ticker Symbol	AZL
Stk Agt	Bank One Arizona	Outstanding Shares	1,850,000
Counsel	NA	E.P.S.	NA
DUNS No.	NA	Shareholders	NA

Business: The groups principle activity is to invest in first mortgage loans. The group operates from the United States. The groups quarterly revenue for 2007 was 0.05 millions of USD.

Primary SIC and add'l.: 6798

CIK No: 0000830748

Officers: Thomas R. Hislop/59/Chmn., CFO, CEO, Barry W. Peacock/70/Pres., Larry P. Staley/65/Dir., VP

Directors: Thomas R. Hislop/59/Chmn., CFO, CEO, Robert L. Blackwell/85/Dir., Burton P. Freireich/82/Dir., David W. Miller/59/Dir.

Owners: Phillip Barkdoll/6.80%, Burton P. Freireich/6.80%, Insiders/8.00%, Larry P. Staley, David W. Miller, Robert L. Blackwell, Thomas R. Hislop

Financial Data: **Fiscal Year End:**12/31 **Latest Annual Data:** 12/31/2006

Year		Sales		Net Income
2006		$445,000		$3,681,000
2005		$385,000		$39,000
2004		$1,024,000		$1,938,000
Curr. Assets:	$2,642,000	Curr. Liab.:	$1,877,000	P/E Ratio: 4.45
Plant, Equip.:	$56,000	Total Liab.:	$1,877,000	Indic. Yr. Divd.: NA
Total Assets:	$6,109,000	Net Worth:	$4,232,000	Debt/ Equity: NA

Arizona Public Service Co

400 N Fifth St., Phoenix, AZ, 85004; *PH:* 1-602-250-1000; *http://* www.aps.com

General - Incorporation	AZ	Stock - Price on:12/24/2007	NA
Employees	NA	Stock Exchange	NA
Auditor	Deloitte & Touche LLP	Ticker Symbol	NA
Stk Agt	Bank of New York	Outstanding Shares	NA
Counsel	NA	E.P.S.	NA
DUNS No.	00-690-1995	Shareholders	NA

Business: The group's principle activities include generating, transmiting and distributing electricity to state of Arizona. It also generates, sell and deliver electricity and energy-related products to wholesale and retail customers in the western United States. The company is a wholly owned subsidiary of pinnacle west capital corporation. The company also provides retail electric services to the entire state of Arizona and currently has more than 931,500 customers. The company operates through two segments namely regulated electricity segment and marketing and trading segment. The group operates from United States.

Primary SIC and add'l.: 4911

CIK No: 0000007286

Subsidiaries: Acoustic Locating Services, LLC, Aegis Technologies, Inc., APACS Holdings LLC, Apex Power LLC, APS Energy L.P., APS Energy Services Company, Inc., APS Foundation, Inc., APSES Holdings, Inc., Arizona Business Accelerator, Arizona Public Service Company, Avimor, LLC(formerly SunCor Idaho, LLC), AXIOM Power Solutions, Inc., AZ PB Partnership, Bixco, Inc., BV at Hayden Ferry Lakeside, LLC 71 Subsidiaries included in the Index

Officers: Jack E. Davis/CEO, Warren Kotzmann/VP - Resource Acquisition, Risk Management, David A. Hansen/VP - Power Marketing, Trading, Nancy Loftin/Sr. VP, General Counsel, Sec., Don Robinson/Sr. VP - Planning, Administration, Chris Froggatt/VP, Controller, Barbara M. Gomez/VP, Treasurer, Denny L. Brown/CIO, VP, Edward Z. Fox/VP, Chief Sustainability Officer, John R. Denman/Sr. VP - Fossil Operations, Steven M. Wheeler/Exec. VP - Customer Service, Regulation, Donald E. Brandt/CFO, Pres., Ajit P. Bhatti/VP - Resource Planning, Bob Bement/VP - Operations, Randy Edington/Exec. VP, Chief Nuclear Officer *(20 Officers included in Index)*

Directors: William J. Post/57/Chmn., Bruce J. Nordstrom/Dir., William L. Stewart/Dir., Edward N. Basha/Dir., Michael L. Gallagher/Dir., Pamela Grant/Dir., Roy A. Herberger/Dir., Martha O. Hesse/Dir., William S. Jamieson/Dir., Humberto S. Lopez/Dir., Kathryn L. Munro/Dir.

Arizona Star Resources Corp (F)

401 Bay St., Ste. 2700, Toronto, ON, M5H 2Y4; *PH:* 1-604-623-4700; *http://* www.arizonastar.com

General - Incorporation: BC
Employees: NA
Auditor: PricewaterhouseCoopers LLP
Stk Agt: Computershare Investor Services LLC
Counsel: NA
DUNS No.: NA

Stock- Price on:12/24/2007: $10.36
Stock Exchange: AMEX
Ticker Symbol: AZS
Outstanding Shares: 42,330,000
E.P.S: -$0.06
Shareholders: NA

Business: The groups principal activity is exploring minerals. The group operates from the United States and Canada.

Primary SIC and add'l.: 8880

CIK No: 0000809103

Subsidiaries: Arizona Star (Bermuda) Ltd., Compaa Minera Casale, Estrella de Oro Limitada, Imperial Gold Corporation

Officers: Paul A. Parisotto/Dir., CEO, Pres., Thomas C. Dawson/Dir., CFO

Directors: Paul A. Parisotto/Dir., CEO, Pres., James S. Anthony/Chmn., Rudi P. Fronk/Dir., Christopher J. Reynolds/Dir., James T. Smolik/Dir., Thomas C. Dawson/Dir., CFO

Financial Data: *Fiscal Year End:*04/30 *Latest Annual Data:* 4/30/2006

Year	Sales	Net Income
2006	NA	-$2,914,000

Curr. Assets:	$4,336,000	**Curr. Liab.:**	$1,955,000		
Plant, Equip.:	NA	**Total Liab.:**	$1,955,000	**Indic. Yr. Divd.:**	NA
Total Assets:	$4,686,000	**Net Worth:**	$2,731,000	**Debt/ Equity:**	NA

Ark Restaurants Corp

85 Fifth Ave., 14th Fl., New York, NY, 10003; *PH:* 1-212-206-8800; *Fax:* 1-212-206-8845; *http://* www.arkrestaurants.com; *Email:* info@arkrestaurants.com

General - Incorporation: NY
Employees: 1,544
Auditor: J. H. Cohn LLP
Stk Agt: Continental Stock Transfer & Trust Co
Counsel: Shack Siegel Katz Flaherty & Goodman
DUNS No.: 14-462-2438

Stock- Price on:12/24/2007: $35.3
Stock Exchange: NDQ
Ticker Symbol: ARKR
Outstanding Shares: 3,590,000
E.P.S: $3.20
Shareholders: NA

Business: The group's principal activity is to own and operate restaurants & bars. The group operates through 24 restaurants and bars, 12 fast food concepts. The restaurants are located in New York, Washington, las vegas, Nevada and Florida. The group also owns and operates four restaurants and four food court facilities at the venetian casino resort and one restaurant and six food court facilities at the aladdin resort and casino and one restaurant within the forum shops at caesar's shopping center. The group also provides management services to restaurants owned by outside parties. Other operations of the group include catering businesses, wholesale and retail bakeries.

Primary SIC and add'l.: 5812 8741

CIK No: 0000779544

Subsidiaries: AFC Restaurant, Inc., Ark 474 Corp., Ark 47th St. Corp., Ark Atlantic City Corp., Ark Atlantic City Restaurant corp, Ark Bryant Park Corp., Ark D.C. Kiosk, Inc., Ark Fifth Avenue Corp., Ark Fremont, Inc., Ark Fulton Street Corp., Ark Islamorada Corp., Ark JMR Corp., Ark Las Vegas Restaurant Corp., Ark of Seaport, Inc., Ark Operating Corp. 42 Subsidiaries included in the Index

Officers: Michael Weinstein/Chmn., CEO, Pres., Walter Rauscher/VP - Corporate Sales, Catering, John Oldweiler/Dir. - Purchasing, Jennifer Sutton/Dir. - Operations, Financial Analysis, Michael Buck/General Counsel, Sec., Vincent Pascal/Dir., Sr. VP - Operations, Marilyn Guy/Dir. - Human Resources, Robert Stewart/CFO, Joe Vasquez/Dir. - Facilities Management, Colleen Hennigan/Dir. - Operations, Washington Division, Robert Towers/Dir., COO, Pres., Treasurer, Nancy Alvarez/Controller, Etty Scaglia/Dir. - Tour, Travel Sales, Paul Gordon/Dir., Sr. VP, Dir. - Las Vegas Operations, Evyette Ortiz/Dir. - Marketing *(16 Officers included in Index)*

Directors: Michael Weinstein/Chmn., CEO, Pres., Ernest Bogen/Chmn. Emeritus, Stephen Novick/Dir., Edward Lowenthal/Owner, Robert Towers/Dir., COO, Pres., Treasurer, Bruce Lewin/Dir., Marcia Allen/Dir., Paul Gordon/Dir., Sr. VP, Dir. - Las Vegas Operations, Vincent Pascal/Dir., Sr. VP - Operations, Steven Shulman/Dir., Arthur Stainman/Dir., Robert Thomas Zankel/Owner

Owners: Edward Lowenthal/1.00%, Vincent Pascal/1.52%, Robert Towers/1.04%, Robert Thomas Zankel/1.00%, Arthur Stainman/1.28%, Bruce R. Lewin/7.45%, Bruce R. Lewin/7.45%, Steven Shulman/1.00%, Michael Weinstein/29.86%, Insiders/43.21%, Robert Stewart/1.00%, Paul Gordon/1.00%, Kirkwood Capital, LP/70.16%

Financial Data: *Fiscal Year End:*10/01 *Latest Annual Data:* 9/30/2006

Year	Sales	Net Income
2006	$115,969,000	$5,220,000
2005	$115,577,000	$6,579,000
2004	$115,698,000	$6,657,000

Curr. Assets:	$16,261,000	**Curr. Liab.:**	$7,863,000	**P/E Ratio:**	10.20
Plant, Equip.:	$24,144,000	**Total Liab.:**	$12,367,000	**Indic. Yr. Divd.:**	$1.760
Total Assets:	$52,120,000	**Net Worth:**	$39,753,000	**Debt/ Equity:**	0.0231

Arkados Group Inc

220 Old New Brunswick Rd. , Piscataway, NJ, 08854; *PH:* 1-732-465-9300; *http://* www.arkados.com; *Email:* info@arkados.com

General - Incorporation: DE
Employees: 12
Auditor: Sherb & Co., LLP
Stk Agt: Interwest Transfer Company, Inc.
Counsel: NA
DUNS No.: NA

Stock- Price on:12/24/2007: $0.43
Stock Exchange: OTC
Ticker Symbol: AKDS
Outstanding Shares: 26,080,000
E.P.S: -$0.23
Shareholders: NA

Business: The groups principle activities include developing and marketing technology that enable broadband communication and networking over standard electrical lines. The group products include ArkTIC, AI-1100. The group marketed its products under the trade name ArkTIC (TM). The customers of the group include Original Equipment Manufacturers. The group operates through four segments namely In-Home networking, consumer audio visual applications or multimedia networking, MDU/MTU net working, broadband power line. The group operates from the United States.

Primary SIC and add'l.: 4813

CIK No: 0001095130

Subsidiaries: Arkados, Inc., CDK Financial Corp., CDKnet, LLC, Creative Technology, LLC, Diversified Capital Holdings, LLC

Officers: Oleg Logvinov/Pres., CEO - Arkados, Inc, Stephen S. Woodman/VP - Worldwide Sales, Business Develop, Arkados, Inc, Michael MacAluso/VP - Engineering, Arkados, Inc, Barbara Kane-Burke/CFO, Assist. Sec., Grant Ogata/Exec. VP - Worldwide Operations

Owners: Andreas Typaldos, William H. Carson, Grant Ogata, Gennaro Vendome, Oleg Logvinov, Barbara Kane-Burke, Insiders

Financial Data: *Fiscal Year End:*05/31 *Latest Annual Data:* 05/31/2007

Year	Sales	Net Income
2007	$132,000	-$6,033,000
2006	$112,000	-$4,025,000
2005	$833,000	-$7,001,000

Curr. Assets:	$558,000	**Curr. Liab.:**	$3,297,000		
Plant, Equip.:	$47,000	**Total Liab.:**	$11,534,000	**Indic. Yr. Divd.:**	NA
Total Assets:	$1,425,000	**Net Worth:**	-$10,109,000	**Debt/ Equity:**	NA

Arkanova Energy Corp

Ste. 300, 21 Waterway, Woodlands, TX, 77381; *PH:* 1-281-362-2787

General - Incorporation: NV
Employees: NA
Auditor: Malone & Bailey, P.C
Stk Agt: Pacific Stock Transfer Company
Counsel: NA
DUNS No.: NA

Stock- Price on:12/24/2007: $1.6
Stock Exchange: OTC
Ticker Symbol: AKVA
Outstanding Shares: NA
E.P.S: NA
Shareholders: NA

Business: The groups principal activity is to explore minerals. The group operates from Canada and the United States.

Primary SIC and add'l.: 1040

CIK No: 0001191359

Officers: Pierre Mulacek/CEO

Owners: Pierre Mulacek/1.33%, Reginald Denny, Erich Hofer/3.54%, Insiders/5.17%

Curr. Assets:	$41,000	**Curr. Liab.:**	$54,000		
Plant, Equip.:	NA	**Total Liab.:**	$54,000	**Indic. Yr. Divd.:**	NA
Total Assets:	$41,000	**Net Worth:**	-$13,000	**Debt/ Equity:**	NA

Arkansas Best Corp

3801 Old Greenwood Rd., Fort Smith, AR, 72903; *PH:* 1-479-785-6000; *Fax:* 1-479-785-6004; *http://* www.arkbest.com; *Email:* info@arkbest.com

General - Incorporation: DE
Employees: 12,665
Auditor: Ernst & Young LLP
Stk Agt: LaSalle Bank N.A
Counsel: NA
DUNS No.: 19-450-1870

Stock- Price on:12/24/2007: $39.09
Stock Exchange: NDQ
Ticker Symbol: ABFS
Outstanding Shares: 25,080,000
E.P.S: $2.28
Shareholders: NA

Business: The groups principle activity is to provide motor carrier transportation operations. The group operates from United States.

Primary SIC and add'l.: 7534 4213 4731

CIK No: 0000894405

Subsidiaries: ABF Aviation, LLC, ABF Cartage, Inc., ABF Farms, Inc., ABF Freight System (B.C.), Ltd., ABF Freight System Canada, Ltd., ABF Freight System de Mexico, Inc., ABF Freight System, Inc., Arkansas Best Airplane Leasing, Inc., Arkansas Underwriters Corporation, CaroTrans Canada, Ltd., CaroTrans de Mexico, S.A. DE C.V., Clipper Exxpress Company, Data-Tronics Corp., FleetNet America, Inc., FreightValue, Inc. 21 Subsidiaries included in the Index

Officers: Robert A. Davidson/Dir., CEO, Pres./$3,331,183.00, John R. Meyers/VP, David Humphrey/Dir. - Investor Relations, Judy R. McReynolds/CFO, Sr. VP, Treasurer/$784,642.00, Lavon J. Morton/VP - Tax, Chief Internal Auditor, David R. Cobb/VP, Controller, David W. Hardt/Pres. - Data, Tronics Corp, Oren C. Summer/Pres. - Fleetnet America, Inc, Christopher D. Baltz/41/ABF Sr. VP - Yield, Management, Strategic Development/$855,015.00, Wesley B. Kemp/61/ABF Sr. VP - Operations/$1,095,494.00, Roy M. Slagle/54/ABF Sr. VP - Sales, Marketing/$951,055.00, Michael R. Johns/VP, General Counsel, Corp. Sec.

Directors: Robert A. Davidson/Dir., CEO, Pres., Robert A. Young/Chmn., Fred A. Allardyce/Dir., John W. Alden/Dir., Alan J. Zakon/Dir., William M. Legg/Dir., Frank Edelstein/Dir., John H. Morris/Dir.

Owners: NFJ Investment Group L.P./6.64%, Insiders/10.00%, Robert A. Davidson, Barclays Global Investors, N.A./8.26%, John H. Morris, William M. Legg, Fred A. Allardyce, Royce & Associates, LLC/14.49%, Robert A. Young/8.60%, Christopher D. Baltz, John W. Alden, Wesley B. Kemp, Roy M. Slagle, Judy R. McReynolds, Frank Edelstein *(17 Owners included in Index)*

Financial Data: *Fiscal Year End:*12/31 *Latest Annual Data:* 12/31/2006

Year	Sales	Net Income
2006	$1,860,477,000	$84,094,000
2005	$1,860,269,000	$104,626,000
2004	$1,715,763,000	$75,529,000

Curr. Assets:	$350,957,000	**Curr. Liab.:**	$258,414,000	**P/E Ratio:**	14.06
Plant, Equip.:	$461,883,000	**Total Liab.:**	$359,321,000	**Indic. Yr. Divd.:**	$0.600
Total Assets:	$938,716,000	**Net Worth:**	$579,395,000	**Debt/ Equity:**	0.0019

Arkona Inc

10757 S River Front Pk.way, Ste. 400, South Jordan, UT, 84095; *PH:* 1-801-501-7100; *http://* www.arkona.com

General - Incorporation: DE
Employees: 91
Auditor: Mantyla McReynolds LLC
Stk Agt: Atlas Stock Transfer Corp
Counsel: NA
DUNS No.: NA

Stock- Price on:12/24/2007: NA
Stock Exchange: NA
Ticker Symbol: NA
Outstanding Shares: NA
E.P.S: NA
Shareholders: NA

Business: The group's principle activity is to develop, market and sell software products for use by new-cars and used-car dealership markets. The group's flagship product, arkona dealer management suite ('adms'), provides automation of all departments of an automobile dealership, including parts department, sales, finance, insurance, customer management and service. Adms is developed to run on IBM's iseries (as400) platform. The group also offers adms in an application service provider ('asp') format, where all

principal functions are performed by servers located at its facilities and can be accessed by the dealership by modem, broadband or other connection. Adms is marketed directly to dealers, through trade shows, seminars, as well as through relationships with third party suppliers, automobile manufacturers and other industry partners.

Primary SIC and add'l.: 7379 7372

CIK No: 0000925662

Subsidiaries: Thorsden acquired Arkona, Inc.

Officers: Alan Rudd/Chmn., CEO, Blake Nielson/VP - Client Services, Lee Boardman/VP - Operations, CFO, Richard Holland/Dir., Pres., Michael Critchfield/VP - Sales, David D. Jenkins/VP - Marketing, Rod Merrill/Contact - OEM, Third Party Integration, Kenny Mills/Regional Sales Mgr. - Southwest Regional Office, Justin Albrecht/Regional Sales Mgr. - Corporate Office, Sherry Arnold/Regional Sales Mgr. - Midwest Regional Office, Troy Clement/Regional Sales Mgr. - Central Regional Office, David Smith/Regional Sales Mgr. - Gulf States Regional Office, Jim Cassidy/Regional Sales Mgr. - Northcentral Regional Office, Steve Windham/Regional Sales Mgr. - Great Lakes Regional Office, Cliff Lavergne/Regional Sales Mgr. - Southeast Regional Office *(17 Officers included in Index)*

Directors: Alan Rudd/Chmn., CEO, Paul Henriod/Dir., Kent A. Misener/Dir., Richard Holland/Dir., Pres., Marc Fuller/Dir.

Arlington Hospitality Inc

2355 S Arlington Hts. Rd. , Ste 400, Arlington Heights, IL, 60005; *PH:* 1-847-228-5400; *http://* www.arlingtonhospitality.com

General - Incorporation	DE	Stock - Price on:12/24/2007	$0.008
Employees	NA	Stock Exchange	OTC
Auditor	Grant Thornton LLP, KPMG LLP	Ticker Symbol	HOST
Stk Agt	Affiliated Stock Transfer Co.	Outstanding Shares	NA
Counsel	NA	E.P.S.	NA
DUNS No.	11-537-1403	Shareholders	NA

Business: The group's principle activity is to develop, construct and sell hotels under the name of amerihost inn. It owns, operates and operates amerihost inn hotels and other hotels. The group has designed three- and four-story amerihost inn & suites prototypes for larger markets. Upon the sale of the amerihost inn and amerihost inn & suites brand names and franchising rights, the group simultaneously entered into franchise agreements with cendant for its amerihost inn hotels. The group offers complete operational and financial management services, including sales, marketing, quality control, training, purchasing and accounting.

Primary SIC and add'l.: 1522 7021 7361 7011 7389

CIK No: 0000778423

Subsidiaries: Altoona, PA 792 Limited Partnership, AP Equities of Florida, Inc., AP Hotels of California, Inc., AP Hotels of Georgia, Inc., AP Hotels of Illinois, Inc., AP Hotels of Iowa, Inc., AP Hotels of Michigan, Inc., AP Hotels of Mississippi, Inc., AP Hotels of Missouri, Inc., AP Hotels of Ohio, Inc., AP Hotels of Oklahoma, Inc., AP Hotels of Pennsylvania, Inc., AP Hotels of Texas, Inc., AP Hotels of Wisconsin, Inc., AP Hotels/Parkersburg, WV, Inc. 41 Subsidiaries included in the Index

Financial Data: *Fiscal Year End:*12/31   *Latest Annual Data:* 12/31/2004

Year	Sales		Net Income
2004	$63,442,000		-$5,637,000
2003	$72,517,000		-$5,619,000
2002	$76,531,000		-$1,710,000
Curr. Assets:	$46,463,000	**Curr. Liab.:**	$52,795,000
Plant, Equip.:	$42,967,000	**Total Liab.:**	$96,609,000	**Indic. Yr. Divd.:** NA
Total Assets:	$103,362,000	**Net Worth:**	$6,507,000	**Debt/ Equity:** 6.9339

Arlington Tankers Ltd

191 Post Rd. W, Westport, CT, 06880; *PH:* 1-203-221-2765; *Fax:* 1-203-221-2763; *http://* www.arlingtontankers.com; *Email:* info@arlingtontankers.com

General - Incorporation	Bermuda	Stock - Price on:12/24/2007	$28.16
Employees	3	Stock Exchange	NYSE
Auditor	KPMG LLP	Ticker Symbol	ATB
Stk Agt	HSBC Bank U.S.	Outstanding Shares	15,500,000
Counsel	NA	E.P.S.	$1.12
DUNS No.	NA	Shareholders	NA

Business: The groups principle activity is to transport crude oil and petroleum products. The groups products include Stena Victory, Stena Vision, Stena Consul and Stena Contest. The groups customers include ChevronTexaco Corporation, the Royal Dutch/Shell Group of Companies, ConocoPhillips and BP plc. The group operates from the United States. The groups quarterly revenue for September 2007 was 17.51 millions of USD.

Primary SIC and add'l.: 4412

CIK No: 0001305507

Subsidiaries: Companion Ltd., Compatriot Ltd., Concept Ltd., Concord Ltd., Consul Ltd., Contest Ltd., Victory Ltd., Vision Ltd.

Officers: Arthur L. Regan/Pres., Co - CEO, Edward Terino/Co - CEO, CFO, Dawna Ferguson/Sec.

Directors: Michael K. Drayton/Chmn., Stephen O. Jaeger/Dep. Chmn., Grant E. Gibbons/Dir.

Owners: Arthur Regan, Stephen O. Jaeger, Kayne Anderson Capital Advisors, L.P./5.10%, Vaughan Nelson Investment Management, L.P./7.80%, Wellington Management Company, LLP/9.80%, Michael K. Drayton, U.S. Trust Corporation/7.60%, Stena and Concordia entities and related persons/14.40%, Insiders

Financial Data: *Fiscal Year End:*12/31   *Latest Annual Data:* 12/31/2006

Year	Sales		Net Income
2006	$69,435,000		$21,464,000
2005	$55,455,000		$21,913,000
2004	$61,246,000		$20,351,000
Curr. Assets:	$17,397,000	**Curr. Liab.:**	$3,289,000	**P/E Ratio:** 25.14
Plant, Equip.:	$344,973,000	**Total Liab.:**	$232,789,000	**Indic. Yr. Divd.:** $2.360
Total Assets:	$363,409,000	**Net Worth:**	$130,620,000	**Debt/ Equity:** 1.8267

ARM Holdings Plc

141 Caspian Ct., Sunnyvale, CA, 94089; *PH:* 1-408-734-5600; *Fax:* 1-408-734-5050; *http://* www.arm.com; *Email:* investor.relations@arm.com

General - Incorporation	UK	Stock - Price on:12/24/2007	$8.4
Employees	1,659	Stock Exchange	NDQ
Auditor	PricewaterhouseCoopers LLP	Ticker Symbol	ARMHY
Stk Agt	Bank of New York	Outstanding Shares	NA
Counsel	Linklaters	E.P.S.	$0.17
DUNS No.	76-354-0937	Shareholders	NA

Business: The group's principle activities are the licensing, marketing, research and development of RISC microprocessor cores, peripheral solutions and system-on-chip designs. Products licensed by the group are used in a range of applications, including automotive, consumer entertainment, digital imaging, mass storage, networking, security and wireless industries. The group has formed partnerships with Philips, Texas Instruments, and Toshiba. Sales offices include six offices in the United States, and offices in Tokyo, Seoul, Taipei, Tel Aviv, Paris, and Munich. Design offices are based in Cambridge, Maidenhead, Sheffield, Blackburn, Sophia Antipolis, Leuven and Austin.

Primary SIC and add'l.: 5045 3674

CIK No: 0001057997

Subsidiaries: ARM Belgium N.V, ARM Consulting (Shanghai) Co. Ltd, ARM Embedded Technologies Pvt. Ltd, ARM France SAS, ARM Germany GmbH, ARM KK, ARM Korea Limited, ARM Limited, ARM Physical IP Asia Pacific Pte Ltd, ARM Physical IP, Inc, ARM Taiwan Limited (99.9% owned), ARM, Inc, Axys Design Automation, Inc, Keil Elektronik GmbH, Keil Software, Inc

Officers: Warren East/Dir., CEO, Simon Segars/Dir., Exec. VP - Sales, Tim Score/Dir., CFO, Mike Inglis/Dir., Exec. VP - Marketing, Mike Muller/Dir., CTO, Tudor Brown/Dir., COO, Bruce Beckloff/VP - Investor Relations, Patricia Alsop/Company Sec., Laura Faid/Investor Relations Co - Ordinator

Directors: Warren East/Dir., CEO, Doug Dunn/Chmn., Mike Muller/Dir., CTO, Mike Inglis/Dir., Exec. VP - Marketing, John Scarisbrick/Non Exec. Dir., Simon Segars/Dir., Exec. VP - Sales, Jeremy Scudamore/Dir., Tim Score/Dir., CFO, Philip Rowley/Dir., Tudor Brown/Dir., COO, Lucio L. Lanza/Dir., Kathleen O'Donovan/Dir., Young Sohn/Dir.

Owners: Capital Group Companies/8.85%, Nordea Investment Management/3.09%, MFS International/3.37%, Fidelity Investments/13.25%, Legal & General Investment Management/6.23%, Janus Capital Corporation/11.04%

Financial Data: *Fiscal Year End:*12/31   *Latest Annual Data:* 12/31/2006

Year	Sales		Net Income
2006	$515,741,000		$88,479,000
2005	$399,051,000		$71,900,000
2004	$294,571,000		$53,900,000
Curr. Assets:	$427,883,000	**Curr. Liab.:**	$143,626,000	
Plant, Equip.:	$27,369,000	**Total Liab.:**	$152,920,000	**Indic. Yr. Divd.:** $0.090
Total Assets:	$1,278,710,000	**Net Worth:**	$1,125,791,000	**Debt/ Equity:** NA

Armitage Mining Corp

8100 E Union Ave, Ste. 1206, Denver, CO, 80237; *PH:* 1-604-687-7178

General - Incorporation	NV	Stock - Price on:12/24/2007	NA
Employees	NA	Stock Exchange	OTC
Auditor	Sherb & Co., LLP	Ticker Symbol	GAHI
Stk Agt	NA	Outstanding Shares	NA
Counsel	NA	E.P.S.	NA
DUNS No.	NA	Shareholders	NA

Business: The group was incorporated in the State of Nevada on 30-Apr-2004 to engage in the acquisition, exploration and development of natural resource properties. The group has just commenced limited business operations, but have not yet realized any income.

Primary SIC and add'l.: 1040

CIK No: 0001303163

Officers: Michael Potts/51/Dir., CEO, CFO, Pres., Treasurer, Sec.

Directors: Michael Potts/51/Dir., CEO, CFO, Pres., Treasurer, Sec.

Owners: Michael Potts/58.17%, Insiders/58.80%

Financial Data: *Fiscal Year End:*09/30   *Latest Annual Data:* 09/30/2006

Year	Sales		Net Income
2006	NA		-$33,000
2005	NA		-$23,000
Curr. Assets:	$6,000	**Curr. Liab.:**	$25,000	
Plant, Equip.:	NA	**Total Liab.:**	$25,000	**Indic. Yr. Divd.:** NA
Total Assets:	$6,000	**Net Worth:**	-$19,000	**Debt/ Equity:** NA

Armor Electric Inc

201 Lomas Santa Fe Dr., Solana Beach, CA, 92075; *PH:* 1-858-720-0123; *http://* www.armorelectric.com

General - Incorporation	FL	Stock - Price on:12/24/2007	$0.055
Employees	NA	Stock Exchange	OTC
Auditor	Braverman International, P.C.	Ticker Symbol	ARME
Stk Agt	Holladay Stock Transfer, Inc.	Outstanding Shares	43,020,000
Counsel	NA	E.P.S.	-$0.03
DUNS No.	NA	Shareholders	NA

Business: The groups principal activities include manufacturing and marketing of new electric vehicles. The group operates through four segments namely transportation, recreation, leisure and riding toys, defense and industrial. The group operates from the United States.

Primary SIC and add'l.: 1731

CIK No: 0001211768

Officers: Merrill W. Moses/55/Chmn., CEO, Pres., Cheryl A. Spousta-Schertzer/Dir., VP - Operations, Chief Financial

Directors: Merrill W. Moses/55/Chmn., CEO, Pres., Cheryl A. Spousta-Schertzer/Dir., VP - Operations, Chief Financial, Laroy Orr/Dir.

Owners: Merrill Moses/2.90%, Insiders/3.80%, Cheryl Spousta-Schertzer, Nu Age Electrical Systems Inc/14.70%

Financial Data: *Fiscal Year End:*06/30   *Latest Annual Data:* 06/30/2007

Year	Sales	Net Income
2007	NA	-$1,377,000
2006	NA	-$824,000
2005	NA	-$189,000

Curr. Assets:	$33,000	**Curr. Liab.:**	$178,000		
Plant, Equip.:	NA	**Total Liab.:**	$551,000	**Indic. Yr. Divd.:**	NA
Total Assets:	$63,000	**Net Worth:**	-$488,000	**Debt/ Equity:**	NA

Armstrong Holdings Inc

2500 Columbia Ave., Lancaster, PA, 17603; ***PH:*** 1-717-397-0611; ***http://*** www.armstrong.com

General - Incorporation....PA
Employees....14,900
Auditor....KPMG LLP
Stk Agt...... American Stock Transfer & Trust Co.
Counsel....NA
DUNS No.....NA

Stock- Price on:12/24/2007....$0.632
Stock Exchange....NA
Ticker Symbol....NA
Outstanding Shares....40,550,000
E.P.S....$27.58
Shareholders....NA

Business: The group's principal activity is to produce flooring products and ceiling systems for use in construction and renovation of residential, commercial and institutional buildings. It operates in five segments: resilient flooring, wood flooring, textiles and sports flooring ('tsf'), building products and cabinets. Resilient flooring includes floor coverings, such as vinyl sheet, vinyl tile, linoleum flooring and luxury vinyl tile. Wood flooring includes solid wood and engineered wood floors in various wood species. Tsf includes carpeting products, artificial turf and other sports surfaces. Building products include suspended mineral fiber, soft fiber, metal and wood ceiling systems. Cabinets include kitchen and bathroom cabinetry and related products. Products are marketed to retailers, builders, contractors, installers, homecenters and others. Customers include the home depot inc and lowe's companies inc. The group operates in America, Europe and Asia-pacific.

Primary SIC and add'l.: 3448 2426 2273 3253 1742 3292 3996

CIK No: 0001109304

Subsidiaries: Armstrong (U.K.) Investments, Armstrong Architectural Products S.L., Armstrong Building Products B.V., Armstrong Building Products Company (Shanghai) Ltd., Armstrong Building Products G.m.b.H., Armstrong Cork Finance Corporation, Armstrong DLW AG, Armstrong DLW Licensing GmbH, Armstrong Hardwood Flooring Company, Armstrong Metal Ceilings Limited, Armstrong Metalldecken AG, Armstrong Metalldecken GmbH, Armstrong Metalldecken Holdings AG, Armstrong Realty Group, Inc., Armstrong Ventures, Inc. 30 Subsidiaries included in the Index

Officers: Frank J. Ready/Pres., CEO - Armstrong Floor Products, AFP North America, Michael D. Lockhart/Chmn., CEO, Rich Wiley/Assoc. Marketing Mgr. - Retail Business, Meg Graham/VP - Corporate Communication, Armstrong, Donald A. McCunniff/Sr. VP - Human Resources, Nicholas F. Grasberger/Sr. VP, CFO, Salvatore A. Abbate/VP - Marketing, ASC Operations, Stephen J. Senkowski/Exec. VP - Armstrong World Industries, John N. Rigas/Sr. VP, General Counsel, William C. Rodruan/VP, Controller, Beth A. Riley/Dir. - Investor Relations, Cathy Putt/Supervisor, Stockholder Services, Carlene Moloney/GM - Marketing Communications, Michele Zelman/Public Relations Consultant Armstrong Flooring Products, Linda Neal/Assist. Marketing Mgr. - Communications

Directors: Michael D. Lockhart/Chmn., CEO, Edward M. Sellers/63/Dir., James J. Gaffney/Dir., James J. O'Connor/Dir., Judith R. Haberkorn/Dir., John J. Roberts/Dir., Robert C. Garland/Dir., Scott D. Miller/Dir., Russel F. Peppet/Dir., Arthur J. Pergament/Dir., Alexander M. Sanders/Dir., Jerre L. Stead/65/Dir.

Owners: William C. Rodruan, Jerre L. Stead, John N. Rigas, S. Muoio & Co LLC & Salvatore Muoio/5.60%, Insiders, Michael D. Lockhart

Financial Data: ***Fiscal Year End:***12/31 ***Latest Annual Data:*** 12/31/2006

Year	Sales	Net Income
2006	NA	$1,226,400,000
2005	$3,558,400,000	$112,100,000
2004	$3,497,300,000	-$80,800,000

Curr. Assets:	$26,400,000	**Curr. Liab.:**	$100,000	**P/E Ratio:**	0.02
Plant, Equip.:	NA	**Total Liab.:**	$100,000	**Indic. Yr. Divd.:**	NA
Total Assets:	$26,400,000	**Net Worth:**	$26,300,000	**Debt/ Equity:**	NA

Armstrong World Industries Inc

2500 Columbia Ave., Lancaster, PA, 17604; ***PH:*** 1-717-397-0611; ***Fax:*** 1-717-396-6133; ***http://*** www.armstrong.com

General - Incorporation....PA
Employees....14,500
Auditor....KPMG LLP
Stk Agt...... American Stock Transfer & Trust Co.
Counsel......... Womble Carlyle Sandridge & Rice
DUNS No.....00-130-7792

Stock- Price on:12/24/2007....$52.39
Stock Exchange....NYSE
Ticker Symbol....AWI
Outstanding Shares....56,500,000
E.P.S....NA
Shareholders....NA

Business: The group designs, manufactures and sells flooring products and ceiling systems around the world. The company also designs, manufactures and sells kitchen and bathroom cabinets. The principal products of the company are resilient flooring, building products, wood flooring, cabinets, textiles and sports floorings. The company's products are sold primarily for use in the finishing, refurbishing and repair of residential, commercial and institutional buildings. The major customers of the company are retailers, builders, contractors, installers, home center chains and industry buying groups. The company's operations are carried on in Americas, Europe, Australia, China and other pacific area.

Primary SIC and add'l.: 2273 3053 1742 2426 3253 3996 6719

CIK No: 0000007431

Subsidiaries: Armstrong (U.K.) Investments, Armstrong Architectural Products S.L., Armstrong Building Products B.V., Armstrong Building Products Company (Shanghai) Ltd., Armstrong Building Products G.m.b.H., Armstrong Cork Finance Corporation, Armstrong DLW AG, Armstrong DLW Licensing GmbH, Armstrong Hardwood Flooring Company, Armstrong Metal Ceilings Limited, Armstrong Metalldecken AG, Armstrong Metalldecken GmbH, Armstrong Metalldecken Holdings AG, Armstrong Realty Group, Inc., Armstrong Ventures, Inc. 30 Subsidiaries included in the Index

Officers: Michael D. Lockhart/Chmn., CEO, Pres., Frank J. Ready/CEO, Pres. - Armstrong Floor Products, AFP North America, Donald A. McCunniff/Sr. VP - Human Resources, Stephen J. Senkowski/Exec. VP, Cathy Putt/Supervisor, Stockholder Services, Carlene Moloney/GM - Marketing Communications, Michele Zelman/Public Relations Consultant Armstrong Flooring Products Cherry Leaf Communications, Linda Neal/Assist. Marketing Mgr. - Communications, Nicholas F. Grasberger/CFO, Sr. VP, William C. Rodruan/VP, Controller, John N. Rigas/Sr. VP, General Counsel, Rich Wiley/Assoc. Marketing Mgr. - Retail Business, Salvatore A. Abbate/VP - Marketing, ASC Operations, Meg Graham/VP - Corporate Communication, Beth A. Riley/Dir. - Investor Relations

Directors: Michael D. Lockhart/Chmn., CEO, Pres., Alexander M. Sanders/Dir., Russel F. Peppet/Dir., Arthur J. Pergament/Dir., John J. Roberts/Dir., James J. Gaffney/Dir., Robert C. Garland/Dir., James J. O'Connor/Dir., James E. Marley/Dir., Judith R. Haberkorn/Dir.

Owners: Armstrong World Industries, Inc. Asbestos Personal Injury Settlement Trust/65.60%, John N. Rigas, Frank J. Ready, Insiders, Nicholas F. Grasberger, Stephen J. Senkowski, Michael D. Lockhart

Financial Data: ***Fiscal Year End:***12/31 ***Latest Annual Data:*** 12/31/2006

Year	Sales	Net Income
2006	$3,425,900,000	$1,358,000,000
2005	$3,558,400,000	$111,100,000
2004	$3,497,300,000	-$79,700,000

Curr. Assets:	$1,371,400,000	**Curr. Liab.:**	$516,600,000		
Plant, Equip.:	$966,200,000	**Total Liab.:**	$1,998,500,000	**Indic. Yr. Divd.:**	NA
Total Assets:	$4,170,700,000	**Net Worth:**	$2,164,700,000	**Debt/ Equity:**	0.3237

Arotech Corp

1229 Oak Valley Dr., Ann Arbor, MI, 48108; ***PH:*** 1-800-281-0356; ***Fax:*** 1-734-761-5368; ***http://*** www.arotech.com; ***Email:*** info@arotech.com

General - Incorporation....DE
Employees....342
Auditor....BDO Seidman, LLP
Stk Agt...... American Stock Transfer & Trust Co.
Counsel....NA
DUNS No.....NA

Stock- Price on:12/24/2007....$3.37
Stock Exchange....NDQ
Ticker Symbol....ARTX
Outstanding Shares....11,980,000
E.P.S....-$0.54
Shareholders....NA

Business: The group's principal activity is to design, develop and market zinc-air technology for primary and reusable battery systems. The group operates in two segments: defense and security products and electric fuel batteries. The defense and security products segment develops manufactures and markets advanced hi-tech multimedia and interactive digital solutions for training of military, law enforcement and security personnel and sophisticated lightweight materials and advanced engineering processes to armor vehicles. The electric fuel batteries segment produces zinc-air fuel cell packs for the U.S. Army's communications electronics command. On 13-Jan-2004, the group acquired faac incorporated, on 14-Jan-2004, epsilor electronic industries ltd and armour of America incorporated on 10-Aug-2004.

Primary SIC and add'l.: 3692 3691

CIK No: 0000916529

Subsidiaries: FAAC Inc

Officers: Robert S. Ehrlich/Chmn., CEO, Pres./$1,106,011.00, Steven Esses/Dir., Exec. VP, COO/$496,561.00, Yoel Gilon/Contact - Electric Vehicles, Yaakov Har-Oz/VP, General Counsel, Corp. Sec., Jonathan Whartman/Sr. VP, William Graham/VP - Government Affairs, Thomas J. Paup/VP - Finance, CFO/$157,956.00, Dean Krutty/Contact

Directors: Robert S. Ehrlich/Chmn., CEO, Pres., Steven Esses/Dir., Exec. VP, COO, Michael Marrus/45/Dir., Elliot Sloyer/44/Dir., Jay M. Eastman/Dir., Edward J. Borey/Dir., Seymour Jones/Dir., Jack E. Rosenfeld/Dir., Lawrence M. Miller/Dir.

Owners: Steven Esses/1.90%, Insiders/7.50%, Edward J. Borey, Lawrence M. Miller, Jay M. Eastman, Jack E. Rosenfeld, Robert S. Ehrlich/4.10%, Seymour Jones, Thomas J. Paup

Financial Data: ***Fiscal Year End:***12/31 ***Latest Annual Data:*** 12/31/2006

Year	Sales	Net Income
2006	$43,121,000	-$15,569,000
2005	$49,045,000	-$24,043,000
2004	$49,954,000	-$9,042,000

Curr. Assets:	$28,209,000	**Curr. Liab.:**	$15,738,000		
Plant, Equip.:	$3,741,000	**Total Liab.:**	$20,087,000	**Indic. Yr. Divd.:**	NA
Total Assets:	$75,068,000	**Net Worth:**	$54,960,000	**Debt/ Equity:**	0.0243

Arqule Inc

19 Presidential Way, Woburn, MA, 01801; ***PH:*** 1-781-994-0300; ***Fax:*** 1-781-376-6019; ***http://*** www.arqule.com; ***Email:*** wboni@arqule.com

General - Incorporation....DE
Employees....98
Auditor....PricewaterhouseCoopers LLP
Stk Agt...... American Stock Transfer & Trust Co.
Counsel....Palmer & Dodge LLP
DUNS No.....80-918-8386

Stock- Price on:12/24/2007....$7.28
Stock Exchange....NDQ
Ticker Symbol....ARQL
Outstanding Shares....35,920,000
E.P.S....-$1.56
Shareholders....NA

Business: The group's principal activities are the research and development of small molecular therapeutics based on its activated checkpoint therapy (sm) platform. The act technology develops small molecule compounds that selectively kill cancer cells and spare normal cells by restoring and activating cellular checkpoints that are defective in cancer cells. The trademarks include arqule, directed array, mapping array, amap, arqule reactor, compass array, custom array, mapmaker, optimal chemical entities, oces, parallel track, and prepqule. The group continues to advance the drug discovery efforts of pharmaceutical collaborators by providing high quality library design and compound production, including collaborations with pfizer inc, sankyo company ltd and novartis biomedical research institute. On 08-Sep-2003, the group acquired cyclis pharmaceuticals inc.

Primary SIC and add'l.: 2834

CIK No: 0001019695

Subsidiaries: Camitro Corporation, Camitro U.K. Ltd.

Officers: Stephen A. Hill/Dir., CEO, Pres./$1,150,275.00, Anthony S. Messina/VP - Human Development, Peter S. Lawrence/Exec. VP, General Counsel, Chief Business Officer/$598,435.00, Nigel J. Rulewski/Chief Medical Officer/$278,768.00, Richard H. Woodrich/Acting CFO, Treasurer/$122,800.00

Directors: Stephen A. Hill/Dir., CEO, Pres., Patrick J. Zenner/Chmn., Werner Cautreels/Member - Scientific Advisory Board, Nancy A. Simonian/Dir., Michael D. Loberg/60/Dir., William G. Messenger/Dir., Chiang J. Li/Member - Scientific Advisory Board, Ronald M. Lindsay/Dir., Timothy C. Barabe/Dir., Alan D'Andrea/Member - Scientific Advisory Board, Gerard I. Evan/Member - Scientific Advisory Board, Alfred L. Goldberg/Member - Scientific Advisory Board, William G. Kaelin/Member - Scientific Advisory Board, Arthur B. Pardee/Member - Scientific Advisory Board, John L. Ryan/Member - Scientific Advisory Board *(17 Directors included in Index)*

Owners: Eastbourne Capital Management, L.L.C./11.70%, Joseph Edelman/6.31%, Insiders/4.90%, Timothy C. Barabe, William G. Messenger, Black Bear Offshore Master Fund, L.P./7.70%, Pfizer Inc/9.14%, Stephen A. Hill/2.10%, Chiang J. Li/2.10%, Richard H. Woodrich

Financial Data: ***Fiscal Year End:***12/31 ***Latest Annual Data:*** 12/31/2006

Year	Sales	Net Income
2006	NA	NA
2005	NA	NA
2004	NA	NA

Curr. Assets:	$97,994,000	**Curr. Liab.:**	$17,437,000		
Plant, Equip.:	$4,549,000	**Total Liab.:**	$24,866,000	**Indic. Yr. Divd.:**	NA
Total Assets:	$104,820,000	**Net Worth:**	$79,954,000	**Debt/ Equity:**	NA

Array Biopharma Inc

3200 Walnut St., Boulder, CO, 80301; ***PH:*** 1-303-381-6600; ***Fax:*** 1-303-386-1390;
http:// www.arraybiopharma.com; ***Email:*** info@arraybiopharma.com

General - Incorporation .... DE
Employees 276
Auditor .... KPMG LLP
Stk Agt..... American Stock Transfer & Trust Co.
Counsel .... NA
DUNS No. .... NA

Stock- Price on:12/24/2007 .... $11.83
Stock Exchange .... NDQ
Ticker Symbol .... ARRY
Outstanding Shares 40,000,000
E.P.S .... -$1.55
Shareholders .... NA

Business: The group's principal activity is to discover and create small molecule drugs through the integration of chemistry, biology and informatics. The group uses the array discovery platform(R) discovery technologies to invent small molecule drugs. The group has collaborations with eli lilly and company, genpath pharmaceuticals inc, icos corporation, intermune inc, Japan tobacco inc, merck and co inc, pfizer inc and takeda chemical industries limited. The products and processes include the optimer building blocks, lead generation and lead optimization. The group offers its products and services throughout the United States, Europe and Japan.

Primary SIC and add'l.: 8731 2834

CIK No: 0001100412

Officers: Robert E. Conway/Dir., CEO/$1,107,245.00, Michael R. Carruthers/CFO/$485,773.00, James Blake/Sr. Research Investigator, Array Biopharma, John Yates/Chief Medical Officer, James D. Winkler/VP - Discovery, Translational Biology, David L. Snitman/Dir., COO, VP - Business Development/$651,257.00, John A. Josey/VP - Discovery Chemistry, Kevin Koch/Dir., Pres., Chief Scientific Officer/$856,398.00, John R. Moore/VP, General Counsel/$461,238.00, Gail S. Eckhardt/Professor, Medicine at The University, Colorado Health Sciences Center, Randall K. Johnson/Independent Consultant, Jonathon Kay/Dir. - Clinical Trials in The MGH Rheumatology Unit, Neil Spector/Dir. - Translational Research in Oncology

Directors: Robert E. Conway/Dir., CEO, Kyle A. Lefkoff/Chmn., Kevin Koch/Dir., Pres., Chief Scientific Officer, David L. Snitman/Dir., COO, VP - Business Development, Francis J. Bullock/Dir., Marvin H. Caruthers/Dir., Gil J. Van Lunsen/Dir., Douglas E. Williams/Dir., John L. Zabriskie/Dir.

Owners: Kevin Koch/2.30%, Francis J. Bullock, John L. Zabriskie, David L. Snitman/3.80%, Kopp Investment Advisors, LLC/6.30%, OrbiMed Advisors, LLC/5.20%, Robert E. Conway/2.30%, Deerfield Management Company, LP/5.60%, R. Michael Carruthers, Gil J. Van Lunsen, Marvin H. Caruthers/1.10%, Douglas E. Williams, Kyle A. Lefkoff, Insiders/10.60%, John R. Moore *(16 Owners included in Index)*

Financial Data: ***Fiscal Year End:***06/30 ***Latest Annual Data:*** 6/30/2006

Year	Sales	Net Income
2006	$45,003,000	-$39,614,000
2005	$45,506,000	-$23,244,000
2004	$34,831,000	-$25,966,000

Curr. Assets:	$74,863,000	**Curr. Liab.:**	$18,856,000		
Plant, Equip.:	$27,309,000	**Total Liab.:**	$33,533,000	**Indic. Yr. Divd.:**	NA
Total Assets:	$102,173,000	**Net Worth:**	$68,641,000	**Debt/ Equity:**	0.3964

Arrhythmia Research Technology Inc

25 Sawyer Passway, Fitchburg, MA, 01420; ***PH:*** 1-978-345-5000; ***Fax:*** 1-978-342-0168;
http:// www.arthrt.com

General - Incorporation .... DE
Employees 97
Auditor .... Carlin, Charron & Rosen, LLP
Stk Agt.......... Continental Stock Transfer & Trust Co
Counsel .... NA
DUNS No. 14-800-1167

Stock- Price on:12/24/2007 .... $12.93
Stock Exchange .... AMEX
Ticker Symbol .... HRT
Outstanding Shares 2,710,000
E.P.S $0.69
Shareholders .... NA

Business: The group's principal activity is to sell and license medical software for monitoring, analyzing and treating heart disease. It also sells and licenses medical software, which acquires data and analyzes electrical impulses of the heart to detect and aid in the treatment of potentially lethal arrhythmias. The group's wholly owned subsidiary, micron products, inc. (micron), manufactures silver plated sensors used in the manufacture of disposable medical electrodes constituting a part of ecg diagnostic and monitoring instruments. Micron also distributes metal snap fasteners used in the manufacture of disposable medical electrodes. The products include signal-averaging electrocardiographic (saecg) software comprising the predictor(R) 7. The group operates in Europe, UK, Canada and Pacific Rim. On 07-May-2004, the group acquired new England molders.

Primary SIC and add'l.: 7372 3845

CIK No: 0000819689

Subsidiaries: Micron Products, Inc.

Owners: Paul F. Walter/2.70%, HealthInvest Global Long/Short Fund/9.30%, David A. Garrison, Julius Tabin/4.30%, Insiders/12.00%, Chambers Medical Foundation/10.20%, James E. Rouse, E. P. Marinos/2.20%, Jason Chambers/1.40%

Financial Data: ***Fiscal Year End:***12/31 ***Latest Annual Data:*** 12/31/2006

Year	Sales	Net Income
2006	$19,318,000	$2,164,000
2005	$12,895,000	$1,578,000
2004	$11,111,000	$1,616,000

Curr. Assets:	$8,325,000	**Curr. Liab.:**	$1,824,000		
Plant, Equip.:	$6,046,000	**Total Liab.:**	$1,984,000	**Indic. Yr. Divd.:**	NA
Total Assets:	$16,404,000	**Net Worth:**	$14,420,000	**Debt/ Equity:**	NA

Arris Group Inc

3871 Lakefield Dr., Suwanee, GA, 30024; ***PH:*** 1-770-622-8400; ***Fax:*** 1-770-622-8770;
http:// www.arrisi.com

General - Incorporation .... DE
Employees 781
Auditor .... Ernst & Young LLP
Stk Agt.......... Bank of New York
Counsel .... NA
DUNS No. .... NA

Stock- Price on:12/24/2007 .... $16.69
Stock Exchange .... NDQ
Ticker Symbol .... ARRS
Outstanding Shares 109,020,000
E.P.S $1.43
Shareholders .... NA

Business: The group's principal activities are to develop and supply equipment and technology for cable system operators and other broadband service providers. It develops advanced cable telephony equipment enabling the delivery of converged services through broadband local access. The group's solutions for Internet protocol and optical transport allow broadband services providers to deliver full range of integrated voice, video and data services to the subscribers. The products of the group include broadband, transmission, optical and outside plant and supplies and services. The group's major customers comcast and cox communications.

Primary SIC and add'l.: 3357 3663

CIK No: 0001141107

Subsidiaries: Arris Interactive LLC, Arris International, Inc

Officers: Robert J. Stanzione/Chmn., CEO, Pres./$3,967,562.00, Harry L. Bosco/Dir., CEO, Pres., John Anderson Craig/Dir. - Business Consultant, John R. Petty/Dir. - Private Investor, Ron Coppock/Pres. - International/$1,011,925.00, David B. Potts/Exec. VP, CFO, CIO/$1,122,696.00, James D. Lakin/Pres. - Broadband/$1,143,381.00, Lawrence A. Margolis/Exec. VP - Strategic Planning, Administration, Chief Counsel, Sec./$1,378,882.00, Bryant Isaacs/Pres. - New Business Ventures, Robert Puccini/Pres. - Telewire Supply, Marc Geraci/54/Treasurer, James A. Bauer/Primary IR Contact, Larry Margolis/Primary IR Contact, Daniel Owens/37/VP, Controller

Directors: Robert J. Stanzione/Chmn., CEO, Pres., Harry L. Bosco/Dir., CEO, Pres., John Anderson Craig/Dir. - Business Consultant, Alex B. Best/Dir., Matthew B. Kearney/Dir., William H. Lambert/Dir., John R. Petty/Dir. - Private Investor

Owners: Barclays Global Fund Advisors/5.50%, John Anderson Craig, James D. Lakin, Wellington Management Company, LLP/7.10%, Neuberger Berman Inc./6.40%, Ronald M. Coppock, Alex B. Best, David B. Potts, The Vanguard Group, Inc/5.00%, Insiders/3.30%, Lawrence A. Margolis, Robert J. Stanzione/1.50%, Harry L. Bosco, John R. Petty, Matthew B. Kearney *(16 Owners included in Index)*

Financial Data: ***Fiscal Year End:***12/31 ***Latest Annual Data:*** 12/31/2006

Year	Sales	Net Income
2006	$891,551,000	$142,287,000
2005	$680,417,000	$51,483,000
2004	$490,041,000	-$28,396,000

Curr. Assets:	$800,952,000	**Curr. Liab.:**	$124,454,000	**P/E Ratio:**	11.51
Plant, Equip.:	$28,287,000	**Total Liab.:**	$418,136,000	**Indic. Yr. Divd.:**	NA
Total Assets:	$1,013,557,000	**Net Worth:**	$595,421,000	**Debt/ Equity:**	0.4272

Arrow Electronics Inc

50 Marcus Dr., Melville, NY, 11747; ***PH:*** 1-631-847-2000; ***Fax:*** 1-631-847-2222;
http:// www.arrow.com; ***Email:*** investor@arrow.com

General - Incorporation .... NY
Employees 12,000
Auditor .... Ernst & Young LLP
Stk Agt .... Mellon Investor Services LLC
Counsel .... NA
DUNS No. 04-915-9957

Stock- Price on:12/24/2007 .... $39.77
Stock Exchange .... NYSE
Ticker Symbol .... ARW
Outstanding Shares 124,160,000
E.P.S $3.40
Shareholders .... NA

Business: The groups principle activity is to provide electronic components and computer products to industrial and commercial customers worldwide. The groups services include materials planning, programming and assembly, inventory management, online supply chain tools and design services. The group operates from United States.

Primary SIC and add'l.: 5065 5045

CIK No: 0000007536

Subsidiaries: Adecom Service S.r.l., Arrow Altech Distribution (Pty) Ltd., Arrow Altech Holdings (Pty) Ltd., Arrow Asia Distribution Limited, Arrow Asia Pac Ltd., Arrow CE Hungary Kerekedelmi Kft, Arrow CE International GmbH, Arrow Components (M)Sdn Bhd, Arrow Components (NZ), Arrow Components Sweden AB, Arrow Computer Products S.N.C., Arrow Denmark, ApS, Arrow Electronics (China) Trading Co. Ltd., Arrow Electronics (CI)Ltd., Arrow Electronics (Delaware), Inc. 174 Subsidiaries included in the Index

Officers: William E. Mitchell/Chmn., CEO, Pres./$6,175,324.00, Germano Fanelli/VP, Chmn. - Arrow Europe, Middle East, Africa, South America, Emeasa/$2,534,820.00, Catherine M. Morris/Sr. VP, Pres. - Arrow Enterprise Computing Solutions, Kevin Gilroy/Sr. VP, Pres. - Arrow Enterprise Computing Solutions, John P. McMahon/Sr. VP - Corporate Human Resources, Albert G. Streber/VP - Global Marketing, Arrow Global Components, Paul J. Reilly/CFO, Sr. VP/$1,273,273.00, Wayne Brody/VP, Assist. Sec., Chief Compliance Officer, Peter S. Brown/Sr. VP, General Counsel, Sec., Vincent Vellucci/VP, Sr. VP - Global Sales Excellence, Arrow Global Components, Peter T. Kong/VP, Pres. - Arrow Asia, Pacific/$1,326,465.00, Vincent Melvin/CIO, VP, Jan M. Salsgiver/VP, Exec. VP - Arrow Europe, Middle East, Africa, South America, Emeasa, Bhawnesh C. Mathur/Sr. VP - Supplier Marketing, Asset Management, Arrow Global Components, Michael J. Long/Sr. VP, Pres. - Arrow Global Components/$1,551,287.00 *(23 Officers included in Index)*

Directors: William E. Mitchell/Chmn., CEO, Pres., John C. Waddell/Vice Chmn., Germano Fanelli/VP, Chmn. - Arrow Europe, Middle East, Africa, South America, Emeasa, Karen Gordon Mills/Dir., Roger King/Dir., John N. Hanson/Dir., Daniel W. Duval/Dir., Richard S. Hill/Dir., Stephen C. Patrick/Dir., Barry W. Perry/Dir., M. F. Keeth/Dir.

Owners: Wellington Management Company, LLP/12.40%, William E. Mitchell/2.40%, Germano Fanelli, Stephen C. Patrick, Barry W. Perry, Paul J. Reilly/2.20%, FMR Corp./14.80%, Barclays Global Investors/5.80%, Roger King, John N. Hanson, Insiders/2.90%, Peter T. Kong, Michael J. Long, John C. Waddell, Mutuelles AXA/8.40% *(17 Owners included in Index)*

Financial Data: ***Fiscal Year End:***12/31 ***Latest Annual Data:*** 12/31/2006

Year	Sales	Net Income
2006	$13,577,112,000	$388,331,000
2005	$11,164,196,000	$253,609,000
2004	$10,646,113,000	$207,504,000

Curr. Assets:	$4,895,621,000	**Curr. Liab.:**	$2,504,110,000		
Plant, Equip.:	$262,373,000	**Total Liab.:**	$3,673,013,000	**Indic. Yr. Divd.:**	NA
Total Assets:	$6,669,572,000	**Net Worth:**	$2,996,559,000	**Debt/ Equity:**	0.4232

Arrow Financial Corp

250 Glen St., Glens Falls, NY, 12801; ***PH:*** 1-518-745-1000; ***Fax:*** 1-518-761-0843;
http:// www.arrowfinancial.com; ***Email:*** information@arrowbank.com

General - Incorporation	NY	Stock - Price on:12/24/2007	$22.21
Employees	438	Stock Exchange	NDQ
Auditor	KPMG LLP	Ticker Symbol	AROW
Stk Agt.... American Stock Transfer & Trust Co.		Outstanding Shares	10,420,000
Counsel	NA	E.P.S	$1.59
DUNS No.	11-972-3401	Shareholders	NA

Business: The group's principle activity is to provide commercial and consumer financial products through its subsidiaries in New York. It acts as a holding company to the glens falls national bank and trust company and the saratoga national bank and trust company. The banks accept demand deposits, regular, money market, savings and time deposits. Lending activities consist of commercial loans, financial and agricultural loans, real estate commercial, construction and residential loans and installment loans to individuals. Target market for these services are consumers and small and mid-sized companies. The group also provides retirement planning, trust and estate administration services for individuals and pension, profit sharing and employee benefit plan administration for corporations. The group's quarterly income for September 2007 was 4.51 millions of USD.

Primary SIC and add'l.: 6712 6021

CIK No: 0000717538

Subsidiaries: A Nationally Chartered Commercial Bank, A New York Corporation, A Non-deposit Trust Company, A Real Estate Investment Trust, A Vermont Corporation, Arrow Capital Statutory Trust II, Arrow Capital Statutory Trust III, Arrow Properties, Inc., Capital Financial Group, Inc., Glens Falls National Bank and Trust Company, Glens Falls National Community Development Corporation, GMB Asset Management, LLC, Headquarters: Glens Falls, NY, Headquarters: Saratoga Springs, NY, Headquarters: Glens Falls, NY 19 Subsidiaries included in the Index

Officers: Terry R. Goodemote/Sr. VP, Accounting Division Head/$106,030.00

Directors: Herbert O. Carpenter/70/Dir.

Owners: David L. Moynehan, Thomas L. Hoy/2.13%, David G. Kruczlnicki, Gerard R. Bilodeau, Richard J. Reisman, Jan-Eric O. Bergstedt, Elizabeth OC. Little, Kenneth C. Hopper, Gary C. Dake, Herbert O. Carpenter, Terry R. Goodemote, Michael B. Clarke, Mary-Elizabeth T. FitzGerald, Insiders/7.39%, John J. Carusone **(17 Owners included in Index)**

Financial Data: *Fiscal Year End:*12/31 *Latest Annual Data:* 12/31/2006

Year	Sales	Net Income
2006	$96,494,000	$16,892,000
2005	$87,075,000	$18,639,000
2004	$81,635,000	$19,478,000

Curr. Assets:	$43,995,000	Curr. Liab.:	$1,359,721,000	P/E Ratio:	13.97
Plant, Equip.	$16,000,000	Total Liab.:	$1,402,087,000	Indic. Yr. Divd.:	$0.960
Total Assets:	$1,520,217,000	Net Worth:	$118,130,000	Debt/ Equity:	0.1689

Arrow International Inc

2400 Bernville Rd. , Reading, PA, 19612; **PH:** 1-610-378-0131; *http://* www.arrowintl.com

General - Incorporation	PA	Stock - Price on:12/24/2007	$38.07
Employees	4,000	Stock Exchange	NDQ
Auditor	PricewaterhouseCoopers LLP	Ticker Symbol	ARRO
Stk Agt	Registrar & Transfer Co	Outstanding Shares	45,140,000
Counsel	NA	E.P.S	$1.33
DUNS No.	07-283-1415	Shareholders	NA

Business: The group's principal activities are to develop, manufacture and market a broad range of clinically advanced, disposable catheters and related products for critical and cardiac care. The critical care products are used principally for central vascular access for administration of fluids, drugs and blood products, patient monitoring and diagnostic purposes, as well as for pain management. The group's products are used primarily by anesthesiologists, critical care specialists, surgeons, emergency and trauma physicians, cardiologists, interventional radiologists, electrophysiologists, pain management specialists and other health care providers. The group sells its products in Japan, Germany, the Netherlands, France, Spain, Greece, Africa, Canada, Mexico, the czech republic and slovakia.

Primary SIC and add'l.: 8731 5122 3841

CIK No: 0000886046

Subsidiaries: AMH (Arrow Medical Holdings) B.V., Arrow Africa (Pty) Ltd., Arrow Deutschland GmbH, Arrow France S.A., Arrow Hellas Commercial A.E, Arrow Iberia, S.A., Arrow Internacional de Chihuahua, S.A. de C.V., Arrow Internacional de Mexico S.A. de C.V., Arrow International CR, A.S, Arrow International EDC NV, Arrow International Export Corporation, Arrow International Investment Corp, Arrow International UK Limited, Arrow Interventional, Inc., Arrow Italy S.r.l 25 Subsidiaries included in the Index

Owners: John C. Long, Frederick J. Hirt, James T. Hatlan, Jerome T. Holleran/1.90%, Marlin Miller/8.50%, R. James Macaleer, Raymond Neag/4.90%, Philip B. Fleck, Anna M. Seal, John H. Broadbent/1.20%, Robert L. McNeil/10.10%, John E. Gurski, Carl G. Anderson/1.30%, Insiders/18.60%, Richard T. Niner/10.20% *(17 Owners included in Index)*

Financial Data: *Fiscal Year End:*10/27 *Latest Annual Data:* 8/31/2006

Year	Sales	Net Income
2006	$481,587,000	$56,009,000
2005	$454,296,000	$39,513,000
2004	$433,134,000	$55,942,000

Curr. Assets:	$389,220,000	Curr. Liab.:	$138,087,000		
Plant, Equip.	$173,853,000	Total Liab.:	$171,889,000	Indic. Yr. Divd.:	$0.840
Total Assets:	$697,437,000	Net Worth:	$525,548,000	Debt/ Equity:	NA

Arrow Resources Development Inc

152 W 57th St., New York, NY, 10019; **PH:** 1-212-262-2300; *http://* www.arrowrd.com

General - Incorporation	DE	Stock - Price on:12/24/2007	$0.08
Employees	NA	Stock Exchange	OTC
Auditor	KBL, LLP	Ticker Symbol	NA
Stk Agt	Jersey Transfer & Trust Co	Outstanding Shares	649,540,000
Counsel	NA	E.P.S	NA
DUNS No.	NA	Shareholders	NA

Business: The groups principal activities include provide marketing, selling, distributing and corporate finance services. The group operates from the United States.

Primary SIC and add'l.: 800

CIK No: 0000795255

Officers: Peter John Frugone/Chmn., CEO, William R. St. George/Sec., Treasurer, Hans Karundeng/Sr. Consultant, Richard M. Levychin/Consultant

Directors: Peter John Frugone/Chmn., CEO, John E. McConnaughy/79/Dir., Rudolph Karundeng/Dir., Robert A. Levinson/Dir.

Curr. Assets:	NA	Curr. Liab.:	$5,562,000		
Plant, Equip.	NA	Total Liab.:	$5,562,000	Indic. Yr. Divd.:	NA
Total Assets:	$125,000,000	Net Worth:	$119,438,000	Debt/ Equity:	NA

Arrowhead Research Corp

201 S Lake Ave., Ste. 703, Pasadena, CA, 91101; **PH:** 1-626-304-3400; **Fax:** 1-626-304-3401; *http://* www.arrowres.com; **Email:** info@arrowres.com

General - Incorporation	DE	Stock - Price on:12/24/2007	$6.08
Employees	63	Stock Exchange	NDQ
Auditor	Rose, Snyder & Jacobs LLP	Ticker Symbol	ARWR
Stk Agt	Computershare Trust Co	Outstanding Shares	35,660,000
Counsel	NA	E.P.S	-$0.83
DUNS No.	60-773-5859	Shareholders	NA

Business: The group's principle activities include research and development, and other business planning activities. The company currently produces no products and is evaluating alternative plans for future operations. Previously, the company developed, manufactured and marketed peripheral hardware products. These products enable users to create and send messages across local area networks and wide area networks of personal computers. The group operates from United States.

Primary SIC and add'l.: 8731 3577

CIK No: 0000879407

Subsidiaries: Aonex Technologies, Inc., Calando Pharmaceuticals, Inc., Insert Therapeutics, Inc., NanoPolaris, Inc.

Officers: Bruce R. Stewart/Chmn., CEO, Founder, Richmond Wolf/Chmn. - Advisory Board, John Miller/VP - Business Development, Marc W. Bockrath/Member - Scientific Advisory Board, Sean Olson/Pres. - Aonex Technologies, Inc, Virginia Dadey/VP - Investor Relations, Joseph T. Kingsley/CFO, Pres., Jane Davidson/VP - Operations, Leon Ekchian/Pres.

Directors: Bruce R. Stewart/Chmn., CEO, Founder, Edward W. Frykman/Dir., Leroy T. Rahn/Dir., Charles P. McKenney/Dir., Thomas A. Tombrello/Member - Scientific Advisory Board, Harry Atwater/Member - Scientific Advisory Board, Mark Davis/Member - Scientific Advisory Board, Charles Patrick Collier/Member - Scientific Advisory Board

Owners: David M. Knott/13.10%, Charles P. McKenney, Edward W. Frykman, JGD Management/14.80%, Joseph T. Kingsley, Insiders/5.10%, LeRoy T. Rahn, Bruce R. Stewart/3.30%

Financial Data: *Fiscal Year End:*09/30 *Latest Annual Data:* 9/30/2006

Year	Sales	Net Income
2006	$595,000	-$18,997,000
2005	$591,000	-$6,625,000
2004	$196,000	-$2,497,000

Curr. Assets:	$28,776,000	Curr. Liab.:	$2,920,000		
Plant, Equip.:	$1,271,000	Total Liab.:	$2,920,000	Indic. Yr. Divd.:	NA
Total Assets:	$34,526,000	Net Worth:	$30,671,000	Debt/ Equity:	NA

Art Boutique Inc

7th Fl., New Henry House, 10 Ice House St., Hongkong;

General - Incorporation	WY	Stock - Price on:12/24/2007	$0.2
Employees	NA	Stock Exchange	OTC
Auditor	Jaspers + Hall, PC	Ticker Symbol	ARTB
Stk Agt	Interstate Transfer Company	Outstanding Shares	NA
Counsel	NA	E.P.S	NA
DUNS No.	NA	Shareholders	NA

Business: The groups principal activity is to operate real estate business. The group operates from the United States.

Primary SIC and add'l.: 8412

CIK No: 0001129458

Subsidiaries: Key Chance International, Ltd., Key Chance, Inc., Micronesian Resorts, Inc.

Officers: Jun Kobayashi/44/Dir., CEO, VP, Tsang Ping Lam/64/Dir., Pres., Tsang Hung Quen Quentin/33/Dir., Sec., Treasurer, Ronald Chi Ho Lui/55/Dir., Treasurer, Sec.

Directors: Jun Kobayashi/44/Dir., CEO, VP, Tsang Ping Lam/64/Dir., Pres., Ken Ukai/39/Dir., Kentaro Ono/39/Dir., Tsang Hung Quen Quentin/33/Dir., Sec., Treasurer, Minoru Hirota/65/Dir., Ronald Chi Ho Lui/55/Dir., Treasurer, Sec.

Owners: Yasuhiro Sakakibaro/21.00%

Financial Data: *Fiscal Year End:*12/31 *Latest Annual Data:* 12/31/2006

Year	Sales	Net Income
2006	NA	$457,000
2005	NA	-$709,000
2004	NA	-$525,000

Curr. Assets:	NA	Curr. Liab.:	$81,000		
Plant, Equip.:	NA	Total Liab.:	$81,000	Indic. Yr. Divd.:	NA
Total Assets:	NA	Net Worth:	-$81,000	Debt/ Equity:	NA

Art Technology Group Inc

1 Main St., Cambridge, MA, 02142; **PH:** 1-617-386-1000; **Fax:** 1-617-386-1111; *http://* www.atg.com; **Email:** ir@atg.com

General - Incorporation	DE	Stock - Price on:12/24/2007	$2.65
Employees	378	Stock Exchange	NDQ
Auditor	Ernst & Young LLP	Ticker Symbol	ARTG
Stk Agt	EquiServe Trust Co N.A	Outstanding Shares	127,920,000
Counsel	Hale & Dorr LLP	E.P.S	$0.00
DUNS No.	NA	Shareholders	NA

Business: The group's principle activities are to offer an integrated suite of Internet customer relationship management and electronic commerce software applications. The group's e-commerce portal and relationship management applications, which feature personalization technology, are built on a flexible framework designed to help organizations to manage, build and integrate solutions that improve the customer interactions and business processes. The group produces e-business solutions that enable organizations to improve the relationships with customers, partners and employees. It also provides related

services, which include consulting, design, application development, integration, training and support services in conjunction with our products. These services are provided through professional services, education and customer support service offerings. The gruop's quarterly revenue for September 2007 was 35.89 millions of USD.

Primary SIC and add'l.: 7373 7372 7375

CIK No: 0001086195

Subsidiaries: Amacis Group, Limited, Amacis Ltd., Amacis Trustees Ltd., Amacis, Inc., Art Technology Group (Canada) Inc., Art Technology Group (Europe) Limited, Art Technology Group Australia Pty Limited, Art Technology Group B.V., Art Technology Group Canada ULC, Art Technology Group GmbH, Art Technology Group, KK, Art Technology Group, S.A.R.L., ATG Global, Inc., ATG Securities Corporation, Broad Daylight, Inc. 18 Subsidiaries included in the Index

Officers: Robert D. Burke/Dir., CEO, Pres./$994,132.00, John Federman/GM - Estara, Patricia O'Neill/Sr. VP - Human Resources, Ken Volpe/Sr. VP - Products, Technology/$516,623.00, Julie Bradley/CFO/$416,548.00, Barry Clark/Sr. VP - Worldwide Sales/$516,623.00, Cliff Conneighton/Sr. VP - Marketing/$492,991.00, Lou Frio/Sr. VP - Services, Drew Reynolds/Sr. VP - Corporate Development

Directors: Robert D. Burke/Dir., CEO, Pres., Dan Regis/Chmn., Rob Held/Dir., Phyllis S. Swersky/Dir., Ilene H. Lang/Dir., Michael A. Brochu/Dir., David B. Elsbree/Dir., Mary E. Makela/Dir., John R. Held/Dir., Daniel C. Regis/Dir.

Owners: David B. Elsbree, Patricia ONeill, Mary E. Makela, John R. Held, Ilene H. Lang, Insiders/4.27%, John Federman, Michael A. Brochu, FMR Corp./7.91%, Barry E. Clark, Louis R. Frio, Clifford J. Conneighton, Daniel C. Regis, Kenneth Z. Volpe, Diker Management, LLC/5.55% *(18 Owners included in Index)*

Financial Data: Fiscal Year End: 12/31   **Latest Annual Data:** 12/31/2006

Year	Sales	Net Income
2006	$103,232,000	$9,695,000
2005	$90,646,000	$5,769,000
2004	$69,219,000	-$9,544,000

Curr. Assets:	$68,278,000	Curr. Liab.:	$43,845,000	P/E Ratio:	265.00
Plant, Equip.:	$5,326,000	Total Liab.:	$44,907,000	Indic. Yr. Divd.:	NA
Total Assets:	$149,981,000	Net Worth:	$105,074,000	Debt/ Equity:	NA

Art's Way Manufacturing Co Inc

5556 Hwy. 9, Armstrong, IA, 50514; *PH:* 1-712-864-3131; *Fax:* 1-712-864-3154; *http://* www.artsway-mfg.com; *Email:* artsway@ncn.net

General - Incorporation	DE	Stock - Price on:12/24/2007	$9.2
Employees	90	Stock Exchange	NDQ
Auditor	Eide Bailley LLP	Ticker Symbol	ARTW
Stk Agt	American Stock Transfer & Trust CO.	Outstanding Shares	1,980,000
Counsel	NA	E.P.S.	$1.11
DUNS No	00-529-5647	Shareholders	NA

Business: The group's principle activity is to manufacture farm machinery products under its own and private labels. Equipment manufactured by the company under its own label includes portable and stationary animal feed processing equipment and related attachments used to mill and mix feed grains into custom animal feed rations. It also manufactures a high bulk mixing wagon to mix animal feeds containing silage, hay, and grain; a line of mowers and stalk shredders; minimum till seed bed preparation equipment; sugar beet and potato harvesting equipment; and a line of land maintenance equipment, edible bean equipment, and grain drill equipment. The company's labeled products are sold by farm equipment dealers throughout the United States. The group operates from United States.

Primary SIC and add'l.: 3523

CIK No: 0000007623

Subsidiaries: Art Way Vessels, Inc

Officers: Don Gates/North Dakota Reps, George Cooper/Texas Reps, Larry Johnson/Florida Reps, Darrel Frey/North Carolina Reps, David Almquist/Illinois Reps, Ronald Reed/Pennsylvania Reps, Joseph Runchey/Nebraska Reps, Don Davis/Tennessee Reps, E. W. Muehlhausen/69/Pres., Principal Executive Officer, Carrie Majeski/32/CFO

Directors: Ward J. McConnell/76/Chmn., Thomas E. Buffamate/55/Dir., James Lynch/62/Dir., Douglas McClellan/57/Dir., David R. Castle/58/Dir., Fred W. Krahmer/37/Dir., Marc H. McConnell/29/Dir.

Owners: Fred Krahmer, James Lynch, Douglas McClellan/1.04%, David R. Castle, Marc H. McConnell, Thomas E. Buffamante, J. Ward McConnell/39.44%, Insiders/41.69%

Financial Data: Fiscal Year End: 11/30   **Latest Annual Data:** 11/30/2006

Year	Sales	Net Income
2006	$19,854,000	$934,000
2005	$14,619,000	$977,000
2004	$12,784,000	$1,402,000

Curr. Assets:	$11,219,000	Curr. Liab.:	$2,717,000		
Plant, Equip.:	$3,185,000	Total Liab.:	$6,569,000	Indic. Yr. Divd.:	$0.100
Total Assets:	$14,614,000	Net Worth:	$8,045,000	Debt/ Equity:	0.4449

Artcraft III Inc

700 Bay St., Toronto, On, M5G 1Z6; *PH:* 1-416-408-1173

General - Incorporation	DE	Stock - Price on:12/24/2007	NA
Employees	NA	Stock Exchange	NA
Auditor	Gately & Assoc. LLC	Ticker Symbol	NA
Stk Agt.		Outstanding Shares	NA
Counsel	NA	E.P.S	NA
DUNS No.	NA	Shareholders	NA

Business: The group's principal activity is to engage in any lawful corporate undertaking, including, but not limited to, selected mergers and acquisitions. The group has been in the developmental stage since inception (07-Jun-2004) and have no operations to date other than issuing shares to our original shareholder.

Primary SIC and add'l.: 9995

CIK No: 0001294611

Artcraft V Inc

Rm. 1131, XianKeJiDian Bldg., BaGuaSi Rd., Futian District, Shenzhen City , 518029; *PH:* 86-755-2399-0959

General - Incorporation	DE	Stock - Price on:12/24/2007	NA
Employees	NA	Stock Exchange	OTC
Auditor	Kabani & Co, Inc	Ticker Symbol	NA
Stk Agt	NA	Outstanding Shares	NA
Counsel	NA	E.P.S.	NA
DUNS No.	NA	Shareholders	NA

Business: The groups principle activity is to provide information searching services. The groups other services include information search engine, online web application and image designing, digital network service, online market research, online promotion and advertising services, and query searches for individuals and businesses. The group operates from United States.

Primary SIC and add'l.: 9995

CIK No: 0001294614

Subsidiaries: Top Interest International Limited

Officers: Li Te Xiao/30/Dir., CEO, CFO, Pres., Sec.

Directors: Li Te Xiao/30/Dir., CEO, CFO, Pres., Sec.

Owners: Zu Da Xu/97.56%, Li Te Xiao/0.35%, Insiders/0.35%

Artcraft VI Inc

3560 Se Marine Dr., Vancouver, V5S 4R6; *PH:* 1-604-734-1607

General - Incorporation	DE	Stock - Price on:12/24/2007	NA
Employees	NA	Stock Exchange	NA
Auditor	NA	Ticker Symbol	NA
Stk Agt	Corporate Stock Transfer, Inc.	Outstanding Shares	NA
Counsel	NA	E.P.S.	NA
DUNS No.	NA	Shareholders	NA

Business: The groups principle activity is to provide a number of services, including information search engine, online Web application and image designing, digital network service, online market research, online promotion and advertising services, and query searches for both individuals and business. The group operates from United States.

Primary SIC and add'l.: 9995

CIK No: 0001294616

Artemis International Solutions Corp

4041 Macarthur Blvd., Ste. 401, Newport Beach, CA, 92660; *PH:* 1-949-660-7100; *http://* www.artemispm.com

General - Incorporation	DE	Stock - Price on:12/24/2007	NA
Employees	NA	Stock Exchange	NA
Auditor	Squar, Milner, Raehl & Williamson	Ticker Symbol	NA
Stk Agt	American Stock Transfer & Trust Co.	Outstanding Shares	NA
Counsel	NA	E.P.S.	NA
DUNS No.	NA	Shareholders	NA

Business: The group's principle activities are to develop and supply comprehensive, project and resource collaboration application software products and consulting services. The services provided by the group include task estimating, scheduling, budgeting, forecasting, resource analysis, cost analysis reporting, proactive business alerts and gateways to other enterprise applications. The group operates in three segments namely services, support revenue and software revenue. The group operates in the United States, the United Kingdom, Japan, France, Germany, Italy, Finland and Asia.

Primary SIC and add'l.: 7375 7379 7372

CIK No: 0001099674

Subsidiaries: Artemis International Solutions Corporation

Officers: Randall Jacops/CEO, Pres., Kaoru Nakamura/Exec. VP - Japan, Christopher Smith/VP - Operations, Sean Fallon/VP - Finance, Carlo Boldi/Exec. VP - EMEA, Robert Stefanovich/43/Contact, Denise Pang/Contact, Johnny Tan/Contact - Asia Pacific, Paulo A. Gomes/Contact - Portugal, Angel Garcia-Villodre/Contact - Spain

Directors: Pekka Pere/Chmn., David Cairns/62/Dir., Mike Murphy/Dir., Olof Odman/Dir., Bengt-Ake Algevik/Dir., Joseph Liemandt/39/Dir.

Artesian Resources Corp

664 Churchmans Rd., Newark, DE, 19702; *PH:* 1-302-453-6900; *Fax:* 1-302-453-6957; *http://* www.artesianwater.com

General - Incorporation	DE	Stock - Price on:12/24/2007	$18.69
Employees	198	Stock Exchange	NDQ
Auditor	KPMG LLP	Ticker Symbol	ARTNA
Stk Agt	Registrar & Transfer Co	Outstanding Shares	6,130,000
Counsel	NA	E.P.S.	$0.97
DUNS No.	00-691-8734	Shareholders	NA

Business: The group's principal activity is to supply water throughout the state of Delaware. It sources water from wells that pump groundwater from aquifers and other natural water-bodies in the Atlantic coastal plain. A part of the supply includes surface water purchased from neighboring water utilities and municipalities through interconnections. The group owns 98 operating and 58 monitoring wells. The group also supplies water to public fire protection service through 3,600 hydrants in its service territories. The consumers include residential, commercial, industrial, governmental, municipal and utility customers throughout Delaware. At 30-Jun-2004, the group had 70,400 metered customers and served a population of approximately 230,000.

Primary SIC and add'l.: 4939 6719 4952 4941

CIK No: 0000863110

Subsidiaries: AquaStructure Delaware, LLC, Artesian Development Corporation, Artesian Resources Corporation, Artesian Utility Development, Inc., Artesian Wastewater Management, Inc., Artesian Water Company, Inc., Artesian Water Pennsylvania, Inc.

Officers: Dian C. Taylor/Chmn., CEO, Pres., Joseph A. Dinunzio/Exec. VP, Sec., John M. Thaeder/Sr. VP - Operations, Nicholle R. Taylor/VP, David B. Spacht/CFO, Treasurer, John J. Schreppler/VP, General Counsel, Assist. Sec., Bruce P. Kraeuter/Sr. VP - Engineering, Planning

Directors: Dian C. Taylor/Chmn., CEO, Pres., John R. Eisenbrey/Dir., Norman H. Taylor/Dir., Kenneth R. Biederman/Dir., William C. Wyer/Dir.

Owners: Kenneth R. Biederman/1.40%, Bruce P. Kraeuter/1.50%, John M. Thaeder/1.20%, Norman H. Taylor/31.10%, John R. Eisenbrey/5.20%, Louisa Taylor Welcher/15.40%, Louisa Taylor Welcher/1.00%, Dian C. Taylor/17.90%, John M. Thaeder, Dian C. Taylor/2.60%, Joseph A. DiNunzio, David B. Spacht/1.10%, Insiders/13.90%, David B. Spacht, Insiders/55.10% *(19 Owners included in Index)*

Financial Data: *Fiscal Year End:*12/31 *Latest Annual Data:* 12/31/2006

Year	Sales	Net Income
2006	$48,587,000	$6,071,000
2005	$45,285,000	$5,035,000
2004	$39,582,000	$4,402,000

Curr. Assets:	$10,245,000	*Curr. Liab.:*	$19,122,000	*P/E Ratio:*	18.69
Plant, Equip.:	$253,489,000	*Total Liab.:*	$207,560,000	*Indic. Yr. Divd.:*	NA
Total Assets:	$269,360,000	*Net Worth:*	$61,800,000	*Debt/ Equity:*	1.8731

Artesyn Technologies Inc

7900 Glades Rd. Ste. 500, Boca Raton, FL, 33434; *PH:* 1-561-451-1000; *http://* www.artesyn.com

General - Incorporation....FL
Employees....127,800
Auditor....Ernst & Young, LLP
Stk Agt....Bank of New York
Counsel....K & L Nicholson Graham LLP
DUNS No.....04-493-0139

Stock- Price on:12/24/2007....$49
Stock Exchange....NA
Ticker Symbol....NA
Outstanding Shares....795,260,000
E.P.S....$2.40
Shareholders....NA

Business: The group's principal activities are to design, manufacture and sell power conversion equipment and board level computing solutions incorporated into embedded communications systems. The operations are carried on in two segments namely power conversion and communications products. The power conversion segment designs, manufactures and sells power supplies and power conversion products. The communications products segment designs, manufactures and sells central processing unit boards, wide area network input/output boards bundled with software protocols. The group operates in the United States, Austria, Ireland, Hong Kong and other foreign countries. Its customers include original equipment manufacturers, within four core market sectors in the communications industry, server and storage, wireless infrastructure, networking and telecommunications.

Primary SIC and add'l.: 3568 3577 3679 3613

CIK No: 0000023071

Subsidiaries: Artesyn Asset Management, Inc., Artesyn Austria GmbH, Artesyn Austria GmbH & Co. KG, Artesyn Cayman LP, Artesyn Communication Products Scandinavia AB, Artesyn Communication Products, Inc., Artesyn Communications Products UK Ltd., Artesyn Delaware LLC, Artesyn Delaware, Inc., Artesyn do Brasil Comercio de Produtos de Conversao de Energia Ltda., Artesyn Elektronische Gerate Beteiligungs-und Verwaltungs-GmbH, Artesyn France S.A.R.L., Artesyn Germany GmbH, Artesyn GmbH & Co. KG, Artesyn Holding GmbH 26 Subsidiaries included in the Index

Officers: Pam Vaughn/Marketing Communications Administrator - Carlsbad, CA, United States, Amanda Vera/Marketing Communications Coordinator, Steve Cheung/VP - Sales, Marketing, Asia, Nick Leatherdale/Media Contact - North America, Canada, Mark Osullivan/International Product Marketing Mgr.

Financial Data: *Fiscal Year End:*12/30 *Latest Annual Data:* 9/30/2006

Year	Sales	Net Income
2006	$20,133,000,000	$1,845,000,000
2005	$17,305,000,000	$1,422,000,000
2004	$15,615,000,000	$1,257,000,000

Curr. Assets:	$7,330,000,000	*Curr. Liab.:*	$5,374,000,000	*P/E Ratio:*	20.42
Plant, Equip.:	$3,220,000,000	*Total Liab.:*	$10,342,000,000	*Indic. Yr. Divd.:*	$1.050
Total Assets:	$18,672,000,000	*Net Worth:*	$8,154,000,000	*Debt/ Equity:*	0.4112

Arthrocare Corp

7500 Rialto Blvd., Bldg. 2, Ste. 100, Austin, TX, 78735; *PH:* 1-512-391-3900; *Fax:* 1-512-391-3901; *http://* www.arthrocare.com; *Email:* info@arthrocare.com

General - Incorporation....DE
Employees....881
Auditor....PricewaterhouseCoopers LLP
Stk Agt....Wells Fargo Bank, N.A.
Counsel....Wilson Sonsini Goodrich & Rosati
DUNS No.....83-457-0533

Stock- Price on:12/24/2007....$43.5
Stock Exchange....NDQ
Ticker Symbol....ARTC
Outstanding Shares....27,510,000
E.P.S....$1.30
Shareholders....NA

Business: The group's principal activities are to develop, manufacture and market medical devices for use in soft-tissue surgery. The products are based on its patented coblation technology that allows surgeons to operate with a high level of precision and accuracy, limiting damage to surrounding tissue and thereby reducing pain and speeding recovery for the patient. This technology is applicable to a broad range of soft-tissue surgical markets that includes sports medicine, spinal surgery, neurosurgery, cosmetic surgery, ear, nose and throat (ent) surgery, gynecology, urology, general surgery and various cardiology applications. The products are marketed in the United States, Europe, Australia, New Zealand, China, Korea, Japan, Taiwan, Canada, Mexico, the Caribbean, north Africa, the Middle East, and Central America. On 25-Apr-2003, the group acquired atlantech medizinische produkte vertriebs gmbh and on 28-Jan-2004, medical device alliance inc.

Primary SIC and add'l.: 3842 3841 2833 5047 3845 8731

CIK No: 0001005010

Subsidiaries: AngioCare Corporation, ArthoCare Europe AB, ArthroCare Corporation Cayman Islands, ArthroCare Costa Rica SRL, ArthroCare Deutschland GmbH, ArthroCare France SRL, ArthroCare International, Inc., ArthroCare Italy SPA, ArthroCare Luxembourg, S.a.r.l., ArthroCare Medical Corporation, ArthroCare U.K. LTD, Atlandtech Medizinishche Produkte Vertreibs, Atlantech Medical Devices (UK) Ltd., Atlantech Medical Devices Ltd., LySonix, Inc. 19 Subsidiaries included in the Index

Officers: Michael Baker/Dir., CEO, Pres./$2,210,909.00, Jack Giroux/Pres. - Arthrocare Sports Medicine, Richard W. Rew/VP - Legal Affairs, Howard Zar/Contact - Media Relations, Bruce Prothro/VP, GM - Coblation Technologies, Regulatory Affairs, Michael Gluk/CFO, Sr. VP/$988,636.00, Sten I. Dahlborg/VP, GM - Arthrocare Europe, David Applegate/VP, GM - Arthrocare Spine, Richard A. Christensen/Sr. VP - Operations/$967,107.00, John H. Giroux/63/Sr. VP, Pres. - Sports Medicine/$902,131.00, John T. Raffle/Sr. VP - Strategic Business Units/$664,270.00, Ross Beam/VP - Sales, Norman R. Sanders/VP - Corporate Development, Chief Medical Officer, Jean Woloszko/VP, Chief Technical, Scientific Officer, Tord B. Lendau/Dir., GM *(17 Officers included in Index)*

Directors: Michael Baker/Dir., CEO, Pres., Peter L. Wilson/Dir., James Foster/Dir., Jerry Widman/Dir., Terrence E. Geremski/Dir., David F. Fitzgerald/Dir., Barbara D. Boyan/Dir., Tord B. Lendau/Dir., GM

Owners: Michael Gluk, Insiders/5.20%, Richard A. Christensen, Peter L. Wilson, Michael A. Baker/2.30%, John H. Giroux, Entities affiliated with AXA Financial, Inc/6.80%, Capital Research and Management Company/7.10%, Terrence E. Geremski, David F. Fitzgerald, John Raffle, James G. Foster, Jerry Widman, Barbara D. Boyan, Tord B. Lendau *(16 Owners included in Index)*

Financial Data: *Fiscal Year End:*12/31 *Latest Annual Data:* 12/31/2006

Year	Sales	Net Income
2006	$263,001,000	$31,675,000
2005	$214,334,000	$23,530,000
2004	$154,148,000	-$26,189,000

Curr. Assets:	$163,417,000	*Curr. Liab.:*	$49,673,000	*P/E Ratio:*	35.66
Plant, Equip.:	$36,071,000	*Total Liab.:*	$52,543,000	*Indic. Yr. Divd.:*	NA
Total Assets:	$375,046,000	*Net Worth:*	$322,503,000	*Debt/ Equity:*	NA

Arthur J Gallagher & Co

The Gallagher Ctr., 2 Pierce Pl., Itasca, IL, 60143; *PH:* 1-630-773-3800; *Fax:* 1-630-285-4000; *http://* www.ajg.com

General - Incorporation....DE
Employees....8,750
Auditor....Ernst & Young LLP
Stk Agt.....Computershare Investor Services LLC
Counsel....NA
DUNS No.....07-442-4540

Stock- Price on:12/24/2007....$29.19
Stock Exchange....NYSE
Ticker Symbol....AJG
Outstanding Shares....98,900,000
E.P.S....$1.40
Shareholders....NA

Business: The group's principal activity is to provide insurance brokerage, risk management and related services to clients in the United States and abroad. In addition, the group specializes in furnishing risk management services. The group operates in three business segments. The insurance brokerage services segment encompasses operations that, for commission or fee compensation, place or arrange to place insurance directly related to clients' managing of risk. The risk management services segment primarily represents the group's third-party administration, loss control and risk management consulting and insurance property appraisal operations. The financial services segment is responsible for the management of the group's diversified investment portfolio. In 2004, the group acquired edwin m. Rollins, inc, specialty advisory services inc, burch marcus pool krupp daniel, babineaux inc, johnsey insurance agency inc, health care insurers inc and strategix, inc.

Primary SIC and add'l.: 6282 6411 8742

CIK No: 0000354190

Subsidiaries: AJG Capital, Inc., AJG Chem Mod Holdings LLC, AJG Coal Indiana LLC, AJG Coal, Inc., AJG Financial Services, Inc., AJG Investments, Inc., AJG Two Pierce, Inc., Artex Insurance Company Ltd, Artex Underwriting Managers Ltd., Arthur J. Gallagher (Aus) Pty Ltd., Arthur J. Gallagher (L)BHD, Arthur J. Gallagher (UK) Limited, Arthur J. Gallagher Asia Limited, Arthur J. Gallagher Asia Pte Ltd, Arthur J. Gallagher Australasia Pty Ltd. 74 Subsidiaries included in the Index

Officers: Patrick J. Gallagher/Dir., Pres., CEO - Arthur J Gallagher, Co/$3,310,098.00, Marsha J. Akin/Primary Investor Relations Officer, David Long/Pres. - AJG Financial Services Inc, Mark Strauch/Exec. VP - AJG Financial Services Inc, Sally Wasikowski/VP - AJG Financial Services Inc, Jack Lazzaro/CFO - AJG Financial Services Inc, Walter D. Bay/Corporate VP, General Counsel, Sec., Douglas K. Howell/CFO, Corporate VP/$1,312,695.00, James S. Gault/Corporate VP, Pres., COO - Brokerage Services Retail Division/$1,555,684.00, John C. Rosengren/Sec., Richard J. McKenna/Corporate VP, Pres. - Gallagher Bassett Services, Inc, David E. McGurn/Corporate VP, Pres. - Specialty Marketing, International Division/$1,108,797.00, James W. Durkin/Corporate VP, Pres. - Gallagher Benefit Services, Inc/$1,735,342.00, Richard C. Cary/45/Controller, Chief Accounting Officer, Elizabeth J. Brinkerhoff/64/VP

Directors: Patrick J. Gallagher/Dir., Pres., CEO - Arthur J Gallagher, Co, David S. Johnson/Dir., Kimball T. Brooker/Dir., Gary P. Coughlan/Dir., Elbert O. Hand/Dir., Kay W. McCurdy/Dir., James R. Wimmer/Dir., Ilene S. Gordon/Dir., William L. Bax/Dir.

Owners: Insiders/2.63%, Elbert O. Hand, Ilene S. Gordon, Capital Research and Management Company/7.50%, Kimball T. Brooker, AMVESCAP PLC/6.10%, Gary P. Coughlan, Douglas K. Howell, David S. Johnson, Kay W. McCurdy, James R. Wimmer, Patrick J. Gallagher, James W. Durkin, David E. McGurn, James S. Gault

Financial Data: *Fiscal Year End:*12/31 *Latest Annual Data:* 12/31/2006

Year	Sales	Net Income
2006	$1,534,000,000	$128,500,000
2005	$1,483,900,000	$30,800,000
2004	$1,521,600,000	$188,500,000

Curr. Assets:	$2,376,200,000	*Curr. Liab.:*	$2,401,300,000	*P/E Ratio:*	20.85
Plant, Equip.:	$103,100,000	*Total Liab.:*	$2,556,000,000	*Indic. Yr. Divd.:*	$1.240
Total Assets:	$3,420,100,000	*Net Worth:*	$864,100,000	*Debt/ Equity:*	NA

Artificial Life Inc

4601, China OnlineCtr., 333 Lockhart Rd, Wanchai; *PH:* 852-31022800; *http://* www.artificial-life.com; *Email:* info@artificial-life.com

General - Incorporation....DE
Employees....42
Auditor....GHP Horwath, P.C
Stk Agt......American Stock Transfer & Trust Co.
Counsel....NA
DUNS No.....92-775-4424

Stock- Price on:12/24/2007....$2.9
Stock Exchange....OTC
Ticker Symbol....ALIF
Outstanding Shares....34,920,000
E.P.S....-$0.06
Shareholders....NA

Business: The group's principle activity is to develop, market and support intelligent software robots called smartbots. Smartbots consist of software programs based on artificial intelligence technology that allows for communication in natural language. They are designed to automate and simplify time consuming and complex business-related functions such as Web navigation, direct sales and marketing, e-mail automation, user profiling, sales response and call center automation, wealth planning and portfolio management. The products include alife-webguide, alife-messenger and life-portfolio manager. Alife-webguide helps users navigate the site by accepting and processing questions. Alife-messenger serves as a natural language-based automated e-mail reply and answering services. Alife-portfolio-manager is developed to monitor an individual's investment portfolio. The group's quarterly revenue for September 2007 was 20,995.00 millions of USD.

Primary SIC and add'l.: 7372

CIK No: 0001070361

Subsidiaries: Neurotec International Corp.

Officers: Eberhard Schoneburg/51/Chmn., CEO, Pres., Treasurer, Michael Rowan/Dir. - M, A, Europe, Madison Lee/Mgr. - Graphic, 3D Design, Stephen Leung/Mgr. - Global Product, Rollout, Maryanna Donaldson/Dir. - Creative, Alice Tat/Mgr. - Finance, Accounting, Ada Fong/Sr. VP - Business Development, Ernest Axelbank/CTO, Kazutoshi Miyake/Dir. - Business Development, Japan, Frank Namyslik/Global Controller, Emily Hanan/Investor Relations Officer, Susan Morgenbesser/Investor Relations Officer

Directors: Eberhard Schoneburg/51/Chmn., CEO, Pres., Treasurer, Ajmal Rahman/43/Chmn. - Corporate Advisory Board, Christian Gloe/44/Member - Corporate Advisory Board, Roxy Meade/49/Member - Corporate Advisory Board, Edouard Bannwart/64/Member - Corporate Advisory Board, Gert Hensel/Dir., Michael March/Member - Corporate Advisory Board, Claudia Alsdorf/Dir., Rene Jaeggi/Dir., Claude Cueni/Member - Corporate Advisory Board

Owners: Eberhard Schoneburg/21.90%, Michael Rowan/4.10%, Gert Hensel/1.70%, Claudia Alsdorf/1.70%, Joint Glory International/2.20%, DKR Capital Partners LP/6.60%, Tong Nguen Khoong/1.20%, Accelera Ventures Ltd./7.40%, Ernest Axelbank/2.10%, Ajmal Rahman/5.90%, Christian Gloe/5.70%, Bukit Kiara Capital Sdn. Bhd/4.40%, Bruno Gabriel/5.10%, Insiders/29.70%

Financial Data: ***Fiscal Year End:***12/31 ***Latest Annual Data:*** 12/31/2006

Year	Sales	Net Income
2006	$856,000	-$2,943,000
2005	$267,000	-$1,684,000
2004	$262,000	-$946,000

Curr. Assets:	$1,632,000	***Curr. Liab.:***	$2,051,000		
Plant, Equip.:	$99,000	***Total Liab.:***	$2,051,000	***Indic. Yr. Divd.:***	NA
Total Assets:	$2,264,000	***Net Worth:***	$212,000	***Debt/ Equity:***	NA

Artistdirect Inc

1601 Cloverfield Blvd., Ste. 400 South, Santa Monica, CA, 90404; ***PH:*** 1-310-956-3300; ***Fax:*** 1-310-956-3301; ***http://*** www.artistdirect.com; ***Email:*** adsales@artistdirect.com

General - Incorporation	DE	***Stock*** - Price on:12/24/2007	$1.81
Employees	74	Stock Exchange	OTC
Auditor	Gumbiner Savett Inc	Ticker Symbol	ARTD
Stk Agt	Mellon Investor Services	Outstanding Shares	10,200,000
Counsel	Brobeck, Phleger & Harrison	E.P.S	$0.70
DUNS No.	NA	Shareholders	NA

Business: The group's principle activity is to provide an integrated online music network for music fans, artists and marketing partners. The group provides music entertainment through artist direct network, an integrated network of Web sites offering multi-media content, music news and information and music-related commerce. The group operates in three segments: media operation, sales generated from online and offline advertising and integrated marketing solution. E-commerce: includes recorded music and music-related merchandise. Record label operation: sales generated from sale of compact discs by artists signed to the imusic record label. The group's network also provides the ultimate band list (ubl), a music search engine and resource for music information. The ubl provides information on more than 100,000 artists, featuring news, concert information, artist biographies, album reviews, contests, promotions, music samples and downloads. The group's quarterly revenue for September 2007 was 5.94 millions of USD.

Primary SIC and add'l.: 7375 3652 7389 7319

CIK No: 0001095079

Subsidiaries: MediaDefender

Officers: Jonathan V. Diamond/Dir., CEO, Pres., Randy Saaf/CEO - Mediadefender, Inc, Octavio Herrera/31/Pres. - Mediadefender, Inc, Robert N. Weingarten/CFO, Sec., Rene Rousselet/52/Corporate Controller

Directors: Jonathan V. Diamond/Dir., CEO, Pres., Frederick W. Field/55/Chmn., Fred Davis/48/Dir., Teymour Boutros-Ghali/52/Dir., Eric Pulier/41/Dir., Dimitri Villard/64/Dir., James N. Lane/56/Dir.

Owners: Octavio Herrera/2.20%, Rene Rousselet, Jonathan V. Diamond/9.10%, Eric Pulier/10.20%, Jonathan M. Glaser/6.10%, Teymour Boutros-Ghali/1.80%, Nicholas Turner, Randy Saaf/2.20%, JMB Capital Partners, L.P./18.80%, WNTO7 Holdings, LLC/12.00%, Robert N. Weingarten/2.90%, James N. Lane/1.00%, CCM Master Qualified Fund, Ltd./22.00%, Dimitri Villard/1.10%, Fred Davis *(18 Owners included in Index)*

Financial Data: ***Fiscal Year End:***12/31 ***Latest Annual Data:*** 12/31/2006

Year	Sales	Net Income
2006	$24,062,000	-$4,890,000
2005	$13,971,000	-$12,105,000
2004	$5,143,000	-$3,311,000

Curr. Assets:	$13,379,000	***Curr. Liab.:***	$64,195,000	***P/E Ratio:***	1.30
Plant, Equip.:	$2,468,000	***Total Liab.:***	$64,658,000	***Indic. Yr. Divd.:***	NA
Total Assets:	$54,972,000	***Net Worth:***	-$9,686,000	***Debt/ Equity:***	NA

Arvana Inc

2610-1066 W Hastings St., Vancouver, BC, V6E 3X2; ***PH:*** 1-604-684-4691; ***Fax:*** 1-604-684-4601; ***http://*** www.arvana.net; ***Email:*** info@arvana.net

General - Incorporation	NV	***Stock*** - Price on:12/24/2007	$0.1164
Employees	NA	Stock Exchange	OTC
Auditor	Dohan and Company, P.A.	Ticker Symbol	ARVI
Stk Agt	Interwest Transfer Company, Inc.	Outstanding Shares	NA
Counsel	NA	E.P.S	NA
DUNS No.	NA	Shareholders	NA

Business: The groups principal activity is to develop telecommunications industry. The groups services include carrier pre-select, call by call pre-select, wholesale traffic handling, calling cards, internet telephony. The group operates from the United States and Canada.

Primary SIC and add'l.: 9995

CIK No: 0001113313

Subsidiaries: Arvana Networks Inc., Arvana Participacoes S.A.

Officers: Teyfik ozcan/Dir., CEO, Pres., Leonard Gordon/Dir., CFO, David Troy/CTO, Iain Drummond/VP - Business Development, Karen Engleson/Corp. Sec.

Directors: Teyfik ozcan/Dir., CEO, Pres., John Baring/Chmn., Robert Russell/Dir., Leonard Gordon/Dir., CFO, Ross Wilmot/Dir.

Owners: Brulex-Consultadoria/17.10%, Karen Engleson, Robert Russell/1.00%, Ross Wilmot/1.50%, Michael Jervis, John Baring/1.60%, Leonard Gordon, Pensbreigh Holdings Ltd./5.20%, Insiders/5.60%

Financial Data: ***Fiscal Year End:***12/31 ***Latest Annual Data:*** 12/31/2006

Year	Sales	Net Income
2006	$2,833,000	-$1,743,000
2005	NA	-$16,493,000
2004	NA	-$4,000

Curr. Assets:	$1,910,000	***Curr. Liab.:***	$3,396,000		
Plant, Equip.:	$731,000	***Total Liab.:***	$3,455,000	***Indic. Yr. Divd.:***	NA
Total Assets:	$5,246,000	***Net Worth:***	$1,791,000	***Debt/ Equity:***	NA

Arvinmeritor Inc

2135 W Maple Rd., Troy, MI, 48084; ***PH:*** 1-248-435-1000; ***Fax:*** 1-248-435-1393; ***http://*** www.arvinmeritor.com; ***Email:*** contact.us@arvinmeritor.com

General - Incorporation	IN	***Stock*** - Price on:12/24/2007	$20.76
Employees	27,500	Stock Exchange	NYSE
Auditor	Vernon G. Baker, II	Ticker Symbol	ARM
Stk Agt	Bank of New York	Outstanding Shares	71,400,000
Counsel	NA	E.P.S	-$3.106
DUNS No.	NA	Shareholders	NA

Business: The groups principle activity is to provide integrated systems, modules and components. The groups products include trailer, bus coach and car and light truck products. The group operates from United States.

Primary SIC and add'l.: 3491 3714 5013 3479

CIK No: 0001113256

Subsidiaries: Ansa Marmitte s.r.l., Arvin Canada Holding Limited, Arvin Cayman Islands, Ltd., Arvin Convertidores Cataliticos S.A. de C.V., Arvin de Mexico S.A. de C.V., Arvin European Holdings (UK) Limited, Arvin European Holdings (UK) Limited French Branch, Arvin Exhaust de Venezuela, Arvin Exhaust India Private Ltd., Arvin Exhaust of Canada Ltd., Arvin Exhaust, s.r.o., Arvin France SAS, Arvin Industries Foreign Sales Corporation, Arvin International (UK) Limited, Arvin International Holdings, LLC 186 Subsidiaries included in the Index

Officers: Charles G. McClure/Chmn., CEO, Pres., Bonnie Wilkinson/VP, Sec., Jeffrey Gammons/Sr. Communications Consultant, Krista McClure/Sr. Dir. - Corporate Communications, Media Relations, Malte Raddatz/Dir. - Europe, Asia, Pacific Communications, Terry Huch/Dir. - Investor Relations, Mike D. Pennington/Sr. Dir. - Global Marketing Communications, Linda M. Cummins/Sr. VP - Communications, James D. Donlon/CFO, Sr. VP, Rakesh Sachdev/Sr. VP, Pres. - Asia Pacific, Jeffrey Craig/Sr. VP, Controller, Mary Lehmann/Sr. VP - Strategic Initiatives, Treasurer, Philip R. Martens/Sr. VP, Pres. - Light Vehicle Systems, Carsten J. Reinhardt/Sr. VP, Pres. - Commercial Vehicle Systems, Vernon Baker/Sr. VP, General Counsel

Directors: Charles G. McClure/Chmn., CEO, Pres., William D. George/Dir., David W. Devonshire/Dir., Victoria B. Jackson/Dir., Joseph B. Anderson/Dir., Rhonda L. Brooks/Dir., James E. Marley/Dir., Steven G. Rothmeier/Dir., Ivor J. Evans/Dir., Andrew Schindler/Dir., William R. Newlin/Dir., Joseph P. Flannery/Dir.

Owners: Capital Management, LLC/5.10%, Rhonda L. Brooks, Charles G. McClure, Insiders/1.39%, Vernon G. Baker, Dimensional Fund Advisors LP/6.55%, Victoria B. Jackson, Philip R. Martens, William R. Newlin, James E. Marley, Japan Limited, Ebisu Prime Square Tower/5.17%, American Century Companies, Inc. and American CenturyInvestment Management, Inc./7.20%, Steven G. Rothmeier, T. Rowe Price Trust Company/2.47%, Carsten J. Reinhardt *(19 Owners included in Index)*

Financial Data: ***Fiscal Year End:***10/02 ***Latest Annual Data:*** 9/30/2006

Year	Sales	Net Income
2006	$9,195,000,000	-$175,000,000
2005	$8,903,000,000	$12,000,000
2004	$8,033,000,000	-$42,000,000

Curr. Assets:	$3,093,000,000	***Curr. Liab.:***	$2,549,000,000		
Plant, Equip.:	$988,000,000	***Total Liab.:***	$4,504,000,000	***Indic. Yr. Divd.:***	$0.400
Total Assets:	$5,513,000,000	***Net Worth:***	$944,000,000	***Debt/ Equity:***	1.3289

ASA Eksportfinans

Dr.onning Maudsgt. 15, Oslo, Vika, 119; ***PH:*** 47-22012201; ***http://*** www.eksportfinans.no

General - Incorporation	.Kingdom Of Norway	***Stock*** - Price on:12/24/2007	NA
Employees	NA	Stock Exchange	NA
Auditor	PricewaterhouseCoopers AS	Ticker Symbol	NA
Stk Agt	NA	Outstanding Shares	NA
Counsel	Cravath, Swaine & Moore LLP	E.P.S	NA
DUNS No.	51-505-2520	Shareholders	NA

Business: The group's principle activity is to provide financing for a broad range of exports and for internationalization of norwegian industry. The group operates from United States.

Primary SIC and add'l.: 6159

CIK No: 0000700978

Subsidiaries: Kommunekreditt Norge AS

Officers: Tor F. Johansen/Dir., CEO, Pres., Tellef K. Tellefsen/Dep. Chmn. - Counsel of Representative, Employee Representative, Frode Alhaug/Chmn. - Council, representative, Kristin Normann/Dep. Chmn. - Counsel of Representative, Jorn Pedersen/Dep. Chmn. - Counsel of Representative, Claudine Smith/Dep. Chmn. - Counsel of Representative, Harry Konterud/Dep. Chmn. - Counsel of Representative, Elisabeth Krokeide/Dep. Chmn. - Counsel of Representative, Sandra Riise/Dep. Chmn. - Counsel of Representative, Benedicte Schilbred Fasmer/Dep. Chmn. - Counsel of Representative, Trond Tostrup/Dep. Chmn. - Counsel of Representative, Finn Haugan/Dep. Chmn. - Counsel of Representative, Harald Ellefsen/Dep. Chmn. - Counsel of Representative, Arvid Jensen/Dep. Chmn. - Counsel of Representative, Monica Salthella/Deputies - Counsel of Representative *(100 Officers included in Index)*

Directors: Tor F. Johansen/Dir., CEO, Pres., Tor ostbo/Dir., Dep. Chmn. - Eksportfinans ASA, Oslo, Baard Syrrist/Dep. Chmn., Erik Borgen/Chmn., Cato A. Holmsen/Dir., Leif Johan Laugen/Dir., Bodil Hollingsater/Dir., Live Haukvik Aker/Dir.

Owners: Halden Sparebank, Sparebanken Vestfold, Handelsbanken, Tingvoll Sparebank, Sparebanken Vest, Sparebank 1. Ntter, Focus Bank ASA, Sparebanken Hedmark, Sparebanken Sogn og Fjordane, Helgeland Sparebank, Ringerike Sparebank, Voss Veksel og Landmandsbank ASA, Modum Sparebank, Sparebanken Mre, Sparebank 1. Midt-Norge *(28 Owners included in Index)*

ASA Ltd

2700 Westhall Ln., Ste 140, Maitland, FL, 32751; ***PH:*** 1-407-875-8040; ***http://*** www.asaltd.com

General - Incorporation

Employees NA
Auditor NA
Stk Agt Computershare Trust Co
Counsel NA
DUNS No. NA

Stock- Price on:12/24/2007 $65.8
Stock Exchange NYSE
Ticker Symbol ASA
Outstanding Shares 9,600,000
E.P.S $6.26
Shareholders NA

Business: The groups principle activities include exploration, mining and processing of gold, silver, platinum, diamonds and other precious minerals. The group operates from the United States. The groups quarterly revenue for September 2007 was 5.14 millions of USD.

Primary SIC and add'l.: 6512

CIK No: 0000007645

Financial Data: Fiscal Year End:11/30 Latest Annual Data: 11/30/2006

Year	Sales	Net Income
2006	$188,182,000	$183,978,000
2005	$71,199,000	$66,036,000

Curr. Assets:	$12,393,000	Curr. Liab.:	$7,019,000	P/E Ratio:	25.14
Plant, Equip.:	NA	Total Liab.:	$8,256,000	Indic. Yr. Divd.:	$4.000
Total Assets:	$720,523,000	Net Worth:	$712,267,000	Debt/ Equity:	NA

Asante Technologies Inc

821 Fox Ln., San Jose, CA, 95131; *PH:* 1-408-435-8388; *http://* www.asante.com

General - Incorporation DE
Employees NA
Auditor Odenberg, Muranishi & Co. LLP
Stk Agt Mellon Investor Services LLC
Counsel NA
DUNS No. 19-706-4066

Stock- Price on:12/24/2007 $0.02
Stock Exchange OTC
Ticker Symbol ASNL
Outstanding Shares NA
E.P.S NA
Shareholders NA

Business: The group's principal activity is to design, manufacture and market network and connectivity products. The products of the group include 10base-t, 100base-t (fast ethernet) and 1000base-t (gigabit ethernet). The client access products include adapter cards and media access adapters, connect pcs, macintoshes and peripheral devices to ethernet networks. The network system products include intelligent and non-intelligent switches, hubs, bridge modules, Internet access devices (routers) and network management software for macintoshes and pcs, interconnect users within and between departmental networks. The company markets the products in the United States, Europe, Canada and Asia-pacific.

Primary SIC and add'l.: 3577

CIK No: 0000913598

Subsidiaries: Lite-on Communications

Officers: Mike Tobin/EMEA Sales Mgr., Guy Brasseur/Sales, Marketing Mgr.

ASAT Holdings Ltd

6701 Koll Ctr. Pkwy., Ste. 200, Pleasanton, CA, 94566; *PH:* 1-925-398-0400; *Fax:* 1-925-398-0388; *http://* www.asat.com

General - Incorporation Cayman Islands
Employees 2,898
Auditor PricewaterhouseCoopers LLP
Stk Agt Bank of New York
Counsel Morrison Foerster
DUNS No. NA

Stock- Price on:12/24/2007 $0.9
Stock Exchange NDQ
Ticker Symbol ASTT
Outstanding Shares 46,380,000
E.P.S -$0.97
Shareholders NA

Business: The group's principal activity is the provision of assembly and testing services of integrated circuits to customers in the semiconductor industry. It also offers a broad selection of semiconductor packages, which include standard and advanced leaded packages and ball grid array. The group introduced several technologies including tape bga, which replaces lead wires with balls of solder. Its customers include analog devices, inc., infineon technologies corporation, lucent technologies, inc., motorola inc., stmicroelectronics n.v., altera corporation, broadcom corporation, conexant systems, inc., commquest technologies (IBM), vitesse semiconductor corporation, philips electronics n.v., Texas instruments inc., vlsi technology inc., adaptec inc. And national semiconductor corporation. Operational activities of the group are located in Hong Kong, United States of America and France.

Primary SIC and add'l.: 3679 3674

CIK No: 0001102384

Subsidiaries: ASAT (Cayman) Limited, ASAT (Finance) LLC, ASAT (S)Pte. Ltd., ASAT GmbH, ASAT Korea Limited, ASAT Limited, ASAT Semiconductor (Dongguan) Limited, ASAT, Inc., New ASAT (Finance) Limited, Timerson Limited

Officers: Tung Lok Li/56/Dir., Acting CEO, Leo M. Higgins/VP - Engineering, Technology, Joseph Martin/Exec. VP - Sales, Marketing, Kei Hong Chua/37/CFO, Exec. VP, Kevin T.S. Kong/VP, General Counsel, Corp. Sec., Ernest Tan/Sr. VP - Operations, Peter Tin/Sr. VP - Quality, Reliability Assurance, Gabby Ang/VP - North American Sales, Corey Miller/Asat Regional VP - Sales

Directors: Tung Lok Li/56/Dir., Acting CEO, Henry C. Montgomery/72/Chmn., Glen G. Possley/68/Dir., Eugene Suh/41/Dir., Kei W. Chua/35/Dir., Stephen M. Shaw/47/Dir., Peter Hopper/49/Dir., Kevin Kit Tong Kwan/49/Dir.

Owners: Chase Asia Investment Partners II (Y), LLC/9.50%, Olympus Capital Holdings Asia related funds/12.80%, QPL International Holdings Limited/42.50%, QPL International Holdings Limited/50.00%, CAIP Co-Investment Fund Parallel Fund (II) C.V./1.60%, CAIP Co-Investment Fund Parallel Fund (I) C.V./1.80%, CAIP Co-Investment Fund Parallel Fund (I) C.V./2.30%, Chase Asia Investment Partners II (Y), LLC/7.40%, Olympus Capital Holdings Asia related funds/10.50%, Asia Opportunity Fund, L.P./23.80%, CAIP Co-Investment Fund Parallel Fund (II) C.V./1.20%, Asia Opportunity Fund, L.P./18.50%

Financial Data: Fiscal Year End:04/30 Latest Annual Data: 4/30/2006

Year	Sales	Net Income
2006	$182,115,000	-$42,431,000
2005	$194,411,000	-$60,425,000
2004	$214,674,000	-$16,717,000

Curr. Assets:	$44,370,000	Curr. Liab.:	$56,562,000		
Plant, Equip.:	$79,582,000	Total Liab.:	$217,655,000	Indic. Yr. Divd.:	NA
Total Assets:	$135,137,000	Net Worth:	-$88,261,000	Debt/ Equity:	NA

Asbury Automotive Group Inc

622 Third Ave., 37th Fl., New York, NY, 10017; *PH:* 1-212-885-2500; *Fax:* 1-212-297-2649; *http://* www.asburyauto.com; *Email:* info@asburyauto.com

General - Incorporation DE
Employees 8,300
Auditor Deloitte & Touche LLP
Stk Agt Computershare Trust Co
Counsel NA
DUNS No. NA

Stock- Price on:12/24/2007 $26.14
Stock Exchange NYSE
Ticker Symbol ABG
Outstanding Shares 32,410,000
E.P.S $1.532
Shareholders NA

Business: The group's principle activity is to provide automotive products and services. The group also provides maintenance and repair services. The group operates from United States.

Primary SIC and add'l.: 5511

CIK No: 0001144980

Subsidiaries: AF Motors LLC, ALM Motors LLC, ANL L.P., Asbury AR Niss LLC, Asbury Arkansas Hund LLC, Asbury Atlanta AC LLC, Asbury Atlanta AU LLC, Asbury Atlanta BM LLC, Asbury Atlanta Chevrolet LLC, Asbury Atlanta Hon LLC, Asbury Atlanta Infiniti LLC, Asbury Atlanta Jaguar LLC, Asbury Atlanta Lex LLC, Asbury Atlanta VL LLC, Asbury Automotive Arkansas Dealership Holdings LLC 180 Subsidiaries included in the Index

Officers: Kenneth B. Gilman/61/Dir., CEO, Pres./$2,774,676.00, John R. Capps/CEO, Pres. - Asbury's St. Louis Dealerships, Charles R. Oglesby/Dir., CEO, Pres., Henry Day/CEO, Pres. - Asburys Southern Region, Michael S. Kearney/CEO, Pres. - Asburys Eastern Region, Tom McCollum/CEO, Pres. - Asburys Western Region, Bobby Gray/CEO, Pres. - Asbury Mississippi Dealerships, Charles B. Tomm/CEO, Pres. - Asburys Florida Region, Clarence V. Nalley/Non - Exec. Chmn. - Asbury Automotive Atlanta - aka Nalley Automotive Group, Daniel L. Herwaldt/Non - Exec. Chmn. - Asburys Northern - Central California Dealerships, Luther Coggin/Non - Exec. Chmn. - Asbury's Automotive Jacksonville - dba Coggin Automotive Group, Hunter Johnson/VP, Treasurer, Ronald J. Avallone/VP - Internal Audit, Gordon Smith/CFO, Sr. VP/$1,855,545.00, John C. Stamm/VP - Dealer Development *(25 Officers included in Index)*

Directors: Charles R. Oglesby/Dir., CEO, Pres., Kenneth B. Gilman/61/Dir., CEO, Pres., Michael J. Durham/Chmn., Thomas F. McLarty/Non - Exec. Chmn. - Asbury's Arkansas Dealerships, Dennis Clements/Dir., John M. Roth/Dir., Jeffrey I. Wooley/Dir., Janet M. Clarke/Dir., Vernon E. Jordan/Dir., Philip F. Maritz/Dir., Juanita James/Dir., Thomas C. Deloach/Dir., Eugene S. Katz/Dir.

Owners: Dennis E. Clements, Eugene S. Katz, FMR Corp./6.10%, Thomas C. DeLoach, Freeman Spogli/17.60%, Dimensional Fund Advisors LP/8.30%, Charles R. Oglesby, Lynne A. Burgess, Charles B. Tomm, Barclays Global Investors, N.A./11.50%, Jeffrey I. Wooley, Janet M. Clarke, Vernon E. Jordan, Kenneth B. Gilman, Philip R. Johnson *(21 Owners included in Index)*

Financial Data: Fiscal Year End:12/31 Latest Annual Data: 12/31/2006

Year	Sales	Net Income
2006	$5,748,331,000	$60,749,000
2005	$5,540,663,000	$61,081,000
2004	$4,971,928,000	$50,073,000

Curr. Assets:	$1,293,064,000	Curr. Liab.:	$881,055,000	P/E Ratio:	18.41
Plant, Equip.:	$202,584,000	Total Liab.:	$1,419,004,000	Indic. Yr. Divd.:	$0.900
Total Assets:	$2,030,837,000	Net Worth:	$611,833,000	Debt/ Equity:	0.8393

Ascend Acquisition Corp

435 Devon Pk. Dr., Wayne, PA, 19087; *PH:* 1-610-293-2512; *http://* www.ascendgrowth.com; *Email:* info@ascendgrowth.com

General - Incorporation DE
Employees NA
Auditor Goldstein Golub Kessler LLP
Stk Agt Continental Stock Transfer & Trust Co
Counsel Patton Boggs, LLP
DUNS No. NA

Stock- Price on:12/24/2007 $5.56
Stock Exchange OTC
Ticker Symbol ASAQ
Outstanding Shares NA
E.P.S $0.03
Shareholders NA

Business: The groups principal activity is to acquire or merge with an operating business through a capital stock exchange. The group operates from the United States.

Primary SIC and add'l.: 6211

CIK No: 0001350773

Officers: Don K. Rice/Chmn., CEO, Stephen L. Brown/Dir., Sec., Arthur Spector/Special Advisor

Directors: Don K. Rice/Chmn., CEO, Stephen L. Brown/Dir., Sec., Russell C. Ball/Dir.

Owners: Insiders/9.10%, Hummingbird Management LLC/4.40%, DEGDeutsche Investitionsund Entwicklungsgeselischaft mbH/6.70%, James R. Thomas/1.00%, Russell C. Ball, Don K. Rice/7.90%, Steve Dezso/1.20%, Richard Brook, David M. Knott/2.60%, Capital International Asia CDPQ, Inc./5.40%, Quilvest Asian Equity Limited/5.40%, Jason Lee, Fir Tree, Inc./4.90%, Pacven Walden Ventures IV, LP/18.20%, Jeffrey L. Blaine/1.10% *(19 Owners included in Index)*

Financial Data: Fiscal Year End:12/31 Latest Annual Data: 12/31/2006

Year	Sales	Net Income
2006	NA	$383,000

Curr. Assets:	$39,816,000	Curr. Liab.:	$1,206,000	P/E Ratio:	92.67
Plant, Equip.:	NA	Total Liab.:	$8,905,000	Indic. Yr. Divd.:	NA
Total Assets:	$39,816,000	Net Worth:	$30,912,000	Debt/ Equity:	NA

Ascendant Solutions Inc

16250 Dallas Pkwy., Ste. 100, Dallas, TX, 75248; *PH:* 1-972-250-0945; *Fax:* 1-972-250-0934; *http://* www.ascendantsolutions.com

General - Incorporation DE
Employees 155
Auditor Hein & Assoc. LLP, BDO Seidman LLP
Stk Agt Bank of New York
Counsel Munsch Hardt Kopf & Harr PC
DUNS No. NA

Stock- Price on:12/24/2007 $0.62
Stock Exchange OTC
Ticker Symbol ASDS
Outstanding Shares 22,600,000
E.P.S $0.13
Shareholders NA

Business: The group is a diversified financial services company seeking to invest in, or acquire, manufacturing, distribution or service companies. It also provides various real estate services and performs real estate advisory services for corporate clients. The group through an affiliate purchases real estate assets as a principal. The group had previously been providing call center, order management and fulfillment services on an outsource basis to retailers and direct marketing companies located in the United States.

Primary SIC and add'l.: 7389 7379 7375

CIK No: 0001080029

Subsidiaries: Ascendant CRESA LLC, Ascendant VTE, LLC, ASDS of Orange County, Inc., ASE Investments Corporation, CRESA Capital Markets Group, L.P., CRESA Partners of Orange County, L.P., DM-ASD Holding, Co., Doughertys Holdings, Inc., Doughertys Pharmacy, Inc., Fairways Frisco, L.P., Park Infusion Services, L.P., Park-Medicine Man, L.P., VTE, L.P.

Officers: David E. Bowe/Dir., CEO, Pres., Mark S. Heil/VP - Finance, CFO

Directors: David E. Bowe/Dir., CEO, Pres., James C. Leslie/Chmn., Will Cureton/Dir., Anthony J. Levecchio/Dir., Curt Nonomaque/Dir.

Owners: Insiders/42.10%, Anthony J. LeVecchio, CLB Partners, Ltd./15.50%, Gary W. Boyd, Will Cureton/15.80%, Michal L. Gayler, James C. Leslie/19.70%, David E. Bowe/5.20%, Curt Nonomaque

Financial Data: Fiscal Year End: 12/31   **Latest Annual Data:** 12/31/2006

Year	Sales	Net Income
2006	$55,417,000	$1,023,000
2005	$43,788,000	$65,000
2004	$39,291,000	$249,000

Curr. Assets:	$11,947,000	**Curr. Liab.:**	$12,033,000	**P/E Ratio:** 6.89
Plant, Equip.:	$1,019,000	**Total Liab.:**	$15,857,000	**Indic. Yr. Divd.:** NA
Total Assets:	$21,039,000	**Net Worth:**	$4,235,000	**Debt/ Equity:** 1.4264

Ascendia Brands Inc

Formerly: Cenuco Inc
100 American Metro Blvd., Ste. 108, Hamilton, NJ, 08619; **PH:** 1-609-219-0930;
http:// www.cenuco.com

General - Incorporation	DE	Stock - Price on:12/24/2007	$1.41
Employees	327	Stock Exchange	AMEX
Auditor	BDO Seidman LLP	Ticker Symbol	ASB
Stk Agt	American Stock Transfer & Trust Co.	Outstanding Shares	13,940,000
Counsel	NA	E.P.S.	NA
DUNS No.	NA	Shareholders	NA

Business: The group operates through two segments namely online distance learning and sale of wireless solutions and Web services. The online distance learning offers licensed certificate and degree programs in a variety of concentrations to students in over 80 countries worldwide. The group's focus is on the international, mid-career adult and corporate training markets. In addition to online training, the group develops wireless applications for schools and enterprise companies. The group established a technology subsidiary called cenuco, inc. That develops wireless e-learning platform and technologies in the academic, consumer and corporate marketplaces. The group also develops and sells wireless solutions and Web services. This includes business-to-business and business-to-customer wireless applications and state of art Web technology and design services.

Primary SIC and add'l.: 8299 7375 9441

CIK No: 0000843494

Subsidiaries: Cenuco Wireless, Hermes Holding Company, Inc

Owners: Coty Inc./12.02%, John D. Wille, Robert Picow, Prencen LLC/9.99%, Dana Holdings, LLC/21.74%, Edward J. Doyle/3.36%, Watershed Capital Partners, L.P./9.99%, Andrew W. Sheldrick, MarNan, LLC/19.02%, Insiders/9.59%, Prencen LLC/100.00%, Elizabeth R. Houlihan, Franco S. Pettinato/3.56%, Kenneth D. Taylor, Francis G. Ziegler

Financial Data: Fiscal Year End: 02/28   **Latest Annual Data:** 02/28/2007

Year	Sales	Net Income
2007	$99,642,000	-$103,603,000
2006	$79,562,000	-$30,212,000
2004	$1,514,000	-$3,622,000

Curr. Assets:	$6,639,000	**Curr. Liab.:**	$1,122,000	
Plant, Equip.:	$128,000	**Total Liab.:**	$2,576,000	**Indic. Yr. Divd.:** NA
Total Assets:	$7,188,000	**Net Worth:**	$4,611,000	**Debt/ Equity:** 3.4643

Ascent Solar Technologies Inc

8120 Shaffer Pkwy., Littleton, CO, 80127; **PH:** 1-303-285-9885; **Fax:** 1-303-285-9882;
http:// www.ascentsolartech.com; **Email:** info@ascentsolar.com

General - Incorporation	DE	Stock - Price on:12/24/2007	$7.56
Employees	18	Stock Exchange	NDQ
Auditor	Hein & Assoc., LLP	Ticker Symbol	ASTI
Stk Agt	Computershare Investor Services LLC	Outstanding Shares	7,590,000
Counsel	NA	E.P.S.	-$1.25
DUNS No.	NA	Shareholders	NA

Business: The groups principal activity is to manufacture roll format photovoltaic modules. The groups product is Copper Indium Gallium diSelenide photovoltaic. Specific customers of the group include air force research laboratory, and the national aeronautics and space administration. The group operates from the United States.

Primary SIC and add'l.: 3629 3674 8731 3692 3699

CIK No: 0001350102

Officers: Matthew Foster/CEO, Pres., Mohan S. Misra/Chmn., Chief Strategy Officer, Chmn. - our Technical Advisory Group, Ashutosh Misra/Sr. VP - Operations, Corporate Affairs, Prem Nath/VP - Manufacturing, Joseph McCabe/VP - Business Development, Janet Casteel/Chief Accounting Officer, Treasurer, Scott R. Burrows/Corp. Sec., Rajeewa R. Arya/Member - Technical Advisory Group, Bruce Lanning/Member - Technical Advisory Group, Jeff Summers/Member - Technical Advisory Group, Joseph Armstrong/CTO, VP

Directors: Mohan S. Misra/Chmn., Chief Strategy Officer, Chmn. - our Technical Advisory Group, Stanley Gallery/Dir., Fraser T.W. Russell/Dir., Richard J. Swanson/Dir., Joel S. Porter/Dir., Amit Kumar/Dir., Einar Glomnes/Dir.

Owners: Mohan S. Misra/20.60%, Insiders/24.40%, ITN Energy Systems,Inc./14.50%, Joseph Armstrong/1.00%, Ashutosh Misra, Stanley Gallery, Fraser T.W. Russell, Norsk Hydro Produksjon AS/23.00%, Matthew Foster/2.10%

Financial Data: Fiscal Year End: 12/31   **Latest Annual Data:** 12/31/2006

Year	Sales	Net Income
2006	NA	-$4,181,000

Curr. Assets:	$10,791,000	**Curr. Liab.:**	$379,000
Plant, Equip.:	$91,000	**Total Liab.:**	$389,000	**Indic. Yr. Divd.:** NA
Total Assets:	$11,290,000	**Net Worth:**	$10,901,000	**Debt/ Equity:** NA

Asconi Corp

2200 Winter Springs Blvd, Ste 106-130, Oviedo, FL, 32765; **PH:** 1-407-679-9463;
Fax: 1-407-246-4536; *http://* www.asconi.com; **Email:** info@asconi.com

General - Incorporation	NV	Stock - Price on:12/24/2007	$0.13
Employees	NA	Stock Exchange	OTC
Auditor	Moore Stephens Lovelace P.A	Ticker Symbol	ASCD
Stk Agt	Manhattan Transfer Registrar Co	Outstanding Shares	NA
Counsel	Cozen O'Connor	E.P.S.	NA
DUNS No.	80-736-1654	Shareholders	NA

Business: The group's principle activity is to produce and distribute wine throughout eastern Europe through its wholly owned subsidiary, asconi s.r.l. The wines are categorized as white or red/rose and either ordinary or aged and are further categorized as either dry, semi-dry, semi-sweet, sweet or dessert wines. The group has 300 separate products derived from 32 varieties of grapes. Some of the major brands include souvenir, antique, gothic, vivat, grand reserve, dekabrist, love story, European collection, classic and French. The group also sells wine in bulk to other wineries in moldova for bottling under their brand name. The group export products to Russia, the United States, Germany, czech republic, slovak republic, Poland, romania, bulgaria, belarus, ukraine, China, kazakhstan, kirghyzstan and Russia.

Primary SIC and add'l.: 5182 2085

CIK No: 0000847917

Subsidiaries: Asconi Holding Company Limited, Asconi S.R.L, Coppett Finance Limited, Moldova lei

Officers: Nicolae Sterbets/Chmn., CEO, Pres., Tatiana Radu/Interim Financial Officer

Directors: Nicolae Sterbets/Chmn., CEO, Pres., Constantin Jitaru/Dir., Anatolie Sirbu/Dir., Nurlan Arinov/Dir., Anatolyi Krupskyi/Dir., Andrew Gani/Dir.

Owners: Anatolie Sirbu/44.90%, Constantin Jitaru/44.90%

Financial Data: Fiscal Year End: 12/31   **Latest Annual Data:** 12/31/2004

Year	Sales	Net Income
2004	$19,319,000	$878,000
2003	$16,356,000	-$37,865,000
2002	$13,952,000	$957,000

Curr. Assets:	$16,347,000	**Curr. Liab.:**	$11,813,000	
Plant, Equip.:	$8,027,000	**Total Liab.:**	$12,284,000	**Indic. Yr. Divd.:** NA
Total Assets:	$24,674,000	**Net Worth:**	$10,909,000	**Debt/ Equity:** 0.0982

ASE Test Ltd

10 W Fifth St., Nantze Export Processing Zone, Kaohsiung; **PH:** 86-287805489;
http:// www.asetest.com; **Email:** ir_asetest@aseglobal.com

General - Incorporation	Singapore	Stock - Price on:12/24/2007	$15.015
Employees	5,630	Stock Exchange	NDQ
Auditor	Deloitte & Touche LLP	Ticker Symbol	ASTSF
Stk Agt	Bank of New York	Outstanding Shares	101,850,000
Counsel	Allen & Gledhill	E.P.S.	$0.85
DUNS No.	65-604-4948	Shareholders	NA

Business: The group's principle activity is to provide a broad range of integrated circuit testing services, including testing logic, mixed-signal and memory functions of packaged integrated circuits, wafer probing and variety of related services. The group operates from United States.

Primary SIC and add'l.: 6719 3674 8734

CIK No: 0001014838

Subsidiaries: ASE (Korea) Inc., ASE Electronics (M) Sdn. Bhd., ASE Inc., ASE Test, Inc., ISE Labs, Inc.

Officers: Tien Wu/50/CEO - ISE Labs, Jason C.S. Chang/Chmn., CEO, Lee Kwai Mun/46/Pres. - ASE Test Malaysia, Raymond Lo/Dir., Pres., Ken Hsiang/38/CFO, Pres. - ISE Labs

Directors: Jason C.S. Chang/Chmn., CEO, Richard H.P. Chang/Vice Chmn., Joseph Tung/Dir., Freddie Liu/43/Dir., Albert Yu/Dir., Sim Guan Seng/Dir., Jeffrey Chen/Dir., David Tsang/Dir., Chin Ko-Chien/Dir., Raymond Lo/Dir., Pres., Alan Cheng/Dir.

Owners: Freddie Liu, Jason C.S. Chang, ASE Inc./50.90%, Insiders/1.40%, Chin Ko-Chien, Richard H.P. Chang/1.00%, Tien Wu, Albert C.S. Yu, Joseph Tung

Financial Data: Fiscal Year End: 12/31   **Latest Annual Data:** 12/31/2006

Year	Sales	Net Income
2006	$517,706,000	$117,318,000
2005	$420,929,000	-$35,446,000
2004	$621,138,000	$17,890,000

Curr. Assets:	$305,554,000	**Curr. Liab.:**	$102,716,000	
Plant, Equip.:	$381,941,000	**Total Liab.:**	$220,817,000	**Indic. Yr. Divd.:** NA
Total Assets:	$853,928,000	**Net Worth:**	$633,111,000	**Debt/ Equity:** NA

Ashford Hospitality Trust Inc

14185 Dallas Pkwy., Ste. 1100, Dallas, TX, 75254; **PH:** 1-972-490-9600; **Fax:** 1-972-980-2705;
http:// www.ahtreit.com

General - Incorporation	MD	Stock - Price on:12/24/2007	$11.53
Employees	43	Stock Exchange	NYSE
Auditor	Ernst & Young LLP	Ticker Symbol	AHT
Stk Agt	EquiServe Trust Co N.A	Outstanding Shares	122,600,000
Counsel	NA	E.P.S.	$0.46
DUNS No.	NA	Shareholders	NA

Business: The groups principle activity is to invest in the hospitality industry. The group invests in direct hotel investments, first mortgages, mezzanine loans, construction loans and sale-leaseback transactions. The group operates through two segments namely, direct hotel investments and hotel financing. The group operates 81 hotel properties located in 26 states with 15,492 rooms in the United States. The group acquired the Pan Pacific San Francisco Hotel in Calfornia in April 2006, Marriott Crystal Gateway hotel in Arlington in July 2006 and the Western OHore hotel in Rosemont in November 2006. The group's quarterly revenue for September 2007 was 336.82 millions of USD.

Primary SIC and add'l.: 6798

CIK No: 0001232582

Subsidiaries: Annapolis Hotel GP LLC, Annapolis Maryland Hotel Limited Partnership, Ashford 1031 General Partner II LLC, Ashford 1031 GP LLC, Ashford 1031 Ground Lessee LLC, Ashford Alpharetta Limited Partnership, Ashford Anaheim LP, Ashford Anchorage GP LLC, Ashford Anchorage LP, Ashford Atlantic Beach LP, Ashford Austin LP, Ashford Bucks County LLC, Ashford Buena Vista LP, Ashford Buford I LP, Ashford Buford II LP 176 Subsidiaries included in the Index

Officers: Montgomery J. Bennett/Dir., CEO, Pres., Douglas A. Kessler/COO, Head - Acquisitions, David A. Brooks/Chief Legal Officer, Head - Transactions, David J. Kimichik/CFO, Treasurer, Mark L. Nunneley/Chief Accounting Officer, Tripp Sullivan/Contact - Investor Relations

Directors: Montgomery J. Bennett/Dir., CEO, Pres., Archie Bennett/Chmn., Martin L. Edelman/Dir., Michael W. Murphy/Dir., Charles P. Toppino/Dir., Wesley D. Minami/Dir., Philip S. Payne/Dir.

Owners: W.D. Minami, Munder Capital Management/9.08%, David A. Brooks, Michael W. Murphy, The Vanguard Group, Inc./5.24%, David Kimichik, Douglas Kessler, Montgomery J. Bennett/5.46%, Mark L. Nunneley, Philip S. Payne, Archie Bennett/5.46%, Security Capital Secured Growth Incorporated/100.00%, Security Capital Research & Management Inc./6.76%, Martin Edelman, Charles P. Toppino (16 Owners included in Index)

Financial Data: *Fiscal Year End:*12/31 *Latest Annual Data:* 12/31/2006

Year	Sales	Net Income
2006	$480,434,000	$37,796,000
2005	$331,650,000	$9,437,000
2004	$116,925,000	$1,419,000

Curr. Assets:	$121,558,000	Curr. Liab.:	$74,693,000	P/E Ratio:	25.07
Plant, Equip.:	$1,754,398,000	Total Liab.:	$1,185,339,000	Indic. Yr. Divd.:	$0.840
Total Assets:	$2,011,912,000	Net Worth:	$641,709,000	Debt/ Equity:	1.7049

Ashland Inc

50 E RiverCtr. Blvd., Covington, KY, 41012; *PH:* 1-859-815-3333; *Fax:* 1-859-815-5053; *http://* www.ashland.com

General - Incorporation	KY	Stock - Price on:12/24/2007	$62.44
Employees	11,700	Stock Exchange	NYSE
Auditor	Ernst & Young LLP	Ticker Symbol	ASH
Stk Agt	National City Bank	Outstanding Shares	62,770,000
Counsel	NA	E.P.S.	$5.79
DUNS No.	NA	Shareholders	NA

Business: The groups principle activities include manufacturing and supplying chemicals and services to the building and construction, packaging and converting, transportation, marine and metal casting industries. The groups products marketed under the brand names includes Valvoline(R), EagleOne(R), Zerex(R), Pyroil(R), MaxLife(R) and Car Brite(R). The group operates through four segments namely, performance materials, distribution, valvoline and water technologies. The groups manufacturing sites located in the United States, Belgium, Denmark, Finland, Italy, Poland, Norway, Portugal, Brazil, China, Spain, England, Austria, Germany, South Korea and Sweden. The group's total revenue in the year 2007 was 2,104.00 millions of USD.

Primary SIC and add'l.: 4226 4731 5169 2899 2869 2891 7549 2992

CIK No: 0001305014

Subsidiaries: ASH GP LLC ("ASH GP"), ASH LP LLC ("ASH LP"), Ashland Brasil Ltda. ("ABL"), Ashland Canada Corp. ("ACC"), Ashland Canada Holdings B.V. ("ACHBV"), Ashland Chemical Hispania, S.L, Ashland Chimie France SAS ("ACF"), Ashland Deutschland GmbH ("ADG"), Ashland Finland Oy, Ashland France SAS ("AF"), Ashland Holdings B.V. ("AHBV"), Ashland International Holdings, Inc. ("AIHI"), Ashland Italia S.p.A, Ashland Nederland B.V., Ashland Polyester SAS 23 Subsidiaries included in the Index

Officers: James J. O'Brien/53/Chmn., CEO, David L. Hausrath/Sr. VP, General Counsel, Marvin J. Quin/CFO, Sr. VP, Walter H. Solomon/VP, Chief Growth Officer, Frank L. Waters/Pres. - Ashland Water Technologies, Ashland Performance Materials, VP, Larry L. Detjen/VP - Business Integration, Kristy J. Folkwein/VP - Information Systems, Luca P. Fontana/CTO, VP, Kevin J. Willis/Treasurer, John F. Guldig/General Auditor, James E. Vitak/Contact - Media, Linda L. Foss/Assist. General Counsel, Corp. Sec., Lamar M. Chambers/VP, Controller, Susan B. Esler/VP - Human Resources, Communications, Theodore L. Harris/Pres. - Ashland Distribution, VP (23 Officers included in Index)

Directors: James J. O'Brien/53/Chmn., CEO, Mannie L. Jackson/68/Dir., Barry W. Perry/61/Dir., George A. Schaefer/62/Dir., Ernest H. Drew/70/Dir., Roger W. Hale/64/Dir., Bernadine P. Healy/63/Dir., Kathleen Ligocki/51/Dir., Theodore M. Solso/60/Dir., John F. Turner/65/Dir., Michael J. Ward/57/Dir.

Owners: George A. Schaefer, John F. Turner, James J. OBrien, Michael J. Ward, Ernest H. Drew, State Street Corporation, Roger W. Hale, David L. Hausrath, The Goldman Sachs Group, Inc., Fidelity Management Trust Company, Insiders, Barry W. Perry, Marvin J. Quin, Samuel J. Mitchell, AXA (22 Owners included in Index)

Financial Data: *Fiscal Year End:*09/30 *Latest Annual Data:* 9/30/2006

Year	Sales	Net Income
2006	$7,277,000,000	$407,000,000
2005	$9,860,000,000	$2,004,000,000
2004	$8,781,000,000	$378,000,000

Curr. Assets:	$4,250,000,000	Curr. Liab.:	$2,041,000,000	P/E Ratio:	10.78
Plant, Equip.:	$950,000,000	Total Liab.:	$3,494,000,000	Indic. Yr. Divd.:	$1.100
Total Assets:	$6,590,000,000	Net Worth:	$3,096,000,000	Debt/ Equity:	0.0229

Ashworth Inc

2765 Loker Ave. W, Carlsbad, CA, 92010; *PH:* 1-760-438-6610; *Fax:* 1-760-476-8417; *http://* www.ashworthInc.com; *Email:* customercare@ashworthinc.com

General - Incorporation	DE	Stock - Price on:12/24/2007	$7.4
Employees	625	Stock Exchange	NDQ
Auditor	KPMG LLP, Moss Adams LLP	Ticker Symbol	ASHW
Stk Agt	Computershare Trust Co	Outstanding Shares	14,520,000
Counsel	Gibson, Dunn & Crutcher LLP	E.P.S.	-$0.6
DUNS No.	18-750-8486	Shareholders	NA

Business: The group's principal activities are to design, market and distribute sports apparel headwear and accessories under the ashworth(R) label. The group has two divisions namely men's division and women's division. The group's men's division designs knit and woven shirts, pullovers, jackets, sweaters, vests, pants, shorts, headwear and accessories. The products are sold through the group's retails stores in California, Texas, Colorado, Arizona, Utah and Nevada and the group's concept store in costa mesa, California. They are also sold through golf pro shops, resorts, upscale department and specialty stores. Internationally, the group operates in Canada, the United Kingdom and virgin islands. Products are also sold in other European countries. On 07-Jul-2004, the group acquired gekko brands llc.

Primary SIC and add'l.: 3949

CIK No: 0000820774

Subsidiaries: Ashworth Acquisition Corp, Ashworth EDC, LLC, Ashworth Store I, Inc., Ashworth Store II, Inc., Ashworth Store III, Inc., Ashworth U.K., Ltd., Gekko Brands, LLC, Kudzu, LLC, The Game, LLC

Officers: Peter M. Weil/CEO, Dir., Greg W. Slack/46/VP, Corporate Controller, Principal Accounting Officer, Gary I. Schneiderman/46/Pres., Peter E. Holmberg/56/Exec. VP - Merchandising, Design, Production, Edward J. Fadel/Pres., Eric R. Hohl/54/Dir., Exec. VP, CFO, Treasurer

Directors: Peter M. Weil/CEO, Dir., James B. Hayes/70/Chmn., Detlef H. Adler/50/Dir., Michael S. Koeneke/61/Dir., John M. Hanson/68/Dir., David M. Meyer/Dir., John W. Richardson/63/Dir., Stephen G. Carpenter/68/Dir., Eric R. Hohl/54/Dir., Exec. VP, CFO, Treasurer

Owners: Stephen G. Carpenter, David M. Meyer, Disciplined Growth Investors, Inc./6.10%, John M. Richardson, Peter M. Weil, Heartland Advisors, Inc./7.10%, Insiders/4.50%, Greg W. Slack, Dimensional Fund Advisors LP/8.30%, Knightspoint Partners II, L.P./14.60%, Gary I. Schneiderman, Peter E. Holmberg, Detlef H. Adler, James G. OConnor, James B. Hayes (18 Owners included in Index)

Financial Data: *Fiscal Year End:*10/31 *Latest Annual Data:* 10/31/2006

Year	Sales	Net Income
2006	$209,600,000	$951,000
2005	$204,788,000	-$727,000
2004	$173,102,000	$8,203,000

Curr. Assets:	$99,095,000	Curr. Liab.:	$37,599,000		
Plant, Equip.:	$39,126,000	Total Liab.:	$55,409,000	Indic. Yr. Divd.:	NA
Total Assets:	$164,043,000	Net Worth:	$108,634,000	Debt/ Equity:	0.1078

ASI Entertainment Inc

101 N Brand Blvd., 17th Fl., Glendale, CA, 91203; *PH:* 1-818-637-5611; *Fax:* 1-818-637-6402; *http://* www.asientertainment.com

General - Incorporation	DE	Stock - Price on:12/24/2007	$0.022
Employees	NA	Stock Exchange	OTC
Auditor	Larry O'Donnell, CPA, P.C.	Ticker Symbol	ASIQ
Stk Agt	Corporate Stock Transfer, Inc.	Outstanding Shares	NA
Counsel	NA	E.P.S.	NA
DUNS No.	NA	Shareholders	NA

Business: The groups principal activity is to develop marketing, software engineering and research. The group services include advertising research, concept research, international research and brand equity. The groups net sale in the year 2005 was $ 62,149. The group operates from the United States and Australia.

Primary SIC and add'l.: 3669 3663 7389 4899

CIK No: 0001067873

Subsidiaries: ASiQ Pty. Ltd.

Officers: Beverly Bolotin/CEO, Elliot Rosenberg/Pres., Guy Duff/CTO, Neal Lavine/Nationwide Theater Dir.

Owners: Ocean View Investments Pty. Ltd./25.13%, Richard Lukso/2.06%, Philip A. Shiels/6.69%, Ronald J. Chapman/10.27%, Insiders/22.22%, Eric P. van der Griend/25.61%, Graham O. Chappell/3.20%

Financial Data: *Fiscal Year End:*06/30 *Latest Annual Data:* 12/31/2006

Year	Sales	Net Income
2006	NA	NA

Curr. Assets:	$81,000	Curr. Liab.:	$468,000		
Plant, Equip.:	NA	Total Liab.:	$468,000	Indic. Yr. Divd.:	NA
Total Assets:	$81,000	Net Worth:	-$387,000	Debt/ Equity:	NA

ASI Technology Corp

980 American Pacific Dr., Ste. 111, Henderson, NV, 89014; *PH:* 1-702-734-1888; *Fax:* 1-702-737-6900; *http://* www.asiplasma.com

General - Incorporation	NV	Stock - Price on:12/24/2007	$0.47
Employees	NA	Stock Exchange	OTC
Auditor	Moss Adams LLP	Ticker Symbol	ASIT
Stk Agt	Transfer Online, Inc.	Outstanding Shares	15,910,000
Counsel	NA	E.P.S.	$0.00
DUNS No.	07-623-0085	Shareholders	NA

Business: The group's principal activity is the development of advanced patented technologies in support of dod and commercial organizations. The group has patented plasma technologies, plasma antenna technology and plasma sound reduction technology for jet engines. Plasma sound reduction technology employs patented techniques to modulate the plasma in a jet engine to reduce noise. The group has acquired a license to third plasma technology for sterilization and decontamination. The group operates in the United States of America.

Primary SIC and add'l.: 8711 8731

CIK No: 0000007951

Officers: Jerry E. Polis/Chmn., CEO, Pres., Eric M. Polis/Dir., Treasurer, Sec., CFO

Directors: Jerry E. Polis/Chmn., CEO, Pres., Eric M. Polis/Dir., Treasurer, Sec., CFO, Dawayne R. Jacobs/Dir., Gerald L. Ehrens/68/Dir., Richard A. Fait/70/Dir.

Owners: Eric M. Polis/2.30%, Jerry E. Polis/41.00%, Insiders/45.50%, Gerald L. Ehrens/2.70%, Richard A. Fait/1.10%

Financial Data: *Fiscal Year End:*12/31 *Latest Annual Data:* 9/30/2006

Year	Sales	Net Income
2006	$262,000	-$14,000
2005	NA	-$267,000
2004	NA	-$716,000

Curr. Assets:	$2,080,000	Curr. Liab.:	$23,000		
Plant, Equip.:	NA	Total Liab.:	$942,000	Indic. Yr. Divd.:	NA
Total Assets:	$2,080,000	Net Worth:	$1,139,000	Debt/ Equity:	0.2353

Asia Automotive Acquisition Corp

2711 Centerville Rd., Ste. 400, Wilmington, DE, 19808; *PH:* 1-248-593-8330

General - Incorporation
Employees NA
Auditor Rothstein & Kass LLP
Stk Agt Continental Stock Transfer & Trust Co
Counsel NA
DUNS No. NA

Stock- Price on:12/24/2007 $7.74
Stock Exchange OTC
Ticker Symbol AAAC
Outstanding Shares NA
E.P.S. $0.12
Shareholders NA

Business: The groups principle activity is to provide recruiting services. The groups service area includes the research and development, engineering, marketing, sales, information technology and manufacturing industries. The group operates from United States.

Primary SIC and add'l.: 6770

CIK No:

Financial Data: *Fiscal Year End:*NA *Latest Annual Data:* 12/31/2006

Year	Sales	Net Income
2006	$1,309,000	-$3,570,000

Curr. Assets:	$384,000	Curr. Liab.:	$12,703,000		
Plant, Equip.:	NA	Total Liab.:	$20,352,000	Indic. Yr. Divd.:	NA
Total Assets:	$39,111,000	Net Worth:	$18,759,000	Debt/ Equity:	NA

Asia Biotechnology Group Inc

Formerly: Echelon Acquisition Corp
No 7 Bohaisan St, Pingfang Indust. Dist., Econ.&amp, Technological Development Areaharbin, Heilongjiang, 150069; *PH:* 86-0451-86810508

General - Incorporation DE
Employees 283
Auditor William Tay
Stk Agt Holladay Stock Transfer, Inc.
Counsel NA
DUNS No. NA

Stock- Price on:12/24/2007 $16.84
Stock Exchange NA
Ticker Symbol NA
Outstanding Shares 39,430,000
E.P.S. -$0.54
Shareholders NA

Business: The group's principle activity is to develop biotechnology applications. The group operates from United States.

Primary SIC and add'l.: 6770

CIK No: 0001302646

Owners: Jiaxin Yang, Hui Wang, Mingshi Qiu, Far Grand

Financial Data: *Fiscal Year End:*12/31 *Latest Annual Data:* 12/31/2006

Year	Sales	Net Income
2006	$57,276,000	-$24,440,000
2005	$74,428,000	-$19,719,000
2004	$109,921,000	$5,272,000

Curr. Assets:	$170,853,000	Curr. Liab.:	$38,433,000		
Plant, Equip.:	$15,188,000	Total Liab.:	$39,701,000	Indic. Yr. Divd.:	NA
Total Assets:	$196,276,000	Net Worth:	$156,575,000	Debt/ Equity:	NA

Asia Electrical Power International Group Inc

6130 ELTON Ave., Las Vegas, NV, 89107; *PH:* 1-702-216-0470; *Fax:* 1-604-697-8898; *http://* www.asiaelectricalpower.com; *Email:* info@EquiComCapital.com

General - Incorporation NV
Employees 108
Auditor Robert G. Jeffrey
Stk Agt NA
Counsel NA
DUNS No. NA

Stock- Price on:12/24/2007 $2.76
Stock Exchange OTC
Ticker Symbol AEPW
Outstanding Shares 51,000,000
E.P.S. -$0.02
Shareholders NA

Business: The groups principle activities include developing, producing and selling of novel and innovative electronic flat panel displays. The group operates from the United States.

Primary SIC and add'l.: 3613

CIK No: 0001306046

Subsidiaries: Shenzhen Naiji Electrical Equipment Co., Ltd.

Officers: Yulong Guo/Chmn., CEO, Pres., Xiaoling Chen/Dir., Sec., CFO

Directors: Yulong Guo/Chmn., CEO, Pres., Xiaoling Chen/Dir., Sec., CFO, Dudley Barrington Delapenha/Dir.

Owners: YuLong Guo/46.00%, XiaoLing Chen/10.00%, Ying Yang/9.00%, Insiders/56.00%

Financial Data: *Fiscal Year End:*12/31 *Latest Annual Data:* 12/31/2006

Year	Sales	Net Income
2006	$8,081,000	$477,000

Curr. Assets:	$7,688,000	Curr. Liab.:	$3,681,000	P/E Ratio:	276.00
Plant, Equip.:	$2,824,000	Total Liab.:	$4,055,000	Indic. Yr. Divd.:	NA
Total Assets:	$10,579,000	Net Worth:	$6,524,000	Debt/ Equity:	NA

Asia Global Holdings Corp

834 S Broadway Fl 5, Los Angeles, CA, 90014; *PH:* 1-213-243-1503; *http://* www.asiaglobalholdings.com; *Email:* ir@asiaglobalholdings.com

General - Incorporation NV
Employees NA
Auditor Hlb Hodgson Impey Cheng
Stk Agt Signature Stock Transfer, Inc.
Counsel NA
DUNS No. NA

Stock- Price on:12/24/2007 $0.0685
Stock Exchange OTC
Ticker Symbol AAGH
Outstanding Shares NA
E.P.S. NA
Shareholders NA

Business: The groups principle activities include advertising, media services and products. The groups services include Internet marketing, search engine marketing, email marketing and print advertising. The group products include TradeDragon and DragonDynamics (TM).The group marketed its products under the trade name DragonDynamics (TM). The group operates through two segments namely product sale and advertising and list rental. The group operates from Hon Kong and China. The group's quarterly revenue for September 2007 was 3.84 millions of USD.

Primary SIC and add'l.: 7311

CIK No: 0001171689

Subsidiaries: Sino Trade - Intelligent Development Corp. Limited., Wah Mau Corporate Planning Development (Shenzhen) Company Limited

Officers: Michael Mak/Dir., CEO, Interim CFO, John Leper/Dir., Sec.

Directors: Michael Mak/Dir., CEO, Interim CFO, John Leper/Dir., Sec.

Owners: Standford International Holding Corporation/57.90%, Michael Mak/57.90%, Insiders/57.90%, Ernest Cheung/11.84%

Financial Data: *Fiscal Year End:*12/31 *Latest Annual Data:* 12/31/2006

Year	Sales	Net Income
2006	$5,179,000	-$6,111,000
2005	$2,189,000	-$382,000
2004	$4,466,000	$474,000

Curr. Assets:	$4,399,000	Curr. Liab.:	$2,099,000		
Plant, Equip.:	$52,000	Total Liab.:	$2,253,000	Indic. Yr. Divd.:	NA
Total Assets:	$4,763,000	Net Worth:	$2,510,000	Debt/ Equity:	0.0374

Asia Premium Television Group Inc

2 N Tuanjiehu St., Ste. 602, Chaoyang District, Beijing, 100026; *PH:* 86-10-6582-7900

General - Incorporation NV
Employees NA
Auditor HJ Assoc. & Consultants LLP
Stk Agt American Stock Transfer & Trust Co.
Counsel NA
DUNS No. 60-349-5508

Stock- Price on:12/24/2007 NA
Stock Exchange OTC
Ticker Symbol ATVG
Outstanding Shares NA
E.P.S. NA
Shareholders NA

Business: The group's principal activity is to acquire and develop film rights for distribution through television broadcasting contracts and cable distribution agreements. The group also market products directly to consumers through various television broadcasting contracts, cable distribution. It is currently broadcasting programs using the transmission and distribution facilities of sun television cybernetworks holdings ltd into Hong Kong, Taiwan and mainland China. It began broadcasting on a limited basis by performing test product valuations and fulfillment service evaluations on its home shopping and general entertainment programs through satellite transmission on its own channel. The group acquired shandong hongzhi advertising, ltd., lee and brothers international advertising, ltd. And Beijing young fu century advertising consultancy co, ltd. In jul 2004.

Primary SIC and add'l.: 6719 4841

CIK No: 0000860543

Subsidiaries: Beijing Asia Hongzhi Advertising Co., Ltd., Beijing Asia Qiangshi Media Advertising Co., Ltd., Beijing Hongzhi Century Advertising Co., Ltd, Shandong Hongzhi Communications and Career Advertising Co., Ltd., Tibet Asia Culture Media Co., Ltd., Tibet Hongzhi Advertising Co., Ltd.

Officers: Yan Gong/44/Dir., CEO, Hongmei Zhang/43/Finance Mgr., Chuan He/Media Planning Mgr., Dapeng Sun/Mgr. - Customer Service

Directors: Yan Gong/44/Dir., CEO, Li Li/45/Chmn., Jing Xing/41/Dir., Huiyang Yu/Dir., Douglas J. Toth/47/Dir.

Owners: Faithhill Investments Limited/12.65%, Capital Holdings, LLC/5.18%, Beijing Shengshi Chuanren Advertising Co., Ltd./5.99%, Global Women Multi-Media Co., Ltd./29.05%, Hershop.com Ltd/17.43%, Vesto Pacific Holdings, Ltd./12.39%, Sun New Media Inc./6.17%

Financial Data: *Fiscal Year End:*03/31 *Latest Annual Data:* 03/31/2006

Year	Sales	Net Income
2006	$61,794,000	$1,116,000
2005	$48,228,000	$340,000

Curr. Assets:	$15,045,000	Curr. Liab.:	$16,088,000		
Plant, Equip.:	$1,006,000	Total Liab.:	$16,088,000	Indic. Yr. Divd.:	NA
Total Assets:	$16,052,000	Net Worth:	-$36,000	Debt/ Equity:	NA

Asia Satellite Telecommunications Holdings Ltd

17th Floor, The Lee Gardens, 33 Hysan Ave., Causeway Bay; ; *http://* www.asiasat.com; *Email:* as-mkt@asiasat.com

General - Incorporation Bermuda
Employees 102
Auditor PricewaterhouseCoopers LLP
Stk Agt Bank of New York
Counsel Catherine Chang
DUNS No. NA

Stock- Price on:12/24/2007 $19.95
Stock Exchange NYSE
Ticker Symbol SAT
Outstanding Shares 39,030,000
E.P.S. $1.52
Shareholders NA

Business: The group's principle activity is the provision of high-quality satellite transponder capacity and the provision of services to broadcasting and telecommunications markets. The group has three satellites which are positioned over the Asian landmass and offer its customers coverage of close to 70% of the world's population. AsisSat 4 is a Boeing 601 HP satellite and has commenced commerical service in July 2003. The had purchased a plot of land at the Tai Po Industrial Estates in Hong Kong to build a new satellite earth station which was completed in January 2004. The group earns revenue fom customers in Hong Kong, Greater China, including Taiwan, USA, British Virgin Islands, Singapore and other contries.

Primary SIC and add'l.: 4899 4813 7359 5065

CIK No: 0001015276

Subsidiaries: Asia Satellite Telecommunications Company Limited, AsiaSat BVI Limited, Hanbury International Limited, Skywave TV Company Limited

Officers: Peter Jackson/Executive Dir., CEO, Fai Wong Ko/Non Exec. Dir., Sabrina Cubbon/46/GM - Marketing, Catherine Chang/40/Legal Counsel, Barry Turner/GM - Engineering, Liqun Chen/57/GM - China, William Wade/Executive Dir., Ching Siu Yeung/Company Sec., Ya Hui Chiu/58/GM - Operation

Directors: Peter Jackson/Executive Dir., CEO, Xin Zeng Mi/Chmn., Ronald J. Herman/Dep. Chmn., Nancy Ku/Non Exec. Dir., Yu Cheng Ding/42/Dir., Min Wei Ju/Non Exec. Dir., James Watkins/Dir., John F. Connelly/Non Exec. Dir., Mark Chen/Non Exec. Dir., Edward Chen/Dir., William Wade/Executive Dir., Cheng Yu Ding/Non Exec. Dir., Robert Sze/Dir.

Owners: Insiders, Bowenvale Limited/68.75%

Financial Data: *Fiscal Year End:*12/31 *Latest Annual Data:* 12/31/2006

Year	Sales	Net Income
2006	$119,218,000	$57,221,000
2005	$112,783,000	$46,002,000
2004	$128,844,000	$54,369,000

Curr. Assets:	$269,161,000	**Curr. Liab.:**	$42,121,000		
Plant, Equip.:	$341,685,000	**Total Liab.:**	$86,761,000	**Indic. Yr. Divd.:**	$0.210
Total Assets:	$657,103,000	**Net Worth:**	$570,342,000	**Debt/ Equity:**	NA

AsiaInfo Holdings Inc

5201 Great America Pkwy., Ste. 429, Santa Clara, CA, 95054; ***PH:*** 1-408-970-9788; ***Fax:*** 1-408-970-9366; ***http://*** www.asiainfo.com; ***Email:*** info@asiainfo.com

General - Incorporation	DE	**Stock**- Price on:12/24/2007	$9.35
Employees	1,800	Stock Exchange	NDQ
Auditor	Deloitte Touche Tohmatsu CPA Ltd	Ticker Symbol	ASIA
Stk Agt	Bank of New York	Outstanding Shares	43,150,000
Counsel	T&C Law Firm	E.P.S	$0.39
DUNS No.	NA	Shareholders	NA

Business: The group's principal activities are to provide services for telecommunications network integration and software solutions. The group operates under two segments: communications solutions and operation support system. Communications solutions include network solutions, service application solutions, network security solutions and network monitoring solutions. Operation support system includes software customer care and billing, order fulfillment and customer relationship management. The group's customers are China Telecom, China Netcom Group, China Mobile, China Unicom and China Railcom. The group provides telecommunication services in China. On 06-Feb-2002, the group acquired Bonson.

Primary SIC and add'l.: 6719 7379 4813 7372 7373

CIK No: 0001100969

Subsidiaries: AsiaInfo (H.K.) Systems Co. Limited, AsiaInfo H.K. Limited, AsiaInfo Management Software,Inc., AsiaInfo Technologies (Chengdu),Inc., AsiaInfo Technologies (China), Inc., Beijing Star VATS Technologies, Inc., Bonson Information TechnologyLimited, Lenovo Computer System and Technology Services Limited, Lenovo Security Technologies (Beijing), Inc., Lenovo-AsiaInfo Technologies, Inc., Times AsiaInfo Technologies (Beijing), Inc. (1)

Officers: Steve Zhang/Dir., CEO, Pres./$2,037,941.00, Jian Qi/47/CEO, Pres. - Lenovo, Asiainfo Division, Louis Lau/Chmn., Pres., Yinhu Zhang/46/VP, GM - Human Resources, Administration, Eileen Chu/Investor Relations Officer, Ying Li/Human Resources Department, Zhou Yan/Internal Auditor, Ying Han/CFO, Exec. VP/$361,465.00, Jason Zhang/VP, GM - Human Resources, Organization Development, Asiainfo Holdings, Inc, Feng Liu/36/VP, GM - Research, Development, Asiainfo Technologies Division

Directors: Steve Zhang/Dir., CEO, Pres., Louis Lau/Chmn., Pres., Michael Zhao/Dir., Anders Cheung/Dir., Qing Yu/Partner, Alan Bickell/Dir., Yichen Zhang/44/Dir., Yungang Lu/Dir., James Ding/Dir., Chang Sun/Dir., Tao Long/Dir., Edward Tian/Dir., Davin A. MacKenzie/Dir., Tom Manning/Dir.

Owners: CITIC Capital MB Investment Ltd./9.19%, Tao Long, Feng Liu, Ying Han/1.44%, Steve Zhang/1.72%, Tom Manning, James Ding/5.63%, Edward Tian/17.05%, Yinhu Zhang, Lenovo IT Alliance Limited/9.39%, Sansar Capital Special Opportunity Master Fund, L.P./5.34%, Insiders/26.62%, Yungang Lu, Davin A. Mackenzie, Jian Qi

Financial Data: ***Fiscal Year End:***12/31 ***Latest Annual Data:*** 12/31/2006

Year	Sales	Net Income
2006	$109,583,000	$5,831,000
2005	$93,900,000	-$37,169,000
2004	$106,677,000	$9,791,000

Curr. Assets:	$216,585,000	**Curr. Liab.:**	$81,701,000	**P/E Ratio:**	34.63
Plant, Equip.:	$1,857,000	**Total Liab.:**	$81,701,000	**Indic. Yr. Divd.:**	NA
Total Assets:	$244,162,000	**Net Worth:**	$162,461,000	**Debt/ Equity:**	NA

Asiamart Inc

Rm. 1508-1509, Peninsula Sq., 18 Sung On St., Hung Hom; ***PH:*** 852-25113873; ***Fax:*** 852-35808818; ***http://*** www.asiamartinc.com; ***Email:*** financials@asiamartinc.com

General - Incorporation	DE	**Stock**- Price on:12/24/2007	$0.8
Employees	NA	Stock Exchange	OTC
Auditor	Moore Stephens Wurth F & T LLP	Ticker Symbol	AAMA
Stk Agt	Continental Stock Transfer & Trust Co	Outstanding Shares	NA
Counsel	NA	E.P.S	NA
DUNS No.	NA	Shareholders	NA

Business: The groups principle activity is to operate retail and trading outlets. The group s services include consumer electronics, health food, skin care products, cosmetics, perfumes, leather goods, eyewear and fashion. The group operates through two segments namely trading and retail. In the year 2005, the group acquired by Central Class Holdings Limited. The group operates from Hon Kong and China.

Primary SIC and add'l.: 5331

CIK No: 0001072702

Officers: Alex Chun Shan Yue/51/Chmn., CEO, Danny Leung/Dir., COO, Anita Mei Kam Yeung/41/Dir., Corp. Sec., Cary Shek/Executive Dir., Ricky Kee Kwong Tsoi/Founder - Advisor, Albert Chi Wai Wong/CFO, Noelle Hon/Chief Investor Relations Officer

Directors: Alex Chun Shan Yue/51/Chmn., CEO, Danny Leung/Dir., COO, Anita Mei Kam Yeung/41/Dir., Corp. Sec., Cary Shek/Executive Dir., Ricky Kee Kwong Tsoi/Founder - Advisor

Owners: Ricky Kee Kwong Tsoi, Alex Chun Shan Yue, Forever Rise Holdings Limited, Insiders

Financial Data: ***Fiscal Year End:***12/31 ***Latest Annual Data:*** 12/31/2006

Year	Sales	Net Income
2006	$53,145,000	$3,149,000
2005	NA	$1,421,000
2004	NA	-$2,744,000

Curr. Assets:	$9,678,000	**Curr. Liab.:**	$4,264,000		
Plant, Equip.:	$679,000	**Total Liab.:**	$4,609,000	**Indic. Yr. Divd.:**	NA
Total Assets:	$11,692,000	**Net Worth:**	$7,083,000	**Debt/ Equity:**	NA

Asian Dragon Group Inc

475 Howe St., Ste.1100, Vancouver, BC, V6C 2B3; ***PH:*** 1-604-801-5995; ***http://*** www.asiandragongroup.net; ***Email:*** info@asiandragongroup.net

General - Incorporation	NV	**Stock**- Price on:12/24/2007	$2.3
Employees	NA	Stock Exchange	OTC
Auditor	Schumacher & Associates, Inc.	Ticker Symbol	AADG
Stk Agt	NA	Outstanding Shares	NA
Counsel	NA	E.P.S	NA
DUNS No.	NA	Shareholders	NA

Business: The groups principal activity is to explore minerals. The group operates from Canada and the United States.

Primary SIC and add'l.: 1081

CIK No: 0001314259

Subsidiaries: Galaxy Telnet

Officers: John Karlsson/Dir., CEO, Pres., Yang Dali/Chief Chinese Advisor, Christian Derosier/Sr. Technical Advisor

Directors: John Karlsson/Dir., CEO, Pres., Daniel Hachey/Dir., Jacques Trottier/Dir.

Owners: Insiders/18.50%, John Karlsson/18.50%

Financial Data: ***Fiscal Year End:***08/31 ***Latest Annual Data:*** 08/31/2006

Year	Sales	Net Income
2006	NA	-$95,000

Curr. Assets:	$2,000	**Curr. Liab.:**	$177,000		
Plant, Equip.:	NA	**Total Liab.:**	$177,000	**Indic. Yr. Divd.:**	NA
Total Assets:	$2,000	**Net Worth:**	-$175,000	**Debt/ Equity:**	NA

ASM International

3440 E University Dr., Phoenix, AZ, 85034; ***PH:*** 1-602-470-5700; ***Fax:*** 1-602-437-1403; ***http://*** www.asm.com; ***Email:*** investor.relations@asm.com

General - Incorporation	Netherlands	**Stock**- Price on:12/24/2007	$26.33
Employees	10,868	Stock Exchange	NDQ
Auditor	Deloitte Accountants B.V	Ticker Symbol	ASMI
Stk Agt	Citibank N.A	Outstanding Shares	53,920,000
Counsel	NA	E.P.S	$1.12
DUNS No.	NA	Shareholders	NA

Business: The group's principal activity is the design, manufacture and sale of equipment and materials used to produce semiconductor devices or integrated circuits. The group also provides solutions for the main areas of semiconductor production, namely wafer processing, assembly and packaging. Products fall into two categories: front end: semiconductor wafer fabrication equipment, such as epitaxial reactors, cluster tools, vertical furnaces, rapid thermal process equipment, atomic layer cvd tools; back end: equipment for assembly of integrated circuits, such as die attach tools, wire bonders, trim and form equipment, encapsulation mould tools, assembly automation & test equipment.

Primary SIC and add'l.: 3559 3469 3479

CIK No: 0000351483

Subsidiaries: Advanced Semiconductor Materials, Cayman Islands limited liability

Officers: Arthur H. Del Prado/Chmn., CEO, Lee Wai Kwong/Member - Management Board, CEO - ASM Pacific Technology Ltd, W. K. Lee/CEO - ASM Pacific Technology Ltd, Peter Lo Tsan Yin/Vice Chmn. - ASM Pacific Technology Ltd, James Chow Chuen/Dir., COO - ASM Pacific Technology Ltd, Arnold J.M. Van Der Ven/Member - Management Board, CFO, Richard W. Bowers/Chief Legal Officer Front - end Operations, Eric Tang Koon Hung/Dir., CFO - ASM Pacific Technology Ltd, Yam Mo Wong/CTO - ASM Pacific Technology Ltd, Lies Rijnveld/Investor Relations Officer - Netherlands, Mary Jo Dieckhaus/Investor Relations Officer - USA, Patrick Lam See Pong/VP - Asian Operations, MD - ASM Pacific Technology Ltd, Charles D. Del Prado/Member - Management Board, Regional Mgr. Front, end Operations USA And Pres., GM ASM America - Inc, Fukumi Tomino/Regional Mgr. - Front, end Operations Asia, MD - ASM Japan KK, Hans Van Selm/Group Controller, Dir. - Finance, Front - end *(18 Officers included in Index)*

Directors: Arthur H. Del Prado/Chmn., CEO, Lee Wai Kwong/Member - Management Board, CEO - ASM Pacific Technology Ltd, Peter Lo Tsan Yin/Vice Chmn. - ASM Pacific Technology Ltd, Paul C. Van Den Hoek/69/Chmn. - Supervisory Board, Berend C. Brix/59/Member - Supervisory Board, Han F.M. Westendorp/Member - Management Board, COO - Front, end Operations, Charles D. Del Prado/Member - Management Board, Regional Mgr. Front, end Operations USA And Pres., GM ASM America - Inc, Johan M.R. Danneels/59/Member - Supervisory Board, Eric Tang Koon Hung/Dir., CFO - ASM Pacific Technology Ltd, Heinrich W. Kreutzer/59/Member - Supervisory Board, Eric A. Van Amerongen/55/Member - Supervisory Board, Leon P.E.M. Van Den Boom/56/Member - Supervisory Board, Arnold J.M. Van Der Ven/Member - Management Board, CFO, James Chow Chuen/Dir., COO - ASM Pacific Technology Ltd

Owners: Insiders/22.00%, Fursa Alternative Strategies LLC/8.30%, Hermes Focus Asset Management Europe Ltd/10.00%, Arthur H. del Prado/21.30%

Financial Data: ***Fiscal Year End:***12/31 ***Latest Annual Data:*** 12/31/2006

Year	Sales	Net Income
2006	$1,158,551,000	$45,331,000
2005	$860,369,000	-$47,633,000
2004	$1,029,092,000	$32,799,000

Curr. Assets:	$813,989,000	**Curr. Liab.:**	$310,685,000	**P/E Ratio:**	34.63
Plant, Equip.:	$199,715,000	**Total Liab.:**	$733,874,000	**Indic. Yr. Divd.:**	NA
Total Assets:	$1,098,882,000	**Net Worth:**	$365,007,000	**Debt/ Equity:**	NA

ASML Holding

8555 S River Pkwy., Tempe, AZ, 85284; ***PH:*** 1-480-383-4422; ***Fax:*** 1-480-383-3995; ***http://*** www.asml.com; ***Email:*** corpcom@asml.com

General - Incorporation	Netherlands	**Stock**- Price on:12/24/2007	$27.44
Employees	5,594	Stock Exchange	NDQ
Auditor	Deloitte Accountants B.V	Ticker Symbol	ASML
Stk Agt	JPMorgan Service Center	Outstanding Shares	477,100,000
Counsel	NA	E.P.S	$2.49
DUNS No.	41-846-0788	Shareholders	NA

Business: The group's principal activities are the production and distribution of lithographic technology including wafer steppers and step and scan systems. The group also offers equipment options and software upgrades. The products are for use in the telecommunications, industrial, automotive and consumer electronics sectors. The group has technological agreements with leading ic manufacturers and research and development institutions in Europe, the us and the Asian/pacific region and is a member of jessi and esprit.

Primary SIC and add'l.: 3559 5084

CIK No: 0000937966

Subsidiaries: ASML (Tianjin) Co. Ltd., ASML (UK)Ltd., ASML Capital US, Inc., ASML Equipment Malaysia Sdn. Bhd., ASML Finance B.V., ASML France S.a.r.l., ASML Germany GmbH, ASML Hong Kong Ltd., ASML Ireland Ltd., ASML Israel (2001)Ltd., ASML Italy S.r.l., ASML Japan Co. Ltd., ASML Korea Co. Ltd., ASML Macau Commercial Offshore Ltd., ASML MaskTools B.V. 22 Subsidiaries included in the Index

Officers: Eric Meurice/Chmn., CEO, Pres., Martin Van Den Brink/Exec. VP - Marketing, Technology, Peter Wennink/CFO, Exec. VP, Klaus Fuchs/Exec. VP - Operations, Franki D'Hoore/Dir. - European Investor Relations, Asml Veldhoven, Rob Van Vliet/Mgr. - Investor Relations, Asml Veldhoven, Annie Prinsen/Assist. Mgr. Investor Relations - Asml Veldhoven, Craig Deyoung/VP - Investor Relations, Asml Tempe, Michael Pullen/Assist. Mgr. Investor Relations - Asml Tempe

Directors: Eric Meurice/Chmn., CEO, Pres., Arthur P.M. Van Der Poel/60/Member - Supervisory Board, Jan A. Dekker/Member - Supervisory Board, O. B. Bilous/70/Member - Supervisory Board, Fritz W. Frohlich/66/Member - Supervisory Board, Leke C.J. Van Den Burg/56/Member - Supervisory Board, Jos W.B. Westerburgen/66/Member - Supervisory Board

Owners: FMR Corp/14.80%, Capital Group International, Inc/11.70%, Capital Research and Management Company/10.40%, Insiders

Financial Data: Fiscal Year End:12/31   Latest Annual Data: 12/31/2006

Year	Sales	Net Income
2006	$4,749,256,000	$824,777,000
2005	$2,995,309,000	$368,898,000
2004	$3,363,773,000	$321,262,000

Curr. Assets:	$4,523,398,000	Curr. Liab.:	$1,559,820,000	P/E Ratio:	34.63
Plant, Equip.:	$357,656,000	Total Liab.:	$2,369,384,000	Indic. Yr. Divd.:	NA
Total Assets:	$5,216,552,000	Net Worth:	$2,847,168,000	Debt/ Equity:	NA

ASP Ventures Corp

1066 W Hastings St., Vancouver, BC, V6E3X2; *PH:* 1-604-602-1717

General - Incorporation	FL	Stock - Price on:12/24/2007	$0.015
Employees	NA	Stock Exchange	OTC
Auditor	Dale Matheson Carr-Hilton LaBonte LLP	Ticker Symbol	APVE
Stk Agt	Interwest Transfer Company, Inc.	Outstanding Shares	NA
Counsel	NA	E.P.S.	NA
DUNS No.	NA	Shareholders	NA

Business: The groups principle activity is to provide recruiting services. The groups service area includes the research and development, engineering, marketing, sales, information technology and manufacturing industries. The group operates from United States.

Primary SIC and add'l.: 9995

CIK No: 0001101298

Officers: Nora Coccaro/50/Dir., CEO, CFO, Principal Accounting Officer/$24,000.00

Directors: Nora Coccaro/50/Dir., CEO, CFO, Principal Accounting Officer

Owners: Shafiq Nazerali/8.30%, Abdul Majeed Ismail Ali Al Fahim/12.20%

Financial Data: Fiscal Year End:12/31   Latest Annual Data: 12/31/2006

Year	Sales	Net Income
2006	NA	-$194,000
2005	NA	-$222,000
2004	NA	-$763,000

Curr. Assets:	$1,000	Curr. Liab.:	$1,071,000		
Plant, Equip.:	NA	Total Liab.:	$1,071,000	Indic. Yr. Divd.:	NA
Total Assets:	$1,000	Net Worth:	-$1,069,000	Debt/ Equity:	NA

Aspect Medical Systems Inc

1 Upland Rd., Norwood, MA, 02062; *PH:* 1-617-559-7000; *Fax:* 1-617-559-7400; *http://* www.aspectms.com; *Email:* bis_info@aspectms.com

General - Incorporation	DE	Stock - Price on:12/24/2007	$15.37
Employees	288	Stock Exchange	NDQ
Auditor	Ernst & Young LLP	Ticker Symbol	ASPM
Stk Agt	Computershare Investor Services LLC	Outstanding Shares	22,440,000
Counsel	Hale & Dorr LLP	E.P.S.	$1.53
DUNS No.	NA	Shareholders	NA

Business: The group's principal activity is to develop, manufacture and market an anesthesia monitoring system called bis(R) system. This system enables anesthesia providers to assess and manage a patient's level of consciousness during surgery. The bis(R) system is based on the group's patented core technology, the bispectral index (the bis index). The bis(R) system provides information that allows clinicians to better assess and manage a patient's level of consciousness in the operating room and intensive care settings and administer the precise amount of anesthesia needed by each patient. The bis(R) system includes the bis monitor or bis module kit and the single-use, disposable bis sensors. The group's customers include anesthesia providers, hospitals, outpatient surgical centers and individual practitioners. The group's products are available in more than 160 countries.

Primary SIC and add'l.: 3845

CIK No: 0000886235

Subsidiaries: Aspect Medical Systems International B.V., Aspect Medical Systems UK Limited

Officers: Nassib G. Chamoun/Dir., CEO, Pres./$1,051,309.00, Margery Ahearn/VP - Human Resources, Michael Falvey/VP, CFO, Sec./$665,933.00, Paul J. Manberg/VP - Clinical, Regulatory, Quality Assurance, Boudewijn L.P.M Bollen/Dir., Pres. - International Operations/$774,679.00, Marc Davidson/VP - Engineering, Philip H. Devlin/VP, GM - Neuroscience, William Floyd/VP - Sales, Marketing/$579,509.00, Scott D. Kelley/VP, Medical Dir./$549,750.00, John Coolidge/VP - Manufacturing Operations

Directors: Nassib G. Chamoun/Dir., CEO, Pres., Breckenridge J. Eagle/Chmn., Michael A. Esposito/Dir., Donald R. Stanski/Dir., James J. Mahoney/Dir., Boudewijn L.P.M Bollen/Dir., Pres. - International Operations, Edwin M. Kania/Dir., David Feigal/Dir., John J. Oconnor/Dir.

Owners: Michael A. Esposito, Edwin M. Kania, Coghill Capital Management L.L.C./8.10%, Michael Falvey, William H. Floyd, John J. OConnor, Nassib G. Chamoun/3.30%, Boudewijn L.P.M. Bollen, Breckenridge J. Eagle/1.90%, Donald R. Stanski, FMR Corp./15.10%, Massachusetts Financial Services Company/7.70%, Scott D. Kelley/1.00%, David W. Feigal, James J. Mahoney *(17 Owners included in Index)*

Financial Data: Fiscal Year End:12/31   Latest Annual Data: 12/31/2006

Year	Sales	Net Income
2006	$91,334,000	$37,089,000
2005	$76,995,000	$8,475,000
2004	$55,564,000	$303,000

Curr. Assets:	$79,598,000	Curr. Liab.:	$12,218,000	P/E Ratio:	9.98
Plant, Equip.:	$7,798,000	Total Liab.:	$15,716,000	Indic. Yr. Divd.:	NA
Total Assets:	$124,964,000	Net Worth:	$109,248,000	Debt/ Equity:	NA

Aspen Exploration Corp

2050 S Oneida St., Ste. 208, Denver, CO, 80224; *PH:* 1-303-639-9860; *Fax:* 1-303-639-9863; *http://* www.aspenexploration.com; *Email:* accorp2@qwest.net

General - Incorporation	DE	Stock - Price on:12/24/2007	$3.7
Employees	2	Stock Exchange	OTC
Auditor	Gordon Hughes & Banks LLP	Ticker Symbol	ASPN
Stk Agt	Computershare Investor Services LLC	Outstanding Shares	7,260,000
Counsel	NA	E.P.S.	$0.11
DUNS No.	13-321-0310	Shareholders	NA

Business: The group's principal activities are to acquire, explore and develop oil and gas and other mineral properties. The group operates in three business segments: oil and gas exploration and development, mineral exploration and development and electrical generation construction. The oil and gas segment acquires interests in producing oil or gas properties and participating in drilling operations. The mineral exploration and development segment includes mining of minerals and precious metals. Currently, the group has curtailed the operations of the mining segment. The electrical generation construction segment designs, constructs and/or operates gas turbine or other electrical generation projects. As of Dec 31, 2002, the group ceased operations and no further business activity is anticipated in this segment. The major customers include calpine corporation and slawson corporation. The group operates in the United States.

Primary SIC and add'l.: 4911 3295 1382

CIK No: 0000319458

Subsidiaries: Aspen Power Systems, LLC

Officers: Robert A. Cohan/52/CEO, Pres., R. V. Bailey/76/Chmn., VP, Sec.

Directors: R. V. Bailey/76/Chmn., VP, Sec., Kevan B. Hensman/52/Dir.

Owners: Kevan B. Hensman/0.14%, Robert A. Cohan/8.43%, Insiders/26.93%, R. V. Bailey/18.37%

Financial Data: Fiscal Year End:06/30   Latest Annual Data: 6/30/2006

Year	Sales	Net Income
2006	$5,979,000	$2,970,000
2005	$4,127,000	$1,487,000
2004	$1,824,000	$201,000

Curr. Assets:	$9,946,000	Curr. Liab.:	$6,073,000	P/E Ratio:	12.33
Plant, Equip.:	$8,224,000	Total Liab.:	$9,090,000	Indic. Yr. Divd.:	$0.050
Total Assets:	$19,191,000	Net Worth:	$10,101,000	Debt/ Equity:	NA

Aspen Group Resources Corp

1000 - 910 7th Ave. SW, Calgary, AB, T2P 3N8; ; *http://* www.aspengroupresources.com

General - Incorporation	Canada	Stock - Price on:12/24/2007	$0.1
Employees	NA	Stock Exchange	OTC
Auditor	Lane Gorman Trubitt LLP	Ticker Symbol	ASRPF
Stk Agt	Equity Transfer & Trust Co.	Outstanding Shares	84,070,000
Counsel	Hall Estill Hardwick Gable Et Al	E.P.S.	-$0.122
DUNS No.	NA	Shareholders	NA

Business: The group's principle activity are to acquire, explore, develop and operate oil and gas properties. The oil and gas properties are located in eleven states with a predominate focus on Oklahoma, Kansas and Texas. The recoverability of the amounts capitalized for oil and gas is dependent upon the identification of economically recoverable reserves and necessary financing to exploit such reserves. The group's quarterly revenue for September 2007 was 0.62 millions of USD.

Primary SIC and add'l.: 1311 1321 3533

CIK No: 0001023947

Subsidiaries: Aspen Endeavour Resources Inc., Aspen Energy Group, Inc.

Officers: Robert L. Calentine/Dir., CEO, Ronald L. Mercer/VP

Directors: Robert L. Calentine/Dir., CEO, Robert C. Cudney/Dir., Wayne T. Egan/Dir., James A. Unger/Dir.

Financial Data: Fiscal Year End:12/31   Latest Annual Data: 12/31/2003

Year	Sales	Net Income
2003	$9,720,000	-$2,718,000
2001	$4,253,000	-$869,000

Curr. Assets:	$5,189,000	Curr. Liab.:	$19,296,000	P/E Ratio:	12.33
Plant, Equip.:	$40,371,000	Total Liab.:	$19,713,000	Indic. Yr. Divd.:	NA
Total Assets:	$45,624,000	Net Worth:	$25,910,000	Debt/ Equity:	NA

Aspen Insurance Holdings Ltd

Aspen Specialty Insurance Company, 600 Atlantic Ave., Ste. 2100, Boston, MA, 02210; *PH:* 1-617-531-5100; *Fax:* 1-617-532-7314; *http://* www.aspen.bm; *Email:* info@aspen.bm

General - Incorporation	Bermuda	Stock - Price on:12/24/2007	$28.18
Employees	444	Stock Exchange	NYSE
Auditor	KPMG Audit Plc	Ticker Symbol	AHL
Stk Agt	Mellon Investor Services LLC	Outstanding Shares	88,140,000
Counsel	NA	E.P.S.	$4.42
DUNS No.	NA	Shareholders	NA

Business: The groups principle activity is to provide insurance service. The groups services include property, casualty and specialty insurance. The group operates from United States.

Primary SIC and add'l.: NA

CIK No: 0001267395

Subsidiaries: AIUK Trustees Limited, Aspen (UK) Holdings Limited, Aspen Insurance Limited, Aspen Insurance U.S. Services Inc., Aspen Insurance UK Limited, Aspen Insurance UK Services Limited, Aspen Re America, Inc., Aspen Specialty Insurance Company, Aspen Specialty Insurance Management Inc., Aspen U.S. Holdings, Inc.

Officers: Christopher O'Kane/Dir., CEO, Ian Campbell/Group Chief Accountant, Head - Group Finance, Stuart Sinclair/Dir., COO, Pres. - Aspen, Richard Houghton/Dir., CFO, David Curtin/General Counsel, James Few/Head - Property Reinsurance, Group Underwriting Officer - Aspen Insurance, Brian Boornazian/Head - Reinsurance, Pres. - Aspen Re America, Karen Green/Head - Strategy, Oliver Peterken/Chief Risk Officer, Chris Woodman/Head - Human Resources, Kate Vacher/Underwriting Dir.

Directors: Christopher O'Kane/Dir., CEO, Paul Myners/Chmn., Julian Avery/62/Dir., Liaquat Ahamed/Dir., Prakash Melwani/Dir., Kamil M. Salame/Dir., Ian Cormack/Dir., Heidi Hutter/Dir., David Kelso/Dir., Norman L. Rosenthal/Dir., Julian Cusack/Dir., Glyn Jones/Dir., John Cavoores/Dir., Stuart Sinclair/Dir., COO, Pres. - Aspen, Richard Houghton/Dir., CFO *(17 Directors included in Index)*

Owners: Heidi Hutter, Snow Capital Management, L.P./6.25%, FMR Corp/10.42%, Ian Cormack, Credit Suisse/5.06%, Christopher OKane/1.00%, Stuart Sinclair, Insiders/2.22%, Paul Myners, Julian Cusack, The Blackstone Group/13.00%, David Kelso, Candover Investments plc, its/6.92%, Norman Rosenthal, Brian Boornazian *(16 Owners included in Index)*

Financial Data: *Fiscal Year End:*12/31 *Latest Annual Data:* 12/31/2006

Year	Sales	Net Income
2006	$1,859,500,000	$378,100,000
2005	$1,649,100,000	-$177,800,000
2004	$1,297,600,000	$195,100,000

Curr. Assets:	$2,438,900,000	**Curr. Liab.:**	$276,300,000	**P/E Ratio:**	6.38
Plant, Equip.:	$24,600,000	**Total Liab.:**	$4,250,800,000	**Indic. Yr. Divd.:**	$0.600
Total Assets:	$6,640,100,000	**Net Worth:**	$2,389,300,000	**Debt/ Equity:**	0.1097

Aspen Technology Inc

200 Wheeler Rd., Burlington, MA, 01803; *PH:* 1-781-221-6400; *Fax:* 1-617-949-1030; *http://* www.aspentec.com; *Email:* info@aspentech.com

General - Incorporation	DE	**Stock**- Price on:12/24/2007	$14.12
Employees	1,292	Stock Exchange	NDQ
Auditor	Deloitte & Touche LLP	Ticker Symbol	AZPN
Stk Agt	American Stock Transfer & Trust Co.	Outstanding Shares	88,090,000
Counsel	Hale & Dorr LLP	E.P.S	$0.42
DUNS No.	04-551-4031	Shareholders	NA

Business: The group's principal activities are to provide integrated software and services to the process industries. The group develops two types of software to design, operate, manage and optimize its customers' key business processes; engineering software and manufacturing/supply chain software. It operates through three - license, consulting services and maintenance and training. The license segment develops and licenses the software. The consulting services segment offers implementation, advanced process control, real-time optimization and other consulting services in order to provide customers with complete solutions. The maintenance and training segment provides customers with a wide range of support services that include on-site support, telephone support, software updates and various forms of training.

Primary SIC and add'l.: 7372 7379

CIK No: 0000929940

Subsidiaries: Aspen Tech Australia, P.T.Y, Aspen Technology (Asia), Inc., Aspen Technology Receivables I LLC, Aspen Technology Receivables II LLC, Aspen Technology S.L., Aspen Technology S.r.l., AspenTech Asia, Ltd., AspenTech Canada Ltd., AspenTech EMEA, Inc., AspenTech Securities Corporation, Coppermine LLC, EA Systems, Inc., Hunter Acquisition Corporation, ICARUS Corporation, Petrolsoft Corporation 17 Subsidiaries included in the Index

Officers: Mark E. Fusco/Dir., CEO, Pres., Antonio Pietri/Exec. VP - Field Operations, Willie K. Chan/VP - Research, Development, Bradley T. Miller/Sr. VP, CFO, Henry Lau/Sr. VP, MD - Regional Sales, Services, Apac, Michele Triponey/Sr. VP - Global Customer Support, Training, Aspen Professional Services, Richard Packwood/Sr. VP - Business Development, Blair Wheeler/Sr. VP - Marketing, Manolis Kotzabasakis/Sr. VP - Sales, Strategy, Hedwig Veith Whitney/Sr. VP - Human Resources, Steve Pringle/Sr. VP - Aspenone, Frederic G. Hammond/Sr. VP, General Counsel, David Woodruff/Sr. VP - Regional Sales, Services, Americas

Directors: Mark E. Fusco/Dir., CEO, Pres., Stephen M. Jennings/Chmn., David McKenna/Dir., Michael Pehl/Dir., Joan C. McArdle/Dir., Don Casey/Dir., Gary E. Haroian/Dir.

Owners: David M. McKenna, Charles F. Kane, David M. McKenna, Insiders, Advent International Corporation/100.00%, Michael Pehl, Blair F. Wheeler, Insiders/3.43%, Smithfield Fiduciary LLC/100.00%

Financial Data: *Fiscal Year End:*06/30 *Latest Annual Data:* 6/30/2006

Year	Sales	Net Income
2006	$293,148,000	$12,823,000
2005	$269,567,000	-$69,372,000
2004	$332,996,000	-$21,806,000

Curr. Assets:	$165,255,000	**Curr. Liab.:**	$140,512,000	**P/E Ratio:**	33.62
Plant, Equip.:	$8,674,000	**Total Liab.:**	$163,716,000	**Indic. Yr. Divd.:**	NA
Total Assets:	$274,636,000	**Net Worth:**	-$14,555,000	**Debt/ Equity:**	NA

Aspenbio Inc

1585 S Perry St., Castle Rock, CO, 80104; *PH:* 1-303-794-2000; *http://* www.aspenbioinc.com

General - Incorporation	CO	**Stock**- Price on:12/24/2007	$4.7
Employees	11	Stock Exchange	NDQ
Auditor	GHP Horwath, P.C	Ticker Symbol	APPY
Stk Agt	Corporate Stock Transfer, Inc.	Outstanding Shares	27,780,000
Counsel	Patton Boggs LLP	E.P.S	-$0.212
DUNS No.	NA	Shareholders	NA

Business: The group's principle activities include manufacturing and developing human and animal diagnostic antigens. It manufactures over thirty human antigens and tumor markers, which are used as standards and controls in diagnostic test kits, antibody purification and in research projects. The company develops products using purified proteins for diagnosis and treatment of animals. It also develops quine proteins to diagnose and treat problems or potential enhancements to fertility, lactation, thyroid and wounds. The company's products are human antigen, cea carcinoembryonic antigen, ungulate pregnancy test, insulin/pzi and equine proteins. The major customers of the company include biorad, golden west biologics and clinga. The group operates from United States.

Primary SIC and add'l.: 2835

CIK No: 0001167419

Subsidiaries: IDEXX Pharmaceuticals, Inc

Officers: Richard G. Donnelly/Dir., CEO, Pres., Gregory Pusey/Chmn., Sec., Jeffrey G. McGonegal/CFO, Lori Rafferty/Accounting Payable, Scott Wathen/Mgr. - Antigen Sales

Directors: Richard G. Donnelly/Dir., CEO, Pres., Gregory Pusey/Chmn., Sec., David E. Welch/Dir., Douglas I. Hepler/Dir., Gail S. Schoettler/Dir.

Owners: Gregory Pusey/5.30%, Richard G. Donnelly/3.20%, 1837 Partners, L.P./10.30%, Insiders/12.50%, The Peierls Foundation, Inc./10.00%, David E. Welch/0.60%, Roaring Fork Capital SBIC, L.P./6.90%, Gail S. Schoettler/1.00%, Panacea Fund, L.L.C./10.10%, Douglas I. Hepler/1.20%, Jeffrey G. McGonegal/1.90%

Financial Data: *Fiscal Year End:*12/31 *Latest Annual Data:* 12/31/2006

Year	Sales	Net Income
2006	$1,190,000	-$3,109,000
2005	$860,000	-$2,114,000
2004	$804,000	-$2,092,000

Curr. Assets:	$4,305,000	**Curr. Liab.:**	$700,000		
Plant, Equip.:	$3,308,000	**Total Liab.:**	$4,323,000	**Indic. Yr. Divd.:**	NA
Total Assets:	$8,748,000	**Net Worth:**	$4,425,000	**Debt/ Equity:**	0.4267

Aspire Japan Inc

Formerly: 511410 Inc

4695 MacArthur Ct., 11th Fl., Newport Beach, CA, 92660; *PH:* 1-949-798-6138

General - Incorporation	DE	**Stock**- Price on:12/24/2007	NA
Employees	NA	Stock Exchange	NA
Auditor	Webb & Co., P.A.	Ticker Symbol	NA
Stk Agt	Corporate Stock Transfer, Inc.	Outstanding Shares	NA
Counsel	Anslow & Jaclin, LLP	E.P.S	NA
DUNS No.	NA	Shareholders	NA

Business: The group's principal activity is providing a method for a foreign or domestic private company to become a reporting ("public") company whose securities are qualified for trading in the United States secondary market. The company is engaged in any lawful corporate undertaking, including, but not limited to, selected mergers and acquisitions. It has been in the developmental stage since inception and has no operations to date other than issuing shares to our original shareholders.

Primary SIC and add'l.: 6770

CIK No: 0001317838

Officers: Ken Osako/36/Chmn., CEO, CFO, Pres.

Directors: Ken Osako/36/Chmn., CEO, CFO, Pres.

Owners: Insiders, Kenji Osako

Aspreva Pharmaceuticals Corp

4464 Markham St., Ste. 1203, Victoria, BC, V8Z 7X8; *PH:* 1-250-744-2488; *http://* www.aspreva.com

General - Incorporation	BC	**Stock**- Price on:12/24/2007	$20.12
Employees	133	Stock Exchange	NDQ
Auditor	Ernst & Young LLP	Ticker Symbol	ASPV
Stk Agt	Computershare Investor Services LLC	Outstanding Shares	35,180,000
Counsel	NA	E.P.S	$3.49
DUNS No.	NA	Shareholders	NA

Business: The groups principle activities include identifying, developing, commercializing existing approved drugs and drug candidates for new indications. The group operates from Canada, Switzerland, the United States and the United Kingdom.

Primary SIC and add'l.: 2899 8731

CIK No: 0001314026

Subsidiaries: Aspreva Pharmaceuticals Ltd., Aspreva Pharmaceuticals S.A., Aspreva Pharmaceuticals, Inc.

Officers: William J. Freytag/Chmn., CEO, Paul Brennan/Sr. VP - Business Development, Noel Hall/Co - Founder, Dir., Pres., Bruce Cousins/CFO, Exec. VP, Usman Azam/Chief Medical Officer, Exec. VP, Rick Goulburn/Exec. VP - Global Pharmaceutical Operations

Directors: William J. Freytag/Chmn., CEO, William Hunter/Dir., Richard M. Glickman/Dir., Noel Hall/Co - Founder, Dir., Pres., Kirk K. Calhoun/Dir., Ronald M. Hunt/Dir., Julia G. Levy/Dir., Hector R. MacKay-Dunn/Dir., George M. Milne/Dir., Arnold L. Oronsky/Dir.

Owners: Hbm Bioventures (Cayman) Ltd/9.10%, Hector R. MacKay-Dunn, Charles F. Goulburn, Bruce G. Cousins, Entities Affiliated with InterWest Partners/5.70%, Julia G. Levy, Noel F. Hall/3.50%, Ronald M. Hunt/8.40%, Richard M. Glickman/3.60%, Kirk K. Calhoun, Insiders/21.90%, William L. Hunter, George M. Milne, Arnold L. Oronsky/5.80%, Entities And Persons Affiliated With The Sprout Group/8.40%

Financial Data: *Fiscal Year End:*12/31 *Latest Annual Data:* 12/31/2006

Year	Sales	Net Income
2006	$214,784,000	$124,156,000
2005	$76,480,000	$19,667,000
2004	NA	-$22,493,000

Curr. Assets:	$320,886,000	**Curr. Liab.:**	$44,107,000	**P/E Ratio:**	6.17
Plant, Equip.:	$4,736,000	**Total Liab.:**	$45,419,000	**Indic. Yr. Divd.:**	NA
Total Assets:	$327,057,000	**Net Worth:**	$281,638,000	**Debt/ Equity:**	0.0002

Asset Acceptance Capital Corp

28405 Van Dyke Ave., Warren, MI, 48093; *PH:* 1-586-939-9600; *Fax:* 1-586-446-7837; *http://* www.assetacceptance.com; *Email:* customerservice@assetacceptance.com

General - Incorporation	DE	**Stock**- Price on:12/24/2007	$16.69
Employees	1,615	Stock Exchange	NDQ
Auditor	Shumaker, Loop & Kendrick, LLP	Ticker Symbol	AACC
Stk Agt	LaSalle Bank N.A	Outstanding Shares	34,700,000
Counsel	NA	E.P.S	$1.10
DUNS No.	NA	Shareholders	NA

Business: The group's principal activity is to purchase and collect charged-off accounts receivable portfolios from consumer credit originators. Charged-off receivables are the unpaid obligations of individuals to credit originators, such as credit card issuers, consumer finance companies, retail merchants and telecommunications and other utility providers as well as from resellers and other holders of consumer debt.

Primary SIC and add'l.: 6153

CIK No: 0001264707

Subsidiaries: AAC Investors, Inc., Asset Acceptance Holdings LLC, Asset Acceptance, LLC, Consumer Credit, LLC, RBR Holding Corp., Rx Acquisitions, LLC

Owners: Mark A. Redman/2.60%, Nathaniel F. Bradley/12.20%, Eugene Lockhart, William F. Pickard, Insiders/51.60%, Anthony R. Ignaczak/35.70%, Donald Haider, Jennifer L. Adams, Terrence D. Daniels/35.70%, William I. Jacobs, Deborah L. Everly, Phillip L. Allen

Financial Data: *Fiscal Year End:* 12/31 *Latest Annual Data:* 06/30/2007

Year	Sales	Net Income
2007	NA	NA
2006	$254,873,000	$45,518,000
2005	$252,684,000	$51,267,000

Curr. Assets:	$315,383,000	**Curr. Liab.:**	$16,693,000	**P/E Ratio:**	14.03
Plant, Equip.:	$12,709,000	**Total Liab.:**	$94,405,000	**Indic. Yr. Divd.:**	NA
Total Assets:	$350,583,000	**Net Worth:**	$256,178,000	**Debt/ Equity:**	0.0265

Assisted Living Concepts Inc New

1810 E 12th St. Ofc, York, NE, 68467; *PH:* 1-402-362-5538; *http://* www.alcco.com

General - Incorporation	NV	**Stock**- Price on:12/24/2007	$10.97
Employees	4,600	Stock Exchange	NYSE
Auditor	Grant Thornton, LLP	Ticker Symbol	ALC
Stk Agt	American Stock Transfer & Trust Co.	Outstanding Shares	NA
Counsel	NA	E.P.S.	$0.25
DUNS No.	NA	Shareholders	NA

Business: The groups principal activity is to operate living home-like residences for older adults. The group operates 207 residences in 17 states in the United States.

Primary SIC and add'l.: 6513

CIK No: 0000929994

Subsidiaries: ALC Indiana, Inc., ALC Iowa, Inc., ALC McKinney Partners, LP, ALC Nebraska, Inc., ALC Nevada McKinney, Inc., ALC Nevada Paris, Inc., ALC Nevada Plano, Inc., ALC North Woods Operating LLC, ALC North Woods Real Estate LLC, ALC Ohio, Inc., ALC Operating, LLC, ALC Paris Partners, LP, ALC Plano Partners, LP, ALC Properties II, Inc., ALC Properties, Inc. 42 Subsidiaries included in the Index

Officers: Laurie A. Bebo/37/Dir., CEO, Pres./$720,715.00, John Buono/44/Sr. VP, CFO, Treasurer/$71,200.00, Eric B. Fonstad/60/Sr. VP, General Counsel, Sec./$36,529.00, Walter A. Levonowich/52/VP, Controller/$233,860.00, Terrance Usher/Divisional VP - Midwest, Central

Directors: Laurie A. Bebo/37/Dir., CEO, Pres., Mel Rhinelander/57/Vice Chmn., David J. Hennigar/68/Chmn., Graham Day/74/Dir., Alan Bell/59/Dir., Derek H.L. Buntain/66/Dir., Malen S. Ng/56/Dir., Charles H. Roadman/63/Dir., Jesse C. Brotz/34/Dir., Michael J. Spector/68/Dir.

Owners: Derek H.L. Buntain, David M. Dunlap, Laurie A. Bebo, David J. Hennigar, Graham Day, Melvin A. Rhinelander, Charles H. Roadman, Jesse C. Brotz, John Buono, Insiders/1.06%, Alan Bell, Jesse C. Brotz, Graham Day, Eric B. Fonstad, David J. Hennigar *(23 Owners included in Index)*

Financial Data: *Fiscal Year End:* 12/31 *Latest Annual Data:* 12/31/2006

Year	Sales	Net Income
2006	$231,148,000	$9,009,000
2003	$168,012,000	$157,000
2002	$146,269,000	-$4,414,000

Curr. Assets:	$40,498,000	**Curr. Liab.:**	$27,746,000	**P/E Ratio:**	10.78
Plant, Equip.:	$374,612,000	**Total Liab.:**	$130,502,000	**Indic. Yr. Divd.:**	NA
Total Assets:	$447,340,000	**Net Worth:**	$316,838,000	**Debt/ Equity:**	0.2774

Associated Banc-Corp

1200 Hansen Rd., Green Bay, WI, 54304; *PH:* 1-920-491-7000; *http://* www.associatedbank.com

General - Incorporation	WI	**Stock**- Price on:12/24/2007	$33.13
Employees	5,101	Stock Exchange	NDQ
Auditor	KPMG LLP	Ticker Symbol	ASBC
Stk Agt	National City Bank	Outstanding Shares	127,530,000
Counsel	NA	E.P.S.	NA
DUNS No.	07-478-8803	Shareholders	NA

Business: The groups principle activity is to provide banking services. The group also provides online banking services. In the year 2007 the group acquired First National Bank of Hudson. The group operates from United States.

Primary SIC and add'l.: 6021 6712

CIK No: 0000007789

Subsidiaries: ASBC Investment Corp., Associated Bank, National Association, Associated Commercial Finance, Inc., Associated Community Development, LLC, Associated Financial Group, LLC, Associated Green Bay Investment Corp., Associated Illinois Investment Corp., Associated Illinois Real Estate Corp., Associated Investment Management, LLC, Associated Investment Partnership I, LLC, Associated Investment Partnership II, LLC, Associated Investment Services, Inc., Associated Minnesota Investment Corp., Associated Minnesota Real Estate Corp., Associated Mortgage Reinsurance, Inc. 27 Subsidiaries included in the Index

Officers: Paul S. Beideman/Chmn., CEO/$1,809,196.00, Nancy Maas/Exec. VP, Chief Marketing Officer, Brian R. Bodager/Chief Administrative Officer, General Counsel, Corp. Sec., Arthur E. Olsen/56/Exec. VP, General Auditor - Assoc.d, David Stein/Exec. VP, Dir. - Retail Banking, John P. Evans/Exec. VP, Dir. - Business Banking, Gordon J. Weber/Dir. - Corporate Banking Division/$820,237.00, Teresa A. Rosengarten/Dir. - Consumer Banking, Mark Quinlan/CIO, Exec. VP, Joseph B. Selner/CFO/$725,548.00, David A. Baumgarten/Exec. VP, Dir. - Regional Banking/$607,948.00, Judith M. Docter/Exec. VP, Dir. - Human Resources, Gordon King/Exec. VP, Chief Credit Officer, Mark J. McMullen/Exec. VP, Dir. - Wealth Management/$696,479.00, Jared Johnson/Residential Loan Officer *(16 Officers included in Index)*

Directors: Paul S. Beideman/Chmn., CEO, John C. Seramur/Vice Chmn., Richard T. Lommen/Dir., Carlos E. Santiago/Dir., Karen T. Beckwith/Dir., Ruth M. Crowley/Dir., Jack C. Rusch/Dir., Robert C. Gallagher/Dir., Eileen A. Kamerick/Dir., John Charles Meng/Dir., William R. Hutchinson/Dir., Ronald Richard Harder/Dir., Harry B. Conlon/Dir., Douglas J. Quick/Dir.

Owners: Joseph B. Selner, Associated Trust Company/6.04%, John C. Seramur, Richard T. Lommen, Insiders/3.69%, Robert C. Gallagher, Karen T. Beckwith, Barclays Global Investors Japan Trust/5.58%, John C. Meng, David A. Baumgarten, Ruth M. Crowley, William R. Hutchinson, Mark J. McMullen, Douglas J. Quick, Jack C. Rusch *(18 Owners included in Index)*

Financial Data: *Fiscal Year End:* 12/31 *Latest Annual Data:* 12/31/2006

Year	Sales	Net Income
2006	$1,574,880,000	$316,645,000
2005	$1,385,111,000	$320,161,000
2004	$977,369,000	$258,286,000

Curr. Assets:	$482,036,000	**Curr. Liab.:**	$16,544,749,000	**P/E Ratio:**	14.12
Plant, Equip.:	$210,407,000	**Total Liab.:**	$18,615,891,000	**Indic. Yr. Divd.:**	$1.240
Total Assets:	$20,861,384,000	**Net Worth:**	$2,245,493,000	**Debt/ Equity:**	0.7795

Associated Estates Realty Corp

1 AEC Pkwy., Richmond Heights, OH, 44143; *PH:* 1-216-261-5000; *Fax:* 1-216-289-9600; *http://* www.aecrealty.com

General - Incorporation	OH	**Stock**- Price on:12/24/2007	$14.97
Employees	650	Stock Exchange	NYSE
Auditor	PricewaterhouseCoopers LLP	Ticker Symbol	AEC
Stk Agt	National City Bank	Outstanding Shares	17,500,000
Counsel	NA	E.P.S.	$1.77
DUNS No.	NA	Shareholders	NA

Business: The group is real estate company engaged in property acquisition, advisory, development, management, disposition, operation, and ownership activities. The group operates through four segments namely, acquisition/disposition multifamily properties, market-rate multifamily properties, affordable housing multifamily properties and management and service operations. The group acquired Vista Lago property in March 2005 and Cambridge at Buckhead in October 2005. The group operates from the United States. The group's quarterly revenue for September 2007 was 39.37 millions of USD.

Primary SIC and add'l.: 6798

CIK No: 0000911635

Subsidiaries: AERC Arbor Landings, LLC, AERC Arbor, Inc., AERC Arrowhead Station, Inc., AERC Avon LLC, AERC Barrington, Inc., AERC Bay Club, Inc., AERC Bedford Commons, Inc., AERC Bennell, Inc., AERC Bradford, Inc., AERC Broker of Texas, Inc., AERC Brook, Inc., AERC Central Park Place, LLC, AERC Central Park, Inc., AERC Christopher Wren, Inc., AERC Clinton Place, LLC 110 Subsidiaries included in the Index

Officers: Jeffrey I. Friedman/Chmn., CEO, Pres./$1,550,585.00, John T. Shannon/Sr. VP - Operations/$522,820.00, Lou Fatica/CFO, VP, Treasurer/$451,811.00, Martin A. Fishman/VP, General Counsel, Sec./$482,192.00, Patrick Duffy/VP - Strategic Marketing, Kara Florack/VP - Human Resources, Michael K. Lawson/VP - Investor Relations, Corp Communications, Jenee McClain-Bankhead/Regional VP, Miria C. Rabideau/Regional VP, Beth L. Stoll/VP - Operations, James M. Delaney/72/Dir. - Consultant

Directors: Jeffrey I. Friedman/Chmn., CEO, Pres., Richard T. Schwarz/55/Dir., Albert T. Adams/56/Dir., James M. Delaney/72/Dir. - Consultant, Michael E. Gibbons/56/Dir., Mark L. Milstein/44/Outside Affiliated Dir., James A. Schoff/62/Dir.

Owners: James A. Schoff, John T. Shannon, Mark L. Milstein/4.50%, Third Avenue Management LLC/7.70%, James M. Delaney, Lou Fatica/1.10%, Michael E. Gibbons, Loomis, Sayles& Co., L.P./8.00%, Insiders/18.37%, Martin A. Fishman/1.90%, Richard T. Schwarz, Albert T. Adams, Jeffrey I. Friedman/9.00%

Financial Data: *Fiscal Year End:* 12/31 *Latest Annual Data:* 12/31/2006

Year	Sales	Net Income
2006	$145,761,000	$27,021,000
2005	$150,428,000	$36,206,000
2004	$160,399,000	$3,324,000

Curr. Assets:	$41,148,000	**Curr. Liab.:**	$34,095,000	**P/E Ratio:**	21.08
Plant, Equip.:	$591,520,000	**Total Liab.:**	$536,778,000	**Indic. Yr. Divd.:**	NA
Total Assets:	$648,829,000	**Net Worth:**	$112,051,000	**Debt/ Equity:**	NA

Associated Materials Inc

3773 State Rd. , Cuyahoga Falls, OH, 44223; *PH:* 1-330-929-1811; *http://* www.associatedmaterials.com

General - Incorporation	DE	**Stock**- Price on:12/24/2007	NA
Employees	NA	Stock Exchange	NA
Auditor	Ernst & Young LLP	Ticker Symbol	NA
Stk Agt	Chase Mellon Shareholder Services LLC	Outstanding Shares	NA
Counsel	NA	E.P.S.	NA
DUNS No.	10-730-1319	Shareholders	NA

Business: The group's principle activities of the group are to manufacture and distribute exterior residential building products and electrical cable products. The company operates through its two divisions, alside and amercable. Alside manufactures vinyl sidings, windows, fencing, decking and garage doors and amercable manufactures jacketed electrical cable utilized in mining, shipboard, marine, offshore, drilling and transportation industries. The company markets its products through wholesalers and supply centers. The company's alside has a nationwide distribution network of 69 supply centers which markets manufactured products and other complementary building products to more than 30,000 professional home improvement and new construction contractors.

Primary SIC and add'l.: 1521 1731

CIK No: 0000802967

Subsidiaries: Associated Materials Holdings Inc. (Holdings), Simon Acquisition Corp

Officers: Thomas N. Chieffe/CEO, Pres., Cynthia L. Sobe/VP - Finance, Interim CFO, Treasurer, Sec., Robert M. Franco/54/Pres. - Alside Supply Centers, Christine Bianco/Human Resources, Greg Hartman/Operations Mgr. Lexington - Kentucky, Bonnie White/Operations Mgr. Dallas - Texas, Chris Bilger/Operations Mgr. Dayton - Ohio, Keith D. Lavanway/43/VP, CFO, Treasurer, Sec.

Directors: Ira D. Kleinman/51/Chmn., Dennis W. Vollmershausen/64/Dir., Kevin M. Hayes/39/Dir., Thomas J. Sullivan/45/Dir., Dana R. Snyder/61/Dir.

Owners: Harvest Funds, Associated Equity Limited/16.00%, Sipco Limited/100.00%, Insiders, AM Investments Limited/16.00%, Investcorp Coinvestment Partners II, L.P/7.30%, Investcorp Coinvestment Partners I, L.P/6.70%, Ira D. Kleinman, AM Equity Limited/16.00%, Associated Investments Limited/16.00%, Investcorp 2005 AMH Holdings II Portfolio Limited Partnership/21.90%, Investcorp S.A/100.00%

Assuranceamerica Corp

5500 Interstate N Pkwy., Ste. 600, Atlanta, GA, 30328; *PH:* 1-770-952-0200; *Fax:* 1-770-952-0258; *http://* www.assuranceamerica.com

General - Incorporation	NV	Stock - Price on:12/24/2007	$1
Employees	268	Stock Exchange	OTC
Auditor	Miller Ray, Houser & Stewart LLP	Ticker Symbol	ASAM
Stk Agt.	Fidelity Transfer Co	Outstanding Shares	61,400,000
Counsel	NA	E.P.S.	$0.06
DUNS No.	NA	Shareholders	NA

Business: The group's principal activity is to solicit, underwrite and retain risks associated with private passenger non standard automobile insurance. The group was previously involved in funding and business consulting services to early-stage technology companies. It develops, invests in the companies, acquires and operates such companies. The group works with universities, corporations, research laboratories, government economic authorities and individual investors in order to commercialize new concepts and technologies. On 01-Apr-2003, it acquired assuranceamerica corp and discontinued the funding and business consulting services.

Primary SIC and add'l.: 6331

CIK No: 0000008497

Subsidiaries: AAC Merger Corp II, Apple Insurance Mall of Boynton Beach, Inc., Apple Insurance Mall of Bradenton, Inc., Apple Insurance Mall of Clearwater, Inc., Apple Insurance Mall of Countryside, Inc., Apple Insurance Mall of Englewood, Inc., Apple Insurance Mall of Lake Park, Inc., Apple Insurance Mall of Lake Worth, Inc., Apple Insurance Mall of Orlando, Inc., Apple Insurance Mall of Pinellas Park, Inc., Apple Insurance Mall of Port Charlotte, Inc., Apple Insurance Mall of Regency, Inc., Apple Insurance Mall of Rockledge, Inc., Apple Insurance Mall of Sarasota, Inc., Apple Insurance Mall of Southside, Inc. 42 Subsidiaries included in the Index

Officers: Lawrence Stumbaugh/CEO, Pres./$242,880.00, David H. Anthony/VP - Information Technology, Mark H. Hain/Sr. VP, General Counsel, Sec. Assuranceamerica Corporation, Scott Nelson/VP - Product Development, Elise Quadrozzi/VP - Claims, Joseph J. Skruck/Exec. VP/$213,013.00, Courtney Wright/Pres. - Trustway, Tony Pepsoski/Regional VP - Product Development, Barry Allen Schwartz/VP - Sales

Directors: Guy Millner/Chmn., Donald Ratajczak/Dir., John E. Cay/Dir., Quill O. Healey/Dir., John Ray/Dir., Kaaren J. Street/Dir., Sam Zamarripa Zamarripa/Dir.

Owners: Quill O. Healey, Donald Ratajczak, Joseph J. Skruck, John Ray/18.30%, Sam Zamarripa, Kaaren J. Street, Insiders, John E. Cay, Guy W. Millner/55.50%, Insiders/80.20%, Lawrence Stumbaugh/9.00%, Sam Zamarripa, Heritage Assurance Partners, LLP, John Ray, Heritage Assurance Partners, LLP/16.30%

Financial Data: Fiscal Year End:12/31 Latest Annual Data: 12/31/2006

Year	Sales	Net Income
2006	$53,723,000	$4,732,000
2005	$37,115,000	$2,330,000
2004	$24,187,000	-$48,000

Curr. Assets:	$64,676,000	Curr. Liab.:	$24,104,000	P/E Ratio:	14.29
Plant, Equip.:	$2,482,000	Total Liab.:	$80,648,000	Indic. Yr. Divd.:	NA
Total Assets:	$95,745,000	Net Worth:	$15,097,000	Debt/ Equity:	0.7302

Assurant Inc

1 Chase Manhattan Plz., 41st Fl., New York, NY, 10005; **PH:** 1-212-859-7000; **Fax:** 1-212-859-7010; **http://** www.assurant.com

General - Incorporation	DE	Stock - Price on:12/24/2007	$58.19
Employees	13,400	Stock Exchange	NYSE
Auditor	PricewaterhouseCoopers LLP	Ticker Symbol	AIZ
Stk Agt.	Mellon Investor Services	Outstanding Shares	121,010,000
Counsel	NA	E.P.S.	$5.79
DUNS No.	05-290-8241	Shareholders	NA

Business: The groups' principle activities are to provide creditor-placed homeowners insurance, credit insurance, group dental insurance and life insurance. The operations as carried on in four segments solutions, health, employee benefits and preneed. Solutions segment provides credit insurance, including life, disability and unemployment, creditor-placed homeowners insurance and manufactured housing homeowners insurance. Health segment provides individual, short-term and small group health insurance. Employee benefits segment provides employee-paid dental insurance and employer-paid dental, disability and life insurance products and related services. Preneed segment provides life insurance policies and annuity products that provide benefits to fund pre-arranged funerals. The group operates primarily in the United States and Canada. The group's quarterly revenue for September 2007 was 2,148.19 millions of USD.

Primary SIC and add'l.: 6719 6321 6311

CIK No: 0001267238

Subsidiaries: ABIG Holding de Espana, S.L., ALOC Holdings ULC, American Association For Financial Institution Services, American Bankers Capital, Inc., American Bankers Dominicana S.A., American Bankers Financial Services, LLC, American Bankers General Agency, Inc., American Bankers Insurance Company of Florida, American Bankers Insurance Group, Inc., American Bankers International Division, Inc, American Bankers Life Assurance Company Of Florida, American Bankers Management Company, Inc., American Bankers Sales Corporation, Inc., American Memorial Life Insurance Company, American Reliable Insurance Company 106 Subsidiaries included in the Index

Officers: Kerry J. Clayton/Interim CEO, Pres. - Assurant, Donald Hamm/CEO, Exec. VP, Pres. - Assurant Health, Robert B. Pollock/53/Dir., CEO, Pres., John S. Roberts/Interim CEO, Pres. - Assurant Employee Benefits, Craig S. Lemasters/CEO, Pres. - Assurant Solutions, John B. Owen/47/CEO, Pres. - Assurant Specialty Property, Philip Bruce Camacho/CFO, Exec. VP, John A. Sondej/43/Sr. VP, Controller, Principal Accounting Officer, Peter Duckler/Contact - Media, Melissa Kivett/Sr. VP - Investor Relations, Gene Mergelmeyer/Pres. - Assurant Specialty Property, John Egan/VP - Investor Relations, Drew Guthrie/Mgr. - Communications, Media Relations, Michael J. Peninger/Exec. VP, Interim Chief Financial, Jerome A. Atkinson/Exec. VP, Chief Compliance (18 Officers included in Index)

Directors: Robert B. Pollock/53/Dir., CEO, Pres., John Michael Palms/72/Chmn., Robert J. Blendon/65/Dir., Charles John Koch/61/Dir., Michele Coleman Mayes/58/Dir., Allen R. Freedman/68/Dir., Juan N. Cento/56/Dir., Carroll H. MacKin/67/Dir., Beth L. Bronner/56/Dir., David B. Kelso/55/Dir., Howard L. Carver/63/Dir., Michel Baise/59/Dir.

Owners: Donald Hamm, Robert B. Pollock, Carroll H. Mackin, Allen R. Freedman, Kerry J. Clayton, Charles J. Koch, Fortis Insurance N.V./18.80%, Craig S. Lemasters, FMR Corp./10.00%, JPMorgan Chase& Co./9.10%, John Michael Palms, Insiders/1.30%, Beth L. Bronner, Howard L. Carver, Juan N. Cento (20 Owners included in Index)

Financial Data: Fiscal Year End:12/31 Latest Annual Data: 12/31/2006

Year	Sales	Net Income
2006	$8,070,584,000	$717,418,000
2005	$7,497,675,000	$479,355,000
2004	$7,403,464,000	$350,560,000

Curr. Assets:	$5,828,769,000	Curr. Liab.:	$5,120,832,000	P/E Ratio:	10.05
Plant, Equip.:	$275,201,000	Total Liab.:	$21,310,391,000	Indic. Yr. Divd.:	$0.480
Total Assets:	$25,165,148,000	Net Worth:	$3,832,597,000	Debt/ Equity:	0.3947

Assure Energy Inc

521 3rd Ave. SW, Ste 800, Calgary, AB, T2P 1G2; **PH:** 1-403-266-4975; **http://** www.assure-energy.com; **Email:** info@geocan.com

General - Incorporation	AB	Stock - Price on:12/24/2007	NA
Employees	NA	Stock Exchange	OTC
Auditor	BDO Dunwoody LLP	Ticker Symbol	ASURF
Stk Agt.	Continental Stock Transfer & Trust Co	Outstanding Shares	NA
Counsel	NA	E.P.S.	NA
DUNS No.	NA	Shareholders	NA

Business: The group's principal activity is to explore for, develop and produce oil and natural gas properties in the Canadian provinces of alberta, saskatchewan and british columbia. The group operates through its subsidiaries, assure oil & gas corp ('assure o&g'), westerra 2000 inc ('westerra') and quarry oil & gas ltd ('quarry'). Assure o&g explores for, develops, acquires and produces petroleum and natural gas properties, primarily located in western Canada. Westerra owns natural gas and oil interests in approximately five sections of land in the lloydminster area along the provincial border of alberta and saskatchewan. The group conducts all of its operations in Canada.

Primary SIC and add'l.: 1311 1382

CIK No: 0001136609

Subsidiaries: Assure Oil & Gas Corp., Westerra 2000 Inc.

Assured Guaranty Ltd

1325 Ave. of the Americas, 18th Fl., New York, NY, 10019; **PH:** 1-212-974-0100; **Fax:** 1-212-581-3268; **http://** www.assuredguaranty.com; **Email:** info@assuredguaranty.com

General - Incorporation	Bermuda	Stock - Price on:12/24/2007	$28.92
Employees	135	Stock Exchange	NYSE
Auditor	PricewaterhouseCoopers LLP	Ticker Symbol	AGO
Stk Agt.	Mellon Investor Services LLC	Outstanding Shares	67,780,000
Counsel	NA	E.P.S.	$2.25
DUNS No.	NA	Shareholders	NA

Business: The group operates through its subsidiary whose principle activity is to provide financial guaranty and credit enhancement products to investors, financial institutions and other participants in the global capital markets. The groups services include public and structured finance. The group operates through two segments namely financial guaranty direct and financial guaranty reinsurance. The group operates from United States.

Primary SIC and add'l.: NA

CIK No: 0001273813

Subsidiaries: AG Financial Products Inc., AG Intermediary Inc., Assured Guaranty (UK) Ltd., Assured Guaranty (UK) Services Ltd., Assured Guaranty Barbados Holdings Ltd., Assured Guaranty Corp., Assured Guaranty Finance Overseas Ltd., Assured Guaranty Mortgage Insurance Company, Assured Guaranty Overseas US Holdings Inc., Assured Guaranty Re Ltd., Assured Guaranty Re Overseas Ltd., Assured Guaranty US Holdings Inc., Assured Value Insurance Company, Cedar Personnel Ltd.

Officers: Dominic J. Frederico/Dir., CEO, Pres./$7,671,699.00, Michael J. Schozer/Pres. - Assured Guaranty Corp, Sabra R. Purtill/MD - Investor Relations, Strategic Planning, Assured Guaranty Corp, Robert B. Mills/CFO, James M. Michener/General Counsel, Sec./$2,552,727.00, Paul R. Livingstone/MD - Structured Credit, CDO Group, Assured Guaranty Corp, John Trahan/MD - Public Finance, Assured Guaranty Corp, Craig Welch/MD - Underwriting, Risk Management, Assured Guaranty Corp, Nicholas Moy/MD - Underwriting, Risk Management, Assured Guaranty Corp, Donald L. Paston/MD, Treasurer - Assured Guaranty Corp, Andrew H. Pickering/MD, Chief Surveillance Officer - Assured Guaranty Corp, John W. Gray/MD - Mortgage Backed Securities, Assured Guaranty Corp, Jeffrey Nabi/MD - Consumer, Mortgage Backed Securities Group, Assured Guaranty Corp, Craig Lee/MD - Asia Pacific, Assured Guaranty, UK Ltd, Sam Nakhleh/VP - Consumer, Mortgage, Backed Securities (31 Officers included in Index)

Directors: Walter A. Scott/Chmn., Neil Baron/Dir., Donald H. Layton/Dir., Michael T. Okane/Dir., John Heimann/78/Dir., Stephen A. Cozen/Dir., Robin Monro-Davies/Dir., Patrick W. Kenny/Dir., Lawrence G. Buhl/Dir., Francisco L. Borges/Dir.

Owners: Walter A. Scott, Lawrence G. Buhl, Ariel Capital Management, LLC/10.97%, Robert B. Mills, Donald H. Layton, Dominic J. Frederico, Michael T. OKane, Robert A. Baileson, ACE Limited/27.90%, Insiders, Michael J. Schozer, Patrick W. Kenny, Stephen A. Cozen, James M. Michener

Financial Data: Fiscal Year End:12/31 Latest Annual Data: 12/31/2006

Year	Sales	Net Income
2006	$322,058,000	$159,734,000
2005	$294,534,000	$188,448,000
2004	$347,915,000	$182,788,000

Curr. Assets:	$198,803,000	Curr. Liab.:	$50,389,000	P/E Ratio:	12.85
Plant, Equip.:	NA	Total Liab.:	$1,284,579,000	Indic. Yr. Divd.:	$0.160
Total Assets:	$2,935,340,000	Net Worth:	$1,650,761,000	Debt/ Equity:	0.2048

Assured Pharmacy Inc

17935 Sky Pk. Cir., Ste. F, Irvine, CA , 92614; **PH:** 1-949-222-9971; **Fax:** 1-949-222-0978; **http://** www.assuredpharmacy.com

General - Incorporation	NV	Stock - Price on:12/24/2007	$0.285
Employees	23	Stock Exchange	OTC
Auditor	Miller, Ellin & Co., LLP	Ticker Symbol	APHY
Stk Agt.	Pacific Stock Transfer Company	Outstanding Shares	53,850,000
Counsel	Cane & Associates, LLP	E.P.S.	-$0.06
DUNS No.	NA	Shareholders	NA

Business: The groups principle activity is to operate pharmacies that dispense regulated pain medication. Customers of the group include governmental agency, workers compensation, a private employer and health maintenance organization. In the year 2006, the group acquired TPG Partners, L.L.C. The group operates from the United States. The groups quarterly revenue for September 2007 was 3.68 millions of USD.

Primary SIC and add'l.: 5912

CIK No: 0001100592

Subsidiaries: Assured Pharmacies Northwest, Inc., Assured Pharmacies, Inc., Assured Pharmacy DME, Corp., Assured Pharmacy Gresham, Inc., Assured Pharmacy Irvine, Inc., Assured Pharmacy Los Angeles 1, Inc., Assured Pharmacy Plus, Corp.

Officers: Robert J. Delvecchio/Dir., CEO, Haresh Sheth/Dir., CFO, Eric John Mutter/CTO, Dir. - Pharmacy

Directors: Robert J. Delvecchio/Dir., CEO, Richard Falcone/Chmn., James Manfredonia/Dir., Haresh Sheth/Dir., CFO

Owners: Richard Falcone, Insiders/25.10%, Haresh Sheth/8.60%, James Manfredonia, John Eric Mutter/1.50%, Robert DelVecchio/13.20%, Mosaic Capital Advisors, LLC/19.00%

Financial Data: *Fiscal Year End:*12/31 *Latest Annual Data:* 12/31/2006

Year	Sales	Net Income
2006	$7,897,000	-$4,502,000
2005	$3,837,000	-$4,797,000
2004	$1,165,000	-$8,011,000

Curr. Assets:	$2,134,000	Curr. Liab.:	$3,092,000		
Plant, Equip.:	$443,000	Total Liab.:	$4,655,000	Indic. Yr. Divd.:	NA
Total Assets:	$3,277,000	Net Worth:	-$1,378,000	Debt/ Equity:	NA

Asta Funding Inc

210 Sylvan Ave., Englewood Cliffs, NJ, 07632; *PH:* 1-201-567-5648; *Fax:* 1-201-569-4595; *http://* www.astafunding.com

General		Stock	
Incorporation	DE	Price on:12/24/2007	$39.13
Employees	166	Stock Exchange	NDQ
Auditor	Eisner LLP	Ticker Symbol	ASFI
Stk Agt	American Stock Transfer & Trust Co.	Outstanding Shares	13,900,000
Counsel	NA	E.P.S.	$3.56
DUNS No.	92-980-4482	Shareholders	NA

Business: The group's principal activity is to purchase, manage, service and sell distressed consumer receivables. The group also liquidates previously purchased automobile loan receivables. Distressed consumer receivables are unpaid debts that are owed by individuals to banks, finance companies and other credit providers. The group's receivables include mastercard and visa credit card accounts which are charged-off by the issuing bank for non-payments. The group operates in the United States of America.

Primary SIC and add'l.: 6159 6141

CIK No: 0001001258

Subsidiaries: Asta Commercial, LLC, Asta Funding Acquisition I, LLC, Asta Funding Acquisition II, LLC, Asta Funding Acquisition IV, LLC, Asta Funding, Inc., Asta Funding.com, LLC, Cliffs Portfolio Acquisition I, LLC, Computer Finance, LLC, Emce Pal Auto LLC, Option Card, LLC, Palisades Acquisition I, LLC, Palisades Acquisition II, LLC, Palisades Acquisition IV, LLC, Palisades Acquisition IX, LLC, Palisades Acquisition V, LLC 22 Subsidiaries included in the Index

Officers: Nan Bellinson/Contact

Owners: David Slackman, Harvey Leibowitz, Insiders/16.60%, Arthur Stern/4.60%, Barbara Marburger/3.20%, Alan Rivera, GMS Family Investors LLC/6.30%, Mitchell Cohen, Asta Group, Incorporated/6.10%, Herman Badillo, Louis A. Piccolo, Stern Family Investors LLC/5.00%, Edward Celano, Judith R. Feder/11.40%, Gary Stern/10.40%

Financial Data: *Fiscal Year End:*09/30 *Latest Annual Data:* 9/30/2006

Year	Sales	Net Income
2006	$101,979,000	$45,765,000
2005	$69,479,000	$30,996,000
2004	$51,175,000	$22,237,000

Curr. Assets:	$10,888,000	Curr. Liab.:	$16,429,000	P/E Ratio:	10.87
Plant, Equip.:	$1,101,000	Total Liab.:	$103,578,000	Indic. Yr. Divd.:	$0.160
Total Assets:	$287,840,000	Net Worth:	$184,262,000	Debt/ Equity:	0.5597

Astea International Inc

240 Gibraltar Rd., Ste. 300, Horsham, PA, 19044; *PH:* 1-215-682-2500; *Fax:* 1-215-682-2515; *http://* www.astea.com

General		Stock	
Incorporation	DE	Price on:12/24/2007	$6.47
Employees	193	Stock Exchange	NDQ
Auditor	BDO Seidman LLP	Ticker Symbol	ATEA
Stk Agt	First City Transfer Co	Outstanding Shares	3,590,000
Counsel	Pepper Hamilton LLP	E.P.S.	$0.15
DUNS No.	07-358-0201	Shareholders	NA

Business: The group's principal activity is to develop, market and support customer relationship management software solutions. The software solutions are licensed to companies that sell and service equipment, or sell and deliver professional services. The group's products and services are used in information technology, healthcare, industrial controls and instrumentation, retail systems, office automation, imaging systems, facilities management and telecommunications industries. The group's software has been licensed to approximately 580 companies worldwide. The group provides customers with an array of professional consulting, training and customer support services to implement its products, integrate them with other corporate systems. Customers range from mid-size organizations to large, multinational corporations with geographically dispersed locations around the globe.

Primary SIC and add'l.: 7372 7378

CIK No: 0000945989

Subsidiaries: FC Acquisition Corp

Officers: Zack B. Bergreen/Chmn., CEO, Pres./$305,725.00, Frank Fesnak/VP - Strategic Alliances, Paul Buzby/MD - Asia Pacific, Mark Solomon/VP - Client Services, Fredric Etskovitz/CFO, Treasurer, Danny Klein/VP - Development, Mark Kolibas/VP - Sales, Americas, Debbie Geiger/VP - Marketing, John Tobin/Pres./$304,038.00, Mark L. Kent/MD - EMEA, Ariel Katz/VP - Research, Development, GM - Astea Israel

Directors: Zack B. Bergreen/Chmn., CEO, Pres., Thomas J. Reilly/Dir., Eric Scott Siegel/Dir., Adrian A. Peters/Dir.

Owners: Adrian Peters/0.60%, Thomas J. Reilly, Insiders/41.00%, Zack Bergreen/37.80%, Eric Siegel/0.30%, Walrus Partners, LLC/5.20%, Rick Etskovitz/0.80%, John Tobin/0.80%

Financial Data: *Fiscal Year End:*12/31 *Latest Annual Data:* 12/31/2006

Year	Sales	Net Income
2006	$20,284,000	-$4,982,000
2005	$22,765,000	$1,828,000
2004	$19,317,000	$2,134,000

Curr. Assets:	$10,628,000	Curr. Liab.:	$11,917,000		
Plant, Equip.:	$648,000	Total Liab.:	$11,953,000	Indic. Yr. Divd.:	NA
Total Assets:	$18,059,000	Net Worth:	$6,106,000	Debt/ Equity:	NA

Astec Industries Inc

1725 Shepherd Rd., Chattanooga, TN, 37421; *PH:* 1-423-899-5898; *Fax:* 1-423-899-4456; *http://* www.astecindustries.com

General		Stock	
Incorporation	TN	Price on:12/24/2007	$42.41
Employees	3,241	Stock Exchange	NDQ
Auditor	Ernst & Young, LLP	Ticker Symbol	ASTE
Stk Agt	Mellon Investor Services LLC	Outstanding Shares	21,870,000
Counsel	Chambliss, Bahner & Stophel	E.P.S.	$2.27
DUNS No.	06-130-8649	Shareholders	NA

Business: The group's principal activities are to design, engineer, manufacture, market and financing equipment and components used primarily in road building and related construction activities. The group's products are used in each phase of road building from quarrying and crushing the aggregate to application of the road surface. In addition it also manufactures certain equipment and components unrelated to road construction including trenching, auger boring, directional drilling, environmental remediation and industrial heat transfer equipment and sampling and testing equipment for the asphalt mix and aggregate processing industries. The group's products are marketed both domestically and internationally.

Primary SIC and add'l.: 3531 3532

CIK No: 0000792987

Subsidiaries: American Augers, Inc., Astec Insurance Company, Astec Mobile Screens, Inc., Astec Underground, Inc., Astec, Inc., Breaker Technology Ltd., Breaker Technology, Inc., Buckeye Underground, Inc., Carlson Paving Products, Inc., CEI Enterprises, Inc., Heatec, Inc., Johnson Crushers International, Inc., Kolberg-Pioneer, Inc., Osborn Engineered Products SA (Pty) Ltd., Roadtec, Inc. 16 Subsidiaries included in the Index

Officers: Don J. Brock/Chmn., Principal Executive Officer, Pres./$1,028,511.00, Rick Worth/Contact - Parts Sales, Troy Norris/Service Support Coordinator, Jeff Simpson/Service Support Coordinator, Neal J. Ferry/55/Exec. VP/$548,113.00, Mckamy F. Hall/CFO, VP, Treasurer/$317,967.00, Mark Hudsonc/Contact - Parts Technician, Tony Martin/Contact - Parts Sales, Aimie Bates/Sales Coordinator, Steve Munson/Regional Sales Mgr. - TN, KY, OH, MI, Lower, Dave Hampton/Mgr. - International Projects, Richard J. Dorris/Exec. Officer, Richard A. Patek/Exec. Officer, Frank D. Cargould/65/Exec. Officer, Jeffery J. Elliott/54/Exec. Officer *(99 Officers included in Index)*

Directors: Don J. Brock/Chmn., Principal Executive Officer, Pres., William D. Gehl/Dir., William B. Sansom/Dir., Daniel K. Frierson/Dir., Albert E. Guth/Dir., Glen E. Tellock/Dir., Robert G. Stafford/Dir., Ronald F. Green/Dir., Phillip E. Casey/Dir.

Owners: J. Don Brock/13.50%, Albert E. Guth, McKamy F. Hall, Jeffrey L. Gendell/11.80%, Insiders/18.30%, Lynne W. Brock/7.50%, AXA Mutuelle Group/5.60%

Financial Data: *Fiscal Year End:*12/31 *Latest Annual Data:* 12/31/2006

Year	Sales	Net Income
2006	$710,607,000	$39,588,000
2005	$616,068,000	$28,094,000
2004	$504,554,000	$19,053,000

Curr. Assets:	$283,018,000	Curr. Liab.:	$104,869,000		
Plant, Equip.:	$113,914,000	Total Liab.:	$124,997,000	Indic. Yr. Divd.:	NA
Total Assets:	$421,863,000	Net Worth:	$296,166,000	Debt/ Equity:	NA

Asthmatx Inc

1340 Space Pk. Way, Mountain View, CA, 94043; *PH:* 1-650-810-1100; *Fax:* 1-650-810-1101; *http://* www.asthmatx.com

General		Stock	
Incorporation		Price on:12/24/2007	NA
Employees	NA	Stock Exchange	NDQ
Auditor	NA	Ticker Symbol	AZMA
Stk Agt	Computershare Investor Services LLC	Outstanding Shares	NA
Counsel	NA	E.P.S.	NA
DUNS No.	NA	Shareholders	NA

Business: The groups principal activities include designing, developing and manufacturing catheter based medical devices. The product of the group is Alair(R)System. The group operates from the United States.

Primary SIC and add'l.: 3841

CIK No: 0001286294

Officers: Glendon E. French/45/Dir., CEO, Pres., Gary S. Kaplan/41/Sr. VP - Technology, Operations, Christopher P. Lowe/Contact - Investor, Karen Passafaro/47/Contact - Press, Debera M. Brown/54/VP - Regulatory Affairs, Narinder S. Shargill/52/VP - Clinical Affairs

Directors: Glendon E. French/45/Dir., CEO, Pres., Michael D. Laufer/49/Dir., Annette J. Campbell-White/60/Dir., Brian E. Chee/41/Dir., James W. Fitzsimmons/51/Dir., Thomas C. McConnell/53/Dir., Beat R. Merz/46/Dir., Lowell E. Sears/56/Dir.

Astoria Financial Corp

1 Astoria Federal Plz., Lake Success, NY, 11042; *PH:* 1-516-327-3000; *Fax:* 1-516-327-7461; *http://* www.astoriafederal.com; *Email:* ir@astoriafederal.com

General		Stock	
Incorporation	DE	Price on:12/24/2007	$25.52
Employees	1,516	Stock Exchange	NYSE
Auditor	KPMG LLP	Ticker Symbol	AF
Stk Agt	Mellon Investor Services LLC	Outstanding Shares	97,320,000
Counsel	NA	E.P.S.	$1.53
DUNS No.	15-608-3990	Shareholders	NA

Business: The group's principal activity is the acceptance of deposits and investing them in loans, securities and other funds. It acts as the holding company of astoria federal savings and loan association and its subsidiaries and directs, plans and coordinates their business activities. The group invests primarily in one-to-four family mortgage loans, mortgage-backed securities, multi-family mortgage loans and commercial real estate loans. On a smaller scale, it also invests in construction loans, consumer loans and other loans. In addition the group invests in us government and federal agency securities and other investments permitted by federal laws and regulations. It also provides insurance products through contractual agreements with various third party marketing organizations. The operations are conducted through 86 full-service banking offices.

Primary SIC and add'l.: 6712 6035

CIK No: 0000910322

Subsidiaries: AF Agency, Inc., AF Insurance Agency, Inc., Astoria Capital Trust I, Astoria Federal Mortgage Corp, Astoria Federal Savings and Loan Association, Astoria Federal Savings and Loan Association a/k/a Astoria Federal Savings or Astoria Federal, Astoria Preferred Funding Corporation, Entrust Holding Corp., Federal Savings and Loan Association, Fidata Service Corp., Revocable Grantor Trust, Star Preferred Holding Corporation, Suffco Service Corporation

Officers: George L. Engelke/69/Chmn., CEO, Pres./$2,703,052.00, Gerard C. Keegan/61/Vice Chmn., Chief Administrative Officer/$1,258,784.00, Alan P. Eggleston/54/Exec. VP, Sec., General Counsel/$1,037,848.00, Gary T. McCann/54/Exec. VP, Arnold K. Greenberg/67/Exec. VP, Assist. Sec./$1,640,300.00, Monte N. Redman/57/CFO, Exec. VP/$1,507,256.00

Directors: George L. Engelke/69/Chmn., CEO, Pres., Gerard C. Keegan/61/Vice Chmn., Chief Administrative Officer, Andrew M. Burger/73/Dir., Denis J. Connors/66/Dir., Thomas J. Donahue/67/Dir., Peter C. Haeffner/69/Dir., Ralph F. Palleschi/61/Dir., Leo J. Waters/73/Dir.

Owners: John J. Conefry, Monte N. Redman/2.10%, Alan P. Eggleston/1.47%, Arnold K. Greenberg/1.90%, Thomas V. Powderly, Gerard C. Keegan, Leo J. Waters, Andrew M. Burger, Association ESOP/10.77%, Thomas J. Donahue, EARNEST Partners, LLC/9.98%, Ralph F. Palleschi, Denis J. Connors, LSV Asset Management/5.74%, George L. Engelke/4.65% *(18 Owners included in Index)*

Financial Data: *Fiscal Year End:*12/31 *Latest Annual Data:* 12/31/2006

Year	Sales	Net Income
2006	$1,178,164,000	$174,897,000
2005	$1,185,186,000	$233,803,000
2004	$1,142,505,000	$219,537,000

Curr. Assets:	$284,471,000	**Curr. Liab.:**	$19,790,683,000	**P/E Ratio:**	16.25
Plant, Equip.:	$145,858,000	**Total Liab.:**	$20,338,765,000	**Indic. Yr. Divd.:**	$1.040
Total Assets:	$21,554,519,000	**Net Worth:**	$1,215,754,000	**Debt/ Equity:**	0.4838

Astralis Ltd

75 Passaic Ave., Fairfield, NJ, 07004; ***PH:*** 1-973-227-7168; ***Fax:*** 1-973-227-7169; ***http://*** www.astralisltd.com; ***Email:*** info@astralisltd.com

General -		**Stock** -	
Incorporation	DE	Price on:12/24/2007	$0.021
Employees	1	Stock Exchange	OTC
Auditor	L J Soldinger Assoc. LLC	Ticker Symbol	ASTR
Stk Agt	American Stock Transfer & Trust Co.	Outstanding Shares	91,450,000
Counsel	NA	E.P.S	$0.00
DUNS No.	NA	Shareholders	NA

Business: The group's principal activity is to research and develop drugs for the treatment of immune system disorders and skin diseases. The group's initial product is psoraxine, a protein extract used for the treatment of the skin disease psoriasis. Psoraxine is a synthesized immuno-therapeutic agent, presented in liquid form and is packed in 0.5 mg ampules for intra-muscular injection. The group's second product is for the treatment of leishmaniasis. The group is a development stage company.

Primary SIC and add'l.: 2834

CIK No: 0001099066

Officers: Michael Garone/CEO, CFO, Interim Pres., Jose Antonio O'Daly/Chmn., Pres. - Research, Development, Samuel Barnett/Non Exec. Dir.

Directors: Jose Antonio O'Daly/Chmn., Pres. - Research, Development, Gerald Krueger/Member - Medical Advisory Board, Michael Ashton/Non Exec. Dir., James Leyden/Member - Medical Advisory Board

Owners: Insiders/81.42%, Jose Antonio O'Daly/15.60%, Blue Cedar/42.40%, Manuel Tarabay, SkyePharma/39.80%

Financial Data: *Fiscal Year End:*12/31 *Latest Annual Data:* 12/31/2006

Year	Sales	Net Income
2006	NA	-$979,000
2005	NA	-$3,914,000
2004	NA	-$9,288,000

Curr. Assets:	$313,000	**Curr. Liab.:**	$464,000		
Plant, Equip.:	$6,000	**Total Liab.:**	$534,000	**Indic. Yr. Divd.:**	NA
Total Assets:	$324,000	**Net Worth:**	-$210,000	**Debt/ Equity:**	NA

Astrata Group Inc

950 S Coast Dr., Ste. 265, Costa Mesa, CA, 92626; ***PH:*** 1-310-282-8646; ***Fax:*** 1-310-226-8553; ***http://*** www.astratagroup.com; ***Email:*** info@astratagroup.com

General -		**Stock** -	
Incorporation	NV	Price on:12/24/2007	$1.06
Employees	NA	Stock Exchange	OTC
Auditor	Squar, Rrrhl & Williamson, LLP	Ticker Symbol	ATTG
Stk Agt	Interwest Transfer Company, Inc.	Outstanding Shares	20,850,000
Counsel	NA	E.P.S	NA
DUNS No.	NA	Shareholders	NA

Business: The groups principle activities include designing and implementing of GPS positioning and integrated communications. The group operates through two segments namely geomatics and telematics. The group operates from North America, Europe and South East Asia.

Primary SIC and add'l.: 3829

CIK No: 0001071157

Subsidiaries: Astrata (B) Sdn Bhd, Astrata (Malaysia) Sdn Bhd, Astrata (New Zealand) Ltd, Astrata (Singapore) Pte Ltd, Astrata Asia Pacific Pte Ltd,, Astrata Europe Ltd, Astrata Geomatics (Pty) Ltd, Astrata GeoTrax Sdn Bhd, Astrata South Africa (Pty) Ltd, Astrata Systems (Pty) Ltd, Barloworld Optron Technologies (Pty) Ltd,, CyberPro Software Solutions (Pty) Ltd

Officers: Martin Euler/Dir., CEO, CFO, Sec./$215,000.00, Robin Littau/MD Asia Pacific - Middle East, Hoyt Layson/CTO/$100,000.00, Richard Nelson/MD - Corporate Communications

Directors: Martin Euler/Dir., CEO, CFO, Sec., Anthony Harrison/48/Chmn., Anthony J.A. Bryan/84/Vice Chmn., Stephanie Powers/Dir., William Corn/63/Dir., Paul Barril/61/Dir., Bill Corn/Dir., Capitaine Paul Barril/Dir.

Owners: Westminster Securities/8.40%, Pointe Capital Limited/9.90%, Paul Barril, Robin Littau/6.20%, Insiders/29.70%, Stephanie Powers, Anthony J.A. Bryan, Vision Opportunity Master Fund/9.90%, Martin Euler/9.90%, Anthon J. Harrison/16.10%, William Corn/9.80%, Wick Trust/9.90%, Walter Jared Frost/5.90%, Infomax Co. Ltd./9.90%

Curr. Assets:	$2,045,000	**Curr. Liab.:**	$11,554,000		
Plant, Equip.:	$684,000	**Total Liab.:**	$11,664,000	**Indic. Yr. Divd.:**	NA
Total Assets:	$3,070,000	**Net Worth:**	-$8,595,000	**Debt/ Equity:**	NA

AstraZeneca Plc

1800 Concord Pike, Wilmington, DE, 19803; ***PH:*** 1-302-886-3000; ***http://*** www.astrazeneca.com

General -		**Stock** -	
Incorporation	England And Wales	Price on:12/24/2007	$52.09
Employees	66,000	Stock Exchange	NYSE
Auditor	KPMG Audit Plc	Ticker Symbol	AZN
Stk Agt	Lloyds TSB Registrars	Outstanding Shares	1,510,000,000
Counsel	NA	E.P.S	$3.79
DUNS No.	23-079-0719	Shareholders	NA

Business: The group's principal activities are the research, development and marketing of medicines for serious health conditions. The group focused on seven important areas of healthcare such as gastrointestinal, cardiovascular, oncology, respiratory and inflammation, central nervous system, pain control and infection. The group has 31 manufacturing sites in 20 countries. Brands include losec/prilosec, nexium, seloken/toprol-xl, plendil, zoladex, casodex, arimidex, nolvadex, pulmicort, oxis, symbicort, accolate, rhinocort, seroquel, zomig, diprivan, naropin, xylocaine, atacand, zestril, and merrem/meronem. The group operates in the United Kingdom, Belgium, France, Germany, Italy, Spain, Sweden, the Netherlands, Canada, Puerto Rico, the United States of America, Australia and Japan.

Primary SIC and add'l.: 2834

CIK No: 0000901832

Subsidiaries: AstraZeneca AB, AstraZeneca BV, AstraZeneca Canada Inc., AstraZeneca Dunkerque Production SCS, AstraZeneca Farmaceutica Spain SA, AstraZeneca GmbH, AstraZeneca Holding GmbH, AstraZeneca Insurance Company Limited, AstraZeneca KK, AstraZeneca LP, AstraZeneca Pharmaceuticals LP, AstraZeneca Pty Limited, AstraZeneca SAS, AstraZeneca SpA, AstraZeneca Treasury Limited 19 Subsidiaries included in the Index

Officers: David Brennan/Exec. Dir., CEO, David Mott/CEO - Medimmune, David Smith/Exec. VP - Operations, John Patterson/Exec. Dir. - Development, Tony Bloxham/Exec. VP - Human Resources, Peter Bonfield/63/Sr. Non - Exec. Dir., Martin Nicklasson/Exec. VP - Global Marketing, Jan Lundberg/Exec. VP - Discovery Research, Bruno Angelici/Exec. VP - Europe, Japan, Asia Pacific, ROW, Jonathan Symonds/Exec. Dir., CFO, Tony Zook/Exec. VP - North America, Lynn Tetrault/Exec. VP - Human Resources, Corporate Affairs, Simon Lowth/Exec. Dir., CFO

Directors: David Brennan/Exec. Dir., CEO, Louis Schweitzer/Non - Exec. Chmn., Hakan Mogren/Non - Exec. Dep. Chmn., Dame Nancy Rothwell/Non - Exec. Dir., Michele Hooper/Non - Exec. Dir., Marcus Wallenberg/Non - Exec. Dir., Jonathan Symonds/Exec. Dir., CFO, Jane Henney/Non - Exec. Dir., Joe Jimenez/48/Non - Exec. Dir., John Varley/Non - Exec. Dir., John Buchanan/Non - Exec. Dir., Bo Angelin/Non - Exec. Dir., Simon Lowth/Exec. Dir., CFO

Financial Data: *Fiscal Year End:*12/31 *Latest Annual Data:* 12/31/2006

Year	Sales	Net Income
2006	$26,475,000,000	$4,392,000,000
2005	$23,950,000,000	$3,884,000,000
2004	$21,960,000,000	$3,051,000,000

Curr. Assets:	$16,936,000,000	**Curr. Liab.:**	$9,447,000,000	**P/E Ratio:**	12.85
Plant, Equip.:	$12,108,000,000	**Total Liab.:**	$16,314,000,000	**Indic. Yr. Divd.:**	$1.750
Total Assets:	$48,781,000,000	**Net Worth:**	$32,467,000,000	**Debt/ Equity:**	NA

Astris Energi Inc

2175 Dunwin Dr., Unit 6, Mississauga, ON, L5L 1X2; ; ***http://*** www.astris.ca

General -		**Stock** -	
Incorporation	Canada	Price on:12/24/2007	$0.028
Employees	NA	Stock Exchange	NA
Auditor	Danziger & Hochman	Ticker Symbol	NA
Stk Agt	Equity Transfer Services Inc	Outstanding Shares	NA
Counsel	NA	E.P.S	NA
DUNS No.	NA	Shareholders	NA

Business: The group's principal activity is to develop affordable fuel cells, fuel cell power generators, and related small products. These products are used for industrial, commercial, educational, scientific, transportation and similar applications. Fuel cells are electrochemical devices, similar to batteries that supply electricity for a wide variety of requirements, presently served by gasoline and diesel generators. The group's products include demonstration and educational fuel cells and accessories, scientific products such as electrochemical test cells, associated electronic and computer based test equipment, fuel cells and batteries and sub-kilowatt fuel cells and stacks. The products are sold in North America and Europe.

Primary SIC and add'l.: 3629

CIK No: 0001022518

Subsidiaries: Astris s.r.o.

Officers: Jiri K. Nor/Chmn., CEO, Pres., Josef Soltys/Industrial Systems Specialist, Radek Kotoucek/GM - Astris sro, Peter K. Nor/VP - Marketing - Corporate Development, Anthony Durkacz/Dir., VP - Finance, Treasurer, Sec.

Directors: Jiri K. Nor/Chmn., CEO, Pres., Brian D. Clewes/Dir., Michael M. Liik/Dir., Anthony Durkacz/Dir., VP - Finance, Treasurer, Sec., Gary G. Brandt/Member - Advisory Board, Arthur E. Laudenslager/Dir.

Owners: Jiri K. Nor/26.50%, Acme Global Inc./7.71%

Financial Data: *Fiscal Year End:*12/31 *Latest Annual Data:* 12/31/2006

Year	Sales	Net Income
2006	$74,000	-$1,820,000
2005	$250,000	-$4,574,000
2004	$74,000	-$2,875,000

Curr. Assets:	$170,000	**Curr. Liab.:**	$1,138,000		
Plant, Equip.:	$498,000	**Total Liab.:**	$1,561,000	**Indic. Yr. Divd.:**	NA
Total Assets:	$1,516,000	**Net Worth:**	-$46,000	**Debt/ Equity:**	NA

Astro Med Inc

600 E Greenwich Ave., West Warwick, RI, 02893; ***PH:*** 1-401-828-4000; ***Fax:*** 1-401-822-2430; ***http://*** www.astro-medinc.com

General -		**Stock** -	
Incorporation	RI	Price on:12/24/2007	$11
Employees	400	Stock Exchange	NDQ
Auditor	Ernst & Young, LLP	Ticker Symbol	ALOT
Stk Agt	Registrar & Transfer Co	Outstanding Shares	6,880,000
Counsel	Hinckley, Allen & Snyder	E.P.S	$0.81
DUNS No.	04-798-6898	Shareholders	NA

Business: The group's principal activities are to develop and manufacture electronic data processing systems. The group operates through three segments quicklabel systems, grass-telefactor and test and measurement. Qls digital systems and media products create product and packaging labels and tags in

one or many colors. Grass-telefactor products electronically record signals that reflect the physiological status of living creatures for digital or analog access. T&m data acquisition systems record scientific signals and print the output onto charts or electronic media. The group supplies all range of products that include the hardware, software and supplies to variety of industrial customers.

Primary SIC and add'l.: 3577

CIK No: 0000008146

Subsidiaries: Astro-Med GMBH, Astro-Med SRL, AWO, Inc., Grass Properties, Inc., Grass Telefactor Corporation

Officers: Albert W. Ondis/Chmn., CEO/$755,298.00, Everett V. Pizzuti/Dir., COO, Pres./$516,672.00, Michael J. Sullivan/CTO, VP/$183,539.00, Michael Morawetz/VP - Branch Operations, John D. McGuinness/VP, Corporate Controller, Stephen M. Petrarca/VP - Instrument Manufacturing, Joseph P. Oconnell/Sr. VP, CFO/$274,760.00, Elias G. Deeb/VP - Media Sales, Manufacturing/$190,845.00, Gordon Bentley/VP - Information Technology

Directors: Albert W. Ondis/Chmn., CEO, Graeme MacLetchie/70/Dir., Jacques V. Hopkins/77/Dir., Everett V. Pizzuti/Dir., COO, Pres., Hermann Viets/65/Dir.

Owners: Albert W. Ondis/28.40%, Jacques V. Hopkins, Insiders/42.20%, Elias G. Deeb/1.60%, Eliot Rose Asset Management, LLC/9.80%, Everett V. Pizzuti/7.20%, Hermann Viets/2.70%, Michael J. Sullivan/1.00%, Kern Capital Management, LLC/6.40%, Graeme MacLetchie/1.20%, Joseph P. OConnell/4.00%

Financial Data: Fiscal Year End:01/31   **Latest Annual Data:** 1/31/2007

Year	Sales	Net Income
2007	$65,519,000	$6,059,000
2006	$59,301,000	$2,551,000
2005	$55,975,000	$2,710,000

Curr. Assets:	$44,168,000	**Curr. Liab.:**	$9,874,000	**P/E Ratio:**	13.58
Plant, Equip.:	$7,964,000	**Total Liab.:**	$12,042,000	**Indic. Yr. Divd.:**	$0.200
Total Assets:	$58,001,000	**Net Worth:**	$45,958,000	**Debt/ Equity:**	NA

Astronics Corp

130 Commerce Way, East Aurora, NY, 14052; **PH:** 1-716-805-1599; **Fax:** 1-716-805-1286; **http://** www.astronics.com; **Email:** invest@astronics.com

General - Incorporation .... NY	**Stock**- Price on:12/24/2007 ....$28.2981
Employees....................................787	Stock Exchange..NDQ
Auditor .... Ernst & Young LLP	Ticker Symbol..ATRO
Stk Agt..... American Stock Transfer & Trust Co.	Outstanding Shares 8,060,000
Counsel..... Hodgson Russ Andrews Woods Et Al	E.P.S..NA
DUNS No. 04-982-9302	Shareholders..NA

Business: The group's principal activity is to design and manufacture specialised lighting and electronic control systems for the global aerospace industry. The products consist of electro-luminescent lamps used for backlight liquid crystal displays and emergency lighting systems like escape path markers and exit locators, which are used in aircraft cockpits, cabins and exteriors. The products are sold to major aircraft manufacturers, avionics companies and aircraft operators around the world. The group also manufactures durable keyboards and illuminated switch panels for military and industrial purposes. On 14-Mar-2003, the group spun off its wholly owned subsidiary, mod-pac corp.

Primary SIC and add'l.: 3647

CIK No: 0000008063

Subsidiaries: Astronics Advanced Electronics Systems Corp., Astronics Air, LLC, LSI Europe B.V.B.A., Luminescent Systems Canada, Inc., Luminescent Systems, Inc.

Officers: Peter J. Gundermann/Dir., CEO, Pres./$480,679.00, David C. Burney/CFO, VP/$281,131.00, Frank G. Johns/VP - Luminescent Systems, Inc, James S. Kramer/VP - Luminescent Systems, Inc, Richard M. Miller/VP - Luminescent Systems, Inc, Mark Peabody/Exec. VP - Astronics Advanced Electronic Systems

Directors: Peter J. Gundermann/Dir., CEO, Pres., Kevin T. Keane/Chmn., Raymond W. Boushie/Dir., John B. Drenning/Dir., Robert T. Brady/Dir., Robert J. McKenna/Dir.

Owners: David C. Burney, John B. Drenning/1.90%, Robert T. Brady/2.40%, Peter J. Gundermann/4.30%, Insiders/48.90%, David C. Burney, FMR Corp./5.80%, Robert J. McKenna, Kevin T. Keane/37.10%, John B. Drenning/5.40%, Robert T. Brady/1.40%, Athena Capital Management, Inc./5.00%, Robert J. McKenna, Lewis Capital Management, LLC/5.60%, Peter J. Gundermann/3.60% **(19 Owners included in Index)**

Financial Data: Fiscal Year End:12/31   **Latest Annual Data:** 12/31/2006

Year	Sales	Net Income
2006	$110,767,000	$5,736,000
2005	$74,354,000	$2,237,000
2004	$34,696,000	-$734,000

Curr. Assets:	$51,656,000	**Curr. Liab.:**	$34,219,000		
Plant, Equip.:	$23,436,000	**Total Liab.:**	$51,190,000	**Indic. Yr. Divd.:**	NA
Total Assets:	$82,538,000	**Net Worth:**	$31,348,000	**Debt/ Equity:**	NA

Asure Software

Formerly: Forgent Networks Inc
108 Wild Basin Rd. , Austin, TX, 78746; **PH:** 1-512-437-2700; **http://** www.forgent.com

General - Incorporation .... DE	**Stock**- Price on:12/24/2007 ....$0.9869
Employees....................................37	Stock Exchange..NDQ
Auditor .... Ernst & Young LLP	Ticker Symbol..NA
Stk Agt..... American Stock Transfer & Trust Co.	Outstanding Shares 25,600,000
Counsel................... Godwin Gruber LLP	E.P.S..$0.47
DUNS No. 14-713-4548	Shareholders..NA

Business: The group's principle activity is to provide automation software solutions and professional services. The group operates in two segments: intellectual property licensing and software and professional services. The intellectual property licensing segment generates license revenues relating to the group's data compression technology. Software and professional services segment provides customers with enterprise meeting automation software as well as software customization, installation, training, network consulting, hardware devices, and other comprehensive related services. In fiscal 2003, the group discontinued its integration and videoconferencing hardware services businesses. On 06-Oct-2003, the group acquired network simplicity software inc. The group's total revenue for the year 2007 was 40.41 millions of USD.

Primary SIC and add'l.: 7372 7379 7373

CIK No: 0000884144

Subsidiaries: Compression Labs, Inc., Forgent Networks Canada, Inc., VTEL Australia, PTY LTD, VTEL Germany, GmbH

Officers: Richard N. Snyder/Chmn., CEO, Nancy Harris/VP, GM - Netsimplicity, Jay Peterson/CFO, VP, Hala Elsherbini/Investor Contact, Snehal Shah/VP, GM - Iemployee, Fenil Shah/VP, GM - Iemployee

Directors: Richard N. Snyder/Chmn., CEO, Richard J. Agnich/Dir., Ray Rajko Miles/Dir., Lou Mazzucchelli/Dir., Kathleen A. Cote/Dir., James H. Wells/Dir.

Owners: Richard J. Agnich, Insiders/6.56%, Dimensional Fund Advisors Inc./5.34%, Ray R. Miles, Richard N. Snyder/3.62%, Jay C. Peterson, Lou Mazzucchelli, James H. Wells, Kathleen A. Cote, Nancy L. Harris

Financial Data: Fiscal Year End:07/31   **Latest Annual Data:** 07/31/2007

Year	Sales	Net Income
2007	$40,407,000	$12,248,000
2006	$14,896,000	-$3,555,000
2005	$9,906,000	-$6,568,000

Curr. Assets:	$17,194,000	**Curr. Liab.:**	$6,081,000	**P/E Ratio:**	2.60
Plant, Equip.:	$788,000	**Total Liab.:**	$7,869,000	**Indic. Yr. Divd.:**	NA
Total Assets:	$17,989,000	**Net Worth:**	$10,120,000	**Debt/ Equity:**	0.0635

ASV Inc

840 Lily Ln., Grand Rapids, MN, 55744; **PH:** 1-218-327-3434; **Fax:** 1-218-327-9122; **http://** asvi.com; **Email:** investorrelations@asvi.com

General - Incorporation .... MN	**Stock**- Price on:12/24/2007 ....$18.6
Employees....................................284	Stock Exchange..NDQ
Auditor .... Grant Thornton LLP	Ticker Symbol..ASVI
Stk Agt .... Wells Fargo Bank Minnesota N.A	Outstanding Shares 26,660,000
Counsel................... Dorsey & Whitney LLP	E.P.S..$0.42
DUNS No. 11-622-6242	Shareholders..NA

Business: The group's principal activity is to design, manufacture and distribute track-driven all-season vehicles. It manufactures three principal product lines. They are the posi-track (TM) line, the r-series line and the multi-terrain loaders undercarriage line. All products use the rubber track suspension system. They are used in the industries of construction, agriculture, landscaping, trail grooming and maintenance, vineyards, military, wildlife management and other applications. The group jointly manufactures the multi-terrain loaders in alliance with caterpillar. It also entered into a licensing agreement to sell its rubber track, all-surface utility loader through polaris industries inc. Track truck, posi-track, rc-30, r-50, rc-50, maximum traction support system, posi-turn and snow saver are trademarks of the group. It has a manufacturing facility in grand rapids, Minnesota and its products are sold in United States, Canada, Australia, New Zealand and Portugal.

Primary SIC and add'l.: 3714 3711

CIK No: 0000926763

Subsidiaries: A.S.V. Distribution, Inc., Loegering Mfg. Inc.

Officers: Richard A. Benson/Chmn., CEO, Principal Executive Officer/$245,340.00, Mark S. Glasnapp/52/Pres./$848,787.00, Thomas R. Karges/47/CFO, Sec./$345,161.00

Directors: Richard A. Benson/Chmn., CEO, Principal Executive Officer, Leland T. Lynch/Dir., Kenneth J. Zika/Dir., Karlin S. Symons/Dir., James H. Dahl/Dir., Bruce D. Iserman/Dir., Jerome T. Miner/Dir.

Owners: Wellington Management Co. LLC/5.20%, Insiders/7.60%, Caterpillar Inc./23.60%, Gary D. Lemke/3.90%, Jerome T. Miner/2.70%, Transamerica Investment Management, LLC/7.90%, Richard A. Benson, James H. Dahl/2.60%, Kenneth J. Zika, Karlin S. Symons, Bruce D. Iserman, Leland T. Lynch, Thomas R. Karges/1.10%, Mark S. Glasnapp, Neuberger Berman Inc./10.40%

Financial Data: Fiscal Year End:12/31   **Latest Annual Data:** 12/31/2006

Year	Sales	Net Income
2006	$246,137,000	$22,047,000
2005	$245,082,000	$27,898,000
2004	$160,873,000	$17,175,000

Curr. Assets:	$138,621,000	**Curr. Liab.:**	$20,716,000	**P/E Ratio:**	38.75
Plant, Equip.:	$29,342,000	**Total Liab.:**	$22,386,000	**Indic. Yr. Divd.:**	NA
Total Assets:	$198,588,000	**Net Worth:**	$176,202,000	**Debt/ Equity:**	0.0104

Asyst Technologies Inc

46897 Bayside Pkwy., Fremont, CA, 94538; **PH:** 1-510-661-5000; **Fax:** 1-510-661-5166; **http://** www.asyst.com; **Email:** info@asyst.com

General - Incorporation .... CA	**Stock**- Price on:12/24/2007 ....$7.11
Employees....................................1,046	Stock Exchange..NDQ
Auditor .... PricewaterhouseCoopers LLP	Ticker Symbol..ASYT
Stk Agt .... EquiServe Trust Co N.A	Outstanding Shares 49,470,000
Counsel................... Cooley Godward LLP	E.P.S..$0.00
DUNS No. 10-297-1777	Shareholders..NA

Business: The group's principal activity is to provide integrated automation systems for the semiconductor manufacturing industry. The group's systems help semiconductor manufacturers to increase their manufacturing productivity and protect their investment in silicon wafers during the manufacture of integrated circuits, or ics. The integrated automation systems consist of isolation systems, work-in-process materials management, wafer-handling robotics, automated transport and loading systems and equipment connectivity software and services. The group markets its products in the United States, Taiwan, Japan, Europe and other Asian countries.

Primary SIC and add'l.: 3599

CIK No: 0000909326

Subsidiaries: Asyst Japan, Inc., Asyst Shinko, Inc., Asyst Technologies (Far East) Pte. Ltd., Asyst Technologies (Taiwan) Ltd., Asyst Technologies Europe, Ltd., Asyst Technologies GmbH, Asyst Technologies Malaysia Sdn. Bhd., Korea Asyst Ltd., SMIF Equipment (Tianjin) Co., Ltd.

Officers: Stephen S. Schwartz/Chmn., CEO, Pres./$1,744,682.00, Anthony C. Bonora/CTO, Exec. VP - Asyst Fellow/$962,812.00, Alan Lowe/Sr. VP - Global Business Solutions/$942,374.00, John Swenson/VP - Investor Relations, Corporate Communications, Steve Debenham/46/VP, General Counsel, Sec., Michael A. Sicuro/Sr. VP, CFO/$244,109.00, Paula C. Lupriore/51/Sr. VP - Automated Solutions Group/$1,047,185.00, Thomas R. Leitzke/59/Sr. VP - Global Operations

Directors: Stephen S. Schwartz/Chmn., CEO, Pres., Tsuyoshi Kawanishi/Dir., Stanley Grubel/Dir., Walter W. Wilson/Dir., Anthony E. Santelli/Dir., Robert A. McNamara/Dir., William Simon/Dir.

Owners: Stephen S. Schwartz/2.10%, Alexandra Global Master FundLtd./9.70%, Tsuyoshi E. Kawanishi, Alan S. Lowe, Anthony E. Santelli, Michael A. Sicuro, Barclays Global Investors, NA./5.50%, Stanley Grubel, Paula C. LuPriore, Insiders/5.90%, Walter W. Wilson, Robert A. McNamara, Anthony C. Bonora, William Simon, Defiance Asset Management, LLC/5.10% (*16 Owners included in Index*)

Financial Data: Fiscal Year End:03/31 Latest Annual Data: 3/31/2007

Year		Sales		Net Income
2007		$492,473,000		-$38,000
2006		$459,221,000		-$104,000
2005		$612,987,000		-$17,542,000
Curr. Assets:	$305,275,000	Curr. Liab.:	$255,780,000	
Plant, Equip.:	$25,138,000	Total Liab.:	$370,875,000	Indic. Yr. Divd.: NA
Total Assets:	$465,686,000	Net Worth:	$94,681,000	Debt/ Equity: 1.5314

AT&T Inc

One AT&T Way, Bedminster, NJ, 07921; *PH:* 1-908-221-2000; *http://* www.att.com

General - Incorporation	NY	Stock - Price on:12/24/2007	$40.43
Employees	302,000	Stock Exchange	NYSE
Auditor	PricewaterhouseCoopers LLP	Ticker Symbol	T
Stk Agt	Computershare Trust Co	Outstanding Shares	6,170,000,000
Counsel	NA	E.P.S.	$1.951
DUNS No.	00-698-0080	Shareholders	NA

Business: The group's principle activity is to provide IP-based communications services to business. The group also provides wireless, high speed Internet access, local and long distance voice, and directory publishing and advertising services. In November 2007, the group acquired Dobson Communications Corporation. The group operates from United States.

Primary SIC and add'l.: 4822 4813

CIK No: 0000005907

Subsidiaries: ACC Corp., Alascom, Inc., AT&T Capital Holdings, Inc. ., AT&T Communications of California, Inc., AT&T Communications of Delaware, LLC., AT&T Communications of Hawaii, Inc., AT&T Communications of Illinois, Inc., AT&T Communications of Indiana, G.P, AT&T Communications of Maryland, LLC., AT&T Communications of Michigan, Inc., AT&T Communications of Nevada, Inc., AT&T Communications of New England, Inc, AT&T Communications of New York, Inc., AT&T Communications of Ohio, Inc., AT&T Communications of Pennsylvania, LLC. 38 Subsidiaries included in the Index

Officers: Randall L. Stephenson/Chmn., CEO, Ralph De La Vega/CEO, Pres. - AT, T Mobility, Forrest E. Miller/Group Pres. - Corporate Strategy, Development, Ronald E. Spears/Group Pres. - Global Business Services, John T. Stankey/Group Pres. - Telecom Operations, James W. Callaway/Sr. Exec. VP - Exec. Operations, William A. Blase/Sr. Exec. VP - Human Resources, Catherine M. Coughlin/Sr. Exec. VP, Global Marketing Officer, Wayne D. Watts/Sr. Exec. VP, General Counsel, Ray Carpenter/Mgr. - Institutional Investors, Kent Evans/Mgr. - Institutional Investors, James W. Cicconi/Sr. Exec. VP - External, Legislative Affairs, James D. Ellis/Sr. Exec. VP, General Counsel, James S. Kahan/Sr. Exec. VP - Corporate Development, Richard G. Lindner/CFO, Sr. Exec. VP (*25 Officers included in Index*)

Directors: Randall L. Stephenson/Chmn., CEO, Joyce M. Roche/Dir., Laura D'Andrea Tyson/Dir., Patricia P. Upton/Dir., Lynn M. Martin/Dir., John B. McCoy/Dir., Mary S. Metz/Dir., Toni Rembe/Dir., Reuben V. Anderson/Dir., James H. Blanchard/Dir., James P. Kelly/Dir., William F. Aldinger/Dir., Gilbert F. Amelio/Dir., August A. Busch/Dir., Charles F. Knight/Dir. (*16 Directors included in Index*)

Financial Data: Fiscal Year End:12/31 Latest Annual Data: 12/31/2006

Year		Sales		Net Income
2006		$63,055,000,000		$7,356,000,000
2005		$43,862,000,000		$4,786,000,000
2004		$40,787,000,000		$5,887,000,000
Curr. Assets:	$25,553,000,000	Curr. Liab.:	$40,482,000,000	P/E Ratio: 20.72
Plant, Equip.:	$94,596,000,000	Total Liab.:	$155,094,000,000	Indic. Yr. Divd.: NA
Total Assets:	$270,634,000,000	Net Worth:	$115,540,000,000	Debt/ Equity: 0.4865

ATA Holdings Corp

7337 W Washington St. , Indianapolis, IN, 46231; *PH:* 1-317-247-4000

General - Incorporation	IN	Stock - Price on:12/24/2007	$0.007
Employees	NA	Stock Exchange	NA
Auditor	Ernst & Young LLP	Ticker Symbol	NA
Stk Agt	Medallion Program	Outstanding Shares	NA
Counsel	NA	E.P.S.	NA
DUNS No.	10-222-5307	Shareholders	NA

Business: The group's principal activity is to provide airline-related services. It operates in four segments: scheduled services, charter services, ground package services and other services. The scheduled services segment provides airline services to destinations primarily from its gateways at Chicago-midway and indianapolis. The charter services segment provides commercial charter services and military/government charter services. The ground package services include the sale of hotel, car rental, cruise, vacation packages and other accommodations in conjunction with air transportation. The group's other services include sale of ground arrangements, airframe and power plant mechanic training, helicopter charter services and cargo services.

Primary SIC and add'l.: 4512 4581 4522

CIK No: 0000898904

Subsidiaries: Ambassadair Travel Club, Inc., Amber Travel, Inc., America Trans Air ExecuJet, Inc., ATA Airlines, Inc., ATA Cargo, Inc., ATA Leisure Corp., Chicago Express Airlines, Inc.

Officers: Brian Hunt/Chief Administrative Officer, Sr. VP - ATA Airlines, Inc, Gary E. Ellmer/Sr. VP - Operations, GM - Charter

Atari Inc

417 5th Ave., New York, NY, 10016; *PH:* 1-212-726-6500; *http://* www.atari.com

General - Incorporation	DE	Stock - Price on:12/24/2007	$2.91
Employees	329	Stock Exchange	NDQ
Auditor	Deloitte & Touche LLP	Ticker Symbol	ATAR
Stk Agt	American Stock Transfer & Trust Co.	Outstanding Shares	13,480,000
Counsel	NA	E.P.S.	-$6.08
DUNS No.	80-918-5903	Shareholders	NA

Business: The group's principal activity is to develop, publish and distribute interactive entertainment software for leisure entertainment, gaming enthusiasts and children's markets for a variety of platforms. This includes PC's, sony playstation, nintendo game boy, microsoft xbox and sega dreamcast. Publishing is conducted in three main studios located at santa monica, California; beverly, Massachusetts and minneapolis, Minnesota. Distribution activities include the sale of games produced by software publishers unrelated to the group.

Primary SIC and add'l.: 7372

CIK No: 0001002607

Subsidiaries: ATARI Asia Pacific Pty Ltd., GT Interactive Europe Holdings BV, GT Interactive Software Europe Ltd., GT Interactive Software France SARL, GT Interactive Software GmbH, Reflections Interactive Limited

Officers: David Pierce/CEO, Pres./$415,805.00, Ann E. Kronen/Dir., Independent Consultant, Kristina K. Pappa/Sec., Jean-Marcel Nicolai/Sr. VP - Worldwide Product Development, CTO/$565,105.00, Arturo Rodriguez/Acting CFO, VP, Controller, Investor Relations Officer

Directors: Michael G. Corrigan/Chmn., Ronald C. Bernard/Dir., Ann E. Kronen/Dir., Independent Consultant, Evence-Charles Coppee/Dir., Jean-Michel Perbet/Dir., James Ackerly/Dir., Thomas Schmider/Dir., Denis Guyennot/Dir.

Owners: The Vanguard Group, Inc., Michael G. Corrigan, Denis Guyennot, James Ackerly, Insiders, Ann E. Kronen, Infogrames Entertainment S. A, Jean-Marcel Nicolai, CCM Master Qualified Fund, Ltd., California U.S. Holdings, Inc., Thomas Schmider, Ronald C. Bernard, David Pierce

Financial Data: Fiscal Year End:03/31 Latest Annual Data: 03/31/2007

Year		Sales		Net Income
2007		$122,285,000		-$69,711,000
2006		$218,661,000		-$68,986,000
2005		$395,165,000		$5,692,000
Curr. Assets:	$66,078,000	Curr. Liab.:	$69,789,000	
Plant, Equip.:	$6,364,000	Total Liab.:	$70,458,000	Indic. Yr. Divd.: NA
Total Assets:	$143,670,000	Net Worth:	$73,212,000	Debt/ Equity: NA

ATC Healthcare Inc

1983 Marcus Ave., Lake Success, NY, 11042; *PH:* 1-516-750-1600; *Fax:* 1-516-750-1755; *http://* www.atchealthcare.com

General - Incorporation	DE	Stock - Price on:12/24/2007	$0.36
Employees	6,100	Stock Exchange	AMEX
Auditor	Goldstein Golub Kessler LLP	Ticker Symbol	AHN
Stk Agt	American Stock Transfer & Trust Co.	Outstanding Shares	46,660,000
Counsel	NA	E.P.S.	-$0.06
DUNS No.	11-316-7142	Shareholders	NA

Business: The group's principal activity is to provide medical supplemental staffing services to health care facilities. The group offers qualified health care associates in over 60 job categories. These health care associates ranges from the highest level of specialty nurse including critical care, neonatal, labor and delivery. The group also provides associates in medical administrative staff, including third party billers, administrative assistants, claims processors, collection personnel and medical records clerks. At 29-Feb-2004, the group had 52 offices of supplemental staffing to health care facilities in 23 states. It markets its supplemental staffing services through service trademark and atc(R) logo. The group also operates a travel nurse program whereby qualified nurses, physical therapists and occupational therapists are recruited on behalf of the clients who require such services on a long-term basis. The group operates solely in the United States.

Primary SIC and add'l.: 7363

CIK No: 0000720480

Subsidiaries: ATC Funding, LLC, ATC Healthcare Services, Inc, ATC Healthcare, Inc, ATC Staffing Services, Inc

Officers: David Savitsky/CEO/$546,071.00, Stephen Savitsky/Chmn., Pres./$455,315.00, Daniel Pess/Sr. VP/$144,226.00, David Kimbell/Sr. VP, CFO

Directors: Stephen Savitsky/Chmn., Pres., Jonathan J. Halpert/63/Dir., Bernard J. Firestone/58/Dir., Martin Schiller/71/Dir.

Owners: Stephen Savitsky/6.34%, Insiders/11.98%, David Savitsky/45.00%, Roaring Fork Capital SBIC L.P./100.00%, Enable Growth Partners LP/6.94%, Roaring Fork Capital SBIC L.P./12.01%, Stephen Savitsky/45.00%, David Savitsky/5.64%, Insiders/90.00%

Financial Data: Fiscal Year End:02/28 Latest Annual Data: 02/28/2007

Year		Sales		Net Income
2007		$89,401,000		-$2,159,000
2006		$71,528,000		-$2,332,000
2005		$67,937,000		-$10,404,000
Curr. Assets:	$32,459,000	Curr. Liab.:	$12,763,000	
Plant, Equip.:	$848,000	Total Liab.:	$69,674,000	Indic. Yr. Divd.: NA
Total Assets:	$74,727,000	Net Worth:	$5,053,000	Debt/ Equity: NA

Atherogenics Inc

8995 Westside Pkwy., Alpharetta, GA, 30004; *PH:* 1-678-336-2500; *Fax:* 1-678-336-2501; *http://* www.atherogenics.com

General - Incorporation	GA	Stock - Price on:12/24/2007	$2.37
Employees	127	Stock Exchange	NDQ
Auditor	Ernst & Young LLP	Ticker Symbol	AGIX
Stk Agt	American Stock Transfer & Trust Co.	Outstanding Shares	39,490,000
Counsel	Brown & Wood LLP	E.P.S.	-$1.371
DUNS No.	NA	Shareholders	NA

Business: The group's principal activity is to discover, develop and commercialize drugs for the treatment of chronic inflammatory diseases. These drugs are used in the treatment of atherosclerosis, heart disease, asthma, organ transplant rejection and rheumatoid arthritis. Its main products, the agi-1067 is an oral drug to benefit patients with coronary artery disease, agix-4207 i.v. To treat rheumatoid arthritis patients in whom the rapid attainment of target drug levels in the blood is desirable, agix-4207 for rheumatoid arthritis and agi-1096 designed to both diminish the organ transplant response to inflammation and to directly protect the blood vessels to the transplanted organ through its v-protectanttm activity . Group depends on a third party manufacturer for the supply of agi-1067 bulk drug substance and formulated drug products. Oxykine, design, agi and aatherogenics are the registered trademarks of the group.

Primary SIC and add'l.: 8731 2834

CIK No: 0001107601

Officers: Russell M. Medford/Dir., Scientific Co - Founder, CEO, Pres./$1,677,807.00, Charles W. Montgomery/Sr. VP - Business Development, Alliance Management/$762,876.00, Mark P. Colonnese/Exec. VP - Commercial Operations, CFO/$928,706.00, Joseph M. Gaynor/Sr. VP, General Counsel/$478,152.00, Robert A.D. Scott/Exec. VP - Research, Development, Chief Medical Officer/$964,646.00

Directors: Russell M. Medford/Dir., Scientific Co - Founder, CEO, Pres., Michael A. Henos/58/Chmn., William A. Scott/67/Dir., David Bearman/62/Dir., Arthur M. Pappas/60/Dir., Wayne R. Alexander/66/Dir., Samuel L. Barker/Dir., Vaughn D. Bryson/69/Dir., Forcht T. Dagi/59/Dir., Margaret E. Grayson/Dir.

Owners: Barclays Global Investors, NA/5.30%, Vaughn D. Bryson, Arthur M. Pappas, Atticus Capital, LP/14.10%, Margaret E. Grayson, Eastbourne Capital Management, LLC./11.40%, Wellington Management Company, LLP/14.00%, Mark P. Colonnese, Bank of America Corporation./6.10%, Joseph M. Gaynor, David Bearman, Forcht T. Dagi, William A. Scott, OppenheimerFunds, Inc./14.40%, Russell M. Medford/4.60% *(23 Owners included in Index)*

Financial Data: *Fiscal Year End:*12/31 *Latest Annual Data:* 12/31/2006

Year	Sales	Net Income
2006	$31,675,000	-$67,322,000
2005	NA	-$82,554,000
2004	NA	-$69,589,000

Curr. Assets:	$163,030,000	**Curr. Liab.:**	$44,244,000		
Plant, Equip.:	$9,685,000	**Total Liab.:**	$332,327,000	**Indic. Yr. Divd.:**	NA
Total Assets:	$178,340,000	**Net Worth:**	-$153,988,000	**Debt/ Equity:**	NA

Atheros Communications Inc

5480 Great America Pkwy., Santa Clara, CA, 95054; ***PH:*** 1-408-773-5200; ***Fax:*** 1-408-773-9940; ***http://*** www.atheros.com; ***Email:*** info@atheros.com

General - Incorporation	DE	***Stock***- Price on:12/24/2007	$29.99
Employees	660	Stock Exchange	NDQ
Auditor	Deloitte & Touche LLP	Ticker Symbol	ATHR
Stk Agt	Computer share & Trust Co.	Outstanding Shares	55,270,000
Counsel	NA	E.P.S	$0.43
DUNS No.	NA	Shareholders	NA

Business: The group's is a developer of semiconductor system solutions for wireless communications products. It combine our wireless systems expertise with high-performance radio frequency, mixed signal and digital semiconductor design skills to provide highly integrated chipsets that are manufacturable on low-cost, standard complementary metal-oxide semiconductor processes. A broad base of leading customers, including personal computer and networking equipment manufacturers is using the group's technology. The group's trademarks are atheros, the atheros logo, super g, super a/g, wake-on-wireless and wake-on-theft. The group's wireless networking solutions incorporate semiconductors, software and system level reference designs to enable customers to deliver advanced products that provide users with high-performance, as measured by integration of standards, throughput, power consumption and range, at lower cost.

Primary SIC and add'l.: 3674

CIK No: 0001140486

Subsidiaries: Atheros (Shanghai) Co., Ltd, Atheros Communications International, LLC, Atheros Communications K.K., Atheros Hong Kong Limited, Atheros India, LLC, Atheros International Ltd., Atheros Technology (Macao Commercial Offshore) Limited, Atheros Technology Ltd.

Officers: Craig H. Barratt/Dir., CEO, Pres./$763,688.00, Richard G. Bahr/VP - Engineering/$766,615.00, Adam H. Tachner/VP, General Counsel, Paul G. Franklin/VP - Operations, Dave D. Torre/VP, Chief Accounting Officer, Dakota Lee/Sr. Mgr. - Corporate Communications, Greg Wood/Dir., Sr. Accounting Supervisor, Sam Endy/VP, GM - Mobile Wireless Business Unit, Edward L. Martin/VP - Global Human Resources, Ben Naskar/VP, GM - Wireless Networking Business Unit, Jack R. Lazar/CFO, VP, Corp. Sec./$1,211,599.00, Todd D. Antes/VP - Marketing/$672,849.00, Ali Hariri/VP - Business Development, William J. McFarland/CTO, Kenneth P. McKeithan/VP - Software Engineering *(18 Officers included in Index)*

Directors: Craig H. Barratt/Dir., CEO, Pres., John L. Hennessy/55/Chmn., Marshall L. Mohr/Dir., Forest Baskett/64/Dir., Andrew S. Rappaport/Dir., Willy C. Shih/Dir., Teresa H. Meng/Co - Founder, Greg Wood/Dir., Sr. Accounting Supervisor, Daniel A. Artusi/53/Dir.

Owners: Forest Baskett, Richard G. Bahr, FMR Corp./14.30%, Marshall L. Mohr, Fred Alger Management, Inc./6.00%, Willy C. Shih, Teresa H. Meng/1.10%, Andrew S. Rappaport, Gary Szilagyi, Daniel A. Artusi, Insiders/4.30%, T. Rowe Price Associates, Inc./5.00%, Todd Antes, Craig H. Barratt/1.70%, John L. Hennessy *(16 Owners included in Index)*

Financial Data: *Fiscal Year End:*12/31 *Latest Annual Data:* 12/31/2006

Year	Sales	Net Income
2006	$301,691,000	$18,678,000
2005	$183,485,000	$16,688,000
2004	$169,607,000	$10,824,000

Curr. Assets:	$268,446,000	**Curr. Liab.:**	$63,981,000	**P/E Ratio:**	85.69
Plant, Equip.:	$8,994,000	**Total Liab.:**	$83,116,000	**Indic. Yr. Divd.:**	NA
Total Assets:	$364,058,000	**Net Worth:**	$280,942,000	**Debt/ Equity:**	NA

Atlantic American Corp

4370 Peachtree Rd., NE, Atlanta, GA, 30319; ***PH:*** 1-404-266-5500; ***Fax:*** 1-404-266-5702; ***http://*** www.atlam.com

General - Incorporation	GA	***Stock***- Price on:12/24/2007	$4.12
Employees	253	Stock Exchange	NDQ
Auditor	BDO Seidman, LLP	Ticker Symbol	AAME
Stk Agt	American Stock Transfer & Trust CO.	Outstanding Shares	21,590,000
Counsel	Jones, Day, Reavis & Pogue	E.P.S	NA
DUNS No.	04-758-4941	Shareholders	NA

Business: The group's principal activities are to provide life, health, property and casualty insurance services. The casualty operations include workers' compensation insurance policies and coverage for automobile, property and general damage liabilities. The life and health operations consist of life and supplemental health products including, non-participating individual term and whole life insurance policies, medical care supplement policies, ordinary life, medicare supplement, cancer, accident and other supplemental health coverage. The operations are carried out through four segments. The American southern, association casualty, bankers fidelity segment and Georgia casualty segment.

Primary SIC and add'l.: 6321 6311 6331 6719

CIK No: 0000008177

Subsidiaries: American Safety Insurance Company, American Southern Insurance Company, Association Casualty Insurance Company, Association Risk Management General Agency, Inc., Bankers Fidelity Life Insurance Company, Georgia Casualty & Surety Company, Self-Insurance Administrators, Inc.

Officers: Hilton H. Howell/Dir., CEO, Pres./$785,000.00, Scott G. Thompson/Dir., CEO, Pres. - American Southern Insurance Company, Samuel E. Hudgins/Dir., Consultant, Robert J. Foskey/Assist. VP - Property, Casualty Actuarial Services, Katherine L. Slonina/Assist. VP - Property, Casualty Compliance Services, Eugene Choate/Pres. - Bankers Fidelity Life Insurance Company, John G. Sample/CFO, Sr. VP/$561,803.00, James A. Lynn/VP - Information Services, Barbara B. Snyder/VP - Human Resources, Michael J. Brasser/VP - Internal Audit, Casey B. Hudson/Assist. VP, Controller, Janie L. Ryan/Corp. Sec., Robert B. Deuben/Assist. VP - Corporate Communications

Directors: Hilton H. Howell/Dir., CEO, Pres., Scott G. Thompson/Dir., CEO, Pres. - American Southern Insurance Company, Mack J. Robinson/Chmn., Calvin L. Wall/Chmn. - American Southern Insurance Company, Raymond D. Riddle/74/Dir., William H. Whaley/Dir., Dom H. Wyant/Dir., Edward E. Elson/Dir., Harold K. Fischer/Dir., Mark C. West/Dir., Samuel E. Hudgins/Dir., Consultant, Harriett J. Robinson/Dir.

Owners: Raymond D. Riddle, John G. Sample, Harriett J. Robinson, Hilton H. Howell, Mark C. West, Scott G. Thompson, Harold K. Fischer, Insiders, William H. Whaley, Samuel E. Hudgins, Mack J. Robinson, Dom H. Wyant, Edward E. Elson

Financial Data: *Fiscal Year End:*12/31 *Latest Annual Data:* 12/31/2006

Year	Sales	Net Income
2006	$179,532,000	$8,936,000
2005	$185,085,000	-$3,175,000
2004	$190,102,000	$5,017,000

Curr. Assets:	$116,763,000	**Curr. Liab.:**	$42,949,000		
Plant, Equip.:	NA	**Total Liab.:**	$364,444,000	**Indic. Yr. Divd.:**	NA
Total Assets:	$458,632,000	**Net Worth:**	$94,188,000	**Debt/ Equity:**	0.4309

Atlantic Bancgroup Inc

1315 S 3rd St., Jacksonville Beach, FL, 32250; ***PH:*** 1-904-247-9494; ***Fax:*** 1-904-247-9402; ***http://*** www.oceansidebank.com

General - Incorporation	FL	***Stock***- Price on:12/24/2007	$40.1
Employees	47	Stock Exchange	NDQ
Auditor	Stevens, Powell & Co. P.A	Ticker Symbol	ATBC
Stk Agt	Registrar & Transfer Co	Outstanding Shares	1,250,000
Counsel	NA	E.P.S	$1.32
DUNS No.	NA	Shareholders	NA

Business: The group's principle activities are to provide general commercial banking services to businesses and individuals. The deposit services include demand deposit accounts, negotiable order of withdrawal accounts, money market accounts, certificates of deposit and various retirement accounts. The lending services include real estate loans, commercial loans and consumer and other loans. Other services provided by the group include check collections, purchase of federal funds, security safekeeping, investment services, coin and currency supplies, over line and liquidity loan participation and sales of loans to or participation with correspondent banks.

Primary SIC and add'l.: 6712 6022

CIK No: 0001087790

Subsidiaries: Oceanside Bank

Officers: Barry W. Chandler/Dir., CEO, Pres./$263,271.00, David L. Young/62/Exec. VP, CFO, Corp. Sec./$159,803.00, Gwen Dasher/Branch Mgr., Assist. VP, Lisa Harmon/Branch Mgr., Judy Kehrig/Branch Mgr., Banking Officer, Robin Leuthold/Branch Mgr., Assist. VP

Directors: Barry W. Chandler/Dir., CEO, Pres., Donald F. Glisson/48/Chmn., Frank J. Cervone/Dir., Conrad L. Williams/Dir., Jimmy D. Dubberly/Dir., Dennis M. Wolfson/Dir., Robin Scheiderman/Dir., Keith G. Watson/Dir., Gordon K. Watson/58/Dir.

Owners: Insiders/19.10%, Robin H. Scheiderman/4.09%, Jimmy D. Dubberly/0.65%, Barry W. Chandler/1.20%, Gordon K. Watson/6.41%, Donald F. Glisson/3.26%, Grady R. Kearsey/0.29%, Conrad L. Williams/0.49%, David L. Young/0.59%, Dennis M. Wolfson/0.95%, Frank J. Cervone/1.17%

Financial Data: *Fiscal Year End:*12/31 *Latest Annual Data:* 12/31/2006

Year	Sales	Net Income
2006	$16,580,000	$1,918,000
2005	$12,128,000	$1,478,000
2004	$9,164,000	$1,166,000

Curr. Assets:	$18,922,000	**Curr. Liab.:**	$219,904,000	**P/E Ratio:**	25.87
Plant, Equip.:	$3,960,000	**Total Liab.:**	$226,246,000	**Indic. Yr. Divd.:**	NA
Total Assets:	$243,497,000	**Net Worth:**	$17,251,000	**Debt/ Equity:**	0.3036

Atlantic City Electric Co

PO Box 231, Wilmington, DE, 19899; ***PH:*** 1-202-872-2000; ***http://*** www.conectiv.com

General - Incorporation	NJ	***Stock***- Price on:12/24/2007	NA
Employees	NA	Stock Exchange	NA
Auditor	PricewaterhouseCoopers LLP	Ticker Symbol	NA
Stk Agt	Bank of New York	Outstanding Shares	NA
Counsel	NA	E.P.S	NA
DUNS No.	00-697-1618	Shareholders	NA

Business: The group's principal activities are to generate, purchase, deliver and sell electricity throughout the United States. The regulated service area covers about 2,700 square miles within the southern one-third of New Jersey and has a population of approximately 0.9 million. The electricity is delivered to customers consisting of residents, commercials, industries and others. The group supplies electricity to customers within its service area with power purchased from other suppliers and electricity generated by its power plants.

Primary SIC and add'l.: 4911

CIK No: 0000008192

Subsidiaries: Delmarva Power & Light Company, Mirant Corporation, Pepco Holdings

Officers: Paul H. Barry/Sr. VP, CFO

Atlantic Coast Federal Corp

505 Haines Ave., Waycross, GA, 31501; *PH:* 1-912-283-4711; *Fax:* 1-912-284-2284; *http://* www.acfederal.net

General - Incorporation	Federal	**Stock**- Price on:12/24/2007	$16.79
Employees	162	Stock Exchange	NDQ
Auditor	Crowe, Chizek and Company LLC	Ticker Symbol	ACFC
Stk Agt	Registrar & Transfer Co	Outstanding Shares	13,680,000
Counsel	NA	E.P.S.	$0.23
DUNS No.	NA	Shareholders	NA

Business: The group operates through its subsidiaries whose principle activity is to provide financial services. The groups services include lending, deposits and borrowings. The financial products of the group include residential first and second mortgage loans, home equity loans, land and multifamily real estate loans, commercial real estate loans, construction loans. The group operates from Waycross, Douglas and Garden City, Georgia. The assets of the group for the year 2006 were $842,825 (thousands).

Primary SIC and add'l.: 6035 6712

CIK No: 0001284077

Subsidiaries: Atlantic Coast Bank, Atlantic Coast Holdings, Inc., Coastal Properties, Inc., First Community Financial Services, Inc.

Officers: Robert J. Larison/Dir., CEO, Pres., Thomas B. Wagers/COO, Carl W. Insel/Marketing Pres. - Florida, Phillip S. Buddenbohm/Sr. VP - Credit Administration, Jon C. Parker/Dir., Sr. VP, CFO, Tricia H. Echols/Marketing Pres. - Georgia, Philip S. Hubacher/Treasurer, Patrick J. Watson/Sr. VP - Principal, Marsha A. Boyette/Sr. VP - Administration, Dawna Miller/Sr. VP, CFO, Pamela T. Saxon/Sec.

Directors: Robert J. Larison/Dir., CEO, Pres., Charles E. Martin/Chmn., Thomas F. Beeckler/Dir., Jon C. Parker/Dir., Sr. VP, CFO, Eric W. Palmer/Dir., Forrest W. Sweat/Dir., Frederick D. Franklin/Dir., Robert J. Smith/Dir., Dennis H. Woods/Dir.

Owners: Jon C. Parker, Phillip S. Buddenbohm, W. Eric Palmer, H. Dennis Woods, Frederick D. Franklin, Robert J. Smith, Robert J. Larison, Thomas B. Wagers, Insiders, Carl W. Insel, Forrest W. Sweat, Thomas F. Beeckler, Charles E. Martin, Philip S. Hubacher, Atlantic Coast Federal, MHC 505 *(17 Owners included in Index)*

Financial Data: Fiscal Year End:12/31   Latest Annual Data: 12/31/2006

Year	Sales	Net Income
2006	$54,575,000	$5,129,000
2005	$44,748,000	$4,689,000
2004	$37,132,000	$3,192,000

Curr. Assets:	$45,756,000	**Curr. Liab.:**	$751,992,000	**P/E Ratio:**	57.90
Plant, Equip.:	$22,261,000	**Total Liab.:**	$751,992,000	**Indic. Yr. Divd.:**	$0.600
Total Assets:	$843,079,000	**Net Worth:**	$91,087,000	**Debt/ Equity:**	0.5947

Atlantic Liberty Financial Corp

186 Montague St. , Brooklyn, NY, 11201; ; *http://* www.atlanticlibertysavings.com

General - Incorporation	DE	**Stock**- Price on:12/24/2007	$16.66
Employees	260	Stock Exchange	NA
Auditor	Miller Ellin & Co. LLP	Ticker Symbol	NA
Stk Agt	Computershare Trust Co	Outstanding Shares	21,120,000
Counsel	Hughes Hubbard & Reed LLP	E.P.S.	$1.03
DUNS No.	NA	Shareholders	NA

Business: The group's principal activity is to accept retail deposits and provide loans. The deposits offered include passbook savings accounts, money market accounts, fixed-term certificates of deposit, and individual retirement accounts. The group offers one to four family residential mortgage loans, multi-family and commercial real estate loans. The group also invests in mortgage-related securities and various other securities. The banking services are provided at two locations in brooklyn, New York.

Primary SIC and add'l.: 6712 6035

CIK No: 0001172095

Subsidiaries: Atlantic Liberty Savings, F.A.

Financial Data: Fiscal Year End:03/31   Latest Annual Data: 12/31/2006

Year	Sales	Net Income
2006	$168,179,000	$21,639,000
2005	$139,733,000	$23,542,000
2004	$124,767,000	$22,649,000

Curr. Assets:	$42,583,000	**Curr. Liab.:**	$1,968,295,000	**P/E Ratio:**	15.28
Plant, Equip.:	$23,042,000	**Total Liab.:**	$2,618,106,000	**Indic. Yr. Divd.:**	$0.480
Total Assets:	$2,836,521,000	**Net Worth:**	$218,415,000	**Debt/ Equity:**	2.7826

Atlantic Pacific Bank

3725 Westwind Blvd, Ste. 100, Santa Rosa, CA, 95403; *PH:* 1-707-543-2700; *http://* www.apbconnect.com

General - Incorporation	NA	**Stock**- Price on:12/24/2007	$9.9
Employees	NA	Stock Exchange	OTC
Auditor	Perry-Smith, LLP	Ticker Symbol	APFB
Stk Agt	U.S. Stock Transfer Corp	Outstanding Shares	NA
Counsel	NA	E.P.S.	NA
DUNS No.	NA	Shareholders	NA

Business: The groups principal activity is banking operations. The group financial products include real estate financing, on line banking, personal banking, saving and fixed deposits. The group operates from the United States.

Primary SIC and add'l.: 6022

CIK No:

Officers: Charles O. Hall/Dir., CEO, Pres., Allen R. Christenson/CFO, Exec. VP, Jeanne Marie Reade/Exec. VP, Chief Credit Officer, Sheila Thomas Moran/Sr. VP, Dir. - Operations, Sean K. Olhan/Sr. VP, Chief Risk Officer, Terry Richter/Sr. VP, Branch Mgr., Sarah Davies/Sr. VP - Corporate Banking

Directors: Charles O. Hall/Dir., CEO, Pres., Timothy J. Jorstad/Chmn., Catherine H. Munson/Dir., Randall J. Verrue/Dir., Joseph C. Zils/Dir., Randy M. Decaminada/Dir., Richard A. Dowd/Dir., Robin R. Goble/Dir.

Atlantic Southern Financial Group Inc

1701 Bass Rd., Macon, GA, 31210; *PH:* 1-478-757-8181

General - Incorporation	GA	**Stock**- Price on:12/24/2007	NA
Employees	NA	Stock Exchange	NDQ
Auditor	Porter Keadle Moore, LLP	Ticker Symbol	ASFN
Stk Agt	Registrar & Transfer Co	Outstanding Shares	NA
Counsel	NA	E.P.S.	$1.85
DUNS No.	NA	Shareholders	NA

Business: The groups principal activity is to provide banking services. The group financial products include commercial real estate and construction loans, deposits like saving, mortgage loans, CD and Iras. The group operates from the United States. The groups asset in the year 2006 was $78,038,853.

Primary SIC and add'l.: 6712

CIK No: 0001313730

Subsidiaries: Atlantic Southern Bank, Sapelo Bancshares, Inc

Owners: Donald L. Moore, Raymond O. Ballard/1.17%, Peter R. Cates, Michael C. Griffin, George Waters, Thomas J. McMichael, Brandon L. Mercer, Carl E. Hofstadter/1.83%, Russell J. Lipford/1.40%, Hugh F. Smisson/3.82%, Laudis H. Lanford, Douglas J. Dunwody, Mark A. Stevens, Gary P. Hall, Tyler J. Rauls/2.68% *(19 Owners included in Index)*

Financial Data: Fiscal Year End:12/31   Latest Annual Data: 12/31/2006

Year	Sales	Net Income
2006	$39,577,000	$5,964,000
2005	$22,810,000	$3,885,000

Curr. Assets:	$48,481,000	**Curr. Liab.:**	$598,534,000		
Plant, Equip.:	$17,425,000	**Total Liab.:**	$608,844,000	**Indic. Yr. Divd.:**	NA
Total Assets:	$671,075,000	**Net Worth:**	$62,232,000	**Debt/ Equity:**	NA

Atlantic Syndication Network Inc

1800 Century Pk. E, Ste. 200, Los Angeles, CA, 90067; *PH:* 1-310-895-7778; *http://* www.thestockshow.com

General - Incorporation	NV	**Stock**- Price on:12/24/2007	$0.02
Employees	2	Stock Exchange	OTC
Auditor	Larry O'donnell, CPA, P.C	Ticker Symbol	ASNI
Stk Agt	OTC Corporate Transfer Service Co	Outstanding Shares	40,490,000
Counsel	Carmine Bua	E.P.S.	-$0.011
DUNS No.	NA	Shareholders	NA

Business: The group's principle activities are to develop, produce and distribute television programs and specific projects created for domestic and international markets. The television programs include entertainment, educational and informational programs. The group's productions include master of the martial arts, ninjaerobics(tm), the stock show(tm) and intervention shatters alcohol and drug addiction. It also produces and distributes commercials, infomercials and commissioned projects and provides third party consulting services. The consulting services are pertaining to project development, script, layout, production and editing and distribution of the product. The group also provides third party video production and postproduction services and videotape sales.

Primary SIC and add'l.: 7812

CIK No: 0001085129

Officers: Kent G. Wyantt/Dir., CEO, Pres. - Execitive Producer, Michael Ewards/Dir. - Boardcast , Producer, Sho Kosugi/Dir. - Boardcast , Producer, Thom Keith/Broadcast Dir., Producer, David Bergen/Broadcast Consultant, Broadcast Dir., Producer, Brandon Scott/Host, Commentator, Tony Dicarlo/Investor Relations Officer, Sarah E. Wyatt/68/Dir., Corp. Sec., Glen Schlosser/60/CFO

Directors: Kent G. Wyantt/Dir., CEO, Pres. - Execitive Producer, Thom Keith/Broadcast Dir., Producer, Sarah E. Wyatt/68/Dir., Corp. Sec.

Owners: Kent G. Wyatt/29.78%, Glen Schlosser/1.10%, Sarah E. Wyatt/14.92%, Michael S. Edward, Insiders/48.88%

Financial Data: Fiscal Year End:02/28   Latest Annual Data: 2/28/2007

Year	Sales	Net Income
2007	$16,000	-$449,000
2006	$6,000	-$439,000
2005	$5,000	-$293,000

Curr. Assets:	$0	**Curr. Liab.:**	$939,000		
Plant, Equip.:	NA	**Total Liab.:**	$960,000	**Indic. Yr. Divd.:**	NA
Total Assets:	$0	**Net Worth:**	-$960,000	**Debt/ Equity:**	NA

Atlantic Tele-Network Inc

10 Derby Sq., Salem, MA, 01970; *PH:* 1-978-619-1300; *Fax:* 1-978-744-3951; *http://* www.atni.com

General - Incorporation	DE	**Stock**- Price on:12/24/2007	$28.5
Employees	797	Stock Exchange	NDQ
Auditor	PricewaterhouseCoopers LLP	Ticker Symbol	ATNI
Stk Agt	Bank of New York	Outstanding Shares	15,190,000
Counsel	NA	E.P.S.	$2.12
DUNS No.	18-356-5613	Shareholders	NA

Business: The group's principle activity is to provide telecommunication services. The group operates through its subsidiaries: the Guyana Telephone and Telegraph Company, LTD (GT and T), Atlantic Tele-Center Inc (ATC), Bermuda Digital Communications, LTD (BDC), Choice Communications, LLC, ATN (Haiti) S.A. and Call Home Telecom, LLC. GT&T provides public telecommunications services in Guyana. It also provides yellow pages and other directory services and sales and service of telecommunication equipment. ATC is developing a call-center business in Guyana to provide services to businesses in the United States. BDC provides cellular telephone service in Bermuda under the name Cellular One. Choice Communications provides Internet service, specialized mobile radio, paging and wireless cable television services the U.S. Virgin Islands. The group provides Internet access and radio paging in Haiti. The group's quarterly revenue for September 2007 was 46.96 millions of USD.

Primary SIC and add'l.: 4813 4812

CIK No: 0000879585

Subsidiaries: Atlantic Tele-Center,Inc., ATN (Haiti) S.A., ATN (Haiti),Inc., Call Home Telecom, LLC., Chama Wireless, LLC, Choice Communications, LLC, Commnet Four Corners, LLC, Commnet Illinois, LLC, Commnet of California, LLC, Commnet of Missouri, LLC, Commnet Wireless, LLC, Elbert County Wireless, LLC, Excomm, LLC, Guyana Telephone and Telegraph Company Limited, Transnet S.A.

Officers: Michael T. Prior/CEO, Pres./$767,732.00, Cornelius B. Prior/Chmn., Exec. Officer/$338,750.00, Douglas J. Minster/VP, General Counsel, Andrew S. Fienberg/Chief Accounting Officer, Justin D. Benincasa/CFO, Treasurer/$680,443.00, John P. Audet/VP - Financial Analysis, Planning/$368,683.00, William F. Kreisher/Sr. VP - Corporate Development

Directors: Cornelius B. Prior/Chmn., Exec. Officer, Charles J. Roesslein/Dir., Henry U. Wheatley/Dir., Ernst A. Burri/63/Dir., Martin L. Budd/Dir., Brian A. Schuchman/Dir.

Owners: Justin D. Benincasa, Charles J. Roesslein, FMR Corp./7.90%, Steven J. Parrish, Insiders/38.00%, Ernst A. Burri, Henry U. Wheatley, Martin L. Budd, Michael T. Prior, Cornelius B. Prior/36.90%, John P. Audet, Brian A. Schuchman

Financial Data: Fiscal Year End: 12/31   **Latest Annual Data:** 12/31/2006

Year	Sales	Net Income
2006	$155,358,000	$23,500,000
2005	$102,281,000	$13,598,000
2004	$89,252,000	$12,117,000

Curr. Assets:	$91,139,000	**Curr. Liab.:**	$35,041,000		
Plant, Equip.:	$138,573,000	**Total Liab.:**	$123,844,000	**Indic. Yr. Divd.:**	$0.640
Total Assets:	$302,614,000	**Net Worth:**	$178,770,000	**Debt/ Equity:**	0.2709

Atlantic Wine Agencies Inc

Golden Cross House, 8 Duncannon St., London, WC2N 4JF; **PH:** 44-2074845005;
Fax: 44-2074844957; **http://** www.atlanticwineagencies.com; **Email:** info@atlanticwineagencies.com

General - Incorporation	FL	**Stock**- Price on:12/24/2007	$0.02
Employees	NA	Stock Exchange	OTC
Auditor	Meyler & Company, LLC	Ticker Symbol	AWNA
Stk Agt.	NA	Outstanding Shares	NA
Counsel	NA	E.P.S.	NA
DUNS No.	NA	Shareholders	NA

Business: The groups principle activity is to produce wine. The group operates from the United States and the United Kingdom. The groups quarterly revenue for September 2007 was 0.07 millions of USD.

Primary SIC and add'l.: 5182 6552

CIK No: 0001142790

Subsidiaries: Atlantic Wine Agencies Limited, Mount Rozier Estates Pty Ltd, Mount Rozier Properties Pty Ltd

Officers: Adam Mauerberger/Dir., CEO, CFO, Pres., Andy Bayley/Dir., Sr. VP - Sales, Marketing, Christopher Burr/Exec. Consultant, Larry Cherubino/Exec. Consultant

Directors: Adam Mauerberger/Dir., CEO, CFO, Pres., Andy Bayley/Dir., Sr. VP - Sales, Marketing

Owners: Crayson Properties Ltd/9.80%, Insiders/23.88%, Willowcreek International Ltd/23.81%, Adam Mauerberger/23.76%, Andy Bayley/0.12%

Financial Data: Fiscal Year End: 03/31   **Latest Annual Data:** 03/31/2007

Year	Sales	Net Income
2007	$197,000	-$1,565,000
2006	$1,132,000	-$2,270,000
2005	$121,000	-$1,651,000

Curr. Assets:	$919,000	**Curr. Liab.:**	$1,905,000		
Plant, Equip.:	$2,946,000	**Total Liab.:**	$1,905,000	**Indic. Yr. Divd.:**	NA
Total Assets:	$3,866,000	**Net Worth:**	$1,961,000	**Debt/ Equity:**	NA

Atlantica Inc

4685 S Highland Dr., Ste. 202, Salt Lake City, UT, 84117; **PH:** 1-801-278-9424

General - Incorporation	UT	**Stock**- Price on:12/24/2007	NA
Employees	NA	Stock Exchange	OTC
Auditor	HJ & Associates, LLC	Ticker Symbol	ATTC
Stk Agt.	Interwest Transfer Company, Inc.	Outstanding Shares	NA
Counsel	NA	E.P.S.	NA
DUNS No.	NA	Shareholders	NA

Business: The groups principal activity is to investigate assets, property or businesses to acquire business. The group operates from the United States.

Primary SIC and add'l.: 8742

CIK No: 0001062506

Subsidiaries: Allied Equities, Inc., Keys Equities, Inc

Officers: Alan D. Gordon/CEO, Pres., Shelley Goff/47/Dir., CFO, Sec., Duane S. Jenson/63/Dir., Pres., Terry Jenson/58/Dir., VP

Directors: Duane S. Jenson/63/Dir., Pres., Terry Jenson/58/Dir., VP, Shelley Goff/47/Dir., CFO, Sec.

Owners: Thomas J. Howells, Duane S. Jenson, Terry Jenson, Leonard W. Burningham, Travis T. Jenson

Atlantis Business Development Corp

6302 Mesedge Dr., Coloradosprings, CO, 80919; **PH:** 1-719-598-2469; **http://** www.atlantisbdc.com

General - Incorporation	NV	**Stock**- Price on:12/24/2007	NA
Employees	NA	Stock Exchange	OTC
Auditor	Bagell, Levine & Company, LLC	Ticker Symbol	ATNO
Stk Agt.	Signature Stock Transfer, Inc.	Outstanding Shares	NA
Counsel	NA	E.P.S.	NA
DUNS No.	NA	Shareholders	NA

Business: The groups principal activity is to provide managerial, accounting and financial advices. In the year 2005, the group merged with a Nevada corporation. The group operates from the United States.

Primary SIC and add'l.: 6799

CIK No: 0000812805

Subsidiaries: 727 Communications, Inc, E-Direct Inc.

Officers: Tim Deherrera/Chmn., CEO, Pres.

Directors: Tim Deherrera/Chmn., CEO, Pres., Gerald Jacoby/Dir., Frank Ganem/Dir.

Owners: Tim Deherrera, Insiders, Gerald Jacoby

Curr. Assets:	$6,000	**Curr. Liab.:**	$18,000		
Plant, Equip.:	NA	**Total Liab.:**	$18,000	**Indic. Yr. Divd.:**	NA
Total Assets:	$6,000	**Net Worth:**	-$12,000	**Debt/ Equity:**	NA

Atlantis Plastics Inc

1870 The Exchange, Ste. 200, Atlanta, GA, 30339; **PH:** 1-770-953-4567; **Fax:** 1-770-618-7080;
http:// www.atlantisplastics.com

General - Incorporation	DE	**Stock**- Price on:12/24/2007	$3.82
Employees	1,381	Stock Exchange	NDQ
Auditor	Ernst & Young LLP	Ticker Symbol	ATPL
Stk Agt	American Stock Transfer & Trust Co.	Outstanding Shares	8,260,000
Counsel	Greenberg Traurig	E.P.S.	-$0.924
DUNS No.	14-410-9170	Shareholders	NA

Business: The group's principal activity is to manufacture specialty and custom plastic products. The group operates in three segments: atlantis plastic films ('plastic films'), injection molding and profile extrusion. Plastic films segment manufactures stretch films, which are multilayer plastic films used principally to wrap pallets of materials for shipping or storage and custom film products that include high-grade laminating films, embossed films and specialty film products targeted primarily to industrial and packaging markets. Injection molding segment manufactures injection molded thermoplastic parts that are sold primarily to original equipment manufacturers and a variety of extruded plastic parts for trim and functional applications (profile extrusion) that are incorporated into a broad range of consumer and commercial products.

Primary SIC and add'l.: 2821 3089 3081 2671

CIK No: 0000811828

Officers: Earl W. Powell/69/Chmn., CEO, Lisa Pieper/National Sales Mgr., V. M. Philbrook/54/COO, Pres./$388,037.00, David Probst/GM, Paul Saari/CFO/$309,072.00, Ken Comer/National Sales Mgr., Tom Gifford/Dir. - Agency Sales, Proprietary Products, Brad Bastin/Marketing Dir. - Custom Films

Directors: Earl W. Powell/69/Chmn., CEO, Cesar L. Alvarez/60/Dir., Larry D. Horner/74/Dir., Charles D. Murphy/64/Dir., Jay Shuster/53/Dir., Chester B. Vanatta/72/Dir., Peter Vandenberg/52/Dir.

Owners: Earl W. Powell/57.20%, Insiders/57.20%, Chester B. Vanatta, Phillip T. George/10.40%, Phillip T. George/37.30%, Charles D. Murphy, Insiders/26.40%, Larry D. Horner, Jay Shuster, Cesar L. Alvarez, V. M. Philbrook, Earl W. Powell/23.20%, Peter Vandenberg, Stadium Capital Management, LLC/13.40%, Paul G. Saari

Financial Data: Fiscal Year End: 12/31   **Latest Annual Data:** 12/31/2006

Year	Sales	Net Income
2006	$418,667,000	-$4,146,000
2005	$424,326,000	$6,671,000
2004	$347,802,000	$11,515,000

Curr. Assets:	$94,644,000	**Curr. Liab.:**	$33,338,000		
Plant, Equip.:	$68,979,000	**Total Liab.:**	$251,081,000	**Indic. Yr. Divd.:**	NA
Total Assets:	$226,888,000	**Net Worth:**	-$24,193,000	**Debt/ Equity:**	NA

Atlas Air Worldwide Holdings Inc

2000 Westchester Ave., Purchase, NY, 10577; **PH:** 1-914-701-8000; **Fax:** 1-914-701-8444;
http:// www.atlasair.com; **Email:** info@atlasair.com

General - Incorporation	DE	**Stock**- Price on:12/24/2007	$58.28
Employees	1,840	Stock Exchange	NDQ
Auditor	Ernst& Young LLP	Ticker Symbol	AAWW
Stk Agt	Bank of New York	Outstanding Shares	21,280,000
Counsel	NA	E.P.S.	$3.27
DUNS No.	NA	Shareholders	NA

Business: The group operates through its subsidiaries whose principle activity is to provide aircraft operations and related services. The groups service is air cargo. The groups operates through four segments namely ACMI, scheduled service, AMC charter and commercial charter. Specific customers of the group include The International Airline of United Arab Emirates, British Airways, Qantas, Air New Zealand, Panalpina Airfreight Management, Lan Cargo and Instone Air Services, Inc. The group operates from the Asia, Europe, the Middle East, South America and the United States. The group's quarterly revenue for September 2007 was 395.94 millions of USD.

Primary SIC and add'l.: 4522 4512

CIK No: 0001135185

Subsidiaries: Atlas Air, Inc., Liege Global Cargo, Polar Air Cargo Worldwide, Inc., Polar Air Cargo, Inc.

Officers: William J. Flynn/Dir., CEO, Pres./$2,187,882.00, John W. Dietrich/COO, Exec. VP/$963,815.00, Ronald L. Lane/Sr. VP - Special Advisor/$795,266.00, Adam R. Kokas/Sr. VP, General Counsel, Sec., William C. Bradley/VP, Treasurer, James R. Cato/VP - Flight Operations, Labor Relations/$561,624.00, James Forbes/VP - Worldwide Ground Operations, Facilities, Properties, Lawrence B. Gibbons/VP - Procurement, Jason Grant/CFO, Sr. VP, Gordon L. Hutchinson/VP, Controller, Michael T. Steen/Sr. VP, Chief Marketing Officer, William E. Kelley/VP - Safety, Regulatory Compliance, Mark S. Swearingin/VP - Technical Operations, Gary Wade/VP - Security, Ken Johnson/VP - Charter Sales, Marketing, Charter Business Unit *(17 Officers included in Index)*

Directors: William J. Flynn/Dir., CEO, Pres., Eugene I. Davis/Chmn., Robert F. Agnew/Dir., Timothy J. Bernlohr/Dir., Keith E. Butler/Dir., Jeffrey H. Erickson/Dir., James S. Gilmore/Dir., Carol B. Hallett/Dir., Frederick McCorkle/Dir.

Owners: Robert F. Agnew, William J. Flynn, Carol B. Hallett, Ore Hill Partners LLC/5.90%, Jeffrey H. Erickson, Michael L. Barna, John W. Dietrich, Keith E. Butler, Insiders/2.50%, Eugene I. Davis, James S. Gilmore, Timothy J. Bernlohr, James R. Cato, Frederick McCorkle, JGD Management Corp./6.90% *(18 Owners included in Index)*

Financial Data: Fiscal Year End: 12/31   **Latest Annual Data:** 12/31/2006

Year	Sales	Net Income
2006	$1,476,330,000	$59,781,000
2005	$1,617,897,000	$73,861,000
2004	$1,414,661,000	$50,956,000

Curr. Assets:	$463,879,000	**Curr. Liab.:**	$209,872,000	**P/E Ratio:**	17.82
Plant, Equip.:	$583,271,000	**Total Liab.:**	$646,937,000	**Indic. Yr. Divd.:**	NA
Total Assets:	$1,119,780,000	**Net Worth:**	$472,843,000	**Debt/ Equity:**	0.8005

Atlas America Inc

311 Rouser Rd., Moon Township, PA, 15108; *PH:* 1-412-262-2830; *Fax:* 1-412-262-7430;
http:// www.atlasamerica.com

General - Incorporation	........DE	Stock- Price on:12/24/2007 ......$54.73
Employees	517	Stock Exchange........NDQ
Auditor	...Grant Thornton LLP	Ticker Symbol.......ATLS
Stk Agt.....	American Stock Transfer & Trust Co.	Outstanding Shares.......26,850,000
Counsel	...NA	E.P.S.......NA
DUNS No.	...NA	Shareholders.......NA

Business: The group's principal activities are the development, production and transportation of natural gas and oil in the appalachian basin. It conducts its natural gas transportation operations through atlas pipeline partners, l p. The group finance its drilling operations principally through funds raised from investors in its public and private drilling investment partnerships. Major customer of the group include first energy solutions corporation. On 16-Jul-2004, the group acquired spectrum field services, inc.

Primary SIC and add'l.: 1382 1381 1321

CIK No: 0001279228

Subsidiaries: AED Investments, Inc., AIC, Inc., Anthem Securities, Inc., APC Acquisition, LLC, ARD Investments, Inc., Atlas America Mid-Continent, Inc., Atlas Energy Corporation, Atlas Information Management, LLC, Atlas Noble Corp., Atlas Pipeline Mid-Continent LLC, Atlas Pipeline New York, LLC, Atlas Pipeline Ohio, LLC, Atlas Pipeline Operating Partnership, L.P., Atlas Pipeline Partners GP, LLC, Atlas Pipeline Partners, L.P. 26 Subsidiaries included in the Index

Officers: Edward E. Cohen/Chmn., CEO, Pres., Lisa Washington/Sec., Nancy J. McGurk/Chief Accounting Officer, Matthew A. Jones/CFO, Freddie M. Kotek/Exec. VP, Jeffrey C. Simmons/Exec. VP, Michael L. Staines/Exec. VP, Frank P. Carolas/Exec. VP, Bruce Bundy/Contact - Regional Marketing Dir. - Central, James M. O'Mara/Contact - Regional Marketing Dir. - Northeast, Vicki Burbridge/Contact - Regional Marketing Dir. - West, Robert J. Gourlay/Contact - Regional Marketing Dir. - Southeast

Directors: Edward E. Cohen/Chmn., CEO, Pres., Jonathan Z. Cohen/Vice Chmn., Donald W. Delson/Dir., Nicholas Dinubile/Dir., William R. Bagnell/Dir., Dennis A. Holtz/Dir., Harmon S. Spolan/72/Dir., Carlton M. Arrendell/Dir.

Owners: Freddie M. Kotek, Cobalt Capital Management, Inc./11.46%, Matthew A. Jones, Insiders/18.50%, Magnetar Financial LLC/10.05%, Edward E. Cohen/10.73%, Harmon S. Spolan, Jonathan Z. Cohen/5.65%, Donald W. Delson, Frank P. Carolas, Leon G. Cooperman/7.91%, Michael L. Staines, Nicholas A. DiNubile, Carlton M. Arrendell, Nancy J. McGurk *(18 Owners included in Index)*

*Financial Data: Fiscal Year End:*09/30 *Latest Annual Data:* 12/31/2006

Year	Sales	Net Income
2006	$749,306,000	$16,001,000
2005	$474,511,000	$32,940,000
2004	$180,856,000	$21,187,000

Curr. Assets:	$104,310,000	Curr. Liab.:	$181,118,000		
Plant, Equip.:	$505,967,000	Total Liab.:	$449,238,000	Indic. Yr. Divd.:	$0.030
Total Assets:	$759,711,000	Net Worth:	$120,351,000	Debt/ Equity:	7.5388

Atlas America Series 25-2004 A LP

311 Rouser Rd., Moon Township, PA, 15108; *PH:* 1-412-262-2830; *http://* www.atlasamerica.com

General - Incorporation	........DE	Stock- Price on:12/24/2007 ......NA
Employees	...NA	Stock Exchange.......NA
Auditor	...Grant Thornton LLP	Ticker Symbol.......NA
Stk Agt.	...American Stk Excng	Outstanding Shares.......NA
Counsel	...NA	E.P.S.......NA
DUNS No.	...NA	Shareholders.......NA

Business: The group is a Delaware limited partnership with Atlas Resources, Inc. as its managing general partner. On the final closing on May 31, 2004, the group had 635 investors who purchased Units (the "participants"). Units mean limited partner units and investor general partner units, which will be automatically converted into limited partner units once our wells are drilled and completed. In accordance with the terms of the offering, 1,077.56 Units were sold at $25,000 per Unit, 21.62 Units were sold at $23,000 per Unit to selling agents and their registered representatives and principals and a client of a registered investment advisor. 6.58 Units were sold at $21,625 per Unit to the managing general partner, its officers, directors and affiliates, and investors who bought Units through the officers and directors of the managing general partner. Also, one Unit was sold at $22,500.

Primary SIC and add'l.: 1311

CIK No: 0001283810

Subsidiaries: Atlas America, Inc.

Atlas America Series 25-2004 B LP

311 Rouser Rd., Moon Township, PA, 15108; *PH:* 1-412-262-2830; *http://* www.atlasamerica.com

General - Incorporation	........DE	Stock- Price on:12/24/2007 ......NA
Employees	...NA	Stock Exchange.......NA
Auditor	...Grant Thornton LLP	Ticker Symbol.......NA
Stk Agt.	...NA	Outstanding Shares.......NA
Counsel	...NA	E.P.S.......NA
DUNS No.	...NA	Shareholders.......NA

Business: The groups principle activities include developing, producing and transporting of natural gas. The group operates from United States.

Primary SIC and add'l.: 1311

CIK No: 0001294208

Officers: Freddie M. Kotek/Exec. VP, Chmn., CEO, Pres., Edward E. Cohen/Chmn., CEO, Pres., Matthew A. Jones/CFO, Jeffrey C. Simmons/49/Sr. VP - Operations, Jack L. Hollander/51/Sr. VP - Direct Participation Programs, Frank P. Carolas/Exec. VP, Nancy J. McGurk/52/Chief Accounting Officer, VP, Michael L. Staines/58/Dir., Exec. VP

Directors: Edward E. Cohen/Chmn., CEO, Pres., Jonathan Z. Cohen/Vice Chmn., Carlton M. Arrendell/Dir., Michael L. Staines/58/Dir., Exec. VP, William R. Bagnell/Dir., Donald W. Delson/Dir., Nicholas Dinubile/Dir., Dennis A. Holtz/Dir.

Atlas Mining Co

Atlas Mining Company, Osburn, ID, 83849; *PH:* 1-208-783-0270; *Fax:* 1-208-556-6741;
http:// www.atlasmining.com; *Email:* admin@atlasmining.com

General - Incorporation	...ID	Stock- Price on:12/24/2007 ......$2.629
Employees	...14	Stock Exchange.......OTC
Auditor	...Chisholm Bierwolf & Nilson LLC	Ticker Symbol.......ALMI
Stk Agt.	...Cottonwood Stock Transfer	Outstanding Shares.......53,090,000
Counsel	...Law Offices of Gary L. Blum	E.P.S.......NA
DUNS No.	...NA	Shareholders.......NA

Business: The group's principal activities are to acquire, explore and develop resource properties in the states of Idaho and Utah. It also provides contract-mining services and specialized civil construction services for mine operators, exploration companies and the construction and natural resources industries. In addition, the group has harvestable timber resources on its exploration properties in northern Idaho.

Primary SIC and add'l.: 1499 1081 2421

CIK No: 0000008328

Subsidiaries: Dragon Mine

Officers: Robert Dumont/CEO, Pres., Barbara Suveg/CFO, Frank Fausett/Operations Supervisor, Ron Short/Operations Mgr.

Directors: William T. Jacobson/Chmn.

Owners: Ronald R. Price, Kurt Hoffman, Marqueta Martinez, William T. Jacobson/3.30%, Insiders/3.60%, John Harvey

*Financial Data: Fiscal Year End:*12/31 *Latest Annual Data:* 12/31/2006

Year	Sales	Net Income
2006	$3,800,000	-$1,993,000
2005	$628,000	-$3,780,000
2004	$1,035,000	-$946,000

Curr. Assets:	$1,282,000	Curr. Liab.:	$638,000		
Plant, Equip.:	$2,978,000	Total Liab.:	$855,000	Indic. Yr. Divd.:	NA
Total Assets:	$4,310,000	Net Worth:	$3,403,000	Debt/ Equity:	0.0637

Atlas Pipeline Holdings LP

311 Rouser Rd., Moon Township, PA, 15108; *PH:* 1-412-262-2830; *Fax:* 1-412-262-2820;
http:// www.atlaspipelineholdings.com

General - Incorporation	........DE	Stock- Price on:12/24/2007 ......$39.94
Employees	...NA	Stock Exchange.......NYSE
Auditor	...Grant Thornton LLP	Ticker Symbol.......AHD
Stk Agt.....	American Stock Transfer & Trust Co.	Outstanding Shares.......21,100,000
Counsel	...NA	E.P.S.......$0.078
DUNS No.	...NA	Shareholders.......NA

Business: The groups principle activities include transmitting, gathering and processing of natural gas. The group operates through two segments namely, mid-continent operations and appalachia operations. The group acquired Atlas Arkansas Pipeline LLC in October 2005 and NOARK Pipeline System, Limited Partnership in May 2006. The group operates from the United States. The group's quarterly revenue for September 2007 was 242.30 millions of USD.

Primary SIC and add'l.: 4922

CIK No: 0001347218

Subsidiaries: Atlas Arkansas Pipeline LLC, Atlas Pipeline Finance Corp., Atlas Pipeline Mid-Continent LLC, Atlas Pipeline New York, LLC, Atlas Pipeline Ohio, LLC, Atlas Pipeline Operating Partnership, L.P., Atlas Pipeline Partners GP, LLC, Atlas Pipeline Partners, L.P., Atlas Pipeline Pennsylvania, LLC, Elk City Oklahoma GP, LLC, Elk City Oklahoma Pipeline, L.P., Mid-Continent Arkansas Pipeline, LLC, NOARK Energy Services, LLC, NOARK Pipeline System, Limited Partnership, Ozark Gas Gathering, LLC 16 Subsidiaries included in the Index

Officers: Edward E. Cohen/68/Chmn., CEO, Robert R. Firth/52/Dir., COO, Pres., Matthew A. Jones/45/Dir., CFO, Lisa Washington/39/Chief Legal Officer, Sec., Sean P. McGrath/35/Chief Accounting Officer, Daniel C. Herz/30/VP - Corporate Development, Brian Begley/VP - Investor Relations

Directors: Edward E. Cohen/68/Chmn., CEO, Jonathan Z. Cohen/36/Vice Chmn., Robert R. Firth/52/Dir., COO, Pres., Matthew A. Jones/45/Dir., CFO, William G. Karis/58/Dir., Harvey G. Magarick/67/Dir., Jeffrey C. Key/Dir.

Owners: Robert R. Firth, Atlas America, Inc./82.90%, Insiders

*Financial Data: Fiscal Year End:*12/31 *Latest Annual Data:* 12/31/2006

Year	Sales	Net Income
2006	$465,061,000	$18,538,000

Curr. Assets:	$76,403,000	Curr. Liab.:	$75,496,000		
Plant, Equip.:	$607,097,000	Total Liab.:	$794,144,000	Indic. Yr. Divd.:	$1.280
Total Assets:	$787,134,000	Net Worth:	-$7,010,000	Debt/ Equity:	NA

Atlas Pipeline Partners LP

311 Rouser Rd., Moon Township, PA, 15108; *PH:* 1-412-262-2830; *Fax:* 1-412-262-2820;
http:// www.atlaspipelinepartners.com

General - Incorporation	........DE	Stock- Price on:12/24/2007 ......$54
Employees	...NA	Stock Exchange.......NYSE
Auditor	...Grant Thornton LLP	Ticker Symbol.......APL
Stk Agt.....	American Stock Transfer & Trust Co.	Outstanding Shares.......13,080,000
Counsel	...NA	E.P.S.......-$3.16
DUNS No.	...NA	Shareholders.......NA

Business: The groups principle activities include transmitting, gathering and processing of natural gas. The group operates through two segments namely, mid-continent operations and appalachia operations. The group acquired Atlas Arkansas Pipeline LLC in October 2005 and NOARK Pipeline System, Limited Partnership in May 2006. The group operates from the United States. The group's quarterly revenue for September 2007 was 242.30 millions of USD.

Primary SIC and add'l.: 4922

CIK No: 0001092914

Subsidiaries: Atlas Arkansas Pipeline LLC, Atlas Pipeline Finance Corp., Atlas Pipeline Mid-Continent LLC, Atlas Pipeline New York, LLC, Atlas Pipeline Ohio, LLC, Atlas Pipeline Operating Partnership, L.P., Atlas Pipeline Pennsylvania, LLC, Elk City Oklahoma GP, LLC, Elk City Oklahoma Pipeline, L.P., Mid-Continent Arkansas Pipeline, LLC, NOARK Energy Services, LLC, NOARK Pipeline System, Limited Partnership, Ozark Gas Gathering, LLC, Ozark Gas Transmission, LLC

Officers: Edward E. Cohen/Chmn., CEO, Robert R. Firth/52/Pres., CEO - Atlas Pipeline Mid, Continent, LLC, Jonathan Z. Cohen/Vice Chmn. - Managing Board, Michael L. Staines/Dir., COO, Pres., MD, Matthew A. Jones/CFO, Sean P. McGrath/Chief Accounting Officer, Frank Carolas/VP, Jeffrey C. Simmons/VP, Daniel C. Herz/VP, Lisa Washington/Chief Legal Officer, Sec.

Directors: Edward E. Cohen/Chmn., CEO, Jonathan Z. Cohen/Vice Chmn. - Managing Board, Michael L. Staines/Dir., COO, Pres., MD, Tony C. Banks/Dir., Curtis D. Clifford/Dir., Gayle P.W. Jackson/Dir., Martin Rudolph/Dir.

Owners: Michael L. Staines, Jonathan Z. Cohen, Edward E. Cohen, Tony C. Banks, Elliott Associates, L.P./7.46%, Martin Rudolph, Insiders, Matthew A. Jones, Gayle P.W. Jackson, Robert R. Firth, Atlas Pipeline Partners GP, LLC/12.55%, Kayne Anderson Capital Advisors/Richard A. Kayne/7.13%, Curtis D. Clifford

Financial Data: Fiscal Year End:12/31 Latest Annual Data: 12/31/2006

Year	Sales	Net Income
2006	$464,692,000	$33,665,000
2005	$371,500,000	$25,752,000
2004	$91,291,000	$18,334,000

Curr. Assets:	$76,469,000	Curr. Liab.:	$75,233,000		
Plant, Equip.:	$607,097,000	Total Liab.:	$407,750,000	Indic. Yr. Divd.:	$3.640
Total Assets:	$786,884,000	Net Worth:	$379,134,000	Debt/ Equity:	0.9634

Atlas South Sea Pearl Ltd

Formerly: Atlas Pacific Ltd
43 York St., Subiaco Western, 6008; *PH:* 61-8933-67955; *http://* www.atlaspacific.com.au

General - Incorporation	Australia	Stock- Price on:12/24/2007	$8.16
Employees	NA	Stock Exchange	NDQ
Auditor	BDO Chartered Accountants	Ticker Symbol	APCFY
Stk Agt	NA	Outstanding Shares	NA
Counsel	NA	E.P.S.	NA
DUNS No.	75-756-6153	Shareholders	NA

Business: The group's principal activity is the development and management of a pearl farming business located in Australia and Indonesia.

Primary SIC and add'l.: 0919

CIK No: 0001011974

Subsidiaries: Tansim Pty Ltd

Officers: Joseph James Uel Taylor/Dir., MD, CEO, Jan Seir Jorgensen/42/Mgr. - Pearl Production, Simon Charles Bunbury Adams/CFO, Company Sec.

Directors: Joseph James Uel Taylor/Dir., MD, CEO, George Robert Warwick Snow/Chmn., Ian Mckenzie Murchison/Dir., Stephen John Arrow/Dir., Stephen Paul Birkbeck/Dir.

Owners: Stephen Paul Birkbeck/0.88%, Joseph James Uel Taylor/1.35%, Jan Seir Jorgensen/0.83%, Ian McKenzie Murchison/0.77%, Stephen John Arrow/2.17%, Simon Charles Bunbury Adams/0.56%, George Robert Warwick Snow/15.97%

Financial Data: Fiscal Year End:12/31 Latest Annual Data: 12/31/2006

Year	Sales	Net Income
2006	$10,439,000	$2,554,000
2005	$7,190,000	$1,514,000
2004	$5,334,000	-$2,666,000

Curr. Assets:	$11,204,000	Curr. Liab.:	$3,373,000		
Plant, Equip.:	$2,109,000	Total Liab.:	$3,412,000	Indic. Yr. Divd.:	NA
Total Assets:	$17,738,000	Net Worth:	$14,326,000	Debt/ Equity:	NA

Atlas Technology Group Inc

Formerly: Tribeworks Inc
2001 152nd Ave. Ne, Redmond, WA, 98052; *PH:* 1-425-458-2360

General - Incorporation	DE	Stock- Price on:12/24/2007	$1
Employees	31	Stock Exchange	NA
Auditor	Williams & Webster, P.S	Ticker Symbol	NA
Stk Agt	Holladay Stock Transfer	Outstanding Shares	26,330,000
Counsel	NA	E.P.S.	-$0.09
DUNS No.	NA	Shareholders	NA

Business: The groups principle activities include selling software and through two main distributions channel the graphics software tools business and the enterprise application development business. The group markets its product under the tradename iShell(R). Customers of the group include graphic industry professionals. In January 2006, the group acquired TakeCareofIT Holdings Ltd. The group operates from the United States.

Primary SIC and add'l.: 7374

CIK No: 0001093636

Subsidiaries: TakeCareofIT (NZ) Limited, TakeCareofIT (US) Inc., TakeCareofIT Holdings Limited, TakeCareofIT Limited, Tribeworks Development Corporation

Officers: Peter Jacobson/Dir., CEO - Sales, Marketing Officer/$100,000.00, Robert Altinger/Exec. Chmn./$145,000.00, Michael Murphy/COO, B. S.P. Marra/Dir., CFO/$100,000.00

Directors: Peter Jacobson/Dir., CEO - Sales, Marketing Officer, Robert Altinger/Exec. Chmn., B. S.P. Marra/Dir., CFO, Gordon W. Blankstein/Dir., Robert C. Gardner/Dir., Andrew Berger/Dir.

Owners: Pharaoh Properties Corporation/7.50%, Gordon W. Blankstein/2.30%, Robert Altinger/5.90%, Robert C. Gardner/1.90%, Michael T. Murphy/16.40%, Insiders/25.00%, Robert Blankstein/8.10%, WebConsult Limited/8.30%, Peter Jacobson/5.90%

Financial Data: Fiscal Year End:12/31 Latest Annual Data: 12/31/2006

Year	Sales	Net Income
2006	$40,000	-$1,992,000
2005	$594,000	-$176,000
2004	$822,000	-$194,000

Curr. Assets:	$206,000	Curr. Liab.:	$900,000		
Plant, Equip.:	$210,000	Total Liab.:	$900,000	Indic. Yr. Divd.:	NA
Total Assets:	$1,672,000	Net Worth:	$772,000	Debt/ Equity:	NA

ATM Financial Corp

2533 North Carson St., Carson, NV, 89706; *PH:* 1-775-841-7018

General - Incorporation	NV	Stock- Price on:12/24/2007	$0.75
Employees	NA	Stock Exchange	OTC
Auditor	Vellmer & Chang	Ticker Symbol	AFIC
Stk Agt	Signature Stock Transfer, Inc.	Outstanding Shares	5,730,000
Counsel	NA	E.P.S.	$0.00
DUNS No.	NA	Shareholders	NA

Business: The groups principal activity is to provide shared cash dispensing and related services to independent operators of automated teller machines. The group operates from the United States.

Primary SIC and add'l.: 7389

CIK No: 0001221554

Officers: Viktoria Vynnyk/Dir., CEO, CFO, Pres.

Directors: Viktoria Vynnyk/Dir., CEO, CFO, Pres.

Owners: Viktoria Vynnyk/70.00%, Insiders/70.00%

Financial Data: Fiscal Year End:12/31 Latest Annual Data: 12/31/2006

Year	Sales	Net Income
2006	NA	-$16,000
2005	NA	-$19,000

Curr. Assets:	$103,000	Curr. Liab.:	$27,000		
Plant, Equip.:	$3,000	Total Liab.:	$27,000	Indic. Yr. Divd.:	NA
Total Assets:	$106,000	Net Worth:	$79,000	Debt/ Equity:	NA

Atmel Corp

2325 Orchard Pkwy., San Jose, CA, 95131; *PH:* 1-408-441-0311; *Fax:* 1-408-436-4314; *http://* www.atmel.com; *Email:* invest@atmel.com

General - Incorporation	DE	Stock- Price on:12/24/2007	$5.44
Employees	7,992	Stock Exchange	NDQ
Auditor	PricewaterhouseCoopers LLP	Ticker Symbol	ATML
Stk Agt	Chase Mellon Shareholder Services	Outstanding Shares	488,840,000
Counsel	NA	E.P.S.	$0.06
DUNS No.	12-138-5264	Shareholders	NA

Business: The group's principal activity is to design, develop, manufacture and sell integrated circuit ('ic') products. It operates in four segments: application specific integrated circuit ('asic'), microcontrollers, nonvolatile memories and radio frequency ('rf') and automotive. Asic segment includes custom ics designed to meet specialized single-customer requirements. Microcontrollers segment includes proprietary and standard microcontrollers. Nonvolatile memories segment includes serial and parallel interface flash memories, eeproms and eproms. Rf and automotive segment includes radio frequency and analog circuits. Products are marketed in the communications, consumer electronics computing, storage and printing, security, automotive, military and aerospace industries. Customers include ericsson, matsushita, microsoft, hewlett-packard, schlumberger, daimler-chrysler and raytheon. International operations are in the United Kingdom, France, Japan, China and Germany.

Primary SIC and add'l.: 3674

CIK No: 0000872448

Subsidiaries: ACP Test Company, Inc., APT Property Investments, Inc., Atmel Acquisition Corporation, Atmel Asia Limited, Atmel B.V., Atmel Duisburg GmbH, Atmel Europe SARL, Atmel Finance Inc., Atmel France SARL, Atmel FSC, Inc., Atmel Germany GmbH, Atmel Grenoble S.A.S., Atmel Hellas A.E., Atmel Holding GmbH, Atmel Irving LLC 46 Subsidiaries included in the Index

Officers: Steven Laub/Dir., CEO, Pres./$1,129,046.00, Robert Valiton/VP - Americas Sales, Global Sales Operations, Jean Vaylet/VP, GM - Biometry Business Unit, Walter Lifsey/Sr. VP - Operations, Michel Thouvenin/VP - European Sales, Chih Jen/Exec. VP, GM - Asia, Japan Operations, Ken Kwong/VP - Corporate Marketing, Steve Schumann/VP - Engineering, Rod Erin/VP - Non - Volatile Memories Business Unit, Patrick Reutens/Chief Legal Officer, Graham Turner/VP, GM - Microcontroller Business Unit/$666,931.00, Robert Avery/VP - Finance, CFO/$842,076.00, Bernard Pruniaux/VP, GM - Asic Business Unit/$669,156.00, Robert McConnell/VP, GM - RF, Automotive Business Unit, Tsung-Ching Wu/Dir., Exec. VP - Office, Pres./$963,544.00 *(16 Officers included in Index)*

Directors: Steven Laub/Dir., CEO, Pres., David Sugishita/Chmn., Tsung-Ching Wu/Dir., Exec. VP - Office, Pres., Pierre Fougere/Dir., Papken Der Torossian/Dir., Jack L. Saltich/Dir., Peter T. Thomas/Dir., Chaiho Kim/Dir.

Owners: Steven Laub, Insiders/2.67%, Graham Turner, Papken Der Torossian, Tsung-Ching Wu/1.71%, Pierre Fougere, T. Peter Thomas, Goldman Sachs Asset Management, L.P./10.02%, David Sugishita, Chaiho Kim, Robert Avery, George Perlegos/5.29%, Bernard Pruniaux, FMR Corp./12.07%

Financial Data: Fiscal Year End:12/31 Latest Annual Data: 12/31/2006

Year	Sales	Net Income
2006	$1,670,887,000	$14,650,000
2005	$1,675,715,000	-$32,898,000
2004	$1,649,722,000	-$2,434,000

Curr. Assets:	$1,152,539,000	Curr. Liab.:	$567,376,000	P/E Ratio:	90.67
Plant, Equip.:	$638,146,000	Total Liab.:	$864,645,000	Indic. Yr. Divd.:	NA
Total Assets:	$1,818,539,000	Net Worth:	$953,894,000	Debt/ Equity:	0.2350

ATMI Inc

7 Commerce Dr., Danbury, CT, 06810; *PH:* 1-203-794-1100; *Fax:* 1-203-792-8040; *http://* www.atmi.com; *Email:* info@atmi.com

General - Incorporation	DE	Stock- Price on:12/24/2007	$31.89
Employees	806	Stock Exchange	NDQ
Auditor	Ernst & Young LLP	Ticker Symbol	ATMI
Stk Agt	BankBoston, N.A	Outstanding Shares	34,510,000
Counsel	Kramer, Levin, Naftalis & Frankel	E.P.S.	$1.07
DUNS No.	15-725-4749	Shareholders	NA

Business: The group's principal activity is to supply materials, materials delivery systems and high-putiy materials packaging products used in the manufacture of semiconductor devices. The group caters front-end semiconductor markets, which includes processes used to convert bare silicon wafers into fully functional wafers that contain copies of a semiconductor chip. On 14-Jul-2003, the group acquired all of the outstanding capital stock of esc, inc. In 2004, the group completed the sale of gallium nitride materials business.

Primary SIC and add'l.: 8731 3559

CIK No: 0001041577

Subsidiaries: Advanced Delivery & Chemical Systems Holdings, LLC, Advanced Delivery & Chemical Systems Manager, Inc., Advanced Delivery & Chemical Systems Nevada, Inc., Advanced Delivery & Chemical Systems Operating, LLC, Advanced Technology Materials, Inc., ATMI Acquisition BVBA, ATMI Belgium Holdings, Inc., ATMI Belgium, LLC, ATMI Ecosys Corporation, ATMI Fab Services Ireland, Ltd, ATMI GmbH, ATMI International Holdings, Inc., ATMI International Trading Co. Ltd., ATMI Japan KK, ATMI Korea Co. Ltd. 23 Subsidiaries included in the Index

Officers: Douglas Neugold/Dir., CEO, Pres./$2,042,302.00, Kevin Laing/CIO, VP, Tod Higinbotham/Exec. VP - Process Solutions/$859,231.00, Tim Carlson/Exec. VP, CFO, Treasurer, Tom McGowan/VP - Human Resources, Organizational Development, Cynthia Shereda/47/Exec. VP, Chief Legal Officer, Sec./$723,107.00, Dan Sharkey/Exec. VP - Business Development/$935,531.00, Paul Hohlstein/Sr. VP - Supply Chain, Operations, Stephen Curtis/Sr. VP - Sales

Directors: Douglas Neugold/Dir., CEO, Pres., Gene Banucci/Chmn., Stephen Mahle/Dir., Frederick Flynn/Dir., Cheryl Shavers/Dir., Mark Adley/Dir., Douglas C. Marsh/Dir., Robert Hillas/Dir.

Owners: Ziff Brothers Investments LLC/6.80%, Mark A. Adley, Gerald Catenacci/7.70%, Cheryl L. Shavers, Frederick C. Flynn, Stephen H. Mahle, Daniel P. Sharkey, T. Rowe Price Associates, Inc./5.20%, Eugene G. Banucci/1.30%, Robert S. Hillas, Tod A. Higinbotham, Douglas A. Neugold/1.10%, Insiders/4.90%, FMR Corp/10.20%, Cynthia L. Shereda *(16 Owners included in Index)*

Financial Data: Fiscal Year End:12/31 Latest Annual Data: 12/31/2006

Year	Sales	Net Income
2006	$325,913,000	$39,961,000
2005	$281,754,000	$30,722,000
2004	$246,291,000	$31,502,000

Curr. Assets:	$332,234,000	Curr. Liab.:	$50,872,000	P/E Ratio: 29.80
Plant, Equip.:	$92,719,000	Total Liab.:	$52,541,000	Indic. Yr. Divd.: NA
Total Assets:	$488,037,000	Net Worth:	$435,496,000	Debt/ Equity: NA

Atmos Energy Corp

3 Lincoln Ctr., 5430 LBJ Fwy., Ste. 1800, Dallas, TX, 75240; *PH:* 1-972-934-9227; *Fax:* 1-972-855-3040; *http://* www.atmosenergy.com

General - Incorporation	TX	**Stock**- Price on:12/24/2007	$30.22
Employees	4,632	Stock Exchange	NYSE
Auditor	Ernst & Young LLP	Ticker Symbol	ATO
Stk Agt	American Stock Transfer & Trust Co.	Outstanding Shares	88,810,000
Counsel	NA	E.P.S.	$2.09
DUNS No.	10-820-3241	Shareholders	NA

Business: The group's principle activity is to provide natural gas. The group operates from United States.

Primary SIC and add'l.: 4924 4911

CIK No: 0000731802

Subsidiaries: Atmos Energy Holdings, Inc., Atmos Energy Marketing, LLC, Atmos Energy Services, LLC, Atmos Exploration And Production, Inc., Atmos Gathering Company, LLC, Atmos Pipeline And Storage, LLC, Atmos Power Systems, Inc., Blue Flame Insurance Services, Ltd, Egasco, LLC, Energas Energy Services Trust, Enermart Energy Services Trust, Legendary Lighting, LLC, Mississippi Energies, Inc., Pdh I Holding Company, Inc, Straight Creek Gathering Gp, LLC 22 Subsidiaries included in the Index

Officers: Robert W. Best/Chmn., CEO, Pres., Gary W. Gregory/Pres. - West Texas Division, Doug Hill/Mgr. - Public Affairs, Richard A. Erskine/Pres. - Mid, Tex Division, Pres. - Atmos Pipeline, Texas, Ray Granado/Contact - Media Relations, Rand Lavonn/Contact - Public Communications, Darwin Winfield/Mgr. - Public Affairs, David Park/Mgr. - Public Affairs, Mark H. Johnson/Sr. VP - Nonutility Operations, Pres. - Atmos Energy Marketing, LLC, Ron W. McDowell/VP - New Business Ventures, Pres. - Atmos Energy Services, Atmos Power Systems, Gary L. Schlessman/Pres. - Colorado, Kansas Division, Susan Kappes Giles/VP - Investor Relations, Fred E. Meisenheimer/VP, Controller, Conrad E. Gruber/VP - Strategic Planning, Verlon R. Aston/VP - Governmental, Public Affairs *(49 Officers included in Index)*

Directors: Robert W. Best/Chmn., CEO, Pres., Thomas C. Meredith/Dir., Richard Ware/Dir., Nancy K. Quinn/Dir., Charles K. Vaughan/Dir., Richard W. Douglas/Dir., Phillip E. Nichol/Dir., Dan Busbee/Dir., Thomas J. Garland/Dir., Lee E. Schlessman/Dir., Stephen R. Springer/Dir., Travis W. Bain/Dir., Richard K. Gordon/Dir., Richard W. Cardin/Dir.

Owners: John P. Reddy, Robert W. Best, Phillip E. Nichol, Barclays Global Investors, NA/5.50%, Mark H. Johnson, Travis W. Bain, Dan Busbee, Charles K. Vaughan, Richard W. Cardin, Franklin Resources, Inc./7.80%, Louis P. Gregory, Richard Ware, Thomas J. Garland, Stephen R. Springer, Thomas C. Meredith *(19 Owners included in Index)*

Financial Data: Fiscal Year End:09/30 Latest Annual Data: 9/30/2006

Year	Sales	Net Income
2006	$6,152,363,000	$147,737,000
2005	$4,973,326,000	$135,785,000
2004	$2,920,037,000	$86,227,000

Curr. Assets:	$1,117,545,000	Curr. Liab.:	$1,119,161,000	P/E Ratio: 14.46
Plant, Equip.:	$3,629,156,000	Total Liab.:	$4,071,449,000	Indic. Yr. Divd.: $1.280
Total Assets:	$5,719,547,000	Net Worth:	$1,648,098,000	Debt/ Equity: 0.9289

Atmospheric Glow Technologies Inc

924 Corridor Pk. Blvd, Knoxville, TN, 37932; *PH:* 1-865-777-3776; *Fax:* 1-865-777-3767; *http://* www.a-gtech.com; *Email:* info@atmosphericglow.com

General - Incorporation	DE	**Stock**- Price on:12/24/2007	$0.025
Employees	28	Stock Exchange	OTC
Auditor	Coulter & Justus, P.C	Ticker Symbol	AGWT
Stk Agt	Mid-US Bk of Louisville & Trust Co	Outstanding Shares	237,540,000
Counsel	NA	E.P.S.	-$0.01
DUNS No.	15-898-6732	Shareholders	NA

Business: The group's principal activity is to develop commercial applications for the one atmosphere uniform glow discharge plasma, a process of non-thermal, atmospheric pressure processing for use in areas such as sterilization, decontamination, surface cleaning and etching. The group's technology is a simple, lower cost plasma generation technique. Atmospheric plasma is created by electrically energizing air at standard atmospheric pressure and ambient temperature generating highly reactive, short lived chemistry that can be used in a variety of commercial applications. The group is a development stage company.

Primary SIC and add'l.: 2834

CIK No: 0001020676

Subsidiaries: LandOak Company, LLC, Tice Engineering and Sales, Inc.

Officers: Scott W. McDonald/CEO, Carolyn Young/Administrative Support, John Halliwell/Sr. Electrical Engineer, Chris Coleman/Mechanical Engineer, Jim Davis/Laboratory Technician, Charles K. Brown/Machine Shop Supervisor, Rancy C. Merritt/Machine Shop Assist., Melissa A. Preston/Administrative Assist., Suzanne L. South/Co - Founder, Member - Agt's Management Team, Jacque Young/Sr. Microbiologist, Holly Brown/Microbiologist, William R. Schmidt/Plasma Laboratory Supervisor, Marty Brown/Sr. Technician, Glen Bailey/Sr. Electronic Technician, Kimberly Kelly-Wintenberg/COO, Pres. *(16 Officers included in Index)*

Directors: Patrick L. Martin/Chmn., Steven D. Harb/Dir., Thomas W. Reddoch/Dir., Suzanne L. South/Co - Founder, Member - Agt's Management Team, Al R. Anderson/Dir., Joseph B. Byrum/Dir., Russell J. Mothershed/Dir.

Owners: Russell J. Mothershed, Kimberly Kelly-Wintenberg, Kimberly Kelly-Wintenberg, Patrick L. Martin, Insiders, Michael A. Atkins, Thomas W. Reddoch, Scott W. McDonald, Atmospheric Plasma Holdings, LLC, Suzanne L. South, Atmospheric Plasma Holdings, LLC, Daniel M. Sherman, Patrick L. Martin, Joseph B. Byrum, Suzanne L. South *(18 Owners included in Index)*

Financial Data: Fiscal Year End:03/31 Latest Annual Data: 03/31/2007

Year	Sales	Net Income
2007	$1,910,000	-$2,674,000
2006	$1,642,000	-$2,579,000
2005	$1,885,000	-$1,849,000

Curr. Assets:	$324,000	Curr. Liab.:	$2,493,000	
Plant, Equip.:	$550,000	Total Liab.:	$3,092,000	Indic. Yr. Divd.: NA
Total Assets:	$2,317,000	Net Worth:	-$775,000	Debt/ Equity: NA

Atomic Guppy Inc

Formerly: XTX Energy Inc

4610 So. Ulster St., Ste. 150, Denver, CO, 80237; *PH:* 1-303-495-3684; *http://* www.xtxenergy.com

General - Incorporation	NV	**Stock**- Price on:12/24/2007	$0.18
Employees	NA	Stock Exchange	NA
Auditor	Jewett, Schwartz & Associates	Ticker Symbol	NA
Stk Agt	Nevada Agency & Trust Company	Outstanding Shares	NA
Counsel	NA	E.P.S.	NA
DUNS No.	NA	Shareholders	NA

Business: The groups principle activity is in the natural resources development and acquisition business. The group was founded as a mining exploration group with mineral claims. The group operates from the United States and Canada.

Primary SIC and add'l.: 7389

CIK No: 0001122991

Officers: Adam Bauman/50/Dir., CEO, Pres., Qui Sung Poon/Dir., Sec. Treasurer, Albert Folsom/Dir., CFO, Sec., Michael Fisher/Dir., Pres., David A. Carter/58/Sec., Neal Lenarsky/51/Sr. VP - Business Development

Directors: Adam Bauman/50/Dir., CEO, Pres., Leigh Rothschild/56/Chmn., Lawrence Moskowitz/43/Dir., Mark Hanna/60/Dir., Albert Folsom/Dir., CFO, Sec., Michael Fisher/Dir., Pres., Qui Sung Poon/Dir., Sec. Treasurer, John Watson/Dir., Jay Howard Linn/74/Dir.

Owners: Insiders, Neal Lenarsky, Leigh Rothschild, Jerrold Dean Burden, Irrevocable Trust III, David A. Carter, Adam Bauman

Financial Data: Fiscal Year End:10/31 Latest Annual Data: 10/31/2006

Year	Sales	Net Income
2006	$49,000	-$279,000
2005	$6,000	-$67,000

Curr. Assets:	$5,000	Curr. Liab.:	$225,000	
Plant, Equip.:	NA	Total Liab.:	$225,000	Indic. Yr. Divd.: NA
Total Assets:	$7,000	Net Worth:	-$218,000	Debt/ Equity: NA

ATP Oil & Gas Corp

4600 Post Oak Pl., Ste. 200, Houston, TX, 77027; *PH:* 1-713-622-3311; *Fax:* 1-713-622-5101; *http://* www.atpog.com; *Email:* atpinfo@atpog.com

General - Incorporation	TX	**Stock**- Price on:12/24/2007	$46.77
Employees	59	Stock Exchange	NDQ
Auditor	Deloitte & Touche, LLP	Ticker Symbol	ATPG
Stk Agt	American Stock Transfer & Trust Co.	Outstanding Shares	30,290,000
Counsel	NA	E.P.S.	-$0.038
DUNS No.	NA	Shareholders	NA

Business: The group's principal activities are to acquire, develop and produce natural gas and oil properties. The operations are carried out in the outer continental shelf of the gulf of Mexico in the shallow-deep waters of the gulf of Mexico and in the southern gas basin of the north sea. The group develops properties with proved undeveloped reserves that are economically attractive but are not strategic to major oil and gas companies. On 31-Dec-2003, the group had leasehold and other interests in 50 offshore blocks, 26 platforms and 62 wells, including six subsea wells. The group had net proved reserves of 303 billion cubic feet of equivalent of natural gas and oil.

Primary SIC and add'l.: 1311

CIK No: 0001123647

Subsidiaries: ATP Energy, ATP Oil & Gas (U.K.) Limited, Gulf of Mexico

Officers: Paul T. Bulmahn/Chmn., Pres./$4,877,475.00, Gerald W. Schlief/Sr. VP/$1,051,344.00, Albert L. Reese/CFO, Treasurer/$732,023.00, Ross G. Frazer/VP - Engineering, Keith R. Godwin/Chief Accounting Officer/$700,458.00, Isabel M. Plume/Chief Communications Officer, Corp. Sec., Leland E. Tate/COO/$1,107,104.00, John E. Tschirhart/General Counsel, Sr. VP - International, Robert M. Shivers/VP - Projects, Mickey W. Shaw/VP - Production Operations, Pauline Van Der Sman-Archer/VP - Administration, Scott D. Heflin/VP, Controller, Timothy P. McGinty/VP - Business Development, Scott A. Bellaire/VP - Drilling, Brian C. Nelson/VP - Finance

Directors: Paul T. Bulmahn/Chmn., Pres., Robert C. Thomas/Dir., Burt A. Adams/Dir., Robert J. Karow/Dir., Gerard J. Swonke/Dir., Arthur H. Dilly/Dir., Chris A. Brisack/Dir., Walter Wendlandt/Dir., George R. Edwards/Dir.

Owners: Touradji Capital Management, LP/8.69%, Arthur H. Dilly, Keith R. Godwin, Albert L. Reese/1.22%, Chris A. Brisack, Walter Wendlandt, Leland Tate, George R. Edwards, Robert J. Karow, Gerard J. Swonke, Insiders/29.46%, Robert C. Thomas, Gerald W. Schlief/3.94%, Paul T. Bulmahn/23.89%, Anchorage Capital Master Offshore, Ltd./6.00% *(17 Owners included in Index)*

Financial Data: Fiscal Year End:12/31 Latest Annual Data: 12/31/2006

Year	Sales	Net Income
2006	$419,821,000	$6,877,000
2005	$146,674,000	-$2,716,000
2004	$116,123,000	$1,356,000

Curr. Assets:	$327,333,000	**Curr. Liab.:**	$249,829,000		
Plant, Equip.:	$1,096,724,000	**Total Liab.:**	$1,411,140,000	**Indic. Yr. Divd.:**	NA
Total Assets:	$1,447,058,000	**Net Worth:**	$35,918,000	**Debt/ Equity:**	18.8845

AtriCure Inc

6033 Schumacher Pk. Dr., West Chester, OH, 45069; ***PH:*** 1-513-755-4100; ***Fax:*** 1-513-755-4108; ***http://*** www.atricure.com

General - Incorporation .... DE
Employees 176
Auditor .... Deloitte& Touche LLP
Stk Agt...... American Stock Transfer & Trust Co.
Counsel .... NA
DUNS No. .... NA

Stock- Price on:12/24/2007 .... $9.5
Stock Exchange .... NDQ
Ticker Symbol .... ATRC
Outstanding Shares 12,300,000
E.P.S. .... -$1.08
Shareholders .... NA

Business: The groups principle activities include developing, manufacturing and selling surgical devices design. The groups services include medicare and medicaid. The group products sold under the trade name Isolator(TM) and Synergy(TM). In August 2005, the group acquired Enable Medical Corporation. The group operates from the United States and International. The group's quarterly revenue for September 2007 was 12.05 millions of USD.

Primary SIC and add'l.: 3841

CIK No: 0001323885

Subsidiaries: AtriCure Europe, B.V.

Officers: David J. Drachman/Dir., CEO, Pres., James L. Lucky/VP - Quality Assurance, Healthcare Compliance, Julie A. Piton/VP - Finance, Administration, CFO, Elsa C. Abruzzo/VP - Regulatory, Clinical Affairs, Frederick Preiss/VP - Operations, Salvatore Privitera/VP - Business Development, Research, Maureen A. Shaffer/VP - Marketing, Jon Sherman/VP - Product Development, Stewart W. Strong/VP - United States Sales

Directors: David J. Drachman/Dir., CEO, Pres., Richard M. Johnston/Chmn., Michael D. Hooven/Dir., Donald C. Harrison/Dir., Elizabeth D. Krell/Dir., Mark R. Lanning/Dir., Karen P. Robards/Dir., Lee R. Wrubel/Dir.

Owners: Insiders/29.90%, Lee R. Wrubel/4.10%, Michael D. Hooven/6.50%, Donald C. Harrison/7.50%, Norman R. Weldon/5.10%, Charter Ventures/5.70%, Camden Partners/7.50%, Stephen S. Cambridge, Kairos Partners III Limited Partnership/9.80%, Mark R. Lanning, Massachusetts Financial Services Company/6.20%, Karen P. Robards/1.50%, TimesSquare Capital Management, LLC/8.40%, Richard M. Johnston/7.60%, U.S. Venture Partners/18.30%

Financial Data: **Fiscal Year End:**12/31 **Latest Annual Data:** 12/31/2006

Year	Sales	Net Income
2006	$38,243,000	-$13,717,000
2005	$30,957,000	-$12,683,000
2004	$19,157,000	-$9,452,000

Curr. Assets:	$30,688,000	**Curr. Liab.:**	$7,657,000		
Plant, Equip.:	$3,643,000	**Total Liab.:**	$8,434,000	**Indic. Yr. Divd.:**	NA
Total Assets:	$39,128,000	**Net Worth:**	$30,694,000	**Debt/ Equity:**	0.0217

Atrion Corp

1 Allentown Pkwy., Allen, TX, 75002; ***PH:*** 1-972-390-9800; ***Fax:*** 1-972-396-7581; ***http://*** www.atrioncorp.com; ***Email:*** ir-info@atrioncorp.com

General - Incorporation .... DE
Employees 486
Auditor .... Grant Thornton LLP
Stk Agt...... American Stock Transfer & Trust Co.
Counsel .... NA
DUNS No. 11-920-2877

Stock- Price on:12/24/2007 .... $93.2
Stock Exchange .... NDQ
Ticker Symbol .... ATRI
Outstanding Shares 1,890,000
E.P.S. $6.02
Shareholders .... NA

Business: The group's principal activities are to design, develop, manufacture, sell and distribute medical products and components for the health care industry. The group's products include ophthalmology, cardiovascular products, fluid delivery devices, contract manufacturing and kitting services. The group also has a line of non-medical components that are used in aviation and marine safety products. It owns and maintains a gaseous oxygen pipeline and the same has been leased. It's products include soft contact lens storage, disinfection cases, pressure monitoring kits used and lacricath product line that is used in the treatment of nasolacrimal duct obstruction. It is a registered pharmaceutical reseller providing custom packaging and labelling. The group operates in the United States, Canada and the United Kingdom.

Primary SIC and add'l.: 3851 2835 3494 3841

CIK No: 0000701288

Subsidiaries: AlaTenn Pipeline Company LLC, Atrion Leasing Company LLC, Atrion Medical Products, Inc, Halkey-Roberts Corporation, Quest Medical, Inc

Officers: Emile A. Battat/Chmn., CEO/$709,578.00, Jeffery Strickland/CFO, VP/$284,142.00, David A. Battat/COO, Pres., Lane Johnson/Human Resources

Directors: Emile A. Battat/Chmn., CEO, John P. Stupp/Dir., Hugh J. Morgan/Dir., Roger F. Stebbing/Dir., Ronald N. Spaulding/Dir.

Owners: Emile A. Battat/12.07%, Jeffery Strickland/1.79%, Insiders/24.49%, T. Rowe Price Associates, Inc./8.92%, Roger F. Stebbing/1.52%, Oak Forest Investment Management, Inc/6.99%, Hugh J. Morgan/1.06%, Royce & Associates, LLC/7.94%, John P. Stupp/8.64%

Financial Data: **Fiscal Year End:**12/31 **Latest Annual Data:** 12/31/2006

Year	Sales	Net Income
2006	$81,020,000	$10,765,000
2005	$72,089,000	$8,958,000
2004	$66,081,000	$6,470,000

Curr. Assets:	$30,658,000	**Curr. Liab.:**	$6,923,000	**P/E Ratio:**	15.48
Plant, Equip.:	$51,442,000	**Total Liab.:**	$24,877,000	**Indic. Yr. Divd.:**	$0.800
Total Assets:	$95,772,000	**Net Worth:**	$70,895,000	**Debt/ Equity:**	0.0877

ATS Medical

3905 Annapolis Ln., Ste. 105, Minneapolis, MN, 55447; ***PH:*** 1-763-553-7736; ***Fax:*** 1-763-557-2244; ***http://*** www.atsmedical.com; ***Email:*** info@atsmedical.com

General - Incorporation .... MN
Employees 254
Auditor .... Ernst & Young LLP
Stk Agt .... Wells Fargo Shareowner Services
Counsel .... Dorsey & Whitney LLP
DUNS No. 17-759-5899

Stock- Price on:12/24/2007 .... $2.02
Stock Exchange .... NDQ
Ticker Symbol .... ATSI
Outstanding Shares 49,210,000
E.P.S. .... -$0.9
Shareholders .... NA

Business: The group's principal activity is to manufacture and market a mechanical bileaflet heart valve with a patented open pivot design. The heart valve manufactured is used to treat heart valvular diseases caused by the natural aging process, rheumatic heart disease, prosthetic valve failure and congenital defects. The group's product is designed to advance the standard of existing mechanical heart valves by combining a proprietary open pivot design and other innovative features with the widely accepted biocompatibility and durability of pyrolytic carbon. The group holds an exclusive, royalty-free, worldwide license to an open pivot, bileaflet mechanical heart valve design. The group markets its products in the United States, Europe, Japan, Canada and Australia.

Primary SIC and add'l.: 3842

CIK No: 0000824068

Subsidiaries: ATS Medical France, SARL, ATS Medical Gmbh, ATS Medical Sales, Inc.

Officers: Michael D. Dale/47/Chmn., CEO, Pres. ATS Medical - Inc/$722,056.00, Jeremy J. Curtis/VP - Worldwide Marketing, Richard A. Curtis/VP - Marketing, Business Development/$308,032.00, Steven M. Anderson/44/Dir., VP, David R. Elizondo/VP - Research, Development, GM - Tissue Operations, Allen W. Putnam/VP - Regulatory, Clinical, Quality

Directors: Michael D. Dale/47/Chmn., CEO, Pres. ATS Medical - Inc, Steven M. Anderson/44/Dir., VP, Robert E. Munzenrider/62/Dir., Guy P. Nohra/Dir., Theodore C. Skokos/59/Dir.

Owners: Insiders/9.00%, John R. Judd, SF Capital Partners, Ltd./5.50%, Potomac Capital Management LLC/5.30%, Michael R. Kramer, Maria-Teresa Ajamil, Deborah K. Chapman, Richard A. Curtis, Accipiter Life Sciences Funds/10.00%, Perceptive Life Sciences Master Fund, Ltd./6.50%, Eric W. Sivertson, Marc R. Sportsman, Michael D. Dale/1.10%, Steven M. Anderson, Robert E. Munzenrider *(16 Owners included in Index)*

Financial Data: **Fiscal Year End:**12/31 **Latest Annual Data:** 12/31/2006

Year	Sales	Net Income
2006	$40,449,000	-$27,674,000
2005	$34,636,000	-$14,394,000
2004	$28,015,000	-$16,643,000

Curr. Assets:	$42,338,000	**Curr. Liab.:**	$9,362,000		
Plant, Equip.:	$8,213,000	**Total Liab.:**	$27,950,000	**Indic. Yr. Divd.:**	NA
Total Assets:	$85,840,000	**Net Worth:**	$57,890,000	**Debt/ Equity:**	0.2658

ATSI Communications Inc

8600 Wurzbach Rd., Ste. 700 W, San Antonio, TX, 78240; ***PH:*** 1-210-614-7240; ***Fax:*** 1-210-614-7264; ***http://*** www.atsi.net; ***Email:*** investorinfo@atsi.net

General - Incorporation .... NV
Employees 8
Auditor .... Malone & Bailey, P.C
Stk Agt ....Chase Mellon Shareholder Services
Counsel .... NA
DUNS No. .... NA

Stock- Price on:12/24/2007 .... $0.21
Stock Exchange .... OTC
Ticker Symbol .... ATSX
Outstanding Shares 37,110,000
E.P.S. $0.00
Shareholders .... NA

Business: The group's principal activity is to provide telecommunication services and Internet e-commerce services in the United States, Latin America and Mexico. It offers termination services to American and latin American carriers in Mexico. It also provides network services like data, voice and fax transmission and Internet to multi-national and latin American corporates. The group retail services like integrated prepaid services without operator assistance and international collect, person-to-person, third party, calling card, and credit card calls with operator assistance. The group ceased operations of two subsidiaries atsi-Texas and telespan inc in fiscal 2003.

Primary SIC and add'l.: 4813 4812

CIK No: 0001014052

Subsidiaries: American TeleSource International, Inc, ATSI Comunicaciones, S.A. de C.V., ATSI de CentroAmerica, S.A., ATSI Merger Corporation, Canadian corporation, Digerati Networks, Inc, Latin America Telecomm, Inc, Sistema de Telefonia Computarizada, S.A. de C.V., Telefamilia Communications, Inc

Officers: Arthur L. Smith/CEO, Pres., Antonio Estrada/Corporate Controller, Ruben Caraveo/Sr. VP - Sales, Operations, Kathleen Keller/Mgr. - Administration, Human Resources

Owners: Antonio Estrada/2.70%, Arthur L. Smith/4.30%, John R. Fleming/2.60%, Murray R. Nye/2.60%, Insiders/1.50%, Ruben R. Caraveo/2.70%

Financial Data: **Fiscal Year End:**07/31 **Latest Annual Data:** 07/31/2007

Year	Sales	Net Income
2007	$31,692,000	-$257,000
2006	$14,696,000	$947,000
2005	$6,011,000	$10,407,000

Curr. Assets:	$690,000	**Curr. Liab.:**	$3,490,000		
Plant, Equip.:	$102,000	**Total Liab.:**	$4,234,000	**Indic. Yr. Divd.:**	NA
Total Assets:	$792,000	**Net Worth:**	-$3,442,000	**Debt/ Equity:**	NA

Attunity Ltd

70 Blanchard Rd., Burlington, MA, 01803; ***PH:*** 1-781-213-5200; ***Fax:*** 1-781-213-5240; ***http://*** www.attunity.com; ***Email:*** info-emea@attunity.com

General - Incorporation .... Israel
Employees 110
Auditor .... Kost Forer Gabbay & Kasierer
Stk Agt ..... American Stock Transfer & Trust Co.
Counsel .... Efrati, Galili & Co
DUNS No. .... NA

Stock- Price on:12/24/2007 .... $1.1001
Stock Exchange .... NDQ
Ticker Symbol .... ATTU
Outstanding Shares 23,200,000
E.P.S. .... -$0.31
Shareholders .... NA

Business: The group's principle activities include developing, marketing and supporting computer software productivity tools which currently operate on dec vax/vms platforms; and provides software development and consulting services, including product evaluations, quality assurance reviews and software development services. The group operates from United States.

Primary SIC and add'l.: 7372

CIK No: 0000893821

Subsidiaries: Attunity (France) S.A., Attunity (Hong Kong) Limited, Attunity (UK) Limited, Attunity Inc., Attunity Israel (1992) Ltd., Attunity Pty. Limited, Attunity Singapore PTE Ltd., Attunity Software Services (1991) Ltd.

Officers: Aki Ratner/Dir., CEO, Zafrir Ron/VP - Research, Development, World Wide Support, Ofer Segev/48/CFO, Andy Bailey/VP - Worldwide Marketing, Nirit Barnea/VP - Human Resources, Dror Elkayam/VP - Finance, Mel Passarelli/VP - Sales North America

Directors: Aki Ratner/Dir., CEO, Shimon Alon/Chmn., Ron Zuckerman/Dir., Zamir Bar-Zion/Dir., Dov Biran/Dir., Dan Falk/Dir., Anat Segal/Dir.

Owners: Rimon Investment Master Fund L.P./5.10%, Aki Ratner/5.20%, Ron Zuckerman/5.70%, Ofer Segev, Arie Gonen/7.90%, Insiders/20.70%, Dov Biran/3.90%, Shimon Alon/5.90%

Financial Data: *Fiscal Year End:*12/31 *Latest Annual Data:* 12/31/2006

Year	Sales	Net Income
2006	$13,348,000	-$6,484,000
2005	$15,149,000	-$3,790,000
2004	$17,637,000	-$4,040,000

Curr. Assets:	$8,717,000	**Curr. Liab.:**	$7,336,000		
Plant, Equip.:	$939,000	**Total Liab.:**	$9,041,000	**Indic. Yr. Divd.:**	NA
Total Assets:	$21,353,000	**Net Worth:**	$12,312,000	**Debt/ Equity:**	NA

Atwood Oceanics Inc

15835 Pk. Ten Pl. Dr., Houston, TX, 77084; *PH:* 1-281-749-7800; *Fax:* 1-281-492-7871; *http://* www.atwd.com

General - Incorporation	TX	**Stock**- Price on:12/24/2007	$68.1
Employees	1,100	Stock Exchange	NYSE
Auditor	PricewaterhouseCoopers LLP	Ticker Symbol	ATW
Stk Agt	Continental Stock Transfer & Trust Co	Outstanding Shares	31,480,000
Counsel	NA	E.P.S	$4.37
DUNS No.	04-821-9539	Shareholders	NA

Business: The group's principal activities are the international offshore exploration and developmental oil and gas wells in offshore areas. It also provides related support management and consulting services. The group has 8 premium offshore mobile drilling units located in five areas of the United States, southeast Asia, the Mediterranean Sea, Africa and Australia. The major customers of the group include exxonmobil production Malaysia, inc., esso exploration angola, woodside energy ltd., burullus gas company and rashid petroleum company. The group operates in the United States, southeast Asia, Mediterranean Sea, Australia, and India.

Primary SIC and add'l.: 8741 1389 1381

CIK No: 0000008411

Subsidiaries: Alpha Offshore Drilling Services, ATW Management, Inc., Atwood Deep Seas, Ltd., Atwood Drilling, Inc., Atwood Hunter Co., Atwood Management, Inc., Atwood Oceanics (M) Sdn Bhd, Atwood Oceanics Australia Pty Limited, Atwood Oceanics Drilling Pty. Ltd., Atwood Oceanics International Limited, Atwood Oceanics Leasing Limited, Atwood Oceanics Management, LP, Atwood Oceanics Pacific Limited, Atwood Oceanics Platforms Pty. Ltd., Atwood Oceanics Services 25 Subsidiaries included in the Index

Officers: John R. Irwin/CEO, Pres., Corey H. Beckman/Dir. - Atwood Oceanics Pacific Limited, James A. Nowotny/Mgr. - Operations, Atwood Eagle, David Alexander/Mgr. - Operations, Southern Cross, Ronnie Hall/GM - Operations, Rodney Mallams/General Counsel, Emmanuel Deligeorges/Mgr. - Area Accounting, Finance, Australia, Richard Morgan/Employee Relations Representative, UK, Dir. - Atwood Oceanics Pacific Limited, Barry Smith/GM - Technical, Darryl R. Smith/VP - Operations, Michael Koenig/Mgr. - Marine Operations Support, James E. Gillenwater/Mgr. - Human Resources, Alan Quintero/VP - Engineering, Glen P. Kelley/Sr. VP - Marketing, Administration, David Petrusek/Mgr. - Purchasing *(33 Officers included in Index)*

Directors: Deborah A. Beck/60/Dir., George S. Dotson/67/Dir., William J. Morrissey/80/Dir., Robert W. Burgess/66/Dir., Larry W. Holloway/Dir. - Atwood Oceanics Pacific Limited, Nigel Richardson/Dir. - Atwood Oceanics Pacific Limited, Hans Helmerich/49/Dir., James R. Montague/60/Dir.

Owners: William J. Morrissey, Glen P. Kelley, Deborah A. Beck, Hans Helmerich, John R. Irwin, Insiders/2.04%, James M. Holland, H&PIDC/12.87%, George S. Dotson, James R. Montague, Robert W. Burgess, Columbia Wanger Asset Management, L.P./10.00%

Financial Data: *Fiscal Year End:*09/30 *Latest Annual Data:* 9/30/2006

Year	Sales	Net Income
2006	$276,625,000	$86,122,000
2005	$176,156,000	$26,011,000
2004	$163,454,000	$7,587,000

Curr. Assets:	$147,673,000	**Curr. Liab.:**	$61,365,000	**P/E Ratio:**	19.76
Plant, Equip.:	$436,166,000	**Total Liab.:**	$134,935,000	**Indic. Yr. Divd.:**	NA
Total Assets:	$593,829,000	**Net Worth:**	$458,894,000	**Debt/ Equity:**	NA

AU Optronics Corp

1 Li Hsin Rd. 2, Science-Based Industrial Pk., Hsinchu, 300; ; *http://* www.auo.com

General - Incorporation	Taiwan	**Stock**- Price on:12/24/2007	$17.67
Employees	24,327	Stock Exchange	NYSE
Auditor	KPMG LLP	Ticker Symbol	AUO
Stk Agt	National Securities Corp	Outstanding Shares	757,400,000
Counsel	NA	E.P.S	$1.00
DUNS No.	NA	Shareholders	NA

Business: The group's principal activity is the manufacture of thin film transistor liquid crystal display (TFT-LCD) and other electrical, and electronic supplies. TFT-LCD are used in notebook computers, desktop monitors, televisions, digital cameras, DVD players, mobile phones, portable games, car navigation systems and other appliances. The group's operations are carried out in Taiwan, Asia and in other countries. Its products are exported in Taiwan, Asia and in other countries.

Primary SIC and add'l.: 5065 3699

CIK No: 0001172494

Subsidiaries: AU Optronics (L) Corp., AU Optronics (Shanghai) Corp., AU Optronics (Suzhou) Corp., AU Optronics Corporation America, AU Optronics Corporation Japan, AU Optronics Europe B.V., AU Optronics Korea Ltd., Darwin Precisions (L) Corp, Darwin Precisions (Suzhou) Corp., Konly Venture Corp., Raydium Semiconductor Corporation

Officers: K.y. Lee/56/Chmn., CEO, Paul Peng/Sr. VP, GM - Information Technology Display Business Group, C. T. Liu/VP, GM - Consumer Product Display Operation, F. C. Hsiang/Sr. VP, GM - Global Supply Chain Management, Global Manufacturing, L. J. Chen/COO, Pres., Max Cheng/CFO, VP, David Su/Sr. VP, GM - TV Display, Consumer Product Display Business Groups, Shin Chen/Supervisor, B.D. Liu/VP - AUO Technology Center, Fang-Chen Chen/CTO, VP, Frank Wu/VP - Administration

Directors: K.y. Lee/56/Chmn., CEO, Chee-Chun Leung/58/Vice Chmn., Ching-Shih Han/Dir., Tze-Kaing Yang/Dir., Michael Wang/54/Dir., T. J. Huang/62/Dir., Hui Hsiung/Dir., Hsuan Bin Chen/Dir., Vivien Huey-Juan Hsieh/Dir., Chieh-Chien Chao/Dir., Cheng-Chu Fan/56/Dir., Hsi-Hua Sheaffer Lee/53/Dir., Ko-Yung Yu/Dir.

Owners: BenQ/8.47%, Quanta Computer Inc./5.31%, Insiders/9.18%

Financial Data: *Fiscal Year End:*12/31 *Latest Annual Data:* 12/31/2006

Year	Sales	Net Income
2006	$8,993,764,000	$35,999,000
2005	$6,627,695,000	$264,579,000
2004	$5,296,521,000	$570,654,000

Curr. Assets:	$4,686,795,000	**Curr. Liab.:**	$5,133,994,000		
Plant, Equip.:	$11,616,919,000	**Total Liab.:**	$10,698,605,000	**Indic. Yr. Divd.:**	$0.020
Total Assets:	$18,020,426,000	**Net Worth:**	$7,321,821,000	**Debt/ Equity:**	NA

Auburn National Bancorp Inc

100 N Gay St., Auburn, AL, 36830; *PH:* 1-334-821-9200; *Fax:* 1-334-887-2772; *http://* www.auburnbank.com

General - Incorporation	DE	**Stock**- Price on:12/24/2007	$27
Employees	137	Stock Exchange	NDQ
Auditor	KPMG LLP	Ticker Symbol	AUBN
Stk Agt	Registar and Transfer Co.	Outstanding Shares	3,730,000
Counsel	Arnold W. Umbach Jr.	E.P.S	$1.76
DUNS No.	08-780-0025	Shareholders	NA

Business: The group's principal activity is that of a holding company for auburnbank, an Alabama state member bank. The group accepts demand, savings and transaction deposits, including certificate of deposits from consumers, business and other institutions. It primarily offers residential mortgage loans. Other offerings include commercial, financial, agricultural, real estate construction and consumer loans. The group also provides automated teller services in east Alabama with 14 locations. Its tiger teller ATM cards can be used internationally through the cirrus(R) network. In addition, it also offers visa checkcards, debit cards with a visa logo that can be used anywhere visa is accepted. The banking operations are conducted in east Alabama and the lee county and surrounding areas through its main office in auburn and seven branches in auburn, opelika and hurtsboro.

Primary SIC and add'l.: 6712 6022

CIK No: 0000750574

Subsidiaries: AUB Holdings Corp., AUB, Inc., Auburn Mortgage Corporation, Auburn National Bancorporation Capital Trust I, AuburnBank, Banc of Auburn, Inc.

Officers: Robert W. Dumas/Dir., CEO, Pres. - Auburnbank/$224,376.00, E. L. Spencer/Chmn., CEO, Pres., Edward Lee Spencer/Chmn., CEO, Pres., Christy A. Young/Loan Review Officer - Auburnbank, Sam S. Rainer/Marketing Officer - Auburnbank, Brandi Black/Contact - Opelika Wal, Mart, Terrell E. Bishop/Sr. VP, Sr. Mortgage Lending Officer - Auburnbank, Joann Hall/COO, Exec. VP, Thomas W. Johnson/Sr. VP - Sr. Lender, Auburnbank, James E. Dulaney/Sr. VP - Business Development, Marketing, Auburnbank, Eddie C. Smith/Sr. VP, City Pres. - Opelika, Auburnbank, Patty Allen/VP - Commercial, Consumer Loans, Opelika Branch, Auburnbank, Kris Blackmon/VP - Asset, Liability Mgr., Chief Investment Officer - Auburnbank, Mark S. Bridges/VP - Commercial, Consumer Loans, Auburnbank, Laura Carrington/VP, Human Resources Officer - Auburnbank *(39 Officers included in Index)*

Directors: E. L. Spencer/Chmn., CEO, Pres., Edward Lee Spencer/Chmn., CEO, Pres., Robert W. Dumas/Dir., CEO, Pres. - Auburnbank, David E. Housel/Dir., William F. Ham/Dir., Winifred H. Boyd/Dir. Emeritus - Auburnbank, Tutt J. Barrett/Member - Opelika Branch Advisory Board, William H. Brown/Member - Opelika Branch Advisory Board, William G. Dyas/Member - Opelika Branch Advisory Board, Hugh Dean Fuller/Member - Opelika Branch Advisory Board, Emil F. Wright/Dir., J. E. Evans/Dir., Anne M. May/Dir., Terry W. Andrus/Dir., Robert G. Young/Member - Opelika Branch Advisory Board *(22 Directors included in Index)*

Owners: Insiders/34.46%, Thomas W. Johnson, E. L. Spencer/19.13%, Wayne C. Alderman, Eddie C. Smith, Emil F. Wright/10.62%, William F. Ham/0.07%, Terrell E. Bishop/1.10%, Ann Jo Hall, J. E. Evans/0.48%, Edward Lee Spencer/0.22%, Anne M. May/0.82%, James E. Dulaney/0.11%, David E. Housel/0.07%, Terry W. Andrus/0.04% *(16 Owners included in Index)*

Financial Data: *Fiscal Year End:*12/31 *Latest Annual Data:* 12/31/2006

Year	Sales	Net Income
2006	$40,274,000	$6,585,000
2005	$36,293,000	$6,470,000
2004	$34,092,000	$6,510,000

Curr. Assets:	$17,026,000	**Curr. Liab.:**	$486,304,000	**P/E Ratio:**	15.34
Plant, Equip.:	$5,796,000	**Total Liab.:**	$586,708,000	**Indic. Yr. Divd.:**	$0.700
Total Assets:	$635,126,000	**Net Worth:**	$48,418,000	**Debt/ Equity:**	1.8047

Aucxis Corp

666 Burrard St., Ste. 500, Vancouver, BC, V6C 3P6; *PH:* 1-604-639-3109; *http://* www.aucxis.com

General - Incorporation	NV	**Stock**- Price on:12/24/2007	$0.006
Employees	NA	Stock Exchange	OTC
Auditor	Manning Elliott LLP	Ticker Symbol	AUCX
Stk Agt	Interwest Transfer Company, Inc.	Outstanding Shares	NA
Counsel	NA	E.P.S	NA
DUNS No.	NA	Shareholders	NA

Business: The group's principal activity is to develop e-business services for perishable commodity in Europe. The group has temporarily suspended development of e-business services for the perishable commodity marketplace pending further review of the opportunities in this area. The group is currently inactive. It currently has a wholly owned subsidiary, e-auction (barbados), which in turn has one wholly owned subsidiary, aucxis corp. (Canada). Both of these companies are inactive that have not conducted any active business from inception to date.

Primary SIC and add'l.: 8999

CIK No: 0001102233

Subsidiaries: e-Auction Global Trading Inc., i-Three Inc

Financial Data: *Fiscal Year End:*12/31 *Latest Annual Data:* 12/31/2004

Year	Sales	Net Income
2004	NA	-$289,000
2002	$4,718,000	-$1,226,000
2001	$7,442,000	-$14,728,000

Curr. Assets:	$2,000	**Curr. Liab.:**	$1,942,000		
Plant, Equip.:	NA	**Total Liab.:**	$1,942,000	**Indic. Yr. Divd.:**	NA
Total Assets:	$2,000	**Net Worth:**	-$6,156,000	**Debt/ Equity:**	NA

Audible Inc

1 Washington Pk., Newark, NJ, 07102; ***PH:*** 1-973-820-0400; ***Fax:*** 1-973-820-0505; ***http://*** www.audible.com; ***Email:*** investor_relations@audible.com

General - Incorporation .... DE
Employees 152
Auditor .... KPMG LLP
Stk Agt...... American Stock Transfer & Trust Co.
Counsel .... NA
DUNS No. .... NA

Stock- Price on:12/24/2007 .... $9.81
Stock Exchange .... NDQ
Ticker Symbol .... ADBL
Outstanding Shares 24,280,000
E.P.S .... NA
Shareholders .... NA

Business: The group's principal activity is to provide subscription based, premium spoken audio content over the Internet. The services include: Web site, audible.com; collection of digital audio content; software for securing, downloading, managing, scheduling and playing audio selections; a variety of audibleready(R) players; and other services. Its Web site, audible.com, delivers a large and diverse selection of premium digital spoken audio content in a secure format through the Internet. The group's digital audio content includes more than 5,000 digital audiobooks and more than 12,000 other audio selections. Audibleready(R) players are electronic devices that have a speaker or an audio output jack to play back audio content. Other services include the provision of audible(R) service to over 50 public library and school library systems.

Primary SIC and add'l.: 7372 7375 5731 7373

CIK No: 0001077926

Subsidiaries: Audible Limited

Officers: Donald R. Katz/Chmn., CEO/$1,146,750.00, Guy Story/Chief Scientist, Sr. VP - Business Development/$421,482.00, Glenn Rogers/COO/$559,439.00, Helene Godin/Corporate Counsel, Will Lopes/VP - Customer Experience, Brian M. Fielding/Exec. VP - Content, Legal Affairs/$436,866.00, Beth Anderson/Sr. VP - Publisher, Foy C. Sperring/Exec. VP - Customer Acquisition, William H. Mitchell/CFO/$54,090.00

Directors: Donald R. Katz/Chmn., CEO, William H. Washecka/Dir., Jim Bankoff/Dir., Richard Sarnoff/Dir., Johannes Mohn/Dir., Oren Zeev/Dir., Gary L. Ginsberg/Dir.

Owners: Brian M. Fielding, Johannes Mohn, Random House, Inc./5.60%, William H. Washecka, Oren Zeev, Glenn M. Rogers, AXA Financial, Inc./14.90%, Andrew P. Kaplan, Gary L. Ginsberg, Insiders/6.00%, Apax Managers, Inc./24.00%, Donald R. Katz/3.60%, Richard Sarnoff, Alan J. Patricof, Guy A. Story

Financial Data: **Fiscal Year End:**12/31 **Latest Annual Data:** 12/31/2006

Year	Sales	Net Income
2006	$82,350,000	-$8,680,000
2005	$64,243,000	-$653,000
2004	$34,320,000	$2,025,000

Curr. Assets:	$73,846,000	**Curr. Liab.:**	$31,445,000		
Plant, Equip.:	$8,149,000	**Total Liab.:**	$32,310,000	**Indic. Yr. Divd.:**	NA
Total Assets:	$82,776,000	**Net Worth:**	$50,466,000	**Debt/ Equity:**	NA

AudioCodes Ltd

2099 Gateway Pl., Ste. 500, San Jose, CA, 95110; ***PH:*** 1-408-441-1175; ***Fax:*** 1-408-451-9520; ***http://*** www.audiocodes.com; ***Email:*** info@audiocodes.com

General - Incorporation .... Israel
Employees 522
Auditor .... Kost Forer Gabbay & Kasierer
Stk Agt...... American Stock Transfer & Trust Co.
Counsel .... Fulbright & Jaworski LLP
DUNS No. .... NA

Stock- Price on:12/24/2007 .... $5.73
Stock Exchange .... NDQ
Ticker Symbol .... AUDC
Outstanding Shares 42,310,000
E.P.S .... -$0.06
Shareholders .... NA

Business: The group's principle activity is to provide network equipment providers and system integrators with voice over packet media gateway and media processing technology and systems solutions. The company is a market leader in voice compression technology and the key originator of the ITU G.723.1 standard for the emerging voice over IP market. Its products include media gateway systems, VOIP communication boards, VOIP media gateway modules, VOP chip processors, and analog media gateways for access and enterprise solutions. Its customers include the leading global telecom and datacom network equipment providers. Audiocodes' international headquarters and R&D facilities are located in Israel, with U.S. Headquarters in San Jose, California and additional offices in, Boston, Dallas, Chicago and Beijing. The company's shares have been traded on Nasdaq National Market since May, 1999 and on the Tel Aviv Stock Exchange since Oct, 2001. The group operates from United States.

Primary SIC and add'l.: 3669 3679 5065

CIK No: 0001086434

Subsidiaries: AudioCodes Argentina SA, AudioCodes Brasil Equipamentos de Voz sobre IP Ltda, AudioCodes Europe Limited, AudioCodes France SAS, AudioCodes Germany GmbH, AudioCodes Inc, AudioCodes India Private Limited, AudioCodes Korea Co. Ltd., AudioCodes National Inc., AudioCodes Russ Ltd, AudioCodes USA Inc

Officers: Shabtai Adlersberg/Chmn., CEO, Pres., Lior Aldema/VP - Marketing, Nachum Falek/CFO, VP, Gary Drutin/VP - Sales EMEA, Channel Operations, Marketing, Tal Dor/VP - Human Resources, Eli Nir/VP - Research, Development, Ben Rabinowitz/VP, GM - Session Border Controllers, Media Server Business Lines, Eyal Frishberg/VP - Operations, David Eliel Perez/VP - Sales, Asia Pacific, Yehuda Hershkovits/VP - Systems, Moshe Tal/VP, GM - Blade Business Line, Hanan Maoz/VP - Business Operations, Shirley Nakar/Dir. - Investor Relations, Corporate Communications

Directors: Shabtai Adlersberg/Chmn., CEO, Pres., Doron Nevo/Dir., Joseph Tenne/Dir., Eyal Kishon/Dir., Karen Sarid/Dir.

Owners: Shabtai Adlersberg/13.40%

Financial Data: **Fiscal Year End:**12/31 **Latest Annual Data:** 12/31/2006

Year	Sales	Net Income
2006	$147,353,000	$6,877,000
2005	$115,827,000	$13,436,000
2004	$82,756,000	$5,006,000

Curr. Assets:	$134,436,000	**Curr. Liab.:**	$36,982,000		
Plant, Equip.:	$7,847,000	**Total Liab.:**	$172,371,000	**Indic. Yr. Divd.:**	NA
Total Assets:	$337,056,000	**Net Worth:**	$164,685,000	**Debt/ Equity:**	NA

Audiovox Corp

180 Marcus Blvd., Hauppauge, NY, 11788; ***PH:*** 1-631-231-7750; ***Fax:*** 1-631-434-3995; ***http://*** www.audiovox.com

General - Incorporation .... DE
Employees .... NA
Auditor .... Grant Thornton LLP
Stk Agt .... Continental Stock Transfer & Trust Co
Counsel .... Levy & Stopol
DUNS No. 04-469-4040

Stock- Price on:12/24/2007 .... $13.13
Stock Exchange .... NDQ
Ticker Symbol .... VOXX
Outstanding Shares 22,900,000
E.P.S $0.41
Shareholders .... NA

Business: The group's principal activity is to design and market handsets and accessories for wireless communications and to provide services for wireless carriers, automotive entertainment and security products, automotive electronic accessories and consumer electronics. The trademarks of the group include audiovox (R), prestige (R), pursuit(R) and rampage(tm). The group licenses its trade names to ten retail outlets under the name quintex (r). Customers of the group include bell Atlantic, air airtouch communications, gte mobilnet, primeco personal communications lp, frontier, ameritech and vodafone. Its products are sold through a distribution network covering the United States, Canada and other foreign markets. During the year 2003, the group acquired certain assets of recoton corporation & recoton german holdings gmbh.

Primary SIC and add'l.: 3651 3639 3661 5064 5065 5731 5013

CIK No: 0000807707

Subsidiaries: American Radio Corp., Audiovox Communications Canada Co., Audiovox Communications Corp., Audiovox Electronics Corporation, Audiovox German Holdings GmbH, Audiovox Holding Corp., Audiovox Venezuela C.A., Code Systems, Inc., Quintex Mobile Communications Corp.

Officers: Patrick M. Lavelle/Dir., CEO, Pres./$1,018,245.00, Charles M. Stoehr/Dir., Sr. VP, CFO/$442,012.00, Chris L. Johnson/VP, Sec., Richard A. Maddia/Sr. VP, Loriann Shelton/Sr. VP/$344,741.00, Thomas C. Malone/Sr. VP/$616,080.00, James Gordon/Sr. VP/$408,426.00, David C. Geise/Sr. VP

Directors: Patrick M. Lavelle/Dir., CEO, Pres., John J. Shalam/Chmn., Charles M. Stoehr/Dir., Sr. VP, CFO, Philip Christopher/Dir., Dennis F. McManus/Dir., Paul C. Kreuch/Dir., Peter A. Lesser/Dir.

Owners: Philip Christopher/3.80%, Barclays Global Investors, NA/5.06%, John J. Shalam/19.80%, Donald Smith & Co., Inc./9.71%, Insiders/26.30%, Dennis F. McManus, James Gordon, Aegis Financial Corp./6.30%, Patrick M.Lavelle/1.30%, Charles M.Stoehr, Kahn Brothers & Co., Inc./11.18%, Loriann Shelton, Thomas C. Malone, Paul C. Kreuch, Tracer Capital Management L.P./5.78% *(16 Owners included in Index)*

Financial Data: **Fiscal Year End:**11/30 **Latest Annual Data:** 2/28/2007

Year	Sales	Net Income
2007	$456,690,000	$2,936,000
2005	$539,716,000	-$9,591,000
2004	$567,077,000	$77,200,000

Curr. Assets:	$375,345,000	**Curr. Liab.:**	$72,732,000	**P/E Ratio:**	82.06
Plant, Equip.:	$18,019,000	**Total Liab.:**	$91,411,000	**Indic. Yr. Divd.:**	NA
Total Assets:	$495,773,000	**Net Worth:**	$404,362,000	**Debt/ Equity:**	0.0274

August Technology Corp

4900 W 78th St. , Bloomington, MN, 55435; ***PH:*** 1-952-820-0080; ***http://*** www.augusttech.com

General - Incorporation .... MN
Employees .... NA
Auditor .... KPMG LLP
Stk Agt ..... American Stock Transfer & Trust Co.
Counsel .... Fredrikson & Byron
DUNS No. .... NA

Stock- Price on:12/24/2007 .... NA
Stock Exchange .... NDQ
Ticker Symbol .... AUGT
Outstanding Shares .... NA
E.P.S .... NA
Shareholders .... NA

Business: The group's principal activity is to conduct research, design, develop, manufacture, sell and distribute automated defect inspection systems. The group provides machine vision solutions for a variety of devices manufacturing applications. The products include the nsx series of automated wafer inspection systems and the cassette verification systems and cv series. The automated defect inspection system provide manufacturers with information, which enables process-enhancing decisions, ultimately lowering costs, improving time-to-Market and enhancing the performance of their products. The customers are located in North America, Taiwan, southeast Asia, South Korea, Europe and Japan. On 15-Apr-2003, the group acquired semiconductor technologies and instruments inc and on 03-Jul-2003, counterpoint solutions inc.

Primary SIC and add'l.: 3827 3812

CIK No: 0001063527

Subsidiaries: August Technology International LLC, August Technology Korea Ltd., August Technology Limited, Semiconductor Technologies & Instruments, Inc.

Aurelio Resource Corp

5554 Prince St., Ste. 200, Littleton, CO, 80120; ***PH:*** 1-303-795-3030; ***Fax:*** 1-303-945-7270; ***http://*** www.aurelioresources.com

General - Incorporation .... NV
Employees .... NA
Auditor .... Mason Russell West, LLC
Stk Agt .... NA
Counsel .... NA
DUNS No. .... NA

Stock- Price on:12/24/2007 .... $1.04
Stock Exchange .... OTC
Ticker Symbol .... AULO
Outstanding Shares .... NA
E.P.S .... NA
Shareholders .... NA

Business: The groups principal activity is to explore minerals and natural gas. The group acquired Aurelio Resources Inc. Minera Milenium in the year 2006 and Minera Holmex S.A in Aug 26, 2005. The group operates from the United States and Canada.

Primary SIC and add'l.: 1000

CIK No: 0001295803

Subsidiaries: Aurelio Resources, Inc., Bolsa Resources, Inc., Minera Milenium, S.A. de C.V.

Officers: Fred W. Warnaars/Dir., CEO, Pres., Stephen B. Doppler/Chmn., Corp. Sec., David S. Johnson/General Counsel, Dir., David C. Jonson/VP - Exploration, Allan J. Marter/Dir., CFO, Stephen R. Stine/Dir., Future COO, Diane G. Dudley/Investor Relations, Earl H. Detra/VP - Exploration

Directors: Fred W. Warnaars/Dir., CEO, Pres., Stephen B. Doppler/Chmn., Corp. Sec., David S. Johnson/General Counsel, Dir., Allan J. Marter/Dir., CFO, Stephen R. Stine/Dir., Future COO

Owners: Insiders/30.90%, David S. Johnson/1.50%, Frederik Warnaars/20.20%, Allan J. Marter/0.80%, David C. Jonson/5.00%, Stephen R. Stine/1.20%, Stephen Doppler/2.00%

Financial Data: Fiscal Year End:05/31 Latest Annual Data: 5/31/2006

Year	Sales	Net Income
2006	NA	-$37,000
2005	NA	-$7,000

Curr. Assets:	$25,000	Curr. Liab.:	$12,000		
Plant, Equip.:	NA	Total Liab.:	$12,000	Indic. Yr. Divd.:	NA
Total Assets:	$25,000	Net Worth:	$14,000	Debt/ Equity:	3.5910

Auriga Laboratories Inc

2029 Century Pk. E, Ste. 1130, Los Angeles, CA, 90067; **PH:** 1-678-282-1600; **http://** www.aurigalabs.com

General - Incorporation	CO	**Stock** - Price on:12/24/2007	$1.07
Employees	24	Stock Exchange	OTC
Auditor	Williams & Webster, P.S	Ticker Symbol	ARGA
Stk Agt	Computershare Trust Co	Outstanding Shares	42,130,000
Counsel	NA	E.P.S.	-$0.313
DUNS No.	NA	Shareholders	NA

Business: The groups principle activity is to unique solutions for the respiratory, dermatology and psychiatry markets. The group products include Aquoral(TM), Zinx(TM), Akurza(TM), Xyralid(TM), Extendryl(R) and Levall(R). The group marketed its products under the trade names Extendryl(R) and Levall(R). The group operates from the United States. In the year 2006, the group acquired by Multi-Link.The groups quarterly revenue for September 2007 was 0.33 millions of USD.

Primary SIC and add'l.: 5122

CIK No: 0001072313

Subsidiaries: Auriga Laboratories, Inc., Auriga Operations, Inc.,, Auriga Pharmaceuticals, LLC

Officers: Philip S. Pesin/Chmn., CEO/$927,422.00, Steven D. Gallopo/VP - Business Development, Andrew D. Shales/COO/$743,256.00, Alan T. Roberts/Chief Scientific Officer/$313,071.00, Patrick Hayes/Relationship Mgr., Richard K. Sampson/National Sales Dir., Mischelle M. Hall/VP - Marketing, Jae C. Yu/VP - Corporate Development, Frank R. Greico/CFO, Rick C. Coulon/VP - Consumer Brands

Directors: Philip S. Pesin/Chmn., CEO, Dayne Wagoner/42/Dir., Brian P. Alleman/51/Dir., Stephen C. Glover/48/Dir., Trevor K. Pokorney/Dir., Leonhard Dreimann/Dir., Thomas G. Heck/Dir., Elliot M. Maza/Dir.

Owners: Trevor K. Pokorney, Elliot Maza, Frank Greico, Insiders/11.92%, Leon Dreimann, Philip S. Pesin/18.11%

Financial Data: Fiscal Year End:09/30 Latest Annual Data: 12/31/2006

Year	Sales	Net Income
2006	$3,174,000	-$11,713,000
2005	NA	-$125,000
2004	NA	-$19,000

Curr. Assets:	$2,412,000	Curr. Liab.:	$6,289,000	P/E Ratio:	0.62
Plant, Equip.:	$327,000	Total Liab.:	$7,039,000	Indic. Yr. Divd.:	NA
Total Assets:	$10,600,000	Net Worth:	$3,561,000	Debt/ Equity:	NA

Aurizon Mines Ltd

666 Burrard St., Ste. 3120, Pk. Pl., Vancouver, BC, V6C 2X8; **PH:** 1-604-687-6600; **http://** www.aurizon.com; **Email:** info@aurizon.com

General - Incorporation	BC	**Stock** - Price on:12/24/2007	$3.38
Employees	66	Stock Exchange	AMEX
Auditor	PricewaterhouseCoopers LLP	Ticker Symbol	AZK
Stk Agt	Computershare Investor Services LLC	Outstanding Shares	146,420,000
Counsel	NA	E.P.S.	$0.06
DUNS No.	24-760-5132	Shareholders	NA

Business: The group's principal activities are gold mining and other exploration activities in the gold producing abitibi region of north-western quebec. The properties of the group include, the sleeping giant mine and douay and douay west properties. The la reyna property is located in the state of sinaloa, Mexico. The principal two uses of gold are product fabrication and bullion investment. In the fabrication category there are a wide variety of end uses including caret jewelry, official coins, electronics, dentistry, medals and medallions.

Primary SIC and add'l.: 1041

CIK No: 0000913955

Officers: David P. Hall/Chmn., CEO, Pres., Julie A. Stokke Kemp/Corp. Sec., Ian S. Walton/Dir., Exec. VP, CFO, Michel Gilbert/VP, Gilles Brousseau/GM, Mining Manager, Dir., Chris McLean/Corporate Controller

Directors: David P. Hall/Chmn., CEO, Pres., Richard Faucher/Dir., Frank A. Lang/Dir., Ian S. Walton/Dir., Exec. VP, CFO, Brian S. Moorhouse/Dir., Robert Normand/Dir., Gilles Brousseau/GM, Mining Manager, Dir., Sargent H. Berner/Dir., Louis Dionne/Dir., Diane Francis/Dir.

Financial Data: Fiscal Year End:12/31 Latest Annual Data: 12/31/2006

Year	Sales	Net Income
2006	$1,063,000	-$12,421,000
2005	$642,000	$1,277,000
2004	$15,240,000	-$4,203,000

Curr. Assets:	$37,309,000	Curr. Liab.:	$11,308,000		
Plant, Equip.:	$144,887,000	Total Liab.:	$87,871,000	Indic. Yr. Divd.:	NA
Total Assets:	$187,108,000	Net Worth:	$99,236,000	Debt/ Equity:	NA

Aurora Gold Corp

30 Ledgar Rd., Balcatta, 6021; **PH:** 61-9240 2836; **Fax:** 61-9240 2406; **http://** www.aurora-gold.com; **Email:** admin@aurora-gold.com

General - Incorporation	DE	**Stock** - Price on:12/24/2007	$0.3
Employees	NA	Stock Exchange	OTC
Auditor	Peterson Sullivan, PLLC	Ticker Symbol	ARXG
Stk Agt	StockTrans, Inc.	Outstanding Shares	NA
Counsel	NA	E.P.S.	NA
DUNS No.	NA	Shareholders	NA

Business: The group's principal activities are to locate, acquire, explore and develop mineral resources. The group explores gold, silver, base metal and industrial minerals. It also evaluates, locates and provides finance for joint ventures and option agreements. All the mineral properties in which the group has an interest are in the exploration stage. The group has its operations in Canada, Mexico, South America and the United States of America.

Primary SIC and add'l.: 1041 1044

CIK No: 0001037049

Subsidiaries: Aurora Gold Mineracao

Officers: Klaus Eckhof/49/Dir., CEO, Pres., Cameron Richardson/55/Dir., Sec., CFO, Lars Pearl/46/Dir., Pres., Michael Montgomery/Executive Dir.

Directors: Klaus Eckhof/49/Dir., CEO, Pres., Cameron Richardson/55/Dir., Sec., CFO, Antonino G. Cacace/61/Dir., Lars Pearl/46/Dir., Pres., Michael Montgomery/Executive Dir.

Owners: Insiders/7.63%, Klaus P. Eckhof/7.61%, Antonino G. Cacace

Financial Data: Fiscal Year End:12/31 Latest Annual Data: 12/31/2006

Year	Sales	Net Income
2006	NA	-$5,464,000
2005	NA	-$457,000
2004	NA	-$224,000

Curr. Assets:	$321,000	Curr. Liab.:	$1,156,000		
Plant, Equip.:	$103,000	Total Liab.:	$1,156,000	Indic. Yr. Divd.:	NA
Total Assets:	$423,000	Net Worth:	-$732,000	Debt/ Equity:	NA

Aurora Metals (BVI) Ltd

349 W Georgia St., Vancouver, BC, V6B 3Z1; **PH:** 1-303-727-8609; **Fax:** 1-303-936-0333; **http://** www.aurorametals.net

General - Incorporation British Virgin Islands		**Stock** - Price on:12/24/2007	$0.09
Employees	NA	Stock Exchange	OTC
Auditor	Peterson Sullivan PLLC	Ticker Symbol	AURMF
Stk Agt	Holladay Stock Transfer, Inc.	Outstanding Shares	NA
Counsel	Salley Bowes Harwardt	E.P.S.	NA
DUNS No.	NA	Shareholders	NA

Business: The groups principal activity is to explore minerals. The group operates from the United States and Canada.

Primary SIC and add'l.: 1031 1099 1021

CIK No: 0001117073

Subsidiaries: Crystal Coding Limited

Officers: Cameron A. Richardson/55/Dir., CEO, CFO, Sec., John A.A. James/Dir., Pres., Melika Kassar/Member - Authorized Representative in Tunisia

Directors: Cameron A. Richardson/55/Dir., CEO, CFO, Sec., John A.A. James/Dir., Pres.

Owners: A. Cameron Richardson/5.29%, John A.A. James/13.21%, International Mining & Finance Corporation/6.51%, Insiders/18.50%

Financial Data: Fiscal Year End:12/31 Latest Annual Data: 12/31/2006

Year	Sales	Net Income
2006	NA	-$120,000
2005	NA	-$239,000
2004	NA	-$177,000

Curr. Assets:	$28,000	Curr. Liab.:	$112,000		
Plant, Equip.:	NA	Total Liab.:	$112,000	Indic. Yr. Divd.:	NA
Total Assets:	$28,000	Net Worth:	-$84,000	Debt/ Equity:	NA

Aurora Oil & Gas Corp

4110 Copper Ridge Dr., Ste. 100, Traverse City, MI, 49684; **PH:** 1-231-941-0073; **Fax:** 1-231-933-0757; **http://** www.auroraogc.com

General - Incorporation	UT	**Stock** - Price on:12/24/2007	$2.15
Employees	88	Stock Exchange	AMEX
Auditor	Rachlin Cohen & Holtz LLP	Ticker Symbol	AOG
Stk Agt	Mellon Investor Services LLC	Outstanding Shares	101,640,000
Counsel	NA	E.P.S.	-$0.02
DUNS No.	NA	Shareholders	NA

Business: The groups principle activities include exploring, exploiting and developing natural gas properties. In the year 2005, the group acquired Aurora Energy, Ltd. The group operates from the United States. The groups quarterly revenue for September 2007 was 7.23 millions of USD.

Primary SIC and add'l.: 1311

CIK No: 0000933157

Subsidiaries: Aurora Antrim North, LLC, Aurora Energy, Ltd., Aurora Holdings, LLC, Aurora Operating, LLC, Bach Services& Manufacturing Company, L.L.C., Celebration Mining Company, Hudson Pipeline & Processing Co., LLC, Indiana Royalty Trustory, LLC, Kingsley Development Company, L.L.C.

Officers: William W. Deneau/64/Chmn., CEO, Pres., Ronald E. Huff/53/CFO, Pres., Inside Dir., Dean A. Swift/56/General Counsel, Corp. Sec., John V. Miller/50/VP - Business, Corporate Development, Thomas W. Tucker/65/VP - Exploration, Jeffrey W. Deneau/Investor Relations Officer, John C. Hunter/57/VP - Exploration, Production

Directors: William W. Deneau/64/Chmn., CEO, Pres., Ronald E. Huff/53/CFO, Pres., Inside Dir., Richard M. Deneau/62/Outside Affiliated Dir., Gary J. Myles/63/Dir., Wayne G. Schaeffer/62/Dir., Kevin D. Stulp/52/Dir., Earl V. Young/67/Dir.

Owners: Crestview Capital Master, LLC/6.00%, John V. Miller/3.00%, Thomas W. Tucker/3.00%, Gary J. Myles, FMR Corp./15.00%, Kevin D. Stulp, Nathan A. Low Roth IRA and affiliates/8.00%, Earl V. Young, Insiders/12.00%, Lorraine M. King, William W. Deneau/4.00%, Ronald E. Huff, Richard M. Deneau

Financial Data: Fiscal Year End:09/30 Latest Annual Data: 12/31/2006

Year	Sales	Net Income
2006	$23,117,000	-$1,945,000
2005	$7,363,000	-$516,000

Curr. Assets:	$14,464,000	Curr. Liab.:	$18,118,000	P/E Ratio:	4.45
Plant, Equip.:	$170,515,000	Total Liab.:	$72,656,000	Indic. Yr. Divd.:	NA
Total Assets:	$212,387,000	Net Worth:	$139,731,000	Debt/ Equity:	NA

Austin Chalk Oil & Gas Ltd

5868 Westheimer, Ste. 233, Houston, TX, 77057; *PH:* 1-713-780-7633;
http:// www.austinchalkoil.com

General - Incorporation .... NV
Employees .... NA
Auditor .... Chisholm Bierwolf & Nilson LLC
Stk Agt .... Madison Stock Transfer, Inc.
Counsel .... NA
DUNS No. .... NA

Stock- Price on:12/24/2007 .... $0.025
Stock Exchange .... OTC
Ticker Symbol .... ACKO
Outstanding Shares .... NA
E.P.S. .... NA
Shareholders .... NA

Business: The group's principle activity is to provide microsoft consulting and training as well as telecommunications consulting, training and outsourcing. The group operates from United States.

Primary SIC and add'l.: 4899 7375 7379

CIK No: 0001098590

Financial Data: *Fiscal Year End:*12/31 **Latest Annual Data:** 12/31/2004

Year	Sales	Net Income
2004	NA	-$224,000
2003	NA	-$454,000
2002	NA	-$294,000

Curr. Assets:	$45,000	Curr. Liab.:	$44,000		
Plant, Equip.:	$75,000	Total Liab.:	$44,000	Indic. Yr. Divd.:	NA
Total Assets:	$119,000	Net Worth:	$75,000	Debt/ Equity:	NA

Austral Pacific Energy Ltd

PO Box 5337, Lambton Quay, Wellington, 6145; *PH:* 64-44950888; *http://* www.austral-pacific.com

General - Incorporation .... Canada
Employees 8
Auditor .... KPMG LLP
Stk Agt .... KPMG LLP
Counsel .... NA
DUNS No. .... NA

Stock- Price on:12/24/2007 .... $1.04
Stock Exchange .... AMEX
Ticker Symbol .... AEN
Outstanding Shares 27,960,000
E.P.S. .... -$0.73
Shareholders .... NA

Business: The group's principal activities are to acquire, explore and develop oil and gas properties. The group's exploration and production activities are focused in the Australia-pacific region. The group's interests are held in twenty permits in Australia, New Zealand and papua new guinea.

Primary SIC and add'l.: 1311

CIK No: 0001041829

Subsidiaries: Austral Pacific Energy (NZ) Limited, Coral Sea Drilling Limited, Indo-Pacific Energy Australia Pty Limited, Kanuka Energy Limited, Millennium Oil & Gas Limited, Odyssey International Pty Limited, Rata Energy Limited, Source Rock Holdings Limited, Totara Energy Limited, Trans-Orient Petroleum (Aust) Pty Limited, Trans-Orient Petroleum (PNG) Limited, Zoca 96-16 Pty Ltd.

Officers: Thompson Jewell/Dir., CEO, Derek Gardiner/CFO, Andy Price/Projects Mgr., David McKeogh/Acting CFO, Jeanette Watson/Company Sec., Carey Mills/Exploration Mgr., Joe Johnston/Petroleum Engineering Mgr., Warren Player/Mgr. - Joint Venture, Government Relations, Irene Bocock/Financial Controller, Chris McKeown/Commercial Mgr.

Directors: Peter Hill/Chmn., Ronald Bertuzzi/Dir., Bernhard Zinkhofer/Dir., David Newman/Dir., Douglas Ellenor/Dir.

Owners: Carey Mills/0.13%, Douglas Ellenor/0.23%, Joseph Johnston/0.12%, Ronald Bertuzzi/0.16%, Peter Hill/1.08%, David Newman/0.18%

Financial Data: *Fiscal Year End:*12/31 **Latest Annual Data:** 12/31/2006

Year	Sales	Net Income
2006	$871,000	-$13,174,000
2005	$1,705,000	-$2,641,000
2004	$212,000	-$9,435,000

Curr. Assets:	$9,749,000	Curr. Liab.:	$11,230,000		
Plant, Equip.:	$21,089,000	Total Liab.:	$23,898,000	Indic. Yr. Divd.:	NA
Total Assets:	$35,994,000	Net Worth:	$12,096,000	Debt/ Equity:	NA

Australia & New Zealand Banking GRP

100 Queen St., Melbourne, 3000; ; *http://* www.anz.com.au

General - Incorporation .... Australia
Employees 32,256
Auditor .... KPMG
Stk Agt .... Bank of New York
Counsel .... NA
DUNS No. 75-368-2830

Stock- Price on:12/24/2007 .... $124.17
Stock Exchange .... OTC
Ticker Symbol .... ANZBY
Outstanding Shares 368,940,000
E.P.S. $8.83
Shareholders .... NA

Business: The group's principal activities are the provision of general banking services, mortgage lending, life insurance, leasing, hire purchase and general finance, international and investment banking, investment and portfolio management and advisory services, nominee and custodian services and executor and trustee services. The group operates within Australia, New Zealand and overseas markets.

Primary SIC and add'l.: 6411 6282 6726 6099 6311 6211 6029

CIK No: 0000859994

Subsidiaries: ANZ Holdings (New Zealand) Limited, ANZ StEPS, ASB Bank Limited, Bank of New Zealand, Samson Funding Limited, UDC Finance Limited, Westpac Trust Corporation

Officers: John McFarlane/60/Dir., CEO, Robert Bell/CEO, Graham Hodges/Dir., CEO - ANZ National Bank Limited, John Harries/MD - Banking Products, Geoff Cohen/MD - Investment, Insurance Products, Shane Freeman/GM - People Capital, Breakout, Peter Marriott/CFO, Mark Ellis/MD - Private Bank, Owen Wilson/MD - International Partnerships, Paul Edwards/Head - Corporate Communications, Jenny Fagg/MD - Consumer Finance, Gilles Plante/MD - Markets, Mark Whelan/MD - Markets, Chris Cooper/MD - Debt, Transaction Services, Neil Shilbury/MD - Corporate Banking *(36 Officers included in Index)*

Directors: Graham Hodges/Dir., CEO - ANZ National Bank Limited, John McFarlane/60/Dir., CEO, Charles B. Goode/69/Chmn., D. M. Gonski/54/Dir., D. E. Meiklejohn/66/Dir., G. J. Clark/65/Dir., J. P. Morschel/65/Dir., M. A. Jackson/55/Dir., J. K. Ellis/70/Dir., I. J. MacFarlane/61/Dir.

Owners: Citicorp Nominees Pty Limited, Citicorp Nominees Pty Limited, ANZ Nominees Limited, Chase Manhattan Nominees Limited, Chase Manhattan Nominees Limited, National Nominees Limited, National Nominees Limited, National Nominees Limited, ANZ Nominees Limited, Citicorp Nominees Pty Limited, Westpac Custodian Nominees Limited, Westpac Custodian Nominees Limited, Westpac Custodian Nominees Limited, Chase Manhattan Nominees Limited, Insiders *(16 Owners included in Index)*

Financial Data: *Fiscal Year End:*09/30 **Latest Annual Data:** 9/30/2006

Year	Sales	Net Income
2006	$18,905,989,000	$2,731,048,000
2005	$15,950,334,000	$2,412,432,000
2004	$12,549,734,000	$1,998,438,000

Curr. Assets:	$36,570,049,000	Curr. Liab.:	$161,340,165,000		
Plant, Equip.:	$1,295,698,000	Total Liab.:	$236,212,839,000	Indic. Yr. Divd.:	$5.150
Total Assets:	$250,735,113,000	Net Worth:	$14,496,882,000	Debt/ Equity:	NA

Australian Canadian Oil Royalties Ltd

1301 Ave. M, Cisco, TX, 76437; *PH:* 1-254-442-2638; *Fax:* 1-254-442-3843;
http:// www.aussieoil.com; *Email:* acor@aussieoil.com

General - Incorporation .... Canada
Employees 3
Auditor .... Killman, Murrell & Co. P.C
Stk Agt .... NA
Counsel .... NA
DUNS No. .... NA

Stock- Price on:12/24/2007 .... $0.3
Stock Exchange .... OTC
Ticker Symbol .... AUCAF
Outstanding Shares 13,520,000
E.P.S. .... -$0.02
Shareholders .... NA

Business: The group's principal activity is to purchase, hold and sell producing and non-producing oil and gas royalty interests in Australia, Canada and the United States. The group is making a study of available oil and gas development acreage in Australia. The group selects and applies for the exploration permit on the area that demonstrates a high probability of success with the maximum rate of return for dollars invested. The group employs third parties for leasing operations in various countries.

Primary SIC and add'l.: 6792

CIK No: 0001061288

Officers: Andre Sakhai/27/Dir., CEO, Pres., Robert Kamon/Dir., Sec., Bernard Lipton/CFO

Directors: Andre Sakhai/27/Dir., CEO, Pres., Ely Sakhai/57/Dir., Robert Kamon/Dir., Sec., Kenneth W. Campbell/77/Dir., Howard Siegel/65/Dir.

Owners: Ken Campbell/1.85%, Insiders/49.11%, Robert Kamon/15.77%, Andre Sakhai/1.19%, Jan Soleimani/6.29%, Ely Sakhai/23.36%, Howard Siegel/0.22%, Tensleep Oil & Production, Inc./6.72%

Financial Data: *Fiscal Year End:*12/31 **Latest Annual Data:** 12/31/2006

Year	Sales	Net Income
2006	$42,000	-$620,000
2005	$21,000	-$615,000
2004	$26,000	-$393,000

Curr. Assets:	$14,000	Curr. Liab.:	$346,000		
Plant, Equip.:	$1,071,000	Total Liab.:	$346,000	Indic. Yr. Divd.:	NA
Total Assets:	$1,086,000	Net Worth:	$740,000	Debt/ Equity:	NA

Australian Forest IN

9974 Huntington Pk. Dr., Strongsville, OH, 44136; *Fax:* 1-440-759-7470

General - Incorporation ....
Employees .... NA
Auditor .... NA
Stk Agt .... Transfer Online, Inc.
Counsel .... NA
DUNS No. .... NA

Stock- Price on:12/24/2007 .... $0.1
Stock Exchange .... OTC
Ticker Symbol .... AUFI
Outstanding Shares .... NA
E.P.S. .... NA
Shareholders .... NA

Business: The groups principle activity is to operate pine saw milling and timber facility. The group operates from Australia and the United States. The groups quarterly revenue for September 2007 was 0.48 millions of USD.

Primary SIC and add'l.: 2421

CIK No:

Officers: Michael Timms/57/Chmn., CEO, Pres., Colin Baird/49/Dir., CFO, Tony Esplin/Exec. VP - Marketing, Dir., Roger Timms/52/Exec. VP - Engineering, Dir.

Directors: Michael Timms/57/Chmn., CEO, Pres., Colin Baird/49/Dir., CFO

Owners: Insiders/93.39%, Timbermans Group Pty Ltd/54.47%, Tony Esplin/7.78%, Michael Timms/7.78%, Colin Baird/7.78%, Roger Timms/7.78%, Norman Backman/7.78%

Financial Data: *Fiscal Year End:*NA **Latest Annual Data:** 12/31/2006

Year	Sales	Net Income
2006	$15,327,000	-$6,233,000
2005	$13,500,000	-$2,611,000
2004	$12,991,000	-$868,000

Curr. Assets:	$2,272,000	Curr. Liab.:	$22,846,000		
Plant, Equip.:	$17,929,000	Total Liab.:	$27,778,000	Indic. Yr. Divd.:	NA
Total Assets:	$20,943,000	Net Worth:	-$6,834,000	Debt/ Equity:	NA

Australian Oil & Gas Corp

Level 25, 500 Collins St., Melbourne, Victoria State, 3000; *PH:* 928-778-1450; *Fax:* 61-386104799;
http:// www.ausoil.com

General - Incorporation .... DE
Employees .... NA
Auditor .... Demetrius & Company, L.L.C
Stk Agt .... Holladay Stock Transfer, Inc.
Counsel .... NA
DUNS No. .... NA

Stock- Price on:12/24/2007 .... $0.1
Stock Exchange .... OTC
Ticker Symbol .... AOGC
Outstanding Shares 35,900,000
E.P.S. .... -$0.02
Shareholders .... NA

Business: The groups principal activity is to explore minerals and natural gas. The group operates from the United States and Canada.

Primary SIC and add'l.: 1311

CIK No: 0001080634

Subsidiaries: Alpha Oil & Natural Gas Pty Ltd, Gascorp, Inc., Nations LNG, Inc., Nations Natural Gas Pty Ltd

Officers: Geoffrey E. Albers/CEO, CFO, Pres., Treasurer, Dir., William Ray Hill/Dir., VP, Mark Anthony Muzzin/Dir., VP

Directors: Geoffrey E. Albers/CEO, CFO, Pres., Treasurer, Dir., E. G. Albers/Chmn., William Ray Hill/Dir., VP, Mark Anthony Muzzin/Dir., VP

Owners: Insiders/58.99%, William Ray Hill, Ernest Geoffrey Albers/58.70%

Financial Data: Fiscal Year End:12/31 **Latest Annual Data:** 12/31/2006

Year	Sales	Net Income
2006	NA	-$163,000
2005	NA	-$321,000
2004	NA	-$100,000

Curr. Assets:	$737,000	Curr. Liab.:	$98,000		
Plant, Equip.:	NA	Total Liab.:	$374,000	Indic. Yr. Divd.:	NA
Total Assets:	$737,000	Net Worth:	$363,000	Debt/ Equity:	NA

Authentidate Holding Corp

Connell Corporate Ctr., 3 Connell Dr., Berkeley Heights, NJ, 07922; *PH:* 1-908-787-1700; *Fax:* 1-908-673-9920; *http://* www.authentidatehc.com

General - Incorporation	DE	**Stock**- Price on:12/24/2007	$1.55
Employees	141	Stock Exchange	NDQ
Auditor	Eisner LLP	Ticker Symbol	ADAT
Stk Agt	Continental Stock Transfer & Trust Co	Outstanding Shares	34,430,000
Counsel	Goldstein & Digioia	E.P.S.	-$0.448
DUNS No.	15-413-4753	Shareholders	NA

Business: The group develops, assembles and sells document imaging software and systems, authentication and security software products, integration of computer systems and related peripheral equipment, components, and accessories and the provides network and Internet services. The group operates through docstar division and its subsidiaries djs marketing group inc, authentidate inc, authentidate international ag and trac medical solutions inc. The group operates in the United States and Germany.

Primary SIC and add'l.: 3577 3571 7373

CIK No: 0000885074

Subsidiaries: Authentidate International, AG, Authentidate, Inc., DJS Marketing Group, Inc., Trac Medical Solutions, Inc.

Officers: Surendra B. Pai/45/Dir., CEO, Pres., Jan C.E. Wendenburg/CEO - Authentidate International AG, Suren Pai/CEO, Pres., Benjamin O'Connell/VP - Products, Technology, Jakes Srinivasan/44/VP - Corporate Development, William Marshall/CFO, Treasurer, Joan Rothman/VP - Marketing, Paul Skinner/VP - Sales, Oconnell Benjamin/59/VP - Products, Technology

Directors: Surendra B. Pai/45/Dir., CEO, Pres., Ross F. Johnson/Chmn., David J. Luce/Dir., Edward J. Sheridan/73/Dir., Roger O. Goldman/Dir., John Waters/Dir., Charles C. Johnston/Dir., Ranjit C. Singh/Dir.

Owners: Charles C. Johnston, Roger O. Goldman, John J. Waters, Clint Coghill CCM Master Qualified Fund, Ltd./9.90%, NWQ Investment Management Company, LLC/5.20%, Ranjit C. Singh, Ross F. Johnson, Jan C. Wendenburg, Edward J. Sheridan, William A. Marshall, David J. Luce/2.90%, Surendra B. Pai/1.90%, Morgan Stanley/7.60%, Insiders/8.10%

Financial Data: Fiscal Year End:06/30 **Latest Annual Data:** 6/30/2006

Year	Sales	Net Income
2006	$16,572,000	-$17,823,000
2005	$17,553,000	-$19,184,000
2004	$19,242,000	-$15,669,000

Curr. Assets:	$50,008,000	Curr. Liab.:	$7,970,000		
Plant, Equip.:	$3,945,000	Total Liab.:	$8,199,000	Indic. Yr. Divd.:	NA
Total Assets:	$64,534,000	Net Worth:	$56,335,000	Debt/ Equity:	NA

Auto Underwriters of America Inc

2755 Campus Dr., Ste 155, San Mateo, CA, 94403; *PH:* 1-650-377-4381; *http://* www.autounderwriter.com

General - Incorporation	CA	**Stock**- Price on:12/24/2007	$3.5
Employees	46	Stock Exchange	OTC
Auditor	Malone & Bailey P.C., Clancy & Co.	Ticker Symbol	ADWT
Stk Agt	NA	Outstanding Shares	7,040,000
Counsel	NA	E.P.S.	-$0.88
DUNS No.	07-314-1129	Shareholders	NA

Business: The groups principle activity is to sale used vehicles. The group generates non-prime vehicle lender, originating and servicing auto loans via the Internet for consumers with less than perfect credit. The group also provides financial services. The group operates from United States.

Primary SIC and add'l.: 3661

CIK No: 0000726747

Officers: William J. Kellagher/45/Dir., Exec. VP, Divina Viray/42/Dir., Sec., Dean Antonis/42/Dir., Pres., Principal Executive Officer, Principal Financial, Accounting Officer, Michele H. Clark/47/Dir., Sec.

Directors: William J. Kellagher/45/Dir., Exec. VP, Divina Viray/42/Dir., Sec., Dean Antonis/42/Dir., Pres., Principal Executive Officer, Principal Financial, Accounting Officer, Robert Vaughan/70/Dir., Michele H. Clark/47/Dir., Sec.

Owners: Michele H. Clark/1.40%, Lawrence E. Gunnels/10.80%, Dean Antonis/11.20%, Insiders/23.26%, Timothy Hassell/11.00%, William J. Kellagher/10.70%

Financial Data: Fiscal Year End:06/30 **Latest Annual Data:** 6/30/2006

Year	Sales	Net Income
2006	$13,992,000	-$6,574,000
2005	$15,221,000	-$1,528,000
2004	$7,061,000	$172,000

Curr. Assets:	$51,000	Curr. Liab.:	$1,726,000		
Plant, Equip.:	$423,000	Total Liab.:	$14,125,000	Indic. Yr. Divd.:	NA
Total Assets:	$9,230,000	Net Worth:	-$4,896,000	Debt/ Equity:	NA

Autobytel Inc

18872 MacArthur Blvd., Irvine, CA, 92612; *PH:* 1-949-225-4500; *Fax:* 1-949-225-4557; *http://* www.autobytel.com; *Email:* consumercare@autobytel.com

General - Incorporation	DE	**Stock**- Price on:12/24/2007	$4.22
Employees	364	Stock Exchange	NDQ
Auditor	Mcgladrey & Pullen, LLP	Ticker Symbol	ABTL
Stk Agt	U.S. Stock Transfer Corp	Outstanding Shares	43,400,000
Counsel	NA	E.P.S.	-$0.23
DUNS No.	NA	Shareholders	NA

Business: The group's principal activity is to provide automotive marketing services over the Internet. It provides the services through four Web-sites it owns and operates: autobytel.com, autoweb.com, carsmart.com and autosite.com. The sites help automobile dealers to sell cars using marketing and customer relationship management tools and programs. Dealers subscribe to the new car marketing programs and the used vehicle cyberstore program on the sites on a contractual basis. The group directs consumers visiting the sites to appropriate dealers based on their location and preferences. The sites also help consumers in research, comparison and configuration of vehicles. On 31-Jan-2004, the group had 29,100 dealer relationships covering major manufacturers like bmw, daimlerchrysler, ford, general motors, honda and toyota. On 04-Jun-2003, the group acquired applied virtual vision inc, on 09-Apr-2004, acquired idriveonline, inc and on 15-Apr-2004, acquired stoneage corp.

Primary SIC and add'l.: 7375

CIK No: 0001023364

Subsidiaries: A.I.N. Corporation, Auto-By-Tel Acceptance Corporation, Auto-By-Tel Insurance Services, Inc., Autobytel Acquisition Corp., Autobytel Columbia Corp., Autobytel Information Services Inc., Autobytel Services Corporation, Autoweb.com, Inc., AVV, Inc., Car.com, Inc., e~autosdirect.com inc., Retention Performance Marketing, Inc., Stoneage Financial Corporation

Officers: James Riesenbach/Dir., CEO, Pres./$2,069,709.00, Ariel Amir/48/Exec. VP, Chief Legal, Administrative Officer, Sec./$649,973.00, Michael Schmidt/CFO, Exec. VP/$1,033,704.00, Melanie Webber/VP - Corporate Communications, Russell L. Bartlett/38/Sr. VP - CRM, Data Services/$466,639.00, Mark A. Garms/43/Sr. VP - Dealer Operations, Strategy/$566,539.00, Monty Houdeshell/CFO, Exec. VP, Crystal Hartwell/Mgr. - Corporate Communications

Directors: James Riesenbach/Dir., CEO, Pres., Mark R. Ross/Vice Chmn., Michael J. Fuchs/62/Chmn., Jeffrey H. Coats/Dir., Robert S. Grimes/Dir., Mark N. Kaplan/Dir., Jeffrey M. Stibel/Dir.

Owners: Michael J. Fuchs, Robert S. Grimes/2.10%, Richard Walker/1.20%, Morgan Stanley/8.30%, Jeffrey H. Coats, Dimensional Fund Advisors LP/7.80%, James E. Riesenbach, BC Advisors, LLC/5.60%, Russell Bartlett, Insiders/10.30%, Mark R. Ross/1.20%, Mark Garms, Richard A. Post, Ariel Amir/1.70%, Michael F. Schmidt *(18 Owners included in Index)*

Financial Data: Fiscal Year End:12/31 **Latest Annual Data:** 06/30/2007

Year	Sales	Net Income
2007	NA	NA
2006	$111,090,000	-$31,468,000
2005	$125,269,000	-$6,258,000

Curr. Assets:	$45,174,000	Curr. Liab.:	$20,499,000		
Plant, Equip.:	$7,954,000	Total Liab.:	$20,694,000	Indic. Yr. Divd.:	NA
Total Assets:	$124,696,000	Net Worth:	$103,818,000	Debt/ Equity:	NA

Autocarbon Inc

89 Ravine Edge Dr., Richmond Hill, ON, L4E 4J6; *PH:* 1-905-787-8225

General - Incorporation	DE	**Stock**- Price on:12/24/2007	$0.8
Employees	NA	Stock Exchange	NA
Auditor	Aaron Stein CPA	Ticker Symbol	NA
Stk Agt	Florida Atlantic Stock Transfer, Inc.	Outstanding Shares	NA
Counsel	Loeb & Loeb LLP	E.P.S.	NA
DUNS No.	NA	Shareholders	NA

Business: The group's principle activities include developing, marketing and distributing cosmetic products for the construction industry for blocking fiberglass insulation fibers from becoming lodged on a workman's skin. As of Mar 31, 2004, the company acquired our subsidiary, ncn. Ncn sells its product through its Website www.newconceptsnutra.com. The group operates from United States.

Primary SIC and add'l.: 2844

CIK No: 0001157300

Subsidiaries: Changchun Xiandai Technology, Jilin BenCao Tang Pharmacy Co Ltd.

Officers: Lianqin Qu/52/Chairwoman, CEO, Pres., Tom Du/52/Dir., CTO, Joseph J. Levinson/31/Dir., CFO, Zongsheng Zhang/CFO

Directors: Lianqin Qu/52/Chairwoman, CEO, Pres., Xiaobo Sun/50/Dir., Tom Du/52/Dir., Joseph J. Levinson/31/Dir., CFO

Owners: Insiders/84.96%, Lianqin Qu/63.50%, Zhenyou Zhang/21.51%

Financial Data: Fiscal Year End:12/31 **Latest Annual Data:** 12/31/2006

Year	Sales	Net Income
2006	$2,376,000	-$1,234,000
2005	$3,085,000	$201,000
2002	$11,000	-$426,000

Curr. Assets:	$174,000	Curr. Liab.:	$343,000		
Plant, Equip.:	$26,000	Total Liab.:	$343,000	Indic. Yr. Divd.:	NA
Total Assets:	$200,000	Net Worth:	-$142,000	Debt/ Equity:	0.2361

Autocorp Equities Inc

2500 Legacy Dr., Ste. 226, Frisco, TX, 75034; *PH:* 1-214-618-6400

General - Incorporation	NV	**Stock**- Price on:12/24/2007	$0.009
Employees	4	Stock Exchange	NA
Auditor	Friedman LLP	Ticker Symbol	NA
Stk Agt	Holladay Stock Transfer, Inc.	Outstanding Shares	198,640,000
Counsel	NA	E.P.S.	-$0.016
DUNS No.	NA	Shareholders	NA

Business: The group's principal operations consist of providing services to the finance industry. The finance services include the purchase of automobile finance receivables, collateralized by used automobiles from franchised and independent automobile retailers. The automobile finance receivables are sold to banks and credit unions. The services include the purchasing, sale and loan servicing of prime and non-prime automobile loans on behalf of banks and credit unions. Additionally, the group provides re-Marketing services to banks and credit unions. On 30-Jun-2003 the group acquired pacific auto group, inc.

Primary SIC and add'l.: 6141 5521

CIK No: 0000790066

Subsidiaries: ACE Motor Company, AutoCorp Financial Services, Inc., Pacific Auto Group, Inc.

Officers: Peter Ubaldi/Dir., CEO, Pres., Terri Ashley/VP - Investor Relations, Roy Pardini/Dir., Exec. VP, Jay Doleh/Special Projects Consultant, Anthony Santora/CTO

Directors: Peter Ubaldi/Dir., CEO, Pres., Charles Norman/50/Dir., Roy Pardini/Dir., Exec. VP

Owners: Charles Norman/23.25%, Insiders, Charles Norman, Roy Pardini/3.11%, AutoCorp Acquisition Partners/0.00%, Jay Doleh/1.14%, Peter Ubaldi/25.32%, Securities Acquisition New York/5.07%, William Merritt/5.20%, Peter Ubaldi, Insiders, Terri Ashley/1.72%, AutoCorp Acquisition Partners, Donna Blohm/1.05%, Roderick Michael Johnson/6.47% *(20 Owners included in Index)*

Financial Data: ***Fiscal Year End:***12/31 ***Latest Annual Data:*** 12/31/2006

Year	Sales	Net Income
2006	$64,000	-$2,966,000
2005	$318,000	-$5,195,000
2004	$542,000	-$3,142,000

Curr. Assets:	$2,000	***Curr. Liab.:***	$4,458,000		
Plant, Equip.:	$13,000	***Total Liab.:***	$4,458,000	***Indic. Yr. Divd.:***	NA
Total Assets:	$15,000	***Net Worth:***	-$4,443,000	***Debt/ Equity:***	NA

Autodesk Inc

111 McInnis Pkwy., San Rafael, CA, 94903; ***PH:*** 1-415-507-5000; ***Fax:*** 1-415-507-5100; ***http://*** usa.autodesk.com

General - Incorporation	DE	***Stock***- Price on:12/24/2007	$47.1
Employees	5,169	Stock Exchange	NDQ
Auditor	Ernst & Young LLP	Ticker Symbol	ADSK
Stk Agt	Computershare Investor Services LLC	Outstanding Shares	231,200,000
Counsel	Wilson Sonsini Goodrich & Rosati	E.P.S.	$1.47
DUNS No.	06-970-1282	Shareholders	NA

Business: The group's principal activities are to provide integrated and interoperable design software, Internet services, and wireless development platforms and point-of-location applications. The group operates through two segments: design solutions and discreet segment. Design solutions segment markets design software products and services for professionals and consumers who design, build, manage and own building projects or manufactured goods. It also markets mapping and geographic information systems technology to public and private users. The discreet segment develops, integrates, markets, sells and supports film and television compositing systems, high definition and standard definition broadcast editorial and finishing systems, digital cinema production systems for color grading and film finishing and animation, visualization, and streaming media products.

Primary SIC and add'l.: 7372 7373

CIK No: 0000769397

Subsidiaries: ADSKCanadaInc., Alias Systems GmbH, Alias Systems Inc., Alias Systems KK, Alias Systems Limited, Alias Systems SAS, Alias Systems Singapore Pte. Ltd., Alias Systems Srl., AliasSystemsKoreaLimitedCompany, Autodesk (EMEA) S.a.r.l., Autodesk (Europe) S.A., Autodesk AB, Autodesk Asia Pte Ltd., Autodesk Australia Pty Ltd., Autodesk B.V. 48 Subsidiaries included in the Index

Officers: Carl Bass/Dir., CEO, Pres./$6,082,677.00, Carol Bartz/Executive Chmn./$6,059,996.00, Sue Pirri/VP - Investor Relations, Mary Alice Taylor/Dir., Independent Business Executive, Ken Bado/Exec. VP - Worldwide Sales, Global Accounting, Jan Becker/Sr. VP - Human Resources/$1,388,980.00, Andrew Miller/VP - Finance, Chief Accounting Officer, Alfred Castino/Sr. VP, CFO/$1,584,233.00, Jay Bhatt/Sr. VP - Architecture, Engineering, Construction Solutions, Chris Bradshaw/Sr. VP - Worldwide Marketing, Moonhie Chin/Sr. VP - Strategic Planning, Operations, Pascal W. Di Fronzo/Sr. VP, General Counsel, Sec., Amar Hanspal/Sr. VP - Platform Solutions, Emerging Business, Robert Kross/Sr. VP - Manufacturing Solutions, Marc Petit/Sr. VP - Media, Entertainment

Directors: Carl Bass/Dir., CEO, Pres., Carol Bartz/Executive Chmn., Per-Kristian Halvorsen/Dir., Mark Bertelsen/Dir., Michael J. Fister/Dir., Crawford W. Beveridge/Dir., Hallam J. Dawson/Dir., Larry Wangberg/Dir., Mary Alice Taylor/Dir., Independent Business Executive

Owners: Carol A. Bartz/1.40%, TCW Asset Management Co./5.84%, Hallam J. Dawson, Mark A. Bertelsen, ClearBridge Advisors, LLC/5.34%, T. Rowe Price Associates, Inc./8.48%, Michael J. Fister, Wellington Management Co. LLP/5.33%, Alfred J. Castino, Crawford W. Beveridge, Carl Bass, Insiders/2.53%, George M. Bado, Jan Becker, Per-Kristian Halvorsen *(16 Owners included in Index)*

Financial Data: ***Fiscal Year End:***01/31 ***Latest Annual Data:*** 1/31/2007

Year	Sales	Net Income
2007	$1,839,800,000	$289,700,000
2006	$1,523,200,000	$328,900,000
2005	$1,233,767,000	$221,508,000

Curr. Assets:	$1,189,700,000	***Curr. Liab.:***	$574,200,000	***P/E Ratio:***	34.63
Plant, Equip.:	$65,600,000	***Total Liab.:***	$682,500,000	***Indic. Yr. Divd.:***	NA
Total Assets:	$1,797,500,000	***Net Worth:***	$1,115,000,000	***Debt/ Equity:***	0.0352

Autoimmune Inc

1199 Madia St., Pasadena, CA, 91103; ***PH:*** 1-626-792-1235; ***Fax:*** 1-626-792-1236; ***http://*** www.autoimmuneinc.com

General - Incorporation	DE	***Stock***- Price on:12/24/2007	$1.35
Employees	NA	Stock Exchange	OTC
Auditor	PricewaterhouseCoopers LLP	Ticker Symbol	AIMM
Stk Agt	Computershare Trust Co	Outstanding Shares	16,980,000
Counsel	Nutter McClennen & Fish	E.P.S.	-$0.003
DUNS No.	78-562-6888	Shareholders	NA

Business: The group's principle activities include developing and marketing pharmaceutical products for the treatment of autoimmune and other cell-mediated inflammatory diseases. The products are based on the principles of mucosal tolerance. Mucosal tolerance utilizes the natural immune system mechanisms associated with the gut, nasal passages, lungs and other mucosally lined tissues. The products consist of drugs for the treatment of rheumatoid arthritis, type 1 diabetes and multiple sclerosis. The group operates from United States.

Primary SIC and add'l.: 2834 8099

CIK No: 000879106

Officers: Robert C. Bishop/Chmn., CEO/$94,600.00, Suzanne Glassburn/Sec.

Directors: Robert C. Bishop/Chmn., CEO, John R. Fletcher/62/Dir.

Owners: Allan R. Ferguson, Arnhold and S. Bleichroeder Advisers, LLC/6.60%, Eastbourne Capital Management, L.L.C./6.10%, BVF Partners L.P./21.10%, Andrew H. Tisch/7.70%, Lloyd I. Miller/5.30%, R. John Fletcher, Insiders/6.70%, Hugh A. DAndrade, Diane M. McClintock, Robert C. Bishop/4.60%, Dane Andreeff/7.00%

Financial Data: ***Fiscal Year End:***12/31 ***Latest Annual Data:*** 12/31/2006

Year	Sales	Net Income
2006	$401,000	-$481,000
2005	$179,000	-$666,000
2004	$130,000	-$761,000

Curr. Assets:	$8,951,000	***Curr. Liab.:***	$128,000		
Plant, Equip.:	NA	***Total Liab.:***	$128,000	***Indic. Yr. Divd.:***	NA
Total Assets:	$8,951,000	***Net Worth:***	$8,823,000	***Debt/ Equity:***	NA

Autoinfo Inc

6413 Congress Ave., Ste. 260, Boca Raton, FL, 33487; ***PH:*** 1-561-988-9456; ***Fax:*** 1-561-994-8033; ***http://*** www.sunteckransport.com

General - Incorporation	DE	***Stock***- Price on:12/24/2007	$0.78
Employees	45	Stock Exchange	OTC
Auditor	Dworken, Hillman, LaMorte & Sterczala	Ticker Symbol	AUTO
Stk Agt	American Stock Transfer & Trust Co.	Outstanding Shares	32,470,000
Counsel	NA	E.P.S.	$0.06
DUNS No.	09-889-6756	Shareholders	NA

Business: The group's principal activities are transportation from coast to coast, local pick up and delivery, warehousing, air freight and ocean freight. The group's services include arranging for the transport of customers' freight from the shippers' location to the designated destination. The group does not own any trucking equipment and relies on independent carriers for the movement of customers' freight. The group has strategic alliances with less than truckload, truckload, air, rail and ocean common carriers to provide services. It has six regional operating centers providing brokerage services and representatives in 15 states and Canada. As of 01-Mar-2004 it had five regional offices providing contract carrier services and 43 independent owner-operators. Each operations office markets the full range of supply chain services to existing customers and pursues new customers within their local markets.

Primary SIC and add'l.: 4731

CIK No: 0000351017

Subsidiaries: Sunteck Transport & Logistics, Inc., Sunteck Transport Co., Inc.

Officers: Harry M. Wachtel/Chmn., CEO, Pres./$519,000.00, Mark Weiss/Dir. - Autoinfo, Inc, Exec. VP - Sunteck Transport Group/$137,000.00, William I. Wunderlich/CFO/$404,000.00, Michael P. Williams/COO, General Counsel - Sunteck Transport Group, Dave Dallas/VP - Marketing, Sunteck Transport Group, Jonathan M. Gloss/CTO - Sunteck Transport Group

Directors: Harry M. Wachtel/Chmn., CEO, Pres., Peter C. Einselen/68/Dir., Thomas C. Robertson/62/Dir.

Owners: Thomas C. Robertson/1.70%, Mark Weiss/3.30%, James T. Martin/ Listan Ltd./18.30%, Insiders/26.70%, Harry Wachtel/20.50%, Peter C. Einselen/2.10%, Wasatch Advisors, Inc/9.90%, William I. Wunderlich/4.80%, Kinderhook Partners, LP/18.50%

Financial Data: ***Fiscal Year End:***12/31 ***Latest Annual Data:*** 12/31/2006

Year	Sales	Net Income
2006	$84,111,000	$3,628,000
2005	$68,040,000	$3,608,000
2004	$46,492,000	$1,466,000

Curr. Assets:	$18,921,000	***Curr. Liab.:***	$11,826,000	***P/E Ratio:***	7.80
Plant, Equip.:	$324,000	***Total Liab.:***	$11,826,000	***Indic. Yr. Divd.:***	NA
Total Assets:	$23,822,000	***Net Worth:***	$11,996,000	***Debt/ Equity:***	NA

Autoline Group Inc

280 W River Pk. Dr., Provo, UT, 84604; ***PH:*** 1-801-623-4751

General - Incorporation	UT	***Stock***- Price on:12/24/2007	$0.67
Employees	5	Stock Exchange	NA
Auditor	Mantyla McReynolds	Ticker Symbol	NA
Stk Agt	Atlas Stock Transfer Corp	Outstanding Shares	45,670,000
Counsel	NA	E.P.S.	-$0.02
DUNS No.	NA	Shareholders	NA

Business: The group's principle activity is to sell used cars in the retail and wholesale market. The company provides access to the national wholesale market to the national wholesale market. Used car retail sales occurs through either manufacturer's franchised new car dealerships that sell used cars or through independent used car dealerships. The company purchases vehicles through auctions or a variety of other discount channels and resells in the retail market.

Primary SIC and add'l.: 5521

CIK No: 0001145328

Subsidiaries: GeNOsys, Inc.

Officers: John W.R. Miller/Dir., Pres./$120,000.00, Michael J. Holman/CFO/$8,462.00

Directors: John W.R. Miller/Dir., Pres.

Owners: Smith Consulting Services, Inc./7.30%, John W. R. Miller/54.90%, Christie Melanie Woodruff Jones, Insiders/81.00%, Clark M. Mower/18.30%

Financial Data: ***Fiscal Year End:***11/30 ***Latest Annual Data:*** 11/30/2006

Year	Sales	Net Income
2006	NA	-$1,179,000
2005	NA	-$200,000
2004	$288,000	-$26,000

Curr. Assets:	$989,000	***Curr. Liab.:***	$60,000		
Plant, Equip.:	$177,000	***Total Liab.:***	$60,000	***Indic. Yr. Divd.:***	NA
Total Assets:	$1,173,000	***Net Worth:***	$1,114,000	***Debt/ Equity:***	NA

Autoliv Inc

1320 Pacific Dr., Auburn Hills, MI, 48326; ***PH:*** 1-248-475-9000; ***Fax:*** 1-248-475-9838; ***http://*** www.autoliv.com; ***Email:*** info@autoliv.com

General - Incorporation	DE	***Stock***- Price on:12/24/2007	$57.88
Employees	35,700	Stock Exchange	NYSE
Auditor	Ernst & Young LLP	Ticker Symbol	ALV
Stk Agt	Computershare Trust Co	Outstanding Shares	79,610,000
Counsel	NA	E.P.S.	$3.73
DUNS No.	60-251-1248	Shareholders	NA

Business: The group's principle activity is to provide automotive safety systems. Specific customers of the group include Ford, Volvo and Mazda. The group operates from United States.

Primary SIC and add'l.: 3714
CIK No: 0001034670
Subsidiaries: Autoliv AB, Autoliv ASP, Inc.
Officers: Jan Carlson/47/CEO, Pres., Steve Fredin/46/VP - Engineering, Svante Mogefors/53/VP - Quality, Michael S. Anderson/Acting VP - Legal Affairs, General Counsel, Sec., Lars Sjobring/VP - Legal Affairs, General Counsel, Sec., Hans-Goran Patring/59/VP - Human Resources, Jorgen I. Svensson/46/Pres. - Legal Affairs, General Counsel, Sec./$620,559.00, Mats odman/58/VP - Corporate Communications, Jan Olsson/54/VP - Research, Benoit Marsaud/56/COO/$976,995.00, Halvar Jonzon/58/VP - Purchasing/$665,698.00, Magnus Lindquist/45/CFO, VP/$739,861.00, Ray Pekar/Investor Relations Officer
Directors: Lars Westerberg/60/Chmn., Robert W. Alspaugh/61/Dir., Sune Carlsson/67/Dir., Walter Kunerth/68/Dir., Kazuhiko Sakamoto/63/Dir., Jay S. Stewart/70/Dir., Per Welin/72/Dir., Tetsuo Sekiya/73/Dir., George A. Lorch/67/Dir., William E. Johnston/68/Dir., Lars Nyberg/57/Dir., James M. Ringler/62/Dir.
Owners: Lars Westerberg, Magnus Lindquist, William E. Johnston, Insiders, James M. Ringler, Per-Olof Aronson, Halvar Jonzon, Tetsuo Sekiya, Benot Marsaud, George A. Lorch, Per Welin, Jrgen I. Svensson, Sune Carlsson, Jay S. Stewart
Financial Data: Fiscal Year End:12/31 Latest Annual Data: 12/31/2006

Year	Sales	Net Income
2006	$6,188,000,000	$402,300,000
2005	$6,204,900,000	$292,600,000
2004	$6,143,900,000	$326,300,000

Curr. Assets:	$2,098,400,000	Curr. Liab.:	$1,531,600,000	P/E Ratio:	13.15
Plant, Equip.:	$1,160,400,000	Total Liab.:	$2,707,900,000	Indic. Yr. Divd.:	$1.560
Total Assets:	$5,110,800,000	Net Worth:	$2,402,900,000	Debt/ Equity:	0.3909

Automatic Data Processing Inc

1 ADP Blvd., Roseland, NJ, 07068; ***PH:*** 1-973-974-5000; ***Fax:*** 1-973-974-3334; ***http://*** www.adp.com

General - Incorporation	DE	**Stock**- Price on:12/24/2007	$49.17
Employees	46,000	Stock Exchange	NYSE
Auditor	Deloitte & Touche LLP	Ticker Symbol	ADP
Stk Agt	American Stock Transfer & Trust CO.	Outstanding Shares	553,240,000
Counsel	Paul Weiss Rifkind Wharton & Garrison	E.P.S	$2.93
DUNS No.	00-191-5172	Shareholders	NA

Business: The groups principle activity is to provide computerized transaction processing and data communication services. The group operates through three segments namely employer, brokerage and dealer services. The group operates from United States.
Primary SIC and add'l.: 7374 7375 7291 8721
CIK No: 0000008670
Subsidiaries: 71 Hanover Florham Park Associates LLC, ADP Atlantic, Inc., ADP Belgium CVA, ADP Broker-Dealer, Inc., ADP Brokerage International Limited, ADP Canada Co., ADP Clearing & Outsourcing Services, Inc., ADP Clearing do Brasil Ltda., ADP Commercial Leasing, LLC, ADP Dealer Services Deutschland GmbH, ADP Dealer Services France SAS, ADP Dealer Services Italia s.r.l., ADP Dealer Services UK Limited, ADP East, Inc., ADP Employer Services GmbH 48 Subsidiaries included in the Index
Officers: Gary C. Butler/Dir., CEO, Pres./$9,507,457.00, Kris D. Borkovich/Corporate VP, Benito Cachinero/Corporate VP, Laurie J. Eldridge/Corporate VP, George I. Stoeckert/Pres. - Employer Services, International/$2,125,157.00, Jan Siegmund/Corporate VP, Regina R. Lee/Corporate VP, Michael S. Martone/COO/$4,339,890.00, Steven J. Anenen/Corporate VP, John J. Gleason/Corporate VP, Daniel A. Zaccardo/Staff VP, Stephen A. Doherty/Staff VP, James B. Benson/General Counsel, Sec./$2,350,312.00, Campbell B. Langdon/Corporate VP, Raymond L. Colotti/Corporate VP *(24 Officers included in Index)*
Directors: Gary C. Butler/Dir., CEO, Pres., Gregory D. Brenneman/Dir., Frederic V. Malek/Dir., Gregory L. Summe/Dir., Leslie A. Brun/Dir., Leon G. Cooperman/Dir., John P. Jones/Dir., Glenn R. Hubbard/Dir., Eric C. Fast/Dir., Henry Taub/Dir.
Owners: George I. Stoeckert, James B. Benson, Gregory D. Brenneman, Gary C. Butler, Dan Sheldon, Christopher R. Reidy, Henry Taub, Frederic V. Malek, Arthur F. Weinbach, Insiders/2.10%, Leslie A. Brun, John P. Jones, Leon G. Cooperman, Glenn R. Hubbard, Michael S. Martone
Financial Data: Fiscal Year End:06/30 Latest Annual Data: 6/30/2006

Year	Sales	Net Income
2006	$8,881,500,000	$1,554,000,000
2005	$8,499,100,000	$1,055,400,000
2004	$7,754,942,000	$935,570,000

Curr. Assets:	$4,760,100,000	Curr. Liab.:	$2,592,700,000	P/E Ratio:	16.78
Plant, Equip.:	$782,400,000	Total Liab.:	$21,478,500,000	Indic. Yr. Divd.:	NA
Total Assets:	$27,490,100,000	Net Worth:	$6,011,600,000	Debt/ Equity:	0.0072

Autonation Inc FL

110 SE 6th St., Fort Lauderdale, FL, 33301; ***PH:*** 1-954-769-6000; ***Fax:*** 1-954-769-6537; ***http://*** www.autonation.com

General - Incorporation	DE	**Stock**- Price on:12/24/2007	$22.47
Employees	26,000	Stock Exchange	NYSE
Auditor	Deloitte & Touche, LLP	Ticker Symbol	AN
Stk Agt	Computershare Investor Services LLC	Outstanding Shares	209,840,000
Counsel	NA	E.P.S	$1.46
DUNS No.	04-589-3054	Shareholders	NA

Business: The groups principle activity is to provide automotive products and services. The groups products include new vehicles and used vehicles. The groups services include vehicle maintenance and repair, parts and extended service contracts. In the year 2006, the group acquired five automobile retail franchises and other related assets. The group operates from United States.
Primary SIC and add'l.: 3714 7515 5511
CIK No: 0000350698
Subsidiaries: 7 Rod Real Estate North, a Limited Liability Company, 7 Rod Real Estate South, a Limited Liability Company, A&R Insurance Enterprises, Inc., Abraham Chevrolet-Tampa, Inc., ACER Fiduciary, Inc., Al Maroone Ford, LLC, Albert Berry Motors, Inc., All-State Rent A Car, Inc., Allison Bavarian, American Way Motors, Inc., AN Cadillac of WPB, LLC, AN California Region Management, LLC, AN Chevrolet Arrowhead, Inc., AN Chevrolet of Phoenix, LLC, AN CJ Valencia, Inc. 435 Subsidiaries included in the Index

Officers: Mike Jackson/Chmn., CEO/$4,513,617.00, Kevin P. Westfall/Sr. VP - Sales/$1,040,172.00, Alan T. Haig/Sr. VP - Corporate Development, John M. Zimmerman/VP - Investor Relations, Jonathan P. Ferrando/Exec. VP, General Counsel, Sec./$1,780,359.00, Michael E. Maroone/Dir., COO, Pres./$3,706,955.00, Marc Cannon/Sr. VP - Corporate Communications, Gary Marcotte/Sr. VP - eCommerce, Donna Parlapiano/Sr. VP - Regional Operations, Industry Relations, Michael J. Short/CFO, Exec. VP
Directors: Mike Jackson/Chmn., CEO, William C. Crowley/Dir., Wayne H. Huizenga/Founder, Michael E. Maroone/Dir., COO, Pres., Carlos A. Migoya/Dir., Robert J. Brown/Dir., Rick L. Burdick/Dir., Robert R. Grusky/Dir., Kim C. Goodman/Dir.
Owners: Jonathan P. Ferrando, Carlos A. Migoya, Robert J. Brown, ESL Investments, Inc./23.70%, Goldman Sachs Asset Management, L.P/8.10%, Kevin P. Westfall, Rick L. Burdick, Insiders/26.90%, Barclays Global Investors, NA/17.00%, Edward S. Lampert/23.80%, Robert R. Grusky, Michael E. Maroone/2.60%, Mike Jackson, Irene B. Rosenfeld, William C. Crowley/23.80%
Financial Data: Fiscal Year End:12/31 Latest Annual Data: 12/31/2006

Year	Sales	Net Income
2006	$18,988,600,000	$316,900,000
2005	$19,253,400,000	$496,500,000
2004	$19,424,700,000	$433,600,000

Curr. Assets:	$3,385,800,000	Curr. Liab.:	$3,030,500,000		
Plant, Equip.:	$1,929,600,000	Total Liab.:	$4,894,300,000	Indic. Yr. Divd.:	NA
Total Assets:	$8,607,000,000	Net Worth:	$3,712,700,000	Debt/ Equity:	0.3535

AutoZone Inc

123 S Front St., Memphis, TN, 38103; ***PH:*** 1-901-495-6500; ***Fax:*** 1-901-495-8300; ***http://*** www.autozoneinc.com; ***Email:*** investor.relations@autozone.com

General - Incorporation	NV	**Stock**- Price on:12/24/2007	$137.1
Employees	30,210	Stock Exchange	NYSE
Auditor	Ernst & Young LLP	Ticker Symbol	AZO
Stk Agt	Computershare Investor Services LLC	Outstanding Shares	67,290,000
Counsel	NA	E.P.S	$8.53
DUNS No.	15-723-3511	Shareholders	NA

Business: The group's principle activity is to provide automotive parts and accessories. The group operates from United States.
Primary SIC and add'l.: 5531
CIK No: 0000866787
Subsidiaries: Alldata LLC, AutoZone de Mexico, S. de R.L. de C.V., AutoZone Development Corporation, AutoZone Northeast, Inc. fka ADAP, Inc., AutoZone Parts, Inc., AutoZone Puerto Rico, Inc., AutoZone Stores, Inc., AutoZone Texas, L.P., AutoZone West, Inc. fka Chief Auto Parts Inc., AutoZone.com, Inc.
Officers: William C. Rhodes/43/Dir., CEO, Pres., Robert D. Olsen/Exec. VP - Retail, Commercial Operations, Mexico, Thomas B. Newbern/Sr. VP - Store Operations, Timothy W. Briggs/Sr. VP - Human Resources, Larry Roesel/Sr. VP - Commercial, Harry L. Goldsmith/Exec. VP, Sec., General Counsel, Lisa R. Kranc/Sr. VP - Marketing, Charlie Pleas/VP, Controller, James A. Shea/Exec. VP - Merchandising, Marketing, William T. Giles/CFO, Exec. VP, William W. Graves/Sr. VP - Supply Chain
Directors: William C. Rhodes/43/Dir., CEO, Pres., Charles M. Elson/Dir., Andrew W. McKenna/60/Dir., Gerry N. House/Dir., Sue E. Gove/Dir., J. R. Hyde/63/Dir., Earl G. Graves/Dir., George R. Mrkonic/55/Dir., Theodore W. Ullyot/41/Dir.
Owners: N. Gerry House, James A. Shea, Andrew W. McKenna, Harry L. Goldsmith, Theodore W. Ullyot, Earl G. Graves, Sue E. Gove, Charles M. Elson, William T. Giles, George R. Mrkonic, Insiders/2.30%, J. R. Hyde, Robert D. Olsen, William C. Rhodes
Financial Data: Fiscal Year End:08/27 Latest Annual Data: 8/26/2006

Year	Sales	Net Income
2006	$5,948,355,000	$569,275,000
2005	$5,710,882,000	$571,019,000
2004	$5,637,025,000	$566,202,000

Curr. Assets:	$1,755,757,000	Curr. Liab.:	$1,818,115,000	P/E Ratio:	16.52
Plant, Equip.:	$1,790,089,000	Total Liab.:	$3,741,172,000	Indic. Yr. Divd.:	NA
Total Assets:	$3,912,565,000	Net Worth:	$171,393,000	Debt/ Equity:	4.2210

Aux (USA) Inc

566 E Yinzhou Rd., Ningbo, 10005; ***PH:*** 86-574-882-20636; ***http://*** www.heritagecapitalgroup.com

General - Incorporation	DE	**Stock**- Price on:12/24/2007	NA
Employees	NA	Stock Exchange	NA
Auditor	Paritz & Co P.A	Ticker Symbol	NA
Stk Agt	NA	Outstanding Shares	NA
Counsel	NA	E.P.S	NA
DUNS No.	NA	Shareholders	NA

Business: The group's principle activity is to seek, investigate and if such investigation warrants, merge or acquire an interest in business opportunities presented to it by persons or companies who or which desire to seek the perceived advantages of a Securities Exchange Act of 1934 registered corporation. The group operates from United States.
Primary SIC and add'l.: 6770
CIK No: 0001289277
Subsidiaries: AUX Group

Auxilio Inc

27401 Los Altos, Ste. 100, Mission Viejo, CA, 92691; ***PH:*** 1-949-614-0700; ***Fax:*** 1-949-614-0701; ***http://*** www.auxilioinc.com

General - Incorporation	NV	**Stock**- Price on:12/24/2007	$0.72
Employees	60	Stock Exchange	OTC
Auditor	Haskell & White LLP	Ticker Symbol	AUXO
Stk Agt	Colonial Stock Transfer Co Inc	Outstanding Shares	16,120,000
Counsel	NA	E.P.S	-$0.03
DUNS No.	NA	Shareholders	NA

Business: The group's principle activity is to provide human capital management ("Hcm") solutions to fortune-1000 enterprises, mid-size companies, organization development and human resource consultants and governmental institutions. The group provides real- time decision support tools and

services to better manage human capital in the organization. The primary product suite, known as actionable insightst, includes employee climate assessment, skills inventory assessments, and 360 multi-rator assessments. The group provides its products and solutions to dell computer, haliburton, sharp healthcare, storagetek, northwestern mutual and electronic data systems, among others. The group's quarterly revenue for September 2007 was 5.00 millions of USD.

Primary SIC and add'l.: 9999

CIK No: 0001011432

Subsidiaries: Auxilio Solutions, Inc.

Officers: Etienne Weidemann/CEO, Pres./$227,170.00, John D. Pace/Chmn., Chief Strategy Officer, Jacques Terblanche/Exec. VP, Paul Anthony/CFO, Corp. Sec./$245,520.00

Directors: John D. Pace/Chmn., Chief Strategy Officer, Michael Vanderhoof/Dir., Edward Case/Dir., Max Poll/Dir., Michael J. Joyce/Dir., Mark St. Clare/Dir., Joseph J. Flynn/Dir.

Owners: Robert L. Krakoff, Etienne Weidemann/2.90%, Max Poll, Michael Vanderhoof/6.90%, Insiders/14.50%, Joseph J. Flynn/3.60%, John Pace, Edward B. Case, Paul Anthony/2.20%

Financial Data: Fiscal Year End: 12/31 **Latest Annual Data:** 03/31/2007

Year	Sales	Net Income
2007	NA	NA
2006	$10,248,000	-$3,903,000
2005	$4,291,000	-$3,359,000

Curr. Assets:	$2,765,000	Curr. Liab.:	$3,303,000		
Plant, Equip.:	$304,000	Total Liab.:	$5,206,000	Indic. Yr. Divd.:	NA
Total Assets:	$5,516,000	Net Worth:	$310,000	Debt/ Equity:	2.2243

Auxilium Pharmaceuticals Inc

40 Valley Stream Pkwy., Malvern, PA, 19355; **PH:** 1-484-321-5900; **Fax:** 1-484-321-5999; **http://** www.auxilium.com

General - Incorporation	DE	**Stock** - Price on:12/24/2007	$14.67
Employees	269	Stock Exchange	NDQ
Auditor	KPMG LLP	Ticker Symbol	AUXL
Stk Agt	StockTrans, Inc.	Outstanding Shares	36,230,000
Counsel	Morgan, Lewis & Bockius LLP	E.P.S.	-$1.35
DUNS No.	NA	Shareholders	NA

Business: The group's principal activity is to develop and market pharmaceutical products that focus on urology and sexual health. In addition to the development of follow-on products for androgen replacement, the group is pursuing product opportunities for other disorders. Major brands of the group are testim and auxilium logo. The group entirely operates in United States.

Primary SIC and add'l.: 8731

CIK No: 0001182129

Officers: Armando Anido/Dir., CEO, Pres., Jennifer Evans Stacey/Exec. VP, General Counsel - Human Resources, Sec., James E. Fickenscher/CFO, Roger D. Graham/Exec. VP - Sales, Marketing, Jyrki Mattila/Exec. VP - Business Development, Research & Development, and Technical Operations

Directors: Armando Anido/Dir., CEO, Pres., Oliver Fetzer/Dir., Renato Fuchs/Dir., Dennis J. Purcell/Dir., Al Altomari/Dir., Edwin A. Bescherer/Dir., Rolf Classon/Dir., Philippe O. Chambon/Dir., Winston Churchill/Dir.

Owners: Philippe O. Chambon/12.20%, Davidson Kempner Partners/8.40%, Visium Asset Management LLC/8.40%, Oliver S. Fetzer, Armando Anido, Sprout Capital IX L.P./12.20%, Roger D. Graham, Edwin A. Bescherer, James E. Fickenscher, Winston J. Churchill/5.20%, FMR Corp./5.60%, Dennis J. Purcell, Jennifer Evans Stacey, Insiders/19.30%, Millennium Management/5.50% (22 Owners included in Index)

Financial Data: Fiscal Year End: 12/31 **Latest Annual Data:** 12/31/2006

Year	Sales	Net Income
2006	$68,490,000	-$45,948,000
2005	$42,804,000	-$38,258,000
2004	$27,025,000	-$28,518,000

Curr. Assets:	$69,512,000	Curr. Liab.:	$22,693,000		
Plant, Equip.:	$4,732,000	Total Liab.:	$34,430,000	Indic. Yr. Divd.:	NA
Total Assets:	$76,759,000	Net Worth:	$42,329,000	Debt/ Equity:	NA

Avalon Holdings Corp

1 American Way, Warren, OH, 44484; **PH:** 1-330-856-8800; **Fax:** 1-330-856-8480; **http://** www.avalonholdings.com

General - Incorporation	OH	**Stock** - Price on:12/24/2007	$9.06
Employees	152	Stock Exchange	AMEX
Auditor	Grant Thornton LLP	Ticker Symbol	AWX
Stk Agt	American Stock Transfer & Trust Co.	Outstanding Shares	3,800,000
Counsel	NA	E.P.S.	$0.42
DUNS No.	61-512-2942	Shareholders	NA

Business: The group's principal activities are classified into three business segments: transportation services, waste management services and golf and related operations. The transportation services segment provide transportation of hazardous and nonhazardous waste, transportation of general and bulk commodities and the brokerage and management of transportation services. The transportation services are provided to industrial, commercial, municipal and governmental customers primarily in selected northeastern and midwestern United States market. Waste management services assist customers with managing and disposing of wastes at approved treatment and disposal sites based on customer's needs. Golf and related operation segment owns and operates a pete dye designed championship golf course located in warren, Ohio.

Primary SIC and add'l.: 6719 4212 7992 4953 8748

CIK No: 0001061069

Subsidiaries: American Landfill Management, Inc., American Waste Management Services, Inc., Avalon Golf and Country Club, Inc., Avalon Lakes Golf, Inc., Avalon Travel, Inc., TBG, Inc.

Officers: Timothy C. Coxson/CFO, Treasurer, Assist. Sec./$147,900.00

Directors: Kurtis D. Gramley/Dir., David G. Bozanich/Dir.

Owners: Insiders/5.40%, Moloco Capital Partners LLC/5.30%, Timothy C. Coxson, Ronald E. Klingle/5.30%, Anil C. Nalluri, M.D., Inc./12.70%, Frances R. Klingle, Frank Lamanna, Advisory Research, Inc./14.90%, Frances R. Klingle, Dimension Fund Advisors LP/5.80%, Robert M. Arnoni, Insiders, Ronald E. Klingle, Raffles Associates, L.P./6.20%

Financial Data: Fiscal Year End: 12/31 **Latest Annual Data:** 12/31/2006

Year	Sales	Net Income
2006	$39,329,000	$1,327,000
2005	$34,157,000	$390,000
2004	$30,002,000	$902,000

Curr. Assets:	$21,370,000	Curr. Liab.:	$7,656,000	P/E Ratio:	22.10
Plant, Equip.:	$24,512,000	Total Liab.:	$7,973,000	Indic. Yr. Divd.:	NA
Total Assets:	$45,951,000	Net Worth:	$37,978,000	Debt/ Equity:	0.0080

Avalon Oil & Gas Inc

310 4th Ave. S, Minneapolis, MN, 55415; **PH:** 1-952-746-9655; **Fax:** 1-952-746-5216; **http://** www.avalonoilinc.com

General - Incorporation	NV	**Stock** - Price on:12/24/2007	NA
Employees	1	Stock Exchange	OTC
Auditor	Murrell, Hall, Mcintosh & Co., PLLP	Ticker Symbol	AOGN
Stk Agt	Corporate Stock Transfer, Inc.	Outstanding Shares	NA
Counsel	NA	E.P.S.	-$0.262
DUNS No.	NA	Shareholders	NA

Business: The group's principle activity is to distribut high-end European outdoor apparel and equipment for the outdoor enthusiast. The group operates from United States.

Primary SIC and add'l.: 5699 5091

CIK No: 0000918573

Officers: Kent Rodriguez/47/Dir., CEO, Pres., Menno Wiebe/Advisor to Avalon, Jill Allison/VP, Gary Browning/Advisor to Avalon

Directors: Kent Rodriguez/47/Dir., CEO, Pres., Douglas Barton/Dir., Thad Kaplan/Dir., William D. Anderson/Member - Advisory Board, Glen P. Harrod/Member - Advisory Board, John Rhodes/Member - Advisory Board, Mark Oliver/Member - Advisory Board, Billy D. Graham/Member - Advisory Board

Owners: Insiders/43.80%, Thad Kaplan/0.56%, UTEK Corporation/19.00%, Trinity Bui/6.76%, Douglas Barton/0.56%, Kent Rodriguez/42.68%

Financial Data: Fiscal Year End: 03/31 **Latest Annual Data:** 3/31/2006

Year	Sales	Net Income
2006	NA	-$499,000
2005	NA	-$212,000
2004	NA	-$300,000

Curr. Assets:	$1,040,000	Curr. Liab.:	$202,000		
Plant, Equip.:	$584,000	Total Liab.:	$232,000	Indic. Yr. Divd.:	NA
Total Assets:	$2,993,000	Net Worth:	$2,762,000	Debt/ Equity:	NA

Avalon Pharmaceuticals Inc

20358 Seneca Meadows Pkwy., Germantown, MD, 20876; **PH:** 1-301-556-9900; **Fax:** 1-301-556-9910; **http://** www.avalonrx.com; **Email:** info@avalonrx.com

General - Incorporation	DE	**Stock** - Price on:12/24/2007	$5
Employees	56	Stock Exchange	NDQ
Auditor	Ernst & Young LLP	Ticker Symbol	AVRX
Stk Agt	American Stock Transfer & Trust Co.	Outstanding Shares	13,140,000
Counsel	NA	E.P.S.	-$1.67
DUNS No.	NA	Shareholders	NA

Business: The groups principle activities include discovering and developing cancer therapeutics. The product of the group is AvalonRx(R). The group operates from United States.

Primary SIC and add'l.: 2836 8731 3826 2834

CIK No: 0001162192

Officers: Kenneth C. Carter/Dir., CEO, Pres./$1,128,328.00, Thomas G. David/General Counsel, Sr. VP - Operations/$431,858.00, Gary Lessing/CFO, Exec. VP/$669,109.00, David K. Bol/Sr. VP - Product, Pharmaceutical Development/$457,693.00, David D. Muth/Exec. VP, Chief Business Officer/$203,162.00, Eric C. Winzer/CFO, Exec. VP, Michael J. Hamilton/Chief Medical Officer, Steve K. Horrigan/VP - Research

Directors: Kenneth C. Carter/Dir., CEO, Pres., Bradley G. Lorimier/Chmn., Todd Golub/Chmn. - Scientific Advisory Board, William H. Washecka/Dir., Paul Workman/Member - Scientific Advisory Board, Brian Druker/Member - Scientific Advisory Board, Michael R. Kurman/Dir., Ivor Royston/Dir., William A. Scott/Dir., Alan G. Walton/Dir., Carmen Allegra/Member - Scientific Advisory Board, Kenneth C. Anderson/Member - Scientific Advisory Board, Otis Brawley/Member - Scientific Advisory Board, Edward A. Sausville/Member - Scientific Advisory Board, Chris H. Takimoto/Member - Scientific Advisory Board (17 Directors included in Index)

Owners: Michael J. Hamilton, David K. Bol, Entities affiliated with Forward Ventures IV Associates, LLC/4.60%, Entities affiliated with EuclidSR Partners, L.P./5.80%, Entities affiliated with GIMV N.V./6.80%, Insiders/29.50%, Thomas G. David, Raymond J. Whitaker/6.00%, James H. Meade, Entities affiliated with OBP Management III, L.P./6.50%, Kenneth C. Carter/3.90%, Alan G. Walton/6.70%, Michael R. Kurman, David S. Kabakoff, Bradley G. Lorimier (22 Owners included in Index)

Financial Data: Fiscal Year End: 12/31 **Latest Annual Data:** 12/31/2006

Year	Sales	Net Income
2006	$2,724,000	-$17,102,000
2005	$1,544,000	-$19,292,000
2004	$1,900,000	-$13,659,000

Curr. Assets:	$14,722,000	Curr. Liab.:	$5,641,000		
Plant, Equip.:	$8,923,000	Total Liab.:	$13,517,000	Indic. Yr. Divd.:	NA
Total Assets:	$31,391,000	Net Worth:	$17,874,000	Debt/ Equity:	0.3162

AvalonBay Communities Inc

2900 Eisenhower Ave., Ste. 300, Alexandria, VA, 22314; **PH:** 1-703-329-6300; **Fax:** 1-703-329-1459; **http://** www.avalonbay.com

General - Incorporation	MD	**Stock** - Price on:12/24/2007	$125.48
Employees	1,767	Stock Exchange	NYSE
Auditor	Ernst & Young LLP	Ticker Symbol	AVB
Stk Agt	Bank of New York	Outstanding Shares	79,650,000
Counsel	NA	E.P.S.	$3.34
DUNS No.	NA	Shareholders	NA

Business: The groups principle activities include developing, redeveloping, acquiring, owning and operating multifamily apartment communities. The group operates through three segments namely established communities, other stabilized communities and development/redevelopment communities. The group operates 151 apartments containing 43,533 homes in 10 states and 2,381 apartment homes under reconstruction in the United States. The group's quarterly revenue for September 2007 was 208.12 millions of USD.

Primary SIC and add'l.: 6798

CIK No: 0000915912

Subsidiaries: 4100 Massachusetts Avenue Associates, L.P., 4600 Eisenhower Avenue, LLC, Acton FS, LLC, AIV I, LLC, Albee Residential, LLC, AMP Apartments, LLC, AMV I, LLC, AMV II, LLC, AMV III, LLC, AMV IV, LLC, Aria at Hathorne Hill, LLC, Aria at Laurel Hill, LLC, Arna Valley View Limited Partnership, Avalon Alfran North Bergen, LLC, Avalon 4100 Massachusetts Avenue, Inc. 166 Subsidiaries included in the Index

Officers: Bryce Blair/Chmn., CEO/$4,768,803.00, David W. Bellman/Sr. VP - Construction, Shannon E. Brennan/VP - Property Operations, Sean J. Breslin/Sr. VP - Investments, Alfred Brockunier/VP - Construction, Duane W. Carlson/VP - Construction, Darren R. Carrington/VP - Investments, Deborah A. Coombs/Sr. VP - Property Operations, Jonathan B. Cox/Sr. VP - Development, Scott W. Dale/VP - Development, Lili F. Dunn/Sr. VP - Investments/$884,719.00, Mark J. Forlenza/VP - Development, Brian E. Fritz/VP - Development, Frederick S. Harris/Sr. VP - Development, Lawrence A. Scott/45/Sr. VP - Development *(48 Officers included in Index)*

Directors: Bryce Blair/Chmn., CEO, Timothy J. Naughton/Dir., Pres., Bruce A. Choate/Dir., John J. Healy/Dir., Gilbert M. Meyer/Dir., Lance R. Primis/Dir., Allan D. Schuster/Dir., Jay H. Sarles/Dir., Amy P. Williams/Dir., Peter S. Rummell/Dir.

Owners: Cohen & Steers, Inc./6.39%, Lili F. Dunn, Thomas J. Sargeant, Insiders/3.36%, Morgan Stanley/5.35%, John J. Healy, Gilbert M. Meyer/1.69%, Bryce Blair, Timothy J. Naughton, Leo S. Horey, LaSalle Investment Management, Inc./6.43%, Bruce A. Choate, Jay H. Sarles, Allan D. Schuster, Amy P. Williams *(18 Owners included in Index)*

Financial Data: ***Fiscal Year End:*** 12/31 ***Latest Annual Data:*** 12/31/2006

Year	Sales	Net Income
2006	$737,300,000	$266,546,000
2005	$670,680,000	$322,378,000
2004	$648,454,000	$219,745,000

Curr. Assets:	$8,567,000	**Curr. Liab.:**	$385,455,000	**P/E Ratio:**	46.86
Plant, Equip.:	$5,510,362,000	**Total Liab.:**	$3,272,337,000	**Indic. Yr. Divd.:**	$3.400
Total Assets:	$5,845,491,000	**Net Worth:**	$2,573,154,000	**Debt/ Equity:**	NA

Avanex Corp

40919 Encyclopedia Cir., Fremont, CA, 94538; ***PH:*** 1-510-897-4188; ***Fax:*** 1-510-897-4189; ***http://*** www.avanex.com

General - Incorporation	DE	**Stock** - Price on:12/24/2007	$1.775
Employees	610	Stock Exchange	NDQ
Auditor	Deloitte & Touche, LLP	Ticker Symbol	AVNX
Stk Agt	EquiServe Trust Co N.A	Outstanding Shares	225,620,000
Counsel	Wilson Sonsini Goodrich & Rosati	E.P.S	-$0.1
DUNS No.	NA	Shareholders	NA

Business: The group's principal activity is to manufacture and market fiber optic-based products, known as photonic processors. These processors are designed to increase the performance of optical networks. The group provides photonic processing solutions in six product families: powerfilter wavelength separators, powermux wavelength channel processors, powerexchanger optical add/drop processors, powerexpress amplification processors, powerequalizer dynamic gain equalizers and powershaper dispersion management processors. The photonic processing solutions are used by fiber optic transmission systems providers and their network carrier customers to enhance system performance and increase network speed and efficiency. On 31-Jul-2003, the group acquired alcatel optronics France sa.

Primary SIC and add'l.: 3674

CIK No: 0001056794

Subsidiaries: Avanex (Thailand) Limited, Avanex Cayman, Avanex Communication Technologies Co. Ltd, Avanex France S.A., Avanex International Corporation, Avanex U.S.A. Corporation, LambdaFlex, Inc., Pearl Acquisition Corp.

Officers: Jo Major/Chmn., CEO, Pres., Yves Lemaitre/Chief Marketing Officer, Giovanni Barbarossa/CTO, Patrick Edsell/Sr. VP, GM, Bradley Kolb/Sr. VP - Operations, Marla Sanchez/CFO, Sr. VP, Maria Riley/Dir. - Communications

Directors: Jo Major/Chmn., CEO, Pres., Greg Dougherty/Dir., Vinton G. Cerf/Dir., Joel A. Smith/Dir., Susan Wang/Dir.

Owners: Insiders/2.06%, Alcatel/12.42%, Susan Wang, Vinton Cerf, Joel A. Smith, Marla Sanchez, Kings Road Investments Ltd./9.71%, Anthony Riley, Yves LeMaitre, Trivium Capital Management, LLC/6.70%, Jo S. Major, Greg Dougherty, Brad Kolb

Financial Data: ***Fiscal Year End:*** 06/30 ***Latest Annual Data:*** 06/30/2007

Year	Sales	Net Income
2007	$212,755,000	-$30,605,000
2006	$162,944,000	-$54,692,000
2005	$160,695,000	-$108,371,000

Curr. Assets:	$145,397,000	**Curr. Liab.:**	$63,033,000		
Plant, Equip.:	$5,668,000	**Total Liab.:**	$92,220,000	**Indic. Yr. Divd.:**	NA
Total Assets:	$165,558,000	**Net Worth:**	$73,338,000	**Debt/ Equity:**	NA

Avani International Group Inc

17 Fawcett Rd., Ste. 328, Coquitlam, BC, V3K 6V2; ***PH:*** 1-604-913-2386; ***http://*** www.avaniwater.com; ***Email:*** marketing@avaniwater.com

General - Incorporation	NV	**Stock** - Price on:12/24/2007	$0.2835
Employees	NA	Stock Exchange	OTC
Auditor	BDO Dunwoody LLP	Ticker Symbol	AVIT
Stk Agt	Computershare Trust Co	Outstanding Shares	NA
Counsel	NA	E.P.S	NA
DUNS No.	NA	Shareholders	NA

Business: The group's principle activities include developing, manufacturing and distributing oxygen enriched, purified bottled water under the Avani brandname. The group operates from United States.

Primary SIC and add'l.: 2086

CIK No: 0001048701

Subsidiaries: Avani International Marketing Corporation., Avani Oxygen Water Corporation

Officers: Robert Wang/60/Dir., Pres., Principal Executive Officer/$120,298.00, Dennis Robinson/67/Dir., Sec., Treasurer, Principal Financial Officer

Directors: Robert Wang/60/Dir., Pres., Principal Executive Officer, Dennis Robinson/67/Dir., Sec., Treasurer, Principal Financial Officer, Jeffrey Lightfoot/50/Dir.

Owners: Tee Ah Siew/24.80%, Chin Yen Ong/64.30%

Financial Data: ***Fiscal Year End:*** 12/31 ***Latest Annual Data:*** 12/31/2006

Year	Sales	Net Income
2006	$99,000	-$321,000
2005	$307,000	$66,000
2004	$2,488,000	-$948,000

Curr. Assets:	$975,000	**Curr. Liab.:**	$1,013,000		
Plant, Equip.:	$21,000	**Total Liab.:**	$1,299,000	**Indic. Yr. Divd.:**	NA
Total Assets:	$1,017,000	**Net Worth:**	-$282,000	**Debt/ Equity:**	NA

Avanir Pharmaceuticals

101 Enterprise, Ste. 300, Aliso Viejo, CA, 92656; ***PH:*** 1-949-389-6700; ***Fax:*** 1-949-643-6800; ***http://*** www.avanir.com

General - Incorporation	CA	**Stock** - Price on:12/24/2007	$3.04
Employees	150	Stock Exchange	NDQ
Auditor	Deloitte & Touche LLP	Ticker Symbol	AVNR
Stk Agt	American Stock Transfer & Trust Co.	Outstanding Shares	42,600,000
Counsel	Heller Ehrman White & McAuliffe LLP	E.P.S	-$1.53
DUNS No.	19-841-3080	Shareholders	NA

Business: The group's principle activities consist of research, development, commercialization, licensing and sales of innovative drug products and antibody generation services. The group's subsidiary xenerex biosciences is developing completely human antibody products to target antigens causing various ailments. The group also carries out clinical development of neurodex a drug for treatment of several central nervous systems disorders. Other researches include for the treatment of allergies, asthma and cholesterol reduction. The group has entered into marketing license agreements with glaxosmithkline in North America, boryung pharmaceuticals in South Korea and cts chemical industries in Israel. The group's total revenue for year 2007 was 9.22 millions of USD.

Primary SIC and add'l.: 8731 2834

CIK No: 0000858803

Subsidiaries: Avanir Holding Company, Xenerex Biosciences

Officers: Eric K. Brandt/Dir., CEO, Pres., Gregory P. Hanson/VP - Finance, Chief Accounting Officer, Sec., Keith A. Katkin/36/Sr. VP - Sales, Marketing, Jagadish C. Sircar/VP - Drug Discovery, Michael J. Puntoriero/Sr. VP - Finance, CFO, Theresa Hope-Reese/VP - Human Resources, Randall E. Kaye/Sr. VP - Clinical Research - Medical Affairs, Chief Medical Officer, Martin J. Sturgeon/VP, Interim CFO, Gregory J. Flesher/VP - Business Development, Eric S. Benevich/VP - Communications

Directors: Eric K. Brandt/Dir., CEO, Pres., Craig A. Wheeler/Chmn., Paul G. Thomas/Dir., David J. Mazzo/Dir., Jonathan T. Silverstein/Dir., Charles A. Mathews/Dir., Scott M. Whitcup/Dir., Dennis G. Podlesak/Dir., Stephen G. Austin/Dir.

Owners: David J. Mazzo, Keith Katkin, Michael J. Puntoriero, Jonathan T. Silverstein/4.63%, Gregory P. Hanson, Dennis G. Podlesak, Charles A. Mathews, Steven G. Austin, Randall Kaye, Eric K. Brandt, Jagadish Sircar, Insiders/6.15%

Financial Data: ***Fiscal Year End:*** 09/30 ***Latest Annual Data:*** 9/30/2006

Year	Sales	Net Income
2006	$15,186,000	-$62,553,000
2005	$16,691,000	-$30,607,000
2004	$3,589,000	-$28,155,000

Curr. Assets:	$29,333,000	**Curr. Liab.:**	$36,303,000		
Plant, Equip.:	$6,395,000	**Total Liab.:**	$77,137,000	**Indic. Yr. Divd.:**	NA
Total Assets:	$71,462,000	**Net Worth:**	-$5,675,000	**Debt/ Equity:**	NA

Avant Immunotherapeutics Inc

119 4th Ave., Needham, MA, 02494; ***PH:*** 1-781-433-0771; ***Fax:*** 1-781-433-0262; ***http://*** www.avantimmune.com; ***Email:*** info@avantimmune.com

General - Incorporation	DE	**Stock** - Price on:12/24/2007	$0.81
Employees	86	Stock Exchange	NDQ
Auditor	PricewaterhouseCoopers LLP	Ticker Symbol	AVAN
Stk Agt	EquiServe Trust Co N.A	Outstanding Shares	74,180,000
Counsel	NA	E.P.S	-$0.31
DUNS No.	11-885-1765	Shareholders	NA

Business: The group's principal activity is to discover, develop and commercialize pharmaceutical products to prevent and treat diseases. The group is developing a portfolio of vaccines against viral and bacterial diseases, including single-dose oral vaccines aimed at protecting travelers and people in endemic regions from cholera, typhoid fever and other illnesses. The group's current collaborations encompass the development of an oral human rotavirus vaccine, vaccines to combat threats of biological warfare and vaccines addressing human food safety and animal health. In addition, the group is conducting clinical studies of a proprietary vaccine candidate for cholesterol management.

Primary SIC and add'l.: 8731 2834

CIK No: 0000744218

Subsidiaries: Megan Health Inc.

Officers: Una S. Ryan/Dir., CEO, Pres./$1,741,990.00, Ronald W. Ellis/55/Sr. VP - Research, Development/$314,603.00, Timothy M. Cooke/COO, Sr. VP/$398,994.00, Avery W. Catlin/Sr. VP, CFO/$277,399.00, Henry C. Marsh/VP - Research/$220,755.00, Taha Keilani/VP - Medical, Regulatory Affairs/$287,762.00

Directors: Una S. Ryan/Dir., CEO, Pres., Barrie J. Ward/Chmn., Harry H. Penner/Dir., Alf A. Lindberg/Dir., Francis R. Cano/Dir., Peter A. Sears/Dir., Larry Ellberger/Dir., Karen Shoos Lipton/Dir.

Owners: M. Timothy Cooke, Alf A. Lindberg, Karen Shoos Lipton, Una S. Ryan/2.66%, Francis R. Cano, J. Barrie Ward, Peter A. Sears, Avery W. Catlin, Insiders/4.57%, Larry Ellberger, Taha Keilani, Harry H. Penner, Ronald W. Ellis, Henry C. Marsh

Financial Data: ***Fiscal Year End:*** 12/31 ***Latest Annual Data:*** 12/31/2006

Year	Sales	Net Income
2006	$4,931,000	-$20,374,000
2005	$3,088,000	-$18,097,000
2004	$6,859,000	-$13,204,000

Curr. Assets:	$42,403,000	**Curr. Liab.:**	$10,084,000		
Plant, Equip.:	$13,968,000	**Total Liab.:**	$59,318,000	**Indic. Yr. Divd.:**	NA
Total Assets:	$61,480,000	**Net Worth:**	$2,161,000	**Debt/ Equity:**	NA

Avantair Inc

Formerly: Ardent Acquisition Corp
4311 General Howard Dr, Clearwater, FL, 33762; ***PH:*** 1-727-539-0071

General - Incorporation	DE	**Stock**- Price on:12/24/2007	$4.6
Employees	264	Stock Exchange	NA
Auditor	J.H. Cohn, LLP	Ticker Symbol	NA
Stk Agt	Continental Stock Transfer & Trust Co	Outstanding Shares	15,220,000
Counsel	NA	E.P.S	NA
DUNS No.	NA	Shareholders	NA

Business: The groups principle activity is to provide aircraft services. The group operates from the United States.

Primary SIC and add'l.: 6799

CIK No: 0001303849

Owners: Jonathan Auerbach, Steven Santo, Robert J. Lepofsky, Kevin McKamey, Clinton A. Allen, Fred B. Barbara, John Waters, Paul J. Solit, Jeff Feinberg, Tracy Chaplin, Arthur H. Goldberg, Allison Roberto, Barry J. Gordon, Jeffrey Kirby, Paul Sonkin *(17 Owners included in Index)*

Avantogen Oncology Inc

2121 Ave. of the Stars, Ste. 2550, Los Angeles, CA, 90067; ***PH:*** 1-646-723-8944;
Fax: 1-310-772-0538; ***http://*** www.avantogen.com; ***Email:*** info@avantogen.com

General - Incorporation	NV	**Stock**- Price on:12/24/2007	NA
Employees	NA	Stock Exchange	OTC
Auditor	Singer Lewak Greenbaum & Goldstein	Ticker Symbol	AVTO
Stk Agt	National Stock Transfer, Inc.	Outstanding Shares	NA
Counsel	NA	E.P.S	-$0.04
DUNS No.	NA	Shareholders	NA

Business: The groups principal activities include acquiring, developing and seeking to Commercialize novel compounds to treat various types of cancer. The group products include RP101, Pentrys (TM), and GP1- 0100,Revisys (TM). The group marketed its products under the trade name Pentrys(TM). The group operates from the United States and Australia.

Primary SIC and add'l.: 9995

CIK No: 0000894538

Subsidiaries: Cynat Oncology Limited, Cynat Oncology, Inc., Innovate Oncology, Inc, Innovative Oncology Limited, Resistys, Inc.

Officers: William Ardrey/42/Chmn., CEO, Angela Bronow Davanzo/44/CFO, Sec.

Directors: William Ardrey/42/Chmn., CEO, Michael Hillmeyer/45/Dir., Lee J. Cole/47/Dir.

Owners: Avantogen Limited/43.10%, Angela Bronow Davanzo, Insiders, Gardant Pharmaceuticals, Inc./22.60%, Chopin Opus One LP/16.90%, Christopher Nowers

Financial Data: ***Fiscal Year End:***12/31 ***Latest Annual Data:*** 12/31/2006

Year	Sales	Net Income
2006	NA	-$5,206,000
2005	NA	-$5,015,000
2004	NA	-$1,120,000

Curr. Assets:	$117,000	**Curr. Liab.:**	$2,380,000		
Plant, Equip.:	$8,000	**Total Liab.:**	$2,380,000	**Indic. Yr. Divd.:**	NA
Total Assets:	$170,000	**Net Worth:**	-$2,210,000	**Debt/ Equity:**	NA

Avasoft Inc

Formerly: Ventures United Inc
2206 Plz. Dr., Rocklin, CA, 95765; ***PH:*** 1-916-771-0900

General - Incorporation	UT	**Stock**- Price on:12/24/2007	NA
Employees	NA	Stock Exchange	OTC
Auditor	Pritchett, Siler & Hardy, P.C	Ticker Symbol	AVAF
Stk Agt	NA	Outstanding Shares	NA
Counsel	NA	E.P.S	NA
DUNS No.	NA	Shareholders	NA

Business: The groups principle activities include developing its cartridge technology, entering into strategic partnerships to produce its ice cream system and building its sales and distribution infrastructure. The group operates from the United States.

Primary SIC and add'l.: 6770

CIK No: 0000789878

Officers: Jim Wheeler/Dir., CEO, Art Morley/VP - Sales, Robert Duncan/Dir., CFO, John Quereto/COO, Jacque Taylor/63/Sec., Richard Carpenter/Capital Group Communications

Directors: Jim Wheeler/Dir., CEO, Robert Duncan/Dir., CFO, Terry Worley/Dir.

Owners: Gary Littler/41.32%, Jacque Taylor/5.80%, Tryant, LLC/21.20%, Gary Crandall, Insiders/11.70%, Robert Taylor/5.80%

Financial Data: ***Fiscal Year End:***12/31 ***Latest Annual Data:*** 12/31/2006

Year	Sales	Net Income
2006	NA	-$34,000

Curr. Assets:	$0	**Curr. Liab.:**	$11,000		
Plant, Equip.:	NA	**Total Liab.:**	$11,000	**Indic. Yr. Divd.:**	NA
Total Assets:	$0	**Net Worth:**	-$11,000	**Debt/ Equity:**	NA

Avatar Holdings Inc

201 Alhambra Cir., Coral Gables, FL, 33134; ***PH:*** 1-305-442-7000; ***Fax:*** 1-305-448-9927;
http:// www.avatarhomes.com

General - Incorporation	DE	**Stock**- Price on:12/24/2007	$78.36
Employees	483	Stock Exchange	NDQ
Auditor	Ernst & Young LLP	Ticker Symbol	AVTR
Stk Agt	Mellon Investor Services LLC	Outstanding Shares	8,290,000
Counsel	Weil, Gotshal & Manges LLP	E.P.S	$11.14
DUNS No.	04-526-0007	Shareholders	NA

Business: The group's principal activity is the development and sale of active adult and residential communities. The communities are being developed in poinciana, central Florida, harbor islands on Florida's east coast and rio rico, south of tucson, Arizona. Development also includes storm-water management facilities, drainage work, irrigation facilities, water and wastewater utilities and offsite roadways. Other activities of the group include operations of amenities, cable television operations, title insurance agency, the development, leasing and management of improved commercial properties and the sale of industrial properties. In feb 2004 the group discontinued the operations of harbor islands marina.

Primary SIC and add'l.: 1531 6552

CIK No: 0000039677

Subsidiaries: Avatar Asset Management, Inc., Avatar Communities, Inc., Avatar Condominium Management Inc., Avatar Development Corporation, Avatar Finance, Inc., Avatar Homes of Arizona, Inc., Avatar New Homes of Florida, Inc., Avatar Ocean Palms, Inc., Avatar Poinciana, Inc., Avatar Properties at Doral, Inc., Avatar Properties Inc., Avatar Realty Inc., Avatar Realty of Arizona, Inc., Avatar Regalia, Inc., Avatar Retirement Communities, Inc. 33 Subsidiaries included in the Index

Officers: Gerald D. Kelfer/Vice Chmn., CEO, Pres./$7,093,066.00, Juanita I. Kerrigan/VP, Sec., Michael F. Levy/Exec. VP, COO - Avatar Properties Inc/$5,640,298.00, Jonathan Fels/Pres. - Avatar Properties Inc/$5,642,530.00, Patricia K. Fletcher/Exec. VP, General Counsel, Randy L. Kotler/Exec. VP, CFO, Treasurer

Directors: Gerald D. Kelfer/Vice Chmn., CEO, Pres., Joshua Nash/Chmn., Fred Stanton Smith/Dir., Joel M. Simon/Dir., Eduardo Brea/Dir., Milton H. Dresner/Dir., Roger W. Einiger/Dir., Kenneth T. Rosen/Dir., Beth A. Stewart/Dir., Paul D. Barnett/Dir.

Owners: Leon Levy Foundation/8.50%, Beth A. Stewart, Michael Levy, Roger W. Einiger, Joel M. Simon, Joshua Nash/25.50%, Insiders/27.74%, Milton Dresner, Dennis J. Getman, Highbridge International LLC/6.00%, William G. Spears, Private Capital/21.80%, Dimensional Fund Advisors LP/5.60%, Eduardo A. Brea, Gerald D. Kelfer *(22 Owners included in Index)*

Financial Data: ***Fiscal Year End:***12/31 ***Latest Annual Data:*** 12/31/2006

Year	Sales	Net Income
2006	$835,079,000	$174,726,000
2005	$516,848,000	$63,127,000
2004	$337,399,000	$29,559,000

Curr. Assets:	$231,326,000	**Curr. Liab.:**	$84,098,000	**P/E Ratio:**	5.16
Plant, Equip.:	$503,581,000	**Total Liab.:**	$245,716,000	**Indic. Yr. Divd.:**	NA
Total Assets:	$751,072,000	**Net Worth:**	$505,356,000	**Debt/ Equity:**	NA

Avatar Systems Inc TX

2801 Network Blvd., Ste. 210, Frisco, TX, 75034; ***PH:*** 1-972-720-1800; ***Fax:*** 1-972-720-1900;
http:// www.avatarsystems.net

General - Incorporation	TX	**Stock**- Price on:12/24/2007	NA
Employees	NA	Stock Exchange	OTC
Auditor	Whitley Penn LLP	Ticker Symbol	AVSY
Stk Agt	Securities Transfer Corp	Outstanding Shares	NA
Counsel	NA	E.P.S	NA
DUNS No.	NA	Shareholders	NA

Business: The group's principal activities are to provide solutions for accounting and financial management, production and land management, oil and gas marketing and electronic data exchange on both a licensed and asp basis to the petroleum industry. The group provides technology products and services to support the ongoing management of an upstream petroleum business and to facilitate the processing of oil and gas transactions through the back office systems. The group offers a full line of accounting and resource management software for the petroleum industry including avatar400, petroware2000 and remote access private integrated datalink services. The products offer a variety of applications specific to the accounting, billing, financial analysis and land, royalty and production management functions of a petroleum company. The group provides software services for acccounting and financial management.

Primary SIC and add'l.: 7379 7378 7373 7372

CIK No: 0000707063

Subsidiaries: Hospitality Companies, Inc.

Officers: Robert C. Shreve/Chmn., CEO, CFO, Pres., Leah Spears/Contact - Sales, Scott White/Contact - Sales, Jo Ann Loftin/Contact - Sales, Cindy Skelton/49/Sec., Kellie Williams/Contact - Sales, Integra Energy

Directors: Robert C. Shreve/Chmn., CEO, CFO, Pres., Allen D. Farris/Dir., Stephen A. Komlosy/Dir., John J. May/Dir.

Owners: Insiders/18.30%, Orville Gregory Allen/26.60%, Charles Timothy Allen/27.10%, Robert C. Shreve/18.20%, PSG Solutions Plc/18.60%, Stephen A. Komlosy/0.20%

Curr. Assets:	$1,117,000	**Curr. Liab.:**	$1,134,000		
Plant, Equip.:	$457,000	**Total Liab.:**	$3,210,000	**Indic. Yr. Divd.:**	NA
Total Assets:	$6,514,000	**Net Worth:**	$3,304,000	**Debt/ Equity:**	0.3637

Avatech Solutions Inc

10715 Red Run Blvd., Ste. 101, Owings Mills, MD, 21117; ***PH:*** 1-410-581-8080;
Fax: 1-410-753-1591; ***http://*** www.avatechsolutions.com; ***Email:*** info@avat.com

General - Incorporation	DE	**Stock**- Price on:12/24/2007	$1.2
Employees	235	Stock Exchange	OTC
Auditor	Stegman & Co.	Ticker Symbol	AVSO
Stk Agt	American Stock Transfer & Trust Co.	Outstanding Shares	15,040,000
Counsel	Neuberger Et Al	E.P.S	NA
DUNS No.	18-208-5126	Shareholders	NA

Business: The group's principal activities are to design and engineer technology solutions. The group provides these solutions with specialization in cad software, data management and process optimisation capabilities for the manufacturing, engineering, building design and facilities management industries. It specializes in software integration, standards development and deployment, education and technical support. Solutions offered by the group include product lifecycle management [plm] and integration of autodesk software. The group serves 18,000 clients worldwide. The customers of the group include aol time warner, at&t, bell Atlantic, champion industries, ford motor company and general electric.

Primary SIC and add'l.: 7372

CIK No: 0000852437

Subsidiaries: Facilities Resources, Inc.

Officers: George Davis/Dir., CEO, Pres., Jean Schaeffer/VP - Marketing, Bill Zavadil/Sr. VP - Services, Lawrence Rychlak/CFO, Bruce White/Sr. VP - Sales, Kim Valdes/VP - Sales Operations, Todd Stuart/National Support Center Mgr., Jeff Lotan/Autocad Technical Support Specialist, Nick Fuller/Architectural Technical Support Specialist, Brian Grunder/Mechanical Technical Support Specialist, Daren Chung/Technical Support Specialist, Allen Hudson/Applications Engineer

Directors: George Davis/Dir., CEO, Pres., Thom Waye/Chmn., Garnett Y. Clark/Vice Chmn., George Cox/Dir., Robert Post/Dir., Jim W. Hindman/Dir., David Reymann/Dir., Eugene Fischer/Dir.

Owners: W. James Hindman, The Tail Wind Fund Ltd./13.90%, George M. Davis, Insiders/27.90%, Garnett Y. Clark/1.50%, George W. Cox/1.50%, Eugene Fischer/8.10%, Thom Waye/15.50%, Sigma Opportunity Fund LLC/15.00%, Capstone Ventures SBIC, L.P./8.10%, Robert J. Post, Henry D. Felton/6.20%, Lawrence Rychlak/1.30%

Financial Data: *Fiscal Year End:*06/30 *Latest Annual Data:* 6/30/2006

Year	Sales	Net Income
2006	$39,620,000	$2,203,000
2005	$34,144,000	$1,934,000
2004	$27,950,000	-$927,000

Curr. Assets:	$8,091,000	*Curr. Liab.:*	$8,452,000		
Plant, Equip.:	$870,000	*Total Liab.:*	$8,570,000	*Indic. Yr. Divd.:*	NA
Total Assets:	$16,850,000	*Net Worth:*	$4,651,000	*Debt/ Equity:*	0.0004

Avax Technologies Inc

4520 Main St., Ste. 930, Kansas City, MO, 64112; *PH:* 1-215-241-9760; *http://* www.avax-tech.com

General - Incorporation	DE	**Stock**- Price on:12/24/2007	$0.201
Employees	24	Stock Exchange	OTC
Auditor	Briggs, Bunting & Dougherty LLP	Ticker Symbol	AVXT
Stk Agt	UMB Bank, N.A.	Outstanding Shares	142,600,000
Counsel	Shook, Hardy & Bacon	E.P.S.	-$0.06
DUNS No.	96-400-6548	Shareholders	NA

Business: The group's principal activity is to develop and market individualized therapies and small molecules for the treatment of cancer and other life-threatening diseases. The group also offers biological manufacturing services to other biotechnology and pharmaceutical companies. The group's patented autologous cell technology ac vaccine attempts to stimulate a patient's own immune system to recognize, contain and eliminate cancer cells. The ac vaccine products include m-vax and o-vax. M-vax is designed as an immunotherapy for the post-surgical treatment of late stages melanoma. O-vax is designed as an immunotherapy for the treatment of ovarian cancer. The group is a development stage and operates in the United States, France & Australia.

Primary SIC and add'l.: 8731 2836

CIK No: 0001015441

Subsidiaries: AVAX America, Inc., AVAX Australia Holdings Pty Limited, AVAX Australia Manufacturing Pty Limited, AVAX Australia Pty Limited, AVAX International Holdings, Inc., AVAX International IP Holdings, Inc., AVAX International Services, Inc., AVAX Technologies Holdings ApS, Denmark Offshore Holding Company, Genopoietic, S.A., GPH, S.A., United States Incorporation

Officers: Richard P. Rainey/Pres., Sec., CEO, Andres Crespo/GM - Genopoietic Subsidiary, David Berd/Chief Medical Officer, Henry E. Schea/Dir. - Quality Systems

Directors: John K.A. Prendergast/Chmn., Andrew W. Dahl/Dir., Edson D. De Castro/Dir., Carl Spana/Dir.

Owners: Carl Spana, BioCentive Limited/0.11%, John K.A. Prendergast, David Berd, Yoshinoro SHIRONO/0.60%, Richard P. Rainey, Carmignac Innovation/0.62%, Aqua RIMCO LTD/0.60%, Edson D. de Castro, JFE Hottinger/0.14%, Andrew W. Dahl, Insiders/0.10%, Firebird Global Master Fund, LTD/0.74%

Financial Data: *Fiscal Year End:*12/31 *Latest Annual Data:* 12/31/2006

Year	Sales	Net Income
2006	$735,000	-$5,356,000
2005	$1,624,000	-$3,704,000
2004	$1,691,000	-$3,458,000

Curr. Assets:	$1,977,000	*Curr. Liab.:*	$2,700,000		
Plant, Equip.:	$879,000	*Total Liab.:*	$2,700,000	*Indic. Yr. Divd.:*	NA
Total Assets:	$3,044,000	*Net Worth:*	$344,000	*Debt/ Equity:*	NA

Avaya Inc

211 Mount Airy Rd. , Basking Ridge, NJ, 07920; *PH:* 1-908-953-6000; *http://* www.avaya.com

General - Incorporation	DE	**Stock**- Price on:12/24/2007	$17.01
Employees	19,000	Stock Exchange	NYSE
Auditor	PricewaterhouseCoopers LLP	Ticker Symbol	AV
Stk Agt	Bank of New York	Outstanding Shares	449,860,000
Counsel	NA	E.P.S.	$0.48
DUNS No.	NA	Shareholders	NA

Business: The group's principle activity is to provide communication systems, applications and services. The group also provides voice, converged voice and data, customer relationship management, messaging, multi-service networking and structured cabling products and services. the groups servicing areas include businesses, government agencies and other organizations. The group operates from United States, Europe, Asia and Australia.

Primary SIC and add'l.: 3669 4899 7372 4812 3661

CIK No: 0001116521

Subsidiaries: 3102455 Nova Scotia Company, Agile Software NZ Limited, Avaya (China) Communications Co., Ltd., Avaya (Gibraltar) Investments Limited, Avaya (Malaysia) Sdn. Bhd., Avaya (Mauritus) Ltd., Avaya - Tenovis GmbH& Co. KG, Avaya - Tenovis Management GmbH, Avaya - Tenovis Service GmbH, Avaya Argentina S.R.L., Avaya Asia Pacific Inc., Avaya Australia Pty. Ltd., Avaya Austria GmbH, Avaya Belgium SPRL, Avaya Beteiligungs GmbH 107 Subsidiaries included in the Index

Officers: Louis J. D'Ambrosio/Dir., CEO, Pres., Jocelyne J. Attal/Chief Marketing Officer, Li Li/Research Scientist, Feng Liu/Research Scientist, Qian Yang/Research Scientist, Edward L. Peebles/Engineer, P. Krishnan/Research Scientist, Juan Jenny Li/Research Scientist, Eniko Kovacs/Research Scientist, Reinhard Klemm/Research Scientist, Colin Mallows/Research Scientist, Subrata Mazumdar/Research Scientist, Karyn Mashima/Sr. VP - Strategy, Technology, Roger Gaston/Sr. VP - Human Resources, Caroline Dorsa/CFO *(59 Officers included in Index)*

Directors: Louis J. D'Ambrosio/Dir., CEO, Pres., Bruce R. Bond/Dir., Frank J. Fanzilli/Dir., Joseph P. Landy/Dir., Mark Leslie/Dir., Philip A. Odeen/Dir., Hellene S. Runtagh/Dir., Daniel C. Stanzione/Dir., Paula Stern/Dir., Anthony P. Terracciano/Dir., Richard F. Wallman/Dir., Ronald L. Zarrella/Dir., James M. Landwehr/Dir. - Data Analysis Research, Venkatesh Krishnaswamy/Dir. - IP Communications Research, Anjur S. Krishnakumar/Dir. - Networked Systems Research

Owners: Paula Stern, Daniel C. Stanzione, Hellene S. Runtagh, Louis J. D'Ambrosio, Ronald L. Zarrella, Frank J. Fanzilli, Mark Leslie, Bruce R. Bond, Philip A. Odeen, Pamela F. Craven, Insiders/1.60%, Michael C. Thurk, Joseph P. Landy, Lord Abbett & Co., LLC/5.60%, Caroline Dorsa *(18 Owners included in Index)*

Financial Data: *Fiscal Year End:*09/30 *Latest Annual Data:* 9/30/2006

Year	Sales	Net Income
2006	$5,148,000,000	$201,000,000
2005	$4,902,000,000	$921,000,000
2004	$4,069,000,000	$296,000,000

Curr. Assets:	$2,359,000,000	*Curr. Liab.:*	$1,387,000,000	*P/E Ratio:*	35.44
Plant, Equip.:	$668,000,000	*Total Liab.:*	$3,114,000,000	*Indic. Yr. Divd.:*	NA
Total Assets:	$5,200,000,000	*Net Worth:*	$2,086,000,000	*Debt/ Equity:*	0.0035

Aventine Renewable Energy Holdings Inc

1300 S 2nd St., Pekin, IL, 61555; *PH:* 1-309-347-9200; *Fax:* 1-309-346-0742; *http://* www.aventinerei.com

General - Incorporation	DE	**Stock**- Price on:12/24/2007	$14.09
Employees	321	Stock Exchange	NYSE
Auditor	Ernst & Young LLP	Ticker Symbol	AVR
Stk Agt	American Stock Transfer & Trust Co.	Outstanding Shares	41,910,000
Counsel	NA	E.P.S.	$1.02
DUNS No.	NA	Shareholders	NA

Business: The groups principal activities include manufacturing, producing and marketing fuel-grade ethanol. In the year 2006, the group acquired Advanced BioEnergy, LLC. The specific customers of the groups are BP and Exxon/Mobil. The group operates from the United States.

Primary SIC and add'l.: 2869 5169 2865 5169 2865 2869

CIK No: 0001285043

Subsidiaries: Aventine Power, LLC, Aventine Renewable Energy Aurora West, LLC, Aventine Renewable Energy Mt Vernon, LLC, Aventine Renewable Energy, Inc., Aventine Renewable Energy, LLC, Nebraska Energy, LLC

Officers: Ronald H. Miller/Dir., CEO, Pres., Ajay Sabherwal/CFO, William J. Brennan/Chief Accounting, Compliance Officer, Roger E. Bushue/VP - Business Resources, Administration, Kenneth R. Eckhardt/Sec., John R. Gray/VP - Global Supply, Distribution, James M. Redding/VP - External Relations, James R. Sneed/VP - Biofuels Marketing, Jerry L. Weiland/VP - Operations, Les Nelson/Dir. - Investor Relations, Daniel R. Trunfio/COO, Lynn K. Landman/VP, General Counsel, Sec., Jeffrey A. Moery/VP - Technical Services

Directors: Ronald H. Miller/Dir., CEO, Pres., Bobby L. Latham/Chmn., Leigh J. Abramson/Dir., Richard A. Derbes/Dir., Farokh S. Hakimi/Dir., Arnold M. Nemirow/Dir., Michael C. Hoffman/Dir., Wayne D. Kuhn/Dir.

Owners: Touradji Capital Management, LP/8.90%, Richard A. Derbes, Leigh Abramson, Bobby L. Latham, Jerry L. Weiland, Wayne D. Kuhn, Michael C. Hoffman, Ronald H. Miller, Paul Touradji/8.90%, Aventine Holdings LLC/28.30%, Capital Research and Management Company/7.60%, Insiders/1.40%, Touradji Global Resources Master FundLtd./8.30%, Farokh S. Hakimi, Ajay Sabherwal *(17 Owners included in Index)*

Financial Data: *Fiscal Year End:*12/31 *Latest Annual Data:* 12/31/2006

Year	Sales	Net Income
2006	$1,592,420,000	$54,901,000
2005	$935,468,000	$32,182,000
2004	$858,876,000	$29,245,000

Curr. Assets:	$286,491,000	*Curr. Liab.:*	$83,244,000	*P/E Ratio:*	10.06
Plant, Equip.:	$115,645,000	*Total Liab.:*	$103,973,000	*Indic. Yr. Divd.:*	NA
Total Assets:	$408,136,000	*Net Worth:*	$304,163,000	*Debt/ Equity:*	0.9343

Aventura Holdings Inc

Formerly: Sun Network Group Inc

2650 Biscayne Blvd., First Fl., Miami, FL, 33137; *PH:* 1-305-937-2000

General - Incorporation	FL	**Stock**- Price on:12/24/2007	$0.0005
Employees	1	Stock Exchange	NA
Auditor	Jewett, Schwartz, Wolfe & Assoc.	Ticker Symbol	NA
Stk Agt	Corporate Stock Transfer, Inc.	Outstanding Shares	3,040,000,000
Counsel	NA	E.P.S.	$0.00
DUNS No.	NA	Shareholders	NA

Business: The group's principal activity is the production and distribution of television programs. It produces the television versions of top rated radio programs through its wholly owned subsidiary radiotv network inc. The television shows will be initially distributed via local broadcast stations. Radio x is a nationally syndicated radio network that will develop, produce and syndicate radio programs to young male population.

Primary SIC and add'l.: 4833

CIK No: 0000878802

Subsidiaries: Radio X Network, Inc.

Officers: Craig A. Waltzer/46/Chmn., CEO

Directors: Craig A. Waltzer/46/Chmn., CEO, Jere J. Lane/53/Dir., Sean Josiah/37/Dir.

Owners: Melissa Apple, Trustee of the Maria Lopez/48.92%, Horvath Holdings, LLC/13.14%

Financial Data: *Fiscal Year End:*12/31 *Latest Annual Data:* 12/31/2006

Year	Sales	Net Income
2006	$47,000	-$496,000
2005	$5,000	-$2,961,000
2004	$8,000	-$5,278,000

Curr. Assets:	$152,000	*Curr. Liab.:*	$278,000		
Plant, Equip.:	NA	*Total Liab.:*	$500,000	*Indic. Yr. Divd.:*	NA
Total Assets:	$413,000	*Net Worth:*	-$87,000	*Debt/ Equity:*	NA

Avenue Entertainment Group Inc

10 W 66th St., New York, NY, 10023; *PH:* 1-212-769-3814; *http://* www.avenue-entertainment.com

General - Incorporation	DE	**Stock** - Price on:12/24/2007	$0.06
Employees	NA	Stock Exchange	OTC
Auditor ... Singer Lewak Greenbaum & Goldstein		Ticker Symbol	PIXG
Stk Agt........Harris Trust Company of New York		Outstanding Shares	NA
Counsel	NA	E.P.S.	NA
DUNS No.	18-385-5295	Shareholders	NA

Business: The group's principal activity is to produce feature films, television films, series for televisions, cable movies made for televisions and one hour profiles of hollywood stars both domestically and internationally. The group develops and produces motion pictures for theatrical exhibition, television and other ancillary markets, both domestically and internationally.

Primary SIC and add'l.: 7812

CIK No: 0001023298

Subsidiaries: Avenue Pictures, Inc., Wombat Productions, Inc.

Owners: GP Strategies Corporation/20.00%, Hammer International Foundation/18.00%, Cary Brokaw/49.00%

Financial Data: *Fiscal Year End:*12/31 *Latest Annual Data:* 12/31/2004

Year	Sales	Net Income
2004	$995,000	-$63,000
2003	$637,000	-$884,000
2002	$1,516,000	-$634,000

Curr. Assets:	$215,000	*Curr. Liab.:*	$402,000		
Plant, Equip.:	$3,000	*Total Liab.:*	$2,214,000	*Indic. Yr. Divd.:*	NA
Total Assets:	$223,000	*Net Worth:*	-$1,990,000	*Debt/ Equity:*	NA

Avenue Group Inc

405 Lexington Ave., 26th Fl., New York, NY, 10174; *PH:* 1-888-612-4188; *Fax:* 1-347-952-3683; *http://* www.Ave.groupinc.com; *Email:* ir@Ave.groupinc.com

General - Incorporation	DE	**Stock** - Price on:12/24/2007	$0.015
Employees	2	Stock Exchange	OTC
Auditor	Sherb & Co., LLP	Ticker Symbol	AVNU
Stk Agt..... American Stock Transfer & Trust CO.		Outstanding Shares	247,590,000
Counsel	NA	E.P.S.	-$0.005
DUNS No.	NA	Shareholders	NA

Business: The group's principle activity is the exploration and development of oil and gas. It operates in three segments: oil and gas, digital media and e-commerce. The group's oil and gas operations are conducted through its subsidiary, avenue energy inc ('avenue energy'). Avenue energy operates predominantly in the republic of turkey, where it has entered into agreements with the sayer group. Pursuant to these agreements, avenue energy currently has a 50% interest in the karakalise licenses and has options to acquire similar interests in 31 other oil and gas properties in turkey. The group's oil and gas exploration and development, e-commerce and digital media businesses are conducted through its operating subsidiaries avenue energy inc, stampville.com and videodome.com networks inc. The group is a development stage enterprise with limited sales. The group's quarterly revenue for September 2007 was 0.01 millions of USD.

Primary SIC and add'l.: 7372 7375

CIK No: 0001100006

Subsidiaries: Avenue Energy, Inc., I.T. Technology Pty. Ltd.

Officers: Levi Mochkin/Chmn., CEO, Mendel Mochkin/Exec. VP, Vladimir Gerchikov/Geologist

Directors: Levi Mochkin/Chmn., CEO, Uri Bar Ner/Dir.

Owners: Levi Mochkin/22.20%, Shaya Boymelgreen/8.40%, Fawdon Investments Limited/16.80%, Uri Bar Ner, Langley Park Investment Trust PLC/16.40%, Insiders/24.00%, Norman J. Singer, Instanz Nominees Pty Ltd/7.00%, Mendel Mochkin/2.50%

Financial Data: *Fiscal Year End:*12/31 *Latest Annual Data:* 12/31/2006

Year	Sales	Net Income
2006	$61,000	-$472,000
2005	$35,000	-$6,025,000
2004	$86,000	-$12,458,000

Curr. Assets:	$722,000	*Curr. Liab.:*	$492,000		
Plant, Equip.:	$459,000	*Total Liab.:*	$504,000	*Indic. Yr. Divd.:*	NA
Total Assets:	$1,189,000	*Net Worth:*	$309,000	*Debt/ Equity:*	NA

Averion International Corp

Formerly: IT&E International Group
225 Tpke. Rd., Southborough, MA, 01772; *PH:* 1-508-597-6000; *http://* www.iteinternational.com

General - Incorporation	DE	**Stock** - Price on:12/24/2007	$0.13
Employees	227	Stock Exchange	NA
Auditor	Schneider Downs & Co., Inc.	Ticker Symbol	NA
Stk Agt...... American Stock Transfer & Trust Co.		Outstanding Shares	498,500,000
Counsel	NA	E.P.S.	-$0.04
DUNS No.	NA	Shareholders	NA

Business: The groups principle activity is to provide validation and clinical services. The group also provides validation services include systems configuration and implementation, network infrastructure, corporate systems, document management systems configuration, lab systems and instrument qualification, clinical adverse event systems. The groups clinical services include regulatory planning, data management, biometrics, medical affairs, clinical trails monitoring and project management, and medical affairs. The group operates from United States.

Primary SIC and add'l.: NA

CIK No: 0001193940

Officers: Alastair McEwan/52/Dir., Interim CEO, Philip T. Lavin/61/Dir., CEO, Anthony Allocca/64/VP - Operations, Gene Resnick/59/Chief Medical Officer, Christopher Codeanne/40/CFO, Glenn E. Deegan/41/VP, General Counsel, Sec., Faith Kolb/41/CTO, Mark Levine/49/VP - Business Development, Marketing, George Van Lear/66/Pres. - Information Technology, E International Division, John Shillingford/58/Pres. - Averion Europe

Directors: Alastair McEwan/52/Dir., Interim CEO, Philip T. Lavin/61/Dir., CEO, Fred Sancilio/58/Dir., Michael Falk/46/Dir., Robert D. Tucker/74/Dir., Cecilio M. Rodriguez/48/Dir.

Owners: Philip T. Lavin, Kelly Alberts, Insiders, Anthony Allocca, Peter Sollenne, Robert D. Tucker, Fred Sancilio, Michael Falk, Alastair McEwan, Gene Resnick

Financial Data: *Fiscal Year End:*12/31 *Latest Annual Data:* 12/31/2006

Year	Sales	Net Income
2006	$27,256,000	-$5,126,000
2005	$18,438,000	-$2,869,000
2004	$13,843,000	-$467,000

Curr. Assets:	$16,602,000	*Curr. Liab.:*	$9,944,000		
Plant, Equip.:	$1,434,000	*Total Liab.:*	$16,199,000	*Indic. Yr. Divd.:*	NA
Total Assets:	$44,762,000	*Net Worth:*	$28,562,000	*Debt/ Equity:*	0.2274

Averox Inc

39555 Orchard Hill Pl., Ste. 600, Crystal Glen Ctr., Novi, MI, 48375; *PH:* 1-248-449-2972; *Fax:* 1-248-348-5760; *http://* www.averox.com

General - Incorporation	NV	**Stock** - Price on:12/24/2007	$7
Employees	NA	Stock Exchange	OTC
Auditor Morgenstern, Svoboda & Baer CPA's PC		Ticker Symbol	AVOX
Stk Agt	NA	Outstanding Shares	NA
Counsel	NA	E.P.S.	NA
DUNS No.	NA	Shareholders	NA

Business: The groups principle activity is to provide customized development services. The group provides e-commerce solutions, enterprise resource planning, IT strategy and consulting, project management, web based applications such as content management systems, Internet and intranet application. The groups servicing areas include voice compression, telecom billing, lawful interception, fraud management, mediation, CDMA/GSM/ PSTN/VOIP, network design, network deployment & network optimization. The group operates from United States.

Primary SIC and add'l.: 9995

CIK No: 0001096656

Officers: Salman Mahmood/Chmn., CEO, Dir. - Resident, Christopher Baker/Sr. VP - Development, Dir., Maajid Maqbool/Sr. VP - Operations, Dir., Graham Hill/Sr. VP - Sales, Yasser Ahmad/31/Acting CFO

Directors: Salman Mahmood/Chmn., CEO, Dir. - Resident, Christopher Baker/Sr. VP - Development, Dir., Maajid Maqbool/Sr. VP - Operations, Dir.

Owners: Salman Mahmood/65.00%, Insiders/65.00%

Financial Data: *Fiscal Year End:*12/31 *Latest Annual Data:* 06/30/2007

Year	Sales	Net Income
2007	$3,612,000	-$640,000

Curr. Assets:	$1,561,000	*Curr. Liab.:*	$614,000		
Plant, Equip.:	$129,000	*Total Liab.:*	$715,000	*Indic. Yr. Divd.:*	NA
Total Assets:	$1,701,000	*Net Worth:*	$986,000	*Debt/ Equity:*	NA

Avery Dennison Corp

150 N Orange Grove Blvd., Pasadena, CA, 91103; *PH:* 1-626-304-2000; *Fax:* 1-626-792-7312; *http://* www.averydennison.com; *Email:* corporate.communications@averydennison.com

General - Incorporation	DE	**Stock** - Price on:12/24/2007	$66.61
Employees	22,700	Stock Exchange	NYSE
Auditor	PricewaterhouseCoopers LLP	Ticker Symbol	AVY
Stk Agt	Computershare Trust Co	Outstanding Shares	106,550,000
Counsel	Latham & Watkins	E.P.S.	$3.77
DUNS No.	00-825-6364	Shareholders	NA

Business: The group's principle activity is to manufacture pressure sensitive components through embossing, printing, stamping and die cutting. The groups manufacturing products include binders, organizing systems, markers, fasteners, business forms, tickets, tags, and imprinting equipment. The group operates from United States.

Primary SIC and add'l.: 2679 2672 2891

CIK No: 0000008818

Subsidiaries: A.v. Chemie Gmbh, Adc Philippines, Inc., Adespan S.r.l., Adespan U.k. Limited, Aeac, Inc., Austracote Pty Ltd., Avery (china)company Limited, Avery Corp., Avery De Mexico S.a. De C.v., Avery Dennison (asia)holdings Limited, Avery Dennison (bangladesh)ltd., Avery Dennison (fiji)limited, Avery Dennison (fuzhou)converted Products Limited, Avery Dennison (guangzhou)co. Ltd., Avery Dennison (guangzhou)converted Products Limited 188 Subsidiaries included in the Index

Officers: Dean A. Scarborough/Dir., CEO, Pres./$5,276,154.00, Daniel R. O'Bryant/CFO, Exec. VP - Finance/$2,789,045.00, Robert G. Van Schoonenberg/Exec. VP, Chief Legal Officer, Sec., General Counsel/$4,069,942.00, Christian A. Simcic/Group VP - Roll Materials/$1,938,444.00, Timothy S. Clyde/Group VP - Specialty Materials, Converting, David N. Edwards/CTO, Terrence L. Hemmelgarn/Group VP - Retail Information Services Group, Anne Hill/Sr. VP, Chief Human Resources Officer, Mitchell R. Butier/VP, Controller, Chief Accounting Officer, Susan C. Miller/VP, General Counsel, Richard P. Randall/VP - Corporate Governance, Assoc. General Counsel, Assist. Sec., Greg E. Temple/VP - Global Operations, Supply Chain, Robert M. Malchione/Sr. VP - Corporate Strategy, Technology/$1,804,883.00, Diane B. Dixon/Sr. VP - Worldwide Communications, Advertising, Karyn E. Rodriguez/VP, Treasurer (16 Officers included in Index)

Directors: Dean A. Scarborough/Dir., CEO, Pres., Kent Kresa/Chmn., Ken C. Hicks/Dir., Charles D. Miller/Dir. Emeriti, Russell H. Smith/Dir. Emeriti, Richard M. Ferry/70/Dir., Peter W. Mullin/Dir., David E.I. Pyott/Dir., Julia A. Stewart/Dir., Peter K. Barker/Dir., John T. Cardis/Dir., Rolf Borjesson/Dir., Patrick T. Siewert/Dir.

Owners: Robert M. Malchione, Rolf Borjesson, Peter K. Barker, Patrick T. Siewert, Peter W. Mullin, Richard M. Ferry, Dean A. Scarborough, John T. Cardis, Robert G. van Schoonenberg, Kent Kresa, Daniel R. OBryant, Christian A. Simcic, Insiders/1.30%, Julia A. Stewart, David E. I. Pyott

Financial Data: *Fiscal Year End:*12/31 *Latest Annual Data:* 12/30/2006

Year	Sales	Net Income
2006	$5,575,900,000	$367,200,000
2005	$5,473,500,000	$226,400,000

Curr. Assets:	$1,558,300,000	*Curr. Liab.:*	$1,525,600,000		
Plant, Equip.:	$1,295,700,000	*Total Liab.:*	$2,692,000,000	*Indic. Yr. Divd.:*	$1.600
Total Assets:	$4,203,900,000	*Net Worth:*	$1,511,900,000	*Debt/ Equity:*	0.2915

AVI BioPharma

1 SW Columbia, Ste. 1105, Portland, OR, 97258; *PH:* 1-503-227-0554; *Fax:* 1-503-227-0751; *http://* www.antivirals.com; *Email:* avi@avibio.com

General - Incorporation	OR
Employees	117
Auditor	KPMG LLP
Stk Agt.	Mellon Investor Services LLC
Counsel	NA
DUNS No.	83-254-6196

Stock - Price on:12/24/2007	$2.94
Stock Exchange	NDQ
Ticker Symbol	AVII
Outstanding Shares	53,630,000
E.P.S.	-$0.63
Shareholders	NA

Business: The group's principle activity is to develop therapeutic products for the treatment of life-threatening diseases. It is in the development stage. The products have initial applications in cardiovascular disease, colorectal cancer, pancreatic cancer, polycystic kidney disease, and drug metabolism. These are based on two distinct core technologies, neugeneo antisense and avicineo cancer vaccine. These compounds have the potential to provide safe and effective treatment for a wide range of human diseases. The company has entered into alliances with supergen, inc, abgenix, inc and exelixis, inc for product development and marketing. It has licensed medtronic, inc to use its antisense compounds in conjunction with medtronic devices. The group operates from United States.

Primary SIC and add'l.: 2833 2834 8731

CIK No: 0000873303

Officers: Denis R. Burger/Chmn., CEO/$1,191,557.00, James B. Hicks/Dir., CEO, Jenny Moede/Press Contact - Waggener Edstrom Bioscience, Alan P. Timmins/Dir., COO, Pres./$1,051,073.00, Ray R. Cummings/VP - Business Development, Dwight D. Weller/Dir., Sr. VP - Chemistry, Manufacturing/$579,283.00, Michael C. Hubbard/Dir. - Investor Relations, Bruce Voss/MD - Lippert, Heilshorn, Associates Inc, Jody Cain/VP - Lippert, Heilshorn, Associates Inc, Janet Rose Christensen/VP - Regulatory Affairs, Quality, Patrick L. Iversen/Dir., Sr. VP - Research, Development/$630,006.00, Mark M. Webber/CFO, CIO/$563,873.00, Peter D. O'Hanley/Sr. VP - Clinical Development, Regulatory Affairs

Directors: Denis R. Burger/Chmn., CEO, James B. Hicks/Dir., CEO, Jack L. Bowman/Chmn. - AVI Biopharma, Alan P. Timmins/Dir., COO, Pres., John C. Hodgman/Dir., Patrick L. Iversen/Dir., Sr. VP - Research, Development, Dwight D. Weller/Dir., Sr. VP - Chemistry, Manufacturing, Michael K. Forrest/Dir., Michael D. Casey/Dir., John W. Fara/Dir.

Owners: Denis R. Burger/2.50%, John C. Hodgman, James B. Hicks, Michael D. Casey, Jack L. Bowman, John W. Fara, Mark M. Webber, Dwight D. Weller/1.40%, George W. Haywood/8.50%, Michael K. Forrest, Alan P. Timmins/1.40%, Patrick L. Iversen, Peter D. OHanley, Insiders/7.20%

Financial Data: Fiscal Year End:12/31 Latest Annual Data: 12/31/2006

Year	Sales	Net Income
2006	$115,000	-$31,073,000
2005	$4,784,000	-$16,676,000
2004	$430,000	-$24,778,000

Curr. Assets:	$33,940,000	Curr. Liab.:	$8,343,000		
Plant, Equip.:	$4,330,000	Total Liab.:	$8,343,000	Indic. Yr. Divd.:	NA
Total Assets:	$40,863,000	Net Worth:	$32,519,000	Debt/ Equity:	NA

Aviall Inc

2750 Regent Blvd., Dallas Airport, TX, 75261; **PH:** 1-972-586-1000; **http://** www.aviall.com

General - Incorporation	DE
Employees	NA
Auditor	PricewaterhouseCoopers LLP
Stk Agt.	Wells Fargo Bank, N.A.
Counsel	NA
DUNS No.	80-996-8902

Stock - Price on:12/24/2007	NA
Stock Exchange	NA
Ticker Symbol	NA
Outstanding Shares	NA
E.P.S.	NA
Shareholders	NA

Business: The group's principal activity is the distribution of new and aftermarket aviation parts and supplies. Its aviall services business resells aviation parts, components and supplies procured from 180 manufacturers through 40 customer service centers in North America, Europe, Asia, New Zealand and Australia. It also operates a central warehouse at the Dallas/fort worth international airport. The inventory locator service brings buyers and sellers together into a global electronic marketplace serving the aviation, marine and defense industries. Principal suppliers include honeywell, goodrich, scott aviation and transdigm. The group is the exclusive service provider of rolls-royce model t56 engine parts. Its customers include military, passenger and freight air carriers, overhaul facilities, helicopter fleet operators and governmental agencies.

Primary SIC and add'l.: 5088 7375

CIK No: 0000701650

Subsidiaries: Aviall (Canada) Ltd., Aviall (UK) Limited, Aviall Airstocks Limited, Aviall Asia Limited, Aviall Australia Pty Ltd, Aviall de Mexico, S.A. de C.V., Aviall Foreign Sales Corporation, Aviall Japan Limited, Aviall New Zealand Limited, Aviall Product Repair Services, Inc., Aviall Pte Ltd, Aviall S.A.R.L., Aviall Services, Inc., Aviall, Inc., ILS eBusiness Services, Inc. 17 Subsidiaries included in the Index

Officers: Paul Fulchino/Chmn., CEO, Pres., Jim Quinn/Sr. VP - Sales, Marketing, Jeff Murphy/Sr. VP - Law, Human Resources, Sec., General Counsel, Charles Kienzle/Sr. VP - Operations, Tim White/Contact - United Kingdom, Ireland, Gale McCoy/Mgr. - Atlanta, Frank Previte/Contact - Boston, Massachusetts, Jose Benayas/Contact - France, Spain, Portugal, Catherine Testart/Contact - France, Haggai Mazursky/Contact - Eastern Europe, Russia, Baltics, Israel, Turkey, Greece, Christian Brandi/Contact - Scandinavia, Joe Piorico/Contact - Italy, Sloan Gray/Contact - Boston, New England, Tom Evans/Mgr. - Denver, David Saenz/Mgr. - Dallas Export, Mexico (82 Officers included in Index)

Directors: Paul Fulchino/Chmn., CEO, Pres.

Aviation Upgrade Technologies Inc

Aviation Upgrade Technologies, 24040 Camino Del Avion, Monarch Beach, CA, 92629; **PH:** 1-949-499-6665; **Fax:** 1-815-301-3844; **http://** www.aviationupgrade.com; **Email:** sales@aviationupgrade.com

General - Incorporation	NV
Employees	NA
Auditor	Stan J.h. Lee, Cpa
Stk Agt.	NA
Counsel	NA
DUNS No.	NA

Stock - Price on:12/24/2007	NA
Stock Exchange	OTC
Ticker Symbol	AVUG
Outstanding Shares	NA
E.P.S.	-$0.01
Shareholders	NA

Business: The groups principle activity is to manufacture the valve cap. The group product is Air Alert Valve Cap. The group operates from the United States.

Primary SIC and add'l.: 5085

CIK No: 0001094847

Subsidiaries: Automotive Upgrade Technologies, Inc.

Owners: Jack A. Tuszynski/7.00%, Alexander Ruckdaeschel, James Wemett/16.50%, Insiders/46.00%, Tamas Bakos, Alexander L. Weis/25.60%, Wexford Spectrum Trading Ltd./10.40%, Kay Noel, CAMOFI Master LDC/10.80%, Biomed Solutions, LLC/7.10%, Technology Innovations/9.40%, OncoVentures, LLC/5.00%, Corey Levenson/3.40%, Robert Patterson

Financial Data: Fiscal Year End:12/31 Latest Annual Data: 12/31/2006

Year	Sales	Net Income
2006	$180,000	-$235,000
2005	$148,000	-$274,000

Curr. Assets:	$41,000	Curr. Liab.:	$1,858,000		
Plant, Equip.:	$9,000	Total Liab.:	$1,858,000	Indic. Yr. Divd.:	NA
Total Assets:	$49,000	Net Worth:	-$1,809,000	Debt/ Equity:	NA

Avicena Group Inc

228 Hamilton Ave. Fl 3, 3rd Fl., Palo Alto, CA, 94301; **PH:** 1-415-397-2880; **Fax:** 1-415-397-2898; **http://** www.avicenagroup.com; **Email:** info@avicenagroup.com

General - Incorporation	DE
Employees	4
Auditor	Vitale, Caturano & Company, Ltd
Stk Agt.	Computershare Trust Co
Counsel	NA
DUNS No.	NA

Stock - Price on:12/24/2007	$4.5
Stock Exchange	OTC
Ticker Symbol	AVGO
Outstanding Shares	51,000,000
E.P.S.	-$0.17
Shareholders	NA

Business: The groups principle activities include developing and commercializing drug, cosmetic and nutritional products. The group products include Nurigene(TM) and Neotine(R). The group marketed its products uder the trade names Nurigene(TM) and Neotine(R). The group operates from the United States.

Primary SIC and add'l.: 8731

CIK No: 0001317092

Officers: Belinda Tsao-Nivaggioli/Chmn., CEO, Leslie S.T. Fang/Dir., Chmn. - Scientific Advisory Board, Chief Scientific Officer, Steven Hersch/Member - Participating Clinicians - Harvard Medical School, Massachusetts General Hospital, Jeffrey Rosenfeld/Member - Participating Clinicians, Dir. - Carolinas ALS Center, Charlotte, North Carolina, Mark A. Tarnopols/Member - Participating Clinicians, Associate Professor - Departments, Pediatrics, Medicine, Mcmaster University, Hamilton, Ontario, Paul Gordon/Member - Research Alliances, Merit Cudkowicz/Member - Research Alliances, Jeremy Shefner/Member - Research Alliances, Peter Hespel/Member - Research Alliances, Karl Kieburtz/Member - Research Alliances, Robert Chetlin/Member - Research Alliances, Laurie Gutmann/Member - Research Alliances, Sophia Chun/Member - Research Alliances, Michael Sullivan/Acting CFO, Bolko Zu Stolberg/VP - Marketing, Business Strategy (28 Officers included in Index)

Directors: Belinda Tsao-Nivaggioli/Chmn., CEO, Leslie S.T. Fang/Dir., Chmn. - Scientific Advisory Board, Chief Scientific Officer, Nasser Menhall/51/Chmn., Andrew Gertler/Dir., Paul Schimmel/67/Dir., Uri Sagman/Dir., Flint M. Beal/Co - Founder, Member - Scientific Advisory Board, Dir. - Cornell Medical School, Rima Kaddurah-Daouk/Member - Scientific Advisory Board, Co - Founder - Avicena Group

Owners: Paul Schimmel/2.00%, Leslie S. T. Fang/1.30%, Insiders/11.80%, Andrew M. Gertler, Karen Georgiou/9.60%, Belinda Tsao Nivaggioli/5.90%, Nasser Menhall/2.50%

Financial Data: Fiscal Year End:12/31 Latest Annual Data: 12/31/2006

Year	Sales	Net Income
2006	$375,000	-$5,528,000

Curr. Assets:	$1,222,000	Curr. Liab.:	$372,000		
Plant, Equip.:	$3,000	Total Liab.:	$5,376,000	Indic. Yr. Divd.:	NA
Total Assets:	$2,981,000	Net Worth:	-$2,935,000	Debt/ Equity:	NA

Avici Systems Inc

101 Billerica Ave., Bldg. 2, North Billerica, MA, 01862; **PH:** 1-978-964-2000; **Fax:** 1-978-964-2100; **http://** www.avici.com; **Email:** info@avici.com

General - Incorporation	DE
Employees	104
Auditor	Ernst & Young LLP
Stk Agt.	Mellon Investor Services LLC
Counsel	Choate, Hall & Stewart LLP
DUNS No.	83-595-0395

Stock - Price on:12/24/2007	$7.55
Stock Exchange	NDQ
Ticker Symbol	AVCI
Outstanding Shares	14,100,000
E.P.S.	$2.46
Shareholders	NA

Business: The group's principal activity is to provide high-speed data networking equipment and routing solutions. The products optimize bandwidths of network through dynamic management enabling the transmission of high volumes of information. The group's routing product family, include the terabit switch router(R) and the stackable switch router (TM) that are marketed to telecommunications companies and Internet service providers. The customers of the group include incumbent local exchange carriers, inter-exchange carriers, postal telephone, telegraph operators, international competitive carriers, Internet service providers and agencies of the United States government. The group outsources raw material procurement, assembly of the systems and their testing from celestica corporation and the sanmina-sci corporation. The products and solutions are offered through regional partners in Japan, the republic of Korea and southeast Asia.

Primary SIC and add'l.: 3663 3669

CIK No: 0001094895

Subsidiaries: Avici Systems Europe B.V, Avici Systems France sarl, Avici Systems Germany GmbH, Avici Systems International, Inc, Avici Systems KK, Avici Systems Texas, Inc., Avici Systems Texas, L.P.

Officers: William Leighton/CEO, Pres./$1,028,454.00, Jo-Ann Mendles/Chief Business Officer/$715,244.00, Larry Dennison/Founder, CTO, William J. Stuart/CFO, Sr. VP - Finance, Administration/$419,164.00, Esmeralda Swartz/VP - Marketing, T. S. Ramesh/41/Principal Accounting Officer, VP - Finance/$292,443.00

Directors: Richard Liebhaber/Chmn., Robert Schechter/Dir., Larry Dennison/Founder, CTO, Bill Ingram/Dir., William Ingram/51/Dir.

Owners: T. S. Ramesh, Robert P. Schechter, Citadel Limited Partnership/8.84%, Renaissance Technologies Corp./7.90%, Coghill Capital Management LLC/5.83%, William Ingram, Insiders/2.60%, William J. Leighton/1.37%, Richard T. Liebhaber, William J. Stuart

Financial Data: Fiscal Year End:12/31 Latest Annual Data: 12/31/2006

Year	Sales	Net Income
2006	$82,236,000	$8,285,000
2005	$35,095,000	-$24,654,000
2004	$24,492,000	-$35,425,000

Curr. Assets:	$71,249,000	**Curr. Liab.:**	$18,506,000	**P/E Ratio:**	5.39
Plant, Equip.:	$4,937,000	**Total Liab.:**	$18,506,000	**Indic. Yr. Divd.:**	NA
Total Assets:	$84,690,000	**Net Worth:**	$66,184,000	**Debt/ Equity:**	NA

Avid Technology Inc

Avid Technology Pk., 1 Pk. W, Tewksbury, MA, 01876; *PH:* 1-978-640-6789; *Fax:* 1-978-640-3366; *http://* www.avid.com

General - Incorporation .... DE
Employees 2,792
Auditor .... Ernst & Young, LLP
Stk Agt..... Computershare Investor Services LLC
Counsel .... NA
DUNS No. 19-988-0659

Stock- Price on:12/24/2007 .... $33.94
Stock Exchange .... NDQ
Ticker Symbol .... AVID
Outstanding Shares 41,290,000
E.P.S .... -$1.57
Shareholders .... NA

Business: The group's principal activities are to develop, market, sell and support a wide range of software and systems for creating and manipulating digital media content. The group's digital, nonlinear video and film editing systems are designed to improve the productivity of video and film editing. The group develops and sells a range of image manipulation products that allow users in the video and film post-production and broadcast markets to create graphics and special effects. The group also develops and sells digital audio systems for professional audio market. The operations are conducted in Germany and other foreign countries. During dec 2003, the group acquired assets of bomb factory digital inc, on 26-Jan-2004, the group acquired Munich based nxn software ag and on 20-Aug-2004 m-audio.

Primary SIC and add'l.: 7379 7372

CIK No: 0000896841

Subsidiaries: 1117 Acquisition Corporation, Avid Benelux B.v., Avid C.v. LLC, Avid General Partner B.v., Avid Internet Media Group, Inc., Avid Nordic Ab, Avid North Asia Limited, Avid Technology (australia) Pty Ltd, Avid Technology (s.e. Asia) Pte Ltd, Avid Technology C.v., Avid Technology Europe Limited, Avid Technology Gmbh, Avid Technology Holding B.v., Avid Technology Holdings Gmbh, Avid Technology Iberia Ltd 43 Subsidiaries included in the Index

Officers: Nancy Hawthorne/Dir., CEO - Interim, David A. Krall/47/Dir., CEO, Pres./$2,240,258.00, David M. Lebolt/VP, GM - Digidesign/$708,490.00, Sharad Rastogi/VP - Corporate Development/$784,349.00, Michael J. Rockwell/CTO/$793,731.00, Joel E. Legon/CFO, VP, Greg Estes/VP, Chief Marketing Officer, Graham Sharp/VP, GM - Avid Video, Greg Munster/CIO, VP - Business Transformation, Paige Parisi/VP, General Counsel, Corp. Sec., Lynne D. Richer/Acting VP - Human Resources, Dean Ridlon/Dir. - Investor Relations, Patricia A. Baker/60/VP - Human Resources, Jeffrey S. Hastings/43/VP, GM - Consumer

Directors: Nancy Hawthorne/Dir., CEO - Interim, David A. Krall/47/Dir., CEO, Pres., Pamela F. Lenehan/Chmn., John H. Park/Dir., George H. Billings/Dir., Elizabeth Monk Daley/Dir., John V. Guttag/Dir., Youngme E. Moon/Dir.

Owners: John V. Guttag, Michael J. Rockwell, George H. Billings, Private Capital Management, L.P./11.90%, T. Rowe Price Associates, Inc./9.70%, PRIMECAP Management Company/5.30%, Insiders/2.50%, Paul J. Milbury, Columbia Wanger Asset Management, L.P./14.60%, David A. Krall/1.30%, Nancy Hawthorne, Youngme E. Moon, Elizabeth M. Daley, David M. Lebolt, Blum Capital Partners, L.P./15.30% *(19 Owners included in Index)*

Financial Data: *Fiscal Year End:*12/31 *Latest Annual Data:* 12/31/2006

Year	Sales	Net Income
2006	$910,578,000	-$42,927,000
2005	$775,443,000	$33,980,000
2004	$589,605,000	$71,701,000

Curr. Assets:	$483,939,000	**Curr. Liab.:**	$196,182,000		
Plant, Equip.:	$40,483,000	**Total Liab.:**	$216,653,000	**Indic. Yr. Divd.:**	NA
Total Assets:	$997,034,000	**Net Worth:**	$780,381,000	**Debt/ Equity:**	NA

Avigen Inc

1301 Harbor Bay Pkwy., Alameda, CA, 94502; *PH:* 1-510-748-7150; *Fax:* 1-510-748-7155; *http://* www.avigen.com; *Email:* info@avigen.com

General - Incorporation .... DE
Employees 33
Auditor .... Odenberg, Muranishi & Co. LLP
Stk Agt..... American Stock Transfer & Trust Co.
Counsel .... Cooley Godward LLP
DUNS No. 80-374-4051

Stock- Price on:12/24/2007 .... $6.35
Stock Exchange .... NDQ
Ticker Symbol .... AVGN
Outstanding Shares 29,150,000
E.P.S .... -$0.9
Shareholders .... NA

Business: The group's principal activity is to develop pharmaceutical products for serious and chronic hematological and neurological diseases. The group has developed proprietary dna-based drug delivery technologies including gene delivery platform based on adeno-associated virus (aav) vectors. The dna drug-based delivery technologies are used to develop products designed to treat hematological and neurological diseases that are difficult to treat using conventional pharmaceutical drugs. The group's advanced product development programs are designed to utilize aav vector technology to deliver dna into the cells of patients in order to generate the expression of therapeutic proteins to treat hemophilia and Parkinson's disease.

Primary SIC and add'l.: 8731 2834

CIK No: 0000932903

Subsidiaries: Amarin Pharmaceuticals, Inc

Officers: Kenneth Chahine/Dir., CEO, Pres./$777,465.00, Christina Thomson/VP, Corporate Counsel/$451,346.00, Kirk W. Johnson/VP - Preclinical Development/$479,707.00, Michael D. Coffee/Chief Business Officer/$514,658.00, Andrew A. Sauter/VP - Finance, Principal Financial, Accounting Officer/$359,208.00

Directors: Kenneth Chahine/Dir., CEO, Pres., Zola Horovitz/Chmn., Richard Wallace/Dir., Jan K. ohrstrom/Dir., Stephen G. Dilly/Dir., Daniel Vapnek/Dir., John K.A. Prendergast/Dir., Yuichi Iwaki/Dir.

Owners: Ridgeback Capital Investments Ltd./4.99%, Yuichi Iwaki, Zola Horovitz, Michael Coffee, Andrew Sauter, Insiders/5.58%, BVF, Inc./8.73%, Kirk Johnson, Richard Wallace, Kenneth Chahine/2.03%, Federated Investors, Inc./14.29%, Daniel Vapnek, John Prendergast, Davidson Kempner Partner/5.56%, Christina M. Thomson *(16 Owners included in Index)*

Financial Data: *Fiscal Year End:*12/31 *Latest Annual Data:* 12/31/2006

Year	Sales	Net Income
2006	$103,000	-$24,256,000
2005	$12,026,000	-$14,696,000
2004	$2,195,000	-$23,923,000

Curr. Assets:	$69,437,000	**Curr. Liab.:**	$9,970,000		
Plant, Equip.:	$2,709,000	**Total Liab.:**	$11,540,000	**Indic. Yr. Divd.:**	NA
Total Assets:	$75,017,000	**Net Worth:**	$63,477,000	**Debt/ Equity:**	NA

Avino Silver & Gold Mines Ltd

455 Granville St., Ste. 400, Vancouver, BC, V6C 1T1; *PH:* 1-604-682-3701; *Fax:* 1-604-682-3600; *http://* www.avino.com; *Email:* ir@avino.com

General - Incorporation .... BC
Employees .... NA
Auditor .... Manning Elliott LLP
Stk Agt .... Pacific Stock Transfer Company
Counsel .... Salley Bowes Harwardt
DUNS No. .... NA

Stock- Price on:12/24/2007 .... $1.67
Stock Exchange .... OTC
Ticker Symbol .... ASGMF
Outstanding Shares .... NA
E.P.S .... NA
Shareholders .... NA

Business: The groups principal activity is to explore minerals and natural gas. The group operates from the United States and Canada.

Primary SIC and add'l.: 1081

CIK No: 0000316888

Subsidiaries: Cia Minera Mexicana de Avino, S.A. de C.V.

Officers: Louis Wolfin/Founder, Dir., CEO, David Wolfin/Dir., Pres., Principal Executive Officer, Principal Financial Officer, Connie Lillico/Corp. Sec., Kevin Bales/CFO, Mimy Fernandez-Maldonado/Corp. Sec.

Directors: Louis Wolfin/Founder, Dir., CEO, Lloyd Andrews/Chmn., Michael Baybak/Dir., David Wolfin/Dir., Pres., Principal Executive Officer, Principal Financial Officer, Gary Robertson/Dir.

Owners: Michael Bayback, Gary Robertson, Louis Wolfin, Lloyd Andrews, Connie Lillico, David Wolfin

Financial Data: *Fiscal Year End:*01/31 *Latest Annual Data:* 01/31/2007

Year	Sales	Net Income
2007	NA	-$11,811,000
2006	NA	-$2,095,000

Curr. Assets:	$9,503,000	**Curr. Liab.:**	$1,229,000		
Plant, Equip.:	$859,000	**Total Liab.:**	$3,205,000	**Indic. Yr. Divd.:**	NA
Total Assets:	$10,614,000	**Net Worth:**	$7,409,000	**Debt/ Equity:**	NA

Avis Budget Group Inc

Formerly: Cendant Corp
6 Sylvan Way, Parsippany, New Jersey, 07054; *PH:* 1-973-496-4700; *http://* www.cendant.com

General - Incorporation .... DE
Employees 19,000
Auditor .... Deloitte & Touche LLP
Stk Agt .... Mellon Investor Services LLC
Counsel .... NA
DUNS No. 06-250-6134

Stock- Price on:12/24/2007 .... $29.8
Stock Exchange .... NYSE
Ticker Symbol .... CAR
Outstanding Shares 102,030,000
E.P.S .... -$9.58
Shareholders .... NA

Business: The group operates through its subsidiaries whose principle activity is to provide vehicles on rent basis. The group operates through two segments include Avis and Budget. The group operates from United States, Canada, Australia and New Zealand.

Primary SIC and add'l.: 6411 6794 4724 7299 7389 6531

CIK No: 0000723612

Subsidiaries: 9805 Willows Avenue, LLC, Aesop Leasing Corporation, AFS Mortgage, Allmon, Tiernan& Ely, Inc., American Home Settlement Services, LLC, American TitleCompany of Houston, Amerihost Franchise Systems, Inc., Apanage B.V., Apex Marketing, Inc., APEX Real Estate Information Services Alabama, LLC, Apex Real Estate Information Services LLP, Apollo Galileo USA Partnership, Apollo Galileo USA SubI, Inc., Apollo Galileo USA SubII, Inc., Apple Ridge Services Corporation 339 Subsidiaries included in the Index

Officers: Ronald L. Nelson/55/Chmn., CEO/$15,301,240.00, John T. McClain/46/Chief Accounting Officer, Sr. VP/$1,251,916.00, Leonard S. Coleman/59/Presiding Dir., Patric T. Siniscalchi/Exec. VP - International Operations, David B. Wyshner/40/CFO, Exec. VP, Treasurer/$2,842,193.00, Robert F. Salerno/56/Dir., COO, Pres./$3,259,008.00, Larry De Shon/48/Exec. VP - Operations, Jean M. Sera/Sec., Karen Sclafani/56/Exec. VP, General Counsel, Scott W. Deaver/56/Exec. VP - Strategy, Mark J. Servodidio/42/Chief Human Resources Officer, Exec. VP/$1,208,884.00

Directors: Ronald L. Nelson/55/Chmn., CEO, Martin L. Edelman/66/Dir., Robert F. Salerno/56/Dir., COO, Pres., Sheli Z. Rosenberg/66/Dir., Stender E. Sweeney/69/Dir., Mary C. Choksi/57/Dir., Lynn Krominga/57/Dir.

Financial Data: *Fiscal Year End:*12/31 *Latest Annual Data:* 12/31/2006

Year	Sales	Net Income
2006	$5,689,000,000	-$1,994,000,000
2005	$18,236,000,000	$1,341,000,000
2004	$19,785,000,000	$2,082,000,000

Curr. Assets:	$1,806,000,000	**Curr. Liab.:**	$1,884,000,000		
Plant, Equip.:	$7,535,000,000	**Total Liab.:**	$10,828,000,000	**Indic. Yr. Divd.:**	NA
Total Assets:	$13,271,000,000	**Net Worth:**	$2,443,000,000	**Debt/ Equity:**	1.0528

Avista Corp

1411 E Mission Ave., Spokane, WA, 99202; *PH:* 1-509-489-0500; *Fax:* 1-509-495-8725; *http://* www.avistacorp.com; *Email:* corpcomm@avistacorp.com

General - Incorporation .... WA
Employees 1,995
Auditor .... Deloitte & Touche LLP
Stk Agt .... Bank of New York
Counsel .... NA
DUNS No. 00-794-3764

Stock- Price on:12/24/2007 .... $22.37
Stock Exchange .... NYSE
Ticker Symbol .... AVA
Outstanding Shares 52,750,000
E.P.S $1.08
Shareholders .... NA

Business: The group's principle activities are to generate, transmit and distribute energy and other energy related businesses. It operates in four segments: avista utilities, energy trading and marketing, avista advantage and other segment. The avista utilities segment generates, transmits and distributes electricity and distributes natural gas. It also engages in wholesale purchases and sales of electric capacity and energy. The energy trading and marketing segment engages in electricity and natural gas marketing and trading business. Avista advantage provides utility bill processing, payment and information services. Other segment is responsible for investing in business opportunities. The group's quarterly revenue for September 2007 was 267.66 millions of USD.

Primary SIC and add'l.: 4939 7374 3629

CIK No: 0000104918

Subsidiaries: Advanced Manufacturing and Development, Inc., AVA Capital Trust III, Avista Advantage, Inc., Avista Capital II, Avista Capital, Inc., Avista Development, Inc., Avista Energy Canada LTD, Avista Energy, Inc., Avista Power, LLC, Avista Rathdrum, LLC, Avista Receivables Corporation, Avista Ventures, Inc., Bay Area Manufacturing, Inc., CoPac Management, Inc., Pentzer Corporation 17 Subsidiaries included in the Index

Officers: Stu Stiles/Pres., CEO - Avista Advantage, Gary G. Ely/Chmn., CEO, Pres./$3,325,275.00, Dennis Vermillion/VP - Avista Corp, VP - Energy Resources, Avista Utilities, Malyn Malquist/CFO, Exec. VP/$1,096,256.00, Marian Durkin/Sr. VP, General Counsel, Chief Compliance Officer/$724,126.00, Don Kopczynski/VP Avista Corp, VP - Transmission, Distribution Operations, Avista Utilities, Karen Eastwood/Contact - Shareholder Services, Jessie Wuerst/Mgr. - Communications, Christy Burmeister-Smith/VP, Controller, Principal Accounting Officer, James M. Kensok/CIO, VP, Scott L. Morris/Dir., COO, Pres./$1,115,496.00, David J. Meyer/VP, Chief Counsel Regulatory - Governmental Affairs/$692,620.00, Ronald Peterson/VP - Avista Corp, VP - Customer Solutions, Avista Utilities, Kelly Norwood/VP - Avista Corp, VP State - Federal Regulations, Avista Utilities, Fred Valentine/Journeyman gas Measurement Technician *(26 Officers included in Index)*

Directors: Gary G. Ely/Chmn., CEO, Pres., Roy Lewis Eiguren/Dir., John R. Taylor/Dir., John F. Kelly/Dir., Michael L. Noel/Dir., Erik J. Anderson/Dir., Jack W. Gustavel/Dir., Heidi B. Stanley/51/Dir., Kristianne Blake/Dir., Lura J. Powell/Dir.

Owners: John F. Kelly, Insiders, Malyn K. Malquist, Heidi B. Stanley, Kristianne Blake, Gary G. Ely, Lura J. Powell, Jack W. Gustavel, Erik J. Anderson, David J. Meyer, Michael L. Nol, John R. Taylor, Scott L. Morris, Roy Lewis Eiguren, Marian M. Durkin

Financial Data: ***Fiscal Year End:***12/31 ***Latest Annual Data:*** 12/31/2006

Year	Sales	Net Income
2006	$1,506,311,000	$73,133,000
2005	$1,359,607,000	$45,168,000
2004	$1,151,580,000	$35,154,000

Curr. Assets:	$1,032,274,000	***Curr. Liab.:***	$945,209,000	***P/E Ratio:***	20.71
Plant, Equip.:	$2,290,932,000	***Total Liab.:***	$3,139,662,000	***Indic. Yr. Divd.:***	$0.600
Total Assets:	$4,056,508,000	***Net Worth:***	$916,846,000	***Debt/ Equity:***	1.1590

Avistar Communications Corp

1875 S Grant St., 10th Fl., San Mateo, CA, 94402; ***PH:*** 1-650-525-3300; ***Fax:*** 1-650-525-1360; ***http://*** www.avistar.com; ***Email:*** info@avistar.com

General		***Stock***	
Incorporation	DE	Price on:12/24/2007	$1.36
Employees	88	Stock Exchange	NDQ
Auditor	Burr, Pilger & Mayer, LLP	Ticker Symbol	AVSR
Stk Agt	EquiServe Trust Co N.A	Outstanding Shares	35,430,000
Counsel	Wilson Sonsini Goodrich & Rosati	E.P.S	-$0.07
DUNS No.	NA	Shareholders	NA

Business: The group's principal activity is to develop, market and support a suite of networked video communication services. The group operates through two segments, the integrated suite consists of video and data collaboration applications and management software. It is managed by the avistarvostm video operating system and is used by enterprises for interactive video calling, content creation and publishing, video-on demand and for integrated data sharing. The group's wholly owned subsidiary, collaboration properties inc, develops, maintains, supports and licenses the intellectual property used in the systems. The systems are sold directly to enterprises in select markets in 42 countries in North America, western Europe and Asia. The group's customers include jp morgan chase, deutsche bank, goldman sachs, ubs warburg llc.

Primary SIC and add'l.: 7379 7373 7372

CIK No: 0001111632

Subsidiaries: Avistar Corporation, Avistar Financial Corporation, Avistar Systems Corporation, Collaboration Properties, Inc.

Officers: Gerald J. Burnett/Chmn., CEO/$261,750.00, William L. Campbell/Dir., Dir. - Strategic Development, Stephen F. Arisco/49/VP - Operations, Customer Service, Rima Vanhill/Dir. - Contracts, Assist. Corp. Sec., Lester F. Ludwig/VP - Collaboration Properties, Anton F. Rodde/Pres. - Intellectual Property Division/$306,663.00, Robert Habig/CFO/$310,747.00, Robert T. Garrigan/47/VP - Sales/$296,904.00, Chris Lauwers/Chief Technology, Products Officer/$309,580.00, Simon Moss/Pres., Gary Stager/VP - Engineering

Directors: Gerald J. Burnett/Chmn., CEO, Stephen R. Heinrichs/Dir., Craig F. Heimark/Dir., Robert M. Metcalfe/Dir., James W. Zeigon/Dir., William L. Campbell/Dir., Dir. - Strategic Development

Owners: Chris J. Lauwers/2.80%, William L. Campbell/5.80%, Robert M. Metcalfe, Insiders/56.30%, James W. Zeigon, Robert P. Latta, Robert J. Habig/1.90%, Gerald J. Burnett/43.20%, Robert Garrigan, Stephen R. Heinrichs/15.60%, Anton Rodde, Craig F. Heimark, Fuller& Thaler Asset Management,Inc./10.10%

Financial Data: ***Fiscal Year End:***12/31 ***Latest Annual Data:*** 12/31/2006

Year	Sales	Net Income
2006	$13,225,000	-$8,149,000
2005	$6,911,000	-$5,174,000
2004	$6,896,000	-$8,706,000

Curr. Assets:	$11,765,000	***Curr. Liab.:***	$14,340,000		
Plant, Equip.:	$256,000	***Total Liab.:***	$24,648,000	***Indic. Yr. Divd.:***	NA
Total Assets:	$14,699,000	***Net Worth:***	-$9,949,000	***Debt/ Equity:***	NA

Avitar Inc

65 Dan Rd., Canton, MA, 02021; ***PH:*** 1-781-821-2440; ***Fax:*** 1-781-821-4458; ***http://*** www.avitarinc.com; ***Email:*** investorrelations@avitarinc.com

General		***Stock***	
Incorporation	DE	Price on:12/24/2007	$0.0095
Employees	67	Stock Exchange	OTC
Auditor	BDO Seidman LLP	Ticker Symbol	AVTI
Stk Agt	Continental Stock Transfer & Trust Co	Outstanding Shares	27,280,000
Counsel	Dolgenos, Newman & Cronin	E.P.S	-$0.355
DUNS No.	18-715-9900	Shareholders	NA

Business: The group's principal activities are to develop, manufacture and market diagnostic test products and proprietary medical-grade hydrophilic polyurethane foam disposables. These products are designed for medical, diagnostic, dental and consumer use. The products include oralscreen (TM), an oral fluid-based, rapid on-site assay system for detecting drugs of abuse. Hairscreen(tm), is a hair-based test that detects both short and long-term drug abuse. The child guard(tm) tests provide the ability to detect a child's exposure to drugs and possible drug abuse through testing of a child's hair. The group also operates a certified laboratory and provides specialized drug testing services primarily utilizing hair and meconium as the samples. On 16-Dec-2003, the group disposed its wholly owned subsidiary, United States drug testing laboratories, inc.

Primary SIC and add'l.: 3826 2835

CIK No: 0000814008

Subsidiaries: Avitar Technologies, Inc, BJR Security, Inc, United States Drug Testing Laboratories, Inc

Officers: Peter P. Phildius/Chmn., CEO, Peter N. Cholakis/VP - Marketing, Jay C. Leatherman/CFO, Douglas W. Scott/COO, Pres.

Directors: Peter P. Phildius/Chmn., CEO

Owners: Jay C. Leatherman, Neil R.Gordon, Charles R. McCarthy, Peter Cholakis, Insiders, Peter P. Phildius, PK&S, Douglas W. Scott

Financial Data: ***Fiscal Year End:***09/30 ***Latest Annual Data:*** 9/30/2006

Year	Sales	Net Income
2006	$4,925,000	-$3,703,000
2005	$4,509,000	-$2,433,000
2004	$4,049,000	-$2,969,000

Curr. Assets:	$1,296,000	***Curr. Liab.:***	$4,338,000		
Plant, Equip.:	$324,000	***Total Liab.:***	$7,314,000	***Indic. Yr. Divd.:***	NA
Total Assets:	$2,346,000	***Net Worth:***	-$8,184,000	***Debt/ Equity:***	NA

Aviza Technology Inc

440 Kings Village Rd., Scotts Valley, CA, 95066; ***PH:*** 1-831-438-2100; ***http://*** www.avizatechnology.com

General		***Stock***	
Incorporation	DE	Price on:12/24/2007	$5.63
Employees	675	Stock Exchange	NDQ
Auditor	Deloitte & Touche LLP	Ticker Symbol	AVZA
Stk Agt	American Stock Transfer & Trust Co.	Outstanding Shares	20,820,000
Counsel	Latham & Watkins	E.P.S	-$0.62
DUNS No.	NA	Shareholders	NA

Business: The groups principle activities include designing, manufacturing, selling and supporting semiconductor capital equipment and process technologies. The products of the group include silicon, 3-D packaging and power integrated circuits, physical vapor deposition and chemical vapor deposition. The group products sold under the trade names Celsior(TM), Verano(TM) 5500 and Sigma fxP(TM). In December 2005, the group merged with Trikon Technologies, Inc. Specific customers of the group include Winbond Electronics Corp., Inotera Memories Inc, and Infineon Technologies AG. The group operates from Asia Pacific, Europe and North America. The group's quarterly revenue for September 2007 was 50.18 millions of USD.

Primary SIC and add'l.: 3567 3559

CIK No: 0001311396

Subsidiaries: Aviza Europe Limited, Aviza Technologies (Israel) Limited, Aviza Technology (Cayman) Ltd., Aviza Technology (Scotland) Ltd., Aviza Technology (Shanghai) Inc., Aviza Technology GmbH, Aviza Technology International, Inc., Aviza Technology International, Inc., Taiwan Branch, Aviza Technology K.K., Aviza Technology Korea Co., Ltd, Aviza Technology Limited, Aviza Technology Pte. Ltd., Aviza Technology S.A.S., Aviza Technology Sdn. Bhd., Aviza, Inc. 23 Subsidiaries included in the Index

Officers: Jerauld J. Cutini/49/Chmn., CEO, Pres., Patrick C. O'Connor/CFO, Exec. VP, John MacNeil/CTO, Exec. VP, Rick O'Malley/VP - Worldwide Sales, Costomer Support, John Villadsen/VP - Worldwide Operations, May Su/VP, GM - ALD, Thermal Business Unit, Kevin Crofton/VP, GM - PVD, CVD, Etch Business Unit, Michael Martinez/VP - Worldwide Corporate Marketing, Nitin Shah/VP - Business Development

Directors: Jerauld J. Cutini/49/Chmn., CEO, Pres., Robert R. Anderson/Chmn., Klaus Wiemer/Dir., David Fries/Dir., Richard Conn/Dir., Dana Ditmore/Dir., Richard C. Neely/Dir.

Owners: Caisse de dpt et placement du Qubec/15.00%, Klaus C. Wiemer, Robert R. Anderson, Dana C. Ditmore, Richard C. Neely, Richard M. Conn, Insiders/8.90%, John Macneil, Affiliates of VantagePoint Venture Partners/35.30%, Patrick C. OConnor/3.10%

Financial Data: ***Fiscal Year End:***09/29 ***Latest Annual Data:*** 9/29/2006

Year	Sales	Net Income
2006	$160,860,000	-$14,688,000
2005	$171,209,000	-$16,013,000

Curr. Assets:	$66,952,000	***Curr. Liab.:***	$72,534,000		
Plant, Equip.:	$19,569,000	***Total Liab.:***	$111,647,000	***Indic. Yr. Divd.:***	NA
Total Assets:	$90,909,000	***Net Worth:***	-$31,738,000	***Debt/ Equity:***	0.0131

Avnet Inc

2211 S 47th St., Phoenix, AZ, 85034; ***PH:*** 1-480-643-2000; ***Fax:*** 1-480-643-7370; ***http://*** www.avnet.com; ***Email:*** investorrelations@avnet.com

General		***Stock***	
Incorporation	NY	Price on:12/24/2007	$41.1
Employees	10,900	Stock Exchange	NYSE
Auditor	KPMG LLP	Ticker Symbol	AVT
Stk Agt	American Stock Transfer & Trust Co.	Outstanding Shares	149,470,000
Counsel	NA	E.P.S	NA
DUNS No.	00-699-5419	Shareholders	NA

Business: The groups principle activity is to provide electronic components, enterprise network, computer equipment and embedded subsystems. The group also provides engineering design, materials management and logistics services, system integration and configuration, and supply chain advisory services. In the year 2007, the group acquired ChannelWorx Pty Ltd. The group operates from United States, Europe, and Middle East.

Primary SIC and add'l.: 5065 5064 5045

CIK No: 0000008858

Subsidiaries: Avnet, Inc., incorporated

Officers: Roy Vallee/Chmn., CEO/$9,780,761.00, David Birk/Sr. VP, General Counsel, Sec./$2,004,835.00, Steven C. Church/59/Sr. VP, Chief Human Resources Development Officer, Harley Feldberg/55/Corporate VP, Pres. - Avnet Electronic Marketing/$2,335,329.00, Kirsten Klatt/Dir. - Communications, Avnet Technology Solutions, Europe, Peggy Lee/Marketing Programs Mgr. - Channels, AAC, Asia, Sonia Bovio/VP, Sabine Huckmann/Managing Partner, Allen Maag/VP,

Chief Communications Officer, Steven R. Phillips/45/CIO, VP, James N. Smith/62/Pres. - Avnet Logistics Services, Bob Brown/VP, Dir. - Corporate Audit, John Clark/VP, Dir. - Credit, Edward Kamins/59/Corporate Sr. VP, Chief Operational Excellence Officer, Raymond Sadowski/CFO, Sr. VP, Assist. Sec./$1,740,412.00 *(42 Officers included in Index)*

Directors: Roy Vallee/Chmn., CEO, Gary L. Tooker/Dir., Frank R. Noonan/Dir., Ray M. Robinson/Dir., Eleanor Baum/Dir., Lawrence W. Clarkson/Dir., Ehud Houminer/Dir., James A. Lawrence/Dir., Veronica J. Biggins/Dir.

Owners: Harley Feldberg, First Pacific Advisors LLC/7.20%, David R. Birk, Insiders/1.87%, AXA Financial, Inc. et al/5.70%, Ray M. Robinson, James A. Lawrence, Veronica J. Biggins, Ehud Houminer, Barclays Global Investors, NA./14.03%, Frank R. Noonan, Gary L. Tooker, Lawrence W. Clarkson, Eleanor Baum, Raymond Sadowski *(18 Owners included in Index)*

Financial Data: *Fiscal Year End:*07/02 *Latest Annual Data:* 7/1/2006

Year	Sales	Net Income
2006	$14,253,630,000	$204,547,000
2005	$11,066,816,000	$168,239,000
2004	$10,244,741,000	$72,897,000

Curr. Assets:	$3,483,986,000	**Curr. Liab.:**	$1,644,993,000	
Plant, Equip.:	$187,339,000	**Total Liab.:**	$2,910,225,000	**Indic. Yr. Divd.:** NA
Total Assets:	$4,863,651,000	**Net Worth:**	$1,953,426,000	**Debt/ Equity:** 0.3640

Avocent Corp

4991 Corporate Dr., Huntsville, AL, 35805; *PH:* 1-256-430-4000; *Fax:* 1-256-430-4030; *http://* www.avocent.com

General - Incorporation	DE	**Stock**- Price on:12/24/2007	$29.76
Employees	1,707	Stock Exchange	NDQ
Auditor	PricewaterhouseCoopers LLP	Ticker Symbol	AVCT
Stk Agt.	American Stock Transfer & Trust CO.	Outstanding Shares	50,460,000
Counsel	NA	E.P.S.	NA
DUNS No.	NA	Shareholders	NA

Business: The group's principle activities are to design, manufacture and market switching systems and remote access products for the client/server computing market. The group's products provide plug and play switching systems for many network administrations, management and storage problems faced by customers using client/server architecture. It also offers visual display products for high information-content digital display solutions. The groups major trademarks are apex, amworks, amx, avocent, autoview, cstation, cybex, ds1800, dsr, equinox, longview, superserial, switchview and xp4000. The group's international sales are within Europe, Asia and the Pacific Rim through the utilization of the sales offices in China, England, France, Holland, Korea, Ireland, Germany, Japan, Hong Kong and Singapore. The group's quarterly revenue for September 2007 was 162.07 millions of USD.

Primary SIC and add'l.: 3613 7373 7372 3679

CIK No: 0001109808

Subsidiaries: Apex International, Inc, Apex PC Solutions, Ltd, Avocent California Corp, Avocent Canada Holding Corp, Avocent China LTD, Avocent Computertechnik GmbH, Avocent France SARL, Avocent Huntsville Corp, Avocent International, Ltd, Avocent Ireland Holdings Ltd, Avocent Netherlands B.V., Avocent Nevada LLC, Avocent Redmond Corp, Avocent Services Corporation, Avocent Texas I, LLC 22 Subsidiaries included in the Index

Officers: John R. Cooper/Chmn., CEO/$2,187,642.00, Mitch Friend/Sr. VP, GM - Avocent Connectivity, Control Division, Everett Brooks/VP - Analyst, Investor Relations, Bill Neiland/VP - Product Management, Services, Samuel F. Saracino/Exec. VP - Legal, Corporate Affairs, General Counsel, Sec., Steve Daly/Exec. VP - Avocent, GM - Landesk Division, Eugene F. Mulligan/Sr. VP - Global Operations/$867,644.00, David C. Perry/Exec. VP, GM - Avocent Management Systems Division/$993,635.00, Doyle C. Weeks/Dir., COO, Pres./$1,347,061.00, Edward H. Blankenship/Sr. VP - Finance, CFO/$705,856.00, Tom Miller/Sr. VP - OEM Sales, Kieran MacSweeney/Sr. VP, GM - Avocent Desktop Solutions Division, MD - Avocent International, Douglas E. Pritchett/Exec. VP - Corporate Strategy, William A. Dambrackas/Exec. VP - Advanced Technology, Dudley Devore/Sr. VP - Global Branded Markets *(19 Officers included in Index)*

Directors: John R. Cooper/Chmn., CEO, Edwin L. Harper/Dir., Francis A. Dramis/Dir., William H. McAleer/Dir., Doyle C. Weeks/Dir., COO, Pres., David P. Vieau/Dir., Stephen F. Thornton/Dir., Harold D. Copperman/Dir.

Owners: Edwin L. Harper, Francis A. Dramis, Insiders/5.75%, John R. Cooper, Harold D. Copperman, David C. Perry, Stephen F. Thornton/1.30%, David P. Vieau, William H. McAleer, Eugene F. Mulligan, Barclays Global Investors, NA/5.50%, Edward H. Blankenship, Doyle C. Weeks

Financial Data: *Fiscal Year End:*12/31 *Latest Annual Data:* 12/31/2006

Year	Sales	Net Income
2006	$519,195,000	$45,532,000
2005	$369,888,000	$48,349,000
2004	$365,255,000	$18,040,000

Curr. Assets:	$300,025,000	**Curr. Liab.:**	$133,342,000	**P/E Ratio:** 44.42
Plant, Equip.:	$38,004,000	**Total Liab.:**	$325,011,000	**Indic. Yr. Divd.:** NA
Total Assets:	$1,158,854,000	**Net Worth:**	$833,843,000	**Debt/ Equity:** 0.1826

Avon Products Inc

1345 Ave. of the Americas, New York, NY, 10105; *PH:* 1-212-282-5000; *Fax:* 1-212-282-6049; *http://* www.avoncompany.com

General - Incorporation	NY	**Stock**- Price on:12/24/2007	$38.45
Employees	40,300	Stock Exchange	NYSE
Auditor	PricewaterhouseCoopers LLP	Ticker Symbol	AVP
Stk Agt.	First Chicago Trust	Outstanding Shares	438,860,000
Counsel	NA	E.P.S.	$1.28
DUNS No.	00-146-8693	Shareholders	NA

Business: The groups principle activities include manufacturing and marketing beauty and related products. The group operates through six geographical segments namely North America; Latin America, western Europe, Middle East and Africa, Central and Eastern Europe, Asia Pacific, and China. The group operates from United States.

Primary SIC and add'l.: 3421 2389 2844 3961 5961

CIK No: 0000008868

Subsidiaries: Albee Dublin Finance Company, Arlington Limited, Avon (Windsor) Limited, Avon Aliada LLC, Avon Americas, Ltd., Avon Asia Holdings Co., Avon Beauty Products Co. (ABPC) Russia, Avon Beauty Products India PVT. LTD., Avon Beauty Products, SARL, Avon Canada, Inc., Avon Capital Corporation, Avon Colombia Holdings I, Avon Colombia Holdings II, Avon Colombia Ltda., Avon Component Manufacturing, Inc. 111 Subsidiaries included in the Index

Officers: Andrea Jung/Chmn., CEO/$13,320,570.00, Nancy Glaser/Sr. VP - Global Communications, Geralyn R. Breig/Sr. VP, Global Brand Pres., Charles Cramb/Exec. VP - Finance, Technology, CFO/$2,357,260.00, Bennett Gallina/29/Sr. VP - China, Western Europe, The Middle East, Africa, John F. Owen/Sr. VP - Global Supply Chain, Lucien Alziari/Sr. VP - Human Resources, Brian C. Connolly/Exec. VP - Global Sales Strategy/$3,074,997.00, Elizabeth A. Smith/Pres./$3,299,890.00, Harriet Edelman/Sr. VP - Business Transformation, CIO, John Higson/Sr. VP - Central, Eastern Europe, James C. Wei/Sr. VP - Asia Pacific, Renee W. Johansen/Contact - Institutional Investors, Equity Analysts, Rob Foresti/Contact - Institutional Investors, Equity Analysts, Gilbert L. Klemann/Sr. VP, General Counsel *(19 Officers included in Index)*

Directors: Andrea Jung/Chmn., CEO, Edward T. Fogarty/Dir., Ann S. Moore/Dir., Lawrence A. Weinbach/Dir., Paula A. Stern/Dir., Maria Elena Lagomasino/Dir., Don W. Cornwell/Dir., Gary M. Rodkin/Dir., Fred Hassan/Dir., Paul S. Pressler/Dir.

Owners: Edward T. Fogarty, Lawrence A. Weinbach, Dodge & Cox/5.30%, Maria Elena Lagomasino, Elizabeth Smith, Stanley C. Gault, Ann S. Moore, Paula Stern, Susan J. Kropf, Insiders, Fred Hassan, Brian Connolly, FMR Corp./11.20%, Don W. Cornwell, Charles W. Cramb *(18 Owners included in Index)*

Financial Data: *Fiscal Year End:*12/31 *Latest Annual Data:* 12/31/2006

Year	Sales	Net Income
2006	$8,763,900,000	$477,600,000
2005	$8,149,600,000	$847,600,000
2004	$7,747,800,000	$846,100,000

Curr. Assets:	$3,334,400,000	**Curr. Liab.:**	$2,550,100,000	**P/E Ratio:** 30.04
Plant, Equip.:	$1,100,200,000	**Total Liab.:**	$4,410,800,000	**Indic. Yr. Divd.:** $0.740
Total Assets:	$5,238,200,000	**Net Worth:**	$790,400,000	**Debt/ Equity:** 1.5152

AVP

6100 Ctr Dr., 9th Fl., Los Angeles, CA, 90045; *PH:* 1-310-426-8000; *http://* www.avp.com

General - Incorporation	DE	**Stock**- Price on:12/24/2007	$1.22
Employees	29	Stock Exchange	OTC
Auditor	Mayer Hoffman Mccann, P.C	Ticker Symbol	AVPI
Stk Agt	U.S. Stock Transfer Corp	Outstanding Shares	19,820,000
Counsel	NA	E.P.S.	-$0.01
DUNS No.	25-104-3212	Shareholders	NA

Business: The group's principal activity is to seek an opportunity to merge with or acquire a private entity. The group provided an Internet based search engine for digital entertainment, music and for exchanging electronic files. In 2001, the board of directors approved a plan to shut down all unnecessary operations. As a result, the group currently, has no business operations.

Primary SIC and add'l.: 7375 7372

CIK No: 0000930817

Subsidiaries: AVP Pro Beach Volleyball Tour, Inc.

Officers: Leonard Armato/Chmn., CEO, Dir. - Tour Commissioner, Andrew Reif/42/CFO, COO, Sec., Bruce Binkow/Dir., Chief Marketing Officer, Thomas Torii/41/Controller, William J. Chardavoyne/Dir., CFO, Jeffrey G. Benz/Exec. VP, General Counsel, Sec.

Directors: Leonard Armato/Chmn., CEO, Dir. - Tour Commissioner, Bruce Binkow/Dir., Chief Marketing Officer, Philip Guarascio/Dir., Jack Kemp/Dir., Scott Painter/Dir., Kathy Vrabeck/Dir., William J. Chardavoyne/Dir., CFO, Brett D. Yormark/Dir.

Owners: Insiders, Kathy Vrabeck, Brett Yormark, Amtrust Financial Group, Bruce Binkow, Thomas Torii, FOX, Andrew Reif, Philip Guarascio, Diker Micro Value Fund, LP, Highbridge/39.40%, William J. Chardavoyne, Scott Painter, AEG, Highbridge *(17 Owners included in Index)*

Financial Data: *Fiscal Year End:*12/31 *Latest Annual Data:* 12/31/2006

Year	Sales	Net Income
2006	$21,472,000	-$337,000
2005	$15,581,000	-$8,964,000
2004	$12,309,000	-$2,873,000

Curr. Assets:	$8,250,000	**Curr. Liab.:**	$2,636,000	
Plant, Equip.:	$340,000	**Total Liab.:**	$2,827,000	**Indic. Yr. Divd.:** NA
Total Assets:	$8,695,000	**Net Worth:**	$5,869,000	**Debt/ Equity:** NA

avVaa World Health Care Products Inc

1710 Shuswap Ave., Lumby, BC, V0E-2G0; *PH:* 1-250-547-2048; *Fax:* 1-250-547-2067; *http://* www.avvaa.com

General - Incorporation	NV	**Stock**- Price on:12/24/2007	$0.0006
Employees	NA	Stock Exchange	OTC
Auditor	Davidson & Company LLP	Ticker Symbol	AVVW
Stk Agt	Signature Stock Transfer, Inc.	Outstanding Shares	NA
Counsel	Anslow & Jaclin, LLP	E.P.S.	NA
DUNS No.	NA	Shareholders	NA

Business: The group is a global biotechnology company specializing in providing all natural, therapeutic skin care products. The group operates from Lumby, British Columbia, and Canada.

Primary SIC and add'l.: 2834 2833 2844

CIK No: 0001092534

Subsidiaries: 648311 B.C. Ltd, AVVAA World Health Care Products Canada Ltd., Mind Your Own Skin Products Inc

Officers: Jack Farley/Chmn., Founder, CEO, Merle Goertz/Investor Relations Officer, Mark Alden/VP - Research - Development, Lorie Campbell-Farley/Exec. VP - Sales - Marketing, Advisor to The Board, James W. Haney/VP - Manufacturing - Distribution, Donald Scott/Executive Officer - Institutional Sales, Robert Brian Buchanan/Executive Officer - Corporate Development, Ruth Brennan/Controller, Dustin Thomson/Executive Officer - Systems, Internet Sales, Stephanie Tambellini/Graphic Design, Merchandising, Barb Hazell/VP - Animal Care, Frances Tourand/Administrative Accounting Assist., Brenda Fex/Customer Sales, Service Mgr.

Directors: Jack Farley/Chmn., Founder, CEO, James MacDonald/Dir., Lorie Campbell-Farley/Exec. VP - Sales - Marketing, Advisor to The Board

Owners: John Farley/1.80%, Insiders/20.30%

Financial Data: *Fiscal Year End:*05/31 *Latest Annual Data:* 5/31/2006

Year	Sales	Net Income
2006	$19,000	-$4,035,000
2005	$13,000	-$3,146,000
2004	$9,000	-$2,307,000

Curr. Assets:	$1,000,000	Curr. Liab.:	$3,747,000		
Plant, Equip.:	$328,000	Total Liab.:	$3,747,000	Indic. Yr. Divd.:	NA
Total Assets:	$1,712,000	Net Worth:	-$2,035,000	Debt/ Equity:	NA

AVX Corp

801 17th Ave. S., Myrtle Beach, SC, 29578; *PH:* 1-843-448-9411; *Fax:* 1-843-916-7751;
http:// www.avxcorp.com

General - Incorporation	DE	**Stock**- Price on:12/24/2007	$17.91
Employees	13,000	Stock Exchange	NYSE
Auditor	Deloitte & Touche, LLP	Ticker Symbol	AVX
Stk Agt	American Stock Transfer & Trust Co.	Outstanding Shares	171,770,000
Counsel	Parker Poe Adams & Bernstein	E.P.S	$0.90
DUNS No.	05-889-5921	Shareholders	NA

Business: The group's principle activities are to manufacture and supply a broad line of passive electronic components and interconnect products. The passive electronic component products include ceramic and tantalum capacitors, film capacitors, varistors and non-linear resistors. These products are marketed to multi-national original equipment manufacturers and contract equipment manufacturers. The group also manufactures electronic connectors and inter-connect systems for use in the telecommunications, information technology hardware, automotive electronics, medical device, military and aerospace industries. The group operates in the United States, Europe, Asia, Latin America and Israel. The group's total revenue for year 2007 was 1,498.49 millions of USD.

Primary SIC and add'l.: 3678 3675

CIK No: 0000859163

Subsidiaries: Avio Excelente, S.A. DE C.V., AVX Components DA Amazonia Ltda., AVX Corporation, AVX Czech Republic s.r.o., AVX Electronics (Tianjin) Co. Ltd., AVX Filters Corporation, AVX Industries. Pte. Ltd., AVX Israel Limited, AVX Limited, AVX Tantalum Corporation, AVX/Kyocera Asia Ltd., AVX/Kyocera Pt. Ltd., Elco Europe GmbH, Elco USA, Inc., Kyocera Electronic Devices, LLC 17 Subsidiaries included in the Index

Officers: John S. Gilbertson/Dir., CEO, Pres./$1,395,764.00, Carl Eggerding/CTO, VP, Keith Thomas/VP, Pres. - Kyocera Electronic Devices, Peter Venuto/VP - North American, Europe Sales/$504,140.00, John Lawing/VP - Advanced Products, Kurt Cummings/VP, CFO, Treasurer, Sec./$421,654.00, John Sarvis/VP - Ceramic Products, Peter Collis/VP - Tantalum/$825,549.00, S. M. Chan/VP - Sales, Marketing, Asia, Marshall C. Jackson/Exec. VP - Sales, Marketing/$615,720.00

Directors: John S. Gilbertson/Dir., CEO, Pres., Benedict P. Rosen/Chmn., Masahiro Umemura/Dir., Yuzo Yamamura/Dir., Donald B. Christiansen/Dir., Joseph Stach/Dir., Kauzuo Inamori/Dir., Rodney Lanthorne/Dir., Makoto Kawamura/Dir., Noboru Nakamura/Dir., David Decenzo/Dir.

Owners: Yuzo Yamamura, Peter Venuto, John S. Gilbertson, Kazuo Inamori, Richard Tressler, Peter Collis, Insiders/1.49%, Kensuke Itoh, Kurt Cummings, Masahiro Umemura, Rodney N. Lanthorne, Marshall C. Jackson, Benedict P. Rosen, Joseph Stach, Donald B. Christiansen

Financial Data: Fiscal Year End:03/31 Latest Annual Data: 3/31/2007

Year	Sales	Net Income
2007	$1,498,495,000	$153,865,000
2006	$1,333,208,000	$81,752,000
2005	$1,283,202,000	$55,732,000

Curr. Assets:	$1,203,772,000	Curr. Liab.:	$171,030,000	P/E Ratio:	20.12
Plant, Equip.:	$232,950,000	Total Liab.:	$227,099,000	Indic. Yr. Divd.:	$0.160
Total Assets:	$1,675,208,000	Net Worth:	$1,448,109,000	Debt/ Equity:	NA

Aware Inc

40 Middlesex Tpke., Bedford, MA, 01730; *PH:* 1-781-276-4000; *Fax:* 1-781-276-4001;
http:// www.aware.com; *Email:* info@aware.com

General - Incorporation	MA	**Stock**- Price on:12/24/2007	$5.5
Employees	117	Stock Exchange	NDQ
Auditor	PricewaterhouseCoopers LLP	Ticker Symbol	AWRE
Stk Agt	Computershare Trust CO.	Outstanding Shares	23,700,000
Counsel	Foley, Hoag & Eliot LLP	E.P.S	$0.04
DUNS No.	18-898-5071	Shareholders	NA

Business: The group's principle activity is to develop and market intellectual property for broadband communications. The group licenses the intellectual property to semiconductor companies that build integrated circuits based on the technology. The group offers digital subscriber line (DSL) technology for the telecommunications industry. Dsl enables telephone companies to use their existing copper telephone lines to offer broadband services. The group's DSL offers a technology package for asymmetric digital subscriber line (adsl). Adsl is a broadband service that is primarily targeted at residential telephone customers for high-speed Internet accesses. The group licenses the intellectual property worldwide through direct sales force. The group's semiconductor customers are analog devices, inc., infineon technologies, ag and intel corporation. The group's quarterly revenue for September 2007 was 7.46 millions of USD.

Primary SIC and add'l.: 7372 7373

CIK No: 0001015739

Subsidiaries: Aware Security Corporation

Officers: Michael A. Tzannes/Dir., CEO/$568,751.00, Edmund C. Reiter/Dir., Pres./$496,400.00, Keith Farris/CFO, VP/$179,870.00, Richard W. Gross/Sr. VP - Engineering/$324,890.00

Directors: Michael A. Tzannes/Dir., CEO, John K. Kerr/Chmn., Frederick D. D'Alessio/Dir., Edmund C. Reiter/Dir., Pres., David G. Forney/Dir., Adrian F. Kruse/Dir., Mark G. McGrath/Dir.

Owners: Michael A. Tzannes/6.20%, Dimensional Fund Advisors Inc/6.70%, Insiders/17.80%, Frederick D. D'Alessio, Richard W. Gross/1.40%, John K. Kerr/3.70%, Mark G. McGrath, John S. Stafford/11.40%, State of Wisconsin Investment Board/5.20%, Edmund C. Reiter/4.30%, Adrian F. Kruse, David G. Forney, Keith A. Farris

Financial Data: Fiscal Year End:12/31 Latest Annual Data: 12/31/2006

Year	Sales	Net Income
2006	$24,056,000	$1,034,000
2005	$15,667,000	-$2,468,000
2004	$16,485,000	-$1,367,000

Curr. Assets:	$44,258,000	Curr. Liab.:	$2,886,000	P/E Ratio:	183.33
Plant, Equip.:	$8,123,000	Total Liab.:	$3,216,000	Indic. Yr. Divd.:	NA
Total Assets:	$54,586,000	Net Worth:	$51,370,000	Debt/ Equity:	NA

AXA

1290 Ave. of the Americas, New York, NY, 10104; *PH:* 1-212-554-1234; *Fax:* 1-212-707-1805;
http:// www.axa.com; *Email:* management@axa-assistance.com

General - Incorporation	France	**Stock**- Price on:12/24/2007	$44.69
Employees	78,800	Stock Exchange	NYSE
Auditor	PricewaterhouseCoopers LLP	Ticker Symbol	AXA
Stk Agt	Axa Financial Inc	Outstanding Shares	NA
Counsel	NA	E.P.S.	$3.92
DUNS No.	38-479-8021	Shareholders	NA

Business: The group's principle activity is to provide insurance and related financial services. The company operates through four divisions: life insurance (range of life insurance products with an emphasis on investment linked and savings products); non life insurance (products for the automobile, domestic and commercial property sectors, as well as for transport, general liability and construction); asset management and other financial services (asset management, investment banking, securities trading, brokerage, real estate and other financial activities) and holding companies. The group operates from United States.

Primary SIC and add'l.: 6029 6311 6512 6331 6371 6719 6321

CIK No: 0000898427

Subsidiaries: AllianceBernsteins largest client, global investment management

Officers: Henri De Castries/54/Chmn., CEO, Nicolas Moreau/Chmn. - AXA Investment Mgr., CEO - AXA UK, Ireland, Francois Pierson/61/Member - Management Board, Claude Brunet/51/Member - Management Board, Etienne Bouas-Laurent/Sr. VP, Head - Investor Relations, Kevin Byrne/CIO, Sr. VP - AXA Financial, Relations With US Investors, Emmanuel Touzeau/VP - Financial Transactions, Rating Agencies, Marie-Elodie Bazy/Financial Analyst, Financial Transactions, Rating Agencies, Paul-Antoine Cristofari/VP - Accounting Releases, Gilbert Chahine/Financial Analyst, Accounting Releases, Laurence Letty/Event Management, Investor Meetings, Conferences, Similar Events, Sandra Allou/Team Assist., Sylvie Maurey/Team Assist., George Guerrero/VP - Relations With US Investors, Sara Gori/Financial Analyst *(17 Officers included in Index)*

Directors: Henri De Castries/54/Chmn., CEO, Jean-Rene Fourtou/69/Vice Chmn. - Supervisory Board, Claude Bebear/73/Chmn. - Supervisory Board, David Dautresme/74/Member - Supervisory Board, Ezra Suleiman/67/Member - Supervisory Board, Michel Pebereau/66/Member - Supervisory Board, Christopher Condron/61/Member - Management Board, Henri Hottinguer/73/Member - Supervisory Board, Dominique Reiniche/53/Member - Supervisory Board, Jacques Tabourot/63/Member - Supervisory Board, Jacques De Chateauvieux/57/Member - Supervisory Board, Leo Apotheker/55/Member - Supervisory Board, Denis Duverne/55/Member - Management Board, Gerard Mestrallet/59/Member - Supervisory Board, Henri Lachmann/70/Member - Supervisory Board *(20 Directors included in Index)*

Owners: Grard Mestrallet, Anthony Hamilton, Jean-Ren Fourtou, Denis Duverne, Franois Pierson, Norbert Dentressangle, David Dautresme, Jacques Tabourot, Claude Brunet, Claude Bbar, Michel Pbereau, Leo Apotheker, Henri Hottinguer, Henri De Castries, Henri Lachmann *(18 Owners included in Index)*

Financial Data: Fiscal Year End:12/31 Latest Annual Data: 12/31/2006

Year	Sales	Net Income
2006	$104,006,633,000	$5,716,899,000
2005	$84,887,132,000	$6,196,781,000
2004	$133,401,481,000	$4,413,834,000

Curr. Assets:	$89,602,160,000	Curr. Liab.:	$109,258,786,000	P/E Ratio:	13.15
Plant, Equip.:	$29,673,743,000	Total Liab.:	$908,714,959,000	Indic. Yr. Divd.:	$1.210
Total Assets:	$962,746,916,000	Net Worth:	$54,031,957,000	Debt/ Equity:	NA

AXA Equitable Life Insurance Co

1290 Ave. Of The Americas, New York, NY, 10104; *PH:* 1-212-554-1234;
http:// www.equitable.com; *Email:* jeffrey.tolvin@axa-financial.com

General - Incorporation	NY	**Stock**- Price on:12/24/2007	NA
Employees	78,800	Stock Exchange	NA
Auditor	PricewaterhouseCoopers LLP , KPMG LLP	Ticker Symbol	NA
Stk Agt	NA	Outstanding Shares	NA
Counsel	NA	E.P.S	NA
DUNS No.	00-698-3365	Shareholders	NA

Business: The group's principal activity is to provide diversified financial services including insurance, investment management and asset management services through its subsidiaries. The insurance products offered by the group includes traditional, variable and interest sensitive life insurance products and variable and fixed-interest annuity products to individuals, small and medium-size businesses, state and local governments and not-for-profit organizations. The group also provides diversified investment management and related services to individual and institutional investors and also private clients. Insurance segment products are offered on a retail basis in all 50 states, the district of columbia, Puerto Rico and the U.S. Virgin islands. The group is a wholly owned subsidiary of axa financial, inc.

Primary SIC and add'l.: 6289 6321

CIK No: 0000727920

Subsidiaries: AXA Advisors, LLC, AXA Distributors, LLC, AXA Life Inc, AXA Network, LLC

Officers: Christopher M. Condron/Chmn., CEO, Mary Taylor/Media Contact, Jennifer L. Blevins/Exec. VP - Human Resources, Barbara Goodstein/Chief Innovation Officer, Exec. VP - Marketing, Robert S. Jones/Exec. VP, Head - Retail Distribution, Kevin E. Murray/CIO, Exec. VP, Richard V. Silver/Exec. VP, General Counsel, Andrew McMahon/Exec. VP, COO - Retail Distribution, Mary Beth Beth Farrell/Exec. VP - Service Delivery, Richard S. Dziadzio/CFO

Directors: Christopher M. Condron/Chmn., CEO

AXA Financial Inc

1290 Ave. of the Americas, New York, NY, 10104; *PH:* 1-212-554-1234; *Fax:* 1-212-314-4480;
http:// www.axa-financial.com

General - Incorporation	DE	**Stock**- Price on:12/24/2007	NA
Employees	NA	Stock Exchange	NA
Auditor	KPMG LLP	Ticker Symbol	NA
Stk Agt	Mellon Investor Services	Outstanding Shares	NA
Counsel	NA	E.P.S	NA
DUNS No.	79-080-2383	Shareholders	NA

Business: The group's principle activity is to provide financial services offering a broad spectrum of financial advisory, insurance, investment banking and brokerage and investment management services. The financial advisory/insurance group offers a variety of traditional, variable and interest-sensitive life insurance products, variable and fixed-interest annuity products, mutual fund and other investment products and asset management services to individuals, small groups, small and medium-size businesses, state and local governments and not-for-profit organizations, as well as financial planning services to individuals. The group operates from United States.

Primary SIC and add'l.: 6311 6211 6282

CIK No: 0000888002

Subsidiaries: AXA Advisors, LLC, AXA Distributors, LLC, AXA Financial (Bermuda) Ltd., AXA Insurance Holding Co., Ltd., AXA Life and Annuity Company, AXA Network, LLC, MONY Life Insurance Company of America, The Advest Group, Inc., U.S. Financial Life Insurance Company

Officers: Christopher M. Condron/Dir., CEO, Pres., Alvin H. Fenichel/Sr. VP, Controller, Richard S. Dziadzio/CFO, Exec. VP

Directors: Christopher M. Condron/Dir., CEO, Pres., Henri De Castries/Chmn., Charlynn Goins/Dir., Lorie A. Slutsky/Dir., Ezra Suleiman/Dir., Denis Duverne/Dir., Peter J. Tobin/Dir., Scott D. Miller/Dir., Bruce W. Calvert/Dir., Mary R. Henderson/Dir., Joseph H. Moglia/Dir., James F. Higgins/Dir., Anthony J. Hamilton/Dir.

Axcan Pharma Inc

22 Inverness Ctr. Pkwy., Birmingham, AL, 35242; ***PH:*** 1-205-991-8085; ***Fax:*** 1-612-991-8176; ***http://*** www.axcan.com

General - Incorporation	Canada	***Stock***- Price on:12/24/2007	$18.8
Employees	425	Stock Exchange	NDQ
Auditor	Raymond Chabot Grant Thornton LLP	Ticker Symbol	AXCA
Stk Agt	Computershare Trust Co of Canada	Outstanding Shares	46,070,000
Counsel	NA	E.P.S.	$1.11
DUNS No.	NA	Shareholders	NA

Business: The group's principal activities are developing, manufacturing and distributing pharmaceutical products in the field of gastroenterology. The major products of the group include amphojel, adeks, canasa, cortenema, endospray, flutter, lansoyl, modulon, mucaine, scandishake, salofalk, photofrin, viokase, ultrase and urso 250. The group also operates in United States, Europe and other foreign countries.

Primary SIC and add'l.: 2834 8731

CIK No: 0001116094

Subsidiaries: DELURSAN

Officers: Frank A.G.M. Verwiel/Dir., CEO, Pres., Francois Martin/Sr. Advisor, Scientific Affairs, Roddie Thurman/Customer Service Mgr. - United States, North America, Daniel Belanger/Dir. - Human Resources, Canada, Joel Morley/Dir. - Business Development, US, David W. Mims/COO, Exec. VP, Martha Donze/VP - Corporate Administration, Steve Gannon/Sr. VP, CFO, Jean-Francois Hebert/VP - Global Procurement, Manufacturing Operations, Michael E. Thiel/VP - North American Marketing Operations, Isabelle Adjahi/Sr. Dir. - Investor Relations, Communications, Axcan Pharma Inc, Alexandre P. Lebeaut/Chief Scientific Officer, Sr. VP, Jocelyn Pelchat/Sr. VP - International Commercial Operations, Richard Tarte/VP - Corporate Development, General Counsel, Jean Vezina/VP - Finance *(20 Officers included in Index)*

Directors: Frank A.G.M. Verwiel/Dir., CEO, Pres., Leon F. Gosselin/Chmn., Jacques Gauthier/Dir., Colin R. Mallet/Dir., Francois Painchaud/Dir., Rolland E. Dickson/Dir., Michael M. Tarnow/Dir., Claude Sauriol/Dir., Mary C. Ritchie/Dir., Louis P. Lacasse/Dir.

Financial Data: ***Fiscal Year End:***09/30 ***Latest Annual Data:*** 9/30/2006

Year	***Sales***	***Net Income***
2006	$292,317,000	$39,119,000
2005	$251,343,000	$26,425,000
2004	$243,634,000	$48,728,000

Curr. Assets:	$262,378,000	***Curr. Liab.:***	$64,617,000	***P/E Ratio:***	53.56
Plant, Equip.:	$28,817,000	***Total Liab.:***	$228,393,000	***Indic. Yr. Divd.:***	NA
Total Assets:	$695,817,000	***Net Worth:***	$467,424,000	***Debt/ Equity:***	NA

Axcelis Technologies Inc

108 Cherry Hill Dr., Beverly, MA, 01915; ***PH:*** 1-978-787-4000; ***Fax:*** 1-978-787-3000; ***http://*** www.axcelis.com

General - Incorporation	DE	***Stock***- Price on:12/24/2007	$6.36
Employees	1,632	Stock Exchange	NDQ
Auditor	Ernst & Young LLP	Ticker Symbol	ACLS
Stk Agt	EquiServe Trust Co.	Outstanding Shares	101,650,000
Counsel	Palmer & Dodge LLP	E.P.S.	$0.14
DUNS No.	NA	Shareholders	NA

Business: The group's principal activity is to produce ion implantation, dry strip, thermal processing and curing equipment used in the fabrication of semiconductor chips. The group also provides after aftermarket service and support, including spare parts, equipment upgrades, maintenance services and customer training. The group has joint venture with sumitomo heavy industries ltd in Japan that licenses ion implantation technology and manufactures and sells the products in Japan. Products of the group are sold in the United States, Taiwan, South Korea, China, Israel, Germany, Singapore, and Italy. These products are sold directly as well as through distributors and manufacturing representatives. Customers of the group include samsung, micron and IBM. On 07-Jul-2003, the group acquired matrix integrated systems inc.

Primary SIC and add'l.: 3559 3674

CIK No: 0001113232

Subsidiaries: Axcelis Technologies , Inc, Axcelis Technologies B.V., Axcelis Technologies Limited, Axcelis Technologies Ltd., Axcelis Technologies Pte. Ltd., Axcelis Technologies Semiconductor Trading Co., Ltd., Axcelis Technologies, GmbH, Axcelis Technologies, KK, Axcelis Technologies, Ltd., Axcelis Technologies, S.r.L, Axcelis Technologies, Sarl, Fusion Investments, Inc., Fusion Systems Corporation, Fusion Technology International, Inc., High Temperature Engineering Corporation 17 Subsidiaries included in the Index

Officers: Mary G. Puma/Chmn., CEO/$1,510,199.00, Craig M. Halterman/CIO, Sr. VP, Mark Namaroff/Sr. VP - Marketing, Stephen G. Bassett/CFO, Exec. VP/$587,771.00, Kevin Brewer/Sr. VP - Manufacturing Operations/$566,617.00, Lynnette C. Fallon/Exec. VP, General Counsel - Human Resources/$694,994.00, Matthew Flynn/Sr. VP - Global Customer Operations/$683,457.00, Bill Bintz/Sr. VP - Marketing

Directors: Mary G. Puma/Chmn., CEO, John Fletcher/Dir., Stephen R. Hardis/Dir., Michio Naruto/Dir., William C. Jennings/Dir., Brian H. Thompson/Dir., Patrick H. Nettles/Dir., Geoffrey Wild/Dir.

Owners: Dimensional Fund Advisors LP/8.10%, Lynnette C. Fallon, Brian H. Thompson, Matthew P. Flynn, William C. Jennings, Stephen G. Bassett, FMR Corp/15.00%, John R. Fletcher, Michio Naruto, Donald Smith & Co., Inc/9.90%, Insiders/2.90%, Patrick H. Nettles, Stephen R. Hardis, Barclays Global Investors, NA/5.30%, Mary G. Puma/1.50% *(16 Owners included in Index)*

Financial Data: ***Fiscal Year End:***12/31 ***Latest Annual Data:*** 12/31/2006

Year	***Sales***	***Net Income***
2006	$461,717,000	$40,770,000
2005	$372,540,000	-$3,855,000
2004	$507,976,000	$74,175,000

Curr. Assets:	$475,051,000	***Curr. Liab.:***	$190,141,000	***P/E Ratio:***	15.14
Plant, Equip.:	$66,678,000	***Total Liab.:***	$276,431,000	***Indic. Yr. Divd.:***	NA
Total Assets:	$753,993,000	***Net Worth:***	$477,562,000	***Debt/ Equity:***	0.1604

Axcess International Inc TX

3208 Commander Dr., Carrollton, TX, 75006; ***PH:*** 1-972-407-6080; ***Fax:*** 1-972-407-9085; ***http://*** www.axsi.com

General - Incorporation	DE	***Stock***- Price on:12/24/2007	$1.4
Employees	17	Stock Exchange	OTC
Auditor	Hein & Assoc. LLP	Ticker Symbol	AXSI
Stk Agt	American Stock Transfer & Trust Co.	Outstanding Shares	28,730,000
Counsel	NA	E.P.S.	-$0.26
DUNS No.	NA	Shareholders	NA

Business: The group's principal activity is to provide advanced security and asset management systems, which locate, identify, track, monitor and protect assets. The group's product line includes digital video and radio frequency identification. Digital video system is used for transmitting and viewing applications and digital video recording. Radio frequency identification technology is used to track and monitor people, assets, inventory and vehicles and also provides custom alerts in the form of streaming video, e-mail, or messages delivered to wireless devices.

Primary SIC and add'l.: 3829 3825

CIK No: 0000710597

Subsidiaries: Sandia Imaging Systems Corporation

Officers: Allan Griebenow/Dir., CEO, Pres., Robert F. Hussey/Dir. - Entrepreneur, Private Investor, Allan Frank/CFO, VP - Operations, Ben Donohue/VP - Business Development, Raj Bridgelall/CTO, VP - Engineering, Ray Cavanagh/VP - Worldwide Sales, Jordan Darrow/Contact - Investor Relations, Darrow Associates

Directors: Allan Griebenow/Dir., CEO, Pres., Richard C.E. Morgan/Chmn., Robert J. Bertoldi/Dir., Paul J. Coleman/Dir., Robert F. Hussey/Dir. - Entrepreneur, Private Investor

Owners: Richard C.E. Morgan, Amphion Group, Richard C.E. Morgan, Paul J. Coleman, Allan Griebenow, Robert J. Bertoldi, Robert J. Bertoldi, Richard C.E. Morgan, Richard C.E. Morgan, Insiders/12.20%, Paul J. Coleman, Robert J. Bertoldi, Amphion Group, Richard C.E. Morgan/12.20%, Insiders *(23 Owners included in Index)*

Financial Data: ***Fiscal Year End:***12/31 ***Latest Annual Data:*** 12/31/2006

Year	***Sales***	***Net Income***
2006	$1,501,000	-$3,359,000
2005	$1,080,000	-$3,256,000
2004	$912,000	-$3,417,000

Curr. Assets:	$1,088,000	***Curr. Liab.:***	$4,752,000		
Plant, Equip.:	$18,000	***Total Liab.:***	$4,752,000	***Indic. Yr. Divd.:***	NA
Total Assets:	$1,278,000	***Net Worth:***	-$3,474,000	***Debt/ Equity:***	NA

Axeda Systems Inc

25 Forbes Blvd., Ste. 3, Foxborough, MA, 02035; ***PH:*** 1-508-337-9200

General - Incorporation	DE	***Stock***- Price on:12/24/2007	NA
Employees	NA	Stock Exchange	NA
Auditor	KPMG LLP	Ticker Symbol	NA
Stk Agt	EquiServe Trust Co N.A	Outstanding Shares	NA
Counsel	NA	E.P.S.	NA
DUNS No.	NA	Shareholders	NA

Business: The group's principle activity is to provide an emerging category of business software known as device relationship management. The group's flagship product, the axeda device relationship management system, is a distributed software solution designed to enable businesses to remotely monitor, manage and service intelligent devices. This product allows the businesses to optimize their service, development, sales and manufacturing operations. The group's customers include global 2000 original equipment manufacturers in the medical instrument, enterprise technology, printer and copier and industrial and building automation industries. The group sells its products in the United States, Europe and Japan.

Primary SIC and add'l.: 7379 3429 7376

CIK No: 0001052593

Subsidiaries: Axeda Systems B.V., Axeda Systems GmbH:, Axeda Systems KK: a Japanese corporation, Axeda Systems Limited, Axeda Systems Ltd., Axeda Systems Operating Company, Inc., Axeda Systems S.A.S., eMation R&D, Inc, Ravisent British Columbia:, Ravisent Nova Scotia:, Viona Vervatungs GmbH:

Officers: Dale E. Calder/CEO, Pres., David Bennett/VP - Worldwide Sales, James R. Hansen/CTO, Brian Anderson/VP - Marketing, Richard MacKeen/Sr. VP - Research - Development, Services, Rachael T. McCarthy/CFO, David Canavan/VP - OEM Sales, Business Development

Axesstel Inc

6815 Flanders Dr., Ste. 210, San Diego, CA, 92121; ***PH:*** 1-858-625-2100; ***Fax:*** 1-858-625-2110; ***http://*** www.axesstel.com

General - Incorporation	NV	***Stock***- Price on:12/24/2007	$1.3899
Employees	87	Stock Exchange	AMEX
Auditor	Gumbiner Savett Inc	Ticker Symbol	AFT
Stk Agt	Transfer Online, Inc.	Outstanding Shares	22,870,000
Counsel	NA	E.P.S.	-$0.196
DUNS No.	NA	Shareholders	NA

Business: The group's principal activities are to develop, design and market telecommunication products. The products of the group include telecommunication carrier-grade subscriber terminals such as fixed wireless telephones, wireless hybrid products and enhanced wireless devices. The group operates

through san diego-based organization and a Korea-based development and design facility. The san diego office is responsible for activities such as marketing communications, product planning, management and customer support. The Korea facility designs and produces advanced cdma wireless products. The group's products are classified into three categories namely wireless local loop terminal products, hybrid and enhanced wireless products and strategic original design and manufacturing product development. The group also develops and distributes mp3 player, multi-line phone amplifier, FM hands-free kit for the cellular phone and 900 mhz digital spread spectrum pbx phone receiver.

Primary SIC and add'l.: 3669 3661 3663

CIK No: 0001092492

Subsidiaries: Axess Telecom Co., Ltd., Axesstel R&D Center Co., Ltd.

Officers: Marvin Tseu/Dir., CEO/$531,401.00, Clark Hickock/COO/$321,162.00, Patrick Gray/CFO/$238,752.00, David Kim/VP - Product Marketing, Management, Stephen Sek/CTO/$54,107.00, Murray Kawchuk/Sr. VP - Sales, Corporate Marketing/$174,356.00

Directors: Marvin Tseu/Dir., CEO, Mike Kwon/43/Founder, Honorary Chmn., Jai Bhagat/Vice Chmn., Bryan B. Min/Chmn., Osmo A. Hautanen/Dir., Ake Persson/62/Dir., Seung Taik Yang/Dir.

Owners: Osmo A. Hautanen, Insiders/17.30%, Patrick Gray, Bryan B. Min, Lixin Cheng, Seung Taik Yang, Marvin Tseu/1.10%, Entities affiliated with ComVentures/16.70%, ke Persson, Potomac Capital Management LLC/7.40%, Mike H. Kwon/13.70%, Robeco USA LLC/7.50%, Stephens Investment Management/9.80%, Jai Bhagat, Clark H. Hickock/1.30%

Financial Data: *Fiscal Year End:* 12/31 *Latest Annual Data:* 12/31/2006

Year	Sales	Net Income
2006	$95,520,000	-$6,636,000
2005	$94,666,000	-$10,201,000
2004	$62,565,000	-$8,270,000

Curr. Assets:	$46,387,000	**Curr. Liab.:**	$40,154,000		
Plant, Equip.:	$1,905,000	**Total Liab.:**	$43,223,000	**Indic. Yr. Divd.:**	NA
Total Assets:	$52,721,000	**Net Worth:**	$9,498,000	**Debt/ Equity:**	NA

Axia Group Inc

1324 N Magnolia Ave., El Cajon, CA, 92020; ***PH:*** 1-619-444-1919; ***http://*** www.axiagroup.info

General - Incorporation	NV	**Stock** - Price on:12/24/2007	NA
Employees	NA	Stock Exchange	OTC
Auditor	HJ Assoc. & Consultants LLP	Ticker Symbol	AXGO
Stk Agt	Signature Stock Transfer, Inc.	Outstanding Shares	NA
Counsel	NA	E.P.S	NA
DUNS No.	14-431-9621	Shareholders	NA

Business: The group's principle activity is to consider business opportunities either through merger or acquisition that might create value for shareholders. The group is in the development stage and currently has no operations. Its earlier operations were carried out through two segments: real estate holdings and financial consulting services. On 27-Jul-2004, the group acquired d&r crane inc. The group operates from United States.

Primary SIC and add'l.: 9999

CIK No: 0000788738

Subsidiaries: D & R. Crane, Inc.

Financial Data: *Fiscal Year End:* 09/30 *Latest Annual Data:* 09/30/2004

Year	Sales	Net Income
2004	$866,000	-$599,000
2003	NA	-$815,000
2002	NA	-$4,265,000

Curr. Assets:	NA	**Curr. Liab.:**	$376,000		
Plant, Equip.:	$1,000	**Total Liab.:**	$376,000	**Indic. Yr. Divd.:**	NA
Total Assets:	$1,000	**Net Worth:**	-$380,000	**Debt/ Equity:**	NA

Axial Vector Engine Corp

One World Trade Ctr., 121 SW Salmon St., Ste. 1100, Portland, OR, 97204; ***PH:*** 1-503-471-1348; ***http://*** www.axialvectorengine.com; ***Email:*** info@axialvectorengine.com

General - Incorporation	NV	**Stock** - Price on:12/24/2007	$0.17
Employees	4	Stock Exchange	OTC
Auditor	Bagell, Levine & Company, LLC	Ticker Symbol	AXVC
Stk Agt	Int Registrar and Transfer Agency	Outstanding Shares	36,780,000
Counsel	NA	E.P.S	NA
DUNS No.	NA	Shareholders	NA

Business: The groups principal activities include developing, licensing revolutionary internal combustion engine and electric power generator technologies for use in automotive, power generation, appliance, and military application. The group product is stereo lithographic. The group operates from the United States.

Primary SIC and add'l.: 3724 3714

CIK No: 0001144130

Officers: Ahmed Khalifa/CEO, Oyvin Haugan/Engineering Mgr.

Directors: Benjamin Langford/58/Dir.

Owners: Insiders/60.10%, Samuel J. Higgins/54.80%, Raymond Brouzes/6.90%

AXIS Capital Holdings Ltd

AXIS House, 92 Pitts Bay Rd., Pembroke, HM; ***PH:*** 441-496-2600; ***http://*** www.axis.bm; ***Email:*** neera.dunleavy@axiscapital.com

General - Incorporation	Bermuda	**Stock** - Price on:12/24/2007	$39.98
Employees	570	Stock Exchange	NYSE
Auditor	Deloitte & Touche LLP	Ticker Symbol	AXS
Stk Agt	Bank of New York	Outstanding Shares	153,750,000
Counsel	Leboeuf, Lamb, Greene Et Al	E.P.S	$5.81
DUNS No.	NA	Shareholders	NA

Business: The group's principle activity is to provide specialty insurance and treaty reinsurance services. Its specialty coverage includes terrorism, aviation and marine war, and political risk; commercial property; aviation; marine; and onshore and offshore energy. AXIS Capital's reinsurance products include marine and aviation; professional liability; workers' compensation, personal accident, and life;and property. The group operates from United States.

Primary SIC and add'l.: NA

CIK No: 0001214816

Subsidiaries: AXIS Insurance Company, AXIS Re Limited, AXIS Reinsurance Company, AXIS Specialty Holdings Ireland Limited, AXIS Specialty Insurance Company, AXIS Specialty Ireland Limited, AXIS Specialty Limited, AXIS Specialty U.S. Holdings,Inc., AXIS Specialty U.S. Services,Inc., AXIS Specialty UK Holdings Limited, AXIS Surplus Insurance Company, Combined Specialty Group,Inc.

Officers: John R. Charman/Dir., CEO, Pres./$10,875,050.00, John Gressier/Chmn. - Axis Insurance/$4,276,868.00, Richard H. Blum/Chmn. - Axis Specialty US Holdings, Inc, Raymond Karrenbauer/Exec. VP - Axis Capital - Cism, Csap CIO, Brian W. Goshen/Chief Human Resources Officer, Richard Richard Strachan/Chief Claims Officer, Richard T. Gieryn/Corp. Sec., General Counsel, Anders C. Anderson/Chief Audit Exec., Karl Mayr/Pres., William A. Fischer/Exec. VP/$4,223,340.00, Michael E. Morrill/Exec. VP, Dennis B. Reding/COO, Marshall F. Turner/Pres. - Axis Insurance, Glenn E. Gardner/Sr. VP, Chief Technology Offi cer, Lorraine S. Mariano/Sr. VP, Chief Human Resources *(22 Officers included in Index)*

Directors: John R. Charman/Dir., CEO, Pres., Michael A. Butt/Chmn., Andrew Large/Dir., Geoffrey Bell/Dir., Christopher V. Greetham/Dir., Jurgen Grupe/Dir., Maurice A. Keane/Dir., Henry B. Smith/Dir., Frank J. Tasco/Dir., Charles A. Davis/Dir., Robert L. Friedman/Dir., Donald J. Greene/Dir.

Owners: Christopher V. Greetham, Neuberger Berman Inc/5.70%, Andrew Cook, FMR Corp./9.50%, David B. Greenfield, Donald J. Greene, Insiders/6.90%, Robert L. Friedman, Barclays Global Investors, NA/7.80%, Trident II, L.P./14.70%, Geoffrey Bell, John Gressier, Henry B. Smith, AXA Financial Inc and related entities/9.20%, William A. Fischer *(19 Owners included in Index)*

Financial Data: *Fiscal Year End:* 12/31 *Latest Annual Data:* 12/31/2006

Year	Sales	Net Income
2006	$3,078,561,000	$963,060,000
2005	$2,788,398,000	$94,440,000
2004	$2,205,356,000	$494,998,000

Curr. Assets:	$4,793,051,000	**Curr. Liab.:**	$1,550,918,000	**P/E Ratio:**	6.88
Plant, Equip.:	NA	**Total Liab.:**	$9,252,640,000	**Indic. Yr. Divd.:**	$0.660
Total Assets:	$13,665,287,000	**Net Worth:**	$4,412,647,000	**Debt/ Equity:**	0.1075

AXM Pharma Inc

7251 W Lake Mead Blvd., Ste. 300, Las Vegas, NV, 89128; ***PH:*** 1-702-562-4155; ***Fax:*** 1-702-562-4157; ***http://*** www.axmpharma.com

General - Incorporation	NV	**Stock** - Price on:12/24/2007	$0.18
Employees	150	Stock Exchange	OTC
Auditor	Lopez, Blevins, Bork & Assoc. LLP	Ticker Symbol	AXMP
Stk Agt	Signature Stock Transfer	Outstanding Shares	22,410,000
Counsel	NA	E.P.S	-$0.6
DUNS No.	NA	Shareholders	NA

Business: The group's principal activity is to sell over-the-counter and prescription pharmaceutical products in the People's Republic of China. The products are currently produced by third-party manufacturers and sold through third-party distributors. On 14-Mar-2003, the group acquired werke pharmaceuticals inc.

Primary SIC and add'l.: 5399

CIK No: 0001113643

Subsidiaries: AXM Pharma (Shenyang) Inc.

Officers: Wang Wei Shi/Chmn., CEOr

Directors: Wang Wei Shi/Chmn., CEOr, Chaoying Li/Dir., Baozhong Zhang/Dir., Elliot M. Maza/Dir., Tracey Oneill/Dir.

Financial Data: *Fiscal Year End:* 12/31 *Latest Annual Data:* 12/31/2005

Year	Sales	Net Income
2005	$2,022,000	-$11,088,000
2004	$2,116,000	-$13,990,000
2003	$10,026,000	-$3,708,000

Curr. Assets:	$4,060,000	**Curr. Liab.:**	$9,640,000		
Plant, Equip.:	$7,558,000	**Total Liab.:**	$9,640,000	**Indic. Yr. Divd.:**	NA
Total Assets:	$13,729,000	**Net Worth:**	$4,089,000	**Debt/ Equity:**	NA

Axonyx Inc

11085 N Torrey Pines Rd., Ste. 300, La Jolla, CA, 92037; ***PH:*** 1-858-623-5665; ***http://*** www.axonyx.com

General - Incorporation	NV	**Stock** - Price on:12/24/2007	$7.15
Employees	43	Stock Exchange	NA
Auditor	Ernst & Young, LLP	Ticker Symbol	NA
Stk Agt	Nevada Agency & Trust Company	Outstanding Shares	15,700,000
Counsel	Brobeck, Phleger & Harrison	E.P.S	-$1.71
DUNS No.	NA	Shareholders	NA

Business: The group's principal activities are to discover, develop and acquire pharmaceutical compounds for the treatment of memory and cognitive disorders. The group identifies and acquires novel post-discovery central nervous system drug candidates. It acquires the patent rights to these candidates and advances the compounds through clinical development towards regulatory approval. The group has acquired worldwide exclusive patent rights to three main classes of therapeutic compounds designed for the treatment of alzheimer's disease, mild cognitive impairment and related diseases. These patent rights were licensed from the New York university via a sublicense from the national institutes of health and the national institute of aging. Phenserine is its main product, which is used for treating alzheimer's disease. On 15-Jan-2004, the group acquired oxis international inc.

Primary SIC and add'l.: 8731 2836

CIK No: 0001070698

Subsidiaries: Axonyx Europe BV

Owners: Insiders/46.50%, Entities affiliated with GIMV NV/16.30%, Patrick Van Beneden/16.30%, Jason S. Fisherman/9.80%, Evelyn A. Graham, Craig A. Johnson, Michael F. Murphy, Gosse B. Bruinsma, Paul M. Feuerman, S. Colin Neill, Louis G. Cornacchia, Peter Davis, Steven B. Ratoff, Jean Deleage/16.40%, Steven H. Ferris *(21 Owners included in Index)*

Financial Data: *Fiscal Year End:* 12/31 *Latest Annual Data:* 12/31/2006

Year	Sales	Net Income
2006	$9,850,000	-$25,377,000
2005	$403,000	-$28,614,000
2004	$2,275,000	-$28,780,000

Curr. Assets:	$55,964,000	**Curr. Liab.:**	$12,270,000		
Plant, Equip.:	$796,000	**Total Liab.:**	$18,866,000	**Indic. Yr. Divd.:**	NA
Total Assets:	$63,435,000	**Net Worth:**	$44,569,000	**Debt/ Equity:**	0.0861

AXS-One Inc

301 Rte. 17 N, Rutherford, NJ, 07070; ***PH:*** 1-201-935-3400; ***Fax:*** 1-201-935-7678; ***http://*** www.axsone.com; ***Email:*** info@axsone.com

General - Incorporation .... DE
Employees 135
Auditor .... Amper, Politziner & Mattia P.c
Stk Agt .... Computershare Investor Services LLC
Counsel .... NA
DUNS No. 07-773-4499

Stock- Price on:12/24/2007 .... $0.72
Stock Exchange .... OTC
Ticker Symbol .... NA
Outstanding Shares 36,010,000
E.P.S. $0.04
Shareholders .... NA

Business: The group's principle activity is to provide business solutions that allow an organization to achieve efficiency in its business processes. The group is organized into three business segments: axs-one enterprise solutions, axspoint solutions and tivity solutions. Axs-one provides enterprise resource planning solutions to global 2000 companies. Axspoint is developing core technology for solutions that enable organizations to share knowledge, both within the enterprise and with their customers and other business partners. Tivity provides solutions to professional services organizations that decrease the time and effort involved in the billing and revenue recognition processes, while increasing the utilization of knowledge workers. The registered trademarks of the group include axs one(R), axspoint(R), transaxs(R) and computron(R). The group's quarterly revenue for September 2007 was 2.49 millions of USD.

Primary SIC and add'l.: 7379 7371 7373

CIK No: 0000947427

Subsidiaries: AXS-One Limited, AXS-One Proprietary Limited, AXS-One Pte Ltd, AXS-One Pty Ltd., Computron Holdings, Inc., Hospitality Warehouse Proprietary Ltd

Officers: William P. Lyons/Chmn., CEO/$965,743.00, Al Clegg/MD - EMEA, Europe, Middle East, Africa, Joseph P. Dwyer/CFO, Exec. VP/$465,622.00, David Thompson/VP - Asia Pacific, Matt Hayden/Contact, Phil Kufal/Mgr. - Product, Axspoint, South Africa, Dorethea Horak/Dir. - Finance, South Africa, Malcolm Hobden/Mgr. - Product, Workflow, Technical, South Africa, Diederik Jordaan/GM - Professional Services, Antonet Coetzer/Financial Mgr. - South Africa, Michael Fortune/Exec. - New Business Development, Phil Rugani/Exec. VP - Field Operations, Marie-Charlotte Patterson/VP - Corporate Marketing, Product Management

Directors: William P. Lyons/Chmn., CEO, Daniel H. Burch/Dir., Elias Typaldos/Dir., Anthony H. Bloom/Dir., Allan Weingarten/Dir., Harold D. Copperman/Dir., Robert J. Migliorino/Dir., Timothy P. Bacci/Dir., Monica Hutton/Member - Advisory Board

Owners: Daniel H. Burch, Anthony H. Bloom, RIT Capital Partners plc/6.40%, Joseph Dwyer/1.60%, William P. Lyons/5.40%, Harold D. Copperman/1.50%, Gennaro Vendome/4.30%, Timothy P. Bacci/13.60%, Robert Milks, Elias Typaldos/2.50%, Allan Weingarten, BlueLine Partners, LLC/13.60%, Philip L. Rugani/5.40%, Jurika Family Trust/13.40%, Robert Migliorino *(16 Owners included in Index)*

Financial Data: **Fiscal Year End:**12/31 **Latest Annual Data:** 12/31/2006

Year	Sales	Net Income
2006	$10,296,000	$5,501,000
2005	$32,808,000	-$8,998,000
2004	$38,436,000	-$5,212,000

Curr. Assets:	$11,012,000	**Curr. Liab.:**	$8,078,000		
Plant, Equip.:	$419,000	**Total Liab.:**	$8,122,000	**Indic. Yr. Divd.:**	NA
Total Assets:	$11,533,000	**Net Worth:**	$3,411,000	**Debt/ Equity:**	NA

Axsys Technologies Inc

175 Capital Blvd., Ste. 103, Rocky Hill, CT, 06067; ***PH:*** 1-860-257-0200; ***Fax:*** 1-860-594-5750; ***http://*** www.axsys.com; ***Email:*** inquire@axsys.com

General - Incorporation .... DE
Employees 765
Auditor .... Ernst & Young LLP
Stk Agt .... Mellon Investor Services LLC
Counsel .... NA
DUNS No. 04-318-9620

Stock- Price on:12/24/2007 .... $20.54
Stock Exchange .... NDQ
Ticker Symbol .... AXYS
Outstanding Shares 10,670,000
E.P.S. $1.11
Shareholders .... NA

Business: The group's principal activities are carried out by three segments: aerospace and defense, commercial products and distributed products. Aerospace and defense segment designs, manufactures and sells high-end components such as precision position sensors, high-performance motors, precision metal optics, precision machined light-weight structures and opto-mechanical and electro-mechanical subassemblies. The commercial product segment designs, manufactures and sells airbearing scanners, micro-positioning stages and laser-based distance measuring interferometers and autofocus. The distributed product division distributes precision ball bearings which are used in a variety of industrial automation and commercial markets acquired from various domestic and international sources, to original equipments manufacturers and maintenance repair operations distributors. On 8-Apr-2004, the group acquired telic optics, inc.

Primary SIC and add'l.: 3562 3812 3679 5085 3678 3621

CIK No: 0000206030

Subsidiaries: Diversified Optical Products, Inc., Precision Aerotech,Inc., Speedring Systems,Inc., Speedring,Inc., Telic Optics,Inc.

Officers: Stephen W. Bershad/Chmn., CEO/$828,551.00, Peter Kornik/Customer Contact - OEM Optics, Worldwide, Cynthia J. McNickle/Sec., Jake Soujah/Customer Contact - Axsys Technologies, Eurasia Fzco, Scott B. Conner/VP - Strategic Planning, Corporate Development/$507,991.00, David A. Almeida/VP - Finance, Administration, CFO/$573,229.00, Geoffrey Ling/Dir. - Investor Relations, Gary Browning/Customer Contact - Investor Relations Officer Cameras - Worldwide, Alex Giuffrida/Customer Contact - Stabilized Camera Systems, Andy Healey/Customer Contact - Axsys Technologies, EMEA, Stabilized Camera Systems, John Brower/Customer Contact - Eastern North America, Europe, Imaging Systems, George Murray/Customer Contact - Western North America, Asia, Dennis Reilly/Customer Contact - Precision Positioners, Pan, Tilt Mechanisms, Motion Control Products, Al Mejia/Customer Contact - Western United States, Motion Control Products, Mark Emmet/Customer Contact - Central United States, Motion Control Products *(17 Officers included in Index)*

Directors: Stephen W. Bershad/Chmn., CEO, Eliot M. Fried/Dir., Robert G. Stevens/Dir., Anthony J. Fiorelli/Dir., Richard F. Hamm/Dir.

Owners: Insiders/20.20%, David A. Almeida/1.40%, Albert Fried & Company, LLC/6.60%, Wellington Management Co, LLP/11.30%, Richard F. Hamm, Eliot M. Fried, AWM Investment Co., Inc/5.10%, Anthony J. Fiorelli, Robert G. Stevens, Luther King Capital Management Corporation/6.50%, Scott B. Conner, Stephen W. Bershad/17.70%, Dimensional Fund Advisor, LP/6.50%

Financial Data: **Fiscal Year End:**12/31 **Latest Annual Data:** 12/31/2006

Year	Sales	Net Income
2006	$156,347,000	$10,265,000
2005	$133,543,000	$7,323,000
2004	$103,530,000	$8,664,000

Curr. Assets:	$76,631,000	**Curr. Liab.:**	$35,331,000	**P/E Ratio:**	18.50
Plant, Equip.:	$22,860,000	**Total Liab.:**	$41,157,000	**Indic. Yr. Divd.:**	NA
Total Assets:	$172,345,000	**Net Worth:**	$131,188,000	**Debt/ Equity:**	NA

AXT Inc

4281 Technology Dr., Fremont, CA, 94538; ***PH:*** 1-510-683-5900; ***Fax:*** 1-510-353-0668; ***http://*** www.axt.com; ***Email:*** sales@axt.com

General - Incorporation .... DE
Employees 1,022
Auditor .... Burr, Pilger & Mayer LLP
Stk Agt .... American Stock Transfer & Trust CO.
Counsel .... Gary Cary Ware & Frederick
DUNS No. 19-674-1979

Stock- Price on:12/24/2007 .... $4.1
Stock Exchange .... NDQ
Ticker Symbol .... AXTI
Outstanding Shares 29,890,000
E.P.S. $0.22
Shareholders .... NA

Business: The group's principal activities are to design, develop, manufacture and distribute compound semiconductor substrates. These semiconductor substrates comprises of gallium arsenide (gaas), indium phosphide (inp) and germanium (ge). The group's substrate products are used primarily in fiber optic communications, wireless communications and lighting display applications. The major customers for substrates include united epitaxy company, motorola, agilent technologies, samsung, emcore, kopin, iqe and sumika. On 27-Sep-2003, the group discontinued its opto-electronics business.

Primary SIC and add'l.: 3674

CIK No: 0001051627

Subsidiaries: AXT-Japan

Officers: Philip C.S. Yin/Dir., CEO/$446,857.00, Wilson W. Cheung/CFO, Corp. Sec./$313,444.00, Minsheng Lin/COO/$355,824.00, Davis Zhang/Pres. - Joint Venture Operation/$394,994.00, John J. Cerilli/VP - Global Sale, Marketing/$275,471.00, Hani Badawi/VP - Application Engineering, Robert G. Ochrym/VP - Business Development, Raymond A. Low/VP, Corporate Controller

Directors: Philip C.S. Yin/Dir., CEO, Jesse Chen/Chmn., Morris S. Young/Dir., David C. Chang/Dir., Leonard J. Leblanc/Dir.

Owners: Leonard LeBlanc, David C. Chang, Jesse Chen, Davis Zhang/1.83%, State of Wisconsin Investment Board/10.27%, Philip C.S. Yin, Morris S. Young/5.34%, John J. Cerilli, Dimensional Fund Advisors LP/6.21%, Minsheng Lin, Insiders/8.94%, Wilson W. Cheung

Financial Data: **Fiscal Year End:**12/31 **Latest Annual Data:** 12/31/2006

Year	Sales	Net Income
2006	$44,445,000	$944,000
2005	$26,536,000	-$12,215,000
2004	$35,454,000	-$13,633,000

Curr. Assets:	$74,109,000	**Curr. Liab.:**	$7,750,000	**P/E Ratio:**	18.64
Plant, Equip.:	$12,775,000	**Total Liab.:**	$17,132,000	**Indic. Yr. Divd.:**	NA
Total Assets:	$98,332,000	**Net Worth:**	$81,200,000	**Debt/ Equity:**	0.0763

AZCO Mining Inc

7239 N El Mirage Rd., Glendale, AZ, 85307; ***PH:*** 1-623-935-0774; ***http://*** www.azco.com

General - Incorporation .... DE
Employees 1
Auditor .... Stark Winter Schenkein & Co. LLP
Stk Agt .... Colonial Stock Transfer Co Inc
Counsel .... NA
DUNS No. 19-498-6915

Stock- Price on:12/24/2007 .... NA
Stock Exchange .... NA
Ticker Symbol .... NA
Outstanding Shares .... NA
E.P.S. .... -$0.04
Shareholders .... NA

Business: The group's principal activity is to acquire and develop mineral properties with current focus on producing muscovite mica. The black canyon mica project includes a mineral property of mica ore and a pilot processing plant located near phoenix, Arizona. The piedras verdes project is located in southern sonora, Mexico. The group has established a strategic partnership with phelps dodge corporation on the piedras verdes copper project. The group also has mineral interests located in foreign countries including Mexico, Indonesia and mali.

Primary SIC and add'l.: 1021 1499

CIK No: 0000851726

Subsidiaries: AZCO Mica, Inc., Cobre de Suaqui Verde, S.A. de C.V., Sanou Mining Corporation

Officers: Pierce W. Carson/Dir., CEO, Pres., Ryan P. Carson/Mgr. - Legal Affairs, Stephen J. Antol/Acting CFO

Directors: Pierce W. Carson/Dir., CEO, Pres., Lawrence G. Olson/Chmn., John E. Frost/Dir.

Owners: Pierce W. Carson/15.40%, John E. Frost/0.01%, Lawrence G. Olson/9.60%, Christian Mustad/6.90%, Insiders/23.90%

Financial Data: **Fiscal Year End:**06/30 **Latest Annual Data:** 06/30/2006

Year	Sales	Net Income
2006	$16,000	-$5,383,000
2005	$55,000	-$1,596,000
2004	$168,000	-$7,810,000

Curr. Assets:	$1,607,000	**Curr. Liab.:**	$7,146,000		
Plant, Equip.:	$3,442,000	**Total Liab.:**	$10,752,000	**Indic. Yr. Divd.:**	NA
Total Assets:	$5,228,000	**Net Worth:**	-$5,524,000	**Debt/ Equity:**	NA

Aztar Corp

2390 E Camelback Rd. Ste. 400, Phoenix, AZ, 85016; *PH:* 1-602-381-4100; *http://* www.aztar.com

General - Incorporation	DE	Stock- Price on:12/24/2007	NA
Employees	NA	Stock Exchange	NA
Auditor	PricewaterhouseCoopers LLP	Ticker Symbol	NA
Stk Agt	Mellon Investor Services LLC	Outstanding Shares	NA
Counsel	NA	E.P.S.	NA
DUNS No.	60-693-7886	Shareholders	NA

Business: The group's principal activities are to develop and operate casino hotels and riverboat casinos. Its principal casinos are tropicana Atlantic city in New Jersey, tropicana las vegas in las vegas and ramada express in laughlin, Nevada. Its riverboat casinos are casino aztar evansville in Indiana and casino aztar caruthersville in Missouri. The casinos offer table games, slot machines, food and beverages, theatre showrooms, indoor and outdoor swimming pools, health and fitness clubs, jogging tracks, gymnasiums and other recreational facilities.

Primary SIC and add'l.: 7999 7993 7011 5812

CIK No: 0000852807

Subsidiaries: Adamar Garage Corporation, Adamar of Nevada, Adamar of New Jersey, Inc., Atlantic-Deauville, Inc., Aztar Development Corporation, Aztar Indiana Gaming Company, LLC, Aztar Missouri Riverboat Gaming Company, LLC, Hotel Ramada of Nevada, Ramada Express, Inc., Ramada New Jersey Holdings Corporation, Ramada New Jersey, Inc., Tropicana Enterprises, a general partnership

Owners: Insiders/5.20%, John B. Bohle, Linda C. Faiss, Robert M. Haddock/3.40%, Gordon M. Burns, Frank J. Brady, Joe C. Cole, Nelson W. Armstrong, Meridith P. Sipek, Barclays Global Investors, NA/5.20%, John A. Spencer, Citadel Limited Partnership/5.60%, Neil A. Ciarfalia, Private Capital Management, L.P./10.10%

Aztec Oil & Gas Inc

1207 Quarrier St., Charleston, WV, 25301; *PH:* 1-304-343-7142; *http://* www.aztecoil-gas.com

General - Incorporation	NV	Stock- Price on:12/24/2007	NA
Employees	5	Stock Exchange	OTC
Auditor	Malone & Bailey, PC	Ticker Symbol	AZGS
Stk Agt	Cottonwood Stock Transfer	Outstanding Shares	29,760,000
Counsel	NA	E.P.S.	NA
DUNS No.	NA	Shareholders	NA

Business: The groups principal activity is to explore minerals and natural gas. The group operates from the United States.

Primary SIC and add'l.: 1382

CIK No: 0000789606

Subsidiaries: Golden Circle Broadcasting Inc., Lloyd Communications, Inc.

Officers: Franklin C. Fisher/68/Chmn., CEO, Pres., Tony Drake/Investor Relations Officer

Directors: Franklin C. Fisher/68/Chmn., CEO, Pres.

Owners: Mark Vance, Insiders/38.56%, Ken Lehrer/1.38%, Larry Hornbrook, Kathryn E. Parks, Franklin C. Fisher/33.77%

Curr. Assets:	$27,000	Curr. Liab.:	$273,000		
Plant, Equip.:	$305,000	Total Liab.:	$273,000	Indic. Yr. Divd.:	NA
Total Assets:	$335,000	Net Worth:	$62,000	Debt/ Equity:	NA

Azur Holdings Inc

633 S.E. 3rd Ave., Ste. 203, Ft. Lauderdale, FL, 33301; *PH:* 1-954-763-1515; *Fax:* 1-954-763-1516; *http://* www.azurholdings.com; *Email:* info@azurholdings.com

General - Incorporation	DE	Stock- Price on:12/24/2007	NA
Employees	NA	Stock Exchange	OTC
Auditor	Baum & Company, P.A	Ticker Symbol	AZHIE
Stk Agt	Olde Monmouth Stk Trnsfer Co. Inc.	Outstanding Shares	NA
Counsel	NA	E.P.S.	NA
DUNS No.	NA	Shareholders	NA

Business: The groups principle activity is real estate business. The group operates from the United States.

Primary SIC and add'l.: 6770

CIK No: 0000785544

Subsidiaries: Azur Shell Landing Resort, Inc., The Grand Shell Landing, Inc.

Officers: Donald H. Goree/Chmn., CEO, Don C. Winfrey/Dir., Pres., Albert J. Lazo/General Counsel, Corp. Sec., Jeffrey A. Grene/COO - US, Carl Crawford/Pres., Ulrich Ansin/Dir. - Creative, Albert A. Lazo/In House Counsel

Directors: Donald H. Goree/Chmn., CEO, Don C. Winfrey/Dir., Pres., Tony Sharp/Dir., Frederick Trowman-Rose/Dir.

AZZ Inc

1300 S University Dr. University Ctr. 1200, Fort Worth, TX, 76107; *PH:* 1-817-810-0095; *Fax:* 1-817-336-5354; *http://* www.azzincorporated.com; *Email:* info@azz.com

General - Incorporation	TX	Stock- Price on:12/24/2007	$29.88
Employees	1,301	Stock Exchange	NYSE
Auditor	BDO Seidman, LLP	Ticker Symbol	AZZ
Stk Agt	Computershare Investor Services LLC	Outstanding Shares	11,650,000
Counsel	Shannon, Gracey, Ratliff & Miller	E.P.S.	$1.825
DUNS No.	00-801-2148	Shareholders	NA

Business: The group's principal activities are to manufacture electrical equipment and components and to provide galvanizing services. The group operates through two segments: electrical and industrial products and galvanizing services. Electrical and industrial products segment manufactures highly engineered specialty electrical product as well as lighting and tubular products. The specialty components are used in power generation, transmission and distribution. Lighting and tubular products are used in petrochemical and industrial applications. Galvanizing services segment provides hot dip galvanizing services to the steel fabrication industry. This segment serves fabricators and manufacturers involved in the highway construction, electrical utility, transportation, water treatment, agriculture, petrochemical and chemical, pulp and paper industries and numerous original equipment manufacturers. The group primarily operates in the United States.

Primary SIC and add'l.: 3479 3648 3559

CIK No: 0000008947

Officers: David H. Dingus/60/Dir., CEO, Pres./$820,776.00, John V. Petro/62/VP - Electrical, Industrial Products Segment/$412,622.00, Clement H. Watson/VP - Sales, Electrical Products Group/$307,465.00, Fred L. Wright/67/Sr. VP - Galvanizing Services Segment/$415,158.00, Dana L. Perry/59/Dir., Sr. VP - Finance, CFO, Sec./$437,012.00, Tim E. Pendley/46/VP - Operations - Galvanizing Services Segment, Richard W. Butler/42/VP, Corporate Controller, Robert D. Ruffin/67/VP - Human Resources

Directors: David H. Dingus/60/Dir., CEO, Pres., Sam Rosen/72/Dir., Dana L. Perry/59/Dir., Sr. VP - Finance, CFO, Sec., Daniel E. Berce/54/Dir., Kirk H. Downey/65/Dir., Robert H. Johnson/83/Dir., Kevern R. Joyce/61/Dir., R. J. Schumacher/79/Dir., Martin C. Bowen/64/Dir., Daniel R. Feehan/57/Dir., Peter A. Hegedus/Dir.

Owners: R. J. Schumacher, FMR Corp./9.20%, Kevern R. Joyce, Insiders/7.20%, Dana L. Perry/2.50%, Dimensional Fund Advisors LP/8.00%, Bear Stearns Asset Management Inc./11.10%, Daniel E. Berce, Daniel R. Feehan, Martin C. Bowen, David H. Dingus/2.40%, Fred L. Wright, Sam Rosen, Robert H. Johnson, Kirk H. Downey *(16 Owners included in Index)*

Financial Data: Fiscal Year End:02/28 Latest Annual Data: 2/28/2007

Year	Sales	Net Income
2007	$260,344,000	$21,604,000
2006	$187,184,000	$7,827,000
2005	$152,428,000	$4,812,000

Curr. Assets:	$111,967,000	Curr. Liab.:	$49,715,000		
Plant, Equip.:	$46,628,000	Total Liab.:	$89,759,000	Indic. Yr. Divd.:	NA
Total Assets:	$200,908,000	Net Worth:	$111,148,000	Debt/ Equity:	0.3166

B Fast Corp

660 Newtown Yardley Rd. , Newtown, PA, 18940; *PH:* 1-215-860-5600; *http://* www.bfast.com

General - Incorporation	LA	Stock- Price on:12/24/2007	$0.07
Employees	5	Stock Exchange	OTC
Auditor	WithumSmith & Brown, P.C	Ticker Symbol	BFTC
Stk Agt	Mellon Investor Services LLC	Outstanding Shares	8,000,000
Counsel	NA	E.P.S.	$0.04
DUNS No.	00-820-2608	Shareholders	NA

Business: The group's principal activity is to provide ground support services to corporate and other general aviation aircraft at the harrisburg international airport located in middletown, Pennsylvania. The group provides on demand line services for the general aviation fleet that includes the fueling, ground handling and storage of aircraft along with the subleasing of hangar and office space to tenants. Along with these services, it also provides amenities for the passengers and crews of the aircraft, such as passenger and pilot lounges, flight planning assistance and weather information facilities, conference facilities, arranging of travel and hotel accommodations, aircraft catering and ground transportation. It also provides, on a contractual basis, ground support services for commercial airlines, which primarily include fueling and de-icing.

Primary SIC and add'l.: 4581

CIK No: 0000350200

Owners: Insiders, Alinco S.A./4.10%, Transtech Holding Company, Inc./50.89%, Cesamar, S.A./4.10%, Transtech Holding Company, Inc./71.80%, John F. Bricker Estate/5.00%, Project Bond Limited/4.10%

Financial Data: Fiscal Year End:09/30 Latest Annual Data: 9/30/2006

Year	Sales	Net Income
2006	NA	$483,000
2005	$4,526,000	-$1,119,000
2004	$4,119,000	-$955,000

Curr. Assets:	$2,464,000	Curr. Liab.:	$29,359,000	P/E Ratio:	1.75
Plant, Equip.:	$2,000	Total Liab.:	$29,747,000	Indic. Yr. Divd.:	NA
Total Assets:	$8,607,000	Net Worth:	-$21,140,000	Debt/ Equity:	NA

B&D Food Corp

575 Madison Ave., Ste. 1006, New York, NY, 10022; *PH:* 1-212-937-8456; *Fax:* 1-212-412-9034; *http://* www.bdfcorp.com; *Email:* info@bdfcorp.com

General - Incorporation	DE	Stock- Price on:12/24/2007	$0.04
Employees	20	Stock Exchange	OTC
Auditor	Schwartz Levitsky Feldman LLP	Ticker Symbol	BDFC
Stk Agt	OTC Stock Transfer, Inc.	Outstanding Shares	108,400,000
Counsel	NA	E.P.S.	NA
DUNS No.	NA	Shareholders	NA

Business: The groups principle activities include manufacturing and marketing coffee. The group products include Brazilian Best, Samba Caf, Torino and Vivenda. The group marketed its products under the trade names Brazilian Best, Samba Caf, Torino and Vivenda. In the year 2005, the group acquired BDFC Brazil Alimentos LTDA. The group operates from Brazil and the United States.

Primary SIC and add'l.: 2090

CIK No: 0000743241

Subsidiaries: BDFC Brasil Alimentos LTDA.

Officers: Yaron Arbell/50/Dir., CEO, Daniel Ollech/50/Chmn., CFO, Pres., Jacques Ollech/41/Dir., Exec. VP

Directors: Yaron Arbell/50/Dir., CEO, Daniel Ollech/50/Chmn., CFO, Pres., Jacques Ollech/41/Dir., Exec. VP

Owners: Yaron Arbell/2.30%, Insiders/3.80%, Emerdale Enterprises Ltd/7.40%, Jacques Ollech, Daniel Ollech, Rolf Investments LTD/6.60%, Yossi Haras, Livorno Investments S.A./69.30%

Curr. Assets:	$130,000	Curr. Liab.:	$6,686,000		
Plant, Equip.:	$1,862,000	Total Liab.:	$17,868,000	Indic. Yr. Divd.:	NA
Total Assets:	$2,252,000	Net Worth:	-$15,616,000	Debt/ Equity:	NA

B&G Foods Inc

4 Gatehall Dr., Ste. 110, Parsippany, NJ, 07054; *PH:* 1-973-401-6500; *http://* www.reddevilsauce.com

General - Incorporation	DE	Stock- Price on:12/24/2007	$20.73
Employees	744	Stock Exchange	NYSE
Auditor	KPMG LLP	Ticker Symbol	BGF
Stk Agt	Bank of New York	Outstanding Shares	NA
Counsel	NA	E.P.S.	NA
DUNS No.	NA	Shareholders	NA

Business: The group's principle activities include manufacturing, marketing and distributing diversified portfolio of shelf-stable branded food products, such as pickles, relishes, peppers, olives, molasses, maple syrup, hot sauces, salad dressings and other gourmet products. The group operates from United States.

Primary SIC and add'l.: 2035 2033

CIK No: 0001049172

Subsidiaries: BGH Holdings,Inc., Bloch& Guggenheimer,Inc., Heritage Acquisition Corp., Les Produits Alimentaires Jacques et Fils,Inc., Maple Grove Farms of Vermont,Inc., Ortega HoldingsInc., Polaner,Inc., Trappey Fine Foods,Inc., William Underwood Company

Officers: Scott E. Lerner/VP, General Counsel, Sec., Albert J. Soricelli/Exec. VP - Marketing, Strategic Planning

Directors: Stephen C. Sherrill/Chmn., Cynthia T. Jamison/Dir., Dennis M. Mullen/Dir.

Financial Data: Fiscal Year End:01/01   Latest Annual Data: 12/30/2006

Year	Sales	Net Income
2006	$411,306,000	$11,573,000
2005	$379,262,000	$8,005,000

Curr. Assets:	$150,826,000	Curr. Liab.:	$46,990,000		
Plant, Equip.:	$40,190,000	Total Liab.:	$510,901,000	Indic. Yr. Divd.:	NA
Total Assets:	$594,175,000	Net Worth:	$83,274,000	Debt/ Equity:	5.7069

B+H Ocean Carriers Ltd

19 Burnside St., Bristol, RI, 02809; *PH:* 1-401-410-1100; *Fax:* 1-401-410-1122; *http://* www.bhocean.com; *Email:* info@bhcousa.com

General - Incorporation	Liberia	Stock - Price on:12/24/2007	$17.62
Employees	212	Stock Exchange	AMEX
Auditor	Ernst & Young LLP	Ticker Symbol	BHO
Stk Agt	American Stock Transfer & Trust Co.	Outstanding Shares	7,040,000
Counsel	NA	E.P.S.	$1.75
DUNS No.	NA	Shareholders	NA

Business: The group's principle activity is to invests in, own and operate vessels and product tanker vessels for dry bulk and liquid cargo, refined petroleum products, vegetable oils, caustic soda and molasses transportation. The group operates from United States.

Primary SIC and add'l.: 4499

CIK No: 0000835540

Subsidiaries: Acushnet Shipping Corp., Agawam Shipping Corp., Algonquin Shipping Corp., Anawan Shipping Corp., Aquidneck Shipping Corp., Bhobo One Ltd., Bhobo Three Ltd., Bhobo Two Ltd., Cliaship Holdings Ltd., Isabelle Shipholdings Corp., Obo Holdings Ltd., Rmj Shipping Ltd., Sachuest Shipping Ltd., Sagamore Shipping Corp., Sakonnet Shipping Ltd. 17 Subsidiaries included in the Index

Owners: Michael S. Hudner, Goldman Sachs, Anthony R. Dalzell, Insiders, Fundamental Securities International Ltd., Trevor J. Williams, Caiano Ship AS, Dean Investments Ltd., Northampton Holdings Ltd., Harbor Holdings Corp., Goldman Sachs International, HBK Investments L.P., Devonport Holdings Ltd.

Financial Data: Fiscal Year End:12/31   Latest Annual Data: 12/31/2006

Year	Sales	Net Income
2006	$96,879,000	$18,774,000
2005	$71,903,000	$20,099,000
2004	$51,363,000	$4,424,000

Curr. Assets:	$85,871,000	Curr. Liab.:	$63,688,000	P/E Ratio:	6.88
Plant, Equip.:	$261,687,000	Total Liab.:	$230,842,000	Indic. Yr. Divd.:	NA
Total Assets:	$366,822,000	Net Worth:	$135,980,000	Debt/ Equity:	NA

B2 Digital Inc

9171 Wilshire Blvd, Ste B, Beverly Hills, CA, 90210; *PH:* 1-310-281-2571; *Fax:* 1-310-278-0457; *http://* www.b2digital.com

General - Incorporation	DE	Stock- Price on:12/24/2007	$0.052
Employees	6	Stock Exchange	OTC
Auditor	Larry O'donnell, CPA, P.C	Ticker Symbol	BTDG
Stk Agt	Manhattan Transfer Registrar Co	Outstanding Shares	107,500,000
Counsel	NA	E.P.S.	NA
DUNS No.	NA	Shareholders	NA

Business: The group's principle activities are to provide software systems and services that deliver a range of audiovisual services & entertainment to the hospitality and property management industry and develop high compression video technology for movie viewing and teleconferencing though the Internet channel. The group installs and operates a comprehensive hotel entertainment system (movies, interactive guest services) in hotel properties. Cost projections demonstrate the capability to install, sell and provide free-to-guest (ftg) cable/satellite television programming at highly competitive per room cost. The group's products are fully integrated with the hotel property management (pms) and back office billing systems which manage collection, minimize administration and optimize revenue for the group and their customers.

Primary SIC and add'l.: 3663

CIK No: 0000725929

Officers: Robert C. Russell/41/Dir., CEO, Pres., Marcia A. Pearlstein/52/Dir., Interim CFO, Corp. Sec., Paul La Barre/62/Dir., COO, VP

Directors: Robert C. Russell/41/Dir., CEO, Pres., Marcia A. Pearlstein/52/Dir., Interim CFO, Corp. Sec., Paul La Barre/62/Dir., COO, VP

Owners: Insiders/43.60%, Paul LaBarre/1.05%, Robert Russell/52.94%, Insiders/1.00%, Paul LaBarre/47.06%, Robert Russell/14.18%, Igor Loginov, Marcia A. Pearlstein/28.34%

Financial Data: Fiscal Year End:03/31   Latest Annual Data: 03/31/2007

Year	Sales	Net Income
2007	$287,000	-$1,190,000
2006	$511,000	-$1,363,000
2005	$684,000	-$4,802,000

Curr. Assets:	$48,000	Curr. Liab.:	$1,100,000		
Plant, Equip.:	$95,000	Total Liab.:	$2,939,000	Indic. Yr. Divd.:	NA
Total Assets:	$143,000	Net Worth:	-$2,795,000	Debt/ Equity:	NA

BAB Inc

500 Lake Cook Rd., Ste. 475, Deerfield, IL, 60015; *PH:* 1-847-948-7520; *Fax:* 1-847-405-8140; *http://* www.babcorp.com; *Email:* bab@babcorp.com

General - Incorporation	DE	Stock - Price on:12/24/2007	$1.05
Employees	23	Stock Exchange	OTC
Auditor	Altschuler, Melvoin & Glasser LLP	Ticker Symbol	BABB
Stk Agt	LaSalle Bank N.A	Outstanding Shares	7,260,000
Counsel	NA	E.P.S.	$0.10
DUNS No.	NA	Shareholders	NA

Business: The group's principal activity is to operate, franchise and license bagel, muffin and coffee retail units. The group-owned stores under the big apple bagels brand franchise, features daily baked bagels, flavored cream cheeses, premium coffees, gourmet bagel sandwiches and other related products. Licensed big apple bagels units serve par-baked frozen bagel products, freshly baked daily and related products. The group's 'my favorite muffin' units feature freshly baked muffins, coffees and related products under the 'my favorite muffin' brand. In addition, the group derives income through nontraditional channels of distribution, including licensing agreements with mrs. Fields famous brands, alonti cafe and kohr bros. Frozen custard, as well as direct home delivery of specialty muffin gift baskets and coffee.

Primary SIC and add'l.: 5499 5461

CIK No: 0001123596

Subsidiaries: BAB Operations, Inc., BAB Systems, Inc., Brewsters Franchise, My Favorite Muffin Too, Inc.

Officers: Michael W. Evans/51/Dir., CEO, Pres., Michael K. Murtaugh/63/Dir., VP, General Counsel, Jeffrey M. Gorden/52/CFO, Treasurer

Directors: Michael W. Evans/51/Dir., CEO, Pres., Steven G. Feldman/Dir., James A. Lentz/60/Dir., Michael K. Murtaugh/63/Dir., VP, General Counsel

Owners: Insiders, Holdings Investment,, James A. Lentz, Michael W. Evans, Steven G. Feldman, Jeffrey M. Gorden, Michael K. Murtaugh

Financial Data: Fiscal Year End:11/30   Latest Annual Data: 11/30/2006

Year	Sales	Net Income
2006	$3,917,000	$717,000
2005	$5,125,000	$693,000
2004	$5,708,000	$652,000

Curr. Assets:	$2,303,000	Curr. Liab.:	$1,458,000	P/E Ratio:	10.50
Plant, Equip.:	$101,000	Total Liab.:	$1,756,000	Indic. Yr. Divd.:	$0.080
Total Assets:	$6,719,000	Net Worth:	$4,964,000	Debt/ Equity:	0.0492

BabyUniverse Inc

150 S U.S Hwy 1, Ste. 500, Jupiter, FL, 33347; *PH:* 1-954-771-5160; *Fax:* 1-954-523-9881; *http://* www.babyuniverse.com

General - Incorporation	FL	Stock - Price on:12/24/2007	$8.6
Employees	87	Stock Exchange	NDQ
Auditor	Singer Lewak Greenbaum & Goldstein	Ticker Symbol	POSH
Stk Agt	American Stock Transfer & Trust Co.	Outstanding Shares	5,690,000
Counsel	NA	E.P.S.	-$1
DUNS No.	NA	Shareholders	NA

Business: The groups principle activity is to provide online retailer of baby, toddler and maternity products. The group provides services through PoshTots.com, BabyUniverse.com, DreamtimeBaby.com and PoshLiving.com websites. The group acquired Posh Tots, LLC in the year 2006 and Huta Duna, Inc in the year 2005. The group operates from the United States. The group's quarterly revenue for September 2007 was 16.20 millions of USD.

Primary SIC and add'l.: 5641 5621 5632 5945 5999

CIK No: 0001325118

Subsidiaries: Huta Duna, Inc., Posh Tots, Inc.

Officers: John C. Textor/Chmn., CEO, Georgianne K. Brown/Exec. VP - Marketing, Susan Lindeman/Pres. - Luxury Brands, Andrea Edmunds/Pres. - Content, Social Networking, John Studdard/Exec. VP - New Media, Michael R. Hull/CFO, Barry Hollingsworth/Investor Relations Contact

Directors: John C. Textor/Chmn., CEO, Lauren Krueger/Dir., Michael J. Wagner/Dir., John Schaefer/Dir., Edward Ulbrich/Dir., Frank Rosales/Dir., Pam Abrams/Dir., Michael Bay/Member - Advisory Board, Kenneth Goore/Member - Advisory Board, Dan Marino/Member - Advisory Board

Owners: John C. Textor/8.60%, Christopher H. Cummings, Gilder, Gagnon, Howe& Co, LLC/5.60%, Georgianne K. Brown, Michael R. Hull, Michael J. Wagner/1.10%, Frederick L. Hurley, D. E. Shaw Laminar Acquisition Holdings3, L.L.C/63.30%, Wyndcrest Baby Universe Holdings III, LLC/5.00%, John Studdard, Insiders/10.70%, Stuart Goffman/1.50%, Robert Brown, Craig K. Currie

Financial Data: Fiscal Year End:12/31   Latest Annual Data: 12/31/2006

Year	Sales	Net Income
2006	$35,550,000	-$3,344,000
2005	$23,702,000	-$492,000
2004	$14,277,000	$221,000

Curr. Assets:	$6,585,000	Curr. Liab.:	$6,630,000		
Plant, Equip.:	$1,937,000	Total Liab.:	$12,597,000	Indic. Yr. Divd.:	NA
Total Assets:	$30,304,000	Net Worth:	$17,706,000	Debt/ Equity:	0.3322

Back Yard Burgers Inc

1657 N Shelby Oaks Dr., Ste. 105, Memphis, TN, 38134; *PH:* 1-901-367-0888; *Fax:* 1-901-367-0999; *http://* www.backyardburgers.com

General - Incorporation	DE	Stock- Price on:12/24/2007	$6.33
Employees	1,000	Stock Exchange	NDQ
Auditor	PricewaterhouseCoopers LLP	Ticker Symbol	BYBI
Stk Agt	Registrar & Transfer Co	Outstanding Shares	5,130,000
Counsel	Henke, Heaton & Bufkin	E.P.S.	$0.11
DUNS No.	18-190-5605	Shareholders	

Business: The group's principal activity is to operate and franchise quick service in 17 states throughout the southeast region of the United States. The restaurants specialize in charbroiled, freshly prepared food. The menu features made-to-order gourmet 100% black angus hamburgers and chicken sandwiches - charbroiled over an open flame, fresh salads, chili and other special entrees as well as hand-dipped milkshakes, fresh-made lemonade and fresh-baked cobblers. At 03-Jan-2004, the group had 42 company-operated restaurants and 90 franchised restaurants. It also provides construction support services to its franchisees. The trademarks include great little burger and back yard burgers.

Primary SIC and add'l.: 5812

CIK No: 0000901495

Subsidiaries: Atlanta Burgers BYB Corporation, BYB Properties, Inc, Little Rock Back Yard Burgers

Officers: Lattimore M. Michael/Chmn., CEO, Joseph L. Weiss/48/Dir., COO, Michael G. Webb/39/CFO, Exec. VP

Directors: Lattimore M. Michael/Chmn., CEO, William B. Raiford/47/Dir., Joseph L. Weiss/48/Dir., COO, Kurt W. Henke/50/Dir., Jim L. Peterson/72/Dir., Dane C. Andreeff/42/Dir., Gina A. Balducci/46/Dir.

Owners: Dane C. Andreeff/7.60%, Kurt W. Henke, Insiders/30.70%, Joseph L. Weiss/9.50%, Lattimore M. Michael/11.30%, William B. Raiford, BBAC, LLC/8.50%, Michael G. Webb/1.30%, Jim L. Peterson/1.50%

Financial Data: *Fiscal Year End:*12/31 *Latest Annual Data:* 12/30/2006

Year	Sales	Net Income
2006	$44,710,000	$876,000
2005	$41,001,000	-$44,000

Curr. Assets:	$5,316,000	**Curr. Liab.:**	$4,010,000	**P/E Ratio:**	57.55
Plant, Equip.:	$23,035,000	**Total Liab.:**	$16,339,000	**Indic. Yr. Divd.:**	NA
Total Assets:	$31,641,000	**Net Worth:**	$15,302,000	**Debt/ Equity:**	0.4636

BackWeb Technologies Ltd

2077 Gateway Pl., Ste 500, San Jose, CA, 95110; ***PH:*** 1-972-933-1763; ***http://*** www.backweb.com

General -		**Stock** -	
Incorporation	Israel	Price on:12/24/2007	NA
Employees	46	Stock Exchange	OTC
Auditor	Grant Thornton LLP	Ticker Symbol	BWEBF
Stk Agt	American Stock Transfer & Trust Co.	Outstanding Shares	NA
Counsel	Naschitz Brandes & Co	E.P.S	NA
DUNS No.	NA	Shareholders	NA

Business: The group's principle acitivity is to provide Internet communication infrastructure software and application-specific software which enables companies to communicate business-critical, time-sensitive information throughout their extended enterprise of customers, partners and employees.

Primary SIC and add'l.: 7372 7375

CIK No: 0001082064

Subsidiaries: BackWeb Canada Inc, BackWeb K.K. Ltd., BackWeb Technologies (U.K.) Ltd., BackWeb Technologies A.B., BackWeb Technologies B.V., BackWeb Technologies Europe Limited, BackWeb Technologies GmbH, BackWeb Technologies S.a.r.l., BackWeb Technologies, Inc

Officers: William Heye/Dir., CEO, David Collins/Contact - Investor Relation, Boaz Hamo/VP - Research - Development, Ken Holmes/42/VP - Finance

Directors: William Heye/Dir., CEO, Eli Barkat/Chmn., Co - Founder, Uday Bellary/Dir., Amir Makleff/Dir., Kara Andersen/Dir.

Owners: Kara Andersen, EliBarkat Holdings Ltd./8.10%, 8 Hamarpe Street Har Hotzvim Jerusalem 91450 Israel NirBarkat Holdings Ltd./8.10%, Insiders/14.60%, Amir Makleff, Uday Bellary, William Heye/2.50%, Ken Holmes, 8 Hamarpe Street Har Hotzvim Jerusalem 91450 Israel Yuval 63 Holdings (1995) Ltd./8.10%, Eli Barkat/11.80%

Bad Toys Holdings Inc

2344 Woodridge Ave., Kingsport, TN, 37664; ***PH:*** 1-423-247-9560; ***http://*** www.badtoysinc.com

General -		**Stock** -	
Incorporation	NV	Price on:12/24/2007	$0.25
Employees	457	Stock Exchange	NA
Auditor	T. Alan Walls P.C	Ticker Symbol	NA
Stk Agt	Nevada Agency & Trust Company	Outstanding Shares	22,310,000
Counsel	NA	E.P.S	$0.04
DUNS No.	NA	Shareholders	NA

Business: The group's principal activity is to manufacture to customers' orders v-twin harley-davidson type motorcycles from component parts, maintains a customizing and motorcycle servicing operation and special orders premium accessories, parts and apparel related to harley-davidson motorcycles. The component parts are manufactured in five basic styles: the phoenix, the concorde, the taos, the rigid flame and the tour glide. The pricing is based on its costs plus a retail and overhead markup. The prices may vary if a motorcycle is customized.

Primary SIC and add'l.: 3714 3751

CIK No: 0001200268

Subsidiaries: Bad Toys, Inc., Southland Health Services, Inc.

Officers: Larry N. Lunan/67/Dir., CEO, Pres., Alan T. Walls/47/CFO, Sec.

Directors: Larry N. Lunan/67/Dir., CEO, Pres., Roger A. Warren/43/Dir., Clinton Hubbard/60/Dir.

Owners: Larry N. Lunan, Roger A. Warren, Susan H. Lunan, T. Alan Walls, Clinton L. Hubbard, Insiders

Financial Data: *Fiscal Year End:*12/31 *Latest Annual Data:* 12/31/2006

Year	Sales	Net Income
2006	$43,546,000	$1,977,000
2005	$44,667,000	$3,856,000
2004	$3,721,000	-$2,101,000

Curr. Assets:	$13,894,000	**Curr. Liab.:**	$15,114,000	**P/E Ratio:**	6.25
Plant, Equip.:	$3,587,000	**Total Liab.:**	$17,870,000	**Indic. Yr. Divd.:**	NA
Total Assets:	$25,399,000	**Net Worth:**	$7,529,000	**Debt/ Equity:**	0.1709

Badger Meter Inc

4545 W Brown Deer Rd., Milwaukee, WI, 53223; ***PH:*** 1-414-355-0400; ***Fax:*** 1-414-371-5956; ***http://*** www.badgermeter.com

General -		**Stock** -	
Incorporation	WI	Price on:12/24/2007	$28.13
Employees	1,113	Stock Exchange	AMEX
Auditor	Ernst & Young LLP	Ticker Symbol	BMI
Stk Agt	American Stock Transfer & Trust Co.	Outstanding Shares	14,230,000
Counsel	NA	E.P.S	$0.41
DUNS No.	00-606-9710	Shareholders	NA

Business: The group's principal activities are to manufacture and market flow-measurement meters and control technologies. Its product line includes residential, commercial and industrial water meters, automotive fluid meters, small precision valves and industrial process meters. The customers of the group include water utilities, original equipment manufacturers and various industrial customers primarily operating in the water, wastewater and process waters, energy and petroleum, food and beverage, pharmaceutical, chemical and concrete markets. The group has manufacturing facilities at milwaukee, tulsa and rio rico in the United States, nogales in Mexico and brno in czech republic. It also has facilities for assembly at stuggart in Germany and nancy in France.

Primary SIC and add'l.: 3823

CIK No: 0000009092

Subsidiaries: Badger Meter Canada, Inc., Badger Meter Czech Republic, Badger Meter de las Americas, SA de CV, Badger Meter de Mexico, SA de CV, Badger Meter Europe, GmbH, Badger Meter France SAS, Badger Meter International, Inc., Badger Meter Slovakia, MecaPlus Equipements SAS

Officers: Richard A. Meeusen/53/Chmn., CEO, Pres./$775,905.00, Dennis J. Webb/60/VP - Sales, Marketing, Engineering/$435,455.00, Scott Berry/Mgr. - Accounting, Steve Portlance/Mgr. - Accounting, Scott Jones/Mgr. - Accounting, Barb Kesselhon/Customer Service Representative, Therese Martin/Customer Service Representative, Paul Fecht/Mgr. - Accounting, Rob Sears/Mgr. - Accounting, Eric Foley/National Accounting Mgr., Maria Klasinski/Mgr. - Accounting, Chuck Tindall/Mgr. - Accounting, Bruce Lackey/Distributor Mgr., Tom Watts/Mgr. - Accounting, Daniel D. Zandron/59/VP - Business Development/$428,045.00 *(46 Officers included in Index)*

Directors: Richard A. Meeusen/53/Chmn., CEO, Pres., John J. Stollenwerk/68/Dir., Ulice Payne/52/Dir., James O. Wright/87/Dir., Steven J. Smith/58/Dir., Ronald H. Dix/63/Dir., Sr. VP - Administration, Kenneth P. Manning/66/Dir., Thomas J. Fischer/60/Dir., Andrew J. Policano/58/Dir.

Owners: Insiders/9.00%, John J. Stollenwerk, T. Rowe Price Associates, Inc./5.70%, Andrew J. Policano, Kenneth P. Manning, Thomas J. Fischer, Heartland Advisors, Inc./5.70%, Richard E. Johnson/1.70%, Ulice Payne, AMVESCAP PLC/9.40%, Dennis J. Webb, Ronald H. Dix/2.20%, Daniel D. Zandron, Steven J. Smith, Marshall & Ilsley Corporation/7.30% *(17 Owners included in Index)*

Financial Data: *Fiscal Year End:*12/31 *Latest Annual Data:* 12/31/2006

Year	Sales	Net Income
2006	$229,754,000	$7,548,000
2005	$216,654,000	$13,253,000
2004	$205,010,000	$9,633,000

Curr. Assets:	$79,359,000	**Curr. Liab.:**	$45,711,000		
Plant, Equip.:	$44,709,000	**Total Liab.:**	$67,564,000	**Indic. Yr. Divd.:**	NA
Total Assets:	$139,383,000	**Net Worth:**	$71,819,000	**Debt/ Equity:**	0.0723

Baidu.com Inc

12/F, Ideal International Plz., No. 58 WN 4th Ring, Beijing, Hebei, 100080; ***PH:*** 86-1082621188; ***Fax:*** 86-1082607007; ***http://*** www.baidu.com; ***Email:*** ir@baidu.com

General -		**Stock** -	
Incorporation	Cayman Islands	Price on:12/24/2007	$154.45
Employees	NA	Stock Exchange	NDQ
Auditor	Ernst & Young LLP	Ticker Symbol	BIDU
Stk Agt	Bank of New York	Outstanding Shares	33,700,000
Counsel	NA	E.P.S	NA
DUNS No.	NA	Shareholders	NA

Business: The groups principle activity is to provide Chinese language Internet search. The groups services include Baidu Web Search, Baidu Post Bar, Baidu Information, Baidu Knows, Baidu Image Search. The group operates from the United States. The group's quarterly revenue for September 2007 was 496.53 millions of USD.

Primary SIC and add'l.: 7375 7379

CIK No: 0001329099

Subsidiaries: Baidu (China) Co., Ltd., Baidu Holdings Limited, Baidu Netcom Science Technology Co., Ltd., Baidu Online Network Technology (Beijing) Co. Ltd., Beijing Perusal Technology Co., Ltd

Officers: Robin Li/Chmn., CEO, Shawn Wang/CFO, William Chang/Chief Scientist, Jun Yu/VP - Products, Xuyang Ren/VP - Marketing, Business Development, Hailong Xiang/VP - Sales, Haoyu Shen/VP - Business Operations

Directors: Robin Li/Chmn., CEO, William Decker/Dir., James Ding/Dir., Greg Penner/Dir., Nobuyuki Idei/Dir.

Owners: FMR Corp./6.20%, James Ding, Shawn Wang, Robin Yanhong Li/21.50%, William Chang, William Decker, Asad Jamal, David Hongbo Zhu, Handsome Reward Limited/16.30%, Greg Penner/5.10%, Insiders/28.20%

Financial Data: *Fiscal Year End:*12/31 *Latest Annual Data:* 12/31/2006

Year	Sales	Net Income
2006	$107,359,000	$38,668,000
2005	$39,555,000	$5,899,000
2004	$13,401,000	$1,450,000

Curr. Assets:	$163,855,000	**Curr. Liab.:**	$38,569,000	**P/E Ratio:**	115.26
Plant, Equip.:	$24,568,000	**Total Liab.:**	$39,827,000	**Indic. Yr. Divd.:**	NA
Total Assets:	$213,743,000	**Net Worth:**	$173,916,000	**Debt/ Equity:**	NA

Bairnco Corp

300 Primera Blvd., Ste. 432, Lake Mary, FL, 32746; ***PH:*** 1-407-875-2222; ***http://*** www.bairnco.com

General -		**Stock** -	
Incorporation	DE	Price on:12/24/2007	NA
Employees	878	Stock Exchange	NA
Auditor	Grant Thornton LLP	Ticker Symbol	NA
Stk Agt	Trust Co Bank	Outstanding Shares	NA
Counsel	NA	E.P.S	NA
DUNS No.	01-828-8621	Shareholders	NA

Business: The group's principal activities are design, manufacture, market and sell laminated and coated products and also meat-room products. The group operates under three segments: arlon coated materials, arlon electronic materials and components and kasco replacement products and services. The aem and acm segments are into design, manufacture, marketing of laminated and coated products to the

electronic, industrial and commercial. Products include printed circuit boards, custom-engineered laminates, coated products and silicone rubber materials used in consumer, industrial and commercial products. Kasco products include saw blades for cutting meat, fish, wood and metal, grinder plates and knives for grinding meat, seasoning products. These are distributed to supermarkets, deli operations and meat, poultry and fish processing plants through out the United States, Canada and Europe.

Primary SIC and add'l.: 3081 3425 2822 3670 3556

CIK No: 0000350750

Subsidiaries: Arlon Adhesives & Films, Inc., Arlon Material Technologies Co. Ltd., Arlon Materials for Electronics Co. Ltd., Arlon MED International, LLC, Arlon Partners, Inc., Arlon Signtech, Ltd., Arlon Viscor, Ltd., Arlon, Inc., Atlantic Service Co. (UK) Ltd., Atlantic Service Co. Ltd., Bertram & Graf GmbH, EuroKasco S.A., Kasco Corporation, Kasco Ensambly S.A. de C.V., Kasco Mexico LLC

Officers: Luke E. Fichthorn/66/Chmn., CEO, Kenneth L. Bayne/VP - Finance, CFO, Lawrence C. Maingot/48/Corporate Controller, Larry D. Smith/VP - Administration, Sec.

Directors: Luke E. Fichthorn/66/Chmn., CEO, Gerald L. Degood/Dir., William F. Yelverton/Dir., Charles T. Foley/Dir., James A. Wolf/Dir.

Owners: Insiders/11.51%, Luke E. Fichthorn/5.97%, Kenneth L. Bayne, William F. Yelverton, Marvin Schwartz/10.34%, Gerald L. DeGood, Larry D. Smith, FMR Corp./5.81%, Lawrence C. Maingot, Charles T. Foley/3.51%, James A. Wolf, Steel PartnersII, L.P./15.23%

Baker Boyer Bancorp

7 W Main St., Walla Walla, WA, 99362; ***PH:*** 1-509-525-2000; ***Fax:*** 1-509-525-1034; ***http://*** www.bakerboyer.com; ***Email:*** *callcenter@bakerboyer.com*

General - Incorporation		**Stock**- Price on:12/24/2007	$60
Employees	173	Stock Exchange	OTC
Auditor	NA	Ticker Symbol	BBBK
Stk Agt	NA	Outstanding Shares	1,300,000
Counsel	NA	E.P.S	NA
DUNS No.	NA	Shareholders	NA

Business: The groups principal activity is to provide banking business. The group financial products include savings and fixed deposits, on line, personal, commercial lending and business banking. The group operates from the United States.

Primary SIC and add'l.: 6733 6712 6021

CIK No:

Officers: Megan Clubb/CEO, Pres., Rita Van Schoiack/Tri, Cities Wealth Management, Business Banking, Jon Bren/Exec. VP, Mgr. - Division, Wealth Management Services, Lyle Hansen/Exec. VP, Mgr. - Banking Division, Mark Hess/COO, Exec. VP, Chris Avey/Investment Exec., Baker Boyer Investor Services, Tyson Graves/Investment Exec., Baker Boyer Bank

Baker Hughes Inc

2929 Allen Pkwy. Ste. 2100, Houston, TX, 77019; ***PH:*** 1-713-439-8600; ***Fax:*** 1-713-439-8699; ***http://*** www.bakerhughes.com; ***Email:*** info@bakerhughes.com

General - Incorporation	DE	**Stock**- Price on:12/24/2007	$87.53
Employees	34,600	Stock Exchange	NYSE
Auditor	Deloitte & Touche LLP	Ticker Symbol	BHI
Stk Agt	Mellon Investor Services LLC	Outstanding Shares	320,330,000
Counsel	NA	E.P.S	$4.36
DUNS No.	17-498-7909	Shareholders	NA

Business: The groups principle activity is to provide oilfield products and services. The group operates through two segments namely oilfield and process industries segment. The group operates from United States.

Primary SIC and add'l.: 3532 3531 3533 3594

CIK No: 0000808362

Subsidiaries: Baker Hughes Asia Pacific Ltd., Baker Hughes Canada Company, Baker Hughes Canada Holdings B.V., Baker Hughes EHHC, Inc., Baker Hughes Finance International S.r.l., Baker Hughes Financing Company, Baker Hughes GmbH, Baker Hughes International Branches, Inc., Baker Hughes Limited, Baker Hughes Nederland Holdings B.V., Baker Hughes Norge A/S, Baker Hughes Oilfield Operations, Inc., Baker Petrolite Corporation, JDI International Leasing Limited, Latin America Finance S.r.l. 20 Subsidiaries included in the Index

Officers: Chad C. Deaton/55/Chmn., CEO/$8,004,199.00, Mike F. Davis/VP, Pres. - Baker Hughes Russia, Christopher P. Beaver/VP, Pres. - Baker Oil Tools, Gene H. Shiels/Assist. Dir. - Investor Relations, Gary G. Rich/VP, Pres. - Hughes Christensen, Charles S. Wolley/VP, Pres. - Centrilift, Peter Ragauss/CFO, Sr. VP/$1,985,076.00, Steve Palmer/VP - Business Development, Integrated Operations, Stephen K. Ellison/VP, Pres. - Baker Atlas, William D. Marsh/Dir. - Enterprise Risk Strategy, Deputy General Councel, Didier Charreton/VP - Human Resources, Russell J. Cancilla/Chief Security Officer, Halina Caravello/Dir. - HS, E, Joe Vandevier/Pres. - Productionquest, Gary R. Flaharty/Dir. - Investor Relations *(28 Officers included in Index)*

Directors: Chad C. Deaton/55/Chmn., CEO, Edward P. Djerejian/68/Dir., Anthony G. Fernandes/62/Dir., Pierre H. Jungels/64/Dir., Claire W. Gargalli/65/Dir., Clarence P. Cazalot/57/Dir., James F. McCall/73/Dir., James A. Lash/63/Dir., Larry J. Nichols/65/Dir., John H. Riley/67/Dir., Francios Stieger/Dir., Charles L. Watson/58/Dir., Larry D. Brady/65/Dir.

Owners: Alan R. Crain, James R. Clark, Charles L. Watson, Douglas J. Wall, Clarence P. Cazalot, Larry J. Nichols, James F. McCall, Larry D. Brady, Anthony G. Fernandes, Insiders, Stephen G. Finley, David H. Barr, John H. Riley, Pierre H. Jungels, Peter A. Ragauss *(19 Owners included in Index)*

Financial Data: ***Fiscal Year End:***12/31 ***Latest Annual Data:*** 12/31/2006

Year	**Sales**	**Net Income**
2006	$9,027,400,000	$2,419,000,000
2005	$7,185,500,000	$878,400,000
2004	$6,103,800,000	$528,600,000

Curr. Assets:	$4,967,800,000	**Curr. Liab.:**	$1,621,900,000	**P/E Ratio:**	20.08
Plant, Equip.:	$1,800,500,000	**Total Liab.:**	$3,462,800,000	**Indic. Yr. Divd.:**	NA
Total Assets:	$8,705,700,000	**Net Worth:**	$5,242,900,000	**Debt/ Equity:**	0.1929

Baker Michael Corp

Airside Business Pk., 100 Airside Dr., Moon Township, PA, 15108; ***PH:*** 1-412-269-6300; ***Fax:*** 1-412-375-3980; ***http://*** www.mbakercorp.com; ***Email:*** energy@mbakercorp.com

General - Incorporation	PA	**Stock**- Price on:12/24/2007	$37.51
Employees	4,737	Stock Exchange	AMEX
Auditor	Deloitte & Touche, LLP	Ticker Symbol	BKR
Stk Agt	American Stock Transfer & Trust Co.	Outstanding Shares	8,710,000
Counsel	Reed Smith Shaw & McClay	E.P.S	$3.09
DUNS No.	00-791-6968	Shareholders	NA

Business: The group's principal activity is to provide engineering and energy expertise for public and private sector clients. It operates three segments: engineering, energy and non-core. The engineering segment provides a variety of design and related consulting services. Services include design-build, construction management, consulting, program management, site assessment and restoration, strategic regulatory analysis, regulatory compliance and advanced management systems. The energy segment specializes in providing a full range of total asset management services for operating energy production facilities. Services include training, personnel recruitment, pre-operations engineering, maintenance management systems, field operations and maintenance, procurement and supply chain management. The non-core segment consists of buildings and transportation construction operations. The group has operations in Texas, Louisiana, Wyoming, Montana and the gulf of Mexico.

Primary SIC and add'l.: 8711 8712 4231 1541

CIK No: 0000009263

Subsidiaries: Baker Construction, Inc., Baker Energy International, Ltd., Baker Engineering NY, Inc., Baker Engineering, Inc., Baker Environmental, Inc., Baker Global Project Services, Inc., Baker Heavy & Highway, Inc., Baker Holding Corporation, Baker Mellon Stuart Construction, Inc., Baker O&M International, Ltd., Baker Program Management, Inc., Baker/MO Services, Inc., Baker/OTS International, Inc., Baker/OTS Ltd., Baker/OTS, Inc. 30 Subsidiaries included in the Index

Officers: Richard L. Shaw/Chmn., CEO/$452,631.00, William P. Mooney/CFO, Exec. VP/$286,378.00, David G. Higie/VP - Corporate Communications, James H. McKnight/Exec. VP, General Counsel, Sec./$279,655.00, Bradley L. Mallory/Pres. - Baker Engineering/$250,058.00, John D. Whiteford/Corporate Exec. VP/$260,479.00, Andrew P. Pajak/Executive Program Dir./$318,228.00

Directors: Richard L. Shaw/Chmn., CEO, Robert N. Bontempo/Dir., Nicholas P. Constantakis/Dir., William J. Copeland/Dir., John E. Murray/Dir., Pamela S. Pierce/Dir., Roy V. Gavert/Dir., Robert H. Foglesong/Dir.

Owners: Richard L. Shaw, William P. Mooney, Pamela S. Pierce, Donald P. Fusilli, Jeffrey Gendell/9.74%, William J. Copeland, Roy V. Gavert, James H. McKnight, Bradley L. Mallory, Nicholas P. Constantakis, Robert H. Foglesong, Wellington Management Company LLP/6.01%, Andrew P. Pajak, John E. Murray, Baker 401(k) Plan/17.18% *(18 Owners included in Index)*

Financial Data: ***Fiscal Year End:***12/31 ***Latest Annual Data:*** 12/31/2006

Year	**Sales**	**Net Income**
2006	$651,012,000	$11,831,000
2005	$579,278,000	$5,051,000
2004	$550,751,000	$12,292,000

Curr. Assets:	$221,589,000	**Curr. Liab.:**	$152,863,000		
Plant, Equip.:	$21,323,000	**Total Liab.:**	$171,003,000	**Indic. Yr. Divd.:**	NA
Total Assets:	$266,123,000	**Net Worth:**	$95,120,000	**Debt/ Equity:**	0.0677

Bakers Footwear Group Inc

2815 Scott Ave., St. Louis, MO, 63103; ***PH:*** 1-314-621-0699; ***Fax:*** 1-314-621-0708; ***http://*** www.bakersshoes.com

General - Incorporation	MO	**Stock**- Price on:12/24/2007	$7.05
Employees	700	Stock Exchange	NDQ
Auditor	Ernst & Young LLP	Ticker Symbol	BKRS
Stk Agt	Continental Stock Transfer & Trust Co	Outstanding Shares	6,490,000
Counsel	NA	E.P.S	-$0.24
DUNS No.	NA	Shareholders	NA

Business: The group's principal activity is to sell distinctive footwear and accessories for young women seeking the latest in fashion footwear. It sells private label and national brand dress, casual, and sport shoes, boots, sandals and accessories. The group operates over 200 stores in 36 states.

Primary SIC and add'l.: 5661

CIK No: 0001171032

Owners: Wellington Management Company, LLP/13.59%, Austin W. Marxe and David M. Greenhouse and affiliates/9.02%, Harry E. Rich, Scott C. Schnuck, Joseph R. Vander Pluym, Searock Capital Management, LLC and affiliates/5.64%, Insiders/16.48%, Timothy F. Finley, Stanley K. Tusman, Bernard A. Edison/5.36%, Royce& Associates, LLC/8.83%, Lawrence L. Spanley, Andrew N. Baur, Peter A. Edison/11.79%, Wells Fargo& Company and affiliates/15.75% *(17 Owners included in Index)*

Financial Data: ***Fiscal Year End:***01/28 ***Latest Annual Data:*** 2/3/2007

Year	**Sales**	**Net Income**
2007	$204,753,000	-$1,543,000
2006	$194,780,000	$6,553,000
2005	$150,515,000	$1,428,000

Curr. Assets:	$30,810,000	**Curr. Liab.:**	$32,519,000		
Plant, Equip.:	$51,021,000	**Total Liab.:**	$41,993,000	**Indic. Yr. Divd.:**	NA
Total Assets:	$83,159,000	**Net Worth:**	$41,167,000	**Debt/ Equity:**	0.0007

Balaton Power Inc

1651 W 15th St., Vancouver, BC, V7P 1N3; ***PH:*** 1-604-987-2850; ***Fax:*** 1-604-691-1784; ***http://*** www.lunadesign.org

General - Incorporation	BC	**Stock**- Price on:12/24/2007	$0.27
Employees	NA	Stock Exchange	OTC
Auditor	Harris & Partners, LLP	Ticker Symbol	BPWRF
Stk Agt	Mellon Investor Services LLC	Outstanding Shares	83,790,000
Counsel	NA	E.P.S	NA
DUNS No.	NA	Shareholders	NA

Business: The groups principal activity is to exploration of minerals. The group operates from the United States and Canada.

Primary SIC and add'l.: 9995

CIK No: 0001132704

Subsidiaries: Continental Resources (USA) Ltd., Snoqualmie River Hydro Inc

Officers: Michael Rosa/73/Dir., CEO, Pres., Robert Wyllie/44/Dir., CFO

Directors: Michael Rosa/73/Dir., CEO, Pres., Robert Wyllie/44/Dir., CFO, David C. Wynn/40/Dir., Nicole Bouthillier/57/Dir.

Owners: David C. Wynn, Michael Rosa, Robert Wyllie, Nicole Bouthillier

Financial Data: Fiscal Year End:12/31 Latest Annual Data: 12/31/2006

Year	Sales	Net Income
2006	NA	-$1,074,000
2005	NA	-$1,149,000
2004	NA	-$1,193,000

Curr. Assets:	$29,000	**Curr. Liab.:**	$1,039,000		
Plant, Equip.:	NA	**Total Liab.:**	$1,039,000	**Indic. Yr. Divd.:**	NA
Total Assets:	$230,000	**Net Worth:**	-$809,000	**Debt/ Equity:**	NA

Balchem Corp

52 Sunrise Pk. Rd., New Hampton, NY, 10958; *PH:* 1-845-326-5600; *Fax:* 1-845-326-5742; *http://* www.balchem.com

General - Incorporation	MD	**Stock**- Price on:12/24/2007	NA
Employees	200	Stock Exchange	NDQ
Auditor	McGladrey & Pullen LLP	Ticker Symbol	BCPC
Stk Agt	Registrar & Transfer Co	Outstanding Shares	NA
Counsel	Duane, Morris LLP	E.P.S	NA
DUNS No.	04-199-2728	Shareholders	NA

Business: The group's principal activity is to manufacture and market specialty performance ingredients for food, feed and medical sterilization industries. The group operates in three segments: specialty products, encapsulated products / nutritional products and unencapsulated feed supplements. The specialty products segment sells ethylene oxide, propylene oxide and methyl chloride gases. They are used to sterilize medical and surgical devices, bacteria reduction in spice treatment and in herbicides, fertilizers and pharmaceuticals. Encapsulated products segment makes performance ingredients for use in food and animal products to enhance processing, mixing, packaging and shelf life improvement. The unencapsulated feed supplements segment manufactures and supplies choline chloride for use in animal health, poultry and swine industries.

Primary SIC and add'l.: 2899 2819

CIK No: 0000009326

Subsidiaries: Balchem Minerals Corporation, BCP Ingredients, Inc., Chelated Minerals Corporation

Officers: Dino A. Rossi/Chmn., CEO, Pres./$770,715.00, Robert T. Miniger/VP - Human Resources/$277,305.00, Matthew Houston/General Counsel, Sec., Paul Richardson/VP - Research, Development/$3,013,428.00, David F. Ludwig/VP, GM - ARC Specialty Products/$377,312.00, Frank J. Fitzpatrick/CFO, Treasurer, Assist. Sec./$406,517.00, Karin McCaffery/Investor Contact

Directors: Dino A. Rossi/Chmn., CEO, Pres., John Televantos/Dir., Kenneth P. Mitchell/Dir., Hoyt Ammidon/Dir., Elaine R. Wedral/Dir., Edward McMillan/Dir.

Owners: Robert T. Miniger, Hoyt Ammidon, Frank Fitzpatrick, Royce & Associates/5.00%, Paul Richardson, Elaine R. Wedral, Kayne Anderson Rudnick Investment Management, LLC/7.90%, Segall, Bryand & Hamill/4.90%, Kenneth P. Mitchell, Edward L. McMillan, Dino A. Rossi/2.00%, Insiders/5.20%, John Televantos, Ashford Capital Management, Inc./9.70%, David F. Ludwig

Curr. Assets:	$28,855,000	**Curr. Liab.:**	$9,560,000		
Plant, Equip.:	$31,313,000	**Total Liab.:**	$16,971,000	**Indic. Yr. Divd.:**	NA
Total Assets:	$92,333,000	**Net Worth:**	$75,362,000	**Debt/ Equity:**	NA

Baldor Electric Co

5711 R. S Boreham, Jr. St., Fort Smith, AR, 72901; *PH:* 1-479-646-4711; *Fax:* 1-479-648-5792; *http://* www.baldor.com

General - Incorporation	MO	**Stock**- Price on:12/24/2007	$49.09
Employees	3,700	Stock Exchange	NYSE
Auditor	Ernst & Young LLP	Ticker Symbol	BEZ
Stk Agt	Continental Stock Transfer & Trust Co	Outstanding Shares	45,770,000
Counsel	Thompson Coburn LLP	E.P.S	NA
DUNS No.	00-633-8537	Shareholders	NA

Business: The group's principal activities are to design, manufacture and sell electric motors, drives, generators and related products. The products of the group include power generators, speed reducers, industrial grinders, buffers, polishing lathes, stampings, castings and repair parts. The group manufactures many of the components used in its products including laminations, motor hardware and aluminum die-castings. Group's products are marketed throughout the United States and in more than 60 foreign countries, principally in Canada, Mexico, Europe, Australia, the Far East and Latin America. On 13-Feb-2003, the group acquired energy dynamics, inc.

Primary SIC and add'l.: 3621 3679 3629 3625

CIK No: 0000009342

Subsidiaries: Australian Baldor Pty Limited, Baldor ASR AG, Baldor ASR GmbH fur Antriebstechnik, Baldor ASR U.K. Limited, Baldor de Mexico, S.A. de C.V., Baldor Electric (Asia) PTE, Ltd., Baldor Electric India Pvt Ltd, Baldor Holdings, Inc., Baldor International, Inc., Baldor Investments, LLC, Baldor Italia S.r.l., Baldor Japan Corporation, Baldor of Arkansas, Inc., Baldor of Nevada, Inc., Baldor of Texas, L.P. 23 Subsidiaries included in the Index

Officers: John McFarland/Chmn., CEO/$1,331,479.00, Ronald Thurman/VP, Engineering Officer, Gene Hagedorn/Exec. VP - Materials/$435,817.00, Roger Bullock/VP, Drives Officer, Tracy Long/VP - Investor Relations, Assist. Sec. Officer, Randall Breaux/VP, Marketing Officer, Randy Colip/Exec. VP, Sales Officer, Edward Ralston/Exec. VP, Business Integration Officer, Ronald Tucker/COO, Pres., Sec. Officer/$789,461.00, Michael Cinquemani/Exec. VP - Sales, William Fowler/VP - Information Services - Reliance, Dodge, Terry Fulmer/VP - Manufacturing - Reliance, Jason Green/VP - Human Resources, Tom Mascari/VP - Business Integration, George Moschner/CFO *(23 Officers included in Index)*

Directors: John McFarland/Chmn., CEO, Jean Mauldin/Dir., Richard Jaudes/Dir., Jefferson Asher/Dir., Merlin Augustine/Dir., Robert Messey/Dir., Robert Proost/Dir., R. L. Qualls/Dir., Barry Rogstad/Dir.

Owners: Richard E. Jaudes, Gene J. Hagedorn, T. Rowe Price Associates, Inc./5.10%, Merlin J. Augustine, Lord, Abbett& Co. LLC/3.80%, Jefferson W. Asher, Employees Profit Sharing and Savings Plan/6.00%, Steven A. Cohen/6.10%, R. L. Qualls, Barry K. Rogstad, Robert L. Proost, Ronald E. Tucker, Insiders/3.80%, Robert J. Messey, Charles H. Cramer *(18 Owners included in Index)*

Financial Data: Fiscal Year End:12/31 Latest Annual Data: 12/30/2006

Year	Sales	Net Income
2006	$811,280,000	$48,118,000
2005	$721,569,000	$43,021,000

Curr. Assets:	$294,617,000	**Curr. Liab.:**	$105,662,000		
Plant, Equip.:	$140,295,000	**Total Liab.:**	$205,147,000	**Indic. Yr. Divd.:**	NA
Total Assets:	$504,602,000	**Net Worth:**	$299,455,000	**Debt/ Equity:**	1.9847

Baldwin & Lyons Inc

1099 N Meridian St., Indianapolis, IN, 46204; *PH:* 1-317-636-9800; *Fax:* 1-317-632-9444; *http://* www.baldwinandlyons.com

General - Incorporation	IN	**Stock**- Price on:12/24/2007	$25.5
Employees	279	Stock Exchange	NYSE
Auditor	Ernst & Young LLP	Ticker Symbol	BWINB
Stk Agt	National City Bank	Outstanding Shares	15,140,000
Counsel	NA	E.P.S	NA
DUNS No.	04-282-3336	Shareholders	NA

Business: The group's principle activities are to market and underwrite property and casualty insurance for motor carrier industry. The insurance products consist of fleet trucking insurance, voluntary assumption reinsurance, private passenger automobile insurance, small fleet trucking insurance and small business workers' compensation insurance. The fleet trucking segment provides multiple line insurance coverage to large trucking fleets. The non-standard private passenger automobile segment provides motor vehicle liability and physical damage coverage to individuals. The reinsurance assumed segment accepts retrocession from selected reinsurance companies, reinsuring against catastrophes. The group, through its subsidiaries, is licensed to do business in all the 50 states of the United States, all the Canadian provinces and Bermuda. The group's quarterly revenue for September 2007 was 57.28 millions of USD.

Primary SIC and add'l.: 6321 6211 6331

CIK No: 0000009346

Subsidiaries: B & L Insurance, Ltd., Baldwin & Lyons, California, Protective Insurance Company, Sagamore Insurance Company

Officers: Gary Wayne Miller/Chmn., CEO/$1,266,593.00, James William Good/Exec. VP/$1,122,098.00, Joseph James Devito/Dir., COO, Pres./$1,010,538.00, Patrick G. Corydon/CFO, Sr. VP/$653,095.00, James Edward Kirschner/Sr. VP, Sec./$631,156.00

Directors: Gary Wayne Miller/Chmn., CEO, James William Good/Exec. VP, Joseph James Devito/Dir., COO, Pres., John M. O'Mara/Dir., John A. Pigott/Dir., Norton Shapiro/Dir., John D. Weil/Dir., Stuart Douglas Bilton/Dir., Otto N. Frenzel/Dir., Thomas H. Patrick/Dir., Robert Shapiro/Dir., Nathan Shapiro/Dir., Kenneth D. Sacks/Dir., Steven A. Shapiro/Dir.

Owners: John A. Pigott, Otto N. Frenzel, Joseph J. DeVito, John D. Weil, Otto N. Frenzel, Steven A. Shapiro, Steven A. Shapiro, Insiders, Jon Mills, Norton Shapiro, John M. O'Mara, Thomas H. Patrick, G. Patrick Corydon, Thomas H. Patrick, John A. Pigott *(32 Owners included in Index)*

Baldwin Technology Co Inc

2 Trap Falls Rd., Ste. 402, Shelton, CT, 06484; *PH:* 1-203-402-1000; *Fax:* 1-203-402-5500; *http://* www.baldwintech.com

General - Incorporation	DE	**Stock**- Price on:12/24/2007	$6.1
Employees	513	Stock Exchange	AMEX
Auditor	PricewaterhouseCoopers LLP	Ticker Symbol	BLD
Stk Agt	Registrar & Transfer Co	Outstanding Shares	15,340,000
Counsel	Morgan, Lewis & Bockius LLP	E.P.S	$0.40
DUNS No.	18-337-9239	Shareholders	NA

Business: The group's principal activity is to manufacture controls and accessories equipment for the printing industry. The group's products include cleaning systems, fluid management and ink control systems, Web press protection systems, drying systems and newspaper inserter equipment. The customers of the group are printing press manufacturers and printers. The group sells its products in The Americas, Europe and Asia.

Primary SIC and add'l.: 3555

CIK No: 0000805792

Subsidiaries: Acrotec UK Ltd., Baldwin (UK) Ltd., Baldwin Americas Corporation, Baldwin Americas do Brasil Ltda, Baldwin Asia Pacific Corporation, Baldwin Europe Consolidated BV, Baldwin Europe Consolidated Inc., Baldwin France Sarl, Baldwin Germany GmbH, Baldwin Globaltec Ltd., Baldwin Graphic Equipment BV, Baldwin Graphic Equipment Pty. Ltd., Baldwin Graphic Systems, Inc., Baldwin India Private, Ltd., Baldwin Italy Srl 25 Subsidiaries included in the Index

Officers: Gerald A. Nathe/Chmn., CEO, Vijay C. Tharani/CFO, VP, Treasurer, Leon Richards/Controller, Helen P. Oster/Dir. - Investor Relations, Shaun Kilfoyle/Pres. - America, Peter Tkachuk/MD - Australia, Dominique Durand/Technical Service - Australia, Alexandre Menezes/Dir. - Service, Brazil, Martin Buttlar/MD - Central Eastern Europe, Hans Wendt/Sales Mgr. - Central, Eastern Europe, Peter Loew/Sales Mgr. - Central, Eastern Europe, Werner Kettl/Technical Service - Central, Eastern Europe, Chan Sui Man/Technical Service, Samir Gupta/Operations Mgr. - Technical Services, India, Aldo Parodi/Dir. - Italy *(38 Officers included in Index)*

Directors: Gerald A. Nathe/Chmn., CEO, Samuel B. Fortenbaugh/Dir., Judith A. Mulholland/Dir., Rolf Bergstrom/Dir., Mark T. Becker/Dir., Ronald B. Salvagio/Dir., Akira Hara/Dir., Ralph R. Whitney/Dir., Karl S. Puehringer/Dir., COO, Pres., Frederick J. Westlake/Dir.

Owners: Dimensional FundAdvisors Inc./5.53%, John P. Jordan, Gerald A. Nathe/3.03%, Shaun J. Kilfoyle, Royce& Associates, LLC/6.53%, Rolf Bergstrom, Ronald B. Salvagio, Gabelli Asset Management, Inc./11.05%, Ralph R. Whitney, Mark T. Becker, Judith A. Mulholland, Karl S. Puehringer/1.41%, Insiders/10.40%, Akira Hara/3.47%, Red Oak Partners, LLC/5.61% *(18 Owners included in Index)*

Financial Data: Fiscal Year End:06/30 Latest Annual Data: 6/30/2006

Year	Sales	Net Income
2006	$179,380,000	$6,258,000
2005	$173,185,000	$5,035,000
2004	$158,110,000	$6,986,000

Curr. Assets:	$82,779,000	**Curr. Liab.:**	$53,014,000	**P/E Ratio:**	19.06
Plant, Equip.:	$3,617,000	**Total Liab.:**	$66,830,000	**Indic. Yr. Divd.:**	NA
Total Assets:	$112,763,000	**Net Worth:**	$45,933,000	**Debt/ Equity:**	0.5060

Ball Corp

10 Longs Peak Dr., Broomfield, CO, 80021; *PH:* 1-303-469-3131; *Fax:* 1-303-460-2127; *http://* www.ball.com; *Email:* corpinfo@ball.com

General - Incorporation	IN	**Stock**- Price on:12/24/2007	$54.59
Employees	15,500	Stock Exchange	NYSE
Auditor	PricewaterhouseCoopers LLP	Ticker Symbol	BLL
Stk Agt	EquiServe Trust Co N.A	Outstanding Shares	102,100,000
Counsel	NA	E.P.S	$3.50
DUNS No.	00-641-9147	Shareholders	NA

Business: The groups principle activity is to manufacture metal and plastic packaging, primarily for beverages and foods, and a supplier of aerospace and other technologies and services to government and commercial customers. Specific customers of the group include Sab Miller Plc and Pepsico, Inc. The group operates from United States.

Primary SIC and add'l.: 3769 8711 3679 3812 3411 3221

CIK No: 0000009389

Subsidiaries: Ball (France) Holdings, S.A.S., Ball (France) Investment Holdings, S.A.S., Ball (Luxembourg) Finance S.a.r.l., Ball (UK) Holdings, Ltd., Ball Asia Pacific Beijing Metal Container Limited, Ball Asia Pacific Holdings Limited, Ball Asia Pacific Hubei Metal Container Limited, Ball Asia Pacific Limited, Ball Asia Pacific Shenzhen Metal Container Limited, Ball Asia Services Limited, Ball Capital Corp. II, Ball Company Ltd., Ball Europe Ltd., Ball European Holdings S.a.r.l., Ball Holdings S.a.r.l. 38 Subsidiaries included in the Index

Officers: Terence P. Voce/59/Chmn., CEO - Ball Asia Pacific Limited, David L. Taylor/CEO, Pres. - Ball Aerospace, Technologies Corp, David R. Hoover/63/Chmn., CEO, Pres./$6,285,504.00, Michael W. Feldser/57/Pres. - Ball Metal Food, Household Packaging Division, Americas, Charles E. Baker/51/VP, General Counsel, David A. Westerlund/58/Exec. VP - Administration, Corp. Sec./$1,694,572.00, Harold L. Sohn/62/Sr. VP - Corporate Relations, Douglas K. Bradford/51/VP, Controller, John R. Friedery/52/COO, Sr. VP - Packaging Products, Americas/$1,726,837.00, Scott C. Morrison/46/VP, Treasurer, John A. Hayes/43/Sr. VP, Pres. - Ball Packaging Europe/$1,599,378.00, Michael D. Herdman/58/Pres. - Metal Beverage Container Operations, Ann Scott/Primary Investor Relations Officer, Lisa A. Pauley/VP - Administration, Compliance, Leroy J. Williams/VP - Information Technology, Services *(17 Officers included in Index)*

Directors: David R. Hoover/63/Chmn., CEO, Pres., Jan Nicholson/Dir., Stuart A. Taylor/Dir., Hanno C. Fiedler/Dir., George A. Sissel/Dir., Georgia Nelson/Dir., Howard M. Dean/Dir., Erik H. Van Der Kaay/Dir., John F. Lehman/Dir., Theodore M. Solso/61/Dir., George M. Smart/Dir., John W. Fisher/Dir.

Owners: Stuart A. Taylor, Jan Nicholson, David R. Hoover/1.50%, Theodore M. Solso, Erik H. van der Kaay, John R. Friedery, Georgia R. Nelson, Hanno C. Fiedler, Iridian Asset Management LLC/6.40%, Raymond L. Seabrook, David A. Westerlund, George M. Smart, Lord Abbett& Co./8.70%, Howard M. Dean, John F. Lehman *(20 Owners included in Index)*

Financial Data: **Fiscal Year End:**12/31 **Latest Annual Data:** 12/31/2006

Year	Sales	Net Income
2006	NA	NA
2005	NA	NA
2004	NA	NA

Curr. Assets:	$1,761,300,000	**Curr. Liab.:**	$1,454,300,000	**P/E Ratio:**	19.06
Plant, Equip.:	$1,876,000,000	**Total Liab.:**	$4,674,500,000	**Indic. Yr. Divd.:**	$0.400
Total Assets:	$5,840,900,000	**Net Worth:**	$1,165,400,000	**Debt/ Equity:**	NA

Ballantyne of Omaha Inc

4350 McKinley St., Omaha, NE, 68112; ***PH:*** 1-402-453-4444; ***Fax:*** 1-402-453-7238; ***http://*** www.ballantyne-omaha.com

General - Incorporation	DE	**Stock**- Price on:12/24/2007	$6.17
Employees	197	Stock Exchange	AMEX
Auditor	KPMG LLP	Ticker Symbol	BTN
Stk Agt	First Chicago Trust Co.	Outstanding Shares	13,800,000
Counsel	Marks Clare & Richards	E.P.S	$0.004
DUNS No.	08-582-6485	Shareholders	NA

Business: The group's principal activity is to design, develop, manufacture and distribute commercial motion picture equipment, lighting systems, audiovisual equipment and restaurant equipment. The group's lighting segment manufactures and distributes lighting equipment under the names strong (R), xenotech(R) and sky-tracker (r). Strong is a supplier of long-range follow spotlights. Xenotech is a supplier of high intensity searchlights and computer-based lighting systems for the motion picture production, television, live entertainment, theme park and architectural industries. Sky-tracker sells and rents computer and manually operated high intensity searchlights. The audiovisual segment provides audiovisual services to the hotel and convention industries. The group' products are marketed through a network of over 100 domestic and international dealers.

Primary SIC and add'l.: 5043 3648 3589

CIK No: 0000946454

Subsidiaries: Design & Manufacturing, Inc, Strong Westrex, Inc

Officers: John P. Wilmers/Dir., CEO, Pres./$266,295.00, Ray F. Boegner/Sr. VP/$182,104.00, Kevin S. Herrmann/Sec. Treasurer, CFO/$113,983.00, Chris D. Stark/VP - Operations, Paul Rabinovitz/VP - Lighting, P. L. Wong/GM - Strong Westrex, Thomas A. McLaughlin/Controller, Gerhard Marburg/VP - Manufacturing, Brian Hendricks/GM - Design, Manufacturing

Directors: John P. Wilmers/Dir., CEO, Pres., William F. Welsh/Chmn., Alvin Abramson/Dir., Marc E. Lebaron/Dir., Mark D. Hasebroock/Dir., Christopher E. Beach/Dir.

Owners: William F. Welsh/1.10%, Marc E. LeBaron, Ray F. Boegner, Alvin Abramson, Pequot Capital Management,Inc./10.90%, Insiders/6.90%, Kevin S. Herrmann, Cramer Rosenthal McGlynn, LLC/8.90%, John P. Wilmers/2.10%, Christopher E. Beach/1.90%, Mark D. Hasebroock

Financial Data: **Fiscal Year End:**12/31 **Latest Annual Data:** 12/31/2006

Year	Sales	Net Income
2006	$49,732,000	$1,568,000
2005	$53,857,000	$4,309,000
2004	$49,145,000	$5,073,000

Curr. Assets:	$42,061,000	**Curr. Liab.:**	$7,087,000	**P/E Ratio:**	293.81
Plant, Equip.:	$4,855,000	**Total Liab.:**	$7,518,000	**Indic. Yr. Divd.:**	NA
Total Assets:	$49,908,000	**Net Worth:**	$42,389,000	**Debt/ Equity:**	NA

Ballard Power Systems Inc

9000 Glenlyon Pkwy., Burnaby, BC, V5J 5J8; ***PH:*** 1-604-454-0900; ***http://*** www.ballard.com; ***Email:*** investors@ballard.com

General - Incorporation	Canada	**Stock**- Price on:12/24/2007	$4.94
Employees	1,300	Stock Exchange	NDQ
Auditor	KPMG LLP	Ticker Symbol	BLDP
Stk Agt	Computershare Trust Co of Canada	Outstanding Shares	114,370,000
Counsel	Lang Michener	E.P.S	-$1.49
DUNS No.	25-327-7073	Shareholders	NA

Business: The group's principle activities are to develop, manufacture and market proton exchange membrane fuel cells, fuel cell engines, sub-systems, electric drives and power electronic products. The group operates in three business segments: fuel cells, fuel cell and other systems and carbon products. The fuel cells segment develops, manufactures and markets proton exchange membrane fuel cells. The fuel cell and other systems segment provides power for transportation engines and stationary power plants. The carbon products segment develops, manufactures and markets carbon materials for automotive and fuel cell applications. The group operates in the United States, Japan, Germany and other countries. The group's quarterly revenue for September 2007 was 17.57 millions of USD.

Primary SIC and add'l.: 3629 5989

CIK No: 0000933777

Subsidiaries: Ballard GmbH, Ballard Material Products Inc., Ballard Power Systems Corporation, Ebara Ballard Corporation

Officers: John Sheridan/CEO, Pres., W. G. Douglas/Dir. - Whitehead, British Columbia, Canada, David J. Smith/Dir., VP, CFO, Nick Kovics/Contact - Investor Relations, Lee Craft/VP - Operations, Christopher Guzy/CTO, VP, Noordin Nanji/VP, Chief Customer Officer, Peter Stickler/VP - Human Resources, Lori Vetter/Contact - Investor Relations, Rebecca Young/Contact - Media Relations

Directors: David J. Smith/Dir., VP, CFO, Ian A. Bourne/Dir., Ed Kilroy/Dir., David Prystash/Dir., Gerhard Schmidt/Dir., Gerri Sinclair/Dir., David B. Sutcliffe/Dir., Mark Suwyn/Dir., Thomas Weber/Dir., C. S. Park/Dir., Hans-Joachim Schopf/Dir., Douglas W.G. Whitehead/Dir.

Financial Data: **Fiscal Year End:**12/31 **Latest Annual Data:** 12/31/2006

Year	Sales	Net Income
2006	$49,823,000	-$181,137,000
2005	$53,733,000	-$86,983,000
2004	$81,373,000	-$169,157,000

Curr. Assets:	$221,153,000	**Curr. Liab.:**	$34,004,000		
Plant, Equip.:	$51,280,000	**Total Liab.:**	$44,945,000	**Indic. Yr. Divd.:**	NA
Total Assets:	$350,038,000	**Net Worth:**	$305,093,000	**Debt/ Equity:**	NA

Ballistic Recovery Systems Inc

300 Airport Rd., South St. Paul, MN, 55075; ***PH:*** 1-651-457-7491; ***Fax:*** 1-651-457-8651; ***http://*** www.brsparachutes.com; ***Email:*** info@brsparachutes.com

General - Incorporation	MN	**Stock**- Price on:12/24/2007	$1.65
Employees	50	Stock Exchange	OTC
Auditor	Virchow, Krause & Co. LLP	Ticker Symbol	BRSI
Stk Agt	Registrar & Transfer Co	Outstanding Shares	10,170,000
Counsel	NA	E.P.S	$0.01
DUNS No.	03-629-7273	Shareholders	NA

Business: The group's principle activities include designing, manufacturing and marketing emergency parachute recovery systems for use in the general aviation and recreational aircraft. These systems are designed to bring down the entire aircraft and its occupants under the parachute canopy in the event of an in-air emergency. Recreational aviation products include products designed and manufactured for use on unregistered aircraft such as ultralights and aircraft that registered with the federal aviation administration as experimental. The products are sold directly to individuals and through dealers and distributors. The group's quarterly revenue for June 2007 was 2.61 millions of USD. The group operates from United States.

Primary SIC and add'l.: 8731 3728

CIK No: 0000801907

Subsidiaries: BRS de Mexico S.A. de C.V.

Officers: Larry E. Williams/Dir., CEO, Pres., John M. Gilmore/VP - Sales, Don R. Hedquist/CFO, Frank Hoffmann/VP - Engineering, Gary Moore/VP - International Operations, Government Sales, Randy Bakeberg/Mgr. - Production, Ken Marek/Purchasing Mgr., Peter Truitt/Quality Assurance

Directors: Larry E. Williams/Dir., CEO, Pres., Robert L. Nelson/Chmn., Edward L. Underwood/Dir., Boris Popov/61/Dir., Thomas H. Adams/71/Dir., Darrel D. Brandt/64/Dir.

Owners: John M. Gilmore, Insiders/34.00%, Larry E. Williams, Thomas H. Adams/1.90%, Don Hedquist, Fernando Caralt/11.90%, Cirrus Design Corporation/10.20%, CIMSA Ingenieria de Sistemas, S.A./11.90%, Edward L. Underwood, Darrel D. Brandt/15.00%, Boris Popov/4.10%, Robert L. Nelson

Financial Data: **Fiscal Year End:**09/30 **Latest Annual Data:** 9/30/2006

Year	Sales	Net Income
2006	$9,192,000	$27,000
2005	$8,116,000	-$1,120,000
2004	$6,559,000	$301,000

Curr. Assets:	$3,359,000	**Curr. Liab.:**	$1,363,000	**P/E Ratio:**	165.00
Plant, Equip.:	$585,000	**Total Liab.:**	$2,412,000	**Indic. Yr. Divd.:**	NA
Total Assets:	$5,415,000	**Net Worth:**	$3,003,000	**Debt/ Equity:**	0.0596

Ballston Spa Bancorp Inc

87 Front St., Ballston Spa, NY, 12020; ***PH:*** 1-518-885-6781; ***Fax:*** 1-518-885-6711; ***http://*** www.bsnb.com

General - Incorporation		**Stock**- Price on:12/24/2007	$38.75
Employees	NA	Stock Exchange	OTC
Auditor	NA	Ticker Symbol	BSPA
Stk Agt	NA	Outstanding Shares	NA
Counsel	NA	E.P.S	NA
DUNS No.	NA	Shareholders	NA

Business: The groups principle activity is to provide community banking products and services. The groups convenience services include online banking and bill pay, telephone banking, ATM, debit cards and deposit services. The groups personal services include checking, savings, premier plan, mortgages and home equity, consumer loans and credit cards. The group operates from United States.

Primary SIC and add'l.: 6021

CIK No: 0001227652

Bally Technologies Inc

Formerly: Alliance Gaming Corp

6601 S Bermuda Rd., Las Vegas, NV, 89119; ***PH:*** 1-702-584-7700; ***http://*** www.ballytech.com

General - Incorporation	NV	**Stock**- Price on:12/24/2007	$25.79
Employees	NA	Stock Exchange	NYSE
Auditor	Deloitte & Touche LLP	Ticker Symbol	BYI
Stk Agt	American Stock Transfer & Trust Co.	Outstanding Shares	NA
Counsel	NA	E.P.S	NA
DUNS No.	07-723-4177	Shareholders	NA

Business: The group's principle activities are to design, manufacture and distribute gaming machine and computerized monitoring systems for gaming machines at casinos. The group operates in two segments: gaming equipment and systems and casino operations. The gaming equipment and systems designs, manufactures and distributes gaming machines and computerized monitoring systems. The casino unit owns and operates two regional casinos. It has operations primarily in the United States with a significant sales and distribution office in Germany. The group's quarterly revenue for September 2007 was 15.20 millions of USD.

Primary SIC and add'l.: 7993 3999 7011 7999

CIK No: 0000002491

Subsidiaries: ACSC Acquisitions,Inc., Advanced Casino Systems Corporation, Alliance Holding Company, APT Games,Inc., Arcade Planet,Inc., Bally Gaming Africa (Proprietary) Ltd., Bally Gaming and Systems UK Limited, Bally Gaming and Systems, S.A., Bally Gaming de Puerto Rico,Inc., Bally Gaming Hong Kong Limited, Bally Gaming International GmbH, Bally Gaming International,Inc., Bally Gaming Macau Limited, Bally Gaming,Inc., BGI Acquisition Company 31 Subsidiaries included in the Index

Officers: Richard Haddrill/Dir., CEO, Pres., Rich Soltys/Sr. VP - TMS Product Group, Tom Doyle/VP - Product Management, Tom Reilly/VP - Systems Sales, East Coast, Srini Raghavan/VP, MD - Bally Technologies Systems Division India, Vijay Vanarase/VP - System Development, Joan Konsdorf/VP - Global Client Services, Catherine Burns/VP, MD Bally Pan - Asia, Denise Fritz/Dir. - Operations Support, Denyse Moore/Dir. - Client Services, Sridhar Laveti/Sr. Dir. - Client Services, Cheryl Miedema/Sr. Dir. - Client Services, Derik Mooberry/VP - Systems Sales, West Coast, Ramesh Srinivasan/Exec. VP, Robert Luciano/CTO *(22 Officers included in Index)*

Directors: Richard Haddrill/Dir., CEO, Pres., David Robbins/Chmn., Jacques Andre/Dir., Robert L. Guido/Dir., Kevin Verner/Dir.

Owners: Stephen Race, Robert Guido, Mark Lipparelli, Kevin Verner, Columbia Wanger Assets Management LP/7.34%, Robert Luciano/3.15%, Steven Des Champs, Insiders/13.66%, Ramesh Srinivasan, Robert L. Saxton, David Robbins/1.17%, Alfred Wilms/7.01%, Joel Kirschbaum/4.58%, Jacques Andr, FMR Corp/9.41% *(17 Owners included in Index)*

Financial Data: *Fiscal Year End:*06/30 *Latest Annual Data:* 6/30/2006

Year	Sales	Net Income
2006	$547,144,000	-$46,071,000
2005	$483,107,000	-$22,563,000
2004	$488,876,000	$84,514,000

Curr. Assets:	$329,354,000	**Curr. Liab.:**	$198,837,000		
Plant, Equip.:	$111,872,000	**Total Liab.:**	$543,119,000	**Indic. Yr. Divd.:**	NA
Total Assets:	$687,881,000	**Net Worth:**	$144,078,000	**Debt/ Equity:**	2.1896

Bally Total Fitness Holding Corp

8700 W Bryn Mawr Ave., Chicago, IL, 60631; ***PH:*** 1-773-380-3000; ***Fax:*** 1-773-693-2982; ***http://*** www.ballyfitness.com

General - Incorporation	DE	**Stock**- Price on:12/24/2007	NA
Employees	NA	Stock Exchange	OTC
Auditor	Alixpartners, LLP	Ticker Symbol	BFTH
Stk Agt	NA	Outstanding Shares	NA
Counsel	NA	E.P.S	NA
DUNS No.	NA	Shareholders	NA

Business: The groups principal activity is to operate fitness centers. The group also provides additional services including personal training, its branded apparel, nutrition products and weight management program. The group operates from the North America and Canada

Primary SIC and add'l.: 3949 7999 2844 7991

CIK No: 0000770944

Subsidiaries: 59thStreet Gym LLC, 708 Gym LLC, Ace LLC, Bally ARA Corporation, Bally Fitness Franchising, Inc., Bally Franchise RSC, Inc., Bally Franchising Holdings, Inc., Bally Matrix Fitness Center Ltd., Bally Real Estate I LLC, Bally Real EstateII LLC, Bally Real EstateIII LLC, Bally Real EstateIV LLC, Bally REFS West Hartford, LLC, Bally Sports Clubs, Inc., Bally Total Fitness Corporation 63 Subsidiaries included in the Index

Officers: Don R. Kornstein/56/Interim Chmn., Chief Restructuring Officer, Teresa R. Willows/49/Sr. VP - Customer Care, Member Services, Mike Divello/Assist. Dir. - Personal Training, Sharon Knecht/Dir. - Training, Education The Northern Ohio, Pittsburgh, Charles Little/Assist. Dir. - Fitness Education, Robert Stockwell/Assoc. Trainer, Norris Tomlinson/National Dir. - Training, David Van Daff/Dir. - Personal Training Operations, Julie Adams/62/Sr. VP - Membership Services, Marc D. Bassewitz/51/Sr. VP, Sec., General Counsel, Ronald G. Eidell/64/Sr. VP, CFO, William G. Fanelli/46/Sr. VP - Corporate Development, Gail J. Holmberg/52/CIO, Sr. VP, Thomas S. Massimino/48/Sr. VP - Operations, Harold Morgan/51/Sr. VP, Chief Administrative Officer *(18 Officers included in Index)*

Directors: Don R. Kornstein/56/Interim Chmn., Chief Restructuring Officer, Barry R. Elson/67/Dir., Charles J. Burdick/56/Dir.

Owners: Emanuel R. Pearlman/11.20%, Marc D. Bassewitz, Carl Landeck, S.A.C. Capital Advisors LLC/6.70%, John H. Wildman, Paul A. Toback/1.66%, Pardus Capital Management L.P./14.80%, James A. McDonald, Dimensional FundAdvisors Inc./7.60%

Curr. Assets:	$76,333,000	**Curr. Liab.:**	$959,798,000	**P/E Ratio:**	3.78
Plant, Equip.:	$247,797,000	**Total Liab.:**	$1,797,193,000	**Indic. Yr. Divd.:**	NA
Total Assets:	$396,771,000	**Net Worth:**	-$1,400,422,000	**Debt/ Equity:**	NA

Balsam Ventures Inc

1480 Gulf Rd., Ste. 204, Point Roberts, WA, 98281; ***PH:*** 1-360-305-5012

General - Incorporation	NV	**Stock**- Price on:12/24/2007	$0.11
Employees	1	Stock Exchange	OTC
Auditor	Telford Sadovnick, PLLC	Ticker Symbol	BLSV
Stk Agt	Pacific Stock Transfer Company	Outstanding Shares	36,230,000
Counsel	NA	E.P.S	$0.00
DUNS No.	NA	Shareholders	NA

Business: The group's principle activities include developing and marketing a Web site on the Internet atwww.usacitizenship. .net designed to provide information on the processof immigrating int o the United States from foreign countries. The group operates from United States.

Primary SIC and add'l.: 7375

CIK No: 0001103092

Officers: John Boschert/38/CEO, Pres., Sec., Treasurer, Dir., CFO

Directors: John Boschert/38/CEO, Pres., Sec., Treasurer, Dir., CFO

Owners: John Boschert/23.20%, NorPac Technologies, Inc./15.20%

Financial Data: *Fiscal Year End:*12/31 *Latest Annual Data:* 12/31/2006

Year	Sales	Net Income
2006	NA	-$419,000
2005	NA	-$154,000
2004	NA	-$307,000

Curr. Assets:	$2,000	**Curr. Liab.:**	$366,000		
Plant, Equip.:	NA	**Total Liab.:**	$366,000	**Indic. Yr. Divd.:**	NA
Total Assets:	$2,000	**Net Worth:**	-$363,000	**Debt/ Equity:**	NA

Baltia Air Lines Inc

6325 Saunders St. Apt 7i, Rego Park, NY, 11374; ***PH:*** 1-718-275-5205; ***http://*** www.baltia.com

General - Incorporation	NY	**Stock**- Price on:12/24/2007	$0.046
Employees	4	Stock Exchange	OTC
Auditor	Michael F. Cronin, CPA	Ticker Symbol	BLTA
Stk Agt	Continental Stock Transfer & Trust Co	Outstanding Shares	130,480,000
Counsel	NA	E.P.S	-$0.04
DUNS No.	NA	Shareholders	NA

Business: The groups principal activity is to provide air transportation. The group operates from the United States and Moscow.

Primary SIC and add'l.: 4512

CIK No: 0000869187

Officers: Igor Dmitrowsky/CEO, Pres., Steffanie Lewis/General Counsel, Jeffrey Fessler/Securities Counsel, Steven Orlikoff/Of Counsel, Larry Hecker/VP - Operations, Victoria Charlton/VP - International Relations, Andris Rukmanis/VP - Europe, Bob Storm/VP - Public Relations, Barry Clare/Dir. - Investor Relations, Steven Reiss/Dir. - Telemarketing, Nick Oppegard/Dir. - General Planning, Rita Gurvich/Dir. - Personnel, Nina Morozova/Dir. - Accounting, Kari Tkkanen/Dir. - Cargo Sales, Hans Wolf/Dir. - Cargo Handling *(19 Officers included in Index)*

Directors: Anita Schiff-Spielman/53/Dir.

Owners: Anita Schiff-Spielman, Andris Rukmanis, Steffanie J. Lewis/5.24%, Walter Kaplinsky/3.73%, Igor Dmitrowsky/39.58%, Insiders/44.63%

Financial Data: *Fiscal Year End:*12/31 *Latest Annual Data:* 12/31/2006

Year	Sales	Net Income
2006	NA	-$1,209,000
2005	NA	-$721,000
2004	NA	-$338,000

Curr. Assets:	$4,000	**Curr. Liab.:**	$1,000		
Plant, Equip.:	$3,000	**Total Liab.:**	$1,000	**Indic. Yr. Divd.:**	NA
Total Assets:	$7,000	**Net Worth:**	$6,000	**Debt/ Equity:**	NA

Baltimore Gas and Electric Co

750 E Pratt St., Baltimore, MD, 21202; ***PH:*** 1-410-783-2800; ***Fax:*** 1-410-712-9323; ***http://*** www.bge.com

General - Incorporation	MD	**Stock**- Price on:12/24/2007	$89.25
Employees	9,645	Stock Exchange	NYSE
Auditor	PricewaterhouseCoopers LLP	Ticker Symbol	NA
Stk Agt	American Stock Transfer & Trust Co.	Outstanding Shares	180,310,000
Counsel	NA	E.P.S	$5.60
DUNS No.	15-617-1464	Shareholders	NA

Business: The group's principle activities include producing, purchasing and selling electrical energy; purchases, transports, brokers and sells natural gas; holdsinterests in power generation p rojects which operate, maintain and sell electrical energy; holds interests in various financial investments including security portfolios, financial guarantee company, senior living projects, and other real estate projects; sells, installs and services commercial and residential heating, air conditioning, and plumbing systems, as well as various gas and electrical appliances; and provides kitchen remodeling services, lighting and mechanical engineering services, and brokering and associated financial contracts services. The group operates from United States.

Primary SIC and add'l.: 4923 6211 4931 1711 6512

CIK No: 0000009466

Subsidiaries: Baltimore Gas and Electric Company., BGE Capital Trust II, BGE Home Products& Services,Inc., Calvert Cliffs Nuclear Power Plant,Inc., CEG Acquisition, LLC, Constellation Energy Commodities Group,Inc., Constellation Energy Projects and Services Group,Inc., Constellation Enterprises,Inc., Constellation Generation Group, LLC, Constellation Holdings,Inc., Constellation Investments,Inc., Constellation NewEnergy, Inc, Constellation Nuclear Services,Inc., Constellation Power Source Generation,Inc., Constellation Power Source Holdings,Inc. 20 Subsidiaries included in the Index

Officers: Mayo A. Shattuck/53/Chmn., CEO, Pres., Kenneth W. Defontes/53/Dir., CEO, Pres., Johnny Magwood/Sr. VP - Customer Relations, Accounting Services, Mark Case/Sr. VP - Strategy, Regulatory Affairs, Follin E. Smith/48/CFO, Sr. VP, Chief Administrative Officer, Thomas Valenti/Sr. VP - Logistics Management Services, Carol Dodson/VP - Business Transformation, Malinda Small/VP - BGE Communications, Stephen Woerner/Sr. VP - Electric Business Operations, Planning, Jeannette Mills/Sr. VP - Gas Business Operations, Planning, Christopher A. Burton/Sr. VP - Asset Management Services, Brian Daschbach/Sr. VP - Integrated Field Services

Directors: Kenneth W. Defontes/53/Dir., CEO, Pres., Mayo A. Shattuck/53/Chmn., CEO, Pres., Yves C. De Balmann/Dir., Douglas L. Becker/Dir., James R. Curtiss/Dir., Freeman A. Hrabowski/Dir., Michael D. Sullivan/Dir., Robert J. Lawless/Dir., Nancy Lampton/Dir.

Financial Data: *Fiscal Year End:*12/31 *Latest Annual Data:* 12/31/2006

Year	Sales	Net Income
2006	$19,284,900,000	$936,400,000
2005	$17,132,000,000	$623,100,000
2004	$12,549,700,000	$539,700,000

Curr. Assets:	$6,254,800,000	**Curr. Liab.:**	$6,605,500,000		
Plant, Equip.:	$10,385,500,000	**Total Liab.:**	$15,657,800,000	**Indic. Yr. Divd.:**	$1.740
Total Assets:	$20,199,300,000	**Net Worth:**	$4,519,600,000	**Debt/ Equity:**	NA

BancFirst Corp

101 N Broadway, Ste. 200, Oklahoma City, OK, 73102; ***PH:*** 1-405-270-1086; ***Fax:*** 1-405-270-1089; ***http://*** www.bancfirst.com

General - Incorporation ....OK
Employees 1,400
Auditor ....Grant Thornton LLP
Stk Agt............BancFirst Trust & Investment Mgt
Counsel ....NA
DUNS No. 14-495-6158

Stock- Price on:12/24/2007 ....$44
Stock Exchange............NDQ
Ticker Symbol............BANF
Outstanding Shares 15,760,000
E.P.S............$3.15
Shareholders............NA

Business: The group's principal activities are to provide retail and commercial banking services which includes commercial, real estate, agricultural and consumer lending; depository and funds transfer services; collections; safe deposit boxes, cash management services, retail brokerage services and other services. The group also offers trust services and acts as executor, administrator, trustee, transfer agent and in various other fiduciary capacities, item processing, research and other correspondent banking services to financial institutions and government units. The group provides a full range of commercial banking services to retail customers and small to medium-sized businesses through 86 banking locations serving 44 communities of Oklahoma region. On 14-Oct-2003, the group acquired Lincoln National Bancorporation.

Primary SIC and add'l.: 6712 6022

CIK No: 0000760498

Subsidiaries: BancFirst, BancFirst Agency, Inc., BancFirst Community Development Corporation, BFC Capital Trust I, BFC Capital Trust II, Century Life Assurance Company, Citibanc Insurance Agency, Inc., Council Oak Investment Corporation, Council Oak Partners, LLC, Lender Collection Corporation, Park State Bank, Wilcox & Jones, Inc.

Officers: David Rainbolt/CEO/$379,370.00, Randy Foraker/Exec. VP

Owners: William O. Johnstone/0.10%, Joe T. Shockley, Paul B. Odom, Insiders/48.33%, William H. Crawford/2.20%, Robert A. Gregory/0.03%, Dave R. Lopez/0.04%, John C. Hugon/0.64%, Melvin Moran/0.86%, Dennis L. Brand/0.24%, Donald B. Halverstadt/0.05%, BancFirst Corporation/6.35%, Darryl Schmidt/0.16%, G. Rainey Williams, J. Ralph McCalmont/1.24% *(24 Owners included in Index)*

Financial Data: **Fiscal Year End:**12/31 **Latest Annual Data:** 12/31/2006

Year	Sales	Net Income
2006	$271,649,000	$49,352,000
2005	$225,990,000	$42,835,000
2004	$196,856,000	$37,176,000

Curr. Assets:	$515,637,000	**Curr. Liab.:**	$3,005,545,000	**P/E Ratio:**	14.33
Plant, Equip.:	$83,715,000	**Total Liab.:**	$3,070,219,000	**Indic. Yr. Divd.:**	NA
Total Assets:	$3,418,574,000	**Net Worth:**	$348,355,000	**Debt/ Equity:**	0.0778

Banco Bilbao Vizcaya Argentaria

1345 Ave. of the Americas, 45th Fl., New York, NY, 10105; *PH:* 1-212-728-1500; *Fax:* 1-212-333-2906; *http://* www.bbv.es; *Email:* atencion.clientes@grupobbva.com

General - Incorporation ....Spain
Employees 98,553
Auditor ....Deloitte, S.L.
Stk Agt............Bank of New York
Counsel............Mario Fernandez Pelaz
DUNS No. 46-106-4446

Stock- Price on:12/24/2007 ....$24.66
Stock Exchange............NYSE
Ticker Symbol............BBV
Outstanding Shares 3,550,000,000
E.P.S............$1.94
Shareholders............NA

Business: The group's principle activity is to provide retail, corporate banking and other financial services in Europe , north, central and South America. As of 09/01/2003 the company reduced its business areas in the following manner retail banking; Spanish asset management, investment services and insurance activities. Wholesale and investment banking which include real estate and private equity areas and America area which accounts for all banking, pensions and insurance activities in the region, including bbva bancomer. The group operates from United States.

Primary SIC and add'l.: 6021

CIK No: 0000842180

Subsidiaries: Adm. De Fondos Para El Retiro-bancomer, S.a. De C.v., Administradora De Fondos De Pensiones Provida (afp Provida), Advera, S.a., Afp Genesis Administradora De Fondos, S.a., Afp Horizonte, S.a., Afp Prevision Bbv-adm. De Fondos De Pensiones, S.a., Almacenadora Financiera Provincial, Almacenadora Internacional, C.a., Almacenes Generales De Deposito, S.a.e. De, Almagrario, S.a., Altitude Investments Limited, Altura Markets, A.v., S.a., Ancla Investments, S.a., Anida Desarrollos Inmobiliarios, S.l., Anida Grupo Inmobiliario, S.l. 336 Subsidiaries included in the Index

Officers: Francisco Gonzalez Rodriguez/64/Chmn., CEO, Angel Boix Angel/44/Representing Dir. - Telefonica de Espana, Jose Maldonado Ramos/Dir., Sec., Jose Sevilla alvarez/49/Dir., Eduardo Arbizu Lostao/Head - Legal Tax, Audit, Compliance Department, Jose Ignacio Goirigolzarri Tellaeche/54/Dir., COO, Pres.

Directors: Francisco Gonzalez Rodriguez/64/Chmn., CEO, Roman Knorr Borras/69/Dir., Tomas Alfaro Drake/57/Dir., Enrique Medina Fernandez/Dir., Jose Maldonado Ramos/Dir., Sec., Ignacio Ferrero Jordi/63/Dir., Ricardo Lacasa Suarez/72/Dir., Juan Carlos Alvarez Mezquiriz/49/Dir., Telefonica D. Espana/Dir., Susana Rodriguez Vidarte/Dir., Richard C. Breeden/59/Dir., Carlos Loring Martinez De Irujo/61/Dir., Jose Ignacio Goirigolzarri Tellaeche/54/Dir., COO, Pres., Ramon Bustamante Y De La Mora/60/Dir., Jose Antonio Fernandez Rivero/59/Dir.

Owners: Charles W. Daniel, Ray G. Stone, Carl J. Gessler, Tranum Fitzpatrick, George M. Boltwood, Lee E. Harris, Paul D. Jones/1.50%, Insiders/4.00%, John S. Stein, Gregory P. Deming, Jerry W. Powell, William Eugene Davenport, Clayton D. Pledger, James D. Barri, Garrett R. Hegel *(19 Owners included in Index)*

Financial Data: **Fiscal Year End:**12/31 **Latest Annual Data:** 12/31/2006

Year	Sales	Net Income
2006	$40,078,483,000	$6,564,125,000
2005	$27,381,060,000	$2,389,750,000
2004	$23,405,323,000	$4,223,286,000

Curr. Assets:	$111,799,197,000	**Curr. Liab.:**	$382,066,732,000	**P/E Ratio:**	6.88
Plant, Equip.:	$5,156,326,000	**Total Liab.:**	$515,590,544,000	**Indic. Yr. Divd.:**	$0.680
Total Assets:	$555,808,425,000	**Net Worth:**	$40,217,880,000	**Debt/ Equity:**	NA

Banco Bradesco S.A.

Av. Paulista, 1.450 - 1 - CEP, So Paulo, NY, 01310-917; *PH:* 1-113-684-3311; *http://* www.bradescori.com.br/site/default.asp?menuid=168

General - Incorporation ....
Employees 79,306
Auditor ....NA
Stk Agt ....Citibank N.A
Counsel............NA
DUNS No. ....NA

Stock- Price on:12/24/2007 ....$25.26
Stock Exchange............NYSE
Ticker Symbol............BBD
Outstanding Shares 2,000,000,000
E.P.S............$1.64
Shareholders............NA

Business: The groups principal activity is to provide banking and financial products and services. The groups services and products including lending and deposit taking, credit card issuance, leasing, payment collection and processing. The group operates through two segments namely, banking services and saving plan services. The group operates from the Brazil. The groups total assts in the year 2005 was $206,594 (millions).

Primary SIC and add'l.: 6081

CIK No: 0001035683

Officers: Marico Arthur Laurelli Cypriano/Dir., CEO, Laercio Albino Cezar/Exec. VP, Arnaldo Alves Vieira/Exec. VP, Luiz Carlos Trabuco Cappi/Exec. VP, Sergio Socha/Exec. VP, Julio De Siqueira Carvallho De Araujo/54/Exec. VP, Milton Almicar Silva Vargas/Exec. VP, Jose Luiz Acar Pedro/Exec. VP, Norberto Pinto Barbedo/Exec. VP, Armando Trivelato Filho/MD, Carlos Alberto Rodriques Guilherme/MD, Jose Alcides Munhoz/MD, Jose Guilherme De Faria/MD, Luiz Pasteur Vasconcellos Machado/MD, Milton Matsumoto/MD *(21 Officers included in Index)*

Directors: Marico Arthur Laurelli Cypriano/Dir., CEO, Lazaro De Mello Brandao/Chmn., Antonio Bornia/Vice Chmn., Mario Da Silveira Teixeira/Dir., Ricardo Espirito Santo Silva Salgado/Dir., Joao Aguiar Alvarez/Dir., Denise Aguiar Alvarez Valente/Dir., Raul Santoro De Mattos Almeida/Dir.

Financial Data: **Fiscal Year End:**NA **Latest Annual Data:** 12/31/2006

Year	Sales	Net Income
2006	$25,629,605,000	$3,030,032,000
2005	$20,991,545,000	$2,710,776,000
2004	$14,305,082,000	$1,252,283,000

Curr. Assets:	$53,694,208,000	**Curr. Liab.:**	$62,133,471,000	**P/E Ratio:**	10.06
Plant, Equip.:	$1,406,700,000	**Total Liab.:**	$109,163,202,000	**Indic. Yr. Divd.:**	$0.090
Total Assets:	$121,572,172,000	**Net Worth:**	$12,408,970,000	**Debt/ Equity:**	NA

Banco De Chile

535 Madison Ave., 9th Fl., New York, NY, 10022; *PH:* 1-212-758-0909; *Fax:* 1-212-705-4450; *http://* www.bancochile.cl

General - Incorporation ..... Republic Of Chile
Employees 10,157
Auditor ....Ernst & Young LLP
Stk Agt ....Banco De Chile
Counsel............NA
DUNS No. ....NA

Stock- Price on:12/24/2007 ....$48.31
Stock Exchange............NYSE
Ticker Symbol............BCH
Outstanding Shares 117,610,000
E.P.S............$0.004
Shareholders............NA

Business: The group's principal activity is the provision of general banking services which include granting of loans, financing of foreign trade, dealing in money markets, syndicating and trading foreign loans, and accepting and placing deposits primarily with a diversified customer base, consisting of latin American, European, Asian and United States customers.

Primary SIC and add'l.: 6021

CIK No: 0001161125

Subsidiaries: Banchile Administradora General de Fondos S.A., Banchile Asesoria Financiera S.A., Banchile Corredores de Bolsa S.A., Banchile Corredores de Seguros Limitada, Banchile Factoring S.A., Banchile Securitizadora S.A., Banchile Trade Services Limited, Promarket S.A., Socofin S.A.

Officers: Fernando Canas Berkowitz/CEO, Marcelo Caracci Lagos/Operations, Technology Division Mgr., Julio Guzman Herrera/Corporate, International Division Mgr., Jacqueline Barrio/FVP, Dir. - Investor Relations, Oscar Mehech Castellon/Global Compliance Officer, Allan Becker/Sr. Analyst, Eduardo Ebensperger Orrego/Large Companies Division Mgr., Pedro Bolados Morales/Risk Control Division Mgr., Jorge Diaz Vial/Adviser, Gonzalo Rios Diaz/Marketing Division Mgr., Mauricio Baeza Letelier/Credit Risk Division Mgr., Jennie Coleman Alvarez/Mgr. - Human Resources Division, Francisco Garces Garrido/Adviser to The Board, Maximo Silva Bafalluy/Adviser to The Board, Arturo Concha Ureta/Finance Division Mgr. *(19 Officers included in Index)*

Directors: Andronico Luksic Craig/Vice Chmn., Pablo Granifo Lavin/Chmn., Jorge Awad Mehech/Dir., Guillermo Luksic Craig/Dir., Jorge Ergas Heymann/Alternate Dir., Jacob Ergas Ergas/Dir., Rodrigo Manubens Moltedo/Dir., Hernan Buchi Buc/Dir., Jaime Estevez Valencia/Dir., Fernando Quiroz Robles/Dir., Gonzalo Menendez Duque/Dir., Francisco Perez MacKenna/Dir., Thomas Furst Freiwirth/Alternate Dir.

Owners: Insiders/0.02%, SM-Chile S.A./58.26%, Jacob Ergas/6.41%, Quienco S.A./21.11%

Financial Data: **Fiscal Year End:**12/31 **Latest Annual Data:** 12/31/2006

Year	Sales	Net Income
2006	$1,828,902,000	$328,388,000
2005	$1,729,916,000	$328,327,000
2004	$1,278,137,000	$264,442,000

Curr. Assets:	$4,727,535,000	**Curr. Liab.:**	$16,730,239,000	**P/E Ratio:**	6.88
Plant, Equip.:	$385,962,000	**Total Liab.:**	$20,597,089,000	**Indic. Yr. Divd.:**	$1.950
Total Assets:	$23,402,283,000	**Net Worth:**	$2,805,194,000	**Debt/ Equity:**	NA

Banco Itau Holding Financeira S.A. (Holding Co)

Praa Alfredo Egydio de Souza Aranha 100, Torre Conceicao - 11, Sao Paulo, Rio de Janeiro; *PH:* 55-1150191549; *Fax:* 55-1150191133; *http://* www.itau.com

General - Incorporation ....Federative Republic of Brazil
Employees 59,921
Auditor ....PricewaterhouseCoopers LLP
Stk Agt ....Bank of New York
Counsel............Mr. Luciano da Silva Amaro
DUNS No. ....NA

Stock- Price on:12/24/2007 ....$45.37
Stock Exchange............NYSE
Ticker Symbol............ITU
Outstanding Shares 1,200,000,000
E.P.S............$1.82
Shareholders............NA

Business: The groups principle activity is to provide banking services. The groups services include credit cards, asset management and insurance, private retirement plans and capitalization plans and savings plan. The group operates from the Brazil and Argentina.

Primary SIC and add'l.: 6022

CIK No: 0001132597

Subsidiaries: Afinco Amricas Madeira, SGPS, Soc. Unipessoal Lda., Akbar Marketing e Servios Lda., Banco Fiat S.A., Banco Ita Buen Ayre S.A., Banco Ita S.A., Banco Ita-BBA S.A., Banco Itaucred Financiamentos S.A., Cia Ita de Capitalizao, Cia Itauleasing de Arrendamento Mercantil, Fiat Administradora de Consrcios Ltda, Financeira Americanas Ita S.A - Crdito, Financiamento e Investimento, Financeira Ita CBD S.A - Crdito, Financiamento e Investimento, Intrag Distribuidora de Ttulos e Valores Mobilirios Ltda., Ita Administradora de Consrcios Ltda., Ita Bank, Ltd. 22 Subsidiaries included in the Index

Officers: Roberto Egydio Setubal/54/Vice Chmn., CEO, Member - Board Of Executive Officers, International Member - Advisory Board, Luciano Da Silva Amaro/Legal Counsel, Rodolfo Henrique Fischer/Executive Officer, Iran Siqueira Lima/64/Pres. - Fiscal Counsel, Alberto Sozin Furuguem/65/Councilors, Silvio De Carvalho/Executive Officer, Jackson Ricardo Gomes/MD, Marco Antonio Antunes/49/MD, Wagner Roberto Pugliesi/50/MD, Fernando Alves De Almeida/56/Councilor, Member - Fiscal Counsel, Alfredo Egydio Setubal/50/Dir., Exec. VP, Candido Botelho Bracher/50/Exec. VP

Directors: Roberto Egydio Setubal/54/Vice Chmn., CEO, Member - Board Of Executive Officers, International Member - Advisory Board, Olavo Egydio Setubal/85/Chmn., Alfredo Egydio Arruda Villela Filho/Vice Chmn., Jose Carlos Moraes Abreu/86/Vice Chmn., Rubens Antonio Barbosa/Member - International Advisory Board, Fernando De Almeida Nobre Neto/Member - Advisory Board, Artur Eduardo Brochado Dos Santos Silva/Member - International Advisory Board, Luiz Eduardo Campello/Member - Advisory Board, Liciox Licio Meirelles Ferreira/Member - Advisory Board, Alcides Lopes Tapias/66/Dir., Carlos Da Camara Pestana/77/Dir., Fernao Carlos Botelho Bracher/73/Dir., Geraldo Jose Carbone/Dir., Guillermo Alejandro Cortina/Dir., Gustavo Jorge Laboissiere Loyola/56/Dir. *(22 Directors included in Index)*

Owners: PREVI - Caixa de Previdncia dos, Others/10.00%, ItasaInvestimentos Ita S.A., Bank of America Corporation/3.28%, PREVI - Caixa de Previdncia dos/6.74%, Bank of America Corporation/11.51%, Others/78.42%, Treasury Stock, Treasury Stock/3.32%, ItasaInvestimentos Ita S.A./85.30%

Financial Data: *Fiscal Year End:*12/31 *Latest Annual Data:* 12/31/2006

Year	Sales	Net Income
2006	$19,685,360,000	$2,764,634,000
2005	$14,389,452,000	$2,342,609,000
2004	$10,018,262,000	$1,744,238,000

Curr. Assets:	$37,775,522,000	**Curr. Liab.:**	$51,407,852,000	**P/E Ratio:**	10.06
Plant, Equip.:	$1,468,126,000	**Total Liab.:**	$77,520,424,000	**Indic. Yr. Divd.:**	$0.340
Total Assets:	$90,376,255,000	**Net Worth:**	$12,855,831,000	**Debt/ Equity:**	NA

Banco Macro S.A.

Sarmiento 401, Buenos Aires, 1041; *PH:* 54-1152226500; *http://* www.bansud.com.ar; *Email:* relacionesinstitucionales@macro.com.ar

General - Incorporation		**Stock**- Price on:12/24/2007	$34.44
Employees	NA	Stock Exchange	NYSE
Auditor	NA	Ticker Symbol	BMA
Stk Agt	Bank of New York	Outstanding Shares	683,900,000
Counsel	NA	E.P.S	$0.22
DUNS No.	NA	Shareholders	NA

Business: The groups principal activity is to provide traditional commercial banking products and services. The group also provides payroll services, lending, corporate credit care, mortgage finance, transaction processing and foreign exchange. In the year 2007, the group merged with Nuevo Banco Suquia S.A. The group operates from the Argentina. The groups total assts in the year 2006 was $13,578.01 (millions).

Primary SIC and add'l.: 6081 6029

CIK No:

Officers: Jorge Scarinci/Finance Officer, Officer in Charge - Investor Relations, Mario Eduardo Lanusse/Administrative Mgr., Eduardo Covello/Operations Mgr., Miguel Gurfinkiel/Government Banking Mgr., Rodolfo Lehmann/Money Laundering Prevention Mgr., Milagro Medrano/Management Control Mgr., Pablo Martijena/Investors Relations, Paola Gayoso/Investors Relations, Constanza Brito/Human Resources Mgr., Guillermo Goldberg/Deputy GM, Maria Begona Perez De Solay/Personal Banking Mgr., Francisco Sguera/Legal Affairs Mgr., Daniel Violatti/Accounting, Tax Mgr., Carmen Estevez/Internal Audit Officer, Ana Maria Marcet/Credit Risk Mgr. *(17 Officers included in Index)*

Directors: Jorge Horacio Brito/Chmn., D. J. Ezequiel Carballo/Vice Chmn., Carlos Enrique Videla/Dir., Juan Pablo Brito Devoto/Dir., Luis Carlos Cerolini/Dir., Jorge Pablo Brito/Dir., Roberto Julio Eilbaum/Dir., Alejandro MacFarlane/Dir., Guillermo Eduardo Stanley/Dir., Mario Eduardo Bartolome/Alternate Dir., Ernesto Eduardo Medina/Alternate Dir.

Financial Data: *Fiscal Year End:*NA *Latest Annual Data:* 12/31/2006

Year	Sales	Net Income
2006	$524,812,000	$130,450,000
2005	$346,961,000	$152,820,000

Curr. Assets:	$920,537,000	**Curr. Liab.:**	$3,293,983,000	**P/E Ratio:**	10.06
Plant, Equip.:	$137,069,000	**Total Liab.:**	$3,985,398,000	**Indic. Yr. Divd.:**	$0.490
Total Assets:	$4,623,915,000	**Net Worth:**	$638,517,000	**Debt/ Equity:**	NA

Banco Santander S.A

Formerly: Banco Santander Central Hispano

28660 Boadilla Del Monte, Madrid; ; *http://* www.gruposantander.com

General - Incorporation	Spain	**Stock**- Price on:12/24/2007	$18.6399
Employees	129,749	Stock Exchange	NYSE
Auditor	Deloitte, S.L.	Ticker Symbol	STD
Stk Agt	Morgan ADR Service Center	Outstanding Shares	6,250,000,000
Counsel	NA	E.P.S	$2.16
DUNS No.	56-399-2809	Shareholders	NA

Business: The group's principal activity is to operate as a bank, whose branch network covers the whole of Spain and it's main areas of concentration being Europe and Latin America. The company's main business areas are commercial banking, investment and pension funds, investment banking, corporate banking, Internet and telephone banking and treasury and capital markets.

Primary SIC and add'l.: 6021

CIK No: 0000891478

Subsidiaries: Abbey National Financial, Abbey National Offshore Holdings Limited, Banco Santa Cruz., Gibraltar Abbey National (Gibraltar) Limited., Puerto Rico, Santander BanCorp, Santander Consumer Finance S.A, Wells Fargo, Whitewick Limited

Officers: Alfredo Saenz/Vice Chmn., CEO, Alfredo Saenz Abad/66/Vice Chmn., CEO, David Arce/65/Exec. VP - Internal Auditing, Juan Manuel Cendoya/41/Exec. VP - Communications, Research, Jesus M. Zabalza/50/Exec. VP - America, Cesar Ortega/54/Exec. VP - General Secretariat, Fermin Colomes/59/Exec. VP - Operations, Juan Guitard/48/Exec. VP - General Secretariat, Marcial Portela/63/Exec. VP - America, Juan R. Inciarte/56/Exec. VP - Consumer Finance, Jorge Maortua/47/Exec. VP - Global Wholesale Banking, Joan-David Grima/55/Exec. VP - Asset Management, Insurance, Ignacio Benjumea Cabeza De Vaca/General Secretary, Sec., Jose Manuel Tejon/57/Exec. VP - Financial Accounting, Control, Jorge Moran/44/Exec. VP - Insurance *(27 Officers included in Index)*

Directors: Alfredo Saenz/Vice Chmn., CEO, Alfredo Saenz Abad/66/Vice Chmn., CEO, Matias Rodriguez Inciarte/60/Vice Chmn., Manuel Soto Serrano/68/Vice Chmn., Fernando De Asua/76/Vice Chmn., Emilio Botin/74/Chmn., Luis Angel Rojo Duque/74/Non Exec. Dir., Luis Alberto Salazar-Simpson Bos/68/Non Exec. Dir., Jay S. Sidhu/57/Non Exec. Dir., Assicurazioni Generali/Dir., Ana P. Botin/48/Dir., Javier Botin/35/Dir., Mutua Madrilena Automovilista/67/Non Exec. Dir. - Proprietary, Isabel Tocino Biscarolasaga/59/Non Exec. Dir., Juan Guitard Marin/Deputy General Secretary, Deputy Sec. *(25 Directors included in Index)*

Owners: Abel Matutes/0.00%, Fernando de Asa/0.00%, Isabel Tocino, Antonio Basagoiti/0.01%, Assicurazioni Generali S.p.A/1.31%, Antonio Escmez/0.01%, Mutua Madrilena Automovilista/1.17%, Luis Alberto Salazar-Simpson/0.00%, Rodrigo Echenique/0.01%, Luis ngel Rojo, Matas R. Inciarte/0.01%, Francisco Luzn/0.02%, Alfredo Senz/0.03%, Lord Burns, Manuel Soto/0.00% *(19 Owners included in Index)*

Financial Data: *Fiscal Year End:*12/31 *Latest Annual Data:* 12/31/2006

Year	Sales	Net Income
2006	$77,101,001,000	$9,789,458,000
2005	$52,440,168,000	$7,483,584,000
2004	$19,371,297,000	$5,376,918,000

Curr. Assets:	$327,124,143,000	**Curr. Liab.:**	$669,513,072,000	**P/E Ratio:**	6.88
Plant, Equip.:	$11,471,413,000	**Total Liab.:**	$1,046,675,592,000	**Indic. Yr. Divd.:**	$0.570
Total Assets:	$1,110,978,876,000	**Net Worth:**	$64,303,284,000	**Debt/ Equity:**	NA

Banco Santander-Chile

Bandera 140, Santiago; *PH:* 56-23202000; *http://* www.bsantander.cl

General - Incorporation	Chile	**Stock**- Price on:12/24/2007	$49.31
Employees	8,184	Stock Exchange	NYSE
Auditor	Deloitte & Touche LLP	Ticker Symbol	SAN
Stk Agt	Customary Among Chilean Co	Outstanding Shares	181,370,000
Counsel	NA	E.P.S	$3.32
DUNS No.	NA	Shareholders	NA

Business: The group's principal activities are carried out through two business units: retail banking: provides lending in the form of consumer loans, credit cards, auto loans, commercial loans, foreign trade financing and residential mortgage loans to individuals, medium and small companies and micro-businesses. Wholesale banking: provides commercial lending, leasing, factoring, infrastructure construction financing, trade financing and financial advisory, payment and cash management services to medium-sized real estate companies and large domestic and multinational companies. It also provides a diversified range of treasury and risk management products to these customers. As of 31-Dec-2003, the group owned 345 total branches, 64 of which operated under the banefe brand name and 35 under the santiago express brand name. The remaining 246 branches are operated under the newly created santander santiago brand name.

Primary SIC and add'l.: 6211 6029 6021

CIK No: 0001027552

Subsidiaries: Santander S.A. Agente de Valores

Officers: Oscar Von Chrismar/CEO, Jose Alberto Garcia Matanza/Corp. Dir. - Credit Risk, Fernando Massu/Mgr. - Global Banking, Guillermo Sabater/Corporate Financial Controller, Ignacio Centenera/Corp. Dir. - Internal Audit, Jose Miguel Silva/Contact - Banefe Consumer Division, Claudio Melandri/Corp. Dir. - Human Resources, Juan Fernandez/Administration, Operations, Roberto Jara/Chief Accounting Officer, Andres Roccatagliata/Retail Banking, Ramon Sanchez/Corp. Dir. - Internal Audit, Andres Heusser/Sr. Management - Middle, Marketing Banking, Alejandro Cuevas/Mgr. - Banefe Consumer Division, Jose Manuel Manzano/Corp. Dir. - Credit Risk, Gonzalo Romero/General Counsel

Directors: Carlos Olivos Marchant/Vice Chmn., Marcial Portela Alvarez/Vice Chmn., Mauricio Larrain Garces/Chmn., Raimundo Monge Zegers/Alternate Dir., Juan Manuel Hoyos Martinez De Irujo/Dir., Marco Colodro Hadjes/Dir., Lucia Santa Cruz Sutil/Dir., Claudia Bobadilla Ferrer/Dir., Benigno Rodriguez Rodriguez/Dir., Roberto Zahler Mayanz/Dir., Victor Arbulu Crousillat/Dir., Roberto Mendez Torres/Dir., Jesus Zabalza Lotina/Alternate Dir.

Owners: Santander Chile Holding/35.46%, Teatinos Siglo XXI S.A./41.45%

Financial Data: *Fiscal Year End:*12/31 *Latest Annual Data:* 12/31/2006

Year	Sales	Net Income
2006	$2,625,549,000	$448,242,000
2005	$2,380,314,000	$429,480,000
2004	$1,792,390,000	$358,072,000

Curr. Assets:	$2,140,859,000	**Curr. Liab.:**	$19,814,882,000	**P/E Ratio:**	6.88
Plant, Equip.:	$506,365,000	**Total Liab.:**	$24,061,615,000	**Indic. Yr. Divd.:**	NA
Total Assets:	$27,898,965,000	**Net Worth:**	$3,837,350,000	**Debt/ Equity:**	NA

Bancolombia

1111 Brickell Ave., Ste. 1550, Miami, FL, 33131; *PH:* 1-305-373-3969; *Fax:* 1-305-373-6853; *http://* www.bancolombia.com; *Email:* investorrelations@bancolombia.com

General - Incorporation	Colombia	**Stock**- Price on:12/24/2007	$34.16
Employees	16,222	Stock Exchange	NYSE
Auditor	Deloitte & Touche Ltd	Ticker Symbol	CIB
Stk Agt	Fiducolombia	Outstanding Shares	181,960,000
Counsel	Sullivan & Cromwell	E.P.S	$2.21
DUNS No.	NA	Shareholders	NA

Business: The group's principal activity is the holding and execution of all operations, businesses, acts and services legally permitted to bank establishments of a commercial character/nature with subjection to the requisites and limitations of Colombian law. It has 364 offices located in more than 116 cities and a network of 760 electronic cash machines.

Primary SIC and add'l.: 6162 6211 6029

CIK No: 0001071371

Subsidiaries: Bancolombia Cayman S.A., Future Net S.A., Sinesa Holding Company Limited, Sistema de Inversiones y Negocios S.A

Officers: Gonzalo Toro Bridge/48/VP - Corporate - Government Banking, Federico G. Ochoa Barrera/61/Exec. VP - Services, Juan Esteban Toro Valencia/Mgr. - Investor Relations, Juan Carlos Mora Uribe/43/VP - Risk Management, Jaime Alberto Velasquez Botero/48/VP - Financial, Sergio Restrepo Isaza/47/Exec. VP - Corporate Development, Margarita Maria Mesa Mesa/48/VP, Company Sec., Jairo Burgos De La Espriella/43/VP - Human Resources, Luis Arturo Penagos Londono/58/VP - Internal Audit, Jorge Ivan Toro Villegas/60/VP - Technology, Hernan Dario Ramirez Giraldo/50/Administrative VP, Luis Fernando Montoya Cusso/54/VP - Operations, Luis Fernando Munoz Serna/52/VP - Mortgage Banking, Olga Botero De Duque/VP - Technology, Engineer, Augusto Restrepo Gomez/VP - Aministrative *(17 Officers included in Index)*

Directors: David Emilio Bojanini Garcia/52/Chmn., Carlos Raul Yepes Jimenez/44/Dir., Juan Sebastian Betancur Escobar/65/Alternate Dir., Carlos Mario Giraldo Moreno/48/Alternate Dir., Jose Alberto Velez Cadavid/58/Dir., Carlos Enrique Piedrahita Arocha/54/Dir., Juan Camilo Restrepo Salazar/62/Dir., Alejandro Gaviria Uribe/43/Dir., Francisco Jose Moncaleano Botero/50/Dir., Luis Alberto Zuleta Jaramillo/62/Alternate Dir., Maria Angelica Arbelaez Restrepo/43/Alternate Dir., Gonzalo Alberto Perez Rojas/Dir., Ricardo Sierra Moreno/57/Dir.

Owners: ADR Program/70.00%, Suramericana de Inversiones and Subsidiaries, Inversiones Argos S.A./14.20%, Suramericana de Inversiones and Subsidiaries/45.30%, Fondo de Pensiones Obligatorias Proteccion S.A./10.60%, Fondo de Pensiones Obligatorias Proteccion S.A./1.10%, Inversiones Argos S.A./3.50%

Financial Data: *Fiscal Year End:*12/31 *Latest Annual Data:* 12/31/2006

Year	Sales	Net Income
2006	$1,689,477,000	$376,473,000
2005	$1,705,524,000	$356,448,000
2004	$1,001,711,000	$256,850,000

Curr. Assets:	$1,129,701,000	**Curr. Liab.:**	$10,234,548,000	**P/E Ratio:**	6.88
Plant, Equip.:	$361,673,000	**Total Liab.:**	$12,336,834,000	**Indic. Yr. Divd.:**	$0.940
Total Assets:	$14,156,441,000	**Net Worth:**	$1,819,607,000	**Debt/ Equity:**	NA

Bancorp Bank Inc (The)

405 Silverside Rd., Wilmington, DE, 19809; ***PH:*** 1-302-385-5000; ***Fax:*** 1-302-385-5194; ***http://*** www.thebancorp.com; ***Email:*** info@thebancorp.com

General - Incorporation	DE	**Stock**- Price on:12/24/2007	$23.5
Employees	181	Stock Exchange	NDQ
Auditor	Grant Thornton LLP	Ticker Symbol	TBBK
Stk Agt	American Stock Transfer & Trust Co.	Outstanding Shares	13,780,000
Counsel	NA	E.P.S.	$0.91
DUNS No.	11-058-1787	Shareholders	NA

Business: The group's principle activity is to provide retail and commercial banking services, including checking, savings and other interest-bearing accounts. The business lending services focus on secured loans and lines of credit, construction loans and customized equipment and vehicle leasing programs. The consumer lending services focus on home equity loans, personal and home equity lines of credit, personal installment loans and vehicle leasing. It also provides banking services for affinity groups through a private-label Website under the affinity group's name. It provides its services to small to mid-size businesses and their principals in the philadelphia-wilmington market area. It operates through 12 countries surrounding philadelphia and wilmington and includes: philadelphia, Delaware, chester, montgomery, bucks and lehigh countries in Pennsylvania, new castle county in Delaware and mercer, burlington, camden, ocean and cape may countries in New Jersey. The group operates from United States.

Primary SIC and add'l.: 6035

CIK No: 0001295401

Subsidiaries: The Bancorp, Inc.

Officers: Betsy Z. Cohen/Dir., CEO, Frank M. Mastrangelo/Dir., COO, Pres., Scott R. Megargee/Exec. VP - Consumer Lending, Leasing, Donald F. McGraw/Exec. VP, Chief Credit Officer, Arthur M. Birenbaum/Exec. VP - Commercial Lending, Martin F. Egan/CFO, Sr. VP

Directors: Betsy Z. Cohen/Dir., CEO, Daniel Gideon Cohen/Chmn., Frank M. Mastrangelo/Dir., COO, Pres., Leon A. Huff/Dir., Michael J. Bradley/Dir., Steven N. Stein/Dir., William H. Lamb/Dir., Joan Specter/Dir., Matthew Cohn/Dir., James J. McEntee/Dir., Linda Schaeffer/Dir., Walter T. Beach/Dir.

Owners: Royce & Associates LLC/6.46%, James J. McEntee, Walter T. Beach/5.05%, Matthew Cohn, Daniel G. Cohen/3.27%, Steven Stein/1.38%, Scott R. Megargee, Leon A. Huff, Insiders/19.99%, Goldman Sachs Asset Management, L.P./7.73%, Linda Schaeffer, Frank M. Mastrangelo/1.03%, Donald F. McGraw, Joan Specter, William H. Lamb *(20 Owners included in Index)*

Financial Data: *Fiscal Year End:*12/31 *Latest Annual Data:* 12/31/2006

Year	Sales	Net Income
2006	$86,006,000	$12,500,000
2005	$51,457,000	$7,447,000
2004	$33,577,000	$3,718,000

Curr. Assets:	$145,658,000	**Curr. Liab.:**	$1,183,876,000	**P/E Ratio:**	25.82
Plant, Equip.:	$3,951,000	**Total Liab.:**	$1,185,930,000	**Indic. Yr. Divd.:**	NA
Total Assets:	$1,334,838,000	**Net Worth:**	$148,908,000	**Debt/ Equity:**	NA

Bancorp Rhode Island Inc

1 Turks Head Pl., Providence, RI, 02903; ***PH:*** 1-401-456-5000; ***Fax:*** 1-401-456-5059; ***http://*** www.bankri.com

General - Incorporation	RI	**Stock**- Price on:12/24/2007	$37.25
Employees	228	Stock Exchange	NDQ
Auditor	KPMG LLP	Ticker Symbol	BARI
Stk Agt	Registrar & Transfer Co	Outstanding Shares	4,840,000
Counsel	Hinckley, Allen & Snyder	E.P.S.	$1.85
DUNS No.	NA	Shareholders	NA

Business: The group's principal activities are to provide commercial banking services to individuals and small to mid-sized businesses in Rhode Island. The group accepts demand deposits, now accounts, money market accounts, savings accounts and certificate of deposit accounts. The deposits are insured by the federal deposit insurance corporation. Loans comprise of commercial real estate and multi-family loans, non-real estate commercial loans, small business loans, construction loans, residential mortgage loans and consumer lines of credit. The group also offers non-deposit investment products, online banking services, automated teller machines, debit cards and related products and services. Its subsidiary, bri investment corp, manages and maintains intangible investments and the collection and distribution of the income from such investments. The group operates through thirteen full service branches with nine located in the providence county and four in the kent county.

Primary SIC and add'l.: 6022 6712

CIK No: 0001109525

Subsidiaries: Acorn Insurance Agency, Bank Rhode Island, BRI Investment Corp., Macrolease Corporation

Officers: Merrill W. Sherman/Dir., CEO, Pres., James V. Derentis/Chief Business Officer, Linda Haber Simmons/CFO, Treasurer

Directors: Merrill W. Sherman/Dir., CEO, Pres., Malcolm G. Chace/Chmn., Karen Adams/Dir., Pablo Rodriguez/Dir., Meredith A. Curren/Dir., Ernest J. Chornyei/Dir., John R. Berger/Dir., Mark R. Feinstein/Dir., Cheryl Watkins Snead/Dir., Anthony F. Andrade/Dir., Bogdan Nowak/Dir., Edward J. Mack/Dir., John A. Yena/Dir., Michael E. McMahon/Dir., Richard L. Bready/Dir.

Owners: James V. DeRentis, Mendon Capital Advisors Corp./8.20%, Malcolm G. Chace/11.00%, Richard A. Grills/5.20%, Linda H. Simmons, Mark R. Feinstein, Cheryl W. Snead, Anthony F. Andrade/1.10%, John A. Yena, Meredith A. Curren, Jeffrey W. Angus, Edward J. Mack, Merrill W. Sherman/5.90%, Richard L. Bready, Michael E. McMahon *(24 Owners included in Index)*

Financial Data: *Fiscal Year End:*12/31 *Latest Annual Data:* 06/30/2007

Year	Sales	Net Income
2007	$23,979,000	$2,194,000
2006	$91,049,000	$7,711,000
2005	$78,794,000	$9,569,000

Curr. Assets:	$68,519,000	**Curr. Liab.:**	$1,092,764,000	**P/E Ratio:**	22.04
Plant, Equip.:	$13,736,000	**Total Liab.:**	$1,367,014,000	**Indic. Yr. Divd.:**	$0.640
Total Assets:	$1,479,099,000	**Net Worth:**	$112,085,000	**Debt/ Equity:**	0.1608

BancorpSouth Inc

1 Mississippi Plz., 201 S. Spring St., Tupelo, MS, 38804; ***PH:*** 1-662-680-2000; ***Fax:*** 1-662-678-7299; ***http://*** www.bancorpsouth.com

General - Incorporation	MS	**Stock**- Price on:12/24/2007	$24.75
Employees	4,100	Stock Exchange	NYSE
Auditor	KPMG LLP	Ticker Symbol	BXS
Stk Agt	Suntrust Bank	Outstanding Shares	82,200,000
Counsel	J. Patrick Caldwell	E.P.S.	$1.51
DUNS No.	10-629-1446	Shareholders	NA

Business: The group's principle activities are that of a commercial bank, providing commercial and retail banking services, personal and corporate trust, agency and investment services, consumer lending, credit life insurance, investment brokerage and sale of insurance products. The department offers a variety of services including personal trust and estate services, certain employee benefit accounts and plans, including individual retirement accounts, and limited corporate trust functions. The group is a holding company with commercial banking and financial services operations in Mississippi, Tennessee, Alabama, Arkansas, Texas and Louisiana. The group operates 41 offices located in 39 communities in Mississippi and Tennessee. The principal subsidiary is bancorpsouth bank.

Primary SIC and add'l.: 6361 6311 6141 6022 6712

CIK No: 0000701853

Subsidiaries: American State Capital Trust, BancorpSouth Bank, BancorpSouth Capital Trust, BancorpSouth Insurance Services, Inc., BancorpSouth Investment Services, Inc., BancorpSouth Municipal Development Corporation, Business Holding Company Trust, Century Credit Life Insurance Company, Personal Finance Corporation, Premier Bancorp Capital Trust, Risk Advantage, Inc.

Officers: Aubrey B. Patterson/Dir., Chmn., CEO - Bancorpsouth Bank/$2,459,759.00, Gregg Cowsert/Exec. VP, Vice Chmn., Chief Lending Officer - Bancorpsouth Bank/$681,487.00, Nash L. Allen/Treasurer, CFO, Exec. VP/$501,371.00, Gary R. Harder/Exec. VP, Cathy M. Robertson/Exec. VP, Cathy S. Freeman/Sr. VP, Corp. Sec., Larry Bateman/Exec. VP, James V. Kelley/Dir., COO, Pres./$1,023,368.00, Michael L. Sappington/Exec. VP/$732,375.00, James Threadgill/Exec. VP

Directors: Aubrey B. Patterson/Dir., Chmn., CEO - Bancorpsouth Bank, Madison R. Murphy/Dir., Cal Partee/Dir., Robert C. Nolan/Dir., Alan W. Perry/Dir., Hassell H. Franklin/Dir., Travis E. Staub/Dir., Larry G. Kirk/Dir., James V. Kelley/Dir., COO, Pres., W. G. Holliman/Dir., Guy W. Mitchell/Dir., Turner O. Lashlee/Dir.

Owners: Robert C. Nolan, James V. Kelley, Aubrey B. Patterson/1.33%, Cal W. Partee, Hassell H. Franklin/1.33%, Michael L. Sappington, Insiders/7.15%, BancorpSouth, Inc./8.00%, Gregg W. Cowsert, Guy W. Mitchell, Nash L. Allen, Madison R. Murphy, Alan W. Perry, W. G. Holliman, Larry G. Kirk *(17 Owners included in Index)*

Financial Data: *Fiscal Year End:*12/31 *Latest Annual Data:* 12/31/2006

Year	Sales	Net Income
2006	$887,985,000	$125,194,000
2005	$758,748,000	$115,199,000
2004	$681,809,000	$110,620,000

Curr. Assets:	$686,498,000	**Curr. Liab.:**	$10,619,286,000	**P/E Ratio:**	16.39
Plant, Equip.:	$287,215,000	**Total Liab.:**	$11,013,936,000	**Indic. Yr. Divd.:**	$0.840
Total Assets:	$12,040,521,000	**Net Worth:**	$1,026,585,000	**Debt/ Equity:**	0.2802

Bancshares of Florida Inc

1185 Immokalee Rd., Naples, FL, 34110; ***PH:*** 1-239-254-2100; ***Fax:*** 1-239-254-2107; ***http://*** www.bankofloridaonline.com

General - Incorporation	FL	**Stock**- Price on:12/24/2007	$17.52
Employees	200	Stock Exchange	NDQ
Auditor	KPMG LLP	Ticker Symbol	BOFL
Stk Agt	Registrar & Transfer Co	Outstanding Shares	12,680,000
Counsel	NA	E.P.S.	$0.39
DUNS No.	NA	Shareholders	NA

Business: The group's principal activities are the provision of commercial and consumer banking services in naples, Florida. The group provides the services in its capacity as a holding company for bank of Florida, n.a., the bank of Florida and Florida trust company. Depository activities include interest bearing and non-interest bearing accounts, including commercial and retail checking accounts, money market accounts, individual retirement accounts, regular interest bearing statement savings accounts and certificates of deposit. The lending products include commercial loans, real estate loans, home equity loans, consumer and installment loans. It also provides consumer services consisting of us savings bonds, traveler's checks, cashiers checks, safe deposit boxes, bank by mail services, direct deposit, automatic teller services and wealth management services. The primary market areas include the collier, lee, broward, dade and palm beach counties of Florida.

Primary SIC and add'l.: 6712 6021

CIK No: 0001082368

Subsidiaries: Bank of Florida, Bank of Florida Tampa Bay, Bank of Florida Trust Company

Subsidiaries: Bank of Florida, Bank of Florida Tampa Bay, Bank of Florida Trust Company

Officers: Michael L. McMullan/Dir., CEO, Pres./$368,918.00, John B. James/Dir., Sr. Exec. VP, Chief Administrative Officer/$216,205.00, Tracy L. Keegan/CFO, Exec. VP/$253,084.00, John S. Chaperon/Dir., Exec. VP, Corporate Risk Officer, Craig D. Sherman/Exec. VP, Chief Loan Officer, Sharon I. Hill/Chief Accounting Officer, Sr. VP, Daniel W. Taylor/Exec. VP, Dir. - Bank Operations, Technology

Directors: Michael L. McMullan/Dir., CEO, Pres., Earl L. Frye/Chmn. Emeritus, Joe B. Cox/Vice Chmn., Donald R. Barber/Dir., Wayne H. Huizenga/Dir., Lavonne Johnson/Dir., John S. Chaperon/Dir., Exec. VP, Corporate Risk Officer, John B. James/Dir., Sr. Exec. VP, Chief Administrative Officer, Edward Kaloust/Dir., Harry K. Moon/Dir., Michael T. Putziger/Dir., Richard C. Rochon/Dir., Ramon A. Rodriguez/Dir., Terry W. Stiles/Dir., Pierce T. Neese/Dir.

Owners: Times Square Capital Management, LLC/5.27%, LaVonne Johnson/2.97%, John B. James/0.75%, Harry K. Moon, John S. Chaperon/0.21%, Ashford Capital Management, Inc./7.52%, Tracy L. Keegan/0.03%, Ramon A. Rodriguez/0.40%, Michael T. Putziger/1.53%, Edward Kaloust/0.36%, Donald R. Barber/0.76%, Terry W. Stiles/2.01%, Joe B. Cox/1.18%, Insiders/14.76%, Patricia L. Frost/0.94% *(19 Owners included in Index)*

Financial Data: ***Fiscal Year End:***12/31 ***Latest Annual Data:*** 12/31/2006

Year	Sales	Net Income
2006	$56,572,000	$2,319,000
2005	$31,750,000	$4,883,000
2004	$16,943,000	-$2,880,000

Curr. Assets:	$32,160,000	***Curr. Liab.:***	$736,597,000		
Plant, Equip.:	$7,304,000	***Total Liab.:***	$747,597,000	***Indic. Yr. Divd.:***	NA
Total Assets:	$883,102,000	***Net Worth:***	$135,505,000	***Debt/ Equity:***	0.0802

Banctec Inc

2701 E Grauwyler Rd. , Irving, TX, 75061; ***PH:*** 1-972-821-4000; ***http://*** www.banctec.com; ***Email:*** inquiries@banctec.com

General - Incorporation	DE	***Stock*** - Price on:12/24/2007	NA
Employees	NA	Stock Exchange	NA
Auditor	KPMG LLP	Ticker Symbol	NA
Stk Agt	NA	Outstanding Shares	NA
Counsel	NA	E.P.S	NA
DUNS No.	06-411-2683	Shareholders	NA

Business: The group's principle activty is to provide automated solutions that captures, processes and archives paper and electronic forms, as well as provides complete check and exception processing systems, and manufactures high-apeed check processing equipment that is distributed to other system builders around the globe. The group operates from United States.

Primary SIC and add'l.: 7374 7373 3577 7378 7371

CIK No: 0000318378

Subsidiaries: BancTec (Canada),Inc., BancTec (Export),Inc. (dormant), BancTec (Puerto Rico),Inc., BancTec A/S, BancTec AB, BancTec B.V., BancTec GmbH, BancTec Holding N.V., BancTec Iberica S.A., BancTec Limited, BancTec S.A., BancTec Service Belgium, SPRL, BancTec Service Canada, BancTec Service Europe, B.V., BancTec Service France, SAS 24 Subsidiaries included in the Index

Officers: Coley J. Clark/Dir., CEO, Pres., Jeffrey D. Cushman/Sr. VP, CFO, Mark D. Fairchild/CTO, Sr. VP, Michael D. Fallin/Sr. VP - Corporate Marketing, Pres. - Americas, Emerging Markets, Lin M. Held/Sr. VP, Chief Administrative Officer, Brendan P. Keegan/Sr. VP, Pres. - Information Technology Service Management, Mike Peplow/Sr. VP, Pres. - Europe, Middle East, Africa, EMEA

Directors: Coley J. Clark/Dir., CEO, Pres., Robert A. Minicucci/55/Chmn., Gary J. Fernandes/64/Dir., Eric J. Lee/36/Dir., Sanjay Swani/41/Dir.

Owners: Cheyne Special Situations Fund LP/6.90%, Coley J. Clark, Michael D. Peplow, Brendan P. Keegan, Michael D. Fallin, Jeffrey D. Cushman, CR Intrinsic Investments LLC/5.30%, Citadel Equity Fund, Ltd./8.00%, Paulson& Co./9.60%

Banctrust Financial Group Inc

100 St. Joseph St., Mobile, AL, 36602; ***PH:*** 1-251-431-7800; ***Fax:*** 1-251-431-7851; ***http://*** www.banctrustfinancialgroupinc.com

General - Incorporation	AL	***Stock*** - Price on:12/24/2007	$20.83
Employees	419	Stock Exchange	NDQ
Auditor	KPMG LLP	Ticker Symbol	BTFG
Stk Agt	Registrar & Transfer Co	Outstanding Shares	11,190,000
Counsel	NA	E.P.S	$0.83
DUNS No.	14-786-7345	Shareholders	NA

Business: The group's principal activity is that of a bank holding company. The subsidiaries are banktrust, banktrust of brewton, the monroe county bank, south Alabama trust company inc, the commercial bank of demopolis, wewahitchka state bank and sweet water state bank. The banking services include business and personal checking accounts, money market accounts, saving accounts, certificates of deposits and overdraft protection. They also include business and personal loans, mortgages on commercial and residential real estate, credit card privileges, letters of credit, safe deposit box facilities, mutual funds, annuities, insurance products etc. The group also provides general banking advice and consultation to the public and community oriented services. It operates in the counties of escambia, mobile, marengo and baldwin of Alabama. In 2003 the group acquired eufaula bank and santa rosa beach bank and on 30-Dec-2003 commercesouth inc..

Primary SIC and add'l.: 6022 6712

CIK No: 0000783739

Subsidiaries: BancTrust Company, Inc., BankTrust, BankTrust of Alabama

Officers: Bibb W. Lamar/Dir., CEO, Pres./$693,445.00, Michael D. Fitzhugh/59/Exec. VP/$281,065.00, Raymond F. Lynn/Sr. VP, Trust Mgr., Alexis J. Malloy/VP, Employee Benefits Mgr., Michael F. Johnson/62/CFO, Exec. VP, Sec./$346,490.00, O. G. Rester/VP - Trust Administration, Jason E. Walker/VP - Trust Administration, Bruce C. Finley/59/Sr. VP, Sr. Loan Officer/$253,833.00, Daniel Britton/Pres., Carolyn L. Bollenbacher/VP, Mgr. - Trust Operations, Elaine M. Catoe/VP, Trust Administrator, Robert E. Hardin/Sr. VP, Mgr. - Trust Investment

Directors: Bibb W. Lamar/Dir., CEO, Pres., Stephen J. Nelson/Chmn., Robert M. Dixon/Dir., David C. De Laney/Dir., Tracy T. Conerly/Dir., John G. Lewis/Dir., James A. Faulkner/Dir., Dwight W. Harrigan/Dir., John H. Lewis/Dir., Harris V. Morrissette/Dir., Dennis A. Wallace/Dir., Clifton C. Inge/Dir., Stephen G. Crawford/Dir., James P. Hayes/Dir., Paul D. Owens/Dir. *(17 Directors included in Index)*

Owners: Michael D. Fitzhugh/0.26%, David C. De Laney/0.65%, Broox G. Garrett, Insiders/13.19%, Stephen G. Crawford/1.40%, Earl H. Weaver/0.83%, Dwight W. Harrigan/1.90%, Bruce C. Finley, Michael F. Johnson, Greg B. Faison/0.89%, John H. Lewis, Harris V. Morrissette/0.33%, Tracy T. Conerly/0.03%, Paul D. Owens/2.94%, Robert M. Dixon *(21 Owners included in Index)*

Financial Data: ***Fiscal Year End:***12/31 ***Latest Annual Data:*** 12/31/2006

Year	Sales	Net Income
2006	$99,852,000	$13,286,000
2005	$83,892,000	$15,119,000
2004	$64,891,000	$11,301,000

Curr. Assets:	$134,465,000	***Curr. Liab.:***	$1,108,249,000	***P/E Ratio:***	25.10
Plant, Equip.:	$47,324,000	***Total Liab.:***	$1,214,883,000	***Indic. Yr. Divd.:***	$0.520
Total Assets:	$1,353,406,000	***Net Worth:***	$138,523,000	***Debt/ Equity:***	NA

BancWest Corp

999 Bishop St., 29th Fl., Honolulu, HI, 96813; ***PH:*** 1-808-525-7000; ***Fax:*** 1-808-525-7086; ***http://*** www.bancwestcorp.com

General - Incorporation	DE	***Stock*** - Price on:12/24/2007	NA
Employees	NA	Stock Exchange	NA
Auditor	PricewaterhouseCoopers LLP	Ticker Symbol	NA
Stk Agt	American Stock Transfer & Trust CO.	Outstanding Shares	NA
Counsel	NA	E.P.S	NA
DUNS No.	00-922-7000	Shareholders	NA

Business: The group's principle activities of the group are to provide general, commercial and consumer banking services. The group also provides commercial, equipment and vehicle leasing, trust and insurance products. The group operates 221 offices in the state of Hawaii, California, Oregon, Washington, Idaho, guam and saipan.

Primary SIC and add'l.: 6021 6712

CIK No: 0000036377

Subsidiaries: 1897 Services Corporation, BancWest Capital I, BancWest Investment Services, Inc., Bank of the West, Bishop Street Capital Management Corporation, BW Insurance Agency, Inc., BW Leasing, Inc., BW Mortgage, LLC, Center Club, Inc., CFB Capital III, CFB Capital IV, CFB Community Development Corporation, CIC/HCM Asset Management, Inc., Community First Holdings, Inc., Community First Home Mortgage, Inc. 37 Subsidiaries included in the Index

Officers: Don J. McGrath/Dir., CEO, Vanessa Washington/Corp. Sec., Thibault Fulconis/CFO, Gilles Karpowicz/Risk Mgr.

Directors: Don J. McGrath/Dir., CEO, Frank Bonetto/57/Dir., Robert A. Fuhrman/83/Dir., Rodney R. Peck/62/Dir., Jacques Henri Wahl/76/Dir., Bert T. Kobayashi/68/Dir., Pierre Mariani/51/Dir., Gerard A. Denot/Dir., Donald G. Horner/Dir., Walter A. Dods/Dir., Ewan A. MacDonald/66/Dir., Didier Balme/Dir., Jean Thomazeau/Dir., Francois Dambrine/59/Dir., Michael J. Shepherd/Dir.

Bandag Inc

2905 N Hwy. 61, Bandag Headquarters, Muscatine, IA, 52761; ***PH:*** 1-563-262-1400; ***http://*** www.bandag.com

General - Incorporation	IA	***Stock*** - Price on:12/24/2007	NA
Employees	3,788	Stock Exchange	NYSE
Auditor	Ernst & Young LLP	Ticker Symbol	BDG
Stk Agt	Computershare Trust Co	Outstanding Shares	NA
Counsel	NA	E.P.S	NA
DUNS No.	00-526-9758	Shareholders	NA

Business: The group's principal activities are to manufacture, sell and maintain new and retread tires to commercial and industrial customers. The group operates in two segments namely the manufacture and sale of precured tread rubber and equipment and sale and maintenance of new and retread tires. The company and its licensees have 1,020 franchisees worldwide, with 33% located in the United States and 67% internationally. The traditional business can be divided into two main areas: manufacturing the tread rubber and bonding the tread to a tire casing. It manufactures over 500 separate tread designs & sizes, treads specifically designed for various applications, allowing fleet managers to fine-tune their tire programs. The group also offers tire management services including line of new tires and 24-hour road service and alignment.

Primary SIC and add'l.: 3011 7534

CIK No: 0000009534

Subsidiaries: Bandag A.G., Bandag B.V., Bandag Canada Ltd., Bandag de Mexico, S.A. de C.V., Bandag do Brasil Ltda, Bandag Europe N.V., Open Road Technologies, Inc., Speedco, Inc., Tire Distribution Systems, Inc.

Officers: Martin G. Carver/59/Chmn., CEO, Pres., Warren W. Heidbreder/61/VP, CFO, Sec., Jeffrey C. Pattison/52/VP, Corporate Controller

Directors: Martin G. Carver/59/Chmn., CEO, Pres., Gary E. Dewel/65/Dir., Phillip J. Hanrahan/68/Dir., Roy J. Carver/64/Dir., James R. Everline/66/Dir., Amy P. Hutton/45/Dir., Stephen R. Newman/64/Dir.

Owners: Amy P. Hutton/36.90%, Amy P. Hutton, R. Stephen Newman, Warren W. Heidbreder/0.01%, Frederico U. Kopittke, John C. McErlane/0.01%, Insiders/0.47%, Michael A. Tirona, Martin G. Carver/31.50%, Phillip J. Hanrahan, James R. Everline, Roy J. Carver/30.20%, R. Stephen Newman, Phillip J. Hanrahan/42.10%

Bangla Property Mgmt Inc

89 Changan Middle Rd., Yangming International Tower, Yangming International Tower, Flrs. 26/27, Xian, 26/27; ***PH:*** 86-298-525-7560; ***http://*** www.jiahuigroup.com

General - Incorporation	CO	***Stock*** - Price on:12/24/2007	$1.5
Employees	NA	Stock Exchange	NA
Auditor	Kempisty & Co	Ticker Symbol	NA
Stk Agt	Pacific Stock Transfer Co.	Outstanding Shares	NA
Counsel	NA	E.P.S	NA
DUNS No.	NA	Shareholders	NA

Business: The groups principle activity is to provide property management and customer support services to residential property owners. The group operates from Canada.

Primary SIC and add'l.: NA

CIK No: 0001174741

Subsidiaries: Jiahui Real Estate Co., Ltd

Officers: Pingan Wu/Chmn., CEO, Pres., Steven Lou/Dir., CFO, Exec. VP, Yingming Wang/Dir., VP, COO, Howard Li/Board Advisor

Directors: Pingan Wu/Chmn., CEO, Pres., Steven Lou/Dir., CFO, Exec. VP, Yingming Wang/Dir., VP, COO, Xingguo Wang/Dir., Ren Mingchuan/Dir., Yuan Qianfei/Dir., Mingchuan Ren/47/Dir., Qianfei Yuan/42/Dir.

Owners: Yingming Wang/1.60%, Lin Wu/8.10%, Shuo Lou/1.60%, Insiders/18.50%, Rong Wu/8.10%, Zhendong Wu/8.10%, Xingguo Wang/1.10%, Pingan Wu/14.30%

Financial Data: *Fiscal Year End:* 12/31 *Latest Annual Data:* 12/31/2006

Year	Sales	Net Income
2006	$4,734,000	-$124,000
2005	$37,000	$7,000

Curr. Assets:	$13,000	Curr. Liab.:	$15,000		
Plant, Equip.:	$56,000	Total Liab.:	$55,000	Indic. Yr. Divd.:	NA
Total Assets:	$69,000	Net Worth:	$15,000	Debt/ Equity:	8.4937

Bank Holdings

9990 Double R Blvd., Reno, NV, 89521; *PH:* 1-775-853-8600; *Fax:* 1-775-853-2068; *http://* www.thebankholdings.com

General - Incorporation	NV	Stock - Price on:12/24/2007	$16.1
Employees	116	Stock Exchange	NDQ
Auditor	McGladrey & Pullen LLP	Ticker Symbol	TBHS
Stk Agt..... American Stock Transfer & Trust CO.		Outstanding Shares	5,830,000
Counsel	NA	E.P.S.	$0.52
DUNS No.	NA	Shareholders	NA

Business: The group principal activities are to provide consumer and commercial banking services primarily to the business and professional community and individuals. The group operates through 74 banking offices, including 47 offices of 3 major chain banks (bank of America, us bank and wells fargo), operating within washoe county. The lending activities of the group includes commercial lines of credit and term loans, credit lines to individuals, checking overdraft credit lines, professional loans, sba loans, equipment loans, accounts receivable financing and real estate and construction loans. The operations of the group are conducted through its subsidiary Nevada security bank. The group also offers a wide range of deposit instruments consisting of personal and business checking accounts and savings accounts, interest-bearing negotiable order of withdrawal accounts, money market accounts and time certificates of deposit.

Primary SIC and add'l.: 6712 6022

CIK No: 0001234383

Subsidiaries: Bank Holdings Statutory Trust, Granite Exchange Inc, Nevada Security Bank

Officers: Harold Giomi/Chmn., CEO, John Donovan/Exec. VP, Chief Credit Officer, Joseph Bourdeau/Pres., Jack B. Buchold/CFO, Exec. VP

Directors: Harold Giomi/Chmn., CEO, Edward Allison/Dir., Marybel Batjer/Dir., Edward Coppin/Dir., David A. Funk/Dir., Jesse Haw/Dir., Kelvin Moss/Dir., James L. Pfrommer/Dir., Lance M. Faulstich/38/Dir., Mark W. Knobel/53/Dir.

Owners: Edward Coppin/1.28%, The Jeffrey Barker Bank Stock Trust/6.10%, James Pfrommer, Jack Buchold, Hal Giomi/1.57%, Insiders/11.13%, Lance Faulstich, Edward Allison, John Donovan, NAI Insurance Agency, Inc./5.75%, Jesse Haw/1.68%, The Devere Barker Bank Stock Trust/5.42%, Mark Knobel, Joseph Bourdeau/1.45%, Marybel Batjer *(17 Owners included in Index)*

Financial Data: *Fiscal Year End:* 12/31 *Latest Annual Data:* 12/31/2006

Year	Sales	Net Income
2006	$32,721,000	$2,083,000
2005	$17,938,000	$1,412,000
2004	$11,075,000	$281,000

Curr. Assets:	$33,723,000	Curr. Liab.:	$534,371,000	P/E Ratio:	30.96
Plant, Equip.:	$7,857,000	Total Liab.:	$576,545,000	Indic. Yr. Divd.:	NA
Total Assets:	$651,540,000	Net Worth:	$73,568,000	Debt/ Equity:	0.3879

Bank McKenney

20718 1st St., McKenney, VA, 23872; *PH:* 1-804-478-4434; *Fax:* 1-804-478-4704; *http://* www.bankofmckenney.com

General - Incorporation		Stock - Price on:12/24/2007	$9.75
Employees	61	Stock Exchange	NDQ
Auditor	NA	Ticker Symbol	BOMK
Stk Agt.	Fleet Bank of New York	Outstanding Shares	1,930,000
Counsel	NA	E.P.S.	NA
DUNS No.	NA	Shareholders	NA

Business: The groups principal activity is to provide banking and financial services. The groups products include real estate, construction, commercial loan and Lines of Credit. The group operates from the United States.

Primary SIC and add'l.: 6022

CIK No:

Officers: Richard M. Liles/Dir., CEO, Pres., James B. Neville/CFO, Exec. VP, Ruth Wray/First VP - Human Resources, Lynda Cunningham/First VP - Operations, Mark Stevens/First VP - Credit Administration

Directors: Richard M. Liles/Dir., CEO, Pres., William D. Allen/Chmn., Edward B. Titmus/Dir., Meade L. Harrison/Dir., Harry D. Baird/Dir., Joseph W. Lyle/Dir., Rudy L. Hawkins/Dir., Joan Clarke/Dir., Channing F. Baskerville/Dir. Emeritus, Louis J. Blaha/Dir.

Bank Mutual Corp

4949 W Brown Deer Rd., Milwaukee, WI, 53223; *PH:* 1-414-354-1500; *Fax:* 1-414-354-5450; *http://* www.bankmutualcorp.com

General - Incorporation	WI	Stock - Price on:12/24/2007	$11.47
Employees	692	Stock Exchange	NDQ
Auditor	Ernst & Young LLP	Ticker Symbol	BKMU
Stk Agt.	Registrar & Transfer Co	Outstanding Shares	55,320,000
Counsel	NA	E.P.S.	$0.31
DUNS No.	NA	Shareholders	NA

Business: The group's principal activity is to provide financial services to individuals and businesses primarily located in the state of Wisconsin. The activities consists of accepting retail deposits from the general public and investing those deposits, together with funds generated from other operations, in residential mortgage loans, consumer loans, commercial real estate loans and commercial business loans. The loans include primarily adjustable rate mortgage loans for the group's own portfolio. It also invests in various mortgage-related securities and investment securities. The group operates through 70 banking offices located in 28 counties in Wisconsin, in addition to an office in Minnesota.

Primary SIC and add'l.: 6712 6035

CIK No: 0001123270

Subsidiaries: Arrowood Development LLC, BancMutual Financial & Insurance Services, Inc, Bank Mutual, First Northern Investments, Inc., MC Development LTD, Mutual Investment Corporation, Savings Financial Corporation

Owners: Eugene H. Maurer, Robert B. Olson, Christopher J. Callen, Thomas J. Lopina, David J. Rolfs, Thomas H. Buestrin, Michael T. Crowley/3.90%, Advisory Research, Inc./5.20%, Rick B. Colberg, Gus J. Swoboda, Mark C. Herr, Barclays Global Investors, NA./5.30%, Insiders/12.00%, Terry P. Anderegg, Raymond W. Dwyer *(16 Owners included in Index)*

Financial Data: *Fiscal Year End:* 12/31 *Latest Annual Data:* 12/31/2006

Year	Sales	Net Income
2006	$191,439,000	$20,597,000
2005	$181,651,000	$28,026,000
2004	$165,096,000	$29,554,000

Curr. Assets:	$58,967,000	Curr. Liab.:	$2,158,641,000	P/E Ratio:	34.76
Plant, Equip.:	$51,746,000	Total Liab.:	$2,915,088,000	Indic. Yr. Divd.:	$0.340
Total Assets:	$3,451,385,000	Net Worth:	$533,779,000	Debt/ Equity:	1.7590

Bank of America Corp

Bank Of America Corporate Ctr., 100 N Tryon St, Charlotte, NC, 28255; *PH:* 1-704-386-8486; *http://* www.bankamerica.com

General - Incorporation	DE	Stock - Price on:12/24/2007	$49.89
Employees	203,425	Stock Exchange	NYSE
Auditor	PricewaterhouseCoopers LLP	Ticker Symbol	BAC
Stk Agt	Computershare Trust Co	Outstanding Shares	4,440,000,000
Counsel	NA	E.P.S.	$4.78
DUNS No.	00-894-1528	Shareholders	NA

Business: The group's principle activity is to provide wide range of banking and non-banking financial services. The group's products and services include checking, credit cards, mortgages, home equity, personnel loans and investment services. The group operates from United States.

Primary SIC and add'l.: 6411 6021 6712 6162 6282

CIK No: 0000070858

Subsidiaries: 100 Federal Street Limited Partnership, 1784 S.a. Sociedad Gerente De Fondos Comunes De Inversion, A/M Properties, Inc., Abilene Park, Inc., Abn Amro Merchant Services, LLC, ACO Limitada, AdFleet, Inc., Administradora Blue 2234 S. de R.L. de C.V., AF&L, Inc., Aguila Corp S.A.C., Airlease Management Services, Inc., Alamo Funding II, Inc., Alamo Funding LLC, Alie Street Investments 10 Limited, Alie Street Investments 11 Limited 1117 Subsidiaries included in the Index

Officers: Kenneth D. Lewis/60/Chmn., CEO, Pres. - Bank, America Corporation/$27,873,350.00, Gene Taylor/Vice Chmn., Pres. - Global Corporate, Investment Banking, Bank, America Corporation, Neil A. Cotty/Chief Accounting Officer, Sr. VP, Barbara J. Desoer/Chief Technology, Operations Officer - Bank, America Corporation/$10,436,130.00, Liam E. McGee/Pres. - Global Consumer, Small Business Banking, Bank, America Corporation/$10,533,960.00, Brian T. Moynihan/Pres. - Global Wealth, Investment Management, Bank, America Corporation/$10,882,990.00, Amy Woods Brinkley/Global Risk Exec., Bank, America Corporation/$10,392,520.00, Steele J. Alphin/Chief Administrative Officer, William J. Mostyn/Deputy General Counsel, Corp. Sec., Joe L. Price/CFO - Bank, America Corporation, Wendy Tan/Media Relations, Asia, Christiana Marran/Head - International Media Relations, Elizabeth Wood/Media Relations, EMEA

Directors: Kenneth D. Lewis/60/Chmn., CEO, Pres. - Bank, America Corporation, Jackie M. Ward/69/Dir., Patricia E. Mitchell/65/Dir., Thomas J. May/60/Dir., Paul Fulton/Dir., Monica C. Lozano/51/Dir., Thomas M. Ryan/55/Dir., Temple O. Sloan/69/Dir., William Barnet/65/Dir., Walter E. Massey/69/Dir., Robert L. Tillman/64/Dir., Meredith R. Spangler/70/Dir., John T. Collins/61/Dir., Gary L. Countryman/68/Dir., Frank P. Bramble/59/Dir. *(18 Directors included in Index)*

Owners: Alvaro G. deMolina, Robert L. Tillman, Temple O. Sloan, Paul Fulton, Walter E. Massey, Tommy R. Franks, Eugene R. Taylor, William Barnet, Liam E. McGee, Gary L. Countryman, Thomas M. Ryan, Brian T. Moynihan, Steven W. Jones, Meredith R. Spangler, Kenneth D. Lewis *(25 Owners included in Index)*

Financial Data: *Fiscal Year End:* 12/31 *Latest Annual Data:* 12/31/2006

Year	Sales	Net Income
2006	$117,017,000,000	$21,133,000,000
2005	$83,980,000,000	$16,465,000,000
2004	$63,324,000,000	$14,143,000,000

Curr. Assets:	$338,911,000,000	Curr. Liab.:	$1,094,456,000,000	P/E Ratio:	10.64
Plant, Equip.:	$9,255,000,000	Total Liab.:	$1,324,465,000,000	Indic. Yr. Divd.:	$2.560
Total Assets:	$1,459,737,000,000	Net Worth:	$135,272,000,000	Debt/ Equity:	1.2643

Bank of Commerce Holdings

1951 Churn Creek Rd., Redding, CA, 96002; *PH:* 1-530-224-3333; *Fax:* 1-530-224-3337; *http://* www.reddingbankofcommerce.com; *Email:* main@reddingbankofcommerce.com

General - Incorporation	CA	Stock - Price on:12/24/2007	$10.9
Employees	115	Stock Exchange	NDQ
Auditor	Moss Adams LLP	Ticker Symbol	BOCH
Stk Agt	Mellon Investor Services LLC	Outstanding Shares	8,910,000
Counsel	NA	E.P.S.	$0.71
DUNS No.	NA	Shareholders	NA

Business: The group's principal activity is to provide traditional commercial banking services to small and medium sized businesses, professionals and individuals. The group provides a wide range of financial services and products through its subsidiaries. The products include deposits such as checking, interest bearing checking and savings accounts and money market deposit accounts. The group's lending activities include commercial and real estate construction. The loans offered by the group are single and multi family residential loans, equity lines of credit and commercial real estate loans. The other services provided by the group include traveler's checks, safe deposit boxes, collection services and electronic banking activities. The group operates in the counties of butte, el dorado, placer, shasta and sacramento in the California state.

Primary SIC and add'l.: 6712 6022

CIK No: 0000702513

Subsidiaries: Bank of Commerce Holdings Trust, Bank of Commerce Holdings Trust I, Bank of Commerce Holdings Trust II, Bank of Commerce Mortgage, RBC Mortgage Services, Redding Bank of Commerce

Officers: Patrick J. Moty/CEO, Pres., Exec. VP, Chief Credit Officer/$247,950.00, Randall S. Eslick/Regional Pres. - Roseville Division/$233,442.00, Robert A. Matranga/Sr. VP, Group Mgr. - Lending, Linda J. Miles/CFO, Exec. VP/$363,701.00, Caryn A. Blais/CIO, Sr. VP, Debbie A. Sylvester/Sr. VP, Chief Administrative Officer, Theodore Cumming/Sr. VP, Group Mgr. - Lending, Samuel Jimenez/Sr. VP, Dir. - Risk Management, Robert J. O'Neil/Sr. VP, Regional Credit Mgr. - Roseville Bank, Commerce/$208,000.00

Directors: Kenneth R. Gifford/Chmn., Lyle L. Tullis/Vice Chmn., Harry L. Grashoff/Dir., Orin N. Bennett/Dir., Welton L. Carrel/Dir., Russell L. Duclos/Dir., John C. Fitzpatrick/Dir., Jon W. Halfhide/Dir., David H. Scott/Dir.

Owners: Randall S. Eslick/0.27%, Robert J. ONeil/0.37%, Kenneth R. Gifford/2.76%, John C. Fitzpatrick/6.00%, Russell L. Duclos/1.74%, Jon Halfhide, Patrick J. Moty/0.77%, David H. Scott/1.03%, Robert C. Anderson/6.19%, Orin Bennett/0.35%, Linda J. Miles/0.36%, Welton L. Carrel/3.60%, Michael C. Mayer/2.02%, Insiders/31.86%, Lyle L. Tullis/0.62% *(16 Owners included in Index)*

Financial Data: *Fiscal Year End:*12/31 *Latest Annual Data:* 12/31/2006

Year	Sales	Net Income
2006	$39,709,000	$6,568,000
2005	$29,989,000	$6,278,000
2004	$23,192,000	$4,978,000

Curr. Assets:	$42,713,000	**Curr. Liab.:**	$519,204,000	**P/E Ratio:**	15.35
Plant, Equip.:	$8,595,000	**Total Liab.:**	$539,526,000	**Indic. Yr. Divd.:**	$0.320
Total Assets:	$583,442,000	**Net Worth:**	$43,916,000	**Debt/ Equity:**	0.3407

Bank of Granite Corp

23 N Main St., Granite Falls, NC, 28630; *PH:* 1-828-496-2027; *Fax:* 1-828-496-2077; *http://* www.bankofgranite.com

General - Incorporation	DE	**Stock**- Price on:12/24/2007	$17.35
Employees	337	Stock Exchange	NDQ
Auditor	Dixon Hughes PLLC	Ticker Symbol	GRAN
Stk Agt	Registrar & Transfer Co	Outstanding Shares	15,990,000
Counsel	NA	E.P.S	$0.87
DUNS No.	03-583-1478	Shareholders	NA

Business: The group's principal activities are that of a commercial bank. The group accepts demand, savings, now and money market deposit accounts and provides real estate construction, mortgage, commercial, financial, agricultural and consumer loans. The group conducts its banking business from 3 offices located in charlotte metropolitan area and in 20 offices in caldwell, catawba, burke watauga, wilkes and mecklenburg counties in North Carolina. The mortgage banking business is conducted through 11 offices in the central and southern piedmont and catawba valley regions of North Carolina and in jilton head island. The group's majority of customers are individuals and small businesses.

Primary SIC and add'l.: 6712 6022

CIK No: 0000810689

Subsidiaries: Bank of Granite, Granite Mortgage, Inc

Officers: Charles M. Snipes/Chmn., CEO/$555,273.00, Gary L. Lackey/Pres., CEO - Granite Mortgage/$194,740.00, Kirby A. Tyndall/Exec. VP, Sec., Treasurer, CFO/$287,906.00, Scott R. Anderson/COO, Pres./$346,245.00, Samuel M. Black/Sr. VP, Karen B. Warlick/Sr. VP, Dir. - Human Resources, John S. Gabriel/Special Assets Officer, W. C. Upchurch/Sr. VP, Office Administrator, Terry N. Freeman/Sr. VP, Karen C. Stroup/Banking Officer, Samuel B. Stephenson/Banking Officer, Dana F. Watson/Banking Officer, Adam M. Wingler/Assist. VP, Randell M. Dula/Collections Officer, Wayne G. Bass/VP, Chief Auditor *(64 Officers included in Index)*

Directors: Charles M. Snipes/Chmn., CEO, John N. Bray/Vice Chmn., Hugh R. Gaither/Dir., Boyd C. Wilson/Dir., James Y. Preston/Dir., Lelia N. Erwin/Dir., Joseph D. Crocker/Dir., Paul M. Fleetwood/Dir.

Owners: John A. Forlines/5.33%, Hugh R. Gaither, Charles M. Snipes/1.42%, Kirby A. Tyndall, Mark D. Stephens, Boyd C. Wilson, Scott R. Anderson, John N. Bray, James Y. Preston, Insiders/3.21%, Paul M. Fleetwood/1.11%, Gary L. Lackey, Leila N. Erwin, Joseph D. Crocker

Financial Data: *Fiscal Year End:*12/31 *Latest Annual Data:* 12/31/2006

Year	Sales	Net Income
2006	$99,049,000	$18,032,000
2005	$80,070,000	$15,010,000
2004	$66,523,000	$12,718,000

Curr. Assets:	$58,602,000	**Curr. Liab.:**	$998,316,000	**P/E Ratio:**	19.94
Plant, Equip.:	$13,426,000	**Total Liab.:**	$1,053,339,000	**Indic. Yr. Divd.:**	$0.520
Total Assets:	$1,199,772,000	**Net Worth:**	$146,434,000	**Debt/ Equity:**	0.0849

Bank of Hawall Corp

130 Merchant St., Honolulu, HI, 96813; *PH:* 1-888-643-3888; *Fax:* 1-808-537-8440; *http://* www.boh.com

General - Incorporation	DE	**Stock**- Price on:12/24/2007	$51.69
Employees	2,600	Stock Exchange	NYSE
Auditor	Ernst & Young LLP	Ticker Symbol	BOH
Stk Agt	Computershare Investor Services LLC	Outstanding Shares	49,560,000
Counsel	NA	E.P.S	$3.87
DUNS No.	00-692-6752	Shareholders	NA

Business: The group's principal activities are to provide a wide range of banking financial services and products. The group is engaged in equipment leasing, insurance services, securities brokerage and investment services. The group's operations are conducted through its business segments retail banking, commercial banking, investment services group and treasury and other corporate. The retail banking segment provides residential mortgage loans, home equity lines of credit, automobile loans and checking and time deposit accounts. The commercial banking segment offers products like commercial real estate loans, lease financing, auto dealer financing, cash management and casualty insurance products. The investment services group offers trust services and asset management services. The treasury and other corporate segment consists of asset and liability management activities. The group has operating facilities located in Hawaii and the pacific islands comprising 88 branches.

Primary SIC and add'l.: 6021 6022 6712

CIK No: 0000046195

Subsidiaries: Bancorp Hawaii Capital Trust I, Bank Of Hawaii, Bank of Hawaii Insurance Services,Inc. (Insurance), Bank of Hawaii International,Inc., Bank of Hawaii Leasing,Inc. (Parent)(Leasing), Bankoh Investment Partners, LLC, Bankoh Investment Services,Inc. (Brokerage), BNE Airfleets Corporation, Pacific Century Advisory Services,Inc.(Advisory Services), Pacific Century Insurance Services,Inc. (Captive Insurance), Pacific Century Leasing International, LLC, Pacific Century Life Insurance Corporation (Insurance), RGA Corp., Triad Insurance Agency,Inc. (Insurance)

Officers: Allan R. Landon/Chmn., CEO, Pres./$2,274,759.00, Peter S. Ho/Vice Chmn., Chief Banking Officer - Bank, Hawaii/$1,052,174.00, Shelley B. Thompson/Vice Chmn., Chief Fiduciary Officer, David W. Thomas/Vice Chmn., COO - Bank, Hawaii/$1,939,986.00, Daniel C. Stevens/Vice Chmn., CFO, Mark A. Rossi/Vice Chmn., Chief Administrative Officer, Brian T. Stewart/Exec. VP, Controller

Directors: Allan R. Landon/Chmn., CEO, Pres., David W. Thomas/Vice Chmn., COO - Bank, Hawaii, Mary E. Sellers/Vice Chmn. - Corporate Risk, Donna A. Tanoue/Vice Chmn. - Bank, Hawaii, Shelley B. Thompson/Vice Chmn., Chief Fiduciary Officer, Alton T. Kuioka/Vice Chmn. - Bank, Hawaii, Peter S. Ho/Vice Chmn., Chief Banking Officer - Bank, Hawaii, Clinton R. Churchill/Dir., Michael J. Chun/Dir., Barbara J. Tanabe/Dir., Donald M. Takaki/Dir., Robert W. Wo/Dir., Mary G. Bitterman/Dir., Robert Huret/Dir., Haunani Apoliona/Dir. *(18 Directors included in Index)*

Owners: Clinton R. Churchill, Allan R. Landon, Peter S. Ho, Robert W. Wo, Insiders/2.30%, Donald M. Takaki, Haunani S. Apoliona, Kent T. Lucien, Michael J. Chun, David A. Heenan, David W. Thomas, Robert Huret, Barbara J. Tanabe, Neal C. Hocklander, Mary G.F. Bitterman *(19 Owners included in Index)*

Financial Data: *Fiscal Year End:*12/31 *Latest Annual Data:* 12/31/2006

Year	Sales	Net Income
2006	$788,848,000	$180,359,000
2005	$715,756,000	$181,561,000
2004	$660,902,000	$173,339,000

Curr. Assets:	$526,214,000	**Curr. Liab.:**	$9,443,566,000	**P/E Ratio:**	14.36
Plant, Equip.:	$126,332,000	**Total Liab.:**	$9,852,395,000	**Indic. Yr. Divd.:**	$1.760
Total Assets:	$10,571,815,000	**Net Worth:**	$719,420,000	**Debt/ Equity:**	NA

Bank of Ireland (The)

75 Holly Hill Ln., Greenwich, CT, 06830; *PH:* 1-203-869-0111; *Fax:* 1-203-869-0268; *http://* www.bankofireland.ie

General - Incorporation		**Stock**- Price on:12/24/2007	$86.32
Employees	NA	Stock Exchange	NYSE
Auditor	NA	Ticker Symbol	IRE
Stk Agt	Computershare Investor Services LLC	Outstanding Shares	238,850,000
Counsel	n	E.P.S	$9.21
DUNS No.	NA	Shareholders	NA

Business: The groups principal activities include banking and other financial services. The groups products include current account, overdrafts, loans, leasing, invoice discounting and deposit accounts. In the year 2006, the group acquired Guggenheim Advisors. The group operates from the United States. The groups total assts in the year 2006 was $177,843 (millions).

Primary SIC and add'l.: 6029

CIK No: 0000800179

Officers: Brian J. Goggin/Group Chief Executive, Des Crowley/Dir., Chief Executive - UK Financial Services, Derek Collins/Dir. - New Business, Letitia Kelly/Mgr. - New Business, Louise Millward/Treasury, New Business UK, Henry Cleary/Treasury, New Business Ukscott Cowan, Scott Cowan/Treasury, New Business UK, George Magan/Deputy Governor, John Barry/Treasury, New Business UK, Conor Haugh/Treasury, New Business Ireland, John Kelly/Treasury, New Business Ireland, Tom Fuller/Treasury, New Business Ireland, Seamus Creaven/Treasury, New Business Ireland, Ann O'Meara/Treasury, New Business Ireland, Lorraine Spillane/Treasury, New Business Ireland *(21 Officers included in Index)*

Directors: Des Crowley/Dir., Chief Executive - UK Financial Services, David Dilger/Non Exec. Dir., Paul Haran/Non Exec. Dir., Dennis Holt/Non Exec. Dir., Declan McCourt/Non Exec. Dir., Terry Neill/Non Exec. Dir., Heather Ann McSharry/46/Non Exec. Dir., Jerome Kennedy/59/Non Exec. Dir., Rose Hynes/50/Non Exec. Dir., Richie Boucher/Dir., Chief Executive - Retail Financial Services Ireland, Denis Donovan/Dir., Chief Executive - Capital Markets, John O'Donovan/Dir., Group CFO

Financial Data: *Fiscal Year End:* *Latest Annual Data:* 03/31/2007

Year	Sales	Net Income
2007	$16,000,667,000	$2,206,943,000
2006	$11,061,616,000	$969,703,000
2005	$7,301,415,000	$1,061,695,000

Curr. Assets:	$4,231,430,000	**Curr. Liab.:**	$116,908,963,000	**P/E Ratio:**	16.93
Plant, Equip.:	$1,325,945,000	**Total Liab.:**	$189,570,254,000	**Indic. Yr. Divd.:**	$2.840
Total Assets:	$195,633,615,000	**Net Worth:**	$6,009,018,000	**Debt/ Equity:**	NA

Bank of Kentucky Financial Corp

111 Lookout Farm Dr., Crestview Hills, KY, 41017; *PH:* 1-859-371-2340; *Fax:* 1-859-578-2487; *http://* www.bankofky.com

General - Incorporation	KY	**Stock**- Price on:12/24/2007	$25.8
Employees	251	Stock Exchange	OTC
Auditor	Crowe Chizek & Co. LLC	Ticker Symbol	BKYF
Stk Agt	Firstar Corporation	Outstanding Shares	5,780,000
Counsel	Ziegler & Schneider	E.P.S	$1.91
DUNS No.	61-738-7279	Shareholders	NA

Business: The group's principal activity is to provide community-oriented consumer and commercial financial services to customers throughout northern Kentucky. The group is a holding company for the bank of Kentucky inc whose activity consists of accepting consumer and commercial deposits and using such deposits to fund residential and non-residential real estate loans and commercial, consumer, construction and land development loans. The federal deposit insurance corporation has insured the deposits. The group also makes construction and equipment loans to the municipalities of Kentucky. The group operates through its subsidiary primarily in boone, campbell, grant and kenton counties in northern Kentucky.

Primary SIC and add'l.: 6712 6022

CIK No: 0000934547

Subsidiaries: The Bank of Kentucky, Inc.

Officers: Robert W. Zapp/Dir., CEO, Pres./$600,753.00, Martin J. Gerrety/44/CFO, Treasurer, Assist. Sec./$210,292.00

Directors: Robert W. Zapp/Dir., CEO, Pres., Rodney S. Cain/69/Chmn., R. C. Durr/88/Chmn. Emeritus, Barry G. Kienzle/Dir., Mary Sue Rudicill/Dir., John E. Miracle/Dir., Ruth Seligman-Doering/67/Dir., Ruth Seligman Doering/Dir., John P. Williams/Dir., Harry J. Humpert/Dir., Charles M. Berger/Dir., Herbert H. Works/Dir.

Owners: John E. Miracle/1.91%, Mary Sue Rudicill/1.54%, John P. Williams, Charles M. Berger/1.22%, Herbert H. Works, Martin J. Gerrety, Harry J. Humpert, Barry C. Kienzle, Ruth Seligman-Doering/2.14%, Insiders/43.56%, Robert W. Zapp/3.65%, R. C. Durr/16.52%, Rodney S. Cain/15.52%

Financial Data: Fiscal Year End: 12/31 **Latest Annual Data:** 12/31/2006

Year	Sales	Net Income
2006	$75,405,000	$10,452,000
2005	$59,840,000	$10,127,000
2004	$49,862,000	$10,058,000

Curr. Assets:	$67,875,000	Curr. Liab.:	$940,773,000	P/E Ratio:	13.95
Plant, Equip.:	$17,069,000	Total Liab.:	$964,680,000	Indic. Yr. Divd.:	$0.480
Total Assets:	$1,051,563,000	Net Worth:	$86,883,000	Debt/ Equity:	0.2725

Bank of Louisiana

300 St. Charles Ave., New Orleans, LA, 70130; *PH:* 1-504-889-9400; *Fax:* 1-504-592-0606; *http://* www.bankoflouisiana.com

General - Incorporation	LA	Stock - Price on:12/24/2007	NA
Employees	NA	Stock Exchange	NA
Auditor	Laporte, Sehrt, Romig & Hand	Ticker Symbol	NA
Stk Agt	NA	Outstanding Shares	NA
Counsel	NA	E.P.S.	NA
DUNS No.	36-441-8335	Shareholders	NA

Business: The group's principal activities are to provide commercial banking and related services. The services offered by the group include checking accounts, negotiable order of withdrawal accounts, individual retirement accounts, savings and other time deposits of various types and business, real-estate, personal use, home improvement, automobile and a variety of other loans. Other services of the group include letters of credit, safe deposit boxes, money orders, traveler's checks, credit cards, wire transfer, electronic banking, night deposit and drive-in facilities. The group's operations are conducted through offices at 6 locations in the state of Louisiana.

Primary SIC and add'l.: 6712 6022

CIK No: 0000832818

Officers: Peggy L. Schaefer/55/CFO, Sr. VP, Treasurer, Jefferson Parish/Contact - Metairie, Orleans Parish/Contact - Main Office, Tammany Parish/Contact - Slidell

Directors: Harrison G. Scott/84/Chmn., Johnny C. Crow/57/Dir., Henry L. Klein/63/Dir., Franck F. Labiche/62/Dir., Sharry R. Scott/37/Dir.

Owners: Franck F. LaBiche, Edward J. Soniat/5.79%, Scott Family, LLP/31.25%, Harrison G. Scott/23.11%, Johnny C. Crow, Harrison G. Scott/7.55%, Henry L. Klein, Insiders/55.88%, Insiders/7.68%, Edward J. Soniat/12.32%

Bank of Marin

Pell Plz., 504 Redwood Blvd., Ste. 100, Novato, CA, 94947; *PH:* 1-415-763-4520; *http://* www.bankofmarin.com

General - Incorporation		Stock - Price on:12/24/2007	$32.99
Employees	194	Stock Exchange	NDQ
Auditor	NA	Ticker Symbol	BMRC
Stk Agt	Registrar & Transfer Co	Outstanding Shares	5,190,000
Counsel	NA	E.P.S.	NA
DUNS No.	NA	Shareholders	NA

Business: The groups principal activity is to provide banking and financial services. The groups products include Commercial Real Estate Loans, Construction Loans and Lines of Credit. The group operates from the United States.

Primary SIC and add'l.: 6712 6022

CIK No: 0000890479

Officers: Russell A. Colombo/Dir., CEO, Pres., Peter Pelham/Exec. Officer, Nancy R. Boatright/Exec. Officer, Christina Cook/Exec. Officer, Michael Besselievre/Exec. Officer, Roy Dotto/Organizer, William A. Gleason/Organizer, Peter J. Hunt/Organizer, Kevin Coonan/Exec. Officer, Hector A. Rubini/Organizer, Judi Cole/Corp. Officer, Chris Colliver/Corp. Officer, Neils Schultz/Organizer, Gimi Sessi/Organizer, Nancy Jones/Corp. Officer *(89 Officers included in Index)*

Directors: Russell A. Colombo/Dir., CEO, Pres., Joel Sklar/Chmn., Judith O'Connell Allen/Dir., Stuart Lum/Dir., James D. Kirsner/Dir., Patrick J. Hunt/Dir., William H. McDevitt/Dir., James E. Deitz/Dir., Joe Martino/Dir., Brian M. Sobel/Dir., Norma J. Howard/Dir., Dietrich J. Stroeh/Dir., Robert Heller/Dir., Jan Yanchiro/Dir.

Financial Data: Fiscal Year End: NA **Latest Annual Data:** 12/31/2006

Year	Sales	Net Income
2006	$62,283,000	$11,883,000
2005	$53,193,000	$11,737,000
2004	$41,232,000	$9,518,000

Curr. Assets:	$67,004,000	Curr. Liab.:	$782,053,000		
Plant, Equip.:	$8,446,000	Total Liab.:	$787,053,000	Indic. Yr. Divd.:	NA
Total Assets:	$876,578,000	Net Worth:	$89,525,000	Debt/ Equity:	0.0762

Bank of Montreal

1 First Canadian Pl., 21st Fl. , Toronto, ON , M5X 1A1 ; *PH:* 1-312-461-2121; *Fax:* 1-312-461-3869; *http://* www.bmo.com; *Email:* corp.secretary@bmo.com

General - Incorporation	Canada	Stock - Price on:12/24/2007	$63.29
Employees	34,942	Stock Exchange	NYSE
Auditor	KPMG LLP	Ticker Symbol	BMO
Stk Agt	Computershare Trust Co of Canada	Outstanding Shares	499,830,000
Counsel	NA	E.P.S.	$4.14
DUNS No.	25-721-2316	Shareholders	NA

Business: The group's principle activities are to provide a range of retail banking, wealth management and investment banking products and solutions. The group serves clients across Canada and in the United States through its Canadian retail arm BMO Bank of Montreal, Chicago-based Harris Bank,

a United States mid-west financial services organization which also has wealth management offices and branches across the United States and BMO Nesbitt Burns, a North America's full-service investment firm. The group's financial division is made up of three client groups: personal and commercial client group (p&c), private client group (pcg) and investment banking group (ibg).

Primary SIC and add'l.: 6021

CIK No: 0000927971

Subsidiaries: Bank of Montreal Holding Enterprise Inc., Bmo (us) Funding, LLC, Bmo (us) Lending, LLC, BMO Financial Group, BMO Financial, Inc, BMO Global Capital Solutions, Inc., BMO Holding Finance, LLC, BMO Nesbitt Burns Equity Group (U.S.), Inc, BMO, Efs (u.s.), Inc, Harris Bancorp Insurance Services, Inc, Harris Bankcorp, Inc, Harris Financial Corp, Harris Investment Management, Inc., Harris Nesbitt Corp 17 Subsidiaries included in the Index

Officers: Yvan J.P. Bourdeau/CEO - BMO Capital Markets, Head - Investment Banking Group, William A. Downe/55/Dir., CEO, Pres., Ellen M. Costello/CEO - Harris Bankcorp, Inc, Michael R.P. Rayfield/Vice Chmn. - Investment, Corporate Banking, BMO Capital Markets, Pamela J. Robertson/Exec. VP - Personal, Commercial Delivery, BMO Bank, Montreal, Robert McGlashan/Exec. VP, Chief Risk Officer - Enterprise Risk, Portfolio Management, BMO Financial Group, Dina Palozzi/Exec. VP - Client Relations, BMO Nesbitt Burns, Sr. VP, Chief Privacy Officer - BMO Financial Group, Penny Somerville/Exec. VP, Sr. Marketing Risk Officer - BMO Financial Group, Eric C. Tripp/Co - Pres. - BMO Capital Markets, Viki Lazaris/Sr. VP - Investor Relations, Steve Bonin/Dir. - Investor Relations, Krista White/Sr. Mgr. - Investor Relations, Melissa Wynne/Events Coordinator, Investor Relations, Neil R. MacMillan/Exec. VP, Sr. Risk Officer - Investment Banking Group, BMO Financial Group , Barry K. Gilmour/Group Head - Technology, Operations *(28 Officers included in Index)*

Directors: William A. Downe/55/Dir., CEO, Pres., David A. Galloway/64/Chmn., Eva Lee Kwok/65/Dir., Harold N. Kvisle/55/Dir., Robert M. Astley/63/Dir., Stephen E. Bachand/69/Dir., David R. Beatty/65/Dir., Robert Chevrier/64/Dir., George A. Cope/Dir., Ronald H. Farmer/57/Dir., Bruce H. Mitchell/61/Dir., Philip S. Orsino/53/Dir., Martha Piper/Dir., Robert J.S. Prichard/58/Dir., Jeremy H. Reitman/62/Dir. *(17 Directors included in Index)*

Owners: Jerome M. Edquist, James J. Rothenbach, Patti Nettesheim, Scott L. Anderson, Daniel J. Haislmaier/2.10%, Dean W. Fitting/8.30%, Richard J. Krier, M. D. Hepburn/14.40%, Insiders/30.30%, Larry R. Dalton/1.90%, William C. Werner, Peter T. Barry, William R. Arpe, George F. Roth/2.80%, Duane F. Stroebel *(16 Owners included in Index)*

Financial Data: Fiscal Year End: 10/31 **Latest Annual Data:** 10/31/2006

Year	Sales	Net Income
2006	$16,197,922,000	$2,325,334,000
2005	$12,935,122,000	$1,934,828,000
2004	$10,842,447,000	$1,839,637,000

Curr. Assets:	$102,635,024,000	Curr. Liab.:	$238,320,838,000		
Plant, Equip.:	$1,860,446,000	Total Liab.:	$280,714,011,000	Indic. Yr. Divd.:	$2.570
Total Assets:	$294,558,938,000	Net Worth:	$13,844,927,000	Debt/ Equity:	NA

Bank of Napa NA CA

2007 Redwood Rd., Ste. 101, Napa, CA, 94558; *PH:* 1-707-257-7777; *Fax:* 1-707-257-1497; *http://* www.thebankofnapa.com

General - Incorporation		Stock - Price on:12/24/2007	$9.56
Employees	NA	Stock Exchange	OTC
Auditor	NA	Ticker Symbol	BNNP
Stk Agt	NA	Outstanding Shares	NA
Counsel	NA	E.P.S.	NA
DUNS No.	NA	Shareholders	NA

Business: The groups principle activity is to provide banking services, The groups services include online banking, personal, and business services. The groups personal banking services include personal checking account, harvest checking account, personal internet checking, certificate of deposits, direct deposit checking and spirit checking. The group operates from United States.

Primary SIC and add'l.: 6022

CIK No:

Officers: Thomas M. Lemasters/Exec. VP, CFO, Interim CEO, Diane Bishofberger/Sr. VP, Bank Sales Mgr., Donna Cordeiro/Business Development Officer, Lise Tarner/VP, Relationship Mgr., Ruth Appleby/VP, Relationship Mgr., Cheryl Payan/Customer Service Mgr., Lisa Gallo/Investor Relations Officer, John Cavender/Investor Relations Officer

Directors: Dick Anderson/Dir., Greg Bennett/Dir., Michael Livingston/Dir., Malcolm A. MacKenzie/Dir., John K. Meras/Dir., Leroy Moore/Dir., Harold Moskowite/Dir., Lisa R. Paul/Dir., Kent D. Payne/Dir., Ernest A. Rota/Dir.

Bank of New Canaan (The)

156 Cherry St., New Canaan, CT, 06840; *PH:* 1-203-972-3838; *http://* www.bankofnewcanaan.com; *Email:* bnc@bankofnewcanaan.com

General - Incorporation		Stock - Price on:12/24/2007	$20.75
Employees	NA	Stock Exchange	OTC
Auditor	NA	Ticker Symbol	BNFI
Stk Agt	Registrar & Transfer Co	Outstanding Shares	NA
Counsel	NA	E.P.S.	NA
DUNS No.	NA	Shareholders	NA

Business: The groups principal activity is to provide banking business. The group financial products include savings and fixed deposits, on line, personal, commercial lending and business banking. The group operates from the United States.

Primary SIC and add'l.: 6022

CIK No:

Bank of New York Co Inc

1 Wall St., 10th Fl., New York, NY, 10286; *PH:* 1-212-495-1784; *Fax:* 1-212-809-9528; *http://* www.bankofny.com

General - Incorporation	NY	Stock - Price on:12/24/2007	$41.96
Employees	22,961	Stock Exchange	NYSE
Auditor	Ernst & Young LLP	Ticker Symbol	BK
Stk Agt	Mellon Investor Services	Outstanding Shares	758,520,000
Counsel	NA	E.P.S.	$3.96
DUNS No.	00-698-5873	Shareholders	NA

Business: The groups principle activity is to provide financial services. The groups services include wealth management, asset management and advisor service. The group operates from United States.

Primary SIC and add'l.: 6712 6022

CIK No: 0000009626

Subsidiaries: New York State Chartered Bank, Pershing Group LLC

Officers: Richard Brueckner/CEO - Pershing, Brian G. Rogan/CEO - Issuer, Treasury Services The Bank, New York Mellon/$5,516.00, Robert P. Kelly/Dir., CEO, David F. Lamere/CEO - BNY Mellon Wealth Management, Ronald P. O'Hanley/CEO - BNY Mellon Asset Management, James P. Palermo/Co - CEO - BNY Mellon Asset Servicing, Karen B. Peetz/CEO - Bank, New York Mellon Corporate Trust, Timothy F. Keaney/Co - CEO - BNY Mellon Asset Servicing, Thomas A. Renyi/Exec. Chmn./$13,634.00, Donald R. Monks/Vice Chmn., Co - Head - Integration/$6,230.00, Steven G. Elliott/Sr. Vice Chmn., Co - Head - Integration, John M. Liftin/64/Vice Chmn., General Counsel, Torry Berntsen/Chief Client Management Officer, Carl Krasik/General Counsel, Lisa B. Peters/Chief Human Resources Officer *(34 Officers included in Index)*

Directors: Robert P. Kelly/Dir., CEO, Steven G. Elliott/Sr. Vice Chmn., Co - Head - Integration, Thomas A. Renyi/Exec. Chmn., John M. Liftin/64/Vice Chmn., General Counsel, Michael J. Kowalski/Dir., Nicholas M. Donofrio/Dir., John C. Malone/Dir., Gerald L. Hassell/Dir., Pres., Brian L. Roberts/Dir., Richard C. Vaughan/Dir., Frank J. Biondi/Dir., Richard J. Kogan/Dir., Catherine A. Rein/Dir., William C. Richardson/Dir., Ruth E. Bruch/Dir. *(22 Directors included in Index)*

Owners: Richard J. Kogan, Brian L. Roberts, Gerald L. Hassell, Frank J. Biondi, John C. Malone, William C. Richardson, Samuel C. Scott, John A. Luke, Paul Myners, Nicholas M. Donofrio, Catherine A. Rein, Brian G. Rogan, Donald R. Monks, Thomas A. Renyi, Leslie V. Godridge *(21 Owners included in Index)*

Financial Data: Fiscal Year End:12/31 Latest Annual Data: 12/31/2006

Year	Sales	Net Income
2006	$9,062,000,000	$3,011,000,000
2005	$8,312,000,000	$1,571,000,000
2004	$7,144,000,000	$1,440,000,000

Curr. Assets:	$31,072,000,000	**Curr. Liab.:**	$75,746,000,000	**P/E Ratio:**	10.60
Plant, Equip.:	$1,068,000,000	**Total Liab.:**	$91,777,000,000	**Indic. Yr. Divd.:**	$0.960
Total Assets:	$103,370,000,000	**Net Worth:**	$11,593,000,000	**Debt/ Equity:**	0.8969

Bank of Nova Scotia (The)

55 Ontario St. s, Milton, ON, L9T 2M3; *PH:* 1-905-878-4173; *http://* www.scotiabank.com; *Email:* email@scotiabank.com

General - Incorporation	Canada	**Stock** - Price on:12/24/2007	$49.62
Employees	53,251	Stock Exchange	NYSE
Auditor	KPMG LLP	Ticker Symbol	BNS
Stk Agt	Computershare Trust Co	Outstanding Shares	989,730,000
Counsel	NA	E.P.S	$4.06
DUNS No.	NA	Shareholders	NA

Business: The groups principal activity is to provide banking services. The group operates from Canada.

Primary SIC and add'l.: 6021

CIK No: 0000009631

Subsidiaries: BNS Capital Trust, BNS International (Barbados) Limited, BNS Investments Inc., BNSII Group, Corporacion Interfin, Grupo BNS de Costa Rica, S.A., Grupo Financiero Scotiabank, S.A. de C.V. (97%), Maple Trust Company, Montreal Trust Company of Canada, MontroServices Corporation, National Trust Company, National Trustco Inc., Nova Scotia Inversiones Limitada, RoyNat Inc., Scotia Capital (USA)Inc. 46 Subsidiaries included in the Index

Officers: Stephen D. McDonald/Co - Chmn., Co - CEO - Scotia Capital, Head - Global Corporate, Investment Banking, John C. Schumacher/Co - Chmn., Co - CEO - Scotia Capital, Head - Global Capital Markets, Sarabjit S. Marwah/Vice Chmn., Chief Administrative Officer, Robert L. Brooks/Vice Chmn., Group Treasurer, Deborah M. Alexander/Exec. VP, General Counsel, Sec., Alberta G. Cefis/Exec. VP, Group Head - Global Transaction Banking, Sylvia D. Chrominska/Exec. VP - Human Resources, Public, Corporate, Government Affairs, Wendy Hannam/Exec. VP - Domestic Personal Banking, Distribution, Timothy P. Hayward/Exec. VP, Chief Administrative Officer - International Banking, Christopher J. Hodgson/Exec. VP, Head - Domestic Personal Banking, Dieter W. Jentsch/Exec. VP - Domestic Commercial Banking, Barb Mason/Exec. VP - Wealth Management, Luc A. Vanneste/CFO, Exec. VP, Robin S. Hibberd/Exec. VP - Domestic Personal Lending, Insurance, Ann Derabbie/Sr. Mgr. - Public Affairs *(21 Officers included in Index)*

Directors: Sarabjit S. Marwah/Vice Chmn., Chief Administrative Officer, Robert L. Brooks/Vice Chmn., Group Treasurer, Ashleigh N. Everett/Dir., John C. Kerr/Dir., Ronald A. Brenneman/Dir., C. J. Chen/Dir., Barbara S. Thomas/Dir., Richard E. Waugh/Dir., Michael J.L. Kirby/Dir., Laurent Lemaire/Dir., John T. Mayberry/Dir., Barbara J. McDougall/Dir., Elizabeth Parr-Johnston/Dir., Alexis E. Rovzar De La Torre/Dir., Arthur R.A. Scace/Dir. *(18 Directors included in Index)*

Financial Data: Fiscal Year End:10/31 Latest Annual Data: 10/31/2006

Year	Sales	Net Income
2006	$20,060,689,000	$3,173,019,000
2005	$15,584,033,000	$2,773,876,000
2004	$13,542,387,000	$2,500,461,000

Curr. Assets:	$76,766,354,000	**Curr. Liab.:**	$236,702,206,000	**P/E Ratio:**	10.06
Plant, Equip.:	NA	**Total Liab.:**	$335,660,060,000	**Indic. Yr. Divd.:**	$1.810
Total Assets:	$351,894,566,000	**Net Worth:**	$16,234,506,000	**Debt/ Equity:**	NA

Bank of Oak Ridge

105 N Oak St., Oak Ridge, LA, 71264; *PH:* 1-318-244-6560; *http://* www.bankofoakridge.com

General - Incorporation		**Stock** - Price on:12/24/2007	$11.2
Employees	64	Stock Exchange	NDQ
Auditor	NA	Ticker Symbol	BKOR
Stk Agt	First Citizens Bank & Trust Co	Outstanding Shares	1,790,000
Counsel	NA	E.P.S	$0.46
DUNS No.	NA	Shareholders	NA

Business: The groups principal activity is to provide banking and financial services. The group operates from the United States.

Primary SIC and add'l.: 6022

CIK No:

Officers: Ronald O. Black/Dir., CEO, Pres., Thomas W. Wayne/Sr. VP, Chief Finanical Officer, William L. Vasaly/VP, Relationship Mgr.

Directors: Ronald O. Black/Dir., CEO, Pres., Douglas G. Boike/Chmn., Herbert M. Cole/Dir., Craig S. Fleming/Dir., Billy R. Kanoy/Dir., Francis R. Disney/Dir., Stephen S. Neal/Dir., Manuel L. Perkins/Dir., James W. Hall/Dir., Lynda J. Lengyel/Dir., John S. Olmsted/Dir.

Financial Data: Fiscal Year End:NA Latest Annual Data: 12/31/2006

Year	Sales	Net Income
2006	$14,950,000	$1,259,000
2005	$10,283,000	$794,000
2003	$4,717,000	-$263,000

Curr. Assets:	$12,874,000	**Curr. Liab.:**	$174,232,000		
Plant, Equip.:	$5,022,000	**Total Liab.:**	$190,683,000	**Indic. Yr. Divd.:**	NA
Total Assets:	$207,136,000	**Net Worth:**	$16,453,000	**Debt/ Equity:**	0.9651

Bank of Salem OR

100 W Fourth St., Salem, MO, 65560; *PH:* 1-573-729-3137; *Fax:* 1-573-729-2668; *http://* www.thebankofsalem.com; *Email:* bank@thebankofsalem.com

General - Incorporation		**Stock** - Price on:12/24/2007	$19
Employees	NA	Stock Exchange	OTC
Auditor	NA	Ticker Symbol	BSOG
Stk Agt	NA	Outstanding Shares	NA
Counsel	NA	E.P.S	NA
DUNS No.	NA	Shareholders	NA

Business: The groups principle activity is to provide banking products and services. The groups banking products include deposits, loans, insurance and deposits. The group also provides Internet banking and telephone banking services. The group operates from United States.

Primary SIC and add'l.: 6022

CIK No:

Officers: Scott D. Ball/Dir., Pres., Michael E. Douglas/Dir., Exec. VP, John D. Casey/Sr. VP, Denny J. Pogue/Sr. VP, Peggy L. Cubbage/VP, Leona F. McDaniels/Cashier, S. N. Ball/VP, Shericia J. Cook/Assist., Loan Officer, Barbara E. Medlock/Assist., Loan Officer, Gerriann C. Ball/Marketing Officer, Penny S. Cox/Information Technology Officer, Shirley E. Larson/Assist., Loan Officer

Directors: James L. Coffman/Chmn., Sanborn N. Ball/Vice Chmn., William E. Seay/Dir., George Alan Barnitz/Dir., Robert Coffman/Dir., Scott D. Ball/Dir., Pres., Michael E. Douglas/Dir., Exec. VP

Bank of South Carolina Corp

256 Meeting St., Charleston, SC, 29401; *PH:* 1-843-724-1500; *Fax:* 1-843-724-1513; *http://* www.banksc.com; *Email:* information@banksc.com

General - Incorporation	SC	**Stock** - Price on:12/24/2007	$15.3
Employees	67	Stock Exchange	NDQ
Auditor	KPMG LLP	Ticker Symbol	BKSC
Stk Agt	Computershare Investor Services LLC	Outstanding Shares	3,930,000
Counsel	Warren & Sinkler	E.P.S	$1.03
DUNS No.	15-421-0074	Shareholders	NA

Business: The group's principal activity is to provide consumer and commercial banking services to individuals and small to medium-sized businesses. The deposit products include regular non-interest bearing checking accounts as well as interest bearing negotiable order of withdrawal accounts, savings and certificate of deposit. The lending services include commercial, personal and mortgage loans. The group provides credit cards (through correspondent banking services) including mastercard (TM) and visa (TM) along with a personal checking account related line of credit. Other services provided include safe deposit boxes, letters of credit, travelers checks, direct deposit of payroll, social security and dividend payments and automatic payment of insurance premiums and mortgage loans. The group operates a courier service as part of its deposit services for commercial customers and provides a safekeeping brokerage service through one of its correspondent banks.

Primary SIC and add'l.: 6712 6022

CIK No: 0001007273

Officers: Hugh C. Lane/60/Dir., CEO, Pres./$213,130.50, William L. Hiott/63/Dir., Exec. VP, Treasurer/$187,534.00, Rhett D. Bearden/Assist. VP, Nancy Batchelder/Accounting Officer, Valerie Stone/Assist. VP, Helene Mixon/VP, Rovina Andrade/Branch Mgr., Fleetwood S. Hassell/Dir., Exec. VP - Advisory Board/$135,228.00, Lucy E. Ashley/VP, Jennifer A. Arato/Assist. VP, Sally I. Altman/Sr. VP, Ellen J. Cox/Assist. VP, Lynn C. Christian/VP, Liz Ryan/Loan Officer, Carlos Torres/Loan Officer *(35 Officers included in Index)*

Directors: Hugh C. Lane/60/Dir., CEO, Pres., Alan I. Nussbaum/56/Dir., Member - Advisory Board, William L. Hiott/63/Dir., Exec. VP, Treasurer, Charles G. Lane/53/Dir., Edmund Rhett/60/Dir., Malcolm M. Rhodes/49/Dir., Member - Advisory Board, Thomas C. Stevenson/57/Dir., Steve D. Swanson/40/Dir., Richard W. Hutson/50/Dir., Sec., Katherine M. Huger/66/Dir., Ronald C. Coward/72/Dir., Graham M. Eubank/40/Dir., Louise J. Maybank/68/Dir., Linda J. Bradley-Mckee/57/Dir., Dean T. Harton/62/Dir. *(31 Directors included in Index)*

Owners: Louise J. Maybank/1.11%, Alan I. Nussbaum, William L. Hiott/3.57%, Dean T. Harton, Fleetwood S. Hassell/1.38%, Thomas C. Stevenson, Glen B. Haynes, Hugh C. Lane/12.92%, Linda J. Bradley-McKee, Charles G. Lane/5.82%, Graham M. Eubank, Malcolm M. Rhodes, Richard W. Hutson, Steve D. Swanson/0.04%, Katherine M. Huger/0.20% *(18 Owners included in Index)*

Financial Data: Fiscal Year End:12/31 Latest Annual Data: 12/31/2006

Year	Sales	Net Income
2006	$17,660,000	$3,928,000
2005	$14,172,000	$3,185,000
2004	$9,653,000	$1,846,000

Curr. Assets:	$38,089,000	**Curr. Liab.:**	$219,833,000	**P/E Ratio:**	14.71
Plant, Equip.:	$2,662,000	**Total Liab.:**	$219,833,000	**Indic. Yr. Divd.:**	$0.640
Total Assets:	$243,473,000	**Net Worth:**	$23,640,000	**Debt/ Equity:**	NA

Bank of the Carolinas Corp

135 Boxwood Village Dr., Mocksville, NC, 27028; *PH:* 1-336-751-5755; *Fax:* 1-336-751-4222; *http://* www.bankofthecarolinas.com

General - Incorporation	NC	**Stock** - Price on:12/24/2007	$11.97
Employees	NA	Stock Exchange	NDQ
Auditor	Dixon Hughes PLLC	Ticker Symbol	BCAR
Stk Agt	First Citizens Bank & Trust Co	Outstanding Shares	3,830,000
Counsel	NA	E.P.S	$0.88
DUNS No.	NA	Shareholders	NA

Business: The group operates through its subsidiaries whose principle activity is to provide financial services. The groups services include deposits, loans, lending and, commercial and consumer banking services. The group operates from Asheboro, Cleveland, Landis, Harrisburg, Lexington and King. The assets of the group for the year 2006 were $37,906 (thousands).

Primary SIC and add'l.: 6022

CIK No: 0001365997

Officers: Robert Marziano/Chmn., CEO, Stephen R. Talbert/Vice Chmn., Branch Mgr. - Landis, Robin H. Smith/COO, Exec. VP, Lilliayn Arnette/Office Mgr., Banking Officer - Winston, Salem, Sheila M. Everhart/VP, Branch Mgr. - Lexington, Ed Jordan/Pres. - Advance, Harry Hill/Exec. VP - Mocksville, Eric Rhodes/Sr. VP, CFO - Mocksville, Rick James/VP, Branch Mgr. - Harrisburg, Wayne Jarrell/VP, Branch Mgr. - Harrisburg, Nelson Smith/VP, Branch Mgr. - King, Deborah B. Wright/VP, Mortgage Officer - Asheboro, Greg M. Cunningham/Sr. VP, Slayton Harpe/Sr. VP - Regional Executive, George Jarvis/Sr. VP *(20 Officers included in Index)*

Directors: Robert Marziano/Chmn., CEO, Stephen R. Talbert/Vice Chmn., Branch Mgr. - Landis

Owners: Lynne Scott Safrit/0.46%, Thomas G. Fleming/0.81%, Salem Investment Counselors, Inc/3.86%, Eric E. Rhodes/0.01%, Jerry W. Anderson/0.61%, Henry H. Land/0.51%, Alan M. Bailey/0.89%, Stephen R. Talbert/0.93%, Robert E. Marziano/1.62%, Michael D. Larrowe/0.59%, Steven G. Laymon/0.85%, John A. Drye/0.67%, George E. Jordan/0.10%, Wellington Management Company, LLP/3.52%, John W. Googe/0.48% *(20 Owners included in Index)*

Financial Data: Fiscal Year End:12/31 **Latest Annual Data:** 12/31/2006

Year	Sales	Net Income
2006	$32,650,000	$3,474,000
2005	$21,897,000	$2,333,000
2004	$14,316,000	$1,459,000

Curr. Assets:	$22,301,000	**Curr. Liab.:**	$416,864,000	**P/E Ratio:**	13.60
Plant, Equip.:	$12,142,000	**Total Liab.:**	$416,864,000	**Indic. Yr. Divd.:**	NA
Total Assets:	$454,578,000	**Net Worth:**	$37,714,000	**Debt/ Equity:**	0.5983

Bank of the James Financial Group Inc

828 Main St., Lynchburg, VA, 24504; **PH:** 1-434-846-2000; **Fax:** 1-434-846-4450; *http://* www.bankofthejames.com

General - Incorporation	VA	**Stock**- Price on:12/24/2007	$19.13
Employees	107	Stock Exchange	OTC
Auditor	Yount, Hyde & Barbour, P.C	Ticker Symbol	BOJF
Stk Agt	StockTrans, Inc.	Outstanding Shares	2,550,000
Counsel	NA	E.P.S.	$0.78
DUNS No.	NA	Shareholders	NA

Business: The group operates thru its subsidiary whose principal activity is banking operations. The group products include real estate loans, commercial real estate loans, home equity lines-of-credit, construction and land loans and deposits. The group operates from the United States. The groups asset in the year 2006 was $207,395.

Primary SIC and add'l.: 6022 6712

CIK No: 0001275101

Subsidiaries: Bank of the James, BOTJ Investment Group, Inc.

Officers: Robert R. Chapman/Dir., CEO, Pres., Todd J. Scruggs/Dir., Sec., Treasurer, CFO, Exec. VP, Martin E. Waltemyer/COO, Exec. VP, Garry L. Friend/Sr. VP, Retail Branch Administrator, Donna W. Guthrie/Sr. VP, Consumer Loan Officer, Chris P. Taylor/Sr. VP, Commercial Loan Officer, Harry P. Umberger/Sr. VP, Sr. Credit Officer, Rhonda R. Buracker/VP, Loan Administration Officer, Brian E. Cash/VP, Mgr. - Bank, James Mortgage, Brandon P. Farmer/VP, Information Technology Officer, Brenda P. Gray/VP, Business Development Officer, Angelia R. Johnson/VP, Regional Mgr., Katrina Y. Rice/VP, Commercial Loan Officer, Wilma K.E. Rucker/VP, Operations Officer, Lisa S. Light/Accounting, Financing Officer *(53 Officers included in Index)*

Directors: Robert R. Chapman/Dir., CEO, Pres., Kenneth S. White/Chmn., Thomas Watts Pettyjohn/Vice Chmn., Todd J. Scruggs/Dir., Sec., Treasurer, CFO, Exec. VP, Lewis C. Addison/Dir., William C. Bryant/Dir., Donna Schewel Clark/Dir., James F. Daly/Dir., Watt R. Foster/Dir., Donald M. Giles/Dir., Augustus A. Petticolas/Dir., Richard R. Zechini/Dir.

Owners: Augustus A. Petticolas, Watt R. Foster/1.85%, Kenneth S. White/1.32%, Robert R. Chapman/3.80%, James F. Daly/1.20%, Martin E. Waltemyer/1.55%, Insiders/16.63%, Richard R. Zechini/1.37%, Todd J. Scruggs/2.10%, Thomas W. Pettyjohn, Donald M. Giles/1.53%, William C. Bryant, Donna S. Clark/1.22%, Lewis C. Addison

Financial Data: Fiscal Year End:12/31 **Latest Annual Data:** 12/31/2006

Year	Sales	Net Income
2006	$16,994,000	$1,765,000
2005	$14,119,000	$1,791,000
2000	$3,233,000	-$86,000

Curr. Assets:	$11,186,000	**Curr. Liab.:**	$210,653,000		
Plant, Equip.:	$5,644,000	**Total Liab.:**	$210,778,000	**Indic. Yr. Divd.:**	NA
Total Assets:	$232,709,000	**Net Worth:**	$21,931,000	**Debt/ Equity:**	NA

Bank of the Ozarks

10500 Stonepoint Pl, Duluth, GA, 30097; **PH:** 1-678-584-2229; *http://* www.bankozarks.com

General - Incorporation	AR	**Stock**- Price on:12/24/2007	NA
Employees	NA	Stock Exchange	NDQ
Auditor	Crowe, Chizek and Company LLC	Ticker Symbol	OZRK
Stk Agt	Union Planters National Bank	Outstanding Shares	NA
Counsel	NA	E.P.S.	$1.84
DUNS No.	NA	Shareholders	NA

Business: The group operates through its subsidiaries whose principle activity is to provide retail and commercial banking services. The groups services include deposit, Lending, Leasing, mortgage lending, cash management, trust services, safety deposit boxes, real estate appraisals, credit related life and disability insurance, ATMs and telephone banking. The group operates from Charlotte, North Carolina, Little Rock, Arkansas, Tulsa and Oklahoma. The assets of the group for the year 2006 were $2.53 (billion).

Primary SIC and add'l.: 6021

CIK No: 0001038205

Subsidiaries: Bank of the Ozarks, Ozark Capital Statutory Trust II, Ozark Capital Statutory Trust III, Ozark Capital Statutory Trust IV, Ozark Capital Statutory Trust V

Officers: George Gleason/Chmn., CEO/$774,064.00, Mark Ross/Vice Chmn., COO, Pres./$293,098.00, Paul Moore/CFO, Chief Accounting Officer/$204,604.00, Fred Campbell/Pres. - Eastern Division, Danny Criner/Pres. - Northern Division, John Davis/Pres. - Hot Springs Division, C.

E. Dougan/Pres. - Western Division, Scott Hastings/Pres. - Leasing Division, Gene Holman/Pres. - Mortgage Division/$203,611.00, Dennis James/Pres. - Metro Dallas Division, Rex Kyle/Pres. - Trust Division, Shannon White/Pres. - Northwest Division, Brad Payne/Pres. - Russellville Division, Dan Rolett/Exec. VP, Darrel Russell/Pres. - Central Division/$192,892.00 *(19 Officers included in Index)*

Directors: George Gleason/Chmn., CEO, Mark Ross/Vice Chmn., COO, Pres., Steven Arnold/Dir., Richard Cisne/Dir., Robert East/Dir., Linda Gleason/Dir., Henry Mariani/Dir., James Matthews/Dir., John Mills/Dir., R. L. Qualls/Dir., Kennith Smith/Dir., Robert Trevino/Dir., Jean Arehart/Dir., Ian Arnof/Dir.

Owners: Richard Cisne, Steven Arnold, Darrel Russell, Fidelity Management & Research/9.96%, Wasatch Advisors, Inc./8.62%, Jean Arehart, John Mills, Mark Ross/2.20%, R. L. Qualls, Gene Holman, Henry Mariani, Robert Trevino, Kennith Smith, Robert East, George and Linda Gleason/22.70% *(21 Owners included in Index)*

Financial Data: Fiscal Year End:12/31 **Latest Annual Data:** 12/31/2006

Year	Sales	Net Income
2006	$178,429,000	$31,693,000
2005	$132,133,000	$31,489,000
2004	$103,456,000	$25,883,000

Curr. Assets:	$60,118,000	**Curr. Liab.:**	$2,095,156,000	**P/E Ratio:**	16.48
Plant, Equip.:	$117,086,000	**Total Liab.:**	$2,354,767,000	**Indic. Yr. Divd.:**	NA
Total Assets:	$2,529,400,000	**Net Worth:**	$174,633,000	**Debt/ Equity:**	NA

Bank of Tokyo-Mitsubishi

7-1 Marunouchi 2-chome, Chiyoda-Ku, Tokyo; ; *http://* www.bk.mufg.jp

General - Incorporation	Japan	**Stock**- Price on:12/24/2007	NA
Employees	NA	Stock Exchange	NA
Auditor	Deloitte Touche Tohmatsu	Ticker Symbol	NA
Stk Agt	Mitsubishi UFJ Trust & Banking Corp	Outstanding Shares	NA
Counsel	NA	E.P.S.	NA
DUNS No.	NA	Shareholders	NA

Business: The group's principle activity is to provider retail banking, commercial banking, corporate banking, investment banking and asset management services. The group operates from United States.

Primary SIC and add'l.: 6021

CIK No: 0000852743

Subsidiaries: Union Bank of California, N.A., UnionBanCal Corporation

Officers: Tatsuo Tanaka/59/Managing Exec. Officer, Deputy Chief Exec., Global Business Unit CEO - Asia, Oceania Exec. Officer China, Tadashi Shiraishi/55/Managing Exec. Officer, CEO - Europe, Middle East, Africa, Jun Sato/57/Managing Exec. Officer, Deputy CEO - Americas, Takashi Morimura/56/Managing Exec. Officer, CEO - Europe, Middle East, Africa, Ryosuke Tamakoshi/61/Dep. Chmn., Dir. - Internal Audit, Credit Examination Division, Kiyoshi Sono/55/Managing Exec. Officer, Group Head - Osaka Corporate Banking Group, Toshiaki Arai/54/Exec. Officer, GM - Nihonbashi Commercial Banking Office, Nobushige Kamei/56/Managing Exec. Officer, Kazuo Sassa/61/Dir., Deputy Pres., Takao Kawanishi/60/MD, Sohei Sasaki/58/MD, Chief Exec. - Global Markets Unit, Bank, Htatsunori Imagawa/65/Corporate Auditor, Kazuhiko Hasegawa/56/Corporate Auditor, Tsutomu Takasuka/66/Corporate Auditor, Kotaro Muneoka/68/Corporate Auditor *(68 Officers included in Index)*

Directors: Shigemitsu Miki/73/Chmn., Ryosuke Tamakoshi/61/Dep. Chmn., Dir. - Internal Audit, Credit Examination Division, Katsunori Nagayasu/61/Dir., Deputy Pres. - Business, Systems Integration Division, Norimichi Kanari/62/Dir., Kazuo Sassa/61/Dir., Deputy Pres., Kunio Ishihara/65/Dir., Teruo Ozaki/64/Dir., Nobuo Kuroyanagi/Dir., Pres., Takamune Okihara/57/Dir.

Owners: Mitsubishi UFJ Financial Group, Inc/65.56%, Bank of Tokyo-Mitsubishi UFJ/100.00%, Mitsubishi UFJ Financial Group, Inc./100.00%, Bank of Tokyo-Mitsubishi UFJ/100.00%, Mitsubishi UFJ Financial Group, Inc./99.93%, Mitsubishi UFJ Trust and Banking/0.07%, Bank of Tokyo-Mitsubishi UFJ/34.44%

Bank Of Virginia

11730 Hull St. Rd., Midlothian, VA, 23112; **PH:** 1-804-774-7576; **Fax:** 1-804-774-2306; *http://* www.bankofva.com

General - Incorporation		**Stock**- Price on:12/24/2007	$8.01
Employees	NA	Stock Exchange	NDQ
Auditor	NA	Ticker Symbol	BOVA
Stk Agt	Computershare Trust Co	Outstanding Shares	3,030,000
Counsel	NA	E.P.S.	NA
DUNS No.	NA	Shareholders	NA

Business: The groups principle activity is to provide recruiting services. The groups service area includes the research and development, engineering, marketing, sales, information technology and manufacturing industries. The group operates from United States.

Primary SIC and add'l.: 6021

CIK No:

Officers: Frank Bell/Dir., CEO, Pres., Sandra Krajacich/Assist. VP, Branch Mgr., Scott Rowe/Assist. VP - Commercial Loans, Bruce T. Brockwell/Sr. VP, Chief Credit Officer, Kenneth P. Mulkey/Sr. VP, CFO, Ann-Cabell Williams/Sr. VP - Retail Banking Executive, Thomas L. Adams/VP - Commercial Loans, Ellen L. Allen/VP - Loan Operations, Lisa S. Carter/Compliance Officer, Assist. VP, Nancy R. Coffman/VP - Human Resources, Tammy F. Ferguson/Bank Officer, Branch Mgr., Rene T. Metz/VP - Construction Loans, Kim D. Norwood/Bank Officer, Deposit Operations Mgr., Donald J. Seeterlin/Bank Officer, Information Technology Dir., Jane H. Wagner/Assist. VP, Branch Mgr. *(19 Officers included in Index)*

Directors: Frank Bell/Dir., CEO, Pres., Vernon E. Laprade/Chmn., H. E. Richeson/Vice Chmn., Gary W. Fenchuk/Dir., Waddy G. Garrett/Dir., Thomas L. Gordon/Dir., Michael J. Jarvis/Dir., Jack W. Miller/Dir., Claiborne G. Thomasson/Dir.

Bank Reale WA

5205 N Road 68, Pasco, WA, 99301; **PH:** 1-509-545-6360; *http://* www.bankreale.com

General - Incorporation		**Stock**- Price on:12/24/2007	$24
Employees	NA	Stock Exchange	OTC
Auditor	NA	Ticker Symbol	BKRL
Stk Agt	NA	Outstanding Shares	NA
Counsel	NA	E.P.S.	NA
DUNS No.	NA	Shareholders	NA

Business: The groups principle activity is to provide banking services. The group provides personal, business and online services. The groups services include checking accounts, saving accounts and certificate of deposit. The group operates from United States.

Primary SIC and add'l.: 6022

CIK No:

Officers: Dorian F. Corliss/CEO, Chuck Steltenpohl/Pres., Chief Lending Officer, Susie Gadd/Customer Service, Mardie Heilbrun/Operations Assist., Daniel Corliss/Mortgage Division Mgr., Raymond Flores/Personal Banker, Megan Hiner/Operations Mgr., Tea Trump/Loan Officer, Sloan W. Kimball/CFO, Eugene Astley/Officer, Jose Gonzalez/Officer, Rj Hoch/Officer, Richard Moeller/Officer, Keith Sattler/Officer, Dale A. Walter/Officer *(18 Officers included in Index)*

Directors: Dennis D. Gisi/Chmn.

Bank Santa Clarita

27441 Tourney Rd., Santa Clarita, CA, 91355; *PH:* 1-661-362-6000; *Fax:* 1-661-799-0427; *http://* www.bankofsantaclarita.com

General - Incorporation		Stock- Price on:12/24/2007	$14.25
Employees	NA	Stock Exchange	OTC
Auditor	NA	Ticker Symbol	BSCA
Stk Agt.	NA	Outstanding Shares	NA
Counsel	NA	E.P.S.	NA
DUNS No.	NA	Shareholders	NA

Business: The groups principle activity is to provide online banking services. The groups banking services include accounts, business banking services, cash management and applications. The group operates from United States.

Primary SIC and add'l.: 6022

CIK No:

Officers: James D. Hicken/Dir., CEO, Pres., Carol Morrissey/First VP, Client Service Mgr., Eric R. Jensen/First VP, Mgr. - Information Services, Julie F. Tunnell/Sr. VP, Dir. - Enterprise Risk Management, Stephanie M. Stephens/First VP, Controller, John S. Carlson/VP, Commercial Loan Officer, Jeffrey L. Johnson/Sr. VP, Dir. - Client Services, Barbara Andriuzzo/First VP, Consumer Loan Mgr., Ida Juliana/VP, Commercial Loan Officer, Joni Nelson/First VP, Central Operations Mgr., Janet Olmos/First VP, Client Service Mgr., Mary Hernandez/First VP, Note Department Mgr., Julie E. Canning/First VP, Client Service Mgr., Kimberly A. Altobello/Exec. VP, Chief Administrative Officer, Elizabeth Hopp/Sr. VP, Regional Mgr. *(16 Officers included in Index)*

Directors: James D. Hicken/Dir., CEO, Pres., Frank D. Di Tomaso/Vice Chmn., Robert W. King/Chmn., David Finkelstein/Dir., Bruce C. Jay/Dir., Carl J. Kanowsky/Dir., Margaret L. Lauffer/Dir., Thomas Pelino/Dir., Thomas J. Phillips/Dir. Emeritus, Steve Sansone/Dir., Shawn C. Shambaugh/Dir., Sharon K. Skinner/Dir., Thomas J. Bulger/Dir. Emeritus

Bank Utica NY

222 Genesee St., Utica, NY, 13502; *PH:* 1-315-797-2700; *http://* www.bankofutica.com; *Email:* info@bankofutica.com

General - Incorporation		Stock- Price on:12/24/2007	$470
Employees	NA	Stock Exchange	OTC
Auditor	NA	Ticker Symbol	BKUT
Stk Agt.	Bank Utica NY	Outstanding Shares	NA
Counsel	NA	E.P.S.	NA
DUNS No.	NA	Shareholders	NA

Business: The groups principle activity is to provide banking products and services. The group provides services include Internet banking, personal banking, commercial banking and 24 hour banking. The group operates from United States.

Primary SIC and add'l.: 6022

CIK No:

BankAtlantic Bancorp Inc

2100 W Cypress Creek Rd., Fort Lauderdale, FL, 33309; *PH:* 1-954-940-5000; *Fax:* 1-954-940-5250; *http://* www.bankatlanticbancorp.com; *Email:* info@bankatlanticcenter.com

General - Incorporation		Stock- Price on:12/24/2007	$8.71
Employees	2,433	Stock Exchange	NYSE
Auditor	PricewaterhouseCoopers LLP	Ticker Symbol	BBX
Stk Agt.	American Stock Transfer & Trust Co.	Outstanding Shares	60,120,000
Counsel	NA	E.P.S.	-$0.24
DUNS No.	84-923-8902	Shareholders	NA

Business: The group's principal activity is to provide traditional retail banking services, commercial banking products and related financial services. The group operates 73 branch offices located primarily in miami-dade, broward, hillsborough, palm beach, martin, st. Lucie and Indian river counties in the state of Florida. Banking activities include accepting checking and savings deposits from the public and general business customers, originating commercial real estate and business loans, consumer and small business loans and making other investments in mortgage-backed securities, tax certificates and other securities.

Primary SIC and add'l.: 6712 6035

CIK No: 0000921768

Subsidiaries: BA Community Development Corporation, BA Financial Services, LLC, BA Title Insurance Agency, Inc., Ba-hd, LLC, BAH Corp., BankAtlantic, BankAtlantic Mortgage Partners, Inc., BBC Capital Statutory Trust III, BBC Capital Statutory Trust IV, BBC Capital Statutory Trust VII, BBC Capital Statutory Trust X, BBC Capital Trust II, BBC Capital Trust IX, BBC Capital Trust V, BBC Capital Trust VI 55 Subsidiaries included in the Index

Officers: Alan B. Levan/Chmn., CEO/$1,303,173.00, Jarett S. Levan/Dir., Pres., Jay C. McClung/Exec. VP, Chief Risk Officer, Marcia K. Snyder/Exec. VP - Commercial Lending, Susan D. McGregor/Exec. VP, Dir. - Human Resources, Lewis F. Sarrica/Exec. VP, Chief Investment Officer, Leo Hinkley/Investor Relations Officer, Donna Rouzeau/Contact - Investor Relations, Corporate Communications, Lloyd Devaux/COO, Exec. VP/$1,126,470.00, Mark Begelman/Exec. VP, Chief Marketing Officer, Valerie C. Toalson/CFO, Exec. VP

Directors: Alan B. Levan/Chmn., CEO, John E. Abdo/Vice Chmn., Willis N. Holcombe/Dir., David A. Lieberman/Dir., Keith D. Cobb/Dir., John J. Stollenwerk/68/Dir., Ronald H. Dix/63/Dir., Thomas J. Fischer/60/Dir., Richard A. Meeusen/53/Dir., Ulice Payne/52/Dir., Andrew J. Policano/58/Dir., Steven J. Smith/58/Dir., Kenneth P. Manning/66/Dir., Bruno L. Digiulian/Dir., Mary E. Ginestra/Dir. *(18 Directors included in Index)*

Owners: Charlie C. Winningham, Insiders/100.00%, Willis N. Holcombe, Mellon Financial Corporation/5.78%, D. Keith Cobb, James A. White, Lloyd B. DeVaux, Alan B. Levan/1.82%, John E. Abdo/1.22%, BFC Financial Corporation/15.12%, Insiders/20.89%, Jarett S. Levan, Steven M. Coldren, Jay R. Fuchs, David A. Lieberman *(17 Owners included in Index)*

Financial Data: Fiscal Year End:12/31 Latest Annual Data: 12/31/2006

Year	Sales	Net Income
2006	$510,775,000	$15,387,000
2005	$701,504,000	$59,182,000
2004	$605,344,000	$70,768,000

Curr. Assets:	$381,968,000	Curr. Liab.:	$5,518,052,000	P/E Ratio:	29.03
Plant, Equip.:	$241,464,000	Total Liab.:	$5,970,680,000	Indic. Yr. Divd.:	$0.160
Total Assets:	$6,495,662,000	Net Worth:	$524,982,000	Debt/ Equity:	0.5594

Bankers Store Inc

1535 Memphis Junction Rd., Bowling Green, KY, 42101; *PH:* 1-270-781-8453; *Fax:* 1-270-782-9639; *http://* www.bankstore.com

General - Incorporation	NY	Stock- Price on:12/24/2007	$0.1
Employees	19	Stock Exchange	OTC
Auditor	Marmann, Mccrary & Assoc.	Ticker Symbol	BSTR
Stk Agt.	Continental Stock Transfer & Trust Co	Outstanding Shares	14,950,000
Counsel	NA	E.P.S.	-$0.01
DUNS No.	NA	Shareholders	NA

Business: The group's principal activities are the buying, selling, trading and refurbishing financial equipment for banks and other financial institutions. The principal products and services include bank-related equipment, remote drive-up and walk-up teller systems, automated teller machines (ATMs), vaults, safe deposit boxes, safes, filing systems and counter lines. It also provides all types of physical security systems including access control, master key systems and electronic locks, closed circuit television and security systems to its customers. The other operations include office equipment and furniture retail business. The customer base includes traditional bank locations, pharmacies and super drug stores, utilities, shipping departments in factories and hospitals. The group conducts it's operations throughout the United States.

Primary SIC and add'l.: 7629

CIK No: 0000027850

Officers: Vincent C. Buckman/Dir., CEO, Pres., Cynthia A. Hayden/Dir., Sec., Sam Stone/Dir., CFO

Directors: Vincent C. Buckman/Dir., CEO, Pres., Sam Stone/Dir., CFO

Owners: Cynthia A. Hayden/2.20%, Paul D. Clark/83.60%, Vincent C. Buckman, Roberta W. Clark/83.60%, Samuel J. Stone, Insiders/86.90%

Financial Data: Fiscal Year End:05/31 Latest Annual Data: 05/31/2007

Year	Sales	Net Income
2007	$2,622,000	-$218,000
2006	$2,456,000	$59,000
2005	$2,879,000	$101,000

Curr. Assets:	$1,345,000	Curr. Liab.:	$831,000		
Plant, Equip.:	$95,000	Total Liab.:	$833,000	Indic. Yr. Divd.:	NA
Total Assets:	$1,460,000	Net Worth:	$628,000	Debt/ Equity:	NA

BankFinancial Corp

15W060 N Frontage Rd., Burr Ridge, IL, 60527; *PH:* 1-630-242-7700; *Fax:* 1-708-675-6699; *http://* www.bankfinancial.com

General - Incorporation	MD	Stock- Price on:12/24/2007	$16.25
Employees	420	Stock Exchange	NDQ
Auditor	Crowe, Chizek and Company LLC	Ticker Symbol	BFIN
Stk Agt.	Computershare Trust Co	Outstanding Shares	23,180,000
Counsel	NA	E.P.S.	$0.35
DUNS No.	NA	Shareholders	NA

Business: The groups principal activity is to provide commercial, family and personal banking services. The products of the group include loan, deposit, cash management, merchant processing, funds transfers, bill payment and online banking transactions, automated teller machines, safe deposit boxes, wealth management, and insurance. In April 2006 the group acquired University National Bank. The group operates from Cook, DuPage, Lake, Will Counties and Illinois. The assets of the group for the year 2006 were $1,613,122 (thousands).

Primary SIC and add'l.: 6035 6712

CIK No: 0001303942

Subsidiaries: BankFinancial Asset Recovery Corporation, BankFinancial, F.S.B., Financial Assurance Services

Officers: Morgan F. Gasior/Chmn., CEO, Pres., Elizabeth A. Doolan/Sr. VP, Controller, Gregg T. Adams/48/Exec. VP - Marketing, Sales, James J. Brennan/57/Sec., General Counsel, Christa N. Calabrese/59/Pres. - Banks Northern Region, Paul A. Cloutier/44/CFO, Treasurer, Mark W. Collins/57/Exec. VP - Information Systems Division, Bank, Robert J. OShaughnessy/69/Chief Credit Officer, Patricia M. Smith/45/Exec. VP - Human Resources Division, Donald F. Stelter/55/Exec. VP - General Services Division, Bank, Thad F. Stewart/46/Exec. VP - Internal Audit Division

Directors: Morgan F. Gasior/Chmn., CEO, Pres., Glen R. Wherfel/58/Dir., John M. Hausmann/53/Dir., Joseph A. Schudt/70/Dir., Cassandra J. Francis/42/Dir., Sherwin R. Koopmans/66/Dir., Terry R. Wells/49/Dir.

Owners: John G. Manos, Sherwin R. Koopmans, Patricia M. Smith, Gregg T. Adams, F. Morgan Gasior/1.10%, Keeley Asset Management Corp./8.04%, Glen R. Wherfel, John M. Hausmann, Mark W. Collins, Thad F. Stewart, Joseph A. Schudt, Donald F. Stelter, James J. Brennan, Insiders/5.44%, Robert OShaughnessy *(22 Owners included in Index)*

Financial Data: Fiscal Year End:12/31 Latest Annual Data: 12/31/2006

Year	Sales	Net Income
2006	$105,088,000	$10,046,000
2005	$89,385,000	$11,073,000

Curr. Assets:	$75,206,000	Curr. Liab.:	$1,140,674,000	P/E Ratio:	41.67
Plant, Equip.:	$35,005,000	Total Liab.:	$1,287,107,000	Indic. Yr. Divd.:	$0.280
Total Assets:	$1,613,122,000	Net Worth:	$326,015,000	Debt/ Equity:	0.4338

BankGreenville Financial Corp

499 Woodruff Rd., Greenville, SC, 29067; ***PH:*** 1-864-271-1245

General - Incorporation	SC	**Stock**- Price on:12/24/2007	$8.85
Employees	11	Stock Exchange	OTC
Auditor	Elliott Davis, LLC	Ticker Symbol	BGVF
Stk Agt	Registrar & Transfer Co	Outstanding Shares	1,180,000
Counsel	NA	E.P.S.	-$0.57
DUNS No.	NA	Shareholders	NA

Business: The group operates through its subsidiary whose principal activity is banking business. The group products include real estate loans, commercial real estate loans, home equity lines-of-credit, construction and land loans and deposits. The group operates from the United States. The groups asset in the year 2005 was $31,656,709.

Primary SIC and add'l.: 6022

CIK No: 0001334679

Subsidiaries: BankGreenville

Owners: Frank B. Halter/1.50%, Roger H. Gower/2.50%, William H. Pelham/2.50%, Insiders/23.00%, Bruce R. Harman/3.70%, Paula S. King/3.10%, Jeffrey L. Dezen/2.10%, David A. Merline/2.10%, Arthur L. Howson/2.00%, Russel T. Williams/3.70%, Jonathan T. McClure/2.00%

Financial Data: ***Fiscal Year End:***12/31 ***Latest Annual Data:*** 12/31/2006

Year	Sales	Net Income
2006	$1,203,000	-$785,000
2005	$17,000	-$242,000

Curr. Assets:	$5,731,000	**Curr. Liab.:**	$21,590,000		
Plant, Equip.:	$2,136,000	**Total Liab.:**	$21,590,000	**Indic. Yr. Divd.:**	NA
Total Assets:	$31,657,000	**Net Worth:**	$10,067,000	**Debt/ Equity:**	NA

Bankrate Inc

11760 U.S Hwy. 1, Ste. 200, North Palm Beach, FL, 33408; ***PH:*** 1-561-630-2400; ***Fax:*** 1-561-625-4540; ***http://*** www.bankrate.com

General - Incorporation	FL	**Stock**- Price on:12/24/2007	$49
Employees	163	Stock Exchange	NDQ
Auditor	KPMG LLP	Ticker Symbol	RATE
Stk Agt	Suntrust Bank	Outstanding Shares	18,270,000
Counsel	NA	E.P.S.	$1.04
DUNS No.	NA	Shareholders	NA

Business: The group's principle activity is to operate an Internet-based consumer banking marketplace. The company operates through two segments: online publishing and print publishing and licensing. The online publishing division sells graphic advertising, sponsorships, and hyperlinks in connection with the company's Internet site, bankrate.com. This flagship site has information on over 250 financial products including mortgages, credit cards, new and used automobile loans, money market accounts, certificates of deposit, checking and ATM fees, home equity loans and online banking fees. The print publishing and licensing segment advertises the consumer mortgage guide rate tables, newsletter subscriptions and licensing of research information. The company also provides financial applications and information to a network of distribution partners and also through national and state publications. The company operates solely in the domestic market. The group operates from United States.

Primary SIC and add'l.: 7375

CIK No: 0001080866

Subsidiaries: Interest.com, Inc, Mortgage Market Information Services, Inc, Wescoco LLC

Officers: Thomas R. Evans/Dir., CEO, Pres./$3,142,542.00, Edward J. Dimaria/Sr. VP, CFO/$1,115,746.00, Bruce J. Zanca/Sr. VP, Chief Marketing, Communications Officer/$667,880.00, Robert J. Defranco/Sr. VP - Finance/$581,987.00, Daniel P. Hoogterp/CTO, Sr. VP, Lynn E. Varsell/Sr. VP - Publisher, Steven L. Horowitz/Sr. VP - Product, Business Development/$633,603.00, Michael J. Ricciardelli/Sr. VP - Consumer Marketing, Donaldson M. Ross/Sr. VP, Chief Revenue Officer

Directors: Thomas R. Evans/Dir., CEO, Pres., Peter C. Morse/Chmn., Richard Pinola/Dir., Randall E. Poliner/Dir., Robert P. Oblock/Dir., William C. Martin/Dir.

Owners: Edward J. DiMaria, Insiders/35.40%, Robert P. OBlock/2.40%, Robert J. DeFranco, Richard J. Pinola, Steven L. Horowitz, Trafelet & Company, LLC/8.80%, Capital Research and Management Company/8.00%, William C. Martin, Randall E. Poliner/2.90%, Peter C. Morse/25.70%, Tracer Capital Management L.P./6.40%, T. Rowe Price Associates, Inc/5.40%, Thomas R. Evans/5.10%, Bruce J. Zanca

Financial Data: ***Fiscal Year End:***12/31 ***Latest Annual Data:*** 06/30/2007

Year	Sales	Net Income
2007	NA	NA
2006	$79,650,000	$10,004,000
2005	$49,049,000	$9,674,000

Curr. Assets:	$128,463,000	**Curr. Liab.:**	$6,306,000	**P/E Ratio:**	69.01
Plant, Equip.:	$1,704,000	**Total Liab.:**	$6,529,000	**Indic. Yr. Divd.:**	NA
Total Assets:	$176,684,000	**Net Worth:**	$170,155,000	**Debt/ Equity:**	NA

Banks.com Inc

Formerly: InterSearch Group Inc

222 Kearny St. Ste. 550, San Francisco, CA, 94108; ***PH:*** 1-415-962-9795; ***Fax:*** 1-415-869-9954; ***http://*** www.intersearch.com; ***Email:*** info@intersearch.com

General - Incorporation	FL	**Stock**- Price on:12/24/2007	$2.47
Employees	31	Stock Exchange	AMEX
Auditor	Hacker, Johnson & Smith PA	Ticker Symbol	IGO
Stk Agt	Transfer Online, Inc.	Outstanding Shares	25,330,000
Counsel	NA	E.P.S.	$0.10
DUNS No.	NA	Shareholders	NA

Business: The group's principle activity is to provide Internet paid search and advertising services. Internet search services and corporate services. In the year 2005, the group acquired DotCom Corporation and La Jolla Internet Properties. The group operates from the United States.

Primary SIC and add'l.: 7375

CIK No: 0001341470

Subsidiaries: Dotted Ventures, Inc., Internet Revenue Services, Inc., InterSearch Corporate Services, Inc., La Jolla Internet Properties, Inc., Overseas Internet Properties, Inc., Walnut Ventures, Inc.

Officers: Daniel M. ODonnell/Chmn., CEO, Pres., Steve Ernst/Exec. VP - Enterprise Architecture, Gary Bogatay/CFO, Sec., Treasurer, Andrew Keery/38/Exec. VP - Product Development, Robert Hoult/Exec. VP - Revenue Development, Kimberly O'Donnell/Exec. VP - Human Resources, Corporate Services, Kate Sidorovich/Investor Relations Officer, John Terlip/Exec. VP - Technology Developmentdan

Directors: Daniel M. ODonnell/Chmn., CEO, Pres., Frank McPartland/Vice Chmn., Jerry Callaghan/Dir., Lawrence J. Gibson/Dir., Charles K. Dargan/Dir.

Owners: Frank McPartland/1.90%, Lawrence J. Gibson, Robert E. Hoult/4.60%, Charles K. Dargan, Barron Partners L.P./30.90%, Insiders/49.30%, Jeremiah Callaghan/1.00%, Andrew Keery/9.80%, Steven Ernst/13.00%, Daniel M. ODonnell/17.00%, Gary W. Bogatay/1.50%

Financial Data: ***Fiscal Year End:***12/31 ***Latest Annual Data:*** 12/31/2006

Year	Sales	Net Income
2006	$25,634,000	$3,417,000
2005	$17,543,000	-$459,000

Curr. Assets:	$4,641,000	**Curr. Liab.:**	$3,373,000		
Plant, Equip.:	$1,416,000	**Total Liab.:**	$9,934,000	**Indic. Yr. Divd.:**	NA
Total Assets:	$21,107,000	**Net Worth:**	$11,173,000	**Debt/ Equity:**	NA

Bankunited Financial Corp

255 Alhambra Cir., Coral Gables, FL, 33134; ***PH:*** 1-305-569-2000; ***Fax:*** 1-305-569-2057; ***http://*** www.bankunitedfla.com

General - Incorporation	FL	**Stock**- Price on:12/24/2007	$22.12
Employees	1,350	Stock Exchange	NDQ
Auditor	PricewaterhouseCoopers LLP	Ticker Symbol	BKUNA
Stk Agt	American Stock Transfer & Trust Co.	Outstanding Shares	36,410,000
Counsel	Camner,Lipsitz & Poller	E.P.S.	$2.15
DUNS No.	12-167-1556	Shareholders	NA

Business: The group's principal activity is to provide a range of banking services through its wholly owned subsidiary, bankunited, fsb. The group accepts deposits from the general public and invests those deposits in originating residential mortgage loans and other loans. The loans originated include one-to-four family residential mortgage loans, commercial real estate mortgage loans, multi-family mortgage loans, commercial business loans and consumer loans. The group also offers various retail and business deposit products, as well as a variety of value-added, fee-based banking services to retail customers and businesses. The group invests primarily in the us government and federal agency securities, mortgage-backed securities and other permitted investments. It operates 45 full-service banking offices located in south Florida.

Primary SIC and add'l.: 6035 6712

CIK No: 0000894490

Subsidiaries: BankUnited Capital, BankUnited Capital II, BankUnited Capital III, BankUnited Financial Corporation owns 100% of:, BankUnited Financial Services, Incorporated, BankUnited Statutory Trust I, BankUnited Statutory Trust II, BankUnited Statutory Trust III, BankUnited Statutory Trust IV, BankUnited Statutory Trust IX, BankUnited Statutory Trust V, BankUnited Statutory Trust VI, BankUnited Statutory Trust VIII, BankUnited, FSB which owns 100% of:, Bay Holdings, Inc. 23 Subsidiaries included in the Index

Officers: Alfred R. Camner/Chmn., CEO, Lawrence H. Blum/Vice Chmn., Sec., Joris Jabouin/Exec. VP, General Auditor Internal Audit - Bankunited FSB, Douglas B. Sawyer/Exec. VP - Bank Services, Bankunited FSB, Ramiro A. Ortiz/Dir., Pres., COO - Bankunited FSB, Carlos R. Fernandez-Guzman/Sr. Exec. VP - Consumer Banking Division, Bankunited, FSB, Bernardo M. Argudin/Exec. VP, Chief Accounting Officer, Felix M. Garcia/Exec. VP, Chief Risk Officer, Roberta R. Kressel/Exec. VP - Human Resources, Bankunited, FSB, Clay F. Wilson/Exec. VP - Commercial Real Estate, Bankunited, FSB, Robert A. Marsden/Exec. VP - Corporate Real Estate Services, Robert L. Green/Exec. VP - Residential Lending, Bankunited, FSB, Abel L. Iglesias/Exec. VP - Corporate, Commercial Banking, Humberto L. Lopez/Sr. Exec. VP, CFO, Hunting F. Deutsch/Exec. VP - Wealth Management *(16 Officers included in Index)*

Directors: Alfred R. Camner/Chmn., CEO, Lawrence H. Blum/Vice Chmn., Sec., Ramiro A. Ortiz/Dir., Pres., COO - Bankunited FSB, Neil H. Messinger/Dir., Albert E. Smith/Dir., Tod Aronovitz/Dir., Hardy C. Katz/Dir., Allen M. Bernkrant/Dir., Lauren R. Camner/Dir., Marc D. Jacobson/Dir., Bradley S. Weiss/Dir.

Owners: Lauren R. Camner, Insiders/98.30%, Abel L. Iglesias, Neil H. Messinger, Alfred R. Camner, Hardy C. Katz, Lauren R. Camner, Allen M. Bernkrant, Marc D. Jacobson, Dimensional Fund Advisors LP/6.56%, Humberto L. Lopez, Robert L. Green, Allen M. Bernkrant/1.90%, Albert E. Smith, Barclays Global Investors/6.02% *(31 Owners included in Index)*

Financial Data: ***Fiscal Year End:***09/30 ***Latest Annual Data:*** 06/30/2007

Year	Sales	Net Income
2007	$249,354,000	$23,209,000
2006	$755,489,000	$83,875,000
2005	$457,784,000	$27,537,000

Curr. Assets:	$138,053,000	**Curr. Liab.:**	$12,409,231,000	**P/E Ratio:**	8.54
Plant, Equip.:	$49,457,000	**Total Liab.:**	$12,817,739,000	**Indic. Yr. Divd.:**	$0.020
Total Assets:	$13,570,899,000	**Net Worth:**	$753,160,000	**Debt/ Equity:**	0.4598

Banner Corp

10 S First Ave., Walla Walla, WA, 99362; ***PH:*** 1-509-527-3636; ***Fax:*** 1-509-526-8898; ***http://*** www.banrbank.com

General - Incorporation	WA	**Stock**- Price on:12/24/2007	$36.03
Employees	855	Stock Exchange	NDQ
Auditor	Moss Adams LLP	Ticker Symbol	BANR
Stk Agt	Computershare Trust Co	Outstanding Shares	13,000,000
Counsel	Breyer & Assocaite PC	E.P.S.	$2.37
DUNS No.	02-024-5940	Shareholders	NA

Business: The group's principal activity is to accept deposits and provide commercial, savings and consumer loans to its customers. It is a holding company and operates through its wholly owned subsidiary, banner bank. The deposits accepted include demand checking, now, money market deposit and regular savings accounts, certificates of deposit and retirement savings plans. The lending activities of the group include origination of one-to four-family, multifamily and commercial real estate loans, construction loans, agricultural and land loans, consumer and other loans. In addition, the group also invests in securities, primarily in the us government and agency securities, municipal bonds, certificates of deposit, marketable corporate debt obligations and mortgage-backed securities. As on 31-Dec-2003, it had 42 branch offices and 9 loan production offices located in 20 counties in Washington, Idaho and Oregon.

Primary SIC and add'l.: 6712 6035

CIK No: 0000946673

Subsidiaries: Banner Bank, Community Financial Corporation
Officers: Michael D. Jones/CEO, Pres./$961,348.00
Owners: JoAnn Walker/5.27%, Mel Hansen/8.26%, Stephen Goodfellow/5.22%, Dan Goodfellow/5.07%, Craig Homchick/2.66%, Debby McDaniel, Insiders/32.89%, Dimitri Mandelis, Don Reichert/3.91%, Terry Sorom/1.60%, Dan Feil/3.35%, John Zapotocky/1.42%, William Miller/1.60%, Peter Spadoni/1.40%, Mike Wade/1.13% *(16 Owners included in Index)*

Financial Data: Fiscal Year End:12/31 **Latest Annual Data:** 12/31/2006

Year	Sales	Net Income
2006	$263,594,000	$32,163,000
2005	$208,006,000	$12,444,000
2004	$173,198,000	$19,340,000

Curr. Assets:	$96,657,000	**Curr. Liab.:**	$3,011,414,000	**P/E Ratio:**	15.14
Plant, Equip.:	$58,921,000	**Total Liab.:**	$3,245,339,000	**Indic. Yr. Divd:**	$0.800
Total Assets:	$3,495,566,000	**Net Worth:**	$250,227,000	**Debt/ Equity:**	0.7762

Banro Corp

1 First Canadian Pl., 100 King St. W, Ste. 7070, Toronto, ON, M5X 1E3; **PH:** 1-416-366-2221; *http://* www.banro.com

General - Incorporation	Canada	**Stock**- Price on:12/24/2007	$10.39
Employees	192	Stock Exchange	AMEX
Auditor	BDO Dunwoody LLP	Ticker Symbol	BAA
Stk Agt.	Equity Transfer Services Inc	Outstanding Shares	39,770,000
Counsel	Macleod Dixon LLP	E.P.S.	-$0.11
DUNS No.	NA	Shareholders	NA

Business: The group's principal activity is to provide acquisition, exploration, and development of precious metal projects including gold projects. The company has to date identified 2.45 million ounces of Measured and Indicated Resources, plus Inferred Resources of 5.48 million ounces. The company's common shares have been approved for listing on the Toronto Stock Exchange (the "TSX"). The company's strategy is to unlock shareholder value by increasing and developing its significant gold assets in a socially and environmentally responsible manner.The area of operations include South Kivu and Maniema provinces of Democratic Republic of the Congo. The company enjoys strong support from institutional investors in North America, the U.K. and Europe.
Primary SIC and add'l.: 1040
CIK No: 0001286597
Subsidiaries: Kamituga Mining SARL, Lugushwa Mining SARL, Twangiza Mining SARL
Officers: Michael Prinsloo/CEO, Geoffrey G. Farr/Corp. Sec., Peter Cowley/Dir., Pres., Arnold T. Kondrat/Dir., Exec. VP, Mike Skead/VP - Exploration, Martin Jones/VP - Corporate Development, Donat K. Madilo/CFO, Dan Bansah/VP - Exploration, Howard Fall/Exploration Mgr., Desire Sangara/VP - Government Relations
Directors: Simon Village/Chmn., Peter Cowley/Dir., Pres., Arnold T. Kondrat/Dir., Exec. VP, John Clarke/Dir., Bernard R. Van Rooyen/Dir., Piers Cumberlege/Dir., Richard Lachcik/Dir.

Financial Data: Fiscal Year End:12/31 **Latest Annual Data:** 12/31/2006

Year	Sales	Net Income
2006	NA	-$26,126,000
2005	NA	-$14,609,000

Curr. Assets:	$52,540,000	**Curr. Liab.:**	$2,859,000		
Plant, Equip.:	$1,210,000	**Total Liab.:**	$2,859,000	**Indic. Yr. Divd:**	NA
Total Assets:	$54,318,000	**Net Worth:**	$51,459,000	**Debt/ Equity:**	NA

Banta Corp

225 Main St. , Menasha, WI, 54952; **PH:** 1-920-751-7777; *http://* www.banta.com

General - Incorporation	WI	**Stock**- Price on:12/24/2007	NA
Employees	8,500	Stock Exchange	NA
Auditor	Ernst & Young LLP	Ticker Symbol	NA
Stk Agt.	American Stock Transfer & Trust Co.	Outstanding Shares	NA
Counsel	Foley & Lardner LLP	E.P.S.	NA
DUNS No.	18-176-6155	Shareholders	NA

Business: The group's principal activities are to provide printing and digital imaging solutions to publishers and direct marketers, advanced digital content management and e-business services. It operates in three segments: print segment: provides products, including digital imaging and services to publishers of educational and general books and magazines and also supplies consumer and business catalogs and direct marketing material. The supply-chain management segment: provides product configuration and manufacturing, procurement, testing, packaging, assembly and worldwide distribution services for computer hardware, consumer electronics and computer software publishers in North America, Europe, and Asia. Healthcare products segment: produces disposable products used in outpatient clinics, dental offices and hospitals. On 24-Feb-2003 group acquired qualipak inc.
Primary SIC and add'l.: 2732 2741 8099 7221 7371 2389 2754
CIK No: 0000009801
Subsidiaries: Banta Direct Marketing, Inc., Banta Europe BV, Banta Europe Corporation, Banta Finance Corporation, Banta Global Turnkey (Singapore) Pte. Ltd., Banta Global Turnkey - Guadalajara Sde RL de CV, Banta Global Turnkey B.V, Banta Global Turnkey Kft, Banta Global Turnkey Ltd., Banta Global Turnkey, Limited, Banta Global Turnkey, Ltd., Banta Healthcare Group, Ltd., Banta Holding Corp., Banta Integrated Media - Cambridge, Inc, Banta Packaging & Fulfillment, Inc. 25 Subsidiaries included in the Index
Owners: John F. Bergstrom, Ronald D. Kneezel, Geoffrey J. Hibner, Pamela J. Moret, Michael B. Allen, Ginger M. Jones, Deutsche Bank AG/9.00%, Henry T. DeNero, Citadel Investment Group, L.L.C./7.20%, Janel S. Haugarth, Frank W. Rudolph, Michael J. Winkler, Stephanie A. Streeter/2.20%, Patrick E. Allen, Insiders/4.80% *(21 Owners included in Index)*

Banyan Corp OR

Ste 500, 1925 Century Pk. E, Los Angeles, CA, 90067; **PH:** 1-800-808-0899; *http://* www.banyancorp.com

General - Incorporation	OR	**Stock**- Price on:12/24/2007	$0.0003
Employees	48	Stock Exchange	OTC
Auditor	Schwartz Levitsky Feldman LLP	Ticker Symbol	BANY
Stk Agt.	Transfer Online, Inc.	Outstanding Shares	2,480,000,000
Counsel	NA	E.P.S.	-$0.007
DUNS No.	NA	Shareholders	NA

Business: The group's principal activities are to provide chiropractic services through three clinics. The clinics are located in lake charles, sulphur and Iowa, Louisiana. The group is focused on investing in and building a network of operating subsidiaries engaged in the development of branded chiropractic clinics throughout North America, providing financing to chiropractors and other health care professionals, and providing support services to chiropractors. The group operates in two business segments, the group owned operation of chiropractic clinics and franchised chiropractic clinics.
Primary SIC and add'l.: 8041
CIK No: 0001086473
Subsidiaries: Banyan Financial Services, Inc, Chiropractic USA, Inc, Diagnostic USA, Inc, Franchise Support Network Inc, Southern Diagnostics, Inc, Southern Health Care, Inc.
Officers: Michael J. Gelmon/45/Dir., CEO, Cory H. Gelmon/48/Dir., CFO, Pres.
Directors: Michael J. Gelmon/45/Dir., CEO, Cory H. Gelmon/48/Dir., CFO, Pres.
Owners: Cory H. Gelmon/17.40%, Michael J. Gelmon/17.40%, Insiders/34.70%

Financial Data: Fiscal Year End:12/31 **Latest Annual Data:** 12/31/2006

Year	Sales	Net Income
2006	$5,451,000	-$4,083,000
2005	$1,091,000	-$4,646,000
2004	$466,000	-$2,460,000

Curr. Assets:	$2,221,000	**Curr. Liab.:**	$2,384,000		
Plant, Equip.:	$89,000	**Total Liab.:**	$4,438,000	**Indic. Yr. Divd:**	$1.120
Total Assets:	$5,232,000	**Net Worth:**	$793,000	**Debt/ Equity:**	2.5901

Bar Harbor Bankshares

82 Main St., Bar Harbor, ME, 04609; **PH:** 1-207-288-3314; **Fax:** 1-207-288-2626; *http://* www.bhbt.com

General - Incorporation	ME	**Stock**- Price on:12/24/2007	$31.5
Employees	159	Stock Exchange	AMEX
Auditor	KPMG LLP	Ticker Symbol	BHB
Stk Agt.	American Stock Transfer & Trust Co.	Outstanding Shares	3,040,000
Counsel	NA	E.P.S.	$2.14
DUNS No.	12-135-6117	Shareholders	NA

Business: The group's principal activity is the provision of banking services to individuals and corporates throughout eastern Maine. The services provided include checking accounts, individual retirement accounts, safe deposit boxes, travelers checks and bank-by-mail and club accounts. The group's lending services include consumer loans in the form of installment loans, overdraft protection and visa credit card accounts. It also offers business loans to individuals, partnerships, corporations and other business entities for capital construction. Other financial services include brokerage and trust and investment management services. The operations are conducted through ten offices located in coastal Maine. The customers of the group include individual customers, seasonal lodging, small retail establishments, campgrounds and restaurants.
Primary SIC and add'l.: 6712 6022
CIK No: 0000743367
Subsidiaries: Bar Harbor Bank & Trust, Bar Harbor Trust Services
Officers: Daniel A. Hurley/Pres., Trust Officer - Bar Harbor Trust Services/$141,352.00, Julie Zimmerman/Assist. Trust Officer - Bar Harbor Trust Services, Greg W. Dalton/Sr. VP - Business Banking/$117,779.00, Kelli Hall/CSR, Head Teller - Lubec, ME, Will Hatt/Regional VP - Business Banking, Machias, ME, Ellsworth Branch, Colleen Maynard/Assist. VP, Branch Mgr. - Southwest Harbor, ME, Lisa Young/Customer Service Representative, Southwest Harbor, ME, Jamie Church/Branch Supervisor - Winter Harbor, ME, Marsha Sawyer/Human Resources, Debra Sanner/Customer Service Mgr., Mischelle Adams/VP, Trust Officer - Bar Harbor Trust Services, Melanie Bowden/VP, Trust Officer - Bar Harbor Trust Services, Faye Geel/VP, Trust Officer - Bar Harbor Trust Services, Joseph Pratt/MD, Trust Officer - Bar Harbor Trust Services, Joshua Radel/VP, Chief Investment Officer - Bar Harbor Trust Services *(38 Officers included in Index)*
Owners: Robert M. Phillips, Gregory W. Dalton, Peter Dodge, David B. Woodside, Martha T. Dudman, Thomas A. Colwell, Gregg S. Hannah, Kenneth E. Smith, Clyde H. Lewis, Scott G. Toothaker, Shufro Rose & Co.,LLC/6.54%, Gerald Shencavitz, Lauri E. Fernald, Daniel A. Hurley, Robert C. Carter *(21 Owners included in Index)*

Financial Data: Fiscal Year End:12/31 **Latest Annual Data:** 12/31/2006

Year	Sales	Net Income
2006	$53,021,000	$6,879,000
2005	$43,610,000	$6,424,000
2004	$38,494,000	$5,732,000

Curr. Assets:	$19,547,000	**Curr. Liab.:**	$671,565,000		
Plant, Equip.:	$11,368,000	**Total Liab.:**	$763,826,000	**Indic. Yr. Divd:**	$0.960
Total Assets:	$824,877,000	**Net Worth:**	$61,051,000	**Debt/ Equity:**	1.3999

Barclays Bank Plc

200 Pk. Ave., New York, NY, 10166; **PH:** 1-212-412-4000; *http://* www.barclays.co.uk; **Email:** internetsecurity@barclays.co.uk

General - Incorporation	UK	**Stock**- Price on:12/24/2007	$59.22
Employees	122,600	Stock Exchange	AMEX
Auditor	PricewaterhouseCoopers LLP	Ticker Symbol	NA
Stk Agt.	Bank of New York	Outstanding Shares	1,630,000,000
Counsel	Howard Trust	E.P.S.	$5.93
DUNS No.	21-002-1523	Shareholders	NA

Business: The group's principle activity is to provide commercial and retail banking operations, investment banking services, trust services, credit card services, international banking , insurance services and other related financial activities. The group operates from United States.
Primary SIC and add'l.: 6282 6029 6211 6141
CIK No: 0000312070
Subsidiaries: Absa Group Limited, Barclays Assurance (Dublin) Limited, Barclays Bank (Suisse) S.A., Barclays Bank Egypt SAE, Barclays Bank of Botswana Limited, Barclays Bank of Ghana Limited, Barclays Bank of Kenya Limited, Barclays Bank of Zimbabwe Limited, Barclays Bank PLC ordinary shares, Barclays Bank SA, Barclays Bank Trust Company Limited, Barclays Capital Inc., Barclays Capital Japan Limited, Barclays Capital Securities Limited, Barclays Global Investors Limited 28 Subsidiaries included in the Index
Officers: John Varley/Dir., Group CEO, Frits Seegers/50/Dir., CEO. - Global Retail, Commercial Banking, Christopher Lucas/48/Dir, Group Dir. - Finance, Bertha Dadson/Contact - International Retail, Commercial Banking, Tania Viarnaud/Contact - International Retail, Commercial Banking, Adrian Walcott/Contact - Central Support, Helen Gallagher/Contact - Central Support, Paul T.

Idzik/COO, Naguib Kheraj/43/Exec. Dir., Group Dir. - Finance, Lawrence Dickinson/Company Sec., Alastair Camp/Corporate Responsibility Dir., Richard Hamilton/Assist. Dir. - Corporate Responsibility, Sue Acton/Head - Diversity, Rachael Barber/Head - Global Community Investment, Philippa Birtwell/Head - Public Issues *(22 Officers included in Index)*

Directors: Frits Seegers/50/Dir., CEO. - Global Retail, Commercial Banking, Marcus Agius/62/Chmn., Nigel Rudd/61/Dep. Chmn., Richard Broadbent/54/Sr. Dir., Naguib Kheraj/43/Exec. Dir., Group Dir. - Finance, Andrew Likierman/65/Non Exec. Dir., Robert E. Diamond/57/Dir., Stephen G. Russell/63/Dir., Richard L. Clifford/61/Dir., Fulvio Conti/61/Dir., John Sunderland/63/Dir., Christopher Lucas/48/Dir, Group Dir. - Finance, Danie Cronje/62/Dir., Dame Sandra Dawson/61/Dir., Leigh Clifford/60/Non - Exec. Dir. *(17 Directors included in Index)*

Owners: Andrew Likierman, Richard Broadbent, Robert E. Diamond, Marcus Agius, John Sunderland, John Varley, Fulvio Conti, Naguib Kheraj, Frits Seegers, Nigel Rudd, Professor Dame Sandra Dawson, Danie Cronj, David Roberts, Matthew W. Barrett, Stephen Russell *(17 Owners included in Index)*

Financial Data: **Fiscal Year End:**12/31 **Latest Annual Data:** 12/31/2006

Year	Sales	Net Income
2006	$62,892,987,000	$8,459,394,000
2005	$47,941,488,000	$5,045,386,000
2003	$33,554,960,000	$3,094,590,000

Curr. Assets:	$901,922,622,000	**Curr. Liab.:**	$1,012,014,246,000	**P/E Ratio:**	6.88
Plant, Equip.:	NA	**Total Liab.:**	$1,765,499,779,000	**Indic. Yr. Divd.:**	$2.990
Total Assets:	$1,818,156,469,000	**Net Worth:**	$39,244,691,000	**Debt/ Equity:**	NA

Barclays Plc

54 Lombard St., London, EC3 P3AH; ***PH:*** 44-2076993130; ***http://*** www.barclays.co.uk; ***Email:*** internetsecurity@barclays.co.uk

General - Incorporation	UK	**Stock**- Price on:12/24/2007	$59.22
Employees	122,600	Stock Exchange	NYSE
Auditor	PricewaterhouseCoopers LLP	Ticker Symbol	BCS
Stk Agt	Bank of New York	Outstanding Shares	1,630,000,000
Counsel	NA	E.P.S.	$5.91
DUNS No.	21-002-1531	Shareholders	NA

Business: The group's principal activities are carried out through the following business groups: personal financial services, barclays private clients, barclaycard, business banking, barclays Africa, barclays capital and barclays global investors. Personal financial service provides products and services to personal customers including current account, saving, mortgages, consumer loans and general insurance. Barclays private clients provides banking and asset management services. Barclaycard offers a full range of credit card services to individual and corporate customers. Business banking serves customers by a network of relationship and industry sector specialty managers. Barclays Africa provides banking services to personal and customers in north Africa, sub-saharan Africa and islands in the Indian ocean. Barclays capital provides financing and risk management need. Barclays global investors provides management products and services.

Primary SIC and add'l.: 6021 6141

CIK No: 0000312069

Subsidiaries: 54 Lombard Street Investments Limited, Abecor (Europe) Limited (In Liquidation 09.09.2005), Absa Group Limited, Afcarme Zimbabwe Holdings (Pvt) Limited, Aix Investment Company Limited, Akela Finance Limited, Albert E Sharp Limited, Allied Provincial P.E.P. (Nominees) Limited, Allied Trust Limited (In liquidation 07/07/05), Am Platzl Nominees GmbH, Antlia Promociones Inmobiliarias SA, Antlia Investments Limited, Antlia Shipping LTD Partnership, Appalachian NPI, LLC, Appleyard Finance Holdings Limited 717 Subsidiaries included in the Index

Officers: John Varley/52/Dir., Group CEO, Robert E. Diamond/57/Dir., Pres., Naguib Kheraj/44/Group Dir. - Finance, Lawrence Dickinson/Company Sec., Chris Lucas/48/Dir., Group Dir. - Finance, Paul Idzik/Dir., COO, Frits Seegers/Exec. Dir.

Directors: John Varley/52/Dir., Group CEO, Nigel Rudd/Dep. Chmn., Gary Hoffman/48/Group Vice Chmn., Marcus Agius/Chmn., Paul Idzik/Dir., COO, Frits Seegers/Exec. Dir., Fulvio Conti/Non Exec. Dir., Andrew Likierman/Non Exec. Dir., Richard Broadbent/Sr. Dir., John Sunderland/Non Exec. Dir., Danie Cronje/62/Non Exec. Dir., Richard Leigh Clifford/Non Exec. Dir., Dame Sandra Dawson/Non Exec. Dir., Robert E. Diamond/57/Dir., Pres., Chris Lucas/48/Dir., Group Dir. - Finance *(18 Directors included in Index)*

Financial Data: **Fiscal Year End:**12/31 **Latest Annual Data:** 12/31/2006

Year	Sales	Net Income
2006	$62,892,987,000	$8,459,394,000
2005	$47,941,488,000	$5,045,386,000
2003	$33,554,960,000	$3,094,590,000

Curr. Assets:	$901,922,622,000	**Curr. Liab.:**	$1,012,014,246,000	**P/E Ratio:**	6.88
Plant, Equip.:	NA	**Total Liab.:**	$1,778,911,778,000	**Indic. Yr. Divd.:**	$2.980
Total Assets:	$1,818,156,469,000	**Net Worth:**	$39,244,691,000	**Debt/ Equity:**	NA

Bare Escentuals Inc

71 Stevenson St., 22nd Fl., San Francisco, CA, 94105; ***PH:*** 1-415-489-5000; ***Fax:*** 1-800-227-3990; ***http://*** www.bareescentuals.com; ***Email:*** beauty@bareescentuals.com

General - Incorporation	DE	**Stock**- Price on:12/24/2007	$34.58
Employees	341	Stock Exchange	NDQ
Auditor	Ernst& Young LLP	Ticker Symbol	BARE
Stk Agt	Bank of New York	Outstanding Shares	89,990,000
Counsel	NA	E.P.S.	$0.68
DUNS No.	NA	Shareholders	NA

Business: The groups principle activities include develop, market and sell cosmetics, skin care, and body care products. The products of the group include blushes, liner shadows, eye shadows and glimmers. The group products sold under the trade names bareMinerals, md formulations, RareMinerals, Mineral Veil and namesake Bare Escentuals. The groups operates through two segments namely retail and wholesale. The group operates from the United States and International. The group's quarterly revenue for September 2007 was 126.64 millions of USD.

Primary SIC and add'l.: 2844

CIK No: 0001295557

Subsidiaries: Bare Escentuals Beauty, Inc., Bare Escentuals Kabushiki Kaisha, ID Direct, Inc., MD Beauty Sales, Inc., MD Formulations, Inc.

Officers: Leslie A. Blodgett/Dir., CEO, Diane M. Miles/Pres. - Wholesale, International, Myles B. McCormick/CFO, COO, Jim Taschetta/Chief Marketing Officer

Directors: Leslie A. Blodgett/Dir., CEO, Ross M. Jones/Chmn., Bradley M. Bloom/Dir., John C. Hansen/Dir., Michael J. John/Dir., Lea Anne Ottinger/Dir., Karen M. Rose/Dir., Glen T. Senk/Dir.

Owners: Karen Rose, JH MDB Investors, L.P., JH Capital Partners IV, LP., Berkshire Partners LLC, Berkshire Fund V, Limited Partnership, Shares beneficially owned by Leslie A. Blodgett, Funds affiliated with Berkshire Partners LLC, JH MDB Investors, L.P. and its affiliates, Lea Anne S. Ottinger, Keith M. Blodgett and Leslie A. Blodgett, trustees of the Blodgett Family Trust, Glen T. Senk, Siberia Investment Company, LLC, John C. Hansen, Berkshire Investors LLC, Myles B. McCormick *(20 Owners included in Index)*

Financial Data: **Fiscal Year End:**12/31 **Latest Annual Data:** 12/31/2006

Year	Sales	Net Income
2006	$394,525,000	$50,198,000

Curr. Assets:	$125,715,000	**Curr. Liab.:**	$59,377,000	**P/E Ratio:**	41.67
Plant, Equip.:	$21,111,000	**Total Liab.:**	$384,357,000	**Indic. Yr. Divd.:**	NA
Total Assets:	$155,835,000	**Net Worth:**	-$228,522,000	**Debt/ Equity:**	NA

Barnes & Noble Inc

122 5th Ave., New York, NY, 10011; ***PH:*** 1-212-633-3300; ***Fax:*** 1-212-675-0413; ***http://*** www.barnesandnobleinc.com; ***Email:*** customerservice@bn.com

General - Incorporation	DE	**Stock**- Price on:12/24/2007	$40.16
Employees	39,000	Stock Exchange	NYSE
Auditor	BDO Seidman LLP	Ticker Symbol	BKS
Stk Agt	Bank of New York	Outstanding Shares	65,800,000
Counsel	Robinson, Silverman, Pearce Et Al	E.P.S.	$2.16
DUNS No.	18-671-6668	Shareholders	NA

Business: The group's principle activity is to sell books on Internet. The group also operates video game and entertainment-software stores. The group operates in two segments include bookstores and video game, and entertainment software stores. The bookstores include trade books, paperbacks, children's books, bargain books, magazines and music. Video game and entertainment software segment consists of video-game hardware and software and PC-entertainment software. The trade names of the groups selling books include B. Dalton Bookseller, Bookstar, Readers' Advantage, Booksavers, Gamestop, Game Informer, Babbage's and Funcoland. The group operates from United States.

Primary SIC and add'l.: 5961 7372 5942

CIK No: 0000890491

Subsidiaries: Altamont Press, Inc, B. Dalton Bookseller, LLC, Barnes & Noble BookQuest, Barnes & Noble Booksellers, Inc, Barnes & Noble Publishing, Inc, Barnes & Noble Purchasing, Inc, Barnes & Noble Services, Inc, barnesandnoble.com inc, barnesandnoble.com LLC, Calendar Club LLC, CCI Holdings, Inc, Chelsea Insurance Company LTD, Doubleday Book Shops, Inc, Marketing Services (Minnesota) Corp., SparkNotes LLC 16 Subsidiaries included in the Index

Officers: Stephen Riggio/Vice Chmn., CEO/$3,110,481.00, Joseph Lombardi/CFO/$1,756,728.00, David S. Deason/VP, Chris Troia/CIO, Mark Bottini/VP, Dir. - Stores, Mary Ellen Keating/Sr. VP - Corporate Communications, Public Affairs, Mitchell S. Klipper/COO/$4,993,847.00, Alan J. Kahn/Pres. - Barnes, Noble Publishing Group, William F. Duffy/Exec. VP - Distribution, Logistics/$1,591,570.00, Michelle Smith/VP - Human Resources, Marie J. Toulantis/Exec. Officer - Barnes, Noblecom/$3,530,724.00, Michael N. Rosen/Dir., Sec., Jennifer Daniels/VP, General Counsel, Corp. Sec.

Directors: Stephen Riggio/Vice Chmn., CEO, Leonard Riggio/Chmn., Michael J. Del Giudice/Dir., William Dillard/Dir., Margaret T. Monaco/Dir., William Sheluck/Dir., Matthew A. Berdon/Dir., Irene R. Miller/Dir., Michael N. Rosen/Dir., Sec., Patricia L. Higgins/Dir., William F. Reilly/Dir., Lawrence S. Zilavy/Dir.

Owners: Patricia L. Higgins, Mitchell S. Klipper/2.10%, William Sheluck, Lawrence S. Zilavy, William F. Reilly, Irene R. Miller, Pershing Square Capital Management, L.P./9.20%, Marie J. Toulantis, Stephen Riggio/3.60%, Matthew A. Berdon, Leonard Riggio/22.90%, William F. Duffy, Joseph J. Lombardi, Margaret T. Monaco, Michael Del Giudice *(18 Owners included in Index)*

Financial Data: **Fiscal Year End:**01/28 **Latest Annual Data:** 2/3/2007

Year	Sales	Net Income
2007	$5,261,254,000	$150,527,000
2006	NA	$5,829,000
2005	$4,873,595,000	$143,376,000

Curr. Assets:	$1,922,440,000	**Curr. Liab.:**	$1,496,998,000	**P/E Ratio:**	19.69
Plant, Equip.:	$806,056,000	**Total Liab.:**	$2,021,273,000	**Indic. Yr. Divd.:**	$0.600
Total Assets:	$3,196,798,000	**Net Worth:**	$1,164,865,000	**Debt/ Equity:**	NA

Barnes Group Inc

123 Main St., Bristol, CT, 06011; ***PH:*** 1-860-583-7070; ***Fax:*** 1-860-589-3507; ***http://*** www.barnesgroupinc.com; ***Email:*** info@barnesgroupinc.com

General - Incorporation	DE	**Stock**- Price on:12/24/2007	$34.3
Employees	6,666	Stock Exchange	NYSE
Auditor	PricewaterhouseCoopers LLP	Ticker Symbol	NA
Stk Agt	Mellon Investor Services LLC	Outstanding Shares	52,840,000
Counsel	NA	E.P.S.	NA
DUNS No.	00-114-5481	Shareholders	NA

Business: The group's principal activities are to manufacture and distribute precision metal parts and distribute industrial supplies. It operates through three business segments: associated spring manufactures precision mechanical and nitrogen gas springs, manifold systems and other close-tolerance engineered metal components. Barnes aerospace produces precision machined and fabricated components and assemblies for original equipment manufacturer turbine engine, airframe and industrial gas turbine builders. Barnes distribution distributes fast moving consumable repair and replacement products for industrial, heavy equipment and transportation maintenance markets. On 06-Feb-2003, the group acquired kar products llc. On 17-Sep-2004, the group acquired de-sta-company.

Primary SIC and add'l.: 3724 5075 3495

CIK No: 0000009984

Subsidiaries: AS Monterrey S. de R.L. de C.V., AS Troy, LLC, Associated Spring (Tianjin) Company, Ltd., Associated Spring (U.K.) Ltd., Associated Spring do Brasil Ltda., Associated Spring Mexico, S.A., Associated Spring-Asia Pte. Ltd., Barnes Financing Delaware LLC, Barnes Group (Bermuda) Limited, Barnes Group (Delaware) LLC, Barnes Group (Germany) GmbH, Barnes Group (Thailand) Ltd., Barnes Group (U.K.) Limited, Barnes Group Canada Corp., Barnes Group Canada Holding Corp. 34 Subsidiaries included in the Index

Officers: Gregory F. Milzcik/Dir., CEO, Pres./$2,789,829.00, Jerry W. Burris/Pres. - Barnes Industrial, Thomas P. Fodell/Pres. - Sales, Associated Spring, Idelle K. Wolf/Pres. - Barnes Distribution, John R. Arrington/Sr. VP - Human Resources/$1,866,201.00, Lawrence W. O'Brien/VP,

Treasurer, Signe S. Gates/Sr. VP, General Counsel, Sec./$1,721,325.00, Francis C. Boyle/VP, Controller, Joseph D. Deforte/VP - Tax, Scott M. Deakin/Sr. VP - Corporate Development, William C. Denninger/Dir., Sr. VP - Finance, CFO, Patrick Dempsey/VP, Barnes Group Inc Pres. - Barnes Aerospace/$136,738.00

Directors: Gregory F. Milzcik/Dir., CEO, Pres., Thomas O. Barnes/Chmn., William C. Denninger/Dir., Sr. VP - Finance, CFO, William S. Bristow/Dir., William J. Morgan/Dir., George T. Carpenter/Dir., John C. Alden/Dir., Frank E. Grzelecki/Dir., Edmund M. Carpenter/Dir., Gary G. Benanav/Dir., Donald W. Griffin/Dir., Mylle H. Mangum/Dir.

Owners: NFJ Investments Group L.P./5.20%, Mylle H. Mangum, Patrick J. Dempsey, William C. Denninger, George T. Carpenter, John R. Arrington, Thomas O. Barnes/6.90%, Barnes Group Inc. Retirement Savings Plan/8.80%, John W. Alden, Bank of America Corporation/15.30%, Gary G. Benanav, Gregory F. Milzcik, Edmund M. Carpenter/4.30%, Thomas O. Barnes/6.90%, Frank E. Grzelecki (21 Owners included in Index)

Financial Data: Fiscal Year End:12/31 Latest Annual Data: 12/31/2006

Year	Sales	Net Income
2006	$1,259,656,000	$73,845,000
2005	$1,102,174,000	$60,517,000
2004	$994,709,000	$33,401,000

Curr. Assets:	$461,214,000	Curr. Liab.:	$295,060,000		
Plant, Equip.:	$209,645,000	Total Liab.:	$816,656,000	Indic. Yr. Divd.:	NA
Total Assets:	$1,336,451,000	Net Worth:	$519,795,000	Debt/ Equity:	0.7305

Barnwell Industries Inc

1100 Alakea St., Ste. 2900, Honolulu, HI, 96813; **PH:** 1-808-531-8400; **Fax:** 1-808-531-7181; http:// www.brninc.com

General - Incorporation	DE	Stock - Price on:12/24/2007	$20.35
Employees	52	Stock Exchange	AMEX
Auditor	KPMG LLP	Ticker Symbol	BRN
Stk Agt..... American Stock Transfer & Trust Co.		Outstanding Shares	8,220,000
Counsel	NA	E.P.S	$0.84
DUNS No.	00-694-8228	Shareholders	NA

Business: The group's principal activities are exploration, development, production and marketing of oil and natural gas primarily in Canada. The group operates in three business segments: oil and natural gas segment, land investment segment and contract drilling segment. Oil and natural gas segment includes exploratory and developmental operations on property and evaluations by third parties on proposals with regard to participation in such exploratory and developmental operations elsewhere. Land investment segment includes investment in leasehold land in Hawaii. Contract drilling includes water and exploratory well drilling, contract labor servicing for geothermal well drilling and workovers, and water pumping system installation and repair in Hawaii.

Primary SIC and add'l.: 1382 1311 1629 1781

CIK No: 0000010048

Subsidiaries: Barnwell Alakea Properties, Inc., Barnwell Financial Corporation, Barnwell Geothermal Corporation, Barnwell Hawaiian Properties, Inc., Barnwell Hilo Corporation, Barnwell Investment Corporation, Barnwell Israel, Ltd., Barnwell Kona Corporation, Barnwell Management Co., Inc., Barnwell Mining Co., Barnwell of Canada, Limited, Barnwell Oil & Gas, Ltd., Barnwell Overseas, Inc., Barnwell Shallow Oil, Inc., Bill Robbins Drilling, Ltd. 23 Subsidiaries included in the Index

Officers: Morton H. Kinzler/Chmn., CEO, Margaret A. Mangan/Assist. VP, Assistant Treasurer, Assistant Sec., Erik Hazelhoff-Roelfzema/Dir. - Investor, Warren D. Steckley/VP - Canadian Operations, Pres., COO - Barnwell, Canada, Limited, Joseph R. Downs/Mgr. - Information Services, Cynthia M. Grillot/Assist. VP, Assistant Sec., Assist. VP, Marketing Mgr. - Barnwell, Canada, Limited, Russell M. Gifford/Dir., Exec. VP, CFO, Treasurer, Sec., Pres. - Water Resources International, Inc, Mark A. Murashige/VP, Controller, Assist. Sec., Murray C. Gardner/Dir., Independent Resource Consultant, Terry Johnston/Dir. - Investor, Alexander C. Kinzler/Dir., COO, Pres., General Counsel, Sheryl A.L. Villanueva/Assist. Controller, Paul Hurst/VP, Exploration Mgr. - Barnwell, Canada, Limited, Albert Hulzebos/VP, Land Mgr. - Barnwell, Canada, Limited, Nancy M. Lee/Controller - Barnwell, Canada, Limited (18 Officers included in Index)

Directors: Morton H. Kinzler/Chmn., CEO, Diane G. Kranz/Dir., Erik Hazelhoff-Roelfzema/Dir. - Investor, Martin Anderson/Dir., Alan D. Hunter/Dir., Kevin K. Takata/Dir., Russell M. Gifford/Dir., Exec. VP, CFO, Treasurer, Sec., Pres. - Water Resources International, Inc, Murray C. Gardner/Dir., Independent Resource Consultant, Alexander C. Kinzler/Dir., COO, Pres., General Counsel, Ahron H. Haspel/Dir.

Owners: Insiders/23.60%, Kevin K. Takata, Russell M. Gifford/2.60%, Martin Anderson, Diane G. Kranz, David R. Sudarsky/8.90%, Mercury Real Estate Advisors LLC/16.30%, Ahron H. Haspel, Alan D. Hunter, Warren D. Steckley/1.40%, Erik Hazelhoff-Roelfzema, Murray C. Gardner, Morton H. Kinzler/16.00%, Alexander C. Kinzler/4.00%, Joseph E. Magaro/15.50% (16 Owners included in Index)

Financial Data: Fiscal Year End:09/30 Latest Annual Data: 9/30/2006

Year	Sales	Net Income
2006	$57,960,000	$14,637,000
2005	$44,210,000	$6,027,000
2004	$37,970,000	$8,710,000

Curr. Assets:	$25,338,000	Curr. Liab.:	$22,112,000	P/E Ratio:	24.23
Plant, Equip.:	$79,217,000	Total Liab.:	$53,950,000	Indic. Yr. Divd.:	$0.200
Total Assets:	$104,555,000	Net Worth:	$50,605,000	Debt/ Equity:	0.2916

Barossa Coffee Company Inc

311 South State St., Ste. 460, Salt Lake City, UT, 84111; **PH:** 1-801-364-9262

General - Incorporation	NV	Stock - Price on:12/24/2007	$0.99
Employees	1	Stock Exchange	OTC
Auditor	Pritchett, Siler & Hardy, P.C.	Ticker Symbol	BSSA
Stk Agt...........Interwest Transfer Company, Inc.		Outstanding Shares	2,060,000
Counsel	NA	E.P.S	NA
DUNS No.	NA	Shareholders	NA

Business: The group opened a retail coffee outlet featuring specialty coffees. The group products include roasted coffee beans and espresso related beverages. The group operates from the United States.

Primary SIC and add'l.: 5810

CIK No: 0001332572

Subsidiaries: Alchemy Coffee Company, Inc

Officers: Adam Gatto/45/Dir., CEO, CFO, Pres.

Directors: Adam Gatto/45/Dir., CEO, CFO, Pres.

Owners: Thomas G. Kimble/26.20%, Insiders/31.10%, Adam Gatto/31.10%, Lynn Dixon/26.20%

Financial Data: Fiscal Year End:06/30 Latest Annual Data: 06/30/2007

Year	Sales	Net Income
2007	NA	-$26,000

Curr. Assets:	$16,000	Curr. Liab.:	$5,000		
Plant, Equip.:	NA	Total Liab.:	$5,000	Indic. Yr. Divd.:	NA
Total Assets:	$16,000	Net Worth:	$11,000	Debt/ Equity:	NA

Barr Pharmaceuticals Inc

223 Quaker Rd., Pomona, NY, 10970; **PH:** 1-845-362-1100; **Fax:** 1-845-362-2774; http:// www.barrlabs.com; **Email:** ir@barrlabs.com

General - Incorporation	DE	Stock - Price on:12/24/2007	$52.12
Employees	8,500	Stock Exchange	NYSE
Auditor	Deloitte & Touche LLP	Ticker Symbol	BRL
Stk Agt	Mellon Investor Services LLC	Outstanding Shares	109,750,000
Counsel	NA	E.P.S	-$7.39
DUNS No.	05-630-6780	Shareholders	NA

Business: The group's principal activities are to develop, manufacture and market generic and proprietary pharmaceutical products. The group manufactures and markets more than 57 pharmaceutical products, representing various dosage strengths and product forms of approximately 54 chemical entities. The product line is focused on proprietary products in oncology, female healthcare, cardiovascular, anti-infectives and psychotherapeutics. The group's major brands include desogen (R), ortho-cept (R), alesse (R), danocrine (R), adderall (R), dexedrine (R), spansule (R), persantine (R), prozac (R), mircette (R), levlite (R), provera (R), rheumatrex (R), aygestin(R) and coumadin (r). The group operates throughout the United States, Puerto Rico and Canada. On 26-Feb-2004, the group acquired women's capital corporation.

Primary SIC and add'l.: 2834

CIK No: 0000010081

Subsidiaries: 2 Quker Rod Inc., 2 Quker Rod LLC, 265 Livingston Street Corp., BMI Inc., BRL Inc., Brr Distribution Compny, Brr Lbortories Europe, Brr Lbortories Inc., Brr Ventures LLC., Copper 380T LLC, Durmed Phrmceuticl Sles Corp., Durmed Phrmceuticls Inc., Durmed Reserch Inc., Womens Cpitl Corp.

Officers: Bruce L. Downey/Chmn., CEO/$2,251,890.00, Frederick G. Wilkinson/Pres., COO - Duramed Pharmaceuticals, Inc/$772,035.00, Timothy P. Catlett/Sr. VP - Generic Sales, Marketing, Catherine F. Higgins/Sr. VP - Human Resources, Christopher J. Mengler/Exec. VP - Global Strategic Planning, Amy C. Niemann/Sr. VP - Proprietary Marketing, Michael J. Bogda/Exec. VP - Global Product Supply, Christine A. Mundkur/Exec. VP - Global Quality, Safety, Regulatory Affairs, Salah U. Ahmed/Exec. VP - Global Research, Development, William T. Mckee/CFO, Exec. VP/$638,190.00, Frederick J. Killion/Exec. VP, General Counsel/$646,378.00, Jane F. Greenman/Exec. VP - Global Human Resources, Marc Kustoff/CIO, Sr. VP, Timothy B. Sawyer/Sr. VP, European Head - Commercial Development, Carol A. Cox/Sr. VP - Global Investor Relations, Corporate Communications (17 Officers included in Index)

Directors: Bruce L. Downey/Chmn., CEO, Richard R. Frankovic/Dir., Peter R. Seaver/Dir., James S. Gilmore/Dir., George P. Stephan/Dir., Harold N. Chefitz/Dir.

Owners: George P. Stephan, Frederick J. Killion, Peter R. Seaver, Insiders/2.95%, James S. Gilmore, Frederick G. Wilkinson, Barclays Global Investors, NA/9.51%, Bruce L. Downey/1.27%, William T. McKee, Richard R. Frankovic, Paul M. Bisaro, Harold N. Chefitz

Financial Data: Fiscal Year End:06/30 Latest Annual Data: 6/30/2006

Year	Sales	Net Income
2006	$1,314,465,000	$336,477,000
2005	$1,047,399,000	$214,988,000

Curr. Assets:	$1,108,982,000	Curr. Liab.:	$187,319,000		
Plant, Equip.:	$275,960,000	Total Liab.:	$230,463,000	Indic. Yr. Divd.:	NA
Total Assets:	$1,921,419,000	Net Worth:	$1,690,956,000	Debt/ Equity:	1.2542

Barrett Business Services Inc

8100 NE Pkwy. Dr., Ste. 200, Vancouver, WA, 98662; **PH:** 1-360-828-0700; **Fax:** 1-360-828-0701; http:// www.barrettbusiness.com

General - Incorporation	MD	Stock - Price on:12/24/2007	$23.74
Employees	32,895	Stock Exchange	NDQ
Auditor	Moss Adams LLP	Ticker Symbol	BBSI
Stk Agt	Mellon Investor Services LLC	Outstanding Shares	11,260,000
Counsel	NA	E.P.S	$1.49
DUNS No.	08-745-9558	Shareholders	NA

Business: The group's principle activity is to provide staffing and professional employer services. The company's range of services and expertise in human resource management encompasses five major categories: payroll processing, employee benefits and administration, worker's compensation coverage, aggressive risk management and workplace safety programs and human resources administration. Staffing services include short term staffing assignments, contract staffing and human resource administration. It operates through a network of 28 branch offices in Oregon, California, Washington, Maryland, Delaware, Arizona and North Carolina. The customers of the company include electronics manufacturers, light-manufacturing industries, agriculture-based companies, food processing, telecommunications, public utilities and professional service firms. The group's quarterly revenue for September 2007 was 82.91 millions of USD.

Primary SIC and add'l.: 7361 8721

CIK No: 0000902791

Officers: William W. Sherertz/Chmn., CEO, Pres./$471,659.00, Michael L. Elich/VP, COO/$239,175.00, Gregory R. Vaughn/VP/$228,566.00, Michael D. Mulholland/VP - Finance, Treasurer, Sec./$265,469.00

Directors: William W. Sherertz/Chmn., CEO, Pres., Roger L. Johnson/Dir., Anthony Meeker/Dir., Jon L. Justesen/Dir., James B. Hicks/Dir., Thomas J. Carley/Dir.

Owners: Jon L. Justesen, William W. Sherertz/25.70%, Michael D. Mulholland, Thomas J. Carley, Gregory R. Vaughn, Michael L. Elich, Manulife Financial Corporation/5.40%, James B. Hicks, Anthony Meeker, Roger L. Johnson, Nancy B. Sherertz/10.90%, Insiders/27.40%

Financial Data: Fiscal Year End:12/31 Latest Annual Data: 12/31/2006

Year	Sales	Net Income
2006	$259,184,000	$16,336,000
2005	$231,389,000	$12,490,000
2004	$194,961,000	$7,371,000

Curr. Assets:	$111,225,000	**Curr. Liab.:**	$47,020,000	**P/E Ratio:**	15.93
Plant, Equip.:	$13,502,000	**Total Liab.:**	$58,481,000	**Indic. Yr. Divd.:**	$0.280
Total Assets:	$162,181,000	**Net Worth:**	$103,700,000	**Debt/ Equity:**	NA

Barrick Gold Corp

136 E S Temple, Ste. 1050, Salt Lake City, UT, 84111; **PH:** 1-801-990-3900; **Fax:** 1-801-359-0875; http:// www.barrick.com

General - Incorporation	ON	**Stock** - Price on:12/24/2007	$29.33
Employees	11,900	Stock Exchange	NYSE
Auditor	PricewaterhouseCoopers LLP	Ticker Symbol	ABX
Stk Agt	CIBC Mellon Trust CO.	Outstanding Shares	865,000,000
Counsel	NA	E.P.S.	$1.29
DUNS No.	NA	Shareholders	NA

Business: The groups principal activities include exploring and developing gold mining properties. The group operates from Canada.

Primary SIC and add'l.: 1041 1021 1044 1081

CIK No: 0000756894

Officers: Gregory C. Wilkins/Dir., CEO, Pres., Peter J. Kinver/COO, Exec. VP, Gordon Fife/Exec. VP - Organization Effectiveness, Jamie C. Sokalsky/CFO, Exec. VP, Alexander J. Davidson/Exec. VP - Exploration, Corporate Development, Patrick Garver/Exec. VP, General Counsel

Directors: Gregory C. Wilkins/Dir., CEO, Pres., Peter Munk/Chmn., William D.C. Birchall/Vice Chmn., Steven J. Shapiro/Dir., Howard L. Beck/Dir., Donald J. Carty/Dir., Gustavo Cisneros/Dir., Marshall A. Cohen/Dir., Peter A. Crossgrove/Dir., John W. Crow/Dir., Robert M. Franklin/Dir., Peter C. Godsoe/Dir., Brett J. Harvey/Dir., Brian Mulroney/Dir., Anthony Munk/Dir.

Financial Data: Fiscal Year End:12/31   Latest Annual Data: 12/31/2006

Year	Sales	Net Income
2006	$5,636,000,000	$1,506,000,000
2005	$2,350,000,000	$401,000,000
2004	$1,932,000,000	$248,000,000
Curr. Assets: $4,796,000,000	**Curr. Liab.:** $1,852,000,000	**P/E Ratio:** 10.06
Plant, Equip.: $8,703,000,000	**Total Liab.:** $7,174,000,000	**Indic. Yr. Divd.:** $0.300
Total Assets: $21,373,000,000	**Net Worth:** $14,199,000,000	**Debt/ Equity:** NA

Barrier Therapeutics Inc

600 College Rd. E, Ste. 3200, Princeton, NJ, 08540; **PH:** 1-609-945-1200; **Fax:** 1-609-945-1212; http:// www.barriertherapeutics.com

General - Incorporation	DE	**Stock** - Price on:12/24/2007	$6.35
Employees	93	Stock Exchange	NDQ
Auditor	Ernst & Young LLP	Ticker Symbol	BTRX
Stk Agt	American Stock Transfer & Trust Co.	Outstanding Shares	29,370,000
Counsel	Morgan, Lewis & Bockius LLP	E.P.S.	-$2.11
DUNS No.	NA	Shareholders	NA

Business: The group's principal activity is the discovery, development and commercialization of a portfolio of innovative pharmaceutical products to address major medical needs in the field of dermatology. The group currently have multiple product candidates in clinical development, with four of these candidates in or entering phase iii clinical trials. Its four most advanced product candidates are sebazole, zimycan, hyphanox and liarozole. The group became publicly held during apr-2004. The group's major trademarks are barrier therapeuticstm, sebazoletm, zimycantm, hyphanoxtm, rambazoletm and hivenyltm.

Primary SIC and add'l.: 8734 8731 2834

CIK No: 0001173657

Subsidiaries: Barrier Therapeutics Canada, Inc, Barrier Therapeutics, NV

Officers: Geert Cauwenbergh/Dir., CEO, Al Altomari/COO, Charles T. Nomides/51/Chief Research, Development Officer, Al C. Bristow/General Counsel, Corp. Sec., Anne Vanlent/Exec. VP, CFO, Treasurer, Joan Chypyha/GM - Canada, Regional Contact, Nicole Eyben/VP - Commercial Operations, Europ, Regional Contact, Braham Shroot/Chief Scientific Officer, Gerrit Dispersyn/Dir. - Business Development, Dennis P. Reilly/50/VP - Finance, Principal Accounting Officer

Directors: Geert Cauwenbergh/Dir., CEO, Peter Ernster/Chmn., Carl Ehmann/Dir., Robert Campbell/Dir., Charles Jacey/Dir., Srinivas Akkaraju/Dir., Nicholas J. Simon/54/Dir., Carol Raphael/Dir., Edward Erickson/Dir.

Owners: Nicholas J. Simon/6.60%, Charles T. Nomides, Dennis P. Reilly, JPMP Capital Corp./9.10%, Perseus-Soros BioPharmaceutical Fund, LP/7.90%, Edward L. Erickson, Columbia Wanger Asset Management, L.P./6.30%, Charles F. Jacey, Insiders/20.10%, Geert Cauwenbergh/2.60%, New Leaf Ventures I, L.P./5.20%, Alfred Altomari, Peter Ernster, Srinivas Akkaraju/9.70%, Carl W. Ehmann (21 Owners included in Index)

Financial Data: Fiscal Year End:12/31   Latest Annual Data: 12/31/2006

Year	Sales	Net Income
2006	$6,738,000	-$52,717,000
2005	$2,540,000	-$45,241,000
2004	$897,000	-$39,743,000
Curr. Assets: $63,744,000	**Curr. Liab.:** $13,688,000	
Plant, Equip.: $873,000	**Total Liab.:** $13,968,000	**Indic. Yr. Divd.:** NA
Total Assets: $67,181,000	**Net Worth:** $53,213,000	**Debt/ Equity:** 0.0059

Baseline Oil & Gas Corp

411 N Sam Houston Pkwy. E, Ste. 300, Houston, TX, 77060; **PH:** 1-281-591-6100; **Fax:** 1-281-445-5888; http:// www.baselineoil.com

General - Incorporation	NV	**Stock** - Price on:12/24/2007	$0.47
Employees	2	Stock Exchange	OTC
Auditor	Malone & Bailey, P.C	Ticker Symbol	BOGA
Stk Agt.	NA	Outstanding Shares	31,440,000
Counsel	NA	E.P.S.	-$0.19
DUNS No.	NA	Shareholders	NA

Business: The groups principal activity is to exploration of minerals. In the year 2005, the group acquired Coastal Energy Services, Inc. The group operates from the United States.

Primary SIC and add'l.: 1311

CIK No: 0001291983

Subsidiaries: PennTex Illinois, Rex Energy

Officers: Thomas Kaetzer/Chmn., CEO, Pres., Patrick H. McGarey/CFO, Amy E. Chavez/Contact - Invester Relations

Directors: Thomas Kaetzer/Chmn., CEO, Pres., Alan Gaines/Vice Chmn., Richard D'Abo/Dir.

Owners: Alan Gaines/23.00%, Thomas Kaetzer/3.70%, Richard d'Abo/3.70%, Superius Securities Group Inc., Lakewood Group LLC/8.70%, Richard Cohen/1.50%, Insiders/29.00%, Barrie Damson/23.00%

Financial Data: Fiscal Year End:12/31   Latest Annual Data: 12/31/2006

Year	Sales	Net Income
2006	NA	-$3,773,000
2005	NA	-$17,699,000
Curr. Assets: $249,000	**Curr. Liab.:** $2,357,000	
Plant, Equip.: NA	**Total Liab.:** $2,357,000	**Indic. Yr. Divd.:** NA
Total Assets: $9,247,000	**Net Worth:** $6,890,000	**Debt/ Equity:** NA

BASF

ZOI - D 100, Ludwigshafen; **PH:** 49-621600; http:// www.basf.com; **Email:** investorrelations@basf-ag.de

General - Incorporation	Germany	**Stock** - Price on:12/24/2007	$129.5
Employees	95,247	Stock Exchange	NA
Auditor	Deloitte & Touche GmbH	Ticker Symbol	NA
Stk Agt	NA	Outstanding Shares	494,700,000
Counsel	NA	E.P.S.	NA
DUNS No.	NA	Shareholders	NA

Business: The group's principle activity is to provide customers a range of high-performance products, including high value chemicals, plastics, colorants and pigments, dispersions, automotive and industrial coatings, agricultural products and fine chemicals as well as crude oil and natural gas. The group's operations are divided into the following five segments: health and nutrition; finishing products; chemicals; plastics and fibres and oil and gas. The group operates from United States.

Primary SIC and add'l.: 3695 3911 2911 2819 2851 2865 2821

CIK No: 0001024148

Subsidiaries: Aislantes y Acusticos de Monterrey, S.A. de C.V., Aislapol S.A., Amylogene Handelsbolaget, ART Automotive Refinish Technologies (PTY) Ltd., Athens, Greece, Aurentum Innovationstechnologien GmbH, Ausbildungsplatzinitiative Pfalz GmbH, Automotive Refinish Technologies, LLC, Automotive Refinish Technology,Inc. (ART), Awiag Ltd., Axaron Bioscience AG, Basanil S.A., BASF (China) Company Ltd., BASF (Ethiopia) Ltd. P. L. C., BASF (Malaysia) Sdn. Bhd. 413 Subsidiaries included in the Index

Officers: Julia Jorder/Exec. Assist. - Investor Relations, Christoph Beumelburg/Mgr. - Investor Relations., USA, Thilo Bischoff/Mgr. - Investor Relations, Rest Europe, Volker Seidl/Mgr. - Investor Relations, UK, Helke Hillebrand/Mgr. - Investor Relations, Kurt W. Bock/50/Dir., CFO, Karlheinz Messmer/Plant Mgr. - Ludwigshafen Site, Basf Aktiengesellschaft, Weisenheim, Ralf-Gerd Bastian/50/Member - Supervisory Board, Magdalena Moll/Sr. VP - Investor Relations, Carolin Trieloff/Junior Mgr. - Investor Relations, Andrea Wentscher/Junior Mgr. - Investor Relations, Markus Zeise/Mgr. - Investor Relations, Nicole Tremmel/Event Mgr., Investor Relations Officer, Jennifer Rieb/Event Mgr. - Investor Relations Officer

Directors: Jurgen Hambrecht/62/Chmn., Robert Oswald/Dep. Chmn. - Supervisory Board, Chmn. - Joint Counsel, Jurgen F. Strube/68/Chmn. - Supervisory Board, Eggert Voscherau/65/Vice Chmn., Ralf Sikorski/47/Member - Supervisory Board, Hermann Scholl/73/Member - Supervisory Board, Friedrich Wirsing/50/Member - Supervisory Board, Hans Dieter Potsch/Member - Supervisory Board, Martin Brudermuller/47/Dir., Tessen Von Heydebreck/Member - Supervisory Board, Robert Studer/70/Member - Supervisory Board, Michael Vassiliadis/Member - Supervisory Board, Michael Diekmann/54/Member - Supervisory Board, Max Dietrich Kley/67/Member - Supervisory Board, Stefan Marcinowski/57/Dir. (27 Directors included in Index)

Financial Data: Fiscal Year End:12/31   Latest Annual Data: 12/31/2006

Year	Sales	Net Income
2006	$69,460,587,000	$4,117,884,000
2005	$50,627,060,000	$3,534,960,000
2004	$50,817,000,000	$2,521,800,000
Curr. Assets: $24,283,618,000	**Curr. Liab.:** $18,458,190,000	**P/E Ratio:** 6.88
Plant, Equip.: $19,674,450,000	**Total Liab.:** $35,269,041,000	**Indic. Yr. Divd.:** NA
Total Assets: $60,255,059,000	**Net Worth:** $24,285,598,000	**Debt/ Equity:** NA

Basic Earth Science Systems Inc

1801 Broadway, Ste. 620, Denver, CO, 80202; **PH:** 1-303-296-3076; **Fax:** 1-303-773-8099; http:// www.basicearth.net/contact.html

General - Incorporation	DE	**Stock** - Price on:12/24/2007	$1.45
Employees	8	Stock Exchange	OTC
Auditor	Hein & Assoc. LLP	Ticker Symbol	BSIC
Stk Agt	Visa Stock Transfer	Outstanding Shares	16,810,000
Counsel	NA	E.P.S.	$0.12
DUNS No.	06-729-4009	Shareholders	NA

Business: The group's principle activities are to explore, acquire, develop, operate, produce and sell crude oil and natural gas. The group operates through the following two segments: oil and gas sales and well services. The operations of the group are located in the williston basin in North Dakota and Montana, south Texas and d-j basin in Colorado. Oil and natural gas is sold to various purchasers in the geographic area of its properties. The group's total revenue for year 2007 was 7.17 millions of USD.

Primary SIC and add'l.: 1382 1311

CIK No: 0000010254

Subsidiaries: Legent Resources Corporation

Officers: Ray Singleton/56/Dir., CEO, Pres., David Flake/52/Dir., CFO, Sec., Treasurer, Patrick J. Russell/General Counsel

Directors: Ray Singleton/56/Dir., CEO, Pres., David Flake/52/Dir., CFO, Sec., Treasurer, Richard K. Rodgers/47/Dir., Monroe W. Robertson/Dir.

Owners: Insiders/30.78%, David Flake/4.43%, Ray Singleton/26.32%, Monroe W. Robertson

Financial Data: Fiscal Year End:03/31   Latest Annual Data: 03/31/2007

Year	Sales	Net Income
2007	$7,167,000	$2,500,000
2006	$6,615,000	$2,815,000
2005	$4,856,000	$1,845,000

Curr. Assets:	$4,046,000	Curr. Liab.:	$1,989,000	P/E Ratio:	11.15
Plant, Equip.:	$11,337,000	Total Liab.:	$4,372,000	Indic. Yr. Divd.:	NA
Total Assets:	$15,452,000	Net Worth:	$11,080,000	Debt/ Equity:	NA

Basic Energy Services Inc

400 W Illinios, Ste. 800, Midland, TX, 79701; *PH:* 1-432-620-5500; *Fax:* 1-432-620-5501; *http://* www.basicenergyservices.com; *Email:* info@basicenergyservices.com

General - Incorporation	DE	Stock- Price on:12/24/2007	$26.53
Employees	4,000	Stock Exchange	NYSE
Auditor	KPMG LLP	Ticker Symbol	BAS
Stk Agt	American Stock Transfer & Trust Co.	Outstanding Shares	40,860,000
Counsel	NA	E.P.S	$2.48
DUNS No.	NA	Shareholders	NA

Business: The groups principle activity is to provide site services to oil and gas drilling and producing companies. The groups services include well servicing, fluid servicing, drilling and completion services, and well site construction services. The group operates through four segments namely, well servicing, fluid services, drilling and completion services, and well site construction services. The group acquired LeBus Oil Field Service Co. in January 2006, G&L Tool, Ltd. in February 2006, Chaparral Service, Inc. in August 2006. The group operates from the United States. The group's quarterly revenue for September 2007 was 229.23 millions of USD.

Primary SIC and add'l.: 1389

CIK No: 0001109189

Subsidiaries: Acid Services, LLC, Basic Energy Services GP, LLC, Basic Energy Services L.P., Basic Energy Services LP, LLC, Basic Marine Services, Inc., First Energy Services Company, Globe Well Service, Inc., JetStar Consolidated Holdings, Inc., JetStar Energy Services, LLC, JS Acquisition LLC, LeBus Oil Field Service Co., Oilwell Fracturing Services, Inc., SCH Disposal, L.L.C.

Officers: Kenneth V. Huseman/Dir., CEO, Pres./$1,836,123.00, Alan Krenek/Sr. VP, CFO, Treasurer, Sec./$713,646.00, Charles W. Swift/Sr. VP - Rig, Truck Operations/$551,552.00, Dub William Harrison/VP - Equipment, Safety/$461,474.00, Mark D. Rankin/VP - Risk Management, James E. Tyner/VP - Human Resources/$342,688.00, Thomas Monroe Patterson/VP - Corporate Development, Rental, Fishing Tool Services

Directors: Kenneth V. Huseman/Dir., CEO, Pres., Steven A. Webster/Chmn., William E. Chiles/Dir., James S. D'Agostino/Dir., Robert F. Fulton/Dir., Sylvester P. Johnson/Dir., H. H. Wommack/Dir., Thomas P. Moore/Dir.

Owners: Ted Collins, David W. Sledge, Kelcy Warren, Patrick J. Collins, JSL Interests, Ltd, Michael Harrison, D-K Stanhope, Brett Smith, BV Investments, LP, Collins & Jones Investments, LLC, Charles Kennan McArthur Jr. and Dana Janet McArthur Family Trust, Atlas Resources, D.B. Zwirn Special Opportunities Fund, L.P, Drawbridge Special Opportunities Fund, LP, Spencer D. Armour *(20 Owners included in Index)*

Financial Data: Fiscal Year End:12/31   Latest Annual Data: 12/31/2006

Year	Sales	Net Income
2006	$730,148,000	$98,830,000
2005	$459,752,000	$44,781,000
2004	$311,502,000	$12,861,000

Curr. Assets:	$209,764,000	Curr. Liab.:	$89,786,000	P/E Ratio:	10.28
Plant, Equip.:	$475,431,000	Total Liab.:	$417,010,000	Indic. Yr. Divd.:	NA
Total Assets:	$796,260,000	Net Worth:	$379,250,000	Debt/ Equity:	0.7569

Basin Water Inc

8731 Prestige Ct., Rancho Cucamonga, CA, 91730; *PH:* 1-909-481-6800; *Fax:* 1-909-481-6801; *http://* www.basinwater.com; *Email:* info@basinwater.com

General - Incorporation	DE	Stock- Price on:12/24/2007	$7.75
Employees	65	Stock Exchange	NDQ
Auditor	Singer Lewak Greenbaum & Goldstein	Ticker Symbol	BWTR
Stk Agt	American Stock Transfer & Trust Co.	Outstanding Shares	19,910,000
Counsel	NA	E.P.S	-$0.7
DUNS No.	NA	Shareholders	NA

Business: The groups principle activity is to provide designing, building and implementing systems for the treatment of contaminated groundwater. The groups services include Design of System, Manufacturing and Assembly, and Permitting and Installation. Customers served by the group include municipalities, real estate developers and other organizations. Specific customers of the group include American Water, Aqua America, California Water Service Group and American States Water Company. The group operates from the United States. The group's quarterly revenue for September 2007 was 5.35 millions of USD.

Primary SIC and add'l.: 4959 3589 8711 1799

CIK No: 0001352045

Officers: Peter L. Jensen/Chmn., CEO, Michael M. Stark/COO, Pres., Thomas C. Tekulve/CFO, Treasurer, Chief Administrative Officer, Pat C. Kelly/GM, Larry W. Rowe/VP - Business Development, Dan Ziol/Dir. - Research, Development, Silvia Jardino/Mgr. - Corporate Administration, Communications

Directors: Peter L. Jensen/Chmn., CEO, Russell C. Ball/Dir., Victor J. Fryling/Dir., Scott A. Katzmann/Dir., Keith R. Solar/Dir., Roger S. Faubel/Dir., Stephen A. Sharpe/Dir.

Owners: Michael M. Stark/1.00%, Scott A. Katzmann/4.51%, Magnetar Capital Partners LP/7.94%, Oppenheimer Capital LLC/5.04%, Insiders/22.04%, Thomas C. Tekulve/1.12%, Roger S. Faubel, Peter L. Jensen/13.22%, Keith R. Solar/1.74%, Victor J. Fryling

Financial Data: Fiscal Year End:12/31   Latest Annual Data: 12/31/2006

Year	Sales	Net Income
2006	$17,114,000	-$11,167,000
2005	$12,231,000	$563,000
2004	$4,307,000	-$556,000

Curr. Assets:	$67,454,000	Curr. Liab.:	$7,490,000		
Plant, Equip.:	$12,227,000	Total Liab.:	$10,315,000	Indic. Yr. Divd.:	NA
Total Assets:	$90,052,000	Net Worth:	$79,737,000	Debt/ Equity:	0.0003

Basset Enterprises Inc

PO Box 110310, Naples, FL, 34108; *PH:* 1-239-598-2300; *http://* www.bassettenterprises.com

General - Incorporation	NV	Stock- Price on:12/24/2007	NA
Employees	NA	Stock Exchange	NA
Auditor	Child, Sullivan & Co	Ticker Symbol	NA
Stk Agt	Manhattan Transfer Registrar Co	Outstanding Shares	NA
Counsel	NA	E.P.S	-$0.11
DUNS No.	NA	Shareholders	NA

Business: The group's principal activities and business opportunities have not been identified. The company has not reached any agreement or understanding with any person concerning an acquisition. The company is in a development stage.

Primary SIC and add'l.: 9995

CIK No: 0001097752

Subsidiaries: Digital Network Alliance International, Inc., Lotus Capital Corp., Medianet Group Technology, Inc., Mid-Am Systems Inc, Oriole, Inc., Our Glass, Inc., Sea Sun Capital Corp.

Financial Data: Fiscal Year End:12/31   Latest Annual Data: 12/31/2006

Year	Sales	Net Income
2006	$434,000	-$1,120,000
2005	$177,000	-$1,073,000
2004	$112,000	-$336,000

Curr. Assets:	$236,000	Curr. Liab.:	$167,000		
Plant, Equip.:	$3,000	Total Liab.:	$167,000	Indic. Yr. Divd.:	NA
Total Assets:	$343,000	Net Worth:	$175,000	Debt/ Equity:	NA

Bassett Furniture Industries Inc

3525 Fairystone Pk. Hwy., Bassett, VA, 24055; *PH:* 1-276-629-6000; *Fax:* 1-276-629-6333; *http://* www.bassettfurniture.com; *Email:* consumer1@bassettfurniture.com

General - Incorporation	VA	Stock- Price on:12/24/2007	$13.67
Employees	1,800	Stock Exchange	NDQ
Auditor	Ernst & Young LLP	Ticker Symbol	BSET
Stk Agt	Wachovia Bank N.A	Outstanding Shares	11,830,000
Counsel	NA	E.P.S	NA
DUNS No.	17-703-9914	Shareholders	NA

Business: The group's principal activities are to manufacture and market home furnishings. The operations comprise of three segments: wood, upholstery and import. The wood segment manufactures wood furniture that includes bedroom and dining suites and accent pieces. The upholstery segment manufactures upholstered frames and cuts with a variety of frame and fabric options, including sofas, chairs, and love seats. The import segment sources the required raw material, principally from Asia, and distributes the finished products through a network of retailers, both independent and those affiliated to the group. The retailers consist of department and furniture stores across the United States. Once such major customer is the jc penney company. The group has eight manufacturing facilities and 101 stores operating in United States.

Primary SIC and add'l.: 2511 2512 2515

CIK No: 0000010329

Subsidiaries: Bassett Direct NC, LLC, Bassett Direct SC, LLC, Bassett Direct Stores, Inc., Bassett Furniture Industries of North Carolina, Inc., Bassett Industries Alternative Asset Fund, L.P., BDP, LC, Bdu Ny, LLC, BFD-Atlanta, LLC, LRG Furniture, LLC, The Accessories Group, Inc., The E.B. Malone Corporation

Officers: Robert H. Spilman/51/Dir., CEO, Pres., Barry C. Safrit/Sr. VP, CFO

Directors: Robert H. Spilman/51/Dir., CEO, Pres., Paul Fulton/73/Chmn., George W. Henderson/59/Dir., Dale C. Pond/61/Dir., William C. Wampler/48/Dir., Peter W. Brown/65/Dir., Howard H. Haworth/73/Dir., William C. Warden/55/Dir.

Owners: Insiders/10.11%, Keith R. Sanders/1.00%, Dimensional Fund Advisors Inc./8.71%, Grace& White, Inc./6.05%, Charles T. King/1.00%, Franklin Resources, Inc./7.57%, Barry C. Safrit/3.89%

Financial Data: Fiscal Year End:11/26   Latest Annual Data: 11/25/2006

Year	Sales	Net Income
2006	$328,214,000	$5,429,000
2005	$335,207,000	$7,563,000
2004	$315,654,000	$8,209,000

Curr. Assets:	$102,677,000	Curr. Liab.:	$38,549,000		
Plant, Equip.:	$93,328,000	Total Liab.:	$76,154,000	Indic. Yr. Divd.:	$0.800
Total Assets:	$297,366,000	Net Worth:	$221,212,000	Debt/ Equity:	0.0924

Bassett Ventures Inc

Formerly: Assistglobal Technologies Corp
1255 W Pender St., Vancouver, BC, V6E 2V1; *PH:* 1-604-687-0879; *http://* www.assistglobal.com

General - Incorporation	BC	Stock- Price on:12/24/2007	$0.18
Employees	NA	Stock Exchange	NA
Auditor	LDMB Advisors Inc	Ticker Symbol	NA
Stk Agt	Pacific Corporate Trust Co	Outstanding Shares	NA
Counsel	NA	E.P.S	NA
DUNS No.	NA	Shareholders	NA

Business: The group's principal activity is to provide and develop Internet commerce services including information access, entertainment, gaming and financial services. Through its subsidiaries, the group offers a complete range of e-commerce services, including real-time Internet credit card processing, a robust reporting facility and access to offshore banking and merchant accounts. The group is able to offer its e-commerce services to companies in a wide variety of industries particularly that of Internet gaming through its offshore subsidiaries. The operations of the group are being carried out in Canada, st. Kitts and Costa Rica.

Primary SIC and add'l.: 7999 7375

CIK No: 0001036140

Subsidiaries: AssistGlobal Inc., AssistGlobal USA Inc.

Officers: Curt Huber/Dir., CEO, Pres., Harpreet Janda/Dir., CFO, Sec.

Directors: Curt Huber/Dir., CEO, Pres., Parmjeet Johal/Dir., Harpreet Janda/Dir., CFO, Sec., Tajinderjit Johal/Dir.

Owners: Jade Petal Investments Inc./9.79%, Hypo Alpe-Adria Bank (Liechtenstein) AG/9.79%

Financial Data: Fiscal Year End:12/31   Latest Annual Data: 12/31/2006

Year	Sales	Net Income
2006	NA	-$94,000
2005	NA	-$174,000
2004	$573,000	-$597,000

Curr. Assets:	$481,000	**Curr. Liab.:**	$135,000		
Plant, Equip.:	$6,000	**Total Liab.:**	$135,000	**Indic. Yr. Divd.:**	NA
Total Assets:	$488,000	**Net Worth:**	$353,000	**Debt/ Equity:**	NA

Battle Mountain Gold Explorations Inc

333 Clay St., 42nd Fl., Houston, TX, 77002; *PH:* 1-713-650-6400; *http://* www.bmegold.com

General - Incorporation	NV	**Stock**- Price on:12/24/2007	$0.4
Employees	2	Stock Exchange	NA
Auditor	Pricewaterhousecoopers LLP	Ticker Symbol	NA
Stk Agt	Pacific Corporate Trust Co.	Outstanding Shares	69,070,000
Counsel	NA	E.P.S.	-$0.04
DUNS No.	NA	Shareholders	NA

Business: The group's principle activities include producing and mining gold properties.The group operates from United States.

Primary SIC and add'l.: 1040

CIK No: 0000771498

Officers: Mark Kucher/Chmn., CEO, David Atkinson/CFO

Directors: Mark Kucher/Chmn., CEO, Brian M. Labadie/Dir., Robert Connochie/Dir., Christopher E. Herald/Dir., Anthony E.W. Crews/Dir.

Financial Data: *Fiscal Year End:*12/31 *Latest Annual Data:* 12/31/2006

Year	Sales	Net Income
2006	$2,395,000	-$2,100,000
2005	NA	-$1,794,000
2004	NA	-$319,000

Curr. Assets:	$1,166,000	**Curr. Liab.:**	$6,497,000	**P/E Ratio:**	12.32
Plant, Equip.:	$18,423,000	**Total Liab.:**	$13,212,000	**Indic. Yr. Divd.:**	NA
Total Assets:	$21,497,000	**Net Worth:**	$8,285,000	**Debt/ Equity:**	NA

Bausch & Lomb Inc

One Bausch & Lomb Pl, Rochester, NY, 14604; *PH:* 1-585-338-6000; *Fax:* 1-585-338-6007; *http://* www.bausch.com

General - Incorporation	NY	**Stock**- Price on:12/24/2007	$68.97
Employees	13,000	Stock Exchange	NYSE
Auditor	PricewaterhouseCoopers LLP	Ticker Symbol	BOL
Stk Agt	Mellon Investor Services LLC	Outstanding Shares	54,380,000
Counsel	NA	E.P.S.	$0.92
DUNS No.	00-220-7751	Shareholders	NA

Business: The group's principal activities are to develop, manufacture and market healthcare products for the eye. The product categories include contact lens, lens care, pharmaceutical, cataract and refractive. The contact lens products include traditional, planned replacement disposable, daily disposable, rigid gas permeable, continuous wear and toric lenses. The lens care products include multipurpose solutions, enzyme cleaners and saline solutions. It manufactures and sells generic and proprietary prescription pharmaceuticals and vision accessories with a strategic emphasis in the ophthalmic field and over-the-counter (otc) ophthalmic medications. The refractive product line includes lasers, microkeratomes, and other products used in refractive surgery. Major trademarks of the group are bausch & lomb, ocuvite and renu multiplus.

Primary SIC and add'l.: 2844 3842 3851 2834 3827

CIK No: 0000010427

Subsidiaries: B&L CRL Inc., B&L Domestic Holdings Corp., B&L Financial Holdings Corp., B&l Spaf Inc., B&l Vplex Holdings, Inc., B.L.J. Company Limited, Bausch & Lomb (Australia) Pty. Limited, Bausch & Lomb (China) Investment Company Limited, Bausch & Lomb (Hong Kong) Limited, Bausch & Lomb (Jersey) Limited, Bausch & Lomb (Malaysia) Sdn. Bhd., Bausch & Lomb (New Zealand) Limited, Bausch & Lomb (Philippines), Inc., Bausch & Lomb (Shanghai) Trading Company Limited, Bausch & Lomb (Singapore) Pte. Ltd. 55 Subsidiaries included in the Index

Officers: Ronald L. Zarrella/Chmn., CEO/$4,920,066.00, Jean F. Geisel/Corp. Sec., Lindsay Brooks/Surgical, Cataract, Vitreoretinal, Refractive, Europe, Anthony Neo/Surgical, Cataract, Vitreoretinal, Refractive, Asia, Pacific, John Heiser/Pharmaceuticals, Rx, Americas, Jabrane Annaki/Pharmaceuticals, Rx, Europe, Grace Chiu/Pharmaceuticals, Rx, Asia, Pacific, Abigail Markward/Surgical, Cataract, Vitreoretinal, Refractive, Americas, Dwain L. Hahs/Sr. VP/$1,341,056.00, Robert D A. Bailey/Assist. Sec., Gerhard Bauer/Sr. VP - Global Operations, Engineering, Alan H. Farnsworth/Sr. VP, Pres. - Europe, Middle East, Africa Region, Dipankar Bhattacharjee/VP, Pres. Asia Pacific Region, Robert J. Moore/VP, Pres. - US Vision Care, Henry C. Tung/VP - Global Surgical *(30 Officers included in Index)*

Directors: Ronald L. Zarrella/Chmn., CEO, Catherine M. Burzik/57/Dir.

Owners: Linda Johnson Rice, Dwain L. Hahs, Ruth R. McMullin, Paul A. Friedman, Barry W. Wilson, Praveen Tyle, Franklin Mutual Advisers, LLC/8.20%, Ronald L. Zarrella, Stephen C. McCluski, Capital Research and Management Company/5.80%, John Loughlin, William H. Waltrip, Insiders/1.00%, Alan M. Bennett, Kenneth L. Wolfe *(17 Owners included in Index)*

Financial Data: *Fiscal Year End:*12/25 *Latest Annual Data:* 03/31/2007

Year	Sales	Net Income
2007	NA	NA
2006	$2,292,400,000	$14,900,000
2005	$2,353,800,000	$19,200,000

Curr. Assets:	$1,627,900,000	**Curr. Liab.:**	$1,010,200,000	**P/E Ratio:**	176.85
Plant, Equip.:	$604,400,000	**Total Liab.:**	$2,108,000,000	**Indic. Yr. Divd.:**	$0.520
Total Assets:	$3,416,400,000	**Net Worth:**	$1,283,900,000	**Debt/ Equity:**	0.4988

BAXL Holdings Inc

Formerly: Allmarine Consultants Corp

8601 Rr 2222, Bldg. 1, Ste. 210, Austin, TX, 78730; *PH:* 1-512-689-7787

General - Incorporation	NV	**Stock**- Price on:12/24/2007	NA
Employees	NA	Stock Exchange	NA
Auditor	LBB & Assoc. Ltd., LLP	Ticker Symbol	NA
Stk Agt	NA	Outstanding Shares	NA
Counsel	David M. Loev	E.P.S.	NA
DUNS No.	NA	Shareholders	NA

Business: The groups principal activities include providing maritime services to ship owners and operators including registration and deletion of merchant vessels, bareboat and registration of mortgage. The group operates from the United States.

Primary SIC and add'l.: 4499

CIK No: 0001343957

Officers: Gus Bottazzi/CEO, David Van Rossum/CFO, Michael Chavez/28/Dir., Pres., Sec., Treasurer, Arthur Stone/64/Dir., VP

Directors: Michael Chavez/28/Dir., Pres., Sec., Treasurer, Arthur Stone/64/Dir., VP

Owners: Insiders/54.20%, DAVID LOEV/28.00%, ARTHUR STONE/27.10%, MICHAEL CHAVEZ/27.10%

Curr. Assets:	$0	**Curr. Liab.:**	$27,000		
Plant, Equip.:	NA	**Total Liab.:**	$27,000	**Indic. Yr. Divd.:**	NA
Total Assets:	$0	**Net Worth:**	-$27,000	**Debt/ Equity:**	NA

Baxter International Inc

1 Baxter Pkwy., Deerfield, IL, 60015; *PH:* 1-847-948-2000; *Fax:* 1-847-948-2016; *http://* www.baxter.com

General - Incorporation	DE	**Stock**- Price on:12/24/2007	$57.7
Employees	48,000	Stock Exchange	NYSE
Auditor	PricewaterhouseCoopers LLP	Ticker Symbol	BAX
Stk Agt	Computershare Investor Services LLC	Outstanding Shares	651,520,000
Counsel	NA	E.P.S.	$2.53
DUNS No.	00-514-6311	Shareholders	NA

Business: The groups principle activity is to provide diversified medical products. The group's are sold under the brand names advate, alyx, aralast, arena, baxter, enlightenedhrbc, exeltra, extraneal, intercept, nanoedge,and premasol. The group operates from United States, Canada and Mexico.

Primary SIC and add'l.: 3841 3845 3842

CIK No: 0000010456

Subsidiaries: Baxter AG, Baxter BioScience Manufacturing Sarl, Baxter Corporation, Baxter Deutschland GmbH, Baxter Deutschland Holding GmbH, Baxter Export Corporation, Baxter Global Holdings II Inc., Baxter Global Holdings Inc., Baxter Handel GmbH, Baxter Healthcare (Asia) Pte Ltd, Baxter Healthcare (Holdings) Limited, Baxter Healthcare Corporation, Baxter Healthcare Corporation of Puerto Rico, Baxter Healthcare Holding GmbH, Baxter Healthcare Limited 39 Subsidiaries included in the Index

Officers: Robert L. Parkinson/57/Chmn., CEO, Pres./$13,582,040.00, Bruce McGillivray/Corporate VP, Pres. - Renal, Jeanne K. Mason/Corporate VP - Human Resources, Karenann Terrell/Corporate VP, CIO, Carlos Alonso/Corporate VP, Pres. - Latin America, Robert J. Hombach/Corporate VP, Treasurer, Peter Nicklin/Corporate VP, Pres. - Europe, Michael James Gatling/Corporate VP - Manufacturing, Robert M. Davis/CFO, Corporate VP/$1,496,533.00, James Michael Gatling/Corporate VP - Manufacturing, Susan R. Lichtenstein/Corporate VP, General Counsel, John J. Greisch/Corporate VP, Pres. - International/$3,939,359.00, Peter J. Arduini/Corporate VP, Pres. - Medication Delivery/$2,438,642.00, Norbert G. Riedel/Corporate VP, Chief Scientific Officer, Joy A. Amundson/Corporate VP, Pres. - Bioscience/$3,455,474.00 *(21 Officers included in Index)*

Directors: Robert L. Parkinson/57/Chmn., CEO, Pres., John D. Forsyth/59/Dir., Wayne T. Hockmeyer/63/Dir., K. J. Storm/64/Dir., Blake E. Devitt/60/Dir., Peter S. Hellman/57/Dir., William B. Graham/91/Dir., Gail D. Fosler/59/Dir., Joseph B. Martin/68/Dir., Thomas T. Stallkamp/60/Dir., Carole Shapazian/63/Dir., Walter E. Boomer/68/Dir., James R. Gavin/61/Dir., Albert P.L. Stroucken/59/Dir.

Owners: Blake E. Devitt, Albert P.L. Stroucken, FMR Corp/6.65%, Carole J. Shapazian, Peter S. Hellman, Robert M. Davis, John D. Forsyth, James R. Gavin, Gail D. Fosler, Joseph B. Martin, Insiders, K. J. Storm, Joy A. Amundson, Robert L. Parkinson, Walter E. Boomer *(18 Owners included in Index)*

Financial Data: *Fiscal Year End:*12/31 *Latest Annual Data:* 12/31/2006

Year	Sales	Net Income
2006	$10,378,000,000	$1,397,000,000
2005	$9,849,000,000	$956,000,000
2004	$9,509,000,000	$388,000,000

Curr. Assets:	$6,970,000,000	**Curr. Liab.:**	$3,610,000,000	**P/E Ratio:**	25.09
Plant, Equip.:	$4,229,000,000	**Total Liab.:**	$8,414,000,000	**Indic. Yr. Divd.:**	$0.870
Total Assets:	$14,686,000,000	**Net Worth:**	$6,272,000,000	**Debt/ Equity:**	0.3216

Bay Banks of Virginia Inc

100 S Main St., Kilmarnick, VA, 22482; *PH:* 1-804-435-1171

General - Incorporation	VA	**Stock**- Price on:12/24/2007	$14
Employees	NA	Stock Exchange	OTC
Auditor	Yount, Hyde & Barbour, P.C	Ticker Symbol	BAYK
Stk Agt	Registrar & Transfer Co	Outstanding Shares	2,370,000
Counsel	Dunton, Simmons & Dunton	E.P.S.	$0.82
DUNS No.	NA	Shareholders	NA

Business: The group's principal activity is to provide a full range of banking and related financial services. The deposit products include checking accounts, savings account and other depository services. The lending activities include commercial and industrial loans, residential and commercial mortgages, home equity loans and consumer installment loans. The group's other services to commercial customers include analysis checking, cash management deposit accounts, wire services, direct deposit payroll service and a full line of commercial lending options. It also provides a broad range of trust and related fiduciary services including testamentary trust, revocable and irrevocable personal, managed agency, custodial trusts and discount brokerage services.

Primary SIC and add'l.: 6022 6712

CIK No: 0001034594

Subsidiaries: Bank of Lancaster, Bay Trust Company

Owners: Walter C. Ayers, Deborah M. Evans, Richard A. Farmar, Ammon G. Dunton/4.00%, Insiders/6.90%, Austin L. Roberts/1.90%, Robert C. Berry, Allen C. Marple, Robert F. Hurliman, Robert J. Wittman

Financial Data: *Fiscal Year End:*12/31 *Latest Annual Data:* 12/31/2006

Year	Sales	Net Income
2006	$21,363,000	$2,329,000
2005	$18,978,000	$2,547,000
2004	$16,875,000	$2,181,000

Curr. Assets:	$12,523,000	**Curr. Liab.:**	$281,897,000	**P/E Ratio:**	15.91
Plant, Equip.:	$10,879,000	**Total Liab.:**	$283,325,000	**Indic. Yr. Divd.:**	$0.680
Total Assets:	$309,693,000	**Net Worth:**	$26,368,000	**Debt/ Equity:**	NA

Bay Commercial Bank CA

2328 W Joppa Rd., Lutherville, MD, 21093; *PH:* 1-410-494-2580; *Fax:* 1-410-494-2589; *http://* www.baycommercialbank.com; *Email:* info@baycommercialbank.com

General		Stock	
Incorporation		Price on:12/24/2007	$11.65
Employees	NA	Stock Exchange	OTC
Auditor	NA	Ticker Symbol	BCML
Stk Agt	StockTrans, Inc.	Outstanding Shares	1,540,000
Counsel	NA	E.P.S	NA
DUNS No.	NA	Shareholders	NA

Business: The groups principal activity is to provide banking business. The group financial products include savings and fixed deposits, on line, personal, commercial lending and business banking. The group operates from the United States.

Primary SIC and add'l.: 6021 6712

CIK No:

Officers: George J. Guarini/Dir., CEO, Keary L. Colwell/CFO, Janet L. King/COO, Brian K. Bray/Chief Credit Officer, Wai-Yew Lam/VP - Marketing, Exchange Officer

Directors: George J. Guarini/Dir., CEO, Bill Caldwell/Chmn., David M. Spatz/Dir., Lloyd W. Kendall/Dir., Jim Apple/Dir., James S. Camp/Dir., A. L. Walburg/Dir., Robert G. Laverne/Dir.

Bay National Corp (Maryland)

2328 W Joppa Rd., Lutherville, MD, 21093; *PH:* 1-410-494-2580; *Fax:* 1-410-494-2589; *http://* www.baynational.com

General		Stock	
Incorporation	MD	Price on:12/24/2007	$16.4199
Employees	57	Stock Exchange	NDQ
Auditor	Stegman & Company	Ticker Symbol	BAYN
Stk Agt	NA	Outstanding Shares	2,130,000
Counsel	NA	E.P.S	$0.892
DUNS No.	NA	Shareholders	NA

Business: The group operates through its subsidiaries whose principle activity is to provide banking and financial services. The groups services include commercial and industrial loans, real estate loans, consumer loans and residential mortgage and home equity loans, ATMs and Deposits. The financial products of the group include business and personal savings and checking accounts, money market demand accounts, and certificates of deposit. The group operates from the United Sates. The assets of the group for the year 2006 were $254,805 (thousands).

Primary SIC and add'l.: 6021

CIK No: 0001089787

Subsidiaries: Bay National Bank, Bay National Capital Trust I, BNB Mortgage, LLC

Officers: Hugh W. Mohler/Chmn., CEO, Pres., Principal Executive Officer/$364,725.00, Richard J. Oppitz/Exec. VP/$198,544.00, Mark A. Semanie/Exec. VP, CFO - Principal Accounting, Financial Officer/$275,615.00, Warren F. Boutilier/Sr. VP, Robert W. Freeman/Sr. VP, Scott Hargest/Member - Advisory Board, Baltimore, Robert F. Scholz/Member - Advisory Board, Batlimore, Gregory J. Olinde/Sr. VP, Robert W. Reilley/Sr. VP, Hugh L. Robinson/Sr. VP - Bay National Bank, Mary Ellen Barthelme/VP, Charles J. Fleury/VP, Curt H.G. Heinfelden/VP - Bay National Bank, Gilbert F. Kennedy/VP - Corporate Banking, Bay National Bank, John C. Wasowicz/VP - Bay National Bank

Directors: Hugh W. Mohler/Chmn., CEO, Pres., Principal Executive Officer, Eugene M. Waldron/Dir., Robert L. Moore/Dir., Carl A.J. Wright/Dir., John R. Lerch/Dir., Henry H. Stansbury/Dir., Donald G. McClure/Dir., Kenneth H. Trout/Dir., James P. O'Conor/Dir., Richard C. Springer/48/Dir., Anthony S. Brandon/Member - Advisory Board, Baltimore, Wayne D. Coffey/Member - Advisory Board, Baltimore, Harold C. Green/Member - Advisory Board, Baltimore, James C. Groschan/Member - Advisory Board, Baltimore, Charles Maskell/Member - Advisory Board, Baltimore *(42 Directors included in Index)*

Owners: Richard J. Oppitz/0.03%, Hugh W. Mohler/4.66%, John R. Lerch/2.23%, Michael R. Gill, Donald G. McClure, James P. OConor/0.25%, NexTier, Inc./8.11%, Insiders/22.82%, Victor H. Rieger/1.44%, Mark A. Semanie/1.01%, Edwin A. Rommel/1.76%, Charles E. Bounds/0.39%, Robert L. Moore/0.49%, Kenneth H. Trout/3.00%, William B. Rinnier/0.67% *(19 Owners included in Index)*

Financial Data: *Fiscal Year End:*12/31 *Latest Annual Data:* 12/31/2006

Year	Sales	Net Income
2006	$20,558,000	$2,430,000
2005	$13,733,000	$2,744,000
2004	$8,162,000	$802,000

Curr. Assets:	$37,049,000	Curr. Liab.:	$227,962,000	P/E Ratio:	13.57
Plant, Equip.:	$1,100,000	Total Liab.:	$235,962,000	Indic. Yr. Divd.:	NA
Total Assets:	$254,805,000	Net Worth:	$18,842,000	Debt/ Equity:	0.4245

Bayer

Bayerwerk, Gebaeude W11, Kaiser-Wilhelm-Allee, Leverkusen, 51368; *PH:* 49-0214301; *http://* www.bayer.com

General		Stock	
Incorporation	Germany	Price on:12/24/2007	$75.89
Employees	106,000	Stock Exchange	OTC
Auditor	PricewaterhouseCoopers LLP	Ticker Symbol	BAYRY
Stk Agt	John Hancock Signature Services, Inc	Outstanding Shares	764,340,000
Counsel	NA	E.P.S	$6.88
DUNS No.	NA	Shareholders	NA

Business: The group's principle activity is to provide health care, nutrition and related services. The group operates through the following four divisions: healthcare, cropscience, polymers and chemicals. The healthcare division comprises of pharmaceuticals, biological products, consumer care, animal health and diagnostics. Cropscience includes the crop protection, environmental science and bioscience business groups. The division polymers is active in the areas of polycarbonate plastics, polyurethanes, coating raw materials and colorants, and includes the subsidiaries h.c. Starck and wolff walsrode.

Primary SIC and add'l.: 2899 3861 3089 2836 2819 2834 3826

CIK No: 0001144145

Subsidiaries: Bayer Corporation, Bayer MaterialScience, Wolff Walsrode AG

Officers: Roland Hartwig/General Counsel, Klaus Kuhn/56/Dir., CFO

Directors: Werner Wenning/62/Chmn., Richard Pott/55/Dir., Thomas Hellmuth/52/Member - Supervisory Board, Paul Achleitner/52/Member - Supervisory Board, Hermann Josef Strenger/Member - Supervisory Board, Manfred Schneider/70/Member - Supervisory Board, Josef Ackermann/60/Member - Supervisory Board, Andreas Becker/49/Member - Supervisory Board, Thomas Fischer/53/Member - Supervisory Board, Peter Hausmann/54/Member - Supervisory Board, Henkel E.H. Hans-Olaf/68/Member - Supervisory Board, Gregor Justen/60/Member - Supervisory Board, Klaus Kleinfeld/Member - Supervisory Board, Martin H.C. Kohlhaussen/73/Member - Supervisory Board, Hubertus Schmoldt/63/Member - Supervisory Board *(33 Directors included in Index)*

Financial Data: *Fiscal Year End:*12/31 *Latest Annual Data:* 12/31/2006

Year	Sales	Net Income
2006	$38,230,607,000	$355,161,000
2005	$32,432,425,000	$1,571,699,000
2004	$40,601,815,000	$890,953,000

Curr. Assets:	$26,398,078,000	Curr. Liab.:	$20,484,455,000	P/E Ratio:	6.88
Plant, Equip.:	$11,707,100,000	Total Liab.:	$56,811,190,000	Indic. Yr. Divd.:	$1.070
Total Assets:	$73,115,573,000	Net Worth:	$16,082,574,000	Debt/ Equity:	NA

Bayer Schering Pharma Aktiengesellschaft

Formerly: Schering
Mullerstrasse 178, Berlin, 13353; ; *http://* www.schering.de

General		Stock	
Incorporation	Germany	Price on:12/24/2007	NA
Employees	NA	Stock Exchange	NA
Auditor	BDO Deutsche Warentreuhand	Ticker Symbol	NA
Stk Agt	NA	Outstanding Shares	NA
Counsel	NA	E.P.S	NA
DUNS No.	NA	Shareholders	NA

Business: The group's principal activities are the development and manufacturing of pharmaceuticals and diagnostic substances. The group operates through four business units: therapeutics (drugs to combat disabling diseases), gynaecology and andrology (oral contraceptives, hormone replacement medication), diagnostics (X-ray, mri and ultrasound contrast media) and dermatology (corticoid creams and other dermatological preparations). The group has subsidiaries worldwide.

Primary SIC and add'l.: 5122 2834 2835

CIK No: 0001124139

Subsidiaries: 1338768 Ontario Inc, 1342077 Ontario Inc, African Metals Ltd, Aluminium Consortium Venezuela B.V., Angola Mining Finance Ltd, Angola Mining Services Ltd, Angola Technical Services Ltd, Atlas Steels Company Ltd, Auvernier Limited (in liquidation), Baniettor Mining (Pty) Ltd, BHP Billiton (BVI) Ltd, BHP Billiton (RA) Limited (in liquidation), BHP Billiton (UK) Limited, BHP Billiton Aluminium Ltd, BHP Billiton Aluminium Projects (Pty) Ltd 156 Subsidiaries included in the Index

Officers: Karin Dorrepaal/Member - Executive Board, Marc Rubin/Member - Executive Board, Ulrich Kostlin/Member - Executive Board, Jorg Spiekerkotter/Member - Executive Board, Sr. Management, Rainer Metternich/Member - Executive Board, Sr. Management

Directors: Giuseppe Vita/Chmn. - Supervisory Board, Berlin, Norbert Deutschmann/Vice Chmn. - The Member - Supervisory Board - Berlin, Hubertus Erlen/Chmn., Arthur J. Higgins/Chmn. - Management Board, Werner Wenning/Chmn. - Supervisory Board, Friedrich Berschauer/Member - Supervisory Board, Roland Hartwig/Member - Supervisory Board, Klaus Kuhn/Member - Supervisory Board, Achim Noack/Member - Supervisory Board, Hans-Georg Bleeck/Member - Supervisory Board, Berlin, Werner Baumann/Member - Board Of Management, Andreas Busch/Member - Board Of Management, Gunnar Riemann/Member - Board Of Management, Johannes Heitbaum/Member - Supervisory Board - Werne, Reiner Hagemann/Member - Supervisory Board, Munich *(22 Directors included in Index)*

Financial Data: *Fiscal Year End:*12/31 *Latest Annual Data:* 12/31/2005

Year	Sales	Net Income
2005	$6,286,795,000	$696,427,000
2004	$6,695,111,000	$642,632,000
2003	$6,309,000,000	$616,000,000

Curr. Assets:	$4,244,890,000	Curr. Liab.:	$1,966,104,000		
Plant, Equip.:	$1,375,088,000	Total Liab.:	$3,340,008,000	Indic. Yr. Divd.:	NA
Total Assets:	$7,298,273,000	Net Worth:	$3,936,946,000	Debt/ Equity:	NA

Baylake Corp

217 N 4th Ave., Sturgeon Bay, WI, 54235; *PH:* 1-920-743-5551; *Fax:* 1-920-746-3984; *http://* www.baylake.com

General		Stock	
Incorporation	WI	Price on:12/24/2007	$14
Employees	336	Stock Exchange	OTC
Auditor	Crowe Chizek & Co. LLC	Ticker Symbol	BYLK
Stk Agt	Registrar & Transfer Co	Outstanding Shares	7,840,000
Counsel	NA	E.P.S	$0.28
DUNS No.	00-794-7740	Shareholders	NA

Business: The group's principal activity is to provide general banking and trust services through its subsidiaries. The subsidiaries are the baylake bank, baylake investments inc, the bank of sturgeon bay building corporation, cornerstone financial inc, arborview llc and baylake insurance agency inc. The group accepts demand deposit accounts, various savings account plans, certificates of deposit and offers real estate, consumer, commercial, industrial and agricultural loans. Other services include transfer agency, personal and corporate trusts, insurance agency, brokerage, financial planning, cash management and electronic banking services. The group's subsidiaries conduct certain non-banking businesses also, including the provision of data and automated teller machine processing services to 73 banks; the operation of a community based residential facility and managing conference facilities.

Primary SIC and add'l.: 6022 6712

CIK No: 0000275119

Subsidiaries: Baylake Bank, Baylake Capital Trust I, Baylake City Center LLC, Baylake Insurance Agency, Inc., Baylake Investments, Inc., United Financial Services, Inc. (49.8% owned)

Officers: Thomas L. Herlache/Chmn., CEO/$707,236.00, Paul Wickmann/Financial Advisor/$201,632.00, Dan Baldwin/Financial Advisor, Ryan Freitag/Financial Advisor, Brian Hartl/Financial Advisor, Pamela J. Lent/Financial Advisor, Suzanne Udoni/Financial Advisor, Park Drescher/Trust Officer, Frederick A. Kohnle/Pres. - Tisch Mills Farm Center, Inc, Charles E. Burnham/Pres. - Marketing, Bay Area Region, Marcia M. Cryderman/55/Sr. VP - Bank, Wide Services, Daniel F. Maggle/Sec., John A. Hauser/VP, David J. Miller/Chief Credit Officer - Baylake Bank, Larry Brunette/Asset Management *(30 Officers included in Index)*

Directors: Thomas L. Herlache/Chmn., CEO, Richard A. Braun/Vice Chmn., Michelle Knaus/Dir., Dir. - Retail, Bay Area Region, George Delveaux/Dir., Dee Geurts-Bengtson/Dir., Robert Cera/Dir., Pres. - Baylake Corp, COO - Baylake Bank, William Parsons/Dir., Kevin Flatley/Dir., John B. Gilman/Dir., Roger G. Ferris/Dir., Robert W. Agnew/Dir., Paul Jay Sturm/Dir., Joseph Morgan/Dir., Henry M. Isaksen/Dir., Jeffrey J. Rabas/Dir. *(29 Directors included in Index)*

Owners: Richard A. Braun/1.30%, Robert J. Cera, Roger G. Ferris, Joseph Morgan, Paul C. Wickmann, Robert A. Agnew, Paul Jay Sturm, William C. Parsons/1.80%, Ellsworth L. Peterson/5.50%, John W. Bunda, Michael J. Gilson, Dee Geurts-Bengtson, George Delveaux, Insiders/8.30%, Sharon A. Haines *(18 Owners included in Index)*

Financial Data: Fiscal Year End:12/31 **Latest Annual Data:** 12/31/2006

Year	Sales	Net Income
2006	$79,751,000	$7,376,000
2005	$73,135,000	$8,903,000
2004	$59,900,000	$10,773,000

Curr. Assets:	$28,868,000	Curr. Liab.:	$1,013,391,000	P/E Ratio:	29.17
Plant, Equip.:	$34,165,000	Total Liab.:	$1,029,491,000	Indic. Yr. Divd.:	$0.640
Total Assets:	$1,111,684,000	Net Worth:	$82,193,000	Debt/ Equity:	NA

Bayou City Exploration Inc

10777 Westheimer, Ste. 170, Houston, TX, 77042; *PH:* 1-832-358-3900; *Fax:* 1-832-358-3903; *http://* www.bcexploration.com

General - Incorporation	NV	Stock - Price on:12/24/2007	$0.19
Employees	5	Stock Exchange	OTC
Auditor	Mountjoy & Bressler, LLP	Ticker Symbol	BYCX
Stk Agt	First American Stock Transfer, Inc.	Outstanding Shares	26,280,000
Counsel	NA	E.P.S.	-$0.1
DUNS No.	NA	Shareholders	NA

Business: The groups principle activity is to exploration of minerals. The group operates from the United States.

Primary SIC and add'l.: 1311

CIK No: 0001050957

Officers: Robert D. Burr/61/Chmn., Pres., Barton C. Birdsall/Consulting Exploration Project Mgr., Jerry Nixon/Consulting Field Operations Mgr.

Directors: Robert D. Burr/61/Chmn., Pres., Harry J. Peters/63/Dir.

Owners: Gregory B. Shea/2.80%, Harry J. Peters/3.70%, Ronald E. Mitchell, Robert D. Burr/14.20%, Insiders/19.80%, Blue Ridge Group, Inc./13.80%

Financial Data: Fiscal Year End:12/31 **Latest Annual Data:** 12/31/2006

Year	Sales	Net Income
2006	$299,000	-$3,891,000
2005	$644,000	-$1,752,000
2004	$624,000	-$1,315,000

Curr. Assets:	$1,769,000	Curr. Liab.:	$1,722,000	P/E Ratio:	425.00
Plant, Equip.:	$595,000	Total Liab.:	$1,855,000	Indic. Yr. Divd.:	NA
Total Assets:	$2,371,000	Net Worth:	$517,000	Debt/ Equity:	0.1257

Baytex Energy Trust

Bow Valley Sq. II, 205 - 5th Ave. SW, Ste. 2200, Calgary, AB, T2P 2V7; *PH:* 1-403-269-4282; *Fax:* 1-403-205-3845; *http://* www.baytex.ab.ca; *Email:* investor@baytex.ab.ca

General - Incorporation	Canada	Stock - Price on:12/24/2007	$19.92
Employees	149	Stock Exchange	NYSE
Auditor	Deloitte & Touche LLP	Ticker Symbol	BTE
Stk Agt	Valient Trust Co	Outstanding Shares	75,860,000
Counsel	Burnet, Duckworth & Palmer	E.P.S.	$1.71
DUNS No.	NA	Shareholders	NA

Business: The group's principal activities are to explore, develop and produce oil and natural gas. The group's operations are carried out in three districts in the western Canadian sedimentary basin. The group focuses on building an asset base through land acquisitions, seismic data interpretation, exploratory and development drilling, as well as property and corporate acquisitions.

Primary SIC and add'l.: 1311

CIK No: 0001279495

Subsidiaries: Baytex Energy Ltd.

Officers: Raymond T. Chan/Dir., CEO, Pres., Randal J. Best/Sr. VP - Corporate Development, Anthony W. Marino/COO, Derek W. Aylesworth/CFO, Shannon M. Gangl/Corp. Sec., Stephen Brownridge/VP - Heavy Oil, Brett J. McDonald/VP - Land, Shaun R. Paterson/VP - Marketing, Mark F. Smith/VP - Conventional Oil, Gas

Directors: Raymond T. Chan/Dir., CEO, Pres., Edward Chwyl/Chmn., John A. Brussa/Dir., Dale O. Shwed/Dir., W.A. Blake Cassidy/Dir., R.E. T. Goepel/Dir., Naveen Dargan/Dir.

Financial Data: Fiscal Year End:12/31 **Latest Annual Data:** 12/31/2006

Year	Sales	Net Income
2006	$404,495,000	$104,921,000
2005	$370,035,000	$58,579,000

Curr. Assets:	$67,756,000	Curr. Liab.:	$188,429,000		
Plant, Equip.:	$690,940,000	Total Liab.:	$1,998,971,000	Indic. Yr. Divd.:	$2.010
Total Assets:	$794,934,000	Net Worth:	-$1,204,038,000	Debt/ Equity:	NA

Baywood International Inc

14950 N 83rd Pl., Ste. 1, Scottsdale, AZ, 85260; *PH:* 1-480-951-3956; *Fax:* 1-480-483-2168; *http://* www.bywd.com; *Email:* customerservice@bywd.com

General - Incorporation	NV	Stock - Price on:12/24/2007	$0.045
Employees	9	Stock Exchange	OTC
Auditor	Epstein Weber & Conover, PLC	Ticker Symbol	BYWD
Stk Agt	American Stock Transfer & Trust CO.	Outstanding Shares	42,670,000
Counsel	NA	E.P.S.	-$0.02
DUNS No.	80-011-7194	Shareholders	NA

Business: The group's principle activities include developing, marketing and distributing natural-based consumer products. The company's products consist of nutraceutical brand lines, purechoice(tm), solutions(tm) and complete la femme(tm). The company's products are distributed through independent and chain health food stores, pharmacies, grocery stores, and other direct-to-consumer channels both internationally and domestically. The company also sells directly to consumers and to health care practitioners through its wholly-owned subsidiary, epipharma, inc. The number of different products within each line varies depending on the types of products that the company decides to develop from time to time. The products are distributed through health food stores, pharmacies, grocery and drug chains. The group operates from United States.

Primary SIC and add'l.: 2834

CIK No: 0000806175

Subsidiaries: EpiPharma Inc

Officers: Neil Reithinger/Chmn., CEO, Pres., Acting Principal Financial Officer, Karl H. Rullich/74/Dir., VP, Sec., Kentish Soobramanien/Dir. - Marketing Operations

Directors: Neil Reithinger/Chmn., CEO, Pres., Acting Principal Financial Officer, Karl H. Rullich/74/Dir., VP, Sec., Lee O. Tawes/60/Dir.

Owners: Thomas Pinkowski/9.10%, Lee O. Tawes/28.20%, Insiders/53.40%, Karl H. Rullich/8.70%, Neil Reithinger/7.50%

Financial Data: Fiscal Year End:12/31 **Latest Annual Data:** 12/31/2006

Year	Sales	Net Income
2006	$1,078,000	-$625,000
2005	$1,225,000	-$435,000
2004	$2,914,000	-$657,000

Curr. Assets:	$209,000	Curr. Liab.:	$3,235,000		
Plant, Equip.:	$28,000	Total Liab.:	$3,235,000	Indic. Yr. Divd.:	NA
Total Assets:	$480,000	Net Worth:	-$2,754,000	Debt/ Equity:	NA

BB Holdings Ltd

Formerly: Carlisle Holdings Ltd
60 Market Sq, Belize City; ; *http://* www.carlisleholdings.com; *Email:* info@bbholdings.commail

General - Incorporation	Belize	Stock - Price on:12/24/2007	NA
Employees	11,000	Stock Exchange	OTC
Auditor	PricewaterhouseCoopers LLP	Ticker Symbol	BBHLF
Stk Agt	The Belize Bank Ltd	Outstanding Shares	NA
Counsel	NA	E.P.S.	$0.88
DUNS No.	NA	Shareholders	NA

Business: The group operates through its subsidiaries whose principle activity is to provide commercial banking operations, credit card services, mortgage banking, international banking and other related financial services. The group also provides management services, cleaning and specialty cleaning of commercial and institutional buildings, cleaning product supply, landscape management, and mechanical and maintenance services, and develop real estate properties; construct leisure and business premises. The group operates from United States.

Primary SIC and add'l.: 7623 6719 7349 0782 0781 7342 6029

CIK No: 0000882505

Subsidiaries: Aaxis Holdings S.a.r.l., Aaxis Investments S.a.r.l., Abacus Recruitment (Holdings) Limited, Abacus Recruitment Limited, Agency Cover Limited, Akita Security Limited, Aspillo Limited, B.B. Holdings Limited, Barker Personnel Services Limited, Belize Corporate Services Limited, Belize Incorporation Services Limited, Belize Nominees Limited, Belize Registration Services Limited, Belize Trust Company Limited, Bhi (bvi) Limited 179 Subsidiaries included in the Index

Officers: Philip Osborne/Company Sec., Philip Johnson/Financial Services, Pres., Peter Gaze/CFO, Exec. VP

Directors: Lord Ashcroft/Chmn., John Searle/Non Exec. Dir., Cheryl Jones/Dir.

Financial Data: Fiscal Year End:03/31 **Latest Annual Data:** 03/31/2005

Year	Sales	Net Income
2005	$1,380,000,000	$34,000,000
2004	$1,179,100,000	$45,200,000
2003	$1,233,700,000	$36,200,000

Curr. Assets:	$302,200,000	Curr. Liab.:	$534,700,000		
Plant, Equip.:	$23,700,000	Total Liab.:	$623,900,000	Indic. Yr. Divd.:	NA
Total Assets:	$1,199,300,000	Net Worth:	$575,400,000	Debt/ Equity:	NA

BB&T Corp

200 W 2nd St., Winston-Salem, NC, 27101; *PH:* 1-336-733-2505; *Fax:* 1-336-733-2509; *http://* www.bbandt.com

General - Incorporation	NC	Stock - Price on:12/24/2007	$41.78
Employees	29,300	Stock Exchange	NYSE
Auditor	PricewaterhouseCoopers LLP	Ticker Symbol	BBT
Stk Agt	BB&T Corporate Trust Services	Outstanding Shares	542,560,000
Counsel	Womble Carlyle Sandridge & Rice	E.P.S.	$2.82
DUNS No.	07-557-6306	Shareholders	NA

Business: The groups principle activity is to provide banking services. The groups services include trust, investment and mutual fund sales, international banking, electronic payment, credit and debit card services. The group operates from United States.

Primary SIC and add'l.: 6021 6712 6726 6411 6733

CIK No: 0000092230

Subsidiaries: Agency Technologies, Inc., Atlantic Wire Company, LLC, Attenta, Inc., BB&T Asset Management, Inc., BB&T Assurance Company, LTD, BB&T Bankcard Corporation, BB&T Capital Partners, LLC, BB&T Capital Partners/Windsor Mezzanine Fund, LLC, BB&T Capital Trust I, BB&T Charitable Foundation, BB&T Collateral Service Corporation, BB&T Collateral Service Corporation (TN), BB&T Collateral Service Corporation (WV), BB&T Credit Services, Inc., BB&T Insurance Services, Inc. 99 Subsidiaries included in the Index

Officers: John A. Allison/60/Chmn., CEO/$8,443,573.00, Ricky K. Brown/Sr. Exec. VP, Mgr. - Banking Network, Steven B. Wiggs/51/Sr. Exec. VP, Chief Marketing Officer, Barbara F. Duck/42/Sr. Exec. VP, Electronic Delivery Systems Mgr., Kelly S. King/60/COO/$4,920,523.00, Leon Wilson/53/Sr. Exec. VP, Operations Division Mgr., Jesse W. Howard/61/Pres. - BB, T, Virginia Greater Washington Group, State Pres., Luis G. Lobo/Washington DC Regional Pres., Robert E. Greene/58/Sr. Exec. VP, Mgr. - Administrative Services/$2,408,309.00, Wes Beckner/50/Group, State Pres., Louisville Metro Regional Pres., Lee F. Hess/62/Central Kentucky Regional Pres., Michael J. Willett/48/Western Regional Pres., Mike R. Brenan/56/Pres. - BB, T, South Carolina, Group, State Pres., Midlands Regional Pres., Frank J. Bullard/49/Coastal Regional Pres., Michael L. Oster/56/Group, State Pres., Baltimore Metro Regional Pres. *(47 Officers included in Index)*

Directors: John A. Allison/60/Chmn., CEO, Tom D. Efird/68/Dir., Anna R. Cablik/55/Dir., Nido R. Qubein/59/Dir., Barry Fitzpatrick/Dir., James H. Maynard/68/Dir., Jennifer S. Banner/48/Dir., Jane P. Helm/65/Dir., Ronald E. Deal/64/Dir., Nelle R. Chilton/68/Dir., Albert O. McCauley/67/Dir., Rhone E. Sasser/70/Dir., Holmes J. Morrison/67/Dir., Vincent L. Hackley/67/Dir., John P. Howe/64/Dir.

Owners: Insiders/1.09%, John P. Howe, Holmes J. Morrison, Jennifer S. Banner, Nido R. Qubein, Vincent L. Hackley, Ronald E. Deal, Anna R. Cablik, Nelle R. Chilton, Tom D. Efird, James H. Maynard, Kendall W. Chalk, Rhone E. Sasser, Jane P. Helm, Christopher L. Henson *(20 Owners included in Index)*

Financial Data: ***Fiscal Year End:***12/31 ***Latest Annual Data:*** 12/31/2006

Year	Sales	Net Income
2006	$9,487,000,000	$1,528,000,000
2005	$7,831,464,000	$1,653,769,000
2004	$6,665,966,000	$1,558,375,000

Curr. Assets:	$5,012,000,000	***Curr. Liab.:***	$93,702,000,000	***P/E Ratio:***	14.82
Plant, Equip.:	$1,410,000,000	***Total Liab.:***	$109,606,000,000	***Indic. Yr. Divd.:***	$1.840
Total Assets:	$121,351,000,000	***Net Worth:***	$11,745,000,000	***Debt/ Equity:***	1.7112

BBVA Banco Frances

Reconquista 199, Buenos Aires; ***PH:*** 54-7595576; ***http://*** www.bancofrances.com; ***Email:*** inversiones@bancofrances.com

General - Incorporation	AR	***Stock***- Price on:12/24/2007	$11.14
Employees	3,692	Stock Exchange	NYSE
Auditor	Deloitte & Co. S.R.L.	Ticker Symbol	BFR
Stk Agt	Bank of New York	Outstanding Shares	157,120,000
Counsel	NA	E.P.S	$0.55
DUNS No.	NA	Shareholders	NA

Business: The group's principal activity is the provision of general banking services to corporate and retail customers including deposits, checking and savings accounts, automatic teller machines, visa credit cards, mortgage financing, commercial loans, credit-logro consumer loans, electronic collections, foreign currency transactions, investment advisory services, and custody of securities and travelers' check, pension and asset management, insurance and other related services. The group operates 241 retail branches, 28 branches specialized in middle market, 2 personal banking and 39 credilogros offices

Primary SIC and add'l.: 6411 6021 6371

CIK No: 0000913059

Subsidiaries: Assurex S.A., Atuel Fideicomisos S.A. and subsidiary, BBVA Seguros S.A., Consolidar AFJP S.A., Consolidar ART S.A., Consolidar Ca. de Seguros de Retiro S.A., Consolidar Seguros de Vida S.A., Credilogros Compaa Financiera S.A., Francs Valores Sociedad de Bolsa S.A., PSA Compaa Financiera S.A., Rombo Compaa Financiera S.A.

Officers: Jorge Carlos Bledel/54/Exec. Chmn., Carlos Eduardo Montoto/51/Dir. - Human Resources, Tomas Deane/41/Dir. - Global Wholesale Banking, Gabriel Milstein/50/Dir. - Media, Marcelo Gustavo Canestri/55/Dir., Dir. - Finance, Oscar Hugo Fantacone/57/Dir. - Retail Banking, Jose Carlos Lopez Alvarez/49/Assist. Exec. Dir. - Accounting, Dir. - Risk Management, Juan Eugenio Rogero Gonzalez/52/Dir. - Risk Management

Directors: Jorge Carlos Bledel/54/Exec. Chmn., Jose Carlos Pla Royo/56/Vice Chmn., Jose Carlos Lopez Alvarez/49/Assist. Exec. Dir. - Accounting, Dir. - Risk Management, Javier Jose D'Ornellas/68/Dir., Marcelo Gustavo Canestri/55/Dir., Dir. - Finance, Oscar Miguel Castro/63/Dir.

Owners: Banco Bilbao Vizcaya Argentaria/45.65%, Inversora Otar S.A./9.40%, Bilbao Vizcaya America BV/20.92%, The Bank of New York/9.82%

Financial Data: ***Fiscal Year End:***12/31 ***Latest Annual Data:*** 12/31/2006

Year	Sales	Net Income
2006	$956,170,000	$319,070,000
2005	$941,715,000	$538,605,000
2004	$585,596,000	$471,554,000

Curr. Assets:	$2,250,306,000	***Curr. Liab.:***	$4,505,327,000		
Plant, Equip.:	$129,873,000	***Total Liab.:***	$5,584,782,000	***Indic. Yr. Divd.:***	$0.110
Total Assets:	$5,982,940,000	***Net Worth:***	$398,158,000	***Debt/ Equity:***	NA

BCB Bancorp Inc

104-110 Ave. C, Bayonne, NJ, 07002; ***PH:*** 1-201-823-0700; ***Fax:*** 1-201-339-0403; ***http://*** bayonnecommunitybank.com

General - Incorporation	NJ	***Stock***- Price on:12/24/2007	$16.43
Employees	69	Stock Exchange	NDQ
Auditor	Beard Miller Co. LLP	Ticker Symbol	BCBP
Stk Agt	NA	Outstanding Shares	4,790,000
Counsel	NA	E.P.S	$1.07
DUNS No.	NA	Shareholders	NA

Business: The group's principal activities are to provide retail FDIC insured deposit products. The group is a community-oriented financial institution. It operates through its subsidiary, bayonne community bank. It invests these deposits in investment securities and loans. The group also provides a wide range of loans, including one-to-four family mortgage loans, home equity loans, construction loans, commercial real estate loans, consumer loans and commercial business loans. The group operates a single branch in bayonne, New Jersey.

Primary SIC and add'l.: 6022

CIK No: 0001228454

Subsidiaries: BCB Equipment Leasing LLC, BCB Holding Company Investment Corp.

Officers: Donald Mindiak/49/Dir., CEO, Pres./$220,631.00, Olivia M. Klim/62/Exec. VP/$147,599.00, James E. Collins/59/Dir., Sr. Lending Officer/$186,588.00, Amer Saleem/53/VP/$155,354.00, Thomas M. Coughlin/48/Dir., CFO/$171,103.00

Directors: Donald Mindiak/49/Dir., CEO, Pres., Mark D. Hogan/42/Chmn., Joseph Tagliareni/53/Dir., Judith Q. Bielan/43/Dir., Alexander Pasiechnik/46/Dir., Joseph Lyga/48/Dir., James E. Collins/59/Dir., Sr. Lending Officer, Robert Ballance/49/Dir., August Pellegrini/48/Dir., Joseph Brogan/69/Dir., Thomas M. Coughlin/48/Dir., CFO

Owners: Joseph Tagliareni, Insiders/27.40%, Olivia Klim, James E. Collins/3.00%, Joseph Lyga/1.70%, Joseph Brogan/4.00%, Donald Mindiak/2.70%, Judith Q. Bielan/2.30%, Thomas M. Coughlin/2.90%, Amer Saleem, Alexander Pasiechnik/1.80%, Mark D. Hogan/3.70%, Robert Ballance/2.10%, August Pellegrini/1.90%

Financial Data: ***Fiscal Year End:***12/31 ***Latest Annual Data:*** 12/31/2006

Year	Sales	Net Income
2006	$32,521,000	$5,567,000
2005	$26,043,000	$4,729,000
2004	$21,379,000	$3,619,000

Curr. Assets:	$29,534,000	***Curr. Liab.:***	$382,747,000		
Plant, Equip.:	$5,885,000	***Total Liab.:***	$458,872,000	***Indic. Yr. Divd.:***	$0.320
Total Assets:	$510,835,000	***Net Worth:***	$51,963,000	***Debt/ Equity:***	1.4129

BCE Inc

1000, rue de La Gauchetire Ouest, Ste. 3700, Montreal, PQ, H3B 4Y7; ***PH:*** 1-514-870-8777; ***Fax:*** 1-514-870-4385; ***http://*** www.bce.ca; ***Email:*** customercare@digitalvoice.bell.ca

General - Incorporation	Canada	***Stock***- Price on:12/24/2007	$36.74
Employees	54,000	Stock Exchange	NYSE
Auditor	Deloitte & Touche LLP	Ticker Symbol	BCE
Stk Agt	Deloitte & Touche LLP	Outstanding Shares	800,900,000
Counsel	NA	E.P.S	$2.84
DUNS No.	24-460-7925	Shareholders	NA

Business: The group's principle activity is to provide telecommunication services. The services include voice, data, wireline and directory communications and satellite entertainment to Canadian customers and integrated information, communications and entertainment services. It also provides voice, data and Internet services including connectivity services to Internet service providers, Internet content providers, application service providers, carriers and global enterprises; and e-commerce infrastructures focusing in transaction-intensive e-health and financial services. In the year 2001, the company discontinued excel communications group and bci latin American clecs and Asia mobile segments. The group operates from United States.

Primary SIC and add'l.: 4810 6099 3663 3661

CIK No: 0000718940

Subsidiaries: Aliant Inc, Bell Canada companies, Bell ExpressVu, Bell Globemedia, Bell Mobility

Officers: Michael J. Sabia/Dir., CEO, Pres., Lawson A.W. Hunter/Exec. VP, Chief Corp. Officer, Bernard Le Duc/Sr. VP - Investor Relation, Lyne Roy/Individual Investor, Martine Turcotte/Chief Legal Officer, Patricia A. Olah/Corp. Sec. - Lead Governance Counsel, Leo W. Houle/Chief Talent Officer, Scott L. Thomson/Exec. VP - Corporate Development, Planning, Siim A. Vanaselja/CFO, Thane Fotopoulos/Dir. - Investor Relations, Victoria Neal/Dir. - Investor Relations, Wayne L. Tunney/Sr. VP - Taxation, William J. Fox/Exec. VP - Communications, Corporate Development

Directors: Michael J. Sabia/Dir., CEO, Pres., Richard J. Currie/Chmn., Andre Berard/Corp. Dir., Ronald A. Brenneman/Dir., Anthony S. Fell/Dir., Donna Soble Kaufman/Dir., Brian M. Levitt/Dir., Edward C. Lumley/Dir., Judith Maxwell/Dir., John H. McArthur/Dir., Thomas C. O'Neill/Dir., James A. Pattison/Dir., Robert C. Pozen/Dir., Paul M. Tellier/Corp. Dir., Victor L. Young/Corp. Dir.

Financial Data: ***Fiscal Year End:***12/31 ***Latest Annual Data:*** 12/31/2006

Year	Sales	Net Income
2006	$15,199,525,000	$3,073,714,000
2005	$16,392,090,000	$1,668,810,000
2004	$15,935,948,000	$1,315,195,000

Curr. Assets:	$3,161,240,000	***Curr. Liab.:***	$4,034,786,000	***P/E Ratio:***	15.44
Plant, Equip.:	$18,945,990,000	***Total Liab.:***	$20,242,579,000	***Indic. Yr. Divd.:***	$1.440
Total Assets:	$30,654,764,000	***Net Worth:***	$10,412,185,000	***Debt/ Equity:***	NA

BCSB Baltimore County Savings Bank

4111 E Joppa Rd., Ste. 300, Baltimore, MD, 21236; ***PH:*** 1-410-256-5000; ***Fax:*** 1-410-256-0261; ***http://*** www.baltcosavings.com; ***Email:*** info@bcsb.net

General - Incorporation	US	***Stock***- Price on:12/24/2007	$10.86
Employees	150	Stock Exchange	NDQ
Auditor	Stegman & Co	Ticker Symbol	BCSB
Stk Agt	American Stock Transfer & Trust Co.	Outstanding Shares	5,920,000
Counsel	Moore, Carney, Ryan & Lattanzi	E.P.S	-$0.5
DUNS No.	02-614-7095	Shareholders	NA

Business: The group's principal activity is that of a holding company for the baltimore county savings bank, fsb. The bank is a federally chartered stock savings bank which operates through sixteen banking offices in the baltimore and harford counties of Maryland. The group accepts deposits from the general public and originates commercial and consumer loans secured by first mortgages on owner-occupied, single-family residences in the baltimore metropolitan area. Other investment areas include real estate loans, commercial and consumer loans and automobile loans.

Primary SIC and add'l.: 6712 6035

CIK No: 0001052101

Subsidiaries: Baltimore County Savings Bank, F.S.B., BCSB Bankcorp Capital Trust I, BCSB Bankcorp Capital Trust II, BCSB Bankcorp, Inc., Ebenezer Road, Inc.

Officers: Joseph J. Bouffard/CEO, Pres., David M. Meadows/Exec. VP, Sec.

Owners: Louis P. Rohe, Henry V. Kahl, Michael J. Klein, John J. Panzer, David M. Meadows, Adrian H. Cox, BCSB Bankcorp, Inc./7.10%, Baltimore County Savings Bank, M.H.C./63.50%, William J. Kappauf, Bonnie M. Klein, William M. Loughran, Insiders/4.50%

Financial Data: ***Fiscal Year End:***09/30 ***Latest Annual Data:*** 09/30/2007

Year	Sales	Net Income
2007	$40,852,000	-$2,921,000
2006	$41,520,000	-$7,393,000
2005	$38,639,000	$601,000

Curr. Assets:	$24,996,000	***Curr. Liab.:***	$644,845,000		
Plant, Equip.:	$11,319,000	***Total Liab.:***	$752,436,000	***Indic. Yr. Divd.:***	$0.500
Total Assets:	$785,857,000	***Net Worth:***	$33,421,000	***Debt/ Equity:***	1.5448

BE Aerospace Inc

1400 Corporate Ctr. Way, Wellington, FL, 33414; ***PH:*** 1-561-791-5000; ***Fax:*** 1-561-791-7900; ***http://*** www.beaerospace.com

General - Incorporation	DE	***Stock***- Price on:12/24/2007	$39.84
Employees	5,058	Stock Exchange	NDQ
Auditor	Deloitte & Touche LLP	Ticker Symbol	BEAV
Stk Agt	EquiServe Trust Co N.A	Outstanding Shares	92,190,000
Counsel	Edmund J. Moriarty	E.P.S	$1.39
DUNS No.	04-412-7439	Shareholders	NA

Business: The group's principle activities are to manufacture cabin interior products for commercial aircrafts and business jets and distribute aerospace fasteners. The group operates in three reportable segments namely, commercial aircraft products, business jet products and fastener distribution. The group's quarterly revenue for September 2007 was 428.20 millions of USD.

Primary SIC and add'l.: 3728 2531 8711

CIK No: 0000861361

Subsidiaries: Acurex, LLC, Advanced Thermal Sciences Corporation, Advanced Thermal Sciences Korea, Advanced Thermal Sciences Shanghai Corporation, Advanced Thermal Sciences Taiwan Corporation, Aerospace Lighting Corporation, Aerospace, Inc., ATS Japan Corporation, B/E Aerospace (Canada) Company, B/E Aerospace (UK) Limited, B/E Aerospace Development Corporation, B/E Aerospace Machined Products, Inc., B/E Aerospace Services B.V., B/E Aerospace Services, LLC, BE Aerospace (France) SARL 45 Subsidiaries included in the Index

Officers: Amin J. Khoury/Chmn., CEO, Founder/$5,566,205.00, Wayne R. Exton/Group VP, GM - Business Jet Segment/$459,339.00, Werner Lieberherr/47/VP, GM - Commercial Aircraft Products Group/$418,869.00, Rj Landry/VP - Human Resources, Edmund J. Moriarty/Corporate VP - Law, General Counsel, Sec., Thomas P. McCaffrey/Sr. VP - Administration, CFO/$1,537,006.00, Jeffrey P. Holtzman/VP - Finance, Treasurer, Mark D. Krosney/61/VP, GM - Business Jet Segment, Robert Marchetti/Group VP, GM - Fastener Distribution Group/$646,790.00, Michael B. Baughan/COO, Pres./$820,316.00, Stephen R. Swisher/VP, Controller, Joseph A. Piegari/Corporate VP - Human Resources

Directors: Amin J. Khoury/Chmn., CEO, Founder, Jim C. Cowart/Dir., Robert J. Khoury/Dir., Richard G. Hamermesh/Dir., David C. Hurley/67/Dir., Brian H. Rowe/Dir., Jonathan M. Schofield/Dir., Wesley W. Marple/Dir., Arthur E. Wegner/Dir., Charles L. Chadwell/67/Dir.

Owners: Jim C. Cowart, Insiders/1.42%, David C. Hurley, Amin J. Khoury, FMR Corp./6.66%, Robert A. Marchetti, Robert J. Khoury, Thomas P. McCaffrey, Arthur E. Wegner, Werner Lieberherr, Wayne Exton, Jonathan M. Schofield, Charles L. Chadwell, Richard G. Hamermesh, American Century Investment Management/8.29% (16 Owners included in Index)

Financial Data: Fiscal Year End:12/31   **Latest Annual Data:** 12/31/2006

Year	Sales	Net Income
2006	$1,128,200,000	$85,600,000
2005	$844,100,000	$84,600,000
2004	$733,500,000	-$22,000,000

Curr. Assets:	$725,700,000	**Curr. Liab.:**	$269,700,000		
Plant, Equip.:	$107,900,000	**Total Liab.:**	$791,700,000	**Indic. Yr. Divd.:**	NA
Total Assets:	$1,497,700,000	**Net Worth:**	$706,000,000	**Debt/ Equity:**	0.4500

BE Semiconductor Industries N.V.

224 E Chilton Dr., Ste. 9, Chandler, AZ, 85225; **PH:** 1-480-497-8190; **Fax:** 1-480-497-9104; http:// www.besi.nl; **Email:** info@besi.nl

General - Incorporation .... Netherlands	Stock - Price on:12/24/2007 ....NA
Employees...1,087	Stock Exchange...OTC
Auditor .... KPMG LLP	Ticker Symbol...BESIY
Stk Agt............................... Bank of New York	Outstanding Shares ....NA
Counsel....................................... Hale & Dorr LLP	E.P.S..NA
DUNS No. 40-952-3602	Shareholders...NA

Business: The group's principal activity is manufacturing semiconductor packaging, plating, die attach and die sort equipment for the semiconductor industry. These equipment are used to produce semiconductor packages, which provide the electronic interface and physical connection between the chip and other electronic components. These equipment also protect the chip from the external environment. The packaging equipment consists of automated molding systems that encapsulate semiconductor devices in epoxy resin. The plant and singulation equipment consists of fully automated tin-lead planting systems. The die attach equipment consists of manual and automated high precision systems which place the contact points of the chip in direct contact with the packaged substrate. The group's customers include Amkor, Lucent Technologies, Motorola and Philips.

Primary SIC and add'l.: 5084 3559

CIK No: 0001003196

Subsidiaries: ASM Fico (F.E.) SDN. BHD., BE Semiconductor Industries USA, Inc., Besi Austria Holding GmbH, Besi Japan Co. Ltd., Besi Korea Ltd., Besi Taiwan Ltd., Besi USA Inc., Datacon Asia Pacific Pte. Ltd., Datacon Beteiligungs GmbH, Datacon Eurotec GmbH, Datacon Hungary Termelo Kft., Datacon Korea Ltd., Datacon North America Inc., Datacon Philippines, Inc., Datacon Technology GmbH 28 Subsidiaries included in the Index

Officers: Richard W. Blickman/54/Chmn., CEO, Pres., Helmut Rutterschmidt/51/CEO Datacon Technology, Executive Dir., Gerard A. Veld/52/MD - Fico Singulation, Claudia Vissers/COO, Executive Dir., Investor Relations Administrator, Hugo F. Menschaar/62/Dir. - Corporate Technology, Cor Te Hennepe/50/Dir. - Finance, Frans J.M. Jonckheere/49/MD - Meco

Directors: Richard W. Blickman/54/Chmn., CEO, Pres., Helmut Rutterschmidt/51/CEO Datacon Technology, Executive Dir., Willem D. Maris/69/Chmn. - Supervisory Board, Evert B. Polak/64/Member - Supervisory Board, Dick Sinninghe Damste/Member - Supervisory Board, Tom De Waard/62/Member - Supervisory Board, Claudia Vissers/COO, Executive Dir., Investor Relations Administrator

Financial Data: Fiscal Year End:12/31   **Latest Annual Data:** 12/31/2005

Year	Sales	Net Income
2005	$194,552,000	-$6,136,000
2004	$171,040,000	-$7,347,000
2003	$107,362,000	-$16,948,000

Curr. Assets:	$202,440,000	**Curr. Liab.:**	$63,637,000		
Plant, Equip.:	$47,847,000	**Total Liab.:**	$141,684,000	**Indic. Yr. Divd.:**	NA
Total Assets:	$356,547,000	**Net Worth:**	$214,863,000	**Debt/ Equity:**	NA

BEA Systems Inc

2315 N 1st St., San Jose, CA, 95131; **PH:** 1-408-570-8000; **Fax:** 1-408-570-8901; http:// www.bea.com

General - Incorporation .... DE	Stock - Price on:12/24/2007 ....$13.54
Employees...3,878	Stock Exchange...NDQ
Auditor .... Ernst & Young LLP	Ticker Symbol...BEAS
Stk Agt....................................... BankBoston, N.A	Outstanding Shares 393,420,000
Counsel.......................... Morrison & Foerster LLP	E.P.S..$0.08
DUNS No. 83-755-6844	Shareholders...NA

Business: The group's principal activity is to provide application infrastructure software and related services. It enables companies build distributed systems that extend investments in existing computer systems and provide the foundation for running an integrated business. The customers use products as a

deployment platform for Internet-based applications, including custom-built and packed applications and as a means for robust enterprise application integration among mainframe, client/server and Internet-based applications. The group's weblogic enterprise platform includes weblogic server tm, weblogic integration tm, weblogic portal tm, weblogic workshop(TM) and weblogic jrockit tm. The products have been adopted in a industries like telecommunications, commerical and invetment banking, securities trading, government, manufacturing, retail, airlines, pharmaceuticals and insurance. The group has operations in Europe, Middle East, Africa and Asia/pacific countries.

Primary SIC and add'l.: 7371 7372

CIK No: 0001031798

Subsidiaries: ADSKCanadaInc., Alias Systems GmbH, Alias Systems Inc., Alias Systems KK, Alias Systems Limited, Alias Systems SAS, Alias Systems Singapore Pte. Ltd., Alias Systems Srl., AliasSystemsKoreaLimitedCompany, Autodesk (EMEA) S.a.r.l., Autodesk (Europe) S.A., Autodesk AB, Autodesk Asia Pte Ltd., Autodesk Australia Pty Ltd., Autodesk B.V. 48 Subsidiaries included in the Index

Officers: Alfred S. Chuang/Founder, Chmn., CEO, Wai Wong/Exec. VP - Products, Rob Levy/CTO, Exec. VP, Lai Hoe/Industry Analysts Asean, Maya Culas/Industry Analysts India, Silvana Kozlovic/Industry Analysts Australia, New Zealand, William M. Klein/Exec. VP - Business Planning, Development, Mark Dentinger/CFO, Exec. VP, Mark Carges/Exec. VP - Business Interaction Division, James Rivas/Business, Product, Technology Public Relations, Marissa Lee/Business Interaction Division, Asako Hatta/Industry Analyst, Sarah Atkinson/Industry Analysts Europe, Middle East, Africa, David L. Gai/Exec. VP - World Wide Services, Richard Geraffo/Exec. VP - Worldwide Sales (23 Officers included in Index)

Directors: Alfred S. Chuang/Founder, Chmn., CEO, Dean Morton/Dir., Stewart Gross/Dir., Dale Crandall/Dir., Bruce A. Pasternack/Dir., Richard T. Schlosberg/Dir., William H. Janeway/Dir., Robin A. Abrams/Dir., Kiran M. Patel/Dir., George Reyes/Dir.

Owners: Stewart K. P Gross, Richard T. Schlosberg, Mark P. Dentinger, Dean O. Morton, William H. Janeway, Wai M. Wong, Private Capital Management Inc., Bruce A. Pasternack, Robin A. Abrams, George Reyes, Thomas M. Ashburn, Alfred S. Chuang, Mark T. Carges, Insiders, AMVESCAP PLC (17 Owners included in Index)

Financial Data: Fiscal Year End:01/31   **Latest Annual Data:** 01/31/2007

Year	Sales	Net Income
2007	$1,402,349,000	$4,500,000
2006	$1,199,845,000	$142,743,000
2005	$1,080,094,000	$131,056,000

Curr. Assets:	$1,802,729,000	**Curr. Liab.:**	$1,136,623,000	**P/E Ratio:**	37.61
Plant, Equip.:	$343,389,000	**Total Liab.:**	$1,365,294,000	**Indic. Yr. Divd.:**	NA
Total Assets:	$2,475,531,000	**Net Worth:**	$1,110,237,000	**Debt/ Equity:**	0.1882

Beach Business Bank CA

1230 Rosecrans Ave., Manhattan Beach, CA, 90266; **PH:** 1-310-536-9270; http:// www.beachbusinessbank.com; **Email:** info@beachbusinessbank.com

General - Incorporation	Stock - Price on:12/24/2007 ....$12.5
Employees...NA	Stock Exchange...OTC
Auditor .... NA	Ticker Symbol...BBBC
Stk Agt....................... Computershare Trust CO.	Outstanding Shares ....NA
Counsel... NA	E.P.S..NA
DUNS No. ....NA	Shareholders...NA

Business: The groups principal activity is to provide banking business. The group financial products include savings and fixed deposits, on line, personal, commercial lending and business banking. The group operates from the United States.

Primary SIC and add'l.: 6022

CIK No:

Officers: Robert M. Franko/Dir., CEO, Pres., Melissa Lanfre/Sr. VP, CFO, Phillip J. Bond/Exec. VP, Chief Credit Officer, Melissa Rickabaugh/Sr. VP, Sr. Operations Officer, Girish Bajaj/Exec. VP, Chief Business Development Officer

Directors: Robert M. Franko/Dir., CEO, Pres., James H. Gray/Co - Chmn., John F. Philips/Co - Chmn., Michael L. Quick/Dir., Frank J. Greskovich/Member - Advisory Board, Daniel L. Orr/Dir., Robb Evans/Dir., John W. Hancock/Dir., Rick A. Jaye/Member - Advisory Board, Fred D. Jensen/Dir.

Beach First National Bancshares Inc

3751 Robert M.Grissom Pkwy., Ste. 100, Myrtle Beach, SC, 29577; **PH:** 1-843-626-2265; **Fax:** 1-843-916-7818; http:// www.beachfirst.com; **Email:** investor@beachfirst.com

General - Incorporation ....SC	Stock - Price on:12/24/2007 ....$22.091
Employees...110	Stock Exchange...NDQ
Auditor ....Elliott Davis LLC	Ticker Symbol...BFNB
Stk Agt .... First-citizens Bank & Trust Co	Outstanding Shares 4,820,000
Counsel...... Nelson Mullins Riley & Scarborough	E.P.S..$1.41
DUNS No. 92-820-4742	Shareholders...NA

Business: The group's principal activity is to provide banking services. It operates through its subsidiary, beach first national bank. The group provides deposit products including checking accounts, now accounts, savings accounts and other time deposits. It emphasizes a range of lending services, including real estate, commercial and consumer loans. In addition, the group provides cash management services, safe deposit boxes, travelers' checks, direct deposit of payroll, social security checks and automatic draft for various accounts. The group also provides mastercard and visa credit cards. It has one automated teller machine located in its main office. The services are provided to businesses, professional concerns and individuals in myrtle beach. The operations are conducted in domestic market.

Primary SIC and add'l.: 6712 6021

CIK No: 0000949228

Subsidiaries: Beach First National Bank, BFNB Trust

Officers: Walter E. Standish/Dir., CEO, Pres./$550,455.00, Julien E. Springs/Exec. VP - Business Development Officer/$269,233.00, Katharine M. Huntley/Exec. VP, Chief Credit Officer, Gary S. Austin/CFO, Exec. VP, Melissa Downs-High/Contact - Investor Relations

Directors: Walter E. Standish/Dir., CEO, Pres., Raymond E. Cleary/Chmn., Rick H. Seagroves/Dir., Joe N. Jarrett/Dir., Richard E. Lester/Dir., Michael D. Harrington/Dir., Leigh Ammons Meese/Dir., Michael Bert Anderson/Dir., Samuel Robert Spann/Dir., Thomas E. Fulmer/Dir., Don J. Smith/Dir., Larkin B. Spivey/Dir., James C. Yahnis/Dir., Bartlett Buie/Dir.

Owners: Samuel Robert Spann/2.18%, Raymond E. Cleary/3.15%, Larkin B. Spivey/1.40%, River Oaks Capital, LLC/6.07%, Walter E. Standish/2.33%, Leigh Ammons Meese/1.02%, Thomas E. Fulmer, Bartlett Buie/1.12%, Julien E. Springs/1.00%, Richard E. Lester/1.59%, Michael Bert Anderson/1.20%, Rick H. Seagroves/2.54%, Richard N. Burch, Michael D. Harrington/4.17%, Don J. Smith/1.49% (18 Owners included in Index)

Financial Data: *Fiscal Year End:*12/31 *Latest Annual Data:* 12/31/2006

Year	Sales	Net Income
2006	$40,477,000	$6,196,000
2005	$22,042,000	$3,360,000
2004	$12,634,000	$1,436,000

Curr. Assets:	$19,210,000	*Curr. Liab.:*	$453,857,000	*P/E Ratio:*	15.78
Plant, Equip.:	$14,344,000	*Total Liab.:*	$474,742,000	*Indic. Yr. Divd.:*	NA
Total Assets:	$520,201,000	*Net Worth:*	$45,460,000	*Debt/ Equity:*	0.3689

Beacon Power Corp

234 Ballardvale St., Wilmington, MA, 01887; *PH:* 1-978-694-9121; *Fax:* 1-978-694-9127;
http:// www.beaconpower.com

General - Incorporation	DE	**Stock**- Price on:12/24/2007	$1.11
Employees	39	Stock Exchange	NDQ
Auditor	Miller Wachman LLP	Ticker Symbol	BCON
Stk Agt	Registar & transfer co.	Outstanding Shares	71,350,000
Counsel	Edwards Angell Palmer & Dodge LLP	E.P.S.	-$0.18
DUNS No.	NA	Shareholders	NA

Business: The group's principal activities are the design and development of flywheel energy storage systems that provide reliable and uninterruptible electric power. The flywheel systems are based on energy storage technologies that can perform the same function as batteries and deliver high amounts of power over a short period of time. They also protect sensitive systems from sags, surges and other temporary interruptions in utility-supplied power. The group currently sells two high-energy flywheel-based products and will introduce a range of uninterruptible power supply (ups) products starting with the smart power(tm) 250 kwh flywheel ups. The ups systems have been approved by the underwriters laboratory and conform to the telcordia safety standards of the telecommunication industry. The products will be marketed directly to customers in commercial facilities, telecommunication, cable and computer networks, Internet service providers and industrial manufacturing plants.

Primary SIC and add'l.: 3621

CIK No: 0001103345

Subsidiaries: Beacon Acquisition Co., Beacon Power Securities Corporation

Officers: William F. Capp/Dir., CEO, Pres./$911,593.00, Chet Lyons/Contact - Sales, Commercial, Industrial, Institutional Markets/$256,010.00, James M. Spiezio/CFO, VP - Finance/$527,517.00, Matthew L. Lazarewicz/CTO/$481,885.00, Matt Polimeno/Contact - Sales, Government, Military, Aerospace, Research Markets, Gene Hunt/Contact- Investor Relations, Corporate Communications, Richard L. Hockney/Chief Engineer/$200,318.00

Directors: William F. Capp/Dir., CEO, Pres., Stephen P. Adik/Dir., Daniel E. Kletter/Dir., Jack Smith/Dir., Virgil G. Rose/Dir., Edward A. Weihman/Dir.

Owners: William E. Stanton, William F. Capp/2.90%, James M. Spiezio/1.40%, Chester B. Lyons, Virgil G. Rose, Matthew L. Lazarewicz/1.50%, Jack P. Smith, Stephen P. Adik, Daniel E. Kletter, Perseus Capital, L.L.C./5.60%, Insiders/6.70%, Lisa W. Zappala, Richard L. Hockney

Financial Data: *Fiscal Year End:*12/31 *Latest Annual Data:* 12/31/2006

Year	Sales	Net Income
2006	$969,000	-$12,163,000
2005	$1,487,000	-$9,312,000
2004	$325,000	-$5,330,000

Curr. Assets:	$6,668,000	*Curr. Liab.:*	$3,358,000		
Plant, Equip.:	$415,000	*Total Liab.:*	$3,358,000	*Indic. Yr. Divd.:*	NA
Total Assets:	$7,258,000	*Net Worth:*	$3,900,000	*Debt/ Equity:*	NA

Beacon Roofing Supply Inc

1 Lakeland Pk. Dr., Peabody, MA, 01960; *PH:* 1-978-535-7668; *Fax:* 1-978-535-7358;
http:// www.beaconroofingsupply.net; *Email:* dgrace@beaconsales.com

General - Incorporation	DE	**Stock**- Price on:12/24/2007	$17.61
Employees	2,641	Stock Exchange	NDQ
Auditor	Ernst & Young LLP	Ticker Symbol	BECN
Stk Agt	Computershare Trust Company, N.A.	Outstanding Shares	NA
Counsel	NA	E.P.S.	$0.56
DUNS No.	NA	Shareholders	NA

Business: The groups principle activity is to distribute residential, non-residential roofing materials and other complementary building materials. The group operates from United States and Canada.

Primary SIC and add'l.: NA

CIK No: 0001124941

Subsidiaries: Beacon Canada, Inc., Beacon Roofing Supply Canada Company, Beacon Sales Acquisition, Inc., Best Distributing Co., JGA Beacon, Inc., Quality Roofing Supply, Inc., SDI Holding, Inc., Shelter Distribution, Inc., The Roof Center, Inc., West End Lumber Company, Inc.

Officers: Robert Buck/Chmn., CEO, Pres., James I. MacKimm/Sr. VP, John C. Smith/Regional VP - Shelter Southwest Region, John Blackburn/VP - Vendor Relations, Jean-Guy Plante/Regional VP - Beacon Canada, David R. Grace/Sr. VP, CFO, Timothy C. Hanks/Regional VP - Shelter Central Plains Region, Robert Keen/Regional VP - Beacon Pacific, Eric C. Swank/Sr. VP - Operations, Ross D. Cooper/Sr. VP, General Counsel, Corp. Sec., Roger P. Deschenes/VP - Finance, Christopher Nelson/CIO, VP, Munroe Best/Regional VP - Best Distributing Co, David Wrabel/VP - Credit, Rick C. Welker/VP, Corporate Controller *(22 Officers included in Index)*

Directors: Robert Buck/Chmn., CEO, Pres., Stuart A. Randle/Dir., Wilson B. Sexton/Dir., Andrew R. Logie/Dir., Arthur H. Bellows/Dir., James J. Gaffney/Dir., Peter Gotsch/Dir.

Owners: Stuart A. Randle, Wellington Management Company, LLP, Eric C. Swank, William Blair& Company, LLC, Scout Capital Partners, L.P., Arthur H. Bellows, Gilder, Gagnon, Howe& Co. LLC, Wilson B. Sexton, David R. Grace, Insiders, Andrew R. Logie, Peter M. Gotsch, James J. Gaffney, Robert R. Buck

Financial Data: *Fiscal Year End:*09/24 *Latest Annual Data:* 06/30/2007

Year	Sales	Net Income
2007	$484,870,000	$11,505,000
2006	$1,500,637,000	$49,311,000
2005	$850,928,000	$32,917,000

Curr. Assets:	$425,645,000	*Curr. Liab.:*	$220,254,000		
Plant, Equip.:	$59,291,000	*Total Liab.:*	$548,721,000	*Indic. Yr. Divd.:*	NA
Total Assets:	$839,890,000	*Net Worth:*	$291,169,000	*Debt/ Equity:*	1.2047

Beaconsfield II Inc

497 Delaware Ave., Buffalo, NY, 14202; *PH:* 1-716-882-2157

General - Incorporation	DE	**Stock**- Price on:12/24/2007	NA
Employees	NA	Stock Exchange	NA
Auditor	Raich Ende Malter & Co. LLP	Ticker Symbol	NA
Stk Agt	NA	Outstanding Shares	NA
Counsel	NA	E.P.S.	NA
DUNS No.	NA	Shareholders	NA

Business: The group's principle activity is to intend to merge with or acquired buiness entity. The group operates from United States.

Primary SIC and add'l.: 6770

CIK No: 0001323924

Beaconsfield III Inc

497 Delaware Ave., Buffalo, NY, 14202; *PH:* 1-716-882-2157

General - Incorporation	DE	**Stock**- Price on:12/24/2007	NA
Employees	NA	Stock Exchange	NA
Auditor	Raich Ende Malter & Co. LLP	Ticker Symbol	NA
Stk Agt	NA	Outstanding Shares	NA
Counsel	NA	E.P.S.	NA
DUNS No.	NA	Shareholders	NA

Business: The group's principle activity is to provide organizational efforts and obtaining initial financing. The group operates from United States.

Primary SIC and add'l.: 6770

CIK No: 0001323925

Bear Lake Recreation Inc

4685 S Highland Dr., Ste. No. 202, Salt Lake City, UT, 84117; *PH:* 1-801-278-9424

General - Incorporation	NV	**Stock**- Price on:12/24/2007	NA
Employees	NA	Stock Exchange	OTC
Auditor	Mantyla McReynolds, LLC	Ticker Symbol	BLKE
Stk Agt	Colonial Stock Transfer Co Inc	Outstanding Shares	NA
Counsel	NA	E.P.S.	NA
DUNS No.	NA	Shareholders	NA

Business: The group principle activities include developing, extracting, refining and marketing of nickel, cobalt and brown coal. In the year 2005, the group acquired Kazakh Metals, Inc and Kyzyl Kain Mamyt (KKM). The group operates from Kazakhstan.

Primary SIC and add'l.: 7999

CIK No: 0001074871

Officers: Wayne Bassham/50/Dir., Pres., Derrick Albiston/29/Dir., VP, Todd Albiston/50/Dir., Sec., Treasurer

Directors: Wayne Bassham/50/Dir., Pres., Derrick Albiston/29/Dir., VP, Todd Albiston/50/Dir., Sec., Treasurer

Owners: Derrick Albiston, Todd Albiston, Wayne Bassham, Thomas J. Howells

Financial Data: *Fiscal Year End:*06/30 *Latest Annual Data:* 6/30/2006

Year	Sales	Net Income
2006	NA	-$9,000

Curr. Assets:	NA	*Curr. Liab.:*	$31,000		
Plant, Equip.:	NA	*Total Liab.:*	$31,000	*Indic. Yr. Divd.:*	NA
Total Assets:	NA	*Net Worth:*	-$31,000	*Debt/ Equity:*	NA

Bear Stearns Cos Inc

383 Madison Ave., New York, NY, 10179; *PH:* 1-212-272-2000; *Fax:* 1-212-272-4785;
http:// www.bearstearns.com

General - Incorporation	DE	**Stock**- Price on:12/24/2007	$142.81
Employees	13,566	Stock Exchange	NYSE
Auditor	Deloitte & Touche LLP	Ticker Symbol	BSC
Stk Agt	Mellon Investor Services LLC	Outstanding Shares	144,750,000
Counsel	Cadwalader, Wickersham & Taft LLP	E.P.S.	$13.35
DUNS No.	14-464-7336	Shareholders	NA

Business: The group operates through its subsidiary whose principle activity is to provide investment banking, securities trading and brokerage services. Customers served by the group include corporations, governments, and institutional and individual investors. The group operates from United States.

Primary SIC and add'l.: 6719 6221

CIK No: 0000777001

Subsidiaries: Bear Hunter Holdings LLC, Bear Stearns Bank plc, Bear Stearns Capital Markets Inc., Bear Stearns Commercial Mortgage, Inc., Bear Stearns Credit Products Inc., Bear Stearns Financial Products Inc., Bear Stearns Forex Inc., Bear Stearns Global Lending Limited, Bear, Stearns & Co. Inc., Bear, Stearns International Limited, Bear, Stearns Securities Corp., Custodial Trust Company, EMC Mortgage Corporation

Officers: James E. Cayne/Chmn., CEO, Warren J. Spector/Co - COO, Pres., Alan D. Schwartz/Dir., Pres., Samuel L. Molinaro/CFO, Exec. VP - Finance, Jeffrey M. Farber/43/Sr. VP - Finance, Michael S. Solender/43/General Counsel, Sec., Kenneth L. Edlow/Dir., Sec., Michael Minikes/64/Treasurer

Directors: James E. Cayne/Chmn., CEO, Alan C. Greenberg/Dir., Paul A. Novelly/Dir., Wesley S. Williams/Dir., Carl D. Glickman/Dir., Kenneth L. Edlow/Dir., Sec., Michael Goldstein/Dir., Henry S. Bienen/Dir., Alan D. Schwartz/Dir., Pres., Frederic V. Salerno/Dir., Donald J. Harrington/Dir., Frank T. Nickell/Dir., Vincent Tese/Dir.

Owners: Frederic V. Salerno, Vincent Tese, Frank T. Nickell, Private Capital Management, L.P./5.90%, Alan C. Greenberg, Warren J. Spector, Samuel L. Molinaro, Wesley S. Williams, James E. Cayne/5.32%, Carl D. Glickman, Insiders/7.68%, Donald J. Harrington, Putnam LLC, d/b/a Putnam Investments and related entities/5.50%, Paul A. Novelly, Alan D. Schwartz *(16 Owners included in Index)*

Financial Data: *Fiscal Year End:*11/30 *Latest Annual Data:* 11/30/2006

Year	Sales	Net Income
2006	$16,551,419,000	$2,053,871,000
2005	$11,552,447,000	$1,462,177,000
2004	$8,421,902,000	$1,344,733,000

Curr. Assets:	$108,231,077,000	**Curr. Liab.:**	$221,472,824,000	**P/E Ratio:**	10.70
Plant, Equip.:	$479,637,000	**Total Liab.:**	$338,303,211,000	**Indic. Yr. Divd.:**	$1.280
Total Assets:	$350,432,595,000	**Net Worth:**	$12,129,384,000	**Debt/ Equity:**	9.9080

Beard Co

5600 N May Ave., Ste. 320, Oklahoma City, OK, 73112; *PH:* 1-405-842-2333; *Fax:* 1-405-842-9901; *http://* www.beardco.com; *Email:* info@beardco.com

General - Incorporation ... OK
Employees ... 69
Auditor ... Cole & Reed P.C
Stk Agt ... Liberty Transfer Co
Counsel ... McAfee & Taft
DUNS No. ... 78-950-5856

Stock- Price on:12/24/2007 ... $0.5
Stock Exchange ... OTC
Ticker Symbol ... BRCO
Outstanding Shares ... 5,590,000
E.P.S ... -$0.26
Shareholders ... NA

Business: The group's principal activity is to explore oil and gas. The activities are carried out through four segments: coal reclamation, carbon dioxide, China and e-commerce. Coal reclamation segment operates coal fines reclamation facilities and provides slurry pond core drilling services, fine coal laboratory analytical services and consulting services. Carbon dioxide segment produces carbon dioxide. China segment pursues environmental opportunities in China, focusing on the installation and construction of facilities, which utilize the patented airlance compost systems(tm) composting technology. E-commerce segment develops Internet payment system and focuses on developing licensing agreements and other fee based agreements with companies implementing technology in conflict with the group's intellectual property. The group operates in the United States and China.

Primary SIC and add'l.: 7375 2813 1241

CIK No: 0000909992

Subsidiaries: Advanced Internet Technologies, LLC, Beard Environmental Engineering, LLC, Beard Oil Company, Beard Pinnacle, LLC, Beard Sino-American Resources Co., Inc., Beard Technologies, Inc., Bee/7hbf, LLC, Beijing Beard Sino-American Bio-Tech Engineering Co., Ltd., starpay. com, LLC, The Beard Company, Xianghe BH Fertilizer Co., Ltd.

Officers: Riza Murteza/CEO, Pres. - Beard Sino, American Resources Co, Inc, W. M. Beard/79/Chmn., CEO/$134,650.00, Mark E. Voth/VP - Beard Sino, American Resources Co, Inc, USA, Eliza Shen/VP - Beard Sino, American Resources Co, Inc, China, Herb Mee/79/Dir., CFO, Pres./$133,650.00, Jack A. Martine/58/Controller, Chief Accounting Officer, Harl R. Dubben/47/Treasurer

Directors: W. M. Beard/79/Chmn., CEO, Herb Mee/79/Dir., CFO, Pres., Allan R. Hallock/Dir., Ford C. Price/Dir., Harlon E. Martin/Dir.

Owners: Herb Mee, Lu Beard, 7HBF, Ltd., Harlon E. Martin, Allan R. Hallock Trust, Ford C. Price, The Beard Group, Allan R. Hallock, William M. Beard, Boatright Family, Insiders, W. M. Beard, John Hancock Financial Services, Inc.

Financial Data: **Fiscal Year End:**12/31 **Latest Annual Data:** 12/31/2006

Year	Sales	Net Income
2006	$2,085,000	-$1,554,000
2005	$1,379,000	-$2,160,000
2004	$972,000	$937,000

Curr. Assets:	$840,000	**Curr. Liab.:**	$1,111,000		
Plant, Equip.:	$1,297,000	**Total Liab.:**	$9,770,000	**Indic. Yr. Divd.:**	NA
Total Assets:	$2,422,000	**Net Worth:**	-$7,348,000	**Debt/ Equity:**	NA

BearingPoint Inc

1676 International Dr., McLean, VA, 22102; *PH:* 1-703-747-3000; *Fax:* 1-703-747-8500; *http://* www.bearingpoint.com

General - Incorporation ... DE
Employees ... NA
Auditor ... PricewaterhouseCoopers LLP
Stk Agt ... Computershare Trust Co
Counsel ... NA
DUNS No. ... NA

Stock- Price on:12/24/2007 ... $7.41
Stock Exchange ... NYSE
Ticker Symbol ... BE
Outstanding Shares ... NA
E.P.S ... -$1.41
Shareholders ... NA

Business: The groups principle activities include designing, implementing and providing consulting application services, technology solutions and managed services. The groups customers are government organizations and Global 2000 companies. The group operates through seven segments namely, public services, commercial services, financial services, EMEA, Asia Pacific, Latin America and corporate. The group operates from the United States, Spain, France, Brazil, Switzerland, Norway, Finland, Sweden, South Korea and Peru. The group's quarterly revenue for September 2007 was 861.90 millions of USD.

Primary SIC and add'l.: 8742 7379 8748 7376 7371 7373

CIK No: 0001113247

Subsidiaries: 800 MHZ Transition Administrator, LLC, Barents Group Egypt, Ltd., BearingPoint (Netherlands Americas) N.V., BearingPoint Hong Kong) Limited, BearingPoint (Asia Pacific) Limited, BearingPoint (Asia Pacific) Pte. Ltd., BearingPoint (ASPAC)Sdn. Bhd., BearingPoint (Thailand) Ltd., BearingPoint 2002 Asia Pacific Pte. Ltd., BearingPoint 2002 Asia Pacific Pty. Ltd., BearingPoint 2002 Australia Pty. Ltd., BearingPoint 2002 Peru SRL, BearingPoint 2002 Singapore Pte. Ltd., BearingPoint Advisors Venezuela C.A., BearingPoint Americas Holdings Limited 127 Subsidiaries included in the Index

Officers: Harry L. You/Dir., CEO/$4,598,528.00, Judy A. Ethell/CFO, Exec. VP/$2,825,497.00, Ed Harbach/COO, Pres., Rick Martino/Exec. VP - Global Human Resources, Michael D. Lyman/Exec. VP, Chief Strategy Officer - Global Management Consulting, Laurent C. Lutz/General Counsel, Sec./$2,325,549.00, Connie K. Weaver/Exec. VP, Chief Marketing Officer, Christopher Formant/Exec. VP - Global Financial Services, Eric Goldfarb/CIO, Exec. VP, Joni Kahn/Exec. VP - Technology Solutions, Robin S. Lineberger/Exec. VP - Global Public Services, Peter Mockler/Exec. VP - Europe, Middle East, Africa, Robin G. Palmer/Exec. VP - Asia Pacific, Mark Vayda/Exec. VP - Global Sales, Francesca Luthi/Investor Relations Officer

Directors: Harry L. You/Dir., CEO, Roderick C. McGeary/Chmn., Richard J. Roberts/Chmn. - Global Public Services, Jill Kanin-Lovers/Dir., Douglas C. Allred/Dir., Betsy Bernard/Dir., Spencer Fleischer/Dir., Wolfgang Kemna/Dir., Albert L. Lord/Dir., Terry J. Strange/Dir.

Owners: Insiders/1.70%, Wolfgang Kemna, J. Terry Strange, Douglas C. Allred, Glenview Capital Management, LLC/10.00%, Richard J. Roberts, Betsy J. Bernard, Spencer C. Fleischer, Harry L. You, Goldman Sachs Asset Management, L.P./6.90%, Ariel Capital Management, LLC/14.90%, Roderick C. McGeary, Albert L. Lord, Judy A. Ethell

Financial Data: **Fiscal Year End:**12/31 **Latest Annual Data:** 12/31/2006

Year	Sales	Net Income
2006	$3,444,003,000	-$213,440,000
2005	$3,388,900,000	-$721,643,000
2004	$3,375,782,000	-$546,226,000

Curr. Assets:	$1,203,986,000	**Curr. Liab.:**	$1,037,611,000		
Plant, Equip.:	$146,392,000	**Total Liab.:**	$2,116,541,000	**Indic. Yr. Divd.:**	NA
Total Assets:	$1,939,240,000	**Net Worth:**	-$177,301,000	**Debt/ Equity:**	NA

Beasley Broadcast Group Inc

3033 Riviera Dr., Ste. 200, Naples, FL, 34103; *PH:* 1-239-263-5000; *Fax:* 1-239-263-8191; *http://* www.beasleybroadcasting.com; *Email:* email@bbgi.com

General - Incorporation ... DE
Employees ... 549
Auditor ... Crowe Chizek & Co. LLC
Stk Agt ... American Stock Transfer & Trust Co.
Counsel ... Latham & Watkins
DUNS No. ... NA

Stock- Price on:12/24/2007 ... $8.461
Stock Exchange ... NDQ
Ticker Symbol ... BBGI
Outstanding Shares ... 23,990,000
E.P.S ... $0.31
Shareholders ... NA

Business: The group's principal activity is to operate radio broadcasting stations. It owns and operates 41 stations, 26 FM and 15 AM. The group's station operates in ten large and mid-sized markets primarily located in the eastern United States. The group's operations are divided into three reportable segments, radio group one includes market clusters located in miami-ft. Lauderdale, west palm beach-boca raton, ft. Myers-naples, and greenville-new bern-jacksonville. Radio group two includes market clusters located in atlanta, Boston, philadelphia, fayetteville, and augusta. Radio group three includes our market cluster located in las vegas. The group sells broadcasting time to local and national spot advertisers and national network advertisers. On 05-Feb-2003, the group completed the sale of wbyu-AM in the new orleans market.

Primary SIC and add'l.: 4832

CIK No: 0001099160

Subsidiaries: Beasley Broadcasting of Augusta, Inc., Beasley Broadcasting of Boston, Inc., Beasley Broadcasting of Coastal Carolina, Inc., Beasley Broadcasting of Eastern North Carolina, Inc., Beasley Broadcasting of Eastern Pennsylvania, Inc., Beasley Broadcasting of Florida, Inc., Beasley Broadcasting of Nevada, Beasley Broadcasting of New Jersey, Inc., Beasley Broadcasting of Southwest Florida, Inc., Beasley Communications, Inc., Beasley FM Acquisition Corp., Beasley Internet Ventures II, LLC, Beasley Internet Ventures, LLC, Beasley Mezzanine Holdings, LLC, Beasley Nevada Holdings, Inc. 46 Subsidiaries included in the Index

Officers: George G. Beasley/75/Chmn., CEO/$1,220,868.00, Brian E. Beasley/48/Dir., VP - Operations/$879,974.00, Caroline B. Beasley/45/Dir., Exec. VP, CFO, Sec./$895,609.00, Bruce G. Beasley/50/Dir., COO, Pres./$913,330.00, Marie Tedesco/VP - Finance, Shaun P. Greening/VP - Financial Reporting, Denyse S. Mesnik/Dir. - Corporate Communications, Patricia Russell/Dir. - Human Resources, Joyce Fitch/General Counsel, Joseph Jaffoni/Investors

Directors: George G. Beasley/75/Chmn., CEO, Allen B. Shaw/64/Vice Chmn., Caroline B. Beasley/45/Dir., Exec. VP, CFO, Sec., Bruce G. Beasley/50/Dir., COO, Pres., Mark S. Fowler/66/Dir., Brian E. Beasley/48/Dir., VP - Operations, Joe B. Cox/68/Dir., Herbert W. McCord/65/Dir.

Owners: Allen B. Shaw, Deephaven Capital Management/24.60%, Westport Asset Management/6.30%, Insiders/92.80%, Insiders/23.50%, George G. Beasley/82.00%, Dimensional Fund Advisors/5.10%, Joe B. Cox, Caroline Beasley/6.10%, Mark S. Fowler, George G. Beasley/6.70%, Gabelli Asset Management/12.50%, Herbert W. McCord, Brian E. Beasley/6.50%, Bruce G. Beasley/6.10% *(21 Owners included in Index)*

Financial Data: **Fiscal Year End:**12/31 **Latest Annual Data:** 06/30/2007

Year	Sales	Net Income
2007	$34,836,000	$2,142,000
2006	$125,190,000	$10,134,000
2005	$124,294,000	$10,705,000

Curr. Assets:	$36,075,000	**Curr. Liab.:**	$15,734,000	**P/E Ratio:**	21.15
Plant, Equip.:	$25,788,000	**Total Liab.:**	$210,377,000	**Indic. Yr. Divd.:**	$0.250
Total Assets:	$297,968,000	**Net Worth:**	$87,592,000	**Debt/ Equity:**	2.2728

Beazer Homes USA Inc

1000 Abernathy Rd., Ste. 1200, Atlanta, GA, 30328; *PH:* 1-770-829-3700; *Fax:* 1-770-481-2808; *http://* www.beazer.com; *Email:* lkratcos@beazer.com

General - Incorporation ... DE
Employees ... 4,234
Auditor ... Deloitte & Touche LLP
Stk Agt ... American Stock Transfer & Trust Co.
Counsel ... C. Lowell Ball
DUNS No. ... 10-183-5189

Stock- Price on:12/24/2007 ... $30.08
Stock Exchange ... NYSE
Ticker Symbol ... BZH
Outstanding Shares ... 39,100,000
E.P.S ... $2.33
Shareholders ... NA

Business: The group operates through its subsidiaries whose principle activities include designing, building and selling single-family homes. The groups projects include design centers to select desired customizations for their homes such as cabinetry, flooring, fixtures, appliances and wall coverings. The group also provides mortgage origination, title and insurance services. The group operates from United States.

Primary SIC and add'l.: 1521 1531 6162

CIK No: 0000915840

Subsidiaries: April Corporation, Arden Park Ventures, LLC, Beazer Allied Companies Holdings, Inc., Beazer Clarksburg, LLC, Beazer Commercial Holdings, LLC, Beazer General Services, Inc., Beazer Homes Corp., Beazer Homes Holdings Corp., Beazer Homes Indiana Holding Corp., Beazer Homes Indiana, LLP, Beazer Homes Investments, LLC, Beazer Homes Michigan, LLC, Beazer Homes Sales, Inc., Beazer Homes Texas Holdings, Inc., Beazer Homes Texas, LP 34 Subsidiaries included in the Index

Officers: Ian J. McCarthy/Dir., CEO, Pres., Michael H. Furlow/COO, Exec. VP, Tony L. Callahan/Sr. VP - National Purchasing, Planning, DesignSr. VP - National Purchasing, Planning, Design, Cindy B. Tierney/CIO, Sr. VP, Martin J. Shaffer/Operating Management, Southeast Region, Thomas W. Bruce/Operating Management, Charlotte Division, David G. Byrnes/Operating Management, Orlando Division, Frank L. Finlaw/Operating Management, Columbia Division, William A. June/Operating Management, Nevada Division, Karl Billisits/Operating Management, Columbus Division, Allan P. Merrill/CFO, Exec. VP, Ken Dohrn/Operating Management, Memphis Division, Kevin Glover/Operating Management, Myrtle Beach Division, Mike Mansfield/Operating Management, Georgia Division, Scott Phillips/Operating Management, Jacksonville Division *(43 Officers included in Index)*

Directors: Ian J. McCarthy/Dir., CEO, Pres., Brian C. Beazer/Chmn., Stephen P. Zelnak/Dir., Larry T. Solari/Dir., Peter G. Leemputte/Dir., Laurent Alpert/Dir., Katie J. Bayne/Dir.

Owners: Brian C. Beazer, Ian J. McCarthy/2.50%, Legg Mason Capital Management,Inc./12.71%, James OLeary, Insiders/4.10%, Michael H. Furlow, Katie J. Bayne, FMR Corp/5.49%, Neuberger Berman Inc./10.41%, Michael T. Rand, Kenneth J. Gary, Capital Group International,Inc./10.14%, Stephen P. Zelnak, Larry T. Solari, Laurent Alpert (18 Owners included in Index)

Financial Data: Fiscal Year End:09/30 Latest Annual Data: 9/30/2006

Year	Sales	Net Income
2006	$5,462,003,000	$388,761,000
2005	$4,995,353,000	$262,524,000
2004	$3,907,109,000	$235,811,000

Curr. Assets:	$4,026,346,000	Curr. Liab.:	$141,131,000		
Plant, Equip.:	$29,465,000	Total Liab.:	$2,857,508,000	Indic. Yr. Divd.:	$0.400
Total Assets:	$4,559,431,000	Net Worth:	$1,701,923,000	Debt/ Equity:	1.0255

Bebe Stores Inc

400 Valley Dr., Brisbane, CA, 94005; *PH:* 1-415-715-3900; *Fax:* 1-415-715-3939; *http://* www.bebe.com

General - Incorporation	CA	Stock- Price on:12/24/2007	$16.79
Employees	1,250	Stock Exchange	NDQ
Auditor	Deloitte & Touche LLP	Ticker Symbol	BEBE
Stk Agt	Computershare Trust Co	Outstanding Shares	93,220,000
Counsel	NA	E.P.S	$0.76
DUNS No	05-459-4957	Shareholders	NA

Business: The group's principal activity is to design, develop and produce a line of contemporary women's apparel and accessories. The group's products include tops, pants, skirts, dresses, suits, logo products, casual sportswear, activewear, outerwear, handbags and other accessories. The group designs and develops the majority of its merchandise in-house. The group markets its products under the bebe and bebe sport brand names through its 180 retail stores located in 32 states in the United States, the district of columbia and Canada. The group stores are designed to create a clean, upscale boutique environment featuring contemporary furnishings and sophisticated details. The group's licensees operate its 16 international stores.

Primary SIC and add'l.: 2337 2331 2339 2335

CIK No: 0001059272

Subsidiaries: bebe management, inc., bebe stores (Canada), inc., bebe studio realty, LLC, bebe studio, inc.

Officers: Gregory Scott/CEO, Barbara Wambach/Chief Administrative Officer, Walter Parks/CFO, COO

Directors: Manny Mashouf/Chmn., Founder

Owners: Susan Peterson, Lawrence Smith, Gregory Scott/3.00%, Walter Parks, Cynthia Cohen, Neda Mashouf/12.00%, Insiders/57.00%, Corrado Federico, Barbara Wambach/1.00%, Caden Wang, Barbara Bass, Manny Mashouf/54.00%

Financial Data: Fiscal Year End:07/02 Latest Annual Data: 07/07/2007

Year	Sales	Net Income
2007	$670,912,000	$77,278,000
2006	$579,073,000	$73,807,000
2005	$509,527,000	$66,332,000

Curr. Assets:	$319,607,000	Curr. Liab.:	$43,890,000	P/E Ratio:	19.99
Plant, Equip.:	$77,753,000	Total Liab.:	$74,303,000	Indic. Yr. Divd.:	$0.200
Total Assets:	$407,546,000	Net Worth:	$333,243,000	Debt/ Equity:	0.0001

Beckman Coulter Inc

4300 N Harbor Blvd., Fullerton, CA, 92834; *PH:* 1-714-871-4848; *Fax:* 1-714-773-8283; *http://* www.beckmancoulter.com

General - Incorporation	DE	Stock- Price on:12/24/2007	$66.53
Employees	10,340	Stock Exchange	NYSE
Auditor	KPMG LLP	Ticker Symbol	BEC
Stk Agt	Computershare Trust Co	Outstanding Shares	61,940,000
Counsel	NA	E.P.S	$3.39
DUNS No	00-825-4708	Shareholders	NA

Business: The groups principle activity is to manufacture biomedical testing instrument systems, tests and supplies to simplify and automate laboratory processes. The group provides laboratory tools to conduct basic research into the fundamental processes of human biology, to develop vaccines and drugs to treat disease, to conduct clinical trials and related research activities, and to perform simple patient blood tests to complex diagnostic testing. The group operates from United States.

Primary SIC and add'l.: 3826 3841

CIK No: 0000840467

Subsidiaries: Beckman Coulter Australia Pty. Ltd., Beckman Coulter Canada Inc., Beckman Coulter France S.A., Beckman Coulter G.m.b.H., Beckman Coulter Hong Kong Ltd., Beckman Coulter International S.A., Beckman Coulter Ireland Inc., Beckman Coulter K.K., Beckman Coulter S.p.A., Beckman Coulter United Kingdom Ltd.

Officers: Scott Garrett/Dir., CEO, Pres./$4,341,779.00, Arnie Pinkston/Sr. VP, General Counsel, Sec./$1,489,409.00, Pam Miller/Sr. VP - Supply Chain Management, Paul Glyer/Sr. VP - Strategy, Business Development, Investor Relations, Robert W. Kleinert/56/Exec. VP - Worldwide Commercial Operations/$1,048,473.00, Russ Bell/Chief Scientific Officer, Sr. VP, Bob Hurley/Sr. VP - Human Resources, Communications, Bob Kleinert/Exec. VP - Worldwide Commercial Operations, Bob Boghosian/Sr. VP - Quality, Regulatory Affairs, Mike Whelan/Group VP - High Sensitivity Testing Group, Scott Atkin/Group VP - Chemistry, Discovery, Automation Business Group, Cindy Collins/Group VP - Cellular Business Group, Charlie Slacik/CFO, Sr. VP - Information Technology, Robert H. Raynor/Dir. - Investor Relations, Cynthia Skoglund/Mgr. - Investor Relations (18 Officers included in Index)

Directors: Scott Garrett/Dir., CEO, Pres., Betty Woods/Chmn., William N. Kelley/Dir., Charles A. Haggerty/Dir., B. Van Honeycutt/Dir., Risa J. Lavizzo-Mourey/53/Dir., Peter B. Dervan/Dir., Kevin Farr/Dir., Robert G. Funari/Dir., James V. Mazzo/Dir., Glenn S. Schafer/Dir.

Owners: C. P. Slacik, G. S. Schafer, K. M. Farr, C. A. Haggerty, B. Woods, S. Garrett, B. D. Spaid, R. W. Kleinert, W. N. Kelley, C. D. Beaver, P. B. Dervan, J. V. Mazzo, J. T. Glover, R. G. Funari, V. B. Honeycutt (19 Owners included in Index)

Financial Data: Fiscal Year End:12/31 Latest Annual Data: 12/31/2006

Year	Sales		Net Income
2006		$2,528,500,000	$186,900,000
2005		$2,443,800,000	$150,600,000
2004		$2,408,300,000	$210,900,000

Curr. Assets:	$1,338,100,000	Curr. Liab.:	$711,600,000	P/E Ratio:	19.63
Plant, Equip.:	$721,000,000	Total Liab.:	$2,137,400,000	Indic. Yr. Divd.:	$0.640
Total Assets:	$3,291,700,000	Net Worth:	$1,154,300,000	Debt/ Equity:	0.7705

Becton Dickinson & Co

1 Becton Dr., Franklin Lakes, NJ, 07417; *PH:* 1-201-847-6800; *Fax:* 1-201-847-6475; *http://* www.bd.com

General - Incorporation	NJ	Stock- Price on:12/24/2007	$75.38
Employees	26,990	Stock Exchange	NYSE
Auditor	Ernst & Young LLP	Ticker Symbol	BDX
Stk Agt	Computershare Trust Co	Outstanding Shares	244,990,000
Counsel	NA	E.P.S	$3.49
DUNS No	00-129-2192	Shareholders	NA

Business: The group's principle activities are to manufacture and sell supplies, devices, laboratory equipment and diagnostic products. Healthcare institutions, life science researchers, clinical laboratories, industry and the public use these products. The group operates in 3 segments: medical systems, clinical lab and biosciences. Medical systems manufacture hypodermic products, prefillable drug delivery systems, infusion therapy products, elastic support products and thermometers, disposable scrubs, specialty needles and surgical blades. Clinical lab does clinical and industrial microbiology products, sample collection products, specimen management systems, hematology instruments and diagnostic systems, consulting services and customized, automated bar-code systems. Biosciences are into flow cytometry systems for cellular analysis, reagents and tissue culture labware. The group's total revenue for year 2007 was 6,359.71 millions of USD.

Primary SIC and add'l.: 3841

CIK No: 0000010795

Subsidiaries: Atto BioScience, Inc., B-D (Cambridge U.K.) Ltd., B-d U.k. Holdings Limited, BD Biosciences, Systems and Reagents Inc., BD Holding S. de R.L. de C.V., BD Matrex Holdings, Inc., BD Norge AS, BD Ophthalmic Systems Limited, BD Ventures LLC, Bdx Ino LLC, Becton Dickinson (Mauritius) Limited, Becton Dickinson (Pty) Ltd., Becton Dickinson (Royston) Limited, Becton Dickinson (Thailand) Limited, Becton Dickinson A/S 108 Subsidiaries included in the Index

Officers: Edward J. Ludwig/Chmn., CEO, Pres., David T. Durack/Sr. VP - Corporate Medical Affairs, Patricia B. Shrader/Sr. VP - Corporate Regulatory, External Affairs, Laureen Higgins/Pres. - North Latin America, Geraldo Barbosa/Pres. - South Latin America, Helen Cunniff/Pres. - BD Asia, Pacific, Jean-Marc Dageville/Pres. - Western Europe, Richard K. Berman/VP, Treasurer, Mark H. Borofsky/VP - Taxes, James R. Brown/VP - Quality Management, Jeffrey S. Sherman/Sr. VP, General Counsel, John A. Hanson/Exec. VP, Scott P. Bruder/CTO, Sr. VP, John R. Considine/CFO, Exec. VP, Vincent A. Forlenza/Exec. VP (23 Officers included in Index)

Directors: Edward J. Ludwig/Chmn., CEO, Pres., Alfred Sommer/Dir., Willard J. Overlock/Dir., Edward F. Degraan/Dir., James E. Perrella/Dir., James F. Orr/Dir., Claire M. Fraser-Liggett/Dir., Marshall O. Larsen/Dir., Adel A.F. Mahmoud/Dir., Gary A. Mecklenburg/Dir., Bertram L. Scott/Dir., Henry P. Becton/Dir., Basil L. Anderson/Dir.

Owners: Bertram L. Scott, Gary M. Cohen, State Street Corporation/5.30%, Claire M. Fraser-Liggett, William A. Kozy, Willard J. Overlock, Alfred Sommer, James E. Perrella, Gary A. Mecklenburg, Edward F. DeGraan, Adel A.F. Mahmoud, Barclays Global Investors, NA/9.90%, Insiders/1.30%, FMR Corporation/12.20%, Henry P. Becton (20 Owners included in Index)

Financial Data: Fiscal Year End:09/30 Latest Annual Data: 06/30/2007

Year	Sales		Net Income
2007	NA		NA
2006		$5,834,827,000	$752,280,000
2005		$5,414,681,000	$722,263,000

Curr. Assets:	$3,185,253,000	Curr. Liab.:	$1,576,329,000	P/E Ratio:	25.13
Plant, Equip.:	$2,133,548,000	Total Liab.:	$2,988,321,000	Indic. Yr. Divd.:	NA
Total Assets:	$6,824,525,000	Net Worth:	$3,836,204,000	Debt/ Equity:	0.2315

Bed Bath & Beyond Inc

650 Liberty Ave., Union, NJ, 07083; *PH:* 1-908-688-0888; *Fax:* 1-908-688-6483; *http://* www.bedbathandbeyond.com

General - Incorporation	NY	Stock- Price on:12/24/2007	$37.32
Employees	33,000	Stock Exchange	NDQ
Auditor	KPMG LLP	Ticker Symbol	BBBY
Stk Agt	American Stock Transfer & Trust Co.	Outstanding Shares	277,130,000
Counsel	NA	E.P.S	$2.11
DUNS No	05-812-7986	Shareholders	NA

Business: The group's principle activity is to operate domestics merchandise and home furnishings stores. The group's domestic merchandise products include bed linens, bath accessories and kitchen textiles. The group's home furnishings products include cookware, dinnerware, glassware and basic house wares. The group's products include food, giftware, health and beauty care items, and infant and toddler merchandise. The group's products sold under the brand name Clad, Braun, Calphalon, Fieldcrest, Kitchenaid, Krups, Cannon and Croscill. The group operates from United States.

Primary SIC and add'l.: 5719

CIK No: 0000886158

Subsidiaries: BBBY Management Corp., Bed n Bath Stores, Inc., Bed Bath & Beyond of California Limited Liability Company, Bed Bath & Beyond Procurement Company Inc., Christmas Tree Shops, Inc., Harmon Stores, Inc.

Officers: Steven H. Temares/Dir., CEO/$6,424,045.00, Charles Bilezikian/CEO - Christmas Tree Shops, Inc, Alan J. Natowitz/VP, General Merchandise Mgr. - Bedding, Window, Ross Richman/VP - Financial Operations Analysis, Christine R. Pirog/VP - Store Operations, Jeffrey W. Mack/VP - Supply Chain Logistics, Robert Claybrook/VP - Business Application Development, Joseph P. Rowland/VP - E, Service Operations, Matthew Fiorilli/Sr. VP - Stores, Timothy P. Brewster/VP - Stores, NYC Region, Michael Callahan/VP, Corporate Counsel, Robyn M. D'Elia/VP, Controller, David S. Denenberg/VP - Merchandise Control, Louis M. Sepe/VP - Application Development, Merchandising Systems, Jeffrey L. Feinstein/VP, Sec., Treasurer - Buy Buy Baby, Inc (50 Officers included in Index)

Directors: Steven H. Temares/Dir., CEO, Leonard Feinstein/Co - Chmn., Warren Eisenberg/Co - Chmn., Jordan Heller/Dir., Fran Stoller/Dir., Victoria A. Morrison/Dir., Patrick Gaston/Dir., Robert S. Kaplan/Dir., Stanley F. Barshay/Dir., Klaus Eppler/Dir., Dean S. Adler/Dir.

Owners: Warren Eisenberg/2.60%, Jordan Heller, Stanley F. Barshay, Leonard Feinstein/2.00%, Fran Stoller, Robert Kaplan, Victoria A. Morrison, Insiders/6.20%, Ruane, Cunniff & Goldfarb Inc./6.40%, Eugene A. Castagna, Steven H. Temares, Arthur Stark, Klaus Eppler, Dean S. Adler

Financial Data: *Fiscal Year End:* 02/25 *Latest Annual Data:* 3/3/2007

Year	Sales	Net Income
2007	$6,617,429,000	$594,244,000
2006	$5,809,562,000	$572,847,000
2005	$5,147,678,000	$504,964,000

Curr. Assets:	$2,698,614,000	**Curr. Liab.:**	$1,145,073,000	**P/E Ratio:**	17.69
Plant, Equip.:	$929,507,000	**Total Liab.:**	$1,310,153,000	**Indic. Yr. Divd.:**	NA
Total Assets:	$3,959,304,000	**Net Worth:**	$2,649,151,000	**Debt/ Equity:**	NA

Bedminster National Corp (A)

90 Washington Valley Rd., Bedminster, NJ, 07921; *PH:* 1-908-719-8941

General - Incorporation	NV	Stock - Price on: 12/24/2007	$0.18
Employees	1	Stock Exchange	OTC
Auditor	Webb & Company, P. A.	Ticker Symbol	BMSTE
Stk Agt	NA	Outstanding Shares	8,680,000
Counsel	NA	E.P.S.	-$0.159
DUNS No.	NA	Shareholders	NA

Business: The groups principle activity is to provide management-consulting services to third party companies. The group operates from the United States.

Primary SIC and add'l.: 8742

CIK No: 0001334314

Subsidiaries: Bedminster Capital Corp, Bedminster Financial Corp.

Owners: Insiders/90.00%, Paul Patrizio/90.00%

Financial Data: *Fiscal Year End:* 12/31 *Latest Annual Data:* 12/31/2006

Year	Sales	Net Income
2006	$26,000	-$356,000

Curr. Assets:	$111,000	**Curr. Liab.:**	$317,000		
Plant, Equip.:	$2,000	**Total Liab.:**	$358,000	**Indic. Yr. Divd.:**	NA
Total Assets:	$113,000	**Net Worth:**	-$245,000	**Debt/ Equity:**	NA

Beeston Enterprises Ltd New

1687 West Broadway, No. 200, Vancouver, BC, V6J 1X2; *PH:* 1-604-738-1143

General - Incorporation	NV	Stock - Price on: 12/24/2007	$0.85
Employees	NA	Stock Exchange	OTC
Auditor	Bagell, Levine & Company, LLC	Ticker Symbol	BESE
Stk Agt	Pacific Stock Transfer Company	Outstanding Shares	NA
Counsel	NA	E.P.S.	NA
DUNS No.	NA	Shareholders	NA

Business: The groups principal activity is to exploration of minerals. The group operates from the United States and Canada.

Primary SIC and add'l.: 1021

CIK No: 0001221548

Officers: Brian Smith/56/Dir., CEO, CFO, Pres., Sec., Treasurer

Directors: Brian Smith/56/Dir., CEO, CFO, Pres., Sec., Treasurer

Owners: Insiders/8.85%, Brian Smith/8.85%

Financial Data: *Fiscal Year End:* 12/31 *Latest Annual Data:* 12/31/2006

Year	Sales	Net Income
2006	NA	-$92,000
2005	NA	-$26,000
2004	NA	-$31,000

Curr. Assets:	$12,000	**Curr. Liab.:**	$12,000		
Plant, Equip.:	$1,000	**Total Liab.:**	$87,000	**Indic. Yr. Divd.:**	NA
Total Assets:	$13,000	**Net Worth:**	-$75,000	**Debt/ Equity:**	NA

Beicang Iron & Steel Inc

Formerly: Alpha Spacecom Inc
8/f Beicang Bldg., 76 Jianshe N Rd., Taiyuan City, 30013; *PH:* 86-351-465-6727; *http://* www.alphaspacecom.com

General - Incorporation	NV	Stock - Price on: 12/24/2007	$0.03
Employees	NA	Stock Exchange	NA
Auditor	De Joya & Co., Kabani & Co.	Ticker Symbol	NA
Stk Agt	Computershare Trust Co	Outstanding Shares	NA
Counsel	NA	E.P.S.	NA
DUNS No.	08-812-5174	Shareholders	NA

Business: The group's principal activity is to develop ka band communication satellite system. Ka band refers to the range of frequency at which a satellite communicates. This system provides broadband telecommunications services to the People's Republic of China and its neighboring countries of Asia-Pacific countries. There are three bands that are commonly used in satellite telecommunications: ku-band, c-band and ka-band. Ku-band is typically used for television broadcast and telecommunications with beam coverage of a subcontinent. C-band satellites are able to reach relatively larger coverage areas but require a receiver dish much larger in diameter. Ka-band is used by broadband multimedia companies, because it has sufficient bandwidth to support the demands of broadband multimedia applications. The group is a development stage company.

Primary SIC and add'l.: 4899

CIK No: 0000763245

Subsidiaries: Alpha Spacecom Company Limited

Officers: Beicang Hou/45/CEO, Dir., CFO, Sec.

Directors: Beicang Hou/45/CEO, Dir., CFO, Sec.

Owners: Insiders/90.00%, Beicang Hou/90.00%

Financial Data: *Fiscal Year End:* 12/31 *Latest Annual Data:* 12/31/2006

Year	Sales	Net Income
2006	$38,388,000	-$2,334,000
2005	NA	-$162,000
2004	NA	-$70,000

Curr. Assets:	$10,273,000	**Curr. Liab.:**	$13,806,000		
Plant, Equip.:	$5,129,000	**Total Liab.:**	$13,806,000	**Indic. Yr. Divd.:**	NA
Total Assets:	$15,876,000	**Net Worth:**	$2,069,000	**Debt/ Equity:**	NA

Beijing Med-Pharm Corp

600 W Germantown Pike, Plymouth Meeting, PA, 19462; *PH:* 1-610-940-1675; *http://* www.beijingmedpharm.com; *Email:* info@beijingmedpharm.com

General - Incorporation	DE	Stock - Price on: 12/24/2007	$10.84
Employees	185	Stock Exchange	NDQ
Auditor	Grant Thornton LLP	Ticker Symbol	BJGP
Stk Agt	Florida Atlantic Stock Transfer, Inc.	Outstanding Shares	NA
Counsel	NA	E.P.S.	-$0.27
DUNS No.	NA	Shareholders	NA

Business: The groups principle activities include marketing and distributing pharmaceutical product. The groups services include clinical trial management, product registration, and market research and pharmaceutical distribution. The products of the group include Propess, Anpo, Misopess and Fentora. In December 2005 the group acquired Beijing Wanwei Pharmaceutical Co., Ltd. The groups operates through two segments namely pharmaceutical distribution and, sales and marketing fees. The group operates from China. The group's quarterly revenue for September 2007 was 8.98 millions of USD.

Primary SIC and add'l.: 5122

CIK No: 0001281696

Subsidiaries: Beijing Med-Pharm Hong Kong Company Ltd., Beijing Medpharm Co. Ltd., Beijing Wanwei Pharmaceutical Co., Ltd.

Officers: David Gao/Dir., CEO, Pres./$531,189.00, Fred Powell/CFO/$323,813.00, Byron Wang/VP - Sales, Marketing, Yong Guo/GM - Beijing Wanwei Pharmaceutical, Robert Wang/New Business Development, Richard Liu/Mgr. - Business Development, Frank Xu/National Sales Mgr., Bin Duan/Marketing Mgr., Amy Zhou/Dir. - Human Resources, China

Directors: David Gao/Dir., CEO, Pres., Martyn Greenacre/Chmn., Michel Y. De Beaumont/Dir., Jack M. Ferraro/Dir., Frank J. Hollendoner/Dir., John W. Stakes/Dir., Albert Yeung/Dir.

Owners: Fred M. Powell, Artis Capital Management, Inc./5.53%, Michel Y. deBeaumont, Insiders/3.37%, John W. Stakes, Martyn D. Greenacre, Abacus Investments Ltd./33.06%, David Gao, Jack M. Ferraro, Frank J. Hollendoner, Ashford Capital Management, Inc./6.79%

Financial Data: *Fiscal Year End:* 12/31 *Latest Annual Data:* 12/31/2006

Year	Sales	Net Income
2006	$24,258,000	-$6,796,000
2005	$4,179,000	-$5,724,000

Curr. Assets:	$26,190,000	**Curr. Liab.:**	$8,830,000		
Plant, Equip.:	$313,000	**Total Liab.:**	$8,957,000	**Indic. Yr. Divd.:**	NA
Total Assets:	$27,517,000	**Net Worth:**	$18,560,000	**Debt/ Equity:**	0.0049

Bekem Metals Inc

875 Donner Way Apt 705, Salt Lake City, UT, 84108; *PH:* 1-801-582-1881; *http://* www.bekem.com

General - Incorporation	UT	Stock - Price on: 12/24/2007	$1.7
Employees	NA	Stock Exchange	OTC
Auditor	Hansen, Barnett & Maxwell P.C.	Ticker Symbol	BKMM
Stk Agt	Interwest Transfer Company, Inc.	Outstanding Shares	NA
Counsel	NA	E.P.S.	NA
DUNS No.	NA	Shareholders	NA

Business: The group principle activities include developing, extracting, refining and marketing of nickel, cobalt and brown coal. In the year 2005, the group acquired Kazakh Metals, Inc and Kyzyl Kain Mamyt (KKM), LLP. The group operates from Kazakhstan.

Primary SIC and add'l.: 1061

CIK No: 0001223550

Subsidiaries: Kazakh Metals, Inc., Kaznickel, LLP, Kyzyl Kain Mamyt, LLP

Officers: Marat Cherdabayev/Chmn., CEO, Pres., Yermek Kudabayev/37/CFO, Abai Turemuratov/COO

Directors: Marat Cherdabayev/Chmn., CEO, Pres., James F. Gunnell/Dir., Dossan Kassymkhanuly/Dir., James Kohler/60/Dir., Timothy Adair/43/Dir., Valery Tolkachev/39/Dir., Nurlan Tajibaev/60/Dir.

Owners: Marat Cherdabayev, Nurlan Tajibaev, GLG Emerging Markets Fund, Hsuih Chi Hun, Central Asian Metals, Inc., Insiders, Brisa Equities Corporation, Yermek Kudabayev, Bekem Metals, Inc., Brilliance Investments Ltd

Financial Data: *Fiscal Year End:* 12/31 *Latest Annual Data:* 12/31/2006

Year	Sales	Net Income
2006	$105,000	-$4,588,000
2005	$149,000	-$2,091,000
2004	NA	-$215,000

Curr. Assets:	$9,740,000	**Curr. Liab.:**	$815,000		
Plant, Equip.:	$13,871,000	**Total Liab.:**	$2,280,000	**Indic. Yr. Divd.:**	NA
Total Assets:	$25,364,000	**Net Worth:**	$23,084,000	**Debt/ Equity:**	NA

Bel Fuse Inc

206 Van Vorst St., Jersey City, NJ, 07302; *PH:* 1-201-432-0463; *Fax:* 1-201-432-9542; *http://* www.belfuse.com; *Email:* belfuse@belfuse.com

General - Incorporation	NJ	Stock - Price on: 12/24/2007	NA
Employees	NA	Stock Exchange	NDQ
Auditor	Deloitte & Touche LLP	Ticker Symbol	BELFA , BELFB
Stk Agt	Continental Stock Transfer & Trust Co	Outstanding Shares	NA
Counsel	NA	E.P.S.	NA
DUNS No.	00-132-1389	Shareholders	NA

Business: The group's principal activity is the design, manufacture and sale of components for local area networking, telecommunication, business equipment and consumer electronic applications. The products include magnetic components and connector modules with combinations of rj45 and usb connectors for signal delay, signal timing, signal conditioning, filtering, impedance matching, electro-magnetic interference suppression etc. They also consist of miniature micro and chip fuses for supplementary circuit protection in televisions, vers and computers and transformers for networking and

telecommunication applications. The group has designed non-isolated dc/dc converters for power low voltage silicon devices. The group manufactures the products in its Far East facilities, which are sold to more than 800 customers throughout northamerica, western Europe and the Far East. Belfuse, bel, belmag, belstack, surfuse etc are the trademarks owned by the group.

Primary SIC and add'l.: 3674 3695 3679 3677 3613

CIK No: 0000729580

Subsidiaries: Bel Components Ltd., Bel Connector Inc., Bel Fuse (Macao Commerical Offshore) Limited, Bel Fuse Delaware Inc., Bel Fuse Europe Ltd., Bel Fuse Limited, Bel Fuse Macau LDA, Bel Power (Hangzhou) Co. Ltd., Bel Power Inc., Bel Power Products Inc., Bel Stewart Gmbh, Bel Stewart Limited, Bel Transformer Inc., Bel Ventures Inc., Netwatch s.r.o. 18 Subsidiaries included in the Index

Officers: Daniel Bernstein/54/CEO, Pres., VP, MD, Treasurer/$341,510.00, Connie Adams/Contact - Media Information, Robert Jacobs/Investor Relations Officer, Joseph Meccariello/58/VP - Manufacturing/$348,391.00, Dennis Ackerman/45/VP - Operations/$251,798.00, Colin Dunn/VP - Finance/$307,976.00, Donna Marganella/Mgr. - Marketing Communications

Directors: Peter Gilbert/60/Dir., Robert H. Simandl/79/Dir., John S. Johnson/78/Dir., John F. Tweedy/62/Dir., Avi Eden/60/Dir.

Owners: Robert H. Simandl, Howard B. Bernstein/3.10%, Robert H. Simandl, Joseph Meccariello, Peter Gilbert, Dennis Ackerman, Dennis Ackerman, Howard B. Bernstein/5.20%, John S. Johnson, Colin Dunn, colin Dunn/3.80%, Insiders/8.90%, John F. Tweedy, Peter Gilbert, Insiders/7.80% *(25 Owners included in Index)*

Financial Data: ***Fiscal Year End:***12/31 ***Latest Annual Data:*** 3/31/2007

Year		Sales		Net Income
2007		$61,807,000		$4,009,000
2006		$73,260,000		$7,745,000
Curr. Assets:	$193,686,000	***Curr. Liab.:***	$52,661,000	
Plant, Equip.:	$43,641,000	***Total Liab.:***	$56,674,000	***Indic. Yr. Divd.:*** NA
Total Assets:	$277,365,000	***Net Worth:***	$220,691,000	***Debt/ Equity:*** NA

Belden Inc

Formerly: Belden CDT Inc

7701 Forsyth Blvd., Ste. 800, St. Louis, MO, 63105; ***PH:*** 1-314-854-8000; ***http://*** www.beldencdt.com

General - Incorporation	DE	***Stock***- Price on:12/24/2007	$59.0993
Employees	4,650	Stock Exchange	NYSE
Auditor	Ernst & Young LLP	Ticker Symbol	BDC
Stk Agt	Computershare Trust Co	Outstanding Shares	45,050,000
Counsel	NA	E.P.S	$2.23
DUNS No.	00-917-8666	Shareholders	NA

Business: The group principal activities are to manufacture high-speed electronic cables and products for the specialty electronics and data networking markets, including connectivity. The business is carried out through five operating divisions: electronics, networking, specialty, European operations and west penn wire.

Primary SIC and add'l.: 3357

CIK No: 0000913142

Subsidiaries: 190 Partnership L.P., Anglo-American Cables Ltd., Belden (Canada) Finco Limited Partnership, Belden (UK) Finco Limited Partnership, Belden - Duna Kabel Kft, Belden Australia Pty Ltd., Belden Brasil Comercial LTDA, Belden CDT (Canada) Inc., Belden CDT European Shared Services B.V., Belden CDT International, Inc., Belden CDT Networking, Inc., Belden CDT Orebro AB, Belden Communications Holding, Inc., Belden Deutschland GmbH, Belden Electronics Argentina S.A. 60 Subsidiaries included in the Index

Officers: John S. Norman/Controller, Chief Accounting Officer, Cathy O. Staples/57/VP - Human Resources, Louis Pace/36/VP - Business Development, Naresh Kumra/37/VP - Operations, Pres. - Asia Pacific Operations, Robert Canny/51/VP - Operations, Pres. - Specialty Products

Directors: David Aldrich/Dir.

Owners: Insiders, David Aldrich, Peter Sheehan, Bernard G. Rethore, Glenn Kalnasy, John M. Monter, Michael F. O. Harris, Lance Balk, Larrie D. Rose, Lorne D. Bain, John Stroup, Gray Benoist, Bryan C. Cressey, Stephen H. Johnson, Kevin Bloomfield

Financial Data: ***Fiscal Year End:***12/31 ***Latest Annual Data:*** 12/31/2006

Year		Sales		Net Income
2006		$1,495,811,000		$65,935,000
2005		$1,352,131,000		$47,558,000
2004		$966,174,000		$15,189,000
Curr. Assets:	$719,436,000	***Curr. Liab.:***	$262,008,000	***P/E Ratio:*** 33.77
Plant, Equip.:	$272,285,000	***Total Liab.:***	$512,067,000	***Indic. Yr. Divd.:*** $0.200
Total Assets:	$1,355,968,000	***Net Worth:***	$843,901,000	***Debt/ Equity:*** 0.5092

Belk Inc

PO Box 960012, Orlando, FL, 32896; ***PH:*** 1-704-357-1000; ***http://*** www.belk.com

General - Incorporation	DE	***Stock***- Price on:12/24/2007	NA
Employees	NA	Stock Exchange	OTC
Auditor	KPMG LLP	Ticker Symbol	BLKIA
Stk Agt	Pacific Stock Transfer Company	Outstanding Shares	NA
Counsel	Ralph A. Pitts	E.P.S	NA
DUNS No.	01-683-6160	Shareholders	NA

Business: The groups principle activity is to operate retail department stores. The groups products include fashion apparel, shoes and accessories for women, men and children, including cosmetics, home furnishings, housewares, gifts and other types of merchandise. The group operates from United States.

Primary SIC and add'l.: 6141 5311

CIK No: 0001051771

Subsidiaries: Belk Accounts Receivable LLC, Belk Administration Company, Belk Department Store LP, Belk Gift Card Company LLC, Belk International, Inc., Belk Merchandising LLC, Belk Stores of Virginia LLC, Belk Stores Services, Inc., Belk Texas Holdings LLC, Belk-Simpson Company, Greenville, South Carolina, The Belk Center, Inc., United Electronic Services, Inc.

Officers: Thomas M. Belk/Chmn., CEO/$2,761,257.00, Belk H.W. McKay/Pres., Chief Merchandising Officer/$2,085,993.00, Ralph A. Pitts/Exec. VP, General Counsel, Sec./$1,479,555.00, Brian T. Marley/CFO, Exec. VP/$1,584,964.00, John R. Belk/Dir., COO, Pres./$2,091,273.00, Adam M. Orvos/Sr. VP - Finance, Controller

Directors: Thomas M. Belk/Chmn., CEO, John M. Belk/Chmn. Emeritus, John R. Belk/Dir., COO, Pres., John R. Thompson/Dir., Elizabeth Valk Long/Dir., Kirk J. Glenn/Dir., John A. Kuhne/Dir., Thomas C. Nelson/Dir., John L. Townsend/Dir., Sarah Belk Gambrell/Honorary Dir.

Owners: McKay H.W. Belk/2.10%, Brian T. Marley/4.50%, Frank Matthews/5.80%, Thomas M. Belk/2.60%, Katherine McKay Belk/12.80%, Insiders/17.50%, Katherine Belk Morris/9.00%, Elizabeth Valk Long, Thomas C. Nelson, John M. Belk, Katherine McKay Belk/6.50%, John R. Belk/7.20%, Insiders/19.50%, John L. Townsend, Sarah Belk Gambrell/20.10% *(26 Owners included in Index)*

Bell Canada

1000, de La Gauchetire Ouest, Bureau 3700, Montral, QC, H3B 4W5; ***PH:*** 1-212-894-8940; ***http://*** www.bce.ca; ***Email:*** bcecomms@bce.ca

General - Incorporation	Canada	***Stock***- Price on:12/24/2007	$0.01
Employees	NA	Stock Exchange	NA
Auditor	Deloitte & Touche LLP	Ticker Symbol	NA
Stk Agt	Computershare Trust Co of Canada	Outstanding Shares	NA
Counsel	NA	E.P.S	NA
DUNS No.	20-211-4617	Shareholders	NA

Business: The group's principle activity is to provide telecommunication services, including local and access services and toll and network services. The group operates from United States.

Primary SIC and add'l.: 4813 2741

CIK No: 0000225090

Subsidiaries: Aliant, Bell ExpressVu, Bell Mobility, Bell Nordiq Group Inc

Officers: Michael J. Sabia/Dir., CEO, Patrick Pichette/Pres. - Operations, Karen H. Sheriff/Pres. - Small, Medium Business, Martine Turcotte/Chief Legal Officer, Patricia A. Olah/Corp. Sec. - Lead Governance Counsel, Leo W. Houle/Chief Talent Officer, George Cope/COO, Pres., Kevin W. Crull/Pres. - Bell Residential Services, Siim A. Vanaselja/CFO, Stephane Boisvert/Pres. - Enterprise, Scott L. Thomson/Exec. VP - Corporate Development, Planning, Wade Oosterman/Pres. - Bell Mobility, BDI, Chief Brand Officer, Eugene Roman/Group Pres. - Systems, Technology

Directors: Michael J. Sabia/Dir., CEO, Victor L. Young/Dir., John H. McArthur/Dir., Judith Maxwell/Dir., James A. Pattison/Dir., Ronald A. Brenneman/Dir., Brian M. Levitt/Dir., Donna Soble Kaufman/Dir., Anthony S. Fell/Dir., Paul M. Tellier/Dir., Richard J. Currie/Dir., Thomas C. Oneill/Dir., Andre Berard/Dir., Edward C. Lumley/Dir., Robert C. Pozen/Dir.

Financial Data: ***Fiscal Year End:***12/31 ***Latest Annual Data:*** 12/31/2002

Year		Sales		Net Income
2002		$146,952,000		$25,389,000
2001		$235,089,000		-$145,120,000
2000		$577,454,000		$54,549,000
Curr. Assets:	$266,774,000	***Curr. Liab.:***	$14,784,000	
Plant, Equip.:	$107,000	***Total Liab.:***	$116,288,000	***Indic. Yr. Divd.:*** NA
Total Assets:	$283,724,000	***Net Worth:***	$167,436,000	***Debt/ Equity:*** NA

Bell Industries Inc

8888 Keystone Crossing, Ste. 1700, Indianapolis, IN, 46240; ***PH:*** 1-317-704-6000; ***Fax:*** 1-317-704-0064; ***http://*** www.bellind.com

General - Incorporation	CA	***Stock***- Price on:12/24/2007	$3.79
Employees	1,150	Stock Exchange	AMEX
Auditor	BKD, LLP	Ticker Symbol	BI
Stk Agt	Computershare Investor Services LLC	Outstanding Shares	8,620,000
Counsel	Irell & Manella	E.P.S	-$1.44
DUNS No.	00-690-5533	Shareholders	NA

Business: The group's principal activities are to provide technology lifecycle and outsourced services, distribute aftermarket products for recreational vehicles, motor cycles, snowmobiles and power boats and manufacture specialty electronic components. The group operates in three reportable business segments: technology solutions, recreational products and electronics components. The technology solutions segment provides integrated technology solutions, such as technology lifecycle services and recurring support services in the midwestern, mideastern and Atlantic regions. The recreational products segment distributes replacement parts and accessories for recreational and other leisure-time vehicles in the us. The electronics components segment manufactures and distributes radio frequency standard and surface mount magnetic products in North America, Europe and Asia.

Primary SIC and add'l.: 5084 7373 3679 5013 5561 5065

CIK No: 0000945489

Subsidiaries: Bell Industries, Inc.

Officers: John A. Fellows/43/Dir., CEO, Pres./$762,294.00, Clinton Colemen/Interim CEO, Pres., Michael R. Barker/Sr. VP, Kevin Thimjon/CFO, Jim Myers/Pres. - Sky Tel, Wireless, Jim Schulteis/Branch Mgr., Mitchell I. Rosen/Contact/$380,018.00, Bob Berwanger/Exec. VP - Operations, Brad Richards/Exec. VP - Skytel, Fred Parker/Sr. VP - Human Resources, Mark J. Kelson/Sec.

Directors: John A. Fellows/43/Dir., CEO, Pres., Mark E. Schwarz/Chmn., James L. Lawson/Dir., Michael R. Parks/Dir.

Owners: Loeb Partners Corporation/11.20%, Dimensional Fund Advisors Inc./6.80%, Kevin J. Thimjon, Mark E. Schwarz/22.30%, Insiders/26.00%, John A. Fellows/4.50%, Royce & Associates, LLC/10.00%, James L. Lawson, Daniel Zeff/8.30%, Michael R. Parks, Advisory Research, Inc./5.20%

Financial Data: ***Fiscal Year End:***12/31 ***Latest Annual Data:*** 12/31/2006

Year		Sales		Net Income
2006		$120,296,000		-$2,893,000
2005		$130,936,000		-$799,000
2004		$143,954,000		-$953,000
Curr. Assets:	$32,781,000	***Curr. Liab.:***	$21,238,000	
Plant, Equip.:	$3,553,000	***Total Liab.:***	$24,860,000	***Indic. Yr. Divd.:*** NA
Total Assets:	$43,114,000	***Net Worth:***	$18,254,000	***Debt/ Equity:*** NA

Bell Microproducts Inc

1941 Ringwood Ave., San Jose, CA, 95131; ***PH:*** 1-408-451-9400; ***Fax:*** 1-408-451-1600; ***http://*** www.bellmicro.com

General - Incorporation	CA	***Stock***- Price on:12/24/2007	$6.52
Employees	1,827	Stock Exchange	NDQ
Auditor	PricewaterhouseCoopers LLP	Ticker Symbol	BELM
Stk Agt	Mellon Investor Services	Outstanding Shares	30,410,000
Counsel	NA	E.P.S	-$0.37
DUNS No.	18-331-2321	Shareholders	NA

General - Incorporation	CA	*Stock*- Price on:12/24/2007	$6.52
Employees	1,827	Stock Exchange	NDQ
Auditor	PricewaterhouseCoopers LLP	Ticker Symbol	BELM
Stk Agt	Mellon Investor Services	Outstanding Shares	30,410,000
Counsel	NA	E.P.S.	-$0.37
DUNS No.	18-331-2321	Shareholders	NA

Business: The group's principle activity is to distribute value-added storage products and systems, computer products, semiconductors and peripherals. The products include semiconductor components such as memory components, microprocessors, peripheral and speciality components and computer products such as disk, tape libraries and optical drives. The group also provides system design, integration, installation, maintenance and other consulting services along with the products. The group handles over 130 brand lines as well as its own brands consisting of rorke data storage products and markvision memory modules. The group markets its products to original equipment manufacturers, value-added resellers and dealers in the United States, Europe, Canada and Latin America. On 15-Oct-2003, the group acquired ebm mayorista and on 22-Jun-2004, it also acquired openpsl ltd.

Primary SIC and add'l.: 5065 5045

CIK No: 0000900708

Subsidiaries: Bell Microproducts (US) Limited, Bell Microproducts AB, Bell Microproducts ApS, Bell Microproducts B.V., Bell Microproducts Brazil Holdings, LLC, Bell Microproducts BVBA, Bell Microproducts Canada Inc., Bell Microproducts Canada—Tenex Data ULC, Bell Microproducts do Brasil, Ltda., Bell Microproducts Europe B.V., Bell Microproducts Europe Export Limited, Bell Microproducts Europe Holding B.V., Bell Microproducts Europe Inc., Bell Microproducts Europe Partners C.V., Bell Microproducts Funding Corporation 37 Subsidiaries included in the Index

Officers: Donald W. Bell/Chmn., CEO, Pres., Robert J. Sturgeon/CIO, VP - Operations, Richard J. Jacquet/Sr. VP - Human Resources, Graeme Watt/Pres. - Bell Microproducts Europe, Jim Illson/COO, Pres. - Americas, Andrew Hughes/VP, General Counsel, Sec., Bill Meyers/CFO, Exec. VP

Directors: Donald W. Bell/Chmn., CEO, Pres., James Ousley/Dir., David M. Ernsberger/Dir., Eugene B. Chaiken/Dir., Gordon Campbell/Dir., Edward L. Gelbach/Dir., Glen E. Penisten/Dir., Mark L. Sanders/Dir., Mike Grainger/Dir.

Financial Data: Fiscal Year End:12/31   Latest Annual Data: 12/31/2005

Year	Sales		Net Income
2005	$3,193,833,000		$481,000
2004	$2,827,777,000		$11,337,000
2003	$2,230,287,000		-$4,474,000
Curr. Assets:	$798,675,000	*Curr. Liab.:*	$452,493,000
Plant, Equip.:	$13,212,000	*Total Liab.:*	$712,951,000	*Indic. Yr. Divd.:*	NA
Total Assets:	$933,332,000	*Net Worth:*	$220,381,000	*Debt/ Equity:*	1.0492

Belo Corp

400 S Record St., Ste. 600, Dallas, TX, 75202; *PH:* 1-214-977-6606; *Fax:* 1-214-977-6603; http:// www.belo.com

General - Incorporation	DE	*Stock*- Price on:12/24/2007	$21.86
Employees	6,200	Stock Exchange	NYSE
Auditor	Ernst & Young LLP	Ticker Symbol	BLC
Stk Agt	Bank of New York	Outstanding Shares	102,250,000
Counsel	NA	E.P.S.	$1.19
DUNS No.	00-734-0078	Shareholders	NA

Business: The groups principle activity is to provide media services. The group operates through two business segments namely the television and the newspaper group. The group operates from United States.

Primary SIC and add'l.: 4833 4841 2711 7375 7812

CIK No: 0000356080

Subsidiaries: Al Dia, Inc., Arizona NewsChannel, LLC, Belo Advertising Customer Services, Inc., Belo Capital Bureau, Inc., Belo CNC, Inc., Belo Company, Belo Enterprises, Inc., Belo Expositions, Inc., Belo Havana Bureau, Inc., Belo HG Company, Inc., Belo HNC General Partner, Inc., Belo HNC Limited Partner, Inc., Belo Holdings, Inc., Belo Interactive, Inc., Belo Investment Corporation 97 Subsidiaries included in the Index

Officers: Robert W. Decherd/Chmn., CEO/$5,739,493.00, James M. Moroney/Publisher, CEO - Dallas Morning News, Guy H. Kerr/Sr. VP, General Counsel, Sec./$1,257,597.00, Carey P. Hendrickson/VP - Human Resources, Richard J. Keilty/Sr. VP, Dennis A. Williamson/60/CFO, Exec. VP/$1,730,610.00, Peter L. Diaz/Sr. VP, Donald F. Cass/Exec. VP, Dunia A. Shive/47/COO, Pres./$1,743,527.00, Marian Spitzberg/59/Sr. VP - Human Resources, Alison K. Engel/VP, Corporate Controller, Anna R. Nicodemus/VP - Internal Audit, David M. Duitch/VP - Capital Bureau, Paul R. Fry/VP - Investor Relations, Corporate Communications, John P. Irvin/VP - Facilities Planning *(20 Officers included in Index)*

Directors: Robert W. Decherd/Chmn., CEO, John L. Sander/Vice Chmn., Lloyd D. Ward/Dir., France A. Cordova/60/Dir., Judith L. Craven/Dir., Louis E. Caldera/Dir., Henry P. Becton/Dir., Anne M. Szostak/Dir., Williams J. McDonald/66/Dir., Douglas G. Carlston/Dir., William T. Solomon/Dir., Wayne R. Sanders/Dir., Laurence E. Hirsch/Dir., Dealey D. Herndon/Dir.

Owners: Henry P. Becton, Judith L. Craven, John L. (Jack) Sander/6.40%, John L. (Jack) Sander, Robert W. Decherd, Dealey D. Herndon, Judith L. Craven, Judith L. Craven, Insiders/85.10%, Anne M. Szostak, John L. (Jack) Sander, Dennis A. Williamson/2.20%, France A. Cordova, Henry P. Becton, Insiders/1.20% *(49 Owners included in Index)*

Financial Data: Fiscal Year End:12/31   Latest Annual Data: 06/30/2007

Year	Sales		Net Income
2007	NA		NA
2006	NA		NA
2005	$1,521,234,000		$127,688,000
Curr. Assets:	$384,163,000	*Curr. Liab.:*	$258,912,000	*P/E Ratio:*	17.49
Plant, Equip.:	$560,494,000	*Total Liab.:*	$2,087,130,000	*Indic. Yr. Divd.:*	$0.500
Total Assets:	$3,614,278,000	*Net Worth:*	$1,527,148,000	*Debt/ Equity:*	0.8386

Bema Gold Corp

3100 Three Bentall Ctr., Vancouver, BC, V7X 1J1; *PH:* 1-604-623-4700; http:// www.bema.com

General - Incorporation	Canada	*Stock*- Price on:12/24/2007	NA
Employees	1,938	Stock Exchange	NA
Auditor	PricewaterhouseCoopers LLP	Ticker Symbol	NA
Stk Agt	Computershare Investor Services LLC	Outstanding Shares	NA
Counsel	Axium Law Corp	E.P.S.	NA
DUNS No.	24-777-3815	Shareholders	NA

Business: The group's principal activities are to explore, mining, extraction, processing and reclamation of gold. The product is produced in Russia and Chile with exploration activities carried out in Canada, Chile and the United States.

Primary SIC and add'l.: 1041

CIK No: 0000879338

Subsidiaries: Arian Resources Limited, Bema Gold (Bermuda) Ltd., Bema Gold (US) Inc., Bema South Africa (Pty) Ltd (Bema SA)., BGO (Bermuda) Ltd., Chimera Mines and Minerals Corp., Chukotka Mining & Geological Company (CMGC), Compania Minera Casale (CMC), Compania Minera Maricunga (Maricunga), Compania Minera San Damian, Consolidated Puma Minerals Corp. (Puma), Consolidated Westview Corporation, EAGC Ventures Corp. (EAGC), Kupol Au-Ag (Barbados) Inc., Kupol Ventures Limited 20 Subsidiaries included in the Index

Bemis Co Inc

1 Neenah Ctr., Neenah, WI, 54957; *PH:* 1-920-727-4100; *Fax:* 1-920-527-7600; http:// www.bemis.com; *Email:* contactbemis@bemis.com

General - Incorporation	MO	*Stock*- Price on:12/24/2007	$33.19
Employees	15,736	Stock Exchange	NYSE
Auditor	PricewaterhouseCoopers LLP	Ticker Symbol	BMS
Stk Agt	Wells Fargo Bank Minnesota N.A	Outstanding Shares	104,590,000
Counsel	Faegre & Benson	E.P.S.	$1.71
DUNS No.	00-647-7061	Shareholders	NA

Business: The groups principle activities include providing flexible packaging and manufacturing pressure sensitive materials for labels, decoration and signage. The group operates from United States.

Primary SIC and add'l.: 2672 2671

CIK No: 0000011199

Subsidiaries: American Packaging S.A., American Plast S.A., Banner Packaging, Inc., Bemis Asia Pacific Sdn Bhd, Bemis Clysar, Inc., Bemis Coordination Center S.A., Bemis Czech Republic, s.r.o., Bemis Deutschland Holdings GmbH, Bemis Elsham Limited, Bemis Epernon S.A.S., Bemis Europe Holdings, S.A., Bemis Flexible Packaging de Mexico, S.A. de C.V., Bemis Flexible Packaging Mexico Servicios, S.A. de C.V., Bemis France Holdings S.A.S., Bemis Hungary Trading Limited Liability Company 79 Subsidiaries included in the Index

Officers: Jeffrey H. Curler/Chmn., CEO, Pres./$5,799,180.00, William F. Austen/VP - Operations/$1,550,103.00, Stanley A. Jaffy/VP, Controller, Melanie E.R. Miller/VP, Treasurer, Gene H. Seashore/VP - Human Resources/$1,381,768.00, James J. Seifert/VP, General Counsel, Sec., Henry J. Theisen/Dir., COO, Exec. VP/$2,639,603.00, Gene C. Wulf/Dir., CFO, Sr. VP/$1,925,618.00, Eugene H. Seashore/58/VP - Human Resources, James W. Ransom/VP - Operations, Robert F. Hawthorne/VP - Operations

Directors: Jeffrey H. Curler/Chmn., CEO, Pres., William J. Scholle/Dir., Roger D. O'Shaughnessy/Dir., Philip G. Weaver/Dir., David S. Haffner/Dir., Barbara L. Johnson/Dir., Edward N. Perry/Dir., William J. Bolton/Dir., Henry J. Theisen/Dir., COO, Exec. VP, Nancy P. McDonald/Dir., Timothy M. Manganello/Dir., Gene C. Wulf/Dir., CFO, Sr. VP, Paul S. Peercy/Dir.

Owners: Roger D. OShaughnessy, Nancy P. McDonald, David S. Haffner, William J. Bolton, Gene C. Wulf, Barbara L. Johnson, Gene H. Seashore, Philip G. Weaver, Insiders/4.40%, Paul S. Peercy, Edward N. Perry, William J. Scholle, William F. Austen, Henry J. Theisen, Timothy M. Manganello *(16 Owners included in Index)*

Financial Data: Fiscal Year End:12/31   Latest Annual Data: 12/31/2006

Year	Sales		Net Income
2006	$3,639,363,000		$176,296,000
2005	$3,473,950,000		$162,529,000
2004	$2,834,394,000		$179,967,000
Curr. Assets:	$1,093,712,000	*Curr. Liab.:*	$555,455,000	*P/E Ratio:*	18.97
Plant, Equip.:	$1,175,959,000	*Total Liab.:*	$1,537,808,000	*Indic. Yr. Divd.:*	$0.840
Total Assets:	$3,039,009,000	*Net Worth:*	$1,472,016,000	*Debt/ Equity:*	0.5232

Ben Franklin Financial Inc

14 N Dryden Pl., Arlington Heights, IL , 33309; *PH:* 1-412-366-8502; http:// www.benfrankbank.com

General - Incorporation	Federal	*Stock*- Price on:12/24/2007	$10.35
Employees	29	Stock Exchange	OTC
Auditor	Crowe Chizek & Co. LLC	Ticker Symbol	BFFI
Stk Agt	Registrar & Transfer Co	Outstanding Shares	NA
Counsel	NA	E.P.S.	$0.02
DUNS No.	NA	Shareholders	NA

Business: The group operates through its subsidiary whose principal activity is banking business. The group products include real estate loans, commercial real estate loans, home equity lines-of-credit, construction and land loans and other loans. The group operates from the United States. The groups asset in the year 2006 was $ 15,712.

Primary SIC and add'l.: 6162

CIK No: 0001366925

Subsidiaries: Ben Franklin Bank of Illinois

Owners: Robert E. DeCelles, Glen A. Miller, John R. Perkins, Ben Franklin Financial, MHC/55.00%, James M. Reninger, Steven C. Sjogren/1.05%, Nicholas J. Raino, Bernadine V. Dziedzic, Robin L. Jenkins, Angie Plesiotis, Insiders/58.90%

Financial Data: Fiscal Year End:12/31   Latest Annual Data: 12/31/2006

Year	Sales		Net Income
2006	$6,588,000		$131,000
Curr. Assets:	$21,140,000	*Curr. Liab.:*	$102,193,000		
Plant, Equip.:	$597,000	*Total Liab.:*	$103,207,000	*Indic. Yr. Divd.:*	NA
Total Assets:	$118,901,000	*Net Worth:*	$15,694,000	*Debt/ Equity:*	NA

Benchmark Bankshares Inc VA

100 S Broad St., Kenbridge, VA, 23944; *PH:* 1-804-676-8444; http:// www.bcbonline.com

General - Incorporation	VA	*Stock*- Price on:12/24/2007	$17
Employees	NA	Stock Exchange	OTC
Auditor	NA	Ticker Symbol	BMBN
Stk Agt	Benchmark Bankshares Inc. VA	Outstanding Shares	2,730,000
Counsel	NA	E.P.S.	$1.36
DUNS No.	NA	Shareholders	NA

Business: The groups principle activity is to provide banking products and services. The group provides services include Internet banking, personal banking, commercial banking and 24 hour banking. The group operates from United States.

Primary SIC and add'l.: 6022

CIK No: 0000804563

Officers: Mike Walker/CEO, Pres., Jay Stafford/Sr. VP, Branch Administrator, Janice Pernell/Sr. VP, Sr. VP, Compliance Officer

Financial Data: ***Fiscal Year End:***12/31 ***Latest Annual Data:*** 12/31/2003

Year	Sales	Net Income
2003	$18,261,000	$3,596,000
2002	$18,442,000	$3,398,000
2001	$18,444,000	$2,736,000

Curr. Assets:	$29,853,000	***Curr. Liab.:***	$254,491,000	***P/E Ratio:***	12.32
Plant, Equip.:	$4,638,000	***Total Liab.:***	$255,273,000	***Indic. Yr. Divd.:***	$0.540
Total Assets:	$283,886,000	***Net Worth:***	$28,613,000	***Debt/ Equity:***	NA

Benchmark Electronics Inc

3000 Technology Dr., Angleton, TX, 77515; ***PH:*** 1-979-849-6550; ***Fax:*** 1-979-848-5270; ***http://*** www.bench.com

General - Incorporation	TX	***Stock***- Price on:12/24/2007	$23.13
Employees	9,548	Stock Exchange	NYSE
Auditor	KPMG LLP	Ticker Symbol	BHE
Stk Agt	Computershare Trust Co	Outstanding Shares	72,630,000
Counsel	Cravath, Swaine & Moore LLP	E.P.S	$1.57
DUNS No.	02-479-2194	Shareholders	NA

Business: The groups principle activity is to provide engineering and manufacturing services. The groups services include account management, product life cycle and product development services. The group operates from United States.

Primary SIC and add'l.: 3672 7373

CIK No: 0000863436

Subsidiaries: ACT Manufacturing Holdings UK Limited, AVEX Constitution, Inc, AVEX Liberty, Inc., BEI Electronics Ireland Ltd., Benchmark BV Holdings, Inc, Benchmark Electronics (Suzhou) Co., Ltd., Benchmark Electronics (Thailand) Public Company Limited, Benchmark Electronics AB, Benchmark Electronics California, Benchmark Electronics Company, Benchmark Electronics de Mexico, Benchmark Electronics Delaware Corp, Benchmark Electronics England, Benchmark Electronics FSC, Inc, Benchmark Electronics GmbH 26 Subsidiaries included in the Index

Officers: Cary T. Fu/Dir., CEO/$1,938,214.00, Steven A. Barton/Dir., Exec. VP, Gayla Delly/Pres./$1,235,528.00, Marco A.F. Aguilar/Contact - Brazil, Jeroen Tuik/GM - Almelo, The Netherlands, Kenneth S. Barrow/Sec., Donald F. Adam/CFO/$307,475.00, Shannon Speers/GM - Angleton, Texas

Directors: Cary T. Fu/Dir., CEO, Donald E. Nigbor/Chmn., Peter G. Dorflinger/Dir., Douglas G. Duncan/Dir., Michael R. Dawson/Dir., Bernee D.L. Strom/Dir., Steven A. Barton/Dir., Exec. VP, Laura W. Lang/Dir.

Owners: FMR Corp./5.50%, Wellington Management Company, LLP/5.70%, Steven A. Barton, Insiders/3.40%, Royce & Associates, LLC/5.30%, Donald E. Nigbor, Douglas G. Duncan, Peter G. Dorflinger, Bernee D.L. Strom, Cary T. Fu/1.80%, EARNEST Partners, LLC/6.10%, Gayla J. Delly, Michael R. Dawson, Laura W. Lang, Donald F. Adam

Financial Data: ***Fiscal Year End:***12/31 ***Latest Annual Data:*** 12/31/2006

Year	Sales	Net Income
2006	$2,907,304,000	$111,677,000
2005	$2,257,225,000	$80,589,000
2004	$2,001,340,000	$70,991,000

Curr. Assets:	$1,170,610,000	***Curr. Liab.:***	$409,718,000	***P/E Ratio:***	14.73
Plant, Equip.:	$110,912,000	***Total Liab.:***	$421,098,000	***Indic. Yr. Divd.:***	NA
Total Assets:	$1,406,120,000	***Net Worth:***	$985,022,000	***Debt/ Equity:***	0.0100

Benetton Group SpA

Villa Minelli, Ponzano, 31050; ***PH:*** 39-422519111; ***http://*** www.benetton.com; ***Email:*** investor@benetton.it

General - Incorporation	Italy	***Stock***- Price on:12/24/2007	$33.89
Employees	7,269	Stock Exchange	OTC
Auditor	PricewaterhouseCoopers S.P.A	Ticker Symbol	BNG
Stk Agt	Morgan ADR Service Center	Outstanding Shares	91,340,000
Counsel	NA	E.P.S	$1.88
DUNS No.	43-052-9545	Shareholders	NA

Business: The group's principle activities include manufacturing and marketing wool, cotton and denim clothing, shoes, accessories. The group is present in approximately 120 countries worldwide. The group operates from United States.

Primary SIC and add'l.: 2321 3949 2389 2329 2281 2331 3149

CIK No: 0000849314

Subsidiaries: Benair S.p.A., Bencom S.r.l., Benetton 2 Retail Comrcio de Produtos Txteis S.A., Benetton Asia Pacific Ltd., Benetton Australia Pty. Ltd., Benetton Austria GmbH, Benetton Beograd D.O.O., Benetton Commerciale Tunisie S. r.l., Benetton Croatia D.O.O., Benetton Denmark A.p.S., Benetton Deutschland GmbH, Benetton France Commercial S.A.S, Benetton France S. r.l., Benetton Giyim Sanayi ve Ticaret A.S., Benetton Holding International N.V. S.A. 54 Subsidiaries included in the Index

Officers: Gerolamo Caccia Dominioni/53/Dir., CEO, Angelo Casa/68/Chmn., Statutory Auditor, Alessandro Benetton/44/Dep. Chmn., Marco Leotta/52/Alternate Statutory Auditor, Maximo Ibarra/40/Dir. - Marketing, Strategy, Adolfo Pastorelli/52/CIO, Mara Di Giorgio/Head - Investor Relations, Piermauro Carabellese/50/Alternate Statutory Auditor, Antonio Cortellazzo/71/Statutory Auditor, Andrea Negrin/45/Chief - Human Resources, Biagio Chiarolanza/46/COO, Ariodante Valeri/53/Dir. - Sales, Vincenzo Scognamiglio/44/Product Mgr. - United Colors, Benetton, The Hip Site Lines, Barbara Razzini/Contact - Investor Relations, Samantha Loy/Investor Relations Assist. *(19 Officers included in Index)*

Directors: Gerolamo Caccia Dominioni/53/Dir., CEO, Luciano Benetton/73/Chmn., Carlo Benetton/65/Dep. Chmn., Alessandro Benetton/44/Dep. Chmn., Ulrich Weiss/72/Dir., Luigi Arturo Bianchi/50/Dir., Giuliana Benetton/71/Dir., Gilberto Benetton/67/Dir., Giorgio Brunetti/71/Dir., Gianni Mion/65/Dir., Robert Singer/56/Dir., Alfredo Malguzzi/46/Dir.

Owners: Edizione Holding S.p.A., Alessandro Benetton, Ulrich Weiss

Financial Data: ***Fiscal Year End:***12/31 ***Latest Annual Data:*** 12/31/2006

Year	Sales	Net Income
2006	$2,523,060,000	$131,774,000
2005	$2,230,241,000	$113,680,000
2004	$2,404,947,000	$145,953,000

Curr. Assets:	$1,688,144,000	***Curr. Liab.:***	$1,463,656,000		
Plant, Equip.:	$1,071,488,000	***Total Liab.:***	$1,616,335,000	***Indic. Yr. Divd.:***	$0.730
Total Assets:	$3,331,105,000	***Net Worth:***	$1,685,344,000	***Debt/ Equity:***	NA

Benihana Inc

8685 NW 53rd Ter., Miami, FL, 33166; ***PH:*** 1-305-593-0770; ***Fax:*** 1-305-592-6371; ***http://*** www.benihana.com

General - Incorporation	DE	***Stock***- Price on:12/24/2007	$22.27
Employees	NA	Stock Exchange	NDQ
Auditor	Deloitte & Touche LLP	Ticker Symbol	BNHN
Stk Agt	American Stock Transfer & Trust Co.	Outstanding Shares	NA
Counsel	Dornbush Mensch Mandelstam	E.P.S	$0.82
DUNS No.	00-394-7512	Shareholders	NA

Business: The group's principal activity is to operate a chain of Japanese concept restaurants. These restaurants offer teppanyaki-style Japanese cooking, which consists of preparation of fresh steak, chicken and seafood. The Haru concept of cooking offers menu of Japanese fusion dishes in an urban atmosphere. In addition to traditional, high quality sushi and sashimi creations, Haru offers raw bar items and Japanese cuisine, including New York strip steak with wasabi croquette, spicy shallots and ginger sauce, garlic shrimp and crispy duck. The group owns and operates 56 dinner house restaurants and franchises 22 restaurants. The group also owns and operates five Haru concept restaurants, four Sushi concept restaurants and one Doraku concept restaurants.

Primary SIC and add'l.: 6794 5812

CIK No: 0000935226

Officers: Joel A. Schwartz/Chmn., CEO, Pres., Darwin C. Dornbush/Sec., Vlad Rogov/Mgr. - Moscow, Taka Yoshimoto/Dir., Exec. VP - Restaurant Operations, Jose Ortega/VP - Finance, CFO, Masanobu Tamura/Mgr. - Toronto, Laureen Kuniyoshi/Mgr. - Seattle, Mike Izutani/Mgr. - Beaverton, Nori Nishihama/Mgr. - Las Vegas, Teddy Kojoh/Mgr. - Anaheim, Bal Tejada/Mgr. - Beverly Hills, June Shimabuku/Mgr. - Burlingame, Hisayo Kimura/Mgr. - Carlsbad, Andrew Wong/Mgr. - City, Industry, Ted Akaosugi/Mgr. - Concord *(87 Officers included in Index)*

Directors: Joel A. Schwartz/Chmn., CEO, Pres., John E. Abdo/Dir., Ronald J. Castell/Dir., Lewis Jaffe/Dir., Kevin Y. Aoki/Dir., Taka Yoshimoto/Dir., Exec. VP - Restaurant Operations, Norman Becker/Dir., Robert B. Sturges/Dir., Joseph J. West/Dir.

Owners: Insiders, Joseph J. West, Norman Becker, John E. Abdo, Michael R. Burris, Lewis Jaffe, Robert B. Sturges, John E. Abdo/1.00%, Grace Aoki, Management, LLC/5.70%, Taka Yoshimoto/1.30%, Insiders/8.00%, Joseph J. West, Ronald J. Castell, Robert B. Sturges *(32 Owners included in Index)*

Financial Data: ***Fiscal Year End:***03/26 ***Latest Annual Data:*** 04/01/2007

Year	Sales	Net Income
2007	$272,649,000	$14,495,000
2006	$272,649,000	$14,495,000
2005	$218,331,000	$7,820,000

Curr. Assets:	$21,534,000	***Curr. Liab.:***	$33,835,000		
Plant, Equip.:	$146,479,000	***Total Liab.:***	$42,446,000	***Indic. Yr. Divd.:***	NA
Total Assets:	$204,289,000	***Net Worth:***	$142,482,000	***Debt/ Equity:***	NA

Benjamin Franklin Bancorp Inc

58 Main St., Franklin, MA, 02038; ***PH:*** 1-508-528-7000; ***Fax:*** 1-508-520-8364; ***http://*** www.benfranklinbank.com

General - Incorporation	MA	***Stock***- Price on:12/24/2007	$15.01
Employees	143	Stock Exchange	NDQ
Auditor	Wolf & Company, P.C.	Ticker Symbol	BFBC
Stk Agt	American Stock Transfer & Trust Co.	Outstanding Shares	8,180,000
Counsel	NA	E.P.S	$0.46
DUNS No.	NA	Shareholders	NA

Business: The group operates through its subsidiaries whose principle activity is to provide financial products and services. The groups services include residential mortgages, commercial real estate loans, construction loans, commercial business loans and consumer loans, and investment and mortgage backed securities and ATMs. The group operates from Franklin, Foxboro, Bellingham, Milford, Medfield, Waltham, Wellesley, and Newton. The assets of the group for the year 2006 were $913,678 (thousands).

Primary SIC and add'l.: 6036 6712

CIK No: 0001302176

Subsidiaries: Benjamin Franklin Bank Capital Trust I, Benjamin Franklin Securities Corp, Creative Strategic Solutions, Inc.

Officers: Thomas R. Venables/Dir., CEO, Pres., Barbara Schrader/Assist. VP, Accounting Mgr., Rose M. Buckley/Sr. VP, Sr. Loan Officer, Brian E. Ledwith/39/VP, Sr. Retail Lending Officer - Benjamin Franklin Bank, Armand A. Fernandez/VP, Business Relationship Mgr., Jason Trepanier/Secondary Marketing Officer, Pasqual Kioumejian/VP, Commercial Loan Officer, Lisa M. Sax/Assist. VP - BSA, Bank Security Officer, Jeffrey R. Guimond/VP - Sr. Retail Lender, Loan Operations, Karen M. Niro/VP - Systems, Operations, Laura Reed/Loan Origination Officer, Mary C. Buck/Loan Origination Officer, Team Leader, Sharon Quinn/Cash Management Dir., Daisy S. Siddiqui/Assist. VP, Community Banking Officer - Wellesley, George M. Ellis/Loan Origination Officer *(52 Officers included in Index)*

Directors: Thomas R. Venables/Dir., CEO, Pres., Alfred H. Wahlers/Chmn., William F. Brady/Vice Chmn., Anne M. King/Dir., Clerk - Corporation, Mary Ambler/Dir., William Bissonnette/Dir., Richard Bolton/Dir., Paul E. Capasso/Dir., Jonathan Haynes/Dir., Charles Yergalian/Dir., Daniel F. O'Brien/Dir., Charles Oteri/Dir., Donald Quinn/Dir., Neil Todreas/Dir.

Owners: Charles F. Oteri, Paul E. Capasso/1.05%, William F. Brady, Richard E. Bolton, Anne M. King, Daniel F. OBrien, Michael J. Piemonte, Neil E. Todreas/1.26%, John C. Fuller, Claire S. Bean, Thomas R. Venables/1.24%, Richard D. Mann, Donald P. Quinn, Wellington Management Company, LLP/8.23%, Insiders/10.48% *(24 Owners included in Index)*

Financial Data: ***Fiscal Year End:***12/31 ***Latest Annual Data:*** 12/31/2006

Year	Sales	Net Income
2006	$50,333,000	$4,740,000
2005	$39,642,000	$431,000
2003	$22,608,000	$1,688,000

Curr. Assets:	$76,075,000	Curr. Liab.:	$643,179,000		
Plant, Equip.:	$5,202,000	Total Liab.:	$804,273,000	Indic. Yr. Divd:	$0.240
Total Assets:	$913,678,000	Net Worth:	$109,405,000	Debt/ Equity:	1.2748

Bennett Environmental Inc

1540 Cornwall Rd., Ste. 208, Oakville, ON, L6J 7W5; *PH:* 1-905-339-1540; *Fax:* 1-905-339-0016; *http://* www.bennettenv.com; *Email:* info@bennettenv.com

General - Incorporation	Canada	**Stock** - Price on:12/24/2007	$0.3333
Employees	79	Stock Exchange	OTC
Auditor	KPMG LLP	Ticker Symbol	BEVFF
Stk Agt	Computershare Trust Co	Outstanding Shares	NA
Counsel	Borden, Ladner, Gervais	E.P.S.	NA
DUNS No.	NA	Shareholders	NA

Business: The group's principal activity is to remediate contaminated soil. The group also designs, manufactures and distributes thermal oxidizing equipment and other pollution control equipment. This equipment is used in remediation of contaminated soils and the incineration of waste materials. The group's operation are spread throughout Canada and the United States.

Primary SIC and add'l.: 3569 0711

CIK No: 0001048295

Subsidiaries: Bennett Environmental New Brunswick Inc., Material Resources Recovery S.R.B.P. Inc, Reupre Sol Inc

Officers: Jack Shaw/Dir., CEO, Pres., Fred Cranston/CFO, Bernd Christmas/Dir., Pres., Wendy Ford/Corporate Controller, Peter Demeter/Sr. Dir. - Canadian Sales, Marketing, Wes Hicks/Dir. - Canadian Sales, Bill Eaton/Dir. - Sales, Marketing, Northern US, Jim Dilts/Dir. - Sales, Marketing, Southeast, US

Directors: Jack Shaw/Dir., CEO, Pres., Christopher S. Wallace/Chmn., Michael F. Blair/Dir., Benoit Bouchard/Dir., Bernd Christmas/Dir., Pres., Michael Fleischer/Dir., Ralph T. Neville/Dir.

Bentley Pharmaceuticals Inc

2 Holland Way, Exeter, NH, 03833; *PH:* 1-603-658-6100; *Fax:* 1-603-658-6101; *http://* www.bentleypharm.com

General - Incorporation	DE	**Stock** - Price on:12/24/2007	$13.25
Employees	442	Stock Exchange	NYSE
Auditor	Deloitte & Touche LLP	Ticker Symbol	BNT
Stk Agt	Mellon Shareholder Services	Outstanding Shares	22,270,000
Counsel	Jenkens & Gilchrist Parker Chapin	E.P.S.	$0.01
DUNS No.	06-966-6733	Shareholders	NA

Business: The group's principle activity is carried out through two segments: research, development and licensing/commercialization of advanced drug delivery technologies and pharmaceutical products and manufacturing and selling of generic and branded pharmaceutical products. The group's research and development segment based in the United States, develops products incorporating proprietary technologies and seeks to form strategic alliances with pharmaceutical and biotechnology companies to facilitate the development and commercialization of its products. The product sales segment based in Spain, manufactures and markets branded and generic pharmaceutical products within four primary therapeutic areas: cardiovascular, gastrointestinal, infectious and neurological diseases. The group's quarterly revenue for September 2007 was 27.35 millions of USD.

Primary SIC and add'l.: 2834

CIK No: 0000821616

Subsidiaries: B.O.G. International Finance,Inc., Belmac A.I.,Inc., Belmac Health Corporation, Belmac Holdings,Inc., Belmac Hygiene,Inc., Belmac Jamaica, Ltd., Bentley A.P.I. S.L., Bentley Healthcare Corporation, Bentley Park, LLC, Bentley Pharmaceuticals Ireland Limited, Laboratorios Belmac S.A., Laboratorios Davur S.L., Laboratorios Rimafar S.L., Pharma de Espana,Inc.

Officers: James R. Murphy/Chmn., CEO/$1,089,980.00, Robert M. Stote/Sr. VP, Chief Medical Officer, Robert P. Hebert/Controller, Assist. Treasurer, Assist. Sec., Adolfo Herrera/MD - European Subsidiaries/$759,571.00, Richard P. Lindsay/VP, CFO, Sec., Treasurer/$106,183.00, Fred Feldman/VP - Research, Development, David C. Brush/VP - Business Development, Strategic Planning, Jim Buckley/Exec. VP - Investor Relations, John A. Sedor/Pres./$687,120.00

Directors: James R. Murphy/Chmn., CEO, Michael McGovern/Vice Chmn., John W. Spiegel/Dir., Charles L. Bolling/Dir., Miguel Fernandez/Dir., Edward J. Robinson/Dir., Ross F. Johnson/Dir.

Owners: James R. Murphy/4.50%, Michael D. Price/1.60%, Adolfo Herrera/1.50%, Michael McGovern/14.40%, John W. Spiegel, John A. Sedor, Ross F. Johnson, Insiders/21.60%, Richard P. Lindsay, Luther King Capital Management Corporation/6.50%, Edward J. Robinson, ClearBridge Advisors, LLC/12.10%, Miguel Fernandez

Financial Data: *Fiscal Year End:*12/31 **Latest Annual Data:** 03/31/2007

Year		Sales		Net Income
2007		$31,391,000		$2,360,000
2006		$27,054,000		$4,414,000
2005		$97,730,000		$10,919,000
Curr. Assets:	$67,690,000	Curr. Liab.:	$27,387,000	P/E Ratio: 132.50
Plant, Equip.:	$48,556,000	Total Liab.:	$34,025,000	Indic. Yr. Divd: NA
Total Assets:	$134,356,000	Net Worth:	$100,331,000	Debt/ Equity: NA

BEO Bancorp OR

250 NW Gale, Heppner, OR, 97836; *PH:* 1-541-676-9125; *Fax:* 1-541-676-5541; *http://* www.beobank.com

General - Incorporation	NA	**Stock** - Price on:12/24/2007	NA
Employees	NA	Stock Exchange	OTC
Auditor	NA	Ticker Symbol	BEOB
Stk Agt	NA	Outstanding Shares	NA
Counsel	NA	E.P.S.	NA
DUNS No.	NA	Shareholders	NA

Business: The groups principal activity is to provide banking business. The group financial products include savings and fixed deposits, on line, personal, commercial lending and business banking. The group operates from the United States.

Primary SIC and add'l.: 6022 6712

CIK No:

Berkeley Technology Ltd

650 California St., 26th Fl., San Francisco, CA, 94108; *PH:* 1-415-249-0450; *http://* www.berkeleyvc.com; *Email:* info@berkeleyvc.com

General - Incorporation	Channel Is.	**Stock** - Price on:12/24/2007	$0.8
Employees	NA	Stock Exchange	OTC
Auditor	BDO Seidman LLP	Ticker Symbol	BKLYY
Stk Agt	Bank of New York	Outstanding Shares	NA
Counsel	NA	E.P.S.	NA
DUNS No.	22-618-8068	Shareholders	NA

Business: The group's principal activities are the provision of life insurance and annuities, and venture capital and consulting.

Primary SIC and add'l.: 6799 6311 6722 6726

CIK No: 0000891377

Subsidiaries: Berkeley (USA) Holdings Limited, Berkeley Institutional Investment, Inc., Berkeley International Advisors, Inc., Berkeley International Asset Management, Berkeley International Capital Corporation, Berkeley International Capital Limited, Berkeley International Limited, Berkeley International Technologies, Inc., Berkeley Technology Limited, Frederick Morgan & Co. Limited, London Pacific Advisers Limited, London Pacific Assurance Limited, London Pacific Secretaries Limited, London Pacific Trust Company Limited, LPAL Investments Limited

Officers: Arthur I. Trueger/Chmn., Founder, Principal Executive Officer/$300,000.00, Robert A. Cornman/Sec., Ian K. Whitehead/CFO/$366,009.00, Halsted W. Wheeler/Principals, Berkeley International Capital Corporation, Michael J. Mayer/Principals, Berkeley International Capital Corporation

Directors: Arthur I. Trueger/Chmn., Founder, Principal Executive Officer, Victor A. Hebert/71/Dep. Chmn., Lord Trenchard/57/Dir., Harold E. Hughes/Dir.

Owners: Fund, L.P./8.70%, The London Pacific Group/20.30%, Harold E. Hughes, The Viscount Trenchard, BVI, Ltd./6.30%, Ian K. Whitehead/2.60%, Arthur I. Trueger/33.00%, Peter Gyllenhammar/6.40%, Victor A. Hebert, Insiders/35.80%

Financial Data: *Fiscal Year End:*12/31 **Latest Annual Data:** 12/31/2006

Year		Sales		Net Income
2006		$1,943,000		-$3,683,000
2005		$2,093,000		-$3,247,000
2004		$6,614,000		-$12,141,000
Curr. Assets:	$6,861,000	Curr. Liab.:	$674,000	
Plant, Equip.:	$17,000	Total Liab.:	$4,314,000	Indic. Yr. Divd: NA
Total Assets:	$20,237,000	Net Worth:	$15,923,000	Debt/ Equity: NA

Berkley Resources Inc

455 Granville St., Ste 400, Vancouver, BC, V6C 1T1; *PH:* 1-604-682-3701; *http://* www.berkleyresources.com; *Email:* ir@berkleyresources.com

General - Incorporation	BC	**Stock** - Price on:12/24/2007	$0.595
Employees	NA	Stock Exchange	OTC
Auditor	Staley, Okada & Partners	Ticker Symbol	BRKDF
Stk Agt	Computershare Trust Co	Outstanding Shares	NA
Counsel	NA	E.P.S.	NA
DUNS No.	24-860-8671	Shareholders	NA

Business: The group's principle activity is to participate in various oil and gas drilling ventures, as an investor. The group's quarterly revenue for September 2007 was 0.32 millions of USD.

Primary SIC and add'l.: 1311 6519 6792

CIK No: 0000870589

Officers: Matt Wayrynen/Exec. Chmn., CEO, David Wolfin/Dir., VP - Finance, Lindsay E. Gorrill/COO, Pres., Jim Obyrne/Dir., VP - Operations, Connie Lillico/Sec.

Directors: Matt Wayrynen/Exec. Chmn., CEO, Lloyd Andrews/Chmn. - Smith Barney Mutal Fund, Louis Wolfin/Dir., David Wolfin/Dir., VP - Finance, Jim Obyrne/Dir., VP - Operations, Phillip Piffer/Dir., Ronald Andrews/Dir., Tyrone Docherty/Dir.

Owners: Matt Wayrynen, Lisa Wayrynen/6.32%

Financial Data: *Fiscal Year End:*12/31 **Latest Annual Data:** 12/31/2006

Year		Sales		Net Income
2006		$1,346,000		-$3,874,000
2005		$1,413,000		-$2,665,000
2004		$913,000		-$605,000
Curr. Assets:	$1,092,000	Curr. Liab.:	$3,829,000	
Plant, Equip.:	$5,097,000	Total Liab.:	$4,746,000	Indic. Yr. Divd: NA
Total Assets:	$7,938,000	Net Worth:	$3,192,000	Debt/ Equity: NA

Berkshire Bancorp Inc

160 Broadway, New York, NY, 10038; *PH:* 1-212-791-5362; *Fax:* 1-212-791-5367; *http://* www.berkbank.com

General - Incorporation	DE	**Stock** - Price on:12/24/2007	$15.52
Employees	101	Stock Exchange	NDQ
Auditor	Grant Thornton LLP	Ticker Symbol	BERK
Stk Agt	American Stock Transfer & Trust Co.	Outstanding Shares	6,910,000
Counsel	NA	E.P.S.	$0.66
DUNS No.	09-995-0776	Shareholders	NA

Business: The group's principal activity is to provide residential and commercial mortgage loans, commercial non-mortgage loans and other banking services. The group acting as a holding company for the berkshire bank accepts deposits from general public and invests them in loans and debt obligations issued by the United States government and mortgaged backed securities. Loans consist of residential and commercial mortgage loans and commercial non-mortgage loans, both unsecured and secured by personal property. The group operates through nine deposit taking offices in New York city, orange and sullivan counties, New York. The group's main office at manhattan provides personal, face to face banking services for professionals and other high balance depositors.

Primary SIC and add'l.: 6712 6022

CIK No: 0000759718

Subsidiaries: Berkshire Agency, Inc., Berkshire Capital Trust I, East 39, LLC, Greater American Finance Group, Inc., The Berkshire Bank

Officers: Moses Krausz/Dir., Pres., CEO - Berkshire Bank/$683,554.00, Steven Rosenberg/Dir. - Berkshire Bank, CEO, CFO, Pres./$457,267.00, Jeanette Kahan/Assist. VP - Berkshire Bank, Gerald T. Loughren/Assist. VP - Berkshire Bank, Chani Sperlin-Simchon/Assist. VP - Berkshire Bank, Paul S. Buenafe/Assist. VP - Berkshire Bank, Dan Kimchi/VP - Berkshire Bank, David W. Lukens/Exec. VP, CFO - Berkshire Bank, Patrick B. Dennehy/VP - Berkshire Bank, Ira Mermelstein/VP - Berkshire Bank, Michael Langner/Assist. VP - Berkshire Bank, Claire Simonetti/Assist. VP - Berkshire Bank, Elizabeth Vivier/Assist. VP - Berkshire Bank, William Corbett/Assist. VP - Berkshire Bank, Frank Pugliese/Assist. VP - Berkshire Bank (29 Officers included in Index)

Directors: Moses Krausz/Dir., Pres., CEO - Berkshire Bank, Steven Rosenberg/Dir. - Berkshire Bank, CEO, CFO, Pres., Moses Marx/Chmn. - Berkshire Bank, Philippe D. Katz/Dir. - Berkshire Bank, Bjorn Bamberger/Dir. - Berkshire Bank, Donald Press/Dir. - Berkshire Bank, Joseph Fink/Dir. - Berkshire Bank, Victor Gartenstein/Dir. - Berkshire Bank, Martin A. Fischer/Dir. - Berkshire Bank, William L. Cohen/Dir. - Berkshire Bank, Randolph B. Stockwell/61/Dir.

Owners: David Lukens, Steven Rosenberg, Moses Krausz/2.10%, Insiders/54.30%, Randolph B. Stockwell, Martin A. Fischer, William L. Cohen, Moses Marx/51.30%

Financial Data: Fiscal Year End:12/31 Latest Annual Data: 12/31/2006

Year	Sales	Net Income
2006	$51,914,000	$4,880,000
2005	$46,262,000	$5,541,000
2004	$41,827,000	$7,502,000
Curr. Assets:	$30,708,000	Curr. Liab.: $752,251,000	P/E Ratio: 23.52
Plant, Equip.:	$9,338,000	Total Liab.: $832,879,000	Indic. Yr. Divd.: $0.180
Total Assets:	$948,656,000	Net Worth: $115,777,000	Debt/ Equity: 0.6514

Berkshire Hathaway Inc

1440 Kiewit Plz., Omaha, NE, 68131; PH: 1-402-346-1400; Fax: 1-402-346-3375; http:// www.berkshirehathaway.com; Email: berkshire@berkshirehathaway.com

General - Incorporation	DE	Stock- Price on:12/24/2007	$108300
Employees	217,000	Stock Exchange	NYSE
Auditor	Deloitte & Touche LLP	Ticker Symbol	BRK-A
Stk Agt	American Stock Transfer & Trust CO.	Outstanding Shares	1,540,000
Counsel	NA	E.P.S.	$7,820.28
DUNS No.	NA	Shareholders	NA

Business: The groups principle activity is to provide insurance services. The groups services include accidental, risk and life insurance. The group operates from United States.

Primary SIC and add'l.: 5139 3635 5944 5451 2273 6331 5712

CIK No: 0001067983

Subsidiaries: Acme Brick Company, Acme Building Brands, Inc., Albecca Inc., Ben Bridge Jeweler, Inc., Benjamin Moore & Co., Benjamin Moore & Co., Limited, Berkshire Hathaway Credit Corporation, Berkshire Hathaway Finance Corporation, Berkshire Hathaway International Insurance Ltd., Berkshire Hathaway Life Insurance Company of Nebraska, BH Finance LLC, BH Shoe Holdings, Inc., BHG Life Insurance Company, BHSF, Inc., Blue Chip Stamps 122 Subsidiaries included in the Index

Officers: Warren E. Buffett/77/Chmn., CEO, Forrest N. Krutter/Sec., Marc D. Hamburg/CFO, VP, Daniel J. Jaksich/Controller

Directors: Warren E. Buffett/77/Chmn., CEO, Charles T. Munger/84/Vice Chmn., Thomas S. Murphy/82/Dir., Charlotte Guyman/51/Dir., Howard G. Buffett/53/Dir., Malcolm G. Chace/73/Dir., William H. Gates/52/Dir., David S. Gottesman/81/Dir., Donald R. Keough/81/Dir., Ronald L. Olson/66/Dir., Walter Scott/76/Dir., Susan L. Decker/45/Dir.

Owners: Insiders/28.70%, Malcolm G. Chace, Thomas S. Murphy, Warren E. Buffett/24.40%, William H. Gates/3.90%, David S. Gottesman/1.50%, Howard G. Buffett, Ronald L. Olson, Walter Scott, Charles T. Munger/1.40%, Thomas S. Murphy, Charlotte Guyman, Malcolm G. Chace, Howard G. Buffett, Susan L. Decker (22 Owners included in Index)

Financial Data: Fiscal Year End:12/31 Latest Annual Data: 12/31/2006

Year	Sales	Net Income
2006	$98,539,000,000	$11,015,000,000
2005	$82,451,000,000	$8,528,000,000
2004	$74,382,000,000	$7,308,000,000
Curr. Assets:	$56,624,000,000	Curr. Liab.: $20,600,000,000	P/E Ratio: 13.85
Plant, Equip.:	$38,599,000,000	Total Liab.: $137,756,000,000	Indic. Yr. Divd.: NA
Total Assets:	$248,437,000,000	Net Worth: $108,419,000,000	Debt/ Equity: 0.3453

Berkshire Hills Bancorp Inc

24 N St., Pittsfield, MA, 01201; PH: 1-413-443-5601; Fax: 1-413-443-3587; http:// www.berkshirebank.com

General - Incorporation	DE	Stock- Price on:12/24/2007	$31.85
Employees	522	Stock Exchange	NDQ
Auditor	Wolf & Co. P.C	Ticker Symbol	BHLB
Stk Agt	Registrar & Transfer Co	Outstanding Shares	8,830,000
Counsel	Muldoon Murphy & Faucette	E.P.S.	$1.65
DUNS No.	NA	Shareholders	NA

Business: The group's principal activity is to provide banking services. It is a holding company for the berkshire bank in Massachusetts, a member of the federal home loan bank system. The bank accepts savings, checking accounts, term certificate accounts and other deposits from the public in the areas surrounding its offices and lends them as loans. The loans consist of residential mortgage loans, commercial business and real estate loans and consumer loans that are principally automobile loans. The group makes investments in us government and agency securities, mortgage and asset-backed securities, collateralized mortgage obligations, debt and equity securities and other investments. In addition, it also provides trust services and insurance products. The group operates through 11 offices mainly in berkshire county in Massachusetts, extending its business into western Massachusetts, northern Connecticut, eastern New York and southern Vermont.

Primary SIC and add'l.: 6035 6712

CIK No: 0001108134

Subsidiaries: Berkshire Bank, Berkshire Hills Capital Trust I., Berkshire Hills Technology, Inc., Woronoco Savings Bank

Officers: Michael P. Daly/Dir., CEO, Pres./$1,016,432.00, Ross D. Gorman/CEO, Pres. - Berkshire Insurance Group, Inc, Michael J. Oleksak/Exec. VP - Commercial Banking, Regional Pres. - Pioneer Valley, Kevin P. Riley/CFO, Exec. VP, Treasurer, Thomas W. Barney/Sr. VP, Gayle P.

Fawcett/Sr. VP, Wayne F. Patenaude/CFO, Sr. VP, Treasurer/$340,412.00, Gerald A. Denmark/Corp. Sec., Ann-Marie Racine/Investment Relations Officer, John S. Millet/42/Sr. VP, Treasurer/$152,734.00, John J. Howard/Exec. VP - Retail Banking, Shepard D. Rainie/Sr. VP, Chief Risk Officer

Directors: Michael P. Daly/Dir., CEO, Pres., Lawrence A. Bossidy/Chmn., Jeffrey D. Templeton/Dir., Wallace W. Altes/Dir., David B. Farrell/Dir., Edward G. McCormick/Dir., Cornelius D. Mahoney/Dir., John B. Davies/Dir., Catherine B. Miller/Dir., Corydon L. Thurston/Dir., Ann H. Trabulsi/Dir., Robert A. Wells/Dir., Rodney C. Dimock/Dir., David E. Phelps/Dir., Susan M. Hill/Dir.

Owners: Daniel X. Stannard, Edgar T. Campbell, David S. Wolk, Katherine P. Mosenthal, Michael A. Powers/1.60%, John R. Hand, Tyler Dann/9.19%, Paul J. Beaulieu/2.35%, Insiders/20.89%, Timothy J. Kononan, Susan M. Hill, Guy H. Boyer/3.82%, Tamara E. Heaton, Robert E. Buzzell, Sheri A. Savage

Financial Data: Fiscal Year End:12/31 Latest Annual Data: 12/31/2006

Year	Sales	Net Income
2006	$133,229,000	$11,263,000
2005	$102,655,000	$8,226,000
2004	$68,845,000	$11,509,000
Curr. Assets:	$30,985,000	Curr. Liab.: $1,521,938,000	P/E Ratio: 24.31
Plant, Equip.:	$29,130,000	Total Liab.: $1,891,481,000	Indic. Yr. Divd.: $0.600
Total Assets:	$2,149,642,000	Net Worth: $258,161,000	Debt/ Equity: 1.3953

Berliner Communications Inc

20 Bushes Ln., Elmwood Park, NJ, 07407; ; http:// www.bcisites.com; Email: berlinerr@bcisites.com

General - Incorporation	DE	Stock- Price on:12/24/2007	$1.05
Employees	155	Stock Exchange	OTC
Auditor	BDO Seidman LLP	Ticker Symbol	BERL
Stk Agt	American Stock Transfer & Trust Co.	Outstanding Shares	17,040,000
Counsel	NA	E.P.S.	NA
DUNS No.	19-150-3697	Shareholders	NA

Business: The group has liquidated all its operating subsidiaries and will not have any revenues until the group is able to re-deploy its cash assets. During the first six months of fiscal 2002, two of the group's indirect wholly-owned subsidiaries, axistel and e.volve, provided telecommunications services. E.volve offered network transport to its customers, primarily qwest, on a wholesale basis. These subsidiaries ceased operations in connection with their plan of liquidation, effective Sept of 2001 and Dec of 2001, respectively. Since that date, neither the group nor any of its debtor subsidiaries have conducted operations or generated revenue. The group is currently not providing any products or services of any kind (including telecommunications services) to any customers. The group's total revenue for year 2007 was 55.13 millions of USD.

Primary SIC and add'l.: 6719 4812

CIK No: 0000826773

Subsidiaries: AxisTel Communications, Inc., BCI Communications, Inc., e.Volve Technology Group, Inc., eVentures Holdings, LLC, eVentures Latin America, Inc., Internet Global Services, Inc., Internet Streaming Video, Inc., Novo Networks Global Services, Inc., Novo Networks International Services, Inc., Novo Networks Metro Services, Inc., Novo Networks Operating Corp.

Officers: Rich Berliner/Chmn., Pres., Bill D'Agostino/VP - BCI West, Abert E. Gencarella/63/CFO, Nicholas Day/General Counsel, Michael Guerriero/COO, Jelani Rucker/GM - Configured Solutions, John Giannella/Regional GM - Philly Region, In, Building, Al Gencarella/CFO, Robert Bradley/VP - New York, New Jersey, Darren Belick/GM - Specialty Communications Services, John Underwood/GM - West Region, Kevin Schenck/General Manger, Florida Marketing, James Davis/Dir. - Marketing - Boston Marketing, Jacob Hornberger/GM - Technical Services, In, Building, Mike Stoloff/Dir. - RF Engineering

Directors: Rich Berliner/Chmn., Pres., Thom Waye/43/Dir., Mark Dailey/50/Dir., Peter J. Mixter/56/Dir., Mehran Nazari/48/Dir., John Stevens Robling/58/Dir., Richard B. Berliner/55/Dir.

Owners: Insiders, Mark S. Dailey, Richard B. Berliner, Old Berliner, Pacific Asset Partners, Albert E. Gencarella, Rock Creek Partners II, LP, Sigma Opportunity Fund, LLC, Sigma Berliner, LLC, Thom Waye, Operis Partners I LLC, CB Private Equity Partners, LP, Mehran Nazari, Nicholas Day, John Stevens Robling (17 Owners included in Index)

Financial Data: Fiscal Year End:06/30 Latest Annual Data: 6/30/2006

Year	Sales	Net Income
2006	$39,325,000	$1,255,000
2005	$10,196,000	-$1,191,000
2004	NA	-$3,633,000
Curr. Assets:	$13,522,000	Curr. Liab.: $10,910,000	P/E Ratio: 9.55
Plant, Equip.:	$566,000	Total Liab.: $11,097,000	Indic. Yr. Divd.: NA
Total Assets:	$14,256,000	Net Worth: $3,158,000	Debt/ Equity: 0.9383

Berman Center Inc

211 E Ontario, Ste 800, Chicago, IL, 60611; PH: 1-312-255-8088; http:// www.bermancenter.com

General - Incorporation	DE	Stock- Price on:12/24/2007	$4
Employees	NA	Stock Exchange	OTC
Auditor	Aj. Robbins, P.C	Ticker Symbol	BRMC
Stk Agt	American Stock Transfer & Trust Co.	Outstanding Shares	NA
Counsel	NA	E.P.S.	-$0.04
DUNS No.	NA	Shareholders	NA

Business: The group's principal activity is to provide an array of female health management products and services marketed through a diversified media platform through its wholly owned subsidiary, Berman Health and Media, Inc. (BHM). Their services include menopause management center and sexual function clinic.

Primary SIC and add'l.: 8000

CIK No: 0000876160

Subsidiaries: Berman Health and Media, Inc, BHM Berman Center, Inc., LB Center, Inc., LBC MergerSub, Inc

Officers: Laura A. Berman/39/Dir., CEO, Pres., Carlos Bernal/39/CFO

Directors: Laura A. Berman/39/Dir., CEO, Pres., Samuel P. Chapman/43/Chmn., Howard Zuker/67/Dir.

Owners: Absolute Return Europe Fund/11.00%, Todd M. Ficeto/22.20%, Corporate Advisors Group/11.00%, Samuel P. Chapman/16.10%, European Catalyst Fund/12.30%, Peter Ondrousek/11.00%, Insiders/16.70%, Esarbee Investments Limited/5.60%

Financial Data: Fiscal Year End:12/31 Latest Annual Data: 12/31/2006

Year	Sales	Net Income
2006	$1,373,000	-$1,347,000
2005	$808,000	-$2,422,000

Curr. Assets:	$384,000	**Curr. Liab.:**	$998,000		
Plant, Equip.:	$336,000	**Total Liab.:**	$1,003,000	**Indic. Yr. Divd.:**	NA
Total Assets:	$720,000	**Net Worth:**	-$283,000	**Debt/ Equity:**	NA

Bernard Chaus Inc

530 7th Ave., New York, NY, 10018; ***PH:*** 1-212-354-1280; ***Fax:*** 1-201-863-6307; ***http://*** www.BernardChaus.com

General - Incorporation	NY	**Stock**- Price on:12/24/2007	$0.85
Employees	223	Stock Exchange	OTC
Auditor	Mahoney Cohen & Co., CPA, P.C.	Ticker Symbol	CHBD
Stk Agt	Chase Mellon Shareholder Services LLC	Outstanding Shares	37,380,000
Counsel	Swidler Berlin Shreff Friedman LLP	E.P.S.	$0.05
DUNS No.	07-771-9045	Shareholders	NA

Business: The group's principal activity is to design and arrange for the manufacture and marketing of a range of women's career and casual sportswear. The group markets its products as coordinated groups of jackets, skirts, pants, blouses, sweaters and related accessories under the brand names of josephine chaus collection, josephine chaus sport, josephine chaus woman and petite collections. The group's products are sold through department store chains, specialty retailers and other retail outlets. Josephine chaus collection consists of tailored suits, dresses, jackets, skirts and pants. Josephine chaus sport consists of casual tops, sweaters, pants, and skirts. Josephine chaus woman and petite collections include large and petite size dresses. The group also sells private label apparel manufactured according to customer's specifications.

Primary SIC and add'l.: 2331 2335

CIK No: 0000793983

Subsidiaries: Bernard Chaus International (Hong Kong), Inc., Bernard Chaus International (Korea), Inc., Bernard Chaus International (Taiwan), Inc., Chaus Retail, Inc., Cynthia Steffe Acquisition, LLC., S.L. Danielle Acquisition, LLC.

Officers: Josephine Chaus/Chairwoman, CEO, Judith Leech/VP - Design, Barton Heminover/CFO, VP, Financial Controller, VP - Finance, David Panitz/COO, Jackie Muldowney/VP - Merchandising, Ed Eskew/VP - Information Technology, Ken Christmann/VP - Logistics

Directors: Josephine Chaus/Chairwoman, CEO

Owners: Lee S. Kling, Insiders/45.51%, Barton Heminover, Harvey M.Krueger, Kenneth Cole Production, Inc./0.16%, Josephine Chaus/0.45%, Philip G. Barach

Financial Data: ***Fiscal Year End:***06/30 ***Latest Annual Data:*** 6/30/2006

Year	Sales	Net Income
2006	$136,827,000	-$4,874,000
2005	$143,255,000	-$1,157,000
2004	$157,107,000	$3,104,000

Curr. Assets:	$33,156,000	**Curr. Liab.:**	$17,224,000	**P/E Ratio:**	17.00
Plant, Equip.:	$3,154,000	**Total Liab.:**	$22,091,000	**Indic. Yr. Divd.:**	NA
Total Assets:	$39,914,000	**Net Worth:**	$17,823,000	**Debt/ Equity:**	0.1276

Berry Petroleum Co CA

5201 Truxtun Ave., Ste. 300, Bakersfield, CA, 93309; ***PH:*** 1-661-616-3900; ***Fax:*** 1-661-616-3881; ***http://*** www.bry.com

General - Incorporation	DE	**Stock**- Price on:12/24/2007	$39.55
Employees	243	Stock Exchange	NYSE
Auditor	PricewaterhouseCoopers LLP	Ticker Symbol	BRY
Stk Agt	Mellon Investor Services LLC	Outstanding Shares	43,990,000
Counsel	Jackson, De Marco & Peckenpaugh	E.P.S.	$2.72
DUNS No.	15-132-1411	Shareholders	NA

Business: The group's principle activities include producing, developing, acquiring and exploring crude oil and natural gas. The company's principal producing properties are located in the san joaquin valley, los angeles and ventura basins in California and the uinta basin in northeastern Utah. At 31-Dec-2003, the group had working interest in 2,757 oil wells and 84 gas wells. The group owns three cogeneration facilities, which are intended to provide an efficient and secure long-term supply of steam that is necessary for the economic production of heavy oil. The group also has electricity generation operation. The group's customers include oil and pipeline companies, refineries and utility companies. The group operates from United States.

Primary SIC and add'l.: 1311 4911

CIK No: 0000778438

Officers: Robert F. Heinemann/54/Dir., CEO, Pres./$3,255,821.00, George T. Crawford/46/VP - California Production, Michael Duginski/42/Exec. VP - Corporate Development, California/$898,844.00, Ralph J. Goehring/50/CFO, Exec. VP/$820,545.00, Daniel G. Anderson/45/VP - Rocky Mountains, Mid, Continent Production/$556,286.00, Walter B. Ayers/VP - Human Resources, Bruce S. Kelso/51/VP - Rocky Mountains, Mid, Continent Exploration/$537,686.00, Shawn M. Canaday/32/Controller, Kenneth A. Olson/52/Corp. Sec., Todd Crabtree/Investor Relations Officer, Steven B. Wilson/Treasurer

Directors: Robert F. Heinemann/54/Dir., CEO, Pres., Martin H. Young/53/Chmn., Stephen L. Cropper/56/Dir., William E. Bush/58/Dir., Joseph H. Bryant/51/Dir., Herbert J. Gaul/62/Dir., Thomas J. Jamieson/63/Dir., Ralph B. Busch/46/Dir., Frank J. Keller/62/Dir., Ronald J. Robinson/61/Dir.

Owners: Frank J. Keller, Daniel G. Anderson, Thomas J. Jamieson, William E. Bush, Martin H. Young, Ralph J. Goehring, Ronald J. Robinson, Herbert J. Gaul, William F. Berry, Ralph B. Busch, William F. Berry/7.10%, Winberta Holdings, Ltd./4.60%, Stephen L. Cropper, Joseph H. Bryant, Insiders *(20 Owners included in Index)*

Financial Data: ***Fiscal Year End:***12/31 ***Latest Annual Data:*** 12/31/2006

Year	Sales	Net Income
2006	$486,338,000	$107,943,000
2005	$406,725,000	$112,356,000
2004	$274,946,000	$69,187,000

Curr. Assets:	$98,809,000	**Curr. Liab.:**	$215,403,000	**P/E Ratio:**	14.54
Plant, Equip.:	$1,080,631,000	**Total Liab.:**	$771,297,000	**Indic. Yr. Divd.:**	$0.300
Total Assets:	$1,198,997,000	**Net Worth:**	$427,700,000	**Debt/ Equity:**	1.1742

Bertucci's Corp

155 Otis St., North Borough, MA, 01532; ***PH:*** 1-508-352-2500; ***http://*** www.bertuccis.com

General - Incorporation	DE	**Stock**- Price on:12/24/2007	NA
Employees	NA	Stock Exchange	NA
Auditor	Deloitte & Touche LLP	Ticker Symbol	NA
Stk Agt	NA	Outstanding Shares	NA
Counsel	NA	E.P.S.	NA
DUNS No.	NA	Shareholders	NA

Business: The group operates through its subsidiaries whose principle activity is to own and operate full service, casual dining restaurants in the northeastern United States.

Primary SIC and add'l.: 6794 6719 5812

CIK No: 0001061588

Owners: James N. Moriarty, Benjamin R. Jacobson/31.20%, Stephen V. Clark/1.50%, Heywood Wilansky, Dennis D. Pedra/7.70%, David G. Lloyd/1.30%, Thomas R. Devlin/10.30%, Insiders/36.90%, Sally M. Dungan, James J. Morgan/1.70%, James R. Parish

Best Buy Co Inc

7601 Penn Ave. S, Richfield, MN, 55423; ***PH:*** 1-612-291-1000; ***Fax:*** 1-612-292-4001; ***http://*** www.bestbuy.com

General - Incorporation	MN	**Stock**- Price on:12/24/2007	$44.92
Employees	140,000	Stock Exchange	NYSE
Auditor	Deloitte & Touche LLP	Ticker Symbol	BBY
Stk Agt	Computershare Trust Co	Outstanding Shares	479,300,000
Counsel	Robins, Kaplan, Miller & Ciresi LLP	E.P.S.	$2.79
DUNS No.	02-305-8159	Shareholders	NA

Business: The group's principle activity is to operate retail stores. The group also sells consumer electronics, home-office products, entertainment software and appliances. The group products are sold under the brand names BestBuy.com, BestBuyCanada.ca, BestBuy.com.cn, Five Star, Future Shop, Geek Squad, Magnolia Audio Video, and Pacific Sales Kitchen and Bath Centers. The group operates from United States.

Primary SIC and add'l.: 5731 5734 5722

CIK No: 0000764478

Subsidiaries: 656956 British Columbia Ltd., 661899 British Columbia Ltd., BBC Insurance Agency,Inc., BBC Investment Co., BBC Property Co., BBCAN Finance Company One, ULC, BBCAN Financial Services, L.P., BBY (Mauritius I) Ltd., BBY (Mauritius II) Ltd., BBY (Mauritius III) Ltd., BBY Business to Business, ULC, BBY Holdings International,Inc., BBY Networks,Inc., Best Buy (AsiaPacific) Ltd., Best Buy Canada Ltd. 41 Subsidiaries included in the Index

Officers: Bruce Chatterley/CEO, Pres. - Speakeasy, Robert A. Willett/CEO - Best Buy International, CIO/$8,592,830.00, Bradbury H. Anderson/59/Vice Chmn., CEO/$5,596,904.00, Elliot S. Kaplan/71/Dir., Sec., Brian J. Dunn/COO, Pres./$4,543,674.00, Shari L. Ballard/Exec. VP - Human Resources, Legal/$2,746,428.00, Thomas C. Healy/Exec. VP - Best Buy Business, Redmong Yeung/COO, Pres. - Best Buy Asia, Joseph M. Joyce/Sr. VP, General Counsel, Assist. Sec., Barry Judge/Sr. VP - Marketing, Darren R. Jackson/CFO, Exec. VP - Finance, Exec. VP - Customer Operating Groups/$3,622,961.00, Kalendu Patel/Exec. VP - Strategy, International, Emerging Business, Julie Gilbert/Sr. VP - Retail Training, Leadership Development, Wolf, Women's Leadership Forum, Susan S. Grafton/VP, Controller, Chief Accounting Officer, John Noble/CFO, Sr. VP - Best Buy International *(27 Officers included in Index)*

Directors: Bradbury H. Anderson/59/Vice Chmn., CEO, Allen U. Lenzmeier/64/Vice Chmn., Richard M. Schulze/68/Chmn., Founder, Matthew H. Paull/56/Dir., Hatim A. Tyabji/63/Dir., Mary A. Tolan/48/Dir., Frank D. Trestman/73/Dir., Elliot S. Kaplan/71/Dir., Sec., Ronald James/57/Dir., Rogelio Rebolledo/63/Dir., James E. Press/61/Dir., Mark Hoffenberg/Pres., Co - Founder - Audiovisions, Kathy J. Higgins Victor/51/Dir.

Owners: Ronald James, Shari L. Ballard, Frank D. Trestman, Insiders/17.10%, Elliot S. Kaplan, Kathy J. Higgins Victor, Rogelio M. Rebolledo, Matthew H. Paull, Hatim A. Tyabji, Richard M. Schulze/15.30%, James E. Press, Capital Researchand Management Co./15.30%, Ari Bousbib, Robert A. Willett, Bradbury H. Anderson/1.00% *(19 Owners included in Index)*

Financial Data: ***Fiscal Year End:***02/25 ***Latest Annual Data:*** 3/3/2007

Year	Sales	Net Income
2007	$35,934,000,000	$1,377,000,000
2006	$30,848,000,000	$1,140,000,000
2005	$27,433,000,000	$984,000,000

Curr. Assets:	$9,081,000,000	**Curr. Liab.:**	$6,301,000,000	**P/E Ratio:**	16.51
Plant, Equip.:	$2,938,000,000	**Total Liab.:**	$7,334,000,000	**Indic. Yr. Divd.:**	$0.400
Total Assets:	$13,570,000,000	**Net Worth:**	$6,201,000,000	**Debt/ Equity:**	0.0951

Bestnet Communications Corp

3725 Lawrenceville-suwanee Rd., Ste. B-7, Suwanee, GA, 30024; ***PH:*** 1-770-831-8818; ***http://*** www.bestnetcall.com

General - Incorporation	NV	**Stock**- Price on:12/24/2007	NA
Employees	NA	Stock Exchange	NA
Auditor	Semple & Cooper LLP	Ticker Symbol	NA
Stk Agt	NA	Outstanding Shares	NA
Counsel	NA	E.P.S.	-$0.12
DUNS No.	15-397-5099	Shareholders	NA

Business: The group's principle activity is to develop, market, sell and sub-license patented Internet-based telecommunication applications, technologies and services. The development activities are performed by softalk, inc. ('softalk'), a Canada-based technology company. This technology is used by the personal computer users to access the world wide Web to make long distance telephone calls at reduced rates. The group's marketing efforts are targeted at international long distance users in Caribbean, North America, Asia-Pacific, central and South America, Europe and Middle East. The Web-enabled long distance service is rendered under the brand name bestnetcall. The bestnetcall suite of products include long-distance calling, conference calling, call me services, sales calls, satellite calls and mobile calling.

Primary SIC and add'l.: 4813 4899 4822 7379

CIK No: 0000799694

Subsidiaries: International Environment Corporation, Interpretel (Canada) Inc., Interpretel, Inc., Telplex International

Officers: Andrew Green/40/Dir., CEO, Pres., Michael Kramarz/CFO, Adam G. Lowe/46/Dir., COO, Andrew Kennedy/44/Dir., Chief Medical Officer

Directors: Andrew Green/40/Dir., CEO, Pres., Stanley L. Schloz/65/Chmn., Andrew Kennedy/44/Dir., Chief Medical Officer, Adam G. Lowe/46/Dir., COO, Judy Lindstrom/63/Dir., Steven Kurtzman/46/Dir.

Owners: Insiders/40.66%, Adam G. Lowe/5.30%, Jeff Franco/19.63%, Anthony Silverman/8.86%, Michael Kramarz/0.36%, Steven Kurtzman, Judy Lindstrom/0.01%, Barry Griffith/0.56%, Andrew M. Green/5.32%, Andrew Kennedy/19.66%, Stanley L. Schloz/1.65%

Financial Data: *Fiscal Year End:* 08/31 *Latest Annual Data:* 08/31/2007

Year	Sales	Net Income
2007	NA	-$7,646,000
2006	$1,174,000	-$6,086,000
2005	$1,546,000	-$774,000

Curr. Assets:	$374,000	**Curr. Liab.:**	$1,950,000		
Plant, Equip.:	$203,000	**Total Liab.:**	$2,638,000	**Indic. Yr. Divd.:**	NA
Total Assets:	$613,000	**Net Worth:**	-$2,025,000	**Debt/ Equity:**	NA

Bestway Coach Express Inc

991 Sta. Rd., Bellport, NY, 11713; *PH:* 1-512-773-8112; *http://* www.bestwaycoach.com; *Email:* info@bestwaycoach.com

General - Incorporation	NY	**Stock** - Price on:12/24/2007	$0.55
Employees	45	Stock Exchange	OTC
Auditor Child, Van Wagoner & Bradshaw, PLLC		Ticker Symbol	BWCX
Stk Agt	Stalt, Inc.	Outstanding Shares	13,730,000
Counsel	NA	E.P.S.	NA
DUNS No.	NA	Shareholders	NA

Business: The group provides motor coach services in the Northeastern United States on both contracted and per seat basis. They use deluxe European style coaches. The company has been providing comprehensive transportation and maintenance solutions to the motor coach industry for many years. The company has an exclusive Van Hool alliance - with comprehensive sales, management and maintenance and backed by Van Hool nationwide parts. The models include the T2145 model with a passenger seating of 61 plus Deluxe Tour Guide Seat, wide viewing area and baggage capacity with acoustically insulated environment. The model comes equipped with independent suspension, disc brakes and an integrated air conditioning system. Transportation needs including an airport transfer, sight seeing; casino charter or any kind of charter is available. Other models include T945.

Primary SIC and add'l.: 4100

CIK No: 0001170016

Officers: Wilson Cheng/36/Founder, Chmn., CEO, Pres., Treasurer, Vivian Cheng/39/VP, Jovi Chen/31/Dir., COO, VP - Sales, Marketing

Directors: Wilson Cheng/36/Founder, Chmn., CEO, Pres., Treasurer, Arthur J. Kremer/Chmn. - Advisory Board, Jovi Chen/31/Dir., COO, VP - Sales, Marketing

Owners: Insiders, Jovi Chen, Wilson Cheng, Xu Kexi, Vivian Cheng

Financial Data: *Fiscal Year End:* 11/30 *Latest Annual Data:* 11/30/2006

Year	Sales	Net Income
2006	NA	NA

Curr. Assets:	$339,000	**Curr. Liab.:**	$4,626,000		
Plant, Equip.:	$5,747,000	**Total Liab.:**	$8,422,000	**Indic. Yr. Divd.:**	NA
Total Assets:	$6,508,000	**Net Worth:**	-$1,914,000	**Debt/ Equity:**	NA

Better Biodiesel Inc

Formerly: Mountain States Holdings Inc
355 S 1550 W, Fork, UT, 84660; *PH:* 1-801-798-7576; *http://* www.mslending.com

General - Incorporation	CO	**Stock** - Price on:12/24/2007	$2.25
Employees	5	Stock Exchange	OTC
Auditor Peterson Sullivan, PLLC		Ticker Symbol	BBDS
Stk Agt Corporate Stock Transfer, Inc.		Outstanding Shares	30,850,000
Counsel	NA	E.P.S.	-$0.1
DUNS No.	NA	Shareholders	NA

Business: The group's principal activities are to provide mortgage finance for borrowers wishing to purchase or refinance a home. The group provides finance through a network of approximately 100 banks and wholesale mortgage lending institutions. The mortgage loan finance includes conventional loans, fha loans, va loans, jumbo loans, construction loans, non-conforming loans and sub-prime loans. The group is also engaged in the business of selling pre-manufactured modular homes. Modular homes define the system of building a conventional home in sections for a specific customer and site. The group intends to purchase undeveloped lots throughout the denver metro area with a focus on aurora and the bennett watkins area about 20 miles east of denver.

Primary SIC and add'l.: 6162

CIK No: 0001157004

Subsidiaries: Mountain Eagle Homes, Inc.

Officers: Ron Crafts/CEO, Suzanne Frank/Loan Officer, Robert Mangas/Loan Officer, Woody Bonger/Loan Officer, Gary Crook/Principal Financial Officer, Jenny Bruso/Assist., Jan L. Peterson/Processor, Cindy Henneck/Office Mgr. - Processor, Mark E. Massa/49/Founder, Pres., Joy Parker/Loan Officer, Terry Neff/Loan Officer, Jeff Koeberle/Loan Officer, Matt Gray/Loan Officer

Directors: Mark E. Massa/49/Founder, Pres.

Owners: Ron Crafts/17.21%, John Crawford/17.21%, Insiders/84.00%, Capital Group Communications, Inc./14.75%, Briton F. McConkie/8.61%, Lynn Dean Crawford/12.31%, David M. Otto/4.92%, Peter Kristensen/8.61%

Financial Data: *Fiscal Year End:* 12/31 *Latest Annual Data:* 9/30/2006

Year	Sales	Net Income
2006	NA	-$421,000
2005	$358,000	-$166,000
2004	$610,000	-$169,000

Curr. Assets:	$192,000	**Curr. Liab.:**	$138,000		
Plant, Equip.:	$265,000	**Total Liab.:**	$138,000	**Indic. Yr. Divd.:**	NA
Total Assets:	$462,000	**Net Worth:**	$325,000	**Debt/ Equity:**	NA

Beverly Hills Bancorp Inc

23901 Calabasas Rd., Ste. 1050, Calabasas, CA, 91302; *PH:* 1-818-223-8084; *Fax:* 1-818-223-9531; *http://* www.fbbh.com

General - Incorporation	DE	**Stock** - Price on:12/24/2007	$7.82
Employees	47	Stock Exchange	NDQ
Auditor Deloitte & Touche LLP		Ticker Symbol	BHBC
Stk Agt Computershare Trust Co		Outstanding Shares	18,780,000
Counsel	NA	E.P.S.	$0.72
DUNS No.	NA	Shareholders	NA

Business: The group's principal banking activity is to conduct banking and lending operations in southern California and surrounding states. It provides mortgage loan servicing operations nationwide through wilshire credit corporation and mortgage investment operations through wilshire funding corporation. Through its subsidiary, first bank of beverly hills, f.s.b. It conducts a banking business primarily on niche products, including the origination and acquisition of commercial and multi-family real estate loans, investments in residential whole loans and investments in primarily aaa-rated and government agency mortgage-backed securities.

Primary SIC and add'l.: 6712 6162 6159 6035

CIK No: 0001024321

Subsidiaries: First Bank of Beverly Hills, WFC Inc., Wilshire Acquisitions Corporation

Officers: Larry B. Faigin/Chmn., CEO/$957,494.00, Takeo K. Sasaki/CFO/$256,056.00

Directors: Larry B. Faigin/Chmn., CEO, William D. King/66/Dir., Howard M. Amster/60/Dir., Kathleen L. Kellogg/55/Dir., Robert H. Kanner/60/Dir., Stephen P. Glennon/64/Dir., John J. Lannan/Dir.

Owners: Dimensional Fund Advisors LP/8.20%, Larry B. Faigin/3.00%, Howard Amster/8.40%, Takeo K. Sasaki, Craig W. Kolasinski, John J. Lannan/2.70%, Kathleen L. Kellogg, Namco Financial, Inc./8.20%, Stephen P. Glennon/3.30%, Capital Research and Management/9.60%, Robert H. Kanner/6.00%, William D. King, Annette J. Vecchio, Insiders/23.60%, Ezri Namvar/8.20% *(18 Owners included in Index)*

Financial Data: *Fiscal Year End:* 12/31 *Latest Annual Data:* 12/31/2006

Year	Sales	Net Income
2006	$98,203,000	$14,810,000
2005	$79,416,000	$15,052,000
2004	$61,730,000	$25,577,000

Curr. Assets:	$35,690,000	**Curr. Liab.:**	$1,422,005,000		
Plant, Equip.:	$1,897,000	**Total Liab.:**	$1,468,398,000	**Indic. Yr. Divd.:**	$0.500
Total Assets:	$1,623,836,000	**Net Worth:**	$155,438,000	**Debt/ Equity:**	0.2952

Beverly National Corp

240 Cabot St., Beverly, MA, 01915; *PH:* 1-978-922-2100; *Fax:* 1-978-524-7858; *http://* www.bevbank.com

General - Incorporation	MA	**Stock** - Price on:12/24/2007	$20.6
Employees	96	Stock Exchange	AMEX
Auditor Semple, Marchal & Cooper, LLP		Ticker Symbol	BNV
Stk Agt Registrar & Transfer Co		Outstanding Shares	2,770,000
Counsel	NA	E.P.S.	NA
DUNS No.	00-695-1412	Shareholders	NA

Business: The group's principal activity is to provide banking services through its banking subsidiary, beverly national bank. It also owns 100% of a Massachusetts business trust, cabot street realty trust. The group operates its business through six full service branches and two educational banking offices located in Massachusetts. The banking services include acceptance of checking, savings and time deposits and the making of commercial, real estate, instalment and other loans. The group also offers a full range of trust services, financial planning, official checks, traveller's checks, safe deposit boxes, automatic teller machines and customary banking services to its customers.

Primary SIC and add'l.: 6712 6022

CIK No: 0000742275

Subsidiaries: Beverly National Bank

Officers: Donat A. Fournier/CEO, Pres./$441,337.00, Martha Lewis/Public Relations Officer - Retail Financial Services, Diane M. Horne/VP - Audit, Finance, Kenneth R. Fisher/Assist. VP - Finance, Susan Doody/Assist. Cashier - Finance, Elizabeth A. Thompson/VP - Operations, Judy E. Curran/Assist. VP, Trust Operations Mgr. - Wealth Management, Investments, Janet Belsky/VP - Marketing, Retail Financial Services, Natasha Astrom/VP, Business Development Officer - Danvers, Ann Giroux/Assist. Branch Mgr. - Danvers, John L. Good/Exec. VP - Retail Financial Services/$203,630.00, Janice Egenberg/Human Resources Representative, Cynthia Funchion/VP, Branch Officer - Manchester, By, The, Sea, Yvonne Donnelly/Office Mgr. - Salem, Meaghan Dragani/Office Mgr. - Topsfield *(50 Officers included in Index)*

Directors: Donat A. Fournier/CEO, Pres., John N. Fisher/67/Dir., Alice B. Griffin/70/Dir., Robert W. Luscinski/66/Dir., Pamela C. Scott/56/Dir., Clark R. Smith/70/Dir., Michael F. Tripoli/50/Dir., Mark B. Glovsky/60/Dir., Kevin M. Burke/60/Dir., Suzanne S. Gruhl/61/Dir., John J. Meany/58/Dir.

Owners: Robert W. Luscinski, John J. Meany, John L. Good, Richard H. Booth, John R. Putney, James E. Rich, Alice B. Griffin, Paul J. Germano, Suzanne S. Gruhl, Donat A. Fournier, Michael O. Gilles, John N. Fisher, Pamela C. Scott, Kevin M. Burke, Clark R. Smith *(18 Owners included in Index)*

Financial Data: *Fiscal Year End:* 12/31 *Latest Annual Data:* 12/31/2006

Year	Sales	Net Income
2006	$28,205,000	$2,546,000
2005	$23,484,000	$2,393,000
2004	$20,219,000	$2,500,000

Curr. Assets:	$27,408,000	**Curr. Liab.:**	$416,230,000		
Plant, Equip.:	$6,285,000	**Total Liab.:**	$420,966,000	**Indic. Yr. Divd.:**	$0.800
Total Assets:	$467,144,000	**Net Worth:**	$46,178,000	**Debt/ Equity:**	NA

Bexil Corp

11 Hanover Sq., New York, NY, 10005; *PH:* 1-212-785-0400; *Fax:* 1-212-363-1101; *http://* www.bexil.com; *Email:* info@bexil.com

General - Incorporation	MD	**Stock** - Price on:12/24/2007	$33.85
Employees	NA	Stock Exchange	OTC
Auditor Tait, Weller & Baker LLP		Ticker Symbol	BXLC
Stk Agt American Stock Transfer & Trust Co.		Outstanding Shares	NA
Counsel	NA	E.P.S.	$23.97
DUNS No.	NA	Shareholders	NA

Business: The group operates through its subsidiaries whose principle activity is to provide banking and insurance services. The group operates from the United States.

Primary SIC and add'l.: 6399 6411

CIK No: 0001023714

Subsidiaries: Specialty Hospital of Northeast Mississippi, Inc

Officers: Thomas B. Winmill/Dir., CEO, Pres., General Counsel/$1,703,218.00, Bassett S. Winmill/Dir., Exec. Chmn./$430,301.00, Thomas O'Malley/CFO, Chief Accounting Officer, VP/$136,060.00, John F. Ramirez/VP, Sec., Chief Compliance Officer

Directors: Thomas B. Winmill/Dir., CEO, Pres., General Counsel, Bassett S. Winmill/Dir., Exec. Chmn., Robert D. Anderson/Vice Chmn., Charles A. Carroll/Dir., Edward G. Webb/Dir., Douglas Wu/Dir.

Owners: Edward G. Webb, Bassett S. Winmill/30.40%, Charles A. Carroll, John F. Ramirez, Douglas Wu, Thomas B. Winmill/10.70%, Insiders/39.70%

Financial Data: Fiscal Year End: 12/31   **Latest Annual Data:** 12/31/2006

Year	Sales	Net Income
2006	NA	NA
2005	NA	NA
2004	NA	NA

BFC Financial Corp

2100 W Cypress Creek Rd. , Fort Lauderdale, FL, 33309; **PH:** 1-954-940-4900; **Fax:** 1-954-940-4910; **http://** www.bfcfinancial.com

General - Incorporation	FL	**Stock** - Price on:12/24/2007	NA
Employees	NA	Stock Exchange	NYSE
Auditor	PricewaterhouseCoopers LLP	Ticker Symbol	BFF
Stk Agt	American Stock Transfer & Trust Co.	Outstanding Shares	NA
Counsel	Stearns Weaver Miller Weissler A & S	E.P.S.	-$0.84
DUNS No.	05-991-0968	Shareholders	NA

Business: The group's principal activity is to provide commercial banking services. The activities include attracting checking and savings deposits from the public and general business customers. The group also purchases wholesale residential loans from third parties and making other investments in mortgage-backed securities, tax certificates and other securities. The group's subsidiary ryan beck provides a full range of investment banking, brokerage and investment management services. The group operates 73 branch offices located primarily in miami-dade, broward, hillsborough, palm beach, martin, st. Lucie and Indian river counties in the state of Florida.

Primary SIC and add'l.: 6531 6712 6035 6282

CIK No: 0000315858

Subsidiaries: ATM Services, LLC, BA HD, LLC, BA Community Development Corporation, BA Financial Services, LLC, BA Title Insurance Agency, Inc., BAH Corp., Banc Servicing Center, LLC, BankAtlantic, BankAtlantic Bancorp Partners, Inc., BankAtlantic Bancorp, Inc., BankAtlantic Factors, LLC, BankAtlantic Financial Technology Venture Partners, LLC, BankAtlantic Financial Ventures II, LLC, BankAtlantic Leasing Inc., BankAtlantic Mortgage Partners, Inc. 135 Subsidiaries included in the Index

Officers: Alan B. Levan/Chmn., CEO, Phil J. Bakes/MD, Glen R. Gilbert/Exec. VP, Greg S. Heller/Dir. - Business Development, Sharon Lyn/Investor Relations Officer, Leo Hinkley/Investor Relations Officer

Directors: Alan B. Levan/Chmn., CEO, John E. Abdo/Vice Chmn., Keith D. Cobb/67/Dir., Earl Pertnoy/82/Dir., Neil Sterling/57/Dir., Oscar Holzmann/66/Dir.

Owners: Oscar Holzmann, Insiders/32.40%, I.R.E. Properties, Inc./5.30%, I.R.E. Realty Advisory Group, Inc./11.80%, I.R.E. Properties, Inc./7.30%, Alan B. Levan/29.60%, Insiders/86.80%, Levan Enterprises, Ltd./1.10%, Earl Pertnoy, I.R.E. Realty Advisory Group, Inc./7.00%, Glen R. Gilbert/3.20%, Herbert A. Wertheim/5.90%, Levan Enterprises, Ltd./0.80%, Neil Sterling, D. Keith Cobb *(26 Owners included in Index)*

Financial Data: Fiscal Year End: 12/31   **Latest Annual Data:** 12/31/2006

Year	Sales	Net Income
2006	$1,094,580,000	-$2,221,000
2005	$1,274,851,000	$12,774,000
2004	$1,166,601,000	$14,230,000
Curr. Assets:	$248,799,000 **Curr. Liab.:** $5,555,201,000	
Plant, Equip.:	$1,167,752,000 **Total Liab.:** $6,729,858,000 **Indic. Yr. Divd.:** NA	
Total Assets:	$7,605,766,000 **Net Worth:** $177,585,000 **Debt/ Equity:** NA	

BFC Financial Corp (B)

2100 W Cypress Creek Rd. , Fort Lauderdale, FL, 33309; **PH:** 1-954-940-4900; **Fax:** 1-954-940-4910; **http://** www.bfcfinancial.com; **Email:** InvestorRelations@BFCFinancial.com

General - Incorporation	FL	**Stock** - Price on:12/24/2007	$3.75
Employees	NA	Stock Exchange	OTC
Auditor	PricewaterhouseCoopers LLP	Ticker Symbol	BFCFB
Stk Agt	American Stock Transfer & Trust Co.	Outstanding Shares	NA
Counsel	Stearns, Weaver, Weissler, A & S	E.P.S.	NA
DUNS No.	NA	Shareholders	NA

Business: The groups principal activity is to provide banking business. The group financial products include savings and fixed deposits, on line, personal, commercial lending and business banking. The group operates from the United States.

Primary SIC and add'l.: 6035 6712 6552 1521 1522 6799 1531

CIK No: 0000315858

Subsidiaries: ATM Services, LLC, Avalon Park by Levitt and Sons, LLC, BA Community Development Corporation, BA Equity Ventures, LLC, BA Financial Services, LLC, BA-GR, LLC, BA-HD, LLC, BA-SL, LLC, BA-TOL, LLC, BAH Corp., Banc Servicing Center, LLC, BankAtlantic, BankAtlantic Bancorp Partners, Inc., BankAtlantic Bancorp, Inc., BankAtlantic Factors, LLC 214 Subsidiaries included in the Index

Officers: Alan B. Levan/Chmn., CEO, Phil Bakes/MD, Greg S. Heller/Dir. - Business Development, Sharon Lyn/Investor Relations Officer, Leo Hinkley/Investor Relations Officer, George P. Scanlon/Exec. VP

Directors: Alan B. Levan/Chmn., CEO, John E. Abdo/Vice Chmn.

Owners: Oscar Holzmann, I.R.E. Realty Advisory Group, Inc./7.00%, Insiders/86.80%, Neil Sterling, Florida Partners Corporation/1.90%, Herbert A. Wertheim/9.80%, Levan Enterprises, Ltd./1.10%, Glen R. Gilbert/3.20%, John E. Abdo/41.80%, I.R.E. Realty Advisory Group, Inc./11.80%, Alan B. Levan/29.60%, Levan Enterprises, Ltd., Earl Pertnoy/1.20%, Insiders/32.40%, I.R.E. Properties, Inc./5.30% *(26 Owners included in Index)*

BG Group Plc

Thames Valley Pk. , Reading, RG6 1PT; ; **http://** www.bg-group.com; **Email:** box.info@bg-group.com

General - Incorporation	UK	**Stock** - Price on:12/24/2007	$78.81
Employees	4,766	Stock Exchange	NYSE
Auditor	PricewaterhouseCoopers LLP	Ticker Symbol	BRG
Stk Agt	Lloyds TSB Registrars	Outstanding Shares	681,400,000
Counsel	NA	E.P.S.	$4.88
DUNS No.	NA	Shareholders	NA

Business: The group's principal activities are carried out through exploration and production, liquefied natural gas (lng), transmission and distribution and power generation. The exploration and production segment explores, develops, produces and markets hydrocarbons with a focus on gas. The lng segment combines the development and use of lng import and export facilities with the purchase, shipping and sale of lng and regasified natural gas. The transmission and distribution segment develops, owns and operates major pipelines and distribution networks and supplies gas through these to the end customer. The power generation segment develops, owns and operates natural gas-fired power generation plants. The group operates in the north west Europe, South America, Asia and Middle East, North America and trinidad, and the mediterranean basin and Africa.

Primary SIC and add'l.: 1320 4920 4931 1389 4923 1311

CIK No: 0000805260

Subsidiaries: Atlantic LNG 2/3 Company of Trinidad and, Atlantic LNG Company of Trinidad and Tobago, BG Asia Pacific Pte Limited, BG Bolivia Corporation, BG Canada Exploration and Production, Inc., BG E&P Brasil Ltda, BG Egypt S.A., BG Energy Holdings Limited, BG Exploration and Production India Limited, BG Gas Marketing Limited, BG International (CNS) Limited, BG International (NSW) Limited, BG International Limited, BG Karachaganak Limited, BG LNG Services, LLC 36 Subsidiaries included in the Index

Officers: William Friedrich/59/Deputy CEO, Frank Chapman/54/CEO, Martin Houston/50/Exec. VP, MD North America - Caribbean, Global LNG, Ben Mathews/39/Company Sec., Jorn Berget/55/Exec. VP, MD BG Advance - India, The Middle East, Charles Bland/59/Exec. VP - Policy, Corporate Affairs, Peter Hughes/50/Exec. VP - Group Strategy, Development, Keith Hubber/Acting General Counsel, Alan McCulloch/Acting Company Sec., Chris Lloyd/Head - Investor Relations, Helen Parris/Mgr. - Investor Relations, Siobhan Andrews/Mgr. - Investor Relations, Sylvia Radbourn/General Investor Relations Enquiries, Stefan Ricketts/39/General Counsel, Mark Carne/49/Exec. VP, MD - Europe, Central Asia *(20 Officers included in Index)*

Directors: Robert Wilson/64/Chmn., Dame S. Rimington/70/Non - Exec. Dir., John Coles/70/Non - Exec. Dir., Lord Sharman/65/Non - Exec. Dir., Peter Backhouse/56/Non - Exec. Dir., Jurgen Dormann/68/Non - Exec. Dir., Baroness Hogg/61/Non - Exec. Dir., Philippe Varin/55/Non - Exec. Dir., John Hood/56/Non - Exec. Dir., Paul Collins/71/Non - Exec. Dir.

Owners: Paul Collins, Lord Sharman, Philippe Varin, Peter Backhouse, William Friedrich, John Coles, Jrgen Dormann, Baroness Hogg

Financial Data: Fiscal Year End: 12/31   **Latest Annual Data:** 12/31/2006

Year	Sales	Net Income
2006	$15,034,133,000	$4,119,987,000
2005	$9,657,130,000	$1,958,270,000
2004	$8,322,912,000	$1,408,345,000
Curr. Assets:	$8,108,715,000 **Curr. Liab.:** $5,522,703,000	
Plant, Equip.:	$11,842,760,000 **Total Liab.:** $12,191,480,000 **Indic. Yr. Divd.:** $0.730	
Total Assets:	$24,637,642,000 **Net Worth:** $12,246,334,000 **Debt/ Equity:** NA	

BH Re LLC

3325 N Service Rd. , Unit 105 Burlington, Ontario, Canada, NY, 10022; **PH:** 1-905-332-3110; **Fax:** 1-905-332-2068; **http://** www.cleanwatts.com

General - Incorporation	NV	**Stock** - Price on:12/24/2007	NA
Employees	NA	Stock Exchange	NA
Auditor	Ernst & Young LLP	Ticker Symbol	NA
Stk Agt	Computershare Trust Co. Inc.	Outstanding Shares	NA
Counsel	NA	E.P.S.	NA
DUNS No.	NA	Shareholders	NA

Business: The group's principal activities are hotel and resorts business.

Primary SIC and add'l.: 7011

CIK No: 0001281657

Subsidiaries: EquityCo, LLC, MezzCo, LLC, OpBiz, LLC

Officers: Michael V. Mecca/59/CEO, Pres., Donna Lehmann/38/CFO, Treasurer, Robert Earl/56/Mgr., Douglas P. Teitelbaum/42/Mgr.

BHIT Inc

Formerly: Banyan Hotel Investment Fund
7005 Stadium Dr., Ste. 100, Brecksville, OH, 44141; **PH:** 1-212-895-3526

General - Incorporation	DE	**Stock** - Price on:12/24/2007	$0.23
Employees	NA	Stock Exchange	OTC
Auditor	Grant Thornton LLP	Ticker Symbol	VHTI
Stk Agt	Computershare Investor Services LLC	Outstanding Shares	14,990,000
Counsel	NA	E.P.S.	-$0.01
DUNS No.	NA	Shareholders	NA

Business: The groups principle activities include servicing cash investment portfolio and maximizing existing capital with stable interest generating instruments. The group operates from the United States.

Primary SIC and add'l.: 6798

CIK No: 0000764897

Officers: Andrew H. Scott/40/Interim CEO, Paul S. Dennis/70/Interim CFO

Directors: Harvey J. Polly/79/Chmn., Gary O. Marino/63/Dir.

Owners: Paul S. Dennis/6.40%, Andrew H. Scott/4.20%, Harvey J. Polly/8.80%, Insiders/21.20%, Gary O. Marino/2.90%

Financial Data: Fiscal Year End: 12/31   **Latest Annual Data:** 12/31/2006

Year	Sales	Net Income
2006	$72,000	-$49,000
2005	$49,000	-$71,000
2004	$23,000	-$78,000

Curr. Assets:	$1,440,000	Curr. Liab.:	$48,000		
Plant, Equip.:	NA	Total Liab.:	$48,000	Indic. Yr. Divd.:	NA
Total Assets:	$1,440,000	Net Worth:	$1,392,000	Debt/ Equity:	NA

BHP Billiton Ltd

180 Lonsdale St., Melbourne, Victoria, 3000; ; *http://* www.bhpbilliton.com;
Email: investor.relations@bhpbilliton.com

General - Incorporation	Australia	**Stock**- Price on:12/24/2007	$59.57
Employees	33,184	Stock Exchange	NYSE
Auditor	KPMG LLP	Ticker Symbol	BHP
Stk Agt	JP Morgan Chase Bank, N.A.	Outstanding Shares	2,970,000,000
Counsel	NA	E.P.S	$4.09
DUNS No.	75-316-8160	Shareholders	NA

Business: The group's principal activities are minerals exploration, production and processing (particularly alumina, aluminium, copper, iron ore, metallurgical coal, ferroalloys, energy coal, nickel, diamonds and titanium minerals), oil and gas exploration and development and production.

Primary SIC and add'l.: 1311 1031 3312 1221 1021 1011 1044

CIK No: 0000811809

Subsidiaries: 1338768 Ontario Inc, 1342077 Ontario Inc, 141 Union Company, African Metals Ltd, Aluminium Consortium Venezuela B.V., Angola Mining Finance Ltd, Angola Mining Services Ltd, Angola Technical Services Ltd, Araguaia Participaes Ltda, Atlas Steels Company Ltd, Auvernier Limited (in liquidation), Baniettor Mining (Pty) Ltd, Beswick Pty Ltd (in liquidation), Bhp (usa) Investments Inc, BHP Asia Pacific Nickel Pty Ltd 480 Subsidiaries included in the Index

Officers: Marius Kloppers/45/Dir., CEO, Alexandre Vanselow/Group Executive, CFO, Marcus Randolph/52/Group Executive, Chief Executive Ferrous - Coal, Karen Wood/52/Group Executive, Chief People Officer, Alberto Calderon/48/Group Executive, Chief Commercial Officer, Rebecca McDonald/Pres. Gas - Power, Michael J. Yeager/55/Group Pres. - Energy, Jane McAloon/Dir., Company Sec.

Directors: Marius Kloppers/45/Dir., CEO, Don Argus/70/Chmn., Jane McAloon/Dir., Company Sec., Charles Goodyear/50/Dir., Carlos Cordeiro/52/Dir., Paul Anderson/63/Dir., David Jenkins/69/Dir., Jacques Nasser/60/Dir., David Brink/69/Dir., John Buchanan/65/Dir., David Crawford/64/Dir., John Schubert/65/Dir., Gail De Planque/Dir.

Owners: HSBC Custody Nominees (Australia) Limited/0.55%, Bond Street Custodians Limited/0.33%, UBS Nominees Pty Ltd/0.62%, Potter Warburg Nominees Pty Ltd/0.50%, Suncorp Custodian Services Pty Limited/0.34%, J P Morgan Nominees Australia Limited/11.11%, Queensland Investment Corporation/1.22%, Tasman Asset Management Ltd/0.19%, National Nominees Ltd/9.65%, ANZ Nominees Ltd/3.70%, Perpetual Trustee Australia Group/0.25%, RBC Dexia Investor Services Australia Nominees Pty Ltd/1.14%, Citicorp Nominees Pty Ltd/13.12%, Australian Reward Investment Alliance/0.40%, Australian Mutual Provident Society/3.09% *(20 Owners included in Index)*

Financial Data: *Fiscal Year End:*06/30 **Latest Annual Data:** 6/30/2006

Year	Sales	Net Income
2006	$35,891,000,000	$9,783,000,000
2005	$29,587,000,000	$6,388,000,000
2004	$22,887,000,000	$2,716,000,000

Curr. Assets:	$8,776,000,000	Curr. Liab.:	$8,861,000,000		
Plant, Equip.:	$33,116,000,000	Total Liab.:	$24,061,000,000	Indic. Yr. Divd.:	$1.120
Total Assets:	$52,137,000,000	Net Worth:	$27,839,000,000	Debt/ Equity:	NA

BHP Billiton Plc

Neathouse Pl., Victoria, London, SW1V 1LH; *PH:* 44-2078024000; *http://* www.bhpbilliton.com

General - Incorporation	UK	**Stock**- Price on:12/24/2007	$54.71
Employees	33,184	Stock Exchange	NYSE
Auditor	KPMG	Ticker Symbol	BBL
Stk Agt	JP Morgan Chase Bank, N.A.	Outstanding Shares	2,970,000,000
Counsel	NA	E.P.S	$4.58
DUNS No.	NA	Shareholders	NA

Business: The group's principal activities are carried out through the seven customer sector groups: petroleum, produces crude oil and condensates, natural gas, lng, lpg and ethane. Aluminium, produces primary aluminum, foundry alloy, extrusion billet, rolling slab, wire rod, bauxite and alumina. Base metals, produces copper, lead, zinc, silver and gold. Carbon steel materials, supplies iron and manganese ore, manganese alloys, metallurgical coal and hot briquetted iron to the international steel industry. Diamonds and specialty products, produces diamonds, titanium minerals, aluminium and stainless steel products. Energy coals, provides steaming coal for use in the electric power generation industry and general industrial activities such as cement production. Stainless steel materials, produces nickel, ferrochrome, chrome ores and cobalt. It operates in Australia, Europe, Japan, North America, South Korea, southern Africa, South America and in other Asian countries.

Primary SIC and add'l.: 1099 3313 3341 3312

CIK No: 0001171264

Subsidiaries: 1338768 Ontario Inc, 1342077 Ontario Inc, 141 Union Company, African Metals Ltd, Aluminium Consortium Venezuela B.V., Angola Mining Finance Ltd, Angola Mining Services Ltd, Angola Technical Services Ltd, Araguaia Participaes Ltda, Atlas Steels Company Ltd, Auvernier Limited (in liquidation), Baniettor Mining (Pty) Ltd, Beswick Pty Ltd (in liquidation), Bhp (usa) Investments Inc, BHP Asia Pacific Nickel Pty Ltd 485 Subsidiaries included in the Index

Officers: Charles Goodyear/50/Dir., CEO, Marcus Randolph/52/Group Executive, Chief Executive Ferrous - Coal, Samantha Evans/Contact - Media Relations, Australia, Alexandre Vanselow/46/CFO - Group Executive, Karen Wood/52/Chief Governance Officer, Group Company Sec., Michael J. Yeager/55/Group Executive, Chief Executive Petroleum, Illtud Harri/Contact - Media Relations, United Kingdom, Tracey Whitehead/Contact - Investor, Media Relations, United States, Alison Gilbert/Contact - Investor Relations, South Africa

Directors: Charles Goodyear/50/Dir., CEO, Don Argus/70/Chmn., Marius Kloppers/45/Dir., Gail De Planque/Dir., Jane McAloon/44/Dir., David Crawford/64/Dir., David Jenkins/69/Dir., Jacques Nasser/60/Dir., John Schubert/65/Dir., Paul Anderson/63/Dir., David Brink/68/Dir., John Buchanan/Dir., Carlos Cordeiro/52/Dir.

Owners: Insiders/0.02%, Legal and General Investment Management Limited/3.53%, Old Mutual Plc/4.82%

Financial Data: *Fiscal Year End:*06/30 **Latest Annual Data:** 6/30/2005

Year	Sales	Net Income
2005	$29,587,000,000	$6,398,000,000

Curr. Assets:	$9,877,000,000	Curr. Liab.:	$8,994,000,000		
Plant, Equip.:	$30,347,000,000	Total Liab.:	$24,795,000,000	Indic. Yr. Divd.:	$1.080
Total Assets:	$41,948,000,000	Net Worth:	$17,153,000,000	Debt/ Equity:	NA

Bi-Optic Ventures Inc

1030 West Georgia St., Ste.No. 1518, Vancouver, BC, V6E 2Y3; *PH:* 1-604-689-2646

General - Incorporation	BC	**Stock**- Price on:12/24/2007	$0.25
Employees	NA	Stock Exchange	OTC
Auditor	Manning Elliott LLP	Ticker Symbol	BOVKF
Stk Agt	Pacific Stock Transfer Company	Outstanding Shares	NA
Counsel	NA	E.P.S	NA
DUNS No.	NA	Shareholders	NA

Business: The groups principle activity is to provide recruiting services. The groups service area includes the research and development, engineering, marketing, sales, information technology and manufacturing industries. The group operates from United States.

Primary SIC and add'l.: 8731

CIK No: 0001168960

Officers: Harry Chew/47/Dir., CEO, Pres., Terrance G. Owen/62/Dir., Corp. Sec.

Directors: Harry Chew/47/Dir., CEO, Pres., Sonny Chew/39/Dir., David J.L. Williams/54/Dir., Terrance G. Owen/62/Dir., Corp. Sec.

Owners: David J.L. Williams/1.40%, Insiders/9.30%, Sonny Chew/1.00%, Harry Chew/6.90%

Financial Data: *Fiscal Year End:*02/28 **Latest Annual Data:** 2/28/2007

Year	Sales	Net Income
2007	NA	-$351,000
2006	NA	-$174,000
2005	NA	-$237,000

Curr. Assets:	$11,000	Curr. Liab.:	$63,000		
Plant, Equip.:	$12,000	Total Liab.:	$63,000	Indic. Yr. Divd.:	NA
Total Assets:	$23,000	Net Worth:	-$40,000	Debt/ Equity:	NA

Bidville Inc

601 Cleveland St., Ste 120, Clearwater, FL, 33755; *PH:* 1-727-442-9669; *Fax:* 1-727-210-1459; *http://* www.bidville.com; *Email:* investorrelations@bidville.com

General - Incorporation	NV	**Stock**- Price on:12/24/2007	NA
Employees	NA	Stock Exchange	OTC
Auditor	Stark Winter Schenkein & Co. LLP	Ticker Symbol	PEDI
Stk Agt	Pacific Stock Transfer Company	Outstanding Shares	NA
Counsel	NA	E.P.S	NA
DUNS No.	NA	Shareholders	NA

Business: The group's principal activity is to provide Internet users with an active Website that facilitates auctions and fixed-price e-commerce between unrelated third parties. The group currently has approximately 145,000 active members, with over 3,500 active sellers. The group's on-line auction and fixed price offering allows buyers and sellers to bypass traditionally expensive, regionally fragmented intermediaries and provides a venue to transact business twenty-four hours a day, seven days a week, and 365 days a year. The group currently has over 1.3 million daily listings, ranging from electronics to baseball cards, and supports a growing community, evidenced by its active message boards. On 11-Dec-2003, the group acquired bidville inc and on 25-Mar-2004, it acquired 3 2 1 play inc and its wholly-owned subsidiary buy sell connect inc.

Primary SIC and add'l.: 7372 7375 2721

CIK No: 0001081275

Subsidiaries: Buy Sell Connect.com, Inc., Greatestescapes Corp.

Officers: Michael Palandro/Dir., CEO, Pres., Robert W. Pearce/Dir., Corp. Sec., Kimberly Cullen/Dir. - Marketing

Directors: Michael Palandro/Dir., CEO, Pres., Gerald C. Parker/Chmn., John C. Dewey/Dir., Robert W. Pearce/Dir., Corp. Sec., Edward Orlando/Dir.

Financial Data: *Fiscal Year End:*12/31 **Latest Annual Data:** 12/31/2004

Year	Sales	Net Income
2004	$92,000	-$8,262,000
2003	$46,000	-$38,396,000

Curr. Assets:	$268,000	Curr. Liab.:	$1,348,000		
Plant, Equip.:	$70,000	Total Liab.:	$1,348,000	Indic. Yr. Divd.:	NA
Total Assets:	$338,000	Net Worth:	-$1,010,000	Debt/ Equity:	NA

Bidz.com Inc

3562 Eastham Dr., Culver City, CA, 90232; *PH:* 1-310-280-7373; *Fax:* 1-310-280-7375; *http://* www.bidz.com; *Email:* customerservice@bidz.com

General - Incorporation	CA	**Stock**- Price on:12/24/2007	NA
Employees	NA	Stock Exchange	NDQ
Auditor	Stonefield Josephson, Inc	Ticker Symbol	BIDZ
Stk Agt	Registrar & Transfer Co	Outstanding Shares	NA
Counsel	NA	E.P.S	NA
DUNS No.	NA	Shareholders	NA

Business: The group's principal activity is providing online auctions services. The company has 3 Minute Auctions. It offers free shipping services for customers paying online. The company features various products categories like extremely expensive products, ornaments, fine arts, art & antiques, auto parts, collectibles, coins & stamps, sports cards, computers, electronics, real estate, slot machines, tools and wholesale products.

Primary SIC and add'l.: 7389

CIK No: 0001324105

Officers: David Zinberg/CEO, Pres., Lawrence Kong/CFO, Larry Russell/CCO, Controller, Claudia Liu/COO, Marina Zinberg/VP, Executive Sec., Vilius Zukauskas/Auctions Mgr., Jorge L. Gonzalez/Customer Service Mgr.

Directors: David Zinberg/CEO, Pres.

Owners: Peter G. Hanelt, David Zinberg/33.10%, Man Jit Singh, Saied Aframian/5.70%, Marina Zinberg/33.10%, Insiders/34.90%, Lawrence Y. Kong/2.90%, Claudia Y. Liu/2.90%

Big 5 Sporting Goods Corp

2525 E El Segundo Blvd., El Segundo, CA, 90245; *PH:* 1-310-536-0611; *Fax:* 1-310-297-7585;
http:// www.big5sportinggoods.com

General - Incorporation	DE	Stock - Price on:12/24/2007	$26.17
Employees	8,100	Stock Exchange	NDQ
Auditor	KPMG LLP	Ticker Symbol	BGFV
Stk Agt	U.S. Stock Transfer Corp	Outstanding Shares	22,690,000
Counsel	NA	E.P.S.	$1.39
DUNS No.	NA	Shareholders	NA

Business: The group's principal activity is retail sale of sporting goods and apparel in the western United States. As of 27-Jun-2004, the group operated 295 stores in California, Washington, Arizona, Oregon, Texas, New Mexico, Nevada, Utah, Idaho and Colorado under the name "Big 5 Sporting Good". The group's products include athletic shoes, apparel and accessories, outdoor and athletic equipment for team sports, fitness, camping, hunting, fishing, tennis, golf, snowboarding and in-line skating.

Primary SIC and add'l.: 5941 6719 5661

CIK No: 0001156388

Subsidiaries: Big 5 Corp., Big 5 Services Corp

Officers: Steven Miller/Chmn., CEO, Pres./$1,249,005.00, Barry Emerson/Sr. VP, CFO, Treasurer/$677,802.00, John Mills/Primary Investor Relations Officer, Shane O. Starr/50/Sr. VP - Operations, Gary Meade/Sr. VP, General Counsel, Sec./$394,752.00, Richard Johnson/Sr. VP - Store Operations/$525,250.00, Jeffrey Fraley/Sr. VP - Human Resources, Thomas Schlauch/Sr. VP - Buying/$568,676.00

Directors: Steven Miller/Chmn., CEO, Pres., Jennifer Holden Dunbar/Dir., Sandra Bane/Dir., Michael G. Brown/Dir., David Jessick/Dir., Michael Miller/Dir.

Owners: Richard A. Johnson, Steven G. Miller/5.80%, Michael D. Miller/1.20%, FMR Corp./9.00%, Sandra N. Bane, David R. Jessick, Insiders/8.40%, Barry D. Emerson, Wasatch Advisors, Inc./6.80%, Jennifer Holden Dunbar, Gary S. Meade, Thomas J. Schlauch, G. Michael Brown

Financial Data: *Fiscal Year End:*01/01 *Latest Annual Data:* 12/31/2006

Year	Sales		Net Income
2006	$876,805,000		$30,835,000
2005	$782,215,000		$33,519,000
Curr. Assets:	$262,605,000	Curr. Liab.: $161,056,000	P/E Ratio: 18.30
Plant, Equip.:	$88,159,000	Total Liab.: $263,639,000	Indic. Yr. Divd.: $0.360
Total Assets:	$364,099,000	Net Worth: $100,460,000	Debt/ Equity: 0.6606

Big Bear Mining Corp

1728 Yew St., Ste. 8, Vancouver, BC, V6K 3E9; *PH:* 1-604-376-7468;
http:// www.bigbearmining.com

General - Incorporation	WV	Stock - Price on:12/24/2007	NA
Employees	NA	Stock Exchange	OTC
Auditor	NA	Ticker Symbol	BGBR
Stk Agt.	NA	Outstanding Shares	NA
Counsel	NA	E.P.S.	NA
DUNS No.	NA	Shareholders	NA

Business: The groups principle activity is to provide recruiting services. The groups service area includes the research and development, engineering, marketing, sales, information technology and manufacturing industries. The group operates from United States.

Primary SIC and add'l.: 1000

CIK No: 0001274951

Officers: Aaron Hall/CEO, Pres.

Big Cat Energy Corp

201 W Lakeway, Ste. 1000, Gillette, WY, 82718; ; *http://* www.bigcatenergy.com;
Email: investor@bigcatenergy.com

General - Incorporation	NV	Stock - Price on:12/24/2007	$2.2
Employees	NA	Stock Exchange	OTC
Auditor	Hein & Assoc., LLP	Ticker Symbol	BCTE
Stk Agt.	Nevada Agency & Trust Company	Outstanding Shares	29,540,000
Counsel	NA	E.P.S.	-$0.14
DUNS No.	NA	Shareholders	NA

Business: The groups principal activity is to provide new technology, which allows Coal Bed Methane operators to re-inject produced water at a fraction of the cost of current technology. The group operates from the United States.

Primary SIC and add'l.: 1040

CIK No: 0001089272

Officers: Tim Barritt/Dir., Petroleum Engineer, CEO, Pres., Dick Stockdale/Dir., Licensed Geohydrologist, VP, Ray Murphy/Dir., Licensed Geologist, COO, Robert Goodale/46/Sec., Principal Financial Officer, Principal Accounting Officer, Treasurer, Richard G. Stockdale/64/Dir., VP, Timothy J. Barritt/58/Dir., Pres., Principal Exec. Officer, Richard G. Stifel/CFO, Sec.

Directors: Tim Barritt/Dir., Petroleum Engineer, CEO, Pres., Dick Stockdale/Dir., Licensed Geohydrologist, VP, Ray Murphy/Dir., Licensed Geologist, COO, Charles W. Peck/Dir., George L. Hampton/Dir., Richard G. Stockdale/64/Dir., VP, Timothy J. Barritt/58/Dir., Pres., Principal Exec. Officer

Owners: Big Cat Energy Corporation/66.67%, Richard Stockdale/1.70%, Timothy G. Barritt/1.70%, Insiders/5.00%, Raymond Murphy/10.30%, Ray Murphy/1.70%

Financial Data: *Fiscal Year End:*04/30 *Latest Annual Data:* 04/30/2007

Year	Sales		Net Income
2007	NA		-$2,639,000
2006	NA		-$145,000
2005	NA		-$23,000
Curr. Assets:	$1,164,000	Curr. Liab.: $10,000	
Plant, Equip.:	$1,804,000	Total Liab.: $10,000	Indic. Yr. Divd.: NA
Total Assets:	$3,016,000	Net Worth: $3,006,000	Debt/ Equity: NA

Big Dog Holdings Inc

121 Gray Ave., Santa Barbara, CA, 93101; *PH:* 1-805-963-8727; *Fax:* 1-805-962-9460;
http:// www.bigdogs.com

General - Incorporation	DE	Stock - Price on:12/24/2007	$16.65
Employees	1,100	Stock Exchange	NDQ
Auditor ... Singer Lewak Greenbaum & Goldstein		Ticker Symbol	BDOG
Stk Agt	U.S. Stock Transfer Corp	Outstanding Shares	9,360,000
Counsel	NA	E.P.S.	-$0.09
DUNS No.	79-027-6331	Shareholders	NA

Business: The group's principal activities are to develop, market and retail branded, lifestyle collection of unique, high-quality, popular-priced consumer products, including activewear, casual sportswear, accessories and gifts. The group's products includes graphic t-shirts, shorts, knit and woven shirts, fleece items, loungewear and boxer shorts. The group also sells a line of non-apparel products, including plush animals, stationery and pet products, which feature big dog graphics and are developed to complement group's apparel. The group operates in 201 stores in 42 states and 2 stores in Puerto Rico. The trademarks of the group include big dogs(R), big dog sportswear(R), dog logo, big dog(R), little big dogs(R) and big big dogs(R) .the group acquired the walking company on 08-Mar-2004.

Primary SIC and add'l.: 5961 5399 5641 5611 5621 5699

CIK No: 0001019439

Officers: Andrew Feshbach/Dir., CEO/$627,178.00, Michael Grenley/50/Sr. VP/$354,913.00, Anthony J. Wall/52/Exec. VP - Business Affairs, General Counsel, Sec./$408,514.00, Roberta J. Morris/48/CFO, Treasurer, Assist. Sec./$315,821.00, Jamie Gilles/Sponsorship Information, Douglas N. Nilsen/59/Exec. VP/$359,077.00, Lee M. Cox/39/Sr. VP - Retail Operations/$337,346.00

Directors: Andrew Feshbach/Dir., CEO, Fred Kayne/Chmn., David J. Walsh/48/Dir.

Owners: Anthony J. Wall/2.30%, Roberta J. Morris/1.40%, Steven C. Good, Douglas N. Nilsen/1.60%, Fred Kayne/56.90%, David C. Walsh, Lee M. Cox/1.30%, Michael Grenley, Insiders/69.10%, Andrew R. Feshbach/9.80%, Skip R. Coomber

Financial Data: *Fiscal Year End:*12/31 *Latest Annual Data:* 12/31/2006

Year	Sales		Net Income
2006	$218,604,000		$971,000
2005	$179,115,000		$4,723,000
2004	$161,358,000		$3,688,000
Curr. Assets:	$68,617,000	Curr. Liab.: $46,027,000	
Plant, Equip.:	$24,174,000	Total Liab.: $53,533,000	Indic. Yr. Divd.: NA
Total Assets:	$102,661,000	Net Worth: $49,128,000	Debt/ Equity: 0.1064

Big Lots Inc

300 Phillipi Rd., Columbus, OH, 43228; *PH:* 1-614-278-6800; *Fax:* 1-614-278-6676;
http:// www.biglots.com

General - Incorporation	OH	Stock - Price on:12/24/2007	$29.13
Employees	15,467	Stock Exchange	NYSE
Auditor	Deloitte & Touche LLP	Ticker Symbol	BIG
Stk Agt	National City Bank	Outstanding Shares	106,880,000
Counsel	NA	E.P.S.	$1.25
DUNS No.	19-059-2519	Shareholders	NA

Business: The group's principle activity is to operate closeout retail stores. The groups selling products include consumables, home, seasonal and toys. The groups consumable category includes food, health and beauty, plastics, paper and pet departments. Seasonal and toys includes toys, lawn and garden, trim-a-tree and various holiday-oriented departments. The group operates from United States.

Primary SIC and add'l.: 5331

CIK No: 0000768835

Subsidiaries: Barn Acquisition Corporation, Big Lots Capital, Inc., Big Lots Stores, Inc., BLSI Property, LLC, C.S. Ross Company, Capital Retail Systems, Inc., Closeout Distribution, Inc., Consolidated Property Holdings, Inc., CSC Distribution, Inc., DTS, Inc., Durant DC, LLC, Fashion Barn of Florida, Inc., Fashion Barn of Georgia, Inc., Fashion Barn of Indiana, Inc., Fashion Barn of Missouri, Inc. 41 Subsidiaries included in the Index

Officers: Steven S. Fishman/Chmn., CEO, Pres./$3,989,590.00, Charles W. Haubiel/42/Sr. VP, General Counsel, Corp. Sec., Brad A. Waite/50/Exec. VP - Human Resources, Loss Prevention, Real Estate, Risk Management/$1,631,308.00, John C. Martin/57/Exec. VP - Merchandising/$1,224,955.00, Lisa M. Bachmann/46/Sr. VP - Merchandise Planning, Allocation, CIO/$973,049.00, Joe R. Cooper/50/CFO, Sr. VP/$920,061.00, Donald A. Mierzwa/58/Exec. VP - Store Operations, Timothy A. Johnson/40/VP - Strategic Planning, Investor Relations, Paul A. Schroeder/42/VP, Controller, Robert C. Claxton/53/Sr. VP - Marketing, Norman J. Rankin/51/Sr. VP, General Merchandise Mgr., Harold A. Wilson/59/Sr. VP - Distribution, Transportation Services

Directors: Steven S. Fishman/Chmn., CEO, Pres., Sheldon M. Berman/67/Dir., Russell Solt/60/Dir., David T. Kollat/69/Dir., James R. Tener/58/Dir., Brenda J. Lauderback/57/Dir., Dennis B. Tishkoff/64/Dir., Philip E. Mallott/50/Dir., Jeffrey P. Berger/58/Dir.

Owners: Sheldon M. Berman, Joe R. Cooper, Westport Asset Management, Inc./5.58%, American Century Companies, Inc./5.40%, Putnam, LLC./5.00%, Dennis B. Tishkoff, State Street Bank and Trust Company/11.70%, Russell Solt, Steven S. Fishman, James R. Tener, Insiders/1.45%, Goldman Sachs Asset Management, L.P./9.30%, Brenda J. Lauderback, Cooke & Bieler, L.P./6.00%, David T. Kollat (21 Owners included in Index)

Financial Data: *Fiscal Year End:*01/28 *Latest Annual Data:* 2/3/2007

Year	Sales		Net Income
2007	$4,743,048,000		$124,045,000
2006	$4,429,905,000		-$10,088,000
2005	$4,375,072,000		$23,763,000
Curr. Assets:	$1,149,047,000	Curr. Liab.: $474,232,000	P/E Ratio: 23.30
Plant, Equip.:	$505,647,000	Total Liab.: $590,823,000	Indic. Yr. Divd.: NA
Total Assets:	$1,720,526,000	Net Worth: $1,129,703,000	Debt/ Equity: NA

Big Sky Energy Corp

Formerly: China Energy Ventures Corp
440 2nd Ave. Sw, Ste. 750, Calgary, AB, T2P 5E9; *PH:* 1-403-234-8282

General - Incorporation	NV	**Stock**- Price on:12/24/2007	$169.38
Employees	64	Stock Exchange	NA
Auditor	Deloitte & Touche LLP	Ticker Symbol	NA
Stk Agt	Interwest Transfer Company, Inc.	Outstanding Shares	160,750,000
Counsel	NA	E.P.S	-$0.429
DUNS No.	NA	Shareholders	NA

Business: The group's principal activity is to provide equipment and technical services to support Internet usage. These services are provided to major urban markets throughout the People's Republic of China. It operates through its wholly owned subsidiary chengdu technology services which had 210 corporate subscribers. The group also resells Internet access service purchased from authorized Internet providers. On 12-Jan-2004, the group acquired big sky energy kazakhstan ltd.

Primary SIC and add'l.: 7379 7375

CIK No: 0001075247

Subsidiaries: Big Sky Network Canada Ltd.

Officers: S. A. Sehsuvaroglu/52/Dir., CEO, Pres., Barry R. Swersky/68/Co - Chmn., VP - New Developments, Matthew J. Heysel/Executive Chmn., Bruce H. Gaston/42/Dir., CFO, Daming Yang/Consultant

Directors: S. A. Sehsuvaroglu/52/Dir., CEO, Pres., Barry R. Swersky/68/Co - Chmn., VP - New Developments, Matthew J. Heysel/Executive Chmn., Guglielmo A.C. Moscato/71/Dir., Servet Harunoglu/62/Dir., Daniel Caleb Feldman/37/Dir., Philip D. Pardo/51/Dir., Bruce H. Gaston/42/Dir., CFO

Owners: Daniel Caleb Feldman, Servet Harunoglu, Insiders/9.34%, S.A. Sehsuvaroglu/4.35%, ARC Energy Fund/5.97%, Philip Pardo, Bruce Gaston/1.24%, Guglielmo Antonio Claudio Moscato, Matthew Heysel/3.18%, Ingalls & Snyder/7.82%, Barry Swersky, ABT Ltd LLP/9.30%

Financial Data: *Fiscal Year End:*12/31 *Latest Annual Data:* 12/31/2005

Year	Sales	Net Income
2005	$526,000	-$44,664,000
2004	NA	-$6,792,000
2003	$184,000	-$3,130,000

Curr. Assets:	$28,962,000	**Curr. Liab.:**	$26,079,000		
Plant, Equip.:	$21,481,000	**Total Liab.:**	$28,604,000	**Indic. Yr. Divd.:**	NA
Total Assets:	$50,444,000	**Net Worth:**	$21,840,000	**Debt/ Equity:**	NA

Bigstring Corp

3 Harding Rd., Ste. F, Red Bank, NJ, 07701; ***PH:*** 1-732-741-2840; ***Fax:*** 1-732-741-2842; ***http://*** www.bigstring.com

General - Incorporation	DE	**Stock**- Price on:12/24/2007	$0.27
Employees	8	Stock Exchange	OTC
Auditor	Wiener, Goodman & Company, P.C.	Ticker Symbol	BSGC
Stk Agt	Registrar & Transfer Co	Outstanding Shares	47,270,000
Counsel	NA	E.P.S	-$0.07
DUNS No.	NA	Shareholders	NA

Business: The groups principle activity is to provide an email service for both individuals and businesses that is recallable and changeable. The group products include POP3 server, email service solution, and text-based message through BigStrings server. In the year 2006, the group acquired DailyLOL.com. The group operates from the United States. The groups quarterly revenue for September 2007 was 0.01 millions of USD.

Primary SIC and add'l.: 7389

CIK No: 0001335282

Subsidiaries: BigString Interactive, Inc, Email Emissary, Inc

Officers: Darin M. Myman/Dir., CEO, Pres., Robert S. Demeulemeester/CFO, Treasurer, Dir., Adam M. Kotkin/Dir., COO, Sec.

Directors: Darin M. Myman/Dir., CEO, Pres., Robert S. Demeulemeester/CFO, Treasurer, Dir., Adam M. Kotkin/Dir., COO, Sec., Marc Dutton/Dir., Lee Rosenberg/Dir., Todd M. Ross/Dir.

Owners: Lee Rosenberg/2.40%, Insiders/31.04%, Darin M. Myman/19.00%, Deborah K. Daniels/8.44%, Todd M. Ross/3.67%, Robert S. DeMeulemeester/1.65%, Adam M. Kotkin/4.06%, Marc W. Dutton/1.63%, Paul Tudor Jones/9.93%, Jo Myman/19.00%, David L. Daniels/8.44%, Alfred L. Pantaleone/13.34%, Mark Shefts/5.07%

Financial Data: *Fiscal Year End:*12/31 *Latest Annual Data:* 12/31/2006

Year	Sales	Net Income
2006	$14,000	-$3,114,000

Curr. Assets:	$523,000	**Curr. Liab.:**	$213,000		
Plant, Equip.:	$215,000	**Total Liab.:**	$213,000	**Indic. Yr. Divd.:**	NA
Total Assets:	$3,726,000	**Net Worth:**	$3,513,000	**Debt/ Equity:**	NA

Bill Barrett Corp

1099 18th St., Ste. 2300, Denver, CO, 80202; ***PH:*** 1-303-293-9100; ***Fax:*** 1-303-291-0420; ***http://*** www.billbarrettcorp.com

General - Incorporation	DE	**Stock**- Price on:12/24/2007	$38.31
Employees	216	Stock Exchange	NYSE
Auditor	Deloitte & Touche LLP	Ticker Symbol	BBG
Stk Agt	Mellon Investor Services LLC	Outstanding Shares	44,360,000
Counsel	NA	E.P.S	$0.79
DUNS No.	NA	Shareholders	NA

Business: The groups principle activities include exploring, developing and producing crude oil and natural gas. The group operates from the Rocky Mountain region of the United States. The groups quarterly revenue for September 2007 was 82.25 millions of USD.

Primary SIC and add'l.: 1311

CIK No: 0001172139

Subsidiaries: Bill Barrett CBM Corporation, Bill Barrett Production Company, Bill Barrett Properties Inc

Officers: Fredrick J. Barrett/Chmn., CEO, Joseph N. Jaggers/Dir., COO, Pres., Francis B. Barron/Sr. VP, General Counsel, Sec., Terry R. Barrett/Sr. VP - Exploration, Northern Division, Kurt M. Reinecke/Sr. VP - Exploration, Southern Division, Wilfred Roy Roux/Sr. VP - Geophysics, Huntington T. Walker/Sr. VP - Land, Lynn Boone Henry/VP - Reservoir Engineering, Kevin Finnegan/VP - Information Systems, David R. MacOsko/VP - Accounting, Duane J. Zavadil/VP - Government, Regulatory Affairs, Robert W. Howard/CFO, Treasurer, Scot R. Woodall/Sr. VP - Operations, Jennifer Martin/Dir. - Investor Relations

Directors: Fredrick J. Barrett/Chmn., CEO, Joseph N. Jaggers/Dir., COO, Pres., James M. Fitzgibbons/Dir., Randy A. Foutch/Dir., Jeffrey A. Harris/Dir., Roger L. Jarvis/54/Dir., Philippe S.E. Schreiber/Dir., Randy Stein/Dir., Michael E. Wiley/Dir., Jim W. Mogg/Dir.

Owners: AMVESCAP PLC./5.90%, Capital Research and Management Company./8.60%, Philippe S.E. Schreiber, Warburg Pincus Private Equity VIII, L.P./22.80%, Randy Stein, James M. Fitzgibbons, T. Rowe Price Associates, Inc./9.30%, State Farm Mutual Automobile Insurance Co./9.90%, Kurt M. Reinecke, Roger Jarvis, Jeffrey A. Harris/22.80%, Insiders/25.50%, Terry R. Barrett, Fredrick J. Barrett, Michael E. Wiley *(17 Owners included in Index)*

Financial Data: *Fiscal Year End:*12/31 *Latest Annual Data:* 12/31/2006

Year	Sales	Net Income
2006	$375,329,000	$62,011,000
2005	$288,759,000	$23,805,000
2004	$169,980,000	-$5,266,000

Curr. Assets:	$138,507,000	**Curr. Liab.:**	$119,795,000		
Plant, Equip.:	$1,038,595,000	**Total Liab.:**	$431,004,000	**Indic. Yr. Divd.:**	NA
Total Assets:	$1,187,401,000	**Net Worth:**	$756,397,000	**Debt/ Equity:**	NA

Bio Imaging Technologies Inc

826 Newtown-Yardley Rd., Newtown, PA, 18940; ***PH:*** 1-267-757-3000; ***Fax:*** 1-267-757-3010; ***http://*** www.bioimaging.com; ***Email:*** general@bioimaging.com

General - Incorporation	DE	**Stock**- Price on:12/24/2007	$6.95
Employees	283	Stock Exchange	NDQ
Auditor	PricewaterhouseCoopers LLP	Ticker Symbol	BITI
Stk Agt	North American Transfer Co	Outstanding Shares	11,590,000
Counsel	Hale & Dorr LLP	E.P.S	$0.15
DUNS No.	78-807-9473	Shareholders	NA

Business: The group's principal activities are to provide services that support product development process of pharmaceutical, biotechnology and medical device industries. The group assists the clients in the design and management of the medical imaging component of clinical trials for all modalities, which consist of computerized tomography, magnetic resonance imaging, x-rays, dual energy X-ray absorptiometry, position emission tomography single photon emission computerized tomography and ultrasound. It provides medical imaging management services for clinical development purposes. The imaging core laboratory facilities in the United States and Europe provide centralized image data collection, processing, analysis and archival services for clinical trials. The computer assisted masked reading systems offer numerous advantages over conventional film-based medical image reading scenarios, including increased reading speed, greater standardization of image reading.

Primary SIC and add'l.: 8071 7389

CIK No: 0000822418

Subsidiaries: Bio-Imaging Technologies Holding B.V, Oxford Bio-Imaging Research

Officers: Mark L. Weinstein/Dir., CEO, Pres./$721,289.00, David A. Pitler/Sr. VP - Operations/$285,538.00, John Blank/MD - Bio, Imaging Technologies, BV, Ted I. Kaminer/Sr. VP, CFO, Sec./$328,143.00, Colin G. Miller/Sr. VP - Business Development/$272,442.00, Bioman /Company Representative, Andrew Reiter/VP - Technical Services, Andrea M. Perrone/VP - Clinical Operations, Medical Dir., Klaus Noever/Dir. - Business Development, Clinical Affairs, European Sales, Mark Endres/VP - Sales, Domestic Sale, Cornelis Van Kuijk/Member - Scientific Advisory Board, Curtis W. Hayes/Member - Scientific Advisory Board, George Patrick Heyrich/Member - Scientific Advisory Board, Johan H.C. Reiber/Member - Scientific Advisory Board, Larry Schwartz/Member - Scientific Advisory Board *(20 Officers included in Index)*

Directors: Mark L. Weinstein/Dir., CEO, Pres., David E. Nowicki/Chmn., James A. Taylor/Dir., E. M. Davidoff/Dir., Richard F. Cimino/Dir., David M. Stack/Dir., Jeffrey H. Berg/Dir., Paula B. Stafford/Dir., Martin E. Davidoff/56/Dir.

Owners: Jeffrey H. Berg/1.00%, Ted I. Kaminer/1.00%, Insiders/13.30%, David E. Nowicki/1.50%, Martin E. Davidoff, Covance Inc/20.30%, David A. Pitler/1.40%, David M. Stack/1.20%, Healthinvest Partners AB/9.20%, Paula B. Stafford, James A. Taylor/1.00%, Colin G. Miller/1.00%, Mark L. Weinstein/5.30%, Royce & Associates LLC/7.60%

Financial Data: *Fiscal Year End:*12/31 *Latest Annual Data:* 12/31/2006

Year	Sales	Net Income
2006	$40,519,000	$1,004,000
2005	$30,486,000	-$2,545,000
2004	$29,691,000	$949,000

Curr. Assets:	$25,179,000	**Curr. Liab.:**	$14,961,000	**P/E Ratio:**	46.33
Plant, Equip.:	$5,908,000	**Total Liab.:**	$15,266,000	**Indic. Yr. Divd.:**	NA
Total Assets:	$34,108,000	**Net Worth:**	$18,842,000	**Debt/ Equity:**	0.0020

Bio Key International Inc

3349 Hwy. 138, Bldg. D, Ste. B, Wall, NJ, 07719; ***PH:*** 1-732-359-1100; ***Fax:*** 1-732-359-1101; ***http://*** www.bio-key.com; ***Email:*** information@bio-key.com

General - Incorporation	DE	**Stock**- Price on:12/24/2007	$0.2
Employees	100	Stock Exchange	OTC
Auditor	Carlin, Charron & Rosen, LLP	Ticker Symbol	BKYI
Stk Agt	American Stock Transfer & Trust Co.	Outstanding Shares	57,480,000
Counsel	NA	E.P.S	-$0.04
DUNS No.	82-491-6787	Shareholders	NA

Business: The group's principal activity is to develop and market biometric fingerprint technology solutions. Biometric technology is the science of analyzing specific human characteristics which are unique to each individual in order to identify a specific person from a broader population. The group's target market includes Internet application service providers, Internet based retailers and other operators of private networks and entities where security and identification applications are required, including the aviation industry. The products include sdk and Web-key(tm). Sdk is a software developers toolkit that can be deployed in both Internet and non-Internet applications. Web-key(tm) is a biometric identification solution designed to secure Web based applications through the use of a Web based browser plug-in and a server side plug-in. On 31-Mar-2004, the group acquired public safety group inc.

Primary SIC and add'l.: 7382 7372

CIK No: 0001019034

Subsidiaries: BIO-key Acquisition Corp., BIO-key International, Inc., Public Safety Group, Inc.

Officers: Mike Depasquale/Dir., CEO, Frank Cusick/CFO, Randy Fodero/VP - Sales, Kenneth S. Souza/GM - Law Enforcement Business Unit, Sr. VP - Development, CTO, Anthony Barone/VP, GM - Fire Safety Business Unit, Mira K. Lacous/VP - Technology, Development, Biometrics, Roy Wicklund/VP - Programs, Customer Service, Charles Yanak/VP - Marketing, Augustine Okwu/Investor Relations Officer

Directors: Mike Depasquale/Dir., CEO, Thomas J. Colatosti/Chmn., John Schoenher/Dir., Charlie Romeo/Dir., Jeffrey J. May/Dir.

Owners: Michael W. DePasquale/2.30%, Insiders/6.90%, John Schoenherr, Kingdon Capital Management, LLC/4.80%, Charles P. Romeo, Kenneth S. Souza, Thomas J. Colatosti/1.90%, Jeffrey May, Trellus Management Company, LLC/15.80%, Randy Fodero, Francis J. Cusick

Financial Data: Fiscal Year End:12/31 Latest Annual Data: 12/31/2006

Year	Sales	Net Income
2006	$15,194,000	-$11,081,000
2005	$14,226,000	-$3,673,000
2004	$5,558,000	-$7,237,000

Curr. Assets:	$5,163,000	Curr. Liab.:	$13,812,000		
Plant, Equip.:	$429,000	Total Liab.:	$17,149,000	Indic. Yr. Divd.:	NA
Total Assets:	$20,465,000	Net Worth:	-$2,743,000	Debt/ Equity:	NA

Bio Logic Systems Corp

One Bio Logic Plaza, Mundelein, IL, 60060; PH: 1-847-949-5200; http:// www.natus.com

General		Stock	
Incorporation	DE	Price on:12/24/2007	$16.12
Employees	360	Stock Exchange	NA
Auditor	Grant Thornton LLP	Ticker Symbol	NA
Stk Agt	Wells Fargo Shareowner Services	Outstanding Shares	21,570,000
Counsel	Fenwick & West LLP	E.P.S.	$0.29
DUNS No.	06-162-4656	Shareholders	NA

Business: The group's principal activities are to design, develop, assemble and market computer-based electro-diagnostic systems for hospitals, clinics, universities and physicians. The electro-diagnostic system procedures include automated auditory brainstem response used for infant hearing screening, evoked response testing, otoacoustic emissions testing, polysomnography, digital electroencephalography for routine and long-term monitoring, and other quantitative eeg analyses. These systems conducted tests are used by medical practitioners specializing in neurology, otolaryngology, audiology, anesthesiology, pulmonology and psychiatry. The group also develops software that enables medical personnel to administer diagnostic tests to control various aspects of testing and to record and process data generated by the tests. The products are sold to the health care industry in North America, Europe and the Far East.

Primary SIC and add'l.: 3845

CIK No: 0000355007

Subsidiaries: Bio-logic Holding Inc, Bio-logic Systems Corp., Ltd.

Officers: James B. Hawkins/Dir., CEO, Pres., Steven J. Murphy/VP - Finance, CFO, William L. Mince/VP - Operations, Kenneth M. Traverso/VP - Marketing, Sales, Christopher D. Chung/VP - Medical Affairs, Research & Development, and Engineering

Directors: James B. Hawkins/Dir., CEO, Pres., Robert A. Gunst/Chmn., William M. Moore/Dir., Kenneth E. Ludlum/Dir., Mark D. Michael/Dir., Doris Engibous/Dir.

Financial Data: Fiscal Year End:02/28 Latest Annual Data: 12/31/2006

Year	Sales	Net Income
2006	$89,915,000	-$927,000
2005	$43,045,000	$6,152,000
2004	$36,506,000	-$2,407,000

Curr. Assets:	$51,596,000	Curr. Liab.:	$20,793,000	P/E Ratio:	62.00
Plant, Equip.:	$7,897,000	Total Liab.:	$23,137,000	Indic. Yr. Divd.:	NA
Total Assets:	$124,163,000	Net Worth:	$101,026,000	Debt/ Equity:	NA

Bio Rad Laboratories Inc

1000 Alfred Nobel Dr., Hercules, CA, 94547; PH: 1-510-724-7000; Fax: 1-510-741-5817; http:// www.bio-rad.com

General		Stock	
Incorporation	DE	Price on:12/24/2007	$72.37
Employees	5,400	Stock Exchange	AMEX
Auditor	Deloitte & Touche LLP	Ticker Symbol	BIO
Stk Agt	Computershare Investor Services LLC	Outstanding Shares	26,650,000
Counsel	NA	E.P.S.	NA
DUNS No.	00-912-7663	Shareholders	NA

Business: The group's principal activities are to manufacture and supply products and systems for life science research and clinical diagnostics. The operations are organized into two business segments: life science and clinical diagnostics. The life science segment develops, manufacture and sells liquid chromatography, electrophoresis, gene amplification and transformation, imaging and image analysis, dna sequencing and sample preparation products. The clinical diagnostics segment manufactures and sells automated test systems, informatics systems, test kits and specialized reference laboratories. It also sells hospital laboratories, state newborn screening facilities and insurance and forensic testing laboratories. The products are manufactured in the United States, England, Italy, France, Germany and Belgium and are sold in 34 countries across the world.

Primary SIC and add'l.: 3826 3829 3841

CIK No: 0000012208

Subsidiaries: ADIL Instruments , Bio-Metrics Ltd., Bio-Metrics Properties, Limited, Bio-Rad, Bio-Rad China Limited, Bio-Rad France Holding, Bio-Rad Fujirebio Inc, Bio-Rad Holdings LLC, Bio-Rad Hungary Trading Ltd, Bio-Rad Korea Limited, Bio-Rad Laboratoires-Aparelhos e Reagentes Hospitalares, LDA, Bio-Rad Laboratories (Canada) Limited, Bio-Rad Laboratories (Israel) Inc., Bio-Rad Laboratories (Pty) Limited, Bio-Rad Laboratories (Shanghai) Limited 49 Subsidiaries included in the Index

Officers: Giovanni Magni/51/VP, International Sales Mgr.

Directors: Louis Drapeau/64/Dir.

Owners: Steven Schwartz, Insiders, Steven Schwartz/0.80%, Blue Raven Partners, L.P., Norman Schwartz, Private Capital Management, Inc./6.70%, Ariel Capital Management, LLC/9.60%, Sanford S. Wadler/0.10%, Albert J. Hillman, Ruediger Naumann-Etienne, Norman Schwartz/1.00%, James J. Bennett, Insiders/16.60%, John Goetz/0.30%, Albert J. Hillman *(17 Owners included in Index)*

Financial Data: Fiscal Year End:12/31 Latest Annual Data: 12/31/2006

Year	Sales	Net Income
2006	$1,273,930,000	$103,263,000
2005	$1,180,985,000	$81,553,000
2004	$1,090,012,000	$68,242,000

Curr. Assets:	$1,129,777,000	Curr. Liab.:	$319,533,000		
Plant, Equip.:	$189,627,000	Total Liab.:	$776,630,000	Indic. Yr. Divd.:	NA
Total Assets:	$1,596,168,000	Net Worth:	$819,538,000	Debt/ Equity:	0.4943

Bio Reference Laboratories Inc

481 Edward H. Ross Dr., Elmwood Park, NJ, 07407; PH: 1-201-791-2600; Fax: 1-201-791-1941; http:// www.bioreference.com

General		Stock	
Incorporation	NJ	Price on:12/24/2007	$26.68
Employees	1,156	Stock Exchange	NDQ
Auditor	Moore Stephens, P.C	Ticker Symbol	BRLI
Stk Agt	American Stock Transfer & Trust Co.	Outstanding Shares	13,660,000
Counsel	Tolins & Lowenfels	E.P.S.	$0.92
DUNS No.	12-157-1798	Shareholders	NA

Business: The group's principal activities are to provide clinical laboratory testing services to a range of healthcare providers. The group offers a range of laboratory testing services including blood and urine analysis, blood chemistry, hematology services, serology, toxicology, pap smears, tissue pathology and other tissue analysis. Healthcare providers utilize these tests in the detection, diagnosis, evaluation, monitoring and treatment of diseases. The clinical laboratory testing business consists of routine testing and esoteric testing. Routine tests measure various health parameters such as the functions of the heart, kidney, liver, thyroid and other organs. Esoteric tests require sophisticated equipment, materials, highly skilled personnel and professional attention are ordered less frequently than routine tests.

Primary SIC and add'l.: 7375 8071

CIK No: 0000792641

Subsidiaries: CareEvolve.com, Inc., Medilabs, Inc.

Officers: Marc D. Grodman/Chmn., CEO, Pres., John W. Littleton/VP, Dir. - Sales, James Weisberger/VP, Chief Medical Officer, Dir. - Laboratory, Cory Fishkin/Careevolve, Pres., Richard L. Faherty/CIO, Pres. - Psimedica, Nicholas Papazicos/VP - Financial Operations, Charles T. Todd/Sr. VP - Sales, Marketing, Warren Erdmann/VP, GM, Sally Howlett/VP - Billing, Sam Singer/Dir., CFO, VP, Howard Dubinett/Dir., COO, Exec. VP, Nick Cetani/VP, Laboratory Mgr., Scott Fein/Sr. VP, Azmy Awad/Sr. VP, Kara Sheffel/Coordinator, Investor Relations

Directors: Marc D. Grodman/Chmn., CEO, Pres., Harry Elias/Dir., Gary Lederman/Dir., Sam Singer/Dir., CFO, VP, Howard Dubinett/Dir., COO, Exec. VP, John Roglieri/Dir., Joseph Benincasa/58/Dir.

Owners: Paradigm Capital Management, LLC, Gary Lederman, Marc D. Grodman, Howard Dubinett, Sam Singer, John Roglieri, Insiders

Financial Data: Fiscal Year End:10/31 Latest Annual Data: 10/31/2006

Year	Sales	Net Income
2006	$193,134,000	$11,291,000
2005	$163,896,000	$7,621,000
2004	$136,184,000	$8,516,000

Curr. Assets:	$84,576,000	Curr. Liab.:	$44,582,000	P/E Ratio:	29.00
Plant, Equip.:	$12,084,000	Total Liab.:	$51,694,000	Indic. Yr. Divd.:	NA
Total Assets:	$120,473,000	Net Worth:	$68,779,000	Debt/ Equity:	0.1339

Bio Solutions Manufacturing Inc

1161 James St. , Hattiesburg, MS, 39403; PH: 1-888-262-1600; http:// www.biosolutionsmfg.com

General		Stock	
Incorporation	NY	Price on:12/24/2007	NA
Employees	7	Stock Exchange	OTC
Auditor	Sherb & Co., LLP	Ticker Symbol	BSLM
Stk Agt	Pacific Stock Transfer Company	Outstanding Shares	NA
Counsel	NA	E.P.S.	-$0.086
DUNS No.	NA	Shareholders	NA

Business: The group's principle activity is to obtain customers such as large merchant accounts processing a high volume of credit card transactions and merchant associations with numerous members. The group also operate as a corporate independent sales organization for the purpose of developing merchant accounts and recruiting and providing support services to other independent sales organization. To date the group has been unsuccessful in developing these businesses. The group has discontinued the operation of marketing and leasing electronic transaction equipment in 2003, operated by its subsidiary single source electronic transactions inc.

Primary SIC and add'l.: 7389 5065 5044

CIK No: 0001128581

Subsidiaries: Bio Solutions Production, Inc., CardReady of New York, Inc, Single Source Electronic Transactions, Inc.

Officers: Patricia Spreitzer/Dir., Sec., Treasurer, David S. Bennett/Dir., Pres.

Directors: David S. Bennett/Dir., Pres., Patricia Spreitzer/Dir., Sec., Treasurer

Owners: Loewen Global Fund, Ltd/9.30%, Innovative Industries, LLC/17.14%, Bio Solutions Franchise Corp./17.14%, Insiders/1.12%, Interstellar Holdings, LLC/4.90%, Wayne N. Wade/17.14%, Marjolein Imfeld/2.40%, Patricia M. Spreitzer, David S. Bennett, Louis Elwell/17.14%, T&T Vermogensverwaltung AG, Loewen Global Fund Ltd./4.70%

Financial Data: Fiscal Year End:10/31 Latest Annual Data: 10/31/2006

Year	Sales	Net Income
2006	$144,000	-$2,740,000
2005	$206,000	-$1,025,000
2004	$191,000	-$657,000

Curr. Assets:	$192,000	Curr. Liab.:	$1,377,000		
Plant, Equip.:	$459,000	Total Liab.:	$1,377,000	Indic. Yr. Divd.:	NA
Total Assets:	$794,000	Net Worth:	-$582,000	Debt/ Equity:	NA

Bio-Bridge Science Inc

1211 W 22nd St. Ste. 615, Ste. 615, Oak Brook, IL, 60523; PH: 1-630-928-0869; http:// www.bio-bridge-science.com; Email: info@Bio-Bridge-Science.com

General		Stock	
Incorporation	DE	Price on:12/24/2007	$1
Employees	26	Stock Exchange	OTC
Auditor	Weinberg & Company, P.A.	Ticker Symbol	BGES
Stk Agt	Registrar & Transfer Co	Outstanding Shares	33,730,000
Counsel	NA	E.P.S.	-$0.09
DUNS No.	NA	Shareholders	NA

Business: The groups principal activity is to development of biological products for the prevention and treatment of human infectious diseases.The group products include HIV-PV VACCINE I, and HIV-1 Gag. The group operates from China, Japan and the United States.

Primary SIC and add'l.: 2834

CIK No: 0001309304

Officers: Liang Qiao/Chmn., CEO, Wenhui Qiao/Dir., Pres., Chuen Huei Lee/CFO

Directors: Liang Qiao/Chmn., CEO, Wenhui Qiao/Dir., Pres., Isao Arimoto/Dir., Shyh-Jing Chiang/Dir., Katherine Knight/Member - Scientific Advisory Board, Greg T. Spear/Member - Scientific Advisory Board, Toshihiro Komoike/Dir., Trevor Roy/Dir., Anthony Cheung/Dir., Cheung Hin Shun Anthony/53/Dir.

Owners: Shyh-Jing Chiang/2.40%, Isao Arimoto/9.90%, Lee Huei Chuen, Anthony Hin Shun Cheung/5.30%, Toshihiro Komoike/2.20%, Insiders/68.20%, Liang Qiao/37.20%, Trevor Roy/5.30%, Wenhui Qiao/5.20%

Financial Data: *Fiscal Year End:*12/31 *Latest Annual Data:* 12/31/2006

Year	Sales	Net Income
2006	$2,000	-$1,324,000
2005	NA	-$1,253,000

Curr. Assets:	$206,000	Curr. Liab.:	$649,000		
Plant, Equip.:	$1,750,000	Total Liab.:	$649,000	Indic. Yr. Divd.:	NA
Total Assets:	$2,316,000	Net Worth:	$1,668,000	Debt/ Equity:	NA

Bio-Life Labs Inc

9911 W Pico Blvd, Ste. 1410, Los Angeles, CA, 90035; *PH:* 1-310-943-6445; *http://* www.biolifelabs.com

General - Incorporation	NV	Stock- Price on:12/24/2007	$0.006
Employees	NA	Stock Exchange	OTC
Auditor	Robison, Hill & Co	Ticker Symbol	BLFE
Stk Agt.	Interwest Transfer Company, Inc.	Outstanding Shares	NA
Counsel	NA	E.P.S.	NA
DUNS No.	NA	Shareholders	NA

Business: The group's principal activity is to pursue investment, development and distribution opportunities in the field of biometrics. The products of the group include a line of biometric door locks, computer access control devices, digital video surveillance and time and attendance devices. The group has secured a master resellers agreement with biothentica corporation, a distributor of biometric identification hardware and security solutions for home and business. On 10-Jun-2003, the group discontinued its prior operations of publishing and selling of books and toys related to the character manfred moose. During 2003, the group acquired tecscan international inc.

Primary SIC and add'l.: 7372 7382

CIK No: 0000899049

Financial Data: *Fiscal Year End:*06/30 *Latest Annual Data:* 6/30/2004

Year	Sales	Net Income
2004	NA	-$445,000
2003	NA	-$428,000
2002	$107,000	-$87,000

Curr. Assets:	$131,000	Curr. Liab.:	$79,000		
Plant, Equip.:	$13,000	Total Liab.:	$79,000	Indic. Yr. Divd.:	NA
Total Assets:	$429,000	Net Worth:	$349,000	Debt/ Equity:	NA

Bio-Matrix Scientific Group Inc

Formerly: Tasco International Inc
8885 Rehco Rd., San Diego, CA, 92121; *PH:* 1-619-398-3517; *http://* www.tasco360.com

General - Incorporation	DE	Stock- Price on:12/24/2007	$0.64
Employees	8	Stock Exchange	NA
Auditor	Chang G. Park, Cpa	Ticker Symbol	NA
Stk Agt.		Outstanding Shares	19,300,000
Counsel	NA	E.P.S.	-$0.13
DUNS No.	NA	Shareholders	NA

Business: The group's principle activity is to provide virtual reality technology for CD-ROM, media and Internet presentations. The company is a development stage company. The company plans to provide both business and consumers solutions that enable the company to deliver digital media content to Web sites. The company initially plans to use and develop collective resources within the digital media arena to provide production of visual content, particularly of providing images in the 360-degree format whereby users can easily navigate on a computer screen by moving a cursor inside the image. The company has initially targeted the global vertical markets like real estate, travel and hospitality, automotive and entertainment. The group operates from United States.

Primary SIC and add'l.: 7375

CIK No: 0001079282

Officers: Geoffrey O'Neill/58/Chief Scientific Advisor

Owners: David R. Koos, BMXP Holdings Shareholder Business Trust, Brian Pockett, Insiders

Financial Data: *Fiscal Year End:*09/30 *Latest Annual Data:* 9/30/2006

Year	Sales	Net Income
2006	NA	-$31,383,000
2005	NA	-$7,000

Curr. Assets:	$43,000	Curr. Liab.:	$1,453,000		
Plant, Equip.:	$341,000	Total Liab.:	$1,453,000	Indic. Yr. Divd.:	NA
Total Assets:	$413,000	Net Worth:	-$1,041,000	Debt/ Equity:	NA

Bio-Solutions International Inc

2 Ridgedale Ave., Ste. 217, Cedar Knolls, NJ, 07927; *PH:* 1-973-993-8001

General - Incorporation	NV	Stock- Price on:12/24/2007	NA
Employees	2	Stock Exchange	NA
Auditor	Russell Bedford Stefanou Mirchandani	Ticker Symbol	NA
Stk Agt.	Interwest Transfer Company, Inc.	Outstanding Shares	178,730,000
Counsel	NA	E.P.S.	-$0.02
DUNS No.	NA	Shareholders	NA

Business: The group's principal activity is to provide biological solutions to industries that desire an environment friendly form of waste remediation. The products are developed to digest the waste products effectively and in an environmentally safe and responsible manner. The products help complex waste products to break down into simple, harmless and elemental substances. The group's products include bio-clear pond formula, bp310 powder - bio plumber, bp310 plus - bio plumber plus, bp410 - bio-clear wastewater formula, bp610 - bio sewage septic, bp710 - bio-clear solid waste treatment formula, bp810 - bio-clear algae formula and others.

Primary SIC and add'l.: 2819

CIK No: 0000842013

Subsidiaries: Medefile, Inc.

Officers: Milton Hauser/Chmn., CEO, Pres., Acting CFO, Eric Rosenfeld/CIO, David Dorrance/VP - Digital Imaging, Peter Loprimo/VP - Marketing, Kevin Hauser/Dir. - New Business Development

Directors: Milton Hauser/Chmn., CEO, Pres., Acting CFO, Peter Leveton/Dir., William Cullen/Dir., John R. Bason/62/Dir.

Owners: Insiders/0.27%, Milton Hauser/0.25%, David Dorrance, Anthony Paquin, Eric Rosenfeld/0.01%, Vantage Holding Ltd./0.52%

Financial Data: *Fiscal Year End:*12/31 *Latest Annual Data:* 12/31/2006

Year	Sales	Net Income
2006	$37,000	-$3,609,000
2005	NA	-$63,000

Curr. Assets:	$45,000	Curr. Liab.:	$604,000		
Plant, Equip.:	NA	Total Liab.:	$604,000	Indic. Yr. Divd.:	NA
Total Assets:	$45,000	Net Worth:	-$559,000	Debt/ Equity:	NA

Bioanalytical Systems Inc

2701 Kent Ave., West Lafayette, IN, 47906; *PH:* 1-765-463-4527; *Fax:* 1-765-497-1102; *http://* www.bioanalytical.com

General - Incorporation	IN	Stock- Price on:12/24/2007	$7.45
Employees	370	Stock Exchange	NDQ
Auditor	Crowe Chizek & Co. LLC	Ticker Symbol	BASI
Stk Agt.	National City Bank	Outstanding Shares	4,910,000
Counsel	NA	E.P.S.	$0.09
DUNS No.	04-029-4803	Shareholders	NA

Business: The group's principal activity is to provide a broad range of value-added services and products on chemical analysis to pharmaceutical, medical device and biotechnology industries. The group operates in two principal segments: research services and research products. The research services unit provides screening, pharmacological testing, preclinical safety testing, formulation development, regulatory compliance and quality control testing. The research products unit provides liquid chromatography, electrochemical and physiological monitoring products to pharmaceutical companies, universities, government research centers and medical research institutions. The group has 18 established distributors covering Japan, the pacific basin, South America, the Middle East, India, South Africa and eastern Europe. The group acquired pharmakinetics laboratories inc on 26-May-2003 and lc resources inc on 13-Dec-2002.

Primary SIC and add'l.: 3821 8734

CIK No: 0000720154

Subsidiaries: BAS Analytics, Ltd., BAS Evansville, Inc., BAS Instruments, Ltd., BASi Maryland, Inc., BASi Northwest Laboratory, Inc., Bioanalytical Systems, Ltd.

Officers: Richard M. Shepperd/Dir., CEO, Pres., Peter T. Kissinger/Chmn., Chief Scientific Officer, Candice B. Kissinger/56/Dir., Sr. VP, Dir. - Research, Sec., Michael R. Cox/CFO, VP - Finance, Ronald E. Shoup/COO - Basi Contract Research Services, Lisa Sanford/Contract Services Inquiries, Regional Business Mgr. - Southeast, Jim Gitzen/Contract Services Inquiries, Regional Business Mgr. - Midwest, Christina Nocernino/Contract Services Inquiries, Regional Business Mgr. - Northwest, Diana Kelsey/Contract Services Inquiries, Regional Business Mgr. - Southwest, Andy Brown/Contract Services Inquiries, Regional Business Mgr. - Europe, UK, Edward M. Chait/Exec. VP

Directors: Richard M. Shepperd/Dir., CEO, Pres., Peter T. Kissinger/Chmn., Chief Scientific Officer, Candice B. Kissinger/56/Dir., Sr. VP, Dir. - Research, Sec., David W. Crabb/Dir., William E. Baitinger/Dir., Leslie B. Daniels/Dir., Larry S. Boulet/Dir.

Owners: Richard M. Shepperd, William B. Baitinger/3.10%, Leslie B. Daniels/1.30%, Michael R. Cox/0.70%, Ronald E. Shoup/2.30%, Edward M. Chait, Candice B. Kissinger/25.20%, Insiders/33.80%

Financial Data: *Fiscal Year End:*09/30 *Latest Annual Data:* 9/30/2006

Year	Sales	Net Income
2006	$43,048,000	-$2,610,000
2005	$42,395,000	-$101,000
2004	$37,152,000	-$203,000

Curr. Assets:	$13,663,000	Curr. Liab.:	$10,110,000		
Plant, Equip.:	$25,766,000	Total Liab.:	$24,961,000	Indic. Yr. Divd.:	NA
Total Assets:	$42,314,000	Net Worth:	$17,354,000	Debt/ Equity:	0.5147

BioChem Solutions Inc

Formerly: Normexsteel Inc
Bay & Deveax St.s, Nassau, CR 5464; *PH:* 242-328-1110; *http://* www.norarc.com

General - Incorporation	FL	Stock- Price on:12/24/2007	$26
Employees	1	Stock Exchange	NA
Auditor	North American Liability Group, Inc	Ticker Symbol	NA
Stk Agt.	NA	Outstanding Shares	NA
Counsel	NA	E.P.S.	NA
DUNS No.	NA	Shareholders	NA

Business: The group's principal activity was to provide education and franchiser of the ed-vancement centers, a network that provided a comprehensive range of educational and tutorial services to individuals of all ages. The group developed and published a variety of specialized educational programs including computer global Internet educational campus in various languages. The group also developed a variety of educational programs for children of all ages for both video and television production. Through its subsidiary, the group intends to provide services to professional groups seeking to obtain affordable professional liability insurance rates, through the creation of captive insurance companies. The services include evaluation, development, and management of captive insurance programs. On 02-Oct-2003, the group acquired nor-american liability corporation

Primary SIC and add'l.: 7389 6411

CIK No: 0001085115

Subsidiaries: North American Liability Group, Inc., North-American Liability Corporation

Officers: Francois Leblane/Pres.

Owners: Island Rock Investment/99.00%

Financial Data: *Fiscal Year End:*12/31 *Latest Annual Data:* 12/31/2005

Year	Sales	Net Income
2005	NA	-$933,000
2004	NA	-$1,181,000
2003	NA	-$316,000

Curr. Assets:	$0	**Curr. Liab.:**	$1,689,000		
Plant, Equip.:	$3,000	**Total Liab.:**	$1,689,000	**Indic. Yr. Divd.:**	NA
Total Assets:	$3,000	**Net Worth:**	-$1,686,000	**Debt/ Equity:**	NA

Biocoral Inc

c/o Corporation Service Company, 2711 Centerville Rd., Ste. 400, Wilmington, DE, 19808;
PH: 1-33-147579843; *http://* www.biocoral.com; *Email:* biocoralinc@biocoral.com

General - Incorporation	DE	**Stock**- Price on:12/24/2007	$28.2
Employees	NA	Stock Exchange	OTC
Auditor	Moore & Assoc.	Ticker Symbol	BCRA
Stk Agt	U.S. Stock Transfer Corp	Outstanding Shares	NA
Counsel	NA	E.P.S	NA
DUNS No.	NA	Shareholders	NA

Business: The group's principal activities are to research, develop and commercialize biotechnology and biomaterial in the health care area. The group through its subsidiaries manufactures and markets bone graft substitute and other patented biomaterials. The group has developed autologous fibrin glue that utilizes the patient's own blood, there by eliminating the risk of viral transmission. The group has developed a product biocoral(R) for treatment of bone fractures due to osteoporosis. The group has begun clinical trials of its products. The group has patient applications in various countries such as Europe, Canada, the United States, Japan, Australia and Switzerland.

Primary SIC and add'l.: 8731 2836 2834

CIK No: 0000919605

Subsidiaries: Bio Holdings

Officers: Nasser Nassiri/Chmn., CEO, Yuhko Grossmann/Dir., Sec., Treasurer

Directors: Nasser Nassiri/Chmn., CEO, Lhocine Yahia/Member - Scientific Advisory Board, Jean Darondel/Dir., Member - Scientific Advisory Board, R. Eloy/Member - Scientific Advisory Board, Genevieve Guillemin/Member - Scientific Advisory Board, Roland Schmitthauesler/Member - Scientific Advisory Board, Yves Cirotteau/Member - Scientific Advisory Board, A. Jussmann/Member - Scientific Advisory Board, Yuhko Grossmann/Dir., Sec., Treasurer, Yann Lepetitcorps/Member - Scientific Advisory Board

Owners: Insiders, Yuhko Grossman, Jean Darondel, Nasser Nassiri

Financial Data: *Fiscal Year End:*12/31 *Latest Annual Data:* 03/31/2007

Year	Sales	Net Income
2007	NA	NA
2006	$408,000	-$1,473,000
2005	$316,000	-$886,000

Curr. Assets:	$736,000	**Curr. Liab.:**	$1,231,000		
Plant, Equip.:	$25,000	**Total Liab.:**	$4,687,000	**Indic. Yr. Divd.:**	NA
Total Assets:	$1,325,000	**Net Worth:**	-$3,362,000	**Debt/ Equity:**	NA

Biocryst Pharmaceuticals Inc

2190 Pkwy. Lake Dr., Birmingham, AL, 35244; *PH:* 1-205-444-4600; *Fax:* 1-205-444-4640;
http:// www.biocryst.com; *Email:* info@biocryst.com

General - Incorporation	DE	**Stock**- Price on:12/24/2007	$7.39
Employees	85	Stock Exchange	NDQ
Auditor	Ernst & Young LLP	Ticker Symbol	BCRX
Stk Agt	American Stock Transfer & Trust Co.	Outstanding Shares	29,360,000
Counsel	Brobeck, Phleger & Harrison	E.P.S	-$1.41
DUNS No.	61-819-4609	Shareholders	NA

Business: The group's principle activity is to develop pharmaceuticals for the treatment of infections, inflammatory and cardiovascular diseases and disorders. The group uses structured-based drug design technologies to develop small-molecule pharmaceuticals for the treatment of diseases and disorders. Some of the projects under development include Neuraminidase Inhibitor, PNP Inhibitor, Tissue Factor, Complement Component C1s inhibitors, Hepatitis C Polymerase Iinhibitors. The group markets its products through collaborators and licensees. The group operates from United States.

Primary SIC and add'l.: 8731 2836 2834

CIK No: 0000882796

Subsidiaries: 3-Dimensional Pharmaceuticals, Inc

Officers: Jon P. Stonehouse/Dir., CEO, Pres., Stuart Grant/Sr. VP, CFO, James W. Alexander/Sr. VP - Clinical, Regulatory Operations, Chief Medical Officer/$654,640.00, Jonathan M. Nugent/VP - Corporate Communications, Claude J. Bennett/COO/$531,048.00, Yarlagadda S. Babu/VP - Drug Discovery, Randall B. Riggs/Sr. VP - Business Development/$619,657.00, Michael A. Darwin/VP - Finance/$352,080.00, David S. McCullough/VP - Strategic Planning, Commercialization

Directors: Jon P. Stonehouse/Dir., CEO, Pres., Charles Bugg/Chmn., Albert F. Lobuglio/Member - Scientific Advisory Board, Gordon N. Gill/Member - Scientific Advisory Board, Lorraine J. Gudas/Member - Scientific Advisory Board, Herbert A. Hauptman/Member - Scientific Advisory Board, Hamilton O. Smith/Member - Scientific Advisory Board, Stephen R. Biggar/37/Dir., Zola P. Horovitz/73/Dir., Joseph H. Sherrill/67/Dir., William M. Spencer/87/Dir., Randolph C. Steer/58/Dir., John L. Higgins/38/Dir., Beth C. Seidenberg/51/Dir., William W. Featheringill/65/Dir.

Owners: Insiders/31.90%, Michael A. Darwin, Joseph H. Sherrill/2.00%, Felix J. and Julian C. Baker/6.00%, Charles E. Bugg/2.00%, Stephens Investment Management, LLC/6.10%, James W. Alexander, Jon P. Stonehouse, John L. Higgins, Randolph C. Steer, Jonathan M. P. Nugent, William W. Featheringill/9.60%, Claude J. Bennett/1.00%, Beth C. Seidenberg, William M. Spencer/2.20%
(20 Owners included in Index)

Financial Data: *Fiscal Year End:*12/31 *Latest Annual Data:* 12/31/2006

Year	Sales	Net Income
2006	$6,212,000	-$43,618,000
2005	$152,000	-$26,099,000
2004	$337,000	-$21,104,000

Curr. Assets:	$45,790,000	**Curr. Liab.:**	$10,735,000		
Plant, Equip.:	$3,029,000	**Total Liab.:**	$47,331,000	**Indic. Yr. Divd.:**	NA
Total Assets:	$68,485,000	**Net Worth:**	$21,155,000	**Debt/ Equity:**	NA

BioCurex Inc

215-7080 River Rd., Richmond, BC, V6X 1X5; *PH:* 1-604-207-9150; *Fax:* 1-604-922-5919;
http:// www.biocurex.com; *Email:* sales@curex.net

General - Incorporation		**Stock**- Price on:12/24/2007	$0.62
Employees	NA	Stock Exchange	OTC
Auditor	NA	Ticker Symbol	BOCX
Stk Agt	Securities Transfer Corp	Outstanding Shares	NA
Counsel	NA	E.P.S	NA
DUNS No.	NA	Shareholders	NA

Business: The groups principle activities include developing and manufacturing cancer detection technologies. The groups technologies include BioCurexs Histo-RECAF(TM) and Serum-RECAF(TM). The group operates from United States.

Primary SIC and add'l.: 3841

CIK No:

Officers: Ricardo Moro-Vidal/CEO, Pres., Gerald Wittenberg/Chmn., Sec., Treasurer

Directors: Gerald Wittenberg/Chmn., Sec., Treasurer, Phil Gold/Chmn. - Scientific Advisory Board, Jose Uriel/Member - Scientific Advisory Board, M. J. Villacampa/Member - Scientific Advisory Board, T. Tamaoki/Member - Scientific Advisory Board, E. Alpert/Member - Scientific Advisory Board, Michel Sadelain/Member - Scientific Advisory Board, Strath Wilson/Member - Scientific Advisory Board, Garri Abelev/Member - Scientific Advisory Board

Financial Data: *Fiscal Year End:*NA *Latest Annual Data:* 12/31/2006

Year	Sales	Net Income
2006	NA	-$2,081,000
2005	$200,000	-$1,756,000
2004	$209,000	-$1,406,000

Curr. Assets:	$879,000	**Curr. Liab.:**	$780,000		
Plant, Equip.:	NA	**Total Liab.:**	$780,000	**Indic. Yr. Divd.:**	NA
Total Assets:	$1,208,000	**Net Worth:**	$428,000	**Debt/ Equity:**	NA

Biodelivery Sciences International Inc

801 Corporate Ctr. Dr., Ste. 210, Raleigh, NC, 27607; *PH:* 1-919-582-9050; *Fax:* 1-919-582-9051;
http:// www.bdsinternational.com

General - Incorporation	IN	**Stock**- Price on:12/24/2007	$4.17
Employees	12	Stock Exchange	NDQ
Auditor	Aidman, Piser & Co. P.A	Ticker Symbol	BDSI
Stk Agt	American Stock Transfer & Trust Co.	Outstanding Shares	18,830,000
Counsel	Ellenoff Grossman & Schole LLP	E.P.S	-$2.02
DUNS No.	NA	Shareholders	NA

Business: The group's principal activity is to develop and design drug delivery technology for pharmaceuticals, vaccines and over-the-counter drugs. The proposed drug delivery technology encapsulates or wraps the selected drug in a jellyroll-like structure termed as a cochleate cylinder. These drugs may be marketed under the brand name bioral. The group operates in the United States. On 24-Aug-2004, the group acquired arius pharmaceuticals inc.

Primary SIC and add'l.: 2834

CIK No: 0001103021

Subsidiaries: Arius Pharmaceuticals, Inc, Bioral Nutrient Delivery, LLC

Officers: Mark A. Sirgo/54/Dir., CEO, Pres./$314,690.00, Andrew L. Finn/58/Exec. VP - Clinical Development, Regulatory Affairs/$259,459.00, Raphael J. Mannino/61/Dir., Exec. VP, Chief Scientific Officer/$153,917.00, James A. McNulty/57/Sec., Treasurer, CFO/$127,050.00, James Carbonara/Investor Relations Group Contact, Joseph Kessler/Investor Relations Group Contact, Albert J. Medwar/VP - Marketing, Niraj Vasisht/VP - Product Development

Directors: Mark A. Sirgo/54/Dir., CEO, Pres., Frank E. Odonnell/57/Chmn., Raphael J. Mannino/61/Dir., Exec. VP, Chief Scientific Officer, William B. Stone/63/Dir., John J. Shea/80/Dir., William S. Poole/60/Dir., Thomas W. D'Alonzo/Dir.

Owners: William B. Stone, Laurus Master Fund. Ltd./4.99%, CDC IV, LLC/18.52%, The Francis E. ODonnell, Jr. Irrevocable Trust/20.50%, Insiders/34.92%, William S. Poole, Raphael J. Mannino/1.81%, Mark A. Sirgo/4.74%, Francis E. ODonnell/21.11%, John J. Shea, James A. McNulty, Thomas DAlonzo, Hopkins Capital Group II, LLC/19.61%, Andrew L. Finn/4.40%

Financial Data: *Fiscal Year End:*12/31 *Latest Annual Data:* 12/31/2006

Year	Sales	Net Income
2006	$2,776,000	-$19,895,000
2005	$850,000	-$10,079,000
2004	$1,779,000	-$2,827,000

Curr. Assets:	$2,404,000	**Curr. Liab.:**	$12,053,000		
Plant, Equip.:	$380,000	**Total Liab.:**	$16,056,000	**Indic. Yr. Divd.:**	NA
Total Assets:	$9,842,000	**Net Worth:**	-$6,214,000	**Debt/ Equity:**	NA

Bioenvision Inc

345 Pk. Ave., 41st Fl., New York, NY, 10154; *PH:* 1-212-750-6700; *Fax:* 1-212-750-6777;
http:// www.bioenvision.com; *Email:* info@bioenvision.com

General - Incorporation	DE	**Stock**- Price on:12/24/2007	$5.59
Employees	33	Stock Exchange	NDQ
Auditor	J.H. Cohn, LLP	Ticker Symbol	BIVN
Stk Agt	Liberty Transfer Co	Outstanding Shares	55,040,000
Counsel	NA	E.P.S	-$0.81
DUNS No.	NA	Shareholders	NA

Business: The group's principal activity is the acquisition, development and distribution of drugs in treatment of cancer. The drugs for cancer tumor include, breast, prostate, colorectal, pancreatic and bladder. The hematologic malignancies include drugs for acute myeloid leukemia, acute lymphocytic leukemia, chronic lymphocytic leukemia and lymphoma. The group is also planning to develop products for other therapeutic areas. The product portfolio of the group includes purine nucleoside technology; selective steroid receptor modulation technology; oligon(R) technology; methylene blue technology; gene therapy technology; cytostatic technology and animal health products. The group's products are marketed and distributed in North America and Europe.

Primary SIC and add'l.: 8731 2834

CIK No: 0001028205

Subsidiaries: Biotechnology & Healthcare Ventures Limited

Officers: Henk Doude Van Troostwijk/Country Mgr. - Benelux, Olivier Pilley/Country Mgr. - France, Adriaan J. Fluks/Country Mgr. - Germany, Austria, Switzerland, Giancarlo Parisi/Country Mgr. - Italy, Henrik Luning/Country Mgr. - Nordic Area, Claire Bastien/Country Mgr. - Spain, Portugal, Mark Fisher/Country Mgr. - UK, Ireland, James S. Scibetta/CFO, Lauren Bullaro/Chief Accounting Officer

Owners: Genzyme Corporation, Lehman Brothers Holdings Inc., Joseph Edelman, Michael Kauffman, Robert Sterling, Christopher B. Wood, James S. Scibetta, Thomas Scott Nelson, Federated Investors, Kristen Dunker, David P. Luci, Ian Abercrombie, Insiders, Hugh Griffith, SCO Capital Partners LLC

Financial Data: Fiscal Year End:06/30 **Latest Annual Data:** 6/30/2006

Year		Sales		Net Income
2006		$5,309,000		-$23,899,000
2005		$4,651,000		-$24,263,000
2004		$3,102,000		-$10,651,000
Curr. Assets:	$48,657,000	Curr. Liab.:	$8,592,000	
Plant, Equip.:	$274,000	Total Liab.:	$15,663,000	Indic. Yr. Divd.: NA
Total Assets:	$62,250,000	Net Worth:	$46,588,000	Debt/ Equity: NA

Bioethics Ltd

8092 South Juniper Ct., South Weber, UT, 84405; **PH:** 1-801-476-8110

General - Incorporation	NV	**Stock** - Price on:12/24/2007	$0.25
Employees	NA	Stock Exchange	OTC
Auditor	Pritchett, Siler & Hardy, P.C.	Ticker Symbol	BOTH
Stk Agt	National Stock Transfer, Inc.	Outstanding Shares	NA
Counsel	Cathy Mikus, Esq	E.P.S	$0.00
DUNS No.	NA	Shareholders	NA

Business: The groups principle activity is to provide recruiting services. The groups service area includes the research and development, engineering, marketing, sales, information technology and manufacturing industries. The group operates from United States.

Primary SIC and add'l.: 6770

CIK No: 0000894560

Officers: Mark Cowan/39/Dir., CEO, CFO, Pres., Sec., Treasurer

Directors: Mark Cowan/39/Dir., CEO, CFO, Pres., Sec., Treasurer

Owners: Windsor Development/18.00%, Insiders/23.00%, Mark Cowan/23.00%

Financial Data: Fiscal Year End:12/31 **Latest Annual Data:** 12/31/2006

Year		Sales		Net Income
2006		NA		-$16,000
2005		NA		-$7,000
2004		NA		-$6,000
Curr. Assets:	$7,000	Curr. Liab.:	NA	
Plant, Equip.:	NA	Total Liab.:	NA	Indic. Yr. Divd.: NA
Total Assets:	$7,000	Net Worth:	$7,000	Debt/ Equity: NA

Biofield Corp

1025 N Nine Dr., Ste. M, Alpharetta, GA, 30004; **PH:** 1-770-740-8180; **Fax:** 1-770-740-9366; **http://** www.biofield.com; **Email:** ir@biofield.com

General - Incorporation	DE	**Stock** - Price on:12/24/2007	$0.07
Employees	2	Stock Exchange	OTC
Auditor	Russell Bedford Stefanou Mirchandani	Ticker Symbol	BZET
Stk Agt	American Stock Transfer & Trust Co.	Outstanding Shares	40,840,000
Counsel	NA	E.P.S	-$0.02
DUNS No.	79-489-8494	Shareholders	NA

Business: The group's activity is to develop a system that assists in detecting breast cancer in a non-invasive and objective procedure. The group's breast cancer diagnostic device, the biofield diagnostic system, employs single-use sensors of our own design and a measurement device to detect and analyze changes associated with the development of epithelial cancers, such as breast cancer. The group operates mainly in the United States.

Primary SIC and add'l.: 3845

CIK No: 0001007018

Subsidiaries: Biofield International, Inc.

Officers: Michael Antonoplos/56/Dir., CEO, Joseph Repko/59/CFO, Michael Yom/Dir., COO, Ram B. Roy/Scientific Advisor

Directors: Michael Antonoplos/56/Dir., CEO, James MacKay/Chmn., Michael Yom/Dir., COO, Kenny Lau/47/Dir.

Owners: MacKay Group Limited, James MacKay

Financial Data: Fiscal Year End:12/31 **Latest Annual Data:** 12/31/2006

Year		Sales		Net Income
2006		NA		-$809,000
2005		NA		-$2,225,000
2004		$11,000		-$3,847,000
Curr. Assets:	$11,000	Curr. Liab.:	$6,506,000	
Plant, Equip.:	$0	Total Liab.:	$6,506,000	Indic. Yr. Divd.: NA
Total Assets:	$11,000	Net Worth:	-$6,495,000	Debt/ Equity: NA

Biogen Idec Inc

14 Cambridge Ctr., Cambridge, MA, 02142; **PH:** 1-617-679-2000; **Fax:** 1-617-679-2617; **http://** www.biogenidec.com

General - Incorporation	DE	**Stock** - Price on:12/24/2007	$51.43
Employees	3,750	Stock Exchange	NDQ
Auditor	PricewaterhouseCoopers LLP	Ticker Symbol	BIIB
Stk Agt	Computershare Ltd.	Outstanding Shares	342,160,000
Counsel	John M. Dunn	E.P.S	NA
DUNS No.	12-137-6230	Shareholders	NA

Business: The groups principle activities include developing, manufacturing and commercializing therapies in the areas of oncology, neurology and immunology. The groups products include AVONEX, FUMADERM, ZEVALIN and TYSABRI. The group operates from United States.

Primary SIC and add'l.: 2834 2836 8731

CIK No: 0000875045

Subsidiaries: Biogen Idec (Bermuda) Investments II Limited, Biogen Idec (Bermuda) Investments Limited, Biogen Idec (Denmark) A/S, Biogen Idec (Denmark) Manufacturing ApS, Biogen Idec (RTP) Realty LLC, Biogen Idec Australia Pty Ltd, Biogen Idec Austria GmbH, Biogen Idec B.V., Biogen Idec Belgium SA/NV, Biogen Idec Canada Inc., Biogen Idec Finland Oy, Biogen Idec GmbH, Biogen Idec Holding I Inc., Biogen Idec Holding II Inc., Biogen Idec Iberia, SL 38 Subsidiaries included in the Index

Officers: James C. Mullen/Dir., CEO, Pres./$12,201,580.00, Mark C. Wiggins/Exec. VP - Corporate, Business Development, John M. Dunn/Exec. VP - New Ventures, Craig Eric Schneier/Exec. VP - Human Resources, Public Affairs, Corporate Communications/$3,597,837.00, Burt A. Adelman/Exec. VP - Portfolio Strategy/$3,500,465.00, Susan H. Alexander/Exec. VP, General Counsel, Corp. Sec., Cecil Pickett/Dir., Pres. - Research, Development, Paul J. Clancy/CFO, Exec. VP, Peter N. Kellogg/51/CFO, Exec. VP - Finance/$3,412,215.00, Robert A. Hamm/Exec. VP - Pharmaceutical Operations, Technology, Hans Peter Hasler/Exec. VP - Global Neurology, Head - International, Michael F. MacLean/Sr. VP, Chief Accounting Officer, Controller, Faheem Hasnain/Exec. VP - Oncology Rheumatology Strategic Business, Tim Hunt/VP - Media, Naomi Aoki/Dir. - Media *(16 Officers included in Index)*

Directors: James C. Mullen/Dir., CEO, Pres., Bruce R. Ross/Chmn., Mary L. Good/Dir., Robert W. Pangia/Dir., William D. Young/Dir., Cecil Pickett/Dir., Pres. - Research, Development, Lynn Schenk/Dir., Lawrence C. Best/Dir., Marijn E. Dekkers/Dir., Thomas F. Keller/Dir., Alan B. Glassberg/Dir., Phillip A. Sharp/Dir., Alan Belzer/Dir.

Owners: Alan Belzer, PRIMECAP Management Company/9.50%, James C. Mullen, Robert W. Pangia, Phillip A. Sharp, ClearBridge Advisors, LLC/11.20%, FMR Corp./11.20%, Insiders/1.70%, Peter N. Kellogg, Robert A. Hamm, Craig Eric Schneier, Burt A. Adelman, Thomas F. Keller, Lynn Schenk

Financial Data: Fiscal Year End:12/31 **Latest Annual Data:** 12/31/2006

Year		Sales		Net Income
2006		$2,683,049,000		$217,511,000
2005		$2,422,500,000		$160,711,000
2004		$2,211,562,000		$25,086,000
Curr. Assets:	$1,712,567,000	Curr. Liab.:	$582,855,000	P/E Ratio: 77.92
Plant, Equip.:	$1,280,385,000	Total Liab.:	$1,403,030,000	Indic. Yr. Divd.: NA
Total Assets:	$8,552,808,000	Net Worth:	$7,149,778,000	Debt/ Equity: 0.0070

Bioject Medical Technologies Inc

20245 SW 95th Ave., Tualatin, OR, 97062; **PH:** 1-503-692-8001; **Fax:** 1-503-692-6698; **http://** www.bioject.com; **Email:** investorrelations@bioject.com

General - Incorporation	OR	**Stock** - Price on:12/24/2007	$1.57
Employees	81	Stock Exchange	NDQ
Auditor	Moss Adams LLP	Ticker Symbol	BJCT
Stk Agt	American Stock Transfer & Trust Co.	Outstanding Shares	15,010,000
Counsel	Stoel Rives LLP	E.P.S	-$0.34
DUNS No.	15-690-9038	Shareholders	NA

Business: The group's principal activity is to develop, manufacture and market jet injection systems for needle-free drug administration. The technology allows healthcare professionals to inject medications through the skin, both intramuscularly and subcutaneously without the risk of needlestick injuries and blood-borne pathogen transmission. Bioject(R) is a hand-held and reusable jet injector and a sterile, single-use, disposable plastic syringe. Vitajet(R) is a spring-powered, needle-free and self-injection device. The products are sold directly to healthcare providers and are licensed to pharmaceutical and biotechnology companies.

Primary SIC and add'l.: 6794 3841

CIK No: 0000810084

Officers: Ralph Makar/CEO, Pres., Jerald S. Cobbs/Chmn., Interim Pres., Christine Farrell/VP - Administration, Controller - Principal Financial, Accounting Officer/$149,823.00, Richard Stout/VP - Clinical Affairs

Directors: Jerald S. Cobbs/Chmn., Interim Pres., David S. Tierney/Dir., Brigid Makes/Dir., John Gandolfo/Dir., John Ruedy/Dir., Randal D. Chase/Dir., Joseph F. Bohan/Dir.

Owners: Randal D. Chase, James C. OShea/5.10%, Christine M. Farrell, John P. Gandolfo/2.70%, Jerald S. Cobbs, Edward Flynn/8.60%, Joseph F. Bohan, Insiders/6.40%, Life Sciences Opportunities Fund II, L.P. and Life Sciences/31.70%, John Ruedy, Michael J. Redmond/1.10%

Financial Data: Fiscal Year End:12/31 **Latest Annual Data:** 12/31/2006

Year		Sales		Net Income
2006		$10,795,000		-$6,997,000
2005		$12,288,000		-$6,589,000
2004		$9,486,000		-$9,081,000
Curr. Assets:	$6,355,000	Curr. Liab.:	$4,965,000	
Plant, Equip.:	$2,984,000	Total Liab.:	$5,542,000	Indic. Yr. Divd.: NA
Total Assets:	$10,624,000	Net Worth:	$5,082,000	Debt/ Equity: 0.0230

BioKey Identification Inc

Formerly: Demco Industries Inc
Arcade At Royal Palm 1, 950 S Pine Island Rd., Ste. 150a, Plantation, FL, 33324; **PH:** 1-954-727-8393

General - Incorporation	FL	**Stock** - Price on:12/24/2007	NA
Employees	NA	Stock Exchange	NA
Auditor	Rotenberg & Co. LLP	Ticker Symbol	NA
Stk Agt	NA	Outstanding Shares	NA
Counsel	NA	E.P.S	NA
DUNS No.	NA	Shareholders	NA

Business: The groups principle activity is to employ and distribute its technology by way of contracting to governments and commercial operations and through licensing regional offices and organizations around the world. The group operates from United States.

Primary SIC and add'l.: 1700

CIK No: 0001242388

BioLargo Inc

Formerly: Nuway Medical Inc
2603 Main St., Ste. 1155, Irvine, CA, 92614; **PH:** 1-949-643-9540; **http://** www.nuwaymedical.net

General - Incorporation	DE	**Stock**- Price on:12/24/2007	NA
Employees	2	Stock Exchange	NA
Auditor	Jeffrey S. Gilbert	Ticker Symbol	NA
Stk Agt	American Stock Transfer & Trust Co.	Outstanding Shares	NA
Counsel	NA	E.P.S	NA
DUNS No.	82-489-5510	Shareholders	NA

Business: The group's principal activity is to offer medical and health related technology products and services based on the needs of the sports industry. The group's primary product is its player record library system ('prls'). The prls is an electronic medical record and workflow process software application designed to address the information technology needs of the sports industry relating to player's health. It also helps to electronically acquire and archive player medical data and images in a digital format that helps in medical diagnosis. The records are accessible over a private network or the Internet, and can be displayed, analyzed, and interpreted by team doctors and other authorized officials. The group discontinued its operations of slot machine rental, distribution and sale of premium brand cigars and oil and gas exploration in 2002. The group purchased certain assets from genesis health tech, inc. On 28-Jun-2002.

Primary SIC and add'l.: 7379 7372 7371

CIK No: 0000880242

Subsidiaries: NuWay Sports, LLC

Officers: Dennis Calvert/45/Chmn., CEO, CFO, Pres./$184,800.00, Kenneth R. Code/CTO, Robert Szolomayer/Dir. - Corporate Development, Jeffrey C. Wallace/Dir. - Sales, Marketing, Joseph Provenzano/Dir., VP - Operations/$101,200.00, Ted Toch/Corporate Accounting Development Representative, Member - Business Advisory Board

Directors: Dennis Calvert/45/Chmn., CEO, CFO, Pres., Joseph Provenzano/Dir., VP - Operations, Dennis E. Marshall/Dir., Gary Cox/Dir., Ted Toch/Corporate Accounting Development Representative, Member - Business Advisory Board

Owners: Dennis Calvert/6.90%, Gary A. Cox/1.00%, Dennis E. Marshall/0.40%, Kenneth R. Code/57.40%, Joseph Provenzano/1.50%, Insiders/67.10%

Financial Data: *Fiscal Year End:*12/31 *Latest Annual Data:* 12/31/2006

Year	Sales	Net Income
2006	NA	-$1,311,000
2005	NA	-$1,187,000
2004	NA	-$1,218,000

Curr. Assets:	$246,000	**Curr. Liab.:**	$6,115,000		
Plant, Equip.:	NA	**Total Liab.:**	$6,115,000	**Indic. Yr. Divd.:**	NA
Total Assets:	$246,000	**Net Worth:**	-$5,869,000	**Debt/ Equity:**	NA

BIOLASE Technology Inc

4 Cromwell, Irvine, CA, 92618; ***PH:*** 1-949-361-1200; ***Fax:*** 1-949-273-6677; ***http://*** www.biolase.com; ***Email:*** dentists@biolase.com

General - Incorporation	DE	**Stock**- Price on:12/24/2007	$6.55
Employees	199	Stock Exchange	NDQ
Auditor	BDO Seidman, LLP	Ticker Symbol	BLTI
Stk Agt	U.S. Stock Transfer Corp	Outstanding Shares	23,810,000
Counsel	NA	E.P.S	-$0.18
DUNS No.	15-216-5700	Shareholders	NA

Business: The group's principal activities are to design, manufacture and market dental, cosmetic and surgical lasers and related products. The system allows dentists, oral surgeons and other specialists to perform a broad range of common dental procedures, including cosmetic applications. The group's waterlase system is used for hard and soft tissue dental procedures. The lasersmile system is used for a range of soft issue procedures and tooth whitening. The diolase and pulsemaster systems are primarily used for soft tissue procedures. The group also manufactures and markets accessories and disposable, such as handpieces, laser tips and tooth whitening gel, for use with dental laser systems. The group markets the laser system in the United States, Canada, Australia and various countries throughout Europe and the Pacific Rim. On 21-May-2003, the group acquired the American dental laser product line from American medical technologies, inc and paclive in fiscal 2004.

Primary SIC and add'l.: 8731 3845 3843

CIK No: 0000811240

Subsidiaries: BIOLASE Europe

Officers: Jeffrey W. Jones/Vice Chmn., CEO, Pres./$507,716.00, Keith G. Bateman/Exec. VP - Global Sales, Marketing/$318,263.00, Richard L. Harrison/CFO, Exec. VP, Sec./$330,506.00, Scott Jorgensen/VP - Business Development, Susan Vassallo/Dir. - Corporate Communications

Directors: Jeffrey W. Jones/Vice Chmn., CEO, Pres., George V. D'Arbeloff/Chmn., Federico Pignatelli/Dir., Robert M. Anderton/Dir., Daniel S. Durrie/Dir., Neil J. Laird/Dir.

Owners: Federico Pignatelli/4.40%, Insiders/12.20%, Daniel S. Durrie, Jeffrey W. Jones/4.30%, Capital Research and Management Company/7.00%, George V. dArbeloff/1.30%, Neil J. Laird, Keith G. Bateman/1.40%, Absolute Return Europe Fund/5.00%, FMR Corp. and related entities/10.70%

Financial Data: *Fiscal Year End:*12/31 *Latest Annual Data:* 12/31/2006

Year	Sales	Net Income
2006	$69,700,000	-$4,689,000
2005	$62,060,000	-$17,510,000
2004	$60,651,000	-$23,214,000

Curr. Assets:	$38,989,000	**Curr. Liab.:**	$22,063,000		
Plant, Equip.:	$4,851,000	**Total Liab.:**	$26,612,000	**Indic. Yr. Divd.:**	NA
Total Assets:	$48,578,000	**Net Worth:**	$21,966,000	**Debt/ Equity:**	NA

BioLife Solutions Inc

171 Front St., Owego, NY, 13827; ***PH:*** 1-607-687-4487; ***Fax:*** 1-607-687-6683; ***http://*** www.biolifesolutions.com; ***Email:*** info@biolifesolutions.com

General - Incorporation	DE	**Stock**- Price on:12/24/2007	$0.1
Employees	9	Stock Exchange	OTC
Auditor	Aronson & Co	Ticker Symbol	BLFS
Stk Agt	American Stock Transfer & Trust Co.	Outstanding Shares	69,610,000
Counsel	NA	E.P.S	-$0.023
DUNS No.	61-940-3405	Shareholders	NA

Business: The group's principle activitity to research, develop, manufacture and market low temperature technologies for use in the cryoablation of cancerous tissue and in preserving and prolonging the viability of cellular and genetic material for use in cell therapy and tissue engineering. The products of the group include accuprobe, single use probes and other disposables used with the accuprobe and also offers service contracts. The group markets accuprobe system through a direct sales force and through distributors to hospitals, surgeons and radiologists in the United States and abroad. The group's quarterly revenue for September 2007 was 0.24 millions of USD.

Primary SIC and add'l.: 3841 8731

CIK No: 0000834365

Subsidiaries: Cryomedical Sciences, Inc

Officers: Michael Rice/Chmn., CEO, Andrew Hinson/Dir. - Scientific Advisor, Matthew Snyder/VP - Sales, Aby J. Mathew/Sr. Scientist, Shelly Heimfeld/Scientific Advisor, Dayong Gao/Scientific Advisor, Darin Weber/Scientific Advisor, Scott R. Burger/Scientific Advisor, Erik J. Woods/Scientific Advisor, Matt Clawson/Contact - Investor Relations

Directors: Michael Rice/Chmn., CEO, Howard S. Breslow/Dir., Roderick De Greef/Dir., Thomas Girschweiler/Dir., Raymond Cohen/Dir., Andrew Hinson/Dir. - Scientific Advisor

Owners: Raymond Cohen/0.20%, Thomas Girschweiler/20.30%, Howard S. Breslow/3.70%, Walter Villiger/27.40%, Insiders/31.70%, Roderick de Greef/7.50%, Beskivest Chart LTD/10.60%, John G. Baust/6.40%

Financial Data: *Fiscal Year End:*12/31 *Latest Annual Data:* 12/31/2006

Year	Sales	Net Income
2006	$603,000	-$1,134,000
2005	$615,000	-$619,000
2004	$627,000	-$743,000

Curr. Assets:	$516,000	**Curr. Liab.:**	$380,000		
Plant, Equip.:	$45,000	**Total Liab.:**	$380,000	**Indic. Yr. Divd.:**	NA
Total Assets:	$560,000	**Net Worth:**	$180,000	**Debt/ Equity:**	NA

BioMarin Pharmaceutical Inc

105 Digital Dr., Novato, CA, 94949; ***PH:*** 1-415-506-6700; ***Fax:*** 1-415-382-7889; ***http://*** www.biomarinpharm.com; ***Email:*** ir@bmrn.com

General - Incorporation	DE	**Stock**- Price on:12/24/2007	$17.35
Employees	410	Stock Exchange	NDQ
Auditor	KPMG LLP	Ticker Symbol	BMRN
Stk Agt	Mellon Investor Services LLC	Outstanding Shares	95,800,000
Counsel	Paul, Hastings, Janofsky & Walker LLP	E.P.S	-$0.3
DUNS No.	NA	Shareholders	NA

Business: The group's principal activities are to develop & commercialize first-to-Market biopharmaceuticals to improve the lives of people living with life-threatening diseases or serious medical conditions. It develops enzyme-based therapeutics for the treatment of a variety of diseases and conditions.the products consist of three clinical stage product candidates including two in phase 3 development products: aryplasetm for the treatment of mps vi and neutralasetm for the reversal of anticoagulation by heparin in coronary artery bypass graft surgery. The groups trademarks are Biomarin, Aryplase, Vibrilase, Phenoptin, Neutralase, Phenylase & Neuro Trans. On 2-Jan-03, the group sold certain assets of Glyko Inc. On 18-May-04 the group acquired Ascent Pediatrics.

Primary SIC and add'l.: 2834 8731

CIK No: 0001048477

Subsidiaries: BioMarin Clinical Ltd., BioMarin Delivery Canada Inc., BioMarin Europe Ltd., BioMarin Genetics, Inc., BioMarin Holding (Lux) S.a.r.l., BioMarin Holding Ltd., BioMarin Holdings (Nova Scotia) Company, BioMarin Pharmaceutical (Canada) Inc., BioMarin/Genzyme LLC, BioMarinAcquisition(NovaScotia)Company, BioMarinPharmaceuticalDeliveryNovaScotiaCompany, BioMarinPharmaceuticalNovaScotiaCompany, Glyko Biomedical Ltd., Glyko,Inc.

Officers: Jean-Jacques Bienaime/CEO, Louis Drapeau/Sr. VP - Finance, Stephen Aselage/Sr. VP - Global Commercial Development, Baffi Robert/Sr. VP - Technical Operations/$680,208.00, Steven Jungles/VP - Supply Chain, Daniel P. Maher/VP - Product Development, Victoria Sluzky/VP - Quality, Analytical Chemistry, Stuart J. Swiedler/Sr. VP - Clinical Affairs, Amy Waterhouse/VP - Regulatory, Government Affairs, Christopher M. Starr/Chief Scientific Officer, Sr. VP, Andrew R. Ramelmeier/VP - Manufacturing, Process Development, Eric G. Davis/VP, General Counsel, Sec., Robert A. Baffi/Sr. VP - Technical Operations, Jeffrey H. Cooper/Sr. VP, CFO, Emil D. Kakkis/Sr. VP, Chief Medical Officer/$794,929.00 *(18 Officers included in Index)*

Directors: Joseph Klein/Dir., John Urquhart/Member - Science Advisory Board, Pierre Lapalme/Dir., Michael Grey/Dir., Elaine Heron/Dir., Larry J. Shapiro/Member - Science Advisory Board, David L. Rimoin/Member - Science Advisory Board, Joseph Loscalzo/Member - Science Advisory Board, Robert Langer/Member - Science Advisory Board, Jeffrey Borer/Member - Science Advisory Board, Randy Meier/Dir., Bryan V. Lawlis/Dir., Erich Sager/Dir., Alan Lewis/Dir., Member - Science Advisory Board

Owners: Insiders/2.30%, OrbiMed Advisors LLC / OrbiMed Capital LLC/6.40%, PRIMECAP Management Company/7.10%, Stephen Aselage, Pierre Lapalme, Jeffrey H. Cooper, Alan Lewis, Jean-Jacques Bienaim, Michael Grey, Robert Baffi, Elaine Heron, Emil D. Kakkis, Joseph Klein, Richard A. Meier, FMR Corp./11.00%

Financial Data: *Fiscal Year End:*12/31 *Latest Annual Data:* 12/31/2006

Year	Sales	Net Income
2006	$84,209,000	-$28,533,000
2005	$25,669,000	-$74,270,000
2004	$18,641,000	-$187,443,000

Curr. Assets:	NA	**Curr. Liab.:**	NA		
Plant, Equip.:	NA	**Total Liab.:**	NA	**Indic. Yr. Divd.:**	NA
Total Assets:	NA	**Net Worth:**	NA	**Debt/ Equity:**	1.9009

Biomed Realty Trust

17140 Bernardo Ctr. Dr., Ste. 222, San Diego, CA, 92128; ***PH:*** 1-858-485-9840; ***Fax:*** 1-858-485-9843; ***http://*** www.biomedrealty.com; ***Email:*** info@biomedrealty.com

General - Incorporation	MD	**Stock**- Price on:12/24/2007	$26.01
Employees	87	Stock Exchange	NYSE
Auditor	KPMG LLP	Ticker Symbol	BMR
Stk Agt	Bank of New York	Outstanding Shares	65,450,000
Counsel	NA	E.P.S	$0.85
DUNS No.	NA	Shareholders	NA

Business: The groups principle activities include acquiring, developing, owning, leasing and managing laboratory and office space for the life science industry. The group operates from the United States. The groups quarterly revenue for September 2007 was 64.83 millions of USD.

Primary SIC and add'l.: 6798

CIK No: 0001289236

Subsidiaries: BioMed Realty, L.P.

Officers: Alan D. Gold/Chmn., CEO, Pres., Gary A. Kreitzer/Dir., Exec. VP, General Counsel, Sec., John F. Wilson/Exec. VP, Kent R. Griffin/CFO, Matthew G. McDevitt/Regional Exec. VP, Chris Elmendorf/Dir. - Acquisitions, Leasing, San Diego, Bill Hunter/Dir. - Acquisitions, Leasing, Pennsylvania, Greg N. Lubushkin/VP, Chief Accounting Officer, Jonathan P. Klassen/VP - Legal, Assist. Sec., Karen A. Sztraicher/VP - Finance, Treasurer, William A. Gartner/Sr. VP - Real Estate Operations

Directors: Alan D. Gold/Chmn., CEO, Pres., Gary A. Kreitzer/Dir., Exec. VP, General Counsel, Sec., Barbara R. Cambon/Dir., Edward A. Dennis/Dir., Mark J. Riedy/Dir., Theodore D. Roth/Dir., Faye M. Wilson/Dir.

Owners: John F. Wilson, Barbara R. Cambon, Mark J. Riedy, Kent R. Griffin, The Vanguard Group, Inc./5.90%, Edward A. Dennis, Alan D. Gold/2.30%, Matthew G. McDevitt, Insiders/4.90%, Gary A. Kreitzer/1.40%, ING Groep N.V./5.40%, Faye M. Wilson, Cohen& Steers, Inc./7.90%, Theodore D. Roth

Financial Data: *Fiscal Year End:*12/31 *Latest Annual Data:* 12/31/2006

Year	Sales			Net Income
2006	$221,410,000			$35,033,000
2005	$138,856,000			$17,046,000
2004	$32,368,000			$5,783,000
Curr. Assets:	$58,521,000	Curr. Liab.:	$90,153,000	P/E Ratio: 30.60
Plant, Equip.:	NA	Total Liab.:	$1,458,610,000	Indic. Yr. Divd.: $1.240
Total Assets:	$2,692,642,000	Net Worth:	$1,214,713,000	Debt/ Equity: 0.8468

Biomerica Inc

1533 Monrovia Ave., Newport Beach, CA, 92663; *PH:* 1-949-645-2111; *Fax:* 1-949-722-6674; *http://* www.biomerica.com; *Email:* bmra@biomerica.com

General - Incorporation	DE	Stock- Price on:12/24/2007	$0.78
Employees	24	Stock Exchange	OTC
Auditor	PKF	Ticker Symbol	BMRA
Stk Agt.	Interwest Transfer Company, Inc.	Outstanding Shares	5,940,000
Counsel	Jeffers, Shaff & Falk	E.P.S.	$0.07
DUNS No.	06-764-7321	Shareholders	NA

Business: The group's principal activities are to develop, manufacture and distribute various orthodontic products and medical diagnostic test products. The medical diagnostic products are designed for the early detection and monitoring of chronic diseases and medical conditions. The diagnostic test kits are used to analyze blood or urine from patients in the diagnosis of various diseases and other medical complications. The group's orthodontic products include preformed bands, direct bonding pads, various brackets, buccal tubes, lingual attachments and related accessories. The group has about 300 customers for its diagnostic business including distributors, hospital and clinical laboratories, medical research institutions, medical schools, pharmaceutical companies, chain drugstores, wholesalers and physicians' offices. Trademarks include fortel, isletest, nimbus and gap.

Primary SIC and add'l.: 3843 3841

CIK No: 0000073290

Subsidiaries: Lancer Orthodontics,Inc

Officers: Zackary S. Irani/42/Chmn., CEO/$167,143.00, Janet Moore/57/Dir., CFO, Sec., Treasurer/$91,953.00, Patrick Garcia/Dir. - Sales, Marketing

Directors: Zackary S. Irani/42/Chmn., CEO, Janet Moore/57/Dir., CFO, Sec., Treasurer, Allen Barbieri/50/Dir., Francis R. Cano/61/Dir., Jane Emerson/54/Dir., John Roehm/49/Dir.

Owners: Janet Moore/13.60%, John Roehm/0.20%, Francis R. Cano/1.60%, Jane Emerson/0.20%, Allen Barbieri/1.80%, Keith A. Cannon/7.00%, Insiders/28.50%, Francis Capitanio/2.60%, Zackary Irani/11.70%, Joseph L. Rink/7.00%

Financial Data: *Fiscal Year End:*05/31 *Latest Annual Data:* 5/31/2006

Year	Sales			Net Income
2006	$7,185,000			$230,000
2005	$9,274,000			$162,000
2004	$9,169,000			-$223,000
Curr. Assets:	$2,610,000	Curr. Liab.:	$1,412,000	P/E Ratio: 11.14
Plant, Equip.:	$168,000	Total Liab.:	$1,472,000	Indic. Yr. Divd.: NA
Total Assets:	$3,225,000	Net Worth:	$1,753,000	Debt/ Equity: NA

Biomet Inc

56 E Bell Dr, Warsaw, IN, 46582; *PH:* 1-574-267-6639; *http://* www.biomet.com

General - Incorporation	IN	Stock- Price on:12/24/2007	$45.6
Employees	6,357	Stock Exchange	NA
Auditor	Ernst & Young LLP	Ticker Symbol	NA
Stk Agt.	American Stock Transfer & Trust Co.	Outstanding Shares	245,490,000
Counsel	NA	E.P.S.	$1.37
DUNS No.	08-678-2224	Shareholders	NA

Business: The group's principle activity is manufacture surgical and nonsurgical medical devices. The group's products include reconstructive products (hips, knees, and shoulders), fixation devices (bone screws and pins), orthopedic support devices, dental implants and operating-room supplies. The group operates from United States.

Primary SIC and add'l.: 3842 3841

CIK No: 0000351346

Subsidiaries: American OsteoMedix Corp., Arthrotek, Inc., Arthrovision Sport GmbH, Biolectron, Inc., Biomet Acquisitions Limited, Biomet Argentina S.A., Biomet Australia Pty. Ltd., Biomet Austria GmbH, Biomet Belgium BVBA, Biomet Biologics, Inc., Biomet Bridgend B.V., Biomet C Z S.r.o., Biomet Canada, Inc., Biomet Cementing Technologies AB, Biomet Chile, S.A. de C.V. 92 Subsidiaries included in the Index

Officers: Jeffrey R. Binder/Dir., CEO, Pres., Roger P. Van Broeck/VP - Biomet, Inc, Pres. - International Operations, Robert E. Durgin/Corporate VP - Global Regulatory Affairs, Darlene K. Whaley/51/Sr. VP - Human Resources, Daniel P. Florin/CFO, Sr. VP, Steven F. Schiess/VP - Biomet, Inc, Bradley J. Tandy/Sr. VP, General Counsel, Sec. - Biomet, Inc, Richard J. Borror/Sr. VP - Manufacturing Operations, Greg W. Sasso/Sr. VP, Pres. - Biomet SBU Operations , Biomet International, Canada, Latin America, Asia, Pacific, Kevin Haskew/CIO, Glen A. Kashuba/Sr. VP, Pres. - Biomet Trauma, Biomet Spine, Lance Perry/Corporate VP - Global Product Development, Reconstructive Devices, William C. Kolter/Sr. VP - Commercial Operations, Biomet Orthopedics, Inc, David A. Nolan/Pres. - Biomet Sports Medicine, Inc, Stuart G. Kleopfer/Pres. - Biomet Biologics, Inc *(21 Officers included in Index)*

Directors: Jeffrey R. Binder/Dir., CEO, Pres., Gene L. Tanner/75/Dir., Kenneth V. Miller/60/Dir., Dane A. Miller/Founder, Dir., Chinh E. Chu/Dir., Jonathan J. Coslet/Dir., Michael Dal Bello/Dir., Sean Fernandes/Dir., Adrian Jones/Dir., Michael Michelson/Dir., John Saer/Dir., Todd Sisitsky/Dir., Jerry L. Miller/Dir.

Owners: Scott C. Harrison, Charles E. Niemier, Gene L. Tanner, Adrian Jones, LVB Acquisition, Inc./84.74%, Daniel P. Hann, Kenneth V. Miller, Sean Fernandes, Dane A. Miller/2.50%, Insiders/2.80%, Gregory D. Hartman, State Farm Mutual Automobile Insurance Company/7.70%, Roger Van Broeck

Financial Data: *Fiscal Year End:*05/31 *Latest Annual Data:* 5/31/2006

Year		Sales		Net Income
2006		$2,025,739,000		$405,908,000
2005		$1,879,950,000		$351,616,000
2004		$1,615,253,000		$325,627,000
Curr. Assets:	$1,334,153,000	Curr. Liab.:	$535,462,000	P/E Ratio: 33.28
Plant, Equip.:	$357,632,000	Total Liab.:	$562,453,000	Indic. Yr. Divd.: $0.300
Total Assets:	$2,282,647,000	Net Worth:	$1,720,194,000	Debt/ Equity: NA

bioMETRX Inc

500 N Broadway Ste. 204, Jericho, NY, 11753; *PH:* 1-516-937-2828; *http://* www.biometrx.net

General - Incorporation	DE	Stock- Price on:12/24/2007	$1.5
Employees	NA	Stock Exchange	OTC
Auditor	Wolinetz, Lafazan & Company, P.C.	Ticker Symbol	BMRX
Stk Agt.	PacWest Transfer LLC	Outstanding Shares	NA
Counsel	Sommer & Schneider, LLP	E.P.S.	-$0.83
DUNS No.	NA	Shareholders	NA

Business: The group principal activities include designing, developing, engineering and marketing biometrics-based products for the consumer home security, consumer electronics, medical records and medical products markets. The groups products include smart touch GDO, smart lock, smart stat, and smart stick. The group marketed its product under the trade names SMARTTOUCH(TM) and MasterLock (TM). The group operates from the United States.

Primary SIC and add'l.: 3699

CIK No: 0000774657

Subsidiaries: BioMETRX Technologies, Inc., smartTOUCH Consumer Products, Inc., smartTOUCH Medical, Inc.

Officers: Mark R. Basile/49/Chmn., CEO, Lorraine Yarde/COO, Richard Iler/CFO

Directors: Mark R. Basile/49/Chmn., CEO

Owners: Lorraine Yarde, The Naples Trust, Mark Basile, Alpha Capital Aktiengesellschaft, Russell Kuhn, Whalehaven Capital Fund, Richard J. Iler, BridgePointe Master Fund Ltd., Linden Growth Partners Master Fund, LP, Insiders

Financial Data: *Fiscal Year End:*12/31 *Latest Annual Data:* 12/31/2006

Year		Sales		Net Income
2006		NA		-$10,837,000
2005		NA		-$12,174,000
2004		$287,000		-$144,000
Curr. Assets:	$513,000	Curr. Liab.:	$1,352,000	
Plant, Equip.:	$92,000	Total Liab.:	$2,046,000	Indic. Yr. Divd.: NA
Total Assets:	$636,000	Net Worth:	-$1,410,000	Debt/ Equity: NA

BioMimetic Therapeutics Inc

389-A Nichol Mill Ln., Franklin, TN, 37067; *PH:* 1-615-844-1280; *Fax:* 1-615-844-1281; *http://* www.biomimetics.com

General - Incorporation	DE	Stock- Price on:12/24/2007	$17.41
Employees	61	Stock Exchange	NDQ
Auditor	Ernst & Young LLP	Ticker Symbol	BMTI
Stk Agt.	American Stock Transfer & Trust Co.	Outstanding Shares	18,170,000
Counsel	NA	E.P.S.	-$1.33
DUNS No.	NA	Shareholders	NA

Business: The groups principle activities include developing and commercializing bioactive drug device combination products. The groups provide their product for periodontal, orthopedic, spine sports injury and cranio maxillofacial. The group products sold under the trade name GEM 21(R), GEM 21A(TM), GEM OS(R), GEM(R), GEM C(TM), GEM LT(TM) and OsteoMimetic(TM). The group operates from the United States. The group's quarterly revenue for September 2007 was 1.67 millions of USD.

Primary SIC and add'l.: 2834 3841

CIK No: 0001138400

Subsidiaries: BioMimetic Therapeutics Limited, BioMimetic Therapeutics Pty Ltd

Officers: Samuel E. Lynch/Founder, Dir., CEO, Pres./$461,438.00, William Beasley/Dir. - Clinical Affairs, Russ Pagano/VP - Regulatory, Clinical Affairs, Kearstin Patterson/Contact - Corporate Communications, Larry Bullock/CFO/$348,116.00, Mark Citron/58/Sr. VP - Regulatory Affairs, Quality Systems, Earl Douglas/General Counsel/$272,003.00, Charles E. Hart/Chief Scientific Officer, VP/$324,824.00, Steve Hirsch/COO, Exec. VP - Orthopedics/$533,185.00, James Monsor/VP - Operations/$279,392.00

Directors: Samuel E. Lynch/Founder, Dir., CEO, Pres., Larry W. Papasan/Chmn., Thomas Dyrberg/53/Dir., Charles Federico/Dir., Jim Murphy/Dir., Doug Watson/Dir., Chris Ehrlich/Dir., Gary Friedlaender/Dir., Member - Orthopedic, Scientific Advisory Board, Edward Akelman/Member - Orthopedic Scientific Advisory Board, Arnold Caplan/Member - Orthopedic Scientific Advisory Board, Michael Ehrlich/Member - Orthopedic Scientific Advisory Board, Jeffrey Hollinger/Member - Orthopedic Scientific Advisory Board, Periodontal Member - Scientific Advisory Board, Joseph Lane/Member - Orthopedic Scientific Advisory Board, Kevin Foley/Member - Orthopedic Scientific Advisory Board, Alexander Vaccaro/Member - Orthopedic Scientific Advisory Board *(18 Directors included in Index)*

Owners: Larry W. Papasan, Douglas Watson, FMR Corporation/11.20%, ClearBridge Advisors, LLC/10.10%, Gary Friedlaender, Thomas Dyrberg/13.10%, Novo A/S, Denmark/13.10%, Mark Citron, Samuel E. Lynch/6.90%, Charles E. Hart, GLG Partners LP/5.40%, Steven N. Hirsch, James A. Monsor, Larry Bullock, Chris Ehrlich/4.90% *(17 Owners included in Index)*

Financial Data: *Fiscal Year End:*12/31 *Latest Annual Data:* 12/31/2006

Year		Sales		Net Income
2006		$4,134,000		-$17,064,000
2005		$4,517,000		-$11,676,000
2004		$5,601,000		-$1,043,000

Curr. Assets:	$53,915,000	Curr. Liab.:	$5,344,000		
Plant, Equip.:	$3,933,000	Total Liab.:	$20,394,000	Indic. Yr. Divd.:	NA
Total Assets:	$65,395,000	Net Worth:	$45,001,000	Debt/ Equity:	0.0005

Biomira Inc

221 E 6th St., Tucson, AZ, 85705; **PH:** 1-520-622-5552; **Fax:** 1-520-622-5553;
http:// www.biomira.com; **Email:** ir@biomira.com

General - Incorporation	Canada	**Stock**- Price on:12/24/2007	$1.08
Employees	NA	Stock Exchange	NDQ
Auditor	Deloitte & Touche LLP	Ticker Symbol	BIOM
Stk Agt	Computershare Investor Services LLC	Outstanding Shares	116,920,000
Counsel	Pepper Hamilton LLP	E.P.S.	-$0.17
DUNS No.	24-582-7571	Shareholders	NA

Business: The group's principle activity is to develop cancer therapeutics by applying technology in immunotherapy and organic chemistry. The company is focused on synthetic therapeutic vaccines and innovative strategies for immunotherapy of cancer. The products of the company include theratope vaccine for breast cancer, blp25 vaccine for lung cancer, autologous vaccine for lymphoma and liposomal interleukin-2, designed to boost the general immune system. The company has its operations in Canada, the United States, barbados and Europe.

Primary SIC and add'l.: 2834 2836 8731

CIK No: 0000877984

Subsidiaries: Biomira, Biomira B.V, Biomira International Inc., Biomira USA Inc.

Officers: Robert L. Kirkman/Dir., CEO, Pres., Marilyn Olson/VP - Clinical, Regulatory Affairs, Edward A. Taylor/VP - Finance, Administration, CFO, Rao R. Koganty/VP, GM - Synthetic Biologics, Lynn D. Kirkpatrick/Chief Scientific Officer, Gary Christianson/COO

Directors: Robert L. Kirkman/Dir., CEO, Pres., Christopher S. Henney/Chmn., Richard L. Jackson/Dir., Robert S. Blair/Dir., Michael C. Welsh/Dir., Vickery W. Stoughton/Dir.

Financial Data: Fiscal Year End:12/31 Latest Annual Data: 12/31/2006

Year	Sales	Net Income
2006	$3,873,000	-$35,174,000
2005	$3,755,000	-$15,264,000
2004	$7,424,000	-$9,669,000

Curr. Assets:	$5,459,000	Curr. Liab.:	NA		
Plant, Equip.:	NA	Total Liab.:	NA	Indic. Yr. Divd.:	NA
Total Assets:	$5,459,000	Net Worth:	NA	Debt/ Equity:	0.0103

Biomoda Inc

PO Box 11342, Albuquerque, NM, 87192; **PH:** 1-505-821-0875; **http://** www.biomoda.com

General - Incorporation	NM	**Stock**- Price on:12/24/2007	$0.21
Employees	3	Stock Exchange	OTC
Auditor	Malone & Bailey, PC	Ticker Symbol	BMOD
Stk Agt.	NA	Outstanding Shares	11,160,000
Counsel	NA	E.P.S.	-$0.24
DUNS No.	NA	Shareholders	NA

Business: The groups principal activities include developing assays, or tests, to detect cancer. The group product is Tetrakis Carboxy Phenyl Porphine. The group operates from the United States.

Primary SIC and add'l.: 8731

CIK No: 0001058767

Subsidiaries: Biomoda Holdings, Inc.

Officers: John J. Cousins/Dir., Pres., Treasurer, CFO, Controller, Herbert L. Whitaker/Dir., Exec. VP, Leslie S. Robins/Dir., VP, Sec., Robin E. Neft/Dir. - Research, Development, Lewis White/52/Control Person

Directors: John J. Cousins/Dir., Pres., Treasurer, CFO, Controller, Herbert L. Whitaker/Dir., Exec. VP, Leslie S. Robins/Dir., VP, Sec., Jeffrey L. Garwin/57/Dir.

Owners: Insiders/15.46%, Irving Weiman/9.35%, Advanced Optics/29.54%, Lewis White/10.41%, June Garwin/4.68%, Jeffrey Garwin/4.68%, John Cousins/5.39%, Leslie Robins/4.29%

Financial Data: Fiscal Year End:12/31 Latest Annual Data: 12/31/2006

Year	Sales	Net Income
2006	NA	-$1,807,000

Curr. Assets:	$3,000	Curr. Liab.:	$2,109,000		
Plant, Equip.:	$6,000	Total Liab.:	$2,109,000	Indic. Yr. Divd.:	NA
Total Assets:	$244,000	Net Worth:	-$1,865,000	Debt/ Equity:	NA

Biophan Technologies Inc

150 Lucius Gordon Dr., Ste. 215, West Henrietta, NY, 14586; **PH:** 1-585-214-2441;
Fax: 1-585-427-2433; **http://** www.biophan.com; **Email:** info@biophan.com

General - Incorporation	NV	**Stock**- Price on:12/24/2007	$0.16
Employees	22	Stock Exchange	OTC
Auditor	Goldstein Golub Kessler LLP	Ticker Symbol	BIPH
Stk Agt	Continental Stock Transfer & Trust Co	Outstanding Shares	108,020,000
Counsel	NA	E.P.S.	NA
DUNS No.	NA	Shareholders	NA

Business: The groups principle activity is to develop novel, patent-protected technologies to provide competitive advantages to companies in the medical device market. The group product is MYO-VAD(TM). The group marketed its product under the trade name MYO-VAD(TM). The group operates from the United States. The groups quarterly revenue for September 2007 was 0.16 millions of USD.

Primary SIC and add'l.: 3845 3841 5047 3842

CIK No: 0001084000

Subsidiaries: Biophan Europe GmbH, LTR Antisense Technology, Inc., Myotech, LLC, Nanolution, LLC, TE Bio LLC

Officers: John F. Lanzafame/CEO/$188,077.00, Robert J. Wood/CFO, Michael L. Weiner/60/Dir., Pres./$271,758.00, Darryl L. Canfield/61/VP, Treasurer, Sec./$180,000.00, Stuart G. MacDonald/VP - Research, Development/$175,000.00, Jeffrey L. Helfer/55/VP - Engineering/$180,000.00

Directors: Guenter H. Jaensch/Chmn., Theodore A. Greenberg/Dir., Michael L. Weiner/60/Dir., Pres., Bonnie Labosky/Dir., Bonita L. Labosky/65/Dir., Stan Yakatan/Dir., Bradford C. Berk/Member - Scientific Advisory Board, Dave Glocker/Member - Scientific Advisory Board, Herbert Hauptman/Member - Scientific Advisory Board, Ray Kurzweil/Member - Scientific Advisory Board,

Mark E. Ladd/Member - Scientific Advisory Board, Andreas Melzer/Member - Scientific Advisory Board, Kevin Parker/Member - Scientific Advisory Board, Harald H. Quick/Member - Scientific Advisory Board, Frank G. Shellock/Member - Scientific Advisory Board (17 Directors included in Index)

Owners: Technology Innovations, LLC/5.45%, Insiders/5.60%, Guenter H. Jaensch/1.46%, Stuart G. MacDonald/1.34%, Stan Yakatan, Biomed Solutions, LLC/5.17%, John F. Lanzafame/1.41%, Bonita L. Labosky, Robert J. Wood/1.16%, Michael L. Weiner/7.02%, Theodore A. Greenberg

Curr. Assets:	$2,632,000	Curr. Liab.:	$7,419,000		
Plant, Equip.:	$418,000	Total Liab.:	$32,107,000	Indic. Yr. Divd.:	NA
Total Assets:	$28,896,000	Net Worth:	-$3,210,000	Debt/ Equity:	NA

BioProgress Plc

15-17 Cambridge Science Pk., Milton Road, CB4 0FQ; ; **http://** www.bioprogress.com

General - Incorporation	England And Wales	**Stock**- Price on:12/24/2007	NA
Employees	63	Stock Exchange	OTC
Auditor	Grant Thornton UK LLP	Ticker Symbol	BPRGY
Stk Agt	Fidelity Transfer Co	Outstanding Shares	NA
Counsel	NA	E.P.S.	NA
DUNS No.	NA	Shareholders	NA

Business: The group's principal activity is the manufacture and distribution of products that use water soluble and biodegradable films. The products are applied in the dietary supplement, pharmaceutical, recreational and cosmetic industries and in other applications. The group also distributes flushable and biodegradable products for the medical and hygiene industries. The group is developing the XGEL(TM) Film System, for producing soft capsules that contain non-aqueous fillings in a variety of shapes and sizes. The non-aqueous filling is in either ingestible form in products such as vitamin, herbal and mineral supplements and in non-ingestible form in products such as paintballs and toiletries. Flushable and biodegradable products include ostomy products for female personal hygiene. The group's manufacturing facilities are located at Cambridgeshire, England. Osotomy products are sourced from Dambi in Wales, the United Kingdom and in the United States.

Primary SIC and add'l.: NA

CIK No: 0001210959

Subsidiaries: BioCustom Limited, BioProgress Technology Inc., BioProgress Technology International, Inc., BioProgress Technology Limited, BioTec Films LLC, D.H.A Nutrition Limited, Dexo BioGenerics Limited, Dexo BioPharm France SAS, Dexo LLC, Laboratoires Pharmaceutiques Dexo SA

Officers: Richard Trevillion/Dir., CEO, Alberto Mussio/GM - Italy, Peter Keen/Executive Dir., Dir. - Finance, Steve Martin/Dir., Dir. - Commercial Development, Hiral Patel/Dir., Group Dir. - Finance, Keith Hemming/Head - Operations

Directors: Richard Trevillion/Dir., CEO, Peter Ibbetson/Non Exec. Chmn., Barry Muncaster/Member - Advisory Board, Giancarlo Mennella/Member - Advisory Board, Alan Clarke/Non Exec. Dir., Anthony Knight/Non Exec. Dir., Steve Martin/Dir., Dir. - Commercial Development, John Dowell/Member - Advisory Board, Jonathan Hadgraft/Member - Advisory Board, Christopher Mugglestone/Member - Advisory Board, Jim Murray/Non Exec. Dir.

Biopure Corp

11 Hurley St., Cambridge, MA, 02141; **PH:** 1-617-234-6500; **Fax:** 1-617-234-6505;
http:// www.biopure.com; **Email:** ir@biopure.com

General - Incorporation	DE	**Stock**- Price on:12/24/2007	$0.65
Employees	76	Stock Exchange	NDQ
Auditor	Ernst & Young LLP	Ticker Symbol	BPUR
Stk Agt	American Stock Transfer & Trust Co	Outstanding Shares	77,960,000
Counsel	Hogan & Hartson LLP	E.P.S.	-$0.45
DUNS No.	NA	Shareholders	NA

Business: The group's principal activity is to develop, manufacture and market oxygen therapeutics. The products include hemopure and oxyglobin. Hemopure is an alternative to red blood cell transfusions as well as for use in the treatment of other critical care conditions. Oxyglobin is similar to hemopure except for its molecular distribution and has the same advantage over red blood cells. Oxyglobin is used in the treatment of canine anemia, mainly for veterinary purposes. Biopure (R), hemopure(R) and oxyglobin(R) are the registered trademarks of the group. The group's products are marketed through advertising, direct mail, educational seminars, conference calls, lectures at congresses and attendance at trade shows. The group has 24 patents and 11 applications pending relating to our oxygen therapeutics.

Primary SIC and add'l.: 2834 2836

CIK No: 0000815508

Subsidiaries: Biopure Netherlands, BV, Biopure South Africa, Pty, Ltd., DeNovo Technologies Corporation, Reperfusion Systems Incorporated

Officers: Zafiris G. Zafirelis/61/Chmn., CEO, Pres., Barry L. Scott/VP - Business Development, Francis H. Murphy/CFO, Gerson A. Greenburg/VP - Medical Affairs, Richard W. Light/VP - Technology Development, Jane Kober/Sr. VP, General Counsel, Sec., Geoffrey J. Filbey/VP - Engineering, Virginia T. Rentko/VP - Preclinical Development

Directors: Zafiris G. Zafirelis/61/Chmn., CEO, Pres., David N. Judelson/75/Vice Chmn., Martin B. Leon/Chmn. - Scientific Advisory Board, Howard A. Cohen/Member - Scientific Advisory Board, Guido J. Neels/Dir., Jay B. Pieper/62/Dir., Daniel P. Harrington/48/Dir., Everett C. Koop/87/Dir., Spencer B. King/Member - Scientific Advisory Board, David R. Holmes/Member - Scientific Advisory Board, William W. O'Neill/Member - Scientific Advisory Board, Kenneth Ouriel/Member - Scientific Advisory Board, Allan Ferguson/Dir.

Owners: Jay B. Pieper, Geoffrey J. Filbey, Francis H. Murphy, Jane Kober, Guido Neels, Zafiris Zafirelis, Daniel P. Harrington, Everett C. Koop, David N. Judelson, Allan Ferguson/1.54%, Barry L. Scott, Insiders/3.58%

Financial Data: Fiscal Year End:10/31 Latest Annual Data: 10/31/2006

Year	Sales	Net Income
2006	$1,715,000	-$26,454,000
2005	$2,110,000	-$28,671,000
2004	$3,750,000	-$41,665,000

Curr. Assets:	$10,621,000	Curr. Liab.:	$4,216,000		
Plant, Equip.:	$22,406,000	Total Liab.:	$5,290,000	Indic. Yr. Divd.:	NA
Total Assets:	$33,832,000	Net Worth:	$28,542,000	Debt/ Equity:	NA

Biosante Pharmaceuticals Inc

111 Barclay Blvd., Lincolnshire, IL, 60069; *PH:* 1-847-478-0500; *Fax:* 1-847-478-9152; *http://* www.biosantepharma.com

General - Incorporation .... DE	Stock - Price on:12/24/2007 .... $6.55
Employees 8	Stock Exchange.................................NDQ
Auditor ....Deloitte & Touche LLP	Ticker Symbol.................................BPAX
Stk Agt..... Computershare Investor Services LLC	Outstanding Shares 23,480,000
Counsel..... Oppenheimer Wolff & Donnelly LLP	E.P.S.................................$0.12
DUNS No. ....NA	Shareholders.................................NA

Business: The group's principal activity is to develop prescription pharmaceutical products, vaccines and vaccine adjuvants using nanoparticle technology. In addition, it is also developing a pipeline of hormone replacement products to treat hormone deficiencies in men and women. Since its inception, it has been in the development stage.

Primary SIC and add'l.: 8731 2834

CIK No: 0001023024

Subsidiaries: Structured Biologicals Inc., Teva Pharmaceuticals USA, Inc., Unimed Pharmaceuticals, Inc.

Officers: Stephen M. Simes/Vice Chmn., CEO, Pres./$641,166.00, Phillip B. Donenberg/CFO, Treasurer, Sec./$392,608.00, Steven J. Bell/VP - Research, Pre, Clinical Development

Directors: Stephen M. Simes/Vice Chmn., CEO, Pres., Louis W. Sullivan/Chmn., Ross J. Mangano/Dir., Peter Kjaer/Dir., Fred Holubow/Dir., Edward C. Rosenow/Dir.

Owners: Phillip B. Donenberg, Marcus Jebsen/12.80%, Louis W. Sullivan/25.60%, Insiders/16.00%, Stephen M. Simes/2.10%, JO & Co/7.60%, Victor Morgenstern/3.10%, Hans Michael Jebsen/25.60%, Marcus Jebsen, Louis W. Sullivan, Hans Michael Jebsen/2.30%, Angela Ho, Peter Kjaer, Ross Mangano/9.20%, Insiders/25.60% *(18 Owners included in Index)*

*Financial Data: Fiscal Year End:*12/31 *Latest Annual Data:* 12/31/2006

Year	Sales	Net Income
2006	$14,439,000	$2,791,000
2005	$258,000	-$9,651,000
2004	$78,000	-$12,016,000

Curr. Assets:	$22,208,000	Curr. Liab.:	$4,300,000	P/E Ratio:	38.53
Plant, Equip.:	$137,000	Total Liab.:	$4,300,000	Indic. Yr. Divd.:	NA
Total Assets:	$22,371,000	Net Worth:	$18,071,000	Debt/ Equity:	NA

Bioscrip Inc

100 Clearbrook Rd., Elmsford, NY, 10523; *PH:* 1-914-460-1600; *Fax:* 1-914-460-1660; *http://* www.bioscrip.com; *Email:* investor@bioscrip.com

General - Incorporation............ DE	Stock - Price on:12/24/2007 .... $4.33
Employees 838	Stock Exchange.................................NDQ
Auditor ....Ernst & Young LLP	Ticker Symbol.................................BIOS
Stk Agt..... American Stock Transfer & Trust Co.	Outstanding Shares 37,490,000
Counsel..............................King & Spalding LLP	E.P.S.................................-$0.73
DUNS No. 95-712-6931	Shareholders.................................NA

Business: The group's principal activity is to deliver innovative pharmacy benefit management, specialty pharmaceutical management and distribution and other pharmacy-related healthcare solutions. It provides pharmacy benefits and pharmacy products and services to individual enrollees receiving health benefits through health insurers, labor unions, self-funded employer groups, government agencies. The pharmacy benefit management and mail services offers plan sponsors a range of pbm services designed to promote the cost-effective delivery of clinically appropriate pbm services. The specialty pharmacy distribution and clinical management services are offered to the chronically ill and genetically impaired. It also includes the distribution of biotech and other prescription medications and the provision of pharmacy-related clinical management services. On 30-Jan-2004, it acquired curascript pharmacy inc and on 02-Feb-2004, it acquired natural living inc.

Primary SIC and add'l.: 8099 6324

CIK No: 0001014739

Subsidiaries: BioScrip Infusion Services, LLC, BioScrip Nursing Services, LLC, BioScrip PBM Services, LLC, BioScrip Pharmacy (NY), BioScrip Pharmacy Services, Inc, BioScrip Pharmacy, Inc., Chronimed Service Corporation, Chronimed Wholesale Inc., Chronimed, Inc, Intravenous Therapy Services, Inc., JPD, Inc., Los Feliz Drugs Inc., MEDgenesis Inc, MIM Funding, LLC, MIM Health Plans of Puerto Rico 18 Subsidiaries included in the Index

Officers: Richard H. Friedman/Chmn., CEO/$1,604,540.00, Brian J. Reagan/Exec. VP - Infusion Division/$392,608.00, Douglas A. Lee/CIO, VP, Thomas Ordemann/VP - Community Pharmacy Operations, Jeff Vigh/VP - Managed Markets, Healthcare Payors, Healthcare Payors, Elizabeth Engelhardt/Dir. - New Marketing Development, Healthcare Payors, Lois Murray/Sr. VP - Pharmaceutical Relations, Clinical Services, Drug Manufacturers, Randi Abramowitz/VP - Physician Sales, Health Care Providers, Dan Colucci/VP - PBM Services, Healthcare Payors, PBM Programs, Barry A. Posner/Exec. VP, Sec., General Counsel/$550,704.00, Alfred Carfora/Exec. VP - Mail Service, PBM Division, Russel J. Corvese/VP - Mail Operations, Stanley Rosenbaum/Exec. VP, CFO, Treasurer/$331,411.00, Scott W. Friedman/Exec. VP - Sales, Marketing/$410,304.00

Directors: Richard H. Friedman/Chmn., CEO, Steven K. Schelhammer/Dir., Stuart A. Samuels/Dir., David R. Hubers/Dir., Charlotte W. Collins/Dir., Martin Kooper/Dir., Myron Z. Holubiak/Dir., Louis T. Difazio/Dir., Richard L. Robbins/Dir.

Owners: Barry A. Posner, Dimensional Fund Advisors Inc./7.20%, Insiders/9.05%, David R. Hubers, Louis T. DiFazio, Richard H. Friedman/5.92%, Gregory H. Keane, Stuart A. Samuels, Richard L. Robbins, Byram Capital Management LLC/5.19%, Myron Z. Holubiak, Michael Kooper, Brian J. Reagan, Stanley G. Rosenbaum, Wells Fargo & Company/5.47% *(19 Owners included in Index)*

*Financial Data: Fiscal Year End:*12/31 *Latest Annual Data:* 12/31/2006

Year	Sales	Net Income
2006	$1,152,459,000	-$38,289,000
2005	$1,073,235,000	-$23,847,000
2004	$630,516,000	$7,033,000

Curr. Assets:	$170,700,000	Curr. Liab.:	$133,677,000		
Plant, Equip.:	$10,409,000	Total Liab.:	$143,623,000	Indic. Yr. Divd.:	NA
Total Assets:	$305,456,000	Net Worth:	$161,833,000	Debt/ Equity:	NA

Biosite Inc

11030 Roselle St. , San Diego, CA, 92121; *PH:* 1-619-455-4808; *http://* www.biosite.com

General - Incorporation .... DE	Stock - Price on:12/24/2007 .... $92.34
Employees 1,036	Stock Exchange.................................NA
Auditor ....Ernst & Young LLP	Ticker Symbol.................................NA
Stk Agt...... American Stock Transfer & Trust Co.	Outstanding Shares 17,090,000
Counsel..............................Cooley Godward LLP	E.P.S.................................$2.17
DUNS No. 19-485-4949	Shareholders.................................NA

Business: The group's principal activity is to develop, manufacture and market diagnostic products. The group provides rapid immunoassays or antibody-based diagnostic tests for the diagnosis of critical diseases through several product platforms. Another product triage panel for drugs of abuse is capable of detecting a broad spectrum of commonly overdosed prescription and illicit drugs in approximately 10 minutes. Triage parasite panel is designed to simultaneously detect three common waterborne parasites, giardia lamblia, cryptosporidium parvum and entamoeba histolytica/dispar, that can cause gastrointestinal infections. Triage cardiac system aids in the diagnosis of acute myocardial infarction. The group's trademarks are biosite (R), triage (R), omniclonal(R) and new dimensions in diagnosis (r).

Primary SIC and add'l.: 3826 2835 8731

CIK No: 0000834306

Subsidiaries: Biosite B.V., Biosite BVBA, Biosite France S.A.S., Biosite GmbH, Biosite Ltd, Biosite S.r.l., Biosite sarl

Officers: Kim D. Blickenstaff/Chmn., CEO, Robin G. Weiner/VP - Regulatory, Government Affairs, John Cajigas/VP - Finance, Christopher J. Twomey/Sr. VP - Finance, CFO, Sec., Kenneth F. Buechler/Dir., Pres., Chief Scientific Officer, Elaine S. Walton/VP - Quality Assurance, Program Management, Thomas G. Blassey/VP - US Sales, Michael A. Whittaker/VP - Intellectual Properties, Robert B. Anacone/Sr. VP - Worldwide Marketing, Sales, Christopher R. Hibberd/Sr. VP - Corporate Development, Paul H. McPherson/VP - Research, Development, Gary A. King/VP - International Operations, Gunars E. Valkirs/Sr. VP - Biosite Discovery, David B. Berger/VP - Legal Affairs, Stephen M. Lesefko/VP - Engineering

Directors: Kim D. Blickenstaff/Chmn., CEO, Howard E. Greene/Dir., Kenneth F. Buechler/Dir., Pres., Chief Scientific Officer, Timothy J. Wollaeger/Dir., Lonnie M. Smith/Dir., Anthony Demaria/Dir.

Owners: Insiders/16.60%, Smith Barney Fund Management LLC and its affiliates/7.40%, Christopher R. Hibberd, Kenneth F. Buechler/3.60%, Barclays Global Investors, NA and its affiliates/6.90%, Howard E. Greene/1.80%, Lonnie M. Smith, Timothy J. Wollaeger, Christopher J. Twomey/1.80%, Gunars E. Valkirs/3.20%, Anthony DeMaria, FMR Corp. and its affiliates/15.30%, Kim D. Blickenstaff/3.90%, Neuberger Berman Inc. and its affiliates/15.10%, Wellington Management Company, LLP/5.50%

*Financial Data: Fiscal Year End:*12/31 *Latest Annual Data:* 12/31/2006

Year	Sales	Net Income
2006	$308,592,000	$39,994,000
2005	$287,699,000	$54,029,000
2004	$244,942,000	$41,448,000

Curr. Assets:	$145,599,000	Curr. Liab.:	$34,669,000	P/E Ratio:	42.55
Plant, Equip.:	$157,945,000	Total Liab.:	$46,432,000	Indic. Yr. Divd.:	NA
Total Assets:	$326,587,000	Net Worth:	$280,155,000	Debt/ Equity:	0.0131

Biospecifics Technologies Corp

35 Wilbur St., Lynbrook, NY, 11563; *PH:* 1-516-593-7000; *Fax:* 1-516-593-7039; *http://* www.biospecifics.com; *Email:* biospe-info@biospecifics.com

General - Incorporation .... DE	Stock - Price on:12/24/2007 .... $4.63
Employees ....NA	Stock Exchange.................................OTC
Auditor ....Tabriztchi & Co., CPA, P.C	Ticker Symbol.................................BSTC
Stk Agt.........OTC Corporate Transfer Service Co	Outstanding Shares ....NA
Counsel..............................Fred Frank Harris	E.P.S.................................NA
DUNS No. ....NA	Shareholders.................................NA

Business: The group's principle activities are to conduct research, develop and produce collagenase abc enzyme. Collagenase abc, is an enzyme that digests collagen, the body's principal connective tissue. The drug is approved for topical enzymatic debridement of dermal ulcers (wounds), such as pressure ulcers and second and third degree burns. Collagenase abc enzyme powder is the active pharmaceutical ingredient of a topical ointment. The group has operations in North America, South America and Europe. The group's quarterly revenue for September 2007 was 0.37 millions of USD.

Primary SIC and add'l.: 6794 8731 2834

CIK No: 0000875622

Officers: Thomas L. Wegman/53/Pres. - Principal Executive, Financial Officer/$382,311.00

Directors: Henry Morgan/87/Dir., Michael Schamroth/68/Dir., Paul Gitman/67/Dir., Toby Wegman/73/Dir., Mark Wegman/58/Dir.

Owners: Michael Schamroth/3.80%, Edwin H. Wegman/41.10%, Insiders/17.70%, Mark Wegman/1.00%, Paul Gitman/3.30%, Toby Wegman, Thomas L. Wegman/6.90%, Henry Morgan/2.70%, Jeffrey K. Vogel/9.30%

*Financial Data: Fiscal Year End:*12/31 *Latest Annual Data:* 12/31/2005

Year	Sales	Net Income
2005	$5,478,000	-$1,297,000
2003	$4,079,000	-$2,925,000
2002	$8,210,000	-$257,000

Curr. Assets:	$4,463,000	Curr. Liab.:	$3,742,000		
Plant, Equip.:	$68,000	Total Liab.:	$7,799,000	Indic. Yr. Divd.:	NA
Total Assets:	$4,531,000	Net Worth:	-$3,269,000	Debt/ Equity:	NA

Biosphere Medical Inc

1050 Hingham St., Rockland, MA, 02370; *PH:* 1-781-681-7900; *Fax:* 1-781-792-2745; *http://* www.biospheremed.com; *Email:* info@biospheremed.com

General - Incorporation .... DE	Stock - Price on:12/24/2007 .... $7.12
Employees 83	Stock Exchange.................................NDQ
Auditor ....Ernst & Young LLP	Ticker Symbol.................................BSMD
Stk Agt..........................Mellon Investor Services	Outstanding Shares 17,980,000
Counsel..............................Hale & Dorr LLP	E.P.S.................................-$0.14
DUNS No. 82-502-2254	Shareholders.................................NA

Business: The group's principal activity is to develop, market and manufacture medical device products for the treatment of hypervascularized tumors and arteriovenous malformations during embolotherapy. Embolotherapy is a procedure in which embolic materials such as microspheres are injected through a catheter into the blood vessels to inhibit blood flow to tumors and arteriovenous malformations. The group's patented platform technology also has applications in tissue bulking, tissue repair and drug delivery. The products include embosphere(R) microspheres, embogold (TM)

microspheres, hepasphere sap (TM) microspheres, temprx (TM) microspheres, etc. In addition to embolotherapic products, the group also sells barium delivery kits and other ancillary products in the European union. Barium kits are purchased from guerbet medical inc and resold for use in gastrointestinal medical testing.

Primary SIC and add'l.: 3826 3841 3823

CIK No: 0000919015

Subsidiaries: Biosphere Medical S.A.

Officers: Richard J. Faleschini/Dir., CEO, Pres., Martin Joseph Joyce/CFO, Exec. VP - Finance, Administration/$498,325.00, Gary M. Saxton/47/COO, Exec. VP, Peter Chandler Sutcliffe/54/VP - Manufacturing

Directors: Richard J. Faleschini/Dir., CEO, Pres., Timothy J. Barberich/Dir., Alexander M. Klibanov/Dir., David P. Southwell/Dir., Jack MacKinnon/Dir., William M. Cousins/Dir., Marian L. Heard/Dir., John H. MacKinnon/Dir., Riccardo Pigliucci/Dir.

Owners: Gary M. Saxton, Stephen Feinberg/15.00%, John H. MacKinnon, Sepracor Inc./23.63%, David P. Southwell, Peter C. Sutcliffe, Alexander M. Klibanov, Insiders/5.69%, Riccardo Pigliucci, Richard J. Faleschini/2.14%, William M. Cousins, Martin J. Joyce, Timothy J. Barberich, Management LLC/6.87%, Clough Capital Partners L.P./7.82%

Financial Data: Fiscal Year End:12/31 **Latest Annual Data:** 12/31/2006

Year	Sales	Net Income
2006	$22,891,000	-$2,324,000
2005	$18,484,000	-$2,801,000
2004	$14,158,000	-$6,841,000

Curr. Assets:	$29,643,000	Curr. Liab.:	$4,924,000	
Plant, Equip.:	$929,000	Total Liab.:	$5,114,000	Indic. Yr. Divd.: NA
Total Assets:	$32,079,000	Net Worth:	$26,965,000	Debt/ Equity: 0.0009

Biosynergy Inc

1940 E Devon Ave., Elk Grove Village, IL, 60007; **PH:** 1-847-956-0471; **Fax:** 1-847-956-6050; http:// www.biosynergyinc.com

General - Incorporation	IL	Stock - Price on:12/24/2007	$0.0001
Employees	5	Stock Exchange	OTC
Auditor	Blackman Kallick Bartelstein LLP	Ticker Symbol	BSYN
Stk Agt.	NA	Outstanding Shares	14,220,000
Counsel	NA	E.P.S.	$0.009
DUNS No.	07-069-8154	Shareholders	NA

Business: The group's principle activities include manufacturing and marketing disposable medical, laboratory and industrial thermometric and thermographic cholesteric liquid crystal devices. The company's customers include hospitals, clinical end-users, laboratories and product dealers. The company also distributes certain blood bank and laboratory products manufactured by third parties to specifications of the company. The company's primary distributor in the United States medical market is the fisher scientific company. In addition, the company is developing certain compounds intended for use as bacteria growth retardant agents for use in food and other products. The group operates from United States.

Primary SIC and add'l.: 5047 3829 8731 3841

CIK No: 0000715812

Owners: Fred K. Suzuki, Mary K. Friske, James F. Schembri, Laurence C. Mead, Insiders, Beverly R. Suzuki, Lauane C. Addis, F.K. Suzuki

Financial Data: Fiscal Year End:04/30 **Latest Annual Data:** 04/30/2007

Year	Sales	Net Income
2007	$980,000	$132,000
2006	$817,000	$29,000
2005	$764,000	-$29,000

Curr. Assets:	$454,000	Curr. Liab.:	$61,000	P/E Ratio: 0.01
Plant, Equip.:	$32,000	Total Liab.:	$61,000	Indic. Yr. Divd.: NA
Total Assets:	$555,000	Net Worth:	$493,000	Debt/ Equity: NA

Biotech Holdings Ltd

3751 Shell Rd., Ste. 160, Richmond, BC, V6W 2X2; **PH:** 1-604-295-1119; **Fax:** 1-604-295-1110; http:// www.biotechltd.com

General - Incorporation	Canada	Stock - Price on:12/24/2007	$0.165
Employees	NA	Stock Exchange	OTC
Auditor	HLBCinnamon Jang Willoughby & Co.	Ticker Symbol	BIOHF
Stk Agt.	Pacific Corporate Trust Co	Outstanding Shares	NA
Counsel	Borden Ladner Gervais LLP	E.P.S.	NA
DUNS No.	25-647-5757	Shareholders	NA

Business: The group's principal activities are to develop, manufacture and market pharmaceutical, personal care and health products. The products of the group are otc drug, topical creams and lotions, personal care and nutritional products like sunscreens and skincare. Its products also include drugs for the treatment of type ii diabetes in China and Asian countries. The operations of the group are carried out in Canada, the United States, South America and China.

Primary SIC and add'l.: 2844 2834

CIK No: 0001018153

Subsidiaries: Biotech Laboratories Inc.

Officers: Robert B. Rieveley/Chmn., CEO, Pres., Lorne D. Brown/CFO, Gale V. Belding/Dir., Exec. VP, Luis M. Ornelas/VP - Latin American Operations, Borden Ladner Gervais/Legal Counsel, Austin Rand/Sr. Office Staff

Directors: Robert B. Rieveley/Chmn., CEO, Pres., Johan De Rooy/Dir., Gale V. Belding/Dir., Exec. VP, Geoffrey F. Herring/Dir., Cheryl A. Rieveley/Dir., Art Cowie/Dir., Ross M. Wilmot/Dir.

Owners: Art Cowie/0.10%, Rieveley Family Trust/100.00%, Robert Rieveley/100.00%, Rieveley Family Trust/22.00%, Johan de Rooy/1.40%, Gale Belding/0.30%, Insiders/23.80%, Insiders/100.00%, Robert Rieveley/22.00%, Lorne Brown

Financial Data: Fiscal Year End:03/31 **Latest Annual Data:** 03/31/2007

Year	Sales	Net Income
2007	$291,000	-$1,328,000
2006	$414,000	-$1,659,000
2005	NA	-$1,245,000

Curr. Assets:	$210,000	Curr. Liab.:	$1,995,000	
Plant, Equip.:	$110,000	Total Liab.:	$2,187,000	Indic. Yr. Divd.: NA
Total Assets:	$682,000	Net Worth:	-$1,506,000	Debt/ Equity: NA

Biotel Inc

1285 Corporate Ctr. Dr., Ste. 150, Eagan, MN, 55121; **PH:** 1-952-890-5135; **Fax:** 1-952-882-6550; http:// www.biotelinc.com; **Email:** info@biotelinc.com

General - Incorporation	MN	Stock - Price on:12/24/2007	$3.37
Employees	52	Stock Exchange	OTC
Auditor	Elliott Davis LLC	Ticker Symbol	BTEL
Stk Agt	Valley Forge Software Corp	Outstanding Shares	2,670,000
Counsel	NA	E.P.S.	$0.12
DUNS No.	NA	Shareholders	NA

Business: The group's principal activity is to provide contract medical devices, software and research services primarily used by medical corporations to satisfy their various outsourcing needs. The company holds four operating subsidiaries consising of Braemar, Inc., Carolina Medical, Inc., Agility Centralized Research Services, Inc., and Advanced Biosensor Inc. The company's subsidiaries operate as OEM distribution companies for medical devices, designing and manufacturing 24- and 48-hour Holter recorders, 30-day ECG event recorders, liposuction components, and other products which are sold to medical corporations to be used in their product lines. Advanced Biosensor Inc. sells diagnostic cardiology systems to end users in hospitals and clinics.

Primary SIC and add'l.: 3841

CIK No: 0001300128

Subsidiaries: Carolina Medical, Inc.

Officers: Steve Springrose/CEO, Pres., Sec., Judy E. Naus/CFO, Harry Strandquist/Pres. - Braemar, Inc

Owners: Cardiac Science Corporation/6.80%, Insiders/23.90%, Roger C. Jones/8.50%, Steven B. Springrose/9.30%, Harold A. Strandquist/3.50%, David A. Heiden, Elk Corporation/6.70%, Charles Moyer/10.00%, Spencer M. Vawter, Stanley N. Bormann/1.10%, Judy E. Naus/1.70%, Donna Horschmann Moyer/10.90%, John L. Ankney

Financial Data: Fiscal Year End:06/30 **Latest Annual Data:** 6/30/2006

Year	Sales	Net Income
2006	$10,223,000	$452,000
2005	$10,169,000	$444,000

Curr. Assets:	$3,773,000	Curr. Liab.:	$1,642,000	P/E Ratio: 28.08
Plant, Equip.:	$702,000	Total Liab.:	$1,884,000	Indic. Yr. Divd.: NA
Total Assets:	$5,194,000	Net Worth:	$3,311,000	Debt/ Equity: 0.0591

Biotime Inc

6121 Hollis St., Emeryville, CA, 94608; **PH:** 1-510-350-2940; **Fax:** 1-510-350-2948; http:// www.biotimeinc.com

General - Incorporation	CA	Stock - Price on:12/24/2007	$0.46
Employees	9	Stock Exchange	OTC
Auditor	Rothstein, Kass & Co., P.C	Ticker Symbol	BTIM
Stk Agt	American Stock Transfer & Trust Co.	Outstanding Shares	22,830,000
Counsel	Lippenberger, Thompston, Welch Et Al	E.P.S.	-$0.09
DUNS No.	78-107-8977	Shareholders	NA

Business: The group's principle activity is the research and development of synthetic solutions used during low temperature surgery and organ preservation solutions. The products enable the substitution of blood plasma volume expanders and blood replacement solutions during the hypothermic surgery. Currently in its development stages, the company is also developing a specially formulated hypothermic blood for the replacement of very large volumes of a patient's blood during cardiac surgery, neurosurgery and other surgeries. Hextend (TM), the first product of the company is a physiologically balanced blood plasma volume expander, for the treatment of hypovolemia. The company is also developing pentalyte, a penta-starch based synthetic plasma expander and hetacool, a modified formulation of hextend specifically designed for use at low temperatures. It has provided an exclusive license to abbott laboratories to manufacture and sell hextend. The group operates from United States.

Primary SIC and add'l.: 8731 2836

CIK No: 0000876343

Officers: Jeffrey B. Nickel/62/VP - Business Development, Marketing, Judith Segall/53/Dir., VP - Operations, Corp. Sec, Pres., Steven A. Seinberg/39/CFO, Treasurer, Hal Sternberg/54/Dir., VP - Research, Harold D. Waitz/64/Dir., VP - Engineering, Regulatory Affairs, Office, Pres.

Directors: Valeta A. Gregg/54/Dir., Michael D. West/54/Dir., Judith Segall/53/Dir., VP - Operations, Corp. Sec, Pres., Hal Sternberg/54/Dir., VP - Research, Harold D. Waitz/64/Dir., VP - Engineering, Regulatory Affairs, Office, Pres., Jeffrey S. Freed/Member - Scientific Advisory Board, Eugene M. Breznock/Member - Scientific Advisory Board, Harry J. Buncke/Member - Scientific Advisory Board, Paul Cianci/Member - Scientific Advisory Board, Harriett Williams Hopf/Member - Scientific Advisory Board, Roger Jacobs/Member - Scientific Advisory Board, Reid Rubsamen/Member - Scientific Advisory Board, Lewis G. Shepler/Member - Scientific Advisory Board, Paola S. Timiras/Member - Scientific Advisory Board

Owners: Alfred D. Kingsley/38.50%, George Karfunkel/9.80%, Neal C. Bradsher/13.80%, Cyndel & Co., Inc/7.60%

Financial Data: Fiscal Year End:12/31 **Latest Annual Data:** 12/31/2006

Year	Sales	Net Income
2006	$1,162,000	-$1,865,000
2005	$903,000	-$2,074,000
2004	$688,000	-$3,085,000

Curr. Assets:	$619,000	Curr. Liab.:	$616,000	
Plant, Equip.:	$11,000	Total Liab.:	$2,516,000	Indic. Yr. Divd.: NA
Total Assets:	$651,000	Net Worth:	-$1,865,000	Debt/ Equity: NA

Biovail Corp

7150 Mississauga Rd., Mississauga, ON, 08807; **PH:** 1-905-286-3000; **Fax:** 1-905-286-3050; http:// www.biovail.com

General - Incorporation	Canada	Stock - Price on:12/24/2007	$24.96
Employees	1,734	Stock Exchange	NYSE
Auditor	Ernst & Young LLP	Ticker Symbol	BVF
Stk Agt	Mellon Trust Co (Canada)	Outstanding Shares	160,850,000
Counsel	Stikeman Elliott	E.P.S.	$2.15
DUNS No.	24-514-1858	Shareholders	NA

Business: The group's principle activities are developing, manufacturing and distributing pharmaceutical products. The group develops generic formulations of medications for the treatment of chronic medical conditions. The services of the group include pharmaceutical development, from research and development, through clinical testing and regulatory filings to full-scale manufacturing. The group's quarterly revenue for September 2007 was 188.89 millions of USD.

Primary SIC and add'l.: 2834 8731

CIK No: 0000885590

Subsidiaries: Biovail Americas Corp, Biovail Distribution Corporation, Biovail Insurance Incorporated., Biovail Laboratories Incorporated, Biovail Laboratories International SRL, Biovail Pharmaceuticals,Inc., Biovail Technologies (Ireland) Limited, Biovail TechnologiesLtd.

Officers: Douglas J.P. Squires/Chmn., CEO, Kenneth G. Howling/Sr. VP, CFO, Mark Durham/VP - Corporate Human Resources, John Miszuk/VP, Controller, Assist. Sec., John Sebben/VP - Manufacturing, Wendy Kelley/Sr. VP, General Counsel, Corp. Sec., Gilbert Godin/Sr. VP - Technical Operations, Drug Delivery, Peter Silverstone/Sr. VP - Medical, Scientific Affairs, Chris Bovaird/VP - Corporate Taxation, Adrian A. De Saldanha/VP - Finance, Treasurer, Gregory Gubitz/Sr. VP, Kathleen Brown/44/VP, Assoc. General Counsel, Chief Compliance Officer

Directors: Douglas J.P. Squires/Chmn., CEO, Jamie Wohlstadter/Dir., Wilfred G. Bristow/Dir., Laurence E. Paul/Dir., Michael V. Every/Dir., Sheldon Plener/Dir., William Wells/Dir.

Owners: Eugene N. Melnyk/12.60%, Barclays Global Investors/6.40%, Phillips Hager & North Investments/5.90%, Insiders/13.00%

Financial Data: Fiscal Year End:12/31   Latest Annual Data: 12/31/2006

Year	Sales	Net Income
2006	$1,067,722,000	$211,626,000
2005	$935,536,000	$236,221,000
2004	$886,543,000	$160,994,000

Curr. Assets:	$1,057,624,000	Curr. Liab.:	$410,287,000		
Plant, Equip.:	$211,979,000	Total Liab.:	$890,185,000	Indic. Yr. Divd.:	$1.500
Total Assets:	$2,192,442,000	Net Worth:	$1,302,257,000	Debt/ Equity:	NA

Bioveris Corp

16020 Indl. Dr., Gaithersburg, MD, 20877; *PH:* 1-301-869-9800; *http://* www.bioveris.com

General - Incorporation	DE	Stock - Price on:12/24/2007	$21.43
Employees	206	Stock Exchange	NA
Auditor	PricewaterhouseCoopers LLP	Ticker Symbol	NA
Stk Agt.	Computershare Investor Services LLC	Outstanding Shares	27,250,000
Counsel	NA	E.P.S.	-$1.13
DUNS No.	NA	Shareholders	NA

Business: The group's principal activities are to develop, manufacture and market its m-series(R) family of products. These products serve as a platform for diagnostic systems to be used for the detection and measurement of biological or chemical substances. The group incorporates its technologies into its instrument systems, tests and reagents, which are the biological and chemical components used to perform such tests. The products are used in clinical diagnostics and non-clinical diagnostics markets. In the clinical diagnostics markets the products are used for testing of patient samples to measure the presence of disease and monitor medical conditions. In the non-clinical diagnostics the products are used for the biodefense, life science and industrial markets including for detection of bacteria, discovery and development and detection of foodborne and waterborne disease. The group operates in the United States and the United Kingdom.

Primary SIC and add'l.: 2835

CIK No: 0001264899

Subsidiaries: BioVeris Europe Corporation, BioVeris K.K.

Owners: Joop Sistermans, Samuel J. and Nadine Wohlstadter/19.60%, William J. Crowley, John Quinn, Richard J. Massey/4.20%, Anthony Rees, Insiders/25.00%, Gem Partners, LP/8.20%, George V. Migausky/1.10%

Financial Data: Fiscal Year End:03/31   Latest Annual Data: 3/31/2007

Year	Sales	Net Income
2007	$24,063,000	-$30,486,000
2006	$20,615,000	-$27,853,000
2005	$26,299,000	-$77,573,000

Curr. Assets:	$58,517,000	Curr. Liab.:	$12,206,000		
Plant, Equip.:	$3,617,000	Total Liab.:	$20,522,000	Indic. Yr. Divd.:	NA
Total Assets:	$80,365,000	Net Worth:	$59,843,000	Debt/ Equity:	NA

Biovest International Inc

Biotech Bldg. 4, 377 Plantation St., Worcester, MA, 01605; *PH:* 1-508-793-0001; *Fax:* 1-508-798-0899; *http://* www.biovest.com; *Email:* info@biovest.com

General - Incorporation	DE	Stock - Price on:12/24/2007	$0.86
Employees	84	Stock Exchange	OTC
Auditor	Lazar Levine & Felix LLP	Ticker Symbol	BVTI
Stk Agt.	American Stock Transfer & Trust CO.	Outstanding Shares	94,470,000
Counsel	NA	E.P.S.	-$0.44
DUNS No.	04-298-1506	Shareholders	NA

Business: The group's principal activities are to supply cell culture instrumentation and services to the biotechnology industry and bioprocessing market. The group focuses principally on the development, assembly and marketing of instruments used for the growth of mammalian cells and for the related production of cell-derived bioproducts. The cells and bioproducts produced by the group's instruments, are used by the group's customers to manufacture products designed to diagnose or treat human and animal disease. The group markets its products and services to pharmaceutical, biotechnology and other industrial companies.

Primary SIC and add'l.: 2836 3841 8731 2835

CIK No: 0000704384

Subsidiaries: Biovax, Inc.

Officers: Steve Arikian/Chmn., CEO, James J. Carroll/GM - Biovest Advanced Instrumentation Division, Mark Hirschel/Chief Scicintific Officer, Samuel S. Duffey/Dir., General Counsel, Sam Duffey/General Counsel, James A. McNulty/CFO

Directors: Steve Arikian/Chmn., CEO, Raphael Mannino/Dir., Ronald E. Osman/Dir., Samuel S. Duffey/Dir., General Counsel, John Sitilides/Dir., Peter J. Pappas/Dir., Jeffrey Scott/Dir., Robert D. Weiss/Dir., Christopher Chapman/Dir.

Owners: Raphael Mannino, Samuel Duffey, Martin Baum, Jeffrey Scott, Peter J. Pappas, Insiders, Stephane Allard, Robert Weiss, Francis E. ODonnell, Christopher Kyriakides, Othon Mourkakos, Christopher Chapman, Accentia, Inc., Nicholas Leb, James A. McNulty *(16 Owners included in Index)*

Financial Data: Fiscal Year End:09/30   Latest Annual Data: 9/30/2006

Year	Sales	Net Income
2006	$7,298,000	-$13,652,000
2005	$5,077,000	-$11,479,000

Curr. Assets:	$4,260,000	Curr. Liab.:	$13,266,000		
Plant, Equip.:	$898,000	Total Liab.:	$15,364,000	Indic. Yr. Divd.:	NA
Total Assets:	$8,444,000	Net Worth:	-$16,520,000	Debt/ Equity:	NA

Birch Branch Inc

2560 W Main St., Ste. 200, Littleton, CO, 80120; *PH:* 1-303-794-9450

General - Incorporation	CO	Stock - Price on:12/24/2007	NA
Employees	NA	Stock Exchange	OTC
Auditor	Miller & McCollom	Ticker Symbol	BRBH
Stk Agt.	Corporate Stock Transfer, Inc.	Outstanding Shares	NA
Counsel	NA	E.P.S.	-$0.09
DUNS No.	NA	Shareholders	NA

Business: The group's priciple activity is to provide real estate services. The group operates from United States.

Primary SIC and add'l.: 6532

CIK No: 0000857872

Subsidiaries: Birch Branch, Pride Holdings, Inc., Pride, Inc., Prime Rate Income & Dividend Enterprises, Inc., USMS

Officers: Earnest Mathis/48/Dir., CEO, Robert Lazzeri/47/Dir., CFO

Directors: Earnest Mathis/48/Dir., CEO, Robert Lazzeri/47/Dir., CFO

Owners: Lazzeri Family Trust, Mathis Family Partners, LTD, Insiders, La Mirage Trust, Brasel Family Partners, LTD

Financial Data: Fiscal Year End:06/30   Latest Annual Data: 06/30/2006

Year	Sales	Net Income
2006	NA	-$80,000

Curr. Assets:	$7,000	Curr. Liab.:	$36,000		
Plant, Equip.:	NA	Total Liab.:	$36,000	Indic. Yr. Divd.:	NA
Total Assets:	$7,000	Net Worth:	-$29,000	Debt/ Equity:	NA

Birch Financial Inc

20946 Devonshire St., Ste. 200, Chatsworth, CA, 91311; *PH:* 1-800-959-3701; *Fax:* 1-800-959-3702; *http://* www.birchfinancial.com; *Email:* info@birchfinancial.com

General - Incorporation	NV	Stock - Price on:12/24/2007	NA
Employees	NA	Stock Exchange	NA
Auditor	Mantyla McReynolds	Ticker Symbol	NA
Stk Agt.	Standard Registrar & Transfer Co Inc.	Outstanding Shares	NA
Counsel	NA	E.P.S.	-$0.18
DUNS No.	NA	Shareholders	NA

Business: The group's principal activity is of insurance premium financing and equipment financing. Insurance premium financing is for landscapers, nurseries, golf courses and other members of the green industry. The premium financing loans are relatively short term, generally with maturities of approximately nine months. Insurance premium finacing services is done for landscape contractor insurance, inc. Wholly owned subsidiary of golden oak cooperative corporation, oak creek insurance and ackerman insurance. The equipment financing includes financing for truck and trailer equipment, lawnmowers, tractors and other construction equipment. The initial terms for truck and trailer equipment typically will range from 24 months to 60 months. At 31-Dec-2003, the group had 60 outstanding contracts, with total outstanding balances of $882,719. The contracts will be made exclusively with business users.

Primary SIC and add'l.: 6159

CIK No: 0001125119

Subsidiaries: Birch Missouri

Officers: Nelson L. Colvin/CEO, Pres., CFO, Keith Walton/Dir., VP, Sec., Treasurer

Directors: Barry L. Cohen/Chmn., Jon Alsdorf/Dir., Mickey Strauss/Dir., Richard Angelo/Dir., Timothy Nord/Dir., Lebo Newman/Dir., Ronald Dietz/Dir., Keith Walton/Dir., VP, Sec., Treasurer, Frank Quaresma/Dir.

Financial Data: Fiscal Year End:12/31   Latest Annual Data: 06/30/2006

Year	Sales	Net Income
2006	NA	-$80,000

Curr. Assets:	$3,000	Curr. Liab.:	$37,000		
Plant, Equip.:	$454,000	Total Liab.:	$493,000	Indic. Yr. Divd.:	NA
Total Assets:	$457,000	Net Worth:	-$35,000	Debt/ Equity:	NA

Birch Mountain Resources Ltd

250 6th Ave. SW, Ste. 300, Calgary, AB, T2P 3H7; *PH:* 1-403-262-1838; *Fax:* 1-403-263-9888; *http://* www.birchmountain.com

General - Incorporation	AB	Stock - Price on:12/24/2007	$3.56
Employees	27	Stock Exchange	AMEX
Auditor	Meyers Norris Penny LLP	Ticker Symbol	BMD
Stk Agt.	Computershare Trust Co of Canada	Outstanding Shares	82,780,000
Counsel	NA	E.P.S.	-$0.248
DUNS No.	NA	Shareholders	NA

Business: The groups principle activities include exploring, exploiting and developing mineral properties. The group operates from the Canada. The groups quarterly revenue for September 2007 was 0.52 millions of CAD.

Primary SIC and add'l.: 1011 1422 1041 1044 1031 1061

CIK No: 0001006224

Subsidiaries: Birch Mountain Minerals Ltd.,

Officers: Douglas J. Rowe/Dir., Pres., Chief Executive, Donald L. Dabbs/Co - Founder, Dir., Sr. VP, Derrick Kershaw/Dir., Sr. VP, Hugh Abercrombie/VP - Business Development, Russ Gerrish/VP - Engineering, Operations, David E. Reid/VP - Facilities Engineering, Hansine Ullberg/CFO, VP, Joel Jarding/Dir., Pres., COO - Calgary, Alberta

Directors: Kerry E. Sully/Chmn., Douglas Annable/Dir., Larry Shelley/Dir., Douglas J. Rowe/Dir., Pres., Chief Executive, Charles Hopper/Dir., Donald L. Dabbs/Co - Founder, Dir., Sr. VP, Lanny K. McDonald/Dir., Derrick Kershaw/Dir., Sr. VP

Owners: Hugh Abercrombie/0.42%, Donald L. Dabbs/0.74%, Larry Shelley/0.13%, Douglas J. Rowe/1.29%, Lanny K. McDonald/0.46%, Charles Hopper/0.55%, Dan J. Rocheleau, David Reid/0.01%, Derrick Kershaw/0.02%, Hansine Ullberg/0.02%, Kerry E. Sully/0.39%, Russell Gerrish/0.18%

Financial Data: *Fiscal Year End:*12/31 *Latest Annual Data:* 12/31/2006

Year		Sales		Net Income	
2006		$1,322,000		-$19,478,000	
2005		NA		-$12,803,000	
2004		NA		-$3,385,000	
Curr. Assets:	$14,800,000	**Curr. Liab.:**	$7,021,000	**P/E Ratio:**	4.45
Plant, Equip.:	$31,982,000	**Total Liab.:**	$42,366,000	**Indic. Yr. Divd.:**	NA
Total Assets:	$50,411,000	**Net Worth:**	$8,046,000	**Debt/ Equity:**	NA

Birds Eye Foods Inc

90 Linden Oaks, Rochester, NY, 14625; ***PH:*** 1-585-383-1850; ***http://*** www.birdseyefoods.com

General - Incorporation	DE	**Stock**- Price on:12/24/2007	NA
Employees	NA	Stock Exchange	NA
Auditor	Deloitte & Touche LLP	Ticker Symbol	NA
Stk Agt	NA	Outstanding Shares	NA
Counsel	NA	E.P.S.	NA
DUNS No.	00-221-2611	Shareholders	NA

Business: The group's principle activity is to produce and market processed food products. Its operations are carried out in three segments: branded frozen, branded dry, and non-branded products. Branded frozen includes traditional frozen vegetables and value added products marketed under recognizable consumer brands. Branded dry markets products under brands including comstock and wilderness, well-known fruit fillings and toppings consumer brands. The company also markets snack items through regional brands including snyder of berlin, husman and tim's. Non-branded includes food service, industrial and export product offerings. Major customers of the company's includes albertson's, aldi, inc., associated wholesale grocers, bj's, safeway, supervalu, wal-Mart/sam's, wegmans, western family, and winn-dixie. On 24-Sep-2004, the group acquired California &Washington company. The group operates from United States.

Primary SIC and add'l.: 2035 5142 2096 2037 2033

CIK No: 0000026285

Subsidiaries: A NewYork corporation, BEMSA Holding, Inc., Birds Eye de Mexico, S.A. de C.V., Holdings Inc, Kennedy Endeavors, Incorporated, Linden Oaks Corporation, Pro-Fac Cooperative, Inc.

Officers: Neil Harrison/Chmn., CEO, Pres. - Rochester, New York, Robert G. Montgomery/Sr. VP - Frozen Sales, Rochester, New York, Earl L. Powers/CFO, Exec. VP - Business Optimization, Rochester, New York, Lois Warlick-Jarvie/Sr. VP - Administration, Rochester, New York, Carl Caughran/Exec. VP - Specialty Foods Group, Rochester, New York, Ron Trine/Sr. VP - Frozen Supply Chain - Rochester, New York

Directors: Neil Harrison/Chmn., CEO, Pres. - Rochester, New York

Birks & Mayors Inc

5870 N Hiatus Rd., Tamarac, FL, 33321; ***PH:*** 1-514-397-2511; ***http://*** www.birksandmayors.com

General - Incorporation	Canada	**Stock**- Price on:12/24/2007	$7.82
Employees	NA	Stock Exchange	AMEX
Auditor	KPMG LLP	Ticker Symbol	BMJ
Stk Agt	SunTrust Bank	Outstanding Shares	11,230,000
Counsel	NA	E.P.S.	$1.03
DUNS No.	NA	Shareholders	NA

Business: The groups principle activities include designing, developing, making and retailing fine jewelry, sterling silver and gifts. The group operates from the retail and other. The group operates from the Canada, Mary Land and Georgia. The group's quarterly revenue for September 2007 was 59.85 millions of USD.

Primary SIC and add'l.: 5094 5944 3915 3911 3873 3914

CIK No: 0001179821

Subsidiaries: Exclusive Diamonds International Ltd., Henry Birks& Sons U.S., Inc., Jan Bell Marketing/Puerto Rico Inc., JBM Retail Company Inc., JBM Venture Co. Inc., Mayors Jewelers Intellectual Property Holding Co., Mayors Jewelers of Florida Inc., Mayors Jewelers, Inc., Regal Diamonds International (T.A. Ltd.)

Officers: Thomas A. Andruskevich/Dir., CEO, Pres., Al Rahm/Sr. VP - Retail Store Operations, Joseph A. Keifer/COO, Exec. VP, Daisy Chin-Lor/Exec. VP, Chief Marketing Officer, Michael Rabinovitch/Sr. VP, CFO, John Orrico/Sr. VP, Supply Chain Officer, Aida Alvarez/Sr. VP - Merchandising, Randolph Dirth/Sr. VP - Merchandising, Carlo Coda-Nunziante/Group VP - Strategy, Business Development, Jocelyn Desy/Group VP - Corporate Sales, Helene Messier/Group VP - Human Resources, Miranda Melfi/Group VP - Legal Affairs, Corp. Sec., Milt Thacker/Group VP, CIO, Marco Pasteris/Group VP - Finance, Treasurer, Jeff Morris/Group VP - Accounting, Corporate Controller

Directors: Thomas A. Andruskevich/Dir., CEO, Pres., Lorenzo Rossi Di Montelera/Chmn., Margherita Oberti/Dir., Filippo Recami/Dir., Emily Berlin/Dir., Alain Benedetti/Dir., Shirley A. Dawe/Dir., Elizabeth M. Eveillard/Dir., Massimo Ferragamo/Dir., Ann Spector Lieff/Dir., Peter O'Brien/Dir.

Owners: Elizabeth Eveillard, Thomas A. Andruskevich, Ann Spector Lieff, Randolph Dirth, Montrovest BV, Emily Berlin, Alain Benedetti, Shirley A. Dawe, Daisy Chin-Lor, Goldfish Trust, Peter R. OBrien, Michael Rabinovitch, Diamond A. Partners, LP, Massimo Ferragamo, Rohan Private Trust Company Limited *(22 Owners included in Index)*

Financial Data: *Fiscal Year End:*03/31 *Latest Annual Data:* 03/31/2007

Year		Sales		Net Income	
2007		$294,282,000		$13,123,000	
Curr. Assets:	$181,118,000	**Curr. Liab.:**	$151,147,000	**P/E Ratio:**	4.45
Plant, Equip.:	$34,964,000	**Total Liab.:**	$171,019,000	**Indic. Yr. Divd.:**	NA
Total Assets:	$252,516,000	**Net Worth:**	$81,497,000	**Debt/ Equity:**	NA

Birmingham Bloomfield Bancshares Inc

33583 Woodward Ave., Birmingham, MI, 48009; ***PH:*** 1-248-593-6455; ***http://*** www.bankofbirmingham.net

General - Incorporation	MI	**Stock**- Price on:12/24/2007	$9.5
Employees	22	Stock Exchange	OTC
Auditor	Plante & Moran, PLLC	Ticker Symbol	BBBI
Stk Agt	Registrar & Transfer Co	Outstanding Shares	1,800,000
Counsel	NA	E.P.S.	-$1.7
DUNS No.	NA	Shareholders	NA

Business: The group operates through its subsidiary, whose principle activity is banking operations. The group financial products include real estate loans, commercial loans., consumer loans and investments. The group operates from the United States.

Primary SIC and add'l.: 6022

CIK No: 0001335792

Subsidiaries: Bank of Birmingham

Officers: Robert E. Farr/Dir., Pres., CEO - Bank, Birmingham/$135,000.00, Donald J. Abood/Dir. - Organizer, Bnk, Birmingham, Linda Alvey/Sr. VP - Residential Mortgage - Bank, Birmingham, Jaime Cogan/Loan Operations Coordinator, Bank, Birmingham, Maggie Currier/Sales, Marketing, Bank, Birmingham, John Danilowicz/VP, Operations Officer - Bank, Birmingham, Amy Depriest/Assist. Branch Mgr. - Bank, Birmingham, Lori Glesmann/Loan Operations Support Specialist - Bank, Birmingham, Lindsay Humenny/Assist. Branch Mgr. - Bank, Birmingham, Chris Johnson/Credit Specialist - Bank, Birmingham, Lance Krajacic/Exec. VP, Chief Credit Officer - Bank, Birmingham, Bari Livsey/Sr. VP, Sr. Relationship Mgr. - Bnak, Birmingham, Bank, Birmingham, Jenny Meier/VP - Sr. Credit Officer - Bank, Birmingham, Barbar Riopelle/Customer, Shareholder Liaison, Bank, Girmingham, Peggy Shields/Sr. VP, Sr. Relationship Mgr. - Bank, Girmingham *(20 Officers included in Index)*

Directors: Robert E. Farr/Dir., Pres., CEO - Bank, Birmingham, William R. Aikens/Chmn. - Bank, Birmingham, Harry Cendrowski/Dir., Donald J. Abood/Dir. - Organizer, Bnk, Birmingham, Donald E. Copus/Dir., Charles Kaye/Dir., Daniel P. O Donnell/Dir., Charles T. Pryde/Dir., Donald Ruff/Dir., Walter G. Schwartz/Dir., Henry Spellman/Dir., Scott McCallum/48/Dir., Richard J. Miller/Dir., Exec. VP, CFO - Bank, Birmingham

Owners: Daniel P. ODonnell/0.90%, Harry Cendrowski/1.07%, Charles Kaye, Charles T. Pryde/0.09%, Lance N. Krajacic/1.00%, Robert E. Farr/0.97%, Jane L. Brodsky/0.90%, Richard J. Miller/1.07%, Donald Ruff, Walter G. Schwartz/0.90%, Insiders/13.53%, Donald E. Copus/0.96%, William R. Aikens/1.93%, John M. Farr/0.87%, Henry G. Spellman/1.07% *(16 Owners included in Index)*

Financial Data: *Fiscal Year End:*12/31 *Latest Annual Data:* 12/31/2006

Year		Sales		Net Income	
2006		$392,000		-$2,963,000	
Curr. Assets:	$8,666,000	**Curr. Liab.:**	$10,366,000		
Plant, Equip.:	$2,319,000	**Total Liab.:**	$10,366,000	**Indic. Yr. Divd.:**	NA
Total Assets:	$23,704,000	**Net Worth:**	$13,338,000	**Debt/ Equity:**	NA

Birner Dental Mgmt Services Inc

3801 E Florida Ave., Ste. 508, Denver, CO, 80210; ***PH:*** 1-303-691-0680; ***Fax:*** 1-303-691-0889; ***http://*** www.bdms-perfecteeth.com

General - Incorporation	CO	**Stock**- Price on:12/24/2007	$21.9
Employees	566	Stock Exchange	NDQ
Auditor	Hein & Assoc. LLP	Ticker Symbol	BDMS
Stk Agt	Computershare Trust Co	Outstanding Shares	2,120,000
Counsel	NA	E.P.S.	$1.05
DUNS No.	93-899-1411	Shareholders	NA

Business: The group's principal activity is to acquire, develop and manage geographically dense dental practice networks in select markets. It operates and markets in Colorado, New Mexico and Arizona. The group provides a solution to the needs of dentists, patients, and third-party payors by allowing the group's affiliated dentists to provide high-quality, efficient dental care in patient-friendly, family practice settings. The group also provides management services, which are designed to improve the efficiency and profitability of the dental practices. As of 31-Dec-2003, the group managed 54 offices, of which 37 were acquired and 17 were developed internally.

Primary SIC and add'l.: 8021

CIK No: 0000948072

Officers: Frederic W.J. Birner/50/Chmn., CEO/$656,637.00, Mark A. Birner/48/Dir., Pres./$509,417.00, Dennis N. Genty/50/CFO, Sec., Treasurer/$509,417.00

Directors: Frederic W.J. Birner/50/Chmn., CEO, Mark A. Birner/48/Dir., Pres., Thomas D. Wolf/53/Dir., Paul E. Valuck/51/Dir., Brooks G. O'Neil/51/Dir.

Financial Data: *Fiscal Year End:*12/31 *Latest Annual Data:* 12/31/2006

Year		Sales		Net Income	
2006		$39,387,000		$2,323,000	
2005		$36,716,000		$2,164,000	
2004		$32,170,000		$1,380,000	
Curr. Assets:	$4,775,000	**Curr. Liab.:**	$5,711,000	**P/E Ratio:**	21.47
Plant, Equip.:	$5,593,000	**Total Liab.:**	$13,274,000	**Indic. Yr. Divd.:**	$0.600
Total Assets:	$22,822,000	**Net Worth:**	$9,548,000	**Debt/ Equity:**	0.5222

Bison Instruments Inc

7725 Vasserman Trail, Chanhassen, Minneapolis, MN, 55317; ***PH:*** 1-952-938-1055

General - Incorporation	MN	**Stock**- Price on:12/24/2007	$0.4
Employees	NA	Stock Exchange	OTC
Auditor	Eide Bailly LLP	Ticker Symbol	BSOI
Stk Agt	Cibc Mellon Trust Co.	Outstanding Shares	NA
Counsel	NA	E.P.S.	-$0.05
DUNS No.	NA	Shareholders	NA

Business: The groups principal activities include manufacturing and selling electronic instruments. The group operates from the United States.

Primary SIC and add'l.: 9995

CIK No: 0001093683

Officers: Edward G. Lampman/62/Dir., CEO, CFO, Lawrence M. Martin/66/Dir., GM

Directors: Edward G. Lampman/62/Dir., CEO, CFO, Lawrence M. Martin/66/Dir., GM, Barrie D. Rose/77/Dir., Allan D. Erickson/65/Dir.

Owners: Barrie D. Rose/67.05%

Financial Data: *Fiscal Year End:*10/31 *Latest Annual Data:* 10/31/2006

Year	Sales	Net Income
2006	NA	-$36,000
2005	NA	-$60,000
2004	$0	-$32,000

Curr. Assets:	$2,000	Curr. Liab.:	$1,000		
Plant, Equip.:	NA	Total Liab.:	$118,000	Indic. Yr. Divd.:	NA
Total Assets:	$2,000	Net Worth:	-$116,000	Debt/ Equity:	NA

Bisys Group Inc (The)

105 Eisenhower Pkwy., Roseland, NJ, 07068; *PH:* 1-973-461-2500; *http://* www.bisys.com

General - Incorporation .... DE
Employees 5,000
Auditor .... PricewaterhouseCoopers LLP
Stk Agt...... American Stock Transfer & Trust Co.
Counsel .... NA
DUNS No. 78-771-6331

Stock- Price on:12/24/2007 .... $11.79
Stock Exchange .... NA
Ticker Symbol .... NA
Outstanding Shares 121,260,000
E.P.S $0.04
Shareholders .... NA

Business: The group's principal activity is to provide business process outsourcing solutions for the financial services sector. The group distributes and administers approximately 2,200 mutual funds, hedge funds, private equity funds and other investment products and provides retirement plan record keeping services to more than 18,000 companies. It also provides insurance distribution solutions, professional certification training and licensing and continuing education and investment industry consulting services. The group acquired lifesource, uhlemeyer services, inc. On 12-Jan-2004, usa insurance group inc. On 10-Nov-2003 in fiscal 2004.

Primary SIC and add'l.: 7374 6411 6282

CIK No: 0000883587

Subsidiaries: Ascensus Insurance Services, Inc, BISYS Commercial Insurance Services, Inc, BISYS Document Solutions LLC, BISYS Financial Services Ltd., BISYS Financing Company, BISYS Fund Services Ohio, Inc, BISYS Fund Services, Inc., BISYS Fund Services, LP, BISYS Hedge Fund Services (Ireland) Ltd., BISYS Hedge Fund Services Limited, BISYS Hedge Fund Services, Inc, BISYS Information Solutions L.P., BISYS Insurance Services Holding Corp., BISYS Insurance Services, Inc, BISYS Management Company 25 Subsidiaries included in the Index

Owners: Sterling Capital Management/5.55%, John M. Howard, Robert J. Jones, Joseph J. Melone, Bruce D. Dalziel, Denis A. Bovin, Thomas A. Cooper, Wellington Management Company LLP/13.79%, Ahmet H. Okumus, and Okumus Capital LLC/10.81%, Richard J. Haviland, Robert J. Casale, Insiders/1.86%, Russell P. Fradin, John Lyons, S.A.C. Capital Advisors/5.59% *(16 Owners included in Index)*

Financial Data: *Fiscal Year End:*06/30 *Latest Annual Data:* 6/30/2006

Year	Sales	Net Income
2006	$842,852,000	$232,162,000
2005	$1,063,055,000	$6,107,000
2004	$1,037,302,000	$63,580,000

Curr. Assets:	$483,642,000	Curr. Liab.:	$404,589,000	P/E Ratio:	294.75
Plant, Equip.:	$42,100,000	Total Liab.:	$457,129,000	Indic. Yr. Divd.:	NA
Total Assets:	$1,398,743,000	Net Worth:	$941,614,000	Debt/ Equity:	0.0017

Bitstream Inc

245 1st St., 17th Fl., Cambridge, MA, 02142; *PH:* 1-617-497-6222; *Fax:* 1-617-868-0784; *http://* www.bitstream.com

General - Incorporation .... DE
Employees 63
Auditor .... PricewaterhouseCoopers LLP
Stk Agt .... EquiServe Trust Co.
Counsel... Rubin Baum Levin Constant Friedman
DUNS No. 05-060-2689

Stock- Price on:12/24/2007 .... $7.99
Stock Exchange .... NDQ
Ticker Symbol .... BITS
Outstanding Shares 9,650,000
E.P.S $0.32
Shareholders .... NA

Business: The group's principal activities are to develop, market and support software products and technologies to enhance creation, transport, viewing and printing of electronic documents. The group operates through three segments: type, myfonts and pageflex segment. The type and technology division segment license products and technologies to original equipment manufacturers and independent software vendors for inclusion in their output devices. The myfonts.com segment provides Internet display fonts in an e-commerce Web site. Pageflex segment provides software that produces customized data sheets and brochures directly from xml text. The group also sells custom and other type products directly to end users such as graphic artists, desktop publishers and corporations.

Primary SIC and add'l.: 7372 7379 7375

CIK No: 0000818813

Subsidiaries: Bitstream World Trade, Inc., Bitstream, B.V., MyFonts.com, Inc., Pageflex, Inc.

Officers: Anna M. Chagnon/Dir., CEO, Pres./$547,995.00, Costas Kitsos/VP - Engineering/$279,645.00, James P. Dore/CFO, VP/$285,827.00, Sampo Kaasila/VP - Research, Development/$269,639.00, John Collins/CTO, VP/$239,190.00, Bob Thomas/Dir. - Product Management, Kate Devagno/Mgr. - Thunderhawk Product Marketing, Browsing, Thunderhawk, Marion Williams-Bennett/Marketing Specialist

Directors: Anna M. Chagnon/Dir., CEO, Pres., Charles Ying/Chmn., David G. Lubrano/Dir., Amos Kaminski/Dir., George B. Beitzel/Dir.

Owners: Costas Kitsos, Amos Kaminski/4.01%, Insiders/23.20%, John S. Collins/1.00%, AIGH Investment Partners, LLC/6.58%, Charles Ying/5.95%, George B. Beitzel/4.36%, Bjurman, Barry & Associates/6.22%, Oppenheimer Funds, Inc/5.79%, Anna M. Chagnon/2.96%, David G. Lubrano/4.54%, Sampo Kaasila, James P. Dore/1.04%

Financial Data: *Fiscal Year End:*12/31 *Latest Annual Data:* 12/31/2006

Year	Sales	Net Income
2006	$20,248,000	$3,234,000
2005	$15,653,000	$1,034,000
2004	$11,632,000	-$615,000

Curr. Assets:	$13,351,000	Curr. Liab.:	$3,992,000	P/E Ratio:	24.97
Plant, Equip.:	$402,000	Total Liab.:	$4,091,000	Indic. Yr. Divd.:	NA
Total Assets:	$14,717,000	Net Worth:	$10,626,000	Debt/ Equity:	NA

BIW Ltd

230 BeAve.r St., Ansonia, CT, 06401; *PH:* 1-203-735-1888; *Fax:* 1-203-732-2616; *http://* www.buiweb.com

General - Incorporation .... CT
Employees 40
Auditor .... Dworken, Hillman, LaMorte & Sterczala
Stk Agt...... American Stock Transfer & Trust Co.
Counsel .... Wiggin & Dana LLP
DUNS No. 06-135-6986

Stock- Price on:12/24/2007 .... $16.1
Stock Exchange .... AMEX
Ticker Symbol .... BIW
Outstanding Shares 1,670,000
E.P.S $0.55
Shareholders .... NA

Business: The group's principal activity is to collect and distribute water for domestic, commercial and industrial uses and fire protection. It provides water related services in Ansonia and Derby, Connecticut and Seymour. The group is a specially chartered Connecticut public service corporation. The current sources of the group's water are wells located in Derby and Seymour and interconnections with the south central Connecticut regional water authority's system. Birmingham utilities' properties consist chiefly of land, wells, reservoirs, and pipelines. The group has approximately 11,270 customers principally residential and commercial.

Primary SIC and add'l.: 4499 4941

CIK No: 0001169237

Subsidiaries: Birmingham H2O Services Inc., Birmingham Utilities, Inc., Eastern Connecticut Regional Water Company, Inc.

Officers: Betsy Henley-Cohn/Chairwoman, CEO, John S. Tomac/Dir., Pres., Treasurer, CFO, Henrietta Vitale/Sec., Linda B. Batten/Controller, Assist. Treasurer

Directors: Betsy Henley-Cohn/Chairwoman, CEO, Charles T. Seccombe/Dir. Emeritus, Alvaro Da Silva/Dir., Michael J. Adanti/Dir., Kenneth E. Schaible/Dir., Aldore J. Rivers/Dir., John S. Tomac/Dir., Pres., Treasurer, CFO, Themis Klarides/Dir., Mary Jane Burt/Dir., James E. Cohen/Dir., Lance B. Sauerteig/Dir., Juri Henley-Cohn/Dir.

Owners: Group consisting of Betsy Henley-Cohn,/11.80%, Mary Jane Burt/1.20%, Alvaro da Silva, Betsy Henley-Cohn/11.80%, Kenneth E. Schaible, John S. Tomac, Themis Klarides, James E. Cohen/4.80%, Juri Henley-Cohn/3.30%, TowerView LLC/5.70%, Insiders/22.30%, B. Lance Sauerteig

Financial Data: *Fiscal Year End:*12/31 *Latest Annual Data:* 12/31/2006

Year	Sales	Net Income
2006	$9,256,000	$649,000
2005	$9,055,000	$659,000
2004	$9,866,000	$511,000

Curr. Assets:	$2,165,000	Curr. Liab.:	$8,580,000	P/E Ratio:	34.26
Plant, Equip.:	$32,324,000	Total Liab.:	$25,092,000	Indic. Yr. Divd.:	$0.680
Total Assets:	$36,487,000	Net Worth:	$11,395,000	Debt/ Equity:	0.8024

BJ Services Co

4601 Westway Pk. Blvd., Houston, TX, 77092; *PH:* 1-713-462-4239; *Fax:* 1-713-895-5851; *http://* www.bjservices.com; *Email:* shareowner-svcs@bankofny.com

General - Incorporation .... DE
Employees 16,000
Auditor .... Deloitte & Touche LLP
Stk Agt .... Bank of New York
Counsel .... NA
DUNS No. 11-743-6816

Stock- Price on:12/24/2007 .... $28.85
Stock Exchange .... NYSE
Ticker Symbol .... BJS
Outstanding Shares 293,330,000
E.P.S $2.761
Shareholders .... NA

Business: The group's principle activity is to provide pressure pumping and oilfield services to the petroleum industry. The group's pressure pumping services includes stimulation, cementing, sand control, coiled tubing, fracturing, acidizing and tools services. Other oilfield services include specialty chemicals, tubular services and process and pipeline services. The group also provides commissioning, leak detection and inspection services to refineries, pipelines and offshore platforms and chemical services. The group operates from United States, Canada, Latin America, Europe, Asia, Africa, the Middle East, Russia and China.

Primary SIC and add'l.: 1382 1389

CIK No: 0000864328

Subsidiaries: Aspac Region Pte. Ltd., B.j. Petroleum Services International Limited, Biarritz Overseas Limited, Bj - Rotary Petroleum Services Company Limited, Bj Canada Technical Services Limited, Bj Chemical Products (beijing) Limited, Bj General Holdings, Bj General Holdings Secs LLC, Bj Holdings (russia) Limited, Bj Oilwell Services (m) Sdn. Bhd., Bj Petroleum Services (china) Limited, Bj Petroleum Services Limited, Bj Process & Pipeline Services (australia) Pty Ltd, Bj Process & Pipeline Services Limited, Bj Process & Pipeline Services Pte. Ltd. 123 Subsidiaries included in the Index

Officers: James W. Stewart/Chmn., CEO, Pres., Margaret B. Shannon/VP, General Counsel, Corp. Sec., David D. Dunlap/COO, Exec. VP, Douglas Bret Wells/VP, Treasurer, Chief Tax Officer, Susan E. Douget/VP - Human Resources, Brian T. McCole/VP, Controller, Jeffrey E. Smith/CFO, VP - Finance, Alasdair I. Buchanan/VP - International Pressure Pumping Services, Paul F. Yust/CIO, VP, Ronald F. Coleman/VP - North American Pressure Pumping Operations, Jeff Hibbeler/VP - Technology, Logistics

Directors: James W. Stewart/Chmn., CEO, Pres., Don D. Jordan/Dir., William L. Heiligbrodt/Dir., John R. Huff/Dir., William H. White/Dir., Michael E. Patrick/Dir., James L. Payne/Dir.

Owners: William L. Heiligbrodt, J. W. Stewart/1.30%, Alasdair Buchanan, James L. Payne, Margaret B. Shannon, John R. Huff, Don D. Jordan, William H. White, Insiders/2.20%, T. Rowe Price Associates, Inc./8.90%, Capital Research and Management Company/7.20%, David Dunlap, Michael E. Patrick, Jeffrey E. Smith

Financial Data: *Fiscal Year End:*09/30 *Latest Annual Data:* 9/30/2006

Year	Sales	Net Income
2006	$4,367,864,000	$804,610,000
2005	$3,243,186,000	$453,042,000
2004	$2,600,986,000	$361,041,000

Curr. Assets:	$1,458,860,000	Curr. Liab.:	$947,936,000	P/E Ratio:	10.45
Plant, Equip.:	$1,392,926,000	Total Liab.:	$1,715,348,000	Indic. Yr. Divd.:	$0.200
Total Assets:	$3,862,288,000	Net Worth:	$2,146,940,000	Debt/ Equity:	0.1982

BJ's Restaurants Inc

7755 Ctr. Ave., Ste. 300, Huntington Beach, CA, 92647; *PH:* 1-714-500-2400; *http://* www.bjsbrewhouse.com; *Email:* investorrelations@bjsbrewhouse.com

General - Incorporation .... CA
Employees 6,438
Auditor .... Ernst & Young LLP
Stk Agt .... U.S. Stock Transfer Corp
Counsel.... Jeffer Mangels Butler & Mamaro LLP
DUNS No. .... NA

Stock- Price on:12/24/2007 .... $18.49
Stock Exchange .... NDQ
Ticker Symbol .... BJRI
Outstanding Shares 26,090,000
E.P.S $0.39
Shareholders .... NA

Business: The group's principal activity is to own and operate 31 restaurants located in California, Arizona, Oregon, Colorado, Texas and Nevada. It also receives fees from one licensed restaurant in lahaina, maui. These restaurants operate as either a bj's restaurant and brewery, a bj's pizza and grill, a bj's restaurant and brewhouse or a pietro's pizza restaurant. The menus offered by the group's bj's restaurants include deep-dish pizza, bj's own hand-crafted beers, appetizers, entrees, pastas, sandwiches, speciality salads and desserts. The ten bj's restaurant and brewery restaurants have in-house brewing facilities where bj's hand-crafted beers are produced. On 15-Mar-2004 the group's sold its three pietro's pizza restaurants. The group purchases its food products from several wholesale distributors.

Primary SIC and add'l.: 5812 5813

CIK No: 0001013488

Subsidiaries: Chicago America Holding LLC, Chicago Pizza Hospitality Holding Inc., Chicago Pizza Management LLC, Chicago Pizza Northwest Inc., Chicago Pizza Restaurant Holding Inc., Chicago Pizza& Brewery LP

Officers: Gerald W. Deitchle/Dir., CEO, Pres./$864,924.00, Paul Motenko/Co - Chmn., VP, Sec./$388,785.00, Robert Deliema/Pres. - Bj's Restaurants Foundation, Alex Puchner/Sr. VP - Brewing Operations, Greg Levin/CFO/$503,816.00, Rana Schirmer/VP - Accounting, Controller, Nanette McWhertor/VP - Operations Support, Restaurant Openings, Brian Pearson/VP - Information Services, Lon Ledwith/Sr. VP - Restaurant Operations, Greg Lynds/Chief Development Officer/$501,292.00, John Allegretto/Chief Supply Chain Officer/$461,532.00, Jeff Williams/Dir. - Brewing Operations, New Brewery Operations, John M. Oliver/Mgr. - Production, Regional Brewmaster, Cal South, Derek Osborne/Mgr. - Procedures,Regional Brewmaster, East, Dan Pedersen/Mgr. - QA, Regional Brewmaster, Northwest *(29 Officers included in Index)*

Directors: Gerald W. Deitchle/Dir., CEO, Pres., Jerry Hennessy/Co - Chmn., Paul Motenko/Co - Chmn., VP, Sec., John Grundhofer/Dir., James Dal Pozzo/Dir., Larry D. Bouts/Dir., Shann Brassfield/Dir., Roger J. King/Dir., Peter A. Bassi/Dir.

Owners: FMR Corp./6.40%, Insiders/25.08%, T. Rowe Price Associates, Inc./6.44%, Gregory S. Lynds, Peter A. Bassi, Golden Resorts, Inc./13.32%, Morgan Stanley/7.88%, Gerald W. Deitchle, Paul A. Motenko/1.81%, John D. Allegretto, Shann M. Brassfield/2.52%, Roger J. King, Larry D. Bouts, Next Century Growth Investors, LLC/6.72%, John F. Grundhofer *(19 Owners included in Index)*

Financial Data: **Fiscal Year End:**01/03 **Latest Annual Data:** 1/2/2007

Year	Sales	Net Income
2007	$238,928,000	$9,845,000
2006	$178,210,000	$8,351,000
2005	$129,049,000	$6,265,000

Curr. Assets:	$58,231,000	**Curr. Liab.:**	$26,405,000		
Plant, Equip.:	$99,773,000	**Total Liab.:**	$34,059,000	**Indic. Yr. Divd.:**	NA
Total Assets:	$163,958,000	**Net Worth:**	$129,899,000	**Debt/ Equity:**	NA

BJ's Wholesale Club Inc

1 Mercer Rd., Natick, MA, 01760; ***PH:*** 1-508-651-7400; ***Fax:*** 1-508-651-6114; ***http://*** www.bjswholesale.com; ***Email:*** investor@bjs.com

General - Incorporation .... DE
Employees 21,200
Auditor .... PricewaterhouseCoopers LLP
Stk Agt .... Bank of New York
Counsel .... NA
DUNS No. 15-908-2692

Stock- Price on:12/24/2007 .... $37.15
Stock Exchange .... NYSE
Ticker Symbol .... BJ
Outstanding Shares 66,080,000
E.P.S $1.07
Shareholders .... NA

Business: The groups principle activity is to operate warehouse clubs. The group also provides optical stores, food courts, on-site photo service, a selection of garden sheds, and patios and sunrooms. The group operates from United States.

Primary SIC and add'l.: 5145 5147 5143 5399 5141 5142 5144

CIK No: 0001037461

Subsidiaries: BJs Charitable Foundation Inc., BJs FL Distribution Center, Inc., BJs MA Distribution Center, Inc., BJs NJ Distribution Center, LLC, BJs Uxbridge Business Trust, BJs Uxbridge, LLC, BJME Operating Corp., BJNH Operating Co., LLC., CWC Beverages Corp., FWC Beverages Corp., JWC Beverages Corp., Mercer Holdings 2002 Business Trust, Mercer Mortgage Holdings, Inc., Mormax Beverages Corp., Mormax Corporation 71 Subsidiaries included in the Index

Officers: Herbert J. Zarkin/Chmn., CEO/$3,614,751.00, Frank D. Forward/53/CFO, Exec. VP/$962,414.00, Laura Sen/51/Exec. VP - Merchandising, Logistics, Lon F. Povich/48/Sr. VP, General Counsel, Sec., Henry Ragin/Contact - Supplier Inquiries Movies, Music, Video Games, Electronics, Automotive, Sporting Goods, Computers, Office Supplies, Bruce Graham/Contact - Supplier Inquiries Foods, Sundries, Jim Hilson/Contact - Supplier Inquiries Domestics, Books, Seasonal, Appliances, Lawn, Garden, Furniture, Toys, Collectibles, Giftware, Housewares, Diane Faranda/Contact - Supplier Inquiries Apparel, Jewelry, Brian Riccio/Contact - Supplier Inquiries Fresh Foods, Thomas F. Gallagher/56/Exec. VP - Club Operations/$473,741.00

Directors: Herbert J. Zarkin/Chmn., CEO, Helen Frame Peters/Dir., Paul Danos/Dir., Ronald R. Dion/Dir., James S. Coppersmith/Dir., Thomas J. Shields/Dir., Lorne R. Waxlax/Dir., Edmond J. English/Dir.

Owners: Edward F. Giles, FMR Corp./11.46%, Lorne R. Waxlax, Paul M. Bass, Thomas F. Gallagher, Hotchkis and Wiley Capital Management, LLC/6.88%, Helen Frame Peters, Frank D. Forward, Ronald R. Dion, Herbert J. Zarkin/1.67%, Thomas J. Shields, Barclays Global Investors, NA./6.73%, S. James Coppersmith, Insiders/2.40%, Paul Danos *(16 Owners included in Index)*

Financial Data: **Fiscal Year End:**01/28 **Latest Annual Data:** 2/3/2007

Year	Sales	Net Income
2007	$8,480,281,000	$72,016,000
2006	$7,949,934,000	$128,533,000
2005	$7,375,301,000	$114,401,000

Curr. Assets:	$1,069,578,000	**Curr. Liab.:**	$866,578,000		
Plant, Equip.:	$900,148,000	**Total Liab.:**	$972,924,000	**Indic. Yr. Divd.:**	NA
Total Assets:	$1,992,811,000	**Net Worth:**	$1,019,887,000	**Debt/ Equity:**	0.0155

Black & Decker Corp

101 Schilling Rd., Hunt Valley, MD, 21031; ***PH:*** 1-410-716-3900; ***Fax:*** 1-410-716-2933; ***http://*** www.blackanddecker.com; ***Email:*** investor.relations@bdk.com

General - Incorporation .... MD
Employees 25,500
Auditor .... Ernst & Young LLP
Stk Agt .... EquiServe Trust Co N.A
Counsel .... NA
DUNS No. 00-131-7189

Stock- Price on:12/24/2007 .... $86.89
Stock Exchange .... NYSE
Ticker Symbol .... BDK
Outstanding Shares 65,970,000
E.P.S $6.32
Shareholders .... NA

Business: The groups principle activities include manufacturing and marketing power tools and accessories, hardware and home improvement products and technology based fastening systems. The group operates through three segments namely power tools and accessories manufactures and markets power tools, electric lawn, garden tools, electric cleaning and lighting products. The group operates from United States, Canada, and Europe.

Primary SIC and add'l.: 3452 3429 3546 3524

CIK No: 0000012355

Subsidiaries: Anzi Masterfix Tool Ltd., Aven Tools Limited, B.B.W. Bayrische Bohrerwerke G.m.b.H., Baldwin Hardware Corporation, Baltimore Financial Services Company, Baltimore Insurance Limited, Bandhart, Bandhart Overseas, BD Beteiligungs G.m.b.H. & Co. K.G., Belco Investments Company, Biesemeyer Manufacturing Corporation, Black & Decker, Black & Decker (Australia) Pty. Ltd., Black & Decker (Belgium) N.V., Black & Decker (Czech) S.R.O. 133 Subsidiaries included in the Index

Officers: Nolan D. Archibald/Chmn., CEO, Pres./$10,336,440.00, Thomas D. Koos/44/Group VP/$1,783,675.00, James R. Raskin/VP - Business Development, Robert I. Rowan/VP - Corporate, Pres. - Construction Tools, Industrial Products Group, Power Tools, Accessories Group, Natalie A. Shields/VP, Corp. Sec., Ben S. Sihota/VP - Corporate, Pres. - Asia, Pacific, Power Tools, Accessories Group, Michael A. Tyll/Group VP - Corporate, Pres. - Fastening, Assembly Systems Group, John W. Schiech/Group VP - Corporate, Pres. - Industrial Products Group, Power Tools, Accessories Group/$1,950,441.00, James T. Caudill/Group VP - Corporate, Pres. - Hardware, Home Improvement Group, Les H. Ireland/VP - Corporate, Pres. - Europe, Middle East, Africa Power Tools, Accessories Group, Mark M. Rothleitner/VP - Investor Relations, Treasurer, Christina M. McMullen/VP, Controller, Bruce W. Brooks/Group VP - Corporate, Pres. - Consumer Products Group Power Tools, Accessories Group, Edward J. Scanlon/VP - Corporate, Pres. - Commercial Operations, North, South America, Power Tools, Accessories Group, Michael D. Mangan/CFO, Sr. VP/$2,822,160.00 *(18 Officers included in Index)*

Directors: Nolan D. Archibald/Chmn., CEO, Pres., Mark H. Willes/Dir., Norman R. Augustine/Dir., Barbara L. Bowles/Dir., George W. Buckley/Dir., Anthony M. Burns/Dir., Benjamin H. Griswold/Dir., Manuel A. Fernandez/Dir., Kim B. Clark/Dir., Robert L. Ryan/Dir., Anthony Luiso/Dir.

Owners: Kim B. Clark, Paul F. McBride, George W. Buckley, Mark H. Willes, Barbara L. Bowles, Charles E. Fenton, John W. Schiech, Manuel A. Fernandez, Nolan D. Archibald, Anthony Luiso, Michael D. Mangan, Thomas D. Koos, Benjamin H. Griswold, Robert L. Ryan, Norman R. Augustine *(17 Owners included in Index)*

Financial Data: **Fiscal Year End:**12/31 **Latest Annual Data:** 12/31/2006

Year	Sales	Net Income
2006	$6,447,300,000	$486,100,000
2005	$6,523,700,000	$543,900,000
2004	$5,398,400,000	$456,000,000

Curr. Assets:	$2,703,400,000	**Curr. Liab.:**	$1,779,600,000	**P/E Ratio:**	12.89
Plant, Equip.:	$622,200,000	**Total Liab.:**	$4,084,100,000	**Indic. Yr. Divd.:**	$1.680
Total Assets:	$5,247,700,000	**Net Worth:**	$1,163,600,000	**Debt/ Equity:**	0.9990

Black Box Corp

1000 Pk. Dr., Lawrence, PA, 15055; ***PH:*** 1-724-746-5500; ***Fax:*** 1-724-746-0746; ***http://*** www.blackbox.com; ***Email:*** info@blackbox.com

General - Incorporation .... DE
Employees 3,300
Auditor .... BDO Seidman LLP
Stk Agt ..... American Stock Transfer & Trust Co.
Counsel .... Buchanan Ingersoll P.C.
DUNS No. 08-225-4871

Stock- Price on:12/24/2007 .... $36.4
Stock Exchange .... NDQ
Ticker Symbol .... BBOX
Outstanding Shares 17,360,000
E.P.S .... NA
Shareholders .... NA

Business: The group's principal activities are to build, design and maintain network infrastructure systems. The group provides technical support and network services to the clients on the phone, on-site and on-line in 132 countries with 117 offices throughout the world. The clients include manufacturers, retailers, financial and educational institutions and government. The products and services are marketed under the brand name black box (r). The operations are carried out in North America, Europe and other countries.

Primary SIC and add'l.: 7373 6719 4822 3577 4841

CIK No: 0000849547

Subsidiaries: A.T.S., Inc., Advanced Communications Corporation, Advanced Network Technologies, Inc., American Telephone Wiring Company, Associated Network Solutions, Inc., Atimco Network Services, Inc., Bainbridge Communications, Inc., BB Technologies, Inc., BBC Acquisition, LLC, BBox Holding Company, BCI of Tampa, LLC, Black Box A/S, Black Box AB, Black Box Canada Corporation, Black Box Chile S.A. 102 Subsidiaries included in the Index

Officers: Terry R. Blakemore/51/Interim CEO, Pres./$803,568.00, Francis W. Wertheimber/55/Sr. VP - Pacific Rim, Far East/$677,069.00, Michael McAndrew/CFO, VP, Sec., Treasurer, Principal Accounting Officer/$456,319.00, Roger E.M. Croft/Sr. VP/$493,450.00

Directors: Thomas G. Greig/60/Chmn., Richard L. Crouch/61/Dir., Thomas W. Golonski/65/Dir., William F. Andrews/76/Dir., Edward A. Nicholson/68/Dir.

Owners: LSV Asset Management/5.10%, William F. Andrews, Fred C. Young/8.30%, Edward A. Nicholson, Francis W. Wertheimber/1.20%, Terry R. Blakemore, Thomas W. Golonski, Royce& Associates, LLC/6.00%, Roger E. M. Croft, Thomas G. Greig, Dimensional FundAdvisors LP/8.30%, Michael McAndrew, AXA/5.80%, FMR Corp./11.30%, Insiders/10.80% *(18 Owners included in Index)*

Financial Data: **Fiscal Year End:**03/31 **Latest Annual Data:** 03/31/2007

Year	Sales	Net Income
2007	$1,016,310,000	$35,609,000
2006	$721,335,000	$37,358,000
2005	$535,076,000	$29,912,000

Curr. Assets:	$231,124,000	**Curr. Liab.:**	$127,868,000		
Plant, Equip.:	$35,124,000	**Total Liab.:**	$258,834,000	**Indic. Yr. Divd.:**	$0.240
Total Assets:	$799,734,000	**Net Worth:**	$540,900,000	**Debt/ Equity:**	0.4522

Black Hills Corp

625 9th St., Rapid City, SD, 57701; *PH:* 1-605-721-1700; *Fax:* 1-605-721-2599; *http://* www.blackhillscorp.com; *Email:* bhc@blackhillscorporation.com

General - Incorporation	SD	**Stock**- Price on:12/24/2007	$40.51
Employees	819	Stock Exchange	NYSE
Auditor	Deloitte & Touche LLP	Ticker Symbol	BKH
Stk Agt	Wells Fargo Shareowner Services	Outstanding Shares	37,670,000
Counsel	NA	E.P.S	$2.86
DUNS No.	NA	Shareholders	NA

Business: The group's principal activities are to produce and market power and fuel and provide broadband communication services. The group operates through three business units: integrated energy, electric utility and communications. The integrated energy unit produces and markets power and fuel in a number of markets, with a strong emphasis on the western United States. Electric utility serves approximately 61,000 customers in South Dakota, Wyoming and Montana. The communications unit offers state-of-the-art broadband communication services to residential and business customers in rapid city and the northern black hills region of South Dakota. On 10-Mar-2003, the group acquired mallon resources corporation.

Primary SIC and add'l.: 1311 3568 4939 4911 4899 1222

CIK No: 0001130464

Subsidiaries: Black Hills Artesia, LLC, Black Hills Cabresto Pipeline, Black Hills Colorado, LLC, Black Hills Energy Pipeline, LLC, Black Hills Energy Resources, Inc, Black Hills Energy Terminal, LLC, Black Hills Energy, Inc, Black Hills Exploration and Production, Inc., Black Hills Fountain Valley II, LLC, Black Hills Fountain Valley, LLC, Black Hills Gas Holdings Corp., Black Hills Gas Resources, Inc., Black Hills Generation, Inc., Black Hills Idaho Operations, Black Hills Independent Power Fund, Inc. 56 Subsidiaries included in the Index

Officers: David R. Emery/45/Chmn., CEO, Pres./$1,707,710.00, Maurice T. Klefeker/Sr. VP - Strategic Planning, Development, James Williams/VP, GM - Wyodak Resources, Dale T. Jahr/Dir. - Investor Relations, Perry S. Krush/VP, Controller, Roxann R. Basham/VP - Governance, Corp. Sec., Kyle D. White/VP - Corporate Affairs, Tim Hopkins/VP, GM - Black Hills Exploration, Production, Thomas M. Ohlmacher/Pres., COO - Wholesale Business/$1,326,597.00, Kurt Kittleson/VP - Energy Marketing, GM Enserco Energy, Mark Lux/VP - Power Delivery, Black Hills Generation, Stuart Wevik/VP - Retail Operations, Garner M. Anderson/VP, Treasurer, Chief Risk Officer, James M. Mattern/Sr. VP - Corporate Administration, Compliance, Mark T. Thies/CFO, Exec. VP/$703,412.00 *(17 Officers included in Index)*

Directors: David R. Emery/45/Chmn., CEO, Pres., Warren L. Robinson/57/Dir., David C. Ebertz/62/Dir., John R. Howard/67/Dir., Stephen D. Newlin/55/Dir., Thomas J. Zeller/60/Dir., Jack W. Eugster/62/Dir., Gary L. Pechota/58/Dir., Kay S. Jorgensen/57/Dir., John B. Vering/58/Dir.

Owners: Barclays Global Investors, NA and Barclays Global Fund/9.00%, David R. Emery, Kay S. Jorgensen, Richard Korpan, Warren L. Robinson, Steven J. Helmers, Linden R. Evans, T. Rowe Price Associates, Inc./6.90%, John B. Vering, Lord, Abbett & Co. LLC/8.70%, Mark T. Thies, Insiders/1.90%, David C. Ebertz, Jack W. Eugster, Thomas J. Zeller *(18 Owners included in Index)*

Financial Data: *Fiscal Year End:*12/31 *Latest Annual Data:* 12/31/2006

Year	Sales	Net Income
2006	$656,882,000	$81,019,000
2005	$1,391,644,000	$33,420,000
2004	$1,121,701,000	$57,973,000

Curr. Assets:	$474,501,000	**Curr. Liab.:**	$528,978,000	**P/E Ratio:**	14.16
Plant, Equip.:	$1,646,367,000	**Total Liab.:**	$1,449,477,000	**Indic. Yr. Divd.:**	$1.360
Total Assets:	$2,244,676,000	**Net Worth:**	$790,041,000	**Debt/ Equity:**	0.6389

Black Hills Power Inc

409 Deadwood Ave., Rapid City, SD, 57702; *PH:* 1-605-721-2660; *Fax:* 1-605-721-2573; *http://* www.blackhillspower.com

General - Incorporation	SD	**Stock**- Price on:12/24/2007	$40.58
Employees	819	Stock Exchange	NA
Auditor	Deloitte & Touche LLP	Ticker Symbol	NA
Stk Agt	Hanover Trust Co	Outstanding Shares	37,670,000
Counsel	NA	E.P.S	NA
DUNS No.	00-792-0333	Shareholders	NA

Business: The group operates through its subsidiaries whose principle activity is to generate, purchase, transmit, distribute and sell electric power; mine and sell low sulfur sub-bituminous coal; and explore for and produce oil and natural gas. The group operates from United States.

Primary SIC and add'l.: 1311 6719 4931 1221

CIK No: 0000012400

Officers: David R. Emery/Chmn., CEO, Pres., Kristy Schmitz/Dir. - Customer Service, Mark T. Thies/Exec. VP, CFO - Principal Financial, Accounting Officer, Lee Delange/Business Mgr., Monni Karim/Southern Hills Business Mgr. - Edgemont Office, Hot Springs Office, Jim Bunch/Business Mgr. - Newcastle Wyoming Office, Jim Keck/Energy Services Supervisor, Keith Gade/Marketing Services Supervisor, Gene Mantei/Energy Services Representative, Tom Berry/Energy Services Advisor, Tom Ohlmacher/VP - Power Supply, Michael Fredrich/Contact, Vern Schild/Dir. - Power Generation

Directors: David R. Emery/Chmn., CEO, Pres., John B. Vering/Dir., Jack W. Eugster/Dir., David C. Ebertz/Dir., Stephen D. Newlin/Dir., Kay S. Jorgensen/Dir., Richard Korpan/Dir., John R. Howard/Dir., Thomas J. Zeller/Dir.

Financial Data: *Fiscal Year End:*12/31 *Latest Annual Data:* 12/31/2006

Year	Sales	Net Income
2006	$656,882,000	$81,019,000
2005	$1,391,644,000	$33,420,000
2004	$1,121,701,000	$57,973,000

Curr. Assets:	$474,501,000	**Curr. Liab.:**	$528,978,000	**P/E Ratio:**	15.85
Plant, Equip.:	$1,646,367,000	**Total Liab.:**	$1,449,477,000	**Indic. Yr. Divd.:**	$1.360
Total Assets:	$2,244,676,000	**Net Worth:**	$790,041,000	**Debt/ Equity:**	0.6389

Blackbaud Inc

2000 Daniel Island Dr., Charleston, SC, 29492; *PH:* 1-843-216-6200; *Fax:* 1-843-216-6111; *http://* www.blackbaud.com

General - Incorporation	DE	**Stock**- Price on:12/24/2007	$22.53
Employees	1,165	Stock Exchange	NDQ
Auditor	PricewaterhouseCoopers LLP	Ticker Symbol	BLKB
Stk Agt	Wachovia Bank, N.A	Outstanding Shares	43,950,000
Counsel	NA	E.P.S	$0.68
DUNS No.	10-121-9228	Shareholders	NA

Business: The group's principal activity is to provide software and related services designed specifically for nonprofit organizations. The products and services enable nonprofit organizations to increase donations, reduce fundraising costs, improve communications with constituents, manage their finances and optimize internal operations. In 2003, the group had over 12,500 active customers distributed across multiple verticals within the nonprofit market including religion; education; foundations; health and human services; arts and cultural; public and societal benefits; environment and animal welfare and international and foreign affairs.

Primary SIC and add'l.: 7379 7372

CIK No: 0001280058

Officers: Marc Chardon/CEO, Pres., Jay B. Love/Pres., CEO - Etapestry, John Mistretta/VP - Human Resources, Lee W. Gartley/Sr. VP, Charles L. Longfield/Chief Scientist, Gerard J. Zink/VP - Customer Support, Richard S. Braddock/39/VP - Marketing, Charles T. Cumbaa/VP - Products, Services, Heidi H. Strenck/VP, Controller, Louis J. Attanasi/VP - Products, Christopher R. Todd/VP - Sales, Timothy V. Williams/CFO, Sr. VP - Finance, Administration

Directors: Marco W. Hellman/Chmn., Andrew M. Leitch/Dir., George Ellis/Dir., John McConnell/Dir., Timothy Chou/Dir., Carolyn Miles/Dir.

Owners: Timothy V. Williams, Waddell & Reed Financial Inc./6.50%, Munder Capital Management/5.90%, Insiders/3.20%, Marco W. Hellman, Andrew M. Leitch, Richard S. Braddock, Gerard J. Zink, George H. Ellis, Marc E. Chardon, FMR Corp./10.30%, Christopher R. Todd, John P. McConnell

Financial Data: *Fiscal Year End:*12/31 *Latest Annual Data:* 12/31/2006

Year	Sales	Net Income
2006	$191,380,000	$30,153,000
2005	$166,296,000	$33,301,000
2004	$138,745,000	$12,641,000

Curr. Assets:	$111,631,000	**Curr. Liab.:**	$97,506,000	**P/E Ratio:**	33.13
Plant, Equip.:	$10,524,000	**Total Liab.:**	$99,651,000	**Indic. Yr. Divd.:**	$0.340
Total Assets:	$195,009,000	**Net Worth:**	$95,358,000	**Debt/ Equity:**	0.0108

Blackboard Inc

1899 L St. NW, 5th Fl., Washington, DC, 20036; *PH:* 1-202-463-4860; *Fax:* 1-202-463-4863; *http://* www.blackboard.com

General - Incorporation	DE	**Stock**- Price on:12/24/2007	$42.27
Employees	765	Stock Exchange	NDQ
Auditor	Ernst & Young LLP	Ticker Symbol	BBBB
Stk Agt	American Stock Transfer & Trust Co.	Outstanding Shares	28,570,000
Counsel	NA	E.P.S	$0.03
DUNS No.	01-613-1430	Shareholders	NA

Business: The group's principal activity is to provide enterprise software applications and related services to the education industry. The products consist of five software applications: blackboard learning system, blackboard portal systems, blackboard content system, blackboard transaction system and blackboard one bundled in two suites, the blackboard academic suite and blackboard commerce suite. The customers of the group include colleges, universities, school, other educational providers, textbook publishers and student-focused merchants.

Primary SIC and add'l.: 7372

CIK No: 0001106942

Subsidiaries: Bb Acquisition Corp., Bb Management Co. LLC, Blackboard (Beijing) Co., Ltd., Blackboard Acquisition Company, LLC, Blackboard CampusWide of Texas, Inc., Blackboard Corp., Blackboard iCollege, Inc., Blackboard International B.V., Blackboard International Holdings Inc., Blackboard International LP, Blackboard Japan KK, Blackboard Tennessee, LLC, College Acquisition Sub, Inc.

Officers: Michael L. Chasen/Dir., CEO, Pres./$1,740,657.00, Timothy L. Hill/Pres. - Professional Education Solutions, Michael Beach/CFO/$570,134.00, Karen Gage/VP - Blackboard Beyond Initiative, Melissa Chotiner/Public Relations Mgr., Craig Chanoff/Sr. VP - Client Support, Information Technology, David Sample/Sr. VP - Sales/$663,063.00, John Kinzer/Sr. VP - Finance, David Marr/Sr. VP - Global Services, Neil Allison/Dir. - Product Marketing, Melissa Anderson/Pegagogical Advisor, Tom Bell/VP - Industry Relations, Juan Lucca/Pres. - International Business, Russ C. Carlson/Pres. - Blackboard Commerce Business, Jessie Woolley-Wilson/Pres. - K12 at Blackboard Inc *(23 Officers included in Index)*

Directors: Michael L. Chasen/Dir., CEO, Pres., Matthew S. Pittinsky/Chmn., Beth Kaplan/Dir., Frank Gatti/Dir., William Raduchel/Dir., Roger Novak/Dir., Joseph L. Cowan/Dir., Thomas Kalinske/Dir.

Owners: Waddell& Reed Investment Management Company/10.70%, ICG Holdings, Inc./7.70%, Peter Repetti, David Sample, Rogers E. Novak, Frank Gatti, Matthew H. Small, Insiders/4.30%, William Raduchel, Michael J. Beach, ClearBridge Advisors, LLC/5.10%, BlackRock, Inc./7.90%, Michael L. Chasen/1.70%, Arthur Levine, Matthew L. Pittinsky/1.70%

Financial Data: *Fiscal Year End:*12/31 *Latest Annual Data:* 12/31/2006

Year	Sales	Net Income
2006	$183,063,000	-$10,737,000
2005	$135,664,000	$41,853,000
2004	$111,403,000	$10,049,000

Curr. Assets:	$104,370,000	**Curr. Liab.:**	$141,346,000		
Plant, Equip.:	$12,761,000	**Total Liab.:**	$167,178,000	**Indic. Yr. Divd.:**	NA
Total Assets:	$307,299,000	**Net Worth:**	$140,121,000	**Debt/ Equity:**	0.1255

Blackhawk Bancorp Inc

400 Broad St., Beloit, WI, 53511; *PH:* 1-864-335-2200; *http://* www.blackhawkbank.com

General - Incorporation	WI	**Stock**- Price on:12/24/2007	$11.05
Employees	NA	Stock Exchange	OTC
Auditor	McGladrey & Pullen LLP	Ticker Symbol	BHWB
Stk Agt	NA	Outstanding Shares	NA
Counsel	NA	E.P.S	NA
DUNS No.	NA	Shareholders	NA

Business: The groups principle activity is to provide online banking, personal, business, mortgage, wealth management services. The groups services include checking, savings, Money Market Accounts, Certificate of Deposits, Health Savings Accounts, Loans, Business Banking Services, Health Savings Accounts, ATMs and Online Application. The group operates from United States.

Primary SIC and add'l.: 6712 6022 6035

CIK No: 0000857853

Officers: Richard R. Bastian/Dir., Pres., CEO - Blackhawk Bank, Stephen P. Carter/Dir. - Blackhawk Bank, Rocio Ivens/Contact - Belvidere, Blackhawk Bank, Todd J. James/Dir., Sec., Treasurer - Blackhawk Bancorp, Inc, Exec. VP, CFO - Blackhawk Bank, Monica Diaz/Contact - Capron, Blackhawk Bank, Charles Hart/Dir. - Blackhawk Bank, James D. Metz/Dir. - Blackhawk Bank, Merritt J. Mott/Dir. - Blackhawk Bank, Maria Gloria/Contact - Belvidere, Blackhawk Bank, Kristina Gomez/Contact - Belvidere, Blackhawk Bank, Leo Prieto/Contact - Rockford, Blackhawk Bank, Cindy Arellano/Contact - Belvidere, Blackhawk Bank, Mireya Gloria/Contact - Belvidere, Blackhawk Bank, Sabrina Olivez/Contact - Belvidere, Blackhawk Bank, Laura Pena/Contact - Machesney, Blackhawk Bank *(46 Officers included in Index)*

Financial Data: Fiscal Year End: 12/31   **Latest Annual Data:** 12/31/2003

Year	Sales	Net Income
2003	$21,556,000	$1,211,000
2002	$22,194,000	$1,236,000
2001	$25,370,000	$864,000

Curr. Assets:	$26,211,000	**Curr. Liab.:**	$333,125,000	
Plant, Equip.:	$9,981,000	**Total Liab.:**	$392,422,000	**Indic. Yr. Divd.:** NA
Total Assets:	$425,185,000	**Net Worth:**	$25,763,000	**Debt/ Equity:** 2.7617

Blackhawk Capital Group BDC Inc

14 Wall St. 11th Fl., New York, NY, 10005; **PH:** 1-212-566-8300

General - Incorporation	DE	**Stock**- Price on:12/24/2007	$0.49
Employees	2	Stock Exchange	OTC
Auditor	Eisner LLP	Ticker Symbol	BHCG
Stk Agt	NA	Outstanding Shares	30,510,000
Counsel	NA	E.P.S.	-$0.01
DUNS No.	NA	Shareholders	NA

Business: The group's principal activities are investing in other companies financially and to give support in areas such as marketing, management, finance, production and overhead. The company intends to offer managerial assistance to eligible portfolio companies in which it invests. The company serves small & large private companies, new and developing companies, even more mature privately and publicly held companies some of which may be experiencing financial difficulties, but which have potential for further development or revitalization, and which, in the long-term, could experience growth and achieve profitability. The group does not intend to limit its acquisitions to a single line of business or industry. The group does not intend to limit its acquisitions to a single line of business or industry. The company is a development stage company.

Primary SIC and add'l.: 6199

CIK No: 0001294345

Owners: Insiders/11.97%, Robert M. Fujii/1.64%, The Concorde Group, Inc./33.38%, Doreen McCarthy/7.69%, Craig A. Zabala/6.01%, Mick Woodwards/4.33%

Financial Data: Fiscal Year End: 12/31   **Latest Annual Data:** 12/31/2006

Year	Sales	Net Income
2006	$0	-$387,000

Curr. Assets:	NA	**Curr. Liab.:**	$202,000	
Plant, Equip.:	NA	**Total Liab.:**	$306,000	**Indic. Yr. Divd.:** NA
Total Assets:	$10,000	**Net Worth:**	-$296,000	**Debt/ Equity:** NA

BlackHawk Fund (The)

1802 N Carson St., Carson City, NV, 89701; **PH:** 1-775-887-0670; **http://** www.blackhawkfund.com; **Email:** contact@blackhawkfund.com

General - Incorporation	NV	**Stock**- Price on:12/24/2007	$0.01
Employees	2	Stock Exchange	OTC
Auditor	Gruber & Co., LLC	Ticker Symbol	BHWF
Stk Agt	Pacific Stock Transfer Company	Outstanding Shares	191,880,000
Counsel	NA	E.P.S.	-$0.018
DUNS No.	NA	Shareholders	NA

Business: The group's principle activity is to provide agency services for the commercial transactions between vietnamese purchasers and U.S. Manufacturers. The group acts as an intermediary in exporting and importing industrial and consumer goods to and from vietnam. The group identifies suitable U.S. Suppliers for vietnamese buyers, facilitates communication between the parties. The group also assists vietnamese buyers with the preparation of letter of credit documentation and submitting of such to the seller for approval. The group participates in the bidding process for the purchase of goods by vietnamese governmental agencies and associated entities and seeks to extend its business so as to provide similar services to private enterprises throughout vietnam. It generates revenue in the form of finder fees or sales commissions based upon a percentage of the overall procurement order. The group's quarterly revenue for September 2007 was 0.04 millions of USD.

Primary SIC and add'l.: 7389

CIK No: 0001096768

Officers: Steve Bonenberger/51/Dir., CEO, Pres., Brent Fouch/38/Dir., Sec., CFO

Directors: Steve Bonenberger/51/Dir., CEO, Pres., Brent Fouch/38/Dir., Sec., CFO

Owners: Palomar Enterprises/95.00%, Palomar Enterprises/100.00%, Palomar Enterprises/100.00%

Financial Data: Fiscal Year End: 12/31   **Latest Annual Data:** 12/31/2006

Year	Sales	Net Income
2006	$149,000	-$564,000
2005	$24,000	-$4,780,000
2004	NA	-$29,477,000

Curr. Assets:	$12,000	**Curr. Liab.:**	$592,000	
Plant, Equip.:	$1,693,000	**Total Liab.:**	$2,088,000	**Indic. Yr. Divd.:** NA
Total Assets:	$1,704,000	**Net Worth:**	-$384,000	**Debt/ Equity:** NA

Blackrock Inc

40 E 52nd St., New York, NY, 10022; **PH:** 1-212-754-5560; **http://** www.blackrock.com

General - Incorporation	DE	**Stock**- Price on:12/24/2007	$160.26
Employees	5,113	Stock Exchange	NYSE
Auditor	Deloitte & Touche LLP	Ticker Symbol	BLK
Stk Agt	Mellon Investor Services LLC	Outstanding Shares	116,090,000
Counsel	Skadden, Arps	E.P.S.	$6.39
DUNS No.	NA	Shareholders	NA

Business: The groups principle activity is to provide global investment management services. Customers served by the group include institutional and individual investors. The group also provides risk management, investment system outsourcing and financial advisory services to institutional investors under the BlackRock Solutions brand name. The group operates from United States.

Primary SIC and add'l.: 6282 6211 6719 6799

CIK No: 0001060021

Subsidiaries: BlackRock Advisors, Inc., BlackRock Financial Management, Inc., BlackRock Institutional Management Corporation, SSRM Holdings, Inc., State Street Research& Management Company

Officers: Laurence D. Fink/Chmn., CEO, Susan L. Wagner/Vice Chmn., COO, Barbara G. Novick/Vice Chmn., Head - Accounting Management, Robert C. Doll/Vice Chmn., Chief Investment Officer - Global Equities, Blackrock, Inc, Robert Fairbairn/Vice Chmn., Chmn. - Europe, Middle East, Africa, Australia, Charles S. Hallac/Vice Chmn., Head - Blackrock Solutions, Keith T. Anderson/Vice Chmn., Global CIO - Fixed Income, Peter R. Fisher/MD, Randolph B. Brown/MD, David E. Byrket/MD, Eileen Byrne/MD, Katherine S. Cahill/MD, Thomas P. Callan/MD, Laurence J. Carolan/MD, Stewart J. Carracher/MD *(105 Officers included in Index)*

Directors: Laurence D. Fink/Chmn., CEO, Susan L. Wagner/Vice Chmn., COO, Robert Fairbairn/Vice Chmn., Chmn. - Europe, Middle East, Africa, Australia, Stanley E. ONeal/Dir., Thomas H. O'Brien/Dir., James E. Rohr/Dir., Mathis Cabiallavetta/Dir., Dennis D. Dammerman/Dir., Gregory J. Fleming/Dir., Deryck Maughan/Dir., James Grosfeld/Dir., Murry S. Gerber/Dir., William S. Demchak/Dir., Rob S. Kapito/Dir., Pres., David H. Komansky/Dir. *(18 Directors included in Index)*

Financial Data: Fiscal Year End: 12/31   **Latest Annual Data:** 12/31/2006

Year	Sales	Net Income
2006	$2,097,976,000	$322,602,000

Curr. Assets:	$2,362,145,000	**Curr. Liab.:**	$2,048,948,000	
Plant, Equip.:	$214,784,000	**Total Liab.:**	$8,578,520,000	**Indic. Yr. Divd.:** $2.680
Total Assets:	$20,469,492,000	**Net Worth:**	$10,781,880,000	**Debt/ Equity:** 0.0230

BlackRock Kelso Capital Corp

40 E 52nd St., New York, NY, 10022; **PH:** 1-212-810-5800; **Fax:** 1-212-810-5801; **http://** www.blackrockkelso.com; **Email:** info@blackrockkelso.com

General - Incorporation	DE	**Stock**- Price on:12/24/2007	NA
Employees	NA	Stock Exchange	NDQ
Auditor	Deloitte & Touche LLP	Ticker Symbol	BKCC
Stk Agt	PFPC Inc	Outstanding Shares	NA
Counsel	NA	E.P.S.	NA
DUNS No.	NA	Shareholders	NA

Business: The group's principal activities include providing of global investment management, consulting/risk management, and advisory services. The group manages assets in multiple assets classes including a variety of equity, fixed income, liquidity alternative investment products & real estate strategies & options. The group's customer includes institutions, corporate, public, and Taft-Hartley pension plans, insurance companies, mutual funds, endowments, foundations, nuclear decommissioning trusts, corporations, banks, and individuals worldwide. In addition, the group provides risk management, investment system outsourcing and financial advisory services to a growing number of institutional investors. As of September 30, 2005, BlackRock assets under management total $428 billion across various assets. On 31/01/2005, BlackRock acquired SSRM Holdings Inc., the holding company of State Street Research and Management and State Street Realty. BlackRock

Primary SIC and add'l.: 6799

CIK No: 0001326003

Subsidiaries: BlackRock Financial Management, Inc.

Officers: James R. Maher/Chmn., CEO, Vincent B. Tritto/Chief Compliance Officer, Sec., Frank D. Gordon/CFO, Michael B. Lazar/COO, Kevin J. Kraska/MD, Peter S. MacDonald/MD, Jason A. Mehring/MD, Marshall R. Merriman/MD, Basil Palmeri/MD, Stephen N. Sachman/MD, Scott J. Booth/Assoc., Vikas M. Keswani/Assoc., Cindy Cao/Analyst, Ryan K. Carroll/Assoc., Christopher Ferraro/Analyst *(19 Officers included in Index)*

Directors: James R. Maher/Chmn., CEO, Jerrold B. Harris/Dir., William E. Mayer/Dir., France De Saint Phalle/Dir., Maureen K. Usifer/Dir., Brian J. Moncrief/Dir., Francois De Saint/Dir.

Owners: Jerrold B. Harris, Summer Street BRK Investors, L.L.C./15.06%, Performance Equity Management, LLC/18.83%, Frank D. Gordon, Vincent B. Tritto, William E. Mayer, James R. Maher/1.87%, Franois de Saint Phalle, Virginia Retirement System/37.66%, Maureen K. Usifer, Michael B. Lazar, First Plaza Group Trust/18.83%, Insiders/3.19%

Blacksands Petroleum Inc

645 7th Ave., Ste. 1250, Calgary, AB, T2P 4G8; **PH:** 1-403-870-2220

General - Incorporation	NV	**Stock**- Price on:12/24/2007	$2.2
Employees	NA	Stock Exchange	OTC
Auditor	Sherb & Co., LLP	Ticker Symbol	BSPE
Stk Agt	Continental Stock & Transfer Co	Outstanding Shares	NA
Counsel	NA	E.P.S.	NA
DUNS No.	NA	Shareholders	NA

Business: The groups principle activity is to provide recruiting services. The groups service area includes the research and development, engineering, marketing, sales, information technology and manufacturing industries. The group operates from United States.

Primary SIC and add'l.: 1311

CIK No: 0001308137

Subsidiaries: Maha San Lam Liang Co. Ltd.

Officers: Darren R. Stevenson/36/Dir., CEO, CFO, Pres., Sec.

Directors: Darren R. Stevenson/36/Dir., CEO, CFO, Pres., Sec., Bruno Mosimann/64/Dir.

Owners: Darren R. Stevenson/1.10%, Insiders/1.10%

Financial Data: Fiscal Year End: 10/31   **Latest Annual Data:** 10/31/2006

Year	Sales	Net Income
2006	NA	-$309,000
2005	NA	-$14,000

Curr. Assets:	$11,651,000	Curr. Liab.:	$100,000		
Plant, Equip.:	$31,000	Total Liab.:	$100,000	Indic. Yr. Divd.:	NA
Total Assets:	$11,693,000	Net Worth:	$11,593,000	Debt/ Equity:	NA

Blair Corp

220 Hickory St. , Warren, PA, 16366; PH: 1-814-723-3600; http:// www.blair.com

General - Incorporation	DE	Stock - Price on:12/24/2007	NA
Employees	1,900	Stock Exchange	NA
Auditor	Ernst & Young LLP	Ticker Symbol	NA
Stk Agt	National City Bank	Outstanding Shares	NA
Counsel	NA	E.P.S	NA
DUNS No.	00-791-7560	Shareholders	NA

Business: The group's principal activity is to market fashion apparel for men and women, as well as home furnishings, primarily through mail and the Internet. Catalogs and letters depicting the current styles of women and men's wear and home products are mailed directly to existing and prospective customers in the United States. The apparel line consists of coordinates, dresses, tops, pants, skirts, lingerie, sportswear, suits and shoes for women and men suits, shirts, outerwear and active wear for men. Home products include linen, furniture, bath accessories, kitchenware, gifts and personal care items. Popular brands include the crossing pointe line and the Jane Seymour Signature Collection. The group also operates three retail stores, two in Pennsylvania and one in Delaware. The group markets products manufactured by domestic, as well as international suppliers that are sourced through international trade offices located in Singapore, Hong Kong, Taiwan, India, Korea and China.

Primary SIC and add'l.: 5136 5961 5719 2339

CIK No: 0000071525

Subsidiaries: Allegheny Trail Corporation, Blair Credit Services Corp, Blair Factoring Company, Blair Holdings Incorporated, Blair International Holding, Inc, Blair International Limited, Blair International Singapore Pte. Ltd, Blair Payroll LLC, JLB Service Bank

Owners: Jewelcor Companies/5.11%, Michael A. Schuler, John O. Hanna, Randall A. Scalise, Robert W. Blair/5.88%, Insiders/7.59%, Murray K. McComas/1.19%, Dimensional Fund Advisors LP/6.60%, Harriet Edelman, Ronald L. Ramseyer, Cynthia A. Fields, John E. Zawacki/3.14%, Shelley J. Seifert, Jerel G. Hollens, Lawrence R. Vicini *(19 Owners included in Index)*

Blast Energy Services Inc

14550 Torrey Chase Blvd., Ste. 330, Houston, TX, 77014; PH: 1-281-453-2888; Fax: 1-281-453-2899; http:// www.blastenergyservices.com

General - Incorporation	CA	Stock - Price on:12/24/2007	$0.15
Employees	42	Stock Exchange	OTC
Auditor	Malone & Bailey, P.C	Ticker Symbol	BESV
Stk Agt	American Stock Transfer & Trust CO.	Outstanding Shares	67,610,000
Counsel	NA	E.P.S	-$0.7
DUNS No.		Shareholders	NA

Business: The group's principle activity is to provide services to the oil and gas industry. The company operates in two segments: drilling services and satellite services. The drilling services segment provides a service that enhances the recovery of oil and gas from new and existing wells. The satellite services segment provides services that allow its customers to remotely monitor and control wellhead, pipeline and drilling operations. Customers include amvest osage inc, esperada energy partners llc and maxim energy inc for drilling services and apache corporation, british petroleum and noble energy for satellite services. The company's services are provided to customers in the United States and Canada. The company merged with verdisys inc on 18-Jul-2003. The group operates from United States.

Primary SIC and add'l.: 1381 1389 1382

CIK No: 0001141197

Subsidiaries: Berg McAfee Energy, LLC, Energy 2000 NGC, Inc.

Officers: John O'Keefe/CEO, David M. Adams/56/Pres., Andrew Wilson/VP, GM - Satellite Business, John MacDonald/CFO, Corp Sec.

Directors: James O. Woodward/70/Chmn., Scott W. Johnson/56/Dir., Jeffrey R. Pendergraft/60/Dir., Roger P. Herbert/59/Dir., John R. Block/71/Dir., Joseph J. Penbera/58/Dir., Frederick R. Ruiz/62/Dir.

Owners: Berg McAfee Companies LLC/14.00%, Frederick R. Ruiz, Roger P. Herbert, O. James Woodward, Insiders/7.40%, Alberta Energy Partners/5.60%, Eric A. McAfee/15.80%, John R. Block, John OKeefe/1.70%, Scott W. Johnson, Laurus Master Fund/15.30%, Thornton Business Security Trust/24.30%, Jeffrey R. Pendergraft, David M. Adams/1.70%, John A. MacDonald *(16 Owners included in Index)*

Financial Data: Fiscal Year End:12/31 Latest Annual Data: 12/31/2006

Year	Sales	Net Income
2006	$3,243,000	-$38,073,000
2005	$1,159,000	-$2,862,000
2004	$1,453,000	-$8,766,000

Curr. Assets:	$4,398,000	Curr. Liab.:	$46,055,000		
Plant, Equip.:	$42,208,000	Total Liab.:	$50,747,000	Indic. Yr. Divd.:	NA
Total Assets:	$51,930,000	Net Worth:	$1,182,000	Debt/ Equity:	NA

Blastgard International Inc

12900 Automobile Blvd, Ste D, Clearwater, FL, 33762; PH: 1-727-592-9400; Fax: 1-727-592-9402; http:// www.blastgardintl.com; Email: sales@blastgardintl.com

General - Incorporation	CO	Stock - Price on:12/24/2007	$0.4
Employees	5	Stock Exchange	OTC
Auditor	Cordovano & Honeck LLP	Ticker Symbol	BLGA
Stk Agt	Corporate Stock Transfer, Inc.	Outstanding Shares	35,570,000
Counsel	NA	E.P.S	-$0.131
DUNS No.	NA	Shareholders	NA

Business: The groups principal activity is to develop Internet application which consists the medical information of the customer. The Website of the group can be accessed by the patient or an authorized person to input the patient's medical history on the Internet. The data input mode is designed to be user

friendly. The patient can either go into the input mode and type the data directly or go through a question and answer session with "Dr. E-Med", a computerized assistant that helps the patient to input their medical histories. The patient can enter the data by using the scroll bars and prompts. On 05-Feb-2002, the group acquired tooltrust corp.

Primary SIC and add'l.: 6719 7375

CIK No: 0001102358

Subsidiaries: BlastGard Technologies, Inc.

Officers: James F. Gordon/Chmn., CEO, Michael J. Gordon/Dir., VP - Corporate Administration, CFO, John L. Waddell/Dir., COO, Pres., James A. Burke/Consultant, Kevin J. Sharpe/VP - Engineering, Product Development

Directors: James F. Gordon/Chmn., CEO, Joel L. Gold/Dir., Michael J. Gordon/Dir., VP - Corporate Administration, CFO, John L. Waddell/Dir., COO, Pres., Arnold I. Burns/Dir., Ambassador Bremer/Dir., Paul Bremer/66/Dir.

Owners: Insiders/34.40%, Michael J. Gordon/5.90%, Paul L. Bremer/1.80%, James F. Gordon/12.40%, John L. Waddell/13.30%, Kevin J. Sharpe/1.00%, Andrew R. McKinnon, Joel Gold/1.40%

Financial Data: Fiscal Year End:12/31 Latest Annual Data: 12/31/2006

Year	Sales	Net Income
2006	$926,000	-$2,451,000
2005	$1,129,000	-$1,771,000
2004	$1,000	-$2,951,000

Curr. Assets:	$340,000	Curr. Liab.:	$1,198,000		
Plant, Equip.:	$36,000	Total Liab.:	$1,728,000	Indic. Yr. Divd.:	NA
Total Assets:	$654,000	Net Worth:	-$1,074,000	Debt/ Equity:	NA

Blockbuster Inc

1201 Elm St., Dallas, TX, 75270; PH: 1-214-854-3000; Fax: 1-214-254-3677; http:// www.blockbuster.com

General - Incorporation	DE	Stock - Price on:12/24/2007	$4.54
Employees	33,600	Stock Exchange	NYSE
Auditor	PricewaterhouseCoopers LLP	Ticker Symbol	BBI
Stk Agt	EquiServe Trust Co N.A	Outstanding Shares	192,040,000
Counsel	Hughes Hubbard & Reed LLP	E.P.S	-$0.01
DUNS No.	NA	Shareholders	NA

Business: The group's principle activity is to provide entertaining services. The group provides in-home rental and retail movie and games. The group provides their services by traditional retail outlets, online retailers, and cable and satellite providers. The group operates from United States.

Primary SIC and add'l.: 5735 7841 6794

CIK No: 0001085734

Subsidiaries: Ardnasillagh Ltd., Blockbuster Argentina, S.A., Blockbuster Australia Pty. Ltd., Blockbuster BEI Taiwan Ltd., Blockbuster Canada Co., Blockbuster Canada Inc., Blockbuster de Mexico, SA de CV, Blockbuster Distribution, Inc., Blockbuster Entertainment (Ireland) Limited, Blockbuster Entertainment Limited, Blockbuster Global Services Inc., Blockbuster Holdings Ireland, Blockbuster International (Taiwan) B.V., Blockbuster International Spain Inc., Blockbuster Investments LLC 33 Subsidiaries included in the Index

Officers: John F. Antioco/58/Chmn., CEO/$16,328,660.00, Frank G. Paci/50/Exec. VP - Strategic Planning, Business Development/$1,667,541.00, Larry J. Zine/53/CFO, Exec. VP, Chief Administrative Officer/$2,278,271.00, Nicholas P. Shepherd/49/Exec. VP, Pres. - Worldwide Stores/$3,316,642.00, Andi Yorio/Assist. Sec.

Directors: John F. Antioco/58/Chmn., CEO, Jackie M. Clegg/45/Dir., Edward Bleier/78/Dir., Carl C. Icahn/72/Dir., Robert A. Bowman/52/Dir., Gary J. Fernandes/64/Dir., Strauss Zelnick/50/Dir., James W. Crystal/70/Dir., Jules Haimovitz/57/Dir.

Owners: Gary J. Fernandes, Chris Wyatt, JPMorgan Chase& Co./6.40%, Morgan Stanley/7.20%, The TCW Group, Inc., on behalf of the TCW Business Unit/5.10%, Deutsche Bank AG/9.60%, HighRiverLimited/7.70%, Jackie M. Clegg, UBS AG/9.50%, HBK Investments L.P./6.90%, Barclays Global Investors, NA/5.70%, John F. Antioco, Robert A. Bowman, John F. Antioco/3.60%, Dimensional Fund Advisors LP/6.80% *(30 Owners included in Index)*

Financial Data: Fiscal Year End:12/31 Latest Annual Data: 12/31/2006

Year	Sales	Net Income
2006	$5,523,500,000	$54,700,000
2005	$5,864,400,000	-$588,100,000
2004	$6,053,200,000	-$1,248,800,000

Curr. Assets:	$1,565,600,000	Curr. Liab.:	$1,395,300,000		
Plant, Equip.:	$580,100,000	Total Liab.:	$2,394,800,000	Indic. Yr. Divd.:	NA
Total Assets:	$3,137,200,000	Net Worth:	$742,400,000	Debt/ Equity:	1.2660

Blonder Tongue Laboratories Inc

1 Jake Brown Rd., Old Bridge, NJ, 08857; PH: 1-732-679-4000; Fax: 1-732-679-4353; http:// www.blondertongue.com; Email: information@blondertongue.com

General - Incorporation	DE	Stock - Price on:12/24/2007	$1.55
Employees	250	Stock Exchange	AMEX
Auditor	Marcum & Kliegman, LLP	Ticker Symbol	BDR
Stk Agt	American Stock Transfer & Trust Co.	Outstanding Shares	6,220,000
Counsel	Stadley Ronon Stevens & Young	E.P.S	-$0.12
DUNS No.	00-213-6265	Shareholders	NA

Business: The group's principal activity is to design, manufacture and supply electronics and systems equipment for cable television industry. The group's products include headend products, distribution products, subscriber products, microwave products and fiber products. These products are used to acquire, distribute and protect the broad range of communications signals carried on fiber optic, coaxial cable and wireless distribution systems. The customers of the group are communication services industry including television, high-speed data (Internet) and telephony, to single family dwellings, multiple dwelling units, the lodging industry and institutions such as hospitals, prisons, schools and marinas.

Primary SIC and add'l.: 3669 3663

CIK No: 0001000683

Subsidiaries: Blonder Tongue Far East, LLC, Master Gain International Industrial Limited

Officers: James A. Luksch/CEO/$512,351.00, Peter F. Daly/Sr. VP - Sales, Marketing/$221,673.00, Emily M. Nikoo/Sr. VP - Operations, Eric S. Skolnik/CFO, Sr. VP/$179,113.00, Robert J. Palle/COO, Pres., Sec./$380,433.00, Allen Horvath/VP - Manufacturing, Norman A. Westcott/Sr. VP - Operational Services, Kant Mistry/VP - Engineering/$203,857.00, Ed Curreri/Dir. - Sales, Eastern Region, Tom Lowden/Inside Sales Representative - Eastern Region, Jeff Smith/Dir. - Sales, Western Region, Pattie Homeny/Western Region, Inside Sales Representative

Directors: Robert B. Mayer/Dir., John E. Dwight/Dir., Robert E. Heaton/Dir., Gary P. Scharmett/Dir., James F. Williams/Dir., James H. Williams/50/Dir.

Owners: James A. Luksch/16.72%, Kant Mistry/1.31%, Robert B. Mayer, James F. Williams/1.81%, FMR Corp./6.95%, Robert E. Heaton, Insiders/44.98%, Eric S. Skolnik, Al Frank Asset Management, Inc./7.25%, Robert J. Pall/20.01%, Peter F. Daly, Gary P. Scharmett/1.05%, John E. Dwight/1.89%

Financial Data: *Fiscal Year End:*12/31 *Latest Annual Data:* 12/31/2006

Year	Sales	Net Income
2006	$35,775,000	$342,000
2005	$36,468,000	-$5,500,000
2004	$39,233,000	-$3,122,000

Curr. Assets:	$14,942,000	**Curr. Liab.:**	$5,431,000		
Plant, Equip.:	$9,589,000	**Total Liab.:**	$6,990,000	**Indic. Yr. Divd.:**	NA
Total Assets:	$27,222,000	**Net Worth:**	$20,232,000	**Debt/ Equity:**	0.0770

Blount International Inc

4909 SE International Way, Portland, OR, 97222; *PH:* 1-503-653-8881; *Fax:* 1-503-653-4612; *http://* www.blount.com

General - Incorporation	DE	**Stock**- Price on:12/24/2007	$13.32
Employees	3,400	Stock Exchange	NYSE
Auditor	PricewaterhouseCoopers LLP	Ticker Symbol	BLT
Stk Agt	EquiServe Trust Co.	Outstanding Shares	47,280,000
Counsel	NA	E.P.S.	$0.72
DUNS No.	09-984-4185	Shareholders	NA

Business: The group's principal activities are carried out through two divisions: outdoor products and industrial and power equipment. Outdoor products include wide variety of cutting chain, chain saw guide bars, cutting chain drive sprockets and maintenance tools. They are used on portable gasoline and electric chain saws, and mechanical timber harvesting equipment. Industrial and power equipment segment manufactures equipment for the timber harvesting industry and for industrial use components, industrial tractors for land and utility right-of-way clearing and power transmission components. The users include logging contractors, harvesters, utility contractors, building materials distributors, scrap yard operators and original equipment manufacturers of hydraulic equipment. The group operates in Brazil, Canada, Europe, Japan, Russia and in the United States.

Primary SIC and add'l.: 3546 3599 3714

CIK No: 0001001606

Subsidiaries: Blount Holdings Ltd., Blount Industrial LTDA, Blount, Inc., Dixon Industries, Inc., Frederick Manufacturing Corporation

Officers: James S. Osterman/Chmn., CEO/$1,693,300.00, Dennis E. Eagan/Group Pres. - Industrial, Power Equipment/$859,756.00, Leonard J. Sillis/Corporate Sr. VP - Marketing, Logistics, Jake Vanderzanden/Pres. - ICS, Dale C. Johnson/VP - Corporate Human Resources, Richard H. Irving/Sr. VP, General Counsel, Sec./$852,706.00, Calvin E. Jenness/Sr. VP, CFO/$657,069.00, Kenneth O. Saito/Group Pres. - Oregon Cutting Systems/$934,301.00, Mark V. Allred/VP, Controller

Directors: James S. Osterman/Chmn., CEO, Eliot M. Fried/Dir., Daniel E. James/Dir., Harold E. Layman/Dir., Eugene R. Cartledge/Dir., Thomas J. Fruechtel/Dir., Joshua L. Collins/Dir., Robert D. Kennedy/Dir.

Owners: Wellington Management Company, LLP, Harold E. Layman, Lehman Brothers Holdings Inc., Kenneth O. Saito, Thomas J. Fruechtel, Davis Selected Advisers, L.P., Joshua L. Collins, R. Eugene Cartledge, Insiders, Richard H. Irving, Arnhold & S. Bleichroeder Advisers, LLC, Eliot M. Fried, James S. Osterman, Robert D. Kennedy, Ariel Capital Management *(16 Owners included in Index)*

Financial Data: *Fiscal Year End:*12/31 *Latest Annual Data:* 12/31/2006

Year	Sales	Net Income
2006	$651,064,000	$42,546,000
2005	$756,627,000	$106,615,000
2004	$692,600,000	$6,300,000

Curr. Assets:	$216,681,000	**Curr. Liab.:**	$98,819,000	**P/E Ratio:**	15.86
Plant, Equip.:	$102,365,000	**Total Liab.:**	$535,757,000	**Indic. Yr. Divd.:**	NA
Total Assets:	$430,466,000	**Net Worth:**	-$105,291,000	**Debt/ Equity:**	NA

Blue Coat Systems Inc

420 N Mary Ave., Sunnyvale, CA, 94085; *PH:* 1-408-220-2200; *Fax:* 1-408-220-2250; *http://* www.bluecoat.com; *Email:* info@bluecoat.com

General - Incorporation	DE	**Stock**- Price on:12/24/2007	$49.14
Employees	NA	Stock Exchange	NDQ
Auditor	Ernst & Young LLP	Ticker Symbol	BCSI
Stk Agt	BankBoston, N.A	Outstanding Shares	14,810,000
Counsel	NA	E.P.S.	$0.26
DUNS No.	NA	Shareholders	NA

Business: The group's principal activities are to design, develop, market and support proxy appliances. The group's products are designed to enable enterprises to minimize security risks and reduce the management costs and complexity of their Web infrastructure. The products include proxysg 400 series, proxysg 800 series and the proxysg 8000 series. These three models of proxysg appliances are very similar in terms of functionality and differ mainly in terms of their performance characteristics and scalability. The group currently licenses three separate software products, url filtering software, anti-virus software and blue coat reporter, which are used in conjunction with the proxysg and proxyav appliances. It also manufactures an appliance called director, which is used primarily to manage large numbers of proxysg appliances in a customer's environment. The group sells its products in North America, Europe and Asia. On 14-Nov-2003, the group acquired ositis software, inc.

Primary SIC and add'l.: 7372 7373 3572 7371

CIK No: 0001095600

Subsidiaries: Blue Coat Systems Canada, Inc., Blue Coat Systems Hong Kong Ltd., Blue Coat Systems International, Inc., Blue Coat Systems K.K. (Japan), Blue Coat Systems Latvia, SIA, Blue Coat Systems Ltd. (UK), Blue Coat Systems, Belgium B.V.B.A., CacheFlow Australia Pty. Ltd., CacheFlow Netherlands B.V., Cerberian, Inc., Entera Corporation, Riga Corporation

Officers: Brian Nesmith/Dir., CEO, Pres., Kevin S. Royal/Sr. VP, CFO, Bethany Mayer/Sr. VP - Worldwide Marketing, Nigel Hawthorn/Contact - Media Industry Community, Steve Schick/Contact - Media, Analyst, Corporate, North America, David A. De Simone/52/Sr. VP - Corporate Operations, Betsy E. Bayha/Sr. VP, General Counsel, Sec., Kevin Biggs/Sr. VP - Worldwide Sales

Directors: Brian Nesmith/Dir., CEO, Pres., David Hanna/Chmn., Keith Geeslin/Dir., Timothy Howes/Dir., Jim Barth/Dir.

Owners: Keith Geeslin/60.00%, Brian M. NeSmith/3.80%, David A. de Simone, Entities affiliated with Francisco Partners/8.40%, David W. Hanna/1.70%, Insiders/60.00%, Timothy A. Howes, Insiders/14.70%, Ergates Capital Management LLC/12.30%, James A. Barth, Thomas B. Ayers, Stephen P. Mullancy, Entities affiliated with Sequoia Capital/40.00%, Kevin S. Royal, Entities affiliated with Sequoia Capital/5.80% *(17 Owners included in Index)*

Financial Data: *Fiscal Year End:*04/30 *Latest Annual Data:* 04/30/2007

Year	Sales	Net Income
2007	$177,700,000	-$7,198,000
2006	$141,722,000	$2,940,000
2005	$96,186,000	$5,375,000

Curr. Assets:	$84,801,000	**Curr. Liab.:**	$44,076,000		
Plant, Equip.:	$8,059,000	**Total Liab.:**	$54,206,000	**Indic. Yr. Divd.:**	NA
Total Assets:	$164,164,000	**Net Worth:**	$109,958,000	**Debt/ Equity:**	NA

Blue Dolphin Energy Co

801 Travis, Ste. 2100, Houston, TX, 77002; *PH:* 1-713-227-7660; *Fax:* 1-713-227-7626; *http://* www.blue-dolphin.com

General - Incorporation	DE	**Stock**- Price on:12/24/2007	$3.11
Employees	7	Stock Exchange	NDQ
Auditor	UHY Mann Frankfort Stein & Lipp LLP	Ticker Symbol	BDCO
Stk Agt	Securities Transfer Corp	Outstanding Shares	11,560,000
Counsel	Vinson & Elkins LLP	E.P.S.	-$0.034
DUNS No.	11-435-5613	Shareholders	NA

Business: The group's principal activity is to explore and produce oil and gas in the western and central gulf of Mexico. The group operates in two business segments: oil and gas exploration and production and pipeline operations. The oil and gas exploration and production activities include the exploration, acquisition, development, operation and disposition of oil and gas properties. The pipeline operations include the group's developmental-stage mid-stream projects. The group's operations are carried out through its subsidiaries. The group's major customers include spinnaker exploration company and houston exploration and production company.

Primary SIC and add'l.: 4612 4922 1311 1382

CIK No: 0000793306

Subsidiaries: Blue Dolphin Exploration Company, Blue Dolphin Petroleum Company, Blue Dolphin Pipe Line Company, Blue Dolphin Services Co., Petroport, Inc.

Officers: Ivar Siem/Chmn., CEO/$60,000.00, Michael J. Jacobson/Pres./$205,000.00, Gregory W. Starks/VP, Treasurer, Sec./$116,181.00, Larry Turpin/Mgr. - Pipelines, Terminals, Alvin W. Childs/Production Superintendent, William J. Driscoll/Mgr. - Geology, Thomas W. Heath/Exec. VP

Directors: Ivar Siem/Chmn., CEO, Laurence N. Benz/Dir., Harris A. Kaffie/Dir., Erik Ostbye/Dir., John N. Goodpasture/Dir.

Owners: Ivar Siem/5.50%, Gregory W. Starks, Columbus Petroleum Limited, Inc./7.90%, Michael J. Jacobson, Michael S. Chadwick, John N. Goodpasture, Spencer Finance Corp. and Arne Blystad/7.30%, Laurence N. Benz, Erik Ostbye, Spencer Energy AS/5.10%, Insiders/14.40%, Harris A. Kaffie/7.00%

Financial Data: *Fiscal Year End:*12/31 *Latest Annual Data:* 12/31/2006

Year	Sales	Net Income
2006	$4,299,000	$913,000
2005	$4,511,000	$541,000
2004	$1,436,000	-$2,500,000

Curr. Assets:	$7,011,000	**Curr. Liab.:**	$358,000	**P/E Ratio:**	77.75
Plant, Equip.:	$4,912,000	**Total Liab.:**	$2,372,000	**Indic. Yr. Divd.:**	NA
Total Assets:	$11,944,000	**Net Worth:**	$9,572,000	**Debt/ Equity:**	NA

Blue Earth Refineries Inc

Unit 803, 8/f Dina House, Ruttonjee Ctr, 11 Duddell St., Central; *PH:* 852-253-73613

General - Incorporation	Canada	**Stock**- Price on:12/24/2007	$1.95
Employees	NA	Stock Exchange	OTC
Auditor	Deloitte & Touche, LLP	Ticker Symbol	BUERF
Stk Agt	Mellon Investor Services LLC	Outstanding Shares	NA
Counsel	NA	E.P.S.	NA
DUNS No.	NA	Shareholders	NA

Business: The groups principle activity is to operate a cobalt project located in southwest Uganda and recovers cobalt from a pyrite stockpile at a former copper mine. The group also provides metal refining operations, bioleaching of pyrite concentrate, solvent extraction of the dissolved cobalt and recovery through electro-winning. The group operates from United States.

Primary SIC and add'l.: 3330

CIK No: 0001299795

Subsidiaries: Blue Earth Refineries (Canada) Inc., Kasese Cobalt Company Limited

Officers: Michael J. Smith/59/Dir., CEO, Pres., Principal Financial Officer, Sec.

Directors: Michael J. Smith/59/Dir., CEO, Pres., Principal Financial Officer, Sec., Rajesh Kumar Singhal/45/Dir., Nowroz Jal Cama/63/Dir.

Owners: Mass Financial Corp./10.00%, Lloyd I. Miller/12.30%, Peter Kellogg/31.40%, Michael J. Smith/10.60%, The PNC Financial Services Group, Inc./6.80%

Financial Data: *Fiscal Year End:*06/30 *Latest Annual Data:* 6/30/2006

Year	Sales	Net Income
2006	$18,134,000	-$3,324,000
2005	$15,881,000	-$2,890,000

Curr. Assets:	$11,655,000	**Curr. Liab.:**	$2,077,000		
Plant, Equip.:	$33,393,000	**Total Liab.:**	$3,085,000	**Indic. Yr. Divd.:**	NA
Total Assets:	$46,747,000	**Net Worth:**	$43,662,000	**Debt/ Equity:**	NA

Blue Holdings Inc

5804 E Slauson Ave., Commerce, CA, 90040; *PH:* 1-323-278-6600; *Fax:* 1-323-725-5504;
http:// www.blueholdings.com

General - Incorporation............................NV	**Stock**- Price on:12/24/2007 ....$1.22
Employees.....................................126	Stock Exchange...NDQ
Auditor .... Weinberg & Company, P.A.	Ticker Symbol..BLUE
Stk Agt............. Pacific Stock Transfer Company	Outstanding Shares 26,060,000
Counsel...NA	E.P.S..-$0.2
DUNS No..NA	Shareholders...NA

Business: The groups principle activities include designing, manufacturing and marketing fashion jeans, apparel and accessories. The products of the group include jeans, jackets, belts, purses and T-shirts. The group products sold under the trade names Antik Denim, Taverniti So Jeans, Yanuk and Faith Connexion. The group operates from the United States, Canada, Japan, Italy and Spain. The group's quarterly revenue for September 2007 was 9.46 millions of USD.

Primary SIC and add'l.: 2325 3144 5137 2339 3143 2387

CIK No: 0001139683

Subsidiaries: Antik Denim, LLC, LR Acquisition Corporation, Taverniti So Jeans, LLC

Officers: Glenn Palmer/CEO, Pres., Larry Jacobs/60/CFO, Sec., Scott Drake/59/Pres. - Sales, COO

Directors: Paul Guez/Chmn., Kevin R. Keating/Dir., Gary Freeman/Dir., Harry Haralambus/59/Dir., Leonard Hecht/72/Dir.

Owners: Philippe Naouri/2.30%, Insiders/78.60%, Alexandre Caugant/4.10%, Kevin R. Keating, Leonard Hecht, Harry Haralambus, Gary Freeman, Paul Guez/71.90%

Financial Data: *Fiscal Year End:*12/31 *Latest Annual Data:* 12/31/2006

Year	Sales	Net Income
2006	$48,996,000	-$4,761,000
2005	$36,365,000	$5,140,000
2004	NA	-$159,000

Curr. Assets:	$19,467,000	**Curr. Liab.:**	$17,835,000		
Plant, Equip.:	$1,611,000	**Total Liab.:**	$17,835,000	**Indic. Yr. Divd.:**	NA
Total Assets:	$21,078,000	**Net Worth:**	$3,243,000	**Debt/ Equity:**	NA

Blue Nile Inc

705 5th Ave. S, Ste. 900, Seattle, WA, 98104; *PH:* 1-206-336-6700; *Fax:* 1-206-336-6750;
http:// www.bluenile.com

General - Incorporation............................DE	**Stock**- Price on:12/24/2007 ....$61.6
Employees.....................................159	Stock Exchange...NDQ
Auditor ....Deloitte & Touche, LLP	Ticker Symbol...NA
Stk Agt.................Mellon Investor Services LLC	Outstanding Shares 15,720,000
Counsel...NA	E.P.S..$0.82
DUNS No..NA	Shareholders...NA

Business: The group's principle activities are leading online retailing of high quality diamonds and fine jewelry. It has built a well respected consumer brand by employing an informative sales process that empowers their customers while offering a broad selection of high quality jewelry at competitive prices. The group's Web site at www.bluenile.com showcases over 30,000 independently certified diamonds and more than 1,000 styles of fine jewelry, including rings, wedding bands, earrings, necklaces, pendants, bracelets and watches. The group's quarterly revenue for September 2007 was 67.36 millions of USD.

Primary SIC and add'l.: 5944

CIK No: 0001091171

Officers: Mark Vadon/Chmn., CEO, Pres./$2,114,839.00, Terri Maupin/VP - Finance, Controller, Susan Bell/Sr. VP/$433,261.00, Robin Easton/CFO, Dwight Gaston/Sr. VP/$457,430.00, Darrell Cavens/Sr. VP/$496,098.00, Diane Irvine/Dir., Pres./$1,114,660.00

Directors: Mark Vadon/Chmn., CEO, Pres., Joanna Strober/Dir., Mary Alice Taylor/Dir., Diane Irvine/Dir., Pres., Joseph Jimenez/Dir., Eric W. Carlborg/Dir., Anne Saunders/46/Dir.

Owners: M.A.M. Investments LTD/9.20%, Morgan Stanley/14.70%, Mary Alice Taylor, Baron Capital Group, Inc./11.00%, Maverick Capital, Ltd./5.90%, Joseph Jimenez, W. Eric Carlborg, Anne Saunders, Diane Irvine/1.80%, Darrell Cavens, Capital Research and Management Company/7.10%, Mark Vadon/10.30%, FMR Corp./13.00%, Dwight Gaston, Barclays Global Investors, NA/5.80% *(20 Owners included in Index)*

Financial Data: *Fiscal Year End:*01/01 *Latest Annual Data:* 12/31/2006

Year	Sales	Net Income
2006	$251,587,000	$13,064,000
2005	$169,242,000	$9,987,000

Curr. Assets:	$116,018,000	**Curr. Liab.:**	$74,137,000		
Plant, Equip.:	$3,391,000	**Total Liab.:**	$74,803,000	**Indic. Yr. Divd.:**	NA
Total Assets:	$122,106,000	**Net Worth:**	$47,303,000	**Debt/ Equity:**	NA

Blue Ridge Real Estate Co

PO Box 707, Blakeslee, PA, 18610; *PH:* 1-570-443-8433; *http://* www.mtncountryrealestate.com

General - Incorporation............................PA	**Stock**- Price on:12/24/2007 ....$34
Employees.....................................22	Stock Exchange...OTC
Auditor ....Parente Randolph LLC	Ticker Symbol...BLRGZ
Stk Agt.................................HSBC Bank U.S.	Outstanding Shares 2,440,000
Counsel...NA	E.P.S..$0.18
DUNS No 06-403-1180	Shareholders...NA

Business: The group's principle activity is to own and lease investment properties in northeastern Pennsylvania. The group owns 18,581 acres of land located in the pocono mountains. The lands are held entirely as investment property. Income is derived from these lands through leases, selective timbering by others, condemnation, sales and other dispositions. The group owns and leases other investments. These investments include jack frost mountain ski area, a 225-site campground; a retail store leased to wal-Mart and a shopping center. Jack frost mountain ski area consists of twenty-one slopes and trails, snowmobile course, snowtubing hill, various chairlifts and buildings. The group's quarterly revenue for July 2007 was 2.74 millions of USD.

Primary SIC and add'l.: 7011 7999 6519

CIK No: 0000012779

Subsidiaries: Boulder Creek Resort Company, BRRE Holdings, Inc., Cobble Creek, LLC, Coursey Commons Shopping Center, LLC, Coursey Creek, LLC, Jack Frost Mountain Company, Jack Frost National Golf Course, Inc., Moseywood Construction Company, Northeast Land Company, Oxbridge Square Shopping Center, LLC

Officers: Daniel Kaylor/Owner, Developer, Matt Butler/Realtor, Julie Rhodes/Realtor, Kristi Ray/Realtor, Missy Ware/Realtor, Lindakay Benka/Realtor, Joann Magee/Assoc. Broker

Directors: Holly Kaylor/Owner

Owners: Patrick M. Flynn, Milton Cooper, Michael J. Flynn, Insiders, Kimco Realty Corporation, Eldon D. Dietterick, Richard T. Frey

Financial Data: *Fiscal Year End:*10/31 *Latest Annual Data:* 04/30/2007

Year	Sales	Net Income
2007	NA	NA
2006	$13,330,000	$2,831,000
2005	$13,062,000	$1,932,000

Curr. Assets:	$1,010,000	**Curr. Liab.:**	$3,355,000	**P/E Ratio:**	20.61
Plant, Equip.:	$61,461,000	**Total Liab.:**	$33,970,000	**Indic. Yr. Divd.:**	NA
Total Assets:	$71,814,000	**Net Worth:**	$37,845,000	**Debt/ Equity:**	0.6017

Blue River Bancshares Inc

29 E Washington St., Shelbyville, IN, 46176; *PH:* 1-317-398-9721; *Fax:* 1-317-835-0306;
http:// www.shelbycountybank.com

General - Incorporation............................IN	**Stock**- Price on:12/24/2007 ....$5.52
Employees.....................................56	Stock Exchange...OTC
Auditor .... Crowe Chizek & Co. LLC	Ticker Symbol...BRBI
Stk Agt............Continental Stock Transfer & Trust Co	Outstanding Shares 3,510,000
Counsel.................................Krieg Devault LLP	E.P.S..$0.13
DUNS No 02-366-5545	Shareholders...NA

Business: The group's principal activity is to provide retail deposit and lending services. The group operates through its main office in shelbyville and three other branch offices in shelbyville, morristown and st. Paul, Indiana. The group's retail strategy is to provide basic banking products and services to its customers. Its commercial strategy centers on small to medium sized businesses.

Primary SIC and add'l.: 6035

CIK No: 0001055870

Subsidiaries: First Tier One Corporation, Paramount Bank, Shelby County Bank, The Shelby Group, Inc

Officers: Russell Breeden/Chmn., CEO, Pres./$225,442.00, Randy J. Collier/Exec. VP, Sec./$249,699.00, Patrice M. Lima/VP, Controller/$107,665.00, Richard E. Walke/VP, Auditor

Directors: Russell Breeden/Chmn., CEO, Pres., Steven R. Abel/Vice Chmn., Wendell L. Bernard/Dir., Peter G. Deprez/Dir., John Eckart/Dir., Wayne C. Ramsey/61/Dir., Robert J. Owens/Dir., Robert J. Salyers/Dir.

Owners: Wendell L. Bernard/0.42%, Insiders/29.23%, Peter G. DePrez/0.99%, Robert J. Salyers/0.43%, Steven R. Abel/1.40%, Patrice Lima/0.19%, John Eckart/0.34%, Randy J. Collier/0.91%, John R. Owens/0.35%

Financial Data: *Fiscal Year End:*12/31 *Latest Annual Data:* 12/31/2006

Year	Sales	Net Income
2006	$15,877,000	$599,000
2005	$13,387,000	$1,573,000
2004	$11,268,000	-$283,000

Curr. Assets:	$14,505,000	**Curr. Liab.:**	$201,477,000	**P/E Ratio:**	42.46
Plant, Equip.:	$2,411,000	**Total Liab.:**	$208,694,000	**Indic. Yr. Divd.:**	NA
Total Assets:	$226,514,000	**Net Worth:**	$17,820,000	**Debt/ Equity:**	0.4006

Blue Square Israel Ltd

2 Amal St. Afek, Industrial Pk., Rosh Ha Ayin, 48092; *PH:* 972-39282222; *http://* www.coop.co.il

General - Incorporation............................Israel	**Stock**- Price on:12/24/2007 ....$17
Employees.....................................3,195	Stock Exchange...NYSE
Auditor ....Ernst & Young LLP	Ticker Symbol...BSI
Stk Agt.........................Bank of New York	Outstanding Shares 41,280,000
Counsel...NA	E.P.S..$0.96
DUNS No 60-037-4987	Shareholders...NA

Business: The group's principal activity is the operation of chains of supermarkets, department stores and other retail chains in Israel. At 31-Dec.-2003, the group owned and operated 161 supermarkets under the brand names Mega, Super Center, Co-Op, Super Center City, Shefa Shuk and other. The group had a total of 290,800 sqm of selling space in 2003. The group's shares are traded on the Tel Aviv and the New York Stock Exchanges.

Primary SIC and add'l.: 5311 5499 5411

CIK No: 0001016837

Subsidiaries: Blue Square Real Estate Ltd., Hamachsan Hamerkazi Kfar Hashaashuim Ltd., Radio Non Stop Ltd., The Blue Square Chain (Hyper Hyper) Ltd., The Blue Square Chain Investments & Properties Ltd.

Officers: Zeev Stein/55/CEO - Blue Square Real Estate Ltd, Gershon Lewinsky/Internal Auditor, Uri Kaminsky/52/Mgr., Elli Levinson Sela/General Counsel, Corp. Sec., Rafi Messiah/Chain Mgr. - Mega, Eli Gayer/Chain Mgr. - Super Center, Daniel Magen/Supply Chain Mgr., Moshe Shatz/Head - Human Resources Division, Ilan Buchris/VP - Planning - Maintenance Division, Uri Falach/VP - Trade, Shay Lifshitz/Head - Staff, Trade Division, Gil Unger/Pres., Oren Lahat/Head - Property, Development Division, Odelia Levanon/Head - Information Technology Division, CIO, Dror Moran/VP - Finance, CFO

Directors: David Wiessman/53/Chmn., Yitzhak Bader/62/Dir., Erez Meltzer/51/Dir., Shlomo Even/51/Dir., Shaul Gliksberg/46/Dir., Diana Bogoslavsky/49/Dir., David Alphandary/73/Dir., Uzi Baram/71/Dir.

Owners: Clal Insurance Enterprises Holdings Ltd./5.60%, Alon Retail/70.60%

Financial Data: *Fiscal Year End:*12/31 *Latest Annual Data:* 12/31/2006

Year	Sales	Net Income
2006	$1,546,669,000	$39,580,000
2005	$1,267,808,000	$19,320,000
2004	$1,241,106,000	$10,463,000

Curr. Assets:	$468,230,000	**Curr. Liab.:**	$385,489,000		
Plant, Equip.:	$461,324,000	**Total Liab.:**	$736,729,000	**Indic. Yr. Divd.:**	$1.290
Total Assets:	$971,548,000	**Net Worth:**	$234,820,000	**Debt/ Equity:**	NA

Blue Valley Ban Corp

11935 Riley, Overland Park, KS, 66225; *PH:* 1-913-338-1000; *Fax:* 1-913-338-2801; *http://* www.bankbv.com

General - Incorporation	KS	**Stock**- Price on:12/24/2007	$38
Employees	224	Stock Exchange	OTC
Auditor	BKD LLP	Ticker Symbol	BVBC
Stk Agt	Computershare Trust Co	Outstanding Shares	2,430,000
Counsel	NA	E.P.S	$2.43
DUNS No.	NA	Shareholders	NA

Business: The group's principal activities are to provide banking and mortgage services to individuals and corporate customers. It operates through the wholly owned subsidiary, bank of blue valley. The deposit products include demand deposits, interest-bearing transaction accounts, money market accounts, saving deposits and time deposits. The lending activities include commercial and industrial lending, commercial real estate lending, construction lending, indirect lending, leasing, residential mortgage lending and origination services. The other services provided by the group include deposit and cash management services, investment brokerage services and trust services. The group operates banking centers located in johnson county, overland park, olathe and shawnee and supermarket banking facilities in leawood and shawnee.

Primary SIC and add'l.: 6021 6712

CIK No: 0000901842

Subsidiaries: Bank of Blue Valley, BBV Accommodations, LLC, Blue Valley Building Corp., Blue Valley Insurance Services, Inc., Blue Valley Investment Corporation, BVBC Capital Trust II, BVBC Capital Trust III

Officers: Robert D. Regnier/Chmn., CEO, Pres., Megan Stutler/Mortgage Closing Mgr., Bonnie A. Kay/Investment Services Officer, Jennifer Rowe/Personal Banking Officer, Mark A. Fortino/Sr. VP, CFO, Treasurer/$210,087.00, Gary Sherrer/Sr. VP - Mortgage Division, Patricia L. Day/VP, Corporate Controller, Ralph J. Schramp/Sr. VP - Commercial, Mortgage Loans, Bank, Blue Valley/$192,218.00, Trish Williams/VP - Trust, Renee Gier/AVP - Cashier, Rebecca Leon/AVP - Internal Audit, Bethany Rambo/AVP - Merchant Bankcard Sales, Ann Sooksengdao/AVP - Commercial Loan Operations, Joanne Wilson/AVP - Internal Audit, Matt Bennett/Credit Officer *(83 Officers included in Index)*

Directors: Robert D. Regnier/Chmn., CEO, Pres., Suzanne Dotson/Dir., Charles H. Hunter/Dir., Donald H. Alexander/Dir., Harvey S. Bodker/Dir., Dick Bond/Dir.

Owners: Robert D. Taylor/0.29%, Wayne A. Henry/5.04%, Robert D. Regnier/31.50%, Thomas A. McDonnell/6.56%, Sheila C. Stokes/0.38%, Ralph J. Schramp/0.13%, Insiders/50.54%, Michael J. Brown/0.02%, Donald H. Alexander/6.24%, Mark A. Fortino/0.38%

Financial Data: *Fiscal Year End:*12/31 *Latest Annual Data:* 12/31/2006

Year	Sales	Net Income
2006	$57,713,000	$6,923,000
2005	$51,690,000	$4,569,000
2004	$45,643,000	$1,930,000

Curr. Assets:	$31,430,000	**Curr. Liab.:**	$541,822,000	**P/E Ratio:**	13.52
Plant, Equip.:	$18,670,000	**Total Liab.:**	$638,399,000	**Indic. Yr. Divd.:**	$0.300
Total Assets:	$692,219,000	**Net Worth:**	$53,820,000	**Debt/ Equity:**	1.2043

Blue Wireless & Data Inc

3001 Knox St., Ste. 401, Dallas, TX, 75205; *PH:* 1-469-227-7605; *http://* www.bluewirelessdata.com

General - Incorporation	DE	**Stock**- Price on:12/24/2007	$0.017
Employees	NA	Stock Exchange	OTC
Auditor	Davis, Kinard & Co. P.C	Ticker Symbol	BWDT
Stk Agt	Executive Registrar & Transfer, Inc.	Outstanding Shares	NA
Counsel	NA	E.P.S	NA
DUNS No.	NA	Shareholders	NA

Business: The group's principal activity is to offer video entertainment on-demand and video communication products. Its technology is based on new and emerging custom chips and video compression algorithms, which are used in the wireless delivery technologies mode. The activities are based upon wireless Internet services to residential and commercial clients in rural and semi-rural areas where broadband access is offered at a limited access or termination bandwidth rate. The group operates in the United States. On 15-Mar-2004, the group acquired bold communication networks l.l.c.

Primary SIC and add'l.: 3661

CIK No: 0001086519

Financial Data: *Fiscal Year End:*09/30 *Latest Annual Data:* 9/30/2004

Year	Sales	Net Income
2004	$215,000	-$1,327,000
2003	$52,000	-$1,048,000
2002	$51,000	-$1,747,000

Curr. Assets:	$100,000	**Curr. Liab.:**	$1,041,000		
Plant, Equip.:	$494,000	**Total Liab.:**	$1,121,000	**Indic. Yr. Divd.:**	NA
Total Assets:	$2,031,000	**Net Worth:**	$911,000	**Debt/ Equity:**	NA

Bluebook International Holding Co

21098 Bake Pkwy., Ste. 100, Lake Forest, CA, 92630; *PH:* 1-949-470-9534; *Fax:* 1-949-470-9563; *http://* www.bluebook.net; *Email:* customercare@bluebook.net

General - Incorporation	DE	**Stock**- Price on:12/24/2007	$0.11
Employees	9	Stock Exchange	OTC
Auditor	Weinberg & Co. P.a	Ticker Symbol	BBKH
Stk Agt	Global Securities Transfer, Inc	Outstanding Shares	9,340,000
Counsel	NA	E.P.S	NA
DUNS No.	NA	Shareholders	NA

Business: The group's principal activity is to develop, market, and sell software solutions and information services to the insurance and construction industries. The software solutions and services automate, integrate, manage and quicken claims processing and communication among participants in claims handling process. The bluebook, in both desk and pocket sizes, contains the information of the average unit costs attendant to the cleaning, reconstruction and repair industries. The distribution also includes the software version named the bluebook estimating systems technology. It allows subscribers to retrieve the data and calculate the cost to clean, reconstruct or repair. The customers include property and casualty insurance companies and construction, reconstruction, repair and service companies. Blue book for adjusters & contractors, deejay advertising, bluebook of cleaning, reconstruction and repair costs, b.e.s.t. Are the trademarks owned by the group.

Primary SIC and add'l.: 7372 7375 2741 6719 7379

CIK No: 0001126577

Subsidiaries: Bluebook International, Inc.

Officers: Mark A. Josipovich/CEO, Pres., Marilyn Bartholomew/Administrative Officer, Michela Di Carlo/Sales Mgr., Daniel T. Josipovich/COO

Directors: Dorothy Josipovich/Co - Founder, Daniel E. Josipovich/Co - Founder

Financial Data: *Fiscal Year End:*12/31 *Latest Annual Data:* 12/31/2005

Year	Sales	Net Income
2005	$620,000	-$2,711,000
2004	$570,000	-$1,985,000
2003	$706,000	-$1,560,000

Curr. Assets:	$118,000	**Curr. Liab.:**	$2,772,000		
Plant, Equip.:	$67,000	**Total Liab.:**	$2,774,000	**Indic. Yr. Divd.:**	NA
Total Assets:	$889,000	**Net Worth:**	-$1,885,000	**Debt/ Equity:**	NA

Bluefly Inc

42 W 39th St., 9th Fl., New York, NY, 10018; *PH:* 1-212-944-8000; *Fax:* 1-212-354-3400; *http://* www.bluefly.com; *Email:* flyrep@bluefly.com

General - Incorporation	DE	**Stock**- Price on:12/24/2007	$1.02
Employees	95	Stock Exchange	NDQ
Auditor	PricewaterhouseCoopers LLP	Ticker Symbol	BFLY
Stk Agt	American Stock Transfer & Trust Co.	Outstanding Shares	130,930,000
Counsel	NA	E.P.S	-$0.11
DUNS No.	78-264-7879	Shareholders	NA

Business: The group's principal activity is the retail distribution of designer apparel and home accessories through the Internet at discount prices. The group markets over 350 brands of designer apparel, accessories and home products at discounts upto 75% off retail value. These products are offered through the group's Web site www.bluefly.com. The group buys merchandise directly from designers as well as from retailers and other third party distributors. The products are advertised through multiple channels that include traditional and online advertising, direct marketing and print advertising. The group operates in the United States. During 2003, the group offered over 80,000 different types of items for sale in categories such as men's, women's and accessories as well as house and home accessories.

Primary SIC and add'l.: 5699

CIK No: 0001030896

Subsidiaries: Time Warner, Inc

Officers: Melissa Payner-Gregor/CEO/$6,167,333.00, Patrick Barry/CFO - Investor/$4,905,363.00, Martin Keane/43/Sr. VP - E, Commerce/$529,000.00, Bradford Matson/50/Chief Marketing Officer/$740,000.00

Directors: David Wassong/37/Dir., Interim Chmn., Christopher G. McCann/47/Dir., Barry Erdos/64/Dir., Ann Jackson/56/Dir., Martin Miller/78/Dir., Neal Moszkowski/42/Dir., Michael Gross/32/Dir., Alex Rafal/37/Dir.

Owners: SFM Domestic Investments LLC, Martin Keane, Ann Jackson, Quantum Industrial Partners LDC, Insiders, Michael Gross, S.A.C. Capital Associates, LLC, Michael Zimmerman, Maverick Fund, L.D.C., Melissa Payner, Martin Miller, David Wassong, Patrick C. Barry, Prentice Capital Offshore, Ltd., Christopher G. McCann *(23 Owners included in Index)*

Financial Data: *Fiscal Year End:*12/31 *Latest Annual Data:* 12/31/2006

Year	Sales	Net Income
2006	$77,062,000	-$12,193,000
2005	$58,811,000	-$3,820,000
2004	$43,799,000	-$3,791,000

Curr. Assets:	$48,606,000	**Curr. Liab.:**	$14,603,000		
Plant, Equip.:	$3,573,000	**Total Liab.:**	$14,603,000	**Indic. Yr. Divd.:**	NA
Total Assets:	$52,430,000	**Net Worth:**	$37,827,000	**Debt/ Equity:**	NA

Bluegreen Corp

4960 Conference Way N, Ste. 100, Boca Raton, FL, 33431; *PH:* 1-561-912-8000; *Fax:* 1-561-912-8100; *http://* www.bluegreenonline.com

General - Incorporation	MA	**Stock**- Price on:12/24/2007	$11.37
Employees	5,342	Stock Exchange	NYSE
Auditor	Ernst & Young LLP	Ticker Symbol	BXG
Stk Agt	Mellon Investor Services LLC	Outstanding Shares	30,980,000
Counsel	Choate, Hall & Stewart LLP	E.P.S	$1.061
DUNS No.	06-129-9855	Shareholders	NA

Business: The group's principal activity is to market vacation and residential lifestyle choices. The group operates in two segments: bluegreen resorts and bluegreen communities. Bluegreen resorts develops, markets and markets timeshare interests in the group's resorts, primarily through the club, and provides resort management services to resort property owners associations. Bluegreen communities acquires large tracts of real estate, which are subdivided, improved and marketed, typically on a retail basis as home sites. On 21-Jan-2004, the group acquired marathon resort and marina and on 10-Jun-2004, the group acquired the vacation club & resort.

Primary SIC and add'l.: 6141 6531 6552

CIK No: 0000778946

Subsidiaries: Big Cedar Jv Interiors, LLC, Bluegreen Asset Management Corporation, Bluegreen Bahamas Ltd., Bluegreen Carolina Lands, LLC, Bluegreen Communities Of Georgia Realty, Inc., Bluegreen Communities Of Georgia, LLC, Bluegreen Communities Of Texas, Lp, Bluegreen Corporation, Bluegreen Corporation Of Tennessee, Bluegreen Corporation Of The Rockies, Bluegreen Golf Clubs, Inc., Bluegreen Guaranty Corporation, Bluegreen Holding Corporation (texas), Bluegreen Interiors, LLC, Bluegreen Properties N.v. 55 Subsidiaries included in the Index

Officers: John M. Maloney/CEO, Pres./$1,252,055.00, Daniel C. Koscher/Pres., Sr. VP/$1,069,708.00, Douglas O. Kinsey/Sr. VP - Acquisitions, Development/$675,159.00, Sheila B. Donahoe/CIO, Sr. VP, James R. Martin/Sr. VP, General Counsel, Clerk/$486,264.00, Anthony M. Puleo/CFO, Sr. VP, Treasurer/$599,543.00, Raymond S. Lopez/VP, Chief Accounting Officer, Allan J. Herz/Sr. VP - Mortgage Operations, Susan J. Saturday/Sr. VP, Chief Human Resources Officer, Lani M. Liber/Sr. VP - Owner Relations, Lisa Thornhill/Contact - Media Relations, David L. Pontius/Sr. VP, Pres. - Bluegreen Resorts, Devin Sullivan/Investor Relations Officer

Directors: Alan B. Levan/Chmn., John E. Abdo/Vice Chmn., Norman H. Becker/Dir., Robert F. Dwors/Dir., Larry J. Rutherford/Dir., John Laguardia/Dir., Scott W. Holloway/Dir., Arnold Sevell/Dir., Mark A. Nerenhausen/Dir., Lawrence A. Cirillo/Dir., Joseph C. Abeles/Dir. Emeritus

Owners: Arnold Sevell, Central Florida Investments, Lawrence A. Cirillo, Daniel C. Koscher, Dimensional Fund Advisors Inc., George F. Donovan, John Laguardia, Larry J. Rutherford, Mark A. Nerenhausen, John E. Abdo, John M. Maloney, Anthony M. Puleo, Scott W. Holloway, Levitt Corporation, Insiders *(18 Owners included in Index)*

Financial Data: *Fiscal Year End:*12/31 *Latest Annual Data:* 12/31/2006

Year	Sales	Net Income
2006	NA	NA
2005	NA	NA
2004	NA	NA

Curr. Assets:	$225,627,000	**Curr. Liab.:**	$67,923,000	**P/E Ratio:** 10.72
Plant, Equip.:	$441,778,000	**Total Liab.:**	$486,487,000	**Indic. Yr. Divd.:** NA
Total Assets:	$854,212,000	**Net Worth:**	$353,023,000	**Debt/ Equity:** 0.8611

Bluelinx Holdings Inc

4300 Wildwood Pkwy., Atlanta, GA, 30339; *PH:* 1-770-953-7000; *Fax:* 1-770-221-8902; *http://* www.bluelinxco.com; *Email:* investor.relations@bluelinxco.com

General - Incorporation	DE	**Stock**- Price on:12/24/2007	$11.01
Employees	3,300	Stock Exchange	NDQ
Auditor	Ernst & Young LLP	Ticker Symbol	BXC
Stk Agt	Registrar & Transfer Co	Outstanding Shares	31,210,000
Counsel	NA	E.P.S.	$0.05
DUNS No.	NA	Shareholders	NA

Business: The groups principal activity is to distribute building products. The groups products include plywood, rebar and remesh, lumber, roofing, insulation and vinyl products. The group operates from the United States. The groups net sales in the year 2006 were $479,807 (thousands).

Primary SIC and add'l.: 5039 5031 5033 5211

CIK No: 0001301787

Subsidiaries: ABP AL (Midfield)LLC, ABP AR (Little Rock) LLC, ABP CA (City of Industry) LLC, ABP CA (National City) LLC, ABP CA (Newark)LLC, ABP CA (North Highlands) LLC, ABP CA (Riverside)LLC, ABP CO I (Denver)LLC, ABP CO II (Denver)LLC, ABP CT (Newton)LLC, ABP FL (Lake City) LLC, ABP FL (Miami)LLC, ABP FL (Pensacola)LLC, ABP FL (Tampa)LLC, ABP FL (Yulee)LLC 73 Subsidiaries included in the Index

Officers: Stephen E. MacAdam/Dir., CEO, George R. Judd/COO, Pres., Lynn A. Wentworth/CFO, Sr. VP, Treasurer, David J. Dalton/Sr. VP - West, Duane G. Goodwin/Sr. VP - Supply Chain, Steven G. Skinner/Sr. VP - Industrials, Barbara V. Tinsley/Sr. VP, General Counsel, Sec., Dean A. Adelman/VP - Human Resources, Daniel J. Richards/Mgr. - Supplier Diversity, Jim Storey/Contact - Media, Trade Publications

Directors: Stephen E. MacAdam/Dir., CEO, Jeffrey J. Fenton/Chmn., Richard S. Grant/Dir., Charles H. McElrea/Dir., Richard B. Marchese/Dir., Steven F. Mayer/Dir., Alan H. Schumacher/Dir., Mark A. Suwyn/Dir., Lenard B. Tessler/Dir., Robert G. Warden/Dir., Howard S. Cohen/Dir.

Owners: Alan H. Schumacher, Steven G. Skinner, David J. Dalton, Richard S. Grant, Barclays Global Investors, NA/6.27%, Insiders/5.08%, Jeffrey J. Fenton, Richard B. Marchese, Barbara V. Tinsley, Duane G. Goodwin, Stephen E. Macadam, Stephen Feinberg/57.99%, George R. Judd/1.86%, Lynn A. Wentworth, Dean A. Adelman *(16 Owners included in Index)*

Financial Data: *Fiscal Year End:*12/30 *Latest Annual Data:* 12/30/2006

Year	Sales	Net Income
2006	NA	NA
2005	NA	NA

Curr. Assets:	$948,068,000	**Curr. Liab.:**	$418,085,000	**P/E Ratio:** 57.95
Plant, Equip.:	$184,049,000	**Total Liab.:**	$973,788,000	**Indic. Yr. Divd.:** $0.500
Total Assets:	$1,157,640,000	**Net Worth:**	$183,852,000	**Debt/ Equity:** NA

BluePhoenix Solutions Ltd

8000 Regency Pky., Ste. 300, Cary, NC, 27518; *PH:* 1-919-380-5100; *Fax:* 1-919-380-5111; *http://* www.bphx.com; *Email:* usa@bphx.com

General - Incorporation	Israel	**Stock**- Price on:12/24/2007	$10.88
Employees	615	Stock Exchange	NDQ
Auditor	Ziv Haft	Ticker Symbol	BPHX
Stk Agt	Blue Phoenix Solutions USA Inc	Outstanding Shares	15,370,000
Counsel	NA	E.P.S.	$0.03
DUNS No.	NA	Shareholders	NA

Business: The group's principle activities include developing and marketing software tools, and providing consulting services, including conversion of various information systems from one operating system to another, various programming language upgrades and data field expansion conversions, for the implementation of complex conversion projects, primarily for mainframe computer systems. The group operates from United States.

Primary SIC and add'l.: 7371 7372 7379

CIK No: 0001029581

Subsidiaries: Alexandria Migration Technologies Ltd., ASE Advanced Systems Eourope B.V, BluePhoenix Solutions B.V, BluePhoenix Solutions GmbH, BluePhoenix Solutions Italia SRL, BluePhoenix Solutions Ltd., BluePhoenix Solutions Nordic, AS, BluePhoenix Solutions Pty Ltd., BluePhoenix Solutions S.R.L, BluePhoenix Solutions U.K Limited, BluePhoenix Solutions U.S.A Inc, Burford International Applications Ltd., Burford management services PTE, Ce-Post Ltd., Crystal America Inc. 34 Subsidiaries included in the Index

Officers: Arik Kilman/Dir., CEO, Iris Yahal/CFO, Tsipora Cohen/VP - Worldwide Marketing, Eliezer Harkavi/VP - Research & Development and Delivery, Theis Eichel/VP, GM Nordic Operations, Mario Zerini/VP - Sales, Southern, Central, Eastern Europe, Asia Regional Dept, Varda Sagiv/CFO, David Leichner/Chief Marketing Officer, Thomas O'Connell/VP - Research, Development, Tzvia Shmuelevich/VP - Worldwide Delivery, Pesach Galon/VP - Presales, Greg Schottland/VP - Sales, North America

Directors: Arik Kilman/Dir., CEO, Michael Chill/Dir., Aaron Crystal/Dir., Amira Berkovitz-Amir/Dir., Shai Beilis/Dir., Gur Shomron/55/Dir.

Owners: Formula Systems (1985) Ltd./52.30%, Arie Kilman/8.00%, Aaron Crystal/3.80%

Financial Data: *Fiscal Year End:*12/31 *Latest Annual Data:* 12/31/2006

Year	Sales	Net Income
2006	$68,004,000	$4,672,000
2005	$58,947,000	$1,789,000
2004	$57,186,000	$2,846,000

Curr. Assets:	$42,265,000	**Curr. Liab.:**	$24,404,000	**P/E Ratio:** 155.43
Plant, Equip.:	$2,147,000	**Total Liab.:**	$67,517,000	**Indic. Yr. Divd.:** NA
Total Assets:	$127,466,000	**Net Worth:**	$59,949,000	**Debt/ Equity:** NA

Bluepoint Linux Software Corp

4 Floor, Xinyang Bldg, Bagua 4th Rd, Shenzhen , Guangdong, 518029; *PH:* 86-7552450750; *http://* www.bluepoint.com.cn

General - Incorporation	IN	**Stock**- Price on:12/24/2007	NA
Employees	NA	Stock Exchange	OTC
Auditor	Moores Rowland Mazars	Ticker Symbol	BLPT
Stk Agt	Signature Stock Transfer, Inc.	Outstanding Shares	NA
Counsel	NA	E.P.S.	NA
DUNS No.	NA	Shareholders	NA

Business: The group's principal activity is to provide embedded linux solutions and related service and support. The group has developed an operating system called bluepoint. It licenses its software bluepoint linux to original equipment manufacturers of personal computers and sells bluepoint linux software packages to software retailers in the People's Republic of China.

Primary SIC and add'l.: 7372

CIK No: 0001081376

Subsidiaries: Shenzhen Sinx Software Co. Ltd

Officers: Xin Liu/40/Dir., CEO, Pres., Frank K. Shing/34/Dir., CFO

Directors: Xin Liu/40/Dir., CEO, Pres., Frank K. Shing/34/Dir., CFO, Jun Liu/38/Dir.

Owners: Insiders, Xin Liu, Jun Liu

Financial Data: *Fiscal Year End:*12/31 *Latest Annual Data:* 12/31/2006

Year	Sales	Net Income
2006	NA	-$19,000
2005	NA	-$219,000
2004	$209,000	-$344,000

Curr. Assets:	$0	**Curr. Liab.:**	$547,000	
Plant, Equip.:	NA	**Total Liab.:**	$547,000	**Indic. Yr. Divd.:** NA
Total Assets:	$0	**Net Worth:**	-$547,000	**Debt/ Equity:** NA

Bluestar Health Inc

19901 Swest Fwy., Ste. 205, Sugar Land, TX, 77479; *PH:* 1-281-207-5485; *Fax:* 1-281-207-5486; *http://* www.bluestarhealth.biz

General - Incorporation	CO	**Stock**- Price on:12/24/2007	$0.1
Employees	NA	Stock Exchange	OTC
Auditor	LBB & Assoc. Ltd., LLP	Ticker Symbol	BLSH
Stk Agt	ComputerShare Investor Services LLC	Outstanding Shares	NA
Counsel	NA	E.P.S.	-$0.06
DUNS No.	NA	Shareholders	NA

Business: The group's principal activity is to acquire, develop, and operate licensed outpatient physical therapy clinics nationwide. The clinics provide post-operative care and treatment for a variety of orthopedic related disorders and sports-related injuries on an outpatient basis. The group is a development stage company with limited operating history. On 12-Jun-2003, the group merged with bluestar physical therapy. On 31-Oct-2003, it acquired healthquest inc.

Primary SIC and add'l.: 8093

CIK No: 0000225926

Subsidiaries: Bluestar Physical Therapy, Inc., PT Centers, Inc

Officers: Linda Solz/Contact - Investor Relations, Peter Wokoun/Contact - Investor Relations, Alfred Oglesby/40/Dir., Pres., Chief Accounting Officer, Sec., Thomas Redmon/60/Pres., Sec., Dir., Richard M. Greenwood/CFO, Pres.

Directors: Alfred Oglesby/40/Dir., Pres., Chief Accounting Officer, Sec., Thomas Redmon/60/Pres., Sec., Dir.

Owners: Alfred L. Oglesby/55.60%, Richard M. Greenwood/15.30%, Insiders/15.30%

Financial Data: *Fiscal Year End:*09/30 *Latest Annual Data:* 9/30/2005

Year	Sales	Net Income
2005	$362,000	-$1,031,000
2004	$302,000	-$407,000
2003	NA	-$584,000

Curr. Assets:	$0	**Curr. Liab.:**	$398,000	
Plant, Equip.:	NA	**Total Liab.:**	$458,000	**Indic. Yr. Divd.:** NA
Total Assets:	$0	**Net Worth:**	-$458,000	**Debt/ Equity:** NA

Blyth Inc

1 E WeAve.r St., Greenwich, CT, 06831; *PH:* 1-203-661-1926; *Fax:* 1-203-661-1969; *http://* www.blyth.com

General - Incorporation	DE	**Stock**- Price on:12/24/2007	$27.26
Employees	4,000	Stock Exchange	NYSE
Auditor	Deloitte & Touche LLP	Ticker Symbol	BTH
Stk Agt	Computer Share Investor Services	Outstanding Shares	39,440,000
Counsel	NA	E.P.S.	-$1.54
DUNS No.	09-680-0578	Shareholders	NA

Business: The group's principal activities are to design, market and distribute an extensive array of candles, home fragrance products, decorative accessories, seasonal decorations and household convenience items, as well as tabletop lighting and chafing fuel for the away from home or food service trade. The group operates in five segments the direct selling segment, the wholesale home fragrance segment, the wholesale creative expressions segment, the catalog and Internet segment, and the all other segment. The products of the group are sold under the brand names like partylite(R), ambria(R), colonialtm1, colonial candle of cape cod(R) and colonial at home(r). The group operates in the United States, Canada and Europe, with additional activity in Mexico, Australia and the Far East. On 01-Apr-2003, the group acquired miles kimball company, on 20-Jun-2003, acquired kaemingk b.v and on 22-Dec-2003, acquired walter drake.

Primary SIC and add'l.: 3999 2869

CIK No: 0000921503

Subsidiaries: Adam Gies GmbH, Asp-Holmblad A/S, Beejay, Ltd., Blyth Asia Limited, Blyth Catalog and Internet Holdings,Inc., Blyth Direct Selling Holdings,Inc., Blyth Holding B.V., Blyth Home Expressions,Inc., Blyth HomeScents International de Mexico S.A. de C.V., Blyth HomeScents International GmbH, Blyth HomeScents International Servicios S.A. de C.V., Blyth HomeScents International UK Limited, Blyth Wholesale Europe Holdings,Inc., Blyth Wholesale North America Holdings,Inc., Blyth Wholesale Worldwide,Inc. 66 Subsidiaries included in the Index

Officers: Robert B. Goergen/Chmn., CEO, Tyler P. Schuessler/VP - Organizational Development, Investor Relations, Jane F. Casey/VP, Treasurer, Robert H. Barghaus/CFO, VP/$702,002.00, Michael S. Novins/VP, General Counsel, Sec., Edward J. Scannell/VP - Internal Audit, Joseph T. Cirillo/VP - Reporting, Planning, Anne M. Butler/VP, Pres. - Partylite Worldwide

Directors: Howard E. Rose/Dir., Roger A. Anderson/Dir., Neal I. Goldman/Dir., Pamela M. Goergen/Dir., Carol J. Hochman/Dir., John W. Burkhart/Dir., Wilma H. Jordan/Dir., Jim McTaggart/Dir., Anne M. Busquet/Dir.

Owners: Pamela M. Goergen/28.80%, Carol J. Hochman, James M. McTaggart, Robert B. Goergen/28.80%, Robert B. Goergen/4.70%, Neal I. Goldman, Insiders/35.90%, Robert H. Barghaus, Roger A. Anderson, Wilma H. Jordan, Howard E. Rose, Frank P. Mineo, John W. Burkhart/1.40%

Financial Data: ***Fiscal Year End:***01/31 ***Latest Annual Data:*** 1/31/2007

Year	Sales	Net Income
2007	$1,220,611,000	-$103,173,000
2006	$1,573,076,000	$24,857,000
2005	$1,586,297,000	$96,514,000

Curr. Assets:	NA	***Curr. Liab.:***	NA		
Plant, Equip.:	NA	***Total Liab.:***	NA	***Indic. Yr. Divd.:***	$0.540
Total Assets:	NA	***Net Worth:***	NA	***Debt/ Equity:***	0.5905

BMB Munai Inc

324 S 400 W Ste. 250, Salt Lake City, UT, 84101; ***PH:*** 1-800-355-2227; ***http://*** www.bmbmunai.com; ***Email:*** usoffice@bmbmunai.com

General - Incorporation	NV	***Stock*** - Price on:12/24/2007	$5.9
Employees	199	Stock Exchange	AMEX
Auditor	BDO Kazakhstanaudit LLP	Ticker Symbol	KAZ
Stk Agt	OTC Stock Transfer, Inc.	Outstanding Shares	44,690,000
Counsel	NA	E.P.S.	$0.18
DUNS No.	NA	Shareholders	NA

Business: The group's principal activity is exploration development, exploitation and production of crude oil and natural gas. The group operates in one segment , natural gas and oil exploration and development. The group is in its development stage. The group operates through emir oil, its wholly owned subsidiary. The group carries its activities within aksaz, dolinnoe and in amir oil fields. On 01-Dec-2003, the group acquired bmb holding inc.

Primary SIC and add'l.: 6211 6282

CIK No: 0000924805

Subsidiaries: Emir Oil

Officers: Gamal Kulumbetov/CEO, COO/$385,469.00, Askar Tashtitov/Pres./$437,843.00, Sanat Kasymov/CFO/$494,316.00

Directors: Boris Cherdabayev/Chmn., Leonard M. Stillman/Dir., Troy F. Nilson/Dir., Georges Benarroch/Dir., Valery Tolkachev/Dir., Steeve Smoot/Dir.

Owners: Gamal Kulumbetov, Boris Cherdabayev/15.00%, Valery Tolkachev, Troy Nilson, Sanat Kasymov, Stephen Smoot, Insiders/16.00%, Askar Tashtitov

Financial Data: ***Fiscal Year End:***03/31 ***Latest Annual Data:*** 3/31/2007

Year	Sales	Net Income
2007	$15,786,000	$1,039,000
2006	$5,957,000	-$5,344,000
2005	$974,000	-$3,286,000

Curr. Assets:	$29,972,000	***Curr. Liab.:***	$9,120,000	***P/E Ratio:***	32.78
Plant, Equip.:	$110,170,000	***Total Liab.:***	$19,234,000	***Indic. Yr. Divd.:***	NA
Total Assets:	$144,796,000	***Net Worth:***	$125,562,000	***Debt/ Equity:***	NA

BMC Software Inc

2101 City W Blvd., Houston, TX, 77042; ***PH:*** 1-713-918-8800; ***Fax:*** 1-713-918-8000; ***http://*** www.bmc.com

General - Incorporation	DE	***Stock*** - Price on:12/24/2007	$31.26
Employees	6,000	Stock Exchange	NYSE
Auditor	Ernst & Young LLP	Ticker Symbol	BMC
Stk Agt	Computershare Trust CO.	Outstanding Shares	200,550,000
Counsel	NA	E.P.S.	$1.03
DUNS No.	01-158-9751	Shareholders	NA

Business: The group's principal activities are to develop and deliver comprehensive systems software solutions to enterprises. The group's software solutions enhance the availability, performance and recoverability of the customers' business-critical applications. The group's solutions fall into the following broad categories: enterprise data management software, enterprise systems management software, professional services & other software solutions. The group's integrated software solutions address the technology layers within the it enterprise; operating systems, databases, middleware, storage and network devices, Web application servers, transaction servers and the applications themselves. The group acquired it masters international s.a and assets of remedy during fiscal 2003 and acquired dgi on 23-Jun-2003. On 15-Jul-2004, the group acquired marimba inc.

Primary SIC and add'l.: 7372 7377 7379

CIK No: 0000835729

Subsidiaries: ASA Knowledge PTY Ltd, BMC Finance (dba, BMC Software, Inc.), BMC Financial Services Co. (dba, Software Credit LP), BMC Receivable Corporation II B.V., BMC Receivables Corporation No.2, BMC Receivables Corporation No.3, BMC Receivables Corporation No.4, BMC Receivables Corporation No.5, BMC Software (China) Limited, BMC Software (Eagle Eye) Ltd., BMC Software (Hong Kong) Limited, BMC Software (New Zealand), BMC Software (Philippines) Inc., BMC Software (Thailand) Limited, BMC Software A/S (Denmark) 79 Subsidiaries included in the Index

Officers: Robert E. Beauchamp/Dir., CEO, Pres./$7,762,977.00, Jae W. Chung/47/Sr. VP - Business Operations, Cory T. Bleuer/38/VP, Controller, Chief Accounting Officer

Directors: Robert E. Beauchamp/Dir., CEO, Pres., Garland Cupp/Chmn., Meldon K. Gafner/Dir., Thomas P. Jenkins/Dir., Tom C. Tinsley/Dir., L. W. Gray/Dir., Jon E. Barfield/Dir., Kathleen O'Neil/Dir., George F. Raymond/Dir., Gary Bloom/Dir., Thomas J. Smach/48/Dir.

Owners: Garland B. Cupp, State Street Bank/6.60%, Stephen Solcher, George F. Raymond, Cosmo Santullo, Robert E. Beauchamp/1.30%, Dodge& Cox/9.60%, Dan Barnea, Denise M. Clolery, Meldon K. Gafner, John W. Barter, Lew W. Gray, Thomas J. Smach, Tom C. Tinsley, Jon E. Barfield *(19 Owners included in Index)*

Financial Data: ***Fiscal Year End:***03/31 ***Latest Annual Data:*** 3/31/2007

Year	Sales	Net Income
2007	$1,580,400,000	$215,900,000
2006	$1,498,400,000	$102,000,000
2005	$1,463,000,000	$75,300,000

Curr. Assets:	$1,789,500,000	***Curr. Liab.:***	$1,232,900,000	***P/E Ratio:***	26.95
Plant, Equip.:	$88,300,000	***Total Liab.:***	$2,210,900,000	***Indic. Yr. Divd.:***	NA
Total Assets:	$3,260,000,000	***Net Worth:***	$1,049,100,000	***Debt/ Equity:***	NA

BMX Entertainment Corp

PO Box 10857, Stamford, CT, 06904; ***PH:*** 1-203-524-2697; ***http://*** www.bmxentertainment.com

General - Incorporation	DE	***Stock*** - Price on:12/24/2007	NA
Employees	NA	Stock Exchange	NA
Auditor	NA	Ticker Symbol	NA
Stk Agt	Registrar & Transfer Co	Outstanding Shares	NA
Counsel	NA	E.P.S.	NA
DUNS No.	NA	Shareholders	NA

Business: The group's principal activity is to identify and develop musical artists and produce their music and music videos to sell in traditional retail outlets and online outlets. The company is a prerecorded music supplier of cassette, CD, DVD. Its vision is to captivate the market share worldwide in getting its product to its customers. The company intends to manufacture in house when its new facilities are operational. The new facilities have capacity for producing digital business cards, compact discs, DVDs, videos, cassettes, and a full service graphic arts department for color printing services. The group also intends to launch its subsidiary company to service corporations with graphic arts design, color printing, and other fulfillment. The group's services include printing color brochures, magazines in high quality standards.

Primary SIC and add'l.: 7812

CIK No: 0001218249

BNC Bancorp

831 Julian Ave., Thomasville, NC, 27360; ***PH:*** 1-336-476-9200; ***Fax:*** 1-336-476-5818; ***http://*** www.bankofnc.com

General - Incorporation	NC	***Stock*** - Price on:12/24/2007	$17.65
Employees	181	Stock Exchange	NDQ
Auditor	Cherry, Bekaert & Holl&, L.l.p.	Ticker Symbol	BNCN
Stk Agt	Registrar & Transfer Co	Outstanding Shares	6,840,000
Counsel	NA	E.P.S.	$1.034
DUNS No.	NA	Shareholders	NA

Business: The group's principle activity is to provide commercial banking products and services to individuals and small to medium size business. The company accepts deposits from the general public and provides consumer and commercial loans. The products offered by the company include statement savings accounts, money market demand accounts, non interest-bearing accounts and fixed interest rate certificates. As of 31-Dec-2003, the company had 58 branch offices located at thomasville and lexington in davidson county, archdale in randolph county, kernersville in forsyth county and oak ridge in guilford county. The group operates from United States.

Primary SIC and add'l.: 6022 6712

CIK No: 0001210227

Subsidiaries: Bank of North Carolina, BNC Bancorp Capital Trust I, BNC Capital Trust II, BNC Capital Trust III.

Officers: Swope W. Montgomery/Dir., CEO, Pres., Richard D. Callicutt/48/Dir., COO, Exec. VP, Ralph N. Strayhorn/53/Dir., Chief Administrative Officer, Exec. VP, Richard F. Wood/63/Dir., Sec., David B. Spencer/45/CFO, Exec. VP

Directors: Swope W. Montgomery/Dir., CEO, Pres., Joseph M. Coltrane/61/Dir., Lenin J. Peters/56/Dir., Robert A. Team/51/Dir., Richard D. Callicutt/48/Dir., COO, Exec. VP, Ralph N. Strayhorn/53/Dir., Chief Administrative Officer, Exec. VP, Thomas R. Sloan/63/Dir., Charles T. Hagan/59/Dir., Randall R. Kaplan/51/Dir., Larry L. Callahan/60/Dir., Groome W. Fulton/69/Dir., Thomas R. Smith/59/Dir., Colon E. Starrett/69/Dir., Vann D. Williford/60/Dir., Richard F. Wood/63/Dir., Sec.

Owners: Richard F. Wood/0.49%, Swope W. Montgomery/2.36%, Lenin J. Peters/7.88%, Groome Fulton/3.96%, Vann D. Williford/1.04%, Thomas R. Smith/1.17%, Ralph N. Strayhorn/1.15%, Thomas R. Sloan/2.08%, Colon E. Starrett/0.37%, Charles T. Hagan, Larry L. Callahan, Joseph M. Coltrane, Richard D. Callicutt/1.30%, Robert A. Team, Randall R. Kaplan/1.12% *(17 Owners included in Index)*

Financial Data: ***Fiscal Year End:***12/31 ***Latest Annual Data:*** 03/31/2007

Year	Sales	Net Income
2007	$18,046,000	$1,917,000
2006	$57,032,000	$6,170,000
2005	$36,355,000	$4,505,000

Curr. Assets:	$29,510,000	***Curr. Liab.:***	$797,495,000	***P/E Ratio:***	16.34
Plant, Equip.:	$19,622,000	***Total Liab.:***	$879,208,000	***Indic. Yr. Divd.:***	$0.180
Total Assets:	$951,731,000	***Net Worth:***	$72,523,000	***Debt/ Equity:***	1.1737

BNCCORP Inc

322 E Main Ave., Bismarck, ND, 58501; ***PH:*** 1-701-250-3040; ***Fax:*** 1-701-222-3653; ***http://*** www.bnccorp.com

General - Incorporation	DE	***Stock*** - Price on:12/24/2007	$18.41
Employees	308	Stock Exchange	NDQ
Auditor	KPMG LLP	Ticker Symbol	BNCC
Stk Agt	American Stock Transfer & Trust Co.	Outstanding Shares	3,600,000
Counsel	NA	E.P.S.	$0.56
DUNS No.	18-335-2301	Shareholders	NA

Business: The group's principal activity is to provide banking and financial services to small and mid-sized businesses, private banking clients and consumers. The activities are carried out through 21 facilities located in Arizona, Minnesota & North Dakota. The services include commercial and industrial loans, real estate mortgage loans, real estate construction loans, agricultural loans, lease financing and

consumer loans. The group offers customary range of depository products that include checking, savings and money market deposits. It offers 24-hour telephone banking services through its voice response system, bnc bankline. The group also provides Internet banking and cash management services through its Internet banking site. The group is a holding company for bnc national bank.

Primary SIC and add'l.: 6021 9999 6712

CIK No: 0000945434

Subsidiaries: Bismarck Properties, Inc., BNC Asset Management, Inc., (a Subsidiary of BNC National Bank), BNC Capital Trust I, BNC Insurance Services, Inc. (a Subsidiary ofBNC National Bank), BNC National Bank, BNC Statutory Trust II

Officers: Gregory K. Cleveland/Dir., CEO, Pres./$404,503.00, Richard W. Milne/53/Exec. Officer/$359,554.00, Cleveland Goll Shawn/39/Exec. Officer, Neil M. Brozen/Exec. VP - Retirement Services/$258,411.00, Annette Eckroth/Sec.

Directors: Gregory K. Cleveland/Dir., CEO, Pres., Tracy J. Scott/Chmn., Shawn Cleveland Goll/Dir. - BNC National Bank, Mark W. Sheffert/Dir., Timothy J. Franz/CFO, Dir. - BNC National Bank, Jess Roman/Dir. - BNC National Bank, Jerry D. Renk/Dir. - BNC National Bank, Mark E. Peiler/Dir. - BNC National Bank, Ghylin Gaylen/Dir., Stephen H. Roman/Dir., Thomas E. Welch/Dir. - BNC National Bank, Dave Hoekstra/Dir. - BNC National Bank, Jerry R. Woodcox/Dir., Richard M. Johnsen/Dir., Gaylen Ghylin/60/Dir.

Owners: Gregory K. Cleveland/3.67%, Thomas E. Welch, Gaylen Ghylin, Financial Stocks Capital Partners IV, L.P./9.37%, Tracy Scott/3.89%, Insiders/14.48%, Richard M. Johnson, Kenneth H. Johnson/10.64%, Richard W. Milne/3.82%, Jerry R. Woodcox, Timothy J. Franz, BNC National Bank, Neil Brozen, Terrence M. Scali/6.50%

Financial Data: ***Fiscal Year End:***12/31 ***Latest Annual Data:*** 12/31/2006

Year	Sales	Net Income
2006	$66,283,000	$3,621,000
2005	$62,214,000	$4,103,000
2004	$53,591,000	$3,404,000

Curr. Assets:	$45,527,000	**Curr. Liab.:**	$601,161,000	**P/E Ratio:**	13.24
Plant, Equip.:	$24,286,000	**Total Liab.:**	$636,674,000	**Indic. Yr. Divd.:**	NA
Total Assets:	$692,276,000	**Net Worth:**	$55,602,000	**Debt/ Equity:**	0.3891

BNL Financial Corp

7010 Hwy 71 W, Ste. 100, Austin, TX, 78735; ***PH:*** 1-515-383-0220

General - Incorporation	IA	**Stock**- Price on:12/24/2007	NA
Employees	NA	Stock Exchange	NA
Auditor	Smith, Carney & Co., P.c.	Ticker Symbol	NA
Stk Agt	BNL Financial Corp	Outstanding Shares	NA
Counsel	NA	E.P.S	NA
DUNS No.	18-618-1400	Shareholders	NA

Business: The group's principal activity is to provide life, accident and health insurance on individual and group basis through its subsidiaries. The products of the group include 10-year level term policy, group life, hospital indemnity policy and group dental insurance. The major operations of the group are through brokers national life assurance company. At 31-Dec-2003, the group had 4,590 general agents and brokers in 34 states to market its policies. The group operates solely in the domestic market.

Primary SIC and add'l.: 6719 6321 6311

CIK No: 0000757641

Subsidiaries: BNL Brokerage Corporation, BNL Equity Corporation, Brokers National Life Assurance Company, Consumers Protective Association

Officers: Wayne E. Ahart/67/Chmn., CEO/$430.27, Pamela Randolph/Sec., Barry N. Shamas/60/Dir., CFO, COO, Exec. VP, Treasurer/$310,905.00, Kenneth Tobey/49/Dir., Pres./$236,926.00

Directors: Wayne E. Ahart/67/Chmn., CEO, Donald C. Byrd/66/Vice Chmn., James C. McCormick/82/Dir., Kenneth Tobey/49/Dir., Pres., Stanley L. Schoelerman/82/Dir., Barry N. Shamas/60/Dir., CFO, COO, Exec. VP, Treasurer, Eugene A. Cernan/73/Dir., James A. Mullins/74/Dir., Cecil L. Alexander/71/Dir., Richard L. Barclay/70/Dir., Hayden Fry/78/Dir., John E. Miller/78/Dir., Roy E. Ledbetter/77/Dir., John Greig/72/Dir., Orville Sweet/83/Dir. *(16 Directors included in Index)*

Owners: Hayden Fry/0.44%, Barry N. Shamas/17.88%, Richard L. Barclay/0.29%, Stanley L. Schoelerman, John Greig/0.32%, Kenneth Tobey/7.07%, John E. Miller/0.30%, Robert R. Rigler/0.02%, Orville Sweet/0.32%, Wayne E. Ahart/30.07%, James C. McCormick, Insiders/70.48%, James A. Mullins/0.32%, Roy E. Ledbetter/0.24%, Donald C. Byrd/11.55% *(17 Owners included in Index)*

BNP Residential Properties Inc

301 S College St., Ste.3850, Charlotte, NC, 28202; ***PH:*** 1-704-944-0100;
http:// www.bnp-residential.com

General - Incorporation	MD	**Stock**- Price on:12/24/2007	NA
Employees	NA	Stock Exchange	AMEX
Auditor	Grant Thornton LLP	Ticker Symbol	BNP
Stk Agt	American Stock Transfer & Trust Co.	Outstanding Shares	NA
Counsel	NA	E.P.S	NA
DUNS No.	NA	Shareholders	NA

Business: The groups principle activities include owning and operating in apartment communities. In the year 2005, the group acquired Boddie Investment Company. The group operates from North Carolina, South Carolina and Virginia.

Primary SIC and add'l.: 6798

CIK No: 0000812150

Officers: Scott D. Wilkerson/Dir., CEO, Pres., Pamela B. Bruno/VP, Treasurer, CFO, Alex S. Burris/VP - Operations, Eric S. Rohm/VP, Sec., General Counsel, Teresa M. Sandman/VP - Property Management, Andrea Burris/Dir. - Investor Relations

Directors: Scott D. Wilkerson/Dir., CEO, Pres., Philip S. Payne/Chmn., Mayo B. Boddie/Chmn. Emeritus, Michael W. Gilley/Dir., Peter J. Weidhorn/Dir., Stephen R. Blank/Dir., Paul G. Chrysson/Dir.

Owners: Pamela B. Bruno, Cliffwood Partners LLC and affiliates/9.00%, Michael W. Gilley/2.70%, Scott D. Wilkerson/1.60%, Stephen R. Blank, Peter J. Weidhorn/4.50%, Philip S. Payne/2.50%, Paul G. Chrysson/2.80%, Kensington Investment Group Inc./5.90%, Insiders/14.20%, Eric S. Rohm

BNS Holding Inc

25 Enterprise Ctr., Ste. 104, Middletown, RI, 02842; ***PH:*** 1-401-848-6300; ***Fax:*** 1-401-848-6444;
http:// www.bnsco.com

General - Incorporation	DE	**Stock**- Price on:12/24/2007	$11.7
Employees	NA	Stock Exchange	OTC
Auditor	Mcgladrey & Pullen, LLP	Ticker Symbol	BNSSA
Stk Agt	Computershare Investor Services LLC	Outstanding Shares	3,040,000
Counsel	NA	E.P.S	$1.88
DUNS No.	00-119-1246	Shareholders	NA

Business: The group's principle activity is real estate management deriving rental revenues from an owned office and industrial building in north kingstown, Rhode Island. The group also owns a gravel extraction and landfill property in the United Kingdom, from which it derives royalty income, and holds vacant land adjacent to its north kingstown building. The north kingstown, Rhode Island property consists of an industrial and office building of approximately 734,000 square feet, and approximately 169 acres of undeveloped commercially zoned land. The group's quarterly revenue for July 2007 was 92.59 millions of USD.

Primary SIC and add'l.: 6512 6514

CIK No: 0000014637

Subsidiaries: BNS Co., BNS International, Ltd., and Bath Road Holdings, Limited, Xygent Inc

Owners: James Henderson, Dimensional Fund Advisors Inc./5.65%, Insiders/2.50%, Robert J. Held, Kenneth N. Kermes/1.60%, Steel Partners II, L.P./41.70%, Warren B. Kanders/5.80%, Jack Howard

Financial Data: ***Fiscal Year End:***12/31 ***Latest Annual Data:*** 10/31/2006

Year	Sales	Net Income
2006	$309,867,000	$8,144,000
2005	NA	-$1,176,000
2004	NA	$8,770,000

Curr. Assets:	$21,185,000	**Curr. Liab.:**	$1,358,000	**P/E Ratio:**	6.22
Plant, Equip.:	$7,000	**Total Liab.:**	$1,358,000	**Indic. Yr. Divd.:**	NA
Total Assets:	$22,255,000	**Net Worth:**	$20,897,000	**Debt/ Equity:**	4.3688

BNSF Railway Co

2650 Lou Menk Dr., Fort Worth, TX, 76131; ***PH:*** 1-800-795-2673; ***Fax:*** 1-817-352-7171;
http:// www.bnsf.com

General - Incorporation	DE	**Stock**- Price on:12/24/2007	$87.05
Employees	41,000	Stock Exchange	NA
Auditor	PricewaterhouseCoopers LLP	Ticker Symbol	NA
Stk Agt	Computershare Investor Services LLC	Outstanding Shares	356,120,000
Counsel	NA	E.P.S	$4.91
DUNS No.	04-834-1788	Shareholders	NA

Business: The group's principle activity is to provide rail and road transportation services. The company transports bulk commodities such as grain, low-sulphur coal, intermodal containers, automobiles and packed commodities across 28 states and 2 Canadian provinces. The company is also engaged in transportation of coal, agricultural commodities, chemicals, forest products, consumer goods, metals, minerals, automobiles and automobile parts.

Primary SIC and add'l.: 4013 4011

CIK No: 0000015511

Subsidiaries: Santa Fe Receivables Corporation

Officers: Matthew K. Rose/Chmn., CEO, Pres., Marsha K. Morgan/VP - Investor Relations, John P. Lanigan/Exec. VP, Chief Marketing Officer, Jeffrey J. Campbell/VP - Technology Services, CIO, Steve Forsberg/General Dir. - Public Affairs, Shelley J. Venick/VP - General Tax Counsel, David W. Stropes/VP - Corporate Audit Services, James H. Gallegos/VP, Corporate General Counsel, Amy Hawkins/VP - Federal Government Affairs, Paul R. Hoferer/VP, General Counsel, Linda J. Hurt/Treasurer, Richard E. Weicher/VP, Sr. Regulatory Counsel, Carl R. Ice/COO, Exec. VP, Thomas N. Hund/CFO, Exec. VP, Joe Faust/Dir. - Public Affairs *(33 Officers included in Index)*

Directors: Matthew K. Rose/Chmn., CEO, Pres., Alan L. Boeckmann/Dir., Steven J. Whisler/Dir., Roy S. Roberts/Dir., Donald G. Cook/Dir., Vilma S. Martinez/Dir., Marc J. Shapiro/Dir., J. C. Watts/Dir., Robert H. West/Dir., Edward E. Whitacre/Dir., Marc F. Racicot/Dir.

Financial Data: ***Fiscal Year End:***12/31 ***Latest Annual Data:*** 12/31/2006

Year	Sales	Net Income
2006	$14,985,000,000	$1,887,000,000
2005	$12,987,000,000	$1,531,000,000
2004	$10,946,000,000	$791,000,000

Curr. Assets:	$2,181,000,000	**Curr. Liab.:**	$3,326,000,000	**P/E Ratio:**	17.48
Plant, Equip.:	$27,676,000,000	**Total Liab.:**	$21,247,000,000	**Indic. Yr. Divd.:**	$1.280
Total Assets:	$31,643,000,000	**Net Worth:**	$10,396,000,000	**Debt/ Equity:**	0.6615

Boardwalk Bancorp Inc

201 Shore Rd., Linwood, NJ, 08221; ***PH:*** 1-609-601-0600; ***Fax:*** 1-609-601-8554;
http:// www.boardwalkbank.com

General - Incorporation	NJ	**Stock**- Price on:12/24/2007	$16.51
Employees	67	Stock Exchange	NDQ
Auditor	KPMG LLP	Ticker Symbol	BORD
Stk Agt	Stock Transfer & Trust Co	Outstanding Shares	NA
Counsel	NA	E.P.S	NA
DUNS No.	NA	Shareholders	NA

Business: The group operates through its subsidiaries whose principle activity is to provide banking services. The groups financial product is loan. The groups financial services include commercial loans, mortgage loans, consumer loans, Marina Loans, Hotel, Motel and Bed and Breakfast Inn Loans, and Restaurant Loans. Customers served by the group include commercial and retail. The group operates from the United States. The assets of the group for the year 2006 were $453,280,000.

Primary SIC and add'l.: 6022 6099 6712

CIK No: 0001354835

Subsidiaries: Boardwalk Bank

Officers: Michael D. Devlin/Chmn., CEO, Pres./$216,473.00, Wayne S. Hardenbrook/CFO, Exec. VP/$160,502.00, Joan B. Ditmars/Corp. Sec., Don K. Dodson/Sr. VP, Commercial Loan Officer, John Charles/VP, Commercial Loan Officer, David Plummer/VP, Construction Loan Officer, Rick Simone/VP, Commercial Loan Officer, Fran Goldstein/VP, Commercial Loan Officer, Guy

Hackney/VP, Controller, Lee Van Horn/VP - Retail Banking, Mark Welzel/VP - Residential Mortgages, Michael Steffens/Assist. VP - Merchant Services, Brian R. Maund/Information Technology Mgr., VP, Joanna Marositz/Branch Mgr. - Linwood, Joann Calvarese/Branch Mgr. - Galloway *(32 Officers included in Index)*

Directors: Michael D. Devlin/Chmn., CEO, Pres., Joseph M. Brennan/Dir., Arthur R. Coslop/Dir., Agostino R. Fabietti/Dir., James L. Fraser/Dir., Thomas L. Glenn/Dir., Roy Goldberg/Dir., Carol Nugent Harris/Dir., Pravin Khatiwala/Dir., Patricia C. Koelling/Dir., Thomas S. Rittenhouse/Dir., Thomas K. Ritter/Dir., Arthur J. Galletta/Dir., Rudolph Chiorazzo/Dir. - Boardwalk Bank, Mark A. Benevento/Dir.

Owners: Roy Goldberg/1.10%, Thomas S. Rittenhouse, Wayne S. Hardenbrook, Jacobs Asset Management, LLC/6.81%, Michael D. Devlin/2.60%, Mark A. Benevento, Arthur R. Coslop/1.00%, Agostino R. Fabietti/1.10%, Pravin Khatiwala, Carol Nugent Harris/1.40%, Thomas K. Ritter/3.20%, Insiders/16.30%, Guy A. Deninger, Arthur J. Galletta/1.10%, Thomas L. Glenn/1.20% *(18 Owners included in Index)*

Financial Data: **Fiscal Year End:** 12/31 **Latest Annual Data:** 12/31/2006

Year	Sales	Net Income
2006	$27,648,000	$3,025,000
2005	$19,718,000	$2,600,000
2004	$13,378,000	$2,071,000

Curr. Assets:	$13,288,000	**Curr. Liab.:**	$310,514,000		
Plant, Equip.:	$16,186,000	**Total Liab.:**	$402,153,000	**Indic. Yr. Divd.:**	$0.400
Total Assets:	$453,280,000	**Net Worth:**	$51,127,000	**Debt/ Equity:**	NA

BOB Evans Farms Inc

3776 S High St., Columbus, OH, 43207; ***PH:*** 1-614-491-2225; ***Fax:*** 1-614-492-4949; ***http://*** www.bobevans.com

General - Incorporation	DE	**Stock** - Price on:12/24/2007	$36.48
Employees	50,810	Stock Exchange	NDQ
Auditor	Ernst & Young LLP	Ticker Symbol	BOBE
Stk Agt	Bob Evans Farms Inc	Outstanding Shares	35,140,000
Counsel	Vorys, Sater, Seymour & Pease	E.P.S	$1.76
DUNS No.	00-428-6407	Shareholders	NA

Business: The groups principle activity is to operate restaurants. The groups products include pork sausages, buttermilk biscuits, and sausage patties hot, sandwiches and grocery products. The group operates from United States.

Primary SIC and add'l.: 2013 5812

CIK No: 0000033769

Subsidiaries: BEF Aviation Co., Inc., BEF Holding Co., Inc., BEF RE Holding Co., Inc., Bef Reit, Inc., Bob Evans Farms, Inc., Bob Evans Restaurants of Michigan, Inc., Bob Evans Restaurants, Inc., Bob Evans Transportation Company, LLC, Mimi's Cafe Kansas, Inc., Mimi's Cafe, LLC, Owens Country Foods, Inc., Owens Country Sausage, Inc., Owens Foods, Inc., SWH Corporation, SWH Liquor Company 18 Subsidiaries included in the Index

Officers: Steven A. Davis/Chmn., CEO/$2,385,531.00, Roger D. Williams/Pres. - Bob Evans Restaurants/$1,777,553.00, Donald J. Radkoski/CFO, Treasurer, Sec./$977,320.00, Randall A. Hicks/Exec. VP - Bob Evans Restaurants/$591,242.00, Dan Dillon/COO - Mimi's Cafe, Mike Townsley/VP - Food Products Division, Mary L. Garceau/35/VP, General Counsel, Assist. Sec., Richard D. Hall/52/Sr. VP - Corporate Procurement, VP - Food Products Operations, Tod P. Spornhauer/42/Sr. VP - Finance, Controller, Assist. Treasurer, Assist. Sec.

Directors: Steven A. Davis/Chmn., CEO, Mary L. Cusick/52/Dir., Larry C. Corbin/Dir., E. W. Ingram/Dir., Daniel A. Fronk/Dir., Cheryl L. Krueger/Dir., Bryan G. Stockton/Dir., Michael J. Gasser/Dir., Robert G. Lucas/Dir., Russell Bendel/54/Dir.

Owners: Capital Research and Management Company/6.40%, Barclays Global Investors, NA/6.70%, Bryan G. Stockton, Russell W. Bendel, Daniel A. Fronk, Cheryl L. Krueger, Steven A. Davis, Robert G. Lucas, Donald J. Radkoski, Ariel Capital Management, LLC/8.70%, E. W. Ingram, Advisory Research, Inc./6.80%, Dimensional Fund Advisors LP/7.70%, Michael J. Gasser, Randall L. Hicks *(18 Owners included in Index)*

Financial Data: **Fiscal Year End:** 04/28 **Latest Annual Data:** 04/27/2007

Year	Sales	Net Income
2007	$1,654,460,000	$60,542,000
2006	$1,584,819,000	$54,774,000
2005	$1,460,195,000	$36,968,000

Curr. Assets:	$47,472,000	**Curr. Liab.:**	$145,847,000	**P/E Ratio:**	21.98
Plant, Equip.:	$783,397,000	**Total Liab.:**	$238,070,000	**Indic. Yr. Divd.:**	$0.560
Total Assets:	$868,233,000	**Net Worth:**	$630,163,000	**Debt/ Equity:**	NA

BOC Group Plc

Chertsey Rd., Windlesham, GU20 6HJ; ***PH:*** 44-012-764-7722; ***http://*** www.boc.com

General - Incorporation	UK	**Stock** - Price on:12/24/2007	$109
Employees	NA	Stock Exchange	NA
Auditor	PricewaterhouseCoopers LLP	Ticker Symbol	NA
Stk Agt	NA	Outstanding Shares	NA
Counsel	NA	E.P.S	NA
DUNS No.	21-004-2594	Shareholders	NA

Business: The group's principal activity is the supply of industrial gases by pipeline, on-site production units, or in liquid form by tanker. The group is organised in three lines of business: process gas solutions, provides tailored solutions for the customers' process needs. Industrial and special products, provides metal welding and cutting services. Boc edwards, concentrates on the needs of the semiconductor industry. It also has two specialist businesses: gist and afrox hospitals.

Primary SIC and add'l.: 3559 8062 3563 8742 2813

CIK No: 0000715095

Subsidiaries: 177470 Canada Inc, 177472 Canada Inc, 3 Shires (Cutting & Welding Automated) Limited, 3 Shires Cutting & Welding Limited, 44001 Ontario Limited, 9155-2257 Quebec Inc, A-TEC Ltd, African Oxygen Limited, Afrox (Transkei)(Pty) Limited, Afrox African Investments (Pty) Limited, Afrox Educational Services (Pty) Limited, Afrox Finance Limited, Afrox Gas & Engineering Supplies (Botswana), Afrox International Limited, Afrox Lesotho (Pty) Limited 492 Subsidiaries included in the Index

Bodisen Biotech Inc

N Part Of Xinquia Rd, Yang Ling Ag, High-Tech Industries Demonstration Zone, Yang Ling, 712100; ***PH:*** 86-2987074957; ***http://*** www.bodisen.com; ***Email:*** info@bodisen.com

General - Incorporation	DE	**Stock** - Price on:12/24/2007	NA
Employees	543	Stock Exchange	OTC
Auditor	Kabani & Co, Inc	Ticker Symbol	BBCZ
Stk Agt	Interwest Transfer Company, Inc.	Outstanding Shares	NA
Counsel	Sichenzia Ross Friedman Ference LLP	E.P.S	NA
DUNS No.	NA	Shareholders	NA

Business: The groups principle activities include developing, manufacturing and selling organic fertilizers and pesticides. The group operates from China..

Primary SIC and add'l.: NA

CIK No: 0001178552

Subsidiaries: Bodisen Holdings, Inc., Technology Development Company Limited, Yang Ling Bodisen Biology Science

Officers: Bo Chen/50/Chmn., CEO, Pres., Wang Chunsheng/45/COO, Yiliang Lai/43/CFO - Bodisen, Yang Ling, Junyan Tong/37/CFO

Directors: Bo Chen/50/Chmn., CEO, Pres., Wang Qiong/43/Chmn., Patrick McManus/53/Dir., David Gatton/54/Dir., Linzhang Zhu/57/Dir., Qiong Wang/43/Dir.

Owners: Bo Chen/3.70%, Patrick McManus, Insiders/7.60%, Qiong Wang/3.90%, David Gatton

Financial Data: **Fiscal Year End:** 12/31 **Latest Annual Data:** 12/31/2006

Year	Sales	Net Income
2006	$43,627,000	$13,731,000
2005	$30,975,000	$7,421,000
2004	$16,226,000	$5,027,000

Curr. Assets:	$46,240,000	**Curr. Liab.:**	$1,370,000		
Plant, Equip.:	$8,865,000	**Total Liab.:**	$1,370,000	**Indic. Yr. Divd.:**	NA
Total Assets:	$69,197,000	**Net Worth:**	$67,826,000	**Debt/ Equity:**	NA

BOE Financial Services of Virginia Inc

1325 Tappahannock Blvd., Tappahannock, VA, 22560; ***PH:*** 1-804-443-4343; ***Fax:*** 1-804-443-9472; ***http://*** www.bankofessex.com

General - Incorporation	VA	**Stock** - Price on:12/24/2007	$29
Employees	92	Stock Exchange	NDQ
Auditor	Yount, Hyde & Barbour, P.C	Ticker Symbol	BSXT
Stk Agt	Bank of Essex	Outstanding Shares	1,210,000
Counsel	McGuire Woods Battle & Boothe	E.P.S	$2.41
DUNS No.	NA	Shareholders	NA

Business: The group's principal activity is to provide commercial banking and other financial services to individuals and corporate customers. The group is a bank holding company, which owns all of the stock of its sole subsidiary, bank of essex. The products include commercial, residential and consumer loans and a variety of deposit products to its customers in the northern neck, middle peninsula and richmond regions of Virginia. The group operates six full service offices located in tappahannock, king william county, hanover county and henrico county, Virginia.

Primary SIC and add'l.: 6022 6712

CIK No: 0001109848

Subsidiaries: Bank of Essex, BOE Statutory Trust I, Essex Services, Incorporated

Officers: George M. Longest/Dir. - Bank, Essex, CEO, Pres./$178,522.00, Alexander F. Dillard/Dir., Chmn. - Bank, Essex, Suzanne S. Rennolds/Sr. VP - Human Resources, Bruce E. Thomas/Sr. VP, CFO/$122,613.00, Robert Harding Ball/Dir. - Bank, Essex, Gwendolyn S. Cook/Mortgage Officer - Bank, Essex, Saint George B. Pinckney/Sr. Credit Analyst, Bank, Essex, Sharon C. James/Assist. VP - Loan Administration, Bank, Essex, George B. Elliott/Dir. - Bank, Essex, Kevin P. Dolan/VP - Bank, Essex, Frances H. Ellis/Dir. - Bank, Essex, William E. Saunders/VP - Risk Management, Tyler R. Bland/Dir. - Bank, Essex, Mccauley L. Chenault/Dir. - Bank, Essex, Lisa L. Roccaforte/VP - Essex Services, Bank, Essex *(34 Officers included in Index)*

Directors: Philip T. Minor/Dir. - Bank, Essex, Emerson P. Hughes/Dir. - Bank, Essex

Owners: Tyler R. Bland, Frances H. Ellis, Philip T. Minor/1.19%, George M. Longest, Bruce E. Thomas, Page Emerson Hughes, Alexander F. Dillard/1.83%, McCauley L. Chenault, George B. Elliott, Harding R. Ball, Terrell D. Vaughan, Wayne K. Aylor, Banc Fund V L.P./6.18%, Insiders/6.63%

Financial Data: **Fiscal Year End:** 12/31 **Latest Annual Data:** 12/31/2006

Year	Sales	Net Income
2006	$18,997,000	$3,123,000
2005	$15,943,000	$3,101,000
2004	$14,502,000	$2,885,000

Curr. Assets:	$6,883,000	**Curr. Liab.:**	$246,923,000	**P/E Ratio:**	11.98
Plant, Equip.:	$10,454,000	**Total Liab.:**	$253,331,000	**Indic. Yr. Divd.:**	NA
Total Assets:	$281,378,000	**Net Worth:**	$28,047,000	**Debt/ Equity:**	0.1453

Boeing

100 N Riverside, Chicago, IL, 60606; ***PH:*** 1-312-544-2000; ***Fax:*** 1-312-544-2078; ***http://*** www.boeing.com; ***Email:*** boeing2@boeing.com

General - Incorporation	DE	**Stock** - Price on:12/24/2007	$97.64
Employees	154,000	Stock Exchange	NYSE
Auditor	Deloitte & Touche LLP	Ticker Symbol	BA
Stk Agt	Computershare Investor Services LLC	Outstanding Shares	787,400,000
Counsel	NA	E.P.S	$5.21
DUNS No.	00-925-6819	Shareholders	NA

Business: The group's principle activity is to manufacture commercial jetliners and military aircraft combined. The group also designs and manufactures rotorcraft, electronic and defense systems, missiles, satellites, launch vehicles, and advanced information and communication systems. The group operates from United States.

Primary SIC and add'l.: 6159 4581 3761 3724

CIK No: 0000012927

Subsidiaries: Boeing Phantom Works Investments, Inc., Boeing Pharmacy, Inc., Boeing Precision Gear, Inc., Boeing Realty Corporation, Boeing Research& Technology Europe, S.L., Boeing Russia, Inc., Boeing Sales Corporation, Boeing Satellite Systems International, Inc., Boeing Satellite Systems, Inc., Boeing Service Company, Boeing Space Operations Company, Boeing Spain, Ltd., Boeing Stellar Holdings B.V., Boeing Stores, Inc., Boeing Superannuation Pty. Ltd. 148 Subsidiaries included in the Index

Officers: James W. McNerney/Chmn., CEO, Pres./$19,414,980.00, Laurette T. Koellner/54/Pres. - Boeing International/$7,009,014.00, Harry S. McGee/VP - Finance, Corporate Controller, James C. Johnson/Corp. Sec., Scott E. Carson/62/Exec. VP, Shephard W. Hill/56/Sr. VP - Business Development, Strategy, Michael J. Luttig/Sr. VP, General Counsel, John J. Tracy/Sr. VP - Engineering, Operations, Technology, Christopher D. Raymond/VP - Business Development, Tim Copes/Pres. - Shared Services Group, Richard Stephens/Sr. VP - Human Resources, Administration/$4,134,702.00, Tod R. Hullin/65/Sr. VP - Public Policy, Bonnie W. Soodik/57/Sr. VP - Office, Internal Governance, James A. Bell/CFO, Exec. VP - Finance/$5,908,486.00, James F. Albaugh/58/Exec. VP/$6,804,689.00 *(32 Officers included in Index)*

Directors: James W. McNerney/Chmn., CEO, Pres., Rozanne L. Ridgway/Dir., John E. Bryson/Dir., John H. Biggs/Dir., William M. Daley/Dir., Richard Nanula/47/Dir., John F. McDonnell/Dir., Arthur D. Collins/Dir., James L. Jones/Dir., Edward M. Liddy/Dir., Kenneth M. Duberstein/Dir., Linda Z. Cook/Dir., Mike S. Zafirovski/Dir.

Owners: Richard D. Stephens, Kenneth M. Duberstein, AXA Assurances I.A.R.D. Mutuelle/5.90%, James A. Bell, Mike S. Zafirovski, John E. Bryson, James F. Albaugh, John F. McDonnell, Insiders, Alan R. Mulally, State Street Bank and Trust Company/10.80%, John H. Biggs, Richard D. Nanula, William M. Daley, Linda Z. Cook *(18 Owners included in Index)*

Financial Data: *Fiscal Year End:* 12/31 *Latest Annual Data:* 12/31/2006

Year	Sales	Net Income
2006	$61,530,000,000	$2,215,000,000
2005	$54,845,000,000	$2,572,000,000
2004	$52,457,000,000	$1,872,000,000

Curr. Assets:	$22,983,000,000	**Curr. Liab.:**	$29,701,000,000	**P/E Ratio:**	31.91
Plant, Equip.:	$7,675,000,000	**Total Liab.:**	$47,055,000,000	**Indic. Yr. Divd.:**	$1.600
Total Assets:	$51,794,000,000	**Net Worth:**	$4,739,000,000	**Debt/ Equity:**	1.5072

Boeing Capital Corp

500 Naches Ave. SW, 3rd Fl., Renton, WA, 98057; *PH:* 1-425-965-4002; *Fax:* 1-425-965-4085; *http://* www.boeing.com

General - Incorporation	DE	**Stock** - Price on:12/24/2007	$97.42
Employees	154,000	Stock Exchange	NA
Auditor	Deloitte & Touche LLP	Ticker Symbol	NA
Stk Agt	Computershare Investor Services LLC	Outstanding Shares	787,400,000
Counsel	NA	E.P.S	$4.65
DUNS No.	05-981-9219	Shareholders	NA

Business: The group's principal activity is to provide equipment financing and leasing arrangements to a diversified range of customers and industries. The group's primary operations include two principal financial reporting segments: the aircraft financial services and commercial financial services. Aircraft financial services provides financing to buy or lease commercial jet airplanes. These services are extended to buy new and used boeing and non-boeing airplanes. The commercial financial services specializes in leasing and financing of commercial equipment.

Primary SIC and add'l.: 6159 7359

CIK No: 0000711513

Subsidiaries: Boeing Capital Services Corporation (BCSC)

Officers: Walter E. Skowronski/60/Pres., Russell A. Evans/CFO, VP, Kevin J. Murphy/Controller

Directors: James A. Bell/Chmn., James C. Johnson/Dir., Paul R. Kinscherff/Dir.

Financial Data: *Fiscal Year End:* 12/31 *Latest Annual Data:* 12/31/2006

Year	Sales	Net Income
2006	$61,530,000,000	$2,215,000,000
2005	$54,845,000,000	$2,572,000,000
2004	$52,457,000,000	$1,872,000,000

Curr. Assets:	$22,983,000,000	**Curr. Liab.:**	$29,701,000,000	**P/E Ratio:**	31.84
Plant, Equip.:	$7,675,000,000	**Total Liab.:**	$47,055,000,000	**Indic. Yr. Divd.:**	$1.400
Total Assets:	$51,794,000,000	**Net Worth:**	$4,739,000,000	**Debt/ Equity:**	1.5072

BofI Holding Inc

12777 High Bluff Dr., Ste. 100, San Diego, CA, 92130; *PH:* 1-858-350-6200; *Fax:* 1-858-350-0443; *http://* www.bofiholding.com; *Email:* investors@bankofinternet.com

General - Incorporation	DE	**Stock** - Price on:12/24/2007	$7.35
Employees	24	Stock Exchange	NDQ
Auditor	Crowe, Chizek and Company LLC	Ticker Symbol	BOFI
Stk Agt	U.S. Stock Transfer Corp	Outstanding Shares	8,280,000
Counsel	NA	E.P.S	$0.36
DUNS No.	NA	Shareholders	NA

Business: The group operates through its subsidiaries whose principle activity is to provide consumer banking services. The groups services include loan and deposit. The products of the group include single-family loans, commercial loans, consumer loans, atms, debit cards and automated clearinghouse funds. The group operates from the United States. The assets of the group for the year 2006 were $737.8 (million).

Primary SIC and add'l.: 6035 6712

CIK No: 0001299709

Subsidiaries: Bank of Internet USA

Officers: Gregory Garrabrants/CEO, Kenn Darling/Chief Loan Officer, VP, Gary Lewis Evans/Dir., Pres., Mike Berengolts/CTO, VP, Barbara D. Fronek/VP - Internet Development, Andrew J. Micheletti/CFO, VP

Directors: Jerry Englert/Chmn., Gary Lewis Evans/Dir., Pres., Ted Allrich/Dir., John Gary Burke/Dir., Michael Chipman/Dir., Paul Grinberg/Dir., Thomas J. Pancheri/Dir., Michelle Paulus/Dir., Gordon L. Witter/Dir., Connie M. Paulus/48/Dir.

Owners: Insiders/31.29%, Michael Berengolts, Michael A. Chipman/9.26%, Michelle C. Paulus/2.19%, Gordon L. Witter/1.29%, Jerry F. Englert/7.72%, Paul Grinberg, Thomas J. Pancheri/2.00%, Kenneth Darling, John Gary Burke/5.64%, Andrew J. Micheletti/1.16%, Theodore Allrich/1.11%, Gary Lewis Evans/2.57%

Financial Data: *Fiscal Year End:* 06/30 *Latest Annual Data:* 6/30/2006

Year	Sales	Net Income
2006	$34,055,000	$3,266,000
2005	$23,388,000	$2,869,000
2004	$16,962,000	$2,175,000

Curr. Assets:	$45,154,000	**Curr. Liab.:**	$662,434,000		
Plant, Equip.:	$222,000	**Total Liab.:**	$667,589,000	**Indic. Yr. Divd.:**	NA
Total Assets:	$737,835,000	**Net Worth:**	$70,246,000	**Debt/ Equity:**	0.0706

Bois d'Arc Energy Inc

600 Travis St., Ste. 5200, Houston, TX, 77002; *PH:* 1-713-228-0438; *Fax:* 1-713-228-1759; *http://* www.boisdarcenergy.com; *Email:* investorrelations@boisdarcenergy.com

General - Incorporation	NV	**Stock** - Price on:12/24/2007	$17.01
Employees	23	Stock Exchange	NYSE
Auditor	Ernst& Young LLP	Ticker Symbol	BDE
Stk Agt	American Stock Transfer & Trust Co.	Outstanding Shares	66,430,000
Counsel	NA	E.P.S	$0.93
DUNS No.	NA	Shareholders	NA

Business: The groups principle activities include exploring, developing and producing oil and natural gas. The group operates from the United States and Gulf of Mexico. The groups specific customers are Coral Energy Resources LP and National Energy & Trading, LP. The groups quarterly revenue for September 2007 was 87.99 millions of USD.

Primary SIC and add'l.: 1311

CIK No: 0001304069

Subsidiaries: Bois dArc Holdings, LLC(1), Bois dArc Offshore, Ltd.(2), Bois dArc Oil & Gas Company, LLC(1), Bois dArc Properties, LP(3)

Officers: Wayne L. Laufer/Dir., CEO, Gary W. Blackie/Dir., Pres., Roland O. Burns/Dir., Sr. VP, CFO, Sec., Greg T. Martin/VP - Operations, William E. Holman/VP - Exploration, Karen S. Acree/VP - Accounting, Controller, James P. Perkins/Mgr. Offshore Land - Business Development

Directors: Wayne L. Laufer/Dir., CEO, Jay M. Allison/Chmn., Gary W. Blackie/Dir., Pres., Roland O. Burns/Dir., Sr. VP, CFO, Sec., John L. Duvieilh/Dir., Michael D. Harris/Dir., David K. Lockett/Dir., Cecil E. Martin/Dir., David W. Sledge/Dir.

Owners: Michael D. Harris, Comstock Resources, Inc./48.50%, Cecil E. Martin, Wayne L. Laufer/14.20%, Jay M. Allison/1.10%, David W. Sledge, Roland O. Burns/1.10%, Insiders/25.80%, John L. Duvieilh, David K. Lockett, Gary W. Blackie/9.30%

Financial Data: *Fiscal Year End:* 12/31 *Latest Annual Data:* 12/31/2006

Year	Sales	Net Income
2006	$254,710,000	$55,024,000
2005	$184,436,000	-$51,672,000

Curr. Assets:	$56,794,000	**Curr. Liab.:**	$68,868,000	**P/E Ratio:**	57.95
Plant, Equip.:	$827,795,000	**Total Liab.:**	$368,891,000	**Indic. Yr. Divd.:**	NA
Total Assets:	$885,501,000	**Net Worth:**	$516,610,000	**Debt/ Equity:**	NA

BOK Financial Corp

Bank of Oklahoma Tower, Tulsa, OK, 74192; *PH:* 1-918-588-6000; *Fax:* 1-918-588-6853; *http://* www.bokf.com

General - Incorporation	OK	**Stock** - Price on:12/24/2007	$51.169
Employees	3,958	Stock Exchange	NDQ
Auditor	Ernst & Young LLP	Ticker Symbol	BOKF
Stk Agt	Computershare Investor Services LLC	Outstanding Shares	67,220,000
Counsel	Frederic Dorwart Lawyers	E.P.S	$3.22
DUNS No.	78-054-2882	Shareholders	NA

Business: The group's principal activities are to provide financial services. The group serves commercial and industrial customers, other financial institutions and consumers. The services provided by the group include depository and cash management, lending and lease financing, mortgage banking and underwriting and other. It operates in four principal line of business: corporate banking: provides credit and lease financing, deposit and cash management, and international collection services. Consumer banking: provides direct and indirect consumer loans and deposit services. Mortgage banking: provides full range of mortgage products and services. Trust services: provide financial services to both individual and corporate clients. Regional banks include bank of Arkansas, bank of albuquerque and bank of Texas. The areas of operations include Oklahoma, northwest Arkansas, north Texas and New Mexico. On 10-Sep-2003, the group acquired Colorado funding company.

Primary SIC and add'l.: 6712 6021

CIK No: 0000875357

Subsidiaries: Affiliated BancServices, Inc., Affiliated Financial Holding Company, Affiliated Financial Insurance Agency, Inc., Arizona Bancorp, Ltd., BancOklahoma Agri-Service Corporation, BancOklahoma Mortgage Corporation, Bank of Albuquerque, National Association, Bank of Arizona, National Association, Bank of Arkansas, National Association, Bank of Oklahoma, National Association, Bank of Texas, National Association, BOK Capital Services Corporation BOSC, Inc., BOK Delaware, Inc., BOK Funding Trust, BOKF Equipment Finance, Inc. 23 Subsidiaries included in the Index

Officers: Stanley A. Lybarger/Dir., CEO, Pres./$6,700,074.00, Don T. Parker/47/CIO, Exec. VP, Steven E. Nell/CFO, Exec. VP/$894,095.00, John C. Morrow/Sr. VP, Dir. - Financial Accounting, Reporting, Frederic Dorwart/Sec., Barron D. Beal/41/Exec. VP - Wealth Management, Scott C. Grauer/43/Sr. VP, Mgr. - Investment Center, Marc C. Maun/49/Sr. VP, Mgr. - Corporate Banking, James H. Holloman/56/Exec. VP, Mark W. Funke/52/Pres., Charles E. Cotter/54/Exec. VP, James L. Huntzinger/56/Chief Investment Officer, Jeffery R. Dunn/45/Sr. VP - Commercial Lending, Steven G. Bradshaw/48/Sr. Exec. VP/$944,223.00, Jeffrey W. Pickry/56/Sr. Exec. VP - Regional Banks/$1,033,646.00 *(20 Officers included in Index)*

Directors: Stanley A. Lybarger/Dir., CEO, Pres., George B. Kaiser/Chmn., Burns V. Hargis/Vice Chmn., Paula Marshall/Dir., Frederick C. Ball/Dir., William E. Durrett/Dir., Sharon J. Bell/Dir., David F. Griffin/Dir., Peter C. Boylan/Dir., Carey E. Joullian/Dir., Chester Edward Cadieux/Dir., Gregory S. Allen/Dir., Steven J. Malcolm/Dir., Robert G. Greer/73/Dir., Judith Z. Kishner/Dir. *(19 Directors included in Index)*

Owners: Steven J. Malcolm, Steven G. Bradshaw, Steven E. Nell, Peter C. Boylan, Daniel H. Ellinor, William E. Durrett, Burns V. Hargis, George B. Kaiser/66.10%, Fred C. Ball, David F. Griffin, Thomas L. Kivisto, Judith Z. Kishner, Insiders/67.10%, Robert J. LaFortune, Paula Marshall *(23 Owners included in Index)*

Financial Data: *Fiscal Year End:* 12/31 *Latest Annual Data:* 12/31/2006

Year	Sales	Net Income
2006	$1,359,624,000	$212,977,000
2005	$1,123,775,000	$201,505,000
2004	$927,736,000	$179,023,000

Curr. Assets:	$952,638,000	**Curr. Liab.:**	$14,883,586,000	**P/E Ratio:**	16.45
Plant, Equip.:	$196,527,000	**Total Liab.:**	$16,338,602,000	**Indic. Yr. Divd.:**	$0.800
Total Assets:	$18,059,624,000	**Net Worth:**	$1,721,022,000	**Debt/ Equity:**	0.7770

Bolivar Mining Corp

Formerly: Kingdom Ventures Inc
3028 Commercial Ave, Northbrook, IL, 60062; *PH:* 1-734-686-0137;
http:// www.kingdomventures.org

General - Incorporation .... NV
Employees .... NA
Auditor .... E. Randall Gruber CPA, P.C
Stk Agt....... Olde Monmouth Stk Trnsfer Co. Inc.
Counsel .... NA
DUNS No. .... NA

Stock- Price on:12/24/2007 .... $0.013
Stock Exchange .... NA
Ticker Symbol .... NA
Outstanding Shares 36,840,000
E.P.S. .... -$0.04
Shareholders .... NA

Business: The group's principal activities are to help churches and their people to grow. The group's primary media property is christian times today, a nationally impacting monthly newspaper distributed by and to churches, leaders, and business settings across the country. The current circulation is in excess of 300,000 monthly. Iexalt.com provides a variety of chat groups and news information in an electronic format. The product activities are focused on jobasic, an Internet charity shopping network. Jobasic provides e-commerce fundraising potential for every non-profit group in America. It also owns mr. Roy productions, inc. A northern Nevada silk screen, embroidery and production facility. The roy productions, inc serves a local clientele and provides product support for each of the group's other activities, including the distribution of yahwear, a line of christian clothing sold in e-commerce, direct mail, and at selected christian music festivals.

Primary SIC and add'l.: 7375 5735 5944 5945 5942 5999

CIK No: 0001130951

Subsidiaries: AACC Acquisition Corporation, Inc, Blue Hill Media, Inc., Kingdom Communications Group, Inc, Visionquest Ministries, Inc.

Officers: Larry Cheng/Dir. - Investments, Anthony Dewitt/Dir. - Technology

Directors: Tony Campolo/Member - Advisory Board, Craig Hammon/Member - Advisory Board, Jim Morris/Member - Advisory Board

Owners: Debbie Leibovitz/100.00%, Debbie Leibovitz/24.50%, Insiders/100.00%, Insiders/25.18%, Eric Joffe/0.68%

Financial Data: *Fiscal Year End:*01/31 *Latest Annual Data:* 1/31/2006

Year	Sales	Net Income
2006	NA	-$192,000
2005	NA	-$2,557,000
2004	$821,000	-$3,188,000

Curr. Assets:	NA	**Curr. Liab.:**	$924,000		
Plant, Equip.:	NA	**Total Liab.:**	$924,000	**Indic. Yr. Divd.:**	NA
Total Assets:	NA	**Net Worth:**	-$924,000	**Debt/ Equity:**	NA

Bolt Technology Corp

4 Duke Pl., Norwalk, CT, 06854; *PH:* 1-203-853-0700; *Fax:* 1-203-854-9601;
http:// www.bolt-technology.com; *Email:* sales@bolt-technology.com

General - Incorporation .... CT
Employees 100
Auditor .... McGladrey & Pullen LLP
Stk Agt .... Mellon Investor Services LLC
Counsel .... Levett Rockwood
DUNS No. 00-259-0883

Stock- Price on:12/24/2007 .... $41.25
Stock Exchange .... AMEX
Ticker Symbol .... BTJ
Outstanding Shares 5,610,000
E.P.S. $2.12
Shareholders .... NA

Business: The group's principle activities are carried out through two business segments: geophysical equipment and industrial products. The geophysical equipment segment develops, manufactures and markets marine seismic energy sources. The industrial products segment manufactures and markets miniature industrial clutches, brakes and sub-fractional horsepower electric motors. The principal customers for the group's geophysical equipment are seismic contractors. The principal customers for industrial products are original equipment manufacturers (OEMs). The products of the group are sold in the United States, Canada, Europe and other countries. The group's total revenue for year 2007 was 50.46 millions of USD.

Primary SIC and add'l.: 3829

CIK No: 0000354655

Subsidiaries: A-G Geophysical Products, Inc., Custom Products Corporation

Officers: Raymond M. Soto/Chmn., CEO, Pres., Joseph Espeso/66/Dir., CFO, Sr. VP - Finance, Joseph Mayerick/66/Dir., Sr. VP - Marketing, Sec.

Directors: Raymond M. Soto/Chmn., CEO, Pres., Joseph Espeso/66/Dir., CFO, Sr. VP - Finance, Joseph Mayerick/66/Dir., Sr. VP - Marketing, Sec., Kevin M. Conlisk/63/Dir., Michael H. Flynn/70/Dir., George R. Kabureck/69/Dir., Stephen F. Ryan/73/Dir., Gerald H. Shaff/Dir., Gerald A. Smith/62/Dir., Michael C. Hedger/53/Dir.

Owners: Gerald A. Smith, Raymond M. Soto, Michael H. Flynn, George R. Kabureck, Kevin M. Conlisk, Robert Sussman/8.80%, Gerald H. Shaff, Stephen F. Ryan, Bridgeway Capital Management, Inc./5.70%, Joseph Espeso, Insiders/1.80%

Financial Data: *Fiscal Year End:*06/30 *Latest Annual Data:* 6/30/2006

Year	Sales	Net Income
2006	$32,591,000	$4,845,000
2005	$18,796,000	$1,659,000
2004	$14,806,000	$853,000

Curr. Assets:	$20,898,000	**Curr. Liab.:**	$5,843,000	**P/E Ratio:**	26.44
Plant, Equip.:	$2,603,000	**Total Liab.:**	$6,279,000	**Indic. Yr. Divd.:**	NA
Total Assets:	$34,611,000	**Net Worth:**	$28,332,000	**Debt/ Equity:**	NA

Bombay Company Inc (The)

550 Bailey Ave., Ste 700, Fort Worth, TX, 76107; *PH:* 1-817-347-8200;
http:// www.bombaycompany.com; *Email:* customer_service@us.bombayco.com

General - Incorporation .... DE
Employees 1,900
Auditor .... PricewaterhouseCoopers LLP
Stk Agt .... Computershare Ltd.
Counsel .... NA
DUNS No. 02-032-8753

Stock- Price on:12/24/2007 .... $0.671
Stock Exchange .... OTC
Ticker Symbol .... BBAO
Outstanding Shares 36,880,000
E.P.S. .... -$1.453
Shareholders .... NA

Business: The group's principal activities are to design, source and market classic and traditional furniture, wall decor and accessories. Furniture includes both wood and metal ready-to-assemble furniture focusing on the bedroom, living room, dining room and home office. Accessories include both functional and decorative accessories like lamps, jewellery, candles, crystal, ceramics, textiles, etc. Wall decor includes prints, mirrors and sconces. At 31-Jul-04, it operates through 472 retail stores in 42 states in the United States and 56 stores in nine Canadian provinces through mail order and over the Internet. It has also provided licenses to stores being operated in the Dominican Republic, Puerto Rico and kuwait. The group sources its merchandise from contract manufacturers in over 20 countries located in Asia and North America and operates branch offices in Taiwan, Malaysia, Indonesia, China and vietnam.

Primary SIC and add'l.: 5719 5712

CIK No: 0000096287

Subsidiaries: Wells Fargo Retail Finance, LLC

Officers: David B. Stewart/69/Dir., CEO, Elaine D. Crowley/Sr. VP, CFO, Treasurer, Michael J. Veitenheimer/Sr. VP, Sec., General Counsel, Scott L. Binger/VP - Visual Merchandising, Concept Development, Vicki L. Bradley/Pres. - Bombay Furniture Company, Canada, Inc, Donald V. Roach/Sr. VP - Operations, Steven G. Sherlock/VP - Store Operations, Alicia Miller/Merchandise Administration Mgr., Joseph Marin/Counsel, Robert D. Albergotti/Attorney, Ian T. Peck/Attorney, John D. Penn/Attorney, Paul Myrick/41/VP - Real Estate

Directors: David B. Stewart/69/Dir., CEO, Paul V. Higham/Dir., Susan T. Groenteman/Dir., Laurie M. Shahon/Dir., Nigel Travis/Dir., Paul J. Raffin/Dir., Julie L. Reinganum/Dir., Bruce R. Smith/Dir.

Owners: Elaine D. Crowley, Michael J. Veitenheimer, Royce & Associates/5.13%, Laurie M. Shahon, Julie L. Reinganum, Wells Fargo & Company/8.56%, Paul V. Higham, Steven C. Woodward, Susan T. Groenteman, Bruce R. Smith, Dimensional Fund Advisors, LP/8.26%, Insiders, Paul J. Raffin, Nigel Travis, Donald V. Roach

Financial Data: *Fiscal Year End:*01/28 *Latest Annual Data:* 2/3/2007

Year	Sales	Net Income
2007	$536,325,000	-$52,781,000
2006	$565,074,000	-$46,731,000

Curr. Assets:	$147,580,000	**Curr. Liab.:**	$64,028,000		
Plant, Equip.:	$84,651,000	**Total Liab.:**	$103,004,000	**Indic. Yr. Divd.:**	NA
Total Assets:	$238,741,000	**Net Worth:**	$135,737,000	**Debt/ Equity:**	NA

Bon Ton Stores Inc

2801 E Market St., York, PA, 17402; *PH:* 1-717-757-7660; *Fax:* 1-717-751-3108;
http:// www.bonton.com; *Email:* ir@bonton.com

General - Incorporation .... PA
Employees 33,000
Auditor .... KPMG LLP
Stk Agt ..... American Stock Transfer & Trust Co.
Counsel.. Wolf Block Schorr & Solis-Cohen LLP
DUNS No. 00-791-2173

Stock- Price on:12/24/2007 .... $44.09
Stock Exchange .... NDQ
Ticker Symbol .... BONT
Outstanding Shares 17,130,000
E.P.S. $1.97
Shareholders .... NA

Business: The groups principle activity is to operate departmental stores. The groups products include fashion apparel and accessories for women, men and children, including footwear, cosmetics, home furnishings and other goods. The group operates from United States.

Primary SIC and add'l.: 5311

CIK No: 0000878079

Subsidiaries: Bon-Ton Distribution, Inc., Bonstores Holdings One, LLC, Bonstores Holdings Two, LLC, Bonstores Realty One, LLC, Bonstores Realty Two, LLC, Capital City Commons Realty, Inc., Carson Pirie Scott II, Inc., Carson Pirie Scott, Inc., Elder-Beerman Holdings, Inc., Elder-Beerman Operations, LLC, Elder-Beerman West Virginia, Inc., Herberger's Department Stores, LLC, McRIL, LLC, The Bon-Ton Department Stores, Inc., The Bon-Ton Giftco, Inc. 26 Subsidiaries included in the Index

Officers: Byron L. Bergren/61/Dir., CEO, Pres./$4,093,357.00, Anthony J. Buccina/Vice Chmn., Pres. - Merchandising/$3,747,096.00, Stephen R. Byers/Vice Chmn. - Stores, Operations, Private Brand, Planning, Allocation, Internet Marketing, Tim Grumbacher/68/Exec. Chmn./$2,533,930.00, David B. Zant/Vice Chmn. - Private Brands, Planning, Allocation, Internet Marketing/$1,340,720.00, Keith E. Plowman/CFO, Exec. VP, Principal Accounting Officer/$770,157.00, Dennis R. Clouser/Exec. VP - Human Resources, Edward P. Carroll/Exec. VP - Sales Promotion, Marketing, Robert E. Stern/VP, General Counsel, Sec., James M. Zamberlan/Exec. VP - Stores, Visual

Directors: Byron L. Bergren/61/Dir., CEO, Pres., Anthony J. Buccina/Vice Chmn., Pres. - Merchandising, Tim Grumbacher/68/Exec. Chmn., Shirley A. Dawe/61/Dir., Robert E. Salerno/60/Dir., Philip M. Browne/48/Dir., Lucinda M. Baier/43/Dir., Thomas K. Hernquist/50/Dir., Todd C. McCarty/42/Dir., Marsha M. Everton/56/Dir., Robert B. Bank/61/Dir., Michael L. Gleim/66/Dir.

Owners: M. Thomas Grumbacher Trust/1.42%, Marsha M. Everton, Byron L. Bergren/1.26%, Keith E. Plowman, Buckingham Capital Management Inc./9.06%, David B. Zant, Dimensional Fund Advisors LP/5.70%, Philip M. Browne, Robert E. Salerno, Michael L. Gleim/10.66%, Insiders, Michael L. Gleim, Henry F. Miller, Trafelet Capital Management, L.P./13.31%, Henry F. Miller/9.07% *(23 Owners included in Index)*

Financial Data: *Fiscal Year End:*01/28 *Latest Annual Data:* 2/3/2007

Year	Sales	Net Income
2007	$3,455,810,000	$46,883,000
2006	$1,307,595,000	$26,014,000
2005	$1,319,623,000	$20,162,000

Curr. Assets:	$914,809,000	**Curr. Liab.:**	$512,395,000	**P/E Ratio:**	26.09
Plant, Equip.:	$897,886,000	**Total Liab.:**	$1,788,403,000	**Indic. Yr. Divd.:**	$0.200
Total Assets:	$2,134,799,000	**Net Worth:**	$346,396,000	**Debt/ Equity:**	4.1370

Bonso Electronics International Inc

Unit 1106 - 1110, 11/f, Star House, 3 Salisbury Rd., Tsimshatsui, Kowloon; *PH:* 852-26055822;
http:// www.bonso.com; *Email:* info@bonso.com

General - Incorporation. British Virgin Islands
Employees 3,460
Auditor ....PricewaterhouseCoopers LLP
Stk Agt....U.S. Stock Transfer Corp
Counsel.... Schlueter & Associates P.C.
DUNS No. 68-611-7565

Stock- Price on:12/24/2007 ....$3.8
Stock Exchange....NDQ
Ticker Symbol....BNSO
Outstanding Shares 5,580,000
E.P.S....$0.00
Shareholders....NA

Business: The group operates through its with subsidiaries whose principle activities include designing, development, manufactuinge and marketing of electronic scales, weighing instruments and electronic consumer and health products such as blood pressure meters, electronic thermometers, bicycle computers, pedometers and joysticks. The group also develops and manufactures digital telecommunications products including 900mhz cordless telephone. The group's services include search and development, and repairing services. The group operates from United States.

Primary SIC and add'l.: 3829 3596 7629 8731 6719

CIK No: 0000846546

Subsidiaries: Bonso Electronics (Shenzhen) Company Limited, Bonso Electronics Limited, Bonso Investment Limited

Officers: Anthony So/65/Chmn., CEO, Pres., Kim Wah Chung/50/Dir., Dir. - Engineering, Research, Development, Henry F. Schlueter/57/Dir., Assist. Sec., Henry Wan Chong Ma/46/CFO, Sec., Treasurer

Directors: Anthony So/65/Chmn., CEO, Pres., Kim Wah Chung/50/Dir., Dir. - Engineering, Research, Development, Woo-Ping Fok/59/Dir., Stewart J. Jackson/72/Dir., Henry F. Schlueter/57/Dir., Assist. Sec.

Owners: Insiders/55.34%, Cathy Kit Teng Pang/2.64%, Henry F. Schlueter/1.32%, Royce & Associates LLC/5.32%, Anthony So/36.41%, Kim Wah Chung/3.67%, Douglas W. Moreland/8.99%, Woo-Ping Fok/2.03%, Stewart J. Jackson/9.27%

Financial Data: ***Fiscal Year End:***03/31 ***Latest Annual Data:*** 3/31/2006

Year	Sales	Net Income
2006	$64,543,000	$484,000
2005	$69,602,000	$3,350,000
2004	$74,707,000	$2,269,000

Curr. Assets:	$32,504,000	**Curr. Liab.:**	$15,657,000	**P/E Ratio:**	32.78
Plant, Equip.:	$12,834,000	**Total Liab.:**	$15,677,000	**Indic. Yr. Divd.:**	$0.050
Total Assets:	$49,479,000	**Net Worth:**	$33,802,000	**Debt/ Equity:**	NA

Bontan Corp Inc

47 Ave. Rd., Ste 200, Toronto, ON, M5N 2C5; ***PH:*** 1-877-859-5200;
http:// www.bontancorporation.com

General - Incorporation....Canada
Employees ....NA
Auditor ....Sloan Partners LLP
Stk Agt....Equity Transfer Services Inc
Counsel....NA
DUNS No.....NA

Stock- Price on:12/24/2007 ....$0.38
Stock Exchange....OTC
Ticker Symbol....BNTNF
Outstanding Shares ....NA
E.P.S....NA
Shareholders....NA

Business: The groups principle activity is to provide oil and gas exploration and development services. The group operates from Canada.

Primary SIC and add'l.: 2099

CIK No: 0001095435

Subsidiaries: 1388755 Ontario Inc., Bontan Diamond Corporation, Bontan Oil & Gas Corporation, Foodquest Inc.

Officers: Kam Shah/Chmn., CEO, CFO

Directors: Kam Shah/Chmn., CEO, CFO, Dean Bradley/Dir., Brett D. Rees/Dir.

Owners: Pinetree Resource Partnership/10.86%, Current Capital Corp./7.00%, Kam Shah, John Robinson, Terence Robinson, Damian Lee

Financial Data: ***Fiscal Year End:***03/31 ***Latest Annual Data:*** 03/31/2007

Year	Sales	Net Income
2007	$644,000	-$45,000
2006	$1,592,000	-$3,933,000
2005	$330,000	-$4,306,000

Curr. Assets:	$3,994,000	**Curr. Liab.:**	$102,000		
Plant, Equip.:	NA	**Total Liab.:**	$102,000	**Indic. Yr. Divd.:**	NA
Total Assets:	$3,994,000	**Net Worth:**	$3,892,000	**Debt/ Equity:**	NA

Boo Koo Holdings In

Formerly: Captech Financial Group Inc
10200 W 44th Ave., Ste. 210-e, Wheat Ridge, CO, 80033; ***PH:*** 1-303-432-7703;
http:// www.captec.com

General - Incorporation....FL
Employees ....NA
Auditor ....Larry Wolfe
Stk Agt....Interwest Transfer Company, Inc.
Counsel....NA
DUNS No.....NA

Stock- Price on:12/24/2007 ....NA
Stock Exchange....NA
Ticker Symbol....NA
Outstanding Shares ....NA
E.P.S....-$0.25
Shareholders....NA

Business: The group intends to provide investment banking, institutional sales and trading, specialised asset management & financial products & services. On 16-May-2003, the company changed its name from e-travel store network, inc.

Primary SIC and add'l.: 7375

CIK No: 0001201259

Officers: Daniel Y. Lee/CEO, Patrick L. Beach/Chmn., CEO, Redgie Green/54/Dir., Sec., Stephen C. Ruffini/CFO, COO, Sec., Joanna E. Zabriskie/MD, Kenneth S. Milne/MD, Jennifer L. Davis/Credit Mgr., Wesley F. Whiting/74/Dir., Pres.

Directors: Patrick L. Beach/Chmn., CEO, Wesley F. Whiting/74/Dir., Pres., Redgie Green/54/Dir., Sec.

Owners: John Raby/85.20%

Financial Data: ***Fiscal Year End:***12/31 ***Latest Annual Data:*** 12/31/2006

Year	Sales	Net Income
2006	NA	-$5,000
2005	NA	-$14,000
2004	NA	-$17,000

Curr. Assets:	NA	**Curr. Liab.:**	$32,000		
Plant, Equip.:	NA	**Total Liab.:**	$32,000	**Indic. Yr. Divd.:**	NA
Total Assets:	NA	**Net Worth:**	-$32,000	**Debt/ Equity:**	NA

Bookham Inc

2584 Junction Ave., San Jose, CA, 95134; ***PH:*** 1-408-383-1400; ***Fax:*** 1-408-919-6083;
http:// www.bookham.com; ***Email:*** sales@bookham.com

General - Incorporation ....DE
Employees....2,123
Auditor ....Ernst & Young LLP
Stk Agt....Bank of New York
Counsel...... Wilmer Cutler Pickering H & D LLP
DUNS No.....NA

Stock- Price on:12/24/2007 ....$2.1
Stock Exchange....NDQ
Ticker Symbol....BKHM
Outstanding Shares 83,270,000
E.P.S....-$0.93
Shareholders....NA

Business: The groups principle activities include designing, manufacturing and marketing optical components, modules and subsystems. The products of the group include transmitters, transceivers, receivers, amplifiers, pump laser chips, transponder modules and thin film filters. Customers served by the group include telecommunications systems vendors, data communications, military, aerospace, industrial and manufacturing industries. The group operates through two segments namely optics and, research and industrial. In the year 2006 the group acquired Avalon Photonics. Specific customers of the group include Nortel Networks, Huawei and Cisco. The group operates from Canada, the United States, China, Europe, Asia and the United Kingdom.

Primary SIC and add'l.: 3679 3661 3674 3679 3661 3674

CIK No: 0001110647

Subsidiaries: Avalon Photonics AG, Bookham (Canada) Inc., Bookham (Switzerland) AG, Bookham (US)Inc., Bookham International Ltd., Bookham Nominees Ltd., Bookham Technology (Shenzhen) (FFTZ)Co. Ltd., Bookham Technology KK, Bookham Technology plc, Focused Research Inc., Forthaven Limited, Globe Y. Technology Inc., Ignis Optics Inc., New Focus FSC Inc., New Focus GmbH 17 Subsidiaries included in the Index

Officers: Alain Couder/CEO, Pres., Thomas Kelley/General Counsel, Steve Abely/CFO/$696,655.00, Jim Haynes/COO, Acting Technology Officer/$630,662.00, Steve Turley/Chief Commercial Officer/$522,932.00, Adrian Meldrum/VP - Sales, Marketing/$531,304.00

Directors: Peter F. Bordui/Chmn., Joseph Cook/Dir., Arthur W. Porter/Dir., Lori Holland/Dir., David Simpson/Dir.

Owners: Jim Haynes, Insiders/2.10%, GLG Partners LP/7.20%, FMR Corp/5.00%, Stephen Abely, Stephen Turley, Adrian Meldrum, David Simpson, Lori Holland, Granahan Investment Management, Inc/5.00%, Tennenbaum Capital Partners, LLC/5.10%, Peter Bordui, Joseph Cook, Alain Couder, W. Arthur Porter

Financial Data: ***Fiscal Year End:***07/01 ***Latest Annual Data:*** 7/1/2006

Year	Sales	Net Income
2006	$231,649,000	-$87,497,000
2005	$200,256,000	-$247,972,000
2004	$79,763,000	-$67,371,000

Curr. Assets:	$226,320,000	**Curr. Liab.:**	$72,928,000		
Plant, Equip.:	$72,369,000	**Total Liab.:**	$137,435,000	**Indic. Yr. Divd.:**	NA
Total Assets:	$468,025,000	**Net Worth:**	$330,590,000	**Debt/ Equity:**	NA

Books A Million Inc

402 Industrial Ln., Birmingham, AL, 35211; ***PH:*** 1-205-942-3737; ***Fax:*** 1-205-942-6601;
http:// www.bamm.com

General - Incorporation ....DE
Employees....3,000
Auditor ....Deloitte & Touche LLP
Stk Agt....Bank of New York
Counsel....NA
DUNS No. 03-159-5309

Stock- Price on:12/24/2007 ....$16.11
Stock Exchange....NDQ
Ticker Symbol....BAMM
Outstanding Shares 16,820,000
E.P.S....NA
Shareholders....NA

Business: The group's principal activity is the retail distribution of books. The group operates bookstores and newsstands. The group also operates as a wholesaler of books to bookstores, wholesale clubs, supermarkets, department stores and mass merchandisers. The group operates in two segments: retail/wholesale trade: operates in the retail trade of book merchandise and group's distribution center's. Electronic commerce trade: operates business over the Internet. The trademarks include books-a-million, bam!, books & co., bookland, millionaire's club, sweet water press, thanks-a-million, night reader, read & save rebate, readables accessories for reader, kids-a-million, teachers first, the write-price and big fat coloring book. The group currently operates 202 retail bookstores including 164 superstores located in 18 states and the district of columbia in southeastern United States.

Primary SIC and add'l.: 5942 5192

CIK No: 0000891919

Subsidiaries: American Internet Service, Inc., American Wholesale Book Company, NetCentral, Inc.

Officers: Sandra B. Cochran/Dir., CEO, Pres., Sec./$1,186,066.00, Clyde B. Anderson/Exec. Chmn./$835,218.00, Terrance G. Finley/Pres. - Books, A, Million, Inc Merchandising Group/$746,318.00, Douglas G. Markham/CFO/$166,317.00

Directors: Clyde B. Anderson/Exec. Chmn., Albert C. Johnson/Dir., Ronald G. Bruno/Dir., Terry C. Anderson/Dir., William H. Rogers/Dir., Barry Mason/Dir.

Owners: Charles C. Anderson/12.50%, William H. Rogers, Terrance G. Finley/1.10%, Clyde B. Anderson, First Anderson Grandchildrens Trust, Fourth Anderson Grandchildrens Trust, Albert C. Johnson, Alexandra Ruth Anderson Irrevocable Trust, Terrence C. Anderson/9.50%, Third Anderson Grandchildrens Trust, Charles C. Anderson/12.50%, Bear Stearns Asset Management, Inc./11.10%, J. Barry Mason, Ronald G. Bruno, Second Anderson Grandchildrens Trust *(28 Owners included in Index)*

Financial Data: ***Fiscal Year End:***01/28 ***Latest Annual Data:*** 2/3/2007

Year	Sales	Net Income
2007	$520,416,000	$18,887,000
2006	$503,751,000	$13,067,000
2005	$475,226,000	$10,199,000

Curr. Assets:	$248,934,000	**Curr. Liab.:**	$131,197,000	**P/E Ratio:**	13.89
Plant, Equip.:	$51,471,000	**Total Liab.:**	$147,003,000	**Indic. Yr. Divd.:**	NA
Total Assets:	$304,037,000	**Net Worth:**	$157,034,000	**Debt/ Equity:**	0.0454

Boots & Coots Intl Well Control Inc

7908 N Sam Houston Pkwy. W, Ste. 500, Houston, TX, 77064; *PH:* 1-281-931-8884; *Fax:* 1-281-931-8392; *http://* www.bootsandcoots.com; *Email:* Venezuela@bncg.com

General - Incorporation .... DE
Employees 392
Auditor .UHY Mann Frankfort Stein & Lipp LLP
Stk Agt............ Mellon Investor Services LLC
Counsel............ Thompson, Knight, Brown Et Al
DUNS No. 83-788-8486

Stock- Price on:12/24/2007 .... $1.8
Stock Exchange .... AMEX
Ticker Symbol .... WEL
Outstanding Shares 75,030,000
E.P.S $0.182
Shareholders .... NA

Business: The group's principal activity is to provide oil and gas services. The group responds and controls oil and gas well emergencies including blowouts and well fires. The group operates in two segments: prevention and response. The prevention segment consists of non-event services designed to reduce the number and severity of critical well events to oil and gas operators. The response segment consists of personnel and equipment services provided during an emergency response. It has the capacity to supply the equipment, expertise and personnel necessary to contain the oil and hazardous materials spills and discharges and restore affected oil and gas wells to production. Through its proprietary insurance program wellsure(r). The group provides contracting and high-risk management services to the program's insured clients. It has a strategic alliance with halliburton energy services.

Primary SIC and add'l.: 1389

CIK No: 0000833845

Subsidiaries: Boots & Coots Canada, Ltd., Boots & Coots Services de, Boots & Coots Services, Inc., Boots & Coots/IWC, De Venezuela, S.A., HWC Limited, HWCES International, IWC Services, LLC, Mexico S. de R.L. de C.V., Overseas, Inc.

Officers: Jerry Winchester/CEO, Dir./$550,135.00, Bill Markus/Safety, Fire Specialist, Juan Moran/Sr. Well Control Specialist, Allen Duke/VP - Safeguard International, Ashley Evans/Administrative Assist. - Wellsure, Glenda Spence/Human Resources Specialist, Shelly Blest/Mgr. - Accounting, Amy Raymon/Administrative Assist. - Business Development, Sharon McCoy/Office Mgr., Liliana Quebodeaux/Administrative Assist., Dewitt H. Edwards/Exec. VP/$616,151.00, Gabriel Aldape/CFO/$445,873.00, Brian Keith/General Counsel, Larry Burleson/VP - Business Development, Andrew Schiro/Global Technical Support Operations, Sales *(36 Officers included in Index)*

Directors: Jerry Winchester/CEO, Dir., Douglas E. Swanson/Chmn., Robert S. Herlin/Dir., Kirk K. Krist/Dir., Richard W. Anderson/Dir., E. J. Dipaolo/Dir., Cindy B. Taylor/Dir., Robert G. Croyle/Dir., Bo Burris/Dir. - Wellsure

Owners: Robert S. Herlin, Insiders/2.60%, Dewitt H. Edwards, Richard W. Anderson, Robert G. Croyle, Oil States Energy Services, Inc./15.30%, Gabriel Aldape, Jerry L. Winchester/1.20%, E. J. DiPaolo, Kirk K. Krist, Don B. Cobb

Financial Data: **Fiscal Year End:**12/31 **Latest Annual Data:** 12/31/2006

Year	Sales	Net Income
2006	$97,030,000	$11,165,000
2005	$29,537,000	$2,779,000
2004	$24,175,000	-$248,000

Curr. Assets:	$52,347,000	**Curr. Liab.:**	$26,835,000		
Plant, Equip.:	$43,790,000	**Total Liab.:**	$62,595,000	**Indic. Yr. Divd.:**	NA
Total Assets:	$101,017,000	**Net Worth:**	$38,422,000	**Debt/ Equity:**	0.7521

Borders Group Inc

100 Phoenix Dr., Ann Arbor, MI, 48108; *PH:* 1-734-477-1100; *Fax:* 1-734-477-1285; *http://* www.bordersgroupinc.com; *Email:* ccare@bordersstores.com

General - Incorporation .... MI
Employees 16,600
Auditor .... Ernst & Young LLP
Stk Agt............ Computershare Trust Co
Counsel............ NA
DUNS No. 87-772-9368

Stock- Price on:12/24/2007 .... $19.56
Stock Exchange .... NYSE
Ticker Symbol .... BGP
Outstanding Shares 58,810,000
E.P.S .... -$5.04
Shareholders .... NA

Business: The group's principle activity is to operate book and music superstores, mall-based bookstores and other bookstores. The group operates superstores in the United Kingdom, Australia, Puerto Rico, Singapore and New Zealand.

Primary SIC and add'l.: 5963 5942 5735

CIK No: 0000940510

Subsidiaries: Bgi (uk) Limited, Bgp (uk) Limited, Books Etc Properties Limited, Borders (UK) Limited, Borders Australia PTY, Limited, Borders Books Ireland Limited, Borders Bookstore (M) SDN.BHD, Borders Development, Inc., Borders Fulfillment, Inc., Borders International Services, Inc., Borders Management, LLC, Borders New Zealand Limited, Borders Online, Inc., Borders Online, LLC, Borders Outlet, Inc. 30 Subsidiaries included in the Index

Officers: George L. Jones/Dir., CEO, Pres./$1,681,807.00, Cedric J. Vanzura/43/Exec. VP - Emerging Business - Technology, Chief Strategy Officer/$605,914.00, Edward W. Wilhelm/CFO, Exec. VP/$570,643.00, Daniel T. Smith/Sr. VP - Human Resources/$379,627.00, Thomas D. Carney/Sr. VP, General Counsel, Sec., Robert P. Gruen/Exec. VP - Merchandising, Marketing, Kenneth H. Armstrong/Exec. VP - Borders Stores US, Pamela Empie/Investor Relations Officer

Directors: George L. Jones/Dir., CEO, Pres., Larry Pollock/Non - Exec. Chmn., Joel J. Cohen/Dir., Donald G. Campbell/Dir., Amy B. Lane/Dir., Victor L. Lund/Dir., Brian T. Light/Dir., Edna Greene Medford/Dir., Michael Weiss/Dir.

Owners: Deutsche Bank AG/10.30%, Amy B. Lane, Victor L. Lund, Brian T. Light, Lawrence I. Pollock, Vincent E. Altruda, Edna Greene Medford, Donald G. Campbell, Michael Weiss, Dreman Value Management, L.L.C./12.90%, George L. Jones, Cedric J. Vanzura, Pershing Square Capital Management, L. P./11.60%, Insiders/1.70%, Daniel T. Smith *(20 Owners included in Index)*

Financial Data: **Fiscal Year End:**01/28 **Latest Annual Data:** 2/3/2007

Year	Sales	Net Income
2007	$4,113,500,000	-$151,300,000
2006	$4,079,200,000	$101,000,000
2005	$3,903,000,000	$131,900,000

Curr. Assets:	$1,723,600,000	**Curr. Liab.:**	$1,595,900,000		
Plant, Equip.:	$707,700,000	**Total Liab.:**	$1,969,400,000	**Indic. Yr. Divd.:**	$0.440
Total Assets:	$2,613,400,000	**Net Worth:**	$642,000,000	**Debt/ Equity:**	0.0086

Borgwarner Inc

3850 Hamlin Rd., Auburn Hills, MI, 48326; *PH:* 1-248-754-9200; *Fax:* 1-248-754-9397; *http://* www.bwauto.com

General - Incorporation .... DE
Employees 17,400
Auditor .... Deloitte & Touche LLP
Stk Agt .... Mellon Investor Services LLC
Counsel............ NA
DUNS No. 00-134-4191

Stock- Price on:12/24/2007 .... $85.1
Stock Exchange .... NYSE
Ticker Symbol .... BWA
Outstanding Shares 58,030,000
E.P.S .... -$0.068
Shareholders .... NA

Business: The group's principle activities include manufacturing and marketing engineered systems and components for vehicle power train applications. The groups products are sold to original equipment manufacturers of passenger cars, sport utility vehicles, trucks and commercial transportation products. The group operates from United States, Europe and Asia.

Primary SIC and add'l.: 3714

CIK No: 0000908255

Subsidiaries: AG Kuhnle, Kopp & Kausch, B 80 S.r.l., Beru AG, BERU Automotive Co., Ltd., BERU Corp., BERU Diesel Start Systems Pvt. Ltd., Beru Electronics Gmbh, BERU Eyquem SAS, BERU F1 Systems Ltd., BERU Italia S.r.l., BERU Japan Corp., BERU Mexico S.A. de C.V., BERU Microelectronica S.A., Beru Motorsport Holdings Ltd., Beru SAS 88 Subsidiaries included in the Index

Officers: Timothy M. Manganello/Chmn., CEO/$2,627,594.00, Jeffrey L. Obermayer/VP, Controller, Robin J. Adams/Dir., CFO, Exec. VP, Chief Administrative Officer, Chief Administrative Officer/$1,294,875.00, Kenneth P. Lamb/Mgr. - Investor Relations, Alfred Weber/VP/$1,041,208.00, Mark A. Perlick/VP - Advanced Product Technology, Jamal M. Farhat/CIO, VP, Angela D'Aversa/VP - Human Resources, Scott Gallett/Dir. - Global Sales, Emissions Systems, Mike McCabe/Product Mgr. - Morsetec, Drivetrain Products, Wolfgang Bullmer/VP - Engine Products, Morsetec, Engine Products, Keith Pierson/Dir. - Commercial Sales, Thermal Systems, Ulli Froehn/VP - Sales, Marketing, Turbochargers, Commercial Vehicles, Lou Bogart/VP - Sales, Marketing, 4WD Transfer Cases, Steve Gifford/VP - Sales, Marketing, Worldwide, Automatic Transmission Products, Components, Systems *(25 Officers included in Index)*

Directors: Timothy M. Manganello/Chmn., CEO, Richard O. Schaum/Dir., David T. Brown/Dir., Robin J. Adams/Dir., CFO, Exec. VP, Chief Administrative Officer, Chief Administrative Officer, Ernest J. Novak/Dir., Thomas T. Stallkamp/Dir., Phyllis Bonanno/Dir., Alexis P. Michas/Dir., Jere A. Drummond/Dir., Paul E. Glaske/Dir.

Owners: UBS AG/13.20%, Alfred Weber, Alexis P. Michas, AXA Financial, Inc./12.80%, Ernest J. Novak, Robin J. Adams, Richard O. Schaum, Roger J. Wood, Jere A. Drummond, Paul E. Glaske, Timothy M. Manganello, Insiders/1.20%, Phyllis O. Bonanno, Thomas T. Stallkamp, Cynthia Niekamp *(16 Owners included in Index)*

Financial Data: **Fiscal Year End:**12/31 **Latest Annual Data:** 12/31/2006

Year	Sales	Net Income
2006	$4,585,400,000	$211,600,000
2005	$4,293,800,000	$239,600,000
2004	$3,525,300,000	$218,300,000

Curr. Assets:	$1,437,500,000	**Curr. Liab.:**	$1,034,800,000	**P/E Ratio:**	23.19
Plant, Equip.:	$1,460,700,000	**Total Liab.:**	$2,546,500,000	**Indic. Yr. Divd.:**	$0.440
Total Assets:	$4,584,000,000	**Net Worth:**	$1,875,400,000	**Debt/ Equity:**	0.2979

Borland Software Corp

8303 N Mopac Expressway, Ste. A-300, Austin, TX, 78759; *PH:* 1-512-340-2200; *http://* www.borland.com

General - Incorporation .... DE
Employees 1,168
Auditor .... PricewaterhouseCoopers LLP
Stk Agt .... Mellon Investor Services LLC
Counsel............ NA
DUNS No. 10-276-0501

Stock- Price on:12/24/2007 .... $5.7
Stock Exchange .... NDQ
Ticker Symbol .... BORL
Outstanding Shares 72,700,000
E.P.S .... -$0.42
Shareholders .... NA

Business: The group's principal activity is to provide software development technologies and application infrastructure software. For the development of the software application, it offers jbuilder, delphi, kylix and c++builder products, as well as recently introduced teamsource dsp service. The deployment and integration products include borland enterprise server family of application servers, including appserver edition, visibroker edition and the entry level Web edition databases. To manage applications, it offers borland appcenter technology. The professional service organization provides consulting, training and support. On 08-Jan-2003, the group acquired remaining interest of starbase corporation and on 15-Jan-2003, togethersoft corporation.

Primary SIC and add'l.: 8748 7372 7379

CIK No: 0000853273

Subsidiaries: Borland (japan) Co., Ltd., Borland France Sarl, Borland Gmbh, Starbase Corporation

Officers: Tod Nielsen/Dir., CEO, Pres./$5,404,148.00, Jonathan Schoonmaker/Sr. VP - Human Resources, David Packer/Sr. VP - Field Operations, Rick Jackson/Chief Marketing Officer, Sr. VP - Corporate Strategy, Peter Morowski/Sr. VP - Research, Development/$468,819.00, Erik E. Prusch/CFO/$212,495.00, Gregory J. Wrenn/Sr. VP, General Counsel/$132,923.00

Directors: Tod Nielsen/Dir., CEO, Pres., John F. Olsen/Chmn., William K. Hooper/Dir., Michael T. Nevens/Dir., Charles F. Kane/Dir., Bryan Leblanc/Dir., Robert Tarkoff/Dir.

Owners: Michael T. Nevens, Erik E. Prusch, Gregory J. Wrenn, Tod Nielsen, John F. Olsen, Dimensional FundAdvisors LP/7.61%, Timothy J. Stevens, William K. Hooper, Insiders, Silver Point Capital, L.P./5.70%, Third Avenue Management LLC/11.87%, Robert M. Tarkoff, Wells Fargo& Company/5.45%, Kenneth R. Hahn, Squared Technology, LLC/6.64% *(19 Owners included in Index)*

Financial Data: **Fiscal Year End:**12/31 **Latest Annual Data:** 12/31/2006

Year	Sales	Net Income
2006	$304,660,000	-$51,953,000
2005	$276,743,000	-$29,832,000
2004	$309,548,000	$11,370,000

Curr. Assets:	$132,141,000	**Curr. Liab.:**	$142,730,000		
Plant, Equip.:	$11,176,000	**Total Liab.:**	$158,419,000	**Indic. Yr. Divd.:**	NA
Total Assets:	$443,899,000	**Net Worth:**	$285,480,000	**Debt/ Equity:**	NA

BOS Better Online Solutions Ltd

Beit Rabin, Teradyon Industrial Pk., Misgav, 20179; *PH:* 972-49907555; *http://* www.bosweb.com; *Email:* contactbos@boscom.com

General - Incorporation	Israel	**Stock**- Price on:12/24/2007	$2.7
Employees	53	Stock Exchange	NDQ
Auditor	Kost Forer Gabbay & Kasierer	Ticker Symbol	BOSC
Stk Agt	American Stock Transfer & Trust Co.	Outstanding Shares	6,520,000
Counsel	NA	E.P.S	-$0.17
DUNS No.	60-028-5977	Shareholders	NA

Business: The group's principle activties include designing, developing, manufacturing, selling and supporting connectivity and networking products primarily designed for use with IBM mid-range computers and for personal computers users communicating with IBM midrange computers. The group operates from United States.

Primary SIC and add'l.: 7372 7373

CIK No: 0001005516

Subsidiaries: Better On-Line Solutions Ltd., Better On-Line Solutions S.A.S, BOS Delaware Inc., BOScom Ltd, Dean Tech Technologies Associates, LLC., IP Gear Ltd., Lynk USA Inc., Odem Electronic Technologies 1992 Ltd., PacInfo, Quasar Communication Systems Ltd., Quasar Telecom (2004) Ltd., Ruby-Tech Inc, Texan corporation

Officers: Shmuel Koren/CEO, Pres., Shai Sadeh/Sr. VP - Software Division, Eyal Cohen/CFO, Sari Ellenberg/VP - Resources

Directors: Edouard Cukierman/Chmn., Andrea Mandel-Mantello/49/Dir., Avishai Gluck/36/Dir., Ronen Zavlik/47/Dir., Yael Ilan/59/Dir., Adi Raveh/Dir., Joel Adler/Dir., Jean-Marc Bally/37/Dir., Amir Ohad/Dir., Joshua Zoller/Dir., Dan Hoz/Dir.

Owners: Joel Adler, Jacob Neuhof, Touareg Consulting Ltd., Avidan Zelicovsky, Edouard Cukierman, Catalyst Fund, LP/19.73%, D.S Apex Holdings Ltd./8.87%

Financial Data: *Fiscal Year End:*12/31 *Latest Annual Data:* 12/31/2006

Year		Sales			Net Income
2006		$20,917,000			$92,000
2005		$27,053,000			-$3,605,000
2004		$8,282,000			-$2,053,000
Curr. Assets:	$12,540,000	**Curr. Liab.:**	$9,494,000	**P/E Ratio:**	6.88
Plant, Equip.:	$520,000	**Total Liab.:**	$12,180,000	**Indic. Yr. Divd.:**	NA
Total Assets:	$24,529,000	**Net Worth:**	$12,349,000	**Debt/ Equity:**	NA

Boss Holdings Inc

221 W 1st St., Kewanee, IL, 61443; *PH:* 1-309-852-2131; *Fax:* 1-309-852-0848; *http://* www.bossgloves.com; *Email:* bossmfg1893@bossgloves.com

General - Incorporation	DE	**Stock**- Price on:12/24/2007	$7.35
Employees	210	Stock Exchange	OTC
Auditor	McGladrey & Pullen LLP	Ticker Symbol	BSHI
Stk Agt	North American Transfer Co	Outstanding Shares	2,010,000
Counsel	NA	E.P.S	$1.89
DUNS No.	86-746-5304	Shareholders	NA

Business: The group's principal activities are to import and distribute protective wear including gloves, boots and rainwear products. The group operates under work gloves and protective wear and pet supplies divisions. It sells its products through mass merchandisers, hardware stores and other retailers in the United States and Canada. The group also sells its products directly to the commercial users in the agricultural, automotive, energy, construction and lumber industries. Pet products division imports and markets a line of pet supplies including dog and cat toys, collars, leads, chains and rawhide products in the United States.

Primary SIC and add'l.: 3199 2385 2381 5999

CIK No: 0000916802

Subsidiaries: Boss Balloon Company, Boss Canada Inc., Boss Manufacturing Company, Boss Manufacturing Holdings Inc., Boss Manufacturing Real Estate Inc., Boss Pet Products Inc., Galaxy Balloons Incorporated

Officers: Steven G. Pont/53/VP - Finance

Owners: Advisory Research, Inc./6.88%, Richard Bern/1.41%, Paul A. Novelly/5.64%, Ginarra Partners, LLC/28.73%, Louis G. Graziadio/13.24%, James F. Sanders, Perry A. Lerner/3.85%, Graziadio Family Trust/20.46%, Lee E. Mikles/1.35%, Insiders/67.30%

Financial Data: *Fiscal Year End:*10/31 *Latest Annual Data:* 12/30/2006

Year		Sales			Net Income
2006		$53,663,000			$3,894,000
2005		$54,150,000			$690,000
2004		$43,474,000			$3,723,000
Curr. Assets:	$27,122,000	**Curr. Liab.:**	$4,553,000	**P/E Ratio:**	4.18
Plant, Equip.:	$3,799,000	**Total Liab.:**	$9,763,000	**Indic. Yr. Divd.:**	NA
Total Assets:	$35,441,000	**Net Worth:**	$25,678,000	**Debt/ Equity:**	0.0709

Boston Beer Co Inc

1 Design Ctr. Pl., Ste. 850, Boston, MA, 02110; *PH:* 1-617-368-5000; *Fax:* 1-617-368-5500; *http://* www.samadams.com

General - Incorporation	MA	**Stock**- Price on:12/24/2007	$39.47
Employees	433	Stock Exchange	NYSE
Auditor	Ernst & Young LLP	Ticker Symbol	SAM
Stk Agt	Mellon Investor Services LLC	Outstanding Shares	14,310,000
Counsel	NA	E.P.S	$1.24
DUNS No.	83-710-5725	Shareholders	NA

Business: The group's principal activity is brewing and selling malt beverages and cider throughout the United States and in selected international markets. The group's brands include samuel adams Boston lager (R), sam adams light(tm) , hardcore(R) crisp hard cider, twisted tea (TM) etc. The beverages consist of beers with full-flavor and without adjuncts such as rice, corn, stabilizers and without water dilution. The group produced a total of 15 beers under the Boston beer group name, two cider products under the hardcore cider group name and two alternative malt beverage products under the twisted tea brewing group name during 2002. It owns breweries in cincinnati, Ohio and Boston, Massachusetts and contracts breweries in lehigh valley, Pennsylvania, tumwater, Washington and rochester, New York. The group sells its products through distributors to pubs, restaurants, grocery chains, package stores and other retail outlets.

Primary SIC and add'l.: 2082 5181

CIK No: 0000949870

Subsidiaries: BBC Brands, LLC, BBC Keg Company, LLC, Boston Beer Corporation, Boston Beer Corporation Canada Inc., Boston Brewing Company, Inc., SABC Investments Limited Partnership, SABC Realty, Ltd., Samuel Adams Brewery Company, Ltd.

Officers: Martin F. Roper/Dir., CEO, Pres./$2,431,431.00, James C. Koch/Chmn., Clerk/$572,287.00, William F. Urich/CFO, Treasurer/$754,865.00, Jeffrey D. White/50/COO/$466,963.00, Robert H. Hall/VP - Brand Development/$619,991.00, Frederick H. Grein/General Counsel, Thomas W. Lance/VP - Operations, John C. Geist/VP - Sales

Directors: Martin F. Roper/Dir., CEO, Pres., James C. Koch/Chmn., Clerk, Charles Joseph Koch/Dir., David A. Burwick/Dir., Pearson C. Cummin/Dir., Jay Margolis/Dir., Jean-Michel Valette/Dir.

Owners: James C. Koch/31.60%, William F. Urich, Jean-Michel Valette, Robert H. Hall, Renaissance Technologies Corp./7.30%, Martin F. Roper, Pearson C. Cummin, Barclays Global Investors, NA/10.80%, David A. Burwick, Insiders/35.20%, FMR Corp./5.00%, Jeffrey D. White, Charles J. Koch, Jay Margolis

Financial Data: *Fiscal Year End:*12/31 *Latest Annual Data:* 12/30/2006

Year		Sales			Net Income
2006		$285,431,000			$18,192,000
2005		$238,304,000			$15,559,000
2004		$217,208,000			$12,502,000
Curr. Assets:	$89,189,000	**Curr. Liab.:**	$28,739,000	**P/E Ratio:**	27.41
Plant, Equip.:	$26,525,000	**Total Liab.:**	$33,075,000	**Indic. Yr. Divd.:**	NA
Total Assets:	$119,054,000	**Net Worth:**	$85,979,000	**Debt/ Equity:**	NA

Boston Communications Group Inc

55 Middlesex Tpke., Bedford, MA, 01730; *PH:* 1-781-904-5000; *http://* www.bcgi.net

General - Incorporation	MA	**Stock**- Price on:12/24/2007	$1.55
Employees	504	Stock Exchange	NDQ
Auditor	Ernst & Young LLP	Ticker Symbol	BCGI
Stk Agt	Computershare Trust Co	Outstanding Shares	17,910,000
Counsel	Ropes & Gray LLP	E.P.S	-$0.7
DUNS No.	60-401-3631	Shareholders	NA

Business: The group's principal activity is to provide real-time subscriber management services to the wireless industry. The group utilizes its proprietary software applications and a carrier-class hosted environment to provide services to approximately 70 wireless carriers and resellers. The operations are divided into three segments. The prepaid wireless services segment serves national and regional carriers on a service bureau basis. The roaming services segment provides for roaming in the carriers' service areas for subscribers who are not covered under traditional roaming agreements. The prepaid systems business delivers prepaid wireless calling solutions on a turnkey basis primarily to international customers like cable and wireless, ss8 networks and nortel networks. Other customers of the group include verizon wireless, cingular wireless, at&t wireless etc. In Mar 2004, the group discontinued its roaming services segment.

Primary SIC and add'l.: 4813 4899

CIK No: 0001012887

Subsidiaries: BCG De Mexico, BCG Securities Corp., BCGI Billing Services, Inc., BCGI Wireless Private Limited, Cellular Express, Inc., PureSight Technologies, LTD, Wireless Funding Solutions, Inc.

Officers: Joseph Mullaney/CFO, Acting CEO, Timothy Donovan/General Counsel, Mike Palackdharry/VP - Sales, Patricia Travaline/Investor Relation Officer, James Anderson/Chief Sales Officer, Ersin Galioglu/COO

Directors: Brian E. Boyle/Vice Chmn., Paul J. Tobin/Chmn., Miguel Horta E Costa/Dir., Paul R. Gudonis/50/Dir., James A. Dwyer/Dir., Gerald Segel/Dir., Gerald McGowan/Dir.

Financial Data: *Fiscal Year End:*12/31 *Latest Annual Data:* 12/31/2005

Year		Sales			Net Income
2005		$103,858,000			-$54,162,000
2004		$107,928,000			$17,211,000
2003		$103,191,000			$16,144,000
Curr. Assets:	$99,089,000	**Curr. Liab.:**	$84,477,000		
Plant, Equip.:	$53,283,000	**Total Liab.:**	$88,945,000	**Indic. Yr. Divd.:**	NA
Total Assets:	$175,291,000	**Net Worth:**	$86,346,000	**Debt/ Equity:**	NA

Boston Life Sciences Inc

85 Main St., Hopkinton, MA, 01748; *PH:* 1-508-497-2360; *http://* www.bostonlifesciences.com

General - Incorporation	DE	**Stock**- Price on:12/24/2007	NA
Employees	22	Stock Exchange	NA
Auditor	PricewaterhouseCoopers LLP	Ticker Symbol	NA
Stk Agt	Continental Stock Transfer & Trust Co	Outstanding Shares	NA
Counsel	Ballard Spahr Andrews & Ingersoll LLP	E.P.S	-$1.6
DUNS No.	82-751-9448	Shareholders	NA

Business: The group's principal activity is the research and development of novel therapeutic and diagnostic products to treat chronic debilitating diseases such as cancer and central nervous system disorders. Still in its development stages, the group has eleven technologies in its product portfolio, which were invented or discovered by researchers working at the harvard university and its affiliated hospitals and has been exclusively licensed to the group. They include the altropane(tm) imaging agent, a small molecule being developed as a diagnostic for Parkinson's disease and attention deficit hyperactivity disorder. The group owns the exclusive license for the use of troponin to treat a variety of angiogenic diseases. The group has acquired the rights for inosine and af-1, which are nerve growth factors, specifically promoting axon outgrowth in cns cells.

Primary SIC and add'l.: 2834 8731

CIK No: 0000094784

Subsidiaries: Acumed Pharmaceuticals, Inc., Ara Pharmaceuticals, Inc., Boston Life Sciences International, Inc., Coda Pharmaceuticals, Inc., Neurobiologics, Inc., ProCell Pharmaceuticals, Inc.

Officers: Peter G. Savas/Chmn., CEO/$1,160,790.00, Noel J. Cusack/Sr. VP - Preclinical Development, Frank Bobe/Exec. VP, Chief Business Officer, Susan M. Flint/Sr. VP - Drug Development, Mark Hurtt/Chief Medical Officer, Kenneth L. Rice/CFO, Exec. VP - Finance, Administration, In-House Counsel/$737,645.00, Mark J. Pykett/COO, Pres./$761,621.00, Richard M. Thorn/Sr. VP - Program Operations, James R. Weston/Sr. VP - Regulatory Affairs, Quality

Directors: Peter G. Savas/Chmn., CEO, John T. Preston/Dir., Michael J. Mullen/49/Dir., Robert S. Langer/60/Dir., William L.S. Guiness/68/Dir., Joseph R. Bianchine/Member - Scientific Advisory Board, Henry Brem/Dir., Gary Frashier/Dir.

Owners: Peter G. Savas/3.05%, Michael J. Mullen, John T. Preston, Robert L. Gipson/24.67%, Robert S. Langer, Gary E. Frashier, Arthur Koenig/4.52%, Kenneth L. Rice/1.60%, Mark J. Pykett/1.58%, Insiders/7.59%, Thomas L. Gipson/25.06%, William Guinness, Henry Brem

Financial Data: *Fiscal Year End:*12/31 *Latest Annual Data:* 12/31/2006

Year	Sales	Net Income
2006	NA	-$26,355,000
2005	NA	-$11,501,000
2004	NA	-$11,251,000

Curr. Assets: $1,851,000 **Curr. Liab.:** $18,705,000
Plant, Equip.: $136,000 **Total Liab.:** $18,941,000 **Indic. Yr. Divd.:** NA
Total Assets: $2,369,000 **Net Worth:** -$16,572,000 **Debt/ Equity:** NA

Boston Private Financial Holdings Inc

10 Post Office Sq., Boston, MA, 02109; *PH:* 1-617-912-1900; *Fax:* 1-617-912-4550; *http://* www.bostonprivate.com; *Email:* mchambers@bostonprivate.com

General - Incorporation .... MA
Employees 1,031
Auditor .... KPMG LLP
Stk Agt..... Computershare Investor Services LLC
Counsel .... NA
DUNS No. 61-163-0435

Stock- Price on:12/24/2007 .... $28.26
Stock Exchange .... NDQ
Ticker Symbol .... BPFH
Outstanding Shares 37,040,000
E.P.S $1.23
Shareholders .... NA

Business: The group's principal activity is to provide commercial banking and investment management services. The group acts as holding company for Boston Private Bank, Borel Private Bank and Trust Company, Westfield Capital Management Company, Sand Hill Advisors Inc, Boston Private Value Investors and Rinet Company. Boston Private Bank provides banking, investment, automated teller machine and fiduciary products and services to high net worth individuals, their families and businesses. Borel offers banking services including demand, savings and time deposits and making commercial, real estate and consumer loans. Westfield, BVPI and Sand Hill provide investment management services. Rinet provides fee-only financial planning, tax planning and investment management services to high net worth individuals and their families. The group acquired Dalton, Greiner, Hartman, Maher & Co, LLC on 06-Feb-2004 and First State Bancorp on 17-Feb-2004.

Primary SIC and add'l.: 6021 6712

CIK No: 0000821127

Subsidiaries: Borel Private Bank& Trust Company, Boston Private Bank& Trust Company, Boston Private Value Investors Inc., Dalton, Greiner, Hartman,& Maher& Co. LLC, First Private Bank& Trust, Gibraltar Private Bank& Trust Company, KLS Professional Advisors Group LLC, RINET Company LLC, Sand Hill Advisors Inc, Westfield Capital Management Company LLC

Officers: Timothy L. Vaill/Chmn., CEO/$3,304,003.00, Mark D. Thompson/Dir., CEO - Boston Private Bank, Trust Company, Eugene S. Colangelo/Chmn. - Boston Private Bank, Trust Company, Patricia McGovern/Dir. - Boston Private Financial Holdings, Inc, Michael F. Schiavo/Dir. - Boston Private Financial Holdings, Inc, Alan D. Solomont/Dir. - Boston Private Financial Holdings, Inc, Margaret W. Chambers/48/Exec. VP, General Counsel, James D. Dawson/Pres., COO - Boston Private Bank, Trust Company, James C. Brown/Exec. VP, Chief Lending Officer Commercial Banking - Boston Private Bank, Trust Company, James D. Henderson/Exec. VP - Investment Management, Boston Private Bank, Trust Company, Amy E. Hunter/Exec. VP, Dir. - Marketing, Boston Private Bank, Trust Company, Pilar Pueyo/Sr. VP - Human Resources, Boston Private Bank, Trust Company, Anne L. Randall/Exec. VP, CFO - Boston Private Bank, Trust Company, George G. Schwartz/Exec. VP, Treasurer - Deposit, Cash Management, Boston Private Bank, Trust Company, John J. Sullivan/Exec. VP - Residential Lending, Boston Private Bank, Trust Company *(30 Officers included in Index)*

Directors: Timothy L. Vaill/Chmn., CEO, Allen L. Sinai/68/Dir., Peter C. Bennett/69/Dir., Walter M. Pressey/63/Dir., Pres., William J. Shea/60/Dir., Lynn Thompson Hoffman/59/Dir., Richard I. Morris/Dir., Stephen M. Waters/Dir.

Owners: J. H. Cromarty, Insiders/4.10%, Robert J. Whelan, Jonathan H. Parker, William J. Shea, Walter M. Pressey, Timothy L. Vaill/1.34%, FMR Corp/9.58%, Herbert S. Alexander, Eugene S. Colangelo, Kathleen M. Graveline, Richard I. Morris, Stephen M. Waters, Lynn Thompson Hoffman, Barclays Global Investors, NA,/5.07% *(18 Owners included in Index)*

Financial Data: **Fiscal Year End:**12/31 **Latest Annual Data:** 12/31/2006

Year	Sales	Net Income
2006	NA	NA
2005	NA	NA
2004	NA	NA

Curr. Assets: $290,557,000 **Curr. Liab.:** $4,166,400,000 **P/E Ratio:** 22.98
Plant, Equip.: $35,641,000 **Total Liab.:** $5,128,347,000 **Indic. Yr. Divd.:** $0.360
Total Assets: $5,763,544,000 **Net Worth:** $635,197,000 **Debt/ Equity:** 0.3593

Boston Properties Inc

111 Huntington Ave., Boston, MA, 02199; *PH:* 1-617-236-3300; *Fax:* 1-617-536-5087; *http://* www.bostonproperties.com

General - Incorporation .... DE
Employees 650
Auditor .... PricewaterhouseCoopers LLP
Stk Agt .... Computershare Trust Co
Counsel .... NA
DUNS No. .... NA

Stock- Price on:12/24/2007 .... $109.44
Stock Exchange .... NYSE
Ticker Symbol .... BXP
Outstanding Shares 119,000,000
E.P.S $10.62
Shareholders .... NA

Business: The groups principle activities include owing and developing office properties. In the year 2006, the group acquired Kingstowne Towne Center, Four and Five Cambridge Center and the Cambridge Center East Garage. The group operates 127 office properties, two hotels and two retail properties in the United States. The groups quarterly revenue for September 2007 was 371.51 millions of USD.

Primary SIC and add'l.: 7011 6798

CIK No: 0001037540

Subsidiaries: 101 Carnegie Center Associates, 17M Associates, 191 Spring Street Trust, 206 Associates Limited Partnership, 210 Associates Limited Partnership, 211 Associates Limited Partnership, 30 Shattuck Road LLC, 40-46 Harvard Street Trust, 90 Church Street Limited Partnership, 91 Hartwell Avenue Trust, 92 Hayden Avenue Trust, Big Apple Associates Limited Partnership, Billerica Road LLC, Billerica Road Member LLC, Boston Properties Limited Partnership 165 Subsidiaries included in the Index

Officers: Edward H. Linde/Dir., CEO, Pres./$3,590,287.00, Douglas T. Linde/CFO, Pres., Treasurer/$2,224,937.00, Mitchell E. Norville/COO, Exec. VP/$1,746,246.00, Raymond A. Ritchey/Exec. VP, Head - Washington, DC Office, National Dir. - Acquisitions, Development/$2,271,217.00, Peter D. Johnston/Sr. VP, Regional Mgr. - Washington, DC Office, Bryan J. Koop/Sr. VP, Regional Mgr. - Boston Office, Mitchell S. Landis/Sr. VP, Regional Mgr. - Princeton Office, Robert E. Pester/Sr. VP, Regional Mgr. - San Francisco Office, Robert E. Selsam/Sr. VP, Regional Mgr. - New York Office, Goodwin Procter/Corporate Counsel, Kathleen Dichiara/Mgr. - Investor Relations, Frank D. Burt/49/Sec., Arthur S. Flashman/46/VP, Controller

Directors: Edward H. Linde/Dir., CEO, Pres., Mortimer B. Zuckerman/Chmn., Lawrence S. Bacow/Dir., Zoe Baird/Dir., William Daley/Dir., Carol B. Einiger/Dir., Alan J. Patricof/Dir., Richard E. Salomon/Dir., Martin Turchin/Dir., David A. Twardock/Dir.

Owners: Richard E. Salomon, Zo Baird, Alan J. Patricof, Edward H. Linde/6.53%, Raymond A. Ritchey, Cohen& Steers Capital Management, Inc./6.69%, Mitchell E. Norville, Martin Turchin, Barclays Global Investors, NA/5.45%, Lawrence S. Bacow, Morgan Stanley/5.29%, The Vanguard Group/6.45%, Douglas T. Linde, Cohen& Steers, Inc./6.73%, William M. Daley *(20 Owners included in Index)*

Financial Data: **Fiscal Year End:**12/31 **Latest Annual Data:** 12/31/2006

Year	Sales	Net Income
2006	$1,477,586,000	$873,635,000
2005	$1,437,635,000	$438,292,000
2004	$1,400,465,000	$284,017,000

Curr. Assets: $1,110,177,000 **Curr. Liab.:** $1,008,267,000
Plant, Equip.: $8,160,403,000 **Total Liab.:** $6,471,796,000 **Indic. Yr. Divd.:** $2.720
Total Assets: $9,695,022,000 **Net Worth:** $3,223,226,000 **Debt/ Equity:** 1.3863

Boston Restaurant Assoc Inc

999 Broadway Way, Ste. 400, Saugus, MA, 01906; *PH:* 1-781-231-7575

General - Incorporation .... DE
Employees 425
Auditor .... BDO Seidman LLP
Stk Agt .... Computershare Investor Services LLC
Counsel .... NA
DUNS No. 61-650-1391

Stock- Price on:12/24/2007 .... NA
Stock Exchange .... OTC
Ticker Symbol .... BRAI
Outstanding Shares .... NA
E.P.S $0.01
Shareholders .... NA

Business: The group's principal activity is to operate a chain of eighteen restaurants and twelve fast service pizzerias. The restaurants are operated under the trademark pizzeria regina and polcari's north end. The pizzeria regina restaurants feature the group's signature product, its premium neapolitan style thin crust pizza, prepared in gas-fired brick ovens. Of the fourteen pizzeria regina restaurants, thirteen are food court kiosks. The polcari's north end restaurants are full service Italian/american, family style restaurants.

Primary SIC and add'l.: 6794 5812

CIK No: 0000926295

Financial Data: **Fiscal Year End:**04/25 **Latest Annual Data:** 04/30/2006

Year	Sales	Net Income
2006	$23,535,000	$298,000
2005	$22,629,000	-$429,000
2004	$23,290,000	-$3,437,000

Curr. Assets: $1,627,000 **Curr. Liab.:** $2,802,000
Plant, Equip.: $3,310,000 **Total Liab.:** $6,336,000 **Indic. Yr. Divd.:** NA
Total Assets: $6,391,000 **Net Worth:** $55,000 **Debt/ Equity:** NA

Boston Scientific Corp

One Boston Scientific Pl, Natick, MA, 01760; *PH:* 1-508-650-8000; *http://* www.bsci.com

General - Incorporation .... DE
Employees 28,600
Auditor .... Ernst & Young LLP
Stk Agt .... Mellon Investor Services LLC
Counsel .... NA
DUNS No. 02-171-7889

Stock- Price on:12/24/2007 .... $15.99
Stock Exchange .... NYSE
Ticker Symbol .... BSX
Outstanding Shares 1,480,000,000
E.P.S $0.40
Shareholders .... NA

Business: The groups principle activity is to provide medical devices. The groups products include convoy (R) Advanced Delivery Sheath and PeriVac(TM) Pericardiocentesis Kits. The group operates from United States.

Primary SIC and add'l.: 3841

CIK No: 0000885725

Subsidiaries: Advanced Bionics Corporation, Advanced Bionics GmbH, Advanced Bionics Japan Company Ltd., Advanced Bionics NV, Advanced Bionics SARL, Advanced Bionics SL, Advanced Bionics UK Ltd., Advanced Stent Technologies, Inc., AMS Medinvent S.A., B.I.C. Insurance Company of Vermont, Inc., Boston Scientific (2001) Ltd., Boston Scientific (Malaysia) Sdn. Bhd., Boston Scientific (South Africa) (Proprietary) Limited, Boston Scientific (Thailand) Ltd., Boston Scientific (UK) Limited 114 Subsidiaries included in the Index

Officers: James R. Tobin/Dir., CEO, Pres./$8,360,566.00, Jim Tobin/Dir., CEO, Pres., Gerard Wallace/Pres. - Europe, Samuel R. Leno/Exec. VP - Finance - Information Systems, CFO, David N. McClellan/Pres. - Oncology, David McFaul/Pres. - Asia Pacific, Japan, John B. Pedersen/Pres. - Peripheral Interventions, Michael P. Phalen/Pres. - Endoscopy, William F. McConnell/Sr. VP - Sales - Marketing, Administration CRM, Lucia Luce Quinn/Exec. VP - Human Resources, Paul W. Sandman/Exec. VP, Sec., General Counsel/$2,859,657.00, Lisa D. Earnhardt/Pres. - Cardiac Surgery, Joseph M. Fitzgerald/Pres. - Electrophysiology, Eric Goorno/Pres. - Urology, Gynecology, Jeffrey H. Greiner/Pres. - Neuromodulation Group *(31 Officers included in Index)*

Directors: James R. Tobin/Dir., CEO, Pres., Jim Tobin/Dir., CEO, Pres., Peter M. Nicholas/Chmn., Co - Founder, Raymond J. Elliott/Dir., Joel L. Fleishman/Dir., N. J. Nicholas/Dir., Uwe E. Reinhardt/Dir., Marye Anne Fox/Dir., John E. Pepper/Dir., Ursula M. Burns/Dir., Kristina M. Johnson/Dir., Nancy-Ann Deparle/Dir., John E. Abele/Co - Founder, Dir., Ray J. Groves/Dir., Ernest Mario/Dir. *(16 Directors included in Index)*

Owners: Kristina M. Johnson, Paul A. LaViolette, Paul W. Sandman, Promerica, L.P/5.50%, Ernest Mario, Ursula M. Burns, Insiders/11.00%, Ray J. Groves, Uwe E. Reinhardt, Joel L. Fleishman, John E. Abele/4.00%, Marye Anne Fox, Lawrence C. Best, Fredericus A. Colen, Nancy-Ann DeParle *(20 Owners included in Index)*

Financial Data: **Fiscal Year End:**12/31 **Latest Annual Data:** 12/31/2006

Year	Sales	Net Income
2006	$7,821,000,000	-$3,577,000,000
2005	$6,283,000,000	$628,000,000
2004	$5,624,000,000	$1,062,000,000

Curr. Assets: $4,901,000,000 **Curr. Liab.:** $2,630,000,000 **P/E Ratio:** 39.98
Plant, Equip.: $1,726,000,000 **Total Liab.:** $15,798,000,000 **Indic. Yr. Divd.:** NA
Total Assets: $31,096,000,000 **Net Worth:** $15,298,000,000 **Debt/ Equity:** 0.5722

Botetourt Bankshares Inc

19747 Main St., Buchanan, VA, 24066; *PH:* 1-540-473-1173; *Fax:* 1-540-473-3936;
http:// www.bankofbotetourtonline.com

General - Incorporation	VA	*Stock*- Price on:12/24/2007	$41
Employees	85	Stock Exchange	OTC
Auditor	Larrowe & Co. Plc	Ticker Symbol	BORT
Stk Agt.	Botetourt Bankshares Inc	Outstanding Shares	1,240,000
Counsel	NA	E.P.S.	$2.70
DUNS No.	NA	Shareholders	NA

Business: The group's principal activity is to provide banking services including checking and savings accounts; commercial, installment, mortgage and personal loans; safe deposit boxes and other associated services. The group also provides lending service: real estate, commercial, agricultural and consumer loans. The bank currently operates seven offices in three counties of Virginia. The group wholly operates in the United States.

Primary SIC and add'l.: 6712 6021

CIK No: 0001172229

Subsidiaries: Buchanan Service Corporation

Officers: Watts H. Steger/Chmn., CEO/$354,841.00, Lyn G. Hayth/49/Dir., Sec./$181,697.00, Vicky M. Wheeler/VP - Human Resources, Joanne B. Snyder/Retail Banking Officer, Michelle A. Alexander/CFO/$88,579.00, Duaine P. Fitzgerald/Sr. VP/$120,147.00

Directors: Watts H. Steger/Chmn., CEO, Bruce D. Patterson/57/Dir., Joyce R. Kessinger/55/Dir., Lindsey F. Stinnett/67/Dir., John B. Williamson/53/Dir., Lyn G. Hayth/49/Dir., Sec., Gerald A. Marshall/69/Dir., Tommy L. Moore/58/Dir., Edgar K. Baker/63/Dir.

Owners: Norma P. Wells Marital Trust/0.44%, Lyn G. Hayth, The Norma P. Wells Irrevocable Insurance Trust/1.86%, Norma P. Wells Living Trust/4.73%, Watts H. Steger/4.11%, Insiders/11.19%, Gerald A. Marshall/1.21%, Bruce D. Patterson, Edgar K. Baker, John B. Williamson, Joyce R. Kessinger, Tommy L. Moore/1.24%, Lindsey F. Stinnett/1.37%

Financial Data: Fiscal Year End:12/31 *Latest Annual Data:* 03/31/2007

Year	Sales	Net Income
2007	NA	NA
2006	NA	NA
2005	$15,799,000	$3,210,000

Curr. Assets:	$8,421,000	*Curr. Liab.:*	$229,513,000	*P/E Ratio:*	14.75
Plant, Equip.:	$5,626,000	*Total Liab.:*	$230,759,000	*Indic. Yr. Divd.:*	NA
Total Assets:	$254,382,000	*Net Worth:*	$23,623,000	*Debt/ Equity:*	NA

Bottomline Home Loan Inc

201 E Huntington Dr., Ste. 202, Monrovia, CA, 91016; *PH:* 1-800-520-5626

General - Incorporation	NV	*Stock*- Price on:12/24/2007	NA
Employees	NA	Stock Exchange	OTC
Auditor	Mendoza Berger & Co LLP	Ticker Symbol	BOTM
Stk Agt.	Computershare Investor Services LLC	Outstanding Shares	NA
Counsel	NA	E.P.S.	NA
DUNS No.	NA	Shareholders	NA

Business: The groups principle activities include originating and selling residential mortgage loans. The groups products include Fannie Mae eligible loans, alternate "A" loans, non-prime loans, home equity and second mortgage loans, construction loans and bridge loans. The group operates from United States.

Primary SIC and add'l.: NA

CIK No: 0001017130

Subsidiaries: Bottomline Mortgage, Inc

Officers: Buster Williams/54/Dir., CEO, CFO, Pres., David Williams/32/VP, Dir.

Directors: Buster Williams/54/Dir., CEO, CFO, Pres., David Williams/32/VP, Dir.

Owners: Buster Williams/85.00%, David J. Williams/6.00%, Insiders/91.00%

Bottomline Technologies (DE) Inc

325 Corporate Dr., Portsmouth, NH, 03801; *PH:* 1-603-436-0700; *Fax:* 1-603-436-0300;
http:// www.bottomline.com; *Email:* info@bottomline.com

General - Incorporation	DE	*Stock*- Price on:12/24/2007	$12.16
Employees	481	Stock Exchange	NDQ
Auditor	Ernst & Young LLP	Ticker Symbol	EPAY
Stk Agt.	Computershare Investor Services LLC	Outstanding Shares	24,510,000
Counsel	Hale & Dorr LLP	E.P.S.	-$0.27
DUNS No.	NA	Shareholders	NA

Business: The group's principal activity is to provide financial resource management solutions to companies. It offers its services to financial services, health care, technology, communications, education, media, manufacturing and government. The software products and services enable organizations to more effectively make and collect payments, send and receive invoices and conduct electronic banking. It offers software designed to run on-site at the customer's location and hosted solutions. The group also provides professional services for installation, training, consulting, product enhancement and related equipment and supplies. On 18-Sep-2003 the group acquired create! form international, inc.

Primary SIC and add'l.: 3577 7379 7371

CIK No: 0001073349

Subsidiaries: Bottomline Technologies Europe Limited, Bottomline Technologies Limited, Bottomline Transactional Services Limited, CLS Research Pty Ltd., Create!form International Pty Ltd., Create!form International, Inc., Create!form US, Inc., Fleet Street (US) Corp., HMSL Group, Ltd., Tranmit Plc., Visibillity LLC.

Officers: Robert A. Eberle/Dir., CEO, Pres., Craig Jones/VP, GM - Global Banking, Finance, Andrew Mintzer/Sr. VP - Product Strategy, Delivery, Paul Fannon/MD - Transactional Services, Europe, Eric Campbell/CTO, Kevin Donovan/CFO, Nigel Savory/MD - Europe, Rick Bell/VP, GM - Financial Process Solutions, North America, Chris Peck/Group Sales Dir. - Europe, Peter S. Fortune/COO, Pres. - Bottomline Europe, Tom Gaillard/VP, GM - Transactional Services, North America

Directors: Robert A. Eberle/Dir., CEO, Pres., Joseph L. Mullen/Chmn., John W. Barter/Dir., Joseph L. Barry/Dir., James L. Loomis/Dir., Michael J. Curran/Dir., Garen K. Staglin/Dir., James W. Zilinski/Dir., Daniel M. McGurl/Dir., Jeffrey C. Leathe/Dir.

Owners: Jeffrey C. Leathe, James L. Loomis/2.09%, Insiders/11.56%, T. Rowe Price Associates, Inc./11.54%, Peter S. Fortune/1.06%, Kevin M. Donovan, James W. Zilinski, Daniel M. McGurl/1.35%, Garen K. Staglin, BlackRock, Inc./11.17%, Joseph L. Barry, Joseph L. Mullen/3.01%, Michael J. Curran, Royce& Associates, LLC/5.87%, Robert A. Eberle/2.47%

Financial Data: Fiscal Year End:06/30 *Latest Annual Data:* 06/30/2007

Year	Sales	Net Income
2007	$118,335,000	-$7,030,000
2006	$101,665,000	-$1,834,000
2005	$96,505,000	$5,888,000

Curr. Assets:	$106,404,000	*Curr. Liab.:*	$34,530,000		
Plant, Equip.:	$7,106,000	*Total Liab.:*	$39,226,000	*Indic. Yr. Divd.:*	NA
Total Assets:	$175,834,000	*Net Worth:*	$136,608,000	*Debt/ Equity:*	NA

Boulder Specialty Brands Inc

115 W Century Rd., Ste. 260, Paramus, NJ, 07652; ; *http://* www.boulderspecialtybrands.com

General - Incorporation	DE	*Stock*- Price on:12/24/2007	$9.93
Employees	NA	Stock Exchange	NDQ
Auditor	Ehrhardt Keefe Steiner& Hottman PC	Ticker Symbol	SMBL
Stk Agt.	Continental Stock Transfer & Trust Co	Outstanding Shares	15,950,000
Counsel	NA	E.P.S.	-$3.27
DUNS No.	NA	Shareholders	NA

Business: The groups principal activity is to marketing of functional food products. The group products include Smart Balance(R) and Earth Balance(R). The group marketed its products under the trade names Smart Balance(R) and Earth Balance(R). The group operates from the United States.

Primary SIC and add'l.: 2000

CIK No: 0001331301

Subsidiaries: BSB Acquisition Co., Inc.

Officers: Stephen B. Hughes/Chmn., CEO, James E. Lewis/Vice Chmn. - Principal Financial, Accounting Officer, Michael R. OBrien/Sr. Advisor, John T. Stofko/Senoir Advisor

Directors: Stephen B. Hughes/Chmn., CEO, Robert S. Gluck/Vice Chmn., James E. Lewis/Vice Chmn. - Principal Financial, Accounting Officer, Robert J. Gillespie/Dir., William E. Hooper/Dir., Gerald J. Laber/63/Dir., Robert F. McCarthy/Dir.

Owners: James E. Lewis, Sunset Oasis Trust No. 3, Robyn L. Duda, Stephen B. Hughes, Robert S. Gluck, Caroline Elise Hughes Irrevocable Trust, Grace Warfield Hughes, Earl E. Hoellen, Sunset Oasis Trust No. 2, Robert J. Gillespie and Westmount Investments, L.L.C., Sunset Oasis Trust No. 1, Jeffrey R. Nieder, Henry Thomas Hughes Irrevocable Trust, Robert F. McCarthy, Peter Mazula *(26 Owners included in Index)*

Financial Data: Fiscal Year End:12/31 *Latest Annual Data:* 12/31/2006

Year	Sales	Net Income
2006	NA	-$13,779,000
2005	NA	-$637,000

Curr. Assets:	$102,693,000	*Curr. Liab.:*	$40,863,000		
Plant, Equip.:	NA	*Total Liab.:*	$60,957,000	*Indic. Yr. Divd.:*	NA
Total Assets:	$106,284,000	*Net Worth:*	$45,327,000	*Debt/ Equity:*	NA

Bovie Medical Corp

734 Walt Whitman Rd., Melville, NY, 11747; *PH:* 1-631-421-5452; *Fax:* 1-631-421-5821;
http:// www.boviemedical.com; *Email:* info@boviemedical.com

General - Incorporation	DE	*Stock*- Price on:12/24/2007	$6.3999
Employees	161	Stock Exchange	AMEX
Auditor	Bloom & Co. LLP	Ticker Symbol	BVX
Stk Agt.	Manhattan Transfer & Registrar	Outstanding Shares	15,480,000
Counsel	NA	E.P.S.	$0.17
DUNS No.	10-122-3287	Shareholders	NA

Business: The group's principal activities are to manufacture and market medical products and develop related technologies. The products are marketed through the group's subsidiary, aaron medical industries, inc. The group also manufactures a variety of specialty lighting instruments for use in ophthalmology, general surgery, hip replacement surgery and for the placement of endotracheal tubes. Additionally, the group has original equipment manufacturing agreements with other medical device manufacturers. The products manufactured by the group include battery operated cauteries, electrosurgery products, bovie/aaron 800 and 900 high frequency desiccators, bovie/aaron 950. The products also include bovie/aaron 1250, bovie/aaron 2250, new generators, battery operated medical lights and nerve locator stimulator . The group's products are marketed under the brand name bovie/aaron in the United States, Europe and other countries.

Primary SIC and add'l.: 3841 5049 3679 3821 3641

CIK No: 0000719135

Subsidiaries: Aaron Medical Industries, Inc.

Officers: Andrew Makrides/Chmn., CEO, Pres., Robert J. Saron/Pres. - Aaron Medical Industries, Inc, Moshe Citronowicz/COO, VP, Gary D. Pickett/56/CFO, John Aneralla/Contact - Investor Inquiries, Vera MacElroy/58/Sec., Dir. - Human Resources

Directors: Andrew Makrides/Chmn., CEO, Pres., Randy Rossi/48/Dir., Brian H. Madden/54/Dir., George W. Kromer/68/Dir., Michael Norman/52/Dir.

Owners: George Kromer/2.90%, Bjurman Barry & Associates/5.20%, Robert J. Saron/2.60%, Randy Rossi/0.40%, Insiders/16.80%, The Frost National Bank FBO/6.60%, Andrew Makrides/5.60%, Moshe Citronowicz/4.20%, Mike Norman/0.40%, The Frost National Bank FBO/6.60%, Vera MacElroy, Brian Madden/0.60%

Financial Data: Fiscal Year End:12/31 *Latest Annual Data:* 9/30/2006

Year	Sales	Net Income
2006	$19,751,000	$2,260,000
2005	$20,211,000	$406,000

Curr. Assets:	$9,515,000	*Curr. Liab.:*	$2,011,000	*P/E Ratio:*	42.67
Plant, Equip.:	$3,163,000	*Total Liab.:*	$2,011,000	*Indic. Yr. Divd.:*	NA
Total Assets:	$14,775,000	*Net Worth:*	$12,639,000	*Debt/ Equity:*	NA

Bowater Inc

55 E Camperdown Way, Greenville, SC, 29601; *PH:* 1-864-271-7733; *http://* www.bowater.com

General - Incorporation .... DE
Employees 7,400
Auditor .... KPMG LLP
Stk Agt .... Bank of New York
Counsel .... NA
DUNS No. 00-194-6011

Stock- Price on:12/24/2007 .... $25.45
Stock Exchange .... NYSE
Ticker Symbol .... BOW
Outstanding Shares 57,400,000
E.P.S .... -$3.61
Shareholders .... NA

Business: The groups principle activity is to produce coated and specialty papers and newsprint. The group also makes bleached market pulp and lumber products. The group operates from United States.

Primary SIC and add'l.: 0831 2679 2611 2621

CIK No: 0000743368

Subsidiaries: Alliance Forest Products (2001)Inc., Bowater Alabama Inc., Bowater America Inc., Bowater Asia Pte Ltd., Bowater Canada Finance Corporation, Bowater Canada Inc., Bowater Canadian Forest Products Inc., Bowater Canadian Holdings Incorporated, Bowater Canadian Limited, Bowater Europe Limited, Bowater Finance Company Inc., Bowater Funding Inc., Bowater Maritimes Inc.(1), Bowater Mersey Paper Company Limited(2), Bowater Mississippi LLC 20 Subsidiaries included in the Index

Officers: David J. Paterson/Chmn., CEO, Pres./$2,504,493.00, Eric W. Streed/Exec. VP - Operations, Process Improvement, Pierre Monahan/Exec. VP - Building Products/$1,086,979.00, Ronald T. Lindsay/Exec. VP, General Counsel, Sec., William C. Morris/Sr. VP - Coated, Specialty Papers Sales, Marketing/$656,315.00, Joseph B. Johnson/VP, Controller, Ann Frazier/Contact - Newsprint, Customer Service, Kevin Craig/Contact - Newsprint, North America, Western Region, H. H. Kim/Contact - Newsprint, International Sales, Asia, Seoul, Richard Hobson/Contact - Newsprint, International Sales, United Kingdom, Pedro Bueno/Contact - Newsprint, International Sales, Northern Latin America, Martin Cordi/Contact - Newsprint, International Sales, Continental Europe, Middle East, Peter Benjung/Dir. - Fluff Pulp Business, Glenn Harding/Dir. - North American Sales, John McDonald/Sales Mgr. - Canadian, International Sales *(28 Officers included in Index)*

Directors: David J. Paterson/Chmn., CEO, Pres., Gordon D. Giffin/Dir., Richard B. Evans/Dir., Bruce W. Van Saun/Dir., Ruth R. Harkin/Dir., Jacques L. Menard/Dir., John A. Rolls/Dir., Togo D. West/Dir., Arthur R. Sawchuk/Dir.

Owners: Insiders/1.30%, Ruth R. Harkin, John A. Rolls, Togo D. West, Arnold M. Nemirow, Bruce R. Van Saun, NWQ Investment Management Company, LLC/22.20%, Arthur R. Sawchuk, William C. Morris, Massachusetts Financial Services Company/10.90%, Gordon D. Giffin, Randolph C. Ellington, Iridian Asset Management LLC/6.00%, Wellington Management Company, LLC/12.90%, Franklin Resources, Inc./8.30% *(22 Owners included in Index)*

Financial Data: *Fiscal Year End:*12/31 *Latest Annual Data:* 03/31/2007

Year	Sales	Net Income
2007	NA	NA
2006	$3,529,800,000	-$138,300,000
2005	$3,483,800,000	-$120,600,000

Curr. Assets:	$959,000,000	**Curr. Liab.:**	$446,100,000		
Plant, Equip.:	$2,938,700,000	**Total Liab.:**	$3,754,300,000	**Indic. Yr. Divd.:**	NA
Total Assets:	$4,645,900,000	**Net Worth:**	$832,600,000	**Debt/ Equity:**	2.8216

Bowl America Inc

6446 Edsall Rd. , Alexandria, VA, 22312; ***PH:*** 1-703-941-6300; ***http://*** www.bowl-america.com; ***Email:*** administrator@bowlingparty.com

General - Incorporation .... MD
Employees 750
Auditor .... Aronson & Co
Stk Agt...... American Stock Transfer & Trust Co.
Counsel .... Jerome J. Dick
DUNS No. 00-108-1553

Stock- Price on:12/24/2007 .... $16.83
Stock Exchange .... AMEX
Ticker Symbol .... BWL-A
Outstanding Shares 5,140,000
E.P.S $0.80
Shareholders .... NA

Business: The group's principal activity is to operate bowling centers. These establishments are fully air-conditioned with facilities for service of food and beverages, game rooms, rental lockers and playroom facilities. They also provide shoes for rental, retails bowling accessories and bowling balls are provided free. The group operates 18 centers with a total of 716 lanes located in Washington dc, baltimore, orlando, richmond and jacksonville. Its primary competitors are brunswick corporation and amf bowling worldwide, inc. The group has no foreign operations.

Primary SIC and add'l.: 7933 5812

CIK No: 0000013573

Subsidiaries: Bowl America Duke Inc., Bowl America of Florida Inc., Bowl America Shirley Inc., Falls Church Bowl Inc., Manassas Bowl Inc., Reisterstown Bowl Inc.

Officers: Leslie H. Goldberg/Dir., CEO, Pres., Cheryl A. Dragoo/CFO, Ruth E. MacKlin/Dir., Sr. VP, Treasurer, Irvin Clark/Dir., Sr. VP, GM, Joseph A. Levy/Dir., Sr. VP, Sec.

Directors: Leslie H. Goldberg/Dir., CEO, Pres., Stanley H. Katzman/Dir., Warren T. Braham/Dir., Allan L. Sher/Dir., Merle Fabian/Dir., Ruth E. MacKlin/Dir., Sr. VP, Treasurer, Irvin Clark/Dir., Sr. VP, GM, Joseph A. Levy/Dir., Sr. VP, Sec.

Owners: Merle Fabian, Leslie H. Goldberg, Leslie H. Goldberg, Stanley H. Katzman, Allan L. Sher, Joseph A. Levy, Warren T. Braham, Merle Fabian, Joseph A. Levy, Ruth E. Macklin, Ruth E. Macklin, Insiders, Irvin Clark, Warren T. Braham, Insiders *(16 Owners included in Index)*

Financial Data: *Fiscal Year End:*06/27 *Latest Annual Data:* 7/2/2006

Year	Sales	Net Income
2006	$30,320,000	$3,640,000
2005	$28,607,000	$3,849,000
2003	$29,376,000	$3,583,000

Curr. Assets:	$14,231,000	**Curr. Liab.:**	$3,598,000	**P/E Ratio:**	21.04
Plant, Equip.:	$23,440,000	**Total Liab.:**	$6,358,000	**Indic. Yr. Divd.:**	NA
Total Assets:	$42,549,000	**Net Worth:**	$36,192,000	**Debt/ Equity:**	NA

Bowlin Travel Centers Inc

150 Louisiana NE, Albuquerque, NM, 87108; ***PH:*** 1-505-266-5985; ***Fax:*** 1-505-266-7821; ***http://*** www.bowlintc.com

General - Incorporation .... NV
Employees 134
Auditor .... Neff & Ricci LLP
Stk Agt.......... Wells Fargo Shareowner Services
Counsel .... NA
DUNS No. .... NA

Stock- Price on:12/24/2007 .... $1.55
Stock Exchange .... OTC
Ticker Symbol .... BWTL
Outstanding Shares 4,580,000
E.P.S $0.18
Shareholders .... NA

Business: The group's principal activity is to operate travel centers dedicated to serving the traveling public in rural and smaller metropolitan areas of the southwestern United States. The group currently operates eleven full-service travel centers along interstate highways in Arizona and New Mexico. It advertises its travel centers through a network of approximately 300 outdoor advertising display faces. The group's travel centers offer gasoline, variety of southwestern merchandise and brand name food and beverages, ranging from drinks and snack foods at some locations to full-service restaurants at others for the travelling public. Its food service operations at five of the group's eleven travel centers operate under the dairy queen/brazier or dairy queen trade names. It is an authorized distributor of citgo and exxon petroleum products.

Primary SIC and add'l.: 5541 5812

CIK No: 0001124653

Officers: Michael L. Bowlin/Chmn., CEO, Pres., William J. McCabe/58/Dir., Sr. VP - Management Information Systems, Sec., Treasurer, Nina J. Pratz/56/Dir., CFO, Sr. VP, Kim D. Stake/52/Dir., Chief Administrative Officer, VP

Directors: Michael L. Bowlin/Chmn., CEO, Pres., William J. McCabe/58/Dir., Sr. VP - Management Information Systems, Sec., Treasurer, David B. Raybould/55/Dir., Nina J. Pratz/56/Dir., CFO, Sr. VP, Kim D. Stake/52/Dir., Chief Administrative Officer, VP

Owners: Nina J. Pratz, Michael L. Bowlin, Yorktown Avenue Capital, LLC, William J. McCabe, Insiders, Monica A. Bowlin

Financial Data: *Fiscal Year End:*01/31 *Latest Annual Data:* 1/31/2007

Year	Sales	Net Income
2007	$27,751,000	$604,000
2006	$27,668,000	$650,000
2005	$23,599,000	$439,000

Curr. Assets:	$6,932,000	**Curr. Liab.:**	$1,881,000	**P/E Ratio:**	12.92
Plant, Equip.:	$12,680,000	**Total Liab.:**	$7,359,000	**Indic. Yr. Divd.:**	NA
Total Assets:	$20,006,000	**Net Worth:**	$12,648,000	**Debt/ Equity:**	0.3685

Bowne & Co Inc

55 Water St., New York, NY, 10041; ***PH:*** 1-212-924-5500; ***Fax:*** 1-212-229-3400; ***http://*** www.bowne.com

General - Incorporation .... DE
Employees 3,200
Auditor .... KPMG LLP
Stk Agt .... Bank of New York
Counsel .... NA
DUNS No. 00-126-5230

Stock- Price on:12/24/2007 .... $19.77
Stock Exchange .... NYSE
Ticker Symbol .... BNE
Outstanding Shares 27,590,000
E.P.S $0.97
Shareholders .... NA

Business: The group's principal activity is to offer its customers an integrated way to design and manage their information flows. The process includes creating, sorting, presenting and utilizing information in any combination of paper and electronic forms. The group operates in three segments, namely, financial printing, outsourcing and globalization. Financial printing consists of transactional financial, corporate reporting, mutual fund, commercial and digital printing. Outsourcing consists of document management solutions for the legal and financial communities. Globalization segment provides business processing, technical writing, translation services, software localization and content reengineering of software and technology products. The group conducts operations in the United States, Canada, Europe, Latin America, South America and Asia.

Primary SIC and add'l.: 2754 2759 7389

CIK No: 0000013610

Subsidiaries: Bowne Business Communications, Inc., Bowne Enterprise Solutions, LLC, Bowne International de Mexico, S.A. de C.V., Bowne International Holdings GmbH, Bowne International, LLC, Bowne International, Ltd., Bowne International, SAS, Bowne Japan& Co, Inc., Bowne Litigation Solutions, LP, Bowne MBC, LLC, Bowne of Atlanta, Inc., Bowne of Boston, Inc., Bowne of Canada, Ltd., Bowne of Chicago, Inc., Bowne of Cleveland, Inc. 32 Subsidiaries included in the Index

Officers: David J. Shea/Chmn., CEO, Pres., William J. Coote/VP, Treasurer, Richard Bambach/Chief Accounting Officer, VP, Corporate Controller, Susan W. Cummiskey/Sr. VP - Human Resources, Scott L. Spitzer/Sr. VP, General Counsel, Corp. Sec., Elaine Beitler/Sr. VP, Pres. - Bowne Marketing, Business Communications, Suzanne Grey/Sr. VP - Marketing, Strategy, William P. Penders/Sr. VP, Pres. - Financial Communications, John J. Walker/Sr. VP, CFO

Directors: David J. Shea/Chmn., CEO, Pres., Lisa A. Stanley/Dir., Marshall H. Schwarz/Dir., Gloria M. Portela/Dir., Richard R. West/Dir., Carl J. Crosetto/Dir., Douglas B. Fox/Dir., Philip E. Kucera/Dir., Stephen V. Murphy/Dir., Vincent Tese/Dir., Marcia J. Hooper/Dir.

Owners: Susan W. Cummiskey, Richard Bambach, Stephen V. Murphy, Barclays Global Fund Advisors/6.10%, Lisa A. Stanley, Carl J. Crosetto, Gloria M. Portela, Pzena Investment Management, LLC/8.90%, William P. Penders, Wellington Management Company, LLP/13.10%, Douglas B. Fox, David J. Shea, Goldman, Sachs & Co./5.00%, Richard R. West, Dimensional Fund Advisors Inc./10.00% *(21 Owners included in Index)*

Financial Data: *Fiscal Year End:*12/31 *Latest Annual Data:* 12/31/2006

Year	Sales	Net Income
2006	$832,215,000	-$1,768,000
2005	$694,140,000	-$604,000
2004	$899,011,000	$27,504,000

Curr. Assets:	$300,918,000	**Curr. Liab.:**	$128,527,000	**P/E Ratio:**	79.08
Plant, Equip.:	$132,767,000	**Total Liab.:**	$278,653,000	**Indic. Yr. Divd.:**	$0.220
Total Assets:	$515,401,000	**Net Worth:**	$236,748,000	**Debt/ Equity:**	0.3231

Boxwood Inc

850 Third Ave., Ste. 1801, New York, NY, 10022; ***PH:*** 1-646-218-1400

General - Incorporation .... DE
Employees .... NA
Auditor .... Li & Co., P.C
Stk Agt .... Action Stock Transfer Corp
Counsel .... NA
DUNS No. .... NA

Stock- Price on:12/24/2007 .... NA
Stock Exchange .... OTC
Ticker Symbol .... BXWD
Outstanding Shares .... NA
E.P.S .... NA
Shareholders .... NA

Business: The groups principle activity is to provide recruiting services. The groups service area includes the research and development, engineering, marketing, sales, information technology and manufacturing industries. The group operates from United States.

Primary SIC and add'l.: 6770

CIK No: 0001354636

Officers: Richard Rosenblum/48/Dir., CEO, CFO, Pres., David Stefansky/36/Dir., Sec.

Directors: Richard Rosenblum/48/Dir., CEO, CFO, Pres., David Stefansky/36/Dir., Sec.

Owners: Diverse Trading Ltd/49.50%, Insiders/49.50%, Harborview Master Fund, L.P./49.50%

Boyd Gaming Corp

3883 Howard Hughes Pkwy., 9th Fl., Las Vegas, NV, 89169; **PH:** 1-702-792-7200;
Fax: 1-702-792-7313; **http://** www.boydgaming.com

General - Incorporation	NV	**Stock**- Price on:12/24/2007	$49.96
Employees	18,300	Stock Exchange	NYSE
Auditor	Deloitte & Touche LLP	Ticker Symbol	BYD
Stk Agt	Wells Fargo Shareowner Services	Outstanding Shares	87,360,000
Counsel	NA	E.P.S.	$3.71
DUNS No.	61-736-9335	Shareholders	NA

Business: The groups principle activity is to operate casinos. The group operates from United States.

Primary SIC and add'l.: 7993 7990 7011

CIK No: 0000906553

Subsidiaries: Blue Chip Casino, LLC, Boyd Atlantic City, Inc, Boyd Kenner, Inc, Boyd Louisiana LLC, Boyd Pennsylvania Partners, LP, Boyd Pennsylvania, Inc, Boyd Racing, LLC, Boyd Shreveport, LLC, Boyd Tunica, Inc, California Hotel and Casino, California Hotel Finance Co, Coast Casinos, Inc, Coast Hotels and Casinos, Inc, d.b.a. Sams Town Hotel and Casino, Echelon Resorts Corporation 22 Subsidiaries included in the Index

Officers: Robert L. Boughner/CEO, Pres. - Echelon Resort/$3,411,630.00, William S. Boyd/Chmn., CEO/$7,683,242.00, Marianne Boyd Johnson/Vice Chmn., Sr. VP/$1,443,054.00, Christopher R. Gibase/Sr. VP - Operations, Rob Stillwell/VP - Corporate Communications, Primary Investor Relations Officer, Gina B. Polovina/VP - Government, Community Affairs, Jeffrey G. Santoro/46/VP, Controller, Brian A. Larson/Sr. VP, General Counsel, Sec., Hector Mon/Sr. VP - Operations, Central Regions, William J. Noonan/Sr. VP - Administration, Stephen S. Thompson/Sr. VP - Operations, Nevada Region, Keith E. Smith/COO, Pres., William R. Boyd/VP, Paul J. Chakmak/CFO, Exec. VP, Treasurer/$1,052,792.00

Directors: William S. Boyd/Chmn., CEO, Marianne Boyd Johnson/Vice Chmn., Sr. VP, Billy G. McCoy/Dir., Thomas V. Girardi/Dir., Veronica J. Wilson/Dir., Luther Mack/Dir., Michael O. Maffie/Dir., Frederick J. Schwab/Dir., Peter M. Thomas/Dir.

Owners: Thomas V. Girardi, Peter M. Thomas, William R. Boyd/2.20%, Paul J. Chakmak, Veronica J. Wilson, Keith E. Smith, Insiders/36.60%, Ellis Landau, Luther W. Mack, Marianne Boyd Johnson/15.70%, Frederick J. Schwab, William S. Boyd/17.80%, Private Capital Management, L.P./8.50%, Michael O. Maffie, Marianne Boyd Johnson/15.70% *(17 Owners included in Index)*

Financial Data: Fiscal Year End:12/31   Latest Annual Data: 03/31/2007

Year	Sales	Net Income
2007	$517,030,000	$217,866,000
2006	$2,278,830,000	$116,778,000
2005	$2,223,020,000	$144,610,000

Curr. Assets:	$374,678,000	**Curr. Liab.:**	$331,990,000	**P/E Ratio:**	16.38
Plant, Equip.:	$2,129,445,000	**Total Liab.:**	$2,791,347,000	**Indic. Yr. Divd.:**	$0.600
Total Assets:	$3,901,299,000	**Net Worth:**	$1,109,952,000	**Debt/ Equity:**	1.6262

Boyds Collection Ltd

350 S St. , Mcsherrystown, PA, 17344; **PH:** 1-717-633-9898; **http://** www.boydsstuff.com

General - Incorporation	MD	**Stock**- Price on:12/24/2007	$1
Employees	420	Stock Exchange	OTC
Auditor	Deloitte & Touche LLP	Ticker Symbol	BYDC
Stk Agt	Bank of New York	Outstanding Shares	59,050,000
Counsel	NA	E.P.S.	-$1.85
DUNS No.	NA	Shareholders	NA

Business: The group's principal activities are to design, import and distribute handcrafted collectibles and other specialty giftware products. The products include plush animals, resin figurines, dolls, villages and other giftware products. Huggle-fluffs-tm-, the artisan series-tm-, the mohair bears-tm-, j.b. Bean & associates-tm-, the archive collection-tm- and angels and friends-tm are the trademarks used for the products of plush animals. The group imports substantially all of its products from the manufactures in China through buying agencies.

Primary SIC and add'l.: 5199

CIK No: 0001074530

Financial Data: Fiscal Year End:12/31   Latest Annual Data: 12/31/2005

Year	Sales	Net Income
2005	$78,559,000	-$181,831,000
2004	$103,714,000	$5,439,000
2003	$113,037,000	$10,863,000

Curr. Assets:	$30,824,000	**Curr. Liab.:**	$5,727,000		
Plant, Equip.:	$31,727,000	**Total Liab.:**	$100,907,000	**Indic. Yr. Divd.:**	NA
Total Assets:	$63,010,000	**Net Worth:**	-$37,897,000	**Debt/ Equity:**	NA

Boystoys.com Inc

Alexander House Ling Rd., Tower Pk., Poole, BH12 4NZ; **PH:** 619-895-6900;
Fax: 44-01202733969; **http://** www.boystoys.com

General - Incorporation	DE	**Stock**- Price on:12/24/2007	NA
Employees	NA	Stock Exchange	OTC
Auditor	Armando C. Ibarra, CPA	Ticker Symbol	GRLZ
Stk Agt	Olde Monmouth Stk Trnsfer Co. Inc.	Outstanding Shares	NA
Counsel	NA	E.P.S.	$0.001
DUNS No.	NA	Shareholders	NA

Business: The groups principle activity is to provide recruiting services. The groups service area includes the research and development, engineering, marketing, sales, information technology and manufacturing industries. The group operates from United States.

Primary SIC and add'l.: 5810

CIK No: 0000931799

Officers: Ralph M. Amato/56/Chmn., CEO, CFO, Pres., Tom Perkins/Editor, Phil King/Content Mgr., Christian Dickinson/Advertising Mgr., Iain Manners/Sr. Sales Executive, David Knight/Sales Executive

Directors: Ralph M. Amato/56/Chmn., CEO, CFO, Pres.

Owners: Ralph M. Amato/50.28%

Financial Data: Fiscal Year End:12/31   Latest Annual Data: 12/31/2003

Year	Sales	Net Income
2003	NA	-$144,000
2002	$1,616,000	-$1,694,000
2001	$2,531,000	-$308,000

Curr. Assets:	$569,000	**Curr. Liab.:**	$2,012,000		
Plant, Equip.:	NA	**Total Liab.:**	$2,012,000	**Indic. Yr. Divd.:**	NA
Total Assets:	$602,000	**Net Worth:**	-$1,410,000	**Debt/ Equity:**	NA

BP International Inc

510 W Arizona Ave., Deland, FL, 32720; **PH:** 1-386-943-6222; **Fax:** 1-386-943-4060;
http:// www.ballproducts.com; **Email:** contact@ballproducts.com

General - Incorporation	DE	**Stock**- Price on:12/24/2007	$0.02
Employees	NA	Stock Exchange	OTC
Auditor	Daszkal Bolton LLP	Ticker Symbol	BPIL
Stk Agt	Interwest Transfer Company, Inc.	Outstanding Shares	NA
Counsel	NA	E.P.S.	NA
DUNS No.	NA	Shareholders	NA

Business: The group's principal activities are to manufacture tennis court equipment, industrial fabrics, athletic field and gymnasium equipment, privacy and construction fence screening. The group also manufactures fabric architecture shade structures and cabanas, sports lighting, and custom netting. The group sells these products to sports facilities, support facilities, municipalities, parks, playgrounds, schools, and recreation centers. It distributes the products through authorized dealers, contractors or direct delivery. On 21-Apr-2003, the group acquired ball products inc. On 31-May-2004, the group acquired telas olefines a Mexico corporation.

Primary SIC and add'l.: 3949

CIK No: 0001082737

Subsidiaries: Allergy Acquisition Corporation, Ball Products, Inc

Officers: William C. De Temple/CEO, Pres.

Financial Data: Fiscal Year End:05/31   Latest Annual Data: 5/31/2005

Year	Sales	Net Income
2005	$6,358,000	-$2,748,000
2004	$5,321,000	-$2,602,000
2003	$5,696,000	-$1,289,000

Curr. Assets:	$2,246,000	**Curr. Liab.:**	$3,064,000		
Plant, Equip.:	$1,559,000	**Total Liab.:**	$4,980,000	**Indic. Yr. Divd.:**	NA
Total Assets:	$4,076,000	**Net Worth:**	-$905,000	**Debt/ Equity:**	NA

BP Plc

28100 Torch Pkwy., Warrenville, IL, 60555; **PH:** 1-630-821-2222; **http://** www.bp.com;
Email: ir@bp.com

General - Incorporation	UK	**Stock**- Price on:12/24/2007	$69.27
Employees	97,000	Stock Exchange	NYSE
Auditor	Ernst & Young LLP	Ticker Symbol	BP
Stk Agt	JP Morgan Chase Bank, N.A.	Outstanding Shares	3,220,000,000
Counsel	NA	E.P.S.	$5.98
DUNS No.	21-004-2669	Shareholders	NA

Business: The group's principal activities comprise of exploration and production, gas, power and renewables, refining and marketing, and petrochemicals. Exploration and production activities include oil and natural gas exploration and field development and production, pipeline transportation and natural gas processing. Gas, power and renewables include shipping and trading of liquefied natural gas, funding and building regasification facilities and gas import terminals, gas pipelines and the generation of solar power. Refining and marketing includes selling, transporting and trading of crude oil and petroleum products. Petrochemicals' activities include the manufacturing and marketing of petrochemicals. Brands include bp, AM/pm, aral, arco and castrol. The group operates in Europe, Middle East, Far East, Africa, australasia and United States of America.

Primary SIC and add'l.: 2869 1311 2911 4922

CIK No: 0000313807

Subsidiaries: Amoco Caspian Sea Petroleum, Atlantic Richfield Co., BP America, BP America Production Company, BP Amoco Chemical Company, BP Amoco Exploration (In Amenas), BP Australia Capital Markets, BP Canada Energy, BP Canada Finance, BP Capital, BP Capital Markets, BP Capital Markets America, BP Chemicals, BP Chemicals Investments, BP Company North America 45 Subsidiaries included in the Index

Officers: Robert A. Malone/Chmn., Pres. - BP America, Inc, A. B. Hayward/Executive Dir., Johali Peeck/Administrative Assist., Kenneth Kaminski/Mgr. - US Shareholder Service, Byron Grote/CFO, Iain Conn/Chief Executive - Refining, Marketing, John Manzoni/48/Executive Dir., Andrew G. Inglis/Chief Executive - Exploration, Production, Vivienne Cox/Exec. VP - Gas, Power, Renewables, Integrated Supply, Trading, Sara T. Bott/Exec. VP - Human Resources, David Allen/Group Chief - Staff, Group MD, Peter Bevan/Group General Counsel, Tony Hayward/Chief Executive, Marie Louka/Administrator - Investor Relations, Rachael MacLean/VP - Investor Relations North America *(23 Officers included in Index)*

Directors: P. D. Sutherland/62/Chmn., Ian Prosser/64/Dir., William Castell/Dir., John Manzoni/48/Executive Dir., Deanne S. Julius/59/Non Exec. Dir., Tom McKillop/65/Non Exec. Dir., Walter E. Massey/Non Exec. Dir., A. B. Hayward/Executive Dir., John H. Bryan/71/Dir., A. Burgmans/61/Non Exec. Dir., Erroll B. Davis/63/Non Exec. Dir., Douglas J. Flint/52/Non Exec. Dir.

Owners: The Lord Browne of Madingley, Tom McKillop, J. H. Bryan, Ian Prosser, A. B. Hayward, D. S. Julius, W. E. Massey, A. Burgmans, B. E. Grote, I. C. Conn, D. C. Allen, A. G. Inglis, P. D. Sutherland, E. B. Davis, J. A. Manzoni *(16 Owners included in Index)*

Financial Data: Fiscal Year End:12/31   Latest Annual Data: 12/31/2006

Year	Sales	Net Income
2006	$274,316,000,000	$21,116,000,000
2005	$245,486,000,000	$19,642,000,000
2004	$285,059,000,000	$15,731,000,000

Curr. Assets:	$75,339,000,000	**Curr. Liab.:**	$75,352,000,000	**P/E Ratio:**	32.78
Plant, Equip.:	$90,994,000,000	**Total Liab.:**	$132,914,000,000	**Indic. Yr. Divd.:**	$2.600
Total Assets:	$219,431,000,000	**Net Worth:**	$86,517,000,000	**Debt/ Equity:**	NA

BP Prudhoe Bay Royalty Trust

101 Barclay St., New York, NY, 10286;

General - Incorporation .... DE
Employees .... NA
Auditor .... KPMG LLP
Stk Agt .... Bank of New York
Counsel .... NA
DUNS No. .... NA

Stock- Price on:12/24/2007 .... $70.1
Stock Exchange .... NYSE
Ticker Symbol .... BPT
Outstanding Shares 21,400,000
E.P.S. $8.49
Shareholders .... NA

Business: The groups principle activities include exploring and developing crude oil. The group operates from the United States. The group's quarterly revenue for September 2007 was 44.19 millions of USD.

Primary SIC and add'l.: 6792

CIK No: 0000850033

Subsidiaries: BP Exploration (Alaska) Inc, BP p.l.c., The Standard Oil Company

Officers: Remo Reale/VP

Financial Data: *Fiscal Year End:*12/31 *Latest Annual Data:* 12/31/2006

Year	Sales	Net Income
2006	$184,939,000	$183,882,000
2005	$153,015,000	$151,918,000
2004	$82,693,000	$81,717,000

Curr. Assets:	$1,010,000	**Curr. Liab.:**	$191,000	**P/E Ratio:**	8.26
Plant, Equip.:	NA	**Total Liab.:**	$191,000	**Indic. Yr. Divd.:**	$7.270
Total Assets:	$9,044,000	**Net Worth:**	$8,853,000	**Debt/ Equity:**	NA

BPC Holding Corp

101 Oakley St., Evansville, IN, 47710; *PH:* 1-812-424-2904; *Fax:* 1-812-424-0128; *http://* www.berryplastics.com

General - Incorporation .... DE
Employees .... NA
Auditor .... Deloitte & Touche, LLP
Stk Agt .... NA
Counsel .... NA
DUNS No. 62-332-7731

Stock- Price on:12/24/2007 .... NA
Stock Exchange .... NA
Ticker Symbol .... NA
Outstanding Shares .... NA
E.P.S. .... NA
Shareholders .... NA

Business: The group's principal activities are to manufacture and market rigid plastic packaging products. The products include open-top containers, aerosol overcaps, closures, drink cups and housewares. The group operates through three divisions: containers, closures, and consumer products. Plastic cups are sold mainly to fast food chain restaurants, convenience stores, stadiums, tabletop restaurants and retail stores. Containers are used in the industry that manufactures food products, building products, chemicals and dairy products. During 2003, the group acquired the assets of ccl plastic packaging & apm inc. On 20-Nov-2003, the group acquired landis plastics, inc.

Primary SIC and add'l.: 3089

CIK No: 0000919465

Subsidiaries: AeroCon, Inc., Berry Iowa Corporation, Berry Plastics Acquisition Corporation II, Berry Plastics Acquisition Corporation III, Berry Plastics Acquisition Corporation IX, Berry Plastics Acquisition Corporation V, Berry Plastics Acquisition Corporation VII, Berry Plastics Acquisition Corporation VIII, Berry Plastics Acquisition Corporation X, Berry Plastics Acquisition Corporation XI, Berry Plastics Acquisition Corporation XII, Berry Plastics Acquisition Corporation XIII, Berry Plastics Acquisition Corporation XIV, LLC, Berry Plastics Acquisition Corporation XV, LLC, Berry Plastics Asia Pte. Ltd 39 Subsidiaries included in the Index

Officers: Ira G. Boots/53/Chmn., CEO, Pres., Brent R. Beeler/54/COO, Exec. VP, James M. Kratochvil/51/Exec. VP, CFO, Treasurer, Sec., Adam G. Unfried/Pres. - Rigid Open Top Division

Directors: Ira G. Boots/53/Chmn., CEO, Pres., Robert V. Seminara/35/Dir., Joshua J. Harris/42/Dir., Steven C. Graham/48/Dir., Donald C. Graham/74/Dir., Patrick J. Dalton/39/Dir., Anthony M. Civale/33/Dir.

Owners: Ira G. Boots, Insiders, Graham Berry Holdings, LP, Steven C. Graham, Donald C. Graham, Joshua J. Harris, Patrick J. Dalton, James M. Kratochvil, Brent R. Beeler, Adam G. Unfried, Apollo Investment Fund V, L.P., Anthony M. Civale, Apollo Investment Fund VI, L.P., Robert V. Seminara, Randall J. Hobson *(16 Owners included in Index)*

BPI Energy Holdings Inc

Formerly: BPI Industries Inc
501 E Deyoung St., Marion, IL, 62959; *PH:* 1-618-993-1460; *http://* www.bpi-industries.com; *Email:* info@bpi-industries.com

General - Incorporation .... BC
Employees .... NA
Auditor .... Meaden & Moore Ltd
Stk Agt .... Pacific Stock Transfer Company
Counsel .... Thompson Hine Llp
DUNS No. .... NA

Stock- Price on:12/24/2007 .... NA
Stock Exchange .... AMEX
Ticker Symbol .... BPG
Outstanding Shares .... NA
E.P.S. .... -$0.28
Shareholders .... NA

Business: The group operates through its subsidiaries whose principle activities include exploring, producing and selling coalbed methane. The group operates from the Canada. The groups quarterly revenue for September 2007 was 0.32 millions of USD.

Primary SIC and add'l.: 8711

CIK No: 0001314077

Subsidiaries: BPI Energy, Inc.

Officers: James G. Azlein/59/Dir., CEO, Pres., Randy L. Elkins/41/Acting CFO, Controller, James E. Craddock/49/Dir., COO, Randy Oestreich/53/VP - Field Operations, Dan Anderson/61/Dir. - Property Acquisitions

Directors: James G. Azlein/59/Dir., CEO, Pres., James E. Craddock/49/Dir., COO, Dennis Carlton/58/Dir., William J. Centa/55/Dir., David E. Preng/62/Dir., Costa Vrisakis/74/Dir., Kevin Reimer/Member - Advisory Board, Craig Creel/Member - Advisory Board, William Ginn/Member - Advisory Board, Thomas J. Vessels/Member - Advisory Board, Clyde House/Member - Advisory Board, Luc Berthoud/Member - Advisory Board, Joseph P. McCoy/Dir.

Owners: William J. Centa, James E. Craddock/1.20%, Costa Vrisakis/2.80%, David E. Preng, Dennis Carlton, James G. Azlein/4.70%, Joseph P. McCoy, CFSIL a/c Colonial First State Wholesale Global Resources Fund/6.40%, Insiders/10.30%, Randall L. Elkins, Jennison Associates LLC/10.30%

Financial Data: *Fiscal Year End:*07/31 *Latest Annual Data:* 07/31/2007

Year	Sales	Net Income
2007	$1,204,000	-$20,641,000
2006	$1,126,000	-$8,836,000

Curr. Assets:	$13,334,000	**Curr. Liab.:**	$11,962,000		
Plant, Equip.:	$26,189,000	**Total Liab.:**	$12,124,000	**Indic. Yr. Divd.:**	NA
Total Assets:	$39,843,000	**Net Worth:**	$27,719,000	**Debt/ Equity:**	NA

BPO Management Services

Formerly: netGuru Inc
1290 N Hancock Hills, Anaheim Hills, CA, 92807; *PH:* 1-714-974-2670; *http://* www.netguru.com

General - Incorporation .... DE
Employees 173
Auditor .... Kelly & Co.
Stk Agt .... NA
Counsel .....Mr. Gregg Amber Of Rutan & Tucker
DUNS No. 09-621-1032

Stock- Price on:12/24/2007 .... NA
Stock Exchange .... NA
Ticker Symbol .... NA
Outstanding Shares .... NA
E.P.S. .... -$0.63
Shareholders .... NA

Business: The group's principal activity is to provide integrated Internet and information technology solutions and services. The group's operations are carried out through four segments: engineering and collaborative software products, it services and Internet content, e-commerce and center. Engineering software products include design automation and analysis solutions for use by engineering analysis and design professionals, as well as related maintenance and services. It services include Web-based real-time collaboration/engineering solution for document review and markup. Internet content and e-commerce include Web-based collaboration and communication software solutions, long-distance communication and travel services. The major customers of the group include british telecom, siemens, sun microsystems and hewlett packard, ag. The group operates in the United States, Germany, India, the United Kingdom and France.

Primary SIC and add'l.: 7373 7371 7379 7372

CIK No: 0001015920

Subsidiaries: netGuru Limited, R-Cube Technologies, Inc.

Officers: Patrick Dolan/50/Chmn., CEO, James Cortens/52/Dir., COO, Pres., Sec., Koushik Dutta/CTO, Airat Khasanov/Software Mgr.

Directors: Patrick Dolan/50/Chmn., CEO, James Cortens/52/Dir., COO, Pres., Sec., Dale Paisley/66/Dir.

Owners: Renaissance US Growth Investment Trust PLC, Heller Capital Investments LLC**, Vision Opportunity Master Fund, Ltd.**, Heller Capital Investments LLC**, Russell Cleveland, Koushik Dutta, Russell Cleveland, Don West, US Special Opportunities Trust PLC, Premier RENN US Emerging Growth Fund Ltd., Insiders/100.00%, James Cortens, James Cortens/36.50%, Vision Opportunity Master Fund, Ltd.**, Dale Paisley *(49 Owners included in Index)*

Financial Data: *Fiscal Year End:*03/31 *Latest Annual Data:* 12/31/2006

Year	Sales	Net Income
2006	$4,711,000	-$3,300,000
2005	$15,843,000	-$788,000

Curr. Assets:	$1,860,000	**Curr. Liab.:**	$4,998,000		
Plant, Equip.:	$510,000	**Total Liab.:**	$5,260,000	**Indic. Yr. Divd.:**	NA
Total Assets:	$7,716,000	**Net Worth:**	$2,455,000	**Debt/ Equity:**	0.3419

BPZ Energy Inc

580 Westlake Pk. Blvd., Ste. 525, Houston, TX, 77079; *PH:* 1-281-556-6200; *Fax:* 1-281-556-6377; *http://* www.bpzenergy.com; *Email:* bpz@bpzenergy.com

General - Incorporation .... CO
Employees 23
Auditor .... Johnson Miller & Co. Cpas, P.c.
Stk Agt .... Hein & Assoc. LLP
Counsel .... NA
DUNS No. 80-287-2564

Stock- Price on:12/24/2007 .... NA
Stock Exchange .... AMEX
Ticker Symbol .... BZP
Outstanding Shares .... NA
E.P.S. .... -$0.35
Shareholders .... NA

Business: The group's principal activities are to provide technology solutions and financial and mortgage services. The group operates in three separate business segments: financial services, mortgage services and technology. The financial services segment provides consulting and personnel services to emerging growth micro and small capitalization companies to help them effectively structure transactions to attract public and private capital. The group also provides financial public relations services. The mortgage services segment provides end to end mortgage services from back office processing to mortgage banking services. The technology segment provides quality solutions that enable organizations to manage and secure access to Web applications within the enterprise and across the business value chain. On 11-Sep-2003, the group acquired 80% of northsight mortgage group llc and on 09-Sep-2004, the group acquired bpz energy inc.

Primary SIC and add'l.: 7373 7375 7371 7372 5045

CIK No: 0001023734

Subsidiaries: BPZ Energy, Inc., Navidec Financial Services, Inc., SMC Ecuador, Inc., SMC Ecuador, Inc., Sucursal Ecuador

Officers: Manual Pablo Zuniga Pflucker/47/Dir., CEO, Pres./$137,472.00, Frederic Briens/48/COO/$932,168.00, Edward G. Caminos/45/CFO/$395,371.00, Tomas E. Vargas/64/VP - Geosciences, Rafael Zoeger/59/VP, GM - Peru, Edward Gilliard/53/VP - Finance, Treasurer

Directors: Manual Pablo Zuniga Pflucker/47/Dir., CEO, Pres., Fernando Zuniga Y Rivero/81/Chmn., Gordon Gray/53/Dir., John J. Lendrum/55/Dir., Barger E. Miller/68/Dir., Dennis G. Strauch/58/Dir.

Owners: Dennis G. Strauch/0.20%, John J. Lendrum, Fernando Ziga y Rivero/2.30%, Insiders/13.10%, Frederic Briens/0.60%, Wellington Management Company, LLP/11.00%, Allied Crude Purchasing, Inc./5.00%, International Finance Corporation/8.70%, Manuel Pablo Ziga-Pflcker/4.40%, Barger E. Miller, Gordon Gray/5.00%, Edward G. Caminos/0.20%

Financial Data: *Fiscal Year End:*12/31 *Latest Annual Data:* 12/31/2006

Year	Sales	Net Income
2006	NA	-$15,487,000
2005	NA	-$6,407,000
2004	NA	-$10,653,000

Curr. Assets:	$32,402,000	**Curr. Liab.:**	$10,345,000		
Plant, Equip.:	$38,727,000	**Total Liab.:**	$10,401,000	**Indic. Yr. Divd.:**	NA
Total Assets:	$74,037,000	**Net Worth:**	$63,636,000	**Debt/ Equity:**	NA

Bradley Pharmaceuticals Inc

383 Rte. 46 W, Fairfield, NJ, 07004; *PH:* 1-973-882-1505; *Fax:* 1-973-575-5366; *http://* www.bradpharm.com; *Email:* info@bradpharm.com

General - Incorporation	DE	Stock - Price on:12/24/2007	$20.915
Employees	300	Stock Exchange	NYSE
Auditor	Grant Thornton LLP	Ticker Symbol	BDY
Stk Agt	American Stock Transfer & Trust Co.	Outstanding Shares	16,870,000
Counsel	NA	E.P.S.	$0.04
DUNS No.	NA	Shareholders	NA

Business: The groups principle activities include acquiring, developing and marketing products for dermatology, podiatry, gastroenterology and womens health. The groups products marketed under the brand names include ADOXA(R), ZODERM(R), LIDAMANTLE(R) and ROSULA(R). The group operates through three segments namely, dermatology and podiatry, dermatology and generic. The group operates from the United States. The group's quarterly revenue for September 2007 was 33.55 millions of USD.

Primary SIC and add'l.: 2834

CIK No: 0000864268

Subsidiaries: A. Aarons, Inc., Bioglan Pharmaceuticals Corp., Doak Dermatologics, Inc.

Officers: Daniel Glassman/Dir., CEO, Pres./$913,171.00, Bradley Glassman/Sr. VP - Sales, Marketing/$350,083.00, Alan Goldstein/VP - Corporate Development/$341,515.00, Ralph Landau/VP, Chief Scientific Officer/$292,231.00, Brent R. Lenczycki/CFO, VP/$413,524.00, Cecelia C. Heer/Mgr. - Investor, Public Relations/$361,470.00

Directors: Daniel Glassman/Dir., CEO, Pres., Seth W. Hamot/Interim Non Exec. Chmn., Steven Kriegsman/66/Dir., Michael Fedida/Dir., Douglas E. Linton/Dir., William J. Murphy/Dir., Andre Fedida/52/Dir.

Owners: Gene Goldberg, Seth W. Hamot/9.80%, Daniel Glassman/9.90%, Barclays Global Investors, NA, Barclays Global/7.80%, Insiders/96.20%, Brent R. Lenczycki, Michael Fedida, Andre Fedida, Alan Goldstein, Costa Brava Partnership III L.P./9.80%, William J. Murphy, Daniel Glassman/91.30%, Dimensional Fund Advisors LP./7.40%, Steven Kriegsman, Insiders/22.30% (18 Owners included in Index)

Financial Data: Fiscal Year End:12/31　Latest Annual Data: 12/31/2006

Year		Sales		Net Income
2006		$144,807,000		$9,668,000
2005		$133,382,000		$7,962,000
2004		$96,694,000		$7,954,000
Curr. Assets:	$88,431,000	Curr. Liab.:	$69,452,000	P/E Ratio: 61.51
Plant, Equip.:	$814,000	Total Liab.:	$124,906,000	Indic. Yr. Divd.: NA
Total Assets:	$312,523,000	Net Worth:	$187,616,000	Debt/ Equity: 0.2671

Bradner Ventures Ltd

200 Burrard St. , Ste. 1925, Vancouver, BC, V6C 3L6; *PH:* 1-604-693-0177; *Fax:* 1-604-638-3525; *http://* www.bradnerventures.com

General - Incorporation	BC	Stock - Price on:12/24/2007	NA
Employees	NA	Stock Exchange	OTC
Auditor	Amisano Hanson	Ticker Symbol	BNVLF
Stk Agt	Computershare Trust Co	Outstanding Shares	NA
Counsel	NA	E.P.S.	NA
DUNS No.	NA	Shareholders	NA

Business: The groups principle activity is to provide recruiting services. The groups service area includes the research and development, engineering, marketing, sales, information technology and manufacturing industries. The group operates from United States.

Primary SIC and add'l.: 1081

CIK No: 0001123839

Officers: Richard Coglon/Dir., Sec., Pres., Randy Buchamer/51/Dir., CFO

Directors: Richard Coglon/Dir., Sec., Pres., Randy Buchamer/51/Dir., CFO, Anthony Knott/60/Dir.

Owners: Richard Coglon/34.30%, Randy Buchamer/3.30%, Anthony Knott/1.60%

Financial Data: Fiscal Year End:11/30　Latest Annual Data: 11/30/2006

Year		Sales		Net Income
2006		NA		-$51,000
2005		NA		-$61,000
2004		NA		-$42,000
Curr. Assets:	$16,000	Curr. Liab.:	$8,000	
Plant, Equip.:	NA	Total Liab.:	$8,000	Indic. Yr. Divd.: NA
Total Assets:	$16,000	Net Worth:	$8,000	Debt/ Equity: NA

Brady Corp

6555 W Good Hope Rd., Milwaukee, WI, 53223; *PH:* 1-414-358-6600; *Fax:* 1-800-292-2289; *http://* www.bradycorp.com

General - Incorporation	WI	Stock - Price on:12/24/2007	$36.01
Employees	7,000	Stock Exchange	NYSE
Auditor	Deloitte & Touche LLP	Ticker Symbol	BRC
Stk Agt	Wells Fargo Bank Minnesota N.A	Outstanding Shares	54,020,000
Counsel	NA	E.P.S.	$2.02
DUNS No.	00-607-3027	Shareholders	NA

Business: The group's principal activity is to manufacture and market identification solutions and specialty coated materials. The products include wire and cable markers, high-performance labels and signs, printing systems and software mainly to the electrical, electronic, telecommunications, automotive and general industrial market. The group also manufactures and sells signs, labels, tags, safety devices, printers and accessories for do-it-yourself industrial signage and labels. The group also deals in regulatory training programs and products, accident-prevention tags, other visual warning systems and variety of products to end users via direct-mail catalogs, telemarketing and the Internet. During fiscal 2003, the group acquired tiscor inc, etimark gmbh, and cleere advantage ltd and during fiscal 2004, brandon international inc, prinzing enterprises inc, emed co inc, aztec ltd, b.i.g & ID technologies pte ltd.

Primary SIC and add'l.: 3993 2899

CIK No: 0000746598

Subsidiaries: Accidental Health& Safety Pty. Ltd., AIO Acquisition Inc., AIO Holding Inc., Also Doing Business As:, Ave One, Inc., B.I. Financial Limited, B.i. U.k. Limited, Bakee Metal Manufacturing Company Limited, Balkhausen, Barcodes West, Brady, Brady (Beijing) Co. Ltd., Brady (Shenzhen) Co. Ltd., Brady (Thailand) Co. Ltd., Brady (Turkey) Ltd. 127 Subsidiaries included in the Index

Officers: Frank M. Jaehnert/Dir., CEO, Pres., Robert L. Tatterson/VP - Research & Development, CTO, Barbara G. Bolens/VP, Treasurer, Dir. - Investor Relations, Tom Felmer/Pres. - Direct Marketing Americas, Peter C. Sephton/Pres. - Brady Europe, David Mathieson/Sr. VP, CFO, Matt O. Williamson/Pres. - Brady Americas, David R. Hawke/Exec. VP, Allan J. Klotsche/Pres. - Brady Asia, Pacific, Global Die Cut, Strategic Accounting Mgr., Michael O. Oliver/Sr. VP - Human Resources, Thomas J. Felmer/46/Pres. - Direct Marketing Americas, VP - Brady Corporation, Keith Kaczanowski/VP - Supply Chain Management

Directors: Frank M. Jaehnert/Dir., CEO, Pres., Patrick W. Allender/61/Dir., Conrad G. Goodkind/Dir., Chan Galbato/Dir., Robert C. Buchanan/Dir., Mary K. Bush/Dir., Frank W. Harris/Dir., Roger Peirce/Dir., Richard A. Bemis/Dir., Peter J. Lettenberger/Dir., Gary E. Nei/Dir., Frank R. Jarc/Dir., Elizabeth Pungello/Dir.

Owners: Peter C. Sephton, Gary E. Nei, Mary K. Bush, Barbara Bolens, Conrad G. Goodkind, William H. Brady, Elizabeth P. Pungello, David R. Hawke, Richard A. Bemis, Frank R. Jarc, Frank M. Jaehnert, Matthew O. Williamson, Robert C. Buchanan, Elizabeth P. Pungello, Michael O. Oliver (22 Owners included in Index)

Financial Data: Fiscal Year End:07/31　Latest Annual Data: 7/31/2006

Year		Sales		Net Income
2006		$1,018,436,000		$104,175,000
2005		$816,447,000		$81,947,000
2004		$671,219,000		$50,871,000
Curr. Assets:	$459,157,000	Curr. Liab.:	$218,620,000	P/E Ratio: 18.37
Plant, Equip.:	$139,906,000	Total Liab.:	$619,140,000	Indic. Yr. Divd.: $0.560
Total Assets:	$1,365,186,000	Net Worth:	$746,046,000	Debt/ Equity: 0.5879

Braintech Inc

Braintech Canada Inc., 102 & 104b 930 W, 1st St., North Vancouver, BC, V7P 3N4; *PH:* 1-604-988-6440; *http://* www.braintech.com; *Email:* webservices@braintech.com

General - Incorporation	NV	Stock - Price on:12/24/2007	$0.75
Employees	NA	Stock Exchange	OTC
Auditor	Smythe Ratcliffe LLP	Ticker Symbol	BRHI
Stk Agt	Colonial Stock Transfer Co Inc	Outstanding Shares	NA
Counsel	NA	E.P.S.	NA
DUNS No.	NA	Shareholders	NA

Business: The group's principle activities include developing and supplying custom machine vision systems and has developed specialized software products for use in the development, maintenance and support of machine vision systems. The group operates from United States.

Primary SIC and add'l.: 3823

CIK No: 0001015715

Subsidiaries: Braintech Canada, Inc, Brainware Systems Inc

Officers: Owen L.J Jones/Dir., CEO/CAD144,672.00, Babak Habibi/Dir., COO, Pres., Edward A. White/Dir., CFO, Treasurer, Sec., Jim Dara/Member - Sales Officer

Directors: Owen L.J Jones/Dir., CEO, Babak Habibi/Dir., COO, Pres., James L. Speros/Dir., Edward A. White/Dir., CFO, Treasurer, Sec., Drew Miller/Dir., Clifford G. Butler/Dir.

Owners: Insiders/42.34%, Frederick W. Weidinger/7.27%, Owen L.J. Jones/31.44%, Clifford Butler/7.27%, James L. Speros/5.75%, Edward A. White/1.63%, Babak Habibi/2.48%, Drew Miller/0.28%

Financial Data: Fiscal Year End:12/31　Latest Annual Data: 12/31/2006

Year		Sales		Net Income
2006		$1,756,000		-$5,962,000
2005		$1,203,000		-$2,716,000
2004		$750,000		-$2,860,000
Curr. Assets:	$1,299,000	Curr. Liab.:	$1,408,000	
Plant, Equip.:	$29,000	Total Liab.:	$3,391,000	Indic. Yr. Divd.: NA
Total Assets:	$1,329,000	Net Worth:	-$2,062,000	Debt/ Equity: NA

Bralorne Mining Company

17 Anyuan Rd., Rm. 618, Chaoyang District, Beijing, 100029; *PH:* 86-10-6498-7788

General - Incorporation	NV	Stock - Price on:12/24/2007	$0.022
Employees	NA	Stock Exchange	OTC
Auditor	Keith K. Zhen, Cpa	Ticker Symbol	SMGH
Stk Agt	Pacific Corporate Trust Co.	Outstanding Shares	NA
Counsel	NA	E.P.S.	NA
DUNS No.	NA	Shareholders	NA

Business: The groups principal activity is to exploration of minerals. The group operates from the United States and Canada.

Primary SIC and add'l.: 4813

CIK No: 0001077637

Officers: Zheng Shuying/41/Dir., CEO, CFO

Directors: Zheng Shuying/41/Dir., CEO, CFO, Guan Da Wei/44/Dir., Liu Meifeng/46/Dir.

Owners: Guan Da Wei/78.40%, Insiders/78.40%, Zhang Feng Ming/7.40%

Financial Data: Fiscal Year End:11/30　Latest Annual Data: 12/31/2006

Year		Sales		Net Income
2006		$878,000		-$1,914,000
2005		NA		-$27,000
Curr. Assets:	$126,000	Curr. Liab.:	$145,000	
Plant, Equip.:	$292,000	Total Liab.:	$145,000	Indic. Yr. Divd.: NA
Total Assets:	$421,000	Net Worth:	$276,000	Debt/ Equity: NA

Brampton Crest International Inc

1224 Washington Ave., Miami Beach, FL, 33139; *PH:* 1-305-531-1174

General - Incorporation	NV	Stock - Price on:12/24/2007	$0.11
Employees	NA	Stock Exchange	OTC
Auditor	Berenfeld Spritzer Shechter & Sheer	Ticker Symbol	BRCI
Stk Agt	NA	Outstanding Shares	51,520,000
Counsel	NA	E.P.S.	NA
DUNS No.	NA	Shareholders	NA

Business: The groups principle activities include marketing and selling consumer cosmetics and non-prescription dermatology products. The group operates from United States.

Primary SIC and add'l.: 2844
CIK No: 0001321002
Subsidiaries: Hamilton PNG
Officers: Robert Wineberg/53/Dir., CEO, Principle Accounting Officer, Brad Hacker/48/CFO
Directors: Robert Wineberg/53/Dir., CEO, Principle Accounting Officer, Joseph I. Emas/53/Dir.
Owners: Robert Wineberg, Murray Bacal, Joseph I. Emas, Brampton Crest International, LLC., Insiders
Financial Data: *Fiscal Year End:* 12/31 *Latest Annual Data:* 12/31/2006

Year	Sales	Net Income
2006	$5,000	-$75,000
2005	$3,000	-$239,000

Curr. Assets:	$867,000	**Curr. Liab.:**	$23,000		
Plant, Equip.:	$1,000	**Total Liab.:**	$23,000	**Indic. Yr. Divd.:**	NA
Total Assets:	$868,000	**Net Worth:**	$845,000	**Debt/ Equity:**	NA

Branded Media Corp

425 Madison Ave., Penthouse, New York, NY, 10017; *PH:* 1-212-230-1941;
http:// www.brandedmedia.com

General - Incorporation	NV	**Stock**- Price on:12/24/2007	$0.01
Employees	9	Stock Exchange	OTC
Auditor	Friedman LLP	Ticker Symbol	BMCP
Stk Agt	American Stock Transfer & Trust Co.	Outstanding Shares	34,240,000
Counsel	NA	E.P.S.	NA
DUNS No.	NA	Shareholders	NA

Business: The group's principle activity of the group is delivering timely editorial on all disciplines of business-to-business marketing for marketing strategists. The company provides more than 45,000 subscribers with the information and analysis they need to develop a winning integrated marketing strategy for their companies. They have a branch in Chicago as well. The group also publishes Media Business, the magazine for business publishing executives. The company is a brand-building, marketing and production company that develops our clients' consumer products through a proprietary strategy that they refer to as Branded Media(TM). Branded Media(TM) is designed to capture the attention of targeted consumers and materially increase sales of our client's products by exposing their clients' brands through television and related internet programming created by them.
Primary SIC and add'l.: 6532
CIK No: 0000080751
Subsidiaries: Executive Media Network Inc.
Owners: Insiders/19.00%, James J. Cahill/1.90%, Brian Pussilano/2.80%, The Vantage Funds/17.10%, Gary Kucher/5.00%, Michael S. Scofield, Donald C. Taylor/4.50%, Joseph J. Coffey/4.70%

Brandpartners Group Inc

10 Main St., Rochester, NH, 03839; *PH:* 1-603-335-1400; *Fax:* 1-603-332-7429;
http:// www.bptr.com; *Email:* bptrinfo@brandpartners.com

General - Incorporation	DE	**Stock**- Price on:12/24/2007	$0.11
Employees	152	Stock Exchange	OTC
Auditor	Moore Stephens, P.C	Ticker Symbol	BPTR
Stk Agt	Continental Stock Transfer & Trust Co	Outstanding Shares	34,920,000
Counsel	NA	E.P.S.	-$0.02
DUNS No.	13-020-0488	Shareholders	NA

Business: The group's principal activity is to provide merchandising, branch planning and design and creative services through its wholly-owned subsidiary, willey brothers, inc. The services are provided to financial services firms and other service retailers. The group also provides online database solutions with access to market and economic data in user-friendly mapped formats through digital computer software through its majority-owned subsidiary, imapdata.com, inc.
Primary SIC and add'l.: 6719 7372 7379 8742 7374
CIK No: 0000798600
Subsidiaries: BrandPartners Europe, Ltd, BrandPartners Retail, Inc, Building Partners, Inc, Grafico Incorporated
Officers: James Brooks/Chmn., CEO, Pres.
Directors: James Brooks/Chmn., CEO, Pres., Cliff Brune/Dir., Richard Levy/Dir., Weldon J. Chitwood/Dir.
Owners: MicroCapital/8.50%, Richard Levy/1.40%, Anthony Cataldo/13.30%, Clifford D. Brune/2.90%, Heartland Advisors, Inc./4.30%, James F. Brooks/11.00%, Suzanne Verrill/0.50%, Gruber & McBaine Capital Management/7.80%, Longview Fund, L.P./9.10%, Insiders/17.30%, Robert S. Trump/12.80%, Weldon J. Chitwood/1.40%
Financial Data: *Fiscal Year End:* 12/31 *Latest Annual Data:* 12/31/2006

Year	Sales	Net Income
2006	$52,476,000	-$2,324,000
2005	$52,036,000	$1,915,000
2004	$50,613,000	$14,220,000

Curr. Assets:	$10,420,000	**Curr. Liab.:**	$12,860,000		
Plant, Equip.:	$1,374,000	**Total Liab.:**	$19,312,000	**Indic. Yr. Divd.:**	NA
Total Assets:	$36,506,000	**Net Worth:**	$17,195,000	**Debt/ Equity:**	0.3594

Brandywine Operating PArtnership LP

555 E Lancaster Ave., Ste 500, Radnor, PA, 19087; *PH:* 1-610-325-5600; *Fax:* 1-610-325-5622;
http:// www.brandywinerealty.com

General - Incorporation	DE	**Stock**- Price on:12/24/2007	$29.76
Employees	599	Stock Exchange	NA
Auditor	PricewaterhouseCoopers LLP	Ticker Symbol	NA
Stk Agt	Computershare Investor Services LLC	Outstanding Shares	87,050,000
Counsel	NA	E.P.S.	$0.42
DUNS No.	NA	Shareholders	NA

Business: The groups principle activity is to conduct business and its assets. The groups services include acquiring, developing, redeveloping, leasing and managing office and industrial properties, feasibility and economic analysis, municipal and state approval coordination, budget development and administration, design co. The group also produces real estate development projects. The group operates from United States.
Primary SIC and add'l.: 6798
CIK No: 0001060386
Subsidiaries: 100 Arrandale Associates, 111 Arrandale Associates, 1130 Commerce Associates LLC, 440 Creamery Way Associates, 442 Creamery Way Associates, 481 John Young Way Associates, AAP Sub One, AAPOP 1, AAPOP 2, Atlantic American Land Development, Brandywine - Main Street, Brandywine 300 Delaware, Brandywine Ambassador, Brandywine Brokerage Services, Brandywine Byberry LLC 106 Subsidiaries included in the Index
Officers: Gerard H. Sweeney/51/Pres., CEO - Trustee, Beth R. Glassman/VP - Human Resources, Howard M. Sipzner/CFO, Exec. VP, Robert J. Juliano/CIO, VP, Robert K. Wiberg/Exec. VP, Sr. MD - Metro Washington DC Region, Christopher M. Hipps/Exec. VP, MD - Southwest, Southern CA Regions, Daniel K. Cushing/Sr. VP, MD - Northern CA Region, Gregory Imhoff/Sr. VP, Chief Administrative Officer, Anthony S. Rimikis/Sr. VP - Development, Philip M. Schenkel/VP, MD - Northern PA Region, George D. Sowa/Exec. VP, Sr. MD - New Jersey, Delaware Region, Brad A. Molotsky/Sr. VP, General Counsel, Sec., Michael J. Cooper/Sr. VP, MD - Metro DC Region, Jeffrey H. Devuono/Sr. VP, MD - Pennsylvania Region, George D. Johnstone/Sr. VP - Operations *(17 Officers included in Index)*
Directors: Gerard H. Sweeney/51/Pres., CEO - Trustee, Walter D'Alessio/Chmn. - Board of Trustee, Pike D. Aloian/Trustee, Donald E. Axinn/Trustee, Michael J. Joyce/Trustee, Charles P. Pizzi/Trustee, Tom August/Trustee, Wyche Fowler/Trustee, Anthony A. Nichols/Trustee, Mike V. Prentiss/Trustee
Financial Data: *Fiscal Year End:* 12/31 *Latest Annual Data:* 12/31/2006

Year	Sales	Net Income
2006	$662,801,000	$10,482,000
2005	$391,460,000	$42,767,000
2004	$323,592,000	$60,303,000

Curr. Assets:	$139,482,000	**Curr. Liab.:**	$151,160,000	**P/E Ratio:**	70.86
Plant, Equip.:	$4,865,742,000	**Total Liab.:**	$3,486,346,000	**Indic. Yr. Divd.:**	$1.760
Total Assets:	$5,508,263,000	**Net Worth:**	$1,897,926,000	**Debt/ Equity:**	1.7803

Brandywine Realty Trust

555 E Lancaster Ave., Radnor, PA, 19087; *PH:* 1-610-325-5600; *Fax:* 1-610-325-5622;
http:// www.brandywinerealty.com

General - Incorporation	MD	**Stock**- Price on:12/24/2007	NA
Employees	599	Stock Exchange	NYSE
Auditor	PricewaterhouseCoopers LLP	Ticker Symbol	BDN
Stk Agt	Computershare Trust Co	Outstanding Shares	87,050,000
Counsel	NA	E.P.S.	NA
DUNS No.	NA	Shareholders	NA

Business: The groups principle activities include acquiring, developing, redeveloping, leasing and managing office and industrial properties. The group operates through nine geographic segments. The group operates 261 office properties, 23 industrial properties and one mixed-use property in the United States. The group's quarterly revenue for September 2007 was 175.40 millions of USD.
Primary SIC and add'l.: 6798
CIK No: 0000790816
Subsidiaries: 100 Arrandale Associates, L.P, 1000 Chesterbrook Boulevard Partnership, 111 Arrandale Associates, L.P, 440 Creamery Way Associates, L.P, 442 Creamery Way Associates, L.P, 481 John Young Way Associates, L.P, AAP Sub One, Inc, AAPOP 1, L.P, AAPOP 2, L.P, Atlantic American Land Development, Inc, Atlantic American Properties Trust, BDN GP Real Estate Fund I LLC, BDN Properties I Inc, BDN Real Estate Fund I LP, Beltline Associates GP, LLC 189 Subsidiaries included in the Index
Officers: Gerard H. Sweeney/CEO, Pres., Trustee/$3,200,883.00, George D. Sowa/Exec. VP, Sr. MD - New Jersey, Delaware Region/$645,373.00, Christopher Donohoe/VP - Property Management, Northern CA Region, Duane Henley/Sr. VP - Leasing, Southwest Region, Christopher Hipps/Exec. VP, MD - Southwest, Southern CA Regions, Robert K. Wiberg/Exec. VP, Sr. MD - Metro Washington DC Region/$648,912.00, Marge Boccuti/Investor Relations Contact, Ralph Bistline/VP - Leasing, Southwest Region, Gerald Avery Mays/VP - Construction, Southwest Region, Daniel Palazzo/VP - Asset Management, Western, Northern PA Regions, William Reister/VP - Asset Management, Southwest Region, Leon H. Shadowen/VP - New Business Development, Richmond Region, Suzanne K. Stumpf/VP - Asset Management, Richmond Region, Jeffrey R. Weinstein/VP - Construction, Urban Division, Anthony V. Ziccardi/VP - Suburban Development *(34 Officers included in Index)*
Directors: Gerard H. Sweeney/CEO, Pres., Trustee, Walter D'Alessio/Chmn., Anthony A. Nichols/Chmn. Emeritus, Trustee, Mike Prentiss/Trustee, George D. Sowa/Exec. VP, Sr. MD - New Jersey, Delaware Region, David Ryder/52/Sr. VP, MD - Western Pennsylvania Region, Pike D. Aloian/Trustee, Donald E. Axinn/Trustee, Michael J. Joyce/Trustee, Charles P. Pizzi/Trustee, Tom August/Trustee, Wyche Fowler/Trustee
Owners: Security Capital Research& Management Incorporated/6.51%, George D. Sowa, Brad A. Molotsky, The Vanguard Group, Inc/5.86%, Michael V. Prentiss/1.84%, Goldman Sachs Asset Management, L.P/7.38%, Insiders/5.79%, Pike D. Aloian, Michael J. Joyce, Morgan Stanley/10.39%, Walter DAlessio, Cohen& Steers Capital Management, Inc/10.14%, Charles P. Pizzi, AEW Capital Management, L.P/5.07%, Donald E. Axinn/1.04% *(21 Owners included in Index)*

Curr. Assets:	NA	**Curr. Liab.:**	NA		
Plant, Equip.:	NA	**Total Liab.:**	NA	**Indic. Yr. Divd.:**	NA
Total Assets:	NA	**Net Worth:**	NA	**Debt/ Equity:**	NA

Brasil Telecom Participacoes S.A.

One Wall St., New York, NY , 10286; *PH:* 1-212-815-2009; *http://* www.brasiltelecom.com.br

General - Incorporation		**Stock**- Price on:12/24/2007	$60.6801
Employees	NA	Stock Exchange	NYSE
Auditor	NA	Ticker Symbol	BRP
Stk Agt	Bank of New York	Outstanding Shares	72,500,000
Counsel	NA	E.P.S.	$3.00
DUNS No.	NA	Shareholders	NA

Business: The groups principle activity is to provide telecommunications services. The group also provides data transmission services. The group operates through three segments namely, fixed telephony and data transmission, mobile telephony and internet. The group operates from the Brazil, the United States, Venesuela and Bermudas Islands. The group's quarterly revenue for September 2007 was 2,748.27 millions of USD.
Primary SIC and add'l.: 4812 7375 4813 4822 7389 4899 7379
CIK No:

Subsidiaries: 14 Brasil Telecom Celular S.A., Brasil Telecom Cabos Submarinos (HolLDng) Ltda., Brasil Telecom Cabos Submarinos Ltda., Brasil Telecom Comunicao Multimidia Ltda., Brasil Telecom de Venezuela S.A, Brasil Telecom of America Inc., Brasil Telecom Subsea Cable Systems (Bermuda) Ltd, BrT Servios de Internet S.A., Freelance S.A., iBest Espanha Award Espaa S.L., iBest Holding Corporation, iBest Mxico Award Mexico S.A. de C.V., Internet Group (Cayman) Limited, Internet Group do Brasil Ltda., Lokau Mxico de S.A. de C.V. 23 Subsidiaries included in the Index

Officers: Ricardo Knoepfelmacher/42/CEO, Charles Lagana Putz/Investor Relations Officer, Francisco Aurelio Sampaio Santiago/54/Network Executive Officer, Luiz Francisco Tenorio Perrone/66/Human Resources Executive Officer, Paulo Narcelio Simoes Amaral/45/Financial Executive Officer, Investor Relations Officer

Directors: Sergio Spinelli Silva/Chmn., Pedro Paulo Elejalde De Campos/Dir., Elemer Andre Suranyi/Dir., Ricardo Ferraz Torres/Dir., Antonio Cardoso Dos Santos/Dir.

Owners: Antonio Cardoso dos Santos, Elemer Andre Suranyi, Ricardo Ferraz Torres, Eduardo Grande Bittencourt, Pedro Paulo Elejalde de Campos, Insiders, Sergio Spinelli Silva, Insiders, Ricardo Knoepfelmacher

Financial Data: *Fiscal Year End:*NA **Latest Annual Data:** 12/31/2006

Year	Sales		Net Income
2006	$4,828,103,000		$322,275,000
2005	$4,355,579,000		$72,512,000
2004	$3,412,011,000		$107,239,000
Curr. Assets:	$2,820,344,000	**Curr. Liab.:**	$2,164,631,000
Plant, Equip.:	$3,062,089,000	**Total Liab.:**	$4,888,073,000	**Indic. Yr. Divd.:** $0.180
Total Assets:	$8,201,777,000	**Net Worth:**	$3,307,894,000	**Debt/ Equity:** NA

Braskem

Av. Das Naes Unidas, 4777 - Cep, So Paulo, 5477000; *PH:* 55-1134439999; *http://* www.braskem.com.br; *Email:* braskem-ri@braskem.com.br

General - Incorporation	Brazil	Stock - Price on:12/24/2007	$17.78
Employees	3,262	Stock Exchange	NYSE
Auditor	PricewaterhouseCoopers LLP	Ticker Symbol	BAK
Stk Agt	Citibank N.A	Outstanding Shares	357,570,000
Counsel	NA	E.P.S	$0.83
DUNS No.	89-828-8154	Shareholders	NA

Business: The group principal activities are the manufacture, sale, import and export of chemical and petrochemical products. The group is also engaged in the production and sale of products used in the steam and treated water, compressed air and electric power industries. The group provides petrochemical and related products to companies of the northeastern petrochemical complex in bahia.

Primary SIC and add'l.: 2869 2911 4939

CIK No: 0001071438

Subsidiaries: Braskem Cayman Ltd., Braskem Distribuidora de Combustveis Ltda., Braskem Importao e Exportao Ltda., Braskem Incorporated Ltd., Braskem International Ltd., Braskem Participaes S.A., Cetrel, Chemical Fundo de Investimento em Direitos Creditrios (Fundo Chemical II), Chemical Fundo de Investimento em Direitos Creditrios (Fundo Chemical), Cinal, Codeverde, Copesul, CPP - Companhia Petroqumica Paulista (CPP), CSAM Orion Fund Limited (Orion), Fundo Parin 34 Subsidiaries included in the Index

Officers: Jose Carlos Grubisich Filho/CEO, Carlos Jose Fadigas De Souza Filho/VP, Luiz De Mendonca/VP, Mauricio Roberto De Carvalho Ferro/VP, General Counsel, Marcelo Lyra Do Amaral/VP - Institutional Relations, Manoel Carnauba Cortez/VP, Luis Fernando Sartini Felli/VP, Jose Augusto Cardoso Mendes/VP - Planning, Roberto Prisco Paraiso Ramos/VP, Bernardo Afonso De Almeida Gradin/43/VP, Executive Officer, Roberto Lopes Pontes Simoes/VP

Directors: Ruy Lemos Sampaio/57/Alternate Dir., Claudio Melo Filho/40/Alternate Dir., Rubio Fernal Ferreira eSousa/56/Alternate Dir., Yukihiro Funamoto/35/Alternate Dir., Jose Mauro Mettrau Carneiro Da Cunha/Dir., Francisco Teixeira De Sa/Dir., Pedro Augusto Ribeiro Novis/Dir., Lucio Jose Santos/42/Alternate Dir., Guilherme Simoes De Abreu/56/Alternate Dir., Marcos Wilson Spyer Rezende/60/Alternate Dir., Newton Sergio De Souza/Dir., Hilberto Mascarenhas Alves Da Silva Filho/52/Alternate Dir., Marcos Luiz Abreu De Lima/64/Alternate Dir., Alvaro Pereira Novis/Dir., Patrick Horbach Fairon/Dir. (23 Directors included in Index)

Owners: BNDESPAR/5.50%, Insiders, Vera Maria Wolf/3.40%, Petroquisa/7.50%, Beatriz Wolf Wander/6.80%, Liane Maria Wolf, Marcos Juliano Lucas Carvalho, Marcos Juliano Lucas Carvalho, Marcos Juliano Lucas Carvalho/32.40%, Petroquisa/9.80%, Liane Maria Wolf/6.80%, Insiders, ODBPAR Investments/75.40%, Alliance Capital Management L.P./5.00%, ODBPAR Investments/19.80%

Financial Data: *Fiscal Year End:*12/31 **Latest Annual Data:** 12/31/2006

Year	Sales		Net Income
2006	$5,609,638,000		$75,774,000
2005	$5,158,551,000		$316,658,000
2004	$4,589,069,000		$334,168,000
Curr. Assets:	$2,617,822,000	**Curr. Liab.:**	$2,586,687,000	**P/E Ratio:** 32.78
Plant, Equip.:	$3,122,733,000	**Total Liab.:**	$5,591,117,000	**Indic. Yr. Divd.:** $0.300
Total Assets:	$6,982,249,000	**Net Worth:**	$1,391,133,000	**Debt/ Equity:** NA

Bravo Foods International Corp

11300 Us Hwy. 1, Ste. 400, North Palm Beach, FL, 33408; *PH:* 1-561-625-1411; *http://* www.bravobrands.com

General - Incorporation	DE	Stock - Price on:12/24/2007	$0.033
Employees	60	Stock Exchange	NA
Auditor	Lazar Levine & Felix LLP	Ticker Symbol	NA
Stk Agt	American Stock Transfer & Trust Co.	Outstanding Shares	249,970,000
Counsel	NA	E.P.S	-$0.34
DUNS No.	NA	Shareholders	NA

Business: The group's principal activity is to process, market and distribute dairy and juice products. The products include baggie milk, milk powder, aseptic packaged milk, juice products and bottled drinkable yogurt. The flavors include vanilla shake, orange cream, chocolate, strawberry and banana and are branded with bugs bunny, tweety and sylvester, daffy duck, lola bunny, wile e. Coyote and the road runner. The group operates in the United States, Canada, Mexico and China.

Primary SIC and add'l.: 2026

CIK No: 0001061029

Subsidiaries: Bravo! Brands (UK) Ltd., Bravo! Brands International Ltd., China Premium Food Corp (Shanghai) Co. Ltd., Wai Gao Qiao

Officers: Roy Warren/52/Dir., CEO, Roy Toulan/62/VP, Corp. Sec., General Counsel, Michael Edwards/48/Chief Revenue Officer, Benjamin Patipa/52/COO, Tommy Kee/59/Chief Accounting Officer, Jeffrey Kaplan/59/CFO, Stanley Harris/59/Chief Marketing Officer, Michael Comerford/52/Dir. - Sales Operations, Mark Maraist/39/VP, Controller, Joseph Librizzi/60/Dir. - Procurement, Supply Mgmt Operations

Directors: Roy Warren/52/Dir., CEO, Stanley Hirschman/61/Chmn., Arthur Blanding/84/Dir., Robert Cummings/65/Dir., Phillip Pearce/79/Dir., John McCormack/48/Dir., Gerald Bos/68/Dir., Jack Shea/57/Dir. - Business Development, Charles Walton/52/Dir. - Product Development

Owners: Deutsche Bank AG/5.23%, Evolution Capital Management, LLP/9.44%, Jeffrey Kaplan, Phillip Pearce, Lombard Odier Darier Hentsch & Cie/8.15%, Robert Cummings, Michael Edwards, Arthur Blanding, Roy Toulan, Mid-Am Capital, L.L.C./9.97%, Roy Warren/2.62%, Stanley Hirschman, John McCormack, Tommy Kee, Insiders/8.26% (18 Owners included in Index)

Financial Data: *Fiscal Year End:*12/31 **Latest Annual Data:** 12/31/2006

Year	Sales		Net Income
2006	$14,662,000		-$36,697,000
2005	$11,949,000		-$79,529,000
2004	$3,345,000		-$3,800,000
Curr. Assets:	$7,296,000	**Curr. Liab.:**	$61,674,000
Plant, Equip.:	$1,212,000	**Total Liab.:**	$61,742,000	**Indic. Yr. Divd.:** NA
Total Assets:	$30,378,000	**Net Worth:**	-$33,763,000	**Debt/ Equity:** NA

Brazauro Resources Corp

800 Bering Dr., Ste. 208, Houston, TX, 77057; *PH:* 1-713-785-1278; *Fax:* 1-713-785-5247; *http://* www.Brazauroresources.com; *Email:* info@brazauroresources.com

General - Incorporation	BC	Stock - Price on:12/24/2007	$0.75
Employees	24	Stock Exchange	OTC
Auditor	Morgan & Co	Ticker Symbol	BZOFF
Stk Agt	Computershare Investor Services LLC	Outstanding Shares	76,360,000
Counsel	DuMoulin Black	E.P.S	$1.03
DUNS No.	NA	Shareholders	NA

Business: The group's principle activity is to explore and develop mineral resource properties, primarily diamond properties, in Arkansas in the U.S., and in Iceland.

Primary SIC and add'l.: 1499

CIK No: 0000908177

Subsidiaries: A British Columbia corporation

Officers: Mark E. Jones/Chmn., CEO, Leendert G. Krol/Dir., Advisor, Elton Pereira/VP - Exploration

Directors: Mark E. Jones/Chmn., CEO, Leendert G. Krol/Dir., Advisor, Daniel B. Leonard/Dir., Roger David Morton/Dir., Roger Howard Mitchell/Dir., Patrick L. Glazier/Dir., Brian C. Irwin/Dir., Harry Dobson/Dir.

Owners: Roger David Morton, Insiders/12.70%, Brian C. Irwin, Daniel B. Leonard/1.90%, Roger Howard Mitchell, Mark E. Jones/3.80%, Patrick L. Glazier/2.60%, Stephen G. Zahony, Leendert G. Krol/1.90%, Harry W. D. Dobson

Financial Data: *Fiscal Year End:*01/31 **Latest Annual Data:** 01/31/2007

Year	Sales		Net Income
2007	$222,000		-$5,222,000
2006	$156,000		-$8,093,000
Curr. Assets:	$7,811,000	**Curr. Liab.:**	$308,000
Plant, Equip.:	$1,547,000	**Total Liab.:**	$308,000	**Indic. Yr. Divd.:** NA
Total Assets:	$9,364,000	**Net Worth:**	$9,055,000	**Debt/ Equity:** NA

Brazil Fast Food Corp

Av Brazil 6431, Bonsucesso, Rio De Janeiro; *PH:* 55-2125367500; *http://* www.bobs.com.br

General - Incorporation	DE	Stock - Price on:12/24/2007	$5.8
Employees	1,392	Stock Exchange	OTC
Auditor	Grant Thornton LLP	Ticker Symbol	BOBS
Stk Agt	American Stock Transfer & Trust Co.	Outstanding Shares	8,380,000
Counsel	Sonnenschein Nath & Rosenthal LLP	E.P.S	$0.86
DUNS No.	83-592-0323	Shareholders	NA

Business: The group operates through its subsidiary whose principle activity is to operate hamburger fast food restaurants. The group operates from United States.

Primary SIC and add'l.: 6719 5812

CIK No: 0000914537

Subsidiaries: Bigburger Goiania Lanchonetes Ltda., Bigburger Sao Paulo Lanchonetes Ltda.

Owners: Guillermo Hector Pisano, Mexford Resources, Stephen J. Rose, Insiders, Ricardo Figueiredo Bomeny, Gustavo Figueiredo Bomeny, Omar Carneiro da Cunha, Jos Ricardo Bousquet Bomeny, Peter J. F. van Voorst Vader, Rmulo Borges Fonseca

Financial Data: *Fiscal Year End:*12/31 **Latest Annual Data:** 12/31/2006

Year	Sales		Net Income
2006	$45,631,000		$4,658,000
2005	$37,599,000		$1,909,000
2004	$28,504,000		$226,000
Curr. Assets:	$7,415,000	**Curr. Liab.:**	$9,076,000	**P/E Ratio:** 8.66
Plant, Equip.:	$8,184,000	**Total Liab.:**	$17,145,000	**Indic. Yr. Divd.:** NA
Total Assets:	$21,965,000	**Net Worth:**	$4,819,000	**Debt/ Equity:** NA

Brazil Telecom Co

Sia/sul Asp, Lote D Bloco B, Setor de Industria, Brasilia; *PH:* 55-614151140; *http://* www.brasiltelecom.net.br

General - Incorporation	Brazil	Stock - Price on:12/24/2007	$60.13
Employees	6,872	Stock Exchange	NA
Auditor	KPMG LLP	Ticker Symbol	NA
Stk Agt	Bank of New York	Outstanding Shares	72,500,000
Counsel	NA	E.P.S	NA
DUNS No.	NA	Shareholders	NA

Business: The group's principal activity is the provision of voice, text, data and image transmission services for both private and public sectors via fixed telecommunications networks. The group operates in the states of acre, rondonia, mato grosso, mato grosso do sul, tocantins, goias, santa catarina, parana and rio grande do sul with the exception of the city of londrina.

Primary SIC and add'l.: 4899 7389 4813 4822 4812

CIK No: 0001160846

Subsidiaries: 14 Brasil Telecom Celular S.A., Brasil Telecom Cabos Submarinos (HolLDng) Ltda., Brasil Telecom Cabos Submarinos Ltda., Brasil Telecom Comunicao Multimidia Ltda., Brasil Telecom de Venezuela S.A., Brasil Telecom of America Inc., Brasil Telecom Subsea Cable Systems (Bermuda) Ltd., BrT Servios de Internet S.A., Freelance S.A., iBest Espanha Award Espaa S.L., iBest Holding Corporation, iBest Mxico Award Mexico S.A. de C.V., Internet Group (Cayman) Limited, Internet Group do Brasil Ltda., Lokau Mxico de S.A. de C.V. 23 Subsidiaries included in the Index

Officers: Ricardo Knoepfelmacher/CEO, Paulo Narcelio Simoes Amaral/CFO, Investor Relations Officer, Carlos Alberto Caser/Member - Fiscal Counsel, Eduardo Grande Bittencourt/Member - Fiscal Counsel, Flavia Menezes/Mgr. - Investor Relations, Giovanni Foragi/Dir. - Human Resources, Francisco Aurelio Sampaio Santiago/COO, Luiz Francisco Tenorio Perrone/Human Resources Officer, Rosalia Maria Tereza Sergi Agati Camello/Member - Fiscal Counsel, Marcel Cecchi Vieira/Member - Fiscal Counsel, Jose Arthur Escodro/Member - Fiscal Counsel, Hiram Bandeira Pagano Filho/Member - Fiscal Counsel, Roberto Henrique Gremler/Member - Fiscal Counsel, Bruno Oliva Girardi/Member - Fiscal Counsel

Directors: Sergio Spinelli Silva/Chmn., Pedro Paulo Elejal De Campos/Vice Chmn., Kevin Michael Altit/Dir., Alberto Ribeiro Guth/Dir., Elemer Andre Suranyi/Dir., Renato Carvalho Do Nascimento/Dir., Ricardo Ferraz Torres/Dir., Adriana Duarte Chagastelles/Dir., Antonio Cardoso Dos Santos/Dir., Gregorio Mancebo Rodriguez/Dir., Mariana Sarmento Meneghetti/Dir., Jose Luiz Rodrigues/Dir.

Owners: Insiders, Sergio Spinelli Silva, Elemer Andre Suranyi, Ricardo Knoepfelmacher, Ricardo Ferraz Torres, Eduardo Grande Bittencourt, Pedro Paulo Elejalde de Campos, Insiders, Antonio Cardoso dos Santos

Financial Data: *Fiscal Year End:* 12/31 *Latest Annual Data:* 12/31/2006

Year	Sales	Net Income
2006	$4,828,103,000	$322,275,000
2005	$4,355,579,000	$72,512,000
2004	$3,412,011,000	$107,239,000

Curr. Assets:	$2,820,344,000	**Curr. Liab.:**	$2,164,631,000	**P/E Ratio:**	8.66
Plant, Equip.:	$3,062,089,000	**Total Liab.:**	$4,888,073,000	**Indic. Yr. Divd.:**	NA
Total Assets:	$8,201,777,000	**Net Worth:**	$3,307,894,000	**Debt/ Equity:**	NA

Brazilian Distribution Co Companhia Brasileira De Distr CBD

Formerly: Brazilian Distribution Co

Av Brigadeiro Luiz Antonio 3126 1, Andar, SAO PAULO, 01402-901; *PH:* 011-886-0814

General - Incorporation	Brazil	**Stock**- Price on:12/24/2007	$38.92
Employees	63,607	Stock Exchange	NYSE
Auditor	PricewaterhouseCoopers LLP	Ticker Symbol	NA
Stk Agt	Bank of New York	Outstanding Shares	113,770,000
Counsel	NA	E.P.S	NA
DUNS No.	NA	Shareholders	NA

Business: The group's principal activity is the operation of retail food, home appliance and clothing in 497 stores among which there are supermarkets, department stores, and other specialised stores in 12 brazilian states.

Primary SIC and add'l.: 5399 5720 5731 5411 5311

CIK No: 0001038572

Officers: Cassio Casseb Lima/CEO, Daniela Sabbag/Investor Relations Officer, Caio Racy Mattar/Investment, Construction Officer, Maria Aparecida Fonseca/Human Resources Officer, Eneas Cesar Pestana Neto/CFO, Antonio Ramatis Fernandes Rodrigues/Commercial, Food Exec. Officer, Claudia Jordao Ribeiro Pagnano/Marketing Exec. Officer, Pedro Barcellos Janot Marinho/Commercial - Non - Food Exec. Officer, Alexandre Lodygensky Junior/International Commerce Exec. Officer, Hugo Antonio Jordao Bethlem/Hypermarkets, Comprebem Supermarkets Officer, Jose Roberto Coimbra Tambasco/Pao de Acucar Supermarket Officer

Directors: Abilio Dossantos Diniz/Chmn., Valentim Dossantos Diniz/Honorable Chmn., Hakim Laurent Aouani/Dir., Maria Silvia Bastos Marques/Dir., Jean-Charles Henri Naouri/Dir., Henri Philippe Reichstul/Dir., Gerald Dinu Reiss/Dir., Francis Andre Mauger/Dir., Anamaria Falleiros Dos Santos Diniz DAvila/Dir., Geyze Marchesi Diniz/Dir., Candido Botelho Bracher/Dir., Joaopaulo Falleiros Dos Santos Diniz/Dir., Pedro Paulo Falleiros Dos Dos Santos Diniz/Dir., Michel Alain Maurice Favre/Dir., Xavier Michel Marie Jacques Desjobert/Dir.

Financial Data: *Fiscal Year End:* 12/31 *Latest Annual Data:* 12/31/2006

Year	Sales	Net Income
2006	$6,508,521,000	$6,798,000
2005	$4,530,905,000	$116,251,000
2004	$4,729,472,000	$184,019,000

Curr. Assets:	$2,287,489,000	**Curr. Liab.:**	$1,793,031,000	**P/E Ratio:**	8.66
Plant, Equip.:	$2,010,403,000	**Total Liab.:**	$3,149,136,000	**Indic. Yr. Divd.:**	$0.090
Total Assets:	$5,393,466,000	**Net Worth:**	$2,184,116,000	**Debt/ Equity:**	NA

Brazilian Petroleum Corp

750 Lexington Ave., 43rd Fl., New York, NY, 10022; *PH:* 1-212-829-1517; *Fax:* 1-212-832-5300; *http://* www.petrobras.com.br

General - Incorporation	Brazil	**Stock**- Price on:12/24/2007	$120.83
Employees	62,266	Stock Exchange	NA
Auditor	Ernst & Young LLP	Ticker Symbol	NA
Stk Agt	Citibank N.A	Outstanding Shares	1,100,000,000
Counsel	NA	E.P.S	$3.48
DUNS No.	NA	Shareholders	NA

Business: The group's principal activities are the research, exploration, mining, distribution, import, export, production, refining, transportation and sale of oil and it's byproducts, such as light distillates (gasoline, naphtha), medium distillates (diesel oil, kerosene), bottom settlings (fuel oil, aromatic) and other related activities. The group is organized into 4 business divisions, 2 support divisions and 7 corporate units.

Primary SIC and add'l.: NA

CIK No: 0001119639

Subsidiaries: 5283 Participaes Ltda., Baixada Santista Energia Ltda., BEAR Insurance Company Limited, Blade Securities Limited, Braspetro Oil Company, Braspetro Oil Services Company, Charter Development, Cia. De Desenvolvimento e Modernizao de Plantas Industriais, Codajs Coari Participaes Ltda., Downstream Participaes S.A., FAFEN Energia S.A., Fundo de Investimento Imobilirio, Gasene Participaes Ltda., Manaus Gerao Termeltrica Participaes Ltda, Petrobras Distribuidora S.A. 24 Subsidiaries included in the Index

Officers: Jose Sergio Gabrielli De Azevedo/56/Dir., CEO, Pres., Daniel Lima De Oliveira/Chmn., CEO - Pifco, Gabrielli J.S De Azevedo/59/Dir., CEO, Pres., Helio Shiguenobu Fujikawa/General Sec., Maria Lucia De Oliveira Falcon/Member - Fiscal Counsel, Marcus Pereira Aucelio/Member - Fiscal Counsel, Tulio Luiz Zamin/Member - Fiscal Counsel, Nelson Rocha Augusto/Member - Fiscal Counsel, Gerson Luiz Goncalves/55/Auditor Mgr. - Pifco, Almir Guilherme Barbassa/CFO, Dir. - Investor Relations, Guilherme De Oliveira Estrella/Dir. - Exploration, Production, Paulo Roberto Costa/Dir. - Downstream, Ildo Luis Sauer/Dir. - Gas, Energy, Nestor Cunat Cervero/International Dir., Renato De Souza Duque/Dir.ervices

Directors: Jose Sergio Gabrielli De Azevedo/56/Dir., CEO, Pres., Daniel Lima De Oliveira/Chmn., CEO - Pifco, Gabrielli J.S De Azevedo/59/Dir., CEO, Pres., Dilma Vana Rousseff/Chmn., Francisco Roberto De Albuquerque/Dir., Guido Mantega/Dir., Silas Rondeau Cavalcante Silva/Dir., Fabio Colletti Barbosa/Dir., Jorge Gerdau Johannpeter/Dir., Arthur Antonio Sendas/Dir., Roger Agnelli/Dir.

Owners: Other Brazilian public sector entities/0.10%, Brazilian government/32.20%, Others/60.10%, BNDES Participaes S.A.-BNDESPAR/7.60%, Insiders

Financial Data: *Fiscal Year End:* 12/31 *Latest Annual Data:* 12/31/2005

Year	Sales	Net Income
2005	$56,324,000,000	$10,344,000,000
2004	$37,452,000,000	$6,190,000,000
2003	$42,690,000,000	$6,559,000,000

Curr. Assets:	$25,778,000,000	**Curr. Liab.:**	$18,155,000,000	**P/E Ratio:**	8.66
Plant, Equip.:	$45,920,000,000	**Total Liab.:**	$44,634,000,000	**Indic. Yr. Divd.:**	NA
Total Assets:	$78,625,000,000	**Net Worth:**	$32,917,000,000	**Debt/ Equity:**	NA

BRE Properties Inc

525 Market St., 4th Fl., San Francisco, CA, 94105; *PH:* 1-415-445-6530; *Fax:* 1-415-445-6505; *http://* www.breproperties.com; *Email:* ir@breproperties.com

General - Incorporation	DE	**Stock**- Price on:12/24/2007	$58.42
Employees	836	Stock Exchange	NYSE
Auditor	Ernst& Young LLP	Ticker Symbol	BRE
Stk Agt	Mellon Investor Services LLC	Outstanding Shares	50,690,000
Counsel	NA	E.P.S	$0.99
DUNS No.	NA	Shareholders	NA

Business: The groups principle activities include developing, acquiring and management of multifamily apartment communities. The group operates from the Western United States. The groups quarterly revenue for September 2007 was 87.76 millions of USD.

Primary SIC and add'l.: 6798

CIK No: 0000009677

Officers: Constance B. Moore/Dir., CEO, Pres., Edward F. Lange/48/COO, Exec. VP, Bradley P. Griggs/Exec. VP, Chief Investment Officer, Deirdre A. Kuring/Exec. VP - Asset Management, Craig Swanson/Dir. - Land Acquisitions

Directors: Constance B. Moore/Dir., CEO, Pres., Robert A. Fiddaman/70/Chmn., Roger P. Kuppinger/67/Dir., Irving F. Lyons/58/Dir., Edward E. MacE/56/Dir., Christopher J. McGurk/51/Dir., Matthew T. Medeiros/51/Dir., Jeanne R. Myerson/54/Dir., Thomas E. Robinson/Dir.

Financial Data: *Fiscal Year End:* 07/31 *Latest Annual Data:* 12/31/2006

Year	Sales	Net Income
2006	$329,968,000	$120,195,000
2005	$298,133,000	$80,948,000
2004	$280,642,000	$73,541,000

Curr. Assets:	$20,703,000	**Curr. Liab.:**	$68,442,000	**P/E Ratio:**	59.01
Plant, Equip.:	$2,758,917,000	**Total Liab.:**	$1,746,102,000	**Indic. Yr. Divd.:**	$2.150
Total Assets:	$2,823,491,000	**Net Worth:**	$976,845,000	**Debt/ Equity:**	1.9133

Breakwater Resources Ltd

95 Wellington St. W, Ste. 950, Toronto, ON, M5J 2N7; *PH:* 1-416-363-4798; *http://* www.breakwater.ca; *Email:* investorinfo@breakwater.ca

General - Incorporation	Canada	**Stock**- Price on:12/24/2007	$2.52
Employees	NA	Stock Exchange	OTC
Auditor	Pricewaterhousecoopers LLP	Ticker Symbol	BWLRF
Stk Agt	Computershare Investor Services LLC	Outstanding Shares	NA
Counsel	Smith Lyons	E.P.S	NA
DUNS No.	24-899-4790	Shareholders	NA

Business: The group's principal activity is to acquire, explore, develop and mine base metal deposits such as zinc, lead, copper, gold and silver in the Americas and north Africa. At 31-Dec-2001, the group owns seven mines: bouchard-hebert mine in quebec, nanisivik mine in nunavut, langlois mine in quebec, caribou mine in new brunswick, bougrine mine in Tunisia, el mochito mine in Honduras and el toqui mine in Chile. The group owns base and precious metal exploration properties in Canada, Honduras, Chile and Tunisia.

Primary SIC and add'l.: 1044 1031

CIK No: 0000782875

Subsidiaries: American Pacific Honduras S.A. de C.V., Breakwater Tunisia S.A., CanZinco Ltd, Consell Marketing Inc., NVI Mining Ltd, Sociedad Contractual Minera El Toqui

Officers: George E. Pirie/Dir., CEO, Pres., Robert Cuttriss/VP - Technical Services, William M. Heath/Exec. VP, Torben Jensen/VP - Engineering, Steven J. Hayes/VP - Commercial, Fred Herman/Sr. VP - Sustainability, Wes Roberts/VP - Corporate Development, Ann E. Wilkinson/VP - Investor Relations, Leroy A. Fong/Controller, Dave Langille/VP - Finance, CFO, Jason C. Stevens/Exec. VP - Legal, Corporate Affairs, Sec., Bertrand Boivin/VP - Canada, Daniel Goffaux/VP - Latin America, Robert R. Carreau/VP - CSR, Sustainability

Directors: George E. Pirie/Dir., CEO, Pres., Garth A.C. MacRae/Chmn., Jonathan C. Goodman/Dir., John W. Murray/Dir., Donald K. Charter/Corp. Dir., Ned Goodman/Dir., Joanne Ferstman/Dir., John W. Ivany/Dir., Grant A. Edey/Dir., Murray A. Sinclair/Dir.

Financial Data: *Fiscal Year End:* 12/31 *Latest Annual Data:* 12/31/2006

Year	Sales	Net Income
2006	$278,356,000	$146,256,000
2005	$268,524,000	$10,913,000
2004	$199,520,000	$4,952,000

Curr. Assets:	$175,801,000	Curr. Liab.:	$78,404,000		
Plant, Equip.:	$171,586,000	Total Liab.:	$181,086,000	Indic. Yr. Divd.:	NA
Total Assets:	$454,001,000	Net Worth:	$272,915,000	Debt/ Equity:	NA

Breda Telephone Corp

112 E Main, Breda, IA, 51436; **PH:** 1-712-673-2311; **Fax:** 1-712-673-2800; **http://** www.win-4-u.com

General - Incorporation.............................. IA	**Stock** Price on:12/24/2007 ....NA
Employees ....NA	Stock Exchange.......................................NA
Auditor .... Kiesling Assoc. LLP	Ticker Symbol...NA
Stk Agt...NA	Outstanding Shares ....NA
Counsel..NA	E.P.S ....NA
DUNS No...NA	Shareholders..NA

Business: The group's principle actiivty is to provide telecommunications exchange and local access services, cable television services, Internet services and telecommunications equipment in a service area located primarily in western Iowa. The group operates from United States.

Primary SIC and add'l.: 4841 7375 4813

CIK No: 0001084448

Subsidiaries: Westside Independent Telephone Company

Officers: Steve Frickenstein/CEO/$67,239.00, Rick Anthofer/51/Treasurer, Dir., Chuck Diesbeck/COO/$59,328.00, Andrea Haney/Quality Assurance Mgr., Dave Grabner/59/Dir., VP, Jane Morlok/CFO/$135,603.00, Charles Thatcher/56/Dir., Pres., Neil Kanne/61/Dir., Sec., Kevin Skinner/Accounting Department Mgr., Diane Miller/Human Resources Mgr., Mike Ludwig/Plant Mgr., Megan Badding/CSR, Sales, Marketing Mgr.

Directors: Dave Grabner/59/Dir., VP, Clifford Neumayer/58/Dir., Charles Thatcher/56/Dir., Pres., Neil Kanne/61/Dir., Sec., Rick Anthofer/51/Treasurer, Dir., Daniel Nieland/51/Dir., Robert Buelt/49/Dir.

Owners: Robert Buelt/0.43%, Insiders/1.34%, Dave Grabner/0.18%, Neil Kanne/0.01%, Daniel Nieland/0.00%, Clifford Neumayer/0.58%, Charles Thatcher, Rick Anthofer/0.04%

Breeze-Eastern Corp

Formerly: Transtechnology Corp

700 Liberty Ave., Union, NJ, 07083; **PH:** 1-908-686-4000; **http://** www.transtechnology.com

General - Incorporation.............................. DE	**Stock** - Price on:12/24/2007 ....$13.75
Employees 198	Stock Exchange.......................................NA
Auditor .... Deloitte & Touche LLP	Ticker Symbol...NA
Stk Agt........................ EquiServe Trust Co N.A	Outstanding Shares 9,280,000
Counsel........................... Hahn, Loeser & Parks	E.P.S $0.476
DUNS No...................... 00-955-7935	Shareholders..NA

Business: The group's principal activity is to design, develop, manufacture and sell sophisticated lifting equipment for specialty aerospace and defense applications. The products of the group include performance-critical rescue hoists, cargo-hook systems, weapons-handling systems, cargo winches, tie-down equipment and tow-hook assemblies. Its products are sold primarily to military and civilian agencies and aerospace contractors. The group supplies equipment for the United States, Japanese and European multiple-launch rocket systems which use two specialized hoists to load and unload rocket pod containers.

Primary SIC and add'l.: 3537

CIK No: 0000099359

Subsidiaries: Rancho TransTechnology Corporation, Retainers, Inc., SSP Industries, SSP International Sales, Inc., TransTechnology Germany GmbH, TransTechnology International Corporation, TT Connecticut Corporation, TT Minnesota Corporation, Tterusa, Inc.

Owners: Jay R. Harris/11.91%, William J. Recker/3.11%, William M. Shockley, Goldsmith& Harris, Incorporated/12.19%, Robert L. G. White/1.88%, Joseph S. Bracewell, T. Rowe Price Associates, Inc./12.52%, Russell M. Sarachek/1.50%, Jan Cope, Insiders/21.38%, Tinicum Capital Partners II, L.P./26.40%, Thomas V. Chema, Wynnefield Partners Small Cap Value, L.P./22.25%, Gerald C. Harvey/1.03%, Gail F. Lieberman (17 Owners included in Index)

Financial Data: Fiscal Year End:03/31 Latest Annual Data: 3/31/2006

Year	Sales	Net Income
2006	$64,418,000	$1,292,000
2005	$62,932,000	-$2,776,000
2004	$64,606,000	$1,744,000

Curr. Assets:	$38,369,000	Curr. Liab.:	$21,269,000	P/E Ratio:	28.06
Plant, Equip.:	$8,810,000	Total Liab.:	$69,617,000	Indic. Yr. Divd.:	NA
Total Assets:	$81,945,000	Net Worth:	$12,328,000	Debt/ Equity:	NA

BreitBurn Energy Partners LP

515 S Flower St., Ste. 4800, Los Angeles, CA, 90071; **PH:** 1-213-225-5900; **Fax:** 1-213-225-5916; **http://** www.breitburn.com

General - Incorporation.............................. DE	**Stock** - Price on:12/24/2007 ....$34.67
Employees ....NA	Stock Exchange....................................NDQ
Auditor .... PricewaterhouseCoopers LLP	Ticker Symbol....................................BBEP
Stk Agt...... American Stock Transfer & Trust Co.	Outstanding Shares 21,980,000
Counsel..NA	E.P.S ....-$0.23
DUNS No...NA	Shareholders..NA

Business: The groups principle activities include acquiring, exploring and developing oil and gas properties. Customer served by the group is a refiner of crude oil. Specific customers of the group include Marathon Oil Company and ConocoPhillips. In the year 2006 the group acquired BreitBurn Energy Company L.P. The group operates from the United States. The group's quarterly revenue for September 2007 was 24.89 millions of USD.

Primary SIC and add'l.: 1311

CIK No: 0001357371

Subsidiaries: Alamitos Company, BreitBurn Fulton LLC, BreitBurn Operating GP, LLC, BreitBurn Operating L.P., Phoenix Production Company, Preventive Maintenance Services, LLC

Officers: Randall H. Breitenbach/Dir., Co - CEO, Halbert S. Washburn/Dir., Co - CEO, James G. Jackson/CFO, Gregory C. Brown/Exec. VP, General Counsel, Bruce D. McFarland/Treasurer - General Partner, Lawrence C. Smith/Controller - General Partner, Chris E. Williamson/VP - Operations, General Partner, Thurmon Andress/MD - Breitburn Management, Dennis Graue/Mgr. - Exploitation, Breitburn Management, William Fong/Engineer - With Breitburn Management, Jonathan Kuespert/Mgr. - Development, Sr. Geologist, Breitburn Management

Directors: Randall H. Breitenbach/Dir., Co - CEO, Halbert S. Washburn/Dir., Co - CEO, Randall J. Findlay/Chmn., Grant D. Billing/Dir., Greg L. Armstrong/Dir., Gregory J. Moroney/Dir., Thomas W. Buchanan/Dir., John R. Butler/Dir., Charles S. Weiss/Dir.

Owners: Gregory J. Moroney, John R. Butler, Charles S. Weiss, Randall H. Breitenbach/3.05%, Provident Energy Trust/65.55%, Halbert S. Washburn/3.05%, Insiders/3.11%, BreitBurn Corporation/3.05%, Greg L. Armstrong

Financial Data: Fiscal Year End:12/31 Latest Annual Data: 12/31/2006

Year	Sales	Net Income
2006	$138,038,000	$49,919,000

Curr. Assets:	$20,956,000	Curr. Liab.:	$13,458,000	P/E Ratio:	93.70
Plant, Equip.:	$185,870,000	Total Liab.:	$30,036,000	Indic. Yr. Divd.:	$1.770
Total Assets:	$207,244,000	Net Worth:	$177,208,000	Debt/ Equity:	0.2170

Bremer Financial Corp

445 Minnesota St., Ste. 2000, St. Paul, MN, 55101; **PH:** 1-651-227-7621; **Fax:** 1-651-312-3550; **http://** www.bremer.com; **Email:** info@bremer.com

General - Incorporation .... MN	**Stock** - Price on:12/24/2007 ....NA
Employees ....NA	Stock Exchange.......................................NA
Auditor ....Deloitte & Touche LLP	Ticker Symbol...NA
Stk Agt................................ Bremer Trust	Outstanding Shares ....NA
Counsel..NA	E.P.S ....NA
DUNS No 05-607-3711	Shareholders..NA

Business: The group's principal activity is the provision of banking and related products and services through its subsidiaries. The services provided by the group include transaction and savings deposits, commercial, consumer, agricultural and real estate loans and mortgage origination services. In addition, the group also provides asset-based lending and leasing, trust and insurance services to its customers through non-banking subsidiaries and investment services through a third party relation ship. The group operates through 11 banking subsidiaries and 104 offices in the states of Minnesota, Wisconsin and North Dakota.

Primary SIC and add'l.: 6021 6712

CIK No: 0000846616

Subsidiaries: Bremer Bank, National Association (Alexandria, MN), Bremer Bank, National Association (Brainerd, MN), Bremer Bank, National Association (Fargo, ND), Bremer Bank, National Association (Grand Forks, ND), Bremer Bank, National Association (International Falls, MN), Bremer Bank, National Association (Menomonie, WI), Bremer Bank, National Association (South Saint Paul, MN), Bremer Bank, National Association (Willmar, MN), Bremer Business Finance Corporation, Bremer Capital Trust I, Bremer Financial Services, Inc., Bremer Insurance Agencies, Inc., Bremer Life Insurance Company, Bremer Statutory Trust I, Bremer Trust, National Association

Officers: Ruth Molloy/Administrator - Alexandria, MN, Chuck Hiller/Administrator - Crookston, Lawrence Lewandowski/Administrator - Detroit Lakes, Mark Strand/Administrator - Fargo, Deanne Jones/Administrator - Grand Forks, Kevin Weise/Administrator - Minneapolis, St. Paul, Luther Ranheim/Administrator - Minneapolis, St. Paul, Kathleen Metcalf/Administrator - Minneapolis, St. Paul, Cari Dietman/Administrator - St. Cloud, Susan Voeltz/Administrator - St. Cloud, Kyle Fagerland/Administrator - St. Cloud, Keith Finstad/Administrator - St. Cloud, Jeff J. Burak/Loan Officer - Aitkin, Sherrie L. Lessard/Loan Officer - International Falls, Deb J. Blomme/Loan Officer - Marshall (73 Officers included in Index)

Bresler & Reiner Inc

11200 Rockville Pike, Ste. 502, Rockville, MD, 20852; **PH:** 1-301-945-4300; **Fax:** 1-301-945-4301; **http://** www.breslerandreiner.com

General - Incorporation .... DE	**Stock** - Price on:12/24/2007 ....NA
Employees 22	Stock Exchange....................................OTC
Auditor .... Ernst & Young, LLP	Ticker Symbol....................................BRER
Stk Agt.............Continental Stock Transfer & Trust Co	Outstanding Shares ....NA
Counsel............Shaiman, Rovin & Silverman P.C.	E.P.S $1.36
DUNS No 05-518-5763	Shareholders..NA

Business: The group's principal activity is to acquire, develop, own and manage commercial and residential real estate. It also participates in residential land development and hotel management activities. The group operates through the following segments: home and other construction, commercial rental, residential rentals and hotel operations. Home and other construction consists of residential home building as well as renovation projects. Commercial rental operations provide office and retail space for various types of tenants, ranging from retail to governmental agencies. Residential rental segment provides housing throughout the Washington, d.c., metropolitan area. Hotel operations segment manages the ownership of two hotel properties.

Primary SIC and add'l.: 1531 6552 6512 6159 7359 6513 9999

CIK No: 0000014073

Subsidiaries: 14th Street Developers, LLC, 1925 K Street Associates, LLC, 220 West Germantown Pike Owner, LP, 400 South Philadelphia Developers, LLC, 4259 West Swamp Road Owner, LP, 699 North Broad Street Associates, LP, 900 Northbrook Owner, LP, B&r 1105, LLC, B&r 5160 Parkstone Owner, LLC, B&r 919, LLC, B&R Devon Owner, LP, B&R Investment Properties FL, Inc., B&R PA Holdings, Inc., B&R Waterfront Properties, LLC, B-R Holdings, Inc. 37 Subsidiaries included in the Index

Officers: Sidney M. Bresler/Dir., CEO Pres., Jean S. Cafardi/Corp. Sec., Darryl M. Edelstein/CFO, Exec. VP - Finance

Directors: Sidney M. Bresler/Dir., CEO Pres., Charles S. Bresler/Chmn., Burton J. Reiner/Dir., Randall L. Reiner/Dir., Benjamin C. Auger/Dir., Michael W. Malafronte/Dir., Gary F. Bulmash/Dir., John P. Casey/Dir., Gretchen M. Dudney/Dir.

Owners: Charles S. Bresler/38.33%, Michael W. Malafronte, The Burton and Anita Reiner Charitable Remainder Trust/6.09%, Jean S. Cafardi, Burton J. Reiner/30.71%, Fleur S. Bresler/5.16%, Insiders/75.69%, Sidney M. Bresler, Randall L. Reiner/6.29%, Benjamin C. Auger

Financial Data: Fiscal Year End:12/31 Latest Annual Data: 12/31/2006

Year	Sales	Net Income
2006	$100,426,000	$15,708,000
2005	$122,944,000	-$2,249,000
2004	$78,258,000	$4,419,000

Curr. Assets:	$78,222,000	**Curr. Liab.:**	$19,358,000		
Plant, Equip.:	$664,379,000	**Total Liab.:**	$670,901,000	**Indic. Yr. Divd.:**	NA
Total Assets:	$855,621,000	**Net Worth:**	$141,224,000	**Debt/ Equity:**	4.1061

Bridge Bancorp Inc

2200 Montauk Hwy., Bridgehampton, NY, 11932; ***PH:*** 1-631-537-1000; ***Fax:*** 1-631-537-1835; ***http://*** www.bridgenb.com

General - Incorporation .... NY
Employees 128
Auditor .... Ernst & Young, LLP
Stk Agt........ Registrar & Transfer Co
Counsel .... NA
DUNS No. 61-506-4334

Stock- Price on:12/24/2007 .... $24.2
Stock Exchange .... OTC
Ticker Symbol .... BDGE
Outstanding Shares 6,090,000
E.P.S $1.34
Shareholders .... NA

Business: The group's principal activities are to provide commercial, consumer banking and limited trust services. A holding company for the bridgehampton national bank of New York, the group accepts time and demand deposits and invests them in commercial and consumer loans, including auto, personal, home equity, home improvement, residential and guaranteed loans. It also invests in the obligations of New York state and local political subdivisions and U.S. Government agency and treasury securities. Other services include merchant credit and debit card processing, wealth management services, automated teller machines, cash management services, online banking services, safe deposit boxes and individual retirement accounts. The group operates through eight branches located in bridgehampton, east hampton, greenport, mattituck, montauk, sag harbor, southampton and southhold, New York areas.

Primary SIC and add'l.: 6021 6712

CIK No: 0000846617

Subsidiaries: The Bridgehampton National Bank

Officers: Thomas J. Tobin/Dir., Pres., CEO - Bridge Bancorp, Inc, The Bridgehampton National Bank/$673,098.00, Lauren Ditalia/Sr. Systems Analyst, Kevin L. Santacroce/Chief Lending Officer, Steven Bodziner/VP - Bridge Abstract LLC, Patricia F. Horan/Branch Mgr. - Cutchogue, Aidan Wood/Loan Officer - East Hampton, Montauk Marketing Area, Donna Zdanko/Branch Operations Mgr., Jeffrey M. Greenwald/Branch Mgr. - Bridgehampton, Assist. Cashiers, Emily Healy/Branch Mgr. - Greenport, Assist. Cashiers, Peter Hillick/Credit Department Mgr., Assist. Cashiers, Erin D. Kaelin/Training, Development Officer, Assist. Cashiers, Lauren D'Italia/Sr. Systems Analyst, Caroline Kalish/Data Processing Operations Mgr., Margaret Meighan/Branch Manage , East Hampton, Nancy Messer/Loan Officer - North Fork Marketing Area *(33 Officers included in Index)*

Directors: Thomas J. Tobin/Dir., Pres., CEO - Bridge Bancorp, Inc, The Bridgehampton National Bank, Marcia Z. Hefter/Vice Chmn., Raymond Wesnofske/Chmn. - Bridge Bancorp, Inc, The Bridgehampton National Bank, Howard H. Nolan/Dir., Sr. Exec. VP, COO, Charles I. Massoud/Dir., Thomas E. Halsey/Dir., Dennis A. Suskind/Dir., Timothy R. Maran/Dir.

Owners: Insiders/0.08%, Raymond Wesnofske/1.90%, Dennis A. Suskind/1.40%, Thomas J. Tobin/1.50%, R. Timothy Maran/1.10%, Charles I. Massoud/0.10%, Howard H. Nolan/0.10%, Thomas E. Halsey/0.01%, Janet T. Verneuille/0.30%, Marcia Z. Hefter/0.60%

Financial Data: **Fiscal Year End:**12/31 **Latest Annual Data:** 12/31/2006

Year	Sales	Net Income
2006	$36,732,000	$8,168,000
2005	$33,818,000	$9,623,000
2004	$32,363,000	$10,377,000

Curr. Assets:	$15,955,000	**Curr. Liab.:**	$523,867,000	**P/E Ratio:**	18.06
Plant, Equip.:	$18,005,000	**Total Liab.:**	$528,105,000	**Indic. Yr. Divd.:**	$0.920
Total Assets:	$573,644,000	**Net Worth:**	$45,539,000	**Debt/ Equity:**	NA

Bridge Capital Holdings

55 Almaden Blvd., San Jose, CA, 95113; ***PH:*** 1-408-423-8500; ***Fax:*** 1-408-423-8520; ***http://*** www.bridgebank.com; ***Email:*** sanjose@bridgebank.com

General - Incorporation .... CA
Employees 134
Auditor .... Vavrinek, Trine, Day & Co. LLP
Stk Agt...... American Stock Transfer & Trust Co.
Counsel .... NA
DUNS No. .... NA

Stock- Price on:12/24/2007 .... $22.66
Stock Exchange .... NDQ
Ticker Symbol .... BBNK
Outstanding Shares 6,420,000
E.P.S $1.34
Shareholders .... NA

Business: The group's principle activities are to provide a variety of banking services to businesses, governmental units and individuals. The group offers a wide range of deposit accounts designed to attract small and medium size commercial businesses as well as business professionals and retail customers. Accepts passbook savings, money market deposit, now accounts, certificates of deposit and bundled accounts. Other deposit services include oriented services, including direct payroll and social security deposit, post-paid bank-by-mail, and Internet banking, including on-line access to account information. The group lends commercial loans, real estate commercial loans, real estate construction loans and consumer loans. The group also issues cashier's checks, sells traveler's checks and provides other customary banking services.

Primary SIC and add'l.: 6021 6712

CIK No: 0001304740

Subsidiaries: Bridge Bank, National Association, Bridge Capital Holdings Trust I

Officers: Daniel P. Myers/Dir., CEO, Pres., Robert P. Gionfriddo/Dir., Exec. VP, Chief Business Development Officer, Margie McMahon/Sr. VP, Branch Operations Mgr. - Bridge Bank, Palo Alto, Manju Kamboj/VP, Branch Services Mgr. - Bridge Bank, San Jose, Kenneth D. Brenner/Exec. VP, Pres. - Palo Alto Group, Peter Mills/VP, Relationship Mgr. - Bridge Bank, East Bay, Scott Chamberlin/Sr. VP, Marketing Mgr. - Technology Banking Group, Bridge Bank, Michael J. Field/Exec. VP, Division Mgr. - Technology Banking Group, Bridge Bank, Michael Hengl/Sr. VP, Corporate Banking Mgr. - Bridge Bank, East Bay, Ernie Lavagetto/VP, Business Development Officer - Bridge Bank, East Bay, Natalie Taaffe/Exec. VP, Construction Lending Mgr. - Bridge Bank, Kimberly Rysyk/Sr. VP, Construction Loan Officer - Bridge Bank, San Jose, Tony Pare/VP - Operations, Bridge Bank, Specialty Markets, Ed Lambert/Sr. VP, Marketing Mgr. - Technology Banking Group, Bridge Bank, Bill Nay/Sr. VP, Marketing Mgr. - Technology Banking Group, Bridge Bank *(77 Officers included in Index)*

Directors: Daniel P. Myers/Dir., CEO, Pres., Allen C. Kramer/Chmn., Owen Brown/Dir. - Bridge Bank, Robert P. Latta/Dir., David V. Campbell/Dir., Thomas M. Quigg/Dir., David K. Chui/Dir. - Bridge Bank, Barry A. Turkus/Dir., Richard M. Brenner/Dir., Lawrence Owen Brown/Dir., Robert P. Gionfriddo/Dir., Exec. VP, Chief Business Development Officer

Owners: Timothy W. Boothe/1.10%, David V. Campbell/1.26%, Robert Latta/0.29%, Richard M. Brenner/2.51%, Allan C. Kramer/4.56%, Kenneth B. Silveira/0.93%, Daniel P. Myers/3.45%, Thomas M. Quigg/0.31%, Owen Brown/0.16%, Robert P. Gionfriddo/1.92%, Insiders/20.12%, Barry A. Turkus/2.52%, Thomas A. Sa/1.12%

Financial Data: **Fiscal Year End:**12/31 **Latest Annual Data:** 12/31/2006

Year	Sales	Net Income
2006	$56,799,000	$8,634,000
2005	$38,315,000	$5,725,000
2004	$23,312,000	$3,037,000

Curr. Assets:	$122,497,000	**Curr. Liab.:**	$645,305,000	**P/E Ratio:**	16.91
Plant, Equip.:	$3,479,000	**Total Liab.:**	$672,885,000	**Indic. Yr. Divd.:**	NA
Total Assets:	$721,979,000	**Net Worth:**	$49,094,000	**Debt/ Equity:**	0.3341

Bridge Street Financial Inc

44 E Bridge St., Owego, NY, 13126; ***PH:*** 1-315-343-4100; ***http://*** www.ocnb.com

General - Incorporation .... NY
Employees 324
Auditor .... KPMG LLP
Stk Agt ..... American Stock Transfer & Trust Co.
Counsel .... NA
DUNS No. .... NA

Stock- Price on:12/24/2007 .... $26.75
Stock Exchange .... NDQ
Ticker Symbol .... OCNB
Outstanding Shares 4,780,000
E.P.S $1.92
Shareholders .... NA

Business: The group's principal activity is to provide community banking services to individuals and small-to-medium sized businesses through its seven branches in oswego and onondaga counties of New York state. The group conducts its operation through its wholly owned subsidiary, oswego county savings bank, a New York state-chartered stock savings bank. The majority of loans and deposits held by the group are generated within oswego and onondaga counties, a region consisting of a mixture of urban, suburban and rural areas and which includes the cities of oswego, fulton and syracuse. The group has developed and implemented a lending strategy that focuses less on residential real estate lending and more on servicing commercial customers.

Primary SIC and add'l.: 6712 6035

CIK No: 0001182555

Subsidiaries: Oswego County National Bank

Financial Data: **Fiscal Year End:**12/31 **Latest Annual Data:** 12/31/2006

Year	Sales	Net Income
2006	$75,493,000	$7,311,000
2005	$60,724,000	$7,507,000
2004	$49,142,000	$7,255,000

Curr. Assets:	$32,003,000	**Curr. Liab.:**	$938,247,000	**P/E Ratio:**	13.51
Plant, Equip.:	$22,492,000	**Total Liab.:**	$1,163,461,000	**Indic. Yr. Divd.:**	NA
Total Assets:	$1,272,967,000	**Net Worth:**	$109,506,000	**Debt/ Equity:**	1.9634

Bridgford Foods Corp

1308 N Patt St., Anaheim, CA, 92801; ***PH:*** 1-714-526-5533; ***Fax:*** 1-714-526-4360; ***http://*** www.bridgford.com; ***Email:*** info@bridgford.com

General - Incorporation .... CA
Employees 684
Auditor .... Haskell & White LLP
Stk Agt .... Continental Stock T & T Co.
Counsel .... NA
DUNS No. 00-850-6768

Stock- Price on:12/24/2007 .... $7.56
Stock Exchange .... NDQ
Ticker Symbol .... BRID
Outstanding Shares 9,930,000
E.P.S $0.14
Shareholders .... NA

Business: The group's principal activity is to manufacture, market and distribute frozen, refrigerated and snack food products. The products include a variety of sliced luncheon meats and cheeses, wieners, bacon, sandwiches, dry sausages, biscuits, bread dough items and roll dough items. The group also purchases certain food products to be resold again. They include a variety of jerky, cheeses, salads, party dips, Mexican foods, nuts and other delicatessen type food products. The products are sold directly and through brokers, cooperatives, wholesalers and independent distributors. They are sold to approximately 38,000 retail food stores located in 48 states of the United States, Hawaii and Canada.

Primary SIC and add'l.: 2045 2011 5142

CIK No: 0000014177

Subsidiaries: A.S.I. Corporation, American Ham Processors, Inc., Bridgford Food Processing Corporation, Bridgford Food Processing of Texas, L.P., Bridgford Marketing Company, Bridgford Meat Company

Officers: William L. Bridgford/Chmn., Principal Executive Officer, Bruce Bridgford/Pres. - Bridgford Foods, California, Raymond F. Lancy/Exec. VP, CFO, Treasurer, Hugh Wm. Bridgford/Dir., VP, John V. Simmons/Pres., Daniel R. Yost/Sr. VP - Frozen Food Division, Chris Cole/VP, Cindy Matthews-Morales/Sec., Michael Bridgford/Assist. Sec.

Directors: Allan L. Bridgford/Sr. Chmn., William L. Bridgford/Chmn., Principal Executive Officer, Richard A. Foster/Dir., Hugh Wm. Bridgford/Dir., VP, Robert E. Schulze/Dir., Paul R. Zippwald/Dir., Todd C. Andrews/Dir., Gregory D. Scott/Dir.

Owners: Bridgford Industries Incorporated, William L. Bridgford, Bruce H. Bridgford, Todd C. Andrews, Hugh Wm. Bridgford, Paul R. Zippwald, Raymond F. Lancy, John V. Simmons, Robert E. Schulze, D. Gregory Scott, Richard A. Foster, Insiders, Baron R.H. Bridgford, Allan L. Bridgford

Financial Data: **Fiscal Year End:**10/28 **Latest Annual Data:** 11/3/2006

Year	Sales	Net Income
2006	$134,264,000	$1,240,000
2005	$130,845,000	-$943,000
2004	$137,865,000	$24,000

Curr. Assets:	$45,913,000	**Curr. Liab.:**	$14,231,000	**P/E Ratio:**	54.00
Plant, Equip.:	$13,041,000	**Total Liab.:**	$22,745,000	**Indic. Yr. Divd.:**	NA
Total Assets:	$72,931,000	**Net Worth:**	$50,186,000	**Debt/ Equity:**	NA

Briggs & Stratton Corp

12301 W Wirth St., Wauwatosa, WI, 53222; ***PH:*** 1-414-259-5333; ***Fax:*** 1-414-259-5773; ***http://*** www.briggsandstratton.com

General - Incorporation .... WI
Employees 8,701
Auditor .... PricewaterhouseCoopers LLP
Stk Agt .... National City Bank
Counsel .... NA
DUNS No. 00-608-2531

Stock- Price on:12/24/2007 .... $31.45
Stock Exchange .... NYSE
Ticker Symbol .... BGG
Outstanding Shares 49,460,000
E.P.S. .... -$0.08
Shareholders .... NA

Business: The groups principle activity is to produce air cooled gasoline engines for outdoor power equipment. The group operates through two business segments namely engines and power products. The group operates from United States.

Primary SIC and add'l.: 3519 3429

CIK No: 0000014195

Subsidiaries: Briggs & Stratton (Chongqing) Engine Co., Ltd., Briggs & Stratton (Czech) Power Products, s.r.o., Briggs & Stratton (Shanghai) International Trading Co., Ltd., Briggs & Stratton (Shanghai) Power Products Co., Ltd., Briggs & Stratton AG, Briggs & Stratton Australia Pty. Limited, Briggs & Stratton Austria GmbH, Briggs & Stratton Canada Inc., Briggs & Stratton CZ, s.r.o., Briggs & Stratton France, S.A.R.L., Briggs & Stratton Germany GmbH, Briggs & Stratton Iberica, S.L., Briggs & Stratton International Sales Corp., Briggs & Stratton International, Inc., Briggs & Stratton Italy S.r.l. 27 Subsidiaries included in the Index

Officers: John S. Shiely/Chmn., CEO, Pres./$4,713,552.00, James E. Brenn/CFO, Sr. VP/$1,351,375.00, Todd J. Teske/COO, Exec. VP/$1,033,384.00, Thomas R. Savage/Sr. VP - Administration/$1,216,727.00, Harold L. Redman/VP, Pres. - Home Power Products Group, David J. Rodgers/Controller, Carita R. Twinem/Treasurer, William H. Reitman/Sr. VP - Sales, Marketing/$648,054.00, Vincent R. Shiely/Sr. VP, Pres. - Yard Power Products Group, Joseph C. Wright/Sr. VP, Pres. - Engine Power Products Group, Mark R. Hazeltine/VP, Sales Mgr. - Consumer Products, Michael D. Schoen/Sr. VP, Pres. - International Power Products Group, Robert F. Heath/Sec., David G. Debaets/VP, GM - Large Engine Division

Directors: John S. Shiely/Chmn., CEO, Pres., Robert J. Otoole/Dir., Charles I. Story/Dir., Brian C. Walker/Dir., William F. Achtmeyer/Dir., David L. Burner/Dir., Mary K. Bush/Dir., Michael E. Batten/Dir., Keith R. McLoughlin/Dir.

Owners: Thomas R. Savage, Robert J. OToole, Todd J. Teske, Van Den Berg Management Inc./8.64%, Michael E. Batten, Fidelity Management & Research/15.56%, John S. Shiely/2.80%, James E. Brenn, William H. Reitman, Mac-Per-Wolf Company/5.63%, Barclays Global Investors, N.A./6.47%, David L. Burner, William F. Achtmeyer, Mary K. Bush, Brandes Investment Partners, L.P./5.08% *(19 Owners included in Index)*

Financial Data: ***Fiscal Year End:***07/03 ***Latest Annual Data:*** 07/01/2007

Year	Sales	Net Income
2007	$2,157,233,000	$146,000
2006	$2,542,171,000	$102,346,000
2005	$2,654,875,000	$136,567,000

Curr. Assets:	$1,119,205,000	**Curr. Liab.:**	$352,668,000		
Plant, Equip.:	$434,830,000	**Total Liab.:**	$1,109,782,000	**Indic. Yr. Divd.:**	$0.880
Total Assets:	$1,998,968,000	**Net Worth:**	$889,186,000	**Debt/ Equity:**	0.2969

Brigham Exploration Co

6300 Bridge Point Pkwy. Building 2 Ste. 500, Austin, TX, 78730; ***PH:*** 1-512-427-3300; ***Fax:*** 1-512-427-3400; ***http://*** www.bog3d.com; ***Email:*** hr@bexp3d.com

General - Incorporation	DE	***Stock***- Price on:12/24/2007	$6.07
Employees	66	Stock Exchange	NDQ
Auditor	KPMG LLP	Ticker Symbol	BEXP
Stk Agt	American Stock Transfer & Trust Co.	Outstanding Shares	45,620,000
Counsel	Thompson & Knight	E.P.S	$0.29
DUNS No.	79-178-9126	Shareholders	NA

Business: The group's principal activity is to explore, develop and produce domestic oil and natural gas. The group applies three-dimensional seismic imaging and other advanced technologies like caex for the systematic exploration of onshore domestic oil and natural gas. The exploration activities are concentrated in the anadarko basin of western Oklahoma and the Texas panhandle, the onshore Texas gulf coast and west Texas. Major oil and gas customers of the group are highland energy company and lantern petroleum corporation. The group also acquires digital land grids, log curves, geologic studies and two-dimesnional seismic data to integrate with the 3-D data on its caex workstations and create maps of producing and productive reservoirs.

Primary SIC and add'l.: 1382 1381

CIK No: 0001034755

Subsidiaries: Brigham Oil & Gas, L.P

Officers: Ben M. Brigham/Chmn., CEO, Pres./$855,503.00, Malcom Brown/VP, Controller, Harold D. Carter/67/Dir., Consultant, Jeffery E. Larson/Exec. VP - Exploration/$604,497.00, David T. Brigham/Exec. VP - Land, Administration/$630,981.00, Eugene B. Shepherd/CFO, Exec. VP/$790,667.00, Lance A. Langford/Exec. VP - Operations/$613,691.00, Eric E. Sigsbey/General Counsel, Corp. Sec., Rob Roosa/Finance Mgr., Toffee Wilson/Investor Relation Officer

Directors: Ben M. Brigham/Chmn., CEO, Pres., Graham R. Whaling/51/Dir., Hobart A. Smith/69/Dir., Stephen P. Reynolds/54/Dir., Harold D. Carter/67/Dir., Consultant, Stephen C. Hurley/56/Dir.

Owners: Insiders/9.80%, Millennium Partners II, L.P., MBP III Plan Investors, L.P., Lazard Asset Management LLC/5.60%, DLJ ESC II, L.P., DW Merchant Banking III, L.P., DLJ MB Partners III GmbH & Co., KG, Harold D. Carter, DLJ Merchant Banking III, Inc.,, David T. Brigham, Ben M. Brigham/6.80%, DLJ Merchant Banking Partners III, L.P./16.50%, Lance A. Langford, FUNDING III, DLJ Merchant Banking III, Inc., *(22 Owners included in Index)*

Financial Data: ***Fiscal Year End:***12/31 ***Latest Annual Data:*** 12/31/2006

Year	Sales	Net Income
2006	$106,297,000	$19,788,000
2005	$97,040,000	$27,435,000
2004	$72,228,000	$19,650,000

Curr. Assets:	$31,218,000	**Curr. Liab.:**	$57,453,000	**P/E Ratio:**	18.97
Plant, Equip.:	$486,461,000	**Total Liab.:**	$246,471,000	**Indic. Yr. Divd.:**	NA
Total Assets:	$522,587,000	**Net Worth:**	$266,015,000	**Debt/ Equity:**	0.6906

Bright Horizons Family Solutions Inc

200 Talcott Ave. S, Watertown, MA, 02472; ***PH:*** 1-617-673-8000; ***Fax:*** 1-617-673-8001; ***http://*** www.brighthorizons.com; ***Email:*** ir@brighthorizons.com

General - Incorporation	DE	***Stock***- Price on:12/24/2007	$38.39
Employees	18,000	Stock Exchange	NDQ
Auditor	Deloitte & Touche LLP	Ticker Symbol	BFAM
Stk Agt	Wells Fargo Bank, N.A.	Outstanding Shares	26,160,000
Counsel	NA	E.P.S	$1.67
DUNS No.	NA	Shareholders	NA

Business: The group's principle activity is to provide workplace services for employers and families. These services include childcare, early education and strategic work and life consulting. Each childcare and early education center provides a number of services designed to meet the business objectives of the client and the family needs of the sponsor's employees. The group's services are designed to address employers' ever-changing workplace needs, enhance employee productivity, improve recruitment and retention of employees and help project the image as the employer of choice within the employer's industry. The group operates 509 childcare and early education centers for over 400 clients. The group serves more than 59,200 children in 37 states, the district of columbia, Canada, guam, Ireland and the United Kingdom. The group's quarterly revenue for September 2007 was 189.53 millions of USD.

Primary SIC and add'l.: 8351

CIK No: 0001060559

Subsidiaries: Access Management, Inc., Allmont Ltd., BHFS One Limited, BHFS Three Limited, BHFS Two Limited, Bright Horizons Children's Centers, Inc., Bright Horizons Family Solutions Ireland, Ltd., Bright Horizons Family Solutions, Ltd., Bright Horizons Limited Partnership, Bright Horizons Livingston, Ltd., Bright Horizons Support Services, Ltd., Bright Horizons, Inc., ChildrenFirst Ltd., ChildrenFirst, Inc., CorporateFamily SB, Inc. 29 Subsidiaries included in the Index

Officers: David H. Lissy/Dir., CEO/$1,411,080.00, Susan Brenner/Sr. VP - Operations, Jim Greenman/Sr. VP - Education, Programs, Gary O'Neil/Sr. VP - Marketing, Client Relations, Elizabeth Boland/CFO/$632,057.00, Sandy Wells/Sr. VP - Client Services, Jackie Legg/Sr. VP - Operations, Danroy T. Henry/Sr. VP - Human Resources, Michael Day/Sr. VP - Client Services, Fatima Tavares/Regional Mgr., Geoff Beckett/Canadian Client Services Dir., Linda Harris/Foundation Assist. - Bright Horizons Foundation Children, Europe, Lawrence Armstrong/Finance Mgr. - Bright Horizons Foundation Children, Europe, Dave Shaby/Sr. VP - Business Operations, Ann Pickens/Sr. VP - Strategic Planning *(28 Officers included in Index)*

Directors: David H. Lissy/Dir., CEO, Roger H. Brown/Founder, Vice Chmn., Linda A. Mason/Chmn., Founder, Stewart D. Friedman/Member - Advisory Board, Donna Klein/Member - Advisory Board, Mary Ann Tocio/Dir., COO, Pres., Sharon Lynn Kagan/Member - Advisory Board, Dwayne Crompton/Member - Advisory Board, Alice Honig/Member - Advisory Board, Josu Cruz/Member - Advisory Board, Bettye Caldwell/Member - Advisory Board, Ian M. Rolland/Dir., Sara Lawrence-Lightfoot/Dir., Marguerite W. Sallee/Dir., Joanne Brandes/Dir. *(31 Directors included in Index)*

Owners: Mary Ann Tocio, David Gergen, Elizabeth J. Boland, Stephen I. Dreier, E. Townes Duncan, Marguerite W. Kondracke, Fred K. Foulkes, Insiders/3.61%, Roger H. Brown, Linda A. Mason, Joshua Bekenstein, JoAnne Brandes, David H. Lissy, Sara Lawrence-Lightfoot, Ian M. Rolland

Financial Data: ***Fiscal Year End:***12/31 ***Latest Annual Data:*** 12/31/2006

Year	Sales	Net Income
2006	NA	NA
2005	NA	NA
2004	NA	NA

Curr. Assets:	$79,506,000	**Curr. Liab.:**	$151,359,000	**P/E Ratio:**	23.27
Plant, Equip.:	$137,312,000	**Total Liab.:**	$185,532,000	**Indic. Yr. Divd.:**	NA
Total Assets:	$409,370,000	**Net Worth:**	$223,838,000	**Debt/ Equity:**	NA

Brightec Inc

8C Pleasant St., South Natick, MA, 01760; ***PH:*** 1-508-647-9710; ***http://*** www.brightec.com; ***Email:*** info@brightec.com

General - Incorporation	NV	***Stock***- Price on:12/24/2007	$0.035
Employees	3	Stock Exchange	OTC
Auditor	Rotenberg Meril Solomon	Ticker Symbol	NA
Stk Agt	National Stock Transfer, Inc.	Outstanding Shares	128,940,000
Counsel	NA	E.P.S	-$0.025
DUNS No.	NA	Shareholders	NA

Business: The groups principal activities include developing and marketing luminescent films incorporating luminescent or phosphorescent pigments. The group marketed its products under the trade names Brightec and Be Brilliant. The group operates from the United States and Switzerland.

Primary SIC and add'l.: 3081

CIK No: 0000894537

Subsidiaries: Brightec SA

Officers: Patrick Planche/44/Founder, CEO, Treasurer, CFO

Directors: Patrick Planche/44/Founder, CEO, Treasurer, CFO, David Geffen/53/Dir.

Owners: Jeffrey A. Stern/6.89%, Jose Canales la Rosa/5.29%, James J. Galvin/6.19%, Insiders/45.30%, Patrick Planche/28.12%, David J. Geffen/18.63%

Financial Data: ***Fiscal Year End:***12/31 ***Latest Annual Data:*** 12/31/2006

Year	Sales	Net Income
2006	$12,000	-$2,290,000
2005	$132,000	-$774,000
2004	$222,000	-$1,644,000

Curr. Assets:	$205,000	**Curr. Liab.:**	$1,035,000		
Plant, Equip.:	NA	**Total Liab.:**	$1,035,000	**Indic. Yr. Divd.:**	NA
Total Assets:	$219,000	**Net Worth:**	-$816,000	**Debt/ Equity:**	NA

Brightpoint Inc

2601 Metropolis Pkwy., Ste. 210, Plainfield, IN, 46168; ***PH:*** 1-317-707-2355; ***Fax:*** 1-317-707-2512; ***http://*** www.brightpoint.com; ***Email:*** info@brightpoint.com

General - Incorporation	IN	***Stock***- Price on:12/24/2007	$14.48
Employees	2,112	Stock Exchange	NDQ
Auditor	Ernst & Young LLP	Ticker Symbol	CELL
Stk Agt	American Stock Transfer & Trust Co.	Outstanding Shares	50,860,000
Counsel	Blank Rome Tenzer Greenblatt	E.P.S	$0.76
DUNS No.	61-199-1373	Shareholders	NA

Business: The groups principle activity is to distribute wireless devices and accessories to the wireless industry. The groups products include PDAs and handheld devices, modems, and integrated devices. The groups services include activation, logistics and subscriber, and advanced wireless services. The group operates from United States.

Primary SIC and add'l.: 5065

CIK No: 0000918946

Subsidiaries: Axess Communication Sp. z o. o, Brightpoint (South Africa) (Proprietary) Limited, Brightpoint Activation Services LLC, Brightpoint Asia Limited, Brightpoint Australia Pty Ltd., Brightpoint B.V., Brightpoint de Colombia Limited, Brightpoint de Mexico, S.A. de C.V., Brightpoint de Venezuela, C.A., Brightpoint EMA B.V., Brightpoint EMA Limited., Brightpoint Finland Oy, Brightpoint Germany GmbH, Brightpoint GmbH, Brightpoint Holdings B.V 35 Subsidiaries included in the Index

Officers: Robert J. Laikin/Chmn., CEO/$2,816,423.00, Steen F. Pedersen/Pres. - Brightpoint Europe, Mark J. Howell/Co - COO, Pres. - Brightpoint Americas/$1,309,963.00, Bruce R. Thomlinson/Pres. - Brightpoint Asia, Pacific/$1,149,682.00, John Alexander Du Plessis Currie/43/Pres. - Emerging Markets/$1,272,655.00, Michael Koehn Milland/Co - COO, Pres. - Brightpoint International, Steven E. Fivel/Exec. VP, General Counsel, Sec./$991,873.00, Anthony MacKle/VP - Internal Audit, Vincent Donargo/VP, Chief Accounting Officer, Controller, Anurag Gupta/Sr. VP - Global Strategy, Investor, Public Relations, Annette Cyr/Sr. VP - Human Resources, Jac Currie/Pres. - Emerging Markets, Anthony Boor/CFO, Exec. VP, Treasurer/$735,182.00, David P. O'Connell/VP - Taxation, Global Credit, Risk Management

Directors: Robert J. Laikin/Chmn., CEO, Richard W. Roedel/Dir., Stephen H. Simon/42/Dir., Marisa E. Pratt/Dir., William V. Hunt/63/Dir., Kari-Pekka Wilska/Dir., Jan Gesmar-Larsen/Dir., Jorn P. Jensen/Dir., Thorleif Krarup/Dir., Eliza Hermann/Dir., Jerre L. Stead/Dir., Robert F. Wagner/73/Dir.

Owners: Trivium Capital Management LLC/4.10%, John Alexander Du Plessis Currie, Barclays Global Investors, NA/3.50%, Kari-Pekka Wilska, Robert F. Wagner, S. A. C. Capital Advisors LLC/3.10%, Steven E. Fivel, Marisa E. Pratt, Goldman Sachs Group, Inc./6.10%, Eliza Hermann, Richard W. Roedel, LSV Asset Management/3.40%, Anthony W. Boor, William V. Hunt, Robert J. Laikin (22 Owners included in Index)

Financial Data: Fiscal Year End:12/31   **Latest Annual Data:** 12/31/2006

Year	Sales	Net Income
2006	$2,425,373,000	$35,610,000
2005	$2,140,177,000	$10,440,000
2004	$1,859,355,000	$13,770,000

Curr. Assets:	$727,498,000	Curr. Liab.:	$567,738,000	P/E Ratio:	19.31
Plant, Equip.:	$37,904,000	Total Liab.:	$583,525,000	Indic. Yr. Divd.:	NA
Total Assets:	$778,353,000	Net Worth:	$194,828,000	Debt/ Equity:	0.4275

Brightstar Information Technology Gp Inc

6160 Stoneridge Mall Rd., Ste. 250, Pleasanton, CA, 94588; **PH:** 1-925-251-0000; **Fax:** 1-925-251-0001; **http://** www.brightstar.com; **Email:** info@brightstar.com

General - Incorporation	DE	Stock - Price on:12/24/2007	NA
Employees	31	Stock Exchange	OTC
Auditor	Stonefield Josephson, Inc	Ticker Symbol	BTSR
Stk Agt	American Stock Transfer & Trust Co.	Outstanding Shares	NA
Counsel	Gusov Ofsink LLC	E.P.S.	-$0.009
DUNS No.	00-802-6119	Shareholders	NA

Business: The group's principal activities are to provide application outsourcing and systems integration services to global 2000 companies and public sector organizations. The group deploys solutions in areas of supply chain management (scm), customer relationship management (crm), enterprise resource management (erp) and application outsourcing services. For erp, the group implements sap and peoplesoft applications, covering a complete range of business processes, from manufacturing and finance to human resources, procurement and supply chain planning. The group's services are provided to various industries including communications, consumer products, energy, healthcare, technology and to state and local governments.

Primary SIC and add'l.: 7375 7372 7373

CIK No: 0001050025

Subsidiaries: BrightStar Information Technology Services, Inc., NYNEX

Officers: Jim Cahill/45/CEO, John Coogan/CFO, Jordan Loewer/Corp. Sec.

Directors: Ian Scott-Dunne/Chmn.

Financial Data: Fiscal Year End:12/31   **Latest Annual Data:** 12/31/2005

Year	Sales	Net Income
2005	$2,463,000	-$406,000
2004	$3,634,000	-$2,355,000
2003	$5,852,000	-$138,000

Curr. Assets:	$581,000	Curr. Liab.:	$610,000		
Plant, Equip.:	$20,000	Total Liab.:	$1,969,000	Indic. Yr. Divd.:	NA
Total Assets:	$601,000	Net Worth:	-$1,368,000	Debt/ Equity:	NA

Brillian Corp

1600 N Desert Dr., Tempe, AZ, 85281; **PH:** 1-602-389-8888

General - Incorporation	DE	Stock - Price on:12/24/2007	$5.01
Employees	225	Stock Exchange	NDQ
Auditor	Ernst & Young, LLP	Ticker Symbol	BRLC
Stk Agt	Bank of New York	Outstanding Shares	62,780,000
Counsel	Greenberg Traurig	E.P.S.	$0.28
DUNS No.	NA	Shareholders	NA

Business: The group's principle activities include designing and developing microdisplay products. Microdisplays are thumbnail-sized displays that create high-resolution images, including full motion video and computer screen content. Microdisplay devices are used in rear-projection, high-definition televisions, home theatre projectors and head-mounted monocular or binocular headsets. It is also used for industrial, medical, military, commercial, and consumer applications. The company markets hdtvs under the brand names of retailers, including consumer electronics retailers, consumer retail stores, personal computer manufacturers, and high-end audio/video manufacturers.the company spun-off from three-five systems inc on Sept 15, 2003. The group operates from United States.

Primary SIC and add'l.: 8711 3674 3679

CIK No: 0001232229

Subsidiaries: Syntax Corporation, Syntax Groups Corporation

Officers: James Ching Hua Li/41/Dir., CEO, Pres., Vincent F. Sollitto/Executive Chmn., John S. Hodgson/56/Exec. VP, CFO, Treasurer, Dir., Michael Chan/Sec., Man Kit Chow/47/Dir., Chief Procurement Officer

Directors: James Ching Hua Li/41/Dir., CEO, Pres., Vincent F. Sollitto/Executive Chmn., David P. Chavoustie/65/Dir., John S. Hodgson/56/Exec. VP, CFO, Treasurer, Dir., Shih-Jye Cheng/49/Dir., Man Kit Chow/47/Dir., Chief Procurement Officer, Max Fang/55/Dir., Christopher C.L. Liu/59/Dir.

Owners: Insiders/11.80%, Yasushi Chikagami, Shih-Jye Cheng, Christopher C.L. Liu/5.60%, Taiwan Kolin Co. Ltd. and affiliates/6.30%, Wayne A. Pratt, Vincent F. Sollitto, David P. Chavoustie, John S. Hodgson, Max Fang, Man Kit Chow/2.20%, Robert L. Melcher, James Ching Hua Li/1.20%, Michael Chan/1.60%, Bruce I. Berkoff

Financial Data: Fiscal Year End:12/31   **Latest Annual Data:** 6/30/2006

Year	Sales	Net Income
2006	$192,990,000	-$18,879,000
2004	$2,688,000	-$32,897,000
2003	$2,194,000	-$18,744,000

Curr. Assets:	$80,458,000	Curr. Liab.:	$53,036,000	P/E Ratio:	17.89
Plant, Equip.:	$16,703,000	Total Liab.:	$59,422,000	Indic. Yr. Divd.:	NA
Total Assets:	$127,656,000	Net Worth:	$64,802,000	Debt/ Equity:	NA

Brilliance China Automotive Holdings Ltd

Stes 1602-05, Chater House, 8connaught Rd. Central, Wanchai, 23036; **PH:** 852-25237227; **http://** www.brillianceauto.com; **Email:** cba@brillianceauto.com

General - Incorporation	Bermuda	Stock - Price on:12/24/2007	$23.99
Employees	11,000	Stock Exchange	NA
Auditor	Moores Rowland Mazars	Ticker Symbol	NA
Stk Agt	Reid Management Ltd	Outstanding Shares	36,680,000
Counsel	Shearman & Sterling LLP	E.P.S.	-$1.4
DUNS No.	66-229-9734	Shareholders	NA

Business: The group's principle activities are the manufacturing and distribution of minibuses for passenger and commercial use, automobile window molding, stripping, other automotive components and passenger sedan. It also manufactures gasoline engines for use in passenger vehicles and light duty trucks. Major brands include toyota and zhonghua.

Primary SIC and add'l.: 3799 3999 3714 3710

CIK No: 0000891765

Subsidiaries: Beston Asia Investment Limited, BMW Brilliance Automotive Ltd., Brilliance China Automotive Finance Ltd., China Brilliance Automotive Components Group Limited, Chongqing Baosheng Automotive Sale and Service Co., Ltd., Chongqing FuHua Automotive Sales Service Co., Ltd., Key Choices Group Limited, Mianyang Brilliance Ruian Automotive Components Co., Ltd., Mianyang Xinchen Engine Co., Ltd., Ningbo Brilliance Ruixing Auto Components Co., Ltd., Ningbo Yuming Machinery Industrial Co., Ltd., Pure Shine Limited, Shanghai Hidea Auto Design Co., Ltd., Shenyang Aerospace Mitsubishi Motors Engine Manufacturing Co., Ltd, Shenyang Brilliance Dongxing Automotive Component Co., Ltd. 25 Subsidiaries included in the Index

Officers: Qi Yu Min/48/Dir., CEO, Lin C. Xiaogang/CFO, Huang Yu/34/Accountant

Directors: Qi Yu Min/48/Dir., CEO, Wu Xiao An/46/Chmn., Song Jian/51/Dir., Wang Shi Ping/51/Dir., He Guo Hua/57/Dir., Xu Bing Jin/68/Dir., Jiang Bo/48/Dir.

Owners: Brandes Investment Partners, L.P./9.10%, Huachen Automotive Group Holdings Company Limited/39.42%, The Northern Trust Company/5.18%, Templeton Asset Management Ltd./6.06%, Deutsche Bank Aktiengesellschaft/6.88%

Financial Data: Fiscal Year End:12/31   **Latest Annual Data:** 12/31/2005

Year	Sales	Net Income
2005	$678,155,000	-$83,240,000
2004	$791,582,000	$147,000
2003	$1,223,256,000	$94,482,000

Curr. Assets:	$881,661,000	Curr. Liab.:	$999,419,000	P/E Ratio:	8.66
Plant, Equip.:	$540,982,000	Total Liab.:	$1,009,290,000	Indic. Yr. Divd.:	NA
Total Assets:	$1,821,846,000	Net Worth:	$761,321,000	Debt/ Equity:	NA

Brilliant Digital Entertainment Inc

14011 Ventura Blvd., Ste. 501, Sherman Oaks, CA, 91423; **PH:** 1-818-386-2180; **Fax:** 1-818-386-2179; **http://** www.brilliantdigital.com

General - Incorporation	DE	Stock - Price on:12/24/2007	$0.14
Employees	8	Stock Exchange	OTC
Auditor	Vasquez & Co. LLP	Ticker Symbol	BDLN
Stk Agt	U.S. Stock Transfer Corp	Outstanding Shares	NA
Counsel	Troop Meisinger Steuber & Pasich	E.P.S.	$0.19
DUNS No.	95-944-3284	Shareholders	NA

Business: The group's principal activity is to develop media advertising serving technologies, software authoring tools and content for three dimensional animation on the world wide Web. The group licenses its media advertising server technologies to Web sites to enable advertisers and Web sites to display the rich media 3D advertising banners. It offers proprietary media authoring tools b3d studio and b3d studio pro for creating digital animation that could be streamed easily and efficiently via the Internet. B3d studio is the centerpiece of the content development and production process. B3d studio is an object-oriented environment that collects and integrates source files from scripnav and talktrack with graphics, sound and animation, and makes them available for lay-up, editing and final output. The group operates in the United States and Australia.

Primary SIC and add'l.: 4833 7812 7372

CIK No: 0001022844

Subsidiaries: Altnet, Inc

Financial Data: Fiscal Year End:12/31   **Latest Annual Data:** 12/31/2005

Year	Sales	Net Income
2005	$5,970,000	-$4,030,000
2004	$8,775,000	-$4,784,000
2003	$5,655,000	-$9,518,000

Curr. Assets:	$2,208,000	Curr. Liab.:	$4,790,000		
Plant, Equip.:	$92,000	Total Liab.:	$4,840,000	Indic. Yr. Divd.:	NA
Total Assets:	$2,649,000	Net Worth:	-$2,191,000	Debt/ Equity:	NA

Brilliant Technologies Corp

211 Madison Ave., New York, NY, 10016; **PH:** 1-212-532-2736; **Fax:** 1-212-532-2904; **http://** www.ltdnetwork.com; **Email:** enquiries@blln.net

General - Incorporation	DE	Stock - Price on:12/24/2007	NA
Employees	NA	Stock Exchange	OTC
Auditor	Marcum & Kliegman LLP	Ticker Symbol	BLLN
Stk Agt	Interwest Transfer Company, Inc.	Outstanding Shares	NA
Counsel	NA	E.P.S.	-$0.039
DUNS No.	NA	Shareholders	NA

Business: The groups principle activity is to provide banking products and services. The group provides services include Internet banking, personal banking, commercial banking and 24 hour banking. The group operates from United States.

Primary SIC and add'l.: 2874

CIK No: 0001054825

Subsidiaries: Alfa-Pro Products GmbH, LTDnetwork Pty Ltd, LTDnetwork, Inc., Reseal, Ltd

Officers: Allan Klepfisz/CEO, Chmn. - New York, Brilliant Office/$365,000.00, Kenneth R. Parks/44/COO/$339,833.00, Rick Riccobono/Expert, Pioneer in Digital Distribution, Chai Ong/Dir. - Melbourne Office, Arie Baalbergen/Dir. Brilliant - Ltdnetwork, CFO - Melbourne Office

Directors: Allan Klepfisz/CEO, Chmn. - New York, Brilliant Office, Arie Baalbergen/Dir. Brilliant - Ltdnetwork, CFO - Melbourne Office

Owners: Chai Ong, Insiders/2.70%, Allan Klepfisz, Arie Baalbergen/1.80%

Financial Data: Fiscal Year End:12/31 Latest Annual Data: 12/31/2006

Year	Sales	Net Income
2006	NA	-$14,239,000
2005	NA	$1,751,000
2004	NA	-$28,548,000

Curr. Assets:	$204,000	Curr. Liab.:	$21,589,000		
Plant, Equip.:	$59,000	Total Liab.:	$21,589,000	Indic. Yr. Divd.:	NA
Total Assets:	$2,502,000	Net Worth:	-$19,087,000	Debt/ Equity:	NA

Brinker International Inc

6820 LBJ Fwy., Ste. 200, Dallas, TX, 75240; *PH:* 1-972-980-9917; *Fax:* 1-972-770-9593; *http://* www.brinker.com

General - Incorporation	DE	**Stock** - Price on:12/24/2007	$30.23
Employees	110,800	Stock Exchange	NYSE
Auditor	KPMG LLP	Ticker Symbol	EAT
Stk Agt	Wells Fargo Bank Minnesota N.A	Outstanding Shares	113,480,000
Counsel	NA	E.P.S.	$1.84
DUNS No.	02-332-8248	Shareholders	NA

Business: The group's principle activities include owning, operating, developing and franchising concept restaurant chains. The group's operating restaurants include Chili's Grill And Bar, Romano's Macaroni Grill, On The Border Mexican Grill & Cantina, Cozymel's Coastal Grill, Maggiano's Little Italy, The Corner Bakery Cafe and The Big Bowl Asian Kitchen. The group operates from United States, Australia, Great Britain, Latin America, South America, the Middle East and Asia.

Primary SIC and add'l.: 6794 5812

CIK No: 0000703351

Subsidiaries: Brinker Alabama, Inc., Brinker Arkansas, Inc., Brinker Connecticut Corporation, Brinker Delaware, Inc., Brinker Florida, Inc., Brinker Freehold, Inc., Brinker Georgia, Inc., Brinker Indiana, Inc., Brinker Iowa, Inc., Brinker Kentucky, Inc., Brinker Louisiana, Inc., Brinker Massachusetts Corporation, Brinker Michigan, Inc., Brinker Mississippi, Inc., Brinker Missouri, Inc. 53 Subsidiaries included in the Index

Officers: Douglas H. Brooks/Chmn., CEO, Pres./$4,945,930.00, Wyman Roberts/Pres. - Maggiano's Little Italy, Jean M. Birch/Pres. - Romano's Macaroni Grill, Michael B. Webberman/Exec. VP - Brand Solutions/$1,367,248.00, Charles M. Sonsteby/CFO, Exec. VP/$3,057,913.00, Valerie L. Davisson/Exec. VP - Peopleworks, Todd E. Diener/Pres. - Chili's Grill, Bar/$3,159,599.00, Rebeca M. Johnson/Exec. VP, Chief Marketing, Branding Officer, David M. Orenstein/Pres. - On The Border Mexican Grill, Cantina, Roger F. Thomson/Exec. VP, Chief Administrative Officer, General Counsel, Sec./$2,088,272.00, Greg Walther/Pres. - Global Business Development

Directors: Douglas H. Brooks/Chmn., CEO, Pres., Erle Nye/Dir., James E. Oesterreicher/Dir., Cece Smith/Dir., Marvin J. Girouard/Dir., Rosendo G. Parra/Dir., George R. Mrkonic/Dir., Ron Kirk/Dir., John W. Mims/Dir.

Owners: Ronald Kirk, Mellon Financial Corporation/5.87%, Earnest Partners, LLC/7.74%, Marvin J. Girouard, Insiders/2.88%, Todd E. Diener, FMR Corp./10.11%, Erle Nye, George R. Mrkonic, James E. Oesterreicher, Barclays Global Investors, NA/11.00%, Charles M. Sonsteby, John W. Mims, Cece Smith, Lord, Abbett & Co. LLC/7.10% *(20 Owners included in Index)*

Financial Data: Fiscal Year End:06/29 Latest Annual Data: 6/28/2006

Year	Sales	Net Income
2006	$4,151,291,000	$212,395,000
2005	$3,912,850,000	$160,219,000
2004	$3,707,486,000	$150,918,000

Curr. Assets:	$400,920,000	Curr. Liab.:	$379,162,000	P/E Ratio:	17.47
Plant, Equip.:	$1,566,846,000	Total Liab.:	$1,196,964,000	Indic. Yr. Divd.:	$0.360
Total Assets:	$2,207,386,000	Net Worth:	$1,010,422,000	Debt/ Equity:	0.5632

Brinks Co

1801 Bayberry Ct., Richmond, VA, 23226; *PH:* 1-804-289-9600; *Fax:* 1-804-289-9770; *http://* www.brinkscompany.com; *Email:* info@brinkscompany.com

General - Incorporation	VA	**Stock** - Price on:12/24/2007	$62.27
Employees	50,200	Stock Exchange	NYSE
Auditor	KPMG LLP	Ticker Symbol	BCO
Stk Agt	American Stock Transfer & Trust Co.	Outstanding Shares	48,500,000
Counsel	NA	E.P.S.	$4.47
DUNS No.	78-727-5296	Shareholders	NA

Business: The groups principle activity is to provide business and security services. The groups services include armored car transportation, ATM servicing, currency and coin processing and other value-added services to banks, retailers, and other commercial and governmental agencies. The group also provides security alarm monitoring services for residential and commercial properties security alarm monitoring services for residential and commercial properties. The group operates from United States.

Primary SIC and add'l.: 1221 4513 1041 7381 2421 3812

CIK No: 0000078890

Subsidiaries: A.c.n. 081 163 108 Pty Ltd, Addington, Inc., Aero Sky Panama, S.A., Aeropanamericano, C.A., Allied Couriers Limited, American Eagle Coal Company, Apollo Acropolis Holdings, B.V., Appalachian Mining, Inc., Armonia Gie, Artes Graficas Avanzadas 98, C.A., Athena Marathon Holdings, B.V., BAX Finance Inc., BAX Holding Company, BGS - Agenciamento de Carga e Despacho Aduaneiro Ltda, BI is Settlor of Trust) 204 Subsidiaries included in the Index

Officers: Michael T. Dan/58/Chmn., CEO, Pres./$7,090,672.00, James B. Hartough/VP - Corporate Finance, Treasurer/$1,347,589.00, Arthur E. Wheatley/VP - Risk Management, Insurance, Matthew A.P. Schumacher/Controller, Frank T. Lennon/VP, Chief Administrative Officer/$2,059,386.00, Austin F. Reed/VP, General Counsel, Sec./$2,038,054.00, Robert T. Ritter/CFO, VP/$1,902,257.00

Directors: Michael T. Dan/58/Chmn., CEO, Pres., Murray D. Martin/60/Dir., John S. Brinzo/66/Dir., James L. Broadhead/Dir., Roger G. Ackerman/69/Dir., Betty C. Alewine/60/Dir., James R. Barker/72/Dir., Marc C. Breslawsky/65/Dir., Lawrence J. Mosner/66/Dir., Carl S. Sloane/71/Dir., Ronald L. Turner/62/Dir., Thomas R. Hudson/42/Dir., Timothy Smart/50/Dir.

Owners: Frank T. Lennon, Ronald L. Turner, Murray D. Martin, Pirate Capital LLC/8.50%, Lawrence J. Mosner, Michael T. Dan/1.59%, John S. Brinzo, Carl S. Sloane, Betty C. Alewine, Steel Partners II, L.P./8.00%, Roger G. Ackerman, Robert T. Ritter, Marc C. Breslawsky, James R. Barker, James L. Broadhead *(23 Owners included in Index)*

Financial Data: Fiscal Year End:12/31 Latest Annual Data: 12/31/2006

Year	Sales	Net Income
2006	$2,837,600,000	$587,200,000
2005	$2,549,000,000	$142,400,000
2004	$4,718,100,000	$121,500,000

Curr. Assets:	$750,800,000	Curr. Liab.:	$606,700,000	P/E Ratio:	13.96
Plant, Equip.:	$981,900,000	Total Liab.:	$1,382,400,000	Indic. Yr. Divd.:	$0.400
Total Assets:	$2,188,000,000	Net Worth:	$753,800,000	Debt/ Equity:	NA

Brinx Resources Ltd

820 Piedra Vista Rd. NE, Albuquerque, NM, 87123; *PH:* 1-505-291-0158; *Fax:* 1-505-291-0158; *http://* www.brinxresources.com; *Email:* ir@brinxresources.com

General - Incorporation	NV	**Stock** - Price on:12/24/2007	NA
Employees	1	Stock Exchange	OTC
Auditor	Gordon, Hughes & Banks, LLP	Ticker Symbol	BNXR
Stk Agt	NA	Outstanding Shares	NA
Counsel	NA	E.P.S.	-$0.01
DUNS No.	NA	Shareholders	NA

Business: The groups principal activity is to exploration of minerals. In the year 2005, the group acquired Ranken Energy Corporation's Owl Creek Project and Vector Exploration Inc.'s. The group operates from the United States and Canada.

Primary SIC and add'l.: 1040

CIK No: 0001212641

Officers: Leroy Halterman/Pres., Sec., Treasurer, Dir. - Principal Executive, Financial and Accounting Officer, Jesse Keller/Contact - Investor Relations

Directors: Kenneth A. Cabianca/Dir.

Owners: Leroy Halterman/1.01%, Insiders/12.33%, Torito Business Corp./6.61%, Ritornello Group SA/7.01%, Kenneth A. Cabianca/11.41%, Scott Cabianca/5.10%

Financial Data: Fiscal Year End:10/31 Latest Annual Data: 10/31/2006

Year	Sales	Net Income
2006	$624,000	-$397,000
2005	NA	-$75,000
2004	NA	-$34,000

Curr. Assets:	$610,000	Curr. Liab.:	$96,000		
Plant, Equip.:	NA	Total Liab.:	$168,000	Indic. Yr. Divd.:	NA
Total Assets:	$2,419,000	Net Worth:	$2,251,000	Debt/ Equity:	NA

Bristol Myers Squibb Co

345 Pk. Ave., New York, NY, 10154; *PH:* 1-212-546-4000; *Fax:* 1-212-546-4020; *http://* www.bms.com

General - Incorporation	DE	**Stock** - Price on:12/24/2007	$31.68
Employees	43,000	Stock Exchange	NYSE
Auditor	Deloitte & Touche, LLP	Ticker Symbol	BMY
Stk Agt	Mellon Investor Services LLC	Outstanding Shares	1,970,000,000
Counsel	NA	E.P.S.	$1.08
DUNS No.	00-128-8497	Shareholders	NA

Business: The groups principle activities include discovering, developing, manufacturing and distributing pharmaceuticals and healthcare-related products. The groups products include Atripla(TM), Abilify(R) and Avapro(R). The group operates through three segments namely pharmaceuticals, nutritionals and other health care. The group operates from United States.

Primary SIC and add'l.: 3842 2844 8099 2834 2023

CIK No: 0000014272

Subsidiaries: 2309 Realty Corporation, 3130827 Canada Inc., 345 Park Corporation, 77 Wilson St., Corp., A.G. Medical Services, P.A., Alive& Well, Inc., Allard Laboratories, Inc., Allard Labs Acquisition LLC, Allied Medical Services (UK) Ltd., AMCARE Limited, Apothecon, Inc., Apothecon, S.L., B-MS GeneRx, Bioenhance Medicines, Inc., Blisa Acquisition LLC 284 Subsidiaries included in the Index

Officers: Andrew R.J. Bonfield/CFO, Exec. VP/$3,439,770.00, Sandra Leung/Sr. VP, General Counsel, Tony Plohoros/Contact - Corporate, Financial Communications, Jeff MacDonald/Contact - Financial Communications, Jennifer Fron Mauer/Contact - Research & Development Communications, Laura Hortas/Contact - Policy Communications, Ken Dominski/Contact - Cardiovasculars, Metabolics, David Rosen/Contact - Neuroscience, Metabolics, Biologics, John E. Celentano/Pres. - Health Care Group, Sonia Choi/Contact - Oncology, Virology, Marilyn Tretler/Contact - Technical Operations, Manufacturing, Brian Henry/Contact - Europe, Middle East, Africa, Stephen Haynes/Contact - Asia Pacific, Pete Paradossi/Contact - Health Care Group, Medical Imaging, Joseph C. Caldarella/52/VP, Corporate Controller *(21 Officers included in Index)*

Directors: Laurie H. Glimcher/Dir., Leif Johansson/Dir., Sanders R. Williams/Dir., Vicki L. Sato/Dir., James M. Cornelius/Dir., Vance D. Coffman/Dir., Lewis B. Campbell/Dir., Robert E. Allen/Dir., James D. Robinson/Dir., Michael Grobstein/Dir., Louis J. Freeh/Dir.

Owners: R. E. Allen, J. M. Cornelius, J. D. Robinson, R. S. Williams, A. R. J. Bonfield, U. S. Trust Corporation/6.67%, P. R. Dolan, Capital Research and Management Company/10.10%, E. Sigal, L. H. Glimcher, V. D. Coffman, A. C. Hooper, Insiders, L. Johansson, L. Andreotti *(19 Owners included in Index)*

Financial Data: Fiscal Year End:12/31 Latest Annual Data: 12/31/2006

Year	Sales	Net Income
2006	$17,914,000,000	$1,585,000,000
2005	$19,207,000,000	$3,000,000,000
2004	$19,380,000,000	$2,388,000,000

Curr. Assets:	$10,302,000,000	Curr. Liab.:	$6,496,000,000	P/E Ratio:	39.60
Plant, Equip.:	$5,673,000,000	Total Liab.:	$15,584,000,000	Indic. Yr. Divd.:	$1.240
Total Assets:	$25,575,000,000	Net Worth:	$9,991,000,000	Debt/ Equity:	0.6950

Bristol West Holdings Inc

5701 Stirling Rd., Davie, FL, 33314; *PH:* 1-954-316-5200; *http://* www.bristolwest.com

General - Incorporation .... DE	Stock - Price on:12/24/2007 .... $22.28
Employees 1,154	Stock Exchange .... NYSE
Auditor .... Deloitte & Touche LLP	Ticker Symbol .... BRW
Stk Agt .... Bank of New York	Outstanding Shares 29,540,000
Counsel .... NA	E.P.S. $1.16
DUNS No. .... NA	Shareholders .... NA

Business: The group's principal activity is to provide non-standard private passenger automobile insurance and related services. Non-standard automobile insurance offers coverage to drivers who find it difficult to purchase standard automobile insurance because of their driving record, vehicle age, claims history or limited financial resources. As of 31-Dec-2003, the group is licensed in thirty-five states and the district of columbia. The group also provides non-insurance services like policy servicing and installment payment plans.

Primary SIC and add'l.: 6321 6719

CIK No: 0001272957

Subsidiaries: Apex Adjustment Bureau, Inc., Bayview Adjustment Bureau, Inc., Bristol West Casualty Insurance Company, Bristol West Insurance Company, Bristol West Insurance Services of California, Inc., Bristol West Insurance Services of Georgia, Inc., Bristol West Insurance Services of Pennsylvania, Inc., Bristol West Insurance Services of Texas, Inc., Bristol West Insurance Services, Inc. of Florida, BWIS of Nevada, Inc., Coast National General Agency, Inc., Coast National Holding Company, Coast National Insurance Company, GP, LLC, Insurance Data Systems, G.P. 16 Subsidiaries included in the Index

Officers: Jeffrey J. Dailey/Dir., CEO, Pres., George G. Obrien/Chief Legal Officer, Corp. Sec., Robert D. Sadler/Sr. VP, CFO

Directors: Jeffrey J. Dailey/Dir., CEO, Pres., Perry Golkin/Dir., Cary R. Blair/Dir., Richard T. Delaney/Dir., Todd A. Fisher/Dir., James R. Fisher/Dir., Mary R. Hennessy/Dir., Arthur J. Rothkopf/Dir., Eileen Hilton/Dir., James N. Meehan/61/Dir., Allan W. Ditchfield/Dir.

Owners: Insiders, Allan W. Ditchfield, Jeffrey J. Dailey, Cary R. Blair, Bristol West Associates LLC, Eileen Hilton, Stadium Capital Management LLC, Arthur J. Rothkopf, Robert D. Sadler, Simon J. Noonan, Perry Golkin, James R. Fisher, Richard T. Delaney, Mary R. Hennessy, T. Rowe Price Associates, Inc. *(18 Owners included in Index)*

Financial Data: *Fiscal Year End:* 12/31 *Latest Annual Data:* 12/31/2006

Year	Sales	Net Income
2006	$661,079,000	$42,136,000
2005	$677,549,000	$54,702,000
2004	$410,901,000	$61,137,000

Curr. Assets:	$265,826,000	Curr. Liab.:	$49,123,000	P/E Ratio:	19.21
Plant, Equip.:	$20,036,000	Total Liab.:	$587,808,000	Indic. Yr. Divd.:	$0.320
Total Assets:	$944,559,000	Net Worth:	$356,751,000	Debt/ Equity:	0.2773

Bristow Group Inc

2000 W Sam Houston Pkwy. S, Ste. 1700, Houston, TX, 77042; *PH:* 1-713-267-7600; *Fax:* 1-713-267-7620; *http://* www.bristowgroup.com

General - Incorporation .... DE	Stock - Price on:12/24/2007 .... $51.15
Employees 4,159	Stock Exchange .... NYSE
Auditor .... KPMG LLP	Ticker Symbol .... BRS
Stk Agt .... Mellon Investor Services LLC	Outstanding Shares 23,590,000
Counsel .... NA	E.P.S. $2.74
DUNS No. .... NA	Shareholders .... NA

Business: The groups principle activity is to provide helicopter transportation services to the oil and gas industry. The group operates through two segments namely, helicopter services and production management services. The group operates from the United States, Brazil, China, Nigeria, Russia, Trinidad, Gulf of Mexico and the North Sea. The group's quarterly revenue for September 2007 was 273.34 millions of USD.

Primary SIC and add'l.: 4522 1389

CIK No: 0000073887

Subsidiaries: Aeroleo Taxi Aereo S/A, Air Logistics of Alaska, Inc., Air Logistics, LLC, Aircopter Maintenance International, Inc., Airlog International, Inc., Airlog International, Ltd., ALN, Inc., Atyrau-Bristow Airways Services, Aviashelf, Brilog Leasing Limited, Bristow Aviation Holdings Limited, Bristow Caribbean Ltd., Bristow Helicopter Group Limited, Bristow Helicopters Australia Pty. Ltd., Bristow Helicopters BV 53 Subsidiaries included in the Index

Officers: William E. Chiles/Dir., CEO, Pres./$1,966,004.00, Perry L. Elders/CFO, Exec. VP/$954,608.00, Richard D. Burman/Sr. VP - Eastern Hemisphere/$664,812.00, Michael R. Suldo/Sr. VP - Western Hemisphere/$658,014.00, Mark B. Duncan/Sr. VP - Global Business Development/$606,275.00, Randall A. Stafford/VP, General Counsel, Corp. Sec., Joseph A. Baj/VP, Treasurer, Elizabeth D. Brumley/VP, Chief Accounting Officer, William H. Hopkins/VP - Global Standards, Gavin Sinclair/VP - Compliance, Michael J. Simon/Sr. VP - Production Management, Patrick Corr/Sr. VP - Global Training, Mark Frank/VP - Planning, Hilary Ware/VP - Global Human Resources

Directors: William E. Chiles/Dir., CEO, Pres., Tom Knudson/Chmn., Thomas N. Amonett/Dir., Charles F. Bolden/Dir., Peter N. Buckley/Dir., Michael A. Flick/Dir., Stephen J. Cannon/Dir., Jonathan H. Cartwright/Dir., Ken C. Tamblyn/Dir.

Owners: Jonathan H. Cartwright/7.00%, Peter N. Buckley/7.00%, Michael R. Suldo, Caledonia Investments plc/8.30%, Franklin Resources, Inc./9.30%, Barclays Global Investors NA/5.14%, Ken C. Tamblyn, Thomas C. Knudson, Insiders/9.00%, Charles F. Bolden, Stephen J. Cannon, Thomas N. Amonett, FMR Corp./10.67%, Richard D. Burman, North Run Capital LP/5.80% *(21 Owners included in Index)*

Financial Data: *Fiscal Year End:* 03/31 *Latest Annual Data:* 3/31/2007

Year	Sales	Net Income
2007	$897,861,000	$74,172,000
2006	$768,940,000	$57,809,000
2005	$673,646,000	$51,560,000

Curr. Assets:	$535,974,000	Curr. Liab.:	$167,968,000	P/E Ratio:	18.67
Plant, Equip.:	$891,908,000	Total Liab.:	$628,701,000	Indic. Yr. Divd.:	NA
Total Assets:	$1,505,803,000	Net Worth:	$871,657,000	Debt/ Equity:	0.2916

British Airways Plc

75-20 Astoria Blvd., Jackson Heights, NY, 11370; *PH:* 1-347-418-4000; *Fax:* 1-347-418-4204; *http://* www.british-airways.com

General - Incorporation .... UK	Stock - Price on:12/24/2007 .... NA
Employees 49,957	Stock Exchange .... OTC
Auditor .... Ernst & Young LLP	Ticker Symbol .... BAIRY
Stk Agt .... Computershare Investor Services LLC	Outstanding Shares .... NA
Counsel .... NA	E.P.S. .... NA
DUNS No. 22-531-1612	Shareholders .... NA

Business: The group's principal activities are the operation of international and domestic scheduled and charter air services for the carriage of passengers, freight and mail and the provision of ancillary services. The group's global alliance includes new code share arrangements agreed with finnair, iberia and cathay pacific. The group operates in such geographical areas as the United Kingdom, continental Europe, the Americas, Africa, Middle East, Far East, australasia and Indian sub-continent.

Primary SIC and add'l.: 4512 4581 4522 4513

CIK No: 0000809023

Subsidiaries: Air Miles Travel Promotions Ltd, BA & AA Holdings Ltd, BA Connect Ltd, Britair Holdings Ltd, British Airways 777 Leasing Ltd, British Airways Capital Ltd, British Airways CitiExpress, British Airways Holdings Ltd, British Airways Holidays Ltd, British Airways Leasing Limited, British Airways Maintenance Cardiff Ltd, British Airways Regional Ltd, British Airways Travel Shops Ltd, British Regional Air Lines Group Plc, CityFlyer Express Ltd 17 Subsidiaries included in the Index

Officers: William Walsh/Dir., CEO, Keith Williams/Dir., CFO, George Stinnes/Head - Investor Relations, Ceinwen Williams/Mgr. - Investor Relations, Robert Boyle/Commercial Dir., Paul Coby/CIO, Lloyd Cromwell Griffiths/Dir. - Flight Operations, Geoff Want/Dir. - Ground Operations UK, Overseas, Robert Webb Qc/General Counsel, Roger Maynard/Dir. - Investments, Alliances, Jim Lawrence/Non Exec. Dir., Garry Copeland/Dir. - Engineering, Gareth Kirkwood/Dir. - Operations, Alison Marshall/Sec. to Head - Investor, Sarah Billington/Mgr. - Shareholder Services

Directors: William Walsh/Dir., CEO, Martin Broughton/Chmn., Maarten Van Den Bergh/Non Exec. Dir., Keith Williams/Dir., CFO, Martin Read/Non Exec. Dir., Alison Reed/Non Exec. Dir., Ken Smart/Non Exec. Dir., Baroness Symons/Non Exec. Dir., Chumpol Nalamlieng/Non Exec. Dir., Baroness Kingsmill/Non Exec. Dir.

British American Tobacco Industries Plc

Globe House, 4 Temple Pl., London, WC2R 2PG; *PH:* 44-2078451000; *http://* www.bat.com

General - Incorporation	Stock - Price on:12/24/2007 .... $66.06
Employees 97,431	Stock Exchange .... AMEX
Auditor .... NA	Ticker Symbol .... BTI
Stk Agt .... NA	Outstanding Shares 1,020,000,000
Counsel .... NA	E.P.S. .... NA
DUNS No. .... NA	Shareholders .... NA

Business: The groups principle activity is to manufacture tobacco products. The groups products include cigars, and pipe tobacco. The group's products sold under the brand name include Dunhill, Kent, Lucky Strike and Pall Mall. The group operates from United States.

Primary SIC and add'l.: 2100

CIK No: 0001303523

Officers: Paul Adams/54/Dir., Chief Executive, Paul Rayner/53/Dir. - Finance, Antonio Monteiro De Castro/62/Dir., COO, Flavio De Andrade/59/Dir. - Latin America, Caribbean, John Daly/51/Dir. - Asia, Pacific, Nicandro Durante/51/Dir. - Africa, Middle East, Rudi Kindts/50/Dir. - Human Resources, Michael Prideaux/57/Dir. - Corporate, Regulatory Affairs, Jimmi Rembiszewski/57/Dir. - Marketing, Ben Stevens/48/Dir. - Europe, Peter Taylor/55/Dir. - Operations, Information Technology, Neil Withington/51/Dir. - Legal, General Counsel, Mark Cobben/Dir. - Latin America, Caribbean, Nicky Snook/Company Sec.

Directors: Jan Du Plessis/54/Chmn., Kenneth Clarke/67/Dep. Chmn., Nicholas Scheele/64/Non Exec. Dir., Antonio Monteiro De Castro/62/Dir., COO, Piet Beyers/58/Dir., Paul Adams/54/Dir., Chief Executive, Robert Lerwill/56/Non Exec. Dir., Rupert Pennant-Rea/60/Non Exec. Dir., Ana Maria Llopis/57/Non Exec. Dir., Anthony Ruys/60/Non Exec. Dir., Thys Visser/53/Non Exec. Dir., Karen De Segundo/Non Exec. Dir., Christine Morin-Postel/Non Exec. Dir.

British Sky Broadcasting Group Plc

Grant Way, Isleworth, TW7 5QD; *PH:* 44-2077053000; *http://* www.sky.com; *Email:* investor-relations@bskyb.com

General - Incorporation ...England And Wales	Stock - Price on:12/24/2007 .... NA
Employees 10,617	Stock Exchange .... NDQ
Auditor .... Deloitte & Touche LLP	Ticker Symbol .... BSY
Stk Agt .... Lloyds TSB Registrars	Outstanding Shares 438,250,000
Counsel .... Herbert Smith	E.P.S. $2.10
DUNS No. 39-934-3466	Shareholders .... NA

Business: The group's principal activity is the operation of a pay television broadcasting service to customers in the United Kingdom and the republic of Ireland. The group also offers Internet services via digital satellite. Programs include sky one, sky news, sky sports and sky movies.

Primary SIC and add'l.: 4841 7812 4833

CIK No: 0000932789

Subsidiaries: British Interactive Broadcasting Holdings Limited (BIB), British Sky Broadcasting Limited (BSkyB Limited), British Sky Broadcasting SA, BSkyB Finance Limited, BSkyB Finance UK plc, BSkyB Investments Limited, Easynet Group Plc, Hestview Limited, Marketing Contributions Limited, Sky Broadband Services Limited (Sky Broadband), Sky In-Home Services Limited, Sky Interactive Limited, Sky New Media Ventures Limited, Sky Subscribers Services, Sky Television Limited 17 Subsidiaries included in the Index

Officers: James Murdoch/Dir., CEO, Vic Wakeling/65/MD - Sky Sports, Sky News, Beryl Cook/47/Dir. - People, Organisational Development, Mike Darcey/43/COO, Jeff Hughes/38/Exec. VP, Robin Crossley/49/Strategic Adviser, Technology, Alun Webber/42/Group Dir. - Strategic Project Delivery, James Conyers/43/General Counsel, Jeremy Darroch/Dir., CFO, Matthew Anderson/42/Group Dir. Communications - Brand Marketing, David Rowe/49/MD - Enterprise Business, Sophie Turner Laing/47/MD - Entertainment, David Gormley/45/Group Company Sec.

Directors: James Murdoch/Dir., CEO, Lord Rothschild/Dep. Chmn., Rupert Murdoch/Chmn., David Devoe/Non Exec. Dir., Chase Carey/Non Exec. Dir., Andrew Higginson/Dir., Lord Wilson/Dir., Jacques Nasser/Dir., David Evans/Dir., Arthur Siskind/Non Exec. Dir., Gail Rebuck/Non Exec. Dir., Nicholas Ferguson/Non Exec. Dir., Jeremy Darroch/Dir., CFO, Allan Leighton/Non Exec. Dir.

Owners: Templeton Global Advisors Limited/5.89%, The Capital Group Companies, Inc./3.10%, News UK Nominees Limited/39.14%, Brandes Investment Partners L.P./3.12%, Janus Capital Management LLC/3.07%

Financial Data: Fiscal Year End:06/30   Latest Annual Data: 06/30/2007

Year	Sales	Net Income
2007	$9,119,749,000	$959,868,000
2006	$7,534,012,000	$1,000,781,000
2005	$7,426,752,000	$1,041,370,000

Curr. Assets:	$4,146,613,000	Curr. Liab.:	$2,784,388,000	P/E Ratio:	8.66
Plant, Equip.:	$942,660,000	Total Liab.:	$6,647,658,000	Indic. Yr. Divd.:	NA
Total Assets:	$8,026,230,000	Net Worth:	$1,378,572,000	Debt/ Equity:	NA

British Telecommunications Plc

Bt Ctr., 81 Newgate St., London, EC1A 7 AJ; **PH:** 44-2073565000; **http://** www.bt.com; **Email:** kevan@lloydstsb-registrars.co.uk

General - Incorporation	UK	**Stock**- Price on:12/24/2007	$63.84
Employees	NA	Stock Exchange	NYSE
Auditor	PricewaterhouseCoopers LLP	Ticker Symbol	NA
Stk Agt.	NA	Outstanding Shares	NA
Counsel	NA	E.P.S.	NA
DUNS No.	NA	Shareholders	NA

Business: The group's principle activities are the provision of local, long distance and international telecommunication services, Internet services and it solutions. It comprises the following divisions: bt ignite: focuses primarily on corporate and wholesale markets. Btopenworld: an international mass-Market Internet business. Bt retail: serving end-business and residential customers and the prime channel to market for other bt businesses. Bt wholesale: runs bt telecommunications plc networks and sells network capacity and call terminations to other carriers. On 18-Apr-2001, the group acquired 49.5% interest in esat digifone.

Primary SIC and add'l.: 7389

CIK No: 0000820534

Subsidiaries: BT Group plc

Officers: Larry Stone/51/Company Sec., Hanif Lalani/46/Dir., Group Dir. - Finance, Ben Verwaayen/56/Chief Executive, Dir., Ian Livingston/44/Chief Executive - BT Retail, Dir., Paul Reynolds/51/Chief Executive - BT Wholesale, Andy Green/52/Chief Executive - Group Strategy, Operations, Dir., Francois Barrault/47/Chief Executive - BT Global Services, Dir.

Directors: Maarten Van Den Bergh/66/Dep. Chmn., Christopher Bland/70/Chmn., Ben Verwaayen/56/Chief Executive, Dir., Clayton Brendish/61/Non Exec. Dir., Hanif Lalani/46/Dir., Group Dir. - Finance, Baroness Jay/68/Non Exec. Dir., John Nelson/61/Non Exec. Dir., Carl G. Symon/62/Non Exec. Dir., Andy Green/52/Chief Executive - Group Strategy, Operations, Dir., Phil Hodkinson/50/Non Exec. Dir., Matti Alahuhta/56/Non Exec. Dir., Francois Barrault/47/Chief Executive - BT Global Services, Dir., Deborah Lathen/Non Exec. Dir.

Financial Data: Fiscal Year End:03/31   Latest Annual Data: 3/31/2006

Year	Sales	Net Income
2006	$34,345,392,000	$1,849,407,000
2005	$35,313,926,000	$2,437,063,000
2004	$34,540,747,000	$1,612,535,000

Curr. Assets:	$11,694,936,000	Curr. Liab.:	$16,481,125,000	P/E Ratio:	8.66
Plant, Equip.:	$25,160,988,000	Total Liab.:	$41,562,081,000	Indic. Yr. Divd.:	NA
Total Assets:	$41,377,663,000	Net Worth:	-$274,888,000	Debt/ Equity:	NA

Britton & Koontz Capital Corp

500 Main St., Natchez, MS, 39120; **PH:** 1-601-445-5576; **Fax:** 1-601-445-2488; **http://** www.bkbank.com; **Email:** answers@bkbank.com

General - Incorporation	MS	**Stock**- Price on:12/24/2007	$19.02
Employees	100	Stock Exchange	NDQ
Auditor	Hannis T. Bougeois LLP	Ticker Symbol	BKBK
Stk Agt.	American Stock Transfer & Trust Co.	Outstanding Shares	2,120,000
Counsel	NA	E.P.S.	$1.33
DUNS No.	00-890-5978	Shareholders	NA

Business: The group's principal activity is to provide full banking services and trust services through its subsidiary britton & koontz first national bank. The services offered include personal and commercial checking accounts, savings and time deposits, money market deposit accounts, money transfer and safe deposit facilities. The group is a full-service residential and commercial mortgage lender. It also provides other commercial and consumer lending services including issuance of visa and mastercard credit cards. The group's operations are conducted through its main office and three branch offices in Mississippi and Louisiana. The group's trust department offers a range of trust services, acting as trustee, executor, administrator, custodian, guardian and agent.

Primary SIC and add'l.: 6712 6021

CIK No: 0000707604

Subsidiaries: B&K Title Insurance Agency, Inc., Britton & Koontz Bank, National Association, Britton & Koontz Statutory Trust # I

Officers: Page W. Ogden/CEO, Pres./$254,388.00

Owners: A. J. Ferguson, Andrew R. Patty, William M. Salters, Jarrett E. Nicholson, George R. Kurz, W. W. Allen, Page W. Ogden/2.80%, Robert J. Punches, Hot Creek Capital, L.L.C., Hot Creek Investors, L.P./7.00%, Bethany L. Overton, Vinod K. Thukral/2.10%, Britton & Koontz Capital Corporation Employee/4.20%, Craig A. Bradford/1.10%, Insiders/8.30%

Financial Data: Fiscal Year End:12/31   Latest Annual Data: 12/31/2006

Year	Sales	Net Income
2006	$26,200,000	$3,579,000
2005	$24,451,000	$3,228,000
2004	$22,452,000	$2,844,000

Curr. Assets:	$9,314,000	Curr. Liab.:	$330,164,000	P/E Ratio:	14.30
Plant, Equip.:	$8,976,000	Total Liab.:	$335,721,000	Indic. Yr. Divd.:	$0.720
Total Assets:	$369,318,000	Net Worth:	$33,597,000	Debt/ Equity:	0.1534

Broadband Wireless International Corp

8290 W Sahara, Ste. 270, Las Vegas, NV, 89117; **PH:** 1-702-314-6900; **http://** www.bbanwireless.com

General - Incorporation	NV	**Stock**- Price on:12/24/2007	$0.0011
Employees	NA	Stock Exchange	OTC
Auditor	Shelley International CPA	Ticker Symbol	BBAN
Stk Agt.	Broadband Wireless International Corp	Outstanding Shares	367,780,000
Counsel	NA	E.P.S.	-$0.001
DUNS No.	NA	Shareholders	NA

Business: The group's principal activity is to provide wireless Internet services in the greater Oklahoma city geographical market. The group conducted test applications of the wireless operations in edmond and norman, Oklahoma. These tests were successfully completed and, on 23-Feb-2001 and 19-Mar-2001, the group entered into agreements with the American bank & trust company of edmond, Oklahoma and republic bank of norman, Oklahoma respectively, to provide wireless communication services for those banks to and from their branch offices in central Oklahoma. On 27-Dec-2001, the group filed an application to reorganize under chapter 11 of the bankruptcy code. The current business plan is to set up wireless systems for customers and also to do target advertising over the Internet for the music industry.

Primary SIC and add'l.: 7375

CIK No: 0000012388

Owners: Insiders/4.40%, Michael Williams/4.40%

Financial Data: Fiscal Year End:03/31   Latest Annual Data: 3/31/2006

Year	Sales	Net Income
2006	$23,000	-$224,000
2005	$26,000	-$1,788,000
2004	NA	-$804,000

Curr. Assets:	$1,000	Curr. Liab.:	$733,000		
Plant, Equip.:	$4,000	Total Liab.:	$733,000	Indic. Yr. Divd.:	NA
Total Assets:	$5,000	Net Worth:	-$728,000	Debt/ Equity:	NA

Broadcast International Inc

7050 Union Pk. Ave., Ste. 600, Salt Lake City, UT, 84047; **PH:** 1-801-562-2252; **Fax:** 1-801-562-1773; **http://** www.brin.com; **Email:** info@brin.com

General - Incorporation	UT	**Stock**- Price on:12/24/2007	$1.1
Employees	35	Stock Exchange	OTC
Auditor	Deloitte & Touche, LLP	Ticker Symbol	BCST
Stk Agt.	Interwest Transfer Company, Inc.	Outstanding Shares	30,000,000
Counsel	NA	E.P.S.	-$0.53
DUNS No.	NA	Shareholders	NA

Business: The group's principal activity is to integrate broadband delivery technologies, such as satellite, Internet streaming and wi-fi. The group's provides satellite uplink services and related equipment service, Web hosting services, and video production services. It also offers services such as internal business applications, external business applications, satellite-based services, streamed video hosting services and production and content development services. The group serves large retailers, other businesses, and to a third party provider of in-store music and video.

Primary SIC and add'l.: 7375 4899

CIK No: 0000740726

Subsidiaries: BI Acquisitions, Inc., Interact Devices, Inc.

Officers: Rod Tiede/CEO, Pres., Ken Moore/VP - Technical Services, Randy Turner/VP - Finance, Robert J. Chipman/VP - Sales, Marketing, Mary K. Hall/VP - Client Services, Reed L. Benson/CFO, General Counsel, Sec., Dan Mabey/VP - International Development, Renae Hambly/VP - Operations

Directors: Rod Tiede/CEO, Pres., William Davidson/56/Chmn., James E. Solomon/56/Dir., Kirby D. Cochran/53/Dir.

Owners: James E. Solomon, Renae Hambly/5.90%, Leon Frenkel/17.10%, Randy L. Turner/5.60%, Kirby D. Cochran, William H. Davidson, Yang Lan Studio Ltd/5.50%, Reed L. Benson/3.30%, Insiders/17.70%, Kenneth Moore/5.60%, Rodney M. Tiede/12.40%

Financial Data: Fiscal Year End:12/31   Latest Annual Data: 12/31/2006

Year	Sales	Net Income
2006	$13,894,000	-$15,598,000
2005	$5,381,000	-$5,582,000
2004	$5,386,000	-$16,489,000

Curr. Assets:	$3,106,000	Curr. Liab.:	$6,828,000		
Plant, Equip.:	$387,000	Total Liab.:	$8,876,000	Indic. Yr. Divd.:	NA
Total Assets:	$5,191,000	Net Worth:	-$3,685,000	Debt/ Equity:	NA

Broadcaster Inc

9201 Oakdale Ave., Ste. 200, Chatsworth, CA, 91311; **PH:** 1-818-206-0598; **Fax:** 1-818-206-9371; **http://** www.broadcaster.com

General - Incorporation	CA	**Stock**- Price on:12/24/2007	$1.21
Employees	43	Stock Exchange	OTC
Auditor	Choi, Kim & Park, LLP	Ticker Symbol	BCAS
Stk Agt.	American Stock Transfer & Trust Co.	Outstanding Shares	102,550,000
Counsel	NA	E.P.S.	-$0.63
DUNS No.	NA	Shareholders	NA

Business: The groups principle activity is to provide downloadable media and content over the Internet. House plans and access media. The group operates through two segments namely house plans and access media. In the year 2005, the group acquired Weinmaster. In the year 20063, the group merged with Access Media. The group operates from the United States. The group's quarterly revenue for September 2007 was 0.60 millions of USD.

Primary SIC and add'l.: 4899 7372

CIK No: 0000814929

Subsidiaries: AccessMedia Networks, Inc., Houseplans, Inc., IMSI Australia PTY, Media Zone, LTD, MyVod, Inc., PeopleCaster, Inc., Value Investments, Inc., Weinmaster Homes, Limited.

Officers: Susan Morgenbesser/Investor Relations Officer, Mike Graff/Contact - Media, Peter Wang/Chief Analytics Officer - Broadcaster

Directors: Paul Goodman/47/Dir., Vincent F. Orza/58/Dir.

Owners: Insiders, Software People, LLC, Paul Goodman, Martin Wade, Vincent F. Orza, Trans Global Media, LLC, Nolan Quan, Richard Berman, Blair Mills, Broadcaster, LLC, Michael Gardner

Financial Data: **Fiscal Year End:**06/30 **Latest Annual Data:** 06/30/2007

Year	Sales	Net Income
2007	$6,913,000	-$19,993,000
2006	$8,203,000	$848,000
2005	$13,874,000	-$1,754,000

Curr. Assets:	$10,760,000	**Curr. Liab.:**	$5,149,000		
Plant, Equip.:	$363,000	**Total Liab.:**	$10,481,000	**Indic. Yr. Divd.:**	NA
Total Assets:	$94,757,000	**Net Worth:**	$84,276,000	**Debt/ Equity:**	0.0030

Broadcom Corp

5300 California Ave., Irvine, CA, 92617; *PH:* 1-949-926-5000; *Fax:* 1-949-926-5203; *http://* www.broadcom.com

General - Incorporation .... CA
Employees 5,233
Auditor .... Ernst & Young LLP
Stk Agt............ U.S. Stock Transfer Corp
Counsel............ Brobeck, Phleger & Harrison
DUNS No............ 79-987-0605

Stock- Price on:12/24/2007 .... $30.51
Stock Exchange .... NDQ
Ticker Symbol .... BRCM
Outstanding Shares 541,000,000
E.P.S. $0.29
Shareholders .... NA

Business: The groups principle activity is to provide system-on-a-chip and software solutions to manufacturers of computing and networking equipment, digital entertainment and broadband access products, and mobile devices. The groups products include bluetooth, cable, cellular and GPS navigation products. The group operates from United States.

Primary SIC and add'l.: 3674 5065

CIK No: 0001054374

Subsidiaries: Broadcom International Limited, Broadcom Singapore Pte Ltd, ServerWorks Corporation, ServerWorks International Ltd

Officers: Scott A. McGregor/Dir., CEO, Pres./$9,898,390.00, Henry Samueli/Chmn., CTO, Co - Founder/$787,848.00, David A. Dull/Sr. VP - Business Affairs, General Counsel, Sec./$2,569,469.00, Vahid Manian/Sr. VP - Global Manufacturing Operations/$3,161,366.00, Thomas F. Lagatta/Sr. VP - Worldwide Sales/$2,683,472.00, Edward H. Frank/VP - Research, Development, Robert A. Rango/Sr. VP, GM - Wireless Connectivity Group, Eric K. Brandt/CFO, Sr. VP, Jeremy Hyatt/Mobile, Wireless, Europe Contact - Media Relations, Gennis Lafayette/Contact - Business Networks, Mike He/Conntact, Asia Media Relations, Peter Andrew/Investor Relations Officer, Vince Brocato/Contact - Sales, Alabama, Keith Zalkin/Contact - Sales, Texas, Mike Goh/Sales Offices, Australia, New Zealand *(41 Officers included in Index)*

Directors: Scott A. McGregor/Dir., CEO, Pres., Henry Samueli/Chmn., CTO, Co - Founder, George L. Farinsky/Dir., Maureen E. Grzelakowski/Dir., Nancy H. Handel/Dir., Alan E. Ross/Dir., Werner F. Wolfen/Dir., John Major/Dir., Robert E. Switz/Dir.

Owners: George L. Farinsky, Maureen E. Grzelakowski, Vahid Manian, Henry Samueli/7.18%, Thomas F. Lagatta, William J. Ruehle, Robert E. Switz, Alan E. Ross, Nicholas Broadcom Trust, Wellington Management Company, LLP/4.98%, Nancy H. Handel, Scott A. McGregor, David A. Dull, The AXA Group/12.57%, Insiders *(26 Owners included in Index)*

Financial Data: **Fiscal Year End:**12/31 **Latest Annual Data:** 12/31/2006

Year	Sales	Net Income
2006	$3,667,818,000	$379,041,000
2005	$2,670,788,000	$367,089,000
2004	$2,400,610,000	$218,745,000

Curr. Assets:	$3,351,788,000	**Curr. Liab.:**	$678,701,000	**P/E Ratio:**	70.95
Plant, Equip.:	$164,699,000	**Total Liab.:**	$685,100,000	**Indic. Yr. Divd.:**	NA
Total Assets:	$4,876,766,000	**Net Worth:**	$4,191,666,000	**Debt/ Equity:**	NA

Broadpoint Securities Group Inc

Formerly: First Albany Cos Inc
677 Brdway, Albany, NY, 12207; *PH:* 1-518-447-8500; *http://* www.fac.com

General - Incorporation .... NY
Employees 284
Auditor .... PricewaterhouseCoopers LLP
Stk Agt...... American Stock Transfer & Trust Co.
Counsel .... NA
DUNS No............ 00-208-8607

Stock- Price on:12/24/2007 .... $1.61
Stock Exchange .... NDQ
Ticker Symbol .... FACT
Outstanding Shares 16,370,000
E.P.S. .... -$2.3
Shareholders .... NA

Business: The group's principle activity is to act as an independent investment bank and asset management firm serving the institutional market, corporate middle market and public institutions. The group operates through taxable fixed-income, municipal and equity capital markets divisions by providing its clients with strategic, research-based, innovative investment opportunities. The group offers a diverse range of products and advisory services in the areas of corporate and public finance as well as fixed income and equity sales and trading. The group provides venture capital, management and guidance for companies in the emerging growth sectors of information technology and energy technology. The group has 19 offices in 12 states in the United States. The group's quarterly revenue for Sep'07 was 11.77 millions of USD.

Primary SIC and add'l.: 6282 6211

CIK No: 0000782842

Subsidiaries: Descap Securities Inc, FA Asset Management Inc, FA Technology Ventures Corporation, Fac Management Corporation, First Albany Capital Inc., First Albany Capital Limited, First Albany Enterprise Funding, Inc

Officers: Lee Fensterstock/Chmn., CEO, Brian Coad/CFO/$445,438.00, Patricia Arciero-Craig/General Counsel, Scott Coburn/Dir. - Equity Capital Markets, Christina Rizopoulos Valauri/Dir. - Equity Research, David Reed/Dir. - Investment Banking, Peter Lukas/Dir. - Equity Sales Trading, Mark Palamountain/Dir. - Equity Trading, Robert Tirschwell/Head - Trading, Broadpoint Descap, Eric Kirby/Dir. - Equity Sales, Peter McNierney/Dir., COO, Pres./$2,080,412.00, Robert Fine/Pres. - Broadpoint Descap, David Hughes/Chief Technology, Operations Officer

Directors: Lee Fensterstock/Chmn., CEO, Mark Patterson/Dir., Christopher R. Pechock/Dir., Frank Plimpton/Dir., Robert Yingling/Dir., Carl P. Carlucci/Dir., Dale Kutnick/Dir., George C. McNamee/Dir., Peter McNierney/Dir., COO, Pres.

Owners: Gordon J. Fox, MatlinPatterson FA Acquisition LLC, George C. McNamee, David J. Matlin, Alan P. Goldberg, Paul W. Kutey, Brian Coad, Insiders, Peter J. McNierney, Carl P. Carlucci, Mark R. Patterson, Dale Kutnick

Financial Data: **Fiscal Year End:**12/31 **Latest Annual Data:** 12/31/2006

Year	Sales	Net Income
2006	$138,295,000	-$43,981,000
2005	$178,983,000	-$10,217,000
2004	$181,837,000	-$3,587,000

Curr. Assets:	$43,932,000	**Curr. Liab.:**	$284,824,000		
Plant, Equip.:	$4,516,000	**Total Liab.:**	$305,541,000	**Indic. Yr. Divd.:**	NA
Total Assets:	$357,118,000	**Net Worth:**	$51,577,000	**Debt/ Equity:**	0.4057

Broadview Media Inc

4455 W 77th St., Minneapolis, MN, 55435; *PH:* 1-612-835-4455; *http://* www.broadviewmedia.com

General - Incorporation .... MN
Employees 79
Auditor .... Lurie Besikof Lapidus & Co. LLP
Stk Agt ..... American Stock Transfer & Trust Co.
Counsel .... Fredrikson & Byron
DUNS No. 04-815-7259

Stock- Price on:12/24/2007 .... $2.15
Stock Exchange .... OTC
Ticker Symbol .... BVII
Outstanding Shares 8,110,000
E.P.S. $0.07
Shareholders .... NA

Business: The group's principal activity is to create and produce a broad range of communication products, primarily video and film based products and related services. The group operates in one segment: through entertainment, media production and education. The entertainment segment creates and produces television shows for cable networks. The media production segment develops communication products for corporations, associations and other organizations. The education segment creates and produces educational products for large publishers and proprietary products for sale through third party vendors. The other services offered include designing rich media e-mail, creating Web sites, authoring interactive content and streaming video over enterprise networks and the Internet. The group operates production and post-production facilities in minneapolis and Chicago.

Primary SIC and add'l.: 7812 7819

CIK No: 0000073048

Subsidiaries: Broadview Media/Chicago, Inc., C Square Educational Enterprises, Utah Career College

Officers: Terry L. Myhre/63/Chmn., CEO, Laurence S. Zipkin/68/Dir., COO, Michael H. Blair/63/Investor Relations, Business Affairs, Mark White/55/Contact

Directors: Terry L. Myhre/63/Chmn., CEO, Laurence S. Zipkin/68/Dir., COO, Robert A. Kramarczuk/68/Dir., Richard W. Letsche/65/Dir., Norman H. Winer/71/Dir.

Owners: Norman H. Winer/1.80%, Terry Myhre/64.30%, Insiders/66.10%, Roger Kuhl/18.00%, Thomas Tucker

Financial Data: **Fiscal Year End:**03/31 **Latest Annual Data:** 03/31/2007

Year	Sales	Net Income
2007	$9,160,000	$164,000
2006	$9,907,000	-$486,000
2005	$3,348,000	-$757,000

Curr. Assets:	$1,175,000	**Curr. Liab.:**	$570,000	**P/E Ratio:**	35.83
Plant, Equip.:	$1,403,000	**Total Liab.:**	$699,000	**Indic. Yr. Divd.:**	NA
Total Assets:	$3,321,000	**Net Worth:**	$2,622,000	**Debt/ Equity:**	NA

Broadvision Inc

1600 Seaport Blvd., Ste. 550, Redwood City, CA, 94063; *PH:* 1-650-331-1000; *Fax:* 1-650-364-3425; *http://* www.broadvision.com; *Email:* irl@broadvision.com

General - Incorporation .... DE
Employees 181
Auditor .... BDO Seidman, LLP
Stk Agt .... Computershare Investor Services LLC
Counsel............ Cooley Godward LLP
DUNS No. 80-963-9065

Stock- Price on:12/24/2007 .... NA
Stock Exchange .... OTC
Ticker Symbol .... BVSN
Outstanding Shares .... NA
E.P.S. $0.18
Shareholders .... NA

Business: The group's principal activity is to develop, market and support personalized self-service Web applications. The group's portal applications are a set of cross-industry and industry-specific applications, designed to Web-enable specific business processes. This includes broadvision one-to-one commerce, broadvision one-to-one portal and broadvision one-to-one content. The group's portal framework unifies and integrates the appropriate technologies necessary for companies to deploy content-rich, process-aware and user-centric portals. This includes broadvision one-to-one enterprise, broadvision command center, broadvision deployment center and others. The group provides services such as implementation, training, education and technical support. As of Dec 31, 2003, the group had licensed its products to over 1,000 end-user customers and partners. The group operates in the United States, Europe and Asia-Pacific.

Primary SIC and add'l.: 7379 8742 7372

CIK No: 0000920448

Officers: Pehong Chen/Chmn., CEO, Pres./$414,848.00, Lisa Joy Rosner/VP - Worldwide Marketing, Shin-Yuan Tzou/Chief - Staff, Albert Chen/VP - Worldwide Operations, David Boyer/Sr. VP - Engineering, Technical Support, Andrea Rubei/GM - EMEA Operations, Sandra Adams/Sec., General Counsel

Directors: Pehong Chen/Chmn., CEO, Pres., Francois Stieger/Dir., Bob Lee/Dir., James D. Dixon/Dir.

Owners: William Meyer, Micro Cap Partners, L.P., Palo Alto Investors LLC, Robert Lee, Honu Holdings, LLC, Palo Alto Investors, James D. Dixon, William Leland Edwards, Francois Stieger, Palo Alto Fund II, L.P., Pehong Chen, Insiders

Financial Data: **Fiscal Year End:**12/31 **Latest Annual Data:** 12/31/2006

Year	Sales	Net Income
2006	$51,984,000	$15,016,000
2005	$60,121,000	-$38,966,000
2004	$78,004,000	$20,635,000

Curr. Assets:	$49,214,000	**Curr. Liab.:**	$30,259,000		
Plant, Equip.:	$1,144,000	**Total Liab.:**	$33,688,000	**Indic. Yr. Divd.:**	NA
Total Assets:	$76,942,000	**Net Worth:**	$43,254,000	**Debt/ Equity:**	NA

Broadway Financial Corp

4800 Wilshire Blvd., Los Angeles, CA, 90010; *PH:* 1-323-634-1700; *Fax:* 1-323-634-1717; *http://* www.broadwayfederalbank.com

General - Incorporation DE
Employees 62
Auditor Crowe Chizek & Co. LLC
Stk Agt US Stock Transfer
Counsel NA
DUNS No. 96-240-0263

Stock- Price on:12/24/2007 $11.02
Stock Exchange NDQ
Ticker Symbol BYFC
Outstanding Shares 1,640,000
E.P.S $0.80
Shareholders NA

Business: The group's principal activity is to accept retail deposits from the general public and invest those deposits together with borrowings and other funds in multi-family and single-family residential mortgage loans. The group is a community-oriented saving institution dedicated to serving the african-american, hispanic and other communities of mid-city and south central los angeles, California. It also invests in non-residential real estate loans secured primarily by church properties and commercial properties. In addition, the group invests in securities issued by the federal government and agencies, mortgage-backed securities, mortgage-related mutual funds and other investments. The group conducts its business through three banking offices in los angeles and one banking office located in the city of inglewood.

Primary SIC and add'l.: 6035 6712

CIK No: 0001001171

Subsidiaries: Broadway Federal Bank, Broadway Financial Funding, LLC, Broadway Service Corporation

Officers: Paul C. Hudson/Chmn., CEO/$342,805.00, Kellogg Chan/Dir. - Broadway Federal Bank, Rick McGill/Dir. - Broadway Federal Bank, Sam Sarpong/VP, Internal Auditor, Chief Compliance Officer - Broadway Federal Bankbroadway Federal/$158,284.00, Robert C. Davidson/Dir., Dir. - Broadway Federal Bank, Daniel A. Medina/Dir. - Broadway Federal Bank, Cindy Yoshida/VP, Dir. - Savings Operations, Retail Banking Department, Broadway Federal Bank, Elrick Williams/Dir. - Broadway Federal Bank, Wilbur McKesson/Sr. VP, Chief Loan Officer - Broadway Federal Bank, Candis Hurdle Noel/Sr. VP, Chief Retail Banking Officer - Broadway Federal Bank, Mildred Cayton/VP, Controller - Administration, Broadway Federal Bank, Emmanuel Boateng/VP, Dir. - Internal Audit, Administration, Broadway Federal Bank, Daniele Johnson/Corp. Sec. - Administration, Broadway Federal Bank, Kim Johnson/Human Resources, Administration, Broadway Federal Bank, Karen E. Hudson/Public Relations, Administration, Broadway Federal Bank *(30 Officers included in Index)*

Directors: Paul C. Hudson/Chmn., CEO, Odell A. Maddox/Dir. - Broadway Federal Bank

Owners: Rick McGill/0.06%, Stanley C. Cruden/5.22%, Elrick Williams/6.11%, Insiders/17.49%, First Financial Fund, Inc./7.89%, A. Odell Maddox/1.01%, Virgil Roberts/0.44%, Kellogg Chan/1.60%, Cathay General Bancorp/13.13%, Daniel A. Medina/0.48%, Paul C. Hudson/7.10%, Sam Sarpong/0.27%, Broadway Federal Bank/5.70%, Robert C. Davidson

Financial Data: *Fiscal Year End*:12/31 *Latest Annual Data:* 12/31/2006

Year	Sales	Net Income
2006	$18,600,000	$1,663,000
2005	$17,323,000	$1,662,000
2004	$15,430,000	$1,708,000

Curr. Assets:	$6,786,000	**Curr. Liab.:**	$271,452,000	**P/E Ratio:**	13.12
Plant, Equip.:	$5,263,000	**Total Liab.:**	$280,970,000	**Indic. Yr. Divd.:**	$0.200
Total Assets:	$300,995,000	**Net Worth:**	$20,025,000	**Debt/ Equity:**	0.2942

Brocade Communications Systems Inc

1745 Technology Dr., San Jose, CA, 95110; ***PH:*** 1-408-333-8000; ***Fax:*** 1-408-333-8101; ***http://*** www.brocade.com; ***Email:*** info@brocade.com

General - Incorporation DE
Employees 1,440
Auditor KPMG LLP
Stk Agt Wells Fargo Shareowner Services
Counsel NA
DUNS No. NA

Stock- Price on:12/24/2007 $8.521
Stock Exchange NDQ
Ticker Symbol BRCD
Outstanding Shares 400,910,000
E.P.S $0.21
Shareholders NA

Business: The group's principal activity is to design, develop, market, sell and support data storage networking products and services. The group delivers products and provides education and services that allow companies to implement available, scalable, manageable and secure environments for business-critical storage applications. The silkworm family of fibre channel fabric switches enables customers to create san fabric to support the interconnection of hundreds of server and storage devices. This is compatible with existing and recently introduced products, providing investment protection for the customer. The products are sold through OEM partners, distributors, system integrators and resellers. On 27-Jan-2003, the group acquired rhapsody networks inc, a privately held technology company based in fremont, California. The group's registered trademarks are brocade, silkworm, and the brocade logo.

Primary SIC and add'l.: 3679

CIK No: 0001009626

Subsidiaries: Brocade Communications Canada Corp., Brocade Communications Denmark Aps, Brocade Communications France Sas, Brocade Communications Gmbh, Brocade Communications Italy Srl, Brocade Communications Luxembourg Sarl, Brocade Communications Services Switzerland Sarl, Brocade Communications Singapore Pte. Ltd., Brocade Communications Spain, S.l., Brocade Communications Switzerland Sarl, Brocade Communications Systems (shenzhen) Co. Ltd., Brocade Communications Systems Austria Gmbh, Brocade Communications Systems Belgium S.p.r.l, Brocade Communications Systems Hk Ltd., Brocade Communications Systems International Fsc 23 Subsidiaries included in the Index

Officers: Michael Klayko/Dir., CEO, Luc Moyen/VP - Operations, Don Jaworski/VP - Product Development, Ian Whiting/VP - Worldwide Sales, Services, Tom Buiocchi/VP - Worldwide Marketing, T. J. Grewal/VP - Corporate Development, Richard Deranleau/VP - Finance, CFO, Michelle Lindeman/Contact - Public Relations, Charlie Foo/Contact - Public Relations, Singapore, Saeko Hashimura/Contact - Public Relations, Japan, Honglin Yang/Contact - Public Relations, Greater China, Virginie Cooney/Contact - Public Relations, Southern EMEA, Chris Gibbs/Contact - Public Relations, United Kingdom, Erhard Ruettimann/Contact - Public Relation, Switzerland, Sophie Perrette-bryant Comvitamin/Contact - Public Relation, France *(20 Officers included in Index)*

Directors: Michael Klayko/Dir., CEO, Dave House/Chmn., Glenn Jones/Dir., Sanjay Vaswani/Dir., William L. Krause/Dir., Mike Rose/Dir., Robert R. Walker/Dir., Renato Dipentima/Dir., John W. Gerdelman/Dir.

Financial Data: *Fiscal Year End*:10/29 *Latest Annual Data:* 10/28/2006

Year	Sales	Net Income
2006	$750,592,000	$67,629,000
2005	$574,120,000	$43,121,000
2004	$596,265,000	-$33,694,000

Curr. Assets:	$606,814,000	**Curr. Liab.:**	$172,652,000		
Plant, Equip.:	$124,701,000	**Total Liab.:**	$541,730,000	**Indic. Yr. Divd.:**	NA
Total Assets:	$987,382,000	**Net Worth:**	$445,652,000	**Debt/ Equity:**	0.1224

Bronco Drilling Company Inc

16217 N May Ave., Edmond, OK, 73013; ***PH:*** 1-405-242-4444; ***Fax:*** 1-405-285-0478; ***http://*** broncodrill.com

General - Incorporation DE
Employees 2,050
Auditor Grant Thornton LLP
Stk Agt Computershare Trust Co
Counsel NA
DUNS No. NA

Stock- Price on:12/24/2007 $16.31
Stock Exchange NDQ
Ticker Symbol BRNC
Outstanding Shares 26,020,000
E.P.S $1.84
Shareholders NA

Business: The groups principle activity is to provide land drilling services. The group acquired Eagle Well Services, Inc for September 2007, Big A Drilling L.L.C. in the year 2006 and Strata Drilling and Strata Property, Eagle Drilling L.L.C and Thomas Drilling Company in the year 2005. Specific customers of the group include Chesapeake Energy Corporation, Comstock Oil and Gas, New Dominion, L.L.C, Chesapeake Energy Corporation, Carl E. Gungoll Exploration, L.L.C, Western Oil and Gas Development Co and XTO Energy. The group operates from Oklahoma, Kansas, Texas, Colorado and North Dakota. The group's quarterly revenue for September 2007 was 76.29 millions of USD.

Primary SIC and add'l.: 1381

CIK No: 0001328650

Subsidiaries: Elk Hill Drilling, Inc.

Officers: Frank D. Harrison/Dir., CEO, Pres., Bob Jarvis/Primary Investor Relations Officer, Zachary M. Graves/CFO, Larry Bartlett/Sr. VP - Rig Operations, Mark Dubberstein/Pres., Steven R. Starke/Chief Accounting Officer

Directors: Frank D. Harrison/Dir., CEO, Pres., Mike Liddell/Chmn., David L. Houston/Dir., William R. Snipes/Dir., Gary C. Hill/Dir.

Owners: Zachary M. Graves, Frank D. Harrison, William R. Snipes, Insiders/1.10%, Gary C. Hill, David L. Houston, Larry L. Bartlett, Wellington Management Company, LLP/9.10%

Financial Data: *Fiscal Year End*:12/31 *Latest Annual Data:* 12/31/2006

Year	Sales	Net Income
2006	$285,828,000	$59,833,000
2005	$77,885,000	$5,131,000

Curr. Assets:	$73,372,000	**Curr. Liab.:**	$35,804,000		
Plant, Equip.:	$381,922,000	**Total Liab.:**	$142,503,000	**Indic. Yr. Divd.:**	NA
Total Assets:	$482,488,000	**Net Worth:**	$339,985,000	**Debt/ Equity:**	0.1816

Brookdale Senior Living Inc

330 N Wabash, Ste. 1400, Chicago, IL, 60611; ***PH:*** 1-312-977-3700; ***Fax:*** 1-312-977-3701; ***http://*** www.brookdaleliving.com; ***Email:*** info@brookdaleliving.com

General - Incorporation DE
Employees 21,000
Auditor Ernst & Young LLP
Stk Agt American Stock Transfer & Trust Co.
Counsel NA
DUNS No. NA

Stock- Price on:12/24/2007 $45.76
Stock Exchange NYSE
Ticker Symbol BKD
Outstanding Shares 101,510,000
E.P.S -$1.48
Shareholders NA

Business: The groups principle activity is to provide residents on monthly fees. The group operates through four segments namely independent living, assisted living, retirement centers and management services. In the year 2006, the group acquired American Retirement Corporation and Southern Assisted Living Inc. The group operates from the United States. The group's quarterly revenue for September 2007 was 464.59 millions of USD.

Primary SIC and add'l.: 8051 8052 8361 8059

CIK No: 0001332349

Subsidiaries: 2010 Union L.P., 2960 Beverage Corporation, Abingdon Place of Gastonia Limited Partnership, Abingdon Place of Greensboro Limited Partnership, Abingdon Place of Lenoir Limited Partnership, AH Battery Park Member, LLC, AH Battery Park Owner, LLC, AH Illinois Owner, LLC, AH Michigan CGP, Inc., AH Michigan Owner Limited Partnership, AH Michigan Subordinated, LLC, AH North Carolina Owner, LLC, AH Ohio-Columbus Owner, LLC, AH Pennsylvania CGP, Inc., AH Pennsylvania Owner Limited Partnership 638 Subsidiaries included in the Index

Officers: Mark J. Schulte/Co - CEO, Bill E. Sheriff/Co - CEO, Mark W. Ohlendorf/CFO, Co - Pres., John P. Rijos/Co - Pres., Stanley R. Young/55/Exec. VP, Kristin A. Ferge/Exec. VP, Chief Administrative Officer, Treasurer, Andrew T. Smith/Exec. VP, Sec., General Counsel, Todd H. Kaestner/Exec. VP - Development, Gregory B. Richard/Exec. VP - Operations, Bryan D. Richardson/Exec. VP, Chief Accounting Officer, Paul Froning/Exec. VP, Chief Investment Officer, Francie Nagy/Contact - Investor Relations, Ross Roadman/Contact - Investor Relations, George T. Hicks/Exec. VP - Finance, Mark A. Kultgen/49/Exec. VP - Finance

Directors: Wesley R. Edens/Chmn., William B. Doniger/Vice Chmn., Jackie M. Clegg/Dir., Frank M. Bumstead/Dir., Jeffrey G. Edwards/Dir., Samuel Waxman/Dir., Jeffrey R. Leeds/Dir.

Owners: Insiders, Jackie M. Clegg, Mark W. Ohlendorf, Deborah C. Paskin, John P. Rijos, W.E. Sheriff, Jeffrey G. Edwards, Mark J. Schulte, Fortress Operating Entity I LP, William B. Doniger, R. Stanley Young, Jeffrey R. Leeds, Paul A. Froning, Wesley R. Edens, FMR Corp. *(17 Owners included in Index)*

Financial Data: *Fiscal Year End*:12/31 *Latest Annual Data:* 12/31/2006

Year	Sales	Net Income
2006	$1,309,913,000	-$108,087,000
2005	$790,577,000	-$50,986,000

Curr. Assets:	$270,232,000	**Curr. Liab.:**	$508,905,000		
Plant, Equip.:	$3,658,788,000	**Total Liab.:**	$2,978,443,000	**Indic. Yr. Divd.:**	$2.000
Total Assets:	$4,742,455,000	**Net Worth:**	$1,764,012,000	**Debt/ Equity:**	1.1533

Brooke Corp

10950 Grandview Dr., Ste. 600, Overland Park, KS, 66210; ***PH:*** 1-913-661-0123; ***Fax:*** 1-913-451-3183; ***http://*** www.brookecorp.com; ***Email:*** askbrooke@brookecorp.com

General - Incorporation KS
Employees 538
Auditor Summers, Spencer & Callison, Cpas
Stk Agt American Stock Transfer & Trust CO.
Counsel Wilson Sonsini Goodrich & Rosati
DUNS No. NA

Stock- Price on:12/24/2007 $14.9
Stock Exchange NDQ
Ticker Symbol BXXX
Outstanding Shares 12,690,000
E.P.S $0.882
Shareholders NA

Business: The group's principal activities are to sell insurance and financial services through franchisees or franchise agents. The group operates in three business segments namely insurance franchise, insurance brokerage and facilitator services. The insurance franchise segment includes the sale of insurance on a retail basis primarily through franchise agents in the states of Arizona, Colorado, Florida, Georgia, Iowa, Illinois, Kansas, Louisiana, Missouri, Nebraska, Nevada, New Mexico, Oklahoma, Tennessee, Texas and Utah. The insurance brokerage segment includes the sale of insurance on a wholesale basis through franchise agents and other unaffiliated agents. The facilitator services segment includes the sale of lending and consulting services which facilitate the transfer of insurance agency ownership. The group acquired ace insurance services inc & Texas all risk general agency inc in 2004.

Primary SIC and add'l.: 6411 6153

CIK No: 0000834408

Subsidiaries: Brooke Acceptance Company LLC, Brooke Agency Services Company LLC, Brooke Agency Services Company of Nevada, LLC, Brooke Agency, Inc., Brooke Bancshares, Inc., Brooke Brokerage Corporation, Brooke Canada Funding, Inc., Brooke Capital Company, LLC, Brooke Captive Credit Company 2003, LLC, Brooke Credit Corporation, Brooke Credit Funding, LLC, Brooke Franchise Corporation, Brooke Funeral Services Company, LLC, Brooke Investments, Inc., Brooke Life and Health, Inc. 23 Subsidiaries included in the Index

Officers: Robert D. Orr/Chmn., CEO/$250,572.00, Anita Larson/Dir., COO, Pres., Primary Investor Relations Officer, Leland Orr/45/Dir., CFO, Treasurer, Assist. Sec./$220,600.00, Stephanie Felder/Communications, Public Relations, Lisa Solomon/Communications, Public Relations, Shawn T. Lowry/33/Pres., Michael S. Lowry/Pres., James H. Ingraham/General Counsel, Sec./$165,000.00

Directors: Robert D. Orr/Chmn., CEO, Anita Larson/Dir., COO, Pres., Primary Investor Relations Officer, Joe L. Barnes/Dir., John Allen/Dir., Leland Orr/45/Dir., CFO, Treasurer, Assist. Sec., Derrol Hubbard/Dir., Mitchell G. Holthus/50/Dir.

Owners: Anita F. Larson/1.38%, Mitchell G. Holthus/0.03%, Michael S. Hess/1.98%, James H. Ingraham/0.01%, Leland G. Orr/10.16%, Robert D. Orr/46.53%, Insiders/55.03%, Kyle L. Garst/1.38%, Derrol D. Hubbard/0.19%, Shawn T. Lowry/1.35%, John L. Allen/0.19%, Joe L. Barnes/0.39%

Financial Data: Fiscal Year End:12/31   Latest Annual Data: 12/31/2006

Year	Sales	Net Income
2006	$179,695,000	$10,742,000
2005	$145,418,000	$9,705,000
2004	$101,923,000	$6,694,000

Curr. Assets:	$285,972,000	Curr. Liab.:	$196,607,000	P/E Ratio:	16.89
Plant, Equip.:	$18,127,000	Total Liab.:	$261,397,000	Indic. Yr. Divd.:	$0.720
Total Assets:	$323,389,000	Net Worth:	$56,528,000	Debt/ Equity:	1.0906

Brookfield Asset Mgmt Inc

3 World Financial Ctr., 11th Fl., New York, NY, 10281; **PH:** 1-212-417-7000; **Fax:** 1-212-417-7196; http:// www.brookfield.com

General - Incorporation	Canada	Stock - Price on:12/24/2007	$38.58
Employees	5,500	Stock Exchange	NYSE
Auditor	Deloitte & Touche LLP	Ticker Symbol	BAM
Stk Agt.	Mellon Trust Co	Outstanding Shares	581,820,000
Counsel	NA	E.P.S	$1.69
DUNS No.	24-193-3886	Shareholders	NA

Business: The group's principle acitivities include developing, and operating hydroelectric and other power generating facilities principally in Canada; investment activities, which include the receipt of interest and dividends on the company's financial assets as well as gains realized on investment transaction. The group operates from United States.

Primary SIC and add'l.: 4911

CIK No: 0001001085

Subsidiaries: BPO Properties Limited, Brascade Corporation, Brascan Brasil, S.A., Brookfield Homes Corporation (Brookfield Homes), Brookfield Power Inc. (Brookfield Power), Brookfield Properties Corporation (Brookfield Properties), Great Lakes Hydro Income Fund

Officers: Bruce J. Flatt/Dir. - Managing Partner, CEO, Harry Goldgut/Managing Partner, CEO - Brookfield Power, Richard Legault/Managing Partner, Pres., Co - CEO - Brookfield Power, Clifford Lai/Managing Partner, Public Securities, Joe Freedman/Managing Partner, General Counsel, Bruce K. Robertson/Managing Partner, Funds Development, Lori A. Pearson/Sr. VP - Human Resources, Alan V. Dean/Sr. VP, Sec., Katherine C. Vyse/Sr. VP - Global Marketing, Client Communications, Brian D. Lawson/Managing Partner, CFO, Richard Clark/Managing Partner, Commercial Properties, Samuel J. Pollock/Managing Partner, George E. Myhal/Managing Partner, Joyce Shapiro/Global Head - Client Relationship Management, Barry Blattman/Managing Partner, US Operations *(22 Officers included in Index)*

Directors: Bruce J. Flatt/Dir. - Managing Partner, CEO, Jack L. Cockwell/Dir., Robert J. Harding/Dir., Marcel R. Coutu/Dir., William A. Dimma/Dir., Trevor J. Eyton/Dir., James K. Gray/Dir., David W. Kerr/Dir., Lance M. Liebman/Dir., Philip B. Lind/Dir., Roy MacLaren/Dir., Wallace F. McCain/Dir., Frank J. McKenna/Dir., James A. Pattison/Dir., George S. Taylor/Dir. *(16 Directors included in Index)*

Financial Data: Fiscal Year End:12/31   Latest Annual Data: 12/31/2006

Year	Sales	Net Income
2006	$3,776,000,000	$1,517,000,000
2005	$2,355,000,000	$1,743,000,000
2004	$4,027,000,000	$636,000,000

Curr. Assets:	$7,155,000,000	Curr. Liab.:	$6,497,000,000		
Plant, Equip.:	$28,082,000,000	Total Liab.:	$34,457,000,000	Indic. Yr. Divd.:	$0.480
Total Assets:	$41,186,000,000	Net Worth:	$6,729,000,000	Debt/ Equity:	NA

Brookfield Homes Corp

12865 Pointe Del Mar, Ste. 200, Del Mar, CA, 92014; **PH:** 1-858-481-8500; **Fax:** 1-858-794-6185; http:// www.brookfieldhomes.com; **Email:** infosdrv@brookfieldhomes.com

General - Incorporation	DE	Stock - Price on:12/24/2007	$31.97
Employees	591	Stock Exchange	NYSE
Auditor	Deloitte & Touche LLP	Ticker Symbol	BHS
Stk Agt.	Wells Fargo Shareowner Services	Outstanding Shares	26,630,000
Counsel	NA	E.P.S	$3.67
DUNS No.	NA	Shareholders	NA

Business: The group's principal activities are to design, construct and market single-family and multi-family homes mainly to move-up and luxury homebuyers. It also develops land for sale to other homebuilders. The group operates through local business units, which are involved in all phases of the planning and building of the group's master-planned communities and infill developments. The operations of the group are focused primarily in five markets: the san francisco bay area; southland / los angeles area; san diego / riverside; sacramento and northern Virginia.

Primary SIC and add'l.: 1520

CIK No: 0001202157

Subsidiaries: Brookfield Asset Management Inc., Brookfield Bay Area Holdings LLC, Brookfield Homes Holdings Inc, Brookfield Properties Corporation, Brookfield Sacramento LLC, Brookfield San Diego Holdings LLC, Brookfield Southland Holdings LLC, Brookfield Washington LLC

Officers: Ian G. Cockwell/Dir., CEO, Pres./$-2,296,918.00, Paul G. Kerrigan/CFO, Exec. VP, Treasurer/$-830,413.00, Shane D. Pearson/VP, Sec., Robert A. Ferchat/Corp. Dir., Jessica Caldwell/VP, Corporate Controller, Lenis Quan/VP, Treasurer, Richard T. Whitney/Pres. - Brookfield California Land Holdings LLC, John J. Ryan/Pres. - Brookfield Bay Area Holdings LLC, Robert Hubbell/Pres. - Brookfield Washington LLC, John Stewart/Regional Pres., Adrian Foley/Pres. - Brookfield Southland Holdings LLC, Stephen P. Doyle/Pres. - Brookfield San Diego Holdings LLC, William B. Seith/Exec. VP - Risk Management/$190,569.00, Linda T. Northwood/Dir. - Investor Relations

Directors: Ian G. Cockwell/Dir., CEO, Pres., Bruce J. Flatt/Chmn., Joan H. Fallon/Dir., Alan Norris/Dir., Bruce T. Lehman/Dir., Michael D. Young/Dir., David M. Sherman/Dir., Robert L. Stelzl/Dir.

Owners: Ian G. Cockwell, Robert L. Stelzl, Brookfield Asset Management Inc, Paul G. Kerrigan, Alan Norris, Michael D. Young, Insiders, David M. Sherman, Baron Capital Group, Inc., William B. Seith, Morgan Stanley, Alson Capital Partners, LLC, Bruce J. Flatt, Robert A. Ferchat

Financial Data: Fiscal Year End:12/31   Latest Annual Data: 03/31/2007

Year	Sales	Net Income
2007	$107,946,000	$28,660,000
2006	$336,244,000	$58,823,000
2005	$1,231,052,000	$218,740,000

Curr. Assets:	$123,840,000	Curr. Liab.:	$160,896,000	P/E Ratio:	5.46
Plant, Equip.:	$1,134,573,000	Total Liab.:	$937,992,000	Indic. Yr. Divd.:	$0.400
Total Assets:	$1,401,453,000	Net Worth:	$371,406,000	Debt/ Equity:	1.7714

Brookfield Properties Corp

Three World Financial Ctr., 200 Vesey St., 11th Fl., New York, NY, 10281; **PH:** 1-212-417-7000; **Fax:** 1-212-417-7214; http:// www.brookfieldproperties.com

General - Incorporation	Canada	Stock - Price on:12/24/2007	$25.5
Employees	2,014	Stock Exchange	NYSE
Auditor	Deloitte & Touche LLP	Ticker Symbol	BPO
Stk Agt	Mellon Trust Co	Outstanding Shares	397,180,000
Counsel	NA	E.P.S	$0.39
DUNS No.	NA	Shareholders	NA

Business: The group's principle activities are to own, develop and manage north American office properties. The portfolio of the group comprises 50 commercial properties and development sites totaling 45 million square feet, including landmark properties such as the world financial center in New York and bce place in toronto.

Primary SIC and add'l.: 1540 6530 1520

CIK No: 0001085359

Subsidiaries: 1445750 Ontario Inc., 1452917 Ontario Limited/1262004 Ontario, 1464255 Ontario Limited, 1523605 Ontario Limited, 200 Broadway Joint Venture Co. LLC, 2012769 Ontario Limited, 2072790 Ontario Inc., 2072792 Ontario Inc., 6447376 Canada Inc., 6451217 Canada Inc., 70 York Street Limited, Bay Street Canada Holdings Company, BCE Place (Wellington) Limited, Bfp 1625 Eye Co. LLC, BFP 245 Park Co. LLC 84 Subsidiaries included in the Index

Officers: Alan Norris/CEO, Pres. - Residential Operations, Richard B. Clark/Dir., CEO, Pres., Tom Farley/COO, Exec. VP - Canadian Commercial Operations, Craig Laurie/CFO, Sr. VP, Rael L. Diamond/VP, Controller, Dennis Friedrich/COO, Pres. - US Commercial Operations, Michael P. Sullivan/VP - Risk Management, Lawrence F. Graham/Exec. VP - Development, Bryan Davis/CFO, Sr. VP, Mark G. Brown/Sr. VP - Finance, Melissa J. Coley/VP - Investor Relations, Communications, Nga T. Trinh/VP, Treasurer, Keith P. Hyde/VP - Taxation, Kathleen Kane/Sr. VP, General Counsel, Brett M. Fox/Sr. VP, Corporate Counsel, Assist. Sec. *(16 Officers included in Index)*

Directors: Richard B. Clark/Dir., CEO, Pres., Gordon E. Arnell/Chmn., John E. Zuccotti/Co - Chmn., William C. Wheaton/Dir., Linda Rabbitt/Dir., Paul D. McFarlane/Dir., Roderick D. Fraser/Dir., Allan S. Olson/Dir., Jack L. Cockwell/Dir., Samuel P.S. Pollock/83/Dir., William T. Cahill/Dir., Robert L. Stelzl/Dir., Diana L. Taylor/Dir., Bruce J. Flatt/Dir.

Financial Data: Fiscal Year End:12/31   Latest Annual Data: 12/31/2006

Year	Sales	Net Income
2006	$1,028,000,000	$138,000,000
2005	$823,000,000	$173,000,000
2004	$814,000,000	$259,000,000

Curr. Assets:	$1,372,000,000	Curr. Liab.:	$923,000,000		
Plant, Equip.:	$16,325,000,000	Total Liab.:	$16,202,000,000	Indic. Yr. Divd.:	$0.560
Total Assets:	$19,139,000,000	Net Worth:	$2,937,000,000	Debt/ Equity:	NA

Brookline Bancorp Inc

160 Washington St., Brookline, MA, 02447; **PH:** 1-617-730-3500; **Fax:** 1-617-730-3552; http:// www.brooklinebank.com

General - Incorporation	DE	Stock - Price on:12/24/2007	$11.91
Employees	208	Stock Exchange	NDQ
Auditor	KPMG LLP	Ticker Symbol	BRKL
Stk Agt	American Stock Transfer & Trust Co.	Outstanding Shares	61,310,000
Counsel	NA	E.P.S	$0.32
DUNS No.	00-695-3590	Shareholders	NA

Business: The group's principal activity is to accept deposits, originate mortgage loans on residential and commercial real estate, commercial and consumer loans, and investment in debt securities, mortgage-backed securities and other financial instruments. The group is a holding company that operates through its wholly owned subsidiaries, brookline, lighthouse and brookline securities corp (bsc). Brookline includes its wholly owned subsidiaries, 160 associates, inc. (associates) and bbs investment

corporation (bbs). Brookline securites and bbs investment corporation are into buying, selling and holding investment securities. The associates provide marketing services and owns brookline preferred capital corporation, a real estate investment trust. The operations of the group are conducted through five full service banking offices in brookline and one in newton, Massachusetts.

Primary SIC and add'l.: 6712 6035

CIK No: 0001049782

Subsidiaries: 160 Associates, Inc

Officers: Michael J. Fanger/Dir., CEO, Pres. - Eastern Funding LLC/$295,502.00, Richard P. Chapman/73/Chmn., CEO, Pres./$1,672,278.00, Warren Ramirez/VP - Commercial Lending, William Henning/VP, Mgr. - Relationship, George C. Caner/82/Sec., Paul R. Bechet/68/CFO, Sr. VP, Treasurer/$647,368.00, Charles Peck/Pres., Sr. Loan Officer/$831,404.00, Joseph Cavallini/Sr. VP - Commercial Lending, William R. MacKenzie/Sr. VP - Commercial Banking, Wesley K. Blair/Sr. VP, Lori Leeth/VP, Mgr. - Relationship, Douglas Stevens/VP - Commercial Lending, Gretchen Annese/VP - Commercial Lending, David J. Pallin/68/Sr. VP/$336,702.00

Directors: Michael J. Fanger/Dir., CEO, Pres. - Eastern Funding LLC, Richard P. Chapman/73/Chmn., CEO, Pres., Dennis S. Aronowitz/76/Dir., Franklin Wyman/86/Dir., David C. Chapin/71/Dir., William G. Coughlin/75/Dir., John L. Hall/68/Dir., John J. McGlynn/86/Dir., Hollis W. Plimpton/77/Dir., Joseph J. Slotnik/71/Dir., William V. Tripp/69/Dir., Rosamond B. Vaule/70/Dir., Peter O. Wilde/68/Dir.

Owners: Hollis W. Plimpton, Dimensional Fund Advisors LP/6.70%, Richard P. Chapman/2.70%, Joseph J. Slotnik/0.40%, John J. McGlynn, Dennis S. Aronowitz, David J. Pallin, William G. Coughlin/0.50%, Insiders/8.70%, Franklin Wyman, Barclays Global Investors, N.A./5.30%, William V. Tripp, Private Capital Management, L.P./8.50%, Peter O. Wilde/0.30%, Rosamond B. Vaule/0.30% *(25 Owners included in Index)*

Financial Data: *Fiscal Year End:*12/31 *Latest Annual Data:* 12/31/2006

Year	Sales	Net Income
2006	$136,500,000	$20,812,000
2005	$112,393,000	$22,030,000
2004	$77,320,000	$17,767,000

Curr. Assets:	$162,964,000	Curr. Liab.:	$1,307,760,000		
Plant, Equip.:	$9,335,000	Total Liab.:	$1,788,772,000	Indic. Yr. Divd.:	$0.340
Total Assets:	$2,373,040,000	Net Worth:	$582,893,000	Debt/ Equity:	0.7894

Brooklyn Cheesecake & Desert Com

20 Passaic Ave, Fairfield, NJ, 07004; ***PH:*** 1-973-808-8248

General - Incorporation	NY	Stock- Price on:12/24/2007	$0.25
Employees	33	Stock Exchange	OTC
Auditor	Sherb & Co. LLP	Ticker Symbol	BCKE
Stk Agt	American Securities T & T Inc.	Outstanding Shares	NA
Counsel	NA	E.P.S	-$0.2
DUNS No.	87-762-7893	Shareholders	NA

Business: The group's principal activity is to manufacture baking and confectionery products, which are sold to supermarkets, food distributors, educational institutions, restaurants, mail order and to the public. The group offers a broad line of premium quality pastries, cakes, pies, cookies and other assorted desserts, which are produced at its baking facility. The products are marketed and distributed on a wholesale basis to supermarkets, restaurants and institutional dining facilities. The chatterley desserts subsidiary markets a full line of premium quality baked products such as cheesecakes, mousse cakes and tart shells as well complete gourmet line of muffins. The group operates solely in the United States.

Primary SIC and add'l.: 6719 2051 5149 5142

CIK No: 0000949721

Subsidiaries: Brooklyn Cheesecake & Desserts Company

Owners: Donald OToole/1.40%, Insiders/15.20%, Wachovia Corporation/5.10%, Liberio Borsellino/1.60%, Anthony J. Merante/8.70%, Carmelo L. Foti/1.90%, Ronald L. Schutt/18.30%, David Rabe/1.60%

Financial Data: *Fiscal Year End:*12/31 *Latest Annual Data:* 12/31/2006

Year	Sales	Net Income
2006	$13,000	-$115,000
2005	$2,224,000	-$1,064,000
2004	$3,035,000	-$574,000

Curr. Assets:	$13,000	Curr. Liab.:	$926,000		
Plant, Equip.:	NA	Total Liab.:	$926,000	Indic. Yr. Divd.:	NA
Total Assets:	$74,000	Net Worth:	-$852,000	Debt/ Equity:	NA

Brooklyn Federal Bancorp Inc

81 Ct. St., Brooklyn, NY, 11201; ***PH:*** 1-718-855-8500; ***Fax:*** 1-718-858-5174; ***http://*** www.brooklynbank.com

General - Incorporation	Federal	Stock- Price on:12/24/2007	$15.4
Employees	59	Stock Exchange	NDQ
Auditor	Beard Miller Company LLP	Ticker Symbol	BFSB
Stk Agt	NA	Outstanding Shares	13,400,000
Counsel	NA	E.P.S	$0.29
DUNS No.	NA	Shareholders	NA

Business: The group operates through its subsidiaries whose principle activity is to provide financial services. The groups services include construction loans and loans secured by commercial real estate, multi family real estate, land loans and deposit accounts. The group operates from the United States. The assets of the group for the year 2006 were $408,045 (thousands).

Primary SIC and add'l.: 6712 6035

CIK No: 0001310313

Subsidiaries: 3D Holding Corp., Inc., BFS Reit, Inc, Brooklyn Bancorp MHC

Officers: Angelo J. Di Lorenzo/Dir., CEO, Pres., Richard A. Kielty/CFO, Exec. VP, Marilyn Alberici/Sr. VP, Loan Servicing Officer, Marc Leno/Chief Lending Officer, Sr. VP, Salvatore Gargaro/VP, Sr. Retail Banking Officer, Operations Officer, Ralph Walther/VP, Controller, Rosemary Demeo/VP, Retail Banking Officer, Operations Officer, Sandra Weiss/VP, Sec., Commercial Lending Officer, Joseph Raucci/Assist VP, Assist. Financial Officer, Natalya Khandros/Assist. VP, Loan Servicing Mgr., Richard Maher/Assist. VP, Commercial Loan Officer, Erica Minott/Assist. VP, Assistant Controller, Edward Bolmarcich/VP, Residential Mortgage Officer

Directors: Angelo J. Di Lorenzo/Dir., CEO, Pres., John A. Loconsolo/Chmn., Vincent E. Caccese/Dir., John C. Gallin/Dir., Daniel O. Reich/Dir., Robert J.A. Zito/Dir.

Owners: Insiders, Daniel O. Reich, Angelo J. DiLorenzo, Salvatore M. Salibello, John A. Loconsolo, John C. Gallin, BFS Bancorp, MHC/70.00%, Vincent E. Caccese

Financial Data: *Fiscal Year End:*09/30 *Latest Annual Data:* 9/30/2006

Year	Sales	Net Income
2006	$24,371,000	$4,558,000
2005	$19,463,000	$3,780,000

Curr. Assets:	$13,230,000	Curr. Liab.:	$318,472,000	P/E Ratio:	55.00
Plant, Equip.:	$1,245,000	Total Liab.:	$328,082,000	Indic. Yr. Divd.:	$0.200
Total Assets:	$408,045,000	Net Worth:	$79,963,000	Debt/ Equity:	0.0616

Brookmount Explorations Inc

World Trade Ctr., 404 - 999 Canada Pl., Vancouver, BC, V6C 3E2; ***PH:*** 1-604-676-5244; ***Fax:*** 1-604-632-3717; ***http://*** www.brookmount.com; ***Email:*** info@brookmount.com

General - Incorporation	NV	Stock- Price on:12/24/2007	$0.07
Employees	NA	Stock Exchange	OTC
Auditor	Dale Matheson Carr-Hilton LaBonte LLP	Ticker Symbol	BMXI
Stk Agt	Brookmount Explorations, Inc.	Outstanding Shares	NA
Counsel	NA	E.P.S	NA
DUNS No.	NA	Shareholders	NA

Business: The groups principal activity is to exploration of minerals. The group operates from the United States and Canada.

Primary SIC and add'l.: 1041

CIK No: 0001122993

Officers: Peter Flueck/Chmn., CEO, Pres., Victor Stilwell/VP, Zaf Sungur/55/Dir., CFO, COO, Richard Scott-Ram/Advisor to The Board, Adrin G. Mann/Advisor to The Board, David E. Danovitch/Legal Counsel, Corporate Securities Lawyer, Gregory S. Yanke/Legal Counsel

Directors: Peter Flueck/Chmn., CEO, Pres., Zaf Sungur/55/Dir., CFO, COO, David Dadon/Dir.

Owners: Zaf Sungur/15.96%, Peter Flueck/27.69%, Insiders/43.65%

Financial Data: *Fiscal Year End:*11/30 *Latest Annual Data:* 05/31/2007

Year	Sales	Net Income
2007	NA	NA
2006	NA	-$1,403,000
2005	NA	-$2,511,000

Curr. Assets:	$24,000	Curr. Liab.:	$233,000		
Plant, Equip.:	$1,000	Total Liab.:	$233,000	Indic. Yr. Divd.:	NA
Total Assets:	$25,000	Net Worth:	-$208,000	Debt/ Equity:	NA

Brooks Automation Inc

15 Elizabeth Dr., Chelmsford, MA, 01824; ***PH:*** 1-978-262-2400; ***Fax:*** 1-978-262-2500; ***http://*** www.brooks.com; ***Email:*** hr@brooks.com

General - Incorporation	DE	Stock- Price on:12/24/2007	$18.66
Employees	2,400	Stock Exchange	NDQ
Auditor	PricewaterhouseCoopers LLP	Ticker Symbol	BRKS
Stk Agt	EquiServe Trust Co N.A	Outstanding Shares	75,820,000
Counsel	Brown Rudnick Berlack Israels LLP	E.P.S	$2.05
DUNS No.	60-319-9688	Shareholders	NA

Business: The group's principle activities are to provide integrated tool and factory automation solutions for the global semiconductor and related industries. It includes the data storage and flat panel display manufacturing industries and other precision electronics manufacturing industries. The group's products include hardware and software products and services include tool control application consulting services, software customization and spare parts sales. The customers of the group are based in the United States, Europe, Japan, Singapore, South Korea and Taiwan. The group's total revenue for year 2007 was 743.26 millions of USD.

Primary SIC and add'l.: 3569 3674 3559

CIK No: 0000933974

Subsidiaries: 1045060 Ontario Limited, 1325949 Ontario Inc, Autosimulations UK Limited, AutoSoft Corporation Limited, Brooks — PRI Automation Holding Belgium BVBA, Brooks Automation (Canada) Inc., Brooks Automation (Delaware) LLC, Brooks Automation (France) SAS, Brooks Automation (Germany) GmbH, Brooks Automation (Ireland) Ltd, Brooks Automation (Japan) KK, Brooks Automation (Singapore) PTE LTD, Brooks Automation (Taiwan) Company Ltd, Brooks Automation (the Netherlands) BV, Brooks Automation (UK) Ltd 41 Subsidiaries included in the Index

Officers: Robert J. Lepofsky/Dir., CEO, Robert E. Anastasi/Exec. VP, Mark Chung/Dir. - Investor Relations, Jason Kolbenson/Contact - Factory, Tool Automation, Richard C. Small/Sr. VP, Corporate Controller, Thomas S. Grilk/Sr. VP, General Counsel, Sec., Robert W. Woodbury/CFO, Sr. VP, James Gentilcore/COO, Pres. - Semiconductor Products Group, Jake Bornstein/Contact - Factory, Tool Automation, Mike Gillis/Contact - Factory, Tool Automation

Directors: Robert J. Lepofsky/Dir., CEO, Joseph R. Martin/Chmn., Clinton A. Allen/Dir., John K. McGillicuddy/Dir., Edward C. Grady/Dir., Krishna G. Palepu/Dir., Alfred Woollacott/Dir., Mark Stephen Wrighton/Dir., Marvin Schorr/Dir., Kirk P. Pond/Dir.

Owners: Insiders/2.50%, Krishna G. Palepu, Clinton A. Allen, Mark S. Wrighton, T. Rowe Price Associates, Inc./8.40%, John K. McGillicuddy, Mazama Capital Management/12.10%, Thomas S. Grilk, Alfred Woollacott, Joseph R. Martin, James Gentilcore, Nierenberg Investment Management Company, Inc./5.80%, Marvin G. Schorr, Joseph M. Bellini, Robert J. Lepofsky *(17 Owners included in Index)*

Financial Data: *Fiscal Year End:*09/30 *Latest Annual Data:* 9/30/2006

Year	Sales	Net Income
2006	$692,870,000	$25,930,000
2005	$463,746,000	-$11,612,000
2004	$539,769,000	$17,721,000

Curr. Assets:	$432,812,000	Curr. Liab.:	$180,179,000	P/E Ratio:	8.29
Plant, Equip.:	$78,833,000	Total Liab.:	$193,049,000	Indic. Yr. Divd.:	NA
Total Assets:	$992,577,000	Net Worth:	$799,134,000	Debt/ Equity:	NA

Brookside Technology Holdings Corp

Formerly: Cruisestock Inc

5313-b Fm, 1960 W Ste. 224, Houston, TX, 77069; ***PH:*** 1-281-350-1173

General - Incorporation .... TX
Employees 15
Auditor .... PMB Helin Donovan, LLP
Stk Agt...... American Stock Transfer & Trust Co.
Counsel........ Shumaker, Loop & Kendrick, LLP
DUNS No. .... NA

Stock- Price on:12/24/2007 .... $1.79
Stock Exchange .... NA
Ticker Symbol .... NA
Outstanding Shares 11,500,000
E.P.S. .... -$0.24
Shareholders .... NA

Business: The groups principle activity is to provide turnkey converged voice and data solutions. The group services include Voice, Data, IP, long distance, and IP-MPLS solutions. The group acquired Brookside in the 2007. The group operates from the United States.

Primary SIC and add'l.: 1731

CIK No: 0001367001

Subsidiaries: Brookside Technology Partners, Inc.

Officers: Michael Nole/42/Dir., CEO, Bryan McGuire/42/CFO, Michael Dance/47/Pres. - Brookside

Directors: Michael Nole/42/Dir., CEO

Owners: Insiders/57.00%, Michael Nole/21.70%, Michael Dance/34.80%, Apogee Financial Investments, Inc./22.60%

Financial Data: *Fiscal Year End:*08/31 *Latest Annual Data:* 12/31/2006

Year	Sales	Net Income
2006	$3,103,000	-$110,000

Curr. Assets:	$419,000	**Curr. Liab.:**	$1,329,000	**P/E Ratio:**	19.89
Plant, Equip.:	$63,000	**Total Liab.:**	$1,329,000	**Indic. Yr. Divd.:**	NA
Total Assets:	$483,000	**Net Worth:**	-$846,000	**Debt/ Equity:**	NA

Brown & Brown Inc

PO Box 1348, Tampa, FL, 33601; ***PH:*** 1-813-222-4182; ***http://*** www.poebrown.com

General - Incorporation .... FL
Employees 4,733
Auditor .... Deloitte & Touche LLP
Stk Agt...... American Stock Transfer & Trust Co.
Counsel .... Cobb Cole & Bell
DUNS No. 00-442-9478

Stock- Price on:12/24/2007 .... $25.91
Stock Exchange .... NYSE
Ticker Symbol .... BRO
Outstanding Shares 140,400,000
E.P.S. $1.39
Shareholders .... NA

Business: The group's principle activity is to provide property and casualty insurance products and services. The group operates in four divisions. The retail division provides insurance products and services to commercial, governmental, professional and individual customers. The national programs division provides professional liability and related package products for certain professionals, as well as products and services designated for specific industries, trade groups and market niches. The services division provides insurance-related services, employee benefit self-insurance and managed healthcare services. The brokerage division markets and sells excess and surplus commercial insurance and reinsurance. The group acquired the remaining 25% of Florida intracoastal underwriters limited company in 2003 and proctor financial insurance in 2004 and balcones-southwest, inc. The group's quarterly revenue for September 2007 was 237.28 millions of USD.

Primary SIC and add'l.: 6411 6282

CIK No: 0000079282

Subsidiaries: Acumen Re Management Corporation (DE), AFC Insurance, Inc., American Specialty Insurance & Risk Services, Inc. (IN), Axiom Re, Inc., Azure IV Acquisition Corporation, B & B Insurance Services, Inc., B & B Protector Plans, Inc., Balcones-Southwest, Inc., Braishfield Associates, Inc., Brown & Brown Agency of Insurance Professionals, Inc. (OK), Brown & Brown Disaster Relief Foundation, Inc., Brown & Brown Insurance Agency of Virginia, Inc. (VA), Brown & Brown Insurance Benefits, Inc. (TX), Brown & Brown Insurance of Arizona, Inc. (AZ), Brown & Brown Insurance of Georgia, Inc. (GA) 92 Subsidiaries included in the Index

Officers: Cory T. Walker/CEO, Sr. VP, Treasurer/$536,931.00, Hyatt J. Brown/Chmn., CEO/$1,765,221.00, Jim W. Henderson/Vice Chmn., COO/$1,504,926.00, Roy C. Bridges/Regional Exec. VP, Powell J. Brown/Pres., Kenneth Kirk/Regional Pres./$1,162,877.00, Charles Lydecker/Regional Exec. VP, Kenneth Masters/Regional Exec. VP, Robert W. Lloyd/VP, Chief Litigation Officer, Laurel Grammig/VP, Sec., General Counsel, Scott J. Penny/Regional Exec. VP, Linda Downs/Exec. VP - Leadership Development, Thomas Riley/Regional Pres./$1,346,425.00, Thomas Donegan/VP, Assist. Sec., Assist. General Counsel, Richard Freebourn/VP - Internal Operations

Directors: Hyatt J. Brown/Chmn., CEO, Jim W. Henderson/Vice Chmn., COO, Hugh M. Brown/Dir., Theodore J. Hoepner/Dir., Samuel P. Bell/Dir., Bradley Currey/Dir., John R. Riedman/Dir., David H. Hughes/Dir., Jan E. Smith/Dir., Chilton D. Varner/Dir., Toni Jennings/Dir.

Owners: Hyatt J. Brown/15.29%, Insiders/20.39%, David H. Hughes, Cory T. Walker, Jim W. Henderson, Select Equity Group, Inc/6.91%, Hugh M. Brown, Jan E. Smith, Thomas E. Riley, Ruane, Cunniff & Goldfarb, Inc/8.47%, Theodore J. Hoepner, Toni Jennings, Bradley Currey, John R. Riedman, Kenneth D. Kirk *(17 Owners included in Index)*

Financial Data: *Fiscal Year End:*12/31 *Latest Annual Data:* 12/31/2006

Year	Sales	Net Income
2006	$878,004,000	$172,350,000
2005	$785,807,000	$150,551,000
2004	$646,934,000	$128,843,000

Curr. Assets:	$648,206,000	**Curr. Liab.:**	$590,667,000	**P/E Ratio:**	20.09
Plant, Equip.:	$44,170,000	**Total Liab.:**	$878,607,000	**Indic. Yr. Divd.:**	$0.280
Total Assets:	$1,807,952,000	**Net Worth:**	$929,345,000	**Debt/ Equity:**	NA

Brown Forman Corp

850 Dixie Hwy., Louisville, KY, 40210; ***PH:*** 1-502-585-1100; ***Fax:*** 1-502-774-7876; ***http://*** www.brown-forman.com

General - Incorporation .... DE
Employees 3,350
Auditor .... PricewaterhouseCoopers LLP
Stk Agt........ National City Bank
Counsel........ Ogden, Newell & Welch
DUNS No. 00-637-9812

Stock- Price on:12/24/2007 .... $73.23
Stock Exchange .... NYSE
Ticker Symbol .... BFB
Outstanding Shares 123,130,000
E.P.S. $3.13
Shareholders .... NA

Business: The groups principle activities include producing and marketing consumer beverage products. The groups products are sold under the brand names Southern Comfort, Finlandia, Tequila Herradura and el Jimador Tequila. The company also provides beverage alcohol products including Tennessee, Canadian and Kentucky whiskies. The group operates from United States.

Primary SIC and add'l.: 3161 3262 2085 5182 2449 3229

CIK No: 0000014693

Subsidiaries: Amercain Investments C.V., AMG Trading, LLC, B-F Korea, LLC, BFC Tequila Limited, Brooks & Bentley Limited, Brown-Forman Arrow Continental Europe, LLC, Brown-Forman Beverages Australia Pty. Ltd., Brown-Forman Beverages Edinburgh, Brown-Forman Beverages Europe, Ltd., Brown-Forman Beverages Japan, LLC, Brown-Forman Beverages North Asia, LLC, Brown-Forman Beverages Worldwide,Comercio de Bebidas Ltda., Brown-Forman Czech & Slovak Republics, s.r.o., Brown-Forman Korea Ltd., Brown-Forman Polska Sp. z o.o. 41 Subsidiaries included in the Index

Officers: Paul C. Varga/Chmn., CEO, Michael B. Crutcher/64/Vice Chmn., General Counsel, Sec., James S. Welch/Vice Chmn., Vice Chmn. - Strategy, Human Resources, Phoebe A. Wood/Vice Chmn., CFO, Paul Gross/CIO, Sr. VP, Bruce Cote/VP, Dir. - Human Resources Employee Services, Jane C. Morreau/49/Sr. VP, Controller, T. J. Graven/VP, Dir. - Investor Relations, Phil Lichtenfels/Sr. VP, Chief - Staff, Phil Lynch/VP, Dir. - Corporate Communications, Jill Jones/Dir. - Global Production, James Lloyd Bareuther/COO, Exec. VP, William A. Blodgett/Sr. VP, Deputy General Counsel, James B. Chiles/Sr. VP - Global Production, Mark I. McCallum/Chief Brands Officer, Exec. VP *(16 Officers included in Index)*

Directors: Paul C. Varga/Chmn., CEO, Phoebe A. Wood/Vice Chmn., CFO, James S. Welch/Vice Chmn., Vice Chmn. - Strategy, Human Resources, Michael B. Crutcher/64/Vice Chmn., General Counsel, Sec., Barry D. Bramley/Dir., William M. Street/Dir., Donald G. Calder/Dir., Matthew R. Simmons/Dir., Patrick Bousquet-Chavanne/Dir., Martin S. Brown/Dir., Sandra A. Frazier/Dir., Garvin Brown/Dir., William E. Mitchell/Dir., Richard P. Mayer/Dir., Owsley Brown/Dir. *(16 Directors included in Index)*

Owners: Laura Lee Gastis, Dace Brown Stubbs, William M. Street/2.90%, Garvin Brown, Lyons W. L. Brown, Owsley Brown/13.70%, Campbell P. Brown, Matthew R. Simmons, Donald G. Calder, Phoebe A. Wood, Sandra A. Frazier/8.60%, Owsley Brown, Alanson B. Houghton, Garvin Brown, Donald G. Calder *(47 Owners included in Index)*

Financial Data: *Fiscal Year End:*04/30 *Latest Annual Data:* 04/30/2007

Year	Sales	Net Income
2007	$2,806,000,000	$389,000,000
2006	$2,444,000,000	$320,000,000
2005	$2,729,000,000	$308,000,000

Curr. Assets:	$1,610,000,000	**Curr. Liab.:**	$569,000,000	**P/E Ratio:**	22.67
Plant, Equip.:	$430,000,000	**Total Liab.:**	$1,165,000,000	**Indic. Yr. Divd.:**	$1.210
Total Assets:	$2,728,000,000	**Net Worth:**	$1,563,000,000	**Debt/ Equity:**	0.2064

Brown Shoe Co Inc

8300 Maryland Ave., St. Louis, MO, 63105; ***PH:*** 1-314-854-4000; ***Fax:*** 1-314-854-4274; ***http://*** www.browngroup.com

General - Incorporation .... NY
Employees 12,700
Auditor .... Ernst & Young LLP
Stk Agt .... Mellon Investor Services
Counsel .... NA
DUNS No. 00-626-6787

Stock- Price on:12/24/2007 .... $25.69
Stock Exchange .... NYSE
Ticker Symbol .... BWS
Outstanding Shares 44,160,000
E.P.S. $1.49
Shareholders .... NA

Business: The groups principle activity is to operate retail shoe stores. The group operates through two business segments namely retail operations and wholesale operations. The groups products are sold under the brand names Naturalizer, Via Spiga, Franco Sarto and LifeStride. The group operates from United States.

Primary SIC and add'l.: 5661 5139

CIK No: 0000014707

Subsidiaries: Bennett Footwear Group, LLC, Brown California, Inc., Brown Cayman Ltd., Brown Group Dublin Limited, Brown Group Retail, Inc., Brown Missouri, Inc., Brown Retail Development Company, Brown Shoe Company of Canada Ltd, Brown Shoe de Mexico, S.A. de C.V., Brown Shoe International Corporation, Brown Shoe International Sales and Licensing Limited, Brown Shoe International Sales and Licensing S.r.l., Brown Shoe Investment Company, Inc., Brown Texas, Inc., Buster Brown & Co. 40 Subsidiaries included in the Index

Officers: Ronald A. Fromm/Chmn., CEO/$4,277,334.00, Michael I. Oberlander/Sr. VP, General Counsel, Corp. Sec., Douglas Koch/Sr. VP, Chief Talent Officer, Richard M. Ausick/Pres. - Brown New York Division, Gary M. Rich/Pres. - Brown Shoe Wholesale Division/$1,484,341.00, Joseph W. Wood/Pres. - Brown Shoe Retail/$1,996,094.00, Richard C. Schumacher/Chief Accounting Officer, Sr. VP, Diane M. Sullivan/Dir., COO, Pres./$2,998,194.00, Mark E. Hood/CFO, Sr. VP/$213,339.00, Sheri Wilson-Gray/Sr. VP, Chief Marketing Officer, Joe Caro/CIO, Sr. VP

Directors: Ronald A. Fromm/Chmn., CEO, Patricia G. McGinnis/Dir., Julie C. Esrey/Dir., Hal J. Upbin/Dir., Joseph L. Bower/Dir., Steven W. Korn/Dir., Carla Hendra/Dir., Patrick W. McGinnis/Dir., Michael F. Neidorff/Dir., Ward Klein/Dir.

Owners: Patrick W. McGinnis, FMR Corp./5.17%, Goldman Sachs Asset Management, L.P./5.76%, Michael F. Neidorff, Steven W. Korn, Insiders/3.25%, Ronald A. Fromm/1.05%, Joseph L. Bower, Joseph W. Wood, Mark E. Hood, Diane M. Sullivan, Julie C. Esrey, Hal J. Upbin, Andrew M. Rosen, Gary M. Rich *(17 Owners included in Index)*

Financial Data: *Fiscal Year End:*01/28 *Latest Annual Data:* 2/3/2007

Year	Sales	Net Income
2007	$2,470,930,000	$65,708,000
2006	$2,292,057,000	$41,000,000
2005	$1,941,804,000	$43,305,000

Curr. Assets:	$638,360,000	**Curr. Liab.:**	$334,516,000	**P/E Ratio:**	17.24
Plant, Equip.:	$138,164,000	**Total Liab.:**	$575,412,000	**Indic. Yr. Divd.:**	$0.280
Total Assets:	$1,099,057,000	**Net Worth:**	$523,645,000	**Debt/ Equity:**	0.2758

Brownie's Marine Group Inc

Formerly: United Companies Corp
940 NW 1st St., Ft Lauderdale, FL, 33311; ***PH:*** 1-954-462-5570; ***http://*** www.browniedive.com

General - Incorporation .... NV
Employees 16
Auditor .... LL Bradford & Co
Stk Agt .... Transfer Online, Inc.
Counsel .... NA
DUNS No. .... NA

Stock- Price on:12/24/2007 .... $0.038
Stock Exchange .... NA
Ticker Symbol .... NA
Outstanding Shares 160,130,000
E.P.S. $0.003
Shareholders .... NA

Business: The group has no on-going operations. The group is presently seeking for potential operating businesses and business opportunities. The group is in development stage. On 17-Feb-2004, the group acquired trebor industries inc.

Primary SIC and add'l.: NA

CIK No: 0001166708

Subsidiaries: Avid Sportswear & Golf Corp., Trebor Industries, Inc
Officers: Robert M. Carmichael/Chmn., CEO, CFO, Pres.
Directors: Robert M. Carmichael/Chmn., CEO, CFO, Pres.
Owners: Insiders/57.80%, Joshua William Arvin/10.20%, Jeffrey Morris/14.70%, Robert Carmichael/57.80%
Financial Data: Fiscal Year End:12/31 Latest Annual Data: 12/31/2006

Year	Sales	Net Income
2006	$4,203,000	$566,000
2005	$2,936,000	-$96,000
2004	$2,974,000	-$511,000

Curr. Assets:	$937,000	Curr. Liab.:	$765,000	P/E Ratio:	12.67
Plant, Equip.:	$30,000	Total Liab.:	$1,396,000	Indic. Yr. Divd.:	NA
Total Assets:	$996,000	Net Worth:	-$400,000	Debt/ Equity:	NA

BRT Realty Trust

60 Cutter Mill Rd., Ste. 303, Great Neck, NY, 11021; *PH:* 1-516-466-3100; *Fax:* 1-516-466-3132; *http://* www.brtrealty.com

General		Stock	
Incorporation	MA	Price on:12/24/2007	$27.26
Employees	NA	Stock Exchange	NYSE
Auditor	Ernst& Young LLP	Ticker Symbol	BRT
Stk Agt	American Stock Transfer & Trust Co.	Outstanding Shares	11,090,000
Counsel	NA	E.P.S	$3.33
DUNS No.	NA	Shareholders	NA

Business: The groups principal activity is to provide loan services. The groups loan services include mortgage loans, acquisition loans, renovation loans and participation loans. The group operates from the United States
Primary SIC and add'l.: 6798
CIK No: 0000014846
Subsidiaries: 2190 Boston Post Road Realty Corp., Blue Realty Corp., BRT Funding Corp., BRT Joint Venture No. 1 LLC, BRT Realty Trust Statutory Trust I, BRT Realty Trust Statutory Trust II, Forest Green Corporation, TRB 69th Street Corp., TRB Ashbourne Road Corp., TRB Charlotte Apartments LLC, TRB Hartford Corp., TRB Lawrence Realty Corp., TRB New York Corp., TRB No. 1 Corp., TRB No. 3 Owners Corp. 18 Subsidiaries included in the Index
Officers: Jeffrey A. Gould/Trustee, CEO, Pres., Matthew J. Gould/Trustee, Sr. VP, Mitchell K. Gould/36/Exec. VP, Israel Rosenzweig/Sr. VP, David W. Kalish/Sr. VP - Finance, Simeon Brinberg/Sr. VP, Sec., George E. Zweier/CFO, VP, Mark H. Lundy/Sr. VP, Alysa Block/Acting Treasurer
Directors: Jeffrey A. Gould/Trustee, CEO, Pres., Fredric H. Gould/Chmn., Gary Hurand/Trustee, Louis C. Grassi/Trustee, Jeffrey Rubin/Trustee, Kenneth F. Bernstein/Trustee, Matthew J. Gould/Trustee, Sr. VP, Alan H. Ginsburg/Trustee, Jonathan H. Simon/Trustee
Owners: Simeon Brinberg/3.08%, David Heiden, Kenneth F. Bernstein, Henry Moskowitz/5.17%, Mitchell Gould, Gary Hurand/2.10%, Matthew J. Gould/21.73%, Patrick J. Callan, Insiders/36.92%, George Zweier, Alan H. Ginsburg, Louis C. Grassi, Jonathan H. Simon, Jeffrey Rubin, Gould Investors L.P./19.08% *(17 Owners included in Index)*
Financial Data: Fiscal Year End:09/30 Latest Annual Data: 9/30/2006

Year	Sales	Net Income
2006	$37,488,000	$20,071,000
2005	$25,715,000	$16,214,000
2004	$18,583,000	$12,002,000

Curr. Assets:	$8,393,000	Curr. Liab.:	$15,970,000	P/E Ratio:	5.91
Plant, Equip.:	$6,175,000	Total Liab.:	$216,607,000	Indic. Yr. Divd.:	$2.480
Total Assets:	$371,042,000	Net Worth:	$154,435,000	Debt/ Equity:	0.4505

Bruker Biosciences Corp

40 Manning Rd., Billerica, MA, 01821; *PH:* 1-978-663-3660; *Fax:* 1-978-667-5993; *http://* www.bruker-biosciences.com; *Email:* info@bruker-biosciences.com

General		Stock	
Incorporation	DE	Price on:12/24/2007	$9
Employees	1,905	Stock Exchange	NDQ
Auditor	Ernst & Young LLP	Ticker Symbol	BRKR
Stk Agt	American Stock Transfer & Trust Co.	Outstanding Shares	105,310,000
Counsel	NA	E.P.S	$0.26
DUNS No.	13-450-5978	Shareholders	NA

Business: The group's principal activities are to design, manufacture and market life science systems, process analysis systems and analytical instruments based on mass spectrometry technology. Mass spectrometers are the devices that measure the mass or weight of a molecule and provide information about the structure of materials. The customers consist of pharmaceutical, biotechnology, proteomics, molecular diagnostics, fine chemical companies, commercial, government and university laboratories and not-for-profit research institutes. The group sells through distributors including affiliated companies like agilent technologies inc, sequenom inc, geneprot inc and others. The group has representatives in South Korea, Portugal, Israel, Latin America and eastern Europe. On 01-Jul-2003, the group acquired bruker axs inc.
Primary SIC and add'l.: 3826 8731
CIK No: 0001109354
Subsidiaries: Bruker (Pty) Ltd., Bruker AXS GmbH, Bruker AXS Inc., Bruker AXS KK, Bruker AXS Ltd., Bruker AXS Microanalysis GmbH, Bruker AXS Pte Ltd (Singapore), Bruker AXS SA, Bruker AXS SrL, Bruker BioSciences S.A., Bruker BioSciences Security Corp., Bruker Daltonics Australia Pty. Ltd., Bruker Daltonics B.V., Bruker Daltonics Chusik Hoesa, Bruker Daltonics GmbH 31 Subsidiaries included in the Index
Officers: Frank H. Laukien/Chmn., CEO, Pres./$626,440.00, Brian Monahan/Corporate Controller/$211,472.00, William J. Knight/CFO/$437,489.00, Michael Willett/Dir. - Investor Relations, Public Relations, Dirk D. Laukien/Sr. VP/$2,902,700.00, Richard M. Stein/Sec., Christopher M. Canavan/Dir. - Financial Consultant
Directors: Frank H. Laukien/Chmn., CEO, Pres., Christopher M. Canavan/Dir. - Financial Consultant, Taylor J. Crouch/Dir., Daniel S. Dross/Dir., Collin J. Dsilva/Dir., Richard D. Kniss/Dir., Jorg C. Laukien/Dir., William A. Linton/Dir., Bernhard Wangler/Dir., Wolf-Dieter Emmerich/Dir.
Owners: Brian P. Monahan, William A. Linton, M.Christopher Canavan, Isolde Laukien-Kleiner/6.80%, Richard Kniss, Insiders/38.30%, Taylor J. Crouch, Collin J. DSilva, Joerg C. Laukien/8.70%, Bernhard Wangler, Richard M. Stein, Daniel S. Dross, Marc M. Laukien/7.30%
Financial Data: Fiscal Year End:12/31 Latest Annual Data: 12/31/2006

Year	Sales	Net Income
2006	$435,834,000	$18,481,000
2005	$297,569,000	$3,646,000
2004	$284,416,000	-$7,831,000

Curr. Assets:	$294,744,000	Curr. Liab.:	$195,128,000	P/E Ratio:	47.37
Plant, Equip.:	$90,349,000	Total Liab.:	$241,482,000	Indic. Yr. Divd.:	NA
Total Assets:	$433,187,000	Net Worth:	$191,466,000	Debt/ Equity:	0.1061

Brunswick Bancorp

439 Livingston Ave., New Brunswick, NJ, 08901; *PH:* 1-732-247-5800; *Fax:* 1-732-247-5996; *http://* www.brunswickbank.com

General		Stock	
Incorporation	NJ	Price on:12/24/2007	NA
Employees	48	Stock Exchange	OTC
Auditor	Michael R. Ferraro, CPA	Ticker Symbol	BRBW
Stk Agt	NA	Outstanding Shares	NA
Counsel	NA	E.P.S	$0.60
DUNS No.	00-697-3960	Shareholders	NA

Business: The group's principal activity is to provide commercial banking and related financial services to its customers. The operations of the group are conducted through its head office & five branch offices that are located in monmouth and middlesex counties, New Jersey. These services include checking, savings, time deposit account and certificates of deposit. The group provides trust services and originates secured and unsecured personal loans, commercial, residential and commercial real estate loans. The group is a holding company, which operates through brunswick bank and trust company.
Primary SIC and add'l.: 6022 6712
CIK No: 0000771614
Subsidiaries: Brunswick Bank & Trust
Officers: Roman T. Gumina/Chmn., CEO, Pres., Christine A. Cioffi/VP, COO, Thomas Fornale/Sr. VP, Sec., CFO, Russell J. Jaeschke/Chief Lending Officer, Sr. VP, Joanne Chek/Assist. Treasurer, Branch Mgr., Patricia Gerhartz/VP, Assist. Sec., Pearl Lin/Assist. Treasurer, Branch Mgr., Michael A. Studney/CIO, Sr. VP, Kamrul H. Chowdhury/VP, Chief Auditor, Kathryn Neu/Assist. Sec., Dir. - Executive Administration, Frank J. Gumina/VP - Bank Counsel, Compliance, BSA Officer, Lenore Umali/Assist. Treasurer, Branch Mgr., Margeret Keeling/Assist. Treasurer, Branch Mgr., Marie Alfrey/Assist. VP
Directors: Roman T. Gumina/Chmn., CEO, Pres., Frederick H. Perrine/Vice Chmn., Robert P. Sica/Dir., Michael Kaplan/Dir., Joseph Demarco/Dir., Edwin Leavitt-Gruberger/Dir., Dominick Faraci/Dir., Richard A. Malouf/Dir., James Gassaro/Dir., Phillip W. Barrood/Dir., Frank Gumina/Dir.
Financial Data: Fiscal Year End:12/31 Latest Annual Data: 12/31/2005

Year	Sales	Net Income
2005	$8,089,000	$1,763,000
2004	$7,370,000	$1,505,000
2003	$7,665,000	$1,839,000

Curr. Assets:	$56,029,000	Curr. Liab.:	$124,548,000		
Plant, Equip.:	$939,000	Total Liab.:	$124,931,000	Indic. Yr. Divd.:	NA
Total Assets:	$160,182,000	Net Worth:	$35,251,000	Debt/ Equity:	NA

Brunswick Corp

1 N Field Ct., Lake Forest, IL, 60045; *PH:* 1-847-735-4700; *Fax:* 1-847-735-4765; *http://* www.brunswick.com; *Email:* services@brunswick.com

General		Stock	
Incorporation	DE	Price on:12/24/2007	$33.72
Employees	28,000	Stock Exchange	NYSE
Auditor	Ernst & Young LLP	Ticker Symbol	BC
Stk Agt	Brunswick	Outstanding Shares	90,360,000
Counsel	NA	E.P.S	$1.20
DUNS No.	00-130-7636	Shareholders	NA

Business: The groups principle activities include manufacturing and marketing marine engines, pleasure boats, fitness equipment, bowling products and billiards. The group's products include ball, bags, shoes and apparels. The group operates from United States, Europe, Pacific Rim, and Canada.
Primary SIC and add'l.: 3519 3732 3949 7933
CIK No: 0000014930
Subsidiaries: Advanced Exercise Equipment, LLC, Albemarle Boats, Inc., Appletree Ltd., Ashland City Land & Brand Partners, G.P., Askeladden Marine AS, Attwood Corporation, Baja Marine Corporation, BBG Logistics, Inc., BCMM Holdings, Inc., Bella-Veneet Oy, Bluewater Marine Group, Inc., BNT Marine Limited, Boston Whaler, Inc., BRIG Holdings, Inc., Brunswick Acceptance Company, LLC 162 Subsidiaries included in the Index
Officers: Dustan E. McCoy/Chmn., CEO/$3,575,958.00, Judith P. Zelisko/VP - Tax, Marschall I. Smith/63/VP, General Counsel, Sec./$1,061,472.00, Kathryn J. Chieger/VP - Corporate, Investor Relations, John E. Stransky/VP, Pres. - Life Fitness Division, Peter G. Leemputte/CFO, Sr. VP/$1,504,936.00, Warren N. Hardie/VP, Pres. - Brunswick Bowling, Billiards, Lloyd C. Chatfield/VP, General Counsel, Sec., Andrew E. Graves/VP, Pres. - Brunswick Outboard Boat Group, Mark Schwabero/VP, Pres. - Mercury Marine Outboard Business Unit, Richard C. Stone/VP, Pres. - Sea Ray Group, Russell B. Lockridge/VP, Chief Human Resources Officer, Kevin S. Grodzki/VP, Pres. - Mercury Mercruiser, William J. Gress/VP, Pres. - Brunswick Latin America Group, William L. Metzger/VP, Treasurer *(18 Officers included in Index)*
Directors: Dustan E. McCoy/Chmn., CEO, Lawrence A. Zimmerman/Dir., Jeffrey L. Bleustein/Dir., Manuel A. Fernandez/Dir., Nolan D. Archibald/Dir., Graham H. Phillips/Dir., Ralph C. Stayer/Dir., Michael J. Callahan/Dir., Cambria W. Dunaway/Dir., Steven J. Whisler/Dir.
Owners: Putnam, LLC/0.06%, Barclays Global Investors, NA/0.09%, Eminence Capital, LLC/0.05%
Financial Data: Fiscal Year End:12/31 Latest Annual Data: 12/31/2006

Year	Sales	Net Income
2006	$5,665,000,000	$133,900,000
2005	$5,923,800,000	$385,400,000
2004	$5,229,300,000	$269,800,000

Curr. Assets:	$2,078,400,000	Curr. Liab.:	$1,293,200,000		
Plant, Equip.:	$1,047,700,000	Total Liab.:	$2,578,500,000	Indic. Yr. Divd.:	$0.600
Total Assets:	$4,450,300,000	Net Worth:	$1,871,800,000	Debt/ Equity:	0.3824

Brush Engineered Materials Inc

17876 St. Clair Ave., Cleveland, OH, 44110; *PH:* 1-216-486-4200; *Fax:* 1-216-383-4091; *http://* www.beminc.com; *Email:* bwi-sales@brushwellman.com

General - Incorporation	OH	**Stock**- Price on:12/24/2007	$40.45
Employees	2,185	Stock Exchange	NYSE
Auditor	Ernst & Young LLP	Ticker Symbol	BW
Stk Agt	LaSalle Bank, N.A	Outstanding Shares	20,300,000
Counsel	NA	E.P.S.	$3.43
DUNS No.	NA	Shareholders	NA

Business: The group's principal activity is to manufacture high-performance engineered materials. The group operates in two segments: the group operates in two segments: metal systems and microelectronics. The metal systems group comprises of strip and bulk alloy (primarily copper beryllium), beryllium products and engineered materials. Microelectronics group manufactures products such as precious and non-precious vapor deposition materials, other precious and non-precious metal products, ceramics, electronic packages, powdered metals and circuitry. The group serves the global telecommunications and computer, optical media, automotive electronics, industrial components, aerospace and defense and appliance markets.

Primary SIC and add'l.: 3369 3364 3339

CIK No: 0001104657

Subsidiaries: BEM Services, Inc., Brush Ceramic Products Inc., Brush International, Inc., Brush Resources Inc., Brush Wellman (Japan), Ltd., Brush Wellman (Singapore) Pte Ltd., Brush Wellman GmbH, Brush Wellman Inc., Brush Wellman Limited, CERAC incorporated, Circuits Processing Technology, Inc., OMC Scientific Holding Limited, Technical Materials, Inc., Thin Film Technology, Inc., Williams Advanced Materials (Netherlands) B. 18 Subsidiaries included in the Index

Officers: Richard J. Hipple/Chmn., CEO, Pres./$2,042,570.00, John D. Grampa/VP - Finance, CFO/$1,222,392.00, Daniel A. Skoch/Sr. VP - Administration/$1,291,298.00, Michael C. Hasychak/VP, Treasurer, Sec., John J. Pallam/VP, General Counsel, Gary W. Schiavoni/Assist. Treasurer, Assist. Sec., James P. Marrotte/VP, Controller

Directors: Richard J. Hipple/Chmn., CEO, Pres., William R. Robertson/Dir., Albert C. Bersticker/Dir., William P. Madar/Dir., William G. Pryor/Dir., John Sherwin/Dir., Joseph P. Keithley/Dir., Mohan N. Reddy/Dir., William B. Lawrence/Dir.

Owners: Daniel A. Skoch, Joseph P. Keithley, John Sherwin, William P. Madar, Bear Stearns Asset Management Inc/6.60%, Albert C. Bersticker, William B. Lawrence, William R. Robertson, Mohan N. Reddy, Jeffrey Gendell, et al./11.60%, John D. Grampa, William G. Pryor, Insiders/2.20%, Richard J. Hipple, Barclays Global Investors, N.A., et al./5.10%

Financial Data: *Fiscal Year End:*12/31 *Latest Annual Data:* 12/31/2006

Year	Sales	Net Income
2006	$763,054,000	$49,603,000
2005	$541,267,000	$17,825,000
2004	$496,276,000	$15,516,000

Curr. Assets:	$271,584,000	**Curr. Liab.:**	$116,442,000	**P/E Ratio:**	12.29
Plant, Equip.:	$175,929,000	**Total Liab.:**	$207,606,000	**Indic. Yr. Divd.:**	NA
Total Assets:	$498,606,000	**Net Worth:**	$291,000,000	**Debt/ Equity:**	0.0955

Bryn Mawr Bank Corp

801 Lancaster Ave., Bryn Mawr, PA, 19010; *PH:* 1-610-525-1700; *Fax:* 1-610-526-2450; *http://* www.bmtc.com

General - Incorporation	PA	**Stock**- Price on:12/24/2007	$23.05
Employees	230	Stock Exchange	NDQ
Auditor	KPMG LLP	Ticker Symbol	BMTC
Stk Agt	Mellon Investor Services LLC	Outstanding Shares	8,540,000
Counsel	McElroy Deutsch Mulaney & Crp LLP	E.P.S.	$1.56
DUNS No.	00-790-9989	Shareholders	NA

Business: The group's principal activity is the provision of retail and commercial banking services. It serves as a holding company for the bryn mawr trust company, a state chartered bank and other subsidiaries. The group's banking operations include accepting demand, time and savings deposits and originating commercial, real estate and consumer loans. The group also provides a full range of investment management and trust services including estate administration, investment advisory services, pension and profit sharing administration, and personal financial planning and tax preparation. It offers investments in mutual funds, annuities, individual stocks and bonds and retirement plans through the bank's branch system. The branches are located in bryn mawr, havertown, wayne, wynnewood, paoli and west conshohocken, Pennsylvania.

Primary SIC and add'l.: 6162 6022 6712 6091

CIK No: 0000802681

Subsidiaries: BMT Mortgage Services, Inc., BMT Settlement Services, Inc., Bryn Mawr Advisors, Inc., Bryn Mawr Brokerage Co., Inc., Bryn Mawr Financial Services, Inc, Insurance Counsellors of Bryn Mawr, Inc., Joseph W. Roskos & Co., Inc., The Bryn Mawr Trust Company

Officers: Frederick C. Peters/Chmn., CEO/$537,995.80, Alison E. Gers/Exec. VP - Retail Banking, Marketing, Support Division/$263,504.20, Duncan J. Smith/CFO, Exec. VP/$243,218.00, Robert J. Ricciardi/Sec., Exec. VP, Chief Credit Policy Officer/$318,539.20, Joseph G. Keefer/49/Exec. VP, Chief Lending Officer/$279,014.20, Matthew G. Waschull/Exec. VP - Wealth Management Division, Ted Peters/Investor Relations Officer

Directors: Frederick C. Peters/Chmn., CEO, David E. Lees/Dir., Andrea F. Gilbert/Dir., Wendell F. Holland/Dir., Francis J. Leto/Dir., Thomas L. Bennett/Dir., Scott M. Jenkins/Dir., Britton H. Murdoch/Dir., Loyall B. Taylor/Dir.

Owners: Duncan J. Smith, Nancy J. Vickers, Alison E. Gers, Britton H. Murdoch, Thomas A. Williams, Insiders/6.97%, George W. Connell/19.57%, Andrea F. Gilbert, Scott M. Jenkins, Frederick C. Peters/2.10%, Joseph G. Keefer, David E. Lees, Loyall B. Taylor, Francis J. Leto, Robert J. Ricciardi *(19 Owners included in Index)*

Financial Data: *Fiscal Year End:*12/31 *Latest Annual Data:* 12/31/2006

Year	Sales	Net Income
2006	$64,267,000	$12,716,000
2005	$56,213,000	$11,350,000
2004	$51,175,000	$9,345,000

Curr. Assets:	$66,237,000	**Curr. Liab.:**	$718,835,000		
Plant, Equip.:	$16,571,000	**Total Liab.:**	$744,277,000	**Indic. Yr. Divd.:**	$0.520
Total Assets:	$826,660,000	**Net Worth:**	$82,383,000	**Debt/ Equity:**	0.1820

BSD Medical Corp

2188 W 2200 S, Salt Lake City, UT, 84119; *PH:* 1-801-972-5555; *Fax:* 1-801-972-5930; *http://* www.bsdmc.com

General - Incorporation	DE	**Stock**- Price on:12/24/2007	$7.02
Employees	36	Stock Exchange	AMEX
Auditor	Pricewaterhousecoopers LLP	Ticker Symbol	BSM
Stk Agt	NA	Outstanding Shares	21,090,000
Counsel	Fulcrum Global Partners	E.P.S.	-$0.16
DUNS No.	08-932-6938	Shareholders	NA

Business: The group's principle activities include developing, producing, marketing and servicing microwave systems used for the treatment of cancer and other benign diseases. It has developed the technology required to approach hyperthermia therapy through three techniques: superficial hyperthermia, interstitial or intercavitary hyperthermia and deep hyperthermia. Superficial hyperthermia systems are used to non-invasively treat tumors within a few centimeters of the surface of the body, typical in conditions of melanoma and recurrent breast cancer. Interstitial hyperthermia is primarily used to treat tumors in combination with popular interstitial and intercavitary ionizing radiation therapy. Deep hyperthermia is used to non-invasively treat tumors deep within the body, including many problematic cancer sites located in the pelvis, abdomen and chest areas. The group operates from United States.

Primary SIC and add'l.: 3845

CIK No: 0000320174

Subsidiaries: TherMatrx, Inc.

Officers: Hyrum A. Mead/60/Dir., CEO, Pres., Paul F. Turner/Chmn., CTO, Sr. VP, Dennis Bradley/Accountant, Sec., Ray Lauritzen/VP - Field Service Operations, Dixie Toolson Sells/VP - Regulatory Affairs, Mark Hagmann/Sr. Engineer, Richard A. White/VP - Business Development, Richard J. Faux/Production, Materials Mgr., Brian L. Ferrand/VP - Sales, Dennis P. Gauger/CFO

Directors: Hyrum A. Mead/60/Dir., CEO, Pres., Paul F. Turner/Chmn., CTO, Sr. VP, Douglas P. Boyd/Dir., Michael Nobel/Dir., Gerhard Sennewald/Dir., Steven G. Stewart/Dir.

Owners: Steven G. Stewart, Insiders/44.80%, Douglas P. Boyd/1.20%, Gerhard W. Sennewald/30.70%, John E. Langdon/6.20%, Hyrum A. Mead/3.50%, Paul F. Turner/10.00%, Michael Nobel/1.30%

Financial Data: *Fiscal Year End:*08/31 *Latest Annual Data:* 8/31/2006

Year	Sales	Net Income
2006	$2,898,000	$9,249,000
2005	$2,021,000	$3,322,000
2004	$1,631,000	$8,413,000

Curr. Assets:	$27,848,000	**Curr. Liab.:**	$2,468,000		
Plant, Equip.:	$303,000	**Total Liab.:**	$2,686,000	**Indic. Yr. Divd.:**	NA
Total Assets:	$28,310,000	**Net Worth:**	$25,624,000	**Debt/ Equity:**	NA

BSML Inc

Formerly: Britesmile Inc
490 N Wiget Ln., Walnut Creek, CA, 94598; *PH:* 1-925-941-6260; *http://* www.britesmile.com

General - Incorporation	UT	**Stock**- Price on:12/24/2007	NA
Employees	101	Stock Exchange	OTC
Auditor	Deloitte & Touche, LLP	Ticker Symbol	BSML
Stk Agt	Continental Stock Transfer & Trust Co	Outstanding Shares	NA
Counsel	NA	E.P.S.	NA
DUNS No.	10-270-8062	Shareholders	NA

Business: The group's principal activities are to develop, produce, market and lease advanced teeth whitening products, services and technology. The products and services are distributed in professional salon-like settings operated by the group, known as britesmile professional teeth whitening centers. The group also offers its products and technologies to existing independent dental offices known as britesmile professional teeth whitening associated centers. The group sells britesmile brand post-whitening maintenance products like toothpaste, mouthwash, whitening chewing gum and electric toothbrushes to consumers in centers, associated centers, and on its Internet site. The group operates in 14 centers located in beverly hills, irvine, walnut creek, palo alto, la jolla, Chicago, phoenix, boca raton, honolulu, atlanta, houston, denver, Boston and New York. The group acquired of certain intellectual property from r. Eric montgomery in 2003.

Primary SIC and add'l.: 3843 2844 8099

CIK No: 0000866734

Subsidiaries: BriteSmile Development, Inc, BriteSmile International, Limited, BriteSmile Leasing, Inc., BriteSmile Management, Inc., BriteSmile Overseas, Inc., BriteSmile Spas, LLC., BriteSmile, Inc.

Officers: Julian Feneley/Dir., CEO/$721,387.00, Richard Deyoung/CFO, Exec. VP

Directors: Julian Feneley/Dir., CEO, John Reed/Vice Chmn., Anthony M. Pilaro/Chmn., Peter Schechter/Dir., Tim Pierce/Dir., Brad Peters/Dir.

Owners: LCO Investment, Julian Feneley, Insiders, Tim L. Pierce, Bradford Peters, Bradford Peters, Harry Thompson, Phillip Powell, Peter Schecter, John Reed, MicroCapital LLC, Anthony M. Pilaro

Curr. Assets:	$25,467,000	**Curr. Liab.:**	$30,025,000		
Plant, Equip.:	$629,000	**Total Liab.:**	$30,293,000	**Indic. Yr. Divd.:**	NA
Total Assets:	$27,842,000	**Net Worth:**	-$2,451,000	**Debt/ Equity:**	NA

Bsquare Corp

110 110th Ave. NE, Ste. 200, Bellevue, WA, 98004; *PH:* 1-425-519-5900; *Fax:* 1-425-519-5999; *http://* www.bsquare.com; *Email:* sales@bsquare.com

General - Incorporation	WA	**Stock**- Price on:12/24/2007	$6.6
Employees	170	Stock Exchange	NDQ
Auditor	Moss Adams LLP	Ticker Symbol	BSQR
Stk Agt	Chase Mellon Shareholder Services	Outstanding Shares	9,790,000
Counsel	Summit Law Group	E.P.S.	$0.224
DUNS No.	NA	Shareholders	NA

Business: The group's principal activity is to provide products and services for the development and deployment of wireless and wireline smart devices that use microsoft windows embedded operating systems. The activities are carried out through two segments: software services and hardware. The software service segment provides professional engineering services such as custom development, product

adaptations, and system quality assurance. The software product segment licenses software products to original equipment manufacturers, distributing products through resellers, and distribution of third-party products. The customers include original equipment manufacturers, original design manufacturers, software developers and network operators.

Primary SIC and add'l.: 7371 7379 7372

CIK No: 0001054721

Subsidiaries: BlueWater Systems, Inc., BSQUARE GmbH, Bsquare Kk, BSQUARE Silicon Valley Corporation, BSQUARE Software Solutions, Inc., BSQUARE Taiwan Corporation, Cory Corporation, Embedded Technologies, Inc.

Officers: Brian Crowley/Dir., CEO, Pres./$280,708.00, Carey E. Butler/VP - Professional Engineering Services/$208,084.00, Larry Stapleton/VP - North American Sales/$282,204.00, Scott Mahan/CFO, VP - Finance/$230,509.00, Steven Yee/Mgr. - Engineering, Software Architect

Directors: Brian Crowley/Dir., CEO, Pres., Donald B. Bibeault/Chmn., Elwood D. Howse/Dir., Scot E. Land/Dir., Elliott H. Jurgensen/Dir., William D. Savoy/Dir., Kendra Vandermeulen/Dir.

Owners: S Squared Technology, LLC/15.40%, Kendra A. VanderMeulen, Scott C. Mahan, Carey E. Butler, Pawan Gupta, Donald B. Bibeault/2.10%, Insiders/9.00%, Elwood D. Howse, Larry C. Stapleton, Elliott H. Jurgensen, Brian T. Crowley/2.10%, Scot E. Land, William D. Savoy

Financial Data: *Fiscal Year End:*12/31 *Latest Annual Data:* 12/31/2006

Year	Sales	Net Income
2006	$49,815,000	-$466,000
2005	$42,923,000	-$1,297,000
2004	$38,920,000	-$7,051,000

Curr. Assets:	$17,497,000	**Curr. Liab.:**	$7,245,000	**P/E Ratio:**	38.82
Plant, Equip.:	$821,000	**Total Liab.:**	$7,600,000	**Indic. Yr. Divd.:**	NA
Total Assets:	$19,676,000	**Net Worth:**	$12,076,000	**Debt/ Equity:**	NA

BT Group Plc

350 Madison Ave., New York, NY, 10017; *PH:* 1-646-487-7400; *Fax:* 1-646-487-3370; *http://* www.btplc.com; *Email:* kevan@lloydstsb-registrars.co.uk

General - Incorporation	UK	**Stock**- Price on:12/24/2007	$63.25
Employees	104,400	Stock Exchange	NYSE
Auditor	PricewaterhouseCoopers LLP	Ticker Symbol	BT
Stk Agt	Morgan ADR Service Center	Outstanding Shares	NA
Counsel	NA	E.P.S	NA
DUNS No.	22-727-0410	Shareholders	NA

Business: The group's principal activities are the provision of local, long distance and international telecommunication services, broadband, Internet products and services, and it solutions. The group is comprised of three lines of business namely bt retail, bt wholesale and bt global services. Bt retail supplies a range of communication products and services and offers a range of managed and packaged communication solutions. Bt wholesale provides network services and solutions. Bt global services provides global reach and a range of ict solutions and services. The group also held stakes in satellite entities, lg telecom, starhub and albacom. During fiscal 2003, the former concert business, customer accounts and networks were returned to its two parent companies with the group and at&t each taking ownership of substantially those parts contributed by them. During the year the group acquired UK trade and nsb retail plc.

Primary SIC and add'l.: 7389

CIK No: 0000756620

Subsidiaries: British Telecommunications plc, PlusNet

Officers: Andy Green/53/CEO - Group Strategy, Operations, Paul Reynolds/51/CEO - BT Wholesale, Ian Livingston/44/CEO - BT Retail, Ben Verwaayen/56/CEO, Larry Stone/51/Company Sec., Hanif Lalani/46/Group Dir. - Finance

Directors: Christopher Bland/70/Chmn., Maarten Van Den Bergh/66/Dep. Chmn., Carl G. Symon/62/Non - Exec. Dir., Phil Hodkinson/50/Non - Exec. Dir., Matti Alahuhta/56/Non - Exec. Dir., Baroness Jay/68/Non - Exec. Dir., John Nelson/61/Non - Exec. Dir., Clayton Brendish/61/Non - Exec. Dir., Deborah Lathen/Non - Exec. Dir.

Financial Data: *Fiscal Year End:*03/31 *Latest Annual Data:* 3/31/2006

Year	Sales	Net Income
2006	$34,345,392,000	$1,849,407,000
2005	$35,313,926,000	$2,437,063,000
2004	$34,540,747,000	$1,612,535,000

Curr. Assets:	$11,694,936,000	**Curr. Liab.:**	$16,481,125,000	**P/E Ratio:**	8.66
Plant, Equip.:	$25,160,988,000	**Total Liab.:**	$41,562,081,000	**Indic. Yr. Divd.:**	NA
Total Assets:	$41,377,663,000	**Net Worth:**	-$274,888,000	**Debt/ Equity:**	NA

BTU International Inc

23 Esquire Rd., North Billerica, MA, 01862; *PH:* 1-978-667-4111; *Fax:* 1-978-667-9068; *http://* www.btu.com; *Email:* sales@btu.com

General - Incorporation	DE	**Stock**- Price on:12/24/2007	$13.76
Employees	348	Stock Exchange	NDQ
Auditor	Vitale, Caturano & Co. Ltd	Ticker Symbol	BTUI
Stk Agt	EquiServe Trust	Outstanding Shares	9,300,000
Counsel	Ropes & Gray LLP	E.P.S	$0.45
DUNS No.	10-118-5908	Shareholders	NA

Business: The group's principal activities are to design and manufacture thermal processing systems used in packaging semiconductors and printed circuit boards. The products include solder reflow systems supplied to the electronics original equipment manufacturers and contract electronics manufacturers. They also include high temperature systems, applied into the manufacture of the ceramics. The users of these products manufacture the high-density printed circuit boards and semiconductor packages used in the advanced electronics industry. The products are also used for the sintering of ceramics, metal brazing and the deposition of thin film coatings. Major customers of the group include electronic manufacturers like celestica, solectron, sci-sanmina and foxconn and original equipment manufactures like intel, IBM, nokia, samsung, lucent technologies, motorola and raytheon. In 2003, the group acquired the assets of sagarus robotics corporation of tempe.

Primary SIC and add'l.: 3823

CIK No: 0000840883

Subsidiaries: BTU Engineering FSC, Inc, BTU Europe LTD, BTU GmbH, BTU Overseas, Limited

Officers: Paul J. Van Der Wansem/Chmn., CEO/$603,805.00, Thomas F. Nash/VP - Global Operations, Marketing/$201,963.00, John E. Beard/Dir., Sec., Thomas P. Kealy/VP, Chief Accounting Officer, Corporate Controller/$176,303.00, James M. Griffin/VP - Global Sales/$178,662.00, Peter Franklin/MD - Europe, Stephen J. Parrott/Dir. - Engineering, Donald A. Seccombe/Dir. - Research Engineering, David J. Fancher/Dir. - Information Technology, Boris Mathiszik/Dir. - Asia Pacific Sales, Jolanda Creech/Mgr. - Corporate Support, Bill Monigle/Investor Relations Officer, Contact - Agency

Directors: Paul J. Van Der Wansem/Chmn., CEO, John E. Beard/Dir., Sec., Joseph F. Wrinn/Dir., Jeffrey Chuan Chu/Dir., Samuel J. Parkhill/Dir., Mead G. Wyman/Dir., Chuan J. Chu/88/Dir.

Owners: Mead G. Wyman, Chuan J. Chu, T. Rowe Price Associates, Inc./8.00%, Thomas F. Nash, James M. Griffin, Wellington Management Co., LLP/14.00%, John E. Beard, Joseph F. Wrinn, Samuel J. Parkhill, Columbia Management Advisors, Inc./7.00%, Thomas P. Kealy, Insiders/18.10%, Paul J. vander Wansem/16.52%

Financial Data: *Fiscal Year End:*12/31 *Latest Annual Data:* 12/31/2006

Year	Sales	Net Income
2006	$78,289,000	$9,222,000
2005	$66,407,000	$4,619,000
2004	$54,639,000	-$4,181,000

Curr. Assets:	$59,134,000	**Curr. Liab.:**	$10,320,000	**P/E Ratio:**	30.58
Plant, Equip.:	$4,156,000	**Total Liab.:**	$20,755,000	**Indic. Yr. Divd.:**	NA
Total Assets:	$65,687,000	**Net Worth:**	$44,932,000	**Debt/ Equity:**	0.2061

BTX Holdings Inc

PO Box 191476, Miami Beach, FL, 33119; *PH:* 1-954-776-6600; *Fax:* 1-954-491-9200; *http://* www.biotexcorp.com; *Email:* info@biotexcorp.com

General - Incorporation	FL	**Stock**- Price on:12/24/2007	$0.04
Employees	3	Stock Exchange	OTC
Auditor	Webb & Company, P. A.	Ticker Symbol	BTXH
Stk Agt	Corporate Stock Transfer, Inc.	Outstanding Shares	35,040,000
Counsel	NA	E.P.S	-$0.18
DUNS No.	NA	Shareholders	NA

Business: The groups principal activates include acquiring, developing and deploying technologies from around the world to process plant derived biomass waste, extract the usable fractions, and then utilize or sell those extractions in further secondary processes. The group products include cellulose, fiber, protein, hemicelluloses, lignin, and ethanol. The group operates from the United States.

Primary SIC and add'l.: 3559

CIK No: 0001268238

Subsidiaries: BioTex Corporation

Officers: Scott J. Silverman/Chmn., CEO, CFO, Pres.

Directors: Scott J. Silverman/Chmn., CEO, CFO, Pres.

Owners: Robert deZanger/5.49%, Mark H. Silverman/14.94%, Insiders/51.16%, Scott J. Silverman/30.73%

Financial Data: *Fiscal Year End:*12/31 *Latest Annual Data:* 12/31/2006

Year	Sales	Net Income
2006	NA	-$741,000
2005	NA	-$1,251,000

Curr. Assets:	$2,000	**Curr. Liab.:**	$631,000		
Plant, Equip.:	$7,000	**Total Liab.:**	$631,000	**Indic. Yr. Divd.:**	NA
Total Assets:	$9,000	**Net Worth:**	-$622,000	**Debt/ Equity:**	NA

BUCA Inc

1300 Nicollet Mall, Ste. 5003, Minneapolis, MN, 55403; *PH:* 1-612-225-3400; *Fax:* 1-612-225-3302; *http://* www.bucainc.com

General - Incorporation	MN	**Stock**- Price on:12/24/2007	$3.94
Employees	6,170	Stock Exchange	NDQ
Auditor	Grant Thornton, LLP	Ticker Symbol	BUCA
Stk Agt	Wells Fargo Bank, N.A.	Outstanding Shares	20,920,000
Counsel	Faegre & Benson LLP	E.P.S	-$0.49
DUNS No.	NA	Shareholders	NA

Business: The group's principal activity is to develop, own and operate southern Italian restaurants under the names buca di beppo and vinny testa's. These restaurants offer immigrant southern Italian cuisine served family-style in large portions in a fun and energetic atmosphere that parodies the decor and ambiance of post-war Italian/american restaurants. The food is based on authentic family recipes enjoyed for generations in the villages of southern Italy and then adapted to American ingredients. The menu features dishes such as garlic bread with mozzarella, pizza arrabiatta, garlic mash potatoes, buca di beppo 1893 salad, spaghetti with half-pound meat balls, tortelloni, chicken marsala, veal parmigiana and tiramisu. Vinny testa's menu features a variety of pasta, meat, poultry and seafood items, appetizers, soups, salads and desserts.

Primary SIC and add'l.: 5812

CIK No: 0001046501

Subsidiaries: BUCA (Kansas), Inc., BUCA (Minneapolis), Inc., BUCA Investments, Inc., BUCA Restaurants 2, BUCA Restaurants 3, Inc, BUCA Restaurants, Inc, BUCA Texas Beverage, Inc, BUCA Texas Restaurants, L.P.

Officers: Wallace B. Doolin/Chmn., CEO/$727,651.00, Pam Thompson/Divisional VP - Operations, Chris Gravel/Divisional VP - Operations, Jeff Friedman/Divisional VP - Operations, Donna Morris/Divisional VP - Operations, John T. Bettin/Pres., Jeff Abramson/VP - Purchasing, David Suddath/Divisional VP - Operations, Richard G. Erstad/General Counsel, Sec., Brian Beers/VP - Operations, Divisional VP - Operations, Off Premise, Franchising, Steve Hickey/Chief Marketing Officer/$412,618.00, Mickey Mills/Sr. VP - Operations, Vittorio Renda/Founding Executive Chef, Bernie Cullen/Divisional VP - Operations, Dennis Goetz/VP, Chief Accounting Officer *(24 Officers included in Index)*

Directors: Wallace B. Doolin/Chmn., CEO, John P. Whaley/Dir., Paul J. Zepf/Dir., Sid Feltenstein/Dir., James T. Stamas/Dir., Fritzi G. Woods/Dir.

Owners: Paul J. Zepf, Cynthia C. Rodahl, Kennedy Capital Management, Inc./5.30%, Peter J. Mihajlov/1.10%, Rutabaga Capital Management LLC/9.70%, Wallace B. Doolin/3.50%, John P. Whaley/6.20%, State of Wisconsin Investment Board/14.40%, Heartland Advisors, Inc./13.60%, Sidney J. Feltenstein, AWM Investment Company, Inc./6.90%, Stephen B. Hickey, James T. Stamas, Prentice Capital Management, LP/8.60%, Dimensional Fund Advisors, Inc./8.10% *(20 Owners included in Index)*

Financial Data: *Fiscal Year End:*12/25 *Latest Annual Data:* 12/31/2006

Year	Sales	Net Income
2006	$253,813,000	-$3,608,000
2005	$238,959,000	-$32,101,000
2004	$258,408,000	-$37,587,000

Curr. Assets:	$17,178,000	**Curr. Liab.:**	$31,215,000		
Plant, Equip.:	$112,189,000	**Total Liab.:**	$70,383,000	**Indic. Yr. Divd.:**	NA
Total Assets:	$137,403,000	**Net Worth:**	$67,020,000	**Debt/ Equity:**	0.2507

Buckeye GP Holdings LP

Five TEK Pk., 9999 Hamilton Blvd., Breinigsville, PA, 18031; *PH:* 1-610-904-4000; *Fax:* 1-484-232-4543; *http://* www.buckeye.com

General - Incorporation: DE; Employees: NA; Auditor: NA; Stk Agt: Computershare Trust Co; Counsel: NA; DUNS No.: NA

Stock - Price on:12/24/2007: NA; Stock Exchange: NYSE; Ticker Symbol: BGH; Outstanding Shares: 28,300,000; E.P.S.: $0.635; Shareholders: NA

Business: The groups principle activities include transporting and storing refine petroleum products for oil companies. The group operates through three segments namely, pipeline operations, terminalling and storage, and other operations. In January 2006, the group acquired Buckeye NGL Pipe Lines LLC. The group operates from the United States. The group's quarterly revenue for September 2007 was 125.65 millions of USD.

Primary SIC and add'l.: 4613

CIK No: 0001359055

Subsidiaries: Buckeye GP LLC, Buckeye Gulf Coast Holdings I, LLC, Buckeye Gulf Coast Holdings II, LLC, Buckeye Gulf Coast Pipe Lines, L.P., Buckeye NGL Pipe Lines LLC, Buckeye Partners, L.P., Buckeye Pipe Line Company, L.P., Buckeye Pipe Line Holdings, L.P., Buckeye Pipe Line Transportation LLC, Buckeye Products Pipe Line, L.P., Buckeye Terminals, LLC, Buckeye Texas Pipe Line Company, L.P., Everglades Pipe Line Company, L.P., Ferrysburg Terminal LLC ., Gulf Coast Pipe Line, L.P. 27 Subsidiaries included in the Index

Officers: William H. Shea/53/Chmn., CEO, Pres., Stephen C. Muther/58/Exec. VP - Administration, Legal Affairs, Robert B. Wallace/46/CFO, Sr. VP - Finance, Eric A. Gustafson/Sr. VP - Operations - Technology

Directors: William H. Shea/53/Chmn., CEO, Pres., Barnes W. Hauptfuhrer/53/Dir., Michael B. Hoffman/57/Dir., Frank S. Sowinski/51/Dir., Andrew W. Ward/40/Dir., Bartow E. Jones/31/Dir.

Owners: Stephen C. Muther/1.50%, Insiders/7.50%, Robert B. Wallace, Frank S. Sowinski, Carlyle/Riverstone BPL Holdings II, L.P./53.70%, Eric A. Gustafson, William H. Shea/4.50%, MainLine Management LLC

Financial Data: Fiscal Year End:12/31 **Latest Annual Data:** 12/31/2006

Year	Sales	Net Income
2006	$461,760,000	$8,734,000

Curr. Assets:	$131,900,000	**Curr. Liab.:**	$102,461,000		
Plant, Equip.:	$1,738,199,000	**Total Liab.:**	$1,971,968,000	**Indic. Yr. Divd.:**	$1.060
Total Assets:	$2,212,585,000	**Net Worth:**	$240,617,000	**Debt/ Equity:**	NA

Buckeye Partners LP

9999 Hamilton Blvd., Breinigsville, PA, 18031; *PH:* 1-610-904-4000; *Fax:* 1-484-232-4543; *http://* www.buckeye.com

General - Incorporation: DE; Employees: NA; Auditor: Deloitte & Touche LLP; Stk Agt: Computershare Trust Co; Counsel: NA; DUNS No.: NA

Stock - Price on:12/24/2007: $51.0699; Stock Exchange: NYSE; Ticker Symbol: BPL; Outstanding Shares: 41,190,000; E.P.S.: $2.92; Shareholders: NA

Business: The groups principle activities include transporting and storing refine petroleum products for oil companies. The group operates through three segments namely, pipeline operations, terminalling and storage, and other operations. In January 2006, the group acquired Buckeye NGL Pipe Lines LLC. The group operates from the United States. The group's quarterly revenue for September 2007 was 125.65 millions of USD.

Primary SIC and add'l.: 4613

CIK No: 0000805022

Subsidiaries: Buckeye Gulf Coast Holdings I, LLC, Buckeye Gulf Coast Holdings II, LLC, Buckeye Gulf Coast Pipe Lines, L.P., Buckeye NGL Pipe Lines LLC, Buckeye Pipe Line Company, L.P., Buckeye Pipe Line Holdings, L.P., Buckeye Pipe Line Transportation LLC, Buckeye Products Pipe Line, L.P., Buckeye Terminals, LLC, Buckeye Texas Pipe Line Company, L.P., Everglades Pipe Line Company, L.P., Ferrysburg Terminal LLC, Gulf Coast Pipe Line, L.P., Gulf Coast/Products GP Holding LLC, Gulf Coast/Products Holding L.P. 23 Subsidiaries included in the Index

Officers: William H. Shea/53/Chmn., CEO, Pres., Robert B. Wallace/46/CFO, Sr. VP - Finance, Eric A. Gustafson/59/Sr. VP - Operations, Technology, Stephen C. Muther/58/Exec. VP - Administration, Legal Affairs

Directors: William H. Shea/53/Chmn., CEO, Pres., Brian F. Billings/69/Dir., Michael B. Hoffman/57/Dir., Bartow E. Jones/31/Dir., Edward F. Kosnik/63/Dir., Joseph A. Lasala/53/Dir., Jonathan Oherron/78/Dir., Andrew W. Ward/40/Dir.

Owners: Michael B. Hoffman, Insiders, Brian F. Billings, Edward F. Kosnik, Robert B. Wallace, William H. Shea, Eric A. Gustafson, Buckeye GP Holdings L.P., Andrew W. Ward, Stephen C. Muther, Bartow E. Jones, Jonathan OHerron

Financial Data: Fiscal Year End:12/31 **Latest Annual Data:** 12/31/2006

Year	Sales	Net Income
2006	$461,760,000	$110,240,000
2005	$408,446,000	$99,958,000
2004	$323,543,000	$82,962,000

Curr. Assets:	$129,427,000	**Curr. Liab.:**	$89,549,000		
Plant, Equip.:	$1,727,222,000	**Total Liab.:**	$1,185,588,000	**Indic. Yr. Divd.:**	$3.300
Total Assets:	$1,995,470,000	**Net Worth:**	$809,882,000	**Debt/ Equity:**	NA

Buckeye Technologies Inc

1001 Tillman St., Memphis, TN, 38112; *PH:* 1-901-320-8100; *Fax:* 1-901-320-8836; *http://* www.bkitech.com; *Email:* info@bkitech.com

General - Incorporation: DE; Employees: 1,600; Auditor: Ernst & Young LLP; Stk Agt: American Stock Transfer & Trust Co.; Counsel: NA; DUNS No.: 79-831-8028

Stock - Price on:12/24/2007: $16.05; Stock Exchange: NYSE; Ticker Symbol: BKI; Outstanding Shares: 38,000,000; E.P.S.: $0.00; Shareholders: NA

Business: The group's principal activities are to manufacture and distribute value-added cellulose-based specialty products used in numerous applications. The product lines of the group include chemical cellulose, customized fibers, fluff pulp and nonwoven materials. Chemical cellulose is used to impart purity, strength and viscosity in the manufacture of diverse products. Customized fibers are used to provide porosity, color permanence, strength and tear resistance in filters, premium letterhead, currency paper and personal stationery. Fluff pulp and nonwoven materials are used to increase absorbency and fluid transport in products such as disposable diapers, feminine hygiene products, adult incontinence products and to enhance fluid management and strength in wipes, tabletop items, food pads and household wipes. The group has operations in the United States, Canada, Germany, Ireland and Brazil. Procter & gamble is one of the major customers of the group.

Primary SIC and add'l.: 2679 2823 2676 2611

CIK No: 0000899597

Subsidiaries: BFC 2 Inc., BFC 3 LLC, BFOL 2 Inc., Bfol 3 LLC, BKI Asset Management Corporation, BKI Finance Corporation, BKI Holding Corporation, BKI International Inc., BKI Lending Inc., BKI South America LLC, Buckeye (U.K.) Limited, Buckeye Americana Ltda., Buckeye Building Fibers, LLC, Buckeye Canada, Buckeye Canada Co. 31 Subsidiaries included in the Index

Officers: John B. Crowe/Chmn., CEO/$1,140,105.00, Kristopher J. Matula/Dir., COO, Pres./$667,733.00, Marko M. Rajamaa/Sr. VP - Nonwovens, Dan R. Moore/VP - Process Technology, Jeffery T. Cook/Sr. VP - Marketing, William M. Handel/Sr. VP - Lean Enterprise/$475,343.00, Elizabeth J. Welter/VP, Chief Accounting Officer, Paul N. Horne/Sr. VP - Product, Marketing Development/$485,911.00, Gray F. Carter/VP - Purchasing, Logistics, Horst Gottsche-Kuhn/VP - Specialty Fibers, Europe, South America, Susan L.H. Crenshaw/VP - Marketing Development, Douglas L. Dowdell/Sr. VP - Specialty Fibers, Charles S. Aiken/Sr. VP - Manufacturing/$448,028.00, Darrell D. Adams/VP - Specialty Fibers, North America, Asia, Steven G. Dean/Sr. VP, CFO/$270,239.00 *(20 Officers included in Index)*

Directors: John B. Crowe/Chmn., CEO, Virginia Wetherell/Dir., Red Cavaney/Dir., Howard R. Cannon/Dir., Kristopher J. Matula/Dir., COO, Pres., Katherine Buckman Gibson/Dir., Lewis E. Holland/Dir., George W. Bryan/Dir., David B. Ferraro/Dir.

Owners: Paul N. Horne, Barclays Global Investors NA/6.60%, Dimensional Fund Advisors Inc./8.30%, Howard R. Cannon, Kristopher J. Matula, David B. Ferraro/1.50%, New South Capital Management, Inc./6.60%, John B. Crowe, Lewis E. Holland, Red Cavaney, George W. Bryan, Insiders/5.80%, Katherine Buckman Gibson, William M. Handel, Charles S. Aiken *(17 Owners included in Index)*

Financial Data: Fiscal Year End:06/30 **Latest Annual Data:** 06/30/2007

Year	Sales	Net Income
2007	$769,321,000	$30,118,000
2006	$728,485,000	$1,980,000
2005	$712,782,000	$20,204,000

Curr. Assets:	$229,872,000	**Curr. Liab.:**	$83,310,000	**P/E Ratio:**	20.32
Plant, Equip.:	$531,898,000	**Total Liab.:**	$659,836,000	**Indic. Yr. Divd.:**	NA
Total Assets:	$949,553,000	**Net Worth:**	$289,717,000	**Debt/ Equity:**	1.3570

Buckeye Ventures Inc

4455 Lamont St., Ste. 3, San Diego, CA, 92109; *PH:* 1-858-272-6600; *Fax:* 1-858—272-9714; *http://* www.beyv.com; *Email:* info@beyv.com

General - Incorporation: MI; Employees: 77; Auditor: Michael T. Studer CPA P.C.; Stk Agt: American Registrar & Transfer Co; Counsel: NA; DUNS No.: NA

Stock - Price on:12/24/2007: $0.18; Stock Exchange: OTC; Ticker Symbol: BEYV; Outstanding Shares: 98,550,000; E.P.S.: $0.00; Shareholders: NA

Business: The groups principle activity is to create a national residential HVAC and plumbing brand. The groups services include Air conditioning service, Air conditioning installation, Plumbing service Plumbing installation, Kitchen and bathroom remodeling. In the year 2005, the group acquired of Heating and Air Conditioning Services, Inc. The group operates from the United States.

Primary SIC and add'l.: 1711 1700 1711

CIK No: 0001005502

Subsidiaries: World Wide Film & Television Institute, World Wide Productions Inc, WWMPC Environmental Services Corporation

Officers: Alan Mintz/Dir., CEO/$150,000.00, Henry S. Leonard/51/VP - Finance, Chief Accounting Officer, Larry Weinstein/60/Exec. VP - Investor Relations/$150,000.00, Stephan Kurz/54/Regional VP

Directors: Alan Mintz/Dir., CEO, Alfred Roach/Chmn., Paul D. Hancock/51/Dir., Larry Epstein/58/Dir., Randy Eakin/46/Dir., Adam Taylor/Dir., Ron Smith/70/Dir.

Owners: Paul D. Hancock/9.43%, Alan J. Mintz/30.99%, Adam Taylor, Al Roach, Insiders/72.33%, Larry Weinstein/30.99%, Randy Eakin, Larry Epstein

Financial Data: Fiscal Year End:12/31 **Latest Annual Data:** 12/31/2006

Year	Sales	Net Income
2006	$2,064,000	-$197,000
2005	$25,000	-$124,000
2004	$42,000	-$73,000

Curr. Assets:	$1,346,000	**Curr. Liab.:**	$2,135,000		
Plant, Equip.:	$415,000	**Total Liab.:**	$6,228,000	**Indic. Yr. Divd.:**	NA
Total Assets:	$7,974,000	**Net Worth:**	$1,746,000	**Debt/ Equity:**	2.3372

Buckle Inc

2407 W 24th St., Kearney, NE, 68845; *PH:* 1-308-236-8491; *Fax:* 1-308-236-4493; *http://* www.buckle.com

General - Incorporation: NE; Employees: 1,300; Auditor: Deloitte & Touche LLP; Stk Agt: American Stock Transfer & Trust Co.; Counsel: Kyle L. Hanson; DUNS No.: 03-505-5219

Stock - Price on:12/24/2007: $39.44; Stock Exchange: NYSE; Ticker Symbol: BKE; Outstanding Shares: 30,050,000; E.P.S.: $1.94; Shareholders: NA

Business: The group's principle activity is the retail of medium to better-priced casual apparel, footwear and accessories for fashion conscious young men and women. At 31-Jan-2004, the company operated 316 retail stores in 38 states throughout the central United States, as well as in the northwest, southeast and southwestern states. The company markets a selection of casual apparel including denims, other casual bottoms, tops, sportswear, outerwear, accessories and footwear. The group emphasizes personalized attention to its customers and provides individual customer services such as free alterations, free gift-wrapping, easy layaways and a frequent shopper program. The trademarks include buckle, the buckle, bkle, reclaim and bke. The group's central office functions, including purchasing, pricing, advertising and distribution, are controlled from its headquarters and distribution center in kearney, Nebraska. The group operates from United States.

Primary SIC and add'l.: 5651

CIK No: 0000885245

Officers: Jo Sear/Contact, Jim Shada/Exec. VP - Sales/$1,497,897.00, Chad /Store Mgr., Scott /District Mgr., Crystal /Store Mgr., Jessica /Store Mgr., Erik /Area Mgr., Linda /District Mgr., Mark /Area Mgr., Rebecca /Area Mgr., Carl /Area Mgr.

Directors: Daniel Hirschfeld/Chmn., David Hirschfeld/Founder

Owners: Bruce L. Hoberman, Robert E. Campbell, Bill L. Fairfield, Daniel J. Hirschfeld/46.02%, Royce & Associates LLC/12.21%, James E. Shada/1.54%, Karen B. Rhoads/1.36%, Dennis H. Nelson/8.87%, Insiders/56.13%, Ralph M. Tysdal

Financial Data: Fiscal Year End:01/28   Latest Annual Data: 2/3/2007

Year	Sales	Net Income
2007	$530,074,000	$55,726,000
2006	$501,101,000	$51,906,000
2005	$470,937,000	$43,229,000

Curr. Assets:	$238,226,000	**Curr. Liab.:**	$49,209,000	**P/E Ratio:**	20.33
Plant, Equip.:	$93,819,000	**Total Liab.:**	$81,611,000	**Indic. Yr. Divd.:**	$0.800
Total Assets:	$368,198,000	**Net Worth:**	$286,587,000	**Debt/ Equity:**	NA

Bucs Financial Corp

10455 Mill Run Cir., Owings Mills, MD, 21117; *PH:* 1-410-998-5961; *http://* www.bucsfederal.com

General - Incorporation	MD	Stock - Price on:12/24/2007	NA
Employees	46	Stock Exchange	NA
Auditor	Stegman & Co	Ticker Symbol	NA
Stk Agt.	Trident Securities	Outstanding Shares	NA
Counsel	NA	E.P.S	NA
DUNS No.	NA	Shareholders	NA

Business: The group's principal activities are to provide banking and non-banking financial services to individuals and commercial enterprises throughout central Maryland. The group operates through its wholly owned subsidiary bucs federal bank. The lending activities include origination of one-to four-family residential mortgage loans, consumer loans, home equity loans, auto and personal loans. The operations are conducted through its branch offices located in owings mills and columbia, Maryland.

Primary SIC and add'l.: 6712 6035

CIK No: 0001125813

Subsidiaries: BUCS Financial Capital Trust I

Officers: Herbert J. Moltzan/62/CEO, Pres., James E. Shinsky/Sr. VP - Systems, Support, William H. Howard/57/Sr. VP, Head - Business Banking Department, Matthew J. Ford/38/Sr. VP - Finance, CFO, Debra J. Vinson/Sr. VP - Financial Services, Brian Bowers/44/Dir., Treasurer, Robin M. Copeland/53/Dir., Sec.

Directors: Joseph Pescrille/70/Chmn., Gregory A. Devou/56/Dir., Allen Maier/59/Dir., Dale Summers/50/Dir., Harry Fox/59/Dir., Joseph J. Mezzanotte/43/Dir., Thomas Markel/54/Dir., Peg Ohrt/59/Dir., Brian Bowers/44/Dir., Treasurer, Virginia A. Wampler/61/Dir., Robin M. Copeland/53/Dir., Sec.

Owners: Gregory A. Devou/0.47%, Virginia A. Wampler/1.69%, Joseph Pescrille/2.83%, William H. Howard/1.07%, Jeffrey L. Gendell/8.92%, James E. Shinsky/1.53%, Harry Fox/0.82%, Thomas Markel/3.22%, Dale Summers/0.91%, Allen Maier/0.70%, Joseph J. Mezzanotte/0.31%, Insiders/24.25%, Debra J. Vinson/2.53%, BUCS Federal Bank/8.54%, Peg Ohrt/0.45% (19 Owners included in Index)

Bucyrus International Inc

1100 Milwaukee Ave., South Milwaukee, WI, 53172; *PH:* 1-414-768-4000; *Fax:* 1-414-768-4474; *http://* www.bucyrus.com

General - Incorporation	DE	Stock - Price on:12/24/2007	NA
Employees	2,400	Stock Exchange	NDQ
Auditor	Deloitte & Touche LLP	Ticker Symbol	BUCY
Stk Agt.	LaSalle Bank N.A	Outstanding Shares	32,080,000
Counsel	NA	E.P.S	$2.47
DUNS No.	00-607-6129	Shareholders	NA

Business: The group's principle activities include designing, manufacturing and marketing large excavation machinery include electric mining shovels and blast hole drills; manufactures and sells replacement parts and components for its mining machines; and provides replacement parts, comprehensive structural and mechanical engineering, non-destructive testing, repairs and rebuilds of machine components. The group operates from United States.

Primary SIC and add'l.: 3532

CIK No: 0000740761

Subsidiaries: Boonville Mining Services, Inc., Bucyrus (Africa) (Proprietary) Limited, Bucyrus (Australia) Proprietary Ltd., Bucyrus (Brasil) Ltda., Bucyrus (Mauritius) Limited, Bucyrus Canada Acquisition, Ltd., Bucyrus Canada Limited, Bucyrus Europe Holdings, Ltd., Bucyrus Europe Limited, Bucyrus India Private Limited, Bucyrus Industries, Inc., Bucyrus International (Chile) Limitada, Bucyrus International (Peru) S.A., BWC Gear, Inc., BWP Gear Inc. 22 Subsidiaries included in the Index

Officers: Timothy W. Sullivan/Dir., CEO, Pres./$3,000,594.00, Craig R. MacKus/CFO, Sec./$1,025,777.00, Kenneth W. Krueger/COO/$1,078,714.00, John F. Bosbous/Treasurer/$534,274.00

Directors: Timothy W. Sullivan/Dir., CEO, Pres., Theodore C. Rogers/Chmn., Robert L. Purdum/Dir., Edward G. Nelson/Dir., Gene Little/Dir., Robert C. Scharp/Dir., Ronald A. Crutcher/Dir., Robert W. Korthals/Dir., Paul W. Jones/Dir.

Owners: Timothy W. Sullivan, Theodore C. Rogers, John F. Bosbous, FMR Corp./7.40%, Edward G. Nelson, Neuberger Berman Inc./11.80%, Ronald A. Crutcher, EARNEST Partners, LLC/12.30%, Robert L. Purdum, Craig R. Mackus, Gene E. Little, Citadel Limited Partnership/6.10%, Kenneth W. Krueger, Insiders, Robert W. Korthals (16 Owners included in Index)

Financial Data: Fiscal Year End:12/05   Latest Annual Data: 12/31/2006

Year	Sales	Net Income
2006	$738,050,000	$70,344,000
2005	$575,042,000	$53,559,000
2004	$454,186,000	$6,084,000

Curr. Assets:	$376,520,000	**Curr. Liab.:**	$170,266,000		
Plant, Equip.:	$125,149,000	**Total Liab.:**	$304,716,000	**Indic. Yr. Divd.:**	$0.200
Total Assets:	$600,712,000	**Net Worth:**	$295,996,000	**Debt/ Equity:**	0.2981

Buenaventura Mining Co Inc

Carlos Villaran 790, Santa Catalina, La Victoria, Lima; ; *http://* www.buenaventura.com; *Email:* recursos@buenaventura.com.pe

General - Incorporation	Peru	Stock - Price on:12/24/2007	$36.61
Employees	2,487	Stock Exchange	NYSE
Auditor	Dongo-soria Gaveglio Y Asociados	Ticker Symbol	NA
Stk Agt.	Bank of New York	Outstanding Shares	127,220,000
Counsel	NA	E.P.S.	$2.66
DUNS No.	NA	Shareholders	NA

Business: The group's principal activities are exploration, extraction, concentration and marketing of polymetallic minerals. It operates 3 mining units located in Julcani, Uchuchacua and Orcopampa in Peru and has control in 4 Peruvian mining companies in Colquijirca, Antapite, Ishihuinca, Shila and Paula. Other activities include transmission of electric energy and provision of engineering services related with the mining industry.

Primary SIC and add'l.: 1041 1044 1031 1021

CIK No: 0001013131

Subsidiaries: Buenaventura Ingenieros S.A., Compaa de Minas Buenaventura S.A.A.

Officers: Roque Benavides/Dir., CEO, Pres., Francois Muths/56/Operations VP, Raul Benavides/VP, Business Development Officer, Carlos E. Galvez/CFO, VP, Cesar Vidal/VP, Chief Explorations Officer, Raul Benavides Ganoza/52/VP - Business Development, Jose Miguel Morales/62/General Counsel, Carlos Humberto Rodriguez/63/Controller, Mario Santillan/VP, COO, Humberto Rodriguez/Controller, Daniel Dominguez/Contact - Investor Relation

Directors: Roque Benavides/Dir., CEO, Pres., Alberto Benavides/87/Chmn., German Suarez Chavez/Dir., Luis Coleridge/Dir., Felipe Ortiz De Zevallos/Dir., Norman Anderson/Dir., Aubrey Laurence Paverd/Dir.

Owners: Insiders/18.91%, AFP, Prima/3.41%, AFP, Integra/4.65%, Fidelity Management & Research/3.54%, Fidelity Low Priced Stock Fund/2.50%, AFP Horizonte/3.37%, Blackrock Investment Management (UK) Ltd./7.36%, Merrill Lynch IIF-World Gold Fund/3.83%, Cia Minera Condesa S.A/7.70%

Financial Data: Fiscal Year End:12/31   Latest Annual Data: 6/27/2006

Year	Sales	Net Income
2006	$344,416,000	$274,259,000
2005	NA	NA
2004	$336,828,000	$209,769,000

Curr. Assets:	$204,321,000	**Curr. Liab.:**	$131,671,000	**P/E Ratio:**	8.66
Plant, Equip.:	$170,003,000	**Total Liab.:**	$388,164,000	**Indic. Yr. Divd.:**	$0.710
Total Assets:	$1,247,841,000	**Net Worth:**	$836,288,000	**Debt/ Equity:**	NA

Buffalo Gold Ltd

24th Fl., 1111 W. Georgia St., Vancouver, BC, V6E 4M3; *PH:* 1-604-685-5492; *http://* www.buffalogold.ca

General - Incorporation	AB	Stock - Price on:12/24/2007	$0.96
Employees	NA	Stock Exchange	OTC
Auditor	Davidson & Company LLP	Ticker Symbol	BYBUF
Stk Agt.	British Controlled Oilfields	Outstanding Shares	NA
Counsel	Miller Thomson LLP	E.P.S	NA
DUNS No.	NA	Shareholders	NA

Business: The group operates from the United States and Canada. In the year 2006, the group acquired Gold Finance and Exploration Pty. Ltd.

Primary SIC and add'l.: 1400

CIK No: 0001090053

Officers: Damien Reynolds/Executive Chmn., CEO, Brian McEwen/CEO, Pres., Mark Dugmore/VP - Corporate Development, Simon Anderson/46/Sec., CFO, Greg Moseley/65/VP - Exploration, Stephen E. Flechner/64/VP, General Counsel, Darryn Hedger/Exploration Mgr. - Australia

Directors: Damien Reynolds/Executive Chmn., CEO, Douglas S. Turnbull/Dir., James G. Stewart/Dir., James Walchuck/Dir., Jeremy Richards/Member - Advisory Board, Thomas A. Allen/Member - Advisory Board, Hein Poulus/Member - Advisory Board

Owners: James Walchuk, Mark Dugmore/1.20%, Damien Reynolds/2.20%, Insiders/6.60%, Douglas Turnbull, Simon Anderson, Brian McEwen, J. G. Stewart/1.20%

Financial Data: Fiscal Year End:12/31   Latest Annual Data: 12/31/2006

Year	Sales	Net Income
2006	NA	-$11,984,000
2005	NA	-$1,201,000
2004	NA	-$67,000

Curr. Assets:	$17,585,000	**Curr. Liab.:**	$786,000	**P/E Ratio:**	425.00
Plant, Equip.:	$7,071,000	**Total Liab.:**	$2,385,000	**Indic. Yr. Divd.:**	NA
Total Assets:	$24,732,000	**Net Worth:**	$22,347,000	**Debt/ Equity:**	NA

Buffalo Wild Wings

1600 Utica Ave. S, Ste. 700, Minneapolis, MN, 55416; *PH:* 1-952-593-9943; *Fax:* 1-952-593-9787; *http://* buffalowildwings.com

General - Incorporation	MN	Stock - Price on:12/24/2007	$44.26
Employees	1,113	Stock Exchange	NDQ
Auditor	KPMG LLP	Ticker Symbol	BWLD
Stk Agt.	Continental Stock Transfer & Trust Co	Outstanding Shares	17,540,000
Counsel	NA	E.P.S	$1.15
DUNS No.	NA	Shareholders	NA

Business: The group's principal activity is to own, operate and franchise restaurants. The restaurants feature boldly flavored, made-to-order menu items including buffalo, New York-style chicken wings spun in one of the group's 12 signature sauces. In addition to fresh chicken wings, the menu also features specialty hamburgers and sandwiches, buffalito soft tacos, finger foods and salads. The restaurants also feature a full bar including approximately 20 domestic and imported beers on tap, bottled beer, wine and liquor. The guests have the option of watching various sporting events or other popular programs on the projection screens or up to 40 additional televisions, playing national trivia network or playing video games. As of 28-Dec-2003, the group owned and operated 84 restaurants and franchised 161 restaurants under the name buffalo wild wings grill & bar.

Primary SIC and add'l.: 6794 5812

CIK No: 0001062449

Subsidiaries: Blazin Wings, Inc, Buffalo Wild Wings International, Inc, Real Wing, Inc.

Officers: Sally J. Smith/CEO, Pres./$1,672,274.00, Judith A. Shoulak/Sr. VP - Operations/$620,360.00, Lee Sanders/55/Sr. VP - Development, Franchising, Linda G. Traylor/Sr. VP - Human Resources, Craig W. Donoghue/46/Sr. VP - Information Systems, Mary J. Twinem/Exec. VP, CFO, Treasurer/$883,346.00, James M. Schmidt/Sr. VP, General Counsel, Sec./$578,266.00, Kathleen M. Benning/Sr. VP - Marketing, Brand Development

Directors: Kenneth H. Dahlberg/90/Chmn., Robert W. MacDonald/Dir., Oliver J. Maggard/Dir., Dale M. Applequist/Dir., Warren E. Mack/Dir., James Damian/Dir., Michael P. Johnson/Dir.

Owners: Oliver J. Maggard, Warren E. Mack, James M. Schmidt, Sally J. Smith/1.20%, Judith A. Shoulak, Tiger Consumer Management, LLC/5.60%, Carefree Capital, Inc./6.20%, Kenneth H. Dahlberg/9.70%, Insiders/13.50%, Lee E. Sanders, Robert W. MacDonald, FMR Corp./5.50%, Michael P. Johnson, Mary J. Twinem, Dale M. Applequist *(16 Owners included in Index)*

Financial Data: ***Fiscal Year End:***12/31 ***Latest Annual Data:*** 12/31/2006

Year	Sales	Net Income
2006	$278,183,000	$16,273,000
2005	$209,700,000	$8,880,000
2004	$171,048,000	$7,201,000

Curr. Assets:	$74,950,000	***Curr. Liab.:***	$25,780,000	***P/E Ratio:***	39.87
Plant, Equip.:	$78,137,000	***Total Liab.:***	$44,967,000	***Indic. Yr. Divd.:***	NA
Total Assets:	$161,183,000	***Net Worth:***	$116,216,000	***Debt/ Equity:***	0.0294

Build-A-Bear Workshop Inc

1954 Innerbelt Business Ctr. Dr., St. Louis, MO, 63114; ***PH:*** 1-314-423-8000; ***Fax:*** 1-314-423-8188; ***http://*** www.buildabear.com; ***Email:*** Guest.Services@buildabear.com

General - Incorporation	DE	***Stock***- Price on:12/24/2007	$22.9766
Employees	1,200	Stock Exchange	NYSE
Auditor	KPMG LLP	Ticker Symbol	BBW
Stk Agt	Mellon Investor Services LLC	Outstanding Shares	20,610,000
Counsel	NA	E.P.S.	$1.37
DUNS No.	NA	Shareholders	NA

Business: The groups principle activity is to provide clothing, shoes and accessories for the stuffed animals. The group also provides clothing for children and adults. The group operates through three segments namely retail, international franchising, and licensing and entertainment. In the year 2006, the group acquired Amsbra Limited and Bear Factory Limited. The group operates from the United States, Japan, Australia, Denmark, Taiwan, Canada, United Kingdom and Ireland. The group's quarterly revenue for September 2007 was 109.77 millions of USD.

Primary SIC and add'l.: 3942 5945 3944

CIK No: 0001113809

Subsidiaries: Amsbra Limited, Build-A-Bear Entertainment, LLC, Build-A-Bear Retail Management, Inc., Build-A-Bear Workshop Canada Ltd., Build-A-Bear Workshop France, SAS, Build-A-Bear Workshop Franchise Holdings, Inc., Build-A-Bear Workshop Ireland Limited, Build-A-Bear Workshop UK Holdings Limited, Hobbies and Models Limited, The Bear Factory Limited

Officers: Maxine Clark/Founder, Chmn., CEO/$965,141.00, Paul Bundonis/Chief Workshop Officer, Dave Finnegan/CIO, Tina Klocke/CFO, Treasurer, Sec./$351,263.00, Teresa Kroll/Chief Marketing Officer/$303,963.00, Scott Seay/COO, Pres./$394,848.00

Directors: Maxine Clark/Founder, Chmn., CEO, Barney Ebsworth/Dir. Emeritus, Mary Lou Fiala/Dir., James Gould/Dir., Louis Mucci/Dir., Coleman Peterson/Dir., William Reisler/Dir., Joan Ryan/Dir.

Owners: Tina Klocke/1.00%, Maxine Clark/15.20%, Buckingham Capital Management Incorporated/8.40%, Scott Seay, James M. Gould, Searock Capital Management, L.L.C./5.00%, William Reisler, Independence Investments, L.L.C./5.80%, S.A.C. Capital Advisors, L.L.C/5.00%, Coleman Peterson, Joan Ryan, Louis Mucci, Paul Bundonis, Teresa Kroll, Mary Lou Fiala *(18 Owners included in Index)*

Financial Data: ***Fiscal Year End:***12/30 ***Latest Annual Data:*** 12/30/2006

Year	Sales	Net Income
2006	$437,072,000	$29,490,000
2005	$361,809,000	$27,314,000

Curr. Assets:	$147,807,000	***Curr. Liab.:***	$81,161,000	***P/E Ratio:***	16.07
Plant, Equip.:	$89,973,000	***Total Liab.:***	$115,751,000	***Indic. Yr. Divd.:***	NA
Total Assets:	$246,108,000	***Net Worth:***	$130,357,000	***Debt/ Equity:***	NA

Builders FirstSource Inc

2001 Bryan St., Ste. 1600, Dallas, TX, 75201; ***PH:*** 1-214-880-3500; ***Fax:*** 1-214-880-3599; ***http://*** www.buildersfirstsource.com; ***Email:*** info@buildersfirstsource.com

General - Incorporation	DE	***Stock***- Price on:12/24/2007	$16.39
Employees	5,900	Stock Exchange	NDQ
Auditor	PricewaterhouseCoopers LLP	Ticker Symbol	BLDR
Stk Agt	LaSalle Bank N.A	Outstanding Shares	35,460,000
Counsel	NA	E.P.S.	$0.01
DUNS No.	NA	Shareholders	NA

Business: The groups principle activities include supplying and manufacturing structural and related building products. The products of the group include prefabricated components, windows and doors, lumber and lumber sheet goods, millwork and, other building products and services. Customers served by the group include national homebuilders, regional homebuilders, and local builders. In the year 2006, the grouop acquired Freeport Truss Company and Waid Home Center, Inc. Specific customers of the group include Centex Corporation, D.R. Horton, Inc., Hovnanian Enterprises, Inc., Pulte Homes, Inc., and The Ryland Group, Inc. The group operates from Atlantic, Southeast and Central. The group's quarterly revenue for September 2007 was 413.92 millions of USD.

Primary SIC and add'l.: 3251 5032 5231 2499 5031 5033 5211 5039 3275 3585 3088

CIK No: 0001316835

Subsidiaries: BFS IP, LLC, BFS Texas, LLC, BFS, LLC, Builders FirstSource Atlantic Group, LLC, Builders FirstSource Colorado Group, LLC, Builders FirstSource Colorado, LLC, Builders FirstSource Dallas, LLC, Builders FirstSource Florida Design Center, LLC, Builders FirstSource Florida, LLC, Builders FirstSource Intellectual Property, L.P., Builders FirstSource MBS, LLC, Builders FirstSource Northeast Group, LLC, Builders FirstSource Raleigh, LLC, Builders FirstSource South Texas, L.P., Builders FirstSource Texas GenPar, LLC 23 Subsidiaries included in the Index

Officers: Floyd F. Sherman/Dir., CEO, Kevin P. O'Meara/COO, Pres., Charles L. Horn/CFO, Sr. VP, Donald F. McAleenan/Sr. VP, General Counsel, Corp. Sec., Morris E. Tolly/Sr. VP - Operations, Frederick B. Schenkel/VP - Manufacturing

Directors: Floyd F. Sherman/Dir., CEO, Paul S. Levy/Chmn., David A. Barr/Dir., Cleveland A. Christophe/Dir., Ramsey A. Frank/Dir., Michael Graff/Dir., Robert C. Griffin/Dir., Kevin J. Kruse/Dir., Brett N. Milgrim/Dir., Craig Steinke/Dir.

Owners: Paul S. Levy, Warburg Pincus Private Equity IX, L.P., Frederick B. Schenkel, Cleveland A. Christophe, Kevin J. Kruse, Barclays Global FundAdvisors, Robert C. Griffin, Floyd F. Sherman, Donald F. McAleenan, Michael Graff, Kevin P. OMeara, JLL Partners FundV, L.P., Insiders, Charles L. Horn, David A. Barr *(16 Owners included in Index)*

Financial Data: ***Fiscal Year End:***12/31 ***Latest Annual Data:*** 12/31/2006

Year	Sales	Net Income
2006	$2,239,454,000	$68,893,000
2005	$2,337,757,000	$48,628,000
2004	$2,058,047,000	$51,581,000

Curr. Assets:	$440,311,000	***Curr. Liab.:***	$144,715,000	***P/E Ratio:***	11.88
Plant, Equip.:	$109,777,000	***Total Liab.:***	$491,651,000	***Indic. Yr. Divd.:***	NA
Total Assets:	$748,515,000	***Net Worth:***	$256,864,000	***Debt/ Equity:***	1.2296

Building Materials Corp of America

1361 Alps Rd., Wayne, NJ, 07470; ***PH:*** 1-973-628-3000; ***Fax:*** 1-973-628-3865; ***http://*** www.gaf.com

General - Incorporation	DE	***Stock***- Price on:12/24/2007	NA
Employees	NA	Stock Exchange	NA
Auditor	Ernst & Young, LLP	Ticker Symbol	NA
Stk Agt	NA	Outstanding Shares	NA
Counsel	NA	E.P.S.	NA
DUNS No.	61-549-9803	Shareholders	NA

Business: The group's principal activity is to manufacture a broad line of asphalt and polymer based roofing products and accessories for the residential and commercial roofing markets. The group also manufactures specialty building products and accessories for the professional and do-it-yourself remodeling and residential construction industries. The group's operations are conducted through three business segments: residential roofing, commercial roofing and specialty building products. Residential roofing segment offers timberline(R) series and the sovereign(R) series. Commercial roofing segment provides a full line of modified bitumen and asphalt built-up roofing products, thermoplastic polyolefin products, liquid applied membrane systems and roofing accessories for use in the application of commercial roofing systems.

Primary SIC and add'l.: 2952

CIK No: 0000927314

Subsidiaries: BMCA Insulation Products Inc., BMCA Quakertown Inc., Building Materials Investment Corporation, Building Materials Manufacturing Corporation, Ductwork Manufacturing Corporation, GAF Leatherback Corp., GAF Materials Corporation (Canada), GAF Premium Products Inc., GAF Real Properties,Inc., GAFTECH Corporation, HBP Acquisition LLC, LL Building Products Inc., Pequannock Valley Claim Service Company,Inc., South Ponca Realty Corp., Wind Gap Real Property Acquisition Corp

Officers: Robert B. Tafaro/57/Dir., CEO, Pres., Kenneth E. Walton/51/Dir., Sr. VP - Operations, John F. Rebele/52/Dir., Sr. VP, CFO, Chief Administrative Officer, David A. Harrison/51/Dir., Chief Marketing Officer, Charles M. Gruber/49/VP - Supply Chain, Douglas Greeff/50/Sr. VP

Directors: Robert B. Tafaro/57/Dir., CEO, Pres., Kenneth E. Walton/51/Dir., Sr. VP - Operations, John F. Rebele/52/Dir., Sr. VP, CFO, Chief Administrative Officer, David A. Harrison/51/Dir., Chief Marketing Officer

Owners: Samuel J. Heyman/100.00%

Building Materials Holding Corp

4 Embarcadero Ctr., Ste. 3200, San Francisco, CA, 94111; ***PH:*** 1-415-627-9100; ***Fax:*** 1-415-627-9119; ***http://*** www.bmhc.com; ***Email:*** info@bmhc.com

General - Incorporation	DE	***Stock***- Price on:12/24/2007	$14.618
Employees	17,000	Stock Exchange	NYSE
Auditor	KPMG LLP	Ticker Symbol	BLG
Stk Agt	Wells Fargo Bank, N.A.	Outstanding Shares	NA
Counsel	Gibson, Dunn & Crutcher LLP	E.P.S.	$0.78
DUNS No.	79-379-1005	Shareholders	NA

Business: The groups principle activity is to provide residential construction services and building products to professional homebuilders and contractors. The group operates through two business segments namely SelectBuild and BMC West. The group operates from United States.

Primary SIC and add'l.: 5211 5231

CIK No: 0001046356

Subsidiaries: 70th and Northern Avenues Holdings, LLC, A-1 Building Components, LLC, BBD Construction, LP, BBP Commercial Company, BBP Concrete Company, BBP Construction Company, BMC Insurance, Inc., BMC Realty, Inc., BMC West Corporation, BMC West Corporation SouthCentral, BMCW SouthCentral, LP, BMCW, LLC, C Construction, Inc., FSC Construction, LLC, HnR Framing Systems, Inc. 31 Subsidiaries included in the Index

Officers: Robert E. Mellor/Chmn., CEO, Pres./$6,236,182.00, Stanley M. Wilson/CEO, Sr. VP, Pres. - BMC West/$2,199,728.00, Paul S. Street/Sr. VP, Chief Administrative Officer, General Counsel, Corp. Sec./$1,676,489.00, Steven H. Pearson/Sr. VP - Human Resources, William M. Smartt/CFO, Sr. VP/$2,201,114.00, Michael D. Mahre/Sr. VP - Corporate Development/$2,696,251.00, Mark R. Kailer/VP, Treasurer, Jeffrey F. Lucchesi/CIO, Sr. VP, Eric R. Beem/VP, Controller, John D. Fa/VP - Real Estate, Terrill F. Rust/VP - Application Services

Directors: Robert E. Mellor/Chmn., CEO, Pres., Eric S. Belsky/46/Dir., Peter S. O'Neill/Dir., Sara L. Beckman/50/Dir., Scott R. Morrison/67/Dir., Norman J. Metcalfe/64/Dir., Richard G. Reiten/67/Dir., James K. Jennings/65/Dir., David M. Moffett/55/Dir., Norman R. Walker/63/Dir.

Owners: Robert E. Mellor/4.40%, Insiders/7.30%, Michael D. Mahre, Paul S. Street, Stanley M. Wilson, William M. Smartt, FMR Corp/14.90%, David M. Moffett, Richard G. Reiten, James K. Jennings, Peter S. ONeill, Eric S. Belsky, Sara L. Beckman, Barclays Global Investors, NA/8.20%, Scott R. Morrison *(16 Owners included in Index)*

Financial Data: Fiscal Year End:12/31 **Latest Annual Data:** 12/31/2006

Year	Sales	Net Income
2006	$3,245,169,000	$102,074,000
2005	$2,912,160,000	$129,507,000
2004	$2,091,025,000	$53,910,000

Curr. Assets:	$566,411,000	Curr. Liab.:	$323,611,000		
Plant, Equip.:	$259,491,000	Total Liab.:	$749,141,000	Indic. Yr. Divd.:	$0.400
Total Assets:	$1,328,911,000	Net Worth:	$572,629,000	Debt/ Equity:	0.7534

Bull Run Corp GA

546 E Main St., Lexington, KY, 40508; *PH:* 1-859-226-4678; *Fax:* 1-859-226-4308; *http://* www.bullruncorp.com

General - Incorporation	GA	Stock- Price on:12/24/2007	$9.34
Employees	666	Stock Exchange	NA
Auditor	PricewaterhouseCoopers LLP	Ticker Symbol	NA
Stk Agt	Computershare Trust Co	Outstanding Shares	5,450,000
Counsel	NA	E.P.S.	-$5.69
DUNS No.	11-974-9000	Shareholders	NA

Business: The group's principal activity is to provide media and marketing services to universities, athletic conferences and various associations. The group though its wholly owned subsidiary Host Communications Inc markets and operates amateur participatory sporting events. The group operates through four divisions. Collegiate Marketing and Production Services provides sports and marketing services and produces publications to universities and conferences in the national collegiate athletic association. Affinity Events produces and manages large participatory sporting events throughout United States and Canada. Affinity Management Services provides management services including association management, financial reporting, lobbying and membership activities to athletic associations. Consulting provides consulting services in connection with acquisitions, dispositions and acquisition financing. In Aug 2003, the group disposed of Datasouth Computer Corporation.

Primary SIC and add'l.: 8748 8742 8743 8699

CIK No: 0000319697

Subsidiaries: BR Holding, Inc., Capital Sports Properties, Inc., Datasouth Computer Corporation, Hoop-It-Up International, Inc., Host Communications, Inc., USA International, S.A.R.L., a corporation organized under the laws of France and a subsidiary of

Financial Data: Fiscal Year End:08/31 **Latest Annual Data:** 6/30/2006

Year	Sales	Net Income
2006	$54,379,000	$4,396,000
2005	$53,823,000	$4,417,000

Curr. Assets:	$15,032,000	Curr. Liab.:	$24,271,000	P/E Ratio:	10.15
Plant, Equip.:	$13,050,000	Total Liab.:	$144,979,000	Indic. Yr. Divd.:	NA
Total Assets:	$163,575,000	Net Worth:	-$2,714,000	Debt/ Equity:	NA

Bullion River Gold Corp

3500 Lakeside Ct., Ste. 200, Reno, NV, 89509; *PH:* 1-775-324-4881; *Fax:* 1-775-324-7893; *http://* www.bullionriver.com; *Email:* info@bullionrivergold.com

General - Incorporation	NV	Stock- Price on:12/24/2007	$0.58
Employees	121	Stock Exchange	OTC
Auditor	HJ & Assoc., LLC	Ticker Symbol	BLRV
Stk Agt	Pacific Stock Transfer Company	Outstanding Shares	63,250,000
Counsel	NA	E.P.S.	-$0.34
DUNS No.	NA	Shareholders	NA

Business: The groups principle activity is to exploration of minerals. The group operates from the United States and Canada. The groups quarterly revenue for September 2007 was 1.23 millions of USD.

Primary SIC and add'l.: 1081

CIK No: 0001168458

Subsidiaries: Antone Canyon Mining Corp., Cimarron Mining Corp, Corcoran Canyon Mining Corp., North Fork (Nevada) Mining Corp, Thomas Creek Mining Corp

Officers: Peter M. Kuhn/CEO, Chief Accounting Officer, Pres., Nancy B. Huber/50/CFO, Glenn C. Blachford/VP - Engineering

Directors: Susan Jeffs/Dir., Lester C. Knight/47/Dir.

Owners: Insiders/3.24%, Peter M. Kuhn/2.04%, Glenn Blachford, Elton Participation Group/20.08%, Nancy B. Huber, Blue Velvet Capital/9.84%, Lester Knight, Susan Jeffs

Financial Data: Fiscal Year End:12/31 **Latest Annual Data:** 12/31/2006

Year	Sales	Net Income
2006	$804,000	-$15,537,000
2005	NA	-$5,420,000
2004	NA	-$2,965,000

Curr. Assets:	$796,000	Curr. Liab.:	$2,490,000		
Plant, Equip.:	$2,557,000	Total Liab.:	$5,014,000	Indic. Yr. Divd.:	NA
Total Assets:	$3,875,000	Net Worth:	-$1,139,000	Debt/ Equity:	NA

Bunge Ltd

50 Main St., 6th Fl., White Plains, NY, 10606; *PH:* 1-914-684-2800; *Fax:* 1-914-684-3499; *http://* www.bunge.com; *Email:* bge.comm@bunge.com

General - Incorporation	Bermuda	Stock- Price on:12/24/2007	$81.28
Employees	22,524	Stock Exchange	NYSE
Auditor	Deloitte & Touche LLP	Ticker Symbol	BG
Stk Agt	Mellon Investor Services LLC	Outstanding Shares	120,730,000
Counsel	NA	E.P.S.	$4.89
DUNS No.	NA	Shareholders	NA

Business: The group's principal activity is to produce and sell agricultural and food products. It operates through four segments: agribusiness, fertilizer, edible oil products and milling products. The agribusiness segment purchases, sells and processes grains and oilseeds. The operations of the fertilizer division include the mining of raw materials to the sale of mixed fertilizer formulas. The edible oil products

division manufactures and markets products derived from vegetable oils such as shortenings, margarine, mayonnaise and other products. The milling products segment manufactures and markets products derived from wheat and corn. The group operates in the United States, Brazil, Canada, Argentina, Asia, Europe and other countries.

Primary SIC and add'l.: 2875 0115 0119 2076 5461

CIK No: 0001144519

Subsidiaries: Afrique Initiatives, AGRI-Bunge, LLC, Agrisat Solucoes Integradas Ltda., Agritrade S.A., Agroproductos Bunge, S.A. de C.V., Almacen Terminal Santana, C.A., Amoniasul Servicos de Refrigeracao Industrial Ltda., Batavia Leasing Co., Biodiesel Bilbao S.L., Black Sea Industries Limited, Brea Commodities Limited, Brunello Ltd., Bunge (Thailand) Ltd., Bunge Agribusiness (M) Sdn. Bhd., Bunge Agribusiness Philippines Inc. 170 Subsidiaries included in the Index

Officers: Raul Padilla/CEO - Bunge Argentina, Andrew J. Burke/Co - CEO - Bunge Global Agribusiness, Christopher White/CEO - Bunge Asia, Alberto Weisser/Chmn., CEO/$7,240,975.00, Sergio Roberto Waldrich/CEO - Bunge Alimentos, Drew Burke/Co - CEO - Bunge Global Agribusiness/$1,283,757.00, Carl Hausmann/CEO - Bunge North America, Mario Barbosa Neto/CEO - Bunge Fertilizantes, Jean-Louis Gourbin/CEO - Bunge Europe, Archie Gwathmey/Co - CEO - Bunge Global Agribusiness/$4,172,113.00, Flavio Sa Carvalho/Chief Personnel Officer, James MacDonald/Sec., Joao Fernando Kfouri/MD - Food Products/$1,969,538.00, Jacqualyn Fouse/CFO

Directors: Alberto Weisser/Chmn., CEO, Jorge Born/Dep. Chmn., Bernard De La Tour D'Auvergne Lauraguais/Dir., Michael H. Bulkin/Dir., Patrick L. Lupo/Dir., Enrique H. Boilini/Dir., William Engels/Dir., Larry G. Pillard/Dir., Ernest G. Bachrach/Dir., Paul H. Hatfield/Dir., Octavio Caraballo/Dir., Francis Coppinger/Dir.

Owners: Jorge Born, Archibald Gwathmey, Flvio S Carvalho, William Wells, Andrew J. Burke, Wellington Management Company, LLP/12.49%, Patrick L. Lupo, Bernard de La Tour dAuvergne Lauraguais, Octavio Caraballo, Francis Coppinger, Capital Research and Management Company/11.33%, William Engels, Insiders/2.40%, Alberto Weisser, Enrique H. Boilini *(20 Owners included in Index)*

Financial Data: Fiscal Year End:12/31 **Latest Annual Data:** 12/31/2006

Year	Sales	Net Income
2006	$26,274,000,000	$521,000,000
2005	$24,275,000,000	$530,000,000
2004	$25,168,000,000	$469,000,000

Curr. Assets:	$8,393,000,000	Curr. Liab.:	$4,515,000,000	P/E Ratio:	21.17
Plant, Equip.:	$3,446,000,000	Total Liab.:	$8,269,000,000	Indic. Yr. Divd.:	$0.680
Total Assets:	$14,347,000,000	Net Worth:	$5,668,000,000	Debt/ Equity:	0.5840

Bunzl Plc

110 Pk. St., London, W1K 6NX; *PH:* 44-2074954950; *http://* www.bunzl.com

General - Incorporation	UK	Stock- Price on:12/24/2007	NA
Employees	10,526	Stock Exchange	NA
Auditor	KPMG Audit Plc	Ticker Symbol	NA
Stk Agt	Computershare Investor Services LLC	Outstanding Shares	NA
Counsel	NA	E.P.S.	NA
DUNS No.	NA	Shareholders	NA

Business: The group's principal activities are carried out through two divisions: outsourcing services: the supplier of a range of products including outsourced food packaging, disposable supplies and cleaning and safety products for supermarkets, redistributors, caterers, food processors, hotels, contract cleaners, non-food retail and other users. Operating across North America, Europe and australasia, filtrona: the supplier of outsourced cigarette filters, ink reservoirs and other bonded fibre products, protection and finishing products, self-adhesive tear tapes and certain security products. It is also a extruder of custom plastic profiles. In 2003, the group acquired enterprise, fibertec, multiline, prolix packaging and o'mahony.

Primary SIC and add'l.: 3089 2676 2679 3999 5111 2656

CIK No: 0001072397

Subsidiaries: NAVTEQ Austria GmbH, Navteq B.v., NAVTEQ Canada Inc., NAVTEQ International, LLC, NAVTEQ Kabushiki Kaisha, Navteq N.v./s.a., NAVTEQ North America, LLC, NAVTEQ Srl

Officers: Pat Larmon/55/Executive Dir., Pres., CEO - North America, Anthony Habgood/61/Chmn., Chief Executive, Michael Roney/53/Non Exec. Dir., Chief Executive, Brian May/43/Dir., Dir. - Finance, P. N. Hussey/Sec.

Directors: Pat Larmon/55/Executive Dir., Pres., CEO - North America, Anthony Habgood/61/Chmn., Chief Executive, Ulrich Wolters/65/Non Exec. Dir., Jeff Harris/59/Non Exec. Dir., Michael Roney/53/Non Exec. Dir., Chief Executive, Charles Banks/67/Non Exec. Dir., Peter Johnson/60/Non Exec. Dir., Brian May/43/Dir., Dir. - Finance

Curr. Assets:	$1,376,812,000	Curr. Liab.:	$1,055,195,000		
Plant, Equip.:	$120,112,000	Total Liab.:	$1,959,131,000	Indic. Yr. Divd.:	NA
Total Assets:	$2,997,462,000	Net Worth:	$1,038,331,000	Debt/ Equity:	NA

Bureau of National Affairs Inc

9435 Key W Ave., Rockville, MD, 20850; *PH:* 1-800-372-1033; *http://* www.bna.com; *Email:* customercare@bna.com

General - Incorporation	DE	Stock- Price on:12/24/2007	NA
Employees	NA	Stock Exchange	NA
Auditor	KPMG LLP	Ticker Symbol	NA
Stk Agt	NA	Outstanding Shares	NA
Counsel	NA	E.P.S.	NA
DUNS No.	00-324-4084	Shareholders	NA

Business: The group's principal activities are to publish and provide specialized legal, regulatory and general business advisory information to business, professional and academic users. The group prepares, publishes and markets subscription information products in print, compact disc, online formats, books, pamphlets and research reports. The customers include lawyers, accountants, labor unions, trade associations, educational institutions, government agencies and libraries. The group operates primarily in the publishing, printing, and software industries. Publishing segment undertakes production and marketing of information products in print and electronic form. Printing operations consist of printing services to internal and outside customers. Software operations consist of the production and marketing of software programs.

Primary SIC and add'l.: 7375 2731 2732 2741

CIK No: 0000015393

Subsidiaries: BNA Holdings Inc., BNA International Inc., BNA Washington Inc., Institute of Management and Administration, Inc., Kennedy Information, Inc., STF Services Corporation, Tax Management Inc., The McArdle Printing Co., Inc.

Officers: Paul N. Wojcik/Chmn., CEO/$638,914.00, Gregory C. McCaffery/COO, Pres./$494,339.00, George Korphage/61/VP/$333,343.00, Cynthia Bolbach/VP, Corp. Sec., Eunice Bumgardner/VP, General Counsel/$237,917.00, Carol Clark/VP - Resource Management/$329,260.00, Elizabeth Brown/Pres. - BNA Washington Inc, Alan Edmunds/Pres. - BNA International Inc, Joseph Bremner/Pres. - BNA Washington Inc, Lisa Arsenault/Pres. - Mcardle Printing Co, Inc, Michael Smith/Pres. - STF Services Corp, Paul A. Blakely/50/Dir., Mgr. - Financial Planning, Analysis, Assist. Treasurer, Margaret Hullinger/43/Publisher, Jonathan Newcomb/61/Dir., Sr. Advisor, Robert P. Ambrosini/CFO, VP *(18 Officers included in Index)*

Directors: Paul N. Wojcik/Chmn., CEO, Leonard L. Silverstein/Chmn. - Advisory Board, Gerald H. Sherman/Dep. Chmn. - Advisory Board, Byrle M. Abbin/Member - Advisory Board, Daniel W. Toohey/68/Dir., Robert Anthoine/Member - Advisory Board, Ronal D. Aucutt/Member - Advisory Board, Kathleen Ford Bay/Member - Advisory Board, Dennis I. Belcher/Member - Advisory Board, Lawrence Brody/Member - Advisory Board, Beverly R. Budin/Member - Advisory Board, Christopher P. Cline/Member - Advisory Board, Richard B. Covey/Member - Advisory Board, Robert T. Danforth/Member - Advisory Board, Julia B. Fisher/Member - Advisory Board *(58 Directors included in Index)*

Owners: Paul A. Blakely/0.48%, Paul N. Wojcik/1.33%, Margaret S. Hullinger/0.32%, Robert L. Velte/0.38%, Gregory C. McCaffery/0.86%, Darren P. McKewen/0.12%, George J. Korphage/2.19%, Cynthia J. Bolbach/0.31%, Sandra C. Degler/3.06%, Neil R. Froemming/1.03%, Eunice Lin Bumgardner/0.43%

Burger King Holdings Inc

5505 Blue Lagoon Dr., Miami, FL, 33126; ***PH:*** 1-305-378-3000; ***Fax:*** 1-305-378-7262; ***http://*** www.burgerking.com

General		***Stock***	
Incorporation	DE	Price on:12/24/2007	$26.65
Employees	37,000	Stock Exchange	NYSE
Auditor	KPMG LLP	Ticker Symbol	BKC
Stk Agt	Bank of New York	Outstanding Shares	134,890,000
Counsel	NA	E.P.S	NA
DUNS No.	NA	Shareholders	NA

Business: The groups principle activity is to operate quick service restaurant. The group operates through three segments namely, United States and Canada, Europe, Middle East and Africa and Asia Pacific (EMEA/APAC), and Latin America. The group operates from the United States, Canada and Latin America. The group's total revenue in the year 2007 was 2,234.00 millions of USD.

Primary SIC and add'l.: 5812

CIK No: 0001352801

Subsidiaries: Administracion de Comidas Rapidas, S.A. de C.V., B.K. Services, Ltd., BK Acquisition, Inc., BK Asiapac, Pte. Ltd., BK Card Company, Inc., BK Grundstucksverwaltungs Beteiligungs GmbH, BK Grundstucksverwaltungs GmbH& Co. KG, Burger King (Gibraltar) Ltd., Burger King (Hong Kong) Limited, Burger King (Luxembourg) S.a r.l., Burger King (Shanghai) Commercial Consulting Co. Ltd., Burger King (Shanghai) Restaurant Company Ltd., Burger King (United Kingdom) Ltd., Burger King A.B, Burger King Asia Pacific P.T.E. Ltd. 62 Subsidiaries included in the Index

Officers: John W. Chidsey/46/Dir., CEO, Ben K. Wells/CFO, Treasurer, Christopher M. Anderson/41/Sr. VP, Controller, Anne Chwat/General Counsel, Corp. Sec., Chuck Fallon/Pres. - North America, Dave Gagnon/Sr. VP - Company Operations, James F. Hyatt/52/COO, Russell B. Klein/Pres. - Global Marketing Strategy, Innovation, Julio Ramirez/Exec. VP - Global Operations, Peter Robinson/Pres. - EMEA, Peter C. Smith/Chief Officer - Human Resources, Peter Tan/Pres. - Asia Pacific, Amy Wagner/Sr. VP - Investor Relations, Global Communications, Raj Rawal/CIO, Sr. VP, Charles M. Fallon/46/Pres. - North America

Directors: John W. Chidsey/46/Dir., CEO, Brian Thomas Swette/54/Non - Exec. Chmn., Brian Thomas/Chmn. - Burger King Brands, Inc, Andrew B. Balson/Dir., Ronald M. Dykes/61/Dir., Sanjeev K. Mehra/49/Dir., Stephen G. Pagliuca/53/Dir., Kneeland C. Youngblood/52/Dir., David Bonderman/Dir., Richard W. Boyce/54/Dir., David A. Brandon/Dir., Peter Raemin Formanek/65/Dir., Manuel A. Garcia/65/Dir., Adrian Jones/44/Dir.

Owners: David M. Brandon, Stephen G. Pagliuca, Kneeland C. Youngblood, Sanjeev K. Mehra, The Goldman Sachs Group, Inc., Insiders, Investment funds affiliated with Bain Capital Investors, LLC, Peter R. Formanek, Manuel A. Garcia, Ronald M. Dykes, Richard W. Boyce, Brian T. Swette, Adrian Jones, TPG BK Holdco LLC, AMVESCAP PLC AIM Advisors, Inc.

Curr. Assets:	$404,000,000	***Curr. Liab.:***	$434,000,000		
Plant, Equip.:	$879,000,000	***Total Liab.:***	$1,801,000,000	***Indic. Yr. Divd.:***	NA
Total Assets:	$2,517,000,000	***Net Worth:***	$716,000,000	***Debt/ Equity:***	NA

Burke & Herbert Bank & Trust Company

100 S Fairfax St., Alexandria, VA, 22314; ***PH:*** 1-703-549-6600; ***Fax:*** 1-703-548-5759; ***http://*** www.burkeandherbertbank.com

General		***Stock***	
Incorporation	VA	Price on:12/24/2007	$1485
Employees	NA	Stock Exchange	OTC
Auditor	NA	Ticker Symbol	BHRB
Stk Agt	NA	Outstanding Shares	NA
Counsel	NA	E.P.S	NA
DUNS No.	NA	Shareholders	NA

Business: The groups principle activity is to provide recruiting services. The groups service area includes the research and development, engineering, marketing, sales, information technology and manufacturing industries. The group operates from United States.

Primary SIC and add'l.: 6022

CIK No: 0001101250

Officers: Charles K. Collum/Chmn., CEO, Hunt E. Burke/Vice Chmn., COO, Pres., Taylor C.S. Burke/Dir., Sr. Exec. VP, Thomas A. Demik/VP, Erik J. Dorn/VP, Elizabeth V. Ellis/VP, Araba A. Brobbey/Assist. VP, Barbara A. Cupp/Assist. VP, Deborah L. Holley/VP, Anthony B. Riolo/VP, Criscella J. Ford/VP, Mary Anne Martins/VP, Ginny Kim/VP, Noble W. Rubenstein/Assist. VP, Trust Officer, Teresa M. Demarco/Assist. VP *(73 Officers included in Index)*

Directors: Charles K. Collum/Chmn., CEO, Hunt E. Burke/Vice Chmn., COO, Pres., Laing S. Hinson/Dir., David M. Burke/Dir., Bernard M. Fagelson/Dir., Julian F. Barnwell/Dir., Hugo A. Blankingship/Dir., Suzanne S. Brock/Dir., Taylor C.S. Burke/Dir., Sr. Exec. VP, Vernon N. Cockrell/Dir., Robert L. Fitton/Dir., Hugh R. Heishman/Dir., Charles F. Holden/Dir., Robert E. Lee/Dir., Louis B. Rodenberg/Dir.

Financial Data: Fiscal Year End:12/31 ***Latest Annual Data:*** 12/31/2002

Year	***Sales***	***Net Income***
2002	$63,623,000	$19,635,000
2001	$45,662,000	$10,451,000
2000	$56,441,000	$11,977,000

Curr. Assets:	$94,386,000	***Curr. Liab.:***	$963,215,000		
Plant, Equip.:	$19,651,000	***Total Liab.:***	$965,793,000	***Indic. Yr. Divd.:***	NA
Total Assets:	$1,078,776,000	***Net Worth:***	$112,983,000	***Debt/ Equity:***	0.0059

Burke Mills Inc

191 Sterling St., NW, Valdese, NC, 28690; ***PH:*** 1-828-874-6341; ***Fax:*** 1-828-879-7188; ***http://*** www.burkemills.com

General		***Stock***	
Incorporation	NC	Price on:12/24/2007	$0.42
Employees	157	Stock Exchange	OTC
Auditor	BDO Seidman, LLP	Ticker Symbol	BMLS
Stk Agt	Union National Bank	Outstanding Shares	2,740,000
Counsel	James, McElroy & Diehl	E.P.S	-$0.8
DUNS No.	00-315-9662	Shareholders	NA

Business: The group's principle activity is to texture, wind, dye, process and sell filament, novelty and spun yarns. The company is also engaged in the dyeing and processing of yarns for others on a commission basis. The principal markets served by the company are apparel, upholstery and industrial uses through the knitting and weaving industry. It markets its products throughout the United States, Caribbean basin, Mexico and Canada. It markets its products in Mexico, Central America and South America through its fifty-percent owned affiliate, fytek, s.a. De c.v. The group operates from United States.

Primary SIC and add'l.: 2282

CIK No: 0000015486

Officers: Humayun N. Shaikh/Chmn., Principal Executive Officer, Thomas I. Nail/Dir., COO, Pres., Principal Financial Officer

Directors: Humayun N. Shaikh/Chmn., Principal Executive Officer, Thomas I. Nail/Dir., COO, Pres., Principal Financial Officer, Richard F. Byers/Dir., Robert P. Huntley/Dir., William T. Dunn/Dir., Robert T. King/Dir., Aehsun Shaikh/Dir.

Financial Data: Fiscal Year End:12/31 ***Latest Annual Data:*** 12/30/2006

Year	***Sales***	***Net Income***
2006	$23,884,000	-$1,877,000
2005	$25,253,000	-$1,922,000

Curr. Assets:	$4,728,000	***Curr. Liab.:***	$1,630,000		
Plant, Equip.:	$4,759,000	***Total Liab.:***	$1,630,000	***Indic. Yr. Divd.:***	NA
Total Assets:	$9,504,000	***Net Worth:***	$7,874,000	***Debt/ Equity:***	NA

Burlington Coat Factory Warehouse Corp

1830 RtE 130, Burlington, NJ, 08016; ***PH:*** 1-609-387-7800; ***Fax:*** 1-609-387-7071; ***http://*** www.coat.com

General		***Stock***	
Incorporation	DE	Price on:12/24/2007	$16.1
Employees	NA	Stock Exchange	NYSE
Auditor	Deloitte & Touche LLP	Ticker Symbol	BCF
Stk Agt	Deloitte & Touche LLP	Outstanding Shares	NA
Counsel	NA	E.P.S	NA
DUNS No.	07-521-5400	Shareholders	NA

Business: The group's principal activity is to operate departmental stores that sell apparel and accessories for men, women and children. The group has two major product segments: apparel and home products. The apparel segment includes departments offering clothing items such as shoes, jewelry, perfumes and watches and apparel accessories for men, women and children. The home products segment includes departments offering linens, home furnishings, gifts, baby furniture and baby furnishings. Stores are operated under the names 'cohoes fashions', 'decelle' and 'luxury linens'. As of 31-Jul-2004, the group operated through 349 departmental stores across 42 states. During the fiscal year ended may 29, 2004, the company discontinued the operations of eight stores.

Primary SIC and add'l.: 5611 5632 5331

CIK No: 0000718916

Subsidiaries: Burlington Coat Factory, Burlington Coat Factory Direct Corporation, Burlington Coat Factory Realty Corp, Burlington Coat Factory Warehouse, Inc, C.F.B., Inc, C.f.i.c. Corporation, C.L.B., Inc, LC Acquisition Corp, Monroe G. Milstein, Inc

Officers: Mark A. Nesci/52/Dir., CEO, Pres., Steven Koster/59/VP, Sr. Divisional Merchandise Mgr. Menswear, Robert L. Lapenta/54/VP, Chief Accounting Officer, Treasurer, Paul C. Tang/55/Exec. VP, General Counsel, Sec., Thomas J. Fitzgerald/47/CFO, Exec. VP, Jack Moore/53/Pres. - Merchandising, Planning, Allocation, Marketing, Elizabeth Williams/54/Exec. VP, Chief Merchandising

Directors: Mark A. Nesci/52/Dir., CEO, Pres., Joshua Bekenstein/49/Dir., Jordan Hitch/41/Dir., John Tudor/38/Dir., Nicholas Nomicos/45/Dir.

Owners: Insiders/1.00%, Robert L. LaPenta, Paul C. Tang, Steven Koster, Mark A. Nesci, Paul C. Tang, Bain Capital, LLC/98.50%, Elizabeth Williams, Robert L. LaPenta, Elizabeth Williams, Bain Capital, LLC/98.50%, Insiders/1.00%, Mark A. Nesci, Steven Koster

Financial Data: Fiscal Year End:05/28 ***Latest Annual Data:*** 10/31/2006

Year	***Sales***	***Net Income***
2006	$55,905,000	$55,035,000

Curr. Assets:	$2,528,000	***Curr. Liab.:***	$14,555,000		
Plant, Equip.:	NA	***Total Liab.:***	$23,515,000	***Indic. Yr. Divd.:***	NA
Total Assets:	$843,798,000	***Net Worth:***	$820,283,000	***Debt/ Equity:***	NA

Burlington Northern Santa FE Corp

2650 Lou Menk Dr., Fort Worth, TX, 76131; ***PH:*** 1-800-795-2673; ***Fax:*** 1-817-352-7171; ***http://*** www.bnsf.com

General		***Stock***	
Incorporation	DE	Price on:12/24/2007	$87.28
Employees	41,000	Stock Exchange	NYSE
Auditor	PricewaterhouseCoopers LLP	Ticker Symbol	BNI
Stk Agt	Computershare Investor Services LLC	Outstanding Shares	356,120,000
Counsel	NA	E.P.S	$5.06
DUNS No.	04-834-1788	Shareholders	NA

Business: The group principle activity is to provide freight rail transportation services. The group operates from United States.

Primary SIC and add'l.: 4013 4011

CIK No: 0000934612

Subsidiaries: Bayport Systems, Inc., BayRail, LLC, BN Leasing Corporation, BNSF Acquisition, Inc., BNSF Equipment Acquisition Company, LLC, BNSF Logistics, LLC, BNSF Railway Company, BNSF Railway International Services, Inc., Burlington Northern (Manitoba) Limited., Burlington Northern Dock Corporation, Burlington Northern Railroad Holdings, Inc., Burlington Northern Santa Fe British Columbia, Ltd., Burlington Northern Santa Fe Insurance Company, Ltd., Burlington Northern Santa Fe Manitoba, Inc., Burlington Northern Santa Fe Properties, LLC 42 Subsidiaries included in the Index

Officers: Matthew K. Rose/Chmn., CEO, Pres./$13,366,750.00, Jeffrey R. Moreland/63/Exec. VP - Public Affairs/$4,854,224.00, Susan Rombach/Shareholder Representative, Steven Forsberg/General Dir. - Public Affairs, James H. Gallegos/VP, Corporate General Counsel, Marsha K. Morgan/VP - Investor Relations, Peter J. Rickershauser/VP - Network Development, Roger Nober/Exec. VP - Law, Sec., Richard E. Weicher/VP - Sr. Regulatory Counsel, Carl R. Ice/COO, Exec. VP/$4,273,002.00, Paul R. Hoferer/VP, General Counsel, Thomas N. Hund/CFO, Exec. VP/$3,853,372.00, David W. Stropes/VP - Corporate Audit Services, Shelley J. Venick/VP - General Tax Counsel, Paul W. Bischler/VP, Controller (27 Officers included in Index)

Directors: Matthew K. Rose/Chmn., CEO, Pres., Marc J. Shapiro/Dir., Alan L. Boeckmann/Dir., Edward E. Whitacre/Dir., Donald G. Cook/Dir., Vilma S. Martinez/Dir., Roy S. Roberts/Dir., J. C. Watts/Dir., Robert H. West/Dir., Steven J. Whisler/Dir., Marc F. Racicot/Dir.

Owners: FMR Corp./6.09%, UBS AG/6.50%, Marsico Capital Management, LLC/8.90%

Financial Data: *Fiscal Year End:* 12/31   *Latest Annual Data:* 12/31/2006

Year	Sales	Net Income
2006	$14,985,000,000	$1,887,000,000
2005	$12,987,000,000	$1,531,000,000
2004	$10,946,000,000	$791,000,000

Curr. Assets:	$2,181,000,000	*Curr. Liab.:*	$3,326,000,000	*P/E Ratio:*	17.78
Plant, Equip.:	$27,676,000,000	*Total Liab.:*	$21,247,000,000	*Indic. Yr. Divd.:*	$1.280
Total Assets:	$31,643,000,000	*Net Worth:*	$10,396,000,000	*Debt/ Equity:*	0.6615

Burlington Resources Inc

717 Texas Ave., Ste. 2100, Houston, TX, 77002; *PH:* 1-713-624-9000; *http://* www.conocophillips.com

General - Incorporation	DE	Stock - Price on: 12/24/2007	$78.2
Employees	38,400	Stock Exchange	NYSE
Auditor	PricewaterhouseCoopers LLP	Ticker Symbol	NA
Stk Agt	Mellon Investor Services LLC	Outstanding Shares	1,630,000,000
Counsel	NA	E.P.S.	$6.54
DUNS No.	19-170-7793	Shareholders	NA

Business: The group's principal activities are to explore, develop, produce and market crude oil, natural gas liquids and natural gas. The group operates through its principal subsidiaries, burlington resources oil & gas company lp, the Louisiana land and exploration company, burlington resources Canada ltd and burlington resources Canada (hunter) ltd and their affiliated companies. The group's customers include local distribution companies, electric utilities, industrial users and marketers. The group operates in the United States and Canada and has projects in northwest Europe, north Africa, China and South America. In may 2003, the group acquired the remaining 50% interest in clam petroleum b.v.

Primary SIC and add'l.: 4925 1311 1321 6719

CIK No: 0000833320

Subsidiaries: BROG GP Inc., BROG LP Inc., Burlington Resources Canada (Hunter) Ltd., Burlington Resources Canada Ltd., Burlington Resources Canada Partnership, Burlington Resources International Inc., Burlington Resources Oil & Gas Company LP, Burlington Resources Trading Inc., Glacier Park Company, The Louisiana Land and Exploration Company

Financial Data: *Fiscal Year End:* 12/31   *Latest Annual Data:* 12/31/2006

Year	Sales	Net Income
2006	$188,523,000,000	$15,550,000,000
2005	$183,364,000,000	$13,529,000,000
2004	$136,916,000,000	$8,129,000,000

Curr. Assets:	$25,066,000,000	*Curr. Liab.:*	$26,431,000,000	*P/E Ratio:*	11.96
Plant, Equip.:	$86,201,000,000	*Total Liab.:*	$80,933,000,000	*Indic. Yr. Divd.:*	$1.640
Total Assets:	$164,781,000,000	*Net Worth:*	$82,646,000,000	*Debt/ Equity:*	0.2590

Burzynski Research Institute Inc

9432 Old Katy Rd. , Ste 200, Houston, TX, 77055; *PH:* 1-713-335-5696; *Fax:* 1-713-935-0649; *http://* www.burzynskiresearch.com; *Email:* info@burzynskiclinic.com

General - Incorporation	DE	Stock - Price on: 12/24/2007	$0.08
Employees	3	Stock Exchange	OTC
Auditor	Fitts, Roberts & Co. P.C	Ticker Symbol	BZYR
Stk Agt	NA	Outstanding Shares	131,390,000
Counsel	NA	E.P.S.	-$0.03
DUNS No.	NA	Shareholders	NA

Business: The group's principle activity is to develop of antineoplaston drugs currently being tested for use in the treatment of cancer. The group also provides consulting services and is currently conducting approximately 36 fda-approved clinical trials. The group holds the exclusive right in the United States, Canada and Mexico to use, manufacture, develop, sell, distribute, sublicense and otherwise exploit all the rights, titles and interest in antineoplaston drugs used in the treatment of cancer, once the drugs are approved for sale by the fda. The group operates from United States.

Primary SIC and add'l.: 2834

CIK No: 0000724445

Officers: Stanislaw R. Burzynski/64/Chmn., CEO, Pres., Sec., Treasurer, Dudley Anderson/CFO

Directors: Stanislaw R. Burzynski/64/Chmn., CEO, Pres., Sec., Treasurer, Barbara Burzynski/67/Dir., Michael H. Driscoll/61/Dir., Carlton Hazlewood/71/Dir.

Owners: Stanislaw R. Burzynski, Barbara Burzynski, Insiders, Michael H. Driscoll

Financial Data: *Fiscal Year End:* 02/28   *Latest Annual Data:* 02/28/2007

Year	Sales	Net Income
2007	NA	-$4,303,000
2006	$54,000	-$4,601,000
2005	NA	-$4,966,000

Curr. Assets:	$11,000	*Curr. Liab.:*	$66,000		
Plant, Equip.:	$2,000	*Total Liab.:*	$66,000	*Indic. Yr. Divd.:*	NA
Total Assets:	$13,000	*Net Worth:*	-$53,000	*Debt/ Equity:*	NA

Business Bank Corp

6085 West Twain Ave., Las Vegas, NV, 89103; *PH:* 1-818-340-6100; *http://* www.bbnv.com

General - Incorporation	NA	Stock - Price on: 12/24/2007	NA
Employees	NA	Stock Exchange	NA
Auditor	NA	Ticker Symbol	NA
Stk Agt	Continental Stock Transfer & Trust Co	Outstanding Shares	NA
Counsel	NA	E.P.S.	NA
DUNS No.	NA	Shareholders	NA

Business: The groups principal activity is to provide banking business. The group financial products include savings and fixed deposits, on line, personal, commercial lending and business banking. The group operates from the United States.

Primary SIC and add'l.: 6021

CIK No: 0001105491

Business Development Solutions Inc

Formerly: Business Development Corp of America
28/f., Citigroup Tower, 33 Huanyuanshiqiao Rd., Pudong, Shanghai, IN, 46914; *PH:* 86-21-5878-7297

General - Incorporation	NV	Stock - Price on: 12/24/2007	NA
Employees	NA	Stock Exchange	NA
Auditor	NA	Ticker Symbol	NA
Stk Agt	Atlas Stock Transfer Corp	Outstanding Shares	NA
Counsel	NA	E.P.S.	NA
DUNS No.	NA	Shareholders	NA

Business: The group's activity is to issue shares to its original shareholders and filing registration statements. The group is at a developmental stage since inception.

Primary SIC and add'l.: 7389

CIK No: 0001296537

Business Objects

3030 Orchard Pkwy., San Jose, CA, 95134; *PH:* 1-408-953-6000; *Fax:* 1-408-953-6001; *http://* www.businessobjects.com

General - Incorporation	France	Stock - Price on: 12/24/2007	$40.19
Employees	5,402	Stock Exchange	NDQ
Auditor	Ernst & Young LLP	Ticker Symbol	BOBJ
Stk Agt	Bank of New York	Outstanding Shares	95,700,000
Counsel	NA	E.P.S.	$0.86
DUNS No.	76-773-7265	Shareholders	NA

Business: The group's principal activities are the development, marketing and support of e-business intelligence software for client/server environments, intranets, extranets and the Internet. The group is spread over 80 countries and has over 24,000 customers. The group acquired Crystal Decisions in Dec 2003.

Primary SIC and add'l.: 8744 7363 7371

CIK No: 0000928753

Subsidiaries: Business Objects (France) S.A.S., Business Objects (UK)Ltd., Business Objects Americas, Business Objects Asia Pacific Pte Ltd., Business Objects Australia Pty Ltd., Business Objects BeLux S.A./N.V., Business Objects Corp., Business Objects Danmark ApS, Business Objects Data Integration, Inc., Business Objects de Brasil Ltda, Business Objects de Mexico S. de R.L. de C.V., Business Objects Deutschland GmbH, Business Objects Finland Ltd., Business Objects Greater China Ltd., Business Objects Iberica S.L. 30 Subsidiaries included in the Index

Officers: John Schwarz/Dir., CEO/$8,919,729.00, Bernard Liautaud/Founder, Chmn., Chief Strategy Officer/$5,889,915.00, Deborah Byron/Sr. VP - Human Resources, Maurizio Carli/Sr. VP, GM EMEA, Greg Wolfe/Sr. VP, GM - Americas Operations, Herve Couturier/Sr. VP - Products, Mark Doll/Sr. VP - Global Services, Sheri Anderson/Group VP, CIO, Susan Wolfe/Sr. VP, General Counsel, Corp. Sec./$965,983.00, Tom Schroeder/Group VP - Corporate Development, Scott Bajtos/Sr. VP - Worldwide Customer Support, Janet Wood/Sr. VP - Global Partnerships, Sales Enablement, Jim Tolonen/58/CFO/$1,138,667.00, Keith Budge/Sr. VP, GM - Asia Pacific, Japan

Directors: John Schwarz/Dir., CEO, Bernard Liautaud/Founder, Chmn., Chief Strategy Officer, Arnold Silverman/Dir., Kurt Lauk/Dir., Gerald Held/Dir., Bernard Charles/Dir., Carl Pascarella/Dir., Jean-Francois Heitz/Dir., David Peterschmidt/Dir.

Owners: Morgan Stanley & Co International Ltd/5.16%, Kurt Lauk, Susan Wolfe, Bernard Charls, Jean-Franois Heitz, Bernard Liautaud/2.02%, John Schwarz, FMR Corp/13.29%, Gerald Held, Insiders/3.08%, James Tolonen, Carl Pascarella, Tudor Investment Corporation/6.21%, Arnold Silverman, David Peterschmidt

Financial Data: *Fiscal Year End:* 12/31   *Latest Annual Data:* 12/31/2006

Year	Sales	Net Income
2006	$1,253,760,000	$75,364,000
2005	$1,077,151,000	$92,625,000
2004	$925,631,000	$47,123,000

Curr. Assets:	$964,563,000	*Curr. Liab.:*	$663,071,000	*P/E Ratio:*	46.73
Plant, Equip.:	$91,091,000	*Total Liab.:*	$692,171,000	*Indic. Yr. Divd.:*	NA
Total Assets:	$2,494,990,000	*Net Worth:*	$1,802,819,000	*Debt/ Equity:*	0.0583

Butler International Inc

The New River Ctr., Ste. 1730, Fort Lauderdale, FL, 33301; *PH:* 1-954-761-2200; *Fax:* 1-954-761-9675; *http://* www5.butler.com

General - Incorporation	MD	Stock - Price on: 12/24/2007	$1.35
Employees	NA	Stock Exchange	OTC
Auditor	Grant Thornton, LLP	Ticker Symbol	BUTL
Stk Agt	American Stock Transfer & Trust Co.	Outstanding Shares	NA
Counsel	NA	E.P.S.	NA
DUNS No.	15-726-1637	Shareholders	NA

Business: The group's principal activity is to provide a wide range of telecommunication and technology solutions and services to companies worldwide. The group operates through four segments: telecommunication services, technology solutions, technical group and fleet services. The telecom services and solutions include integration of optical, wireless and broadband network systems and specialty project services to the voice data and video communications industry. The technology solutions helps companies implement business solutions that harness the power of the Internet to optimize business performance. Technical group provides skilled technical personnel and project management solutions to a wide range of industries. Fleet services provides customized fleet operation services to major ground fleet-holders nationwide.

Primary SIC and add'l.: 8742 7376 7373 7379

CIK No: 0000786765

Subsidiaries: Butler New Jersey Realty Corporation, Butler Service Group, Inc.

Officers: Edward M. Kopko/Chmn., CEO, Pres., Praveen Reddy/MD - India, Thomas J. Considine/Sr. VP, CFO, Mitchell Mendez/Technical Recruiter The Butler Technical Group, John Jones/Technical Recruiter, Butler Technical Group, Kurt Hauser/Dir. - Network Services, Thomas E. Mullin/GM - Network Implementation Services, Renee Ward/Marketing Mgr. - Communications, Tina Shumate/Technical Recruiter, Butler Technical Group, George Georgiou/Sr. VP - Telecom, Charles Neal/GM - Technical Services, James Floody/Technical Marketing Dir., James Von Bampus/VP - Human Resources, Ann Marie MacEachern/Mgr. - Human Resources Planning, Development, Robin Klouda/Contact - Sr. Benefits Specialist - Corp Human Resources *(77 Officers included in Index)*

Directors: Edward M. Kopko/Chmn., CEO, Pres., Ronald Uyematsu/Dir., Hugh G. McBreen/Dir., Walter O. Lecroy/Dir., Frank H. Murray/Dir., Thomas F. Comeau/Dir., Louis F. Petrossi/Dir., Wesley B. Tyler/Dir.

Owners: Louis F. Petrossi, Insiders, Edward M. Kopko, T. Considine, Wesley B. Tyler, C. Tireman, Hugh G. McBreen/23.40%, Frederick H. Kopko/22.40%, Ivan Estes, Prescott Group Capital Management LLC, Walter O. LeCroy, James Beckley, Thomas F. Comeau, M. Koscinski, Charlie Jobson *(25 Owners included in Index)*

Financial Data: Fiscal Year End: 12/31   **Latest Annual Data:** 12/31/2004

Year	Sales		Net Income
2004	$251,325,000		$3,795,000
2003	$208,983,000		-$15,358,000
2002	$263,124,000		-$22,426,000
Curr. Assets:	$46,954,000	**Curr. Liab.:**	$26,034,000
Plant, Equip.:	$11,682,000	**Total Liab.:**	$88,236,000	**Indic. Yr. Divd.:** NA
Total Assets:	$104,233,000	**Net Worth:**	$15,997,000	**Debt/ Equity:** 2.4769

Butler National Corp

19920 W 161st St., Olathe, KS, 66062; **PH:** 1-913-780-9595; **Fax:** 1-913-780-5088; http:// butlernational.com

General - Incorporation	KS	**Stock**- Price on:12/24/2007	$0.425
Employees	82	Stock Exchange	OTC
Auditor	Weaver & Martin LLC	Ticker Symbol	BUKS
Stk Agt	Wells Fargo Shareowner Services	Outstanding Shares	53,050,000
Counsel	NA	E.P.S.	$0.013
DUNS No.	00-625-0609	Shareholders	NA

Business: The group's principle activities are carried out through five segments: aircraft modifications: includes the modification of customer and company owned business-size aircraft from passenger to freighter configuration, addition of aerial photography capability and stability enhancing modifications. Avionics: includes the manufacture, sale and service of airborne electronic switching units and transient suppression devices for fuel tank protection. Gaming: includes business management services and advances to Indian tribes. Monitoring services: includes the monitoring of water and wastewater remote pumping stations through electronic surveillance for municipalities and the private sector. Temporary services: provides temporary employee services for corporate clients. The group's total revenue for year 2007 was 14.68 millions of USD.

Primary SIC and add'l.: 3728

CIK No: 0000015847

Subsidiaries: Avcon Industries Inc., AVT Corporation, BCS Design Inc., Butler National Corporation Inc., Butler National Inc., Butler National Service Corporation, Butler National Services Inc., Butler Temporary Services, Inc., Indian Gaming Corporation, Kansas International Inc.

Officers: Clark D. Stewart/Dir., CEO, Pres., Kathy L. Gorrell/Treasurer, Jeffery H. Shinkle/Pres. - BCS Design, Inc, Curtis Beadle/Pres. - Butler National Services, Inc, Christopher J. Reedy/VP, Larry W. Franke/Pres. - Avcon Industries, Inc, Angela D. Shinabargar/CFO

Directors: Clark D. Stewart/Dir., CEO, Pres., Warren R. Wagoner/Chmn., David B. Hayden/Dir., William E. Logan/Dir.

Owners: William E. Logan/1.50%, Insiders/20.90%, Christopher J. Reedy/0.50%, Angela D. Shinabargar/0.30%, Warren R. Wagoner/7.60%, Larry W. Franke/0.90%, David B. Hayden/2.50%, Clark D. Stewart/7.60%, Warren R. Wagoner/7.60%

Financial Data: Fiscal Year End: 04/30   **Latest Annual Data:** 04/30/2007

Year	Sales		Net Income
2007	$14,681,000		$606,000
2006	$15,307,000		$366,000
2005	$23,390,000		$2,446,000
Curr. Assets:	$12,671,000	**Curr. Liab.:**	$6,465,000
Plant, Equip.:	$2,356,000	**Total Liab.:**	$8,309,000	**Indic. Yr. Divd.:** NA
Total Assets:	$18,138,000	**Net Worth:**	$9,829,000	**Debt/ Equity:** 0.1642

BV Financial Inc MD

1230 Light St., Baltimore, MD, 21230; **PH:** 1-410-477-5000

General - Incorporation	Federal	**Stock**- Price on:12/24/2007	$8.5
Employees	27	Stock Exchange	OTC
Auditor	Beard Miller Company LLP	Ticker Symbol	BVFL
Stk Agt	Registrar & Transfer Co	Outstanding Shares	2,560,000
Counsel	NA	E.P.S.	$0.03
DUNS No.	NA	Shareholders	NA

Business: The group operates through its subsidiary whose principal activity is banking operations. The group products include real estate loans, commercial real estate loans, mobile home loans, home equity lines-of-credit, construction and land loans and deposits. The group operates from the United States. The groups asset in the year 2006 was $18,580 (thousand).

Primary SIC and add'l.: 6035

CIK No: 0001302387

Subsidiaries: Bay-Vanguard Federal Savings Bank, Housing Recovery Corporation

Officers: Frank W. Dingle/34/Dir., VP

Directors: Frank W. Dingle/34/Dir., VP

Owners: Catherine M. Staszak, Edmund T. Leonard/1.28%, Anthony J. Narutowicz, Brian K. McHale, Jerry S. Sopher, Robert R. Kern, Daniel J. Gallagher, Frank W. Dingle, Insiders/5.45%, Carolyn M. Mroz/1.17%, Michael J. Birmingham, Bay-Vanguard, M.H.C./58.90%

Financial Data: Fiscal Year End: 06/30   **Latest Annual Data:** 06/30/2006

Year	Sales		Net Income
2006	$7,471,000		$439,000
2005	$5,906,000		$562,000
Curr. Assets:	$6,094,000	**Curr. Liab.:**	$113,771,000	**P/E Ratio:** 425.00
Plant, Equip.:	$2,404,000	**Total Liab.:**	$115,792,000	**Indic. Yr. Divd.:** $0.200
Total Assets:	$134,010,000	**Net Worth:**	$18,218,000	**Debt/ Equity:** NA

BVR Systems (1998) Ltd

16 Hamelacha St., Afek Industrial Pk., Rosh-ha-ayin, 48091; **PH:** 972-39008000; http:// www.bvrsystems.com; **Email:** human_resources@bvr.co.il

General - Incorporation	Israel	**Stock** - Price on:12/24/2007	$0.17
Employees	80	Stock Exchange	OTC
Auditor	Somekh Chaikin	Ticker Symbol	BVRSF
Stk Agt	American Stock Transfer & Trust Co.	Outstanding Shares	116,860,000
Counsel	NA	E.P.S.	-$0.02
DUNS No.	NA	Shareholders	NA

Business: The group's principle activities include development, manufacturing and marketing computer based simulation systems for military applications. The group operates from United States.

Primary SIC and add'l.: 7373

CIK No: 0001064411

Subsidiaries: Board of iVLab, BVR Pacific PTE, CET Technologies, Koonras Technologies Ltd, Tadiran Spectalink Ltd.

Officers: Ilan Gillies/CEO, Gilad Yavetz/VP - Marketing, Dekel Tzidon/VP - Development, Chief Technological Officer, Reuven Shahar/VP - Finance, CFO

Directors: Aviv Tzidon/Chmn., Yaron Sheinman/Dir., Uri Manor/Dir., Avi Leumi/Dir., Gadi Aviram/Dir., Orit Stav/37/Dir., Eric Chan/Dir., Rimon Ben-Shaoul/Dir., Amnon Harari/57/Dir., Avraham Gilat/61/Dir., Ken Lalo/50/Dir., Nir Dor/44/Dir.

Owners: Bank Leumi Le-Israel B.M./5.23%, H.S.N General Managers Holdings LP/28.18%, CHUN Holdings Limited Partnership/54.03%, Polar Investments House/7.15%

Financial Data: Fiscal Year End: 12/31   **Latest Annual Data:** 12/31/2006

Year	Sales		Net Income
2006	$10,103,000		-$2,353,000
2005	$19,196,000		-$4,000
2004	$12,684,000		-$1,635,000
Curr. Assets:	$11,054,000	**Curr. Liab.:**	$7,567,000	**P/E Ratio:** 46.73
Plant, Equip.:	$865,000	**Total Liab.:**	$9,198,000	**Indic. Yr. Divd.:** NA
Total Assets:	$14,604,000	**Net Worth:**	$5,406,000	**Debt/ Equity:** NA

BWAY Corp

8607 Roberts Dr., Ste 250, Atlanta, GA, 30350; **PH:** 1-309-344-2323; **Fax:** 1-770-645-4810; http:// www.nampac.com; **Email:** sales@bwaycorp.com

General - Incorporation	DE	**Stock**- Price on:12/24/2007	NA
Employees	NA	Stock Exchange	NA
Auditor	Deloitte & Touche LLP	Ticker Symbol	NA
Stk Agt	NA	Outstanding Shares	NA
Counsel	Kirkland & Ellis LLP	E.P.S.	NA
DUNS No.	80-999-3520	Shareholders	NA

Business: The group's principle activity is to develop, manufacture and market steel containers for the general line category of the north American container industry. It also provides related material center services (coating, lithography and metal shearing) to external customers. The products include a wide variety of steel cans and pails used for packaging paint and related products, lubricants, cleaners, roof and driveway sealants, food and household and personal care aerosol products. The group also manufactures steel ammunition boxes and provides material center services. The products are marketed primarily in North America. The group's ammunition boxes are to the U.S. Department of defense as well as to major domestic and foreign producers of ordnance.

Primary SIC and add'l.: 6719 3411 3499 3479

CIK No: 0000943897

Subsidiaries: Armstrong Containers, Inc., North America Packaging Corporation, North America Packaging of Puerto Rico, Inc., SC Plastics, LLC

Officers: Kenneth M. Roessler/CEO, COO, Pres. - Bway Packaging Division Leadership, Jean-Pierre M. Ergas/Exec. Chmn., Thomas K. Linton/COO, Sr. VP, Pres. - Nampac Division, Kevin C. Kern/VP - Administration, CFO, Jeffrey M. OConnell/VP, Treasurer, Sec., Robert Coleman/VP - Sales, Marketing General Line, Sean Fitzgerald/VP - Sales, Marketing Aerosol, Les Bradshaw/VP - GM - Aerosol, Bway Packaging Division, Charles Watling/VP - Engineering, Nampac Division, Hank Harrell/VP - Sales, Marketing, Nampac Division, Danny Byrne/VP, Controller - Finance, Admin, Nampac Division, Dennis Bednar/COO - General Line, Sheila McCafferty/Controller - ICL Industrial Containers, Steven Kenyon/VP - Purchasing, Nampac Division, Alan Houser/VP - Operations, Nampac Division *(16 Officers included in Index)*

Directors: Jean-Pierre M. Ergas/Exec. Chmn., Warren J. Hayford/Non - Exec. Vice Chmn., Lawrence A. McVicker/Dir., David M. Roderick/Dir., David I. Wahrhaftig/Dir., Thomas R. Wall/Dir., Earl L. Mason/Dir.

BWC Financial Corp

1400 Civic Dr., Walnut Creek, CA, 94596; *PH:* 1-925-932-5353; *http://* www.bewc.com

General - Incorporation	CA	**Stock**- Price on:12/24/2007	$53.93
Employees	1,112	Stock Exchange	NA
Auditor	Moss Adams LLP	Ticker Symbol	NA
Stk Agt	American Stock Transfer & Trust Co.	Outstanding Shares	31,110,000
Counsel	NA	E.P.S	NA
DUNS No.	10-808-3346	Shareholders	NA

Business: The group's principal activity is that of a holding company for the bank of walnut creek. It offers commercial banking services to individuals and businesses in the walnut creek, contra costa, alameda and santa clara and solano counties of California. The group accepts deposits, makes construction, mortgage and commercial and installment loans and offers safe deposit services. Deposits consist of money market and now accounts, time certificates of deposit and also an auto deposit pick-up service for business clients. Automatic teller machines are available through the eds, cirrus and star networks with access at locations throughout the United States and Canada. The group also operates a small business administration and a business credit department to provide factoring loans with assignment of receivables. Its subsidiary, bwc real estate, operates a joint venture brokerage service.

Primary SIC and add'l.: 6022 6712

CIK No: 0000353650

Subsidiaries: BWC Real Estate

C&D Technologies Inc

1400 Union Meeting Rd., Blue Bell, PA, 19422; *PH:* 1-215-619-2700; *Fax:* 1-215-619-7840; *http://* www.cdtechno.com; *Email:* iharvie@cdtechno.com

General - Incorporation	DE	**Stock**- Price on:12/24/2007	$5.85
Employees	2,900	Stock Exchange	NYSE
Auditor	PricewaterhouseCoopers LLP	Ticker Symbol	CHP
Stk Agt	Mellon Investor Services LLC	Outstanding Shares	25,650,000
Counsel	Proskauer Rose	E.P.S	-$1.29
DUNS No.	14-841-4600	Shareholders	NA

Business: The group's principal activity is to manufacture integrated reserve power systems for telecommunications, electronic information and industrial applications. The group operates in four segments: the powercom division: manufactures and markets integrated components for the standby power market. The dynasty division: manufactures industrial batteries for the un-interruptible power supply and broadband cable markets. The power electronics division: manufactures dc to dc converters, custom, standard and modified standard embedded high frequency ac to dc switching power supplies and magnetics. The motive power division: markets systems and individual components to power, monitor and test the batteries used in vehicles. The group's products are marketed through trademarks such as c&d(R), dynasty(R) and liberty(r). It operates in the United States and other countries. In fiscal 2004, the group acquired celab limited and datel holding corporation and its subsidiaries.

Primary SIC and add'l.: 3692 3694 3691 3677 3612

CIK No: 0000808064

Subsidiaries: C&D Charter Holdings, Inc., C&D Components Hong Kong, Limited, C&D Dynamo Corporation, C&D Electronic Technology (Shanghai) Co. Ltd, C&D Electronics (GZ) Limited, C&D Holdings Limited, C&D International Investment Holdings, Inc., C&D Power Systems (Canada) ULC, C&D Technologies (CPS) LLC, C&D Technologies (CPS) ULC, C&D Technologies (Datel) GmbH, C&D Technologies (Datel) Inc., C&D Technologies (Datel) SARL, C&D Technologies (HK) Limited, C&D Technologies (Italia), S.r.l. 29 Subsidiaries included in the Index

Officers: Jeffrey A. Graves/Dir., CEO, Pres./$568,100.00, James D. Dee/VP, General Counsel, Corp. Sec./$295,686.00, Neil E. Daniels/VP, Corporate Controller, Treasurer/$378,832.00, Leonard Kiely/VP, GM - Power Systems Divisions/$363,842.00, Ian J. Harvie/CFO, VP

Directors: Jeffrey A. Graves/Dir., CEO, Pres., William Harral/Chmn., Ellen C. Wolf/Dir., Stanley W. Silverman/Dir., John A.H. Shober/Dir., Pamela L. Davies/Dir., Robert I. Harries/Dir., Kevin P. Dowd/Dir., George MacKenzie/Dir., Michael H. Kalb/Dir.

Financial Data: *Fiscal Year End:*01/31 *Latest Annual Data:* 1/31/2007

Year		Sales			Net Income
2007		$524,580,000			-$46,074,000
2006		$497,407,000			-$60,662,000
2005		$414,738,000			-$59,493,000
Curr. Assets:	$194,916,000	**Curr. Liab.:**	$116,943,000		
Plant, Equip.:	$100,815,000	**Total Liab.:**	$308,773,000	**Indic. Yr. Divd.:**	NA
Total Assets:	$400,211,000	**Net Worth:**	$83,890,000	**Debt/ Equity:**	1.7642

C&F Financial Corp

802 Main St., West Point, VA, 23181; *PH:* 1-804-843-2360; *Fax:* 1-804-843-3017; *http://* www.cffc.com

General - Incorporation	VA	**Stock**- Price on:12/24/2007	$41.06
Employees	501	Stock Exchange	NDQ
Auditor	Yount, Hyde & Barbour, P.C	Ticker Symbol	CFFI
Stk Agt	Yount, Hyde & Barfom PC	Outstanding Shares	3,090,000
Counsel	Hudson & Bondurant	E.P.S	$2.97
DUNS No.	05-448-6048	Shareholders	NA

Business: The group's principal activities are to provide general, commercial and mortgage banking services to individuals and small businesses through twelve branch offices. It is a holding company of citizens and farmers bank, which provides various checking and savings deposit accounts and offers business, real estate, development, mortgage, home equity, automobile and other loans. It also offers ATM services, Internet banking services, credit card services, trust services, notary public, wire services and other customary bank services. Through its subsidiaries: c&f title agency inc, c&f investment services inc, c&f insurance services inc and c&f mortgage corporation, the group offers insurance products, investment options and residential mortgages.

Primary SIC and add'l.: 6022 6712

CIK No: 0000913341

Subsidiaries: C&F Finance Company, C&F Financial Statutory Trust I, C&F Insurance Services, Inc., C&F Investment Services, Inc, C&F Mortgage Corporation, C&F Reinsurance LTD, C&F Title Agency, Inc, Certified Appraisals LLC, Citizens and Farmers Bank, Hometown Settlement Services LLC

Officers: Larry G. Dillon/Chmn., CEO, Pres./$424,277.00, Robert L. Bryant/COO, Exec. VP/$334,991.00, Thomas F. Cherry/CFO, Exec. VP, Sec./$311,252.00

Directors: Larry G. Dillon/Chmn., CEO, Pres., J. P. Causey/Dir., Joshua H. Lawson/Dir., Paul C. Robinson/Dir., Barry R. Chernack/Dir., Jim Hudson/Dir., William E. O'Connell/Dir., Elis C. Olsson/Dir., Audrey D. Holmes/Dir.

Owners: Insiders/10.50%, Robert L. Bryant, Paul C. Robinson, Bryan E. McKernon/1.10%, Elis C. Olsson, J. P. Causey/1.40%, James H. Hudson, William E. OConnell, Thomas F. Cherry/1.10%, Audrey D. Holmes, Larry G. Dillon/3.70%, Joshua H. Lawson/1.30%, Barry R. Chernack

Financial Data: *Fiscal Year End:*12/31 *Latest Annual Data:* 12/31/2006

Year		Sales			Net Income
2006		$85,969,000			$12,129,000
2005		$76,354,000			$11,788,000
2004		$65,532,000			$11,198,000
Curr. Assets:	$32,938,000	**Curr. Liab.:**	$547,212,000	**P/E Ratio:**	12.87
Plant, Equip.:	$33,189,000	**Total Liab.:**	$666,462,000	**Indic. Yr. Divd.:**	$1.240
Total Assets:	$734,468,000	**Net Worth:**	$68,006,000	**Debt/ Equity:**	1.6303

C-COR Incorporated

60 Decibel Rd., State College, PA, 16801; *PH:* 1-814-238-2461; *Fax:* 1-814-238-4065; *http://* www.c-cor.net

General - Incorporation	PA	**Stock**- Price on:12/24/2007	$14.45
Employees	1,503	Stock Exchange	NDQ
Auditor	KPMG LLP	Ticker Symbol	CCBL
Stk Agt	American Stock Transfer & Trust Co.	Outstanding Shares	49,560,000
Counsel	NA	E.P.S	$0.61
DUNS No.	NA	Shareholders	NA

Business: The group's principal activity is to provide communications equipment, software solutions and technical services for the full network life cycle of two-way hybrid fiber coax broadband networks. It operates in three segments: broadband communications products (bcp), broadband network services (bns) and broadband management solutions (bms). Bcp provides advanced fiber optic, digital video transport and radio frequency telecommunications equipment. Bns provides technical field services, covering broadband network engineering and design, construction, installation, optimization, certification, maintenance and operations. Bms provides operations support system software solutions to operate and manage multi-service networks. Major customers of the group are cable television operators, telephone companies and broadcast companies. On 07-Sep-2005, it acquired optinel systems inc.

Primary SIC and add'l.: 3669 3663 5065

CIK No: 0000350621

Subsidiaries: Broadband Capital Corporation, Broadband Management Solutions LLC, Broadband Network Services, Inc., Broadband Royalty Corporation, C COR de Mexico, S.A. de C.V., C-COR Argentina, S.R.L., C-COR Broadband Communications Europe GmbH, C-COR Broadband Europe B.V., C-COR Broadband GmbH, C-COR Electronics Canada, Inc., C-COR Europe Holdings B.V., C-COR Iberica, S.L., C-COR Singapore PTE LTD, C-COR Solutions Pvt. Ltd., nCUBE UK Limited 16 Subsidiaries included in the Index

Officers: David A. Woodle/Chmn., CEO, Kenneth A. Wright/CTO, Jo Ann Lehtihet/Public Relations, Press Contact, Sally Thiel/Dir. - Investor Relations, Riki Rau/Marketing Mgr. EMEA - Asiapac, Fred Yang/Sales Dir. - C, COR China, Mary G. Beahm/Corporate VP - Human Resources, Timothy Gropp/Corporate Sr. VP - Global Sales, Worldwide Sales, John O. Caczza/Pres. - Operations Group, Alain Helstroffer/Contact - Technical Marketing EU, William T. Hanelly/CFO, Joseph E. Zavacky/Controller, Assist. Sec., Liz Seidner Davidoff/VP - Global Marketing, Michael J. Pohl/Pres. - Global Strategies Group, Lisa Bousquet/Global Tradeshows, Events *(27 Officers included in Index)*

Directors: David A. Woodle/Chmn., CEO, Steven B. Fink/Dir., James J. Tietjen/Dir., Anthony A. Ibarguen/Dir., John J. Omlor/Dir., James E. Carnes/Dir., Rodney M. Royse/Dir., Rendall I.N. Harper/Dir., James C. Stalder/Dir., Philip L. Walker/Dir. Emeriti, Richard E. Perry/Dir. Emeriti, Donald M. Cook/Dir. Emeriti

Owners: William T. Hanelly, John O. Caezza, Rodney M. Royse, John J. Omlor, Insiders/17.50%, James J. Tietjen, Lawrence J. Ellison/14.60%, James C. Stalder, Steven B. Fink/14.70%, Michael J. Pohl, David A. Woodle/1.20%, Anthony A. Ibargen, James E. Carnes, Barclays Global/4.90%, I.N. Rendall Harper

Financial Data: *Fiscal Year End:*06/24 *Latest Annual Data:* 6/30/2006

Year		Sales			Net Income
2006		$262,526,000			-$27,306,000
2005		$237,260,000			-$25,690,000
2004		$240,918,000			$44,160,000
Curr. Assets:	$149,367,000	**Curr. Liab.:**	$72,981,000	**P/E Ratio:**	27.26
Plant, Equip.:	$20,074,000	**Total Liab.:**	$118,262,000	**Indic. Yr. Divd.:**	NA
Total Assets:	$313,129,000	**Net Worth:**	$194,867,000	**Debt/ Equity:**	0.1618

C. R. Bard Inc

730 Central Ave., Murray Hill, NJ, 07974; *PH:* 1-908-277-8000; *Fax:* 1-908-277-8240; *http://* www.crbard.com

General - Incorporation	NJ	**Stock**- Price on:12/24/2007	$84.84
Employees	9,400	Stock Exchange	NYSE
Auditor	KPMG LLP	Ticker Symbol	BCR
Stk Agt	EquiServe Trust Co.	Outstanding Shares	103,500,000
Counsel	NA	E.P.S	$2.74
DUNS No.	00-697-3408	Shareholders	NA

Business: The groups principle activities include developing, manufacturing, and marketing medical technologies in the fields of vascular, urology, oncology, and surgical specialty products. The groups products include bone biopsy products, allograft tissue, dilation balloons and carotid shunts. The group operates from United States.

Primary SIC and add'l.: 3845 3841 5047

CIK No: 0000009892

Subsidiaries: American Hydro-Surgical Instruments, Inc., Angiomed GmbH, Bard Access Systems, Inc., Bard ASDI, Inc., Bard Australia Pty. Ltd., Bard Benelux N.V., Bard Canada Inc., Bard de Espana, S.A., Bard Devices, Inc., Bard Dublin ITC, Bard European Distribution Center N.V., Bard Financial Services Limited, Bard Finland OY, Bard France S.A.S., Bard Healthcare, Inc. 59 Subsidiaries included in the Index

Officers: Timothy M. Ring/50/Chmn., CEO/$8,134,992.00, Robert L. Mellen/VP - Strategic Planning, Business Development, Jean F. Miller/Assist. Corp. Sec., Christopher D. Ganser/VP - Quality, Environmental Sciences, Safety, Vincent J. Gurnari/VP - Information Technology, John A. Deford/Sr. VP - Science, Technology, Clinical Affairs, Brian P. Kelly/Group VP/$2,071,220.00, Todd

C. Schermerhorn/CFO, Sr. VP/$3,281,591.00, Frank Lupisella/VP, Controller, James M. Howard/VP - Regulatory Sciences, Stephen J. Long/VP, General Counsel, Sec., Amy S. Paul/Group VP/$2,719,787.00, Scott T. Lowry/VP, Treasurer, Bronwen K. Kelly/VP - Human Resources, John H. Weiland/52/Dir., COO, Pres./$6,018,760.00 *(17 Officers included in Index)*

Directors: Timothy M. Ring/50/Chmn., CEO, Gail K. Naughton/Dir., Marc C. Breslawsky/Dir., Kevin T. Dunnigan/Dir., Tommy G. Thompson/Dir., Tony L. White/Dir., Theodore E. Martin/Dir., Herbert L. Henkel/Dir., Anthony Welters/Dir., John H. Weiland/52/Dir., COO, Pres.

Owners: Herbert L. Henkel, Anthony Welters, Tommy G. Thompson, Insiders/3.50%, Tony L. White, FMR Corp/14.00%, Amy S. Paul, Todd C. Schermerhorn, Marc C. Breslawsky, Timothy M. Ring/1.20%, Gail K. Naughton, Capital Research and Management Company/8.80%, Theodore E. Martin, John H. Weiland, Brian P. Kelly *(16 Owners included in Index)*

Financial Data: **Fiscal Year End:** 12/31 **Latest Annual Data:** 12/31/2006

Year	Sales	Net Income
2006	$1,985,500,000	$272,100,000
2005	$1,771,300,000	$337,100,000
2004	$1,656,100,000	$302,800,000

Curr. Assets:	$1,133,900,000	**Curr. Liab.:**	$295,900,000	**P/E Ratio:**	30.96
Plant, Equip.:	$342,700,000	**Total Liab.:**	$579,200,000	**Indic. Yr. Divd.:**	$0.560
Total Assets:	$2,277,200,000	**Net Worth:**	$1,698,000,000	**Debt/ Equity:**	0.0814

C.H. Robinson Worldwide Inc

14701 Charlson Rd., Eden Prairie, MN, 55347; ***PH:*** 1-952-937-8500; ***http://*** www.chrobinson.com

General - Incorporation	DE	**Stock** - Price on:12/24/2007	$54.11
Employees	6,768	Stock Exchange	NDQ
Auditor	Deloitte & Touche LLP	Ticker Symbol	CHRW
Stk Agt	Wells Fargo Shareowner Services	Outstanding Shares	171,160,000
Counsel	Dorsey & Whitney LLP	E.P.S.	$1.79
DUNS No.	19-974-3642	Shareholders	NA

Business: The groups principle activity is to provide transportation and logistic services. In the year 2006, the group acquired Payne, Lynch & Associates, Inc. The group operates from United States.

Primary SIC and add'l.: 4215 4011 4412 4212 4512

CIK No: 0001043277

Subsidiaries: C.H. Robinson (UK) Ltd, C.H. Robinson / Hirdes International GmbH, C.H. Robinson Belgium BVBA, C.H. Robinson Company, C.H. Robinson Company (Canada) Ltd., C.H. Robinson Company LP, C.H. Robinson Company, Inc., C.H. Robinson Czech Republic s.r.o., C.H. Robinson de Mexico, S.A. de C.V., C.H. Robinson Deutschland GmbH, C.H. Robinson Europe B.V., C.H. Robinson Europe BV Ireland, C.H. Robinson France SARL., C.H. Robinson Hungary, LLC, C.H. Robinson Iberica 34 Subsidiaries included in the Index

Officers: John P. Wiehoff/Chmn., CEO/$4,031,255.00, Bryan D. Foe/Pres. - T, Chek, James P. Lemke/VP - Produce, Thomas K. Mahlke/Corporate Controller, Angie Freeman/Dir. - Investor Relations, James V. Larsen/VP, Christopher J. O'Brien/VP, James E. Butts/VP/$1,219,847.00, Jeffrey Scovill/VP - International Forwarding, Scott A. Satterlee/VP/$1,156,379.00, Timothy P. Manning/VP, Laura Gillund/VP - Human Resources, Mark A. Walker/VP/$1,164,376.00, Chad M. Lindbloom/CFO, VP/$1,206,922.00, Steven M. Weiby/VP *(18 Officers included in Index)*

Directors: John P. Wiehoff/Chmn., CEO, Wayne M. Fortun/55/Dir., Brian P. Short/54/Dir., Steve Polacek/48/Dir., Michael W. Wickham/58/Dir., Rebecca Koenig Roloff/51/Dir., Kenneth E. Keiser/55/Dir., Robert Ezrilov/60/Dir., Gerald A. Schwalbach/60/Dir.

Owners: FMR Corp./13.46%, Rebecca Roloff, Wayne M. Fortun, John P. Wiehoff, Michael W. Wickham, Scott Satterlee, Brian P. Short, Insiders/2.17%, Chad Lindbloom, Jim Butts, Ken Keiser, Mark Walker, Robert Ezrilov, Gerald A. Schwalbach

Financial Data: **Fiscal Year End:** 12/31 **Latest Annual Data:** 12/31/2006

Year	Sales	Net Income
2006	$6,556,194,000	$266,925,000
2005	$5,688,948,000	$203,358,000
2004	$4,341,538,000	$137,254,000

Curr. Assets:	$1,256,148,000	**Curr. Liab.:**	$686,949,000	**P/E Ratio:**	33.61
Plant, Equip.:	$82,071,000	**Total Liab.:**	$687,971,000	**Indic. Yr. Divd.:**	$0.880
Total Assets:	$1,631,693,000	**Net Worth:**	$943,722,000	**Debt/ Equity:**	NA

C2 Global Technologies Inc

40 King St. W, Ste. 3200, Toronto, ON, M5H 3Y2; ***PH:*** 1-416-866-3000; ***http://*** www.acceris.com

General - Incorporation	FL	**Stock** - Price on:12/24/2007	$0.4
Employees	5	Stock Exchange	OTC
Auditor	Mintz & Partners LLP	Ticker Symbol	COBT
Stk Agt	American Stock Transfer & Trust Co.	Outstanding Shares	23,090,000
Counsel	NA	E.P.S.	-$0.32
DUNS No.	NA	Shareholders	NA

Business: The group's principal activity is to provide basic and enhanced telecommunication services to customers and subscribers nationwide utilizing Internet protocol. It delivers voice and data services to its partners and customers through wholesale and retail channels, and licenses its enhanced services platform to partners and service providers. The group operates in three segments: retail which offers a broad selection of voice and data telecommunications products and services to residential and commercial customers through a network of independent agents. Enterprise, which offers voice services and fully integrated, fully managed data services. Technologies offers a proven network convergence solution for voice and data in voice over Internet protocol ("Voip") communications technology and holds two foundational patents in the voip space. On 30-Jun-2003, it acquired local telcom holdings llc.

Primary SIC and add'l.: 7371 4813 6794

CIK No: 0000849145

Subsidiaries: I-Link Communications Inc., ITXC Corp., WXC Corp.

Officers: Abby Knowlton/VP - Business Management Regulatory - Legal

Owners: Henry Y.L. Toh, Samuel L. Shimer, Hal B. Heaton, Counsel Corporation and subsidiaries/92.00%, Insiders, Gary H. Taylor, Catherine A. Moran

Financial Data: **Fiscal Year End:** 12/31 **Latest Annual Data:** 12/31/2006

Year	Sales	Net Income
2006	NA	-$7,676,000
2005	NA	-$18,489,000
2004	$113,135,000	-$22,783,000

Curr. Assets:	$73,000	**Curr. Liab.:**	$1,855,000		
Plant, Equip.:	NA	**Total Liab.:**	$1,855,000	**Indic. Yr. Divd.:**	NA
Total Assets:	$1,386,000	**Net Worth:**	-$469,000	**Debt/ Equity:**	NA

CA Inc

Formerly: Computer Assoc International Inc
One Ca Plaza, Islandia, NY, 11749; ***PH:*** 1-631-342-3550; ***http://*** www.cai.com

General - Incorporation	DE	**Stock** - Price on:12/24/2007	$25.59
Employees	14,500	Stock Exchange	NYSE
Auditor	KPMG LLP	Ticker Symbol	CA
Stk Agt	Mellon Investor Services LLC	Outstanding Shares	528,590,000
Counsel	NA	E.P.S.	$0.55
DUNS No.	08-039-9256	Shareholders	NA

Business: The group's principal activities are to design, market, and license computer software products that helps business to run, manage and automate their it operations. Its software products address customers' it requirements in the following areas: enterprise management, security, storage, application life cycle, data and application development, and portal and business intelligence. The products operate with business computer hardware platforms, operating systems, and products marketed by other hardware and software companies. The customers of the group include csc, eds, and IBM global services. The group's products include unicenter(R), etrusttm, brightstor(R), allfusion(R), advantagetm and cleverpathtm. The group operates in North America, Africa, South America, Asia/pacific and Europe. In 2004, the group acquired esecurity online, silent runner and miramar systems inc.

Primary SIC and add'l.: 7379 7373 7372

CIK No: 0000356028

Subsidiaries: AMT (Australia) Pty. Ltd, Aprisma Management Technologies Limited (UK), Aprisma Management Technologies, Inc., Black Lion Investments (Pty) Limited, C.A. Computer Associates Israel Ltd(Ex Memco software Ltd.), C.A. Computer Associates S.A. (Spain), C.A. Foreign Spain, S.L., CA (Hong Kong) Limited, CA Canada Company, CA Computer Associates Cyprus Limited, CA Computer Associates European Holding GmbH, CA Computer Associates GmbH, CA Computer Associates Holding GmbH, CA Computer Associates India Private Limited, CA Computer Associates Technology GmbH 117 Subsidiaries included in the Index

Officers: John Swainson/Dir., CEO, Pres./$8,486,616.00, Russell M. Artzt/Founder, Vice Chmn./$5,600,769.00, George Fischer/Exec. VP, GM - Worldwide Sales, Donald R. Friedman/Exec. VP, Chief Marketing Officer, Andrew Goodman/Exec. VP - Worldwide Human Resources, Michael J. Christenson/COO, Exec. VP/$3,010,278.00, Kenneth V. Handal/Exec. VP - Global Risk, Compliance, Corp. Sec./$3,303,923.00, John Ruthven/Exec. VP - Worldwide Sales Operations, X. Kourakos/VP - Investor Relations, Carol Lu/Program Mgr. - Investor Relations, Bill Hughes/Sr. VP - Corporate Communications, Bill Warren/Sr. VP - Executive Communications, Public Affairs, Dan Kaferle/Sr. VP - Worldwide Public Relations, Bob Gordon/VP - Business Unit Public Relations, Jennifer Hallahan/Dir. - Corporate Public Relations *(22 Officers included in Index)*

Directors: John Swainson/Dir., CEO, Pres., William E. McCracken/Chmn., Lewis S. Ranieri/Dir., Robert E. La Blanc/Dir., Christopher B. Lofgren/Dir., Laura S. Unger/Dir., Walter P. Schuetze/Dir., Ron Zambonini/Dir., Alfonse M. D'Amato/Dir., Jay W. Lorsch/Dir., Raymond J. Bromark/Dir., Gary J. Fernandes/Dir.

Owners: Pzena Investment Management, LLC/6.34%, NWQ Investment Company, LLC/10.14%, Robert Davis, Nancy Cooper, Alfonse M. DAmato, Robert Cirabisi, Private Capital Management, L.P./12.46%, Walter H. Haefner/24.44%, Hotchkis and Wiley Capital Management, LLC/13.14%, Lewis S. Ranieri, Robert E. La Blanc, Walter P. Schuetze, Russell Artzt, Michael Christenson, John A. Swainson *(20 Owners included in Index)*

Financial Data: **Fiscal Year End:** 03/31 **Latest Annual Data:** 3/31/2007

Year	Sales	Net Income
2007	$3,943,000,000	$118,000,000
2006	$3,796,000,000	$159,000,000
2005	$3,560,000,000	-$4,000,000

Curr. Assets:	$3,101,000,000	**Curr. Liab.:**	$3,714,000,000	**P/E Ratio:**	116.32
Plant, Equip.:	$469,000,000	**Total Liab.:**	$6,895,000,000	**Indic. Yr. Divd.:**	$0.160
Total Assets:	$10,585,000,000	**Net Worth:**	$3,690,000,000	**Debt/ Equity:**	0.7075

Cabelas Inc

One Cabela Dr., Sidney, NE, 69162; ***PH:*** 1-308-254-5505; ***Fax:*** 1-308-254-4800; ***http://*** www.cabelas.com; ***Email:*** corporate@cabelas.com

General - Incorporation	DE	**Stock** - Price on:12/24/2007	$21.41
Employees	6,300	Stock Exchange	NYSE
Auditor	Deloitte & Touche LLP	Ticker Symbol	CAB
Stk Agt	Wells Fargo Shareowner Services	Outstanding Shares	65,770,000
Counsel	NA	E.P.S.	$1.25
DUNS No.	03-500-0363	Shareholders	NA

Business: The groups principle activities include marketing and retailing hunting, fishing, camping and related outdoor merchandise. The groups products include hunting, fishing and marine, camping merchandise, casual and outdoor apparel and footwear, optics, vehicle accessories, taxidermy products, gifts and home furnishings. The group operates through four business segments namely direct, retail, financial services and other. The group operates from United States.

Primary SIC and add'l.: 6022 5961 5941

CIK No: 0001267130

Subsidiaries: Cabelas Catalog, Inc., Cabelas Hong Kong, Limited, Cabelas Lodging, LLC, Cabelas Marketing& Brand Management, Inc., Cabelas Outdoor Adventures, Inc., Cabelas Retail GP, LLC, Cabelas Retail LA, LLC, Cabelas Retail MO, LLC, Cabelas Retail TX, L.P., Cabelas Retail, Inc., Cabelas Trophy Properties, LLC, Cabelas Ventures, Inc., Cabelas Wholesale, Inc., Cabelas.com, Inc., CRLP, LLC 23 Subsidiaries included in the Index

Officers: Dennis Highby/Dir., CEO, Pres., Ralph W. Castner/CFO, VP, Michael Callahan/Sr. VP - Retail Operations, Patrick A. Snyder/Sr. VP - Merchandising, Marketing, Brian J. Linneman/COO, VP, Joseph M. Friebe/VP, Chris Gay/Treasurer, Mgr. - Investor Relations, Charles Baldwin/VP, Chief Human Resources Officer

Directors: Dennis Highby/Dir., CEO, Pres., James W. Cabela/Vice Chmn., Richard N. Cabela/Chmn., John Gottschalk/Dir., Theodore M. Armstrong/Dir., Gerald E. Matzke/76/Dir. Emeritus, Michael R. McCarthy/Dir., Reuben Mark/Dir., Stephen P. Murray/Dir., John H. Edmondson/Dir.

Owners: James W. Cabela/18.39%, Michael Callahan, Brian J. Linneman, John Gottschalk, Gerald E. Matzke, Patrick A. Snyder, Reuben Mark, Richard N. Cabela/15.08%, Stephen P. Murray, Michael R. McCarthy/4.78%, Mary A. Cabela/15.06%, Dennis Highby/1.42%, Theodore M. Armstrong, Insiders/40.43%, Ralph W. Castner

Financial Data: **Fiscal Year End:** 12/31 **Latest Annual Data:** 12/30/2006

Year	Sales	Net Income
2006	$2,063,524,000	$85,785,000
2005	$1,799,661,000	$72,569,000

Curr. Assets:	$694,027,000	**Curr. Liab.:**	$548,468,000	**P/E Ratio:**	17.13
Plant, Equip.:	$472,221,000	**Total Liab.:**	$726,427,000	**Indic. Yr. Divd.:**	NA
Total Assets:	$1,366,280,000	**Net Worth:**	$639,853,000	**Debt/ Equity:**	0.3870

CabelTel International Corp

1755 Wittington Pl., Ste. 340, Dallas, TX, 75234; *PH:* 1-972-407-8400; *Fax:* 1-972-407-8435; *http://* www.cabeltel.us

General - Incorporation .... NV
Employees 20
Auditor .... Farmer Fuqua & Huff P.C
Stk Agt ...... American Stock Transfer & Trust Co.
Counsel .... Cable Partners Bulgaria LLC
DUNS No. 01-067-6914

Stock- Price on:12/24/2007 .... $4.65
Stock Exchange .... AMEX
Ticker Symbol .... GBR
Outstanding Shares .... NA
E.P.S $1.18
Shareholders .... NA

Business: The group's principal activity is to own and lease retirement specific real estate and an outlet shopping mall. The group also owns oil and gas leases. It provides housing, general support services and full time personal care services designed to aid elderly residents with the activities of daily living. The group's assisted living services include provision of meals, laundry, transportation, maintenance, security, assisting in bill paying, banking, personal shopping, ambulation, bathing, eating, dressing, personal hygiene and grooming. It also provides alzheimer's and special care services to residents suffering from alzheimer's or other forms of dementia. Through its oil and gas operations segment it seeks to keep producing wells properly maintained and to recondition and bring into production non-operating leases it owns. On 01-Aug-2003, the group acquired gaywood oil and gas llc and on 10-Dec-2003, it acquired gainesville outlet mall llc.

Primary SIC and add'l.: 8059

CIK No: 0000105744

Subsidiaries: American Realty Management, Inc., Big Bear Indian Art, LLC, Crown Pointe, Inc., Finley Equities, Inc., Gainesville Outlet Mall, LLC, Gainesville Partners, LLC, Gainesville Property, LP, Gaywood Oil & Gas II, LLC, Gaywood Oil & Gas, LLC, Greenbriar Financial Corporation, Kellway Corporation, King City Retirement Corporation, Mesquite, LLC, Narisma Holdings Limited, Real Estate Investors, LLC 35 Subsidiaries included in the Index

Officers: Gene S. Bertcher/59/Chmn., CEO, CFO, Pres./$186,000.00, Oscar Smith/Sec.

Directors: Gene S. Bertcher/59/Chmn., CEO, CFO, Pres., Roz Campisi Beadle/52/Dir., James E. Huffstickler/66/Dir., Dan Locklear/56/Dir., Victor L. Lund/80/Dir.

Owners: Insiders/7.29%, Roz Campisi Beadle, HKS Investment Corporation/11.04%, TacCo Financial, Inc./23.17%, Gene S. Bertcher/7.28%, JRG Investments, Inc./15.90%, International Health Products, Inc

Financial Data: *Fiscal Year End:*12/31 *Latest Annual Data:* 12/31/2006

Year	Sales	Net Income
2006	$4,268,000	$1,301,000
2005	$5,821,000	-$986,000
2004	$6,223,000	-$816,000

Curr. Assets:	$1,854,000	**Curr. Liab.:**	$1,127,000	**P/E Ratio:**	3.94
Plant, Equip.:	$6,833,000	**Total Liab.:**	$7,623,000	**Indic. Yr. Divd.:**	NA
Total Assets:	$9,702,000	**Net Worth:**	$2,079,000	**Debt/ Equity:**	NA

Cablevision Systems Corp

1111 Stewart Ave., Bethpage, NY, 11714; *PH:* 1-516-803-2300; *Fax:* 1-516-803-3134; *http://* www.cablevision.com

General - Incorporation .... DE
Employees 13,938
Auditor .... KPMG LLP
Stk Agt .... Mellon Investor Services LLC
Counsel .... Willkie Farr & Gallagher LLP
DUNS No. 80-003-1882

Stock- Price on:12/24/2007 .... $36.14
Stock Exchange .... NYSE
Ticker Symbol CVC
Outstanding Shares 293,230,000
E.P.S $0.64
Shareholders .... NA

Business: The group's principle activity is to provide cable television systems and telecommunication services. The group's products include smarter phone,internet and television. The group operates from United States.

Primary SIC and add'l.: 4841 5731 4813

CIK No: 0001053112

Subsidiaries: 1015 Tiffany Street, Corp., 1047 E 46th Street Corp., 1070 Jericho Turnpike Corp., 11 Penn Tv, LLC, 111 New South Road Corporation, 1111 Stewart Corporation, 1144 Route 109 Corp., 151 S. Fulton Street Corporation, 2234 Fulton Street Corporation, 389 Adams Street Corporation, A-r Cable Services - Ny, Inc., Amc Film Holdings LLC, Amc Movie Companion LLC, Amc New Media LLC, Amc Productions, Inc. 248 Subsidiaries included in the Index

Officers: Joshua Sapan/CEO, Pres. - Rainbow Media Holdings, LLC, James L. Dolan/52/Dir., CEO, Pres./$15,829,850.00, Patrick F. Dolan/56/Dir., Pres. - News 12 Networks, Wilt Hildenbrand/Sr. Advisor, Engineering, Technology, Patricia Armstrong/Sr. VP - Investor Relations, Ken Martin/Mgr. - Investor Relations, Kevin Watson/Sr. VP, Treasurer, Thomas M. Rutledge/COO/$11,036,890.00, John Bickham/Pres. - Cable, Communications, Michael Huseby/CFO, Exec. VP/$2,533,069.00, Victoria D. Salhus/Sr. VP, Deputy General Counsel, Sec., Keith Wm Harper/53/Sr. VP, Controller, Principal Accounting Officer, Thomas C. Dolan/Dir., CIO, Exec. VP, Steve Mills/COO, Pres. - Madison Square Garden Sports, Jonathan D. Schwartz/Exec. VP, General Counsel

Directors: James L. Dolan/52/Dir., CEO, Pres., Charles F. Dolan/81/Chmn., Hank J. Ratner/Vice Chmn., Marianne Dolan Weber/50/Dir., Patrick F. Dolan/56/Dir., Pres. - News 12 Networks, Vincent Tese/65/Dir., Rand V. Araskog/76/Dir., Charles D. Ferris/75/Dir., Leonard Tow/79/Dir., John R. Ryan/62/Dir., Richard H. Hochman/62/Dir., Thomas C. Dolan/Dir., CIO, Exec. VP, Frank J. Biondi/63/Dir., Grover C. Brown/73/Dir., Zachary W. Carter/58/Dir. *(18 Directors included in Index)*

Owners: Matthew J. Dolan, Paul J. Dolan, James L. Dolan, David M. Dolan, Lawrence J. Dolan, Kathleen M. Dolan, Richard H. Hochman, Rand V. Araskog, Mary S. Dolan, Insiders, Thomas C. Dolan, David M. Dolan, Patrick F. Dolan, Charles D. Ferris, Dolan Family Group/3.00% *(43 Owners included in Index)*

Financial Data: *Fiscal Year End:*12/31 *Latest Annual Data:* 12/31/2006

Year	Sales	Net Income
2006	$5,927,462,000	-$126,465,000
2005	$5,175,911,000	$89,320,000
2004	$4,932,864,000	-$676,092,000

Curr. Assets:	$1,667,447,000	**Curr. Liab.:**	$2,430,698,000	**P/E Ratio:**	50.19
Plant, Equip.:	$3,714,842,000	**Total Liab.:**	$15,134,440,000	**Indic. Yr. Divd.:**	NA
Total Assets:	$9,844,857,000	**Net Worth:**	-$5,339,253,000	**Debt/ Equity:**	NA

Cabot Corp

2 Seaport Ln., Ste. 1300, Boston, MA, 02210; *PH:* 1-617-345-0100; *Fax:* 1-617-342-6103; *http://* www.cabot-corp.com

General - Incorporation .... DE
Employees 4,300
Auditor .... Deloitte & Touche, LLP
Stk Agt .... Computershare Trust Co
Counsel .... NA
DUNS No. 00-101-3580

Stock- Price on:12/24/2007 .... $47.9026
Stock Exchange .... NYSE
Ticker Symbol .... CBT
Outstanding Shares 64,390,000
E.P.S $2.015
Shareholders .... NA

Business: The groups principle activity is to provide fine particles products and technology. The groups products include carbon black, fuel cell electrocatalysts, inkjet colorants and niobium. Customers served by the group include the aerospace, agriculture and automotive industries. The group operates from United States.

Primary SIC and add'l.: 2893 4924 2895 3339 2821 2819

CIK No: 0000016040

Subsidiaries: Aizu Holdings K.K., BCB Company, Black Rose Investments Limited, Botsel Limited, Cabot (Bermuda) Ltd., Cabot (China) Limited, Cabot Argentina S.A.I.C., Cabot Asia Investment Corporation, Cabot Australasia Investments Pty. Ltd., Cabot Australasia Pty. Ltd., Cabot B.V., Cabot Bluestar Chemical (Jiangxi) Co., Ltd., Cabot Brasil Industria e Comercio Ltda., Cabot Canada Ltd., Cabot Carbon Limited 74 Subsidiaries included in the Index

Officers: Kennett F. Burnes/64/Chmn., CEO, Pres., Nicholas P. Ballas/VP, GM - Asia Pacific, Eduardo E. Cordeiro/VP, GM - Cabot Supermetals, Brian A. Berube/VP, General Counsel, Dirk L. Blevi/59/Dir., Exec. VP, GM - Europe, Paul J. Gormisky/VP - Corporate Planning, James Belmont/VP, Sean Keohane/VP, GM - Performance Products, Ho-il Kim/VP - Strategic Development, Yakov Kutsovsky/VP - Research, Development, Helmut Lorat/VP - Engineering, Karen M. Morrissey/VP - Corporate Affairs, Martin O'Neill/VP - Safety, Health and Environmental Affairs, Ravijit Paintal/VP, GM - Fumed Metal Oxide, Aerogel, Chang Loo Sih/VP, GM - South America *(32 Officers included in Index)*

Directors: Kennett F. Burnes/64/Chmn., CEO, Pres., Ronaldo H. Schmitz/68/Dir., Juan Enriquez Cabot/48/Dir., Roderick C.G. MacLeod/57/Dir., Gautam S. Kaji/66/Dir., Lydia W. Thomas/63/Dir., Dirk L. Blevi/59/Dir., Exec. VP, GM - Europe, John F. O'Brien/64/Dir., Arthur L. Goldstein/72/Dir., Henry F. McCance/65/Dir., John H. McArthur/73/Dir., Mark S. Wrighton/57/Dir., Shengman Zhang/49/Dir., John S. Clarkeson/65/Dir.

Owners: Brian A. Berube, SPO Advisory Corp./13.06%, Ronaldo H. Schmitz, Jonathan P. Mason, Arthur L. Goldstein, John F. OBrien, Mark S. Wrighton, Franklin Resources,Inc./6.43%, John S. Clarkeson, S.A.C. Capital Associates, LLC/5.28%, Dirk L. Blevi, State Street Bank and Trust Company/10.27%, Gautam S. Kaji, Lydia W. Thomas, John H. McArthur *(21 Owners included in Index)*

Financial Data: *Fiscal Year End:*09/30 *Latest Annual Data:* 9/30/2006

Year	Sales	Net Income
2006	$2,543,000,000	$88,000,000
2005	$2,125,000,000	-$48,000,000
2004	$1,934,000,000	$124,000,000

Curr. Assets:	$1,255,000,000	**Curr. Liab.:**	$505,000,000	**P/E Ratio:**	23.77
Plant, Equip.:	$1,004,000,000	**Total Liab.:**	$1,270,000,000	**Indic. Yr. Divd.:**	$0.720
Total Assets:	$2,534,000,000	**Net Worth:**	$1,196,000,000	**Debt/ Equity:**	0.3418

Cabot Microelectronics Corp

870 N Commons Dr., Aurora, IL, 60504; *PH:* 1-630-375-6631; *http://* www.cabotcmp.com

General - Incorporation .... DE
Employees 742
Auditor .... PricewaterhouseCoopers LLP
Stk Agt .... Computershare Trust Co
Counsel .... Sullivan & Cromwell
DUNS No. .... NA

Stock- Price on:12/24/2007 .... $36.45
Stock Exchange .... NDQ
Ticker Symbol .... CCMP
Outstanding Shares 23,790,000
E.P.S $1.42
Shareholders .... NA

Business: The group's principal activity is to develop, manufacture and supply polishing slurries. This is supplied to the semiconductor industry for usage in chemical mechanical planarization (cmp). Cmp is a polishing process used by ic device manufacturers to planarize many of the multiple layers of material that are built upon silicon wafers to produce advanced devices. The polishing slurries are used in chemical mechanical planarization process to remove excess materials that are deposited on multiple layers that are built upon silicon wafers. Cmp enables ic device manufacturers to produce smaller ic devices with greater density, both of which improve the performance and capabilities of the device. The group markets the products through independent distributors and other industry suppliers. The products of the group are sold in the United States, Europe and Asia.

Primary SIC and add'l.: 3559

CIK No: 0001102934

Subsidiaries: Cabot Microelectronics Global Corporation, Cabot Microelectronics Japan K.K., Cabot Microelectronics Polishing Corporation, Cabot Microelectronics Singapore Pte. Ltd, Nihon Cabot Microelectronics K.K.

Officers: William P. Noglows/Chmn., CEO, Pres., Carol H. Bernstein/VP, Sec., General Counsel, Yumiko Damashek/MD - Japan, William S. Johnson/CFO, VP, David Li/MD - Korea, China, Daniel J. Pike/VP - Corporate Development, Clifford L. Spiro/VP - Research, Development, Daniel S. Wobby/VP - Asia Pacific Region, James Dehoniesto/CIO, Thomas S. Roman/Corporate Controller, Stephen R. Smith/VP - Marketing, Adam F. Weisman/VP - Business Operations, Jean Pol Delrue/VP - Global Sales

Directors: William P. Noglows/Chmn., CEO, Pres., Laurance H. Fuller/68/Dir., Robert J. Birgeneau/64/Dir., John P. Frazee/63/Dir., Edward J. Mooney/65/Dir., Steven V. Wilkinson/65/Dir., Bailing Xia/53/Dir., Albert Y.C. Yu/65/Dir.

Owners: Royce & Associates, LLC/9.20%, William S. Johnson, Snyder Capital Management LP/9.80%, Insiders/8.00%, Steven V. Wilkinson, Carol H. Bernstein/1.10%, Laurance H. Fuller, Adam F. Weisman, Kornitzer Capital Management Inc./7.30%, Albert Y. C. Yu, Clifford L. Spiro, William P. Noglows/1.90%, Legg Mason, Inc./10.60%, Robert J. Birgeneau, Edward J. Mooney *(16 Owners included in Index)*

Financial Data: *Fiscal Year End:*09/30 *Latest Annual Data:* 09/30/2007

Year	Sales	Net Income
2007	$338,205,000	$33,836,000
2006	$320,795,000	$32,948,000
2005	$270,484,000	$32,473,000

Curr. Assets:	$261,505,000	**Curr. Liab.:**	$38,833,000	**P/E Ratio:**	27.61
Plant, Equip.:	$130,176,000	**Total Liab.:**	$44,362,000	**Indic. Yr. Divd.:**	NA
Total Assets:	$412,133,000	**Net Worth:**	$367,771,000	**Debt/ Equity:**	0.0102

Cabot Oil & Gas Corp

1200 EnclAve. Pkwy., Houston, TX, 77077; *PH:* 1-281-589-4600; *Fax:* 1-281-589-4828; *http://* www.cabotog.com

General		**Stock**	
Incorporation	DE	Price on:12/24/2007	$41.31
Employees	374	Stock Exchange	NYSE
Auditor	PricewaterhouseCoopers LLP	Ticker Symbol	COG
Stk Agt	Bank of New York	Outstanding Shares	96,900,000
Counsel	Brown, Drew & Massey LLP	E.P.S	$3.17
DUNS No.	60-792-5757	Shareholders	NA

Business: The group's principal activity is to explore, develop, acquire and exploit oil and gas properties. It also transports, stores, gathers and purchases natural gas for resale. The group operates in three regions: the gulf coast region, the western region and mid-continent areas and the appalachian region. Substantially all of its operations are in the appalachian basin of west Virginia, Pennsylvania and New York, and in the anadarko basin of southwestern Kansas, Oklahoma and the Texas panhandle. As of 31-Dec, 2003, the group drilled 173 gross wells.

Primary SIC and add'l.: 1311 4923

CIK No: 0000858470

Subsidiaries: Big Sandy Gas Company, Cabot Oil& Gas Holding Company, Cabot Oil& Gas Marketing Corporation, Cabot Petroleum Canada Corporation, Cody Energy, LLC, Cody Oil& Gas, Inc., Cody Texas, LP, Cranberry Pipeline Corporation

Officers: Dan O. Dinges/54/Chmn., CEO, Pres./$3,686,079.00, Robert G. Drake/VP - Information Services, Operational Accounting, Jeffrey W. Hutton/VP - Marketing/$923,756.00, Lisa A. MacHesney/VP - Managing Counsel, Corp. Sec., Scott C. Schroeder/CFO, VP/$1,453,893.00, Michael B. Walen/COO, Sr. VP/$2,284,284.00, Abraham D. Garza/VP - Human Resources, Henry C. Smyth/VP, Controller, Treasurer, Scott J. Arnold/VP - Land, Assoc. General Counsel/$1,098,343.00, Les Watson/VP, Thomas S. Liberatore/VP, Regional Mgr. - Eastern Region

Directors: Dan O. Dinges/54/Chmn., CEO, Pres., John G.L. Cabot/73/Dir., Robert Kelley/62/Dir., James G. Floyd/71/Dir., David M. Carmichael/69/Dir., Robert L. Keiser/65/Dir., Dexter P. Peacock/66/Dir., William P. Vititoe/69/Dir.

Owners: Robert Kelley, Dan O. Dinges, Neuberger Berman, Inc./13.40%, Wellington Management Company, LLP/12.40%, Insiders/2.70%, David M. Carmichael, Earnest Partners, LLC/12.30%, James G. Floyd, Robert L. Keiser, Scott C. Schroeder, William P. Vititoe, Dexter P. Peacock, Michael B. Walen, Scott J. Arnold, John G.L. Cabot *(17 Owners included in Index)*

Financial Data: *Fiscal Year End:*12/31 *Latest Annual Data:* 12/31/2006

Year	Sales	Net Income
2006	$761,988,000	$321,175,000
2005	$682,797,000	$148,445,000
2004	$530,408,000	$88,378,000

Curr. Assets:	$315,682,000	**Curr. Liab.:**	$251,027,000	**P/E Ratio:**	13.03
Plant, Equip.:	$1,480,201,000	**Total Liab.:**	$889,293,000	**Indic. Yr. Divd.:**	$0.120
Total Assets:	$1,834,491,000	**Net Worth:**	$945,198,000	**Debt/ Equity:**	0.2174

Cache Inc

1440 Broadway, New York, NY, 10018; *PH:* 1-212-575-3200; *Fax:* 1-212-944-2842; *http://* www.cache-inc.com

General		**Stock**	
Incorporation	FL	Price on:12/24/2007	$13.92
Employees	1,230	Stock Exchange	NDQ
Auditor	Deloitte & Touche LLP	Ticker Symbol	CACH
Stk Agt	Continental Stock Transfer & Trust Co	Outstanding Shares	16,300,000
Counsel	Schulte Roth & Zable	E.P.S	$0.38
DUNS No.	07-847-4756	Shareholders	NA

Business: The group's principal activities are to own and operate two chains of women's apparel specialty stores. The retail stores and an on-line e-commerce Web site, sells women's apparel and accessories. As on 31-Dec-2003 the group operated 227 stores operated cache and 28 lillie rubin stores throughout the United States. The group's merchandise is classified into sportswear, dresses and accessories. Sportswear includes casual wear collections and sportswear separates. Dresses include evening suits and selections suitable for after five and social occasion dressing. Accessories include jewelry, belts, hats and handbags to complement the sportswear and dress selections.

Primary SIC and add'l.: 5632 5621

CIK No: 0000350199

Officers: Brian Woolf/Chmn., CEO, Margaret Feeney/CFO, Exec. VP, Thomas Reinckens/Dir., COO, Pres., Margarita Croasdaile/Mgr. - Human Resources, Allison Malkin/MD - Integrated Corporate Relations, Adrienne Kantor/Exec. VP, Chief Merchandising Officer

Directors: Brian Woolf/Chmn., CEO, Thomas Reinckens/Dir., COO, Pres., Morton J. Schrader/Dir., Andrew M. Saul/Dir., Gene S. Gage/Dir., Arthur S. Mintz/Dir.

Owners: Margaret J. Feeney, Andrew M. Saul and affiliates/9.30%, Palo Alto Investors, LLC/7.90%, Royce and Associates LLC/10.80%, Vardon Capital, LLC and affiliates/8.20%, Thomas E. Reinckens/1.50%, Insiders/13.80%, Morton J. Schrader, Brian Woolf/2.90%

Financial Data: *Fiscal Year End:*12/31 *Latest Annual Data:* 12/30/2006

Year	Sales	Net Income
2006	$278,992,000	$8,271,000
2005	$266,345,000	$13,405,000

Curr. Assets:	$97,260,000	**Curr. Liab.:**	$33,474,000	**P/E Ratio:**	33.95
Plant, Equip.:	$52,760,000	**Total Liab.:**	$51,888,000	**Indic. Yr. Divd.:**	NA
Total Assets:	$150,884,000	**Net Worth:**	$98,996,000	**Debt/ Equity:**	NA

Caci International Inc

1100 N Glebe Rd., Ste. 200, Arlington, VA, 22201; *PH:* 1-703-841-7800; *Fax:* 1-703-841-7882; *http://* www.caci.com

General		**Stock**	
Incorporation	DE	Price on:12/24/2007	$51.9
Employees	10,400	Stock Exchange	NYSE
Auditor	Ernst & Young LLP	Ticker Symbol	CAI
Stk Agt	American Stock Transfer & Trust Co.	Outstanding Shares	30,900,000
Counsel	NA	E.P.S	$2.51
DUNS No.	04-553-4641	Shareholders	NA

Business: The groups principle activity is to provide simulation technology for the IT and communication industries. The groups areas of expertise include systems integration, managed network services, knowledge management and engineering services. In the year 2007 the group acquired The Wexford Group International and Athena Innovative Solutions, Inc. The group operates from United States.

Primary SIC and add'l.: 7373 7372 6719 7379 8711 7371

CIK No: 0000016058

Subsidiaries: CACI Dynamic Systems, Inc, CACI Enterprise Solutions, Inc, CACI Enterprise Solutions, Inc., CACI Limited, Caci Mtl Systems, Inc, CACI Premier Technology, Inc, CACI Systems, Inc., CACI Technologies, Inc, CACI Technology Insights, Inc., Caci, Inc.-commercial, Caci, Inc.-federal, Caci-iss, Inc., Caci-nsr, Inc.

Officers: Gregory R. Bradford/CEO - Caci Limited, Pres. - Information Solutions Group, Paul M. Cofoni/Dir., CEO, Pres., J. P. London/Exec. Chmn., William M. Fairl/Pres. - US Operations, Jody A. Brown/Exec. VP - Public Relations, Business Communications, Ronald A. Schneider/Exec. VP - Business Development, Albert M. Calland/Exec. VP - Security - Intelligence Integration, Deborah B. Dunie/CTO, Exec. VP, Dale E. Luddeke/Exec. VP - Corporate Business Development, Jane Forman/Contact - Homeland Security, Richard F.G. Miller/Exec. VP - Corporate Development, Ryan Wagener/Contact - Intelligence Solutions, David Andrew/Contact - Knowledge Management, Jeff Barsanti/Contact - Logistics, Engineering, Mark Beran/Contact - Media Services *(50 Officers included in Index)*

Directors: Paul M. Cofoni/Dir., CEO, Pres., J. P. London/Exec. Chmn., Warren R. Phillips/Dir., Peter A. Derow/68/Dir., Charles P. Revoile/Dir., Herbert W. Anderson/Dir., Barbara A. McNamara/Dir., Michael J. Mancuso/66/Dir., Richard L. Leatherwood/Dir., Gregory G. Johnson/Dir., Dan R. Bannister/Dir., Hugh H. Shelton/Dir.

Owners: Richard L. Leatherwood, Insiders/2.92%, Gregory G. Johnson, Charles P. Revoile, T. Rowe Price Associates, Inc/5.29%, Kinetics Asset Management, Inc/11.65%, Barbara A. McNamara, William M. Fairl, Paul M. Cofoni, Neuberger Berman, Inc./6.53%, Dan R. Bannister, Herbert W. Anderson, J. P. London/1.18%, Warren R. Phillips, FMR Corp/10.35% *(17 Owners included in Index)*

Financial Data: *Fiscal Year End:*06/30 *Latest Annual Data:* 06/30/2007

Year	Sales	Net Income
2007	$1,937,972,000	$78,532,000
2006	$1,755,324,000	$84,840,000
2005	$1,623,062,000	$85,316,000

Curr. Assets:	$449,829,000	**Curr. Liab.:**	$211,365,000	**P/E Ratio:**	20.43
Plant, Equip.:	$25,082,000	**Total Liab.:**	$622,731,000	**Indic. Yr. Divd.:**	NA
Total Assets:	$1,368,090,000	**Net Worth:**	$745,359,000	**Debt/ Equity:**	0.4050

Cadbury Schweppes Plc

5301 Legacy Dr., Plano, TX, 75024; *PH:* 1-972-673-7000; *Fax:* 1-972-673-7980; *http://* www.cadburyschweppes.com

General		**Stock**	
Incorporation	UK	Price on:12/24/2007	$54.47
Employees	66,702	Stock Exchange	NYSE
Auditor	Deloitte & Touche LLP	Ticker Symbol	CSG
Stk Agt	Morgan ADR Service Center	Outstanding Shares	523,640,000
Counsel	NA	E.P.S	$2.01
DUNS No.	21-052-2751	Shareholders	NA

Business: The group's principal activities are the manufacture, distribution and sale of branded beverages and confectionery products. In confectionery, the group has manufacturing facilities in 37 countries and markets a broad range of chocolates, gum and sugar confectionery brands in over 190 countries in the form of bars, blocks, bagged products, packets, rolls, boxed assortments, chocolate eggs and novelties. In beverages, the group operates both as a manufacturer and as a licensor selling concentrate and syrup to independently owned manufacturers to which it also supplies technical and marketing support. Brands include Cadbury, Halls, Trident, Dentyne, Hollywood, Dr Pepper, 7 Up, Schweppes, Snapple, Hawaiian Punch, Sunkist, A&W, Mott's, Clamato, Clorets, Chiclets, Bubbaloo, Swedish Fish, and Orangina. The group operates in the Americas, Europe, Middle East, Africa and Asia-Pacific. In 2003, the group acquired Adams Confectionery and the Natural Confectionery Co.

Primary SIC and add'l.: 2086 2064

CIK No: 0000744473

Subsidiaries: Adams McCCA Holdings BV, Apollinaris & Schweppes GmbH, Berkeley Re Ltd, Berkeley Square Investments Ltd, Bromor Foods (Pty) Ltd, Cadbury (Swaziland) (Pty) Ltd, Cadbury Adams (Thailand) Ltd, Cadbury Adams Bolivia S.A., Cadbury Adams Brasil Industria e Comercio de Produtos Alimenticios Ltda, Cadbury Adams Canada Inc, Cadbury Adams Colombia SA, Cadbury Adams Costa Rica SA, Cadbury Adams Distribuidora Mexico, SA de CV, Cadbury Adams Dominicana S.A., Cadbury Adams Ecuador SA 95 Subsidiaries included in the Index

Officers: Todd Stitzer/56/CEO, Bob Stack/58/Chief Human Resources Officer, Hester Blanks/55/Group Sec., Ken Hanna/55/CFO

Directors: John Sunderland/63/Non - Exec. Chmn., Raymond G. Viault/63/Non - Exec. Dir., Rosemary Thorne/Non - Exec. Dir., Rick Braddock/Non - Exec. Dir., Wolfgang D. Berndt/65/Non - Exec. Dir., Lord Patten/64/Non - Exec. Dir., Roger Carr/61/Dir., David Thompson/66/Non - Exec. Dir., Sanjiv Ahuja/52/Non - Exec. Dir., Guy Elliott/Non - Exec. Dir., Ellen Marram/61/Non - Exec. Dir.

Owners: Sir John Sunderland, Wolfgang Berndt, David Thompson, Bob Stack, Lord Patten, Roger Carr, Raymond Viault, Ken Hanna, Rosemary Thorne, Rick Braddock, Sanjiv Ahuja, Todd Stitzer

Financial Data: *Fiscal Year End:*01/01 *Latest Annual Data:* 12/31/2006

Year	Sales	Net Income
2006	$14,550,236,000	$2,025,709,000
2005	$12,934,265,000	$827,348,000

Curr. Assets:	$4,966,319,000	**Curr. Liab.:**	$6,713,836,000	**P/E Ratio:**	46.73
Plant, Equip.:	$3,540,094,000	**Total Liab.:**	$12,162,093,000	**Indic. Yr. Divd.:**	NA
Total Assets:	$21,536,386,000	**Net Worth:**	$9,374,294,000	**Debt/ Equity:**	NA

Cadence Design Systems Inc

2655 Seely Ave., Bldg. 5, San Jose, CA, 95134; *PH:* 1-408-943-1234; *Fax:* 1-408-428-5001; *http://* www.cadence.com; *Email:* investor_relations@cadence.com

General		**Stock**	
Incorporation	DE	Price on:12/24/2007	$22.59
Employees	5,200	Stock Exchange	NDQ
Auditor	KPMG LLP	Ticker Symbol	CDNS
Stk Agt	Mellon Investor Services LLC	Outstanding Shares	278,340,000
Counsel	NA	E.P.S	$0.65
DUNS No.	10-406-8093	Shareholders	NA

Business: The group's principal activity is to license electronic design automation, or eda, software, sell or lease hardware technology and to provide design and methodology services throughout the world to help accelerate and manage customers' electronic product development processes. The group operates through three segments: products segment develops and markets software and hardware technologies to customers. Maintenance segment services the ongoing, after-sale support requirements of those products through technical support and software updates. Services segment provides customers with educational services on training customers for the efficient and effective use of technologies, methodology services to assist customers in optimizing the use of technologies within their design activities. During the year the group acquired celestry design technologies inc, get2chip.com inc, certain assets from innotech corporation and verplex systems inc.

Primary SIC and add'l.: 7371 7373 7378

CIK No: 0000813672

Subsidiaries: 849 College Avenue, Inc., Ambit Design Systems, Inc., Axis Systems Europe SARL, Axis Systems International Holding Limited Partnership, Axis Systems LLC, Beijing Cadence Electronics Technology Co., Ltd., Cadence China Ltd., Cadence Credit Corporation, Cadence Design (Israel) II, Ltd., Cadence Design Foundry UK Ltd., Cadence Design Services YK, Cadence Design Systems (Canada) Limited, Cadence Design Systems (Cyprus) Limited, Cadence Design Systems (India) Private Ltd., Cadence Design Systems (Ireland) Limited 68 Subsidiaries included in the Index

Officers: Michael J. Fister/Dir., CEO, Pres./$13,737,610.00, Kevin Bushby/Exec. VP - Worldwide Field Operations/$4,001,027.00, Ted Vucurevich/CTO, Sr. VP - Advanced Research, Development, Moshe Gavrielov/Exec. VP, GM - Verification Division/$2,363,283.00, Debi Muchow/Sr. VP - Global Human Resources, Lung Chu/AP Pres., Corporate VP, Ryoichi Kawashima/Pres. - Cadence Japan, Aki Fujimura/Sr. VP - New Business Incubation, Smith R.L. McKeithen/Sr. VP, General Counsel, Jan Willis/Sr. VP - Industry Alliances, Dean Solov/Contact - Virtuoso, Dan Holden/Contact - DFM, Low Power, Encounter, Jennifer Jordan/Corporate VP, Alan Lindstrom/Dir. - Investor Relations, Therese Papenfuss/Sr. Financial Analyst, Investor Relations (29 Officers included in Index)

Directors: Michael J. Fister/Dir., CEO, Pres., John B. Shoven/Chmn., George M. Scalise/Dir., Donald L. Lucas/Dir., Alberto Sangiovanni-Vincentelli/Dir., Lip-Bu Tan/Dir., Roger S. Siboni/Dir., John A.C. Swainson/Dir.

Owners: John B. Shoven, William Porter, James S. Miller, Kevin Bushby, Insiders/3.52%, Lord, Abbett& Co. LLC/6.86%, Moshe Gavrielov, George M. Scalise, Donald L. Lucas, Alberto Sangiovanni-Vincentelli, Franklin Resources, Inc./11.68%, Lip-Bu Tan, Michael J. Fister/1.55%, Roger S. Siboni, John A.C. Swainson

Financial Data: Fiscal Year End:12/31   Latest Annual Data: 12/30/2006

Year	Sales	Net Income
2006	$1,483,895,000	$142,592,000
2005	$1,329,192,000	$49,343,000

Curr. Assets:	$1,276,302,000	Curr. Liab.:	$605,851,000	P/E Ratio:	34.75
Plant, Equip.:	$356,945,000	Total Liab.:	$1,556,608,000	Indic. Yr. Divd.:	NA
Total Assets:	$3,401,312,000	Net Worth:	$1,844,704,000	Debt/ Equity:	0.3908

Cadence Financial Corp

Formerly: NBC Capital Corp
Nbc Plz., Starkville, MS, 39759; **PH:** 1-601-343-1341; **http://** www.cadencebanking.com

General - Incorporation	MS	Stock - Price on:12/24/2007	NA
Employees	419	Stock Exchange	AMEX
Auditor	T. E. Lott & Co	Ticker Symbol	NA
Stk Agt	Suntrust Bank	Outstanding Shares	NA
Counsel	NA	E.P.S.	NA
DUNS No.	15-650-5745	Shareholders	NA

Business: The group's principal activities are to provide wholesale and retail banking services including mortgage loans and trust services. The group originates commercial, financial and agricultural loans, real estate construction loans, and real estate mortgage and installment loans. It also provides savings accounts, money market accounts and now accounts. The other services provided include insurance services, consumer-financing services and sale of annuity products. The services are provided to customers in the industrial, agricultural, government, educational and individual accounts sectors. The business is carried out through twenty-seven banking facilities and an administration center that serve the communities of aberdeen, amory, brooksville, caledonia, columbus, hamilton, maben, new hope, philadelphia, west point and starkville. On 31-Mar-2004, the group acquired enterprise bancshares inc.

Primary SIC and add'l.: 6021 6712

CIK No: 0000742054

Subsidiaries: Cadence Bank, N.A., Commerce National Insurance Co., Enterprise (TN) Statutory Trust I (See Note 1), Enterprise Bancshares, Inc., Galloway-Chandler-McKinney Insurance Agency, Inc., NBC Capital Corporation (MS) Statutory Trust I (See Note 1), NBC Insurance Services of Alabama, Inc., NBC Service Corporation

Officers: Lewis F. Mallory/Chmn., CEO - Cadence Financial Corporation/$733,608.00, Bobby L. Harper/Dir., Pres. - Columbus Region, Richard T. Haston/CFO, Exec. VP/$314,396.00, Mark A. Abernathy/Dir., COO, Pres./$369,436.00

Directors: Lewis F. Mallory/Chmn., CEO - Cadence Financial Corporation, Allen B. Puckett/Dir. - Cadence Financial Corporation, David C. Byars/Dir. - Cadence Financial Corporation, Robert L. Calvert/Dir. - Cadence Financial Corporation, Mark A. Abernathy/Dir., COO, Pres., Robert A. Cunningham/Dir. - Cadence Financial Corporation, Bobby L. Harper/Dir., Pres. - Columbus Region, Gregory M. Duckett/Dir. - Cadence Financial Corporation, Nutie J. Dowdle/Dir. - Cadence Financial Corporation, Harvey Ronald Foxworthy/Dir. - Cadence Financial Corporation, Hunter M. Gholson/Dir. - Cadence Financial Corporation, Robert S. Jones/Dir., Sammy J. Smith/Dir. - Cadence Financial Corporation, Robert S. Caldwell/Dir. - Cadence Financial Corporation, James C. Galloway/Dir. - Cadence Financial Corporation (20 Directors included in Index)

Owners: Richard T. Haston, Gregory M. Duckett, Dan R. Lee, Shane C. Williams, H. R. Foxworthy, Sammy J. Smith, Lewis F. Mallory/1.20%, Clifton S. Hunt, Robert L. Calvert/1.40%, Allen B. Puckett/1.50%, Stokes H. Smith, Mark A. Abernathy, Nutie J. Dowdle/1.40%, Robert S. Caldwell, James C. Galloway (21 Owners included in Index)

Cadence Pharmaceuticals Inc

12481 High Bluff Dr., Ste. 200, San Diego, CA, 92130; **PH:** 1-858-436-1400; **Fax:** 1-858-436-1401; **http://** www.cadencepharm.com; **Email:** info@cadencepharm.com

General - Incorporation	DE	Stock - Price on:12/24/2007	$12.59
Employees	35	Stock Exchange	NDQ
Auditor	Ernst & Young, LLP	Ticker Symbol	CADX
Stk Agt	American Stock Transfer & Trust Co.	Outstanding Shares	29,130,000
Counsel	NA	E.P.S.	-$2.71
DUNS No.	NA	Shareholders	NA

Business: The groups principal activities include licensing, developing and commercializing proprietary product candidates. The groups services include Medicare and Medicaid. The products of the group include IV APAP and Omigard. The group operates from the United States, Europe and Canada.

Primary SIC and add'l.: 2834

CIK No: 0001333248

Officers: Theodore R. Schroeder/Dir., CEO, Pres., James B. Breitmeyer/Exec. VP - Development, Chief Medical Officer, William S. Craig/Sr. VP - Pharmaceutical Development, Manufacturing, William R. Larue/Sr. VP, CFO, Mike A. Royal/VP - Clinical Development, Analygesics, David Socks/VP - Business Development, Hazel M. Aker/Sr. VP, General Counsel, Catherine J. Hardalo/VP - Clinical Development, Malvina Laudicina/VP - Regulatory Affairs, Quality Assurance, Anna Gralinska/Investor Relations Contact

Directors: Theodore R. Schroeder/Dir., CEO, Pres., Cam L. Garner/Chmn., Brian Atwood/Dir., Samuel L. Barker/Dir., Michael A. Berman/Dir., James C. Blair/Dir., Alan Frazier/Dir., Christopher J. Twomey/Dir.

Owners: Funds affiliated with Technology Partners, Michael A. Berman, Insiders, James C. Blair, William R. LaRue, Cam L. Garne, David A. Socks, Frazier HealthcareV, LP, Funds affiliated with Domain Associates, L.L.C., Theodore R. Schroeder, Christopher J. Twomey, Samuel L. Barker, William S. Craig, Alain B. Schreiber, Brian G. Atwood (20 Owners included in Index)

Financial Data: Fiscal Year End:NA   Latest Annual Data: 12/31/2006

Year	Sales	Net Income
2006	NA	-$52,173,000
2005	NA	-$7,523,000

Curr. Assets:	$87,994,000	Curr. Liab.:	$11,790,000		
Plant, Equip.:	$3,559,000	Total Liab.:	$17,913,000	Indic. Yr. Divd.:	NA
Total Assets:	$93,322,000	Net Worth:	$75,409,000	Debt/ Equity:	0.0597

Cadence Resources Corp

4110 Copper Ridge Dr., Ste. 100, Traverse City, MI, 49684; **PH:** 1-231-941-0073

General - Incorporation	UT	Stock - Price on:12/24/2007	NA
Employees	3,300	Stock Exchange	AMEX
Auditor	Rachlin Cohen & Holtz LLP	Ticker Symbol	NA
Stk Agt	OTC Corporate Transfer Service Co	Outstanding Shares	NA
Counsel	NA	E.P.S.	NA
DUNS No.	95-822-1772	Shareholders	NA

Business: The group's principle activities are to acquire, explore and develop oil and gas properties generally through leases of the prospective property. The group is currently in exploration stage and is earning minimal revenue. Prior to this, the group was acquiring and developing mineral properties. The group carries its operations in wilbarger county, Texas, desoto parish, Louisiana and alpena county, Michigan.

Primary SIC and add'l.: 1382

CIK No: 0000933157

Subsidiaries: Aurora Energy, Ltd., Nevada corporation

Officers: William W. Deneau/63/Chmn., Principal Executive Officer, Pres./$339,424.00, Ronald E. Huff/53/Dir., CFO/$673,921.00, John V. Miller/49/VP - Business, Corporate Development/$191,207.00, Thomas W. Tucker/65/VP - Exploration/$189,332.00

Directors: William W. Deneau/63/Chmn., Principal Executive Officer, Pres., Ronald E. Huff/53/Dir., CFO, Richard M. Deneau/61/Dir., Earl V. Young/67/Dir., Kevin D. Stulp/52/Dir., Gary J. Myles/62/Dir., Wayne G. Schaeffer/61/Dir.

Owners: John V. Miller/3.00%, Kevin D. Stulp, Gary J. Myles, Richard M. Deneau, Earl V. Young, Insiders/12.00%, FMR Corp./15.00%, William W. Deneau/4.00%, Crestview Capital Master, LLC/6.00%, Lorraine M. King, Ronald E. Huff, Thomas W. Tucker/3.00%, Nathan A. Low Roth IRA and affiliates/8.00%

Cadiz Inc

550 S Hope St., Ste. 2850, Los Angeles, CA, 90071; **PH:** 1-213-271-1600; **Fax:** 1-213-271-1614; **http://** www.cadizinc.com

General - Incorporation	DE	Stock - Price on:12/24/2007	$22.94
Employees	9	Stock Exchange	NDQ
Auditor	PricewaterhouseCoopers LLP	Ticker Symbol	CDZI
Stk Agt	Continental Stock Transfer & Trust Co	Outstanding Shares	11,890,000
Counsel	NA	E.P.S.	-$1
DUNS No.	NA	Shareholders	NA

Business: The groups principle activities include acquiring and developing land and water resources. The group operates from the United States.

Primary SIC and add'l.: 6519 6519 4941 6519

CIK No: 0000727273

Subsidiaries: Cadiz Real Estate LLC, Rancho Cadiz Mutual Water Company, SW Estate, Inc.

Officers: Keith Brackpool/Chmn., CEO, Pres./$920,383.00, Richard E. Stoddard/Chmn., CEO - Cadiz Real Estate LLC/$905,392.00, Courtney Degener/Mgr. - Investor Relations, O'Donnell Iselin/CFO, Sec./$431,839.00

Directors: Keith Brackpool/Chmn., CEO, Pres., Richard E. Stoddard/Chmn., CEO - Cadiz Real Estate LLC, Timothy J. Shaheen/Dir., Murray H. Hutchison/Dir., Raymond J. Pacini/Dir., Stephen J. Duffy/Dir., Geoffrey Grant/Dir., Winston Hickox/Dir.

Owners: Bedford Oak Partners, L.P., Pictet Asset Management SA, ODonnell Iselin, ING Groep N.V., Murray Hutchison, Timothy J. Shaheen, ING Groep N.V., Keith Brackpool, Richard E. Stoddard, Peloton Partners, LLP, FMR Corp., Raymond J. Pacini, Insiders

Financial Data: Fiscal Year End:12/31   Latest Annual Data: 12/31/2006

Year	Sales	Net Income
2006	$614,000	-$13,825,000
2005	$1,197,000	-$23,025,000
2004	$47,000	-$16,037,000

Curr. Assets:	$10,941,000	Curr. Liab.:	$833,000		
Plant, Equip.:	$35,190,000	Total Liab.:	$26,714,000	Indic. Yr. Divd.:	NA
Total Assets:	$50,326,000	Net Worth:	$23,612,000	Debt/ Equity:	1.0960

Cadmus Communications Corp

1801 Bayberry Ct., Ste. 200, Richmond, VA, 23226; **PH:** 1-804-287-5680; **http://** www.cadmus.com

Ste. 200, Richmond, VA, 23226; ***PH:*** 1-804-287-5680; ***http://*** www.cadmus.com

General - Incorporation	VA	**Stock**- Price on:12/24/2007	NA
Employees	3,300	Stock Exchange	NDQ
Auditor	BDO Seidman, LLP	Ticker Symbol	CDMS
Stk Agt	Wachovia Bank N.A	Outstanding Shares	NA
Counsel	NA	E.P.S.	NA
DUNS No.	11-906-8542	Shareholders	NA

Business: The group's principal activities are to provide integrated graphic communication services and specialty packaging. The operations are carried out in two segments. The publisher services segment consisting of cadmus professional communications, cadmus specialty publications and cadmus port city press divisions, provides scientific, technical and medical journals, special interest and trade magazines and directories. The services include peer review, content processing and digital management, book and directory database management, production and reprint services. The segment targets non-profit and commercial publishers. The specialty packaging segment consisting of cadmus whitehall produces folding cartons and provides Web and sheet-fed promotional printing, assembly and distribution. Its markets include telecommunications, software, apparel, healthcare and financial services.

Primary SIC and add'l.: 2741 2657 2721 2752

CIK No: 0000745274

Subsidiaries: American Graphics Inc., Cadmus Delaware Inc., Cadmus Direct Marketing Inc., Cadmus Financial Distribution Inc., Cadmus Government Publication Services Inc., Cadmus Hong Kong Limited, Cadmus Interactive Inc., Cadmus International Holdings Inc., Cadmus Investments LLC, Cadmus Journal Services Inc., Cadmus KnowledgeWorks International Ltd., Cadmus Marketing Group Inc., Cadmus Marketing Inc., Cadmus Marketing UK Limited, Cadmus Printing Group Inc. 30 Subsidiaries included in the Index

Owners: Paul K. Suijk, Bruce G. Willis, Thomas C. Norris, Keith Hamill, Gerard P. Lux/1.22%, Martina L. Bradford, Rutabaga Capital Management/8.08%, J.& W. Seligman& Co. Inc./15.11%, Brencourt Advisors, LLC/6.67%, Insiders/24.87%, Nathu R. Puri/18.62%, Edward B. Hutton, Peter R. Hanson, Thomas E. Costello, James E. Rogers *(19 Owners included in Index)*

Cadus Corp

767 Fifth Ave, New York, NY, 10153; ***PH:*** 1-212-702-4367

General - Incorporation	DE	**Stock**- Price on:12/24/2007	$1.85
Employees	NA	Stock Exchange	OTC
Auditor	Holtz Rubenstein Reminick LLP	Ticker Symbol	KDUS
Stk Agt	Herman Group Inc	Outstanding Shares	13,140,000
Counsel	NA	E.P.S.	-$0.05
DUNS No.	NA	Shareholders	NA

Business: The group's principal activity is to seek to license its technologies and realize value from its assets. It also seeks to use a portion of its available cash to acquire technologies or products or to acquire or invest in companies. In Dec 2001, the group organized a wholly owned subsidiary, cadus technologies, inc and transferred its yeast-based drug discovery technologies to the subsidiary. On 19-Dec-2001, the subsidiary licensed its yeast-based drug discovery technologies including various reagents and its library of over 25,000 yeast strains, on a non-exclusive basis to osi pharmaceuticals, inc.

Primary SIC and add'l.: 2836 8731

CIK No: 0000911148

Subsidiaries: Cadus Technologies, Inc

Officers: David Blitz/76/CEO, Pres.

Directors: James R. Broach/60/Dir., Russell D. Glass/45/Dir., Carl C. Icahn/72/Dir., Peter S. Liebert/72/Dir., Jack G. Wasserman/71/Dir.

Owners: Insiders/38.11%, Russell D. Glass, Carl C. Icahn/37.74%, Jack G. Wasserman, GlaxoSmithKline plc/5.03%, Peter S. Liebert

Financial Data: ***Fiscal Year End:***12/31 ***Latest Annual Data:*** 12/31/2006

Year	Sales	Net Income
2006	$100,000	$446,000
2005	$100,000	-$41,000
2004	$100,000	-$394,000

Curr. Assets:	$25,236,000	***Curr. Liab.:***	$61,000		
Plant, Equip.:	NA	***Total Liab.:***	$61,000	***Indic. Yr. Divd.:***	NA
Total Assets:	$26,047,000	***Net Worth:***	$25,985,000	***Debt/ Equity:***	NA

CAE Inc

8585 Cte de Liesse, Saint-Laurent, Quebec, FL, H4T 1G6; ***PH:*** 1-514-341-6780; ***Fax:*** 1-514-341-7699; ***http://*** www.cae.ca; ***Email:*** investor.relations@cae.com

General - Incorporation	Canada	**Stock**- Price on:12/24/2007	$13.74
Employees	NA	Stock Exchange	NYSE
Auditor	PricewaterhouseCoopers LLP	Ticker Symbol	CGT
Stk Agt	Computershare Trust Co of Canada	Outstanding Shares	252,090,000
Counsel	James W. Mccutcheon	E.P.S.	$0.56
DUNS No.	NA	Shareholders	NA

Business: The group's principle activities are to design and produce commercial flight simulators, visual systems and training systems. The group operates in two segments: civil simulation and training and military simulation and marine controls. The civil simulation and training segment supplies civil flight simulators, visual systems and provides business and civil aviation training. The military simulation and marine controls segment supplies military flight and land-based simulators, visual and training systems. This segment also supplies marine controls and training systems.

Primary SIC and add'l.: 3812 3553 3743 3699

CIK No: 0001173382

Subsidiaries: 4025164 Canada Inc, Academia Aeronautica De Evora S.A, B.V. Nationale Luchtvaartschool, CAE (UK) plc, Cae (us) Inc., Cae (us) LLC, CAE Aircrew Training Services plc, CAE Australia Pty Ltd, CAE Aviation Training B.V, CAE Aviation Training Chile Limitada2, CAE Aviation Training International Ltd, CAE Beyss Grundstcksgesellschaft GmbH, CAE Center Amsterdam B.V, CAE Center Brussels N.V, CAE Center Maastricht B.V 54 Subsidiaries included in the Index

Officers: Robert E. Brown/Dir., CEO, Pres., Bill Dolny/VP - Sales, CAE Civil Traning, Services, Dubai, Terri Vassilaros/Customer Service Supervisor - Client Service, Charlotte, Marykate Garcia/Regional Sales Mgr. - Latin America, Richard Dickinson/Regional Sales Mgr. - Sales, Burgess Hill, Jacqueline Van Poeteren/Regional Sales Mgr. - Commercial, Burgess, John Blackwell/Head - Training, Burgess, Nic Anderson/MD - Centre Management, Burgess, Alan Kwong/Regional GM - CAE Aviation Training, Kuala Lumpur, Marie Jose Molaguero/Contact - Planning, Scheduling, Madrid, Vsevolod Shishkin/Deputy Dir. - Aeroflot, Moscow, Alessandro Pinho/Centre Mgr. - Santiago, Lorena Encina/Customer Service Administrator - Client Service, Santiago, Rodolfo Arellana/Regional Sales Mgr. - Santiago, Reyes Jardi/Mgr. - Customer Service, Madrid *(84 Officers included in Index)*

Directors: Robert E. Brown/Dir., CEO, Pres., Lynton R. Wilson/Chmn., Paul Gagne/Dir., Brian E. Barents/Dir., Robert Lacroix/Dir., John Lenyo/Dir. - CAE USA, Ellis D. Parker/Dir. - CAE USA, Leighton W. Smith/Dir. - CAE USA, Lawrence N. Stevenson/Dir., James W. McCutcheon/Dir., James A. Grant/Dir., John A. Craig/Dir., Anthony S. Fell/Dir., Garfield H. Emerson/Dir., James F. Hankinson/Dir. *(21 Directors included in Index)*

Financial Data: ***Fiscal Year End:***03/31 ***Latest Annual Data:*** 03/31/2007

Year	Sales	Net Income
2007	$1,077,028,000	$116,150,000
2006	$948,649,000	$63,832,000
2005	$810,656,000	-$164,482,000

Curr. Assets:	$468,413,000	***Curr. Liab.:***	$493,431,000		
Plant, Equip.:	$724,167,000	***Total Liab.:***	$946,250,000	***Indic. Yr. Divd.:***	$0.040
Total Assets:	$1,477,295,000	***Net Worth:***	$531,045,000	***Debt/ Equity:***	NA

Cagle's Inc

2000 Hills Ave. NW, Atlanta, GA, 30318; ***PH:*** 1-404-355-2820; ***Fax:*** 1-404-355-9326; ***http://*** www.cagles.net; ***Email:*** marketing@caglesinc.com

General - Incorporation	GA	**Stock**- Price on:12/24/2007	$7.8
Employees	1,850	Stock Exchange	AMEX
Auditor	Ernst & Young, LLP	Ticker Symbol	CGL-A
Stk Agt	Registrar & Transfer Agent Trust Co.	Outstanding Shares	4,710,000
Counsel	Byrne, Moore & Davis	E.P.S.	$0.82
DUNS No.	00-349-2519	Shareholders	NA

Business: The group's principal activity is to produce, market and distribute a wide range of fresh and frozen poultry products. The operations consist of breeding, hatching and growing of chicken and processing the chicken into deboned breast and thigh meat, cut-up marinated raw breaded chicken, government school lunch product, fast-food cuts, individually quick frozen products, and mechanically deboned chicken meat. The products are sold to independent and chain supermarkets, food distributors and food processing companies, fast-food chains, restaurants, schools and distributors. The group owns two hatcheries located in dalton and forsyth, Georgia and sources its broiler chicken stock from its own breeder flock maintained at 54 contract grower farms located in north Georgia. The group also mills and processes feed at its three mills in forsyth and rockmart. It owns freezing facilities at atlanta, pine mountain and perry in Georgia and collinsville in Alabama.

Primary SIC and add'l.: 2015

CIK No: 0000016104

Subsidiaries: Cagle Farms, Inc.

Officers: Douglas J. Cagle/78/Chmn., CEO, Pres., Sr. Mgr./$375,098.00, Lavon Waite/Dir. - Human Resources, Alvin B. Harp/64/VP - Live Operations/$192,705.00, Rod Wagner/Sr. Mgr. - Atlanta, GA Division, Randy Long/Sr. Mgr., Ronnie Adrian/Sr. Mgr., Ron Welk/Sr. Mgr., Tim Knight/Sr. Mgr., Spence Jernigen/Sr. Mgr., Chip Webb/Sr. Mgr., Rory M. Morris/55/VP - Processing/$217,784.00, Troydale Tolbert/50/VP - Sales, Marketing, Susan Pelfry/Dir. - Human Resources, Jim Bice/Dir. - Human Resources, O'neal Shaw/Dir. - Human Resources *(18 Officers included in Index)*

Directors: Douglas J. Cagle/78/Chmn., CEO, Pres., Sr. Mgr., Candace Chapman/52/Dir., Panos J. Kanes/55/Dir., Edward J. Rutkowski/65/Dir., George Douglas Cagle/55/Dir., James David Cagle/54/Dir., Mark M. Ham/54/Dir., CFO, Exec. VP, Bland G. Byrne/56/Dir.

Owners: Mark M. Ham, Alvin B. Harp, Bland G. Byrne, Douglas J. Cagle/43.90%, James David Cagle/9.30%, Candace Chapman, FMR Corp./10.00%, Insiders/63.70%, George Douglas Cagle/9.60%, Panos J. Kanes, Advisory Research Inc./6.90%, Cagle Family Holdings, LLC/5.30%

Financial Data: ***Fiscal Year End:***04/01 ***Latest Annual Data:*** 4/1/2006

Year	Sales	Net Income
2006	$237,266,000	-$574,000
2005	$246,343,000	$11,539,000
2003	$313,800,000	-$13,272,000

Curr. Assets:	$32,687,000	***Curr. Liab.:***	$21,477,000	***P/E Ratio:***	9.51
Plant, Equip.:	$44,500,000	***Total Liab.:***	$48,486,000	***Indic. Yr. Divd.:***	NA
Total Assets:	$94,292,000	***Net Worth:***	$45,806,000	***Debt/ Equity:***	0.3655

Caibs International Holding Inc

Formerly: Caibs Holding International Inc

590 Madison Ave., 21st Fl., New York, NY, 10022; ***PH:*** 1-212-521-4421

General - Incorporation	DE	**Stock**- Price on:12/24/2007	NA
Employees	NA	Stock Exchange	NA
Auditor	Gately & Assoc. LLC	Ticker Symbol	NA
Stk Agt	Corporate Stock Transfer	Outstanding Shares	NA
Counsel	NA	E.P.S.	NA
DUNS No.	NA	Shareholders	NA

Business: The group's principal activity is to engage in any lawful corporate undertaking, including, but not limited to, selected mergers and acquisitions. The group has been in the developmental stage since inception and has no operations to date other than issuing shares to their original shareholder. The group was formed to provide a method for foreign or domestic private companies to become reporting ("public") company whose securities are qualified for trading in the United States secondary market.

Primary SIC and add'l.: 6770

CIK No: 0001317832

Cal Alta Auto Glass Inc

8 3927 Edmonton Trl. NE, Calgary, AB, T2E 6T1; ***PH:*** 1-403-291-7020; ***http://*** www.cal-altaautoglass.ca

General - Incorporation	NV	**Stock**- Price on:12/24/2007	NA
Employees	NA	Stock Exchange	OTC
Auditor	Chang G. Park, Cpa	Ticker Symbol	CAAG
Stk Agt	NA	Outstanding Shares	NA
Counsel	NA	E.P.S.	NA
DUNS No.	NA	Shareholders	NA

Business: The groups principle activity is to provide insurance services for auto industry. The group operates from United States.

Primary SIC and add'l.: 7500

CIK No: 0001321724

Subsidiaries: Cal Alta Auto Glass, Ltd.

Officers: Frank Aiello/54/Dir., CEO, Pres., Principal Accounting Officer, Denise Aiello/44/Dir., Sec.

Directors: Frank Aiello/54/Dir., CEO, Pres., Principal Accounting Officer, Denise Aiello/44/Dir., Sec., Mason Graf/28/Dir.

Owners: Insiders/78.00%, Mason Graf/2.50%, Denise Aiello/9.00%, Frank Aiello/66.00%, Michael Kelleher/6.00%

Financial Data: Fiscal Year End:12/31 Latest Annual Data: 12/31/2006

Year	Sales	Net Income
2006	$1,134,000	$29,000

Curr. Assets:	$38,000	Curr. Liab.:	$97,000		
Plant, Equip.:	$10,000	Total Liab.:	$97,000	Indic. Yr. Divd.:	NA
Total Assets:	$149,000	Net Worth:	$52,000	Debt/ Equity:	NA

Cal Bay International Inc

1582 Pkwy Loop, Ste G, Tustin, CA, 92780; *PH:* 1-714-258-7070; *Fax:* 1-760-930-0200; *http://* www.calbayinc.com; *Email:* ir@calbayinternational.com

General - Incorporation	NV	Stock - Price on:12/24/2007	NA
Employees	3	Stock Exchange	OTC
Auditor	Argy & Co	Ticker Symbol	CBAY
Stk Agt.	Pacific Stock Transfer Company	Outstanding Shares	NA
Counsel	NA	E.P.S.	$0.061
DUNS No.	NA	Shareholders	NA

Business: The group's principal activity is to undertake distribution in the process, environmental, safety and laboratory markets. The group operates in three divisions: the representative/distribution division, the systems division and the new products division. The distribution division serves in the process, environmental, safety and laboratory markets. The process control market involves instrumentation and equipment used to help a plant control or improve the operations of specific production or manufacturing processes within the plant. The systems division produces a small number of equipment systems which incorporate a variety of products and parts from numerous vendors and that are integrated into a completely operational system. The group offers the ems product to fire departments and industrial 02 transfilling operations and the cems product to small industrial plants.

Primary SIC and add'l.: 5099 5162 5198

CIK No: 0001142526

Subsidiaries: Cal-Bay Analytical, Inc., Cal-Bay Controls, Inc., Var-Jazz Entertainment, Inc

Financial Data: Fiscal Year End:12/31 Latest Annual Data: 12/31/2005

Year	Sales	Net Income
2005	$6,000	-$2,442,000
2004	$186,000	-$86,000
2003	$145,000	-$570,000

Curr. Assets:	$533,000	Curr. Liab.:	$3,002,000		
Plant, Equip.:	$10,696,000	Total Liab.:	$3,002,000	Indic. Yr. Divd.:	NA
Total Assets:	$11,454,000	Net Worth:	$8,452,000	Debt/ Equity:	NA

Cal Dive International Inc

400 N Sam Houston Pkwy E, Ste. 1000, Houston, TX, 77060; *PH:* 1-281-618-0400; *Fax:* 1-281-618-0501; *http://* www.caldive.com

General - Incorporation	MN	Stock - Price on:12/24/2007	$40.17
Employees	2,300	Stock Exchange	NYSE
Auditor	Ernst & Young LLP	Ticker Symbol	DVR
Stk Agt.	Wells Fargo Bank Minnesota N.A	Outstanding Shares	91,310,000
Counsel	Fulbright & Jaworski LLP	E.P.S.	$1.33
DUNS No.	09-838-5404	Shareholders	NA

Business: The group's principal activity is to provide services to offshore oil and gas exploration and production and pipeline companies. The services provided by the group include underwater construction, well operations, maintenance and repairs of pipelines and platforms, salvage operations and diving and vessel support services in the shallow water. The group has diversified fleet of 22 vessels and 25 remotely operated vehicles. The customers include major and independent natural gas and oil producers, pipeline transmission companies and offshore engineering and construction firms.

Primary SIC and add'l.: 1382 1311 1623

CIK No: 0000866829

Subsidiaries: Canyon Offshore, Inc.

Officers: Quinn J. Hebert/Dir., CEO, Pres., Dan Schultz/VP - Environment, Health, Safety, Lloyd A. Hajdik/42/VP, Corporate Controller, Chief Accounting Officer/$438,339.00, Michael V. Ambrose/Sr. VP - International Business Development, John A. Sokol/Sr. VP - International, Bart H. Heijermans/41/COO, Exec. VP/$1,934,155.00, Scott T. Naughton/COO, Exec. VP, Kregg G. Lunsford/Exec. VP, Lisa Manget Buchanan/VP, General Counsel, Sec., Steve Brazda/Sr. VP - Pipelay, Christopher Landry/VP - Sales, Marketing, Allan Palmer/VP - Diving, Jack Lounsbury/VP - Singapore, Travis Trahan/VP - Human Resources, Robert P. Murphy/49/Exec. VP - Oil, Gas *(17 Officers included in Index)*

Directors: Quinn J. Hebert/Dir., CEO, Pres., Todd A. Dittman/Dir., William T. Porter/Dir., John V. Lovoi/Dir., Anthony Tripodo/Dir., Bernard J. Duroc-Danner/54/Dir., Martin R. Ferron/Dir., Gordon F. Ahalt/80/Dir., David E. Preng/Dir., James A. Watt/Dir., Owen Kratz/Dir., William L. Transier/Dir.

Owners: Gordon F. Ahalt, Bernard Duroc-Danner, Lloyd A. Hajdik, Wade A. Pursell, Martin R. Ferron, Owen Kratz/5.90%, Bart H. Heijermans, Anthony Tripodo, John V. Lovoi, Greenlight Capital, L.L.C./7.30%, Insiders/7.20%, James A. Watt, William T. Porter, Neuberger Berman, LLC/8.90%, William L. Transier

Financial Data: Fiscal Year End:12/31 Latest Annual Data: 12/31/2006

Year	Sales	Net Income
2006	$509,917,000	$119,414,000
2005	$224,299,000	$37,730,000
2004	$125,786,000	$7,674,000

Curr. Assets:	$168,747,000	Curr. Liab.:	$58,814,000	P/E Ratio:	11.41
Plant, Equip.:	$222,247,000	Total Liab.:	$294,392,000	Indic. Yr. Divd.:	NA
Total Assets:	$452,153,000	Net Worth:	$157,761,000	Debt/ Equity:	0.9531

Cal Maine Foods Inc

3320 Woodrow Wilson Ave., Jackson, MS, 39209; *PH:* 1-601-948-6813; *Fax:* 1-601-969-0905; *http://* www.calmainefoods.com; *Email:* ir@cmfoods.com

General - Incorporation	DE	Stock - Price on:12/24/2007	$15.57
Employees	1,584	Stock Exchange	NDQ
Auditor	Moore Stephens Frost	Ticker Symbol	CALM
Stk Agt.	SunTrust Bank	Outstanding Shares	23,560,000
Counsel	NA	E.P.S.	$3.97
DUNS No.	05-064-3436	Shareholders	NA

Business: The group's principal activity is to produce, grade, package, market and distribute shell eggs. The groups total flock consists of approximately 20 million mature female chickens, 5 million young female chickens and male or female chickens. The group sells majority of shell eggs in 28 states, primarily in the southwestern, southeastern, mid-western and mid-Atlantic regions of the United States. The group also produces and markets value-added specialty shell eggs.

Primary SIC and add'l.: 5154 0241 0252

CIK No: 0000016160

Subsidiaries: American Egg Products, Inc., Cal-Maine Farms, Inc., Cal-Maine Partnership, Ltd., CMF of Kansas, LLC, Hillandale, LLC., South Texas Applicators, Inc., Southern Equipment Distributors, Inc.

Officers: Fred R. Adams/Chmn., CEO/$667,349.00, Bob Scott/VP - Operations, Joe M. Wyatt/VP - Feed Mill Division, James Neeld/General Counsel, Charles J. Hardin/VP - Sales/$374,349.00, Charles F. Collins/VP, Controller/$317,278.00, Jack B. Self/VP - Operations - Production, Timothy A. Dawson/Dir., VP, CFO, Treasurer, Sec./$231,258.00, Adolphus B. Baker/Dir., COO, Pres./$379,186.00, David Jenkins/VP - Operations, Ken Paramore/VP - Sales, Steve Storm/VP - Operations, Jeff Hardin/VP - Sales

Directors: Fred R. Adams/Chmn., CEO, Richard K. Looper/Vice Chmn., Letitia C. Hughes/Dir., Timothy A. Dawson/Dir., VP, CFO, Treasurer, Sec., Jim Poole/Dir., Adolphus B. Baker/Dir., COO, Pres., Faser R. Triplett/Dir.

Owners: Cal-Maine Foods, Inc. Employee Stock Ownership Plan/8.10%, James E. Poole, Fred R. Adams/36.00%, Adolphus B. Baker, Charles F. Collins, Fred R. Adams, Faser R. Triplett, Adolphus B. Baker/1.90%, Richard K. Looper, Timothy A. Dawson, Insiders/39.10%, Insiders, Letitia C. Hughes, Joe M. Wyatt

Financial Data: Fiscal Year End:05/28 Latest Annual Data: 06/02/2007

Year	Sales	Net Income
2007	$598,128,000	$36,656,000
2006	$477,555,000	-$1,013,000
2005	$375,266,000	-$10,358,000

Curr. Assets:	$125,678,000	Curr. Liab.:	$64,878,000	P/E Ratio:	20.22
Plant, Equip.:	$176,275,000	Total Liab.:	$196,424,000	Indic. Yr. Divd.:	$0.050
Total Assets:	$317,118,000	Net Worth:	$119,775,000	Debt/ Equity:	0.6858

Calais Resources Inc

8400 E Crescent Pkwy, No. 675, Greenwood Village, CO, 80111; *PH:* 1-303-258-3806; *Fax:* 1-303-258-0402; *http://* www.calaisresources.com; *Email:* thomassh@earthlink.net

General - Incorporation	Canada	Stock - Price on:12/24/2007	$0.1
Employees	NA	Stock Exchange	OTC
Auditor	KPMG LLP	Ticker Symbol	CAAUF
Stk Agt.	NA	Outstanding Shares	NA
Counsel	NA	E.P.S.	NA
DUNS No.	NA	Shareholders	NA

Business: The group's principal activity is to acquire and explore potential mining properties. The group is in the process of exploring and developing its mineral properties to determine whether these properties contain ore reserves that are economically recoverable. The recoverability of these mineral properties is dependent upon the existence of economically recoverable reserves and the ability of the group to obtain necessary financing to complete their development. The group has operations in Mexico, the United States, Canada and Norway.

Primary SIC and add'l.: 1041

CIK No: 0001044650

Officers: David K. Young/CEO

Financial Data: Fiscal Year End:05/31 Latest Annual Data: 5/31/2004

Year	Sales	Net Income
2004	NA	-$4,990,000
2003	NA	-$727,000
2002	NA	-$628,000

Curr. Assets:	$1,257,000	Curr. Liab.:	$844,000		
Plant, Equip.:	$269,000	Total Liab.:	$9,108,000	Indic. Yr. Divd.:	NA
Total Assets:	$4,216,000	Net Worth:	-$4,892,000	Debt/ Equity:	0.6914

Calamos Asset Management Inc

2020 Calamos Ct., Naperville, IL, 60563; *PH:* 1-630-245-7200; *Fax:* 1-630-245-6335; *http://* www.calamos.com

General - Incorporation	DE	Stock - Price on:12/24/2007	$24.69
Employees	380	Stock Exchange	NDQ
Auditor	KPMG LLP	Ticker Symbol	CLMS
Stk Agt.	Bank of New York	Outstanding Shares	23,320,000
Counsel	NA	E.P.S.	$1.19
DUNS No.	NA	Shareholders	NA

Business: The groups principal activity is to provide investment advisory services. The products of the group include Mutual Funds and Separate Accounts. The groups services include Wealth Management and Investor Services. The group operates from the United States. The assets of the group for the year 2006 were $795,840 (thousands).

Primary SIC and add'l.: 6726 6722 6371 6282

CIK No: 0001299033

Subsidiaries: Calamos Advisors LLC, Calamos Capital LLC, Calamos Financial Services LLC, Calamos Holdings LLC, Calamos Partners LLC, Calamos Property Management LLC

Officers: John P. Calamos/Chmn., CEO, Chief Investment Officer, Nick P. Calamos/Dir., Sr. Exec. VP, Head - Investments, CIO, James F. Baka/Exec. VP, Patrick H. Dudasik/Exec. VP, CFO, COO, Treasurer, James S. Hamman/Exec. VP, General Counsel, Sec., Scott Craven Jones/Exec. VP, Chief Administrative Officer, Philip E. Moriarty/Exec. VP, Head - Distribution, Business Development, Nimish S. Bhatt/Sr. VP, Dir. - Operations, Robert M. Kunimura/CTO, Sr. VP, Peter D. Nash/Dir. - Investor Relations

Directors: John P. Calamos/Chmn., CEO, Chief Investment Officer, Nick P. Calamos/Dir., Sr. Exec. VP, Head - Investments, CIO, Arthur L. Knight/Dir., Bradford G. Bulkley/Dir., Richard W. Gilbert/Dir., Mitchell Feiger/Dir.

Owners: Richard W. Gilbert, Calamos Family Partners/76.75%, Arthur L. Knight, Patrick H. Dudasik, James S. Hamman, Earnest Partners, LLC/3.07%, Torray LLC/1.33%, Insiders/76.86%, Bradford G. Bulkley, Morgan Stanley/4.36%

Financial Data: Fiscal Year End: 12/31   **Latest Annual Data:** 12/31/2006

Year	Sales		Net Income
2006	$485,172,000		$34,008,000
2005	$417,567,000		$29,222,000
2004	$312,147,000		$106,174,000
Curr. Assets:	$608,776,000	Curr. Liab.: $54,897,000	P/E Ratio: 20.75
Plant, Equip.:	$43,615,000	Total Liab.: $581,263,000	Indic. Yr. Divd.: $0.440
Total Assets:	$795,840,000	Net Worth: $214,577,000	Debt/ Equity: 0.6797

Calamp Corp

1401 N Rice Ave., Oxnard, CA, 93030; **PH:** 1-805-987-9000; **Fax:** 1-805-987-8359; *http://* www.calamp.com; **Email:** inquiry@calamp.com

General - Incorporation	DE	**Stock** - Price on:12/24/2007	$4.82
Employees	440	Stock Exchange	NDQ
Auditor	KPMG LLP	Ticker Symbol	CAMP
Stk Agt	American Stock Transfer & Trust CO.	Outstanding Shares	23,630,000
Counsel	NA	E.P.S.	-$1.34
DUNS No.	04-452-6671	Shareholders	NA

Business: The group's principal activities are to design, manufacture and market microwave equipment used in the reception of television programming transmitted from satellites and wireless terrestrial transmission sites and two-way transceivers used for wireless high-speed Internet-broadband service. The satellite business unit designs and markets reception products for the direct broadcast satellite television market in the United States and a line of consumer and commercial products for video and data reception. The wireless access business unit designs and markets integrated reception and two-way transmission equipment for broadband data and video applications. On 12-Apr-2004, the group acquired vytek corporation, a privately-held company that provides hardware and software products and services that enable both wireless and wireline access to video, voice and data.

Primary SIC and add'l.: 3663 3669 3679

CIK No: 0000730255

Subsidiaries: CalAmp Solutions Holdings, Inc., CalAmp Solutions, Inc, California Amplifier SAR, MK NY Service Corp, Vytek Products, Inc

Officers: Fred Sturm/50/Dir., CEO, Pres./$1,116,502.00, Steven Lheureux/Pres. - Solutions Division/$522,514.00, Patrick Hutchins/Pres. - Products Division/$604,229.00, Richard K. Vitelle/CFO/$583,409.00, Michael Burdiek/Exec. VP/$330,876.00, Garo Sarkissian/41/VP - Corporate Development

Directors: Fred Sturm/50/Dir., CEO, Pres., Richard Gold/53/Chmn., Arthur Hausman/84/Dir., A. J. Moyer/64/Dir., Thomas Pardun/64/Dir., Frank Perna/70/Dir.

Owners: Thomas Pardun, Richard Vitelle, Insiders/4.50%, Richard Gold, Quaker Capital Management Corporation/6.50%, Dimensional Fund Advisors Inc./8.00%, Fred Sturm/1.80%, A. J. Moyer, Frank Perna, Patrick Hutchins, Michael Burdiek, Arthur Hausman, Barclay's Global Investors/5.70%

Financial Data: Fiscal Year End: 02/28   **Latest Annual Data:** 2/28/2007

Year	Sales		Net Income
2007	$222,339,000		-$31,188,000
2006	$217,493,000		$14,562,000
2005	$220,027,000		$8,076,000
Curr. Assets:	$113,524,000	Curr. Liab.: $38,637,000	
Plant, Equip.:	$6,308,000	Total Liab.: $78,452,000	Indic. Yr. Divd.: NA
Total Assets:	$229,703,000	Net Worth: $151,251,000	Debt/ Equity: 0.2070

Calavo Growers Inc

1141-A Cummings Rd., Santa Paula, CA, 93060; **PH:** 1-805-525-1245; **Fax:** 1-805-921-3223; *http://* www.calavo.com; **Email:** info@calavo.com

General - Incorporation	CA	**Stock** - Price on:12/24/2007	$11.92
Employees	750	Stock Exchange	NDQ
Auditor	Deloitte & Touche LLP	Ticker Symbol	CVGW
Stk Agt	U.S. Stock Transfer Corp	Outstanding Shares	14,300,000
Counsel	Troy & Gould	E.P.S.	$0.52
DUNS No.	NA	Shareholders	NA

Business: The group's principal activities are procurement and marketing of avocados and other perishable foods. The group also prepares and distributes processed avocado products. The operations are conducted through three business segments: California avocados, processed products and international avocados and perishable food products. The California avocado segment includes distribution of avocados procured in California. The processed products segment includes operations related to the purchase, manufacturing, and distribution of processed avocado products. The international avocados and perishable foods products segment includes operations related to distribution of fresh avocados procured and distribution of other perishable food items. On 14-Nov-2003, the group acquired maui fresh international inc.

Primary SIC and add'l.: 2099

CIK No: 0001133470

Subsidiaries: Calavo de Mexico S.A. de C.V, Calavo Foods de Mexico S.A. de C.V, Calavo Foods, Inc, Maui

Officers: Lecil E. Cole/Chmn., CEO, Pres., Mike Browne/VP - Fresh Operations, Rick Castellano/Area Sales Mgr. - Southern California, Ira McDow/Area Sales Mgr. - Southern California, Mark Nolan/Accounting Executive, Bob Collier/Area Sales Mgr., Don Anthony/Area Sales Mgr., Peter Shore/Area Sales Mgr., Scott Runge/Treasurer, Sandy Eason/Organic Sales Mgr., Joe Navarro/Accounting Executive, Paul Stanke/Produce Sales, Los Angeles, CA, Art Bruno/CFO, COO, Corp. Sec., Al Ahmer/VP - Processed Sales, Operations, Rob Wedin/VP - Fresh Sales, Marketing *(34 Officers included in Index)*

Directors: Lecil E. Cole/Chmn., CEO, Pres., Dorcas H. McFarlane/Dir. - Santa Paula, California, Link J. Leavens/Dir. - Ventura, California, Egidio Carbone/Dir., Fred J. Ferrazzano/Dir. - Escondido, California, Donald Sanders/Dir. - Escondido, California, John M. Hunt/Dir. - Goleta, California, Scott N. Van Der Kar/Dir. - Carpenteria, California, Harold S. Edwards/42/Dir., Alan Van Wagner/63/Dir., Alva V. Snider/Dir. - Fallbrook, California, Michael D. Hause/Dir. - Santa Paula, Californiab, George H. Barnes/Dir. - Valley Center, California

Owners: George H. Barnes, Scott Van Der Kar/1.10%, Robert J. Wedin, Dorcas H. McFarlane, Insiders/22.60%, Fred J. Ferrazzano, John M. Hunt, Link J. Leavens/3.30%, Michael D. Hause, Michael A. Browne, Alan C. Ahmer, Limoneira Company/7.00%, Donald M. Sanders, Egidio Carbone, Alva V. Snider *(18 Owners included in Index)*

Financial Data: Fiscal Year End: 10/31   **Latest Annual Data:** 10/31/2006

Year	Sales		Net Income
2006	$273,910,000		$5,788,000
2005	$258,822,000		$3,322,000
2004	$274,218,000		$6,210,000
Curr. Assets:	$45,777,000	Curr. Liab.: $33,754,000	P/E Ratio: 20.91
Plant, Equip.:	$19,908,000	Total Liab.: $48,551,000	Indic. Yr. Divd.: $0.350
Total Assets:	$107,494,000	Net Worth: $58,943,000	Debt/ Equity: 0.1681

Calbatech Inc

15375 Barranca Pkwy., Ste. I-101, Irvine, CA, 92618; **PH:** 1-949-450-9910; **Fax:** 1-949-450-9954; *http://* www.calbatech.com

General - Incorporation	NV	**Stock** - Price on:12/24/2007	$0.015
Employees	16	Stock Exchange	OTC
Auditor	De Joya & Co	Ticker Symbol	CLBE
Stk Agt	Transfer Online, Inc.	Outstanding Shares	121,270,000
Counsel	NA	E.P.S.	-$0.034
DUNS No.	NA	Shareholders	NA

Business: The group's principle activities are to acquire, incubate and develop life science based technologies. The group was designing and marketing traffic and industrial signal products. The products called unilights use light emitting diodes to produce universally recognized symbols in a single lens unit. The products are categorized under two major groups: permanently installed signals and portable or temporary signals. It also sells ancillary items purchased from other manufacturers, such as batteries, solar power chargers and remote controls, which are standard products requiring little or no modification to work with the its signals. The products are sold both directly and through a network of independent sales representatives and distributors. It is a development stage company. The group's quarterly revenue for September 2007 was 0.29 millions of USD.

Primary SIC and add'l.: 3669 8731 3648

CIK No: 0001156293

Subsidiaries: acquired Molecula Research Laboratories, LLC, KD Medical, Inc, LifeStem, Inc., Molecularware, Inc.

Officers: James Deolden/Dir., CEO, John Gordon/Dir., CTO, VP, Ed H. Deese/Dir., COO, Pres.

Directors: James Deolden/Dir., CEO, John Gordon/Dir., CTO, VP, Kary Mullis/Member - Scientific Advisory Board, David O'Bryan/Member - Scientific Advisory Board, Paul Heaney/Member - Scientific Advisory Board, Gerald Huth/Member - Scientific Advisory Board, Jason Van Tassel/Member - Scientific Advisory Board, Ed H. Deese/Dir., COO, Pres., John A. Drews/Member - Scientific Advisory Board

Owners: John F. Gordon/8.05%, James DeOlden/7.49%, Insiders/23.59%, Edward H. Deese/8.05%

Financial Data: Fiscal Year End: 12/31   **Latest Annual Data:** 12/31/2006

Year	Sales		Net Income
2006	$1,250,000		$14,000
2005	$1,292,000		-$5,011,000
2004	$301,000		-$2,701,000
Curr. Assets:	$349,000	Curr. Liab.: $2,388,000	
Plant, Equip.:	$124,000	Total Liab.: $5,275,000	Indic. Yr. Divd.: NA
Total Assets:	$520,000	Net Worth: -$4,754,000	Debt/ Equity: NA

Calcasieu Real Estate and Oil CO Inc

PO Box 899, Lake Charles, LA, 70602; **PH:** 1-318-494-4256

General - Incorporation	LA	**Stock** - Price on:12/24/2007	$14.36
Employees	NA	Stock Exchange	AMEX
Auditor	McElroy, Quirk & Burch	Ticker Symbol	NA
Stk Agt	Mellon Investor Services LLC	Outstanding Shares	1,940,000
Counsel	NA	E.P.S.	$0.88
DUNS No.	02-148-2302	Shareholders	NA

Business: The group's principal activity is to lease properties for mineral, agriculture and raising timber. The group collects rents and royalties from leased properties. It has mineral interests in the parishes of allen, beauregard, calcasieu, cameron, jefferson davis, lafourche, sabine, st. Landry and vermilion in Louisiana. The customers of the group are cox and perkins, riceland petroleum company, neumin production and kerr-mcgee.

Primary SIC and add'l.: 6519 6792

CIK No: 0000352955

Officers: Arthur Hollins/77/Dir., CEO, Pres., Charles D. Viccellio/74/Dir., VP, Sec., Brian R. Jones/46/CFO, Treasurer

Directors: Arthur Hollins/77/Dir., CEO, Pres., William D. Blake/Dir., Laura A. Leach/68/Dir., Frank O. Pruitt/79/Dir., James B. Reaves/73/Dir., Mary Watkins Savoy/68/Dir., William Gray Stream/28/Dir., Charles D. Viccellio/74/Dir., VP, Sec., Mary Leach Werner/40/Dir., Henry E. Blake/69/Dir.

Owners: Mary Leach Werner/1.07%, Brian R. Jones/0.01%, Charles D. Viccellio/0.79%, Ottley Properties, LLC/5.10%, Frank O. Pruitt/1.03%, William Gray Stream/2.09%, Laura A. Leach/4.00%, Henry E. Blake/0.51%, B. James Reaves/1.06%, Insiders/18.07%, Arthur Hollins/2.55%, Mary Watkins Savoy/0.88%

Financial Data: Fiscal Year End: 12/31   **Latest Annual Data:** 12/31/2006

Year	Sales		Net Income
2006	$2,691,000		$1,533,000
2005	$2,650,000		$1,561,000
2004	$2,720,000		$1,576,000
Curr. Assets:	$3,010,000	Curr. Liab.: $2,238,000	P/E Ratio: 18.18
Plant, Equip.:	$4,503,000	Total Liab.: $2,405,000	Indic. Yr. Divd.: $0.280
Total Assets:	$10,128,000	Net Worth: $7,724,000	Debt/ Equity: NA

CalciTech Ltd

Par-La-Ville Pl., 14 Par-La-Ville Rd., Hamilton; ; http:// www.calcitech.com

General - Incorporation	Bermuda	Stock- Price on:12/24/2007	$0.315
Employees	NA	Stock Exchange	OTC
Auditor	H W Fisher & Co.	Ticker Symbol	CLKTF
Stk Agt	Computershare Investor Services LLC	Outstanding Shares	NA
Counsel	NA	E.P.S.	NA
DUNS No.	NA	Shareholders	NA

Business: The groups principle activity is to develop a revolutionary new and patented environmental technology for the conversion of industrial lime waste and carbon dioxide into synthetic calcium carbonate. The group products include CalciSG (TM), CalciRG(TM), and CalciLS(TM). The group marketed its products under the trade names CalciSG (TM), CalciRG(TM), and CalciLS (TM). The group operates from Germany and the United States.

Primary SIC and add'l.: 2810

CIK No: 0000889431

Subsidiaries: CalciTech Deutschland GmbH, CalciTech Group Services SA, CalciTech Holding ApS, CalciTech Odda AS, CalciTech Synthetic Minerals Ltd

Officers: Roger A. Leopard/65/CEO, Pres., Marc Lakmaaker/Dir. - Corporate Communications, Robert Higgs/Sales Dir. - Polymer Applications, Yvan Hequet/Mgr. - Raw Materials Sourcing, Nicholas Meadmore/57/CFO, Francois Roux/Product Development Dir., Charles Kunesh/Business Development Dir. - Americas, Christoph Jensen/Project Dir., Jean-Claude Masson/Marketing Mgr. Food - Pharma

Directors: John Smith/Non Exec. Dir., Alan Perkins/Non Exec. Dir., Howard Edmund Browning/64/Non Exec. Dir.

Owners: Alan Edward Perkins, John M. Smith, Roger A. Leopard

Financial Data: Fiscal Year End:02/28 Latest Annual Data: 2/28/2006

Year	Sales	Net Income
2006	$60,000	-$4,277,000
2005	$75,000	-$2,314,000
2004	$51,000	-$2,928,000

Curr. Assets:	$316,000	Curr. Liab.:	$2,164,000		
Plant, Equip.:	$629,000	Total Liab.:	$8,108,000	Indic. Yr. Divd.:	NA
Total Assets:	$1,036,000	Net Worth:	-$7,072,000	Debt/ Equity:	NA

Caledonia Mining Corp

2145 Dunwin Dr., Unit 9, Mississauga, ON, L5L 4L9; PH: 1-905-607-7543; http:// www.caledoniamining.com; Email: info@caledoniamining.com

General - Incorporation	ON	Stock- Price on:12/24/2007	$0.149
Employees	NA	Stock Exchange	OTC
Auditor	Ernst & Young, LLP	Ticker Symbol	CALVF
Stk Agt	Equity Transfer Services Inc	Outstanding Shares	NA
Counsel	Borden Ladner Gervais LLP	E.P.S.	NA
DUNS No.	20-863-0202	Shareholders	NA

Business: The group's principle activities include acquiring, exploring and developing mineral properties for the exploitation of base and precious metals. The company acquires properties and projects early in the development cycle and then adds value by operating or disposing of the asset. The company owns properties in Canada, zambia, South Africa, and democratic republic of congo with excellent exploration potential for gold, diamond, platinum group metals, nickel, copper and cobalt. The group operates from United States.

Primary SIC and add'l.: 1499 5094 1741

CIK No: 0000766011

Subsidiaries: Barbrook Mines Ltd, Caledonia Nama Limited, Caledonia Western Limited, Eersteling Gold Mining Company Limited, Fintona Investments (Proprietary) Limited, Greenstone Management Services (Proprietary) Limited, Motapa Exploration Limited, Motapa Mining Limited

Officers: Stefan E. Hayden/Dir., CEO, Pres., Carl R. Jonsson/Dir., Company Sec., Jeff Smith/VP - Exploration, Steve Curtis/VP - Finance, CFO

Directors: Stefan E. Hayden/Dir., CEO, Pres., Rupert G. Pardoe/Chmn., James Johnstone/Dir., Carl R. Jonsson/Dir., Company Sec., Roland Fasel/Dir., Christopher Harvey/Dir., Robert Liverant/Dir.

Owners: Ian W. Forrest, Christopher F. Harvey, Carl R. Jonsson

Financial Data: Fiscal Year End:12/31 Latest Annual Data: 12/31/2006

Year	Sales	Net Income
2006	$11,658,000	-$5,435,000
2005	$2,267,000	-$10,056,000
2004	$698,000	-$8,623,000

Curr. Assets:	$7,528,000	Curr. Liab.:	$5,062,000		
Plant, Equip.:	$14,804,000	Total Liab.:	$6,110,000	Indic. Yr. Divd.:	NA
Total Assets:	$22,426,000	Net Worth:	$16,317,000	Debt/ Equity:	NA

Calgon Carbon Corp

400 Calgon Carbon Dr., Pittsburgh, PA, 15205; PH: 1-412-787-6700; Fax: 1-412-787-4511; http:// www.calgoncarbon.com

General - Incorporation	DE	Stock- Price on:12/24/2007	$11.64
Employees	972	Stock Exchange	NYSE
Auditor	Deloitte & Touche LLP	Ticker Symbol	CCC
Stk Agt	First Chicago Trust	Outstanding Shares	40,360,000
Counsel	NA	E.P.S.	-$0.06
DUNS No.	00-431-9810	Shareholders	NA

Business: The group's principal activity is to provide services and solutions for purifying water and air, food, beverage, and industrial process streams. The group's operates in four business segments: activated carbon, service, engineered solutions and consumer. The activated carbon and service segments rely on activated carbon as a base material, while engineered solutions relies on a variety of other methods and materials that do not involve activated carbon. The service segment reactivates spent carbon and the leasing, monitoring and maintenance of mobile carbon absorption equipment. The engineered solutions segment provides solutions to air and water process problems. The consumer health segment provides purification technologies directly to the customers. The group's products are sold in the United States, Europe, Japan, Canada and Asia. On 18-Feb-2004, the group acquired assets of waterlink inc.

Primary SIC and add'l.: 3823 2819

CIK No: 0000812701

Subsidiaries: Barnebey Sutcliffe Corporation

Officers: John S. Stanik/Chmn., CEO, Pres./$872,868.00, Dennis M. Sheedy/VP, General Counsel, Sec., James G. Fishburne/Sr. VP - Asia/$331,623.00, Gail A. Gerono/VP - Investor Relations - Communications, Human Resources, Robert P. O'Brien/Sr. VP - Americas/$370,423.00, C. H.S. Majoor/Sr. VP - Europe/$650,360.00

Directors: John S. Stanik/Chmn., CEO, Pres., William R. Newlin/Dir., Robert W. Cruickshank/Dir., Julie S. Roberts/Dir., Robert L. Yohe/Dir., Timothy G. Rupert/Dir., Seth E. Schofield/Dir., John P. Surma/Dir.

Owners: Julie S. Roberts, Timothy G. Rupert, William R. Newlin, Pictet Asset Management SA/8.80%, Robert P. OBrien, The Goldman Sachs Group, Inc./6.00%, ICM Asset Management, Inc./5.60%, Thomas A. McConomy/7.60%, Seth E. Schofield, John S. Stanik, Linden Capital LP/5.10%, Kees C.H.S. Majoor, Robert L. Yohe, John P. Surma, Insiders/12.30% (21 Owners included in Index)

Financial Data: Fiscal Year End:12/31 Latest Annual Data: 12/31/2006

Year	Sales	Net Income
2006	$316,122,000	-$7,798,000
2005	$290,835,000	-$7,416,000
2004	$336,567,000	$5,888,000

Curr. Assets:	$148,712,000	Curr. Liab.:	$55,526,000		
Plant, Equip.:	$106,101,000	Total Liab.:	$174,491,000	Indic. Yr. Divd.:	NA
Total Assets:	$322,364,000	Net Worth:	$147,873,000	Debt/ Equity:	0.0872

Calibre Mining Corp

Formerly: TLC Ventures Corp
1250 - 999 W Hastings St., Vancouver, BC, V6C 2W2; ; http:// www.tlcventurescorp.com

General - Incorporation	Canada	Stock- Price on:12/24/2007	NA
Employees	NA	Stock Exchange	NA
Auditor	Pricewaterhousecoopers LLP	Ticker Symbol	NA
Stk Agt	Pacific Corporate Trust Co	Outstanding Shares	NA
Counsel	NA	E.P.S.	NA
DUNS No.	NA	Shareholders	NA

Business: The groups principle activities include exploring and developing copper and gold projects. The group operates from South America and Australia.

Primary SIC and add'l.: 1400

CIK No: 0001280797

Subsidiaries: Cybele Resources Inc., Gold Fields Ltd.

Officers: Robert D. Brown/Dir., CEO, Pres., David Heberlein/VP - Exploration, David Toyoda/Corp. Sec., Edward Farrauto/Dir., CFO, Rob Smillie/Australian Country Mgr., Andrew Alliborne/Chief Geologist

Directors: Robert D. Brown/Dir., CEO, Pres., Douglas Forster/Chmn., Edward Farrauto/Dir., CFO, John Reynolds/Dir., Jeffrey P. Franzen/Dir., Blayne Johnson/Dir.

Owners: John Reynolds/1.22%, Insiders/32.68%, David Heberlein/2.03%, Blayne Johnson/10.55%, Jeffrey P. Franzen/4.26%, Edward Farrauto/2.57%, Douglas B. Forster/9.53%, Robert Brown/3.04%

California Business Bank

800 W 6th St. Ste. 1000, Los Angeles, CA, 90017; PH: 1-213-688-9668; http:// www.californiabusinessbank.com; Email: info@californiabusinessbank.com

General - Incorporation		Stock- Price on:12/24/2007	$11.5
Employees	NA	Stock Exchange	OTC
Auditor	NA	Ticker Symbol	CABB
Stk Agt	U.S. Stock Transfer Corp	Outstanding Shares	NA
Counsel	NA	E.P.S.	NA
DUNS No.	NA	Shareholders	NA

Business: The group's principle activity is to provide banking services. The group's products include credit card, loans and deposits. The group operates from United States.

Primary SIC and add'l.: 6022

CIK No:

Officers: Charles R. Wood/Dir., CEO, Pres., Yu-Ching Lau/Dir., Exec. VP, CFO, Charles E. Fenton/Exec. VP, Chief Credit Officer, Keith R. Ellis/Sr. VP, Corporate Banking Mgr., Virginia A. Reid/Sr. VP, Operations Administrator, Theresa Ko/Sr. VP, Controller, Ana Alvarez/Contact - Operations, Maryann Canchola/Contact - Loans

Directors: Charles R. Wood/Dir., CEO, Pres., Raffi D. Krikorian/Chmn., Steve S. Hong/Vice Chmn., Mladen Buntich/Dir., Gary K. Cross/Dir., Thomas J. Holthus/Dir., Ellwood W. Johnston/Dir., Yu-Ching Lau/Dir., Exec. VP, CFO, Michael F. Maluccio/Dir., Aaron M. Yashouafar/Dir., William W. Naylor/Dir., Kenneth D. Thompson/Dir.

California Coastal Communities Inc

6 Executive Cir., Ste. 250, Irvine, CA, 92614; PH: 1-949-250-7700; Fax: 1-949-250-7705; http:// www.californiacoastalcommunities.com

General - Incorporation	DE	Stock- Price on:12/24/2007	$16.92
Employees	59	Stock Exchange	NDQ
Auditor	Deloitte & Touche LLP	Ticker Symbol	CALC
Stk Agt	Chase Mellon Shareholder Services	Outstanding Shares	10,860,000
Counsel	NA	E.P.S.	-$0.08
DUNS No.	02-874-1593	Shareholders	NA

Business: The group's principal activities are to obtain zoning and other entitlements for land and improving the land for residential development. The group has its properties located primarily in southern California. It also provides residential real estate development and single-family constructions. The group sells improved and unimproved land to other developers or homebuilders and participates in joint ventures with other developers, investors or homebuilders to finance and construct infrastructure and homes.

Primary SIC and add'l.: 1522 1531 1521

CIK No: 0000840216

Subsidiaries: Air Correction International, Inc., Calumet Real Estate Inc., Hearthside Holdings, Inc., Hearthside Homes Oxnard, LLC, Hearthside Homes, Inc., Hearthside Residential Corp., Henley Facilities, Inc., Henley Investments, Inc. Two, Henley/KNO Holding Inc., HHI Chandler, LLC, HHI Chino II, LLC, HHI Chino Reserve, LLC, HHI Crosby, LLC, HHI Hellman, LLC, HHI Jasper, LLC 27 Subsidiaries included in the Index

Officers: Raymond J. Pacini/52/Dir., CEO, Pres./$599,600.00, Ed Mountford/52/Sr. VP - Hearthside Homes, Inc/$291,600.00, Doug Woodyard/48/VP - Hearthside Homes, Inc, John W. Marshall/Sr. VP - Hearthside Homes, Inc/$221,600.00, Michael J. Rafferty/COO, Pres. - Hearthside Homes, Inc/$304,600.00, Sandra G. Sciutto/48/CFO, Sr. VP, Treasurer, Corp. Sec./$366,600.00, Steve Ritz/60/VP - Hearthside Homes, Inc

Directors: Raymond J. Pacini/52/Dir., CEO, Pres., Thomas W. Sabin/Chmn., Geoffrey W. Arens/Dir., Phillip R. Burnaman/Dir.

Owners: Phillip R. Burnaman, Dimensional Fund Advisors LP/6.70%, John W. Marshall, Mercury Real Estate Advisors LLC/8.90%, Thomas W. Sabin/2.58%, River Road Asset Management, LLC/6.10%, Ed Mountford, Insiders/7.23%, Geoffrey W. Arens, Michael J. Rafferty, ING Capital LLC/15.00%, Sandra G. Sciutto, Fursa Alternative Strategies LLC/8.00%, Merrill Lynch& Co,Inc./9.60%, Raymond J. Pacini/3.45%

Financial Data: *Fiscal Year End:*12/31   *Latest Annual Data:* 12/31/2006

Year	Sales	Net Income
2006	$95,700,000	$5,600,000
2005	$129,500,000	$28,400,000
2004	$76,000,000	$4,800,000

Curr. Assets:	$290,500,000	**Curr. Liab.:**	$13,100,000		
Plant, Equip.:	NA	**Total Liab.:**	$208,800,000	**Indic. Yr. Divd.:**	NA
Total Assets:	$332,300,000	**Net Worth:**	$123,500,000	**Debt/ Equity:**	1.6595

California Commun CA

800 W Valley Pkwy.., Ste. 100, Escondido, CA, 92025; *PH:* 1-760-888-1100; *Fax:* 1-760-888-1189; *http://* www.calcommunitybank.com

General - Incorporation		Stock - Price on:12/24/2007	$15.5
Employees	NA	Stock Exchange	OTC
Auditor	NA	Ticker Symbol	CABK
Stk Agt	U.S. Stock Transfer Corp	Outstanding Shares	2,090,000
Counsel	NA	E.P.S.	NA
DUNS No.	NA	Shareholders	NA

Business: The groups principle activity is to provide personal banking, business banking and business lending services. The groups business lending services include accounts receivable and inventory financing, business lines of credit and term loans, professional loans and lines, equipment loans, commercial real estate loans, construction financing, and small business administration loans. The groups personal banking services include basic checking, standard checking, interest checking, senior checking, money market accounts, savings accounts, certificates of deposits, debit cards, online banking, check imaging, wire transfers, telephone banking, auto and vehicle loans. The group operates from United States.

Primary SIC and add'l.: 6021 6035

CIK No:

California First National Bancorp

18201 Von Karman Ave., Ste. 800, Irvine, CA, 92612; *PH:* 1-949-255-0500; *Fax:* 1-949-255-0501; *http://* www.calfirstbancorp.com

General - Incorporation	CA	Stock - Price on:12/24/2007	$14.87
Employees	171	Stock Exchange	NDQ
Auditor	PricewaterhouseCoopers LLP	Ticker Symbol	CFNB
Stk Agt	Mellon Investor Services LLC	Outstanding Shares	11,210,000
Counsel	NA	E.P.S.	$0.86
DUNS No.	NA	Shareholders	NA

Business: The group's principal activity is to provide financial services. The group is a holding company operating through its subsidiaries, Amplicon Inc. and California first leasing corporation. The group operates in two segments namely, leasing and banking. The leasing segment provides lease financing for capital assets. The banking segment includes products such as certificates of deposits, money market checking accounts, ATM cards and online bill payment. The customers of the leasing segment include middle-market companies, subsidiaries and divisions of Fortune 1000 companies in the United States.

Primary SIC and add'l.: 7377 6022 6712

CIK No: 0000803016

Subsidiaries: Amplicon, Inc.

Officers: Patrick E. Paddon/57/Dir., CEO, Pres., Peter Aharonyan/59/CEO, Pres. - Calfirst Bank, Glen T. Tsuma/55/Dir., COO, VP, Sec., Leslie S. Jewett/53/CFO, VP - Finance, Michael L. McClendon/60/Sr. VP - Credit, California First Leasing Corp

Directors: Patrick E. Paddon/57/Dir., CEO, Pres., Glen T. Tsuma/55/Dir., COO, VP, Sec., Michael H. Lowry/63/Dir., Harris Ravine/65/Dir., Danilo Cacciamatta/62/Dir.

Owners: Michael L. McClendon, Danilo Cacciamatta, S. Leslie Jewett/2.00%, Insiders/70.80%, Patrick E. Paddon/57.30%, Glen T. Tsuma/12.20%, Bedros Aharonyan, Michael H. Lowry, Donald P. Moriarty/9.50%, Aegis Financial Corporation/5.10%, Harris Ravine

Financial Data: *Fiscal Year End:*06/30   *Latest Annual Data:* 06/30/2007

Year	Sales	Net Income
2007	$36,065,000	$9,888,000
2006	$35,858,000	$10,722,000
2005	$34,537,000	$8,175,000

Curr. Assets:	$47,396,000	**Curr. Liab.:**	$102,665,000		
Plant, Equip.:	$41,726,000	**Total Liab.:**	$120,828,000	**Indic. Yr. Divd.:**	$0.480
Total Assets:	$314,355,000	**Net Worth:**	$193,527,000	**Debt/ Equity:**	0.0350

California Micro Devices Corp

490 N McCarthy Blvd., Ste. 100, Milpitas, CA, 95035; *PH:* 1-408-263-3214; *Fax:* 1-408-263-7846; *http://* www.calmicro.com; *Email:* ir@calmicro.com

General - Incorporation	CA	Stock - Price on:12/24/2007	$4.78
Employees	94	Stock Exchange	NDQ
Auditor	Grant Thornton LLP	Ticker Symbol	CAMD
Stk Agt	Mellon Investor Services LLC	Outstanding Shares	23,200,000
Counsel	Pillsbury Winthrop LLP	E.P.S.	$0.00
DUNS No.	01-093-8165	Shareholders	NA

Business: The group's principle activities include designing, manufacturing and marketing application specific integrated passive devices or asip (TM) and complementary analog semiconductors. The products provide signal integrity, electromagnetic interference filtering, electrostatic discharge

protection and power management solutions to original equipment manufacturers and contract manufacturers. It also designs and manufactures active analog semiconductors that include power management and usb transceiver solutions as well as low voltage, low power operational amplifiers that we enhance by adding passive devices. The products are marketed to original equipment and contract manufacturers in the mobile electronics, computing, led lighting, medical and other industries. The group's customers include dell inc, hewlett-packard company, kyocera wireless corp, lg electronics, motorola, inc, royal philips electronics nv, samsung electronics co ltd, and sony corporation. The group operates from United States.

Primary SIC and add'l.: 5065 3674 3675

CIK No: 0000800460

Subsidiaries: ARQ Acquisition Corporation

Officers: Robert V. Dickinson/Dir., CEO, Pres./$777,507.00, Juergen Lutz/VP - Engineering/$502,758.00, Kyle Baker/VP - Marketing/$405,727.00, Manuel H. Mere/VP - Operations, Information Systems/$371,073.00, Kevin Berry/CFO/$387,154.00, David Casey/VP - Sales, Mary O'Sullivan/Contact - North America, Kelly Miller/Contact - North America, Steve Bull/Contact - Europe, Middle East, Africa, Bryan Hung/Contact - Causeway Bay, Hong Kong, Hiroki Teraoka/Contact - Tokyo, Japan, Simon Ahn/Contact - Kangnam, ku, Seoul

Directors: Robert V. Dickinson/Dir., CEO, Pres., Wade Meyercord/Chmn., Ed Ross/Dir., David Sear/Dir., John L. Sprague/Dir., David L. Wittrock/Dir.

Owners: Edward C. Ross, David L. Wittrock, Manuel Mere, Insiders/6.26%, Wade F. Meyercord, FMR Corp./8.98%, Juergen Lutz, S Squared Technology, LLC/5.32%, T. Rowe Price Associates, Inc./7.19%, Kevin J. Berry, Kyle D. Baker, Robert V. Dickinson/2.76%, Royce& Associates, LLC/7.78%, David W. Sear, John L. Sprague

Financial Data: *Fiscal Year End:*03/31   *Latest Annual Data:* 3/31/2007

Year	Sales	Net Income
2007	$68,006,000	-$81,000
2006	$70,241,000	$10,035,000
2005	$65,869,000	$4,042,000

Curr. Assets:	$69,710,000	**Curr. Liab.:**	$11,852,000	**P/E Ratio:**	119.50
Plant, Equip.:	$3,961,000	**Total Liab.:**	$11,860,000	**Indic. Yr. Divd.:**	NA
Total Assets:	$73,732,000	**Net Worth:**	$61,872,000	**Debt/ Equity:**	NA

California Oil & Gas Corp

260, 600 - 6 Ave. SW, Calgary, AB, T2P 0S5; ; *http://* www.caloilandgas.com; *Email:* info@caloilandgascorp.com

General - Incorporation	NV	Stock - Price on:12/24/2007	$0.46
Employees	NA	Stock Exchange	OTC
Auditor	Lopez, Bork & Associates, LLP	Ticker Symbol	COGC
Stk Agt	Nevada Agency & Trust Company	Outstanding Shares	NA
Counsel	NA	E.P.S.	NA
DUNS No.	NA	Shareholders	NA

Business: The groups principal activity is to explore minerals and natural gas. In the year 2006, the group acquired California Oil & Gas Corporation .The group operates from the United States and Canada.

Primary SIC and add'l.: 1040

CIK No: 0001213109

Officers: John G.F. McLeod/Dir., Pres., Sec., Treasurer, Principal Exec. Officer, Norman S. Johnson/CFO, Ryan Mulhern/Investor Relations Officer

Owners: Rush and Co/6.19%, Insiders/20.34%, Ernie Pratt/2.54%, EH&P Investments/5.65%, John G.F. McLeod/15.24%, Mel Trethart/1.27%, Norman S. Johnson/1.27%

Financial Data: *Fiscal Year End:*11/30   *Latest Annual Data:* 11/30/2006

Year	Sales	Net Income
2006	NA	-$324,000
2005	NA	-$8,000
2004	NA	-$111,000

Curr. Assets:	$878,000	**Curr. Liab.:**	$156,000		
Plant, Equip.:	$601,000	**Total Liab.:**	$156,000	**Indic. Yr. Divd.:**	NA
Total Assets:	$1,729,000	**Net Worth:**	$1,573,000	**Debt/ Equity:**	NA

California Petroleum Transport Corp

One Internatonal Pl., Room5/20, Boston, MA, 02110; *PH:* 1-617-951-7727

General - Incorporation	DE	Stock - Price on:12/24/2007	NA
Employees	12,900	Stock Exchange	NA
Auditor	Grant Thornton LLP	Ticker Symbol	NA
Stk Agt	NA	Outstanding Shares	NA
Counsel	NA	E.P.S.	NA
DUNS No.	NA	Shareholders	NA

Business: The group's principle activity is to issue serial mortgage and term mortgage notes as an agent on behalf of the owners and loan the proceeds of the notes to the owners. It is a special purpose corporation that has been organized solely for the above purpose. The owners of the group are calpetro tankers limited, calpetro tankers (bahamas ii) limited, calpetro tankers (bahamas iii) limited and calpetro tankers (iom) limited. The group operates from United States.

Primary SIC and add'l.: 6159

CIK No: 0000923649

Officers: Franklin P. Collazo/28/Sec., Douglas R. Donaldson/66/Treasurer, Nancy I. Depasquale/41/Dir., Pres., Louise E. Colby/60/Dir., Assist. Sec., Geraldine St-Louis/32/VP

Directors: Nancy I. Depasquale/41/Dir., Pres., Louise E. Colby/60/Dir., Assist. Sec.

Owners: The California Trust/100.00%

California Pizza Kitchen Inc

6053 W Century Blvd., 11th Fl., Los Angeles, CA, 90045; *PH:* 1-310-342-5000; *Fax:* 1-310-342-4640; *http://* www.cpk.com

General - Incorporation	DE	Stock - Price on:12/24/2007	$21.16
Employees	13,900	Stock Exchange	NDQ
Auditor	Ernst & Young LLP	Ticker Symbol	CPKI
Stk Agt	American Stock Transfer & Trust Co.	Outstanding Shares	29,080,000
Counsel	Pillsbury Winthrop LLP	E.P.S.	$0.68
DUNS No.	NA	Shareholders	NA

Business: The group's principal activity is the operation of a casual dining restaurant chain in the premium pizza segment. The restaurants feature an exhibition style kitchen centered on an open-flame oven and serve traditional, American-style, tomato sauce-based pizzas or authentic, Italian-style neapolitan pizzas. They include premium pizzas like bbq chicken pizza, philly cheesesteak pizza, grilled garlic shrimp pizza, jamaican jerk chicken pizza, caramelized pear and gorgonzola pizza. The restaurants also serve pastas, salads, soups, appetizers and desserts. At 12-Mar-2004, the group had 168 restaurants in 27 states, the district of columbia and five foreign countries with 139 of them owned and 29 operated under franchise or license arrangements. The group has made franchise agreements in the United States, Singapore, Malaysia, Indonesia, Hong Kong and the Philippines.

Primary SIC and add'l.: 5812

CIK No: 0000789356

Subsidiaries: California Pizza Kitchen of Illinois, Inc., CPK Management Company, Inc.

Officers: Larry S. Flax/Co - Chmn., Co - Pres., Co - CEO, Co - Founder/$1,510,913.00, Richard L. Rosenfield/Co - Chmn., Co - Pres., Co - CEO, Co - Founder/$1,510,913.00, Susan M. Collyns/CFO, Sr. VP - Finance, Sec./$753,206.00, Thomas P. Beck/Sr. VP - Construction, Tom Beck/Sr. VP - Construction/$443,812.00, Rudy Sugueti/Sr. VP - Asap Operations/$404,050.00, Sarah G. Grover/Sr. VP - Marketing, Public Relations/$426,402.00

Directors: Larry S. Flax/Co - Chmn., Co - Pres., Co - CEO, Co - Founder, Richard L. Rosenfield/Co - Chmn., Co - Pres., Co - CEO, Co - Founder, William C. Baker/Dir., Henry Gluck/Dir., Steven C. Good/Dir., Dick Poladian/Dir., Alan I. Rothenberg/Dir., Avedick Poladian/56/Dir., Charles G. Phillips/Dir.

Owners: Larry S. Flax/5.20%, Rudy Sugueti/0.20%, Insiders/12.30%, FMR Corp./10.20%, Henry Gluck/0.20%, Sarah Goldsmith Grover/0.40%, Charles G. Phillips/0.30%, William C. Baker/0.20%, Avedick B. Poladian/0.10%, Wells Fargo & Company/5.70%, Thomas Beck/0.20%, Barclays Global Investors/5.10%, Alan I. Rothenberg, Baron Capital Group/9.10%, Tiger Consumer Management/5.20% *(19 Owners included in Index)*

Financial Data: *Fiscal Year End:* 01/01 *Latest Annual Data:* 12/31/2006

Year	Sales	Net Income
2006	$554,601,000	$21,000,000
2005	$422,452,000	$17,816,000

Curr. Assets:	$37,917,000	**Curr. Liab.:**	$66,001,000	**P/E Ratio:**	31.12
Plant, Equip.:	$255,382,000	**Total Liab.:**	$102,170,000	**Indic. Yr. Divd.:**	NA
Total Assets:	$310,513,000	**Net Worth:**	$208,343,000	**Debt/ Equity:**	NA

California United Bank

15821 Ventura Blvd, Encino, CA, 91436; *PH:* 1-818-257-7700;
http:// www.californiaunitedbank.com; *Email:* info@californiaunitedbank.com

General - Incorporation		**Stock** - Price on:12/24/2007	$18.75
Employees	NA	Stock Exchange	OTC
Auditor	McGladrey & Pullen LLP	Ticker Symbol	CUNB
Stk Agt	Transfer Online, Inc.	Outstanding Shares	NA
Counsel	NA	E.P.S	NA
DUNS No.	NA	Shareholders	NA

Business: The groups principal activity is to provide banking services. Services of the group include business deposit service, personal deposits, cash management, lending, international banking, investments, loans and private banking. The group operates from the United States.

Primary SIC and add'l.: 6022

CIK No:

Officers: David Rainer/Dir., CEO, Pres., Robert Dennen/CFO, Exec. VP, Anne Williams/Exec. VP, Chief Credit Officer, Anita Wolman/Sr. VP - Legal Counsel, Debby Hart/Sr. VP - Bank Operations, Emily Hamilton/Sr. VP, Dir. - Human Resources, Bart Aikman/VP, Relationship Mgr., Aileen Garrigues/VP, Relationship Mgr., Alon Haim/VP, Relationship Mgr., Sam Kunianski/Sr. VP - Commercial Banking, William Sloan/Sr. VP, Relationship Mgr., Max Bruno/Sr. VP, Relationship Mgr., Lessie McMullen/VP - Operations, Richard Hernandez/VP, Relationship Mgr., Pat Irueta/VP, Relationship Mgr. *(23 Officers included in Index)*

Directors: David Rainer/Dir., CEO, Pres., Stephen G. Carpenter/Chmn., Roberto E. Barragan/Dir., Charles Sweetman/Dir., Kenneth L. Bernstein/Dir., Robert C. Bills/Dir., Ronald W. Jones/Dir., Daniel F. Selleck/Dir., Roy A. Salter/Dir.

California Water Service Group

1720 N 1st St., San Jose, CA, 95112; *PH:* 1-408-367-8200; *Fax:* 1-408-367-8430;
http:// www.calwatergroup.com

General - Incorporation	DE	**Stock** - Price on:12/24/2007	$35.69
Employees	869	Stock Exchange	NYSE
Auditor	KPMG LLP	Ticker Symbol	CWT
Stk Agt	American Stock Transfer & Trust CO.	Outstanding Shares	20,670,000
Counsel	NA	E.P.S	$1.43
DUNS No.	00-644-8992	Shareholders	NA

Business: The group's principal activity is to provide water supply and related services through its subsidiaries. The operations include production, purchase, storage, purification, distribution and sale of water. The group services industrial, public and irrigation uses and for fire protection. The group provides water service to 446,000 residential, commercial, public authority and industrial customers in 75 cities. On 30-Apr-2003, it acquired kaanapali water corporation. The group operates in the san francisco bay area, sacramento valley, salinas valley, san joaquin valley, los angeles area, New Mexico and Washington. On 03-May-2004, the group acquired national utility company.

Primary SIC and add'l.: 6719 4941

CIK No: 0001035201

Subsidiaries: California Water Service Company, CWS Utility Services California, CWS Utility Services New Mexico, Hawaii Water Service Company, Inc., New Mexico Water Service Company, Washington Water Service Company, Water Service Company New Mexico, Water Service Company Washington

Officers: Peter C. Nelson/60/Dir., CEO, Pres./$1,337,420.00, Francis S. Ferraro/VP - Regulatory, Corporate Relations/$522,715.00, Robert R. Guzzetta/VP - Operations/$368,137.00, Martin A. Kropelnicki/CFO, VP, Treasurer/$294,331.00, Michael J. Rossi/VP - Engineering, Water Quality, Calvin L. Breed/Controller, Assist. Sec., Assist. Treasurer, Christine L. McFarlane/VP - Human Resources, Paul G. Ekstrom/VP - Customer Service, Information Systems, Lynne McGhee/Acting Corp. Sec.

Directors: Peter C. Nelson/60/Dir., CEO, Pres., Robert W. Foy/71/Chmn., George A. Vera/64/Dir., David N. Kennedy/71/Dir., Douglas M. Brown/70/Dir., Edward D. Harris/70/Dir., Richard P. Magnuson/52/Dir., Linda R. Meier/67/Dir., Bonnie G. Hill/66/Dir.

Owners: Martin A. Kropelnicki, Robert W. Foy, Richard P. Magnuson, Robert R. Guzzetta, David N. Kennedy, Douglas M. Brown, Linda R. Meier, Insiders, Peter C. Nelson, Edward D. Harris, Francis S. Ferraro, George A. Vera, Bonnie G. Hill

Financial Data: *Fiscal Year End:* 12/31 *Latest Annual Data:* 12/31/2006

Year	Sales	Net Income
2006	$334,717,000	$25,580,000
2005	$320,728,000	$27,223,000
2004	$315,567,000	$26,026,000

Curr. Assets:	$109,624,000	**Curr. Liab.:**	$70,225,000	**P/E Ratio:**	25.31
Plant, Equip.:	$941,475,000	**Total Liab.:**	$783,242,000	**Indic. Yr. Divd.:**	$1.160
Total Assets:	$1,165,019,000	**Net Worth:**	$381,777,000	**Debt/ Equity:**	0.7720

Caliper Life Sciences Inc

68 Elm St., Hopkinton, MA, 01748; *PH:* 1-508-435-9500; *Fax:* 1-508-435-3439;
http:// www.caliperls.com

General - Incorporation	DE	**Stock** - Price on:12/24/2007	$4.5001
Employees	550	Stock Exchange	NDQ
Auditor	Ernst & Young LLP	Ticker Symbol	CALP
Stk Agt	Wells Fargo Bank Minnesota, N.A.	Outstanding Shares	47,170,000
Counsel	NA	E.P.S	NA
DUNS No.	NA	Shareholders	NA

Business: The group's principal activities are to develop, manufacture and selling of labchip systems to pharmaceutical and other companies. Labchip system provides microfluidic lab-on-a-chip technologies that miniaturize integrate and automate many laboratory processes. Each chip contains a network of microscopic channels through which fluids and chemicals are moved, using electricity or pressure, in order to perform experiments. Labchip also includes reagents, instruments, software that together control and read the chips.on 14-Jul-2003 the group acquired zymark corporation. The group has three systems the caliper 250, the ams 90 se is an automated electrophoresis system and the caliper 42 is a microfluidics applications development workstation. The group has two channels of distribution for products direct to end-user and through commercial partners.

Primary SIC and add'l.: 3821 3826 3577

CIK No: 0001014672

Subsidiaries: Caliper Life Sciences AG, Caliper Life Sciences Benelux NV, Caliper Life Sciences Europe, Caliper Life Sciences GmbH, Caliper Life Sciences Ltd., Caliper Life Sciences S.A., Marizyme Corporation, NovaScreen Biosciences Corporation, Oceanix Biosciences Company

Officers: Kevin Hrusovsky/Dir., CEO, Pres./$1,812,532.00, Mark T. Roskey/VP - Reagents, Applied Biology, Thomas T. Higgins/Exec. VP, CFO, Investor Relations Officer/$665,260.00, William C. Kruka/Sr. VP - Corporate Development, Jean-Louis Rufener/Sr. VP, Bruce Bal/Sr. VP - Operations/$556,503.00, Bradley W. Rice/VP - Instrumentation and Biophotonic Imaging Research & Development, Andrea W. Chow/VP - Microfludics, Research & Development and Chip Manufacturing, Cathy Portanova/Investor Relations Officer, Paula J. Cassidy/VP - Human Resources, Stephen E. Creager/Sr. VP, General Counsel, Sec./$530,830.00, David M. Manyak/Exec. VP - Drug Discovery Services/$432,380.00, Stacey Holifield/Contact - Media, John S. Dellisanti/Exec. VP, Chief Commercial Officer, Enrique Bernal/VP - Automation Business Development

Directors: Kevin Hrusovsky/Dir., CEO, Pres., David Milligan/Vice Chmn. - Board, Daniel L. Kisner/Chmn., Kathryn Tunstall/Dir., Robert C. Bishop/Dir., Van Billet/Dir., Allan L. Comstock/Dir., David Carter/Dir.

Owners: Robert C. Bishop, Allan L. Comstock, Platinum Asset Management Limited/9.96%, Bruce J. Bal, The Berwind Company LLC/6.68%, Thomas T. Higgins, Manning & Napier/5.46%, Insiders/13.37%, Van Billet, David V. Milligan, Millennium Management LLC/6.25%, Royce & Associates, LLC/10.18%, Abingworth Management Ltd./5.87%, Kathryn A. Tunstall, Kevin E. Hrusovsky/1.94% *(21 Owners included in Index)*

Financial Data: *Fiscal Year End:* 12/31 *Latest Annual Data:* 12/31/2006

Year	Sales	Net Income
2006	$107,871,000	-$28,934,000
2005	$87,009,000	-$14,457,000
2004	$80,127,000	-$31,556,000

Curr. Assets:	NA	**Curr. Liab.:**	NA		
Plant, Equip.:	NA	**Total Liab.:**	NA	**Indic. Yr. Divd.:**	NA
Total Assets:	NA	**Net Worth:**	NA	**Debt/ Equity:**	0.0545

Call Now Inc

1 Retama Pkwy., Selma, TX, 78154; *PH:* 1-210-651-7145; *http://* www.retamapark.com;
Email: run@retamapark.com

General - Incorporation	NV	**Stock** - Price on:12/24/2007	$17
Employees	210	Stock Exchange	OTC
Auditor	Akin, Doherty, Klein & Feuge P.C	Ticker Symbol	CLNW
Stk Agt	NA	Outstanding Shares	3,160,000
Counsel	NA	E.P.S	-$0.37
DUNS No.	82-485-1448	Shareholders	NA

Business: The group's principle activity is to operate and manage retama park racetrack in selma, Texas. The group reimburses its operating expenses of the track from the revenues generated at the track. Operations are carried on through its wholly owned subsidiaries, arn communications corp, national communications network inc and retama entertainment group inc. The group's quarterly revenue for Spetember 2007 was 1.26 millions of USD.

Primary SIC and add'l.: 7948

CIK No: 0000869484

Subsidiaries: Retama Entertainment Group, Inc.

Officers: Bryan P. Brown/CEO, Dir. - Retama Entertainment Group Inc/$204,000.00, Joe Straus/Chmn. - Retama Entertainment Group Inc, Kenneth Fleenor/Dir. - Retama Entertainment Group Inc, Thomas R. Johnson/Dir. - Retama Entertainment Group Inc/$155,923.00, George Wolff/Dir. - Retama Entertainment Group Inc, Robert W. Pollock/GM - Retama Entertainment Group, Inc, Lisa L. Medrano/CFO - Retama Entertainment Group, Inc, James C. Leatherman/Racing Sec. - Retama Entertainment Group, Inc, Gina Holt/Dir. - Food, Beverage, Catering Operations, Retama Entertainment Group, Inc, Jesse L. Cardenas/Track Superintendent, Retama Entertainment Group, Inc, Angela C. Cooper/Dir. - Human Resources, Retama Entertainment Group, Inc, Richard L. Cole/Dir. - Security, Retama Entertainment Group, Inc, Jackie F. Hart/Dir. - Mutuels, Retama Entertainment Group, Inc, Aaron E. Morris/Dir. - Maintenance, Retama Entertainment Group, Inc, Steven M. Ross/Dir. - Simulcasting, Retama Entertainment Group, Inc *(17 Officers included in Index)*

Owners: Insiders/92.67%, Christopher J. Hall/89.70%, Thomas R. Johnson/2.97%

Financial Data: *Fiscal Year End:* 12/31 *Latest Annual Data:* 12/31/2006

Year	Sales	Net Income
2006	$5,326,000	$103,000
2005	$5,195,000	-$21,000
2004	$4,743,000	$143,000

Curr. Assets:	$34,760,000	**Curr. Liab.:**	$18,981,000		
Plant, Equip.:	NA	**Total Liab.:**	$18,981,000	**Indic. Yr. Divd.:**	NA
Total Assets:	$42,207,000	**Net Worth:**	$23,222,000	**Debt/ Equity:**	NA

Callaway Golf Co

2180 Rutherford Rd., Carlsbad, CA, 92008; ***PH:*** 1-760-931-1771; ***Fax:*** 1-760-930-5015; ***http://*** www.callawaygolf.com; ***Email:*** cg_customer.service@callawaygolf.com

General - Incorporation .... DE
Employees 3,000
Auditor .... Deloitte & Touche LLP
Stk Agt............ Mellon Investor Services LLC
Counsel............ Gibson, Dunn & Crutcher LLP
DUNS No. 05-557-1012

Stock- Price on:12/24/2007 .... $18.34
Stock Exchange .... NYSE
Ticker Symbol .... ELY
Outstanding Shares 72,160,000
E.P.S $0.694
Shareholders .... NA

Business: The group's principal activity is to design, develop, manufacture and market golf clubs and golf balls. The group manufactures and markets golf clubs that include drivers, fairway woods, irons, wedges and putters and golf balls. The other golf accessories sold include golf bags, golf gloves, golf headwear, travel covers and bags, golf towels and golf umbrellas. The primary products include great big bertha, hawk eye, titanium metal woods and tungsten injected titanium irons and a distinctive range of putters. The products are sold in the United States and throughout 100 countries around the world. The products are designed for both amateur and professional golfers. Golfers generally purchase the group's products on the basis of performance, ease of use and appearance. The group acquired top-flite golf company on 15-Sep-2003.

Primary SIC and add'l.: 3949 5091

CIK No: 0000837465

Subsidiaries: All-American Golf LLC, Callaway Golf Canada Ltd., Callaway Golf Europe Ltd., Callaway Golf K.K., Callaway Golf Korea Ltd., CallawayGolf(Germany)GmbH, CallawayGolfInteractive,Inc., CallawayGolfSalesCompany, CallawayGolfSouthPacificPtyLtd., CGV, Inc., The Top-Flite Golf Company

Officers: George Fellows/64/Dir., CEO, Pres./$3,414,311.00

Directors: George Fellows/64/Dir., CEO, Pres., Ronald S. Beard/68/Chmn., Samuel H. Armacost/68/Dir., John C. Cushman/66/Dir., Yotaro Kobayashi/73/Dir., Richard L. Rosenfield/61/Dir., Anthony S. Thornley/60/Dir.

Owners: Ronald S. Beard, David A. Laverty, Insiders/3.15%, Steven C. McCracken/1.13%, Yotaro Kobayashi, George Fellows, Robert A. Penicka, Royce & Associates, LLC/5.44%, Union Bank of California, N.A./5.91%, Samuel H. Armacost, FMR Corporation/5.43%, Anthony S. Thornley, Thomas Yang, Richard L. Rosenfield, Goodman & Company, Investment Counsel Ltd./6.39% *(17 Owners included in Index)*

Financial Data: *Fiscal Year End:*12/31 *Latest Annual Data:* 12/31/2006

Year	Sales	Net Income
2006	$1,017,907,000	$23,290,000
2005	$998,093,000	$13,284,000
2004	$934,564,000	-$10,103,000

Curr. Assets:	$493,200,000	**Curr. Liab.:**	$223,455,000	**P/E Ratio:**	26.43
Plant, Equip.:	$131,224,000	**Total Liab.:**	$266,843,000	**Indic. Yr. Divd.:**	$0.280
Total Assets:	$845,947,000	**Net Worth:**	$577,117,000	**Debt/ Equity:**	0.0356

Callidus Software Inc

160 W Santa Clara St., Ste. 1500, San Jose, CA, 95113; ***PH:*** 1-408-808-6400; ***Fax:*** 1-408-271-2662; ***http://*** www.callidussoftware.com

General - Incorporation .... DE
Employees 355
Auditor .... KPMG LLP
Stk Agt...... American Stock Transfer & Trust Co.
Counsel .... NA
DUNS No. .... NA

Stock- Price on:12/24/2007 .... $7.93
Stock Exchange .... NDQ
Ticker Symbol .... CALD
Outstanding Shares 28,900,000
E.P.S .... -$0.33
Shareholders .... NA

Business: The group's principle activity is to develop and market enterprise software. The group provides enterprise incentive management (eim) software systems to global companies across multiple industries. Large enterprises use eim systems to administer, analyze and report on pay-for-performance plans, which are designed to align sales and channel tactics with targeted business objectives. The software products of the group enable companies to access applicable transaction data and accurately report on compensation results. The group has over 75 customers in the insurance, retail banking, telecommunications, manufacturing and technology industries. The customers include, allstate, j.p. Morgan chase & co., at&t wireless and apple computer. The registered trademarks of the group are callidus software(R), the callidus software logo and truecomp(r). The group's quarterly revenue for September 2007 was 25.37 millions of USD.

Primary SIC and add'l.: 7373 7372

CIK No: 0001035748

Subsidiaries: Callidus Software GbmH, Callidus Software Ltd., Callidus Software Pty. Limited

Officers: Robert H. Youngjohns/Dir., CEO, Pres./$1,607,658.00, William B. Binch/Executive Chmn., Bryan Burkhart/VP - Sales The Americas, Shanker S. Trivedi/Sr. VP - Corporate Development, Richard D. Furino/Sr. VP - Worldwide Client Services/$767,348.00, Ronald J. Fior/Sr. VP - Finance, Operations, CFO/$653,167.00, Leslie J. Stretch/Sr. VP - Global Sales, Marketing, On, Demand Business/$762,532.00, Andrew Armstrong/VP, International GM, Holly V. Albert/Sr. VP, General Counsel, Corp. Sec.

Directors: Robert H. Youngjohns/Dir., CEO, Pres., William B. Binch/Executive Chmn., George B. James/Dir., Michael A. Braun/Dir., David B. Pratt/Dir., Charles M. Boesenberg/Dir., Michele Vion/Dir.

Owners: David B. Pratt/1.09%, Invesco Private Capital, Inc./9.84%, Insiders/8.48%, Ronald J. Fior/1.05%, Robert H. Youngjohns/2.09%, David Knott of Dorsett Management/7.65%, William B. Binch, Robert W. Warfield/1.10%, Leslie J. Stretch, George B. James, Charles M. Boesenberg, Crosspoint Venture Partners/23.48%, Richard D. Furino, Michael A. Braun, Michele Vion

Financial Data: *Fiscal Year End:*12/31 *Latest Annual Data:* 06/30/2007

Year	Sales	Net Income
2007	NA	NA
2006	$76,108,000	-$8,721,000
2005	$61,453,000	-$8,605,000

Curr. Assets:	$79,942,000	**Curr. Liab.:**	$24,993,000		
Plant, Equip.:	$4,086,000	**Total Liab.:**	$27,814,000	**Indic. Yr. Divd.:**	NA
Total Assets:	$85,194,000	**Net Worth:**	$57,380,000	**Debt/ Equity:**	NA

Callisto Pharmaceuticals Inc

420 Lexington Ave., Ste. 1609, New York, NY, 10170; ***PH:*** 1-212-297-0010; ***Fax:*** 1-212-297-0020; ***http://*** www.callistopharma.com; ***Email:*** jacob@callistopharma.com

General - Incorporation .... DE
Employees 9
Auditor .... BDO Seidman LLP
Stk Agt............ Stock Transfer & Trust Co
Counsel .... NA
DUNS No. .... NA

Stock- Price on:12/24/2007 .... $0.69
Stock Exchange .... AMEX
Ticker Symbol .... KAL
Outstanding Shares 39,690,000
E.P.S .... NA
Shareholders .... NA

Business: The groups principal activity is to develop biopharmaceutical products. The group operates from the United States.

Primary SIC and add'l.: 2834 2836 3845 2833 2835 3843 3841

CIK No: 0001142380

Subsidiaries: Callisto Pharma GmbH, Callisto Research Labs LLC, IgX Ltd., Synergy Pharmaceuticals Inc.

Officers: Gary S. Jacob/Dir., CEO, Chief Scientific Officer/$417,772.00, Geoffrey Henson/Consultant, Robert C. Shepard/Chief Medical Officer, Arthur Sytkowski/Clinical Trial Advisor, Consultant, Kunwar Shailubhai/Sr. VP - Drug Discovery, Synergy Pharmaceuticals, Inc, Bernard F. Denoyer/VP - Finance/$122,037.00, Dan D'Agostino/Chief Business Officer/$207,814.00, Craig Talluto/Dir. - Clinical Operations

Directors: Gary S. Jacob/Dir., CEO, Chief Scientific Officer, Gabriele M. Cerrone/Chmn., Christoph Bruening/Dir., John P. Brancaccio/Dir., Stephen K. Carter/Dir., Randall K. Johnson/Dir., Riccardo Dalla-Favera/Dir., Moshe Talpaz/Member - Scientific Advisory Board, Kenneth C. Anderson/Member - Scientific Advisory Board, Roman Perez-Soler/Member - Scientific Advisory Board

Owners: Bernard Denoyer, Insiders/12.90%, Randall K. Johnson, Christoph Bruening/1.40%, Daniel S. DAgostino, John Brancaccio, Gabriele M. Cerrone/8.30%, Gary S. Jacob/2.40%, Riccardo Dalla-Favera, Stephen Carter, Panetta Partners Ltd./5.40%

Financial Data: *Fiscal Year End:*12/31 *Latest Annual Data:* 12/31/2006

Year	Sales	Net Income
2006	NA	-$12,919,000
2005	NA	-$11,779,000
2004	NA	-$7,543,000

Curr. Assets:	$3,971,000	**Curr. Liab.:**	$3,201,000		
Plant, Equip.:	$6,000	**Total Liab.:**	$3,201,000	**Indic. Yr. Divd.:**	NA
Total Assets:	$4,051,000	**Net Worth:**	$850,000	**Debt/ Equity:**	NA

Callon Petroleum Co

200 N Canal St., Natchez, MS, 39120; ***PH:*** 1-601-442-1601; ***Fax:*** 1-601-446-1410; ***http://*** www.callon.com; ***Email:*** terryt@callon.com

General - Incorporation .... DE
Employees 86
Auditor .... Ernst & Young LLP
Stk Agt ..... American Stock Transfer & Trust Co.
Counsel............ Haynes & Boone
DUNS No. 05-711-3318

Stock- Price on:12/24/2007 .... $14.33
Stock Exchange .... NYSE
Ticker Symbol .... CPE
Outstanding Shares 20,750,000
E.P.S $0.77
Shareholders .... NA

Business: The group's principal activity is to explore, develop, acquire and produce oil and gas properties. It also provides natural gas transmission and oil and gas property management services for other investors. The properties are geographically concentrated primarily offshore in the gulf of Mexico and onshore in Louisiana and Alabama. During fourth quarter of 2003, the group's first two deepwater projects, the medusa and habanero fields, began production.

Primary SIC and add'l.: 1311

CIK No: 0000928022

Subsidiaries: Callon Offshore Production, Inc, Mississippi Marketing, Inc.

Officers: Fred L. Callon/Chmn., CEO, Clark H. Smith/CIO, B. F. Weatherly/Dir., CFO, Exec. VP/$243,733.00, Stephen F. Woodcock/VP - Exploration/$477,673.00, Thomas E. Schwager/VP - Engineering, Operations/$419,640.00, Rodger W. Smith/Corporate Controller, Treasurer/$338,241.00, Robert A. Mayfield/Corp. Sec.

Directors: Fred L. Callon/Chmn., CEO, B. F. Weatherly/Dir., CFO, Exec. VP, John C. Wallace/Dir., Richard L. Flury/Dir., Richard O. Wilson/Dir.

Owners: Kennedy Capital Management, Inc./5.93%, Richard L. Flury, Barclays Global Investors, NA/7.02%, Dimensional Fund Advisors LP/8.14%, Thomas E. Schwager, Fred L. Callon/2.75%, B. F. Weatherly, Rodger W. Smith, New York Life Investment Management, LLC./5.13%, Wellington Management Company, LLP/6.27%, Stephen F. Woodcock, Richard O. Wilson, Insiders/5.76%, John C. Wallace

Financial Data: *Fiscal Year End:*12/31 *Latest Annual Data:* 12/31/2006

Year	Sales	Net Income
2006	$182,268,000	$40,560,000
2005	$141,290,000	$26,776,000
2004	$119,802,000	$21,501,000

Curr. Assets:	$57,652,000	**Curr. Liab.:**	$61,179,000	**P/E Ratio:**	12.79
Plant, Equip.:	$549,023,000	**Total Liab.:**	$344,164,000	**Indic. Yr. Divd.:**	NA
Total Assets:	$625,527,000	**Net Worth:**	$281,363,000	**Debt/ Equity:**	0.8015

Callwave Inc

136 W Canon Perdido St., Ste. A, Santa Barbara, CA, 93101; ***PH:*** 1-805-690-4000; ***Fax:*** 1-805-690-4241; ***http://*** investor.callwave.com

General - Incorporation .... DE
Employees 91
Auditor .... Ernst & Young LLP
Stk Agt .... Mellon Investor Services LLC
Counsel .... NA
DUNS No. .... NA

Stock- Price on:12/24/2007 .... $3.66
Stock Exchange .... NDQ
Ticker Symbol .... CALL
Outstanding Shares 20,860,000
E.P.S .... -$0.4
Shareholders .... NA

Business: The groups principle activity is to provide convergence services. The group also manages to calls across their existing landline, mobile and Internet networks. The products and services include CallWave Internet Answering Machine, CallWave Fax, CallWave Mobile, CallWave Web 2.0 Widgets, CallWave Vtxt and PhonePage. The group operates from United States.

Primary SIC and add'l.: NA

CIK No: 0001115091

Subsidiaries: CallWave Long Distance, LLC, Liberty Telecom, LLC

Officers: Jeffrey Cavins/Dir., CEO, Pres., Joshua Fraser/36/VP - Business Development, Patrick Todd/Dir. - Investor Relations, David A. Giannini/VP - Engineering, Colin D. Kelley/CTO, David S. Trandal/Dir., Co - Founder, VP - Operations, Mark Stubbs/CFO

Directors: Jeffrey Cavins/Dir., CEO, Pres., Peter V. Sperling/Chmn., Co - Founder, David S. Trandal/Dir., Co - Founder, VP - Operations, Jerry Murdock/Dir., Jeffrey O. Henley/Dir., Raj Raithatha/Dir., Osmo A. Hautanen/Dir.

Owners: David A. Giannini/0.90%, Mark Stubbs/0.30%, Osmo Hautanen/0.10%, Insight Venture Associates IV, LLC/14.50%, Capital Research and Management Company/6.40%, Insiders/40.20%, Jeffrey O. Henley/0.50%, Peter V. Sperling/18.60%, Raj Raithatha/0.10%, Jerry Murdock/14.80%, David F. Hofstatter/9.50%, Wheatley Partners/6.30%, David S. Trandal/3.40%, Colin Kelley/0.90%, New Millennium Partners/5.80%

Financial Data: *Fiscal Year End:* 06/30 *Latest Annual Data:* 06/30/2007

Year	Sales	Net Income
2007	$25,201,000	-$7,472,000
2006	$36,594,000	-$1,983,000
2005	$45,518,000	$11,602,000

Curr. Assets:	$64,842,000	Curr. Liab.:	$2,793,000		
Plant, Equip.:	$2,014,000	Total Liab.:	$2,793,000	Indic. Yr. Divd.:	NA
Total Assets:	$67,455,000	Net Worth:	$64,662,000	Debt/ Equity:	NA

Calpetro Tankers (BAHAMAS III) Ltd

One Intl. Pl., Rm 619, Boston, MA, 02109;

General - Incorporation	Bahamas	Stock- Price on:12/24/2007	NA
Employees	NA	Stock Exchange	NA
Auditor	Grant Thornton, LLP	Ticker Symbol	NA
Stk Agt	NA	Outstanding Shares	NA
Counsel	NA	E.P.S	NA
DUNS No.	05-168-5956	Shareholders	NA

Business: The group's principle activity is to acquire and charters petroleum tankers. The group operates from United States.

Primary SIC and add'l.: 4412

CIK No: 0000923656

Subsidiaries: California Tankers Investments Limited, CalPetro Holdings Limited, Independent Tankers Corporation

Officers: Kate Blankenship/43/Dir., Sec., Principal Financial Officer, Tor O. Troim/45/Dir., Pres., Principal Executive Officer

Directors: Kate Blankenship/43/Dir., Sec., Principal Financial Officer, Tor O. Troim/45/Dir., Pres., Principal Executive Officer

Calpetro Tankers (IOM) Ltd

Ragnall House, 18 Peel Rd., Douglas, D7 00000;

General - Incorporation	Isle Of Man	Stock- Price on:12/24/2007	NA
Employees	NA	Stock Exchange	NA
Auditor	Grant Thornton LLP	Ticker Symbol	NA
Stk Agt	NA	Outstanding Shares	NA
Counsel	NA	E.P.S	NA
DUNS No.	NA	Shareholders	NA

Business: The group's principle acitvity is to provide charters petroleum tankers. The group operates from United States.

Primary SIC and add'l.: 4412

CIK No: 0000923657

Subsidiaries: California Tankers Investments, CalPetro Holdings Limited, Chevron, Frontline Ltd, Independent Tankers Corporation

Officers: Tor Olav Troim/45/Dir., Pres., Principal Executive Officer, Kate Blankenship/43/Dir., Sec., Principal Financial Officer

Directors: Tor Olav Troim/45/Dir., Pres., Principal Executive Officer, Kate Blankenship/43/Dir., Sec., Principal Financial Officer, John Michael Killip/63/Dir.

Calpetro Tankers Bahamas I Ltd

One Intl. Pl., Rm 619, Boston, MA, 02109;

General - Incorporation	Bahamas	Stock- Price on:12/24/2007	NA
Employees	NA	Stock Exchange	NA
Auditor	Grant Thornton, Ernst & Young	Ticker Symbol	NA
Stk Agt	NA	Outstanding Shares	NA
Counsel	NA	E.P.S	NA
DUNS No.	NA	Shareholders	NA

Business: The group's principle activity is to to acquire and charters petroleum tankers. The group operates from United States.

Primary SIC and add'l.: 4412

CIK No: 0000923652

Subsidiaries: California Tankers Investments Limited, Frontline Ltd., Independent Tankers Corporation

Officers: Kate Blankenship/43/Dir., Sec., Principal Financial Officer, Tor Olav Troim/45/Dir., Pres., Principal Executive Officer

Directors: Kate Blankenship/43/Dir., Sec., Principal Financial Officer, Tor Olav Troim/45/Dir., Pres., Principal Executive Officer

Calpetro Tankers Bahamas II Ltd

One Intl. Pl., Rm 619, Boston, MA, 02109;

General - Incorporation	Bahamas	Stock- Price on:12/24/2007	NA
Employees	3,265	Stock Exchange	NA
Auditor	Grant Thornton LLP	Ticker Symbol	NA
Stk Agt	NA	Outstanding Shares	NA
Counsel	NA	E.P.S	NA
DUNS No.	NA	Shareholders	NA

Business: The group's principle activity is to acquire and charters petroleum tankers. The group operates from United States.

Primary SIC and add'l.: 4412

CIK No: 0000923655

Subsidiaries: California Tankers Investments Limited

Officers: Kate Blankenship/43/Dir., Sec., Principal Financial Officer, Tor Olav Troim/45/Dir., Pres., Principal Executive Officer

Directors: Kate Blankenship/43/Dir., Sec., Principal Financial Officer, Tor Olav Troim/45/Dir., Pres., Principal Executive Officer

Calpine Corp

50 W San Fernando St., San Jose, CA, 95113; *PH:* 1-408-995-5115; *Fax:* 1-408-995-0505; *http://* www.calpine.com; *Email:* investor-relations@calpine.com

General - Incorporation	DE	Stock- Price on:12/24/2007	$3.33
Employees	2,306	Stock Exchange	OTC
Auditor	PricewaterhouseCoopers LLP	Ticker Symbol	CPNLQ
Stk Agt	Chicago Trust Co.	Outstanding Shares	503,110,000
Counsel	NA	E.P.S	$5.16
DUNS No.	11-271-0876	Shareholders	NA

Business: The group's principle activity is to generate electricity in the United States, Canada and the United Kingdom. The group generates revenue from three segments: electric generation and marketing, oil and gas production and marketing and corporate and other activities. It also develops, constructs, owns and operates power generation facilities and the sale of electricity and its by-product, thermal energy primarily in the form of steam. The group also has 12 gas-fired projects and 1 project expansion currently under construction collectively having a net capacity of 7,685 mw. The California department of water resources is one of the major customers of the group. The group sold alvin south field oil and gas assets and the specialty data center engineering business in 2003 and its 50% interest in the lost pines 1 energy center in 2004. The group's quarterly revenue for September 2007 was 2,239.00 millions of USD.

Primary SIC and add'l.: 4924 4961 4931

CIK No: 0000916457

Subsidiaries: 1066917 Ontario Inc., 1071931 Ontario Inc., 3094479 Nova Scotia Company, 3538982 Canada Inc., Acadia Partners Pipeline, LLC, Acadia Power Partners, LLC, Amelia Energy Center, LP, Anacapa Land Company, LLC, Anderson Springs Energy Company, Androscoggin Energy, Inc., Auburndale Peaker Energy Center, LLC, Augusta Development Company, LLC, Aviation Funding Corp., Basento Energia S.r.l, Baytown Energy Center, LP 171 Subsidiaries included in the Index

Officers: Robert P. May/Dir., CEO, Peter Cartwright/76/Chmn., CEO, Pres., Ann B. Curtis/55/Vice Chmn., Exec. VP, Corp. Sec., James J. Shield/Sr. VP - Power Operations, East, Peter Gilmore/VP, Steve Hodkinson/VP, Joseph E. Ronan/Sr. VP - Government, Regulatory Affairs, Eric N. Pryor/40/Sr. VP, Deputy CFO, Corporate Risk Officer, Dennis Fishback/CIO, Sr. VP, Lisa Bodensteiner/44/Exec. VP, General Counsel, Melissa A. Brown/Sr. VP - Strategy, Financial Planning, Analysis, Gregory L. Doody/Exec. VP, General Counsel, Sec., Robert E. Fishman/56/Exec. VP - Power Operations, Dennis J. Gilles/Sr. VP - Power Operations, Geothermal, Casey L. Gunnell/Exec. VP - Shared Services *(51 Officers included in Index)*

Directors: Robert P. May/Dir., CEO, Peter Cartwright/76/Chmn., CEO, Pres., Kenneth Derr/Chmn., William J. Keese/Dir., Walter L. Revell/Dir., George J. Stathakis/Dir., David C. Merritt/Dir., Susan Wang/Dir., Glenn H. Hiner/Dir.

Owners: Robert E. Fishman, George J. Stathakis, Susan Wang, Insiders, Walter L. Revell, Kenneth Derr, Eric N. Pryor, William J. Keese, James E. Macias

Financial Data: *Fiscal Year End:* 12/31 *Latest Annual Data:* 12/31/2006

Year	Sales	Net Income
2006	$6,705,760,000	-$1,764,907,000
2005	$10,112,658,000	-$9,939,208,000
2004	$9,229,888,000	-$242,461,000

Curr. Assets:	$3,168,329,000	Curr. Liab.:	$6,057,947,000	P/E Ratio:	1.83
Plant, Equip.:	$13,603,202,000	Total Liab.:	$25,476,873,000	Indic. Yr. Divd.:	NA
Total Assets:	$18,590,265,000	Net Worth:	-$7,152,900,000	Debt/ Equity:	NA

Calton Inc

2050 40th Ave., Ste. 1, Vero Beach, FL, 32960; *PH:* 1-772-794-1414; *Fax:* 1-772-794-2828; *http://* www.caltoninc.com

General - Incorporation	NJ	Stock- Price on:12/24/2007	$0.23
Employees	10	Stock Exchange	OTC
Auditor	Aidman, Piser & Co. P.A	Ticker Symbol	CTON
Stk Agt	First City Transfer Co	Outstanding Shares	9,630,000
Counsel	Giordano, Halleran & Ciesla	E.P.S	-$0.22
DUNS No.	04-750-9526	Shareholders	NA

Business: The group's principal activity is to operate in three segments: homebuilding and consulting: constructs single-family residential homes in Florida, through homes by calton, llc. The group acts as a general contractor in the construction of residences at the riverside at the island club community. Internet development: provides Internet strategy consulting services and develops comprehensive Internet-based solutions for its clients. The segment provides its services to small and medium size companies in various industries. It also operates a technology based consulting and staffing operation specializing in network design and management. Credit card loyalty business: includes installation of customer loyalty and co-branded credit card programs for the retail automobile industry in the United States.

Primary SIC and add'l.: 7375 1521 7379

CIK No: 0000717216

Subsidiaries: eCalton.com, Inc., Homes by Calton, LLC, PrivilegeONE Networks, LLC

Officers: Anthony J. Caldarone/Chmn., CEO, Pres., Vicky F. Savage/VP, Acting CFO, Treasurer

Directors: Anthony J. Caldarone/Chmn., CEO, Pres.

Owners: Maria F. Caldarone, John G. Yates, Anthony J. Caldarone, Ernest J. Brophy, Anthony J. Caldarone, Laura A. Camisa, Frank Cavell Smith, Kenneth D. Hill, Insiders, John G. Yates, Maria F. Caldarone, Joyce P. Caldarone, Mark N. Fessel

Financial Data: Fiscal Year End: 11/30   **Latest Annual Data:** 11/30/2006

Year	Sales	Net Income
2006	$6,631,000	-$1,406,000
2005	$13,848,000	$1,134,000
2004	$12,202,000	$561,000

Curr. Assets:	$8,658,000	Curr. Liab.:	$5,815,000		
Plant, Equip.:	$171,000	Total Liab.:	$5,815,000	Indic. Yr. Divd.:	NA
Total Assets:	$8,849,000	Net Worth:	$3,034,000	Debt/ Equity:	0.3696

Calumet Specialty Products Partners LP

2780 Waterfront Pkwy. E Dr., Ste. 200, Indianapolis, IN, 46214; **PH:** 1-317-328-5660; **Fax:** 1-317-328-5668; **http://** www.calumetlubricants.com; **Email:** info@calumetlubricants.com

General - Incorporation	DE	**Stock** - Price on: 12/24/2007	$49.92
Employees	360	Stock Exchange	NDQ
Auditor	Ernst & Young LLP	Ticker Symbol	CLMT
Stk Agt	Mellon Investor Services LLC	Outstanding Shares	29,430,000
Counsel	NA	E.P.S.	$5.07
DUNS No.	NA	Shareholders	NA

Business: The groups principle activity is to produce hydrocarbon products. The group operates through two segments namely specialty products and fuel products. The products of the group include lubricating oils, solvents, waxes, asphalt, fuels, gasoline, diesel and jet fuel. The group operates from the United States. The group's quarterly revenue for September 2007 was 428.08 millions of USD.

Primary SIC and add'l.: 5172 2999 2911 2992 5171

CIK No: 0001340122

Subsidiaries: Calumet LP GP, LLC, Calumet Lubricants Co., Limited Partnership, Calumet Operating, LLC, Calumet Sales Company Incorporated, Calumet Shreveport Fuels, LLC, Calumet Shreveport Lubricants & Waxes, LLC, Calumet Shreveport, LLC

Officers: William F. Grube/Dir., CEO, Pres., Allan A. Moyes/Exec. VP - General Partner, Predecessor, Patrick R. Murray/CFO, VP, Sec., Robert M. Mills/VP - Crude Oil Supply, Jeffrey D. Smith/VP - Planning, Economics, General Partner, Predecessor, William A. Anderson/VP - Sales, Marketing, General Partner, Predecessor

Directors: William F. Grube/Dir., CEO, Pres., Fred M. Fehsenfeld/Chmn., James S. Carter/Dir., William S. Fehsenfeld/Dir., Robert E. Funk/Dir., Nicholas J. Rutigliano/Dir., Michael L. Smith/Dir.

Owners: Kayne Anderson Capital Advisors, L.P./8.47%, Allan A. Moyes, Robert E. Funk, Robert M. Mills, Williams, Jones& Associates, LLC/9.17%, James S. Carter, Goldman, Sachs& Co./9.82%, William S. Fehsenfeld, Insiders/2.57%, Michael L. Smith, Janet K. Grube/7.21%, Patrick R. Murray, Jeffrey D. Smith, Fred M. Fehsenfeld/1.13%, Osterweis Capital Management, Inc./6.36% (20 Owners included in Index)

Financial Data: Fiscal Year End: 12/31   **Latest Annual Data:** 12/31/2006

Year	Sales	Net Income
2006	$1,641,048,000	$93,882,000
2005	$1,289,072,000	$11,328,000

Curr. Assets:	$335,209,000	Curr. Liab.:	$102,489,000	P/E Ratio:	10.11
Plant, Equip.:	$191,732,000	Total Liab.:	$151,489,000	Indic. Yr. Divd.:	$2.520
Total Assets:	$530,174,000	Net Worth:	$378,685,000	Debt/ Equity:	0.1492

Calwest Bancorp CA

22342 Avenida Empresa, Rancho Santa Margarita, CA, 92688; **PH:** 1-949-766-3000

General - Incorporation	CA	**Stock** - Price on: 12/24/2007	$12.72
Employees	NA	Stock Exchange	OTC
Auditor	NA	Ticker Symbol	CALW
Stk Agt	U.S. Stock Transfer Corp	Outstanding Shares	NA
Counsel	NA	E.P.S.	NA
DUNS No.	NA	Shareholders	NA

Business: The groups principle activity is to provide recruiting services. The groups service area includes the research and development, engineering, marketing, sales, information technology and manufacturing industries. The group operates from United States.

Primary SIC and add'l.: 6021 6712

CIK No: 0001257580

Calypte Biomedical Corp

5 Ctr.pointe Dr., Ste. 400, Lake Oswego, OR, 97035; **PH:** 1-971-204-0282; **Fax:** 1-971-204-0284; **http://** www.calypte.com; **Email:** customerservice@calypte.com

General - Incorporation	DE	**Stock** - Price on: 12/24/2007	$0.08
Employees	9	Stock Exchange	OTC
Auditor	Odenberg, Muranishi & Co. LLP	Ticker Symbol	CBMC
Stk Agt	American Stock Transfer & Trust Co.	Outstanding Shares	341,510,000
Counsel	Parker Chapin	E.P.S.	$0.08
DUNS No.	18-629-1910	Shareholders	NA

Business: The group's principal activity is to develop and distribute urine-based diagnostic products and services. It has developed a test for the detection of antibodies to the human immunodeficiency virus, type 1 (HIV-1), sexually transmitted diseases and other infectious diseases. The products of the group include screening enzyme immunoassay (eia) and supplemental western blot tests. The products are fda-approved HIV-1 antibody tests that can be used on urine samples. The group sells these products to community-based organizations, public health laboratories, reference laboratories and the life insurance markets located in the United States of America, Indonesia, the republic of South Africa, the People's Republic of China and Malaysia.

Primary SIC and add'l.: 2834 2836 3841

CIK No: 0000899426

Subsidiaries: Beijing Marr

Officers: Roger I. Gale/Chmn., CEO, Pres., Andrew Hellman/Contact - CEO Cast, Christopher P. Kafka/VP - Business Development, Richard J. George/Scientific, Government Affairs Advisor, Richard Brounstein/Exec. VP, Jerrold D. Dotson/VP - Finance, Administration, Ronald W. Mink/Chief Science Officer

Directors: Roger I. Gale/Chmn., CEO, Pres., John J. Dipietro/Dir., Julius R. Krevans/Dir., Paul Freiman/Dir., Maxim A. Soulimov/Dir., Adel Karas/Dir.

Owners: Roger I. Gale, Ahmed Abdalla Deemas Alsuwaidi, Maxim A. Soulimov, Adel Karas, David Khidasheli, Richard D. Brounstein, Jerrold D. Dotson, Marr Technologies BV, John J. DiPietro, Mohamed Yousif Ahmed Saleh Sulaiman, Mohamed Ahmed, Theodore R. Gwin, Paul E. Freiman, Insiders, SF Capital Partners Ltd. (16 Owners included in Index)

Financial Data: Fiscal Year End: 12/31   **Latest Annual Data:** 12/31/2006

Year	Sales	Net Income
2006	$547,000	-$13,750,000
2005	$427,000	-$8,763,000
2004	$3,297,000	-$17,266,000

Curr. Assets:	$970,000	Curr. Liab.:	$5,798,000		
Plant, Equip.:	$1,359,000	Total Liab.:	$13,594,000	Indic. Yr. Divd.:	NA
Total Assets:	$8,018,000	Net Worth:	-$9,398,000	Debt/ Equity:	NA

Cam Commerce Solutions Inc

17075 Newhope St., Ste. A, Fountain Valley, CA, 92708; **PH:** 1-714-241-9241; **Fax:** 1-714-241-9893; **http://** www.camcommerce.com; **Email:** cam32@camcommerce.com

General - Incorporation	DE	**Stock** - Price on: 12/24/2007	$27.62
Employees	188	Stock Exchange	NDQ
Auditor	Ernst & Young, LLP	Ticker Symbol	CADA
Stk Agt	American Stock Transfer & Trust Co.	Outstanding Shares	4,050,000
Counsel	Lundell & Spadafore	E.P.S.	$0.93
DUNS No.	10-666-0731	Shareholders	NA

Business: The group's principle activity is to provide total commerce solutions for small to medium size, traditional retailers and Web retailers. These solutions are based on the open architecture software products for managing inventory, point of sale, sales transaction processing and accounting. The group also provides hardware, installation, training and consulting services. It offers five turn key systems: cam32, profit$, retail star. Retail ice and microbiz. The cam32 is designed for hard goods retailers. The profit$ is designed for apparel and shoe retailers. The retail star incorporates multiple functions of both the cam and profit$ systems. The microbiz is designed for single store hard goods retailers. Turnkey systems help in automated pricing, printing of customer invoice and tracking of inventory. The group's total revenue for year 2007 was 32.23 millions of USD.

Primary SIC and add'l.: 7373 7379

CIK No: 0000819334

Officers: Geoffrey D. Knapp/49/Chmn., CEO, Sec., Paul Caceres/47/CFO, Chief Accounting Officer

Directors: Geoffrey D. Knapp/49/Chmn., CEO, Sec., Walter W. Straub/64/Dir., David A. Frosh/49/Dir., Donald A. Clark/57/Dir.

Owners: Walter W. Straub/2.90%, Donald Clark, Bares Capital Management/9.60%, Insiders/15.60%, Paul Caceres, Geoffrey D. Knapp/11.20%, Ken Templeton/15.10%, David Frosh

Financial Data: Fiscal Year End: 09/30   **Latest Annual Data:** 9/30/2006

Year	Sales	Net Income
2006	$27,212,000	$2,647,000
2005	$24,936,000	$1,774,000
2004	$23,634,000	$2,241,000

Curr. Assets:	$27,109,000	Curr. Liab.:	$3,752,000	P/E Ratio:	29.70
Plant, Equip.:	$484,000	Total Liab.:	$3,752,000	Indic. Yr. Divd.:	$0.800
Total Assets:	$28,145,000	Net Worth:	$24,393,000	Debt/ Equity:	NA

Cambex Corp

115 Flanders Rd., Westborough, MA, 01581; **PH:** 1-508-983-1200; **Fax:** 1-508-983-0255; **http://** www.cambex.com

General - Incorporation	MA	**Stock** - Price on: 12/24/2007	$0.16
Employees	14	Stock Exchange	OTC
Auditor	Sullivan Bille P.C.	Ticker Symbol	CBEX
Stk Agt	American Stock Transfer & Trust Co.	Outstanding Shares	23,430,000
Counsel	NA	E.P.S.	$0.02
DUNS No.	04-590-8217	Shareholders	NA

Business: The group's principal activity is to design and supply fibre channel hardware and software products used to build storage area networks (sans). The products offered include host bus adapters, hubs, disk arrays and software. A host bus adapter is a printed circuit card that plugs into the motherboard of servers and workstations and enables these devices to connect to other fibre channel devices in a san. Fibre channel hub interconnects servers with storage devices and is targeted at workgroup and small enterprise san applications. Raid disk arrays allow users to store large amounts of online information in high availability, high performance environments. The software provided is designed to provide very high availability for enterprise level, mission-critical san deployments. The group operates in the United States, the Netherlands, Germany, England and France.

Primary SIC and add'l.: 7374 3572

CIK No: 0000016590

Subsidiaries: Cambex Securities Corporation, Cambex UK Ltd.

Officers: Joseph F. Kruy/76/Chmn., Pres., Principal Financial Officer, CEO, Treasurer, Lois P. Lehberger/51/Clerk, VP, Controller

Directors: Joseph F. Kruy/76/Chmn., Pres., Principal Financial Officer, CEO, Treasurer, C. V. Ramamoorthy/81/Dir., Robert J. Spain/70/Dir.

Owners: Joseph F. Kruy/23.20%, Peter J. Kruy/6.60%, Terry H. Snowday/6.70%, Robert J. Spain/1.10%, Lois P. Lehberger, Insiders/27.20%, Estate of Richard E. Calvert/9.70%, C. V. Ramamoorthy/2.60%, Bruce D. Rozelle/5.30%

Financial Data: Fiscal Year End: 12/31   **Latest Annual Data:** 12/31/2006

Year	Sales	Net Income
2006	$2,345,000	$907,000
2005	$2,272,000	$230,000
2004	$3,317,000	$1,245,000

Curr. Assets:	$337,000	Curr. Liab.:	$3,094,000	P/E Ratio:	8.00
Plant, Equip.:	$3,000	Total Liab.:	$3,094,000	Indic. Yr. Divd.:	NA
Total Assets:	$340,000	Net Worth:	-$2,754,000	Debt/ Equity:	NA

Cambior Inc

1111 St. Charles St. W, East Tower, Ste. 750, Longueuil, QC, J4K 5G4; *PH:* 1-450-677-0040; *http://* www.cambior.com

General - Incorporation	Canada	**Stock**- Price on:12/24/2007	$7.67
Employees	NA	Stock Exchange	NA
Auditor	Raymond Chabot Grant Thornton LLP	Ticker Symbol	NA
Stk Agt	Mellon Trust Co	Outstanding Shares	292,980,000
Counsel	Robert Lavalliere	E.P.S	-$0.19
DUNS No.	20-778-6195	Shareholders	NA

Business: The group's principal activities are mining, exploration and development of mining properties, principally gold, located in North America and South America.

Primary SIC and add'l.: 1021 1041 1099

CIK No: 0000922354

Subsidiaries: CBJ Caiman S.A.S., Niobec mine, OMAI Bauxite Mining Inc., OMAI Gold Mines Limited, Rosebel Gold Mines N.V, Rosebel Mine, Rouanda Mines Inc, Sociedad Minera Cambior Peru S. A., VSM Exploration Inc

Financial Data: *Fiscal Year End:*12/31 *Latest Annual Data:* 12/31/2006

Year	Sales	Net Income
2006	$332,219,000	$65,175,000
2005	$145,241,000	$13,317,000
2004	$135,021,000	$12,011,000

Curr. Assets:	$318,567,000	**Curr. Liab.:**	$216,511,000		
Plant, Equip.:	$1,273,800,000	**Total Liab.:**	$501,613,000	**Indic. Yr. Divd.:**	$0.060
Total Assets:	$2,236,231,000	**Net Worth:**	$1,730,906,000	**Debt/ Equity:**	NA

Cambrex Corp

1 Meadowlands Plz., East Rutherford, NJ, 07073; *PH:* 1-201-804-3000; *Fax:* 1-201-804-9852; *http://* www.cambrex.com

General - Incorporation	DE	**Stock**- Price on:12/24/2007	$13.51
Employees	1,916	Stock Exchange	NYSE
Auditor	PricewaterhouseCoopers LLP	Ticker Symbol	CBM
Stk Agt	American Stock Transfer & Trust Co.	Outstanding Shares	28,670,000
Counsel	NA	E.P.S	$6.51
DUNS No.	15-059-6716	Shareholders	NA

Business: The group's principal activities are carried out through three segments: human health, bioproducts and biopharma. The human health consists of pharmaceutical ingredients derived from organic chemistry. The bioproducts consists of cell culture products, endotoxin detection products, electrophoresis and chromatography products, and contract biopharmaceutical manufacturing services at clinical and commercial scale for the biotechnology and pharmaceutical industries. The biopharma consists ofgroup's contract biopharmaceutical process development and manufacturing business. Trademarks include poietics(tm) , clonetics(R), seaplaque(R), nusieve(R), reliant(R), latitude(R), pager(R), metaphor(R), accugene(R) and biowhittaker(tm). During the year 2003 the group discontinued rutherford chemicals segment.

Primary SIC and add'l.: 2834 2865 2879 2833 2819

CIK No: 0000820081

Subsidiaries: Cambrex Bio Science Baltimore, Inc., Cambrex Bio Science Clermont Ferrand SAS, Cambrex Bio Science Copenhagen ApS, Cambrex Bio Science Hopkinton, Inc., Cambrex Bio Science Nottingham Limited, Cambrex Bio Science Rockland, Inc., Cambrex Bio Science Verviers Sprl, Cambrex Bio Science Walkersville, Inc. ., Cambrex Charles City, Inc, Cambrex Cork Limited, Cambrex Karlskoga AB, Cambrex North Brunswick, Inc, Cambrex Profarmaco Landen NV, Cambrex Profarmaco Milano S.r.l

Officers: James A. Mack/69/Chmn., CEO, Pres./$1,901,482.00, Gerard Scarlato/Sales, Business Development Mgr. - Northwest, Canada, United States, Max Yeh/Sales, Business Development Mgr. - Southwest, Asia, United States, asa Backman/Marketing Mgr. - Communications, Europe, Jonathan Knight/VP - Sales, Europe, Peter Berg/Sales, Business Development Mgr. - Germany, Austria, Switzerland, Mark Hoggan/Sales, Business Development Mgr. - UK, Eire, Alain Denis/Sales, Business Development Mgr. - Southern Europe, France, Italy, Benelux, Spain, Portugal, Alexandra Englund/Sales, Business Development Mgr. - Scandinavia, Margaretha Eriksson/Customer Service, Stephanie Lafiura/Investor Relations, Per Almskog/Dir. - Purchasing, Cambrex Karlskoga, Europe, Jonas Ekroth/Purchasing Mgr. - Cambrex Karlskoga, Europe, Jan-Erik Mansson/Purchasing Mgr. - Cambrex Karlskoga, Europe, Rick Janssen/Mgr. - Material Resources, Cambrex Charles City, North America *(33 Officers included in Index)*

Directors: James A. Mack/69/Chmn., CEO, Pres., William B. Korb/66/Dir., Leon J. Hendrix/65/Dir., Ilan Kaufthal/59/Dir., David R. Bethune/66/Dir., Rosina B. Dixon/64/Dir., Roy W. Haley/60/Dir., Kathryn Rudie Harrigan/55/Dir., John R. Miller/69/Dir., Peter Tombros/64/Dir.

Owners: Ilan Kaufthal, Roy W. Haley, David R. Bethune, Gary L. Mossman/1.08%, Peter Tombros, Paolo Russolo, Steven M. Klosk, William B. Korb, Luke M. Beshar, Kathryn Rudie Harrigan, John R. Miller, Snyder Capital Management, L.P./8.50%, Leon J. Hendrix, Thomas N. Bird, Rosina B. Dixon *(17 Owners included in Index)*

Financial Data: *Fiscal Year End:*12/31 *Latest Annual Data:* 06/30/2007

Year	Sales	Net Income
2007	$62,855,000	$2,274,000
2006	$97,319,000	-$25,367,000
2005	$455,097,000	-$110,458,000

Curr. Assets:	$224,750,000	**Curr. Liab.:**	$107,134,000		
Plant, Equip.:	$227,024,000	**Total Liab.:**	$359,730,000	**Indic. Yr. Divd.:**	NA
Total Assets:	$606,376,000	**Net Worth:**	$246,646,000	**Debt/ Equity:**	NA

Cambridge Antibody Technology Group Plc

Milstein Bldg., Granta Pk., Cambridge, CB21 6GH; *PH:* 44-1223-471-471; *http://* www.cambridgeantibody.com

General - Incorporation	UK	**Stock**- Price on:12/24/2007	NA
Employees	NA	Stock Exchange	NA
Auditor	Deloitte & Touche LLP	Ticker Symbol	NA
Stk Agt	NA	Outstanding Shares	NA
Counsel	NA	E.P.S	NA
DUNS No.	NA	Shareholders	NA

Business: The group's principal activities are the research, developments and exploitation of products in the field of molecular engineering. Products include trabio, cat 123, cat 354, metelimumab, gc 1008, humira, abt 874, lymphostat-b, trail-r1mab, and abthrax with amgen amrad, elan, and genzyme as co-development partners. Product licensees include abbot laboratories, amgen, chugai, roche, human genome sciences, merck, pfizer and wyeth. Patent licensees include afimed, crucell, dyax, enzn, micromet, morphosys, and xoma.

Primary SIC and add'l.: 8731 2834 2835

CIK No: 0001067386

Subsidiaries: Optein Inc., Tagred Limited

Officers: Patrick Round/Sr. VP - Development, Hamish Cameron/Chief Executive, Adrian Kemp/General Counsel, Lizzie Dant/VP - Finance, Alex Duncan/Sr. VP - Discovery, Lynn Lester/Sr. VP - Human Resources - Business Operations

Directors: Gwyn Morgan/Member - Scientific Advisory Board, Christopher Marshall/Member - Scientific Advisory Board, Aaron Klug/Member - Scientific Advisory Board, John Forrester/Member - Scientific Advisory Board, Markus Grutter/Member - Scientific Advisory Board, Stephen Holgate/Member - Scientific Advisory Board, Stephen O'Rahilly/Member - Scientific Advisory Board, Ashok Venkitaraman/Member - Scientific Advisory Board, Chris Brightling/Member - Scientific Advisory Board

Cambridge Bancorp

1336 Massachusetts Ave., Cambridge, MA, 02138; *PH:* 1-617-876-5500; *Fax:* 1-617-441-1421; *http://* www.cambridgetrust.com

General - Incorporation		**Stock**- Price on:12/24/2007	$28.98
Employees	NA	Stock Exchange	OTC
Auditor	NA	Ticker Symbol	CATC
Stk Agt	NA	Outstanding Shares	3,850,000
Counsel	NA	E.P.S	NA
DUNS No.	NA	Shareholders	NA

Business: The groups principle activity is to provide recruiting services. The groups service area includes the research and development, engineering, marketing, sales, information technology and manufacturing industries. The group operates from United States.

Primary SIC and add'l.: 6022 6712 6282

CIK No:

Officers: Joseph V. Roller/Dir., Pres., CEO - Cambridge Trust Company, Colt Navins/Branch Mgr. - Lincoln Center, Cambridge Trust Company, Ping Wong/Branch Mgr. - University Park at MIT, Cambridge Trust Company, Lynne Linnehan/Branch Mgr. - Weston Center, Cambridge Trust Company, Carol Bartalussi/Branch Mgr. - Concord Center, Cambridge Trust Company, David G. Strachan/Contact - Wealth Management, Cambridge Trust Company, Albert R. Rietheimer/Sr. VP, CFO - Cambridge Trust Company, Robert MacAllister/Contact - Wealth Management, Cambridge Trust Company, James F. Spencer/Sr. VP, Chief Investment Officer - Cambridge Trust Company, Robert N. Siegrist/VP, Marketing Dir. - Cambridge Trust Company, Donna Petro/Branch Mgr. - Beacon Street, Cambridge Trust Company, Maria Montgomery/Branch Mgr., Lynne M. Burrow/CIO, Exec. VP - Cambridge Trust Company, Michael A. Duca/Exec. VP - Wealth Management, Cambridge Trust Company, Noreen A. Briand/Sr. VP, Personnel Officer - Cambridge Trust Company *(22 Officers included in Index)*

Directors: Joseph V. Roller/Dir., Pres., CEO - Cambridge Trust Company, Anne M. Thomas/Dir. - Cambridge Trust Company, Leon A. Palandjian/Dir. - Cambridge Trust Company, Robert S. Peterkin/Dir. - Cambridge Trust Company, Arthur D. Bond/Dir. - Cambridge Trust Company, James F. Dwinell/Dir., Jasper M. Evarts/Dir. - Cambridge Trust Company, Jean K. Mixer/Dir. - Cambridge Trust Company, David A. Thomas/Dir. - Cambridge Trust Company, David C. Warner/Dir. - Cambridge Trust Company, Linda Whitlock/Dir. - Cambridge Trust Company, Kathryn A. Willmore/Dir. - Cambridge Trust Company, Byron E. Woodman/Dir. - Cambridge Trust Company, Colyer M. Crum/Honorary Dir. - Cambridge Trust Company, Leo H. Dworsky/Honorary Dir. - Cambridge Trust Company *(16 Directors included in Index)*

Cambridge Display Technology Inc

2020 Cambourne Business Pk., Building 2020, Cambridge, CB3 6DW; ; *http://* www.cdtltd.co.uk

General - Incorporation	DE	**Stock**- Price on:12/24/2007	$5.92
Employees	114	Stock Exchange	NA
Auditor	Ernst& Young LLP	Ticker Symbol	NA
Stk Agt	Bank of New York	Outstanding Shares	21,630,000
Counsel	NA	E.P.S	-$1.28
DUNS No.	NA	Shareholders	NA

Business: The groups principle activities include producting, manufacturing and commercializing P OLED technology. The group operates through six segments namely the United Kingdom, European, the United States, North American and South America, Japan, and Asia Pacific. In January 2007, the group acquired Next Sierra Inc. The group operates from the United Kingdom, Europe, the United States, North American and South America, Japan, and Asia Pacific.

Primary SIC and add'l.: 2899 3679

CIK No: 0001297968

Subsidiaries: Cambridge Display Technology Limited, CDT Holdings Limited, CDT Licensing Limited, CDT Oxford Limited, Opsys Limited

Officers: David Fyfe/Chmn., CEO, Jeremy Burroughes/CTO, Scott Brown/VP - Research, Technology, Stephen Chandler/VP - Legal, Intellectual Property, Michael Black/Principal Financial, Accounting Officer, Emma Jones/VP - Human Resources, Facilities, Jim Veninger/VP - Technology Development, Ian Chao/VP - Commercial, Hilary Charles/General Counsel

Directors: David Fyfe/Chmn., CEO, Frank K. Bynum/Dir., Joseph Carr/Dir., Malcolm J. Thompson/Dir., Thomas Rosencrants/Dir.

Owners: Michael Black, Powershares Capital Management LLC/5.80%, KEP VI, LLC/40.00%, Sumitomo Chemical Co., Ltd., Kelso Investment Associates VI, L.P./40.00%, David Fyfe, Fidelity Growth Company Fund/5.80%, Malcolm J. Thompson, Joseph Carr, SB Cha, Insiders/40.70%

Financial Data: *Fiscal Year End:*12/31 *Latest Annual Data:* 12/31/2006

Year	Sales	Net Income
2006	$7,936,000	-$27,533,000
2005	$18,093,000	-$13,815,000
2004	$13,286,000	-$34,785,000

Curr. Assets:	$23,025,000	**Curr. Liab.:**	$13,944,000		
Plant, Equip.:	$9,579,000	**Total Liab.:**	$14,733,000	**Indic. Yr. Divd.:**	NA
Total Assets:	$103,969,000	**Net Worth:**	$89,236,000	**Debt/ Equity:**	NA

Cambridge Heart Inc

1 Oak Pk. Dr., Bedford, MA, 01730; *PH:* 1-781-271-1200; *Fax:* 1-781-275-8431;
http:// www.cambridgeheart.com

General - Incorporation	DE	**Stock** - Price on:12/24/2007	$4.19
Employees	34	Stock Exchange	OTC
Auditor	Vitale, Caturano & Co. Ltd	Ticker Symbol	CAMH
Stk Agt	American Stock Transfer & Trust Co.	Outstanding Shares	64,360,000
Counsel	Hale & Dorr LLP	E.P.S	-$0.023
DUNS No.	83-110-1324	Shareholders	NA

Business: The group's principal activity is to conduct research and develop and market products for the non-invasive diagnosis of cardiac disease. The group has developed two products, the ch 2000 and the heartwave system in addition to micro-v alternans sensors. Heartwave system is used to perform a microvolt t-wave alternans test, a non-invasive measurement of extremely subtle beat-to-beat fluctuation in a patient's heartbeat. Ch 2000 performs conventional cardiac stress tests using the t-wave alternans technology. All the products are cleared by the federal drug administration for sale in the United States and have received the ce mark for sale in Europe. Targeted at leading cardiology medical centers, the products are primarily sold to hospitals, research institutions and cardiovascular specialists. In 2001, the group granted an exclusive distributorship of ch 2000 to philips medical systems in the United States and a non-exclusive distribution right outside the country.

Primary SIC and add'l.: 3845

CIK No: 0000913443

Officers: Robert P. Khederian/Chmn., Interim CEO, Interim Pres./$42,261.00, Ali Haghighi-Mood/COO, CTO, Exec. VP, Roderick Degreef/47/CFO, VP - Finance, Administration,Corp. Sec., Investor Relations Officer/$227,358.00, Mark S. Florence/VP - Sales, Marketing/$214,541.00, Vincenzo Licausi/CFO, VP - Finance, Administration/$288,260.00

Directors: Robert P. Khederian/Chmn., Interim CEO, Interim Pres., Richard J. Cohen/Dir., Kenneth Hachikian/Dir., Reed Malleck/Dir., Laurence Blumberg/Dir.

Owners: David A. Chazanovitz, Kenneth V. Hachikian, Laurence J. Blumberg, St. Jude Medical, Inc./6.10%, Leaf Offshore Investment Fund Ltd., J. Leighton Read, AFB Fund LLC/8.69%, Jeffrey J. Langan, Insiders/12.38%, Leaf Offshore Investment Fund Ltd., St. Jude Medical, Inc./100.00%, Roderick de Greef, J. Leighton Read, Robert P. Khederian, Robert P. Khederian/9.16% *(17 Owners included in Index)*

Financial Data: **Fiscal Year End:** 12/31 **Latest Annual Data:** 12/31/2006

Year	Sales	Net Income
2006	$7,438,000	-$10,609,000
2005	$4,199,000	-$2,636,000
2004	$5,108,000	-$3,703,000

Curr. Assets:	$10,701,000	**Curr. Liab.:**	$2,176,000		
Plant, Equip.:	$136,000	**Total Liab.:**	$2,433,000	**Indic. Yr. Divd.:**	NA
Total Assets:	$10,922,000	**Net Worth:**	$8,489,000	**Debt/ Equity:**	0.0063

Cambridge Holdings Ltd

106 S University Blvd. No. 14, Denver, CO, 80209; *PH:* 1-214-877-3337;
http:// www.cambridgeinc.com

General - Incorporation	CO	**Stock** - Price on:12/24/2007	$0.17
Employees	NA	Stock Exchange	OTC
Auditor	Cordovano & Honeck LLP	Ticker Symbol	CDGD
Stk Agt	Corporate Stock Transfer, Inc.	Outstanding Shares	3,510,000
Counsel	NA	E.P.S	$0.04
DUNS No.	19-270-6901	Shareholders	NA

Business: The group's principle activity is to invest in the stock market, real estate development and other business investments. The company also explores other business acquisitions, opportunities and investments. The group operates from United States.

Primary SIC and add'l.: 6519

CIK No: 0000712757

Officers: Gregory Pusey/56/Dir., CEO, Pres., Treasurer, Jeffrey G. McGonegal/57/Dir., CFO, Sr. VP - Finance, Sec.

Directors: Gregory Pusey/56/Dir., CEO, Pres., Treasurer, Scott Menefee/43/Dir., Jeffrey G. McGonegal/57/Dir., CFO, Sr. VP - Finance, Sec.

Owners: Jeffrey E. Peierls/8.60%, Insiders/55.20%, Jeffrey G. McGonegal/4.00%, Gregory Pusey/48.30%, Brian Peierls/6.20%, Scott Menefee/2.90%

Financial Data: **Fiscal Year End:** 06/30 **Latest Annual Data:** 6/30/2006

Year	Sales	Net Income
2006	$765,000	$108,000
2005	$49,000	-$277,000
2004	$87,000	-$64,000

Curr. Assets:	$649,000	**Curr. Liab.:**	$336,000	**P/E Ratio:**	4.25
Plant, Equip.:	$2,000	**Total Liab.:**	$336,000	**Indic. Yr. Divd.:**	NA
Total Assets:	$651,000	**Net Worth:**	$315,000	**Debt/ Equity:**	NA

Camco Financial Corp

6901 Glenn Hwy., Cambridge, OH, 43725; *PH:* 1-740-435-2020; *Fax:* 1-740-435-2021;
http:// www.camcofinancial.com

General - Incorporation	DE	**Stock** - Price on:12/24/2007	$12.43
Employees	286	Stock Exchange	NDQ
Auditor	Plante & Moran, PLLC	Ticker Symbol	CAFI
Stk Agt	Registrar & Transfer Co	Outstanding Shares	7,420,000
Counsel	NA	E.P.S	$0.67
DUNS No.	07-500-0299	Shareholders	NA

Business: The group's principal activity is to provide financial services in Ohio, Kentucky and west Virginia. The group accepts interest and non-interest-bearing checking accounts, money market deposit accounts, regular passbook savings accounts and term certificate accounts. It originates conventional fixed-rate and variable-rate mortgage loans for the acquisition, construction or refinancing of single-family homes and construction and permanent mortgage loans on condominiums, two- to four-family, multi-family and nonresidential properties. In addition, it also provides consumer loans. Other activities include provision of title insurance agency and retirement savings plans. The savings association insurance fund administered by the federal deposit insurance corporation insures the group's deposit accounts. On 20-Aug-2004, the group acquired london financial corporation.

Primary SIC and add'l.: 6035 6712

CIK No: 0000016614

Subsidiaries: Advantage Bank, Cambridge Savings Bank, Camco Mortgage Corporation, Camco Title Agency, Inc, Camco Title Insurance Agency, Inc, First Bank for Savings, First Savings Bank, Marietta Savings Bank, Westwood Homestead Savings Bank

Officers: Richard C. Baylor/53/CEO, Pres./$467,172.00, Edward D. Rugg/53/Sec./$245,423.00, Mark A. Severson/54/Treasurer/$255,843.00, Eric Nadeau/CFO, Sr. VP, Treasurer

Directors: Susan J. Insley/62/Dir., Terry A. Feick/58/Dir., Paul D. Leake/66/Dir., Robert C. Dix/68/Dir., Carson K. Miller/62/Dir., Jeffrey T. Tucker/50/Dir., Timothy J. Young/61/Dir., Douglas F. Mock/52/Dir., Edward D. Goodyear/60/Dir.

Owners: Robert C. Dix, Richard C. Baylor/1.45%, Mark A. Severson, Susan J. Insley, David S. Caldwell, Carson K. Miller, Edward D. Goodyear, Paul D. Leake/1.12%, Edward A. Wright, Jeffrey T. Tucker, Timothy J. Young, Edward D. Rugg/1.88%

Financial Data: **Fiscal Year End:** 12/31 **Latest Annual Data:** 12/31/2006

Year	Sales	Net Income
2006	$68,343,000	$5,874,000
2005	$63,693,000	$8,766,000
2004	$66,656,000	-$2,536,000

Curr. Assets:	$33,044,000	**Curr. Liab.:**	$949,391,000	**P/E Ratio:**	16.36
Plant, Equip.:	$17,156,000	**Total Liab.:**	$957,124,000	**Indic. Yr. Divd.:**	$0.600
Total Assets:	$1,048,216,000	**Net Worth:**	$91,092,000	**Debt/ Equity:**	NA

Camden National Corp

2 Elm St., Camden, ME, 04843; *PH:* 1-207-236-8821; *Fax:* 1-207-236-6256;
http:// www.camdennational.com

General - Incorporation	ME	**Stock** - Price on:12/24/2007	$40
Employees	320	Stock Exchange	AMEX
Auditor	Berry, Dunn, Mcneil & Parker	Ticker Symbol	CAC
Stk Agt	American Stock Transfer & Trust Co.	Outstanding Shares	6,620,000
Counsel	NA	E.P.S	$3.00
DUNS No.	14-426-2888	Shareholders	NA

Business: The group's principle activity is that of a commercial bank. The group provides financial services to individuals and companies in mid-coast and central Maine. As a multi-bank holding company of camden national bank and the unitedkingfield bank, the group accepts deposits from the general public. The group also originates residential mortgage loans, commercial business loans, commercial real estate loans and a variety of consumer loans. The group provides these services through its two banking subsidiaries at 29 branches. It also provides brokerage and insurances services through acadia financial consultants, which operates as a division of the two banking subsidiaries. The group also provides wealth management services and employee benefit administration through its other subsidiary acadia trust.

Primary SIC and add'l.: 6712 6021

CIK No: 0000750686

Subsidiaries: Acadia Trust, Camden National Bank, UnitedKingfield Bank

Officers: Robert W. Daigle/Dir., CEO, Pres./$488,666.00, Robin Melancon-Quimby/Mgr. - Madison, Wendy Hurlburt/Mgr. - Hermon, Nancy Richard/Mgr. - Lewiston, Claude Carbonneau/Sr. VP - Commercial, Wholesale Deposit Products Mgr. - Camden National Bank, Cale Burger/VP - Waldo, Hancock Counties, Union, Camden National Bank, Tammy Bryant/VP - Lincoln County, Camden National Bank, Dottie Gagne/Mgr. - Greenville, Sean G. Daly/CFO/$178,569.00, Susan M. Westfall/Corporate Controller, Laurel J. Bouchard/Chief Administrative Officer/$230,656.00, Richard Littlefield/Sr. VP - Southern Maine, Camden National Bank, Mike Jones/VP - Rockland, Thomaston, Vinalhaven, Camden National Bank, Vera Rand/VP - Camden, Rockport, Camden National Bank, Jayne Crosby Giles/VP - Belfast, Union, Camden National Bank *(57 Officers included in Index)*

Directors: Robert W. Daigle/Dir., CEO, Pres., Rendle Jones/Chmn., David C. Flanagan/Dir., Ann W. Bresnahan/Dir., Rosemary B. Weymouth/Dir. - Camdel National Bank, John W. Holmes/Dir., Ward Irving Graffam/Dir., Robin A. Sawyer/Dir., Robert J. Campbell/Dir., Winfield F. Robinson/Dir.

Owners: Peter A. Blyberg, Sandra H. Collier, John P. Lynch, Paul L. Tracy, Robert W. Spear, Karen W. Stanley, Stephen C. Shea/2.62%, Samuel G. Cohen, Estate of Fitz Eugene Dixon, Jr./5.51%, Timothy R. Maynard, James L. Markos, Blake B. Brown, Rebecca J. Sargent, Peter A. Clapp, Insiders/4.49% *(17 Owners included in Index)*

Financial Data: **Fiscal Year End:** 12/31 **Latest Annual Data:** 12/31/2006

Year	Sales	Net Income
2006	$118,867,000	$20,276,000
2005	$100,103,000	$21,380,000
2004	$84,776,000	$19,493,000

Curr. Assets:	$40,846,000	**Curr. Liab.:**	$1,565,969,000	**P/E Ratio:**	13.33
Plant, Equip.:	$17,720,000	**Total Liab.:**	$1,662,834,000	**Indic. Yr. Divd.:**	$0.960
Total Assets:	$1,769,886,000	**Net Worth:**	$107,052,000	**Debt/ Equity:**	1.0412

Camden Property Trust

3 Greenway Plz., Ste. 1300, Houston, TX, 77046; *PH:* 1-713-354-2500; *Fax:* 1-713-354-2700;
http:// www.camdenliving.com

General - Incorporation	TX	**Stock** - Price on:12/24/2007	$68.59
Employees	1,920	Stock Exchange	NYSE
Auditor	Deloitte & Touche LLP	Ticker Symbol	CPT
Stk Agt	American Stock Transfer & Trust Co.	Outstanding Shares	56,820,000
Counsel	NA	E.P.S	$3.41
DUNS No.	NA	Shareholders	NA

Business: The groups principle activities include owning, developing, constructing and managing multifamily apartment communities. In the year 2006, the group acquired Camden-Delta Westwind, LLC and Camden Stoneleigh. The group operates from Texas, the United States. The groups quarterly revenue for September 2007 was 155.02 millions of USD.

Primary SIC and add'l.: 6798 8741

CIK No: 0000906345

Subsidiaries: Camden Builders, Inc., Camden Development, Inc., Camden Operating, L.P., Camden Realty, Inc., Camden Summit Partnership, L.P., Camden Summit, Inc., Camden USA, Inc., Summit Apartment Builders, Inc., Summit Management Company

Officers: Richard J. Campo/Chmn., CEO/$4,059,384.00, Malcolm H. Stewart/Exec. VP, Chief Investment Officer - Real Estate Investments/$1,343,687.00, Steven K. Eddington/Sr. VP - Operations, Kimberly Callahan/VP - Investor Relations, Asset Management, Tom Sloan/Regional VP - Southeast, Mid, Atlantic Region, Keith D. Oden/Dir., COO, Pres., Trust Mgr./$4,038,024.00, Dennis M. Steen/Sr. VP - Finance, CFO, Sec./$961,619.00, Bob Herr/VP - Accounting, William B.

McGuire/Dir., Mgr. - Board Of Trust, Steven A. Webster/Dir., Mgr. - Board Of Trust, Michael P. Gallagher/VP, Chief Accounting Officer, Ed Malone/Regional VP - Eastern Region, Terry McKinney/VP - Legal Services, John Selindh/VP - Marketing, Mark Bucci/VP - Construction *(40 Officers included in Index)*

Directors: Richard J. Campo/Chmn., CEO, Keith D. Oden/Dir., COO, Pres., Trust Mgr., Lewis A. Levey/Dir., Mgr. - Board Of Trust, William F. Paulsen/Dir., Mgr. - Board Of Trust, William R. Cooper/Dir., Mgr. - Board Of Trust, Scott S. Ingraham/Dir., Mgr. - Board Of Trust, William B. McGuire/Dir., Mgr. - Board Of Trust, Gardner F. Parker/Dir., Mgr. - Board Of Trust, Steven A. Webster/Dir., Mgr. - Board Of Trust

Owners: Scott S. Ingraham, William R. Cooper/1.40%, William F. Paulsen, James M. Hinton, George A. Hrdlicka, Keith D. Oden/2.50%, Lewis A. Levey, Dennis M. Steen, Richard J. Campo/2.50%, Insiders/9.70%, Malcolm H. Stewart, The Vanguard Group, Inc./6.00%, Barclays Global Investors, NA/5.20%, Steven A. Webster, ING Groep N.V./8.80% *(17 Owners included in Index)*

Financial Data: *Fiscal Year End:*12/31   *Latest Annual Data:* 12/31/2006

Year	Sales	Net Income
2006	$634,960,000	$232,846,000
2005	$568,581,000	$199,086,000
2004	$431,231,000	$41,341,000

Curr. Assets:	$39,925,000	**Curr. Liab.:**	$191,208,000	**P/E Ratio:**	20.11
Plant, Equip.:	$4,370,211,000	**Total Liab.:**	$2,851,694,000	**Indic. Yr. Divd.:**	$2.760
Total Assets:	$4,586,050,000	**Net Worth:**	$1,734,356,000	**Debt/ Equity:**	1.4336

Cameco Corp

2121 11th St. W, Saskatoon, SK, S7M 1J3; *PH:* 1-306-956-6200; *http://* www.cameco.com

General - Incorporation	Canada	**Stock**- Price on:12/24/2007	$54.7243
Employees	2,446	Stock Exchange	NYSE
Auditor	KPMG LLP	Ticker Symbol	CCJ
Stk Agt	Mellon Trust Co	Outstanding Shares	353,400,000
Counsel	NA	E.P.S.	$1.08
DUNS No.	20-843-3953	Shareholders	NA

Business: The group's principle activities are exploration, development, mining, refining and conversion of uranium. The company's uranium products are used for generating electricity in nuclear power reactors in Canada and other countries. The company also mines gold and explores for uranium and gold in North America, Australia and Asia. Gold business consists primarily of its mining operations through kumtor gold company and operates the kumtor gold mine in kyrgyzstan, central Asia. The group's quarterly revenue for September 2007 was 681.07 millions of CAD.

Primary SIC and add'l.: 1094 1041

CIK No: 0001009001

Officers: Gerald W. Grandey/61/Dir., CEO, Pres., Tim S. Gitzel/COO, Sr. VP, Kim O. Goheen/Sr. VP, CFO, Gary M.S. Chad/Sr. VP - Governance - Legal, Regulatory Affairs, Corp. Sec., George B. Assie/Sr. VP - Marketing, Business Development, Rita M. Mirwald/Sr. VP - Corporate Services

Directors: Gerald W. Grandey/61/Dir., CEO, Pres., Victor J. Zaleschuk/65/Chmn., James R. Curtiss/54/Dir., Harry D. Cook/64/Dir., George J.W. Ivany/70/Dir., Robert W. Peterson/71/Dir., Neil A. McMillan/56/Dir., Oyvind Hushovd/58/Dir., Nancy E. Hopkins/54/Dir., Joe F. Colvin/65/Dir., George S. Dembroski/74/Dir., John S. Auston/71/Dir., John H. Clappison/62/Dir., Anne McLellan/Dir.

Financial Data: *Fiscal Year End:*12/31   *Latest Annual Data:* 12/31/2006

Year	Sales	Net Income
2006	$1,571,773,000	$307,384,000
2005	$1,126,258,000	$200,120,000
2004	$870,559,000	$235,134,000

Curr. Assets:	$1,162,231,000	**Curr. Liab.:**	$430,739,000		
Plant, Equip.:	$2,842,158,000	**Total Liab.:**	$2,058,622,000	**Indic. Yr. Divd.:**	$0.200
Total Assets:	$4,411,002,000	**Net Worth:**	$2,352,380,000	**Debt/ Equity:**	NA

Camelot Corp

6757 Arapaho Rd., Ste. 711, Dallas, TX, 75248; *PH:* 1-972-458-1767

General - Incorporation	CO	**Stock**- Price on:12/24/2007	$0.035
Employees	NA	Stock Exchange	OTC
Auditor	Comiskey & Co. P.C	Ticker Symbol	CAML
Stk Agt	Stock Transfer Co of America Inc	Outstanding Shares	49,240,000
Counsel	NA	E.P.S.	$0.00
DUNS No.	07-037-9854	Shareholders	NA

Business: The group's principal activities are research and development of Internet software, hardware and retailing of computer software over the Internet. Discontinued operations of the subsidiaries were involved in selling software products through retail stores located in the Dallas. The software services provided were Internet services, video marketing and distribution and financial services. The group is now inactive and all its subsidiaries have discontinued their operations.

Primary SIC and add'l.: 6719

CIK No: 0000013033

Subsidiaries: Beecher Energy, Ltd.

Officers: Daniel Wettreich/56/Chmn., CEO, Pres.

Directors: Daniel Wettreich/56/Chmn., CEO, Pres., Jeanette Fitzgerald/Dir.

Owners: Insiders/87.33%, Daniel Wettreich/87.33%

Financial Data: *Fiscal Year End:*04/30   *Latest Annual Data:* 04/30/2007

Year	Sales	Net Income
2007	NA	-$22,000
2006	NA	-$9,000
2005	NA	-$7,000

Curr. Assets:	$0	**Curr. Liab.:**	$114,000		
Plant, Equip.:	NA	**Total Liab.:**	$114,000	**Indic. Yr. Divd.:**	NA
Total Assets:	$0	**Net Worth:**	-$114,000	**Debt/ Equity:**	NA

Camelot Entertainment Group Inc

2020 Main St., Ste. 990, Irvine, CA, 92614; *PH:* 1-949-777-1080; *Fax:* 1-949-777-1091; *http://* www.camelotfilms.com

General - Incorporation		**Stock**- Price on:12/24/2007	$0.0249
Employees	2	Stock Exchange	OTC
Auditor	Epstein Weber & Conover, PLC	Ticker Symbol	CMEG
Stk Agt	Transfer Online, Inc.	Outstanding Shares	114,810,000
Counsel	NA	E.P.S.	-$0.02
DUNS No.	NA	Shareholders	NA

Business: The groups principal activity is to provide banking services. The services of the group include trust and deposit services, private banking, asset management, commercial lending and corporate and institutional trust services. The group operates from the United States.

Primary SIC and add'l.: 7812

CIK No:

Subsidiaries: Camelot Distribution Group, Inc., Camelot Films, Inc, Camelot Films, Inc., Ferris Wheel Films, Inc.

Officers: Robert Atwell/Chmn., CEO, Pres., Michael B. Ellis/Dir., COO, George Jackson/CFO

Directors: Robert Atwell/Chmn., CEO, Pres., Michael B. Ellis/Dir., COO, Rounsevelle Shaum/Dir., Jane Olmstead/Dir.

Owners: Jane Olmstead/1.62%, Rounsevelle Schaum, George Jackson/3.10%, Insiders/100.00%, Michael Ellis/1.47%, Robert P. Atwell/58.28%, Insiders/100.00%, Robert P. Atwell/100.00%, Robert P. Atwell/58.28%, Insiders/100.00%

Financial Data: *Fiscal Year End:*12/31   *Latest Annual Data:* 12/31/2006

Year	Sales	Net Income
2006	NA	-$2,348,000
2005	NA	-$4,500,000
2004	NA	-$1,265,000

Curr. Assets:	$534,000	**Curr. Liab.:**	$577,000		
Plant, Equip.:	NA	**Total Liab.:**	$1,815,000	**Indic. Yr. Divd.:**	NA
Total Assets:	$620,000	**Net Worth:**	-$1,195,000	**Debt/ Equity:**	NA

Camera Platforms International Inc

10909 Vanowen St., North Hollywood, CA, 91605; *PH:* 1-818-623-1700; *Fax:* 1-818-623-1710; *http://* www.shotmaker.com

General - Incorporation	DE	**Stock**- Price on:12/24/2007	$0.04
Employees	2	Stock Exchange	OTC
Auditor	Rose, Snyder & Jacobs	Ticker Symbol	CPFR
Stk Agt	U.S. Stock Transfer Corp	Outstanding Shares	23,740,000
Counsel	NA	E.P.S.	$0.01
DUNS No.	15-539-3606	Shareholders	NA

Business: The group's principle activities are to design, manufacture, rent and lease a wide variety of production equipment to the film and video industries. The group rents three varieties of camera cars, akela, pegasus and enlouva cranes, panther dollies, jib arms, and dolly track. The group's marketing efforts are primarily conducted by direct sales efforts, limited advertisements in trade publications, and participation in various trade exhibitions. The shotmaker, akela, and enlouva are trademarks that are registered in the United States, Canada, and Japan.

Primary SIC and add'l.: 7359 3861

CIK No: 0000775714

Officers: Martin Perellis/64/Chmn., CEO, CFO

Directors: Martin Perellis/64/Chmn., CEO, CFO, Rick Hicks/64/Dir., William O. Fleischman/62/Dir.

Owners: Herbert Wolas/27.30%, Insiders/51.00%, William O. Fleischman/23.70%, Rick Hicks, Martin Perellis/27.30%

Financial Data: *Fiscal Year End:*12/31   *Latest Annual Data:* 12/31/2006

Year	Sales	Net Income
2006	$343,000	-$87,000
2005	$326,000	-$85,000
2004	$644,000	-$117,000

Curr. Assets:	$79,000	**Curr. Liab.:**	$2,370,000		
Plant, Equip.:	NA	**Total Liab.:**	$2,370,000	**Indic. Yr. Divd.:**	NA
Total Assets:	$101,000	**Net Worth:**	-$2,269,000	**Debt/ Equity:**	NA

Cameron International Corp

Formerly: Cooper Cameron Corp
1333 W Loop S, Ste. 1700, Houston, TX, 77027; *PH:* 1-713-513-3322; *http://* www.c-a-m.com

General - Incorporation	DE	**Stock**- Price on:12/24/2007	$73.68
Employees	12,400	Stock Exchange	NYSE
Auditor	Ernst & Young LLP	Ticker Symbol	CAM
Stk Agt	EquiServe Trust Co N.A	Outstanding Shares	110,140,000
Counsel	NA	E.P.S.	$2.05
DUNS No.	87-904-1309	Shareholders	NA

Business: The groups principle activity is to manufacture oil and gas pressure control and separation equipment. The groups products include valves, wellheads, controls, centrifugal air compressors, integral and separable gas compressors and turbochargers, chokes, and blowout preventers. The group operates from United States.

Primary SIC and add'l.: 3491 3563 3533

CIK No: 0000941548

Subsidiaries: Barton Instrument Systems Limited, Cameron Al Rushaid Ltd., Cameron Algerie (1 share owned by CCPEGI), Cameron Angola Prestaao de Servios, Limitada (1 share owned by CCPEGI), Cameron Argentina S.A.I.C. (122,700 shares owned by CCPEGI), Cameron Australasia Pty. Ltd., Cameron B.V., Cameron France, S.A.S., Cameron Gabon, S.A. (1 share owned by Chairman), Cameron GmbH, Cameron Integrated Services Limited, Cameron Ireland Limited, Cameron Norge AS, Cameron Offshore Engineering Limited, Cameron Offshore Systems Nigeria Limited 87 Subsidiaries included in the Index

Officers: Sheldon R. Erikson/Chmn., CEO, Pres./$11,298,490.00, Scott R. Amann/VP - Investor Relations, Dalton L. Thomas/58/VP - Operations Support, Charles M. Sledge/VP, Corporate Controller, Jack B. Moore/COO, Pres./$1,769,527.00, John Carne/Sr. VP, Pres. - Drilling, Production Systems/$1,505,428.00, Robert J. Rajeski/VP, Pres. - Compression Systems, William C. Lemmer/Sr. VP, General Counsel, Sec./$1,454,950.00, Erik Peyrer/VP - Business Development, Asia Pacific, Middle East, Franklin Myers/CFO, Sr. VP - Finance/$2,545,708.00, Joseph H. Mongrain/VP - Human Resources, John Bartos/VP - Development, Technology, Lorne E. Phillips/VP, Treasurer, Jim E. Wright/VP, Pres. - Valves, Measurement

Directors: Sheldon R. Erikson/Chmn., CEO, Pres., Nathan M. Avery/Dir., Bruce W. Wilkinson/Dir., Michael E. Patrick/Dir., Baker C. Cunningham/Dir., Peter J. Fluor/Dir., Lamar Norsworthy/Dir., David Ross/Dir.

Owners: David Ross, John D. Carne, FMR Corp/6.23%, Michael E. Patrick, Insiders/2.50%, William C. Lemmer, Jack B. Moore, Baker C. Cunningham, Sheldon R. Erikson/1.60%, T. Rowe Price Associates, Inc./7.00%, Bruce W. Wilkinson, Peter J. Fluor, Franklin Myers, Nathan M. Avery

Financial Data: *Fiscal Year End:* 12/31 *Latest Annual Data:* 12/31/2006

Year	Sales	Net Income
2006	$3,742,907,000	$317,816,000
2005	$2,517,847,000	$171,130,000
2004	$2,092,845,000	$94,415,000

Curr. Assets:	$2,907,652,000	**Curr. Liab.:**	$1,628,212,000	**P/E Ratio:**	20.70
Plant, Equip.:	$648,785,000	**Total Liab.:**	$2,609,311,000	**Indic. Yr. Divd.:**	NA
Total Assets:	$4,350,750,000	**Net Worth:**	$1,741,439,000	**Debt/ Equity:**	0.4341

Caminosoft Corp

600 Hampshire Rd., Ste. 105, Westlake Village, CA, 91361; *PH:* 1-805-370-3100; *Fax:* 1-805-370-3200; *http://* www.caminosoft.com; *Email:* info@caminosoft.com

General - Incorporation	CA	**Stock**- Price on:12/24/2007	$0.15
Employees	11	Stock Exchange	OTC
Auditor	Weinberg & Co. P.A	Ticker Symbol	CMSF
Stk Agt	U.S. Stock Transfer Corp	Outstanding Shares	14,260,000
Counsel	NA	E.P.S.	-$0.15
DUNS No.	11-504-7425	Shareholders	NA

Business: The group's principal activity is to develop and sell storage migration software and hardware that enables multi-tiered hierarchical storage management on PC server based computer networks. The products provide increased efficiencies in the customer's data storage and network infrastructure and thereby reduces customer costs by extending the life span of existing storage systems. The highway server hierarchical storage management (hsm) software provides a unique solution for addressing the increasing need for sophisticated management data. The group's managed software is designed to meet the data storage management requirements for local area networks (LAN), wide area networks (wan) and intranet environments.

Primary SIC and add'l.: 7373 3577 3572

CIK No: 0000907686

Subsidiaries: CM Medical Systems, Inc.

Officers: Michael Skelton/Dir., CEO, Stephen Crosson/Dir., CFO, COO, Neil Murvin/CTO, Richard Krueger/VP - Marketing, Alliances

Directors: Michael Skelton/Dir., CEO, Robert Degan/Chmn., Lisa Hart/Member - Advisory Board, Stephen Crosson/Dir., CFO, COO, Russell Cleveland/Dir., Robert Pearson/Dir., Lee Pryor/Dir.

Owners: Renaissance US Growth/29.32%, Lee Pryor/0.24%, Insiders/15.99%, Stephen Crosson/8.06%, Michael Skelton/7.13%, Robert Degan/2.08%, BFSUS Special Opportunities/38.31%, Renaissance Capital Growth &/33.17%

Financial Data: *Fiscal Year End:* 09/30 *Latest Annual Data:* 03/31/2007

Year	Sales	Net Income
2007	NA	NA
2006	$1,773,000	-$1,712,000
2005	$2,637,000	-$770,000

Curr. Assets:	$690,000	**Curr. Liab.:**	$2,560,000		
Plant, Equip.:	$18,000	**Total Liab.:**	$3,699,000	**Indic. Yr. Divd.:**	NA
Total Assets:	$830,000	**Net Worth:**	-$2,869,000	**Debt/ Equity:**	NA

Campbell Resources Inc

1155 rue University, Ste. 1405, Montreal, PQ, H3B 3A7; *PH:* 1-514-875-9033; *http://* www.ressourcescampbell.com; *Email:* invest@campbellresources.com

General - Incorporation	Canada	**Stock**- Price on:12/24/2007	$0.1418
Employees	NA	Stock Exchange	OTC
Auditor	Samson Belair / Deloitte & Touche	Ticker Symbol	CBLRF
Stk Agt	Computershare Trust Co. of Canada	Outstanding Shares	NA
Counsel	Mccarthy Tetrault LLP	E.P.S.	NA
DUNS No.	20-111-7322	Shareholders	NA

Business: The group's principle activities include exploring, developing, mining and processing precious metals such as gold and copper. During the year 2001, the company disposed off the panama and the Mexico operations. During the year 2001, the company acquired msv resources inc and geonova explorations inc. The group operates from United States.

Primary SIC and add'l.: 1021 1041

CIK No: 0000718053

Subsidiaries: Controlled by Campbell Resources Inc.:, Controlled by Meston Resources Inc, GeoNova Explorations Inc., Meston Resources Inc., MSV Resources Inc, Sotula Gold Corporation Inc

Officers: Andre Fortier/Dir., CEO, Pres., Michel Blouin/Dir., Corp. Sec., James Raymond/Dir., Private Investor, Alain Blais/VP, GM - Operations, Real Savoie/VP - Finance

Directors: Andre Fortier/Dir., CEO, Pres., James McCartney/70/Chmn., Michel Blouin/Dir., Corp. Sec., Graham Clow/Dir., G. E. Pralle/Dir., James Raymond/Dir., Private Investor, Louis Archambault/Dir., Rene Galipeau/Dir., Warren Holmes/Dir.

Financial Data: *Fiscal Year End:* 12/31 *Latest Annual Data:* 12/31/2006

Year	Sales	Net Income
2006	$9,370,000	-$35,512,000
2005	$15,679,000	-$21,335,000
2004	$16,989,000	-$6,651,000

Curr. Assets:	$55,947,000	**Curr. Liab.:**	$76,050,000		
Plant, Equip.:	$29,417,000	**Total Liab.:**	$88,501,000	**Indic. Yr. Divd.:**	NA
Total Assets:	$88,850,000	**Net Worth:**	$349,000	**Debt/ Equity:**	NA

Campbell Soup Co

12 Clock Tower Pl., Maynard, MA, 01754; *PH:* 1-978-461-3111; *Fax:* 1-978-897-3739; *http://* shareholder.com

General - Incorporation	NJ	**Stock**- Price on:12/24/2007	$39.22
Employees	24,000	Stock Exchange	NYSE
Auditor	PricewaterhouseCoopers LLP	Ticker Symbol	CPB
Stk Agt	Computershare Investor Services LLC	Outstanding Shares	387,440,000
Counsel	NA	E.P.S.	$2.13
DUNS No.	00-128-8042	Shareholders	NA

Business: The groups principle activities include manufacturing and marketing branded food products. The group operates through four segments namely four segments namely U.S. Soup, sauces and beverages, baking and snacking, and international soup and sauces. The group operates from United States.

Primary SIC and add'l.: 2035 2038 2032 2051 2052

CIK No: 0000016732

Subsidiaries: AB Australasia Pty Ltd, Arnotts Biscuit Company Singapore Pte. Ltd., Arnotts Biscuits (PNG)Pty Limited, Arnotts Biscuits Holdings (PNG)Pty Limited, Arnotts Biscuits Limited, Arnotts New Zealand Limited, Arnotts Philippines Inc, Arnotts Sales Pty Limited, Arnotts SBAH Pty Ltd, Arnotts SBF Pty Ltd, Arnotts SBH Pty Ltd, Arnotts SBI Pty Ltd, Arnotts Snackfoods, Arnotts Biscuits Holdings Pty Ltd, Arnotts Ltd 80 Subsidiaries included in the Index

Officers: Douglas R. Conant/Dir., CEO, Pres., George Dowdie/Sr. VP - Global Research, Development, Quality, Mark Alexander/Pres. - Asia Pacific, Chris Delaney/Pres. - Emerging Markets, Arthur B. Anderson/Sr. VP - Global Research, Development, Quality, Jerry S. Buckley/Sr. VP - Public Affairs, Patrick J. Callaghan/Pres. - Pepperidge Farm, Anthony Disilvestro/VP, Controller, Jim Goldman/Pres. - Godiva Worldwide, Carl M. Johnson/Sr. VP, Chief Strategy Officer, Robert A. Schiffner/CFO, Sr. VP, Denise Morrison/Sr. VP, Pres. - North America Soup, Nancy A. Reardon/Sr. VP, Chief Human Resources, Communications Officer, Ellen Oran Kaden/Sr. VP - Law, Government Affairs, Mark A. Sarvary/49/Exec. VP *(19 Officers included in Index)*

Directors: Douglas R. Conant/Dir., CEO, Pres., Harvey Golub/Chmn., Edmund M. Carpenter/Dir., Randall W. Larrimore/Dir., Sara Mathew/Dir., Bennett Dorrance/Dir., Mary Alice D. Malone/Dir., George Strawbridge/Dir., Charlotte C. Weber/Dir., Kent B. Foster/Dir., Philip E. Lippincott/Dir., David C. Patterson/Dir., Charles R. Perrin/Dir., Paul R. Charron/Dir., Les C. Vinney/Dir. *(16 Directors included in Index)*

Owners: Charlotte C. Weber/4.00%, Douglas R. Conant, Larry S. McWilliams, Mary Alice D. Malone/14.10%, A. Barry Rand, Kent B. Foster, Bennett Dorrance/12.50%, Mark A. Sarvary, David C. Patterson/9.00%, Phillip E. Lippincott, George Strawbridge/2.10%, Les C. Vinney, Harvey Golub, Ellen O. Kaden, Edmund M. Carpenter *(21 Owners included in Index)*

Financial Data: *Fiscal Year End:* 07/31 *Latest Annual Data:* 07/29/2007

Year	Sales	Net Income
2007	$7,867,000,000	$854,000,000
2006	$7,343,000,000	$766,000,000
2005	$7,548,000,000	$707,000,000

Curr. Assets:	$1,481,000,000	**Curr. Liab.:**	$2,339,000,000	**P/E Ratio:**	18.86
Plant, Equip.:	$1,901,000,000	**Total Liab.:**	$5,801,000,000	**Indic. Yr. Divd.:**	$0.800
Total Assets:	$6,675,000,000	**Net Worth:**	$874,000,000	**Debt/ Equity:**	1.3129

Camtek Ltd

Ramat Gavriel Industrial Zone, Migdal Haemek; ; *http://* www.camtek.co.il

General - Incorporation	Israel	**Stock**- Price on:12/24/2007	$3.14
Employees	265	Stock Exchange	NDQ
Auditor	Somekh Chaikin	Ticker Symbol	CAMT
Stk Agt	American Stock Transfer & Trust Co.	Outstanding Shares	30,040,000
Counsel	Skadden, Meagher & Flom LLP	E.P.S.	-$0.33
DUNS No.	NA	Shareholders	NA

Business: The group's principal activities include designing, development, manufacturing and marketing of intelligent optical inspection systems and related products for high-end printed circuit board industry. The group also provides products for semiconductor packaging and microelectronics industry. The group operates from United States.

Primary SIC and add'l.: 3679

CIK No: 0001109138

Subsidiaries: Camtek USA, Inc

Officers: Rafi Amit/Chmn., GM, CEO, Jacob Yavor/VP, PCB Division Mgr., Bruce Patterson/Sales, Midwest, Terry Voorheis/Sales, TX, Southwest, Moshe Amit/Exec. VP, Ronit Dulberg/CFO, Yotam Stern/Dir., Exec. VP - Business, Strategy, Vaughn Yu/Representative, Sales, Semiconductors, China South, China North, Hong Kong, Alyssa Song/Representative, Services, Korea, Alson Ng/Representative, Sales, PCB, Singapore, Johan Kiew/Representative, Sales, ME, Singapore, Philip Boey/Representative, Services, Singapore, Cliff Yang/Representative, Sales, PCB, Taiwan, Kevin Luan/Representative, Services, Taiwan, Thomas Moelders/MEP, Sales, Customer Support *(49 Officers included in Index)*

Directors: Rafi Amit/Chmn., GM, CEO, Meir Ben-Shoshan/Dir., Eran Bendoly/Dir., Haim Horowitz/Dir., Yotam Stern/Dir., Exec. VP - Business, Strategy, Gabi Heller/Dir., Rafi Koriat/Dir.

Owners: Priortech Ltd., Insiders, Rafi Amit, Yotam Stern

Financial Data: *Fiscal Year End:* 12/31 *Latest Annual Data:* 12/31/2006

Year	Sales	Net Income
2006	$100,055,000	$11,603,000
2005	$63,032,000	$2,702,000
2004	$67,419,000	$10,797,000

Curr. Assets:	$98,922,000	**Curr. Liab.:**	$25,446,000	**P/E Ratio:**	46.73
Plant, Equip.:	$10,729,000	**Total Liab.:**	$30,668,000	**Indic. Yr. Divd.:**	NA
Total Assets:	$110,806,000	**Net Worth:**	$80,138,000	**Debt/ Equity:**	NA

CAN Financial Corp

333 S Wabash, Chicago, IL, 60604; *PH:* 1-312-822-5000; *Fax:* 1-312-822-6419; *http://* www.cna.com; *Email:* cna_help@cna.com

General - Incorporation	DE	**Stock**- Price on:12/24/2007	$50.48
Employees	9,800	Stock Exchange	NYSE
Auditor	Deloitte & Touche LLP	Ticker Symbol	NA
Stk Agt	Computershare Trust Co	Outstanding Shares	271,510,000
Counsel	NA	E.P.S.	$4.31
DUNS No.	04-206-4808	Shareholders	NA

Business: The group's principle activity is to provide insurance products, which include property and casualty coverage. The group operates in two operating segments : standard lines and specialty lines. Standard lines includes standard property and casualty coverages sold to small and middle market commercial businesses. Specialty lines provides a broad array of professional, financial and specialty

property and casualty products and services. The services of the group include risk management, information services, health care management, claims administration and employee leasing/payroll processing. Insurance products include property and casualty coverage, life, accident and health insurance and retirement products and annuities.

Primary SIC and add'l.: 6719 6311 6321 6331

CIK No: 0000021175

Subsidiaries: CNA Surety Corporation, Encompass Insurance Company of America (EICA

Officers: Stephen W. Lilienthal/Chmn., CEO/$5,274,745.00, James R. Lewis/Pres., CEO - CNA Property, Casualty Operations CNA Insurance Companies/$3,174,795.00, John Golden/CIO, Exec. VP, Thomas Pontarelli/Exec. VP, Chief Administration Officer, George R. Fay/Exec. VP - Worldwide P, C Claim, Michael Fusco/Exec. VP, Chief Actuary, Chief Risk Officer/$1,782,691.00, Jonathan D. Kantor/Exec. VP, General Counsel, Sec./$3,916,066.00, Craig D. Mense/CFO, Exec. VP/$2,529,591.00, Peter W. Wilson/Exec. VP - Specialty Lines, John J. Hanrahan/Contact - Analyst, David Adams/Contact - Analyst, Katrina Parker/Contact - Media, Dennis Barger/Pres. - Field Operations East, Steve Stonehouse/Pres. - Field Operations West, Naveen Anand/Sr. VP - Commercial Insurance

Directors: Stephen W. Lilienthal/Chmn., CEO, Andrew H. Tisch/Dir., Don M. Randel/Dir., Joseph Rosenberg/Dir., James S. Tisch/Dir., Marvin Zonis/Dir., Paul J. Liska/Dir., Brenda J. Gaines/Dir., Jose Montemayor/Dir.

Owners: Andrew H. Tisch, Loews Corporation, Michael Fusco, Jonathan D. Kantor, Insiders, Stephen W. Lilienthal, Craig D. Mense, Marvin Zonis, James R. Lewis, James S. Tisch, Joseph Rosenberg

Financial Data: Fiscal Year End:12/31 Latest Annual Data: 12/31/2006

Year	Sales	Net Income
2006	$10,376,000,000	$1,108,000,000
2005	$9,862,000,000	$264,000,000
2004	$9,936,000,000	$446,000,000

Curr. Assets:	$18,025,000,000	Curr. Liab.:	$800,000,000	P/E Ratio:	11.71
Plant, Equip.:	$277,000,000	Total Liab.:	$50,180,000,000	Indic. Yr. Divd.:	NA
Total Assets:	$60,283,000,000	Net Worth:	$9,768,000,000	Debt/ Equity:	0.5000

Can-Cal Resources Ltd

2500 Vista Mar Dr., Las Vegas, NV, 89128; **PH:** 1-702-243-1849; **Fax:** 1-702-243-1869; *http://* www.can-cal.com

General - Incorporation	NV	**Stock**- Price on:12/24/2007	$0.6
Employees	1	Stock Exchange	OTC
Auditor	De Joya Griffith & Co LLC	Ticker Symbol	CCRE
Stk Agt	Pacific Stock Transfer Company	Outstanding Shares	24,140,000
Counsel	NA	E.P.S.	-$0.02
DUNS No.	NA	Shareholders	NA

Business: The group's principal activity is the acquisition and exploration of precious metals minerals properties. The group's gold exploration projects are located in California and Arizona. In 2002, the group evaluated the feasibility of processing dump materials on its cerbat property in Arizona. The group has performed external and in-house fire assays on material from its owl canyon property. An assay is a test performed on a sample of minerals to determine the quantity of one or more elements contained in the sample. The group has processed and tested mineralized materials and produced very small amounts of precious metals on a testing basis from the pisgah volcanic cinders property and the owl canyon property.

Primary SIC and add'l.: 1044 1041

CIK No: 0001083848

Subsidiaries: 305856 B.c., Ltd, British Pubs USA, Inc, Sierra Madre, Sierra Madre Resources S.A. de C.V., W. Electric Carriage Company

Officers: Ronald D. Sloan/Chmn., CEO, CFO, Pres., Treasurer, John Brian Wolfe/Sec., a Dir.

Directors: Ronald D. Sloan/Chmn., CEO, CFO, Pres., Treasurer, John Brian Wolfe/Sec., a Dir., James Dacyszyn/76/Dir.

Owners: Ronald D. Sloan/16.70%, James Dacyszyn/4.20%, John Brian Wolfe/4.20%, Insiders/25.10%

Financial Data: Fiscal Year End:12/31 Latest Annual Data: 12/31/2006

Year	Sales	Net Income
2006	NA	-$621,000
2005	$12,000	-$422,000
2004	$33,000	-$1,030,000

Curr. Assets:	$423,000	Curr. Liab.:	$1,038,000		
Plant, Equip.:	$19,000	Total Liab.:	$1,038,000	Indic. Yr. Divd.:	NA
Total Assets:	$491,000	Net Worth:	-$546,000	Debt/ Equity:	NA

Canadian Imperial Bank of Commerce

425 Lexington Ave., 3rd Fl., New York, NY, 10017; **PH:** 1-212-856-4000; **Fax:** 1-212-667-4590; *http://* www.cibc.com

General - Incorporation	Canada	**Stock**- Price on:12/24/2007	$91.9
Employees	37,016	Stock Exchange	NYSE
Auditor	NA	Ticker Symbol	CM
Stk Agt	CIBC Mellon Trust CO.	Outstanding Shares	42,190,000
Counsel	NA	E.P.S.	$74.39
DUNS No.	NA	Shareholders	NA

Business: The groups principal activity is to provide banking services. The group operates from the Canada.

Primary SIC and add'l.: 6159 6211 6082 6282 6081 6162 6289

CIK No: 0001045520

Subsidiaries: CIBC World Markets plc

Officers: Gerald T. McCaughey/Dir., CEO, Pres., Brian Shaw/Chmn., CEO - Cibc World Markets Inc, Ken Kilgour/Sr. Exec. VP, Chief Risk Officer - Risk Management, Cibc, Rob McLeod/Contact - Media Relations, Doug Maybee/Contact - Media Relations, Sonia A. Baxendale/Sr. Exec. VP - Cibc World Markets Inc, Michael G. Capatides/Exec. VP, General Counsel - Legal, Regulatory Compliance, Ron Lalonde/Sr. Exec. VP - Administration, Technology, Operations, Chris Anderson/Contact - Media Relations, Cibc World Markets, Richard E. Venn/Sr. Exec. VP - Corporate Development, Tom Woods/Sr. Exec. VP, CFO

Directors: Gerald T. McCaughey/Dir., CEO, Pres., William A. Etherington/Chmn., Stephen G. Snyder/Dir., Ivan E.H. Duvar/Dir., Charles Sirois/Dir., Cynthia M. Trudell/Dir., Gordon D. Giffin/Dir., Ronald W. Tysoe/Dir., Leslie Rahl/Dir., William L. Duke/Dir., Gary F. Colter/Dir., John P. Manley/Dir., Brent S. Belzberg/Dir., Linda S. Hasenfratz/Dir., Jalynn H. Bennett/Dir. *(16 Directors included in Index)*

Financial Data: Fiscal Year End:10/31 Latest Annual Data: 10/31/2006

Year	Sales	Net Income
2006	$17,994,122,000	$2,570,716,000
2005	$15,975,079,000	$175,971,000
2004	$13,709,851,000	$1,782,995,000

Curr. Assets:	$98,194,047,000	Curr. Liab.:	$227,717,638,000	P/E Ratio:	20.11
Plant, Equip.:	$1,813,154,000	Total Liab.:	$260,945,997,000	Indic. Yr. Divd.:	$3.460
Total Assets:	$272,468,267,000	Net Worth:	$11,522,270,000	Debt/ Equity:	NA

Canadian National Railway Co

17641 S Ashland Ave., Homewood, IL, 60430; **PH:** 1-708-332-3500; *http://* www.cn.ca; **Email:** contact@cn.ca

General - Incorporation	Canada	**Stock**- Price on:12/24/2007	$53.2
Employees	21,540	Stock Exchange	NYSE
Auditor	KPMG LLP	Ticker Symbol	CNI
Stk Agt	Computershare Trust Co of New York	Outstanding Shares	507,400,000
Counsel	NA	E.P.S.	$3.58
DUNS No.	20-213-5729	Shareholders	NA

Business: The group's principle activities are to provide rail transportation and deliver products to customers including industrial , forest , grain and grain products, coal, sulphur and fertilizers, intermodal and automotive. The group's quarterly revenue for September 2007 was 2,023.00 millions of USD.

Primary SIC and add'l.: 4011

CIK No: 0000016868

Subsidiaries: Grand Trunk Corporation, Grand Trunk Western Railroad Incorporated (GTW), Illinois Central Corporation (IC or Illinois Central), Illinois Central Railroad Company (ICRR), Wisconsin Central Limited, Wisconsin Central Transportation Corporation (WC)

Officers: Tullio Cedraschi/CEO, Pres. - CN Investment Division, Hunter E. Harrison/Dir., CEO, Pres., Les Dakens/Sr. VP, Keith E. Creel/Sr. VP - Eastern Canada Region, Karen B. Phillips/VP - North American Government Affairs, Gordon T. Trafton/Sr. VP - Southern Region, John Dalzell/VP - Risk Management, Sameh Fahmy/Sr. VP - Engineering, Mechanical, Supply Management, Kimberly A. Madigan/VP - Labour Relations, North America, Paul C. Miller/VP, Chief Safety Officer, David Ferryman/VP - System Engineering, Jerry Boland/VP - Sales, Industrial Products, Anita Ernesaks/VP, Global MD - CN Worldwide, Harvey Joel/VP - Logistics Solutions, Ghislain Houle/VP - Financial Planning *(38 Officers included in Index)*

Directors: Hunter E. Harrison/Dir., CEO, Pres., David G. McLean/Chmn., Maureen Kempston Darkes/Dir., Denis Losier/Dir., James K. Gray/Dir., Charles A. Baillie/Dir., Michael Ralph Armellino/Dir., Robert Pace/Dir., Hugh J. Bolton/Dir., Purdy Crawford/Dir., Raymond J.V. Cyr/Dir., Gordon D. Giffin/Dir., Edith E. Holiday/Dir., Robert H. Lee/Dir., Edward C. Lumley/Dir.

Financial Data: Fiscal Year End:12/31 Latest Annual Data: 12/31/2006

Year	Sales	Net Income
2006	$6,621,100,000	$1,790,855,000
2005	$7,240,000,000	$1,603,000,000
2004	$6,548,000,000	$1,258,000,000

Curr. Assets:	$1,146,422,000	Curr. Liab.:	$1,814,023,000		
Plant, Equip.:	$18,065,579,000	Total Liab.:	$12,167,858,000	Indic. Yr. Divd.:	$0.830
Total Assets:	$20,597,832,000	Net Worth:	$8,429,974,000	Debt/ Equity:	NA

Canadian Natural Resources Ltd

855 - 2 St. SW, Ste. 2500, Calgary, AB, T2P 4J8; **PH:** 1-403-517-6700; *http://* www.cnrl.com

General - Incorporation	AB	**Stock**- Price on:12/24/2007	$66.54
Employees	3,700	Stock Exchange	NYSE
Auditor	PricewaterhouseCoopers LLP	Ticker Symbol	CNQ
Stk Agt	Computershare Trust Co of Canada	Outstanding Shares	539,260,000
Counsel	NA	E.P.S.	$3.98
DUNS No.	20-913-7967	Shareholders	NA

Business: The group's principal activities are exploring, developing, producing, marketing and sale of oil and natural gas. The group acquires interests in oil and natural gas rights. The group's operations are focused in North America, the north sea and offshore west Africa. On 01-Jul-2002, the group acquired rio alto exploration ltd.

Primary SIC and add'l.: 1311

CIK No: 0001017413

Subsidiaries: CNR International (U.K.) Limited

Officers: Jeff W. Wilson/Sr. VP - Exploration, Christopher M. Kean/VP - Utilities, Offsites, Real J.H. Doucet/Sr. VP - Oil Sands, Philip A. Keele/VP - Mining, Corey B. Bieber/VP - Finance, Investor Relations, Cameron S. Kramer/VP - Development Operations, Real M. Cusson/Sr. VP - Marketing, Allen M. Knight/Sr. VP - International, Corporate Development, Terry J. Jocksch/VP - International, MD - CNR International, UK Limited, Bruce E. McGrath/Corp. Sec., Bill R. Peterson/VP - Production, West, Gordon M. Coveney/54/VP - Exploration, East, Tim S. Mckay/Sr. VP - North American Operations, Richard P. Lock/VP - Bitumen Production, Steve C. Suche/VP - Information, Corporate Services *(42 Officers included in Index)*

Directors: Allan P. Markin/Chmn., John G. Langille/Vice Chmn., Murray N. Edwards/Vice Chmn., Gary A. Filmon/Dir., Frank J. McKenna/Dir., Eldon R. Smith/Dir., Norman F. McIntyre/Dir., Keith A.J. MacPhail/Dir., James S. Palmer/Dir., Steve W. Laut/Dir., COO, Pres., Principal Executive Officer, David A. Tuer/Dir., Gordon D. Giffin/Dir., Catherine M. Best/Dir.

Financial Data: Fiscal Year End:12/31 Latest Annual Data: 12/31/2006

Year	Sales	Net Income
2006	$8,922,524,000	$2,226,770,000
2005	$7,499,778,000	$888,030,000
2004	$5,426,841,000	$1,175,705,000

Curr. Assets:	$2,033,697,000	Curr. Liab.:	$2,660,968,000		
Plant, Equip.:	$26,477,534,000	Total Liab.:	$19,320,122,000	Indic. Yr. Divd.:	$0.340
Total Assets:	$28,668,263,000	Net Worth:	$9,348,141,000	Debt/ Equity:	NA

Canadian Pacific Railway Ltd

401-9th Ave. SW, Ste. 500, Calgary, AB, T2P 4Z4; *PH:* 1-403-319-7000; *Fax:* 1-888-333-6370; *http://* www.cpr.ca

General - Incorporation	Canada	**Stock**- Price on:12/24/2007	$69.93
Employees	15,327	Stock Exchange	NYSE
Auditor	PricewaterhouseCoopers LLP	Ticker Symbol	CP
Stk Agt	Computershare Trust Co of New York	Outstanding Shares	155,200,000
Counsel	Paul Guthrie	E.P.S.	$4.85
DUNS No.	NA	Shareholders	NA

Business: The group's principal activity is to provide rail freight transportation. The group has over 14,000 mile railway network and serves most of the principal centres of Canada as well as the midwestern and northeastern United States. The group transports commodities like grain, coal, lumber and potash and products like cars, household appliances, food and furniture.

Primary SIC and add'l.: 4011

CIK No: 0001166893

Subsidiaries: Canadian Pacific Railway Company, Delaware and Hudson Railway Company, Inc, Soo Line Corporation, Soo Line Railroad Company

Officers: Frederic J. Green/Dir., CEO, Pres., Fred J. Green/Dir., CEO, Pres., Donald B. Campbell/VP - Corporate Planning Calgary, Alberta, Mike Lambert/CFO, Exec. VP, Brock Winter/Sr. VP - Operations, Paul A. Guthrie/VP - Law, Mike Waites/Exec. VP, Marcella Szel/Sr. VP - Marketing, Sales, Janet Weiss/Assist. VP - Investor Relations, Eric Thoms/Mgr. - Investor Relations, Jonathan Legg/VP - Strategic Sourcing, Breanne Feigel/Contact - Western Canada, Jeff Johnson/Contact - US Midwest, Soo Line, Kathryn McQuade/COO, Exec. VP, Mark Seland/Dir. - Communications, Public Affairs *(27 Officers included in Index)*

Directors: Frederic J. Green/Dir., CEO, Pres., Fred J. Green/Dir., CEO, Pres., John E. Cleghorn/Chmn., Linda J. Morgan/Dir., Michael W. Wright/Dir., Krystyna T. Hoeg/Dir., Hartley T. Richardson/Dir., Roger Phillips/Dir., Michael E.J. Phelps/Dir., Madeleine Paquin/Dir., John P. Manley/Dir., Tim W. Faithfull/Dir., Stephen E. Bachand/Dir.

Financial Data: *Fiscal Year End:*12/31   *Latest Annual Data:* 12/31/2006

Year	Sales	Net Income
2006	$3,932,844,000	$661,681,000
2005	$3,767,993,000	$459,030,000
2003	$2,828,623,000	$275,699,000

Curr. Assets:	$862,305,000	**Curr. Liab.:**	$1,063,186,000	**P/E Ratio:**	16.77
Plant, Equip.:	$7,828,360,000	**Total Liab.:**	$5,628,621,000	**Indic. Yr. Divd.:**	$0.920
Total Assets:	$9,795,984,000	**Net Worth:**	$4,167,363,000	**Debt/ Equity:**	NA

Canadian Solar Inc

Xin Zhuang Industry Pk., Suzhou, Jiangsu, 215562; *PH:* 86-8651252477677; *http://* www.csisolar.com; *Email:* Inquire@csisolar.com

General - Incorporation	Canada	**Stock**- Price on:12/24/2007	$10.35
Employees	284	Stock Exchange	NDQ
Auditor	Deloitte Touche Tohmatsu Cpa Ltd.	Ticker Symbol	CSIQ
Stk Agt	Bank of New York	Outstanding Shares	27,270,000
Counsel	NA	E.P.S.	-$0.287
DUNS No.	NA	Shareholders	NA

Business: The groups principal activities include designing, manufacturing and selling solar module products. The products of the group include solar power station, GPS system, battery charger for cars and led lightning. The group operates from China.

Primary SIC and add'l.: 3692 3629 3674

CIK No: 0001375877

Subsidiaries: Changshu CSI Advanced Solar Inc, CSI Central Solar Power Co Ltd, CSI Solar Manufacture Inc, CSI Solar Technologies Inc, CSI Solarchip International Co Ltd, CSI Solartronics (Changhsu) Co Ltd.

Officers: Shawn Qu/Chmn., CEO, Pres., Bing Zhu/Dir., CFO, Arthur Chien/Dir., VP - Finance, Gregory Spanoudakis/VP - International Sales, Marketing, Robert Patterson/VP - Corporate, Product Development, Brian Lu/GM - China Operations, Bencheng Li/GM - CSI Luoyang, Chengbai Zhou/Chief Engineer - CSI Solartronics, Xiaohu Wang/Deputy GM - Commerce, CSI Solartronics, Shanglin Shi/Deputy GM - China Operations, Lingjun Zhang/Technical Dir. - CSI Solar Technologies, Guoxin Zhang/Deputy GM - Manufacturing, CSI Solar Manufacturing, Genmao Chen/Dir. - Research, Development, David Pasquale/Exec. VP

Directors: Shawn Qu/Chmn., CEO, Pres., Bing Zhu/Dir., CFO, Arthur Chien/Dir., VP - Finance, Robert McDermott/Dir., Lars-Eric Johansson/Dir., Michael G. Potter/Dir., Yan Zhuang/Dir.

Owners: Lingjun Zhang/0.07%, Lars-Eric Johannson/0.19%, Chengbai Zhou/0.10%, ATS Automation Tooling Systems Inc./6.80%, HSBC HAV2 (III) Limited/9.70%, Gregory Spanoudakis/0.52%, JAFCO Asia Technology Fund II (Barbados) Limited/5.00%, Bencheng Li/0.10%, Shanglin Shi/0.04%, Columbia Wanger Asset Management, L.P./10.31%, Robert Patterson/0.08%, Xiaohu Wang/0.11%, Shawn Qu/49.83%, Arthur Chien/0.08%, Guoxin Zhang/0.06% *(19 Owners included in Index)*

Financial Data: *Fiscal Year End:*12/31   *Latest Annual Data:* 12/31/2006

Year	Sales	Net Income
2006	$68,212,000	-$9,430,000
2005	$18,324,000	$3,804,000
2004	$9,685,000	$1,457,000

Curr. Assets:	$116,943,000	**Curr. Liab.:**	$15,855,000		
Plant, Equip.:	$7,910,000	**Total Liab.:**	$16,730,000	**Indic. Yr. Divd.:**	NA
Total Assets:	$129,634,000	**Net Worth:**	$112,904,000	**Debt/ Equity:**	NA

Canadian Superior Energy Inc

2700 5th Ave. SW, Ste. 605, Calgary, AB, T2P 3H5; *PH:* 1-403-294-1411; *http://* www.cansup.com

General - Incorporation	AB	**Stock**- Price on:12/24/2007	$3.51
Employees	43	Stock Exchange	AMEX
Auditor	Meyers Norris Penny LLP	Ticker Symbol	SNG
Stk Agt	Computershare Trust Co of Canada	Outstanding Shares	131,960,000
Counsel	McCarthy Tetrault LLP	E.P.S.	-$0.04
DUNS No.	NA	Shareholders	NA

Business: The group's principle activities include exploring and producing oil and natural gas in Canada. Its properties are located in Atlantic Canada on the scotian shelf, offshore nova scotia and in western CanAm, in alberta, saskatchewan and british columbia. The group operates from United States.

Primary SIC and add'l.: 1382

CIK No: 0001177470

Officers: Greg Noval/Chmn., CEO, Mark Gillis/VP - Offshore Drilling, Michael E. Coolen/Dir., Pres. COO, Leigh Bilton/Exec. VP, Roger Harman/CFO, Dennis Erickson/VP - Operations, Western Canada, Ed Chau/Exploration Mgr., Patrick Maris/Engineering Mgr. - Trinidad, Tobago, Tony Sartorelli/Mgr. - Geophysics, David R. Cassidy/Land Mgr., Roger De Freitas/Country Mgr. - Trinidad, Tobago

Directors: Greg Noval/Chmn., CEO, Michael E. Coolen/Dir., Pres. COO, Charles Dallas/Dir., Kaare Idland/Dir., Alex Squires/Dir., Richard Watkins/Dir., Thomas J. Harp/Dir.

Financial Data: *Fiscal Year End:*12/31   *Latest Annual Data:* 12/31/2006

Year	Sales	Net Income
2006	$42,414,000	-$7,780,000
2005	$47,381,000	$9,372,000
2004	$27,299,000	-$4,832,000

Curr. Assets:	$21,656,000	**Curr. Liab.:**	$22,231,000		
Plant, Equip.:	$133,370,000	**Total Liab.:**	$30,367,000	**Indic. Yr. Divd.:**	NA
Total Assets:	$167,730,000	**Net Worth:**	$137,363,000	**Debt/ Equity:**	NA

Canal Capital Corp

717 Fifth Ave, Ste. 407, New York, NY, 10022; *PH:* 1-212-826-6040

General - Incorporation	DE	**Stock**- Price on:12/24/2007	$0.081
Employees	75	Stock Exchange	OTC
Auditor	Todman & Co. CPAs,P.C	Ticker Symbol	COWP
Stk Agt	American Stock Transfer & Trust Co.	Outstanding Shares	4,330,000
Counsel	NA	E.P.S.	-$0.2
DUNS No.	00-693-3071	Shareholders	NA

Business: The group's principle activity is to provide renting, leasing, selling and managing real estate properties. Thje group operates three central public stockyards which provide markets for all categories of livestock; and acquires art for resale such as antiquities primarily from ancient mediterranean cultures and contemporary art. The group operates from United States.

Primary SIC and add'l.: 6230

CIK No: 0000101821

Subsidiaries: Canal Arts Corporation, Canal Capital Corporation, Omaha Livestock Market, Inc., Sioux City Stockyards, Sioux Falls Stockyards Company, St. Joseph Stockyards, St. Paul Union Stockyards

Owners: Michael E. Schultz/1.36%, Insiders/45.50%, Asher B. Edelman/44.13%, Reginald Schauder, William G. Walters/5.42%

Financial Data: *Fiscal Year End:*10/31   *Latest Annual Data:* 10/31/2006

Year	Sales	Net Income
2006	$4,404,000	-$322,000
2005	$6,467,000	$716,000
2004	$4,199,000	-$577,000

Curr. Assets:	$2,283,000	**Curr. Liab.:**	$606,000		
Plant, Equip.:	$3,012,000	**Total Liab.:**	$3,729,000	**Indic. Yr. Divd.:**	NA
Total Assets:	$5,459,000	**Net Worth:**	$1,731,000	**Debt/ Equity:**	1.5053

CanAlaska Uranium Ltd

2303 W 41st Ave., Vancouver, BC, V6M2A3; *PH:* 1-604-685-1870; *Fax:* 1-604-685-8045; *http://* www.canalaska.com

General - Incorporation	BC	**Stock**- Price on:12/24/2007	NA
Employees	NA	Stock Exchange	OTC
Auditor	PricewaterhouseCoopers LLP	Ticker Symbol	CVVUF
Stk Agt	CIBC Mellon Trust Co.	Outstanding Shares	NA
Counsel	NA	E.P.S.	NA
DUNS No.	NA	Shareholders	NA

Business: The groups principal activity is to explore minerals. The group operates from Canada.

Primary SIC and add'l.: 1000

CIK No: 0001023109

Officers: Peter Dasler/Dir., CEO, Pres., Bill T. Cohan/Uranium Consultants, Ralph Newson/Uranium Consultants, Jack C. Moore/Uranium Consultants, Emil Fung/VP - Corporate Development, Dir., Taryn Downing/Corp. Sec., Gord Steblin/CFO, Karl Schimann/VP - Exploration, Jim Kermeen/Mgr. - Joint Venture Development, John Royall/Uranium Consultants

Directors: Peter Dasler/Dir., CEO, Pres., Emil Fung/VP - Corporate Development, Dir., Hubert Marleau/Dir., Colin Bird/Dir., Jean Luc Roy/Dir., Ambassador Thomas Graham/Dir.

Owners: CDS & Company/89.60%, Cede & Co./7.90%

Financial Data: *Fiscal Year End:*04/30   *Latest Annual Data:* 04/30/2007

Year	Sales	Net Income
2007	NA	-$9,363,000
2006	NA	-$7,075,000
2005	NA	-$2,605,000

Curr. Assets:	$12,394,000	**Curr. Liab.:**	$1,195,000		
Plant, Equip.:	$729,000	**Total Liab.:**	$1,195,000	**Indic. Yr. Divd.:**	NA
Total Assets:	$14,202,000	**Net Worth:**	$13,007,000	**Debt/ Equity:**	NA

CanAm Uranium Corp

4th Floor, Crown Plz. Building, 114 W. Magnolia St., Ste. No.424, Bellingham, WA, 98225; *PH:* 1-206-274-7598; *Fax:* 1-206-299-3484; *http://* www.canamuranium.com; *Email:* Info@CanAmUranium.com

General - Incorporation	NV	**Stock**- Price on:12/24/2007	$0.63
Employees	NA	Stock Exchange	OTC
Auditor	MacKay LLP	Ticker Symbol	CAUI
Stk Agt	NA	Outstanding Shares	84,190,000
Counsel	NA	E.P.S.	-$0.012
DUNS No.	NA	Shareholders	NA

Business: The groups principal activity is to exploration of minerals. The group operates from the United States.

Primary SIC and add'l.: 1000

CIK No: 0001310685

Officers: Ryan Anthony Gibson/Chmn., CEO, Pres., David C. Hayes/Dir., CFO

Directors: Ryan Anthony Gibson/Chmn., CEO, Pres., David C. Hayes/Dir., CFO, Charles Rendina/Dir., Michael Hitch/45/Dir., Roger Connors/38/Dir., Stuart R. Angus/Member - Advisory Board, Dave Billard/Member - Advisory Board, Paul T. Sarjeant/47/Dir., Peter Born P. Geo/Dir., Thomas E. Puzzo/41/Dir.

Owners: Roger Connors, Insiders/73.97%, Ryan Gibson/72.64%, David Hayes, Charles Rendina

Financial Data: *Fiscal Year End:*10/31 *Latest Annual Data:* 10/31/2006

Year	Sales	Net Income
2006	NA	-$370,000

Curr. Assets:	$309,000	**Curr. Liab.:**	$66,000		
Plant, Equip.:	$1,000	**Total Liab.:**	$66,000	**Indic. Yr. Divd.:**	NA
Total Assets:	$310,000	**Net Worth:**	$245,000	**Debt/ Equity:**	NA

Canandaigua National Corp

72 S Main St., Canandaigua, NY, 14424; *PH:* 1-585-394-4260; *Fax:* 1-585-394-4001; *http://* www.cnbank.com

General - Incorporation	NY	**Stock**- Price on:12/24/2007	NA
Employees	87	Stock Exchange	OTC
Auditor	KPMG LLP	Ticker Symbol	CNND
Stk Agt	NA	Outstanding Shares	NA
Counsel	NA	E.P.S	NA
DUNS No.	00-697-6914	Shareholders	NA

Business: The group's principal activities are acceptance of deposits, lending, trust, investment and insurance services. The categories of deposits provided by the group include time, demand and savings deposits, now accounts, regular savings accounts, money market deposits, fixed rate certificates of deposit and club accounts. The lending services of the group include secured and unsecured commercial and consumer loans, financing commercial transactions, residential mortgage loans, revolving credit loans with overdraft checking protection, small business loans and student loans. The services are provided to retail, commercial and municipal customers through community banking offices. The facilities at the branch offices include drive-up facilities, automatic teller machines, customer call center, Internet, safe deposit facilities and other remote cash-dispensing machines.

Primary SIC and add'l.: 6021 6712

CIK No: 0000759458

Subsidiaries: Canandaigua National Statutory Trust I, Greater Funding of New York d/b/a Greater Funding, The Mortgage Company, Home Town Funding, Inc. d/b/a CNB Mortgage Company, The Canandaigua National Bank and Trust Company

Officers: George W. Hamlin/Pres., CEO - Trust, CRA Officer - Canandaigua National Bank, Trust Co/$499,876.00, Sandra U. Roberts/45/Sr. VP - Information Technology, Steven H. Swartout/50/Sr. VP - Corporate Risk Operations, Security, General Counsel/$172,885.00, Mark Mazzochetti/IRA Officer - Retirement Services Team, Canandaigua National Bank, Trust, Corinne Tepedino/Mortgage Consultant, Canandaigua National Bank, Trust, David White/Mortgage Consultant, Canandaigua National Bank, Trust, Sue Wood/Mortgage Consultant, Canandaigua National Bank, Trust, Gary L. Babbitt/51/Sr. VP - Commercial Services, Richard H. Hawks/VP - Trust, Estate Services Team, Canandaigua National Bank, Trust, Paul R. Callaway/VP - Trust, Estate Services Team, Canandaigua National Bank, Trust, Mary Jo Derose/Mortgage Consultant, Canandaigua National Bank, Trust, Ron Kraft/Mortgage Consultant, Canandaigua National Bank, Trust, Lauri Mattle/Mortgage Consultant, Canandaigua National Bank, Trust, Lindsey Michaels/Mortgage Consultant, Canandaigua National Bank, Trust, Jason Proietti/Mortgage Consultant, Canandaigua National Bank, Trust *(43 Officers included in Index)*

Directors: James S. Fralick/65/Chmn., Daniel P. Fuller/57/Dir., Thomas S. Richards/64/Dir., Patricia A. Boland/72/Dir., Caroline C. Shipley/68/Dir., Sue S. Stewart/65/Dir., Frank H. Hamlin/35/Dir., Alan J. Stone/67/Dir., Richard P. Miller/64/Dir., Stephen D. Hamlin/71/Dir.

Owners: Steven H. Swartout/0.11%, Robert G. Sheridan/0.94%, The National Bank and Trust Company/8.60%, Lawrence A. Heilbronner/0.09%, Frank H. Hamlin/0.22%, Sue S. Stewart/0.02%, Thomas S. Richards/0.02%, George W. Hamlin/6.23%, The National Bank and Trust Company held in various fiduciary capacities/8.60%, James S. Fralick/0.06%, Insiders/21.59%, Richard P. Miller, Caroline C. Shipley/0.12%, Daniel P. Fuller/0.14%, Patricia A. Boland/0.03% *(18 Owners included in Index)*

Canarc Resource Corp

850 W Hastings St., Ste. 800, Vancouver, BC, V6C 1E1; *PH:* 1-604-685-9700; *http://* www.canarc.net; *Email:* invest@canarc.net

General - Incorporation	BC	**Stock**- Price on:12/24/2007	$0.558
Employees	NA	Stock Exchange	OTC
Auditor	KPMG LLP	Ticker Symbol	CRCUF
Stk Agt	Computershare Investor Services LLC	Outstanding Shares	NA
Counsel	Stewart Lockwood Vector	E.P.S	NA
DUNS No.	24-861-2251	Shareholders	NA

Business: The group's principal activities are to acquire, explore and develop precious metal properties in british columbia, suriname, Mexico and Costa Rica. The group is in development stage and has not yet developed any commercial mineral products.

Primary SIC and add'l.: 1041 1099

CIK No: 0000868822

Subsidiaries: Minera Aztec Silver Corp., Sara Kreek Resource Corporation N.V

Officers: Bradford Cooke/Chmn., CEO, James Moors/VP - Exploration, Gregg Wilson/Mgr. - Investor Relations, Leonard Harris/Dir., Dir. - Metallurgical Engineer, Bruce Bried/COO, Pres., Philip Yee/Mgr. - Finance, Controller, Stewart Lockwood/Sec. - Legal Counsel, Godfrey Walton/Consultant, Garry Biles/VP - Mining

Directors: Bradford Cooke/Chmn., CEO, Chris Theodoropoulos/Dir., Derek W. Bullock/Dir., William Price/Dir., Bill Price/Dir.

Owners: Insiders/9.65%, CDS & Co./47.60%, William Price/8.08%, CEDE & Co./41.44%

Financial Data: *Fiscal Year End:*12/31 *Latest Annual Data:* 12/31/2006

Year	Sales	Net Income
2006	NA	-$4,875,000
2005	NA	-$374,000
2004	NA	-$3,088,000

Curr. Assets:	$2,944,000	**Curr. Liab.:**	$235,000		
Plant, Equip.:	$3,913,000	**Total Liab.:**	$235,000	**Indic. Yr. Divd.:**	NA
Total Assets:	$7,966,000	**Net Worth:**	$7,731,000	**Debt/ Equity:**	NA

CanArgo Energy Corp

60 State St., Ste. 700, Boston, MA, 02109; *PH:* 1-617-973-6401; *Fax:* 1-617-973-6406; *http://* www.canargo.com; *Email:* info@canargo.com

General - Incorporation	DE	**Stock**- Price on:12/24/2007	$0.77
Employees	187	Stock Exchange	AMEX
Auditor	L J Soldinger Assoc. LLC	Ticker Symbol	CNR
Stk Agt	Signature Stock Transfer, Inc.	Outstanding Shares	238,500,000
Counsel	Kelly Lytton Mintz & Vann	E.P.S	-$0.23
DUNS No.	60-693-8355	Shareholders	NA

Business: The group's principal activities are the exploration, development and production of oil and gas. The activities also include refining and marketing oil and gas in the east European nation of Georgia. The group is a member of three production sharing arrangements, the ninotsminda, manavi and west rustavi production sharing contract, the nazvrevi production sharing contract and the norio and north kumisi production sharing agreement. It also has exploratory and developmental oil and gas properties in Georgia and ukraine in the stynawske oilfield and the bugruvativske oilfield. It addition, it has interests in a refinery and a chain of petrol stations located in and around tbilisi, Georgia.

Primary SIC and add'l.: 1311 3533

CIK No: 0000310316

Subsidiaries: CanArgo Acquisition Corporation, CanArgo Georgia Limited, CanArgo Limited, CanArgo Norio Limited, CanArgo Samgori Limited, Cypriot corporation, Georgian Oil Samgori Limited, Kazakhstan through Tethys Petroleum, Lateral Vector Resources Inc., Ninotsminda Oil Company Limited, Westrade Alliance LLC

Officers: Vincent McDonnell/COO, CEO, Chief Commercial Officer/$765,550.00, Liz Landles/47/Corp. Sec./$317,121.00, Sabin Rossi/VP - External Affairs, Investor Relations Officer

Directors: Vincent McDonnell/COO, CEO, Chief Commercial Officer, David Robson/Chmn., Nils Trulsvik/Non - Exec. Dir., Russ Hammond/Non - Exec. Dir., Michael C. Ayre/Non - Exec. Dir.

Owners: Jeffrey Wilkins, Liz Landles, David Robson/1.37%, Vincent McDonnell, Persistency Capital, LLC/11.85%, Russ Hammond, Insiders/3.29%, BlackRock, Inc./10.15%, Persistency/11.64%, Ingalls & Snyder Value Partners, L.P./6.52%, Nils Trulsvik, Michael Ayre, Andrew Morris/11.86%

Financial Data: *Fiscal Year End:*12/31 *Latest Annual Data:* 12/31/2006

Year	Sales	Net Income
2006	$6,527,000	-$60,541,000
2005	$7,582,000	-$12,335,000
2004	$9,575,000	-$4,757,000

Curr. Assets:	$24,329,000	**Curr. Liab.:**	$12,701,000		
Plant, Equip.:	$110,546,000	**Total Liab.:**	$57,116,000	**Indic. Yr. Divd.:**	NA
Total Assets:	$136,485,000	**Net Worth:**	$79,369,000	**Debt/ Equity:**	0.5136

Candela Corp

530 Boston Post Rd., Wayland, MA, 01778; *PH:* 1-508-358-7400; *Fax:* 1-508-358-5602; *http://* www.candelalaser.com; *Email:* info@candelalaser.com

General - Incorporation	DE	**Stock**- Price on:12/24/2007	$11.67
Employees	334	Stock Exchange	NDQ
Auditor	BDO Seidman LLP	Ticker Symbol	CLZR
Stk Agt	Computershare Trust Co	Outstanding Shares	23,120,000
Counsel	Leboeuf,Lamb,Greene & Macrae LLP	E.P.S	$0.39
DUNS No.	05-346-8385	Shareholders	NA

Business: The group's principal activity is to develop, manufacture and market lasers used to perform aesthetic and cosmetic procedures. Manufactured at the group's facility at wayland, Massachusetts, the products include the gentlelase(R) family of hair removal lasers, the vbeam(R) pulsed dye laser for treating vascular lesions and alexlazr(tm) for treating pigmented lesions and tattoos. They also include the smoothbeam(tm) diode laser for the remodeling of periorbital wrinkles and the c-beam(tm) pulsed dye laser, for psoriasis and surgical scars. The major customer base for the products consists of dermatologists, plastic and cosmetic surgeons and vascular surgeons. The group sells directly and distributes the products from western Europe, Japan, latin and South America, the Middle East and the Pacific Rim to customers in 78 countries.

Primary SIC and add'l.: 3845

CIK No: 0000793279

Subsidiaries: Candela Deutschland GmbH, Candela France SARL, Candela Iberica S.A., Candela Italia, Candela KK, Candela Skin Care Centers of Boston, Inc., Candela Skin Care Centers of Scottsdale, Inc.

Officers: Gerard E. Puorro/Dir., CEO, Pres., James C. Hsia/CTO, Peter C. Mara/VP - Western Regional Sales, Dennis S. Herman/Sr. VP - North American Sales, Marketing, Service, Nancy L. Compton/VP - Human Resources, Charles A. Johnson/VP - Development Engineering, Catherine A. Kniker/Sr. VP - Corporate Strategic Development, Paul R. Lucchese/Sr. VP, General Counsel, Corp. Sec., Toshio Mori/Pres. - Candela KK, VP - Candela Corp, Anthony F.L. Shaw/VP - Asia Pacific Sales, Marketing, Service, Robert J. Wilber/Sr. VP - International Operations, Joseph Zapata/VP - Latin American Operations, Kathleen McMillan/VP - Research, Robert E. Quinn/Treasurer, Corporate Controller, Michael F. Moore/VP - International Marketing *(18 Officers included in Index)*

Directors: Gerard E. Puorro/Dir., CEO, Pres., Kenneth D. Roberts/Chmn., George A. Abe/Dir., Ben Bailey/Dir., Nancy Nager/Dir., Douglas W. Scott/Dir.

Owners: Kenneth D. Roberts/0.90%, JPMorgan Chase & Co./14.10%, Gerard E. Puorro/1.30%, Ben Bailey, Douglas W. Scott, HealthInvest Partners AB/6.20%, Nancy E. Nager, Robert E. Quinn, Paul F. Broyer, James C. Hsia, Dennis S. Herman, Third Point LLC/9.75%, George A. Abe, Insiders/3.80%, Paul R. Lucchese

Financial Data: *Fiscal Year End:*06/02 *Latest Annual Data:* 7/1/2006

Year	Sales	Net Income
2006	$149,466,000	$14,934,000
2005	$123,901,000	$7,323,000
2004	$104,438,000	$8,119,000

Curr. Assets:	$88,604,000	**Curr. Liab.:**	$27,217,000	**P/E Ratio:**	29.92
Plant, Equip.:	$3,406,000	**Total Liab.:**	$33,710,000	**Indic. Yr. Divd.:**	NA
Total Assets:	$100,479,000	**Net Worth:**	$66,769,000	**Debt/ Equity:**	NA

Canetic Resources Trust

1900, 255 - 5th Ave. SW, Calgary, AB, T2P 3G6; *PH:* 1-403-539-6300; *Fax:* 1-403-539-6499; *http://* canetictrust.com; *Email:* info@canetictrust.com

General - Incorporation	AB
Employees	540
Auditor	Deloitte & Touche, LLP
Stk Agt	Computershare Trust Co
Counsel	NA
DUNS No.	NA

Stock - Price on:12/24/2007	$16.51
Stock Exchange	NYSE
Ticker Symbol	CNE
Outstanding Shares	227,200,000
E.P.S.	-$1.41
Shareholders	NA

Business: The groups principal activities include acquiring, producing, processing, transporting and marketing crude oil and natural gas liquids. In the year 2005, the group acquired APF Energy Trust, Nexen Inc. and EnCana Corporation. The group operates from Alberta, British Columbia, Saskatchewan, Manitoba, North Dakota, Montana and Wyoming in the United States and Canada.

Primary SIC and add'l.: 6792 1311

CIK No: 0001349237

Officers: Paul J. Charron/Dir., CEO, Pres., Brian K. Keller/VP - Exploitation, Canetic, David Broshko/CFO, VP, Mark Fitzgerald/VP - Operations, Richard J. Tiede/COO, Brian D. Evans/VP, General Counsel, Sec., Keith S. Rockley/VP - Human Resources, Corporate Administration, David Sterna/VP - Corporate Planning, Marketing, Don Robson/VP - Land

Directors: Paul J. Charron/Dir., CEO, Pres., Robert G. Brawn/Chmn. Emeritus, Jack C. Lee/Chmn., Gregory R. Rich/Dir., Daryl Gilbert/Dir., Nancy M. Laird/Dir., Peter W. Comber/Dir., Murray Frame/Dir.

Financial Data: Fiscal Year End:12/31   Latest Annual Data: 12/31/2006

Year	Sales	Net Income
2006	$986,381,000	-$260,896,000

Curr. Assets:	$254,122,000	Curr. Liab.:	$282,063,000	P/E Ratio:	20.11
Plant, Equip.:	$3,278,045,000	Total Liab.:	$4,469,544,000	Indic. Yr. Divd.:	$2.390
Total Assets:	$4,336,359,000	Net Worth:	-$133,186,000	Debt/ Equity:	NA

Caneum Inc

170 Newport Ctr. Dr., Ste. 220, Newport Beach, CA, 92660; *PH:* 1-949-273-4000; *Fax:* 1-949-273-4001; *http://* www.caneum.com; *Email:* info@caneum.com

General - Incorporation	NV
Employees	7
Auditor	Haskell & White LLP
Stk Agt	Interwest Transfer Company, Inc.
Counsel	NA
DUNS No.	NA

Stock - Price on:12/24/2007	NA
Stock Exchange	OTC
Ticker Symbol	CANM
Outstanding Shares	NA
E.P.S.	-$0.4
Shareholders	NA

Business: The groups principle activity is to provide business process and information technology outsourcing services. The groups markets include technology, energy, government, transportation, financial services, education and healthcare. The group operates from United States, Europe and Asia Pacific.

Primary SIC and add'l.: NA

CIK No: 0001118961

Subsidiaries: Tier One Consulting, Inc.

Officers: Jesper Lindorff/CEO - Caneum India Pvt Ltd, Mike Woods/VP - Application Services, Neeraj Sehgal/CTO, Michael Willner/Sr. VP, Robert Morris/Sr. VP, Gary D. Allhusen/COO, Exec. VP, Sukhbir Singh Mudan/Dir., Pres.

Directors: Alan S. Knitowski/Chmn., Luan Dang/Vice Chmn., Robert F. Mitro/Dir., Avtar Singh Ranshi/Dir., Sukhbir Singh Mudan/Dir., Pres., Roger Goulette/Member - Board of Advisor, Romir Bosu/Member - Advisory Board, Paul McNulty/Member - Advisory Board, David Oppenheimer/Member - Advisory Board, Andrew Quintero/Member - Advisory Board, Jack Wells/Member - Advisory Board

Owners: Michael A. Willner, Luan Dang, Iain Stuart Allison, Sukhbir Singh Mudan, Gary D. Allhusen, Avtar Singh Ranshi, Insiders, Robert J. Morris, Alan S. Knitowski, Robert F. Mitro

Financial Data: Fiscal Year End:12/31   Latest Annual Data: 12/31/2006

Year	Sales	Net Income
2006	$6,988,000	-$2,041,000
2005	$2,175,000	-$1,275,000
2004	$535,000	-$1,357,000

Curr. Assets:	$2,249,000	Curr. Liab.:	$2,109,000		
Plant, Equip.:	$194,000	Total Liab.:	$2,826,000	Indic. Yr. Divd.:	NA
Total Assets:	$4,851,000	Net Worth:	$1,794,000	Debt/ Equity:	0.3712

Cangold Ltd

1177 West Hastings St. , Ste. 2100, Vancouver, BC, V6E 2K3; *PH:* 1-604-608-1766; *Fax:* 1-604-608-1744; *http://* www.cangold.ca; *Email:* info@cangold.ca

General - Incorporation	Canada
Employees	NA
Auditor	KPMG LLP
Stk Agt	Pacific Corporate Trust Co
Counsel	M. Michael Sikula Law Corp
DUNS No.	NA

Stock - Price on:12/24/2007	$0.144
Stock Exchange	OTC
Ticker Symbol	CGLJF
Outstanding Shares	NA
E.P.S.	NA
Shareholders	NA

Business: The groups principle activity is to focus on precious metals including gold, silver and platinum group metals. The group operates from United States.

Primary SIC and add'l.: 1400

CIK No: 0001308931

Officers: Robert A. Archer/CEO, Pres., Kaare G. Foy/Chmn., CFO, Wendy Ratcliffe/Corp. Sec., Robert Brown/Dir., VP - Exploration, Kareen McKinnon/VP - Corporate Development, Adrian Bray/Exploration Mgr., Michael M. Sikula/Legal Advisor

Directors: Kaare G. Foy/Chmn., CFO, Bryan J. Frost/Dir., Richard Revelins/Dir., Robert Brown/Dir., VP - Exploration

Cano Petroleum Inc

309 W 7th St., Ste. 1600, Fort Worth, TX, 76102; *PH:* 1-817-698-0900; *Fax:* 1-817-698-0796; *http://* www.canopetro.com; *Email:* info@canopetro.com

General - Incorporation	DE
Employees	95
Auditor	Hein & Associates LLP
Stk Agt	Interwest Transfer Company, Inc.
Counsel	NA
DUNS No.	NA

Stock - Price on:12/24/2007	$5.9164
Stock Exchange	AMEX
Ticker Symbol	CFW
Outstanding Shares	32,680,000
E.P.S.	-$0.14
Shareholders	NA

Business: The groups principle activities include acquiring, developing and operating oil and natural gas properties. The group operates from the United States. The groups quarterly revenue for September 2007 was 8.72 millions of USD.

Primary SIC and add'l.: 1311

CIK No: 0001253710

Subsidiaries: Ladder Companies, Inc., Pantwist, LLC, Square One Energy, Inc., Tri-Flow, Inc., W.O. Energy of Nevada, Inc, W.O. Operating Company, Ltd., W.O. Production Company, Ltd., WO Energy, Inc.

Officers: Jeff Johnson/Chmn., CEO, Sam Smith/Investor Relations Officer, Morris B. Smith/Sr. VP, CFO, Pat McKinney/Sr. VP - Engineering, Operations, Michael J. Ricketts/VP, Principal Accounting Officer, John Marting/Sr. Petroleum Engineer, Keith Flowers/Controller, Carolyn Carroll/Mgr. - Human Resources, Administration, Phillip Feiner/Corp. Sec., Assist. General Counsel, Jayme Wollison/Dir. - Operations

Directors: Jeff Johnson/Chmn., CEO, Robert L. Gaudin/Dir., Randall Boyd/Dir., Don D. Dent/Dir., Gerald W. Haddock/Dir., Donald W. Niemiec/Dir., William O. Powell/Dir.

Owners: Gerald W. Haddock, Donnie D. Dent, D. E. Shaw Laminar Portfolios, LLC/5.40%, Jeffrey S. Johnson/4.00%, Patrick McKinney, Randall Boyd, GLG North American Opportunity Fund/6.90%, Wellington Management Company, LLP/12.40%, Donald W. Niemiec, Morris B. Smith, William Herbert Hunt Trust Estate/3.50%, Trapeze Asset Management,Inc./13.50%, Michael J. Ricketts/1.10%, Insiders/8.10%

Financial Data: Fiscal Year End:06/30   Latest Annual Data: 06/30/2007

Year	Sales	Net Income
2007	$28,353,000	-$790,000
2006	$18,408,000	-$1,844,000
2005	$5,482,000	-$2,973,000

Curr. Assets:	$7,613,000	Curr. Liab.:	$10,990,000		
Plant, Equip.:	$185,189,000	Total Liab.:	$132,608,000	Indic. Yr. Divd.:	NA
Total Assets:	$201,469,000	Net Worth:	$68,861,000	Debt/ Equity:	0.0364

Canon Inc

1 Canon Plz., Lake Success, NY, 11042; *PH:* 1-516-328-5000; *Fax:* 1-516-328-5069; *http://* www.usa.canon.com

General - Incorporation	Japan
Employees	118,499
Auditor	KPMG Azsa & Co
Stk Agt	JP Morgan
Counsel	NA
DUNS No.	69-054-9662

Stock - Price on:12/24/2007	$59.56
Stock Exchange	NYSE
Ticker Symbol	CAJ
Outstanding Shares	1,320,000,000
E.P.S.	$3.39
Shareholders	NA

Business: The group's principal activity is to develop, produce, sell office machines, cameras and optical products. Operations are carried out through the following divisions: office machines such as copying machines, laser beam and bubble jet printers, image scanners and personal copying machines; cameras including single-lens reflex cameras, compact cameras, digital cameras, video camcorders, LCD projectors and lenses; optical equipment/other including semiconductor production equipment, medical equipment, TV lenses for broadcasting use and medical equipment.

Primary SIC and add'l.: 3577 5047 3579 3827 3861

CIK No: 0000016988

Subsidiaries: Canon Europa N.V., Canon Precision Inc, Canon Sales Co., Inc., Canon U.S.A., Inc., Hirosaki Precision, Inc

Officers: Fujio Mitarai/Chmn., CEO, Tsuneji Uchida/Dir., COO, Pres., Teruomi Takahashi/Dir., Corporate Auditor, Junji Ichikawa/Dir., Sr. MD, Tomonori Iwashita/Dir., MD, Kunio Watanabe/Dir., MD, Kunihiro Nagata/Dir., Corporate Auditor, Yasuo Mitsuhashi/Dir., MD, Akiyoshi Moroe/Dir., MD, Hajime Tsuruoka/Dir., MD, Yoshinobu Shimizu/Dir., Corporate Auditor, Minoru Shishikura/Dir., Corporate Auditor, Nobuyoshi Tanaka/Dir., Sr. MD, Shigeyuki Matsumoto/Dir., MD, Yoroku Adachi/Dir., MD (18 Officers included in Index)

Directors: Fujio Mitarai/Chmn., CEO, Tsuneji Uchida/Dir., COO, Pres., Junji Ichikawa/Dir., Sr. MD, Haruhisa Honda/Dir., Toshio Homma/Dir., Shunichi Uzawa/Dir., Keijiro Yamazaki/Dir., Teruomi Takahashi/Dir., Corporate Auditor, Nobuyoshi Tanaka/Dir., Sr. MD, Shigeyuki Matsumoto/Dir., MD, Ryoichi Bamba/Dir., Yoroku Adachi/Dir., MD, Tadashi Ohe/Dir., Corporate Auditor, Toshio Honma/59/Dir., Masahiro Osawa/Dir., MD (33 Directors included in Index)

Owners: BNP Paribas Securities (Japan) Ltd/1.60%, Masaki Nakaoka, Tetsuro Tahara, Kunihiro Nagata, The Dai-Ichi Mutual Life Insurance Co./7.00%, Yoroku Adachi, Masahiro Osawa, Toshizo Tanaka, Keijiro Yamazaki, Nobuyoshi Tanaka, State Street Bank and Trust Company 505103/2.60%, Sompo Japan Insurance Inc/1.70%, Katsuichi Shimizu, Toshio Honma, Nomura Securities Co., Ltd./2.00% (42 Owners included in Index)

Financial Data: Fiscal Year End:12/31   Latest Annual Data: 12/31/2006

Year	Sales	Net Income
2006	$34,916,776,000	$3,824,730,000
2005	$31,910,624,000	$3,264,816,000
2004	$33,638,174,000	$3,330,437,000

Curr. Assets:	$23,371,732,000	Curr. Liab.:	$9,771,779,000		
Plant, Equip.:	$10,637,970,000	Total Liab.:	$12,896,596,000	Indic. Yr. Divd.:	$0.860
Total Assets:	$37,984,086,000	Net Worth:	$25,087,490,000	Debt/ Equity:	NA

Cantel Medical Corp

150 Clove Rd., 9th Fl., Little Falls, NJ, 07424; *PH:* 1-973-890-7220; *Fax:* 1-973-890-7270; *http://* www.cantelmedical.com

General - Incorporation	DE
Employees	794
Auditor	Ernst & Young LLP
Stk Agt	American Stock Transfer & Trust Co.
Counsel	NA
DUNS No.	01-114-1033

Stock - Price on:12/24/2007	$17.22
Stock Exchange	NYSE
Ticker Symbol	CMN
Outstanding Shares	16,040,000
E.P.S.	$0.52
Shareholders	NA

Business: The group's principle activities are to design, develop, manufacture and distribute infection prevention and control products. They include specialized medical devices for diagnostic imaging and therapeutics, consisting of dialysis products, endoscopy and surgical products, endoscope

reprocessing products, filtration and separation products and scientific products. The group markets its products through a direct sales force and distributors. Its subsidiary, minntech corporation distributes the products in Europe, Japan, Singapore and Asia/pacific. Olympus America inc is a supplier and also a major distributor of the endoscopy products for the group. The group's total revenue for year 2007 was 219.04 millions of USD.

Primary SIC and add'l.: 3841 7699 5047 5084

CIK No: 0000019446

Subsidiaries: Biolab Equipment Ltd., Carsen Group Inc., Crosstex International, Inc., Mar Cor Purification, Inc., Minntech B.V., Minntech Corporation, Minntech Japan K.K., Saf-T-Pak, Inc.

Officers: Roy K. Malkin/62/Pres., CEO - Minntech Corporation, Scott R. Jones/Dir., CEO, Pres., Richard Allen Orofino/69/Pres., CEO - Crosstex International, Inc, Curtis Weitnauer/45/Pres., CEO - Cor Purification, Inc, Craig A. Sheldon/CFO, Sr. VP, Joanna Zisa Albrecht/Assist. Sec., Seth R. Segel/Sr. VP - Corporate Development, Andrew A. Krakauer/COO, Exec. VP, Steven C. Anaya/VP, Controller, Eric W. Nodiff/Sr. VP, General Counsel

Directors: Scott R. Jones/Dir., CEO, Pres., Alan J. Hirschfield/Vice Chmn., Charles M. Diker/Chmn., Robert L. Barbanell/Dir., Elizabeth McCaughey/Dir., Darwin C. Dornbush/Dir., Joseph M. Cohen/Dir., Alan R. Batkin/Dir., Spencer Foreman/Dir., Bruce Slovin/Dir., Mark N. Diker/42/Dir.

Owners: Seth R. Segel, Bruce Slovin/1.80%, Darwin C. Dornbush, Craig A. Sheldon, Insiders/28.90%, R. Scott Jones, James P. Reilly/3.50%, Joseph M. Cohen, Andrew A. Krakauer, Alan J. Hirschfield/1.90%, Charles M. Diker/19.70%, Independence Investments LLC/6.20%, Alan R. Batkin, Mark N. Diker, Dimensional Fund Advisors Inc./8.10% (18 Owners included in Index)

Financial Data: Fiscal Year End:07/31   Latest Annual Data: 07/31/2007

Year	Sales	Net Income
2007	$219,044,000	$8,446,000
2006	$192,179,000	$23,697,000
2005	$197,402,000	$15,505,000

Curr. Assets:	$82,448,000	Curr. Liab.:	$39,097,000	P/E Ratio:	13.67
Plant, Equip.:	$38,104,000	Total Liab.:	$97,422,000	Indic. Yr. Divd.:	NA
Total Assets:	$238,227,000	Net Worth:	$140,805,000	Debt/ Equity:	NA

Canterbury Park Holding Corp

1100 Canterbury Rd., Shakopee, MN, 55379; **PH:** 1-952-445-7223; **Fax:** 1-952-496-6400; *http://* www.canterburypark.com; **Email:** investorrelations@canterburypark.com

General - Incorporation	MN	**Stock** - Price on:12/24/2007	$12.7
Employees	398	Stock Exchange	AMEX
Auditor	Deloitte & Touche LLP	Ticker Symbol	ECP
Stk Agt	Wells Fargo Shareowner Services	Outstanding Shares	4,110,000
Counsel	Lindquist & Vennum PLLP	E.P.S.	$0.731
DUNS No.	84-990-5633	Shareholders	NA

Business: The group's principal activity is to hosts pari-mutuel wagering on live thoroughbred and quarter horse racing at its facilities in shakopee, Minnesota and pari-mutuel wagering on races held at out-of-state racetracks that are televised simultaneously at the racetrack. It operates through these segments: the card club segment includes operations of the canterbury card club. It is open 24 hours per day, seven days per week, offering two types of unbanked card games: poker games and casino games. The horse racing segment includes simulcast and live racing operations. The concessions segment represents food and beverage services for simulcast and live racing, the card club and during special events. The group's other activities include admissions and parking fees, as well as from the sale of food and beverage, programs, and other racing publications. It also offers advertising signage space similar to that appearing at many sports stadiums.

Primary SIC and add'l.: 7999 7948

CIK No: 0000926761

Subsidiaries: Canterbury Park Concessions, Inc., Shakopee Valley RV Park Acquisition Company, LLC

Officers: Randall D. Sampson/Dir., CEO, Pres./$311,591.00, Mark A. Erickson/VP - Facilities, Michael J. Garin/VP - Hospitality, Assist. Sec./$134,998.00, Kip Rakos/Corporate Partnership Mgr., David C. Hansen/VP - Finance, CFO, Sec./$207,398.00, Eric Halstrom/VP - Racing, Simulcasting, John R. Harty/VP - Marketing/$145,580.00, Jerry Fuller/VP - Card Club Operations, Michele Dahl/Primary Investor Relations Officer, Vickey Wickenhauser/Banquet Mgr., Mary Kay Dropps/Group Sales Staff, Dale Runge/Mgr. - Food, Beverage

Directors: Randall D. Sampson/Dir., CEO, Pres., Curtis A. Sampson/Chmn., Dale H. Schenian/Vice Chmn., Patrick R. Cruzen/Dir., Carin J. Offerman/Dir., Burton F. Dahlberg/Dir.

Owners: David C. Hansen, Burton F. Dahlberg, Michael J. Garin/2.30%, Jerrold J. Fuller, Dale H. Schenian/11.30%, Randall D. Sampson/6.70%, John R. Harty, Carin J. Offerman/2.10%, Gabelli Asset Management, Inc./10.20%, River Road Asset Management/5.30%, Curtis A. Sampson/22.20%, Patrick R. Cruzen, Insiders/46.10%

Financial Data: Fiscal Year End:12/31   Latest Annual Data: 12/31/2006

Year	Sales	Net Income
2006	$55,840,000	$3,125,000
2005	$55,223,000	$3,053,000
2004	$54,899,000	$3,862,000

Curr. Assets:	$9,427,000	Curr. Liab.:	$7,031,000	P/E Ratio:	17.16
Plant, Equip.:	$24,904,000	Total Liab.:	$7,492,000	Indic. Yr. Divd.:	NA
Total Assets:	$34,351,000	Net Worth:	$26,860,000	Debt/ Equity:	NA

Canton Bancorp Inc PA

5 W Main St., Canton, PA, 17724; **PH:** 1-570-673-5127

General - Incorporation	PA	**Stock** - Price on:12/24/2007	$240
Employees	NA	Stock Exchange	OTC
Auditor	NA	Ticker Symbol	CBPA
Stk Agt	Computershare Investor Services LLC	Outstanding Shares	NA
Counsel	Sky Financial's	E.P.S.	NA
DUNS No.	NA	Shareholders	NA

Business: The groups principle activity is to provide recruiting services. The groups service area includes the research and development, engineering, marketing, sales, information technology and manufacturing industries. The group operates from United States.

Primary SIC and add'l.: 6712

CIK No: 0001022336

Financial Data: Fiscal Year End:12/31   Latest Annual Data: 12/31/2002

Year	Sales	Net Income
2002	$3,688,000	$375,000
2001	$3,791,000	$351,000
2000	$3,708,000	$557,000

Curr. Assets:	$3,970,000	Curr. Liab.:	$47,480,000		
Plant, Equip.:	$1,491,000	Total Liab.:	$48,137,000	Indic. Yr. Divd.:	NA
Total Assets:	$55,062,000	Net Worth:	$6,925,000	Debt/ Equity:	NA

CanWest Global Communications Corp

3100 CanWest Global Pl., 201 Portage Ave., Winnipeg, MB, R3B 3L7; **PH:** 1-204-956-2025; *http://* www.canwestglobal.com; **Email:** inquiries@canwestinteractive.com

General - Incorporation	Canada	**Stock** - Price on:12/24/2007	NA
Employees	NA	Stock Exchange	NA
Auditor	PricewaterhouseCoopers LLP	Ticker Symbol	NA
Stk Agt	Computershare Investor Services LLC	Outstanding Shares	NA
Counsel	Pitblado	E.P.S.	NA
DUNS No.	24-852-3870	Shareholders	NA

Business: The group's principle activities are television broadcasting, radio, specialty cable channels, production and distribution of film and television programming and Internet websites. The group's quarterly revenue for September 2007 was 678.65 millions of CAD.

Primary SIC and add'l.: 7375 4841 4833

CIK No: 0001003565

Subsidiaries: CanWest Media Inc, CanWest MediaWorks (NZ) Limited, CBL Amalco, Global Communications Ltd, TEN Group, TV3 Ireland

Officers: Leonard J. Asper/Dir., CEO, Pres., Nick Falloon/Executive Chmn. - Network TEN, Grace Palombo/Sr. VP - Human Resources Canwest Global Communications, Richard M. Leipsic/Sr. VP, General Counsel, John P. Culligan/VP - Corporate Development, Gail S. Asper/Dir., Corp. Sec., Thomas S. Strike/Pres. - Corporate Development, Strategy Implementation, John E. Maguire/CFO, Rick Hetherington/Pres. - European Operations, Kathleen Dore/Pres. - Television Canwest Mediaworks Inc, Dennis Skulsky/Pres. - Canwest Mediaworks Publications Inc, Debbie Hutton/Sr. VP - Corporate Communications

Directors: Leonard J. Asper/Dir., CEO, Pres., Derek H. Burney/Chmn., Frank W. King/Dir., David W. Kerr/Corp. Dir., David A. Leslie/Corp. Dir., Lisa Pankratz/Dir., Ronald J. Daniels/Dir., Lloyd I. Barber/Dir., Paul V. Godfrey/Dir., Gail S. Asper/Dir., Corp. Sec., David Drybrough/Corp. Dir., David A. Asper/Dir.

Canyon Bancorp CA

1711 E Palm Canyon Dr., Palm Springs, CA, 92264; **PH:** 1-760-325-4442; *http://* www.canyonnational.com; **Email:** info@CanyonNational.com

General - Incorporation	CA	**Stock** - Price on:12/24/2007	$25
Employees	NA	Stock Exchange	OTC
Auditor	Vavrinek, Trine, Day & Co.,LLP	Ticker Symbol	CYBA
Stk Agt	Computershare Trust Co., N.A.	Outstanding Shares	2,300,000
Counsel	NA	E.P.S.	$1.68
DUNS No.	NA	Shareholders	NA

Business: The group operates through its subsidiary whose principal activity is banking operations. The group financial products include Internet banking, lock box processing, direct deposit of payroll and social security funds, and postage-paid bank-by-mail, and mortgage real estate loans. The group operates from the United State. The groups asset in the year 2006 was $24,423.

Primary SIC and add'l.: 6712

CIK No: 0001363569

Subsidiaries: Canyon National Bank

Officers: Stephen G. Hoffmann/Dir., CEO, Pres./$564,562.00

Directors: Stephen G. Hoffmann/Dir., CEO, Pres., Michael D. Harris/Chmn., Robert M. Fey/Vice Chmn., Lynne C. Bushore/Dir., Milton W. Jones/Dir., Kipp I. Lyons/Dir., Richard Shalhoub/Dir., Mark Benedetti/Dir., Max Ross/Dir., Marshall M. Gelfand/Dir. Emeritus

Owners: Kipp I. Lyons/2.03%, Mark Benedetti/1.05%, Stephen G. Hoffmann/2.14%, Robert M. Fey/2.46%, Jeffrey D. Gobble/0.27%, Lynne C. Bushore/0.29%, Richard Shalhoub/4.32%, Jonathan J. Wick/0.52%, Michael D. Harris/2.07%, Insiders/17.97%, Milton W. Jones/3.41%, Max R. Ross/0.34%

Financial Data: Fiscal Year End:09/30   Latest Annual Data: 12/31/2006

Year	Sales	Net Income
2006	$22,164,000	$4,257,000
2002	$9,021,000	$1,355,000
2001	$8,631,000	$1,016,000

Curr. Assets:	$24,034,000	Curr. Liab.:	$226,430,000		
Plant, Equip.:	$4,548,000	Total Liab.:	$227,945,000	Indic. Yr. Divd.:	NA
Total Assets:	$252,368,000	Net Worth:	$24,423,000	Debt/ Equity:	NA

Canyon Copper Corp

No. 408 - 1199 W Pender St., Vancouver, BC, V6E 2R1; **PH:** 1-888-331-9326; *http://* www.canyoncc.com; **Email:** info@canyoncc.com

General - Incorporation	NV	**Stock** - Price on:12/24/2007	$0.31
Employees	NA	Stock Exchange	OTC
Auditor	Manning Elliott LLP	Ticker Symbol	CYOO
Stk Agt	Manning Elliott LLP	Outstanding Shares	NA
Counsel	NA	E.P.S.	NA
DUNS No.	NA	Shareholders	NA

Business: The groups principal activity is to explore minerals. The group operates from Canada.

Primary SIC and add'l.: 1000

CIK No: 0001112706

Owners: Bryan Wilson/1.00%, Clarion Finanz AG/5.10%, Anthony Harvey/7.70%, Mark A. Reynolds/12.20%, DRS Investments Ltd./11.30%, Kurt Bordian, Milton Datsopoulos/1.40%, Insiders/12.90%, John Carlesso/2.70%

Financial Data: Fiscal Year End:06/30   Latest Annual Data: 06/30/2007

Year	Sales	Net Income
2007	NA	-$2,177,000

Curr. Assets:	$50,000	**Curr. Liab.:**	$1,140,000		
Plant, Equip.:	NA	**Total Liab.:**	$1,140,000	**Indic. Yr. Divd.:**	NA
Total Assets:	$50,000	**Net Worth:**	-$1,090,000	**Debt/ Equity:**	NA

Canyon Resources Corp

14142 Denver W Pkwy., Ste. 250, Golden, CO, 80401; ***PH:*** 1-303-278-8464; ***Fax:*** 1-303-279-3772; ***http://*** www.canyonresources.com

General - Incorporation	DE	**Stock**- Price on:12/24/2007	$0.57
Employees	19	Stock Exchange	AMEX
Auditor	Ehrhardt Keefe Steiner & Hottman P.C	Ticker Symbol	CAU
Stk Agt	Computershare Trust Co	Outstanding Shares	44,130,000
Counsel	Perkins Coie LLP	E.P.S.	-$0.09
DUNS No.	03-744-1573	Shareholders	NA

Business: The group's principal activities are to explore, acquire, develop and mine precious metals and other mineral properties. The group's mining operations include all phases from early stage exploration, exploration drilling, development drilling, feasibility studies and permitting, through construction, operation and final closure of mining properties. The group has gold production operations in the western United States and conducts exploration activities in the search for additional valuable mineral properties in the western United States and in a number of areas in Latin America and Africa. During 2003, the group sold its gold produce primarily to standard bank london limited and it's silver produce to metalor usa refining corporation.

Primary SIC and add'l.: 1041

CIK No: 0000739460

Subsidiaries: CR Briggs Corporation, CR International Corporation, CR Kendall Corporation, CR Minerals Corporation, CR Montana Corporation, Judith Gold Corporation

Officers: James K.B. Hesketh/Dir., CEO, Pres./$301,767.00, David Suleski/CFO, VP, Treasurer, Corp. Sec./$208,640.00, Valerie Kimball/Investor Relations Contact, Stephen Zahony/VP - Exploration, Richard T. Phillips/Controller, Treasurer, Corp. Sec.

Directors: James K.B. Hesketh/Dir., CEO, Pres., David K. Fagin/Chmn., Richard F. Mauro/Dir., Ronald D. Parker/Dir., Leland O. Erdahl/Dir., Richard H. De Voto/Dir.

Financial Data: *Fiscal Year End:*12/31 *Latest Annual Data:* 12/31/2006

Year	Sales	Net Income
2006	$1,270,000	-$2,744,000
2005	$4,140,000	-$15,648,000
2004	$11,814,000	-$17,386,000

Curr. Assets:	$4,427,000	**Curr. Liab.:**	$2,392,000		
Plant, Equip.:	$8,720,000	**Total Liab.:**	$6,304,000	**Indic. Yr. Divd.:**	NA
Total Assets:	$16,825,000	**Net Worth:**	$10,520,000	**Debt/ Equity:**	0.0973

Cap Rock Energy Corp

500 W Wall St., Ste. 400, Midland, TX, 79701; ***PH:*** 1-432-683-5422; ***Fax:*** 1-432-684-0334; ***http://*** www.caprockenergy.com; ***Email:*** corporate@caprockenergy.com

General - Incorporation	TX	**Stock**- Price on:12/24/2007	NA
Employees	38	Stock Exchange	NA
Auditor	KPMG LLP	Ticker Symbol	NA
Stk Agt	Computershare Investor Services LLC	Outstanding Shares	NA
Counsel	NA	E.P.S.	NA
DUNS No.	NA	Shareholders	NA

Business: The group's principle activity is to distribute electricity in the state of Texas. The group purchases all electricity from southwest public service company, dynegy power marketing, inc, lower Colorado river authority and garland power and light and distributes it to over 35,000 meters in 28 counties of Texas. The group provides management services to the farmersville municipal electric system. The group invests in the real estate business, the oil and gas business and the petroleum distribution business with investments in certain limited partnerships. Real estate investments consist of building and land related to the electric business. The group's predecessor was incorporated as an electric cooperative. The co-operative's assets and liabilities were transferred to the group in 2002. The group operates from United States.

Primary SIC and add'l.: 4911 4932

CIK No: 0001129162

Subsidiaries: NewCorp Resources Electric Cooperative, Inc

Officers: Melissa D. Davis/CEO, Pres., Ronald W. Lyon/Exec. VP, General Counsel, Sec., Sammy C. Prough/COO, Exec. VP

Capco Energy Inc

5555 San Felipe, Ste. 725, Houston, TX, 77056; ***PH:*** 1-713-622-5550; ***Fax:*** 1-713-622-5552; ***http://*** www.capcoenergy.net

General - Incorporation	CO	**Stock**- Price on:12/24/2007	$0.06
Employees	38	Stock Exchange	OTC
Auditor	Stonefield Josephson, Inc.	Ticker Symbol	CGYN
Stk Agt	Computershare Trust Co	Outstanding Shares	116,080,000
Counsel	NA	E.P.S.	-$0.029
DUNS No.	06-335-4930	Shareholders	NA

Business: The group's principal activity is to acquire, explore, develop and produce oil and natural gas reserves. The group also invests in the equity securities of other public companies involved in similar activities. The group's activities are located principally in the United States of America.

Primary SIC and add'l.: 1311 5541

CIK No: 0000354767

Subsidiaries: Bison Energy Company

Officers: Ilyas M. Chaudhary/Chmn., CEO, Pres., Robert Thomasson/COO, Walton Vance/Controller, William J. Hickey/Dir., Sec., Pat McInturff/VP - Operations, Imran Jattala/CFO

Directors: Ilyas M. Chaudhary/Chmn., CEO, Pres., Irwin Kaufman/Dir., Paul L. Hayes/66/Dir., William J. Hickey/Dir., Sec.

Financial Data: *Fiscal Year End:*12/31 *Latest Annual Data:* 12/31/2005

Year	Sales	Net Income
2005	$3,572,000	-$3,613,000
2004	$6,229,000	$725,000
2003	$3,148,000	-$1,948,000

Curr. Assets:	$1,677,000	**Curr. Liab.:**	$4,329,000		
Plant, Equip.:	$15,720,000	**Total Liab.:**	$11,572,000	**Indic. Yr. Divd.:**	NA
Total Assets:	$30,881,000	**Net Worth:**	$18,948,000	**Debt/ Equity:**	NA

Cape Fear Bank Corp

1117 Military Cutoff Rd., Wilmington, NC, 28405; ***PH:*** 1-910-509-2000; ***Fax:*** 1-910-509-1542; ***http://*** www.capefearbank.com; ***Email:*** info@capefearbank.com

General - Incorporation	NC	**Stock**- Price on:12/24/2007	$9.9
Employees	92	Stock Exchange	NDQ
Auditor	Dixon Hughes PLLC	Ticker Symbol	CAPE
Stk Agt	Registrar & Transfer Co	Outstanding Shares	3,590,000
Counsel	NA	E.P.S.	$0.49
DUNS No.	NA	Shareholders	NA

Business: The group operates through its subsidiaries whose principle activity is to provide banking services. The groups services include deposit and loans. The group operates from Wilmington, North Carolina in the United States. The assets of the group for the year 2006 were $396,272 (thousands).

Primary SIC and add'l.: 6022 6712

CIK No: 0001334872

Subsidiaries: BKWW Statutory Trust I

Officers: Cameron Coburn/Chmn., CEO, Pres., Betty Norris/Sr. VP, CFO, Larry W. Flowers/66/Exec. VP, Chief Credit Officer, Lynn Burney/COO, Sr. VP, James MacLaren/Sr. VP, Chief Credit Officer, Mark Tyler/Sr. VP, Chief Banking Officer

Directors: Cameron Coburn/Chmn., CEO, Pres., Walter Lee Crouch/51/Vice Chmn., John Davie Waggett/52/Dir., Lee W. Crouch/Dir., Windell Daniels/Dir., Craig S. Relan/Dir., Jerry D. Sellers/Dir., Davie J. Waggett/Dir., Walter O. Winter/Dir., Jesse M. Coburn/Dir. Emeritus

Owners: Windell Daniels/0.75%, Cameron Coburn/5.40%, Mark A. Tyler, Walter Lee Crouch/2.75%, Lynn M. Burney/0.88%, River Oaks Capital LLC/9.17%, Betty V. Norris/0.97%, The Banc Funds Company, LLC/5.97%, James R. MacLaren, Larry W. Flowers/1.06%, Jerry D. Sellers/0.29%, Walter O. Winter/0.89%, John Davie Waggett/0.34%, Craig S. Relan/0.89%, Insiders/14.18%

Financial Data: *Fiscal Year End:*12/31 *Latest Annual Data:* 12/31/2006

Year	Sales	Net Income
2006	$29,349,000	$2,272,000
2005	$17,470,000	$1,682,000

Curr. Assets:	$11,341,000	**Curr. Liab.:**	$359,523,000	**P/E Ratio:**	17.37
Plant, Equip.:	$3,570,000	**Total Liab.:**	$397,833,000	**Indic. Yr. Divd.:**	NA
Total Assets:	$424,885,000	**Net Worth:**	$27,052,000	**Debt/ Equity:**	1.3911

Cape Systems Group Inc

Formerly: Vertex Interactive Inc
3619 Kennedy Rd., South Plainfield, NJ, 07080; ***PH:*** 1-908-756-2000; ***http://*** www.capesystems.com

General - Incorporation	NJ	**Stock**- Price on:12/24/2007	NA
Employees	29	Stock Exchange	NA
Auditor	J. H. Cohn LLP	Ticker Symbol	NA
Stk Agt	Continental Stock Transfer & Trust Co	Outstanding Shares	NA
Counsel	NA	E.P.S.	-$0.015
DUNS No.	07-543-2443	Shareholders	NA

Business: The group's principal activity is to provide supply chain management solutions and services. The solutions include enterprise software systems and applications, advance planning and scheduling capabilities and software integration. They enable customers to manage their order, inventory, warehouse and transportation needs, consultative services and software and hardware service and maintenance. The group's enterprise solutions include a suite of java (TM)-architected software applications. The group also provides a full range of software and hardware services and maintenance round the clock.

Primary SIC and add'l.: 7379 7372

CIK No: 0000779681

Subsidiaries: Renaissance Software, Inc., XeQute Solutions, Inc

Officers: Nicholas Toms/Dir., CEO, Hugo Biermann/Exec. Chmn., David Sasson/COO, CTO, Peter Ayling/Head - International Marketing, Brad Leonard/VP - Group Sales, Heidi Larsen/VP - Software Sales, Moshud Bello/European Technical Services Mgr., Victoria Ayling/European Sales, Marketing Mgr., Colin Lacey/European Sales Support Mgr.

Directors: Nicholas Toms/Dir., CEO, Hugo Biermann/Exec. Chmn., Otto Leistner/Dir.

Owners: O'Brien Ltd Partnership0/5.62%, David Sasson, Pitney Bowes, Inc./100.00%, MidMark Capital L.P., Paine Webber Custodian, Joseph Robinson, Nicholas R. H. Toms, Brad Leonard, Otto Leistner, O'Brien Ltd Partnership, Paine Webber Custodian/5.62%, Hugo H. Biermann, Insiders, Barbara Martorano, MidMark Capital II L.P./78.40% *(19 Owners included in Index)*

Financial Data: *Fiscal Year End:*09/30 *Latest Annual Data:* 09/30/2006

Year	Sales	Net Income
2006	$3,524,000	-$1,690,000
2005	$3,779,000	-$6,795,000
2004	$2,567,000	-$2,185,000

Curr. Assets:	$842,000	**Curr. Liab.:**	$26,783,000		
Plant, Equip.:	$33,000	**Total Liab.:**	$26,783,000	**Indic. Yr. Divd.:**	NA
Total Assets:	$2,044,000	**Net Worth:**	-$24,739,000	**Debt/ Equity:**	NA

Capella Education Company

225 S 6th St., 9th Fl., Minneapolis, MN, 55402; ***PH:*** 1-612-339-8650; ***Fax:*** 1-612-977-5060; ***http://*** www.capellauniversity.edu; ***Email:*** investorrelations@capella.edu

General - Incorporation	MN	**Stock**- Price on:12/24/2007	$42.49
Employees	130	Stock Exchange	NDQ
Auditor	Ernst & Young LLP	Ticker Symbol	CPLA
Stk Agt	Wells Fargo Shareowner Services	Outstanding Shares	16,650,000
Counsel	NA	E.P.S.	$1.17
DUNS No.	NA	Shareholders	NA

Business: The groups principle activity is to provide online post secondary education services. The groups services include academic, administrative, library career and counseling. The group operates from the United States. The group's quarterly revenue for September 2007 was 55.53 millions of USD.

Primary SIC and add'l.: 8299 7379 8221

CIK No: 0001104349

Subsidiaries: Capella University, Inc.

Officers: Stephen G. Shank/Chmn., CEO/$1,193,668.00, Scott M. Henkel/Interim Sr. VP - Operations, Business Transformation, CIO, Lois M. Martin/Sr. VP, CFO/$797,487.00, Michael J. Offerman/Sr. VP/$583,400.00, Elizabeth M. Rausch/VP - Human Resources, Paul A. Schroeder/48/Sr. VP - Operations, Business Transformation/$583,003.00, Kenneth J. Sobaski/COO, Pres./$928,451.00, Gregory W. Thom/VP, General Counsel, Sec., Reed A. Watson/Sr. VP - Marketing, Irene Silber/Dir. - Public Relations, Michael Walsh/Public Relations Mgr., Heide Erickson/Dir. - Investor Relations, Amy L. Drifka/VP, Controller, Sally B. Chial/VP Human Resources

Directors: Stephen G. Shank/Chmn., CEO, Gordon A. Holmes/39/Dir., Joshua S. Lewis/Dir., Jody G. Miller/Dir., James A. Mitchell/Dir., Jon Q. Reynolds/Dir., David W. Smith/Dir., Jeffrey W. Taylor/Dir., Sandra E. Taylor/Dir., Darrell R. Tukua/Dir., Andrew M. Slavitt/Dir.

Owners: Stephen G. Shank/15.50%, Entities affiliated with Technology Crossover Ventures/12.20%, David W. Smith, Forstmann Little entities/6.90%, Joshua S. Lewis/8.40%, Maveron entities/6.60%, Darrell R. Tukua, Michael J. Offerman, Jon Q. Reynolds/12.20%, Jody G. Miller, Kenneth J. Sobaski, Salmon River and Insight entities/8.50%, Sandra Taylor, Lois M. Martin, Paul A. Schroeder/1.00% *(19 Owners included in Index)*

Financial Data: ***Fiscal Year End:***12/31 ***Latest Annual Data:*** 12/31/2006

Year	Sales	Net Income
2006	$179,881,000	$13,411,000
2005	$149,240,000	$10,250,000
2004	$117,689,000	$18,785,000

Curr. Assets:	$100,565,000	***Curr. Liab.:***	$31,418,000	***P/E Ratio:***	17.37
Plant, Equip.:	$28,749,000	***Total Liab.:***	$35,569,000	***Indic. Yr. Divd.:***	NA
Total Assets:	$129,314,000	***Net Worth:***	$93,745,000	***Debt/ Equity:***	NA

Capital Alliance Income Trust Ltd

100 Pine St., Ste. 2450, San Francisco, CA, 94111; ***PH:*** 1-415-288-9595; ***Fax:*** 1-415-288-9590; ***http://*** www.caitreit.com

General - Incorporation	DE	***Stock***- Price on:12/24/2007	$7.85
Employees	1	Stock Exchange	AMEX
Auditor	Rothstein, Kass & Company, P.C.	Ticker Symbol	CAA
Stk Agt	Computershare Trust Co	Outstanding Shares	NA
Counsel	NA	E.P.S	-$6.09
DUNS No.	NA	Shareholders	NA

Business: The groups principle activities include investing and operating in real estate properties. The group operates from the United States. The groups quarterly revenue for September 2007 was 0.25 millions of USD.

Primary SIC and add'l.: 6798 6798

CIK No: 0001021422

Officers: Richard Wrensen/53/Dir., CEO, CFO, Pres., Gregory Bronshvag/39/VP, Corp. Sec., Andrea Barney/34/Principal Accounting Officer, Controller

Directors: Richard Wrensen/53/Dir., CEO, CFO, Pres., Thomas Swartz/Chmn., Dennis Konczal/57/Dir., James Grainer/Dir., Alan Jones/Dir., Ace Blackburn/Dir.

Owners: Dennis R. Konczal, Thomas B. Swartz, Ace J. Blackburn, Thomas B. Swartz/1.30%, Alan R. Jones, Dennis R. Konczal/4.60%, Gregory Bronshvag, Richard J. Wrensen/22.40%, Insiders/3.40%, Insiders/35.40%, Richard J. Wrensen, Thomas Morford/8.30%

Financial Data: ***Fiscal Year End:***12/31 ***Latest Annual Data:*** 12/31/2006

Year	Sales	Net Income
2006	$2,479,000	-$1,631,000
2005	$3,798,000	-$307,000
2004	$2,126,000	$670,000

Curr. Assets:	$1,494,000	***Curr. Liab.:***	NA		
Plant, Equip.:	$245,000	***Total Liab.:***	$7,050,000	***Indic. Yr. Divd.:***	NA
Total Assets:	$18,204,000	***Net Worth:***	$11,154,000	***Debt/ Equity:***	0.6178

Capital Bancorp Inc TN

1816 Hayes St., Nashville, TN, 37203; ***PH:*** 1-615-327-9000; ***http://*** www.capitalbk.com

General - Incorporation	TN	***Stock***- Price on:12/24/2007	$32.66
Employees	121	Stock Exchange	NA
Auditor	Porter Keadle Moore, LLP	Ticker Symbol	NA
Stk Agt	Registrar & Transfer Co	Outstanding Shares	3,670,000
Counsel	NA	E.P.S	$1.10
DUNS No.	NA	Shareholders	NA

Business: The groups principal activity is to provide banking services. The group financial products include accepting time and demand deposits, Investment services, making secured, unsecured commercial and consumer loans, personalized service, on-line banking, direct deposit and travelers checks. The group operates from the United States. The groups asset in the year 2006 was $ 564,442.

Primary SIC and add'l.: 6021

CIK No: 0001136303

Subsidiaries: Capital Bancorp Capital Trust I, Capital Bank & Trust Company

Officers: Rick R. Hart/59/Chmn., CEO, Pres., John W. Gregory/57/COO, Exec. VP, Sally P. Kimble/54/Exec. VP, Chief Financial, Accounting Officer

Directors: Rick R. Hart/59/Chmn., CEO, Pres., Newton H. Lovvorn/Dir., Albert J. Dale/Dir., Robert W. Doyle/Dir., Michael D. Shmerling/Dir.

Owners: John W. Gregory/3.12%, Newton H. Lovvorn/1.65%, Mary Bennie Wilson, Insiders/20.37%, Sally P. Kimble, Sam Allen, Michael D. Shmerling/3.78%, Albert J. Dale/2.06%, Rick R. Hart/3.48%, C. M. Gatton/8.59%, Robert W. Doyle/5.39%

Financial Data: ***Fiscal Year End:***12/31 ***Latest Annual Data:*** 12/31/2006

Year	Sales	Net Income
2006	$39,947,000	$4,181,000
2005	$29,005,000	$3,224,000
2004	$19,934,000	$3,373,000

Curr. Assets:	$13,997,000	***Curr. Liab.:***	$512,561,000	***P/E Ratio:***	29.69
Plant, Equip.:	$6,588,000	***Total Liab.:***	$529,473,000	***Indic. Yr. Divd.:***	NA
Total Assets:	$564,442,000	***Net Worth:***	$34,969,000	***Debt/ Equity:***	0.3537

Capital Bank Corp

333 Fayetteville, Ste. 700, Raleigh, NC, 27601; ***PH:*** 1-919-645-6400; ***Fax:*** 1-919-645-6435; ***http://*** www.capitalbank-nc.com

General - Incorporation	NC	***Stock***- Price on:12/24/2007	$29.1
Employees	585	Stock Exchange	NDQ
Auditor	Grant Thornton LLP	Ticker Symbol	CBKN
Stk Agt	Registrar & Transfer Co	Outstanding Shares	7,880,000
Counsel	NA	E.P.S	$0.96
DUNS No.	NA	Shareholders	NA

Business: The group's principal activity is to provide commercial banking services in North Carolina to individuals and small to medium size businesses. The group is a holding company for capital bank and capital bank investment services, inc. The banking services include checking accounts, savings accounts, now accounts, money market accounts and certificates of deposit. The group provides loans for real estate acquisition, businesses, agriculture, personal uses, home improvement and automobiles and equity lines of credit. Other services include safe deposit boxes, credit cards, retirement accounts, electronic funds transfer services and free notary services. The investment services provided by the group include full-service securities brokerage, asset management and financial planning and retirement planning services. The group operates in the wake, chatham, northampton, granville, warren and lee counties of North Carolina through 21 branches.

Primary SIC and add'l.: 6022 6712

CIK No: 0001071992

Subsidiaries: Capital Bank Investment Services, Inc., Capital Bank Statutory Trust I, Capital Bank Statutory Trust II, Capital Bank Statutory Trust III

Officers: Grant B. Yarber/Dir., CEO, Pres./$595,231.00, Jennifer Benefield/Support Services Exec., Chris McCoy/Compliance, Reporting Exec., Mark Redmond/Chief Credit Officer/$237,329.00, Christine A. Baker/CFO/$238,613.00, Robert W. Malburg/Operations Exec., George Nicholson/Chief Accounting Officer, Willard Ross/Exec. - Marketing, Training, Development, David Morgan/Chief Banking Officer, Roger F. Plott/Dir. - Commercial Services, Teresa White/Dir. - Human Resources, Fairfax Reynolds/Central Regional Pres.

Directors: Grant B. Yarber/Dir., CEO, Pres., Oscar A. Keller/Chmn., John F. Grimes/Dir., Charles F. Atkins/Dir., Robert L. Jones/Dir., Carl H. Ricker/Dir., William C. Burkhardt/Member - Triangle Region Advisory Board, Samuel J. Wornom/Dir., James D. Moser/Dir., George R. Perkins/Dir., James A. Barnwell/Dir., L. I. Cohen/Dir., Ernest A. Koury/Dir., Richard H. Shirley/Dir., Rex J. Thomas/Dir. *(82 Directors included in Index)*

Owners: Insiders/12.76%, Don W. Perry, Leopold I. Cohen, James G. McClure, Christine A. Baker, Mark J. Redmond, Charles F. Atkins, George R. Perkins/1.05%, Carl H. Ricker/2.58%, O. A. Keller/1.18%, Robert L. Jones, Maurice J. Koury/7.92%, Tontine Financial Partners, LP and Tontine Management, LLC/6.02%, Rex J. Thomas, Ernest A. Koury *(23 Owners included in Index)*

Financial Data: ***Fiscal Year End:***12/31 ***Latest Annual Data:*** 12/31/2006

Year	Sales	Net Income
2006	$96,285,000	$12,338,000
2005	$57,480,000	$6,699,000
2004	$49,616,000	$5,311,000

Curr. Assets:	$54,332,000	***Curr. Liab.:***	$1,089,447,000	***P/E Ratio:***	10.17
Plant, Equip.:	$23,125,000	***Total Liab.:***	$1,260,703,000	***Indic. Yr. Divd.:***	$0.320
Total Assets:	$1,422,384,000	***Net Worth:***	$161,681,000	***Debt/ Equity:***	0.4862

Capital Beverage Corp

700 Columbia St., Erie Basin, Bldg. 302, Brooklyn, NY, 11231; ***PH:*** 1-718-488-8500; ***http://*** www.beveragecapital.com

General - Incorporation	DE	***Stock***- Price on:12/24/2007	$0.24
Employees	1	Stock Exchange	OTC
Auditor	Sherb & Co. LLP	Ticker Symbol	CBEV
Stk Agt	Continental Stock Transfer & Trust Co	Outstanding Shares	3,790,000
Counsel	NA	E.P.S	-$0.13
DUNS No.	93-261-9125	Shareholders	NA

Business: The group's principal activity is to distribute beer and other beverages. The group has two distributor agreements with pittsburgh brewing company to distribute on an exclusive basis in the entire state of New York. The brands under the agreements include: brigade, brigade light, brigade ice, prime, time lager, prime time malt liquor, iron city, iron city, light twist acapulco lime, iron city twist, rio, cherry, old german, augustiner, evil eye ale, evil eye, black jack, evil eye amber lager and evil eye honey brown.

Primary SIC and add'l.: 5181

CIK No: 0001020186

Subsidiaries: CAP Communications, Ltd

Owners: Carmine Stella/18.80%, Insiders/50.00%, Anthony Stella/6.30%, Michael Matrisciani/6.30%, Monty Matrisciani/6.30%, Casimir Capital L.P./20.90%, Daniel Matrisciani/6.30%, Alex Matrisciani/6.30%

Financial Data: ***Fiscal Year End:***12/31 ***Latest Annual Data:*** 12/31/2006

Year	Sales	Net Income
2006	NA	-$329,000
2005	NA	$3,850,000
2004	$27,615,000	-$4,277,000

Curr. Assets:	$804,000	***Curr. Liab.:***	$796,000		
Plant, Equip.:	NA	***Total Liab.:***	$796,000	***Indic. Yr. Divd.:***	NA
Total Assets:	$807,000	***Net Worth:***	$11,000	***Debt/ Equity:***	NA

Capital City Bank Group Inc

217 N Monroe St., Tallahassee, FL, 32301; ***PH:*** 1-850-671-0300; ***Fax:*** 1-850-878-9150; ***http://*** www.ccbg.com

General - Incorporation	FL	***Stock***- Price on:12/24/2007	$32.0001
Employees	1,056	Stock Exchange	NDQ
Auditor	KPMG LLP	Ticker Symbol	CCBG
Stk Agt	American Stock Transfer & Trust Co.	Outstanding Shares	18,290,000
Counsel	Ausley & Mcmullen	E.P.S	$1.76
DUNS No.	11-974-9604	Shareholders	NA

Business: The group's principal activity is to provide commercial and retail banking business. This includes accepting demand, savings and time deposits, extending credit, originating residential mortgage loans and providing data processing services, asset management services, trust services, retail brokerage

services. It also provides financial services to corporate and individual customers, governmental entities and correspondent banks. The trust services include asset management for individuals and personal investment management. Brokerage services offer a full line of retail securities products such as stocks, mutual funds, annuities and long-term health care. On 25-Mar-2004, the group acquired quincy state bank.

Primary SIC and add'l.: 6021 6712

CIK No: 0000726601

Subsidiaries: Capital City Bank, Capital City Securities, Inc., Capital City Services Company, Capital City Trust Company, CCBG Capital Trust I, CCBG Capital Trust II, First Insurance Agency of Grady County, Inc, FNB Financial Services, Inc, Southern Oaks, Inc.

Officers: William G. Smith/Chmn., CEO, Pres./$934,199.00, Cynthia Pyburn/Exec. VP, Pres. - Capital City Services Company, Randolph M. Pople/Pres. - Capital City Trust Company, Edwin N. West/Exec. VP - Sales Leadership, Kimbrough J. Davis/CFO, Exec. VP/$478,471.00, Beth Corum/Exec. VP, Chief People Officer, Bill Moor/Pres. - Capital City Banc Investments, Karen H. Love/Exec. VP - Residential Lending, William D. Colledge/Exec. VP - Metrocommunity Banking, Edward G. Canup/Exec. VP - Commercial Real Estate Lending, Mitchell R. Englert/Exec. VP - Community Banking, Dale A. Thompson/Exec. VP - Credit Administration, Randolph K. Briley/Exec. VP - Corporate, Professional Banking, Thomas A. Barron/Pres. - Capital City Bank/$587,470.00, Flecia Braswell/Exec. VP, Chief Brand Officer

Directors: William G. Smith/Chmn., CEO, Pres.

Owners: DuBose Ausley/3.84%, Private Capital Management, L.P./5.41%, Kimbrough J. Davis, Robert H. Smith/16.84%, Lina S. Knox, Frederick Carroll, Henry Lewis, Cader B. Cox/2.18%, Everitt J. Drew, Ruth A. Knox, Insiders/30.65%, Thomas A. Barron/1.62%, William G. Smith/18.25%, John K. Humphress/2.78%, McGrath L. Keen/3.13%

Financial Data: Fiscal Year End: 12/31 **Latest Annual Data:** 12/31/2006

Year	Sales	Net Income
2006	$221,474,000	$33,265,000
2005	$189,251,000	$30,281,000
2004	$152,078,000	$29,371,000

Curr. Assets:	$177,564,000	Curr. Liab.:	$2,146,677,000	P/E Ratio:	18.08
Plant, Equip.:	$86,538,000	Total Liab.:	$2,282,140,000	Indic. Yr. Divd.:	$0.700
Total Assets:	$2,597,910,000	Net Worth:	$315,770,000	Debt/ Equity:	0.3406

Capital Corp of the West

550 W Main, Merced, CA, 95340; **PH:** 1-209-725-2269; **Fax:** 1-209-725-4550; **http://** www.ccow.com

General - Incorporation	CA	Stock - Price on:12/24/2007	$24.46
Employees	421	Stock Exchange	NDQ
Auditor	KPMG LLP	Ticker Symbol	CCOW
Stk Agt	LaRea Crespi	Outstanding Shares	10,780,000
Counsel	NA	E.P.S.	NA
DUNS No.	93-366-7230	Shareholders	NA

Business: The group's principal activity is to provide full range of commercial banking services to individual and business customers. The group accepts demand, savings and time deposits and offers commercial, agriculture, real estate, personal, home improvement, home mortgage, automobile, credit card and other installment and term loans. Other services include travelers' checks, safe deposit boxes, banking-by-mail, drive-up facilities and automated teller machines. In addition, the group invests in us government securities, mortgage-backed securities, collateralized mortgage obligations, corporate bonds and municipal bonds. The group has sixteen full service branches located in fresno, madera, mariposa, merced, san francisco, san joaquin, stanislaus, tulare and tuolomne counties of California.

Primary SIC and add'l.: 6712 6022

CIK No: 0001004740

Subsidiaries: Capital West Group, Inc., County Asset Advisors, Inc., County Bank, County Investment Trust, County Statutory Trust I, County Statutory Trust II, Merced Area Investment and Development, Inc.

Officers: Thomas T. Hawker/Dir., CEO/$863,637.00, Dale R. McKinney/Contact - Investor Relations, Ed J. Rocha/Pres., COO - County Bank/$514,214.00, John Incandela/Exec. VP, Chief Credit Officer - County Bank/$343,657.00, David A. Heaberlin/Exec. VP, Treasurer, CFO - County Bank/$326,837.00, Katherine Wohlford/Exec. VP, Chief Administrative Officer - County Bank/$343,162.00, Richard De La Pena/Exec. VP, General Counsel, Denise Butler/Corp. Sec., David A. Curtis/56/Controller, Acting CFO/$129,176.00

Directors: Thomas T. Hawker/Dir., CEO, John Fawcett/Vice Chmn., Jerry Callister/Chmn., Curtis Grant/Dir., Michael Graves/Dir., David Bonnar/Dir., Curtis Riggs/Dir., Gerald Tahajian/Dir., Dorothy Bizzini/Dir., Tom Van Groningen/73/Dir., Donald T. Briggs/Dir., Katherine L. Albiani/Dir.

Owners: Cramer Rosenthal McGlynn/6.01%, Banc Funds Company, L.L.C/6.60%, Wellington Management Company, LLP/7.10%, 1867 Western Financial Corporation/11.50%

Financial Data: Fiscal Year End: 12/31 **Latest Annual Data:** 12/31/2006

Year	Sales	Net Income
2006	$134,287,000	$22,676,000
2005	$100,366,000	$20,954,000
2004	$76,976,000	$12,323,000

Curr. Assets:	$205,702,000	Curr. Liab.:	$1,630,302,000		
Plant, Equip.:	$42,320,000	Total Liab.:	$1,813,959,000	Indic. Yr. Divd.:	NA
Total Assets:	$1,961,539,000	Net Worth:	$147,580,000	Debt/ Equity:	1.0371

Capital Crossing Preferred Corp

101 Summer St. , Boston, MA, 02110; **PH:** 1-617-880-1000; **http://** www.capitalcrossing.com

General - Incorporation	MA	Stock - Price on:12/24/2007	NA
Employees	18	Stock Exchange	NDQ
Auditor	KPMG LLP	Ticker Symbol	CCPCN
Stk Agt	NA	Outstanding Shares	NA
Counsel	Goodwin, Procter & Hoar	E.P.S.	NA
DUNS No.	18-415-5232	Shareholders	NA

Business: The group's principal activities are to provide a variety of financial services primarily purchasing and originating loans and leases. The group operates through its wholly owned subsidiary capital crossing bank. The deposits accepted by the group include certificates of deposit, money market accounts and borrowed funds. The lending activities include originating commercial real estate, multi-family and one-to-four family residential real estate loans, and secured commercial loans. It offers

commercial lending and leasing services to business customers through multiple delivery channels, including the Internet and personal bankers. The group also provides lease financing, which consists of leasing small-ticket business equipment to small business and individuals. The group conducts its business through its executive office in Boston and a branch in chestnut hill, Massachusetts

Primary SIC and add'l.: 6712 6022 6798

CIK No: 0001072806

Subsidiaries: Dolphin Capital Corp.

Officers: Nicholas W. Lazares/56/Chmn., Co - CEO, Richard Wayne/55/Dir., Co - CEO, Pres., Bradley M. Shron/51/VP, Clerk, Edward F. Mehm/43/Dir., VP, Treasurer, Principal Financial Officer, Nancy E. Coyle/Chief Accounting Officer, Controller

Directors: Nicholas W. Lazares/56/Chmn., Co - CEO, Richard Wayne/55/Dir., Co - CEO, Pres., Edward F. Mehm/43/Dir., VP, Treasurer, Principal Financial Officer, John Lapidus/51/Dir., Kirk Sykes/49/Dir., Jeffrey Ross/63/Dir.

Owners: Nicholas W. Lazares, John Lapidus, John Lapidus, Edward F. Mehm, Insiders, Insiders, Capital Crossing Bank/96.10%, Richard Wayne, Nicholas W. Lazares, Capital Crossing Bank/100.00%, Richard Wayne, Insiders

Capital Gold Corp

76 BeAve.r St., 26th Fl., New York, NY, 10005; **PH:** 1-212-344-2785; **Fax:** 1-212-344-4537; **http://** www.capitalgoldcorp.com; **Email:** info@capitalgoldcorp.com

General - Incorporation	NV	Stock - Price on:12/24/2007	$0.405
Employees	18	Stock Exchange	OTC
Auditor	Wolinetz, Lafazan & Co. P.C	Ticker Symbol	CGLD
Stk Agt	American Stock Transfer & Trust Co.	Outstanding Shares	165,630,000
Counsel	Richard Feiner	E.P.S.	NA
DUNS No.	15-771-2027	Shareholders	NA

Business: The group's principle activity is to explore gold and other minerals from its properties. The group owns rights to property located in the California mining district, lake county, Colorado and in the state of sonora, Mexico. The group's mining activities are substantially performed in Mexico. the group's quarterly revenue for October 2007 was 6.53 millions of USD.

Primary SIC and add'l.: 1099

CIK No: 0000726845

Subsidiaries: Leadville Mining & Milling Holding Corp., Minera Santa Rita S. de R.L. de C.V., Oro de Altar S. de R. L. de C.V.

Officers: Gifford A. Dieterle/Chmn., CEO, Pres., Treasurer, Scott Hazlitt/VP - Mine Development, Robert Roningen/Dir., Sr. VP, Jeffrey W. Pritchard/Dir., VP - Investor Relations, Sec., Randy Hubbard/Legal Counsel, Richard Feiner/Legal Counsel, Josephine Scott/Assist. to Pres., Christopher M. Chipman/CFO, John Brownlie/Dir., COO

Directors: Gifford A. Dieterle/Chmn., CEO, Pres., Treasurer, Jeffrey W. Pritchard/Dir., VP - Investor Relations, Sec., Roger A. Newell/Dir., Robert Roningen/Dir., Sr. VP, John Brownlie/Dir., COO, Ian A. Shaw/Dir., John Postle/Dir., Mark T. Nesbitt/Dir.

Owners: Standard Bank PLC/8.40%, Roger A. Newell, Jeffrey W. Pritchard, Scott Hazlitt, Strategic Precious Metal Fund/7.10%, Ian A. Shaw, Gifford A. Dieterle/1.60%, Robert Roningen/1.00%, Christopher Chipman, John Brownlie, Mark T. Nesbitt, Van Eck International Investors/5.70%, SPGP/6.50%, John Postle, Insiders/5.70%

Curr. Assets:	$7,647,000	Curr. Liab.:	$616,000		
Plant, Equip.:	$1,036,000	Total Liab.:	$616,000	Indic. Yr. Divd.:	NA
Total Assets:	$9,546,000	Net Worth:	$8,930,000	Debt/ Equity:	0.7916

Capital Growth Systems Inc

50 E Commerce Dr., Ste. A, Aschaumburg, IL, 60173; **PH:** 1-630-872-5800

General - Incorporation		Stock - Price on:12/24/2007	$0.65
Employees	150	Stock Exchange	OTC
Auditor	NA	Ticker Symbol	CGSY
Stk Agt	NA	Outstanding Shares	21,710,000
Counsel	NA	E.P.S.	-$2.17
DUNS No.	NA	Shareholders	NA

Business: The groups principle activity is to provide recruiting services. The groups service area includes the research and development, engineering, marketing, sales, information technology and manufacturing industries. The group operates from United States.

Primary SIC and add'l.: 6141

CIK No: 0001384265

Financial Data: Fiscal Year End: NA **Latest Annual Data:** 12/31/2006

Year	Sales	Net Income
2006	$14,821,000	-$11,580,000

Curr. Assets:	$5,742,000	Curr. Liab.:	$34,013,000		
Plant, Equip.:	$4,750,000	Total Liab.:	$35,473,000	Indic. Yr. Divd.:	NA
Total Assets:	$37,381,000	Net Worth:	$1,908,000	Debt/ Equity:	0.1799

Capital Hill Gold Inc

Ste. 508 Huan Tai Plz., No. A12, Zhong Guan Cun S St., Haidian District, Beijing; **PH:** 86-10851-89080

General - Incorporation	FL	Stock - Price on:12/24/2007	NA
Employees	21,000	Stock Exchange	NA
Auditor	Jimmy C.H. Cheung & Co	Ticker Symbol	NA
Stk Agt	Standard Registrar & Transfer Co Inc.	Outstanding Shares	NA
Counsel	NA	E.P.S.	-$0.01
DUNS No.	NA	Shareholders	NA

Business: The groups principle activities include developing and exploring gold properties. The groups name has been changed to Amerimine resources Inc. in September 2007. The group operates from United States.

Primary SIC and add'l.: NA

CIK No: 0001075861

Subsidiaries: CAGI Transition, Inc

Officers: Christian Lillieroos/48/Dir., CEO, CFO, Pres., Charlie Peng/CEO, Lin Bi/CEO, Pingshan Guo/53/Sr. VP - China Affairs, Dir., Daniel Enright/Pres., Arthur Garrison/Pres.

Directors: Christian Lillieroos/48/Dir., CEO, CFO, Pres., Zhenkai Jiang/44/Chmn., Pingshan Guo/53/Sr. VP - China Affairs, Dir., Rodger Spainhower/63/Dir.

Owners: Christian Lillieroos/2.20%, Sure Form Investments/35.20%, Guo Pingshan/1.40%, Insiders/37.60%

Financial Data: Fiscal Year End:12/31   Latest Annual Data: 12/31/2006

Year	Sales	Net Income
2006	$3,034,000	-$1,790,000
2005	NA	-$364,000
2004	NA	-$481,000

Curr. Assets:	$3,245,000	Curr. Liab.:	$4,008,000		
Plant, Equip.:	$216,000	Total Liab.:	$4,360,000	Indic. Yr. Divd.:	NA
Total Assets:	$3,461,000	Net Worth:	-$898,000	Debt/ Equity:	NA

Capital Mineral Investors Inc

101 Convention Centre Dr., Ste. 700, Las Vegas, NV, 89109; **PH:** 1-702-284-5848

General - Incorporation	NA	Stock - Price on:12/24/2007	NA
Employees	NA	Stock Exchange	OTC
Auditor	NA	Ticker Symbol	CMIV
Stk Agt.	NA	Outstanding Shares	NA
Counsel	NA	E.P.S.	-$0.03
DUNS No.	NA	Shareholders	NA

Business: The groups principle activity is to provide recruiting services. The groups service area includes the research and development, engineering, marketing, sales, information technology and manufacturing industries. The group operates from United States.

Primary SIC and add'l.: 1400

CIK No:

Officers: Jerry Dibble/63/Dir., CEO, CFO, Pres., Principal Accounting Officer

Directors: Jerry Dibble/63/Dir., CEO, CFO, Pres., Principal Accounting Officer

Owners: Insiders/37.51%, Jerry Dibble/34.63%, Gary Benson/2.88%

Financial Data: Fiscal Year End:NA   Latest Annual Data: 12/31/2006

Year	Sales	Net Income
2006	NA	-$236,000
2005	NA	-$40,000

Curr. Assets:	$2,000	Curr. Liab.:	$89,000		
Plant, Equip.:	$4,000	Total Liab.:	$89,000	Indic. Yr. Divd.:	NA
Total Assets:	$6,000	Net Worth:	-$83,000	Debt/ Equity:	NA

Capital One Financial Corp

1680 Capital One Dr., McLean, VA, 22102; **PH:** 1-703-720-1000; **Fax:** 1-804-284-5728; http:// www.capitalone.com

General - Incorporation	DE	Stock - Price on:12/24/2007	$80.9
Employees	31,800	Stock Exchange	NYSE
Auditor	Ernst & Young LLP	Ticker Symbol	COF
Stk Agt.	Computershare Trust Co	Outstanding Shares	415,590,000
Counsel	NA	E.P.S.	$6.58
DUNS No.	87-818-5453	Shareholders	NA

Business: The groups principle activity is to provide banking services. The groups services include credit card, auto, personnel, home loans and health care finance. The group operates through four segments namely U.S. card, auto finance, global financial services and banking. In the year 2006, the group acquired North Fork Bancorporation, Inc. The group operates from United States.

Primary SIC and add'l.: 6035 7389 6719

CIK No: 0000927628

Subsidiaries: Capital One Auto Finance, Inc., Capital One Bank, Capital One, F.S.B., Hibernia National Bank

Officers: Richard D. Fairbank/Chmn., CEO, Founder./$37,438,700.00, Jory Berson/37/Pres. - US Card, Spencer Gagnet/Contact - Debt Capital Markets, Stephanie F. Tyner/Contact - Hedge Strategy, Peter A. Schnall/44/Chief Risk Officer, Matthew W. Schuyler/42/Chief Human Resources Officer, Gregor S. Bailar/44/CIO/$4,522,681.00, Larry Klane/Exec. VP - Global Financial Services, United Kingdom, Laura K. Watts/Contact - Loan Syndications, David R. Reid/Contact - Energy, Tim Guillory/Mgr. - Commercial Real Estate Lending, Texas, Gary L. Perlin/60/CFO/$5,577,426.00, John G. Finneran/58/General Counsel, Corp. Sec./$9,458,792.00, Katherine Carlson/Sr. Dir., Head - Enterprise Risk Management, Europe *(33 Officers included in Index)*

Directors: Richard D. Fairbank/Chmn., CEO, Founder., John A. Kanas/61/Dir., Pres. - Banking, E. R. Campbell/67/Dir., Ronald W. Dietz/65/Dir., Patrick W. Gross/63/Dir., Ann F. Hackett/54/Dir., Lewis Hay/52/Dir., Pierre E. Leroy/59/Dir., Mayo A. Shattuck/53/Dir., Stanley Westreich/71/Dir., Adam Broadbent/Non - Exec. Dir., Tim Jones/Non - Exec. Dir.

Owners: Insiders/2.94%, Dodge & Cox/5.80%, Gary L. Perlin, John A. Kanas, Patrick W. Gross, Mayo A. Shattuck, Pierre E. Leroy, Gregor S. Bailar, Ann Fritz Hackett, Ronald W. Dietz, Stanley Westreich, John G. Finneran, Richard D. Fairbank/2.04%, Herbert J. Boydstun, David R. Lawson *(17 Owners included in Index)*

Financial Data: Fiscal Year End:12/31   Latest Annual Data: 12/31/2006

Year	Sales	Net Income
2006	$15,190,961,000	$2,414,493,000
2005	$12,084,986,000	$1,809,147,000
2004	$10,694,577,000	$1,543,482,000

Curr. Assets:	$5,476,922,000	Curr. Liab.:	$86,345,655,000	P/E Ratio:	12.29
Plant, Equip.:	$2,203,280,000	Total Liab.:	$124,504,079,000	Indic. Yr. Divd.:	$0.110
Total Assets:	$149,739,285,000	Net Worth:	$25,235,206,000	Debt/ Equity:	1.1406

Capital Pacific Bank

805SW Bordway, Ste. 780, Portland, OR, 97205; **PH:** 1-503-796-0100; http:// www.capitalpacificbank.com

General - Incorporation		Stock - Price on:12/24/2007	NA
Employees	NA	Stock Exchange	OTC
Auditor	NA	Ticker Symbol	CPBO
Stk Agt.	NA	Outstanding Shares	NA
Counsel	NA	E.P.S.	NA
DUNS No.	NA	Shareholders	NA

Business: The groups principal activities include providing banking by offering personalized services of a community bank along with the convenience and security. Services of the group include community banking, free checking, savings account, Loans and Mortgages and financial calculations, credit cards, debit cards, housing loan and personal loans. The group operates from the United States.

Primary SIC and add'l.: 6029

CIK No:

Officers: Mark Stevenson/Dir., CEO, Robert Krueger/Dir., Pres., Felice Belfiore/CFO - Investor Inquires, Harlan Barcus/Chief Credit Officer, Tyson Smith/CIO, Robert Countryman/Exec. VP - Business Development - Client Service

Directors: Mark Stevenson/Dir., CEO, Thomas Tomjack/Chmn., Richard Alexander/Vice Chmn., Robert Krueger/Dir., Pres., Frances Matson/Dir., Stephen Mitchell/Dir., Werner G. Nistler/Dir., Ronald Shellan/Dir., Karen Whitman/Dir.

Capital Properties Inc

100 Dexter Rd., East Providence, RI, 02914; **PH:** 1-401-435-7171; **Fax:** 1-401-435-7179; http://www.stepan.com

General - Incorporation	RI	Stock - Price on:12/24/2007	$22.8
Employees	10	Stock Exchange	AMEX
Auditor	Lefkowitz, Champi & DeRienzo P.C	Ticker Symbol	CPI
Stk Agt.	Computershare Investor Services LLC	Outstanding Shares	3,300,000
Counsel	Mayer Brown Rowe & Maw LLP	E.P.S.	$0.49
DUNS No.	01-292-4254	Shareholders	NA

Business: The group's principle activities are to own, lease and operate real estate properties and petroleum storage facilities. The group's operations are conducted through two business segments: leasing and petroleum facilities. The group owns approximately 18 acres of land in the capital center project area in downtown providence, Rhode Island which it leases or is holding for lease to third parties. The group also owns a 330-car parking garage adjacent to a rail passenger station in downtown providence, Rhode Island, together with the underlying land, which is leased under a short-term cancelable lease to a firm experienced in parking operations. The group through its subsidiary, owns a 524,500 barrel petroleum storage facility and operates the petroleum facilities under a five-year agreement with a petroleum distribution company at a fixed monthly rate. The group's quarterly revenue for September 2007 was 1.56 millions of USD.

Primary SIC and add'l.: 4226 6519

CIK No: 0000202947

Subsidiaries: Capital Terminal Company, Dunellen, LLC, Tri-State Displays, Inc.

Officers: Robert H. Eder/75/Chmn., CEO/$229,000.00, Avery L. Noe/64/Pres. - Capital Terminal Company/$151,844.00, Barbara J. Dreyer/79/Treasurer/$166,625.00, Ronald P. Chrzanowski/65/Dir., Pres./$188,125.00, Stephen J. Carlotti/Sec.

Directors: Robert H. Eder/75/Chmn., CEO, Ronald P. Chrzanowski/65/Dir., Pres., Alfred J. Corso/71/Dir., Roy J. Nirschel/55/Dir., Harris N. Rosen/75/Dir.

Owners: Roy J. Nirschel, Harris N. Rosen, Alfred J. Corso, Lance S. Gad/5.80%, Ronald P. Chrzanowski, Robert H. Eder/52.30%, Insiders/52.80%, Barbara J. Dreyer, Avery L. Noe

Financial Data: Fiscal Year End:12/31   Latest Annual Data: 12/31/2006

Year	Sales	Net Income
2006	$5,789,000	$1,319,000
2005	$6,463,000	$1,663,000
2004	$7,075,000	$1,561,000

Curr. Assets:	$3,036,000	Curr. Liab.:	$535,000	P/E Ratio:	46.53
Plant, Equip.:	$18,471,000	Total Liab.:	$5,841,000	Indic. Yr. Divd.:	$0.240
Total Assets:	$21,858,000	Net Worth:	$16,017,000	Debt/ Equity:	NA

Capital Reserve Canada Ltd

4304-74 Ave., Edmonton, AB, T6B 2K3; **PH:** 1-780-428-6026; http:// capitalreservecanada.com

General - Incorporation	AB	Stock - Price on:12/24/2007	$0.16
Employees	NA	Stock Exchange	OTC
Auditor	Child, Van Wagoner & Bradshaw, PLLC	Ticker Symbol	CRSVF
Stk Agt.	NA	Outstanding Shares	NA
Counsel	NA	E.P.S.	NA
DUNS No.	NA	Shareholders	NA

Business: The groups principal activity is to explore minerals and natural gas. In the year 2005, the group acquired of KCP Innovative Services Inc. The group operates from the United States and Canada.

Primary SIC and add'l.: 1382

CIK No: 0001230622

Subsidiaries: Capital Reserve Canada Projects Ltd., KCP Innovative Services Inc, Two Hills Environmental Inc.

Officers: Ken Pearson/57/Dir., CEO, Pres., Rocky Rombs/Dir., Pres. - Two Hills

Directors: Ken Pearson/57/Dir., CEO, Pres., Donald Getty/Chmn., Rocky Rombs/Dir., Pres. - Two Hills

Owners: Robert Hawkes, Rocky Rombs, Insiders/17.00%, Ken Pearson/13.40%, Donald Getty/2.40%

Financial Data: Fiscal Year End:12/31   Latest Annual Data: 12/31/2006

Year	Sales	Net Income
2006	$1,472,000	-$162,000
2005	$305,000	-$221,000

Curr. Assets:	$655,000	Curr. Liab.:	$385,000		
Plant, Equip.:	$5,211,000	Total Liab.:	$1,124,000	Indic. Yr. Divd.:	NA
Total Assets:	$6,117,000	Net Worth:	$4,993,000	Debt/ Equity:	NA

Capital Senior Living Corp

14160 Dallas Pkwy., Ste. 300, Dallas, TX, 75254; **PH:** 1-972-770-5600; **Fax:** 1-972-770-5666; http:// www.capitalsenior.com

Ste. 300, Dallas, TX, 75254; *PH:* 1-972-770-5600; *Fax:* 1-972-770-5666;
http:// www.capitalsenior.com

General - Incorporation	DE	**Stock** - Price on:12/24/2007	$7.28
Employees	1,914	Stock Exchange	NYSE
Auditor	KPMG LLP	Ticker Symbol	CSU
Stk Agt	Mellon Investor Services LLC	Outstanding Shares	26,460,000
Counsel	NA	E.P.S.	$0.15
DUNS No.	80-287-2028	Shareholders	NA

Business: The group's principal activity is ownership and operation of senior living communities. The services rendered by the group include senior living services, independent living services, assisted living, skilled nursing and home care services. These services include offering daily meals, transportation, social and recreational activities, laundry, housekeeping, and 24-hour staffing, ambulation, bathing, dressing, eating, grooming, personal hygiene, and monitoring or assistance with medications. As on 31-Dec-2003, the group operated 42 senior living communities in 20 states throughout the United States serving 6,900 residents. On 23-Aug-2004, the group acquired cgi management inc.

Primary SIC and add'l.: 8361 8059 8051

CIK No: 0001043000

Subsidiaries: Capital Senior Development, Inc., Capital Senior East Lansing, LLC, Capital Senior Living A, Inc., Capital Senior Living Acquisition, LLC, Capital Senior Living ILM-B, Inc., Capital Senior Living ILM-C, Inc., Capital Senior Living P-B, Inc., Capital Senior Living P-C, Inc., Capital Senior Living Properties 2 NHPT, Inc., Capital Senior Living Properties 2 Gramercy, Inc., Capital Senior Living Properties 2 Veranda Club, Inc., Capital Senior Living Properties 2, Atrium of Carmichael, Inc., Capital Senior Living Properties 2, Crossword Oaks, Inc., Capital Senior Living Properties 2, Heatherwood, Inc., Capital Senior Living Properties 2, Tesson Heights, Inc. 37 Subsidiaries included in the Index

Officers: Lawrence A. Cohen/CEO/$822,229.00, James A. Stroud/Chmn., Sec./$516,332.00, Keith N. Johannessen/COO, Pres./$532,317.00, Ralph A. Beattie/CFO, Exec. VP/$422,729.00, David R. Brickman/49/VP, General Counsel/$263,660.00, Rob L. Goodpaster/58/Exec. VP, David W. Beathard/60/VP - Operations, Glen H. Campbell/63/VP - Development, Gloria Holland/40/VP - Finance, Jerry D. Lee/47/Corporate Controller, Robert F. Hollister/52/Property Controller

Directors: James A. Stroud/Chmn., Sec., Victor W. Nee/72/Dir., Jill M. Krueger/49/Dir., James A. Moore/73/Dir., Craig F. Hartberg/71/Dir.

Financial Data: Fiscal Year End:12/31 **Latest Annual Data:** 12/31/2006

Year	Sales		Net Income
2006	$159,070,000		-$2,600,000
2005	$105,230,000		-$5,354,000
2004	$93,262,000		-$6,758,000
Curr. Assets:	$43,091,000	**Curr. Liab.:** $27,684,000	**P/E Ratio:** 72.80
Plant, Equip.:	$313,569,000	**Total Liab.:** $250,404,000	**Indic. Yr. Divd.:** NA
Total Assets:	$394,488,000	**Net Worth:** $144,084,000	**Debt/ Equity:** 1.3375

Capital Solutions Inc

527 Marquette Ave. S, 17th Fl. Rand Tower, Minneapolis, MN, 55402; *PH:* 1-612-2303100; *Fax:* 1-612-230-3101; *http://* www.capitalsolutionsmn.com

General - Incorporation	DE	**Stock** - Price on:12/24/2007	$1.03
Employees	2	Stock Exchange	OTC
Auditor	Bagell, Levine & Company, LLC	Ticker Symbol	CSNI
Stk Agt	First Global Stock Transfer LLC	Outstanding Shares	NA
Counsel	NA	E.P.S.	NA
DUNS No.	NA	Shareholders	NA

Business: The group's principle activity is to provide learning management and learning content management software and services for corporations, not-for-profit organizations, and educational institutions. The group operates from United States.

Primary SIC and add'l.: 8742

CIK No: 0000061500

Subsidiaries: Bedrock Holdings Corporation, Inc.

Officers: Christopher Astrom/37/CEO, Pres., CFO, Jon D. Goetze/MD, Wilfred F. Becker/MD, Amir A. Berenjian/Analyst, Paul J. Halverson/MD, Deen C. Hubin/Office Mgr., Carrie M. Korf/Analyst, Steven J. Nelson/MD, Christine E. Powell/Analyst, Matthew R. Schubring/Sr. Analyst, Kurri F. Sewich/Industry Research Specialist, Joseph J. Skorczewski/Analyst, Christopher M. Staloch/MD, Dominique A. Staloch/Sr. Analyst, Barbara J. Swenson/Administrative Assist. - Analyst (17 Officers included in Index)

Directors: Richard Astrom/61/Dir.

Owners: Insiders/74.93%, Christopher Astrom/29.97%, Damian Guthrie/6.90%, Richard Astrom/44.96%

Curr. Assets:	$0	**Curr. Liab.:**	$29,000		
Plant, Equip.:	NA	**Total Liab.:**	$29,000	**Indic. Yr. Divd.:**	NA
Total Assets:	$0	**Net Worth:**	-$29,000	**Debt/ Equity:**	NA

Capital Southwest Corp

12900 Preston Rd., Ste. 700, Dallas, TX, 75230; *PH:* 1-972-233-8242; *Fax:* 1-972-233-7362; *http://* www.capitalsouthwest.com; *Email:* cscinfo@capitalsouthwest.com

General - Incorporation	TX	**Stock** - Price on:12/24/2007	$161.7
Employees	7	Stock Exchange	NDQ
Auditor	Grant Thornton LLP	Ticker Symbol	CSWC
Stk Agt	American Stock Transfer & Trust Co.	Outstanding Shares	3,890,000
Counsel	NA	E.P.S.	$33.73
DUNS No.	00-792-5670	Shareholders	NA

Business: The group's principal activity is that of a venture capital investor. The objective of the group is to achieve capital appreciation through long-term investments in businesses having growth potential. The investments consist of early-stage financing, expansion financing, management buyouts and recapitalizations and are made in various industry segments. As of 31-Mar-2004, twelve major investments consisted of the ones in palm harbor homes inc, the rectorseal corporation, skylawn corporation, alamo group inc, encore wire corporation, media recovery, inc, the whitmore manufacturing company, all components, inc., liberty media corporation, petsmart inc and ampro mortgage corporation. The group's portfolio includes major interests as well as marketable securities of these publicly owned companies. In addition to capital investments, the group also provides managerial assistance critical in business development activities to the companies in which it invests.

Primary SIC and add'l.: 6799 6282

CIK No: 0000017313

Subsidiaries: Balco, Inc., Humac Company, Lifemark Group, The RectorSeal Corporation, The Whitmore Manufacturing Company

Officers: William R. Thomas/Chmn., CEO/$281,417.00, Gary L. Martin/Dir., VP/$442,255.00, William M. Ashbaugh/Sr. VP/$393,447.00, Jeffrey G. Peterson/VP/$238,162.00, Tracy L. Morris/Controller

Directors: William R. Thomas/Chmn., CEO, Gary L. Martin/Dir., VP, Donald W. Burton/64/Dir., Graeme W. Henderson/74/Dir., Samuel B. Ligon/69/Dir., John H. Wilson/65/Dir.

Owners: Samuel B. Ligon, Patrick F. Hamner/1.40%, Graeme W. Henderson, William R. Thomas/17.20%, Susan K. Hodgson, First Manhattan Company/6.40%, Insiders/21.90%, Donald W. Burton, John H. Wilson, Gary L. Martin/4.60%, Jeffrey G. Peterson, William M. Ashbaugh/2.30%

Financial Data: Fiscal Year End:03/31 **Latest Annual Data:** 3/31/2007

Year	Sales		Net Income
2007	$119,650,000		$116,911,000
2006	$98,640,000		$96,190,000
2005	$22,738,000		$14,225,000
Curr. Assets:	$39,182,000	**Curr. Liab.:** $231,000	**P/E Ratio:** 5.37
Plant, Equip.:	NA	**Total Liab.:** $215,164,000	**Indic. Yr. Divd.:** $0.400
Total Assets:	$729,507,000	**Net Worth:** $514,344,000	**Debt/ Equity:** NA

Capital Title Group Inc

14648 N Scottsdale Rd., Ste. 125, Scottsdale, AZ, 85254; *PH:* 1-480-624-4200; *http://* www.capitaltitlegroup.com

General - Incorporation	DE	**Stock** - Price on:12/24/2007	$106.02
Employees	13,500	Stock Exchange	NA
Auditor	KPMG LLP	Ticker Symbol	NA
Stk Agt	Continental Stock Transfer & Trust Co	Outstanding Shares	17,110,000
Counsel	Dale A. Head	E.P.S.	$1.54
DUNS No.	94-869-0839	Shareholders	NA

Business: The group's principal activity is to provide escrow services and issue title insurance policies for the real estate industry. In addition, the group is an agent for first American title insurance company, old republic insurance company, stewart information services corporation, fidelity national title and landamerica. The group operates through capital title agency, inc in Arizona, new century title company, national holding group, first California title, united title company and united title insurance company in California and land title of Nevada, inc in Nevada. As of 31-Dec-2003, the group had 120 offices in Arizona, California and Nevada. The group acquired land title of Nevada, inc in jan-2003. On 03-May-2004, the group acquired nationwide appraisal services inc.

Primary SIC and add'l.: 6361 6411 6719

CIK No: 0001017158

Subsidiaries: 1031 Exchangepoint, Inc., AdvantageWare, Inc., Capital Information Services, Inc., Capital Title Agency, Inc., Capital Title Building Company, CTG Real Estate Information Services, Inc., First California Title Company, Land Title of Nevada, Inc., NAC1031 Exchange Services, Inc., Nations Holding Group, Nationwide Appraisal and Title Company of Ohio, Inc., Nationwide Appraisal Services Corporation, Nationwide TotalFlood Services, Inc., New Century Holding Company, New Century Title Company 23 Subsidiaries included in the Index

Officers: Donald R. Head/70/Chmn., CEO, Pres., Mark C. Walker/48/Exec. VP, CFO, COO, Sec., Treasurer, Doug J. Langston/Dir. - Finance, Dale A. Head/GM - Legal Department, James C. Yeager/Corporate Controller

Directors: Donald R. Head/70/Chmn., CEO, Pres., David C. Dewar/46/Dir., Ben T. Morris/62/Dir., Terry S. Jacobs/66/Dir., Theo F. Lamb/65/Dir., Robert B. Liverant/79/Dir., Stephen A. McConnell/55/Dir.

Financial Data: Fiscal Year End:12/31 **Latest Annual Data:** 12/31/2006

Year	Sales		Net Income
2006	$4,015,900,000		$98,800,000
2005	$3,959,600,000		$165,600,000
2004	$3,522,100,000		$146,300,000
Curr. Assets:	$755,700,000	**Curr. Liab.:** $1,018,200,000	
Plant, Equip.:	$164,200,000	**Total Liab.:** $2,779,000,000	**Indic. Yr. Divd.:** $1.200
Total Assets:	$4,174,800,000	**Net Worth:** $1,395,800,000	**Debt/ Equity:** 0.4200

Capital Trust Inc

410 Pk. Ave., 14th Fl., New York, NY, 10022; *PH:* 1-212-655-0220; *Fax:* 1-212-655-0044; *http://* www.capitaltrust.com

General - Incorporation	MD	**Stock** - Price on:12/24/2007	$41.05
Employees	29	Stock Exchange	NYSE
Auditor	Ernst & Young LLP	Ticker Symbol	CT
Stk Agt	American Stock Transfer & Trust Co.	Outstanding Shares	17,460,000
Counsel	NA	E.P.S.	$4.06
DUNS No.	NA	Shareholders	NA

Business: The group's principle activities are to provide structured capital solutions to owner or operators of commercial real estate. It is an investment management and real estate finance group that originates or acquires, for its own account and as investment manager for funds under management, loans and debt-related investments in various types of commercial real estate assets and operating companies. The group has designed and developed a fully integrated platform to provide flexible, value-added financing for large single properties, multiple-asset portfolios and real estate operating companies. The group's investment program emphasizes senior and junior mortgage loans, mezzanine loans secured by pledges of equity interests, and subordinated tranches of commercial mortgage backed securities. The group has been approved as a real estate investment trust by the internal revenue code of 1986. The group's quarterly revenue for September 2007 was 22.46 millions of USD.

Primary SIC and add'l.: 6798 6159 6282

CIK No: 0001061630

Subsidiaries: Capital Trust RE CDO 2004-1 Corp., Capital Trust RE CDO 2004-1 LTD, Capital Trust RE CDO 2005-1 LTD, Capital Trust RE CDO Depositor, Corp., CT BSI Funding Corp., Ct Cdo Iii Corp., Ct Cdo Iii Ltd., Ct Cdo Iii, LLC, CT Investment Management Co., LLC, CT LF Funding Corp., Ct Re Cdo 2004-1 Sub, LLC, Ct Re Cdo 2005-1 Corp., Ct Re Cdo 2005-1 Sub, LLC, Ct-f2-gp, LLC, Ct-f2-lp, LLC 17 Subsidiaries included in the Index

Officers: John R. Klopp/Dir., CEO, Pres./$3,998,018.00, Stephen D. Plavin/COO/$2,926,982.00, Geoffrey G. Jervis/CFO/$1,283,303.00, Matthew Shapiro/Investor Relation Officer, Jay Thailer/39/Dir. - Finance, Accounting

Directors: John R. Klopp/Dir., CEO, Pres., Samuel Zell/Chmn., Henry N. Nassau/Dir., Craig M. Hatkoff/Dir., Edward Hyman/Dir., Thomas E. Dobrowski/Dir., Lynne B. Sagalyn/Dir., Joshua A. Polan/Dir., Martin L. Edelman/Dir.

Owners: Craig M. Hatkoff/1.80%, W. R. Berkley Corporation/11.40%, Geoffrey G. Jervis, Samuel Zell, Martin L. Edelman, Edward S. Hyman, Lynne B. Sagalyn, Thomas C. Ruffing, Vornado Realty, L.P./8.10%, Neuberger Berman Inc./8.70%, Stephen D. Plavin/1.10%, Henry N. Nassau, Insiders/9.70%, John R. Klopp/4.80%, Veqtor Finance Company, L.L.C./5.10% *(16 Owners included in Index)*

Financial Data: **Fiscal Year End:**12/31 **Latest Annual Data:** 12/31/2006

Year	Sales	Net Income
2006	$76,558,000	$54,067,000
2005	$104,828,000	$44,111,000
2004	$57,209,000	$21,976,000

Curr. Assets:	$45,865,000	**Curr. Liab.:**	$742,505,000		
Plant, Equip.:	NA	**Total Liab.:**	$2,222,292,000	**Indic. Yr. Divd.:**	$3.200
Total Assets:	$2,648,564,000	**Net Worth:**	$426,272,000	**Debt/ Equity:**	3.1920

Capitalsource Inc

4445 Willard Ave., 12th Fl., Chevy Chase, MD, 20815; ***PH:*** 1-301-841-2700; ***Fax:*** 1-301-841-2340; ***http://*** www.capitalsource.com; ***Email:*** info@capitalsource.com

General - Incorporation	DE	**Stock**- Price on:12/24/2007	$25.12
Employees	548	Stock Exchange	NYSE
Auditor	Ernst & Young LLP	Ticker Symbol	CSE
Stk Agt	American Stock Transfer & Trust Co.	Outstanding Shares	189,300,000
Counsel	NA	E.P.S	$1.69
DUNS No.	NA	Shareholders	NA

Business: The group's principal activity is to provide loans to small and medium-sized businesses. The group offers a range of senior secured asset-based loans, first mortgage loans, senior-secured cash flow loans and mezzanine loans to its clients. The group finances under three major categories: corporate finance, healthcare finance and structured finance. Corporate finance provides debt financing to small and medium-sized businesses typically sponsored by private equity firms. Healthcare finance provides accounts receivable-based, short-term real estate, equipment and other financing to small and medium-sized businesses in the healthcare market. Structured finance provides debt financing to small and medium-sized businesses that require complex financing alternatives within our targeted sectors of lender finance and real estate. The group operates solely in the domestic market.on 07-Jul-2004, the group acquired cig international llc.

Primary SIC and add'l.: 6159

CIK No: 0001241199

Subsidiaries: Alexander Funding, LLC, Alpha Packaging Associates I, LLC, Boulder City LLC, CapitalSource Advisors LLC, CapitalSource Analytics LLC, CapitalSource Bank, CapitalSource Commercial Loan LLC, 2002-2, CapitalSource Commercial Loan LLC, 2003-1, CapitalSource Commercial Loan LLC, 2003-2, CapitalSource Commercial Loan LLC, 2004-1, CapitalSource Commercial Loan LLC, 2004-2, CapitalSource Commercial Loan LLC, 2005-1, CapitalSource Europe Limited, CapitalSource Finance II Inc., CapitalSource Finance LLC 48 Subsidiaries included in the Index

Officers: John K. Delaney/45/Chmn., CEO, Dean C. Graham/42/COO, Pres., Donald F. Cole/37/Chief Administrative Officer, Steven A. Museles/45/Exec. VP, Chief Legal Officer, Sec., Bryan M. Corsini/47/Chief Credit Officer, Daniel Duffy/47/Co - Pres. - Corporate Finance Business, Jeffrey S. Kilrea/47/Co - Pres., Chris J. Woods/57/CTO, Joe Kenary/Exec. VP - Corporate Lending, Thomas A. Fink/44/CFO, Michael C. Szwajkowski/41/Pres. - Structured Finance Business, James J. Pieczynski/45/Co - Head - Healthcare - Specialty Finance Business, Keith D. Reuben/41/Co - Head - Healthcare - Specialty Finance, David C. Bjarnason/38/Chief Accounting Officer

Directors: John K. Delaney/45/Chmn., CEO, Jason M. Fish/48/Vice Chmn., William G. Byrnes/55/Dir., William C. Hosler/45/Dir., Lawrence C. Nussdorf/61/Dir., Andrew B. Fremder/44/Dir., Timothy M. Hurd/36/Dir., Thomas F. Steyer/48/Dir., Sara L. Grootwassink/38/Dir., Frederick W. Eubank/41/Dir.

Owners: Farallon Partners, L.L.C./5.50%, Insiders/34.80%, Capital Research and Management Company/7.00%, Thomas A. Fink, John K. Delaney/5.10%, Farallon Capital Management, L.L.C./9.30%, Timothy M. Hurd/10.60%, Dean C. Graham, Michael C. Szwajkowski, Frederick W. Eubank, James J. Pieczynski, Thomas F. Steyer/14.80%, Andrew B. Fremder/14.80%, Madison Dearborn Partners III, L.P./10.60%, Sara L. Grootwassink *(20 Owners included in Index)*

Financial Data: **Fiscal Year End:**12/31 **Latest Annual Data:** 12/31/2006

Year	Sales	Net Income
2006	$1,255,088,000	$279,276,000
2005	$666,698,000	$164,672,000
2004	$418,438,000	$124,851,000

Curr. Assets:	$637,055,000	**Curr. Liab.:**	$3,510,768,000	**P/E Ratio:**	15.13
Plant, Equip.:	NA	**Total Liab.:**	$13,061,184,000	**Indic. Yr. Divd.:**	$2.400
Total Assets:	$15,210,574,000	**Net Worth:**	$2,093,040,000	**Debt/ Equity:**	4.4577

CapitalSouth Bancorp

2340 Woodcrest Pl., Ste. 200, Birmingham, AL, 35209; ***PH:*** 1-205-870-1939; ***Fax:*** 1-205-879-3885; ***http://*** www.capitalsouthbank.com

General - Incorporation	DE	**Stock**- Price on:12/24/2007	$15.9
Employees	124	Stock Exchange	NDQ
Auditor	KPMG LLP	Ticker Symbol	CAPB
Stk Agt	NA	Outstanding Shares	2,990,000
Counsel	NA	E.P.S	$1.05
DUNS No.	NA	Shareholders	NA

Business: The group operates through its subsidiaries whose principle activity is to provide commercial banking services. The groups services include Internet banking, direct deposit, ATMs, safe deposit boxes, United States savings bonds and automatic account transfers. In July 2005, the group acquired United Bank of the Gulf Coast. The group operates from Alabama, Atlanta, Georgia Jacksonville, Florida, Birmingham, Huntsville and Montgomery. The assets of the group for the year 2006 were $481,988,863.

Primary SIC and add'l.: 6022 6712

CIK No: 0001338977

Subsidiaries: BOA Mortgage Company LLC, CapitalSouth Bank, CapitalSouth Insurance, Inc., Financial Investors Statutory Trust I, Financial Investors Statutory Trust II, Security Mutual Financial

Officers: Dan W. Puckett/Chmn., CEO - Capitalsouth Bancorp, Charles K. McPherson/External Dir., John Bentley/Sr. VP, Birmingham City Pres., Fred H. Coble/Sr. VP, Jacksonville City Pres., James Cooper/Exec. VP, Chief Credit Officer, Carol Marsh/Sr. VP, CFO, Flake W. Oakley/Dir., Pres.

Directors: Dan W. Puckett/Chmn., CEO - Capitalsouth Bancorp, Bradford H. Dunn/Dir., Stanley L. Graves/External Dir., David W. Wood/External Dir., Flake W. Oakley/Dir., Pres.

Owners: Carol W. Marsh, Charles K. McPherson/3.39%, Dan W. Puckett/5.42%, Insiders/24.48%, David W. Wood/5.95%, Flake W. Oakley, John E. Bentley, Bradford H. Dunn/4.00%, Hot Creek Capital, L.L.C./5.20%, Fred Coble, James Cooper/1.08%, Stanley L. Graves/2.76%

Financial Data: **Fiscal Year End:**12/31 **Latest Annual Data:** 12/31/2006

Year	Sales	Net Income
2006	$34,381,000	$2,928,000
2005	$24,471,000	$2,577,000
2004	$17,270,000	$1,877,000

Curr. Assets:	$7,445,000	**Curr. Liab.:**	$422,430,000	**P/E Ratio:**	15.14
Plant, Equip.:	$10,649,000	**Total Liab.:**	$440,640,000	**Indic. Yr. Divd.:**	$0.240
Total Assets:	$481,989,000	**Net Worth:**	$41,348,000	**Debt/ Equity:**	0.3267

Capitol Bancorp Ltd

Capitol Bancorp Ctr., 200 Washington Sq. North, Lansing, MI, 48933; ***PH:*** 1-517-487-6555; ***Fax:*** 1-517-374-2576; ***http://*** www.capitolbancorp.com

General - Incorporation	MI	**Stock**- Price on:12/24/2007	$28.6699
Employees	1,354	Stock Exchange	NYSE
Auditor	BDO Seidman LLP	Ticker Symbol	CBC
Stk Agt	UMB Bank, N.A.	Outstanding Shares	17,080,000
Counsel	Strobl & Borda PC	E.P.S	NA
DUNS No.	36-452-2581	Shareholders	NA

Business: The group's principal activity is the provision of banking services to individuals, businesses and other customers through affiliates. A holding company for twenty nine banks located in eight states, the group offers commercial, real estate mortgage, installment loans and attracts checking, savings, money market, individual retirement accounts and certificate of deposits. In addition, the group also offers trust and investment services. The group is a member of the federal reserve system and its deposits are insured by the federal deposit insurance. On 01-Apr-2004, the group acquired first carolina state bank.

Primary SIC and add'l.: 6712 6021

CIK No: 0000840264

Subsidiaries: Amera Mortgage Corporation, Inc., Ann Arbor Commerce Bank, Arrowhead Community Bank, Bank of Auburn Hills, Bank of Belleville, Bank of Bellevue, Bank of Escondido, Bank of Las Vegas, Bank of Michigan, Bank of San Francisco, Bank of Santa Barbara, Bank of Tucson, Black Mountain Community Bank, Brighton Commerce Bank, Camelback Community Bank 57 Subsidiaries included in the Index

Officers: Joseph D. Reid/Chmn., CEO/$1,007,839.00, Robert R. Hogan/CEO, Pres. - Capitol Wealth, David D. Fortune/Chief Credit Officer, Lee W. Hendrickson/CFO/$509,778.00, John S. Lewis/Dir., Pres. - Western Regions/$487,995.00, Cristin K. Reid/Corporate Pres., Gregory R. Bixby/42/CIO, Michael M. Moran/Chief - Capital Markets, Investor Relations Contact, Stephen D. Todd/Chief - Bank Performance, Cristin K. Reid-English/Dir., COO/$415,737.00, David J. Dutton/57/CIO, Brian K. English/General Counsel, Bruce A. Thomas/Pres. - Eastern Regions/$405,743.00

Directors: Joseph D. Reid/Chmn., CEO, Michael L. Kasten/Vice Chmn., Robert C. Carr/Vice Chmn., Lyle W. Miller/Vice Chmn., Leonard Maas/Dir., David L. Becker/Dir., David O'Leary/Dir., Michael F. Hannley/Dir., John S. Lewis/Dir., Pres. - Western Regions, Douglas E. Crist/Dir., Kathleen A. Gaskin/Dir., Richard A. Henderson/Dir., James C. Epolito/Dir., Paul R. Ballard/Dir., Joel I. Ferguson/Dir. *(22 Directors included in Index)*

Owners: Bruce A. Thomas, Nicholas H. Genova, Joseph D. Reid/14.96%, Ronald K. Sable, Joel I. Ferguson, Douglas E. Crist, Insiders/26.68%, Michael L. Kasten/1.70%, John S. Lewis, Lyle W. Miller, Richard A. Henderson, Louis G. Allen, David L. Becker, Michael F. Hannley, Lewis D. Johns/1.42% *(26 Owners included in Index)*

Financial Data: **Fiscal Year End:**12/31 **Latest Annual Data:** 12/31/2006

Year	Sales	Net Income
2006	$300,885,000	$42,391,000
2005	$245,487,000	$35,925,000
2004	$198,944,000	$26,716,000

Curr. Assets:	$348,870,000	**Curr. Liab.:**	$3,285,236,000		
Plant, Equip.:	$63,795,000	**Total Liab.:**	$3,577,425,000	**Indic. Yr. Divd.:**	$1.000
Total Assets:	$4,065,816,000	**Net Worth:**	$361,879,000	**Debt/ Equity:**	0.8614

Capitol Federal Financial

700 S Kansas Ave., Topeka, KS, 66603; ***PH:*** 1-785-235-1341; ***Fax:*** 1-785-231-6264; ***http://*** www.capfed.com

General - Incorporation	US	**Stock**- Price on:12/24/2007	$38.06
Employees	596	Stock Exchange	NDQ
Auditor	Deloitte & Touche LLP	Ticker Symbol	CFFN
Stk Agt	Deloitte & Touche LLP	Outstanding Shares	74,270,000
Counsel	NA	E.P.S	$0.44
DUNS No.	NA	Shareholders	NA

Business: The group's principal activity is to provide banking service to customers. The operations are conducted through the group's wholly owned subsidiary, capitol federal savings bank. The group originates real estate, property improvements, auto and other loans. The deposits accepted by the group consists of passbook and statement savings accounts, money market deposit accounts, now and non-interest bearing checking accounts and certificates of deposits. The group is a federally chartered and insured savings bank, which has 28 traditional and 7 in-store banking offices. The metropolitan areas served by the group include topeka, wichita, lawrence, manhattan, emporia and salina, Kansas and a portion of greater Kansas city.

Primary SIC and add'l.: 6035 6712

CIK No: 0001074433

Subsidiaries: Capitol Federal Capitol Federal Capitol Federal, Capitol Federal Savings Bank, Capitol Funds, Inc

Officers: John B. Dicus/47/Dir., CEO, Pres., Judy Bridge/Certified Insurance Counselor, Greater Kansas City Area, Sue Crenshaw/Representative, Wichita, Salina, Manhattan, Mike Toledo/Representative, Greater Kansas City Area, Larry K. Brubaker/61/Exec. VP - Corporate Services, Richard J. Aleshire/Exec. VP - Retail Operations, Ed Cox/Representative, Topeka, Lawrence, Emporia, Kent G. Townsend/47/CFO, Exec. VP

Directors: John B. Dicus/47/Dir., CEO, Pres., John C. Dicus/Chmn., B. B. Andersen/72/Dir., Jeffrey R. Thompson/47/Dir., Jeffrey M. Johnson/42/Dir., Michael T. McCoy/59/Dir., Marilyn S. Ward/68/Dir.

Owners: Jeffrey R. Thompson, Jeffrey M. Johnson, Insiders/2.60%, Michael T. McCoy, Capitol Federal Savings Bank MHC/70.30%, B. B. Andersen, Kent G. Townsend, Larry K. Brubaker, John B. Dicus, Marilyn S. Ward, Richard J. Aleshire, John C. Dicus

Financial Data: *Fiscal Year End:*09/30 *Latest Annual Data:* 09/30/2006

Year	Sales	Net Income
2006	$436,195,000	$48,117,000
2005	$423,455,000	$65,059,000
2004	$408,418,000	-$106,275,000

Curr. Assets:	$623,537,000	**Curr. Liab.:**	$7,234,034,000	**P/E Ratio:**	69.20
Plant, Equip.:	$28,909,000	**Total Liab.:**	$7,335,854,000	**Indic. Yr. Divd.:**	$2.000
Total Assets:	$8,199,073,000	**Net Worth:**	$863,219,000	**Debt/ Equity:**	0.0614

CapLease Inc

Formerly: Capital Lease Funding Inc
1065 Ave. Of The Americas, New York, NY, 10018; *PH:* 1-212-217-6300; *http://* www.caplease.com

General - Incorporation	MD	**Stock**- Price on:12/24/2007	$11.11
Employees	21	Stock Exchange	NYSE
Auditor	Mcgladrey & Pullen, LLP	Ticker Symbol	LSE
Stk Agt	American Stock Transfer & Trust Co.	Outstanding Shares	34,500,000
Counsel	NA	E.P.S	$0.08
DUNS No.	NA	Shareholders	NA

Business: The groups principal activity is to owning and investing in properties. The group also provides loan services include long-term mortgage loans, corporate credit loans and commercial loans. The group operates from the United States. The groups total assets in the year 2006 were $1,575,405 (thousands).

Primary SIC and add'l.: 6798

CIK No: 0001057689

Subsidiaries: CA Portsmouth Investment Trust, Capital Property Associates Limited Partnership, Caplease CDO 2005-1 Corp., Caplease CDO 2005-1, Ltd., Caplease Credit LLC, Caplease Debt Funding, LP, Caplease Investment Management LLC, Caplease Services Corp., Caplease Statutory Trust I, Caplease, LP, CLF 1000 Milwaukee Avenue LLC, CLF 555 N Daniels Way LLC, CLF 6116 GP LLC, CLF Aliso Viejo Business Trust, CLF Arlington GP LLC 52 Subsidiaries included in the Index

Officers: Paul McDowell/Dir., Founder, CEO, William Pollert/Dir., Founder, Pres., Shawn P. Seale/Founder, Sr. VP, CFO, Treasurer, Robert Blanz/Sr. VP, Chief Investment Officer, Paul Hughes/VP, General Counsel, Corp. Sec., Gary Landriau/Contact - Advisory Services, Brad Cohen/Contact - Investor Relation

Directors: Paul McDowell/Dir., Founder, CEO, Lewis Ranieri/Chmn., Shawn P. Seale/Founder, Sr. VP, CFO, Treasurer, William Pollert/Dir., Founder, Pres., Stanley Kreitman/Dir., Jeff Rogatz/Dir., Howard Silver/Dir., Michael Gagliardi/Dir.

Owners: Kensington Investment Group, Inc./6.20%, Jeffrey F. Rogatz, Paul H. McDowell, Snyder Capital Management, LP and/8.90%, Stanley Kreitman, Howard A. Silver, Third Avenue Management LLC/5.10%, Hotchkis and Wiley Capital Management, LLC/12.20%, William R. Pollert, UBS AG,/6.70%, Lewis S. Ranieri/1.60%, Paul C. Hughes, Shawn P. Seale, The Vanguard Group, Inc./5.70%, Robert C. Blanz *(17 Owners included in Index)*

Financial Data: *Fiscal Year End:*12/31 *Latest Annual Data:* 12/31/2006

Year	Sales	Net Income
2006	$124,780,000	$7,249,000
2005	$73,052,000	$5,130,000
2004	$21,004,000	$1,360,000

Curr. Assets:	$31,428,000	**Curr. Liab.:**	$217,634,000	**P/E Ratio:**	138.88
Plant, Equip.:	$1,117,943,000	**Total Liab.:**	$1,336,644,000	**Indic. Yr. Divd.:**	$0.800
Total Assets:	$1,644,300,000	**Net Worth:**	$307,656,000	**Debt/ Equity:**	3.7563

Caprius Inc

1 Parker Plz., Hackensack, NJ, 07601; *PH:* 1-201-592-8838; *Fax:* 1-201-592-0393; *http://* www.caprius.com; *Email:* ir@caprius.com

General - Incorporation	DE	**Stock**- Price on:12/24/2007	$0.8
Employees	17	Stock Exchange	OTC
Auditor	Marcum & Kliegman LLP	Ticker Symbol	CAPS
Stk Agt	American Stock Transfer & Trust Co.	Outstanding Shares	3,790,000
Counsel	NA	E.P.S	-$1.7
DUNS No.	10-791-3154	Shareholders	NA

Business: The group's principal activity is to operate medical imaging systems, healthcare imaging and rehabilitation services and medical infectious waste business. The group manufactures and sells medical diagnostic assays and controls for therapeutic drug monitoring used to assess medication efficacy and safety of therapeutic drug in human bodily fluids. The services provided include breast care for patients through all imaging and diagnostic services in-house, including X-ray mammography, screening ultrasound, ultrasound, stereotactic biopsies, as well as performing bone densitometry to monitor osteoporosis. The products manufactured include sterimed(R) system that destroys biomedical waste into tiny pieces and exposes it to a disinfecting solution called ster-cid(r). During fiscal 2003, the group disposed strax institute business.

Primary SIC and add'l.: 3842 8093

CIK No: 0000722567

Subsidiaries: M.c.m. Environmental Technologies, Inc., M.c.m. Environmental Technologies, Ltd.

Officers: George Aaron/54/Chmn., CEO, Pres., Jonathan Joels/50/Dir., CFO, Treasurer, Sec., Elliott Koppel/63/VP - Sales, Marketing, Beverly Tkaczenko/Dir. - Corporate Communications

Directors: George Aaron/54/Chmn., CEO, Pres., Jonathan Joels/50/Dir., CFO, Treasurer, Sec., Sol Triebwasser/85/Dir., Jeffrey L. Hymes/54/Dir.

Owners: Insiders, Jonathan Joels, Sol Triebwasser, Roger W. Miller, Kenneth C. Leung, Bonanza Master Fund Ltd., Shrikant Mehta, Vision Opportunity Master Fund Ltd., George Aaron, Dolphin Offshore Partners LP, Dwight Morgan

Financial Data: *Fiscal Year End:*09/30 *Latest Annual Data:* 9/30/2006

Year	Sales	Net Income
2006	$1,235,000	-$3,396,000
2005	$849,000	-$2,538,000
2004	$885,000	-$3,356,000

Curr. Assets:	$2,271,000	**Curr. Liab.:**	$618,000		
Plant, Equip.:	$80,000	**Total Liab.:**	$618,000	**Indic. Yr. Divd.:**	NA
Total Assets:	$2,777,000	**Net Worth:**	$2,159,000	**Debt/ Equity:**	NA

Capsource Financial Inc

2305 Canyon Blvd. Ste. 103, Ste. 103, Boulder, CO, 80302; *PH:* 1-303-245-0515; *Fax:* 1-303-245-0521; *http://* www.capsource-financial.com; *Email:* capsource@capsource-financial.com

General - Incorporation	CO	**Stock**- Price on:12/24/2007	$0.86
Employees	25	Stock Exchange	OTC
Auditor	Hernndez Marrn Y Ca, S.C	Ticker Symbol	CPSO
Stk Agt	U.S. Stock Transfer Corp	Outstanding Shares	20,430,000
Counsel	NA	E.P.S	-$0.1
DUNS No.	NA	Shareholders	NA

Business: The groups principle activity is to provide trucking equipment and services. The groups customers include private fleets, for-hire carriers and rental firms. The group operates from United States.

Primary SIC and add'l.: NA

CIK No: 0001173359

Subsidiaries: Mexican-American-Canadian Trailer Rentals, Inc.

Officers: Fred C. Boethling/62/Dir., CEO, Pres., Steven E. Reichert/59/Dir., VP, General Counsel, Steven J. Kutcher/54/CFO, VP

Directors: Fred C. Boethling/62/Dir., CEO, Pres., Randolph M. Pentel/48/Chmn., Lynch Grattan/56/Dir., Steven E. Reichert/59/Dir., VP, General Counsel, Wayne Hoovestol/49/Dir., Bruce Nordin/52/Dir., Scot Malloy/43/Dir.

Owners: Wayne Hoovestal, Lynch Grattan, Insiders, Fred C. Boethling, Steven Kutcher, Randolph Pentel, Whitebox Intermarket Partners L.P., Pandora Select Partners L.P., Steven Reichert

Financial Data: *Fiscal Year End:*12/31 *Latest Annual Data:* 12/31/2006

Year	Sales	Net Income
2006	$36,286,000	-$1,829,000
2005	$20,609,000	-$1,794,000
2004	$7,217,000	-$1,576,000

Curr. Assets:	$17,695,000	**Curr. Liab.:**	$16,015,000		
Plant, Equip.:	$1,135,000	**Total Liab.:**	$17,041,000	**Indic. Yr. Divd.:**	NA
Total Assets:	$19,301,000	**Net Worth:**	$2,259,000	**Debt/ Equity:**	0.3626

Capstead Mortgage Corp

8401 N Central Expwy., Ste. 800, Dallas, TX, 75225; *PH:* 1-214-874-2323; *Fax:* 1-214-874-2398; *http://* www.capstead.com; *Email:* invrel@capstead.com

General - Incorporation	MD	**Stock**- Price on:12/24/2007	$9.64
Employees	12	Stock Exchange	NYSE
Auditor	Ernst & Young LLP	Ticker Symbol	CMO
Stk Agt	Wells Fargo Shareowner Services	Outstanding Shares	19,260,000
Counsel	NA	E.P.S	-$0.48
DUNS No.	NA	Shareholders	NA

Business: The groups principal activity is to invest in real estate properties. The group operates from Delaware, in the United States.

Primary SIC and add'l.: 6798

CIK No: 0000766701

Subsidiaries: Capstead Capital Corporation, Capstead Inc., Capstead Mortgage Corporation, Capstead Mortgage Trust I , Capstead Mortgage Trust II , Capstead Mortgage Trust III , Capstead Securities Corporation IV, CMC Real Estate Capital GP, LLC, CMC Real Estate Capital, L.P., CMC Securities Corporation III, CMC Securities Corporation IV, CMC Securities Holding, LLC

Officers: Andrew F. Jacobs/Dir., CEO, Pres./$582,523.00, Christopher W. Mahowald/Pres., Phillip A. Reinsch/CFO, Exec. VP/$308,772.00, Robert R. Spears/Exec. VP, Dir. - Residential Mortgage Investments/$329,755.00, Michael W. Brown/Sr. VP - Asset, Liability Management/$201,269.00, Anthony R. Page/Sr. VP, Dir. - Commercial Mortgage Investments/$189,431.00

Directors: Andrew F. Jacobs/Dir., CEO, Pres., Paul M. Low/Chmn., Gary Keiser/Dir., Jack Biegler/Dir., Michael G. Oneil/Dir., Mark S. Whiting/Dir.

Owners: Mark S. Whiting, Gary Keiser, Anthony R. Page, Paul M. Low, Jack Biegler, Andrew F. Jacobs/1.46%, Robert R. Spears, UBS AG/6.16%, Insiders/7.03%, Michael W. Brown, Phillip A. Reinsch, Christopher W. Mahowald, Michael G. O'Neil, Howard Rubin/2.60%

Financial Data: *Fiscal Year End:*12/31 *Latest Annual Data:* 12/31/2006

Year	Sales	Net Income
2006	$243,450,000	$3,843,000
2005	$131,415,000	$57,192,000
2004	$102,050,000	$41,805,000

Curr. Assets:	$5,661,000	**Curr. Liab.:**	$4,904,945,000		
Plant, Equip.:	NA	**Total Liab.:**	$5,008,040,000	**Indic. Yr. Divd.:**	$0.160
Total Assets:	$5,348,002,000	**Net Worth:**	$339,962,000	**Debt/ Equity:**	0.2940

Capstone Turbine Corp

21211 Nordhoff St., Chatsworth, CA, 91311; *PH:* 1-818-734-5300; *Fax:* 1-818-734-5320; *http://* www.microturbine.com

General - Incorporation	DE	**Stock**- Price on:12/24/2007	$1.08
Employees	195	Stock Exchange	NDQ
Auditor	Deloitte & Touche LLP	Ticker Symbol	CPST
Stk Agt	Mellon Investor Services LLC	Outstanding Shares	143,990,000
Counsel	Latham & Watkins	E.P.S	-$0.32
DUNS No.	NA	Shareholders	NA

Business: The group's principal activity is to develop, manufacture and market microturbine generator sets used for on-site power production and as an auxillary power source in hybrid electric vehicles. The products of the group include major design features such as patented air-bearing technology, air-cooling, digital power electronics and advanced combustion technology. The model c30 capstone microturbine generates 30 kilowatts of electric power as a stand-alone power source or grid-connected while the capstone 60 family generates 60 kilowatts. They use a broad range of gaseous and liquid fuels

in an environmentally friendly manner. The group also offers various accessories including rotary gas compressors with digital controls, batteries with digital controls for stand-alone or grid-connected operations and packaging options. South coast air quality management district, California and the los angeles department of water and power are two major customers of the group.

Primary SIC and add'l.: 3621 3511

CIK No: 0001009759

Subsidiaries: Capstone Turbine International, Inc

Officers: Darren R. Jamison/Dir., CEO, Pres., Trevor Rainbow/Contact - European Office, Leigh L. Estus/Sr. VP - Operations/$488,891.00, Shelby Ahmann/Sr. VP - Customer Service, James D. Crouse/Exec. VP - Sales, Walter McBride/CFO, Exec. VP, Sec./$744,674.00, Mark Gilbreth/CTO, Exec. VP/$553,374.00, Sohra Yatani/Contact - Capstone Turbine International, Inc Tokyo Branch, Ricardo Nava/Contact - Mexico City Office, Elizabeth M. Reynolds/43/VP, Chief Accounting Officer, Simon Xu/Contact - China Office, Alice Barsoomian/Dir. - Investor, Public Relations, Larry N. Colson/VP - Human Resources

Directors: Darren R. Jamison/Dir., CEO, Pres., Eliot G. Protsch/Chmn., Richard Atkinson/Dir., John Jaggers/Dir., Noam Lotan/Dir., Gary Simon/Dir., Darrell Wilk/Dir.

Owners: Mark G. Gilbreth, Insiders/3.58%, Noam Lotan, Leigh L. Estus, Darrell J. Wilk, Richard K. Atkinson, Eliot G. Protsch/1.11%, John R. Tucker/1.04%, Antonio Rodriquez, John C. Fink, John V. Jaggers, Gary D. Simon, Walter J. McBride

Financial Data: Fiscal Year End:03/31 **Latest Annual Data:** 3/31/2007

Year	Sales	Net Income
2007	$21,018,000	-$36,728,000
2006	$24,103,000	-$47,073,000
2005	$16,968,000	-$39,449,000

Curr. Assets:	$77,515,000	Curr. Liab.:	$17,416,000		
Plant, Equip.:	$7,816,000	Total Liab.:	$18,089,000	Indic. Yr. Divd.:	NA
Total Assets:	$89,717,000	Net Worth:	$71,628,000	Debt/ Equity:	0.0003

Captaris Inc

10885 NE 4th St., Ste. 400, Bellevue, WA, 98004; **PH:** 1-425-455-6000; **Fax:** 1-425-638-1500; http:// www.captaris.com

General - Incorporation	WA	Stock- Price on:12/24/2007	$5
Employees	399	Stock Exchange	NDQ
Auditor	Moss Adams LLP	Ticker Symbol	CAPA
Stk Agt	Mellon Investor Services LLC	Outstanding Shares	27,260,000
Counsel	Perkins Coie LLP	E.P.S.	$0.08
DUNS No.	10-334-7886	Shareholders	NA

Business: The group's principal activity is to provide business information delivery solutions that integrate process and automate the flow of messages, data and documents primarily for medium and large-sized enterprises. The group's products address the fax server, network fax, production fax, e-document delivery, enterprise fax, business process automation/workflow and mobile business markets. The group distributes its products primarily through independent distributors, value-added resellers and a global distribution network in more than 40 countries. Its products run on off-the-shelf server hardware, windows nt, windows 2000, microsoft.net and interface with a wide variety of telephony and computer equipment.

Primary SIC and add'l.: 7372 3661 7379

CIK No: 0000931784

Subsidiaries: Captaris Canada Corporation (NSULC), Captaris GmbH (Deutschland), Captaris International B.V., Captaris International, Inc., Captaris International, PTY Limited, Information Management Research, Inc., MediaTel Corporation, Raven Acquisition Corp.

Officers: David P. Anastasi/51/Dir., CEO, Pres./$640,615.00, Peter Papano/CFO/$373,601.00, Christopher Stanton/Chief Legal Officer, Doug Anderson/Sr. VP - Global Field Operations, Paul Yantus/Exec. VP - Marketing, Product Development, Todd Kehrli/Investor Relations Officer, Jim Byers/Investor Relations Officer

Directors: David P. Anastasi/51/Dir., CEO, Pres., Bruce L. Crockett/64/Chmn., Robert F. Gilb/62/Dir., Patrick J. Swanick/50/Dir., Robert L. Lovely/70/Dir., Daniel R. Lyle/62/Dir., Thomas M. Murnane/61/Dir., Mark E. Siefertson/48/Dir.

Owners: Matthias M. Scheuing/2.08%, Patrick J. Swanick, Robert F. Gilb, David P. Anastasi/4.34%, Mark E. Siefertson, Robert L. Lovely, SACC Partners LP/5.10%, Peter Papano/1.38%, Bruce L. Crockett, Daniel R. Lyle, Insiders/9.17%, Dimensional Fund Advisors LP/7.12%, Thomas M. Murnane

Financial Data: Fiscal Year End:12/31 **Latest Annual Data:** 12/31/2006

Year	Sales	Net Income
2006	$91,986,000	$3,981,000
2005	$86,380,000	-$3,979,000
2004	$78,036,000	$107,000

Curr. Assets:	$46,110,000	Curr. Liab.:	$32,270,000	P/E Ratio:	41.67
Plant, Equip.:	$4,340,000	Total Liab.:	$38,121,000	Indic. Yr. Divd.:	NA
Total Assets:	$135,948,000	Net Worth:	$97,827,000	Debt/ Equity:	NA

Captiva Software Corp

10145 Pacific Hts. Blvd., San Diego, CA, 92121; **PH:** 1-858-320-1000; http:// www.captivasoftware.com

General - Incorporation	DE	Stock- Price on:12/24/2007	$17.99
Employees	31,100	Stock Exchange	NA
Auditor	PricewaterhouseCoopers LLP	Ticker Symbol	NA
Stk Agt	Computershare Investor Services LLC	Outstanding Shares	2,100,000,000
Counsel	NA	E.P.S.	NA
DUNS No.	15-696-7135	Shareholders	NA

Business: The group's principal activity is to develop, market and service information capture software. This software helps to automate and manage the capture of external information into an organization's internal computing systems. The major customers include global 1000 companies and government entities including delta airlines, wachovia bank, fidelity investments, metropolitan life, amgen, prudential and the United States patent office. The software tools are marketed to hardware and software providers under the brand pixel translations. The group acquired adp context inc in feb-2004.

Primary SIC and add'l.: 7379 7372

CIK No: 0000909276

Subsidiaries: Old Captiva

Financial Data: Fiscal Year End:12/31 **Latest Annual Data:** 12/31/2006

Year	Sales	Net Income
2006	$11,155,090,000	$1,223,982,000
2005	$9,663,955,000	$1,133,165,000
2004	$8,229,488,000	$871,189,000

Curr. Assets:	$6,520,587,000	Curr. Liab.:	$3,881,104,000		
Plant, Equip.:	$2,035,559,000	Total Liab.:	$8,240,540,000	Indic. Yr. Divd.:	NA
Total Assets:	$18,566,247,000	Net Worth:	$10,325,707,000	Debt/ Equity:	0.3542

Caraco Pharmaceutical Laboratories Ltd

1150 Elijah McCoy Dr., Detroit, MI, 48202; **PH:** 1-313-871-8400; **Fax:** 1-313-871-8314; http:// www.caraco.com; **Email:** info@caraco.com

General - Incorporation	MI	Stock- Price on:12/24/2007	$15.99
Employees	446	Stock Exchange	AMEX
Auditor	Rehmann Robson P.C	Ticker Symbol	CPD
Stk Agt	American Stock Transfer & Trust Co.	Outstanding Shares	28,120,000
Counsel	Bodman Longley & Dahling	E.P.S.	$0.88
DUNS No.	14-697-4886	Shareholders	NA

Business: The group's principle activities include developing, manufacturing and marketing generic drugs for the ethical and over-the-counter markets. A generic drug is a pharmaceutical product, which is the chemical and therapeutic equivalent of a brand name drug as to which the patent and/or market exclusivity has expired. The company's present product portfolio includes 18 products in 35 strengths in 82 package sizes. The products relate to a variety of therapeutic segments including the central nervous system, cardiology, pain management and diabetes. The customers include wholesalers, buying groups, hospitals, nursing homes and retail pharmacies. The group operates from United States.

Primary SIC and add'l.: 8731 2834

CIK No: 0000887708

Officers: Daniel H. Movens/Dir., CEO/$813,849.00, Jayesh Shah/Dir. - Commercial, Gurpartap Singh/Sr. VP - Business Strategies/$230,200.00, Robert Kurkiewicz/Sr. VP - Regulatory Affairs/$201,291.00, Kaushikkumar Gandhi/VP - Manufacturing, Aaron Miles/Mgr. - Investor Relations, Thomas Larkin/Dir. - Marketing, Daniel Barone/Dir. - Technical, Derrick Mann/Dir. - Regulatory, Mukul Rathi/Interim CFO/$92,760.00, David Risk/Dir. - Business Development, Tammy Bitterman/Dir. - Human Resources, Ann Zajac/Controller, Thomas Versosky/Dir. - Business Strategies

Directors: Daniel H. Movens/Dir., CEO, Dilip S. Shanghvi/Chmn., Sailesh Desai/Dir., Madhava Reddy/Dir., John D. Crissman/Dir., Jitendra N. Doshi/Dir., Georges Ugeux/Dir., Sudhir Valia/Dir., Timothy S. Manney/Dir.

Owners: Timothy S. Manney, Sun Pharma, John D. Crissman, Madhava Reddy, Daniel H. Movens, Robert Kurkiewicz, Georges Ugeux, Insiders, Mukul Rathi, Jitendra N. Doshi, Gurpartap Singh Sachdeva, Sun Global

Financial Data: Fiscal Year End:03/31 **Latest Annual Data:** 03/31/2007

Year	Sales	Net Income
2007	$117,027,000	$26,858,000
2006	$82,789,000	-$10,423,000
2005	$17,337,000	-$4,322,000

Curr. Assets:	$95,439,000	Curr. Liab.:	$19,276,000	P/E Ratio:	19.74
Plant, Equip.:	$19,030,000	Total Liab.:	$19,276,000	Indic. Yr. Divd.:	NA
Total Assets:	$114,469,000	Net Worth:	$95,193,000	Debt/ Equity:	NA

Caraustar Industries Inc

5000 Austell Powder Springs Rd., Ste. 300, Austell, GA, 30106; **PH:** 1-770-948-3101; **Fax:** 1-770-732-3401; http:// www.caraustar.com; **Email:** info@caraustar.com

General - Incorporation	NC	Stock- Price on:12/24/2007	$5.8
Employees	4,190	Stock Exchange	NDQ
Auditor	Deloitte & Touche LLP	Ticker Symbol	CSAR
Stk Agt	Bank of New York	Outstanding Shares	29,110,000
Counsel	Robinson, Bradshaw & Hinson P.A.	E.P.S.	-$1.01
DUNS No.	03-949-7029	Shareholders	NA

Business: The group's principal activity is to manufacture, convert and market recycled paperboard and related products. The group operates in three segments: paperboard, tube, core and composite container and carton and custom packaging. The paperboard segment consists of facilities that manufacture 100% recycled uncoated and clay-coated paperboard. The tube, core and composite container segment produces spiral and convolute-wound tubes, cores and cans for use in cloth cores, paper mill cores, yarn carriers, carpet cores and film, foil and metal cores. The carton segment produces folding cartons and set-up boxes. The group acquired remaining equity of caraustar northwest llc in 2003.

Primary SIC and add'l.: 2655 6719 2657 3275 5093 2631

CIK No: 0000825692

Subsidiaries: Austell Holding Company, LLC, Camden Paperboard Corporation, Caraustar CPB, LLC, Caraustar Custom Packaging Group (Maryland), Inc., Caraustar Custom Packaging Group, Inc., Caraustar Design Tubes, Inc., Caraustar Industrial & Consumer Products Group, Inc., Caraustar Industrial & Consumer Products Group, Ltd., Caraustar Industrial Canada, Inc., Caraustar Integrated Services, S.A. de C.V., Caraustar Mill Group, Inc., Caraustar Paper Tube de Mexico, Caraustar Recovered Fiber Group, Inc., Caraustar, G.P., Chicago Paperboard Corporation 25 Subsidiaries included in the Index

Officers: Michael J. Keough/Dir., CEO, Pres./$1,309,594.00, Janet B. Heilman/Primary Investor Relations Officer, John R. Foster/VP - Sales, Marketing/$539,406.00, Ronald J. Domanico/Dir., Sr. VP, CFO/$673,349.00, Steven L. Kelchen/VP - Converted Products Group/$553,673.00, Barry A. Smedstad/VP - Human Resources, Public Relations, William A. Nix/VP, Chief Accounting Officer, Wilma E. Beaty/VP, General Counsel, Sec., Thomas C. Dawson/VP - Mill Group/$645,581.00, Marinan R. Mays/Assist. Corp. Sec.

Directors: Michael J. Keough/Dir., CEO, Pres., Daniel P. Casey/Chmn., Robert J. Clanin/Dir., Eric R. Zarnikow/Dir., Ronald J. Domanico/Dir., Sr. VP, CFO, James E. Rogers/Dir., Dennis M. Love/Dir., Charles H. Greiner/Dir., Celeste L. Bottorff/Dir., John T. Heald/Dir.

Owners: Wilma E. Beaty, Insiders/4.60%, Dennis M. Love, Barclays Global Investors, N.A./5.40%, Steven L. Kelchen, William A. Nix, Celeste L. Bottorff, James E. Rogers, Daniel P. Casey, Thomas C. Dawson, Dimensional Fund Advisors LP/8.40%, Old Westbury Real Return Fund/8.70%, Jimmy A. Russell, Eric R. Zarnikow, Ronald J. Domanico *(25 Owners included in Index)*

Financial Data: Fiscal Year End:12/31 **Latest Annual Data:** 12/31/2006

Year	Sales	Net Income
2006	$989,918,000	$47,332,000
2005	$862,421,000	-$103,386,000
2004	$1,060,275,000	-$3,979,000

Curr. Assets:	$179,438,000	Curr. Liab.:	$110,474,000		
Plant, Equip.:	$263,605,000	Total Liab.:	$462,689,000	Indic. Yr. Divd.:	NA
Total Assets:	$624,275,000	Net Worth:	$161,586,000	Debt/ Equity:	1.8353

CarBiz Inc

7405 N Tamiami Trl., Sarasota, FL, 34243; **PH:** 1-941-952-9255; **Fax:** 1-941-953-3580;
http:// www.carbiz.com

General - Incorporation ....

General - Incorporation		Stock - Price on:12/24/2007	$0.105
Employees	37	Stock Exchange	OTC
Auditor	NA	Ticker Symbol	CBZFF
Stk Agt	Mellon Trust Co	Outstanding Shares	64,220,000
Counsel	NA	E.P.S.	-$0.1
DUNS No.	NA	Shareholders	NA

Business: The groups principal activity is to provide the dealer community with quality software products and services. The services of the group include software, consulting, training and financing. The group operates from Florida in the United States.

Primary SIC and add'l.: 7373 6141 7371 7379 7389 7372

CIK No: 0001307425

Officers: Carl Ritter/Chmn., CEO, Ross Richard Lye/Dir., Pres., Stanton Heintz/Dir., CFO, Mark Dubois/Regional Mgr., Jennifer Halloran/VP - Finance, Jennifer Downey/Software Operations Mgr., Mike Downey/Business Development Mgr., Virginia Witter/Quality Control Mgr., Diana Fares/Consulting, Don Miller/Consulting, Jose Ramirez/Contact - Sales

Directors: Carl Ritter/Chmn., CEO, Ross Richard Lye/Dir., Pres., Stanton Heintz/Dir., CFO, Ross Quigley/Dir., Ted Popel/Dir., Christopher Bradbury/Dir., Wallace Weylie/Dir., Gene Tomsic/Dir., Vern Haverstock/Dir.

Owners: Richard Lye/1.20%, Christopher Bradbury, Vicis Capital Master Fund/7.30%, Stanton Heintz, Insiders/35.50%, Gene Tomsic, Wallace Weylie, Vernon Haverstock, John Gallucci/5.10%, Medipac International, Inc/7.90%, Theodore Popel/2.80%, Carl Ritter/4.50%, Ross Quigley/26.80%, Jon Kochevar/8.10%

Financial Data: Fiscal Year End:10/31 Latest Annual Data: 1/31/2007

Year	Sales		Net Income
2007	$3,210,000		-$4,754,000
Curr. Assets:	$643,000	Curr. Liab.:	$5,187,000
Plant, Equip.:	$76,000	Total Liab.:	$5,490,000	Indic. Yr. Divd.:	NA
Total Assets:	$768,000	Net Worth:	-$4,722,000	Debt/ Equity:	NA

Carbo Ceramics Inc

6565 MacArthur Blvd., Ste. 1050, Irving, TX, 75039; **PH:** 1-972-401-0090; **Fax:** 1-972-401-0705;
http:// www.carboceramics.com

General - Incorporation	DE	Stock - Price on:12/24/2007	$45.04
Employees	630	Stock Exchange	NYSE
Auditor	Ernst & Young LLP	Ticker Symbol	CRR
Stk Agt	Mellon Investor Services LLC	Outstanding Shares	24,470,000
Counsel	NA	E.P.S.	$2.26
DUNS No.	15-155-2437	Shareholders	NA

Business: The group's principle activity is to produce and supply ceramic proppant for use in the hydraulic fracturing of natural gas and oil wells. In addition, the group provides fracture diagnostic and mapping services, markets fracture simulation software and provides fracture design services to oil and gas companies worldwide. The group manufactures four distinct ceramic proppants: carbohsptm, carbopropgroup, carbolitegroup and carboeconopropgroup. Its products are marketed worldwide through its sales offices in aberdeen, Scotland and through commissioned sales agents located in South America, China and Australia. Customers include bj services company, halliburton energy services inc and schlumberger. The group operates primarily in the United States, Canada and China. The group's quarterly revenue for September 2007 was 84.79 millions of USD.

Primary SIC and add'l.: 3259

CIK No: 0001009672

Subsidiaries: CARBO Ceramics (China) Company Ltd., CARBO Ceramics (Eurasia) LLC, CARBO Ceramics (UK)Limited, CARBO Ceramics Cyprus Ltd., CARBO Ceramics LLC, CARBO Ceramics Mauritius, Inc., Enertech, Ltd., Pinnacle Technologies, Inc., Pinnacle Technologies,Inc.

Officers: Gary Kolstad/CEO, Pres./$688,652.00, Kenn Johnson/Contact - Product Sales, Marketing, Europe, Middle East, Africa, Eduardo Velez/Contact - Product Sales, Marketing, Latin, South America, Simon Hao/Contact - Product Sales, Marketing, International, Albert Malmberg/International Supply Chain Mgr., Gloria Cancienne/Customer Service Representative, Jude Darbonne/Supply Chain, Logistics Analyst, Allie Hewing/Customer Service Representative, Stacy Eschete/Sales Engineer - Southwest Region, Michael Dennis/Field Service Rep, Southeast Region, Thomas H. McGuigan/Dir. - North American Sales, Marketing, Marty Hupp/Sales Engineer - Southeast Region, Mark McGill/Sales Engineer - South Texas Region, John Kullman/Sales Engineer - Northern Region, Jamie Jordan/Sales Engineer - Mid, Continent Region (32 Officers included in Index)

Directors: William C. Morris/69/Chmn., Claude E. Cooke/Dir., Robert S. Rubin/76/Dir., H. E. Lentz/63/Dir., Jesse P. Orsini/68/Dir., James B. Jennings/67/Dir., Randy L. Limbacher/50/Dir., Chad C. Deaton/55/Dir.

Owners: John J. Murphy, Royce & Associates, LLC/5.70%, Insiders/17.40%, Chad C. Deaton, William C. Morris/13.20%, Jesse P. Orsini, H. E. Lentz, Marc Kevin Fisher, Claude E. Cooke, Neuberger Berman, Inc./13.00%, Christopher A. Wright, Gary A. Kolstad, Mark L. Edmunds, Robert S. Rubin/2.90%, Paul G. Vitek

Financial Data: Fiscal Year End:12/31 Latest Annual Data: 12/31/2006

Year	Sales		Net Income
2006	$312,126,000		$54,253,000
2005	$252,673,000		$46,620,000
2004	$223,054,000		$41,673,000
Curr. Assets:	$143,925,000	Curr. Liab.:	$34,246,000
Plant, Equip.:	$231,748,000	Total Liab.:	$61,806,000	Indic. Yr. Divd.:	$0.560
Total Assets:	$404,665,000	Net Worth:	$342,859,000	Debt/ Equity:	NA

Cardero Resource Corp

1177 W Hastings St., Ste. 1901, Vancouver, BC, V6E 2K3; **PH:** 1-604-408-7488;
http:// www.cardero.com; **Email:** info@cardero.com

General - Incorporation	Canada	Stock - Price on:12/24/2007	$1.8199
Employees	5	Stock Exchange	AMEX
Auditor	Smythe Ratcliffe, CA	Ticker Symbol	CDY
Stk Agt	Pacific Corporate Trust Co	Outstanding Shares	47,280,000
Counsel	Gowling, Lafleur, Henderson LLP	E.P.S.	-$0.172
DUNS No.	NA	Shareholders	NA

Business: The group's principal activity is exploration and development of iron-oxide copper, gold properties. The company seeks to identify mineral deposits and facilitate production in the regions of Mexico, Peru and Argentina. The company's exploration focus includes iron, copper, gold.

Primary SIC and add'l.: 1040

CIK No: 0001303936

Officers: Hendrik Van Alphen/CEO, Pres., Mark Cruise/VP - Business Development, Marla K. Ritchie/Corp. Sec., Michael Kinley/CFO, Keith Henderson/VP - Exploration, Tansy O'Connor-Parsons/Sr. Geochemist, Quentin Mai/Contact - Investment, Corporate Communications

Directors: Len J. Harris/Dir., Lawrence W. Talbot/Dir., Murray Hitzman/Dir., Stephan Fitch/Dir., Larry Talbot/Dir.

Financial Data: Fiscal Year End:10/31 Latest Annual Data: 10/31/2006

Year	Sales		Net Income
2006	NA		-$13,101,000
2005	NA		-$10,253,000
2004	NA		-$9,162,000
Curr. Assets:	$5,485,000	Curr. Liab.:	$427,000	P/E Ratio:	70.86
Plant, Equip.:	$94,000	Total Liab.:	$427,000	Indic. Yr. Divd.:	NA
Total Assets:	$13,681,000	Net Worth:	$13,254,000	Debt/ Equity:	NA

Cardiac Science Corp

3303 Monte Villa Pkwy., Bothell, WA, 98021; **PH:** 1-425-402-2000; **Fax:** 1-425-402-2001;
http:// www.cardiacscience.com

General - Incorporation	DE	Stock - Price on:12/24/2007	$10.47
Employees	551	Stock Exchange	NDQ
Auditor	KPMG LLP	Ticker Symbol	CSCX
Stk Agt	Mellon Investor Services LLC	Outstanding Shares	22,690,000
Counsel	Perkins Coie LLP	E.P.S.	$0.26
DUNS No.	NA	Shareholders	NA

Business: The groups principle activities include developing, manufacturing and marketing diagnostic and therapeutic cardiology devices and systems. The groups services include training, maintenance, installation, repair and technical. The products of the group include cardiac monitoring and Defibrillation. The group products sold under the trade names Burdick, Powerheart and Quinton. In the year 2005, the groups acquire Cardiac Science, Inc. The group operates from the United States. The group's quarterly revenue for September 2007 was 45.14 millions of USD.

Primary SIC and add'l.: 3842 3841 3845 5047

CIK No: 0001323115

Subsidiaries: Cardiac Science Holdings UK,, Cardiac Science International A/S, LifeTec Medical Limited, Shanghai Quinton Medical Device Co., Ltd.,

Officers: John R. Hinson/Dir., CEO, Pres., Michael K. Matysik/CFO, Sr. VP, Sec., Allan Criss/Sr. VP - Sales, Marketing, Service, North America, Michael B. Adams/VP - Information Systems, Alfred J. Ford/VP - Sales, Paul E. Kamps/VP, Brian R. Lee/VP - Engineering, Kurt B. Lemvigh/VP - International, Darryl R. Lustig/VP - Cardiology Sales, Feroze D. Motafram/VP - Operations, Garry Norris/VP - Marketing, Cheryl L. Shea/VP - Regulatory Affairs, Quality Assurance, Daphne L. Taylor/VP, Corporate Controller, Chief Accounting Officer, Barbara J. Thompson/VP - Human Resources, Traci Paulk/Contact - Media

Directors: John R. Hinson/Dir., CEO, Pres., Ruediger Naumann-Etienne/Chmn., Robert W. Berg/Dir., Jue Hsien Chern/Dir., Raymond W. Cohen/Dir., Timothy C. Mickelson/Dir., Ray E. Newton/Dir., Jeffrey F. O'Donnell/Dir.

Owners: Wells Fargo & Company/5.60%, Garry D. Norris, Kurt Lemvigh, Raymond W. Cohen/1.20%, Carlo J. Cannell/9.90%, Ruediger Naumann-Etienne/2.10%, Darryl Lustig, John R. Hinson/2.20%, Michael K. Matysik, Robert W. Berg, Jeffrey F. ODonnell, Jue-Hsien Chern, Insiders/7.40%, Entities affiliated with Perseus L.L.C./13.90%, Goldman Sachs Asset Management, L.P./10.80%

Financial Data: Fiscal Year End:12/31 Latest Annual Data: 12/31/2006

Year	Sales		Net Income
2006	$155,429,000		$49,000
2005	$106,650,000		-$1,238,000
Curr. Assets:	$60,977,000	Curr. Liab.:	$31,294,000
Plant, Equip.:	$5,956,000	Total Liab.:	$32,048,000	Indic. Yr. Divd.:	NA
Total Assets:	$247,645,000	Net Worth:	$215,597,000	Debt/ Equity:	NA

Cardica Inc

900 Saginaw Dr., Redwood City, CA, 94063; **PH:** 1-650-364-9975; **Fax:** 1-650-364-3134;
http:// www.cardica.com; **Email:** investors@cardica.com

General - Incorporation	DE	Stock - Price on:12/24/2007	$6.12
Employees	56	Stock Exchange	NDQ
Auditor	Ernst & Young LLP	Ticker Symbol	CRDC
Stk Agt	Computershare Trust Co	Outstanding Shares	11,290,000
Counsel	NA	E.P.S.	-$1.15
DUNS No.	NA	Shareholders	NA

Business: The groups principle activities include designing and manufacturing proprietary automated anastomotic systems. The products of the group include distal and proximal anastomosis system. The group products sold under the trade name C-Port(R) and PAS-Port(R). The group operates from the United States, Japan and Europe. The group's quarterly revenue for September 2007 was 1.35 millions of USD.

Primary SIC and add'l.: 3841

CIK No: 0001178104

Officers: Bernard A. Hausen/Dir., CEO, Pres., Co - Founder, Ryan Welsh/Mid, Atlantic Sales Mgr., Doug Ellison/VP - Worldwide Sales - Marketing, Douglas T. Ellison/VP - Worldwide Sales, Marketing, Bryan D. Knodel/VP - Research, Development, Robert Y. Newell/CFO, VP - Finance, Operations, Ric Ruedy/VP - Regulatory, Clinical, Quality Affairs, Philip Freed/Dir. - Marketing,

Daryl Messinger/Contact - Media, Jannette Buchanan/Contact - Customer Service, Sales Support, Adam Hitch/Ohio Valley Sales Mgr., Anthony Giorgianni/Northwest Sales Mgr., Beth Bacon/Florida Sales Mgr., Bron Marrs/Northeast Sales Representative, Chris Borg/Midwest Sales Mgr. *(18 Officers included in Index)*

Directors: Bernard A. Hausen/Dir., CEO, Pres., Co - Founder, Kevin T. Larkin/Chmn., Richard P. Powers/Dir., Michael J. Egan/Dir., Jeffrey L. Purvin/Dir., Robert C. Robbins/Dir., John Simon/Dir., Stephen A. Yencho/Dir., William H. Younger/Dir.

Owners: John Simon/4.60%, Richard P. Powers, Michael J. Egan/1.72%, Insiders/26.05%, Entities and Persons Affiliated with Wasatch Advisors, Inc./9.63%, Bryan D. Knodel, Richard M. Ruedy, William H. Younger/8.60%, Robert Y. Newell, Bernard A. Hausen/4.76%, Doug T. Ellison, Entities and Persons Affiliated with Allen& Company Incorporated/7.70%, Stephen A. Yencho/4.09%, Robert C. Robbins, Kevin T. Larkin *(18 Owners included in Index)*

Financial Data: Fiscal Year End:06/30 **Latest Annual Data:** 6/30/2006

Year	Sales	Net Income
2006	$2,059,000	-$12,416,000
2005	$2,056,000	-$10,950,000
2004	$836,000	-$10,710,000

Curr. Assets:	$33,247,000	**Curr. Liab.:**	$1,645,000		
Plant, Equip.:	$1,401,000	**Total Liab.:**	$17,481,000	**Indic. Yr. Divd.:**	NA
Total Assets:	$35,158,000	**Net Worth:**	$17,677,000	**Debt/ Equity:**	0.1375

Cardiff Communications Inc

2979 Se Gran Pk. Way, Stuart, FL, 34997; *PH:* 1-772-287-2414

General - Incorporation	NV	**Stock**- Price on:12/24/2007	NA
Employees	NA	Stock Exchange	OTC
Auditor	Chisholm, Bierwolf & Nilson, LLC	Ticker Symbol	LBMH
Stk Agt.	NA	Outstanding Shares	NA
Counsel	NA	E.P.S.	NA
DUNS No.	NA	Shareholders	NA

Business: The groups principle activity is to provide recruiting services. The groups service area includes the research and development, engineering, marketing, sales, information technology and manufacturing industries. The group operates from United States.

Primary SIC and add'l.: 4841

CIK No: 0000017485

Subsidiaries: Summit Media, Inc.

Officers: Rubin Rodriguez/47/Dir., CEO, Pres., Financial Officer, Mark Libratore/57/Founder, CEO, Pres., Bob Davis/61/VP - Finance, John Leger/53/Sr. VP - Operations, Paul Levett/62/VP - Marketing

Directors: Rubin Rodriguez/47/Dir., CEO, Pres., Financial Officer, Mark Libratore/57/Founder, CEO, Pres.

Owners: Rubin Rodriquez/97.00%

Financial Data: Fiscal Year End:09/30 **Latest Annual Data:** 09/30/2006

Year	Sales	Net Income
2006	NA	-$57,000
2004	NA	-$17,000
1999	$1,000	-$2,000

Curr. Assets:	$0	**Curr. Liab.:**	$274,000		
Plant, Equip.:	NA	**Total Liab.:**	$274,000	**Indic. Yr. Divd.:**	NA
Total Assets:	$4,000	**Net Worth:**	-$270,000	**Debt/ Equity:**	NA

Cardiff International Inc

16255 Ventura Blvd., Ste. 525, Encino, CA, 91436; *PH:* 1-818-879-9722

General - Incorporation	CO	**Stock**- Price on:12/24/2007	$0.55
Employees	4	Stock Exchange	OTC
Auditor	Rose, Snyder & Jacobs	Ticker Symbol	CDIF
Stk Agt.	Atlas Stock Transfer Corp	Outstanding Shares	22,570,000
Counsel	Laurence Simons International London	E.P.S.	-$0.04
DUNS No.	NA	Shareholders	NA

Business: The groups principal activity is to develop brilliant tuition cards. In the year 2005, the group acquired Legacy Card Company, Inc. The group operates from the United States.

Primary SIC and add'l.: 6770

CIK No: 0000811222

Owners: Insiders/42.20%, Gary R. Teel/28.40%, Daniel Thompson/13.80%

Financial Data: Fiscal Year End:12/31 **Latest Annual Data:** 12/31/2006

Year	Sales	Net Income
2006	NA	-$1,279,000
2005	NA	-$8,000

Curr. Assets:	NA	**Curr. Liab.:**	$53,000		
Plant, Equip.:	NA	**Total Liab.:**	$53,000	**Indic. Yr. Divd.:**	NA
Total Assets:	NA	**Net Worth:**	-$53,000	**Debt/ Equity:**	NA

Cardima Inc

47266 Benicia St., Fremont, CA, 94538; *PH:* 1-510-354-0300; *Fax:* 1-510-657-4476; *http://* www.cardima.com; *Email:* web.info@cardima.com

General - Incorporation	DE	**Stock**- Price on:12/24/2007	$0.047
Employees	31	Stock Exchange	OTC
Auditor	Marc Lumer & Co, BDO Seidman LLP	Ticker Symbol	CADM
Stk Agt.	U.S. Stock Transfer Corp	Outstanding Shares	102,900,000
Counsel	Pillsbury Winthrop Shaw Pittman LLP	E.P.S.	-$1.42
DUNS No.	80-389-2173	Shareholders	NA

Business: The group's principal activities are to design, develop, manufacture and market microcatheter systems for the mapping and ablation of cardiac arrhythmias. Arrhythmias are abnormal electrical heart rhythms that adversely affect the mechanical activities of the heart and can significantly affect a person's quality of life and be potentially fatal. The microcatheter systems are designed to locate and provide more extensive and less traumatic access to arrhythmia-causing tissue for diagnosing the arrhythmia. It also restores normal heart rhythms by isolating and destroying the arrhythmia-causing tissue using radio frequency energy, referred to as ablation. The microcatheter are also designed with variable stiffness and highly flexible distal tips that enhance access to the vasculature of the heart.

Primary SIC and add'l.: 3841

CIK No: 0001022570

Officers: Robert Cheney/Dir., CEO, John R. Cheney/50/Dir. - Apix International Limited, Eric Chan/Dir., CTO/$238,823.00, Gabriel B. Vegh/Dir., COO, Pres./$278,704.00, Chris Mak/CFO, Corp. Sec.

Directors: Robert Cheney/Dir., CEO, Tony Shum/Dir., Andrew K. Lee/37/Dir., Eric Chan/Dir., CTO, Gabriel B. Vegh/Dir., COO, Pres., Phillip C. Radlick/Dir., Tina Sim/39/Dir.

Owners: Insiders, Andrew K. Lee, Tina Sim, Apix International Limited, Tony Shum, Phillip Radlick, Gabriel B. Vegh, John R. Cheney, Eric K.Y. Chan

Financial Data: Fiscal Year End:12/31 **Latest Annual Data:** 12/31/2006

Year	Sales	Net Income
2006	$1,541,000	-$9,533,000
2005	$1,859,000	-$8,328,000
2004	$2,366,000	-$9,746,000

Curr. Assets:	$1,866,000	**Curr. Liab.:**	$15,010,000		
Plant, Equip.:	$280,000	**Total Liab.:**	$15,094,000	**Indic. Yr. Divd.:**	NA
Total Assets:	$2,217,000	**Net Worth:**	-$12,877,000	**Debt/ Equity:**	NA

Cardinal Bankshares Corp

101 Jacksonville Cir., Floyd, VA, 24091; *PH:* 1-540-745-4191; *Fax:* 1-540-745-4133; *http://* www.bankoffloyd.com; *Email:* bkfloyd@swva.net

General - Incorporation	VA	**Stock**- Price on:12/24/2007	$19.75
Employees	64	Stock Exchange	OTC
Auditor	Larrowe & Co. Plc	Ticker Symbol	CDBK
Stk Agt.	Bank of Floyd	Outstanding Shares	1,540,000
Counsel	NA	E.P.S.	$1.53
DUNS No.	NA	Shareholders	NA

Business: The group's principal activity is to provide comprehensive individual and corporate banking services. The group's deposit service includes demand and time deposits and lending services as installment, mortgage and other consumer. The group makes seasonal and term commercial loans, both alone and in conjunction with other banks or governmental agencies. At 31-Dec-2003 it operates in counties of floyd, carroll, montgomery, and roanoke, Virginia and the city of roanoke, Virginia, through five banking offices.

Primary SIC and add'l.: 6712 6022

CIK No: 0001022759

Subsidiaries: FBC, Inc

Owners: Insiders/8.91%, Dorsey H. Thompson, Stephanie Sigman, Joseph H. Conduff/6.31%, Joseph Howard Conduff/6.31%, William R. Gardner, Ronald Leon Moore, George Harris Warner, Kevin D. Mitchell/1.36%, Hot Creek Capital, L.L.C./7.27%, Carole A. Pratt

Financial Data: Fiscal Year End:12/31 **Latest Annual Data:** 12/31/2006

Year	Sales	Net Income
2006	$12,837,000	$2,511,000
2005	$11,443,000	$2,203,000
2004	$10,689,000	$2,242,000

Curr. Assets:	$34,325,000	**Curr. Liab.:**	$177,493,000	**P/E Ratio:**	11.76
Plant, Equip.:	$4,283,000	**Total Liab.:**	$179,459,000	**Indic. Yr. Divd.:**	$0.560
Total Assets:	$207,849,000	**Net Worth:**	$28,390,000	**Debt/ Equity:**	NA

Cardinal Communications

11025 Dover St., Ste. 100, Broomfield, CO, 80021; *PH:* 1-303-285-5379; *Fax:* 1-720-936-8283; *http://* www.cardinalcomms.com; *Email:* information@cardinalcomms.com

General - Incorporation	NV	**Stock**- Price on:12/24/2007	NA
Employees	115	Stock Exchange	OTC
Auditor	Aj. Robbins, P.C	Ticker Symbol	CDCIE
Stk Agt.	Securities Transfer Corp	Outstanding Shares	NA
Counsel	NA	E.P.S.	NA
DUNS No.	NA	Shareholders	NA

Business: The group's principal activities are to provide video (cable television) and data (Internet) services to business and residential customers. It markets and sells telecommunications-related hardware and software. On 25-Aug-2003, the group acquired the customer base and substantially all of the tangible and intangible assets and rights used in connection with the Internet services from pipeline networks of Colorado, llc. In sep 2003, it acquired certain assets of children's technology, inc. On 21-Apr-2004, the group acquired waveramp, llc. On 28-Jul-2004, the group acquired sunwest communications inc.

Primary SIC and add'l.: 7375

CIK No: 0001035398

Subsidiaries: Cardinal Broadband, LLC, Colorado River KOA, LLC, Connect Paging, Inc, CyberHighway, King Concrete, LLC, Rocky Mountain Panel, LLC, Sovereign Partners, LLC, USURF Telecom, Inc, Usurf TV

Officers: Ronald S. Bass/Principal Accounting Officer

Owners: Ron Bass, Ed Garneau/4.50%, Insiders/53.60%, Jeff Fiebig, Evergreen Venture Partners, LLC/3.60%, Monarch Pointe Fund, Ltd./6.10%, Richard E. Wilson, Crestview Capital MasterLLC/11.50%, Byron T. Young/1.50%, David A. Weisman/4.20%, Craig Cook, Ed Buckmaster/20.20%

Cardinal Financial Corp

8270 Greensboro Dr., Ste. 500, McLean, VA, 22102; *PH:* 1-703-584-3400; *Fax:* 1-703-584-3410; *http://* www.cardinalbank.com

General - Incorporation	VA	**Stock**- Price on:12/24/2007	$9.63
Employees	406	Stock Exchange	NDQ
Auditor	KPMG LLP	Ticker Symbol	CFNL
Stk Agt.	American Stock Transfer & Trust Co.	Outstanding Shares	24,470,000
Counsel	NA	E.P.S.	$0.21
DUNS No.	NA	Shareholders	NA

Business: The group's principal activity is to provide a broad range of banking services to individuals, professionals and small to medium sized businesses in northern Virginia. The services include commercial loans, commercial and residential mortgage loans, construction loans and consumer loans. The deposit

products include commercial and retail checking accounts, money market accounts, individual retirement accounts, regular interest-bearing savings accounts and certificates of deposits. The group also offers credit cards, telephone and Internet banking, automatic teller machines, trust services, insurance services, mortgage services and courier services.

Primary SIC and add'l.: 6022 6712

CIK No: 0001060523

Subsidiaries: Cardinal Bank, Cardinal Statutory Trust I, Cardinal Wealth Services,Inc., George Mason Mortgage, LLC, Wilson/Bennett Capital Management,Inc.

Officers: Bernard H. Clineburg/Chmn., CEO/$467,126.00, Gene D. Merrill/CEO - George Mason Mortgage, LLC, Dennis M. Griffith/Exec. VP - Real Estate Lending, Kevin F. Reynolds/Regional Pres., Betsy Piper/Pres. - Cardinal Trust, Investments, Brian Kennedy/VP - Business Development, Cardinal Trust, Investments, Benjamin J. Hill/VP, Portfolio Mgr. - Cardinal Trust, Investments, Brian F. Burnham/VP, Operations Mgr. - Cardinal Trust, Investments, Steven Collins/VP - Institutional Business Development, Cardinal Trust, Investments, Eleanor D. Schmidt/Exec. VP, Compliance Officer, Robert E. Bradecamp/Exec. VP, Corporate Treasurer, Kendal E. Carson/Pres./$734,033.00, Kim C. Liddell/47/COO, Exec. VP/$244,744.00, Betsy Piper Bach/Pres. - Trust, Investment Services, Christopher W. Bergstrom/Regional Pres., Chief Credit Officer/$245,548.00 *(18 Officers included in Index)*

Directors: Bernard H. Clineburg/Chmn., CEO, John H. Rust/Vice Chmn., Sidney O. Dewberry/Dir., Alice M. Starr/Dir., Alan G. Merten/Dir., George P. Shafran/Dir., Hamilton J. Lambert/Dir., James D. Russo/Dir., B. G. Beck/Dir., William G. Buck/Dir., Michael A. Garcia/Dir., William E. Peterson/Dir.

Owners: Insiders/13.37%, Alice M. Starr, Kendal E. Carson, George P. Shafran, B. G. Beck, Christopher W. Bergstrom, Sidney O. Dewberry, Robert A. Cern, Bernard H. Clineburg/4.35%, Mark A. Wendel, Hamilton J. Lambert, John H. Rust, William G. Buck, Michael A. Garcia, William E. Peterson *(18 Owners included in Index)*

Financial Data: *Fiscal Year End:*12/31 *Latest Annual Data:* 12/31/2006

Year	Sales	Net Income
2006	$109,085,000	$7,388,000
2005	$92,043,000	$9,876,000
2004	$49,932,000	$3,469,000

Curr. Assets:	$50,840,000	**Curr. Liab.:**	$1,238,537,000	**P/E Ratio:**	38.52
Plant, Equip.:	$20,039,000	**Total Liab.:**	$1,482,556,000	**Indic. Yr. Divd.:**	$0.040
Total Assets:	$1,638,429,000	**Net Worth:**	$155,873,000	**Debt/ Equity:**	1.5654

Cardinal Health Inc

7000 Cardinal Pl., Dublin, OH, 43017; *PH:* 1-614-757-5000; *http://* www.cardinal.com

General - Incorporation	OH	**Stock**- Price on:12/24/2007	$70.15
Employees	55,000	Stock Exchange	NYSE
Auditor	Ernst & Young LLP	Ticker Symbol	CAH
Stk Agt	Computershare Trust Co	Outstanding Shares	384,650,000
Counsel	NA	E.P.S.	$4.98
DUNS No.	NA	Shareholders	NA

Business: The groups principle activity is to provide products and services supporting the healthcare industry. The group operates through four segments namely, pharmaceutical services, medical products and services, pharmaceutical technologies and services, and clinical technologies and services. In the year 2006, the group acquired PerMed Pharmaceutical, Inc. The groups specific customers are CVS Corporation and Walgreen Co. The group operates from the United States. The group's total revenue in the year 2007 was 86,852.00 millions of USD.

Primary SIC and add'l.: 2833 2834 5122 2833 5122 2834 2834 5122 2833

CIK No: 0000721371

Subsidiaries: 6464661 Canada, Inc., Abilene Nuclear, LLC, ALARIS Medical 1 (Suisse), S..r.l., ALARIS Medical Cayman Islands, ALARIS Medical Luxembourg II S..r.l., ALARIS Medical Systems Foreign Sales Corporation, Alcon Building Branch, Allcaps Weichgelatinkapseln GmbH & Co. KG, Allcaps Weichgelatinkapseln Verwaltungs GmbH, Allegiance (BVI) Holdings Co. Ltd., Allegiance Corporation, Allegiance Healthcare (Labuan) Pte. Ltd., Allegiance Healthcare Holding B.V., Allegiance Healthcare International GmbH, Allegiance Labuan Holdings Pte. Ltd. 282 Subsidiaries included in the Index

Officers: Kerry R. Clark/Chmn., CEO/$10,822,840.00, Dave Schlotterbeck/CEO - Clinical, Medical Products/$3,250,571.00, Mark Parrish/53/CEO - Healthcare Supply Chain Services/$3,407,759.00, Troy Kirkpatrick/Contact - Media Relations, Scott Storrer/Group Pres. - Healthcare Supply Chain Services, Pharmaceutical, Jim Mazzola/Contact - Media Relations, Mark Rosenbaum/Pres. - Integrated Provider Solutions, Dan Walsh/Exec. VP, Chief Ethics, Compliance Officer, Carole Watkins/Chief Officer - Human Resources, Dwight Winstead/Group Pres. - Clinical Technologies, Services, Tara Schumacher/Contact - Media Relations, Stuart G. Laws/VP, Chief Accounting Officer, Principal Accounting Officer, Vivek Jain/Exec. VP - Strategy, Corporate Development, Robert D. Walter/Exec. Dir./$8,534,485.00, Frank Segrave/Pres. - Generics *(23 Officers included in Index)*

Directors: Kerry R. Clark/Chmn., CEO, Robert D. Walter/Exec. Dir., Calvin Darden/Dir., Gregory Kenny Kenny/Dir., Colleen F. Arnold/Dir., Robert L. Gerbig/Dir., John F. Finn/Dir., Philip L. Francis/Dir., Michael J. Losh/Dir., John B. McCoy/Dir., George H. Conrades/Dir., Richard C. Notebaert/Dir., Michael D. O'Halleran/Dir., David W. Raisbeck/Dir., Jean G. Spaulding/Dir. *(16 Directors included in Index)*

Owners: Dodge & Cox/11.80%, Insiders/2.90%, George H. Conrades, Philip L. Francis, Jeffrey W. Henderson, Jean G. Spaulding, Michael J. Losh, Calvin Darden, Wellington Management Company, LLP/5.70%, Capital Research and Management Company/9.10%, Robert D. Walter/2.00%, Richard C. Notebaert, Michael D. OHalleran, John F. Finn, Matthew D. Walter *(23 Owners included in Index)*

Financial Data: *Fiscal Year End:*06/30 *Latest Annual Data:* 6/30/2006

Year	Sales	Net Income
2006	$81,363,600,000	$1,000,100,000
2005	$74,910,700,000	$1,050,700,000
2004	$65,053,500,000	$1,474,500,000

Curr. Assets:	$14,776,700,000	**Curr. Liab.:**	$11,372,800,000	**P/E Ratio:**	21.45
Plant, Equip.:	$2,584,000,000	**Total Liab.:**	$14,883,400,000	**Indic. Yr. Divd.:**	$0.480
Total Assets:	$23,374,100,000	**Net Worth:**	$8,490,700,000	**Debt/ Equity:**	0.3683

Cardinal State Bank

3710 University Dr., Ste. 100, Durham, NC, 27707; *PH:* 1-919-403-2833; *Fax:* 1-919-403-2783; *http://* cardinalstatebank.com

General - Incorporation	NC	**Stock**- Price on:12/24/2007	$16.95
Employees	37	Stock Exchange	NDQ
Auditor	Larrowe & Co. PLC	Ticker Symbol	CSNC
Stk Agt	Registrar & Transfer Co	Outstanding Shares	2,260,000
Counsel	NA	E.P.S.	NA
DUNS No.	NA	Shareholders	NA

Business: The groups principle activity is to provide commercial banking services. The groups services include checking and savings accounts, commercial, consumer, mortgage and personal loans, and other associated financial services. The group operates from United States.

Primary SIC and add'l.: 6022 6712

CIK No:

Officers: John W. Mallard/CEO, Pres., Lewis A. Bass/Exec. VP, Chief Credit Officer, Wendy B. Wagner/COO, Exec. VP, Harold W. Parker/CFO, Exec. VP, Marlene Jewell/VP - Commercial Lender, Steve Anderson/Sr. VP, Commercial Lending Mgr., Danny Lloyd/First VP - Hillsborough City Executive, James Sansom/First VP - Commercial Lender, Pat Lawrence/VP - Commercial Lender

Cardiodynamics International Corp

6175 Nancy Ridge Dr., Ste. 300, San Diego, CA, 92121; *PH:* 1-858-535-0202; *Fax:* 1-858-535-0055; *http://* www.cardiodynamics.com

General - Incorporation	CA	**Stock**- Price on:12/24/2007	$0.74
Employees	202	Stock Exchange	NDQ
Auditor	Mayer Hoffman Mccann, P.C	Ticker Symbol	CDIC
Stk Agt	American Stock Transfer & Trust Co.	Outstanding Shares	48,830,000
Counsel	NA	E.P.S.	-$0.31
DUNS No.	03-805-9788	Shareholders	NA

Business: The group's principle activities include developing, manufacturing and marketing heart-monitoring devices. These devices provide medical professionals with continuous data on a range of parameters relating to blood flow and heart function. The technology noninvasively monitors the heart's ability to deliver blood to the body and the amount of fluid in the chest. The technology provides the medical professionals in the hospital to effectively assess, diagnose and treat congestive heart failure and hypertension and to evaluate emergency, pacemaker and dialysis patients. The company's primary products include bioz(R) icg monitor, bioztect(R) sensors, bioz(R) icg module, bioz.sim(R) icg simulator, bioz(R) system and bioz.PC system. The group operates from United States.

Primary SIC and add'l.: 3845

CIK No: 0000719722

Subsidiaries: CardioDynamics Management, GmbH, medis Medizinische Messtechnik, GmbH, Vermed, Inc.

Officers: Michael K. Perry/Dir., CEO, Donald J. Brooks/Pres. - Product Development, CTO, Paul R. Jansen/VP - Clinical, Marketing Development, Stephen P. Loomis/VP - Finance, Richard E. Trayler/COO, VP - International Operations, Rhonda F. Rhyne/Pres., Russell H. Bergen/VP - Operations

Directors: Michael K. Perry/Dir., CEO, James C. Gilstrap/Chmn., Robert W. Keith/Dir., Richard O. Martin/Dir., Lynne B. Parshall/Dir., Jay A. Warren/54/Dir.

Owners: Visium Asset Management, LLC/6.30%, Richard E. Trayler, Kairos Partners III Limited Partnership/5.50%, Richard O. Martin, Michael K. Perry/2.20%, J. Michael Paulson/5.90%, James C. Gilstrap/5.00%, Insiders/10.60%, Russell H. Bergen, Rhonda F. Rhyne/1.20%, Steve P. Loomis, Balyasny Asset Management, L.P./10.00%, B. Lynne Parshall, Robert W. Keith, Jay A. Warren *(16 Owners included in Index)*

Financial Data: *Fiscal Year End:*11/30 *Latest Annual Data:* 11/30/2006

Year	Sales	Net Income
2006	$30,342,000	-$6,694,000
2005	$37,005,000	-$14,945,000
2004	$40,988,000	$10,123,000

Curr. Assets:	$15,517,000	**Curr. Liab.:**	$5,884,000		
Plant, Equip.:	$5,456,000	**Total Liab.:**	$10,680,000	**Indic. Yr. Divd.:**	NA
Total Assets:	$36,388,000	**Net Worth:**	$25,406,000	**Debt/ Equity:**	0.1595

Cardiogenesis Corp CA

11 Musick, Irvine, CA, 92618; *PH:* 1-949-420-1800; *Fax:* 1-949-420-1888; *http://* www.eclipsesurg.com; *Email:* info@cardiogenesis.com

General - Incorporation	CA	**Stock**- Price on:12/24/2007	$0.26
Employees	30	Stock Exchange	OTC
Auditor	KMJ Corbin & Co. LLP	Ticker Symbol	CGCP
Stk Agt	Computershare Investor Services LLC	Outstanding Shares	45,270,000
Counsel	NA	E.P.S.	-$0.02
DUNS No.	60-470-3652	Shareholders	NA

Business: The group's principal activity is to design, develop, manufacture and distribute laser-based surgical products and disposable fiber-optic accessories. The group operates in the cardiovascular medical device segment. The products are used for the treatment of advanced cardiovascular disease through transmyocardial revascularization (tmr) and percuteneous myocardial revascularization (ptmr). The group sells its products primarily to hospitals and other healthcare providers in North America, Europe and Asia.

Primary SIC and add'l.: 3842 3845

CIK No: 0000863680

Subsidiaries: CardioGenesis Corporation, Compleat Corporation, Eclipse Surgical Technologies B.V.

Officers: John P. McIntyre/42/VP - Scientific, Regulatory Affairs, Richard P. Lanigan/Pres., Principal Executive Officer/$280,559.00, Charles J. Scarano/46/Sr. VP - Marketing, Business Development/$197,118.00, Gerard A. Arthur/49/Sr. VP - Operations/$194,325.00, William R. Abbott/CFO, Sr. VP, Sec., Treasurer

Directors: Paul J. McCormick/Chmn., Gary S. Allen/Dir., Robert L. Mortensen/Dir., Marvin J. Slepian/Dir., Gregory D. Waller/Dir.

Owners: Perkins Capital Management, Inc./14.00%, Charles J. Scarano, Gary S. Allen/1.00%, Insiders/6.90%, Richard P. Lanigan/1.50%, Paul J. McCormick, Michael J. Quinn/2.40%, Gerard A. Arthur, Robert L. Mortensen, Marvin J. Slepian

Financial Data: *Fiscal Year End:*12/31 *Latest Annual Data:* 12/31/2006

Year	Sales	Net Income
2006	$17,117,000	-$1,979,000
2005	$16,341,000	-$1,857,000
2004	$15,454,000	-$1,319,000

Curr. Assets:	$7,095,000	**Curr. Liab.:**	$4,319,000		
Plant, Equip.:	$617,000	**Total Liab.:**	$4,487,000	**Indic. Yr. Divd.:**	NA
Total Assets:	$7,775,000	**Net Worth:**	$3,288,000	**Debt/ Equity:**	0.0076

Cardiome Pharma Corp

6190 Agronomy Rd., 6th Fl., Vancouver, BC, V6T 1Z3; *PH:* 1-604-677-6905; *Fax:* 1-604-677-6915; *http://* www.cardiome.com

General - Incorporation....Canada
Employees....63
Auditor....Ernst & Young LLP
Stk Agt....Computer share & Trust Co.
Counsel....NA
DUNS No....25-215-7995

Stock- Price on:12/24/2007....$9.75
Stock Exchange....NDQ
Ticker Symbol....CRME
Outstanding Shares....63,240,000
E.P.S....-$1.03
Shareholders....NA

Business: The group's principal activities are to discover and develop proprietary drugs used in prevention of cardiac diseases. The group focuses on four projects designed to prevent or treat atrial and ventricular arrhythmia namely: RSD1235, RSD1122 and KV1.5 and Oxypurinol. On 8-Mar-2002, the group acquired Paralex, Inc.

Primary SIC and add'l.: 8731 2834

CIK No: 0001036141

Officers: Robert W. Rieder/Chmn., CEO, Donald A. McAfee/Chief Scientific Officer, Charles Fisher/Chief Medical Officer - Executive Vice Presidant, Clinical, Regulatery Affairs, Curtis Sikorsky/CFO, Doug G. Janzen/Dir., Pres., Chief Business Officer, Gregory N. Beatch/Vice Presidant, Scientific Affairs, Guy F. Cipriani/Vicepresidant, Buisness Development, Sheila M. Grant/VP - Product Development, Vernakalant, Taryn Boivin/VP - Pharmaceutical Sciences, Manifacturing, Karim Lalji/Sr. VP - Commercial Affairs, Peter K. Hofman/Investor Relation Officer

Directors: Robert W. Rieder/Chmn., CEO, Doug G. Janzen/Dir., Pres., Chief Business Officer, Harold H. Shlevin/Dir., Jackie M. Clegg/Dir., Peter W. Roberts/Dir., Richard M. Glickman/Dir., William L. Hunter/Dir.

Financial Data: **Fiscal Year End:**12/30 **Latest Annual Data:** 12/31/2006

Year	Sales	Net Income
2006	$17,981,000	-$30,692,000
2005	$13,831,000	-$47,081,000
2004	$21,923,000	-$23,140,000

Curr. Assets:	$52,260,000	**Curr. Liab.:**	$12,718,000		
Plant, Equip.:	$3,851,000	**Total Liab.:**	$13,692,000	**Indic. Yr. Divd.:**	NA
Total Assets:	$58,443,000	**Net Worth:**	$44,751,000	**Debt/ Equity:**	NA

Cardiotech International Inc

229 Andover St., Wilmington, MA, 01887; *PH:* 1-978-657-0075; *Fax:* 1-978-657-0074; *http://* www.cardiotech-inc.com; *Email:* general-info@cardiotech-inc.com

General - Incorporation....MA
Employees....164
Auditor....Ernst & Young LLP
Stk Agt......American Stock Transfer & Trust Co.
Counsel............Ellenof Grossman & Schole LLP
DUNS No....94-724-0008

Stock- Price on:12/24/2007....$1.39
Stock Exchange....AMEX
Ticker Symbol....CTE
Outstanding Shares....20,010,000
E.P.S....-$0.22
Shareholders....NA

Business: The group's principal activity is to develop and manufacture small bore vascular grafts or synthetic blood vessels. The vascular grafts, made of chronoflex, are used to replace, bypass or provide a new lining or arterial wall for occluded, damaged, dilated or severely diseased arteries. The group also provides routine vascular access for patients undergoing hemodialysis treatments. The group also develops and manufactures polyurethane-based biomaterials for use in acute and chronically implanted devices. On 07-Apr-2003, the group acquired gish biomedical inc.

Primary SIC and add'l.: 3841 3842 8731

CIK No: 0001011060

Subsidiaries: CardioTech Realty, LLC, Catheter and Disposables Technology,Inc., Dermaphylyx,Inc., Gish Biomedical,Inc.

Officers: Michael F. Adams/Dir., CEO, Pres./$219,985.00, Eric G. Walters/CFO, VP/$186,847.00, Andrew M. Reed/VP - Science, Technology/$140,001.00, Phil A. Beck/VP, GM/$101,863.00

Directors: Michael F. Adams/Dir., CEO, Pres., William J. O'Neill/Chmn., Anthony J. Armini/Dir., Michael A. Barretti/Dir., Jeremiah E. Dorsey/Dir.

Owners: Philip A. Beck, Anthony J. Armini, Michael Szycher/13.20%, Insiders/5.40%, Michael F. Adams/1.20%, Jeremiah E. Dorsey, Andrew M. Reed/1.00%, William J. ONeill, Michael L. Barretti/1.00%, Eric G. Walters/1.00%

Financial Data: **Fiscal Year End:**03/31 **Latest Annual Data:** 03/31/2007

Year	Sales	Net Income
2007	$21,151,000	-$2,962,000
2006	$22,381,000	-$5,069,000
2005	$21,841,000	-$1,595,000

Curr. Assets:	$14,953,000	**Curr. Liab.:**	$2,818,000		
Plant, Equip.:	$4,059,000	**Total Liab.:**	$2,947,000	**Indic. Yr. Divd.:**	NA
Total Assets:	$20,451,000	**Net Worth:**	$17,504,000	**Debt/ Equity:**	NA

CardioVascular BioTherapeutics Inc

1635 Village Ctr. Cir., Ste. 250, Las Vegas, NV, 89134; *PH:* 1-702-839-7200; *Fax:* 1-702-304-2120; *http://* www.cvbt.com

General - Incorporation....DE
Employees....25
Auditor ...Singer Lewak Greenbaum & Goldstein
Stk Agt......American Stock Transfer & Trust Co.
Counsel....NA
DUNS No....NA

Stock- Price on:12/24/2007....$1.01
Stock Exchange....OTC
Ticker Symbol....CVBT
Outstanding Shares....130,890,000
E.P.S....-$0.24
Shareholders....NA

Business: The groups principal activity is to develop new drugs for the treatment of cardiovascular diseases. The group products include CVBT-141A, CVBT-141B and CVBT-141C. The group operates from the United State.

Primary SIC and add'l.: 2834 2836

CIK No: 0001303497

Officers: Daniel C. Montano/Co - Chmn., CEO, Pres., Thomas J. Stegmann/Dir., Co - Founder, Chief Medical Officer, Member - Scientific Advisory Board, Mickael A. Flaa/Dir., VP, CFO, John William Jacobs/Dir., COO, Chief Scientific Officer, Member - Scientific Advisory Board, Kenneth A. Thomas/VP - Research, Development, Member - Scientific Advisory Board

Directors: Daniel C. Montano/Co - Chmn., CEO, Pres., Ralph A. Bradshaw/Chmn. - Scientific Advisory Board, Grant Gordon/Vice Chmn., Wolfgang Priemer/Dir., Thomas L. Ingram/Dir., Robert Levin/Dir., John William Jacobs/Dir., COO, Chief Scientific Officer, Member - Scientific Advisory Board, Thomas J. Stegmann/Dir., Co - Founder, Chief Medical Officer, Member - Scientific Advisory Board, Gary B. Abromovitz/Dir., Joong Ki Baik/Dir.

Owners: Joong Ki Baik/1.18%, Thomas Stegmann/22.54%, Thomas L. Ingram, Gary B. Abromovitz, Grant Gordon/4.16%, Mickael A. Flaa, Wolfgang Priemer/11.27%, Robert Levin, Daniel C. Montano/23.07%, Insiders/63.69%, John W. Jacobs

Financial Data: **Fiscal Year End:**12/31 **Latest Annual Data:** 12/31/2006

Year	Sales	Net Income
2006	NA	-$5,571,000
2005	NA	-$12,366,000
2004	NA	-$8,013,000

Curr. Assets:	$9,979,000	**Curr. Liab.:**	$1,910,000		
Plant, Equip.:	$887,000	**Total Liab.:**	$15,317,000	**Indic. Yr. Divd.:**	NA
Total Assets:	$12,427,000	**Net Worth:**	-$2,890,000	**Debt/ Equity:**	NA

Cardium Therapeutics Inc

3611 Valley Ctr. Dr., Ste. 525, San Diego, CA, 92130; *PH:* 1-858-436-1000; *Fax:* 1-858-436-1001; *http://* www.cardiumthx.com; *Email:* investorrelations@cardiumthx.com

General - Incorporation....DE
Employees....56
Auditor....Marcum & Kliegman, LLP
Stk Agt....Computershare Trust Co
Counsel....NA
DUNS No....NA

Stock- Price on:12/24/2007....$2.45
Stock Exchange....OTC
Ticker Symbol....CDTP
Outstanding Shares....40,910,000
E.P.S....-$0.59
Shareholders....NA

Business: The groups principle activity activities include developing and commercializing of novel biologic therapeutics, medical devices for cardiovascular and ischemic disease. The groups products include Generx, Corgentin, and Genvascor, The group marketed its products under the trade names Generx(TM) Excellarate(TM). In the year 2005, the group acquired AG Group in the year 2005 and Tissue Repair Company in the year 2006. The group operates from the United States. The groups quarterly revenue for September 2007 was 0.36 millions of USD.

Primary SIC and add'l.: 2836 3841

CIK No: 0000772320

Subsidiaries: Aries Ventures, Inc., Innercool Therapies, Inc., Tissue Repair Company

Officers: Christopher J. Reinhard/Chmn., CEO, Pres., Treasurer/$350,000.00, Gabor M. Rubanyi/Chief Scientific Officer, Chmn. - Scientific Advisory Board, Anthony Andrasfay/VP - Clinical Operations, Robert L. Engler/Chief Medical Advisor, Mark McCutchen/VP - Business Development, Tyler M. Dylan/Dir., Chief Business Officer, General Counsel, Exec. VP, Sec./$325,000.00, Dennis M. Mulroy/CFO, Randall W. Moreadith/Chief Medical Officer, Exec. VP/$1,255,858.00, Patricia L. Novak/VP - Program Development, Barbara K. Sosnowski/VP - Biologics Development, Jennifer A. Spinella/VP - Regulatory Affairs, Quality Assurance, Ted Williams/VP - Manufacturing, Technical Operations, Bonnie Ortega/Dir. - Investor Relations, Public Relations

Directors: Christopher J. Reinhard/Chmn., CEO, Pres., Treasurer, Tyler M. Dylan/Dir., Chief Business Officer, General Counsel, Exec. VP, Sec., Edward William Gabrielson/Dir., Gerald J. Lewis/Dir., Murray Hunter Hutchison/Dir., Lon Edward Otremba/Dir., Ronald I. Simon/Dir., Wolfgang Schaper/Dir., Member - Scientific Advisory Board, Seppo Yla-Herttuala/Dir., Member - Scientific Advisory Board, Claudio Basilico/Dir., Member - Scientific Advisory Board, William Sessa/Dir., Member - Scientific Advisory Board, Daniel H. Perez/Dir., Member - Scientific Advisory Board, Andrew M. Leitch/Dir.

Owners: Insiders/19.93%, Tyler M. Dylan/6.23%, Edward W. Gabrielson, Christopher J. Reinhard/7.22%, Randall W. Moreadith, Michael L. Magers, Ronald I. Simon, Murray H. Hutchison, Dennis M. Mulroy, Lon E. Otremba, Gabor M. Rubanyi/4.89%, Gerald J. Lewis

Financial Data: **Fiscal Year End:**12/31 **Latest Annual Data:** 12/31/2006

Year	Sales	Net Income
2006	$756,000	-$18,593,000
2005	NA	-$200,000

Curr. Assets:	$2,543,000	**Curr. Liab.:**	$96,000		
Plant, Equip.:	NA	**Total Liab.:**	$96,000	**Indic. Yr. Divd.:**	NA
Total Assets:	$2,543,000	**Net Worth:**	$2,448,000	**Debt/ Equity:**	NA

Cardtrend International Inc

Formerly: Asia Payment Systems Inc
800 5thave., Ste. 4100, Seattle, wa, 98104; *PH:* 1-206-447-1379; *http://* www.asiapayinc.com

General - Incorporation....NV
Employees....NA
Auditor....Grant Thornton, LLP
Stk Agt............ Pacific Stock Transfer Company
Counsel....NA
DUNS No....NA

Stock- Price on:12/24/2007....NA
Stock Exchange....OTC
Ticker Symbol....CDTR
Outstanding Shares....NA
E.P.S....NA
Shareholders....NA

Business: The groups principle activities include credit card transaction processing and merchant acquiring services. The groups services include payment processing, credit card clearing s, e-commerce, online billing, and web based virtual POS terminal used for capturing bankcard transactions by call center staff. The group operates from the United States and China.

Primary SIC and add'l.: 7389

CIK No: 0001085113

Subsidiaries: Asia Payment Systems (HK) Ltd., Asia Payments, Inc, WOFE

Officers: King K. Ng/Executive Dir., CEO/$145,695.00, Charlie Rodriquez/Executive Dir., Sec., Treasurer/$72,000.00, Kok Keng Low/Executive Dir., COO/$38,604.00, Thomas Wong/CFO, Simon Ao/Head - Business Development, China Marketing

Directors: King K. Ng/Executive Dir., CEO, Robert G. Clarke/Chmn., Charlie Rodriquez/Executive Dir., Sec., Treasurer, Rosaline Tam/Dir., Michael J. Oliver/Dir., Jee Sam Choo/Dir., Kok Keng Low/Executive Dir., COO

Owners: Insiders/18.16%, Michael J. Oliver, Rosaline Tam, Charlie Rodriguez/1.40%, Leong Chee Wong, Kau King Ng/18.12%, Insiders/36.00%, Insiders/19.42%, Keng Kok Low/36.00%, Sam Jee Choo, Robert Clarke/14.59%, Kau King Ng/2.08%, Keng Kok Low, Bayview International Group Limited/3.80%, Indigo Capital Limited/4.00%

Curr. Assets:	$644,000	**Curr. Liab.:**	$2,254,000		
Plant, Equip.:	$313,000	**Total Liab.:**	$2,254,000	**Indic. Yr. Divd.:**	NA
Total Assets:	$2,223,000	**Net Worth:**	-$80,000	**Debt/ Equity:**	NA

Careadvantage Inc

485-C Rte. 1 S, Iselin, NJ, 08830; **PH:** 1-732-362-5000; **Fax:** 1-732-362-5005;
http:// www.careadvantage.com

General - Incorporation	DE	**Stock**- Price on:12/24/2007	$0.014
Employees	17	Stock Exchange	OTC
Auditor	Eisner LLP	Ticker Symbol	CADV
Stk Agt	American Stock Transfer & Trust Co.	Outstanding Shares	56,780,000
Counsel	NA	E.P.S.	$0.00
DUNS No.	87-827-7912	Shareholders	NA

Business: The group's principal activities are to provide management and health care cost containment services to health care insurers and other health service organizations. The group's management and consulting services have been provided to integrated health care delivery systems and other care management organizations. The group provided certain health care cost containment services, including utilization review, case management and disease management and independent reviews to horizon bcbsnj and another blue cross blue shield organization the subsidiaries of the group are careadvantage health systems, inc and contemporary health care management, inc.

Primary SIC and add'l.: 8099

CIK No: 0000937252

Subsidiaries: CareAdvantage Health Systems, Inc, Contemporary HealthCare Management, Inc.

Officers: Dennis J. Mouras/CEO, Pres., Robert Immitt/VP - Client Services, William Vennart/VP - Medical Management, National Medical Dir., Ellen S. Freedman/Dir. - Data Analytics, Richard Bernstein/Sr. Medical Dir., Silvana Pate-Latorre/Dir. - Human Resources, Stacy Percell/Contact, Sheila Van Daly/Sr. Accounting Mgr.

Owners: David G. Noone/5.70%, Dennis J. Mouras/13.79%, David J. McDonnell/2.46%, Insiders/20.15%, Credit Suisse Asset Management, LLC/13.27%

Financial Data: Fiscal Year End:12/31   Latest Annual Data: 12/31/2006

Year	Sales	Net Income
2006	$4,402,000	-$151,000
2005	$2,844,000	-$1,635,000
2004	$2,350,000	-$1,813,000

Curr. Assets:	$992,000	**Curr. Liab.:**	$497,000		
Plant, Equip.:	$232,000	**Total Liab.:**	$992,000	**Indic. Yr. Divd.:**	NA
Total Assets:	$1,392,000	**Net Worth:**	$400,000	**Debt/ Equity:**	0.3575

Career Education Corp

2895 Greenspoint Pkwy., Ste. 600, Hoffman Estates, IL, 60169; **PH:** 1-847-781-3600; **Fax:** 1-847-781-3610; http:// www.careered.com

General - Incorporation	DE	**Stock**- Price on:12/24/2007	$33.66
Employees	8,830	Stock Exchange	NDQ
Auditor	Ernst & Young LLP	Ticker Symbol	CECO
Stk Agt	Harris Trust and saving bank	Outstanding Shares	95,010,000
Counsel	NA	E.P.S.	$0.75
DUNS No.	88-473-6273	Shareholders	NA

Business: The groups principle activity is to provide educational services. The group operates from United States.

Primary SIC and add'l.: 8299 8249 8222 8221

CIK No: 0001046568

Subsidiaries: ABS Educational Heritage, LLC, AI Collins Graphic Design School, Ltd., AIU Educational Heritage, LLC, AIU Online, LLC, Allentown Business School, Ltd, American European Middle East Corporation, LLC, American InterContinental University,Inc., American Intercontinental University-London, Limited U.S., American Intercontinental University-London, Ltd., bassin de lat Villette) SAS, Briarcliffe College,Inc., Briarcliffe Educational Heritage, LLC, Brooks College, Ltd, Brooks Institute of Photography, LLC, Brown Institute, Ltd. 96 Subsidiaries included in the Index

Officers: Gary E. McCullough/Dir., CEO, Pres., Michael J. Graham/CFO, Exec. VP, Karen M. King/VP - Investor Relations, Casey Darby/Analyst - Investor Relations, Todd H. Steele/Pres. - International, Startup Divisions/$969,076.00, Paul Ryan/Pres. - Culinary, Health Education Divisions, Stephen C. Fireng/Pres. - University Group, College, Academy Divisions/$979,248.00, Steven M. Calbi/Chief Internal Auditor, Sr. VP, Robert M. McNamara/Chief Compliance Officer, Sr. VP, Patrick K. Pesch/51/Exec. VP, CFO, Assist. Sec./$1,342,057.00, Thomas G. Budlong/Sr. VP - Organization Effectiveness, Administration, Donna L. Gray/VP - Academic Affairs

Directors: Gary E. McCullough/Dir., CEO, Pres., Robert E. Dowdell/Chmn., Patrick K. Pesch/51/Exec. VP, CFO, Assist. Sec., Thomas B. Lally/Dir., Keith Ogata/Dir., Dennis H. Chookaszian/Dir., Patrick W. Gross/Dir., Leslie T. Thornton/Dir., Steven H. Lesnik/Dir.

Owners: Gary E. McCullough, Steven H. Lesnik, Patrick W. Gross, John M. Larson, Barclays Global Investors, NA/8.20%, Keith K. Ogata, Todd H. Steele, Leslie T. Thornton, FMR Corp./11.30%, Blum Capital Partners, L.P./8.30%, Dennis H. Chookaszian, Prudential Financial,Inc./5.30%, Steven B. Sotraidis, Thomas B. Lally, Robert E. Dowdell *(19 Owners included in Index)*

Financial Data: Fiscal Year End:12/31   Latest Annual Data: 12/31/2006

Year	Sales	Net Income
2006	$1,785,619,000	$46,569,000
2005	$2,034,555,000	$233,878,000
2004	$1,728,532,000	$179,619,000

Curr. Assets:	$662,443,000	**Curr. Liab.:**	$312,503,000	**P/E Ratio:**	42.08
Plant, Equip.:	$349,414,000	**Total Liab.:**	$443,262,000	**Indic. Yr. Divd.:**	NA
Total Assets:	$1,425,663,000	**Net Worth:**	$982,401,000	**Debt/ Equity:**	0.0033

CareGuide Inc

4401 NW 124th Ave., Coral Springs, FL, 33065; **PH:** 1-954-344-2444; **Fax:** 1-954-796-3703; http:// www.ptisys.com; **Email:** investorrelations@careguide.com

General - Incorporation	DE	**Stock**- Price on:12/24/2007	$0.47
Employees	206	Stock Exchange	OTC
Auditor	McGladrey & Pullen LLP	Ticker Symbol	CGDE
Stk Agt	Continental Stock Transfer & Trust Co	Outstanding Shares	67,540,000
Counsel	NA	E.P.S.	-$0.13
DUNS No.	NA	Shareholders	NA

Business: The groups principal activity is to deliver the next generation of health optimizing solutions. The groups product is Care Team Connect(TM). The groups services include understand, plan and merge eldercare, integrated health and care management, innova care soluion. The group operates from the United States.

Primary SIC and add'l.: 8099

CIK No: 0001017813

Subsidiaries: CareGuide, Inc., CBCA Care Management, Inc, CCS Consolidated, Inc, CCS Merger Corp, CCS New Jersey, Inc., CCS/CG Holdings, Inc., Coordinated Care Solutions IPA, Inc, Coordinated Care Solutions of Connecticut, Inc, Coordinated Care Solutions of Connecticut, Inc., Coordinated Care Solutions of Texas, Inc., Coordinated Care Solutions, Inc, Coordinated Physicians Solutions, Inc, IHS Network Services, Inc., PATY Acquisition Corp, Professional Review Network, Inc.

Officers: Chris E. Paterson/Dir., CEO, Rex M. Dendinger/55/CIO, Sr. VP, Julie A. Meek/COO, Exec. VP, Kent A. Tapper/51/VP - Finance, Thomas L. Tran/CFO, Pres., John R. Pegues/Exec. VP, Chief Marketing Officer, Kim Braxl/Sec.

Directors: Chris E. Paterson/Dir., CEO, Albert S. Waxman/Chmn., John Pappajohn/Vice Chmn., Daniel C. Lubin/48/Dir., Mark L. Pacala/Dir., Derace Schaffer/Dir., William C. Stapleton/Dir., Michael J. Barber/Dir.

Owners: Roger L. Chaufournier, Hickory Venture Capital Corporation/13.40%, Chris E. Paterson/1.50%, Derace L. Schaffer/1.70%, Albert S. Waxman/10.30%, Christine St. Andre, Entities affiliated with Essex Woodlands Health Ventures/2.30%, Principal Life Insurance Company/5.50%, Entities affiliated with Psilos Group Partners/9.50%, Ashford Capital Management, Inc./5.60%, Glen A. Spence, Radius Venture Partners I, L.P./9.80%, John Pappajohn/12.50%, Daniel C. Lubin/9.80%, Insiders/35.70%

Financial Data: Fiscal Year End:03/31   Latest Annual Data: 12/31/2006

Year	Sales	Net Income
2006	$41,338,000	$69,000
2005	$11,057,000	-$5,376,000

Curr. Assets:	$15,742,000	**Curr. Liab.:**	$22,826,000		
Plant, Equip.:	$2,948,000	**Total Liab.:**	$30,460,000	**Indic. Yr. Divd.:**	NA
Total Assets:	$58,190,000	**Net Worth:**	$27,730,000	**Debt/ Equity:**	NA

Caremark Rx Inc

3000 Galleria Tower, Ste. 1000, Birmingham, AL, 35244; **PH:** 1-205-733-8996; http:// www.medpartners.com

General - Incorporation	DE	**Stock**- Price on:12/24/2007	NA
Employees	13,628	Stock Exchange	NA
Auditor	Ernst & Young, LLP	Ticker Symbol	NA
Stk Agt	American Stock Transfer & Trust Co.	Outstanding Shares	NA
Counsel	King & Spalding LLP	E.P.S.	NA
DUNS No.	80-441-4852	Shareholders	NA

Business: The group's principle activities are to provide pharmaceutical services in the United States through its wholly-owned indirect subsidiary, caremark inc. These services are referred to as pharmacy benefit management services and involve the design and administration of programs aimed at reducing the costs and improving the safety, effectiveness and convenience of prescription drug use. The group dispenses prescription drugs to customers through a network of about 55,000 retail pharmacies and automated mail service pharmacies located in phoenix, Arizona, westin, Florida, mount prospect, Illinois, san antonio and Texas. The customers of the group include sponsors of health benefit plans such as employers, insurance companies, unions, government employee groups and managed care organizations and other individuals.

Primary SIC and add'l.: 8082

CIK No: 0001000736

Subsidiaries: AdvancePCS Holding Corporation, ADVP Consolidation, LLC, Caremark Inc., Caremark International Inc., CaremarkPCS, CaremarkPCS Health Systems, LLC, CaremarkPCS Health, L.P.

Officers: Mac E. Crawford/Chmn., CEO, Pres., Peter J. Clemens/CFO, Exec. VP, Mark S. Weeks/Sr. VP, Controller, Principal Accounting Officer, Edward L. Hardin/Dir., Exec. VP, General Counsel

Directors: Mac E. Crawford/Chmn., CEO, Pres., Harris Diamond/Dir., Roger L. Headrick/Dir., Kristen E. Gibney Williams/Dir., David C. Brown/55/Dir., Edward L. Hardin/Dir., Exec. VP, General Counsel, Edwin M. Banks/44/Dir., Michael D. Ware/Dir., Colleen Conway-Welch/Dir., Jean-Pierre Millon/Dir., Lance C.A. Piccolo/Dir.

Caribbean Exploration Inc

3001 Knox St., Ste. 403, Dallas, TX, 75205; **PH:** 1-214-389-9800

General - Incorporation	TX	**Stock**- Price on:12/24/2007	NA
Employees	NA	Stock Exchange	NA
Auditor	NA	Ticker Symbol	NA
Stk Agt	NA	Outstanding Shares	NA
Counsel	NA	E.P.S.	NA
DUNS No.	NA	Shareholders	NA

Business: The group's activity is to discover and recover archeologically and historically significant shipwrecks and artifacts. The group expects to sell recovered cargo and artifacts. The group also expects to raise revenues by conducting exhibitions of artifacts, and produces associated documentaries and films and exploiting their findings through travel tours to shipwreck sites. The group is at a developmental stage.

Primary SIC and add'l.: 7900

CIK No: 0001310118

Caribou Coffee Company Inc

3900 Lakebreeze Ave. N, Minneapolis, MN, 55429; **PH:** 1-763-592-2200; **Fax:** 1-763-592-2300; http:// www.cariboucoffee.com

. N, Minneapolis, MN, 55429; *PH:* 1-763-592-2200; *Fax:* 1-763-592-2300;
http:// www.cariboucoffee.com

General - Incorporation	MN	**Stock**- Price on:12/24/2007	$6.97
Employees	1,793	Stock Exchange	NDQ
Auditor	Ernst & Young LLP	Ticker Symbol	CBOU
Stk Agt	Wells Fargo Bank, N.A.	Outstanding Shares	19,320,000
Counsel	NA	E.P.S	-$0.91
DUNS No.	NA	Shareholders	NA

Business: The groups principle activity is to provide gourmet coffee. The products of the group include teas, baked goods and whole bean coffee. The group products sold under the trade name Caribou Coffee, Reindeer Blend, Natural Decaf and Caribou Cooler. Customers served by the group include grocery stores and mass merchandisers, office coffee providers, airlines, hotels and entertainment venues. The group operates from the United States. The group's quarterly revenue for September 2007 was 61.98 millions of USD.

Primary SIC and add'l.: 5812 5812 2095 2095

CIK No: 0001332602

Subsidiaries: Caribou Coffee Development Company, Inc., Caribou MSP Airport, Caribou on Piedmont, Inc., Caribou Ventures, L.L.C.

Officers: Michael J. Coles/Chmn., CEO, Pres., George E. Mileusnic/CFO, Henry A. Stein/VP - Business Development, Commercial Sales, Chad Trewick/Sr. Dir. - Coffee, Tea, Mike Peterson/VP, Controller, Treasurer, Dan E. Lee/VP, General Counsel, Sec., Chris Rich/VP - Global Franchise, Karen McBride/VP - Human Resources, Michael Larson/Sr. Dir. - Information Systems, Kathy F. Hollenhorst/VP - Marketing, Julie Wolleat/Dir. - Real Estate, Amy O'Neil/Sr. VP - Store Operations, Paul Turek/VP - Support Operations, Deb Jones/VP - Training, Kathleen Heaney/Investor Relations Contact *(18 Officers included in Index)*

Directors: Michael J. Coles/Chmn., CEO, Pres., Wallace B. Doolin/Dir., Charles L. Griffith/Dir., Jeffrey C. Neal/Dir., Charles H. Ogburn/Dir., Kip R. Caffey/Dir.

Owners: Insiders, Caribou Holding Company Limited, Wallace B. Doolin, Charles H. Ogburn, Charles L. Griffith, Kip R. Caffey, Arcapita Investment Management Limited, George E. Mileusnic, Jeffrey C. Neal, Arcapita Bank B.S.C., Amy K. ONeil, Michael J. Coles, Christopher B. Rich, Janet D. Astor

Financial Data: ***Fiscal Year End:***01/01 ***Latest Annual Data:*** 12/31/2006

Year	Sales	Net Income
2006	$236,229,000	-$9,059,000
2005	$160,871,000	-$2,074,000

Curr. Assets:	$29,819,000	**Curr. Liab.:**	$32,221,000		
Plant, Equip.:	$104,755,000	**Total Liab.:**	$47,905,000	**Indic. Yr. Divd.:**	NA
Total Assets:	$136,308,000	**Net Worth:**	$88,402,000	**Debt/ Equity:**	NA

Carlisle Companies Inc

13925 Ballantyne Corporate Pl., Ste. 400, Charlotte, NC, 28277; *PH:* 1-704-501-1100;
Fax: 1-704-501-1190; *http://* www.carlisle.com

General - Incorporation	DE	**Stock**- Price on:12/24/2007	$45.9
Employees	11,000	Stock Exchange	NYSE
Auditor	Ernst& Young LLP	Ticker Symbol	CSL
Stk Agt	Computershare Investor Services LLC	Outstanding Shares	62,070,000
Counsel	NA	E.P.S	$3.98
DUNS No.	NA	Shareholders	NA

Business: The group operates through its subsidiaries whose principal activities include manufacturing and distributing products. The groups products include heavy-duty friction blocks, brake shoes, castings, pistons, springs, bearings, trucks and disc linings. The group operates through five segments namely, construction materials, industrial components, specialty products, transportation products and general industry. In the year 2005, the group acquired Zhejiand Kete and ArvinMeritor, Inc. The group operates from North America, Europe and China. Of the total net sales in the year 2006, the construction materials segment accounted for $1,111,184, industrial components $764,506, specialty products $187,578, transportation products $183,006 and general industry $326,236 (thousands).

Primary SIC and add'l.: 3556 3452 3421 3357 3715 3799 3061 3081 5093 5046 3715 5093 3452 3081 3713 3421 3061 3069 3052 3965 5072 5072 3089 3965 3429 3556 3496 3429 3496 5063 3089 3357 3799 3713 5046 3069 5078 5063 5078 3052 3060

CIK No: 0000790051

Subsidiaries: Carlisle Asia Pacific Limited, Carlisle Brake Products (Hangzhou) Co., Ltd., Carlisle Brake Products (UK) Limited, Carlisle Canada, a general partnership, Carlisle Coatings& Waterproofing Incorporated, Carlisle Corporation, Carlisle Engineered Products,Inc., Carlisle Europe BV, Carlisle Europe Off-Highway BV, Carlisle Europe On-Highway BV, Carlisle Financial Services BV, Carlisle Flight Services,Inc., Carlisle FoodService Products Europe BV, Carlisle FoodService Products Incorporated, Carlisle Hardcast Europe BV 46 Subsidiaries included in the Index

Officers: Richmond D. McKinnish/58/CEO, Pres./$5,279,081.00, Steven J. Ford/48/VP, Sec., General Counsel, Carol P. Lowe/42/CFO, VP/$886,424.00, Michael D. Popielec/46/Group Pres. - Diversified Components/$1,933,926.00, John W. Altmeyer/Group Pres. - Construction Materials/$1,728,260.00, Barry Littrell/53/Group Pres. - Industrial Components/$1,160,133.00, Kevin G. Forster/Pres. - Asia, Pacific

Directors: Stephen P. Munn/65/Chmn., Anthony W. Ruggiero/66/Dir., Peter L.A. Jamieson/69/Dir., Peter F. Krogh/71/Dir., Donald G. Calder/70/Dir., Robin S. Callahan/61/Dir., Eriberto R. Scocimara/72/Dir., Paul J. Choquette/69/Dir., Lawrence A. Sala/45/Dir., Magalen C. Webert/56/Dir.

Owners: Barry Littrell, John W. Altmeyer, Insiders/4.16%, Lawrence A. Sala, Magalen C. Webert, Peter L.A. Jamieson, Lord, Abbett& Co., LLC/6.90%, Peter F. Krogh, JPMorgan Chase& Co./6.20%, Cramer Rosenthal McGlynn, LLC/6.50%, Anthony W. Ruggiero, Donald G. Calder, Stephen P. Munn, Franklin Advisory Services, LLC/10.60%, Robin S. Callahan *(20 Owners included in Index)*

Financial Data: ***Fiscal Year End:***12/31 ***Latest Annual Data:*** 12/31/2006

Year	Sales	Net Income
2006	$2,572,510,000	$215,689,000
2005	$2,209,610,000	$106,365,000
2004	$2,227,614,000	$79,612,000

Curr. Assets:	$978,241,000	**Curr. Liab.:**	$466,686,000	**P/E Ratio:**	21.45
Plant, Equip.:	$462,707,000	**Total Liab.:**	$935,608,000	**Indic. Yr. Divd.:**	$0.580
Total Assets:	$1,877,817,000	**Net Worth:**	$942,209,000	**Debt/ Equity:**	NA

Carmanah Technologies Corp

Building 4, 203 Harbour Rd., Victoria, BC, V7H 1A1; *PH:* 1-250-380-0052;
http:// www.carmanah.com; *Email:* info@carmanah.com

General - Incorporation	Canada	**Stock**- Price on:12/24/2007	$2.1278
Employees	NA	Stock Exchange	OTC
Auditor	KPMG LLP	Ticker Symbol	CMHXF
Stk Agt	Pacific Corporate Trust Co	Outstanding Shares	NA
Counsel	NA	E.P.S	NA
DUNS No.	NA	Shareholders	NA

Business: The groups principle activity is to develop renewable technology solutions namely solar-powered light emitting diode, lighting, solar power systems, and LED illuminated signage. The group also provides renewable energy system solutions for industrial, residential and recreational power applications. The group operates from Canada.

Primary SIC and add'l.: 9999

CIK No: 0001085105

Subsidiaries: AVVA Technologies Inc., Carmanah Signs Inc., Carmanah Technologies Inc, Soltek Powersource Ltd.

Officers: Art Aylesworth/Dir., CEO, Brad Neufeld/VP - Sales, Matthew Watson/COO, Richard Sowter/VP - Sales, Marketing, UK, Europe, Peeyush Varshney/41/Corp. Sec., Philippe Favreau/COO, Roland Sartorius/CFO, Richard Chesson/VP - Business Strategy, Andrea Voysey/VP - Marketing, Bob Boulter/VP - Finance

Directors: Art Aylesworth/Dir., CEO, David R. Green/Chmn., Don Hargreaves/Dir., Mark Komonoski/47/Dir., David Egles/Dir., Kelly Edmison/Dir., Praveen K. Varshney/Dir., Irene Schamhart/Dir., Derek Frohloff/Dir., Divesh Sisodraker/Dir., Julian Elliott/Dir., Robert J. Logan/Dir.

Owners: Kelly Edmison, Mark Komonoski, David Green/5.79%, Art Aylesworth/3.01%, Peeyush Varshney, Divesh Sisodraker, Insiders/11.98%, Dave Egles/1.27%, Praveen K. Varshney

Financial Data: ***Fiscal Year End:***12/31 ***Latest Annual Data:*** 12/31/2006

Year	Sales	Net Income
2006	$53,585,000	$211,000
2005	$33,230,000	$650,000
2004	$13,198,000	$123,000

Curr. Assets:	$32,575,000	**Curr. Liab.:**	$9,135,000		
Plant, Equip.:	$2,580,000	**Total Liab.:**	$9,139,000	**Indic. Yr. Divd.:**	NA
Total Assets:	$46,069,000	**Net Worth:**	$36,930,000	**Debt/ Equity:**	NA

CarMax Inc

12800 Tuckahoe Creek Pkwy., Richmond, VA, 23238; *PH:* 1-804-747-0422; *Fax:* 1-804-217-6819;
http:// www.carmax.com

General - Incorporation	VA	**Stock**- Price on:12/24/2007	$25.61
Employees	13,736	Stock Exchange	NYSE
Auditor	KPMG LLP	Ticker Symbol	KMX
Stk Agt	Wells Fargo Bank, N.A.	Outstanding Shares	216,050,000
Counsel	NA	E.P.S	$0.92
DUNS No.	NA	Shareholders	NA

Business: The group's principle activity is to provide used cars and light trucks. The group also sells used cars under the brand names Mitsubishi, Nissan, Toyota, Ford and General Motors. The group operates from United States.

Primary SIC and add'l.: 5511

CIK No: 0001170010

Subsidiaries: CarMax Auto Superstores California, LLC, CarMax Auto Superstores Services, Inc., CarMax Auto Superstores West Coast, Inc., CarMax Auto Superstores, Inc., CarMax Business Services, LLC, Glen Allen Insurance, LTD

Officers: Thomas J. Folliard/Dir., CEO, Pres., Jeremy Byrnes/Assist. VP - Carmax Auto Finance, Mike Callahan/Assist. VP - Carmax Auto Finance, Bill Nash/VP - Auction Services, Ed Hill/VP - Service Operations, Laura Donahue/VP - Advertising, Keith D. Browning/Dir., CFO, Exec. VP, Corp. Sec., Dan Bickett/VP - Construction, Facilities, Michelle Halasz/Assist. VP, Deputy General Counsel, Barbara Harvill/VP - Managment Information Systems, Kim Orcutt/VP, Controller, Tom Wulf/Assist. VP - Store Operations, Veronica Hinckle/Assist. VP, Assist. Controller, Lynn Mussatt/Assist. VP - Business Operations, Natalie Wyatt/Assist. VP, Assist. Controller *(39 Officers included in Index)*

Directors: Thomas J. Folliard/Dir., CEO, Pres., William R. Tiefel/Chmn., Robert W. Grafton/Dir., Hugh G. Robinson/Dir., Vivian M. Stephenson/Dir., Beth A. Stewart/Dir., James F. Clingman/Dir., Edgar H. Grubb/Dir., Shira D. Goodman/Dir., Jeffrey E. Garten/Dir., Thomas G. Stemberg/Dir., Keith D. Browning/Dir., CFO, Exec. VP, Corp. Sec., William S. Kellogg/Dir.

Owners: Stephen F. Mandel/6.30%

Financial Data: ***Fiscal Year End:***02/28 ***Latest Annual Data:*** 2/28/2007

Year	Sales	Net Income
2007	$7,465,656,000	$198,597,000
2006	$6,364,294,000	$148,055,000
2005	$5,260,262,000	$112,928,000

Curr. Assets:	$1,150,516,000	**Curr. Liab.:**	$512,022,000	**P/E Ratio:**	27.96
Plant, Equip.:	$651,850,000	**Total Liab.:**	$638,198,000	**Indic. Yr. Divd.:**	NA
Total Assets:	$1,885,573,000	**Net Worth:**	$1,247,375,000	**Debt/ Equity:**	0.0270

Carmike Cinemas Inc

1301 First Ave., Columbus, GA, 31901; *PH:* 1-706-576-3400; *Fax:* 1-706-576-2812;
http:// www.carmike.com

General - Incorporation	DE	**Stock**- Price on:12/24/2007	$24.43
Employees	560	Stock Exchange	NDQ
Auditor	Deloitte & Touche, LLP	Ticker Symbol	CKEC
Stk Agt	Registrar & Transfer Co	Outstanding Shares	12,610,000
Counsel	NA	E.P.S	-$5.4
DUNS No.	00-679-4630	Shareholders	NA

Business: The group's principal activity is the operation of motion picture theatres. The group has operated in 299 theatres with 2,253 screens located in 35 states. The theatres are primarily located in small to mid-sized non urban markets. The theatres include electronic video games located in or adjacent to the lobby. It operates two family entertainment centres under the name hollywood connection, which feature multiplex theatres and other forms of family entertainment. The trademarks of the group include cinemas(R) and hollywood connection(r).

Primary SIC and add'l.: 7832

CIK No: 0000799088

Subsidiaries: Conway Theatres, LLC, Eastwynn Theatres, Inc., George G. Kerasotes Corporation, GKC Indiana Theatres, Inc., GKC Michigan Theatres, Inc., GKC Theatres, Inc., Military Services, Inc.

Officers: Michael W. Patrick/Chmn., CEO, Pres./$5,229,513.00, Fred W. Van Noy/50/Dir., COO, Sr. VP/$763,161.00, Patricia A. Wilson/56/Dir., Private Attorney, Jeffrey A. Cole/47/Assist. VP, Controller, Chief Accounting Officer, Richard B. Hare/Sr. VP - Finance, Treasurer, CFO/$595,522.00, Anthony J. Rhead/Sr. VP - Entertainment, Digital Cinema/$684,653.00, Gary F. Krannacker/VP - Operations, Madison H. Shirley/Sr. VP - Concessions, Assist. Sec., Larry B. Collins/VP - Film

Directors: Michael W. Patrick/Chmn., CEO, Pres., Alan J. Hirschfield/72/Dir., David S. Passman/55/Dir., Carl L. Patrick/60/Dir., Roland C. Smith/52/Dir., Fred W. Van Noy/50/Dir., COO, Sr. VP, Patricia A. Wilson/56/Dir., Private Attorney, Kevin D. Katari/37/Dir.

Owners: Roland C. Smith, Richard B. Hare, Patricia A. Wilson, Avenue Capital Management II, L.P./8.10%, Fine Capital Partners, L.P./8.10%, FMR Corp./10.20%, Lee Champion, Carl L. Patrick, Stadium Capital Management, Inc./7.00%, Dimensional Fund Advisors LP/5.90%, Fred W. Van Noy, Insiders/6.00%, S. David Passman, Anthony J. Rhead, Watershed Asset Management, L.L.C./6.60% *(18 Owners included in Index)*

Financial Data: ***Fiscal Year End:***12/31 ***Latest Annual Data:*** 12/31/2006

Year	Sales	Net Income
2006	$495,499,000	-$19,389,000
2005	$468,894,000	$177,000
2004	$494,475,000	$28,427,000

Curr. Assets:	$47,163,000	***Curr. Liab.:***	$70,699,000		
Plant, Equip.:	$549,258,000	***Total Liab.:***	$516,923,000	***Indic. Yr. Divd.:***	$0.700
Total Assets:	$720,561,000	***Net Worth:***	$203,638,000	***Debt/ Equity:***	2.2229

Carnival Corp

3655 NW 87th Ave., Miami, FL, 33178; ***PH:*** 1-305-599-2600; ***Fax:*** 1-305-406-4700; ***http://*** www.carnivalcorp.com

General - Incorporation	Panama	***Stock***- Price on:12/24/2007	$49.46
Employees	NA	Stock Exchange	NYSE
Auditor	PricewaterhouseCoopers LLP	Ticker Symbol	CCL
Stk Agt	Computershare Trust CO.	Outstanding Shares	836,490,000
Counsel	Carnival Corp	E.P.S	$2.842
DUNS No.	05-613-4315	Shareholders	NA

Business: The group's principal activity is to provide global vacation and leisure travel. It operates 12 cruise lines under the brand names: carnival cruise lines, princess cruises, Holland America line, windstar cruises, seabourn cruise line, costa cruises, cunard line, p&o cruises, ocean village, swan hellenic, aida and p&o cruises. The group also operates two tour companies under the brand names Holland America tours and princess tours. The tour business of the group operates 17 hotels in Alaska and the Canadian yukon, 500 motorcoaches used for sightseeing and charters in the states of Washington and Alaska and in british columbia, Canada and the Canadian yukon. It also operates 20 domed rail cars which are run on the Alaska railroad between anchorage and fairbanks and two luxury dayboats offering tours to the glaciers of Alaska and the yukon river. On 17-Apr-2003, it acquired p&o princess cruises plc.

Primary SIC and add'l.: 7999 7011 4489 4481 4725 4729

CIK No: 0000815097

Subsidiaries: Costa Crociere, S.p.A., HAL Antillen N.V., Holland America Line N.V., Princess Bermuda Holdings Ltd., Princess Cruise Lines Ltd., Sitmar International Srl (Sitmar), Sunshine Shipping Corp. (Sunshine)

Officers: Ann Sherry/CEO - Carnival Australia, Micky Arison/57/Chmn., CEO, David K. Dingle/CEO - Carnival UK, Pamela C. Conover/CEO, Pres. - Seabourn Cruise Line, John Parker/64/Chmn. - National Grid plc, The Peninsular, Oriental Steam Navigation Company, Howard S. Frank/66/Vice Chmn., COO, Carol Marlow/MD, Pres., Stein Kruse/Pres., Ian J. Gaunt/Sr. VP - International, Richard D. Ames/Sr. VP - Shared Services, Alan B. Buckelew/Pres., Michael Thamm/44/Pres. - Aida Cruises, Gianni Onorato/Pres. - Costa Crociere SpA, Arnaldo Perez/Sr. VP, General Counsel, Sec., Beth Roberts/VP - Investor Relations *(16 Officers included in Index)*

Directors: Micky Arison/57/Chmn., CEO, Howard S. Frank/66/Vice Chmn., COO, Baroness Hogg/60/Dir., Richard G. Capen/72/Dir., Robert H. Dickinson/Dir., Kirk A. Lanterman/Dir., Peter G. Ratcliffe/58/Dir., Laura Weil/Dir., Uzi Zucker/71/Dir., Richard J. Glasier/61/Dir., Arnold W. Donald/52/Dir., Modesto A. Maidique/67/Dir., Pier Luigi Foschi/60/Dir., Stuart Subotnick/65/Dir.

Owners: Nickel 2003 GRAT, Robert H. Dickinson, Howard S. Frank, Artsfare 2006 Trust No. 2, MA 1994 B Shares, L.P., Insiders, Artsfare 2003 Trust, James M. Dubin, Knight Protector, Inc., John J. ONeil, Richard J. Glasier, Citigroup Inc., Peter G. Ratcliffe, Eternity Two Trust, Artsfare 2006 Trust No. 1 *(40 Owners included in Index)*

Financial Data: ***Fiscal Year End:***11/30 ***Latest Annual Data:*** 11/30/2006

Year	Sales	Net Income
2006	$11,839,000,000	$2,279,000,000
2005	$11,087,000,000	$2,257,000,000
2004	$9,727,000,000	$1,854,000,000

Curr. Assets:	$1,995,000,000	***Curr. Liab.:***	$5,415,000,000	***P/E Ratio:***	17.40
Plant, Equip.:	$23,458,000,000	***Total Liab.:***	$12,342,000,000	***Indic. Yr. Divd.:***	$1.400
Total Assets:	$30,552,000,000	***Net Worth:***	$18,210,000,000	***Debt/ Equity:***	0.3365

Carnival Plc

3655 NW 87th Ave., Miami, FL, 33178; ***PH:*** 1-305-599-2600; ***Fax:*** 1-305-406-4700; ***http://*** www.carnivalcorp.com

General - Incorporation	England And Wales	***Stock***- Price on:12/24/2007	$49.55
Employees	67,000	Stock Exchange	NYSE
Auditor	PricewaterhouseCoopers LLP	Ticker Symbol	CUK
Stk Agt	Suntrust Bank	Outstanding Shares	836,490,000
Counsel	NA	E.P.S	$2.91
DUNS No.	NA	Shareholders	NA

Business: The group's principle activity is the operation of cruise ships. The group offers a range of holiday vacation products to a customer base that is broadly varied in terms of cultures, language and leisure-time preferences. The group operates with a portfolio of 12 cruise brands which includes carnival cruise lines, princess cruises, Holland America line, windstar cruises, seabourn cruise line; p&o cruises cunard line, ocean village, swan hellenic , aida , costa cruises and p&o cruises. The group operates in countries such as North America, United Kingdom, Germany, Europe and Australia. The group's quarterly revenue for September 2007 was 3,124.00 millions of USD.

Primary SIC and add'l.: 4481

CIK No: 0001125259

Subsidiaries: Costa Crociere, S.p.A., HAL Antillen N.V., Holland America Line N.V., Princess Bermuda Holdings Ltd., Princess Cruise Lines Ltd, Sitmar International Srl, Sunshine Shipping Corp.

Officers: Micky Arison/57/Chmn., CEO, Ann Sherry/CEO - Carnival Australia, David K. Dingle/MD, CEO - Carnival UK, Gerald R. Cahill/CEO, Pres. - Carnival Cruise Lines, Howard S. Frank/66/Vice Chmn., COO, Richard G. Capen/72/Corp. Dir. - Author, Business Consultant, Richard D. Ames/Sr. VP - Shared Services, Ian J. Gaunt/Sr. VP - International, Arnaldo Perez/Sr. VP, General Counsel, Sec., Micahel Thamm/44/Pres. - Aida Cruises, Gianni Onorato/Pres. - Costa Crociere SpA, David Bernstein/CFO, Sr. VP, Beth Roberts/Investor Relations Officer, Michele Andjel/Investor Relations Officer

Directors: Micky Arison/57/Chmn., CEO, Howard S. Frank/66/Vice Chmn., COO, Pier Luigi Foschi/60/Dir., Uzi Zucker/71/Dir., Richard J. Glasier/61/Dir., Richard G. Capen/72/Corp. Dir. - Author, Business Consultant, Peter G. Ratcliffe/58/Dir., Robert H. Dickinson/Dir., Modesto A. Maidique/67/Dir., Stuart Subotnick/65/Dir., Arnold W. Donald/52/Dir., Baroness Sarah Hogg/60/Dir., Laura Weil/Dir., John Parker/64/Non - Exec. Dir.

Owners: John Parker, Baillie Gifford & Co./7.90%, The Capital Group Companies, Inc./10.00%, Pier Luigi Foschi, Legal & General Group plc/6.60%, Barones Hogg, Insiders

Financial Data: ***Fiscal Year End:***11/30 ***Latest Annual Data:*** 11/30/2006

Year	Sales	Net Income
2006	$11,839,000,000	$2,279,000,000
2005	$11,087,000,000	$2,257,000,000
2004	$9,727,000,000	$1,854,000,000

Curr. Assets:	$1,995,000,000	***Curr. Liab.:***	$5,415,000,000	***P/E Ratio:***	17.57
Plant, Equip.:	$23,458,000,000	***Total Liab.:***	$12,342,000,000	***Indic. Yr. Divd.:***	$1.600
Total Assets:	$30,552,000,000	***Net Worth:***	$18,210,000,000	***Debt/ Equity:***	0.3365

Carolina Bank Holdings Inc

528 College Rd., Greensboro, NC, 27410; ***PH:*** 1-336-288-1898; ***Fax:*** 1-336-286-5553; ***http://*** www.carolinabank.com

General - Incorporation	NC	***Stock***- Price on:12/24/2007	$13.1432
Employees	69	Stock Exchange	NDQ
Auditor	Cherry, Bekaert & Holland LLP	Ticker Symbol	CLBH
Stk Agt	Registrar & Transfer Co	Outstanding Shares	3,270,000
Counsel	NA	E.P.S	$0.85
DUNS No.	NA	Shareholders	NA

Business: The group's principal activities are to provide commercial and consumer banking services. The deposits accepted include personal, commercial checking, savings, money market accounts, certificates of deposit, individual retirement accounts and individual banking services. The lending activities include commercial loans to small-to-medium sized businesses, installment loans, credit card products, mortgage loans and equity lines of credit. The group's primary service area consists of the cities of greensboro and asheboro, which are located in guilford and randolph counties, North Carolina.

Primary SIC and add'l.: 6712 6022

CIK No: 0001127160

Subsidiaries: Carolina Bank, Carolina Capital Trust

Officers: Robert T. Braswell/Dir., CEO, Pres./$359,466.00, Pamela Sparks/VP, Branch Mgr. - Carolina Bank, Tom Wray/VP - Investment Services Consultant, Carolina Bank, Wayne J. Handy/VP, Mortgage Loan Officer, William M. Johnson/Sr. VP - Marketing Executive ~ Asheboro, Daniel D. Hornfeck/Sr. VP, Chief Credit Officer/$133,224.00, Sharon A. Williams/VP, Deposit Operations Mgr., Gunnar N.R. Fromen/Exec. VP, Sr. Loan Officer/$220,205.00, Bob Callicutt/VP, Branch Mgr. - Carolina Bank, Chris Clemmons/VP, Commercial Loan Officer - Carolina Bank, Jessica L. Gourley/Information Technology Officer - Carolina Bank, Marion Lyndon/Assist. VP, Mortgage Loan Officer - Carolina Bank, Ren Stewart/Assist. VP, Branch Mgr. - Carolina Bank, Allen T. Liles/CFO/$204,783.00, Phyllis Rainey/VP, Controller - Carolina Bank *(30 Officers included in Index)*

Directors: Robert T. Braswell/Dir., CEO, Pres., John D. Cornet/Chmn., Julius L. Young/Dir., Kenneth C. Mayer/Dir., Gray T. McCaskill/Dir., Alexander J.S Barrett/Dir., George E. Carr/Dir., James E. Hooper/Dir., Marlene H. Cato/Dir., Gary N. Brown/63/Dir., Wayne D. Thomas/Dir.

Owners: Insiders/13.14%, Gray T. McCaskill, Hot Creek Capital, L.L.C./5.22%, Marlene H. Cato/0.73%, Robert T. Braswell/3.26%, Julius L. Young/0.59%, George E. Carr/0.63%, James E. Hooper/1.48%, Gunnar N.R. Fromen/1.73%, J. Alexander S. Barrett, Daniel Hornfeck/0.34%, John D. Cornet/1.42%, Kenneth C. Mayer, Allen T. Liles/1.43%, Gary N. Brown/1.97%

Financial Data: ***Fiscal Year End:***12/31 ***Latest Annual Data:*** 12/31/2006

Year	Sales	Net Income
2006	$28,631,000	$2,811,000
2005	$20,180,000	$2,037,000
2004	$14,038,000	$1,633,000

Curr. Assets:	$4,983,000	***Curr. Liab.:***	$371,354,000		
Plant, Equip.:	$10,078,000	***Total Liab.:***	$385,663,000	***Indic. Yr. Divd.:***	NA
Total Assets:	$411,592,000	***Net Worth:***	$25,929,000	***Debt/ Equity:***	0.3848

Carolina National Corp

1350 Main St., Columbia, SC, 29201; ***PH:*** 1-803-779-0411; ***Fax:*** 1-803-779-0722; ***http://*** www.carolinanationalbank.com

General - Incorporation	SC	***Stock***- Price on:12/24/2007	$16.78
Employees	41	Stock Exchange	NDQ
Auditor	Elliot Davis LLC	Ticker Symbol	CNCP
Stk Agt	NA	Outstanding Shares	2,580,000
Counsel	NA	E.P.S	$0.78
DUNS No.	NA	Shareholders	NA

Business: The groups principle activity is to provide banking services. The groups services include savings accounts, retirement accounts, checking accounts, money market accounts, and time certificates of deposit. The group operates from United States.

Primary SIC and add'l.: NA

CIK No: 0001157648

Subsidiaries: Carolina National Bank and Trust Company

Officers: Roger B. Whaley/61/Dir., CEO, Pres./$227,485.00, Jack W. McElveen/COO/$142,283.00, Harry Brown/CFO/$105,032.00

Directors: Roger B. Whaley/61/Dir., CEO, Pres., Charlotte J. Berry/76/Dir., Joel A. Smith/62/Dir., Leevy I.S. Johnson/65/Dir., Kirkman Finlay/37/Dir., William P. Cate/63/Dir., Whitaker C. Moore/60/Dir., William H. Stern/51/Dir., Robert E. Staton/61/Dir., Joe E. Taylor/49/Dir., Leon Joseph Pinner/73/Dir., Angus B. Lafaye/64/Dir., R. C. McEntire/64/Dir.

Owners: Angus B. Lafaye, R. C. McEntire/2.44%, Roger B. Whaley/4.15%, Charlotte J. Berry, Leon Joseph Pinner, W. Jack McElveen, Joe E. Taylor/4.81%, I. S. Leevy Johnson, William H. Stern/4.61%, C. Whitaker Moore/1.18%, Kirkman Finlay/3.25%, Joel A. Smith/1.16%, William P. Cate/1.09%, Insiders/26.50%, Robert E. Staton/1.00%

Financial Data: *Fiscal Year End:* 12/31 *Latest Annual Data:* 12/31/2006

Year	Sales	Net Income
2006	$13,961,000	$1,929,000
2005	$8,398,000	$647,000
2004	$4,199,000	-$433,000

Curr. Assets:	$13,154,000	**Curr. Liab.:**	$178,114,000	**P/E Ratio:**	21.51
Plant, Equip.:	$1,486,000	**Total Liab.:**	$178,319,000	**Indic. Yr. Divd.:**	NA
Total Assets:	$208,912,000	**Net Worth:**	$30,593,000	**Debt/ Equity:**	NA

Carolina Power & Light Co

410 S Wilmington St., Raleigh, NC, 27601; *PH:* 1-919-546-6111; *http://* www.progress-energy.com

General - Incorporation	NC	**Stock** - Price on:12/24/2007	$47.43
Employees	11,000	Stock Exchange	NA
Auditor	Deloitte & Touche LLP	Ticker Symbol	NA
Stk Agt	Computershare Investor Services LLC	Outstanding Shares	257,860,000
Counsel	NA	E.P.S	NA
DUNS No.	00-699-7217	Shareholders	NA

Business: The group's principle actiivties include generating, transmitting, distributing and selling electricity in portions of North Carolina and South Carolina. The group operates from United States.

Primary SIC and add'l.: 4911

CIK No: 0000017797

Officers: Lloyd M. Yates/CEO, Pres., Fred N. Day/64/CEO, Pres./$1,717,523.00, Hilda Pinnix-Ragland/VP - Northern Region, Robert A. Sipes/VP - Western Region, Jeffrey M. Stone/46/Chief Accounting Officer, Erik R. Hansen/VP - System Planning, Operations, Peter M. Scott/58/CFO, Exec. VP/$4,197,537.00, Robert H. Bazemore/VP, Mark A. Myers/VP - Corporate Planning, John R. McArthur/Sr. VP, Sec./$1,115,726.00, Jackie Joyner/VP - Eastern Region, Robert F. Caldwell/VP - Regulated Commercial Operations, C. S. Hinnant/Sr. VP, Chief Nuclear Officer Nuclear Generation/$1,693,477.00, Charles M. Gates/VP, Emerson F. Gower/VP - Southern Region *(26 Officers included in Index)*

Directors: Robert B. McGehee/65/Chmn., Robert W. Jones/57/Dir., James E. Bostic/60/Dir., David L. Burner/68/Dir., Richard L. Daugherty/72/Dir., Harris E. Deloach/63/Dir., Steven W. Jones/56/Dir., Marie E. McKee/57/Dir., John H. Mullin/66/Dir., Carlos A. Saladrigas/59/Dir., Theresa M. Stone/63/Dir., Alfred C. Tollison/65/Dir.

Owners: Progress Energy, Inc./100.00%, W. D. Frederick, James E. Bostic, Edwin B. Borden, Richard L. Daugherty, Marie E. McKee, Jean Giles Wittner, Robert B. McGehee, Peter M. Scott, Insiders, John H. Mullin, Carlos A. Saladrigas, John R. McArthur, Theresa M. Stone, Alfred C. Tollison *(21 Owners included in Index)*

Financial Data: *Fiscal Year End:* 12/31 *Latest Annual Data:* 12/31/2006

Year	Sales	Net Income
2006	$9,570,000,000	$571,000,000
2005	$10,108,000,000	$697,000,000
2004	$9,772,000,000	$759,000,000

Curr. Assets:	$3,585,000,000	**Curr. Liab.:**	$2,818,000,000	**P/E Ratio:**	14.92
Plant, Equip.:	$15,732,000,000	**Total Liab.:**	$17,312,000,000	**Indic. Yr. Divd.:**	$2.440
Total Assets:	$25,701,000,000	**Net Worth:**	$8,379,000,000	**Debt/ Equity:**	1.0331

Carolina Trust Bank

901 E Main St., Lincolnton, NC, 28092; *PH:* 1-704-735-1104; *Fax:* 1-704-735-1258; *http://* www.carolinatrust.com

General - Incorporation		**Stock** - Price on:12/24/2007	$17
Employees	NA	Stock Exchange	NDQ
Auditor	NA	Ticker Symbol	CART
Stk Agt	NA	Outstanding Shares	1,570,000
Counsel	NA	E.P.S	NA
DUNS No.	NA	Shareholders	NA

Business: The groups principal activity is to provide community banking services. The products of the group include business loans, real estate loans, commercial loans and equipment & collateral loans. The group operates from Lincolnton, West Lincoln, Denver and Vale.

Primary SIC and add'l.: 6011 6712

CIK No:

Officers: Michael J. Cline/CEO, Pres., Donald J. Boyer/CFO, Sr. VP, Treva J. Carey/Sr. VP, Richard M. Rager/Sr. VP, Chief Credit Officer, Mort M. Wadsworth/Sr. VP - Sr. Lender

Carolyn River Projects Ltd

Formerly: Quorum Ventures Inc

2640 Tempe Knoll Dr., North Vancouver, BC, V6C 1V5; *PH:* 1-604-908-0233

General - Incorporation	NV	**Stock** - Price on:12/24/2007	NA
Employees	NA	Stock Exchange	OTC
Auditor	Dale Matheson Carr-Hilton LaBonte LLP	Ticker Symbol	CRPL
Stk Agt	NA	Outstanding Shares	NA
Counsel	NA	E.P.S	NA
DUNS No.	NA	Shareholders	NA

Business: The groups principal activity is engaged in the acquisition, and exploration of mineral properties with a view to exploiting any mineral deposits discover that demonstrate economic feasibility. The group operates from the United States.

Primary SIC and add'l.: 1000

CIK No: 0001305452

Officers: Steven Bolton/38/Dir., CEO, Pres., Bryan Markert/39/Dir., Sec., Treasurer

Directors: Steven Bolton/38/Dir., CEO, Pres., Bryan Markert/39/Dir., Sec., Treasurer

Owners: Steve Bolton/35.46%, Bryan Markert/35.46%, Insiders/70.92%

Financial Data: *Fiscal Year End:* 05/31 *Latest Annual Data:* 05/31/2007

Year	Sales	Net Income
2007	NA	-$18,000

Curr. Assets:	$4,000	**Curr. Liab.:**	$45,000		
Plant, Equip.:	NA	**Total Liab.:**	$45,000	**Indic. Yr. Divd.:**	NA
Total Assets:	$4,000	**Net Worth:**	-$40,000	**Debt/ Equity:**	NA

Carpenter Technology Corp

2 Meridian Blvd., Wyomissing, PA, 19610; *PH:* 1-610-208-2000; *Fax:* 1-610-208-3716; *http://* www.cartech.com

General - Incorporation	DE	**Stock** - Price on:12/24/2007	$132.26
Employees	3,990	Stock Exchange	NYSE
Auditor	PricewaterhouseCoopers LLP	Ticker Symbol	CRS
Stk Agt	American Stock Transfer & Trust Co.	Outstanding Shares	26,160,000
Counsel	John R. Welty	E.P.S	$4.46
DUNS No.	00-234-4315	Shareholders	NA

Business: The group's principle activities are to manufacture, fabricate and distribute specialty metals and two engineered products. The group operates in two segments namely, specialty metals and engineered products. The specialty metals segment deals with manufacture and distribution of titanium, high temperature alloys, electronic alloys, tool steels and other alloys in billet, bar, wire, rod, strip and powder forms. The engineered products segment deals with the manufacture and sale of structural ceramic products, ceramic cores for the casting industry, metal-injection molded products, tubular metal products for nuclear and aerospace applications, custom shaped bar and ultra hard wear materials. The major products of the group include stainless steels, special alloys, ceramics and other materials, titanium products, tools and other steel. The group's total revenue for year 2007 was 1,944.80 millions of USD.

Primary SIC and add'l.: 3312 3325 3264 3443

CIK No: 0000017843

Subsidiaries: Carpenter Investments, Inc., CRS Holdings, Inc., CRS Investments, Inc., Dynamet Incorporated, Talley Industries, Inc.

Officers: Anne L. Stevens/Chmn., CEO, Pres., Management Dir./$1,655,934.00, Sabina Colling/Europe, Dynamet, Laura B. Scott/CIO, VP, Mitchell Allenspach/Western US Sales, Dynamet, Andrew McElwee/VP - Bar Business Group, Jaime Vasquez/VP, Treasurer, Primary Investor Relations Officer, Mark S. Kamon/Sr. VP - Advanced Metals Operations, Sunil Y. Widge/CTO, Sr. VP, Kathleen T. Hanley/Sr. VP - Organizational Effectiveness, Strategy, Corporate Staffs, Shor Michael/Sr. VP - Engineered Products Operations, William W. Beible/VP - Advanced Manufacturing, Engineering, David L. Strobel/VP - Manufacturing, Christiansen David/VP, General Counsel, Sec./$1,079,080.00, Michael L. Shor/Sr. VP - Premium Alloys Operations/$2,013,842.00, Richard L. Simons/VP, Corporate Controller/$615,372.00 *(28 Officers included in Index)*

Directors: Anne L. Stevens/Chmn., CEO, Pres., Management Dir., Jeffrey Wadsworth/Dir., Peter N. Stephans/Dir., Kathryn C. Turner/Dir., Stephen M. Ward/Dir., Carl G. Anderson/Dir., Gregory A. Pratt/Dir., Martin I. Inglis/Dir., Phillip M. Anderson/Dir., Robert R. McMaster/Dir.

Owners: Ward S. M., Anderson P. M., G. A. Pratt, FMR Corp. Fidelity Investments/8.50%, Simons R. L., Insiders/1.00%, McMaster R. R., Inglis I. M., P. N. Stephan, Anderson C. G., Shor M. L., D. A. Christiansen, State Street Corporation/5.40%, Oates D. M., Stevens A. L. *(18 Owners included in Index)*

Financial Data: *Fiscal Year End:* 06/30 *Latest Annual Data:* 06/30/2007

Year	Sales	Net Income
2007	$1,944,800,000	$227,200,000
2006	$1,568,200,000	$211,800,000
2005	$1,314,200,000	$135,500,000

Curr. Assets:	$999,300,000	**Curr. Liab.:**	$271,400,000	**P/E Ratio:**	14.94
Plant, Equip.:	$541,100,000	**Total Liab.:**	$941,600,000	**Indic. Yr. Divd.:**	$1.200
Total Assets:	$1,887,900,000	**Net Worth:**	$946,300,000	**Debt/ Equity:**	0.2990

Carreker Corp

4055 Valley View Ln., Ste. 1000, Dallas, TX, 75244; *PH:* 1-972-458-1981; *http://* www.carreker.com

General - Incorporation	DE	**Stock** - Price on:12/24/2007	NA
Employees	495	Stock Exchange	NDQ
Auditor	Ernst & Young LLP	Ticker Symbol	CANI
Stk Agt	Mellon Investor Services LLC	Outstanding Shares	NA
Counsel	Locke Liddell & Sapp LLP	E.P.S	NA
DUNS No.	09-993-1313	Shareholders	NA

Business: The group's principle activity is to provide consulting and software solutions to the financial institutions. The group conducts its operations through three segments; global payments technologies, revenue enhancement and global payments consulting. Global payments technologies segment designs, develops, sells and supports the payment technology solutions and comprised of more than 126 software products and solutions. Revenue enhancement segment includes tactical consulting solutions, a licensable software product and sales management methodology. Global payments consulting segment provides banks with applied thought leadership related to payments. The group operates in the United States, Canada, Australia, Latin America, South Africa, Europe, and the United Kingdom.

Primary SIC and add'l.: 7372 7376 7379 7378 7371

CIK No: 0001057709

Subsidiaries: Carreker Canada, Inc., Carreker Holdings Australia Pty, Ltd., Carreker SAS, Carreker, Ltd., Carretek LLC, Mastek Carreker Pvt. Limited

Officers: John D. Carreker/63/Chmn., CEO, Lisa Peterson/Exec. VP, Treasurer, CFO, Blake Williams/Exec. VP, Pres. - Revenue Enhancement, John Davis/Exec. VP, General Counsel, Sec., Suzette Massie/Exec. VP, Pres. - Global Payments Consulting, Michael Inman/Exec. VP, MD, John D. Carreker/Exec. VP, Pres. - Global Payments Technologies, Ann Cain/Strategic Communications Dir.

Directors: John D. Carreker/63/Chmn., CEO, Donald House/64/Dir., James Erwin/62/Dir., Robert Olson/Dir., Gregory B. Tomlinson/66/Dir., David Sias/68/Dir., James D. Carreker/58/Dir., Coley J. Clark/60/Dir., W. C. Hammett/60/Dir., Jeff Watkins/46/Dir.

Carriage Services Inc

3040 Post Oak Blvd., Ste. 300, Houston, TX, 77056; *PH:* 1-713-332-8400; *Fax:* 1-713-332-8401; *http://* www.carriageservices.com

General - Incorporation	DE	**Stock** - Price on:12/24/2007	$8.03
Employees	714	Stock Exchange	NYSE
Auditor	KPMG LLP	Ticker Symbol	CSV
Stk Agt	American Stock Transfer & Trust Co.	Outstanding Shares	NA
Counsel	NA	E.P.S	$0.32
DUNS No.	78-212-8367	Shareholders	NA

Business: The group's principal activity is to provide death care services in the United States. It operates 139 funeral homes and 30 cemeteries in 29 states as on 31-Dec-2003. The group's operations are divided into two segments: funeral operations and cemetery operations. The funeral home provides services and products to meet the needs of families of the deceased, including consultation, removal and preparation of cremations. The group also provides sale of caskets and related funeral merchandise, the use of funeral home facilities for visitation and religious services and transportation services. The cemetery products and services include interment services, the rights to interment in cemetery sites including gravesites, mausoleum crypts and niches and related cemetery merchandise such as memorials and vaults.

Primary SIC and add'l.: 7261

CIK No: 0001016281

Subsidiaries: Barnett, Demrow & Ernst, Inc., Carriage Cemetery Services of California, Inc., Carriage Cemetery Services, Inc., Carriage Funeral Holdings, Inc., Carriage Funeral Services of California, Inc., Carriage Funeral Services of Idaho, Inc., Carriage Funeral Services of Kentucky, Inc., Carriage Funeral Services of Michigan, Inc., Carriage Holding Company, Inc., Carriage Insurance Agency of Massachusetts, Inc., Carriage Internet Strategies, Inc., Carriage Investments, Inc., Carriage Life Events, Inc., Carriage Management, L.P., Carriage Merger I, Inc. 39 Subsidiaries included in the Index

Officers: Melvin C. Payne/Chmn., CEO, Pres./$749,741.00, Joseph Saporito/CFO, Exec. VP, Sec./$542,638.00, George Klug/Sr. VP - Information Systems, CIO/$312,238.00, Terry Sanford/Sr. VP, Chief Accounting Officer, Treasurer - Carriage/$229,380.00, Clark W. Harlow/VP - Corporate Development/$206,623.00, Bradley J. Green/VP - Human Resources, General Counsel, Kevin Musico/VP - Strategic Development

Directors: Melvin C. Payne/Chmn., CEO, Pres., Vincent D. Foster/Dir., Joe R. Davis/Dir., Ronald A. Erickson/Dir., Gary Forbes/Dir.

Owners: Vincent D. Foster, Joe R. Davis, Dimensional Fund Advisors, Inc./8.00%, First Wilshire Securities Management, Inc./6.80%, Melvin C. Payne/7.20%, Zazove Associates, LLC/7.00%, George J. Klug, Joseph Saporito, Ronald A. Erickson, Mark F. Wilson/1.90%, FMR Corp./14.10%, Terry E. Sanford, Clark W. Harlow, Insiders/13.10%

Financial Data: *Fiscal Year End:*12/31 *Latest Annual Data:* 12/31/2006

Year	Sales	Net Income
2006	$151,086,000	-$1,416,000
2005	$155,034,000	-$21,865,000
2004	$150,206,000	$9,234,000

Curr. Assets:	$61,462,000	**Curr. Liab.:**	$25,707,000		
Plant, Equip.:	$157,692,000	**Total Liab.:**	$337,100,000	**Indic. Yr. Divd.:**	NA
Total Assets:	$564,996,000	**Net Worth:**	$96,373,000	**Debt/ Equity:**	2.3141

Carrier Access Corp

5395 Pearl Pkwy., Boulder, CO, 80301; *PH:* 1-303-442-5455; *Fax:* 1-303-443-5908; *http://* www.carrieraccess.com; *Email:* investors@carrieraccess.com

General - Incorporation	DE	Stock - Price on:12/24/2007	$4.84
Employees	304	Stock Exchange	NDQ
Auditor	Hein & Assoc. LLP	Ticker Symbol	CACS
Stk Agt	Computershare Investor Services LLC	Outstanding Shares	34,410,000
Counsel	Wilson Sonsini Goodrich & Rosati	E.P.S.	-$1.23
DUNS No.	NA	Shareholders	NA

Business: The group's principal activity is to manufacture high-performance equipment for telecommunication carriers. It provides broadband digital access equipment to communication service providers, including local exchange carriers, isps, iocs, interexchange carrier (ixc's) and wireless service providers. These broadband digital access equipment are used to enhance voice and high-speed Internet services to end-users like small and medium-sized businesses and government and educational institutions. The group's products include access bank(R), wide bank (R), access navigator(R), adit(tm), broadmore(tm), valet(tm), networkvalet(tm) and axxius(tm). The group markets its products through distributors and directly to end-user customers. On 25-Nov-2003, the group acquired paragon networks international inc.

Primary SIC and add'l.: 3661 4813

CIK No: 0001018074

Subsidiaries: CA Worldwide CV, Carrier Access Distribution Company, Carrier Access Holding Company, Carrier Access Operations Company, Nevko, Inc., Paragon Networks Canada Ltd., Paragon Networks International, Inc.

Officers: Ralph Loeffler/Wireline Sales Contact

Directors: John W. Barnett/Dir., Nancy Pierce/Dir., David R. Laube/Dir., Thomas C. Lamming/Dir., Lance W. Lord/61/Dir.

Owners: David R. Laube, John W. Barnett, Mark A. Floyd

Financial Data: *Fiscal Year End:*12/31 *Latest Annual Data:* 12/31/2006

Year	Sales	Net Income
2006	$75,416,000	-$14,836,000
2005	$75,628,000	-$6,632,000
2004	$95,493,000	-$1,779,000

Curr. Assets:	$146,759,000	**Curr. Liab.:**	$22,324,000		
Plant, Equip.:	$10,471,000	**Total Liab.:**	$22,436,000	**Indic. Yr. Divd.:**	NA
Total Assets:	$168,867,000	**Net Worth:**	$146,431,000	**Debt/ Equity:**	NA

Carrington Laboratories Inc

2001 Walnut Hill Ln., Irving, TX, 75038; *PH:* 1-972-518-1300; *Fax:* 1-972-518-1020; *http://* www.carringtonlabs.com; *Email:* info@carringtonlabs.com

General - Incorporation	TX	Stock - Price on:12/24/2007	$1.4399
Employees	260	Stock Exchange	OTC
Auditor	Weaver & Tidwell, L.l.p.	Ticker Symbol	CARN
Stk Agt	American Stock Transfer & Trust Co.	Outstanding Shares	10,900,000
Counsel	Thompson & Knight	E.P.S.	-$0.8
DUNS No.	06-898-3857	Shareholders	NA

Business: The group's principal activity is to develop, manufacture and market naturally-derived complex carbohydrates and therapeutics products. The products are used in the treatment of major illness, dressing, management of wounds and nutritional supplements. It operates through two business segments: medical services division and consumer products division. Medical services division offers a comprehensive line of wound management products to hospitals, alternate care facilities, cancer centers and the home health care market. The consumer products division markets or license consumer products and bulk raw materials utilizing the group's patented complex carbohydrate technology into the consumer health and nutritional products markets.

Primary SIC and add'l.: 2835 2834

CIK No: 0000718007

Subsidiaries: Caraloe, Inc., Carrington Laboratories International, Inc., DelSite Biotechnologies, Inc., Finca Savila, S.A., Hilcoa Corporation, Sabila Industrial, S.A.

Officers: Carlton E. Turner/Dir., CEO, Pres./$397,981.00, Doug Talley/Dir. - Quality Control, Jose Zuniga/VP - Operations, Carrington, Robert W. Schnitzius/CFO/$198,008.00, Doug Golwas/VP - Corporate Sales, Marketing/$147,806.00, Carol Kitchell/Dir. - Human Resources

Directors: Carlton E. Turner/Dir., CEO, Pres., George Demott/Chmn., Selvi Vescovi/Dir., Thomas J. Marquez/Dir., Dale R. Bowerman/Dir., Edwin Meese/Dir., Ronald R. Blanck/Dir.

Financial Data: *Fiscal Year End:*12/31 *Latest Annual Data:* 12/31/2006

Year	Sales	Net Income
2006	$27,406,000	-$7,607,000
2005	$27,961,000	-$5,336,000
2004	$30,821,000	$36,000

Curr. Assets:	$7,097,000	**Curr. Liab.:**	$6,061,000		
Plant, Equip.:	$6,093,000	**Total Liab.:**	$9,806,000	**Indic. Yr. Divd.:**	NA
Total Assets:	$13,998,000	**Net Worth:**	$4,192,000	**Debt/ Equity:**	0.8933

Carrizo Oil & Gas Inc

1000 Louisiana St., Ste. 1500, Houston, TX, 77002; *PH:* 1-713-328-1000; *Fax:* 1-713-328-1035; *http://* www.carrizo.cc

General - Incorporation	TX	Stock - Price on:12/24/2007	$44.95
Employees	68	Stock Exchange	NDQ
Auditor	Pannell Kerr Forster Of Texas, P.c.	Ticker Symbol	CRZO
Stk Agt	Computershare Trust Co	Outstanding Shares	26,000,000
Counsel	NA	E.P.S.	$0.35
DUNS No.	80-983-7313	Shareholders	NA

Business: The group's principal activities are the exploration, development and production of natural gas and crude oil. The operations are currently conducted on proven oil and gas producing trends along the gulf coast, primarily in Texas and Louisiana in the miocene, wilcox, frio and vicksburg trends. The group other interests include properties in east Texas, a coalbed methane investment in the rocky mountains and, recently, the barnett shale trend in north Texas. The group has acquired licenses for over 8,700 square miles of 3-D seismic data for processing and evaluation. As on 31-Dec-2003, the group operated 94 producing oil and natural gas wells.

Primary SIC and add'l.: 1382 1381 1311

CIK No: 0001040593

Subsidiaries: CCBM, Inc, Pinnacle Gas Resources, Inc

Officers: S. P. Johnson/CEO, Pres./$833,969.00, Gregory E. Evans/V P, Exploration/$680,748.00, Paul F. Boling/V P, CFO, Sec., Treasurer/$680,322.00, Allen B. Connel/V P, Dir. - Investor Relations, Bradley J. Fisher/V P, COO/$902,603.00, Dick Smith/V P, Land, Deborah Soho/Human Resources Inquiries

Directors: Steven A. Webster/Chmn.

Owners: Frank A. Wojtek, Advisory Research, Inc./8.40%, Thomas L. Carter, Richard H. Smith, Steven A. Webster/9.80%, Gregory E. Evans, Neuberger Berman Inc./7.90%, Insiders/15.10%, J. Bradley Fisher, S. P. Johnson/3.00%, Paul B. Loyd, Paul F. Boling, Centennial Energy Partners, L.L.C./5.30%, Roger A. Ramsey, F. Gardner Parker

Financial Data: *Fiscal Year End:*12/31 *Latest Annual Data:* 12/31/2006

Year	Sales	Net Income
2006	$82,945,000	$18,248,000
2005	$78,155,000	$10,634,000
2004	$52,397,000	$11,114,000

Curr. Assets:	$41,057,000	**Curr. Liab.:**	$58,071,000	**P/E Ratio:**	128.43
Plant, Equip.:	$445,447,000	**Total Liab.:**	$282,521,000	**Indic. Yr. Divd.:**	NA
Total Assets:	$494,795,000	**Net Worth:**	$212,274,000	**Debt/ Equity:**	1.0445

Carrollton Bancorp

344 N Charles St., Ste. 300, Baltimore, MD, 21201; *PH:* 1-410-536-4600; *Fax:* 1-410-625-0355; *http://* www.carrolltonbank.com

General - Incorporation	MD	Stock - Price on:12/24/2007	$16.51
Employees	138	Stock Exchange	NDQ
Auditor	Rowles & Co. LLP	Ticker Symbol	CRRB
Stk Agt	American Stock Transfer & Trust Co.	Outstanding Shares	2,830,000
Counsel	NA	E.P.S.	$0.80
DUNS No.	00-694-9853	Shareholders	NA

Business: The group's principal activity is to provide commercial and consumer banking products and services to individuals, businesses, professionals and governments. Carrollton bank is the principal subsidiary of the group. It operates through a network of 10 branches located in baltimore city, baltimore county and anne arundel county, Maryland and operates 155 ATM machines in Maryland, Virginia, west Virginia and Delaware. The group offers commercial loans for businesses, commercial and residential real estate loans, consumer loans and loans guaranteed by the United States small business administration. Its deposit products include money market deposits, demand deposits, now accounts and certificates of deposit. The group also provides credit and debit card services, merchant credit card deposit servicing, safe deposit boxes and brokerage services.

Primary SIC and add'l.: 6712 6022

CIK No: 0000859222

Subsidiaries: Carrollton Bank, Carrollton Community Development Corp., Carrollton Financial ServicesInc., Carrollton Mortgage Services,Inc.

Officers: Robert A. Altieri/46/CEO, Pres./$240,205.00, Gary M. Jewell/61/Sr. VP - Electronic Banking/$169,858.00, James M. Uveges/Sr. VP, CFO, Investor Relations Officer/$159,602.00, Lola B. Stokes/50/Sr. VP - Compliance, CRA Dir. - Bank, Edward R. Bootey/61/Sr. VP - Automation, Technology, Robert F. Hickey/Sr. VP - Branch Administration/$129,337.00, John A. Giovanazi/Sr. VP - Subsidiary/$154,521.00

Directors: Albert R. Counselman/Chmn., Howard S. Klein/Dir., David P. Hessler/Dir., Steven K. Breeden/Dir., Harold I. Hackerman/Dir., Charles E. Moore/Dir., John Paul Rogers/Dir., Ben F. Mason/Dir., Francis X. Ryan/Dir., William C. Rogers/Dir., William L. Hermann/Dir.

Financial Data: *Fiscal Year End:*12/31 *Latest Annual Data:* 12/31/2006

Year	Sales	Net Income
2006	$32,027,000	$2,585,000
2005	$29,790,000	$2,458,000
2004	$24,281,000	$888,000

Curr. Assets:	$15,337,000	**Curr. Liab.:**	$313,524,000	**P/E Ratio:**	20.64
Plant, Equip.:	$6,983,000	**Total Liab.:**	$315,114,000	**Indic. Yr. Divd.:**	$0.480
Total Assets:	$349,825,000	**Net Worth:**	$34,711,000	**Debt/ Equity:**	NA

Carters Inc

The Proscenium, 1170 Peachtree St. NE, Ste. 900, Atlanta, GA, 30309; *PH:* 1-404-745-2700; *Fax:* 1-404-892-0968; *http://* www.carters.com

General - Incorporation .... DE
Employees 2,959
Auditor .... PricewaterhouseCoopers LLP
Stk Agt...... American Stock Transfer & Trust Co.
Counsel .... NA
DUNS No. .... NA

Stock - Price on:12/24/2007 .... $26.53
Stock Exchange .... NYSE
Ticker Symbol .... CRI
Outstanding Shares 58,420,000
E.P.S .... -$1.23
Shareholders .... NA

Business: The group's principal activity is to market and manufacture baby apparel. The baby and sleepwear products include bodysuits, pajamas, blanket sleepers, gowns, bibs, towels, washcloths and receiving blankets. The group's playclothes products include knit and woven cotton apparel for everyday use in sizes 3 months to 7 and other products include bedding, outerwear, shoes, socks, diaper bags, gift sets, toys, room decor, and hair accessories. The group sells the products under the carter's and carter's classics brands in the wholesale channel, which includes over 370 department stores, national chain and specialty store accounts. The group operates 169 carter's retail stores located primarily in premier outlet centers throughout the United States. The group changed it's name from carter holdings inc in 2003.

Primary SIC and add'l.: 5641 5611

CIK No: 0001060822

Subsidiaries: Carters Retail, Inc., OBG Distribution Company, LLC, OshKosh BGosh Operations, LLC, OshKosh BGosh, Inc., The William Carter Company, TWCC Product Development and Sales, Inc.

Officers: Frederick J. Rowan/Chmn., CEO/$4,022,775.00, Joseph Pacifico/Pres./$2,365,172.00, Charles E. Whetzel/Exec. VP, Chief Sourcing Officer/$1,205,720.00, David A. Brown/COO, Exec. VP/$1,163,571.00, Michael D. Casey/CFO, Exec. VP/$1,213,919.00, Eric Martin/VP - Investor Relations

Directors: Frederick J. Rowan/Chmn., CEO, Bradley M. Bloom/Dir., John R. Welch/Dir., Paul Fulton/Dir., Elizabeth Smith/Dir., David Pulver/Dir., Thomas E. Whiddon/Dir., William J. Montgoris/Dir.

Owners: Insiders/9.60%, Charles E. Whetzel/1.50%, Thomas E. Whiddon, David A. Brown/1.40%, David Pulver, Paul Fulton, Michael D. Casey/1.20%, Columbia Wanger Asset Management, L.P./6.00%, Frederick J. Rowan/3.40%, Bradley M. Bloom, Elizabeth A. Smith, John R. Welch, The Guardian Life Insurance Company of America/8.00%, AMVESCAP PLC/10.40%, Baron Capital Group, Inc./9.60% *(16 Owners included in Index)*

Financial Data: **Fiscal Year End:**12/31 **Latest Annual Data:** 12/30/2006

Year	Sales	Net Income
2006	$1,343,467,000	$87,220,000
2005	$1,121,358,000	$47,202,000

Curr. Assets:	$399,045,000	**Curr. Liab.:**	$156,603,000		
Plant, Equip.:	$79,458,000	**Total Liab.:**	$730,083,000	**Indic. Yr. Divd.:**	NA
Total Assets:	$1,116,727,000	**Net Worth:**	$386,644,000	**Debt/ Equity:**	0.6910

Carver Bancorp Inc

75 W 125th St., New York, NY, 10027; *PH:* 1-212-876-4747; *Fax:* 1-212-426-6159; *http://* www.carverbank.com

General - Incorporation .... DE
Employees 126
Auditor .... KPMG LLP
Stk Agt...... American Stock Transfer & Trust Co.
Counsel .... Thacher Proffitt & Wood LLP
DUNS No. 07-521-9659

Stock - Price on:12/24/2007 .... $15.9
Stock Exchange .... NDQ
Ticker Symbol .... CARV
Outstanding Shares 2,510,000
E.P.S $1.78
Shareholders .... NA

Business: The group's principal activity is to attract deposits and invest in mortgage loans and other investments. Deposit services offered by the group include passbook savings accounts, money market savings accounts, now accounts and certificates of deposit. The loan products include commercial business loans, commercial real estate loans, construction loans and consumer loans including home equity loans, automobile loans, student loans, credit card loans, cash collateral personal loans and unsecured personal loans. At 31-Mar-2004, the group operated through six branch offices located in New York.

Primary SIC and add'l.: 6035 6712

CIK No: 0001016178

Subsidiaries: Carver Federal Savings Bank

Officers: Deborah C. Wright/Chmn., CEO, Pres./$788,771.00, David A. Hargraves/Sr. VP, Chief Retail Officer, Roy Swan/CFO, Exec. VP/$412,802.00, Carmelo Felix/Sr. VP, Dir. - Audit, Compliance, James H. Bason/51/Chief Lending Officer, Sr. VP/$264,518.00, Margaret D. Roberts/Sr. VP, Chief Human Resources Officer/$211,370.00, Frank J. Deaton/Sr. VP - Operations/$170,612.00, Charles F. Koehler/Exec. VP - Lending, Gina Lauren Bolden-Rivera/Sr. VP, Pres. - Carver Community Development Corporation, Susan M. Ifill/Sr. VP, Chief - Retail Banking

Directors: Deborah C. Wright/Chmn., CEO, Pres., Robert Holland/Dir., Edward B. Ruggiero/Dir., Carol Ann Baldwin Moody/Dir., Pazel G. Jackson/Dir., David Livingston Hinds/Dir., Samuel J. Daniel/Dir., Robert R. Tarter/Dir.

Owners: Wellington Management Company, LLP/9.70%, Samuel J. Daniel, Third Avenue Management LLC/8.70%, James H. Bason, Margaret Roberts, Donald Leigh Koch/8.30%, RASARA Strategies, Inc./8.10%, David L. Hinds, Gina Bolden-Rivera, Edward B. Ruggiero, Robert Holland, Strauss Zelnick, Deborah C. Wright/7.70%, Robert R. Tarter, Carol Baldwin-Moody *(19 Owners included in Index)*

Financial Data: **Fiscal Year End:**03/31 **Latest Annual Data:** 03/31/2007

Year	Sales	Net Income
2007	$46,043,000	$2,583,000
2006	$37,726,000	$3,770,000
2005	$34,168,000	$2,649,000

Curr. Assets:	$25,874,000	**Curr. Liab.:**	$598,430,000	**P/E Ratio:**	17.47
Plant, Equip.:	$13,194,000	**Total Liab.:**	$612,296,000	**Indic. Yr. Divd.:**	$0.360
Total Assets:	$660,993,000	**Net Worth:**	$48,697,000	**Debt/ Equity:**	NA

Cas Medical Systems Inc

44 E Industrial Rd., Branford, CT, 06405; *PH:* 1-203-488-6056; *Fax:* 1-203-488-9438; *http://* www.casmed.com; *Email:* custsrv@casmed.com

General - Incorporation .... DE
Employees 151
Auditor .... UHY LLP
Stk Agt...... American Stock Transfer & Trust Co.
Counsel .... Wiggin & Dana LLP
DUNS No. 12-221-1543

Stock - Price on:12/24/2007 .... $7.25
Stock Exchange .... NDQ
Ticker Symbol .... CASM
Outstanding Shares 10,700,000
E.P.S $0.09
Shareholders .... NA

Business: The group's principle activities include designing, manufacturing and marketing diagnostic equipment and medical products for use in the healthcare and medical industry. The products include blood pressure measurement equipment, apnea monitoring equipment and neonatal intensive care. The company offers two monitors for use in the emergency medical service (ems) marketplace. It also has a line of monitors for the hospital, alternate site and home care marketplaces. These monitors offer the basic monitoring parameters of non-invasive blood pressure, pulse oximetry and predictive temperature. The trademarks include casr, pedisphygr, oscillomater, neoguardr, tuff-cuffr, limboardr, klear-tracer and the heart shaped mark for use as a thermal reflector. The group operates from United States.

Primary SIC and add'l.: 3841 6794

CIK No: 0000764579

Subsidiaries: Statcorp, Inc

Officers: Andrew E. Kersey/Dir., CEO, Pres./$299,146.00, John Capodanno/Contact - Financial Dynamics Business Communications, Jeffery Baird/CFO/$276,411.00

Directors: Andrew E. Kersey/Dir., CEO, Pres., Louis P. Scheps/Chmn., Lawrence S. Burstein/Dir., Jerome S. Baron/Dir., Saul S. Milles/Dir.

Owners: Potomac Capital Management LLC/6.60%, Jeffery A. Baird/1.10%, Sanford J. Davis/9.50%, Lawrence S. Burstein/1.90%, Insiders/13.80%, Andrew E. Kersey/1.40%, Jerome Baron/1.10%, BMI Capital Corporation/17.10%, Louis P. Scheps/8.50%, Myron L. Cohen/6.10%

Financial Data: **Fiscal Year End:**12/31 **Latest Annual Data:** 12/31/2006

Year	Sales	Net Income
2006	$35,202,000	$1,747,000
2005	$26,884,000	$1,815,000
2004	$19,922,000	$1,205,000

Curr. Assets:	$14,108,000	**Curr. Liab.:**	$5,012,000		
Plant, Equip.:	$3,324,000	**Total Liab.:**	$8,819,000	**Indic. Yr. Divd.:**	NA
Total Assets:	$21,443,000	**Net Worth:**	$12,625,000	**Debt/ Equity:**	0.2823

Cascade Bancorp

1100 NW Wall St., Bend, OR, 97701; *PH:* 1-541-385-6205; *Fax:* 1-541-382-8780; *http://* www.botc.com; *Email:* info@amstock.com

General - Incorporation .... OR
Employees 573
Auditor .... Symonds, Evans & Co. P.C
Stk Agt...... American Stock Transfer & Trust Co.
Counsel .... Karnopp Petersen Noteboom Et Al
DUNS No. 82-644-8052

Stock - Price on:12/24/2007 .... $22.86
Stock Exchange .... NDQ
Ticker Symbol .... CACB
Outstanding Shares 28,460,000
E.P.S $1.41
Shareholders .... NA

Business: The group's principal activity is to provide commercial and personal banking services to businesses and consumers. As a holding company for the bank of the cascades, the group accepts checking, money market, and time deposit accounts and provides commercial, real estate and consumer loans. These loans include commercial real estate loans, construction and development loans, commercial and industrial loans as well as consumer installment, lines-of-credit and home equity loans. Lending activities serve small to medium-sized business, professional and consumer accounts. The federal deposit insurance corporation insures the group's deposits. Trust and investment services provided by the group include living and testamentary trust, asset and financial management and fiduciary services. Non banking services consist of cash management, lock box, Internet banking and electronic bill payment. On 01-Jan-2004, the group acquired community bank of grants pass.

Primary SIC and add'l.: 6022 6712

CIK No: 0000865911

Subsidiaries: Bank of the Cascades, Cascade Bancorp Trust I

Officers: Patricia L. Moss/Dir., CEO, William A. Haden/Exec. VP - Southern Oregon, Regional Mgr., Frank I. Wheeler/Exec. VP - Mortgage Center, Michael M. Mooney/Pres. - Idaho Region, Peggy L. Biss/Chief Human Resources Officer, Exec. VP, Michael J. Delvin/COO, Pres./$651,513.00, Frank R. Weis/Chief Credit Officer, Exec. VP, Gregory D. Newton/CFO, Exec. VP, Debbie C. Amerongen/Chief Deposit Officer, Exec. VP, Julie A. Miller/Exec. VP - Central Oregon, Regional Mgr., Walter O. Krumbholz/Exec. VP - Northwest Oregon, Regional Mgr.

Directors: Patricia L. Moss/Dir., CEO, Gary L. Hoffman/Chmn., Jerry E. Andres/Vice Chmn., Judith A. Johansen/Dir., James E. Petersen/Dir., Henry H. Hewitt/Dir., Gary L. Capps/Dir., Ryan R. Patrick/Dir., Clarence Jones/Dir., Thomas M. Wells/Dir.

Owners: Clarence Jones/0.07%, Insiders/4.12%, Patricia L. Moss/1.10%, David F. Bolger/21.07%, Peggy L. Biss/0.47%, Thomas M. Wells/0.10%, Henry Hewitt/0.02%, James E. Petersen/0.37%, Frank R. Weis/0.46%, Gary L. Hoffman/0.38%, Ryan R. Patrick/0.13%, Gary L. Capps/0.26%, Michael M. Mooney/0.04%, Barclays Global Investors/5.22%, Jerol E. Andres/0.08% *(19 Owners included in Index)*

Financial Data: **Fiscal Year End:**12/31 **Latest Annual Data:** 12/31/2006

Year	Sales	Net Income
2006	$156,752,000	$35,677,000
2005	$85,906,000	$22,436,000
2004	$63,851,000	$16,008,000

Curr. Assets:	$83,311,000	**Curr. Liab.:**	$1,748,390,000	**P/E Ratio:**	16.21
Plant, Equip.:	$40,553,000	**Total Liab.:**	$1,988,238,000	**Indic. Yr. Divd.:**	$0.360
Total Assets:	$2,249,314,000	**Net Worth:**	$261,076,000	**Debt/ Equity:**	0.9186

Cascade Corp

2201 NE 201st Ave., Fairview, OR, 97024; *PH:* 1-503-669-6300; *Fax:* 1-503-669-6716; *http://* www.cascorp.com; *Email:* sales@cascorp.com

General - Incorporation	OR	***Stock***- Price on:12/24/2007	$84.32
Employees	2,100	Stock Exchange	NYSE
Auditor	PricewaterhouseCoopers LLP	Ticker Symbol	CAE
Stk Agt	Mellon Shareholder Services LLC	Outstanding Shares	11,830,000
Counsel	NA	E.P.S	$4.88
DUNS No.	00-903-1378	Shareholders	NA

Business: The group's principle activity is to manufacture materials handling devices. The products are sold under the trade names of cascade and cascade-kenhar. The products provide forklift trucks and construction and agricultural vehicles with the capability of engaging, lifting, carrying and depositing various types of loads. The products are sold to original equipment manufacturers and dealers of lift trucks and construction, mining, agricultural and industrial mobile equipment. The sales are made throughout North America, Latin America, Europe, Asia, Africa, Australia and the Middle East. The group's headquarters are in fairview, Oregon and at its manufacturing facility in guelph, Canada. The group's total revenue for year 2007 was 478.85 millions of USD.

Primary SIC and add'l.: 3537

CIK No: 0000018061

Subsidiaries: Cascade (Africa) Pty. Ltd., Cascade (Australia) Pty. Ltd., Cascade (Canada) Ltd., Cascade (France) S.A.R.L., Cascade (Japan) Limited, Cascade (Scandinavia) Hydraulik A.B., Cascade (U.K.) Limited, Cascade France MHP, S.A.R.L., Cascade GmbH, Cascade Hispania S.A., Cascade IFSC Ltd., Cascade Italia S.r.l., Cascade Kenhar Ltd., Cascade Korea Limited, Cascade NV 17 Subsidiaries included in the Index

Officers: Robert C. Warren/Dir., CEO, Pres./$1,583,533.00, Herre Hoekstra/Regional VP, MD - Europe, Joseph G. Pointer/VP - Finance, Corp. Sec./$674,898.00, Michael E. Kern/VP - MHP Marketing, Sales, John A. Cushing/Treasurer, Jeffrey K. Nickoloff/VP - Corporate Manufacturing, Ken Antone/Contact - US, Sally Jones/Contact - US, Paul Murdock/Contact - Team Leader, Scott Garfield/Contact, Tom Chiovitti/Contact - Canada, Parts Sales Representative, Connie Storer/Contact - US, Latin America, Parts Sales Representative, Dani Hill/Contact - US, Latin America, Parts Sales Representative, Gary Snyder/Contact - US, Latin America, Parts Sales Representative, Jennifer Harber/Contact - US, Latin America, Parts Sales Representative *(127 Officers included in Index)*

Directors: Robert C. Warren/Dir., CEO, Pres., James S. Osterman/Chmn., Nicholas R. Lardy/Dir., Duane C. McDougall/Dir., Nancy A. Wilgenbusch/Dir., Henry W. Wessinger/Dir.

Owners: /7.00%, Barclays Global Investors/6.30%, Joseph G. Pointer, Terry H. Cathey, FMR Corp./10.60%, Nancy A. Wilgenbusch, Royce& Associates, LLC. ./7.20%, Nicholas R. Lardy, Richard S. Anderson, Gregory S. Anderson, T. Rowe Price Associates, Inc./7.00%, Robert J. Davis Family/5.80%, Insiders/19.80%, Duane C. McDougall, James S. Osterman *(18 Owners included in Index)*

Financial Data: ***Fiscal Year End:***01/31 ***Latest Annual Data:*** 1/31/2007

Year	Sales	Net Income
2007	$478,850,000	$45,481,000
2006	$450,503,000	$42,051,000
2005	$385,719,000	$28,490,000

Curr. Assets:	$182,955,000	***Curr. Liab.:***	$69,825,000	***P/E Ratio:***	18.70
Plant, Equip.:	$84,151,000	***Total Liab.:***	$125,796,000	***Indic. Yr. Divd.:***	$0.720
Total Assets:	$397,432,000	***Net Worth:***	$271,636,000	***Debt/ Equity:***	0.1419

Cascade Financial Corp

2828 Colby Ave., Everett, WA, 98201; ***PH:*** 1-425-339-5500; ***Fax:*** 1-425-259-8512; ***http://*** www.cascadebank.com

General - Incorporation	WA	***Stock***- Price on:12/24/2007	NA
Employees	212	Stock Exchange	NDQ
Auditor	Moss Adams LLP	Ticker Symbol	CASB
Stk Agt	Mellon Shareholder Services LLC	Outstanding Shares	12,060,000
Counsel	Anderson Hunter Law Firm	E.P.S	$1.22
DUNS No.	87-622-5095	Shareholders	NA

Business: The group's principal activity is to provide banking and other financial services. A holding company for the cascade bank and cascade capital trust i, the group accepts checking accounts, interest bearing accounts and originates business, real estate and consumer loans. The group markets annuity products, mutual funds and insurance products to customers and non-customers in the bank's market areas. The cascade capital trust has issued trust preferred and common securities and used the proceeds to acquire the group's junior subordinated debentures. The group serves its customers from fifteen full service offices, ten in snohomish county and five in king county. On 03-Jun-2004, the group acquired issaquah bancshares.

Primary SIC and add'l.: 6712 6022

CIK No: 0000928911

Subsidiaries: Cascade Bank, Cascade Capital Trust I, Cascade Capital Trust II, Cascade Investment Services, Inc.

Officers: Carol K. Nelson/Dir., CEO, Pres., Lars H. Johnson/CFO, Robert G. Disotell/Chief Credit Officer, Leanne M. Frank/Chief Administrative Officer, Robert F. Wojcik/Exec. VP - Business Banking, Debbie E. McLeod/Exec. VP - Retail Banking, Steven R. Erickson/Real Estate Lending Executive

Directors: Carol K. Nelson/Dir., CEO, Pres., Brandt G. Westover/Vice Chmn., David W. Duce/Chmn., Janice Halladay/Dir., Katherine M. Lombardo/Dir., Jim Gaffney/Dir., Richard L. Anderson/Dir., Craig G. Skotdal/Dir., David R. O'Connor/Dir., Ronald E. Thompson/Dir., Dwayne R. Lane/Dir., Dennis R. Murphy/Dir.

Owners: Arthur W. Skotdal/7.30%, Dennis R. Murphy, Ronald E. Thompson, Dwayne R. Lane, Jim Gaffney, Lars H. Johnson, Debbie E. McLeod, David R. OConnor/1.30%, Richard L. Anderson, Steven R. Erickson, Craig G. Skotdal/7.30%, Robert F. Wojcik, Brandt G. Westover, Insiders/16.00%, David W. Duce *(18 Owners included in Index)*

Financial Data: ***Fiscal Year End:***12/31 ***Latest Annual Data:*** 12/31/2006

Year	Sales	Net Income
2006	$88,711,000	$13,355,000
2005	$74,135,000	$13,046,000
2004	$60,063,000	$10,785,000

Curr. Assets:	$53,870,000	***Curr. Liab.:***	$1,203,577,000		
Plant, Equip.:	$12,003,000	***Total Liab.:***	$1,230,055,000	***Indic. Yr. Divd.:***	$0.360
Total Assets:	$1,345,254,000	***Net Worth:***	$115,199,000	***Debt/ Equity:***	0.2389

Cascade Microtech Inc

2430 NW 206th Ave., Beaverton, OR, 97006; ***PH:*** 1-503-601-1000; ***Fax:*** 1-503-601-1002; ***http://*** www.cascademicrotech.com; ***Email:*** sales@cmicro.com

General - Incorporation	OR	***Stock***- Price on:12/24/2007	$12.51
Employees	366	Stock Exchange	NDQ
Auditor	KPMG LLP	Ticker Symbol	CSCD
Stk Agt	Mellon Investor Services LLC	Outstanding Shares	12,740,000
Counsel	Ater Wynne LLP	E.P.S	$0.16
DUNS No.	NA	Shareholders	NA

Business: The groups principle activities include designing, developing and manufacturing wafer probing solutions. The products of the group include engineering probe stations, analytical probes, production probe cards, and application software and services. Customers served by the group include semiconductor manufacturers, test subcontractors, research organizations and designers. The group operates through two business segments namely engineering products division and pyramid probe division. Specific customers of the group include Advanced Micro Devices, Avago, Broadcom, Chartered Semiconductor, Fujitsu, Hitachi, IBM, Infineon, Intel, Micron Technology, Nanya Technology and Philips. The group operates from the United State, Japan and Taiwan. The group's quarterly revenue for September 2007 was 21.34 millions of USD.

Primary SIC and add'l.: 3825 3559

CIK No: 0000864559

Subsidiaries: Cascade International Trading (Shanghai) Co., Ltd., Cascade Microtech Europe,Ltd., Cascade Microtech Foreign SalesInc., Cascade Microtech Japan, K.K., Cascade Microtech Taiwan Co., Ltd.

Officers: Eric W. Strid/Chmn., CEO, Co - Founder/$307,485.00, Steven Sipowicz/CFO/$420,669.00, Bruce A. McFadden/62/VP - Corporate Development/$321,585.00, John E. Pence/VP, GM - Engineering Products Division/$381,001.00, Willis Damkroger/VP, GM - Production Products Division, Reed K. Gleason/Co - Founder, VP - Advanced Development, Cascade Microtech, Inc/$154,120.00, Art Smith/Dir. - Human Resources, Akshay Gupta/VP - Research & Development and Marketing, Engineering Products Division, Wayne Poe/Dir. - Worldwide Sales, Applications, Production Products Division, Tariq Alam/VP - Worldwide Sales, Engineering Products Division, Mike Kondrat/VP - Marketing, Production Products Division

Directors: Eric W. Strid/Chmn., CEO, Co - Founder, Art Smith/Dir. - Human Resources, George O'Leary/Dir., Paul F. Carlson/Dir., William R. Spivey/Dir., Keith Barnes/Dir., Raymond Link/Dir.

Owners: Royce & Associates, LLC/7.30%, Reed K. Gleason/13.50%, Steven Sipowicz, Keith L. Barnes, George P. OLeary/1.30%, Raymond A. Link, Insiders/34.00%, Bruce McFadden/1.40%, Eric W. Strid/14.70%, John Pence, Paul F. Carlson/1.40%, William R. Spivey/1.10%, Discovery Group I, LLC/9.40%

Financial Data: ***Fiscal Year End:***12/31 ***Latest Annual Data:*** 12/31/2006

Year	Sales	Net Income
2006	$84,852,000	$3,610,000
2005	$73,637,000	$8,319,000
2004	$64,415,000	$4,707,000

Curr. Assets:	$80,865,000	***Curr. Liab.:***	$12,223,000	***P/E Ratio:***	37.91
Plant, Equip.:	$6,818,000	***Total Liab.:***	$13,593,000	***Indic. Yr. Divd.:***	NA
Total Assets:	$103,786,000	***Net Worth:***	$90,193,000	***Debt/ Equity:***	0.0002

Cascade Natural Gas Corp

222 Fairview Ave. N, Seattle, WA, 98109; ***PH:*** 1-206-624-3900; ***http://*** www.cngc.com

General - Incorporation	WA	***Stock***- Price on:12/24/2007	$26.43
Employees	374	Stock Exchange	NA
Auditor	Deloitte & Touche LLP	Ticker Symbol	NA
Stk Agt	Bank of New York	Outstanding Shares	11,510,000
Counsel	NA	E.P.S	$1.10
DUNS No.	00-794-2584	Shareholders	NA

Business: The group's principal activity is to distribute natural gas to customers in the states of Washington and Oregon. Core customers are principally residential and small commercial and industrial customers who take traditional 'bundled' natural gas service, which includes supply, peaking service, and upstream interstate pipeline transportation. Non-core customers are generally large industrial and institutional customers who have chosen 'unbundled' service, meaning that they select from among several supplies and upstream pipeline transportation options, independent of the group's distribution service.

Primary SIC and add'l.: 4923

CIK No: 0000018072

Subsidiaries: Cascade Land Leasing Co., CGC Energy, Inc., CGC Properties, Inc, CGC Resources, CGC Resources, Inc

Owners: Rick Davis, Larry L. Pinnt, Thomas E. Cronin, Scott M. Boggs, Insiders/1.38%, David W. Stevens, David A. Ederer, Larry C. Rosok, Michael J. Gardner, Brooks G. Ragen, Jon T. Stoltz, Carl Burnham, Douglas G. Thomas, Pirkko H. Borland

Financial Data: ***Fiscal Year End:***09/30 ***Latest Annual Data:*** 9/30/2006

Year	Sales	Net Income
2006	$455,964,000	$12,489,000
2005	$326,500,000	$9,247,000
2004	$318,078,000	$13,302,000

Curr. Assets:	$85,973,000	***Curr. Liab.:***	$81,878,000	***P/E Ratio:***	24.03
Plant, Equip.:	$341,628,000	***Total Liab.:***	$334,579,000	***Indic. Yr. Divd.:***	$0.960
Total Assets:	$456,706,000	***Net Worth:***	$122,127,000	***Debt/ Equity:***	1.4169

Cascades Inc

404 Marie-Victorin Blvd., Kingsey Falls, QC, J0A 1B0; ***PH:*** 1-819-363-5100; ***http://*** www.cascades.com; ***Email:*** info@cascades.com

General - Incorporation	QC	***Stock***- Price on:12/24/2007	$10.5
Employees	NA	Stock Exchange	OTC
Auditor	PricewaterhouseCoopers LLP	Ticker Symbol	CADNF
Stk Agt	Computershare Investor Services	Outstanding Shares	NA
Counsel	Jones Day	E.P.S	NA
DUNS No.	NA	Shareholders	NA

Business: The groups principle activities include producing, transforming and marketing packaging and tissue products. The group operates from Canada.

Primary SIC and add'l.: 2611

CIK No: 0001225525

Subsidiaries: Cascades Fine Papers Group Inc., Cascades Rollpack, Qubec Inc.

Officers: Marc-Andre Depin/CEO, Pres. - Norampac Inc, Suzanne Blanchet/CEO, Pres. - Cascades Tissue Group, Alain Lemaire/Dir., CEO, Pres., Laurent Lemaire/Exec. Vice Chmn., Eric Laflamme/COO, Pres. - North America, Cascades Boxboard Group, Norman Boisvert/VP -

Administration, Claude Cossette/VP - Organizational Development, Alain Ducharme/Corporate VP, Jean-Luc Bellemare/VP - Information Technology, Purchasing, Leon Marineau/VP - Environment, Thomas Roberts/VP - Business Development, Patrick Lemaire/COO, Pres. - Boralex inc, Marc Jasmin/Investor Relations Officer, Didier Filion/Investor Relations Officer, Hubert Bolduc/VP - Communications, Public Affairs (20 Officers included in Index)

Directors: Alain Lemaire/Dir., CEO, Pres., Bernard Lemaire/Chmn., Laurent Lemaire/Exec. Vice Chmn., Laurent Verreault/Exec. Vice Chmn., David McAusland/Dir., Paul R. Bannerman/Dir., Michel Desbiens/Dir., Robert Chevrier/Dir., James B.C. Doak/Dir., Louis Garneau/Dir., Andre Desaulniers/Dir., Sylvie Lemaire/Dir., Martin P. Pelletier/Dir.

Financial Data: *Fiscal Year End:* 12/31 *Latest Annual Data:* 12/31/2006

Year	Sales	Net Income
2006	$2,920,114,000	-$3,432,000
2005	$2,968,680,000	-$87,516,000
2004	$2,701,796,000	$13,285,000

Curr. Assets:	$1,057,179,000	**Curr. Liab.:**	$564,630,000
Plant, Equip.:	$1,770,260,000	**Total Liab.:**	$2,376,079,000	**Indic. Yr. Divd.:** NA
Total Assets:	$3,376,624,000	**Net Worth:**	$1,000,545,000	**Debt/ Equity:** NA

Cascadia International Resources Inc

715 5 Ave. SW, Ste 1530, Calgary, AB, T2P 2X6x; *PH:* 1-403-262-9177; *Fax:* 1-403-262-8284; *http://* www.cascadiaintl.com; *Email:* info@cascadiaintl.com

General - Incorporation	Canada	Stock - Price on: 12/24/2007	NA
Employees	NA	Stock Exchange	NA
Auditor	Meyers Norris Penny LLP	Ticker Symbol	NA
Stk Agt	Mellon Trust Co	Outstanding Shares	NA
Counsel	Burstall Winger LLP	E.P.S.	NA
DUNS No.	NA	Shareholders	NA

Business: The group is involved in exploring properties for mineral content. During Fiscal 2000, 2001 and 2002 the group searched unsuccessfully for properties to explore for mineral content.

Primary SIC and add'l.: 1400

CIK No: 0001317430

Officers: James G. Evaskevich/Dir., CEO, Richard Osmond/Dir., COO, Pres., Meyers Norris Penny/Auditor, Trish Olynyk/VP - Business Development, CFO

Directors: James G. Evaskevich/Dir., CEO, Richard Osmond/Dir., COO, Pres., Glenn Mullen/Dir., Gordon A. Bowerman/Dir., Steve Balch/Dir.

Case Financial Inc

7720 El Camino Real, Ste. 2E, Carlsbad, CA, 92009; ; *http://* www.agfinance.com

General - Incorporation	DE	Stock - Price on: 12/24/2007	$0.11
Employees	2	Stock Exchange	OTC
Auditor	Kabani & Co, Inc	Ticker Symbol	CSEF
Stk Agt	Computershare Trust Co of Canada	Outstanding Shares	28,300,000
Counsel	NA	E.P.S.	$0.024
DUNS No.	NA	Shareholders	NA

Business: The group's principal activity is to provide litigation funding services to attorneys and plaintiffs involved in personal injury and other lawsuit. The group performs an internal underwriting as to the merits of each case, the likelihood of success, and the estimated settlement value. The group acceded to the operations of Asia Web holdings, inc. By way of a reverse acquisition on 24-May-2002.

Primary SIC and add'l.: 7389

CIK No: 0001096841

Subsidiaries: Case Financial Funding, Inc., I. F. Propco Holdings (Ontario) 32, Ltd.

Officers: Michael A. Schaffer/65/Chmn., CEO, Lawrence C. Schaffer/39/Dir., CFO, Pres., Waddy Stephenson/47/Dir., Sec., William J. Rappaglia/60/Dir., COO

Directors: Michael A. Schaffer/65/Chmn., CEO, Lawrence C. Schaffer/39/Dir., CFO, Pres., Waddy Stephenson/47/Dir., Sec., William J. Rappaglia/60/Dir., COO

Owners: Sam D. Schwartz/14.29%, Michael Schaffer/6.35%, Canadian Commercial Workers Industry Pension Plan/6.53%, Lawrence Schaffer/5.84%, William Rapaglia/7.12%, Waddy Stephenson/2.80%, Insiders/21.26%

Financial Data: *Fiscal Year End:* 09/30 *Latest Annual Data:* 9/30/2006

Year	Sales	Net Income
2006	NA	$3,157,000
2005	NA	-$1,586,000
2004	$738,000	-$2,578,000

Curr. Assets:	$2,028,000	**Curr. Liab.:**	$3,271,000	**P/E Ratio:** 3.67
Plant, Equip.:	$2,000	**Total Liab.:**	$3,271,000	**Indic. Yr. Divd.:** NA
Total Assets:	$2,030,000	**Net Worth:**	-$1,241,000	**Debt/ Equity:** NA

Casella Waste Systems Inc

25 Greens Hill Ln., Rutland, VT, 05701; *PH:* 1-802-775-0325; *Fax:* 1-802-775-6198; *http://* www.casella.com

General - Incorporation	DE	Stock - Price on: 12/24/2007	$10.5
Employees	2,900	Stock Exchange	NDQ
Auditor	Vitale, Caturano & Co., Ltd.	Ticker Symbol	CWST
Stk Agt	Computershare Trust CO.	Outstanding Shares	25,320,000
Counsel	Boston EquiServe Hale	E.P.S.	-$0.74
DUNS No.	94-913-9281	Shareholders	NA

Business: The group's principal activity is to provide vertically integrated regional solid waste services in the United States. The activities of the eastern, central and western segments include, the collection, transfer, recycling and disposal of non-hazardous solid waste. The fcr recycling and brokerage segment integrates waste handling services, including processing and recycling of wood, paper, metal, aluminum and glass. As on 14-Jun-2004, the group owns and operates eight subtitle d landfills, two landfills permitted to accept construction and demolition materials, 37 solid waste collection operations, 34 transfer stations, 39 recycling facilities and one waste-to-energy facility. In fiscal 2004 the group acquired 10 solid waste hauling operations and 1 construction and demolition processing facility.

Primary SIC and add'l.: 4953 4911

CIK No: 0000911177

Subsidiaries: All Cycle Waste,Inc., Atlantic Coast Fibers,Inc., B. and C. Sanitation Corporation, Better Bedding Corp., Blasdell Development Group,Inc., Blue Mountain Recycling LLC, Bristol Waste Management,Inc., C.V. Landfill,Inc., Casella Insurance Company, Casella Major Account Services LLC, Casella NH Investors Co. LLC, Casella NH Power Co., LLC, Casella RTG Investors Co., LLC, Casella Transportation,Inc., Casella Waste Management of Cape Cod,Inc. 93 Subsidiaries included in the Index

Officers: John W. Casella/Chmn., CEO, Sec./$405,954.00, Richard A. Norris/Sr. VP, CFO, Treasurer/$325,325.00, Donald A. Wallgren/Sr. VP - Permitting, Compliance, Engineering, Construction, David L. Schmitt/VP, General Counsel, James W. Bohlig/Dir., COO, Pres./$381,477.00, Brian G. Oliver/Regional VP, Gary R. Simmons/VP - Fleet Management, Christopher Hubbard/VP - Information Systems, Alan N. Sabino/Regional VP, Christopher M. Desroches/VP - Selection, Training, Timothy A. Cretney/Regional VP, Larry B. Lackey/VP - Permits, Compliance, Engineering, Michael J. Wall/Regional VP, Charles E. Leonard/Sr. VP - Solid Waste Operations/$337,220.00, Joseph S. Fusco/VP - Communications (18 Officers included in Index)

Directors: John W. Casella/Chmn., CEO, Sec., James F. Callahan/Dir., James W. Bohlig/Dir., COO, Pres., Gregory B. Peters/Dir., James McManus/Dir., Douglas R. Casella/Dir., John F. Chapple/Dir., Joseph G. Doody/Dir., Randolph D. Peeler/Dir.

Owners: John W. Casella/4.60%, Insiders/16.70%, John W. Casella/50.00%, D. Randolph Peeler/2.10%, Franklin Advisors, Inc./5.80%, T. Rowe Price Associates, Inc./10.80%, Insiders/100.00%, James W. Bohlig/3.60%, James P. McManus, Gregory B. Peters, John F. Chapple, James F. Callahan, Charles E. Leonard/1.10%, BlackRock, Inc./5.00%, Buckhead Capital Management, Inc./15.00% (21 Owners included in Index)

Financial Data: *Fiscal Year End:* 04/30 *Latest Annual Data:* 04/30/2007

Year	Sales	Net Income
2007	$546,990,000	-$17,883,000
2006	$525,928,000	$11,104,000
2005	$481,964,000	$7,269,000

Curr. Assets:	$78,974,000	**Curr. Liab.:**	$94,765,000
Plant, Equip.:	$481,284,000	**Total Liab.:**	$591,191,000	**Indic. Yr. Divd.:** NA
Total Assets:	$811,111,000	**Net Worth:**	$149,490,000	**Debt/ Equity:** 3.1941

Caseys General Stores Inc

1 Convenience Blvd., Ankeny, IA, 50021; *PH:* 1-515-965-6100; *Fax:* 1-515-965-6160; *http://* www.caseys.com

General - Incorporation	IA	Stock - Price on: 12/24/2007	$27.94
Employees	6,024	Stock Exchange	NDQ
Auditor	KPMG LLP	Ticker Symbol	CASY
Stk Agt	UMB Bank, N.A.	Outstanding Shares	50,220,000
Counsel	NA	E.P.S.	$1.68
DUNS No.	02-201-0664	Shareholders	NA

Business: The groups principle activity is to operate convenience stores. The groups products include beverages, tobacco products, health and beauty aids, automotive products, and other nonfood items. The group operates from United States.

Primary SIC and add'l.: 5331 5541 5411 5461

CIK No: 0000726958

Subsidiaries: First Heartland Captive Insurance Company, Inc

Officers: Robert J. Myers/Dir., CEO, Pres./$861,619.00, Terry W. Handley/COO/$347,580.00, John G. Harmon/Sr. VP, Sec./$532,130.00, Julia L. Jackowski/VP - Human Resources, Eli J. Wirtz/VP, Corporate Counsel, Bradley G. Heyer/VP - Information Systems, Darryl F. Bacon/VP - Food Services, Cleo R. Kuhns/VP - Real Estate, Store Development, Michael R. Richardson/VP - Marketing, Sam J. Billmeyer/Sr. VP - Transportation, Support Operations/$234,970.00, Hal D. Brown/VP - Support Services, William J. Walljasper/CFO, Sr. VP/$287,790.00, Russell D. Sukut/VP, Treasurer, Robert C. Ford/VP - Store Operations, Bob Ford/VP - Store Operations

Directors: Robert J. Myers/Dir., CEO, Pres., Ronald M. Lamb/Chmn., Donald F. Lamberti/Dir., Kenneth H. Haynie/Dir., John R. Fitzgibbon/Dir., Johnny Danos/Dir., Patricia Clare Sullivan/Dir., William C. Kimball/Dir., Jack P. Taylor/Dir., Diana C. Bridgewater/Dir.

Owners: William C. Kimball, Robert J. Myers, Terry W. Handley, Patricia Clare Sullivan, William J. Walljasper, Ronald M. Lamb/1.60%, Barclays Global Investors, NA/6.48%, T. Rowe Price Associates, Inc./6.10%, Donald F. Lamberti/4.07%, John G. Harmon, Sam J. Billmeyer, Diane C. Bridgewater, Johnny Danos, John R. Fitzgibbon, Insiders/6.86% (17 Owners included in Index)

Financial Data: *Fiscal Year End:* 04/30 *Latest Annual Data:* 04/30/2007

Year	Sales	Net Income
2007	$4,024,010,000	$61,891,000
2006	$3,515,145,000	$60,468,000
2005	$2,810,485,000	$36,753,000

Curr. Assets:	$191,406,000	**Curr. Liab.:**	$243,696,000	**P/E Ratio:** 22.90
Plant, Equip.:	$774,825,000	**Total Liab.:**	$464,349,000	**Indic. Yr. Divd.:** $0.260
Total Assets:	$987,539,000	**Net Worth:**	$523,190,000	**Debt/ Equity:** NA

Cash America International Inc

1600 W 7th St., Fort Worth, TX, 76102; *PH:* 1-817-335-1100; *Fax:* 1-817-570-1225; *http://* www.cashamerica.com; *Email:* investor_relations@cashamerica.com

General - Incorporation	TX	Stock - Price on: 12/24/2007	$40.91
Employees	5,152	Stock Exchange	NYSE
Auditor	PricewaterhouseCoopers LLP	Ticker Symbol	CSH
Stk Agt	Mellon Investor Services LLC	Outstanding Shares	29,700,000
Counsel	NA	E.P.S.	$2.194
DUNS No.	04-330-5796	Shareholders	NA

Business: The group's principal activity is to acquire, establish and operate pawnshops, which advance money on the security of pledged tangible personal property. It offers secured non-recourse loans, commonly referred to as pawn loans, to individuals through its lending operations. As an alternative to a pawn loan, the group offers small consumer cash advances in selected lending locations and on behalf of a third-party financial institution in other locations. The group also provides check-cashing services through its subsidiaries.

Primary SIC and add'l.: 6794 5932

CIK No: 0000807884

Subsidiaries: Bronco Pawn and Gun, Inc., Cash America Acquisition Company, Inc., Cash America Advance, Inc., Cash America Financial Services, Inc., Cash America Franchising, Inc., Cash America Holding, Inc., Cash America International, Inc., Cash America Management L.P., Cash America of Missouri, Inc., Cash America Pawn L.P., Cash America Pawn, Inc. of Ohio, Cash America, Inc., Cash America, Inc. of Alabama, Cash America, Inc. of Colorado, Cash America, Inc. of Illinois 38 Subsidiaries included in the Index

Officers: Daniel R. Feehan/Dir., CEO, Pres./$1,299,420.00, Robert D. Brockman/Exec. VP - Administration, Curtis J. Linscott/Exec. VP, General Counsel, Corp. Sec., Albert Goldstein/Pres. - Internet Lending Services, Thomas A. Bessant/CFO, Exec. VP/$557,093.00, James H. Kauffman/Exec. VP - Business Development/$668,613.00, Michael D. Gaston/Exec. VP - Business Development/$521,147.00, Jerry A. Wackerhagen/Pres. - Retail Lending Services, John A. McDorman/Pres. - Shared Services

Directors: Daniel R. Feehan/Dir., CEO, Pres., Jack R. Daugherty/Chmn. - Board, A. R. Dike/Dir., Daniel E. Berce/Dir., James H. Graves/Dir., Alfred M. Micallef/Dir., Timothy J. McKibben/Dir., B. D. Hunter/Dir.

Owners: B. D. Hunter/0.14%, A. R. Dike, Michael D. Gaston/0.25%, Alfred M. Micallef, Thomas A. Bessant, Jack R. Daugherty, Daniel R. Feehan/1.81%, James H. Graves, Daniel E. Berce, James H. Kauffman/0.58%, Timothy J. McKibben/0.10%, Jerry D. Finn, Insiders/3.69%

Financial Data: ***Fiscal Year End:***12/31 ***Latest Annual Data:*** 12/31/2006

Year	Sales	Net Income
2006	$693,214,000	$60,940,000
2005	$594,346,000	$45,018,000
2004	$469,478,000	$56,835,000

Curr. Assets:	$377,971,000	***Curr. Liab.:***	$118,158,000		
Plant, Equip.:	$119,261,000	***Total Liab.:***	$335,516,000	***Indic. Yr. Divd.:***	$0.140
Total Assets:	$776,244,000	***Net Worth:***	$440,728,000	***Debt/ Equity:***	0.3966

Cash Systems Inc

7350 Dean Martin Dr., Ste. 309, Las Vegas, NV, 89139; ***PH:*** 1-702-987-7169; ***Fax:*** 1-702-987-7168; ***http://*** www.cashsystemsinc.com; ***Email:*** info@cashsystemsinc.com

General		***Stock***	
Incorporation	DE	Price on:12/24/2007	$6.31
Employees	289	Stock Exchange	NDQ
Auditor	Virchow, Krause & Co. LLP	Ticker Symbol	CKNN
Stk Agt	American Registrar & Transfer Co	Outstanding Shares	18,440,000
Counsel	NA	E.P.S.	-$0.63
DUNS No.	NA	Shareholders	NA

Business: The group's principal activity is to develop and provide cash access services to the casino and retail industries. The group provides three primary products: credit/debit card cash advances, automatic teller machines (ATM) and check cashing solutions. The credit/debit card cash advances product has been installed at over 90 casinos throughout the United States. Credit/debit card cash advances products allow casino patrons to obtain cash from their credit card, checking account in case of debit transactions, through the use of software and equipment. Atm services are provided to retailers and casinos. The check cashing services provides check cashing services in the casinos. In addition, the group also sells ATM, provides ATM vault cash, maintenance and armored car services. It provides casinos and the customers with full service check cashing and check guarantee facilities. The operations of the group are carried out in the United States.

Primary SIC and add'l.: 7381 7379 6099

CIK No: 0000861050

Subsidiaries: Cash Access Mxico, S. de R.L. de C.V., Cash Systems Mexico I, LLC, Cash Systems Mexico II, LLC, Cash Systems of Canada, Inc.

Officers: Michael D. Rumbolz/Chmn., CEO, Pres./$429,123.00, John F. Glaser/Exec. VP - Sales, Marketing /$249,032.00, Andrew J. Cashin/43/CFO, Exec. VP, Treasurer/$305,554.00, Katherine W. Bloomfield/CIO/$169,894.00, Carmalen Gillilan/VP - Administration, Sec., Zev E. Kaplan/General Counsel/$177,982.00, Charles S. Crawford/Exec. VP - Operations

Directors: Michael D. Rumbolz/Chmn., CEO, Pres., Patricia W. Becker/Dir., Donald D. Synder/Dir., Patrick R. Cruzen/Dir., Don R. Kornstein/Dir.

Owners: Stadia Capital LLC/7.20%, Forstmann-Leff Associates, LLC/5.70%, Patricia W. Becker, Zev Kaplan, Michael D. Rumbolz/2.40%, Donald D. Snyder, Bridger Management, LLC/5.30%, Andrew Cashin, John Glaser, Gruber and McBaine Capital Management, LLC/7.60%, Katherine Bloomfield, Patrick R. Cruzen, Baron Capital Group, Inc./8.10%, Insiders/8.70%, Don R. Kornstein

Financial Data: ***Fiscal Year End:***12/31 ***Latest Annual Data:*** 12/31/2006

Year	Sales	Net Income
2006	$96,039,000	-$10,018,000
2005	$63,166,000	-$3,765,000
2004	$48,411,000	$2,183,000

Curr. Assets:	$56,012,000	***Curr. Liab.:***	$42,415,000		
Plant, Equip.:	$7,408,000	***Total Liab.:***	$62,450,000	***Indic. Yr. Divd.:***	NA
Total Assets:	$76,516,000	***Net Worth:***	$14,065,000	***Debt/ Equity:***	1.2845

Cash Technologies Inc

1434 W 11th St., Los Angeles, CA, 90015; ***PH:*** 1-213-745-2000; ***Fax:*** 1-213-745-2005; ***http://*** www.cashtechnologies.com

General		***Stock***	
Incorporation	DE	Price on:12/24/2007	$0.86
Employees	169	Stock Exchange	AMEX
Auditor	Vasquez & Co. LLP	Ticker Symbol	TQ
Stk Agt	American Stock Transfer & Trust Co.	Outstanding Shares	22,490,000
Counsel	NA	E.P.S.	-$0.53
DUNS No.	87-980-7238	Shareholders	NA

Business: The group's principal activities are to develop and market e-commerce data processing systems and to provide coin and currency processing services. The coin processing service includes sorting, counting and wrapping functions to cash-intensive businesses. The coinbank machines are automated self-service coin counting and processing machines designed to accept and count loose coins for a fee. Emma (e-commerce message management architecture) is designed to interface with various e-commerce partners and connect with financial networks, particularly the ATM network, the credit card network, the automated clearing house network and cash. On 05-Aug-2004, the group acquired certain assets of heuristic technologies, llc.

Primary SIC and add'l.: 7375 7389

CIK No: 0001022964

Subsidiaries: Cintelia Systems Inc, CoinBank Automated Systems, Inc, National Cash Processors, Inc

Owners: Richard Miller/2.76%, Bruce Korman/12.47%, Kevin Walls/1.09%, Robin Richards/0.58%, Peter& Irene Gauld/5.66%, Robert B. Fagenson/8.70%, Insiders/37.25%, Eric Butlein/11.40%, Edmund King/2.42%

Financial Data: ***Fiscal Year End:***05/31 ***Latest Annual Data:*** 05/31/2007

Year	Sales	Net Income
2007	$314,000	-$3,065,000
2005	$5,719,000	$3,656,000
2004	$81,000	-$4,383,000

Curr. Assets:	$11,185,000	***Curr. Liab.:***	$9,317,000		
Plant, Equip.:	$689,000	***Total Liab.:***	$9,331,000	***Indic. Yr. Divd.:***	NA
Total Assets:	$14,111,000	***Net Worth:***	$4,146,000	***Debt/ Equity:***	0.0016

Caspian Services Inc

257 E 200 S., Ste. 340, Salt Lake City, UT, 84101; ***PH:*** 1-801-746-3700; ***Fax:*** 1-801-746-3701; ***http://*** www.caspianservicesinc.com; ***Email:*** genenquiries@caspianservices.kz

General		***Stock***	
Incorporation	NV	Price on:12/24/2007	$3
Employees	365	Stock Exchange	OTC
Auditor	Hansen, Barnett & Maxwell	Ticker Symbol	CSSV
Stk Agt	Interwest Transfer Company, Inc.	Outstanding Shares	42,070,000
Counsel	NA	E.P.S.	$0.09
DUNS No.	NA	Shareholders	NA

Business: The group's principal activity is to provide and operate vessels for use in the oil and gas industry in the kazakhstan sector of the caspian sea. The services provided include maintenance and upkeep of the vessels, staffing of vessels, providing accommodation and meals for customers & personnel on the vessels and laundry and other services. The group also operates desalinization plant that purifies and markets drinking water in bulk and in bottles.

Primary SIC and add'l.: 1381

CIK No: 0001093430

Subsidiaries: Balykshi LLP, Bautino Development Company, Caspian Geophysic Ltd. BVI, Caspian Real Estate Ltd., BVI, Caspian Services Group Limited, BVI, CJSC Bauta, Kazmorgeophysica CJSC, TatArka, LLP

Officers: Laird Garrard/CEO, Pres., Arjan Goris/MD - Caspian Services Group Ltd, John Scott/COO, Alexey Kotov/General Counsel, Caspian Services Inc, Terrance J. Powell/VP - Investor Relations - Caspian Services Inc, Azhar Stirewalt/Mgr. - Human Resources, John Baile/CFO

Owners: Insiders/44.50%, Firebird Management LLC/16.40%, James Passin/8.20%, Paul Roberts/6.10%, Laird Garrard/6.30%, Mirgali Kunayev/28.60%, Valery Tolkachev, Petroleum Group Services Limited/25.10%

Financial Data: ***Fiscal Year End:***09/30 ***Latest Annual Data:*** 9/30/2006

Year	Sales	Net Income
2006	$43,043,000	-$1,919,000
2005	$23,789,000	$2,177,000
2004	$14,562,000	-$195,000

Curr. Assets:	$23,848,000	***Curr. Liab.:***	$17,007,000		
Plant, Equip.:	$32,778,000	***Total Liab.:***	$18,403,000	***Indic. Yr. Divd.:***	NA
Total Assets:	$61,038,000	***Net Worth:***	$39,136,000	***Debt/ Equity:***	0.0070

Cass Information Systems Inc

13001 Hollenberg Dr., Bridgeton, MO, 63044; ***PH:*** 1-314-506-5500; ***Fax:*** 1-314-506-5955; ***http://*** www.cassinfo.com

General		***Stock***	
Incorporation	MO	Price on:12/24/2007	$32.84
Employees	659	Stock Exchange	NDQ
Auditor	KPMG LLP	Ticker Symbol	CASS
Stk Agt	Mellon Investor Services LLC	Outstanding Shares	8,370,000
Counsel	Armstrong Teasdale LLP	E.P.S.	$1.88
DUNS No.	11-903-8354	Shareholders	NA

Business: The group is a bank holding corporation with the principal activity to provide payment and information processing services to large manufacturing, distribution and retail enterprises across the United States. Its subsidiary, cass commercial bank, is a federally insured commercial bank. Due to this the group is a bank holding corporation. The group accepts checking, savings and time deposit accounts, originates commercial, industrial, real estate and installment loans and provides cash management services. The banking services are provided to businesses, churches and consumers throughout the metropolitan st. Louis area.

Primary SIC and add'l.: 6712 9999 6141 6022

CIK No: 0000708781

Subsidiaries: Cass Commercial Bank, Cass Information Systems, Inc.

Officers: Lawrence A. Collett/64/Chmn., CEO/$1,143,631.00, John J. Vallina/Vice Chmn., Interim Pres. - Cass Commercial Bank, John F. Pickering/COO - Transportation Information Systems, Eric H. Brunngraber/50/Dir., VP, Sec./$457,616.00, Harry M. Murray/Exec. VP/$371,323.00, Gary B. Langfitt/COO - Utility Information Systems/$277,019.00, Stephen P. Appelbaum/CFO/$171,667.00

Directors: Lawrence A. Collett/64/Chmn., CEO, Harry J. Krieg/82/Dir., Bryan S. Chapell/52/Dir., Eric H. Brunngraber/50/Dir., VP, Sec., Wayne J. Grace/66/Dir., Andrew J. Signorelli/67/Dir., Dane K. Brooksher/68/Dir., Robert A. Ebel/51/Dir., Benjamin F. Edwards/51/Dir., Franklin D. Wicks/53/Dir., James J. Lindemann/52/Dir., John L. Gillis/68/Dir.

Owners: Harry J. Krieg/2.95%, Robert A. Ebel, Wayne J. Grace, Harry M. Murray, Gary B. Langfitt, Bryan S. Chapell, Stephen P. Appelbau, Franklin D. Wicks, Andy J. Signorelli/3.45%, Lawrence A. Collett/2.32%, Jake Nania/10.69%, Irving A. Shepard, Benjamin F. Edwards, Dane K. Brooksher, Eric H. Brunngraber *(17 Owners included in Index)*

Financial Data: ***Fiscal Year End:***12/31 ***Latest Annual Data:*** 12/31/2006

Year	Sales	Net Income
2006	$89,874,000	$15,066,000
2005	$76,904,000	$10,946,000
2004	$69,937,000	$8,005,000

Curr. Assets:	$196,504,000	***Curr. Liab.:***	$758,468,000	***P/E Ratio:***	18.24
Plant, Equip.:	$12,898,000	***Total Liab.:***	$774,550,000	***Indic. Yr. Divd.:***	$0.480
Total Assets:	$858,471,000	***Net Worth:***	$83,921,000	***Debt/ Equity:***	0.0424

Castelle

855 Jarvis Dr., Morgan Hill, CA, 95037; ***PH:*** 1-408-852-8000; ***http://*** www.castelle.com

General - Incorporation	CA	Stock- Price on:12/24/2007	$3.91
Employees	40	Stock Exchange	NA
Auditor	Grant Thornton LLP	Ticker Symbol	NA
Stk Agt.	Computershare Trust Co	Outstanding Shares	4,090,000
Counsel	NA	E.P.S.	$0.15
DUNS No.	18-489-5506	Shareholders	NA

Business: The group's principal activity is to design, develop and market server appliances providing office messaging solutions and other shared services. Its products are focused on two areas: fax and integrated messaging products including a range of software enhancements and print servers. The group's products include faxpress, an integrated hardware/software network faxing solution, officedirect, an integrated fax/email messaging system, infopress, an enterprise-level fax-on-demand software product and lanpress print servers. The products are marketed in 40 foreign countries through 50 international distributors through a two-tier, domestic and international distribution network. The customers are value-added resellers, system integrators, e-commerce retailers and other resellers in the United States, Europe and the Pacific Rim.

Primary SIC and add'l.: 7372 3577

CIK No: 0000908605

Officers: Scott C. McDonald/Dir., CEO, Pres., Eric C. Chen/Sr. VP - Engineering, Business Development, Paul Cheng/VP - Finance, Administration, CFO, Sec., Edward Heinze/Sr. VP - Worldwide Sales, Michael Petrovich/VP - North American Sales, Richard Fernandez/VP - Operations, Nicole Calbreath/Inside Sales Mgr. - Castelle Sales, Northern Region, Karin Reak/Dir. - Marketing, Luis Lopez/Contact - Employment Opportunities at Castelle

Directors: Scott C. McDonald/Dir., CEO, Pres., Donald L. Rich/Chmn., Robert O. Smith/Dir., Peter R. Tierney/Dir., Robert H. Hambrecht/Dir.

Owners: Robert O. Smith, Paul Cheng/2.30%, Richard Fernandez/1.50%, Peter R. Tierney/1.40%, Eric Chen/3.40%, Entities affiliated with Daniel Zeff/24.60%, Entities affiliated with Barclays Bank Plc/7.20%, Insiders/25.10%, Robert H. Hambrecht/1.50%, dward J. Heinze, Michael Petrovich/1.20%, Donald L. Rich/5.20%, Scott C. McDonald/11.80%

Financial Data: Fiscal Year End:12/31   Latest Annual Data: 12/31/2006

Year	Sales	Net Income
2006	$10,590,000	$669,000
2005	$10,832,000	$579,000
2004	$10,457,000	$2,119,000

Curr. Assets:	$10,630,000	Curr. Liab.:	$2,884,000	P/E Ratio:	26.07
Plant, Equip.:	$280,000	Total Liab.:	$2,884,000	Indic. Yr. Divd.:	NA
Total Assets:	$11,979,000	Net Worth:	$9,095,000	Debt/ Equity:	NA

Castle Arch Real Estate Investment Co LLC

9595 Wilshire Blvd., Penthouse 1000, Beverly Hills, CA, 90212; **PH:** 1-310-385-5970; **Fax:** 1-310-385-5975; **http://** www.castlearch.com; **Email:** invest@castlearch.com

General - Incorporation	CA	Stock- Price on:12/24/2007	NA
Employees	NA	Stock Exchange	NA
Auditor	Bouwhuis, Morrill & Co LLC	Ticker Symbol	NA
Stk Agt.	NA	Outstanding Shares	NA
Counsel	David S. Hunt, Esq.	E.P.S.	NA
DUNS No.	NA	Shareholders	NA

Business: The group's principal activity is to focus on the professional growth and management of high value real estate development opportunities. Types of projects include the development of raw land into residential neighbourhoods, multi-family housing, retail centres, offices and industrial facilities. The company is a publicly reporting, non-trading company. The group focuses on locating and acquiring undeveloped land parcels in high growth geographic locations. The group has established long-standing relationships with brokers, builders, developers, local government and other business leaders in high growth areas across the nation, particularly in the states of California, Tennessee, Texas, New Mexico, Colorado, Utah and Arizona. The group is headquartered in Beverly Hills, California.

Primary SIC and add'l.: 6552

CIK No: 0001321742

Officers: Kirby D. Cochran/Chmn., CEO, Robert D. Geringer/Dir., COO, Pres., Douglas W. Child/Dir., CFO, Jeff Austin/Dir., Sr. VP - Business Development

Directors: Kirby D. Cochran/Chmn., CEO, Robert D. Geringer/Dir., COO, Pres., Douglas W. Child/Dir., CFO, Jeff Austin/Dir., Sr. VP - Business Development, William Warwick/Dir., William H. Davidson/Dir.

Owners: Robert D. Geringer/17.05%, Douglas W. Child/3.53%, Jeff Austin/10.42%, Insiders/64.65%, Kirby D. Cochran/33.65%

Castle Brands Inc

570 Lexington Ave., 29th Fl., New York, NY, 10022; **PH:** 1-646-356-0235; **Fax:** 1-646-356-0222; **http://** www.castlebrandsinc.com; **Email:** ir@castlebrandsinc.com

General - Incorporation	DE	Stock- Price on:12/24/2007	$5.8019
Employees	51	Stock Exchange	AMEX
Auditor	Eisner LLP	Ticker Symbol	ROX
Stk Agt.	Continental Stock Transfer & Trust Co	Outstanding Shares	12,120,000
Counsel	NA	E.P.S.	-$1.18
DUNS No.	NA	Shareholders	NA

Business: The groups principle activities include developing and marketing spirits. The groups spirits include vodka, rum, Irish whiskey and cordials. The group operates through three segments namely, distilled spirits, wine and beer. In the year 2005, the group acquired Gosling-Castle Partners, Inc. The group operates from the United States.

Primary SIC and add'l.: 2084 2085 2084 2080 2085

CIK No: 0001311538

Subsidiaries: Castle Brands (USA) Corp., Castle Brands Spirits Company (GB) Limited, Castle Brands Spirits Company Limited, Castle Brands Spirits Group Limited, Castle Brands Spirits Marketing and Sales Company Limited, Castle Brands Whiskey Company Limited, Gosling-Castle Partners Inc., The Boru Vodka Company Limited, The Clontarf Irish Whiskey Company Limited, The Roaring Water Bay Spirits Company (NI) Limited

Officers: Mark Andrews/Chmn., CEO/$536,596.00, Keith A. Bellinger/COO, Pres., Sec./$685,184.00, John Soden/Sr. VP, MD - International Operations/$479,022.00, Kelley T. Spillane/Sr. VP - US Sales/$325,976.00, Claes Fick/Chief Commercial, Marketing Officer, Seth B. Weinberg/Sr. VP, General Counsel/$400,015.00, Amelia Gary/VP - Investor Relations, Corporate Affairs

Directors: Mark Andrews/Chmn., CEO, John F. Beaudette/Dir., Robert J. Flanagan/Dir., Phillip Frost/71/Dir., Colm Leen/Dir., Richard C. Morrison/Dir., Frederick M.R. Smith/Dir., Kevin P. Tighe/Dir., Gill Jefferson/Dir.

Owners: Kevin P. Tighe, Colm Leen, FURSA SPV LLC/13.50%, State Teachers Retirement System of Ohio/7.70%, John Soden, Seth B. Weinberg, John Beaudette, Massachusetts Financials Services Company/9.40%, Richard C. Morrison, Robert J. Flanagan/5.80%, Mark Andrews/8.70%, John A. Murphy/9.60%, Phillip Frost/5.30%, Keith A. Bellinger, Knappogue Corp/7.60% (18 Owners included in Index)

Financial Data: Fiscal Year End:03/31   Latest Annual Data: 03/31/2007

Year	Sales	Net Income
2007	$25,164,000	-$16,557,000
2006	$21,150,000	-$13,084,000
2005	$12,618,000	-$12,528,000

Curr. Assets:	$25,734,000	Curr. Liab.:	$8,650,000		
Plant, Equip.:	$644,000	Total Liab.:	$30,973,000	Indic. Yr. Divd.:	NA
Total Assets:	$54,526,000	Net Worth:	$23,553,000	Debt/ Equity:	0.6567

Castle Energy Corp

One Radnor Corporate Ctr Ste. 250, 100 Matsonford Rd., Radnor, PA, 19087; **PH:** 1-610-995-9400

General - Incorporation	DE	Stock- Price on:12/24/2007	$21.07
Employees	122	Stock Exchange	NA
Auditor	KPMG LLP	Ticker Symbol	NA
Stk Agt.	American Stock Transfer & Trust Co.	Outstanding Shares	65,690,000
Counsel	Duane, Morris LLP	E.P.S.	-$2.36
DUNS No.	11-312-8920	Shareholders	NA

Business: The group's principal activity is to produce and explore oil and gas. The group acquired 166 appalachian gas properties on Mar 30 and 31, 2004. The group owned no oil and gas properties from Sept 2002 to Mar 30, 2004.

Primary SIC and add'l.: 9999

CIK No: 0000709355

Subsidiaries: Castle Exploration Company, Inc., Castle Oil and Gas L.P., CEC, Inc., Indian Oil Company, Indian Refining & Marketing I Inc.

Financial Data: Fiscal Year End:09/30   Latest Annual Data: 12/31/2006

Year	Sales	Net Income
2006	$181,361,000	$435,000
2005	$94,707,000	$15,050,000

Curr. Assets:	$27,034,000	Curr. Liab.:	$54,150,000		
Plant, Equip.:	$473,550,000	Total Liab.:	$276,746,000	Indic. Yr. Divd.:	NA
Total Assets:	$512,983,000	Net Worth:	$221,623,000	Debt/ Equity:	0.8557

Castleguard Energy Inc

17768 Preston Rd., Dallas, TX, 75252; **PH:** 1-214-647-2110

General - Incorporation	FL	Stock- Price on:12/24/2007	NA
Employees	NA	Stock Exchange	OTC
Auditor	Whitley Penn LLP	Ticker Symbol	MOAT
Stk Agt.	Interwest Transfer Company, Inc.	Outstanding Shares	NA
Counsel	NA	E.P.S.	-$0.01
DUNS No.	NA	Shareholders	NA

Business: The groups principle activities include acquiring, developing, exploring and operating crude oil and natural gas properties, and the producing crude oil and natural gas. The group operates from North America.

Primary SIC and add'l.: 1311

CIK No: 0001077924

Officers: Harvey Jury/Dir., Pres., Chief Executive, Financial Officer

Directors: Harvey Jury/Dir., Pres., Chief Executive, Financial Officer

Financial Data: Fiscal Year End:12/31   Latest Annual Data: 12/31/2005

Year	Sales	Net Income
2005	$214,000	-$74,000
2004	$364,000	-$4,000
2003	$487,000	-$123,000

Curr. Assets:	$44,000	Curr. Liab.:	$326,000		
Plant, Equip.:	NA	Total Liab.:	$358,000	Indic. Yr. Divd.:	NA
Total Assets:	$1,219,000	Net Worth:	$862,000	Debt/ Equity:	NA

Casual Male Retail Group Inc

555 Tpke. St., Canton, MA, 02021; **PH:** 1-781-828-9300; **Fax:** 1-781-821-6094; **http://** www.casualmalexl.com; **Email:** info@casualmale.com

General - Incorporation	DE	Stock- Price on:12/24/2007	$10.8682
Employees	1,748	Stock Exchange	NDQ
Auditor	Ernst & Young LLP	Ticker Symbol	CMRG
Stk Agt.	American Stock Transfer & Trust Co.	Outstanding Shares	41,520,000
Counsel	NA	E.P.S.	NA
DUNS No.	08-653-0011	Shareholders	NA

Business: The group's principal activity is the retailing of big and tall men's apparel in the United States. It operates through two segments: casual male business: includes its 489 casual male big and tall retail and outlet stores, along with its e-commerce sites and the catalog business. The e-commerce websites include www.casualmale.com and www.reppbigandtall.com. The group's catalog business offers an assortment of casual merchandise such as sportcoats, suit separates and other tailored clothing. Other branded apparel businesses: includes the operations of the group's levi's(R)/dockers(R) outlet stores and its ecko unltd.(R) outlet stores. The major servicemarks and trademarks include casual male big and tall(R), harbor bay(R), gf sport by george foremantm, comfort zone by george foremantm, george foreman signature collectiontm and signature collection by george foremantm.

Primary SIC and add'l.: 5651

CIK No: 0000813298

Subsidiaries: Capture, LLC, Casual Male Canada Inc., Casual Male Direct, LLC, Casual Male RBT, LLC, Casual Male RBT, LLC, Casual Male Retail Store, LLC, Casual Male Store, LLC, Designs Apparel, Inc., LP Innovations, Inc., Securex LLC

Officers: David A. Levin/Dir., CEO, Pres., James Metscher/Sr. VP, General Merchandise Mgr., Pres. - Footwear, Living Xl, Peter Schmitz/Sr. VP - Real Estate, Store Development, Linda B. Carlo/61/Exec. VP - Business Development, Direct, to, Consumer/$360,495.00, Dennis R. Hernreich/CFO, COO, Exec. VP, Treasurer/$1,332,962.00, Mark Bean/Sr. VP, Dir. - Store Sales, Operations, Ric Della Bernarda/Sr. VP, Chief Marketing Officer, Wayne Diller/Exec. VP, Chief Merchandising Officer, Bill Hoeller/Sr. VP - Planning, Allocation, Casual Male Division, Sheri A. Knight/Sr. VP - Finance, Corporate Controller, Roger Mayerson/VP - Global Sourcing, Jack McKinney/CIO, Sr. VP/$267,986.00, Walter Sprague/Sr. VP - Human Resources/$238,300.00, Jeffrey Unger/VP - Investor Relations, Jared Margolis/Pres. - Jared M Custom Clothing

Directors: David A. Levin/Dir., CEO, Pres., Seymour Holtzman/Chmn., Robert L. Sockolov/Dir., Alan Bernikow/Dir., Jesse Choper/Dir., Ward Mooney/Dir., Mitchell Presser/Dir., George T. Porter/Dir.

Owners: George T. Porter, Jack McKinney, Robert L. Sockolov, Walter E. Sprague, Alan S. Bernikow, Baron Capital Group/6.27%, FMR Corp./10.53%, David A. Levin/2.80%, S.A.C. Capital Advisors/5.40%, Insiders/17.41%, Ward K. Mooney, Chilton Investment Company/20.68%, Jesse Choper, Mitchell S. Presser, Bear Stearns Asset Management Inc./5.28% *(18 Owners included in Index)*

Financial Data: ***Fiscal Year End:***01/28 ***Latest Annual Data:*** 2/3/2007

Year	Sales	Net Income
2007	$467,512,000	$42,632,000
2006	NA	NA
2005	$365,047,000	$1,524,000

Curr. Assets:	$141,723,000	***Curr. Liab.:***	$74,942,000	***P/E Ratio:***	11.62
Plant, Equip.:	$59,063,000	***Total Liab.:***	$102,390,000	***Indic. Yr. Divd.:***	NA
Total Assets:	$320,436,000	***Net Worth:***	$218,046,000	***Debt/ Equity:***	NA

Catalina Marketing Corp

200 Carillon Pkwy., St Petersburg, FL, 33716; ***PH:*** 1-727-579-5000; ***http://*** www.catalinamktg.com

General - Incorporation	DE	***Stock***- Price on:12/24/2007	$31.71
Employees	1,200	Stock Exchange	NA
Auditor	PricewaterhouseCoopers LLP	Ticker Symbol	NA
Stk Agt	Mellon Investor Services LLC	Outstanding Shares	47,020,000
Counsel	Paul, Hastings, Janofsky & Walker LLP	E.P.S	$1.30
DUNS No.	11-281-7440	Shareholders	NA

Business: The group's principal activity is to provide targeted marketing solutions for consumer goods companies, pharmaceutical manufacturers and their respective retailers. The services provided by the group include discount coupons, loyalty marketing programs, sampling, advertising, in-store instant-win games and other incentives. The group's services enable retailers and manufacturers to impact purchase decisions before, during and after the purchase using a variety of strategic, targeted programs. It operates in the United States, the United Kingdom, France, Italy and Japan. At 31-Mar-2004, the group's network was installed in 17,604 retail stores and 11,929 pharmacies throughout the United States.

Primary SIC and add'l.: 7389 8742

CIK No: 0000883977

Subsidiaries: Catalina Electronic Clearing Services, Inc., Catalina Health Resource, LLC, Catalina Marketing C.V., Catalina Marketing Deutschland GmbH, Catalina Marketing Direct Marketing Services, Inc., Catalina Marketing France, S.A.S., Catalina Marketing International B.V., Catalina Marketing Italia s.r.l., Catalina Marketing Japan KK, Catalina Marketing Loyalty Holdings, Inc., Catalina Marketing Research Solutions, Inc., Catalina Marketing U.K., LTD., Catalina Marketing Worldwide, Inc., Catalina-Pacific Media, LLC, CMJ Investments, LLC 18 Subsidiaries included in the Index

Officers: Dick L. Buell/Dir., CEO, Cynthia J. McCloud/Exec. VP, Deborah Booth/Exec. VP, Edward C. Kuehnle/Exec. VP, Eric Williams/CIO, Exec. VP, Jay Parsons/Exec. VP, Tom Buehlmann/Exec. VP, Rick Frier/CFO, Exec. VP, Cary Siegel/Exec. VP, Chief Development Officer, Craig Scott/Exec. VP, Joanne Freiberger/VP - Finance

Directors: Dick L. Buell/Dir., CEO, Frederick W. Beinecke/Chmn., Edward Dunn/Dir., Evelyn V. Follit/Dir., Eugene P. Beard/Dir., Peter T. Tattle/Dir., Robert Tobin/Dir., Jeffrey W. Ubben/45/Dir.

Owners: ValueAct Capital/15.42%, Tom Buehlmann, Robert G. Tobin, T. Rowe Price Associates, Inc./12.21%, Dick L. Buell, Jeffrey W. Ubben/15.42%, Evelyn V. Follit, Craig H. Scott, Cooke & Bieler LP/6.43%, Antaeus Enterprises, Inc./6.01%, Wellington Management Company, LLP/7.32%, Insiders/25.05%, Edward C. Kuehnle, Edward S. Dunn, Frederick W. Beinecke/6.58% *(16 Owners included in Index)*

Financial Data: ***Fiscal Year End:***03/31 ***Latest Annual Data:*** 3/31/2006

Year	Sales	Net Income
2006	$417,746,000	$71,616,000
2005	$410,062,000	$65,452,000

Curr. Assets:	$113,152,000	***Curr. Liab.:***	$121,696,000	***P/E Ratio:***	29.64
Plant, Equip.:	$128,501,000	***Total Liab.:***	$193,938,000	***Indic. Yr. Divd.:***	$0.300
Total Assets:	$337,095,000	***Net Worth:***	$143,157,000	***Debt/ Equity:***	0.6138

Catalyst Lighting Group Inc

7700 Wyatt Dr., Forth Worth, TX, 76108; ***PH:*** 1-817-738-8181; ***Fax:*** 1-817-926-5003; ***http://*** www.catalystlighting.com; ***Email:*** investorrelations@catalystlighting.com

General - Incorporation	DE	***Stock***- Price on:12/24/2007	$0.07
Employees	NA	Stock Exchange	OTC
Auditor	Hein & Assoc. LLP	Ticker Symbol	CYSU
Stk Agt	Corporate Stock Transfer, Inc.	Outstanding Shares	4,190,000
Counsel	NA	E.P.S	-$0.8
DUNS No.	NA	Shareholders	NA

Business: The group's principle activity is to manufacture and market steel and aluminium outdoor lighting poles and accessories. It also designs poles and completes specification and stress calculations. The poles are directly sold to original equipment manufacturers and indirectly to other third parties through its own contracted sales representatives in the United States. The group operates through its wholly owned subsidiary, whitco company lp.

Primary SIC and add'l.: 3446

CIK No: 0001161582

Financial Data: ***Fiscal Year End:***12/31 ***Latest Annual Data:*** 9/30/2004

Year	Sales	Net Income
2004	$16,358,000	-$1,533,000

Curr. Assets:	$4,974,000	***Curr. Liab.:***	$7,414,000		
Plant, Equip.:	$163,000	***Total Liab.:***	$9,328,000	***Indic. Yr. Divd.:***	NA
Total Assets:	$10,454,000	***Net Worth:***	$1,126,000	***Debt/ Equity:***	NA

Catalyst Pharmaceutical Partners Inc

355 Alhambra Cir., Ste. 1370, Coral Gables, FL, 33134; ***PH:*** 1-305-529-2522; ***Fax:*** 1-305-529-0933; ***http://*** www.catalystpharma.com

General - Incorporation	DE	***Stock***- Price on:12/24/2007	$4.44
Employees	5	Stock Exchange	NDQ
Auditor	Grant Thornton, LLP	Ticker Symbol	CPRX
Stk Agt	Continental Stock Transfer & Trust Co	Outstanding Shares	12,530,000
Counsel	NA	E.P.S	-$0.33
DUNS No.	NA	Shareholders	NA

Business: The groups principal activities include developing and commercializing prescription drugs. The group The group products sold under the trade name Sabril. In September 2006, the group merged with Catalyst Pharmaceutical Partners, Inc. operates from the United States.

Primary SIC and add'l.: 2834

CIK No: 0001369568

Officers: Patrick J. McEnany/Co - Founder, Chmn., CEO, Pres., Charles W. Gorodetzky/Chief Medical Officer, Alicia Grande/Chief Accounting Officer, Corporate Controller, Jack Weinstein/VP, Treasurer, CFO, Douglas M. Winship/VP - Regulatory Operations, Steven R. Miller/VP - Pharmaceutical Development, Project Management

Directors: Patrick J. McEnany/Co - Founder, Chmn., CEO, Pres., Stephen L. Dewey/Chmn. - Scientific Advisory Board, Jonathan Brodie/Member - Scientific Advisory Board, David S. Tierney/Dir., Milton J. Wallace/Dir., Philip H. Coelho/Dir., Hubert E. Huckel/Co - Founder, Dir., Charles B. O'Keeffe/Dir., Robert D. Fechtner/Member - Scientific Advisory Board, Donald R. Jasinski/Member - Scientific Advisory Board, Thomas Kosten/Member - Scientific Advisory Board, Eugene Laska/Member - Scientific Advisory Board, Richard A. Rawson/Member - Scientific Advisory Board

Owners: Milton J. Wallace/2.70%, Insiders/50.50%, Charles B. OKeeffe/2.70%, Pequot Capital Management, Inc./6.90%, Patrick J. McEnany/29.80%, David S. Tierney/1.50%, Philip H. Coelho/1.80%, Hubert E. Huckel/14.20%, Jack Weinstein/3.40%

Financial Data: ***Fiscal Year End:***12/31 ***Latest Annual Data:*** 12/31/2006

Year	Sales	Net Income
2006	NA	-$2,729,000
2005	NA	-$1,805,000
2004	NA	-$540,000

Curr. Assets:	$20,588,000	***Curr. Liab.:***	$773,000	***P/E Ratio:***	37.91
Plant, Equip.:	$20,000	***Total Liab.:***	$773,000	***Indic. Yr. Divd.:***	NA
Total Assets:	$20,619,000	***Net Worth:***	$19,847,000	***Debt/ Equity:***	NA

Catalyst Semiconductor Inc

2975 Stender Way, Santa Clara, CA, 95054; ***PH:*** 1-408-542-1000; ***Fax:*** 1-408-542-1200; ***http://*** www.catsemi.com; ***Email:*** info@catsemi.com

General - Incorporation	DE	***Stock***- Price on:12/24/2007	$4.28
Employees	155	Stock Exchange	NYSE
Auditor	PricewaterhouseCoopers LLP	Ticker Symbol	CATS
Stk Agt	EquiServe Trust Co N.A	Outstanding Shares	16,410,000
Counsel	Wilson Sonsini Goodrich & Rosati	E.P.S	-$0.69
DUNS No.	14-822-2136	Shareholders	NA

Business: The group's principal activities are to design, develop and market nonvolatile memory semiconductor products serving the micro-controller applications market. The products of the group include communication, computing, industrial automation, consumer and automotive applications. The product portfolio includes serial and parallel flash/electrically erasable programmable read only memories (eeprom), programmable micro-controller supervisory and voltage reference circuits and mixed signal devices. The group sells its products through distributors in Japan, Europe and Far East. The customers of the group include hewlett packard inc., jabil circuit inc., lg electronics inc.,v tech communications ltd and samsung Asia ltd. The group currently offers flash memory in small number of densities. The group at present has eight distrubutors and seven resellers in north and South America and a network of 28 distrubutors and 7 resellers to support international business.

Primary SIC and add'l.: 3674

CIK No: 0000899636

Subsidiaries: Catalyst Semiconductor Romania S.R.L., Nippon Catalyst K.K.

Officers: Gelu Voicu/Dir., CEO, Pres./$765,268.00, Scott Brown/VP - Marketing - Analog, Mixed, Signal Products/$335,922.00, Sorin Georgescu/VP - Technology, George Smarandoiu/VP - Design/$332,071.00, Irvin W. Kovalik/VP - Strategic Accounting/$323,223.00, David Eichler/CFO, VP - Finance, Administration, Daniel Hauck/VP - Worldwide Sales, Sherry Hill/Dir. - Marketing Communications

Directors: Gelu Voicu/Dir., CEO, Pres., Henry Montgomery/Chmn., Garrett Garrettson/Dir., Glen Possley/Dir., Roland Duchatelet/Dir.

Owners: FMR Corp./14.30%, Garrett A. Garrettson, Insiders/18.90%, Individuals and entities affiliated with Seligman Spectrum Focus/5.20%, Elex N.V./5.30%, Thomas E. Gay/1.50%, Individuals and entities affiliated with Royce & Associates, LLC/6.20%, Scott Brown, George Smarandoiu/1.30%, Irvin W. Kovalik/1.70%, Gelu Voicu/6.10%, Individuals and entities affiliated with Wellington Management Company LLP/12.10%, Henry C. Montgomery/1.20%, Glen G. Possley, Roland Duchtelet/5.30% *(16 Owners included in Index)*

Financial Data: ***Fiscal Year End:***04/30 ***Latest Annual Data:*** 04/29/2007

Year	Sales	Net Income
2007	$66,350,000	-$429,000
2006	$60,217,000	$2,556,000
2005	$62,320,000	$3,821,000

Curr. Assets:	$56,158,000	***Curr. Liab.:***	$12,890,000		
Plant, Equip.:	$9,408,000	***Total Liab.:***	$12,890,000	***Indic. Yr. Divd.:***	NA
Total Assets:	$70,420,000	***Net Worth:***	$57,530,000	***Debt/ Equity:***	NA

Catalytica Energy Systems Inc

430 Ferguson Dr., Mountain View, CA, 94043; *PH:* 1-650-960-3000;
http:// www.catalyticaenergy.com

General - Incorporation	DE	**Stock** - Price on:12/24/2007	$1.39
Employees	24	Stock Exchange	NDQ
Auditor	Ernst & Young LLP	Ticker Symbol	CESI
Stk Agt	Mellon Investor Services LLC	Outstanding Shares	18,310,000
Counsel	Wilson Sonsini Goodrich & Rosati	E.P.S.	$0.57
DUNS No.	NA	Shareholders	NA

Business: The group's principal activity is to design, develop and manufacture advanced catalytic products for the energy and transportation industries with a focus on cost-effective solutions for improved performance and reduced emissions from combustion sources. The proprietary technologies include the application of catalysts to combustion systems and next-generation fuel processing applications to mitigate the environmental impact of power generation and transportation systems. The group's product xonon cool combustion(TM) , a breakthrough pollution prevention technology that enables natural gas-fired turbines to achieve ultra-low emissions power production.

Primary SIC and add'l.: 3629 8731

CIK No: 0001053361

Subsidiaries: Catalytica NovoTec,Inc., CESI-SCR,Inc., CESI-Tech Technologies,Inc., GENXON Power Systems, LLC, SCR-Tech, LLC

Officers: Robert M. Worsley/Chmn., CEO - Renegy Holdings, Inc, Scott K. Higginson/Sr. VP - Business Development, Public Affairs, Michael Cooper/Dir. - Research, Process Development, SCR, Tech, Howard N. Franklin/Dir. - Technology, SCR, Tech, Ralph A. Dalla Betta/CTO, VP - Technology, Robert W. Zack/CFO, Exec. VP, William J. McMahon/Pres. - SCR, Tech, David K. Yee/VP - Product Development, Kevin J. Lane/VP - Finance, Corporate Controller, Michael F. Mattes/VP - Sales, Marketing, SCR, Tech, Megan F. Meloni/Dir. - Investor Relations, Marketing Communications, Richard M. Weinroth/Sec., Corporate Counsel, Frank Wenz/GM - Production, Plant Operations, SCR, Tech

Directors: Robert M. Worsley/Chmn., CEO - Renegy Holdings, Inc, William B. Ellis/Dir., Susan F. Tierney/Dir., Ricardo B. Levy/Dir., Richard A. Abdoo/Dir.

Owners: William J. McMahon, AWM Investment Company, Inc./21.86%, William B. Ellis, Richard A. Abdoo, Susan F. Tierney, David F. Merrion, Howard I. Hoffen/18.85%, Insiders/23.59%, Ricardo B. Levy/2.27%, Robert W. Zack/1.54%, Farallon Capital Management, L.L.C/12.44%, Metalmark Capital LLC/18.51%

Financial Data: Fiscal Year End:12/31   Latest Annual Data: 12/31/2006

Year	Sales	Net Income
2006	$7,383,000	-$3,819,000
2005	$3,529,000	-$13,466,000
2004	$5,601,000	-$13,269,000

Curr. Assets:	$21,019,000	Curr. Liab.:	$1,879,000		
Plant, Equip.:	$976,000	Total Liab.:	$1,894,000	Indic. Yr. Divd.:	NA
Total Assets:	$27,571,000	Net Worth:	$25,677,000	Debt/ Equity:	NA

Catapult Communications Corp

160 S Whisman Rd., Mountain View, CA, 94041; *PH:* 1-650-960-1025; *Fax:* 1-650-960-1029;
http:// www.catapult.com; *Email:* info@catapult.com

General - Incorporation	NV	**Stock** - Price on:12/24/2007	$9.95
Employees	220	Stock Exchange	NDQ
Auditor	Deloitte & Touche, LLP	Ticker Symbol	CATT
Stk Agt	Chase Mellon Shareholder Services	Outstanding Shares	13,930,000
Counsel	NA	E.P.S.	-$0.32
DUNS No.	14-821-6328	Shareholders	NA

Business: The group's principal activity is to design, develop, manufacture, market and support advanced software-based test systems. It offers integrated suites of testing applications for the global telecommunications industry. The advanced software and hardware of the group assist customers in the design, integration, installation and acceptance testing of a broad range of digital telecommunications equipment and services. The group's dct, mgts and lance test systems enable equipment manufacturers and network operators to deliver complex digital telecommunications equipment and services more quickly and cost-effectively. Major customers of the group include at&t wireless services, alcatel, bellsouth corporation, cisco systems, fujitsu, lm ericsson, evolium sas, lucent technologies, motorola, nec corporation, nextel, nokia and siemens. The group operates in the United States, Canada, the United Kingdom, Europe, Japan and Australia.

Primary SIC and add'l.: 3825 3829 3663

CIK No: 0001063085

Subsidiaries: Catapult Communications (China) Co. Limited, Catapult Communications International Limited, Catapult Communications K.K, Catapult Communications Limited, Tekelec Limited

Officers: Richard A. Karp/Chmn., Founder, CEO, Chris Stephenson/CFO, VP, Kalyan Sundhar/VP - Engineering, Adam Fowler/VP - Strategic Product Management, Sean Kelly/VP - Sales, Glenn Stewart/CTO, Terry Eastham/VP - Marketing, David Mayfield/COO, Pres., Kathy Omaye-Sosnow/VP - Human Resources, Guy R. Simpson/VP - Applications Engineering, Barbara J. Fairhurst/VP - Operations

Directors: Richard A. Karp/Chmn., Founder, CEO, Peter Cross/Dir., Henry P. Massey/Dir., Nancy Karp/Dir., John Scandalios/Dir., Chuck Waggoner/Dir., Stephen R. Heinrichs/Dir.

Owners: Charles L. Waggoner, John M. Scandalios, Sean Kelly, Royce & Associates LLC/5.13%, Henry P. Massey, Insiders/36.40%, Glenn Stewart/1.29%, Fidelity Management & Research/13.35%, T. Rowe Price Associates, Inc./9.82%, Nancy H. Karp/9.81%, Richard A. Karp/21.26%

Financial Data: Fiscal Year End:09/30   Latest Annual Data: 9/30/2006

Year	Sales	Net Income
2006	$47,384,000	-$10,666,000
2005	$64,948,000	$14,148,000
2004	$58,018,000	$13,911,000

Curr. Assets:	$84,991,000	Curr. Liab.:	$12,295,000		
Plant, Equip.:	$1,912,000	Total Liab.:	$15,075,000	Indic. Yr. Divd.:	NA
Total Assets:	$136,807,000	Net Worth:	$121,732,000	Debt/ Equity:	NA

Catcher Holdings Inc

44084 Riverside Pkwy., Ste. 320, Leesburg, VA, 20176; *PH:* 1-540-882-3087;
http:// www.catcherinc.com; *Email:* info@catcherinc.com

General - Incorporation	DE	**Stock** - Price on:12/24/2007	NA
Employees	NA	Stock Exchange	OTC
Auditor	Stonefield Josephson, Inc.	Ticker Symbol	CTHH
Stk Agt	U.S. Stock Transfer Corp	Outstanding Shares	NA
Counsel	NA	E.P.S.	-$0.75
DUNS No.	NA	Shareholders	NA

Business: The groups principal activities include developing, manufacturing and distributing the CATCHER (TM) device, wireless handheld computing and communications device. In the year 2005, the group acquired U.S. Telesis Holdings, Inc. The group operates from the United States.

Primary SIC and add'l.: 3571

CIK No: 0001230802

Subsidiaries: Catcher, Inc

Officers: Robert Hal Turner/59/Chmn., CEO, Ira Tabankin/Vice Chmn., Sr. VP - Corporate Development, CTO/$356,613.00, Denis McCarthy/CFO/$643,852.00, Kyle S. Brown/VP - Marketing, Michael T. Grady/VP - Sales, Gary Rogers/VP - Engineering, Operations, Charles F. Strasburger/Sr. VP - Sales, Marketing

Directors: Robert Hal Turner/59/Chmn., CEO, Ira Tabankin/Vice Chmn., Sr. VP - Corporate Development, CTO, Harry L. Casari/Dir., Cathal Flynn/Dir.

Owners: Gary Haycox/4.00%, Cathal Flynn, Aequitas Capital Management, Inc./9.30%, Salzwedel Financial Communications, Inc./4.90%, Robert H. Turner/5.50%, Rawleigh Ralls/7.70%, Sandor Capital Master Fund LP/5.10%, Ira Tabankin/7.70%, Charles Sander/7.00%, Insiders/19.50%, John Lemak/6.20%, Jeff Gilford/3.40%, Allan Rakos/2.10%, Harry L. Casari, Denis McCarthy

Financial Data: Fiscal Year End:12/31   Latest Annual Data: 12/31/2006

Year	Sales	Net Income
2006	$100,000	-$12,625,000
2005	NA	-$8,150,000
2004	NA	-$56,000

Curr. Assets:	$4,265,000	Curr. Liab.:	$1,377,000		
Plant, Equip.:	$166,000	Total Liab.:	$1,377,000	Indic. Yr. Divd.:	NA
Total Assets:	$4,468,000	Net Worth:	$3,090,000	Debt/ Equity:	NA

Caterpillar Financial Services Corp

2120 W End Ave., Nashville, TN, 37203; *PH:* 1-615-341-1000; *Fax:* 1-615-341-5022;
http:// finance.cat.com

General - Incorporation	DE	**Stock** - Price on:12/24/2007	$81.38
Employees	94,593	Stock Exchange	NA
Auditor	PricewaterhouseCoopers LLP	Ticker Symbol	NA
Stk Agt	Mellon Investor Services LLC	Outstanding Shares	640,400,000
Counsel	NA	E.P.S.	$4.92
DUNS No.	04-941-9112	Shareholders	NA

Business: The group's principal activities are to provide retail and wholesale financing alternatives to customers and dealers. The group is the wholly-owned finance subsidiary of caterpillar inc. The group also purchases short-term dealer receivables. The retail financing services include tax financing, equipment financing and installment sale contract. The wholesale financing services include inventory financing and short term financing to dealers. The group operates in the United States, Europe, Australia and Asia.

Primary SIC and add'l.: 7359 6153 6159

CIK No: 0000764764

Officers: Kent M. Adams/Dir., CEO, Pres., Mike Sposato/General Counsel - Legal Services, Edward Scott/CFO, Exec. VP, Steven R. Elsesser/Controller, Ed Foley/Exec. VP - North America Operations, Joel Anquetil/VP - European Operations, Ed Goodrich/VP - Diversified Services, Dave Walton/VP - Asia Pacific Operations, Tom Frautschy/VP - Caterpillar Redistribution Services Inc, Garry Monaghan/Territory Mgr. - Canada, Nuno Portela/Territory Mgr. - Western Europe, Africa, The Middle East, Jorge Cervera/Territory Mgr. - Mexico, Central America, The Caribbean, Alexander Tumanov/Territory Mgr. - Russia, CIS, Eastern, Northern Europe, Ricardo Erasso/Territory Mgr. - South America, Kathy Ott/Territory Mgr. - Florida, Mountain Region *(28 Officers included in Index)*

Directors: Kent M. Adams/Dir., CEO, Pres., Steven H. Wunning/Dir.

Financial Data: Fiscal Year End:12/31   Latest Annual Data: 12/31/2006

Year	Sales	Net Income
2006	$41,517,000,000	$3,537,000,000
2005	$36,339,000,000	$2,854,000,000
2004	$30,251,000,000	$2,035,000,000

Curr. Assets:	$23,093,000,000	Curr. Liab.:	$19,252,000,000	P/E Ratio:	16.54
Plant, Equip.:	$8,851,000,000	Total Liab.:	$44,020,000,000	Indic. Yr. Divd.:	NA
Total Assets:	$50,879,000,000	Net Worth:	$6,859,000,000	Debt/ Equity:	2.2713

Caterpillar Inc

100 NE Adams St., Peoria, IL, 61629; *PH:* 1-309-675-1000; *Fax:* 1-309-675-1182;
http:// www.cat.com

General - Incorporation	DE	**Stock** - Price on:12/24/2007	$81.85
Employees	94,593	Stock Exchange	NYSE
Auditor	PricewaterhouseCoopers LLP	Ticker Symbol	CAT
Stk Agt	Mellon Investor Services LLC	Outstanding Shares	640,400,000
Counsel	NA	E.P.S.	$5.19
DUNS No.	00-507-0479	Shareholders	NA

Business: The group's principle activity is to manufacture construction and mining equipment, diesel and natural gas engines, and industrial gas turbines. The group's products include machine, engine and work tools. The group's services include maintenance and support, financial and rental services. The group operates from United States.

Primary SIC and add'l.: 3531 3510 6159 3537 3532 3519

CIK No: 0000018230

Subsidiaries: 10G LLC, A.S.V., Inc., Ace Power Embilipitiya Private Limited, Acefun S.A. de C.V., Aceros Fundidos Internacionales LLC, Aceros Fundidos Internacionales S. de R.L. de C.V., Advanced Filtration Systems Inc., AE-Steam SA, Aiwa Co., Ltd., Akoya, Inc., Amberly Investments, Anchor Coupling Inc., Arch Development Fund I L.P., Asia Power Systems (Tianjin) Ltd., AsiaTrak (Tianjin) Ltd. 424 Subsidiaries included in the Index

Officers: James W. Owens/62/Chmn., CEO/$14,818,620.00, Stuart L. Levenick/Group Pres./$3,865,121.00, Douglas R. Oberhelman/Group Pres./$4,334,118.00, William P. Ainsworth/VP, Gary A. Stampanato/VP, Tana L. Utley/VP, Ed Scott/Chief Ethics, Compliance Officer, Marcus

Watson/Communications Representative, Gerald L. Shaheen/Group Pres./$5,373,275.00, Gerard R. Vittecoq/Group Pres./$6,375,508.00, Steven H. Wunning/Group Pres., Exec. Office Member/$5,215,169.00, Stephen L. Fisher/VP, Robert T. Williams/VP, Robin D. Beran/Assist. Treasurer, Tinkie E. Demmin/Assist. Sec. *(46 Officers included in Index)*

Directors: James W. Owens/62/Chmn., CEO, Daniel M. Dickinson/46/Dir., Edward B. Rust/56/Dir., Joshua I. Smith/66/Dir., David R. Goode/66/Dir., Peter A. Magowan/65/Dir., William A. Osborn/59/Dir., Charles D. Powell/65/Dir., Frank W. Blount/68/Dir., John R. Brazil/61/Dir., John T. Dillon/68/Dir., Eugene V. Fife/67/Dir., Gail D. Fosler/59/Dir., Juan Gallardo/59/Dir.

Financial Data: *Fiscal Year End:*12/31 *Latest Annual Data:* 12/31/2006

Year	Sales	Net Income
2006	$41,517,000,000	$3,537,000,000
2005	$36,339,000,000	$2,854,000,000
2004	$30,251,000,000	$2,035,000,000

Curr. Assets:	$23,093,000,000	**Curr. Liab.:**	$19,252,000,000	**P/E Ratio:**	15.74
Plant, Equip.:	$8,851,000,000	**Total Liab.:**	$44,020,000,000	**Indic. Yr. Divd.:**	$1.440
Total Assets:	$50,879,000,000	**Net Worth:**	$6,859,000,000	**Debt/ Equity:**	2.2713

Cathay General Bancorp

777 N Broadway, Los Angeles, CA, 90012; *PH:* 1-626-582-7380; *Fax:* 1-213-625-1368; *http://* www.cathaybank.com

General		Stock	
Incorporation	DE	Price on:12/24/2007	$33.694
Employees	1,051	Stock Exchange	NDQ
Auditor	KPMG LLP	Ticker Symbol	CATY
Stk Agt	T.C. Realty Inc	Outstanding Shares	51,180,000
Counsel	NA	E.P.S	$2.34
DUNS No.	00-965-9483	Shareholders	NA

Business: The group's principal activity is to provide commercial banking services including acceptance of checks, money market savings and time deposits. The group also lends commercial, real estate, personal, home improvement, automobile and other installment and term loans. The other services provided by the group include accepting checks, savings, letter of credit, wire transfer, spot and forward contracts time deposits and makes commercial, real estate, personal, home improvement, automobile, and other installment and term loans. The group conducts its operations through 12 branches in southern California, seven branches in northern California, three branches in New York state, one branch in houston, Texas and two representative office, one in Hong Kong and one in China. On 20-Oct-2003, the group merged with gbc bancorp and changed its name to cathay general bancorp.

Primary SIC and add'l.: 6712 6022

CIK No: 0000861842

Subsidiaries: Cathay Bank, Cathay Capital Trust I, Cathay Capital Trust II, Cathay Investment Company, Cathay Real Estate Investment Trust, Cathay Statutory Trust I, Cathay Trade Services, Asia Limited, GB Capital Trust II, GBC Investment& Consulting Company, Inc., GBC Real Estate Investments, Inc., GBC Venture Capital, Inc.

Officers: Dunson K. Cheng/Chmn., CEO, Pres., Peter Wu/Dir., Executive Vice Chmn., COO, Monica Chen/Assist. Sec. - Cathay Bank, Perry P. Oei/Sr. VP, General Counsel, Michael M.Y. Chang/Dir., Sec., Heng W. Chen/Exec. VP, CFO, Treasurer, Anthony M. Tang/Dir., Exec. VP

Directors: Dunson K. Cheng/Chmn., CEO, Pres., Peter Wu/Dir., Executive Vice Chmn., COO, Wilbur K. Woo/Vice Chmn. Emeritus, George T.M. Ching/Vice Chmn. Emeritus, Anthony M. Tang/Dir., Exec. VP, Joseph C.H. Poon/Dir., Ting Y. Liu/Dir., Thomas C.T. Chiu/Dir., Michael M.Y. Chang/Dir., Sec., Kelly L. Chan/Dir., Nelson Chung/Dir., Thomas G. Tartaglia/Dir., Patrick S.D. Lee/Dir.

Owners: Kelly L. Chan, Anthony M. Tang/1.82%, Insiders/11.73%, Irwin Wong, Peter Wu/2.58%, FMR Corp/10.02%, Michael M.Y. Chang/1.16%, Thomas C.T. Chiu, Nelson Chung, Ting Y. Liu, Dunson K. Cheng/3.14%, Patrick S.D. Lee, Heng W. Chen, Thomas G. Tartaglia, Joseph C.H. Poon

Financial Data: *Fiscal Year End:*12/31 *Latest Annual Data:* 06/30/2007

Year	Sales	Net Income
2007	NA	$8,500,000
2006	$512,982,000	$117,570,000
2005	$373,147,000	$104,091,000

Curr. Assets:	$220,793,000	**Curr. Liab.:**	$6,867,026,000	**P/E Ratio:**	14.40
Plant, Equip.:	$78,193,000	**Total Liab.:**	$7,074,934,000	**Indic. Yr. Divd.:**	$0.420
Total Assets:	$8,026,508,000	**Net Worth:**	$943,074,000	**Debt/ Equity:**	0.1920

Cathay Merchant Group Inc

Formerly: Equidyne Corp

Unit 803, Dina House, Ruttonjee Ctr., 11 Duddell St. Central, Hong Kong Sar, F4 200070; *PH:* 86-852-253-73613

General		Stock	
Incorporation	DE	Price on:12/24/2007	$0.47
Employees	126	Stock Exchange	NA
Auditor	RSM Hammelrath Gmbh	Ticker Symbol	NA
Stk Agt	American Stock Transfer & Trust Co.	Outstanding Shares	18,890,000
Counsel	NA	E.P.S	-$0.09
DUNS No.	07-870-1752	Shareholders	NA

Business: The group's principal activity is to develop, manufacture and sell the injex system, a patented, needle-free drug delivery system. The injex system consists of a hand-held, spring-powered device that injects drugs from a needle-free syringe through the skin as a narrow, high-pressure stream of liquid. The group presently operates through two wholly owned subsidiaries: equidyne systems inc & equidyne holdings. The group's customers include pharmacy chains and distributors to such chains.

Primary SIC and add'l.: 3841 3845

CIK No: 0000352281

Subsidiaries: AFM Aluminiumfolie Merseburg, AWP Aluminium Walzprodukte GmbH, Cathay Merchant Group (Nevada), Inc., Cathay Merchant Group (Shanghai) Wind Energy Co., Ltd., Cathay Merchant Group Ltd., MAW Mansfelder Aluminiumwerke GmbH

Owners: Michael J. Smith/27.70%, Mass Financial Corp./27.70%, Lloyd Miller/10.60%

Financial Data: *Fiscal Year End:*12/31 *Latest Annual Data:* 12/31/2006

Year	Sales	Net Income
2006	$100,162,000	-$2,515,000
2005	$5,723,000	-$736,000

Curr. Assets:	$15,952,000	**Curr. Liab.:**	$15,463,000		
Plant, Equip.:	$991,000	**Total Liab.:**	$25,988,000	**Indic. Yr. Divd.:**	NA
Total Assets:	$37,468,000	**Net Worth:**	$11,480,000	**Debt/ Equity:**	1.1884

Cato Corp (The)

8100 Denmark Rd. , Charlotte, NC, 28273; *PH:* 1-704-554-8510; *http://* www.catocorp.com

General		Stock	
Incorporation	DE	Price on:12/24/2007	$21.77
Employees	10,400	Stock Exchange	NYSE
Auditor	PricewaterhouseCoopers LLP	Ticker Symbol	CTR
Stk Agt	American Stock Transfer & Trust Co.	Outstanding Shares	31,680,000
Counsel	Robinson, Bradshaw & Hinson P.A.	E.P.S	$1.62
DUNS No.	02-446-7763	Shareholders	NA

Business: The group's principal activity is to offer quality fashion apparel and accessories at low prices. The group operates through two segments namely: women's fashion specialty stores and a credit card division. The specialty stores operate under the names 'cato', 'cato fashions', 'cato plus' and 'it's fashion!' and are located primarily in strip shopping centers in the southeast. The stores feature a broad assortment of apparel and accessories, including casual and dressy sportswear, dresses, careerwear, coats, hosiery, shoes, costume jewelry, handbags and millinery. Under credit card division, the group offers credit card to the customers and all credit authorizations, payment processing, and collection efforts are performed by a separate subsidiary of the group. The group operates 1,102 women's fashion specialty stores in 28 states.

Primary SIC and add'l.: 5621 6153 5632

CIK No: 0000018255

Subsidiaries: CaDel LLC, Cato of Texas L.P., Cato Southwest, Inc., catocorp.com, LLC, CatoSouth LLC, CatoWest LLC, Cedar Hill National Bank, CHW LLC, Providence Insurance Company, Limited

Officers: John P. Derham Cato/Chmn., CEO, Pres., Robert C. Brummer/Sr. VP - Human Resources, Assist. Sec., Michael T. Greer/Exec. VP, Dir. - Stores, Howard A. Severson/Exec. VP, Chief Real Estate, Store Development Officer, Assist. Sec., Allen B. Weinstein/Exec. VP, Chief Merchandising Officer, Shawn Smith/Sr. VP, General Counsel, Sec., Thomas W. Stoltz/CFO, Exec. VP, Tim Greer/Exec. VP, Dir. - Stores, Stuart L. Uselton/Exec. VP, Chief Administrative Officer

Directors: John P. Derham Cato/Chmn., CEO, Pres., James H. Shaw/Dir., Grant L. Hamrick/Dir., George S. Currin/Dir., William H. Grigg/Dir., Robert W. Bradshaw/Dir., Harding D. Stowe/Dir., A. F. Sloan/Dir.

Owners: John P. D. Cato/100.00%, Insiders/1.40%, Royce & Associates, LLC/10.10%, Thomas W. Stoltz, Grant L. Hamrick, Allen B. Weinstein, John P. D. Cato, Barclays Global Investors N.A., et al./5.70%, Howard A. Severson, George S. Currin, Michael T. Greer, Robert W. Bradshaw, NFJ Investment Group, L.P./6.30%, William H. Grigg, Insiders/100.00% *(17 Owners included in Index)*

Financial Data: *Fiscal Year End:*01/28 *Latest Annual Data:* 2/3/2007

Year	Sales	Net Income
2007	$875,885,000	$51,450,000
2006	$836,381,000	$44,829,000
2005	$789,604,000	$34,841,000

Curr. Assets:	$299,513,000	**Curr. Liab.:**	$123,049,000	**P/E Ratio:**	13.44
Plant, Equip.:	$128,461,000	**Total Liab.:**	$155,529,000	**Indic. Yr. Divd.:**	$0.660
Total Assets:	$432,322,000	**Net Worth:**	$276,793,000	**Debt/ Equity:**	NA

Catuity Inc

300 Preston Ave., Ste. 302, Charlottesville, VA, 22902; *PH:* 1-434-979-0724; *Fax:* 1-734-293-4213; *http://* www.catuity.com; *Email:* sales@catuity.com

General		Stock	
Incorporation	DE	Price on:12/24/2007	$0.91
Employees	35	Stock Exchange	OTC
Auditor	BDO Seidman LLP	Ticker Symbol	CTTY
Stk Agt	Computershare Investor Services LLC	Outstanding Shares	2,340,000
Counsel	Jaffe Raitt Heuer & Weiss	E.P.S	-$2.42
DUNS No.	NA	Shareholders	NA

Business: The group's principal activity is to develop and market an application software that allows for the provision of loyalty programs and incentives integrated into the payment system. The product is provided to retailers, card issuing banks and processors for consumer purchases in stores as well as over the Internet. The product consists of network system software that directly connects the seller and the buyer across all purchasing channels. It works with magnetic swipe cards and credit and debit cards that have a computer chip with a portion of the software loaded on them. The product is sold through retail stores, Internet merchants, banks and credit card issuers, public transport providers and membership organizations.

Primary SIC and add'l.: 8731 7372 7379

CIK No: 0001109740

Subsidiaries: Chip Application Technologies (Australia) Proprietary Limited, CIT Cards (Australia) Proprietary Limited, Loyalty Magic (Australia) Proprietary Limited

Officers: Alfred H. Racine/43/Dir., CEO, Pres., Debra Hoopes/47/Sr. VP, CFO, Treasurer, Sec.

Directors: Alfred H. Racine/43/Dir., CEO, Pres., Alexander S. Dawson/Chmn., Donald C. Campion/Dir., Clifford Chapman/Dir., Geoffrey C. Wild/68/Dir.

Owners: John H. Lowry/1.50%, Donald C. Campion, Alexander S. Dawson/1.70%, Insiders/11.80%, A&B Venture Fund/11.20%, Geoffrey C. Wild, Alfred H. Racine/4.70%, Clifford W. Chapman/1.10%, Chris P. Leach/1.70%

Financial Data: *Fiscal Year End:*12/31 *Latest Annual Data:* 12/31/2006

Year	Sales	Net Income
2006	$1,949,000	-$4,233,000
2005	$981,000	-$2,981,000
2004	$759,000	-$3,607,000

Curr. Assets:	$3,011,000	**Curr. Liab.:**	$1,205,000		
Plant, Equip.:	$294,000	**Total Liab.:**	$1,244,000	**Indic. Yr. Divd.:**	NA
Total Assets:	$8,253,000	**Net Worth:**	$7,009,000	**Debt/ Equity:**	NA

Cavalier Homes Inc

PO Box 300, Addison, AL, 35540; *PH:* 1-256-747-9800; *Fax:* 1-256-747-3044; *http://* www.cavalierhomebuilders.com

General		Stock	
Incorporation	DE	Price on:12/24/2007	$4.6501
Employees	1,771	Stock Exchange	AMEX
Auditor	Carr, Riggs & Ingram, LLC	Ticker Symbol	CAV
Stk Agt	Mellon Shareholder Services LLC	Outstanding Shares	18,410,000
Counsel	Lowe Mobley & Lowe	E.P.S	-$0.35
DUNS No.	62-279-1341	Shareholders	NA

Business: The group's principal activity is to design and produce manufactured homes. The group also provides retail installment sale financing and related insurance products for manufactured homes sold through dealers. The group operates through four segments: home manufacturing, retail, financial services and other. The home manufacturing segment designs and manufacture homes. The retail segment owns retail lots and sells homes to individuals. The financial services segment provides retail installment sale financing and related insurance products for manufactured homes. The other segments are primarily supplying companies who sell their products to the manufacturing segment and as well as other manufacturers. The group operates solely in the United States of America.

Primary SIC and add'l.: 1521 6162 6141 6411

CIK No: 0000789863

Subsidiaries: BRC Components, Inc., an corporation, Cavalier Home Builders, LLC, Cavalier Properties, Inc., Cavalier Real Estate Co., Inc., CIS Financial Services, Inc., Quality Housing Supply, LLC, Ridge Pointe Manufacturing, LLC, The Home Place of Nashville, Inc., The Home Place, LLC

Officers: David A. Roberson/Dir., CEO, Pres./$442,992.00, Michael R. Murphy/CFO/$264,302.00, Gregory A. Brown/COO/$314,017.00

Directors: David A. Roberson/Dir., CEO, Pres., Barry Donnell/Chmn., Don J. Williams/Dir., Bobby Tesney/Dir., Lee Roy Jordan/Dir., John W. Lowe/Dir., Thomas A. Broughton/Dir.

Owners: Bobby Tesney, Michael R. Murphy, Thomas A. Broughton, Don J. Williams, David A. Roberson/2.03%, Insiders/9.83%, Gregory A. Brown, GAMCO Investors, Inc./12.07%, Barry B. Donnell/5.16%, Dimensional Fund Advisors LP/6.74%, Paloma International L.P., et al/6.38%, John W. Lowe, Lee Roy Jordan, T. Rowe Price Associates, Inc./8.69%

Financial Data: *Fiscal Year End:* 12/31 *Latest Annual Data:* 12/31/2006

Year	Sales	Net Income
2006	$227,937,000	$172,000
2005	$272,032,000	$10,915,000
2004	$234,161,000	$3,241,000

Curr. Assets:	$59,102,000	**Curr. Liab.:**	$33,794,000		
Plant, Equip.:	$28,010,000	**Total Liab.:**	$38,306,000	**Indic. Yr. Divd.:**	NA
Total Assets:	$96,706,000	**Net Worth:**	$58,400,000	**Debt/ Equity:**	0.0800

Cavarlry Bancorp Inc

114 W College, Murfreesboro, TN, 37130; ***PH:*** 1-615-893-1234; ***http://*** www.cavalrybanking.com

General - Incorporation	TN	**Stock**- Price on:12/24/2007	$29.57
Employees	397	Stock Exchange	NA
Auditor	Rayburn, Bates & Fitzgerald, P.C	Ticker Symbol	NA
Stk Agt	Mellon Investor Services LLC	Outstanding Shares	15,530,000
Counsel	NA	E.P.S	$1.32
DUNS No.	05-151-9213	Shareholders	NA

Business: The group's principle activity is to accept deposits and provide mortgage, consumer, construction and commercial loans to the general public through its retail banking offices. The group is a bank holding company, which operates through its wholly owned subsidiary, cavalry banking. The group accepts now, demand deposit, money market, regular passbook savings and term certificate accounts. It originates fixed and variable mortgage, construction, and acquisition and development loans, in addition to commercial real estate, business and consumer and other non-real estate loans. The group's non-banking services include trust and investment advisory services, brokerage and employee benefit services such as the self-directed individual retirement accounts.

Primary SIC and add'l.: 6712 6411 6022

CIK No: 0001049535

Subsidiaries: Cavalry Banking, Miller & Loughry Insurance and Services, Inc.

Financial Data: *Fiscal Year End:* 12/31 *Latest Annual Data:* 12/31/2006

Year	Sales	Net Income
2006	$125,483,000	$17,927,000
2005	$51,701,000	$8,055,000
2004	$33,152,000	$5,319,000

Curr. Assets:	$103,538,000	**Curr. Liab.:**	$1,822,105,000	**P/E Ratio:**	22.40
Plant, Equip.:	$36,286,000	**Total Liab.:**	$1,886,170,000	**Indic. Yr. Divd.:**	NA
Total Assets:	$2,142,187,000	**Net Worth:**	$256,017,000	**Debt/ Equity:**	0.1960

Cavco Industries Inc

1001 N Central Ave., 8th Fl., Phoenix, AZ, 85004; ***PH:*** 1-602-256-6263; ***Fax:*** 1-602-256-6189; ***http://*** www.cavco.com; ***Email:*** info@cavco.com

General - Incorporation	DE	**Stock**- Price on:12/24/2007	$34.35
Employees	1,320	Stock Exchange	NDQ
Auditor	Ernst & Young LLP	Ticker Symbol	CVCO
Stk Agt	Mellon Investor Services LLC	Outstanding Shares	6,400,000
Counsel	NA	E.P.S	$1.15
DUNS No.	00-901-5264	Shareholders	NA

Business: The group's principal activity is to produce and sell manufactured homes. The homes are built to the standards promulgated by the U.S. Department of housing and urban development. Homes range in size from 640 to 2,720 square feet and typically include two to five bedrooms, a living room, dining room, kitchen and two or more full bathrooms. The group also produces commercial structures for a variety of purposes, including portable school classrooms, retail showrooms and offices. The group sells manufactured homes through 311 independent retail outlets in 15 states and 25 group-owned retail outlets, primarily in Arizona and Texas. In Jun 2003, the group spun-off from centex corporation.

Primary SIC and add'l.: 6321 6515 7519 2452 3448 5999

CIK No: 0000278166

Subsidiaries: CRG Holdings, LLC, CRG Mortgage, LLC, CRG Real Estate Brokerage, LLC

Officers: Tim Gage/GM, Mike Spiker/Regional Sales Mgr., Tyler Maddux/Regional Sales Mgr., Justin Lopinski/Commercial Division

Owners: Columbia Wanger Asset Management LP/11.78%, Jack Hanna, Neuberger Berman LLC/7.40%, Steven G. Bunger, Wachovia Corporation/5.80%, GAMCO Investors, Inc./13.42%, Joseph H. Stegmayer/9.48%, Royce & Associates LLC/5.18%, Michael H. Thomas, T. Rowe Price Associates, Inc./7.60%, Insiders/10.95%, Jacqueline Dout

Financial Data: *Fiscal Year End:* 03/31 *Latest Annual Data:* 3/31/2007

Year	Sales	Net Income
2007	$169,114,000	$11,549,000
2006	$189,503,000	$15,049,000
2005	$157,435,000	$10,127,000

Curr. Assets:	$91,989,000	**Curr. Liab.:**	$21,285,000	**P/E Ratio:**	19.74
Plant, Equip.:	$12,802,000	**Total Liab.:**	$34,045,000	**Indic. Yr. Divd.:**	NA
Total Assets:	$172,137,000	**Net Worth:**	$138,092,000	**Debt/ Equity:**	NA

Cavit Sciences Inc

100 E Linton Blvd, Delray Beach, FL, 33483; ***PH:*** 1-561-278-7856; ***http://*** www.cavitsciences.com

General - Incorporation	FL	**Stock**- Price on:12/24/2007	$0.43
Employees	1	Stock Exchange	OTC
Auditor	Infante & Co.	Ticker Symbol	CVIT
Stk Agt	Gulf Registrar & Trnsfer Corp	Outstanding Shares	NA
Counsel	NA	E.P.S	NA
DUNS No.	NA	Shareholders	NA

Business: The groups principal activities include developing and commercializing intellectual property rights to treat and prevent major diseases. The group operates from the United States.

Primary SIC and add'l.: 2834

CIK No: 0001368502

Subsidiaries: Hard to Treat Diseases, Inc.

Officers: Colm J. King/Dir., CEO, Pres., Emanuel Cheraskin/Investigator, Physician, Julio De Leon/Dir., CFO, Joseph P. D'Angelo/Scientific Researcher, Serge Sira/Scientific Advisor, Consultant, Jay Weitz/Pharmaceutical Advisor, Linus Pauling/Biologist

Directors: Colm J. King/Dir., CEO, Pres., Raymond S. Bazley/Dir., Christopher H. Brown/47/Dir., Harvey Judkowitz/63/Dir., Julio De Leon/Dir., CFO

Owners: Colm J. King/16.74%, Harvey Judkowitz/2.05%, Raymond Bazley/9.01%, Insiders/47.95%, Christopher Brown/14.79%, Julio De Leon/5.36%

Financial Data: *Fiscal Year End:* 09/30 *Latest Annual Data:* 12/31/2006

Year	Sales	Net Income
2006	NA	-$593,000

Curr. Assets:	$39,000	**Curr. Liab.:**	$116,000		
Plant, Equip.:	NA	**Total Liab.:**	$116,000	**Indic. Yr. Divd.:**	NA
Total Assets:	$39,000	**Net Worth:**	-$77,000	**Debt/ Equity:**	NA

CB Financial SVC IPA

3710 Nash St. North, Wilson, North Carolina, 27896;

General - Incorporation		**Stock**- Price on:12/24/2007	$16.5
Employees	NA	Stock Exchange	OTC
Auditor	NA	Ticker Symbol	CBFV
Stk Agt	Community Bank National Association	Outstanding Shares	NA
Counsel	NA	E.P.S	NA
DUNS No.	NA	Shareholders	NA

Business: The groups principle activity is to provide recruiting services. The groups service area includes the research and development, engineering, marketing, sales, information technology and manufacturing industries. The group operates from United States.

Primary SIC and add'l.: 6162

CIK No:

CB Richard Ellis Group Inc

11150 Santa Monica Blvd., Ste. 1600, Los Angeles, CA, 90025; ***PH:*** 1-310-405-8900; ***http://*** www.cbre.com; ***Email:*** info@cbre.com

General - Incorporation	DE	**Stock**- Price on:12/24/2007	$38.07
Employees	24,000	Stock Exchange	NYSE
Auditor	Deloitte & Touche LLP	Ticker Symbol	CBG
Stk Agt	Bank of New York	Outstanding Shares	228,660,000
Counsel	NA	E.P.S	$1.65
DUNS No.	61-760-8104	Shareholders	NA

Business: The groups principle activity is to provide commercial real estate services. The groups services include strategic advice and execution, property leasing and sales, property, facilities and project management; corporate services, debt and equity financing, investment management, valuation and appraisal, research investment strategy and consulting. The group operates from United States, Europe, Asia, Middle East and Africa. .

Primary SIC and add'l.: 6531 7389 6211

CIK No: 0001138118

Subsidiaries: CB Richard Ellis Limited, CB Richard Ellis Real Estate Services, LLC, CB Richard Ellis Services, Inc, CB Richard Ellis, Inc., CBRE Melody of Texas, L.P., CBRE Melody& Company, Insignia Financial Group, LLC, Relam Amsterdam Holdings B.V.

Officers: Brett White/CEO, Pres./$3,645,834.00, Vance G. Maddocks/CEO - CB Richard Ellis Investors, Mary Ann Tighe/CEO - New York Tri, State Region, William Concannon/Vice Chmn. - Global Corporate Services, Joann Young/Mgr. - Facilities, Christine M. Yagersz/Sr. Real Estate Mgr., Donald B. Goldstein/CIO - Information Technology, Brian F. Stoffers/Pres. - Capital Markets, Robert H. Zerbst/Pres. - CB Richard Ellis Investors, William H. Harris/COO - Cbre Investors, Jack Van Berkel/Sr. VP - Human Resources, James A. Reid/Pres. - Eastern Division, Christopher Ludeman/Pres. - US Brokerage, Bill Chillingworth/Pres. - Western Division, Robert W. McGrath/Sr. Dir. - Corporate Communications *(44 Officers included in Index)*

Directors: Richard C. Blum/Chmn., Ray Wirta/Vice Chmn., Stephen Siegel/Chmn. - Global Brokerage, Gary L. Wilson/Dir., Robert E. Sulentic/Dir., Curtis F. Feeny/Dir., Jane J. Su/Dir., Patrice Marie Daniels/Dir., Thomas A. Daschle/Dir., Bradford M. Freeman/Dir., Michael Kantor/Dir., Frederic V. Malek/Dir., John G. Nugent/Dir.

Owners: Richard C. Blum/10.80%, Kenneth J. Kay, Jane J. Su/10.80%, John G. Nugent, Bradford M. Freeman, Insiders/14.60%, Ray Wirta/3.10%, Brett White, Frederic V. Malek, Gary L. Wilson, Blum Strategic Partners II GmbH & Co. KG/10.80%, Thomas A. Daschle, Patrice Marie Daniels, Michael Kantor, Robert Blain *(17 Owners included in Index)*

Financial Data: *Fiscal Year End:* 12/31 *Latest Annual Data:* 12/31/2006

Year	Sales	Net Income
2006	$4,032,027,000	$318,571,000
2005	$2,910,641,000	$217,341,000
2004	$2,365,096,000	$64,725,000

Curr. Assets:	$2,212,013,000	**Curr. Liab.:**	$1,906,013,000	**P/E Ratio:**	30.70
Plant, Equip.:	$519,347,000	**Total Liab.:**	$4,684,854,000	**Indic. Yr. Divd.:**	NA
Total Assets:	$5,944,631,000	**Net Worth:**	$1,181,641,000	**Debt/ Equity:**	1.8573

Cbeyond Inc

320 Interstate N Pkwy. SE, Ste. 300, Atlanta, GA, 30339; *PH:* 1-678-424-2400;
Fax: 1-678-424-2500; *http://* www.cbeyond.net; *Email:* info@cbeyond.net

General - Incorporation .... DE	Stock- Price on:12/24/2007 ....$39.97
Employees 905	Stock Exchange...............................NDQ
Auditor ....Ernst & Young LLP	Ticker Symbol.....................................CBEY
Stk Agt...... American Stock Transfer & Trust Co.	Outstanding Shares 27,930,000
Counsel...NA	E.P.S...$0.45
DUNS No. ....NA	Shareholders.....................................NA

Business: The groups principle activity is to provide Internet Protocol based communications services. The groups services include local and long distance voice services, broadband Internet access, mobile voice and data, email, voicemail, web hosting, secure backup and file sharing, fax-to-email and virtual private network. Customers served by the group include Physicians, legal offices, banking institutions, consulting firms, accounting firms and real estate. The groups operates through six segments namely Atlanta, Dallas, Denver, Houston, Chicago and Los Angeles. The group operates from Atlanta, Dallas, Denver, Houston, Chicago and Los Angeles. The group's quarterly revenue for September 2007 was 72.42 millions of USD.

Primary SIC and add'l.: 4899 7389 4812 7375 7374 4813

CIK No: 0001205727

Subsidiaries: Cbeyond Communications, LLC

Officers: James F. Geiger/Chmn., CEO, Robert J. Fugate/CFO, Exec. VP, Robert R. Morrice/Exec. VP, Pres. - Sales, Service, Richard J. Batelaan/VP, COO, Christopher C. Gatch/CTO, VP, Henry C. Lyon/VP, Chief Accounting Officer, Joseph A. Oesterling/CIO, VP, Brooks A. Robinson/VP, Chief Marketing Officer, Kurt Abkemeier/VP - Finance, Treasurer, Cleveland A. Lewis/VP - Sales, Brent N. Cobb/VP - Product Management, GM - Mobile, Mary N. Ford/VP - Marketing, Joan L. Tolliver/VP - Human Resources, Terry S. Trout/VP - Customer Experience, Minaz K. Vastani/VP - Operations Support Systems *(16 Officers included in Index)*

Directors: James F. Geiger/Chmn., CEO, John Chapple/Dir., Douglas C. Grissom/Dir., Scott D. Luttrell/Dir., James N. Perry/Dir., David Rogan/Dir., Robert Rothman/Dir.

Owners: James F. Geiger/3.38%, Brent N. Cobb, Christopher C. Gatch, Terry S. Trout, Kurt J. Abkemeier, David A. Rogan, James N. Perry/15.62%, Madison Dearborn Partners III, L.P./15.62%, Douglas C. Grissom/15.62%, Joseph A. Oesterling, John R. Fugate, Robert Rothman/2.01%, VantagePoint Venture Partners/9.55%, Scott D. Luttrell/1.93%, Brooks A. Robinson *(20 Owners included in Index)*

*Financial Data: Fiscal Year End:*12/31 *Latest Annual Data:* 12/31/2006

Year	Sales		Net Income
2006	$213,886,000		$7,780,000
2005	$159,097,000		$3,736,000
2004	$113,311,000		-$11,456,000
Curr. Assets:	$68,528,000	*Curr. Liab.:* $52,625,000	*P/E Ratio:* 111.03
Plant, Equip.:	$72,790,000	*Total Liab.:* $53,285,000	*Indic. Yr. Divd.:* NA
Total Assets:	$144,393,000	*Net Worth:* $91,108,000	*Debt/ Equity:* NA

CBL & Associates Properties Inc

2030 Hamilton Pl. Blvd., Ste. 500, Chattanooga, TN, 37421; *PH:* 1-423-855-0001;
Fax: 1-423-490-8390; *http://* www.cblproperties.com

General - Incorporation .... DE	Stock- Price on:12/24/2007 ....$39.47
Employees 790	Stock Exchange...............................NYSE
Auditor ....Deloitte & Touche LLP	Ticker Symbol.....................................CBL
Stk Agt...............................Bank of Boston	Outstanding Shares 65,630,000
Counsel...NA	E.P.S...$1.27
DUNS No. ....NA	Shareholders.....................................NA

Business: The groups principle activities include owning, developing, acquiring, leasing, managing, and operating real estates property. The group operates through three segments namely, malls, associated centers and community centers. In the year 2005, the group acquired opened eight malls, two open-air centers and three associated centers. The group operates from the Southeastern and Midwestern United States. The group's quarterly revenue for September 2007 was 251.22 millions of USD.

Primary SIC and add'l.: 6798

CIK No: 0000910612

Subsidiaries: Acadiana Expansion Parcel, LLC, Acadiana Mall of Delaware, LLC, Acadiana Outparcel, LLC, Akron Mall Land, LLC, Alamance Crossing, LLC, APWM, LLC, Arbor Place GP, Inc., Arbor Place II, LLC, Arbor Place Limited Partnership, Asheville, LLC, Bonita Lakes Mall Limited Partnership, Brannen Street Crossing, LLC, Brookfield Square Joint Venture, Brookfield Square Parcel, LLC, Burnsville Minnesota II, LLC 327 Subsidiaries included in the Index

Officers: Charles B. Lebovitz/Chmn., CEO/$1,857,984.00, John N. Foy/Vice Chmn., CFO, Treasurer/$1,469,410.00, Stephen D. Lebovitz/Dir., Pres., Sec./$1,456,090.00, Augustus N. Stephas/COO, Sr. VP/$799,117.00, Ben S. Landress/Exec. VP - Management, Victoria S. Berghel/Sr. VP, General Counsel, Jay Wiseman/VP - Acquisitions, Katie Reinsmidt/Dir. - Investor Relations, Jerry L. Sink/Sr. VP - Mall Management, Eric P. Snyder/Sr. VP, Dir. - Corporate Leasing/$851,842.00, Stephen R. Tingle/Sr. VP - Development, Charles W.A. Willett/Sr. VP - Real Estate Finance, Tom Carter/VP - Mall Projects, Andrew F. Cobb/VP, Dir. - Accounting, Jeff Gregerson/VP - Specialty Retail *(33 Officers included in Index)*

Directors: Charles B. Lebovitz/Chmn., CEO, John N. Foy/Vice Chmn., CFO, Treasurer, Claude M. Ballard/Dir., Stephen D. Lebovitz/Dir., Pres., Sec.

Owners: Winston W. Walker, Affiliates of Jacobs Realty Investors Limited Partnership/19.75%, American Century Investment Management, Inc./2.85%, Martin J. Cleary, Eric P. Snyder, Matthew S. Dominski, Gary L. Bryenton, Vanguard Group, Inc/3.02%, CBL & Associates, Inc/15.19%, Stephen D. Lebovitz, John N. Foy, Leo Fields, Barclays Global Investors, NA/4.61%, FMR Corporation/8.43%, Charles B. Lebovitz/16.52% *(18 Owners included in Index)*

*Financial Data: Fiscal Year End:*12/31 *Latest Annual Data:* 12/31/2006

Year	Sales		Net Income
2006	$1,002,141,000		$117,501,000
2005	$907,459,000		$162,475,000
2004	$759,164,000		$121,111,000
Curr. Assets:	$109,929,000	*Curr. Liab.:* $309,969,000	*P/E Ratio:* 21.45
Plant, Equip.:	$6,094,251,000	*Total Liab.:* $5,433,954,000	*Indic. Yr. Divd.:* $2.020
Total Assets:	$6,518,810,000	*Net Worth:* $1,084,856,000	*Debt/ Equity:* NA

CBOT Holdings Inc

141 W Jackson Blvd., Chicago, IL, 60604; *PH:* 1-312-435-3500; *http://* www.cbot.com

General - Incorporation .... DE	Stock- Price on:12/24/2007 ....$209.47
Employees 662	Stock Exchange...............................NA
Auditor ....Rowe & Maw LLP	Ticker Symbol.....................................NA
Stk Agt .... Computershare Investor Services LLC	Outstanding Shares 52,840,000
Counsel...............................CBOT Holdings	E.P.S...NA
DUNS No. ....NA	Shareholders.....................................NA

Business: The group operates through its subsidiaries whose principle activity is to trade agriculture, grains and U.S. treasury products. The groups products include wheat, corn, soybeans and rough rice. The group operates through two segments namely, exchange trading and real estate operations. The group operates from the United States, London, Paris, Amsterdam and Singapore.

Primary SIC and add'l.: 6200

CIK No: 0001161448

Subsidiaries: Board of Trade of the City of Chicago, Inc., C-B-T Corporation

Officers: James Bennett/53/Sr. VP - Technical Solutions, Robert D. Ray/54/Sr. VP - Business Development

Owners: Charles M. Wolin, John L. Pietrzak, Christopher Malo, C. C. Odom, James A. Donaldson, Christopher Stewart, James P. McMillin, Insiders/1.00%, Kevin J. P.OHara, Joseph Niciforo, Mark E. Cermak, Bernard W. Dan, Michael D. Walter, Bryan T. Durkin, John E. Callahan *(23 Owners included in Index)*

*Financial Data: Fiscal Year End:*12/31 *Latest Annual Data:* 12/31/2006

Year	Sales		Net Income
2006	$621,091,000		$172,242,000
2005	$466,573,000		$76,543,000
2003	$381,302,000		$30,707,000
Curr. Assets:	$564,496,000	*Curr. Liab.:* $80,281,000	*P/E Ratio:* 21.45
Plant, Equip.:	$224,277,000	*Total Liab.:* $102,910,000	*Indic. Yr. Divd.:* NA
Total Assets:	$811,330,000	*Net Worth:* $708,420,000	*Debt/ Equity:* NA

CBRE Realty Finance Inc

185 Asylum St., 37th Fl., Hartford, CT, 06103; *PH:* 1-860-275-6200; *Fax:* 1-860-275-6225;
http:// www.cbre.com

General - Incorporation .... MD	Stock- Price on:12/24/2007 ....$12.85
Employees ....NA	Stock Exchange...............................NYSE
Auditor ....Ernst & Young, LLP	Ticker Symbol.....................................CBF
Stk Agt ..... American Stock Transfer & Trust Co.	Outstanding Shares 30,720,000
Counsel...NA	E.P.S...-$1.63
DUNS No. ....NA	Shareholders.....................................NA

Business: The groups principle activities include originating and acquiring loan services. The groups services include whole loans, subordinate interests in whole loans, bridge loans, mezzanine loans, joint loans. The group operates from the United States. The groups quarterly revenue for September 2007 was 41.12 millions of USD.

Primary SIC and add'l.: 6798

CIK No: 0001330969

Subsidiaries: CBRE Realty Finance CDO 2006-1 Depositor, LLC, CBRE Realty Finance CDO 2006-1, LLC, CBRE Realty Finance CDO 2006-1, Ltd., CBRE Realty Finance Holdings CDO Funding, LLC, CBRE Realty Finance Holdings II, LLC, CBRE Realty Finance Holdings III, LLC, CBRE Realty Finance Holdings IV, LLC, CBRE Realty Finance Holdings, LLC, CBRE Realty Finance TRS Warehouse Funding II, LLC, CBRE Realty Finance TRS Warehouse Funding III, LLC, CBRE Realty Finance TRS Warehouse Funding, LLC, CBRE Realty Finance TRS, Inc., CBRE Realty Finance TRS, LLC, CBRE Realty Finance Trust I

Officers: Kenneth J. Witkin/Dir., CEO, Pres., Thomas Podgorski/Exec. VP - Mortgage, Structured Loan, Michael Angerthal/CFO, Exec. VP, Treasurer, Paul Martin/Exec. VP - Portfolio, CDO Management

Directors: Kenneth J. Witkin/Dir., CEO, Pres., Ray Wirta/Chmn., Vincent J. Costantini/Dir., Douglas C. Eby/Dir., David P. Marks/Dir., Michael J. Melody/Dir., Richard Koenigsberger/Dir.

Owners: Keith Gollenberg, Paul Martin, Michael Angerthal, Wallace R. Weitz & Company/6.60%, Insiders/2.90%, Ricardo Koenigsberger, James Evans, Dreman Value Management, LLC/6.90%, Vincent Costantini, Douglas Eby/1.30%, David Marks, Ray Wirta, Baron Capital Group, Inc./6.10%, CB Richard Ellis, Inc./5.10%, Michael Melody *(17 Owners included in Index)*

*Financial Data: Fiscal Year End:*12/31 *Latest Annual Data:* 12/31/2006

Year	Sales		Net Income
2006	$74,053,000		$13,743,000
Curr. Assets:	$84,109,000	*Curr. Liab.:* $444,703,000	
Plant, Equip.:	$66,277,000	*Total Liab.:* $1,110,819,000	*Indic. Yr. Divd.:* $0.680
Total Assets:	$1,522,689,000	*Net Worth:* $411,870,000	*Debt/ Equity:* 1.5546

CBRL Group Inc

305 Hartmann Dr., Lebanon, TN, 37088; *PH:* 1-615-444-5533; *Fax:* 1-615-443-9476;
http:// www.cbrlgroup.com

General - Incorporation .... TN	Stock- Price on:12/24/2007 ....$44.73
Employees 74,031	Stock Exchange...............................NDQ
Auditor ....Deloitte & Touche LLP	Ticker Symbol.....................................CBRL
Stk Agt ... American Stock Transfer & Trust CO.	Outstanding Shares 24,460,000
Counsel...............................James F. Blackstock	E.P.S...$5.52
DUNS No. ....NA	Shareholders.....................................NA

Business: The groups principle activity is to operate restaurants and retail concepts. The group also operates from United States.

Primary SIC and add'l.: 5812 5947 6719 6794

CIK No: 0001067294

Subsidiaries: CBOCS Distribution, Inc, CBOCS Properties, Inc, CBOCS West, Inc, Cracker Barrel Old Country Store, Inc., Logans Roadhouse, Inc., Rocking Chair, Inc

Officers: Michael A. Woodhouse/63/Chmn., CEO, Pres., Lawrence E. White/CFO, Sr. VP - Finance, Patrick A. Scruggs/44/VP - Accounting, Tax, Chief Accounting Officer, Forrest N.B. Shoaf/58/Sr. VP, General Counsel, Edward A. Greene/53/Sr. VP - Strategic Initiatives, Simon Turner/53/Sr. VP - Marketing, Innovation, Chief Marketing Officer, Diana S. Wynne/53/Sr. VP - Corporate Affairs, Doug Barber/51/Sr. VP - Restaurant Operations, Robert J. Harig/58/Sr. VP - Human Resources, Terry Maxwell/49/Sr. VP - Retail

Directors: Michael A. Woodhouse/63/Chmn., CEO, Pres., Andrea M. Weiss/53/Dir., Jimmie D. White/67/Dir., James D. Carreker/61/Dir., Robert V. Dale/72/Dir., Richard J. Dobkin/63/Dir., Robert C. Hilton/71/Dir., Charles E. Jones/64/Dir., B. F. Lowery/71/Dir., Martha M. Mitchell/68/Dir., Erik Vonk/55/Dir.

Owners: Terry A. Maxwell, Charles E. Jones, Lawrence E. White, Robert C. Hilton, Forrest N.B. Shoaf, Robert V. Dale, James D. Carreker, Jack F.B Lowery, Insiders/6.10%, Barclays Global Investors, NA/12.84%, Douglas E. Barber, Martha M. Mitchell, Andrea M. Weiss, Jimmie D. White, Michael A. Woodhouse/3.60% *(17 Owners included in Index)*

Financial Data: Fiscal Year End:07/29 Latest Annual Data: 08/03/2007

Year	Sales	Net Income
2007	$2,351,576,000	$162,065,000
2006	$2,642,997,000	$116,291,000
2005	$2,567,548,000	$126,640,000

Curr. Assets:	$203,040,000	Curr. Liab.:	$242,235,000	P/E Ratio:	8.84
Plant, Equip.:	$1,118,573,000	Total Liab.:	$562,368,000	Indic. Yr. Divd.:	$0.560
Total Assets:	$1,435,704,000	Net Worth:	$873,336,000	Debt/ Equity:	7.9791

CBS Corp

51 W 52nd St., New York, NY, 10019; *PH:* 1-212-975-4321; *Fax:* 1-212-975-4516; *http://* www.cbscorporation.com

General - Incorporation		Stock - Price on:12/24/2007	
	NA		NA
Employees	NA	Stock Exchange	NYSE
Auditor	NA	Ticker Symbol	CBS
Stk Agt	Bank of New York	Outstanding Shares	NA
Counsel	NA	E.P.S.	$1.74
DUNS No.	NA	Shareholders	NA

Business: The groups principle activity is to broadcast cable networks, television stations and radio stations. The group operates through four segments namely, television, radio, outdoor and publishing. In the year 2005, the group acquired KIFR-FM and KOVR-TV. The group operates in the United States. The group's quarterly revenue for September 2007 was 3,281.40 millions of USD.

Primary SIC and add'l.: 7312 4833 4841 8999 2721 7812 2731 7312 2721 7383 4841 4832 2731 4833 8999 4832 7383 7812

CIK No:

Subsidiaries: 1020917 Ontario Inc., 13 Radio Corporation, 14 Hours Productions Inc., 1554994 Ontario Inc., 3171193 Nova Scotia Limited, 3171194 Nova Scotia Limited, 4400 Productions Inc., 559733 British Columbia Ltd., 90210 Productions, Inc., A-R Acquisition Corp., A.S. Payroll Company, Inc., Aaron Spelling Productions, Inc., Abaco Farms Limited, Acorn Pipe Line Company, Acorn Properties, Inc. 624 Subsidiaries included in the Index

Officers: Leslie Moonves/Dir., CEO, Pres., Dan Mason/CEO, Pres. - CBS Radio, Clive Punter/CEO - CBS Outdoor International, Matthew C. Blank/Chmn., CEO - Showtime Networks Inc, Wally Kelly/Chmn., CEO - CBS Outdoor, Jack Romanos/CEO, Pres. - Simon, Schuster, Brian T. Bedol/CEO, Pres. - Cstv Networks, Inc, Tom Kane/CEO, Pres. - CBS Television Stations, Roger M. King/CEO - CBS Television Distribution, CBS Paramount Television, Sumner M. Redstone/Founder, Exec. Chmn., Carl D. Folta/Office Chmn., Exec. VP, Martin D. Franks/Exec. VP - Policy, Planning, Government Relations, Susan C. Gordon/Chief Accounting Officer, Sr. VP, Corporate Controller, Joseph R. Ianniello/Sr. VP - Finance, Treasurer, Anthony G. Ambrosio/Exec. VP - Human Resources, Administration *(57 Officers included in Index)*

Directors: Leslie Moonves/Dir., CEO, Pres., Matthew C. Blank/Chmn., CEO - Showtime Networks Inc, Wally Kelly/Chmn., CEO - CBS Outdoor, Carl D. Folta/Office Chmn., Exec. VP, Sumner M. Redstone/Founder, Exec. Chmn., Shari Redstone/Vice Chmn., Linda Griego/Dir., Arnold Kopelson/Dir., Doug Morris/Dir., Fred Salerno/Dir., David R. Andelman/Dir., Joseph A. Califano/Dir., Bruce S. Gordon/Dir., Leonard Goldberg/Dir., William S. Cohen/Dir. *(17 Directors included in Index)*

Owners: Leslie Moonves, Shari Redstone, Leonard Goldberg, Susan C. Gordon, David R. Andelman, Sumner M. Redstone, Susan C. Gordon, NAIRI, Inc./National Amusements, Inc., William S. Cohen, Mario J. Gabelli, Charles K. Gifford, Insiders, Bruce S. Gordon, Fredric G. Reynolds, Frederic V. Salerno *(21 Owners included in Index)*

Financial Data: Fiscal Year End:NA Latest Annual Data: 12/31/2006

Year	Sales	Net Income
2006	$14,320,200,000	$1,660,500,000
2005	$14,536,400,000	-$7,089,100,000
2004	$22,525,900,000	-$17,462,200,000

Curr. Assets:	$8,144,100,000	Curr. Liab.:	$4,399,500,000		
Plant, Equip.:	$2,813,800,000	Total Liab.:	$19,986,300,000	Indic. Yr. Divd.:	$1.000
Total Assets:	$43,508,800,000	Net Worth:	$23,522,500,000	Debt/ Equity:	NA

CBT Financial Corp

11 N 2nd St., Clearfield, PA, 16830; *PH:* 1-814-765-7551; *Fax:* 1-814-765-2943; *http://* www.cbtfinancial.com

General - Incorporation		Stock - Price on:12/24/2007	$26
Employees	NA	Stock Exchange	OTC
Auditor	NA	Ticker Symbol	CBTC
Stk Agt	NA	Outstanding Shares	NA
Counsel	NA	E.P.S.	NA
DUNS No.	NA	Shareholders	NA

Business: The groups principal activity is to provide banking services. The services of the group include personal banking, business banking, trust and investment and online banking. The group operates from Pennsylvania in the United States.

Primary SIC and add'l.: 6712 6022

CIK No: 0001267316

Officers: William E. Wood/Chmn., CEO, Pres., Shelly K. Folmar/Investor Relations Contact, William A. Shiner/Sec., Richard W. Ogden/Treasurer

Directors: William E. Wood/Chmn., CEO, Pres., Robert W. Dotts/Dir., Craig L. Hile/Dir., Barbara J. Hugney-Shope/Dir., Charles R. Johnston/Dir., Andrew J. Kohlhepp/Dir., Robert M. Kurtz/Dir., Michael R. Lytle/Dir., Robert B. Murray/Dir., John G. Soult/Dir.

CCA Industries Inc

200 Murray Hill Pkwy., East Rutherford, NJ, 07073; *PH:* 1-201-330-1400; *Fax:* 1-201-842-6014; *http://* www.ccaindustries.com; *Email:* amberyoung@ccaindustries.com

General - Incorporation	DE	Stock - Price on:12/24/2007	$8.97
Employees	154	Stock Exchange	AMEX
Auditor	KGS LLP	Ticker Symbol	CAW
Stk Agt	American Stock Transfer & Trust Co.	Outstanding Shares	7,000,000
Counsel	Berman & Murray	E.P.S.	$0.65
DUNS No.	10-677-1041	Shareholders	NA

Business: The group's principal activity is to manufacture and distribute health and beauty aid products. The products include oral health-care products, skin-care products, hair-care products, dietary products, foot-care products, sun-care products, lipsticks and perfumes. These products are marketed under the brand and trademark names plus+white, sudden change, bikini zone, mood magic, mega t, cloud dance, cherry vanilla and scar zone. The products are marketed to major drug and food chains, mass merchandisers and wholesale beauty-aids distributors throughout the United States and Canada. The group's customers are wal-Mart, walgreen, rite aid, cvs, albertson and eckerd.

Primary SIC and add'l.: 2844

CIK No: 0000721447

Officers: David Edell/CEO, Dunnan Edell/COO, Pres., Drew Edell/Exec. VP - Research, Elias Ciudad/Exec. VP - Information Technologies

Directors: Ira Berman/Chmn.

Owners: Dunnan Edell, Drew Edell, Stephen A. Heit, Costa Brava Partnership III LP, David Edell, Stanley Kreitman, David Edell, Jack Polak, Insiders, Ira W. Berman, Ira W. Berman, Insiders

Financial Data: Fiscal Year End:11/30 Latest Annual Data: 11/30/2006

Year	Sales	Net Income
2006	$64,100,000	$5,604,000
2005	$63,721,000	$3,786,000
2004	$61,518,000	$5,797,000

Curr. Assets:	$31,305,000	Curr. Liab.:	$9,009,000	P/E Ratio:	12.71
Plant, Equip.:	$562,000	Total Liab.:	$9,132,000	Indic. Yr. Divd.:	$0.280
Total Assets:	$36,517,000	Net Worth:	$27,385,000	Debt/ Equity:	0.0053

CCC Information Services Group Inc

World Trade Ctr. Chicago, 444 Merchandise Mart, Chicago, IL, 60654; *PH:* 1-312-222-4636; *http://* www.cccis.com

General - Incorporation	DE	Stock - Price on:12/24/2007	$26.51
Employees	NA	Stock Exchange	NYSE
Auditor	PricewaterhouseCoopers LLP	Ticker Symbol	CCCG
Stk Agt	Computershare Investor Services LLC	Outstanding Shares	NA
Counsel	NA	E.P.S.	NA
DUNS No.	10-393-5383	Shareholders	NA

Business: The group's principal activity is to supply automobile claims, information and processing services, claims management software and communication services. The group is a holding company that operates through its subsidiary, ccc information services inc. It develops, markets and supplies automobile claim product and services which enable customers in the automobile claims industry, including automobile insurance companies, collision repair facilities, independent appraisers, automobile dealers and consumers, to manage the automobile claim and vehicle restoration process. The customers of the group include automobile insurance companies and automobile dealers. On 26-Feb-2003, the group acquired assets of comp-est estimating solutions.

Primary SIC and add'l.: 6411 7549 7372

CIK No: 0001017917

Subsidiaries: CCC Consumer Services Inc., CCC Consumer Services Southeast Inc., CCC Information Services Inc., CCC Partsco Holdings, Inc.Enterstand Limited, Certified Collateral Corporation of Canada, Ltd., Rayfield Limited (d/b/a CCC International)

Officers: Githesh Ramamurthy/Chmn., CEO, John Harris/Executive Editor, Mark Fincher/Editorial Contributor, Susanna Gotsch/Editorial Contributor, Chrisa Hickey/Editorial Contributor, Jeanene Obrien/Editorial Contributor, Jerry Rozmiarek/Editorial Contributor, Scott Stein/Editorial Contributor, Daniel F. Chan/Design, Art Direction, Jo Mills/Design, Art Direction, James A. Dickens/Editor In Chief, Joe Allen/Editorial Contributor, Mike Barber/Editorial Contributor, Michael Croxton/Editorial Contributor, Debbie Day/Editorial Contributor

Directors: Githesh Ramamurthy/Chmn., CEO

CCE Spinco Inc

9348 Civic Ctr. Dr., Beverly Hills, CA, 90210; *PH:* 1-310-867-7200; *http://* www.livenation.com

General - Incorporation	DE	Stock - Price on:12/24/2007	$23.03
Employees	4,400	Stock Exchange	NYSE
Auditor	Ernst & Young LLP	Ticker Symbol	NA
Stk Agt	Bank of New York	Outstanding Shares	65,520,000
Counsel	NA	E.P.S.	-$1.19
DUNS No.	NA	Shareholders	NA

Business: The groups principle activity is to manage live concerts. The group also promotes and produces tours for artists. The group operates through three segments namely events, venues and sponsorship, and digital distribution. The group operates from United States.

Primary SIC and add'l.: 7900

CIK No: 0001335258

Subsidiaries: 1283220 Ontario Inc., 2037004 Ontario Limited, 3471276 Canada, Inc., A.H. Enterprises, Inc., Addicted LLC, Adventure Sport Events Ltd., AKG, Inc., American Artists Limited, Inc., American Broadway, Inc., American Theatre License, LLC, Amphitheater Entertainment Partnership, Annestown Limited, Anti-Concerts B.V., Anti-Concerts Holding B.V., Anti-Concerts Investments N.V. 453 Subsidiaries included in the Index

Officers: Jason Garner/CEO - North American Music, Michael Rapino/Dir., CEO, Pres., Alan Ridgeway/CEO - International Music, Bruce Eskowitz/49/CEO - North American Music, Arthur Fogel/Chmn. - Global Music, CEO - Global Touring, David I. Lane/47/Chmn. - Global Theatre, CEO - European Theatre, Steve K. Winton/46/CEO - North American Theater Division, Thomas Johansson/Chmn. - International Music, Carl B. Pernow/46/Pres. - International Music, Bryan Perez/Pres. - Global Digital, Michael G. Rowles/Exec. VP, General Counsel, Kathy Willard/CFO, Exec. VP, Lee Ann Gliha/Investor Relations Officer, John Vlautin/Contact - Press

Directors: Michael Rapino/Dir., CEO, Pres., Mark P. Mays/Vice Chmn., Randall T. Mays/Chmn., Harvey Weinstein/Dir., James S. Kahan/Dir., Henry Cisneros/Dir., Robert Ted Enloe/Dir., Ariel Emanuel/Dir., Michael Cohl/Dir., Jeffrey T. Hinson/Dir., Lowry L. Mays/Dir., Connie McCombs McNab/Dir., John N. Simons/47/Dir., Timothy P. Sullivan/Dir.

Owners: Charles Walker, Connie McCombs McNab, Bruce Eskowitz, FMR Corp./14.90%, Alan Ridgeway, Barclays Global Investors, NA./5.20%, Jeffrey T. Hinson, Randall T. Mays, Insiders/7.00%, Michael Rowles, Michael Rapino, John N. Simons, Lowry L. Mays/5.40%, Robert Ted Enloe, Mark P. Mays *(19 Owners included in Index)*

Financial Data: Fiscal Year End:12/31 Latest Annual Data: 12/31/2006

Year	Sales	Net Income
2006	$3,691,559,000	-$31,442,000
2005	$2,936,845,000	-$130,619,000

Curr. Assets:	$738,109,000	Curr. Liab.:	$773,960,000		
Plant, Equip.:	$876,172,000	Total Liab.:	$1,546,340,000	Indic. Yr. Divd.:	NA
Total Assets:	$2,225,002,000	Net Worth:	$638,662,000	Debt/ Equity:	1.0625

CCF Holding Co

101 N Main St., Jonesboro, GA, 30236; *PH:* 1-770-478-8881; *Fax:* 1-678-284-3315; *http://* www.heritage24.com

General - Incorporation	GA	Stock - Price on:12/24/2007	$18.45
Employees	109	Stock Exchange	NDQ
Auditor	Thigpen, Jones, Seaton & Co. P.C	Ticker Symbol	CCFH
Stk Agt	Registrar & Transfer Co	Outstanding Shares	3,650,000
Counsel	Edwin, Kemp, Jr., Esq	E.P.S.	$1.315
DUNS No.	92-681-2629	Shareholders	NA

Business: The group's principal activity is to accept deposits from the general public and offer commercial, residential and consumer loans. The deposits accepted include demand deposits, checking accounts, savings deposits, money market deposits, term certificate accounts and individual retirement accounts. The group also invests in specified short-term securities, mortgage backed securities, certain other investments and the common stock of the federal home loan bank of atlanta. The services are provided through the main office located at jonesboro, Georgia and four other branch offices located in clayton, fayette and henry counties.

Primary SIC and add'l.: 6712 6022

CIK No: 0000943033

Subsidiaries: CCF Capital Trust I, CCF Capital Trust II, Heritage Bank

Officers: David B. Turner/59/Dir., CEO, Pres./$588,454.00, Mary Jo Rogers/47/CFO, Sr. VP/$166,443.00, Leonard A. Moreland/46/VP, Chief Administrative Officer, John C. Bowdoin/58/Exec. VP/$225,794.00, John L. Westervelt/52/Sr. Exec. VP/$232,521.00

Directors: David B. Turner/59/Dir., CEO, Pres., John B. Lee/80/Chmn., John T. Mitchell/67/Dir., Roy V. Hall/62/Dir., Edwin S. Kemp/60/Dir., Charles S. Tucker/81/Dir., Stephen E. Boswell/61/Dir.

Owners: Wellington Management Company, LLP/9.30%, Heritage Bank Employee Stock Ownership Plan/5.60%, Banc Fund V L.P. and Banc Fund VI L.P./7.40%, Roy V. Hall/1.10%, Charles S. Tucker/1.20%, Leonard A. Moreland/3.60%, John T. Mitchell/4.10%, Edwin S. Kemp/3.10%, John C. Bowdoin/1.50%, David B. Turner/6.90%, Stephen E. Boswell, John L. Westervelt, First Financial Fund, Inc./9.30%, Insiders/28.10%, John B. Lee/1.40% *(16 Owners included in Index)*

Financial Data: Fiscal Year End:12/31 Latest Annual Data: 12/31/2006

Year	Sales	Net Income
2006	$33,283,000	$5,191,000
2005	$24,943,000	$3,270,000
2004	$20,616,000	$2,747,000

Curr. Assets:	$27,160,000	Curr. Liab.:	$384,337,000	P/E Ratio:	12.99
Plant, Equip.:	$7,395,000	Total Liab.:	$396,840,000	Indic. Yr. Divd.:	$0.380
Total Assets:	$425,886,000	Net Worth:	$29,046,000	Debt/ Equity:	0.2901

CCFNB Bancorp Inc

232 E St., Bloomsburg, PA, 17815; *PH:* 1-570-784-4400; *Fax:* 1-570-387-4049; *http://* www.ccfnb.com; *Email:* info@ccfnb.com

General - Incorporation	PA	Stock - Price on:12/24/2007	$27.75
Employees	95	Stock Exchange	OTC
Auditor	J. H. Williams & Co. LLP	Ticker Symbol	CCFN
Stk Agt	American Stock Transfer & Trust Co.	Outstanding Shares	1,240,000
Counsel	NA	E.P.S.	$1.99
DUNS No.	60-341-2644	Shareholders	NA

Business: The group's principal activity is to provide banking services through its wholly owned subsidiary, the columbia county farmers national bank. It provides a range of commercial banking services to individuals, small and medium sized businesses by accepting deposits and providing loans. The group accepts time, demand and savings deposits and provides secured and unsecured commercial, real estate and consumer loans. At 31-Dec-2003, the bank had six branch banking offices which are located in bloomsburg, benton, lightstreet, millville, orangeville and south centre, columbia county.

Primary SIC and add'l.: 6021 6712

CIK No: 0000731122

Subsidiaries: Columbia County Farmers National Bank, Neighborhood Group, Inc.

Officers: Lance O. Diehl/42/Dir., CEO, Pres., Virginia D. Kocher/Treasurer, Principal Financial Officer, Edward L. Campbell/69/Dir., Sec., Edwin A. Wenner/COO, Exec. VP, Jacob S. Trump/Sr. VP, Financial Planning Officer

Directors: Lance O. Diehl/42/Dir., CEO, Pres., Elwood R. Harding/61/Vice Chmn., Paul E. Reichart/70/Chmn., Edward L. Campbell/69/Dir., Sec., Robert M. Brewington/57/Dir., Willard H. Kile/53/Dir., Charles E. Long/72/Dir., Frank D. Gehrig/62/Dir., Bruce W. McMichael/48/Dir.

Owners: Virginia D. Kocher, Willard H. Kile, W. Bruce McMichael, Paul E. Reichart, Edwin A. Wenner, Charles E. Long, Robert M. Brewington, Jacob S. Trump, Lance O. Diehl, Insiders/4.95%, Edward L. Campbell, Elwood R. Harding/1.27%, Frank D. Gehrig

Financial Data: Fiscal Year End:12/31 Latest Annual Data: 12/31/2006

Year	Sales	Net Income
2006	$15,102,000	$2,412,000
2005	$13,155,000	$2,226,000
2004	$12,373,000	$2,217,000

Curr. Assets:	$16,525,000	Curr. Liab.:	$200,332,000	P/E Ratio:	13.94
Plant, Equip.:	$5,049,000	Total Liab.:	$211,671,000	Indic. Yr. Divd.:	$0.800
Total Assets:	$241,920,000	Net Worth:	$30,249,000	Debt/ Equity:	0.3697

CCI Group Inc

405 Pk. Ave., 10th Fl., New York, NY, 10022; *PH:* 1-212-421-1400; *Fax:* 1-631-537-1541; *http://* www.caribbeanclubs.net; *Email:* info@caribbeanclubs.net

General - Incorporation	UT	Stock - Price on:12/24/2007	NA
Employees	36	Stock Exchange	OTC
Auditor	Hansen, Barnett & Maxwell	Ticker Symbol	CCIGE
Stk Agt	Atlas Stock Transfer Corp	Outstanding Shares	NA
Counsel	NA	E.P.S.	NA
DUNS No.	NA	Shareholders	NA

Business: The group's principal activity is to develop a network of 'members only' resorts located in the Caribbean. The group intends to acquire, operate, boutique style resorts and sell membership plans to its acquired properties. The group is in the development stage and plans to develop resorts located on the tropical island and intends to offer amenities and comforts expected by an upscale membership clientele, while maintaining the flavor and uniqueness of the property and island setting.

Primary SIC and add'l.: 7011

CIK No: 0001117034

Subsidiaries: Beach Properties Barbuda Limited, Caribbean Clubs International, Inc.

Officers: Fred W. Jackson/Chmn., CEO, Founder, Melanie Brandman/Pres. - Caribbean Clubs, Grace Grillo/Presiden, Caribbean Clubs, Mark C. Casolo/MD - Corporate Finance

Directors: Fred W. Jackson/Chmn., CEO, Founder, Mark C. Casolo/MD - Corporate Finance

Financial Data: Fiscal Year End:12/31 Latest Annual Data: 12/31/2005

Year	Sales	Net Income
2005	$1,732,000	-$11,605,000
2004	$294,000	-$5,745,000
2003	NA	-$3,482,000

Curr. Assets:	$391,000	Curr. Liab.:	$2,906,000		
Plant, Equip.:	$3,664,000	Total Liab.:	$9,176,000	Indic. Yr. Divd.:	NA
Total Assets:	$6,191,000	Net Worth:	-$2,985,000	Debt/ Equity:	NA

CCSB Financial Corp

1178 W 152 Hwy, Liberty, MO, 64068;

General - Incorporation	DE	Stock - Price on:12/24/2007	$14.2
Employees	31	Stock Exchange	OTC
Auditor	BKD LLP	Ticker Symbol	CCFC
Stk Agt	Registrar & Transfer Co	Outstanding Shares	NA
Counsel	Luse Gorman Pomerenk & Schick PC	E.P.S.	NA
DUNS No.	NA	Shareholders	NA

Business: The group's principal activity is to offer a variety of financial products and services. The group is a community-oriented institution, business consisting of attracting retail deposits from the general public. These deposits are invested, together with funds generated from operations and borrowings, primarily in one-to four-family residential mortgage loans, construction loans, multi-family and commercial real estate loans, mortgage related securities and various other securities. The group also invests in commercial business loans, consumer and other loans, including home equity and automobile loans. The group serves the communities located in clay and platte counties and in surrounding counties in Missouri from its main office in liberty and its branch offices in liberty, kearney and smithville.

Primary SIC and add'l.: 6035 6712

CIK No: 0001189356

Financial Data: Fiscal Year End:09/30 Latest Annual Data: 9/30/2005

Year	Sales	Net Income
2005	$4,847,000	$113,000
2004	$4,109,000	-$13,000
2003	$4,523,000	$157,000

Curr. Assets:	$3,700,000	Curr. Liab.:	$80,286,000		
Plant, Equip.:	$4,864,000	Total Liab.:	$80,947,000	Indic. Yr. Divd.:	NA
Total Assets:	$94,895,000	Net Worth:	$13,949,000	Debt/ Equity:	NA

CD&I Inc

80 Wesley St., South Hackensack, NJ, 07606; *PH:* 1-201-487-7740; *http://* www.cdl.net

General - Incorporation	DE	Stock - Price on:12/24/2007	$2.99
Employees	NA	Stock Exchange	NA
Auditor	J.H. Cohn, LLP	Ticker Symbol	NA
Stk Agt	NA	Outstanding Shares	NA
Counsel	Lowenstein Sandler PC	E.P.S.	NA
DUNS No.	86-113-8592	Shareholders	NA

Business: The group's principal activity is to provide customized, time-critical, delivery services to a wide range of commercial, industrial, retail and e-commerce based customers. The group's delivery services include rush delivery service, dedicated contract logistics and routed services and facilities management. Rush delivery services deliver time-sensitive packages, such as critical machine parts or emergency medical devices, from-point-to-point on an as-needed basis. Dedicated contract logistics provides a comprehensive solution to major corporations wanting the control, flexibility and image of an in-house fleet with all the economic benefits of outsourcing. Routed services delivers products from pharmaceutical suppliers to pharmacies and from manufacturers to retailers. Facilities management provides and supervises mailroom personnel, mail and package sorting services. The group operates from 67 leased facilities and 34 customer owned facilities in 22 states.

Primary SIC and add'l.: 4513 4215

CIK No: 0001000779

Subsidiaries: Clayton/National Courier Systems, Inc., Click Messenger Service, Inc., KBD Services, Inc., Olympic Courier Systems, Inc., Securities Courier Corporation, Silver Star Express, Inc., SureWay Air Traffic Corporation

Officers: Albert W. Van Ness/Chmn., CEO, Stuart Hyden/VP - Sales, Marketing, Marty Galinsky/VP, Region Mgr. - Field Operations, Mark T. Carlesimo/VP, General Counsel, Sec., Dominick Simone/VP, Region Mgr. - Banking Division, Dan Ayer/VP, Region Mgr. - Northeast Region, Field Operations, David Kronick/CIO, VP, Michael N. Brooks/Dir., Group Pres. - Ground Operations, Paul Calabro/VP, Region Mgr. - West Region, Field Operations, William T. Brannan/Dir., COO, Pres., Russell J. Reardon/CFO, VP, Curtis Hight/VP, Region Mgr. - New York City, Mathew Morahan/Dir. - Private Investor, Jim Cosentino/VP, Corporate Controller

Directors: Albert W. Van Ness/Chmn., CEO, John S. Wehrle/Dir., Jon F. Hanson/Dir., Michael N. Brooks/Dir., Group Pres. - Ground Operations, Thomas E. Durkin/Dir., Marilu Marshall/Dir., William T. Brannan/Dir., COO, Pres., John A. Simourian/Dir., Mathew Morahan/Dir. - Private Investor

CDC Corp

33/F Citicorp Ctr., 18 Whitfield Rd., Causeway Bay, 30329; **PH:** 1-852-2893-8200; **Fax:** 852-2893-5245; **http://** www.cdccorporation.net; **Email:** media@cdccorporation.net

General - Incorporation..........Cayman Islands	Stock - Price on:12/24/2007 ....$8.5499
Employees 2,451	Stock Exchange..NDQ
Auditor ....Deloitte Touche Tohmatsu	Ticker Symbol..CHINA
Stk Agt.............................Bank of New York	Outstanding Shares 113,230,000
Counsel............................Paul Hastings Janofski	E.P.S. ....-$0.12
DUNS No. ....NA	Shareholders..NA

Business: The group's principle activities are carried out through three divisions: e-business solutions: provides Web site design, hosting and maintenance services and Internet strategy consulting services for companies seeking to utilize the Internet to facilitate their business processes online. Advertising services: provides online advertising through the sale of advertisements for the network of Web sites, electronically delivering such advertisements and tracking the number of such advertisements delivered, and offline advertising and marketing services. It products: distributes computer hardware and software products. Other activities of the group include provision of booking services and provision of ticketing solutions to the transportation industry.

Primary SIC and add'l.: 7311 7379 7373 7372

CIK No: 0001076770

Subsidiaries: c360 Solutions Incorporated, CDC Software Asia Pacific Limited, CDC Software Global Holdings Limited, China.com Inc., chinadotcom Portals Limited, Equity Pacific Limited (holds 17game), Group Team Investments Limited, IMI Global Holdings Ireland Limited, Ion Global (BVI) Limited, Palmweb Inc., Pivotal Corporation, PK Information Systems Pty Ltd., Platinum China Holdings Inc., Praxa Limited, R.N.R. International Marketing Group (Australia) Pty 19 Subsidiaries included in the Index

Officers: James Park/CEO - CDC Games Corporation, South Koera, Eric Musser/Pres., CEO - CDC Software, Peter Yip/Vice Chmn., CEO, Antony Ip/29/Vice Chmn. - CDC Games, Chief Strategy Officer - CDC Games, Arthur Masseur/VP - Finance, CDC Software EMEA, Oscar Pierre/Sr. VP - Latin America, CDC Software, Kim Liou/39/General Counsel - CDC Corporation, Per Norling/Pres. - CDC Software, Michael Kah Meng Chan/VP - Strategy, Business Development, CDC Games Interactive Limited, Xiaowei Chen/Dir., Pres. - CDC Game, Chinacom, Dick De Haan/VP - Enterprise Services, CDC Software, Antony Yip/Chief Strategy Officer - CDC Games, Keith Chau/Chief Accounting Officer - CDC Games, Donglei Fang/COO - CDC Games, Michael Latimore/CFO *(27 Officers included in Index)*

Directors: Peter Yip/Vice Chmn., CEO, Raymond Ch'Ien/Chmn., Antony Ip/29/Vice Chmn. - CDC Games, Chief Strategy Officer - CDC Games, Michael Chan/39/VP - Business Development, Strategy, CDC Games International, Thomas M. Britt/Dir., Fang Xin/55/Dir., John Clough/Dir., Wong Kwong Chi/56/Dir., Simon Wong/Dir., Fred Wang/Dir., Xin Fang/Dir., Carrick John Clough/60/Dir., Chung Kiu Wong/Dir. - CDC Software, Frank K. Au/Dir. - CDC Software, Sin Just Wong/Dir. - CDC Games *(16 Directors included in Index)*

Financial Data: Fiscal Year End:12/31 Latest Annual Data: 12/31/2006

Year		Sales		Net Income
2006		$309,528,000		$10,840,000
2005		$244,874,000		-$3,514,000
2004		$182,683,000		-$9,333,000
Curr. Assets:	$383,472,000	Curr. Liab.:	$142,594,000	P/E Ratio: 31.26
Plant, Equip.:	$9,540,000	Total Liab.:	$402,810,000	Indic. Yr. Divd.: NA
Total Assets:	$857,433,000	Net Worth:	$454,623,000	Debt/ Equity: NA

CDEX Inc

4555 S Palo Verde Rd. , Ste. 123, Tucson, AZ, 85714; **PH:** 1-520-745-5172; **Fax:** 1-520-514-6394; **http://** www.cdex-inc.com; **Email:** Cdexmanagement@cdex-inc.com

General - Incorporation..............................NV	Stock - Price on:12/24/2007 ....$0.17
Employees ....NA	Stock Exchange...OTC
Auditor ....Aronson & Co	Ticker Symbol...CEXI
Stk Agt...........Nevada Agency & Trust Company	Outstanding Shares 41,680,000
Counsel..NA	E.P.S. ....-$0.08
DUNS No. 12-259-7532	Shareholders..NA

Business: The group's principle activities include developing and marketing technologies. The groups markets include market areas including medical, homeland security, brand protection, anit-counterfeiting and drug detection. The group operates from United States.

Primary SIC and add'l.: NA

CIK No: 0001173738

Officers: Malcolm H. Philips/Chmn., CEO, Pres., Wade M. Poteet/Principal Scientist, Timothy D. Shriver/Dir., Sr. VP - Manufacturing Operations, Dir.

Directors: Malcolm H. Philips/Chmn., CEO, Pres., George E. Dials/Dir., B. D. Liaw/70/Dir., Donald W. Strickland/Dir., Timothy D. Shriver/Dir., Sr. VP - Manufacturing Operations, Dir., Carmen Conicelli/Dir.

Owners: George Dials/0.48%, Timothy Shriver/3.38%, James Griffin/0.07%, Insiders/11.48%, B. D. Liaw, Malcolm H. Philips/7.08%

Financial Data: Fiscal Year End:10/31 Latest Annual Data: 10/31/2006

Year		Sales		Net Income
2006		$283,000		-$3,400,000
2005		$179,000		-$5,221,000
2004		$4,000		-$5,978,000
Curr. Assets:	$358,000	Curr. Liab.:	$1,924,000	
Plant, Equip.:	$47,000	Total Liab.:	$1,924,000	Indic. Yr. Divd.: NA
Total Assets:	$458,000	Net Worth:	-$1,489,000	Debt/ Equity: NA

CDG Investments Inc

No. 500 - 926 - 5th Ave. SW, Calgary, AB, T2P 0N7; **PH:** 1-403-233-7898; **http://** www.gold.ca; **Email:** inquiries@cdginvestments.ca

General - Incorporation ....Canada	Stock - Price on:12/24/2007 ....$0.03
Employees ....NA	Stock Exchange...OTC
Auditor ....Grant Thornton LLP	Ticker Symbol..CDGEF
Stk Agt..........Computershare Trust Company of Canada	Outstanding Shares ....NA
Counsel.........Lang Michener Lawrence & Shaw	E.P.S. ....NA
DUNS No. 24-272-0910	Shareholders..NA

Business: The group's principal activity is to invest in mineral exploration investment portfolios. Previously the group explored and developed precious metal properties in western Canada and Mexico. During the current year 2002 the group is negotiating to sell saskatchewan mineral property portfolio and change its business to an investment company. The group's subsidiaries are gr capital corporation, golden rule resources, inc., manson creek resources ltd., northern abitibi mining corp. And waddy lake resources inc.

Primary SIC and add'l.: 1041

CIK No: 0000920543

Subsidiaries: Tyler Resources Inc.

Officers: Barbara O'Neill/Sec., Robert G. Ingram/Dir., Pres., Gregory Smith/Dir., CFO

Directors: Robert G. Ingram/Dir., Pres., Gregory Smith/Dir., CFO, Calvin Fairburn/Dir., Kerry Brown/Dir.

Financial Data: Fiscal Year End:09/30 Latest Annual Data: 9/30/2006

Year		Sales		Net Income
2006		$487,000		$10,986,000
2005		$2,233,000		-$166,000
2004		$19,000		$1,259,000
Curr. Assets:	$1,830,000	Curr. Liab.:	$293,000	
Plant, Equip.:	NA	Total Liab.:	$293,000	Indic. Yr. Divd.: NA
Total Assets:	$1,830,000	Net Worth:	$1,537,000	Debt/ Equity: NA

CDI Corp

1717 Arch St., 35th Fl., Philadelphia, PA, 19103; **PH:** 1-215-569-2200; **Fax:** 1-215-569-1300; **http://** www.cdicorp.com

General - Incorporation ....PA	Stock - Price on:12/24/2007 ....$32.34
Employees 17,700	Stock Exchange..NYSE
Auditor ....KPMG LLP	Ticker Symbol...CDI
Stk Agt.................Mellon Investor Services LLC	Outstanding Shares 20,140,000
Counsel..NA	E.P.S. $1.64
DUNS No. 00-259-9934	Shareholders..NA

Business: The group's principle activity is to provide staffing, project management and permanent placement services. The group's revenues are derived primarily from Fortune 1000 companies primarily in the United States. It operates in four segments: professional services, project management, todays staffing and management recruiters. The professional services segment consists of the technical services staffing business, the information technology services staffing business and the group's anderselite operations in the United Kingdom. The project management operating segment consists of information technology and telecommunications project management business. The todays staffing segment provides temporary administrative and office support staff. The management recruiters segment provides permanent employment positions with its customers. The group's quarterly revenue for September 2007 was 298.71 millions of USD.

Primary SIC and add'l.: 7361 8744 7363 8711

CIK No: 0000018396

Subsidiaries: Asset Computer Personnel Corporation, Browns Canyon Corporation, Brownshill Corporation, Brownshill Holdings Limited, C.D.I. Professional Services Group, S. de R.L. de C.V., CDI AndersElite Australia Pty Limited, CDI AndersElite Limited, CDI Corporation, CDI Engineering Solutions, Inc., CDI Marine Company, CDI Orchard Financial Services Limited, CDI Professional Services, Ltd., Franchise Services of Ohio, Inc., Greenhill LLC, Liquid Medium, LLC 24 Subsidiaries included in the Index

Officers: Roger H. Ballou/Dir., CEO, Pres./$1,207,056.00, Joseph R. Seiders/Sr. VP, General Counsel, Sec./$421,469.00, Robert Giorgio/Pres. - CDI Engineering Solutions, Bill Lage/Sr. VP - Information Technology Staffing, Mark Kerschner/CFO, Exec. VP/$527,123.00, Vincent Webb/VP - Investor Relations, Andrew D. Cvitanov/Pres. - CDI Information Technology Solutions, Michael Jalbert/Pres. - Management Recruiters International Inc, MRI, Paul Hampton/MD - CDI Anderselite Limited, Ted Collins/VP - Technology, CDI, Life Sciences, Eduardo Guzman/VP - Puerto Rico Operations, CDI, Life Sciences, Brian J. White/Business Development Mgr. - CDI, Life Sciences, Mark Balawejder/Sr. VP - Solutions Delivery, Joel Reffner/Sr. Technical Recruiter, CDI, Life Sciences, Pat Murray/VP - Alternative Fuels, CDI, Process, Industrial *(28 Officers included in Index)*

Directors: Roger H. Ballou/Dir., CEO, Pres., Michael J. Emmi/66/Dir., Walter R. Garrison/81/Dir., Lawrence C. Karlson/65/Dir., Ronald J. Kozich/69/Dir., Constantine N. Papadakis/62/Dir., Barton J. Winokur/68/Dir.

Owners: Barton J. Winokur/1.00%, Ronald J. Kozich, Van Den Berg Management/10.30%, Insiders/9.70%, Lawrence C. Karlson/0.40%, Mark A. Kerschner, Joseph R. Seiders/0.30%, Michael J. Emmi, Lawrence C. Karlson/23.90%, Walter R. Garrison/6.80%, Roger H. Ballou/0.80%, Cecilia J. Venglarik/0.30%, FMR Corp./14.50%, John Fanelli, Kay Hahn Harrell

Financial Data: Fiscal Year End:12/31 Latest Annual Data: 12/31/2006

Year		Sales		Net Income
2006		$1,265,286,000		$23,263,000
2005		$1,133,584,000		$13,805,000
2004		$1,045,207,000		$7,528,000
Curr. Assets:	$290,684,000	Curr. Liab.:	$104,746,000	P/E Ratio: 24.32
Plant, Equip.:	$39,851,000	Total Liab.:	$113,787,000	Indic. Yr. Divd.: $0.520
Total Assets:	$413,119,000	Net Worth:	$299,332,000	Debt/ Equity: NA

CDKnet.com Inc

220 Old New Brunswick Rd., Ste. 202, Piscataway, NJ, 08854; **PH:** 1-732-465-9300; **http://** www.arkados.com

General - Incorporation ....DE	Stock - Price on:12/24/2007 ....NA
Employees 12	Stock Exchange..NA
Auditor ....Sherb & Co. LLP	Ticker Symbol..NA
Stk Agt............Interwest Transfer Company, Inc.	Outstanding Shares ....NA
Counsel.........Foley, Hoag & Eliot LLP	E.P.S. ....-$0.23
DUNS No. ....NA	Shareholders..NA

Business: The group's principal activity is to provide propietary convergence technology that links audio, video and the worldwide Web on standard compact disks. The multimedia technology enables users to create personalized compact disc by visiting a Website. The customised discs enable high-quality

video and digital technology which can play audio and display video on full-screen. The group targets many industries like entertainment, travel and tourism, professional sports, financial services, education, toys and games, fashion and healthcare. On 25-May-2004, the group acquired home networking and broadb and powerline technology company.

Primary SIC and add'l.: 6719 7372 7375

CIK No: 0001095130

Subsidiaries: Arkados, Inc, CDK Financial Corp. (F/K/A ValueFlash.com, Inc.), CDKnet, LLC, Creative Technology, LLC, Diversified Capital Holdings, LLC

Officers: Oleg Logvinov/CEO, Pres., Michael MacAluso/Sr. VP - Engineering, Steve Woodman/VP - Sales, Business Development, Grant Ogata/Exec. VP - Worldwide Operations, Barbara Kane-Burke/CFO, Jim Allen/VP - Standardization, Advance Planning, George She/VP - Asic Development

Directors: Andreas Typaldos/Chmn., Gennaro Vendome/Dir., William H. Carson/Dir.

Owners: Insiders/49.00%, William H. Carson/2.00%, Andreas Typaldos/41.00%, Barbara Kane-Burke, Gennaro Vendome/4.00%, Oleg Logvinov/6.00%, Grant Ogata

Financial Data: **Fiscal Year End:**05/31 **Latest Annual Data:** 05/31/2007

Year	Sales	Net Income
2007	$132,000	-$6,033,000
2006	$112,000	-$4,025,000
2005	$833,000	-$7,001,000

Curr. Assets:	$9,000	**Curr. Liab.:**	$2,262,000		
Plant, Equip.:	$2,000	**Total Liab.:**	$6,518,000	**Indic. Yr. Divd.:**	NA
Total Assets:	$595,000	**Net Worth:**	-$5,923,000	**Debt/ Equity:**	NA

CDSI Holdings Inc

100 S E Second St., Miami, FL, 33131; *PH:* 1-305-579-8000

General - Incorporation	DE	**Stock**- Price on:12/24/2007	$0.22
Employees	NA	Stock Exchange	OTC
Auditor	Becher Della Torre Gitto & Co P.C	Ticker Symbol	CDSI
Stk Agt	American Stock Transfer & Trust Co.	Outstanding Shares	3,120,000
Counsel	NA	E.P.S.	$0.00
DUNS No.	62-692-3575	Shareholders	NA

Business: The group's principal activity is to seek new Internet-related or other business opportunities. Prior to may 1998, the group's principal business was an on-line electronic delivery information service that transmits name, address, telephone number and other related information digitally to users of personal computers. Until Feb 2000, the group marketed and leased a prepaid, wireless, remote-operated retail inventory control and dispensing system for tobacco products called the coinexx star 10. In 2003, the group acquired cds.

Primary SIC and add'l.: 6719 9999

CIK No: 0001023994

Subsidiaries: Controlled Distribution Systems, Inc

Officers: Richard J. Lampen/54/Dir., CEO, Pres., Bryant J. Kirkland/42/Dir., VP, CFO, Sec., Treasurer

Directors: Richard J. Lampen/54/Dir., CEO, Pres., Bryant J. Kirkland/42/Dir., VP, CFO, Sec., Treasurer, Robert M. Lundgren/49/Dir., Henry Morris/54/Dir.

Owners: Bryant J. Kirkland, Henry Morris, New Valley LLC/47.80%, Insiders/1.40%, Jay Gottlieb/6.50%, Richard J. Lampen, Robert Lundgren

Financial Data: **Fiscal Year End:**12/31 **Latest Annual Data:** 12/31/2006

Year	Sales	Net Income
2006	NA	-$30,000
2005	NA	-$31,000
2004	NA	-$35,000

Curr. Assets:	$62,000	**Curr. Liab.:**	$8,000		
Plant, Equip.:	NA	**Total Liab.:**	$8,000	**Indic. Yr. Divd.:**	NA
Total Assets:	$62,000	**Net Worth:**	$54,000	**Debt/ Equity:**	NA

CDW Corp

200 N Milwaukee Ave, Vernon Hills, IL, 60061; *PH:* 1-847-465-6000; *http://* www.cdw.com

General - Incorporation	IL	**Stock**- Price on:12/24/2007	$85.05
Employees	5,500	Stock Exchange	NA
Auditor	PricewaterhouseCoopers LLP	Ticker Symbol	NA
Stk Agt	American Stock Transfer & Trust Co.	Outstanding Shares	79,170,000
Counsel	NA	E.P.S.	$0.31
DUNS No.	10-762-7952	Shareholders	NA

Business: The groups principle activity is to provide multi brand computer products and technology. The groups product line includes hardware, software and accessories. The group products are sold under the brand names Fujitsu, Hewlett-Packard, IBM, Lenovo, Microsoft, and Panasonic. In the year 2007, the group acquired Madison Dearborn Partners, LLC and Providence Equity Partners Inc. The group operates from United States.

Primary SIC and add'l.: 9999 5045

CIK No: 0000899171

Subsidiaries: CDW Canada, Inc., CDW Capital Corporation, CDW Corporation, CDW Direct, LLC, CDW Government, Inc., Cdw Isfe, LLC, CDW Logistics, Inc., Cdw Sac, Inc.

Officers: John A. Edwardson/Chmn., CEO/$4,550,368.00, Paul S. Shain/Sr. VP, Vickey Bunker/Investor Relations Specialist, Anne B. Ireland/VP - Business Development, Barbara A. Klein/CFO, Sr. VP/$1,313,526.00, Cindy T. Klimstra/VP - Investor Relations, James J. Lillis/VP - Services, Sandra M. Rouhselang/VP, Controller, Steven M. Schuldt/VP, Christine A. Leahy/Sr. VP, General Counsel, Corp. Sec., James R. Shanks/Exec. VP/$2,060,558.00, Matthew A. Troka/VP - Product, Partner Management, Robert J. Welyki/VP, Treasurer, Assist. Sec., Jonathan J. Stevens/CIO, Sr. VP, Dennis G. Berger/Sr. VP, Chief Coworker Services Officer *(19 Officers included in Index)*

Directors: John A. Edwardson/Chmn., CEO, Daniel S. Goldin/67/Dir., Michael J. Dominguez/Dir., George A. Peinado/Dir., Susan D. Wellington/49/Dir., Brian E. Williams/57/Dir., Benjamin D. Chereskin/Dir., Glenn M. Creamer/Dir., Donald P. Jacobs/80/Dir., Thomas J. Hansen/59/Dir., Stephan A. James/61/Dir., Michelle L. Collins/48/Dir., Michael P. Krasny/54/Dir., Casey G. Cowell/55/Dir., Terry L. Lengfelder/70/Dir.

Owners: Barclays Global Investors NA/7.90%, Circle of Service Foundation, Inc./5.80%, Terry L. Lengfelder, Michael P. Krasny/16.30%, Casey G. Cowell, Thomas J. Hansen, Donald P. Jacobs, James R. Shanks, Madison Dearborn Partners, LLC/22.00%, Brian E. Williams, Capital Research and Management Company/7.50%, Douglas E. Eckrote, Barbara A. Klein, Michelle L. Collins, John A. Edwardson/2.60% *(20 Owners included in Index)*

Financial Data: **Fiscal Year End:**12/31 **Latest Annual Data:** 12/31/2006

Year	Sales	Net Income
2006	$6,785,473,000	$266,080,000
2005	$6,291,845,000	$272,092,000
2004	$5,737,774,000	$241,445,000

Curr. Assets:	$1,549,536,000	**Curr. Liab.:**	$529,381,000	**P/E Ratio:**	23.69
Plant, Equip.:	$171,448,000	**Total Liab.:**	$564,262,000	**Indic. Yr. Divd.:**	NA
Total Assets:	$1,951,427,000	**Net Worth:**	$1,387,165,000	**Debt/ Equity:**	NA

CE Casecnan Water & Energy Co Inc

24th Fl., 6750 Building, Ayala Ave. Makati, Metro Manila; *PH:* 63-289-20276

General - Incorporation	Philippines	**Stock**- Price on:12/24/2007	NA
Employees	NA	Stock Exchange	NA
Auditor	Isla Lipana & Co	Ticker Symbol	NA
Stk Agt	NA	Outstanding Shares	NA
Counsel	Belinda E. Dugan	E.P.S.	NA
DUNS No.	71-879-6972	Shareholders	NA

Business: The group's principle activities include designing, development, construction of hydroelectric power plant and the related facilities for conversion into electricity of water. The group operates from United States.

Primary SIC and add'l.: 4911 4971

CIK No: 0001006402

Subsidiaries: CE Casecnan Ltd

Officers: Joseph L. Sullivan/53/Dir., CEO, Pres., GM, Brian K. Hankel/45/VP, Treasurer, Patrick J. Goodman/41/Dir., CFO, Sr. VP, Douglas L. Anderson/49/Dir., Sr. VP, General Counsel, Assist. Sec., Mitchell L. Pirnie/49/VP

Directors: Joseph L. Sullivan/53/Dir., CEO, Pres., GM, David L. Sokol/51/Chmn., Gregory E. Abel/45/Vice Chmn., Patrick J. Goodman/41/Dir., CFO, Sr. VP, Douglas L. Anderson/49/Dir., Sr. VP, General Counsel, Assist. Sec., Trinity S. Gatuz/41/Dir., Scott Laprairie/50/Dir., Linda B. Castillo/48/Dir., Belinda E. Dugan/39/Dir., Suzy Lyn A. Bayona/32/Dir., Pearl T. Liu/52/Dir.

Owners: CE Casecnan II, Inc./70.00%, CE Casecnan Ltd./30.00%

CE Franklin Ltd

300 - 5th Ave. SW, Ste. 1900, Edmonton, Calgary, AB, T2P 3C4; *PH:* 1-403-531-5600; *http://* www.cefranklin.com; *Email:* info@cefranklin.com

General - Incorporation	Canada	**Stock**- Price on:12/24/2007	$12.78
Employees	427	Stock Exchange	AMEX
Auditor	PricewaterhouseCoopers LLP	Ticker Symbol	CFK
Stk Agt	PricewaterhouseCoopers LLP	Outstanding Shares	18,280,000
Counsel	Macleod Dixon LLP	E.P.S.	$0.89
DUNS No.	20-075-9306	Shareholders	NA

Business: The group's principal activities are in the distribution of supplies for the drilling, producing, processing and pipelining of hydrocarbons. The group also manufactures, assembles, sells and rents progressive cavity pumps and air and gas compressors. The other activities include selling pipes, valves, fitting and maintenance supplies and provides customer inventory procurement and management services. The group owns and operates 41 service centers in Canada. The group's quarterly revenue for September 2007 was 116.82 millions of USD.

Primary SIC and add'l.: 5084 3563

CIK No: 0000912151

Subsidiaries: CE Franklin, CEF Technologies Ltd.

Officers: Michael S. West/Chmn., CEO, Pres., Tim Ritchie/VP - Strategic Initiatives, Roy MacDonald/Branch Mgr. - Edmonton, AB, DC, David Bentley/Branch Mgr. - Edson, AB, Jim Baumgartner/VP - Commercial Initiatives, Rod Tatham/VP - Operations, Ron Koper/VP - Business Effectiveness, Brent Greenwood/VP - Marketing, Supply, Kevin Hughes/Branch Mgr. - Fort Mcmurray, AB, Mike Spears/Branch Mgr. - Edmonton, AB, DC, Dan Solvey/Branch Mgr. - Port Coquitlam, BC, Mark Stoddart/Branch Mgr. - Taber, AB, Doug Schaffner/Branch Mgr. - Viking, AB, Tim Beatty/Branch Mgr. - Estevan, SK, Emile Bourassa/Branch Mgr. - Lloydminster, SK *(51 Officers included in Index)*

Directors: Michael S. West/Chmn., CEO, Pres., Michael Hogan/Dir., Robert McClinton/Dir., Victor J. Stobbe/Dir., Douglas L. Rock/Dir., David A. Dyck/Dir., John J. Kennedy/Dir.

Owners: Smith International/52.60%, Bear Stearns Asset Management Inc./5.30%

Financial Data: **Fiscal Year End:**12/31 **Latest Annual Data:** 12/31/2006

Year	Sales	Net Income
2006	$476,440,000	$19,516,000
2005	$413,902,000	$16,185,000
2004	$281,223,000	$5,077,000

Curr. Assets:	$161,125,000	**Curr. Liab.:**	$87,602,000		
Plant, Equip.:	$4,759,000	**Total Liab.:**	$88,328,000	**Indic. Yr. Divd.:**	NA
Total Assets:	$175,076,000	**Net Worth:**	$86,748,000	**Debt/ Equity:**	NA

CEC Entertainment Inc

4441 W Airport Fwy., Irving, TX, 75062; *PH:* 1-972-258-8507; *Fax:* 1-972-258-5524; *http://* www.chuckecheese.com; *Email:* investor@cecentertainment.com

General - Incorporation	KS	**Stock**- Price on:12/24/2007	$37.83
Employees	18,395	Stock Exchange	NYSE
Auditor	Deloitte & Touche LLP	Ticker Symbol	CEC
Stk Agt	EquiServe Trust Co N.A	Outstanding Shares	32,490,000
Counsel	NA	E.P.S.	$2.11
DUNS No.	03-712-1845	Shareholders	NA

Business: The group's principal activity is to operate family restaurants and entertainment center business. The restaurants offer a variety of pizzas, salad bars, sandwiches and desserts and feature musical and comic entertainment by life-size, computer-controlled robotic characters, family oriented games, rides and arcade-style activities. The group's restaurants contain a family oriented playroom area offering approximately 45 coin and token-operated attractions, including arcade-style games, kiddie rides, a toddler play area, video games, skill oriented games and other similar entertainment. The group owns and operates 420 restaurants in 48 states. Trademarks of the group include chuck e. Cheese and t.j. Hartford's.

Primary SIC and add'l.: 5812 5813 6794 7999

CIK No: 0000813920

Subsidiaries: International Association of CEC Entertainment, Inc.

Officers: Richard M. Frank/Chmn., CEO/$3,132,925.00, Richard T. Huston/Dir., Exec. VP - Marketing/$581,759.00, Mike H. Magusiak/Dir., Pres./$1,803,577.00, Marshall R. Fisco/Corp. Sec., Roger J. Cardinale/48/Exec. VP - Development, Purchasing/$569,624.00, Gene F. Cramm/50/Exec. VP - Games, Concept Evolution, Christopher D. Morris/37/CFO, Exec. VP/$899,876.00, Thomas W. Oliver/68/Exec. VP, General Counsel

Directors: Richard M. Frank/Chmn., CEO, Walter Tyree/Dir., Tim T. Morris/Dir., Richard T. Huston/Dir., Exec. VP - Marketing, Cynthia I. Pharr/Dir., Louis P. Neeb/Dir., Raymond E. Wooldridge/Dir., Mike H. Magusiak/Dir., Pres., Larry T. McDowell/Dir.

Owners: Tim T. Morris, Christopher D. Morris, Barclays Global Investors, NA/5.30%, Richard M. Frank/5.00%, Royce & Associates, LLC/6.70%, Insiders/11.90%, Richard T. Huston, Roger J. Cardinale, Larry T. McDowell, Michael H. Magusiak/3.20%, FMR Corp./11.50%, Walter Tyree, Louis P. Neeb, Cynthia I. Pharr Lee, Raymond E. Wooldridge *(16 Owners included in Index)*

Financial Data: *Fiscal Year End:*01/01 *Latest Annual Data:* 12/31/2006

Year	Sales	Net Income
2006	$774,154,000	$68,257,000
2005	$728,079,000	$82,532,000

Curr. Assets:	$64,764,000	**Curr. Liab.:**	$74,803,000	**P/E Ratio:**	17.93
Plant, Equip.:	$637,560,000	**Total Liab.:**	$344,979,000	**Indic. Yr. Divd.:**	NA
Total Assets:	$704,185,000	**Net Worth:**	$359,206,000	**Debt/ Equity:**	0.3865

Cecil Bancorp Inc

127 N St., Elkton, MD, 21921; *PH:* 1-410-398-1650; *Fax:* 1-410-392-3128; *http://* www.cecilfederal.com

General		**Stock**	
Incorporation	MD	Price on:12/24/2007	$9.05
Employees	87	Stock Exchange	OTC
Auditor	Stegman & Co	Ticker Symbol	CECB
Stk Agt	Registrar & Transfer Co	Outstanding Shares	3,680,000
Counsel	William B. Calvert	E.P.S	$0.85
DUNS No.	07-745-4999	Shareholders	NA

Business: The group's principal activity is to originate loans and accept deposits, primarily in cecil and harford counties, Maryland. The group operates through its subsidiary cecil federal bank. It offers loans on commercial and multi-family real estate, construction loans on one-to four-family residences, home equity loans and land loans. The group also makes consumer loans including education loans, personal and commercial lines of credit, automobile loans and loans secured by deposit accounts. The deposits are accepted in the form of certificates of deposit, savings accounts, checking, now, passbook and money market deposit accounts. The operations are conducted through the main office in elkton and branches in elkton and north east, Maryland.

Primary SIC and add'l.: 6712 6035

CIK No: 0000926865

Subsidiaries: Cecil Bancorp Capital Trust I, Cecil Federal Bank Maryland, Cecil Financial Services Corporation, Cecil Service Corporation, Cecil Ventures, LLC, Cecil Ventures, LLCMaryland

Officers: Mary B. Halsey/Dir., CEO, Pres./$256,727.00, Brian L. Lockhart/VP, Business Development Officer, Brian J. Hale/COO, Exec. VP, Sandra D. Feltman/Sr. VP, Dir. - Lending, John R. Ness/Consumer Loan Officer, Lee R. Whitehead/CFO, VP, John E. Hughes/VP - Commercial Lending, Anthony M. Moss/VP - Commercial Lending, Sally E. Wallace/Assist. VP - Branch Administration, Matthew J. Mullen/Commercial Lending, Robin W. Brueckman/VP - Accounting Executive, Marc E. Corvino/Business Development, Commercial Lending Officer

Directors: Mary B. Halsey/Dir., CEO, Pres., Charles F. Sposato/Chmn., Donald F. Angert/Dir., Leslie McFadden/Dir., Matthew G. Bathon/Dir., Allen J. Fair/Dir., David D. Rudolph/Dir., Mark W. Saunders/Dir., Thomas L. Vaughan/Dir.

Owners: Mary B. Halsey/5.08%, Brian J. Hale/0.60%, Matthew G. Bathon/2.09%, Sandra D. Feltman/0.76%, Insiders/50.08%, Charles Sposato/35.11%, Mark W. Saunders/1.69%, Donald F. Angert/1.35%, Thomas L. Vaughan/1.47%

Financial Data: *Fiscal Year End:*12/31 *Latest Annual Data:* 12/31/2006

Year	Sales	Net Income
2006	$22,950,000	$2,708,000
2005	$16,102,000	$2,062,000
2004	$11,433,000	$1,532,000

Curr. Assets:	$8,270,000	**Curr. Liab.:**	$301,235,000	**P/E Ratio:**	11.46
Plant, Equip.:	$9,208,000	**Total Liab.:**	$323,178,000	**Indic. Yr. Divd.:**	$0.100
Total Assets:	$347,451,000	**Net Worth:**	$24,273,000	**Debt/ Equity:**	0.6816

CECO Environmental

3120 Forrer St., Cincinnati, OH, 45209; *PH:* 1-513-458-2600; *Fax:* 1-513-458-2647; *http://* www.cecofilters.com; *Email:* sales@cecofilters.com

General		**Stock**	
Incorporation	DE	Price on:12/24/2007	$12.11
Employees	649	Stock Exchange	NDQ
Auditor	Battelle & Battelle LLP	Ticker Symbol	CECE
Stk Agt	American Stock Transfer & Trust Co.	Outstanding Shares	NA
Counsel	NA	E.P.S	NA
DUNS No.	25-507-9535	Shareholders	NA

Business: The group operates through its subsidiaries is to provide a wide spectrum of air quality services and products, these include industrial air filters, high performance filter fabrics, environmental maintenance, monitoring and management services, and air quality improvements systems, and is a full-service provider to the steel, aluminum, automotive, aerospace, semiconductor, chemical, cement, metalworking, glass, foundry and virtually all industrial process industries. The group operates from United States.

Primary SIC and add'l.: 6719 3823 3564

CIK No: 0000003197

Subsidiaries: CECO Abatement Systems, Inc., CECO Filters India Pvt. Ltd., CECO Filters, Inc., CECO Group, Inc., CECOaire, Inc., H.M. White, Inc. (f/k/a CECO Energy, Inc.), kbd/Technic, Inc., New Busch Co., Inc., The Kirk& Blum Manufacturing Company

Officers: Phillip Dezwirek/Chmn., CEO, Investor Relations Officer/$340,000.00, Jack Bertoli/Contact - K, B Contracting, Cincinnati, George Nelson/Contact - K, B Contracting, Defiance, William R. Nelson/Contact - K&B Contracting, Indianapolis, Bill Wells/Contact - K&B Contracting, Lexington, Dan Smith/Contact - K&B Contracting, Louisville, Paul Gillespie/Contact - K&B Contracting, Greensboro, Tom Kroeger/Contact - K&B Contracting, Columbia

Directors: Phillip Dezwirek/Chmn., CEO, Investor Relations Officer

Owners: Ronald E. Krieg/0.10%, Donald A. Wright/0.40%, Arthur Cape/0.10%, Thomas J. Flaherty/0.40%, Dennis W. Blazer/0.20%, Jason DeZwirek/28.10%, Richard J. Blum/4.20%, Phillip DeZwirek/25.10%, David D. Blum/2.90%, Insiders/42.00%

Financial Data: *Fiscal Year End:*12/31 *Latest Annual Data:* 12/31/2006

Year	Sales	Net Income
2006	$135,359,000	$3,094,000
2005	$81,521,000	-$435,000
2004	$69,366,000	-$928,000

Curr. Assets:	$42,653,000	**Curr. Liab.:**	$28,342,000		
Plant, Equip.:	$8,530,000	**Total Liab.:**	$48,265,000	**Indic. Yr. Divd.:**	NA
Total Assets:	$63,188,000	**Net Worth:**	$14,923,000	**Debt/ Equity:**	NA

Cedar Fair LP

1 Cedar Point Dr., Sandusky, OH, 44870; *PH:* 1-419-627-2233; *Fax:* 1-419-627-2260; *http://* www.cedarfair.com; *Email:* investing@cedarfair.com

General		**Stock**	
Incorporation	DE	Price on:12/24/2007	$28.1
Employees	1,850	Stock Exchange	NYSE
Auditor	Deloitte & Touche LLP	Ticker Symbol	FUN
Stk Agt	American Stock Transfer & Trust Co.	Outstanding Shares	54,210,000
Counsel	NA	E.P.S	-$0.47
DUNS No.	NA	Shareholders	NA

Business: The groups principle activity is to operate amusement parks, water parks and hotels. In the year 2006, the group acquired Paramount Parks, Inc. The group operates from the United States. The groups quarterly revenue for September 2007 was 567.51 millions of USD.

Primary SIC and add'l.: 5812 7996 7011 7999

CIK No: 0000811532

Subsidiaries: 3147010 Nova Scotia Company, Boeckling, L.P., Canadas Wonderland Company, Cedar Fair, Cedar Point of Michigan, Cedar Point, Inc., Kings Island Company, Knotts Berry Farm, Magnum Management Corporation, Michigans Adventure, Inc., Paramount Parks Experience, Inc., Paramount Parks, Inc., Western Row Properties, Inc.

Officers: Richard L. Kinzel/67/Chmn., CEO, Pres./$3,830,776.00, Stacy Frole/Dir. - Investor Relations, Jacob T. Falfas/56/COO/$1,364,743.00, Peter J. Crage/46/Corporate VP - Finance, CFO/$910,974.00, Robert A. Decker/47/Corporate VP - Planning, Design, Craig J. Freeman/54/VP - Administration, Brian C. Witherow/41/VP, Corporate Controller, Philip H. Bender/52/Regional VP/$441,305.00, John H. Hildebrandt/VP, GM - Cedar Point/$385,941.00, Richard A. Zimmerman/48/Regional VP

Directors: Richard L. Kinzel/67/Chmn., CEO, Pres., Darrel D. Anderson/63/Dir., Richard S. Ferreira/67/Dir., Michael D. Kwiatkowski/60/Dir., David L. Paradeau/65/Dir., Steven H. Tishman/51/Dir., Thomas A. Tracy/76/Dir.

Owners: Michael D. Kwiatkowski, Thomas A. Tracy, Richard L. Kinzel/3.50%, Richard S. Ferreira, Darrel D. Anderson, Insiders/4.70%, Jacob T. Falfas, John H. Hildebrandt, Philip H. Bender, David L. Paradeau, Steven H. Tishman, Peter J. Crage

Financial Data: *Fiscal Year End:*12/31 *Latest Annual Data:* 12/31/2006

Year	Sales	Net Income
2006	$831,389,000	$87,477,000
2005	$568,707,000	$160,852,000
2004	$541,972,000	$78,315,000

Curr. Assets:	$104,508,000	**Curr. Liab.:**	$159,258,000	**P/E Ratio:**	26.26
Plant, Equip.:	$1,985,709,000	**Total Liab.:**	$2,100,306,000	**Indic. Yr. Divd.:**	$1.900
Total Assets:	$2,510,921,000	**Net Worth:**	$410,615,000	**Debt/ Equity:**	5.7212

Cedar Shopping Centers Inc

44 S Bayles Ave., Ste. 304, Port Washington, NY, 11050; *PH:* 1-516-767-6492; *Fax:* 1-516-767-6497; *http://* www.cedarshoppingcenters.com

General		**Stock**	
Incorporation	MD	Price on:12/24/2007	$14.35
Employees	101	Stock Exchange	NYSE
Auditor	Ernst& Young LLP	Ticker Symbol	CDR
Stk Agt	American Stock Transfer & Trust Co.	Outstanding Shares	44,190,000
Counsel	NA	E.P.S	$0.28
DUNS No.	NA	Shareholders	NA

Business: The groups principle activities include developing, redeveloping, renovating, expansion, re-leasing and re-merchandising properties. In the year 2006, the group acquired 13 shopping and convenience centers containing 1.7 million square feet. The group operates from the United States. The groups quarterly revenue for September 2007 was 37.48 millions of USD.

Primary SIC and add'l.: 6798

CIK No: 0000761648

Subsidiaries: Academy Plaza LLC 1, Academy Plaza LLC 2, Cedar Brickyard, LLC, Cedar Camp Hill GP, LLC, Cedar Carbondale, LLC, Cedar Center Holdings L.L.C., Cedar Dubois, LLC, Cedar Golden Triangle LLC, Cedar Halifax II, LLC, Cedar Hamburg, LLC, Cedar Hershey, LLC, Cedar Huntingdon, LLC, Cedar Kenley Village, LLC, Cedar Lake Raystown, LLC, Cedar Lender LLC 166 Subsidiaries included in the Index

Officers: Leo S. Ullman/Chmn., CEO, Pres./$1,168,646.00, Thomas B. Richey/VP - Development, Construction/$711,263.00, Stuart H. Widowski/Sec., General Counsel, Michael Winters/VP - Acquisitions, Jeffrey L. Goldberg/Corporate Controller, Joseph F. Macri/Assist. General Counsel, Assist. Sec., Thomas J. O'Keeffe/CFO/$774,007.00, Brenda J. Walker/Dir., VP - Property Management/$509,060.00, Nancy H. Mozzachio/VP - Leasing/$468,603.00, Ann Maneri/Property Controller, Gaspare Saitta/Chief Accounting Officer, Frank C. Ullman/VP, Brad Cohen/Investor Relations Officer, Bartley Parker/Investor Relations Officer, Liz Brady/Media Relations

Directors: Leo S. Ullman/Chmn., CEO, Pres., Brenda J. Walker/Dir., VP - Property Management, Richard Homburg/Dir., Everett B. Miller/Dir., Roger M. Widmann/Dir., James J. Burns/Dir., Paul G. Kirk/Dir.

Owners: Everett B. Miller, Paul G. Kirk, Leo S. Ullman/1.60%, Lawrence E. Kreider, Insiders/3.00%, Roger M. Widmann, Thomas B. Richey, Snyder Capital Management, L.P. and/6.70%, FMR Corp./9.60%, Richard Homburg, Nancy H. Mozzachio, James J. Burns, Brenda J. Walker, The Vanguard Group, Inc./5.50%, Cohen & Steers Capital Management, Inc./12.80%

Financial Data: *Fiscal Year End:*12/31 *Latest Annual Data:* 12/31/2006

Year	Sales	Net Income
2006	$126,492,000	$15,335,000
2005	$78,941,000	$13,213,000
2004	$51,144,000	$7,860,000

Curr. Assets:	$41,574,000	Curr. Liab.:	$17,435,000	P/E Ratio:	51.25
Plant, Equip.:	$1,177,139,000	Total Liab.:	$673,769,000	Indic. Yr. Divd.:	$0.900
Total Assets:	$1,251,719,000	Net Worth:	$577,950,000	Debt/ Equity:	1.0245

Cedara Software Corp

111 Eighth Ave., New York, NY, 10011; PH: 1-212-894-8940; http:// www.cedara.com

General - Incorporation	Canada	Stock- Price on:12/24/2007	NA
Employees	NA	Stock Exchange	NA
Auditor	KPMG LLP	Ticker Symbol	NA
Stk Agt	KPMG LLP	Outstanding Shares	NA
Counsel	NA	E.P.S.	NA
DUNS No.	NA	Shareholders	NA

Business: The group's principle activity is to provide medical imaging software and serves major healthcare solutions. The medical imaging software enables physicians to diagnose and treat patients accurately and efficiently. The group develops software for medical imaging acquisition, review, distribution, post processing and therapy. Using a business-to-business model, the group markets its products through multi national original equipment manufacturers and value added resellers. The group's products include 2d and 3D medical imaging software applications, components, platforms and custom engineering solutions.

Primary SIC and add'l.: 7374 7372

CIK No: 0000883261

Officers: Loris Sartor/Pres., Peter Bascom/VP - Engineering, Antonia Wells/VP - Customer Operations, Vernon Colaco/VP - Sales

Cedric Kushner Promotions Inc

336 W 37th St., New York, NY, 10018; PH: 1-212-564-1111; http:// www.ckrush.net

General - Incorporation	DE	Stock- Price on:12/24/2007	$0.105
Employees	11	Stock Exchange	OTC
Auditor	Rosenberg Rich Baker Berman & Co	Ticker Symbol	CKRU
Stk Agt	Continental Stock Transfer & Trust Co	Outstanding Shares	112,140,000
Counsel	NA	E.P.S.	-$0.129
DUNS No.	93-299-8875	Shareholders	NA

Business: The group's principal activities are to acquire, adapt, license and market boxing-related programming, either in film or media. The group has two reportable segments: boxing and media. The group functions as a holding company of cedric kushner boxing inc and big content inc. The boxing segment produces and syndicates world championship boxing events for distribution worldwide. The media segment consists primarily of the big content subsidiary and manages the creation, distribution (domestically and internationally), and maintenance of all media holdings, including the group's media library of videotaped boxing events and current original television programming.

Primary SIC and add'l.: 7941 7812 6719 7922

CIK No: 0001064539

Subsidiaries: Beer League Holdings, LLC, Ckrush Direct, Inc., Ckrush Entertainment, Inc., Ckrush Sports, Inc, Identity Films & Company, LLC, TV The Movie Holdings, LLC

Officers: Roy Roberts/Dir., CEO, Jeremy Dallow/Dir., Pres., Jan E. Chason/CFO

Directors: Roy Roberts/Dir., CEO, Jeremy Dallow/Dir., Pres.

Owners: MLC Consultants, LLC/20.80%, Richard Ascher, Jonathan Schwartz, Jan E. Chason/1.90%, Roy Roberts/1.80%, Jeremy Dallow/9.40%, Insiders/12.80%, Jerry Gilbert, Philip Glassman

Financial Data: Fiscal Year End:12/31   Latest Annual Data: 12/31/2006

Year	Sales	Net Income
2006	$1,646,000	-$11,759,000
2005	$704,000	-$7,670,000
2004	$3,013,000	-$12,365,000

Curr. Assets:	-$1,320,811,000	Curr. Liab.:	NA		
Plant, Equip.:	NA	Total Liab.:	NA	Indic. Yr. Divd.:	NA
Total Assets:	-$1,320,811,000	Net Worth:	NA	Debt/ Equity:	NA

Cel-Sci Corp

8229 Boone Blvd., Ste. 802, Vienna, VA, 22182; PH: 1-703-506-9460; Fax: 1-703-506-9471; http:// www.cel-sci.com

General - Incorporation	CO	Stock- Price on:12/24/2007	$0.83
Employees	19	Stock Exchange	AMEX
Auditor	Deloitte & Touche LLP	Ticker Symbol	CVM
Stk Agt	Computershare Investor Services LLC	Outstanding Shares	111,090,000
Counsel	Hart & Trinen LLP	E.P.S.	-$0.177
DUNS No.	10-256-0141	Shareholders	NA

Business: The group's principal activity is to develop novel immune therapy products for cancers and infectious diseases. The group manufactures the product multikine(TM) using proprietary cell culture technologies that involve a combination of natural human interleukin-2 and certain other cytokines. Multikine is developed as a treatment for human papilloma virus (hpv) induced cervical dysplasia in HIV infected women and for head and neck cancer. L.e.a.p.s. is another product, a t-cell modulation technology that is being tested as potential treatment and preventive vaccine against various diseases like aids, chronic genital and oral herpes, malaria, colon cancer, breast cancer and autoimmune myocarditis.

Primary SIC and add'l.: 8731 2834

CIK No: 0000725363

Subsidiaries: Viral Technologies, Inc.

Officers: Geert R. Kersten/Dir., CEO, Treasurer, Maximilian De Clara/Chmn., Pres., John Cipriano/Sr. VP - Regulatory Affairs, Alexander G. Esterhazy/Dir. - Financial Advisor, Patricia B. Prichep/Sr. VP - Operations, Sec., Daniel Zimmerman/Sr. VP - Research, Cellular Immunology, Eyal Talor/Sr. VP - Research, Manufacturing, Gavin De Windt/Contact

Directors: Geert R. Kersten/Dir., CEO, Treasurer, Maximilian De Clara/Chmn., Pres., Alexander G. Esterhazy/Dir. - Financial Advisor, Peter Young/Dir., Richard C. Kinsolving/Dir.

Owners: Maximilian de Clara/0.60%, Richard C. Kinsolving/0.40%, Peter R. Young, Daniel H. Zimmerman/1.10%, Eyal Talor/1.00%, Geert R. Kersten/5.40%, Insiders/10.20%, Alexander G. Esterhazy/0.20%, John Cipriano/0.20%, Patricia B. Prichep/1.50%

Financial Data: Fiscal Year End:09/30   Latest Annual Data: 9/30/2006

Year	Sales	Net Income
2006	$125,000	-$7,939,000
2005	$270,000	-$3,040,000
2004	$325,000	-$4,200,000

Curr. Assets:	$9,048,000	Curr. Liab.:	$1,938,000		
Plant, Equip.:	$92,000	Total Liab.:	$10,584,000	Indic. Yr. Divd.:	NA
Total Assets:	$9,653,000	Net Worth:	-$931,000	Debt/ Equity:	NA

Celadon Group Inc

9503 E 33rd St., Indianapolis, IN, 46235; PH: 1-317-972-7000; Fax: 1-317-890-8099; http:// www.celadontrucking.com; Email: investors@celadontrucking.com

General - Incorporation	DE	Stock- Price on:12/24/2007	$16.47
Employees	3,353	Stock Exchange	NDQ
Auditor	Ernst & Young, LLP	Ticker Symbol	CLDN
Stk Agt	American Stock Transfer & Trust Co.	Outstanding Shares	23,510,000
Counsel	NA	E.P.S.	$0.74
DUNS No.	18-890-5202	Shareholders	NA

Business: The group's principal activity is to provide long haul, full truckload transportation services between the United States, Mexico and Canada. It offers point-to-point, on-time, just-in-time, team service to meet the expectations of the customers. The services are provided through a network of owned and leased tractors and to a lesser extent, independent owner-operators. The group also operates truckersb2b, inc, an e-procurement business that passes on volume purchasing power to more than 11,500 member fleets to provide discounts on fuel, tire and other related services. The group's major customer is daimler chrysler. It transports daimler chrysler original equipment automotive parts primarily between the United States and Mexico and daimler chrysler after-Market replacement parts and accessories within the United States. In Aug 2003, the group purchased certain assets of highway express inc.

Primary SIC and add'l.: 4212 7375

CIK No: 0000865941

Subsidiaries: Celadon Canada, Inc., Celadon E-Commerce, Inc., Celadon Logistics Services, Inc., Celadon Logistics, Inc., Celadon Mexicana, S.A. de C.V., Celadon Trucking Service, Inc., Celadon Trucking Services of Indiana, Inc., RIL Acquisition Corp., Servicios de Transportacion Jaguar, S.A de C.V., Truckers Insurance and Health Benefit Solutions, LLC, TruckersB2B, Inc., Zipp Realty LLC

Officers: Stephen Russell/Founder, Chmn., CEO/$1,435,787.00, Paul A. Will/Vice Chmn., Exec. VP, CFO/$513,332.00, Chris Hines/COO, Pres., Patricia Coady/Customer Service Mgr. - Britishcolumbia, Kelly Crosby/Representative, Pricing, Britishcolumbia, Ron Amos/Representative, Sales, Britishcolumbia, Dave Lord/Representative, Sales, Britishcolumbia, Robert Corbin/Customer Service Mgr. - United States, Gary Crim/Representative, Sales, Antonio Gutierrez/Customer Service Mgr. - Durango, Liz Vazquez/Representative, Pricing, Nicole Black/Representative, Pricing, ME, Marc Pasquini/Representative, Sales, NY, Alejandra Rodriguez/Representative - Customer Service, Durango, Cristina Pena/Representative - Customer Service, Durango *(38 Officers included in Index)*

Directors: Stephen Russell/Founder, Chmn., CEO, Paul A. Will/Vice Chmn., Exec. VP, CFO, Anthony Heyworth/Dir., Michael Miller/Dir., Cathy Langham/Dir., Catherine Langham/50/Dir.

Owners: Paul Will/1.05%, Thompson, Siegel & Walmsley, Inc/5.20%, Sergio Hernandez, Kenneth Core, Anthony Heyworth, Michael Miller, Chris Hines, Thomas Glaser, Insiders/8.01%, Stephen Russell/5.24%

Financial Data: Fiscal Year End:06/30   Latest Annual Data: 06/30/2007

Year	Sales	Net Income
2007	$502,692,000	$22,252,000
2006	$480,194,000	$20,548,000
2005	$436,763,000	$12,580,000

Curr. Assets:	$77,088,000	Curr. Liab.:	$48,206,000		
Plant, Equip.:	$92,836,000	Total Liab.:	$68,614,000	Indic. Yr. Divd.:	NA
Total Assets:	$190,066,000	Net Worth:	$121,427,000	Debt/ Equity:	0.3755

Celebrate Express Inc

11220 120th Ave. NE, Kirkland, WA, 98033; PH: 1-425-250-1064; Fax: 1-425-828-6252; http:// www.celebrateexpress.com; Email: customerservice@celebrateexpress.com

General - Incorporation	WA	Stock- Price on:12/24/2007	$8.72
Employees	456	Stock Exchange	NDQ
Auditor	Grant Thornton LLP	Ticker Symbol	BDAY
Stk Agt	American Securities T & T Inc.	Outstanding Shares	7,920,000
Counsel	NA	E.P.S.	-$0.03
DUNS No.	NA	Shareholders	NA

Business: The groups principle activity is to provide celebration products. The products of the group include birthday express, storybook heirlooms and costume express. The group operates from the United States. The group's quarterly revenue for September 2007 was 17.56 millions of USD.

Primary SIC and add'l.: 5947 5961 2678

CIK No: 0001100124

Officers: Kevin Green/Dir., CEO, Pres./$1,176,378.00, Darin L. White/37/VP - Finance, Sec./$276,175.00, Dennis Everhart/60/VP - Operations/$128,088.00, Lisa Tuttle/51/VP - Information Technology/$183,663.00

Directors: Kevin Green/Dir., CEO, Pres., Kenneth H. Shubin/Dir., Stephen Roseman/Dir., Keith Crandell/Dir., Jean Reynolds/Dir., Donald R. Hughes/Dir., Estelle Demuesy/Dir.

Owners: Keith Crandell, Cramer Rosenthal McGlynn, LLC, Hawkshaw Capital Management, LLC, ARCH Venture Fund IV, L.P., Insiders, Stephen Roseman, Thesis Capital Management, LLC, Kenneth Shubin Stein, Spencer Capital Management, LLC, Midwood Capital Management, LLC, T2 Partners Management, LP

Financial Data: Fiscal Year End:05/31   Latest Annual Data: 5/31/2006

Year	Sales	Net Income
2006	$87,016,000	$405,000
2005	$69,138,000	$2,485,000
2004	$51,939,000	$9,492,000

Curr. Assets:	$44,496,000	Curr. Liab.:	$7,123,000		
Plant, Equip.:	$4,662,000	Total Liab.:	$7,123,000	Indic. Yr. Divd.:	NA
Total Assets:	$57,200,000	Net Worth:	$50,077,000	Debt/ Equity:	NA

Celerity Systems Inc

1005 Glebe Rd., Ste. 550, Arlington, VA, 22201; PH: 1-703-528-7073; http:// www.celerity.com

General - Incorporation DE
Employees 58
Auditor HJ & Assoc. LLC
Stk Agt Worldwide Stock Transfer LLC
Counsel NA
DUNS No. 80-267-2147

Stock- Price on:12/24/2007 $0.0011
Stock Exchange OTC
Ticker Symbol HOMS
Outstanding Shares 4,180,000,000
E.P.S -$0.002
Shareholders NA

Business: The group's principal activity is to operate as a closed-end management investment company. The group currently has two investments, one in a wholly owned subsidiary called celerity systems, inc., a Nevada corporation and the other a minority interest in yorkville advisors management, llc. Prior to 02-Jun-2003, the group's principal activity was to design, develop, integrate, install, operate and support interactive video services hardware and software systems. On 02-Jun-2003, the group elected to become a business development company ("Bdc") that is regulated under the investment company act of 1940, as amended.

Primary SIC and add'l.: 7373 7372 7375

CIK No: 0001006459

Subsidiaries: Nexus Technologies Group, Inc.

Officers: Thomas C. McMillen/Chmn., CEO/$297,193.00, Amanda Koplin/Executive Assist., Sec.

Directors: Thomas C. McMillen/Chmn., CEO, Zev Kaplan/Dir., Philip A. McNeill/Dir., Brian C. Griffin/Dir.

Owners: Cornell Capital Partners, LP/11.30%, Michael T. Brigante/0.70%, Philip A. McNeill/1.40%, Insiders/40.40%, Zev E. Kaplan/1.40%, Brian C. Griffin/0.20%, Thomas C. McMillen/38.50%

Financial Data: *Fiscal Year End:*12/31 *Latest Annual Data:* 12/31/2006

Year	Sales	Net Income
2006	$8,682,000	-$5,838,000
2005	$49,000	-$1,307,000
2004	$964,000	-$353,000

Curr. Assets:	$6,897,000	*Curr. Liab.:*	$10,466,000		
Plant, Equip.:	$499,000	*Total Liab.:*	$14,547,000	*Indic. Yr. Divd.:*	NA
Total Assets:	$8,794,000	*Net Worth:*	-$4,520,000	*Debt/ Equity:*	NA

Celestica Inc

1150 Eglinton Ave. E, Toronto, ON, M3C 1H7; *PH:* 1-416-448-5800; *http://* www.celestica.com; *Email:* contactus@celestica.com

General - Incorporation ON
Employees 33,000
Auditor KPMG LLP
Stk Agt Computershare Trust Co of Canada
Counsel NA
DUNS No. 25-404-7434

Stock- Price on:12/24/2007 $6.5
Stock Exchange NYSE
Ticker Symbol CLS
Outstanding Shares 228,240,000
E.P.S -$0.28
Shareholders NA

Business: The group's principle activities are to provide electronics manufacturing services. These services include design, prototype, assembly, test, product assurance, supply chain management, worldwide distribution and after-sales service. The group offers its services to computer and communications industries. The group operates 34 facilities located in the United States, Canada, Mexico, the United Kingdom, Ireland, Italy, Thailand, China, Hong Kong, czech republic, Brazil, Singapore and Malaysia. The group's quarterly revenue for September 2007 was 2,080.60 millions of USD.

Primary SIC and add'l.: 4961 3672 3674 3679 8734

CIK No: 0001030894

Subsidiaries: 1282087 OntarioInc., Celestica (Thailand) Limited, Celestica (USHoldings)Inc., Celestica (USA)Inc., Celestica Cayman Holdings 1Limited, Celestica Corporation, Celestica Holdings PteLtd., EMS Manufacturing Services (Holdings) Limited, IMS International Manufacturing Services Limited

Officers: Craig H. Muhlhauser/CEO, Pres., John Boucher/Chief Supply Chain, Procurement Officer, Charles M. Kirk/59/Sr. VP, CIO - New Hampshire, US, Anthony P. Puppi/50/Exec. VP, CFO - Ontario, Canada, Rahul Suri/Sr. VP, GM - Enterprise Markets, Betty Delbianco/Sr. VP - Human Resources, Chief Legal Officer, Corp. Sec., Peter J. Bar/Sr. VP, Corporate Controller, Elizabeth L. Delbianco/48/Sr. VP - Human Resources, Chief Legal Officer, Corp. Sec. - Ontario, Canada, Paul Nicoletti/CFO, Dave Tiley/Sr. VP - Global Services, Mike Andrade/Sr. VP - Strategic Business Development, Rob Sellers/Sr. VP, GM - Consumer Markets, Mike McCaughey/Sr. VP, GM - Communications Markets, Peter Lindgren/Sr. VP, GM - Industry Markets, John Peri/Exec. VP - Global Operations

Directors: Robert L. Crandall/Chmn., Anthony R. Melman/Dir., Charles W. Szuluk/Dir., William A. Etherington/Dir., Don Tapscott/Dir., Richard S. Love/Dir., Gerald W. Schwartz/Dir.

Owners: Onex Corporation, Gerald W. Schwartz/13.00%, FMR Corp/8.00%, Gerald W. Schwartz/1.00%, Phillips, Hager& North Investment ManagementLtd/9.40%, Onex Corporation/13.00%

Financial Data: *Fiscal Year End:*12/31 *Latest Annual Data:* 12/31/2006

Year	Sales	Net Income
2006	$8,811,700,000	-$149,300,000
2005	$8,471,000,000	-$42,800,000
2004	$8,839,800,000	-$867,500,000

Curr. Assets:	$3,120,800,000	*Curr. Liab.:*	$1,725,900,000		
Plant, Equip.:	$567,100,000	*Total Liab.:*	$2,591,700,000	*Indic. Yr. Divd.:*	NA
Total Assets:	$4,552,100,000	*Net Worth:*	$1,960,400,000	*Debt/ Equity:*	NA

Celgene Corp

86 Morris Ave., Summit, NJ, 07901; *PH:* 1-908-673-9000; *Fax:* 1-908-673-9001; *http://* www.celgene.com

General - Incorporation DE
Employees 1,287
Auditor KPMG LLP
Stk Agt American Stock Transfer & Trust Co.
Counsel NA
DUNS No. 17-420-1137

Stock- Price on:12/24/2007 $58.04
Stock Exchange NDQ
Ticker Symbol CELG
Outstanding Shares 379,900,000
E.P.S $0.38
Shareholders NA

Business: The group's principal activity is to discover, develop and market pharmaceuticals for treatment of cancer and inflammatory diseases. Its primary focus is on the development of orally administered, small molecule pharmaceuticals that regulate gene and protein modulation. Thalomid, the group's lead product is evaluated in clinical trials for the treatment of solid tumor and hematological cancers as well as serious inflammatory diseases. The drugs are designed to modulate multiple disease-related genes, tnf (alpha) and anti-angiogenic. Tnf (alpha) has been linked to the cause and symptoms of many chronic inflammatory and immunological diseases. Anti-angiogenic drugs inhibit the growth of undesirable blood vessels, including those that promote tumor growth.

Primary SIC and add'l.: 2836 8731 2834

CIK No: 0000816284

Subsidiaries: Anthrogenesis Corp., Celgene Edinburgh Finance, Celgene Europe Ltd., Celgene International SARL, Celgene International, Inc., Celgene Luxembourg Finance Company SARL, Celgene UK Holdings, Limited, Celgene UK Manufacturing II, Limited, Celgene UK Manufacturing, Limited, Signal Pharmaceuticals, Inc.

Officers: Sol J. Barer/Chmn., CEO/$16,084,330.00, Robert J. Hugin/Dir., CFO, COO, Pres., Sr. VP/$7,777,620.00, James R. Swenson/Controller, David W. Gryska/CFO/$263,730.00

Directors: Sol J. Barer/Chmn., CEO, Robert J. Hugin/Dir., CFO, COO, Pres., Sr. VP, Walter L. Robb/Dir., Richard C.E. Morgan/Dir., Arthur Hull Hayes/Dir., Gilla Kaplan/Dir., Michael D. Casey/Dir., Rodman L. Drake/Dir., James Loughlin/Dir., Ernest Mario/Dir.

Owners: Goldman Sachs Asset Management, L.P./5.10%, Rodman L. Drake, Janus Capital Management LLC)/10.10%, Aart Brouwer, Richard C.E. Morgan, FMR Corp./14.50%, Gilla Kaplan, Jack L. Bowman, Walter L. Robb, Arthur Hull Hayes, James J. Loughlin, Sol J. Barer/1.20%, Michael D. Casey, Insiders/2.80%, Robert J. Hugin *(16 Owners included in Index)*

Financial Data: *Fiscal Year End:*12/31 *Latest Annual Data:* 12/31/2006

Year	Sales	Net Income
2006	$898,873,000	$68,981,000
2005	$536,941,000	$63,656,000
2004	$377,502,000	$52,756,000

Curr. Assets:	$2,311,004,000	*Curr. Liab.:*	$239,703,000		
Plant, Equip.:	$146,645,000	*Total Liab.:*	$759,614,000	*Indic. Yr. Divd.:*	NA
Total Assets:	$2,735,791,000	*Net Worth:*	$1,976,177,000	*Debt/ Equity:*	0.1887

Cell Genesys Inc

500 Forbes Blvd., South San Francisco, CA, 94080; *PH:* 1-650-266-3000; *Fax:* 1-650-266-3010; *http://* www.cellgenesys.com; *Email:* ir@cellgenesys.com

General - Incorporation DE
Employees 296
Auditor Ernst & Young LLP
Stk Agt Computershare Ltd.
Counsel Wilson Sonsini Goodrich & Rosati
DUNS No. 60-963-1569

Stock- Price on:12/24/2007 $3.74
Stock Exchange NDQ
Ticker Symbol CEGE
Outstanding Shares 72,950,000
E.P.S -$1.47
Shareholders NA

Business: The group's principal activity is to develop and commercialize novel biological therapies for patients with cancer. It currently has three product platforms: gvax(R) cancer vaccines, oncolytic virus therapies and cancer gene therapies. The group conducts clinical trials in multiple types of cancer utilizing its gvax(R) cancer vaccines and oncolytic virus therapy product platforms. Gvax vaccines consist of irradiated tumor cells, genetically modified to secrete a hormone that stimulates the body's immune response to vaccines. Oncolytic virus therapies, derived from a common cold virus, are designed to replicate in and kill cancer cells, leaving the normal cells unharmed.

Primary SIC and add'l.: 8071

CIK No: 0000865231

Subsidiaries: Cell Genesys Limited

Officers: Stephen A. Sherwin/Chmn., CEO/$1,148,453.00, Joseph J. Vallner/COO, Pres., Carol C. Grundfest/Sr. VP - Regulatory Affairs, Portfolio Management/$628,951.00, Michael W. Ramsay/Sr. VP - Operations, Sharon E. Tetlow/Sr. VP, CFO/$520,533.00, Peter K. Working/Sr. VP - Research, Development, Robert H. Tidwell/Sr. VP - Corporate Development/$602,479.00, Christine McKinley/Sr. VP - Human Resources, Robert J. Dow/Chief Medical Officer/$704,037.00, Kristen M. Hege/VP - Clinical Research

Directors: Stephen A. Sherwin/Chmn., CEO, Nancy M. Crowell/Dir., Bruce Chabner/Member - Medical Advisory Board, Inder M. Verma/Dir., John T. Potts/Dir., Member - Medical Advisory Board, William Nelson/Member - Medical Advisory Board, James M. Gower/Dir., Dennis L. Winger/Dir., Craig Henderson/Member - Medical Advisory Board, Jordan Gutterman/Member - Medical Advisory Board, Eugene L. Step/Dir., David W. Carter/Dir., Thomas E. Shenk/Dir., Ronald Levy/Member - Medical Advisory Board

Owners: Robert J. Dow, Inder M. Verma, James M. Gower, Insiders/5.93%, Robert H. Tidwell, Kopp Holding Co. LLC/5.72%, Nancy M. Crowell, Renaissance Technologies Corp./5.66%, John T. Potts, Carol C. Grundfest, Eugene L. Step, Mazama Capital Management, Inc./5.55%, Legg Mason Capital Management, Inc./6.62%, Thomas E. Shenk, David W. Carter *(19 Owners included in Index)*

Financial Data: *Fiscal Year End:*12/31 *Latest Annual Data:* 03/31/2007

Year	Sales	Net Income
2007	$1,273,000	-$29,449,000
2006	$1,364,000	-$82,929,000
2005	$4,584,000	-$64,939,000

Curr. Assets:	$154,665,000	*Curr. Liab.:*	$51,314,000		
Plant, Equip.:	$129,643,000	*Total Liab.:*	$247,640,000	*Indic. Yr. Divd.:*	NA
Total Assets:	$291,167,000	*Net Worth:*	$43,527,000	*Debt/ Equity:*	6.8626

Cell Robotics International Inc

2715 Brdbent Pkwy NE, Albuquerque, NM, 87107; *PH:* 1-505-343-1131; *Fax:* 1-505-344-8112; *http://* www.cellrobotics.com

General - Incorporation CO
Employees NA
Auditor Stonefield Josephson, Inc.
Stk Agt Corporate Stock Transfer, Inc.
Counsel Neuman, Drennan & Stone
DUNS No. 79-637-8933

Stock- Price on:12/24/2007 $0.009
Stock Exchange OTC
Ticker Symbol CRII
Outstanding Shares NA
E.P.S NA
Shareholders NA

Business: The group's principal activity is to manufacture and market sophisticated laser-based medical device and scientific research instrument. The medical devices have applications in the blood sample and glucose collection and in vitro fertilization markets. The group also develops, produces and markets a scientific research instrument line that increases the usefulness and importance of the conventional laboratory microscope. The customers of the group primarily consist of research institutes, universities, distributors and mail-order business, which serve patients with diabetes as well as the physician community and medical clinics. The group markets its scientific instruments both in domestic and international markets.

Primary SIC and add'l.: 3845 8733 3826 2835

CIK No: 0000845291

Subsidiaries: Cell Robotics, Inc

Financial Data: Fiscal Year End:12/31 Latest Annual Data: 12/31/2004

Year	Sales	Net Income
2004	$309,000	-$2,528,000
2003	$797,000	-$3,444,000
2002	$1,584,000	-$3,007,000

Curr. Assets:	$599,000	Curr. Liab.:	$3,853,000		
Plant, Equip.:	$136,000	Total Liab.:	$3,853,000	Indic. Yr. Divd.:	NA
Total Assets:	$749,000	Net Worth:	-$3,104,000	Debt/ Equity:	NA

Cell Therapeutics Inc

501 Elliott Ave. W, Ste. 400, Seattle, WA, 98119; *PH:* 1-206-282-7100; *Fax:* 1-206-284-6206; *http://* www.cticseattle.com

General - Incorporation	WA	**Stock**- Price on:12/24/2007	$2.88
Employees	197	Stock Exchange	NDQ
Auditor	Grant Thornton LLP	Ticker Symbol	CTIC
Stk Agt... Computershare Investor Services LLC		Outstanding Shares	43,330,000
Counsel	Wilson Sonsini Goodrich & Rosati	E.P.S.	-$3.53
DUNS No.	78-847-9103	Shareholders	NA

Business: The group's principal activity is to develop, acquire and market treatments for cancer. The products of the group include trisenox that is marketed for patients with a type of blood cell cancer called acute promyelocytic leukemia, or apl. The fda to treat patients who have relapsed or refractory acute promyelocytic leukemia has approved trisenox, a pharmaceutical grade arsenic product. The principal products of the group are trisenox, pg-txl, pg-cpt and ct-2584. On 1-Jan-2004 the group acquired novuspharma s.p.a.

Primary SIC and add'l.: 8731 2834

CIK No: 0000891293

Subsidiaries: Cell Therapeutics (Ireland) Holding Limited, Cell Therapeutics Europe S.r.l., CTI Corporate Development, Inc, CTI Technologies, Inc

Officers: James A. Bianco/Principal Founder, Dir., CEO, Pres., Jeff Jacob/CEO - Systems Medicine LLC, Tim Williamson/Chief Business Officer - Systems Medicine LLC, Scott C. Stromatt/50/Exec. VP - Clinical Development, Regulatory Affairs, Leah Grant/Contact - Investors, Security Analysts, Elena Murador/Contact - Italian Investors, Louis A. Bianco/Exec. VP - Finance, Administration, Jack W. Singer/Founder, Dir., Chief Medical Officer, John H. Bauer/Dir., Consultant, Dan Eramian/Exec. VP - Corporate Communications, Gabriella Pezzoni/Scientific Dir. - CTE, Mauro G. Premi/Acting MD, Giovanni Ravaioli/Dir. - Human Resources, CTE

Directors: James A. Bianco/Principal Founder, Dir., CEO, Pres., Phillip M. Nudelman/Chmn., Richard L. Love/Dir., Frederick W. Telling/Dir., Jack W. Singer/Founder, Dir., Chief Medical Officer, Vartan Gregorian/Dir., John H. Bauer/Dir., Consultant, Mary O'neil Mundinger/Dir.

Owners: Frederick W. Telling, Richard L. Love, Mary O. Mundinger, Vartan Gregorian, Louis A. Bianco, Phillip M. Nudelman, James A. Bianco/1.10%, Daniel Eramian, Insiders/3.40%, John H. Bauer, Jack W. Singer, Scott C. Stromatt

Financial Data: Fiscal Year End:12/31 Latest Annual Data: 12/31/2006

Year	Sales	Net Income
2006	$80,000	-$135,819,000
2005	$16,092,000	-$102,505,000
2004	$29,594,000	-$252,298,000

Curr. Assets:	$64,538,000	Curr. Liab.:	$34,372,000		
Plant, Equip.:	$7,915,000	Total Liab.:	$203,425,000	Indic. Yr. Divd.:	NA
Total Assets:	$101,821,000	Net Worth:	-$101,604,000	Debt/ Equity:	NA

Cell Wireless Corp

4625 E Broadway, Tucson, AZ, 85711; ; *http://* www.cellwireless.com

General - Incorporation	NV	**Stock**- Price on:12/24/2007	$0.022
Employees	NA	Stock Exchange	OTC
Auditor ... Russell Bedford Stefanou Mirchandani		Ticker Symbol	CLWL
Stk Agt.	Pacific Stock Transfer Company	Outstanding Shares	NA
Counsel	NA	E.P.S.	NA
DUNS No.	NA	Shareholders	NA

Business: The group's principal activity is to manufacture military aircraft parts for the us air force, navy, coast guard and army and marine corp aviation divisions. The group's products are included in fixed wing and rotary aircraft. The group also provides prototype designs, assembly and subassembly contracting services. The group provides military spare parts to many of the u.s's largest prime contractors such as lockheed martin and northrop grumman. The group's customers include us and foreign private aircraft companies and friendly governments. In 2003, the group acquired Arizona aircraft spares inc and changed its name from American market support network inc.

Primary SIC and add'l.: 3728

CIK No: 0001141880

Subsidiaries: Arizona Aircraft Spares, Inc., Cell Wireless Australia, PTY, LTD

Officers: John Bohringer/Dir., CEO, David Shorey/Dir., CFO

Directors: John Bohringer/Dir., CEO, Sylvia Quintero/48/Dir., Brian Arnold/Dir., David Shorey/Dir., CFO, Michael Featherstone/Dir.

Financial Data: Fiscal Year End:12/31 Latest Annual Data: 12/31/2004

Year	Sales	Net Income
2004	NA	-$4,688,000
2003	$1,008,000	-$123,000
2002	$147,000	-$135,000

Curr. Assets:	$0	Curr. Liab.:	$285,000		
Plant, Equip.:	NA	Total Liab.:	$285,000	Indic. Yr. Divd.:	NA
Total Assets:	$0	Net Worth:	-$284,000	Debt/ Equity:	NA

Cellegy Pharmaceuticals Inc

2085B Quaker Pointe Dr., Quakertown, PA, 18951; *PH:* 1-215-529-6084; *http://* www.cellegy.com

General - Incorporation	DE	**Stock** - Price on:12/24/2007	$0.076
Employees	5	Stock Exchange	OTC
Auditor	Mayer Hoffman Mccann, P.C	Ticker Symbol	CLGY
Stk Agt	Mellon Investor Services LLC	Outstanding Shares	29,830,000
Counsel	Fenwick & West LLP	E.P.S.	$0.413
DUNS No.	61-866-1680	Shareholders	NA

Business: The group's principal activity is the development of prescription drugs and skin care products. The products are for the treatment of gastrointestinal disorders, sexual dysfunction of both men and women and selected conditions affecting women's health. They products of the group include cellegesictm nitroglycerin ointment and tostrex(TM) testosterone gel for chronic anal fissures and male hypogonadism. The drugs have undergone phase iii and phase i/ii trials respectively. In addition, the group has developed skin care and cosmeceutical products like skin moisturizers, protectants and anti-aging lotions and creams. It is presently selling the c79 intensive moisturizer formulation to a major specialty retailer.

Primary SIC and add'l.: 2836 2834

CIK No: 0000887247

Subsidiaries: Cellegy Australia Pty Ltd, Cellegy Canada Inc.

Owners: Thomas M. Steinberg, SJ Strategic Investments, LLC/24.70%, Richard C. Williams/3.30%, Robert J. Caso, Tobi B. Klar, Insiders/5.10%, Anne-Marie Corner/1.10%, Members of the Tisch family/18.50%, Robert B. Rothermel, John Q. Adams

Financial Data: Fiscal Year End:12/31 Latest Annual Data: 12/31/2006

Year	Sales	Net Income
2006	$2,660,000	$9,672,000
2005	$12,835,000	-$5,008,000
2004	$2,596,000	-$28,154,000

Curr. Assets:	$4,145,000	Curr. Liab.:	$756,000	P/E Ratio:	0.18
Plant, Equip.:	NA	Total Liab.:	$1,082,000	Indic. Yr. Divd.:	NA
Total Assets:	$4,145,000	Net Worth:	$3,063,000	Debt/ Equity:	0.1470

Cellular Technical Services Co Inc

20 E Sunrise Hwy., Ste. 200, Valley Stream, NY, 11581; *PH:* 1-516-568-0100; *http://* www.cellulartech.com

General - Incorporation	DE	**Stock**- Price on:12/24/2007	$1.55
Employees	NA	Stock Exchange	OTC
Auditor	Eisner LLP	Ticker Symbol	CTSC
Stk Agt	Continental Stock Transfer & Trust Co	Outstanding Shares	4,590,000
Counsel	NA	E.P.S.	-$0.06
DUNS No.	60-339-6441	Shareholders	NA

Business: The group's principal activity was to develop, market, install and support a diversified mix of products and services for the telecommunications industry. The group had developed technological solutions that focused in the area of wireless communications fraud management and geo-location wireless software applications. In addition, it marketed prepaid long-distance phonecard products, through its majority-owned subsidiary, isis tele-communications, inc. . As on 30-Jun-2004, the group had no operations other than to complete the wind down of operations of isis tele-communications, inc.

Primary SIC and add'l.: 4813 7379 4812 4899 7373

CIK No: 0000876378

Subsidiaries: Isis Tele-Communications, Inc.

Owners: Stewart B. Davis, Kenneth Block, Jeffrey G. Spragens, Phillip Frost, Stephen Katz, Steven D. Rubin, Jane H. Hsiao, Richard Pfenniger, Charles Filipi, Frost Gamma Investments Trust

Financial Data: Fiscal Year End:12/31 Latest Annual Data: 12/31/2006

Year	Sales	Net Income
2006	NA	-$204,000
2005	NA	-$228,000
2004	NA	-$444,000

Curr. Assets:	$3,528,000	Curr. Liab.:	$258,000		
Plant, Equip.:	NA	Total Liab.:	$258,000	Indic. Yr. Divd.:	NA
Total Assets:	$3,528,000	Net Worth:	$3,270,000	Debt/ Equity:	NA

Celsia Technologies Inc

1395 Brickell Ave. Ste. 800, Miami, FL, 33131; *PH:* 1-305-529-6290; *http://* www.icurie.com; *Email:* info@celsiatechnologies.com

General - Incorporation		**Stock**- Price on:12/24/2007	$0.11
Employees	39	Stock Exchange	OTC
Auditor	NA	Ticker Symbol	CSAT
Stk Agt	NA	Outstanding Shares	36,460,000
Counsel	NA	E.P.S.	-$0.307
DUNS No.	NA	Shareholders	NA

Business: The groups principal activities include providing research, development and commercialization of cooling solutions that are built on the patent portfolio in the field of thermofluid nanotechnology. The group markets its products under the tradenames include Celsia NanoSpreaders (TM), Celsias NanoSpreader(TM). The group operates from the United States.

Primary SIC and add'l.: 3443 7359

CIK No:

Officers: Hakan Wretsell/47/Dir., CEO, Pres., Joseph Formichelli/CEO, Jae-Joon Choi/CTO, George A. Meyer/COO, Jorge A. Fernandez/CFO

Directors: Hakan Wretsell/47/Dir., CEO, Pres., Jeff Mandell/Chmn. - Technology Advisory Board, Peter Rugg/Dir., Avram Bar-Cohen/Member - Technology Advisory Board, William Maltz/Member - Technology Advisory Board, David H. Clarke/Dir., Alan Miller/54/Dir., Gregory J. Osborn/Dir., Cathy Biber/Member - Technology Advisory Board, David Saums/Member - Technology Advisory Board, Charles Resnick/Dir., Alan Benaim/Dir.

Owners: George Meyer, Hakan Wretsell/2.09%, Gregory Osborn/1.06%, Michael Karpheden/1.10%, AMF Capital/11.42%, Jorge Fernandez, Alan Miller, Jeong Hyun Lee, David Clarke, Insiders/2.37%, Peter Rugg

Financial Data: Fiscal Year End:NA Latest Annual Data: 12/31/2006

Year	Sales	Net Income
2006	$104,000	-$6,768,000
2005	$19,000	-$7,173,000
2004	NA	-$34,000

Curr. Assets:	$554,000	Curr. Liab.:	$2,133,000		
Plant, Equip.:	$694,000	Total Liab.:	$2,280,000	Indic. Yr. Divd.:	NA
Total Assets:	$2,040,000	Net Worth:	-$240,000	Debt/ Equity:	NA

Celsion Corp

10220 Old Columbia Rd., Ste. L, Columbia, MD, 21046; *PH*: 1-410-290-5390;
Fax: 1-410-290-5394; *http://* www.celsion.com; *Email*: celsion@celsion.com

General - Incorporation.............................DE
Employees...29
Auditor ....Stegman & Co
Stk Agt....... American Stock Transfer & Trust Co.
Counsel ....NA
DUNS No. 07-118-0145

Stock- Price on:12/24/2007 ....$7.05
Stock Exchange...AMEX
Ticker Symbol...CLN
Outstanding Shares.................................10,830,000
E.P.S...$3.58
Shareholders..NA

Business: The group's principle activity is to develop medical treatment systems primarily to treat breast cancer and a chronic prostate enlargement condition, known as benign prostatic hyperplasia (bph). The group uses minimally invasive focused heat technology for treatment. The group currently in late stage clinical development of innovative medical devices to treat both benign prostatic hyperplasia (bph), a prostate condition common in men over age 55 and breast cancer. The group is also working with duke university in the development of heat-sensitive liposome compounds for use in the delivery of chemotherapy drugs to tumor sites, and with sloan-kettering on the development of heat-activated gene therapy compounds. The group operates from United States.

Primary SIC and add'l.: 3845
CIK No: 0000749647
Subsidiaries: Celsion (Canada) Limited
Officers: Michael H. Tardugno/CEO, Pres., Michael Oleck/49/VP - Operations/$283,428.00, Anthony P. Deasey/58/Exec. VP, CFO, COO - Principal Financial, Accounting Officer/$476,324.00, William Hahne/VP - Clinical Development, Medical Affairs/$356,281.00, Nicholas Borys/Chief Medical Officer, VP, Mark Italia/Executive Dir. Quality - Regulatory Affairs, Paul B. Susie/Interim, Chief Accounting Officer, Paul Henning/Contact - Investor Relations
Directors: Max E. Link/Chmn., Kris Venkat/Dir., Gregory Weaver/Dir., Augustine Chow/Dir., Gary W. Pace/Dir., Lawrence S. Olanoff/56/Dir.
Owners: Kris Venkat, Max E. Link/1.12%, Gregory Weaver, William Hahne, Michael Oleck, Anthony P. Deasey/1.44%, Michael H. Tardugno, Gary W. Pace, Boston Scientific Corporation/7.94%, Lawrence S. Olanoff, Insiders/4.18%

Financial Data: Fiscal Year End:12/31 Latest Annual Data: 12/31/2006

Year	Sales		Net Income
2006	$11,251,000		-$7,584,000
2005	$12,320,000		-$8,685,000
2004	$2,506,000		-$13,985,000
Curr. Assets:	$16,023,000	Curr. Liab.:	$4,008,000	P/E Ratio:	1.97
Plant, Equip.:	$515,000	Total Liab.:	$22,131,000	Indic. Yr. Divd.:	NA
Total Assets:	$18,930,000	Net Worth:	-$3,201,000	Debt/ Equity:	NA

CEMEX

840 Gessner, Ste. 1400, Houston, TX, 77024; *PH*: 1-713-650-6200; *Fax*: 1-713-653-6815;
http:// www.cemex.com; *Email*: ir@cemex.com

General - Incorporation......................Mexico
Employees...50,000
Auditor ....Le&ro Castillo Parada
Stk Agt.................................. Vizcaya Argentaria
Counsel ....NA
DUNS No. ....NA

Stock- Price on:12/24/2007 ....$38.88
Stock Exchange...NYSE
Ticker Symbol...CX
Outstanding Shares.................................733,090,000
E.P.S...$2.80
Shareholders..NA

Business: The group's principal activities are the production, distribution and marketing of cement, ready-mix concrete and clinker. Cement products include pozzolana portland cement, white portland cement, masonry cement, and hydraulic lime. At 31-12-2003, the group owned 54 cement plants and 466 ready mix plants. The group's main production facilities are located in Mexico, Spain, venezuela, Colombia, the United States of America, egypt, Philippines, Thailand, Costa Rica, Dominican Republic, panama, nicaragua and Puerto Rico.

Primary SIC and add'l.: 4412 3241 7375 3273 5032 3272 3255
CIK No: 0001076378
Subsidiaries: CEMEX Concretos, S.A. De C.V, CEMEX Corp, CEMEX Espana, S.A, CEMEX Mexico, S.A. De C.V, CEMEX, Inc
Officers: Lorenzo H. Zambrano/Chmn., CEO, Juan Romero/Pres. - South America, Caribbean Region, Victor M. Romo/Exec. VP - Administration, Armando J. Garcia/Dir., Exec. VP - Development, Fernando A. Gonzalez/Pres. - Middle East, Africa, Asia, Australia Region, Rodrigo Trevino/CFO, Ramiro G. Villarreal/General Counsel, Hector Medina/Exec. VP - Planning, Finance, Francisco Garza/Pres. - North America Region, Trading
Directors: Lorenzo H. Zambrano/Chmn., CEO, Alfonso Romo Garza/Dir., Bernardo Quintana Isaac/Dir., Rogelio Zambrano Lozano/Dir., Jose Manuel Rincon Gallardo/Dir., Mauricio Zambrano Villarreal/Dir., Lorenzo Milmo Zambrano/Dir., Roberto Zambrano Villarreal/Dir., Dionisio Garza Medina/Dir., Jorge Garcia Segovia/Dir., Tomas Brittingham Longoria/Dir., Tomas Milmo Santos/Dir., Eduardo Brittingham Sumner/Dir., Rodolfo Garcia Muriel/Dir., Armando J. Garcia/Dir., Exec. VP - Development

Financial Data: Fiscal Year End:12/31 Latest Annual Data: 12/31/2006

Year	Sales		Net Income
2006	$18,290,230,000		$2,354,707,000
2005	$15,131,937,000		$2,056,695,000
2004	$8,143,316,000		$1,611,496,000
Curr. Assets:	$5,172,486,000	Curr. Liab.:	$4,446,605,000	P/E Ratio:	17.57
Plant, Equip.:	$17,548,573,000	Total Liab.:	$17,587,642,000	Indic. Yr. Divd.:	$0.750
Total Assets:	$31,263,949,000	Net Worth:	$13,676,307,000	Debt/ Equity:	0.4735

Centale Inc

191 Main St., East Aurora, NY, 14052; *PH*: 1-716-714-7100

General - Incorporation ....NY
Employees...26
Auditor .... Rotenberg & Co. LLP
Stk Agt...... American Stock Transfer & Trust Co.
Counsel ....NA
DUNS No. ....NA

Stock- Price on:12/24/2007 ....$0.02
Stock Exchange...OTC
Ticker Symbol...CNTL
Outstanding Shares.................................170,620,000
E.P.S...-$0.072
Shareholders..NA

Business: The group's activity is to market desktop software solutions. The group's market strategy includes Phase I, Phase II, Phase III, and Phase IV. Phase I of the plan is marketing desktop software solutions based on proprietary technology. Phase II of the plan is acquiring complementary technologies and businesses. Phase III of the plan is entering into the field of online marketing and utilizing inventory of internet domain names. Phase IV of the plan is integrating business application with online marketing. The group's services include computer and internet services and marketing computers and computer software.

Primary SIC and add'l.: 7389
CIK No: 0001297965
Officers: Thaddeus A. Wier/46/CEO, CFO, Sterling Shepperd/32/VP, Sec.
Directors: Patrick T. Parker/53/Dir., Carlos Huerta/39/Dir., Dan Dearmas/40/Dir.
Owners: Dan DeArmas/0.30%, Insiders/69.50%, Patrick T. Parker/2.00%, Thaddeus A. Wier/45.90%, Carlos Huerta/21.10%

Financial Data: Fiscal Year End:03/31 Latest Annual Data: 3/31/2006

Year	Sales		Net Income
2006	$266,000		-$2,079,000
Curr. Assets:	$45,000	Curr. Liab.:	$1,099,000		
Plant, Equip.:	$45,000	Total Liab.:	$1,099,000	Indic. Yr. Divd.:	NA
Total Assets:	$966,000	Net Worth:	-$132,000	Debt/ Equity:	NA

Centene Corp

7711 Carondelet Ave., Ste. 800, St. Louis, MO, 63105; *PH*: 1-314-725-4477; *Fax*: 1-314-558-2428;
http:// www.centene.com

General - Incorporation .... DE
Employees...2,600
Auditor ....Pricewaterhousecoopers LLP
Stk Agt.................. Mellon Investor Services LLC
Counsel ....NA
DUNS No. ....NA

Stock- Price on:12/24/2007 ....$19.83
Stock Exchange...NYSE
Ticker Symbol...CNC
Outstanding Shares.................................43,610,000
E.P.S...$1.93
Shareholders..NA

Business: The group's principle activity is to provide healthcare services. The group operates through two business segments namely Medicaid managed care and specialty services. The group operates from United States.

Primary SIC and add'l.: 6321
CIK No: 0001071739
Subsidiaries: AirLogix Inc., Bankers Reserve Life Insurance Company of Wisconsin, Buckeye Community Health Plan Inc., CCTX Holdings LLC, CenCorp Consulting Company Inc., Cenpatico Behavioral Health LLC, Cenpatico Behavioral Health of Texas Inc., Cenphiny Management LLC, Centene Company of Texas LP, Centene Holdings LLC, Centene Management Company LLC, Centene Plaza Redevelopment Corporation, CMC Real Estate Company LLC, Coordinated Care Corporation Indiana Inc., FirstGuard Health Plan Inc. 25 Subsidiaries included in the Index
Officers: Michael F. Neidorff/Chmn., CEO, Pres./$8,046,309.00, Cary D. Hobbs/Sr. VP - Business Management, Integration, Keith H. Williamson/Sr. VP, Corp. Sec., General Counsel, Christopher D. Bowers/Sr. VP - Health Plan Business Unit, Karey L. Witty/43/Sr. VP - Health Plan Business Unit/$878,610.00, Marie J. Glancy/Sr. VP - Operational Services, Regulatory Affairs, Robert C. Packman/Sr. VP - Medical Affairs, Carol E. Goldman/Exec. VP, Chief Administrative Officer/$684,401.00, William N. Scheffel/Exec. VP - Specialty Business Unit/$925,553.00, Per J. Brodin/Chief Accounting Officer, Sr. VP/$363,358.00, Glendon A. Schuster/CIO, Sr. VP, Patricia J. Darnley/Sr. VP - Operations, Jesse N. Hunter/Sr. VP - Corporate Development, Edmund E. Kroll/Sr. VP - Finance, Investor Relations, Mary V. Mason/Sr. VP, Chief Medical Officer (*16 Officers included in Index*)
Directors: Michael F. Neidorff/Chmn., CEO, Pres., Pamela A. Joseph/Dir., Frederick H. Eppinger/Dir., Richard A. Gephardt/Dir., John R. Roberts/Dir., Tommy G. Thompson/Dir., Steve Bartlett/Dir., Robert K. Ditmore/Dir., David L. Steward/Dir.
Owners: Per J. Brodin, Robert K. Ditmore, William N. Scheffel, Richard A. Gephardt, John R. Roberts, Tommy Thompson, David L. Steward, Steve Bartlett, Frederick H. Eppinger, Michael F. Neidorff/2.20%, Carol E. Goldman, Karey L. Witty, Earnest Partners LLC/10.10%, Deutsche Bank AG/6.20%, Baron Capital Group, Inc./7.50% (*17 Owners included in Index*)

Financial Data: Fiscal Year End:12/31 Latest Annual Data: 12/31/2006

Year	Sales		Net Income
2006	$2,279,020,000		-$43,629,000
2005	$1,505,864,000		$55,632,000
2004	$1,000,940,000		$44,312,000
Curr. Assets:	$451,821,000	Curr. Liab.:	$387,951,000		
Plant, Equip.:	$110,688,000	Total Liab.:	$568,557,000	Indic. Yr. Divd.:	NA
Total Assets:	$894,980,000	Net Worth:	$326,423,000	Debt/ Equity:	0.5424

Centennial Bank Holdings Inc

1331 17th St., Ste. 300, Denver, CO, 80202; *PH*: 1-303-296-9600; *http://* www.cbhi.com

General - Incorporation .... DE
Employees...518
Auditor ....KPMG LLP
Stk Agt............... Computershare Trust Co., N.A.
Counsel ....NA
DUNS No. ....NA

Stock- Price on:12/24/2007 ....$8.64
Stock Exchange...NDQ
Ticker Symbol...CBHI
Outstanding Shares.................................55,200,000
E.P.S...$0.10
Shareholders..NA

Business: The group operates through its subsidiaries whose principle activity is to provide banking products and services. The groups services include accepting time and demand deposits and originating commercial loans, real estate loans, small business administration guaranteed loans, and consumer loans. The group operates from the United States. The assets of the group for the year 2006 were $2,720,600 (thousands).

Primary SIC and add'l.: 6022 6712 6022 6712
CIK No: 0001324410
Subsidiaries: CenBank Statutory Trust I, CenBank Statutory Trust II, CenBank Statutory Trust III, Centennial Bank of the West, Guaranty Bank and Trust Company, Guaranty Capital Trust III

Officers: Daniel M. Quinn/Dir., CEO, Pres./$1,203,505.00, Zsolt K. Bessko/Exec. VP, General Counsel, Sec./$412,989.00, Sherri L. Heronema/Exec. VP - Human Resources, Administration, Paul W. Taylor/CFO, Exec. VP/$488,364.00, Suzanne R. Brennan/Exec. VP - Operations/$521,402.00, David C. Boyles/Exec. VP, Chief Credit Officer/$1,206,014.00

Directors: Daniel M. Quinn/Dir., CEO, Pres., John M. Eggemeyer/61/Chmn., William R. Farr/Dir., Kathleen Smythe/Dir., Edward B. Cordes/Dir., Stephen D. Joyce/Dir., Stephen B. Shraiberg/Dir., Matthew P. Wagner/Dir., Albert C. Yates/Dir., Gail H. Klapper/Dir.

Owners: Franklin Mutual Advisers, LLC/13.30%, Capital Research and Management Company/7.00%, Paul W. Taylor, Edward B. Cordes, Suzanne R. Brennan, William R. Farr, Zsolt K. Bessk, Stephen D. Joyce, John M. Eggemeyer/3.60%, Kathleen Smythe, Stephen B. Shraiberg, Daniel M. Quinn, Matthew P. Wagner, Insiders/5.50%, Albert C. Yates *(16 Owners included in Index)*

Financial Data: Fiscal Year End:12/31 Latest Annual Data: 12/31/2006

Year	Sales	Net Income
2006	$186,502,000	$24,418,000
2005	$150,688,000	$14,682,000

Curr. Assets:	$49,620,000	**Curr. Liab.:**	$2,022,270,000		
Plant, Equip.:	$75,373,000	**Total Liab.:**	$2,131,141,000	**Indic. Yr. Divd.:**	NA
Total Assets:	$2,720,600,000	**Net Worth:**	$589,459,000	**Debt/ Equity:**	0.1222

Centennial Communications Corp

3349 Rte. 138, Bldg. A, Wall, NJ, 07719; *PH:* 1-732-556-2200; *Fax:* 1-732-556-2242; *http://* www.centennialwireless.com

General - Incorporation	DE	Stock - Price on:12/24/2007	$9.36
Employees	3,400	Stock Exchange	NDQ
Auditor	Deloitte & Touche LLP	Ticker Symbol	CYCL
Stk Agt..... American Stock Transfer & Trust Co.		Outstanding Shares	106,060,000
Counsel	NA	E.P.S.	-$0.22
DUNS No.	NA	Shareholders	NA

Business: The group's principal activity is to provide wireless communications and broadband services in the Caribbean and wireless communications in the United States. It provides wireless and broadband services including switched voice, dedicated (private line), video and other services over its own fiber optic, coaxial and microwave network in the Caribbean. The group also offers its customers Web page design, hosting, Web casting, integration services and a variety of e-commerce design and related services. The group converted the cable network to digital with capacity to support up to 392 channels. As of 31-May-2004, group operated 87 stores and 165 kiosks in the United States. The group owns and operates wireless telephone systems in the United States pursuant to 30 wireless licenses.

Primary SIC and add'l.: 4812 3661

CIK No: 0000879573

Subsidiaries: All America Cables and Radio, Inc., Bauce Communications of Beaumont, Inc., Bauce Communications, Inc., Centennial Beauregard Cellular LLC, Centennial Beauregard Holding Corp., Centennial Benton Harbor Cellular Corp., Centennial Benton Harbor Holding Corp., Centennial Caldwell Cellular Corp., Centennial Caribbean Holding LLC, Centennial Cellular Operating Company LLC, Centennial Cellular Telephone Company of Del Norte, Centennial Cellular Telephone Company of Lawrence, Centennial Cellular Telephone Company of SanFrancisco, Centennial Cellular Tri-State Operating Partnership, Centennial Claiborne Cellular Corp. 50 Subsidiaries included in the Index

Officers: Michael J. Small/Dir., CEO/$1,856,726.00, Steve E. Kunszabo/Dir. - Investor Relations, Tony L. Wolk/Sr. VP, General Counsel, Sec./$691,180.00, Phillip H. Mayberry/Pres. - US Wireless Operations/$1,465,043.00, Carlos T. Blanco/Pres. - Centennial de Puerto Rico/$1,310,982.00, Thomas J. Fitzpatrick/CFO, Exec. VP/$1,273,907.00

Directors: Michael J. Small/Dir., CEO, Thomas E. McInerney/Chmn., Anthony J. De Nicola/Dir., Stephen J. Vanderwoude/Dir., Robert D. Reid/Dir., James P. Pellow/Dir., Raymond A. Ranelli/Dir., Scott N. Schneider/Dir., Darren C. /Dir.

Owners: Welsh, Carson, Anderson & Stowe, Thomas E. McInerney, Tony L. Wolk, Thomas J. Fitzpatrick, Anthony J. de Nicola, Phillip H. Mayberry, Insiders, Carlos T. Blanco, Michael J. Small

Financial Data: Fiscal Year End:05/31 Latest Annual Data: 05/31/2007

Year	Sales	Net Income
2007	$911,896,000	-$31,619,000
2006	$945,728,000	$20,244,000
2005	$882,427,000	$25,621,000

Curr. Assets:	$246,730,000	**Curr. Liab.:**	$223,647,000		
Plant, Equip.:	$647,789,000	**Total Liab.:**	$2,497,522,000	**Indic. Yr. Divd.:**	NA
Total Assets:	$1,435,893,000	**Net Worth:**	-$1,064,859,000	**Debt/ Equity:**	NA

Center Bancorp Inc

2455 Morris Ave., Union, NJ, 07083; *PH:* 1-908-688-9500; *Fax:* 1-908-688-3043; *http://* www.centerbancorp.com

General - Incorporation	NJ	Stock - Price on:12/24/2007	$14.45
Employees	214	Stock Exchange	NDQ
Auditor	KPMG LLP	Ticker Symbol	CNBC
Stk Agt..... American Stock Transfer & Trust CO.		Outstanding Shares	13,910,000
Counsel	NA	E.P.S.	$0.42
DUNS No.	11-307-1906	Shareholders	NA

Business: The group's principal activity is the provision of banking and financial services to commercial, industrial and governmental customers. A holding company for the union center national bank, the group accepts demand deposits, savings accounts and time deposits and offers short and medium term loans, letters of credit, working capital loans and real estate construction loans. The consumer banking services include the acceptance of interest bearing and non-interest bearing checking, savings and money market accounts, certificates of deposit and making secured and unsecured loans, mortgages and home equity lines of credit. The group also deals in us treasury and governmental securities, commercial paper and repurchase agreements. It provides automated teller machines, safe deposit boxes and traveller's checks. The group's business is conducted through eleven locations in springfield township, berkeley heights, vauxhall and summit in the union county.

Primary SIC and add'l.: 6712 6021

CIK No: 0000712771

Subsidiaries: Center Advertising Corporation, Center Bancorp Statutory Trust I, Center Bancorp Statutory Trust II, Center Financial Group, LLC, UCNB Capital Corp., UCNB Investment Corporation, UCNB NJ Investment Corp., Union Center National Bank

Officers: John Joseph Davis/Dir., CEO, Pres./$705,210.00, Julie D'Aloia/VP, Sec., Lori A. Wunder/VP/$173,310.00, John F. McGowan/VP/$201,419.00, Charles E. Nunn/VP/$183,236.00, Mark S. Cardone/VP, Christopher M. Gorey/VP, Anthony C. Weagley/VP, Treasurer, Investor Relations/$246,011.00, Wallace J. Butler/Honorary Dir.

Directors: John Joseph Davis/Dir., CEO, Pres., Alexander A. Bol/Chmn., Kenneth W. Battiato/Dir., Herbert Schiller/Dir., Donald G. Kein/Dir., Hugo Barth/Dir., Stephen J. Lamont/Dir., Norman F. Schroeder/Dir., Eugene V. Malinowski/Dir., Rudi O. Wadle/Honorary Dir., Charles P. Woodward/Honorary Dir., Harold Schechter/Dir., Lawrence B. Seidman/Dir., Raymond Vanaria/Dir., Brenda Curtis/Dir. *(20 Directors included in Index)*

Owners: Donald G. Kein/1.05%, John J. Davis/1.67%, Eugene V. Malinowski/0.36%, Brenda Curtis/0.38%, Hugo Barth, William A. Thompson/0.41%, Alexander A. Bol/0.51%, John J. DeLaney, Norman F. Schroeder/0.81%

Financial Data: Fiscal Year End:12/31 Latest Annual Data: 12/31/2006

Year	Sales	Net Income
2006	$56,523,000	$3,898,000
2005	$54,339,000	$7,646,000
2004	$43,437,000	$7,622,000

Curr. Assets:	$49,295,000	**Curr. Liab.:**	$773,625,000	**P/E Ratio:**	32.11
Plant, Equip.:	$18,829,000	**Total Liab.:**	$953,771,000	**Indic. Yr. Divd.:**	$0.360
Total Assets:	$1,051,384,000	**Net Worth:**	$97,613,000	**Debt/ Equity:**	1.8318

Center Financial Corp

3435 Wilshire Blvd., Ste. 700, Los Angeles, CA, 90010; *PH:* 1-213-251-2222; *Fax:* 1-213-386-6774; *http://* www.centerbank.com

General - Incorporation	CA	Stock - Price on:12/24/2007	$17.22
Employees	344	Stock Exchange	NDQ
Auditor	Grant Thornton LLP	Ticker Symbol	CLFC
Stk Agt	U.S. Stock Transfer Corp	Outstanding Shares	16,660,000
Counsel	NA	E.P.S.	$1.50
DUNS No.	NA	Shareholders	NA

Business: The group's principal activities are to provide a wide range of commercial and consumer banking services. The services provided include commercial real estate loans, commercial loans, working capital lines, sba loans, trade financing, automobile loans, construction loans and other personal loans. The group operates through thirteen full-service branch offices located in los angeles, orange, san bernardino and san diego counties. It serves individuals and small to medium-sized businesses in the los angeles, denver, seattle and phoenix areas. On 23-Apr-2004, the group acquired Chicago branch of Korea exchange bank.

Primary SIC and add'l.: 6022 6712

CIK No: 0001174820

Subsidiaries: CB Capital Trust, Center Capital Trust I, Maryland real estate investment trust

Officers: Jae Whan Yoo/Dir., Pres., CEO - Center Bank, Sang Pil An/Sr. VP - Korea, Downtown Regional Dir., Lonny D. Robinson/Exec. VP, CFO - Center Bank, Lisa Kim Pai/Exec. VP, General Counsel, Chief Risk Officer, Corp. Sec. - Center Bank, Pyung Moo Lee/Sr. VP, Regional Mgr. - Chicago Office, Kwan Sop Song/First VP, Mgr. - Seattle Office, Grace Kim/First VP, Mgr. - Consumer Loan Department, Yi Yong Oh/Sr. VP, Regional Dir. - Expanded Region, Woe Soon Chang/First VP, Mgr. - Valley Office, Insook Park/Sr. VP, Chief Auditor - Audit Department, Jenny Lim/Assist. VP, Mgr. - Irvine Office, Chris Kong/First VP, Mgr. - SBA Department, Brian Kim/FVP, Mgr. - International Department, James Hong/COO, Exec. VP, Angie Yang/Investor Relations Contact - Center Bank *(35 Officers included in Index)*

Directors: Jae Whan Yoo/Dir., Pres., CEO - Center Bank, Peter Y.S. Kim/Chmn., Chung Hyun Lee/Dir., Chang Hwi Kim/Dir., Jin Chul Jhung/Dir., Sang Hoon Kim/Dir., David Z. Hong/Dir.

Owners: Jae Whan Yoo/0.01%, Chung Hyun Lee/3.60%, Kinetics Asset Management, Inc./7.30%, David Z. Hong/4.90%, Sang Hoon Kim/6.10%, Chang Hwi Kim/4.30%, Baron Capital Group, Inc./8.00%, Jin Chul Jhung/1.30%, Peter Y. S. Kim/3.40%, FMR Corp. and Related Entities/10.00%, James Hong/0.10%, Insiders/39.76%

Financial Data: Fiscal Year End:12/31 Latest Annual Data: 12/31/2006

Year	Sales	Net Income
2006	$147,070,000	$26,158,000
2005	$113,356,000	$24,603,000
2004	$78,181,000	$14,224,000

Curr. Assets:	$86,821,000	**Curr. Liab.:**	$1,454,531,000	**P/E Ratio:**	10.97
Plant, Equip.:	$13,322,000	**Total Liab.:**	$1,702,578,000	**Indic. Yr. Divd.:**	$0.200
Total Assets:	$1,843,312,000	**Net Worth:**	$140,734,000	**Debt/ Equity:**	1.7602

Centerline Holding Co

Formerly: CharterMac
625 Madison Ave., New York, NY, 10022; *PH:* 1-212-517-3700; *http://* www.chartermac.com

General - Incorporation	DE	Stock - Price on:12/24/2007	NA
Employees	500	Stock Exchange	NYSE
Auditor	Deloitte & Touche LLP	Ticker Symbol	CHC
Stk Agt	Computershare Trust Co	Outstanding Shares	50,920,000
Counsel	NA	E.P.S.	$0.07
DUNS No.	NA	Shareholders	NA

Business: The groups principle activity is to provide finance in the commercial and multifamily real estate industry. The group also provides capital solutions to real estate developers and owners. The group also provides investment products to retail and institutional investors. The group operates through four segments namely, portfolio investing, fund management, mortgage banking and consolidated partnerships. The group acquired Capri Capital Limited Partnership in March 2005 and ARCap in August 2006. The group operates from the United States.

Primary SIC and add'l.: 6500

CIK No: 0001043325

Subsidiaries: ARCap Investors LLC, ARCap Reit, Inc., Centerbrook Financial LLC, Centerbrook Holdings LLC, CharterMac Capital LLC, CharterMac Capital Company, LLC, CharterMac Corporation, CharterMac Equity Issuer Trust, CharterMac Equity Issuer Trust II, CharterMac Mortgage Capital Corp., Inc., CharterMac Origination Trust I, CM ARCap Investor LLC, CM Holding Trust, CM Holding Trust II, CM Investor LLC 16 Subsidiaries included in the Index

Officers: Marc D. Schnitzer/47/Dir., CEO - Managing Trustee/$2,145,786.00, James L. Duggins/49/Exec. MD/$1,599,923.00, James D. Spound/Sr. MD, Co - Group Mgr. - Commercial Real Estate Group, Andrew J. Weil/Exec. MD, Robert L. Levy/CFO/$1,154,760.00, John D'Amico/Sr. MD, General Counsel, Donald J. Meyer/Chief Investment Officer, Nicholas A.C. Mumford/Exec.

MD, Christopher J. Crouch/Sr. MD, Brenda Abuaf/Dir. - Corporate Communications, Bryan Carr/Sr. MD - Corporate Finance Group, Daryl J. Carter/52/Exec. MD, Larry J. Duggins/Exec. MD, Hilary M. Ginsberg/MD, Dir. - Corporate Communications, Kelly D. Schnur/MD, Dir. - Human Resources *(16 Officers included in Index)*

Directors: Marc D. Schnitzer/47/Dir., CEO - Managing Trustee, Stephen M. Ross/Chmn., Leonard W. Cotton/Vice Chmn., Jeff T. Blau/Managing Trustee, Peter T. Allen/62/Managing Trustee, Robert J. Dolan/Managing Trustee, Nathan Gantcher/Managing Trustee, Jerome Y. Halperin/Managing Trustee, Robert L. Loverd/Managing Trustee, Tom W. White/Managing Trustee, Robert A. Meister/Managing Trustee, Janice Cook Roberts/Managing Trustee

Owners: Insiders/17.60%, Nicholas A.C. Mumford, Daryl J. Carter, Janice Cook Roberts, Related General II L.P./12.80%, Peter T. Allen, Andrew J. Weil, Donald J. Meyer, Stephen M. Ross/13.90%, Leonard W. Cotton, Thomas W. White, Robert A. Meister, Jeff T. Blau/13.00%, James L. Duggins, Robert L. Levy *(20 Owners included in Index)*

Financial Data: *Fiscal Year End:*12/31 *Latest Annual Data:* 12/31/2006

Year	Sales	Net Income
2006	$387,259,000	$41,294,000
2005	$295,000,000	$59,014,000
2004	$232,854,000	$65,363,000

Curr. Assets:	$305,492,000	**Curr. Liab.:**	$84,563,000	**P/E Ratio:**	51.25
Plant, Equip.:	$41,743,000	**Total Liab.:**	$8,738,384,000	**Indic. Yr. Divd.:**	$1.680
Total Assets:	$9,688,516,000	**Net Worth:**	$950,132,000	**Debt/ Equity:**	5.3618

Centerplate Inc

201 E Broad St., Spartanburg, SC, 29306; *PH:* 1-864-598-8600; *Fax:* 1-864-598-8695;
http:// www.centerplate.com

General - Incorporation	DE	**Stock**- Price on:12/24/2007	$17.14
Employees	1,500	Stock Exchange	AMEX
Auditor	Deloitte & Touche LLP	Ticker Symbol	CVP
Stk Agt	Bank of New York	Outstanding Shares	22,520,000
Counsel	NA	E.P.S.	-$0.13
DUNS No.	94-132-1325	Shareholders	NA

Business: The group's principal activity is to provide food and beverage concessions, catering and merchandise services. These services are provided for sports facilities, small- to large-scale banquet catering and food court operations at convention centers and in-facility restaurants and catering. The services are provided at 128 facilities located across the United States and into Canada. The group also provides full facility management services which include a variety of services such as event planning and marketing, maintenance, ticket distribution, program printing, advertising and licensing rights for the facility, and its suites and premium seats.

Primary SIC and add'l.: 5149 7389 5399 5812

CIK No: 0001086774

Subsidiaries: Centerplate of Kansas, Inc., Service America Concessions Corporation, Service America Corporation, Service America Corporation of Wisconsin, Service America of Texas, Inc., Servomation, Inc., V.S.I. of Maryland, Inc., Volume Services America, Inc., Volume Services, Inc.

Officers: Janet L. Steinmayer/Dir., CEO, Pres./$985,460.00

Directors: Janet L. Steinmayer/Dir., CEO, Pres.

Owners: Felix P. Chee, Blackstone/11.50%, Glenn R. Zander, FMR Corp./9.70%, Sue Ling Gin, Hadi K. Monavar, Insiders, David M. Williams, GE Capital/6.50%, Alfred Poe

Financial Data: *Fiscal Year End:*01/03 *Latest Annual Data:* 1/2/2007

Year	Sales	Net Income
2007	$681,120,000	$3,478,000
2006	$643,112,000	-$4,588,000
2004	$607,154,000	$2,320,000

Curr. Assets:	$71,755,000	**Curr. Liab.:**	$70,243,000	**P/E Ratio:**	114.27
Plant, Equip.:	$48,222,000	**Total Liab.:**	$261,172,000	**Indic. Yr. Divd.:**	NA
Total Assets:	$299,046,000	**Net Worth:**	$37,874,000	**Debt/ Equity:**	NA

Centerpoint Energy Inc

1111 Louisiana St., Houston, TX, 77002; *PH:* 1-713-207-1111; *Fax:* 1-713-207-3169;
http:// www.centerpointenergy.com

General - Incorporation	TX	**Stock**- Price on:12/24/2007	$17.31
Employees	8,623	Stock Exchange	NYSE
Auditor	UHY LLP	Ticker Symbol	CNP
Stk Agt	CenterPoint Energy common stock	Outstanding Shares	320,790,000
Counsel	NA	E.P.S.	$1.05
DUNS No.	NA	Shareholders	NA

Business: The groups principle activity is to provide energy services. The group operates through five segments namely electric transmission & distribution, electric generation, natural gas distribution, pipelines and gathering and other operations. The group operates from United States.

Primary SIC and add'l.: 4619 4911 4931 4924

CIK No: 0001130310

Subsidiaries: CenterPoint Energy Houston Electric, LLC, CenterPoint Energy Resources Corp, CNP Investment Management, Inc., Utility Holdings, LLC

Officers: David M. McClanahan/Dir., CEO, Pres./$5,190,463.00, Byron R. Kelley/Sr. VP, Group Pres. - Pipelines, Field Services/$989,425.00, Bryan McCollum/Contact - Sales, Houston, Larry Mundt/Contact - Sales, Houston, Selena Plentl/Contact - Sales, Houston, Wes Dempsey/Contact - Wholesale, Houston, Roger Lee/Contact - Wholesale, Houston, Donald Mauldin/Contact - Wholesale, Houston, Tom Sax/Contact - Wholesale, Houston, David Van Pelt/Contact - Wholesale, Houston, Nick Waters/Contact - Wholesale, Houston, Michelle Crepeau/Contact - Sales, Indiana, Tim Klein/Contact - Sales, Indiana, John Zaharias/Contact - Sales, Indiana, Bruce Tuttle/Contact - Sales, NE, SD *(88 Officers included in Index)*

Directors: David M. McClanahan/Dir., CEO, Pres., Milton Carroll/57/Chmn., Donald R. Campbell/67/Dir., Holcombe O. Crosswell/67/Dir., John T. Cater/Dir., Derrill Cody/69/Dir., Janiece M. Longoria/55/Dir., Thomas F. Madison/72/Dir., Robert T. O'Connell/Dir., Michael E. Shannon/71/Dir., Peter S. Wareing/56/Dir., Sherman M. Wolff/67/Dir.

Owners: Scott E. Rozzell, Thomas F. Madison, Byron R. Kelley, Vanguard Windsor FundsVanguard WindsorII Fund, David M. McClanahan, Horizon Asset Management, Inc., Derrill Cody, Gary L. Whitlock, Northern Trust Corporation, Insiders, Pictet Asset Management SA, O. Holcombe Crosswell, Milton Carroll, John T. Cater, Peter S. Wareing *(21 Owners included in Index)*

Financial Data: *Fiscal Year End:*12/31 *Latest Annual Data:* 12/31/2006

Year	Sales	Net Income
2006	$9,319,000,000	$432,000,000
2005	$9,722,000,000	$252,000,000
2004	$7,999,461,000	-$904,704,000

Curr. Assets:	$2,995,000,000	**Curr. Liab.:**	$4,221,000,000	**P/E Ratio:**	12.02
Plant, Equip.:	$9,204,000,000	**Total Liab.:**	$16,077,000,000	**Indic. Yr. Divd.:**	$0.680
Total Assets:	$17,633,000,000	**Net Worth:**	$1,556,000,000	**Debt/ Equity:**	4.7698

Centerpoint Energy Resources Corp

1111 Louisiana St., Houston, TX, 77002; *PH:* 1-713-207-1111; *Fax:* 1-713-207-3169;
http:// www.centerpointenergy.com

General - Incorporation	DE	**Stock**- Price on:12/24/2007	$17.93
Employees	8,623	Stock Exchange	NA
Auditor	Deloitte & Touche LLP	Ticker Symbol	NA
Stk Agt	NA	Outstanding Shares	320,790,000
Counsel	NA	E.P.S.	$1.04
DUNS No.	04-670-0779	Shareholders	NA

Business: The group's principle activities are to distribute and transport natural gas through interstate pipelines. The group is a wholly owned subsidiary of centerpoint energy inc. The group operates in two segments, natural gas distribution and pipelines and gathering. The natural gas distribution segment consists of intrastate natural gas sales and transportation to commercial, residential and industrial customers in Arkansas, Louisiana, Minnesota, Mississippi, Oklahoma and Texas. The pipelines and gathering segment operates two intrastate natural gas pipelines and provides gathering and pipelines services.

Primary SIC and add'l.: 4923 4932

CIK No: 0001042773

Subsidiaries: CenterPoint Energy Field Services, Inc., CenterPoint Energy Services, Inc., Utility Holding, LLC

Officers: David M. McClanahan/58/Dir., CEO, Pres., Gary Whitlock/CFO, Exec. VP, Johnny Blau/Sr. VP - Business Support Services, Gary Cerny/COO, Pres., Byron R. Kelley/Sr. VP, Group Pres. - Centerpoint Energy Pipelines, Field Services, Georgianna Nichols/Division Pres. - Centerpoint Energy Houston Electric, Scott Rozzell/Exec. VP, General Counsel, Corp. Sec., Tom Standish/Sr. VP, Group Pres. - Regulated Operations, Wayne Stinnett/Division Pres., Dean C. Woods/VP - Human Resources, Joseph B. McGoldrick/Division Pres. - Centerpoint Energy Gas Operations

Directors: David M. McClanahan/58/Dir., CEO, Pres., Milton Carroll/57/Chmn., Donald R. Campbell/67/Dir., Derrill Cody/69/Dir., Holcombe O. Crosswell/67/Dir., Janiece M. Longoria/55/Dir., Thomas F. Madison/72/Dir., Robert T. O'Connell/69/Dir., Michael E. Shannon/71/Dir., Peter S. Wareing/56/Dir.

Financial Data: *Fiscal Year End:*12/31 *Latest Annual Data:* 12/31/2006

Year	Sales	Net Income
2006	$9,319,000,000	$432,000,000
2005	$9,722,000,000	$252,000,000
2004	$7,999,461,000	-$904,704,000

Curr. Assets:	$2,995,000,000	**Curr. Liab.:**	$4,221,000,000	**P/E Ratio:**	17.24
Plant, Equip.:	$9,204,000,000	**Total Liab.:**	$16,077,000,000	**Indic. Yr. Divd.:**	$0.680
Total Assets:	$17,633,000,000	**Net Worth:**	$1,556,000,000	**Debt/ Equity:**	4.7698

CenterStaging Corp

3407 Winona Ave., Burbank, CA, 91504; *PH:* 1-818-559-4333; *Fax:* 1-818-848-4016;
http:// www.centerstaging.com; *Email:* info@centerstaging.com

General - Incorporation	DE	**Stock**- Price on:12/24/2007	$0.56
Employees	99	Stock Exchange	OTC
Auditor	Stonefield Josephson, Inc.	Ticker Symbol	CNSC
Stk Agt	American Stock Transfer & Trust Co.	Outstanding Shares	70,180,000
Counsel	NA	E.P.S.	-$0.291
DUNS No.	NA	Shareholders	NA

Business: The groups principle activities include planning the staging of the musical performances and determining the placement of the equipment. The group operates through two segments namely renting of musical instruments and renting studios for rehearsals and production, and rehearsals.com operations. In the year 2005 the group acquired CenterStaging Musical Productions, Inc. The group operates from the United States.

Primary SIC and add'l.: 7389

CIK No: 0001172939

Subsidiaries: CenterStaging Musical Productions, Inc.

Officers: Roger Paglia/Dir., CEO, Howard Livingston/Dir., CFO

Directors: Roger Paglia/Dir., CEO, Johnny Caswell/Dir., Jan Parent/Dir., Howard Livingston/Dir., CFO

Owners: Jan Parent/15.20%, Howard Livingston/10.10%, Roger Paglia/10.10%, Johnny Caswell/15.20%, Paul Schmidman/4.10%, Insiders/54.70%

Financial Data: *Fiscal Year End:*06/30 *Latest Annual Data:* 6/30/2006

Year	Sales	Net Income
2006	$5,705,000	-$25,299,000
2004	$196,000	-$1,266,000

Curr. Assets:	$914,000	**Curr. Liab.:**	$6,221,000		
Plant, Equip.:	$6,268,000	**Total Liab.:**	$13,199,000	**Indic. Yr. Divd.:**	NA
Total Assets:	$7,387,000	**Net Worth:**	-$5,812,000	**Debt/ Equity:**	NA

Centerstate Banks of Florida Inc

1101 1st St. S, Ste. 202, Winter Haven, FL, 33880; *PH:* 1-863-293-2600; *Fax:* 1-863-291-3994;
http:// www.csflbanks.com

General - Incorporation	FL	**Stock**- Price on:12/24/2007	$17.46
Employees	320	Stock Exchange	NDQ
Auditor	Crowe Chizek & Co. LLC	Ticker Symbol	CSFL
Stk Agt	Continental Stock Transfer & Trust Co	Outstanding Shares	11,180,000
Counsel	NA	E.P.S.	$0.69
DUNS No.	NA	Shareholders	NA

Business: The group's principal activity is to provide a range of consumer and commercial banking services to individuals, businesses and industries. The services offered include: demand interest-bearing and non interest-bearing accounts, money market deposit accounts, time deposits, safe deposit services, cash management, direct deposits, notary services, money orders, night depository, travelers' checks, cashier's checks, domestic collections, savings bonds, bank drafts, automated teller services, drive-in tellers and banking by mail. The group provides secured and unsecured commercial and real estate loans and issues stand-by letters of credit. The group also offers Internet banking services to its customers.

Primary SIC and add'l.: 6022 6021 6712

CIK No: 0001102266

Subsidiaries: CenterState Bank of Florida, CenterState Bank West Florida, First National Bank of Osceola County, First National Bank of Polk County

Officers: Thomas E. White/53/Dir., Pres., CEO - Centerstate Bank Central Florida, NA/$236,249.00, E. S. Pinner/Chmn., CEO, Pres./$721,150.00, Brett Barnhardt/Contact - Winter Haven Area Exec, Paul Gerrard/Contact - Ridge Area Exec, Mark Thompson/Contact - Lakeland Area Exec, Steve Young/CFO, Jennifer Ison/COO, Robert Dodd/Chief Credit Officer, James J. Antal/56/Sr. VP

Directors: Thomas E. White/53/Dir., Pres., CEO - Centerstate Bank Central Florida, NA, E. S. Pinner/Chmn., CEO, Pres., Thomas E. Oakley/Dir., William K. Pou/Dir., Thomas J. Rocker/Dir., Rodney M. Surrency/Dir., George Tierso Nunez/54/Dir., Rulon D. Munns/58/Dir., Gail Gregg-Strimenos/60/Dir., John C. Corbett/Dir., Frank M. Foster/65/Dir., Timothy A. Irby/Dir., Lawrence W. Maxwell/Dir., Bruce A. Davis/Dir., Bruce Ingram/Dir. *(21 Directors included in Index)*

Owners: Wellington Management Co., LLP/8.30%, Insiders/25.07%, James H. Bingham/1.27%, Terry W. Donley/1.06%, George H. Carefoot/1.05%, Rulon D. Munns, Robert G. Blanchard/2.90%, Frank M. Foster, Gail Gregg-Strimenos/1.03%, Thomas E. Oakley/1.51%, Thomas E. White/1.08%, Samuel L. Lupfer, Thomas J. Rocker, Bryan W. Judge/1.05%, Ernest S. Pinner/2.11% *(17 Owners included in Index)*

Financial Data: **Fiscal Year End:**12/31 **Latest Annual Data:** 12/31/2006

Year	Sales	Net Income
2006	$65,249,000	$8,459,000
2005	$45,649,000	$6,330,000
2004	$35,864,000	$4,373,000

Curr. Assets:	$125,056,000	**Curr. Liab.:**	$949,770,000	**P/E Ratio:**	23.59
Plant, Equip.:	$39,879,000	**Total Liab.:**	$959,770,000	**Indic. Yr. Divd.:**	$0.140
Total Assets:	$1,077,102,000	**Net Worth:**	$117,332,000	**Debt/ Equity:**	0.0835

Centex Corp

2728 N Harwood, Dallas, TX, 75201; ***PH:*** 1-214-981-5000; ***Fax:*** 1-214-981-6859; ***http://*** www.centex.com; ***Email:*** ir@centex.com

General - Incorporation	NV	**Stock** - Price on:12/24/2007	$42.84
Employees	11,418	Stock Exchange	NYSE
Auditor	Ernst & Young LLP	Ticker Symbol	CTX
Stk Agt	Chase Mellon Shareholder Services	Outstanding Shares	120,130,000
Counsel	NA	E.P.S.	$2.226
DUNS No.	04-331-3394	Shareholders	NA

Business: The groups principle activity is to provide residential construction and mortgage financing. The group operates from United States.

Primary SIC and add'l.: 6552 1542 1521 3275 6162 3241 3272

CIK No: 0000018532

Subsidiaries: Aaa Holdings, L.p., Abc Homes Limited, Accord Lending, L.p., Adfitech, Inc., Advanced Financial Technology, Inc., Alameda Point Community Partners, LLC, Alpine Insurance Company, American Landmark Mortgage, Ltd., Apartment Protection Systems, Apartment Protection Systems, Inc., Arena Development/centex Construction, LLC, Armor Assurance Company, Armor Indemnity, Inc., A Risk Retention Group, Assurance Financial Services, L.P., Assurance Home Lending Services, L.p. 390 Subsidiaries included in the Index

Officers: Timothy Eller/Chmn., CEO/$12,275,950.00, Matt Moyer/VP - Investor Relations, Robert S. Stewart/Sr. VP - Strategy, Corporate Development/$1,695,907.00, Eric Bruner/Contact - Media, Michael Albright/Sr. VP - Administration, Lawrence Angelilli/Sr. VP - Finance, Joe Bosch/Sr. VP - Human Resources, Mark D. Kemp/Sr. VP, Controller/$1,416,910.00, Brian Woram/Sr. VP, Chief Legal Officer, Cathy R. Smith/CFO, Exec. VP/$1,754,118.00, David L. Barclay/55/Pres. - Western Region/$2,473,270.00

Directors: Timothy Eller/Chmn., CEO, James J. Postl/Dir., Matthew Rose/Dir., Thomas M. Schoewe/Dir., Frederic M. Poses/Dir., Thomas J. Falk/Dir., Ursula O. Fairbairn/Dir., Clint W. Murchison/Dir., David W. Quinn/Dir., Barbara T. Alexander/Dir., Juan L. Elek/Dir.

Owners: Ursula O. Fairbairn, Hotchkis and Wiley Capital Management, LLC/10.20%, James J. Postl, David W. Quinn, Juan L. Elek, Andrew J. Hannigan/1.50%, Robert S. Stewart, David L. Barclay, Neuberger Berman Inc. and Neuberger Berman, LLC/5.35%, Matthew K. Rose, Legg Mason Capital Management, Inc.; Legg Mason Value Trust, Inc.;/13.91%, Thomas M. Schoewe, Catherine R. Smith, Frederic M. Poses, Thomas J. Falk *(22 Owners included in Index)*

Financial Data: **Fiscal Year End:**03/31 **Latest Annual Data:** 3/31/2007

Year	Sales	Net Income
2007	$12,014,567,000	$268,366,000
2006	$14,399,669,000	$1,289,313,000
2005	$12,859,695,000	$1,011,364,000

Curr. Assets:	$10,207,983,000	**Curr. Liab.:**	$2,349,088,000	**P/E Ratio:**	19.25
Plant, Equip.:	$136,172,000	**Total Liab.:**	$7,916,553,000	**Indic. Yr. Divd.:**	$0.160
Total Assets:	$13,205,759,000	**Net Worth:**	$5,112,269,000	**Debt/ Equity:**	1.0890

Centillium Communications Inc

215 Fourier Ave., Fremont, CA, 94539; ***PH:*** 1-510-771-3700; ***Fax:*** 1-510-771-3500; ***http://*** www.centillium.com

General - Incorporation	DE	**Stock** - Price on:12/24/2007	$1.95
Employees	260	Stock Exchange	NDQ
Auditor	Ernst & Young LLP	Ticker Symbol	CTLM
Stk Agt	Mellon Investor Services LLC	Outstanding Shares	41,150,000
Counsel	Wilson Sonsini Goodrich & Rosati	E.P.S.	-$0.63
DUNS No.	NA	Shareholders	NA

Business: The group's principle activity is to develop and manufacture semiconductor devices for equipment manufacturers serving the broadband communications markets. The group is initially developing products designed for the digital subscriber line (DSL) and voice over packet markets. The group derives its revenues from the sale of DSL and voice over packet products, which include the copperlite co, copperlite cpe, optimizer and entropia families of products. The group sells two classes of voice over packet products: entropia co and entropia cpe. Major customers of the group include lucent technologies, sumitomo electric industries, copper mountain networks, nec and nortel networks. The group markets its products in China, Japan, North America, the United Kingdom and South Korea. The group's quarterly revenue for September 2007 was 10.03 millions of USD.

Primary SIC and add'l.: 3661

CIK No: 0001107194

Officers: Faraj Aalaei/47/CEO/$991,110.00, Kris Shankar/VP - Product Line Management, Hassan Parsa/VP - Business Development, Tapan Mohanti/VP - Operations, Manufacturing, Didier Boivin/VP - Marketing, Linda Reddick/CFO

Owners: Robert Hawk, Kamran Elahian/3.10%, Lip-Bu Tan, Riley Investment Management LLC/9.20%, Lloyd I. Miller/5.70%, Jere Drummond, Scott J. Kamsler, Linda Reddick, Insiders/12.20%, Sam Srinivasan, T. Rowe Price Associates, Inc./5.50%, Faraj Aalaei/8.40%, 033 Asset Management, LLC/7.90%

Financial Data: **Fiscal Year End:**12/31 **Latest Annual Data:** 12/31/2006

Year	Sales	Net Income
2006	$64,563,000	-$10,749,000
2005	$76,127,000	-$11,285,000
2004	$71,151,000	-$43,062,000

Curr. Assets:	$69,618,000	**Curr. Liab.:**	$30,872,000		
Plant, Equip.:	$2,702,000	**Total Liab.:**	$32,100,000	**Indic. Yr. Divd.:**	NA
Total Assets:	$72,898,000	**Net Worth:**	$40,798,000	**Debt/ Equity:**	NA

Centra Financial Holdings Inc

990 Elmer Prince Dr., Morgantown, WV, 26505; ***PH:*** 1-304-598-2000; ***http://*** www.centrabank.com

General - Incorporation	WV	**Stock** - Price on:12/24/2007	NA
Employees	286	Stock Exchange	NA
Auditor	Ernst & Young LLP	Ticker Symbol	NA
Stk Agt	NA	Outstanding Shares	NA
Counsel	NA	E.P.S.	NA
DUNS No.	NA	Shareholders	NA

Business: The group operates through its subsidiaries whose principle activity is to perform commercial banking operations and other related financial activities. The group operates from United States.

Primary SIC and add'l.: 6022 6712

CIK No: 0001099932

Subsidiaries: Centra Financial Corporation Martinsburg, Inc, Centra Financial Corporation Morgantown, Inc, Centra Financial Statutory Trust 1, Centra Mortgage I, LLC, Title Services, Inc.

Officers: Doug Leech/Dir., Pres., CEO - Morgantown/$469,959.00, Tim Henry/CEO - Hagerstown, Ed Franczyk/CEO, Pres. - Fayette County, Henry M. Kayes/CEO, Pres. - Martinsburg/$213,101.00, David Dalton/Banking Office Mgr. - Williamsport Pike, Martinsburg, Bob Myers/Contact - Human Resources, Morgantown, Bernard G. Westfall/Dir. - Morgantown, James W. Dailey/Dir. - Martinsburg, Elaine Bobo/Banking Office Mgr. - Foxcroft, Martinsburg, Robert S. Strauch/Dir. - Martinsburg, Barbara Albright/Banking Office Mgr. - Point Marion, Fayette County, Rita D. Tanner/Dir. - Morgantown, Tammie Alexander/General Counsel - Title Services, Morgantown, Sandy Campbell/Branch Administrator - Morgantown, John Fahey/46/VP *(62 Officers included in Index)*

Directors: Doug Leech/Dir., Pres., CEO - Morgantown, Paul T. Swanson/Dir.

Owners: Richard E. Hilleary/1.50%, Bernard G. Westfall, Henry M. Kayes, John T. Fahey, Douglas J. Leech/4.61%, Milan Puskar/2.72%, Karla J. Strosnider, Timothy P. Saab/1.39%, Paul T. Swanson/1.47%, Kevin D. Lemley/1.75%, Mark R. Nesselroad/1.53%, Insiders/22.10%, Edward Franzcyk, Robert A. McMillan/1.71%, Arthur Gabriel *(19 Owners included in Index)*

Centra Software Inc

430 Bedford St., Lexington, MA, 02420; ***PH:*** 1-781-861-7000; ***http://*** www.saba.com

General - Incorporation	DE	**Stock** - Price on:12/24/2007	$5.07
Employees	516	Stock Exchange	NA
Auditor	PricewaterhouseCoopers LLP	Ticker Symbol	NA
Stk Agt	American Stock Transfer & Trust Co.	Outstanding Shares	28,760,000
Counsel	Foley, Hoag & Eliot LLP	E.P.S.	-$0.29
DUNS No.	NA	Shareholders	NA

Business: The group's principle activity is to develop and market software and services for real-time business collaboration. The products and services facilitate product introductions, software deployment and other revenue-generating activities. The centra symposium software is designed for virtual classrooms and highly interactive teamwork. Centra conference enables large-scale Web conferences, seminars, events and corporate communications. Centra knowledge composers enables the development of interactive learning with powerpoint presentations, simulations and online sessions. Major customers of the group include accenture, apl, at&t, cadbury schweppes, century 21, citigroup, domino's pizza and emc corporation.

Primary SIC and add'l.: 7379

CIK No: 0001096658

Subsidiaries: Centra RTP, Inc., Centra Software Australia Pty Ltd, Centra Software Europe Limited, Centra Software Securities Corporation, Centra Software Southern Europe SAS

Officers: Bobby Yazdani/Chmn., CEO, Peter Williams/Exec. VP - Corporate Development, Amar Dhaliwal/Sr. VP - Product Operations Group, Tina Weinfurther/Sr. VP - Saba Corporate Strategy, Gabi Schindler/Chief Marketing Officer, Kazuo Hosoi/VP - Saba North East Asia, Don Bosworth/VP - Sales, North America, Alun Cope-Morgan/Pres. - Saba Europe, Middle East, Africa, Saba Asia, Pacific, Juan Cuadros/VP - Saba Latin America

Directors: Bobby Yazdani/Chmn., CEO, Douglas Ferguson/Dir., Joe E. Kiani/Dir., Lawrence D. Lenihan/Dir., Clifton Thomas Weatherford/Dir., Dow Wilson/Dir.

Financial Data: **Fiscal Year End:**12/31 **Latest Annual Data:** 5/31/2006

Year	Sales	Net Income
2006	$71,147,000	-$6,931,000
2005	$42,210,000	-$3,416,000
2004	$34,471,000	-$12,683,000

Curr. Assets:	$45,231,000	**Curr. Liab.:**	$47,866,000		
Plant, Equip.:	$2,172,000	**Total Liab.:**	$55,187,000	**Indic. Yr. Divd.:**	NA
Total Assets:	$107,034,000	**Net Worth:**	$51,847,000	**Debt/ Equity:**	0.0597

Central Bancorp Inc

399 Highland Ave., Somerville, MA, 02144; *PH:* 1-617-628-4000; *Fax:* 1-617-629-4219; *http://* www.centralbk.com; *Email:* electronicbanker@centralbk.com

General - Incorporation	MA	Stock - Price on:12/24/2007	$27.59
Employees	113	Stock Exchange	NDQ
Auditor	Vitale, Caturano & Co. Ltd	Ticker Symbol	CEBK
Stk Agt	Registrar & Transfer Co	Outstanding Shares	1,640,000
Counsel	Stradley Ronon Stevens & Young LLP	E.P.S.	$0.88
DUNS No.	NA	Shareholders	NA

Business: The group's principal activity is to generate deposits and use such funds to provide mortgage loans. The loans are provided for construction, purchase and refinancing of residential properties and commercial real estate. The group also provides consumer, commercial and industrial loans and home improvement loans. The group's operations are conducted through eight offices located in somerville, arlington, burlington, chestnut hill, malden, melrose and woburn.

Primary SIC and add'l.: 6035 6712

CIK No: 0001076394

Subsidiaries: Central Bancorp Capital Trust I, Central Co-operative Bank, Central Securities Corporation, Central Securities Corporation II

Officers: William P. Morrissey/COO, Exec. VP/$314,184.00, Bryan E. Greenbaum/Sr. VP - Retail Banking, Paul S. Feeley/CFO, Sr. VP, Treasurer/$210,102.00, Rhoda Astone/Clerk, Paula M. Corsetti/VP - Marketing

Owners: Central Co-operative Bank/24.86%, John D. Doherty/14.67%, David W. Kearn/1.76%, William P. Morrissey/2.11%, Jeffrey L. Gendell/9.21%, Insiders/20.83%, Gregory W. Boulos, James F. Linnehan, Paul S. Feeley, Richard E. Stevens, John J. Morrissey, Joseph R. Doherty, Shirley M. Tracy, Edward F. Sweeney, Paul E. Bulman (16 Owners included in Index)

Financial Data: Fiscal Year End:03/31 Latest Annual Data: 03/31/2007

Year		Sales		Net Income
2007		$34,281,000		$1,020,000
2006		$32,338,000		$2,643,000
2005		$29,271,000		$2,463,000
Curr. Assets:	$18,568,000	Curr. Liab.:	$499,019,000	P/E Ratio: 39.41
Plant, Equip.:	$3,870,000	Total Liab.:	$508,086,000	Indic. Yr. Divd.: $0.720
Total Assets:	$547,275,000	Net Worth:	$39,189,000	Debt/ Equity: 0.1839

Central European Distribution Corp

2 Bala Plz., Ste. 300, Bala Cynwyd, PA, 19004; *PH:* 1-610-660-7817; *Fax:* 1-610-667-3308; *http://* www.cedc.com.pl; *Email:* info@cedc.com.pl

General - Incorporation	DE	Stock - Price on:12/24/2007	$36.78
Employees	3,015	Stock Exchange	NDQ
Auditor	PricewaterhouseCoopers Sp. Z O.O.	Ticker Symbol	CEDC
Stk Agt	American Stock Transfer & Trust Co.	Outstanding Shares	40,070,000
Counsel	Hogan & Hartson LLP	E.P.S.	$1.63
DUNS No.	92-698-0970	Shareholders	NA

Business: The group's principal activity is to import and distribute alcoholic and non-alcoholic beverages. The group operates through 47 regional offices located in Poland. The group distributes approximately 800 brands in five categories: beers, spirits, wine, soft drinks and cigars. It imports and distributes eleven international beers, including guinness, corona, miller, foster's, beck's pilsner, bitburger and budweiser budvar. It also distributes 293 spirit products, including leading international brands of scotch, single malt and other whiskeys, rums, bourbons, polish vodkas, tequilas, gins, brandy, cognas, vermouths and specialty liquors. The group imports and distributes 548 wine products. In 2003 the group acquired dako-galant sp z oo, remaining interest in onufry sa and on 09-Sep-2003, the group acquired panta hurt sp z oo.

Primary SIC and add'l.: 5182

CIK No: 0001046880

Subsidiaries: Agis S.A., Astor Sp. z o.o, Bols Sp z o.o., Carey Agri International Poland Sp. z o.o, Dako Galant Sp. z o.o, Damianex S.A., Delikates Sp z o.o., Fine Wines and Spirits, Sp z o.o., Imperial Sp z o.o., Krokus Sp z o.o, Miro Sp z o.o, Multi Trade Company Sp. z o.o, Multi-Ex S.A., Onufry S.A., Panta Hurt Sp z o.o 20 Subsidiaries included in the Index

Officers: William V. Carey/Chmn., CEO, Pres./$1,309,562.00, James Archbold/VP, Sec., Dir. - Investor Relations/$374,188.00, Evangelos Evangelou/VP, COO/$650,287.00, Christopher Biedermann/CFO, VP/$463,406.00, Richard S. Roberts/VP, Export Dir./$141,791.00, Carey Agri/Contact - Cedc, Poland

Directors: William V. Carey/Chmn., CEO, Pres., David Bailey/Dir., Markus Sieger/Dir., Jan W. Laskowski/Dir., Tony Housh/Dir., Scott N. Fine/Dir., Robert P. Koch/Dir.

Owners: Markus Sieger/0.05%, Takirra Investment Corporation N.V./6.33%, David Bailey/0.11%, Chris Biedermann/0.10%, Tony Housh/0.21%, Evangelos Evangelou/0.22%, Botapol Management B.V./6.08%, Charlemagne Capital/4.20%, Richard Roberts/0.11%, Scott N. Fine, James Archbold/0.43%, William V. Carey/10.23%, Jan W. Laskowski/0.22%, Insiders/11.79%, Robert Koch/0.07%

Financial Data: Fiscal Year End:12/31 Latest Annual Data: 12/31/2006

Year		Sales		Net Income
2006		$944,108,000		$55,450,000
2005		$749,415,000		$20,268,000
2004		$580,744,000		$21,830,000
Curr. Assets:	$503,094,000	Curr. Liab.:	$320,826,000	P/E Ratio: 22.56
Plant, Equip.:	$49,801,000	Total Liab.:	$783,665,000	Indic. Yr. Divd.: NA
Total Assets:	$1,326,033,000	Net Worth:	$520,973,000	Debt/ Equity: 0.5599

Central European Media Enterprises Ltd

Clarendon House, Church St, Hamilton; ; *http://* www.cetv-net.com

General - Incorporation	Bermuda	Stock - Price on:12/24/2007	$94.68
Employees	3,347	Stock Exchange	NDQ
Auditor	Deloitte & Touche LLP	Ticker Symbol	CETV
Stk Agt	American Stock Transfer & Trust Co.	Outstanding Shares	40,940,000
Counsel	NA	E.P.S.	$1.55
DUNS No.	87-564-4882	Shareholders	NA

Business: The group's principle activity is to develop and operates national and regional commercial television stations and networks. The group operates from United States.

Primary SIC and add'l.: 4833 7373

CIK No: 0000925645

Subsidiaries: A.R.J. a.s., ADAM a.s., Broadcasting Company Studio 1+1 LLC, Central European Media Enterprises II BV, Central European Media Enterprises N.V., CET 21, s.r.o., CME Cyprus Holding Ltd, CME Czech Republic B.V., CME Czech Republic II B.V., CME Development Corporation, CME Germany B.V., CME Germany GmbH, CME Hungary B.V., CME Media Enterprises B.V., CME Media Investments s.r.o. 53 Subsidiaries included in the Index

Officers: Michael Garin/Dir., CEO/$3,090,067.00, Adrian Sarbu/53/Regional Dir./$1,441,386.00, Mark Wyllie/VP - Corporate Finance, Romana Tomasova/Dir. - Corporate Communications, Yuriy Morozov/61/General Dir., Marina Williams/Exec. VP/$1,704,503.00, Daniel Penn/General Counsel, Sec., Wallace MacMillan/50/CFO/$926,713.00

Directors: Michael Garin/Dir., CEO, Herbert A. Granath/Vice Chmn., Ronald S. Lauder/Non Exec. Chmn., Ann Mather/Dir., Charles R. Frank/Dir., Bruce Maggin/Dir., Eric Zinterhofer/Non Exec. Dir., Alfred W. Langer/58/Dir., Herbert Kloiber/Dir., Frank Ehmer/Dir., Christian Stahl/Dir.

Owners: Michael N. Garin, Morgan Stanley Investment Management, Inc./5.15%, Ann Mather, Herbert A. Granath, Apax Partners Europe Managers Limited, Wallace Macmillan, Alfred W. Langer, Insiders, Eric Zinterhofer, Apax Partners Europe Managers Limited, Morgan Stanley/6.04%, Testora Ltd/10.11%, Eric Semler/8.53%, Ronald S. Lauder, Adrian Sarbu (25 Owners included in Index)

Financial Data: Fiscal Year End:12/31 Latest Annual Data: 12/31/2006

Year		Sales		Net Income
2006		$603,115,000		$20,424,000
2005		$400,978,000		$42,495,000
2004		$182,339,000		$18,531,000
Curr. Assets:	$413,616,000	Curr. Liab.:	$182,961,000	P/E Ratio: 61.08
Plant, Equip.:	$115,805,000	Total Liab.:	$783,234,000	Indic. Yr. Divd.: NA
Total Assets:	$1,819,000,000	Net Worth:	$1,035,766,000	Debt/ Equity: 0.4891

Central Federal Corp

2923 Smith Rd., Fairlawn, OH, 44333; *PH:* 1-330-666-7979; *Fax:* 1-330-666-7959; *http://* www.cfbankonline.com

General - Incorporation	DE	Stock - Price on:12/24/2007	$6.45
Employees	57	Stock Exchange	NDQ
Auditor	Crowe Chizek & Co. LLC	Ticker Symbol	CFBK
Stk Agt	Registrar & Transfer Co	Outstanding Shares	4,560,000
Counsel	NA	E.P.S.	-$0.05
DUNS No.	03-595-7195	Shareholders	NA

Business: The group's principal activities are to provide banking services through four offices in wellsville, Ohio which are primarily light industrial areas. The group attracts deposits from the general public and uses these deposits along with borrowings and other funds to originate mortgage loans and short-term consumer loans. The group also invests in home equity, multi-family, commercial real estate, mortgage-backed securities, construction and land loans. The group is a holding company for central federal savings and loan association.

Primary SIC and add'l.: 6035 6712

CIK No: 0001070680

Subsidiaries: Central Federal Capital Trust I, CFBank

Officers: Mark Allio/Chmn., CEO, Pres./$234,314.00, Raymond E. Heh/COO, Pres. - Cfbank/$153,407.00, Eloise L. MacKus/Sr. VP, General Counsel, Sec. - Fairlawn, Stephen C. Burt/Commercial Banking Officer, Allen C. McConnell/Assist. VP - Commercial Banker, Columbus Office, Carolyn Kibler/Assist. VP, Office Mgr. - Columbus Office, Christopher Creighton/Commercial Loan Support Coordinator, Columbus Office, Courtney Deuser/Client Services Representative, Columbus Office, Therese A. Liutkus/CFO, Treasurer, Marian C. Ferlaino/Office Mgr. - Calcutta Office, Shelly Morrow/Mgr. Commercial Loan Operations - Fairlawn Office, Lisa A. Conkle/Loan Operations, Wellsville Office, Amy D. Dalrymple/Teller, Wellsville Office, Sheryl A. Gibson/Client Service Supervisor, Wellsville Office, Michele R. Guildoo/Human Resources Coordinator, Department Operations Mgr. - Wellsville Office (39 Officers included in Index)

Directors: Mark Allio/Chmn., CEO, Pres., David C. Vernon/Vice Chmn., Jeffrey W. Aldrich/Dir., Thomas P. Ash/Dir., William R. Downing/Dir., Gerry W. Grace/Dir., Jerry F. Whitmer/Dir.

Owners: Mark S. Allio/3.00%, Gerry W. Grace/1.20%, Thomas P. Ash/0.80%, Jeffrey W. Aldrich/0.80%, David C. Vernon/2.40%, William R. Downing/0.80%, Wellington Management Co., LLP/9.40%, Jerry F. Whitmer/0.20%, First Manhattan Co./8.00%, Raymond E. Heh/0.90%, Insiders/12.90%

Financial Data: Fiscal Year End:12/31 Latest Annual Data: 12/31/2006

Year		Sales		Net Income
2006		$14,482,000		-$37,000
2005		$9,557,000		-$3,290,000
2004		$6,736,000		-$1,662,000
Curr. Assets:	$7,198,000	Curr. Liab.:	$201,651,000	P/E Ratio: 80.63
Plant, Equip.:	$4,105,000	Total Liab.:	$206,943,000	Indic. Yr. Divd.: $0.200
Total Assets:	$236,028,000	Net Worth:	$29,085,000	Debt/ Equity: 0.1772

Central Fund of Canada Ltd

Hallmark Estates, 1323-15th Ave. SW, Ste. 805, Calgary, AB, T3C 0X8; *PH:* 1-403-228-5861; *http://* www.centralfund.com; *Email:* info@centralfund.com

General - Incorporation	Canada	Stock - Price on:12/24/2007	$9.27
Employees	NA	Stock Exchange	AMEX
Auditor	Ernst & Young LLP	Ticker Symbol	CEF
Stk Agt	Mellon Trust Co	Outstanding Shares	113,330,000
Counsel	Fraser, Milner, Casgrain LLP	E.P.S.	$0.52
DUNS No.	24-853-9363	Shareholders	NA

Business: The group's principle activity is to invest its assets in gold and silver bullion. The group operates from United States.

Primary SIC and add'l.: 6726

CIK No: 0000784959

Officers: Stefan J.C. Spicer/Dir., CEO, Pres., John S. Elder/Dir., Sec., Catherine A. Spackman/Treasurer, Teresa E. Poper/Assist. Treasurer

Directors: Philip M. Spicer/Chmn., Dale R. Spackman/Vice Chmn., Ian M.T. McAvity/Dir., John S. Elder/Dir., Sec., Douglas E. Heagle/Dir., Malcolm A. Taschereau/Dir., Michael A. Paren/Dir., Robert R. Sale/Dir.

Financial Data: Fiscal Year End:10/31 Latest Annual Data: 10/31/2006

Year	Sales	Net Income
2006	$215,983,000	$212,181,000
2005	$46,120,000	$42,652,000
2004	$46,318,000	$43,916,000

Curr. Assets: $16,902,000 **Curr. Liab.:** $1,867,000
Plant, Equip.: NA **Total Liab.:** $1,867,000 **Indic. Yr. Divd.:** $0.010
Total Assets: $838,196,000 **Net Worth:** $836,329,000 **Debt/ Equity:** NA

Central Garden & Pet Co

1340 Treat Blvd., Ste. 600, Walnut Creek, CA, 94597; *PH:* 1-925-948-4000; *Fax:* 1-925-287-0601; *http://* www.centralgardenandpet.com

General - Incorporation	DE	**Stock**- Price on:12/24/2007	$12.88
Employees	4,670	Stock Exchange	NDQ
Auditor	Deloitte & Touche LLP	Ticker Symbol	CENT
Stk Agt	Mellon Investor Services LLC	Outstanding Shares	71,480,000
Counsel	NA	E.P.S	$0.56
DUNS No.	00-943-9530	Shareholders	NA

Business: The groups principle activities include producing and marketing products for the pet, lawn and garden supplies markets. The groups products include grass seed, wild bird feed, bird feeders, bird houses, grass, ant and other herbicide, insecticide and pesticide products, and decorative outdoor lifestyle and lighting products. The group operates from United States.

Primary SIC and add'l.: 2879 5999 2048 0782

CIK No: 0000887733

Subsidiaries: All-Glass Aquarium Co., Inc., Four Paws Products, Ltd., Gulfstream Home& Garden, Inc., Interpet USA, LLC, Kaytee Products Incorporated, New England Pottery, LLC, Norcal Pottery Products, Inc., Pennington Seed, Inc., Pets International, Ltd., TFH Publications, Inc., Wellmark International

Officers: Glenn W. Novotny/Dir., CEO, Pres., Timothy J. Kane/Dir. - Tax, Assist. Sec., George Rich/VP - Human Resources, Howard MacHek/Corporate Controller, Assist. Sec., James V. Heim/Pres. - Pet Products Division, Bradley P. Johnson/Pres. - Garden Group, John A. Casella/CIO, Brooks M. Pennington/Dir., Corporate Exec. Officer, Stuart W. Booth/CFO, Exec. VP, Roger J. Fieischmann/VP, Treasurer, Assist. Sec., Paul Warburg/VP - Investor Relations, Assist. Sec.

Directors: Glenn W. Novotny/Dir., CEO, Pres., William E. Brown/Chmn., Brooks M. Pennington/Dir., Corporate Exec. Officer, Bruce A. Westphal/Dir., David N. Chichester/Dir., Jack Balousek/Dir., Alfred A. Piergallini/Dir., John B. Balousek/62/Dir.

Owners: William E. Brown, Schroder Investment Management North America Inc., Brooks M. Pennington, Insiders, Insiders, John B. Balousek, David N. Chichester, Glenn W. Novotny, Fidelity Management, John B. Balousek, William E. Brown, Harbinger Capital Partners Master Fund I, Ltd., James V. Heim, Fidelity Management, William E. Brown *(28 Owners included in Index)*

Financial Data: ***Fiscal Year End:***09/24 ***Latest Annual Data:*** 9/30/2006

Year	Sales	Net Income
2006	$1,621,531,000	$65,534,000
2005	$1,380,644,000	$53,787,000
2004	$1,266,526,000	$41,350,000

Curr. Assets: $634,702,000 **Curr. Liab.:** $207,304,000 **P/E Ratio:** 23.00
Plant, Equip.: $162,604,000 **Total Liab.:** $802,297,000 **Indic. Yr. Divd.:** NA
Total Assets: $1,533,823,000 **Net Worth:** $727,359,000 **Debt/ Equity:** 0.9390

Central Hudson Gas & Electric Corp

284 S Ave., Poughkeepsie, NY, 12601; *PH:* 1-914-452-2000; *http://* www2.centralhudson.com

General - Incorporation	NY	**Stock**- Price on:12/24/2007	NA
Employees	NA	Stock Exchange	OTC
Auditor	PricewaterhouseCoopers LLP	Ticker Symbol	CHGEL
Stk Agt	NA	Outstanding Shares	NA
Counsel	NA	E.P.S	NA
DUNS No.	00-699-3695	Shareholders	NA

Business: The group is a holding company, operates through central hudson and ch services. The principle activities of the group are supplying electricity, natural gas, propane, fuel oil and other petroleum products along with energy services. Central hudson gas & electric provides electricity to 276,000 customers and natural gas to 66,000 customers in New York. Ch energy group provides retail and wholesale energy marketing, petroleum product distribution, engineering and construction, electricity generation, and energy management services in the northeast and mid-Atlantic United States.

Primary SIC and add'l.: 4923 4911 4931 6719

CIK No: 0000018647

Subsidiaries: Central Hudson Enterprises Corporation, Central Hudson Gas & Electric Corporation, Griffith Energy Services, Inc., Phoenix Development Company, Inc., SCASCO, Inc.

Officers: Steven V. Lant/Chmn., CEO, Denise D. Vanburen/46/VP - Corporate Communications, Community Relations, Lincoln E. Bleveans/40/Sec., Assist. Treasurer, Carl E. Meyer/60/Dir., COO, Pres., Arthur R. Upright/64/Dir., Sr. VP - Regulatory Affairs, Financial Planning, Accounting, Christopher M. Capone/45/Dir., CFO, Treasurer, Donna S. Doyle/59/VP - Accounting, Controller

Directors: Steven V. Lant/Chmn., CEO, Ernest R. Verebelyi/Dir., Arthur R. Upright/64/Dir., Sr. VP - Regulatory Affairs, Financial Planning, Accounting, Christopher M. Capone/45/Dir., CFO, Treasurer, Carl E. Meyer/60/Dir., COO, Pres., Michel E. Kruse/63/Dir., Jeffrey D. Tranen/61/Dir., Joseph J. Devirgilio/56/Dir., Stanley J. Grubel/65/Dir., Steven M. Fetter/55/Dir., Margarita K. Dilley/50/Dir., Manuel J. Iraola/59/Dir.

Central Illinois Light Co

300 Liberty St., Peoria, IL, 61602; *PH:* 1-309-677-5230; *http://* www.cilco.com

General - Incorporation	IL	**Stock**- Price on:12/24/2007	NA
Employees	7,177	Stock Exchange	NA
Auditor	PricewaterhouseCoopers LLP	Ticker Symbol	NA
Stk Agt	NA	Outstanding Shares	NA
Counsel	NA	E.P.S	NA
DUNS No.	00-693-5258	Shareholders	NA

Business: The group's principal activity is to generate, transmit, distribute and market electric energy. The group also purchases, distributes, transmits and markets natural gas. The group supplies electric energy in an area of approximately 3,700 square miles and natural gas in an area of approximately 4,500 square miles. The group provides electric energy and natural gas for industrial, commercial and residential purposes. The group operates in central and east-central Illinois.

Primary SIC and add'l.: 4911 4923

CIK No: 0000018651

Owners: Warner L. Baxter, Insiders, Daniel F. Cole, Steven R. Sullivan, Scott A. Cisel, Gary L. Rainwater, Thomas R. Voss

Central Illinois Public Service Co

607 E Adams St. , Springfield, IL, 62739; *PH:* 1-217-523-3600

General - Incorporation	IL	**Stock**- Price on:12/24/2007	$50.06
Employees	8,988	Stock Exchange	NA
Auditor	PricewaterhouseCoopers LLP	Ticker Symbol	NA
Stk Agt	NA	Outstanding Shares	207,020,000
Counsel	NA	E.P.S	$3.00
DUNS No.	00-693-6017	Shareholders	NA

Business: The group's principle activities include generating, transmitting and distributing electric energy; and sells and distributes natural gas. The group operates from United States.

Primary SIC and add'l.: 4924 4931

CIK No: 0000018654

Subsidiaries: AFS Development Company, LLC, Agricultural Research& Development Corp., Ameren Corporation, Ameren Development Company, Ameren Energy Communications, Inc., Ameren Energy Development Company, Ameren Energy Fuels and Services Company, Ameren Energy Generating Company, Ameren Energy Marketing Company, Ameren Energy Resources Company, Ameren Energy, Inc., Ameren ERC, Inc., Ameren Services Company, AmerenEnergy Medina Valley Cogen (No. 2) LLC, AmerenEnergy Medina Valley Cogen, (No. 4) LLC 72 Subsidiaries included in the Index

Officers: Scott A. Cisel/54/Chmn., CEO, Pres., Warner L. Baxter/46/Dir., CFO, Exec. VP/$1,270,000.00, Daniel F. Cole/54/Dir., Sr. VP/$751,153.00, Martin J. Lyons/VP, Controller, Principal Accounting Officer

Directors: Scott A. Cisel/54/Chmn., CEO, Pres., Warner L. Baxter/46/Dir., CFO, Exec. VP, Daniel F. Cole/54/Dir., Sr. VP, Gary L. Rainwater/61/Dir., Steven R. Sullivan/47/Dir., Thomas R. Voss/60/Dir., Gordon R. Lohman/Dir.

Owners: Scott A. Cisel, Thomas R. Voss, Warner L. Baxter, Daniel F. Cole, Insiders, Steven R. Sullivan, Gary L. Rainwater

Financial Data: ***Fiscal Year End:***12/31 ***Latest Annual Data:*** 12/31/2006

Year	Sales	Net Income
2006	$6,880,000,000	$547,000,000
2005	$6,780,000,000	$606,000,000
2004	$5,160,000,000	$530,000,000

Curr. Assets: $1,874,000,000 **Curr. Liab.:** $2,202,000,000 **P/E Ratio:** 18.82
Plant, Equip.: $14,299,000,000 **Total Liab.:** $12,766,000,000 **Indic. Yr. Divd.:** $2.540
Total Assets: $19,578,000,000 **Net Worth:** $6,778,000,000 **Debt/ Equity:** 0.8021

Central Jersey Bancorp

627 2nd Ave., Long Branch, NJ, 07740; *PH:* 1-732-571-1300; *Fax:* 1-732-571-1037; *http://* www.mcbna.com

General - Incorporation	NJ	**Stock**- Price on:12/24/2007	$8.2
Employees	147	Stock Exchange	NDQ
Auditor	KPMG LLP	Ticker Symbol	CJBK
Stk Agt	Registrar & Transfer Co	Outstanding Shares	8,670,000
Counsel	NA	E.P.S	$0.06
DUNS No.	NA	Shareholders	NA

Business: The group's principal activity is to provide a full range of retail and commercial banking services to its customers. The services include checking accounts, savings accounts, money market accounts, certificates of deposit, instalment loans, real estate mortgage loans, commercial loans, wire transfers, money orders, traveller's checks, safe deposit boxes, night depository, federal payroll tax deposits, bond coupon redemption, bank by mail, direct deposit and automated teller services, telephone and Internet banking. The bank has six full-service branch facilities located in long branch, spring lake heights, little silver, neptune, neptune city and ocean grove, New Jersey.

Primary SIC and add'l.: 6021 6712

CIK No: 0001172353

Subsidiaries: Central Jersey Bank, National Association, CJB Investment Corp., MCBK Capital Trust I

Officers: James S. Vaccaro/Dir., CEO, Pres., Robert A. Hart/Sr. VP - Consumer Lending, Central Jersey Bank, NA, Anthony J. Denucci/Sr. VP - Information Technology, Central Jersey Bank, NA, Karen Mastria/VP, Branch Mgr. - Central Jersey Bank, NA, Michele Hansen/AC, Finance, Central Jersey Bank, NA, Lisa A. Borghese/Sr. VP - Commercial Lending, Central Jersey Bank, NA, Rosemary Smith/Branch Mgr. - Point Pleasant, Robert K. Wallace/Exec. VP, Sr. Lending Officer - Central Jersey Bank, NA, Michael T. Stocko/VP - Finance, Central Jersey Bank, NA, Donna A. McBain/VP - Audit, Central Jersey Bank, NA, Mary L. Meier/AVP - Operations, Central Jersey Bank, NA, Anne G. Summers/VP, Branch Mgr. - Central Jersey Bank, NA, Jerry Zaleski/Branch Mgr. - Belmar, Luke R. Caverly/Sr. VP - Commercial Lending, Central Jersey Bank, NA, Patricia M. Binkowski/VP, Branch Mgr. - Central Jersey Bank, NA *(37 Officers included in Index)*

Directors: James S. Vaccaro/Dir., CEO, Pres., George S. Callas/Chmn., James G. Aaron/Dir., Nicholas A. Alexander/Dir., John A. Brockriede/Dir., Claire M. French/Dir., William H. Jewett/Dir., Paul A. Larson/Dir., John F. McCann/Dir., Mark G. Solow/Dir., Robert S. Vuono/Dir., Sr. Exec. VP, COO, Sec., Mark R. Aikins/Dir., James P. Dugan/Dir., Carmen M. Penta/Dir.

Owners: Paul A. Larson, Robert K. Wallace/0.69%, Carmen M. Penta/1.19%, Mark R. Aikins/1.30%, Mark G. Solow/2.09%, John A. Brockriede/5.37%, James S. Vaccaro/2.44%, Insiders/25.18%, George S. Callas/2.14%, Nicholas A. Alexander/1.09%, James P. Dugan/1.17%, James G. Aaron/2.72%, Robert S. Vuono/1.24%, Linda J. Brockriede/5.37%, Anthony Giordano *(19 Owners included in Index)*

Financial Data: ***Fiscal Year End:***12/31 ***Latest Annual Data:*** 12/31/2006

Year	Sales	Net Income
2006	$31,159,000	$2,466,000
2005	$26,571,000	$2,632,000
2004	$12,400,000	$1,218,000

Curr. Assets: $43,936,000 **Curr. Liab.:** $428,550,000 **P/E Ratio:** 136.67
Plant, Equip.: $5,357,000 **Total Liab.:** $450,804,000 **Indic. Yr. Divd.:** NA
Total Assets: $516,299,000 **Net Worth:** $65,495,000 **Debt/ Equity:** 0.4351

Central Minera Corp

PO Box 93038, West Vancouver, BC, V7W 3G4; *PH:* 1-604-687-6191;
http:// www.centralminera.com

General - Incorporation......................Canada	Stock- Price on:12/24/2007 ....$0.05
Employees..NA	Stock Exchange...OTC
Auditor .... Pannell Kerr Forster, Steele & Co	Ticker Symbol...CENMF
Stk Agt........... Pannell Kerr Forster, Steele & Co	Outstanding Shares ....NA
Counsel..NA	E.P.S. ....NA
DUNS No. 25-329-8806	Shareholders...NA

Business: The group's principal activities are to design, construct and operate leisure-oriented, amenity-rich master-planned communities. It designs, sells and builds single- and multi-family homes serving move-up, pre-retirement and retirement home buyers. The group also designs, sells and builds luxury residential towers targeting affluent, leisure-oriented home purchasers. On 31-Dec-2003, the group had 30 master-planned communities under development. On 24-May-2004 the group acquired spectrum communities.

Primary SIC and add'l.: 6552 6519 1531 7999

CIK No: 0000927426

Officers: Michael Cytrynbaum/66/Dir., CEO, Pres., Joan Jamieson/63/Dir., Corp. Sec.

Directors: Michael Cytrynbaum/66/Dir., CEO, Pres., Joan Jamieson/63/Dir., Corp. Sec., Barbara West/51/Dir.

Owners: Michael Cytrynbaum/5.30%, Insiders/13.10%, Carlo Civelli/7.70%

Central Pacific Financial Corp

220 S King St., Honolulu, HI, 96813; *PH:* 1-808-544-0500; *Fax:* 1-808-531-2875;
http:// www.cpbi.com

General - Incorporation.............................. HI	Stock- Price on:12/24/2007 ....$34.44
Employees...944	Stock Exchange..NYSE
Auditor ....KPMG LLP	Ticker Symbol..CPF
Stk Agt...........................Wells Fargo Bank, N.A.	Outstanding Shares 30,740,000
Counsel..NA	E.P.S. $2.61
DUNS No. 10-307-9539	Shareholders...NA

Business: The group's principal activity is to provide lending activities including the granting of commercial, consumer and real estate loans. In addition, the group provides inventory and accounts receivable financing, furniture, fixture and equipment financing, short-term operating loans, commercial real estate and construction loans. Consumer loans include home equity lines of credit, loans for automobiles, home improvement and debt consolidation, personal and professional lines of credit and other installment and term loans for other needs. The group operates 78 ATMs throughout the state of Hawaii. It provides other services such as investment and life insurance services, Internet and international banking services, travelers checks and safe deposit boxes. On 15-Sep-2004, the group acquired cb bancshares, inc.

Primary SIC and add'l.: 6712 6022

CIK No: 0000701347

Subsidiaries: CB Technology, Inc., Central Pacific Bank, Central Pacific HomeLoans, Inc., Citibank Properties, Inc., CPB Capital Trust I, CPB Capital Trust II, CPB Capital Trust IV, CPB Real Estate, Inc., CPB Statutory Trust III, CPB Statutory Trust V, Datatronix Financial Services, Inc., Gentry HomeLoans, LLC, Lokahi Mortgage, LLC, Pacific Access Mortgage, LLC, Pacific Island HomeLoans, LLC 16 Subsidiaries included in the Index

Officers: Clint Arnoldus/Vice Chmn., CEO, Pres./$1,392,758.00, Dean K. Hirata/Vice Chmn., CFO/$630,442.00, Denis K. Isono/Exec. VP/$392,492.00, Curtis W. Chinn/Exec. VP/$470,033.00, Hollie Amano/Investor Relations Contact

Directors: Clint Arnoldus/Vice Chmn., CEO, Pres., Blenn A. Fujimoto/Vice Chmn., Ronald K. Migita/Chmn., Dean K. Hirata/Vice Chmn., CFO, Christine H.H. Camp Friedman/Dir., Paul J. Kosasa/Dir., Mike K. Sayama/Dir., Jeannie B. Hedberg/Dir., Dennis I. Hirota/Dir., Dwight L. Yoshimura/Dir., Clayton K. Honbo/Dir., Duane K. Kurisu/Dir., Colbert M. Matsumoto/Dir., Maurice H. Yamasato/Dir., Richard J. Blangiardi/Dir. *(17 Directors included in Index)*

Owners: Dwight L. Yoshimura, Crystal K. Rose, Christine H. H. Camp Friedman, Dean K. Hirata, Maurice H. Yamasato, Barclays Global Investors, N.A./8.39%, Private Capital Management, L.P./8.10%, Earl E. Fry, Dimensional Fund Advisors LP/5.05%, Duane K. Kurisu, Clayton K. Honbo/1.63%, Colbert M. Matsumoto, Denis K. Isono, Clint Arnoldus, Ronald K. Migita *(24 Owners included in Index)*

Financial Data: *Fiscal Year End:*12/31   *Latest Annual Data:* 12/31/2006

Year	Sales	Net Income
2006	$365,047,000	$79,180,000
2005	$304,252,000	$72,459,000
2004	$172,426,000	$37,394,000

Curr. Assets:	$162,370,000	**Curr. Liab.:**	$3,924,244,000	**P/E Ratio:** 13.30
Plant, Equip.:	$77,341,000	**Total Liab.:**	$4,749,053,000	**Indic. Yr. Divd.:** $1.000
Total Assets:	$5,487,192,000	**Net Worth:**	$738,139,000	**Debt/ Equity:** 1.0677

Central Parking Corp

2401 21st Ave. S, Ste. 200, Nashville, TN, 37212; *PH:* 1-615-297-4255; *http://* www.parking.com

General - Incorporation.............................. TN	Stock- Price on:12/24/2007 ....NA
Employees...14,657	Stock Exchange..NA
Auditor ....KPMG LLP	Ticker Symbol..NA
Stk Agt...Suntrust Bank	Outstanding Shares ....NA
Counsel..Harwell Howard Hyne Gabbert Manner	E.P.S. ....NA
DUNS No. 05-066-9670	Shareholders..NA

Business: The group's principal activity is to own, operate and manage parking facilities owned or leased by third parties. It also provides transportation management services and financial and other advisory services to clients in the United States and the United Kingdom. The group operates multi-level parking facilities in the district of columbia, Canada, Puerto Rico, Mexico, Chile, Peru, venezuela, the United Kingdom, the republic of Ireland, Spain, Germany, Poland, Greece and Switzerland. It provides shuttle, valet, and parking meter enforcement and billing and collection services. As of Sept 30, 2003, the group operated 1,714 parking facilities under management contracts and 1,798 parking facilities under leases. The group acquired sterling parking ltd in fiscal 2003.

Primary SIC and add'l.: 7521

CIK No: 0000949298

Subsidiaries: 157166 Canada, Inc., 811462 Ontario, Inc., Allright Auto Parks Canada, Ltd., Allright Carpark, Inc., Allright Corporation, Allright New York Parking, Inc., Allright Park Vancouver, Ltd., Allright Parking Management, Inc., Aparkco Finance, Inc., Aparkco, Inc., Black Angus, LLC, Central Parking Finance Trust, Central Parking System - Airport Services, Inc., Central Parking System Athens, A.e., Central Parking System Birmingham, Ltd. 100 Subsidiaries included in the Index

Officers: Emanuel J. Eads/CEO, Pres., Jeff Heavrin/Sr. VP, CFO, Robert L. Cizek/Sr. VP, Gregory J. Stormberg/Exec. VP, Gregory Maxey/Sr. VP, Benjamin Parrish/Sr. VP, General Counsel, William R. Porter/Sr. VP - Acquisitions, Donald Holmes/Sr. VP - Human Resources, Alan Kahn/Exec. VP, William H. Bodenhamer/Pres. - USA Parking, James H. Bond/Pres. - International Operations

Owners: Lewis Katz/2.20%, Edward G. Nelson, Insiders/33.20%, Monroe J. Carell/19.40%, Dimensional Fund Advisors/9.50%, James H. Bond/1.70%, The Carell Childrens Trust/20.80%, Gregory J. Stormberg, Alan Kahn, William B. Smith, Claude Blankenship, Emanuel J. Eads, Raymond T. Baker, Jeff Heavrin, Columbia Wanger Asset Management/7.50% *(18 Owners included in Index)*

Central Valley Community Bancorp

600 Pollasky Ave., Clovis, CA, 93612; *PH:* 1-559-298-1775; *Fax:* 1-559-221-4376;
http:// www.cvcb.com; *Email:* customerservice@cvcb.com

General - Incorporation .... CA	Stock- Price on:12/24/2007 ....$14.49
Employees...136	Stock Exchange...NDQ
Auditor ....Perry-Smith LLP	Ticker Symbol..CVCY
Stk Agt.......................U.S. Stock Transfer Corp	Outstanding Shares 5,970,000
Counsel..NA	E.P.S. ....NA
DUNS No. ....NA	Shareholders...NA

Business: The group's principal activities are to accept deposits and provide loans. Deposits include demand, savings and time deposits. Loans include commercial, real estate and consumer loans. It also offers installment note collections, issues cashier's checks, sells traveler's checks, provides safe deposits boxes and other customary banking services. The group operates seven full-service banking offices in clovis, fresno, kerman, sacramento and prather, California.

Primary SIC and add'l.: 6022 6712

CIK No: 0001127371

Subsidiaries: Central Valley Community Bank

Officers: Daniel J. Doyle/Dir., CEO, Pres./$1,013,258.00, Charles Jones/VP, Branch Mgr., Bernie Kraus/VP, Commercial Loan Officer, Barbara Gillmore/Dir., VP - Human Resources, Deby Greco/VP, Private Banking Officer, Rod Geist/VP, Branch Mgr., Don Mendenhall/VP, Commercial Loan Officer, Sheryl Michael/VP, Branch Mgr., Jean Ornelas/VP, Real Estate Construction Loan Officer, Elizabeth Salas/VP, Branch Mgr., Theodore Thome/VP, Private Banking Officer, Jennette Williams/VP, Business Development Officer, Carol Worstein/VP, Branch Mgr., Cathy Ponte/Contact, Mari Kroigaard/Mgr. - SBA Department *(41 Officers included in Index)*

Directors: Daniel J. Doyle/Dir., CEO, Pres., Daniel N. Cunningham/Chmn., Sidney B. Cox/Dir., Edwin S. Darden/Dir., Barbara Gillmore/Dir., VP - Human Resources, Steven D. McDonald/Dir., Louis McMurray/Dir., Wanda L. Rogers/Dir., William Smittcamp/Dir., Joseph B. Weirick/Dir.

Owners: Steven D. McDonald/6.65%, Shirley Wilburn, Wanda L. Rogers/3.35%, Louis McMurray/11.15%, Gary Quisenberry, Sidney B. Cox/1.04%, Gayle Graham, Edwin S. Darden/1.84%, Thomas L. Sommer/1.71%, William S. Smittcamp/2.32%, Daniel J. Doyle/4.05%, Insiders/38.95%, Joseph B. Weirick/1.85%, Daniel N. Cunningham/7.06%, David A. Kinross

Financial Data: *Fiscal Year End:*12/31   *Latest Annual Data:* 06/30/2007

Year	Sales	Net Income
2007	NA	NA
2006	$36,109,000	$6,911,000
2005	$29,830,000	$6,044,000

Curr. Assets:	$54,587,000	**Curr. Liab.:**	$450,281,000	**P/E Ratio:** 13.54
Plant, Equip.:	$4,655,000	**Total Liab.:**	$450,281,000	**Indic. Yr. Divd.:** NA
Total Assets:	$500,059,000	**Net Worth:**	$49,778,000	**Debt/ Equity:** NA

Central Vermont Public Service Corp

77 Grove St., Rutland, VT, 05701; *PH:* 1-800-649-2877; *Fax:* 1-802-747-2199;
http:// www.cvps.com; *Email:* cicweb@cvps.com

General - Incorporation .... VT	Stock- Price on:12/24/2007 ....$37.3
Employees...535	Stock Exchange..NYSE
Auditor ....KPMG LLP	Ticker Symbol...CV
Stk Agt............................Deloitte & Touche LLP	Outstanding Shares 10,180,000
Counsel..NA	E.P.S. $1.59
DUNS No. 00-793-9614	Shareholders...NA

Business: The group's principal activity is to purchase, produce, transmit, distribute and market electricity in New Hampshire and Vermont. Its wholly owned subsidiary, Connecticut valley electric company inc, distributes and sells electricity in parts of New Hampshire bordering the Connecticut river. The group also owns a portion of Vermont electric power company inc that owns Vermont's high voltage transmission system and Vermont yankee nuclear power corporation a nuclear generating company. Another wholly owned non-utility subsidiary, catamount resources corporation, holds the group's subsidiaries that invest in unregulated business opportunities. The group owns and operates 20 hydroelectric generating facilities in Vermont with a capacity of 44.7 mw serving 148,164 customers and jointly owns four other facilities. It also owns two oil-fired and one diesel-peaking unit with a combined capacity of 28.9 mw.

Primary SIC and add'l.: 4911

CIK No: 0000018808

Subsidiaries: C.V. Realty, Inc., Catamount Resources Corporation, Custom Investment Corporation, East Barnet Hydroelectric, Inc., Eversant Corporation, Vermont Electric Power Company, Inc., Vermont Yankee Nuclear Power Corporation

Officers: Robert H. Young/60/Dir., CEO, Pres./$951,068.00, Joseph M. Kraus/Sr. VP - Operations, Engineering, Customer Service/$391,452.00, Dale A. Rocheleau/Sr. VP - Legal - Public Affairs, Corp. Sec./$374,669.00, Joan F. Gamble/VP - Strategic Change, Business Services/$319,135.00, Pamela J. Keefe/CFO, VP, Treasurer/$185,755.00

Directors: Robert H. Young/60/Dir., CEO, Pres., Janice B. Case/55/Dir., Robert G. Clarke/57/Dir., Mary Alice McKenzie/50/Dir., Janice L. Scites/57/Dir., Bruce M. Lisman/60/Dir., William R. Sayre/57/Dir., Robert L. Barnett/67/Dir., William J. Stenger/59/Dir., Douglas J. Wacek/56/Dir.

Owners: Insiders/6.40%, Robert L. Barnett, William R. Sayre, Pamela J. Keefe, Dimensional Fund Advisors LP/5.30%, Frederic H. Bertrand, Mary Alice McKenzie, Barclays Global Investors, N.A./6.10%, Douglas J. Wacek, Dale A. Rocheleau, William J. Stenger, Joan F. Gamble, Janice B. Case, Robert H. Young/3.70%, Timothy S. Cobb *(22 Owners included in Index)*

Financial Data: *Fiscal Year End:* 12/31   *Latest Annual Data:* 12/31/2006

Year	Sales	Net Income
2006	$325,738,000	$18,352,000
2005	$311,359,000	$6,346,000
2004	$302,200,000	$23,755,000

Curr. Assets:	$68,567,000	**Curr. Liab.:**	$54,831,000	**P/E Ratio:**	22.47
Plant, Equip.:	$310,436,000	**Total Liab.:**	$310,532,000	**Indic. Yr. Divd:**	$0.920
Total Assets:	$500,938,000	**Net Worth:**	$187,406,000	**Debt/ Equity:**	0.6764

Central Virginia Bankshares Inc

2036 New Dorset Rd., Powhatan, VA, 23139; *PH:* 1-804-403-2000; *Fax:* 1-804-598-5079; *http://* www.centralvabank.com

General - Incorporation	VA	**Stock** - Price on:12/24/2007	$24.7
Employees	107	Stock Exchange	NYSE
Auditor	Mitchell, Wiggins & Co. LLP	Ticker Symbol	CVBK
Stk Agt	Registrar & Transfer Co	Outstanding Shares	2,430,000
Counsel	Williams, Mullen, Clark & Dobbins	E.P.S.	$1.70
DUNS No.	80-897-2194	Shareholders	NA

Business: The group's principal activity is to provide general community and commercial banking business services. It offers a variety of financial services to individuals and corporate customers through its seven branch offices located in the Virginia counties of powhatan, chesterfield, henrico and cumberland. The group offers traditional loan and deposit banking services, Internet banking, telephone banking and debit cards and other related services, such as ATMs, travelers' checks, safe deposit boxes, deposit transfer, notary public, escrow, drive-in facilities and other customary banking services. In addition, the group also provides trust services to its customers through an affiliation with the trust company of Virginia.

Primary SIC and add'l.: 6712 6022

CIK No: 0000804561

Subsidiaries: Central Virginia Bank

Officers: Ralph Larry Lyons/Vice Chmn., CEO, Pres./$333,512.00, Elwood C. May/Dir., Sec., William F. Kid/61/Sr. VP - Cashier, Bank/$158,040.00, Charles F. Catlett/59/Sr. VP, CFO/$199,636.00, Leslie S. Cundiff/59/Sr. VP, Sr. Credit Officer/$190,648.00

Directors: Ralph Larry Lyons/Vice Chmn., CEO, Pres., James T. Napier/Chmn., John B. Larus/Chmn. Emeritus, Roseleen P. Rick/Dir., William C. Sprouse/Dir., Elwood C. May/Dir., Sec., Phoebe P. Zarnegar/Dir., Kemper W. Baker/Dir., Larry D. Wallace/Dir.

Owners: Charles F. Catlett, William C. Sprouse, William F. Kidd, Roseleen P. Rick, Elwood C. May, Phoebe P. Zarnegar, Kemper W. Baker, Ralph Larry Lyons/1.90%, Charles J. Moore/7.18%, James T. Napier, Leslie S. Cundiff, Larry D. Wallace, John B. Larus/2.00%, Insiders/5.85%

Financial Data: *Fiscal Year End:* 12/31   *Latest Annual Data:* 12/31/2006

Year	Sales	Net Income
2006	$31,348,000	$5,150,000
2005	$26,022,000	$4,877,000
2004	$23,156,000	$4,364,000

Curr. Assets:	$42,491,000	**Curr. Liab.:**	$393,687,000		
Plant, Equip.:	$10,592,000	**Total Liab.:**	$400,449,000	**Indic. Yr. Divd.:**	$0.720
Total Assets:	$437,535,000	**Net Worth:**	$37,086,000	**Debt/ Equity:**	0.1350

Central Wireless Inc

2040 Bispham Rd. , Sarasota, FL, 34231; *PH:* 1-941-929-1476; *Fax:* 1-941-929-1534; *http://* www.centralwirelessinc.com

General - Incorporation	UT	**Stock** - Price on:12/24/2007	$0.0001
Employees	NA	Stock Exchange	OTC
Auditor	Moore & Assoc., Chartered	Ticker Symbol	CWIR
Stk Agt	Colonial Stock Transfer Co Inc	Outstanding Shares	NA
Counsel	NA	E.P.S.	NA
DUNS No.	87-977-8819	Shareholders	NA

Business: The group's principal activity is to develop and construct towers including monopole, guy tower, stealth tower designs, and self-support towers for transmission of broadband, cellular and other wireless communications signals. The group also provides related services, including site acquisition, zoning and engineering, antennae and line installation, lease negotiation, assistance in regulatory matters, and tower design. The customers of the group include broadband and wireless telecommunications carriers and individuals or businesses desiring to lease or own telecommunications towers.

Primary SIC and add'l.: 7373 7372 3841

CIK No: 0000814070

Subsidiaries: CareMart, Inc

Officers: Michael Merchant/Chmn., CEO, CFO, Pres.

Directors: Michael Merchant/Chmn., CEO, CFO, Pres.

Owners: Kenneth W. Brand/43.36%, Insiders/43.36%

Financial Data: *Fiscal Year End:* 12/31   *Latest Annual Data:* 12/31/2005

Year	Sales	Net Income
2005	NA	-$790,000
2004	$107,000	-$212,000
2003	$603,000	-$2,767,000

Curr. Assets:	$0	**Curr. Liab.:**	$1,897,000		
Plant, Equip.:	NA	**Total Liab.:**	$1,897,000	**Indic. Yr. Divd.:**	NA
Total Assets:	$0	**Net Worth:**	-$1,897,000	**Debt/ Equity:**	NA

Centrasia Mining Corp

300-1055 W Hasting St., Vancouver, BC, V6E 2E9; *PH:* 1-604-685-9316; *http://* www.centrasiamining.com; *Email:* info@centrasiamining.com

General - Incorporation	Canada	**Stock** - Price on:12/24/2007	$1.15
Employees	NA	Stock Exchange	OTC
Auditor	Davidson & Co. LLP	Ticker Symbol	CTMHF
Stk Agt	Computershare Trust Co	Outstanding Shares	NA
Counsel	NA	E.P.S.	NA
DUNS No.	NA	Shareholders	NA

Business: The group's principle activity is to seek potential business opportunities. The group operates from United States.

Primary SIC and add'l.: 6799

CIK No: 0001123267

Subsidiaries: 0724000 B.c. Ltd., Magellan Gold (BVI) Inc., Magellan Holdings (BVI) Corp.

Officers: Douglas S. Turnbull/CEO, Pres., Nick Demare/CFO, William J. Tafuri/VP - Exploration, James Harris/Sec., Jordan Shapiro/Contact - Investor Relations

Directors: Cary Pinkowski/Dir., Oleg Kim/Dir., Brian McEwen/Dir., Leonid Oparin/Dir., Grigory Aleksenko/Dir., Damien Damien Reynolds/Dir.

Owners: William J. Tafuri/1.61%, Grigory A. Aleksenko/2.44%, Brian McEwen/0.37%, Cary Pinkowski/9.46%, Insiders/18.79%, Douglas Turnbull/4.09%, Leonid Oparin/0.37%, Stargate Solutions Ltd/22.52%, James Harris/0.87%, Oleg Kim/2.44%, Nick DeMare/1.26%

Financial Data: *Fiscal Year End:* 05/31   *Latest Annual Data:* 05/31/2007

Year	Sales	Net Income
2007	NA	-$2,256,000
2006	NA	-$1,485,000
2005	NA	-$87,000

Curr. Assets:	$1,187,000	**Curr. Liab.:**	$141,000	**P/E Ratio:**	69.55
Plant, Equip.:	$130,000	**Total Liab.:**	$141,000	**Indic. Yr. Divd.:**	NA
Total Assets:	$1,656,000	**Net Worth:**	$1,515,000	**Debt/ Equity:**	NA

Centrix Bank & Trust

1 Atwood Ln., Bedford, NH, 03110; *PH:* 1-603-647-4446; *Fax:* 1-603-647-6466; *http://* www.centrixbank.com

General - Incorporation		**Stock**- Price on:12/24/2007	$14.95
Employees	NA	Stock Exchange	OTC
Auditor		Ticker Symbol	CXBT
Stk Agt	Centrix Bank & Trust	Outstanding Shares	2,830,000
Counsel	NA	E.P.S.	NA
DUNS No.	NA	Shareholders	NA

Business: The group's principle activity is to provide banking services. The group's services include international, online and business banking services. The group operates from United States.

Primary SIC and add'l.: 6022

CIK No:

Officers: Joseph B. Reilly/Dir., CEO, Pres., Lucy T. Gobin/Dir., Sr. Exec. VP, CFO, COO - Investor Relations Contact, David Cassidy/Exec. VP, Sr. Loan Officer, Laura J. Okrent/Assist. VP, Customer Response Officer, Joyce P. Baldassare/Sr. VP, Chief Deposit Officer, Donna M. Briggs/VP, Construction Loan Officer, Glenn P. Grande/VP, Commercial Loan Officer, Heather J. Leach/VP, Commercial Loan Officer, Kathleen M. Stevens/VP, Risk Management Officer, Stephen Witt/Sr. VP, Commercial Loan Officer, Debra R. Hallett/Sr. VP - Credit Administration, Wayland C. Elwood/VP, Commercial Loan Officer, Sean E. Fitzgerald/VP, Commercial Loan Officer, Anthony J. Chismark/Sr. VP, Commercial Loan Officer, Brian Lavoie/VP, Commercial Loan Officer *(21 Officers included in Index)*

Directors: Joseph B. Reilly/Dir., CEO, Pres., Lucy T. Gobin/Dir., Sr. Exec. VP, CFO, COO - Investor Relations Contact, Walter W. Hemming/Dir., Gordon H. Lewis/Dir., Michael E. Rubin/Dir., Michael J. Simchik/Dir., Paul D. Spiess/Dir., Ronald C. Thomashow/Dir., William C. Tucker/Dir., John J. Clarke/Dir., Jane E. Hager/Dir.

Centrue Financial Corp

310 S Schuyler Ave, Kankakee, IL, 60901; *PH:* 1-815-937-4440; *http://* www.centrue.com

General - Incorporation	DE	**Stock**- Price on:12/24/2007	NA
Employees	NA	Stock Exchange	NDQ
Auditor	Megladrey & Pullen, LLP	Ticker Symbol	TRUE
Stk Agt	LaSalle Bank N.A	Outstanding Shares	NA
Counsel	NA	E.P.S.	NA
DUNS No.	NA	Shareholders	NA

Business: The group's principal activity is to provide a wide range of general, commercial and mortgage banking services through the subsidiaries. It accepts deposits and originates loans including commercial real estate, consumer, multi-family, commercial business and construction loans. The group provides securities brokerage services, insurance and annuity products. In addition, the group also provides a broad variety of consumer oriented products and services such as visa/mastercard program, debit card services, on-line banking and bill payment services. The group's main office and eighteen branch offices are located ashkum, aviston, bourbonnais, bradley, braidwood, champaign, channahon, coal city (2), diamond, dwight (2) , fairview heights, herscher, manteno, momence, st. Rose and urbana. The group acquired aviston financial corp in 2003 and acquired parish bank and trust company in 2004.

Primary SIC and add'l.: 6035 6712

CIK No: 0000891523

Subsidiaries: Centrue Bank, Centrue Insurance Agency Inc., Centrue Service Corporation, Centrue Statutory Trust II, Kankakee Capital Trust I

Century Aluminum Co

2511 Garden Rd., Bldg. A, Ste. 200, Monterey, CA, 93940; *PH:* 1-831-642-9300; *Fax:* 1-831-642-9399; *http://* www.centuryaluminum.com

General - Incorporation	DE	**Stock**- Price on:12/24/2007	$55.33
Employees	1,530	Stock Exchange	NDQ
Auditor	Deloitte & Touche LLP	Ticker Symbol	CENX
Stk Agt	Computershare Investor Services LLC	Outstanding Shares	40,950,000
Counsel	NA	E.P.S.	-$3.12
DUNS No.	94-226-8202	Shareholders	NA

Business: The group's principal activity is to produce and market aluminum products. It produces primary aluminum products ranging from molten aluminum to premium cast products such as foundry ingot and billet. The products of the group include molten metal, rolling ingot, t-ingot, extrusion billet

and foundry ingot. The group's operating facilities are located in hawesville, Kentucky, ravenswood, west Virginia and mt. Holly, South Carolina. The major customers include pechiney, southwire and glencore. On 01-Apr-2003, the group completed the acquisition of the hawesville facility by acquiring the remaining 20% interest and on 27-Apr-2004, the group acquired nordural hf.

Primary SIC and add'l.: 6719 3353 3355

CIK No: 0000949157

Subsidiaries: Berkeley Aluminum, Inc., Century Alumina, Inc., Century Aluminum Holdings, Inc., Century Aluminum of Kentucky General Partnership, Century Aluminum of Kentucky LLC, Century Aluminum of West Virginia, Inc., Century Bermuda I Limited, Century BermudaII Limited, Century Kentucky, Inc., Century Louisiana, Inc., Hancock Aluminum LLC, Metalsco, Ltd., Nordural ehf., Nordural Holdings I eHf., Nordural HoldingsII eHf. 20 Subsidiaries included in the Index

Officers: Logan W. Kruger/Dir., CEO, Pres./$6,341,599.00, Michael A. Bless/CFO, Exec. VP/$1,765,322.00, Robert R. Nielsen/Exec. VP, General Counsel, Sec./$1,278,540.00, Giulio Casello/Sr. VP - Business Development, David J. Kjos/VP - Operations, Iceland, Peter C. McGuire/VP, Assoc. General Counsel, Steve Schneider/Sr. VP, Chief Accounting Officer, Controller/$599,600.00, Wayne R. Hale/COO, Exec. VP, Shelly Lair/VP, Treasurer - Investor Relations, Jerry E. Reed/VP - Business Development, Michael Dildine/Contact - Media, Cynthia Schadler/Contact - Aluminum Sales, Purchasing, Kip Price/Contact - Aluminum Sales, Purchasing

Directors: Logan W. Kruger/Dir., CEO, Pres., Craig A. Davis/Chmn., Jack E. Thompson/Dir., Robert E. Fishman/Dir., Peter Jones/Dir., John P. O'Brien/Dir., Willy R. Strothotte/Dir., John C. Fontaine/Dir., Jarl Berntzen/Dir.

Owners: John P. OBrien, Craig A. Davis, Robert R. Nielsen, John C. Fontaine, Michael A. Bless, David W. Beckley, Glencore International AG/28.60%, Steve Schneider, Jack E. Gates, Insiders, Prudential Financial, Inc/5.70%, Logan W. Kruger, Gerald J. Kitchen, Citadel Limited Partnership/5.60%, Jack E. Thompson *(16 Owners included in Index)*

Financial Data: **Fiscal Year End:**12/31 **Latest Annual Data:** 12/31/2006

Year	Sales	Net Income
2006	$1,558,566,000	-$40,955,000
2005	$1,132,362,000	-$116,255,000
2004	$1,060,747,000	$27,971,000

Curr. Assets:	$517,639,000	**Curr. Liab.:**	$646,277,000		
Plant, Equip.:	$1,218,777,000	**Total Liab.:**	$2,055,524,000	**Indic. Yr. Divd.:**	NA
Total Assets:	$2,185,234,000	**Net Worth:**	$129,710,000	**Debt/ Equity:**	2.6023

Century Bancorp Inc

400 Mystic Ave., Medford, MA, 02155; *PH:* 1-781-391-4000; *Fax:* 1-781-393-4071; *http://* www.century-bank.com

General - Incorporation	MA	**Stock**- Price on:12/24/2007	$23.07
Employees	281	Stock Exchange	NDQ
Auditor	KPMG LLP	Ticker Symbol	CNBKA
Stk Agt	Registrar And Transfer CO.	Outstanding Shares	5,540,000
Counsel	NA	E.P.S	$0.885
DUNS No.	04-707-0750	Shareholders	NA

Business: The group's principal activity is to provide financial services to commercial enterprises, state and local governments, agencies and individuals in Massachusetts. It acts as a holding company for century bank and trust company, a state chartered financial institution. Through the bank, the group accepts savings, time and demand deposits and provides commercial, real estate and construction and consumer loans. In addition, the group offers automated lock box collection services, cash management services and account reconciliation services and promotes the marketing of these services to the municipal market. Another subsidiary, century financial services inc, provides securities brokerage services in conjunction with commonwealth equity services inc. The group operates through 21 banking offices in 16 cities and towns in Massachusetts serving small and medium-sized businesses, retail customers and local governments.

Primary SIC and add'l.: 6712 6022

CIK No: 0000812348

Subsidiaries: Century Bancorp Capital Trust, Century Bank and Trust Company, Century Financial Services Inc, Century Subsidiary Investments, Inc, Century Subsidiary Investments, Inc. III, Century Subsidiary Investments, Inc.II

Officers: Barry R. Sloane/Co - Pres., co - CEO, Jonathan G. Sloane/Co - Pres., Co - CEO, Cindi Davidson/Branch Mgr. - Braintree, Century Bank, Sandy Jackson/Branch Mgr. - Boston, Century Bank, Carol Melisi/Branch Mgr. - Burlington, Century Bank, Ken Wright/Financial Consultant - Burlington, Century Bank, Sarah O'Toole/Branch Mgr. - Cambridge, Century Bank, Laura Difava/Branch Mgr. - Everett, Century Bank, Paul V. Cusick/63/VP, Treasurer, Principal Financial Officer, David B. Woonton/52/Exec. VP - Century Bank, John Bosco/Branch Mgr. - Allston, Century Bank, Sandra Edey/Branch Mgr. - Beverly, Century Bank, Lisa Gosling/Branch Mgr. - Boston, Century Bank, Brian Pineau/Financial Consultant - Boston, Century Bank, Lina Buttiri/Branch Mgr. - Boston, Century Bank *(27 Officers included in Index)*

Directors: Marshall M. Sloane/Chmn., Roger S. Berkowitz/55/Dir., Henry L. Foster/82/Dir. Emeritus, Marshall I. Goldman/77/Dir., Russell B. Higley/68/Dir., Linda Sloane Kay/46/Dir., Fraser Lemley/67/Dir., Joseph J. Senna/68/Dir., Stephanie Sonnabend/54/Dir., George F. Swansburg/65/Dir., Jon Westling/65/Dir., Jackie Jenkins-Scott/58/Dir., Anthony C. Larosa/Dir., George R. Baldwin/64/Dir.

Owners: Jonathan G. Sloane/0.57%, Fraser Lemley/0.28%, Jon Westling/0.10%, Henry L. Foster, Wellington Management Company, LLP/8.75%, Insiders/90.43%, Endicott Management Company/7.81%, Stephanie Sonnabend/0.07%, Joseph J. Senna/1.36%, Russell B. Higley/0.13%, Castine Capital Management, LLC/5.64%, Paul V. Cusick, Barry R. Sloane/0.09%, Linda S. Kay/0.24%, Jonathan G. Sloane/2.94% *(28 Owners included in Index)*

Financial Data: **Fiscal Year End:**12/31 **Latest Annual Data:** 12/31/2006

Year	Sales	Net Income
2006	$92,072,000	$4,688,000
2005	$83,784,000	$6,880,000
2004	$75,555,000	$8,881,000

Curr. Assets:	$167,040,000	**Curr. Liab.:**	$1,355,925,000	**P/E Ratio:**	26.07
Plant, Equip.:	$22,955,000	**Total Liab.:**	$1,537,472,000	**Indic. Yr. Divd.:**	$0.480
Total Assets:	$1,644,290,000	**Net Worth:**	$106,818,000	**Debt/ Equity:**	0.3312

Century Bank OR

169 W 6th Ave., Eugene, OR, 97401; *PH:* 1-541-684-0515; *http://* www.century-bank.org; *Email:* cbonline@century-bank.org

General - Incorporation		**Stock**- Price on:12/24/2007	$17
Employees	NA	Stock Exchange	OTC
Auditor	NA	Ticker Symbol	CBAO
Stk Agt	U.S. Stock Transfer Corp	Outstanding Shares	1,000,000
Counsel	NA	E.P.S	NA
DUNS No.	NA	Shareholders	NA

Business: The groups principle activity is to provide banking services. The groups business banking services include business checking, business Internet checking, analyzed business checking, money market, century savings and certificate of deposits. The groups cash management products include courier services, credit cards, sweep products, wire transfers and Visa merchant services. The group operates from United States.

Primary SIC and add'l.: 6712

CIK No:

Officers: Thomas P. Widmer/CEO, Pres., Richard T. Re/Sec., Michael J. Nysingh/Sr. VP, CFO, Collin Alspach/Chief Lending Officer, Sr. VP, Melinda Tippets/Sr. VP - Operations - Human Resources

Directors: Marty W. Smith/Chmn., Jeffrey D. Lynn/Vice Chmn., Lee F. Merwin/Dir., Michael R. Curtis/Dir., Kelly R. Richardson/Dir., Kathy Wiltz/Dir.

Century Business Services Inc

6050 Oak Tree Blvd., S, Ste. 500, Cleveland, OH, 44131; *PH:* 1-216-447-9000; *http://* www.cbizinc.com

General - Incorporation	DE	**Stock**- Price on:12/24/2007	$7.33
Employees	5,200	Stock Exchange	NYSE
Auditor	KPMG LLP	Ticker Symbol	CBZ
Stk Agt	Computershare Investor Services LLC	Outstanding Shares	65,010,000
Counsel	Akin, Gump, Strauss, Hauer & Feld LLP	E.P.S	$0.47
DUNS No.	96-573-8701	Shareholders	NA

Business: The group's principle activity is to provide professional business services primarily to small and medium sized businesses and also to individuals, governmental entities and not-for-profit enterprises. These services are provided through three divisions: business solutions, benefits and insurance and national practices. Under business solutions, it offers service in tax planning and preparation, cash flow management, federal, state and local tax return preparation. Under benefits and insurance division, it offers service in employee benefits, insurance brokerage and group life insurance programs. Under national practices, it offers service in payroll processing and administration, tangible and intangible assets and financial securities.

Primary SIC and add'l.: 6351 8742

CIK No: 0000812348

Subsidiaries: Anderson Hunt, LLC, Benmark, Inc., CBIZ Accounting, Tax & Advisory of Atlanta, LLC, CBIZ Accounting, Tax & Advisory of Boca Raton, LLC, CBIZ Accounting, Tax & Advisory of Chicago, LLC, CBIZ Accounting, Tax & Advisory of Colorado, LLC, CBIZ Accounting, Tax & Advisory of Kansas City, Inc., CBIZ Accounting, Tax & Advisory of Maryland, LLC, CBIZ Accounting, Tax & Advisory of New York, LLC, CBIZ Accounting, Tax & Advisory of Northern California, LLC, CBIZ Accounting, Tax & Advisory of Ohio, LLC, CBIZ Accounting, Tax & Advisory of Orange County, LLC, CBIZ Accounting, Tax & Advisory of Phoenix, LLC, CBIZ Accounting, Tax & Advisory of Salt Lake City, LLC, CBIZ Accounting, Tax & Advisory of San Diego, LLC 59 Subsidiaries included in the Index

Officers: Steven L. Gerard/Chmn., CEO/$1,525,256.00, Michael W. Gleespen/General Counsel, Corp. Sec., Ware H. Grove/Sr. VP, CFO/$694,577.00, Jerome P. Grisko/COO, Pres./$1,076,217.00, George A. Dufour/CTO, Sr. VP, Robert A. O'Byrne/Sr. VP - Benefits, Insurance Services/$748,318.00, David Sibits/Pres. - Cbiz Financial Services, Mark Waxman/Chief Marketing Officer

Directors: Steven L. Gerard/Chmn., CEO, Donald V. Weir/Dir., Harve A. Ferrill/Dir., Todd Slotkin/Dir., Rick L. Burdick/Dir., Richard C. Rochon/Dir., Joseph S. Dimartino/Dir., Michael H. Degroote/Dir.

Owners: Ware H. Grove, Insiders/3.84%, Rick L. Burdick, Steven L. Gerard/1.16%, Jerome P. Grisko, Todd J. Slotkin, Robert OByrne, Richard C. Rochon, Michael H. DeGroote, Harve A. Ferrill, Barclays Global Investors, NA & Barclays Global Fund Advisors/6.45%, Leonard Miller, Joseph S. DiMartino, Cardinal Capital Management LLC/5.42%, Donald V. Weir *(16 Owners included in Index)*

Financial Data: **Fiscal Year End:**12/31 **Latest Annual Data:** 12/31/2006

Year	Sales	Net Income
2006	$601,125,000	$24,401,000
2005	$559,269,000	$18,673,000
2004	$520,057,000	$16,051,000

Curr. Assets:	$245,093,000	**Curr. Liab.:**	$175,782,000	**P/E Ratio:**	15.93
Plant, Equip.:	$28,976,000	**Total Liab.:**	$301,704,000	**Indic. Yr. Divd.:**	NA
Total Assets:	$518,282,000	**Net Worth:**	$216,578,000	**Debt/ Equity:**	0.5925

Century Casinos Inc

1263 Lake Plz. Dr., Ste. A, Colorado Springs, CO, 80906; *PH:* 1-719-527-8300; *Fax:* 1-719-527-8301; *http://* www.cnty.com; *Email:* investor@cnty.com

General - Incorporation	DE	**Stock**- Price on:12/24/2007	$8.46
Employees	1,000	Stock Exchange	NDQ
Auditor	Grant Thornton LLP	Ticker Symbol	CNTY
Stk Agt	Computershare Trust Co	Outstanding Shares	23,050,000
Counsel	NA	E.P.S	$0.31
DUNS No.	80-825-6879	Shareholders	NA

Business: The group's principal activity is to own and operate gaming casinos and hotels. In addition to casino, they also provide casino management services and operate casinos in cruises. The group owns and manages casino operations in the United States, South Africa, the czech republic, and international. The group's gaming operations are subject to strict governmental regulations at state and local levels. They regularly pursue additional gaming opportunities internationally and in the United States. At 31-Dec-2003, it has thirteen subsidiaries located in Delaware, Nevada, Austria, Colorado, Missouri and South Africa.

Primary SIC and add'l.: 5813 7011 7999

CIK No: 0000911147

Subsidiaries: Blue Bells Country Club (Pty) Limited, Blue Crane Signature Golf Estate (Pty) Limited, CC Tollgate LLC, Celebrations Accommodation Food Service Management (Pty) Limited, Century Casinos - Nevada, Inc., Century Casinos Africa (Pty) Limited, Century Casinos Caledon

(Pty) Limited, Century Casinos Cripple Creek, Inc., Century Casinos Europe GmbH, Century Casinos Iowa, Inc., Century Casinos Management, Inc., Century Casinos Tollgate, Inc., Century Casinos West Rand (Pty) Limited, Century Resorts Alberta, Inc., Century Resorts International Limited 19 Subsidiaries included in the Index

Officers: Peter Hoetzinger/Vice Chmn., Co - CEO, Pres./$734,398.00, Erwin Haitzmann/Chmn., Co - CEO/$734,398.00, Ray Sienko/Chief Accounting Officer/$127,953.00, Larry J. Hannappel/Sr. VP, Sec., Treasurer/$202,092.00, Niclas Schmiedmaier/Sr. Legal Counsel, Andreas Terler/CIO, Michael Snider/Sec., Reporting Mgr., Ulrike Pichler/Investor Relations, Mgr. - Communications

Directors: Peter Hoetzinger/Vice Chmn., Co - CEO, Pres., Erwin Haitzmann/Chmn., Co - CEO, Robert S. Eichberg/62/Dir., Gottfried Schellmann/Dir., Dinah Corbaci/53/Dir.

Owners: Dinah Corbaci, RS Investment Management Co. LLC, Insiders, Janus Capital Management LLC, Christian Gernert, Robert S. Eichberg, William Blair & Company, L.L.C., Erwin Haitzmann, Larry Hannappel, Thomas Graf, Gottfried Schellmann, Peter Hoetzinger, Cortina Asset Management, LLC, Ray Sienko

Financial Data: Fiscal Year End:12/31   Latest Annual Data: 12/31/2006

Year	Sales		Net Income
2006	$56,285,000		$7,629,000
2005	$37,445,000		$4,481,000
2004	$35,765,000		$4,738,000
Curr. Assets:	$41,167,000	Curr. Liab.: $35,991,000	P/E Ratio: 28.20
Plant, Equip.:	$124,638,000	Total Liab.: $92,027,000	Indic. Yr. Divd.: NA
Total Assets:	$197,860,000	Net Worth: $100,427,000	Debt/ Equity: 0.5475

Century Financial Corp MI

One Century Pl, Rochester, PA, 15074; **PH:** 1-412-774-1872

General - Incorporation	PA	Stock - Price on:12/24/2007	$21
Employees	NA	Stock Exchange	OTC
Auditor	NA	Ticker Symbol	CYFL
Stk Agt.	NA	Outstanding Shares	NA
Counsel	NA	E.P.S.	-$0.12
DUNS No.	NA	Shareholders	NA

Business: The groups principle activity is to provide recruiting services. The groups service area includes the research and development, engineering, marketing, sales, information technology and manufacturing industries. The group operates from United States.

Primary SIC and add'l.: 6021

CIK No: 0000820414

Financial Data: Fiscal Year End:12/31   Latest Annual Data: 12/31/2002

Year	Sales		Net Income
2002	$14,994,000		$2,705,000
2001	$19,112,000		$3,010,000
2000	$20,818,000		$3,759,000
Curr. Assets:	$25,567,000	Curr. Liab.: $193,513,000	
Plant, Equip.:	$6,504,000	Total Liab.: $202,077,000	Indic. Yr. Divd.: NA
Total Assets:	$228,322,000	Net Worth: $26,245,000	Debt/ Equity: 0.2374

Century Petroleum Corp

9595 Six pines Dr., Bldg. 8, level 2, Woodland, TX, 77380; **PH:** 1-303-542-1906; **Fax:** 1-832-631-6059; http:// www.centurypetrol.com; **Email:** info@centurypetrol.com

General - Incorporation	NV	Stock - Price on:12/24/2007	$92
Employees	2	Stock Exchange	OTC
Auditor	Webb & Company, P. A.	Ticker Symbol	CYPE
Stk Agt.	Empire Stock Transfer Inc.	Outstanding Shares	63,780,000
Counsel	NA	E.P.S.	-$0.04
DUNS No.	NA	Shareholders	NA

Business: The groups principal activity is to explore minerals. In the year 2006, the group acquired Som Resources, Inc. The group operates from Canada.

Primary SIC and add'l.: 1311

CIK No: 0001332042

Officers: James B. Hersch/56/Dir., CEO, Pres., Johannes Petersen/CFO, Michael Cochran/Technical Advisor, John N. Seitz/Strategy, Finance Advisor

Directors: James B. Hersch/56/Dir., CEO, Pres.

Owners: Johannes Petersen/40.29%, James B. Hersch/7.78%, Insiders/48.07%, Banque SCS Alliance S.A./8.11%

Financial Data: Fiscal Year End:04/30   Latest Annual Data: 04/30/2007

Year	Sales		Net Income
2007	NA		-$2,012,000
2006	NA		-$51,000
Curr. Assets:	$1,079,000	Curr. Liab.: $200,000	
Plant, Equip.:	$4,000	Total Liab.: $200,000	Indic. Yr. Divd.: NA
Total Assets:	$4,013,000	Net Worth: $3,813,000	Debt/ Equity: NA

CenturyTel Inc

100 CenturyTel Dr., Monroe, LA, 71203; **PH:** 1-318-388-9000; **Fax:** 1-318-388-9064; http:// www.centurytel.com

General - Incorporation	LA	Stock - Price on:12/24/2007	$49.21
Employees	6,400	Stock Exchange	NYSE
Auditor	KPMG LLP	Ticker Symbol	CTL
Stk Agt.	Computershare Investor Services LLC	Outstanding Shares	109,520,000
Counsel	NA	E.P.S.	$3.29
DUNS No.	11-744-4844	Shareholders	NA

Business: The groups principle activity is to provide local exchange, long distance, Internet access and broadband services. In the year 2007, the group acquired Madison River Communications Corp. The group operates from United States.

Primary SIC and add'l.: 4813 4812

CIK No: 0000018926

Subsidiaries: Actel, LLC, Century Business Communications, LLC, CenturyTel Acquisition, LLC, CenturyTel Arkansas Holdings, Inc., CenturyTel Fiber Company II, LLC, CenturyTel Holdings Missouri, Inc., CenturyTel Holdings, Inc., CenturyTel Internet Services, LLC, CenturyTel Investments of Texas, Inc., CenturyTel Investments, LLC, CenturyTel Long Distance, Inc., CenturyTel Midwest - Michigan, Inc., CenturyTel of Adamsville, Inc., CenturyTel of Alabama, LLC, CenturyTel of Arkansas, Inc. 78 Subsidiaries included in the Index

Officers: Glen F. Post/Chmn., CEO/$5,479,228.00, Stacey W. Goff/Sr. VP, General Counsel, Sec./$1,195,042.00, Annmarie Sartor/Mgr. - Communications, Marketing, Tony Davis/VP - Investor Relations, Karen Puckett/COO, Pres./$2,173,736.00, Stewart R. Ewing/CFO, Exec. VP/$2,535,267.00, David D. Cole/Sr. VP - Operations Support/$1,343,709.00, Mike Maslowski/CIO, Sr. VP/$1,396,340.00

Directors: Glen F. Post/Chmn., CEO, Fred R. Nichols/61/Dir., Harvey P. Perry/63/Dir., Jim D. Reppond/66/Dir., Joseph R. Zimmel/54/Dir., William R. Boles/51/Dir., Bruce W. Hanks/53/Dir., C. G. Melville/67/Dir., Virginia Boulet/54/Dir., Calvin Czeschin/72/Dir., James B. Gardner/73/Dir., Gregory J. McCray/45/Dir.

Owners: Jim D. Reppond, Fred R. Nichols, William R. Boles, Karen A. Puckett, Harvey P. Perry, Virginia Boulet, LSV Asset Management/5.40%, David D. Cole, C. G. Melville, Insiders, Michael E. Maslowski, Gregory J. McCray, Stacey W. Goff, Joseph R. Zimmel, Glen F. Post (23 Owners included in Index)

Financial Data: Fiscal Year End:12/31   Latest Annual Data: 12/31/2006

Year	Sales		Net Income
2006	$2,447,730,000		$370,027,000
2005	$2,479,252,000		$334,479,000
2004	$2,407,372,000		$337,244,000
Curr. Assets:	$290,117,000	Curr. Liab.: $617,565,000	
Plant, Equip.:	$3,109,277,000	Total Liab.: $4,240,830,000	Indic. Yr. Divd.: $0.260
Total Assets:	$7,441,007,000	Net Worth: $3,190,951,000	Debt/ Equity: 0.9326

Cenveo Inc

1 Canterbury Green, 201 Broad St., Stamford, CT, 06901; **PH:** 1-203-595-3000; **Fax:** 1-203-595-3070; http:// www.cenveo.com; **Email:** info@cenveo.com

General - Incorporation	CO	Stock - Price on:12/24/2007	$24.63
Employees	6,600	Stock Exchange	NYSE
Auditor	Ernst & Young LLP	Ticker Symbol	CVO
Stk Agt	Computershare Trust CO.	Outstanding Shares	53,690,000
Counsel	NA	E.P.S.	$0.97
DUNS No.	00-705-9488	Shareholders	NA

Business: The group's principal activities are printing and printing related products and value added services. The group operates in two segments: commercial printing and resale. Commercial printing segment operates 66 manufacturing facilities and specializes in the printing of annual reports, car brochures, brand marketing collateral, financial communications, general commercial printing and the manufacture and printing of customized envelopes for billing and remittance and direct mail advertising. Resale business segment operates 20 manufacturing facilities and produces business forms and labels, custom and stock envelopes and specialty packaging and mailers generally sold to third-party dealers such as print distributors, forms suppliers and office-products retail chains.

Primary SIC and add'l.: 2759 2754 2677 5112

CIK No: 0000920321

Subsidiaries: Cenveo Alberta Finance LP, Cenveo Canada Leasing Company Inc., Cenveo Commercial Ohio, LLC, Cenveo Corporation, Cenveo Government Printing, Inc., Cenveo International Holdings, Inc., Cenveo McLaren Morris & Todd Company, Cenveo Resale Ohio, LLC, Cenveo Services, LLC, Cenveo Texas Finance, LP, Cenveo West, Inc., Colorhouse China, Inc., Discount Labels, Inc., Graphic Arts Center de Mexico, Innova Envelope Inc. Enveloppe Innova Inc. 19 Subsidiaries included in the Index

Officers: Robert G. Burton/Chmn., CEO/$6,983,443.00, Thomas W. Oliva/Vice Chmn., Pres., Timothy M. Davis/53/Sr. VP, General Counsel, Sec./$896,392.00, Mark S. Hiltwein/CFO, Exec. VP, Sean S. Sullivan/Pres. - Commercial, Packaging/$1,599,299.00

Directors: Robert G. Burton/Chmn., CEO, Thomas W. Oliva/Vice Chmn., Pres., Robert Obernier/Dir., Patrice M. Daniels/Dir., Leonard C. Green/Dir., Mark J. Griffin/Dir., Robert T. Kittel/Dir.

Owners: Timothy M. Davis, Mark J. Griffin, Ronald Gutfleish/7.80%, Robert G. Burton/6.50%, FMR Corp./12.00%, Robert T. Kittel, Thomas W. Oliva, Robert B. Obernier, Leonard C. Green/1.40%, Patrice M. Daniels, Insiders/9.00%, Harry R. Vinson, Sean S. Sullivan

Financial Data: Fiscal Year End:12/31   Latest Annual Data: 12/31/2006

Year	Sales		Net Income
2006	$1,511,224,000		$118,655,000
2005	$1,749,381,000		-$135,052,000
2004	$1,742,914,000		-$19,708,000
Curr. Assets:	$426,441,000	Curr. Liab.: $227,431,000	P/E Ratio: 21.80
Plant, Equip.:	$251,103,000	Total Liab.: $940,209,000	Indic. Yr. Divd.: NA
Total Assets:	$1,001,950,000	Net Worth: $61,741,000	Debt/ Equity:10.8158

Cephalon Inc

41 Moores Rd., Frazer, PA, 19355; **PH:** 1-610-344-0200; **Fax:** 1-610-738-6590; http:// www.cephalon.com; **Email:** corporatecommunications@cephalon.com

General - Incorporation	DE	Stock - Price on:12/24/2007	$80.04
Employees	2,895	Stock Exchange	NDQ
Auditor	PricewaterhouseCoopers LLP	Ticker Symbol	CEPH
Stk Agt	American Stock Transfer & Trust CO.	Outstanding Shares	66,210,000
Counsel	Morgan, Lewis & Bockius LLP	E.P.S.	$2.18
DUNS No.	18-323-6314	Shareholders	NA

Business: The groups principle activities include developing and marketing products to treat human diseases. The groups products include medications to treat and manage neurological diseases, sleep disorders, cancer, pain and addiction. The group operates from United States.

Primary SIC and add'l.: 8731 2834

CIK No: 0000873364

Subsidiaries: Anesta AG, Anesta Corp., Anesta UK Limited, Cell Therapeutics (UK) Limited, Cephalon (Bermuda) Limited, Cephalon (UK) Limited, Cephalon Development Corporation, Cephalon Financiere Luxembourg S.a.r.l., Cephalon France Holdings SAS, Cephalon France SAS, Cephalon GmbH, Cephalon International Holdings, Inc., Cephalon Investments, Inc., Cephalon Luxembourg S.a.r.l, Cephalon Technologies Partners, Inc. 35 Subsidiaries included in the Index

Officers: Frank Baldino/Chmn., CEO/$11,533,620.00, Jeffry L. Vaught/Exec. VP - Research, Development/$2,595,831.00, Peter E. Grebow/Exec. VP - Worldwide Technical Operations/$2,650,482.00, Carl A. Savini/Exec. VP, Chief Administrative Officer, Robert P. Roche/Exec. VP - Worldwide Pharmaceutical Operations/$2,785,609.00, Kevin J. Buchi/CFO, Exec. VP/$2,716,372.00, John E. Osborn/Exec. VP, General Counsel, Sec., Lesley Russell/Exec. VP - Worldwide Medical, Regulatory Operations, Sheryl L. Williams/VP - Public Affairs, Candace Steele/Sr. Dir. - Product Communications, Jenifer Antonacci/Assoc. Dir. - Product Communications, Stacey Beckhardt/Assoc. Dir. - Product Communications, Karen Boyce McCollum/Sr. Mgr. - Product Communications

Directors: Frank Baldino/Chmn., CEO, William P. Egan/Dir., Vaughn M. Kailian/Dir., Gail R. Wilensky/Dir., Martyn D. Greenacre/Dir., Kevin E. Moley/Dir., Charles A. Sanders/Dir., Dennis L. Winger/Dir.

Owners: Vaughn M. Kailian, Goldman Sachs Asset Management, L.P./7.40%, Charles A. Sanders, William P. Egan, Dennis L. Winger, T. Rowe Price Associates, Inc./13.80%, Wellington Management Company, LLP/13.70%, Gail R. Wilensky, Frank Baldino/1.77%, FMR Corp./12.50%, Jeffry L. Vaught, Robert P. Roche, Insiders/3.50%, Capital Research and Management Company/5.60%, Kevin J. Buchi *(20 Owners included in Index)*

Financial Data: *Fiscal Year End:* 12/31 *Latest Annual Data:* 12/31/2006

Year	Sales	Net Income
2006	$1,764,069,000	$144,816,000
2005	$1,211,892,000	-$174,954,000
2004	$1,015,425,000	-$73,813,000

Curr. Assets:	$1,197,865,000	**Curr. Liab.:**	$1,377,376,000	**P/E Ratio:**	36.72
Plant, Equip.:	$453,010,000	**Total Liab.:**	$1,736,037,000	**Indic. Yr. Divd.:**	NA
Total Assets:	$3,045,497,000	**Net Worth:**	$1,309,460,000	**Debt/ Equity:**	0.1585

Cepheid

904 Caribbean Dr., Sunnyvale, CA, 94089; ***PH:*** 1-408-541-4191; ***Fax:*** 1-408-541-4192; ***http://*** www.cepheid.com

General - Incorporation	CA	**Stock** - Price on:12/24/2007	$13.16
Employees	307	Stock Exchange	NDQ
Auditor	Ernst & Young LLP	Ticker Symbol	CPHD
Stk Agt	Computershare Investor Services LLC	Outstanding Shares	55,090,000
Counsel	Fenwick & West LLP	E.P.S	NA
DUNS No.	NA	Shareholders	NA

Business: The group's principal activities are to develop, manufacture and market fully integrated systems that enable sophisticated genetic and dna analysis of patients and organisms. These systems help in analyzing complex biological samples in disposable cartridges designed to perform rapidly and automatically sophisticated molecular biological procedures. Other functions include automated purification of dna, screening for disease-causing agents, rapid detection of food and water contaminants and generic profiling. The group's products include smart cycler (R), a dna amplification and detection system and the genexpert(R) system, that combines sample preparation with the amplification and detection functions of the smart cycler. The major customers of the group are academic/universities, government and biotechnology/pharmaceutical companies.

Primary SIC and add'l.: 8731 8734 3826

CIK No: 0001037760

Subsidiaries: Cepheid SA

Officers: John L. Bishop/Dir., CEO/$1,213,062.00, Peter J. Dailey/VP - Research, Development, Joseph H. Smith/Sr. VP - Legal, Bussiness Development, General Counsel, Sec./$623,359.00, Sandra Finley/VP - Marketing, Russel K. Enns/Sr. VP - Regulatory Affairs, Quality System, Clinical Affairs, Medical Reimbursement, John R. Sluis/Sr. VP - Finance, CFO/$597,235.00, Lee Christel/VP - Research, System Integration, Emily S. Winn-Deen/VP - Strategic Planning, Business Development, Kerry Flom/VP - Clinical Affairs, Laurie King/VP - Human Resources, David H. Persing/Dir., Exec. VP, Chief Medical, Technology Officer/$891,533.00, Rick Fletcher/VP - Regulatory Compliance, Quality Systems, Michael Myhre/VP, Corporate Controller, Vincent M. Powers/VP - Intellectual Property, Jan Steuperaert/VP - Information Technology *(18 Officers included in Index)*

Directors: John L. Bishop/Dir., CEO, Thomas L. Gutshall/Chmn., Co - Founder, Mitchell D. Mroz/Dir., Hollings C. Renton/Dir., Cristina H. Kepner/Dir., Thomas D. Brown/Dir., Robert J. Easton/Dir., David H. Persing/Dir., Exec. VP, Chief Medical, Technology Officer, Dean Morton/Dir.

Owners: Robert J. Easton, Platinum Asset Management Limited/6.40%, Thomas L. Gutshall/2.27%, Robert J. Koska, Thomas D. Brown, John L. Bishop/1.72%, Hollings C. Renton, Dean O. Morton, Alliance Financial/13.70%, Mitchell Mroz, Cristina H. Kepner, David Persing, Joseph H. Smith, Insiders/6.91%, John R. Sluis *(16 Owners included in Index)*

CepTor Corp

200 Intrntl Cir, Hunt Valley, MD, 21030; ***PH:*** 1-410-527-9998; ***http://*** www.ceptorcorp.com

General - Incorporation	DE	**Stock** - Price on:12/24/2007	$0.0667
Employees	NA	Stock Exchange	OTC
Auditor	Bernstein & Pinchuk, LLP	Ticker Symbol	CEPO
Stk Agt	American Stock Transfer & Trust Co.	Outstanding Shares	15,550,000
Counsel	NA	E.P.S	$0.522
DUNS No.	NA	Shareholders	NA

Business: The groups principal activity is to develop proprietary and cell-targeted therapeutic products for the treatment of neuromuscular and neurodegenerative diseases.The groups product is Myodur. The group operates from the United States.

Primary SIC and add'l.: 8731

CIK No: 0001231472

Officers: Howard Becker/49/Dir., CEO

Directors: Howard Becker/49/Dir., CEO, Tony Coelho/65/Dir.

Owners: William H. Pursley, Ellis International Ltd., Tony Coelho, Alpha Capital Aktiengesellschaft, Len Mudry, Lawrence Zalk, Double U Master Fund, L.P., George Karfunkel, SCG Capital, LLC, Intellect Neurosciences, Inc., The Longview Fund, LP, Brio Capital, L.P., Harbor Trust, Marge Chassman, Trustee, Whalehaven Cap Fund, Joseph Giamanco *(21 Owners included in Index)*

Financial Data: *Fiscal Year End:* 12/31 *Latest Annual Data:* 12/31/2006

Year	Sales	Net Income
2006	NA	-$8,162,000
2005	NA	-$13,268,000
2004	NA	-$14,548,000

Curr. Assets:	$25,000	**Curr. Liab.:**	$14,870,000		
Plant, Equip.:	$36,000	**Total Liab.:**	$14,870,000	**Indic. Yr. Divd.:**	NA
Total Assets:	$1,249,000	**Net Worth:**	-$13,622,000	**Debt/ Equity:**	NA

Ceradyne Inc

3169 Red Hill Ave., Costa Mesa, CA, 92626; ***PH:*** 1-714-549-0421; ***Fax:*** 1-714-549-5787; ***http://*** www.ceradyne.com

General - Incorporation	DE	**Stock** - Price on:12/24/2007	$74.72
Employees	2,205	Stock Exchange	NDQ
Auditor	PricewaterhouseCoopers LLP	Ticker Symbol	CRDN
Stk Agt	American Stock Transfer & Trust Co.	Outstanding Shares	27,190,000
Counsel	Stradling Yocca Carlson & Rauth	E.P.S	$5.31
DUNS No.	05-079-1177	Shareholders	NA

Business: The group's principal activity is to develop, manufacture and market advanced technical ceramic products for defense, industrial, consumer, microwave communications and automotive applications. Its trademarks include ceralloy(R), ceradyne(R) and CD(r). The group operates in three segments each of which has its own manufacturing facilities & administration functions. Advanced technical ceramics can withstand high temperatures and have a high electrical insulation capability. It operates through three divisions: advanced ceramic operations produces armor and orthodontic products and components for semiconductor equipment; semicon associates conducts cathode development and production; thermo materials division produces fused silica products, including missile radomes. The products are sold to contractors and original equipment manufacturers. On 15-May-2004, the group acquired quest technology lp. On 26-Aug-2004, the group acquired esk ceramics gmbh & co.

Primary SIC and add'l.: 3259 3251

CIK No: 0000018937

Subsidiaries: ESK Ceramics

Officers: Joel P. Moskowitz/Chmn., CEO, Pres./$1,270,160.00, Jerrold J. Pellizzon/CFO, Corp. Sec./$712,536.00, Marc King/VP - Armor Operations, Michael Kraft/VP - Nuclear, Semiconductor Business Units/$602,212.00, David P. Reed/VP, Pres. - North American Operations/$727,397.00, Bruce Lockhart/VP, Pres. - Ceradyne Thermo Materials Division, Jeff Waldal/VP, Pres. - Ceradyne Semicon Associates Division, Eagle Hsieh/Representative, Kenneth R. Morris/VP - Operations, Arrigo Borin/Representative, Michael Doring/Representative, Bill Greim/Representative, Michael Staub/Representative, Murray Sheer/Representative, Moti Raviv/Representative *(19 Officers included in Index)*

Directors: Joel P. Moskowitz/Chmn., CEO, Pres., Milton L. Lohr/Dir., Richard A. Alliegro/Dir., Richard A. Kertson/Dir., Frank Edelstein/Dir., William C. Lacourse/Dir.

Owners: Jerrold J. Pellizzon, Insiders/6.70%, Barclays Global Investors, NA/5.40%, Munder Capital Management/6.20%, Richard A. Kertson, Richard A. Alliegro, Joel P. Moskowitz/6.50%, Frank Edelstein, Michael A. Kraft, Milton L. Lohr, David P. Reed

Financial Data: *Fiscal Year End:* 12/31 *Latest Annual Data:* 12/31/2006

Year	Sales	Net Income
2006	$662,888,000	$128,404,000
2005	$368,253,000	$46,778,000
2004	$215,612,000	$27,573,000

Curr. Assets:	$401,975,000	**Curr. Liab.:**	$69,912,000	**P/E Ratio:**	14.42
Plant, Equip.:	$183,011,000	**Total Liab.:**	$207,204,000	**Indic. Yr. Divd.:**	NA
Total Assets:	$613,815,000	**Net Worth:**	$406,611,000	**Debt/ Equity:**	0.2697

Ceragenix Pharmaceuticals Inc

Formerly: Onsource Corp

1444 Wazee St., Ste. 210, Denver, CO, 80202; ***PH:*** 1-720-946-6440

General - Incorporation	DE	**Stock** - Price on:12/24/2007	$1.65
Employees	5	Stock Exchange	NA
Auditor	Ghp Horwath, P.C	Ticker Symbol	NA
Stk Agt	Corporate Stock Transfer, Inc.	Outstanding Shares	16,330,000
Counsel	NA	E.P.S	-$0.03
DUNS No.	NA	Shareholders	NA

Business: The groups principle activities include discovering, developing and commercializing pharmaceuticals products. The groups products used for infectious disease and dermatology. The group also provides technologies include Barrier Repair Technology and Ceragenins(TM). The group operates from United States.

Primary SIC and add'l.: NA

CIK No: 0001180743

Subsidiaries: Alaska Bingo Supply, Inc., Global Alaska Industries, Inc.

Officers: Steven S. Porter/Chmn., CEO, Jeffrey Sperber/CFO, Peter Elias/Chief Scientific Officer, Carl Genberg/Sr. VP - Research, Development, Russell L. Allen/VP - Corporate Development

Directors: Steven S. Porter/Chmn., CEO, Henry F. Chambers/Member - Scientific Advisory Board, Tomas Ganz/Member - Scientific Advisory Board, Richard Gallo/Member - Scientific Advisory Board, Michel Darnaud/Dir., Cheryl A. Hoffman-Bray/Dir., Philippe J.C. Gastone/Dir., Alberto J. Bautista/Dir., Sean P. Gorman/Member - Scientific Advisory Board, Donald Y.M. Leung/Member - Scientific Advisory Board

Owners: Steven S. Porter/5.70%, Philippe J.C. Gastone, Russell Allen/1.20%, Cheryl A. Hoffman Bray, Carl Genberg/3.40%, Insiders/75.40%, Jeffrey S. Sperber/2.50%, Peter Elias/1.00%, Osmotics Corporation/7.20%, Michel Darnaud, Alberto J. Bautista

Financial Data: *Fiscal Year End:* 12/31 *Latest Annual Data:* 12/31/2006

Year	Sales	Net Income
2006	NA	-$4,551,000
2005	NA	-$12,575,000
2004	$2,300,000	$90,000

Curr. Assets:	$587,000	**Curr. Liab.:**	$761,000		
Plant, Equip.:	$81,000	**Total Liab.:**	$2,333,000	**Indic. Yr. Divd.:**	NA
Total Assets:	$667,000	**Net Worth:**	-$1,665,000	**Debt/ Equity:**	NA

Ceragon Networks Ltd

10 Forest Ave., Paramus, NJ, 07652; ***PH:*** 1-201-845-6955; ***Fax:*** 1-201-845-5665; ***http://*** www.ceragon.com; ***Email:*** info@ceragon.com

General - Incorporation	Israel	Stock - Price on:12/24/2007	$10.48
Employees	276	Stock Exchange	NDQ
Auditor	Kost Forer Gabbay & Kasierer	Ticker Symbol	CRNT
Stk Agt	American Stock Transfer & Trust Co.	Outstanding Shares	27,600,000
Counsel	Michael S. Cohen Esq. Nixon Peabody	E.P.S.	$0.02
DUNS No.	NA	Shareholders	NA

Business: The group's principle activities are to design, develop, manufacture and market high-capacity wireless network equipment for cellular operators, communications service providers and enterprises. Its products provide high-speed, fiber-like transmission quality and can be deployed more rapidly and cost effectively than fiber optic lines. These products operate over most of the 7-38 gigahertz (ghz) high-frequency bands, which are licensed by various countries in North America, Europe, the Middle East, Africa, Latin America and the Asia-pacific region. The group markets the products through a direct sales force, systems integrators, original equipment manufacturers, distributors and value-added resellers. To date, the group's products have been commercially deployed in more than 35 countries by communications service providers, including local telephone companies and cellular telephone service providers and large corporate organizations. The group's quarterly revenue for September 2007 was 44.47 millions of USD.

Primary SIC and add'l.: 3661

CIK No: 0001119769

Subsidiaries: BowSteel Corporation, BowSteel of Texas Corporation, Claro Precision, Inc., Earthline Technologies, Inc., Etca G.p., LLC, Etca L.p., Inc., Extrusion Technology Corporation of America, Galt Alloys, Inc., NATI Gas Company

Officers: Ira Palti/CEO, Pres., Naftali Idan/56/CFO, Exec. VP, Norman Kotler/General Counsel, Corp. Sec., Eyal Assa/VP - Business Development, OEM Relations, Paul Obert/Pres. - Ceragon Networks, Inc, US, Uzi Sharabi/VP - Finance, Aviv Ronai/Chief Marketing Officer, Varda Lubling/VP - Operations, Giuseppe Curreri/VP - Customer Service, Ceragon Networks, Inc, Bentzi Laor/VP - EMEA, Simon Altman/VP - Marketing, Sales Vertical Markets, Sharon Ganot/VP - Human Resources, Udi Gordon/VP - Research, Development, Shlomo Tenenberg/Exec. VP - Worldwide Marketing, Sales, Tali Idan/CFO, Exec. VP *(18 Officers included in Index)*

Directors: Zohar Zisapel/59/Chmn., Joseph Atsmon/59/Dir., Yair E. Orgler/68/Dir., Avi Patir/59/Dir., Yael Langer/43/Dir.

Owners: Yehuda Zisapel/10.20%, HarbourVest International Private Equity Partners III Direct Fund, L.P./5.10%, Zohar Zisapel/12.10%

Financial Data: **Fiscal Year End:**12/31 **Latest Annual Data:** 12/31/2006

Year	Sales	Net Income
2006	$108,415,000	-$5,460,000
2005	$73,777,000	-$3,827,000
2004	$54,831,000	$1,614,000

Curr. Assets:	$83,781,000	**Curr. Liab.:**	$36,513,000	**P/E Ratio:**	61.08
Plant, Equip.:	$2,660,000	**Total Liab.:**	$48,790,000	**Indic. Yr. Divd.:**	NA
Total Assets:	$96,351,000	**Net Worth:**	$47,561,000	**Debt/ Equity:**	NA

Cereplast Inc

3421 W El Segundo Blvd, Hawthorne, CA, 90250; ***PH:*** 1-310-676-5000; ***http://*** www.cereplast.com; ***Email:*** info@cereplast.com

General - Incorporation	NV	Stock - Price on:12/24/2007	$0.51
Employees	22	Stock Exchange	OTC
Auditor	HJ Associates & Consultants, LLP	Ticker Symbol	CERP
Stk Agt	Computershare Investor Services	Outstanding Shares	215,990,000
Counsel	NA	E.P.S.	-$0.03
DUNS No.	NA	Shareholders	NA

Business: The groups principal activity is to develop breakthrough technology to produce proprietary bio-based resins. The group products include bowls, plates and utensils. The group operates from the United States.

Primary SIC and add'l.: 2821

CIK No: 0001324759

Officers: Frederic Scheer/Founder, Chmn., CEO, Pres., Principal Financial, Accounting Officer, William Kelly/Sr. VP - Technology, Stephan Garden/Sr. Exec. VP - Finance, Robert Dobbs/39/VP - QSR Sales, Michael Muchin/VP - Sales, Shriram Bagrodia/Sr. VP - Research & Development Blends and Chemistry, Alec Pettigrew/Sr. VP - International Sales, Asia, Europe

Directors: Frederic Scheer/Founder, Chmn., CEO, Pres., Principal Financial, Accounting Officer, Brian Altounian/Dir., Raylan Jensen/66/Dir., Petros G. Kitsos/Dir.

Owners: Stephan Garden, Raylan Jensen, Brian Altounian, Robert L. Dobbs, Insiders/46.10%, Frederic Scheer/44.00%, Michael Muchin, William Kelly

Financial Data: **Fiscal Year End:**12/31 **Latest Annual Data:** 12/31/2006

Year	Sales	Net Income
2006	$726,000	-$3,384,000
2005	$543,000	-$1,119,000

Curr. Assets:	$1,362,000	**Curr. Liab.:**	$1,552,000		
Plant, Equip.:	$1,201,000	**Total Liab.:**	$1,678,000	**Indic. Yr. Divd.:**	NA
Total Assets:	$2,614,000	**Net Worth:**	$936,000	**Debt/ Equity:**	NA

Ceridian Corp

3311 E Old Shakopee Rd., Minneapolis, MN, 55425; ***PH:*** 1-952-853-8100; ***Fax:*** 1-952-853-4430; ***http://*** www.ceridian.com; ***Email:*** information@corporate.ceridian.com

General - Incorporation	DE	Stock - Price on:12/24/2007	$35.58
Employees	8,986	Stock Exchange	NYSE
Auditor	KPMG LLP	Ticker Symbol	CEN
Stk Agt	Bank of New York	Outstanding Shares	143,400,000
Counsel	NA	E.P.S.	$1.259
DUNS No.	NA	Shareholders	NA

Business: The group's principle activities are to provide human resource solutions to employers and transaction processing and related services. The group operates through two segment human resource solutions and comdata. Human resource solutions provide software designed to help employers manage their work forces and information. These products and services include transaction-oriented administrative services, software products, payroll processing, tax filing and enrollment and also provides management support software, human resource administration, regulatory compliance and work-life effectiveness and employee assistance programs. Comdata provides transaction processing and decision support services to the transportation industry, including assistance in obtaining regulatory permits and other services. The group's operations are carried out in the United States, the United Kingdom and Canada.

Primary SIC and add'l.: 8742 7375 7374 7372

CIK No: 0001124887

Subsidiaries: ABR Information Services, Inc., ABR Properties, Inc., Centrefile APS Limited, Ceridian (Mauritius) Ltd., Ceridian Benefits Services, Inc., Ceridian Broker-Dealer, Inc., Ceridian Canada Holdings, Inc., Ceridian Canada Ltd., Ceridian Centrefile Limited, Ceridian Holdings U.K. Limited, Ceridian Limited, Ceridian Performance Partners Limited, Ceridian Recruiting Solutions, Inc., Ceridian Retirement Plan Services, Inc., Ceridian Tax Service, Inc. 28 Subsidiaries included in the Index

Officers: Kathryn V. Marinello/Dir., CEO, Pres., Jim Burns/Exec. VP, Pres. - Ceridian International, Gary M. Nelson/Exec. VP, Chief Administrative Officer, General Counsel, Corp. Sec., Randy W. Strobel/VP - Finance, Controller, Chief Accounting Officer, Gregory J. MacFarlane/CFO, Exec. VP, Perry H. Cliburn/CTO, Exec. VP, Michael F. Shea/Exec. VP - Service Operations, Quality, Kairus K. Tarapore/Exec. VP - Human Resources, Davis Klaila/Sr. Dir. - Strategy, Research

Directors: Kathryn V. Marinello/Dir., CEO, Pres., Gregory A. Pratt/Dir., Richard Szafranski/Dir., George R. Lewis/Dir., White L. Matthews/Dir., William L. Trubeck/Dir., Alan F. White/Dir., John D. Barfitt/Dir., Paul C. Hilal/Dir., Ronald T. Lemay/Dir., Robert J. Levenson/Dir.

Owners: Robert J. Severson, Nicholas D. Chabraja, Pershing Square Capital Management, LP/14.87%, Alan F. White, Douglas C. Neve, Insiders, Gary A. Krow, George R. Lewis, L. White Matthews, Kathryn V. Marinell, William L. Trubeck, Janus Capital Management LLC/9.83%, Michael A. Roth/5.15%, Ronald T. LeMay, Richard Szafranski *(16 Owners included in Index)*

Financial Data: **Fiscal Year End:**12/31 **Latest Annual Data:** 12/31/2006

Year	Sales	Net Income
2006	$1,565,100,000	$173,600,000
2005	$1,459,000,000	$127,900,000
2004	$1,320,400,000	$36,900,000

Curr. Assets:	$1,108,200,000	**Curr. Liab.:**	$721,500,000		
Plant, Equip.:	$110,300,000	**Total Liab.:**	$5,563,200,000	**Indic. Yr. Divd.:**	NA
Total Assets:	$6,934,400,000	**Net Worth:**	$1,371,200,000	**Debt/ Equity:**	3.5938

Cerner Corp

2800 Rockcreek Pkwy., North Kansas City, MO, 64117; ***PH:*** 1-816-221-1024; ***Fax:*** 1-816-474-1742; ***http://*** www.cerner.com; ***Email:*** clientcarecenter@cerner.com

General - Incorporation	DE	Stock - Price on:12/24/2007	$56.28
Employees	7,419	Stock Exchange	NDQ
Auditor	KPMG LLP	Ticker Symbol	CERN
Stk Agt	Computershare Trust CO.	Outstanding Shares	79,130,000
Counsel	Stinson, Mag & Fizzell	E.P.S.	$1.51
DUNS No.	04-241-0688	Shareholders	NA

Business: The group's principal activity is to design, develop, market, install, host and support information technology and content solutions for healthcare organizations and consumers. Cerner(R) solutions give end users secure access to clinical, administrative and financial data in real time. The group's solutions enable healthcare providers to improve operating effectiveness, reduce costs, reduce medical errors, reduce variances and improve quality. The Cerner(R) solutions provide health information and knowledge to care givers, clinicians and consumers. The group's solutions are designed and developed using the Cerner Millennium(TM) architecture, a unified technology infrastructure for combining clinical and management information applications.

Primary SIC and add'l.: 7372 7374

CIK No: 0000804753

Subsidiaries: Cerner (Malaysia) SDN BHD, Cerner Belgium, Inc., Cerner BeyondNow, Inc., Cerner Campus Redevelopment Corporation, Cerner Canada Limited, Cerner Citation, Inc., Cerner Corporation PTY Limited, Cerner Deutschland GmbH, Cerner DHT, Inc., Cerner France SAS, Cerner Health Connections, Inc., Cerner Healthcare Solutions Private Limited, Cerner Iberia, S.L., Cerner Innovation, Inc., Cerner International, Inc. 27 Subsidiaries included in the Index

Officers: Neal L. Patterson/Chmn., Co - Founder, CEO/$3,678,028.00, Marc G. Naughton/Sr. VP, CFO/$793,683.00, Jeffrey A. Townsend/Exec. VP/$1,099,199.00, Amr Mostafa Gad/GM - Middle East, Richard W. Heise/GM - Australia, New Zealand, David Wood/GM - East Asia, Douglas S. McNair/Sr. VP - Knowledge, Discovery, Bryan J. Ince/VP - Knowledge, Discovery, David P. McCallie/VP - Medical Informatics, Rama Nadimpalli/MD - Cerner India, Kelly Lolli/Contact - Sr. Strategist, Industry, Margaret Nelson/Contact - Sr. Strategist, Industry, Kay Hawes/Contact - Corporate, Financial, Kelli Christman/Media Contact - Headquarters, West, Midwest Regions, Lindsay Shannon/Media Contact - National, Northeast Region, Trade Media *(55 Officers included in Index)*

Directors: Neal L. Patterson/Chmn., Co - Founder, CEO, Clifford W. Illig/Co - Founder, Vice Chmn., William D. Zollars/Dir., Gerald E. Bisbee/Dir., Nancy-Ann Deparle/Dir., Michael E. Herman/Dir., William B. Neaves/Dir., John C. Danforth/Dir.

Owners: Nancy-Ann DeParle, John C. Danforth, Michael E. Herman, FMR Corp./14.74%, Marc G. Naughton, Paul M. Black, Clifford W. Illig/6.43%, Earl H. Devanny, Jeff Townsend, Neal L. Patterson/9.14%, Insiders/16.50%, Wellington Management Company, LLP/5.74%, William D. Zollars, The TCW Group, Inc./8.89%, Gerald E. Bisbee *(18 Owners included in Index)*

Financial Data: **Fiscal Year End:**12/30 **Latest Annual Data:** 12/30/2006

Year	Sales	Net Income
2006	$1,378,038,000	$109,891,000
2005	$1,160,785,000	$86,251,000

Curr. Assets:	$651,631,000	**Curr. Liab.:**	$260,090,000		
Plant, Equip.:	$292,608,000	**Total Liab.:**	$541,810,000	**Indic. Yr. Divd.:**	NA
Total Assets:	$1,303,629,000	**Net Worth:**	$760,533,000	**Debt/ Equity:**	0.1931

Cerus Corp

2411 Stanwell Dr., Concord, CA, 94520; ***PH:*** 1-925-288-6000; ***Fax:*** 1-925-288-6001; ***http://*** www.cerus.com; ***Email:*** ir@cerus.com

General - Incorporation	DE	Stock - Price on:12/24/2007	$6.11
Employees	124	Stock Exchange	NDQ
Auditor	Ernst & Young LLP	Ticker Symbol	CERS
Stk Agt	Wells Fargo Shareowner Services	Outstanding Shares	31,800,000
Counsel	Cooley Godward LLP	E.P.S.	-$0.78
DUNS No.	85-899-9485	Shareholders	NA

Business: The group's principle activity is to develop medical systems and therapeutics to provide safer and more effective options to patients. It develops products based on its proprietary helinx(R) technology for controlling biological replication. Its most advanced programs are focused on systems to enhance the safety of the world's blood supply. The intercept blood system inactivates viruses, bacteria, other pathogens and white blood cells. In collaboration with its partner, baxter healthcare corporation, a ce mark has been received for this system. Regulatory submission process to obtain approval in the U.S.

As well as preparations for the U.S. Regulatory submission for the intercept blood system for plasma, which will be followed by a ce mark application for this product, are underway. Phase iii clinical trials for intercept red blood cells are being conducted. Therapeutic applications of helinx technology to treat and prevent serious diseases are being pursued. The group operates from United States.

Primary SIC and add'l.: 3826 2836 8731

CIK No: 0001020214

Officers: Claes Glassell/Dir., CEO, Pres./$1,042,521.00, Lori L. Roll/VP - Administration, Corp. Sec., Laurence M. Corash/Dir., VP, Chief Medical Officer/$610,632.00, William J. Dawson/CFO, VP - Finance/$453,353.00, Howard G. Ervin/VP - Legal Affairs, Thomas W. Dubensky/VP - Vaccine Research, William M. Greenman/Pres. - Cerus Europe/$499,857.00, David N. Cook/Corporate Sr. VP/$576,232.00, Obi Greenman/Pres. - Cerus Europe, Nina Bhardwaj/Member - Immunotherapy Scientific Advisory Board, Myesha Edwards/Contact - Investor Relations

Directors: Claes Glassell/Dir., CEO, Pres., B. J. Cassin/Chmn., Drew Pardoll/Chmn. - Immunotherapy Scientific Advisory Board, Darrell Triulzi/Member - Blood Safety Scientific Advisory Board, Jeffrey McCullough/Member - Blood Safety Scientific Advisory Board, Paul David Mintz/Member - Blood Safety Scientific Advisory Board, Richard Benjamin/Member - Blood Safety Scientific Advisory Board, Laurence M. Corash/Dir., VP, Chief Medical Officer, Timothy B. Anderson/Dir., James P. Aubuchon/Member - Blood Safety Scientific Advisory Board, Morris A. Blajchman/Member - Blood Safety Scientific Advisory Board, Christopher D. Hillyer/Member - Blood Safety Scientific Advisory Board, Paul V. Holland/Member - Blood Safety Scientific Advisory Board, Bruce C. Cozadd/Dir., Elizabeth M. Jaffee/Member - Immunotherapy Scientific Advisory Board *(20 Directors included in Index)*

Owners: Timothy B. Anderson, William M. Greenman, William J. Dawson, B. J. Cassin/2.20%, David M. Knott/6.90%, David N. Cook, Bruce C. Cozadd, Laurence M. Corash/1.90%, T. Rowe Price Associates, Inc./6.20%, William R. Rohn, Insiders/9.20%, AXA Financial, Inc./13.10%, Claes Glassell/1.70%

Financial Data: *Fiscal Year End:*12/31 *Latest Annual Data:* 12/31/2006

Year	Sales	Net Income
2006	$35,580,000	-$4,779,000
2005	$24,371,000	$13,064,000
2004	$13,911,000	-$31,153,000

Curr. Assets:	$102,743,000	**Curr. Liab.:**	$14,814,000		
Plant, Equip.:	$1,627,000	**Total Liab.:**	$14,846,000	**Indic. Yr. Divd.:**	NA
Total Assets:	$115,817,000	**Net Worth:**	$100,971,000	**Debt/ Equity:**	0.0002

CET Services Inc

12503 E Euclid Dr., No. 30, Centennial, CO, 80111; ***PH:*** 1-720-875-9115

General		**Stock**	
Incorporation	CA	Price on:12/24/2007	NA
Employees	4	Stock Exchange	OTC
Auditor	GHP Horwath, P.C	Ticker Symbol	CETR
Stk Agt	U.S. Stock Transfer Corp	Outstanding Shares	NA
Counsel	NA	E.P.S.	-$0.09
DUNS No.	NA	Shareholders	NA

Business: The group's principal activities are to provide environmental consulting, engineering, remediation and related construction activities. It operates in two segments: water/wastewater construction and management and residential housing development and construction. The group has three water/wastewater contracts. The group is engaged in a redevelopment project under an agreement with the city of westminster, Colorado. The project includes the purchase of certain property, the demolition of existing structures, environmental remediation, and construction of 50 new affordable housing units. The group operates in the United States.

Primary SIC and add'l.: 1522 9999 8999

CIK No: 0000944627

Subsidiaries: Community Builders, Inc.

Officers: Steven H. Davis/53/Dir., CEO, Pres., Dale W. Bleck/56/CFO

Directors: Steven H. Davis/53/Dir., CEO, Pres., Craig C. Barto/49/Dir., George Pratt/74/Dir., John D. Hendrick/63/Dir.

Owners: Dale W. Bleck, John D. Hendrick, George Pratt, Ross C. Gordon/6.60%, Ann J. Heckler, Craig C. Barto/12.80%, Steven H. Davis/21.40%, Insiders/35.40%

Financial Data: *Fiscal Year End:*12/31 *Latest Annual Data:* 12/31/2006

Year	Sales	Net Income
2006	$2,981,000	-$339,000
2005	$3,223,000	-$397,000
2004	$4,018,000	-$277,000

Curr. Assets:	$4,657,000	**Curr. Liab.:**	$166,000		
Plant, Equip.:	$3,000	**Total Liab.:**	$1,575,000	**Indic. Yr. Divd.:**	NA
Total Assets:	$4,943,000	**Net Worth:**	$3,367,000	**Debt/ Equity:**	NA

Ceva Inc

2033 Gateway Pl., Ste. 150, San Jose, CA, 95110; ***PH:*** 1-408-514-2900; ***Fax:*** 1-408-514-2995; ***http://*** www.ceva-dsp.com; ***Email:*** info@ceva-dsp.com

General		**Stock**	
Incorporation	DE	Price on:12/24/2007	$8.52
Employees	196	Stock Exchange	NDQ
Auditor	Kost Forer Gabbay & Kasierer	Ticker Symbol	CEVA
Stk Agt	American Stock Transfer & Trust Co.	Outstanding Shares	19,480,000
Counsel	NA	E.P.S.	$0.04
DUNS No.	NA	Shareholders	NA

Business: The group's principal activities are to develop and license designs for programmable digital signal processor cores. A programmable dsp core is a special purpose, software-controlled processor that, through complex mathematical calculations, analyzes, manipulates and enhances voice, audio and video signals. The programmable dsp cores that the group designs are used as the central processor in semiconductor chips made for specific applications. These chips are used in a wide variety of electronic devices, including digital cellular telephones, modems, hard disk drives, mp3 players and digital cameras, and are critical to the performance of the electronic products in which they are used. The group licenses its software to semiconductor companies throughout the world. These semiconductor companies then manufacture, market and sell custom-designed chips to system original equipment manufacturers of a variety of electronic products.

Primary SIC and add'l.: NA

CIK No: 0001173489

Subsidiaries: Ceva (uk) Limited, CEVA Communications Limited, Ceva D.s.p. Limited, CEVA Design Limited, CEVA Development, Inc., Ceva Dsp Technologies LLC, CEVA Holdings B.V., CEVA Inc., CEVA Ireland Limited, CEVA Limited, CEVA Research Limited, CEVA SARL, CEVA Services Limited, CEVA Software Limited, CEVA Systems LLC 18 Subsidiaries included in the Index

Officers: Gideon Wertheizer/CEO/$387,127.00, Yaniv Arieli/CFO/$252,478.00, Issachar Ohana/Exec. VP - World Wide Sales/$415,092.00, Erez Bar-Niv/CTO

Directors: Peter McManamon/Chmn., Eliyahu Ayalon/Dir., Bruce A. Mann/Dir., Dan Tocatly/Dir., Zvi Limon/49/Dir., Louis Silver/54/Dir., Sven-Christer Nilsson/Dir.

Owners: Peninsula Capital Management, LP/5.78%, Louis Silver, Zvi Limon, Brian Long/8.23%, Dimensional Fund Advisors LP/5.15%, Dan Tocatly, Bruce A. Mann, Eliyahu Ayalon/2.78%, Insiders/10.29%, Peter McManamon/2.54%, Ollaberry Limited/7.82%, Sven-Christer Nilsson/1.22%, Issachar Ohana, Yaniv Arieli, Austin W. Marxe and David M. Greenhouse/12.44% *(17 Owners included in Index)*

Financial Data: *Fiscal Year End:*03/31 *Latest Annual Data:* 12/31/2006

Year	Sales	Net Income
2006	$32,505,000	-$98,000
2005	$35,636,000	-$2,266,000
2004	$37,673,000	$1,650,000

Curr. Assets:	$75,722,000	**Curr. Liab.:**	$10,721,000	**P/E Ratio:**	213.00
Plant, Equip.:	$1,706,000	**Total Liab.:**	$14,937,000	**Indic. Yr. Divd.:**	NA
Total Assets:	$121,080,000	**Net Worth:**	$106,143,000	**Debt/ Equity:**	NA

CEZ

Duhova 2/1444, 140 53 Praha 4, Prague; ***PH:*** 420-211041111; ***http://*** www.cez.cz; ***Email:*** cez@cez.cz

General		**Stock**	
Incorporation	Czech Republic	Price on:12/24/2007	NA
Employees	NA	Stock Exchange	NA
Auditor	Ernst & Young LLP	Ticker Symbol	NA
Stk Agt	CT Corporation System	Outstanding Shares	NA
Counsel	NA	E.P.S.	NA
DUNS No.	64-408-0376	Shareholders	NA

Business: The group's principle activity is to involved in generation, purchase and sale of electricity in domestic and export markets. The company's secondary activities are the supply of thermal energy, as well as trading in by-products of electricity and heat generation processes. In Sept 2001, the group launched a new marketing strategy offering seven types of electricity supply. The company has 10 fossil power plants, 13 hydro power plants, 1 nuclear power plants, 1 wind power plants and one solar power plant.

Primary SIC and add'l.: 4911 4961 2819

CIK No: 0001041841

Subsidiaries: Cez Finance B.v., CEZ Logistika, s.r.o., CEZ Sprava majetku, s.r.o.(2), CEZ Zakaznicke sluzby, s.r.o., CEZData, s.r.o., CEZnet, a.s., EN-DATA a.s., Energeticke opravny, a.s., Energetika Vitkovice, a.s., ePRIM, a.s., Hydrocez, A.s., I & C Energo a.s., MSEM, a.s., Prvni energeticka a.s., rpg Energiehandel GmbH 26 Subsidiaries included in the Index

Officers: Martin Roman/39/Chmn., CEO, Jiri Borovec/44/Vice Chmn., Chief Production Officer, Daniel Bene/38/Vice Chmn., COO, Alan Svoboda/36/Chief Sales Officer, Tomas Pleskac/42/Dir., Chief Distribution Officer, Zdenek Pasak/Dir., Chief Personnel Officer, Petr Voboril/58/CFO, Ivan Lapin/43/Chief Administration Officer

Directors: Martin Roman/39/Chmn., CEO, Jiri Borovec/44/Vice Chmn., Chief Production Officer, Daniel Bene/38/Vice Chmn., COO, Martin Kocourek/Chmn. - Supervisory Board, Tomas Huner/49/Vice Chmn. - Supervisory Board, Josef Janecek/56/Member - Supervisory Board, Ivan Fuksa/45/Member - Supervisory Board, Petr Kala/68/Member - Supervisory Board, Zdenek Trojan/72/Member - Supervisory Board, Tomas Pleskac/42/Dir., Chief Distribution Officer, Zdenek Pasak/Dir., Chief Personnel Officer, Zdenek Hruby/52/Member - Supervisory Board, Drahoslav Simek/55/Member - Supervisory Board, Jiri Jedlicka/49/Member - Supervisory Board, Jan Sevr/61/Member - Supervisory Board *(16 Directors included in Index)*

CF Industries Holdings Inc

4 Pkwy. N, Ste. 400, Deerfield, IL, 60015; ***PH:*** 1-847-405-2400; ***Fax:*** 1-847-267-1004; ***http://*** www.cfindustries.com

General		**Stock**	
Incorporation	DE	Price on:12/24/2007	$56.3
Employees	1,400	Stock Exchange	NYSE
Auditor	KPMG LLP	Ticker Symbol	CF
Stk Agt	Bank of New York	Outstanding Shares	55,380,000
Counsel	NA	E.P.S.	$2.08
DUNS No.	NA	Shareholders	NA

Business: The groups principal activities include manufacturing and distributing nitrogen and phosphate fertilizer products. The group operates through two segments namely, nitrogen fertilizers and phosphate fertilizers. The group operates from the North America and Canada. The groups total net sales in the year 2006 were $1,949.5 (millions).

Primary SIC and add'l.: 2875 5191 2874 2873

CIK No: 0001324404

Subsidiaries: CF Industries, Inc.

Officers: Stephen R. Wilson/Chmn., CEO, Pres./$5,623,220.00, Randall W. Selgrad/Treasurer, Anthony Will/VP - Corporate Development, Charles A. Nekvasil/Dir. - Public, Investor Relations, Ernest Thomas/54/CFO, Sr. VP/$1,319,632.00, David J. Pruett/Sr. VP - Operations/$982,186.00, Douglas C. Barnard/VP, General Counsel, Sec./$951,582.00, Frank N. Buzzanca/VP - EHS, Engineering, Wendy Jablow Spertus/VP - Human Resources, Stephen G. Chase/VP - Corporate Planning, William G. Eppel/64/VP - Human Resources, Louis M. Frey/VP, GM - Donaldsonville Nitrogen Complex, Russell A. Holowachuk/VP, GM - Medicine Hat Nitrogen Complex, Philipp P. Koch/VP - Raw Materials Procurement/$814,940.00, Herschel E. Morris/VP - Phosphate Operations *(20 Officers included in Index)*

Directors: Stephen R. Wilson/Chmn., CEO, Pres., Robert C. Arzbaecher/Dir., Wallace W. Creek/Dir., William Davisson/Dir., David R. Harvey/Dir., John D. Johnson/Dir., Edward A. Schmitt/Dir., Stephen A. Furbacher/Dir.

Owners: Wallace W. Creek, Stephen R. Wilson, Ernest Thomas, David J. Pruett, William Davisson, John D. Johnson, Edward A. Schmitt, Douglas C. Barnard, Greenlight Capital, LLC and other reporting entities/6.70%, GROWMARK,Inc./7.70%, Robert C. Arzbaecher, David R. Harvey, Philipp P. Koch, Insiders/1.60%

Financial Data: *Fiscal Year End:*12/31 *Latest Annual Data:* 12/31/2006

Year	Sales	Net Income
2006	$1,949,500,000	$33,300,000
2005	$1,908,400,000	-$39,000,000
2004	$1,650,652,000	$67,732,000

Curr. Assets:	$633,100,000	**Curr. Liab.:**	$353,400,000	**P/E Ratio:**	51.25
Plant, Equip.:	$622,600,000	**Total Liab.:**	$523,400,000	**Indic. Yr. Divd.:**	$0.080
Total Assets:	$1,290,400,000	**Net Worth:**	$767,000,000	**Debt/ Equity:**	NA

CFC International Inc

500 St. ate St., Chicago Heights, IL, 60411; ***PH:*** 1-708-891-3456; ***http://*** www.cfcintl.com

General - Incorporation ... DE
Employees ... 276
Auditor ... PricewaterhouseCoopers LLP
Stk Agt ... Computershare Investor Services LLC
Counsel ... NA
DUNS No. ... 14-835-2198

Stock- Price on:12/24/2007 ... $4.1
Stock Exchange ... NA
Ticker Symbol ... NA
Outstanding Shares ... 278,820,000
E.P.S ... -$0.04
Shareholders ... NA

Business: The group's principle activity is to formulate, manufacture and market chemically complex and multi-layered functional coatings. It produces five types of coated products: holographic products, printed products, pharmaceutical pigmented coatings, security products and simulated metal and other pigmented products. The products serve diversified markets such as furniture and building products, pharmaceutical products, transaction cards, including credit cards, debit cards and access cards, intaglio printing and on sophisticated embossable coatings for holographic packaging and authentication seals. The group has sales, warehousing and finishing operations in the United Kingdom, as well as manufacturing and sales capability in Germany.

Primary SIC and add'l.: 2671

CIK No: 0000949859

Subsidiaries: CFC Europe GmbH, CFC Europe, Ltd., CFC International (Europe) GmbH, CFC Management, Inc., CFC Northern Bank Note Company, LLC

Financial Data: ***Fiscal Year End:***12/31 ***Latest Annual Data:*** 07/31/2006

Year	Sales	Net Income
2006	$87,395,000	$19,388,000
2005	$65,434,000	-$23,789,000
2004	$44,547,000	-$44,842,000

Curr. Assets:	$972,180,000	**Curr. Liab.:**	$40,934,000		
Plant, Equip.:	$8,437,000	**Total Liab.:**	$42,518,000	**Indic. Yr. Divd.:**	NA
Total Assets:	$982,063,000	**Net Worth:**	$939,545,000	**Debt/ Equity:**	NA

CGI Group Inc

4050 Legato Rd., Fairfax, VA, 22033; ***PH:*** 1-703-267-8000; ***Fax:*** 1-703-267-5111; ***http://*** www.cgi.ca

General - Incorporation ... Canada
Employees ... 24,500
Auditor ... Deloitte & Touche LLP
Stk Agt ... Computershare In Canada
Counsel ... NA
DUNS No. ... 24-680-1237

Stock- Price on:12/24/2007 ... $10.83
Stock Exchange ... NYSE
Ticker Symbol ... GIB
Outstanding Shares ... NA
E.P.S ... NA
Shareholders ... NA

Business: The group's principle activity is to provide end-to-end it services and business solutions to more than 3,000 clients worldwide from more than 60 offices. The it services includes consulting, systems integration and the management of business and it functions. The group provides end-to-end it services in six economic sectors telecommunications, financial services, manufacturing/retail/distribution, governments, public utilities and services and healthcare.The group's quarterly revenue for September 207 was 922.85 millions of CAD.

Primary SIC and add'l.: 8742 7371 8999

CIK No: 0001061574

Subsidiaries: CGI Information Systems and Management Consultants Inc., CGI-AMS Inc., Conseillers en gestion et informatique C.G.I. inc

Officers: Michael E. Roach/Dir., CEO, Pres., Serge Godin/Founder, Exec. Chmn., Andre Imbeau/Founder, Executive Vice - Chmn., Corp. Sec., Andre J. Bourque/Exec. VP, Chief Legal Officer, Arnold Langbo/International Advisory Counsel, Yvonne Gibson/Media Contact - Canada, Daniel Rocheleau/Exec. VP, Chief Business Engineering Officer, Donna Morea/Pres. - US Operations, India, Harvey Golub/International Advisory Counsel, Michael Hepher/International Advisory Counsel, David Masse/Assist., Corp. Sec., Jacques Bougie/International Advisory Counsel, David Anderson/CFO, Exec. VP, Linda Odorisio/Contact - United States, Nick Coleman/Contact - Trade Publications, Europe *(23 Officers included in Index)*

Directors: Serge Godin/Founder, Exec. Chmn., Andre Imbeau/Founder, Executive Vice - Chmn., Corp. Sec., Paule Dore/Dir., Robert Chevrier/Dir., Claude Boivin/Dir., Claude Chamberland/Dir. - Companies, Eileen A. Mercier/Dir. - Companies, Gerald T. Squire/Dir. - Companies, Thomas Paul D'Aquino/Dir., Robert Tessier/Dir., C.wesley M. Scott/Dir. - Companies, Jean Brassard/Dir. - Companies, David L. Johnston/Dir.

Financial Data: ***Fiscal Year End:***09/30 ***Latest Annual Data:*** 9/30/2006

Year	Sales	Net Income
2006	$3,122,558,000	$133,945,000
2005	$3,148,569,000	$203,113,000
2004	$2,554,669,000	$171,864,000

Curr. Assets:	$822,695,000	**Curr. Liab.:**	$599,393,000		
Plant, Equip.:	$107,777,000	**Total Liab.:**	$1,745,528,000	**Indic. Yr. Divd.:**	NA
Total Assets:	$3,380,267,000	**Net Worth:**	$1,634,738,000	**Debt/ Equity:**	NA

Ch Energy Group Inc

284 S Ave., Poughkeepsie, NY, 12601; ***PH:*** 1-845-452-2000; ***Fax:*** 1-845-486-5465; ***http://*** www.chenergygroup.com

General - Incorporation ... NY
Employees ... 860
Auditor ... PricewaterhouseCoopers LLP
Stk Agt ... EquiServe Trust Co N.A
Counsel ... Thompson Hine LLP
DUNS No. ... 00-699-3695

Stock- Price on:12/24/2007 ... $45.02
Stock Exchange ... NYSE
Ticker Symbol ... CHG
Outstanding Shares ... 15,760,000
E.P.S ... $2.59
Shareholders ... NA

Business: The group's principal activity is to supply electricity, natural gas, propane, fuel oil and other petroleum products along with energy services. The group is a holding company that operates through Central Hudson and CH services. Central Hudson gas & electric provides electricity to 275,000 customers and natural gas to 65,000 customers in New York. CH Energy Group provides retail and wholesale energy marketing, petroleum product distribution, engineering and construction, electricity generation, and energy management services in the northeast and mid-Atlantic United States.

Primary SIC and add'l.: 4923 4911 6719 4931

CIK No: 0001061393

Subsidiaries: Central Hudson Enterprises Corporation, CH Resources, Inc., Griffith Energy Services, Inc, Phoenix Development Company, Inc.

Officers: Steven V. Lant/50/Chmn., CEO, Pres./$1,556,494.00, Donna S. Doyle/VP - Accounting, Controller, Arthur R. Upright/Dir., Sr. VP/$536,521.00, Denise D. Vanburen/VP - Corporate Communications, Community Relations, Lincoln E. Bleveans/40/Sec., Assist. Treasurer, Christopher M. Capone/CFO, Exec. VP/$480,533.00, Joseph J. Devirgilio/Exec. VP - Corporate Services, Administration/$580,099.00, John E. Gould/Sec., Carl E. Meyer/Exec. VP/$518,369.00, Stacey A. Renner/Treasurer, Joseph B. Koczko/Assist. Sec., Paul J. Gajdos/Contact - Shareholder Services

Directors: Steven V. Lant/50/Chmn., CEO, Pres., Steven M. Fetter/Dir., Margarita K. Dilley/Dir., Stanley J. Grubel/Dir., Manuel J. Iraola/58/Dir., Michel E. Kruse/Dir., Jeffrey D. Tranen/Dir., Ernest R. Verebelyi/Dir.

Owners: Stanley J. Grubel, Christopher M. Capone, E. Michel Kruse, Carl E. Meyer, Joseph J. DeVirgilio, Steven V. Lant, Insiders, Arthur R. Upright, Barclays Global Investors, NA, Edward F. X. Gallagher, Manulife Financial Corporation, Steven M. Fetter, Gabelli Asset Management Inc.

Financial Data: ***Fiscal Year End:***12/31 ***Latest Annual Data:*** 12/31/2006

Year	Sales	Net Income
2006	$993,433,000	$43,084,000
2005	$972,506,000	$44,291,000
2004	$791,512,000	$42,423,000

Curr. Assets:	$265,108,000	**Curr. Liab.:**	$190,088,000	**P/E Ratio:**	14.91
Plant, Equip.:	$860,874,000	**Total Liab.:**	$925,162,000	**Indic. Yr. Divd.:**	$2.160
Total Assets:	$1,460,532,000	**Net Worth:**	$533,889,000	**Debt/ Equity:**	0.6773

CH2M HILL Companies Ltd

40 Manning Rd., Billerica, MA, 01821; ***PH:*** 1-978-663-3660; ***Fax:*** 1-978-667-5993; ***http://*** www.ch2m.com; ***Email:*** power@ch2m.com

General - Incorporation ... OR
Employees ... 1,905
Auditor ... KPMG LLP
Stk Agt ... NA
Counsel ... Holme Roberts & Owen LLP
DUNS No. ... NA

Stock- Price on:12/24/2007 ... $9.19
Stock Exchange ... NA
Ticker Symbol ... NA
Outstanding Shares ... 105,310,000
E.P.S ... $0.21
Shareholders ... NA

Business: The group's principle activity is to provide consulting, design, engineering, procurement, construction, and operations and maintenance services. The groups servicing areas include chemicals, manufacturing, mining, energy, nuclear, power, environmental, transportation, life sciences, government and commercial properties and water, wastewater and water resources. The group operates from United States, Asia, Canada, Europe, Russia, South America and Northern Latin America.

Primary SIC and add'l.: 8999 8711 1541 1629

CIK No: 0000777491

Subsidiaries: Ch2m Hill Constructors, Inc, Ch2m Hill Hanford, Inc., Ch2m Hill Industrial Design & Construction, Inc, Ch2m Hill International , Ltd, Ch2m Hill, Inc, Kaiser-Hill Company, LLC, Lockwood Greene, Inc, Operations Management International

Officers: Ralph R. Peterson/Chmn., CEO/$3,409,649.00, Donald S. Evans/Dir., Group CEO, Pres./$1,427,966.00, Garry Higdem/Pres., Group CEO - EPC Group/$3,190,017.00, Nancy Tuor/Vice Chmn., Pres., Group CEO - Federal Group, Bao Le/VP - Integrated Security Technology, Services, Susan M. Mays/Marketing, Communications Dir., Colleen Campbell/Marketing Mgr., Joan Miller/Dir., Sr. VP - Client Development, Marketing, Industrial Group, Loretta Davis/Marketing Mgr., Mark Lasswell/Dir., Pres. - Operations, Maintenance Business Group, Gabriel Ruiz/MD - Northern Latin America, William T. Dehn/Dir., Pres. - Regional Operations, Scott Prather/Collaborative Solutions Dir., Mahesh Thadhani/Engineer - Procure, Construct, EPC Services, Erin Toelke/Renewable Energy Business Development Leader *(45 Officers included in Index)*

Directors: Ralph R. Peterson/Chmn., CEO, Donald S. Evans/Dir., Group CEO, Pres., Nancy Tuor/Vice Chmn., Pres., Group CEO - Federal Group, Carolyn Chin/Dir., David B. Price/Dir., William T. Dehn/Dir., Pres. - Regional Operations, Robert G. Card/Dir., Michael A. Szomjassy/57/Dir., Sr. VP, Robert W. Bailey/Dir., Jerry D. Geist/Dir., Barry L. Williams/Dir., Samuel H. Iapalucci/Dir., CFO, Exec. VP, Sec., Pres., James J. Ferris/Dir., Susan D. King/Dir., Sr. VP - Operations, Industrial Group, Lee A. McIntire/Dir., COO, Pres. *(17 Directors included in Index)*

Owners: Joan M. Miller, Donald S. Evans, M. Catherine Santee, Michael A. Szomjassy, Samuel H. Iapalucci, Carolyn Chin, David B. Price, William T. Dehn, Mark A. Lasswell, Susan D. King, Lee A. McIntire, Insiders, Robert W. Bailey, Garry M. Higdem, Trustees of the CH2M HILL Retirement and Tax-Deferred Savings Plan/45.30% *(20 Owners included in Index)*

Financial Data: ***Fiscal Year End:***12/31 ***Latest Annual Data:*** 12/31/2006

Year	Sales	Net Income
2006	$435,834,000	$18,481,000
2005	$297,569,000	$3,646,000
2004	$284,416,000	-$7,831,000

Curr. Assets:	$294,744,000	**Curr. Liab.:**	$195,128,000	**P/E Ratio:**	43.76
Plant, Equip.:	$90,349,000	**Total Liab.:**	$241,482,000	**Indic. Yr. Divd.:**	NA
Total Assets:	$433,187,000	**Net Worth:**	$191,466,000	**Debt/ Equity:**	0.1061

Chad Therapeutics Inc

21622 Plummer St., Chatsworth, CA, 91311; ***PH:*** 1-818-882-0883; ***Fax:*** 1-818-882-1809; ***http://*** www.chadtherapeutics.com

General - Incorporation ... CA
Employees ... 115
Auditor ... Rose, Snyder & Jacobs
Stk Agt ... American Stock Transfer & Trust Co.
Counsel ... Morrison & Foerster LLP
DUNS No. ... 10-303-7362

Stock- Price on:12/24/2007 ... $1.62
Stock Exchange ... AMEX
Ticker Symbol ... CTU
Outstanding Shares ... 10,170,000
E.P.S ... -$0.55
Shareholders ... NA

Business: The group's principal activity is to develop, produce and market respiratory care devices. The devices are used by patients with chronic obstructive pulmonary diseases and other respiratory disorders. These devices are designed to improve the efficiency of oxygen delivery systems to patients requiring supplemental oxygen. The group markets products directly to home and hospitals throughout the United States. The trademarks of the group include oxymizer, oxymatic, oxypneumatic, chad, oxycoil and total o2.

Primary SIC and add'l.: 3845 3842

CIK No: 0000713492

Officers: Earl L. Yager/Dir., CEO, Pres./$247,500.00, Oscar J. Sanchez/VP - Business Development, Samuel Patton/VP - Quality Assurance, Regulatory Affairs, Paula O'Connor/Executive Assist., Corp. Sec., Kevin McCulloh/Sr. VP - Engineering, Product Development/$183,607.00, Erika Laskey/Sr. VP - Sales, Marketing/$240,878.00, Tracy A. Kern/CFO/$118,605.00, Alfonso Del Toro/VP - Manufacturing, Dora Rodriguez/International Accounting Mgr., Holly Dysart-Ward/Mgr. - Art, Media, Barbara Muskin/Mgr. - Human Resources, Investor Relations Officer, Lee Duma/Accounting Mgr., Assist. Sec., Beth White/Marketing Administrator, Norma Oviedo/Customer Relations Mgr., Lina Chavez/Postmark Coordinator

Directors: Earl L. Yager/Dir., CEO, Pres., Thomas E. Jones/Chmn., James M. Brophy/Dir., John C. Boyd/Dir., Kathleen M. Fisher Griggs/Dir., Edward Anthony Oppenheimer/Dir., Philip T. Wolfstein/Dir.

Owners: Thomas E. Jones/3.30%, Tracy A. Kern/0.30%, James M. Brophy/0.50%, Philip T. Wolfstein/1.50%, Insiders/13.50%, Kevin Kimberlin/8.20%, Kathleen M. Griggs/0.30%, Erika Laskey/0.30%, Earl L. Yager/2.80%, Kevin McCulloh/0.60%, John C. Boyd/1.60%

Financial Data: Fiscal Year End:03/31 Latest Annual Data: 03/31/2007

Year	Sales	Net Income
2007	$18,981,000	-$3,414,000
2006	$22,354,000	-$673,000
2005	$24,287,000	$1,811,000

Curr. Assets:	$11,763,000	Curr. Liab.:	$1,957,000	
Plant, Equip.:	$950,000	Total Liab.:	$1,961,000	Indic. Yr. Divd.: NA
Total Assets:	$14,356,000	Net Worth:	$12,395,000	Debt/ Equity: NA

Chadmoore Wireless Group Inc

2458 E Russell Rd. , Ste B, Las Vegas, NV, 89120; **PH:** 1-702-740-5633;
http://www.chadmoore.com

General - Incorporation	CO	**Stock** - Price on:12/24/2007	$0.005
Employees	2	Stock Exchange	OTC
Auditor	McGladrey & Pullen LLP	Ticker Symbol	MOORZ
Stk Agt	Computershare Trust Co	Outstanding Shares	47,740,000
Counsel	NA	E.P.S.	-$0.002
DUNS No.	87-686-8399	Shareholders	NA

Business: The group's principal activity was to provide two-way wireless voice communications for business users. On 28-Jan-2002, holders of the group's common stock approved a plan of liquidation. The group is concluding its business activities and is in the process of dissolution.

Primary SIC and add'l.: 4812

CIK No: 0000815755

Officers: Richard M. Brenner/Chief Liquidating Officer

Financial Data: Fiscal Year End:12/31 Latest Annual Data: 12/31/2001

Year	Sales	Net Income
2001	$4,977,000	-$14,610,000
2000	$7,375,000	-$20,404,000
1999	$6,074,000	-$11,763,000

Curr. Assets:	$44,570,000	Curr. Liab.:	$59,990,000	
Plant, Equip.:	$815,000	Total Liab.:	$62,385,000	Indic. Yr. Divd.: NA
Total Assets:	$47,858,000	Net Worth:	-$18,796,000	Debt/ Equity: 0.0267

Chai-Na-Ta Corp

12051 Horseshoe Way, Unit 100, Richmond, BC, V7A 4V4; **PH:** 1-604-272-4118;
Fax: 1-604-272-4113; http://www.chainata.com; **Email:** info@chainata.com

General - Incorporation	BC	**Stock** - Price on:12/24/2007	$0.04
Employees	NA	Stock Exchange	OTC
Auditor	Deloitte & Touche LLP	Ticker Symbol	CCCFF
Stk Agt	Computershare Investor Services LLC	Outstanding Shares	NA
Counsel	Pines McIntyre & Shrieves	E.P.S.	NA
DUNS No.	24-455-8664	Shareholders	NA

Business: The group's principal activities are to farm, process and distribute north American ginseng as bulk root. The group also supplies processed extract powders for the manufacture of value added ginseng-based products.

Primary SIC and add'l.: 0139

CIK No: 0000889329

Subsidiaries: Chai-Na-Ta Farms Ltd., CNT Farms, CNT Nutraceuticals Ltd., CNT Trading, Northfield Laboratories Inc

Officers: Wilman Wong/Dir., CFO, Corp. Sec., Terry Luck/CFO

Directors: William Zen/Chmn., Peter Leung/Dir., Wilman Wong/Dir., CFO, Corp. Sec., Steven Hsieh/Dir., Eric Littley/Dir., Leslie Lumsden/62/Dir., Brent Lau/Dir., Derek Zen/55/Dir.

Owners: Groove Trading Limited/9.13%, ZWP Investments Limited/28.96%, Hover Limited/20.21%

Financial Data: Fiscal Year End:12/31 Latest Annual Data: 12/31/2006

Year	Sales	Net Income
2006	$5,087,000	-$8,099,000
2005	$4,999,000	-$6,667,000
2004	$6,165,000	$264,000

Curr. Assets:	$12,511,000	Curr. Liab.:	$6,066,000	
Plant, Equip.:	$12,948,000	Total Liab.:	$13,244,000	Indic. Yr. Divd.: NA
Total Assets:	$25,459,000	Net Worth:	$12,215,000	Debt/ Equity: NA

Challenger Powerboats Inc

Formerly: Xtreme Companies Inc
300 Wlink Dr., Washington, MO, 63090; **PH:** 1-636-390-9000; http://www.xtremecos.com

General - Incorporation	NV	**Stock** - Price on:12/24/2007	$0.04
Employees	74	Stock Exchange	OTC
Auditor	Jaspers & Hall, P.C	Ticker Symbol	CPBI
Stk Agt	NA	Outstanding Shares	71,510,000
Counsel	NA	E.P.S.	-$0.21
DUNS No.	NA	Shareholders	NA

Business: The group's principal activity design and manufacture high-performance commercial boats used by fire, police, and military personnel for fire, rescue and patrol. The groups products combine innovative designs with power, safety, handling and stability to create boats designed to protect and save lives. The innovative patents and patents-pending that we license, give the boats eye-catching visual market retention, and a competitive advantage in the boating industry, home defense and world markets. Each model of commercial boats comes equipped with mercury marine sport jet 175 xr2 two stroke engines that generate 175 horse power, and mercury marine single stage axial flow jet pumps. The boats come with a two-year warranty on the engine, the fuel system, and the electrical system, and a five-year warranty on the hull.

Primary SIC and add'l.: 4953

CIK No: 0001114908

Subsidiaries: Nuclear Reduction Systems, Inc., Rockwell Power Systems, Inc., Waste Renewal Systems, Inc.

Officers: Jack Clark/59/COO

Owners: Douglas Leighton, eFund Small Cap. Fund LP, Michael Novielli, Fund Capital Partners, LLC, Barrett Evans, Insiders, Dutchess Private Equities Fund, Ltd.

Financial Data: Fiscal Year End:12/31 Latest Annual Data: 12/31/2006

Year	Sales	Net Income
2006	$238,000	-$9,133,000
2005	$1,784,000	-$2,417,000
2004	$165,000	-$1,466,000

Curr. Assets:	$1,992,000	Curr. Liab.:	$5,981,000	
Plant, Equip.:	$1,662,000	Total Liab.:	$17,969,000	Indic. Yr. Divd.: NA
Total Assets:	$4,653,000	Net Worth:	-$13,315,000	Debt/ Equity: NA

Champion Communication Services Inc

1610 Woodstead Ct, Ste 330, The Woodlands, TX, 77380; **PH:** 1-281-362-0144;
Fax: 1-281-364-1901; http://www.champcom.com; **Email:** ccsibro@champcom.com

General - Incorporation	DE	**Stock** - Price on:12/24/2007	$0.31
Employees	2	Stock Exchange	OTC
Auditor	Glo Cpas, LLP	Ticker Symbol	CCMS
Stk Agt	Equity Transfer Services Inc	Outstanding Shares	4,480,000
Counsel	NA	E.P.S.	$0.23
DUNS No.	36-293-0570	Shareholders	NA

Business: The group's principal activity is to provide high-powered community repeater dispatch services to businesses and government agencies throughout the United States. The group's customers are government agencies and private carriers providing telephone service to remote towns and villages with low density populations. The customers of the group primarily consist of businesses and government agencies located in both metropolitan and rural geographic regions. The operations performed by the group include billing, maintenance of subscriber records and federal communications commission licensing activities. As of 31-Dec-2003, the group serves approximately 550 trunked dispatch customers in selected major metropolitan areas utilizing over 10,000 subscriber units in 6 states.

Primary SIC and add'l.: 4812

CIK No: 0001028921

Subsidiaries: Champion Vietnam Wireless B.V., Champion Wireless International B.V., Champion Wireless Systems International N.V., Netherlands Antilles company

Officers: Albert F. Richmond/Chmn., CEO, Pres., Jeff Graber/Technical Operations Mgr., Pamela R. Cooper/Exec. VP, CFO, Controller, Sec., Treasurer

Directors: Albert F. Richmond/Chmn., CEO, Pres.

Owners: Pamela R. Cooper/4.26%, Insiders/52.56%, Albert F. Richmond/51.00%

Financial Data: Fiscal Year End:12/31 Latest Annual Data: 12/31/2006

Year	Sales	Net Income
2006	$1,186,000	-$760,000
2005	$1,400,000	$140,000
2004	$1,884,000	-$1,795,000

Curr. Assets:	$182,000	Curr. Liab.:	$162,000	P/E Ratio: 1.48
Plant, Equip.:	$220,000	Total Liab.:	$186,000	Indic. Yr. Divd.: $0.250
Total Assets:	$437,000	Net Worth:	$252,000	Debt/ Equity: NA

Champion Industries Inc

2450 1st Ave., Huntington, WV, 25728; **PH:** 1-304-528-2700; **Fax:** 1-304-528-2765;
http://www.champion-industries.com; **Email:** champion@champion-industries.com

General - Incorporation	WV	**Stock** - Price on:12/24/2007	$7.1
Employees	730	Stock Exchange	NDQ
Auditor	BKD LLP	Ticker Symbol	CHMP
Stk Agt	National City Bank	Outstanding Shares	9,960,000
Counsel	NA	E.P.S.	$0.56
DUNS No.	79-885-9484	Shareholders	NA

Business: The group's principal activity is to provide a full range of printing services, business forms, office products and office furniture. Its printing services include business cards, books, tags, brochures and posters. It also offers complete bindery and letterpress services. The group provides a full range of office products, office furniture and office design services. The office products include file folders, paper products, pens and pencils, computer paper and laser cartridges. The furniture products include desks, chairs, file cabinets and computer furniture. The design services include space planning, purchasing and installation of office furniture. The products are sold under the trade name 'chapman printing company'. The customers include manufacturers, institutions and professional firms. On 07-Sep-2004, the group acquired syscan corporation.

Primary SIC and add'l.: 5021 2759 5044 5112 2678

CIK No: 0000019149

Subsidiaries: Blue Ridge Printing Co., Inc., Bourque Printing, Inc., Capitol Business Equipment, Inc., Carolina Cut Sheets, Inc., CHMP Leasing, Inc., Dallas Printing Company, Inc., Diez Business Machines, Inc., Donihe Graphics, Inc., Independent Printing Service, Inc., Interform Corporation, Rose City Press, Smith & Butterfield Co., Stationers, Inc., Syscan Corporation, Syscan Furniture Systems, LLC 20 Subsidiaries included in the Index

Officers: Mac J. Aldridge/Sr. VP, Todd R. Fry/Sr. VP, CFO, Walter R. Sansom/Sec., James A. Rhodes/Sr. VP, Toney K. Adkins/COO, Pres., Douglas R. McElwain/Sr. VP

Directors: Neal W. Scaggs/Dir., Louis J. Akers/Dir., Philip E. Cline/Dir., Glenn W. Wilcox/Dir., Harley F. Mooney/Dir., Michael A. Perry/Dir.

Owners: Marshall T. Reynolds/41.50%, Douglas R. McElwain/1.50%, Harley F. Mooney, Glenn W. Wilcox/1.20%, Toney K. Adkins/1.40%, Todd R. Fry/1.30%, James A. Rhodes/1.30%, Michael A. Perry, Philip E. Cline, Neal W. Scaggs, Insiders/52.30%

Financial Data: Fiscal Year End:10/31   Latest Annual Data: 10/31/2006

Year	Sales	Net Income
2006	$145,188,000	$5,474,000
2005	$134,925,000	$1,117,000
2004	$124,402,000	$750,000

Curr. Assets:	$38,931,000	**Curr. Liab.:**	$12,976,000	**P/E Ratio:**	12.68
Plant, Equip.:	$19,046,000	**Total Liab.:**	$21,212,000	**Indic. Yr. Divd.:**	$0.240
Total Assets:	$65,989,000	**Net Worth:**	$44,777,000	**Debt/ Equity:**	0.0919

Champion Mortgage

127 Public Sq., Cleveland, OH, 44114; **PH:** 1-216-689-6300; **Fax:** 1-216-689-0519; http:// www.champion.com

General - Incorporation	MI	**Stock**- Price on:12/24/2007	$35.95
Employees	20,006	Stock Exchange	NYSE
Auditor	Ernst & Young, LLP	Ticker Symbol	NA
Stk Agt	NA	Outstanding Shares	392,300,000
Counsel	NA	E.P.S.	$2.82
DUNS No.	17-520-7422	Shareholders	NA

Business: The group's principal activity is to construct and sell manufactured homes. The group mainly produces single-story, ranch-style homes and also builds one and one-half story and two-story homes, cape cod style homes and multi-family units such as townhouses. It also provides loans to consumers who purchase the group's manufactured homes from both the group-owned and independent retailers. The group operates through two divisions: manufacturing and retail. At 03-Jan-2004, the group operated 30 manufacturing plants in 14 states in the United States and two provinces in western Canada and 78 retail locations in 21 states. In 2003 the group discontinued homepride finance corp, its financial services segment.

Primary SIC and add'l.: 1522 1521

CIK No: 0000814068

Subsidiaries: Champion Development Corp., Champion Enterprises Management Co, Champion Home Builders Co, Champion Homes of Boaz, Inc., Champion Retail, Inc., Covington Estates Limited Partnership, Dutch Housing, Inc, Homes of Merit, Inc., Mhcdc, LLC, Moduline Industries (Canada) Ltd., Moduline International, Inc, New Era Building Systems, Inc, Redman Homes, Inc, Redman Industries, Inc., San Jose Advantage Homes, Inc. 17 Subsidiaries included in the Index

Officers: William C. Griffiths/56/Chmn., CEO, Pres., John J. Collins/56/Sr. VP, General Counsel, Sec., Phyllis A. Knight/45/CFO, Exec. VP, Treasurer, Jeffrey L. Nugent/61/VP - Human Resources

Directors: William C. Griffiths/56/Chmn., CEO, Pres., Robert W. Anestis/62/Dir., Eric S. Belsky/47/Dir., Selwyn Isakow/56/Dir., Brian D. Jellison/62/Dir., Michael G. Lynch/64/Dir., Thomas A. Madden/54/Dir., Shirley D. Peterson/66/Dir., David S. Weiss/47/Dir.

Owners: Barclays Global Investors, NA/5.54%, Borrow, Hanley, Mewhinney& Strauss, Inc./5.83%, GAMCO Asset Management, Inc./6.42%, Eric S. Belsky/0.06%, David S. Weiss/0.04%, William C. Griffiths/0.54%, Selwyn Isakow/0.04%, Columbia Wanger Asset Management, L.P./6.16%, Phyllis A. Knight/0.81%, Insiders/3.22%, Thomas A. Madden/0.02%, Tontine Capital Partners, L.P./7.51%, Michael G. Lynch, Jeffrey L. Nugent/0.13%, First Pacific Advisors, LLC/10.23% (21 Owners included in Index)

Financial Data: Fiscal Year End:12/31   Latest Annual Data: 12/31/2006

Year	Sales	Net Income
2006	$7,507,000,000	$1,055,000,000
2005	$6,695,000,000	$1,129,000,000
2004	$5,564,000,000	$954,000,000

Curr. Assets:	$3,671,000,000	**Curr. Liab.:**	$67,987,000,000	**P/E Ratio:**	12.75
Plant, Equip.:	$1,719,000,000	**Total Liab.:**	$84,634,000,000	**Indic. Yr. Divd.:**	$1.460
Total Assets:	$92,337,000,000	**Net Worth:**	$7,703,000,000	**Debt/ Equity:**	2.1611

Champion Parts Inc

2005 W Ave. B, Hope, AR, 71801; **PH:** 1-870-777-8821; **Fax:** 1-870-777-1379; http:// www.championparts.net; **Email:** info@championparts.net

General - Incorporation	IL	**Stock**- Price on:12/24/2007	$0.66
Employees	291	Stock Exchange	OTC
Auditor	Morison Cogen LLP	Ticker Symbol	CREBE
Stk Agt	Computershare Investor Services LLC	Outstanding Shares	3,660,000
Counsel	Lord, Bissell & Brook	E.P.S.	$2.35
DUNS No.	00-510-5721	Shareholders	NA

Business: The group's principal activity is to remanufacture and sell replacement fuel system components and constant velocity drive assemblies used in automobiles and trucks. The group also remanufactures and sells replacement electrical and mechanical products for passenger car, agricultural and heavy duty truck original equipment applications. The products include carburetors, constant velocity drive assemblies, electrical and mechanical products. The group also prepares and publishes catalogs of its products, including a guide with information as to the various vehicle models. The group makes available to its customers the mema transnet computerized order entry system, which enables the customers to place orders into the group's central computer.

Primary SIC and add'l.: 3592 3714

CIK No: 0000019161

Subsidiaries: C.P.R. Properties, Inc.C5, Champion Productos Reacondicionados, S.A. de C.V., Champion-APR, Inc., Financial Corporation, IMT, Inc., Super Parts, Inc., Western Rebuilders, Inc.

Officers: Jerry A. Bragiel/56/CEO, Pres., Kevin Cain/CFO

Directors: John R. Gross/76/Dir., Raymond F. Gross/69/Dir., Jason W. Guzek/34/Dir., Barry L. Katz/56/Dir., Raymond G. Perelman/90/Dir.

Financial Data: Fiscal Year End:12/31   Latest Annual Data: 12/31/2006

Year	Sales	Net Income
2006	$18,061,000	$10,000
2005	$21,651,000	$37,000
2004	$19,998,000	$715,000

Curr. Assets:	$22,092,000	**Curr. Liab.:**	$10,184,000		
Plant, Equip.:	$2,187,000	**Total Liab.:**	$25,251,000	**Indic. Yr. Divd.:**	NA
Total Assets:	$26,398,000	**Net Worth:**	$1,147,000	**Debt/ Equity:**	12.2284

Championlyte Holdings Inc

600 Bayview Ave., Inwood, NY, 11096; **PH:** 1-516-239-7000

General - Incorporation	FL	**Stock**- Price on:12/24/2007	$0.003
Employees	115	Stock Exchange	OTC
Auditor	Friedman LLP	Ticker Symbol	CPLYE
Stk Agt	Florida Atlantic Stock Transfer, Inc.	Outstanding Shares	1,130,000,000
Counsel	Anslow & Jaclin	E.P.S.	-$0.005
DUNS No.	NA	Shareholders	NA

Business: The group's principal activity is to develop sugar-free, carbohydrate and calorie free isotonic sports beverage. The products are sold under the trademark sweet 'n low(R) and champion lyte (r). The products include the sweet 'n low brand syrup and champion lyte refresher drinks. Sweet 'n low brand syrup is a fat-free, sugar free flavored syrup. The group manufactures and bottles its products under co-packing arrangements with third parties. The principal customers for the syrup are the food retailers, such as supermarkets, drug store chains, discount stores and warehouse centers and institutional entities. On 20-Aug-2003 it acquired old fashioned.

Primary SIC and add'l.: 2087 6719 2066 2086

CIK No: 0001093819

Subsidiaries: Be-Lyte Foods, Inc., Cargo Connection Logistics Holding, Inc., Mid-Coast Management, Inc.

Officers: Jesse Dobrinsky/51/Chmn., CEO, Pres., Scott O. Goodman/48/Dir., CFO, COO, Sec., John L. Udell/52/VP, William F. O'Connell/53/VP - Sales, Marketing, Raymond G. Hunt/61/Sr. VP, Kenneth J. Ryan/60/VP

Directors: Jesse Dobrinsky/51/Chmn., CEO, Pres., Scott O. Goodman/48/Dir., CFO, COO, Sec.

Owners: Insiders/19.02%, Jesse Dobrinsky/6.34%, Scott Goodman/6.34%, John L. Udell/6.34%, Jay Finkelstein/2.11%

Financial Data: Fiscal Year End:12/31   Latest Annual Data: 12/31/2006

Year	Sales	Net Income
2006	$17,928,000	-$5,865,000
2005	$14,662,000	-$4,527,000
2004	$691,000	-$2,334,000

Curr. Assets:	$2,013,000	**Curr. Liab.:**	$10,522,000		
Plant, Equip.:	$327,000	**Total Liab.:**	$12,268,000	**Indic. Yr. Divd.:**	NA
Total Assets:	$3,747,000	**Net Worth:**	-$8,522,000	**Debt/ Equity:**	NA

Champions Biotechnology Inc

Formerly: Champions Sports Inc
2200 Wilson Blvd, Ste. 102-316, Arlington, VA, 22201; **PH:** 1-703-526-0400

General - Incorporation	DE	**Stock**- Price on:12/24/2007	$0.63
Employees	1	Stock Exchange	NA
Auditor	Bagell, Josephs, Levine & Co. LLC	Ticker Symbol	NA
Stk Agt	Integrity Stock Transfer, Inc.	Outstanding Shares	27,620,000
Counsel	NA	E.P.S.	$0.00
DUNS No.	15-363-2369	Shareholders	NA

Business: The group's principal activity is to operate restaurant in san antonio, Texas by the name of champions. This restaurant has a sports theme concept that combines casual dining, sports viewing with strategic marketing and promotions. The group also exclusively supplies sports memorabilia to marriott international inc.

Primary SIC and add'l.: 5812 6794

CIK No: 0000771856

Officers: James M. Martell/61/Chmn., CEO, CFO, Pres., Durwood C. Settles/65/Treasurer, Dir., Manuel Hidalgo/Dir. - Scientific Advisor

Directors: James M. Martell/61/Chmn., CEO, CFO, Pres., Durwood C. Settles/65/Treasurer, Dir., Michael M. Tomic/62/Dir., David Sidransky/48/Dir., Manuel Hidalgo/Dir. - Scientific Advisor

Owners: David Sidransky, Manuel Hidalgo, Insiders, James M. Martell, Michael M. Tomic

Financial Data: Fiscal Year End:04/30   Latest Annual Data: 4/30/2006

Year	Sales	Net Income
2006	NA	-$304,000
2005	$1,797,000	-$247,000
2004	$1,999,000	-$215,000

Curr. Assets:	$1,000	**Curr. Liab.:**	$671,000		
Plant, Equip.:	NA	**Total Liab.:**	$671,000	**Indic. Yr. Divd.:**	NA
Total Assets:	$1,000	**Net Worth:**	-$671,000	**Debt/ Equity:**	NA

Champps Entertainment Inc

10375 Pk. Meadows Dr., Ste. 560, Littleton, CO, 80124; **PH:** 1-303-804-1333; **Fax:** 1-303-804-8477; http:// www.champps.com; **Email:** comments@champps.com

General - Incorporation	DE	**Stock**- Price on:12/24/2007	$4.71
Employees	5,123	Stock Exchange	NDQ
Auditor	KPMG LLP	Ticker Symbol	CMPP
Stk Agt	American Stock Transfer & Trust Co.	Outstanding Shares	13,090,000
Counsel	Brownstein Hyatt & Farber	E.P.S.	-$0.7
DUNS No.	15-978-1327	Shareholders	NA

Business: The group's principal activity is the ownership, operation and franchise of casual dining restaurants under the name of champps Americana. On 28-Mar-2004, the group owned and operated fourty-seven restaurants in twenty one states and had twelve restaurants operating under franchise. The restaurants seat 217 to 360 guests and offer appetizers, main plate salads, sandwiches, specialty burgers and entree selections in traditional American style as well as in a variety of ethnic cuisine. They are built with multiple levels and elements such as Italian tile, slate style floors and wood accents. In addition to food and beverages, they also provide game room for arcade games, sporting events, music and other activities. The restaurants are primarily located in commercial areas, residential housing and high traffic areas, shopping malls and multi-screen movie theaters.

Primary SIC and add'l.: 5812 6794 5813

CIK No: 0001040328

Subsidiaries: Champps Entertainment of Texas, Inc., Champps of Maryland, Inc., Champps Operating Corporation

Officers: Michael P. O'Donnell/52/Chmn., CEO, Pres., Donna L. Depoian/48/VP, Sec., General Counsel, David D. Womack/45/Exec. VP, Treasurer, CFO, David J. Miller/57/VP - Construction, Development, Charles G. Phillips/60/COO

Directors: Michael P. O'Donnell/52/Chmn., CEO, Pres., James Goodwin/52/Dir., Karl S. Okamoto/46/Dir., Stephen F. Edwards/45/Dir., Ian Hamilton/52/Dir.

Owners: Stephen F. Edwards, David D. Womack, David J. Miller, Karl Okamoto, Ian Hamilton, Donna L. Depoian, Atticus Capital, LLC/33.10%, James Goodwin, Dimensional Fund Advisors, Inc./8.40%, Franklin Advisory Services, LLC/7.00%, Insiders/7.40%, Loeb Partners Corp/6.70%, T. Rowe Price Associates, Inc./12.10%, Charles G. Phillips, Michael P. ODonnell/4.00%

Financial Data: Fiscal Year End:07/03 **Latest Annual Data:** 7/2/2006

Year	Sales	Net Income
2006	$209,646,000	-$1,558,000
2005	$218,356,000	-$249,000
2004	$211,502,000	$4,272,000

Curr. Assets:	$17,053,000	Curr. Liab.:	$14,667,000		
Plant, Equip.:	$86,745,000	Total Liab.:	$61,250,000	Indic. Yr. Divd.:	NA
Total Assets:	$137,311,000	Net Worth:	$76,061,000	Debt/ Equity:	NA

Chancellor Group Inc

1800 E Sahara, Ste 107, Las Vegas, NV, 89104; **PH:** 1-702-938-0261;
http:// www.chancellorgroupinc.com

General - Incorporation	NV	Stock- Price on:12/24/2007	$0.12
Employees	NA	Stock Exchange	OTC
Auditor	Ronald R. Chadwick, P.C	Ticker Symbol	CHAG
Stk Agt	NA	Outstanding Shares	64,500,000
Counsel	NA	E.P.S.	-$0.01
DUNS No.	78-490-4682	Shareholders	NA

Business: The group's principal activities are to acquire, explore and develop natural gas and oil properties. The group further examines opportunities in the fields of power generation, minerals development and environmental engineering and remediation.

Primary SIC and add'l.: 4924

CIK No: 0000894544

Subsidiaries: Getty Petroleum, Inc., Lichfield Petroleum America, Inc., Radly Petroleum, Inc.

Officers: Robert Gordon/64/Dir., CEO, Thomas H. Grantham/CFO, Pres.

Directors: Robert Gordon/64/Dir., CEO, Dudley Muth/67/Dir.

Owners: Robert Gordon/7.55%, Insiders/9.78%, John C.Y. Lee/0.41%, Dudley Muth/1.83%, Axis Network, Koala Pictures Proprietary Ltd./36.25%

Financial Data: Fiscal Year End:12/31 **Latest Annual Data:** 12/31/2006

Year	Sales	Net Income
2006	NA	-$66,000
2005	NA	-$11,000
2004	NA	-$20,000

Curr. Assets:	$1,000	Curr. Liab.:	$111,000		
Plant, Equip.:	NA	Total Liab.:	$111,000	Indic. Yr. Divd.:	NA
Total Assets:	$1,000	Net Worth:	-$111,000	Debt/ Equity:	NA

Chandler USA Inc

1010 Manvel Ave., Chandler, OK, 74834; **PH:** 1-405-258-0804; **http://** www.naico.com

General - Incorporation	OK	Stock- Price on:12/24/2007	NA
Employees	85	Stock Exchange	NA
Auditor	Tullius Taylor Sartain & Sartain LLP	Ticker Symbol	NA
Stk Agt	NA	Outstanding Shares	NA
Counsel	Vinson & Elkins LLP	E.P.S.	NA
DUNS No.	NA	Shareholders	NA

Business: The group's principal activity is to provide administrative services through its wholly owned subsidiaries. The group operates in one segment namely, property and casualty insurance. The insurance products offered include property and casualty insurance coverage primarily for businesses in various industries, political divisions and surety bonds for small contractors in the United States of America. The group is wholly owned by chandler insurance (barbados) ltd. .

Primary SIC and add'l.: 6719 6331

CIK No: 0001083750

Subsidiaries: Chandler Capital Trust I, Chandler Capital Trust II, Chandler Insurance Managers, Inc., National American Insurance Company, Network Administrators, Inc.

Officers: Brent W. Lagere/Chmn., CEO, Mark T. Paden/Pres. - Naico, Richard L. Evans/Dir., Sr. VP, Patrick R. Gilmore/General Counsel, Sec., a Sr. VP, Gary Lagere/Sr. VP - Underwriting, Lance A. Lagere/COO

Directors: Brent W. Lagere/Chmn., CEO, Richard L. Evans/Dir., Sr. VP, Robert L. Rice/73/Dir., Scott W. Martin/57/Dir.

Owners: Mark T. Paden/20.00%, Brent W. LaGere/19.90%, Scott W. Martin/3.00%, Brent W. LaGere/80.00%, Insiders/18.10%, Mark T. Paden/4.70%, Richard L. Evans/7.20%, Mark C. Hart/0.90%, Insiders/22.00%, Patrick R. Gilmore/4.60%, Insiders/32.70%, Malinda K. LaGere Laird/59.30%, Insiders/100.00%, Richard L. Evans/13.50%, William T. Keele/19.10%

Chang-On International Inc

Formerly: Gold Standard Inc
514 No. 18 Bldg., High New Technology Development, Harbin, HEILONGJIANG, 150000;
PH: 850-4518-2695010; **http://** www.goldstandardinc.com

General - Incorporation	UT	Stock- Price on:12/24/2007	$0.3
Employees	3	Stock Exchange	OTC
Auditor	Kempisty & Co.	Ticker Symbol	GOLS
Stk Agt	Computershare, Inc.	Outstanding Shares	NA
Counsel	NA	E.P.S	NA
DUNS No.	06-331-0700	Shareholders	NA

Business: The group's principal activities are the exploration, production and sale of gold. The group acquires, leases and sells hard mineral properties and develops those properties, which have the most economic potential. In addition, the group seeks opportunities for joint ventures or other financial arrangements with other companies to develop and/or operate the properties it controls. The group is involved in active exploration programs in the brazilian states of sao paulo and parana. Presently, the group is conducting only exploration activities.

Primary SIC and add'l.: 1041

CIK No: 0000042136

Subsidiaries: Gold Standard Minas, S.A., Tormin, S.A.

Officers: Li Guomin/47/Chmn., CEO, CFO

Directors: Li Guomin/47/Chmn., CEO, CFO, Su Yu/31/Dir., Zhou Qingwei/47/Dir.

Owners: Zhou Qingwei/59.70%, Li Guomin/28.40%, Insiders/97.90%, Su Yu/9.80%

Channell Commercial Corp

26040 Ynez Rd., Temecula, CA, 92591; **PH:** 1-951-719-2600; **Fax:** 1-951-296-2322;
http:// www.channellcomm.com; **Email:** uscustsrv@channellcorp.com

General - Incorporation	DE	Stock- Price on:12/24/2007	$4.48
Employees	568	Stock Exchange	NDQ
Auditor	Deloitte & Touche, LLP	Ticker Symbol	CHNL
Stk Agt	Computershare Investor Services LLC	Outstanding Shares	9,540,000
Counsel	Irell & Manella	E.P.S.	-$0.18
DUNS No.	00-826-2628	Shareholders	NA

Business: The group's principal activity is to design and manufacture telecommunication equipment. The products include thermoplastic and metal fabricated enclosures, advanced copper termination and connectorization products, fiber optic cable management systems, coaxial-based passive rf electronics and heat shrink products. They are supplied to telephone, cable television and power utility network providers worldwide. The products provide cable routing and management, equipment access, heat dissipation and security for the networks. The group also markets third party products, including grade level boxes and cable-in-conduit in order to provide the solutions to meet its customer's outside plant requirements. Major customers include comcast, verizon, time warner, cox and adelphia. The group has operations in the United States, Canada, central and South America, Europe, Africa, Middle East, Australia and Asia. On 02-Aug-2004, the group acquired bushman tanks.

Primary SIC and add'l.: 3829 3669

CIK No: 0001013696

Subsidiaries: AC Egerton Limited, Australian Bushman Tanks Pty Limited, Bushman Engineering Pty Limited, Bushman Group Pty Limited, Channell Bushman Pty Limited, Channell Commercial Canada Inc., Channell Commercial Europe Limited, Channell Commercial Malaysia Sendirian Berhad, Channell de Mexico SA de CV, Channell Hong Kong Limited, Channell Limited, Channell Proprietary Limited, Channell Pty Ltd, Fibercast Limited, Polyrib Tanks Pty Limited

Officers: William H. Channell/Dir., CEO, Pres., Jacqueline M. Channell/Interim Chmn., Sec., Edward J. Burke/52/CTO/$192,592.00, Andrew M. Zogby/Chief Marketing Officer/$207,555.00, Patrick E. McCready/CFO/$63,610.00, Michael Perica/Primary Investor Relations Officer

Directors: William H. Channell/Dir., CEO, Pres., Jacqueline M. Channell/Interim Chmn., Sec., Stephen Gill/Dir., Dana Brenner/65/Dir., Guy Marge/Dir.

Owners: Insiders, Rutabaga Capital Management, The Channell Family Trust, Carlo J. Cannell, The Taylor Family Trust, Carrie S. Channell, Andrew M. Zogby, William H. Channell, Bonanza Capital Ltd., William H. Channell, Jim P. Duvall, Guy Marge, Stephen Gill, Jerry Collazo, Jacqueline M. Channell *(19 Owners included in Index)*

Financial Data: Fiscal Year End:12/31 **Latest Annual Data:** 06/30/2007

Year	Sales	Net Income
2007	$36,722,000	$931,000
2006	$109,138,000	-$6,829,000
2005	$113,530,000	-$6,880,000

Curr. Assets:	$29,457,000	Curr. Liab.:	$29,952,000		
Plant, Equip.:	$18,799,000	Total Liab.:	$30,850,000	Indic. Yr. Divd.:	NA
Total Assets:	$61,878,000	Net Worth:	$30,150,000	Debt/ Equity:	0.0159

Chanticleer Holdings Inc

4201Congress St., Ste. 145, Charlotte, NC, 28209; **PH:** 1-704-366-5122; **Fax:** 1-704-366-2463;
http:// www.chanticleerholdings.com; **Email:** invest@chanticleerholding.com

General - Incorporation	DE	Stock- Price on:12/24/2007	$0.8
Employees	NA	Stock Exchange	OTC
Auditor	Creason & Assoc., PLLC	Ticker Symbol	CEEH
Stk Agt	NA	Outstanding Shares	7,690,000
Counsel	NA	E.P.S.	$0.19
DUNS No.	NA	Shareholders	NA

Business: The groups principal activity is to provide investment. The group operates from the United States.

Primary SIC and add'l.: 6719

CIK No: 0001106838

Officers: Michael D. Pruitt/Chmn., CEO, CFO, Pres., Laura Petty/Investor Relations, Joseph T. Koster/Analyst, Matthew S. Miller/Analyst, Glenn Tobias/Sr. Advisor to Board, Carlton Dean Thomas/Sr. Advisor to Board

Directors: Michael D. Pruitt/Chmn., CEO, CFO, Pres., Brian Corbman/Dir., William Block/69/Dir., Michael Carroll/Dir., Paul I. Moskowitz/Dir.

Owners: Insiders/22.92%, William Block, Brian Corbman, Michael D. Pruitt/21.94%, Michael Carroll, Palisades Master Fund, LP/54.55%

Financial Data: Fiscal Year End:12/31 **Latest Annual Data:** 12/31/2006

Year	Sales	Net Income
2006	$127,000	-$199,000
2005	$5,000	-$172,000

Curr. Assets:	$155,000	Curr. Liab.:	$13,000		
Plant, Equip.:	$33,000	Total Liab.:	$164,000	Indic. Yr. Divd.:	NA
Total Assets:	$2,577,000	Net Worth:	$2,413,000	Debt/ Equity:	NA

Chaparral Resources Inc

2 Gannett Dr., Ste 418, White Plains, NY, 10604; **PH:** 1-866-559-3822; **Fax:** 1-866-700-5091;
http:// www.chaparralresources.com; **Email:** ir@chaparralresources.com

General - Incorporation .... DE
Employees .... NA
Auditor .... Ernst & Young Kazakhstan LLP
Stk Agt..... Computershare Investor Services LLC
Counsel............ Akin, Gump, Strauss, Hauer & Feld LLP
DUNS No. 06-731-1167

Stock- Price on:12/24/2007 .... NA
Stock Exchange .... NA
Ticker Symbol .... NA
Outstanding Shares .... NA
E.P.S .... NA
Shareholders .... NA

Business: The group's principle activity is the exploration, development and production of oil and gas properties. It acquires and develops foreign oil and gas projects in emerging markets, especially the fields with reserves discovered from previous explorations. The group owns a 60% interest in closed type jsc karakudukmunay, a kazakhstan joint stock company, which holds the rights for the exploration, development and production of oil in the karakuduk field in western kazakhstan. It produces crude oil from the karakuduk fields and sells a majority of it on the export market to shell trading international limited. There are six delivery points under the crude oil sales agreement with shell, including three preferred port facilities on the black sea at novorossiisk, odessa, and ventspills and three onshore pipeline facilities at dudkovce, feyeshlitke, and adamovo.

Primary SIC and add'l.: 1311

CIK No: 0000019252

Subsidiaries: CJSC Kaztransoil, LUKOIL Overseas Holding Limited

Chaparral Steel Co

300 Ward Rd., Midlothian, TX, 76065; ***PH:*** 1-972-775-8241; ***http://*** www.chapusa.com

General - Incorporation .... DE
Employees 1,450
Auditor .... Ernst & Young LLP
Stk Agt............ Mellon Investor Services LLC
Counsel............ Robert E. Crawford Jr.
DUNS No. .... NA

Stock- Price on:12/24/2007 .... $71.05
Stock Exchange .... NYSE
Ticker Symbol .... CHAP
Outstanding Shares 46,820,000
E.P.S $5.08
Shareholders .... NA

Business: The group's principle activity is to manufacture structural steel products and steel bar products. The group utilize mini-mill technology in which recycled scrap steel is melted in electric arc furnaces, and continuous casting systems form the molten steel into a broad range of products. The group manufactures over 230 different types, sizes and grades of structural steel and bar products. The groups structural steel products include wide flange beams, channels, piling products and other shapes. The groups steel bar products include specialty bar products, and, to a lesser extent, reinforcing bar. The group operates from United States, Canada and Mexico.

Primary SIC and add'l.: 3310

CIK No: 0001319048

Subsidiaries: 1201/5400 Elm Corporation, Aceros Chaparral, S. de R. L. de C. V., American Materials Transport, Inc., Chaparral (Virginia) Inc., Chaparral Star Recycling LP, Chaparral Steel Holdings, LLC, Chaparral Steel Investments, Inc., Chaparral Steel Midlothian, LP, Chaparral Steel Texas, LLC, Chaparral Steel Trust, Servicios Chaparral, S. de R. L. de C. V.

Owners: James M. Hoak, Ronald J. Gafford, Insiders/1.90%, Ian Wachtmeister, Tommy A. Valenta, Joseph D. Mahaffey, William H. Dickert, Timothy J. Bourcier, Robert E. Crawford, Joseph M. Grant, Eugenio Clariond, Daniel W. Brock, Elizabeth C. Williams, Celtyn J. Hughes

Financial Data: ***Fiscal Year End:***05/31 ***Latest Annual Data:*** 5/31/2005

Year	Sales	Net Income
2005	$1,116,376,000	$78,120,000

Curr. Assets:	$434,724,000	***Curr. Liab.:***	$109,913,000	***P/E Ratio:***	13.99
Plant, Equip.:	$627,253,000	***Total Liab.:***	$800,722,000	***Indic. Yr. Divd.:***	$0.400
Total Assets:	$1,152,242,000	***Net Worth:***	$351,520,000	***Debt/ Equity:***	0.3527

Chapeau Inc

10 Greg St., Sparks, NV, 89431; ***PH:*** 1-916-780-6764

General - Incorporation .... UT
Employees 21
Auditor .... Hansen, Barnett & Maxwell
Stk Agt............ Progressive Transfer Company
Counsel .... NA
DUNS No. 17-795-3684

Stock- Price on:12/24/2007 .... $4.24
Stock Exchange .... OTC
Ticker Symbol .... CPEU
Outstanding Shares 54,730,000
E.P.S .... -$0.43
Shareholders .... NA

Business: The group's principle activity will be to develop, assemble and sell packaged co-generation and power products. The group intends to focus on its resources on the development of a packaged onsite co-generation solution targeting commercial and industrial application requirements. First-generation product is currently based on a well-established natural gas fired, reciprocating engine combined with state-of-the-art proprietary emission control technologies. Initial independent emission testing have yielded favorable results and finalizing commercial configuration is anticipated by the end of 2002. The group continues to evaluate alternative distribution channels for its products including a direct sales force as well as third party distributors. Group's primary target will be principally commercial and industrial power users, as well as gas and electric utilities with application requirements under 1.4 megawatts. The group is in the development stage.

Primary SIC and add'l.: 3621

CIK No: 0000783211

Subsidiaries: Specialized Energy Products, Inc

Officers: Guy A. Archbold/56/Dir., CEO, Steven C. Lagorio/55/CFO, Sec., Neil C. Bokamper/COO, Steve Brandon/50/Pres.

Directors: Guy A. Archbold/56/Dir., CEO, Robert W. Medearis/76/Dir., Gordon V. Smith/76/Dir.

Owners: Calim Bridge IPartners, Guy A. Archbold, Gordon V. Smith5, MFPI, LLC6, Calim Venture Partners, Robert W. Medearis, Steven C. Lagorio, Calim Venture Partners, Calim Venture Partners II, Calim Venture Partners I, Insiders, Gerald H. Dorn, Neil Bokamper, Calim Venture Partners II, Steve Brandon

Financial Data: ***Fiscal Year End:***06/30 ***Latest Annual Data:*** 6/30/2006

Year	Sales	Net Income
2006	$389,000	-$4,704,000
2005	$330,000	-$2,899,000
2004	$171,000	-$3,457,000

Curr. Assets:	$2,925,000	***Curr. Liab.:***	$5,608,000		
Plant, Equip.:	$372,000	***Total Liab.:***	$13,731,000	***Indic. Yr. Divd.:***	NA
Total Assets:	$3,832,000	***Net Worth:***	-$9,899,000	***Debt/ Equity:***	NA

Chardan South China Acquisition Corp

Formerly: Chardan South China Acquisition Corp
625 Brd.way, Ste. 1111, San Diego, CA, 92101; ***PH:*** 1-858-847-9000

General - Incorporation .... DE
Employees .... NA
Auditor .... Goldstein Golub Kessler LLP
Stk Agt .... Continental Stock Transfer & Trust Co
Counsel .... NA
DUNS No. .... NA

Stock- Price on:12/24/2007 .... $8.06
Stock Exchange .... OTC
Ticker Symbol .... CSCA
Outstanding Shares 7,000,000
E.P.S .... -$0.04
Shareholders .... NA

Business: The groups principal is not engage in, any substantive commercial business until the group consummates a business combination. The group operates from the United States.

Primary SIC and add'l.: 6770

CIK No: 0001324298

Owners: Richard D. Propper/9.00%, Kerry Propper/4.50%, Jeffrey L. Feinberg/38.90%, Paul Packer/7.40%, Jiangnan Huang/2.20%, Jack Silver/12.50%, Li Zhang/2.20%, Insiders/18.00%

Financial Data: ***Fiscal Year End:***12/31 ***Latest Annual Data:*** 12/31/2006

Year	Sales	Net Income
2006	NA	$49,000
2005	NA	$69,000

Curr. Assets:	$31,455,000	***Curr. Liab.:***	$604,000		
Plant, Equip.:	NA	***Total Liab.:***	$6,568,000	***Indic. Yr. Divd.:***	NA
Total Assets:	$31,690,000	***Net Worth:***	$25,122,000	***Debt/ Equity:***	NA

Charles & Colvard Ltd

300 Perimeter Pk. Dr., Ste. A, Morrisville, NC, 27560; ***PH:*** 1-919-468-0399; ***Fax:*** 1-919-468-0486; ***http://*** www.moissanite.com

General - Incorporation .... NC
Employees 60
Auditor .... Deloitte & Touche LLP
Stk Agt .... American Stock Transfer & Trust CO.
Counsel .... NA
DUNS No. 00-661-9480

Stock- Price on:12/24/2007 .... $4.8499
Stock Exchange .... NDQ
Ticker Symbol .... CTHR
Outstanding Shares 18,040,000
E.P.S $0.13
Shareholders .... NA

Business: The group's principal activity is to manufacture, market and distribute moissanite jewels. Moissanite is a rare, naturally occurring mineral found primarily in meteorites. The group also develops and markets gemstone test instruments, which are used to distinguish colorless moissanite gemstones from diamond. It sources moissanite gemstones from cree inc, which processes single large crystals of silicon carbide. The group distributes moissanite jewels in substantially all of western Europe and certain territories in southeast Asia.

Primary SIC and add'l.: 3911

CIK No: 0001015155

Subsidiaries: Charles & Colvard (HK) Ltd.

Officers: Jim Braun/CFO/$265,206.00, Dennis M. Reed/Pres. - CMO/$282,363.00

Directors: Robert A. Leggett/50/Dir.

Owners: Earl R. Hines, Lisa A. Gavales, George A. Thornton, James R. Braun, Frederick A. Russ/2.00%, Dennis M. Reed, Geraldine L. Sedlar, Lynn L. Lane, Robert A. Leggett, Robert S. Thomas/9.80%, Laura C. Kendall, Insiders/14.00%, Chester L. F. Paulson/6.50%

Financial Data: ***Fiscal Year End:***12/31 ***Latest Annual Data:*** 12/31/2006

Year	Sales	Net Income
2006	$40,712,000	$6,105,000
2005	$43,544,000	$5,875,000
2004	$23,917,000	$1,612,000

Curr. Assets:	$52,544,000	***Curr. Liab.:***	$6,725,000	***P/E Ratio:***	20.21
Plant, Equip.:	$12,459,000	***Total Liab.:***	$6,725,000	***Indic. Yr. Divd.:***	$0.080
Total Assets:	$66,002,000	***Net Worth:***	$59,277,000	***Debt/ Equity:***	NA

Charles River Assoc Inc

200 Clarendon St., T-33, Boston, MA, 02116; ***PH:*** 1-617-425-3000; ***http://*** www.crai.com

General - Incorporation .... MA
Employees 994
Auditor .... KPMG LLP
Stk Agt .... Computershare Trust Co
Counsel .... Foley Hoag LLP
DUNS No. 07-952-5325

Stock- Price on:12/24/2007 .... $45.97
Stock Exchange .... NDQ
Ticker Symbol .... CRAI
Outstanding Shares 11,700,000
E.P.S $2.32
Shareholders .... NA

Business: The group's principal activity is to provide consulting services. It offers two types of services: legal and regulatory consulting and business consulting. It provides advice to law firms, corporations and governments around the world. As a legal and regulatory consultant, the group works with the law firms on behalf of the companies involved in the litigation or regulatory proceedings. As a business consultant it uses its expertise to establish pricing strategies, estimate market demand, value intellectual property and analyze new sources of supply. The group also offers consultant services for environmental disputes, international trade, transfer pricing, damages and antitrust. The customers include law firms, domestic and foreign corporations, utilities, government agencies, foreign governments and trade associations. The group operates in the United States, United Kingdom, Australia, Mexico, Canada and New Zealand. On 30-Apr-2004, the group acquired Intecap Inc.

Primary SIC and add'l.: 8748

CIK No: 0001053706

Subsidiaries: CRA International (UK) Limited, CRA International de Mexica S.A. de C.V., CRA International Limited, CRA International Pty Ltd, CRA Security Corporation, Economics of Competition and Litigation Limited, InteCap Risk Solutions Limited, Lee & Allen Consulting Limited, Lee & Allen Consulting, Inc., Network Economics Consulting Group PTY LTD, NeuCo, Inc.

Officers: James C. Burrows/Dir., CEO, Pres., Michael Hunter/VP, Henry Ergas/Regional Head - Asia Pacific, Gregory H. Thorpe/VP, Mike Smart/VP, Musadik Malik/VP, Margaret F. Sanderson/VP, James Mellsop/VP, Michael T. Thomas/VP, Frederick Baird/Exec. VP, William Bishop/VP, Tim Allen/VP, Jill Weise/VP, Tim Wilsdon/VP, John R. Woodbury/VP *(188 Officers included in Index)*

Directors: James C. Burrows/Dir., CEO, Pres., Franklin M. Fisher/Vice Chmn., Rowland T. Moriarty/Chmn., Scott Englander/Dir., Carl Shapiro/Dir., Nancy L. Rose/Dir., William F. Concannon/Dir., Steven C. Salop/61/Dir., Basil L. Anderson/Dir., Ronald T. Maheu/Dir.

Owners: Transamerica Investment Management, LLC/6.40%, Franklin M. Fisher, Rowland T. Moriarty, Arnold J. Lowenstein, CNH CA Master Account, L.P./8.60%, Artisan Partner Limited Partnership/6.80%, Basil L. Anderson, Nancy L. Rose, James C. Burrows/2.50%, William F. Concannon, Insiders/8.00%, Carl Shapiro, Paul A. Maleh, Ronald T. Maheu, Steven C. Salop *(17 Owners included in Index)*

Financial Data: ***Fiscal Year End:***11/26 ***Latest Annual Data:*** 11/25/2006

Year	Sales	Net Income
2006	$349,894,000	$27,445,000
2005	$295,474,000	$24,600,000
2004	$216,735,000	$16,344,000

Curr. Assets:	$162,822,000	**Curr. Liab.:**	$61,503,000	**P/E Ratio:**	19.90
Plant, Equip.:	$18,528,000	**Total Liab.:**	$159,600,000	**Indic. Yr. Divd.:**	NA
Total Assets:	$288,811,000	**Net Worth:**	$127,026,000	**Debt/ Equity:**	0.3314

Charles River Laboratories International Inc

251 Ballardvale St., Wilmington, MA, 01887; ***PH:*** 1-978-658-6000; ***Fax:*** 1-978-658-7132; ***http://*** www.criver.com; ***Email:*** comments@crl.com

General - Incorporation .... DE
Employees 8,000
Auditor .... PricewaterhouseCoopers LLP
Stk Agt..... Computershare Investor Services LLC
Counsel .... NA
DUNS No. .... NA

Stock- Price on:12/24/2007 .... $52.34
Stock Exchange .... NYSE
Ticker Symbol .... CRL
Outstanding Shares 67,300,000
E.P.S $2.25
Shareholders .... NA

Business: The group's principal activity is to provide research tools and integrated support services that enable drug discovery and development. The group operates in two segments research models and services (rms) and development and safety testing (dst). Research models and services business is comprised of the commercial production and sale of animal research models, principally purpose-bred rats, mice and other rodents for use by researchers. These research models are bred and maintained in a biosecure environment designed to ensure that the animals are free of specific viral and bacterial agents and other contaminants that can disrupt research operations and distort results. Discovery is followed by development activities, which are directed at demonstrating the safety and efficacy of the selected drug candidates. Discovery and development represent most of the pre-clinical activities in drug development. On 08-Jan-2004, the group acquired river valley farms inc.

Primary SIC and add'l.: 8731 6719 2834 2836

CIK No: 0001100682

Subsidiaries: Alpes S.a., Ballardvale CV, Charles River Consulting GmbH, Charles River Endosafe Limited, Charles River Europe GmbH, Charles River Germany GmbH and Co. KG, Charles River Germany Verwaltungs GmbH, Charles River Holdings LLC, Charles River Japan KK, Charles River Lab Holdings Mass Business Trust, Charles River Laboratories Belgium SA, Charles River Laboratories BioLabs Europe Ltd., Charles River Laboratories Clinical Services GmbH, Charles River Laboratories Clinical Services Inc., Charles River Laboratories Clinical Services International Ltd. 57 Subsidiaries included in the Index

Officers: James C. Foster/Chmn., CEO, Pres./$5,734,178.00, Real H. Renaud/Corporate Exec. VP, GM - Global Research Model Products, Services/$1,912,979.00, Thomas F. Ackerman/Corporate Exec. VP, CFO/$1,806,080.00, David P. Johst/Corporate Exec. VP - Human Resources, Administration/$1,713,908.00, Joanne P. Acford/Corporate Sr. VP, General Counsel, Corp. Sec., Nancy A. Gillett/Corporate Exec. VP, Pres. - Global Preclinical Services/$1,378,719.00, John C. Ho/Corporate Sr. VP - Corporate Strategy, Nicholas Ventresca/Corporate Sr. VP - Information Technology, CIO, Cheri Walker/Corporate Sr. VP - Corporate Development, Stephanie Wells/Corporate Sr. VP - Marketing, Chief Marketing Officer

Directors: James C. Foster/Chmn., CEO, Pres., Douglas E. Rogers/Dir., William Waltrip/Dir., George M. Milne/Dir., George E. Massaro/Dir., Stephen D. Chubb/Dir., Samuel O. Thier/Dir.

Owners: Linda McGoldrick, Insiders, James C. Foster/1.70%, FMR Corp./10.60%, Farallon Capital Partners, L.P/5.00%, William H. Waltrip, Thomas F. Ackerman, Goldman Sachs Asset Management, L.P./6.20%, David P. Johst, Stephen D. Chubb, Samuel O. Thier, George M. Milne, Douglas E. Rogers, Nancy A. Gillett, George E. Massaro *(16 Owners included in Index)*

Financial Data: ***Fiscal Year End:***12/31 ***Latest Annual Data:*** 12/30/2006

Year	Sales	Net Income
2006	$1,058,385,000	-$55,783,000
2005	$1,122,228,000	$141,999,000
2004	$766,917,000	$89,792,000

Curr. Assets:	$419,322,000	**Curr. Liab.:**	$311,412,000	**P/E Ratio:**	44.36
Plant, Equip.:	$399,454,000	**Total Liab.:**	$701,478,000	**Indic. Yr. Divd.:**	NA
Total Assets:	$2,538,209,000	**Net Worth:**	$1,827,013,000	**Debt/ Equity:**	0.3212

Charles Schwab Corp (The)

101 Montgomery St., San Francisco, CA, 94104; ***PH:*** 1-415-636-7000; ***Fax:*** 1-415-636-9820; ***http://*** www.aboutschwab.com; ***Email:*** public.relations@schwab.com

General - Incorporation ....
Employees 12,400
Auditor .... Deloitte & Touche LLP
Stk Agt .... Wells Fargo Bank, N.A.
Counsel .... NA
DUNS No. .... NA

Stock- Price on:12/24/2007 .... $21.79
Stock Exchange .... NDQ
Ticker Symbol .... SCHW
Outstanding Shares 1,250,000,000
E.P.S $2.05
Shareholders .... NA

Business: The groups principle activity is to provide financial services. The group provides services include investing, advice and consultations, and banking and lending. The group operates from United States.

Primary SIC and add'l.: 6029

CIK No: 0001171314

Officers: Charles R. Schwab/70/Chmn., CEO, Peter K. Scaturro/CEO - US, Exec. VP - Trust Corporation, Rebecca Saeger/Chief Marketing Officer, Exec. VP, Randall W. Merk/Exec. VP, Jay L. Allen/Exec. VP - Human Resources, Benjamin L. Brigeman/Exec. VP - Schwab Investor Services, Lisa Kidd Hunt/Exec. VP - Schwab Investor Development, Joseph R. Martinetto/CFO, Exec. VP, Maurisa Sommerfield/Exec. VP - Operational Services, Walter W. Bettinger/COO, Pres. - Charles Schwab Corporation, John S. Clendening/Exec. VP - Solution Services Enterprise, Charles Schwab, Co, Inc, Carrie E. Dwyer/Exec. VP - Corporate Oversight, General Counsel, Charles G. Goldman/COO, Exec. VP - Schwab Institutional, Jan Hier-King/CIO, Exec. VP, James D. McCool/Exec. VP - Schwab Corporate, Retirement Services

Directors: Charles R. Schwab/70/Chmn., CEO, Stephen T. McLin/61/Dir., Frank C. Herringer/65/Dir., Marjorie Magner/58/Dir., William F. Aldinger/60/Dir., Nancy H. Bechtle/70/Dir., Preston C. Butcher/69/Dir., Donald G. Fisher/79/Dir., Paula A. Sneed/60/Dir., Roger O. Walther/72/Dir., Robert N. Wilson/67/Dir., Anthony M. Frank/69/Dir., George P. Shultz/Dir. Emeritus

Financial Data: ***Fiscal Year End:***NA ***Latest Annual Data:*** 12/31/2006

Year	Sales	Net Income
2006	$4,988,000,000	$1,227,000,000
2005	$5,151,000,000	$725,000,000
2004	$4,479,000,000	$286,000,000

Curr. Assets:	$26,946,000,000	**Curr. Liab.:**	$34,532,000,000		
Plant, Equip.:	$602,000,000	**Total Liab.:**	$43,984,000,000	**Indic. Yr. Divd.:**	$0.200
Total Assets:	$48,992,000,000	**Net Worth:**	$5,008,000,000	**Debt/ Equity:**	0.0784

Charlotte Russe Holding Inc

4645 Morena Blvd., San Diego, CA, 92117; ***PH:*** 1-858-587-1500; ***Fax:*** 1-858-587-0902; ***http://*** www.charlotte-russe.com

General - Incorporation .... DE
Employees 2,099
Auditor .... Ernst & Young LLP
Stk Agt........ Mellon Investor Services LLC
Counsel........ Brobeck, Phleger & Harrison
DUNS No. .... NA

Stock- Price on:12/24/2007 .... $27.06
Stock Exchange .... NDQ
Ticker Symbol .... CHIC
Outstanding Shares 25,320,000
E.P.S $1.43
Shareholders .... NA

Business: The group's principal activity is the retail distribution of fashionable, value-priced apparel and accessories. Operating under two distinct store concepts, charlotte russe and rampage, the group offers apparel and accessories targeted at young women aged between 15 and 35. The charlotte russe chain offers fashions that have been tested by the market while the rampage chain retails emerging fashion trends. As of 27-Sep-2003, the group operates 311 stores across 38 states of the United States and Puerto Rico. The merchandise is sourced from 620 third-party vendors with whom the group has established a relationship. It also maintains a buying office in the californiamart in los angeles, the primary apparel center in southern California. The group is currently testing a third store concept, charlotte's room that would cater to the 11 to 17 year age groups.

Primary SIC and add'l.: 2389 2335 5621

CIK No: 0001092006

Officers: Daniel T. Carter/CFO

Owners: Putnam Investment Management, LLC/5.20%, Daniel T. Carter, Insiders/6.90%, Paul R. Del Rossi, Edward Wong, S.A.C. Capital Advisors, LLC/5.00%, Mark J. Rivers, Leonard H. Mogil, Mark A. Hoffman, Apax Funds/5.80%, Jennifer C. Salopek, Allan W. Karp/6.60%

Financial Data: ***Fiscal Year End:***09/24 ***Latest Annual Data:*** 09/29/2007

Year	Sales	Net Income
2007	$740,939,000	$36,304,000
2006	$681,504,000	$25,138,000
2005	$603,756,000	$10,801,000

Curr. Assets:	$152,485,000	**Curr. Liab.:**	$55,141,000	**P/E Ratio:**	14.24
Plant, Equip.:	$177,578,000	**Total Liab.:**	$153,064,000	**Indic. Yr. Divd.:**	NA
Total Assets:	$359,519,000	**Net Worth:**	$206,454,000	**Debt/ Equity:**	NA

Charming Shoppes Inc

450 Winks Ln., Bensalem, PA, 19020; ***PH:*** 1-215-245-9100; ***Fax:*** 1-215-633-4640; ***http://*** www.charmingshoppes.com

General - Incorporation .... PA
Employees 11,000
Auditor .... Ernst & Young LLP
Stk Agt...... American Stock Transfer & Trust Co.
Counsel .... NA
DUNS No. 05-474-4677

Stock- Price on:12/24/2007 .... $11.78
Stock Exchange .... NDQ
Ticker Symbol .... CHRS
Outstanding Shares 128,600,000
E.P.S $0.77
Shareholders .... NA

Business: The groups principle activity is to operate retail apparel stores for women. The groups products include accessories, footwear and gift catalogs. The group operates through two business segments namely retail stores and direct-to-consumer. The group operates from United States.

Primary SIC and add'l.: 5621

CIK No: 0000019353

Subsidiaries: C.s.a.c., Inc., C.S.F., Corp., C.s.i.c., Inc., Catalog Fulfillment Co, Inc., Catalog Receivables, LLC, Catalog Seller, LLC, Catherines C.S.A.C., Inc., Catherines C.S.I.C., Inc., Catherines of California, Inc., Catherines of Nevada, Inc., Catherines of Pennsylvania, Inc., Catherines Partners-Indiana, LLP, Catherines Partners-Texas, L.P., Catherines Partners-Washington, G.P., Catherines Stores Corporation 83 Subsidiaries included in the Index

Officers: Dorrit J. Bern/58/Chmn., CEO, Pres./$8,322,248.00, Michel Bourlon/Exec. VP - Sourcing, Gale H. Varma/Exec. VP - Human Resources, Colin D. Stern/Exec. VP, General Counsel, Sec./$1,296,561.00, John J. Sullivan/Sr. VP, Corporate Controller, Anthony A. Desabato/Exec. VP - Corporate, Labor Relations/$1,160,558.00, Eric M. Specter/CFO, Exec. VP/$1,238,113.00, Joseph M. Baron/COO, Exec. VP/$1,526,051.00, James G. Bloise/Exec. VP - Supply Chain, Technology, Business Services

Directors: Dorrit J. Bern/58/Chmn., CEO, Pres., William O. Albertini/64/Dir., Yvonne M. Curl/53/Dir., Jeannine M. Strandjord/61/Dir., Alan Rosskamm/58/Dir., Charles T. Hopkins/65/Dir., Katherine M. Hudson/61/Dir., Pamela Davies/51/Dir.

Financial Data: ***Fiscal Year End:***01/28 ***Latest Annual Data:*** 2/3/2007

Year	Sales	Net Income
2007	$3,067,517,000	$108,923,000
2006	$2,755,725,000	$99,391,000
2005	$2,332,334,000	$64,526,000

Curr. Assets:	$840,838,000	**Curr. Liab.:**	$397,737,000	**P/E Ratio:**	15.30
Plant, Equip.:	$422,446,000	**Total Liab.:**	$763,404,000	**Indic. Yr. Divd.:**	NA
Total Assets:	$1,710,942,000	**Net Worth:**	$947,538,000	**Debt/ Equity:**	0.3455

Chart Industries Inc

1 Infinity Corporate Ctr. Dr., Ste. 300, Garfield Heights, OH, 44125; ***PH:*** 1-440-753-1490; ***Fax:*** 1-440-753-1491; ***http://*** www.chart-ind.com

General - Incorporation	DE	**Stock**- Price on:12/24/2007	$27.65
Employees	2,703	Stock Exchange	NDQ
Auditor	Ernst& Young LLP	Ticker Symbol	GTLS
Stk Agt	National City Bank	Outstanding Shares	25,650,000
Counsel	NA	E.P.S	$1.36
DUNS No.	NA	Shareholders	NA

Business: The groups principle activity is to manufacture engineered equipment. The products of the group include LNG vacuum insulated pipe, cold boxe,s heat exchangers and cryogenic bulk storage systems. Customers served by the group include production, gas distribution, gas processing, liquid natural gas, and chemical and industrial gas industries. The groups operates through three segments namely energy and chemicals, distribution and storage and biomedical. The group acquired Cooler Service Company, Inc in the year 2006 and Changzhou CEM Cryo Equipment Co., Ltd in the year 2005. Specific customers of the group include The Linde, JGC Corporation or JGC, Bechtel Corporation and Jacobs Engineering Group, Inc. The group operates from New Iberia, Louisiana and Houston and Texas. The group's quarterly revenue for September 2007 was 163.67 millions of USD.

Primary SIC and add'l.: 3443 3441 3845 3585

CIK No: 0000892553

Subsidiaries: CAIRE Inc, Changzhou CEM Cryo Equipment Co., Ltd., Chart Asia, Inc, Chart Australia Pty. Ltd., Chart Biomedical Limited, Chart Cooler Service Company, Inc., Chart Cryogenic Engineering Systems (Changzhou) Co., Ltd., Chart Cryogenic Equipment (Changzhou) Co., Ltd., Chart Energy & Chemicals, Inc., Chart Ferox a.s., Chart Ferox GmbH, Chart Inc., Chart International Holdings, Inc., Chart International, Inc., GTC of Clarksville, LLC 17 Subsidiaries included in the Index

Officers: Samuel F. Thomas/56/Chmn., CEO, Pres./$1,475,022.00, Michael F. Biehl/Exec. VP, CFO, Treasurer/$735,974.00, Matthew J. Klaben/VP, General Counsel, Sec./$554,466.00, James H. Hoppel/Chief Accounting Officer, Controller, Assist. Treasurer/$380,771.00, Steve T. Shaw/Pres. - Biomedical, Marietta, GA, Tom Carey/Pres. - Distribution, Storage Systems, Ball Ground, GA

Directors: Samuel F. Thomas/56/Chmn., CEO, Pres., Timothy H. Day/37/Dir., Richard E. Goodrich/Dir., Steven W. Krablin/Dir., Kenneth W. Moore/38/Dir., Michael W. Press/Dir., James M. Tidwell/Dir.

Owners: First Reserve FundX, L.P/48.40%, Richard E. Goodrich, Michael F. Biehl, Michael W. Press, Capital Research and Management Company/8.90%, Matthew J. Klaben, Samuel F. Thomas/1.90%, James H. Hoppel, Insiders/2.20%

Financial Data: ***Fiscal Year End:***12/31 ***Latest Annual Data:*** 12/31/2006

Year	Sales	Net Income
2006	$537,454,000	$26,895,000
2004	$305,576,000	$22,600,000
2003	$265,587,000	-$7,054,000

Curr. Assets:	$230,635,000	**Curr. Liab.:**	$139,241,000	**P/E Ratio:**	20.33
Plant, Equip.:	$85,723,000	**Total Liab.:**	$505,141,000	**Indic. Yr. Divd.:**	NA
Total Assets:	$724,875,000	**Net Worth:**	$219,734,000	**Debt/ Equity:**	1.2777

Charter Communications Inc

12405 Powerscourt Dr., Ste. 100, St. Louis, MO, 63131; ***PH:*** 1-314-965-0555; ***Fax:*** 1-314-965-9745; ***http://*** www.charter.com

General - Incorporation	DE	**Stock**- Price on:12/24/2007	$4.08
Employees	15,500	Stock Exchange	NDQ
Auditor	KPMG LLP	Ticker Symbol	CHTR
Stk Agt	Mellon Investor Services LLC	Outstanding Shares	408,650,000
Counsel	NA	E.P.S	-$4.21
DUNS No.	NA	Shareholders	NA

Business: The group's principle activity is to provide communication services via cable, Internet and telephone. The groups design solutions include Charter Business Bundle(TM), Charter Business(TM) High-Speed Internet, Charter Business(TM) Telephone, Charter Business(TM) Video and Charter Business(TM) Music. The group operates from United States.

Primary SIC and add'l.: 6719 4841

CIK No: 0001091667

Subsidiaries: 212 Seventh Street, Inc., Adlink Cable Advertising, LLC, American Cable Entertainment Company, LLC, ARH, Ltd., Athens Cablevision, Inc., Ausable Cable TV, Inc., Bend Cable Communications, LLC, Cable Equities Colorado, LLC, Cable Equities of Colorado Management Corp., Cable Systems, Inc., Cc 10, LLC, CC Fiberlink, LLC, CC Holdco I, LLC, CC Michigan, LLC, CC New England, LLC 175 Subsidiaries included in the Index

Officers: Neil Smit/Dir., CEO, Pres./$5,911,425.00, Mary L. White/Divisional Pres. - Central, Eric P. Brown/Divisional Pres. - West, Michael J. Lovett/COO, Exec. VP/$2,022,674.00, Lynne F. Ramsey/Sr. VP - Human Resources, Sueann R. Hamilton/Exec. VP - Programming, Joshua L. Jamison/Divisional Pres. - East, Grier C. Raclin/Exec. VP, General Counsel, Corp. Sec./$1,104,537.00, Marwan Fawaz/CTO, Jeffrey T. Fisher/CFO, Exec. VP/$1,370,793.00, Robert A. Quigley/Exec. VP, Chief Marketing Officer/$1,132,249.00, Mary Jo Moehle/VP - Investor Relations, Communications, Kevin D. Howard/VP, Chief Accounting Officer, Eloise E. Schmitz/Sr. VP - Strategic Planning, Paula Trustdorf/Divisional Pres. - West

Directors: Neil Smit/Dir., CEO, Pres., Paul G. Allen/Chmn., Larry W. Wangberg/Dir., Nathaniel A. Davis/Dir., David C. Merritt/Dir., John H. Tory/Dir., Robert P. May/Dir., Jonathan L. Dolgen/Dir., Rajive Johri/Dir., Marc B. Nathanson/Dir., Jo Allen Patton/Dir., Lance W. Conn/Dir.

Owners: Insiders, Insiders, Paul G. Allen, Wellington Management Company, LLC, Michael J. Lovett, Steelhead Partners, Jo Allen Patton, Lance W. Conn, Edward C. Johnson, FMR Corp., Robert P. May, Fidelity Management & Research Company, Paul G. Allen, Jonathan L. Dolgen, Rajive Johri *(26 Owners included in Index)*

Financial Data: ***Fiscal Year End:***12/31 ***Latest Annual Data:*** 12/31/2006

Year	Sales	Net Income
2006	$5,504,000,000	-$1,370,000,000
2005	$5,254,000,000	-$967,000,000
2004	$4,977,000,000	-$4,341,000,000

Curr. Assets:	$339,000,000	**Curr. Liab.:**	$1,298,000,000		
Plant, Equip.:	$5,217,000,000	**Total Liab.:**	$21,123,000,000	**Indic. Yr. Divd.:**	NA
Total Assets:	$15,100,000,000	**Net Worth:**	-$6,219,000,000	**Debt/ Equity:**	NA

Charter Financial Corp

1233 O.G. Skinner Dr., West Point, GA, 31833; ***PH:*** 1-706-645-1310; ***http://*** www.charterbk.com

General - Incorporation	US	**Stock**- Price on:12/24/2007	NA
Employees	179	Stock Exchange	OTC
Auditor	KPMG LLP	Ticker Symbol	CHFN
Stk Agt	American Stock Transfer & Trust Co.	Outstanding Shares	NA
Counsel	NA	E.P.S	NA
DUNS No.	NA	Shareholders	NA

Business: The group's principal activity is to accept deposits and to provide retail-banking services. The group is a federally chartered corporation registered as a savings and loan holding company. The group provides mortgage loans and a full range of deposit products to individual customers primarily in the states of Georgia and Alabama. The group operates through its wholly owned subsidiaries charterbank and charter insurance company. Charterbank is a service-oriented bank which offers numerous loan products, including residential mortgage loans, commercial real estate loans, commercial loans, home equity loans, second mortgages, and other products. Charterbank also offers deposit products, including consumer and commercial checking accounts, savings accounts, money market accounts, and certificates of deposit. On 21-Feb-2003, the group acquired eba bancshares inc and eagle bank of Alabama.

Primary SIC and add'l.: 6712 6035

CIK No: 0001136796

Subsidiaries: CharterBank

Officers: Robert Lee Johnson/Dir., CEO, Pres., Curtis R. Kollar/Sr. VP, CFO - Chartered Bank, Lee Washam/Exec. VP, Chief Credit Officer - Charterbank, William C. Gladden/Sr. VP, Corp. Sec. - Chartered Bank, William B. Hudson/Dir. - Chartered Bank, David Z. Cauble/Dir. - Chartered Bank

Directors: Robert Lee Johnson/Dir., CEO, Pres., John W. Johnson/Chmn., Founder - Charterbank, Thomas M. Lane/Dir. - Chartered Bank, Jane W. Darden/Dir. - Chartered Bank, David L. Strobel/Dir. - Chartered Bank

Owners: Robert L. Johnson, William C. Gladden, William B. Hudson, ESOP/1.70%, Thomas M. Lane, Lee Washam, First Charter, MHC/82.00%, Curtis R. Kollar, David Z. Cauble, John W. Johnson, David L. Strobel, Jane W. Darden, Insiders/2.50%

Curr. Assets:	$27,999,000	**Curr. Liab.:**	$372,057,000		
Plant, Equip.:	$17,486,000	**Total Liab.:**	$829,613,000	**Indic. Yr. Divd.:**	NA
Total Assets:	$1,097,321,000	**Net Worth:**	$267,709,000	**Debt/ Equity:**	1.2622

Charter Oak Bank CA

600 Trancas St., Napa, CA, 94558; ***PH:*** 1-707-265-2050; ***http://*** www.charteroakbank.com; ***Email:*** info@charteroakbank.com

General - Incorporation		**Stock**- Price on:12/24/2007	$16
Employees	NA	Stock Exchange	OTC
Auditor	NA	Ticker Symbol	CHOB
Stk Agt	U.S. Stock Transfer Corp	Outstanding Shares	NA
Counsel	NA	E.P.S	NA
DUNS No.	NA	Shareholders	NA

Business: The groups principal activity is to provide the front end optical mark sensing and image scanning systems. Customers served by the group include resellers, system integrators and applications developers. The group operates from the United States.

Primary SIC and add'l.: 6022

CIK No:

Officers: Brian J. Kelly/Dir., CEO, Pres., Rod Wiessner/CFO, Exec. VP, Debbie Seaman/Sr. VP - Operations, Michael Ledwich/Exec. VP, Chief Credit Officer, Jody Arnold/Loan Operations Specialist, Evelynn Bekker/Assist. VP, Relationship Officer, Trent Stoppello/Assist. VP, Relationship Officer, Debbie Fay/Assist. VP, Bank Services Officer, Jamie Davidson/Commercial Loan Officer, Al Nuccion/Relationship Officer, Pat Carson/Assist. VP - Loan Operations Supervisor, Lisa Eichler Crump/Marketing Mgr., Tina Grantham/Administrative Coordinator, Belinda Menzel/Loan Operations Specialist, Debbie Vollmer/Assist. VP, Controller *(24 Officers included in Index)*

Directors: Brian J. Kelly/Dir., CEO, Pres., Thomas Nelson/Chmn., Annie Bennett/Vice Chmn., John Dermody/Dir., Joseph Peatman/Dir., William Bacigalupi/Dir., Jeffrey Jaeger/Dir., Richard Kahler/Dir., Joel Tranmer/Dir.

Chartered Semiconductor Mfg Ltd

60 Woodlands Industrial Pk. D, St. Two, 738405; ***PH:*** 65-6362-2838; ***Fax:*** 65-6362-2938; ***http://*** www.charteredsemi.com; ***Email:*** sanjose@charteredsemi.com

General - Incorporation	Singapore	**Stock**- Price on:12/24/2007	$9.02
Employees	4,681	Stock Exchange	NDQ
Auditor	KPMG LLP	Ticker Symbol	CHRT
Stk Agt	Citibank N.A	Outstanding Shares	253,680,000
Counsel	Latham & Watkins	E.P.S	$0.33
DUNS No.	NA	Shareholders	NA

Business: The group's principal activities are the provision of comprehensive wafer fabrication services and technologies to semiconductor suppliers and manufacturers of electronic systems. It provides foundry services to customers that serve high-growth, technologically advanced application, including communications applications such as cable modems, wireless, gigabit ethernet, ATM and adsl. At 31-Dec-2003, the group owned 5 fabrication facilities, all of which are located in Singapore. It offers full turnkey services including packaging, assembly and test. Semiconductor products include logic, mixed-signal and memory. It operates in Singapore and has service operations in 8 countries in North America, Europe and Asia. Its manufacturing operations are solely located in Singapore.

Primary SIC and add'l.: 3674

CIK No: 0001095270

Subsidiaries: Agere Systems Singapore Pte Ltd, Chartered Semiconductor Europe Ltd, Chartered Semiconductor Japan Kabushiki Kaisha, Chartered Semiconductor Manufacturing, Inc., Chartered Semiconductor Taiwan Ltd, Chartered Silicon Partners Pte Ltd, Singapex Investments Pte Ltd

Officers: Chia Song Hwee/Dir., CEO, Pres., Simon Yang/CTO, Sr. VP, Roy Kannan/55/CIO, VP, Tang Yong Ang/VP - Fab Support Operations, Tan Seng Chai/VP - Strategy Resources, George Thomas/Sr. VP, CFO, Michael J. Rekuc/Sr. VP - Worldwide Sales, Marketing, Hsia Liang Choo/Sr. VP - Technology Development, Lim Li Chuen/Dir. - Investor Relations, Ng Seng Huwi/VP - Human Resources, Tony Tsai/VP - Quality, Reliability Assurance, Leow Kim Keat/VP - Customer Support Operations, Supply Management Organization, Baskara Rao Paidithali/CIO, VP, Kevin Meyer/VP - Industry Marketing, Platform Alliances, Suresh Kumar/VP - Investor Relations *(19 Officers included in Index)*

Directors: Chia Song Hwee/Dir., CEO, Pres., James A. Norling/Chmn., Maurizio Ghirga/Dir., Andre Borrel/Dir., Charles E. Thompson/Dir., Tsugio Makimoto/Dir., Tay Siew Choon/Dir., Philip Yuen Fah Tan/Dir., Pasquale Pistorio/Dir., Steven H. Hamblin/Dir., Peter Seah Lim Huat/Dir.

Owners: Temasek Holdings (Private) Limited/59.55%

Financial Data: *Fiscal Year End:*12/31 *Latest Annual Data:* 12/31/2006

Year	Sales	Net Income
2006	$1,435,555,000	$66,754,000
2005	$1,032,734,000	-$159,598,000
2004	$932,131,000	$6,571,000

Curr. Assets:	$1,181,961,000	**Curr. Liab.:**	$613,492,000	**P/E Ratio:** 61.08
Plant, Equip.:	$2,273,119,000	**Total Liab.:**	$1,943,400,000	**Indic. Yr. Divd.:** NA
Total Assets:	$3,618,431,000	**Net Worth:**	$1,428,857,000	**Debt/ Equity:** NA

Chartwell International Inc

100 John Dietsch Blvd., North Attleboro, MA, 02763; *PH:* 1-508-695-1690; *Fax:* 1-508-699-6693; *http://* www.chartwellintl.com; *Email:* info@chartwellintl.com

General - Incorporation	NV	**Stock**- Price on:12/24/2007	$0.75
Employees	6	Stock Exchange	OTC
Auditor	Urish Popeck & Co., LLC	Ticker Symbol	CHWN
Stk Agt	Computershare Trust Co	Outstanding Shares	NA
Counsel	NA	E.P.S	NA
DUNS No.	NA	Shareholders	NA

Business: The groups principle activity is to pursue the waste disposal, transportation and logistics for solid waste disposal business, predominantly concentrating on solid waste from construction debris and general solid waste disposal. The group also provides integrate rail transportation, including construction and service maintenance of rail containers, waste disposal, disposal site management. The group operates from United States.

Primary SIC and add'l.: 4953

CIK No: 0001319048

Subsidiaries: Belville Mining Company, Inc., Cranberry Creek Railroad, Inc, Developing natural resources, Hudson Logistics Loading, Inc, Hudson Logistics, Inc., Kingsley Capital, Inc, Middletown & New Jersey Railway Company, Inc

Officers: Imre Eszenyi/40/Chmn., Acting Pres., VP, Principal Executive Officer, Principal Financial Officer, Paul Biberkraut/47/Chief Financial, Administrative Officer, Sec.

Directors: Imre Eszenyi/40/Chmn., Acting Pres., VP, Principal Executive Officer, Principal Financial Officer, Charles Srebnik/74/Dir., David C. Adams/50/Dir.

Owners: PICIAS Limited/30.62%, David Adams/1.27%, Insiders/5.85%, Charles Srebnik/1.60%, International Kapitalanagegesellsc/14.82%, Bayern Invest Kapitalanagegesellschaft m.b.H/5.42%, Fonditel Velociraptor/10.68%, Imre Eszenyi/2.26%, Gerlach & Company/5.02%, Paul Biberkraut, Faisal A. Alhegelan/5.02%

Financial Data: *Fiscal Year End:*07/31 *Latest Annual Data:* 6/30/2006

Year	Sales	Net Income
2006	$51,000	-$3,298,000
2005	NA	-$973,000
2004	$251,000	-$2,303,000

Curr. Assets:	$9,120,000	**Curr. Liab.:**	$61,000	
Plant, Equip.:	NA	**Total Liab.:**	$61,000	**Indic. Yr. Divd.:** NA
Total Assets:	$9,120,000	**Net Worth:**	$9,059,000	**Debt/ Equity:** 0.7092

Charys Holding Co Inc

1117 Perimeter Ctr W, Ste. N415, Atlanta, GA, 30338; *PH:* 1-678-443-2300; *Fax:* 1-678-443-2320; *http://* www.charys.com; *Email:* info@charys.com

General - Incorporation	DE	**Stock**- Price on:12/24/2007	$1.96
Employees	774	Stock Exchange	OTC
Auditor	Miller Ray, Houser & Stewart LLP	Ticker Symbol	CHYS
Stk Agt	Fidelity Transfer Co	Outstanding Shares	40,260,000
Counsel	NA	E.P.S	NA
DUNS No.	NA	Shareholders	NA

Business: The group's principal activity is to create 'spiderboy's Web' and 'spiderboy's information superhighway, providing an organized system of internal portals linked first geographically and then categorically by content. This system will become much like an information highway with exists and stops for every country and for most major cities in each country. The user will be able to find information that normally would access on the worldwide Web, without tedious search and without the possibility of inadvertently accessing pornographic websites. On 10-Jun-2004, the group acquired ics inc and on 01-Jul-2004, the group acquired personnel resources of Georgia, inc.

Primary SIC and add'l.: 7375

CIK No: 0000845879

Subsidiaries: Ayin Holding Company, Inc., Ayin Tower Management Services, Inc, Berkshire Wireless, Inc., C&B Holding Company, Inc., CCI Telecom, Inc., Contemporary Constructors, Inc., Crochet & Borel Services, Inc., Digital Communication Services, Inc., Integrated Solutions, Inc., LFC, Inc., Method IQ, Inc., Personnel Resources of Georgia, Inc., Viasys Network Services, Inc., Viasys Services, Inc., VSI Real Estate Holdings Inc

Officers: Billy V. Ray/Chmn., CEO, Michael Oyster/Dir., COO, Exec. VP, Raymond J. Smith/56/CFO, Linda L. Rine/VP - Risk Management, Mike Brenner/General Counsel

Directors: Billy V. Ray/Chmn., CEO, Neil L. Underwood/Dir., Gisle Larsen/Dir., Michael Oyster/Dir., COO, Exec. VP, Dennis C. Hayes/Dir., Alec H. McLarty/Dir., David Gergacz/Dir., Michael Brown/Dir.

Financial Data: *Fiscal Year End:*04/30 *Latest Annual Data:* 4/30/2006

Year	Sales	Net Income
2006	$48,571,000	-$1,429,000
2005	$7,483,000	-$799,000
2004	NA	-$1,879,000

Curr. Assets:	$17,866,000	**Curr. Liab.:**	$44,453,000	
Plant, Equip.:	$9,410,000	**Total Liab.:**	$50,439,000	**Indic. Yr. Divd.:** NA
Total Assets:	$58,701,000	**Net Worth:**	$8,262,000	**Debt/ Equity:** NA

Chase Corp

26 Summer St., Bridgewater, MA, 02324; *PH:* 1-508-279-1789; *Fax:* 1-508-697-6419; *http://* www.chasecorp.com; *Email:* pmyers@chasecorp.com

General - Incorporation	MA	**Stock**- Price on:12/24/2007	$31.15
Employees	362	Stock Exchange	AMEX
Auditor	PricewaterhouseCoopers LLP	Ticker Symbol	CCF
Stk Agt	American Stock Transfer & Trust Co.	Outstanding Shares	4,090,000
Counsel	Hughes & Associates	E.P.S	$1.157
DUNS No.	00-135-9769	Shareholders	NA

Business: The group's principal activity is to manufacture industrial products that are used in the wire and cable, construction and electronics industries. It operates through specialized manufacturing and electronic manufacturing services segments. The specialized-manufacturing segment produces protective coatings and trade products that include insulating and conducting materials for wire and cable manufacturers, protective coatings for pipeline applications and moisture protective coatings for electronics and printing services. The electronic manufacturing services segment provides printed circuit board and electro-mechanical assembly services to the electronics industry. The trademarks include humiseal, chase blh2ock and rosphalt50. The products are marketed mainly in the United States and Canada.

Primary SIC and add'l.: 3644 3672

CIK No: 0000830524

Subsidiaries: Chase Export Corporation, Chase Facile,Inc., Chase& Sons Limited, Northeast Quality Products Co.,Inc., RWA,Inc.

Officers: Peter R. Chase/Chmn., CEO, Pres., George M. Hughes/Dir., Corp. Sec., Adam Chase/VP, COO, Terry Jones/VP, Chief Marketing Officer, Kenneth L. Dumas/37/CFO, Treasurer

Directors: Peter R. Chase/Chmn., CEO, Pres., William H. Dykstra/Dir., Brooks J. Fenno/Dir., Ronald Levy/Dir., George M. Hughes/Dir., Corp. Sec., Lewis P. Gack/Dir., Mary Claire Chase/Dir.

Owners: Ronald Levy, FMR LLC/9.79%, Wilen Management Company, Inc./5.11%, Kenneth L. Dumas, Adam P. Chase, George M. Hughes, William H. Dykstra, Athena Capital Management, Inc./6.81%, Royce & Associates, LLC./7.74%, Peter R. Chase/12.53%, Mary Claire Chase, Insiders/15.02%, Edward L. Chase Revocable Trust/15.13%, Terry M. Jones/1.18%, Lewis P. Gack *(16 Owners included in Index)*

Financial Data: *Fiscal Year End:*08/31 *Latest Annual Data:* 8/31/2006

Year	Sales	Net Income
2006	$108,442,000	$6,114,000
2005	$91,389,000	$4,788,000
2004	$87,084,000	$4,627,000

Curr. Assets:	$35,679,000	**Curr. Liab.:**	$17,238,000	**P/E Ratio:** 26.92
Plant, Equip.:	$18,471,000	**Total Liab.:**	$32,763,000	**Indic. Yr. Divd.:** $0.400
Total Assets:	$78,837,000	**Net Worth:**	$46,074,000	**Debt/ Equity:** 0.2155

Chase General Corp

Chase Candy Company, St. Joseph, MO, 64502; *PH:* 1-800-786-1625; *Fax:* 1-816-279-1997; *http://* www.cherrymash.com

General - Incorporation	MO	**Stock**- Price on:12/24/2007	NA
Employees	8,400	Stock Exchange	NA
Auditor	Pricewaterhousecoopers LLP	Ticker Symbol	NA
Stk Agt	NA	Outstanding Shares	NA
Counsel	NA	E.P.S	NA
DUNS No.	10-370-4359	Shareholders	NA

Business: The group's principal activity is to manufacture and sell confectionery products in the midwest region of the United States. The group's wholly owned subsidiary, dye candy company operates in two divisions: chase candy company and poe candy company. Chase candy company produces and sells candy bars under the trade name cherry marsh. Poe candy company produces and sells coconut, peanut, chocolate and fudge confectioneries. The group's products are sold to wholesale candy and tobacco jobbing houses, grocery accounts, vendors, national syndicate accounts and repackers. The group operates in the United States. Its major customers include associated wholesale grocers and wal-Mart and its associates.

Primary SIC and add'l.: 2064 6719

CIK No: 0000015357

Subsidiaries: Chase Candy Company, Dye Candy Company, Poe Candy Company

Officers: Barry M. Yantis/63/Chmn., CEO, CFO, Pres., Treasurer, Brett A. Yantis/40/Dir., VP, Brian A. Yantis/60/Dir., Sec.

Directors: Barry M. Yantis/63/Chmn., CEO, CFO, Pres., Treasurer, Brett A. Yantis/40/Dir., VP, Brian A. Yantis/60/Dir., Sec.

Owners: Brian Yantis/8.40%, Barry Yantis/16.90%

Chatsworth Data Solutions Inc

20710 Lassen St., Chatsworth, CA, 91311; *PH:* 1-818-341-9200; *Fax:* 1-818-341-3002; *http://* www.chatsworthdata.com; *Email:* ir@chatsworthdata.com

General - Incorporation		**Stock**- Price on:12/24/2007	$0.42
Employees	65	Stock Exchange	OTC
Auditor	Weinberg & Co., P.A	Ticker Symbol	CHWD
Stk Agt	NA	Outstanding Shares	NA
Counsel	NA	E.P.S	-$0.16
DUNS No.	NA	Shareholders	NA

Business: The group's principle activity is to provide data capture technology. The groups technology provides testing, gaming, surveying, intelligence gathering and data management solutions. The group also provides impact indicator and impact recording solutions. The group operates from United States.

Primary SIC and add'l.: 3571

CIK No:

Officers: Sidney L. Anderson/61/Chmn., CEO, Pres., Stewart J. Asbury/59/Sec., Clayton E. Woodrum/68/CFO, Dave Young/VP - Sales, Chatsworth Data Corporation, Chuck Warnick/Operations Mgr. - Chatsworth Data Corporation, Steve Mulcahey/Chief Engineer - Electrical Engineering, David Obrien/Chief Engineer - Systems Engineering, Chatsworth Data Corporation, Robert Rischar/Mechanical Engineering, Chatsworth Data Corporation, Joe Alfino/Manufacturing Operations, Chatsworth Data Corporation

Directors: Sidney L. Anderson/61/Chmn., CEO, Pres., William H. Moothart/72/Dir., Gregory A. Nihon/32/Dir., Kerry Stirton/43/Dir., Iain Drummond/37/Dir.

Owners: Gregory A. Nihon, Francis Mailhot/5.50%, Sidney L. Anderson/15.00%, Ashcrete Research & Development, LLC/5.70%, J. Stewart Asbury/1.50%, Clayton E. Woodrum/2.10%, William H. Moothart, Caramat Ltd./9.30%, Iain Drummond, Kerry Stirton, Insiders/19.70%, Vision Opportunity Master Fund Ltd./37.10%, Nite Capital/5.70%

Financial Data: *Fiscal Year End:*NA *Latest Annual Data:* 1/31/2007

Year	Sales	Net Income
2007	$9,267,000	-$586,000
2006	NA	-$50,000

Curr. Assets: $2,505,000 **Curr. Liab.:** $2,475,000
Plant, Equip.: $279,000 **Total Liab.:** $4,389,000 **Indic. Yr. Divd.:** NA
Total Assets: $9,387,000 **Net Worth:** $4,997,000 **Debt/ Equity:** 0.2145

Chattem Inc

1715 W 38th St., Chattanooga, TN, 37409; ***PH:*** 1-423-821-4571; ***Fax:*** 1-423-821-0395; ***http://*** www.chattem.com

General - Incorporation TN
Employees 447
Auditor Grant Thornton, LLP
Stk Agt Computershare Investor Services LLC
Counsel NA
DUNS No. 00-333-6013

Stock- Price on:12/24/2007 $63.02
Stock Exchange NDQ
Ticker Symbol CHTT
Outstanding Shares 18,980,000
E.P.S. $2.60
Shareholders NA

Business: The group's principal activity is to manufacture and market branded consumer products and over the counter healthcare products. The products include medicated powders and lotions, antibiotic ointment and anti-itch creams, topical analgesics, cold sore and fever blister balms, garlic extracts, sleep and digestion aids, facial mask cleansers, shampoo and body wash. They are sold under the brand names of gold bond, flexall, icy hot, aspercreme, pamprin, garlique, phisoderm, dexatrim and bullfrog. Domestically, the products are sold through food, drug and mass merchandiser accounts. Internationally, they are sold by subsidiary companies and national brokers located in Canada and the United Kingdom and by distributors in western Europe. These distributors also sell in central and South America, the Caribbean and the middle and Far East. Major retail-chain customers include wal-Mart stores inc, boots plc in the United Kingdom and shoppers drug mart in Canada.

Primary SIC and add'l.: 2834

CIK No: 0000019520

Subsidiaries: Chattem (Canada) Corp., Chattem (Canada) Holdings, Inc., Chattem (U.K.) Limited, Chattem Canada, Chattem Canada ULC, Chattem Global Consumer Products Limited, HBA Indemnity Insurance, Ltd., Signal Investment & Management Co., SunDex, LLC

Officers: Zan Guerry/Chmn., CEO, Derrill B. Pitts/VP - Operations, Charles M. Stafford/VP - Sales, Theodore K. Whitfield/VP, General Counsel, Sec., Richard W. Kornhauser/VP - Marketing, Ron Galante/VP - New Business Development, Andrea M. Crouch/VP - Brand Management, Robert E. Bosworth/Dir., COO, Pres., Principal Financial Officer, Robert B. Long/Chief Accounting Officer, Blair J. Ramey/VP - Brand Management, Media

Directors: Zan Guerry/Chmn., CEO, Bill W. Stacy/Dir., Philip H. Sanford/Dir., Samuel E. Allen/Dir., Robert E. Bosworth/Dir., COO, Pres., Principal Financial Officer, Ruth W. Brinkley/Dir., Gary D. Chazen/Dir.

Owners: FMR Corp/9.60%, Peter R. Kellogg/10.60%, Gary D. Chazen, Richard W. Kornhauser, Columbia Wanger Asset Management, L.P./5.30%, Derrill B. Pitts, Ruth W. Brinkley, Robert E. Bosworth/4.40%, Samuel E. Allen, Zan Guerry/6.30%, Ron Galante, Insiders/9.20%, Philip H. Sanford, Bill W. Stacy

Financial Data: **Fiscal Year End:**11/30 **Latest Annual Data:** 11/30/2006

Year	Sales	Net Income
2006	$300,548,000	$45,112,000
2005	$279,318,000	$36,047,000
2004	$258,155,000	$1,614,000

Curr. Assets: $161,966,000 **Curr. Liab.:** $27,577,000 **P/E Ratio:** 27.52
Plant, Equip.: $30,353,000 **Total Liab.:** $279,732,000 **Indic. Yr. Divd.:** NA
Total Assets: $415,313,000 **Net Worth:** $135,581,000 **Debt/ Equity:** 3.5398

CHC Helicopter Corp

4740 Agar Dr., Richmond, BC, V7B 1A3; ***PH:*** 1-604-276-7500; ***http://*** www.chc.ca; ***Email:*** communications@chc.ca

General - Incorporation Canada
Employees NA
Auditor Ernst & Young LLP
Stk Agt CT Corporation System
Counsel NA
DUNS No. 24-722-5113

Stock- Price on:12/24/2007 $22.5099
Stock Exchange NYSE
Ticker Symbol FLI
Outstanding Shares 42,790,000
E.P.S. $0.84
Shareholders NA

Business: The group's principle activity is to provide transportation services to the global oil and gas industry. The group provides helicopter transportation services for production and exploration activities and to the emergency medical services and search and rescue sectors. The group also provides repair and overhaul services, which covers all major helicopter components, including engines, rotor heads, gearboxes and blades. The group contracts with customers to provide aircraft for various periods of time. Contracts for helicopter services for oil and gas exploration activities are generally short-term, while contracts for transport of personnel and equipment to oil and gas production sites are generally long-term.

Primary SIC and add'l.: 4522 4581 6719

CIK No: 0000903124

Subsidiaries: 4083423 Canada Inc., Aero Turbine Support Ltd., Canadian Helicopters (UK) Limited, Capital Aviation Services B.V., CHC (Chad) SA, CHC Airways BV, CHC Capital (Barbados) Limited, CHC Composites Inc., CHC Denmark ApS, CHC Helicopters (Africa) Pty. Ltd., CHC Helicopters (Barbados) Limited, CHC Helicopters International Inc., CHC Helicopters Netherlands BV, CHC Helicopters South Africa (Proprietary) Ltd., CHC Helikopter Service AS 32 Subsidiaries included in the Index

Officers: Sylvain Allard/Dir., CEO, Pres., Troy Freeborn/Pres. - CHC Composites, Christine Baird/Pres. - Global Operations, Erik Kjeldsen/GM - CHC Training Centre, Stephen P. Peszel/Head - Training, Licensing, CHC Training Centre, John Hanbury/51/Corporate Treasurer, Blake G. Fizzard/44/Dir. - Taxation, Martin Lockyer/48/VP - Legal Services, Corp. Sec., Frederick Davis/CFO, Sr. VP, Dag S. Johansen/Technical Training Mgr. - CHC Training Centre, Rick Davis/46/VP - Internal Audit, Neil Calvert/Pres. - Heli, One Vancouver, Canada, Keith Mullett/MD - European Operations, James A. Misener/Pres. - CHC Helicopters, Barbados Ltd, Rick O. Green/51/CIO, VP *(23 Officers included in Index)*

Directors: Sylvain Allard/Dir., CEO, Pres., Jack Mintz/Dir., Craig C. Dobbin/Dir., Robert Paul Reid/Dir., Guylaine Saucier/Dir., Mark D. Dobbin/49/Dir., George Gillett/Dir., William W. Stinson/Dir., John J. Kelly/Dir., Donald Carty/Dir.

Owners: Sylvain Allard, Mark D. Dobbin, Mark D. Dobbin, John J. Kelly, Mark D. Dobbin, Guylaine Saucier, Donald Carty, William W. Stinson, Jack M. Mintz

Financial Data: **Fiscal Year End:**04/30 **Latest Annual Data:** 4/30/2006

Year	Sales	Net Income
2006	$905,924,000	$116,982,000
2005	$717,978,000	$43,828,000
2004	$535,344,000	$33,414,000

Curr. Assets: $356,359,000 **Curr. Liab.:** $245,288,000 **P/E Ratio:** 24.76
Plant, Equip.: $830,519,000 **Total Liab.:** $1,102,057,000 **Indic. Yr. Divd.:** $0.440
Total Assets: $1,504,442,000 **Net Worth:** $402,386,000 **Debt/ Equity:** NA

CHDT Corp

Formerly: China Direct Trading Corp
350 Jim Moran Blvd., Ste. 120, Deerfield Beach, FL, 33442; ***PH:*** 1-954-252-3440

General - Incorporation FL
Employees 7
Auditor Robison, Hill & Co
Stk Agt Corporate Stock Transfer, Inc.
Counsel NA
DUNS No. NA

Stock- Price on:12/24/2007 $0.02
Stock Exchange OTC
Ticker Symbol CHDO
Outstanding Shares 560,870,000
E.P.S. $0.00
Shareholders NA

Business: The group's principal activity is to provide software development outsourcing, Web development, custom software development and network systems integration to software programmers. The group has over 30 manufacturing concerns in China for its products. On 01-Dec-2003, it acquired all the issued and outstanding shares of souvenir direct, inc.

Primary SIC and add'l.: 7371 7372

CIK No: 0000814926

Subsidiaries: CPS, SDI, Souvenir Direct, Inc

Officers: Stewart Wallach/56/Dir., CEO

Directors: Stewart Wallach/56/Dir., CEO, Jeffrey Guzy/Dir., Larry Sloven/Dir.

Owners: Stewart Wallach/2.00%, Jeffrey Postal/27.00%, Howard Ullman/72.00%, Jeffrey Postal/0.02%, Laurie Holtz, Laurie Holtz, Insiders/100.00%, Bart Fisher/5.00%, Jeffrey Guzy, Lorenzo Lamadrid, Insiders/57.00%, Gerry McClinton, Margaret Fisher/8.00%, Howard Ullman/51.00%

Financial Data: **Fiscal Year End:**12/31 **Latest Annual Data:** 12/31/2006

Year	Sales	Net Income
2006	$1,547,000	-$79,000
2005	$912,000	-$589,000
2004	$1,062,000	-$270,000

Curr. Assets: $1,066,000 **Curr. Liab.:** $1,543,000
Plant, Equip.: $30,000 **Total Liab.:** $2,365,000 **Indic. Yr. Divd.:** NA
Total Assets: $3,275,000 **Net Worth:** $910,000 **Debt/ Equity:** 0.8602

Check Point Software Technologies Ltd

800 Bridge Pkwy., Redwood City, CA, 94065; ***PH:*** 1-650-628-2000; ***Fax:*** 1-650-654-4233; ***http://*** www.checkpoint.com; ***Email:*** info@checkpoint.com

General - Incorporation Israel
Employees 1,568
Auditor Kost Forer Gabbay & Kasierer
Stk Agt American Stock Transfer & Trust Co.
Counsel Naschitz Brandes & Co
DUNS No. NA

Stock- Price on:12/24/2007 $23.42
Stock Exchange NDQ
Ticker Symbol CHKP
Outstanding Shares 225,690,000
E.P.S. $1.20
Shareholders NA

Business: The group's principle activities are the development, marketing and support of Internet security software solutions for enterprise networks and service providers. These products aim to protect information from unauthorized access and from risks of unauthorized interception through public connections. The company's product offerings also include traffic control/quality of service and ip address management. Its markets include the United States, Europe, great Britain and Japan. The group's quarterly revenue for September 2007 was 184.01 millions of USD.

Primary SIC and add'l.: 7379 7372

CIK No: 0001015922

Subsidiaries: C.p.s.t. Sweden A.b, Check Point Holding (Singapore) PTE Ltd., Check Point Holding (Singapore) PTE Ltd. - US Branch, Check Point Software Technologies (Australia) PTY Ltd., Check Point Software Technologies (Austria) GmbH, Check Point Software Technologies (Belarus) LLC, Check Point Software Technologies (Belgium) S.A, Check Point Software Technologies (Brazil) LTDA, Check Point Software Technologies (Canada) Inc., Check Point Software Technologies (Czech Republic) s.r.o, Check Point Software Technologies (Denmark) ApS, Check Point Software Technologies (Finland) Oy, Check Point Software Technologies (Hong Kong) Ltd., Check Point Software Technologies (Hong Kong) Ltd. Shanghai office, Check Point Software Technologies (India) Private Limited 39 Subsidiaries included in the Index

Officers: Gil Shwed/Founder, Chmn., CEO, Marius Nacht/Founder, Vice Chmn., Sr. VP, Kip E. Meintzer/Dir. - Investor Relations, Eyal Desheh/CFO, Exec. VP, Araceli Roiz/Investor Relations Specialist

Directors: Gil Shwed/Founder, Chmn., CEO, Marius Nacht/Founder, Vice Chmn., Sr. VP, Jerry Ungerman/Vice Chmn., Tal Shavit/Dir., Ray Rothrock/Dir., David Rubner/Dir., Yoav Chelouche/Dir., Irwin Federman/Dir., Guy Gecht/Dir., Dan Propper/Dir.

Owners: Gil Shwed/13.60%, Insiders/23.40%, Marius Nacht/9.10%

Financial Data: **Fiscal Year End:**12/31 **Latest Annual Data:** 12/31/2006

Year	Sales	Net Income
2006	$575,141,000	$278,027,000
2005	$579,350,000	$319,684,000
2004	$515,360,000	$248,393,000

Curr. Assets: $1,255,353,000 **Curr. Liab.:** $358,049,000 **P/E Ratio:** 61.08
Plant, Equip.: $47,192,000 **Total Liab.:** $369,260,000 **Indic. Yr. Divd.:** NA
Total Assets: $2,080,793,000 **Net Worth:** $1,711,533,000 **Debt/ Equity:** NA

Checkers Drive In Restaurants Inc

4300 W Cypress St., Ste. 600, Tampa, FL, 33607; ***PH:*** 1-813-283-7000; ***http://*** www.checkers.com

General - Incorporation DE | **Stock**- Price on:12/24/2007 NA
Employees 10,500 | Stock Exchange NDQ
Auditor Grant Thornton LLP | Ticker Symbol CHKR
Stk Agt American Stock Transfer & Trust Co. | Outstanding Shares NA
Counsel Bush, Ross, Gardner, Warren & Rudy | E.P.S NA
DUNS No. 14-786-7907 | Shareholders NA

Business: The group's principal activity is to operate and franchise restaurants under the names of checkers and rally's hamburgers. The group operates chains of double drive-through restaurants in the United States. The menu includes the original 1/4 pound champ burger(R), white-meat chicken sandwiches, beef hotdogs, chili-cheese dogs and the signature big buford(R), a fully dressed double cheeseburger. In addition, the menu includes checkers famous fries(tm) , soft drinks, super thick shakes and rally's seasoned fries. As of 31-Dec-2003, the group had 784 restaurant locations, consisting of 222 group-owned and 562 franchisee-owned restaurants. Of them, 379 are rally's restaurants operating in 17 different states and 405 are checkers restaurants operating in 20 states, the district of columbia, Puerto Rico and the west bank in the Middle East.

Primary SIC and add'l.: 5812

CIK No: 0000879554

Officers: Enrique Silva/CEO, Pres., Terri Snyder/Exec. VP - CMO, Pat Plumley/Sr. VP, CFO, Treasurer, Wendy Harkness/VP - Human Resources, Ron Levondosky/Exec. VP - Franchise, Adam Noyes/Exec. VP - Company Operations, Services, Brian R. Doster/VP, Corporate Counsel, Sec., Richard Turer/Sr. VP - Marketing, Elizabeth Sheridan/Mgr. - Communications

CheckFree Corp

4411 E Jones Bridge Rd., Norcross, GA, 30092; *PH:* 1-678-375-3000; *Fax:* 1-678-375-1477; *http://* www.checkfreecorp.com

General - Incorporation DE | **Stock**- Price on:12/24/2007 $40.64
Employees 3,450 | Stock Exchange NA
Auditor Deloitte & Touche LLP | Ticker Symbol NA
Stk Agt Wells Fargo Shareowner Services | Outstanding Shares 87,940,000
Counsel Deborah N. Gable | E.P.S $1.36
DUNS No. 15-288-0456 | Shareholders NA

Business: The group's principal activities are to provide financial electronic commerce products and services. The group operates through three segments: electronic commerce, software and investment services. Electronic commerce services provide services that allow customers to receive electronic bills through the Internet, pay any bill electronic or paper to anyone and perform customary banking transactions. Software segment delivers software, maintenance, support and professional services to financial service providers and other companies. The software products include ach solution that provides software and services that are used in automated clearing house payments. Investment services provides investment portfolio management services and investment trading and reporting services to financial institutions, money managers and investment advisors. In fiscal 2004, it acquired heliograph ltd and American payment systems inc.

Primary SIC and add'l.: 6282 7389 8741 6719 7371

CIK No: 0000949341

Subsidiaries: Accurate Software (Australia) PTY Limited, Accurate Software Inc., Accurate Software Limited, Accurate Software S.A., American Payment Holdco, Inc., Bastogne, Inc., CheckFree i-Solutions Corp., CheckFree i-Solutions Limited, CheckFree i-Solutions, Inc., CheckFree Investment Corporation, CheckFree PhonePay Services, Inc., CheckFree Services Corporation, CheckFree Software & Services (UK), Ltd., CheckFreePay Corporation, CheckFreePay Corporation of California 18 Subsidiaries included in the Index

Officers: Peter J. Kight/Chmn., Founder, CEO, David Mangum/CFO, Exec. VP, Leigh Asher/Sr. VP - Corporate Marketing, Laura Binion/Exec. VP, General Counsel, Michael Gianoni/Exec. VP, GM - Investment Services Division, Steve Olsen/CIO, Exec. VP, Judy Derango Wicks/VP - Corporate Communications, Ann Cave/Public Relations Mgr., Kimberly Doan/Events Contact - Meetings, Conferences, Curtis Loveland/Corp. Sec., Jardon Bouska/Exec. VP, GM - Electronic Biller Services Division, Alex Hart/Exec. VP, GM - Electronic Banking Services Division, Sheryl Roehl/Dir. - Public Relations, Afamia Murray/Events Contact - Trade Shows

Directors: Peter J. Kight/Chmn., Founder, CEO, Mark A. Johnson/Vice Chmn., James D. Dixon/Dir., William P. Boardman/Dir., Eugene F. Quinn/Dir., Jeffrey M. Wilkins/Dir., Beth C. Cotner/Dir.

Financial Data: *Fiscal Year End:*06/30 *Latest Annual Data:* 06/30/2007

Year		Sales		Net Income	
2007		$972,644,000		$124,438,000	
2006		$879,402,000		$127,263,000	
2005		$757,832,000		$46,801,000	
Curr. Assets:	$618,467,000	**Curr. Liab.:**	$236,133,000	**P/E Ratio:**	29.66
Plant, Equip.:	$100,217,000	**Total Liab.:**	$274,394,000	**Indic. Yr. Divd.:**	NA
Total Assets:	$1,758,029,000	**Net Worth:**	$1,483,635,000	**Debt/ Equity:**	0.0334

Checkpoint Systems Inc

101 Wolf Dr., Thorofare, NJ, 08086; *PH:* 1-856-848-1800; *Fax:* 1-856-848-0937; *http://* www.checkpointsystems.com

General - Incorporation PA | **Stock**- Price on:12/24/2007 $25.49
Employees 3,213 | Stock Exchange NYSE
Auditor PricewaterhouseCoopers LLP | Ticker Symbol CKP
Stk Agt American Stock Transfer & Trust Co. | Outstanding Shares 39,430,000
Counsel Stradley Ronon Stevens & Young LLP | E.P.S $1.24
DUNS No. 06-184-4015 | Shareholders NA

Business: The group's principal activities are to manufacture and market integrated system solutions for retail security, labeling and merchandising. The group operates through three business segments: security, labeling services and retail merchandising. Security segment products include access control systems, closed circuit television systems and fire and intrusion alarm systems. Labeling services segment products include bar-coding systems, service bureau and radio frequency identification systems. Retail merchandising segment products are hand-held labeling systems and retail merchandising systems. The group manufactures products in the United States of America, the Caribbean, Europe and the Asia-Pacific region.

Primary SIC and add'l.: 3669 3829

CIK No: 0000215419

Subsidiaries: Actron Belgium and Luxemborg N.V., Actron Group Ltd., Actron Sistemas De Seguidad S.A., Actron U.K. Ltd., Checkpoint Canada, Inc., Checkpoint Caribbean Ltd., Checkpoint Caribbean, Inc., Checkpoint de Mexico, S.A. de C.V., Checkpoint do Brasil Ltda., Checkpoint Europe N.V., Checkpoint Export A.G., Checkpoint Holland Holding B.V., Checkpoint Holland Trading B.V., Checkpoint International LLC, Checkpoint International Systems C.V. 60 Subsidiaries included in the Index

Officers: George W. Off/Chmn., CEO/$1,769,963.00, Per Levin/Worldwide Pres. - Shrink Management, Merchandising Solutions/$771,375.00, John E. Davies/Worldwide Pres. - Labels Solutions/$610,387.00, Craig W. Burns/Exec. VP, CFO, Treasurer/$629,690.00, Gail Fiske/Primary Investor Relations Officer, Jennifer Henry/Mgr. - Marketing Services, Farrokh Abadi/Sr. VP - Worldwide Operations, Morag Harmsen/VP, GM - North American Sales, Andre Cote/Sr. Dir. - Business Development, Global Rfid, Alisa Delgaudio/EAS Reseller Channel Sales, Marketing Coordinator, Ioana Barbon/Marketing Assist., Lisa Folker/Source Tagging Communications, Administrator, John R. Van Zile/55/Sr. VP, General Counsel, Sec./$644,367.00, Steve Champeau/Pres. - North America, Bernard Gremillet/Pres. - Europe, Latin America *(16 Officers included in Index)*

Directors: George W. Off/Chmn., CEO, Harald Einsmann/Dir., Alan R. Hirsig/Dir., Jack W. Partridge/Dir., William Smoot Antle/Dir., Keith R. Elliott/Dir., David W. Clark/Dir., Sally Pearson/Dir., George Babich/Dir.

Owners: John E. Davies, Insiders/5.80%, Earnest Partners, LLC/13.50%, Raymond D. Andrews, Per Levin, Craig W. Burns/1.00%, Harald Einsmann, Barclays Global Investors, NA/5.21%, John R. VanZile, Keith R. Elliott, George W. Off/1.60%, George Babich, Sally Pearson, Alan R. Hirsig, David C. Donnan *(20 Owners included in Index)*

Financial Data: *Fiscal Year End:*12/25 *Latest Annual Data:* 12/31/2006

Year		Sales		Net Income	
2006		$687,775,000		$35,922,000	
2005		$721,018,000		$39,405,000	
2004		$778,679,000		-$20,192,000	
Curr. Assets:	$447,597,000	**Curr. Liab.:**	$193,573,000	**P/E Ratio:**	26.01
Plant, Equip.:	$72,042,000	**Total Liab.:**	$306,654,000	**Indic. Yr. Divd.:**	NA
Total Assets:	$781,191,000	**Net Worth:**	$473,581,000	**Debt/ Equity:**	NA

Cheesecake Factory Inc

26901 Malibu Hills Rd., Calabasas Hills, CA, 91301; *PH:* 1-818-871-3000; *Fax:* 1-818-871-3001; *http://* www.thecheesecakefactory.com

General - Incorporation DE | **Stock**- Price on:12/24/2007 $26.89
Employees 29,400 | Stock Exchange NDQ
Auditor PricewaterhouseCoopers LLP | Ticker Symbol CAKE
Stk Agt Computershare Investor Services LLC | Outstanding Shares 71,960,000
Counsel Buchalter, Nemer, Fields & Younger | E.P.S $1.02
DUNS No. 07-621-5003 | Shareholders NA

Business: The group's principal activities are to operate restaurants and a bakery. The group creates, produces and distributes cheesecakes and other baked desserts. These include appetizers, pizza, seafood, steaks, chicken, burgers, pasta, specialty items, salads, sandwiches, omelets and approximately 40 varieties of cheesecake and other baked desserts. The trademarks of the group include 'the cheesecake factory', 'grand lux cafe', 'the cheesecake factory bakery', 'the cheesecake factory express', 'the dream factory' and 'the cheesecake factory bakery cafe'. On 04-Mar-2004, the group operates 75 upscale, full-service, casual dining restaurants under the cheesecake factory(R) mark in 24 states and district of columbia and under the grand lux cafe(R) mark in Chicago, los angeles, and las vegas. The group also operates one self-service and limited menu 'express' foodservices in the United States.

Primary SIC and add'l.: 5142 2053 5812

CIK No: 0000887596

Subsidiaries: C.F.I. Promotions Co. LLC, C.f.r.i. Asset Holdings LLC, C.f.r.i. Texas Restaurants Lp, Cheesecake Factory Restaurants of Kansas LLC, GLC Galleria Club, Inc., Grand Lux Cafe LLC, Hawaii Cheesecake Factory Restaurants Inc., The Cheesecake Factory Assets Co. LLC, The Cheesecake Factory Bakery Incorporated, The Cheesecake Factory Restaurants, Inc., The Houston Cheesecake Factory Corporation

Officers: David Overton/Chmn., CEO/$2,230,059.00, Max S. Byfuglin/Pres. - Cheesecake Factory Bakery Incorporated/$912,403.00, Debby R. Zurzolo/Debby R Zurzolo/$878,520.00, Russell Bendel/Pres., COO - Cheesecake Factory Restaurants, Michael J. Dixon/Sr. VP - Finance, CFO/$696,864.00, Jill Peters/VP - Investor Relations

Directors: David Overton/Chmn., CEO, Thomas L. Gregory/Dir., Agnieszka Winkler/Dir., Wayne H. White/Dir., David R. Klock/Dir., Karl L. Matthies/Dir., Jerome I. Kransdorf/Dir.

Owners: Insiders/6.20%, Wayne H. White, T. Rowe Price Associates, Inc./6.20%, Capital Group International,Inc./5.70%, Michael J. Dixon, Jerome I. Kransdorf, David Overton/5.00%, Thomas L. Gregory, Debby R. Zurzolo, David R. Klock, Baron Capital Group,Inc./7.50%, Peter J. DAmelio, Max S. Byfuglin, Karl L. Matthies

Financial Data: *Fiscal Year End:*01/03 *Latest Annual Data:* 1/2/2007

Year		Sales		Net Income	
2007		$1,315,325,000		$81,282,000	
2006		$1,182,053,000		$87,948,000	
2004		$969,232,000		$66,538,000	
Curr. Assets:	$114,546,000	**Curr. Liab.:**	$109,846,000	**P/E Ratio:**	25.61
Plant, Equip.:	$485,972,000	**Total Liab.:**	$215,865,000	**Indic. Yr. Divd.:**	NA
Total Assets:	$758,717,000	**Net Worth:**	$542,852,000	**Debt/ Equity:**	0.3614

Cheetah Oil & Gas Ltd

PO Box 929 Stn Main, Penticton, BC, V2A 6J9; *PH:* 1-250-491-1723; *http://* www.cheetahoil.com

General - Incorporation NV | **Stock**- Price on:12/24/2007 $0.28
Employees NA | Stock Exchange OTC
Auditor Ernst & Young LLP | Ticker Symbol COGL
Stk Agt Atlas Stock Transfer Corp | Outstanding Shares NA
Counsel NA | E.P.S NA
DUNS No. NA | Shareholders NA

Business: The groups principal activity is to explore minerals and natural gas. The group operates from the United States and Canada.

Primary SIC and add'l.: 1382

CIK No: 0000908821

Subsidiaries: Cheetah Oil and Gas Ltd, Scotia Petroleum Inc

Officers: Jesse Keller/Investor Relations Officer, Isaac Moss/55/Sr. VP, CFO/$21,000.00

Directors: Dean Swanberg/Dir.

Owners: Georgina Martin/66.88%, Insiders/66.88%

Financial Data: Fiscal Year End:12/31 **Latest Annual Data:** 12/31/2006

Year	Sales	Net Income
2006	NA	-$3,592,000
2005	NA	-$3,041,000
2004	NA	-$464,000

Curr. Assets:	$225,000	Curr. Liab.:	$11,381,000		
Plant, Equip.:	$20,971,000	Total Liab.:	$13,489,000	Indic. Yr. Divd.:	NA
Total Assets:	$21,919,000	Net Worth:	$8,430,000	Debt/ Equity:	0.1234

Chelsea Therapeutics International Ltd

666 Fifth Ave., 8th Fl., New York, NY, 10103; ; *http://* chelseatherapeutics.com

General - Incorporation	DE	Stock- Price on:12/24/2007	$5.94
Employees	11	Stock Exchange	NDQ
Auditor	J.H. Cohn LLP	Ticker Symbol	CHTP
Stk Agt.	Corporate Stock Transfer, Inc.	Outstanding Shares	22,390,000
Counsel	NA	E.P.S.	-$0.6
DUNS No.	NA	Shareholders	NA

Business: The groups principal activities include acquiring and developing pharmaceutical products for the treatment of human diseases. The groups product is DROXIDOPA. In February 2005, the group merged with Ivory Capital Corporation. The group operates from the United States.

Primary SIC and add'l.: 8731

CIK No: 0001333763

Subsidiaries: Chelsea Therapeutics, Inc.

Officers: Simon Pedder/Dir., CEO, Pres., Arthur L. Hewitt/VP - Drug Development, Nick J. Richle/VP - Administration, CFO, Keith Schmidt/VP - Marketing, Sales, Michael J. Roberts/Sr. Dir. - Business Development, Cameron Szakacs/Dir. - Drug Development, Roy Freeman/Member - Advisory Board, Neurogenic Orthostatic Hypotension, Kathryn McNeil/Contact - Investor, Media, Art Hewitt/Contact - Clinical Trials

Directors: Simon Pedder/Dir., CEO, Pres., Kevan Clemens/Chmn., Michael Weiser/Dir., Neil Herskowitz/Dir., Johnson Y.N. Lau/Dir., Jason Stein/Dir., Stanley B. Cohen/Member - Advisory Board, Rheumatology, Arthur F. Kavanaugh/Member - Advisory Board, Rheumatology, Edward C. Keystone/Member - Advisory Board, Rheumatology, Joel M. Kremer/Member - Advisory Board, Rheumatology, William Schwieterman/Member - Advisory Board, Rheumatology, Lee Simon/Member - Advisory Board, Rheumatology, Vibeke Strand/Member - Advisory Board, Rheumatology, Horacio Kaufmann/Member - Advisory Board, Neurogenic Orthostatic Hypotension, Phillip Low/Member - Advisory Board, Neurogenic Orthostatic Hypotension *(16 Directors included in Index)*

Owners: Johnson Y.N. Lau, Kevan Clemens, Simon Pedder/3.46%, Insiders/9.40%, RA Capital Management, LLC/4.76%, Lester Lipschutz/16.26%, Arthur L. Hewitt, Jason Stein/2.01%, Neil Herskowitz, HealthCor Management, L.P./11.82%, Michael Weiser/2.32%, El Coronado Holdings, LLC/13.45%, Davidson Kempner Partners/9.82%, Nick J. Riehle

Financial Data: Fiscal Year End:12/31 **Latest Annual Data:** 12/31/2006

Year	Sales	Net Income
2006	NA	-$8,671,000
2005	NA	-$7,916,000

Curr. Assets:	$16,114,000	Curr. Liab.:	$2,034,000		
Plant, Equip.:	$43,000	Total Liab.:	$2,034,000	Indic. Yr. Divd.:	NA
Total Assets:	$16,171,000	Net Worth:	$14,137,000	Debt/ Equity:	NA

Chem RX Corp

Formerly: Paramount Acquisition Corp
787 7th Ave., 48th Fl., New York, NY, 10019; **PH:** 1-212-554-4300

General - Incorporation	DE	Stock - Price on:12/24/2007	$5.55
Employees	NA	Stock Exchange	OTC
Auditor	Marcum & Kliegman LLP	Ticker Symbol	PMQC
Stk Agt.	Continental Stock Transfer & Trust Co	Outstanding Shares	11,900,000
Counsel	NA	E.P.S.	-$0.02
DUNS No.	NA	Shareholders	NA

Business: The groups principal activity is to develop improved therapeutic and diagnostic products. The group operates from the United States.

Primary SIC and add'l.: 6799

CIK No: 0001330487

Owners: Andrew M. Weiss/7.70%, Fir Tree, Inc/6.40%, Arie Belldegrun, Satellite Asset Management, L.P/5.50%, Jay J. Lobell/2.70%, Isaac Kier/1.30%, Morgan Stanley/7.00%, Keith I. Maher/2.70%, Michael Weiser, Insiders/18.30%, Lindsay A. Rosenwald/9.80%

Financial Data: Fiscal Year End:12/31 **Latest Annual Data:** 12/31/2006

Year	Sales	Net Income
2006	NA	-$17,000
2005	NA	$185,000

Curr. Assets:	$54,660,000	Curr. Liab.:	$993,000		
Plant, Equip.:	NA	Total Liab.:	$11,881,000	Indic. Yr. Divd.:	NA
Total Assets:	$54,660,000	Net Worth:	$42,778,000	Debt/ Equity:	NA

Chembio Diagnostics Inc

3661 Horseblock Rd. , Medford, NY, 11763; **PH:** 1-631-924-1135; **Fax:** 1-631-924-6033 ;
http:// www.chembio.com; **Email:** info@chembio.com

General - Incorporation	NV	Stock - Price on:12/24/2007	$0.53
Employees	92	Stock Exchange	OTC
Auditor	Lazar Levine & Felix LLP	Ticker Symbol	CEMI
Stk Agt.	Action Stock Transfer Corp	Outstanding Shares	12,390,000
Counsel	NA	E.P.S.	-$0.67
DUNS No.	NA	Shareholders	NA

Business: The group's principal activity is to de-emphasizing the manufacturing of private label pregnancy tests and focusing on developing products and obtaining applicable clearances or approvals in the areas of rapid tests for HIV, tuberculosis, mad cow disease and dental disease.

Primary SIC and add'l.: 9999

CIK No: 0001092662

Subsidiaries: Chembio Diagnostics (Africa) Limited, Chembio Diagnostics Nigeria Limited, Chembio Diagnostics Systems, Inc

Officers: Lawrence A. Siebert/Chmn., CEO, Pres./$255,332.00, Javan Esfandiari/Sr. VP - Research, Developmentlawrence A Siebert/$208,575.00, Richard J. Larkin/CFO/$182,685.00, Richard Bruce/VP - Operations, Tom Ippolito/VP - Regulatory Affairs, QA, QC, Les Stutzman/VP - Marketing, Matty Arce/Contact - Chembio Investor Relations, Cathy Dudnanski/VP - Marketing

Directors: Lawrence A. Siebert/Chmn., CEO, Pres., Alan Carus/Dir., Gary Meller/Dir., Allen Moore/Member - Advisory Board, Peter Anderson/Member - Advisory Board, Mariano Levin/Member - Advisory Board, Katherine L. Davis/Dir.

Owners: Avi Peloss/0.05%, Richard J. Larkin/0.01%, Mark Baum/0.11%, Lawrence Siebert/0.18%, Gary Meller/0.01%, Javan Esfandiari/0.04%, Crestview Master Fund LLC/0.11%, Alan Carus/0.01%

Financial Data: Fiscal Year End:12/31 **Latest Annual Data:** 12/31/2006

Year	Sales	Net Income
2006	$6,502,000	-$4,995,000
2005	$3,941,000	-$3,252,000
2004	$3,306,000	-$3,099,000

Curr. Assets:	$6,954,000	Curr. Liab.:	$1,840,000		
Plant, Equip.:	$604,000	Total Liab.:	$8,846,000	Indic. Yr. Divd.:	NA
Total Assets:	$7,907,000	Net Worth:	-$940,000	Debt/ Equity:	NA

Chemed Corp

2600 Chemed Ctr., 255 East 5th St., Cincinnati, OH, 45202; **PH:** 1-513-762-6900;
Fax: 1-513-762-6919; *http://* www.chemed.com

General - Incorporation	DE	Stock- Price on:12/24/2007	$66.75
Employees	11,621	Stock Exchange	NYSE
Auditor	PricewaterhouseCoopers LLP	Ticker Symbol	CHE
Stk Agt	Wells Fargo Bank, N.A.	Outstanding Shares	25,300,000
Counsel	Thompson Hine LLP	E.P.S.	$2.40
DUNS No.	05-510-9912	Shareholders	NA

Business: The group's principle activities are to provide residential and commercial repair-and-maintenance-service. The company operates under two segments: roto-rooter group and service America systems inc. Roto-rooter segment provides repair and maintenance services to residential and commercial accounts. These services include plumbing, sewer, drain & pipe cleaning, pipe rehabilitation. Service America provides appliance repair and maintenance services to customers through service contracts and retail sales. This segment sells air conditioning equipment and provides duct cleaning services. The principal markets for the roto-rooter segment are residential, industrial, business/commercial and municipal. The principal markets for the service America segment are retirees, absentee home owners, dual-income households and condominium & home owners' associations. The group's quarterly revenue for September 2007 was 272.50 millions of USD.

Primary SIC and add'l.: 4959 1711

CIK No: 0000019584

Subsidiaries: CCR of Ohio, Inc., Comfort Care Holdings Co., Company; included within the consolidated financial statements as a, Complete Plumbing Services, Inc., Consolidated HVAC, Inc., Hospice Care Incorporated, Hospice, Inc., Inc.; included within the consolidated financial statements as a, Jet Resource, Inc., Nurotoco of Massachusetts, Inc., Nurotoco of New Jersey, Inc., R.r. Uk, Inc., Roto-Rooter Canada, Ltd., Roto-Rooter Corporation, Roto-Rooter Development Company 34 Subsidiaries included in the Index

Officers: Kevin J. McNamara/55/Dir., CEO, Pres/$2,383,382.00, Thomas J. Reilly/51/VP, Thomas C. Hutton/58/Dir., VP, Timothy S. O'Toole/52/Dir., Exec. VP/$1,036,037.00, Lisa A. Reinhard/Chief Administrative Officer

Directors: Kevin J. McNamara/55/Dir., CEO, Pres., Edward L. Hutton/89/Chmn., Charles H. Erhart/83/Dir., George J. Walsh/66/Dir., Sandra E. Laney/65/Dir., Joel F. Gemunder/69/Dir., Thomas C. Hutton/58/Dir., VP, Timothy S. O'Toole/52/Dir., Exec. VP, Frank E. Wood/66/Dir., Walter L. Krebs/75/Dir., Donald E. Saunders/64/Dir., Patrick P. Grace/52/Dir.

Owners: Joel F. Gemunder, David P. Williams, Thomas C. Hutton, Donald E. Saunders, Patrick P. Grace, Frank E. Wood, Timothy S. OToole, Edward L. Hutton, Spencer S. Lee, Donald Breen, Walter L. Krebs, Sandra E. Laney, Arthur V. Tucker, Charles H. Erhart, George J. Walsh *(17 Owners included in Index)*

Financial Data: Fiscal Year End:12/31 **Latest Annual Data:** 12/31/2006

Year	Sales	Net Income
2006	$1,018,587,000	$50,651,000
2005	$926,477,000	$35,817,000
2004	$735,341,000	$27,512,000

Curr. Assets:	$162,113,000	Curr. Liab.:	$166,064,000	P/E Ratio:	32.40
Plant, Equip.:	$70,140,000	Total Liab.:	$371,926,000	Indic. Yr. Divd.:	$0.240
Total Assets:	$793,287,000	Net Worth:	$421,361,000	Debt/ Equity:	0.3613

ChemGenex Pharmaceuticals

3715 HAve.n Ave., Ste. 100, Menlo Park, CA, 94025; **PH:** 1-650-474-9800; **Fax:** 1-650-474-9808;
http:// www.chemgenex.com

General - Incorporation	Australia	Stock- Price on:12/24/2007	$13
Employees	NA	Stock Exchange	NDQ
Auditor	Ernst & Young	Ticker Symbol	CXSP
Stk Agt	Bank of New York	Outstanding Shares	NA
Counsel	NA	E.P.S.	NA
DUNS No.	NA	Shareholders	NA

Business: The groups principle activity is to develop novel therapeutic agents in three diseases including cancer, metabolic syndrome and depression. The group operates from United States.

Primary SIC and add'l.: 2834

CIK No: 0001175965

Subsidiaries: Autogen Research Pty Ltd, ChemGenex Pharmaceuticals, Inc.

Officers: Greg Collier/Dir., MD, CEO, Dennis Brown/Exec. Dir., Pres., James A. Campbell/VP - Operations, Rick Merrigan/CFO, Company Sec., John Blangero/Sr. Dir. - Human Genomics, Member - Scientific Advisory Board, Guy Krippner/Sr. Dir. - Medicinal Chemistry, Eric Humphriss/Sr. Dir. - Clinical Affairs, Jeremy Jowett/Sr. Dir. - Biomarkers, Ken Walder/Sr. Dir. - Drug Discovery, Shawnya Michaels/Sr. Dir. - Cancer Discovery, Tina Herbert/Sr. Dir. - Finance, Hagop Kantarjian/Member - Scientific Advisory Board, Clinical Advisor, Howard Burris/Clinical Advisor, Adam R. Craig/Sr. VP, Chief Medical Officer, Ian Nisbet/VP - Oncology

Directors: Greg Collier/Dir., MD, CEO, Brett J. Heading/Non - Exec. Chmn., Paul Zimmet/Chmn. - Scientific Advisory Board, John Blangero/Sr. Dir. - Human Genomics, Member - Scientific Advisory Board, Patrick Burns/Non - Exec. Dir., Peter Bradfield/Dir., Ian Gust/Member - Scientific Advisory Board, David James/Member - Scientific Advisory Board, Hagop Kantarjian/Member - Scientific Advisory Board, Clinical Advisor, John Hughes/Member - Scientific Advisory Board, George Morstyn/Non - Exec. Dir., Dennis Brown/Exec. Dir., Pres., Elmar J. Schnee/Non - Exec. Dir., Roger V. Byrne/Dir., Geoff Brooke/Non - Exec. Dir. *(16 Directors included in Index)*

Owners: Queensland Investment Corporation/8.10%, GBS Venture Partners Ltd/8.90%, Berne No 132 Nominees Pty Ltd/19.80%, Kinetic Investment Partners Limited/5.10%, Merck Sant/10.10%, Dennis M. Brown/7.40%

Financial Data: *Fiscal Year End:*06/30 *Latest Annual Data:* 6/30/2006

Year	Sales	Net Income
2006	$1,400,000	-$7,625,000
2005	$4,095,000	-$6,187,000

Curr. Assets:	$11,466,000	**Curr. Liab.:**	$1,431,000		
Plant, Equip.:	$240,000	**Total Liab.:**	$1,431,000	**Indic. Yr. Divd.:**	NA
Total Assets:	$11,706,000	**Net Worth:**	$10,275,000	**Debt/ Equity:**	NA

Chemical & Mining Co of Chile Inc

3101 Towercreek Pkwy., Ste. 450, Atlanta, GA, 30339; *PH:* 1-770-916-9400; *Fax:* 1-770-916-9401; *http://* www.sqm.cl

General - Incorporation	Chile	**Stock**- Price on:12/24/2007	$170.06
Employees	3,672	Stock Exchange	NYSE
Auditor	Ernst & Young LLP	Ticker Symbol	SQM
Stk Agt	Bank of New York	Outstanding Shares	26,380,000
Counsel	NA	E.P.S	$6.27
DUNS No.	98-046-4762	Shareholders	NA

Business: The group's principal activities are the production and distribution of fertilizers, industrial chemical products, iodine and lithium. Its products are based on the development of natural resources which include specialty field and water soluble fertilizers, iodine and iodine derivatives, lithium and lithium derivatives, industrial nitrates, sodium sulfate, magnesium chloride and boron.

Primary SIC and add'l.: 2819 2873 2899

CIK No: 0000909037

Subsidiaries: Soquimich Comercial S.A., SQM Europe N.V., SQM Industrial S.A., SQM Nitratos S.A., SQM North America Corp., SQM Salar S.A.

Officers: Patricio G. Contesse/CEO, Pres., Eugenio L. Ponce/Comercial Sr. VP, Camila C. Merino/Sr. VP - Human Resources, Administration, Matias S. Astaburuaga/Legal Counsel, Jaime San L. Martin/Sr. VP - Lithium Operations, Mining Affairs, Mauricio Cabello/Sr. VP - Nitrates, Lodine Operations, Patricio T. De Solminihac/COO, Exec. VP, Pauline D. Vidts/Safety, Health and Environment Sr. VP, Ricardo R. Ramos/CFO, Business Development Sr. VP, Daniel Jimenez/Human Resources, Sr. VP - Administrative, Juan Carlos Barrera/VP - Salar Operations, Christian C. Pubela/Internal Audit Manger

Directors: Wayne R. Brownlee/Vice Chmn., Julio L. Ponce/Chmn., Wolf Von Appen/Dir., Hernan B. Buchi/Dir., Kendrik Taylor Wallace/Dir., Jose Maria Ezapguirre/Dir., Daniel Yarur/Dir., Jose Antonio Silva/Dir.

Owners: Sociedad de Inversiones Pampa Calichera S.A./11.45%, Inversiones El Boldo Ltda./14.50%, Inversiones RAC Chile Ltda./2.24%, Kowa Group/3.71%, The Bank of New York/28.51%, Inversiones El Boldo Ltda./30.71%, Larrain Vial S.A./3.80%, Sociedad de Inversiones Pampa Calichera S.A./40.56%, The Bank of New York/0.06%, Inversiones RAC Chile Ltda./13.44%, A.F.P. Provida S.A./7.00%, Global Mining Investments (Chile) S.A./5.54%, A.F.P. Habitat S.A./7.00%, Larrain Vial S.A./1.04%, Kowa Group/0.04% *(16 Owners included in Index)*

Financial Data: *Fiscal Year End:*12/31 *Latest Annual Data:* 12/31/2006

Year	Sales	Net Income
2006	$1,042,886,000	$154,264,000
2005	$895,970,000	$125,204,000
2004	$788,516,000	$86,826,000

Curr. Assets:	$845,875,000	**Curr. Liab.:**	$197,642,000	**P/E Ratio:**	61.08
Plant, Equip.:	$900,285,000	**Total Liab.:**	$855,311,000	**Indic. Yr. Divd.:**	$2.690
Total Assets:	$1,849,833,000	**Net Worth:**	$994,522,000	**Debt/ Equity:**	NA

Chemical Financial Corp

333 E Main St., Midland, MI, 48640; *PH:* 1-989-839-5350; *Fax:* 1-989-839-5255; *http://* www.chemicalbankmi.com; *Email:* customerservicecenter@chemicalbankmi.com

General - Incorporation	MI	**Stock**- Price on:12/24/2007	$28.07
Employees	1,478	Stock Exchange	NDQ
Auditor	KPMG LLP	Ticker Symbol	CHFC
Stk Agt	Computershare Investor Services LLC	Outstanding Shares	24,810,000
Counsel	NA	E.P.S	NA
DUNS No.	07-635-0529	Shareholders	NA

Business: The group's principal activity is to provide commercial banking and fiduciary services. These include accepting deposits, real estate financing, commercial lending, debit cards, safe deposit box services and corporate and personal trust services. The group accepts deposits including business and personal checking accounts, savings, individual retirement account and time deposits. In addition, it also provides property and casualty insurance agency services, life insurance and annuity products, title insurance and data processing services through its subsidiaries. As of 31-Dec-2003, the group operated 133 banking offices and 2 loan production offices across 33 counties of Michigan. In addition to its banking offices, the group had 139 automated teller machines locations with 39 located off-bank premises.

Primary SIC and add'l.: 6022 6331 6712

CIK No: 0000019612

Subsidiaries: also operates under d/b/a Bailey Financial Services, also operates under d/b/a CFC Investment Centers, CFC Financial Services, Inc., CFC Title Services, Inc., Chemical Bank and Trust Company, Chemical Bank Shoreline, Chemical Bank West, Chemical Loan Management Corporation, Chemical Loan Services, LLC, Chemical Shoreline Loan Management Corporation, Chemical Shoreline Loan Services, LLC, Chemical West Loan Management Corporation, Chemical West Loan Services, LLC, JV Midland No. 1, LLC(50% owned), Shoreline Insurance Services, Inc.

Officers: David B. Ramaker/Chmn., CEO, Pres./$418,033.00, James R. Milroy/47/COO, Exec. VP/$237,915.00, Lori A. Gwizdala/CFO, Treasurer/$260,480.00

Directors: David B. Ramaker/Chmn., CEO, Pres., James A. Currie/Dir., Aloysius J. Oliver/Dir., Gary E. Anderson/Dir., Nancy Bowman/Dir., Thomas T. Huff/Dir., Terence F. Moore/Dir., Daniel J. Bernson/Dir., Michael T. Laethem/Dir., William S. Stavropoulos/Dir., Geoffery E. Merszei/Dir., Larry D. Stauffer/Dir., Franklin C. Wheatlake/Dir.

Owners: G. E. Anderson, F. C. Wheatlake, T. F. Moore, A. J. Oliver, J. A. Currie, D. B. Ramaker, T. W. Kohn, Dimensional FundAdvisors LP/7.27%, T. T. Huff, N. A. Bowman, C. D. Prins, Insiders/4.73%, G. E. Merszei, J. D. Bernson, Chemical Bank/7.50% *(21 Owners included in Index)*

Financial Data: *Fiscal Year End:*12/31 *Latest Annual Data:* 12/31/2006

Year	Sales	Net Income
2006	$258,900,000	$46,844,000
2005	$238,524,000	$52,878,000
2004	$228,579,000	$56,682,000

Curr. Assets:	$244,075,000	**Curr. Liab.:**	$3,136,289,000	**P/E Ratio:**	15.86
Plant, Equip.:	$49,475,000	**Total Liab.:**	$3,281,361,000	**Indic. Yr. Divd.:**	$1.140
Total Assets:	$3,789,247,000	**Net Worth:**	$507,886,000	**Debt/ Equity:**	0.2802

Chemokine Therapeutics Corp

2314 Ralph St. No. 12, Houston, TX, 77006; *PH:* 1-713-630-0782; *Fax:* 1-713-520-0641; *http://* www.chemokine.net; *Email:* devans@chemokine.net

General - Incorporation	DE	**Stock**- Price on:12/24/2007	$0.58
Employees	NA	Stock Exchange	OTC
Auditor	M.D. Sassi Co.	Ticker Symbol	CHKT
Stk Agt	Pacific Corporate Trust Co	Outstanding Shares	NA
Counsel	McCarthy Ttrault LLP	E.P.S	NA
DUNS No.	NA	Shareholders	NA

Business: The groups principle activity is to develop drugs in the field of chemokines. The group products include Neupogen(R) and Epogen(R). The group operates from the United States.

Primary SIC and add'l.: 2833 2836

CIK No: 0001092959

Subsidiaries: Chemokine Therapeutics (BC) Corp.

Officers: Richard C. Piazza/Chmn., CEO, Don Evans/Dir. - Public Relations, Donald Wong/Dir. - Pre, Clinical Drug Development, Bin Huang/VP - Corporate Development, Hassan Salari/Dir., Pres., Chief Scientific Officer/$427,453.00, Bashir Jaffer/CFO/$16,974.00, Guy Ely/Chief Medical Officer, Walter Korz/VP - Drug Development/$132,705.00

Directors: Richard C. Piazza/Chmn., CEO, Hassan Salari/Dir., Pres., Chief Scientific Officer, Michael Evans/Dir., John Osth/Dir., Matthias C. Kurth/Dir., Mohammad Azab/Dir., Shahin Rafii/Member - Scientific Advisory Board, Malcom A.S. Moore/Member - Scientific Advisory Board, Louis M. Pelus/Member - Scientific Advisory Board, Fabio Rossi/Member - Scientific Advisory Board, Edward D. Ball/Member - Advisory Board, Robert Carl Nevin Murray/Member - Advisory Board, Daniel Douglas Von Hoff/Member - Clilnical Advisory Board, William I. Bensinger/Member - Advisory Board, Michael George Boag Smylie/Member - Advisory Board *(17 Directors included in Index)*

Owners: John Osth, Newton Investment Management Limited/10.41%, Bin Huang, RAB Special Situations (Master) FundLimited/3.31%, Mohammad Azab, Michael Evans, Walter Korz, Insiders/8.09%, Matthias C. Kurth, Guy Ely, Bashir Jaffer, Richard C. Piazza, Hassan Salari/8.03%

Financial Data: *Fiscal Year End:*12/31 *Latest Annual Data:* 12/31/2006

Year	Sales	Net Income
2006	NA	-$7,508,000
2005	$275,000	-$6,020,000
2004	NA	-$3,095,000

Curr. Assets:	$6,253,000	**Curr. Liab.:**	$390,000		
Plant, Equip.:	$332,000	**Total Liab.:**	$399,000	**Indic. Yr. Divd.:**	NA
Total Assets:	$6,855,000	**Net Worth:**	$6,456,000	**Debt/ Equity:**	0.0012

Chemung Financial Corp

1 Chemung Canal Plz., Elmira, NY, 14901; *PH:* 1-607-737-3711; *Fax:* 1-607-735-2035; *http://* www.cctc2me.com

General - Incorporation	NY	**Stock**- Price on:12/24/2007	$29.85
Employees	293	Stock Exchange	OTC
Auditor	KPMG LLP	Ticker Symbol	CHMG
Stk Agt	American Stock Transfer & Trust Co.	Outstanding Shares	3,530,000
Counsel	NA	E.P.S	$1.86
DUNS No.	15-650-7782	Shareholders	NA

Business: The group's principal activity is to provide banking and financial services in the New York state. The group operates through its wholly owned subsidiary, chemung canal trust company, a community bank and cfs group inc, a financial services company. It accepts time, demand and savings deposits including now, super now accounts, regular savings account, insured money market accounts, investment certificates, fixed-rate certificates of deposit and club accounts. The group originates secured and unsecured commercial and consumer loans, residential and home equity mortgage loans, revolving credits loans with overdraft checking protection, small business loans and student loans. Non banking services include safe deposit facilities, selling uninsured annuity and mutual fund investment products and the use of networked automated teller facilities. The operations are carried out through 13 branches located in chemung, schuyler, steuben and tioga country

Primary SIC and add'l.: 6712 6022

CIK No: 0000763563

Subsidiaries: CFS Group, Inc., Chemung Canal Trust Company

Officers: Jan P. Updegraff/Vice Chmn., CEO/$521,318.00, John R. Battersby/CFO, Exec. VP, Treasurer/$149,427.00, Melinda A. Sartori/Exec. VP/$142,549.00, Thomas C. Karski/Exec. VP/$196,746.00, James E. Corey/61/Exec. VP/$201,751.00, Ronald M. Bentley/Dir., COO, Pres., Jane H. Adamy/Sec.

Directors: Jan P. Updegraff/Vice Chmn., CEO, Robert H. Dalrymple/Chmn., Clover M. Drinkwater/Dir., Ralph H. Meyer/Dir., Richard W. Swan/Dir., David J. Dalrymple/Dir., William D. Eggers/Dir., John F. Potter/Dir., Robert E. Agan/Dir., Stephen M. Lounsberry/Dir., Thomas K. Meier/Dir., Charles M. Streeter/Dir., Ronald M. Bentley/Dir., COO, Pres.

Owners: Catherine D. Smith/13.17%, John R. Battersby, Clover M. Drinkwater, Thomas K. Meier, David J. Dalrymple/18.17%, Richard W. Swan/2.06%, Ronald M. Bentley, Melinda A. Sartori, John F. Potter/1.21%, Chemung Canal Trust Company/12.97%, Charles M. Streeter, Insiders/28.60%, James E. Corey, William D. Eggers, Robert E. Agan *(20 Owners included in Index)*

Financial Data: *Fiscal Year End:*12/31 *Latest Annual Data:* 12/31/2006

Year	Sales	Net Income
2006	$53,937,000	$6,589,000
2005	$48,973,000	$6,590,000
2004	$50,471,000	$8,733,000

Curr. Assets:	$26,590,000	Curr. Liab.:	$650,188,000	P/E Ratio:	16.14
Plant, Equip.:	$21,722,000	Total Liab.:	$656,409,000	Indic. Yr. Divd.:	$0.960
Total Assets:	$738,170,000	Net Worth:	$81,761,000	Debt/ Equity:	NA

Cheniere Energy Inc

700 Milam St., Ste. 800, Houston, TX, 77002; *PH:* 1-713-659-1361; *Fax:* 1-713-659-5459;
http:// www.cheniere.com; *Email:* info@cheniere.com

General - Incorporation .... DE
Employees 256
Auditor ....UHY Mann Frankfort Stein & Lipp
Stk Agt......................U.S. Stock Transfer Corp
Counsel...........................Andrews & Kurch LLP
DUNS No. 00-860-1684

Stock- Price on:12/24/2007 ....$40.55
Stock Exchange...AMEX
Ticker Symbol... LNG
Outstanding Shares.............................56,270,000
E.P.S. .... -$3.02
Shareholders...NA

Business: The group's principal activity is to explore, develop and exploit oil and gas and to develop liquefied natural gas (lng) receiving terminal business. The group's current oil and gas exploration and development activities are focused on two areas: the cameron project and the offshore Texas project area. It is conducting the exploration for and production of oil and natural gas along the gulf coast of Texas and Louisiana, onshore and in the shallow waters of the gulf of Mexico. The group employs a small staff of experienced oil and gas exploration professionals who utilize third party drilling contractors and others in the oilfield service industry in executing the group's exploration program. It has operations in the United States of America.

Primary SIC and add'l.: 1389 1382 1311

CIK No: 0000003570

Subsidiaries: Cheniere LNG Financial Services, Inc., Cheniere LNG Holdings, LLC, Cheniere LNG Terminals, Inc., Cheniere LNG, Inc., Cheniere LNG-LP Interests, LLC, Sabine Pass LNG, L.P., Sabine Pass LNG-LP, LLC

Officers: Charif Souki/Chmn., CEO/$5,325,191.00, Darron Granger/Sr. VP, Stanley C. Horton/COO, Pres./$2,673,845.00, Graham A. McArthur/VP, Treasurer, Scott Abshire/CIO, VP, Zurab S. Kobiashvili/Sr. VP, General Counsel/$1,402,686.00, Craig K. Townsend/VP, Chief Accounting Officer, Don A. Turkleson/Sr. VP, CFO/$1,214,998.00, Herbert Cole/VP, Controller, Keith R. Teague/Pres. - Cheniere Pipeline Company, Patricia Outtrim/VP - Government Affairs, Meg Gentle/VP - Strategic Planning, Katie Pipkin/VP - Investor Relations, Terence Lynch/VP - Internal Audit, Enrique Mejorada/VP - Risk Management *(21 Officers included in Index)*

Directors: Charif Souki/Chmn., CEO, Walter L. Williams/Vice Chmn., Keith F. Carney/Dir., David B. Kilpatrick/Dir., Robinson J. West/Dir., Vicky A. Bailey/Dir., John Deutch/Dir., Nuno Brandolini/Dir., Paul J. Hoenmans/Dir.

Owners: Stanley C. Horton, Insiders/10.90%, Keith F. Carney, Orbis Asset Management Limited, Vicky A. Bailey, Nuno Brandolini, Walter L. Williams/1.10%, John M. Deutch, Keith M. Meyer, David B. Kilpatrick, SRM Global Master Fund Limited Partnership/9.40%, Gandhara Advisors Europe LLP/5.50%, Perry Corp./8.30%, Zurab S. Kobiashvili, Credit Suisse/6.10% *(20 Owners included in Index)*

Financial Data: Fiscal Year End:12/31 Latest Annual Data: 12/31/2006

Year	Sales	Net Income
2006	$2,371,000	-$145,853,000
2005	$3,005,000	-$29,798,000
2004	$1,998,000	-$24,568,000

Curr. Assets:	$745,687,000	Curr. Liab.:	$64,096,000		
Plant, Equip.:	$624,026,000	Total Liab.:	$1,394,277,000	Indic. Yr. Divd.:	NA
Total Assets:	$1,612,102,000	Net Worth:	$217,825,000	Debt/ Equity:	NA

CHEROKEE

6835 Valjean Ave., Van Nuys, CA, 91406; *PH:* 1-818-908-9868; *Fax:* 1-818-908-9191;
http:// www.cherokeegroup.com

General - Incorporation .... DE
Employees 18
Auditor ....Moss Adams LLP
Stk Agt.........................U.S. Stock Transfer Corp
Counsel.............................Latham & Watkins
DUNS No. 36-440-7510

Stock- Price on:12/24/2007 ....$41.73
Stock Exchange...NDQ
Ticker Symbol..CHKE
Outstanding Shares...............................8,910,000
E.P.S. ....NA
Shareholders...NA

Business: The group's principal activity is the licensing and marketing of brand names and trademarks for apparel, footwear and accessories. The trademarks are spell c, cherokee(R), sideout(R), sideout sport(R), carole little(R), clii(R) , saint tropez-west(R), chorus line(R), all that jazz(R) and molly malloy(R). The sideout brand represents a young active lifestyle and the cherokee brand, casual American lifestyle with traditional values. The group grants licenses to retailers and wholesalers on certain categories of merchandise. The licensees are responsible for designing and manufacturing the merchandise. Target stores in United States and zellers inc in Canada were licensed to use the cherokee brand in specified categories including apparel, sleepwear, fashion accessories, sports bags and cosmetics. As of 31-Jan-2004, the group had 12 continuing license agreements covering both domestic and international markets.

Primary SIC and add'l.: 6794

CIK No: 0000844161

Subsidiaries: Spell C. LLC.

Officers: Robert Margolis/56/Chmn., CEO/$8,760,000.00, Howard Siegel/48/Pres./$397,000.00, Russell Riopelle/41/CFO/$496,000.00, Sandi Stuart/52/Exec. VP - Brand Development/$379,000.00, Carol Gratzke/55/Corp. Sec.

Directors: Robert Margolis/56/Chmn., CEO, Timothy Ewing/43/Dir., Dave Mullen/69/Dir., Keith Hull/51/Dir., Jess Ravich/46/Dir.

Owners: Sandi Stuart, Russell J. Riopelle, Barclays Global Investors, NA/8.60%, Kayne Anderson Rudnick Investment Management, LLC/8.10%, Mark Nawrocki, Keith Hull, Jess Ravich, Dave Mullen, Insiders/16.40%, Howard Siegel, FMR Corp./5.70%, Tim Ewing/1.40%, Robert Margolis/12.10%

Financial Data: Fiscal Year End:01/28 Latest Annual Data: 2/3/2007

Year	Sales	Net Income
2007	$76,627,000	$34,791,000
2006	$42,732,000	$18,277,000
2005	$38,928,000	$17,166,000

Curr. Assets:	$53,830,000	Curr. Liab.:	$26,167,000		
Plant, Equip.:	$216,000	Total Liab.:	$26,167,000	Indic. Yr. Divd.:	$3.000
Total Assets:	$62,302,000	Net Worth:	$36,135,000	Debt/ Equity:	NA

Cherokee International Corp

2841 Dow Ave., Tustin, CA, 92780; *PH:* 1-714-544-6665; *Fax:* 1-714-838-4742;
http:// www.cherokeepwr.com

General - Incorporation .... DE
Employees 1,630
Auditor .... Mayer Hoffman Mccann, P.C
Stk Agt .... Computershare Investor Services LLC
Counsel...Skadden, Arps
DUNS No. 09-915-6259

Stock- Price on:12/24/2007 ....$4.87
Stock Exchange...NDQ
Ticker Symbol..CHRK
Outstanding Shares.............................19,350,000
E.P.S. .... -$0.14
Shareholders...NA

Business: The group's principle activity is to design and manufacture power supply products for original equipment manufacturers. The group's products are used for regulation and distribution of electrical power in electronic equipment. Its products include ac/dc power supplies and dc/dc converters. These products convert alternating current (ac), from a primary source, into a precisely controlled direct current (dc). The major customers of the group include alcatel, brocade communications systems, hewlett-packard, honeywell international, juniper networks, motorola, inc. And nortel networks. The group has operations in North America, Europe, mexco and India. The group's markets its products through local direct sales team, independent sales representatives and in-house account managers in North America and Europe. The group's quarterly revenue for September 2007 was 30.40 millions of USD.

Primary SIC and add'l.: 3629

CIK No: 0001090069

Subsidiaries: Cherokee AB, Cherokee Electronica S.A. de C.V., Cherokee Europe SCA, Cherokee Europe SPRL, Cherokee Germany GmbH, Cherokee India Pvt. Ltd., Cherokee International (China) Power Supply LLC, Cherokee Netherlands B.V., Cherokee Netherlands I B.V., Cherokee Netherlands II B.V., Cherokee Sarl, Cherokee U.K., Powertel India Pvt. Ltd.

Officers: Jeffrey Frank/Dir., CEO, Pres./$715,990.00, Linster W. Fox/CFO, Exec. VP - Finance, Sec./$413,225.00, Eric Brouwers/GM - Cherokee Europe, Bud Patel/Exec. VP/$557,801.00, Mukesh Patel/Exec. VP - Global Operations/$442,993.00, Howard Ribaudo/VP - Sales, Dennis Pouliot/VP - Strategic Accounting, Alex Patel/VP - Engineering/$378,713.00, Michael Wagner/VP - Marketing

Directors: Jeffrey Frank/Dir., CEO, Pres., Raymond Meyer/Chmn., Clark Michael Crawford/Dir., Vincent Cebula/Dir., Daniel Lukas/Dir., Larry Schwerin/Dir., Edward Philip Smoot/Dir.

Owners: F&C Asset Management plc/5.80%, Insiders/56.80%, Mukesh Patel, Linster W. Fox, Green River Management I, L.L.C/5.50%, Raymond Meyer/0.10%, Alex Patel, BC Advisors, LLC/5.40%, Oaktree Capital Management, LLC/24.70%, Bud Patel, GSCP (NJ),Inc./25.80%, Jeffrey Frank/2.00%, Daniel Lukas/25.80%, Vincent Cebula/24.70%, Clark Michael Crawford

Financial Data: Fiscal Year End:01/01 Latest Annual Data: 12/31/2006

Year	Sales	Net Income
2006	$145,028,000	$83,000
2005	$122,079,000	-$3,232,000

Curr. Assets:	$68,778,000	Curr. Liab.:	$27,673,000		
Plant, Equip.:	$19,888,000	Total Liab.:	$81,018,000	Indic. Yr. Divd.:	NA
Total Assets:	$96,893,000	Net Worth:	$15,875,000	Debt/ Equity:	3.2681

Chesapeake Corp

1021 E Cary St., Ste. 2350, Richmond, VA, 23219; *PH:* 1-804-697-1000; *Fax:* 1-804-697-1199;
http:// www.cskcorp.com

General - Incorporation .... VA
Employees 5,553
Auditor ....PricewaterhouseCoopers LLP
Stk Agt .... Computershare Investor Services LLC
Counsel........................Hunton & Williams LLP
DUNS No. 00-310-9634

Stock- Price on:12/24/2007 ....$13.16
Stock Exchange...NYSE
Ticker Symbol..CSK
Outstanding Shares.............................19,920,000
E.P.S. .... -$1.76
Shareholders...NA

Business: The group's principal activity is to design, manufacture and market paperboard and plastic packaging. The group conducts its business in three segments: paperboard packaging, plastic packaging and land development. The paperboard packaging segment manufactures and markets corrugated products, folding cartons, leaflets, labels and rigid fiber boxes primarily for pharmaceuticals, healthcare, food, household, multimedia and technology. The plastic packaging segment designs and manufacturers plastic containers, bottles, preforms and closures primarily to agrochemicals, beverages, pharmaceuticals and healthcare industry. The land development markets land for residential and commercial development, real estate investment and land conservation. The group operates in the United States and in Europe. In 2004, the group discontinued land development segment.

Primary SIC and add'l.: 6552 2631 2653

CIK No: 0000019731

Subsidiaries: Berry Holdings Ltd., BERRYS OF WESTPORT LTD, BERRYS PRINTING WORKS LTD, Bourgeot-etiqso-lesbats Sa, Boxmore Cape (pty) Limited, Boxmore Cleland Ltd, Boxmore Emballage Sa, Boxmore International Ltd, Boxmore Packaging Limited, Boxmore Plastics (mauritius) Limited, Boxmore Plastics (ni) Ltd, Boxmore Plastics International (pty) Ltd, Boxmore Plastics Ltd, Boxmore Technology Limited, Bpg Healthcare Ltd 90 Subsidiaries included in the Index

Officers: Andrew J. Kohut/CEO, Pres./$1,135,550.00, Joel K. Mostrom/CFO, Sr. VP/$521,403.00, Peter L. Lee/VP, Pres. - Chesapeake Asia, Pacific Limited, Neil Rylance/Exec. VP - European Packaging/$770,675.00, Joe Vagi/Mgr. - Corporate Communications, Bob Houghton/Contact - Media, Michael D. Beverly/Assist. Sec., Assoc. General Counsel, Candace Formacek/Treasurer, Richard A. Scully/VP, Dir. - European Finance, J. P. Causey/Exec. VP, Sec., General Counsel/$499,546.00, Michael Jennings/Contact - Westport, Ireland, Lisa Kay/Contact - Lincolnshire, Leen Verschraegen/Contact - Belgium, Gerhard Vetter/Contact - Frankfurt, Germany, Jean Albert Leroux/General Contact *(22 Officers included in Index)*

Directors: David Fell/65/Chmn., Harry H. Warner/72/Dir., Brian Buchan/55/Dir., Joseph P. Viviano/69/Dir., John W. Rosenblum/64/Dir., Beverly L. Thelander/52/Dir., Rafael C. Decaluwe/60/Dir., Henri D. Petit/59/Dir., Jeremy S.G. Fowden/51/Dir., Frank S. Royal/68/Dir.

Owners: Insiders/3.40%, Henri D. Petit, Royce& Associates, LLC/5.40%, Harry H. Warner, John W. Rosenblum, Jeremy S. G. Fowden, Dimensional Fund Advisors LP/8.50%, J. P. Causey, Joseph P. Viviano, T. Rowe Price Associates, Inc./8.70%, Beverly L. Thelander, Barclays Global Investors, Ltd./6.40%, Wells Capital Management Incorporated/10.40%, Neil Rylance, Frank S. Royal *(20 Owners included in Index)*

Financial Data: Fiscal Year End:01/01 Latest Annual Data: 12/31/2006

Year	Sales	Net Income
2006	$995,400,000	-$39,600,000
2005	$1,031,700,000	$10,900,000

Curr. Assets:	$286,900,000	**Curr. Liab.:**	$255,000,000		
Plant, Equip.:	$354,100,000	**Total Liab.:**	$881,100,000	**Indic. Yr. Divd.:**	$0.880
Total Assets:	$1,114,800,000	**Net Worth:**	$233,700,000	**Debt/ Equity:**	1.9729

Chesapeake Energy Corp

6100 N Western Ave., Oklahoma City, OK, 73118; *PH:* 1-405-848-8000; *Fax:* 1-405-843-0573; *http://* www.chkenergy.com

General - Incorporation	OK	**Stock**- Price on:12/24/2007	$37.24
Employees	4,900	Stock Exchange	NYSE
Auditor	Pricewaterhousecoopers LLP	Ticker Symbol	CHK
Stk Agt	UMB Bank, N.A.	Outstanding Shares	460,740,000
Counsel	NA	E.P.S	$3.58
DUNS No.	60-128-5422	Shareholders	NA

Business: The groups principle activity is to produce natural gas. In the year 2007, the group acquired Kerr-McGee Tower. The group operates from United States.

Primary SIC and add'l.: 1381

CIK No: 0000895126

Subsidiaries: Carmen Acquisition, LLC, Chesapeake Acquisition, LLC, Chesapeake Appalachia, LLC, Chesapeake Eagle Canada Corp., Chesapeake Energy Louisiana Corporation, Chesapeake Energy Marketing, Inc., Chesapeake Exploration Limited Partnership, Chesapeake Land Company, LLC, Chesapeake Louisiana, L.P., Chesapeake Operating, Inc., Chesapeake ORC, LLC, Chesapeake Royalty, LLC, Chesapeake Sigma, L.P., Chesapeake South Texas Corp., Columbia Natural Resources Canada, Ltd. 28 Subsidiaries included in the Index

Officers: Aubrey K. McClendon/Chmn., CEO/$15,057,360.00, Marcus C. Rowland/CFO, Exec. VP/$4,564,787.00, Stephen W. Miller/Sr. VP - Drilling, Douglas J. Jacobson/Exec. VP - Acquisitions, Divestitures/$2,827,276.00, Steven C. Dixon/COO, Exec. VP - Operations/$3,143,079.00, Michael A. Johnson/Sr. VP - Accounting, Controller, Chief Accounting Officer, Thomas S. Price/Sr. VP - Corporate Development, Martha A. Burger/Sr. VP - Human, Corporate Resources, Henry J. Hood/General Counsel, Sr. VP - Land, Legal, Jeffrey L. Mobley/Sr. VP - Investor Relations, Research, Mark J. Lester/Exec. VP - Exploration/$3,266,421.00, Jeffrey A. Fisher/Sr. VP - Production, Jim Gipson/Dir. - Media Relations, James C. Johnson/Pres. - Chesapeake Energy Marketing, Inc, Cathy L. Tompkins/Sr. VP - Information Technology *(16 Officers included in Index)*

Directors: Aubrey K. McClendon/Chmn., CEO, Charles T. Maxwell/Dir., Merrill A. Miller/Dir., Breene M. Kerr/Dir., Frank A. Keating/Dir., Frederick B. Whittemore/Dir., Richard K. Davidson/Dir., Donald L. Nickles/Dir.

Owners: Pete Miller, FMR Corp./9.62%, Steven C. Dixon, Tom L. Ward/5.17%, Southeastern Asset Management, Inc./10.10%, Richard K. Davidson, Don Nickles, Frank Keating, Breene M. Kerr, Frederick B. Whittemore, Mark J. Lester, Douglas J. Jacobson, Marcus C. Rowland, Insiders/6.40%, Charles T. Maxwell *(16 Owners included in Index)*

Financial Data: **Fiscal Year End:**12/31 **Latest Annual Data:** 12/31/2006

Year	Sales	Net Income
2006	$7,325,595,000	$2,003,323,000
2005	$4,665,290,000	$948,302,000
2004	$2,709,268,000	$515,155,000

Curr. Assets:	$1,153,869,000	**Curr. Liab.:**	$1,889,809,000	**P/E Ratio:**	10.40
Plant, Equip.:	$21,904,043,000	**Total Liab.:**	$13,165,696,000	**Indic. Yr. Divd.:**	$0.270
Total Assets:	$24,417,167,000	**Net Worth:**	$11,251,471,000	**Debt/ Equity:**	0.6697

Chesapeake Utilities Corp

909 Silver Lake Blvd., Dover, DE, 19904; *PH:* 1-302-734-6799; *Fax:* 1-302-734-6750; *http://* www.chpk.com

General - Incorporation	DE	**Stock**- Price on:12/24/2007	$34.05
Employees	437	Stock Exchange	NYSE
Auditor	PricewaterhouseCoopers LLP	Ticker Symbol	CPK
Stk Agt	Computershare Trust Co	Outstanding Shares	6,730,000
Counsel	NA	E.P.S	$1.95
DUNS No.	04-195-2581	Shareholders	NA

Business: The group's principal activity is to distribute natural gas, propane, and advanced information services, water services and other related businesses. The three natural gas distribution divisions serve residential, commercial and industrial customers in southern Delaware, eastern Maryland and central Florida. The group's subsidiary eastern shore natural gas company operates an interstate pipeline system, transporting gas from Pennsylvania to the Delaware and Maryland as well as to utilities and industrial customers. Information services include Web-related products and the service and support of progress. Water services include conditioning and treatment and bottled water services. In 2003, the group discontinued its six water service business.

Primary SIC and add'l.: 4924 7374 4925 3589 4922 4923

CIK No: 0000019745

Subsidiaries: aQuality Company, Inc, BravePoint, Inc., Chesapeake Investment Company, Chesapeake Service Company, Eastern Shore Natural Gas Company, Eastern Shore Real Estate, Inc., OnSight Energy, LLC, Peninsula Energy Services Company, Inc., Peninsula Pipeline Company, Inc., Sam Shannahan Well Company, Inc., Sharp Energy, Inc., Sharp Water of Idaho, Inc., Sharp Water of Minnesota, Inc., Sharp Water, Inc., Sharpgas, Inc. 18 Subsidiaries included in the Index

Officers: John R. Schimkaitis/Dir., CEO, Pres., Michael P. McMasters/Sr. VP, CFO, Stephen C. Thompson/Sr. VP, Beth W. Cooper/VP, Corp. Sec., Treasurer, Thomas A. Geoffroy/Assist. VP, Heidi W. Watkins/Investor Relations Administrator, Elaine B. Bittner/VP - Eastern Shore Natural GAS, Sydney H. Davis/Mgr. - Communications

Directors: John R. Schimkaitis/Dir., CEO, Pres., Ralph J. Adkins/65/Chmn., Thomas J. Bresnan/55/Dir., Richard Bernstein/65/Dir., Walter J. Coleman/73/Dir., Eugene H. Bayard/61/Dir., Calvert A. Morgan/60/Dir., Joseph E. Moore/65/Dir., Peter J. Martin/68/Dir., Thomas P. Hill/59/Dir.

Owners: Michael P. McMasters, Joseph E. Moore, Robert S. Zola, Ralph J. Adkins, Calvert A. Morgan, Peter J. Martin, Walter J. Coleman, Eugene H. Bayard, Insiders, John R. Schimkaitis, Thomas P. Hill, Thomas J. Bresnan, Beth W. Cooper, Stephen C. Thompson, Paul M. Barbas *(17 Owners included in Index)*

Financial Data: **Fiscal Year End:**12/31 **Latest Annual Data:** 12/31/2006

Year	Sales	Net Income
2006	$231,201,000	$10,507,000
2005	$229,630,000	$10,468,000
2004	$177,955,000	$9,429,000

Curr. Assets:	$77,482,000	**Curr. Liab.:**	$90,461,000	**P/E Ratio:**	17.28
Plant, Equip.:	$240,825,000	**Total Liab.:**	$213,842,000	**Indic. Yr. Divd.:**	$1.180
Total Assets:	$324,994,000	**Net Worth:**	$111,152,000	**Debt/ Equity:**	0.5910

Chestatee Bancshares Inc

6639 Hwy. 53 E, Dawsonville, GA, 30534; *PH:* 1-706-216-2265; *Fax:* 1-706-216-4593; *http://* www.chestateestatebank.com

General - Incorporation	GA	**Stock**- Price on:12/24/2007	$12.25
Employees	67	Stock Exchange	OTC
Auditor	Mauldin & Jenkins LLC	Ticker Symbol	CBNR
Stk Agt	NA	Outstanding Shares	3,450,000
Counsel	NA	E.P.S	$0.86
DUNS No.	NA	Shareholders	NA

Business: The group's principal activity is the provision of commercial banking services including acceptance of deposits and lending loans. The various kinds of deposits accepted by the group includes customary types of time and demand deposits. The categories of loans consist of consumer, commercial and installment loans. The other services offered by the group are money transfers, safe deposit services and investments in U.S. Government and municipal services. The group operates through its wholly owned subsidiaries chestatee state bank, chestatee residential mortgage, inc., and chestatee financial services, inc.

Primary SIC and add'l.: 6712 6022

CIK No: 0001111196

Subsidiaries: Chestatee State Bank

Officers: Philip J. Hester/55/Dir., CEO, Pres./$363,811.00, Deborah F. McLeod/48/CFO, Exec. VP/$232,438.00, James M. Curry/56/Exec. VP

Directors: Philip J. Hester/55/Dir., CEO, Pres., David E. Johnson/Chmn., Glennon C. Grogan/Dir., Alan W. McRae/56/Dir., James H. Grogan/Dir., Ralph Millard Bowen/Dir., Andrew M. Head/54/Dir., Kim M. Mills/Dir., Marcus Calvin Byrd/Dir., John Philip Hester/Dir., Bruce Todd Howard/Dir., William Alan McRae/55/Dir., Millard R. Bowen/65/Dir., Todd B. Howard/41/Dir.

Owners: Andrew M. Head/4.54%, Philip J. Hester/3.84%, Millard R. Bowen/5.47%, Glennon C. Grogan/2.56%, W. Alan McRae/3.28%, Deborah F. McLeod/1.05%, Marcus C. Byrd/4.45%, James H. Grogan/2.81%, James M. Curry/1.16%, Kim M. Mills/1.40%, Todd B. Howard/2.66%, David E. Johnson/4.83%, Insiders/34.56%

Financial Data: **Fiscal Year End:**12/31 **Latest Annual Data:** 12/31/2006

Year	Sales	Net Income
2006	$22,153,000	$2,963,000

Curr. Assets:	$17,885,000	**Curr. Liab.:**	$262,504,000	**P/E Ratio:**	14.41
Plant, Equip.:	$7,296,000	**Total Liab.:**	$271,593,000	**Indic. Yr. Divd.:**	NA
Total Assets:	$299,675,000	**Net Worth:**	$28,082,000	**Debt/ Equity:**	0.2071

Cheviot Financial Corp

3723 Glenmore Ave., Cheviot, OH, 45211; *PH:* 1-513-661-0457; *Fax:* 1-513-389-3312; *http://* www.cheviotsavings.com

General - Incorporation	Federal	**Stock**- Price on:12/24/2007	$13.54
Employees	NA	Stock Exchange	NDQ
Auditor	Grant Thornton LLP	Ticker Symbol	CHEV
Stk Agt	Registrar & Transfer Co	Outstanding Shares	9,270,000
Counsel	Luse Gorman Pomerenk & Schick	E.P.S	$0.16
DUNS No.	NA	Shareholders	NA

Business: The group's principal activity is to attract retail deposits from the general public and investing these funds in loans secured by one-to-four family mortgage loan, multi-family residential loans and construction loans. The group operates through its wholly owned subsidiaries, cheviot savings bank. The operations are conducted through four full service branches in cheviot and hamilton county in Ohio.

Primary SIC and add'l.: 6712 6035

CIK No: 0001248124

Subsidiaries: Cheviot Savings Bank

Officers: Thomas J. Linneman/CEO, Pres./$421,105.00, Jeffrey J. Lenzer/VP - Operations, Cheviot Savings Bank/$264,268.00, Kevin M. Kappa/VP - Compliance, Cheviot Savings Bank/$247,072.00, Deborah A. Fischer/VP - Lending, Cheviot Savings Bank/$129,049.00, Debbie Mundstock/Sr. Loan Officer - Cheviot Branch, Cheviot Savings Bank, George Tenoever/Loan Officer - Cheviot Branch, Cheviot Savings Bank, Scott T. Smith/CFO - Cheviot Savings Bank/$198,912.00, Rick Ahlers/Collection Mgr. - Cheviot Savings Bank, Annie Iverson/Dir. - Marketing, Cheviot Savings Bank, Janet Brown/Branch Mgr. - Cheviot Savings Bank, Kimberly A. Siener/Administrative Assist. - Cheviot Savings Bank, Tricia Walter/Controller - Cheviot Savings Bank, Maureen Monahan/Branch Mgr., Loan Officer - Monfort Heights Branch, Cheviot Savings Bank, Amy E. Case/Branch Mgr., Loan Officer - Bridgetown Branch, Cheviot Savings Bank, Mike Wilson/Branch Mgr., Loan Officer - Harrison Branch, Cheviot Savings Bank *(18 Officers included in Index)*

Directors: Robert Thomas/65/Dir., Steven R. Hausfeld/50/Dir., Edward L. Kleemeier/73/Dir., John T. Smith/63/Dir., James E. Williamson/63/Dir., Exec. Sec.

Financial Data: **Fiscal Year End:**12/31 **Latest Annual Data:** 12/31/2006

Year	Sales	Net Income
2006	$17,068,000	$1,696,000
2005	$14,862,000	$2,153,000
2004	$13,266,000	$1,328,000

Curr. Assets:	$7,067,000	**Curr. Liab.:**	$235,889,000	**P/E Ratio:**	84.63
Plant, Equip.:	$5,397,000	**Total Liab.:**	$237,580,000	**Indic. Yr. Divd.:**	$0.320
Total Assets:	$309,780,000	**Net Worth:**	$72,200,000	**Debt/ Equity:**	NA

Chevron

6001 Bollinger Canyon Rd., San Ramon, CA, 94583; *PH:* 1-925-842-1000; *Fax:* 1-925-842-3530; *http://* www.chevron.com; *Email:* comment@chevron.com

General - Incorporation	DE	**Stock**- Price on:12/24/2007	$82.98
Employees	62,500	Stock Exchange	NYSE
Auditor	PricewaterhouseCoopers LLP	Ticker Symbol	CVX
Stk Agt	Mellon Investor Services LLC	Outstanding Shares	2,150,000,000
Counsel	NA	E.P.S	$8.73
DUNS No.	00-138-2555	Shareholders	NA

Business: The groups principle activity is to provide energy services. The group products are sold under the brand names Texaco and Caltex. The group operates from United States.

Primary SIC and add'l.: 2911 1382 1311 1221 2865

CIK No: 0000093410

Subsidiaries: Bermaco Insurance Company Limited, Cabinda Gulf Oil Company Limited, Caltex (Philippines) Inc., Caltex New Zealand Limited, Caltex Oil (Pakistan) Limited, Caltex Oil (Thailand) Limited, Chevron Asiatic Limited, Chevron Australia Pty Ltd., Chevron Australia Transport Pty Ltd., Chevron Brasil Ltda., Chevron Canada Capital Company, Chevron Canada Finance Limited, Chevron Canada Limited, Chevron Capital Corporation, Chevron Capital U.S.A. Inc. 89 Subsidiaries included in the Index

Officers: David J. OReilly/61/Chmn., CEO/$31,602,890.00, John S. Watson/52/VP, Pres. - Chevron International Exploration, Production/$6,641,585.00, G. P. Luquette/52/VP, Pres. - Chevron North America Exploration, Production Company Since 2006, Michael K. Wirth/48/Exec. VP - Global Downstream, Stephen J. Crowe/61/CFO, VP/$6,036,174.00, Charles A. James/54/VP, General Counsel, George L. Kirkland/58/Exec. VP - Upstream, Gas/$6,902,268.00, John E. Bethancourt/57/Exec. VP - Technology, Services, Randy S. Richards/Sec., Lydia I. Beebe/Sec., Scott A. Swasey/Sec., Patricia E. Yarrington/52/VP, Treasurer, Jim Aleveras/GM, Bill Clutter/Assist. Mgr.

Directors: David J. OReilly/61/Chmn., CEO, Peter J. Robertson/61/Vice Chmn., Robert E. Denham/62/Dir., Donald B. Rice/68/Dir., Robert J. Eaton/68/Dir., Franklyn G. Jenifer/68/Dir., Ronald D. Sugar/59/Dir., Samuel H. Armacost/68/Dir., Linnet F. Deily/62/Dir., Sam Nunn/69/Dir., Charles R. Shoemate/68/Dir., Carl Ware/64/Dir., Kevin W. Sharer/60/Dir., Sam Ginn/70/Dir.

Owners: Robert J. Eaton, Franklyn G. Jenifer, Sam Nunn, John S. Watson, Sam Ginn, George L. Kirkland, Ronald D. Sugar, Insiders, Peter J. Robertson, Carl Ware, Stephen J. Crowe, Donald B. Rice, David J. OReilly, Capital Research and Management Company/6.00%, Linnet F. Deily *(18 Owners included in Index)*

Financial Data: *Fiscal Year End:*12/31 *Latest Annual Data:* 12/31/2006

Year	Sales	Net Income
2006	$210,118,000,000	$17,138,000,000
2005	$198,200,000,000	$14,099,000,000
2004	$155,300,000,000	$13,328,000,000

Curr. Assets:	$36,304,000,000	*Curr. Liab.:*	$28,409,000,000	*P/E Ratio:*	9.51
Plant, Equip.:	$68,858,000,000	*Total Liab.:*	$63,484,000,000	*Indic. Yr. Divd.:*	NA
Total Assets:	$132,628,000,000	*Net Worth:*	$68,935,000,000	*Debt/ Equity:*	0.0857

Chicago Bridge & Iron Company N.V.

2103 Research Forest Dr., The Woodlands, TX, 77380; ***PH:*** 1-832-513-1000; ***Fax:*** 1-832-513-1605; ***http://*** www.cbi.com

General - Incorporation	Netherlands	**Stock** - Price on:12/24/2007	$38.45
Employees	12,101	Stock Exchange	NYSE
Auditor	Ernst & Young LLP	Ticker Symbol	CBI
Stk Agt	Bank of New York	Outstanding Shares	96,440,000
Counsel	NA	E.P.S	$1.65
DUNS No.	38-649-1765	Shareholders	NA

Business: The group's principal activity is providing the services in the field of engineering, procurement and construction. The group offers design, engineering, procurement, fabrication, field construction, mechanical installation and commissioning services. The group operates through the following business segments; process and technology, standard tanks, low temperature cryogenic tanks and systems, repairs and turnarounds, specialty and other structures and pressure vessels. The customers of the group include oil and gas, petrochemical and chemical, power, water and wastewater, metals and mining industries. The group has operations in North America, Europe, Africa, Middle East, Asia-Pacific and central and South America.

Primary SIC and add'l.: 1791 3443

CIK No: 0001027884

Subsidiaries: Arabian CBI Ltd., Arabian CBI Tank Manufacturing Company Limited, Arabian Gulf Material Supply Company Ltd., CB&I (Nigeria) Limited, CB&I Europe B.V., CB&I Finance Company Limited, CB&I Hungary Holding LLC(CBI Hungary Kft), CB&I John Brown Limited, CBI (Malaysia) Sdn. Bhd., CBI (Philippines) Inc., CBI Construcciones S.A., CBI Constructors (PNG)Pty. Ltd., CBI Constructors Limited, CBI Constructors Pty. Ltd., CBI Constructors S.A. (Proprietary) Limited 27 Subsidiaries included in the Index

Officers: Philip K. Asherman/57/CEO, Pres./$4,236,888.00, Jerry H. Ballengee/70/Chmn., Supervisory Dir., Walter G. Browning/60/VP, General Counsel, Sec., Vincent L. Kontny/70/Supervisory Dir., Ronald A. Ballschmiede/52/CFO, Exec. VP/$691,772.00, Marty Spake/Dir. - Investor Relations, Steve Glenn/Contact - Human Resources, Mathew Abraham/Contact - Global Marketing, Ronald E. Blum/58/Exec. VP - Global Business Development/$1,154,595.00, David P. Bordages/57/Supervisory Dir., VP - Human Resources, Administration/$949,918.00, John W. Redmon/59/Exec. VP - Operations, Cbic/$921,780.00, Marsha C. Williams/57/Supervisory Dir., Travis L. Stricker/37/Chief Accounting Officer, Corporate Controller, Samuel C. Leventry/58/Supervisory Dir., VP - Technology Services, Michael Underwood/64/Supervisory Dir. *(20 Officers included in Index)*

Directors: Jerry H. Ballengee/70/Chmn., Supervisory Dir.

Owners: Samuel C. Leventry, Ronald A. Ballschmiede, David P. Bordages, Vincent L. Kontny, Insiders, Marsha C. Williams, John W. Redmon, Charles J. Jennett, Jerry H. Ballengee, FMR Corporation, Ronald E. Blum, Gary L. Neale, Donald L. Simpson, Philip K. Asherman, Richard L. Flury *(16 Owners included in Index)*

Financial Data: *Fiscal Year End:*12/31 *Latest Annual Data:* 12/31/2006

Year	Sales	Net Income
2006	$3,125,307,000	$116,968,000
2005	$2,257,517,000	$15,977,000
2004	$1,897,182,000	$65,920,000

Curr. Assets:	$1,346,388,000	*Curr. Liab.:*	$1,187,758,000	*P/E Ratio:*	28.07
Plant, Equip.:	$194,644,000	*Total Liab.:*	$1,292,575,000	*Indic. Yr. Divd.:*	$0.160
Total Assets:	$1,835,010,000	*Net Worth:*	$542,435,000	*Debt/ Equity:*	NA

Chicago Federal Home Loan Bank

111 E Wacker Dr., Ste. 800, Chicago, IL, 60601; ***PH:*** 1-312-565-5700; ***http://*** www.fhlbc.com

General - Incorporation	Federal	**Stock** - Price on:12/24/2007	NA
Employees	27	Stock Exchange	NA
Auditor	PricewaterhouseCoopers LLP	Ticker Symbol	NA
Stk Agt	NA	Outstanding Shares	NA
Counsel	NA	E.P.S	NA
DUNS No.	NA	Shareholders	NA

Business: The groups principle activity is to provide liquidity, funding and asset-liability management capability to member institutions on a secured basis with minimal credit risk to bank, and to assist them to provide affordable housing and economic development in their communities. The group also promotes housing finance, in partnership with member financial institutions which provide sound and economical home financing throughout America and in all phases of financial and economic cycles. The group operates from United States.

Primary SIC and add'l.: 6111

CIK No: 0001331451

Officers: Mikesell J. Thomas/CEO, Pres., Eldridge Edgecombe/Sr. VP - Community Investment, Charlie A. Huston/Exec. VP - Banking, Peter E. Gutzmer/Exec. VP - Legal, Government Relations, Nancy L. Schachman/VP, Dir. - Communications, Jo-Nell Anton/Bank Support Representative, Sharon Brazelton/Bank Support Representative, Agnes Hardison/Sr. VP, Chief Credit Officer, Jeff Cullerton/Marketing Administration Representative, Cecile Duncan/Sr. Banking Administration Representative, Barbara Barnett/VP, Pat Sommers/Administrative Assist., Debra Pater/VP - Community Investment Consultant, Susan Wohlhart/Assist. VP - Compliance Supervisor, Community Investment, Joann Rudie/Community Investment Operations Mgr. *(45 Officers included in Index)*

Directors: David P. Kuhl/58/Chmn., James K. Caldwell/Vice Chmn., P. D. Kuhl/Dir., Kathleen E. Marinangel/62/Dir., Roger L. Lehmann/66/Dir., Locke/Dir., Rosenbaum/Dir., Thomas L. Herlache/65/Dir., Richard K. McCord/64/Dir., Terry W. Grosenheider/51/Dir., Alex J. Labelle/69/Dir., Gerald J. Levy/75/Dir., James F. McKenna/63/Dir., Thomas M. Goldstein/49/Dir.

Chicago Mercantile Exchange Holdings Inc

20 S Wacker Dr., Chicago, IL, 60606; ***PH:*** 1-312-930-3011; ***http://*** www.cme.com

General - Incorporation	DE	**Stock** - Price on:12/24/2007	NA
Employees	1,430	Stock Exchange	NA
Auditor	Ernst & Young LLP	Ticker Symbol	NA
Stk Agt	Computershare Investor Services LLC	Outstanding Shares	34,890,000
Counsel	NA	E.P.S	NA
DUNS No.	NA	Shareholders	NA

Business: The groups principle activity is to provide products in banking services. The groups product lines include interest rates, equities, foreign exchange and commodities and alternative investments. In the year 2006, the group acquired Swapstream electronic trading platform for interest rate swaps. The group operates from the United States. The groups quarterly revenue for September 2007 was 565.22 millions of USD.

Primary SIC and add'l.: 6200

CIK No: 0001156375

Subsidiaries: Chicago Mercantile Exchange Inc., CME Alternative Marketplace Inc., CME FX Marketplace Inc., CME Global Marketplace Inc., CME Swaps Marketplace Inc., GFX Corporation, Special Technology Investments Limited, Swapstream Limited, Swapstream Operating Services Limited, Swapstream SAS

Officers: Craig S. Donohue/Dir., CEO/$3,522,146.00, Terrence A. Duffy/Executive Chmn., Kimberly S. Taylor/MD, Pres. - CME Clearing House Division/$1,107,360.00, Nancy W. Goble/54/MD, Chief Accounting Officer, Bryan T. Durkin/MD, COO, Julie Holzrichter/MD - Operations, Hilda Harris Piell/MD, Chief Organizational Development Officer, Eileen Beth Keeve/54/MD - Organizational Development, James R. Krause/MD, CIO, Mazen A. Chadid/48/MD - Operations, Kathleen M. Cronin/MD, General Counsel, Corp. Sec., John P. Davidson/MD, Chief Corporate Development Officer/$1,557,824.00, James E. Parisi/MD, CFO/$977,919.00, Richard H. Redding/MD - Products, Services

Directors: Craig S. Donohue/Dir., CEO, Terrence A. Duffy/Executive Chmn., Charles P. Carey/Vice Chmn., Mark E. Cermak/Dir., Jackie Clegg/Dir., Robert F. Corvino/Dir., Phupinder S. Gill/Dir., Robert O. Kabat/72/Dir., John D. Newhouse/62/Dir., Jeffrey R. Carter/45/Dir., James A. Donaldson/Dir., Larry G. Gerdes/Dir., C. C. Odom/Dir., John L. Pietrzak/Dir., Christopher Stewart/Dir. *(33 Directors included in Index)*

Owners: Phupinder S. Gill, Leo Melamed, Dennis H. Chookaszian, Elizabeth Harrington, John P. Davidson, Craig S. Donohue, Insiders/1.00%, Gary M. Katler, John D. Newhouse, James E. Parisi, Alex J. Pollock, Patrick B. Lynch, William P. Miller, Howard J. Siegel, Jeffrey R. Carter *(29 Owners included in Index)*

Financial Data: *Fiscal Year End:*12/31 *Latest Annual Data:* 12/31/2006

Year	Sales	Net Income
2006	$1,089,947,000	$407,348,000
2005	$977,296,000	$306,857,000
2004	$752,802,000	$219,555,000

Chicago Rivet & Machine Co

901 Frontenac Rd., Naperville, IL, 60563; ***PH:*** 1-630-357-8500; ***Fax:*** 1-630-983-9314; ***http://*** www.chicagorivet.com; ***Email:*** info@chicagorivet.com

General - Incorporation	IL	**Stock** - Price on:12/24/2007	$23.7
Employees	261	Stock Exchange	AMEX
Auditor	Grant Thornton LLP	Ticker Symbol	CVR
Stk Agt	Computershare Trust Co	Outstanding Shares	NA
Counsel	NA	E.P.S	$1.27
DUNS No.	00-507-1329	Shareholders	NA

Business: The group's principal activity is to manufacture and market rivets, cold-formed fasteners, screw machine products, automatic rivet setting machines, parts and tools for such machines in the North America. The activities of the group are carried out through two divisions: fastener and assembly equipment. The fastener division manufactures and markets rivets, cold-formed fasteners and parts and screw machine products. The assembly equipment division manufactures automatic rivet setting machines, automatic assembly equipment, parts and tools for such machines and leases automatic rivet setting machines.

Primary SIC and add'l.: 7359 3599 3452

CIK No: 0000019871

Subsidiaries: H & L Tool Company, Inc

Officers: Kimberly A. Kirhofer/49/Sec.

Owners: Dimensional Fund Advisors LP/5.80%, William T. Divane, John A. Morrissey/9.40%, John C. Osterman/0.40%, Advisory Research Inc./7.20%, Poul Erik Madsen/7.70%, Michael J. Bourg/0.02%, Walter W. Morrissey/8.70%, Insiders/18.50%, John R. Madden/0.02%

Financial Data: *Fiscal Year End:*12/31 *Latest Annual Data:* 12/31/2006

Year	Sales	Net Income
2006	$40,370,000	$1,121,000
2005	$39,761,000	-$399,000
2004	$39,233,000	$1,523,000

Curr. Assets: $18,069,000 **Curr. Liab.:** $2,827,000 **P/E Ratio:** 21.94
Plant, Equip.: $9,837,000 **Total Liab.:** $3,903,000 **Indic. Yr. Divd.:** $0.720
Total Assets: $27,906,000 **Net Worth:** $24,003,000 **Debt/ Equity:** NA

Chico's FAS Inc

11215 Metro Pkwy., Fort Myers, FL, 33966; ***PH:*** 1-239-277-6200; ***Fax:*** 1-239-277-5237; ***http://*** www.chicos.com; ***Email:*** investor.relations@chicos.com

General - Incorporation: FL
Employees: 5,250
Auditor: Ernst & Young LLP
Stk Agt: Registrar & Transfer Co
Counsel... Trenam, Kemker, Scharf, Barkin Et Al
DUNS No.: 11-433-2232

Stock- Price on:12/24/2007: $25.54
Stock Exchange: NYSE
Ticker Symbol: CHS
Outstanding Shares: 176,000,000
E.P.S: $0.72
Shareholders: NA

Business: The groups principle activity is to operate retail stores. The groups products include clothing, intimates, sleepwear and activewear complementary accessories and other non-clothing gift items. The groups products are sold under the brand names Chico's, White House/Black Market and Soma. The group operates from United States.

Primary SIC and add'l.: 6794 5621 5632

CIK No: 0000897429

Subsidiaries: Chicos Distribution Services LLC, Chicos Retail Services Inc., FitAppCo Inc., Pazo Inc., Soma by Chicos LLC, White House | Black Market Inc.

Officers: Scott A. Edmonds/51/Chmn., CEO, Pres./$4,932,682.00, Alexander A. Rhodes/49/Sr. VP, General Counsel, Sec., Charles L. Nesbit/52/COO, Exec. VP/$2,162,793.00, Patricia Darrow-Smith/46/Brand Pres. - White House Black Marketing, Patricia Murphy Kerstein/64/Exec. VP/$2,398,834.00, Sher Canada/Sr. VP - Chico's Stores, Mike Elleman/Sr. VP - Real Estate, Terri Meichner/Sr. VP - GMM Soma Intimates, Michael J. Leedy/39/Exec. VP, Chief Marketing Officer, Chuck Nesbit/COO, Exec. VP, Donna Noce Colaco/Brand Pres. - White House | Black Marketing, Kent Kleeberger/CFO, Exec. VP, Treasurer, Mori MacKenzie/Chief Stores Officer, Exec. VP, Gary King/CIO, Exec. VP/$2,009,464.00, Mike Kincaid/Chief Accounting Officer, Sr. VP - Finance *(22 Officers included in Index)*

Directors: Scott A. Edmonds/51/Chmn., CEO, Pres., John W. Burden/71/Dir., Ross E. Roeder/70/Dir., David F. Walker/54/Dir., Charles J. Kleman/57/Dir., Betsy S. Atkins/55/Dir., John J. Mahoney/56/Dir., David F. Dyer/59/Dir., Verna K. Gibson/66/Dir., Michael Weiss/67/Dir.

Owners: David F. Dyer, Michael A. Weiss, Charles J. Kleman, Betsy S. Atkins, Charles L. Nesbit, David F. Walker, Gary King, Patricia Murphy Kerstein, Scott A. Edmonds, Ross E. Roeder, Verna K. Gibson, John W. Burden, Insiders/2.20%

Financial Data: *Fiscal Year End:*01/28 *Latest Annual Data:* 2/3/2007

Year	Sales	Net Income
2007	$1,646,482,000	$166,636,000
2006	$1,404,575,000	$193,981,000
2005	$1,066,882,000	$141,206,000

Curr. Assets: $471,856,000 **Curr. Liab.:** $144,232,000 **P/E Ratio:** 27.46
Plant, Equip.: $456,740,000 **Total Liab.:** $254,203,000 **Indic. Yr. Divd.:** NA
Total Assets: $1,058,134,000 **Net Worth:** $803,931,000 **Debt/ Equity:** NA

Chicopee Bancorp Inc

70 Ctr. St., Chicopee, MA, 01013; ***PH:*** 1-413-594-6692; ***http://*** www.chicopeesavings.com

General - Incorporation: MA
Employees: 100
Auditor: Berry, Dunn, Mcneil & Parker
Stk Agt: Registrar & Transfer Co
Counsel: NA
DUNS No.: NA

Stock- Price on:12/24/2007: $16
Stock Exchange: NDQ
Ticker Symbol: CBNK
Outstanding Shares: 7,440,000
E.P.S: $0.26
Shareholders: NA

Business: The group operates through its subsidiaries whose principle activity is to provide banking services. The groups services include retail deposits and insurance. The financial products of the group include multi-family, commercial real estate, commercial business, construction and development and consumer loans. The group operates from the United States. The assets of the group for the year 2006 were $108,446 (thousands).

Primary SIC and add'l.: 6036

CIK No: 0001355786

Subsidiaries: Cabot Management Corporation, Cabot Realty L.L.C., Chicopee Funding Corporation, Chicopee Savings Bank, CSB Colts, Inc., CSB Investment Corp.

Officers: William J. Wagner/Chmn., CEO, Pres., Guy W. Ormsby/63/Dir., Exec. VP, CFO, Treasurer, Maria J.C. Aigner/Sr. VP - Human Resources, Russell J. Omer/Sr. VP - Lending, Alzira C. Costa/Sr. VP - Operations - Security

Directors: William J. Wagner/Chmn., CEO, Pres., James H. Bugbee/Dir., Louis E. Dupuis/Dir., Edward J. Fitzgerald/Dir., William J. Giokas/Dir., James P. Lynch/Dir., Edmund J. Mekal/Dir., Gregg F. Orlen/Dir., Paul C. Picknelly/Dir., Edwin M. Sowa/Dir., Thomas J. Bardon/Dir., Arthur F. Dubois/Dir., Douglas K. Engebretson/Dir., David P. Fontaine/Dir., Francine Jasinski Hayward/Dir. *(20 Directors included in Index)*

Owners: James H. Bugbee, Anton V. Schutz/6.30%, William J. Wagner, Alzira C. Costa, Edwin M. Sowa, Chicopee Savings Bank Charitable Foundation/7.40%, Gregg F. Orlen, W. Guy Ormsby, Francine Jasinski Hayward, Russell J. Omer, Chicopee Savings Bank Employee Stock Ownership Plan/8.00%, Edmund J. Mekal, John P. Moylan, Daniel S. Och/9.00%, Judith T. Tremble *(28 Owners included in Index)*

Financial Data: *Fiscal Year End:*12/31 *Latest Annual Data:* 12/31/2006

Year	Sales	Net Income
2006	$24,390,000	-$2,534,000

Curr. Assets: $13,429,000 **Curr. Liab.:** $340,602,000
Plant, Equip.: $7,003,000 **Total Liab.:** $341,599,000 **Indic. Yr. Divd.:** NA
Total Assets: $450,045,000 **Net Worth:** $108,446,000 **Debt/ Equity:** NA

Chilco River Holdings Inc

6997 Gypsum Creek Dr., Corona, CA, 92880; ***PH:*** 1-951-371-3900; ***Fax:*** 1-951-371-3904; ***http://*** www.chilcoriverholdings.com; ***Email:*** info@chilcoriverholdings.com

General - Incorporation: NV
Employees: 35
Auditor: Mantyla McReynolds, LLC
Stk Agt: Pacific Corporate Trust Co
Counsel: NA
DUNS No.: NA

Stock- Price on:12/24/2007: NA
Stock Exchange: OTC
Ticker Symbol: CRVH
Outstanding Shares: 48,350,000
E.P.S: -$0.066
Shareholders: NA

Business: The groups principle activity is to operate hotels. The group operates from the United States.

Primary SIC and add'l.: 6719

CIK No: 0001278595

Subsidiaries: Chilco River Holdings, Inc, Kubuk Gaming S.A.C., Kubuk International, Inc., Kubuk Investment S.A.C.

Officers: Tom Liu/Chmn., CEO, Pres., Gavin Roy/Dir., Treasure, Martin Torres Garcia/CFO

Directors: Tom Liu/Chmn., CEO, Pres., Gavin Roy/Dir., Treasure, Yong Yang/Dir., Jack Xu/Dir., Wai Yung Lau/Dir.

Owners: Yong Yang, Lee Kuen Cheung, Blackpool Ltd, Wai Yung Lau, Guoxiu Yan, Insiders, Tom Yu Liu, Gavin Roy, Clear Channel Inc, Jack Xu, David Wong Liu, KC Technology

Financial Data: *Fiscal Year End:*12/31 *Latest Annual Data:* 12/31/2006

Year	Sales	Net Income
2006	$1,598,000	-$3,500,000
2005	$4,508,000	$581,000
2004	NA	-$53,000

Curr. Assets: $1,909,000 **Curr. Liab.:** $3,393,000
Plant, Equip.: $15,632,000 **Total Liab.:** $5,781,000 **Indic. Yr. Divd.:** NA
Total Assets: $25,900,000 **Net Worth:** $20,119,000 **Debt/ Equity:** 0.1186

Children's Internet Inc

110 Ryan Industrial Ct., Ste. 9, San Ramon, CA, 94583; ***PH:*** 1-925-743-9420; ***Fax:*** 1-925-743-9870; ***http://*** www.thechildrensinternet.com; ***Email:*** info@tcimail.net

General - Incorporation: NV
Employees: NA
Auditor: Hunter, Renfro & Whitaker, LLP
Stk Agt: Transfer Online, Inc.
Counsel: NA
DUNS No.: NA

Stock- Price on:12/24/2007: NA
Stock Exchange: OTC
Ticker Symbol: CITC
Outstanding Shares: NA
E.P.S: -$0.04
Shareholders: NA

Business: The groups principal activity is to provide pre-selected and pre-approved educational, and entertaining age appropriate web pages. The group products include Safe Zone Technology(R), The Children's Internet(R), and Family Favorites (TM). The group operates from the United States.

Primary SIC and add'l.: 7372

CIK No: 0001106861

Officers: Sholeh Hamedani/40/Chmn., CEO, CFO, Richard J. Lewis/Cting CEO, Acting CFO, Principal Executive Officer, Principal Financial Officer, Principal Accounting Officer, John J. Heinke/Controller, Tyler Wheeler/Dir., Chief Software Architect - Children's Internet, Jamshid Ghosseiri/68/Dir., Sec., William L. Arnold/61/Pres.

Directors: Sholeh Hamedani/40/Chmn., CEO, CFO, Nasser Hamedani/Chmn. - Advisory Board, Larry Wheeler/Member - Advisory Board, Tyler Wheeler/Dir., Chief Software Architect - Children's Internet, Roger Campos/Member - Advisory Board, Jamshid Ghosseiri/68/Dir., Sec., Dale Boehm/Dir.

Owners: William L. Arnold, Two Dog Net, Inc, Sholeh Hamedani, Tyler Wheeler, Insiders, Shadrack Films, Inc

Financial Data: *Fiscal Year End:*12/31 *Latest Annual Data:* 12/31/2006

Year	Sales	Net Income
2006	$1,000	-$1,087,000
2005	NA	-$1,258,000
2004	NA	-$381,000

Curr. Assets: $40,000 **Curr. Liab.:** $895,000
Plant, Equip.: $7,000 **Total Liab.:** $1,910,000 **Indic. Yr. Divd.:** NA
Total Assets: $49,000 **Net Worth:** -$1,861,000 **Debt/ Equity:** NA

Childrens Place Retail Stores Inc (The)

915 Secaucus Rd., Secaucus, NJ, 07094; ***PH:*** 1-201-558-2400; ***Fax:*** 1-201-558-2630; ***http://*** www.childrensplace.com; ***Email:*** investor_relations@childrensplace.com

General - Incorporation: DE
Employees: 5,000
Auditor: Deloitte & Touche LLP
Stk Agt...... American Stock Transfer & Trust Co.
Counsel: Stroock & Stroock & Lavan
DUNS No.: 19-909-6728

Stock- Price on:12/24/2007: $53.51
Stock Exchange: NDQ
Ticker Symbol: PLCE
Outstanding Shares: NA
E.P.S: $1.49
Shareholders: NA

Business: The groups principle activity is to operate childrens merchandise retail stores. The groups products include apparel and accessories for children from newborn to 10 years of age. The group operates from United States.

Primary SIC and add'l.: 5641

CIK No: 0001041859

Subsidiaries: Hoop Canada Holdings Inc., Hoop Canada Inc., Hoop Holdings LLC, Hoop Retail Stores LLC, TCP Canada Inc., TCP Investment Canada I Corp., TCP Investment Canada II Corp., The Childrens Place (Australia) Pty. Ltd., The Childrens Place (Barbados) Inc., The Childrens Place (Canada) LP, The Childrens Place (Hong Kong) Limited, The Childrens Place (Virginia) LLC, The Childrens Place Canada Holdings Inc., The Childrens Place Charitable Foundation Inc., The Childrens Place International Trading (Shanghai) Co. Ltd. 18 Subsidiaries included in the Index

Officers: Chuck Crovitz/Dir., Interim CEO, Mark L. Rose/Sr. VP, Chief Supply Chain Officer, Richard Flaks/Sr. VP - Planning, Allocation, Information Technology, Amy Hauk/Sr. VP, General Merchandise Mgr. - Disney Store, Neal Goldberg/Pres., Susan Riley/CFO, Sr. VP, Kevin Mead/Sr. VP, Dir. - Children's Place Stores, Tara Poseley/Pres. - Disney Store, Jill Kronenberg/Sr. VP, General Merchandise Mgr., Linda Martin/Sr. VP - Human Resources, Ivy Ross/Sr. VP, Chief Creative Officer Disney Store

Directors: Chuck Crovitz/Dir., Interim CEO, Sally Frame Kasaks/Acting Chmn., Robert Fisch/Dir., Jim Goldman/Dir., Malcolm Elvey/Dir., Ezra Dabah/Dir., Stanley Silverstein/Dir.

Owners: Sally Frame Kasaks, Charles Crovitz, Ezra Dabah/17.20%, Stanley Silverstein/11.60%, Steven Balasiano, Insiders/20.30%, Robert Fisch, Wellington Management Company, LLP/6.80%, Richard Flaks, Mark Rose, Neal Goldberg, Malcolm Elvey

Financial Data: *Fiscal Year End:*01/28 *Latest Annual Data:* 02/03/2007

Year	Sales	Net Income
2007	$2,017,713,000	$87,390,000
2006	$1,668,736,000	$65,575,000
2005	$1,157,548,000	$43,280,000

Curr. Assets:	$199,432,000	**Curr. Liab.:**	$85,157,000		
Plant, Equip.:	$146,707,000	**Total Liab.:**	$102,661,000	**Indic. Yr. Divd.:**	NA
Total Assets:	$359,666,000	**Net Worth:**	$257,005,000	**Debt/ Equity:**	NA

China 3C Group

Formerly: Sun Oil & Gas Corp
368 Hushu Nan Rd., Hangzhou, 310014; *PH:* 86-0571-88381700

General - Incorporation	NV	**Stock**- Price on:12/24/2007	$7.37
Employees	NA	Stock Exchange	OTC
Auditor	Morgenstern & Co., Cpas, P.c.	Ticker Symbol	CHCG
Stk Agt.	Madison Stock Transfer, Inc.	Outstanding Shares	NA
Counsel	NA	E.P.S.	NA
DUNS No.	NA	Shareholders	NA

Business: The group is currently in the process of reviewing potential companies and or businesses to acquire. There is no specified industry that the group is concentrating on. The group is a development stage group. The group operates from United States.

Primary SIC and add'l.: 9999

CIK No: 0001076784

Subsidiaries: Capital Future Development Limited, Hangzhou Wang Da Electronics Company Limited, Yiwu Yong Xin Telecommunication Company Limited, Zhejiang Yong Xin Digital Technology Company Limited

Officers: Zhenggang Wang/38/Chmn., CEO, Xiang Ma/33/Pres., Jian Liu/34/CFO

Directors: Zhenggang Wang/38/Chmn., CEO, Rongjin Weng/43/Dir., Weikang Gu/67/Dir., Mingjun Zhu/39/Dir., Chenghua Zhu/32/Dir., Kenneth T. Berents/60/Dir., Todd L. Mavis/47/Dir.

Owners: Todd L. Mavis, Insiders/18.53%, Yimin Zhang/10.47%, Wen-An Chen/7.62%, Kenneth T. Berents, Weiyi Lv/10.47%, Xiaochun Wang/7.87%, Zhongsheng Bao/5.20%, Huoqing Yang/7.62%

Financial Data: *Fiscal Year End:*12/31 *Latest Annual Data:* 12/31/2006

Year	Sales	Net Income
2006	$148,219,000	$11,277,000
2005	$32,589,000	$1,458,000

Curr. Assets:	$19,573,000	**Curr. Liab.:**	$9,061,000		
Plant, Equip.:	$66,000	**Total Liab.:**	$9,061,000	**Indic. Yr. Divd.:**	NA
Total Assets:	$39,988,000	**Net Worth:**	$30,926,000	**Debt/ Equity:**	NA

China Agritech Inc

Rm.301 No. 11 Building No, Beijing, Hebei, 100020; *PH:* 86-10-5962-1220; *Fax:* 86-1058702108; *http://* www.chinaagritecinc.com

General - Incorporation	DE	**Stock**- Price on:12/24/2007	$3.3
Employees	NA	Stock Exchange	OTC
Auditor	Kabani & Company, Inc.	Ticker Symbol	CAGC
Stk Agt.	Securities Transfer Corp	Outstanding Shares	NA
Counsel	Thelen Reid & Priest LLP	E.P.S.	NA
DUNS No.	NA	Shareholders	NA

Business: The groups principle activates include manufacturing and selling organic liquid compound fertilizers and related agricultural products. The group products include LvLingBao III, LvLingBao IV, and Tailong I. The group operates from China and Honkong.

Primary SIC and add'l.: 6770

CIK No: 0001166389

Subsidiaries: Anhui Agritech Development Co. Ltd., Beijing Agritech Fertilizer Ltd., CAI Investment, Inc., China Tailong Holdings Company Limited, Pacific Dragon Fertilizers Co. Ltd.

Officers: Yu Chang/Chmn., CEO, Pres., Xiaorong Teng/VP - Sales, Marketing, Tak Shing Eddie Wong/VP - Sales, Tik Man Tsoi/VP - Administration, Li Ju Peng/CFO, Controller, Liu Peizhi/Advisors, Chief Consultant, Zhang Zhixiang/Consultant, Ming Fang Zhu/41/VP - Strategic Development, Ji Wei Zhang/39/VP - Administration, Wen Sheng Chen/40/VP - Sales

Directors: Yu Chang/Chmn., CEO, Pres., Tao Liang/43/Dir.

Owners: Yu Chang/41.85%, Xiaorong Teng/2.45%, China Tailong Group Limited/41.85%, Insiders/44.30%

Financial Data: *Fiscal Year End:*12/31 *Latest Annual Data:* 12/31/2006

Year	Sales	Net Income
2006	$29,526,000	$5,349,000
2005	$25,335,000	$3,676,000
2004	NA	-$56,000

Curr. Assets:	$28,513,000	**Curr. Liab.:**	$2,010,000		
Plant, Equip.:	$2,514,000	**Total Liab.:**	$4,171,000	**Indic. Yr. Divd.:**	NA
Total Assets:	$31,027,000	**Net Worth:**	$26,856,000	**Debt/ Equity:**	NA

China Agro Sciences Corp

100 Wall St., 15th Fl., New York, NY, 10005; *PH:* 1-212-232-0120

General - Incorporation	FL	**Stock**- Price on:12/24/2007	NA
Employees	NA	Stock Exchange	OTC
Auditor	Paritz & Company, P.A.	Ticker Symbol	CHAS
Stk Agt.	Island Stock Transfer	Outstanding Shares	NA
Counsel	NA	E.P.S.	NA
DUNS No.	NA	Shareholders	NA

Business: The groups principal activity activities include developing, marketing, and distributing of an interactive travel brochure. The group products include acetochlor, razesor, emamectin benzoate, and clethodim. The group operates from China and the United States.

Primary SIC and add'l.: 7389

CIK No: 0001158420

Subsidiaries: DaLian Acquisition Corp.

Officers: Mark Stewart/Exec. Dir.

Directors: Mark Stewart/Exec. Dir.

Owners: Zhengquan Wang/80.00%, Insiders/80.00%

Financial Data: *Fiscal Year End:*09/30 *Latest Annual Data:* 09/30/2006

Year	Sales	Net Income
2006	$12,750,000	$2,203,000
2005	NA	-$30,000

Curr. Assets:	NA	**Curr. Liab.:**	$22,000		
Plant, Equip.:	NA	**Total Liab.:**	$22,000	**Indic. Yr. Divd.:**	NA
Total Assets:	$25,000	**Net Worth:**	$3,000	**Debt/ Equity:**	NA

China America Holdings Inc

Formerly: SENSE Holdings Inc
4503 NW 103rd Ave., Ste. 200, Sunrise, FL, 33351; *PH:* 1-954-726-1422; *http://* www.senseme.com; *Email:* techsupport@senseme.com

General - Incorporation	FL	**Stock**- Price on:12/24/2007	$0.071
Employees	2	Stock Exchange	OTC
Auditor	Sherb & Co. LLP	Ticker Symbol	SEHO
Stk Agt	American Securities T & T Inc.	Outstanding Shares	58,240,000
Counsel	NA	E.P.S.	NA
DUNS No.	NA	Shareholders	NA

Business: The group's principle activities are to design, develop, manufacture and market biometric security identification systems. The system identifies an employee by comparing his or her unique physical traits such as fingerprints, retina lines, voice waves and palm prints. The access control systems are security systems that permit access to locked buildings, offices or other secured areas only to those whose identity can be verified. In addition, the group develops the smartcard technology that tracks time and attendance of an employee, generates reports and automatically port all payroll information to payroll service. The group's products for time access and access controls are identified by the trade name of checkprint(R) t/a and checkprint(R) a/c. The competitors are kronos, simplex, smartime software, time and tech.com, unitime systems, identix, secugen, veridicom, recognition systems, iridian and visionics.

Primary SIC and add'l.: 7389 3669

CIK No: 0001093903

Subsidiaries: Micro Sensor Technologies, Inc.

Officers: Dore Scott Perler/Chmn., Co - Founder, CEO, Pres., Luis R. Sanchez/Advisory Dir. - Research, Development, Douglas Kilarski/Co - Founder - Company Representative, Andrew S. Goldrich/Dir., VP - Finance, Shawn Tartaglia/Dir., CTO, Alex Schlinkman/Advisory Dir. - Engineering, Chief Design Architect, Joseph Garrity/Corporate Counsel

Directors: Dore Scott Perler/Chmn., Co - Founder, CEO, Pres., Shawn Tartaglia/Dir., CTO, Douglas Kilarski/Co - Founder - Company Representative, Andrew S. Goldrich/Dir., VP - Finance, Robert J. Warmack/Member - Scientific Advisory Board, Lal A. Pinnaduwage/Member - Scientific Advisory Board, Allen Hertz/Member - Scientific Advisory Board, Richard S. Kendall/Member - Scientific Advisory Board

Owners: China Direct Investments, Inc./10.80%, Julie Slater, Aihua Hu/7.50%, Dore Scott Perler/2.60%, Shawn Tartaglia, Insiders/3.30%

Financial Data: *Fiscal Year End:*12/31 *Latest Annual Data:* 03/31/2007

Year	Sales	Net Income
2007	NA	NA
2006	$82,000	-$3,753,000
2005	$501,000	-$1,833,000

Curr. Assets:	NA	**Curr. Liab.:**	NA		
Plant, Equip.:	NA	**Total Liab.:**	NA	**Indic. Yr. Divd.:**	NA
Total Assets:	NA	**Net Worth:**	NA	**Debt/ Equity:**	NA

China Aoxing Pharmaceutical Company Inc

444 Washington Blvd., Unit 2424, Jerseycity, NJ, 07310; *PH:* 1-201-420-1076

General - Incorporation	FL	**Stock**- Price on:12/24/2007	$2.9
Employees	NA	Stock Exchange	OTC
Auditor	Paritz & Company, P.A.	Ticker Symbol	CAXG
Stk Agt	Olde Monmouth Stk Trnsfer Co. Inc.	Outstanding Shares	40,160,000
Counsel	Robert Brantl, Esq	E.P.S.	-$0.11
DUNS No.	NA	Shareholders	NA

Business: The groups principal activities include manufacturing and distributing analgesic drugs. The group products include Naloxone, Pholcodine Syrup, Zhi Ke Bao Pian and Oxycodone. The group operates from China and the United States.

Primary SIC and add'l.: 2834

CIK No: 0001060426

Subsidiaries: Hebei Aoxing Pharmaceutical Group Co., Ltd., Ostar Pharmaceutical

Officers: Zhenjiang Yue/48/Chmn., CEO, CFO, Chief Accounting Officer

Directors: Zhenjiang Yue/48/Chmn., CEO, CFO, Chief Accounting Officer, Richard Wm. Talley/64/Dir., Joseph J. Levinson/31/Dir., Jiaqi Wang/45/Dir., Hui Shao/Dir.

Owners: Huaqin Zhou/5.40%, Richard Wm. Talley, Hui Shao, Joseph J. Levinson, Yumin Yue/7.40%, Jiaqi Wang, Zhenjiang Yue/19.80%, Jinshuan Yue/6.90%, Insiders/20.80%, Yifa Yue/7.40%

Financial Data: *Fiscal Year End:*06/30 *Latest Annual Data:* 6/30/2006

Year	Sales	Net Income
2006	NA	-$1,513,000
2005	$1,412,000	-$367,000
2004	$1,197,000	-$238,000

Curr. Assets:	$157,000	**Curr. Liab.:**	$5,562,000		
Plant, Equip.:	$17,822,000	**Total Liab.:**	$13,461,000	**Indic. Yr. Divd.:**	NA
Total Assets:	$17,979,000	**Net Worth:**	$4,519,000	**Debt/ Equity:**	0.4915

China Automotive Systems Inc

No. 1, Henglong Rd. , Yu Qiao Development Zone, Shashi District, Jing Zhou City, Hubei Province, 434000; *PH:* 86-7168329196; *http://* www.caasauto.com; *Email:* sales@chl.com.cn

General - Incorporation	DE	Stock- Price on:12/24/2007	$7.19
Employees	2,042	Stock Exchange	NDQ
Auditor	Schwartz Levitsky Feldman LLP	Ticker Symbol	CAAS
Stk Agt	Securities Transfer Corp	Outstanding Shares	23,960,000
Counsel	NA	E.P.S.	$0.30
DUNS No.	NA	Shareholders	NA

Business: The group's principal activities are to design, market, sell custom-designed stained glass, leaded glass artifacts and leaded glass windows through a Web site. The group also manufactures, sells automotive systems and components such as rack and pinion power steering gears, integral ball and nut power steering gears for cars, light, heavy-duty vehicles. The group has established a steering systems research institute with tsinghua university, designed to develop the electronic-controlled power steering (eps) and electronic hydraulic steering system (ehps). The group's major customers are brilliance China automotive holdings ltd, beiqi foton motor co ltd and saic chery automobile co ltd.

Primary SIC and add'l.: 3211

CIK No: 0001157762

Subsidiaries: Jingzhou Henglong Automotive Parts Co., Ltd., Jingzhou Henglong Fulida Textile Co., Ltd., Shashi Jiulong Power Steering Gears Co., Ltd., Shenyang Jinbei Henglong Automotive Steering System Co., Ltd., Universal Sensor Application Inc., Zhejiang Henglong & Vie Pump-Manu Co., Ltd.

Officers: Qizhou Wu/CEO, Shengbin Yu/Sr. VP, Shaobo Wang/Sr. VP, Jie Li/CFO

Directors: Hanlin Chen/Chmn., Robert Tung/Dir., Haimian Cai/Dir., William E. Thomson/Dir.

Owners: Insiders/83.00%, Haimian Cai, Robert Tung, Hanlin Chen/64.20%, Qizhou Wu/9.20%

Financial Data: Fiscal Year End:12/31 Latest Annual Data: 12/31/2006

Year	Sales		Net Income
2006	$95,766,000		$4,812,000
2005	$63,572,000		$3,315,000
2004	$58,186,000		$6,867,000
Curr. Assets:	$104,439,000	Curr. Liab.:	$75,302,000	P/E Ratio:	31.26
Plant, Equip.:	$43,489,000	Total Liab.:	$98,728,000	Indic. Yr. Divd.:	NA
Total Assets:	$152,109,000	Net Worth:	$53,380,000	Debt/ Equity:	0.0055

China Bak Battery Inc

Bak Industrial Pk., Kuichong Town, Longgang District, Shenzhen, 518119; *PH:* 86-75589770093; *http://* www.bak.com.cn

General - Incorporation	NV	Stock- Price on:12/24/2007	$3.22
Employees	6,362	Stock Exchange	NDQ
Auditor	PKF	Ticker Symbol	CBAK
Stk Agt	Securities transfer Corp	Outstanding Shares	48,890,000
Counsel	NA	E.P.S.	$0.12
DUNS No.	NA	Shareholders	NA

Business: The group's principle activity is to operate retail coffee shop. The group operates from United States.

Primary SIC and add'l.: 5812

CIK No: 0001117171

Subsidiaries: BAK Battery Co., Ltd., BAK International, Ltd.

Officers: Xiangqian Li/39/Chmn., CEO, Pres., Yongbin Han/VP - Finance, Sec., Huanyu Mao/56/Dir., CTO, COO, Tony Shen/CFO, Sec., Tracy Li/Mgr. - Investor Relations Management Department

Directors: Xiangqian Li/39/Chmn., CEO, Pres., Huanyu Mao/56/Dir., CTO, COO, Richard Goodner/61/Dir., Charlene Spoede Budd/69/Dir., Chunzhi Zhang/46/Dir.

Owners: Xinggang Cao, Yongbin Han, Tony Shen, Huanyu Mao, Insiders/39.70%, Richard Goodner, Charlene Spoede Budd, Chunzhi Zhang, Xiangqian Li/38.70%

Financial Data: Fiscal Year End:09/30 Latest Annual Data: 9/30/2006

Year	Sales		Net Income
2006	$143,829,000		$20,165,000
2005	$101,922,000		$13,497,000
2004	NA		-$15,000
Curr. Assets:	$146,927,000	Curr. Liab.:	$145,722,000	P/E Ratio:	11.50
Plant, Equip.:	$109,406,000	Total Liab.:	$146,027,000	Indic. Yr. Divd.:	NA
Total Assets:	$259,655,000	Net Worth:	$113,628,000	Debt/ Equity:	0.1449

China Biopharma Inc

31 AirPk. Rd. , Princeton, NJ, 08540; *PH:* 1-609-651-8588; *http://* www.techedgeinc.net; *Email:* info@ChinaBiopharma.net

General - Incorporation	DE	Stock- Price on:12/24/2007	$0.071
Employees	56	Stock Exchange	OTC
Auditor	Patrizio & Zhao, LLC	Ticker Symbol	CBPC
Stk Agt	Continental Stock Transfer & Trust Co	Outstanding Shares	90,130,000
Counsel	NA	E.P.S.	-$0.05
DUNS No.	NA	Shareholders	NA

Business: The groups principle activities include to manufacturing and marketing bio-pharmaceutical products. The group products include Influenza, Epidemic Hemorrhagic Fever, Epidemic Japanese Encephalitis, and W135 Meningococcal Polysaccharide. Customers of the group include local hospitals, clinics, and pension fund health programs. The group operates from China and the United States. The group's quarterly revenue for September 2007 was 0.16 millions of USD.

Primary SIC and add'l.: 2836

CIK No: 0001190132

Subsidiaries: China Biopharma Ltd., China Quantum Communications Ltd., Guang Tong Wang Luo (China) Co. Ltd, Hainan CITIC Bio-Pharmaceutical Development Co., Ltd., Zhejiang Tianyuan Biotech Co., Ltd

Officers: Peter Wang/Chmn., CEO, Jean-Denis Shu/Chief Scientist, CEO - China Operations, Chunhui Shu/CFO, Qiumeng Wang/COO, Kenneth Steiner/Medical Affaire Specialist, George Yu/Product Specialist

Directors: Peter Wang/Chmn., CEO, Charles Xue/Dir.

Owners: Qiumeng Wang, Ya Li/1.00%, UTStarcom Inc./13.12%, Insiders/31.19%, PZW Family LLP/20.41%, Pacific Century Fund LLC/17.42%, SB China Holdings PTE Ltd./13.12%, Peter Wang/29.89%, Charles Xue

Financial Data: Fiscal Year End:12/31 Latest Annual Data: 12/31/2006

Year	Sales		Net Income
2006	$1,203,000		-$4,028,000
2005	$381,000		-$2,841,000
2004	$313,000		-$1,446,000
Curr. Assets:	$5,965,000	Curr. Liab.:	$5,151,000		
Plant, Equip.:	$90,000	Total Liab.:	$8,953,000	Indic. Yr. Divd.:	NA
Total Assets:	$7,816,000	Net Worth:	-$1,137,000	Debt/ Equity:	NA

China Biopharmaceuticals Holdings Inc

Rm. 1601, Tower A, Jinshan Mansion, Nanjing, 210009; *PH:* 86-2583205758; *Fax:* 86-2583205759; *http://* www.cbioinc.com; *Email:* info@cbioinc.com

General - Incorporation	DE	Stock- Price on:12/24/2007	$0.32
Employees	NA	Stock Exchange	OTC
Auditor	Moore Stephens Wurth F & T LLP	Ticker Symbol	CHBP
Stk Agt	NA	Outstanding Shares	NA
Counsel	NA	E.P.S.	NA
DUNS No.	06-497-4470	Shareholders	NA

Business: The group invests in restricted securities and securities which are not readily marketable. The company's primary activity is to invest in companies through venture capital investments in new and developing companies. Some of the investee companies are interface systems, inc., kimeragen, inc., repligen corporation, genitope corporation and thermaphore sciences, inc. The group's quarterly revenue for Sep'07 was 8.59 millions of USD.

Primary SIC and add'l.: 6282

CIK No: 0000352868

Subsidiaries: China Biopharmaceuticals Corporation, Nanjing Keyuan Pharmaceutical R&D Co., Ltd., Suzhou Erye Pharmaceutical Limited Company, Suzhou Hengyi Pharmaceuticals of Feedstock Co., Ltd, Suzhou Sintofarm Pharmaceuticals of Feedstock Co., Ltd

Officers: Chris Peng Mao/Chmn., CEO, Lufan An/COO, Pres., Luyong Zhang/CTO, Xiaohao Liu/VP - Sales, Chentai Huang/CFO

Directors: Chris Peng Mao/Chmn., CEO, Stephen E. Globus/Dir., Mingsheng Shi/56/Dir.

Owners: HUANG Chentai/1.10%, ZHANG Luyong/0.55%, QVT Fund LP/5.31%, Chris Peng Mao/9.45%, RimAsia Capital Partners, L.P./24.84%, LIU Xiaohao/6.68%, AN Lufan/8.36%, GCE Property Holdings, Inc./5.36%, Vision Opportunity Master Fund, LTD/5.31%, Stephen E. Globus/1.34%, Insiders/28.43%

Financial Data: Fiscal Year End:12/31 Latest Annual Data: 12/31/2006

Year	Sales		Net Income
2006	$25,981,000		-$2,418,000
2005	$30,949,000		$961,000
Curr. Assets:	$20,282,000	Curr. Liab.:	$21,679,000		
Plant, Equip.:	$12,290,000	Total Liab.:	$30,466,000	Indic. Yr. Divd.:	NA
Total Assets:	$47,604,000	Net Worth:	$13,123,000	Debt/ Equity:	0.6572

China Clean Energy Inc

Fulong Industry Zone, Longtian Town, Fuqing City, Fujian, 350315; *PH:* 86-13801339172; *http://* www.chinacleanenergyinc.com

General - Incorporation	DE	Stock- Price on:12/24/2007	$1.5
Employees	131	Stock Exchange	OTC
Auditor	Michael T. Studer CPA P.C.	Ticker Symbol	CCGY
Stk Agt	Continental Stock T & T Co.	Outstanding Shares	21,510,000
Counsel	NA	E.P.S.	$0.10
DUNS No.	NA	Shareholders	NA

Business: The groups principle activities include developing, manufacturing, and distributing biodiesel and chemical products made from renewable resources. The groups products include dimer acid, biodiesel, polyamide resin, printing ink, fatty acid, stearic acid, and oleic acid. In the year 2006, the group merged with Fujian Zhongde Technology Co., Ltd. The group operates from the United States. The groups quarterly revenue for September 2007 was 5.46 millions of USD.

Primary SIC and add'l.: 2860

CIK No: 0001331444

Subsidiaries: China Clean Energy Resources Limited, Fujian Zhongde Technology Co., Ltd.,

Officers: Tai-Ming Ou/Chmn., CEO, Ri-Wen Xue/Dir., COO, Gary Zhao/CFO, Yun He/Sr. VP - Sales, Distribution, Zicai Liang/Research & Development Advisor, Yu Lin/Chemical Science Advisor, Inks, Printing, Heng Zhang/Oil Chemistry Applications Advisor, Shengxiong Dong/Chemical Science Advisor

Directors: Tai-Ming Ou/Chmn., CEO, Ri-Wen Xue/Dir., COO

Owners: Dian Yang, Tai-ming Ou, Insiders, Nai-ming Yu, Gary Zhao, Yun He, Ri-wen Xue, Qin Yang, Daiyi Chen

Financial Data: Fiscal Year End:12/31 Latest Annual Data: 12/31/2006

Year	Sales		Net Income
2006	$13,499,000		$1,270,000
Curr. Assets:	$5,209,000	Curr. Liab.:	$1,794,000	P/E Ratio:	24.27
Plant, Equip.:	$4,692,000	Total Liab.:	$1,794,000	Indic. Yr. Divd.:	NA
Total Assets:	$12,426,000	Net Worth:	$10,633,000	Debt/ Equity:	NA

China Digital Communication Group

225 S Lake Ave., Ste. 300, Pasadena, CA, 91101; *PH:* 1-626-432-5427; *Fax:* 1-626-432-5435; *http://* www.chinadigitalgroup.com; *Email:* info@chinadigitalgroup.com

General - Incorporation	NV	Stock- Price on:12/24/2007	$0.2
Employees	NA	Stock Exchange	OTC
Auditor	Kabani & Company, Inc.	Ticker Symbol	CHID
Stk Agt	Atlas Stock Transfer Corp	Outstanding Shares	NA
Counsel	NA	E.P.S.	NA
DUNS No.	NA	Shareholders	NA

Business: The groups principle activity activities include manufacturing and distributing lithium battery shells and related products. The group products include Low-Carbon Steel Stretch Series, F6, F8 Nickel Hydrogen and Lithium Ion Duel Functions Series, and Aluminum Square Shell Series. The group operate through two segments namely battery component and hitech communication. In the year 2006, the group acquired Galaxy View Specific customers of the group include Shenzhen Bak Battery Co., Ltd, Shenzhen Yin Si Qi Electronic Co., Ltd and Guizhou Aero Electric Source Tech. Co., Ltd.

Primary SIC and add'l.: 6770

CIK No: 0001144320

Subsidiaries: Billion Electronic Co., Ltd, Galaxy View International Ltd., Shenzhen E'Jenie Technology Development Co., Ltd., Sono Digital Electronic Technologies Co., Ltd.

Officers: Zhongnan Xu/60/Chmn., CEO, Mei Jin Bin/29/Sec., Jiangcheng Wu/48/CFO, Yu Xi Sun/33/Dir., Pres.

Directors: Zhongnan Xu/60/Chmn., CEO, Yu Xi Sun/33/Dir., Pres., Xu Bao Dong/36/Dir.

Owners: Insiders/1.20%, Yu Xi Sun/1.20%

Financial Data: *Fiscal Year End:*12/31 *Latest Annual Data:* 12/31/2006

Year	Sales	Net Income
2006	$12,215,000	-$921,000
2005	$12,742,000	$2,624,000
2004	$2,339,000	$112,000

Curr. Assets:	$5,523,000	**Curr. Liab.:**	$1,271,000		
Plant, Equip.:	$1,121,000	**Total Liab.:**	$1,271,000	**Indic. Yr. Divd.:**	NA
Total Assets:	$18,142,000	**Net Worth:**	$16,872,000	**Debt/ Equity:**	NA

China Digital Media Corp

2505-06, 25/f, Stelux House, 698 Prince Edward Rd. E, Kowloon; ***PH:*** 852-239-8600; ***Fax:*** 852-2127-7515; ***http://*** www.chinadigimedia.com

General - Incorporation	NV	**Stock** - Price on:12/24/2007	$0.45
Employees	NA	Stock Exchange	OTC
Auditor	Jimmy C.H. Cheung & Co	Ticker Symbol	CDGT
Stk Agt	Florida Atlantic Stock Transfer, Inc.	Outstanding Shares	NA
Counsel	NA	E.P.S.	NA
DUNS No.	NA	Shareholders	NA

Business: The group's principal activity is to provide home cleaning services and beauty salon services. The group operates in two segment: residential cleaning service which provides daily residential cleaning services, carpet cleaning and other related services in the south Florida area, retail beauty salons sells its retail cosmetic and beauty through Website and also sells and distributes popular cosmetic, fragrances and beauty products.

Primary SIC and add'l.: 7349 7231

CIK No: 0000821524

Officers: Daniel C.S. Ng/Chmn., CEO, Pres., Tung Zhi Yong/Consultant, Lu Chen/Dir. - Business Development, Billy W.K. Tam/Consultant - Digital Broadcasting Technology Development, Related Strategy, Li Wa Tat Benedict/CFO

Directors: Daniel C.S. Ng/Chmn., CEO, Pres., Zhow Wei Yu/35/Dir., Chen Juan/35/Dir., Chen Lu/38/Dir.

Owners: Modern Delta Holdings Ltd./76.90%, Vision Opportunity Master Fund, Ltd./9.90%, Modern Delta Holdings Ltd./100.00%

Financial Data: *Fiscal Year End:*12/31 *Latest Annual Data:* 12/31/2006

Year	Sales	Net Income
2006	$15,523,000	$2,137,000
2005	$7,862,000	$4,042,000
2004	NA	-$1,224,000

Curr. Assets:	$10,957,000	**Curr. Liab.:**	$12,542,000		
Plant, Equip.:	$12,129,000	**Total Liab.:**	$12,542,000	**Indic. Yr. Divd.:**	NA
Total Assets:	$25,090,000	**Net Worth:**	$12,529,000	**Debt/ Equity:**	NA

China Digital Wireless Inc

429 Guangdong Rd., Shanghai, 200001; ***PH:*** 86-21-6336-8686; ***http://*** www.chinadigitalwireless.com

General - Incorporation	NV	**Stock** - Price on:12/24/2007	NA
Employees	NA	Stock Exchange	OTC
Auditor	Zhong Yi (hong Kong) C.P.A. Co. Ltd.	Ticker Symbol	CREG
Stk Agt	Securities Transfer Corp	Outstanding Shares	NA
Counsel	NA	E.P.S.	NA
DUNS No.	NA	Shareholders	NA

Business: The group's principle activities are to provide value-added information services in China which enables wireless receiver users to access financial information and various entertainment-related services. It operates in three segments namely, product sales, mobile phone service and beep pagers service. It has contract with affiliated wireless service providers to transmit the reformatted content to customers of various network operators. Its financial information software, sifang gutong, enables the customers to access stock and currency exchange information and execute stock trades. The entertainment-related services include icons, screen savers, multiplayer games, western horoscopes, jokes, and sports and entertainment news. These services are ancillary to the financial information services. It distributes nine different samsung electronics company ltd mobile phone models, six of which are compatible with the cdma network and three with the gsm network.

Primary SIC and add'l.: 7375

CIK No: 0000721693

Subsidiaries: Shanghai TCH Data Technology Co., Ltd., Sifang Holdings Co., Ltd.

Officers: Wu Guangyu/36/CEO, Ku Guohua/46/Chmn., Pres., CTO, Mingda Rong/40/Dir., CFO

Directors: Ku Guohua/46/Chmn., Pres., CTO, Zheng Hanqiao/50/Dir., Mingda Rong/40/Dir., CFO

Owners: Hanqiao Zheng/14.00%, Xiaohong Zhang/0.40%, Qianping Huang/0.90%, Insiders/75.20%, Ping Sun/4.30%, Lixia Zhang/2.70%, Guohua Ku/52.90%

Financial Data: *Fiscal Year End:*12/31 *Latest Annual Data:* 12/31/2006

Year	Sales	Net Income
2006	$2,889,000	-$3,463,000
2005	$20,419,000	$1,811,000
2004	$24,521,000	$1,595,000

Curr. Assets:	$4,465,000	**Curr. Liab.:**	$1,118,000		
Plant, Equip.:	NA	**Total Liab.:**	$1,118,000	**Indic. Yr. Divd.:**	NA
Total Assets:	$4,465,000	**Net Worth:**	$3,347,000	**Debt/ Equity:**	NA

China Direct Inc

5301 N Federal Hwy., Ste. 120, Boca Raton, FL, 33487; ***PH:*** 1-561-989-9171; ***Fax:*** 1-561-989-9206; ***http://*** www.cdii.net; ***Email:*** info@cdii.net

General - Incorporation	DE	**Stock** - Price on:12/24/2007	$3.31
Employees	441	Stock Exchange	AMEX
Auditor	Sherb & Co., LLP	Ticker Symbol	CDS
Stk Agt	Olde Monmouth Stk Trnsfer Co. Inc.	Outstanding Shares	13,570,000
Counsel	NA	E.P.S.	$0.27
DUNS No.	NA	Shareholders	NA

Business: The groups principal activity is to provide management and consulting services. The groups services include cross-pacific bridge, advisory service, agent, import and export, and translation services. The group operate through three segments namely lang chemical, chang magnesium and china direct consulting. The group acquired Lang Chemical in the year 2006 and CDI Magnesium Co. Ltd. in 2007. The group operates from China. In the year 2006, land chemical accounted for $11,84,242 and China direct consulting $ 1,627,095.

Primary SIC and add'l.: 8742

CIK No: 0001088787

Subsidiaries: Big Tree Group Corporation, Capital One Resource Co., Ltd., CDI China, Inc., CDI Magnesium Co., Ltd., CDI Shanghai Management Company ,Limited., CDI Wanda Alternative Energy Co., Ltd, China Direct Investments, Inc, Excel Rise Technology Company, Ltd., Jieyang Big Tree Toy Enterprise Co., Ltd, Jinan Alternative Energy Group Corp, Luma Logistic (Shanghai) Co., Ltd, Shanghai Lang Chemical Company, Limited., Taiyuan Chang Magnesium Company, Limited., Taiyuan Changxin YiWei Trading Company, Ltd.

Officers: James Wang/Chmn., CEO, Marc Siegel/Dir., Pres., David Stein/COO, Jenny Liu/VP - Finance, Gary Stuart/General Counsel, Robert Zhuang/GM - CDI Shanghai Management, Frank Zhang/Vice GM - CDI Shanghai Management, Richard Galterio/Exec. VP - Investor Relation

Directors: James Wang/Chmn., CEO, Marc Siegel/Dir., Pres., David Barnes/Dir., Victor Hollander/Dir., Sheldon Steiner/Dir.

Owners: Richard Galterio/8.00%, Yi Liu, Insiders, Marc Siegel/36.00%, David Stein/19.00%, Yuejian Wang/23.00%

Financial Data: *Fiscal Year End:*12/31 *Latest Annual Data:* 12/31/2006

Year	Sales	Net Income
2006	$13,984,000	$169,000
2005	NA	-$1,293,000
2004	$534,000	-$1,327,000

Curr. Assets:	$17,313,000	**Curr. Liab.:**	$10,524,000		
Plant, Equip.:	$2,753,000	**Total Liab.:**	$11,327,000	**Indic. Yr. Divd.:**	NA
Total Assets:	$20,835,000	**Net Worth:**	$5,864,000	**Debt/ Equity:**	NA

China Dongsheng International Inc

Formerly: Paperclip Software Inc

611 Rte. 46, Hasbrouck Heights, NJ, 07604; ***PH:*** 1-201-525-1221; ***http://*** www.paperclip.com; ***Email:*** contactus@paperclip.com

General - Incorporation	DE	**Stock** - Price on:12/24/2007	NA
Employees	16	Stock Exchange	NA
Auditor	Bagell, Josephs, Levine & Co., L.l.c.	Ticker Symbol	NA
Stk Agt	American Stock Transfer & Trust Co.	Outstanding Shares	NA
Counsel	NA	E.P.S.	NA
DUNS No.	78-934-9545	Shareholders	NA

Business: The group's principle activities include developing and distributing computer software for document management and transport of electronic document packages. These are distributed across the public Internet or a private intranet with interoperability, security and tracking capabilities. The company's systems allow users of personal computer networks to scan, file, retrieve, display, print and route documents and other software objects. The products are sold to value added resellers, original equipment manufacturers of personal computers and person computer networks utilized on a corporate level. The products of the company include professional edition, sql edition, paperclip cold, noss and webserver. The group operates from United States. The group operates from United States.

Primary SIC and add'l.: 7372

CIK No: 0000946112

Officers: Aidong Yu/55/Chmn., CEO, CFO, Pres., Suzanne G. Tuck/VP - Sales, Michael Suleski/VP - Research, Development, Michael D. Bridges/Pres.

Directors: Aidong Yu/55/Chmn., CEO, CFO, Pres., Huizhu Xie/61/Dir., Dekui Wang/52/Dir.

Owners: Huizhu Xie/0.09%, Dekui Wang/0.06%, Aidong Yu/53.50%, Chunxiao Zou/5.00%, Dandan Yu/5.00%, Insiders/53.66%

Financial Data: *Fiscal Year End:*12/31 *Latest Annual Data:* 12/31/2005

Year	Sales	Net Income
2005	$1,739,000	-$184,000
2004	$1,421,000	-$258,000
2003	$1,570,000	$454,000

Curr. Assets:	$626,000	**Curr. Liab.:**	$1,228,000		
Plant, Equip.:	$35,000	**Total Liab.:**	$2,096,000	**Indic. Yr. Divd.:**	NA
Total Assets:	$719,000	**Net Worth:**	-$1,377,000	**Debt/ Equity:**	NA

China Eastern Airlines Corp Ltd

2550 Hong Qiao Rd., Hong Qiao International Airport, Shanghai, 200335; ***PH:*** 86-216268; ***http://*** www.ce-air.com; ***Email:*** web_service@ce-air.com

General - Incorporation	China	**Stock** - Price on:12/24/2007	$48.0499
Employees	38,392	Stock Exchange	NYSE
Auditor	PricewaterhouseCoopers LLP	Ticker Symbol	CEA
Stk Agt	Bank of New York	Outstanding Shares	48,670,000
Counsel	NA	E.P.S.	-$5.8
DUNS No.	65-370-7406	Shareholders	NA

Business: The group's principal activities are the operation of common carriage of passengers, civil aviation, air cargo, postal delivery and other extended transportation services. Other activities include the provision of hotel services to crew members, flight training services and investment holding. Some of the group's suppliers are the eastern aviation import and export company and shanghai eastern air catering company ltd. The group's operations are carried out in China, Hong Kong, Japan, United States of America, Europe and other Asian countries.

Primary SIC and add'l.: 4512

CIK No: 0001030475

Subsidiaries: China Cargo Airlines Ltd., China Eastern Airlines Jiangsu Co., Ltd., China Eastern Airlines Wuhan Limited, China Eastern Fudart Transportation Service Co. Ltd., Eastern Airlines Jinjiang Hotel Co., Ltd., Shanghai Eastern Airlines Investment Co., Ltd., Shanghai Eastern Flight Training Co., Ltd., Shanghai Eastern Logistics Co., Ltd., Shanghai Eastern Maintenance Co. Ltd.

Officers: Yang Xingen/55/Supervisor, Zhou Liguo/59/VP, Ba Shengji/49/Supervisor, Zhang Jianzhong/53/VP, Luo Weide/52/CFO, Liu Jiashun/51/Supervisor, Yang Jie/38/Supervisor, Luo Zhuping/55/Dir., Sec., Tong Guozhao/49/VP, Li Yangmin/45/VP, Fan Ru/59/VP

Directors: Li Fenghua/58/Chmn., Luo Zhuping/55/Dir., Sec., Wu Baiwang/65/Dir., Xie Rong/56/Dir., Wan Mingwu/61/Dir., Zhou Ruijin/69/Dir., Cao Jianxiong/49/Dir., Zhong Xiong/62/Dir., Luo Chaogeng/58/Dir., Hu Honggao/54/Dir., Peter Lok/71/Non Exec. Dir.

Owners: HKSCC Nominees Limited/30.70%, CEA Holding/61.64%

Financial Data: Fiscal Year End:12/31 **Latest Annual Data:** 12/31/2006

Year	Sales	Net Income
2006	$4,860,465,000	-$469,336,000
2005	$3,861,355,000	-$171,532,000
2004	$2,564,377,000	$55,016,000

Curr. Assets:	$1,162,693,000	Curr. Liab.:	$4,339,048,000		
Plant, Equip.:	$5,330,812,000	Total Liab.:	$7,716,823,000	Indic. Yr. Divd.:	NA
Total Assets:	$7,959,851,000	Net Worth:	$243,028,000	Debt/ Equity:	NA

China Education Alliance Inc

58 Heng Shan Rd., Kun Lun Shopping Mall, Harbin, 150090; **PH:** 86-45187000662; *http://* chinaeducational.com

General - Incorporation	NC	Stock - Price on:12/24/2007	$0.63
Employees	NA	Stock Exchange	OTC
Auditor	Murrell, Hall, Mcintosh & Co., PLLP	Ticker Symbol	CEUA
Stk Agt	Florida Atlantic Stock Transfer, Inc.	Outstanding Shares	NA
Counsel	NA	E.P.S.	NA
DUNS No.	NA	Shareholders	NA

Business: The groups principle activity is to provide professional education resources. The group also provides educational communication platforms for students and educators. The group provides services include tutoring services, online classroom, on-campus classroom, talent crossroads and wealth island. The group operates from United States.

Primary SIC and add'l.: NA

CIK No: 0001203900

Subsidiaries: Harbin Zhong He Li Da Education Technology, Inc.

Officers: Chunqing Wang/48/Vice Chmn., CFO, Yang Yuhong/42/Exec. Vice Mgr.

Directors: Chunqing Wang/48/Vice Chmn., CFO, Yanzhi Liu/39/Dir., Yuzhong Wu/37/Dir.

Owners: Yanzhi Liu, Yuzhong Wu/1.80%, Xiqun Yu/65.60%, Guilan Feng/6.90%, Chunqing Wang, Insiders/74.30%

Financial Data: Fiscal Year End:12/31 **Latest Annual Data:** 12/31/2006

Year	Sales	Net Income
2006	$8,324,000	$2,625,000
2005	$3,113,000	$1,703,000
2004	$52,000	-$110,000

Curr. Assets:	$3,215,000	Curr. Liab.:	$2,105,000		
Plant, Equip.:	$5,330,000	Total Liab.:	$2,105,000	Indic. Yr. Divd.:	NA
Total Assets:	$9,278,000	Net Worth:	$7,173,000	Debt/ Equity:	NA

China Education Resources Inc

Formerly: China Ventures Inc
1118 Cathedral Pl., 925 W Georgia St., Vancouver, BC, V6C 3L2; **PH:** 1-604-683-6865; *http://* www.chinaeducationresources.com

General - Incorporation	BC	Stock - Price on:12/24/2007	NA
Employees	NA	Stock Exchange	NA
Auditor	Ernst & Young LLP	Ticker Symbol	NA
Stk Agt	Computershare Investor Services Inc.	Outstanding Shares	NA
Counsel	Fraser Milner Casgrain LLP	E.P.S.	NA
DUNS No.	NA	Shareholders	NA

Business: The group's principal activity is to provide education services in China through its traditional distribution business and its recently launched online education resource platform. The group has developed a traditional textbook distribution business through its three Chinese subsidiaries, CEN Smart Networks Ltd. (CEN), Today's Teachers Technology and Culture Ltd. (TTTC), and Northern Education Books Ltd. (NEB), distributors. The focus of their services is primarily on the following subject areas: psychology, information technology, kindergarten curriculum, and high school examination guides. The group's target market is the kindergarten to grade 12 sectors in China. The group is currently developing an education internet portal which will provide educational content to its users. The group is headquartered in Vancouver, Canada.

Primary SIC and add'l.: 2731

CIK No: 0001299878

Subsidiaries: CEN China Education, CEN China Education Network Ltd., CEN Smart Networks Ltd., China Education International Inc., Northern Education Books Ltd., Todays Teachers Technology and Culture Ltd.

Officers: Chengfeng Zhou/Chmn., CEO, Ronald C. Shon/Dir., Pres., Fraser Milner Casgrain/Legal Counsel, Hai Guan/Pres. - Today's Teachers Technology, Culture Ltd, Kathryn Witter/CFO, Corp. Sec., Vivian Pu Chen/CFO - Today's Teachers Technology, Culture, Ltd, Cer's Chinese Operations

Directors: Chengfeng Zhou/Chmn., CEO, Ronald C. Shon/Dir., Pres., William C. Calvin/Dir., Li Wang/Dir., Jeffrey Munks/Dir.

Owners: C. F. Zhou/17.75%, Vivian Pu Chen/0.25%, Ronald Shon/5.79%, Kathryn Witter, Guan Hai/3.00%, Jeffrey Munks, Insiders/30.01%, William Calvin, Wang Li

China Energy & Carbon Black Holdings Inc

Formerly: Huayang International Holdings Inc
B-27c, Construction Plz., No. 26, Guang Ming Rd., Urumqi, Xinjiang; **PH:** 86-991-883-8589; *http://* www.hihi.us

General - Incorporation	NV	Stock - Price on:12/24/2007	NA
Employees	NA	Stock Exchange	OTC
Auditor	Weinberg & Co. P.A	Ticker Symbol	CTTD
Stk Agt	Jersey Transfer & Trust Co	Outstanding Shares	NA
Counsel	Mr. Wang	E.P.S.	NA
DUNS No.	NA	Shareholders	NA

Business: The group's principal activities are to invest in and develop office buildings, apartments and income producing real estate properties. The group currently develops huayang international mansion, which includes mixed-use complex with an area of 163,000 square meters. The building consists of two towers (tower a and b) and two podiums (podium a and b). Tower a is a 22-story construction with 330 office units, 220 business apartments and 66 penthouse apartments. Podium a is a six-story construction totaling 26,912 square meters. Tower b and podium b of the building is operated by starwood hotels & resorts as sheraton shenyang lido hotel.

Primary SIC and add'l.: 6552 6519

CIK No: 0001110569

Subsidiaries: South Xinjiang

China Expert Technology Inc

Rm. 2703-4, Great Eagle Ctr., 23 Harbour Rd., Wanchai; **PH:** 852-28021555; *http://* tech.chinaexpertnet.com; **Email:** info-sz@chinaexpertnet.com

General - Incorporation	NV	Stock - Price on:12/24/2007	$7.31
Employees	NA	Stock Exchange	OTC
Auditor	Bdo Mccabe Lo Ltd.	Ticker Symbol	CXTI
Stk Agt	Madison Stock Transfer, Inc.	Outstanding Shares	NA
Counsel	NA	E.P.S.	NA
DUNS No.	NA	Shareholders	NA

Business: The group seeks to acquire a controlling interest in businesses suitable for acquisition and development by a publicly held group. On 12-Feb-2004, the group acquired China expert network group limited.

Primary SIC and add'l.: 9999

CIK No: 0001039726

Subsidiaries: CEN

Officers: Zhu Xiaoxin/Dir., CEO, Pres., Simon Fu Wan Chung/40/Dir., CFO, Song Feng/44/COO

Directors: Zhu Xiaoxin/Dir., CEO, Pres., Huang Tao/Chmn., Simon Fu Wan Chung/40/Dir., CFO

Owners: Platinum Partners Long Term Growth I, LLC, Tsang Chi Wai Eric, Song Feng, DKR Soundshore Oasis Holding Fund Ltd., China Link Investment Group Limited, Kung Sze Chau, Zhu Xiao Xin, Lai Man Yuk, China Data Holdings Limited, Huang Tao, Insiders

Financial Data: Fiscal Year End:12/31 **Latest Annual Data:** 12/31/2006

Year	Sales	Net Income
2006	$66,235,000	$7,844,000
2005	$35,569,000	$6,503,000
2004	$26,831,000	$4,827,000

Curr. Assets:	$65,917,000	Curr. Liab.:	$8,435,000		
Plant, Equip.:	$16,000	Total Liab.:	$8,435,000	Indic. Yr. Divd.:	NA
Total Assets:	$67,713,000	Net Worth:	$59,277,000	Debt/ Equity:	NA

China Finance Inc

111 Pavonia Ave., Ste 615, Jersey City, NJ, 07310; ; *http://* www.chinafinanceinc.com; **Email:** infous@chinafinanceinc.com

General - Incorporation	UT	Stock - Price on:12/24/2007	$1.15
Employees	13	Stock Exchange	OTC
Auditor	Rotenberg & Co. LLP	Ticker Symbol	CHFI
Stk Agt	Colonial Stock Transfer Co Inc	Outstanding Shares	57,670,000
Counsel	Loeb & Loeb LLP	E.P.S.	$0.27
DUNS No.	NA	Shareholders	NA

Business: The group's principle activity is to sell products at a substantial discount, below wholesale prices for similar products. The group operates from United States. On 08-Sep-2004 the company acquired value global international limited.

Primary SIC and add'l.: 5199

CIK No: 0001123440

Subsidiaries: A Utah Corporation, Shenzhen Shiji Ruicheng Guaranty and Investment Co. Ltd, Value Global International Limited

Officers: Zhi Yong Xu/Chmn., CEO/$90,000.00, Shi Wang/Financial Guarantee Dir., Xinyuan Zhang/Financial Guarantee Dir., Yang Liu/Financial Guarantee Dir., Liang Liao/CFO/$48,000.00, Yong Chen/Financial Guarantee Dir., Wei Wei/VP

Directors: Zhi Yong Xu/Chmn., CEO, Zhongping Wang/Dir., Yifang Li/49/Dir., Denming Yung/41/Dir.

Owners: Shenzhen Li Gao Fa Electronics Limited, China U.S. Bridge Capital Limited, Juxiang Ruan, Zuhong Xu, Xuemei Fang, Top Interest International Limited, Cede & Co.

Financial Data: Fiscal Year End:12/31 **Latest Annual Data:** 12/31/2006

Year	Sales	Net Income
2006	$5,487,000	$4,223,000
2005	$397,000	-$4,149,000
2004	$4,823,000	$3,506,000

Curr. Assets:	$16,583,000	Curr. Liab.:	$88,000	P/E Ratio:	4.26
Plant, Equip.:	$479,000	Total Liab.:	$88,000	Indic. Yr. Divd.:	NA
Total Assets:	$28,538,000	Net Worth:	$28,450,000	Debt/ Equity:	NA

China Finance Online Company Ltd

Corporate Sq., Tower C, 9th Floor, No. 35 Financial St., Xicheng District, Beijing, 100032; **PH:** 86-861058325388; *http://* www.chinafinanceonline.com; **Email:** ir@jrj.com

General - Incorporation	Hong Kong	Stock - Price on:12/24/2007	$9.66
Employees	NA	Stock Exchange	NDQ
Auditor	Deloitte Touche Tohmatsu CPA Ltd.	Ticker Symbol	JRJC
Stk Agt	JP Morgan Chase Bank	Outstanding Shares	21,120,000
Counsel	O' Melveny & Myers	E.P.S.	$0.12
DUNS No.	NA	Shareholders	NA

General - Incorporation	Hong Kong	Stock - Price on:12/24/2007	$9.66
Employees	NA	Stock Exchange	NDQ
Auditor	Deloitte Touche Tohmatsu CPA Ltd.	Ticker Symbol	JRJC
Stk Agt	JP Morgan Chase Bank, N.A.	Outstanding Shares	21,120,000
Counsel	O' Melveny & Myers	E.P.S.	$0.12
DUNS No.	NA	Shareholders	NA

Business: The groups principle activity is to provide online financial and listed company data and information. The groups services include bookkeeping, financial report, securities and payment alert. The group operates from China. The group's quarterly revenue for September 2007 was 7.30 millions of USD.

Primary SIC and add'l.: 4899 7375

CIK No: 0001297830

Subsidiaries: China Finance Online (Beijing) Co., Ltd, Fortune Software (Beijing) Co., Ltd.

Officers: Zhiwei Zhao/Dir., CEO, Jun Wang/CFO

Directors: Zhiwei Zhao/Dir., CEO, Hugo Shong/Chmn., Lee Kheng Nam/Dir., Ling Wang/Dir., Fansheng Guo/Dir.

Owners: Insiders/1.74%, Ling Zhang/8.28%, Jianping Lu/6.78%, IDG Technology Venture Investments, LP/6.37%, IDG Technology Venture Investment, Inc./19.49%, Vertex Technology Fund (III)Ltd./13.72%, Sam Qian/1.00%

Financial Data: Fiscal Year End:12/31 Latest Annual Data: 12/31/2006

Year	Sales		Net Income
2006	$7,128,000		-$601,000
2005	$7,482,000		$4,624,000
2004	$6,016,000		$4,597,000
Curr. Assets:	$46,532,000	Curr. Liab.:	$8,521,000
Plant, Equip.:	$1,697,000	Total Liab.:	$8,666,000	Indic. Yr. Divd.:	NA
Total Assets:	$71,119,000	Net Worth:	$62,453,000	Debt/ Equity:	NA

China Food & Beverage Co

710 W 24th St., Kansas City, MO, 64108; **PH:** 1-877-667-9377

General - Incorporation	NV	Stock - Price on:12/24/2007	$0.03
Employees	NA	Stock Exchange	OTC
Auditor	HJ & Assoc. LLC	Ticker Symbol	CHIF
Stk Agt	Signature Stock Transfer, Inc.	Outstanding Shares	10,400,000
Counsel	NA	E.P.S.	-$0.02
DUNS No.	NA	Shareholders	NA

Business: The group is in development stage company, looking for new business opportunities. The group operates from United States.

Primary SIC and add'l.: 2082

CIK No: 0000717228

Subsidiaries: Victoria Beverage Company Limited

Owners: Anhui Liu An Beer Company/10.00%, Korkor Holdings, Ltd./31.00%, Tiancheng China Corp, Ltd./5.00%, James A. Tilton, Jane Zheng/3.00%, Calder Investments Limited/29.00%

Financial Data: Fiscal Year End:12/31 Latest Annual Data: 12/31/2005

Year	Sales		Net Income
2005	NA		-$234,000
2004	NA		-$205,000
2003	NA		-$211,000
Curr. Assets:	$0	Curr. Liab.:	$449,000
Plant, Equip.:	NA	Total Liab.:	$449,000	Indic. Yr. Divd.:	NA
Total Assets:	$0	Net Worth:	-$449,000	Debt/ Equity:	NA

China Gengsheng Minerals Inc

Formerly: Leadpoint Consolidated Mines Co
211 W Wall St., Midland, TX, 79701; **PH:** 1-432-682-1761

General - Incorporation	WA	Stock - Price on:12/24/2007	NA
Employees	NA	Stock Exchange	OTC
Auditor	S. W. Hatfield, CPA	Ticker Symbol	CHGS
Stk Agt	PacWest Transfer LLC	Outstanding Shares	NA
Counsel	NA	E.P.S.	NA
DUNS No.	NA	Shareholders	NA

Business: The group's principal activities are to provide services for mining and milling processes and producing and dealing in different kinds of ores, metals and minerals. Milling and mining services include concentrating, converting, smelting, treating, preparing for market, manufacturing, buying, selling, and exchanging. The group also produces and deals in ores, metals and minerals and their products and by-products of every kind and description.

Primary SIC and add'l.: 1040

CIK No: 0001338578

Owners: George L. Diamond/5.28%, Insiders/75.50%, David Brigante/5.28%, Timothy P. Halter/5.28%, Marat Rosenberg/5.28%, Shunqing Zhang/70.25%

Financial Data: Fiscal Year End:09/30 Latest Annual Data: 09/30/2006

Year	Sales		Net Income
2006	NA		-$12,000
Curr. Assets:	$154,000	Curr. Liab.:	$0
Plant, Equip.:	NA	Total Liab.:	$0	Indic. Yr. Divd.:	NA
Total Assets:	$154,000	Net Worth:	$154,000	Debt/ Equity:	NA

China Grentech Corp Ltd

Fl.16, Zhongyin Tower, N Caitian Rd., Futian District, Shenzhen, Guangdong, 518026;
PH: 86-75583501796; **http://** www.grentech.com.cn; **Email:** investor@powercn.com

General - Incorporation	Cayman Islands	Stock - Price on:12/24/2007	$12.96
Employees	2,485	Stock Exchange	NDQ
Auditor	NA	Ticker Symbol	GRRF
Stk Agt	Citibank N.A	Outstanding Shares	1,000,000
Counsel	NA	E.P.S.	$16.35
DUNS No.	NA	Shareholders	NA

Business: The groups principle activity is to provide wireless coverage products and services. The products of the group include mobile, unicom, telecom and netcom. The group operates from the China. The group's quarterly revenue for September 2007 was 273.21 millions of USD.

Primary SIC and add'l.: 3663 3669

CIK No: 0001347510

Subsidiaries: GrenTech(BVI) Limited, Quanzhou Lake Communication Co., Ltd., Quanzhou Lake Microwave Co., Ltd., Shenzhen GrenTech Co., Shenzhen Lingxian Technology Co., Ltd.

Officers: Yingjie Gao/Chmn., CEO, Pres., Qingchang Liu/VP, Kunjie Zhuang/Dir., CTO, Rong Yu/Dir., CFO, Xuewei Wu/VP, Liping Mao/Dir., VP, Tianwen Ding/VP, Qi Wang/VP, Guanyu Huang/VP

Directors: Yingjie Gao/Chmn., CEO, Pres., Kunjie Zhuang/Dir., CTO, Huashan Yang/Dir., Rong Yu/Dir., CFO, Liping Mao/Dir., VP, Cuiming Shi/Dir., Xiaohu You/Dir., Kin Kwong Mak/Dir.

Owners: Drag Investments/10.30%, HXY Investments/18.30%, Wells Fargo & Company/7.40%, Actis China/9.90%, Standard Chartered Private Equity/7.70%, Guoren Industrial/24.00%

Financial Data: Fiscal Year End:12/31 Latest Annual Data: 12/31/2006

Year	Sales		Net Income
2006	$106,712,000		$19,072,000
2005	$88,755,000		$22,484,000
Curr. Assets:	$249,665,000	Curr. Liab.:	$111,023,000	P/E Ratio:	53.58
Plant, Equip.:	$21,604,000	Total Liab.:	$113,454,000	Indic. Yr. Divd.:	NA
Total Assets:	$309,560,000	Net Worth:	$196,106,000	Debt/ Equity:	NA

China Health Resource Inc

Formerly: Voice Diary Inc
200 Robbins Ln., Jericho, NY, 11753; **PH:** 1-516-939-0400; **http://** www.voicediary.com;
Email: info@voicediary.com

General - Incorporation	DE	Stock - Price on:12/24/2007	NA
Employees	NA	Stock Exchange	OTC
Auditor	Lake & Assoc. CPA's LLC	Ticker Symbol	CHRI
Stk Agt	Continental Stock Transfer & Trust Co	Outstanding Shares	NA
Counsel	NA	E.P.S.	NA
DUNS No.	NA	Shareholders	NA

Business: The group develop, manufacture and market personal digital assistants ("Pdas") targeted to niche markets. The products have a voice user interface and provide to the user a full range of personal information management applications, including a talking diary, telephone book, daily pad and other features. The groups products are sold in Israel, us, UK, Holland.

Primary SIC and add'l.: 4813

CIK No: 0001173784

Subsidiaries: Aryt Industries Ltd, Israeli corporation

Officers: Jiang Chen/34/Dir., CEO, Jiguang Wang/34/Dir., Pres., Ying Zhong/Dir., CFO

Directors: Jiang Chen/34/Dir., CEO, Jiguang Wang/34/Dir., Pres., Ying Zhong/Dir., CFO, Gewei Wang/39/Dir., Bing Wang/33/Dir.

Owners: Insiders, Li Wang/7.58%, Zhi He/7.25%, Shu Lan Deng/21.00%, Bing Zeng/1.93%, Hua Zhong Lu/2.52%, Shu Lan Deng/1.45%, Jun Rong Zhou/3.96%, Shu Lan Deng/100.00%, Ji Guang Wang, Wen Hui Wang/3.69%, Yuan Lin Ma/2.01%, Shi Ping Kuang/2.76%

Financial Data: Fiscal Year End:12/31 Latest Annual Data: 12/31/2006

Year	Sales		Net Income
2006	$1,039,000		-$155,000
2005	NA		$147,000
2004	$3,000		-$484,000
Curr. Assets:	$1,117,000	Curr. Liab.:	$1,095,000
Plant, Equip.:	$532,000	Total Liab.:	$1,296,000	Indic. Yr. Divd.:	NA
Total Assets:	$1,650,000	Net Worth:	$354,000	Debt/ Equity:	NA

China Holdings Inc

Formerly: China Health Holding Inc
101 Convention Ctr. Dr., Ste. 700, Las Vegas, NV, 89107; **PH:** 1-604-608-6788;
http:// www.chinahealthholding.com

General - Incorporation	NV	Stock - Price on:12/24/2007	NA
Employees	NA	Stock Exchange	OTC
Auditor	Russell Bedford Stefanou Mirchandani	Ticker Symbol	CHHL
Stk Agt	North American Transfer Co.	Outstanding Shares	NA
Counsel	Hong Leong Asia	E.P.S.	NA
DUNS No.	NA	Shareholders	NA

Business: The groups principal activity activities include manufacturing, marketing and distributing natural medical and pharmaceutical medicine. The group products incluc Fanxie Jianfei Yin, Qingshen Yishou Gao, Ershi San, Qingre Sigen Yin, VG-MP, VG-PFI and VG-LZFL. The group operates from China and the United States.

Primary SIC and add'l.: 2834

CIK No: 0001302331

Subsidiaries: China Health World Pharmaceutical Corporation, China Health World Trade Corporation.

Officers: Julianna Lu/Chmn., CEO, CFO, Dahong Li/VP, Xiao Fei Yu/Dir., VP, Zheng-Lun Fan/VP - Research, Development

Directors: Julianna Lu/Chmn., CEO, CFO, Xiao Fei Yu/Dir., VP

Owners: Insiders/67.17%, Insiders/100.00%, Julianna Lu/100.00%, Zheng-Lun Fan, Xiao Fei Yu/8.30%, Julianna Lu/54.22%

Financial Data: Fiscal Year End:12/31 Latest Annual Data: 12/31/2006

Year	Sales		Net Income
2006	NA		-$3,197,000
2005	$2,000		-$3,677,000
Curr. Assets:	$98,000	Curr. Liab.:	$911,000
Plant, Equip.:	$10,000	Total Liab.:	$911,000	Indic. Yr. Divd.:	NA
Total Assets:	$108,000	Net Worth:	-$803,000	Debt/ Equity:	NA

China Housing & Land Development Inc

6 Youyi Dong Lu, Han Yuan 4 Lou, Xi'an, 710054; **PH:** 86-029-82582632

General - Incorporation	NV	Stock - Price on:12/24/2007	$5.05
Employees	NA	Stock Exchange	OTC
Auditor	Moore Stephens Wurth F & T LLP	Ticker Symbol	CHLN
Stk Agt	Holladay Stock Transfer, Inc.	Outstanding Shares	NA
Counsel	NA	E.P.S.	NA
DUNS No.	NA	Shareholders	NA

Business: The groups principle activity is to operate real estate business. The group operates from the United States and China.

Primary SIC and add'l.: 6513

CIK No: 0001303330

Subsidiaries: Xian Tsining Housing Development Co., Ltd.

Officers: Lu Pingji/57/Chmn., CEO, Xiao Genxiang/45/Chief Administrative Officer, Dir., Feng Xiaohong/43/Dir., COO, Wan Yulong/45/CFO, Shi Zhiyong/47/VP, Chief Legal Counsel, Dir.

Directors: Xiao Genxiang/45/Chief Administrative Officer, Dir., Feng Xiaohong/43/Dir., COO, Shi Zhiyong/47/VP, Chief Legal Counsel, Dir.

Owners: Feng Xiaohong/2.00%, Shi Zhiyong, Xiao Genxiang/1.55%, Insiders/15.85%, Wang Yulong, Lu Pingji/11.80%

Financial Data: Fiscal Year End:12/31 **Latest Annual Data:** 12/31/2006

Year	Sales		Net Income
2006	$54,099,000		$9,051,000
2005	NA		-$19,000
Curr. Assets:	$6,033,000	Curr. Liab.:	$29,388,000
Plant, Equip.:	$64,680,000	Total Liab.:	$53,632,000	Indic. Yr. Divd.:	NA
Total Assets:	$72,845,000	Net Worth:	$19,213,000	Debt/ Equity:	1.2619

China Huaren Organic Products Inc

Formerly: Ultradata Systems Inc
100 Wall St., 15th Fl., New York, NY, 10005; *PH:* 1-212-232-0120;
http:// www.ultradatasystems.com

General - Incorporation	DE	Stock - Price on:12/24/2007	NA
Employees	8	Stock Exchange	NA
Auditor	Ms Group Cpa LLC	Ticker Symbol	NA
Stk Agt	American Stock Transfer & Trust Co.	Outstanding Shares	NA
Counsel	NA	E.P.S.	$0.03
DUNS No.	17-416-3717	Shareholders	NA

Business: The group's principle activities include manufacturing and marketing hand-held data retrieval devices. The hand-held data retrieval devices are pocket size computers which guide the travelers with direction and information regarding destination, mileage, gas stations, hotels, motels, hospitals, 24-hour restaurants and highway petrol emergency numbers along the United States interstate highway system. Some of the products are road whiz(tm) plus, road whiz(tm) rv special, aaa tripwizard(R) and others. The products are marketed through catalog companies, department stores, office supply stores, direct mail promotions, luggage stores and selected television shopping channels. The company introduces hand-held travel computer every year with advanced technology that provides maximum information about boarding, lodging distances and driving time between towns etc. The group operates from United States.

Primary SIC and add'l.: 3571 8731

CIK No: 0000931947

Subsidiaries: Ultradata Systems, Incorporated

Officers: Fang Jinzhong/51/Chmn., CEO, CFO, Ernest Clarke/Pres., Zhang Chengcai/45/Dir., VP - Marketing, Sec.

Directors: Fang Jinzhong/51/Chmn., CEO, CFO, Zhang Chengcai/45/Dir., VP - Marketing, Sec., Zhou Huakang/55/Dir.

Owners: American Union Securities, Inc./5.60%, Fang Jinzhong/16.10%, Zhang Chengcai/9.80%, Zhou Huakang/19.40%, Insiders/45.40%

Financial Data: Fiscal Year End:12/31 **Latest Annual Data:** 12/31/2006

Year	Sales		Net Income
2006	$2,188,000		$421,000
2005	$781,000		-$5,872,000
2004	$3,970,000		$318,000
Curr. Assets:	$7,993,000	Curr. Liab.:	$1,219,000
Plant, Equip.:	$44,000	Total Liab.:	$1,219,000	Indic. Yr. Divd.:	NA
Total Assets:	$9,334,000	Net Worth:	$8,115,000	Debt/ Equity:	NA

China Industrial Waste Management Inc

No. 1 Huaihe W Rd., E-t-d-zone, Ste. 314, Dalian, Liaoning, 116600; *PH:* 86-4118-2595339

General - Incorporation	NV	Stock - Price on:12/24/2007	$2.06
Employees	NA	Stock Exchange	OTC
Auditor	Child, Van Wagoner & Bradshaw, PLLC	Ticker Symbol	CIWT
Stk Agt	Interwest Transfer Company, Inc.	Outstanding Shares	NA
Counsel	NA	E.P.S.	NA
DUNS No.	NA	Shareholders	NA

Business: The groups principle activity activities include collecting, disposing and recycling of industrial wastes. The group operates from China and United States.

Primary SIC and add'l.: 4953

CIK No: 0000763846

Subsidiaries: Dalian Acquisition Corp., Dalian Dongtai Industrial Waste Treatment Co., Ltd

Owners: Dong Jinqing/68.80%, American Union Securities, Inc./5.90%, Guo Xin/1.60%, Peter D. Zhou/5.90%, Insiders/72.00%, Li Jun/2.40%

Financial Data: Fiscal Year End:12/31 **Latest Annual Data:** 12/31/2006

Year	Sales		Net Income
2006	$6,383,000		$2,543,000
2005	$4,869,000		$1,126,000
2004	NA		-$1,462,000
Curr. Assets:	$6,860,000	Curr. Liab.:	$751,000
Plant, Equip.:	$2,643,000	Total Liab.:	$1,838,000	Indic. Yr. Divd.:	NA
Total Assets:	$11,620,000	Net Worth:	$9,782,000	Debt/ Equity:	NA

China Kangtai Cactus Bio-tech Inc

NO.99 Taibei Rd., Limin Economy & Technology Developing District, Harbin, Heilongjiang, 150025; *PH:* 86-4515735189; *Fax:* 86-4515735151; *http://* www.biocactus.com

General - Incorporation	NV	Stock - Price on:12/24/2007	$0.83
Employees	NA	Stock Exchange	OTC
Auditor	Michael T. Studer, Cpa, P.c.	Ticker Symbol	CKGT
Stk Agt	NA	Outstanding Shares	NA
Counsel	NA	E.P.S.	NA
DUNS No.	NA	Shareholders	NA

Business: The groups principle activities include selling and marketing of products derived from cacti. The group products include cactus nutriceuticals, cactus nutritional food and drinks, and cactus raw and intermediate materials. In the year 2006 the group acquired Taishan Kangda Food Co., Ltd. The group operates from China and the United States. The groups quarterly revenue for September 2007 was 3.96 millions of USD.

Primary SIC and add'l.: 2834

CIK No: 0001017699

Subsidiaries: Champion Agents Limited, Interchance Limited

Officers: Jinjiang Wang/Chmn., CEO, Pres., Chengzhi Wang/Dir., GM, Hong Bu/Dir., CFO, Ren Hu/VP - North American Operations, Zhimin Zhan/Vice GM, Sr. Engineer, Kexian Wu/Sr. Engineer Research & Development, Dir. - Sino-Mexico Research & Development Center

Directors: Jinjiang Wang/Chmn., CEO, Pres., Chengzhi Wang/Dir., GM, Hong Bu/Dir., CFO, Jiping Wang/47/Dir., Fidel G. Jimenez/Member - Board of Advisor, Ruzhen Tang/Member - Advisory Board, Jiyuan Jin/Member - Board of Advisor, Huisheng Qin/Member - Board of Advisor, Song Yang/34/Dir.

Owners: Hong Bu/4.20%, Chengzhi Wang/21.90%, Jinjiang Wang/27.10%, Song Yang/4.10%, Jiping Wang/4.00%, Insiders/61.30%

Financial Data: Fiscal Year End:12/31 **Latest Annual Data:** 12/31/2006

Year	Sales		Net Income
2006	$10,385,000		$1,435,000
2005	$8,003,000		$795,000
2004	$149,000		-$4,804,000
Curr. Assets:	$9,638,000	Curr. Liab.:	$1,076,000
Plant, Equip.:	$3,445,000	Total Liab.:	$1,076,000	Indic. Yr. Divd.:	NA
Total Assets:	$14,971,000	Net Worth:	$13,895,000	Debt/ Equity:	NA

China Life Insurance Co Ltd

16 Chaowai Ave., Chaoyang District, Beijing, 100020; *PH:* 86-1085659999;
http:// www.chinalife.com.cn; *Email:* serve@e-chinalife.com

General - Incorporation	China	Stock - Price on:12/24/2007	$54.64
Employees	72,900	Stock Exchange	NYSE
Auditor	PricewaterhouseCoopers LLP	Ticker Symbol	LFC
Stk Agt	Morgan ADR Service Center	Outstanding Shares	716,690,000
Counsel	Prc Legal System	E.P.S.	NA
DUNS No.	NA	Shareholders	NA

Business: The group's principal activities are the provision of individual and group life insurance; accident and health insurance and asset management. Operations are carried out in China.

Primary SIC and add'l.: NA

CIK No: 0001268896

Subsidiaries: China Life Asset Management (Hong Kong) Corporation Limited, China Life Insurance Asset Management Company Limited, China Life Pension Company Limited, Property and Casualty Joint Stock Company

Officers: Wan Feng/49/Dir., VP, Acting CEO, Yang Chao/57/Chmn., Pres., Su Hengxuan/44/Assist. to Pres., Daniel Joseph Kunesh/62/Chief Actuary, Liu Jiade/44/VP, Liu Yingqi/49/VP, Liu Tingan/45/Dir., Sec., Heng Kwoo Seng/59/Joint Company Sec., Liu Anlin/45/Chief Information Technology Officer, Shiu Wai Chung/54/Chief Actuary, Liu Lefei/35/Chief Investment Officer, Lin Dairen/48/VP

Directors: Wan Feng/49/Dir., VP, Acting CEO, Yang Chao/57/Chmn., Pres., Xia Zhihua/53/Chmn. - Board of Supervisors, Ma Yongwei/64/Dir., Tian Hui/56/Member - Board Of Supervisors, Liu Tingan/45/Dir., Sec., Zhuang Zuojin/55/NON - Exec. Dir., Ngai Wai Fung/45/Dir., Shi Guoqing/55/Non - Exec. Dir., Cai Rang/50/Dir., Wu Weimin/57/Member - Board Of Supervisors, Chau Tak Hay/64/Dir., Long Yongtu/63/Dir., Sun Shuyi/66/Dir.

Owners: Richbo Investment Limited/5.76%, CLIC/92.80%, Lee Financial Limited/5.76%, Leeworld Limited/5.76%, Shau Kee Financial Enterprises Limited/5.76%, FMR Corp./5.99%, Societe Generale/5.60%, KBC Group N.V./6.00%, Leesons Limited/5.76%, Lee Shau Kee/5.76%, J.P. Morgan Chase & Co./6.72%, Deutsche Bank Aktiengesellschaft/7.99%

Financial Data: Fiscal Year End:12/31 **Latest Annual Data:** 12/31/2006

Year	Sales		Net Income
2006	$18,885,270,000		$2,558,359,000
2005	$12,178,288,000		$1,153,944,000
2004	$9,293,526,000		$867,691,000
Curr. Assets:	$230,280,000	Curr. Liab.:	$1,429,550,000	P/E Ratio:	4.26
Plant, Equip.:	$615,226,000	Total Liab.:	$3,216,697,000	Indic. Yr. Divd.:	$0.270
Total Assets:	$433,282,000	Net Worth:	-$258,312,000	Debt/ Equity:	NA

China Longyi Group International Holdings Ltd

Formerly: Minghua Group International Holdings Ltd
8/f E Area, Century Golden Resources Business Ctr., 69 Banjing Rd., Haidian District, 100089;
PH: 86-108-845-2568

General - Incorporation	NY	Stock - Price on:12/24/2007	$0.05
Employees	NA	Stock Exchange	NA
Auditor	Child, Van Wagoner & Bradshaw, PLLC	Ticker Symbol	NA
Stk Agt	American Stock Transfer & Trust Co.	Outstanding Shares	NA
Counsel	NA	E.P.S.	NA
DUNS No.	NA	Shareholders	NA

Business: The groups principle activities include developing, producing and selling hybrid vehicles. The group operates from the United States.

Primary SIC and add'l.: 7389

CIK No: 0001010566

Subsidiaries: Asia Key Group Limited, Beijing China Cardinal Real Estate Consulting Co., Ltd, Eagle Bus Development Ltd., Euromax International Investments Limited, Good View Bus Manufacturing (Holding) Co. Ltd., Guangzhou City View Bus Installation Co. Ltd., Keytop Holding Limited, Ming Hua Environmental Protection Science and Technology Ltd., Minghua Acquisition Corp., Minghua Group International Holding (Hong Kong) Ltd., Shenzhen Minghua Environmental Protection Vehicles Co. Ltd., Top Team holdings Limited

Officers: Xinmin Pan/62/CFO/$1,125.00

Owners: Chuquan Li, Chang-de Li, Insiders, Beijing Qiang Long Real Estate Development Co. Ltd., Yue Ke International Development, Limited, Wang Wei, Jolly Concept Management Limited, Li Guanglian, Kingsrich Development Limited, China Cardinal Limited

Financial Data: Fiscal Year End:12/31   Latest Annual Data: 12/31/2006

Year	Sales	Net Income
2006	NA	-$346,000
2005	$353,000	-$1,290,000
2004	$84,000	-$11,024,000

Curr. Assets:	$2,071,000	Curr. Liab.:	$2,488,000		
Plant, Equip.:	$1,073,000	Total Liab.:	$2,488,000	Indic. Yr. Divd.:	NA
Total Assets:	$3,151,000	Net Worth:	$663,000	Debt/ Equity:	NA

China Media Group Corp

9901 I.H. 10 W, Ste. 800, San Antonio, TX, 78230; ; *http://* www.chinamediagroup.net;
Email: ir@chinamediagroup.net

General - Incorporation	TX	Stock- Price on:12/24/2007	$0.07
Employees	NA	Stock Exchange	OTC
Auditor	Kabani & Company, Inc.	Ticker Symbol	CHMD
Stk Agt	Nevada Agency & Trust Company	Outstanding Shares	NA
Counsel	NA	E.P.S.	NA
DUNS No.	NA	Shareholders	NA

Business: The groups principle activity is to develop media business. In the 2007,the group acquired Guangzhou Waho Culture Co., Ltd. The group operates from Kuala Lumpur, Malaysia and Hongkong.

Primary SIC and add'l.: 7310

CIK No: 0001211211

Subsidiaries: Ren Ren Media Group Limited

Officers: Con Unerkov/Chmn., CEO, CFO, Alex Te Heng Ho/Dir., Company Sec., Treasurer

Directors: Con Unerkov/Chmn., CEO, CFO, Alex Te Heng Ho/Dir., Company Sec., Treasurer, Luo Qiang/Dir., Zhang Guosheng/Dir.

Owners: Simple Securities Limited, Con Unerkov, Alex Ho, Liu Kang, Tailor-Made Capital Ltd., Insiders, Lam Pui Kit, Zhang Yan Yu, Central High Limited, Maxcom Group International Ltd., Paul Scanlan

Financial Data: Fiscal Year End:12/31   Latest Annual Data: 3/31/2007

Year	Sales	Net Income
2007	$27,000	-$582,000
2006	$25,000	-$191,000
2005	NA	-$132,000

Curr. Assets:	$117,000	Curr. Liab.:	$826,000		
Plant, Equip.:	$15,000	Total Liab.:	$826,000	Indic. Yr. Divd.:	NA
Total Assets:	$270,000	Net Worth:	-$556,000	Debt/ Equity:	0.3736

China Media1 Corp

2020 Main St., Irvine, CA, 92614; **PH:** 1-949-757-0890; *http://* www.chinamedia1corp.com

General - Incorporation	NV	Stock- Price on:12/24/2007	NA
Employees	NA	Stock Exchange	OTC
Auditor	Ernst & Young LLP	Ticker Symbol	CMDA
Stk Agt	Signature Stock Transfer, Inc.	Outstanding Shares	NA
Counsel	Spectrum Law Group Irvine CA	E.P.S.	NA
DUNS No.	NA	Shareholders	NA

Business: The groups principal activity is to own and operates media assets. The group operates from China and the United States.

Primary SIC and add'l.: 4899

CIK No: 0001202081

Officers: Danny C. Hon/CFO, Ernest Cheung/Dir., Pres.

Directors: Han Xiong Cai/Chmn., Ernest Cheung/Dir., Pres.

Owners: Cai Han Li/3.40%, Insiders/52.90%, Hanxiong Cai/46.10%, Zhao Ai Ling/3.40%

Financial Data: Fiscal Year End:12/31   Latest Annual Data: 12/31/2005

Year	Sales	Net Income
2005	NA	-$2,659,000
2004	NA	-$67,000
2003	$13,000	-$25,000

Curr. Assets:	$31,000	Curr. Liab.:	$3,781,000		
Plant, Equip.:	$75,000	Total Liab.:	$3,781,000	Indic. Yr. Divd.:	NA
Total Assets:	$999,000	Net Worth:	-$2,783,000	Debt/ Equity:	NA

China Medical Technologies Inc

No. 24 Yongchang N Rd., Beijing Economic-Technological Development Area, P.R.China, Beijing, Hebei, 100176; **PH:** 86-1067871166; **Fax:** 86-1067889588; *http://* www.chinameditech.com; **Email:** IR@chinameditech.com

General - Incorporation	Cayman Islands	Stock- Price on:12/24/2007	$31.45
Employees	265	Stock Exchange	NDQ
Auditor	KPMG LLP	Ticker Symbol	CMED
Stk Agt	Citibank N.A	Outstanding Shares	27,360,000
Counsel	NA	E.P.S.	$1.55
DUNS No.	NA	Shareholders	NA

Business: The group's principle activities include developing, manufacturing and marketing medical device. The groups operates through two segments namely HIFU therapy system and ECLIA system. Specific customer of the group is Beijing Jia Xing Fang Zhou Trade Co., Ltd. The group operates from the United States. The group's total revenue in the year 2007 was 546.97 millions of USD.

Primary SIC and add'l.: 2835 3826 3841

CIK No: 0001326059

Subsidiaries: Beijing Jin Pu Jia Medical Technologies Co. Ltd., Beijing Yuande Bio-Medical Engineering Co., Ltd, CMED Diagnostics Ltd, CMED Technologies Ltd, Yuande (USA) Corp.

Officers: Xiaodong Wu/Chmn., CEO, Winnie Fan/Investor Relation Officer, Takyung Tsang/Dir., CFO, Feng Zhu/VP

Directors: Xiaodong Wu/Chmn., CEO, Iain Ferguson Bruce/Dir., Cole R. Capener/Dir., Lawrence A. Crum/Dir., Ruyu Du/Dir.

Owners: Chengxuan International Ltd./26.10%, Insiders/26.90%, Xiaodong Wu/26.10%

Financial Data: Fiscal Year End:03/31   Latest Annual Data: 3/31/2006

Year	Sales	Net Income
2006	$46,374,000	$24,824,000
2005	$26,284,000	$14,310,000

Curr. Assets:	$129,253,000	Curr. Liab.:	$16,129,000	P/E Ratio:	115.26
Plant, Equip.:	$13,169,000	Total Liab.:	$16,129,000	Indic. Yr. Divd.:	$0.380
Total Assets:	$171,621,000	Net Worth:	$155,492,000	Debt/ Equity:	NA

China Mobile Hong Kong Ltd

60th Fl., The Ctr., 99 Queens Rd. Central, Hong Kong; ; *http://* www.chinamobileltd.com

General - Incorporation	Hong Kong	Stock- Price on:12/24/2007	$51.61
Employees	111,998	Stock Exchange	NYSE
Auditor	KPMG LLP	Ticker Symbol	CHL
Stk Agt	CT Corporation	Outstanding Shares	4,000,000,000
Counsel	NA	E.P.S.	$2.51
DUNS No.	NA	Shareholders	NA

Business: The group's principal activities are the provision of mobile communications such as cellular telephone and related services in guangdong, zhejiang, jiangsu, fujian, henan, hainan, shandong, liaoning, hebei, anhui, jiangxi, sichuan, hubei, hunan, shaanxi and shanxi provinces, Beijing, shanghai, tianjin and chongqing municipalities and guangxi zhuang autonomous region of the People's Republic of China. Other activity includes investment holding. One of the five largest suppliers is the group's ultimate holding company and its subsidiaries. The group had an aggregate mobile telecommunications subscriber base of 117.7m.

Primary SIC and add'l.: 4812 4813

CIK No: 0001117795

Subsidiaries: Anhui Mobile (BVI) Limited, Anhui Mobile Communication Company Limited, Aspire (BVI) Limited, Aspire Holdings Limited, Beijing Mobile (BVI) Limited, Beijing Mobile Communication Company Limited, Beijing P&T Consulting& Design Institute (BVI) Limited, Beijing P&T Consulting& Design Institute Company Limited, China Mobile (Shenzhen) Limited, China Mobile Communication (BVI) Limited, China Mobile Communication Company Limited, China Mobile Peoples Telephone Company Limited, Chongqing Mobile (BVI) Limited, Chongqing Mobile Communication Company Limited, Fit Best Limited 69 Subsidiaries included in the Index

Officers: Wang Jianzhou/59/Chmn., CEO, Li Yue/49/Executive Dir., VP, Zhang Chenshuang/56/Executive Dir., VP, Xu Long/51/Executive Dir., Madam Xin Fanfei/51/Executive Dir., VP, Wong Wai Lan/Company Sec., Ng Phek Yen/Accountant

Directors: Wang Jianzhou/59/Chmn., CEO, Lo Ka Shui/61/Non Exec. Dir., Frank Wong Kwong Shing/60/Dir., Li Yue/49/Executive Dir., VP, Zhang Chenshuang/56/Executive Dir., VP, Xu Long/51/Executive Dir., Madam Xin Fanfei/51/Executive Dir., VP, Paul Michael Donovan/49/Non Exec. Dir., Frank K.S. Wong/60/Dir., Moses M.C. Cheng/58/Dir.

Financial Data: Fiscal Year End:12/31   Latest Annual Data: 12/31/2006

Year	Sales	Net Income
2006	$37,864,896,000	$8,475,815,000
2005	$30,947,424,000	$6,758,496,000
2004	$24,740,197,000	$5,794,845,000

Curr. Assets:	$21,987,197,000	Curr. Liab.:	$18,025,817,000		
Plant, Equip.:	$35,688,957,000	Total Liab.:	$22,521,407,000	Indic. Yr. Divd.:	$1.020
Total Assets:	$63,417,463,000	Net Worth:	$40,896,056,000	Debt/ Equity:	NA

China Mobility Solutions Inc

789 W Pender St., Ste. 900, Vancouver, BC, V6C 1H2; **PH:** 1-604-632-9638; *http://* www.chinamobilitysolutions.com; **Email:** investors@chinamobilitysolutions.com

General - Incorporation	FL	Stock- Price on:12/24/2007	NA
Employees	NA	Stock Exchange	OTC
Auditor	Moen & Co LLP	Ticker Symbol	CHMS
Stk Agt	NA	Outstanding Shares	NA
Counsel	NA	E.P.S.	NA
DUNS No.	NA	Shareholders	NA

Business: The group's principle activity is to provide Internet services in China. The group operates from United States.

Primary SIC and add'l.: 6719 4813 7375

CIK No: 0001082603

Subsidiaries: Beijing QuickNet Technology Development Corp, Beijing ShiJiYingFu Consultant Corp. Ltd., Infornet Investment Corp., Infornet Investment Ltd., Windsor Education Academy Inc., Xinbiz Corp., Xinbiz Ltd.

Officers: Xiao-Qing Du/38/Dir., CEO, Pres., Ernest Cheung/Dir., Sec., Michael Liu/VP - China Operation, Angela Du/Dir., Pres., Frank Wu/CTO

Directors: Xiao-Qing Du/38/Dir., CEO, Pres., Bryan Ellis/Dir., Ernest Cheung/Dir., Sec., Angela Du/Dir., Pres., John Gaetz/58/Dir.

Owners: Ernest Cheung/1.50%, Insiders/1.50%

Financial Data: Fiscal Year End:12/31   Latest Annual Data: 12/31/2006

Year	Sales	Net Income
2006	$93,000	-$7,879,000
2005	$4,903,000	-$9,163,000
2004	$2,171,000	$3,019,000

Curr. Assets:	$322,000	Curr. Liab.:	$3,875,000		
Plant, Equip.:	$11,000	Total Liab.:	$3,875,000	Indic. Yr. Divd.:	NA
Total Assets:	$511,000	Net Worth:	-$3,364,000	Debt/ Equity:	NA

China Natural Gas, Inc

19th Fl., Bldg. B,Van Metropolis, Tang Yan Rd., Hi-Tech Zone, Xi'an, 710075; *PH:* 403-852600; *http://* www.naturalgaschina.com; *Email:* info@naturalgaschina.com

General - Incorporation	DE	**Stock**- Price on:12/24/2007	$4.18
Employees	NA	Stock Exchange	OTC
Auditor	Kabani & Co, Inc	Ticker Symbol	CHNG
Stk Agt	Interwest Transfer Company, Inc.	Outstanding Shares	NA
Counsel	Crone Rozynko LLP	E.P.S.	NA
DUNS No.	NA	Shareholders	NA

Business: The group's principal activity is to implement a new business plan that is designed to provide management consulting products and services in North America. The group intends to provide these products and services through regionally licensed network operators. The principal products and services include diagnostic assessment, strategic document development, consulting services and coaching services. The group is in the development stage.

Primary SIC and add'l.: 7389

CIK No: 0001120830

Subsidiaries: XXNGC.

Officers: Qinan Ji/Chmn., CEO/$15,000.00, Xiaogang Zhu/CFO/$10,000.00, Yuman Chen/VP - Marketing, Liangzhong Li/VP - Construction

Directors: Qinan Ji/Chmn., CEO, Zhiqiang Wang/Vice Chmn., James A. Garner/Dir., Patrick McManus/55/Dir.

Owners: Insiders/20.30%, Robert K. Moses/6.80%, Xian Sunway Technology & Industry Co. Ltd./9.80%, Yangling Bodisen Biotech Development Co. Ltd./7.10%, Heartland Value Fund/5.10%, Qinan Ji/20.30%

Financial Data: *Fiscal Year End:*12/31   *Latest Annual Data:* 12/31/2006

Year		Sales		Net Income
2006		$18,829,000		$5,451,000
2005		$235,000		$30,000
Curr. Assets:	$23,000	Curr. Liab.:	$161,000	
Plant, Equip.:	$32,000	Total Liab.:	$167,000	Indic. Yr. Divd.: NA
Total Assets:	$56,000	Net Worth:	-$111,000	Debt/ Equity: NA

China Natural Resources Inc

Rm. 2105 W Tower Shun Tak Ctr., 200 Connaught Rd. C, Sheung Wan; *PH:* 86-28107205; *http://* www.chnr.net/feilie.asp

General - Incorporation.British Virgin Islands		**Stock**- Price on:12/24/2007	$7.7899
Employees	383	Stock Exchange	NDQ
Auditor	GHP Horwath, P.C	Ticker Symbol	CHNR
Stk Agt	OTC Stock Transfer, Inc.	Outstanding Shares	11,550,000
Counsel	NA	E.P.S.	$0.69
DUNS No.	66-247-9609	Shareholders	NA

Business: The group operates through its subsidiaries whose principle activity is to purchase, sell and distribute natural rubber; and trade production material, supplies and related commodities, such as fuels and chemicals including fertilizers and pesticides.The group operates from United States.

Primary SIC and add'l.: 5159 6719

CIK No: 0000793628

Officers: Feilie Li/Chmn., CEO, Pres., Tam Cheuk Ho/Dir., CFO, Wong Wah On/Dir., Financial Controller, Sec., Mian Tang/Dir. - Fanchang Zinc, Iron Mine

Directors: Feilie Li/Chmn., CEO, Pres., Tam Cheuk Ho/Dir., CFO, Wong Wah On/Dir., Financial Controller, Sec., Yip Wing Hang/41/Dir.

Owners: Li Feilie/90.20%, Insiders/91.20%, Tam Cheuk Ho, Wong Wah On Edward

Financial Data: *Fiscal Year End:*12/31   *Latest Annual Data:* 12/31/2006

Year		Sales		Net Income
2006		$18,639,000		$9,301,000
2005		$482,000		-$1,718,000
2004		$349,000		-$2,470,000
Curr. Assets:	$18,376,000	Curr. Liab.:	$6,440,000	P/E Ratio: 11.29
Plant, Equip.:	$4,799,000	Total Liab.:	$6,440,000	Indic. Yr. Divd.: NA
Total Assets:	$23,175,000	Net Worth:	$16,735,000	Debt/ Equity: NA

China Netcom Group Corp (Hong Kong) Ltd

Rm. 1020, Bldg. A, No.21, Financial St., Beijing, Xicheng District; *PH:* 852-26268888; *Fax:* 852-26268862; *http://* www.china-netcom.com; *Email:* IR@china-netcom.com

General - Incorporation	Hong Kong	**Stock**- Price on:12/24/2007	$57.25
Employees	140,747	Stock Exchange	NYSE
Auditor	PricewaterhouseCoopers LLP	Ticker Symbol	CN
Stk Agt	Citibank N.A	Outstanding Shares	332,570,000
Counsel	NA	E.P.S.	$5.16
DUNS No.	NA	Shareholders	NA

Business: The groups principle activity is to provide telecommunication services, mobile services, data services and broadband internet access services. In the year 2005, the group acquired China Netcom Group New Horizon Communications Limited. The group operates from the United States, China and Hong Kong. The group's quarterly revenue for September 2007 was 41,508.00 millions of USD.

Primary SIC and add'l.: 4813 4822 4899 7379 7389

CIK No: 0001305755

Subsidiaries: Asia Netcom Corporation Limited, East Asia Netcom Ltd. ("EANL")

Officers: Zuo Xunsheng/Exec. Dir., CEO, Zhang Xiaotie/Exec. Dir., Li Fushen/Exec. Dir., CFO, Joint Company Sec., Mok Kam Wan/45/Joint Company Sec., Fushen Li/45/Exec. Dir., CFO, Joint Company Sec., Jianhua Miao/56/Exec. Dir., Aihua Pei/57/Sr. VP, Li Jianguo/Exec. Dir., Zhao Jidong/Sr. VP, Teng Yong/CTO, Zhu Lijun/VP, Huo Haifeng/VP

Directors: Zuo Xunsheng/Exec. Dir., CEO, Chunjiang Zhang/49/Chmn., Edward Tian Suning/43/Vice Chmn., Zhang Chunjiang/Chmn., Fushen Li/45/Exec. Dir., CFO, Joint Company Sec., Jianhua Miao/56/Exec. Dir., Jose Maria Alvarez-Pallete/43/Non - Exec. Dir., Yan Yixun/Non - Exec. Dir., John Lawson Thornton/Dir., Victor Cha Mou Zing/Dir., Ziqiang Hou/70/Dir., Zhang Xiaotie/Exec. Dir., Li Fushen/Exec. Dir., CFO, Joint Company Sec., Li Jianguo/Exec. Dir., Qian Yingyi/Dir. *(17 Directors included in Index)*

Owners: AllianceBernstein L.P./6.00%, China Network Communications Group Corporation/69.88%

Financial Data: *Fiscal Year End:*12/31   *Latest Annual Data:* 12/31/2006

Year		Sales		Net Income
2006		$11,131,000,000		$1,394,000,000
2005		$10,816,768,000		$1,297,660,000
2004		$7,844,000,000		$833,000,000
Curr. Assets:	$2,313,000,000	Curr. Liab.:	$11,629,000,000	
Plant, Equip.:	$24,568,000,000	Total Liab.:	$17,367,000,000	Indic. Yr. Divd.: NA
Total Assets:	$28,338,000,000	Net Worth:	$10,971,000,000	Debt/ Equity: NA

China North East Petroleum Holdings Ltd

20337 Rimview Pl., Walnut, CA, 91789; *PH:* 1-909-468-1858; *http://* www.cncpetroleum.com

General - Incorporation	NV	**Stock**- Price on:12/24/2007	$0.441
Employees	78	Stock Exchange	OTC
Auditor	Jimmy C.H. Cheung & Co	Ticker Symbol	CNEH
Stk Agt	Interwest Transfer Company, Inc.	Outstanding Shares	29,220,000
Counsel	NA	E.P.S.	$0.06
DUNS No.	NA	Shareholders	NA

Business: The group operates through its wholly-owned subsidiary hong xiang, is engaged in the extraction and production of crude oil. Its current operations are in a portion of the jilin quinan oil field which is located southwest of quinan city in the jilin province of the peoples republic of China

Primary SIC and add'l.: 1311

CIK No: 0000787251

Subsidiaries: Harbin Hong Xiang Petroleum Services Limited, Hong Xiang

Officers: Wang Hong Jun/36/Chmn., Pres., Peng Chong Yao/GM, Xin Chang Ma/Chief General Engineer, Ming Yang Zhu/Chief Accountant, James Jiang/Dir. - Investor Relations, Taylor Zhang/Dir. - Investor Relations, Zhang Yuang/26/CFO, Jiang Chao/28/Sec.

Directors: Wang Hong Jun/36/Chmn., Pres., Wei Guo Ping/40/Dir., Yu Li Guo/35/Dir.

Owners: Wang Hong Jun/35.02%, Wei Guo Ping/0.01%, Insiders/35.03%

Financial Data: *Fiscal Year End:*12/31   *Latest Annual Data:* 12/31/2006

Year		Sales		Net Income
2006		$2,661,000		$926,000
2005		$1,412,000		-$670,000
2004		$1,431,000		$70,000
Curr. Assets:	$363,000	Curr. Liab.:	$10,158,000	P/E Ratio: 7.35
Plant, Equip.:	$16,005,000	Total Liab.:	$13,805,000	Indic. Yr. Divd.: NA
Total Assets:	$16,369,000	Net Worth:	$2,564,000	Debt/ Equity: 0.0458

China Petroleum & Chemical Corp

No.A6 Hui xin E St., Chaoyang District, Beijing, 100029; *PH:* 86-1064990060; *http://* www.sinopec.com.cn

General - Incorporation	China	**Stock**- Price on:12/24/2007	$112.75
Employees	340,886	Stock Exchange	NYSE
Auditor	KPMG	Ticker Symbol	SNP
Stk Agt	NA	Outstanding Shares	867,020,000
Counsel	NA	E.P.S.	$10.80
DUNS No.	NA	Shareholders	NA

Business: The group's principal activities are the exploration, development, and production of crude oil and natural gas. It transports, refines and markets crude oil, natural gas and products by pipelines. Other activities include manufacturing of chemical fibres, plastics, intermediate petrochemical products, synthetic fibres, resins, polyester chips and polyester fibres.

Primary SIC and add'l.: 1311 2999 2911 1382 5171 5541

CIK No: 0001123658

Subsidiaries: Ningbo Yonglian Co., Ltd., Sinopec-usa Co., Ltd

Officers: Cui Guoqi/54/Employee Representative Supervisor, Li Zhonghua/56/Employee Representative Supervisor, Wang Tianpu/45/Dir., Pres., Su Wensheng/51/Employee Representative Supervisor, Zhang Haichao/50/VP, Cai Xiyou/46/Sr. VP, Li Yonggui/67/Independent Supervisor, Zhang Jianhua/43/Dir., Sr. VP, Wang Zhigang/50/Dir., Sr. VP, Zhang Jiaren/Dir., Sr. VP, Jiao Fangzheng/45/VP, Zou Huiping/47/Supervisor, Zhang Jitian/60/Employee Representative Supervisor, Dai Houliang/44/Dir., CFO, Sr. VP, Zhang Kehua/54/VP *(17 Officers included in Index)*

Directors: Wang Zuoran/57/Chmn. - Supervisors, Zhou Yuan/60/Vice Chmn., Zhang Youcai/66/Vice Chmn. - Board Of Supervisors, Chen Tonghai/59/Chmn., Zhang Jiaren/Dir., Sr. VP, Liu Zhongli/73/Dir., Shi Wanpeng/70/Dir., Li Deshui/63/Dir., Yao Zhongmin/55/Dir., Chen Ge/45/Dir., Sec., Wang Zhigang/50/Dir., Sr. VP, Dai Houliang/44/Dir., CFO, Sr. VP, Zhang Jianhua/43/Dir., Sr. VP, Wang Tianpu/45/Dir., Pres., Fan Yifei/44/Dir.

Owners: Sinopec Group Company/75.84%

Financial Data: *Fiscal Year End:*12/31   *Latest Annual Data:* 12/31/2006

Year		Sales		Net Income
2006		$137,994,736,000		$7,033,308,000
2005		$103,161,000,000		$5,529,000,000
2004		$74,885,000,000		$4,830,000,000
Curr. Assets:	$18,648,869,000	Curr. Liab.:	$27,024,816,000	
Plant, Equip.:	$53,689,647,000	Total Liab.:	$44,732,698,000	Indic. Yr. Divd.: $2.080
Total Assets:	$78,359,173,000	Net Worth:	$33,626,475,000	Debt/ Equity: NA

China Pharma Holdings Inc

Formerly: TS Electronics Inc
2nd Fl., No. 17, Jinpan Rd., Haikou, 570216; *PH:* 86-898-668-11730

General - Incorporation	DE	Stock - Price on: 12/24/2007	$1.7
Employees	NA	Stock Exchange	NA
Auditor	Hansen, Barnett & Maxwell	Ticker Symbol	NA
Stk Agt	Securities Transfer Corp	Outstanding Shares	NA
Counsel	Thomas Kenan	E.P.S.	NA
DUNS No.	NA	Shareholders	NA

Business: The group's principle activity is to manufacture a patented rubber product that is used in the road and building construction industries. The products include rubber modules from recycled tires through the process of devulcanization. It uses the levgum process of devulcanization which breaks down the sulfur links across polymer chains in vulcanized rubber which allows the rubber to be used again. Whole tires are inserted into a shredder, reduced to chip rubber, blended with a specially prepared binder element, placed into a custom mold and then pressed into place and locked. These molds are then moved on a conveyor belt through a heated oven where the product cures and comes out at the other end as a rubber-molded product ready for sale. The company has begun an importation business dealing in speciality crumb rubber. The group operates from United States.

Primary SIC and add'l.: 3069

CIK No: 0001106644

Subsidiaries: AsiaNet PE Systems Limited, Onny

Officers: Zhilin Li/55/Dir., CEO, Pres., Xinhua Wu/45/Dir., CFO, Jian Yang/53/Sec.

Directors: Zhilin Li/55/Dir., CEO, Pres., Heung Mei Tsui/51/Dir., Xinhua Wu/45/Dir., CFO

Owners: Zhilin Li/26.86%, Heung Mei Tsui/41.04%, Insiders/67.90%

Financial Data: Fiscal Year End: 06/30   Latest Annual Data: 12/31/2006

Year	Sales	Net Income
2006	$21,843,000	$8,587,000
2005	NA	-$1,842,000

Curr. Assets:	NA	Curr. Liab.:	$4,000		
Plant, Equip.:	NA	Total Liab.:	$4,000	Indic. Yr. Divd.:	NA
Total Assets:	NA	Net Worth:	-$4,000	Debt/ Equity:	NA

China Pharmaceuticals International Corp

Rm. A, 22/f, Noble Ctr., 3rd Fu Zhong Rd., Fu Tian District, Shenzhen, GUANG DONG; PH: 85-2225-50688

General - Incorporation British Virgin Islands		Stock - Price on: 12/24/2007	$0.1
Employees	NA	Stock Exchange	OTC
Auditor	Bongiovanni & Assoc. P.A	Ticker Symbol	CPICF
Stk Agt	Computershare Investor Services LLC	Outstanding Shares	NA
Counsel	NA	E.P.S.	-$0.25
DUNS No.	NA	Shareholders	NA

Business: The group's principal activity is the distribution of packaged entertainment programs. The group operates through two segments, namely, e-trend and langara distribution. E-trend distributes packaged entertainment media, with distribution channels to both online retail e-commerce and traditional bricks and mortar retail outlets. Langara offers business-to-business fulfillment services to electronic commerce companies and third party e-commerce partners. This segment also provides wholesale services to the brick and mortar retailers.

Primary SIC and add'l.: 5032 7389 6799

CIK No: 0001081823

Subsidiaries: E-Trend Networks, Inc.

Officers: Fan Di/Dir., CEO, Pres., Acting CFO, Tai Ching Nam/Exec. VP, Fu Li/Assist. Pres., Corp. Sec.

Directors: Fan Di/Dir., CEO, Pres., Acting CFO, Li Xinggui/Dir.

Owners: Fivestar International Limited/9.65%, Asian Century Development Limited/8.68%, Rich Gush Limited/9.40%, Cede & Co./5.16%, FAN Di/26.04%, Sino Castle Holdings Ltd/9.40%, Mart Burkit Limited/9.40%, Global China Enterprises Limited/9.40%, Mart Express Limited/9.40%

Financial Data: Fiscal Year End: 12/31   Latest Annual Data: 12/31/2006

Year	Sales	Net Income
2006	NA	-$114,000
2005	NA	-$714,000
2004	NA	-$643,000

Curr. Assets:	$25,000	Curr. Liab.:	$677,000		
Plant, Equip.:	$165,000	Total Liab.:	$677,000	Indic. Yr. Divd.:	NA
Total Assets:	$319,000	Net Worth:	-$358,000	Debt/ Equity:	NA

China Print Inc

Formerly: WorldTeq Group International Inc
1300 Pennsylvania Ave Nw, Ste. 700, Washington, DC, 20004; PH: 1-703-294-9933; http:// www.worldteqgroup.com

General - Incorporation	NV	Stock - Price on: 12/24/2007	$0.3
Employees	22	Stock Exchange	NA
Auditor	Traci J. Anderson, CPA	Ticker Symbol	NA
Stk Agt	Corporate Stock Transfer, Inc.	Outstanding Shares	27,100,000
Counsel	NA	E.P.S.	-$0.014
DUNS No.	NA	Shareholders	NA

Business: The group's principle activities are to provide Internet protocol and fiber based communication services including voice, data and related services throughout the United States and Canada. The services include connectivity, electronic mail, electronic commerce, Web hosting, Web site designing and long distance calling cards and related services. It also sells educational courses developed by others over the Internet. The services are marketed through agent network and direct sales force to residential communities, associations, membership-Marketing companies and regional and local Internet service providers. It has developed and launched its own billing system, webbssm (Web enabled back-office business systems) which maintains information regarding customer details, their status, frequently asked questions and customer service issues.

Primary SIC and add'l.: 4899 7375 7372

CIK No: 0001091566

Subsidiaries: CKO Corporation

Officers: Timothy W. Carnahan/40/Chmn., CEO, CFO, Pres., Treasurer, Jeffrey Lieberman/40/Dir., Sec., Dir. - Sales, Operations

Directors: Timothy W. Carnahan/40/Chmn., CEO, CFO, Pres., Treasurer, Jeffrey Lieberman/40/Dir., Sec., Dir. - Sales, Operations

Owners: Jeffrey Lieberman/5.00%, Timothy Carnahan/67.00%

Financial Data: Fiscal Year End: 12/31   Latest Annual Data: 12/31/2006

Year	Sales	Net Income
2006	$1,710,000	-$889,000
2005	$2,299,000	-$272,000
2004	$341,000	-$1,837,000

Curr. Assets:	$106,000	Curr. Liab.:	$624,000		
Plant, Equip.:	NA	Total Liab.:	$624,000	Indic. Yr. Divd.:	NA
Total Assets:	$106,000	Net Worth:	-$518,000	Debt/ Equity:	NA

China Ritar Power Corp

Formerly: Concept Ventures Corp
12890 Hilltop Rd., Argyle, TX, 06226; PH: 1-972-233-0300; http:// www.conceptvc.com

General - Incorporation	UT	Stock - Price on: 12/24/2007	NA
Employees	NA	Stock Exchange	OTC
Auditor	Pritchett, Siler & Hardy, P.C.	Ticker Symbol	CRTP
Stk Agt	Securities Transfer Corp.	Outstanding Shares	NA
Counsel	NA	E.P.S.	NA
DUNS No.	NA	Shareholders	NA

Business: The group's principle activity is to provide international users with telecommunications tools that enable access to in-language content and information services.The group's services include wireless and interpretation. The group operates from United States.

Primary SIC and add'l.: 6799

CIK No: 0000786368

Subsidiaries: Ritar International Group Limited, Ritar Power (Huizhou) Co., Ltd., Shanghai Ritar Power Co., Ltd., Shenzhen Ritar Power Co., Ltd.

Officers: Jiada Hu/Chmn., CEO, Pres., Sec., Treasurer, Zhenghua Cai/37/CFO, Anne Degheest/Mnaging Dir., Julien Nguyen/Mnaging Dir., Jianjun Zeng/40/COO, Degang He/67/CTO

Directors: Jiada Hu/Chmn., CEO, Pres., Sec., Treasurer

Owners: Marat Rosenberg, David Brigante, George L. Diamond, Pope Investments LLC, William P. Wells, Timothy P. Halter, Henying Peng, Jeffrey L. Feinberg, Jianjun Zeng, Jiada Hu, Insiders

Financial Data: Fiscal Year End: 12/31   Latest Annual Data: 12/31/2006

Year	Sales	Net Income
2006	NA	-$43,000
2005	NA	-$14,000
2004	NA	-$30,000

Curr. Assets:	$5,000	Curr. Liab.:	$16,000		
Plant, Equip.:	NA	Total Liab.:	$16,000	Indic. Yr. Divd.:	NA
Total Assets:	$5,000	Net Worth:	-$11,000	Debt/ Equity:	NA

China Security & Surveillance Technology Inc

13/F, Shenzhen Special Zone Press Tower, Shennan Rd., Futian, Shenzhen, 518034; PH: 86-75583765666; http:// www.csst.com

General - Incorporation British Virgin Islands		Stock - Price on: 12/24/2007	$13.6
Employees	NA	Stock Exchange	OTC
Auditor	GHP Horwath, P.C.	Ticker Symbol	CSCT
Stk Agt	Manhattan Transfer Registrar Co	Outstanding Shares	NA
Counsel	NA	E.P.S.	NA
DUNS No.	NA	Shareholders	NA

Business: The groups principle activities include manufacturing, distributing, installing and maintaining security and surveillance systems. The group products include standalone digital video recorders, embedded digital video recorders, mobile digital video recorders, digital cameras and auxiliary apparatus. The customer of the group includes schools, banks, highways, commercial buildings, public security and government entities. The group acquired Safetech in the year 2005, and Jian An Ke, Shenzhen Guangdian, Shenyang Golden, and Jiangxi Golden, Cheng Feng acquired in Nov 2006. The group operates from the United States and China. The groups quarterly revenue for September 2007 was 65.44 millions of USD.

Primary SIC and add'l.: 8741

CIK No: 0001260625

Subsidiaries: China Safetech Holdings Limited, China Security & Surveillance Technology (HK) Ltd., China Security & Surveillance Technology (PRC) Ltd., Golden Group Corporation (Shenzhen) Limited, Shanghai Cheng Feng Digital Technology Co. Ltd.

Officers: Guoshen Tu/Chmn., CEO, Terence Yap/Vice Chmn., CFO, Yong Zhao/CTO, Shufang Yang/COO, Jianguo Jiang/Dir., VP, Lingfeng Xiong/Dir., VP

Directors: Guoshen Tu/Chmn., CEO, Terence Yap/Vice Chmn., CFO, Lingfeng Xiong/Dir., VP, Jianguo Jiang/Dir., VP

Owners: Yong Zhao, Li Zhi Qun, Insiders, Jayhawk China Fund (Cayman) Ltd., Shufang Yang, Lingfeng Xiong, The Pinnacle China Fund, L.P., Runsen Li, Guoshen Tu, Robert Shiver, Jianguo Jiang, Terence Yap, Whitehorse Technology Ltd., Citadel Equity Fund Ltd., The Pinnacle Fund, L.P. (16 Owners included in Index)

Financial Data: Fiscal Year End: 12/31   Latest Annual Data: 12/31/2006

Year	Sales	Net Income
2006	$106,989,000	$22,931,000
2005	$32,689,000	$7,266,000

Curr. Assets:	$86,139,000	Curr. Liab.:	$22,604,000		
Plant, Equip.:	$8,339,000	Total Liab.:	$24,614,000	Indic. Yr. Divd.:	NA
Total Assets:	$114,527,000	Net Worth:	$89,819,000	Debt/ Equity:	0.5846

China Shen Zhou Mining & Resources Inc

No. 166 Fushi Rd., Zeyang Tower, Ste. 305, Shijingshan District, Beijing, 100043; PH: 86-010-68867292

Zeyang Tower, Ste. 305, Shijingshan District, Beijing, 100043; *PH:* 86-010-68867292

General - Incorporation	NV	Stock - Price on:12/24/2007	$4.05
Employees	NA	Stock Exchange	OTC
Auditor	Grobstein, Horwath & Co. LLP	Ticker Symbol	CSZM
Stk Agt	Standard Registrar & Transfer Co Inc.	Outstanding Shares	NA
Counsel	NA	E.P.S.	NA
DUNS No.	NA	Shareholders	NA

Business: The groups principle activity is to explore minerals and natural gas. The group operates from China. The groups quarterly revenue for September 2007 was 4.39 millions of USD.

Primary SIC and add'l.: 6770

CIK No: 0000790024

Officers: Xiaojing Yu/51/Chmn., CEO, Steven Jiao/CFO, Xueming Xu/47/Dir., COO, Pres., Qijiu Song/45/CTO, VP, Ligang Wang/47/VP, Pres. - Qianzhen Mining

Directors: Xueming Xu/47/Dir., COO, Pres., Heling Cui/52/Dir., Youming Yang/53/Dir., Jian Zhang/66/Dir., Feng Bai/37/Dir.

Owners: American Eastern Securities, Inc./10.00%, Xiaojing Yu/65.43%, Qijiu Song, Ligang Wang, Insiders/75.39%, Xueming Xu/8.20%, Helin Cui

*Financial Data: Fiscal Year End:*12/31 *Latest Annual Data:* 12/31/2006

Year	Sales	Net Income
2006	$22,433,000	$1,380,000
2005	NA	-$7,000
2004	NA	-$3,000

Curr. Assets:	$26,873,000	Curr. Liab.:	$12,473,000		
Plant, Equip.:	$16,359,000	Total Liab.:	$39,720,000	Indic. Yr. Divd.:	NA
Total Assets:	$57,182,000	Net Worth:	$17,462,000	Debt/ Equity:	1.6596

China Sky One Medical Inc

8 E Broadway, No. 428, Salt Lake City, UT, 84111; *PH:* 1-801-532-7851; *http://* www.skyonemedical.com

General - Incorporation	NV	Stock - Price on:12/24/2007	$14
Employees	NA	Stock Exchange	OTC
Auditor	E-fang Accountancy Corp. & Cpa	Ticker Symbol	CSKI
Stk Agt	Progressive Transfer Company	Outstanding Shares	NA
Counsel	NA	E.P.S.	NA
DUNS No.	NA	Shareholders	NA

Business: The groups principal activities include developing, manufacturing, marketing and selling medicinal products. The group products include sumei slim patch, pain killer patch, anti-hypertension patch, dysmenorrheal patch, wart removing spray. Customers of the group include retail stores, pharmacies and drug store chains. In the year 2006, the group acquired American California Pharmaceutical Group, Inc., a California corporation. The group operates from China and the United States. Of the total in the year 2006, sprays accounted for 26.45%, patches 32.94%, ointments 7.52%, liquids, creams and powders 4.73% and other products 32.29%.

Primary SIC and add'l.: 2834

CIK No: 0000798985

Subsidiaries: American California Pharmaceutical Group, Inc, Harbin First Bio-Engineering Company Limited, Harbin Tian Di Ren Medical Science and Technology Company, Harbin Tian Qing Biotech Application Company

Officers: Liu Yan-Qing/Chmn., CEO, Pres., Han Xiao-Yan/Dir., CFO, VP, Wang Hai-Feng/Dir., Deputy GM, Steve Wang/Contact, Zhang Yu-Kun/Vice CFO, Kang Kai/Deputy GM, Liu Xing-Han/Chief Research & Development Expert, Zhang Wen-Chao/CTO

Directors: Liu Yan-Qing/Chmn., CEO, Pres., Han Xiao-Yan/Dir., CFO, VP, Wang Hai-Feng/Dir., Deputy GM

Owners: Trang Chong Hung, American Eastern Securities, Inc./1.68%, Insiders/55.32%, American Eastern Group, Inc./4.79%, Han Xiao-yan/12.80%, Liu Yan-qing/42.52%

*Financial Data: Fiscal Year End:*12/31 *Latest Annual Data:* 12/31/2006

Year	Sales	Net Income
2006	$19,882,000	$4,300,000
2005	NA	-$47,000
2004	NA	-$92,000

Curr. Assets:	$10,168,000	Curr. Liab.:	$4,059,000		
Plant, Equip.:	$4,503,000	Total Liab.:	$4,059,000	Indic. Yr. Divd.:	NA
Total Assets:	$19,080,000	Net Worth:	$15,021,000	Debt/ Equity:	NA

China Solar & Clean Energy Solutions Inc

Formerly: Deli Solar (usa) Inc
558 Lime Rock Rd. , Lime Rock, CT, 06039; *PH:* 1-860-435-7000; *http://* www.deli-group.com; *Email:* delisolar@delisolar.com.cn

General - Incorporation	NV	Stock - Price on:12/24/2007	$2.08
Employees	273	Stock Exchange	NA
Auditor Child, Van Wagoner & Bradshaw, PLLC		Ticker Symbol	NA
Stk Agt	Securities Transfer Corp	Outstanding Shares	NA
Counsel	NA	E.P.S.	NA
DUNS No.	10-696-8837	Shareholders	NA

Business: The group's principal activities are to provide research and development in the biomedical industry, with an emphasis on anti-infective drugs. The group has completed various stages of planning and developing products containing its proprietary drugs viraplex(R) and mtch-24(TM). Both of these compounds show positive test results for treatment of a variety of enveloped viruses. An enveloped virus is one in which the infectious particle is surrounded by a coating made of protein, fatty substances and carbohydrate. Mtch-24(TM) which is effective against other enveloped viruses such as influenza, epstein-barr virus, respiratory syncytial virus (a virus which affects the respiratory system), pseudorabies (a specific virus in the rabies family), rhino tracheitis (an infection of the lungs and throat), and cytomegalovirus. Viraplex(R) is administered orally in capsule form as a prescription treatment for orofacial and genital herpes simplex virus infections in humans.

Primary SIC and add'l.: 2834

CIK No: 0000717588

Subsidiaries: Ailiyang, Bazhou Deli Solar Heating Energy Co., Ltd., Beijing Ailiyang Solar energy Technology Co., Ltd., Beijing Deli Solar Technology Development, Ltd., Deli Solar Holding Ltd.

Officers: Deli Du/Chmn., CEO, Jianmin Li/39/Treasurer, Yunjun Luo/Chief Scientific Officer, Gary Lam/CFO

Directors: Deli Du/Chmn., CEO

Owners: Deli Du/50.80%, First Wilshire Securities Management, Inc./6.10%, Insiders/50.80%, David Gelbaum/5.10%

*Financial Data: Fiscal Year End:*12/31 *Latest Annual Data:* 12/31/2006

Year	Sales	Net Income
2006	$21,468,000	$1,240,000
2005	$15,577,000	$1,299,000
2004	$9,380,000	$2,137,000

Curr. Assets:	$5,464,000	Curr. Liab.:	$491,000		
Plant, Equip.:	$5,926,000	Total Liab.:	$491,000	Indic. Yr. Divd.:	NA
Total Assets:	$12,716,000	Net Worth:	$12,225,000	Debt/ Equity:	NA

China Southern Airlines Co Ltd

6300 Wilshire Blvd., Ste. 101, Los Angeles, CA, 90048; *PH:* 1-323-653-8088; *Fax:* 1-323-653-8066; *http://* www.cs-air.com

General - Incorporation	China	Stock - Price on:12/24/2007	$35.3692
Employees	45,575	Stock Exchange	NYSE
Auditor	Ms. Yang Yi Hua	Ticker Symbol	ZNH
Stk Agt	NA	Outstanding Shares	87,480,000
Counsel	Mr. Chen Wei Hua	E.P.S.	$2.00
DUNS No.	65-372-0458	Shareholders	NA

Business: The group's principal activities are the provision of passenger and cargo and mail airline services. It also provides aircraft maintenance, air catering operations, cargo forwarding, pilot training services, aircraft leasing, property development, aviation and advertising. Other activities include aviation supplies, hotel management, travel servicing, financial services, ticket reservation system services and flight logistics services. As of 31-Dec-2003, the group operated a fleet of 132 aircraft consisting primarily of boeing 737-300, 737-500, 737-700, 737-800, 747-400, 757-200, 777-200 and airbus 320-200 and 319-100 aircraft. The group operates 334 routes, of which 274 were domestic, 42 were international and 18 were Hong Kong regional.

Primary SIC and add'l.: 4731 4729 4513 4581 4512

CIK No: 0001041668

Subsidiaries: Airlines Company Limited, Catering Company Limited, China Southern West Australian, Company Limited, Flying College Pty Limited, Guangxi Airlines Company Limited, Guangzhou Air Cargo, Guangzhou Baiyun International Logistic Company Ltd, Guangzhou Nanland Air, Guizhou Airlines, Property Management Limited, Southern Airlines (Group) Shantou, Technology Company Limited, Xiamen Airlines, Xinjiang Civil Aviation 17 Subsidiaries included in the Index

Officers: Liu Qian/42/Chief Pilot, Yang Guang Hua/55/Supervisor, Chen Wei Hua/42/General Counsel, Su Liang/46/Company Sec., Hao Jian Hua/57/VP, Yuan Xin An/51/VP, Si Xian Min/51/Dir., Pres., Xu Jie Bo/43/Dir., CFO, VP, Yang Yi Hua/48/Supervisor, He Zong Kai/57/VP, Liang Zhong Gao/Supervisor, Liu Biao/Supervisor, Dong Su Guang/54/Chief Engineer, Tan Wan Geng/Dir., VP, Lin Guang Yu/Supervisor

Directors: Liu Shao Yong/50/Chmn., Tan Wan Geng/Dir., VP, Chen Zhen You/Dir., Sui Guang Jun/Dir., Gong Hua Zhang/Dir., Wang Quan Hua/54/Dir., Wang Zhi/66/Dir., Wei Ming Hai/Dir., Peter Lok/72/Dir., Si Xian Min/51/Dir., Pres., Xu Jie Bo/43/Dir., CFO, VP, Li Wen Xin/Dir., Zhao Liu An/Dir.

Owners: HKSCC Nominees Limited/26.43%, CSAHC/50.30%

*Financial Data: Fiscal Year End:*12/31 *Latest Annual Data:* 12/31/2006

Year	Sales	Net Income
2006	$5,925,276,000	$27,691,000
2005	$4,748,332,000	-$189,720,000
2004	$2,897,000,000	$29,000,000

Curr. Assets:	$856,761,000	Curr. Liab.:	$4,982,237,000	P/E Ratio:	11.29
Plant, Equip.:	$7,345,604,000	Total Liab.:	$8,384,793,000	Indic. Yr. Divd.:	NA
Total Assets:	$9,656,152,000	Net Worth:	$1,271,359,000	Debt/ Equity:	NA

China Stationery Ltd

Office No.F, 1/F, Sunshine Plz., 17 Sung On St., Hung Hom, Kowloon; *PH:* 852-27966722; *Fax:* 852-27966816; *http://* www.cslchina.com; *Email:* sales@cslchina.com

General - Incorporation	DE	Stock - Price on:12/24/2007	$0.4
Employees	NA	Stock Exchange	OTC
Auditor	Patrizio & Zhao, LLC	Ticker Symbol	CSOF
Stk Agt	NA	Outstanding Shares	NA
Counsel	NA	E.P.S.	NA
DUNS No.	NA	Shareholders	NA

Business: The group operates through its subsidiary whose principal activities include manufacturing and distribution of office supplies and related products. The group products include staplers, seals, pencil sharpeners, correction tapes, hole-punchers, stamps, paper cutters and folders. The group operates through two segments namely stationary and style. The group acquired Dickie Walker Marine, Inc and Ningbo Binbin Stationery Co., Ltd in 2006. The group operates from China. In the year 2006, Stationary accounted for $ 25,927,786 and style $1,792,028.

Primary SIC and add'l.: 2320

CIK No: 0001138724

Officers: Hu Jufen/44/VP, Wei Chengzhao/41/VP

Owners: Wei Chenghui/56.70%, Huaqin Zhou/9.10%, Insiders/56.70%

*Financial Data: Fiscal Year End:*09/30 *Latest Annual Data:* 12/31/2006

Year	Sales	Net Income
2006	$27,720,000	$385,000
2005	$1,703,000	-$2,444,000
2004	$4,465,000	-$1,273,000

Curr. Assets:	$395,000	Curr. Liab.:	$327,000		
Plant, Equip.:	$529,000	Total Liab.:	$621,000	Indic. Yr. Divd.:	NA
Total Assets:	$960,000	Net Worth:	$339,000	Debt/ Equity:	NA

China Sun Group High-Tech Co

Formerly: Capital Resource Funding Inc

1 Hutan St., Zhongshan District, Dalian, Liaoning; *PH*: 86-411-828-97752

General - Incorporation	NC	Stock- Price on:12/24/2007	$1.01
Employees	NA	Stock Exchange	NA
Auditor ...Zhong Yi (hong Kong) C.P.A. Co. Ltd.		Ticker Symbol	NA
Stk Agt.........Island Capital Management, LLC		Outstanding Shares	NA
Counsel	NA	E.P.S.	NA
DUNS No.	NA	Shareholders	NA

Business: The groups principle activities include commercial financing, brokerage and consulting business. The groups financial products include commercial mortgages, asset-based lines of credit, commercial leasing, accounts receivable financing and purchase order financing. The group operates from the United States.

Primary SIC and add'l.: 6153

CIK No: 0001298195

Officers: Bin Wang/43/Chmn., CEO, Pres., Yu-long Wang/44/VP, Ming Fen Liu/56/CFO

Directors: Bin Wang/43/Chmn., CEO, Pres., Zhi Li/37/Dir., Jiao Wang/24/Dir., Fudong Sui/53/Dir., Gang Li/29/Dir., Yefei Liu/31/Dir., Ren Fuqiu/43/Dir.

Owners: Insiders/59.40%, Yu Long Wang, Gang Li, Ming Fen Liu, Bin Wang/58.70%, Zhi Li/58.70%, Yefei Liu, Fudong Sui, Jiao Wang/58.70%

Curr. Assets:	$5,570,000	Curr. Liab.:	$2,603,000		
Plant, Equip.:	$10,774,000	Total Liab.:	$6,598,000	Indic. Yr. Divd.:	NA
Total Assets:	$16,344,000	Net Worth:	$9,746,000	Debt/ Equity:	NA

China SXAN Biotech Inc

Formerly: Advance Technologies Inc

15 N Longspur Dr., The Woodlands, TX, 77380; *PH*: 1-310-213-2143;
http:// www.advancedtechnologiesinc.com

General - Incorporation	NV	Stock- Price on:12/24/2007	$0.0099
Employees	1	Stock Exchange	OTC
Auditor ....Chisholm Bierwolf & Nilson LLC		Ticker Symbol	ADTI
Stk Agt............ Pacific Stock Transfer Company		Outstanding Shares	39,530,000
Counsel	NA	E.P.S.	-$0.001
DUNS No.	NA	Shareholders	NA

Business: The group's principal activity is to develop infrared enhanced vision technology and commercial solutions. The group has a world wide license from hughes aircraft company for a patented advanced infrared imaging system. The group licenses and develops applied infrared enhanced vision solutions for use in diverse industries including aviation, recreational vehicles, commercial trucking, marine, security and fire fighting applications. Currently, the group is developing night vision systems with applications in the commercial sector. The group has an agreement with a Taiwan company wherein they are jointly developing the night vision system for use in class a coaches. In addition, the group is involved in the development of other electro-optical mechanical devices. The group is in the development stage.

Primary SIC and add'l.: 3812

CIK No: 0001081944

Subsidiaries: SeaCrest Industries Corporation

Officers: Paul Thomeer/VP, Dir. - Operations

Directors: Gary E. Ball/70/Dir., James Watson/59/Dir., Gary L. Bane/Dir.

Owners: Huakang Zhou/59.10%

Financial Data: Fiscal Year End:09/30   Latest Annual Data: 9/30/2006

Year	Sales	Net Income
2006	$34,000	-$62,000
2005	$29,000	-$36,000
2004	$149,000	$8,000

Curr. Assets:	$10,000	Curr. Liab.:	$108,000		
Plant, Equip.:	$1,000	Total Liab.:	$108,000	Indic. Yr. Divd.:	NA
Total Assets:	$14,000	Net Worth:	-$95,000	Debt/ Equity:	NA

China TechFaith Wireless Communication Technology Ltd

10 A, Tower D2, IT Pk., Electronic Town, Jiu Xian Qiao North Rd., Chaoyang District, Beijing, 100015; ; *http://* www.techfaithwireless.com; *Email:* ir@TechFaith.cn

General - Incorporation	Cayman Islands	Stock- Price on:12/24/2007	$5.86
Employees	2,400	Stock Exchange	NDQ
Auditor ....Deloitte Touche Tohmatsu CPA Ltd		Ticker Symbol	CNTF
Stk Agt.	Bank of New York	Outstanding Shares	43,310,000
Counsel	Latham & Watkins LLP	E.P.S.	-$0.3
DUNS No.	NA	Shareholders	NA

Business: The groups principle activity is to provide handset design and software solution. The groups services include Mobile Handset Design Services based on Existing Platforms, Successor Model Design and New Platforms. The products of the group include Smart Phones and Pocket PC, wireless modules, PCBs, and Wireless Software and Application. Customer served by the group is a mobile handset brand owner. Specific customers of the group include Eastcom, Lenovo, Haier, Kyocera and CEC Telecom. The group operates from China.

Primary SIC and add'l.: 7389

CIK No: 0001316317

Subsidiaries: STEP Technologies (Beijing) Co., Ltd, Techfaith Intelligent Handset Technology (Beijing) Limited, TechFaith Software (China) Limited, Techfaith Wireless Communication Technology (Beijing) Limited, Techfaith Wireless Communication Technology (Beijing) Limited II, Techfaith Wireless Communication Technology (Shanghai) Limited

Officers: Defu Dong/Chmn., CEO, Baozhuang Huo/Dir., Deputy CEO, Xiaonong Cai/Assist. to CEO, Changke He/CTO, Yibo Fang/39/Pres. - Step Technologies, Jy-Ber Gilbert Lee/52/Dir., COO, Pres., Christopher Holbert/CFO, Gilbert Lee/Dir., COO, Pres.

Directors: Defu Dong/Chmn., CEO, Baozhuang Huo/Dir., Deputy CEO, Ken Lu/Dir., Gilbert Lee./Dir., COO, Pres., Robert Chen/Dir., Ying Han/Dir., Jy-Ber Gilbert Lee/52/Dir., COO, Pres., Hung Hsin Chen/63/Dir., Hui Zhang/34/Dir., Shelley Sui/Dir., Tom Zhang/Dir.

Owners: Insiders/38.40%, Hung Hsin Chen, Defu Dong/38.40%, Jy-Ber Gilbert Lee, Ying Han, Ken Lu, Hui (Tom) Zhang, Christopher Patrick Holbert

Financial Data: Fiscal Year End:12/31   Latest Annual Data: 12/31/2006

Year	Sales	Net Income
2006	$80,804,000	-$8,793,000
2005	$90,110,000	$41,385,000
2004	$46,560,000	$18,244,000

Curr. Assets:	$175,506,000	Curr. Liab.:	$37,123,000		
Plant, Equip.:	$25,092,000	Total Liab.:	$41,364,000	Indic. Yr. Divd.:	NA
Total Assets:	$207,714,000	Net Worth:	$166,350,000	Debt/ Equity:	NA

China Technology Development Group Corp

Rm. 2413-18, Shui On Ctr., 8 Harbour Rd., Wanchai; *PH*: 86-85231128461;
http:// www.chinactdc.com; *Email:* info@chinactdc.com

General - Incorporation British Virgin Islands		Stock- Price on:12/24/2007	$3.67
Employees	130	Stock Exchange	NDQ
Auditor	Friedman LLP	Ticker Symbol	CTDC
Stk Agt ..... American Stock Transfer & Trust Co.		Outstanding Shares	11,270,000
Counsel	NA	E.P.S.	-$1.04
DUNS No.	NA	Shareholders	NA

Business: The groups principle activity is to provide information network security solutions. The products of the group include, security gate, IPSSS, secure channel and secure server, nutraceutical. The groups operates through two segments namely IT operations and nutraceutical operations. In the year 2005, the group acquired Nutraceutical Corporation, Zhejiang Innoessen and Beijing Holdings Limited. The group operates from the China.

Primary SIC and add'l.: 7375 7376 7379 7371 8999 7378 7373 7374 7389 7372

CIK No: 0001027454

Subsidiaries: Anji Science Bio-Product Inc., Beijing BHL Networks Technology Co. Ltd., BHL Networks Technology Co. Ltd., China Natures Technology Inc., Jianou Yingshi Food Technology Ltd, Jing Tai Industrial Investment Co. Ltd., Jingle Technology Co. Ltd., Shenzhen Innoessen Bio-Tech Inc., Zhejiang University (Hangzhou) Innoessen Bio-technology Inc.

Officers: Alan Li/40/Chmn., CEO, Xu Qian/44/Executive Dir., Zhenwei Lu/37/Executive Dir., COO, Ju Zhang/45/Executive Dir., Kang Li/41/Executive Dir., Chief Investment Officer, Brendan Lahiff/Primary Investor Relations Officer, May Li/Primary Investor Relations Officer, Charlene Hua/CFO, Maggie Qiu/Company Sec.

Directors: Alan Li/40/Chmn., CEO, Xu Qian/44/Executive Dir., Zhenwei Lu/37/Executive Dir., COO, Ju Zhang/45/Executive Dir., Loong Cheong Chang/62/Dir., Xiaoping Wang/48/Dir., Xinping Shi/49/Dir., Weidong Wang/48/Dir., Yezhong Ni/38/Dir., Kang Li/41/Executive Dir., Chief Investment Officer, Yu Keung Poon/43/Dir.

Owners: Harvest Smart Overseas Limited/7.07%, Eastern Ceremony Group Limited/5.66%, Insiders/55.26%, China Biotech Holdings Limited/24.74%, Beijing Holdings of Room/14.20%, Great Legend Internet Technology and Service Co., Ltd. of/3.59%

Financial Data: Fiscal Year End:12/31   Latest Annual Data: 12/31/2006

Year	Sales	Net Income
2006	$1,172,000	-$14,371,000
2005	$930,000	-$2,422,000
2004	$807,000	-$1,224,000

Curr. Assets:	$8,207,000	Curr. Liab.:	$1,808,000		
Plant, Equip.:	$90,000	Total Liab.:	$1,808,000	Indic. Yr. Divd.:	NA
Total Assets:	$8,297,000	Net Worth:	$6,489,000	Debt/ Equity:	NA

China Technology Global Corp

Unit 3611, 36/F, West Tower, Shun Tak Ctr., 168-200 Connaught Rd. Central, Hong Kong; ;
http:// www.chinatechglobal.com; *Email:* investors@ChinaTechGlobal.com

General - Incorporation British Virgin Islands		Stock- Price on:12/24/2007	$0.025
Employees	NA	Stock Exchange	OTC
Auditor	Jimmy C.H. Cheung & Co	Ticker Symbol	CTGLF
Stk Agt	BDO McCabe Lo & Co	Outstanding Shares	NA
Counsel	NA	E.P.S.	NA
DUNS No.	NA	Shareholders	NA

Business: The groups principle activity is to manufacture and distribute paper products. The group operates from United States.

Primary SIC and add'l.: 5111

CIK No: 0001021126

Subsidiaries: BVI, DF Paper Guangdong Ltd., DF Paper Jiangsu Limited, DICHAIN Software, DICHAIN Systems Ltd., Guangzhou Dransfield Paper Limited, Jiangsu Dransfield Paper Co. Ltd.

Financial Data: Fiscal Year End:03/31   Latest Annual Data: 3/31/2005

Year	Sales	Net Income
2005	$2,253,000	$148,000
2004	$530,000	-$4,467,000
2003	$703,000	-$13,034,000

Curr. Assets:	$49,052,000	Curr. Liab.:	$19,600,000		
Plant, Equip.:	$208,000	Total Liab.:	$25,404,000	Indic. Yr. Divd.:	NA
Total Assets:	$111,799,000	Net Worth:	$86,395,000	Debt/ Equity:	NA

China Telecom Corp Ltd

31 Jin Rong Ave., Beijing, 100032; *PH*: 86-1066428166; *http://* www.chinatelecom-h.com;
Email: ir@chinatelecom.com.cn

General - Incorporation	China	Stock- Price on:12/24/2007	$60.97
Employees	243,072	Stock Exchange	NYSE
Auditor	KPMG LLP	Ticker Symbol	CHA
Stk Agt	Bank of New York	Outstanding Shares	809,320,000
Counsel	NA	E.P.S.	$4.40
DUNS No.	NA	Shareholders	NA

Business: The group's principal activity is the provision of wireline telecommunications services. The group offers a comprehensive range of wireline telecommunications services to residential and business customers, including local, domestic long distance and international long distance telephone services, Internet and managed data, leased line, and other related services. Its operations are carried out in shanghai municipality, guangdong province, jiangsu province, zhejiang province, anhui province, fujian province, jiangxi province, guangxi zhuang autonomous region, chongqing municipality and sichuan province of the People's Republic of China.

Primary SIC and add'l.: 7375 7389 4899

CIK No: 0001191255

Subsidiaries: Anhui Telecom Company Limited, China Telecom Group Yellow Pages Information Company Ltd., Chongqing Telecom Company Limited, Fujian Telecom Company Limited, Gansu Telecom Company Limited, Guangdong Telecom Company Limited, Guangxi Telecom Company Limited, Guizhou Telecom Company Limited, Hainan Telecom Company Limited, Hubei Telecom Company Limited, Hunan Telecom Company Limited, Jiangsu Telecom Company Limited, Jiangxi Telecom Company Limited, Ningxia Telecom Company Limited, Qinghai Telecom Company Limited 21 Subsidiaries included in the Index

Officers: Wang Xiaochu/50/Chmn., CEO, Li Jinming/56/Non - Exec. Dir., Yang Jie/46/Exec. Dir., Exec. VP, Jacky Yung Shun Loy/45/Assist. CFO, Qualified Accountant, Joint Company Sec., Xu Cailiao/44/Supervisor, William Li/Investor Relations Officer, Lisa Lai/Investor Relations Officer, Zhao Xu/Office - Dir., Wu Andi/53/Exec. Dir., CFO, Exec. VP, Ma Yuzhu/54/Employee Representative Supervisor, Yung Shun Loy Jacky/Assist. CFO, Qualified Accountant, Company Sec., Zhu Lihao/67/Independent Supervisor, Li Ping/54/Exec. Dir., Exec. VP, Leng Rongquan/59/Exec. Dir., COO, Pres., Zhang Jiping/52/Exec. Dir., Exec. VP *(18 Officers included in Index)*

Directors: Wang Xiaochu/50/Chmn., CEO, Shi Wanpeng/71/Dir., Vincent Lo Hong Sui/60/Dir., Zhang Youcai/67/Dir., Yang Jie/46/Exec. Dir., Exec. VP, Vincent Hong Sui Lo/60/Dir., Tse Hau Yin Aloysius/60/Dir., Aloysius Tse Hau Yin/60/Dir., Sun Kangmin/51/Non - Exec. Dir., Li Ping/54/Exec. Dir., Exec. VP, Leng Rongquan/59/Exec. Dir., COO, Pres., Zhang Jiping/52/Exec. Dir., Exec. VP, Xu Erming/58/Dir.

Owners: UBS AG/1.36%, Commonwealth Bank of Australia/1.52%, China Telecom Group/70.89%, Guangdong Rising Assets Management Co., Ltd./6.94%

Financial Data: *Fiscal Year End:*12/31 *Latest Annual Data:* 12/31/2006

Year	Sales	Net Income
2006	$22,446,923,000	$2,826,297,000
2005	$20,979,000,000	$2,798,000,000
2004	$19,478,000,000	$3,107,000,000

Curr. Assets:	$5,071,977,000	Curr. Liab.:	$20,072,915,000	P/E Ratio:	7.35
Plant, Equip.:	$45,535,486,000	Total Liab.:	$27,129,171,000	Indic. Yr. Divd.:	$1.090
Total Assets:	$53,912,715,000	Net Worth:	$26,783,544,000	Debt/ Equity:	NA

China Titanium & Chemical Corp

1530-9th Ave S.e., Calgary, AT, T2G0T7; *PH:* 1-403-693-8000

General - Incorporation	NV	Stock- Price on:12/24/2007	NA
Employees	NA	Stock Exchange	OTC
Auditor Child, Van Wagoner & Bradshaw, PLLC		Ticker Symbol	CTPJA
Stk Agt.	NA	Outstanding Shares	NA
Counsel	NA	E.P.S.	NA
DUNS No.	NA	Shareholders	NA

Business: The group's principal activity was to market technologies and products in the audio industry. The group operates through two wholly owned subsidiaries: white wolf audio video electronics systems (w-waves) inc. And radison acoustique ltee. As of Sept 2003, the group and its subsidiaries ceased operations relating to the marketing of it's technologies and products in the audio industry. Since then it looks out for business opportunities for merger and/or acquisition and to divest itself of its subsidiaries. It is currently in the development stage.

Primary SIC and add'l.: 3679 6719

CIK No: 0000860401

Officers: Michel Bourbonnais/56/Dir., CEO, Pres., Treasurer - PFO, Roger Boileau/56/Dir., Sec.

Directors: Michel Bourbonnais/56/Dir., CEO, Pres., Treasurer - PFO, Roger Boileau/56/Dir., Sec.

Owners: BIC International Ltd./48.72%, Bello Investments (Nassau) Ltd./30.26%, Antonio Care/7.41%

Financial Data: *Fiscal Year End:*12/31 *Latest Annual Data:* 12/31/2006

Year	Sales	Net Income
2006	NA	-$151,000
2005	NA	-$119,000
2004	NA	$164,000

Curr. Assets:	$347,000	Curr. Liab.:	$103,000
Plant, Equip.:	NA	Total Liab.:	$103,000	Indic. Yr. Divd.:	NA
Total Assets:	$347,000	Net Worth:	$244,000	Debt/ Equity:	NA

China TransInfo Technology Corp

Formerly: Intra-Asia Entertainment Corp
07 Fl. E-wing Ctr., No. 113 Zhichunlu, Haidian District, Beijing, 100086; *PH:* 86-1082-671299; http:// www.intra-asia.com

General - Incorporation	NV	Stock- Price on:12/24/2007	$0.65
Employees	2	Stock Exchange	NA
Auditor Simon & Edward, LLP		Ticker Symbol	NA
Stk Agt. Interwest Transfer Company, Inc.		Outstanding Shares	NA
Counsel	NA	E.P.S.	NA
DUNS No.	NA	Shareholders	NA

Business: The group's principal activity is to design and market safety products using electroluminescent technology. Four market segments use the group's technology: vehicle safety, safety apparel, novelty and visual enhancement/emergency lighting. Vehicle safety market includes illumination for bicycles, motorcycles, scooters, wheelchairs, boats and private aircraft. The safety apparel is used by highway construction workers, traffic personnel and police officers. The novelty applications include concert glow jewelry and flashing sports team paraphernalia. On 03-Sep-2003, the group acquired sport technologies, inc and on 19-Dec-2003, the group acquired intra-Asia entertainment corporation. The group sold gti subsidiary, ait subsidiary and sti subsidiary.

Primary SIC and add'l.: 3751 2013

CIK No: 0001081206

Subsidiaries: Intra-Asia Entertainment Corporation

Owners: Insiders, The Pinnacle Fund, L.P., Leguna Verde Investments, Ltd., Karmen Investment Holdings, Ltd, Shudong Xia, Barry M. Kitt, The Pinnacle China Fund, L.P.

Financial Data: *Fiscal Year End:*12/31 *Latest Annual Data:* 12/31/2006

Year	Sales	Net Income
2006	NA	-$5,004,000
2005	$14,852,000	-$10,043,000
2004	$10,864,000	-$1,696,000

Curr. Assets:	$10,286,000	Curr. Liab.:	$1,018,000		
Plant, Equip.:	NA	Total Liab.:	$1,018,000	Indic. Yr. Divd.:	NA
Total Assets:	$10,286,000	Net Worth:	$9,268,000	Debt/ Equity:	NA

China Unicom Ltd

75th Fl., The Ctr., 99 Queens Rd. , Central; *PH:* 852-21262018; http:// www.chinaunicom.com.hk

General - Incorporation	Hong Kong	Stock- Price on:12/24/2007	$16.71
Employees	53,120	Stock Exchange	NYSE
Auditor PricewaterhouseCoopers LLP		Ticker Symbol	CHU
Stk Agt. Hong Kong Registrars Ltd		Outstanding Shares	1,270,000,000
Counsel Sullivan & Cromwell		E.P.S.	$0.50
DUNS No.	NA	Shareholders	NA

Business: The group's principal activity is the provision of telecommunications services which include cellular communications, paging, international and domestic long distance, data and Internet services.

Primary SIC and add'l.: 4813 4899 4812 7375

CIK No: 0001113866

Subsidiaries: China Unicom Corporation Limited, China Unicom International Limited, China United Telecommunications Corporation Limited, China United Telecommunications Satellite Communication Co. Ltd, Unicom BVI, Unicom Huasheng Telecommunications Technology Company Limited, Unicom New Horizon Mobile Telecommunications Company Limited, Unicom Xingye Science and Technology Trade Co

Officers: Chang Xiaobing/50/Chmn., CEO, Yang Xiaowei/44/Executive Dir., VP, Tong Jilu/49/Executive Dir., CFO, Shang Bing/52/Executive Dir., Pres., Li Zhengmao/45/Executive Dir., VP, Li Gang/50/Executive Dir., VP, Zhang Junan/51/Executive Dir., VP, Chu Ka Yee/Qualified Accountant, Company Sec., Li Jianguo/54/Executive Dir.

Directors: Chang Xiaobing/50/Chmn., CEO, Shang Bing/52/Executive Dir., Pres., Tong Jilu/49/Executive Dir., CFO, Shan Weijian/Non Exec. Dir., Li Zhengmao/45/Executive Dir., VP, Li Gang/50/Executive Dir., VP, Zhang Junan/51/Executive Dir., VP, Lu Jianguo/62/Non Exec. Dir., Wu Jinglian/78/Non Exec. Dir., Cheung Wing Lam/59/Non Exec. Dir., Wong Wai Ming/50/Non Exec. Dir., Li Jianguo/54/Executive Dir., Lee Suk Hwan/Non Exec. Dir., Linus Cheung Wing Lam/60/Dir.

Owners: Yang Xiaowei, Shan Weijian, Liu Yunjie, Li Qiuhong, Li Gang, Lo Wing Yan, Tong Jilu, Zhang Junan, Lu Jianguo, Ye Fengping, Wu Jinglian, Li Jianguo, Li Zhengmao, Shang Bing, Chang Xiaobing

Financial Data: *Fiscal Year End:*12/31 *Latest Annual Data:* 12/31/2006

Year	Sales	Net Income
2006	$12,114,924,000	$789,170,000
2005	$10,794,055,000	$621,589,000
2004	$9,599,125,000	$570,235,000

Curr. Assets:	$2,723,658,000	Curr. Liab.:	$6,448,785,000	P/E Ratio:	11.29
Plant, Equip.:	$14,266,855,000	Total Liab.:	$8,331,079,000	Indic. Yr. Divd.:	$0.230
Total Assets:	$18,424,707,000	Net Worth:	$10,093,628,000	Debt/ Equity:	NA

China VoIP & Digital Telecom Inc

4372 Greta St., Burnaby, BC, V5J 1N8; *PH:* 1-506-872-4033; http:// www.chinavoip-telecom.com

General - Incorporation	NV	Stock- Price on:12/24/2007	$1.19
Employees	NA	Stock Exchange	OTC
Auditor Kabani & Co.,Inc.		Ticker Symbol	CVDT
Stk Agt. Island Stock Transfer		Outstanding Shares	NA
Counsel	NA	E.P.S.	NA
DUNS No.	NA	Shareholders	NA

Business: The groups principle activities include developing and selling computer software and hardware, and digital video pictures system. The group products include IP telephone, Analog Gateway: IAD, Video Telephone, Softphone, Wifi Phone, NGN Soft Switch System, and NP PBX. The groups services include government hot line, company customer service center, follow-up service center, integrated information service and media interaction. The group operates through two segments namely telecommunocations and equipments. In the year 2006, the group acquired Jinan YinQuan Technology Co. Ltd. The group operates from the United State. The group's quarterly revenue for September 2007 was 1.90 millions of USD.

Primary SIC and add'l.: 7372

CIK No: 0001337615

Officers: Li Kunwu/Chmn., CEO, Wang Qinghua/Dir., MD, Xu Yinyi/Sr. Economist, Dir., Jiang Yanli/CFO

Directors: Li Kunwu/Chmn., CEO, Kan Kaili/Dir., Wang Qinghua/Dir., MD, Xu Yinyi/Sr. Economist, Dir.

Owners: Li Kunwu/11.98%, Wang Qinghua/11.98%, Xu Yinyi/5.56%, Jiang Yanli

Financial Data: *Fiscal Year End:*04/30 *Latest Annual Data:* 12/31/2006

Year	Sales	Net Income
2006	$1,450,000	-$530,000

Curr. Assets:	$1,817,000	Curr. Liab.:	$158,000		
Plant, Equip.:	$514,000	Total Liab.:	$158,000	Indic. Yr. Divd.:	NA
Total Assets:	$2,355,000	Net Worth:	$2,197,000	Debt/ Equity:	NA

China Water Group Inc

584 Yingbin Rd., Ste. 7a01, Baicheng Bldg., Guangzhou, GUANGDONG, 511430; *PH:* 86-20-3993 4199

General - Incorporation	NV
Employees	NA
Auditor	PKF Witt Mares, PLC
Stk Agt	Pacific Stock Transfer Company
Counsel	NA
DUNS No.	NA

Stock - Price on:12/24/2007	NA
Stock Exchange	OTC
Ticker Symbol	CHWG
Outstanding Shares	NA
E.P.S	NA
Shareholders	NA

Business: The groups principle activity activities include designing, constructing and implementing management of industrial and municipal wastewater treatment facilities. The groups services include turnkey wastewater treatment engineering services. Customers of the group include local governments, food and beverage processing companies and industrial companies. The group operates from China. The groups quarterly revenue for September 2007 was 0.99 millions of USD.

Primary SIC and add'l.: 7389

CIK No: 0001083459

Subsidiaries: Beijing Haotai Shiyuan Water Purification Co., Ltd., Everbury Holdings Limited, Evergreen Asset Group Limited, Evermater Group Limited, Guangdong Xinsheng Environmental Co., Ltd., Haiyang Shengshi Environmental Protection Co., Ltd., Handan Chengsheng Water Service Co., Ltd., Tian Jin Shi Sheng Water Treatment Company Limited

Owners: Vision Opportunity Fund/9.53%, Gao Yongping/7.47%, Shi Rong Jiang/3.75%, Chong Liang Pu/42.30%

Financial Data: *Fiscal Year End:* 12/31 *Latest Annual Data:* 12/31/2005

Year	Sales	Net Income
2005	$6,984,000	-$761,000
2004	$9,367,000	$3,697,000
2003	NA	$1,772,000

Curr. Assets:	$14,186,000	Curr. Liab.:	$17,063,000		
Plant, Equip.:	$344,000	Total Liab.:	$17,885,000	Indic. Yr. Divd.:	NA
Total Assets:	$25,801,000	Net Worth:	$7,916,000	Debt/ Equity:	NA

China West Coal Energy Inc

Formerly: Endo Networks Inc
Rm. 2205, Ste. A, Zhengxin Bldg., No. 5, Gaoxin 1st Rd., Gao Xin District Xian, Shaanxi Province;
PH: 86-298-209-1099; *http://* www.endonetworks.com

General - Incorporation	NV
Employees	NA
Auditor	Schwartz Levitsky Feldman LLP
Stk Agt	Signature Stock Transfer, Inc.
Counsel	NA
DUNS No.	NA

Stock - Price on:12/24/2007	NA
Stock Exchange	NA
Ticker Symbol	NA
Outstanding Shares	NA
E.P.S	NA
Shareholders	NA

Business: The group's principal activity is to build interactive public networks. The group serves as an interactive media, promotion, application and advertising aggregator deploying through wireless capable public access portals to retail and restaurant locations across North America. The component parts deployed consist of in-house TV service (with several strategically placed tvs), a background audio service and various touchscreen interactive devices (kiosks, tablet pcs and others). The company operates through two brands. The endo networks brand (www.endonetworks.com) enables the company to provide interactive network consisting of TV and audio for communication. The streamline media (www.streamlinemedia.com) business encompasses traditional Internet and interactive design/production work. The deployments of network are located in high-traffic public areas like events (i.e. Consumer and trade shows), retail stores, restaurants and government community centers.

Primary SIC and add'l.: 7319 7372

CIK No: 0001120096

Officers: Baowen Ren/38/Chmn., CEO, Pres., Caixia Peng/29/CFO, Treasurer

Directors: Wenjie Zhang/35/Dir., Peng Zhou/39/Dir.

Owners: Wenjie Zhang/4.50%, Insiders/38.50%, Baowen Ren/34.00%

Financial Data: *Fiscal Year End:* 09/30 *Latest Annual Data:* 12/31/2006

Year	Sales	Net Income
2006	NA	-$92,000

Curr. Assets:	NA	Curr. Liab.:	$10,000		
Plant, Equip.:	NA	Total Liab.:	$10,000	Indic. Yr. Divd.:	NA
Total Assets:	NA	Net Worth:	-$10,000	Debt/ Equity:	NA

China Wireless Communications Inc

1746 Cole Blvd., Ste. 225, Golden, CO, 80401; *PH:* 1-303-277-9968; *Fax:* 1-303-484-3794; *http://* www.chinawirelesscommunications.com; *Email:* info@chinawirelesscommunications.com

General - Incorporation	NV
Employees	13
Auditor	Sherb & Co., LLP
Stk Agt	Computershare Trust Co
Counsel	Dill Carr Stonbraker & Hutchings
DUNS No.	NA

Stock - Price on:12/24/2007	$0.014
Stock Exchange	OTC
Ticker Symbol	CWLC
Outstanding Shares	174,390,000
E.P.S	-$0.011
Shareholders	NA

Business: The groups principle activity is to provide network solution to the clients. The group products include system integratio, network security, digital vedio management system and project experience. The group operates from the United States. The groups quarterly revenue for September 2007 was 0.09 millions of USD.

Primary SIC and add'l.: 7379 7373 7371

CIK No: 0001125280

Subsidiaries: CJ Information Technology Company, Strategic Communications Partners Limited, Tianjin Create IT Co. Ltd.

Officers: Pedro E. Racelis/Dir., CEO, Pres., Michael A. Bowden/Dir., VP - Technology, Frank Li/Pres. - Tianjin Create Co, Robert Paradine/Dir. - Finance, Wendy Shi/Dir. - Finance, China, Mark Sisselman/Business Development, Sales Operations, Larry Murphy/Investor Relations Officer

Directors: Pedro E. Racelis/Dir., CEO, Pres., Henry Zaks/Dir., Michael A. Bowden/Dir., VP - Technology, Brad A. Woods/Dir., Robert McElhinney/Dir., Iouri Onoufrienko/Dir.

Owners: Henry Zaks/4.70%, Pedro E. Racelis/6.50%, Michael A. Bowden/5.00%, Insiders/16.20%

Financial Data: *Fiscal Year End:* 12/31 *Latest Annual Data:* 12/31/2006

Year	Sales	Net Income
2006	$478,000	-$3,227,000
2005	$338,000	-$1,961,000
2004	NA	-$4,029,000

Curr. Assets:	$126,000	Curr. Liab.:	$488,000		
Plant, Equip.:	$8,000	Total Liab.:	$488,000	Indic. Yr. Divd.:	NA
Total Assets:	$134,000	Net Worth:	-$354,000	Debt/ Equity:	NA

China World Trade Corp

4th Floor, Goldlion Digital Network Ctr, 138 Tiyu Rd. E, Tianhe, Guangzhou, 510620;
PH: 86-2028860608; *http://* www.chinawtc.com; *Email:* ir@chinawtc.com

General - Incorporation	NV
Employees	NA
Auditor Child, Van Wagoner & Bradshaw, PLLC
Stk Agt	Interwest Transfer Company, Inc.
Counsel	Harold H. Martin, PA in Cornelius, NC
DUNS No.	NA

Stock - Price on:12/24/2007	$0.3
Stock Exchange	OTC
Ticker Symbol	CWTD
Outstanding Shares	NA
E.P.S	NA
Shareholders	NA

Business: The group's principal activity is to provide trade agency business, linking companies in China and the rest of the world. It has four operating arms, namely the Beijing world trade center club (bwtcc); guangzhou world trade center club (gwtcc), infotech enterprises limited (infotech), and general business network (gbn) limited. Bwtcc will be engaged in the establishment of a business club located in Beijing and gwtcc is engaged in the operation with the business club, the prc. Gwtcc provides food and beverages, recreation, business center services, communication and information services, products exhibitions services, commercial and trading brokerage services. Infotech will build a bilingual, English and Chinese, business-to-business portal for the group and providing system integration related services to customers and members. Gbn is an investment holding company, which primarily engages in property investments, advertising and promotional and trading business.

Primary SIC and add'l.: 7375 7997

CIK No: 0001081834

Subsidiaries: British Virgin Islands corporation, CEO Clubs China Limited, Guangzhou World Trade Center Club Limited, Information Service Limited, Main Edge International Limited, Virtual Edge Limited

Officers: Chan Chi Ming/47/Dir., CEO, William Chi Hung Tsang/46/Chmn., Pres./$150,000.00, Chi Ming Chan/42/Dir., GM/$77,062.00, Larry Wei Fan/38/Deputy CFO, Man Ha/45/CFO, Tsang Chi Hung/47/Dir., Pres., Bernard K. Chan/41/Dir., CFO

Directors: Chan Chi Ming/47/Dir., CEO, Zeliang Chen/42/Vice Chmn., Chen Zeliang/42/Vice Chmn., Chi Hung Tsang/43/Chmn., William Chi Hung Tsang/46/Chmn., Pres., Xiao Lei Yang/37/Dir., Chao Ming Luo/55/Dir., Chi Ming Chan/42/Dir., GM, Chi Kin Ho/36/Dir., Hamid R. Seyedin/54/Dir., Tsang Chi Hung/47/Dir., Pres., Ye Xin Long/53/Dir., Luo Chaoming/58/Dir., Bernard K. Chan/41/Dir., CFO, Samuel Yung/47/Dir.

Owners: William Chi Hung Tsang/49.70%, Powertronic Holdings Limited/11.90%, Insiders/53.10%, Chi Ming Chan, John Hui, Chao Ming Luo, Grand Perfection Limited/3.10%

Financial Data: *Fiscal Year End:* 12/31 *Latest Annual Data:* 12/31/2006

Year	Sales	Net Income
2006	$4,339,000	-$10,091,000
2005	$7,839,000	$18,000
2004	$3,093,000	-$7,594,000

Curr. Assets:	$4,573,000	Curr. Liab.:	$2,522,000		
Plant, Equip.:	$66,000	Total Liab.:	$2,540,000	Indic. Yr. Divd.:	NA
Total Assets:	$13,533,000	Net Worth:	$10,993,000	Debt/ Equity:	NA

China Yida Holding Co

Formerly: InteliSys Aviation Systems of America Inc
815 Bombardier St., Shediac, NB, E4P1H9; *PH:* 1-506-532-8515; *Fax:* 1-506-533-1470;
http:// www.intelisys.ca; *Email:* info@intelisys.aero

General - Incorporation	DE
Employees	NA
Auditor	Sherb & Co., LLP
Stk Agt	American Stock Transfer & Trust Co.
Counsel	NA
DUNS No.	NA

Stock - Price on:12/24/2007	$0.0035
Stock Exchange	NA
Ticker Symbol	NA
Outstanding Shares	NA
E.P.S	NA
Shareholders	NA

Business: The groups principle activity is to provide software solutions for regional, mid-sized airlines and fleet operators. The group operates from Canada, United Arab Emirates and the United States.

Primary SIC and add'l.: 7389

CIK No: 0001091325

Officers: Ralph Eisenschmid/42/Dir., CEO, CFO, Pres./$95,224.00, Jock English/58/Dir., COO, VP - Sales, Marketing, Sec./$88,848.00

Directors: Ralph Eisenschmid/42/Dir., CEO, CFO, Pres., Jock English/58/Dir., COO, VP - Sales, Marketing, Sec.

Owners: Chen Minhua/39.20%, Fan Yanling/39.20%, Insiders/78.40%

Financial Data: *Fiscal Year End:* 12/31 *Latest Annual Data:* 12/31/2006

Year	Sales	Net Income
2006	NA	$3,201,000
2005	$1,945,000	-$388,000
2004	$1,620,000	-$3,170,000

Curr. Assets:	NA	Curr. Liab.:	$109,000		
Plant, Equip.:	NA	Total Liab.:	$109,000	Indic. Yr. Divd.:	NA
Total Assets:	NA	Net Worth:	-$109,000	Debt/ Equity:	NA

China Yili Petroleum Co

Formerly: ASAP Show Inc
4349 Baldwin Ave. Ste. A, El Monte, CA, 91731; *PH:* 1-626-636-2530; *http://* www.asapshow.com;
Email: ir@asapshow.com

General - Incorporation	NV
Employees	11
Auditor	Sutton Robinson Freeman & Co., P. C.
Stk Agt	U.S. Stock Transfer Corp
Counsel	The Otto Law Group PLLC
DUNS No.	NA

Stock - Price on:12/24/2007	$0.06
Stock Exchange	NA
Ticker Symbol	NA
Outstanding Shares	8,700,000
E.P.S	-$0.06
Shareholders	NA

Business: The group's principle activity is to organize trade-shows and B2B trade internationally in the apparel industry. The group organizes the ASAP Global Sourcing Show for U.S. buyers to meet hundreds of overseas ready-made garment manufacturers. It is held twice a year in Las Vegas. The groups

buying trips services locates the apparel and textile sources, visit the factories, expand to Asia market and find joint venture partners. The ASAP is arranging a trip to Bangladesh, Pakistan in November 2005, India and Thailand in March 2006 and the second China trip in May 2006. The group's Fashion International Trade Show brings U.S., Canadian and European fashion brands to the largest and fastest growing economy in the world. The group operates from United States.

Primary SIC and add'l.: 7389

CIK No: 0001339854

Officers: Frank S. Yuan/Chmn., CEO, CFO, Haseeb Alam/Contact - Bangladesh, Brown Qiu/Contact - China, Deepak Thadhani/Contact - India, Rajesh S. Kanna/Contact - India, Baki Lee/Contact - Indonesia, Rei Kim/Contact - Korea, Rara Jeon/Contact - Korea, Daniel Jang/Contact - Korea, Pankaj Kumar Jain/Contact - Nepal, Upeksha Karunatilake/Contact - Sri Lanka, Sevket Kandemir/Contact - Turkey, Ethul Kotte/Contact - Sri Lanka, Tharusha Senerath/Contact - Sri Lanka, Buddhi Weerasinghe/Contact - United Kingdom, Europe *(18 Officers included in Index)*

Directors: Frank S. Yuan/Chmn., CEO, CFO, James L. Vandeberg/Dir., Deborah Shamaley/Dir., Charles Rice/Dir., Alvin S. Mirman/Dir.

Owners: Chunshi Li/66.00%, Frank Yuan/0.30%, Insiders/66.30%

Financial Data: Fiscal Year End:05/31   Latest Annual Data: 5/31/2006

Year	Sales		Net Income
2006	$1,993,000		-$685,000
Curr. Assets:	$99,000	Curr. Liab.:	$476,000		
Plant, Equip.:	NA	Total Liab.:	$1,298,000	Indic. Yr. Divd.:	NA
Total Assets:	$109,000	Net Worth:	-$1,189,000	Debt/ Equity:	NA

China Yingxia International Inc

100 Wall St., 15th Fl., New York, NY, 10005; *PH:* 1-212-232-0120; *Fax:* 1-212-785-5867; *http://* www.chinayingxia.com; *Email:* ir@ciccltd.com

General - Incorporation	FL	**Stock**- Price on:12/24/2007	$2.46
Employees	180	Stock Exchange	OTC
Auditor	Bagell, Josephs, Levine & Co., L.Lc.	Ticker Symbol	CYXI
Stk Agt	PacWest Transfer LLC	Outstanding Shares	33,610,000
Counsel	Anslow Jaclin, LLP	E.P.S.	$0.24
DUNS No.	NA	Shareholders	NA

Business: The groups principle activities include developing, producing, and selling of health food products. The group products include Nestle(TM), Soybean, Millet, Cactus. The group operates from the United State.

Primary SIC and add'l.: 2870

CIK No: 0001113546

Subsidiaries: Harbin Yingxia Industrial Group Co., Ltd, Warner Nutraceutical International, Inc.

Officers: Jiao Yingxia/Chmn., CEO, Zhang Ping/COO, Xu Wanhan/Chief Marketing Officer, Chen Weiming/CFO

Directors: Jiao Yingxia/Chmn., CEO, Gerald Montiel/61/Dir., Zhaobo Wang/52/Dir.

Owners: Yingxia Jiao/47.16%, Fuling Jiao/6.59%, Lantin Deng/14.29%, Insiders/61.45%

Financial Data: Fiscal Year End:12/31   Latest Annual Data: 12/31/2006

Year	Sales		Net Income
2006	$8,402,000		$5,340,000
2005	$0		-$715,000
2004	$0		-$1,465,000
Curr. Assets:	$4,843,000	Curr. Liab.:	$910,000		
Plant, Equip.:	$14,991,000	Total Liab.:	$910,000	Indic. Yr. Divd.:	NA
Total Assets:	$20,128,000	Net Worth:	$19,218,000	Debt/ Equity:	NA

China Yuchai International Ltd

16 Raffles Quay No. 26-00, Hong Leong Bldg, 48581; *PH:* 65-63226220; *http://* www.hlcorp.com.sg/cyi

General - Incorporation	Bermuda	**Stock**- Price on:12/24/2007	$10.4
Employees	8,827	Stock Exchange	NYSE
Auditor	KPMG LLP	Ticker Symbol	CYD
Stk Agt	Mellon Investor Services LLC	Outstanding Shares	37,270,000
Counsel	Sullivan & Cromwell	E.P.S.	NA
DUNS No.	NA	Shareholders	NA

Business: The group's principal activities are manufacturing, assembling and selling of diesel engine for light-duty, medium-duty and heavy-duty trucks and buses in the PRC. Its main manufacturing facility is located Yulin City in the Guangxi Zhuang Autonomous Region.

Primary SIC and add'l.: 3519 3714 3621

CIK No: 0000932695

Subsidiaries: Baotou Yuchai Machinery Monopoly Company Limited, Beijing Jingduo Yuchai Trade Company Limited, Cathay Diesel Holdings Ltd., Changsha Yuchai Marketing Company Limited (formerly known as Changsha Yuchai Machinery Monopoly Company Limited), Chengdu Yuchai Marketing Company Limited (formerly known as Chengdu Yuchai Machinery Monopoly Company Limited), Chongqing Yuchai Machinery Monopoly Company Limited, Constellation Star Holdings Limited, Earnest Assets Limited, Goldman Sachs Guangxi Holdings (BVI)Ltd., Guangxi Yuchai Machinery Company Limited, Guangxi Yulin Yuchai Machinery Spare Parts Manufacturing Company Limited, Guangzhou Yuchai Machinery Monopoly Company Limited, Hangzhou Yuchai Machinery Monopoly Company Limited, Hefei Yuchai Machinery Monopoly Company Limited, Hong Leong Technology Systems (BVI)Ltd. 33 Subsidiaries included in the Index

Officers: Teo Tong Kooi/Dir., Pres., Ira Stuart Outerbridge/Sec.

Directors: Gao J. Lin/Dir., Teo Tong Kooi/Dir., Pres., Kwek Leng Peck/Dir., Gan Khai Choon/Dir., Philip Ting Sii Tien/Dir., Wong Hong Ren/Dir.

Owners: Tai Tak Industries Pte Ltd/5.20%, Hong Leong Asia Ltd./21.20%, The Yulin City Government/23.10%

Financial Data: Fiscal Year End:12/31   Latest Annual Data: 12/31/2005

Year	Sales		Net Income
2005	$722,340,000		$8,486,000
2004	$674,451,000		$59,372,000
2003	$552,964,000		$53,020,000
Curr. Assets:	$516,794,000	Curr. Liab.:	$397,912,000	P/E Ratio:	31.26
Plant, Equip.:	$235,734,000	Total Liab.:	$489,052,000	Indic. Yr. Divd.:	NA
Total Assets:	$819,532,000	Net Worth:	$330,480,000	Debt/ Equity:	NA

China-Biotics Inc

No 999 Ningqiao Rd., Jinqiao Export Pro, Pudong, Shanghai, F4 201206; *PH:* 86-21-5834-9748

General - Incorporation		**Stock**- Price on:12/24/2007	$7.5
Employees	NA	Stock Exchange	OTC
Auditor	NA	Ticker Symbol	CHBT
Stk Agt	NA	Outstanding Shares	NA
Counsel	NA	E.P.S.	NA
DUNS No.	NA	Shareholders	NA

Business: The groups principle activity is to provide recruiting services. The groups service area includes the research and development, engineering, marketing, sales, information technology and manufacturing industries. The group operates from United States.

Primary SIC and add'l.: 1400

CIK No:

Subsidiaries: Growing State Limited, Shanghai Shining Biotechnology Co. Ltd, Sinosmart Group Inc.

Financial Data: Fiscal Year End:NA   Latest Annual Data: 03/31/2007

Year	Sales		Net Income
2007	$30,610,000		$10,905,000
Curr. Assets:	$2,000	Curr. Liab.:	NA		
Plant, Equip.:	NA	Total Liab.:	NA	Indic. Yr. Divd.:	NA
Total Assets:	$2,000	Net Worth:	$2,000	Debt/ Equity:	NA

Chinawe Com Inc

Rm. 1304-05, Dongbao Tower, 767 Dongfeng Rd. E, Guangzhou, 510600; *PH:* 86-23810818; *http://* www.chinawe.com

General - Incorporation	CA	**Stock**- Price on:12/24/2007	$0.1
Employees	26	Stock Exchange	OTC
Auditor	Moores Rowland Mazars	Ticker Symbol	CHWE
Stk Agt	Signature Stock Transfer, Inc.	Outstanding Shares	43,800,000
Counsel	NA	E.P.S.	-$0.01
DUNS No.	NA	Shareholders	NA

Business: The group's principle activity is to provide e-commerce services for buyers and suppliers of products made in China. These services will enable buyer and supplier members to efficiently and cost-effectively buy and sell products in an open e-Marketplace. The group provides product and suppliers search engines, a message board, sample sale, factory outlet and business-related services covering the entire product sales lifecycle. The group's quarterly revenue for September 2007 was 0.19 millions of USD.

Primary SIC and add'l.: 7379

CIK No: 0001043222

Subsidiaries: Chinawe Asset Management (PRC) Limited, Chinawe Asset Management Limited, Officeway Technology Limited

Officers: Edward Ziyi/Financial Mgr.

Owners: Man Keung Alan Wai, Barry Yiu, Insiders, Charter One Investments Limited, Gonet Associates Ltd.

Financial Data: Fiscal Year End:12/31   Latest Annual Data: 12/31/2006

Year	Sales		Net Income
2006	$1,477,000		-$96,000
2005	$1,221,000		$213,000
2004	$304,000		$40,000
Curr. Assets:	$686,000	Curr. Liab.:	$1,647,000		
Plant, Equip.:	$87,000	Total Liab.:	$1,674,000	Indic. Yr. Divd.:	NA
Total Assets:	$773,000	Net Worth:	-$901,000	Debt/ Equity:	NA

Chindex International Inc

7201 Wisconsin Ave., Bethesda, MD, 20814; *PH:* 1-301-215-7777; *Fax:* 1-301-215-7719; *http://* www.chindex.com; *Email:* info@chindex.com

General - Incorporation	DE	**Stock**- Price on:12/24/2007	$23.56
Employees	1,699	Stock Exchange	NDQ
Auditor	BDO Seidman LLP	Ticker Symbol	CHDX
Stk Agt	American Stock Transfer & Trust Co.	Outstanding Shares	7,280,000
Counsel	NA	E.P.S.	$0.23
DUNS No.	05-361-8450	Shareholders	NA

Business: The group's principle activity is to market and sell medical equipment, consumable and other healthcare products. It also provides marketing, sales and technical services for the products. The group operates through three segments: healthcare products segment consists of the capital healthcare equipment and the healthcare product distribution market groupings. Healthcare services segment offers family healthcare services, mental health services for men, women and children. In addition to the sale of capital equipment, the group's products distribution business, imports and distributes off-the-shelf healthcare instrumentation and consumable products. Medical capital equipment segment markets, sells and facilitates the export of select capital healthcare equipment and instrumentation. The group's total revenue for year 2007 was 105.92 millions of USD.

Primary SIC and add'l.: 8062 5047 8093 8072 8069

CIK No: 0000922717

Subsidiaries: Beijing United Family Hospital and Clinics (BJU), Chindex Shanghai, Chindex Tianjin, Shanghai United Family Hospital and Clinics (SHU)

Officers: Roberta Lipson/53/Dir., CEO, Pres./$425,109.00, Zhang Pin Qing/VP - Technical Service, Elyse Beth Silverberg/Dir., Exec. VP, Sec./$339,365.00, Lawrence Pemble/Dir., CFO, Exec. VP, Treasurer/$356,260.00, Emilie Lu/GM - Medical Products Distribution Operations, Walter Stryker/Sr. VP - China Administration, Walter Xue/VP - Finance, Controller - China, Daniel Fulton/VP - Information Technology Services, Judy Zakreski/VP - US Operations, Cheryl Chartier/Corporate Controller

Directors: Roberta Lipson/53/Dir., CEO, Pres., Kenneth A. Nilsson/Chmn., Holli Harris/Dir., Julius Y. Oestreicher/Dir., Carol R. Kaufman/Dir., Elyse Beth Silverberg/Dir., Exec. VP, Sec., Lawrence Pemble/Dir., CFO, Exec. VP, Treasurer

Owners: Roberta Lipson/56.80%, General Motors Investment Management Corporation/5.10%, Roberta Lipson/2.70%, Lawrence Pemble/1.20%, Elyse Beth Silverberg/2.90%, Holli Harris, Insiders/100.00%, Anne Marie Moncure, Magenta Magic Limited/17.90%, Julius Y. Oestreicher/1.90%, Elyse Beth Silverberg/33.60%, Andrew Edward Gold/8.80%, Carol R. Kaufman/1.20%, A. Kenneth Nilsson, Insiders/10.10% *(19 Owners included in Index)*

Financial Data: Fiscal Year End:03/31   **Latest Annual Data:** 3/31/2007

Year	Sales			Net Income
2007		$105,921,000		$2,735,000
2006		$90,836,000		-$2,938,000
2005		$100,775,000		-$5,658,000
Curr. Assets:	$34,756,000	**Curr. Liab.:**	$25,748,000	
Plant, Equip.:	$19,119,000	**Total Liab.:**	$34,408,000	**Indic. Yr. Divd.:** NA
Total Assets:	$57,046,000	**Net Worth:**	$22,638,000	**Debt/ Equity:** 0.4016

ChineseWorldNet.com Inc

1199 Pender St. W , Ste. 368, Vancouver, BC, V6E 2R1; **PH:** 1-604-488-8878; **Fax:** 1-604-488-0868; **http://** corp.chineseworldnet.com; **Email:** info@chineseworldnet.com

General - Incorporation	Cayman Islands	Stock- Price on:12/24/2007	$1.25
Employees	NA	Stock Exchange	OTC
Auditor	Vellmer & Chang	Ticker Symbol	CWNOF
Stk Agt	Securities Transfer Corp	Outstanding Shares	NA
Counsel	Baker & McKenzie	E.P.S.	NA
DUNS No.	NA	Shareholders	NA

Business: The groups principle activity is to provide internet financial portal and investor relations. The groups services include summary company profiles, analysts buy/sell ratings, company news; insider trading information, financial statement summary. The group operates from North America and Asia.

Primary SIC and add'l.: 8741

CIK No: 0001145898

Subsidiaries: ChineseWorldNet.com (Hong Kong) Ltd, NAI Interactive Ltd

Officers: Joe K.F. Tai/Dir., Founder, CEO, Pres., Chi Cheong Liu/Dir., Treasurer, John R. Ing/Advisor, Edward Y.K. Wong/Advisor, Gilbert Chan/Sr. VP - Marketing, Investor Relations, Kelvin Szeto/Co - Founder, CFO, COO, Sr. VP - Operations, Lixin Yang/VP - Editing, Frank Feng/Systems Administrator, Karl So/Web Developer, Fornia Lau/Mgr. - Business Development, Vivien Leung/30/Corp. Sec.

Directors: Joe K.F. Tai/Dir., Founder, CEO, Pres., Chi Cheong Liu/Dir., Treasurer, Chi Kong Liu/Dir., Andy S.W. Lam/Dir., Kelvin Szeto/Co - Founder, CFO, COO, Sr. VP - Operations

Owners: Chi Cheong Liu/22.45%, Kelvin Szeto/1.78%, Gilbert Chan/0.60%, Lixin Yang/0.12%, Joe Tai/3.00%, Insiders/34.64%, Chi Kong Liu/6.75%

Financial Data: Fiscal Year End:12/31   **Latest Annual Data:** 12/31/2006

Year	Sales			Net Income
2006		$643,000		-$210,000
Curr. Assets:	$204,000	**Curr. Liab.:**	$439,000	
Plant, Equip.:	$23,000	**Total Liab.:**	$439,000	**Indic. Yr. Divd.:** NA
Total Assets:	$227,000	**Net Worth:**	-$212,000	**Debt/ Equity:** NA

Chino Commercial Bancorp

14345 Pipeline Ave., Chino, CA, 91710; **PH:** 1-909-465-1220; **http://** www.chinocommercialbank.com; **Email:** service@chinocommercialbank.com

General - Incorporation	CA	Stock- Price on:12/24/2007	$25
Employees	27	Stock Exchange	OTC
Auditor	Hutchinson & Bloodgood, LLP	Ticker Symbol	CCBC
Stk Agt	U.S. Stock Transfer Corp	Outstanding Shares	NA
Counsel	NA	E.P.S.	$1.07
DUNS No.	NA	Shareholders	NA

Business: The group operates through its subsidiary whose principal activity is banking operations. The group products include real estate loans, commercial real estate loans, mobile home loans, home equity lines-of-credit, construction, land loans and accepting deposits. The groups asset in the year 2005 was $10,594,862. The group operates from the United States.

Primary SIC and add'l.: 6712

CIK No: 0001365794

Subsidiaries: Chino Statutory Trust I

Officers: Dann H. Bowman/Dir., CEO, Pres., Jeanette L. Young/Dir., Corp. Sec., Polyanna Franks/Dir. - Healthcare Consultant, Roger Caberto/61/Sr. VP, Chief Credit Officer

Directors: Dann H. Bowman/Dir., CEO, Pres., H. H. Kindsvater/Vice Chmn., Jeanette L. Young/Dir., Corp. Sec., Linda M. Cooper/Dir., Polyanna Franks/Dir. - Healthcare Consultant, Richard G. Malooly/Dir., Rick J. Vanderpool/Dir., Thomas A. Woodbury/Dir., Bernard J. Wolfswinkel/Dir.

Owners: Dann H. Bowman/11.64%, Bernard J. Wolfswinkel/4.31%, Jeanette L. Young/2.35%, Roger Caberto, Richard J. Vanderpool/2.27%, Richard G. Malooly/3.06%, H. H. Kindsvater/4.57%, Pollyanna Franks/2.98%, Linda M. Cooper/2.71%, Insiders/34.17%, Thomas A. Woodbury/4.10%, Sandra F. Pender

Financial Data: Fiscal Year End:09/30   **Latest Annual Data:** 12/31/2002

Year	Sales			Net Income
2002		$2,347,000		$203,000
2001		$1,551,000		-$229,000
2000		$233,000		-$219,000
Curr. Assets:	$5,619,000	**Curr. Liab.:**	$36,535,000	**P/E Ratio:** 24.27
Plant, Equip.:	$442,000	**Total Liab.:**	$36,747,000	**Indic. Yr. Divd.:** NA
Total Assets:	$41,683,000	**Net Worth:**	$4,936,000	**Debt/ Equity:** NA

ChipMOS Technologies (Bermuda) Ltd

11F, No. 3, Ln. 91, Dongmei Rd, Hsinchu, 300; **PH:** 886-35716088; **http://** www.chipmos.com.tw; **Email:** chipmos_bermuda@chipmos.com.tw

General - Incorporation	Bermuda	Stock- Price on:12/24/2007	$6.9
Employees	4,905	Stock Exchange	NDQ
Auditor	Moore Stephens	Ticker Symbol	IMOS
Stk Agt	Mellon Investor Services LLC	Outstanding Shares	71,110,000
Counsel	Sullivan & Cromwell	E.P.S.	$0.59
DUNS No.	NA	Shareholders	NA

Business: The groups principle activity is to provide semiconductor and back-end testing services including engineering testing, wafer probing and final testing for memory and mixed-signal semiconductors; as well as testing services for liquid crystal display driver semiconductors. The group operates from United States.

Primary SIC and add'l.: 3674

CIK No: 0001133478

Subsidiaries: ChipMOS TECHNOLOGIES (H.K.) Limited, ChipMOS TECHNOLOGIES (Shanghai) LTD., ChipMOS TECHNOLOGIES INC, Modern Mind Technology Limited, ThaiLin Semiconductor Corp.

Officers: Shih-Jye Cheng/Chmn., CEO, Jesse Huang/42/VP - Assembly Production Group, Jeff Chang/Accounting Deputy Assist. VP - Chipmos Testing Fab, Leo Lin/Accounting Deputy Assist. VP - Chipmos Assembly Fab, Chipmos Gold Bumping Fab, Michael Lee/43/VP - Wafer Sort Business Unit, Robert Tsai/49/VP - Information Technology Management, Ivan Hsu/42/VP - Memory Production Group, Jessie Lin/43/VP - Quality, Reliability, Assurance Center, Joyce Chang/47/VP - Lcdd Production Group, Lafair Cho/Pres. - ThaiLin, F. J. Tsai/Pres. - Chipmos USA, Inc, Shou-Kang Chen/Dir., CFO, Ricky Liu/46/VP - Wafer Bump, Wafer Fab Task Business Unit, Ray Lin/Mgr. - Chipmos Japan INC

Directors: Shih-Jye Cheng/Chmn., CEO, Pierre Laflamme/Dep. Chmn., Shou-Kang Chen/Dir., CFO, Chao-Jung Tsai/Dir., Robert Shen/58/Dir., Antonio R. Alvarez/Dir., Rong Hsu/Dir., Takaki Yamada/Dir., Yeong-Her Wang/Dir., Hsing-Ti Tuan/Dir.

Owners: Siliconware Precision Industries Co., Ltd/14.70%, Mosel Vitelic Inc/23.20%, Insiders/1.30%, Highbridge International LLC/13.60%

Financial Data: Fiscal Year End:12/31   **Latest Annual Data:** 12/31/2006

Year	Sales			Net Income
2006		$625,198,000		$38,451,000
2005		$463,841,000		$24,554,000
2004		$473,718,000		$52,473,000
Curr. Assets:	$436,716,000	**Curr. Liab.:**	$207,041,000	**P/E Ratio:** 7.35
Plant, Equip.:	$942,145,000	**Total Liab.:**	$751,571,000	**Indic. Yr. Divd.:** NA
Total Assets:	$1,409,157,000	**Net Worth:**	$657,586,000	**Debt/ Equity:** NA

Chipotle Mexican Grill Inc

1543 Wazee St., Ste. 200, Denver, CO, 80202; **PH:** 1-303-595-4000; **Fax:** 1-303-595-4014; **http://** www.chipotle.com

General - Incorporation	DE	Stock- Price on:12/24/2007	$83.45
Employees	15,000	Stock Exchange	NYSE
Auditor	Ernst & Young LLP	Ticker Symbol	CMG
Stk Agt	Computershare Trust Co	Outstanding Shares	32,790,000
Counsel	NA	E.P.S.	$1.67
DUNS No.	NA	Shareholders	NA

Business: The groups principle activity is to operate restaurants. The group operates 570 restaurants in 26 states and the District of Columbia, in the United States. The group's quarterly revenue for September 2007 was 286.43 millions of USD.

Primary SIC and add'l.: 5812

CIK No: 0001058090

Subsidiaries: Chipotle International, Limited, Chipotle Mexican Grill of Colorado, LLC, Chipotle Mexican Grill of Kansas, LLC, Chipotle Mexican Grill of Maryland, LLC, Chipotle Mexican Grill Texas Holdings, LLC, Chipotle Texas, LLC, CMGGC, LLC

Officers: Steve Ells/Chmn., CEO/$1,788,480.00, John R. Hartung/Chief Finance, Development Officer/$1,236,779.00, Montgomery F. Moran/Dir., COO, Pres./$2,234,782.00, Robert D. Wilner/Chief Administrative Officer/$946,234.00, Bob Wilner/Chief Administrative Officer

Directors: Steve Ells/Chmn., CEO, Montgomery F. Moran/Dir., COO, Pres., Albert S. Baldocchi/Dir., John S. Charlesworth/Dir., Patrick J. Flynn/Dir., Darlene J. Friedman/Dir., Neil W. Flanzraich/Dir.

Owners: AXA Financial, Inc./9.27%, AXA Financial, Inc., Montgomery Moran, Janus Capital ManagementLLC/4.98%, Robert Wilner, Insiders/6.36%, Albert Baldocchi, Veredus Asset Management,LLC/7.35%, Darlene Friedman, Capital Research& Management Co./5.36%, Patrick Flynn, Darlene Friedman, John Charlesworth, Robert Wilner, Steve Ells *(23 Owners included in Index)*

Financial Data: Fiscal Year End:12/31   **Latest Annual Data:** 12/31/2006

Year	Sales			Net Income
2006		$822,930,000		$41,423,000
2005		$627,695,000		$37,696,000
2004		$470,721,000		$6,126,000
Curr. Assets:	$178,837,000	**Curr. Liab.:**	$61,201,000	**P/E Ratio:** 49.97
Plant, Equip.:	$404,740,000	**Total Liab.:**	$130,251,000	**Indic. Yr. Divd.:** NA
Total Assets:	$604,208,000	**Net Worth:**	$473,957,000	**Debt/ Equity:** 0.0082

Chiquita Brands International Inc

250 E 5th St., Cincinnati, OH, 45202; **PH:** 1-513-784-8000; **Fax:** 1-513-784-8030; **http://** www.chiquita.com

General - Incorporation	NJ	Stock- Price on:12/24/2007	$19.41
Employees	25,000	Stock Exchange	NYSE
Auditor	Ernst & Young LLP	Ticker Symbol	CQB
Stk Agt	Wells Fargo Shareowner Services	Outstanding Shares	NA
Counsel	NA	E.P.S.	-$3.15
DUNS No.	05-154-1597	Shareholders	NA

Business: The group's principle activities include marketing, producing and distributing bananas, pineapples and avocados. The groups products sold under the brand name CHIQUITA. The bananas The group operates from United States.

Primary SIC and add'l.: 0175 0174 5148 2033 2079 0179 2099

CIK No: 0000101063

Subsidiaries: Atlanta Aktiengesllschaft, Atlanta Finanz Service GmbH& Co. KG, Atlanta World Trade GmbH, Bocas Fruit Co. LLC, BVS Ltd., CB Containers, Inc., CDV Ltd., CDY Ltd., Chiquita Banana Company B.V., Chiquita Brands LLC, Chiquita Compagnie des Bananes, Chiquita Far East Holdings B.V., Chiquita Fresh Cut, LLC, Chiquita Fresh North America LLC, Chiquita International Limited 36 Subsidiaries included in the Index

Officers: Steve Warshaw/CEO, Pres., Fernando Aguirre/Chmn., COO, Pres./$3,019,711.00, James E. Thompson/Sr. VP, General Counsel, Sec., Jim Riley/Sr. VP, Kevin Holland/Sr. VP - Human Resources, Manuel Rodriguez/Sr. VP - Government, International Affairs, Corporate Responsibility

Officer, Barbara Wagner/Assoc. General Counsel, Assist. Sec., Tanios E. Viviani/Pres. - Fresh Express/$1,131,609.00, Joseph W. Bradley/VP - Taxation, Michel Loeb/Pres. - Chiquita Fresh Group, Europe, Robert Olson/Sr. VP, General Counsel, Sec./$1,853,862.00, Waheed Zaman/Sr. VP - Supply Chain, Global Procurement, CIO, Robert F. Kistinger/COO, Pres. - Chiquita Fresh Group/$1,668,727.00, Peter Jung/Pres. - Atlanta AG, Brian W. Kocher/VP, Controller, Chief Accounting Officer *(32 Officers included in Index)*

Directors: Fernando Aguirre/Chmn., COO, Pres., Robert W. Fisher/68/Dir., Jaime Serra/54/Dir., Durk I. Jager/62/Dir., Morten Arntzen/50/Dir., Clare M. Hasler/50/Dir., Steven P. Stanbrook/48/Dir., Howard W. Barker/61/Dir.

Owners: Insiders/4.50%, Jeffrey M. Zalla, Jaime Serra, Robert W. Fisher, Dimensional Fund Advisors LP/6.45%, Robert W. Olson, James Gallagher, Robert F. Kistinger/1.30%, Steven P. Stanbrook, FMR Corp./14.89%, Durk I. Jager, Roderick M. Hills, Wells Fargo& Company/5.54%, Clare M. Hasler, Tanios Viviani *(17 Owners included in Index)*

Financial Data: **Fiscal Year End:** 12/31 **Latest Annual Data:** 12/31/2006

Year	Sales	Net Income
2006	$4,499,084,000	-$95,934,000
2005	$3,904,361,000	$131,440,000
2004	$3,071,456,000	$55,402,000

Curr. Assets:	$876,493,000	**Curr. Liab.:**	$629,618,000		
Plant, Equip.:	$573,316,000	**Total Liab.:**	$1,867,717,000	**Indic. Yr. Divd.:**	$0.400
Total Assets:	$2,738,544,000	**Net Worth:**	$870,827,000	**Debt/ Equity:**	1.0956

Chiron Corp

4560 Horton St., Emeryville, CA, 94608; **PH:** 1-510-655-8730; **Fax:** 1-510-655-9910; **http://** www.chiron.com

General - Incorporation	DE	**Stock** - Price on:12/24/2007	NA
Employees	297	Stock Exchange	NDQ
Auditor	Ernst & Young LLP	Ticker Symbol	CHIR
Stk Agt	Computershare Trust Co of New York	Outstanding Shares	NA
Counsel	NA	E.P.S	NA
DUNS No.	04-686-6463	Shareholders	NA

Business: The group's principal activity is to develop, manufacture and market human healthcare products. It operates in three segments: blood testing segment develops and markets a range of blood safety products used by the blood banking and transfusion medicine industry; vaccines segment offers more than 30 vaccines including flu, meningococcal, travel and pediatric vaccines and biophamaceuticals discovers, develops, manufactures and markets a range of therapeutic products. Its products include procleix(R) HIV-1/hcv assay, riba(R) tests, procleix(R) ultriotm assay, procleix(R) wnv assay dtp, diphtheria, tetanus and pertussis (whooping couch) vaccine and oral polio vaccine, tobi(R) (tobramycin solution for inhalation) for pseudomonal lung infections in cystic fibrosis patients and proleukin(R) for cancer. In 2003 it discontinued pa-2794 and research and development of angiozyme. It acquired sagres discovery on 02-Jul-2004 and prion solutions inc on 31-Aug-2004.

Primary SIC and add'l.: 2836 8099 2833

CIK No: 0000706539

Subsidiaries: AlgoRx Pharmaceuticals Inc., Appold Consultadoria E Servios,Sociedade Unipessoal, Lda, Bavarian Nordic AS, Biocent Insurance Company, Inc., Cetus Generic Corporation, Chiron AB, Chiron Alpha Corporation, Chiron B-1 Limited, Chiron B-2 Limited, Chiron B.V., Chiron Behring GmbH & Co KG, Chiron Behring Vaccines Private Limited, Chiron Behring Verwaltungsgesellschaft mbH, Chiron Biotecnologia Limitada Brazil, Chiron Blood Testing (Bermuda) Ltd. 58 Subsidiaries included in the Index

Officers: Gene Walther/Pres.

Chittenden Corp

2 Burlington Sq., Burlington, VT, 05401; **PH:** 1-802-658-4000; **Fax:** 1-802-660-2300; **http://** www.chittendencorp.com

General - Incorporation	VT	**Stock** - Price on:12/24/2007	$28.47
Employees	1,947	Stock Exchange	NYSE
Auditor	PricewaterhouseCoopers LLP	Ticker Symbol	CHZ
Stk Agt	Computershare Ltd.	Outstanding Shares	NA
Counsel	NA	E.P.S	$1.59
DUNS No.	00-793-9515	Shareholders	NA

Business: The group's principal activity is to provide financial services through its banking subsidiaries. The services include offering loans and acceptance of deposits. The loan portfolio includes commercial, real estate and consumer loans. The group also accepts deposits which includes demand, savings negotiable orders of withdrawal, money market and certificates of deposits. Other services rendered by the group includes payroll processing, merchant-processing services, mortgage servicing, business credit card services and automated clearing house for several outside clients. The customers of the group are retail concerns, small manufacturing businesses, larger corporations and political subdivisions. On 28-Feb-2003, the group acquired granite state bankshares, inc.

Primary SIC and add'l.: 6712 6022

CIK No: 0000200138

Subsidiaries: Bank of Western Massachusetts, Flagship Bank and Trust, Granite Bank, Maine Bank & Trust, Ocean National Bank, Vermont National Bank

Officers: Paul A. Perrault/Chmn., CEO, Pres./$1,430,733.00, Eugenie J. Fortin/Assist. Corp. Sec., Assist. VP, Kirk W. Walters/Exec. VP, CFO, Treasurer/$619,178.00, Sheldon F. Prentice/Sr. VP, General Counsel, Corp. Sec., Larry W. MacKinnon/Sr. VP, Chief Credit Officer, Howard L. Atkinson/Chief Auditor, John P. Barnes/CHZ Services Group/$619,117.00

Directors: Paul A. Perrault/Chmn., CEO, Pres., Lyn Hutton/Dir., Mark W. Richards/Dir., James C. Pizzagalli/Dir., Pall D. Spera/Dir., Ernest A. Pomerleau/Dir., Sally W. Crawford/Dir., Philip M. Drumheller/Dir., John K. Dwight/Dir., Owen W. Wells/Dir.

Owners: George A. Vanderheiden/1.00%, Irene S. Kimball/1.47%, Eugene F. Leone/1.14%, Richard A. Rollins/2.02%, Donald A. St. Germain, Thomas A. ODowd/0.78%, Bradford W. Gile/7.96%, Peter B. Alden/1.47%, Gregory A. Roark/6.21%, David Q. Bowers/6.32%, Walter P. Borowski/0.50%, David S. Sands/5.66%, Insiders/28.36%

Financial Data: **Fiscal Year End:** 12/31 **Latest Annual Data:** 12/31/2006

Year	Sales	Net Income
2006	$444,901,000	$85,468,000
2005	$390,206,000	$83,391,000
2004	$344,366,000	$75,127,000

Curr. Assets:	$232,481,000	**Curr. Liab.:**	$5,624,308,000	**P/E Ratio:**	17.91
Plant, Equip.:	$67,036,000	**Total Liab.:**	$5,760,717,000	**Indic. Yr. Divd.:**	$0.880
Total Assets:	$6,431,803,000	**Net Worth:**	$671,086,000	**Debt/ Equity:**	0.3939

Choice Hotels International Inc

10750 Columbia Pike, Silver Spring, MD, 20901; **PH:** 1-301-592-5000; **Fax:** 1-301-592-6157; **http://** www.choicehotels.com

General - Incorporation	DE	**Stock** - Price on:12/24/2007	$40.6
Employees	1,860	Stock Exchange	NYSE
Auditor	PricewaterhouseCoopers LLP	Ticker Symbol	CHH
Stk Agt	Computershare Investor Services LLC	Outstanding Shares	66,120,000
Counsel	NA	E.P.S	$1.63
DUNS No.	00-407-5271	Shareholders	NA

Business: The group's principle activity is to provide hotel franchising services. The group has 4,810 hotel properties and 491 hotels under development representing 388,618 rooms open and 39,877 rooms under development in 44 countries and territories. The group franchises lodging properties under the following brand names comfort inn(R), comfort suites(R), quality(R), clarion(R), sleep inn(R), econo lodge(R), rodeway inn(R), mainstay suites(R) and flag hotels. The group's franchises operate in all 49 states, Puerto Rico and 41 additional countries and territories. The group enters into franchise agreements committing to provide franchisees with various marketing services, a centralized reservation system and limited rights to utilize the company's registered tradenames and trademarks. The group operates from United States.

Primary SIC and add'l.: 7011

CIK No: 0001046311

Subsidiaries: Brentwood Boulevard Hotel Development, LLC, Choice Capital Corp., Choice Hospitality (India) Private Ltd., Choice Hoteles de Mexico S. de R.L. de C.V., Choice Hotels Australasia Pty. Ltd., Choice Hotels Australia Pty. Ltd., Choice Hotels Canada, Inc., Choice Hotels International Services Corp., Choice Hotels Limited, Choice Hotels Netherlands Antilles N.V., Choice Hotels Systems, Inc., Choice International Hospitality Services Licensing Co. B.V, Choice International Hospitality Services, Inc., Dry Pocket Road Hotel Development, LLC, Hotelsupplies.com, LLC 19 Subsidiaries included in the Index

Officers: Charles A. Ledsinger/Vice Chmn., CEO/$5,558,506.00, David L. White/CFO/$442,134.00, David Goldberg/Sr. VP - Brand Value, Janna Morrison/Sr. VP - Customer Care, Technology, Bruce Haase/Sr. VP - Brand Operations, International, Gary Thomson/CIO, Sr. VP, David Pepper/Sr. VP - Franchise Growth, Performance, Thomas Mirgon/Sr. VP - Human Resources, Administration/$1,012,819.00, Mary Beth Beth Knight/Sr. VP - E, Commerce, Paul Mamalian/General Counsel, Scott Oaksmith/Controller, Kevin J. Bradt/Division Pres. - Economy Marketing Brands

Directors: Charles A. Ledsinger/Vice Chmn., CEO, Stewart Bainum/Chmn., Fiona Dias/Dir., William L. Jews/Dir., John T. Schwieters/Dir., Ervin R. Shames/Dir., Gordon A. Smith/Dir., David Sullivan/Dir.

Owners: Insiders, Fiona Dias, Gordon A. Smith, David L. White, David C. Sullivan, Stewart Bainum, Bruce Bainum, John T. Schwieters, Stewart Bainum, Ervin R. Shames, Barbara Bainum, Thomas Mirgon, Barclays Global Investors, N.A., Roberta Bainum, Realty Investment Company, Inc. *(19 Owners included in Index)*

Financial Data: **Fiscal Year End:** 12/31 **Latest Annual Data:** 12/31/2006

Year	Sales	Net Income
2006	$544,662,000	$112,787,000
2005	$477,399,000	$87,565,000
2004	$428,806,000	$74,345,000

Curr. Assets:	$87,082,000	**Curr. Liab.:**	$139,791,000	**P/E Ratio:**	23.47
Plant, Equip.:	$42,802,000	**Total Liab.:**	$365,689,000	**Indic. Yr. Divd.:**	$0.680
Total Assets:	$303,309,000	**Net Worth:**	-$62,380,000	**Debt/ Equity:**	NA

Choiceone Financial Services Inc

109 E Div. St., Sparta, MI, 49345; **PH:** 1-616-887-7366; **Fax:** 1-616-887-7990; **http://** www.choiceone.com; **Email:** ch1info@choiceone.com

General - Incorporation	MI	**Stock** - Price on:12/24/2007	$15.9
Employees	157	Stock Exchange	OTC
Auditor	Plant & Moran, PLLC	Ticker Symbol	COFS
Stk Agt	Registrar & Transfer Co	Outstanding Shares	3,240,000
Counsel	NA	E.P.S	$1.10
DUNS No.	00-890-3247	Shareholders	NA

Business: The group's principal activity is to offer a variety of deposit, payment, credit and other financial services to all types of customers. Its principal banking subsidiary is choiceone bank. The services of the bank include time, savings and demand deposits, safe deposit services and automated transaction machine services. The group's market area consists of portions of kent, muskegon, newaygo and ottawa counties in Michigan. The services are provided through 4 full-service offices and one drive-up facility. In addition, the group markets a full line of insurance policies such as life, health, property and casualty for both commercial and consumer clients. It also offers investment products such as annuities and mutual funds.

Primary SIC and add'l.: 6022 6712

CIK No: 0000803164

Subsidiaries: ChoiceOne Bank, ChoiceOne Insurance Agencies, Inc, ChoiceOne Mortgage Company of Michigan, West Shore Computer Services, Inc

Officers: Kelly Potes/46/Sr. VP, GM - Choiceone Insurance Agencies, Inc/$117,269.00, James A. Bosserd/Dir., CEO, Pres./$235,653.00, Linda R. Pitsch/Sec./$116,627.00, Louis D. Knooihuizen/Sr. VP - Commercial Loans, Bank/$122,074.00, Thomas L. Lampen/CFO, VP/$87,611.00, Mary J. Johnson/44/VP - Bank, Michael E. McHugh/Sr. VP, Sheila Clark/52/Sr. VP - Bank

Directors: James A. Bosserd/Dir., CEO, Pres., Richard L. Edgar/Chmn., Gary Gust/Dir., Jerome B. Arends/Dir., Timothy K. Bull/Dir., Robert C. Humphreys/Dir., Dennis Nelson/Dir., Donald Vansingel/Dir., William F. Cutler/Dir., Andrew W. Zamiara/Dir., Jon E. Pike/Dir., Paul L. Johnson/Dir., Frank G. Berris/Dir., Stuart Goodfellow/Dir., Bruce A. Johnson/Dir.

Owners: Kelly Potes, ChoiceOne Bank 401/5.00%, Linda Pitsch, Dennis Nelson, James A. Bosserd, Jon E. Pike, Richard L. Edgar/2.30%, Stuart Goodfellow/1.40%, Jerome B. Arends/1.50%, Gary Gust/1.80%, Donald VanSingel, Frank G. Berris, Insiders/21.50%, Timothy K. Bull/1.60%, Thomas L. Lampen *(20 Owners included in Index)*

Financial Data: **Fiscal Year End:** 12/31 **Latest Annual Data:** 12/31/2006

Year	Sales	Net Income
2006	$20,548,000	$2,088,000
2005	$15,932,000	$2,166,000
2004	$14,309,000	$1,854,000

Curr. Assets:	$9,936,000	**Curr. Liab.:**	$405,761,000	**P/E Ratio:**	14.45
Plant, Equip.:	$13,396,000	**Total Liab.:**	$415,131,000	**Indic. Yr. Divd.:**	$0.680
Total Assets:	$466,650,000	**Net Worth:**	$51,519,000	**Debt/ Equity:**	NA

ChoicePoint Inc

1000 Alderman Dr., Alpharetta, GA, 30005; *PH:* 1-770-752-6000; *Fax:* 1-770-752-6005;
http:// www.choicepointinc.com

General - Incorporation	GA	*Stock*- Price on:12/24/2007	$41.11
Employees	5,250	Stock Exchange	NYSE
Auditor	Deloitte & Touche LLP	Ticker Symbol	CPS
Stk Agt.... Computershare Investor Services LLC		Outstanding Shares	76,050,000
Counsel	Kong & Spalding	E.P.S.	$1.15
DUNS No.	15-293-0061	Shareholders	NA

Business: The group's principal activity is to provide risk management and fraud prevention information and related technology solutions. Insurance include information products and services used in the underwriting and claim processes by property and casualty insurers, laboratory testing and technology solutions to the life and health insurance market. B&G provide information products and services to Fortune 1000 corporations, service organizations and government agencies. The marketing provides direct marketing that includes data, print fulfillment, database, and Web-based delivery solutions. In 2003 the group acquired National Data Retrieval Inc, Mortgage Asset Research Institute Inc, Citi Network Inc d/b/a Applicant Screening & Processing, Brider systems Inc, Insurance Decisions Inc, TML Information Services Inc, Identico Systems LLC and The List Source Inc d/b/a Kramer Lead Marketing Group; and in 2004, Templar Corporation & Investigation Technologies, LLC.

Primary SIC and add'l.: 9999 7389 6411

CIK No: 0001040596

Subsidiaries: Anacubis Limited, Anacubis, Inc., C.l.u.e. Inc., Charles Jones Inc., ChoicePoint Asset Company, ChoicePoint Capital Inc., ChoicePoint Financial Inc., ChoicePoint Government Services Inc., ChoicePoint Licensing Company, ChoicePoint Police Records Inc., ChoicePoint Precision Marketing Inc., ChoicePoint Public Records Inc., ChoicePoint Services Inc., ChoicePoint UK 1 Limited, ChoicePoint UK 2 Limited 47 Subsidiaries included in the Index

Officers: Derek V. Smith/Chmn., CEO - Choicepoint Inc/$4,964,409.00, Douglas C. Curling/Dir., COO, Pres./$2,422,138.00, David W. Davis/Corp. Sec., Sr. VP - Government Affairs, David E. Trine/CFO/$652,397.00, Chuck Jones/Contact - Media, David T. Lee/Exec. VP, Chief Business Officer/$1,721,664.00, Steven W. Surbaugh/Exec. VP, Chief Administrative Officer/$1,349,307.00, Carol Dibattiste/General Counsel, Chief Privacy Officer, Jeffrey J. Glazer/Sr. VP, GM, John M. Mongelli/Treasurer, VP - Investor Relations, Carey Skinner/Assist. VP - Investor Relations

Directors: Derek V. Smith/Chmn., CEO - Choicepoint Inc, Kenneth G. Langone/Dir., Terrence Murray/Dir., Ray M. Robinson/Dir., John B. McCoy/Dir., Charles I. Story/Dir., Douglas C. Curling/Dir., COO, Pres., John J. Hamre/Dir., Anne M. Szostak/Dir., Renae E. Conley/Dir.

Owners: Oppenheimer Capital LLC/7.00%, Derek V. Smith/3.80%, Kenneth G. Langone/2.60%, Insiders/9.10%, Anne M. Szostak, Baron Capital Group, Inc/12.10%, David E. Trine, Capital Research and Management Company/6.80%, E. Renae Conley, Douglas C. Curling/1.30%, Charles I. Story, Steven W. Surbaugh, Ray M. Robinson, John J. Hamre, David T. Lee *(18 Owners included in Index)*

Financial Data: Fiscal Year End: 12/31   *Latest Annual Data:* 12/31/2006

Year	Sales		Net Income
2006	$1,054,992,000		$16,922,000
2005	$1,057,914,000		$140,656,000
2004	$918,713,000		$147,955,000
Curr. Assets:	$317,519,000	*Curr. Liab.:*	$309,997,000
Plant, Equip.:	$68,167,000	*Total Liab.:*	$679,105,000	*Indic. Yr. Divd.:* NA
Total Assets:	$1,346,092,000	*Net Worth:*	$666,987,000	*Debt/ Equity:* 0.5696

Cholestech Corp

3347 Investment Blvd, Hayward, CA, 94545; *PH:* 1-510-732-7200; *http://* www.cholestech.com

General - Incorporation	CA	*Stock*- Price on:12/24/2007	$22.09
Employees	216	Stock Exchange	NA
Auditor	PricewaterhouseCoopers LLP	Ticker Symbol	NA
Stk Agt..... Computershare Investor Services LLC		Outstanding Shares	15,590,000
Counsel	Wilson Sonsini Goodrich & Rosati	E.P.S.	$0.61
DUNS No.	18-647-8228	Shareholders	NA

Business: The group's principal activity is to manufacture and market diagnostic products. The group manufactures and markets the cholestech ldx(R) and cholestech gdx(tm) systems that assist in assessing the risk of heart disease, diabetes and certain liver diseases outside hospitals and laboratories. It markets and distributes the gdx system under a global distribution agreement with provalis diagnostics ltd. The group markets the products and services in the United States of America, Europe, Asia and South America.

Primary SIC and add'l.: 3821 8071

CIK No: 0000887227

Officers: Warren E. Pinckert/Dir., CEO, Pres., Terry L. Wassmann/VP - Human Resources, John F. Glenn/CFO, Corporate VP - Finance, Treasurer, Sec., Barbara T. McAleer/VP - Quality, Regulatory Affairs, Human Resources, Kenneth F. Miller/VP - Sales, Marketing, Donald P. Wood/VP - Operations, Gregory L. Bennett/VP - Research, Development

Directors: Warren E. Pinckert/Dir., CEO, Pres., John H. Landon/Chmn., Elizabeth H. Davila/Dir., Michael D. Casey/Dir., John L. Castello/Dir., Larry Y. Wilson/Dir., Stuart Heap/Dir.

Owners: Stuart Heap, John H. Landon, FMR Corp./14.97%, Elizabeth H. Dvila, Kenneth F. Miller, John F. Glenn, Larry Y. Wilson, Donald P. Wood, Barbara T. McAleer, Michael D. Casey, Insiders/6.30%, John L. Castello, Peninsula Capital Management, LP/5.00%, Warren E. Pinckert/2.50%

Financial Data: Fiscal Year End: 03/31   *Latest Annual Data:* 3/30/2007

Year	Sales		Net Income
2007	$69,526,000		$9,406,000
2006	$64,093,000		$5,634,000
2005	$52,877,000		$4,148,000
Curr. Assets:	$43,860,000	*Curr. Liab.:*	$6,570,000	*P/E Ratio:* 35.06
Plant, Equip.:	$7,820,000	*Total Liab.:*	$6,570,000	*Indic. Yr. Divd.:* NA
Total Assets:	$80,702,000	*Net Worth:*	$74,132,000	*Debt/ Equity:* NA

Christiana Bank & Trust Company

3801 Kennett Pike E155, Wilmington, DE, 19807; *PH:* 1-302-421-5800;
http:// www.christianatrust.com

General - Incorporation		*Stock*- Price on:12/24/2007	$26.1
Employees	53	Stock Exchange	OTC
Auditor	NA	Ticker Symbol	CBTD
Stk Agt	Registrar & Transfer Co	Outstanding Shares	1,490,000
Counsel	NA	E.P.S.	$1.18
DUNS No.	NA	Shareholders	NA

Business: The groups principal activity is to provide banking services. The services of the group include trust and deposit services, private banking, asset management, commercial lending and corporate and institutional trust services. The group operates from the United States.

Primary SIC and add'l.: 6029

CIK No: 0001312062

Officers: Zissimos A. Frangopoulos/CEO, Pres.

Financial Data: Fiscal Year End: NA   *Latest Annual Data:* 12/31/2002

Year	Sales		Net Income
2002	$8,323,000		$548,000
2001	$7,950,000		$500,000
2000	$7,260,000		$626,000
Curr. Assets:	$5,498,000	*Curr. Liab.:*	$82,450,000	*P/E Ratio:* 17.52
Plant, Equip.:	$3,490,000	*Total Liab.:*	$96,239,000	*Indic. Yr. Divd.:* NA
Total Assets:	$105,907,000	*Net Worth:*	$9,668,000	*Debt/ Equity:* 1.0799

Christie Fun Inc

PO Box 110310, Naples, FL, 34108; *PH:* 1-239-598-2300

General - Incorporation	DE	*Stock*- Price on:12/24/2007	NA
Employees	NA	Stock Exchange	NA
Auditor	Child, Sullivan & Co	Ticker Symbol	NA
Stk Agt	Nevada Agency & Trust Company	Outstanding Shares	NA
Counsel	NA	E.P.S.	NA
DUNS No.	NA	Shareholders	NA

Business: The groups principle activity is to locate a suitable business acquisition candidate and thereafter to complete a business acquisition transaction. The group operates from United States.

Primary SIC and add'l.: 9995

CIK No: 0001300902

Curr. Assets:	$236,000	*Curr. Liab.:*	$167,000	
Plant, Equip.:	$3,000	*Total Liab.:*	$167,000	*Indic. Yr. Divd.:* NA
Total Assets:	$343,000	*Net Worth:*	$175,000	*Debt/ Equity:* NA

Christopher & Banks Corp

2400 Xenium Ln. N, Plymouth, MN, 55441; *PH:* 1-763-551-5000; *Fax:* 1-763-551-5198;
http:// www.christopherandbanks.com; *Email:* info@christopherandbanks.com

General - Incorporation	DE	*Stock*- Price on:12/24/2007	$18.42
Employees	2,200	Stock Exchange	NYSE
Auditor	PricewaterhouseCoopers LLP	Ticker Symbol	CBK
Stk Agt	Wells Fargo Shareholder Services	Outstanding Shares	36,200,000
Counsel	Robins, Kaplan, Miller & Ciresi LLP	E.P.S.	$0.71
DUNS No.	15-758-5878	Shareholders	NA

Business: The group's principal activity is to operate retail specialty stores selling women's apparel in the United States, through its wholly-owned subsidiaries, christopher & banks, inc. And christopher & banks company. As of 30-Apr-2004, the group operated 556 stores in 42 states including 426 christopher & banks stores and 130 c.j. Banks stores. The group's christopher & banks offer distinctive fashions featuring exclusively designed, coordinated assortments of sportswear, sweaters and casual dresses in sizes four to 16. The c.j. Banks stores of the group offers similar assortments of women's specialty apparel in sizes 14w and up. The group operates solely in the domestic market.

Primary SIC and add'l.: 5632 5621

CIK No: 0000883943

Subsidiaries: Christopher & Banks Company, Christopher & Banks Services Company, Christopher & Banks, Inc, Ladbroke Racing Canterbury, Inc.

Officers: Matthew P. Dillon/48/Dir., CEO, Pres./$1,086,622.00, Lorna Nagler/CEO, Pres. - Christopher, Banks, Steve Danker/Sr. VP - Information Systems, Strategy/$173,503.00, Susan Connell/Exec. VP, Chief Merchandise Officer - Christopher, Banks, Inc, James Palczynski/Integrated Corporate Relations, Kim M. Westerham/VP - Merchandise Planning, Distribution, Judy Defrancesco/VP, Dir. - Stores, Christopher, Banks, Kim A. Decker/Sr. VP - Store Operations/$320,532.00, Luke R. Komarek/Sr. VP, General Counsel - Christopher, Banks, Inc, Jillian May/VP - Marketing, Christopher, Banks, Inc, Kipp Sassaman/VP - Human Resources, Christopher, Banks, Inc, Donna Fauchald/VP - Real Estate, Christopher, Banks, Inc, Daniel Fredeen/VP, GM - Christopher, Banks, Inc, Cindy Boden/Dir. - Christopher, Banks, Inc, Monica L. Dahl/COO, Exec. VP/$505,493.00 *(21 Officers included in Index)*

Directors: Matthew P. Dillon/48/Dir., CEO, Pres., Larry C. Barenbaum/61/Chmn., Dorothy Lierman/Dir., Joseph E. Pennington/Dir., Julie M. Rouse/Dir., James J. Fuld/60/Dir., Anne L. Jones/62/Dir., Robert Ezrilov/63/Dir., Donald D. Beeler/72/Dir., Mark A. Cohn/51/Dir.

Owners: Kathryn Gangstee, Joseph Pennington/1.60%, Kornitzer Capital Management, Inc./5.50%, Steven Danker, Anne Jones, T. Rowe Price Associates, Inc./11.20%, Robert Mang, Kim Decker, Andrew Moller/1.20%, Robert Ezrilov, Columbia Wanger Asset Management, L.P./14.70%, Matthew Dillon, James Fuld, Monica Dahl, Larry Barenbaum *(18 Owners included in Index)*

Financial Data: Fiscal Year End: 02/25   *Latest Annual Data:* 3/3/2007

Year	Sales		Net Income
2007	$547,317,000		$33,686,000
2006	$490,508,000		$30,413,000
2005	$438,862,000		$27,015,000
Curr. Assets:	$175,104,000	*Curr. Liab.:*	$46,250,000	*P/E Ratio:* 22.46
Plant, Equip.:	$127,776,000	*Total Liab.:*	$81,558,000	*Indic. Yr. Divd.:* $0.240
Total Assets:	$307,323,000	*Net Worth:*	$225,765,000	*Debt/ Equity:* NA

Chromcraft Revington Inc

1330 Win Hentschel Blvd., Ste. 250, West Lafayette, IN, 47906; *PH:* 1-765-807-2640;
Fax: 1-765-564-3722; *http://* www.prcatalog.com

General - Incorporation: DE
Employees: 904
Auditor: KPMG LLP
Stk Agt: American Stock Transfer & Trust Co.
Counsel: NA
DUNS No.: 78-813-7016

Stock - Price on:12/24/2007: $7.8
Stock Exchange: AMEX
Ticker Symbol: CRC
Outstanding Shares: 6,170,000
E.P.S: -$2.17
Shareholders: NA

Business: The group's principal activities are to design, manufacture and sell residential and commercial furniture. The group operates through its wholly owned subsidiaries chromcraft corporation, peters-revington corporation, silver furniture co. Inc, cochrane furniture company inc and korn industries incorporated. The peters-revington and silver furniture brands of occasional furniture consist of tables, bookcases, modular wall units and curio cabinets in traditional, contemporary and country styles. Cochrane furniture and sumter brands include bedroom furniture in oak, cherry, ash or maple and upholstered sofas, chairs and ottomans. The chromcraft brand of products includes casual dining furniture for use in dining rooms, family rooms and kitchens without formal dining areas. They also include commercial furniture like office chairs, conference room tables and seats for airports and public waiting areas.

Primary SIC and add'l.: 2512 6719 2511

CIK No: 0000884130

Subsidiaries: Chromcraft Corporation, Cochrane Furniture Company, Inc., CRI Capital Corporation, CRI Corporation-Sumter, CRI Realty Company, LLC, Korn Industries, Incorporated, Peters-Revington Corporation, Silver Furniture Co., Inc., Silver Furniture Manufacturing Co., Inc.

Officers: Dennis C. Valkanoff/56/Sr. VP, Richard J. Garrity/49/Sr. VP

Owners: Daniel Zeff/6.80%, Theodore L. Mullett, Chromcraft Revington Employee Stock Ownership Plan Trust/31.90%, Ronald H. Butler, T. Rowe Price Associates, Inc./8.30%, John D. Swift, John R. Hesse, David L. Kolb, Craig R. Stokely, Larry P. Kunz, FMR Corp./15.50%, Frank T. Kane/2.50%, Insiders/4.70%, Benjamin M. Anderson-Ray

Financial Data: *Fiscal Year End:*12/31 *Latest Annual Data:* 12/31/2006

Year	Sales	Net Income
2006	$160,478,000	-$3,393,000
2005	$169,565,000	$7,245,000
2004	$172,393,000	$7,668,000

Curr. Assets:	$64,329,000	**Curr. Liab.:**	$12,678,000		
Plant, Equip.:	$19,212,000	**Total Liab.:**	$15,400,000	**Indic. Yr. Divd.:**	NA
Total Assets:	$85,818,000	**Net Worth:**	$70,418,000	**Debt/ Equity:**	NA

Chubb Corp

15 Mountain View Rd., Warren, NJ, 07059; *PH:* 1-908-903-2000; *Fax:* 1-908-903-2027; *http://* www.chubb.com

General - Incorporation: NJ
Employees: 10,800
Auditor: Ernst & Young LLP
Stk Agt: EquiServe Trust Co N.A
Counsel: NA
DUNS No.: 00-167-1411

Stock - Price on:12/24/2007: $54.06
Stock Exchange: NYSE
Ticker Symbol: CB
Outstanding Shares: 401,480,000
E.P.S: $6.88
Shareholders: NA

Business: The groups principle activity is to provide underwriting of property and casualty insurance, investment in securities and real estate developments. The groups services include multiple peril, casualty, workers compensation, property and marine. The group operates from United States, Canada, Europe, and Australia.

Primary SIC and add'l.: 6331 6531 6321 6719 6552

CIK No: 0000020171

Subsidiaries: Bellemead Development Corporation Delaware, CC Canada Holdings Ltd., Chubb Argentina de Seguros, S.A., Chubb Capital Corporation, Chubb Capital Corporation New Jersey, Chubb Custom Insurance Company, Chubb do Brasil Companhia de Seguros, Chubb Financial Solutions LLCDelaware, Chubb Financial Solutions, Inc. Delaware, Chubb Indemnity Insurance Company, Chubb Insurance Company of Australia Limited, Chubb Insurance Company of Canada, Chubb Insurance Company of Europe, S.A., Chubb Insurance Company of New Jersey, Chubb National Insurance Company 25 Subsidiaries included in the Index

Officers: John D. Finnegan/59/Chmn., CEO, Pres./$16,762,300.00, John J. Degnan/Vice Chmn., Chief Administrative Officer/$6,213,933.00, Thomas F. Motamed/Vice Chmn., COO/$8,182,409.00, Michael OReilly/Vice Chmn., CFO/$6,886,860.00, Robert C. Cox/COO - Chubb Specialty Insurance, Exec. VP - Chubb, Son, Ned Gerstman/Exec. VP, Chief Domestic Investment Officer, Paul J. Krump/COO - Chubb Commercial Insurance, Exec. VP - Chubb, Son/$2,204,572.00, Marjorie D. Raines/Exec. VP, Chief International Investment Officer, Andrew A. McElwee/COO - Chubb Personal Insurance, Exec. VP - Chubb, Son, Henry B. Schram/61/Chief Accounting Officer, Sr. VP, Harold L. Morrison/Exec. VP, US Field Operations Mgr. - Chubb, Son, Janice M. Tomlinson/Exec. VP, International Field Operations Mgr. - Chubb, Son, Maureen Brundage/Exec. VP, General Counsel, Dino E. Robusto/Exec. VP, Chief Claim Officer - Chubb, Son, Georgina Peters/Contact - Media, Chubb Europe *(21 Officers included in Index)*

Directors: John D. Finnegan/59/Chmn., CEO, Pres., John J. Degnan/Vice Chmn., Chief Administrative Officer, Thomas F. Motamed/Vice Chmn., COO, Michael OReilly/Vice Chmn., CFO, Karen Hastie Williams/63/Dir., Alfred W. Zollar/53/Dir., Klaus J. Mangold/64/Dir., David G. Scholey/72/Dir., Lawrence M. Small/66/Dir., Daniel E. Somers/60/Dir., Martin G. Mc Guinn/66/Dir., Joel J. Cohen/70/Dir., Jess Soderberg/64/Dir., Zoe Baird/55/Dir., Sheila P. Burke/57/Dir. *(16 Directors included in Index)*

Owners: Raymond G.H. Seitz, Karen Hastie Williams, Lawrence M. Small, Insiders, Michael OReilly, James I. Cash, John J. Degnan, Dodge& Cox/5.30%, John D. Finnegan, Alfred W. Zollar, David G. Scholey, Thomas F. Motamed, Zo Baird, Joel J. Cohen, Klaus J. Mangold *(19 Owners included in Index)*

Financial Data: *Fiscal Year End:*12/31 *Latest Annual Data:* 12/31/2006

Year	Sales	Net Income
2006	$14,003,000,000	$2,528,000,000
2005	$14,082,300,000	$1,825,900,000
2004	$13,177,200,000	$1,548,400,000

Curr. Assets:	$7,554,000,000	**Curr. Liab.:**	$5,109,000,000	**P/E Ratio:**	8.85
Plant, Equip.:	$564,000,000	**Total Liab.:**	$36,414,000,000	**Indic. Yr. Divd.:**	$1.160
Total Assets:	$50,277,000,000	**Net Worth:**	$13,863,000,000	**Debt/ Equity:**	0.4212

Chugach Electric Association Inc

5601 Electron Dr., Anchorage, AK, 99518; *PH:* 1-907-563-7494; *Fax:* 1-907-762-4678; *http://* www.chugachelectric.com

General - Incorporation: AK
Employees: 1,905
Auditor: KPMG LLP
Stk Agt: NA
Counsel: NA
DUNS No.: 00-389-9341

Stock - Price on:12/24/2007: NA
Stock Exchange: NA
Ticker Symbol: NA
Outstanding Shares: NA
E.P.S: NA
Shareholders: NA

Business: The group's principle activities include generating, transmiting and distributing electricity to approximately 73,500 metered locations in the anchorage and upper kenai peninsula areas. The energy is distributed throughout Alaska's railbelt, with the help of an interconnected regional electrical system. The company provides direct service to retail customers and also supplies power requirements to three wholesale customers, matanuska electric association, homer electric association and the city of seward. The group operates from United States.

Primary SIC and add'l.: 7379 4911

CIK No: 0000878004

Officers: Alex Gimarc/Sec., P. J. Hill/Treasurer

Directors: Uwe Kalenka/Vice Chmn., Liz Vazquez/Chmn., Jeff Lipscomb/Dir., Jim Nordlund/Dir., Rebecca Logan/Dir.

Chunghwa Telecom Co Ltd

21 3 Hsinyi Rd. Section 1, Taipe; *PH:* 86-2234454; *http://* www.cht.com.tw; *Email:* shin@cht.co.th

General - Incorporation: Taiwan
Employees: 25,873
Auditor: Deloitte & Touche LLP
Stk Agt: Taiwan Securities Co Ltd
Counsel: NA
DUNS No.: NA

Stock - Price on:12/24/2007: $18.97
Stock Exchange: NYSE
Ticker Symbol: CHT
Outstanding Shares: 966,780,000
E.P.S: $1.37
Shareholders: NA

Business: The group's principle activity is provide provision of domestic and international telecommunication, and information related services. The groups services include city call, long distance calls, international calls, gsm data communication, Internet services, broadband networking, satellite communication, intelligent network, mobile data and multimedia broadband. The group operates from United States.

Primary SIC and add'l.: NA

CIK No: 0001132924

Subsidiaries: Chunghwa Precision Test Technical Co., Ltd., Chunghwa System Integration, Chunghwa Telecom Global, Inc

Officers: Lawrence Wei/GM - Bangkok Representative Office, Grant Chen/GM - Hcmc Representative Office, Chi-mao Hsieh/54/Exec. VP, Hsiang-yi Chen/56/Exec. VP, Frederick Chang/Vice GM - Hcmc Representative Office, Joseph C.P. Shieh/48/CFO, Sr. VP, Yen-sung Lee/59/Exec. VP, Cheng-lang Huang/59/Exec. VP

Directors: Chao-i Hsieh/60/Dir., Shih-peng Tsai/59/Dir.

Owners: The Republic of China government/35.93%, The Ministry of Transportation and Communications/35.41%

Financial Data: *Fiscal Year End:*12/31 *Latest Annual Data:* 12/31/2006

Year	Sales	Net Income
2006	NA	$3,000,000
2005	NA	NA
2004	NA	NA

Curr. Assets:	$3,096,000,000	**Curr. Liab.:**	$2,059,000,000	**P/E Ratio:**	13.85
Plant, Equip.:	$8,513,000,000	**Total Liab.:**	$2,416,000,000	**Indic. Yr. Divd.:**	$1.050
Total Assets:	$12,236,000,000	**Net Worth:**	$9,820,000,000	**Debt/ Equity:**	NA

Church & Dwight Co Inc

469 N Harrison St., Princeton, NJ, 08543; *PH:* 1-609-683-5900; *Fax:* 1-609-497-7269; *http://* www.churchdwight.com

General - Incorporation: DE
Employees: 3,655
Auditor: Deloitte & Touche LLP
Stk Agt: Mellon Investor Services LLC
Counsel: NA
DUNS No.: 00-121-1952

Stock - Price on:12/24/2007: $48.47
Stock Exchange: NYSE
Ticker Symbol: CHD
Outstanding Shares: 65,790,000
E.P.S: $2.18
Shareholders: NA

Business: The group's principle activities include developing, manufacturing and marketing a range of household, personal care and specialty products. The group operates through three segments namely domestic, consumer international and specialty products. The group operates from United States.

Primary SIC and add'l.: 2841 2819 2879

CIK No: 0000313927

Subsidiaries: Armkel Brasil Cosmeticos Ltda., Armkel Canada (Netherlands) B.V., Armkel Company (France) S.A.S., Armkel Company (Spain), S.r.l., Armkel Company (U.K.) Limited, Armkel Holding (Netherlands) B.V., Brotherton Specialty Products Ltd., Carter Products (N.Z.) Inc., Church & Dwight (Australia) Pty Ltd., Church & Dwight Virginia Co. Inc., Church& Dwight (U.K.) Limited, Church& Dwight Canada Corp., Church& Dwight Chemical Products, Inc., Church& Dwight Company, Church& Dwight de Mexico S. de R.L. de C.V. 18 Subsidiaries included in the Index

Officers: James R. Craigie/Chmn., CEO/$3,721,374.00, Paul A. Siracusa/Exec. VP - Global Research, Development, Gary P. Halker/57/VP - Finance, Treasurer, Louis H. Tursi/VP - Domestic Consumer Sales/$822,167.00, Steven P. Cugine/Exec. VP - Global New Products Innovation, Adrian J. Huns/Exec. VP, Pres. - International Consumer Products/$1,440,671.00, Susan E. Goldy/Exec. VP, Chief Marketing Officer, Joseph A. Sipia/Exec. VP, Pres. - International Consumer Products/$1,008,243.00, Mark G. Conish/Exec. VP - Global Operations, Bruce F. Fleming/Exec. VP, Chief Marketing Officer, Matthew T. Farrell/CFO, Exec. VP - Finance/$886,928.00, Jacquelin J. Brova/Exec. VP - Human Resources

Directors: James R. Craigie/Chmn., CEO, Robert A. Davies/Dir., John O. Whitney/Dir., Rosina B. Dixon/Dir., Robert D. Leblanc/Dir., Rosie T. Albright/Dir., Richard J. Leaman/Dir., Dwight C. Minton/Dir. Emeritus, Robert A. McCabe/Dir., Bradley C. Irwin/Dir., Ravichandra K. Saligram/Dir., Lionel L. Nowell/53/Dir.

Owners: Insiders/1.86%, James R. Craigie, Rosina B. Dixon, Richard J. Leaman, Capital Research& Management Company/5.09%, Louis H. Tursi, Robert D. LeBlanc, Lionel L. Nowell, Joseph A. Sipia, Dwight C. Minton, Matthew T. Farrell, Robert A. Davies, Bradley C. Irwin, John O. Whitney, Neuberger Berman, Inc./12.79% *(17 Owners included in Index)*

Financial Data: *Fiscal Year End:*12/31 *Latest Annual Data:* 12/31/2006

Year	Sales		Net Income
2006	$1,945,661,000		$138,927,000
2005	$1,736,506,000		$122,906,000
2004	$1,462,062,000		$88,808,000

Curr. Assets:	$556,070,000	**Curr. Liab.:**	$444,404,000	**P/E Ratio:**	22.23
Plant, Equip.:	$340,484,000	**Total Liab.:**	$1,470,000,000	**Indic. Yr. Divd.:**	$0.320
Total Assets:	$2,334,154,000	**Net Worth:**	$863,837,000	**Debt/ Equity:**	0.8199

Churchill Downs Inc

700 Central Ave., Louisville, KY, 40208; ***PH:*** 1-502-636-4400;
http:// www.churchilldownsincorporated.com

General - Incorporation	KY	**Stock**- Price on:12/24/2007	$53.49
Employees	1,100	Stock Exchange	NDQ
Auditor	PricewaterhouseCoopers LLP	Ticker Symbol	CHDN
Stk Agt	National City Bank	Outstanding Shares	13,460,000
Counsel	NA	E.P.S.	$1.48
DUNS No.	00-694-5182	Shareholders	NA

Business: The group's principle activities are to conduct pari-mutuel wagering on live race meetings for thoroughbred horses and participate in intrastate and interstate simulcast wagering at its racetracks in Kentucky, California, Florida and Illinois. Through its Indiana subsidiary hoosier park l.p. (hoosier park), it conducts pari-mutuel wagering on live thoroughbred, quarter horse and standardbred horse races and participates in interstate simulcast wagering. The group conducts live horse racing at churchill downs, hollywood park, calder race course, arlington park, hoosier park and ellis park, which generates revenues through pari-mutuel wagering at the group's race tracks. The group's quarterly revenue for September 2007 was 103.91 millions of USD.

Primary SIC and add'l.: 7999 7948

CIK No: 0000020212

Subsidiaries: Arlington International Racecourse, LLCd/b/a Arlington Park, Calder Race Course, Inc., Churchill Downs California Company d/b/a Hollywood Park, Churchill Downs California Fall Operating Company d/b/a Hollywood Park, Churchill Downs Management Company, Ellis Park Race Course, Inc., Hoosier Park, L.P. (limited partnership), Tropical Park, Inc.

Officers: Robert L. Evans/Dir., CEO, Pres./$333,831.00, William C. Carstanjen/Exec. VP, Chief Development Officer/$732,951.00, Donald R. Richardson/Sr. VP - Racing, Steven Sexton/Exec. VP, Pres. - Churchill Downs Racetrack/$503,443.00, Rebecca C. Reed/Sr. VP - Legal Affairs, Corporate Compliance Officer, Sec., Jay Rollins/VP - Information Technology, Randall E. Soth/Sr. VP - Louisiana Operations, Fair Grounds Pres., GM, Michael W. Anderson/VP - Corporate Finance, Treasurer, Dan Leary/Dir. - Communications, Michele Blanco/Dir. - Publicity, Lenny Vangilder/Dir. - Communications Marketing, Tammy Knox/Dir. - Publicity, William E. Mudd/CFO, Exec. VP, Vernon Niven/Exec. VP - Technology Initiatives, Mike Anderson/VP - Corporate Finance, Treasurer *(25 Officers included in Index)*

Directors: Robert L. Evans/Dir., CEO, Pres., Carl F. Pollard/Chmn., Craig J. Duchossois/Dir., David J. Grissom/Dir., Daniel P. Harrington/Dir., Charles W. Bidwill/Dir. Emeriti, Catesby W. Clay/Dir. Emeriti, Frank B. Hower/Dir. Emeriti, Watts G. Humphrey/Dir., Seth W. Hancock/Dir., Thomas H. Meeker/Dir. Emeriti, Darrell R. Wells/Dir., Richard L. Duchossois/Dir., Susan E. Packard/Dir., Robert L. Fealy/Dir. *(18 Directors included in Index)*

Owners: Leonard S. Coleman, Watts G. Humphrey, Andrew G. Skehan, Gamco Investors, Inc. and affiliates/7.04%, Thomas H. Meeker/0.71%, David J. Grissom/0.75%, Craig J. Duchossois/23.47%, Michael E. Miller, Carl F. Pollard/0.99%, Steven P. Sexton/0.22%, C. Kenneth Dunn/0.08%, Duchossois Industries, Inc./23.47%, Susan E. Packard, Darrell R. Wells/1.30%, Seth W. Hancock/0.99% *(18 Owners included in Index)*

Financial Data: ***Fiscal Year End:***12/31 ***Latest Annual Data:*** 12/31/2006

Year	Sales		Net Income
2006	$376,671,000		$29,811,000
2005	$408,801,000		$78,908,000
2004	$463,113,000		$8,915,000

Curr. Assets:	$128,541,000	**Curr. Liab.:**	$126,891,000	**P/E Ratio:**	24.42
Plant, Equip.:	$336,068,000	**Total Liab.:**	$196,249,000	**Indic. Yr. Divd.:**	$0.500
Total Assets:	$546,328,000	**Net Worth:**	$350,079,000	**Debt/ Equity:**	0.0405

Chyron Corp

5 Hub Dr., Melville, NY, 11747; ***PH:*** 1-631-845-2000; ***Fax:*** 1-631-845-3895;
http:// www.chyron.com

General - Incorporation	NY	**Stock**- Price on:12/24/2007	$1.2
Employees	100	Stock Exchange	OTC
Auditor	Pricewaterhousecoopers LLP	Ticker Symbol	CYRO
Stk Agt	American Stock Transfer & Trust Co.	Outstanding Shares	45,660,000
Counsel	Thelen Reid & Priest LLP	E.P.S.	$0.21
DUNS No.	04-617-2946	Shareholders	NA

Business: The group's principle activity is to develop, manufacture and distribute signal distribution and graphic products to broadcasters for use in digital television. The activities are carried through three segments. The graphics segment provides the duet(R) real-time 2d/3D digital video graphics processors that provide television character generator applications and enhance the presentation of live and pre-recorded video. The streaming services segment markets the clarinet dualstreamer(R), a streaming media coder used to encode video and audio for use on the Internet. The group maintains sales offices in the United States, Hong Kong, France, India, Denmark and the United Kingdom. During 2003, the group discontinued the signal distribution and automation segments and sold pro-bel division. The group's quarterly revenue for September 2007 was 8.74 millions of USD.

Primary SIC and add'l.: 3663

CIK No: 0000020232

Subsidiaries: Avid Technologies, Inc, Pro-Bel Limited, Vizrt Ltd

Officers: Michael I. Wellesley-Wesley/Dir. - Presidant, CEO/$680,499.00, Jerry Kieliszak/CFO, Sr. VP/$305,793.00, Kevin Prince/COO, Sr. VP/$278,896.00, Robert S. Matlin/Sec.

Directors: Michael I. Wellesley-Wesley/Dir. - Presidant, CEO, Christopher R. Kelly/Chmn., Eugene M. Weber/Dir., Donald P. Greenberg/Dir., Richard P. Greenthal/Dir., Michael C. Wheeler/Dir.

Owners: Jerry Kieliszak, Michael I. Wellesley-Wesley/7.62%, Michael C. Wheeler, Insiders/23.82%, Eugene M. Weber/1.07%, LMS Capital plc/17.46%, Christopher R. Kelly/13.91%, Kevin Prince, Donald P. Greenberg, Richard P. Greenthal

Financial Data: ***Fiscal Year End:***12/31 ***Latest Annual Data:*** 12/31/2006

Year	Sales		Net Income
2006	$26,246,000		$3,121,000
2005	$25,129,000		$706,000
2004	$23,238,000		$305,000

Curr. Assets:	$10,054,000	**Curr. Liab.:**	$5,005,000	**P/E Ratio:**	15.00
Plant, Equip.:	$984,000	**Total Liab.:**	$7,034,000	**Indic. Yr. Divd.:**	NA
Total Assets:	$12,503,000	**Net Worth:**	$5,469,000	**Debt/ Equity:**	NA

Cia Vale do Rio Doce

546 5th Ave., 12th Fl., New York, NY, 10036; ***PH:*** 1-212-589-9800; ***Fax:*** 1-212-391-4546;
http:// www.cvrd.com.br

General - Incorporation		**Stock**- Price on:12/24/2007	$47.07
Employees	55,819	Stock Exchange	NYSE
Auditor	NA	Ticker Symbol	RIO
Stk Agt	JP Morgan Chase Bank, N.A.	Outstanding Shares	2,410,000,000
Counsel	NA	E.P.S.	$2.24
DUNS No.	NA	Shareholders	NA

Business: The groups principle activities include mining and producing metals. In the year 2006, the group acquired Inco Limited. The group operates from the Brazil, Angola, Argentina, Australia, Chile and South Africa. The groups quarterly revenue for September 2007 was 15,621.00 millions of BRL.

Primary SIC and add'l.: 1011

CIK No:

Officers: Roger Agnelli/CEO, Pres., Fabio Barbosa/CFO, Carla Grasso/Exec. Dir. - Human Resources, Corporate Services, Gabriel Stoliar/Exec. Dir. - Planning, Business Development, Tito Botelho Martins/Exec. Dir. - Corporate Affairs, Energy, Jose Carlos Martins/Exec. Dir. - Ferrous Minerals, Jose Lancaster/Exec. Dir. - Copper, Coal, Aluminum, Eduardo De Salles Bartolomeo/Exec. Dir. - Logistics, Murilo De Oliveira Ferreira/Exec. Dir. - Nickel Business, Marketing, Sales, Copper, Aluminum, Demian Fiocca/Exec. Dir. - Technology, Information Management

Directors: Sergio Ricardo Silva Rosa/Dir., Mario Da Silveira Teixeira/Dir., Hiroshi Tada/Dir., Oscar Augusto De Carmargo Filho/Dir., Francisco Augusto Da Costa E Silva/Dir., Rita De Cassia Paz Andrade Robles/Alternate Dir., Sergio Ricardo Lopes De Farias/Alternate Dir., Joao Moises De Oliveira/Alternate Dir., Hidehiro Takahashi/Alternate Dir., Wanderlei Vicoso Fagundes/Alternate Dir., Jose Mauro Guahyba De Almeida/Alternate Dir., Jose Ricardo Sasseron/Dir., Sandro Kohler Marcondes/Dir., Joao Batista Cavaglieri/Dir., Luiz Mariano Campos/Alternete Dir. *(21 Directors included in Index)*

Financial Data: ***Fiscal Year End:***NA ***Latest Annual Data:*** 12/31/2006

Year	Sales		Net Income
2006	$19,651,000,000		$6,528,000,000
2005	$12,792,000,000		$4,841,000,000
2004	$8,066,000,000		$2,573,000,000

Curr. Assets:	$12,940,000,000	**Curr. Liab.:**	$7,312,000,000	**P/E Ratio:**	49.97
Plant, Equip.:	$38,007,000,000	**Total Liab.:**	$41,281,000,000	**Indic. Yr. Divd.:**	NA
Total Assets:	$60,954,000,000	**Net Worth:**	$19,673,000,000	**Debt/ Equity:**	NA

Ciba Specialty Chemicals Holding Inc

540 White Plains Rd., Tarrytown, NY, 10591; ***PH:*** 1-914-785-2000; ***Fax:*** 1-914-785-2211;
http:// www.cibasc.com; ***Email:*** investors@cibasc.com

General - Incorporation	Switzerland	**Stock**- Price on:12/24/2007	$33.33
Employees	14,130	Stock Exchange	OTC
Auditor	Ernst & Young LLP	Ticker Symbol	CSBHY
Stk Agt	Citibank N.A	Outstanding Shares	134,510,000
Counsel	NA	E.P.S.	-$0.01
DUNS No.	NA	Shareholders	NA

Business: The group's principal activity is the manufacture of chemicals that provide color, performance and care for plastics, coatings, textile, paper, home and personal care. The group operates through five segments: coating effects, plastic additives, water and paper treatment, textile effects and home and personal care. The coating effects segment manufactures organic pigments and supplies photoinitiators and light stabilizers to the coatings, graphic arts and electronic industries. Plastic additives segment develops and markets products and services to the plastic and lubricant industries. The textile effect segment products include dyes and chemicals for dyeing and printing, optical brighteners and textile finishing products for protection and easy care. Home and personal care segment manufactures whiteners and supplies antimicrobials to the personal care market.

Primary SIC and add'l.: 2836 2819 2816 2821 2851 5169 2834

CIK No: 0001035497

Subsidiaries: A/S Alfred Gad, AB CDM, Chemical Insurance Company Ltd., Chemipro Fine Chemical Kaisha Ltd., Ciba Especialidades Qumicas, Ciba Especialidades Qumicas Colon S.A., Ciba Especialidades Qumicas Lda., Ciba Especialidades Qumicas Ltd., Ciba Especialidades Qumicas Ltda., Ciba Especialidades Qumicas Mexico S.A. de C.V., Ciba Especialidades Qumicas S.A., Ciba Especialidades Qumicas S.L., Ciba India Private Ltd., Ciba Specialits Chimiques Monthey SA, Ciba Specialits Chimiques SA 81 Subsidiaries included in the Index

Officers: Armin Meyer/59/Chmn., CEO, Giordano Righini/59/Head - Plastic Additives Segment, Hermann Angerer/61/Head - Coating Effects Segment, Michael Jacobi/55/CFO, Brendan Cummins/57/COO, Jurg Fedier/CFO, Mark Wright/Head - Human Resources, Matthias A. Fankhauser/Investor Relations Officer, Siegfried Schwirzer/Investor Relations Officer, Martin Riediker/56/CTO, James McCummiskey/Head - Water, Paper Treatment Segment, Thomas Koch/Sec., Franz Killer/Head - Product, Process Development, Michael Loechle/CIO, Markus Mayer/Head - Internal Audit *(18 Officers included in Index)*

Directors: Armin Meyer/59/Chmn., CEO, Beat W. Hess/59/Vice Chmn., Utz-Hellmuth Felcht/61/Dir., Erwin W. Heri/54/Dir., Peter Littmann/61/Dir., Gertrud Hohler/67/Dir., Jean-Marie Pierre Lehn/69/Dir., Uli Sigg/62/Dir., Jean-Marie Pierre/Dir.

Financial Data: ***Fiscal Year End:***12/31 ***Latest Annual Data:*** 12/31/2006

Year	Sales		Net Income
2006	$5,211,816,000		-$33,641,000
2005	$5,639,924,000		-$194,611,000
2004	$6,211,165,000		$274,893,000

Curr. Assets:	$2,916,057,000	**Curr. Liab.:**	$1,284,903,000	**P/E Ratio:**	13.85
Plant, Equip.:	$2,113,608,000	**Total Liab.:**	$4,813,874,000	**Indic. Yr. Divd.:**	$1.230
Total Assets:	$7,450,961,000	**Net Worth:**	$2,637,087,000	**Debt/ Equity:**	NA

CIBER Inc

5251 DTC Pkwy., Ste. 1400, Greenwood Village, CO, 80111; *PH:* 1-303-220-0100; *Fax:* 1-303-220-7100; *http://* www.ciber.com

General - Incorporation	DE	**Stock**- Price on:12/24/2007	$8.13
Employees	8,300	Stock Exchange	NYSE
Auditor	Ernst & Young LLP	Ticker Symbol	CBR
Stk Agt	Wells Fargo Bank, N.A.	Outstanding Shares	61,280,000
Counsel	Davis, Graham & Stubbs	E.P.S	$0.47
DUNS No.	07-278-1511	Shareholders	NA

Business: The group's principal activities are to provide information technology (IT) system integration consulting and other it services including reselling of certain hardware and software pdts. The group operates through three segments: custom solutions provides it project solutions and it staffing in custom developed software environments. Package solutions provides enterprise software implementation services including enterprise resource planning, customer relationship management software from software vendors. European operations provides business and technical consulting services including application development, package implementation and systems integration. The clients consist primarily of Fortune 500 and middle market companies. In 2003, the group acquired ecsoft group plc, alphanet solutions inc. In 2004, it also acquired assets & liabilities of fulltilt solutions inc, scb computer technology inc, ascent technology and novasoft ag.

Primary SIC and add'l.: 7371 7373 7379 7376 7372 5734

CIK No: 0000918581

Subsidiaries: Apex Computers Limited, Ascent Technology Group Limited, Ascent Technology Limited, C.i.b.e.r. Sweden Ab, Ciber (uk) Ltd., CIBER Danmark AS, CIBER Europe B.V., CIBER Europe Limited, CIBER European Holdings Limited, CIBER Holding GmbH, CIBER Indiana LLC, CIBER International Holdings C.V., CIBER Nederlands B.V., CIBER Norge AS, CIBER Novasoft ASIA Pte. Ltd. 31 Subsidiaries included in the Index

Officers: Terje Laugerud/CEO - Ciber Europe/$540,008.00, Mac J. Slingerlend/Dir., CEO, Pres., Sec./$1,147,842.00, Peter H. Cheesbrough/Dir., CFO, Exec. VP, Wally Birdseye/Pres. - Federal Solutions/$361,403.00, David E. Girard/53/COO, Exec. VP/$603,773.00, Chris Loffredo/VP, Chief Accounting Officer, Tim Boehm/Pres. - Cibersites, William R. Wheeler/Pres. - Ciber Enterprise Solutions, Peter J. Harris/CFO - Ciber Europe, Ed Burns/Pres. - State Government Solutions, H. K. Katti/MD, Exec. VP - Ciber India, Tony Hadzi/Regional VP - West Region Commercial Operations, Joseph A. Mancuso/Regional VP - Midwest Region, Jennifer J. Matuschek/VP - Investor Relations, Diane Stoner/Mgr. - Public Relations *(23 Officers included in Index)*

Directors: Mac J. Slingerlend/Dir., CEO, Pres., Sec., Bobby G. Stevenson/Chmn., Peter H. Cheesbrough/Dir., CFO, Exec. VP, Jim Wetherbe/Dir., George Sissel/Dir., Archibald J. McGill/Dir., Paul Jacobs/Dir., James C. Spira/Dir.

Owners: Insiders/15.82%, James C. Wetherbe, Mac J. Slingerlend/3.62%, Peter H. Cheesbrough, Paul A. Jacobs, Pzena Investment Management, LLC/8.44%, Wally Birdseye, James C. Spira, Dimensional Fund Advisors LP/8.68%, David E. Girard, Bobby G. Stevenson/10.52%, Artisan Partners Limited Partnership/5.10%, George A. Sissel, Barclays Global Investors, LTD/5.97%, Terje Laugerud *(17 Owners included in Index)*

Financial Data: ***Fiscal Year End:***12/31 ***Latest Annual Data:*** 12/31/2006

Year	Sales	Net Income
2006	$995,837,000	$24,735,000
2005	$956,009,000	$24,707,000
2004	$843,021,000	$29,701,000

Curr. Assets:	$284,142,000	**Curr. Liab.:**	$143,385,000	**P/E Ratio:**	18.07
Plant, Equip.:	$26,521,000	**Total Liab.:**	$362,309,000	**Indic. Yr. Divd.:**	NA
Total Assets:	$779,679,000	**Net Worth:**	$416,122,000	**Debt/ Equity:**	0.4643

Ciena Corp

1201 Winterson Rd., Linthicum, MD, 21090; *PH:* 1-410-865-8500; *Fax:* 1-410-694-5750; *http://* www.ciena.com

General - Incorporation	DE	**Stock**- Price on:12/24/2007	$36.45
Employees	1,485	Stock Exchange	NDQ
Auditor	PricewaterhouseCoopers LLP	Ticker Symbol	CIEN
Stk Agt	Computershare Investor Services LLC	Outstanding Shares	85,390,000
Counsel	Hogan & Hartson LLP	E.P.S	$0.87
DUNS No.	00-758-3495	Shareholders	NA

Business: The group's principal activity is to provide network solutions to telecommunications service providers and enterprise worldwide. The group also offers optical transport and intelligent optical switching systems that enable service providers to manage and deliver bandwidth services to their customers. The optical networking product portfolio is targeted at the critical areas of service provider networks: intelligent optical switching, long-distance optical transport, short-distance optical transport and network management. The customers of the group include long-distance carriers, local exchange carriers, cable operators, Internet service providers, wireless and wholesale carriers, resellers, governments, large businesses and non-profit institutions. The group operates in North America, Europe, Latin America and Asia-Pacific. In 2003, the group acquired wavesmith networks inc and akara corporation and on 03-May-2004, catena networks inc and Internet photonics inc.

Primary SIC and add'l.: 3669 3661

CIK No: 0000936395

Subsidiaries: CIENA Communications, Inc., CIENA Government Solutions, Inc., CIENA Holdings, Inc

Officers: Gary B. Smith/46/Dir., CEO, Pres., Patrick H. Nettles/63/Executive Chmn., Joseph R. Chinnici/Sr. VP - Finance, CFO, Mike Aquino/Sr. VP - Worldwide Sales, Lynn Moore/VP - Global Human Resources, Suzanne Dulong/Chief Communications Officer, Thomas Mock/Sr. VP - Strategic Planning, Arthur Smith/COO, Sr. VP, Francois Locoh-Donou/VP, GM - EMEA, Jesus Leon/Chief Development Officer, Sr. VP, Russell B. Stevenson/Sr. VP, General Counsel, Sec., James Frodsham/Sr. VP - Corporate Development, Stephen B. Alexander/CTO, Sr. VP - Products, Technology, Christopher Smith/VP - Worldwide Services, Support, Andrew C. Petrik/VP, Controller, Treasurer *(18 Officers included in Index)*

Directors: Gary B. Smith/46/Dir., CEO, Pres., Patrick H. Nettles/63/Executive Chmn., Michael J. Rowny/56/Dir., Bruce L. Claflin/55/Dir., Lawton W. Fitt/Dir., Stephen P. Bradley/65/Dir., Gerald H. Taylor/65/Dir., Judith M. O'Brien/Dir., Harvey B. Cash/68/Dir.

Owners: Patrick H. Nettles, Gerald H. Taylor, Judith M. OBrien, Stephen B. Alexander, Gary B. Smith, Michael G. Aquino, Harvey B. Cash, Stephen P. Bradley, FMR Corp./11.00%, Lawton W. Fitt, Michael J. Rowny, Arthur D. Smith, Insiders/2.30%, Joseph R. Chinnici

Financial Data: ***Fiscal Year End:***10/31 ***Latest Annual Data:*** 10/31/2006

Year	Sales	Net Income
2006	$564,056,000	$595,000
2005	$427,257,000	-$435,699,000
2004	$298,707,000	-$789,464,000

Curr. Assets:	$1,098,186,000	**Curr. Liab.:**	$161,603,000	**P/E Ratio:**	98.51
Plant, Equip.:	$44,151,000	**Total Liab.:**	$1,086,087,000	**Indic. Yr. Divd.:**	NA
Total Assets:	$1,839,713,000	**Net Worth:**	$753,626,000	**Debt/ Equity:**	0.3807

Cigna Corp

2 Liberty Pl., 1601 Chestnut St., Philadelphia, PA, 19192; *PH:* 1-215-761-1000; *Fax:* 1-215-761-5515; *http://* www.cigna.com

General - Incorporation	DE	**Stock**- Price on:12/24/2007	$55.15
Employees	27,100	Stock Exchange	NYSE
Auditor	PricewaterhouseCoopers LLP	Ticker Symbol	CI
Stk Agt	Mellon Investor Services LLC	Outstanding Shares	287,790,000
Counsel	Roger Coustry	E.P.S	$3.35
DUNS No.	02-905-3964	Shareholders	NA

Business: The group's principle activity is to provide health care and related benefits offered through the workplace. Key product lines include health care products and services, group disability, life and accident insurance. Health care products and services include medical, pharmacy, behavioral health, clinical information management, dental and vision benefits and disease management. In addition, the group also provides life, accident, health and expatriate employee benefits insurance coverage in selected international markets, primarily in Asia and Europe. The group's quarterly revenue for September 2007 was 4,413.00 millions of USD.

Primary SIC and add'l.: 6321 6719 6282 6371 6311

CIK No: 0000701221

Subsidiaries: Arbor Reinsurance Company Limited, Capstone Government Solutions, LLC, Choicelinx Corporation, Cigna & Cmc Life Insurance Company Limited, CIGNA Apac Holdings Limited, CIGNA Asistencia Administrativa Limitada, CIGNA Behavioral Health, Inc., CIGNA Brasil Participacoes Ltda., CIGNA Brazil Holdings, Inc., CIGNA Compania de Seguros de Vida (Chile) S.A., CIGNA Dental Health of California, Inc., CIGNA Dental Health of Colorado, Inc., CIGNA Dental Health of Delaware, Inc., CIGNA Dental Health of Florida, Inc, CIGNA Dental Health of Illinois, Inc. 100 Subsidiaries included in the Index

Officers: Donna F. Zarcone/50/Dir., CEO, Pres., Eric C. Wiseman/52/Dir., CEO, Pres., Edward H. Hanway/56/Chmn., CEO/$21,014,500.00, David M. Cordani/Pres. - Cigna Healthcare/$3,134,700.00, Nicole S. Jones/Corp. Sec., VP, Chief Counsel - Corporate, Financial Law, Paul E. Hartley/Pres. - Cigna International/$3,497,800.00, Carol Ann Petren/Exec. VP, General Counsel, Ted Detrick/VP - Investor Relations, Prith Ruprai/Financial Analysis Mgr., Joseph Walter/Financial Analysis Sr. Dir. - Investor Relations, John M. Murabito/Exec. VP - Human Resources, Services/$2,690,100.00, Scott A. Storrer/40/Exec. VP - Service Operations, Information Technology, Michael W. Bell/CFO, Exec. VP/$6,068,300.00, Karen S. Rohan/Pres. - Cigna Group Insurance, Cigna Dental, Vision Care

Directors: Donna F. Zarcone/50/Dir., CEO, Pres., Eric C. Wiseman/52/Dir., CEO, Pres., Edward H. Hanway/56/Chmn., CEO, Peter N. Larson/68/Dir., Roman Martinez/60/Dir., Harold A. Wagner/72/Dir., James E. Rogers/60/Dir., Robert H. Campbell/70/Dir., William D. Zollars/60/Dir., Jane E. Henney/61/Dir., Isaiah Harris/55/Dir., Carol Cox Wait/65/Dir.

Owners: Edward H. Hanway/1.10%, Roman Martinez, Carol Cox Wait, John M. Murabito, Robert H. Campbell, Judith E. Soltz, Paul E. Hartley, Michael W. Bell, David M. Cordani, Insiders/1.60%, Peter N. Larson, Harold A. Wagner

Financial Data: ***Fiscal Year End:***12/31 ***Latest Annual Data:*** 12/31/2006

Year	Sales	Net Income
2006	$16,547,000,000	$1,155,000,000
2005	$16,684,000,000	$1,625,000,000
2004	$18,176,000,000	$1,438,000,000

Curr. Assets:	$10,985,000,000	**Curr. Liab.:**	$5,777,000,000	**P/E Ratio:**	16.13
Plant, Equip.:	$632,000,000	**Total Liab.:**	$38,069,000,000	**Indic. Yr. Divd.:**	$0.040
Total Assets:	$42,399,000,000	**Net Worth:**	$4,330,000,000	**Debt/ Equity:**	0.4315

Cignus Ventures Inc

No.206 - 1480 Gulf Rd., Point Roberts, WA, 98281; *PH:* 1-360-483-9517

General - Incorporation	NV	**Stock**- Price on:12/24/2007	NA
Employees	NA	Stock Exchange	OTC
Auditor	Davidson & Co. LLP	Ticker Symbol	CGNV
Stk Agt	Pacific Stock Transfer Company	Outstanding Shares	NA
Counsel	Cementhai Legal Counsel Limited	E.P.S	NA
DUNS No.	NA	Shareholders	NA

Business: The groups principal activity is to exploration of minerals. The group operates from the United States and Canada.

Primary SIC and add'l.: 1000

CIK No: 0001341327

Subsidiaries: CVI Exploration Ltd.

Owners: Insiders/62.50%, David K. Ryan/62.50%

Cilcorp Inc

300 Liberty St. , Ste. 300, Peoria, IL, 61602; *PH:* 1-309-677-5230; *http://* www.cilco.com

General - Incorporation	IL	**Stock**- Price on:12/24/2007	$48.76
Employees	8,988	Stock Exchange	NA
Auditor	PricewaterhouseCoopers LLP	Ticker Symbol	NA
Stk Agt	Continental Stock Transfer & Trust Co	Outstanding Shares	207,020,000
Counsel	Winthrop Stimson Putnam & Roberts	E.P.S	$3.00
DUNS No.	15-212-0093	Shareholders	NA

Business: The group's principle activities include generating, transmitting, distributing and selling electricity energy in an area of approximately 3,700 square miles in central and east-central Illinois, and the purchase, distribution, transportation and sale of natural gas in an area of approximately 4,500 square miles in central and east-central Illinois. The group operates from United States.

Primary SIC and add'l.: 4899 4923 8711 4911

CIK No: 0000762129

Subsidiaries: AFS Development Company, LLC, Agricultural Research& Development Corp., Ameren Corporation, Ameren Development Company, Ameren Energy Communications, Inc., Ameren Energy Development Company, Ameren Energy Fuels and Services Company, Ameren Energy Generating Company, Ameren Energy Marketing Company, Ameren Energy Resources Company, Ameren Energy, Inc., Ameren ERC, Inc., Ameren Services Company, AmerenEnergy Medina Valley Cogen (No. 2) LLC, AmerenEnergy Medina Valley Cogen, LLC 72 Subsidiaries included in the Index

Officers: Gary L. Rainwater/61/Chmn., CEO, Pres., Jerre E. Birdsong/53/VP, Treasurer, Warner L. Baxter/46/CFO, Exec. VP, Martin J. Lyons/41/VP, Steven R. Sullivan/47/VP, General Counsel, Sec., Thomas R. Voss/60/Exec. VP, Daniel F. Cole/54/Sr. VP, Alan R. Kelley/55/Sr. VP

Directors: Gary L. Rainwater/61/Chmn., CEO, Pres., Richard A. Liddy/Dir.

Financial Data: *Fiscal Year End:*12/31 *Latest Annual Data:* 12/31/2006

Year	Sales	Net Income
2006	$6,880,000,000	$547,000,000
2005	$6,780,000,000	$606,000,000
2004	$5,160,000,000	$530,000,000

Curr. Assets:	$1,874,000,000	**Curr. Liab.:**	$2,202,000,000	**P/E Ratio:**	16.76
Plant, Equip.:	$14,299,000,000	**Total Liab.:**	$12,766,000,000	**Indic. Yr. Divd.:**	$2.540
Total Assets:	$19,578,000,000	**Net Worth:**	$6,778,000,000	**Debt/ Equity:**	0.8168

Cimarex Energy Co

1700 Lincoln St., Ste. 1800, Denver, CO, 80203; *PH:* 1-303-295-3995; *Fax:* 1-303-295-3494; *http://* www.cimarex.com

General - Incorporation	DE	**Stock**- Price on:12/24/2007	$41.02
Employees	734	Stock Exchange	NYSE
Auditor	KPMG LLP	Ticker Symbol	XEC
Stk Agt	Continental Stock Transfer & Trust Co	Outstanding Shares	83,290,000
Counsel	NA	E.P.S.	$3.52
DUNS No.	NA	Shareholders	NA

Business: The group's principal activities are to explore, produce and market oil and gas properties. The group operates in two segments: exploration and production segment and natural gas marketing segment. Exploration and production activities include the exploration for and development of productive oil and gas properties located primarily in Oklahoma, Kansas, Texas and Louisiana. The natural gas marketing segment markets most of the natural gas produced by the exploration and production segment as well as natural gas produced by third parties.

Primary SIC and add'l.: 1382 4924

CIK No: 0001168054

Subsidiaries: Belle Isle LLC, Brock Gas Systems & Equipment, Inc., Canvasback Energy, Inc., Cimarex California Pipeline LLC, Cimarex Texas L.P., Cimarex Texas LLC, Columbus Energy Corp., Columbus Energy L.P., Columbus Gas Services, Inc., Columbus Texas, Inc., Conmag Energy Corporation, Cushing Disposal, Inc., Gruy Petroleum Management Co., Hunter Gas Gathering, Inc., Hunter Resources, Inc. 29 Subsidiaries included in the Index

Officers: F. H. Merelli/68/Chmn., CEO, Pres./$3,161,183.00, Paul Korus/CFO, VP, Treasurer/$1,151,474.00, Stephen P. Bell/Sr. VP - Business Development/$1,092,037.00, Joseph R. Albi/Exec. VP - Operations/$1,154,115.00, James H. Shonsey/Chief Accounting Officer, Controller, Gary R. Abbott/VP - Corporate Engineering, Thomas E. Jorden/Exec. VP - Exploration/$1,173,765.00, Richard S. Dinkins/VP - Human Resources, Mark Burford/Investor Relations, Dir. - Capital Markets, Mary Kay Rohrer/Corp. Sec.

Directors: F. H. Merelli/68/Chmn., CEO, Pres., David A. Hentschel/Dir., Jerry W. Box/Dir., Hans Helmerich/45/Dir., Cortland S. Dietler/Dir., Glenn A. Cox/Dir., Paul D. Holleman/Dir., Paul L. Teague/Dir., Michael J. Sullivan/Dir., Monroe W. Robertson/Dir.

Owners: Paul Korus, Michael J. Sullivan, Paul L. Teague, Jerry Box, Paul D. Holleman, Thomas E. Jorden, Monroe W. Robertson, Cortlandt S. Dietler, F. H. Merelli/1.00%, Stephen P. Bell, Glenn A. Cox, Hans Helmerich, Joseph R. Albi, David A. Hentschel, Insiders/2.00% *(16 Owners included in Index)*

Financial Data: *Fiscal Year End:*12/31 *Latest Annual Data:* 12/31/2006

Year	Sales	Net Income
2006	NA	NA
2005	NA	NA
2004	NA	NA

Curr. Assets:	$416,757,000	**Curr. Liab.:**	$354,588,000	**P/E Ratio:**	9.98
Plant, Equip.:	$3,676,634,000	**Total Liab.:**	$1,853,607,000	**Indic. Yr. Divd.:**	$0.160
Total Assets:	$4,829,750,000	**Net Worth:**	$2,976,143,000	**Debt/ Equity:**	0.1684

Cimatron Ltd

26800 Meadowbrook Rd., Ste. 113, Novi, MI, 48377; *PH:* 1-248-596-9700; *Fax:* 1-248-596-9741; *http://* www.cimatron.com; *Email:* info@cimatron.com

General - Incorporation	Israel	**Stock**- Price on:12/24/2007	$2.25
Employees	204	Stock Exchange	NDQ
Auditor	Brightman Almagor & Co	Ticker Symbol	CIMT
Stk Agt	NA	Outstanding Shares	7,840,000
Counsel	Yigal Arnon & Co	E.P.S.	$0.07
DUNS No.	60-002-0176	Shareholders	NA

Business: The groups principle activities include designing, development, manufactuing, marketing of modular, high-performance, fully integrated computer-aided design/computer-aided manufacturing software products. The group operates from United States.

Primary SIC and add'l.: 7373

CIK No: 0001008595

Subsidiaries: Chinese subsidiaries, French subsidiary, German subsidiary, Headquarters in Israel, Japanese subsidiary, North American subsidiary, UK subsidiary

Officers: Sam Golan/CEO, Pres. - Cimatron Technologies, Danny Haran/50/CEO, Pres., Ira Bareket/Corporate VP - Sales, Marketing, Yael Nevat/Investor Relations Officer, Idit Pass Lagziel/Marketing Mgr., Roy Sterenthal/VP - Research - Development, Ilan Erez/CFO, VP - Operations, Kobi Rosenwasser/VP - Asia Pacific

Directors: Rimon Ben-Shaoul/63/Chmn., Yossi Ben Shalom/53/Dir., Kenny Lalo/50/Dir., Ofra Brown/54/Dir., David Golan/67/Dir., Barak Dotan/40/Dir., Rami Entin/57/Dir.

Owners: Insiders/63.91%, Koonras Ltd./31.84%, DBSI Investments Ltd./31.91%

Financial Data: *Fiscal Year End:*12/31 *Latest Annual Data:* 12/31/2006

Year	Sales	Net Income
2006	$21,459,000	$514,000
2005	$20,925,000	-$4,593,000
2004	$23,163,000	-$388,000

Curr. Assets:	$11,425,000	**Curr. Liab.:**	$6,083,000	**P/E Ratio:**	13.85
Plant, Equip.:	$1,010,000	**Total Liab.:**	$9,062,000	**Indic. Yr. Divd.:**	NA
Total Assets:	$17,907,000	**Net Worth:**	$8,845,000	**Debt/ Equity:**	NA

Cimetrix Inc

6979 S High Tech Dr., Salt Lake City, UT, 84047; *PH:* 1-801-256-6500; *Fax:* 1-800-256-6510; *http://* www.cimetrix.com; *Email:* info@cimetrix.com

General - Incorporation	NV	**Stock**- Price on:12/24/2007	$0.3
Employees	42	Stock Exchange	OTC
Auditor	HJ & Assoc., LLC	Ticker Symbol	CMXX
Stk Agt	Colonial Stock Transfer Co Inc	Outstanding Shares	31,930,000
Counsel	Mackey Price & Williams	E.P.S.	-$0.03
DUNS No.	61-502-4353	Shareholders	NA

Business: The group's principal activity is to design, develop and market machine control software products to meet the needs of original equipment manufacturers. The group has three primary machine control software product lines: advanced motion control, general purpose equipment connectivity and specialized connectivity for 300mm semiconductor wafer fabrication facilities. The products include the cimetrix open development environment (code(tm)), cimconnect (TM), gem host manager (TM), testconnect (TM), cim300 (TM), cimfoundation (TM), cim40-process job (TM) and cim90-substrate tracking (TM). The customers of the group include wide variety of technology and manufacturing industries, including smt, semiconductor wafer fabrication, semiconductor back-end, packaging, small parts assembly and robotics.

Primary SIC and add'l.: 7379 7371 7372

CIK No: 0000786620

Subsidiaries: Cimetrix Data Management Solutions, Inc, Cimetrix Europe, Inc., Cimetrix Merger Corporation

Officers: Robert H. Reback/Dir., CEO, Pres./$317,110.00, David P. Faulkner/Exec. VP - Sales, Marketing/$248,991.00, Kourosh Vahdani/VP - Global Services/$232,258.00, Dennis P. Gauger/CFO/$54,219.00, Brian L. Phillips/Sec., Treasurer

Directors: Robert H. Reback/Dir., CEO, Pres., Alan C. Weber/Dir., Michael B. Thompson/Dir., Scott C. Chandler/Dir.

Owners: Tsunami Network Partners Corporation/8.53%, Insiders/6.68%, Robert H. Reback/2.57%, Dennis P. Gauger, David P. Faulkner/1.46%, Alan C. Weber, Securities and Exchange Commission/5.19%, Scott C. Chandler, 1994 Bilzerian Irrevocable Trust/5.16%, Kourosh Vahdani, Michael B. Thompson

Financial Data: *Fiscal Year End:*12/31 *Latest Annual Data:* 12/31/2006

Year	Sales	Net Income
2006	$5,556,000	-$1,149,000
2005	$4,670,000	-$706,000
2004	$4,542,000	$164,000

Curr. Assets:	$1,706,000	**Curr. Liab.:**	$1,170,000		
Plant, Equip.:	$177,000	**Total Liab.:**	$1,616,000	**Indic. Yr. Divd.:**	NA
Total Assets:	$2,538,000	**Net Worth:**	$922,000	**Debt/ Equity:**	0.5463

Cincinnati Bell Inc

221 E 4th St., Cincinnati, OH, 45202; *PH:* 1-513-397-9900; *Fax:* 1-513-397-5092; *http://* www.cincinnatibell.com

General - Incorporation	OH	**Stock**- Price on:12/24/2007	$5.76
Employees	2,950	Stock Exchange	NYSE
Auditor	Pricewaterhousecoopers LLP	Ticker Symbol	CBB
Stk Agt	Computershare Investor Services LLC	Outstanding Shares	247,670,000
Counsel	NA	E.P.S.	$0.33
DUNS No.	00-699-9239	Shareholders	NA

Business: The group's principal activity is to provide diversified communications services. These services are provided through four segments: local communications, broadband, wireless and other. The local communications segment provides local, long distance, data networking and transport, Internet and pay phone services, as well as sale of communication equipment. The broadband segment utilizes an advanced fiber-optic network to provide private line, switched access, data transport, Internet-based and other services to end user customers. The wireless segment provides advanced digital personal communications and sale of related communication equipment. The other segment resells voice long distance and provided public payphone services.

Primary SIC and add'l.: 4813 7389

CIK No: 0000716133

Subsidiaries: BCSIVA Inc., BRCOM Inc., BRFS LLC, BRHI Inc., Cincinnati Bell Any Distance Inc., Cincinnati Bell Complete Protection Inc., Cincinnati Bell Entertainment Inc., Cincinnati Bell Extended Territories LLC, Cincinnati Bell Technology Solutions Inc., Cincinnati Bell Telecommunications Services LLC, Cincinnati Bell Telephone Company LLC, Cincinnati Bell Wireless Company, Cincinnati Bell Wireless Holdings LLC, Cincinnati Bell Wireless LLC, IXC Internet Services, Inc. 20 Subsidiaries included in the Index

Officers: John F. Cassidy/CEO, Pres./$3,726,187.00, Jeff Coleman/VP - Internal Controls, Brian A. Ross/CFO/$1,005,346.00, Michael W. Callaghan/Sr. VP - Corporate Development/$1,249,574.00, Brian G. Keating/VP - Human Resources, Administration, Christopher J. Wilson/VP, General Counsel/$564,121.00, Ann Crable/Sr. VP - Operations, Mark W. Peterson/VP, Treasurer, Rod Dir/COO/$888,667.00, Kurt A. Freyberger/VP, Controller

Directors: Phillip R. Cox/60/Chmn., Alex Shumate/57/Dir., Bruce L. Byrnes/59/Dir., David B. Sharrock/71/Dir., Michael G. Morris/61/Dir., John M. Zrno/69/Dir., Robert W. Mahoney/71/Dir., Daniel J. Meyer/71/Dir.

Owners: Barclays Global Investors, N.A./10.10%, John F. Cassidy/1.80%, Michael G. Morris, Robert W. Mahoney, Christopher J. Wilson, Daniel J. Meyer, Michael W. Callaghan, Phillip R. Cox, Rodney D. Dir, Brian A. Ross, David B. Sharrock, Alex Shumate, Insiders/3.70%, John M. Zrno, Bruce L. Byrnes

Financial Data: *Fiscal Year End:*12/31 *Latest Annual Data:* 12/31/2006

Year	Sales	Net Income
2006	$1,270,100,000	$86,300,000
2005	$1,209,600,000	-$64,500,000
2004	$1,207,100,000	$64,200,000

Curr. Assets:	$347,400,000	**Curr. Liab.:**	$318,900,000	**P/E Ratio:**	17.45
Plant, Equip.:	$818,800,000	**Total Liab.:**	$2,805,400,000	**Indic. Yr. Divd.:**	NA
Total Assets:	$2,013,800,000	**Net Worth:**	-$791,600,000	**Debt/ Equity:**	NA

Cincinnati Financial Corp

6200 S Gilmore Rd., Fairfield, OH, 45014; *PH:* 1-513-870-2000; *Fax:* 1-513-870-2911; *http://* www.cinfin.com

General - Incorporation	OH	**Stock**- Price on:12/24/2007	$45.12
Employees	4,048	Stock Exchange	NDQ
Auditor	Deloitte & Touche LLP	Ticker Symbol	CINF
Stk Agt	Cincinnati Financial Corp	Outstanding Shares	171,680,000
Counsel	NA	E.P.S	$4.60
DUNS No.	05-129-0153	Shareholders	NA

Business: The group's principle activity is to market commercial, personal and life insurance services. The groups insurance services coverage include property, loss of income, general liability, crime, commercial inland marine, machinery and equipment breakdown. The group also offers specialty programs for small businesses, contractors, dentists, financial institutions, garage operations, metalworkers and religious institutions. The group operates from United States.

Primary SIC and add'l.: 6719 6321 6311 6331

CIK No: 0000020286

Subsidiaries: A.M. Cincinnati Life Insurance Company, CFC Investment Company and CinFin Capital Management Company, Fifth Third Bancorp

Officers: John J. Schiff/Chmn., CEO/$2,214,009.00, James E. Benoski/Vice Chmn., COO, Chief Insurance Officer, Pres./$2,486,473.00, Kenneth W. Stecher/CFO, Exec. VP, Sec.,Treasurer/$2,136,214.00, Kenneth S. Miller/Chief Investment Officer, Sr. VP, Assist. Sec., Assist. Treasurer, Eric N. Mathews/VP, Assist. Sec., Assist. Treasurer, Heather J. Wietzel/VP - Investor Relations, Jerry L. Litton/Sec. - Shareholder Services, Joan O. Shevchik/Sr. VP - Corporate Communications

Directors: John J. Schiff/Chmn., CEO, James E. Benoski/Vice Chmn., COO, Chief Insurance Officer, Pres., William F. Bahl/Dir., Michael Brown/Dir., John F. Steele/Dir., Anthony E. Woods/Dir., Gregory T. Bier/Dir., Douglas S. Skidmore/Dir., Gretchen W. Price/Dir., Dirk J. Debbink/Dir., Larry R. Webb/Dir., Rodney W. McMullen/Dir., Thomas R. Schiff/Dir., Kenneth C. Lichtendahl/Dir.

Owners: John M. Shepherd, James E. Benoski/0.28%, Dirk J. Debbink, Eric N. Mathews/0.05%, Rodney W. McMullen, David Popplewell/0.10%, Anthony E. Woods, Kenneth W. Stecher/0.12%, John F. Steele, John J. Schiff/7.22%, Craig W. Forrester/0.05%, Gretchen W. Price/0.01%, Gregory T. Bier, Thomas R. Schiff/5.44%, Kenneth C. Lichtendahl/0.01% *(26 Owners included in Index)*

Financial Data: **Fiscal Year End:**12/31 **Latest Annual Data:** 12/31/2006

Year	Sales	Net Income
2006	$4,550,000,000	$930,000,000
2005	$3,767,000,000	$602,000,000
2004	$3,614,000,000	$584,000,000

Curr. Assets:	$2,229,000,000	**Curr. Liab.:**	NA	**P/E Ratio:**	13.80
Plant, Equip.:	$193,000,000	**Total Liab.:**	$10,414,000,000	**Indic. Yr. Divd.:**	$1.420
Total Assets:	$17,222,000,000	**Net Worth:**	$6,808,000,000	**Debt/ Equity:**	0.1252

Cincinnati Gas & Electric Co

526 S Church St., Ec03t, Charlotte, NC, 28202; *PH:* 1-704-594-6200; *http://* www.duke-energy.com

General - Incorporation	OH	**Stock**- Price on:12/24/2007	NA
Employees	NA	Stock Exchange	NA
Auditor	Deloitte & Touche LLP	Ticker Symbol	NA
Stk Agt	NA	Outstanding Shares	NA
Counsel	NA	E.P.S	NA
DUNS No.	00-699-9189	Shareholders	NA

Business: The group's principle activities include generating, transmiting and distributing electric power in the southwestern portion of Ohio and adjacent areas in Kentucky and Indiana; and sells and transports natural gas. The group operates from United States.

Primary SIC and add'l.: 4931 4922

CIK No: 0000020290

Subsidiaries: 1388368 Ontario Inc., 3036243 Nova Scotia Company, ACcess Broadband, LLC, Attiki Denmark ApS, Attiki Gas Supply Company SA, Avon Energy Partners, LLC, Barre Energy Partners, L.P., Biogas Financial Corporation, Biomass New Jersey, LLC, BMC Energy, LLC, Brickyard Energy Partners, LLC, Brookhaven Energy Partners, LLC, Brown County Energy Associates, LLC, Brown County Landfill Gas Associates, L.P., Brownsville Power I, LLC 233 Subsidiaries included in the Index

Officers: James E. Rogers/Chmn., CEO, Pres., Julia S. Janson/Sr. VP - Ethics, Compliance, Corp. Sec., Marc E. Manly/Group Executive, Chief Legal Officer, Lynn J. Good/Sr. VP, Treasurer, James L. Turner/Group Executive, Pres., COO - US Franchised Electric, Gas, Jim L. Stanley/Pres. - Duke Energy Indiana, R. Sean Trauschke/VP - Investor Relations, Steve Brash/Ohio, Kentucky Media Relations, Duke Energy Electric Operations, Rick Rhodes/Non - Regulated Generation Media Relations - Duke Energy Electric Operations, Henry B. Barron/Group Executive, Chief Nuclear Officer, David L. Hauser/Group Executive, CFO, Sandra P. Meyer/Pres. - Duke Energy Ohio, Duke Energy Kentucky, Thomas C. O'Connor/Group Executive, Pres. - Commercial Businesses, Christopher C. Rolfe/Group Executive, Chief Administrative Officer, Cathy S. Roche/Sr. VP, Chief Communications Officer *(34 Officers included in Index)*

Directors: James E. Rogers/Chmn., CEO, Pres., Mary L. Schapiro/Dir., Michael G. Browning/Dir., Phillip R. Cox/Dir., Dudley S. Taft/Dir., William Barnet/Dir., Alex G. Bernhardt/Dir., Ann Maynard Gray/Dir., James H. Hance/Dir., James T. Rhodes/Dir.

Cinemark USA Inc

3900 Dallas Pkwy, Ste 500, Plano, TX, 75093; *PH:* 1-800-246-3627; *http://* www.cinemark.com

General - Incorporation	TX	**Stock**- Price on:12/24/2007	NA
Employees	NA	Stock Exchange	NA
Auditor	Deloitte & Touche LLP	Ticker Symbol	NA
Stk Agt	NA	Outstanding Shares	NA
Counsel	NA	E.P.S	NA
DUNS No.	08-514-0937	Shareholders	NA

Business: The group's principal activity is to operate motion picture theatres. The group operates 3,142 screens in 294 theatres located in 33 states, Canada, Mexico, Argentina, Brazil, Chile, Ecuador, Peru, Honduras, El Salvador, nicaragua, Costa Rica, panama, Colombia and the United Kingdom, consisting of 2,739 screens in 245 first run theatres and 403 screens in 49 discount theatres.

Primary SIC and add'l.: 7832 7830

CIK No: 0000885975

Subsidiaries: Brainerd Cinema, Ltd., Brasil Holdings, LLC, Bulnes 2215, S.R.L., Canada Theatre Holdings, Inc., Cinema Properties, Inc., Cinemark Argentina, S.R.L., Cinemark Brasil S.A., Cinemark Chile S.A., Cinemark Colombia S.A., Cinemark Costa Rica S.R.L., Cinemark de Mexico, S.A. de C.V., Cinemark del Ecuador S.A., Cinemark del Norte, S.A. de C.V., Cinemark del Peru S.R.L., Cinemark El Salvador Ltda. de C.V. 51 Subsidiaries included in the Index

Officers: Alan W. Stock/CEO, Robert Copple/Exec. VP, Treasurer, CFO, Assist. Sec., Michael Cavalier/Sr. VP, General Counsel, Sec., Tandy Mitchell/Exec. VP, Assist. Sec., Timothy Warner/COO, Pres.

Directors: Lee Roy Mitchell/Chmn., Benjamin D. Chereskin/Dir., Vahe A. Dombalagian/Dir., Enrique F. Senior/Dir., Peter R. Ezersky/Dir., Roger T. Staubach/Dir., Carlos M. Sepulveda/Dir., Raymond W. Syufy/Dir., Donald G. Soderquist/Dir.

Cintas Corp

6800 Cintas Blvd., Cincinnati, OH, 45262; *PH:* 1-513-459-1200; *Fax:* 1-513-573-4130; *http://* www.cintas.com; *Email:* info@cintas.com

General - Incorporation	WA	**Stock**- Price on:12/24/2007	NA
Employees	32,000	Stock Exchange	NDQ
Auditor	Ernst & Young LLP	Ticker Symbol	CFCI
Stk Agt	Wells Fargo Shareowner Services	Outstanding Shares	NA
Counsel	NA	E.P.S	$2.09
DUNS No.	05-648-1716	Shareholders	NA

Business: The groups principle activity is to provide specialized products and services to businesses. The groups products include uniforms and apparel, mats, mops and towels, and flame resistant clothing. The groups services include document shredding and storage, and facility services. The group operates through two business segments namely rentals and Rentals and Other Services. The group operates from United States.

Primary SIC and add'l.: 5699 2329 7213

CIK No: 0000723254

Subsidiaries: 1202327 Ontario, Inc., 3065520 Nova Scotia Company, 3065521 Nova Scotia Company, Affirmed Medical, Inc., American First Aid Company, CDS Equipment Holdings, LLC, Cintas R.U.S., LP, Cintas Canada Investment Limited Partnership, Cintas Canada Limited, Cintas Cleanroom Resources de Mexico S.A. de C.V., Cintas Corp. No. 15, Inc., Cintas Corp. No. 8, Inc., Cintas Corporation No. 2, Cintas Corporation No. 3, Cintas De Honduras, S.A. 26 Subsidiaries included in the Index

Officers: Scott D. Farmer/Dir., CEO, Pres./$1,288,010.00, Thomas E. Frooman/VP, Sec., General Counsel/$669,981.00, William C. Gale/CFO, Sr. VP/$707,207.00, Michael L. Thompson/VP, Treasurer/$440,086.00

Directors: Scott D. Farmer/Dir., CEO, Pres., Robert J. Kohlhepp/Vice Chmn., Richard T. Farmer/Chmn., Founder, David C. Phillips/Dir., Gerald V. Dirvin/Dir., Gerald S. Adolph/Dir., Roger L. Howe/Dir., Joyce Hergenhan/Dir., Paul R. Carter/Dir.

Owners: Michael L. Thompson, William C. Gale, Roger L. Howe, Arnhold& S. Bleichroeder Advisers, LLC/5.20%, Gerald V. Dirvin, Joyce Hergenhan, Insiders/14.40%, David C. Phillips, Richard T. Farmer/11.40%, Paul R. Carter, Gerald S. Adolph, Robert J. Kohlhepp/1.50%, Scott D. Farmer, Thomas E. Frooman

Financial Data: **Fiscal Year End:**05/31 **Latest Annual Data:** 05/31/2007

Year	Sales	Net Income
2007	$3,706,900,000	$334,538,000
2006	$3,403,608,000	$327,178,000
2005	$3,067,283,000	$300,518,000

Curr. Assets:	$1,156,736,000	**Curr. Liab.:**	$403,038,000	**P/E Ratio:**	13.80
Plant, Equip.:	$920,243,000	**Total Liab.:**	$1,402,742,000	**Indic. Yr. Divd.:**	$0.390
Total Assets:	$3,570,480,000	**Net Worth:**	$2,167,738,000	**Debt/ Equity:**	NA

CinTel Corp

7f Msa B/d, 891-43, Daechi-Dong, Kangnam-Gu, Seoul, 135280; *PH:* 82-5026938022; *http://* www.cintel.co.kr; *Email:* info@cintelcorp.net

General - Incorporation	NV	**Stock**- Price on:12/24/2007	$0.44
Employees	10	Stock Exchange	OTC
Auditor	SF Partnership LLP	Ticker Symbol	CNCN
Stk Agt	Corporate Stock Transfer, Inc.	Outstanding Shares	88,630,000
Counsel	NA	E.P.S	-$0.02
DUNS No.	NA	Shareholders	NA

Business: The group's principal activity is to provide various Internet traffic management(itm) solutions to the business world and other consuming public. It introduced Korea's first dynamic server load balancer and involved in marketing of proven itm products, such as packetcurztm icache, i2one, and proximator. The itm solutions of the group helps its customers to improve Internet traffic management, service levels and the user experience. I2one, packetcruz and peertree connect the Web are the registered trademark of the group. Major customers of the group include Korea's ministry of government for administration & home affairs' education Web, sam sung, kt corp, kepco, sk telecom, ktf, lg telecom and hana bank.

Primary SIC and add'l.: 7336 7375

CIK No: 0001191334

Subsidiaries: CinTel Co., Ltd

Officers: Sang Don Kim/41/Dir., CEO, Pres., Kyo Jin Kang/CFO, Principal Accounting Officer, Kwang Hee Lee/Dir., Sec., Treasurer, J. D. Sparks/VP - Strategic Development

Directors: Sang Don Kim/41/Dir., CEO, Pres., Sang Yong Oh/45/Chmn., Kwang Hee Lee/Dir., Sec., Treasurer

Owners: Joung Min Han/7.80%, Insiders/7.90%, Sang Don Kim/5.80%, EMERGING MEMORY & LOGIC Solution Inc../6.70%, KTB China Optinum Fund/10.20%, KTB Network Co., Ltd./4.90%, STS Semiconductor & Telecommunication Co.,Ltd/10.20%, Tai Bok Kim/22.00%, Sang Yong Oh/2.00%

Financial Data: **Fiscal Year End:**12/31 **Latest Annual Data:** 03/31/2007

Year	Sales	Net Income
2007	NA	$8,656,000
2006	$21,135,000	-$1,786,000
2005	$1,605,000	-$2,039,000

Curr. Assets:	$17,111,000	**Curr. Liab.:**	$19,391,000		
Plant, Equip.:	$25,977,000	**Total Liab.:**	$48,376,000	**Indic. Yr. Divd.:**	NA
Total Assets:	$53,149,000	**Net Worth:**	$4,773,000	**Debt/ Equity:**	4.3246

Cipher Holding Corp

104 W Chestnut St., Ste. 315, Hinsdale, IL, 60521; ***PH:*** 1-630-371-5583

General - Incorporation ... DE
Employees ... 3
Auditor ... Frank L. Sassetti & Co.
Stk Agt ... Corporate Stock Transfer, Inc.
Counsel ... NA
DUNS No. ... NA

Stock - Price on:12/24/2007 ... $0.045
Stock Exchange ... NA
Ticker Symbol ... NA
Outstanding Shares ... 68,660,000
E.P.S ... NA
Shareholders ... NA

Business: The group's principal activity is to provide distribution solution to digital content publishers. The group secures and allows access to digital content through proprietary encoding, encryption and authorization technology. The technology and services offered by the group allows publishers and distributors to distribute digital content in a secure format to mass markets. The solution consists of creating campaigns that enable publishers, advertisers and distributors to introduce content, promote products, immediately sell and deliver digital content to end users. The secured digital content is delivered in the form of CD/dvds, diskettes and Internet download. The customers include major and independent film studios, software publishers, monthly magazine and catalog companies, retail stores, Internet retailers, computer manufacturers, Internet service providers and digital content direct marketing companies.

Primary SIC and add'l.: 7373

CIK No: 0001047540

Subsidiaries: Imagin formed Positron Acquisition Corp, Imagin Nuclear Partners Corporation

Officers: Joseph G. Oliverio/38/Dir., CEO, Corey Conn/46/Dir., CFO

Directors: Joseph G. Oliverio/38/Dir., CEO, Neil Sy/38/Chmn., Corey Conn/46/Dir., CFO

Owners: Patrick G. Rooney/22.90%, Insiders/1.73%, Imagin Diagnostic Centers, Inc/11.03%, Corey Conn/1.19%, Neil Sy/0.54%

Financial Data: ***Fiscal Year End:***12/31 ***Latest Annual Data:*** 12/31/2006

Year	Sales	Net Income
2006	$183,000	-$973,000
2005	$3,000	-$75,000
2004	$3,000	-$330,000

Curr. Assets:	$167,000	**Curr. Liab.:**	$848,000		
Plant, Equip.:	$235,000	**Total Liab.:**	$1,054,000	**Indic. Yr. Divd.:**	NA
Total Assets:	$1,989,000	**Net Worth:**	$935,000	**Debt/ Equity:**	0.1897

Ciprico Inc

17400 Medina Rd., Plymouth, MN, 55447; ***PH:*** 1-763-551-4000; ***Fax:*** 1-763-551-4002; ***http://*** www.ciprico.com; ***Email:*** sales@ciprico.com

General - Incorporation ... DE
Employees ... 43
Auditor ... Grant Thornton LLP
Stk Agt ... Wells Fargo Shareowner Services
Counsel ... Fredrikson & Byron
DUNS No. ... 09-841-9500

Stock - Price on:12/24/2007 ... $8.24
Stock Exchange ... NDQ
Ticker Symbol ... CPCI
Outstanding Shares ... 5,090,000
E.P.S ... -$1.23
Shareholders ... NA

Business: The group's principle activity is to design, manufacture and market storage and system solutions for digital media applications. The group's products include disk arrays and digital media appliances that are designed to meet the demanding high availability, data transfer rate and storage capacity expansion needs of visual computing applications. The different types of products include the 7000 fibre channel series, fibrestore(R), talon(tm) and dimeda(tm). The major markets of the group are military and government, broadcast and entertainment media, as well as select other segments. The products are sold principlely to original equipment manufacturers and system integrators through a direct sales force. The group has international sales offices in the United Kingdom. The group's total revenue for year 2007 was 8.61 millions of USD.

Primary SIC and add'l.: 7379 3572

CIK No: 0000720145

Subsidiaries: Ciprico International Limited

Officers: Steven D. Merrifield/CEO, Pres., Monte S. Johnson/Sr. VP, CFO, Donald L. McDonell/VP - Sales, Marketing, Mark J. Moran/Chief Engineer, Andrew Mills/Sr. VP - Marketing, Development

Directors: James W. Hansen/Chmn.

Owners: Insiders, Steven D. Merrifield, Andrew Mills, Coghill Capital Management/7.55%, Gary L. Hokkanen, James D. Gerson, James W. Hansen, Thomas F. Burniece, Dimensional Fund Advisors/7.15%, Mark D. Griffiths, Monte S. Johnson

Financial Data: ***Fiscal Year End:***09/30 ***Latest Annual Data:*** 9/30/2006

Year	Sales	Net Income
2006	$11,932,000	-$3,661,000
2005	$13,213,000	-$2,439,000
2004	$18,081,000	-$7,378,000

Curr. Assets:	$14,582,000	**Curr. Liab.:**	$2,053,000		
Plant, Equip.:	$272,000	**Total Liab.:**	$2,119,000	**Indic. Yr. Divd.:**	NA
Total Assets:	$17,828,000	**Net Worth:**	$15,709,000	**Debt/ Equity:**	NA

CIRCOR International Inc

25 Corporate Dr., Ste. 130, Burlington, MA, 01803; ***PH:*** 1-781-270-1200; ***Fax:*** 1-781-270-1299; ***http://*** www.circor.com

General - Incorporation ... DE
Employees ... 2,800
Auditor ... KPMG LLP
Stk Agt ... American Stock Transfer & Trust CO.
Counsel ... Goodwin, Procter & Hoar
DUNS No. ... NA

Stock - Price on:12/24/2007 ... $40.87
Stock Exchange ... NYSE
Ticker Symbol ... CIR
Outstanding Shares ... 16,360,000
E.P.S ... $1.93
Shareholders ... NA

Business: The group's principal activity is to design, manufacture and distribute valves and related products and services. The group has two major product groups. The instrumentation and thermal fluid control group designs, manufactures and distributes valves, fittings and controls for diverse end-uses. The petrochemical group designs, manufactures and distributes flanged-end and threaded-end floating and trunnion ball valves, needle valves, check valves, butterfly valves, large forged steel ball valves, pipeline closures and strainers for use in oil, gas and chemical processing and industrial applications. The group operates 14 manufacturing facilities, located in the United States, Canada, western Europe and the People's Republic of China. The products are marketed to the oil and gas, aerospace, military and maritime industries. In 2003, the group acquired Texas sampling inc and dqs international bv and on 30-Apr-2004, mallard control company.

Primary SIC and add'l.: 3491 3494 3492

CIK No: 0001091883

Subsidiaries: Aerodyne Controls Inc, CEP Holdings, CEP Holdings Sarl. a Luxembourg limited liability company, Circle Seal Controls Inc., Circle Seal Controls, Inc., Circor (Jersey) Ltd., Circor (Jersey) Ltd., a United Kingdom Company, Circor (Jersey) Ltd.:, CIRCOR Business Trust . A Massachusetts Business Trust, Circor Business Trust:, Circor Energy Products Inc.:, Circor Energy Products (Canada) ULC an Alberta unlimited liability company, Circor Energy Products Inc., Circor German Holdings GmbH& Co. KG, Circor German Holdings LLC: 48 Subsidiaries included in the Index

Officers: David A. Bloss/Chmn., CEO/$2,757,113.00, Alan J. Glass/VP, General Counsel, Sec., Paul M. Coppinger/Group VP - Energy Products/$606,813.00, William A. Higgins/COO, Pres./$787,567.00, Christopher R. Celtruda/VP, GM - Circor Aerospace Products Group, John W. Cope/Group VP - Thermal Fluid Controls/$458,380.00, Jack Kober/VP, Corporate Controller, Susan M. McCuaig/VP - Human Resources, Wayne F. Robbins/VP, GM - Circor Instrumentation Technologies Group, Kenneth W. Smith/Sr. VP, CFO, Treasurer/$900,713.00, Richard A. Broughton/CIO, VP

Directors: David A. Bloss/Chmn., CEO, Jerome D. Brady/Dir., Dewain K. Cross/Dir., David F. Dietz/Dir., Douglas M. Hayes/Dir., Thomas E. Naugle/Dir.

Owners: Insiders/3.50%, Douglas M. Hayes, John W. Cope, David A. Bloss/1.70%, Dewain K. Cross, Gabelli Entities/14.50%, Franklin Resources, Inc./5.80%, Dimensional Fund Advisors Inc./8.40%, David F. Dietz, Keeley Asset Management Corp./9.60%, Thomas E. Naugle, Kenneth W. Smith, Jerome D. Brady, William A. Higgins, Paul M. Coppinger

Financial Data: ***Fiscal Year End:***12/31 ***Latest Annual Data:*** 12/31/2006

Year	Sales	Net Income
2006	$591,711,000	$29,328,000
2005	$450,531,000	$20,383,000
2004	$381,834,000	$11,803,000

Curr. Assets:	$300,950,000	**Curr. Liab.:**	$147,914,000	**P/E Ratio:**	19.10
Plant, Equip.:	$79,039,000	**Total Liab.:**	$248,374,000	**Indic. Yr. Divd.:**	$0.150
Total Assets:	$605,675,000	**Net Worth:**	$357,301,000	**Debt/ Equity:**	0.1790

Circuit City Stores Inc

9950 Mayland Dr., Richmond, VA, 23233; ***PH:*** 1-804-486-4000; ***Fax:*** 1-804-527-4164; ***http://*** www.circuitcity.com; ***Email:*** investor_media@circuitcity.com

General - Incorporation ... VA
Employees ... 46,082
Auditor ... KPMG LLP
Stk Agt ... Wells Fargo Shareowner Services
Counsel ... NA
DUNS No. ... NA

Stock - Price on:12/24/2007 ... $16.1
Stock Exchange ... NYSE
Ticker Symbol ... CC
Outstanding Shares ... 170,740,000
E.P.S ... -$0.85
Shareholders ... NA

Business: The groups principal activity is to retail consumer electronics, home office products, entertainment software and related services. The groups products marketed under the brand name Rogers Plus(R) and Battery Plus(R). The group operates from the United States and Canada. The group operates through two segments namely, domestic and international. Of the total net sales in the year 2006, the domestic segment accounted for $10,974.0 and international $623.7 (millions).

Primary SIC and add'l.: 5946 5734 5945 5735 5731

CIK No: 0000104599

Subsidiaries: CC Distribution Company of Virginia, Inc., Circuit City Global Sourcing Limited, Circuit City Properties, Inc., Circuit City Purchasing Company, LLC, Circuit City Stores West Coast, Inc., Intertan Canada, Ltd., Intertan, Inc., LEI (Hong Kong) Limited, Ventoux International, Inc.

Officers: Philip J. Schoonover/Chmn., CEO, Pres./$6,954,948.00, George D. Clark/Exec. VP - Multi, Channel Sales/$1,561,521.00, Michael E. Foss/50/CFO, Exec. VP/$1,675,893.00, David L. Mathews/48/Exec. VP - Merchandising, Services, Marketing, Ronald G. Cuthbertson/51/Sr. VP - Supply Chain, Inventory Management, Philip J. Dunn/Sr. VP, Treasurer, Controller, Reginald D. Hedgebeth/Sr. VP, General Counsel, Sec./$1,109,129.00, Eric A. Jonas/Sr. VP - Human Resources/$1,167,281.00, John J. Kelly/Sr. VP - Merchandising, Irynne V. MacKay/Sr. VP, Mgr. - General Merchandise, William E. McCorey/CIO, Sr. VP, Steven P. Pappas/Pres. - Small Stores, Sr. VP, Marc J. Sieger/Sr. VP, GM - Services, Peter C. Weedfald/Chief Marketing Officer, Sr. VP, Marshall J. Whaling/Sr. VP - Retail Operations *(18 Officers included in Index)*

Directors: Philip J. Schoonover/Chmn., CEO, Pres., Barbara S. Feigin/Dir., James F. Hardymon/Dir., Alan Kane/Dir., Allen B. King/Dir., Patrick J. Spainhour/Dir., Carolyn Y. Woo/Dir., Ronald L. Turner/Dir., Mikael Salovaara/Dir., Ronald M. Brill/Dir., Carolyn H. Byrd/Dir., Ursula O. Fairbairn/Dir.

Owners: Reginald D. Hedgebeth, Philip J. Schoonover, Allen B. King, James F. Hardymon, George D. Clark, Patrick J. Spainhour, Insiders/1.80%, Michael E. Foss, Carolyn H. Byrd, Eric A. Jonas, Alan Kane, Ronald M. Brill, Mikael Salovaara, Carolyn Y. Woo, Ursula O. Fairbairn *(16 Owners included in Index)*

Financial Data: ***Fiscal Year End:***02/28 ***Latest Annual Data:*** 2/28/2007

Year	Sales	Net Income
2007	$12,429,754,000	-$8,281,000
2006	$11,597,686,000	$139,746,000
2005	$10,472,364,000	$61,658,000

Curr. Assets:	$2,883,512,000	**Curr. Liab.:**	$1,714,029,000		
Plant, Equip.:	$921,027,000	**Total Liab.:**	$2,216,039,000	**Indic. Yr. Divd.:**	$0.160
Total Assets:	$4,007,283,000	**Net Worth:**	$1,791,244,000	**Debt/ Equity:**	0.0281

Circuit Research Labs Inc

7970 S Kyrene Rd., Tempe, AZ, 85284; ***PH:*** 1-480-403-8300; ***Fax:*** 1-480-403-8301; ***http://*** www.crlsystems.com; ***Email:*** sales@orban.com

General		Stock	
Incorporation	AZ	Price on:12/24/2007	$0.28
Employees	75	Stock Exchange	OTC
Auditor	Altschuler, Melvoin & Glasser LLP	Ticker Symbol	CRLI
Stk Agt	Bank One Arizona	Outstanding Shares	8,650,000
Counsel	James S. Freedman	E.P.S	-$0.16
DUNS No.	09-711-9093	Shareholders	NA

Business: The group's principal activity is to develop, manufacture and market electronic audio processing, transmission encoding and noise reduction equipment. The products control the audio quality and range of radio, television, cable and Internet audio reception and allow radio and television stations to broadcast in mono and stereo. The group's orban division manufactures and markets audio processing equipment under the orban, optimod, audicy and opticodec brand names. The product line includes FM series, AM series and other audio post-production workstations. The crl division manufactures and markets audio processing equipment, primarily using analog technology, under the crl, tvs and amigo brand names. The customers include AM and FM radio stations and television stations around the world. The products are exported to Europe, Pacific Rim, latin and South America, Canada and Mexico.

Primary SIC and add'l.: 3663 3651

CIK No: 0000725897

Subsidiaries: CRL International, Inc., CRL Systems, Inc., CRL/Orban Netherlands Holding BV, CRL/Orban Netherlands Operating BV, Orban Europe GmbH

Officers: Charles J. Brentlinger/Chmn., CEO, Pres., Bob Orban/VP, Chief Engineer, Kevin Clayborn/North American Sales Mgr., Charles Hintz/Sr. Engineer - Customer Support, Luis C. Endara/Dir. - Worldwide Sales, John F. Schaab/Orban PC Products Mgr. - Worldwide, David Rusch/Marketing, Advertising, Charlie Rich/Contact, Greg Ogonowski/VP - New Product Development, Peter Lee/VP - European Operations, Gary D. Clarkson/Dir., VP, Sec., Terry Tucker/Marketing Coordinator, Peter Van Beusekom/Sales, Technical Support Engineer, Rebecca Nation/VP - Administrative Operations, Human Resources, Gareth Paredes/MD - Sales, Customer Service *(19 Officers included in Index)*

Directors: Charles J. Brentlinger/Chmn., CEO, Pres., Gary D. Clarkson/Dir., VP, Sec.

Owners: Gary D. Clarkson/1.17%, Phillip T. Zeni/7.33%, Cornelia Burkhardtsmaier/14.50%, Charles Jayson Brentlinger/36.48%, Insiders/63.68%, Greg J. Ogonowski, Robert A. Orban/0.77%, Patricia Humke, Jayson Russell/9.23%, Dialog4 System Engineering GmbH/14.50%, Harman International, Inc./19.00%, Robert W. McMartin/6.12%, Friedrich Maier/14.50%, Christopher M. Kampmeier/0.82%

Financial Data: *Fiscal Year End:*12/31 *Latest Annual Data:* 12/31/2006

Year	Sales	Net Income
2006	$12,677,000	-$2,164,000
2005	$15,190,000	$2,584,000
2004	$13,242,000	-$1,507,000

Curr. Assets:	$3,560,000	**Curr. Liab.:**	$6,262,000		
Plant, Equip.:	$265,000	**Total Liab.:**	$8,394,000	**Indic. Yr. Divd.:**	NA
Total Assets:	$10,728,000	**Net Worth:**	$2,335,000	**Debt/ Equity:**	1.0463

Cirrus Logic Inc

2901 Via Fortuna, Austin, TX, 78746; *PH:* 1-512-851-4000; *Fax:* 1-512-912-3977; *http://* www.cirrus.com

General		Stock	
Incorporation	DE	Price on:12/24/2007	$59.5
Employees	456	Stock Exchange	NDQ
Auditor	Ernst & Young LLP	Ticker Symbol	CRUS
Stk Agt	Computershare Investor Services LLC	Outstanding Shares	88,740,000
Counsel	NA	E.P.S	$0.31
DUNS No.	11-330-3614	Shareholders	NA

Business: The group's principle activity is to develop and market integrated circuits (ics) and embedded software used by original equipment manufacturers (OEMs). The group also provides complete system reference designs based on the technology that enables the customers to market in a timely and cost-effective manner. The products are used in the audio, consumer electronics, automotive entertainment, and other industrial applications. The group offers more than 260 products to over 3,000 customers worldwide, through direct and indirect sales channels. The products of the group are used by the customers in brands such as bose, denon, digi design, harman kardon, kenwood, mackie, marantz, onkyo, panasonic, philips, pioneer, sony, technics, and yamaha. The group has international operations in China, Korea, Japan, Singapore, Taiwan and Europe. The group's total revenue for year 2007 was 182.30 millions of USD.

Primary SIC and add'l.: 3674 3572 7379 3577 3695

CIK No: 0000772406

Officers: Jason Rhode/Dir., CEO, Pres., Keith Cheney/VP, GM - Embedded Products Division, Terry M. Leeder/Sr. VP - Strategic Business Development, Jo-Dee M. Benson/VP - Corporate Communications, Human Resources, Gerald R. Gray/Sr. VP - Worldwide Operations, Gregory Scott Thomas/VP, General Counsel, Corp. Sec./$603,394.00, John J. Paulos/Sr. VP, GM - Industrial Products Division/$614,960.00, Thurman K. Case/CFO, VP - Finance, Treasurer/$353,004.00, Robert A. Kromer/58/VP - Worldwide Sales/$601,026.00, Miroslav Dokic/VP - DSP Business Unit, Wu Bin/VP, GM - Shanghai Power Management Division

Directors: Jason Rhode/Dir., CEO, Pres., Suhas S. Patil/Co - Founder, Chmn. Emeritus, Michael L. Hackworth/Co - Founder, Chmn., James D. Guzy/Dir., Walden C. Rhines/Dir., William D. Sherman/Dir., Robert H. Smith/Dir.

Owners: Jason P. Rhode, Legg Mason Inc./8.50%, Thurman Case, Suhas S. Patil, Robert H. Smith, James D. Guzy, Alfred S. Teo/9.50%, Michael L. Hackworth, Walden C. Rhines, John Kurtzweil, John J. Paulos, David D. French/2.00%, Robert A. Kromer, Royce& Associates, LLC/6.70%, Insiders/4.50% *(17 Owners included in Index)*

Financial Data: *Fiscal Year End:*03/25 *Latest Annual Data:* 3/31/2007

Year	Sales	Net Income
2007	$182,304,000	$27,895,000
2006	$193,694,000	$52,426,000
2005	$194,900,000	-$13,388,000

Curr. Assets:	$321,037,000	**Curr. Liab.:**	$34,620,000	**P/E Ratio:**	191.94
Plant, Equip.:	$11,407,000	**Total Liab.:**	$48,123,000	**Indic. Yr. Divd.:**	NA
Total Assets:	$353,060,000	**Net Worth:**	$304,937,000	**Debt/ Equity:**	0.0444

CirTran Corp

4125 S 6000 W, West Valley City, UT, 84128; *PH:* 1-801-963-5112; *Fax:* 1-801-963-5180; *http://* www.cirtran.com

General		Stock	
Incorporation	NV	Price on:12/24/2007	NA
Employees	110	Stock Exchange	OTC
Auditor	Hansen, Barnett & Maxwell	Ticker Symbol	CIRC
Stk Agt	Interwest Transfer Company, Inc.	Outstanding Shares	NA
Counsel	Sunborne XII	E.P.S	-$0.003
DUNS No.	NA	Shareholders	NA

Business: The group's principal activities are equipment manufacturing in communications, networking, peripherals, gaming, law enforcement, consumer products, telecommunications, automotive, medical and semi-conductor. The group operates through two business segments: electronics assembly and ethernet. The electronics assembly segment manufactures and assembles circuit boards and electronic component cables. The ethernet technology segment designs and manufactures ethernet cards. The group also provides pre-manufacturing, manufacturing and post-manufacturing services. It has operations in the United States, Europe, Africa and the Middle East.

Primary SIC and add'l.: 3672 3679

CIK No: 0000813716

Subsidiaries: CirTran Asia, Inc., CirTran Corporation, CirTran Products Corporation, Diverse Media Group Corporation, Racore Network, Inc.

Officers: Iehab J. Hawatmeh/Chmn., CEO, Pres./$282,807.00, Trevor M. Saliba/34/Dir., Exec. VP - Worldwide Business Development, Marketing/$138,755.00, Shaher Hawatmeh/COO/$157,790.00, Charles Ho/Pres. - Cirtran, Asia/$407,397.00, James Snow/VP - Engineering, Product Development, Patrick L. Gerrard/Corp. Dir. - Quality, Richard Ferrone/CFO/$94,845.00

Directors: Iehab J. Hawatmeh/Chmn., CEO, Pres., Trevor M. Saliba/34/Dir., Exec. VP - Worldwide Business Development, Marketing, Fadi Nora/46/Dir.

Owners: Shaher Hawatmeh/0.15%, Trevor Saliba/1.37%, Insiders/10.68%, Saliba Private Annuity Trust/11.54%, Iehab J. Hawatmeh/9.15%, Raed Hawatmeh/3.63%

Financial Data: *Fiscal Year End:*12/31 *Latest Annual Data:* 12/31/2006

Year	Sales	Net Income
2006	$8,739,000	-$2,854,000
2005	$12,993,000	-$528,000
2004	$8,863,000	-$658,000

Curr. Assets:	$3,624,000	**Curr. Liab.:**	$8,488,000		
Plant, Equip.:	$2,678,000	**Total Liab.:**	$9,511,000	**Indic. Yr. Divd.:**	NA
Total Assets:	$11,130,000	**Net Worth:**	$1,619,000	**Debt/ Equity:**	NA

Cisco Systems Inc

170 W Tasman Dr., Bldg. 10, San Jose, CA, 95134; *PH:* 1-408-526-4000; *Fax:* 1-408-526-4100; *http://* www.cisco.com

General		Stock	
Incorporation	CA	Price on:12/24/2007	$27.15
Employees	49,926	Stock Exchange	NDQ
Auditor	PricewaterhouseCoopers LLP	Ticker Symbol	CSCO
Stk Agt	Computershare Shareholder Ser Inc	Outstanding Shares	6,070,000,000
Counsel	Brobeck, Phleger & Harrison	E.P.S	$1.26
DUNS No.	15-380-4570	Shareholders	NA

Business: The group's principle activities include designing, manufacturing and selling Internet protocol based networking and various products related to the communications and information technology industry. The group's products include interfaces and modules, routers, switches, interoperability systems, wireless LAN controllers, line extenders and software. The group's services include broadband cable, data center, security, storage networking and wireless services. In November 2007, the group acquired Securent, Inc. The group operates from United States.

Primary SIC and add'l.: 7379 3577 7373

CIK No: 0000858877

Subsidiaries: 3010081 Nova Scotia Company, 3045848 Nova Scotia Company, 3048504 Nova Scotia Company, 3120578 Nova Scotia Company, 3801110 Canada Inc., Actona Technologies Ltd., Actona Technologies, Inc., Airespace EMEA Limited, Airespace K.K., Airespace Wireless Networks Private Limited, Airespace, Inc., Aironet Canada Inc., Aironet Canada Limited, Asset Acquisition Corporation, Audium Corporation 215 Subsidiaries included in the Index

Officers: John T. Chambers/Chmn., CEO/$10,984,290.00, Alison Stokes/Contact - Media Relations, Charles H. Giancarlo/Chief Development Officer, Sr. VP/$5,496,240.00, Richard J. Justice/Exec. VP - Worldwide Operations, Business Development/$5,652,581.00, Penny Bruce/Contact - Media Relations, Nancy Darma/Contact - Media Relations, Lee Davis/Contact - Media Relations, Molly Q. Ford/Contact - Media Relations, Terry Alberstein/Contact - Media Relations, Terry Anderson/Contact - Media Relations, Robert Barlow/Contact - Media Relations, Neil Becker/Contact - Media Relations, Willa Black/Contact - Media Relations, Lisa Brooke/Contact - Media Relations, Randy Pond/Exec. VP - Operations, Processes, Systems/$4,677,856.00 *(110 Officers included in Index)*

Directors: John T. Chambers/Chmn., CEO, Michele M. Burns/Dir., Jerry Yang/Dir., Carol Bartz/Dir., Brian L. Halla/Dir., Michael K. Powell/Dir., Richard Kovacevich/Dir., Steven M. West/Dir., Roderick C. McGeary/Dir., Larry R. Carter/Dir., Sr. VP, Michael D. Capellas/Dir., John L. Hennessy/Dir.

Owners: Barclays Global Investors, NA/5.00%, John L. Hennessy, Michael D. Capellas, Richard J. Justice, Roderick C. McGeary, Jerry Yang, Randy Pond, Charles H. Giancarlo, Carol A. Bartz, John T. Chambers, Insiders, Brian L. Halla, Richard M. Kovacevich, Larry R. Carter, Michele M. Burns *(18 Owners included in Index)*

Financial Data: *Fiscal Year End:*07/30 *Latest Annual Data:* 07/28/2007

Year	Sales	Net Income
2007	$34,922,000,000	$7,333,000,000
2006	$28,484,000,000	$5,580,000,000
2005	$24,801,000,000	$5,741,000,000

Curr. Assets:	$14,343,000,000	**Curr. Liab.:**	$8,703,000,000	**P/E Ratio:**	23.21
Plant, Equip.:	$3,290,000,000	**Total Liab.:**	$9,678,000,000	**Indic. Yr. Divd.:**	NA
Total Assets:	$35,594,000,000	**Net Worth:**	$25,826,000,000	**Debt/ Equity:**	0.2271

Cistera Networks Inc

17304 Preston Rd. Ste. 975, Dallas, TX, 75252; *PH:* 1-972-381-4699; *http://* www.cistera.com; *Email:* support@cistera.com

General		Stock	
Incorporation	NV	Price on:12/24/2007	NA
Employees	NA	Stock Exchange	OTC
Auditor	Robison, Hill & Co.	Ticker Symbol	CNWT
Stk Agt	Corporate Stock Transfer, Inc.	Outstanding Shares	9,980,000
Counsel	NA	E.P.S	NA
DUNS No.	NA	Shareholders	NA

Business: The groups principle activity is to develop solutions that help businesses to solve problems and investment in their Internet protocol Telephony Investment. The group products include convergence servers, application platforms and application engines. In the year 2005, the group acquired XBridge Software, Inc. The group operates from the United States. The groups quarterly revenue for September 2007 was 0.89 millions of USD.

Primary SIC and add'l.: 7371

CIK No: 0000821356

Officers: Derek P. Downs/Pres., Interim CEO, Heather Baggett/Cistera Networks, Texas Marketing, Communications, Gregory T. Royal/CTO, Exec. VP, Jim Miller/VP - Operations, Cynthia A. Garr/Dir., CFO, Exec. VP - Corporate Development

Directors: Katrina A. Roche/Dir., Cynthia A. Garr/Dir., CFO, Exec. VP - Corporate Development

Owners: Roaring Fork Capital Management/10.30%, Derek P. Downs/2.00%, Cynthia A. Garr/13.70%, Gregory T. Royal/16.00%, Insiders/31.70%, Kingdon Hughes/15.10%, Artis Capital Management/5.80%

Financial Data: Fiscal Year End:03/31   Latest Annual Data: 03/31/2007

Year	Sales	Net Income
2007	$2,046,000	-$1,174,000

Curr. Assets:	$955,000	Curr. Liab.:	$1,727,000
Plant, Equip.:	$122,000	Total Liab.:	$3,713,000	Indic. Yr. Divd.: NA
Total Assets:	$3,373,000	Net Worth:	-$340,000	Debt/ Equity: 2.7405

CIT Group Inc

505 5th Ave., New York, NY, 10017; *PH:* 1-212-771-0505; *http://* www.cit.com

General - Incorporation	DE	Stock- Price on:12/24/2007	$57.61
Employees	7,345	Stock Exchange	NYSE
Auditor	PricewaterhouseCoopers LLP	Ticker Symbol	CIT
Stk Agt	Bank of New York	Outstanding Shares	191,780,000
Counsel	NA	E.P.S.	$3.09
DUNS No.	15-536-1595	Shareholders	NA

Business: The groups principle activity is to provide financing and advisory services. The groups services include vendor financing, factoring, equipment and transportation financing, small business administration loans. Customers served by the group include manufacturing, transportation, retailing, wholesaling, healthcare, and communications. The group operates from United States.

Primary SIC and add'l.: 6159 6141 7359

CIK No: 0001171825

Subsidiaries: 1020675 Ontario Inc., 1145820 Ontario Limited, 1243029 Ontario Inc., 1244771 Ontario Limited, 1309673 Ontario Limited, 1641964 Ontario Limited, 1663979 Ontario Inc., 2705 Parkhill Drive Limited Partnership, 2937531 Canada Inc., 3918041 Canada Inc., 544211 Alberta Ltd., 555565 Alberta Ltd., 555566 Alberta Ltd., 991102 Alberta Ltd., 991122 Alberta Ltd. 338 Subsidiaries included in the Index

Officers: Jeffrey M. Peek/Chmn., CEO, Lawrence A. Marsiello/Vice Chmn., Chief Lending Officer, Joseph M. Leone/Vice Chmn., CFO, Curtis C. Ritter/Dir. - External Communications, Media Relations, Bhavin Shah/Assist. VP - Investor Relations, Gregg H. Smith/Sr. MD - Investment Banking Services, Ken Brause/Exec. VP - Investor Relations, John F. Daly/Pres. - CIT Commercial Services, Steve Klimas/Sr. VP - Investor Relations, Randall H. Chesler/Pres. - CIT Consumer Finance, Peter Connolly/Exec. VP - CIT Syndicated Loan Group, CIT Capital Markets, Tim Eichenlaub/Sr. MD - CIT Sponsor Finance, James L. Hudak/Sr. MD - CIT Communications, Media, Entertainment, Daryl J. MacLellan/Pres. - CIT Canada, Joseph F. Nemia/Pres. - CIT Commercial, Industrial (53 Officers included in Index)

Directors: Jeffrey M. Peek/Chmn., CEO, Lawrence A. Marsiello/Vice Chmn., Chief Lending Officer, Joseph M. Leone/Vice Chmn., CFO, Thomas B. Hallman/Vice Chmn., Frederick E. Wolfert/53/Vice Chmn. - Commercial Finance, Susan Lyne/Dir., Timothy M. Ring/Dir., Seymour Sternberg/Dir., Lois M. Van Deusen/Dir., Marianne Miller Parrs/Dir., Peter J. Tobin/Dir., Gary C. Butler/Dir., Thomas H. Kean/Dir., William M. Freeman/Dir., John R. Ryan/Dir.

Owners: Jeffrey M. Peek, Gary C. Butler, Barclays Global Investors, NA/17.70%, Insiders/1.80%, Thomas H. Kean, William M. Freeman, Susan Lyne, Seymour Sternberg, Lawrence A. Marsiello, Lois M. Van Deusen, John R. Ryan, Thomas B. Hallman, Timothy Ring, Frederick E. Wolfert, Marianne Miller Parrs (17 Owners included in Index)

Financial Data: Fiscal Year End:12/31   Latest Annual Data: 12/31/2006

Year	Sales	Net Income
2006	$6,942,700,000	$1,046,000,000
2005	$5,652,600,000	$949,100,000
2004	$4,718,100,000	$753,600,000

Curr. Assets:	$6,161,400,000	Curr. Liab.:	$6,840,400,000	P/E Ratio: 11.76
Plant, Equip.:	$14,138,600,000	Total Liab.:	$69,276,900,000	Indic. Yr. Divd.: $1.000
Total Assets:	$77,067,900,000	Net Worth:	$7,751,100,000	Debt/ Equity: 8.3504

Citadel Broadcasting Corp

7201 W Lake Mead Blvd., Ste. 400, Las Vegas, NV, 89128; *PH:* 1-702-804-5200; *Fax:* 1-702-804-5936; *http://* www.citadelbroadcasting.com; *Email:* h.r@citcomm.com

General - Incorporation	DE	Stock- Price on:12/24/2007	$6.59
Employees	2,156	Stock Exchange	NYSE
Auditor	Deloitte & Touche LLP	Ticker Symbol	CDL
Stk Agt	BNY Mellon Shareowner Services	Outstanding Shares	112,130,000
Counsel	Kirkland & Ellis LLP	E.P.S.	$0.23
DUNS No.	NA	Shareholders	NA

Business: The group's principal activitiy is to own and operate radio stations. The group has radio station portfolio that is diversified by programming formats, geographic regions, audience demographics and advertisisng clients. As at 29-Feb-2004, the group owned and operated 145 FM and 58 AM radio stations in 58 markets located in 24 states across the United States. The group's radio stations are primarily located in mid-sized markets.

Primary SIC and add'l.: 4832 6719

CIK No: 0001174527

Officers: Farid Suleman/Chmn., CEO

Directors: Farid Suleman/Chmn., CEO, Herbert J. Siegel/Dir., Charles P. Rose/Dir., Theodore J. Forstmann/Dir., Michael A. Miles/Dir., Wayne Smith/Dir.

Owners: Randy L. Taylor, Insiders, Herbert J. Siegel, Judith A. Ellis, Dimensional Fund Advisors L.P., Katherine Brown, Forstmann Little& Co. Equity Partnership-VII, L.P., Forstmann Little& Co. Equity Partnership-VI, L.P., Jacquelyn J. Orr, Charles P. Rose, Patricia Stratford, Theodore J. Forstmann, Wayne T. Smith, Forstmann Little& Co. Subordinated Debt and Equity Management Buyout Partnership-VII, L.P., Michael A. Miles (19 Owners included in Index)

Financial Data: Fiscal Year End:12/31   Latest Annual Data: 12/31/2006

Year	Sales	Net Income
2006	$432,930,000	-$48,014,000
2005	$419,907,000	$69,757,000
2004	$411,495,000	$74,568,000

Curr. Assets:	$91,184,000	Curr. Liab.:	$40,746,000	
Plant, Equip.:	$83,934,000	Total Liab.:	$1,049,388,000	Indic. Yr. Divd.: $0.720
Total Assets:	$2,173,696,000	Net Worth:	$1,124,308,000	Debt/ Equity: 0.6483

Citadel Security Software Inc

5420 Lyndon B. Johnson Fwy., Ste. 1600, Dallas, TX, 75240; *PH:* 1-214-520-2449; *http://* www.citadel.com

General - Incorporation	DE	Stock - Price on:12/24/2007	NA
Employees	94	Stock Exchange	OTC
Auditor	KBA Group LLP	Ticker Symbol	CWDW
Stk Agt	Computershare Trust Co	Outstanding Shares	NA
Counsel	Ruth R. Lentz	E.P.S.	$0.833
DUNS No.	NA	Shareholders	NA

Business: The group's principle activities are to develop, market and license security line of desktop and network security software products. The security and privacy software is designed to remediate vulnerabilities and address the need for security inside the firewall. Its products include hercules, winshield secure PC and netoff. Hercules provides an automated remediation solution for corporate and government computing environments. Winshield secure PC provides desktop security and access control for computers. Netoff protects a network by shutting down unattended client pcs automatically after a specified period of inactivity. It derives revenues from licensing of software and product support contract. The major customers of the company include sbc communications, IBM global services, Washington mutual bank, merrill lynch, ebsco information services, the U.S. Navy and other health care, education and corporate clients. It operates solely in the domestic market.

Primary SIC and add'l.: 7372

CIK No: 0001164552

Subsidiaries: Citadel Security Software International, LLC

Owners: Mark Rogers/0.71%, Steven B. Solomon/17.76%, Insiders/21.48%, Joe M. Allbaugh/1.09%, John Leide/0.66%, Richard Connelly/0.48%, Chris Economou/1.18%

Financial Data: Fiscal Year End:12/31   Latest Annual Data: 12/31/2005

Year	Sales	Net Income
2005	$10,287,000	-$18,563,000
2004	$15,253,000	-$7,839,000
2003	$5,856,000	-$5,249,000

Curr. Assets:	$4,823,000	Curr. Liab.:	$10,572,000	
Plant, Equip.:	$5,126,000	Total Liab.:	$15,330,000	Indic. Yr. Divd.: $0.500
Total Assets:	$14,465,000	Net Worth:	-$865,000	Debt/ Equity: NA

CITGO Petroleum Corp

1293 Eldridge Pkwy., Houston, TX, 77077; *PH:* 1-832-486-4000; *Fax:* 1-832-486-1814; *http://* www.citgo.com; *Email:* info@citgo.com

General - Incorporation	DE	Stock- Price on:12/24/2007	NA
Employees	NA	Stock Exchange	NA
Auditor	KPMG LLP	Ticker Symbol	NA
Stk Agt	NA	Outstanding Shares	NA
Counsel	NA	E.P.S.	NA
DUNS No.	10-241-7268	Shareholders	NA

Business: The group's principal activities are to refine, market and transport petroleum products including gasoline, diesel fuel, jet fuel, petrochemicals, lubricants, asphalt and refined waxes. The group is wholly owned subsidiaries of pdv America inc. Transportation fuel customers include wholesale marketers, convenience stores and airlines. The customers for asphalt are independent paving contractors and the customers for lubricants are independent marketers, mass marketers and industrial customers. The group owns and operates a crude oil pipeline and three products pipeline systems.

Primary SIC and add'l.: 2911

CIK No: 0001011746

Subsidiaries: CITGO Funding Company LLC, CITGO International, Inc., PDV Midwest Refining, LLC

Officers: Alejandro Granado/Chmn., CEO, Pres., Rafael Gomez Abreu/VP - Strategic Shareholder Relations, Government, Public Affairs, Phil Reedy/VP - Finance, Wladimir Noriega/General Auditor, Bob Kostelnik/VP - Refining, Bill Hatch/VP - Supply, Marketing, Randy Carbo/VP - Lake Charles Manufacturing Complex, Rixio Medina/VP - Health, Safety, Security, Environmental Protection, Shared Services, Maritza Villanueva/Treasurer, Eduardo Assef/VP, GM - Corpus Christi Refinery, John Butts/Corporate Controller, Dean M. Hasseman/General Counsel

Directors: Alejandro Granado/Chmn., CEO, Pres., Juan Carlos Boue/Dir., Bernard Mommer/Dir., Asdrubal Chavez/Dir., Eudomario Carruyo/Dir.

Citi Trends Inc

102 Fahm St., Savannah, GA, 31401; *PH:* 1-912-236-1561; *Fax:* 1-912-443-3663; *http://* www.cititrends.com

General - Incorporation	DE	Stock- Price on:12/24/2007	$42.42
Employees	1,400	Stock Exchange	NDQ
Auditor	KPMG LLP	Ticker Symbol	CTRN
Stk Agt	American Stock Transfer & Trust Co.	Outstanding Shares	13,890,000
Counsel	NA	E.P.S.	$1.13
DUNS No.	NA	Shareholders	NA

Business: The groups principle activity is to provide fashion apparel and accessories. The group products sold under the trade names Citi Steps(TM), Diva Blue(TM) and Urban Sophistication(TM). The products of the group include dresses, sportswear, handbags, hats, jewelry, footwear, toys and belts. Customers served by the group include Womens, Childrens, Mens, and Home dcor. The group operates from Alabama, Arkansas, Florida, Georgia, Louisiana, Maryland and North Carolina. The group's quarterly revenue for September 2007 was 381.92 millions of USD.

Primary SIC and add'l.: 5699 5651 5999 5719 5661

CIK No: 0001318484

Officers: Edward R. Anderson/Chmn., CEO, George A. Bellino/Pres., Chief Merchandising Officer, James A. Dunn/Sr. VP - Store Operations, Bruce D. Smith/Sr. VP, CFO, Ivy D. Council/Sr. VP - Human Resources

Directors: Edward R. Anderson/Chmn., CEO, John S. Lupo/Dir., Patricia M. Luzier/Dir., Lawrence E. Hyatt/Dir.

Owners: Hampshire Equity Partners/45.70%, Insiders/4.60%, Morgan Stanley/13.50%, Lawrence Hyatt, Christopher Bergen, Thomas W. Stoltz, Tracy L. Noll, James A. Dunn, John S. Lupo, George A. Bellino/1.10%, Capital Research and Management Company/11.40%, Patricia M. Luzier, Edward R. Anderson/2.40%

Financial Data: *Fiscal Year End:*01/28 *Latest Annual Data:* 2/3/2007

Year	Sales	Net Income
2007	$381,918,000	$21,351,000
2006	$289,804,000	$14,200,000
2005	$203,442,000	$7,257,000

Curr. Assets:	$158,018,000	**Curr. Liab.:**	$69,650,000	**P/E Ratio:**	29.87
Plant, Equip.:	$34,753,000	**Total Liab.:**	$77,893,000	**Indic. Yr. Divd.:**	NA
Total Assets:	$196,102,000	**Net Worth:**	$118,209,000	**Debt/ Equity:**	0.0206

Citicorp

399 Pk. Ave., New York, NY, 10043; *PH:* 1-212-820-2380; *http://* www.citibank.com

General - Incorporation	DE	**Stock**- Price on:12/24/2007	NA
Employees	NA	Stock Exchange	NA
Auditor	KPMG LLP	Ticker Symbol	NA
Stk Agt	Citibank Shareholder Services	Outstanding Shares	NA
Counsel	NA	E.P.S	NA
DUNS No.	00-698-3704	Shareholders	NA

Business: The group's principle activity is to provide financial services. The group serving the financial needs to individuals, businesses, governments and financial institutions. The group operates from United States.

Primary SIC and add'l.: 6021

CIK No: 0000020405

Subsidiaries: Citigroup Inc

Officers: Robert Morse/MD, CEO - Asia Pacific, Citi Markets, Banking, Institutional Clients Group, William J. Mills/CEO - Europe, Middle East, Africa, Citi Markets, Banking, Institutional Clients Group, Michael Klein/Chmn., Vice Chmn. - Citibank International plc, Co - CEO - Citi Markets, Banking, Institutional Clients Group, Charles D. Johnston/CEO, Pres. - Smith Barney, Citi Global Wealth Management, Citigroup, Douglas L. Peterson/CEO - Citigroup Japan Holdings, Citigroup, Ajay Banga/Chmn., CEO - Global Consumer Group, International, Citigroup, Steven J. Freiberg/Chmn., CEO - Global Consumer Group, North America, Win Bischoff/Chmn. - Citi Europe, Acting CEO - Citi, James A. Forese/Co - CEO - Citi Markets, Banking, Institutional Clients Group, Citigroup, Manuel Medina-Mora/Chmn., CEO - Latin America, Mexico - Citigroup, Yung-Ku Ha/CEO - Citi Korea Inc, Paul S. Galant/CEO - Global Transaction Services, Citi Markets, Banking, Institutional Clients Group, Peter Knitzer/Chmn., CEO - Citibank North America, Global Consumer Group, Steffen W. Parratt/Special Assist. to The CEO - Citi, Fernando Quiroz Robles/CEO - Latin America Citi Markets, Banking, Institutional Clients Group *(119 Officers included in Index)*

Directors: Manuel Medina-Mora/Chmn., CEO - Latin America, Mexico - Citigroup, Vikram A. Atal/Chmn., CEO - Citi Cards Global Consumer Group, Ajay Banga/Chmn., CEO - Global Consumer Group, International, Citigroup, Steven J. Freiberg/Chmn., CEO - Global Consumer Group, North America, Win Bischoff/Chmn. - Citi Europe, Acting CEO - Citi, Stephen R. Volk/Vice Chmn. - Citi, Alan S. MacDonald/Vice Chmn. - Citibank NA, COO - Global Banking, Citi Markets, Banking, Institutional Clients Group, Harry D. Goff/Chmn. - Citifinancial North America, Global Consumer Group, Citigroup, Shengman Zhang/Vice Chmn. - Global Banking, COO - Asia Pacific, Citi Markets, Banking, Institutional Clients Group, Lewis B. Kaden/Vice Chmn. - Citi, Bill Rhodes/Sr. Vice Chmn. - Citi, Robert Druskin/Chmn. - Citi, COO, Member - Office, Sanford I. Weill/Chmn. Emeritus - Citigroup Inc, Judith Rodin/Dir. - Citigroup, Michael C. Armstrong/Dir. - Citigroup *(27 Directors included in Index)*

Citigroup Fairfield Futures Fund LP II

731 Lexington Ave. 25th Fl., New York, NY, 10022; *PH:* 1-212-559-2011

General - Incorporation	NY	**Stock**- Price on:12/24/2007	NA
Employees	NA	Stock Exchange	NA
Auditor	KPMG LLP	Ticker Symbol	NA
Stk Agt	NA	Outstanding Shares	NA
Counsel	NA	E.P.S	NA
DUNS No.	NA	Shareholders	NA

Business: The group's principle activity is to provide financial services. The group operates from United States.

Primary SIC and add'l.: 6221

CIK No: 0001276262

Subsidiaries: Citigroup Global Markets Holdings Inc.

Officers: Jennifer Magro/Dir., CFO, Jerry Pascucci/Dir., Pres., Ihor Rakowsky/Dir., Sec.

Directors: David J. Vogel/Dir., Shelley Ullman/Dir., Jennifer Magro/Dir., CFO, Jerry Pascucci/Dir., Pres., Ihor Rakowsky/Dir., Sec., Daryl Dewbrey/Dir., Raymond Nolte/Dir., Steve Ciampi/Dir.

Owners: Redeemable Units of Limited Partnership Interest/6.60%

Citigroup Global Markets Holdings Inc

388 Greenwich St., New York, NY, 10013; *PH:* 1-212-816-6000; *http://* www.citigroupgcib.com

General - Incorporation	NY	**Stock**- Price on:12/24/2007	NA
Employees	NA	Stock Exchange	AMEX
Auditor	KPMG LLP	Ticker Symbol	NA
Stk Agt	Citicorp Trust Bank	Outstanding Shares	NA
Counsel	NA	E.P.S	NA
DUNS No.	NA	Shareholders	NA

Business: The group's principle activity is to provide investment banking, global securities and commodities trading, and usa oil refining activities. Investment banking activities are conducted by salomon brothers holding company inc and its subsidiaries, including salomon brothers inc.salomon brothers provides capital raising, advisory, research and trading services to its customers, and executes proprietary trading strategies on its own behalf.commodities trading activities are conducted by the phibro division and related affiliates. Commodities traded include crude oil, refined oil products, natural gas, electricity, metals, petrochemicals, ethanol, sugar, cocoa, grains and coffee. The group operates from United States.

Primary SIC and add'l.: 6211 6282 6719

CIK No: 0000200245

Subsidiaries: Citigroup Global Markets Inc, Citigroup Global Markets Limited

Officers: Hal West/Branch Mgr.

Citigroup Inc

399 Pk. Ave., New York, NY, 10043; *PH:* 1-212-559-1000; *Fax:* 1-212-793-3946; *http://* www.citigroup.com

General - Incorporation	DE	**Stock**- Price on:12/24/2007	$54.11
Employees	327,000	Stock Exchange	NYSE
Auditor	KPMG LLP	Ticker Symbol	C
Stk Agt	Citibank Stockholder Services	Outstanding Shares	4,950,000,000
Counsel	NA	E.P.S	$4.19
DUNS No.	NA	Shareholders	NA

Business: The group operates through its subsidiaries whose principle activity is to provide financial services to consumer and corporate customers. The group operates through three segments namely, corporate and investment banking, global wealth management and alternative investments. The group operates from the United States. The groups quarterly net income for September 2007 was 2,212.00 millions of USD.

Primary SIC and add'l.: 6141 6211 6712 6221 6289 6282 6153 6021 6162

CIK No: 0000831001

Subsidiaries: 192 Baker Avenue, LLC, 2490827 Nova Scotia Limited, 3086148 Nova Scotia Company, 3121615 Canada Inc., 44-26 Hunter Street Realty Corporation, 525 Participacoes S.A., ABA SIS, S.A. de C.V., Absolute Value Fund, L.P., ACC CBNA Loan Funding LLC, ACC CFPI Loan Funding LLC, Acciones y Valores Banamex, S.A. de C.V. Casa de Bolsa, Integrante del Grupo Financiero Banamex, Achtundzwanzigste Gamma Trans Leasing Verwaltungs GmbH& Co. Finanzierungs-Management KG, ACONA B.V., Adam Capital Trust I, Adam Capital Trust II 1688 Subsidiaries included in the Index

Officers: James A. Forese/Co - CEO - Citi Markets - Banking, Institutional Clients Group, Win Bischoff/Chmn. - Citi Europe, Acting CEO - Citi, John A. Addison/Co - CEO, COO - Primerica Financial Services, Global Consumer Group, Jonathan Larsen/CEO - Citibank Singapore Ltd, Head - South East Asia, Global Consumer Group, Mgr. - Country Business, Richard D. Williams/Co - CEO, COO - Primerica, Global Consumer Group, Sanjeeb Chaudhuri/CEO - Central, Eastern Europe, Global Consumer Group, Chief Marketing Officer - Europe Middle East, Africa, George M. James/Vice Chmn. - Citi Alternative Investments, Institutional Clients Group, Shengman Zhang/Vice Chmn. - Global Banking, COO - Asia Pacific, Citi Markets, Banking, Institutional Clients Group, Alan S. MacDonald/Vice Chmn. - Citibank NA, COO - Global Banking, Citi Markets, Banking, Institutional Clients Group, Thomas G. Maheras/45/Co - Pres. - Corporate, Investment Banking, Maura Markus/Head - International Retail Banking, Global Consumer Group, Howard D. Marsh/MD, Head - Municipal Securities Division, Citi Markets, Banking, Institutional Clients Group, Mark Mason/CFO - Citi Global Wealth Management, Les Matheson/Division Exec. Pacific Region, Citi Country Officer Australia - Global Consumer Group, Robert S. Matthews/MD, Dir. - Global Wealth Advisory Services, Citi Global Wealth Management *(95 Officers included in Index)*

Directors: Win Bischoff/Chmn. - Citi Europe, Acting CEO - Citi, Robert E. Rubin/Chmn., Lewis B. Kaden/Vice Chmn., Bill Rhodes/Sr. Vice Chmn., Stephen R. Volk/Vice Chmn., Shengman Zhang/Vice Chmn. - Global Banking, COO - Asia Pacific, Citi Markets, Banking, Institutional Clients Group, Sanford I. Weill/Chmn. Emeritus, Robert L. Ryan/Dir., Michael C. Armstrong/Dir., Alain J.P. Belda/Dir., George David/Dir., Kenneth T. Derr/Dir., John M. Deutch/Dir., Roberto Hernandez Ramirez/Dir., Ann Dibble Jordan/Dir. *(22 Directors included in Index)*

Owners: Robert Druskin, Robert E. Rubin, Kenneth T. Derr, Charles Prince, Stephen R. Volk, Sallie L. Krawcheck, Anne M. Mulcahy, Dudley C. Mecum, Klaus C. Kleinfeld, Richard D. Parsons, Ann Dibble Jordan, Alain J.P. Belda, Michael C. Armstrong, Franklin A. Thomas, Roberto Hernandez *(20 Owners included in Index)*

Financial Data: *Fiscal Year End:*12/31 *Latest Annual Data:* 12/31/2006

Year	Sales	Net Income
2006	$146,558,000,000	$21,538,000,000
2005	$120,318,000,000	$24,589,000,000
2004	$108,276,000,000	$17,046,000,000

Curr. Assets:	$790,223,000,000	**Curr. Liab.:**	$1,393,115,000,000		
Plant, Equip.:	NA	**Total Liab.:**	$1,764,535,000,000	**Indic. Yr. Divd.:**	$2.160
Total Assets:	$1,884,318,000,000	**Net Worth:**	$119,783,000,000	**Debt/ Equity:**	2.5455

Citizens & Northern Corp

90-92 Main St., Wellsboro, PA, 16901; *PH:* 1-570-724-3411; *Fax:* 1-570-723-8097; *http://* www.cnbankpa.com

General - Incorporation	PA	**Stock**- Price on:12/24/2007	$20.4
Employees	366	Stock Exchange	NDQ
Auditor	Parente Randolph LLC	Ticker Symbol	CZNC
Stk Agt	American Stock Transfer & Trust Co.	Outstanding Shares	8,920,000
Counsel	NA	E.P.S	$1.23
DUNS No.	01-517-0541	Shareholders	NA

Business: The group's principle activities are to provide banking and mortgage services to individuals and corporate customers in northcentral Pennsylvania. Lending products include mortgage loans, commercial loans, consumer loans and credit cards, as well as instruments such as commercial

letters-of-credit. Deposit products include checking accounts, passbook and statement savings, money market accounts, interest checking accounts, individual retirement accounts and certificates of deposit. The group's trust and financial management services include administration of trusts and estates, retirement plans and other employee benefit plans and investment management services.

Primary SIC and add'l.: 6022 6712

CIK No: 0000810958

Subsidiaries: Bucktail Life Insurance Company, C&N Financial Services Corporation, Canisteo Valley Corporation, Citizens & Northern Bank, Citizens & Northern Investment Corporation, First State Bank

Officers: Craig G. Litchfield/60/Dir., CEO, Pres./$511,913.00, Mark A. Hughes/47/Treasurer/$249,191.00, Jessica R. Brown/Corp. Sec.

Directors: Craig G. Litchfield/60/Dir., CEO, Pres., James E. Towner/61/Dir., Robert R. Decamp/67/Dir., Susan E. Hartley/50/Dir., Ann M. Tyler/63/Dir., Leo F. Lambert/54/Dir., Edward H. Owlett/53/Dir., Karl W. Kroeck/68/Dir., Dennis F. Beardslee/57/Dir., Bruce R. Haner/60/Dir., Leonard Simpson/59/Dir., Edward L. Learn/60/Dir., Jan E. Fisher/53/Dir.

Owners: Raymond R. Mattie, Edward L. Learn, Bruce R. Haner, Deborah E. Scott, James E. Towner, Ann M. Tyler, Susan E. Hartley, Thomas L. Rudy, Karl W. Kroeck, Dawn A. Besse, R. Robert DeCamp, Leo F. Lambert, Craig G. Litchfield, Insiders/3.10%, Mark A. Hughes *(19 Owners included in Index)*

Financial Data: *Fiscal Year End:* 12/31 *Latest Annual Data:* 12/31/2006

Year	Sales	Net Income
2006	$77,818,000	$11,986,000
2005	$72,452,000	$12,984,000
2004	$67,721,000	$14,863,000

Curr. Assets:	$32,205,000	**Curr. Liab.:**	$818,298,000		
Plant, Equip.:	$23,393,000	**Total Liab.:**	$997,480,000	**Indic. Yr. Divd.:**	$0.960
Total Assets:	$1,127,368,000	**Net Worth:**	$129,888,000	**Debt/ Equity:**	1.1659

Citizens Bancorp of Virginia Inc

126 S Main St., Blackstone, VA, 23824; *PH:* 1-434-292-7221; *http://* www.greatbanksva.com

General - Incorporation	VA	Stock- Price on:12/24/2007	$18
Employees	114	Stock Exchange	OTC
Auditor	Yount, Hyde & Barbour, P.C	Ticker Symbol	CZBT
Stk Agt	NA	Outstanding Shares	2,440,000
Counsel	NA	E.P.S.	$1.39
DUNS No.	NA	Shareholders	NA

Business: The group's principal activities are to provide banking and other financial services through its subsidiary. The group's activities include paying and receiving demand deposits, now accounts, savings deposits, certificates of deposit, money market deposits, christmas club deposits and deposits of federal, state and local governments. The group grants and collects installment loans, time and demand loans, and mortgage loans to individuals, partnerships, and corporations. Other services include the issuance and redemption of government savings bonds, receiving of utility payments and other miscellaneous services incidental to the operation of a commercial bank.

Primary SIC and add'l.: 6022

CIK No: 0001277254

Officers: Joseph D. Borgerding/Dir., CEO, Pres., Ronald E. Baron/Sr. VP, CFO, Lynn K. Shekleton/Sr. VP - Human Resources, Branch Administration, Eric J. Roberts/Sr. VP - Credit Administration, Citizens Bank, Trust Company

Directors: Joseph D. Borgerding/Dir., CEO, Pres., Roy C. Jenkins/Chmn., Samuel H. West/Vice Chmn., Joseph F. Morrissette/Dir., Jerome A. Wilson/Dir., Jo Anne Scott Webb/Dir., Irving J. Arnold/Dir., William D. Coleburn/Dir., Walter E. Newman/Dir., Frank P. Beale/Dir., Jo Anne Scott/55/Dir.

Owners: Jerome A. Wilson/3.06%, Samuel H. West/2.60%, Eric J. Roberts, Joseph D. Borgerding, William D. Coleburn, Lynn K. Shekleton, JoAnne Scott Webb/4.08%, Joseph M. H. Irby/1.27%, Walter E. Newman, Irving J. Arnold, Roy C. Jenkins/1.54%, Joseph F. Morrissette, Insiders/13.28%, Ronald E. Baron

Financial Data: *Fiscal Year End:* 12/31 *Latest Annual Data:* 12/31/2006

Year	Sales	Net Income
2006	$18,506,000	$3,367,000
2005	$16,685,000	$3,103,000
2004	$15,467,000	$2,474,000

Curr. Assets:	$14,904,000	**Curr. Liab.:**	$245,857,000	**P/E Ratio:**	12.95
Plant, Equip.:	$8,033,000	**Total Liab.:**	$245,857,000	**Indic. Yr. Divd.:**	$0.640
Total Assets:	$280,915,000	**Net Worth:**	$35,057,000	**Debt/ Equity:**	NA

Citizens Bancorp PA

One Citizens Plz., Providence, RI, 02903; *PH:* 1-401-456-7000; *http://* www.citizensbank.com

General - Incorporation	IN	Stock- Price on:12/24/2007	NA
Employees	NA	Stock Exchange	NA
Auditor	NA	Ticker Symbol	NA
Stk Agt	NA	Outstanding Shares	NA
Counsel	NA	E.P.S.	NA
DUNS No.	NA	Shareholders	NA

Business: The groups principle activity is to provide recruiting services. The groups service area includes the research and development, engineering, marketing, sales, information technology and manufacturing industries. The group operates from United States.

Primary SIC and add'l.: 6211

CIK No: 0001040734

Citizens Bancshares Corp GA

75 Piedmont Ave. NE, Atlanta, GA, 30302; *PH:* 1-404-659-5959; *Fax:* 1-678-406-4039; *http://* www.ctbatlantahb.com

General - Incorporation	GA	Stock- Price on:12/24/2007	$10.5
Employees	133	Stock Exchange	OTC
Auditor	Elliot Davis LLC	Ticker Symbol	CZBS
Stk Agt	SunTrust Bank	Outstanding Shares	2,090,000
Counsel	NA	E.P.S.	$1.37
DUNS No.	78-708-1140	Shareholders	NA

Business: The group's principal activity is to provide general commercial banking and mortgage brokerage services. It is a multi bank holding company, which operates through its subsidiaries the citizens trust bank and citizens trust bank mortgage services inc. The group offers commercial and consumer deposit accounts, lending activities and residential mortgage products and related services. The loan products include consumer/installment loans, home equity lines of credit, construction loans, commercial loans and small business loans. The services are provided to individual and corporate customers in metropolitan atlanta and columbus, Georgia. The group serves its customers through twelve full-service bank branches located in atlanta, lithonia, decatur, stone mountain and columbus, Georgia and birmingham and eutaw, Alabama. On 28-Feb-2003, the group acquired cfs bancshares, inc.

Primary SIC and add'l.: 6712 6022

CIK No: 0000813640

Subsidiaries: Citizens (GA) Statutory Trust, Citizens Trust Bank, grantor trust

Officers: James E. Young/Dir., CEO, Pres./$403,349.00, Mary Rangel-Mattox/Financial Relationship Mgr. - Decatur, GA, Ron A. Garrett/VP, Dekalb Division Mgr. - Citizens Trust Bank, Wanda Nesbit/Sr. VP, Dir. - Human Resources - Citizens Trust Bank, Princess Leigh/Financial Relationship Mgr. - Stone Mountain, GA, Herman Lewis/Financial Relationship Mgr. - Columbus, GA, George Richardson/Financial Relationship Mgr. - Birmingham, AL, Tamara Williams/Financial Relationship Mgr. - Eutaw, AL, Erica W. Bracey/Dir. - Citizens Trust Bank, Frederick L. Daniels/Sr. VP, Commercial Division Mgr., Iris Goodly/VP, Operations Division Mgr. - Citizens Trust Bank, Ardell Walcott/First VP, Retail Banking Mgr. - Citizens Trust Bank, Kenneth R. Gooch/VP, Information Systems Division Mgr. - Citizens Trust Bank, Joseph M. Hopkins/CIA, CBA, CRP, Sr. VP, Internal Audit Mgr. - Citizens Trust Bank, Roger Botwin/Exec. VP, Chief Credit Officer - Citizens Trust Bank/$145,370.00 *(27 Officers included in Index)*

Directors: Ray Robinson/Chmn. Citizens Trust Bank, Mercy P. Owens/Dir., Stephen A. Elmore/Dir., David C. Moody/Dir., Jerome H. Russell/Dir., James Williams/Dir. - Citizens Trust Bank, Donald Ratajczak/Dir. - Citizens Trust Bank, Robert L. Brown/Dir. - Citizens Trust Bank

Owners: Robert L. Brown, Herman J. Russell/29.38%, James E. Young/2.72%, Hot Creek Capital, LLC/7.40%, Stephen A. Elmore, Mercy P. Owens, Donald Ratajczak, Ray Robinson, Jerome H. Russell, James E. Williams, Insiders/7.18%, David C. Moody/2.60%

Financial Data: *Fiscal Year End:* 12/31 *Latest Annual Data:* 12/31/2006

Year	Sales	Net Income
2006	$26,480,000	$3,003,000
2005	$25,246,000	$2,343,000
2004	$25,246,000	$2,305,000

Curr. Assets:	$13,304,000	**Curr. Liab.:**	$299,541,000		
Plant, Equip.:	$7,980,000	**Total Liab.:**	$305,036,000	**Indic. Yr. Divd.:**	NA
Total Assets:	$335,185,000	**Net Worth:**	$30,150,000	**Debt/ Equity:**	0.1792

Citizens Communications Co

3 High Ridge Pk., Stamford, CT, 06905; *PH:* 1-203-614-5600; *Fax:* 1-203-614-4602; *http://* www.czn.net; *Email:* citizens@czn.com

General - Incorporation	DE	Stock- Price on:12/24/2007	$15.24
Employees	5,446	Stock Exchange	NYSE
Auditor	KPMG LLP	Ticker Symbol	CZN
Stk Agt	Illinois Stock Transfer Co	Outstanding Shares	342,420,000
Counsel	NA	E.P.S.	$0.92
DUNS No.	00-691-8296	Shareholders	NA

Business: The groups principle activity is to provide telecommunications services. The group provides regulated and unregulated communications services to residential, business and wholesale customers. In the year 2007 the group acquired Commonwealth Telephone Enterprises Inc., Global Valley Networks Inc. and GVN Services. The group operates from United States.

Primary SIC and add'l.: 4813 4923 4911

CIK No: 0000020520

Subsidiaries: Citizens Cable Company, Citizens Capital Ventures Corp., Citizens Communications Company, Citizens Directory Services Company LLC, Citizens International Management Services Company, Citizens Mohave Cellular Company, Citizens NEWCOM Company, Citizens NEWTEL, LLC, Citizens Pennsylvania Company LLC, Citizens SERP Administration Company, Citizens Southwestern Capital Corporation, Citizens Telecom Services Company LLC, Citizens Telecommunications Company of , Inc., Citizens Telecommunications Company of California Inc., Citizens Telecommunications Company of Colorado 93 Subsidiaries included in the Index

Officers: Maggie Wilderotter/Chmn., CEO/$2,633,683.00, Peter B. Hayes/Exec. VP - Sales, Marketing, Business Development/$976,765.00, John H. Casey/Exec. VP/$2,277,875.00, Daniel McCarthy/COO, Exec. VP/$1,103,920.00, Donald R. Shassian/CFO/$841,446.00, Hilary E. Glassman/Sr. VP, General Counsel, Sec., Cecilia K. McKenney/Sr. VP - Human Resources

Directors: Maggie Wilderotter/Chmn., CEO, Kathleen Quinn Abernathy/Dir., Leroy T. Barnes/Dir., Jeri B. Finard/Dir., Lawton Wehle Fitt/Dir., William M. Kraus/Dir., Howard L. Schrott/Dir., Larraine D. Segil/Dir., Bradley E. Singer/Dir., David H. Ward/Dir., Myron A. Wick/Dir., Peter C.B. Bynoe/Dir., Michael T. Dugan/Dir.

Owners: William M. Kraus, Jerry Elliott, Larraine D. Segil, Insiders, Morgan Stanley/5.50%, Daniel J. McCarthy, Stanley Harfenist, Peter B. Hayes, Myron A. Wick, Kathleen Q. Abernathy, Bradley E. Singer, Lawton Wehle Fitt, David H. Ward, Edwin Tornberg, John H. Casey *(21 Owners included in Index)*

Financial Data: *Fiscal Year End:* 12/31 *Latest Annual Data:* 12/31/2006

Year	Sales	Net Income
2006	$2,025,367,000	$344,555,000
2005	$2,162,479,000	$202,375,000
2004	$2,192,980,000	$72,150,000

Curr. Assets:	$1,272,993,000	**Curr. Liab.:**	$425,643,000	**P/E Ratio:**	13.61
Plant, Equip.:	$2,983,504,000	**Total Liab.:**	$5,733,173,000	**Indic. Yr. Divd.:**	$1.000
Total Assets:	$6,791,205,000	**Net Worth:**	$1,058,032,000	**Debt/ Equity:**	3.6121

Citizens Community Bancorp

2174 Eastridge Ctr., Eau Claire, WI, 57011; *PH:* 1-715-836-9994

General - Incorporation	US	Stock- Price on:12/24/2007	NA
Employees	66	Stock Exchange	NDQ
Auditor	Wipfli LLP	Ticker Symbol	CZWI
Stk Agt	Registrar & Transfer Co	Outstanding Shares	NA
Counsel	NA	E.P.S.	NA
DUNS No.	NA	Shareholders	NA

Business: The groups principle activity is to provide e-banking solutions. The group also provides loan and deposit services. The group operates from United States.

Primary SIC and add'l.: NA

CIK No: 0001273805

Subsidiaries: Citizens Community Federal

Curr. Assets:	$7,990,000	**Curr. Liab.:**	$247,911,000		
Plant, Equip.:	$3,681,000	**Total Liab.:**	$253,908,000	**Indic. Yr. Divd.:**	NA
Total Assets:	$283,990,000	**Net Worth:**	$30,082,000	**Debt/ Equity:**	NA

Citizens Financial Bank

707 Ridge Rd., Munster, IN, 46321; *PH:* 1-219-836-5500; *Fax:* 1-219-836-0265;
http:// www.bankcfs.com

General - Incorporation	IN	**Stock**- Price on:12/24/2007	$14.82
Employees	360	Stock Exchange	NDQ
Auditor	Crowe Chizek & Co. LLC	Ticker Symbol	CITZ
Stk Agt	Illinois Stock Transfer Co	Outstanding Shares	10,980,000
Counsel	Elias, Matz, Tierman & Herrick	E.P.S	$0.65
DUNS No.	NA	Shareholders	NA

Business: The group's principal activity is to provide a full range of financial services in northwest Indiana and Illinois. A holding company for citizens financial services fsb, the group accepts negotiable order of withdrawal, money market, non-interest-bearing checking, passbook and term certificate accounts and originates mortgage loans and invests in securities. The group also originates construction and land development loans, multi family residential real estate loans, commercial real estate loans, home equity loans and other loans. It is a member of the federal home loan bank of indianapolis and the federal deposit insurance corporation insures its deposits. The group's activities are carried out through its executive offices and an insurance and investment center in munster, Indiana and 22 banking centers located in lake and porter counties in northwest Indiana and cook, dupage and will counties in Illinois.

Primary SIC and add'l.: 6035 6712

CIK No: 0001058438

Subsidiaries: CFS Holdings, Ltd., CFS Insurance Agency, Inc, CFS Investment Services, Inc, Suburban Mortgage Services, Inc

Officers: Thomas F. Prisby/66/Chmn., CEO, Charles V. Cole/CFO, Exec. VP/$241,007.00, Thomas L. Darovic/Exec. VP - Commercial Lending/$247,242.00, Zoran Koricanac/50/Sr. VP, Sr. Loan Officer/$232,856.00, Jeffrey C. Stur/59/Sr. VP - Asset Management, Gregg L. Holley/51/Chief Lending Officer, Sr. VP/$190,292.00, Daryl D. Pomranke/Exec. VP, Chief Operating Offi

Directors: Thomas F. Prisby/66/Chmn., CEO, Frank D. Lester/Dir., Gene Diamond/Dir., Gregory W. Blaine/Dir., Robert R. Ross/Dir., Joyce M. Simon/Dir.

Owners: Thomas F. Prisby/5.20%, Gregg L. Holley, Insiders/9.60%, Zoran Koricanac, Robert R. Ross, Gregory W. Blaine, Charles V. Cole, Thomas L. Darovic, CFS Bancorp, Inc./10.60%, Dimensional Fund Advisors, Inc./8.90%, Joyce M. Simon, Gene Diamond, Frank D. Lester

Financial Data: ***Fiscal Year End:***12/31 ***Latest Annual Data:*** 12/31/2006

Year	Sales	Net Income
2006	$87,083,000	$5,340,000
2005	$81,339,000	$5,017,000
2004	$81,614,000	-$6,577,000

Curr. Assets:	$74,690,000	**Curr. Liab.:**	$907,095,000	**P/E Ratio:**	27.44
Plant, Equip.:	$18,118,000	**Total Liab.:**	$1,122,584,000	**Indic. Yr. Divd.:**	$0.480
Total Assets:	$1,254,390,000	**Net Worth:**	$131,806,000	**Debt/ Equity:**	1.5183

Citizens Financial Corp/DE

12910 Shelbyville Rd., Ste. 300, Louisville, KY, 40243; *PH:* 1-502-244-2420; *Fax:* 1-502-254-4059;
http:// www.citizensfinancialcorp.com

General - Incorporation	DE	**Stock**- Price on:12/24/2007	$19.05
Employees	91	Stock Exchange	OTC
Auditor	Yount, Hyde & Barbour, P.C	Ticker Symbol	CIWV
Stk Agt	StockTrans, Inc.	Outstanding Shares	1,830,000
Counsel	Busch & Talbott, John Busch	E.P.S	$1.87
DUNS No.	00-450-1367	Shareholders	NA

Business: The group's principal activity is to provide retail and commercial loans, deposit, trust and brokerage services. The group accepts time, savings deposits, money market deposit accounts, club accounts and certificates of deposits. The group offers commercial loans and lines of credit, residential real estate loans, consumer installment loans and other personal loans and provides safe deposit box rental facility, wire transfer services, telebanking services and automated teller machine services. The group functions as trustee under wills, as executor and administrator of estates, as guardian for estates of minors and incompetents and renders services in various capacities.

Primary SIC and add'l.: 6021 6712

CIK No: 0000764156

Subsidiaries: Citizens National Bank of Elkins

Officers: Robert J. Schoonover/Dir., CEO, Pres., Thomas K. Derbyshire/Treasurer, Principal Financial Officer

Directors: Robert J. Schoonover/Dir., CEO, Pres., Max L. Armentrout/Chmn., William J. Brown/Dir., L. T. Williams/Dir., John A. Yeager/49/Dir., Cyrus K. Kump/61/Dir., John F. Harris/80/Dir., William T. Johnson/Dir., Edward L. Campbell/68/Dir., Robert N. Alday/Dir.

Owners: Thomas K. Derbyshire/0.01%, Robert J. Schoonover/0.10%, Robert N. Alday/3.39%, L. T. Williams/0.29%, Max L. Armentrout/5.05%, Edward L. Campbell/0.11%, John F. Harris/1.32%, William T. Johnson, Insiders/13.02%, John A. Yeager/0.27%, Cyrus K. Kump/0.46%, William J. Brown/0.30%

Financial Data: ***Fiscal Year End:***12/31 ***Latest Annual Data:*** 12/31/2006

Year	Sales	Net Income
2006	$16,999,000	$2,087,000
2005	$14,444,000	$2,047,000
2004	$12,836,000	$1,656,000

Curr. Assets:	$7,488,000	**Curr. Liab.:**	$216,376,000	**P/E Ratio:**	10.19
Plant, Equip.:	$4,331,000	**Total Liab.:**	$222,702,000	**Indic. Yr. Divd.:**	$0.480
Total Assets:	$242,980,000	**Net Worth:**	$20,278,000	**Debt/ Equity:**	0.1530

Citizens Financial Services Inc

15 S Main St., Mansfield, PA, 16933; *PH:* 1-570-662-2121; *Fax:* 1-570-662-3278;
http:// www.firstcitizensbank.com

General - Incorporation	PA	**Stock**- Price on:12/24/2007	$21.5
Employees	184	Stock Exchange	OTC
Auditor	S. R. Snodgrass, A.C.	Ticker Symbol	CZFS
Stk Agt	Illinois Stock Transfer Co	Outstanding Shares	2,820,000
Counsel	NA	E.P.S	$2.17
DUNS No.	15-075-2947	Shareholders	NA

Business: The group's principal activity is to provide general banking services in potter, tioga and bradford counties in north central Pennsylvania and allegany, steuben, chemung and tioga counties in southern New York. The group operates through fifteen full-service banking offices. The banking services include consumer loans, residential real estate loans, commercial loans and loans to various state and municipal entities. Deposit programs include full range of consumer as well as commercial checking and savings accounts, certificates of deposit and individual retirement accounts. The group also provides trust and investment services.

Primary SIC and add'l.: 6712 6021

CIK No: 0000739421

Subsidiaries: First Citizens Insurance Agency, Inc. of Mansfield, First Citizens National Bank of Mansfield

Officers: Randall E. Black/Dir., CEO, Pres./$184,149.00, Chester Reed/VP - Commercial Services, First Citizens National Bank, Kathleen Campbell/Sr. VP, Dir. - Marketing, Training, First Citizens National Bank, Cindy Pazzaglia/VP, Human Resources Mgr. - First Citizens National Bank, Rob Carleton/VP, Western Regional Mgr. - First Citizens National Bank, Jeff Carr/VP, Eastern Regional Mgr. - First Citizens National Bank, Patty Vlajic/VP, Branch Administrator - First Citizens National Bank, Rob Fitzgerald/VP, Business Development Officer - First Citizens National Bank, Doug Whitten/Sr. VP - Operations, Technology Mgr. - First Citizens National Bank/$120,517.00, Tom Lyman/VP - Investment, Strategic Planning, First Citizens National Bank/$137,747.00, Mickey Jones/Exec. VP, CFO - First Citizens National Bank/$114,849.00, Terry B. Osborne/Exec. VP - Credit Administration, First Citizens National Bank/$179,481.00, Chris Landis/VP, Sr. Business Development Officer - First Citizens National Bank, Carol Strong/VP, Professional Development Officer - First Citizens National Bank, Jeffrey Wilson/VP, Business Development Officer - First Citizens National Bank *(20 Officers included in Index)*

Directors: Randall E. Black/Dir., CEO, Pres., Joseph R. Landy/53/Dir., Roger C. Graham/52/Dir., Carol J. Tama/67/Dir., Mark L. Dalton/53/Dir., Rudolph J. Van Der Hiel/68/Dir., Lowell R. Coolidge/67/Dir., Robert W. Chappell/41/Dir., Rinaldo A. Depaola/52/Dir., Gene E. Kosa/61/Dir.

Owners: Insiders/10.40%, Douglas W. Whitten, E. Gene Kosa, Rinaldo A. DePaola, Randall E. Black, Terry B. Osborne, Robert W. Chappell, Roger C. Graham, R. Joseph Landy, Mickey L. Jones, Rudolph J. van der Hiel, John E. Novak, Thomas C. Lyman, Carol J. Tama/2.70%, R. Lowell Coolidge/5.80% *(16 Owners included in Index)*

Financial Data: ***Fiscal Year End:***12/31 ***Latest Annual Data:*** 12/31/2006

Year	Sales	Net Income
2006	$37,567,000	$5,800,000
2005	$33,387,000	$5,274,000
2004	$31,133,000	$5,267,000

Curr. Assets:	$12,473,000	**Curr. Liab.:**	$448,802,000	**P/E Ratio:**	9.91
Plant, Equip.:	$12,892,000	**Total Liab.:**	$528,668,000	**Indic. Yr. Divd.:**	$0.900
Total Assets:	$572,168,000	**Net Worth:**	$43,500,000	**Debt/ Equity:**	1.3221

Citizens First Bancorp Inc

525 Water St., Port Huron, MI, 48060; *PH:* 1-810-987-8300; *Fax:* 1-810-987-7537;
http:// www.cfsbank.com

General - Incorporation	DE	**Stock**- Price on:12/24/2007	$22.52
Employees	411	Stock Exchange	NDQ
Auditor	BDO Seidman LLP	Ticker Symbol	CTZN
Stk Agt	Registrar & Transfer Co	Outstanding Shares	8,420,000
Counsel	NA	E.P.S	$0.64
DUNS No.	NA	Shareholders	NA

Business: The group's principal activities are to provide full range of financial products and services. The group is a holding company for citizens first savings bank and operates as a community-oriented financial institution. The banking services are provided to individuals through 16 full-service branch offices in st. Clair, sanilac, huron and lapeer counties in Michigan. The services include accepting retail deposits from the general public and using those funds, together with funds generated from operations and borrowings, to originate loans. The group originates one-to-four family residential mortgage loans, real estate loans, commercial loans, automobile loans, home equity loans, lines of credit and other consumer loans. The group offers a wide variety of deposit accounts including savings accounts, checking and now accounts, certificates of deposit, individual retirement accounts and money market accounts. On 09-Jan-2004, it acquired metro bancorp inc and metrobank.

Primary SIC and add'l.: 6712 6035

CIK No: 0001127442

Subsidiaries: CFS Insurance Agency, Citizens Financial Services, Inc, Citizens First Mortgage, LLC.

Officers: Ryan Bush/Branch Mgr., Assist. VP, Travis Gostinger/Branch Mgr., Assist. VP, Maria Labie/Regional Mgr. Mortgage - Shelby Township Loan Center, Vitale Plaza, Donna Sears/Branch Mgr., VP, Kate Jackson/Branch Mgr. - Marysville, Diane Moeller/Branch Mgr. - Port Huron, Hancock, Kim Prax/Branch Mgr. - Port Huron, Port Huron Township, Judy Vincent/Branch Mgr., Assist. VP, Terry Souva/Branch Mgr. - Bad Axe, Jason Ma/Branch Mgr. - Chesterfield Township Regional Banking Center, Kim Stencel/Branch Mgr. - Croswell, Kathleen Saelens/Branch Mgr., Assist. VP, Larry Corbett/Mortgage Mgr. - Fort Myers Loan Center, Mark Lundy/Branch Mgr. - Imlay City, Angie Schliter/Branch Mgr., Assist. VP *(20 Officers included in Index)*

Owners: Stephen J. Armstrong, Keeley Asset Management Corp.., Citizens First Savings Bank Employee, Private Capital Management, Douglas E. Brandewie, Ronald W. Cooley, Ronald DiCicco, Janice U. Whipple, Dimensional Fund Advisors LP, Walid Demashkieh, Wellington Management Company, LLP, Marshall J. Campbell, Timothy D. Regan, Citizens First Foundation, Inc., Robert L. Patterson *(16 Owners included in Index)*

Financial Data: ***Fiscal Year End:***12/31 ***Latest Annual Data:*** 12/31/2006

Year	Sales	Net Income
2006	$119,292,000	$9,102,000
2005	$95,862,000	$9,034,000
2004	$78,453,000	$8,229,000

Curr. Assets:	$53,344,000	Curr. Liab.:	$1,597,828,000	P/E Ratio:	19.25
Plant, Equip.:	$43,265,000	Total Liab.:	$1,597,828,000	Indic. Yr. Divd.:	$0.360
Total Assets:	$1,775,142,000	Net Worth:	$177,314,000	Debt/ Equity:	NA

Citizens First Corp

1805 Campbell Ln., Bowling Green, KY, 42104; PH: 1-270-393-0700; Fax: 1-270-393-0716; http:// www.citizensfirstbank.com

General - Incorporation .... KY	Stock- Price on:12/24/2007 .... $13.08
Employees 110	Stock Exchange .... NDQ
Auditor .... Crowe Chizek & Co. LLC	Ticker Symbol .... CZFC
Stk Agt .... Reliance Trust Company	Outstanding Shares 1,980,000
Counsel .... NA	E.P.S. $0.73
DUNS No. .... NA	Shareholders .... NA

Business: The group's principal activities are to provide a full range of banking and mortgage services. The group through its subsidiary, citizens first bank inc, serves individual and corporate customers in bowling green and warren county, Kentucky. The services include non-interest bearing, interest bearing negotiable order of withdrawal accounts, savings and certificate of deposit. The lending services include commercial, personal and mortgage loans. The personal loans offered include secured and unsecured loans for financing automobiles, home improvements and personal investments. The group also offers credit cards facilities and personal checking account related line of credit. Other services include safe deposit boxes, letter of credit, traveler's checks, direct deposit of payroll, social security and dividend. In Jan 2003, the group acquired commonwealth mortgage of bowling green inc and southern Kentucky land title inc.

Primary SIC and add'l.: 6712 6022

CIK No: 0001073475

Subsidiaries: Citizens First Bank, Inc.

Officers: Mary D. Cohron/60/Dir., CEO, Pres./$236,367.00, Steven J. Marcum/51/Exec. VP, CFO, Treasurer/$153,626.00, Kim M. Thomas/37/Exec. VP, Chief Marketing Officer, John T. Perkins/65/Dir., VP, COO, Todd M. Kanipe/39/Exec. VP, Chief Credit Officer/$183,302.00, Carolyn Harp/62/COO, Exec. VP

Directors: Mary D. Cohron/60/Dir., CEO, Pres., Floyd H. Ellis/81/Chmn., Barry D. Bray/62/Dir., Joe B. Natcher/50/Dir., John Kelly/73/Dir., Steve Newberry/45/Dir., Billy J. Bell/74/Dir., Jack Sheidler/51/Dir., Fred Travis/73/Dir., John T. Perkins/65/Dir., VP, COO, Chris B. Guthrie/41/Dir., Jerry Baker/77/Dir., Sarah G. Grise/51/Dir., Wilson Stone/55/Dir.

Owners: Mary D. Cohron/2.96%, Fred Travis, Wellington Management Company, LLP/5.06%, Wellington Trust Company, NA/5.06%, Jack Sheidler/3.20%, Wilson Stone, John T. Perkins, Billy J. Bell/6.00%, Billy J. Bell/4.15%, Steve Newberry, Insiders/18.81%, Insiders/18.00%, Mary D. Cohron/2.00%, Barry D. Bray/3.20%, Floyd H. Ellis/2.00% (26 Owners included in Index)

Financial Data: Fiscal Year End:12/31   Latest Annual Data: 12/31/2006

Year	Sales	Net Income
2006	$16,515,000	$2,153,000
2005	$12,550,000	$2,237,000
2004	$10,085,000	$1,038,000

Curr. Assets:	$32,663,000	Curr. Liab.:	$295,372,000	P/E Ratio:	12.34
Plant, Equip.:	$11,177,000	Total Liab.:	$302,286,000	Indic. Yr. Divd.:	$0.100
Total Assets:	$338,775,000	Net Worth:	$36,489,000	Debt/ Equity:	0.1355

Citizens Holding Co MS

PO Box 209, Philadelphia, MS, 39350; PH: 1-601-656-4692; Fax: 1-601-656-4183; http:// www.thecitizensbankphila.com

General - Incorporation .... MS	Stock- Price on:12/24/2007 .... $22.75
Employees 204	Stock Exchange .... NDQ
Auditor .... Horne LLP	Ticker Symbol .... CIZN
Stk Agt ...... American Stock Transfer & Trust Co.	Outstanding Shares 4,930,000
Counsel .... NA	E.P.S. $1.65
DUNS No. .... NA	Shareholders .... NA

Business: The group's principal activity is to provide commercial and personal banking services through its subsidiary, the citizens bank of philadelphia. The group accepts demand deposits, savings and time deposit accounts; makes secured and unsecured loans; issues letters of credit and originates mortgage loans. The lending services include commercial, real estate, installment and credit card loans. Real estate loans consist of single and multi-family housing, farm, residential and commercial construction and commercial real estate loans. In addition, the group provides personal and corporate trust services; and provides certain services that are closely related to commercial banking such as credit life insurance and title insurance for its loan customers.

Primary SIC and add'l.: 6022 6712

CIK No: 0001075706

Subsidiaries: The Citizens Bank of Philadelphia, Mississippi

Officers: Greg Mckee/Dir., CEO, Pres./$359,958.00, Carolyn Mckee/Sec., Robert T. Smith/Treasurer, CFO/$218,723.00

Directors: Greg Mckee/Dir., CEO, Pres., William M. Mars/Chmn., Karl Brantley/Dir., Don Fulton/Dir., Don Kilgore/Dir., David A. King/Dir., Herbert A. King/Dir., David P. Webb/Dir., A. T. Williams/Dir.

Owners: Don L. Fulton, Insiders/14.80%, Robert T. Smith, Amzie T. Williams, Karl Brantley, David P. Webb, David A. King/1.90%, Greg L. McKee, The Molpus Company/8.00%, Herbert A. King/7.60%, William M. Mars, Daniel Adam Mars, Terrell E. Winstead, Donald L. Kilgore

Financial Data: Fiscal Year End:12/31   Latest Annual Data: 12/31/2006

Year	Sales	Net Income
2006	NA	$1,482,000
2005	NA	$1,358,000
2004	NA	$1,466,000

Curr. Assets:	$36,062,000	Curr. Liab.:	$535,101,000		
Plant, Equip.:	$14,814,000	Total Liab.:	$550,050,000	Indic. Yr. Divd.:	$0.720
Total Assets:	$621,197,000	Net Worth:	$69,665,000	Debt/ Equity:	NA

Citizens Inc

400 E Anderson Ln., Austin, TX, 78752; PH: 1-512-837-7100; Fax: 1-512-836-9785; http:// www.citizensinc.com; Email: postoffice@citizensinc.com

General - Incorporation .... CO	Stock- Price on:12/24/2007 .... $7
Employees 490	Stock Exchange .... NYSE
Auditor .... KPMG LLP	Ticker Symbol .... CIA
Stk Agt .... Computershare Trust CO.	Outstanding Shares 41,310,000
Counsel .... Davis & Davis	E.P.S. $0.31
DUNS No. 60-180-8637	Shareholders .... NA

Business: The group's principal activities are providing life and health insurance and other services through its operating subsidiaries. The subsidiaries, citizens insurance company of America, investors life insurance company and excalibur insurance corporation provide specialty individual accident and health policies to United States residents and ordinary whole-life products on an international basis. Insurance investors inc provides aviation transportation to its parent. Funeral homes of America owns and operates a funeral home in baker, Louisiana. Computing technology inc provides data processing services and acquires and leases furniture and equipment. On 19-Feb-2003, the group acquired first alliance corporation and on 19-Nov-2003, mid American alliance corporation.

Primary SIC and add'l.: 6321 7261 6311 6719 7374 4111

CIK No: 0000024090

Subsidiaries: CICA Life Insurance Company of America (CICA) (fka Citizens Insurance Company of America), Citizens National Life Insurance Company (CNLIC), Citizens USA Life Insurance Company (CUSA), Computing Technology, Inc. (CTI), Funeral Homes of America, Inc. (FHA), Insurance Investors, Inc. (III), KYWIDE Insurance Management, Inc. (KYWIDE), Mid-American Associates Agency, Inc. (MAAAI), Security Alliance Insurance Company (SPFIC), Security Plan Fire Insurance Company (SPFIC), Security Plan Life Insurance Company (SPLIC)

Officers: Geoffrey M. Kolander/32/VP, Corp. Sec., General Counsel, Thomas F. Kopetic/48/VP - Accounting

Owners: Insiders/14.20%, Gala Management Services, Inc., Timothy T. Timmerman, Dean E. Gage, Ray A. Riley/1.30%, Grant G. Teaff, Larry E. Carson, Mark A. Oliver, Harold E. Riley/10.60%, Rick D. Riley/2.20%, Insiders/100.00%, Harold E. Riley/100.00%, Richard C. Scott, Steven F. Shelton, Dimensional Fund Advisors/5.20%

Financial Data: Fiscal Year End:12/31   Latest Annual Data: 12/31/2006

Year	Sales	Net Income
2006	$158,059,000	$8,677,000
2005	$144,315,000	$7,302,000
2004	$102,826,000	$7,732,000

Curr. Assets:	$46,643,000	Curr. Liab.:	$6,443,000	P/E Ratio:	35.00
Plant, Equip.:	$7,350,000	Total Liab.:	$571,573,000	Indic. Yr. Divd.:	NA
Total Assets:	$711,184,000	Net Worth:	$139,611,000	Debt/ Equity:	0.0990

Citizens National Bancorp DE

182 Main St., Putnam, CT, 06260; PH: 1-860-928-7921; http:// www.cnbonlinebank.com

General - Incorporation	Stock- Price on:12/24/2007 .... $105.75
Employees .... NA	Stock Exchange .... OTC
Auditor .... NA	Ticker Symbol .... CTZR
Stk Agt .... NA	Outstanding Shares .... NA
Counsel .... NA	E.P.S. .... NA
DUNS No. .... NA	Shareholders .... NA

Business: The groups principle activity is to provide recruiting services. The groups service area includes the research and development, engineering, marketing, sales, information technology and manufacturing industries. The group operates from United States.

Primary SIC and add'l.: 6712

CIK No:

Officers: Archie McDonnell/CEO, Pres.

Financial Data: Fiscal Year End:NA   Latest Annual Data: 12/31/2002

Year	Sales	Net Income
2002	$12,082,000	$3,322,000
2001	$10,876,000	$2,998,000
2000	$10,332,000	$2,654,000

Curr. Assets:	$15,453,000	Curr. Liab.:	$136,563,000		
Plant, Equip.:	$2,859,000	Total Liab.:	$187,862,000	Indic. Yr. Divd.:	NA
Total Assets:	$216,350,000	Net Worth:	$28,488,000	Debt/ Equity:	2.0257

Citizens National Corp KY

44 Public Sq., Somerset, KY, 41240; PH: 1-606-679-6341; http:// www.cnbsomerset.com; Email: info@cnbsomerset.com

General - Incorporation	Stock- Price on:12/24/2007 .... $71
Employees .... NA	Stock Exchange .... OTC
Auditor .... NA	Ticker Symbol .... CZNL
Stk Agt .... NA	Outstanding Shares .... NA
Counsel .... NA	E.P.S. .... NA
DUNS No. .... NA	Shareholders .... NA

Business: The groups principle activity is to provide banking services. The group also provides overdraft protection, CitizensNET Internet banking and certificates of deposit. The group operates from United States.

Primary SIC and add'l.: 6021

CIK No:

Officers: Clay Parker Davis/Dir., CEO, Pres., Donald E. Bloomer/Sr. VP - Cashier Operations, Personnel, Jerry B. Claunch/Sr. VP - Commercial Lending, George Corder/Sr. VP - Data Processing Supervisor, Mary L. Belcher/Second VP, Auditor, Norma Blevins/VP - Lending Review, Ivalene Dunbar/Assist. Cashier - Commercial Loans, Michelle Gover/Assist. Cashier, Nancy Branch Mgr., Barbara Thompson/Assist. Cashier, Mall Branch Mgr., Charles B. Farris/Exec. VP - Commercial Lending, Jennifer Mink/Assist. Cashier - Audit Department, Brenda Hranicky/Assist. VP - Special Assets, Steve Bray/Assist. Cashier - Mortgage Lending, Ann Dick/Assist. Cashier, Main Office Teller Mgr., Wanda Dykes/Assist. Cashier, Branch Mgr. (31 Officers included in Index)

Directors: Clay Parker Davis/Dir., CEO, Pres., Richard E. Cooper/Chmn., Cy Waddle/Vice Chmn., Lonnie Lawson/Member - Advisory Board, Waitsboro Branch, Jay McShurley/Member - Advisory Board, Waitsboro Branch, Larry Turpen/Member - Advisory Board, Waitsboro Branch, Robert S. Harris/Dir., Charles R. Hembree/Dir., Odell Merrick/Dir., Harris Rakestraw/Dir., Harold D. Rogers/Dir. Emeritus, William J. Wilson/Dir., Nancy Bigelow/Member - Advisory Board, Burnside Branch, Bob Kenison/Member - Advisory Board, Burnside Branch, Darrell Burton/Member - Advisory Board, Burnside Branch (55 Directors included in Index)

Financial Data: Fiscal Year End:NA   Latest Annual Data: 12/31/2002

Year	Sales	Net Income
2002	$1,900,000	$2,859,000
2001	$22,899,000	$1,750,000
2000	$20,770,000	$1,528,000

Curr. Assets:	$495,000	**Curr. Liab.:**	NA		
Plant, Equip.:	NA	**Total Liab.:**	$1,454,000	**Indic. Yr. Divd.:**	NA
Total Assets:	$26,294,000	**Net Worth:**	$24,840,000	**Debt/ Equity:**	0.0356

Citizens Republic Bancorp Inc

Formerly: Citizens Banking Corp

328 S Saginaw St., Flint, MI, 48502; *PH:* 1-810-766-7500; *http://* www.citizensonline.com

General - Incorporation	MI	**Stock**- Price on:12/24/2007	NA
Employees	2,123	Stock Exchange	NDQ
Auditor	Ernst & Young LLP	Ticker Symbol	CRBC
Stk Agt	American Stock Transfer & Trust Co.	Outstanding Shares	NA
Counsel	NA	E.P.S	NA
DUNS No.	05-244-5228	Shareholders	NA

Business: The group's principal activity is to provide banking services, financial services and wealth management services to individuals and businesses. It operates through its subsidiaries, Citizens Bank, F & M Bank and CB Wealth Management, N.A. The group has three segments: commercial banking: provides commercial loans, commercial mortgages, small business loans, letters of credit, deposit accounts, cash management and international trade services to middle-market corporate, small business, government and leasing clients. Consumer banking: provides consumer lending and deposit gathering, electronic banking and residential mortgage loan origination and servicing. Wealth management: provides services to both commercial and consumer clients and offers asset management, estate settlement and administration, deposit and credit products. The group operates 176 banking offices, 194 ATMs and 29 brokerage centers, which are located in Michigan, Illinois, Wisconsin and Iowa.

Primary SIC and add'l.: 6712 6022

CIK No: 0000351077

Subsidiaries: CB Financial Services, Inc., Citizens Bank, Citizens Bank Mortgage Company, LLC, Citizens Bank Wealth Management, N.A., Citizens Service Company, Inc., Citizens Title Services, Inc., F&M BankIowa, Pulaski Capital Corporation, Security Bancservices, Inc.

Officers: William R. Hartman/Dir., CEO, Pres./$3,040,362.00, Randall J. Peterson/Exec. VP, Regional Chmn. - Wisconsin, Iowa, Clinton A. Sampson/Exec. VP, Regional Chmn. - Michigan/$460,630.00, Jeffrey A. Powell/Sr. VP, Controller, Principal Accounting Officer, Thomas W. Gallagher/Sr. VP, General Counsel, Sec., Marilyn K. Allor/Sr. VP, Dir. - Human Resources, John J. Owens/Sr. VP, Chief Marketing Officer, Charles D. Christy/CFO, Exec. VP/$618,792.00, Wendy K. Hemingway/Sr. VP, Dir. - Commercial Products, Sales, Judith L. Klawinski/Sr. VP - Retail Delivery, Arthur G. Heise/Exec. VP, General Auditor, Kristine D. Brenner/Investor Relations Officer, Roy A. Eon/Exec. VP - Operations, Technology, John D. Schwab/Exec. VP, Chief Credit Officer/$497,835.00, James A. Schmelter/Exec. VP - Wealth Management *(19 Officers included in Index)*

Directors: William R. Hartman/Dir., CEO, Pres., Jerry D. Campbell/Chmn., George J. Butvilas/Dir., Richard J. Dolinski/Dir., Stephen J. Lazaroff/Dir., James L. Wolohan/Dir., Benjamin W. Laird/Dir., Joseph P. Day/Dir., William C. Shedd/Dir., Howard J. Hulsman/Dir., Dennis J. Ibold/Dir., Jeoffrey K. Stross/Dir., Gary J. Hurand/Dir., Steven E. Zack/Dir., Dana M. Cluckey/48/Dir. *(18 Directors included in Index)*

Owners: Lizabeth A. Ardisana, Jerry D. Campbell, Benjamin W. Laird, Jeoffrey K. Stross, Barclays Global Investors, N.A/6.80%, John D. Schwab, Cathleen H. Nash, Kendall B. Williams, Richard J. Dolinski, Charles D. Christy, Gary J. Hurand, Dana M. Cluckey, Insiders/4.17%, William C. Shedd, Stephen J. Lazaroff *(22 Owners included in Index)*

Curr. Assets:	$223,950,000	**Curr. Liab.:**	$9,636,940,000		
Plant, Equip.:	$139,490,000	**Total Liab.:**	$12,450,665,000	**Indic. Yr. Divd.:**	NA
Total Assets:	$14,008,351,000	**Net Worth:**	$1,557,686,000	**Debt/ Equity:**	NA

Citizens South Banking Corp

519 S New Hope Rd., Gastonia, NC, 28054; *PH:* 1-704-868-5200; *Fax:* 1-704-868-5226; *http://* www.citizensS.com

General - Incorporation	DE	**Stock**- Price on:12/24/2007	$12.63
Employees	133	Stock Exchange	NDQ
Auditor	Cherry, Bekaert & Holland LLP	Ticker Symbol	CSBC
Stk Agt	Registrar & Transfer Co	Outstanding Shares	7,960,000
Counsel	Luse Gorman Pomerenk & Schick	E.P.S	$0.74
DUNS No.	NA	Shareholders	NA

Business: The group's principal activities are to offers deposits to local customers. These deposits are invested in residential, real estate, commercial and consumer loans, investment securities and mortgage-backed securities. The group also acts as a broker in both the origination of loans secured by one-to-four family dwellings and in the sale of uninsured financial products. The group's provides services through ten branch offices located in North Carolina counties of gaston, rowan and iredell.

Primary SIC and add'l.: 6712 6035

CIK No: 0001051871

Subsidiaries: Citizens South Bank, Citizens South Financial Services, Inc., CSBC Statutory Trust I

Owners: Charles D. Massey/1.40%, Stephen J. Huffstetler, Vance B. Brinson, Kimberly G. Cooke, Eugene R. Matthews/1.33%, David W. Hoyle/2.55%, Ben R. Rudisill/1.72%, James J. Fuller, Michael R. Maguire, Paul L. Teem/2.44%, Gary F. Hoskins/1.54%, David C. McGuirt, Daniel M. Boyd, Mendon Capital Advisors Corp./10.16%, Insiders/17.99% *(17 Owners included in Index)*

Financial Data: *Fiscal Year End:*12/31 *Latest Annual Data:* 12/31/2006

Year	Sales	Net Income
2006	$49,101,000	$5,455,000
2005	$31,389,000	$3,273,000
2004	$25,935,000	$2,955,000

Curr. Assets:	$29,457,000	**Curr. Liab.:**	$569,817,000	**P/E Ratio:**	17.07
Plant, Equip.:	$18,426,000	**Total Liab.:**	$657,408,000	**Indic. Yr. Divd.:**	$0.320
Total Assets:	$743,370,000	**Net Worth:**	$85,961,000	**Debt/ Equity:**	0.8821

Citrix Systems Inc

851 W Cypress Creek Rd., Fort Lauderdale, FL, 33309; *PH:* 1-954-267-3000; *Fax:* 1-954-267-9319; *http://* www.citrix.com

General - Incorporation	DE	**Stock**- Price on:12/24/2007	$33.56
Employees	3,171	Stock Exchange	NDQ
Auditor	Ernst & Young LLP	Ticker Symbol	CTXS
Stk Agt	Computershare Trust Co	Outstanding Shares	180,590,000
Counsel	Testa, Hurwitz & Thibeault	E.P.S	$1.10
DUNS No.	60-459-6346	Shareholders	NA

Business: The group's principal activities are to develop, market and license access infrastructure software and services for enterprise applications. Its products include the citrix metaframe access suite, an integrated set of enterprise access infrastructure products, which provide access to comprehensive information resources from any location, device or connection. These products are designed for microsoft windows(R) operating systems, unix(R) operating systems and Web-based information systems. The trademarks include citrix(R), ica(R), metaframe(R), metaframexp(R), gotomypc(R) and gotoassist(r). Customers include the us department of health and human services, deutsche telecom, banco bilbao vizcaya argentaris and swiss federal railways. The group's products are marketed in the Americas, Europe, the Middle East, Africa and Asia-pacific regions. On 27-Feb-2004, the group acquired expertcity.com inc.

Primary SIC and add'l.: 7376 7373 7372

CIK No: 0000877890

Subsidiaries: Citrix Application Networking LLC, Citrix Capital Corp., Citrix Cayman Finance Group, Ltd., Citrix Cayman Investments, Ltd., Citrix Development Corp., Citrix Gateways, Inc., Citrix Online LLC, Citrix Overseas Holdings B.V., Citrix R&D India Pvt. Ltd., Citrix Sistemas de Argentina, S.R.L., Citrix Sistemas de Chile Limitada, Citrix Sistemas de Mexico S. de RL de CV, Citrix Sistemas do Brasil Ltda., Citrix Systems (Research & Development) Ltd., Citrix Systems Asia Pacific Pty Ltd. 49 Subsidiaries included in the Index

Officers: Mark B. Templeton/Dir., CEO, Pres./$2,646,390.00, Atsuko Kotani/Sr. Mgr. - Marketing, Japan, John C. Burris/Sr. VP - Sales, Service/$1,572,116.00, David Jones/Corporate VP - Business Development, Carrie Shin/Marketing Mgr. - South Korea, Wes Wasson/Sr. VP, Chief Marketing Officer/$937,059.00, Lou Shipley/Group VP, GM - Management Systems Group, Stefan Sjostrom/54/VP - EMEA Sales, GM/$1,139,380.00, Klaus Oestermann/Group VP, Group VP - Application Networking Group, Gordon Payne/Group VP, GM - Advanced Solutions Group, Laura Heisman/Dir. - Product Public Relations, Analyst Relations, Paul Dobson/Public Relations Mgr. - Europe, Middle East, Africa, Ed Bezooijen/Regional Marketing Mgr. - Benelux, Bjorn Riebel/Public Relations Mgr. - Central Europe, Kurt Svenson/Regional Marketing Mgr. - Nordic *(31 Officers included in Index)*

Directors: Mark B. Templeton/Dir., CEO, Pres., Thomas F. Bogan/Chmn., Stephen M. Dow/Dir., Asiff Hirji/Dir., Godfrey R. Sullivan/Dir., Gary E. Morin/Dir., Murray J. Demo/Dir.

Owners: Murray J. Demo, Godfrey R. Sullivan, Insiders/1.84%, Thomas F. Bogan, Stefan Sjstrm, David J. Henshall, Gary E. Morin, Wes R. Wasson, Mark B. Templeton, Stephen M. Dow, Asiff Hirji, PRIMECAP Management Company/8.09%, David R. Friedman, John C. Burris

Financial Data: *Fiscal Year End:*12/31 *Latest Annual Data:* 12/31/2006

Year	Sales	Net Income
2006	$1,134,319,000	$182,997,000
2005	$908,722,000	$166,340,000
2004	$741,157,000	$131,546,000

Curr. Assets:	$811,737,000	**Curr. Liab.:**	$535,543,000	**P/E Ratio:**	31.96
Plant, Equip.:	$92,580,000	**Total Liab.:**	$560,184,000	**Indic. Yr. Divd.:**	NA
Total Assets:	$2,024,473,000	**Net Worth:**	$1,464,289,000	**Debt/ Equity:**	NA

City Bank

14807 Hwy. 99, Lynnwood, WA, 98087; *PH:* 1-425-745-5933; *Fax:* 1-425-742-9797; *http://* www.citybank.com

General - Incorporation		**Stock**- Price on:12/24/2007	$32.21
Employees	NA	Stock Exchange	NDQ
Auditor	NA	Ticker Symbol	CTBK
Stk Agt	National City Bank	Outstanding Shares	15,710,000
Counsel	NA	E.P.S	$2.57
DUNS No.	NA	Shareholders	NA

Business: The groups principal activity is to provide banking services. The groups services include CityBank online banking, VISA check card and money talks 24 hour telephone banking. The products of the group include commercial, construction loan and mortgage loan. The group operates from the United States.

Primary SIC and add'l.: 6022

CIK No:

Financial Data: *Fiscal Year End:*NA *Latest Annual Data:* 12/31/2004

Year	Sales	Net Income
2004	$74,012,000	$19,033,000
2003	$77,491,000	$19,345,000
2002	$75,509,000	$19,664,000

Curr. Assets:	$40,943,000	**Curr. Liab.:**	$422,090,000	**P/E Ratio:**	12.99
Plant, Equip.:	$11,973,000	**Total Liab.:**	$511,227,000	**Indic. Yr. Divd.:**	$0.600
Total Assets:	$667,362,000	**Net Worth:**	$155,694,000	**Debt/ Equity:**	0.5214

City Capital Corp

256 Seabord Ln., Bldg. E, Ste. 101, Franklin, TN, 37067; *PH:* 1-615-503-9900; *Fax:* 1-888-202-4775; *http://* www.citycapitalcorp.net; *Email:* info@citycapitalcorp.net

General - Incorporation	NV	**Stock**- Price on:12/24/2007	$0.43
Employees	NA	Stock Exchange	OTC
Auditor	De Joya Griffith & Co., LLC	Ticker Symbol	CTCC
Stk Agt	Atlas Stock Transfer Corp	Outstanding Shares	25,810,000
Counsel	NA	E.P.S	-$0.17
DUNS No.	NA	Shareholders	NA

Business: The groups principle activity is real estate and investment business. The group operates from the United States.

Primary SIC and add'l.: 6799 8742 6726

CIK No: 0000793986

Subsidiaries: Sarbox Solutions, Inc

Officers: Ephren W. Taylor/Chmn., CEO, Principal Financial Officer, Emerson W. Brantley/Dir., Chief Communications Officer, Gary Borglund/60/Pres., Sec., Dir.

Directors: Ephren W. Taylor/Chmn., CEO, Principal Financial Officer, Emerson W. Brantley/Dir., Chief Communications Officer, Gary Borglund/60/Pres., Sec., Dir., Richard Overdorff/66/Dir., Donald R. McCarthy/Dir., Phillip St. James/Dir.

Owners: Phillip St James, Insiders/39.50%, Ephren Taylor Holdings, LLC/38.40%, Emerson Brantley, Elliott Morgan/5.70%, Grant Dillard/10.40%, Richard Overdorff, Don McCarthy, Gary Borglund

Financial Data: Fiscal Year End:12/31   Latest Annual Data: 12/31/2006

Year	Sales	Net Income
2006	NA	-$582,000
2005	NA	-$466,000
2004	$72,000	-$511,000

Curr. Assets:	$11,000	Curr. Liab.:	NA	P/E Ratio:	24.27
Plant, Equip.:	NA	Total Liab.:	NA	Indic. Yr. Divd.:	NA
Total Assets:	$11,000	Net Worth:	NA	Debt/ Equity:	NA

City Holding Co

25 Gatewater Rd., Cross Lanes, WV, 25313; **PH:** 1-304-769-1100; **Fax:** 1-304-769-1111; http:// www.cityholding.com; **Email:** vikki.evans@cityholding.com

General - Incorporation	WV	**Stock**- Price on:12/24/2007	$38.59
Employees	779	Stock Exchange	NDQ
Auditor	Ernst & Young LLP	Ticker Symbol	CHCO
Stk Agt	Computershare Investor Services LLC	Outstanding Shares	17,160,000
Counsel	John W. Alderman	E.P.S.	$2.99
DUNS No.	14-730-4091	Shareholders	NA

Business: The group's principal activity is to provide community-banking services to consumers and local businesses in west Virginia and Ohio. The group offers credit, deposit services, investment advisory, trust and insurance products and other services to its customers through its subsidiary city national bank of west Virginia. The group deposit services include demand, savings and time accounts and credit offerings consist of commercial, financial and agricultural, residential real estate and instalment loans. It also provides other services, which include automatic teller machines, check cards, telemarketing and interactive voice response systems. The operations are conducted through 51 offices in west Virginia and 2 offices in Ohio.

Primary SIC and add'l.: 6712 6021

CIK No: 0000726854

Subsidiaries: City Financial Corporation, City Holding Capital Trust, City Mortgage Corporation, City National Bank

Officers: Charles R. Hageboeck/Dir., CEO, Pres./$569,257.00, Craig G. Stilwell/Exec. VP - Marketing/$353,388.00, John A. Derito/Exec. VP - Commercial Banking/$296,516.00, John W. Alderman/General Legal Counsel/$244,630.00, Jeffrey D. Legge/CIO, David L. Bumgarner/CFO/$206,726.00

Directors: Charles R. Hageboeck/Dir., CEO, Pres., Samuel M. Bowling/Vice Chmn., Philip L. McLaughlin/Chmn., James L. Rossi/Dir., Oshel B. Craigo/Dir., Hugh R. Clonch/Dir., Dallas C. Kayser/Dir., Tracy W. Hylton/Dir., Robert D. Fisher/Dir., David W. Hambrick/Dir., Edward M. Payne/Dir., James E. Songer/Dir., Sharon Horton Rowe/Dir., William H. File/Dir., Jay C. Goldman/Dir. (16 Directors included in Index)

Owners: David L. Bumgarner, James L. Rossi, Insiders/3.69%, Jay C. Goldman, Dallas C. Kayser, Charles R. Hageboeck, John A. DeRito, Sharon H. Rowe, Tracy W. Hylton, Samuel M. Bowling, Robert D. Fisher, Philip L. McLaughlin, Craig G. Stilwell, James E. Songer, David W. Hambrick (21 Owners included in Index)

Financial Data: Fiscal Year End:12/31   Latest Annual Data: 12/31/2006

Year	Sales	Net Income
2006	$212,321,000	$53,187,000
2005	$185,609,000	$50,288,000
2004	$168,917,000	$46,344,000

Curr. Assets:	$122,785,000	Curr. Liab.:	$2,121,787,000	P/E Ratio:	12.69
Plant, Equip.:	$44,689,000	Total Liab.:	$2,202,500,000	Indic. Yr. Divd.:	$1.240
Total Assets:	$2,507,807,000	Net Worth:	$305,307,000	Debt/ Equity:	0.0723

City National Bancshares Corp

900 Broad St., Newark, NJ, 07102; **PH:** 1-973-624-0865; **Fax:** 1-973-624-5754; http:// www.citynatbank.com

General - Incorporation	NJ	**Stock**- Price on:12/24/2007	NA
Employees	3,171	Stock Exchange	NA
Auditor	KPMG LLP	Ticker Symbol	NA
Stk Agt	Continental Stock Transfer & Trust Co	Outstanding Shares	NA
Counsel	NA	E.P.S.	NA
DUNS No.	15-428-0341	Shareholders	NA

Business: The group's principal activity is to provide retail and commercial banking services through its subsidiary. The group accepts deposits from the communities and neighborhoods in close proximity to its branches. It lends these deposits to its customer base, like that of the urban neighborhoods which it serves, in the form of real estate loans. In addition, it also offers various investment products, including mutual funds. Operations are conducted through nine branch offices located in New Jersey.

Primary SIC and add'l.: 6712 6021

CIK No: 0000714980

Subsidiaries: City National Investments, Inc.

Officers: Louis E. Prezeau/65/Dir., CEO, Pres./$541,157.00, Edward R. Wright/62/Sr. VP, CFO/$187,537.00

Directors: Louis E. Prezeau/65/Dir., CEO, Pres., Eugene Giscombe/67/Chmn., Douglas E. Anderson/58/Dir., Barbara Bell Coleman/57/Dir., Lemar C. Whigham/64/Dir.

Owners: Lemar C. Whigham/7.26%, Edward R. Wright/3.77%, Veronica T. Gilbert, Louis E. Prezeau/17.51%, Carolyn M. Whigham/6.40%, Insiders/39.06%, Eugene Giscombe/7.98%, Raul Oseguera, Douglas Anderson, Stanley M. Weeks, Barbara Bell Coleman

City National Corp

City National Ctr., 400 N. Roxbury Dr., Beverly Hills, CA, 90210; **PH:** 1-310-888-6000; **Fax:** 1-310-888-6045; http:// www.cnb.com

General - Incorporation	DE	**Stock**- Price on:12/24/2007	$77
Employees	2,689	Stock Exchange	NYSE
Auditor	KPMG LLP	Ticker Symbol	CYN
Stk Agt	Continental Stock Transfer & Trust Co	Outstanding Shares	48,770,000
Counsel	NA	E.P.S.	$4.73
DUNS No.	00-690-4395	Shareholders	NA

Business: The group's principle activity is to provide private and business banking services including investment and trust services. The services include a broad range of lending, deposits, cash management, international banking and investment and trust services. The group operates in 12 full-service regional centers, 63 banking offices in southern California and the san francisco bay area. Through reed, conner and birdwell llc and city national investments, the group offers personal and employee benefit trust and estate services, including 401(k) and defined benefit plans. The group also manages and offers mutual funds under the name of cni charter funds.

Primary SIC and add'l.: 6021 6712

CIK No: 0000201461

Subsidiaries: CCM Newco III, Inc., City National Bank, City National Financial Services, Inc, CN Acquisition Corporation, Convergent Capital Management, LLC

Officers: Russell Goldsmith/Dir., CEO, Pres./$4,130,873.00, Christopher J. Warmuth/Dir., Exec. VP/$1,041,079.00, Gwen T. Miller/Exec. VP - Westside Private Banking, City National Bank, Thomas R. Miller/Exec. VP - Marketing, City National Bank, John Pedersen/Exec. VP, Sr. Risk Management Officer, Dan Minkoff/VP - Media Relations, Michael B. Cahill/Exec. VP, General Counsel, Sec. - City National Bank/$664,421.00, Christopher J. Carey/CFO, Exec. VP/$1,207,129.00, John J. Beale/CIO, Exec. VP - City National Bank, Robert H. Brant/Exec. VP - Northern California, City National Bank, Richard D. Byrd/Exec. VP - Wealth Management, City National Bank, Kevin P. Dunigan/Exec. VP - Core Banking, City National Bank, Brian Fitzmaurice/Exec. VP, Chief Credit Officer - City National Bank, Martha Henderson/Exec. VP - Entertainment, City National Bank, Cary Walker/Investor Relations, Sr. VP, Mgr. (22 Officers included in Index)

Directors: Russell Goldsmith/Dir., CEO, Pres., Bram Goldsmith/Chmn., George H. Benter/Vice Chmn. - City National Bank, Kenneth Ziffren/Dir., Ronald L. Olson/Dir., Peter M. Thomas/Dir., Linda Griego/Dir., Ashok Israni/Dir., Bruce Rosenblum/Dir., Kenneth L. Coleman/Dir., Christopher J. Warmuth/Dir., Exec. VP, Richard L. Bloch/Dir., Michael L. Meyer/Dir.

Owners: Michael L. Meyer, Ariel Capital Management, LLC:/8.39%, Michael B. Cahill, Russell Goldsmith/10.58%, Linda Griego, Christopher J. Warmuth, Ronald L. Olson, Peter M. Thomas, Kenneth L. Coleman, Richard L. Bloch, Kenneth Ziffren, Ashok Israni, Christopher J. Carey, Bram Goldsmith/8.02%, Insiders/19.24% (18 Owners included in Index)

Financial Data: Fiscal Year End:12/31   Latest Annual Data: 12/31/2006

Year	Sales	Net Income
2006	$1,073,358,000	$233,523,000
2005	$926,741,000	$234,735,000
2004	$794,478,000	$206,322,000

Curr. Assets:	$762,838,000	Curr. Liab.:	$12,697,121,000	P/E Ratio:	16.28
Plant, Equip.:	$94,745,000	Total Liab.:	$13,365,041,000	Indic. Yr. Divd.:	$1.840
Total Assets:	$14,884,381,000	Net Worth:	$1,490,915,000	Debt/ Equity:	0.3107

City Network Inc

2F-1, No. 16 Jian Ba Road, Chung Ho City; **PH:** 886-282265566; http:// www.citynetwork.com.tw; **Email:** service@citynetwork.com.tw

General - Incorporation	NV	**Stock**- Price on:12/24/2007	NA
Employees	58	Stock Exchange	OTC
Auditor	Simon & Edward LLP	Ticker Symbol	CSNY
Stk Agt	Pacific Stock Transfer Company	Outstanding Shares	NA
Counsel	NA	E.P.S.	NA
DUNS No.	NA	Shareholders	NA

Business: The group's principal activities are to design, manufacture and market a line of broadband and wireless Internet access solutions. The group offers products for several technology platforms including cable and optical product that multiplies bandwidth among all users over tree-based topology coax or optical cables. The other products of the group include xdsl, the technology to connect to Internet. Wireless broadband eliminates the need for phone lines, cables and electrical outlets. Home phone line wiring products allow for networking a home using the existing phone wiring. The group markets its private broadband data systems to domestic and international system integrators who in turn market and sell the products to educational and government institutions, commercial enterprises and to regional competitive service providers and national carriers. The group operates in the United States, Asia and Europe.

Primary SIC and add'l.: 7375 7389

CIK No: 0001140827

Subsidiaries: City Construction Co., Ltd., City Network Inc., City Network Technology, Inc.

Officers: Richard Hill/CEO

City Savings Financial Corp

2000 Franklin St., Michigan City, IN, 46360; **PH:** 1-219-879-5364

General - Incorporation	IN	**Stock**- Price on:12/24/2007	$33.97
Employees	NA	Stock Exchange	NA
Auditor	NA	Ticker Symbol	NA
Stk Agt	US Stock Transfer Corp.	Outstanding Shares	NA
Counsel	City & Suburban Financial Corp	E.P.S.	NA
DUNS No.	NA	Shareholders	NA

Business: The groups principle activity is to provide recruiting services. The groups service area includes the research and development, engineering, marketing, sales, information technology and manufacturing industries. The group operates from United States.

Primary SIC and add'l.: 6712 6036

CIK No: 0001159404

Subsidiaries: City Savings Bank, City Savings Financial Services, Inc.

City Telecom (H.K.) Ltd

39/F, Tower 1Metroplaza, 223 Hing Fong Rd., Kwai Chung, N.t.; **PH:** 852-31454118; http:// www.ctihk.com; **Email:** pr@ctihk.com

General - Incorporation	China	Stock- Price on:12/24/2007	$5.59
Employees	2,565	Stock Exchange	NDQ
Auditor	KPMG LLP	Ticker Symbol	CTEL
Stk Agt	Deutsche Bank Trust Co America	Outstanding Shares	30,710,000
Counsel	State Of NY	E.P.S.	-$0.28
DUNS No.	NA	Shareholders	NA

Business: The group's principal activities are provision of international telecommunications services and fixed telecommunications network services. Other activities include provision of Internet access and media marketing services and investment holding. Operations are carried out in Hong Kong, Japan and Canada.

Primary SIC and add'l.: 7375 6719 4822 4813

CIK No: 0001097086

Officers: Cheung C. Kin/50/Dir., CEO, Lai N. Quiaque/37/CFO, Dir. - Investor Relation, Choy M. Yuk/Dir. - Human Resources

Directors: Cheung C. Kin/50/Dir., CEO, Wong W. Kay/45/Chmn., Cheng M. Chi/57/Non - Exec. Dir., Chan K. Man/48/Non Exec. Dir., Lai N. Quiaque/37/CFO, Dir. - Investor Relation, Peh T. Lu/48/Non Exec. Dir., Lee H. Ying/61/Dir.

Owners: Top Group International Limited, Pak Ka Leung, Cheung Chi Kin Paul, EK Investment Management Limited, Ricky Wai Kay Wong, Andrew Ming Yan Yau

Financial Data: Fiscal Year End:08/31   Latest Annual Data: 8/31/2006

Year	Sales	Net Income
2006	$145,945,000	-$18,269,000
2005	$149,557,000	-$19,195,000
2004	$149,979,000	$6,611,000

Curr. Assets:	$89,972,000	Curr. Liab.:	$36,407,000		
Plant, Equip.:	$175,826,000	Total Liab.:	$158,507,000	Indic. Yr. Divd.:	$0.100
Total Assets:	$273,896,000	Net Worth:	$115,389,000	Debt/ Equity:	NA

Cityfed Financial Corp

4 Youngs Way, Nantucket, MA, 02584; PH: 1-508-228-2366

General - Incorporation	DE	Stock- Price on:12/24/2007	NA
Employees	NA	Stock Exchange	NA
Auditor	Lefkowitz, Champi & DeRienzo P.C	Ticker Symbol	NA
Stk Agt	First City Transfer Co	Outstanding Shares	NA
Counsel	NA	E.P.S.	NA
DUNS No.	62-613-2963	Shareholders	NA

Business: The group's principle activity is to provide savings and loan holding company with subsidiary which performed savings bank operations and other related financial services. The group operates from United States.

Primary SIC and add'l.: 6712 6035

CIK No: 0000744765

Subsidiaries: CFF Services Corp.

Officers: Stephen L. Ranzini/41/Chmn., CEO, Pres., John W. Atherton/64/Dir., VP, CFO, Treasurer

Directors: Stephen L. Ranzini/41/Chmn., CEO, Pres., John W. Atherton/64/Dir., VP, CFO, Treasurer

Owners: John W. Atherton/4.28%, Stephen L. Ranzini/17.56%, John W. Atherton, Insiders, James R. Connacher/1.59%, Peter R. Kellogg/31.76%, Insiders/4.28%, Philadelphia Bourse, Inc./18.57%, Frank A. Constantini/1.59%, John W. Atherton, Peter T. Hyland/1.59%, Insiders/17.57%, Jove Corporation/17.56%

CityView Corp Ltd

Level 9 Bgc Ctr., 28 The Esplanade, Perth Western, Western Australia, 6000; ;
http:// www.cityviewcorp.com; Email: info@cityviewcorp.com

General - Incorporation	Australia	Stock- Price on:12/24/2007	$0.06
Employees	NA	Stock Exchange	OTC
Auditor	BDO Chartered Accountants	Ticker Symbol	CTVWF
Stk Agt	American Securities T & T Inc.	Outstanding Shares	NA
Counsel	NA	E.P.S.	NA
DUNS No.	75-338-6226	Shareholders	NA

Business: The group's principal activities are investments in energy and technology and exploration of oil and gas interests.

Primary SIC and add'l.: 1382

CIK No: 0001023130

Subsidiaries: CityView Asia Pty Ltd

Officers: Peter Mark. Smyth/Dir., CEO, John Henry Jacoby/61/Dir., Company Sec., Paul Williams/Company Sec.

Directors: Peter Mark. Smyth/Dir., CEO, Mahmood Al Ansari/55/Chmn., John Henry Jacoby/61/Dir., Company Sec., Paul Andre De Chazal/Non Exec. Dir., Nicholas Paul Hoexter/Non Exec. Dir., Peter George Hunt Smith/Non Exec. Dir.

Owners: John Jacoby, US Control Account/10.39%, Insiders/7.61%, Mahmood al Ansari, P. M. Smyth, Midwestern Oil Pte Ltd/10.54%

Financial Data: Fiscal Year End:12/31   Latest Annual Data: 12/31/2006

Year	Sales	Net Income
2006	$39,000	-$827,000
2005	$6,000	-$374,000
2004	$13,000	-$767,000

Curr. Assets:	$729,000	Curr. Liab.:	$10,000		
Plant, Equip.:	$9,000	Total Liab.:	$10,000	Indic. Yr. Divd.:	NA
Total Assets:	$2,344,000	Net Worth:	$2,334,000	Debt/ Equity:	NA

Civitas Bankgroup Inc

4 Corporate Ctr., 810 Crescent Centre Drive, Ste. 320, Franklin, TN, 37067; PH: 1-615-383-4758;
http:// www.civitasbankgroup.com

General - Incorporation	TN	Stock- Price on:12/24/2007	NA
Employees	NA	Stock Exchange	NA
Auditor	Crowe Chizek & Co. LLC	Ticker Symbol	NA
Stk Agt	Illinois Stock Transfer Co	Outstanding Shares	NA
Counsel	NA	E.P.S.	NA
DUNS No.	NA	Shareholders	NA

Business: The group's principal activities are to provide banking services through its five subsidiaries. The group operates through twenty three branch offices in twelve markets throughout middle and west Tennessee. The operations of the group involve the provision of a range of customary services that include checking, now accounts, money market, savings accounts and certificate deposits facilities. Lending services include construction, commercial, consumer, residential real estate and home equity improvements. In addition, the banks offer various uninsured, non-deposit products including annuities and mutual funds, brokerage services and secondary market mortgage processing services.

Primary SIC and add'l.: 6022 6712

CIK No: 0001092099

Subsidiaries: Civitas Management Company, Cumberland Bank

Officers: Richard E. Herrington/Dir., CEO, Pres., Lisa Musgrove/CFO, COO, Exec. VP

Directors: Richard E. Herrington/Dir., CEO, Pres., John S. Wilder/Chmn., Danny J. Herron/Dir., Joel H. Porter/Dir., Paul M. Pratt/Dir., William E. Wallace/Dir., John S. Shepherd/Dir., Frank Inman/Dir., Thomas E. Paschal/Dir., Thomas M. Price/Dir., Alexander E. Richmond/Dir., John Stein/Dir.

Owners: Joel Porter/6.05%, C. M. Gatton/6.36%, Danny Herron/0.94%, William Wallace/0.12%, John Stein/5.68%, Ashley Hill/0.30%, Financial Stocks Capital Partners II, LP/5.68%, Richard Herrington/2.71%, Alex Richmond/1.08%, Tom Paschal/1.57%, Tom Price/0.41%, Frank Inman, Insiders/28.19%, John Shepherd/1.95%, Paul Pratt (18 Owners included in Index)

CKE Restaurants Inc

6307 Carpinteria Ave., Ste. A, Carpinteria, CA, 93013; PH: 1-805-745-7500; Fax: 1-714-490-3630;
http:// www.ckr.com

General - Incorporation	DE	Stock- Price on:12/24/2007	$22.469
Employees	30,000	Stock Exchange	NYSE
Auditor	KPMG LLP	Ticker Symbol	CKR
Stk Agt	Chase Mellon Shareholder Services LLC	Outstanding Shares	67,200,000
Counsel	Stradling Yocca Carlson & Rauth	E.P.S.	$0.719
DUNS No.	87-672-0715	Shareholders	NA

Business: The groups principle activity is to operate restaurants. The groups products are sold under the brand names Carls Jr., Hardees and La Salsa Fresh Mexican Grill. The group operates from United States.

Primary SIC and add'l.: 5812 6794

CIK No: 0000919628

Subsidiaries: Aeroways, LLC, Burger Chef Systems, Inc., Carl Karcher Enterprises, Inc., Carls Jr. Region VIII, Inc., Channel Islands Roasting Company, Cke Reit I, Inc, Cke Reit Ii, Inc., Flagstar Enterprises, Inc., GB Franchise Corporation, Hardees Food Systems, Inc., Hardees LTD, Fribourg, Hardees REIT I, Inc., Hardees REIT II, Inc., HED, Inc., La Salsa of Nevada, Inc. 18 Subsidiaries included in the Index

Officers: Andrew F. Puzder/Dir., CEO, Pres./$6,787,074.00, Jeffrey P. Chasney/Exec. VP - Strategic Planning, CIO, John J. Dunion/Exec. VP - Supply Chain Management, Richard E. Fortman/Exec. VP - Carls Jr Operations, Noah J. Griggs/Exec. VP - Carls Jr, Hardees Training/$949,360.00, Theodore Abajian/CFO, Exec. VP/$2,098,322.00, Michael E. Murphy/Chief Administrative Officer, Exec. VP - Franchising, General Counsel/$2,357,753.00, Amir Siddiqi/COO, Exec. VP - Green Burrito, Red Burrito, Michael W. Liby/Exec. VP - Operations Development, Loss Prevention, Brad R. Haley/Exec. VP - Hardees, Carls Jr Marketing/$977,718.00, Richard Buxton/Exec. VP - Real Estate Development, Bob Starke/Exec. VP - Operations, Hardees

Directors: Andrew F. Puzder/Dir., CEO, Pres., Byron Allumbaugh/Chmn., Peter Churm/Dir., Daniel E. Ponder/Dir., Frank P. Willey/Dir., Daniel D. Lane/Dir., Janet E. Kerr/Dir., Carl L. Karcher/Dir., Jerold H. Rubinstein/Dir., Matthew Goldfarb/Dir.

Owners: Theodore Abajian, Michael E. Murphy, Carl L. Karcher, Noah J. Griggs, Frank P. Willey, Janet E. Kerr, Capital Research and Management Company, Andrew F. Puzder, Daniel E. Ponder, Bradford R. Haley, Byron Allumbaugh, Insiders, Matthew Goldfarb, Peter Churm, Jerold H. Rubinstein (18 Owners included in Index)

Financial Data: Fiscal Year End:01/25   Latest Annual Data: 1/31/2007

Year	Sales	Net Income
2007	$1,588,410,000	$50,172,000
2006	$1,518,347,000	$194,582,000
2005	$1,519,881,000	$18,016,000

Curr. Assets:	$152,278,000	Curr. Liab.:	$185,139,000	P/E Ratio:	31.65
Plant, Equip.:	$513,743,000	Total Liab.:	$415,576,000	Indic. Yr. Divd.:	$0.240
Total Assets:	$794,422,000	Net Worth:	$378,846,000	Debt/ Equity:	0.4519

CKF Bancorp Inc

340 W Main St., Danville, KY, 40422; PH: 1-859-236-4181; Fax: 1-859-236-4363;
http:// www.centralkyfsb.com

General - Incorporation	DE	Stock- Price on:12/24/2007	$15.5
Employees	NA	Stock Exchange	OTC
Auditor	NA	Ticker Symbol	CKFB
Stk Agt	Illinois Stock Transfer Co	Outstanding Shares	1,330,000
Counsel	NA	E.P.S.	$0.844
DUNS No.	NA	Shareholders	NA

Business: The groups principal activity is to provide banking services. The services of the group include business checking, business loans, business investments and cash management products, checking accounts, investment products, personal loans and credit lines. The group operates from the United States.

Primary SIC and add'l.: 6712 6035

CIK No: 0000930203

Financial Data: Fiscal Year End:12/31   Latest Annual Data: 12/31/2003

Year	Sales	Net Income
2003	$8,343,000	$1,480,000
2002	$9,383,000	$1,328,000
2001	$8,487,000	$1,063,000

Curr. Assets:	$4,524,000	**Curr. Liab.:**	$128,689,000	**P/E Ratio:**	15.50
Plant, Equip.:	$2,057,000	**Total Liab.:**	$129,916,000	**Indic. Yr. Divd.:**	$0.720
Total Assets:	$144,984,000	**Net Worth:**	$15,068,000	**Debt/ Equity:**	NA

CKX Inc

650 Madison Ave., New York, NY, 10022; ***PH:*** 1-212-838-3100; ***Fax:*** 1-212-872-1473; ***http://*** www.ckx.com

General - Incorporation	DE	**Stock**- Price on:12/24/2007	$14.06
Employees	386	Stock Exchange	NDQ
Auditor	Deloitte & Touche LLP	Ticker Symbol	CKXE
Stk Agt	Bank of New York	Outstanding Shares	97,060,000
Counsel	NA	E.P.S.	$0.03
DUNS No.	19-345-3453	Shareholders	NA

Business: The group's principal activity is to own and operate a retail golf and tennis sporting goods store in las vegas. The store sells golf and tennis equipment such as clubs, golf and tennis shoes, caps, tees, rackets, apparel and other merchandise. These products are sold at a discount compared to prices in other golf and tennis shops. The group also manages and operates family and sports oriented theme park under the name all-american sportpark and operates golf centers. The group owned and operated one retail golf store in las vegas, Nevada and owned approximately 63% of the outstanding shares of common stock and 100% of the convertible preferred stock of all-american sportpark, inc. The group has disposed all the operating businesses.

Primary SIC and add'l.: 5941 7992

CIK No: 0000793044

Subsidiaries: 19 Entertainment Inc., 19 Recording Services Inc., 19 Recordings Inc., 19 Touring LLC, All Girl Productions Inc., Dance Nation Productions Inc., Elvis Anthology, LLC, Elvis Music,Inc., Elvis Presley Enterprises LLC, Elvis Presley Enterprises,Inc., Elvis Presleys Heartbreak Hotel, LLC, Elvis Presleys Memphis LLC, EPE Holding Corporation, Focus Enterprises,Inc., Meadow Oaks Apartments,Inc. 20 Subsidiaries included in the Index

Officers: Simon Fuller/Dir., CEO - Subsidiary, 19 Entertainment Limited/$1,560,794.00, Jack Soden/CEO - Subsidiary, Elvis Presley Enterprises, Inc, Robert F.X. Sillerman/Chmn., CEO/$751,870.00, Kraig G. Fox/Chief Corporate Development Officer, Exec. VP, Sec., Michael G. Ferrel/Dir., Pres./$735,187.00, Mitchell J. Slater/Dir., COO, Sr. Exec VP/$735,187.00, Howard J. Tytel/Dir. - Sr. Exec VP, Dir. - Legal, Governmental Affairs/$735,187.00, Thomas P. Benson/Dir., CFO, Exec. VP, Treasurer/$526,020.00

Directors: Simon Fuller/Dir., CEO - Subsidiary, 19 Entertainment Limited, Robert F.X. Sillerman/Chmn., CEO, Michael G. Ferrel/Dir., Pres., Mitchell J. Slater/Dir., COO, Sr. Exec VP, Howard J. Tytel/Dir. - Sr. Exec VP, Dir. - Legal, Governmental Affairs, Thomas P. Benson/Dir., CFO, Exec. VP, Treasurer, Edwin M. Banks/Dir., Edward Bleier/Dir., Jerry L. Cohen/Dir., Carl D. Harnick/Dir., Jack Langer/Dir., John D. Miller/Dir., Bruce Morrow/Dir., Priscilla Presley/Dir.

Owners: Edwin M. Banks, Simon Fuller/1.60%, Mitchell J. Slater/3.20%, Robert F.X. Sillerman/34.40%, The Huff Alternative Fund, L.P./14.60%, Jack Langer, John D. Miller, Priscilla Presley, Insiders/46.40%, Carl D. Harnick, Edward Bleier, Michael G. Ferrel/2.50%, Howard J. Tytel/2.70%, Bruce Morrow, Jerry L. Cohen *(16 Owners included in Index)*

Financial Data: ***Fiscal Year End:***12/31 ***Latest Annual Data:*** 12/31/2006

Year	Sales	Net Income
2006	$210,153,000	$9,193,000
2005	$120,605,000	-$5,904,000
2004	NA	-$120,000

Curr. Assets:	$72,698,000	**Curr. Liab.:**	$40,063,000	**P/E Ratio:**	468.67
Plant, Equip.:	$35,329,000	**Total Liab.:**	$80,634,000	**Indic. Yr. Divd.:**	NA
Total Assets:	$474,645,000	**Net Worth:**	$371,009,000	**Debt/ Equity:**	0.0070

Claimsnet.com Inc

14860 Montfort Dr., Ste. 250, Dallas, TX, 75254; ***PH:*** 1-972-458-1701; ***Fax:*** 1-972-458-1737; ***http://*** www.claimsnet.com; ***Email:*** admin@claimsnet.com

General - Incorporation	DE	**Stock**- Price on:12/24/2007	$0.11
Employees	12	Stock Exchange	OTC
Auditor	Whitley Penn	Ticker Symbol	CLAI
Stk Agt	Continental Stock Transfer & Trust Co	Outstanding Shares	26,050,000
Counsel	Brock Silverstein	E.P.S.	-$0.02
DUNS No.	96-030-8369	Shareholders	NA

Business: The group's principal activity is to process healthcare transactions for medical and dental industries with the help of Internet. It has developed proprietary software that helps doctors and dentists to prepare and update healthcare claims interactively on the Internet and transmit the claims to the group for processing. This software can be installed only on the servers of the group. The proprietary software provides real time editing of the claims data in the format required by the insurance companies and healthcare management organizations. The software also converts the data to satisfy specific processing requirements and then transmit them to the medical and dental payers electronically. The customers include the healthcare providers submitting claims, the strategic partners and affiliates and the payers accepting claims.

Primary SIC and add'l.: 7374

CIK No: 0001046057

Officers: Don Crosbie/Chmn., CEO, Pres., Laura Bray/CFO, Scott K. Spurlock/40/VP - Development, Gary Austin/COO

Directors: Don Crosbie/Chmn., CEO, Pres., Alfred Dubach/60/Vice Chmn., John C. Willems/52/Dir., Thomas Michel/56/Dir.

Owners: Thomas Michel/100.00%, New York Ventures/2.40%, J. R. Schellenberg/6.90%, Insiders/19.10%, Don Crosbie/7.30%, Alfred Dubach/4.70%, McKesson Corporation/5.80%, Bo W. Lycke/9.90%, John C. Willems, New York Ventures/86.10%, Laura Bray, Thomas Michel/4.50%, Insiders/13.90%, Elmira United Corporation/36.00%, Gary Austin/1.90% *(18 Owners included in Index)*

Financial Data: ***Fiscal Year End:***12/31 ***Latest Annual Data:*** 12/31/2006

Year	Sales	Net Income
2006	$1,464,000	-$389,000
2005	$1,266,000	-$279,000
2004	$1,046,000	-$657,000

Curr. Assets:	$496,000	**Curr. Liab.:**	$1,010,000		
Plant, Equip.:	$230,000	**Total Liab.:**	$1,818,000	**Indic. Yr. Divd.:**	NA
Total Assets:	$726,000	**Net Worth:**	-$1,092,000	**Debt/ Equity:**	NA

Claire's Stores Inc

3 S W 129th Ave, Pembroke Pines, FL, 33027; ***PH:*** 1-954-433-3900; ***http://*** www.clairestores.com

General - Incorporation	FL	**Stock**- Price on:12/24/2007	NA
Employees	7,560	Stock Exchange	NA
Auditor	KPMG LLP	Ticker Symbol	NA
Stk Agt	American Stock Transfer & Trust Co.	Outstanding Shares	NA
Counsel	Greenberg Traurig	E.P.S.	NA
DUNS No.	00-412-4731	Shareholders	NA

Business: The group's principal activity is the retail distribution of fashion accessories and apparel for pre-teens, teenagers and young adults. The group's operations are divided into costume jewelry and fashion accessories. Costume jewelry includes earrings and ear piercing services. Fashion accessories include hair ornaments, totebags and novelty items. The stores operate under the trade names claire's boutiques, claire's accessories, icing by claire's, afterthoughts and the icing. As on 31-Jul-2004, the group operates 2,833 stores throughout the United States, Puerto Rico, Canada, the virgin islands, the United Kingdom, Switzerland, Austria, Germany, France, Ireland and Japan.

Primary SIC and add'l.: 5641 5632 5621 2329

CIK No: 0000034115

Subsidiaries: BMS Distributing Corp., CBI Distributing Corp., Claires Accessories Spain, S.L., Claires Accessories UK, Ltd., Claires Austria GmbH, Claires Belgium B.V.B.A., Claires Boutiques, Inc., Claires Canada Corp., Claires France S.A.S, Claires Germany GmbH, Claires Holding GmbH, Claires International Europe, Ltd., Claires Netherlands B.V., Claires Nippon, Ltd., Claires Puerto Rico Corp. 19 Subsidiaries included in the Index

Officers: Eugene S. Kahn/CEO, Marla L. Schaefer/Co - Chmn., Principal Co - Exec. Officer, Ira D. Kaplan/Dir., Sr. VP, CFO, Marisa F. Jacobs/VP - Corporate Communications, Investor Relations, Bruce Marshall/Sr. VP - Franchise Operations, Rebecca Orand/Sr. VP, Corporate General Counsel, Keith E. Pickens/CIO, Sr. VP, Mary Fitzwilliam/VP - Finance, International Operations, William H. Girard/VP - Finance, David G. Ovis/VP - Taxation, Michael L. Winer/Corporate Treasurer, Lisa Lafosse/Pres., COO - Claire's North America, Joseph A. Defalco/Chief Administrative Officer - Claires North America, Colleen Collins/Sr. VP - Store Operations, Claire's North America, Michael Rosa/Sr. VP - General Merchandise Mana, Claire's North Amierica *(17 Officers included in Index)*

Directors: Rowland Schaefer/Chmn. Emeritus, Marla L. Schaefer/Co - Chmn., Principal Co - Exec. Officer, Bruce G. Miller/Dir., Ira D. Kaplan/Dir., Sr. VP, CFO, Martha C. Goss/Dir., Steven H. Tishman/Dir., Jick D. Todd/Dir., Ann S. Lieff/Dir., Bonnie E. Schaefer/Dir., Carl M. Youngman/Dir.

Owners: Rohit Manocha, Robert J. DiNicola, Mark Smith, Ira D. Kaplan, Ron Marshall, Eugene S. Kahn, Insiders/1.70%, Apollo Management VI, L.P./98.20%, George G. Golleher

Clancy Systems International Inc

2250 S Oneida St., Ste. 308, Denver, CO, 80224; ***PH:*** 1-303-753-0197; ***Fax:*** 1-303-759-4681; ***http://*** www.clancysystems.com

General - Incorporation	CO	**Stock**- Price on:12/24/2007	$0.017
Employees	42	Stock Exchange	OTC
Auditor	Stark Winter Schenkein & Co. LLP	Ticker Symbol	CLSI
Stk Agt	Computershare Investor Services	Outstanding Shares	382,010,000
Counsel	Bingham Dana Ltd	E.P.S.	$0.001
DUNS No.	15-105-2024	Shareholders	NA

Business: The group's principal activity is to design, develop and manufacture automated parking enforcement systems for lease to municipalities, universities and institutions. It also develops and manufactures ticket writing systems, rental car return systems, Internet payment remittance systems and Internet industry guides. The group has installed parking enforcement systems for various clients, towns and universities. It provides computers, printers and software to enable the user to do state department of motor vehicle lookups, maintain citation information storage and recall, generate delinquent notices and have immediate access to files of all tickets previously written. The group also provides hardware and software for special projects.

Primary SIC and add'l.: 7373 7372

CIK No: 0000789318

Subsidiaries: Urban Transit Solutions

Owners: Lizabeth M. Wolfson/34.44%, James R. Nyman/7.10%, Insiders/41.54%

Financial Data: ***Fiscal Year End:***09/30 ***Latest Annual Data:*** 9/30/2006

Year	Sales	Net Income
2006	$3,536,000	$336,000
2005	$3,023,000	$176,000
2004	$3,114,000	$24,000

Curr. Assets:	$1,246,000	**Curr. Liab.:**	$536,000		
Plant, Equip.:	$845,000	**Total Liab.:**	$546,000	**Indic. Yr. Divd.:**	NA
Total Assets:	$3,393,000	**Net Worth:**	$2,847,000	**Debt/ Equity:**	0.0026

CLARCOR Inc

840 Cresent Ctr. Dr., Ste. 600, Franklin, TN, 37067; ***PH:*** 1-615-771-3100; ***Fax:*** 1-615-771-5603; ***http://*** www.clarcor.com; ***Email:*** information@clarcor.com

General - Incorporation	DE	**Stock**- Price on:12/24/2007	$33.78
Employees	5,048	Stock Exchange	NYSE
Auditor	PricewaterhouseCoopers LLP	Ticker Symbol	CLC
Stk Agt	National City Bank	Outstanding Shares	51,280,000
Counsel	NA	E.P.S.	$1.59
DUNS No.	00-516-2417	Shareholders	NA

Business: The group's principal activities are carried out through three principal segments: industrial/environmental filtration, engine/mobile filtration and packaging. The industrial/environmental filtration products are used primarily for commercial, residential and industrial applications. The products include air and antimicrobial treated filters and high efficiency electronic air cleaners, paint spray booths, gas turbine systems, medical facilities, motor vehicle cabins, clean rooms and compressors. Engine/mobile filtration includes filters for oil, air, fuel, coolants and hydraulic fluids for trucks, automobiles, construction, mining and industrial equipment, locomotives, marine and agricultural equipment. The packaging products include a variety of customs styled packaging items used primarily by the food, confectionery, drug, toiletries and chemical specialties industries. On 15-Sep-2004, the group acquired united efp.

Primary SIC and add'l.: 3569 3565 3089 3599 3714 3411

CIK No: 0000020740

Subsidiaries: Airguard Asia Sdn. Bhd., Airklean Engineering Pte. Ltd., Baldwin Filters (Aust.) Pty. Limited, Baldwin Filters Limited, Baldwin Filters N.V., Baldwin Filters, Inc., Baldwin South Africa, Inc., Baldwin-Unifil S.A., Baldwin-Weifang Filters Ltd., CLARCOR Air Filtration Products, Inc., CLARCOR Consumer Products, Inc., CLARCOR Filtration Products, Inc., CLARCOR International, Inc., CLARCOR Total Filtration, Inc., CLARCOR Trading Company 39 Subsidiaries included in the Index

Officers: Norman E. Johnson/60/Chmn., CEO, Pres., David J. Lindsay/52/VP - Administration, Chief Administrative Officer, Bruce A. Klein/60/VP - Finance, CFO, Sam Ferrise/52/Pres. - Baldwin Filters, Richard C. Larson/58/Pres. - Clarcor Air, Clark Filter, UAS, Richard M. Wolfson/41/VP, General Counsel, Corp. Sec.

Directors: Norman E. Johnson/60/Chmn., CEO, Pres., Paul Donovan/Dir., Robert H. Jenkins/Dir., James L. Packard/Dir., Robert J. Burgstahler/Dir., Philip R. Lochner/Dir., Marc J. Adam/Dir., James W. Bradford/Dir.

Owners: Robert H. Jenkins, Insiders/5.64%, James W. Bradford, James L. Packard, David J. Lindsay, Marc J. Adam, Norman E. Johnson/2.94%, Sam Ferrise, Philip R. Lochner, Paul Donovan, GAMCO Investors, Inc./6.30%, Neuberger Berman, LLC/14.70%, Bruce A. Klein, Columbia Wanger Asset Management, L.P./8.40%, Richard M. Wolfson *(16 Owners included in Index)*

Financial Data: *Fiscal Year End:*11/03   *Latest Annual Data:* 12/2/2006

Year	Sales	Net Income
2006	$904,347,000	$82,710,000
2005	$873,974,000	$76,393,000
2004	$787,686,000	$63,997,000

Curr. Assets:	$380,340,000	**Curr. Liab.:**	$118,428,000	**P/E Ratio:** 21.25
Plant, Equip.:	$146,529,000	**Total Liab.:**	$188,351,000	**Indic. Yr. Divd.:** $0.290
Total Assets:	$727,516,000	**Net Worth:**	$537,509,000	**Debt/ Equity:** 0.0287

Clarient Inc

31 Columbia, Aliso Viejo, CA, 92656; *PH:* 1-949-425-5700; *Fax:* 1-949-425-5701; *http://* www.clarientinc.com

General - Incorporation	DE	**Stock** - Price on:12/24/2007	$2.07
Employees	204	Stock Exchange	NDQ
Auditor	KPMG LLP	Ticker Symbol	CLRT
Stk Agt	Mellon Investor Services LLC	Outstanding Shares	71,700,000
Counsel	Gibson, Dunn & Crutcher LLP	E.P.S.	-$0.107
DUNS No.	96-890-8673	Shareholders	NA

Business: The group's principal activities are to develop, manufacture and market automated cellular imaging system. This is a versatile automated digital microscope system with computer-based color imaging technology with the ability to detect, count and classify cells based on color, size and shape to assist pathologists in making critical medical decisions that can affect patient treatment. The group operates as a single segment under the name automated cellular imaging systems (acis). The acis uses specifically developed software to analyze specimens placed on slides and stained with laboratory reagents that impart color to highlight diagnostic features of cells. The customers of the product are classified into two groups: clinical market which includes reference laboratories, pathology practice group and hospitals and research and biotechnology market consisting of pharmaceutical companies, university medical centers and research institutions.

Primary SIC and add'l.: 3841 3845

CIK No: 0001038223

Subsidiaries: Clarient Diagnostic Services, Inc.

Officers: Ronald A. Andrews/CEO, Pres./$835,371.00, James V. Agnello/Sr. VP, CFO/$209,449.00, Anselm Hii/Hematopathologist, Dir. - Consultative Services, Medical Staff, Kenneth J. Bloom/Chief Medical Dir., Alan Wells/Sr. Dir. - Operations, James Wynne/Sales Dir., Michael Nall/Sales Dir., Richard Smooke/Sales Dir., David J. Daly/Sr. VP - Commercial Operations, Michael J. Pellini/COO, Sing-Tsung Chen/Dir. - Hematopathology, Vladislav Chizhevsky/Staff Pathologist, Swati Shah/Sr. Hematopathologist, Claudia Bunting/Sr. Dir. - Anatomical Pathology, Ainura Kyshtoobayeva/QC IHC Dir. *(16 Officers included in Index)*

Directors: James A. Datin/Chmn., Richard J. Cote/Chmn. - Clarient Scientific Advisory Board, Jon R. Wampler/Dir., Craig D. Allred/Member - Scientific Advisory Board, Ruth L. Katz/Member - Scientific Advisory Board, Peter J. Boni/Dir., Frank P. Slattery/Dir., Dennis M. Smith/Dir., Jonathan W. Said/Member - Scientific Advisory Board, Clive R. Taylor/Member - Scientific Advisory Board, Lawrence M. Weiss/Member - Scientific Advisory Board, Gregory D. Waller/Dir.

Owners: Jose de la Torre-Bueno, Irwin Scher, Safeguard Scientifics, Inc./60.91%, Jon R. Wampler, Dennis M. Smith, Insiders/2.84%, Frank P. Slattery, Ronald A. Andrews

Financial Data: *Fiscal Year End:*12/31   *Latest Annual Data:* 06/30/2007

Year	Sales	Net Income
2007	$10,336,000	-$2,801,000
2006	$33,604,000	-$15,926,000
2005	$20,149,000	-$14,802,000

Curr. Assets:	$11,779,000	**Curr. Liab.:**	$13,723,000	
Plant, Equip.:	$10,608,000	**Total Liab.:**	$25,870,000	**Indic. Yr. Divd.:** NA
Total Assets:	$27,030,000	**Net Worth:**	$1,160,000	**Debt/ Equity:** 7.3241

Clarion Technologies Inc

5041 68th, Caledonia, MI, 49316; *PH:* 1-616-454-0055; *Fax:* 1-616-494-8888; *http://* www.clariontechnologies.com

General - Incorporation	DE	**Stock** - Price on:12/24/2007	NA
Employees	800	Stock Exchange	OTC
Auditor	BDO Seidman LLP	Ticker Symbol	CLAR
Stk Agt	Computershare Investor Services LLC	Outstanding Shares	NA
Counsel	NA	E.P.S.	-$0.54
DUNS No.	NA	Shareholders	NA

Business: The group's principal activity is to design and manufacture custom injection molds for automotive, heavy truck, office furniture and consumer goods industries. The group provides mold design models, mold manufacturing, engineering services and post-molding services to customers on a contract basis. The products include automotive interior and exterior trims, wheel covers, door panels, grills, office chair components and refrigerator and other home appliance parts. The parts comprise of thermoplastics manufactured from plastic resins, primarily polycarbonate, polyethylene and polystyrene. In addition to manufacture, the group also provides program management, industrial design, prototyping and tooling from concept through delivery of complete assemblies. Major customers of the group include electrolux and johnson controls inc. The group has four automated custom injection molding plants with in Michigan.

Primary SIC and add'l.: 3089

CIK No: 0000835409

Subsidiaries: Clarion Real Estate, LLC, Clarion Technologies Mexico, LLC, Clarion Technologies de Mexico, S. de R.L. de C.V., CTI Rio Bravo, S. de R.L. de C.V.

Officers: Steven W. Olmstead/Dir., CEO, Pres., William Beckman/Pres., John Brownlow/COO, Jeff Gillesse/CFO

Directors: Steven W. Olmstead/Dir., CEO, Pres., Craig A. Wierda/Chmn., Frank T. Steck/Dir., Anthony Wauterlek/Dir., Frederick A. Sotok/Dir., Jack D. Rutherford/Dir., Kenneth La Grand/Dir.

Financial Data: *Fiscal Year End:*12/31   *Latest Annual Data:* 12/31/2005

Year	Sales	Net Income
2005	$145,515,000	-$5,659,000
2004	$117,698,000	-$1,722,000
2003	$97,668,000	$774,000

Curr. Assets:	$20,019,000	**Curr. Liab.:**	$60,814,000	
Plant, Equip.:	$23,482,000	**Total Liab.:**	$95,340,000	**Indic. Yr. Divd.:** NA
Total Assets:	$68,445,000	**Net Worth:**	-$85,923,000	**Debt/ Equity:** NA

Clark Inc

102 S Wynstone Pk. Dr., Ste. 200, North Barrington, IL, 60010; *PH:* 1-847-304-5800; *http://* www.clarkconsulting.com

General - Incorporation	DE	**Stock** - Price on:12/24/2007	NA
Employees	931	Stock Exchange	NA
Auditor	Ernst & Young LLP	Ticker Symbol	NA
Stk Agt	Bank of New York	Outstanding Shares	NA
Counsel	NA	E.P.S.	NA
DUNS No.	82-557-2209	Shareholders	NA

Business: The group's principle activity is the evaluation, design, implementation and financing of customized compensation and benefit programs for executives, employees and other professionals. Four groups carry out the operations serving corporations, banks and healthcare organizations. The compensation resource group designs, implements, administers and finances non-qualified benefit plans for Fortune 1000 companies and large private companies. The banking practice group offers compensation consulting, executive and director benefits programs and bank-owned life insurance to the bank market. The healthcare group provides compensation and benefit services for large and medium sized non-profit healthcare organizations.

Primary SIC and add'l.: 6411

CIK No: 0001063980

Subsidiaries: Argos Advantage, Inc., CBC Insurance Revenue Securitization LLC, Clark Consulting, Inc., Clark Reinsurance Company Limited, Clark Securities, Inc., Clark Strategic Advisors, Inc., Clark/Bardes of Bermuda, Ltd., Clark/Bardes of Hawaii, LLC, COLI Insurance Agency, Inc., CRG Fiduciary Services, Inc., CRG Insurance Agency, Inc., ECB Insurance Agency, Inc., Executive Benefit Services, Inc., Medex, Inc.

Clarkston Financial Corp

6600 Highland Rd., Ste. 24, Waterford, MI, 48327; *PH:* 1-248-922-6940; *Fax:* 1-248-886-1432; *http://* www.clarkstonstatebank.com

General - Incorporation	MI	**Stock** - Price on:12/24/2007	$12.9
Employees	48	Stock Exchange	OTC
Auditor	Plante & Moran, PLLC	Ticker Symbol	CKSB
Stk Agt	Continental Stock Transfer & Trust Co	Outstanding Shares	1,260,000
Counsel	Honigman Miller Schwartz & Cohn	E.P.S.	-$1.37
DUNS No.	NA	Shareholders	NA

Business: The group's principal activity is to provide full range of commercial and consumer banking services for small to medium size business and individuals. The group is a bank holding company owning all of the outstanding common stock of clarkston state bank. It extends commercial loans, residential real estate loans and consumer loans. The deposit services include checking accounts, now accounts, savings accounts and time deposits. In addition, the group also provides other financial products and services including trust services through third-party service providers. The products and services are provided through five branch offices to Michigan communities in oakland county.

Primary SIC and add'l.: 6712 6022

CIK No: 0001068366

Subsidiaries: Clarkston Capital Trust I, Clarkston State Bank, Huron Valley State Bank

Officers: Edwin L. Adler/70/Chmn., CEO, Grant J. Smith/40/Dir., COO, Pres./$161,583.00, James W. Distelrath/CFO/$101,249.00

Directors: Edwin L. Adler/70/Chmn., CEO, Mark Murvay/68/Dir., Thomas E. Kimble/61/Dir., John H. Welker/67/Dir., William J. Clark/58/Dir., Grant J. Smith/40/Dir., COO, Pres.

Owners: J. Grant Smith/0.30%, Thomas E. Kimble/0.10%, Dawn M. Horner/0.40%, John H. Welker/4.50%, Mark A. Murvay/10.20%, Acadia Master Fund I Limited/7.40%, William J. Clark/0.80%, Bank Fund VI L.P./9.00%, Edwin L. Adler/17.70%

Financial Data: *Fiscal Year End:*12/31   *Latest Annual Data:* 12/31/2006

Year	Sales	Net Income
2006	$14,326,000	-$712,000
2005	$11,875,000	-$24,000
2004	$8,976,000	$1,277,000

Curr. Assets:	$16,699,000	**Curr. Liab.:**	$198,417,000	**P/E Ratio:** 645.00
Plant, Equip.:	$4,730,000	**Total Liab.:**	$202,417,000	**Indic. Yr. Divd.:** NA
Total Assets:	$220,378,000	**Net Worth:**	$14,766,000	**Debt/ Equity:** 0.2665

Clarus Corp

1 Landmark Sq., 22nd Fl., Stamford, CT, 06901; *PH:* 1-203-428-2000; *Fax:* 1-203-428-2020; *http://* www.claruscorp.com; *Email:* info@claruscorp.com

General - Incorporation	DE	**Stock** - Price on:12/24/2007	NA
Employees	6	Stock Exchange	OTC
Auditor	KPMG LLP	Ticker Symbol	CLRS
Stk Agt	American Stock Transfer & Trust Co.	Outstanding Shares	NA
Counsel	NA	E.P.S.	$0.02
DUNS No.	79-129-7658	Shareholders	NA

Business: The group's principle activity is to seek, analyze and evaluate potential merger and acquisition candidates. Prior to the sale of its operating assets in dec-2002, the group developed, marketed and supported Internet-based business-to-business e-commerce software that automated the procurement, sourcing and settlement of goods and services. On 01-Jan-2003, the group sold its cashbook product to an employee group in limerick, Ireland

Primary SIC and add'l.: 7372

CIK No: 0000913277

Officers: Warren B. Kanders/Chmn., CEO/$527,900.00, Susan Luckfield/Controller/$155,381.00, Philip A. Baratelli/40/CFO, Sec., Treasurer, Gary Julien/VP - Corporate Development

Directors: Warren B. Kanders/Chmn., CEO, Burtt R. Ehrlich/Dir., Donald L. House/66/Dir., Nicholas Sokolow/Dir.

Owners: Ashford Capital Management, Inc./11.60%, White Rock Capital Management, L.P./5.60%, Nigel P. Ekern/1.30%, Donald L. House/1.20%, Warren B. Kanders/18.50%, Nicholas Sokolow/1.60%, Burtt R. Ehrlich/1.20%, Susan Luckfield, Insiders/23.90%, Dimensional Fund Advisors Inc./6.40%

Financial Data: Fiscal Year End:12/31 Latest Annual Data: 12/31/2006

Year	Sales	Net Income
2006	NA	-$1,291,000
2005	NA	-$1,291,000
2004	$1,106,000	-$2,889,000
Curr. Assets:	$84,974,000	Curr. Liab.:	$680,000		
Plant, Equip.:	$1,699,000	Total Liab.:	$957,000	Indic. Yr. Divd.:	NA
Total Assets:	$86,673,000	Net Worth:	$85,716,000	Debt/ Equity:	NA

Classified Ad Inc

1016 Clemons St., Ste. 302, Jupiter, FL, 33477; **PH:** 1-561-745-6789

General - Incorporation	FL	Stock - Price on:12/24/2007	NA
Employees	NA	Stock Exchange	NA
Auditor	Wieseneck, Andres & Co P.A	Ticker Symbol	NA
Stk Agt	Florida Atlantic Stock Transfer, Inc.	Outstanding Shares	NA
Counsel	NA	E.P.S.	NA
DUNS No.	NA	Shareholders	NA

Business: The groups principle activity is to provide technology services. The groups technology enables professional advertising agencies, businesses and individuals to send ads to newspapers electronically. The group also provides credit card processing services to the newspaper industry. The group operates from United States.

Primary SIC and add'l.: 9995

CIK No: 0001321499

Officers: Barney A. Richmond/56/Chmn., Pres., Sec., Richard C. Turner/48/Dir., Treasurer

Directors: Barney A. Richmond/56/Chmn., Pres., Sec., Richard C. Turner/48/Dir., Treasurer

Owners: American Capital Holdings, Inc./28.50%, Richard C. Turner/1.50%, United States Financial Group, Inc./9.10%, Barney A. Richmond/18.70%, Insiders/20.20%

Claude Resources Inc

224 4th Ave. S, Ste. 200, Saskatoon, SK, S7K 5M5; **PH:** 1-306-668-7505;
http:// www.clauderesources.com; **Email:** clauderesources@clauderesources.com

General - Incorporation	Canada	Stock - Price on:12/24/2007	$1.45
Employees	NA	Stock Exchange	AMEX
Auditor	KPMG LLP	Ticker Symbol	CGR
Stk Agt	Valient Trust Co	Outstanding Shares	76,980,000
Counsel	NA	E.P.S.	-$0.068
DUNS No.	NA	Shareholders	NA

Business: The groups principle activities include exploring and mining gold, oil and gas. The groups operating projects include Seabee, Porky West Zone, Santoy Area, and Madsen. The group operates from United States.

Primary SIC and add'l.: 9999

CIK No: 0001173924

Officers: Neil McMillan/Dir., CEO, Pres., Rick G. Johnson/CFO, VP - Finance, Brian Groves/VP - Corporate Development

Directors: Neil McMillan/Dir., CEO, Pres., Josef Spross/Chmn., Ronald J. Hicks/Dir., Jon R. MacNeill/Dir., Ted Nieman/Dir., Robert J. Kowalishin/Dir., Ray MacKay/Dir.

Financial Data: Fiscal Year End:12/31 Latest Annual Data: 12/31/2006

Year	Sales	Net Income
2006	$30,616,000	-$2,609,000
2005	$23,080,000	-$7,391,000
2004	$21,447,000	-$497,000
Curr. Assets:	$20,470,000	Curr. Liab.:	$13,906,000	P/E Ratio:	21.78
Plant, Equip.:	$53,358,000	Total Liab.:	$68,767,000	Indic. Yr. Divd.:	NA
Total Assets:	$125,040,000	Net Worth:	$56,272,000	Debt/ Equity:	NA

Claxson Interactive Group Inc

1550 Biscayne Blvd., Miami, FL, 33132; **PH:** 1-305-894-3500; **Fax:** 1-305-894-3606;
http:// www.claxson.com

General - Incorporation British Virgin Islands		Stock - Price on:12/24/2007	$12
Employees	NA	Stock Exchange	NA
Auditor	Deloitte & Touche LLP	Ticker Symbol	NA
Stk Agt	Banco Rio de la Plata S.A	Outstanding Shares	NA
Counsel	Amaya Ariztoy	E.P.S.	NA
DUNS No.	NA	Shareholders	NA

Business: The groups principle activity is to provide branded entertainment content for consumers. The group operates from United States.

Primary SIC and add'l.: 7929

CIK No: 0001132340

Subsidiaries: Carson International Ltd., Claxson Chile S.A., Claxson USA II Inc., CTG Inversora S.A, El Sitio, Inc, Lifford International Co. Ltd, Playboy TV Latin America, LLC

Officers: Roberto Vivo-Chaneton/Chmn., CEO, Ralph Haiek/Chief Strategic Officer, Jose Antonio Ituarte/CFO, Mariano Varela/VP - Sales, MKT, TV Exec., Fernando Gaston/VP - Movies - Series, Music, Infinito, Amaya Ariztoy/General Counsel, Jose Maria Bustamante/Sr. VP - Human Resources, Juan Luis Iramain/Sr. VP - Communications, Public Relations

Directors: Roberto Vivo-Chaneton/Chmn., CEO, Carlos Bardasano/Vice Chmn., Eric C. Neuman/Vice Chmn., Frank Feather/Dir., Marcos Clutterbuck/Dir., Gabriel Montoya/Dir., Ana Teresa Arismendi/Dir., John A. Gavin/Dir., Jose Antonio Rios/Dir., Emilio Romano/Dir., Ricardo Verdaguer/Dir., Luis Villanueva/Dir.

Owners: Hicks Muse, Amaya Ariztoy, Ricardo J. Cisneros, Roberto Vivo-Chaneton, 1947 Carlyle Investments LLC, John A. Gavin, Ricardo Verdaguer, Ezequiel Paz, Eric C. Neuman, Jos Antonio Ituarte, Frank Feather, Ralph Haiek, Mariano Varela, 1945 Carlton Investments LLC, Luis H. Moreno (27 Owners included in Index)

Financial Data: Fiscal Year End:12/31 Latest Annual Data: 12/31/2005

Year	Sales	Net Income
2005	$80,527,000	$6,232,000
2004	$68,184,000	$6,690,000
2003	$81,787,000	$8,337,000
Curr. Assets:	$54,545,000	Curr. Liab.:	$46,856,000		
Plant, Equip.:	$10,583,000	Total Liab.:	$117,309,000	Indic. Yr. Divd.:	NA
Total Assets:	$150,410,000	Net Worth:	$33,101,000	Debt/ Equity:	NA

Clayton Holdings Inc

2 Corporate Dr., Shelton, CT, 06484; **PH:** 1-203-926-5600; **Fax:** 1-203-926-5750;
http:// www.clayton.com

General - Incorporation	DE	Stock - Price on:12/24/2007	$12.16
Employees	589	Stock Exchange	NDQ
Auditor	Grant Thornton LLP	Ticker Symbol	CLAY
Stk Agt	Computershare Trust Co	Outstanding Shares	21,080,000
Counsel	Goodwin Procter LLP	E.P.S.	-$0.09
DUNS No.	NA	Shareholders	NA

Business: The groups principle activity is to provide outsourced services including mortgage related analytics and specialized consulting. The groups services include transaction management, professional staffing, compliance products and oversight and reporting on mortgage backed securities. The groups operates through three segments namely transaction management, special servicing and surveillance. In February 2006, the group acquired MR Network I, Ltd. The group operates from Shelton, Connecticut, Tulsa, Oklahoma; Indianapolis, Indiana, Tampa, Florida, Denver, Colorado, and Costa Mesa and California. The group's quarterly revenue for September 2007 was 31.32 millions of USD.

Primary SIC and add'l.: 7372 7389

CIK No: 0001325228

Subsidiaries: AG NI Holdings, Inc., Clayton Fixed Income Services Inc., Clayton IPS Corporation, Clayton Services, Inc., Clayton Technologies, Inc., First Madison Services, Inc., GRP Holdings, Inc., Quantum Servicing Corporation, TMHC Holdings, Inc.

Officers: Frank P. Filipps/Chmn., CEO, Keith D. Johnson/COO, Pres., Frederick C. Herbst/CFO, Steven L. Cohen/Sr. VP, General Counsel, Sec.

Directors: Frank P. Filipps/Chmn., CEO, David Gilbert/Dir., Roger B. Kafker/Dir., Brian L. Libman/Dir., Frank L. Raiter/Dir., Michael M. Sonderby/Dir., Margaret Sue Allon/Dir., Thomas J. Skelly/Dir.

Owners: Brian L. Libman, Margaret Sue Allon/2.80%, Roger B. Kafker/39.30%, Louis A. Iannaccone, Keith D. Johnson, Frank L. Raiter, Frederick C. Herbst, Frank P. Filipps/2.10%, Todd R. Crockett/39.30%, Steven L. Cohen, Insiders/44.70%

Financial Data: Fiscal Year End:12/31 Latest Annual Data: 12/31/2006

Year	Sales	Net Income
2006	$239,195,000	$7,876,000
2005	$207,502,000	$5,048,000
Curr. Assets:	$92,637,000	Curr. Liab.:	$35,499,000		
Plant, Equip.:	$20,365,000	Total Liab.:	$105,184,000	Indic. Yr. Divd.:	NA
Total Assets:	$262,913,000	Net Worth:	$157,729,000	Debt/ Equity:	0.3804

Clayton Williams Energy Inc

6 Desta Dr., Ste. 3000, Midland, TX, 79705; **PH:** 1-432-682-6324; **Fax:** 1-432-682-1452;
http:// www.claytonwilliams.com

General - Incorporation	DE	Stock - Price on:12/24/2007	$26.07
Employees	180	Stock Exchange	NDQ
Auditor	KPMG LLP	Ticker Symbol	CWEI
Stk Agt	Wells Fargo Bank Minnesota N.A	Outstanding Shares	11,350,000
Counsel	NA	E.P.S.	NA
DUNS No.	80-515-8169	Shareholders	NA

Business: The group's principal activities are exploration, development and production of oil and natural gas primarily in Texas, Louisiana, New Mexico and Mississippi. The group's principal business strategy is to grow oil and gas reserves through exploration activities, leasing the acreage, drilling exploratory wells to determine if recoverable oil and gas reserves exist, drilling developmental wells, and producing and selling any resulting oil and gas production. The group markets its oil and natural gas to various customers and serves as operator in the drilling, completion and operation of oil and gas wells. On 24-May-2004, the group acquired southwest royalties inc and southwest partners l.p.

Primary SIC and add'l.: 1321 1311

CIK No: 0000880115

Subsidiaries: ClayDesta L.P, Clayton Williams Partnership, Ltd, Clayton Williams Ranch Holdings, Inc, CWPLCO, Inc.

Officers: Clayton W. Williams/Chmn. - Board, CEO, Pres./$611,066.00, Mel G. Riggs/Dir., Sr. VP - Finance, Sec., Treasurer, CFO/$480,525.00, Paul L. Latham/Dir., Exec. VP, COO/$529,254.00, Mark T. Tisdale/VP, General Counsel/$302,376.00, Jerry F. Groner/VP - Land, Lease Administration, Robert C. Lyon/VP - Gas Gathering, Marketing, Michael L. Pollard/VP - Accounting, Patrick C. Reesby/VP - Acquisitions, New Ventures/$545,245.00, Greg S. Welborn/VP - Land, Patti Hollums/Dir. - Investor Relations

Directors: Clayton W. Williams/Chmn. - Board, CEO, Pres., Robert L. Parker/Dir., Stanley S. Beard/Dir., Mel G. Riggs/Dir., Sr. VP - Finance, Sec., Treasurer, CFO, Davis L. Ford/67/Dir., Paul L. Latham/Dir., Exec. VP, COO, Jordan R. Smith/Dir., Luann Bolding/Dir. - Human Resources

Owners: Patrick C. Reesby, Williams Childrens Partnership, Ltd./26.70%, BlackRock, Inc./11.40%, Insiders/51.30%, William J. Nasgovitz/6.50%, Robert L. Parker, Mark T. Tisdale, Wellington Management Company, LLP/8.00%, Heartland Advisors, Inc./6.50%, Stanley S. Beard, Mel G. Riggs, Paul L. Latham/26.80%, Davis L. Ford, Jordan R. Smith

Financial Data: ***Fiscal Year End:***12/31 ***Latest Annual Data:*** 12/31/2006

Year	Sales	Net Income
2006	$265,998,000	$17,799,000
2005	$283,599,000	$257,000
2004	$206,330,000	-$14,028,000

Curr. Assets:	$125,998,000	***Curr. Liab.:***	$149,066,000		
Plant, Equip.:	$644,809,000	***Total Liab.:***	$649,379,000	***Indic. Yr. Divd.:***	NA
Total Assets:	$795,433,000	***Net Worth:***	$144,980,000	***Debt/ Equity:***	3.3559

Clean Diesel Technologies Inc

300 Atlantic St., Ste. 702, Stamford, CT, 06901; ***PH:*** 1-203-327-7050; ***Fax:*** 1-203-323-0461; ***http://*** www.cdti.com; ***Email:*** info@cdti.com

General - Incorporation............................ DE
Employees..13
Auditor .... Eisner LLP
Stk Agt...... American Stock Transfer & Trust Co.
Counsel..NA
DUNS No. 93-974-2318

Stock- Price on:12/24/2007 ....NA
Stock Exchange...NDQ
Ticker Symbol..CDTI
Outstanding Shares ....NA
E.P.S...NA
Shareholders...NA

Business: The group's principal activity is to supply fuel additives and systems that reduce harmful emissions from internal combustion engines. The group's two main technology areas include platinum plus(R) fuel borne catalyst and the aris(R) 2000 nox reduction system. Platinum plus takes the catalytic action into engine cylinders where it improves combustion thereby reducing particulates, unburnt hydrocarbons and co emissions as well as improving fuel economy. It helps in emission control and fuel economy improvement in diesel and gasoline-fueled engines. The aris 2000 (advanced reagent injection system) is a patented injection system for the reduction of nox emissions from diesel engines. It is a miniature version of the scr (selective catalytic reduction) injection system. It is designed for volume production and is applicable to both stationary diesel engines for power generation and mobile diesels used in trucks, buses, trains and boats.

Primary SIC and add'l.: 2819 6794

CIK No: 0000949428

Officers: Bernhard Steiner/Dir., CEO, Internal Member - Executive Board - Technology Member - Advisory Board/$356,026.00, Tim Rogers/Exec. VP - International, Internal Member - Executive Board - Technology Member - Advisory Board/$246,739.00, Charles W. Grinnell/Dir., VP, Company Sec., Company Sec., Walter G. Copan/Exec. VP - North American Operations, CTO, Internal Member - Executive Board - Technology Member - Advisory Board/$247,446.00, Michael D. Jackson/Technology Member - Advisory Board, Ann B. Ruple/CFO, VP Administration/$82,135.00

Directors: Bernhard Steiner/Dir., CEO, Internal Member - Executive Board - Technology Member - Advisory Board, Derek R. Gray/Non Exec. Chmn., Charles W. Grinnell/Dir., VP, Company Sec., Company Sec., John Jay McCloy/Dir., John A. De Havilland/Dir., David F. Merrion/Non - Exec. Dir., Member - Technology Advisory Board, Dean Tomazic/Member - Technology Advisory Board, Victor Ghuman/Member - Technology Advisory Board

Owners: Ann B. Ruple, David F. Merrion, Duckworth Esq./5.10%, Ram Ltd./4.00%, Ruffer LLP/14.20%, Kanis SA/4.60%, Avenir Finances S.A./8.00%, Insiders/7.00%, John A. de Havilland, Fuel Tech, Inc./5.00%, Hawkwood Fund Management/6.10%, Walter G. Copan, Positive Securities Limited/5.70%, Timothy Rogers, Udaset Holdings Limited/4.10% *(21 Owners included in Index)*

Curr. Assets:	$8,287,000	***Curr. Liab.:***	$1,070,000		
Plant, Equip.:	$91,000	***Total Liab.:***	$1,070,000	***Indic. Yr. Divd.:***	NA
Total Assets:	$9,018,000	***Net Worth:***	$7,948,000	***Debt/ Equity:***	NA

Clean Harbors Inc

42 Longwater Dr., Norwell, MA, 02061; ***PH:*** 1-781-792-5000; ***Fax:*** 1-781-792-5900; ***http://*** www.cleanharbors.com

General - Incorporation............................ MA
Employees..4,574
Auditor ....Deloitte & Touche LLP
Stk Agt...... American Stock Transfer & Trust Co.
Counsel............. Davis, Malm & D'agostine P.C.
DUNS No. 03-772-9043

Stock- Price on:12/24/2007 ....$47.28
Stock Exchange...NDQ
Ticker Symbol..CLHB
Outstanding Shares 19,830,000
E.P.S...$2.28
Shareholders...NA

Business: The group's principal activity is to provide a wide range of environmental services & solutions to a diversified customer base in the United States, Canada, Mexico & Puerto Rico. The group operates through two business segments: technical services & site services. Technical services include treatment & disposal of industrial wastes; collection, transportation & logistics management & apollo onsite services, which provides customized environmental programs at customer sites. Site services provide highly skilled experts utilizing specialty equipment & resources to provide industrial maintenance, surface remediation, site remediation, oil disposal & analytical testing services. The group has network of 115 locations, including 48 active hazardous waste management properties & also has 59 service centers, satellite & support locations & has eight corporate & regional offices. These properties are located in 36 states, six Canadian provinces, Mexico & Puerto Rico.

Primary SIC and add'l.: 4953 4959

CIK No: 0000822818

Subsidiaries: CH Canada GP, Inc., CH Canada Holdings Corp, CH International Holdings,Inc., Clean Harbors Canada L.P., Clean Harbors Canada,Inc., Clean Harbors Disposal Services,Inc., Clean Harbors Environmental Services,Inc., Clean Harbors Kingston Facility Corporation, Clean Harbors Lone Star Corp., Clean Harbors Mercier,Inc., Clean Harbors of Baltimore,Inc., Clean Harbors of Braintree,Inc., Clean Harbors of Connecticut,Inc., Clean Harbors of Natick,Inc., Clean Harbors of Texas, LLC 20 Subsidiaries included in the Index

Officers: Alan S. Mckim/Chmn., CEO, Pres./$1,100,552.00, Michael J. Twohig/CIO, Sr. VP, James M. Rutledge/CFO, Exec. VP/$697,387.00, Eric W. Gerstenberg/Sr. VP - Disposal Services, George L. Curtis/Sr. VP - Pricing, Proposals, Brian P. Weber/Sr. VP - Transportation, Phillip G. Retallick/Sr. VP - Compliance, Regulatory Affairs, Eugene A. Cookson/Exec. VP - Business Line/$618,285.00, William J. Geary/Exec. VP, General Counsel, Stephen H. Moynihan/Sr. VP, Treasurer, David M. Parry/Sr. VP, Sales, Services/$508,440.00, John R. Beals/VP, Corporate Controller

Directors: Alan S. Mckim/Chmn., CEO, Pres., Lorne R. Waxlax/Dir., John T. Preston/Dir., Andrea Robertson/Dir., John P. Devillars/Dir., John D. Barr/Dir., Gene Banucci/Dir., Jack Kaslow/Dir., Thomas J. Shields/Dir., Daniel J. McCarthy/Dir.

Owners: Alan S. McKim/15.40%, John T. Preston, Insiders/16.90%, John R. Kaslow, FMR Corp./14.90%, James M. Rutledge, Lorne R. Waxlax, Eugene A. Cookson, Eugene Banucci, John D. Barr, Daniel J. McCarthy, Tontine Capital Management, L.L.C./6.20%, Andrea Robertson, David M. Parry, Anthony Pucillo *(18 Owners included in Index)*

Financial Data: ***Fiscal Year End:***12/31 ***Latest Annual Data:*** 12/31/2006

Year	Sales	Net Income
2006	$829,809,000	$46,675,000
2005	$711,170,000	$25,621,000
2004	$643,219,000	$2,600,000

Curr. Assets:	$322,819,000	***Curr. Liab.:***	$198,354,000	***P/E Ratio:***	20.74
Plant, Equip.:	$244,126,000	***Total Liab.:***	$497,622,000	***Indic. Yr. Divd.:***	NA
Total Assets:	$670,808,000	***Net Worth:***	$173,186,000	***Debt/ Equity:***	0.0152

Clean Power Concepts Inc

Formerly: Loma Verde Inc
601 Cordova St., Ste. 290, Vancouver, BC, V6C 1G1; ***PH:*** 1-604-488-0266

General - Incorporation ....NV
Employees..NA
Auditor ....Associates CPAS Inc.
Stk Agt...................... Empire Stock Transfer Inc.
Counsel..NA
DUNS No. ....NA

Stock- Price on:12/24/2007 ....NA
Stock Exchange...OTC
Ticker Symbol..CPOW
Outstanding Shares ....NA
E.P.S...NA
Shareholders...NA

Business: The groups principle activity is to provide recruiting services. The groups service area includes the research and development, engineering, marketing, sales, information technology and manufacturing industries. The group operates from United States.

Primary SIC and add'l.: 8748

CIK No: 0001357594

Subsidiaries: Loma Verde Explorations Ltd

Officers: Cory Turner/Dir., CEO, CFO, Pres., Ken Kelln/VP - Design - Engineering, Ralph Proceviat/CFO

Directors: Cory Turner/Dir., CEO, CFO, Pres.

Owners: Virgilio Santana/14.00%, Peter Hill/14.00%, Belkis Reyes/12.00%

Financial Data: ***Fiscal Year End:***06/30 ***Latest Annual Data:*** 06/30/2007

Year	Sales	Net Income
2007	NA	-$142,000

Curr. Assets:	$128,000	***Curr. Liab.:***	$277,000		
Plant, Equip.:	NA	***Total Liab.:***	$277,000	***Indic. Yr. Divd.:***	NA
Total Assets:	$128,000	***Net Worth:***	-$150,000	***Debt/ Equity:***	NA

Clean Power Technologies Inc

436-35th Ave. N.W., Calgary, AB, T2K 0C1; ***PH:*** 1-403-277-2944; ***Fax:*** 1-403-277-3117; ***http://*** www.cleanpowertech.co.uk; ***Email:*** mail@cleanpowertech.co.uk

General - Incorporation ....NV
Employees..NA
Auditor Child, Van Wagoner & Bradshaw, PLLC
Stk Agt...NA
Counsel..NA
DUNS No. ....NA

Stock- Price on:12/24/2007 ....$1.7
Stock Exchange...OTC
Ticker Symbol..CPWE
Outstanding Shares ....NA
E.P.S...NA
Shareholders...NA

Business: The groups principal activity is to research and development of technology. The group operates from the United States.

Primary SIC and add'l.: 3510

CIK No: 0001282387

Subsidiaries: Clean Energy and Power Solutions Inc, Clean Power Technologies Limited

Officers: Abdul A. Mitha/Dir., CEO, Pres., Martin Smaller/Vehicle Systems Specialist, Diane Glatfelter/42/Dir., CFO, Sec., Fred Bayley/Member - Advisory Board, Inventor, Julie Burns/Executive Assist., Alex Price/Build Engineer, Paul Burns/CAD Engineer, Chris Burns/Build Engineer, Information Technology Specialist, Marco Pereira/Sr. Engine Controls, Instrumentation, John Grist/Controls Engineer, Roger Clooney/Mecganical Engineer

Directors: Abdul A. Mitha/Dir., CEO, Pres., Diane Glatfelter/42/Dir., CFO, Sec., Mike Burns/Dir., Richard Dennis/49/Dir., Fred Bayley/Member - Advisory Board, Inventor, Alastair Fraser/Member - Advisory Board, David Thursfield/63/Dir.

Owners: David Thursfield/0.43%, Seabreeze Capital/5.93%, Richard Schmidt/5.99%, Doosan Babcock/6.85%, Abdul Mitha/7.97%, Diane Glatfelter/0.41%, Richard Dennis/0.09%, Michael Burns/1.71%, Frederick Bayley/1.71%

Financial Data: ***Fiscal Year End:***08/31 ***Latest Annual Data:*** 08/31/2006

Year	Sales	Net Income
2006	NA	-$311,000

Curr. Assets:	$235,000	***Curr. Liab.:***	$609,000		
Plant, Equip.:	$160,000	***Total Liab.:***	$609,000	***Indic. Yr. Divd.:***	NA
Total Assets:	$395,000	***Net Worth:***	-$215,000	***Debt/ Equity:***	NA

Clear Channel Communications Inc

200 E Basse Rd., San Antonio, TX, 78209; ***PH:*** 1-210-822-2828; ***Fax:*** 1-210-822-2299; ***http://*** www.clearchannel.com

General - Incorporation .... TX
Employees..30,900
Auditor ....Ernst & Young LLP
Stk Agt.................................. Bank of New York
Counsel..NA
DUNS No. 06-945-6655

Stock- Price on:12/24/2007 ....$38.28
Stock Exchange...NYSE
Ticker Symbol..CCU
Outstanding Shares 496,370,000
E.P.S...$1.49
Shareholders...NA

Business: The groups principle activity is to provide media services. The group operates through four segments namely radio broadcasting, Americas outdoor advertising, and international outdoor advertising. The group operates from United States.

Primary SIC and add'l.: 4832 4833 7312 7929

CIK No: 0000739708

Subsidiaries: 1567 Media, LLC, 50 2027Th Street LIC, Inc., 701 W. 135th Corp, Ackerley Broadcast Operations, LLC, Ackerley Broadcasting of Fresno, LLC, Ackerley Ventures, Inc., Adcart AB, Adshel (Brazil) Ltda, Adshel Argentina, Adshel Ireland Limited, Adshel Ltd., Adshel Ltda, Adshel NI Ltd., Affitalia, AK Mobile Television, Inc. 298 Subsidiaries included in the Index

Officers: Mark Mays/CEO/$9,311,996.00, Don Perry/56/CEO, Pres. - Clear Channel Television, John Hogan/51/CEO, Pres. - Clear Channel Radio/$3,039,285.00, William Moll/70/Chmn. - Clear Channel Television, Paul Meyer/65/Global COO, Pres. - Clear Channel Outdoor/$1,628,396.00, Bill Hamersly/Sr. VP - Human Resources, Kathryn Johnson/Sr. VP - Corporate Relations, Jessica Marventano/Sr. VP - Government Affairs, Randy Palmer/Sr. VP - Investor Relations, Julie Hill/Sr. VP - Finance, Randall T. Mays/CFO, Pres., Sec./$9,282,382.00, Mary Stich/VP, Assoc. General Counsel, Jared Hand/VP, Dir. - Sales, Lisa Dollinger/Chief Communications Officer, David Wilson/CIO, Sr. VP (28 Officers included in Index)

Directors: Lowry L. Mays/Chmn., John H. Williams/74/Dir., Alan D. Feld/71/Dir., Perry J. Lewis/Dir., B. J. McCombs/80/Dir., Phyllis Riggins/55/Dir., Theodore H. Strauss/83/Dir., J. C. Watts/50/Dir., John B. Zachry/46/Dir.

Owners: John Hogan, Alan D. Feld, Perry J. Lewis, Insiders/7.70%, Theodore H. Strauss, John H. Williams, B. J. McCombs/1.00%, John B. Zachry, FMR Corp/9.70%, J. C. Watts, Paul J. Meyer, Randall T. Mays, Lowry L. Mays/6.30%, Phyllis B. Riggins, Highfields Capital Management LP/5.00% (16 Owners included in Index)

Financial Data: Fiscal Year End:12/31 **Latest Annual Data:** 12/31/2006

Year	Sales	Net Income
2006	$7,066,957,000	$691,517,000
2005	$6,610,418,000	$935,662,000
2004	$9,418,459,000	-$4,038,169,000

Curr. Assets:	$2,205,730,000	Curr. Liab.:	$1,663,846,000	P/E Ratio:	27.15
Plant, Equip.:	$3,220,956,000	Total Liab.:	$10,498,447,000	Indic. Yr. Divd.:	$0.750
Total Assets:	$18,890,179,000	Net Worth:	$8,042,341,000	Debt/ Equity:	0.8531

Clear Channel Outdoor Holdings Inc

2201 E Camelback Rd., Ste. 500, Phoenix, AZ, 85016; **PH:** 1-602-381-5700; **Fax:** 1-602-381-5782; http:// www.clearchanneloutdoor.com

General - Incorporation	DE	**Stock**- Price on:12/24/2007	$28.91
Employees	7,700	Stock Exchange	NYSE
Auditor	Ernst& Young LLP	Ticker Symbol	CCO
Stk Agt.	NA	Outstanding Shares	355,080,000
Counsel	NA	E.P.S.	$0.51
DUNS No.	NA	Shareholders	NA

Business: The groups principle activity is to provide clients with advertising opportunities through billboards, street furniture displays, transit displays and other out-of-home advertising displays. The group operates through two segments namely, Americas and International. In the year 2005, the group acquired Clear Media. The group operates from the United States, France, Canada, Asia, Africa, Australia and the United Kingdom. The groups quarterly revenue for September 2007 was 817.54 millions of USD.

Primary SIC and add'l.: 7312

CIK No: 0001334978

Subsidiaries: 1567 Media, LLC, Adcart AB, Adshel (Brazil) Ltda, Adshel Argentina SRL, Adshel Ireland Limited, Adshel Ltd., Adshel Ltda, Adshel NI Ltd., Affitalia SRL, Allied Outdoor Advertising Ltd., Arcadia Cooper Properties Ltd., Aristex, Barnett And Son Ltd., Bk Studi BV, BPS London Ltd. 219 Subsidiaries included in the Index

Officers: Mark Mays/CEO - Clear Channel Outdoor, Randall T. Mays/CFO - Clear Channel Outdoor, Franklin G. Sisson/55/Global Dir. - Sales, Marketing, Charlie Turner/Exec. VP - Operations, Americas, Paul Meyer/Global COO, Pres. Clear Channel Outdoor, Michael Hudes/Global Dir. - Digital Media, Rocky Sisson/Global Dir. - Sales, Marketing, Tony Jarvis/Exec. VP - Global Research, Jonathan Bevan/International CFO, Dir. - Corporate Development, Augusto Claux/Regional Pres. - Latin America, Michael R. Deeds/Exec. VP - Operations, Rickard Hedlund/Regional Pres. - Northern, Eastern Europe, Gene Leehan/Regional Pres. - Western US, Hubert Janvier/41/Regional Pres. - Southern Europe, Barry Sayer/Regional Pres. - UK, Ireland, Africa (22 Officers included in Index)

Directors: Lowry L. Mays/72/Chmn., Marsha McCombs Shields/53/Dir., William D. Parker/46/Dir., James M. Raines/68/Dir., Dale W. Tremblay/49/Dir.

Owners: James M. Raines, Dale W. Tremblay, Kurt A. Tingey, Tracer Capital Management/9.90%, Franklin G. Sisson, Marsha M. Shields, T. Rowe Price Associates, Inc./13.00%, Clear Channel Communications, Inc., Arnhold & S Bleichroeder Advisers./10.10%, Insiders/1.40%, Paul J. Meyer, Artisan Partners Limited Partnership/9.00%, William D. Parker

Financial Data: Fiscal Year End:12/31 **Latest Annual Data:** 03/31/2007

Year	Sales	Net Income
2007	NA	$181,890,000
2006	$2,897,721,000	$153,072,000
2005	$2,666,078,000	$61,573,000

Curr. Assets:	$1,189,915,000	Curr. Liab.:	$841,509,000	P/E Ratio:	56.69
Plant, Equip.:	$2,191,839,000	Total Liab.:	$3,835,513,000	Indic. Yr. Divd.:	NA
Total Assets:	$5,421,891,000	Net Worth:	$1,586,378,000	Debt/ Equity:	1.5908

Clearant Inc

11111 Santa Monica Blvd., Ste. 650, Los Angeles, CA, 90025; **PH:** 1-310-479-4570; **Fax:** 1-310-691-7150; http:// www.clearant.com; **Email:** investor@clearant.com

General - Incorporation	DE	**Stock**- Price on:12/24/2007	NA
Employees	NA	Stock Exchange	OTC
Auditor	Singer Lewak Greenbaum & Goldstein	Ticker Symbol	CLRA
Stk Agt.	American Stock Transfer & Trust Co.	Outstanding Shares	NA
Counsel	NA	E.P.S.	-$0.48
DUNS No.	NA	Shareholders	NA

Business: The groups principle activities include acquiring, developing and marketing pathogen inactivation technology to produce biological products. The group products include Devitalized musculoskeletal tissue, allograft implants (tissue), Plasma protein therapeutics, and Clearant Process (R). The group operates from the United States.

Primary SIC and add'l.: 2836

CIK No: 0001238579

Officers: Jon M. Garfield/44/Dir., CEO, CFO, Sec./$240,000.00, Don Markley/Investor Relations, Susan Etzel/Controller, Steve Burns/Dir. - Technology Transfer, Manufacturing, Carlo Brigola/Dir. - Sales, Cindy Atkins/Dir. - Sales, Meghan Lake/Mgr. - Product Distribution

Directors: Jon M. Garfield/44/Dir., CEO, CFO, Sec., John S. Wehrle/Chmn., Herve De Kergrohen/Dir., Nolan Sigal/Dir., Alexander Man-kit Ngan/Dir., Warren King/Member - Scientific Advisory Board, Fred Cushner/Member - Scientific Advisory Board, Rowland W. Day/52/Dir., Michael Elek/46/Dir.

Owners: John McGinnis/7.40%, Mel Seid/5.80%, Jon M. Garfield/1.60%, Rowland W. Day/6.40%, Terren S. Peizer/9.60%, Insiders/8.00%, Ursula Azzurrini/4.40%

Financial Data: Fiscal Year End:12/31 **Latest Annual Data:** 12/31/2006

Year	Sales	Net Income
2006	$770,000	-$9,798,000
2005	$541,000	-$11,590,000
2004	$1,000	-$6,000

Curr. Assets:	$1,359,000	Curr. Liab.:	$2,433,000		
Plant, Equip.:	$290,000	Total Liab.:	$2,437,000	Indic. Yr. Divd.:	NA
Total Assets:	$3,021,000	Net Worth:	$584,000	Debt/ Equity:	NA

Clearly Canadian Beverage Corp

2267 10th Ave. W, Vancouver, BC, V6K 211; **PH:** 1-604-922-8100; **Fax:** 1-604-922-8195; http:// www.clearly.ca; **Email:** info@clearly.ca

General - Incorporation	Canada	**Stock**- Price on:12/24/2007	$2.97
Employees	NA	Stock Exchange	OTC
Auditor	KPMG LLP	Ticker Symbol	CCBEF
Stk Agt	Pacific Corporate Trust Co	Outstanding Shares	NA
Counsel	Max Pinsky	E.P.S.	NA
DUNS No.	24-641-9055	Shareholders	NA

Business: The group's principal activities are to produce, distribute and market beverage products and flavoured beverages. The group's products are marketed principally in the united stated and Canada. The major products include clearly Canadian, sparkling flavored water, clearly Canadian o+2, tre limone and reebok beverage. On 22-Feb-2002, the group disposed private label co-pack bottling business, cascade clear business and related production assets.

Primary SIC and add'l.: 2086

CIK No: 0000808464

Subsidiaries: Blue Mountain Springs Ltd., CC Beverage (U.S.) Corporation, Clearly Canadian Beverage (International) Corporation

Officers: Brent Lokash/Dir., CEO, Andrew Strang/Corporate, Legal Affairs, Clearly Canadian Brands, Edwin Fok/CFO - Clearly Canadian Brands, Orlee Muroff/Pres., Brand Mgr. - My Organic Baby, Renella Zahler/VP - Operations, Brand Mgr. - Healthy Snack Division, Jackie Fox/Dir. - Sales, Brand Mgr. - Clearly Canadian Beverages, Max Pinsky/Legal Counsel - Vancouver, British Columbia, Canada, David Reingold/Dir., Pres., Frank Uy/Corporate Controller - Clearly Canadian Brands, Darrell Chin/Dir. - Technical Services, Clearly Canadian Brands

Directors: Brent Lokash/Dir., CEO, Marco Markin/Dir., David Reingold/Dir., Pres., George Reznik/Dir., Brian Obyrne/Member - Advisory Board, Steve Nash/Member - Advisory Board

Owners: Marco P. Markin, Insiders/29.13%, George Reznik, David Reingold/22.60%, James Dines/6.50%, David Reingold/22.63%, Cameron Strang, Brent Lokash/3.70%, David Parkes/1.10%, Robert Genovese/24.70%, Andrew Strang/2.00%, Robert Genovese/100.00%

Financial Data: Fiscal Year End:12/31 **Latest Annual Data:** 12/31/2006

Year	Sales	Net Income
2006	$7,462,000	-$8,247,000
2005	$9,141,000	-$6,007,000
2004	$11,586,000	-$5,012,000

Curr. Assets:	$6,861,000	Curr. Liab.:	$1,616,000		
Plant, Equip.:	$1,153,000	Total Liab.:	$1,629,000	Indic. Yr. Divd.:	NA
Total Assets:	$9,093,000	Net Worth:	$7,464,000	Debt/ Equity:	NA

ClearOne Communications Inc

5225 Wiley Post Way, Ste. 500, Salt Lake City, UT, 84116; **PH:** 1-801-975-7200; **Fax:** 1-801-977-0087; http:// www.clearone.com; **Email:** pr@clearone.com

General - Incorporation	UT	**Stock**- Price on:12/24/2007	$4.71
Employees	123	Stock Exchange	NDQ
Auditor	Jones Simkins, P.c.	Ticker Symbol	CLRO
Stk Agt	American Stock Transfer & Trust Co.	Outstanding Shares	10,890,000
Counsel	NA	E.P.S.	NA
DUNS No.	NA	Shareholders	NA

Business: The groups principle activities include developing, manufacturing, marketing, and servicing audio conferencing products. The group products include RAV(TM), Chat(TM) 50, AccuMic(R), professionally installed audio conferencing systems, tabletop conferencing phones, and personal conferencing devices. The group operates from the United States and Canada. The group operates through two segments namely product and business services. The group's quarterly revenue for September 2007 was 9.44 millions of USD.

Primary SIC and add'l.: 3661 3663

CIK No: 0000840715

Subsidiaries: ClearOne Communications EuMEA GmbH, ClearOne Communications Limited UK, E.mergent, Inc., Gentner Communications, Ltd., Gentner Ventures, Inc.

Officers: Zee Hakimoglu/Chmn., CEO, Pres., Greg A. Leclaire/VP - Finance, Steven P. Andresen/VP - Worldwide Sales, Tracy Bathurst/CTO, Marthes Solamuthu/VP - Operations, Jose Martinez/Contact - Sales, Latin America, Simon Chin/Contact - Sales, Hong Kong, China, Taiwan, Kurt Olsen/Sales Contact - Japan, Australia, New Zealand, K. S. Lee/Sales Contact - South Asia, Malaysia, Singapore, Thailand, Philippines, Vietnam, Indonesia, Charlie Woo/Sales Contact - South Korea, Amit Chowdry/Sales Contact - India, David Wang/Contact - Technical Support

Directors: Zee Hakimoglu/Chmn., CEO, Pres., Brad R. Baldwin/52/Dir., Larry R. Hendricks/65/Dir., Scott M. Huntsman/42/Dir., Harry Spielberg/56/Dir.

Owners: Insiders/6.70%, Marthes Solamuthu, Zee Hakimoglu/1.90%, Greg A. LeClaire, Harry Spielberg, Brad R. Baldwin/1.90%, Edward Dallin Bagley/16.10%, Tracy A. Bathurst, FMR Corp./8.10%, Larry R. Hendricks, Scott M. Huntsman, Royce & Associates Inc./6.10%

Curr. Assets:	$38,317,000	Curr. Liab.:	$9,151,000		
Plant, Equip.:	$2,694,000	Total Liab.:	$10,625,000	Indic. Yr. Divd.:	NA
Total Assets:	$41,063,000	Net Worth:	$30,438,000	Debt/ Equity:	NA

Clearstory Systems Inc

1 Research Dr., Ste. 200 B, Westborough, MA, 01581; *PH:* 1-508-870-4000; *Fax:* 1-508-870-5585;
http:// www.clearstorysystems.com

General - Incorporation	DE	**Stock**- Price on:12/24/2007	$0.06
Employees	72	Stock Exchange	OTC
Auditor	Miller Ellin & Co. LLP	Ticker Symbol	CSYS
Stk Agt	NA	Outstanding Shares	NA
Counsel	NA	E.P.S.	NA
DUNS No.	79-382-1059	Shareholders	NA

Business: The group's principal activity is to provide integrated enterprise software solutions for the electronic content management market. The group's solutions empower clients to better manage electronic content and improve its availability. The solutions also provide storage, access and presentment for mission-critical documents, reports, statements, e-mail and high value digital assets necessary for business functions. The products of the group include active media, digital asset management software and esp+ solutions suite. The customers of the group include unisys, xerox corporation, fuji-xerox, pfpc, agfa and other value added resellers. On 05-Sep-2003, the group acquired certain assets and assumed certain liabilities of webware corporation.

Primary SIC and add'l.: 7373 7371 7379

CIK No: 0000878612

Subsidiaries: InfiniteSpace.com, Corp., Insci (uk) Limited., Lognet 2000, Inc., The Internet Broadcasting Company, Inc., WCORP, Inc.

Officers: Henry F. Nelson/Dir., CEO, Pres., Joshua Duhl/VP - Product Management, Susan Worthy/VP - Marketing, Michael Lam/VP - Technical Solutions, John Sullivan/VP - Sales, Anton Emelianov/VP - Development

Directors: Henry F. Nelson/Dir., CEO, Pres., Yaron Eitan/Chmn., Mitchell Klein/Dir., Thomas G. Rebar/Dir., Robert G. Yablunsky/Dir.

Financial Data: Fiscal Year End:03/31 Latest Annual Data: 3/31/2005

Year	Sales	Net Income
2005	$11,588,000	-$1,242,000
2004	$8,829,000	-$2,324,000
2003	$9,236,000	$1,383,000

Curr. Assets:	$2,205,000	**Curr. Liab.:**	$5,913,000		
Plant, Equip.:	$1,439,000	**Total Liab.:**	$6,519,000	**Indic. Yr. Divd.:**	NA
Total Assets:	$6,905,000	**Net Worth:**	$386,000	**Debt/ Equity:**	NA

Cleco Corp

2030 Donahue Ferry Rd., Pineville, LA, 71360; *PH:* 1-318-484-7400; *Fax:* 1-318-484-7488;
http:// www.cleco.com

General - Incorporation	LA	**Stock**- Price on:12/24/2007	$24.76
Employees	1,167	Stock Exchange	NYSE
Auditor	PricewaterhouseCoopers LLP	Ticker Symbol	CNL
Stk Agt	EquiServe Trust Co N.A	Outstanding Shares	59,680,000
Counsel	NA	E.P.S.	$1.25
DUNS No.	NA	Shareholders	NA

Business: The group's principal activities are to generate, transmit, distribute and sell electric energy. The group operates through its major subsidiaries, cleco power and midstream. Cleco power provides electric generation, transmission, distribution and customer care services to a diversified base of residential, commercial and industrial customers of Louisiana. Midstream develops wholesale generation projects, provides personnel to operate power plants, operates energy marketing and trading business and also operates natural gas pipelines in Louisiana and Texas.

Primary SIC and add'l.: 6719 4911 4924

CIK No: 0001089819

Subsidiaries: Acadia Partners Pipeline LLC, Acadia Power Holdings LLC, Acadia Power Partners, LLC, CLE Intrastate Pipeline Company LLC, Cleco ConnexUs LLC, Cleco Energy LLC, Cleco Evangeline LLC, Cleco Generation Services LLC, Cleco Innovations LLC, Cleco Marketing & Trading LLC, Cleco Midstream Resources LLC, Cleco Power LLC, Cleco Support Group LLC, DeSoto Pipeline Company, Inc., Diversified Lands LLC 20 Subsidiaries included in the Index

Officers: Michael H. Madison/Dir., CEO, Pres./$2,838,715.00, Dilek Samil/52/COO, Pres./$1,208,551.00, Kathleen F. Nolen/Sr. VP, CFO, Treasurer/$826,171.00, Judy P. Miller/50/Corp. Sec., William G. Fontenot/22/GM - Contracts, Analysis/$537,596.00, Russell R. Davis/51/VP, Chief Accounting Officer, Jeffrey W. Hall/Sr. VP - Governmental Affairs, Chief Diversity Officer

Directors: Michael H. Madison/Dir., CEO, Pres., Robert T. Ratcliff/65/Dir., William H. Walker/62/Dir., Sherian G. Cadoria/Dir., Richard B. Crowell/69/Dir., Ben F. James/72/Dir., W. L. Westbrook/Dir., William L. Marks/64/Dir.

Owners: Dilek Samil, Michael H. Madison, ONeal R. Chadwick, William G. Fontenot, Insiders/2.80%, Samuel H. Charlton, Robert T. Ratcliff, Richard B. Crowell, Elton R. King, Patrick J. Garrett, Barclays Global Investors/5.20%, William L. Marks, Mark H. Segura, JPMorgan Chase Bank/94.90%, William H. Walker (28 Owners included in Index)

Financial Data: Fiscal Year End:12/31 Latest Annual Data: 12/31/2006

Year	Sales	Net Income
2006	$996,191,000	$64,828,000
2005	$913,973,000	$59,081,000
2004	$59,084,000	$12,530,000

Curr. Assets:	$415,742,000	**Curr. Liab.:**	$373,676,000	**P/E Ratio:**	13.10
Plant, Equip.:	$1,297,789,000	**Total Liab.:**	$1,377,448,000	**Indic. Yr. Divd.:**	$0.900
Total Assets:	$2,023,852,000	**Net Worth:**	$646,404,000	**Debt/ Equity:**	0.8034

Cleveland BioLabs Inc

73 High St., Buffalo, NY, 14203; *PH:* 1-716-849-6810; *Fax:* 1-716-849-6820;
http:// www.cbiolabs.com; *Email:* info@cbiolabs.com

General - Incorporation	DE	**Stock**- Price on:12/24/2007	$10.59
Employees	35	Stock Exchange	NDQ
Auditor	Meaden & Moore, Ltd.	Ticker Symbol	CBLI
Stk Agt	Continental Stock Transfer & Trust Co	Outstanding Shares	11,890,000
Counsel	NA	E.P.S.	-$1.81
DUNS No.	NA	Shareholders	NA

Business: The groups principal activities include identifying, developing and commercializing drugs. The products of the group include Protectans and Curaxins. The group operates from the United States.

Primary SIC and add'l.: 2834 8731

CIK No: 0001318641

Officers: Michael Fonstein/Dir., CEO, Pres., Andrei Gudkov/Dir., Chief Scientific Officer, Yakov Kogan/Dir., Exec. VP - Business Development, Sec., Jack Marhofer/CFO, Farrel Fort/VP - Drug Development

Directors: Michael Fonstein/Dir., CEO, Pres., Bernard L. Kasten/Chmn., Yakov Kogan/Dir., Exec. VP - Business Development, Sec., Andrei Gudkov/Dir., Chief Scientific Officer, Paul E. Dicorleto/Dir., Daniel H. Perez/Dir., James Antal/Dir., George R. Stark/Member - Scientific Advisory Board, Inder M. Verma/Member - Scientific Advisory Board, Bruce Blazar/Member - Scientific Advisory Board, Ernest Borden/Member - Scientific Advisory Board, Preet M. Chaudhary/Member - Scientific Acvisory Board

Owners: Andrei V. Gudkov/13.00%, James J. Antal, Insiders/31.32%, Bernard L. Kasten, Sunrise Equity Partners, LP/10.47%, Michael Fonstein/11.04%, Daniel H. Perez, Yakov N. Kogan/6.16%, Paul E. DiCorleto, The Cleveland Clinic Foundation/11.01%, John A. Marhofer, ChemBridge Corporation/5.00%, Sunrise Securities Corp./10.47%

Financial Data: Fiscal Year End:12/31 Latest Annual Data: 12/31/2006

Year	Sales	Net Income
2006	$1,708,000	-$7,223,000
2005	$1,139,000	-$2,386,000
2004	$636,000	-$2,523,000

Curr. Assets:	$5,745,000	**Curr. Liab.:**	$773,000		
Plant, Equip.:	$404,000	**Total Liab.:**	$823,000	**Indic. Yr. Divd.:**	NA
Total Assets:	$6,417,000	**Net Worth:**	$5,593,000	**Debt/ Equity:**	NA

Cleveland Cliffs Inc

1100 Superior Ave., Cleveland, OH, 44114; *PH:* 1-216-694-5700; *Fax:* 1-216-694-4880;
http:// www.cleveland-cliffs.com; *Email:* publicrelations@cleveland-cliffs.com

General - Incorporation	OH	**Stock**- Price on:12/24/2007	$76.64
Employees	4,189	Stock Exchange	NYSE
Auditor	Deloitte & Touche LLP	Ticker Symbol	CLF
Stk Agt	Computershare Investor Services LLC	Outstanding Shares	41,020,000
Counsel	NA	E.P.S.	$5.30
DUNS No.	00-790-0269	Shareholders	NA

Business: The groups principle activity is to produce iron ore pellets. The group also supplies metallurgical coal to the global steelmaking industry. In the year 2007 the group acquired PinnOak Resources, LLC. The group operates from United States.

Primary SIC and add'l.: 4731 1011 4432 1081

CIK No: 0000764065

Subsidiaries: CALipso Sales Company, Cleveland-Cliffs Australia Holdings Pty Limited, Cleveland-Cliffs Australia Pty Limited, Cleveland-Cliffs International Holding Company, Cleveland-Cliffs Ore Corporation, Cliffs and Associates Limited, Cliffs Biwabik Ore Corporation, Cliffs Empire, Inc., Cliffs Erie LLC, Cliffs International Management Company LLC, Cliffs Marquette, Inc., Cliffs Mining Company, Cliffs Mining Services Company, Cliffs Minnesota Mining Company, Cliffs Natural Stone, LLC 41 Subsidiaries included in the Index

Officers: Joseph A. Carrabba/56/Chmn., CEO, Pres./$2,773,695.00, Steven M. Raguz/41/VP - Corporate Planning, Strategic Analysis, Treasurer, Ronald K. Aderhold/45/CIO, Laurie Brlas/51/CFO, Sr. VP, Treasurer/$425,074.00, Terrence R. Mee/38/VP - Sales, Transportation, William C. Boor/42/Sr. VP - Business Development, William Brake/48/Exec. VP - Cliffs Metallics, CTO, Kathleen Bardwell/52/VP - Internal Audit, William R. Calfee/61/Exec. VP - Commercial, North America/$2,335,488.00, Randy L. Kummer/52/Sr. VP - Human Resources, Robert J. Leroux/58/VP - Finance, George W. Hawk/52/General Counsel, Sec., Dana W. Byrne/58/VP - Public Affairs, Donald J. Gallagher/56/Pres. - North America/$2,392,709.00, James A. Trethewey/63/Sr. VP - Business Development (18 Officers included in Index)

Directors: Joseph A. Carrabba/56/Chmn., CEO, Pres., Roger Phillips/68/Dir., Barry J. Eldridge/62/Dir., Ronald C. Cambre/70/Dir., Alan Schwartz/68/Dir., Francis R. McAllister/66/Dir., Susan M. Green/49/Dir., Susan M. Cunningham/52/Dir., Richard K. Riederer/64/Dir., James D. Ireland/58/Dir.

Owners: James D. Ireland/1.40%, Bank of America Corporation/5.46%, William R. Calfee, Alan Schwartz, Barclays Global Investors, NA/5.84%, Insiders/1.54%, Ronald C. Cambre, John S. Brinzo, Joseph A. Carrabba, Roger Phillips, LMM LLC/10.44%, Jeffrey L. Gendell/9.87%, Richard K. Riederer, Capital Research and Management Company/5.50%, Susan M. Cunningham (20 Owners included in Index)

Financial Data: Fiscal Year End:12/31 Latest Annual Data: 12/31/2006

Year	Sales	Net Income
2006	$1,933,400,000	$280,100,000
2005	$1,739,500,000	$277,600,000
2004	$1,206,700,000	$323,600,000

Curr. Assets:	$782,300,000	**Curr. Liab.:**	$374,900,000	**P/E Ratio:**	14.46
Plant, Equip.:	$884,900,000	**Total Liab.:**	$935,800,000	**Indic. Yr. Divd.:**	$0.500
Total Assets:	$1,939,700,000	**Net Worth:**	$745,800,000	**Debt/ Equity:**	0.0642

Cleveland Electric Illuminating Co

76 S Main St., Akron, OH, 44308; *PH:* 1-800-736-3402; *http://* www.firstenergycorp.com

General - Incorporation	OH	**Stock**- Price on:12/24/2007	$65.72
Employees	13,739	Stock Exchange	NA
Auditor	PricewaterhouseCoopers LLP	Ticker Symbol	NA
Stk Agt	NA	Outstanding Shares	304,830,000
Counsel	NA	E.P.S.	$4.24
DUNS No.	00-790-0293	Shareholders	NA

Business: The group's principle activity is to provide regulated electric services to northeastern Ohio and western Pennsylvania. The group's retail customers are metered on a cycle basis. Revenue is recognized for unbilled electric service through the end of the year. The group is a wholly owned electric utility operating subsidiary of firstenergy corp. The group provides services to approximately 37,200 square miles in Ohio, New Jersey and Pennsylvania.

Primary SIC and add'l.: 4911

CIK No: 0000020947

Subsidiaries: American Transmission Systems, Inc., Centerior Service Company, FE Acquisition Corp., FELHC, Inc., FirstEnergy Facilities Services Group, LLC, FirstEnergy Foundation, FirstEnergy Nuclear Generation Corp., FirstEnergy Nuclear Operating Company, FirstEnergy Properties Company, FirstEnergy Securities Transfer Company, FirstEnergy Service Company, FirstEnergy Solutions Corp., FirstEnergy Telecom Services, Inc., FirstEnergy Ventures Corp., GPU Capital, Inc. 26 Subsidiaries included in the Index

Officers: Anthony J. Alexander/Dir., CEO, Pres., J. M. Murray/61/Pres. - Ohio Operations, J. F. Pearson/53/VP, Treasurer, Richard R. Grigg/Dir., COO, Exec. VP, L. L. Vespoli/48/Sr. VP, General Counsel, Harvey L. Wagner/VP, Controller, Principal Accounting Officer, Richard H. Marsh/Dir., CFO, Sr. VP, C. E. Jones/52/Sr. VP - Energy Delivery, Customer Service

Directors: Anthony J. Alexander/Dir., CEO, Pres., Richard H. Marsh/Dir., CFO, Sr. VP, Richard R. Grigg/Dir., COO, Exec. VP

Financial Data: *Fiscal Year End:* 12/31 *Latest Annual Data:* 12/31/2006

Year	Sales	Net Income
2006	$11,501,000,000	$1,254,000,000
2005	$11,989,000,000	$861,000,000
2004	$12,453,046,000	$878,175,000

Curr. Assets:	$2,083,000,000	**Curr. Liab.:**	$5,255,000,000	**P/E Ratio:**	16.19
Plant, Equip.:	$14,667,000,000	**Total Liab.:**	$22,161,000,000	**Indic. Yr. Divd.:**	$2.000
Total Assets:	$31,196,000,000	**Net Worth:**	$9,035,000,000	**Debt/ Equity:**	1.0297

Click Commerce Inc

233 N Michigan, 22nd Fl., Chicago, IL, 60601; ***PH:*** 1-312-482-9006; ***http://*** www.clickcommerce.com

General - Incorporation	DE	**Stock**- Price on:12/24/2007	$55.43
Employees	55,000	Stock Exchange	NA
Auditor	BDO Seidman, LLP	Ticker Symbol	NA
Stk Agt	Computershare Investor Services LLC	Outstanding Shares	556,720,000
Counsel	Latham & Watkins	E.P.S.	$3.17
DUNS No.	NA	Shareholders	NA

Business: The group's principal activities are to provide sell-side ebusiness software solutions that connect large, global manufacturing, high-technology and financial services companies with their channel partners. The products use the Internet to connect manufacturing companies with their distributors, dealers and other distribution channel partners. The group builds and maintains customized extranets that provide distribution channel partners with Internet access to product information. The extranets also enable the distribution channel partners to electronically transact business over a secure system with the manufacturer and each other. The products and services are marketed in the United States and Europe. Major customers include delphi automotive systems, equistar, alstom power, American standard and astrazeneca. On 24-Mar-2003, the group acquired allegis corporation and on 06-Jul-2004, btrade inc.

Primary SIC and add'l.: 7375 7372

CIK No: 0001107050

Subsidiaries: Allegis Acquisition, Allegis Corporation, Allegis Ltd., bTrade Inc., Click Commerce BV, Click Commerce GmbH, Click Commerce Ltd., Click Commerce SPO Inc., Click Procure Inc., Click Texas Corp., Click West Coast Corp., Click-Webridge Inc., CWV Acquisition Inc., Elance Software Technologies (India) Private Limited, Elance UK Ltd 23 Subsidiaries included in the Index

Officers: Michael W. Ferro/Chmn., CEO - Click Commerce, Inc, David B. Arney/CFO, Justin Dearborn/GM - Demand Chain Management Solutions, Jim Schoessling/GM - Supply Chain Management Solutions, Marc Stone/GM - Supply Chain Management Solutions, Kushal Dutta/GM - Supply Chain Management Solutions, Gary Whitney/GM - Research, Healthcare Solutions, Stephen J. Cole/Sr. VP - Product Management, Strategy, Grace Feliciano/GM - Demand Chain Management Solutions, Katie Weems/VP - Human Resources, Mike Drazin/Division Controller, Eric Meerschaert/Pres., Jim Walton/GM - Kiwiplan, David Barboro/GM - Service Parts Optimization Solutions, Sampath Gomatam/GM - Contract, Service Management Solutions, Master Data Management Solutions, Secure Communications Solutions

Directors: Michael W. Ferro/Chmn., CEO - Click Commerce, Inc, Andrew J. McKenna/Dir., John F. Sandner/Dir., Samuel K. Skinner/Dir., William J. Devers/Dir. - Click Commerce, Emmanuel A. Kampouris/Dir., June E. Drewry/Dir., Neele E. Stearns/Dir.

Financial Data: *Fiscal Year End:* 12/31 *Latest Annual Data:* 12/31/2006

Year	Sales	Net Income
2006	$14,055,049,000	$1,717,746,000
2005	$12,921,792,000	$1,494,869,000
2004	$11,731,425,000	$1,338,694,000

Curr. Assets:	$5,206,405,000	**Curr. Liab.:**	$2,636,584,000	**P/E Ratio:**	18.00
Plant, Equip.:	$2,053,457,000	**Total Liab.:**	$4,862,931,000	**Indic. Yr. Divd.:**	$0.840
Total Assets:	$13,880,439,000	**Net Worth:**	$9,017,508,000	**Debt/ Equity:**	0.1044

Clicknsettle Com Inc

990 Stewart Ave., 1st Fl., Garden City, NY, 11530; ***PH:*** 1-516-794-8950; ***Fax:*** 1-516-794-8518; ***http://*** www.namadr.com; ***Email:*** customerservice@namadr.com

General - Incorporation	DE	**Stock**- Price on:12/24/2007	$0.111
Employees	NA	Stock Exchange	OTC
Auditor	Bp Audit Group, PLLC	Ticker Symbol	CLIK
Stk Agt	Continental Stock Transfer & Trust Co	Outstanding Shares	9,930,000
Counsel	NA	E.P.S.	-$0.007
DUNS No.	87-768-8069	Shareholders	NA

Business: The group's principal activity is to provide arbitration and mediation services, also known as alternative dispute resolution services and related electronic oversight applications. An alternative dispute resolution proceeding is an alternative forum to the public court system for resolving civil disputes. Arbitration and mediation are the main services offered by the group. In addition, the group offers advisory opinions, mock jury trials and other specialized dispute resolution programs depending on the parties' particular needs. These services are offered principally to insurance companies, law firms, corporations and municipalities.

Primary SIC and add'l.: 8111

CIK No: 0000925741

Subsidiaries: National Arbitration & Mediation, Inc.

Officers: Roy Israel/48/Chmn., CEO, Pres., Patricia Giuliani-Rheaume/50/CFO, VP, Treasurer

Directors: Roy Israel/48/Chmn., CEO, Pres., Willem F. Specht/47/Dir., Corey J. Gottlieb/45/Dir., Randy Gerstenblatt/49/Dir., Kenneth W. Good/61/Dir.

Owners: Randy Gerstenblatt, Insiders/52.20%, M. D. Sabbah/5.90%, Willem F. Specht/1.40%, ISO Investment Holdings, Inc./13.30%, Patricia A. Giuliani-Rheaume/1.40%, Roy Israel/35.50%, Kenneth W. Good/13.30%, Corey J. Gottlieb, Jay Gottlieb/9.90%

Financial Data: *Fiscal Year End:* 06/30 *Latest Annual Data:* 6/30/2006

Year	Sales	Net Income
2006	NA	-$93,000
2005	NA	-$812,000
2004	$3,759,000	-$723,000

Curr. Assets:	$141,000	**Curr. Liab.:**	$25,000		
Plant, Equip.:	NA	**Total Liab.:**	$25,000	**Indic. Yr. Divd.:**	NA
Total Assets:	$141,000	**Net Worth:**	$117,000	**Debt/ Equity:**	NA

ClickSoftware Technologies Ltd

35 Corporate Dr., Ste. 140, Burlington, MA, 01803; ***PH:*** 1-781-272-5903; ***Fax:*** 1-781-272-6409; ***http://*** www.clicksoftware.com

General - Incorporation	Israel	**Stock**- Price on:12/24/2007	$3.41
Employees	194	Stock Exchange	NDQ
Auditor	Brightman Almagor & Co	Ticker Symbol	CKSW
Stk Agt	Computershare Ltd.	Outstanding Shares	27,990,000
Counsel	Skadden Arps Slate Meagher LLP	E.P.S.	$0.11
DUNS No.	NA	Shareholders	NA

Business: The group's principle activity is the provision of Web-based application software that enables companies to efficiently provide service and product delivery in enterprise environments and over the Internet. The group's quarterly revenue for September 2007 was 10.05 millions of USD.

Primary SIC and add'l.: 7372 7379

CIK No: 0001105841

Subsidiaries: ClickSoftware Australia Pty Limited, ClickSoftware Belgium, N.V., ClickSoftware Central Europe GmbH, ClickSoftware Europe, Limited, ClickSoftware, Inc

Officers: Moshe Benbassat/60/Chmn., CEO, Shmuel Arvatz/CFO, Hannan Carmeli/COO, Zvi Piritz/Sr. VP - Worldwide Sales, Udi Keidar/VP - Professional Services, Nigel Clark/VP - Alliances, Israel Beniaminy/Sr. VP - Emerging Business Opportunities, Danny Korach/VP - Research, Development, Simon Morris/VP - Marketing Operations, Steve Lawrence/VP - NA Sales, Noa Schuman/Contact - Investor Relations, Israel, Adam J. Rosen/Contact - Investor Relations, USA

Directors: Moshe Benbassat/60/Chmn., CEO, Dan Falk/Dir., Naomi Atsmon/Dir., Israel Borovich/Dir., Gil Weiser/Dir., Roni A. Einav/Dir., James W. Thanos/Dir.

Owners: Insiders/21.80%, Nicholas G. Farwell/10.70%, Moshe BenBassat/18.70%, Austin W. Marxe/14.80%

Financial Data: *Fiscal Year End:* 12/31 *Latest Annual Data:* 12/31/2006

Year	Sales	Net Income
2006	$32,431,000	$2,138,000
2005	$24,067,000	-$1,993,000
2004	$22,705,000	$913,000

Curr. Assets:	$26,721,000	**Curr. Liab.:**	$11,910,000	**P/E Ratio:**	31.00
Plant, Equip.:	$804,000	**Total Liab.:**	$16,431,000	**Indic. Yr. Divd.:**	NA
Total Assets:	$28,972,000	**Net Worth:**	$12,541,000	**Debt/ Equity:**	NA

Clifton Mining Co

80 W Canyon Crest Rd., Alpine, UT, 84004; ***PH:*** 1-800-756-1414; ***http://*** www.cliftonmining.com; ***Email:*** clifton@cliftonmining.com

General - Incorporation	UT	**Stock**- Price on:12/24/2007	$0.51
Employees	NA	Stock Exchange	OTC
Auditor	Rosenberg Rich Baker Berman & Co	Ticker Symbol	CFTN
Stk Agt	Allied Stock Transfer Inc	Outstanding Shares	NA
Counsel	NA	E.P.S.	NA
DUNS No.	NA	Shareholders	NA

Business: The groups principle activity is to focus on the exploration of precious metals and polymetallic projects. The group operates from United States.

Primary SIC and add'l.: 1040

CIK No: 0000925297

Officers: Keith Moeller/VP, Ken Friedman/Pres.

Owners: Kenneth S. Friedman/2.50%, William D. Moeller/1.20%, Keith W. Moeller/3.50%, Scott S. Moeller/2.20%, Insiders/11.00%, Harold Gunsinger/1.60%

Clifton Savings Bancorp Inc

1433 Van Houten Ave., Clifton, NJ, 07015; ***PH:*** 1-973-473-2200; ***Fax:*** 1-973-473-0451; ***http://*** www.cliftonsavings.com; ***Email:*** info@cliftonsavings.com

General - Incorporation	US	**Stock**- Price on:12/24/2007	$11.08
Employees	82	Stock Exchange	NDQ
Auditor	Beard Miller Co. LLP	Ticker Symbol	CSBK
Stk Agt	Registrar & Transfer Co	Outstanding Shares	28,670,000
Counsel	NA	E.P.S.	$0.09
DUNS No.	NA	Shareholders	NA

Business: The group's principal activity is to provide a wide range of financial services to consumers and businesses in clifton, New Jersey. The group attract deposits from the general public and use those funds to originate one- to four-family, multi-family and commercial real estate and consumer loans. The operations of the group are conducted through its subsidiary clifton savings bank, s l a. The group operates through main office in clifton, New Jersey and nine branch offices in bergen and passaic counties.

Primary SIC and add'l.: 6712 6035

CIK No: 0001240581

Subsidiaries: Clifton Savings Bank, S.L.A.

Officers: Walter Celuch/Pres., Sec., CEO/$507,353.00, Doris Mendez/Assist. Treasurer, Linda Fisher/VP, Loan Officer, Stephen A. Hoogerhyde/Exec. VP, Chief Lending Officer/$318,201.00, Susan L. Horant/VP, Security Officer, Coleen Kelley/VP, IRA Administrator, Bernadette McDonald/VP, Treasurer, Joann M. McGuire/Assist. Treasurer, Ted Munley/VP - Branch Coordinator, Carol Campbell/Assist. VP, Agata Erszkowicz/Assist. Treasurer, Edyta Koc/Assist. Treasurer, Svetlana Milanovic/Assist. Treasurer, Agnieszka Pokoj/Assist. Treasurer, Mary Ann Mac Kinnon/Assist. VP, Branch Mgr. - Richfield *(37 Officers included in Index)*

Directors: John A. Celentano/Chmn., Thomas A. Miller/Dir., Bart D'Ambra/COO, Exec. VP, Cynthia Sisco Parachini/Dir., John H. Peto/Dir., Frank J. Hahofer/Dir. Emeritus, John Stokes/Dir., Joseph C. Smith/Dir., Charles J. Pivirotto/Dir.

Owners: John Stokes, Charles J. Pivirotto, Walter Celuch, Christine R. Piano, Bart D'Ambra, Joseph C. Smith, Stephen A. Hoogerhyde, Insiders/4.23%, John A. Celentano/1.34%, Thomas A. Miller, John H. Peto, Cynthia Sisco Parachini

Financial Data: *Fiscal Year End:*03/31 *Latest Annual Data:* 3/31/2007

Year	Sales	Net Income
2007	$37,893,000	$2,472,000
2006	$35,617,000	$3,667,000
2005	$31,757,000	$5,280,000

Curr. Assets:	$45,544,000	Curr. Liab.:	$612,805,000	P/E Ratio:	123.11
Plant, Equip.:	$8,383,000	Total Liab.:	$620,444,000	Indic. Yr. Divd.:	$0.200
Total Assets:	$805,042,000	Net Worth:	$184,598,000	Debt/ Equity:	NA

Clinical Data Inc

1 Gateway Ctr., Ste. 702, Newton, MA, 02458; *PH:* 1-617-527-9933; *Fax:* 1-617-965-0445; *http://* www.clda.com; *Email:* info@clda.com

General		**Stock**	
Incorporation	DE	Price on:12/24/2007	$21.42
Employees	472	Stock Exchange	NDQ
Auditor	Deloitte & Touche LLP	Ticker Symbol	CLDA
Stk Agt	State Street Bank and Trust Co	Outstanding Shares	9,750,000
Counsel	NA	E.P.S	-$2.49
DUNS No.	05-364-8200	Shareholders	NA

Business: The group's principal activities are to design, manufacture and market scientific instrumentation for use in clinical and analytical laboratories and in process monitoring industry. The group's operations are conducted through three operating subsidiaries located in the Netherlands and Australia. The group's dutch subsidiary, vital scientific nv designs and manufactures scientific instrumentation marketed worldwide through distributors and strategic partnerships. Novachem bv also a dutch subsidiary, develops and markets process monitoring technology for petrochemical and environmental applications. The group's australian subsidiary, vital diagnostics pty ltd., distributes diagnostic instruments and assays in the south pacific. On 29-Apr-2003, it acquired group practice services incorporated and landmark scientific inc.

Primary SIC and add'l.: 3826

CIK No: 0000716646

Subsidiaries: Clinical Data BV, Clinical Data Incorporated, Clinical Data Sales & Service, Inc., Electa Lab s.r.l., Genaissance Pharmaceuticals, Inc., Genome Express S.A., GPSI Acquisition, Inc., Icoria, Inc., Lark Technologies, Inc., NovaChem BV, Spectronetics NV, Vital Diagnostics Ltd., Vital Diagnostics Pty. Ltd., Vital Scientific NV

Officers: Andrew J. Fromkin/41/Dir., CEO, Pres., Evan C. Ballantyne/Sr. VP, CFO, Lynn Ferrucci/VP - Human Resources, Michael Lutz/Sr. VP - Pharmacogenetic Partnerships, Pgxhealth, Caesar J. Belbel/Exec. VP, Chief Legal Officer, Carol Reed/Sr. VP, Chief Medical Officer, John A. Schultz/Sr. VP - Licensing, Strategic Development, Pgxhealth, Robert Bondaryk/Sr. VP, GM - Cogenics, Sephanie Carrington/Investor Contact - Ruth Group

Directors: Andrew J. Fromkin/41/Dir., CEO, Pres., Randal J. Kirk/Chmn., Kevin L. Rakin/47/Dir., Richard J. Wallace/Dir., Arthur B. Malman/Dir., Larry D. Horner/Dir., Burton E. Sobel/Dir.

Owners: Kevin L. Rakin, Third Security, LLC/46.00%, Caesar J. Belbel, Mark D. Shooman, Andrew J. Fromkin/1.37%, Larry D. Horner, Randal J. Kirk/46.00%, Burton E. Sobel, Arthur B. Malman, Evan C. Ballantyne, Insiders/48.61%, Israel M. Stein/3.09%, Carol Reed

Financial Data: *Fiscal Year End:*03/31 *Latest Annual Data:* 03/31/2007

Year	Sales	Net Income
2007	$63,732,000	-$37,522,000
2006	$68,748,000	-$50,881,000
2005	$56,400,000	$3,395,000

Curr. Assets:	$45,003,000	Curr. Liab.:	$27,985,000		
Plant, Equip.:	$6,791,000	Total Liab.:	$36,770,000	Indic. Yr. Divd.:	NA
Total Assets:	$87,490,000	Net Worth:	$50,720,000	Debt/ Equity:	0.1197

Clorox Co (The)

1221 Broadway, Oakland, CA, 94612; *PH:* 1-510-271-7000; *Fax:* 1-510-832-1463; *http://* www.clorox.com

General		**Stock**	
Incorporation	DE	Price on:12/24/2007	$64.59
Employees	7,600	Stock Exchange	NYSE
Auditor	Ernst & Young LLP	Ticker Symbol	CLX
Stk Agt	EquiServe Trust Co N.A	Outstanding Shares	151,760,000
Counsel	NA	E.P.S	$3.12
DUNS No.	00-913-8033	Shareholders	NA

Business: The group's principle activities include non-durable household consumer products. The groups product line includes household cleaning, bleach and home care products, water filtration products, food storage and trash disposal, automotive care, cat litter, insecticides, dressings and sauces. The group operates from North America and Latin America.

Primary SIC and add'l.: 2842

CIK No: 0000021076

Subsidiaries: 1221 Olux, LLC, A & M Products Manufacturing Company, Andover Properties, Inc., BGP Switzerland S. a. r. l., Brita Canada Corporation, Brita Canada Holdings Corporation, Brita GP, Brita LP, Brita Manufacturing Company, Chesapeake Assurance Limited, Clorox (Barbados) Inc., Clorox (Cayman Islands) Ltd., Clorox Africa (Holdings) Pty. Ltd., Clorox Africa Pty. Ltd., Clorox Argentina S.A. 26 Subsidiaries included in the Index

Officers: Donald R. Knauss/57/Chmn., CEO, Laura Stein/Sr. VP, General Counsel, Benno Dorer/VP, GM - Household Division, Robin Evitts/CIO, VP, Charles R. Conradi/VP - Tax, Treasurer, Wayne L. Delker/VP - Research, Development, Warwick Every-Burns/Sr. VP - International, Thomas D. Johnson/VP, Controller, Chief Accounting Officer, Jacqueline P. Kane/Sr. VP - Human Resources, Corporate Affairs, Lawrence S. Peiros/COO, Exec. VP - Clorox North America, Frank A. Tataseo/Exec. VP - Functional Operations, Daniel J. Heinrich/CFO, Sr. VP, Beth Springer/Exec. VP - Strategy, Growth, Tarang Amin/VP - Global Health, Wellness, Tim E. Bailey/VP - Product Supply *(24 Officers included in Index)*

Directors: Donald R. Knauss/57/Chmn., CEO, Robert W. Matschullat/60/Dir., Tully M. Friedman/66/Dir., George Harad/64/Dir., Daniel Boggan/62/Dir., Richard H. Carmona/Dir., Edward A. Mueller/61/Dir., Pamela Thomas-Graham/45/Dir., Gary G. Michael/67/Dir., Jan L. Murley/57/Dir., Michael E. Shannon/71/Dir., Carolyn M. Ticknor/61/Dir.

Owners: Daniel J. Heinrich, Insiders, Robert W. Matschullat, AXA Financial, Inc./8.50%, Frank A. Tataseo, Lawrence S. Peiros, Carolyn M. Ticknor, Tully M. Friedman, Laura Stein, Daniel Boggan, Donald R. Knauss, Jan L. Murley, Gary G. Michael, Michael E. Shannon, George J. Harad *(16 Owners included in Index)*

Financial Data: *Fiscal Year End:*06/30 *Latest Annual Data:* 6/30/2006

Year	Sales	Net Income
2006	$4,644,000,000	$444,000,000
2005	$4,388,000,000	$1,096,000,000
2004	$4,324,000,000	$549,000,000

Curr. Assets:	$1,007,000,000	Curr. Liab.:	$1,130,000,000	P/E Ratio:	20.70
Plant, Equip.:	$1,004,000,000	Total Liab.:	$3,772,000,000	Indic. Yr. Divd.:	$1.600
Total Assets:	$3,616,000,000	Net Worth:	-$156,000,000	Debt/ Equity:	NA

Clover Community Bankshares Inc

PO Box 69, 124 N Main St., Clover Sc, SC, 29710;

General		**Stock**	
Incorporation	SC	Price on:12/24/2007	NA
Employees	NA	Stock Exchange	NA
Auditor	Elliott Davis LLC	Ticker Symbol	NA
Stk Agt	NA	Outstanding Shares	NA
Counsel	NA	E.P.S	NA
DUNS No.	NA	Shareholders	NA

Business: The group's principal activity is to provide general commercial banking services to individuals, small to medium-sized business and professional concerns. It offers deposit services and short to medium term commercial, personal and mortgage loans through a single office located in clover, South Carolina. These services include checking accounts, now accounts, savings accounts and other time deposits ranging from daily money market accounts to longer-term certificates of deposit. Loan services include secured and unsecured loans for working capital, business expansion, purchase of equipment and machinery, financing automobiles, home improvements, education and personal investments. The other services offered include traveler's checks, safe deposit boxes, mastercard and visa accounts, ATM cards and overdraft lines of credit.

Primary SIC and add'l.: 6022 6712

CIK No: 0001057017

Subsidiaries: Clover Community Bank

Officers: Gwen M. Thompson/CEO, Pres., Gerald L. Bolin/COO, Exec. VP, Paige B. McCarter/Sr. VP, Lake Wylie Banking Center Mgr., Earnest A. Robertson/Sr. VP, Chief Credit Officer, Frank Mcc Gadsden/CIO, Sr. VP, Judy Lark/Contact - New Accounting, Misty Adams/Contact - New Accounting, Abbey Holloway/Contact - New Accounting, Ollie Robertson/Contact - Commercial Loans, Donna McSwain/Contact - Consumer Loans, Beverly Good/Contact - Real Estate Loans, Sheila Goss/Contact - New Accounting, Anita Floyd/Contact - New Accounting, Ty Bennett/Lending Contact - Rock Hill, Jim Reno/Lending Contact - Rock Hill

CLP Holdings Ltd

147 Argyle St., Kowloon; *PH:* 852-26788111; *http://* www.clpholdings.com; *Email:* clp_info@clp.com.hk

General		**Stock**	
Incorporation	Hong Kong	Price on:12/24/2007	$6.75
Employees	NA	Stock Exchange	OTC
Auditor	PricewaterhouseCoopers LLP	Ticker Symbol	CLPHF
Stk Agt	NA	Outstanding Shares	NA
Counsel	NA	E.P.S	NA
DUNS No.	66-322-2883	Shareholders	NA

Business: The group's principal activities are the generation and supply of electricity. Other activities of the group are the provision of public lighting and engineering services, property investment, telecommunications and development of other businesses. It supplies electricity to 1.8 million business and residential accounts in kowloon, the new territories and most of the outlying islands of Hong Kong. The group, through its subsidiaries, also develops and operates power business in mainland China and several other Asian countries. Its activities fall into two broad categories: electric utility business operated under clp power in Hong Kong, which is regulated by a scheme of control agreement with the Hong Kong government; and power-related investments and services both in and outside of Hong Kong.

Primary SIC and add'l.: 4939 8731 4911 6798 4899 8711 3612

CIK No: 0001052515

Subsidiaries: CLP Australia Holdings Pty Ltd, CLP Engineering Limited, CLP Power Asia Limited, CLP Power China Limited, CLP Power Hong Kong Limited, CLP Power International Limited, CLP Properties Limited, CLP Research Institute Limited, Guangdong Huaiji Changxin Hydro-electric Power Company Limited, Guangdong Huaiji Gaotang Hydro-electric Power Company Limited, Guangdong Huaiji Weifa Hydro-electric Power Company Limited, Guangdong Huaiji Xinlian Hydro-electric Power Company Limited, Gujarat Paguthan Energy Corporation Private Limited, Hong Kong Nuclear Investment Company Limited, TRUenergy Pty Ltd 16 Subsidiaries included in the Index

Officers: Andrew Clifford Winawer Brandler/52/CEO, Tse Pak Wing Peter/56/Group Executive Dir., CFO, Joe Locandro/48/Dir. - Group Information Technology, Roy Massey/53/Dir. - Group Human Resources, Rajiv Ranjan Mishra/42/MD - India, Poon Wai Yin Paul/55/Dir. - Power Systems, CLP Power Hong Kong, John Stefan Robertsson/43/Group Dir. - Corporate Finance, Development, Stewart Henry Saunders/64/COO - CLP Power Hong Kong, Jane Yuk Yin Lau/49/Dir. - Group Public Affairs, Gail Elizabeth Kendall/55/Dir. - Group Environmental Affairs, MD - CLP Research Institute, Richard Iain James McIndoe/43/Group Dir., MD Australia, Mark Takahashi/49/Group Dir. - Corporate Development, Sheena Brand/52/Dir. - Group Legal Affairs, Peter Albert Littlewood/56/Group Dir. - Operations, Chan Siu Hung/49/Planning Dir. - CLP Power Hong Kong *(26 Officers included in Index)*

Directors: Michael Kadoorie/66/Chmn., William Elkin Mocatta/54/Vice Chmn., Sze Yuen Chung/90/Non Exec. Dir., Rudolf Bischof/66/Non Exec. Dir., Loh Chung Hon Hansen/62/Non Exec. Dir., Jason Holroyd Whittle/40/Non Exec. Dir., Tsui Lam Sin Lai Judy/53/Non Exec. Dir., Roderick Ian Eddington/58/Non Exec. Dir., Lee Yui Bor/61/Dir., John Andrew Harry Leigh/54/Non Exec. Dir., Ronald James McAulay/72/Non Exec. Dir., Ian Duncan Boyce/63/Non Exec. Dir., Lee Ting Chang Peter/54/Non Exec. Dir., Neo Kim Teck/52/Alternate Dir., Vernon Francis Moore/61/Dir. *(18 Directors included in Index)*

Owners: Acorn Holdings Corporation, Kadoorie Muriel, Bermuda Trust (Cayman) Limited, Merlin Investments Limited, J. A. H. Leigh, Oak (Unit Trust) Holdings Limited, Mikado Investments Limited, The Hon. Sir Michael Kadoorie, The Mikado Private Trust Company Limited, Guardian Limited, Jason Whittle, Goshawk Investments Limited, Bermuda Trust Company Ltd, HWR Trustees Limited, Mikado Holding Inc. *(23 Owners included in Index)*

CLP Power Hong Kong Ltd

147 Argyle St., Kowloom; *PH:* 852-26788111; *http://* www.clpgroup.com;
Email: clp_info@clp.com.hk

General - Incorporation	Hong Kong	Stock- Price on:12/24/2007	NA
Employees	NA	Stock Exchange	NA
Auditor	PricewaterhouseCoopers LLP	Ticker Symbol	NA
Stk Agt	NA	Outstanding Shares	NA
Counsel	NA	E.P.S.	NA
DUNS No.	68-609-0606	Shareholders	NA

Business: The group's principal activities are wholly owned subsidiary of CLP Holdings Limited, which is referred to as CLP Holdings in this annual report. We entered into the Scheme of Control in 1964 with the Hong Kong Government and certain other parties to govern electricity-related financial affairs. On January 31, 2005, the Hong Kong Government launched a process of public consultation on post-2008 electricity market arrangements. The commissioning of units 7 and 8 is expected to occur in 2005 and 2006, respectively. See " - Capital Investment programme. Black Point Power Station, when completed, will be one of the largest combined cycle power plants in the world with an expected total capacity of 2,500 MW.

Primary SIC and add'l.: 4911

CIK No: 0001016049

Subsidiaries: CLP Holdings Limited

CLST Holdings Inc

Formerly: Cellstar Corp
15950 N Dallas Pkwy., Tower Ii, No. 400, Dallas, TX, 75248; *PH:* 1-972-361-8426;
http:// www.cellstar.com

General - Incorporation	DE	Stock- Price on:12/24/2007	NA
Employees	730	Stock Exchange	OTC
Auditor	Grant Thornton LLP	Ticker Symbol	CLHI
Stk Agt	Mellon Investor Services LLC	Outstanding Shares	NA
Counsel	Haynes & Boone	E.P.S.	NA
DUNS No.	87-726-9902	Shareholders	NA

Business: The group's principal activity is to distribute and provide value-added logistics services to the wireless communications industry. The group distributes handsets, related accessories, and other wireless products from manufacturers to network operators, agents, resellers, dealers and retailers. It also provides activation services that generate new subscribers for its wireless carrier customers. The group offers its customers value-added services, including Internet-based supply chain services, Internet-based tracking and reporting, inventory management, marketing, prepaid wireless. The services also include product fulfillment, kitting and customized packaging, private labeling, light assembly, accounts receivable management and end-user support services. The group offers wireless handsets and accessories manufactured by OEMs, such as motorola, kyocera, lg, nokia, and sony ericsson. During the year 2003, the group sold both Netherlands and the Sweden operations.

Primary SIC and add'l.: 4899 5065 4812

CIK No: 0000913590

Subsidiaries: A & S Air Service, Inc., Audiomex Export Corp., CellStar Air Services, Inc., CellStar Asia Pacific Corporation, CellStar Asia.com, Inc., CellStar Chile, S.A., CellStar de Colombia Ltda., CellStar de Guatemala S.A., CellStar El Salvador S.A., CellStar Financo, Inc., CellStar Fulfillment, Inc., CellStar Fulfillment, Ltd., CellStar Holding AB, CellStar International Corporation/Asia, CellStar International Corporation/SA 31 Subsidiaries included in the Index

Officers: Robert A. Kaiser/54/CEO

Directors: Dale V. Kesler/69/Chmn., John L. Jackson/76/Dir., Jere W. Thompson/76/Dir., Da Hsuan Feng/Dir.

Owners: Da Hsuan Feng, Jere W. Thompson, Michael A. Roth and Brian J. Stark c/o Stark Investments/15.90%, Insiders/2.40%, Juan Martinez, Dale V. Kesler, Raymond L. Durham, Robert A. Kaiser/1.60%, Michael J. Farrell, John L. Jackson, Elaine Flud Rodriguez, Sherrian Gunn, Timothy S. Durham/9.20%

Financial Data: *Fiscal Year End:*11/30 **Latest Annual Data:** 11/30/2006

Year	Sales		Net Income
2006	$943,140,000		$4,836,000
2005	$987,334,000		-$24,583,000
2004	$1,272,023,000		-$118,117,000
Curr. Assets:	$218,561,000	Curr. Liab.:	$208,135,000
Plant, Equip.:	$2,510,000	Total Liab.:	$219,210,000	Indic. Yr. Divd.: NA
Total Assets:	$235,980,000	Net Worth:	$16,770,000	Debt/ Equity: NA

ClubCorp Inc

3030 Lbj Fwy., Ste. 500, Dallas, TX, 75234; *PH:* 1-972-243-6191; *http://* www.clubcorp.com

General - Incorporation	DE	Stock- Price on:12/24/2007	NA
Employees	87	Stock Exchange	NA
Auditor	KPMG LLP	Ticker Symbol	NA
Stk Agt	NA	Outstanding Shares	NA
Counsel	NA	E.P.S.	NA
DUNS No.	05-637-5835	Shareholders	NA

Business: The group's principal activities are carried out through three principal business segments: country club and golf facilities, business and sports clubs and resorts. The country club and golf facilities segment operates 98 country clubs and golf facilities consisting of 69 private and semi-private golf clubs. The business and sports club segment includes 48 business clubs, 17 business/sports clubs and 4 sports clubs, with about 102,000 memberships as of 30-Dec-2003. The resorts segment offers golf courses, lodging and conference facilities, dining and lounge areas, recreational facilities, European style spas and other resort amenities.

Primary SIC and add'l.: 5812 7011 6552 7997 6719 7992

CIK No: 0000929455

Officers: Eric L. Affeldt/CEO, Pres., Mark Murphy/Sr. VP - Revenue, Daniel T. Tilley/CIO, Exec. VP, Mark Burnett/Exec. VP - Golf, Country, Club Division, Ingrid Keiser/Chief Legal Officer, Sec., Angela A. Stephens/Exec. VP - Finance, William T. Walden/Sr. VP - Purchasing, John H. Longstreet/Exec. VP - People Strategy, Frank C. Gore/Exec. VP - Sales, David B. Woodyard/Exec. VP - Business, Sports Division, Douglas T. Howe/Exec. VP - new Business Development

Directors: Bahram Shirazi/Dir., Patricia Dedman Dietz/Dir., Nancy McMillan Dedman/Dir., John A. Beckert/Dir., James Stern/Dir.

Owners: Insiders, Nancy M. Dedman, Douglas T. Howe, The Cypress Group, James Stern, Patricia Dedman Dietz, Richard N. Beckert, Jeffrey P. Mayer, Robert H. Dedman, John A. Beckert

Clubhouse Videos Inc

2005 Tree Fork Ln, Longwood, FL, 32750; *PH:* 1-407-304-4764

General - Incorporation	FL	Stock- Price on:12/24/2007	NA
Employees	NA	Stock Exchange	NA
Auditor	NA	Ticker Symbol	NA
Stk Agt	Atlantic Stock Transfer, Inc.	Outstanding Shares	NA
Counsel	Mr. Randolph S. Shaw	E.P.S.	NA
DUNS No.	NA	Shareholders	NA

Business: The group's principal activities include marketing and distribution of children's videos and music CD's based upon programming produced for television and E-commerce websites. The group's targets the children and young adult markets. The groups interest also lie in educational children's programming on television and videos, DVD's and music CD's. Clubhouse Videos Inc. is a spinoff and wholly owned subsidiary of Raven Moon Home Video Products LLC. Previously approved by Raven Moon shareholders, Clubhouse is a separately traded corporation.

Primary SIC and add'l.: 7812

CIK No: 0001248218

Subsidiaries: JB Toys, Inc, Raven Moon Home Video Products, LLC

CLX Investment Co Inc

29970 Technology Dr., Ste. 203, Murrieta, CA, 92563; *PH:* 1-951-677-6735; *Fax:* 1-951-677-6573;
http:// www.clxinvestments.com; *Email:* admin@clxinvestments.com

General - Incorporation	CO	Stock- Price on:12/24/2007	$0.012
Employees	1	Stock Exchange	OTC
Auditor	HJ Assoc. & Consultants LLP	Ticker Symbol	CLXN
Stk Agt	Transfer Online, Inc.	Outstanding Shares	118,310,000
Counsel	NA	E.P.S.	-$0.002
DUNS No.	60-544-2482	Shareholders	NA

Business: The group's principle activity is to acquire, explore, develop, sell and to operate oil and gas properties. The oil and gas production is sold to several purchasers in the United States, primarily Colorado, Kansas, Oklahoma and Wyoming. The operations of the company include production of oil and gas wells, the acquisition of producing properties, the acquisition of oil and gas leases and the development of oil and gas drilling prospects. The company's principal products are crude oil and natural gas. The group operates from United States.

Primary SIC and add'l.: 1311

CIK No: 0000317438

Subsidiaries: CLX Energy, Inc.)

Officers: Robert McCoy/Chmn., CEO

Directors: Robert McCoy/Chmn., CEO, James Bickel/Dir.

Owners: Robert McCoy, Insiders/9.00%, Patrick Edgerton/1.00%, James Bickel/5.00%, Vera Leonard/2.00%

Financial Data: *Fiscal Year End:*09/30 **Latest Annual Data:** 9/30/2006

Year	Sales		Net Income
2006	$98,000		-$304,000
2005	$65,000		-$1,065,000
2004	NA		-$24,000
Curr. Assets:	$8,000	Curr. Liab.:	$307,000
Plant, Equip.:	NA	Total Liab.:	$507,000	Indic. Yr. Divd.: NA
Total Assets:	$709,000	Net Worth:	$202,000	Debt/ Equity: NA

Clyvia Inc

1480 Gulf Rd., Ste. 204, Point Roberts, WA, 98281; *PH:* 1-360-306-1133

General - Incorporation	NV	Stock- Price on:12/24/2007	$0.51
Employees	5	Stock Exchange	OTC
Auditor	Davidson & Co. LLP	Ticker Symbol	CLYV
Stk Agt	Grosvenor Explorations Trnsfer Agent	Outstanding Shares	102,350,000
Counsel	Cementhai Legal Counsel Limited	E.P.S.	-$0.03
DUNS No.	NA	Shareholders	NA

Business: The groups principal activity is to produce diesel fuel and heating oil from various forms of recyclable waste materials. The group products include chlorine, fluorine and coke. The group operates from the United States and Germany. In the year 2005, the group acquired Clyvia Technology.

Primary SIC and add'l.: 1081

CIK No: 0001282549

Subsidiaries: Clyvia Technology GmbH

Officers: Walter P.W. Notter/57/Dir., CEO, CFO, Pres., Treasurer, John Boschert/38/Sec., Manfred Sappok/MD - Clyvia Technology Gmbh, Ieter Wagels/MD - Clyvia Technology Gmbh, Dieter Wagels/MD - Clyvia Technology Gmbh

Directors: Walter P.W. Notter/57/Dir., CEO, CFO, Pres., Treasurer

Owners: Inventa Holding GmbH/67.40%, Walter P.W. Notter, Dieter Wagels/2.80%, John Boschert, Insiders/6.30%, Manfred Sappok/2.80%

Financial Data: *Fiscal Year End:*01/31 **Latest Annual Data:** 01/31/2007

Year	Sales		Net Income
2007	NA		-$2,968,000
Curr. Assets:	$345,000	Curr. Liab.:	$331,000
Plant, Equip.:	$2,962,000	Total Liab.:	$529,000	Indic. Yr. Divd.: NA
Total Assets:	$3,307,000	Net Worth:	$2,779,000	Debt/ Equity: 0.0831

CMGI Inc

1100 Winter St., Ste. 4600, Waltham, MA, 02451; *PH:* 1-781-663-5001; *Fax:* 1-781-663-5100;
http:// www.cmgi.com; *Email:* ir@cmgi.com

General - Incorporation	DE	**Stock**- Price on:12/24/2007	$1.99
Employees	3,729	Stock Exchange	NDQ
Auditor	KPMG LLP	Ticker Symbol	CMGI
Stk Agt	American Stock Transfer & Trust Co.	Outstanding Shares	488,600,000
Counsel	Hale & Dorr LLP	E.P.S	$0.14
DUNS No.	13-620-6000	Shareholders	NA

Business: The group's principle activity is to develop, acquire and operate majority-owned subsidiaries focused on Internet technologies and supply chain management services. The group operates through three segments: enterprise software, ebusiness and fulfillment, managed application services. In its enterprise software and services segment, the group leases office, administrative, storage in California, Massachusetts and illionois. In its ebusiness and fulfillment segment, the group leases approximately 1.3 million square feet of office, storage, warehouse, production and assembly, sales and marketing, and operations space, principally in Massachusetts. Managed application services segment increased costs to support the growth of the customer base and network usage at navipath during fiscal year 2001. The group's total revenue for year 2007 was 1.143.03 millions of USD.

Primary SIC and add'l.: 7372 7319 3577 7375 7389

CIK No: 0000914712

Subsidiaries: CMG @ Ventures Capital Corp., CMG @ Ventures Expansion, LLC, CMG @ Ventures II LLC, CMG @ Ventures III, LLC, CMG @ Ventures Securities Corp., CMG @ Ventures, Inc., CMG Securities Corporation, CMGI @ Ventures IV, LLC, Logistix Holdings Europe Limited, Modus Media International (Ireland) Limited, Modus Media International Documentation Services (Ireland) Ltd., Modus Media International Dublin, Modus Media International Financial Services Ltd., Modus Media, Inc., ModusLink (China) Co. Ltd. 49 Subsidiaries included in the Index

Officers: Joseph C. Lawler/Chmn., CEO, Pres., Peter L. Gray/Exec. VP, General Counsel, Sec., James J. Herb/Sr. VP - Human Resources, David S. Wetherell/Consultant, Ventures, David J. Riley/38/Exec. VP - Corporate Development, Steven G. Crane/CFO, Matthew J. Dattilo/CIO, Peter H. Mills/Managing Partner, Ventures, Marc Poirier/General Partner, Ventures

Directors: Joseph C. Lawler/Chmn., CEO, Pres., Michael J. Mardy/Dir., Anthony J. Bay/Dir., Francis J. Jules/Dir., Virginia G. Breen/Dir., Thomas H. Johnson/Dir., Edward E. Lucente/Dir.

Owners: Virginia G. Breen, Thomas H. Johnson, Peter L. Gray, Joseph C. Lawler/1.00%, Francis J. Jules, Steven G. Crane, Edward E. Lucente, Michael J. Mardy, William R. McLennan, Mark J. Kelly, Anthony J. Bay, David J. Riley, Insiders/2.00%

Financial Data: *Fiscal Year End:*07/31 *Latest Annual Data:* 7/31/2006

Year	Sales	Net Income
2006	$1,148,886,000	$14,945,000
2005	$1,069,760,000	$26,525,000
2004	$397,422,000	$86,975,000

Curr. Assets:	$495,610,000	**Curr. Liab.:**	$213,388,000		
Plant, Equip.:	$46,020,000	**Total Liab.:**	$265,304,000	**Indic. Yr. Divd.:**	NA
Total Assets:	$763,219,000	**Net Worth:**	$497,915,000	**Debt/ Equity:**	0.0463

CMS Energy Corp

1 Energy Plz., Jackson, MI, 49201; *PH:* 1-517-788-0550; *Fax:* 1-517-788-1859; *http://* www.cmsenergy.com; *Email:* info@cmsenergy.com

General - Incorporation	MI	**Stock**- Price on:12/24/2007	$16.76
Employees	8,640	Stock Exchange	NYSE
Auditor	Ernst & Young LLP	Ticker Symbol	CMS
Stk Agt	New York Drop-Depository Trust Co.	Outstanding Shares	224,500,000
Counsel	NA	E.P.S	-$1.43
DUNS No.	17-520-6614	Shareholders	NA

Business: The groups principle activity is to provide natural gas and electricity. The group operates through three segments namely electric and gas utility, and enterprises. The group operates from United States.

Primary SIC and add'l.: 4924 4939 1311 4922 4911 4932

CIK No: 0000811156

Subsidiaries: AJD Forest Products Limited Partnership, Atacama Finance Co., Cdec-sing Limitada, Centrales Termica San Nicolas S.A., Centrales Termicas Mendoza, S.A, CMS (Barbados), SRL, CMS (India) Operations & Maintenance Company Private Limited, CMS Antrim Gas LLC, CMS Atacama Company, CMS Bay Area Pipeline, LLC, CMS Capital, LLC, CMS Centrales Termicas S.A, CMS Centrales Termicas S.A., CMS Comercializadora de Energia Ltda, CMS Comercializadora de Energia S.A. 207 Subsidiaries included in the Index

Officers: David W. Joos/Dir., CEO, Pres./$4,872,408.00, Ronn J. Rasmussen/VP - Consumers Energy Company, James E. Brunner/Sr. VP, General Counsel/$1,229,533.00, Joseph P. Tomasik/VP - CMS Enterprises Company, Theodore J. Vogel/VP, Chief Tax Counsel, Jeff Holyfield/Dir. - News, Information, Dan Bishop/Public Information Dir., William E. Garrity/Sr. VP - Electric, James R. Coddington/VP - Generation Operations, Consumers Energy, Jackson L. Hanson/VP - Generation Engineering, Services, Consumers Energy, James P. Pomaranski/VP - Consumers Energy Company, David G. Mengebier/Sr. VP - Governmental, Public Affairs, Chief Compliance Officer, Glenn P. Barba/VP, Controller, Chief Accounting Officer, John G. Russell/COO, Pres. - Consumers Energy/$1,771,862.00, Robert A. Fenech/Sr. VP - Consumers/$1,097,439.00 *(27 Officers included in Index)*

Directors: David W. Joos/Dir., CEO, Pres., Ken Whipple/Chmn., John B. Yasinsky/Dir., Michael T. Monahan/Dir., Joseph F. Paquette/Dir., Jon E. Barfield/Dir., Richard M. Gabrys/Dir., Philip R. Lochner/Dir., Kenneth L. Way/Dir., Percy A. Pierre/Dir., Merribel S. Ayres/Dir.

Owners: Lord, Abbett & Co. LLC/8.60%, Kenneth Whipple, David W. Joos, Michael T. Monahan, John G. Russell, Richard M. Gabrys, Kinnie S. Smith, Joseph F. Paquette, James E. Brunner, Robert A. Fenech, Thomas W. Elward, Philip R. Lochner, Merribel S. Ayres, Jon E. Barfield, FMR Corp/9.60% *(20 Owners included in Index)*

Financial Data: *Fiscal Year End:*12/31 *Latest Annual Data:* 12/31/2006

Year	Sales	Net Income
2006	$6,899,000,000	-$79,000,000
2005	$6,413,000,000	-$84,000,000
2004	$5,587,000,000	$121,000,000

Curr. Assets:	$3,143,000,000	**Curr. Liab.:**	$2,156,000,000		
Plant, Equip.:	$7,976,000,000	**Total Liab.:**	$12,741,000,000	**Indic. Yr. Divd.:**	NA
Total Assets:	$15,371,000,000	**Net Worth:**	$2,495,000,000	**Debt/ Equity:**	2.6533

CN Bancorp Inc MD

7401 Ritchie Hwy., Glen Burnie, MD, 21061; *PH:* 1-410-760-7000; *http://* www.countynational.com

General - Incorporation	MD	**Stock**- Price on:12/24/2007	NA
Employees	NA	Stock Exchange	NA
Auditor	Rowles & Company, LLP	Ticker Symbol	NA
Stk Agt	American Stock Transfer & Trust Co.	Outstanding Shares	NA
Counsel	NA	E.P.S	NA
DUNS No.	NA	Shareholders	NA

Business: The groups principal activity is to provide banking services. The group products include real estate loans, commercial real estate loans, mobile home loans, home equity lines-of-credit, construction, land loans and accepting deposits. The group operates from the United States.

Primary SIC and add'l.: 6021

CIK No: 0001014273

Subsidiaries: County National Bank

Owners: Robert P. Musselman/8.07%, Jan W. Clark/2.28%, Michael T. Storm, LeRoy C. Taylor, John G. Warner/2.10%, Carl L. Hein/2.98%, Insiders/37.39%, Michael L. Derr, Wade H. Ritchie, Daljit S. Sawhney/2.10%, Gerald V. McDonald/2.47%, Paul F. Dorr, Patricia K. Wellford, Creston G. Tate/11.57%, John E. DeGrange/1.88%

CNA Financial Corp

333 S Wabash, Chicago, IL, 60604; *PH:* 1-312-822-5000; *Fax:* 1-312-822-6419; *http://* www.cna.com

General - Incorporation	DE	**Stock**- Price on:12/24/2007	$50
Employees	9,800	Stock Exchange	NYSE
Auditor	Deloitte & Touche LLP	Ticker Symbol	CNA
Stk Agt	Computershare Trust Co	Outstanding Shares	271,510,000
Counsel	NA	E.P.S	$4.24
DUNS No.	NA	Shareholders	NA

Business: The group operates through its subsidiaries whose principle activity is to provide insurance services. The groups services include property insurances and casualty insurances. The group operates through two segments namely, standard lines and specialty lines. The group operates from the United States. The group's quarterly revenue for September 2007 was 2,484.00 millions of USD.

Primary SIC and add'l.: 6321 6331 6311

CIK No: 0000021175

Subsidiaries: Continental Casualty Company, The Continental Corporation

Officers: Stephen W. Lilienthal/Chmn., CEO, James R. Lewis/Pres., Michael Fusco/Exec. VP, Chief Actuary CNA Insurance Companies, Jonathan D. Kantor/Exec. VP - General Counsel, Sec. CNA Financial Corporation, Craig D. Mense/CFO, Exec. VP, George R. Fay/Exec. VP - Worldwide P, C Claim, John Golden/CIO, Exec. VP, Steve Stonehouse/Pres. - Field Operations West, Naveen Anand/Sr. VP - Commercial Insurance, George Eigel/Contact, Daniel Gentile/Contact, Doug Sampson/Contact, Ben Ridgway/Contact, Tom Nolde/Contact, Linda Dickson/Contact *(22 Officers included in Index)*

Directors: Stephen W. Lilienthal/Chmn., CEO, Brenda J. Gaines/Dir., Paul J. Liska/Dir., Jose Montemayor/Dir., Don M. Randel/Dir., Joseph Rosenberg/Dir., Andrew H. Tisch/Dir., James S. Tisch/Dir., Marvin Zonis/Dir.

Owners: Stephen W. Lilienthal, Michael Fusco, Andrew H. Tisch, James R. Lewis, James S. Tisch, Loews Corporation, Marvin Zonis, Jonathan D. Kantor, Insiders, Joseph Rosenberg, Craig D. Mense

Financial Data: *Fiscal Year End:*12/31 *Latest Annual Data:* 12/31/2006

Year	Sales	Net Income
2006	$10,376,000,000	$1,108,000,000
2005	$9,862,000,000	$264,000,000
2004	$9,936,000,000	$446,000,000

Curr. Assets:	$18,025,000,000	**Curr. Liab.:**	$800,000,000	**P/E Ratio:**	11.79
Plant, Equip.:	$277,000,000	**Total Liab.:**	$50,515,000,000	**Indic. Yr. Divd.:**	$0.400
Total Assets:	$60,283,000,000	**Net Worth:**	$9,768,000,000	**Debt/ Equity:**	0.5000

CNA Surety Corp

333 S Wabash Ave., Chicago, IL, 60604; *PH:* 1-312-822-5000; *Fax:* 1-312-755-3737; *http://* www.cnasurety.com; *Email:* info@cnasurety.com

General - Incorporation	DE	**Stock**- Price on:12/24/2007	$19.57
Employees	736	Stock Exchange	NYSE
Auditor	Deloitte & Touche LLP	Ticker Symbol	NA
Stk Agt	EquiServe Trust Co N.A	Outstanding Shares	43,980,000
Counsel	NA	E.P.S	$2.09
DUNS No.	17-955-8770	Shareholders	NA

Business: The group's principle activity is to offer specialty insurance, which includes small fidelity and non-contract surety bonds. The surety bonds include contract surety and commercial surety bonds. Contract surety bonds secure contractor's performance and payment obligation with respect to the construction project. Commercial surety bonds include all surety bonds other than contract and cover obligations required by law and regulation. Fidelity bonds cover losses arising from employee dishonesty. The purchasers of fidelity bonds are law firms, insurance agencies and janitorial service companies. The group writes surety and fidelity bonds in 60 states through a combined network of approximately 34,000 independent agencies. The group's quarterly revenue for September 2007 was 125.01 millions of USD.

Primary SIC and add'l.: 6351 6719

CIK No: 0001044566

Subsidiaries: Capsure Financial Group, Inc., Capsure Holdings Corp. (f/k/a Nucorp, Inc.)., CNA Surety Corporation, NI Acquisition Corp. ., Nucorp Energy of Oklahoma, Inc., SI Acquisition Corp. ., Surety Bonding Company of America., Surewest Financial Corp. ., Troy Fain Insurance, Inc. , Universal Surety Holding Corp. ., Universal Surety of America., Western Surety Company

Officers: John F. Welch/CEO, Pres./$1,852,643.00, John F. Corcoran/Sr. VP, CFO, Treasurer/$546,689.00, Douglas W. Hinkle/Chief Underwriting Officer/$571,441.00, Michael A. Dougherty/CIO, Sr. VP/$468,011.00, Craig D. Mense/56/Exec. VP, William P. Waters/Sr. VP - Contract Surety, Thomas A. Pottle/Sr. VP, Chief Credit Officer, Enid Tanenhaus/Sr. VP, General Counsel, Sec./$492,493.00, Paul T. Bruflat/VP - Commercial Surety, Walter J. Kubalanza/VP, Chief Claims Officer, Barbara A. Wood/VP, Chief Human Resources Officer, Terry J. Reckamp/VP - Commercial Surety, Anthony S. Cleberg/55/Exec. VP

Directors: James R. Lewis/59/Chmn., Philip H. Britt/61/Dir., Robert A. Tinstman/61/Dir., David B. Edelson/48/Dir.

Owners: Insiders/0.40%, Michael A. Dougherty, Adrian M. Tocklin, Douglas W. Hinkle, Thomas A. Pottle, John F. Corcoran, Philip H. Britt, Roy E. Posner, Continental Casualty Company and Affiliates/62.50%, John F. Welch, Dimensional Fund Advisors LP/6.00%, Enid Tanenhaus

Financial Data: *Fiscal Year End:*12/31 *Latest Annual Data:* 06/30/2007

Year	Sales	Net Income
2007	NA	NA
2006	$431,693,000	$82,818,000
2005	$384,082,000	$38,431,000

Curr. Assets:	$302,054,000	**Curr. Liab.:**	$20,413,000	**P/E Ratio:**	10.09
Plant, Equip.:	$24,807,000	**Total Liab.:**	$802,431,000	**Indic. Yr. Divd.:**	NA
Total Assets:	$1,368,333,000	**Net Worth:**	$565,902,000	**Debt/ Equity:**	0.0522

CNB Bancorp Inc

10-24 N Main St. , Gloversville, NY, 12078; *PH:* 1-518-773-7911

General - Incorporation .... NY
Employees 1,321
Auditor .... KPMG LLP
Stk Agt .... NA
Counsel .... NA
DUNS No. 19-976-0661

Stock- Price on:12/24/2007 .... NA
Stock Exchange .... OTC
Ticker Symbol .... CNBV
Outstanding Shares .... NA
E.P.S .... NA
Shareholders .... NA

Business: The group's principal activity is to provide general banking and fiduciary services. The group is a holding company for city national bank and trust company. The services include checking, negotiable orders of withdrawal, savings and certificates of deposit. The group also offers a range of loan products including commercial, real estate and installment loans and provides overdraft-banking lines of credit. In addition, the group also provides various insurance products to businesses and individuals. The group operates through five branch offices located in the county of fulton and one branch located in the county of saratoga.

Primary SIC and add'l.: 6712 6022

CIK No: 0000839928

Subsidiaries: City National Bank And Trust Company, Cnb Reit Corp, Hathaway Agency, Inc

CNB Corp MI

303 N Main St., Cheboygan, MI, 49721; *PH:* 1-231-627-7111; *http://* www.cnbismybank.com

General - Incorporation .... MI
Employees 75
Auditor .... Plant & Moran, PLLC
Stk Agt .... NA
Counsel .... NA
DUNS No. .... NA

Stock- Price on:12/24/2007 .... $40
Stock Exchange .... OTC
Ticker Symbol .... CNBZ
Outstanding Shares 1,240,000
E.P.S $2.63
Shareholders .... NA

Business: The group's principle activity is to provide insurance serevices. The group's services include accidental, disability and life insurance. The group operates from United States.

Primary SIC and add'l.: 6021

CIK No: 0000779125

Officers: James C. Conboy/Dir., CEO, Pres., Marian L. Harrison/VP - Commercial Loans, Sally J. Lacross/Assist. VP - Data Processing, Cyril S. Drier/Assist. VP, Loan Officer, Paul Fisher/Community Advisor, Lisa Renaud-Lapraírie/Community Advisor, Dean Scheerens/Community Advisor, James E. Tamlyn/Community Advisor, Susan J. Cleary/Loan Officer, Michelle J. Ostwald/Loan Officer, Nancy K. Lindsay/Dir. - Marketing, Community Relations, Christina E. Sweet/Mgr. - Internal Audit, Florence Caswell/Assist. Loan Operations Officer, Matthew J. Kavanaugh/Assist. VP, Indian River Branch Mgr., Susan M. Brandt/Banking Officer, Mackinaw City Branch Mgr. *(28 Officers included in Index)*

Directors: James C. Conboy/Dir., CEO, Pres., Vincent J. Hillesheim/Chmn., Steven J. Baker/Dir., Kathleen M. Darrow/Dir., Thomas J. Ellenberger/Dir., John L. Ormsbee/Dir., Francis J. Van Antwerp/Dir., Jeffery R. Swadling/Dir., Kathleen A. Lieder/Dir., Susan A. Eno/Dir.

Owners: Thomas J. Ellenberger/1.09%, Insiders/7.19%, Francis J. VanAntwerp, Vincent J. Hillesheim, Jeffery R. Swadling, Kathleen A. Lieder, John L. Ormsbee/2.38%, Kathleen M. Darrow, Steven J. Baker, James C. Conboy/1.22%, Dessie M. Ormsbee/6.02%

Financial Data: *Fiscal Year End:*12/31 *Latest Annual Data:* 12/31/2006

Year	Sales	Net Income
2006	$16,995,000	$3,323,000
2005	$15,172,000	$3,288,000
2004	$14,084,000	$2,955,000

Curr. Assets:	$14,812,000	**Curr. Liab.:**	$221,365,000	**P/E Ratio:**	15.21
Plant, Equip.:	$6,626,000	**Total Liab.:**	$226,902,000	**Indic. Yr. Divd.:**	NA
Total Assets:	$251,900,000	**Net Worth:**	$24,998,000	**Debt/ Equity:**	NA

CNB Corp/MI

303 N Main St., Cheboygan, MI, 49721; *PH:* 1-231-627-7111; *Fax:* 1-231-627-7283; *http://* www.cnbcmi.com

General - Incorporation .... MI
Employees 3,729
Auditor .... Crowe Chizek & Co. LLC
Stk Agt .... NA
Counsel .... NA
DUNS No. 78-301-6611

Stock- Price on:12/24/2007 .... NA
Stock Exchange .... NA
Ticker Symbol .... NA
Outstanding Shares .... NA
E.P.S .... NA
Shareholders .... NA

Business: The group's principal activity is to provide banking services to individuals, partnerships, corporations and other entities. Services of the group include checking, now accounts, savings, time deposit accounts, money market deposit accounts, safe deposit lockers and money transfers. The group also provides loan products including real estate mortgages, secured and unsecured commercial and consumer loans, lines of credit, home equity loans and construction financing. It also provides agricultural loans, student loans, credit cards, trust and discount brokerage services, mutual fund, annuity and life insurance products. Services are delivered through five full service banking offices and three drive-in branches plus eight automated teller machines in cheboygan, presque isle and emmet counties, Michigan.

Primary SIC and add'l.: 6021 6712

CIK No: 0000779125

Subsidiaries: Citizens National Bank of Cheboygan, CNB Mortgage Corporation

Owners: John L. Ormsbee/2.38%, Kathleen M. Darrow, Steven J. Baker, Dessie M. Ormsbee/6.00%, Vincent J. Hilleseim, James C. Conboy/1.22%, Francis J. VanAntwerp, Jeffery R. Swadling, Thomas J. Ellenberger/1.09%, Kathleen A. Lieder, Insiders/7.19%

CNB Corp/SC

1400 Third Ave., Conway, SC, 29528; *PH:* 1-843-248-5721; *http://* www.conwaynationalbank.com

General - Incorporation .... SC
Employees 8,713
Auditor .... Elliott Davis LLC
Stk Agt .... NA
Counsel .... NA
DUNS No. 61-273-5837

Stock- Price on:12/24/2007 .... NA
Stock Exchange .... NA
Ticker Symbol .... NA
Outstanding Shares .... NA
E.P.S .... NA
Shareholders .... NA

Business: The group's principal activities are to provide a full range of normal commercial banking functions through eleven branch offices. The services provided include checking, now, savings, money market and various types of deposit accounts. Commercial lending operations include various types of credit provided to individuals for personal use, home mortgages, home improvement, automobiles, agricultural purposes and business needs. In addition, the group offers safe deposit boxes, wire transfer services, bank money orders, 24-hour teller machines on the star network, Internet banking, direct deposits and a mastercard/visa program and also brokerage services through a correspondent relationship. The customers of the group are individuals and small to medium-sized businesses.

Primary SIC and add'l.: 6021 6712

CIK No: 0000764581

Officers: Jennings W. Duncan/52/CEO, Pres./$176,086.00, Virginia B. Hucks/VP, Sec., Ford L. Sanders/CFO, Exec. VP/$207,804.00

Directors: Edward T. Kelaher/53/Dir., George F. Sasser/71/Dir., William R. Benson/55/Dir., Howard B. Smith/Dir., James W. Barnette/63/Dir., Harold G. Cushman/48/Dir., Lynn Gatlin Stevens/48/Dir., William O. Marsh/44/Dir., John C. Thompson/77/Dir.

Owners: John C. Thompson/0.13%, Jennings W. Duncan/7.42%, James W. Barnette, Paul R. Dusenbury/0.15%, Lynn Gatlin Stevens/0.04%, Edward T. Kelaher/0.02%, William O. Marsh/0.16%, Insiders/16.98%, Harold G. Cushman/3.23%, George F. Sasser/0.16%, Harold G. Cushman, Ford L. Sanders, Phil R. Hucks, William R. Benson/4.19%

CNB Financial Corp

1 S 2nd St., Clearfield, PA, 16830; *PH:* 1-814-765-9621; *Fax:* 1-814-765-4511; *http://* www.bankcnb.com

General - Incorporation .... PA
Employees 226
Auditor .... Crowe Chizek & Co. LLC
Stk Agt .... Country National Bank
Counsel .... NA
DUNS No. 11-343-1092

Stock- Price on:12/24/2007 .... $14.18
Stock Exchange .... NDQ
Ticker Symbol .... CCNE
Outstanding Shares 8,860,000
E.P.S $1.05
Shareholders .... NA

Business: The group's principle activity is the provision of banking and related services to individual and corporate customers. As a holding company for the county national bank, the group accepts checking, savings, time and deposit accounts and offers real estate, commercial, industrial, residential and consumer loans and other specialized services. The services include the administration of trusts and estates, retirement plans and other employee benefit plans. Through the county reinsurance company, the group provides accidental death and disability and life insurance as a part of lending relationships of the county national bank. It purchases, holds and manages investments through the other non-banking subsidiary, the cnb investment corporation. The group has 18 full service branch offices, 2 limited service branch facility and 2 loan production offices in Pennsylvania. The market consists of the Pennsylvania counties of clearfield, elk, mckean cambria and cameron.

Primary SIC and add'l.: 6712 6021

CIK No: 0000736772

Subsidiaries: CNB Insurance Agency, CNB Investment Corporation, CNB Securities Corporation, Consumer Loan Company, County National Bank, County Reinsurance Company, Holiday Financial Services Corporation, Incorporated in Arizona, Incorporated in Delaware, Incorporated in Pennsylvania, Insurance & Annuity Agency, Investment Holding Company, National Banking Association, Reinsurance Company

Officers: William F. Falger/Dir., CEO, Pres., Charles R. Guarino/CFO, Treasurer/$111,164.00, Mark D. Breakey/Sr. VP, Credit Risk Mgr. - CNB Bank/$228,977.00, Joseph B. Bower/Dir., Sec., Exec. VP, COO/$313,803.00, Richard L. Sloppy/Sr. VP/$207,300.00, Donald E. Shawley/Sr. VP

Directors: William F. Falger/Dir., CEO, Pres., William R. Owens/Chmn., Robert E. Brown/Dir., James J. Leitzinger/Dir., Charles H. Reams/Dir., Deborah Dick Pontzer/Dir., Michael F. Lezzer/Dir. - CNB Bank, Peter F. Smith/Dir., Jeffrey S. Powell/Dir., Joseph B. Bower/Dir., Sec., Exec. VP, COO, Robert W. Montler/Dir., Dennis L. Merrey/Dir., James B. Ryan/Dir.

Owners: Deborah Dick Pontzer, Peter F. Smith, Charles H. Reams, Joseph B. Bower, Donald E. Shawley, William F. Falger, Robert W. Montler, William R. Owens, James J. Leitzinger, Robert E. Brown, Michael F. Lezzer, Richard L. Sloppy, James B. Ryan, Mark D. Breakey, Jeffrey S. Powell *(16 Owners included in Index)*

Financial Data: *Fiscal Year End:*12/31 *Latest Annual Data:* 06/30/2007

Year	Sales	Net Income
2007	NA	NA
2006	NA	NA
2005	$49,463,000	$9,138,000

Curr. Assets:	$33,106,000	**Curr. Liab.:**	$696,261,000	**P/E Ratio:**	13.90
Plant, Equip.:	$16,237,000	**Total Liab.:**	$708,571,000	**Indic. Yr. Divd.:**	$0.640
Total Assets:	$780,850,000	**Net Worth:**	$72,279,000	**Debt/ Equity:**	0.1685

CNE Group Inc

200 W 57th St., Ste. 507, New York, NY, 10019; *PH:* 1-212-977-2200; *http://* www.cnegroupinc.com

General - Incorporation .... DE
Employees .... NA
Auditor .... Kbl Eisner, LLP
Stk Agt .... David W. Dube
Counsel .... NA
DUNS No. .... NA

Stock- Price on:12/24/2007 .... $0.08
Stock Exchange .... NA
Ticker Symbol .... NA
Outstanding Shares 649,540,000
E.P.S .... -$0.01
Shareholders .... NA

Business: The group's principal activity is e-recruiting business through its subsidiary careerengine network, inc. The divisions of the group, careerengine network and careerengine solutions, provide on and off-line companies with products and services addressed to meeting on-line recruiting problems. The group operates 6 portal career sites organized by specific job function and diversity. These sites enable employers and recruiters to post job offerings for specific target areas in one or more of our career specific sites.

Primary SIC and add'l.: 6719 7375 7361

CIK No: 0000795255

Subsidiaries: Arrow Resources Development, Ltd, CareerEngine, Inc.

Financial Data: **Fiscal Year End:** 12/31 **Latest Annual Data:** 12/31/2006

Year	Sales	Net Income
2006	NA	-$3,514,000
2005	NA	-$1,272,000
2004	$2,676,000	-$2,334,000

Curr. Assets:	NA	**Curr. Liab.:**	$5,562,000		
Plant, Equip.:	NA	**Total Liab.:**	$5,562,000	**Indic. Yr. Divd.:**	NA
Total Assets:	$125,000,000	**Net Worth:**	$119,438,000	**Debt/ Equity:**	NA

CNET Networks Inc

235 Second St., San Francisco, CA, 94105; ***PH:*** 1-415-344-2000; ***http://*** www.cnetnetworks.com; ***Email:*** sales@cnet.com

General		**Stock**	
Incorporation	DE	Price on:12/24/2007	$8.59
Employees	2,620	Stock Exchange	NDQ
Auditor	KPMG LLP	Ticker Symbol	CNET
Stk Agt	Computershare Investor Services LLC	Outstanding Shares	151,220,000
Counsel	NA	E.P.S	-$0.14
DUNS No.	80-853-9506	Shareholders	NA

Business: The group's principal activity is to offer products and services providing a platform for advertisers to create brand awareness and sell products to tech-savvy audience. The group operates through three segments: U.S. Media, international media and channel services. U.s. Media consists of an online network, Internet sites providing sources of technology information, shopping services and a technology print publication providing technology news and information. International media includes the delivery of online technology information and several technology print publications in non-U.S. Markets. Channel services includes a product database licensing business and an online technology marketplace for distributors and manufacturers. It operates in the United States, Australia, France, Germany, Singapore, Switzerland and the United Kingdom. On 19-Mar-2004, the group acquired edventure holdings, wgr media on 01-Apr-2004 and twofold photos inc on 02-Aug-2004.

Primary SIC and add'l.: 7812 7375 7319

CIK No: 0001015577

Subsidiaries: A Delaware company, Channel Services S.A., Chuanmei Information Technology (Shanghai) Co. Ltd., Chuanmei Information Technology (Shanghai) Co., Ltd., CNET Investments Inc., CNET Korea Inc., CNET Marketplaces Inc., CNET Networks (France) SAS, CNET Networks Asia Pacific Pte Ltd, CNET Networks Australia Pty Ltd., CNET Networks Deutschland GmbH, CNET Networks Japan KK, CNET Networks Korea Inc., CNET Networks UK Limited, CNET Subsidiary BC Inc. 23 Subsidiaries included in the Index

Officers: Jack Haire/Advisor, Zander Lurie/Sr. VP - Strategy, Development, Jose Martin/Sr. VP - Human Resources, Mickey Mcclay Wilson/Sr. VP - Communications, Brand Development, Joseph Gillespie/Exec. VP - Cnet/$1,029,339.00, Sam Parker/Sr. VP - Network, Neil Ashe/Dir., CFO, Exec. VP/$1,850,887.00, George Mazzotta/CFO/$1,152,385.00, Greg Mason/Sr. VP - Buisness Media, Channel, Adam Power/Pres. - International Media, Andy Sherman/Sr. VP, General Counsel, Corp. Sec.

Directors: Eric Robison/Dir., Betsey Nelson/Dir., John Colligan/Dir., Peter Currie/Dir., Jarl Mohn/Dir., Susanne Lyons/Dir., Mark Rosenthal/Dir.

Owners: Shelby W. Bonnie/6.96%, Mark Rosenthal, Susanne D. Lyons, John C. Colligan, Betsey Nelson, Mazama Capital Management/6.60%, Jarl Mohn, Insiders/8.07%, Eric P. Robison, Barry D. Briggs, Neil M. Ashe, Peter L.S. Currie, Legg Mason Capital Management, Inc./8.79%, Capital Research and Management Company/12.04%, T. Rowe Price Associates, Inc./14.57% *(17 Owners included in Index)*

Financial Data: **Fiscal Year End:** 12/31 **Latest Annual Data:** 12/31/2006

Year	Sales	Net Income
2006	$387,376,000	$6,836,000
2005	$354,209,000	$19,583,000
2004	$291,156,000	$11,685,000

Curr. Assets:	$161,476,000	**Curr. Liab.:**	$164,240,000		
Plant, Equip.:	$72,625,000	**Total Liab.:**	$169,464,000	**Indic. Yr. Divd.:**	NA
Total Assets:	$433,807,000	**Net Worth:**	$264,343,000	**Debt/ Equity:**	0.0188

CNH Global

100 S Saunders Rd., Ste. 200, Lake Forest, IL, 60045; ***PH:*** 1-847-955-4930; ***Fax:*** 1-847-955-3969; ***http://*** www.cnh.com; ***Email:*** wwinvestorrelations@cnh.com

General		**Stock**	
Incorporation	Netherlands	Price on:12/24/2007	$50.49
Employees	25,300	Stock Exchange	NYSE
Auditor	Deloitte & Touche LLP	Ticker Symbol	CNH
Stk Agt	JP Morgan Chase Bank, N.A.	Outstanding Shares	236,600,000
Counsel	NA	E.P.S	$2.02
DUNS No.	40-682-4169	Shareholders	NA

Business: The group's principal activities are the engineering and manufacturing of agricultural equipment such as tractors and combines, as well as construction equipment and machinery. The group operates through three segments: agricultural equipment, construction equipment and financial services. The agricultural equipment segment manufactures and distributes a full line of farm machinery and implements. The construction equipment segment manufactures and distributes a full line of construction equipment such as excavators, crawler dozers, graders, wheel loaders, loader, backhoes, skid steer loaders and trenchers. The financial services segment provides financing facilities to its dealers and end-users. The group products are sold under the brand names: new Holland, case, case ih, fiatallis, fiat-hitachi, o&k, steyr, fermec and link-belt. The group has operations in North America, Europe and Brazil.

Primary SIC and add'l.: 6159 3523 3531

CIK No: 0001024519

Subsidiaries: Al-Ghazi Tractors Ltd., Austoft Industries Ltd., Banco CNH Capital S.A. (), BLI Group, Inc., Blue Leaf I.P., Inc., Brahma Steyr Tractors Limited, Case Brazil Holdings, Inc., Case Canada Receivables, Inc., Case Credit Australia Investments Pty Ltd, Case Credit Holdings Limited, Case Credit Wholesale Pty Ltd, Case Equipment Holdings Limited, Case Equipment International Corporation, Case Europe S.a.r.l., Case Harvesting Systems GmbH 113 Subsidiaries included in the Index

Officers: Harold D. Boyanovsky/64/Dir., CEO, Pres., Randal Wayne Baker/CEO - Case IH Agricultural Equipment Inc, Ugo De Carolis/Pres. - CNH Parts, Service, Roberto Pucci/Sr. VP - Human Resources, Rubin J. McDougal/CFO, Roberto Miotto/Sr. VP, General Counsel, Sec., James E. McCullough/Pres. - Case Construction Equipment, Loris Spaltini/Sr. VP - Strategic Sourcing, Al Trefts/Sr. Dir. - Investor Relations, Capital Markets, Gualberto Ranieri/VP - Communications, Lorenzo Sistino/Pres. - New Holland Agricultural Equipment, Carlo De Bernardi/VP - Internal Audit, Georg Richartz/Sr. VP - Supply Chain, Logistics, Franco Fenoglio/Pres. - New Holland Construction Equipment, Steven Bierman/Pres. - CNH Capital

Directors: Harold D. Boyanovsky/64/Dir., CEO, Pres., Sergio Marchionne/56/Chmn., Leo W. Houle/61/Dir., Rolf M. Jeker/62/Dir., Peter Kalantzis/63/Dir., Ferruccio Luppi/58/Dir., John Lanaway/58/Dir., Jacques Theurillat/49/Dir., Edward A. Hiler/69/Dir., Kenneth Lipper/67/Dir., Paolo Monferino/62/Dir.

Financial Data: **Fiscal Year End:** 12/31 **Latest Annual Data:** 12/31/2006

Year	Sales	Net Income
2006	$12,998,000,000	$292,000,000
2005	$12,575,000,000	$163,000,000
2004	$12,179,000,000	$125,000,000

Curr. Assets:	$8,784,000,000	**Curr. Liab.:**	$6,440,000,000	**P/E Ratio:**	31.00
Plant, Equip.:	$1,632,000,000	**Total Liab.:**	$13,154,000,000	**Indic. Yr. Divd.:**	$0.250
Total Assets:	$18,274,000,000	**Net Worth:**	$5,120,000,000	**Debt/ Equity:**	NA

CNOOC Ltd

65th Fl., Bank Of China Tower, One Garden Rd., Central; ***PH:*** 86-1084521646; ***http://*** www.cnoocltd.com; ***Email:*** xiaozw@cnooc.com.cn

General		**Stock**	
Incorporation	Hong Kong	Price on:12/24/2007	$114.56
Employees	2,929	Stock Exchange	NYSE
Auditor	Ernst & Young LLP	Ticker Symbol	CEO
Stk Agt	Fuji Bank Ltd	Outstanding Shares	433,290,000
Counsel	NA	E.P.S	$9.26
DUNS No.	NA	Shareholders	NA

Business: The group's principal activities are exploration, development, and production of crude oil and natural gas. The group is involved in the petroleum industry's upstream operating activities comprising of production sharing contracts with foreign partners and independent operations.

Primary SIC and add'l.: 5983 1311

CIK No: 0001095595

Subsidiaries: China Offshore Oil Bohai Corporation, CNOOC Africa Limited, CNOOC Belgium BVBA, CNOOC Canada Limited, CNOOC China Limited, CNOOC Finance Corporation Limited, CNOOC International Limited, CNOOC Southeast Asia

Officers: Fu Chengyu/Chmn., CEO, Guangqi Wu/Exec. Dir., Compliance Officer, Wu Guangqi/Compliance Officer, Exec. Dir., Zhou Shouwei/Exec. Dir., Pres., Guohua Zhang/48/Sr. VP, GM - Cnooc China Limited Shanghai Branch, Wei Chen/50/Sr. VP, General Dir., Bi Chen/47/VP, GM - Cnooc China Limited Tianjin Branch, Xin Kang/34/Company Sec., Hua Yang/Exec. Dir., CFO, Exec. VP, Jian Liu/50/Exec. VP, Shouwei Zhou/58/Dir., Pres., Zhang Guohua/Sr. VP, Chen Wei/Sr. VP, Weilin Zhu/VP, GM - Exploration Department, Mingcai Zhu/52/VP, Pres. - Cnooc International Limited *(22 Officers included in Index)*

Directors: Fu Chengyu/Chmn., CEO, Edgar W.K. Cheng/Dir., Guangqi Wu/Exec. Dir., Compliance Officer, Luo Han/Non - Exec. Dir., Chiu Sung Hong/Dir., Aloysius Tse Hau Yin/Dir., Xinghe Cao/Non - Exec. Dir., Zhenfang Wu/56/Non - Exec. Dir., Erwin Schurtenberger/Member - Advisory Board, Shouwei Zhou/58/Dir., Pres., Cao Xinghe/Non - Exec. Dir., Sung Hong Chiu/61/Dir., Lawrence J. Lau/Dir., Wu Zhenfang/Non - Exec. Dir., Zhou Shouwei/Exec. Dir., Pres. *(20 Directors included in Index)*

Owners: CNOOC/66.41%

Financial Data: **Fiscal Year End:** 12/31 **Latest Annual Data:** 12/31/2006

Year	Sales	Net Income
2006	$11,403,042,000	$3,987,480,000
2005	$8,612,512,000	$3,142,552,000
2004	$6,681,870,000	$1,957,356,000

Curr. Assets:	$6,139,764,000	**Curr. Liab.:**	$1,856,513,000	**P/E Ratio:**	31.00
Plant, Equip.:	$13,294,717,000	**Total Liab.:**	$6,098,704,000	**Indic. Yr. Divd.:**	$3.350
Total Assets:	$19,943,379,000	**Net Worth:**	$13,844,675,000	**Debt/ Equity:**	NA

CNS Inc

PO Box 39802, Minneapolis, MN, 55439; ***PH:*** 1-612-820-6696; ***http://*** www.cns.com

General		**Stock**	
Incorporation	DE	Price on:12/24/2007	NA
Employees	58	Stock Exchange	NA
Auditor	KPMG LLP	Ticker Symbol	NA
Stk Agt	Wells Fargo Shareowner Services	Outstanding Shares	NA
Counsel	Lindquist & Vennum PLLP	E.P.S	NA
DUNS No.	10-225-4000	Shareholders	NA

Business: The group's principal activity is to develop and market consumer health care products for better breathing and digestive health. The products include breathe right (R), flair(R) and fiberchoice(R) brands. The breathe right nasal strip improves breathing by reducing nasal airflow resistance and is sold with vicks (R), licensed from procter and gamble. The fiberchoice product is a chewable fiber tablet that offers a supplement for a dietary fiber intake. The flair equine nasal strip that enables horses to breathe more easily during strenuous exercise. The products are sold in chain stores such as wal-Mart, kmart, eckerd, walgreens, riteaid, cvs, and albertson's and warehouse clubs such as sam's club and costco. The group has distributors in Japan, United Kingdom, Italy, Netherlands and Canada.

Primary SIC and add'l.: 3842

CIK No: 0000814258

Owners: Morris J. Siegel, GlaxoSmithKline plc/7.30%, Samuel Reinkensmeyer, Robert H. Hawthorne, Royce & Associates, LLC/6.00%, Larry Muma, Insiders/10.90%, Andrew J. Greenshields, John J. Keppeler, Karen T. Beckwith, Patrick Delaney, Daniel E. Cohen/2.40%, Barclays Global Investors, N.A./5.20%, Linda Kollofski, Richard W. Perkins *(16 Owners included in Index)*

CNX Gas Corp

5 Penn Ctr. W, Ste. 401, Pittsburgh, PA, 15276; ***PH:*** 1-412-200-6730; ***Fax:*** 1-412-200-6761; ***http://*** www.cnxgas.com

General - Incorporation	DE	**Stock**- Price on:12/24/2007	$30.2
Employees	192	Stock Exchange	NYSE
Auditor	PricewaterhouseCoopers LLP	Ticker Symbol	CXG
Stk Agt	National City Bank	Outstanding Shares	150,870,000
Counsel	Buchanan Ingersoll PC	E.P.S.	$0.95
DUNS No.	NA	Shareholders	NA

Business: The groups principle activities include exploring, developing, producing and gathering of natural gas. The group also develops coalbed methane. The group operates through two segments namely Central Appalachia and Northern Appalachia. The group's quarterly revenue for September 2007 was 109.81 millions of USD.

Primary SIC and add'l.: 4925

CIK No: 0001335793

Subsidiaries: Buchanan Generation, LLC, Cardinal States Gathering Company, CNX Gas Company LLC, Coalfield Pipeline Company, Knox Energy, LLC

Officers: Nicholas J. Deluliis/39/Dir., CEO, Pres./$2,195,427.00, Ronald E. Smith/59/COO, Exec. VP/$2,169,988.00, Mark D. Gibbons/49/Sr. VP, CFO, Stephen W. Johnson/49/Exec. VP, General Counsel/$708,574.00, Roland J. Campanelli/VP - Marketing, Daniel J. Zajdel/Dir. - Investor, Public Relations, Gary J. Bench/49/Sr. VP, CFO/$702,900.00, Randall M. /Sr. VP - Emerging Business Units, Deann Craig/Sr. VP - Asset Assessment, Michael J. Onifer/Sr. VP - Established Business Units

Directors: Nicholas J. Deluliis/39/Dir., CEO, Pres., Philip W. Baxter/Chmn., James E. Altmeyer/Dir., Raj K. Gupta/Dir., Brett J. Harvey/Dir., William J. Lyons/Dir., John R. Pipski/Dir., Joseph T. Williams/Dir.

Owners: Philip W. Baxter, Joseph T. Williams, Brett J. Harvey, Gary J. Bench, Insiders, James E. Altmeyer, William J. Lyons, Nicholas J. Deluliis, Stephen W. Johnson, Raj K. Gupta, John R. Pipski, Consolidation Coal Company/81.50%, Ronald E. Smith

Financial Data: *Fiscal Year End:*12/31 *Latest Annual Data:* 12/31/2006

Year	Sales	Net Income
2006	$513,859,000	$159,867,000
2005	$613,441,000	$102,168,000

Curr. Assets:	$172,736,000	**Curr. Liab.:**	$56,912,000	**P/E Ratio:**	31.13
Plant, Equip.:	$918,162,000	**Total Liab.:**	$274,786,000	**Indic. Yr. Divd.:**	NA
Total Assets:	$1,155,001,000	**Net Worth:**	$880,215,000	**Debt/ Equity:**	0.0794

Coach Inc

516 W 34th St., New York, NY, 10001; ***PH:*** 1-212-594-1850; ***Fax:*** 1-212-594-1682; ***http://*** www.coach.com

General - Incorporation	MD	**Stock**- Price on:12/24/2007	$48.63
Employees	2,300	Stock Exchange	NYSE
Auditor	Deloitte & Touche LLP	Ticker Symbol	COH
Stk Agt	Mellon Investor Services LLC	Outstanding Shares	371,130,000
Counsel	NA	E.P.S.	$1.83
DUNS No.	NA	Shareholders	NA

Business: The groups principle activity is to design and market handbags and accessories. The groups product includes womens and mens accessories, footwear, outerwear, business cases, sunwear, watches and travel bags. The group operates from United States.

Primary SIC and add'l.: 5948 2519 3172 3144 3873 3171 3151

CIK No: 0001116132

Subsidiaries: 504-514 West 34th Street Corp, Coach Europe Services S.r.l., Coach International Holdings, Inc., Coach International Limited, Coach Japan Holdings, Inc1, Coach Japan Investments, Inc, Coach Japan, Inc., Coach Leatherware International, Inc, Coach Manufacturing Limited, Coach Services, Inc., Coach Stores Canada Inc, Coach Stores Puerto Rico, Inc.

Officers: Lew Frankfort/Chmn., CEO/$9,865,503.00, Michael Tucci/Pres. - Retail Division, North America/$5,093,334.00, Felice Schulaner/Sr. VP - Human Resources, Carole Sadler/Sr. VP, General Counsel, Sec., Reed Krakoff/Exec. Dir., Pres. - Creative/$17,965,220.00, Keith Monda/COO, Pres./$5,407,439.00, Michael Devine/CFO, Sr. VP/$3,172,074.00, Melanie Hughes/Sr. VP - Human Resources

Directors: Lew Frankfort/Chmn., CEO, Gary Loveman/Dir., Irene Miller/Dir., Joseph Ellis/Dir., Ivan Menezes/Dir., Michael Murphy/Dir., Susan Kropf/Dir., Jide Zeitlin/Dir.

Owners: Ivan Menezes, Jide Zeitlin, Michael Murphy, Insiders/3.64%, Michael Tucci, Lew Frankfort/2.05%, Michael F. Devine, Irene Miller, Susan Kropf, Gary Loveman, Prudential Financial, Inc./5.86%, Keith Monda, Reed Krakoff

Financial Data: *Fiscal Year End:*07/02 *Latest Annual Data:* 06/30/2007

Year	Sales	Net Income
2007	$2,612,456,000	$663,665,000
2006	$2,111,501,000	$494,277,000
2005	$1,710,423,000	$388,652,000

Curr. Assets:	$705,616,000	**Curr. Liab.:**	$181,938,000	**P/E Ratio:**	29.65
Plant, Equip.:	$148,524,000	**Total Liab.:**	$206,174,000	**Indic. Yr. Divd.:**	NA
Total Assets:	$1,028,658,000	**Net Worth:**	$782,286,000	**Debt/ Equity:**	0.0016

Coach Industries Group Inc

12330 SW 53rd St., Ste. 704, Cooper City, FL, 33330; ***PH:*** 1-954-602-1400; ***Fax:*** 1-954-680-7943; ***http://*** www.cigi.cc; ***Email:*** info@cigi.cc

General - Incorporation	NV	**Stock**- Price on:12/24/2007	NA
Employees	60	Stock Exchange	OTC
Auditor	Jewett, Schwartz, & Assoc.	Ticker Symbol	CIGI
Stk Agt	Madison Stock Transfer, Inc.	Outstanding Shares	NA
Counsel	NA	E.P.S.	-$0.235
DUNS No.	NA	Shareholders	NA

Business: The group's principal activity is to manufacture and sell limousines, primarily for the livery industry which modify and custom fabricate stock vehicles that are manufactured by automotive manufacturers.

Primary SIC and add'l.: 7319 7375

CIK No: 0000791115

Subsidiaries: Coach Financial Services, Inc., Commercial Transportation Manufacturing Corporation, Corporate Development Services, Inc., FleetPlan Daily Rental, Inc, FleetPlan LT, FleetPlan OT, SCI Two-Wheel, Inc., Springfield Coach Industries Corporation, Inc, Subcontracting Concepts, Inc.

Financial Data: *Fiscal Year End:*12/31 *Latest Annual Data:* 12/31/2005

Year	Sales	Net Income
2005	$256,166,000	-$5,013,000
2004	$83,596,000	-$6,503,000
2003	$1,068,000	-$1,743,000

Curr. Assets:	$8,188,000	**Curr. Liab.:**	$8,726,000		
Plant, Equip.:	$2,231,000	**Total Liab.:**	$17,337,000	**Indic. Yr. Divd.:**	NA
Total Assets:	$23,084,000	**Net Worth:**	$5,747,000	**Debt/ Equity:**	NA

Coachmen Industries Inc

2831 Dexter Dr., Elkhart, IN, 46514; ***PH:*** 1-574-262-0123; ***Fax:*** 1-574-262-8823; ***http://*** www.coachmen.com

General - Incorporation	IN	**Stock**- Price on:12/24/2007	$9.98
Employees	2,655	Stock Exchange	NYSE
Auditor	Ernst & Young LLP	Ticker Symbol	COA
Stk Agt	National City Bank	Outstanding Shares	15,730,000
Counsel	McDermott Will & Emery	E.P.S.	-$3.54
DUNS No.	00-543-3081	Shareholders	NA

Business: The group's principal activity is to produce recreational vehicles and manufacture modular housing and building. The group operates in two segments. The recreational vehicle segment manufactures and distributes class a and class c motorhomes, travel trailers, fifth wheel, camping trailers, truck campers and related parts and supplies. The housing and buildings segment manufactures and distributes factory-built modules for homes, commercial building and telecommunication shelters. The group operates solely in the United States. Major brands include coachmen, georgie boy, shasta, viking somerset, chaparral, rendezvous and others.

Primary SIC and add'l.: 5561 3714 3716

CIK No: 0000021212

Subsidiaries: All American Building Systems, LLC, All American Homes of Colorado, LLC, All American Homes of Florida, LLC, All American Homes of Indiana, LLC, All American Homes of Iowa, LLC, All American Homes of Kansas, LLC, All American Homes of North Carolina, LLC, All American Homes of Ohio, LLC, All American Homes of Tennessee, LLC, All American Homes, LLC, Carp Construction Management Services, LLC, COA Finance Company, LTD, COA Financial Services, Inc., Coachmen Administrative Services, Inc., Coachmen Industries of California, Inc. 44 Subsidiaries included in the Index

Officers: Richard M. Lavers/CEO/$397,634.00, Colleen A. Zuhl/CFO/$151,129.00, Michael R. Terlep/Pres. - Coachmen Recreational Vehicle Group/$329,348.00, Rick J. Bedell/Pres. - Housing Group, Todd Woelfer/General Counsel, Les G. Thimlar/53/VP - Human Resources

Directors: William P. Johnson/Chmn., Donald W. Hudler/Dir., Robert J. Deputy/Dir., Edwin W. Miller/Dir., Geoffrey B. Bloom/Dir., John A. Goebel/Dir.

Owners: First Pacific Advisors, Inc./14.50%, R. M. Lavers, M. R. Terlep, C. A. Zuhl, R. J. Bedell, G. B. Bloom, Dimensional Fund Advisors, Inc./8.50%, Third Avenue Management LLC/9.70%, P. G. Lux, Donald Smith & Co., Inc./9.80%, J. A. Goebel, D. W. Hudler, L. G.. Thimlar, Insiders/2.70%, W. P. Johnson *(17 Owners included in Index)*

Financial Data: *Fiscal Year End:*12/31 *Latest Annual Data:* 12/31/2006

Year	Sales	Net Income
2006	$564,382,000	-$31,805,000
2005	$702,425,000	-$26,350,000
2004	$865,144,000	$15,334,000

Curr. Assets:	$129,433,000	**Curr. Liab.:**	$66,649,000		
Plant, Equip.:	$57,018,000	**Total Liab.:**	$82,803,000	**Indic. Yr. Divd.:**	$0.120
Total Assets:	$243,134,000	**Net Worth:**	$160,331,000	**Debt/ Equity:**	0.0255

CoActive Marketing Group Inc

75 Ninth Ave., New York, NY, 10011; ***PH:*** 1-212-660-3800; ***Fax:*** 1-212-660-3878; ***http://*** www.coactivemarketing.com; ***Email:*** inquiries@coactivemarketing.com

General - Incorporation	DE	**Stock**- Price on:12/24/2007	$2.51
Employees	235	Stock Exchange	NDQ
Auditor	BDO Seidman LLP	Ticker Symbol	CMKG
Stk Agt	American Stock Transfer & Trust Co.	Outstanding Shares	7,470,000
Counsel	Kronish, Lieb, Weiner & Hellman	E.P.S.	-$0.01
DUNS No.	83-569-5453	Shareholders	NA

Business: The group's principle activities are to design, develop and implement turnkey customized national, regional and local consumer and trade promotion programs. These services are provided to Fortune 600 consumer product companies. The group's marketing and sales promotional services consist of strategic marketing, creative services, broadcast and print media, direct marketing, multi cultural marketing, event marketing, entertainment marketing, in-store sampling and merchandising. It also provides Internet Web site designing and hosting, e-commerce tools, electronic sales tools and computer based training. The principal customers of the group include the procter & gamble company, diageo North America inc, nabisco foods, hillshire farm & kahn's, inc., general motors, starkist seafood company, hewlett-packard company and schieffelin & somerset co. The group's total revenue for year 2007 was 95.88 millions of USD.

Primary SIC and add'l.: 7319

CIK No: 0000886475

Subsidiaries: Bars.com LLC, Digital Intelligence Group LLC, Grupo Hacerlo LLC, Inmark Services LLC, Optimum Group LLC, U.S. Concepts LLC

Officers: Charlie Tarzian/Dir., CEO, Pres./$302,087.00, Paul Amershadian/Dir., Exec. VP - Marketing, Sales, Treasurer/$320,355.00, Susan Murphy/47/Interim CFO, Denise Felitti/44/VP, Controller, Jennifer R. Calabrese/VP, Controller

Directors: Charlie Tarzian/Dir., CEO, Pres., Marc C. Particelli/Chmn., John Ward/Dir., Herbert M. Gardner/Dir., Brian Murphy/48/Dir., John A. Ward/Dir., Paul Amershadian/Dir., Exec. VP - Marketing, Sales, Treasurer, James Feeney/Dir.

Owners: Marc C. Particelli/3.00%, Susan Murphy, Thomas E. Lachenman/6.20%, Charles F. Tarzian/2.80%, Donald A. Bernard/7.90%, James H. Feeney, Rutabaga Capital Management/9.90%, Brian Murphy/9.40%, Herbert M. Gardner/3.80%, Insiders/21.70%, John A. Ward/2.50%, John P. Benfield/8.10%

Financial Data: *Fiscal Year End:*03/31 *Latest Annual Data:* 03/31/2007

Year	Sales	Net Income
2007	$95,880,000	$996,000
2006	$96,941,000	-$1,802,000
2005	$83,951,000	$1,152,000

Curr. Assets:	$24,210,000	**Curr. Liab.:**	$30,800,000	**P/E Ratio:**	17.93
Plant, Equip.:	$4,064,000	**Total Liab.:**	$33,414,000	**Indic. Yr. Divd.:**	NA
Total Assets:	$42,713,000	**Net Worth:**	$8,576,000	**Debt/ Equity:**	NA

Coast Bancorp

500 Marsh St., San Luis Obispo, CA, 93401; ***PH:*** 1-805-541-0400; ***Fax:*** 1-805-541-5758; ***http://*** www.coastnationalbank.com; ***Email:*** sba@coastnationalbank.com

General		**Stock**	
Incorporation	CA	Price on:12/24/2007	$29.9
Employees	70	Stock Exchange	OTC
Auditor	Vavrinek, Trine, Day & Co. LLP	Ticker Symbol	CTBP
Stk Agt	U.S. Stock Transfer Corp	Outstanding Shares	NA
Counsel	NA	E.P.S	$1.77
DUNS No.	NA	Shareholders	NA

Business: The group's principal activity is the provision of loans to small and middle-Market businesses and individuals through its wholly owned subsidiary coast national bank. The services of the group include deposit and savings products, loans for consumers and homeowners as well as local businesses. The group's lending activities include commercial, consumer, real estate and construction loans. The group operates four branches in san luis obispo, arroyo grande, morro bay, and los osos, California.

Primary SIC and add'l.: 6022 6712

CIK No: 0001141575

Subsidiaries: Coast National Bank

Officers: Jack C. Wauchope/Chmn., CEO - Coast National Bank/$243,882.00, James M. Kaney/Dir. - Coast National Bank, Gene D. Mintz/Dir. - Coast National Bank, Jack W. Robasciotti/Dir. - Coast National Bank, Dan H. Wixom/Dir. - Coast National Bank, Ronald R. Olson/Dir. - Coast National Bank, Marilyn M. Britton/Dir. - Coast National Bank, Michael A. Lady/Dir. - Coast National Bank, Davina Palazzo/Exec. VP - Small Business Lending/$165,423.00, Patrick Durkin/VP, Business Developement Officer, Sandy Leyva/Sr. VP, Dir. - Human Resources - Coast National Bank

Directors: Dario A. Domenghini/Dir. - Coast National Bank

Owners: Insiders/20.19%, Davina A. Palazzo/1.10%, Michael A. Lady/0.97%, Jack W. Robasciotti/1.11%, Dan H. Wixom/2.54%, Gene D. Mintz/4.15%, Leah M. Pauly/0.95%, James M. Kaney/1.22%, Ronald R. Olson/2.48%, Marilyn M. Britton/0.54%, Jack C. Wauchope/5.12%, Dario A. Domenghini/1.66%, Karan C. Pohl/0.29%

Financial Data: ***Fiscal Year End:***12/31 ***Latest Annual Data:*** 12/31/2006

Year	Sales	Net Income
2006	$14,743,000	$1,374,000
2005	$11,478,000	$1,098,000
2004	$9,707,000	$1,115,000

Curr. Assets:	$26,540,000	**Curr. Liab.:**	$162,530,000	**P/E Ratio:**	15.49
Plant, Equip.:	$9,740,000	**Total Liab.:**	$168,027,000	**Indic. Yr. Divd.:**	$0.200
Total Assets:	$180,739,000	**Net Worth:**	$12,711,000	**Debt/ Equity:**	0.3965

Coast Distribution System Inc

350 Woodview Ave., Morgan Hill, CA, 95037; ***PH:*** 1-408-782-6686; ***Fax:*** 1-408-782-7790; ***http://*** www.coastdistribution.com; ***Email:*** customerservice@coastdist.com

General		**Stock**	
Incorporation	DE	Price on:12/24/2007	$6.55
Employees	410	Stock Exchange	AMEX
Auditor	Burr, Pilger & Mayer, LLP	Ticker Symbol	CRV
Stk Agt	U.S. Stock Transfer Corp	Outstanding Shares	4,420,000
Counsel	NA	E.P.S	-$0.061
DUNS No.	09-261-8651	Shareholders	NA

Business: The group's principal activities are to supply replacement parts, supplies and accessories for recreational vehicles and boats. The products distributed by the group include awnings, antennae, vents, electrical items, towing equipment and appliances such as air conditioners, refrigerators, ranges and generators, lp gas equipment, portable toilets and plumbing parts, hardware and tools, specialized recreational vehicle housewares and chemicals. The group also distributes ladders, jacks, fans, load stabilizers, mirrors and compressors. As of 31-Dec-2003, the group supplied around 25,000 products and served more than 15,000 customers throughout the United States and Canada. The group operates through 13 regional distribution centers in the United States located in various parts of the United States and 4 distribution centers in Canada. The customers of the group include recreational vehicles and boat dealers, parts and supply stores and service centers.

Primary SIC and add'l.: 5013

CIK No: 0000728303

Subsidiaries: The Coast Distribution System (Canada) Inc, United Sales and Warehouse of Texas, Inc

Officers: Thomas R. McGuire/Chmn., CEO/$409,125.00, Sandra A. Knell/CFO, Exec. VP - Finance/$255,375.00, Dennis A. Castagnola/Exec. VP - Product Development/$219,597.00, David A. Berger/Exec. VP - Operations/$192,858.00, Jim Musbach/COO, Pres./$66,104.00, Stephan Lussier/Pres. - Coast Distribution System, Canada, Inc

Directors: Thomas R. McGuire/Chmn., CEO, Ben A. Frydman/Dir., Robert S. Throop/Dir., Leonard P. Danna/Dir., John W. Casey/Dir.

Owners: Leonard P. Danna, Dennis A. Castagnola/1.70%, James Musbach, David A. Berger/1.30%, Thomas R. McGuire/11.30%, Dimensional Fund Advisors/8.30%, Sandra A. Knell/3.40%, JB Capital Partners, L.P./6.70%, Robert S. Throop, Lone Star RV Sales, Inc./5.70%, Robert E. Robotti/7.10%, Insiders/19.30%, Ben A. Frydman, John W. Casey

Financial Data: ***Fiscal Year End:***12/31 ***Latest Annual Data:*** 12/31/2006

Year	Sales	Net Income
2006	$179,103,000	$2,973,000
2005	$176,341,000	$3,757,000
2004	$171,833,000	$4,406,000

Curr. Assets:	$65,789,000	**Curr. Liab.:**	$13,085,000	**P/E Ratio:**	24.26
Plant, Equip.:	$2,461,000	**Total Liab.:**	$37,647,000	**Indic. Yr. Divd.:**	$0.280
Total Assets:	$69,494,000	**Net Worth:**	$31,847,000	**Debt/ Equity:**	0.7645

Coast Financial Holdings Inc

1301 6th Ave. W, Ste. 300, Bradenton, FL, 34205; ***PH:*** 1-941-752-5900; ***Fax:*** 1-941-748-9199; ***http://*** www.coastbankflorida.com

General		**Stock**	
Incorporation	FL	Price on:12/24/2007	$3.68
Employees	226	Stock Exchange	NDQ
Auditor	Hacker, Johnson & Smith P.A, P.C	Ticker Symbol	CFHI
Stk Agt	Registrar & Transfer Co	Outstanding Shares	6,510,000
Counsel	Carlton Fields, P.A	E.P.S	-$5.746
DUNS No.	NA	Shareholders	NA

Business: The group's principal activity is to provide consumer, commercial banking services to individuals and businesses located in manatee and sarasota counties, Florida. Through its subsidiary, coast bank, the group accepts deposits from the general public and uses those deposits, together with borrowings and other funds, to originate a variety of residential real estate loans, commercial real estate and business loans and consumer loans and to purchase investments. In addition, mortgage banking department originates, closes and services fixed and adjustable rate permanenterally to be sold in the secondary mortgage market. Coast bank has established a subsidiary, coast financial partners, inc., to provide asset and investment management services, insurance products and retirement planning for its customers.

Primary SIC and add'l.: 6022 6712

CIK No: 0001262276

Subsidiaries: Coast Bank of Florida

Officers: Anne V. Lee/Dir., CEO, COO, Acting Pres., Gail Clem/AVP - Commercial Loan Processor, Coast Bank, Florida, George Allen/AVP, Consumer Lending Loan Officer - Coast Bank, Florida, Jan Caro/VP, Training Mgr., IRA Administrator - Coast Bank, Florida, Paul Nidasio/Exec. VP, Chief Credit Officer - Coast Bank, Florida, Denis Durnan/Sr. VP, Dir. - Information Technology, Coast Bank, Florida, April Whitaker/VP, Commercial Lending Loan Operations Mgr. - Coast Bank, Florida, Shirley Walker/VP, Branch Mgr. II - Tuttle Branch, Coast Bank, Florida, Angela Velardi/VP - Business Development, Coast Bank, Florida, Ann Marie Ditoro/VP, Branch Mgr. - Northwood Branch, Coast Bank, Florida, Crystal Doyle/VP, Branch Mgr. - Seminole Branch, Coast Bank, Florida, Sharon Dropp/VP, Branch Mgr. - Dunedin Branch, Coast Bank, Florida, Sandra Goldberg/VP, Branch Mgr. - Lutz Branch, Coast Bank, Florida, Sherry Harris/VP, Branch Mgr. II - Village Green Branch, Coast Bank, Florida, Ben Kleyla/VP, Branch Mgr. - Walsingham Branch, Coast Bank, Florida *(48 Officers included in Index)*

Directors: Anne V. Lee/Dir., CEO, COO, Acting Pres., James K. Toomey/Chmn., Michael T. Ruffino/Vice Chmn., Thomas M. O'Brien/Dir., John R. Reinemeyer/Dir., Brian F. Grimes/Dir., Joseph Gigliotti/Dir., Paul G. Nobbs/Dir., Kennedy Legler/Dir., Alex M. White/Dir.

Owners: Thomas M. OBrien, James V. Dugger, Insiders/9.90%, Kennedy Legler, Paul Nidasio, Alex M. White, Brian F. Grimes, Joseph Gigliotti/1.00%, Anne V. Lee, QVT Financial LP/5.30%, James K. Toomey/5.40%, John R. Reinemeyer, Oz Management, LLC/Daniel S. Och/8.90%, St. Denis J. Villere & Company L.L.C./16.70%, Private Capital Management, LP/7.30% *(18 Owners included in Index)*

Financial Data: ***Fiscal Year End:***12/31 ***Latest Annual Data:*** 12/31/2006

Year	Sales	Net Income
2006	$41,686,000	-$17,280,000
2005	$27,780,000	-$615,000
2004	$20,441,000	$831,000

Curr. Assets:	$18,456,000	**Curr. Liab.:**	$645,572,000		
Plant, Equip.:	$27,598,000	**Total Liab.:**	$662,493,000	**Indic. Yr. Divd.:**	NA
Total Assets:	$719,669,000	**Net Worth:**	$57,176,000	**Debt/ Equity:**	0.2436

Coastal Banking Co Inc

36 Sea Island Pkwy., Beaufort, SC, 29901; ***PH:*** 1-843-522-1228; ***Fax:*** 1-843-524-4510; ***http://*** www.coastalbanking.com; ***Email:*** contact@coastalbanking.com

General		**Stock**	
Incorporation	SC	Price on:12/24/2007	$19.94
Employees	70	Stock Exchange	OTC
Auditor	Mauldin & Jenkins, LLC	Ticker Symbol	CBCO
Stk Agt	First Citizens Bank & Trust Co	Outstanding Shares	2,420,000
Counsel	Nelson Mullins Riley & Scarborough	E.P.S	$1.36
DUNS No.	NA	Shareholders	NA

Business: The group's principal activity is to provide banking services to individuals and small to medium sized businesses in beaufort county, South Carolina. The group's lending activities include consumer loans, commercial loans, equipment loans, home equity loans, small business loans and real estate loans. The group's deposit activities include checking accounts, commercial accounts, savings accounts and other time deposit accounts. The other services provided by the group include ATMs, safe deposit boxes, traveler's checks, direct deposit, U.S. Savings bonds, banking by mail and Internet banking.

Primary SIC and add'l.: 6021 6712

CIK No: 0001093897

Subsidiaries: Coastal Banking Trust I, First National Bank of Nassau County, Lowcountry National Bank

Officers: Randolph C. Kohn/Dir., CEO, Pres./$295,622.00, William Gary Horn/59/Sr. Management, James L. Pate/56/CFO/$164,912.00, Leo Deas/63/Sr. Management

Directors: Randolph C. Kohn/Dir., CEO, Pres., Suellen Rodeffer Garner/52/Chmn., Dennis O. Green/68/Vice Chmn., Ladson F. Howell/65/Vice Chmn., James W. Holden/49/Dir., Michael G. Sanchez/59/Dir., Ron Anderson/64/Dir., Christina H. Bryan/63/Dir., James C. Key/69/Dir., Robert L. Peters/46/Dir., Robert B. Pinkerton/Dir., Edward E. Wilson/57/Dir., Marshall Wood/Dir.

Owners: Dennis O. Green/2.41%, James C. Key/0.98%, James W. Holden/1.46%, Ron Anderson/1.29%, Randolph C. Kohn/3.51%, Robert B. Pinkerton/1.88%, Michael G. Sanchez/2.03%, Robert L. Peters/1.16%, Edward E. Wilson/1.56%, Christina H. Bryan/1.75%, Ladson F. Howell/0.91%, Insiders/20.79%, Total Directors/20.37%, James L. Pate, Suellen Rodeffer Garner/2.76%

Financial Data: ***Fiscal Year End:***12/31 ***Latest Annual Data:*** 12/31/2006

Year	Sales	Net Income
2006	$28,785,000	$3,360,000
2005	$13,067,000	$1,509,000
2004	$7,721,000	$1,111,000

Curr. Assets:	$25,671,000	**Curr. Liab.:**	$342,059,000	**P/E Ratio:**	14.66
Plant, Equip.:	$7,384,000	**Total Liab.:**	$383,039,000	**Indic. Yr. Divd.:**	NA
Total Assets:	$426,210,000	**Net Worth:**	$43,171,000	**Debt/ Equity:**	0.7296

Coastal Caribbean Oils & Minerals Ltd

Clarendon House, Church St, Hamilton 5, Hamilton; ; ***http://*** www.coastalcarib.com; ***Email:*** coastalcarib@mybizz.net

General - Incorporation	Bermuda
Employees	NA
Auditor	James Moore & Co
Stk Agt	Island Stock Transfer
Counsel	Igler & Dougherty
DUNS No.	NA

Stock- Price on:12/24/2007	$0.101
Stock Exchange	OTC
Ticker Symbol	COCBF
Outstanding Shares	NA
E.P.S.	-$0.28
Shareholders	NA

Business: The groups principle activity is to provide exploration of oil, gas and minerals. The groups products include non-producing oil, gas and mineral properties. The group operates from United States.

Primary SIC and add'l.: 1311 1382

CIK No: 0000021239

Subsidiaries: Coastal Petroleum

Officers: Phillip W. Ware/Dir., CEO, Pres., Principal Financial Officer, Robert J. Angerer/Dir., VP, Sec., I. S. Outerbridge/Assist. Sec.

Directors: Phillip W. Ware/Dir., CEO, Pres., Principal Financial Officer, Robert J. Angerer/Dir., VP, Sec., Herbert D. Haughton/Dir., Matthew D. Cannon/Dir., Anthony F. Randazzo/Dir.

Owners: Herbert D. Haughton/0.21%, Anthony F. Randazzo/0.32%, Matthew D. Canon/0.33%, Robert J. Angerer/4.58%, Phillip W. Ware/1.09%, Insiders/6.55%

Financial Data: *Fiscal Year End:*12/31 *Latest Annual Data:* 12/31/2006

Year	Sales	Net Income
2006	$41,000	-$1,621,000
2005	$8,175,000	$6,766,000
2004	$0	-$673,000

Curr. Assets:	$372,000	Curr. Liab.:	$5,000		
Plant, Equip.:	$11,000	Total Liab.:	$5,000	Indic. Yr. Divd.:	NA
Total Assets:	$2,709,000	Net Worth:	$2,704,000	Debt/ Equity:	NA

Coastal Financial Corp

2619 N Oak, Myrtle Beach, SC, 29577; *PH:* 1-843-205-2000; *http://* www.coastalfederal.com

General - Incorporation	DE
Employees	NA
Auditor	KPMG LLP
Stk Agt	Registrar & Transfer Co
Counsel	Muldoon Murphy & Aguggia LLP
DUNS No.	07-370-8240

Stock- Price on:12/24/2007	NA
Stock Exchange	NDQ
Ticker Symbol	CFCP
Outstanding Shares	NA
E.P.S.	NA
Shareholders	NA

Business: The group's principal activity is to accept deposits from the general public and to use these funds to originate various types of loans. The deposits services provided include now checking accounts, money market accounts, regular statement savings and passbook accounts, certificates of deposit and retirement savings plans. The lending activity consists of conventional one-to-four family first mortgage loans, consumer, commercial business loans and commercial real estate loans. It operates through its wholly owned subsidiary, coastal federal savings bank. The operations of the group are conducted through eighteen branch offices in North Carolina and South Carolina.

Primary SIC and add'l.: 6712 6035

CIK No: 0000935930

Subsidiaries: Coastal Federal Bank, Coastal Federal Holding Corporation, Coastal Financial Capital Trust I, Coastal Investor Services, Inc., Coastal Mortgage Bankers and Realty Co., Inc., Coastal Planners Holding Corporation, Coastal Real Estate Investment Corporation, Coastal Retirement Estate and Tax Planners, Inc., Sherwood Development Corporation

Owners: William O. Marsh/0.03%, David G. Bishop/3.59%, Steven J. Sherry/0.85%, Robert J. Calliham/0.07%, Insiders/21.36%, Frank A. Thompson/0.22%, Michael C. Gerald/2.65%, James H. Dusenbury/0.42%, Cecil W. Worsley, James P. Creel/5.21%, Lawton E. Benton/2.81%, Phillip G. Stalvey/1.42%, James T. Clemmons/2.14%, Jimmy R. Graham/1.94%, Jerry L. Rexroad/1.44%

Coastport Capital Inc

3rd Fl., 157 Alexander St., Ste. 501, Vancouver, BC, V6C 2X4; *PH:* 1-604-684-0561; *http://* www.coastportcapital.com; *Email:* info@coastportcapital.com

General - Incorporation	AB
Employees	NA
Auditor	G. Ross Mcdonald
Stk Agt	Pacific Corporate Trust Co
Counsel	NA
DUNS No.	NA

Stock- Price on:12/24/2007	NA
Stock Exchange	NA
Ticker Symbol	NA
Outstanding Shares	NA
E.P.S.	NA
Shareholders	NA

Business: The group's principal activity is capital pooling. The company hopes to hit the mother lode in its new line of business. The capital pool company acquired an interest in a Nicaraguan mining exploration project in 2004. Still in its early stages of development, the San Ramon project will additionally involve operating as a joint venture with Radius Gold Inc. It is believed to contain several major gold quartz veins.

Primary SIC and add'l.: 1040

CIK No: 0001316458

Officers: David Patterson/Pres., Harvey Keats/Technical Advisor, Brent Cook/Special Advisor, Robin Adair/VP - Exploration

Directors: Leonard C. Dennis/Dir., Marc A. Prefontaine/Dir., Laurie W. Sadler/Dir., Mario Szotlender/Dir.

Cobalis Corp

2445 McCabe Way, Ste. 150, Irvine, CA, 92614; *PH:* 1-949-757-0001; *Fax:* 1-949-757-0979; *http://* www.cobalis.com

General - Incorporation	NV
Employees	6
Auditor	Pricewaterhousecoopers LLP
Stk Agt	The Nevada Agency and Trust CO.
Counsel	NA
DUNS No.	NA

Stock- Price on:12/24/2007	$0.37
Stock Exchange	OTC
Ticker Symbol	CLSCE
Outstanding Shares	35,820,000
E.P.S.	-$0.42
Shareholders	NA

Business: The group's principal activity is to develop and commercialise medical products, primarily related to allergic diseases. The major product of the group is prehistin (TM). The group owns the patent for this product.

Primary SIC and add'l.: 2833

CIK No: 0001166414

Subsidiaries: Tykes Acquisition Corp.

Officers: Gerald Yakatan/Dir., CEO, James M. Brodsky/Member - Advisory Board, Pharmd, ND Staff, USC School, Pharmacy, VP - Research - Development, Kevin Pickard/CFO - Interim, Steven Hecht/Cobalis Investor Relations Contact, Anita M. Kirkpatrick/Member - Advisory Board, Certified Specialist - Immunology, Richard E. Danziger/Member - Advisory Board, MD - PhD Board Certified, Allergy, Immunology, Stanley Goldstein/Member - Advisory Board, MD Board Certified - Allergy, Immunology, Charles Jay Siegel/Member - Advisory Board, MD Board Certified - Allergy, Immunology, Bo Cosic/VP - Corporate Administration, Lawrence A. May/Dir., MD, Chairperson - Medical Advisory Boad, Michael J. Noonan/Member - Advisory Board, MD Board Certified - Allergy, Immunology, Chaslav Radovich/Dir., Pres., Lewis Joseph Kanter/Member - Advisory Board, MD Board Certified - Allergy, Immunology, Alvin J. Aubry/Member - Advisory Board, MD Board Certified - Allergy, Immunology, Joseph T. Morgan/Member - Advisory Board, MD Board Certified - Pediatrics *(17 Officers included in Index)*

Directors: Gerald Yakatan/Dir., CEO, Kevin J. Prendiville/Dir., Thomas Stankovich/Dir., Radul Radovich/Dir., Richard E. Danziger/Member - Advisory Board, MD - PhD Board Certified, Allergy, Immunology, Stanley Goldstein/Member - Advisory Board, MD Board Certified - Allergy, Immunology, Charles Jay Siegel/Member - Advisory Board, MD Board Certified - Allergy, Immunology, James M. Brodsky/Member - Advisory Board, Pharmd, ND Staff, USC School, Pharmacy, VP - Research - Development, Lawrence A. May/Dir., MD, Chairperson - Medical Advisory Boad, Michael J. Noonan/Member - Advisory Board, MD Board Certified - Allergy, Immunology, Lyndon E. Mansfield/Member - Medical Advisor Board, Chaslav Radovich/Dir., Pres., Lewis Joseph Kanter/Member - Advisory Board, MD Board Certified - Allergy, Immunology, Alvin J. Aubry/Member - Advisory Board, MD Board Certified - Allergy, Immunology, Joseph T. Morgan/Member - Advisory Board, MD Board Certified - Pediatrics *(19 Directors included in Index)*

Owners: Chaslav Radovich/2.90%, Radul Radovich/25.00%, R & R Development/0.40%, Gene Pharmaceuticals/3.60%, St. Petka Trust/18.40%, Gerald Yakatan/1.50%, Insiders/35.60%, Silver Mountain Promotions/2.10%, Kevin Pickard/0.30%, James Hammer/9.30%, Thomas Stankovich/1.20%, Kevin Prendiville/1.30%, R and R Holdings/1.00%, Ernest Armstrong/0.60%

Financial Data: *Fiscal Year End:*03/31 *Latest Annual Data:* 03/31/2007

Year	Sales	Net Income
2007	NA	-$15,711,000
2006	NA	-$6,603,000
2005	$0	-$8,101,000

Curr. Assets:	$531,000	Curr. Liab.:	$8,718,000		
Plant, Equip.:	$8,000	Total Liab.:	$8,865,000	Indic. Yr. Divd.:	NA
Total Assets:	$1,181,000	Net Worth:	-$8,570,000	Debt/ Equity:	NA

Cobiz Financial Inc

Formerly: CoBiz Inc
821 - 17th St., Ste. 900, Denver, CO, 80202; *PH:* 1-303-293-2265; *https://* www.cobizinc.com

General - Incorporation	CO
Employees	485
Auditor	Deloitte & Touche LLP
Stk Agt	Corporate Stock Transfer, Inc.
Counsel	NA
DUNS No.	10-256-4572

Stock- Price on:12/24/2007	$18.14
Stock Exchange	NDQ
Ticker Symbol	COBZ
Outstanding Shares	23,870,000
E.P.S.	$0.96
Shareholders	NA

Business: The group's principle activity is to provide banking products and services in the denver metropolitan area. American business bank na is a wholly-owned subsidiary of the group which is a full-service business banking institution with nine Colorado locations. The bank provides credit, treasury management, investment, deposit and trust products, as well as employee benefits consulting, insurance brokerage and investment banking services. It accepts certificates of deposit, savings accounts, money market accounts, checking and negotiable order of withdrawal accounts and individual retirement accounts. Lending activity includes the origination of commercial and residential real estate construction loans.

Primary SIC and add'l.: 6022 6712

CIK No: 0001028734

Subsidiaries: CoBiz ACMG, Inc., CoBiz Bank, N.A, CoBiz GMB, Inc., CoBiz Insurance, Inc., Colorado Business Leasing, Inc., Financial Designs, Ltd., Newco Subsidiary LLC

Officers: Steven Bangert/Chmn., CEO/$821,771.00, Richard J. Dalton/Pres./$494,793.00, Lyne B. Andrich/CFO, Exec. VP/$380,313.00, Robert B. Ostertag/47/Exec. VP, Chief Credit Officer/$406,764.00, Gerald W. Chapman/Dir., Independent Consultant, Troy R. Dumlao/VP, Controller

Directors: Steven Bangert/Chmn., CEO, Jonathan C. Lorenz/Vice Chmn., Harold F. Mosanko/Dir., Howard R. Ross/Dir., Noel N. Rothman/Dir., Timothy J. Travis/Dir., Mary White/Dir., Mary Beth Vitale/Dir., Michael B. Burgamy/Dir., Gerald W. Chapman/Dir., Independent Consultant, Evan Makovsky/Dir., Jerry W. Chapman/Dir., Morgan Gust/Dir., Thomas M. Longust/Dir.

Owners: Steven Bangert/5.93%, Thomas M. Longust, Evan Makovsky, Jerry W. Chapman, Estate of Howard R. Ross/5.25%, Noel N. Rothman/6.40%, Mary Beth Vitale, Richard J. Dalton/1.15%, Michael B. Burgamy/1.23%, Morgan Gust, Timothy J. Travis, Jonathan C. Lorenz/1.85%, Insiders/18.93%, Harold F. Mosanko, Mary M. White *(17 Owners included in Index)*

Financial Data: *Fiscal Year End:*12/31 *Latest Annual Data:* 12/31/2006

Year	Sales	Net Income
2006	$166,409,000	$22,826,000
2005	$128,609,000	$20,006,000
2004	$105,068,000	$17,626,000

Curr. Assets:	$48,723,000	Curr. Liab.:	$1,877,582,000		
Plant, Equip.:	$9,033,000	Total Liab.:	$1,949,748,000	Indic. Yr. Divd.:	$0.280
Total Assets:	$2,112,423,000	Net Worth:	$162,675,000	Debt/ Equity:	0.3799

Cobra Electronics Corp

6500 W Cortland St., Chicago, IL, 60707; *PH:* 1-773-889-8870; *Fax:* 1-773-794-1930; *http://* www.cobra.com

General - Incorporation	DE
Employees	181
Auditor	Grant Thornton LLP
Stk Agt	American Stock Transfer & Trust Co.
Counsel	Sidley, Austin, Brown & Wood
DUNS No.	00-506-8986

Stock- Price on:12/24/2007	$9.58
Stock Exchange	NDQ
Ticker Symbol	COBR
Outstanding Shares	6,450,000
E.P.S.	$0.16
Shareholders	NA

Business: The group's principal activities are manufacturing and marketing of two-way mobile communications products. The group's products are citizens band radios, radar detectors, family radio service, two-way radio. The group also includes microtalk frs, gmrs two-way radios, 9 band tm, 10 band tm, 11 band(TM) detectors, highgear(TM) accessories, safety alert transmitters and receivers. The group's products are distributed through network of 300 retailers and distributors located in the United States. The group also market directly through consumer electronics stores, large department store; warehouse clubs, office supply chains, television home-shopping, direct-response merchandisers, home centers and specialty stores. The group's products are purchased from China, Thailand, Hong Kong and South Korea. The group's products are marketed under the cobra brand name in the United States, Canada and Europe.

Primary SIC and add'l.: 5065

CIK No: 0000030828

Subsidiaries: Cobra Electronics Europe Limited, Cobra Electronics Hong Kong Limited

Officers: James R. Bazet/Dir., CEO, Pres./$980,007.00, Anthony A. Mirabelli/Sr. VP - Marketing, Sales/$350,693.00, Gerald M. Laures/VP - Finance, Corp. Sec./$276,943.00, Michael Smith/Sr. VP, CFO/$403,193.00

Directors: James R. Bazet/Dir., CEO, Pres., Carl Korn/Chmn., Robert P. Rohleder/Dir., Ian R. Miller/Dir., William P. Carmichael/Dir., John Lupo/Dir., Sam S. Park/Dir.

Owners: James R. Bazet/5.90%, Robert P. Rohleder, Howson Tattersall Investment Counsel Ltd./7.50%, Eliot Rose Asset Management, LLC/8.00%, William P. Carmichael, Gerald M. Laures/1.20%, Trusco Capital Management, Inc./7.70%, Michael Smith/2.30%, Anthony A. Mirabelli, Insiders/14.10%, Dimensional Fund Advisors Inc./6.10%, Carl Korn/4.10%, Ian R. Miller

Financial Data: **Fiscal Year End:** 12/31 **Latest Annual Data:** 12/31/2006

Year	Sales	Net Income
2006	$153,695,000	-$1,630,000
2005	$133,084,000	$11,984,000
2004	$122,877,000	$2,381,000

Curr. Assets:	$73,243,000	**Curr. Liab.:**	$19,101,000		
Plant, Equip.:	$7,625,000	**Total Liab.:**	$46,985,000	**Indic. Yr. Divd.:**	$0.160
Total Assets:	$116,758,000	**Net Worth:**	$69,769,000	**Debt/ Equity:**	0.2217

Coca-Cola Bottling Co Consolidated

4100 Coca-Cola Plz., Charlotte, NC, 28211; *PH:* 1-704-557-4400; *Fax:* 1-704-551-4646; *http://* www.cokebottling.com; *Email:* investor.relations@ccbcc.com

General -		**Stock** -	
Incorporation	DE	Price on:12/24/2007	$52.07
Employees	5,700	Stock Exchange	NDQ
Auditor	PricewaterhouseCoopers LLP	Ticker Symbol	COKE
Stk Agt	American Stock Transfer & Trust CO.	Outstanding Shares	9,120,000
Counsel	Kennedy Covington Lobdell & Hickman	E.P.S	$3.15
DUNS No.	05-793-1230	Shareholders	NA

Business: The group's principle activity is to produce, market and distribute carbonated and non-carbonated beverages, primarily products of the coca-cola company. The products include carbonated soft drinks, teas, juices, isotonics and bottled water. The group's principal soft drink is coca-cola classic. The products include coca-cola classic, caffeine free coca-cola classic, diet coke, caffeine free diet coke, cherry coke, diet cherry coke, tab, sprite, diet sprite, surge, citra, mello, yello, diet mello yello, minute maid orange etc. The group's soft drink products are sold and distributed directly by the employees to retail stores and other outlets, including food markets, institutional accounts and vending machine outlets. The group also distributes and markets under noncarbonated beverage contracts products such as powerade, dasani and minute maid juices. The group's quarterly revenue for September 2007 was 367.36 millions of USD.

Primary SIC and add'l.: 2086

CIK No: 0000317540

Subsidiaries: Beverage Plus, LLC, CCBC of Wilmington, Inc., CCBCC Operations, LLC, CCBCC Vending, LLC, CCBCC, Inc., Chesapeake Treatment Company, LLC, Coca-Cola Ventures, Inc., Consolidated Beverage Co., Consolidated Real Estate Group, LLC, Data Ventures, LLC, Heath Oil Co., Inc., Piedmont Coca-Cola Bottling Partnership, RVBC, Inc., Tennessee Soft Drink Production Company, TXN, Inc.

Officers: Frank J. Harrison/Chmn., CEO - Coca, Cola Bottling Co Consolidated/$5,011,852.00, Lauren C. Steele/VP - Corporate Affairs, Steven D. Westphal/Sr. VP, CFO/$773,906.00, Jolanta T. Zwirek/CIO, Sr. VP, Kevin A. Henry/Sr. VP - Human Resources, Clifford M. Deal/VP, Treasurer, Umesh M. Kasbekar/Sr. VP - Planning, Administration, William B. Elmore/Dir., Pres., COO - Coca, Cola Bottling Co Consolidated/$1,999,722.00, William J. Billiard/VP, Controller, Chief Accounting Officer, C. Ray Mayhall/Sr. VP - Sales

Directors: Frank J. Harrison/Chmn., CEO - Coca, Cola Bottling Co Consolidated, Henry W. Flint/Vice Chmn. - Coca, Cola Bottling Co Consolidated, James E. Harris/Dir., Dennis A. Wicker/Dir., Sharon A. Decker/Dir., William B. Elmore/Dir., Pres., COO - Coca, Cola Bottling Co Consolidated, H. W. McKay Belk/Dir., Ned R. McWherter/Dir., Deborah S. Harrison/Dir., Carl Ware/Dir., John W. Murrey/Dir.

Owners: H.W. McKay Belk, William B. Elmore, Coca-Cola Enterprises Inc., The Coca-Cola Company, Insiders, Ned R. McWherter, Frank J. Harrison, John W. Murrey

Financial Data: **Fiscal Year End:** 01/01 **Latest Annual Data:** 12/31/2006

Year	Sales	Net Income
2006	$1,431,005,000	$23,243,000
2005	$1,256,482,000	$21,848,000

Curr. Assets:	$247,142,000	**Curr. Liab.:**	$248,942,000	**P/E Ratio:**	16.69
Plant, Equip.:	$454,315,000	**Total Liab.:**	$1,224,512,000	**Indic. Yr. Divd.:**	$1.000
Total Assets:	$1,364,467,000	**Net Worth:**	$93,953,000	**Debt/ Equity:**	7.0941

Coca-Cola Co

One Coca Cola Plz., Atlanta, GA, 30313; *PH:* 1-404-676-2121; *http://* www.cocacola.com

General -		**Stock** -	
Incorporation	DE	Price on:12/24/2007	$51.76
Employees	71,000	Stock Exchange	NYSE
Auditor	Ernst & Young LLP	Ticker Symbol	KO
Stk Agt	EquiServe Trust Co N.A	Outstanding Shares	2,310,000,000
Counsel	NA	E.P.S	$2.25
DUNS No.	00-329-6175	Shareholders	NA

Business: The groups principle activities include producing, marketing and distributing non-alcoholic beverages. The group also provides soft drinks, bottled water sports drinks and energy products. The group operates from United States, Europe, eurasia, Middle East, Africa, Latin America and Asia.

Primary SIC and add'l.: 2033 2086 2087

CIK No: 0000021344

Subsidiaries: 55th& 5th Avenue Corporation, ACCBC Holding Company, Aiftz 2004, Atlantic Industries, Barlan,Inc., Barq's,Inc., Beverage Brands, S.R.L., Beverage Products,Ltd., Beverage ServicesLtd., Bottling Investments Corporation, Caribbean International Sales Corporation,Inc., Caribbean Refrescos,Inc., Carolina Coca-Cola Bottling Investments,Inc., CCDA Waters LLC, CCHBC GroupingInc. 91 Subsidiaries included in the Index

Officers: Neville E. Isdell/Chmn., CEO, Steve K.W. Chan/Chmn. - Coca, Cola China Limited, Paul K. Etchells/Deputy Group Pres. - Pacific Group, Ahmet C. Bozer/Pres., Chief Operationg Officer - Eurasia Group, Dan Sayre/Pres. - Japan Business Unit, Jean-Michel R. Ares/CIO, Sr. VP, Carol Crofoot Hayes/Corp. Sec., Ingrid Saunders Jones/Dir. - Corporate External Affairs, Sr. VP, Connie D. McDaniel/VP, Controller, Kandy Anand/Deputy Division Pres. - Philippines Business Unit, Michael Holm Johansen/Pres. - Central, Southern Europe Business Unit, Eduardo Romo/Dir. - Communications, Dan A. Schafer/VP - Public Affairs, Communications, Brian J. Smith/Presiden, Brazil Business Unit, Xiemar Zarazua/Pres. - Latin Center Business Unit *(52 Officers included in Index)*

Directors: Neville E. Isdell/Chmn., CEO, Masahiko Uotani/Chmn. - Coca, Cola Japan Company, Ltd, CCJC, James B. Williams/Dir., Herbert A. Allen/Dir., Peter V. Ueberroth/Dir., Ronald W. Allen/Dir., Cathleen P. Black/Dir., Barry Diller/Dir., Donald R. Keough/Dir., Donald F. McHenry/Dir., Sam Nunn/Dir., James D. Robinson/Dir.

Owners: Muhtar Kent, James D. Robinson, Berkshire Hathaway Inc./8.62%, Mary E. Minnick, Insiders/5.37%, Gary P. Fayard, Herbert A. Allen, Cathleen P. Black, Peter V. Ueberroth, Sam Nunn, Donald R. Keough, Donald F. McHenry, James B. Williams/4.45%, Ronald W. Allen, Jos Octavio Reyes *(17 Owners included in Index)*

Financial Data: **Fiscal Year End:** 12/31 **Latest Annual Data:** 12/31/2006

Year	Sales	Net Income
2006	$24,088,000,000	$5,080,000,000
2005	$23,104,000,000	$4,872,000,000
2004	$21,962,000,000	$4,847,000,000

Curr. Assets:	$8,441,000,000	**Curr. Liab.:**	$8,890,000,000	**P/E Ratio:**	23.11
Plant, Equip.:	$6,903,000,000	**Total Liab.:**	$12,685,000,000	**Indic. Yr. Divd.:**	$1.360
Total Assets:	$29,963,000,000	**Net Worth:**	$16,920,000,000	**Debt/ Equity:**	0.0844

Coca-Cola Enterprises Inc

2500 Windy Ridge Pkwy., Atlanta, GA, 30339; *PH:* 1-770-989-3000; *Fax:* 1-770-989-3788; *http://* www.cokecce.com; *Email:* ccemail@na.cokecce.com

General -		**Stock** -	
Incorporation	DE	Price on:12/24/2007	$23.48
Employees	74,000	Stock Exchange	NYSE
Auditor	Ernst & Young LLP	Ticker Symbol	CCE
Stk Agt	American Stock Transfer & Trust Co.	Outstanding Shares	480,940,000
Counsel	NA	E.P.S	-$2.54
DUNS No.	11-826-7624	Shareholders	NA

Business: The groups principle activities include selling, manufacturing, and distributing non-alcoholic beverages. The groups products include Diet Coke, Sprite, Dasani and Powerade. The group operates from United States and Canada.

Primary SIC and add'l.: 2086

CIK No: 0000804055

Subsidiaries: 3072009 Nova Scotia Limited, Alabama Coca-Cola Bottling Company, Alexandria Coca-Cola Bottling Company, Amalgamated Beverages Great Britain Ltd. (ABGB), Atlanta Ice Makers, Atlantic Coca-Cola Bottling, Atlantic Coca-Cola Bottling (Embouteillage Coca-Cola Atlantique), Austin Coca-Cola Bottling Company, BCI Coca-Cola Bottling Company of Bellingham, BCI Coca-Cola Bottling Company of Los Angeles (BCI), Beaumont Coca-Cola Bottling Company, BHI Finance LLC(BHI Finance), Big Bend Coca-Cola Bottling Company, Bluegrass Coca-Cola Bottling Company, Bottling Enterprises Management 320 Subsidiaries included in the Index

Officers: John F. Brock/59/Dir., CEO, Pres./$5,751,121.00, Esat Sezer/CIO, Sr. VP, Joseph D. Heinrich/VP, Controller, Chief Accounting Officer, Timothy W. Johnson/VP - Labor, Employee Relations, David M. Katz/VP - Customer Supply Chain, Joyce King-Lavinder/VP, Treasurer, Charles D. Lischer/39/VP, Controller, Chief Accounting Officer, Daniel J. Markle/VP - US Field Sales Operations, Lynn H. Oliver/VP - Tax, Suzanne D. Patterson/VP - Internal Audit, John B. Phillips/VP, Deputy General Counsel, William T. Plybon/VP, Sec., Deputy General Counsel, Terri L. Purcell/VP, Deputy General Counsel, Assist. Sec., Mark W. Schortman/VP - North American Sales, Edward L. Sutter/VP - Supply Chain *(25 Officers included in Index)*

Directors: John F. Brock/59/Dir., CEO, Pres., Lowry F. Kline/67/Chmn., Phillip L. Humann/62/Dir., Summerfield K. Johnston/54/Dir., Calvin Darden/58/Dir., Donna A. James/50/Dir., James E. Copeland/63/Dir., Trevor J. Eyton/Dir., Thomas H. Johnson/58/Dir., Curtis R. Welling/58/Dir., Irial Finan/50/Dir., Paula R. Reynolds/Dir., Marvin J. Herb/70/Dir., Gary P. Fayard/55/Dir., Fernando Aguirre/50/Dir.

Owners: Fernando Aguirre, Insiders/5.57%, Irial Finan, William W. Douglas, Gary P. Fayard, John J. Culhane, Paula R. Reynolds, Trevor J. Eyton, James E. Copeland, Summerfield K. Johnston, Terrance M. Marks, Calvin Darden, Donna A. James, Shaun B. Higgins, John F. Brock *(19 Owners included in Index)*

Financial Data: **Fiscal Year End:** 12/31 **Latest Annual Data:** 12/31/2006

Year	Sales	Net Income
2006	$19,804,000,000	-$1,143,000,000
2005	$18,706,000,000	$514,000,000
2004	$18,158,000,000	$596,000,000

Curr. Assets:	$3,691,000,000	**Curr. Liab.:**	$3,818,000,000		
Plant, Equip.:	$6,698,000,000	**Total Liab.:**	$18,699,000,000	**Indic. Yr. Divd.:**	$0.240
Total Assets:	$23,225,000,000	**Net Worth:**	$4,526,000,000	**Debt/ Equity:**	2.0720

Coca-Cola FEMSA

Guillermo Gonzalez Camarena No. 600, Centro De Ciudad Santa Fe, Delegacion Alvaro Ob, 1210; *PH:* 52-55335300; *http://* www.coca-colafemsa.com; *Email:* krelations@kof.com.mx

General -		**Stock** -	
Incorporation	Mexico	Price on:12/24/2007	$43.93
Employees	56,682	Stock Exchange	NYSE
Auditor	Galaz, Yamazaki, Ruiz Urquiza, S.C	Ticker Symbol	KOF
Stk Agt	Computershare Trust Co	Outstanding Shares	184,650,000
Counsel	Cleary Gottlieb Steen & Hamilton	E.P.S	$3.05
DUNS No.	82-194-8064	Shareholders	NA

Business: The group's principal activity is the production, distribution and marketing of certain Coca-Cola trademark beverages in Mexico, Central America (Guatemala, Nicaragua, Costa Rica and Panama), Colombia, Venezuela, Brazil and Argentina. Other activity includes the acquisition, holding and transferring of all types of bonds, capital stock, shares and marketable securities. Brandnames include Coca-Cola, Sprite, Fanta, Coke Light, Sprite Light, Extra Poma, Etiqueta Azul, Schweppes, Tai, Crush, Kin and Hi-C. On 06-May-2003, the group acquired the outstanding stock of Panamerican Beverages Inc.

Primary SIC and add'l.: 2086

CIK No: 0000910631

Subsidiaries: Administracin y Asesora Integral, S.A. de C.V, Corporacin Interamericana de Bebidas, S.A. de C.V, Kristine Oversease, S.A. de C.V. (holding company of Brazilianoperations), Panamco Bajo, S.A. de C.V, Panamco Mxico, S.A. de C.V, Propimex, S.A. de C.V

Officers: Carlos Salazar Lomelin/57/Dir., CEO, Jose Antonio Fernandez Carbajal/54/Chmn., CEO - Femsa, Ernesto Silva Almaguer/55/COO - Mercosur, Hector Trevino Gutierrez/52/CFO, Administrative Officer, Javier Astaburuaga Sanjines/49/Dir., CFO, Exec. VP - Strategic Development, Alfredo Fernandez/Investor Relations Officer, Julieta Naranjo/Investor Relations Officer, Hermilo Zuart Ruiz/59/COO - Latin Centro, Rafael Suarez Olaguibel/48/Commercial Planning, Strategic Development Officer, Maximilian Zimmermann/Investor Relations Officer, Alejandro Duncan/51/Technical Officer, Ernesto Torres Arriaga/72/VP, Eulalio Cerda Delgadillo/50/Human Resources Officer, John Anthony Santa Maria Otazua/51/COO - Mexico

Directors: Carlos Salazar Lomelin/57/Dir., CEO, Jose Antonio Fernandez Carbajal/54/Chmn., CEO - Femsa, Paulina Garza De Marroquin/36/Dir., Alfonso Garza Garza/46/Dir., Alfonso Gonzalez Migoya/51/Dir., Francisco Zambrano Rodriguez/55/Dir., Charles H. McTier/69/Dir., Daniel Servitje Montul/49/Dir., Gary Fayard/56/Dir., Eduardo Padilla Silva/Dir., Ricardo Guajardo Touche/60/Dir., Federico Reyes Garcia/63/Dir., Enrique Senior/65/Dir., Jose Manuel Canal Hernando/68/Dir., Jose Luis Cutrale/62/Dir. *(37 Directors included in Index)*

Owners: FEMSA/53.70%, The Coca-Cola Company/31.60%, Public/14.70%

Financial Data: Fiscal Year End:12/31   **Latest Annual Data:** 12/31/2006

Year	Sales	Net Income
2006	$5,346,000,000	$468,000,000
2005	$4,668,414,000	$414,315,000
2004	$4,170,960,000	$516,493,000

Curr. Assets:	$1,025,000,000	**Curr. Liab.:**	$1,115,000,000		
Plant, Equip.:	$1,977,000,000	**Total Liab.:**	$3,218,000,000	**Indic. Yr. Divd.:**	$0.740
Total Assets:	$6,947,000,000	**Net Worth:**	$3,729,000,000	**Debt/ Equity:**	NA

CoConnect Inc

480 E 6400 S, Ste. 230, Salt Lake City, UT, 84107; **PH:** 1-801-262-5200; **Fax:** 1-801-262-5261; *http://* www.coconnect.com

General - Incorporation	NV	Stock - Price on:12/24/2007	$0.015
Employees	NA	Stock Exchange	OTC
Auditor	Pollard-Kelley Auditing Services, Inc	Ticker Symbol	CCNN
Stk Agt	Interwest Transfer Company, Inc.	Outstanding Shares	83,410,000
Counsel	NA	E.P.S.	-$0.22
DUNS No.	NA	Shareholders	NA

Business: The groups principal activity is to provide services of voice, video and data. The groups service includes the delivery of voice information in the language of the Internet. The group operates from the United States. In the year 2005, the group acquired Heritage Communications, Inc.

Primary SIC and add'l.: 6770

CIK No: 0001088638

Owners: Richard W. Ferguson/17.98%, Tim Thayne/9.19%, Insiders/22.08%, David Black/6.59%, David Thayne/9.30%, Dean H. Becker/4.10%

Financial Data: Fiscal Year End:12/31   **Latest Annual Data:** 12/31/2006

Year	Sales	Net Income
2006	NA	-$895,000
2005	NA	-$2,754,000
2004	NA	-$279,000

Curr. Assets:	$9,000	**Curr. Liab.:**	$668,000		
Plant, Equip.:	$14,000	**Total Liab.:**	$668,000	**Indic. Yr. Divd.:**	NA
Total Assets:	$23,000	**Net Worth:**	-$646,000	**Debt/ Equity:**	NA

Codatek Corp

8275 South Eastern Ave, Las Vegas, NV, 89123; **PH:** 1-702-938-0460

General - Incorporation	NV	Stock - Price on:12/24/2007	NA
Employees	NA	Stock Exchange	NA
Auditor	Bagell, Josephs, Levine & Co. LLC	Ticker Symbol	NA
Stk Agt	NA	Outstanding Shares	NA
Counsel	NA	E.P.S.	NA
DUNS No.	NA	Shareholders	NA

Business: The group's principle activities include research, designing and developing computer software technologies. The plans of the company are to develop software that code and encode programs, files and to implement the plan by internal development. The company is in development stage and currently has no business operations. The group operates from United States.

Primary SIC and add'l.: 7372

CIK No: 0001080750

Codorus Valley Bancorp Inc

105 Leader Hts. Rd., York, PA, 17405; **PH:** 1-717-747-1519; **Fax:** 1-717-741-9582; *http://* www.peoplesbanknet.com

General - Incorporation	PA	Stock - Price on:12/24/2007	$19.44
Employees	146	Stock Exchange	NDQ
Auditor	Beard Miller Co. LLP	Ticker Symbol	CVLY
Stk Agt	Wells Fargo Bank, N.A.	Outstanding Shares	3,680,000
Counsel	NA	E.P.S.	$1.58
DUNS No.	17-732-6113	Shareholders	NA

Business: The group's principal activity is to provide business and consumer banking services through eleven financial centers located throughout york county, Pennsylvania. It offers investment, insurance, trust and real estate services. The group operates through its subsidiaries, peoplesbank and syc

realty company., inc. The other subsidiaries include syc insurance services, inc. Which provides nondeposit investment products, syc settlement services, inc., provides real estate settlement services and the non banking subsidiary, syc realty company inc provides for the disposal of properties obtained from peoples bank in satisfaction of debts previously contracted.

Primary SIC and add'l.: 6712 6022

CIK No: 0000806279

Subsidiaries: CVB Statutory Trust I, PeoplesBank, A Codorus Valley Company, SYC Realty Company, Inc.

Officers: Larry J. Miller/56/Vice Chmn., CEO, Pres./$437,758.00, Jann Allen Weaver/Treasurer, Assist. Sec./$157,830.00, Scott T. Weaver/58/Treasurer, Assist. Sec., Diane E. Hill/VP, Harry R. Swift/VP, Sec./$260,477.00

Directors: Larry J. Miller/56/Vice Chmn., CEO, Pres., Rodney L. Krebs/67/Chmn., Reed D. Anderson/65/Dir., Donald H. Warner/69/Dir., Michael L. Waugh/Dir.

Owners: Larry J. Miller/2.67%, MacGregor S. Jones/1.35%, Harry R. Swift, Jann Allen Weaver, Insiders/8.02%, Michael L. Waugh, Reed D. Anderson, Diane E. Hill, Donald H. Warner, William H. Simpson, Dallas L. Smith, Rodney L. Krebs/1.29%, PeoplesBank, A Codorus Valley Company/6.20%

Financial Data: Fiscal Year End:12/31   **Latest Annual Data:** 12/31/2006

Year	Sales	Net Income
2006	$38,864,000	$5,322,000
2005	$30,661,000	$4,617,000
2004	$25,095,000	$4,008,000

Curr. Assets:	$35,372,000	**Curr. Liab.:**	$456,645,000		
Plant, Equip.:	$10,495,000	**Total Liab.:**	$505,426,000	**Indic. Yr. Divd.:**	$0.540
Total Assets:	$548,212,000	**Net Worth:**	$42,786,000	**Debt/ Equity:**	0.9719

Coeur d'Alene Mines Corp

400 Coeur d'Alene Mines Bldg., 505 Front Ave., Coeur dAlene, ID, 83816; **PH:** 1-208-667-3511; **Fax:** 1-208-667-2213; *http://* www.coeur.com

General - Incorporation	ID	Stock - Price on:12/24/2007	$3.74
Employees	931	Stock Exchange	NYSE
Auditor	KPMG LLP	Ticker Symbol	CDE
Stk Agt	Mellon Investor Services LLC	Outstanding Shares	278,480,000
Counsel	Foley & Lardner LLP	E.P.S.	$0.18
DUNS No.	00-146-8586	Shareholders	NA

Business: The group's principal activity is to explore, develop and mine silver and gold in the United States and South America. The group directly or through its wholly-owned subsidiaries owns, leases and has interests in certain exploration-stage mining properties located in United States, Chile, Argentina, Bolivia, tanzania and Mexico. The group's major subsidiaries are coeur rochester inc, coeur silver valley inc, coeur Alaska inc, cde cerro bayo ltd, compania minera polimet sa, and empressa minera manquiri sa.

Primary SIC and add'l.: 1044 1041

CIK No: 0000215466

Subsidiaries: Callahan Mining Corporation, CDE Australia Pty. Limited, CDE Chilean Mining Corporation, CDE Mexico, S.A. de C.V, Coeur Alaska, Inc., Coeur Argentina, Coeur Bullion Corporation, Coeur d'Alene Mines Exploration Corporation (Tanzania) Limited, Coeur Explorations, Inc., Coeur Rochester, Inc., Coeur Silver Valley, Inc., Compania Minera CDE Cerro Bayo Limitada, Empresa Minera Manquiri

Officers: Dennis E. Wheeler/Chmn., CEO, Pres./$1,897,946.00, Carolyn S. Turner/Assist. Treasurer, Guy C. Jeske/VP, GM, Richard M. Weston/Sr. VP - Operations, Tim Arnold/VP, GM - Kensington Project, James K. Duff/Pres. - South American Operations/$567,685.00, Kelli C. Kast/VP, General Counsel, Corp. Sec., Gary W. Banbury/Sr. VP, Chief Administrative Officer, Thomas T. Angelos/VP, Controller, Chief Accounting Officer, Chris Harrison/VP - Operations CDE Chilean Mining Corporation Cerro Bayo Ltd, Timothy D. Arnold/VP, GM - Kensington Project, Godfrey Mramba/VP, MD - Coeur Exploration Tanzania, James A. Sabala/53/Exec. VP, CFO, Treasurer/$691,034.00, Scott W. Lamb/VP - Investor Relations, Luke J. Russell/VP - Environmental Services *(22 Officers included in Index)*

Directors: Dennis E. Wheeler/Chmn., CEO, Pres., Sebastian Edwards/Dir., Alex Vitale/Dir., Andrew Lundquist/Dir., Cecil D. Andrus/Dir., James J. Curran/Dir., Robert E. Mellor/Dir., John H. Robinson/Dir., Timothy R. Winterer/Dir., Kenneth J. Thompson/Dir.

Financial Data: Fiscal Year End:12/31   **Latest Annual Data:** 06/30/2007

Year	Sales	Net Income
2007	NA	NA
2006	NA	NA
2005	$172,336,000	$10,551,000

Curr. Assets:	$441,597,000	**Curr. Liab.:**	$58,515,000	**P/E Ratio:**	16.26
Plant, Equip.:	$308,550,000	**Total Liab.:**	$268,632,000	**Indic. Yr. Divd.:**	NA
Total Assets:	$849,626,000	**Net Worth:**	$580,994,000	**Debt/ Equity:**	0.3023

Coffee Holding Co Inc

4401 1st Ave., Ste. 1507, Brooklyn, NY, 11232; **PH:** 1-718-832-0800; **Fax:** 1-718-832-0892; *http://* www.coffeeholding.com; **Email:** info@coffeeholding.com

General - Incorporation	NV	Stock - Price on:12/24/2007	$5.0599
Employees	79	Stock Exchange	AMEX
Auditor	Lazar, Levine & Felix, LLP	Ticker Symbol	JVA
Stk Agt	OTR Transfer Agency	Outstanding Shares	5,530,000
Counsel	NA	E.P.S.	$0.23
DUNS No.	NA	Shareholders	NA

Business: The groups principal activity is to selling coffee roaster. The groups products marketed under the brand names Via Roma, Fifth Avenue, Don Manuel and Caf Caribe. The group operates from the United States.

Primary SIC and add'l.: 2095

CIK No: 0001007019

Officers: Andrew Gordon/46/Dir., CEO, CFO, Pres., Treasurer, David Gordon/43/Dir., Exec. VP - Operations, Sec.

Directors: Andrew Gordon/46/Dir., CEO, CFO, Pres., Treasurer, David Gordon/43/Dir., Exec. VP - Operations, Sec., Gerard Decapua/46/Dir., Robert M. Williams/48/Dir., Daniel Dwyer/51/Dir., Barry Knepper/57/Dir., John Rotelli/49/Dir.

Owners: Insiders/37.30%, Rachelle Gordon/19.90%, John Rotelli, Gerard DeCapua, Sterling Gordon/19.90%, Robert M. Williams, David Gordon/18.50%, Andrew Gordon/18.70%, Daniel Dwyer

Financial Data: Fiscal Year End:10/31   **Latest Annual Data:** 10/31/2006

Year	Sales	Net Income
2006	$51,171,000	$700,000
2005	$41,545,000	$1,185,000
2004	$28,030,000	$875,000

Curr. Assets:	$15,729,000	Curr. Liab.:	$7,372,000	P/E Ratio:	25.30
Plant, Equip.:	$2,139,000	Total Liab.:	$7,641,000	Indic. Yr. Divd.:	NA
Total Assets:	$18,982,000	Net Worth:	$11,342,000	Debt/ Equity:	NA

Coffee Pacifica Inc

2813 7th St., Berkeley, CA, 94710; *PH:* 1-510-204-9424; *http://* www.coffeepacifica.com

General - Incorporation	NV	**Stock**- Price on:12/24/2007	$1.44
Employees	15	Stock Exchange	NA
Auditor	Williams & Webster, P.S	Ticker Symbol	NA
Stk Agt	Integrity Stock Transfer, Inc.	Outstanding Shares	27,920,000
Counsel	NA	E.P.S	-$0.34
DUNS No.	NA	Shareholders	NA

Business: The groups principle activity is to distribute green bean coffee. The group operates through two segments namely roasted beans and green beans operations. Customers of the group include roaster retailers, commercial roasters, coffee brokers and gourmet roasters and retailers. In the year 2005, the group acquired Uncommon Grounds, Inc. The group operates from the United States, Canada and Europe. The group's quarterly revenue for September 2007 was 0.76 millions of USD.

Primary SIC and add'l.: 5499
CIK No: 0001208833
Subsidiaries: Coffee Pacifica PNG Ltd., New Guinea Peaberry Coffee, Inc., Uncommon Grounds, Inc
Officers: Terry Klassen/Dir., CEO/$939,100.00, Shailen Singh/Chmn., Pres., Co Founder/$902,000.00
Directors: Terry Klassen/Dir., CEO, Shailen Singh/Chmn., Pres., Co Founder, Jon V.S. Yogiyo/Co - Founder, Vice Chmn.
Owners: Terry Klassen/2.10%, Shailen Singh/11.20%, James Fraser, CEDE & Co/50.20%, Paul Khakshouri/1.70%, Insiders/24.10%, Jon Yogiyo/8.60%, Rhonda Penner-Dunlop, Brooks Farrell/8.60%

Financial Data: *Fiscal Year End:*12/31 *Latest Annual Data:* 12/31/2006

Year	Sales	Net Income
2006	$2,612,000	-$8,531,000
2005	$750,000	-$3,748,000
2004	$265,000	-$445,000

Curr. Assets:	$949,000	Curr. Liab.:	$296,000		
Plant, Equip.:	$323,000	Total Liab.:	$296,000	Indic. Yr. Divd.:	NA
Total Assets:	$1,332,000	Net Worth:	$1,036,000	Debt/ Equity:	NA

Cogdell Spencer Inc

4401 Barclay Downs Dr., Ste. 300, Charlotte, NC, 28209; *PH:* 1-704-940-2900; *Fax:* 1-704-940-2957; *http://* www.cogdellspencer.com

General - Incorporation	MD	**Stock**- Price on:12/24/2007	$19.84
Employees	118	Stock Exchange	NYSE
Auditor	Deloitte & Touche LLP	Ticker Symbol	CSA
Stk Agt	Continental Stock Transfer & Trust Co	Outstanding Shares	11,950,000
Counsel	NA	E.P.S	-$1.18
DUNS No.	NA	Shareholders	NA

Business: The groups principal actibities include acquiring, developing, redeveloping, and managing medical office buildings and other healthcare related facilities. The group operates through two segments namely, property operations and real estate services. In the year 2006, the group acquired Consera Healthcare Real Estates, LLC. The group operates from the United States. Of the total assets in the year 2006, the property operations accounted for $379,574 and real estate services $8,970 (thousands).

Primary SIC and add'l.: 6798
CIK No: 0001332896
Subsidiaries: Cogdell Spencer LP, CS Business Trust I
Officers: Frank C. Spencer/Dir., CEO, Pres., Charles M. Handy/CFO, Sr. VP, Mary J. Surles/VP - Property Management, Rex A. Noble/VP - Management, Devereaux A. Gregg/VP - Development, Linda M. Irving/Sr. Construction Mgr., Robert S. Oharra/Regional VP, Matthew H. Nurkin/VP - Acquisitions Cogdell Spencer Inc
Directors: Frank C. Spencer/Dir., CEO, Pres., James W. Cogdell/66/Chmn., John Georgius/Dir., Randolph Smoak/Dir., Richard Jennings/Dir., Richard Neugent/Dir., Christopher E. Lee/Dir.
Owners: U.S.Bancorp/4.10%, Christopher E. Lee, JPMorgan Chase& Co./4.00%, Richard C. Neugent, Charles M. Handy, Insiders/17.30%, James W. Cogdell/13.60%, Richard B. Jennings, Morgan Stanley/4.30%, Frank C. Spencer/2.90%, Security Capital Research & Management Inc./5.20%, John R. Georgius, Randolph D. Smoak, Deutsche Bank/7.50%

Financial Data: *Fiscal Year End:*12/31 *Latest Annual Data:* 12/31/2006

Year	Sales	Net Income
2006	$55,777,000	-$9,097,000
2005	$46,366,000	-$1,776,000

Curr. Assets:	$2,011,000	Curr. Liab.:	$14,255,000	P/E Ratio:	31.13
Plant, Equip.:	$357,365,000	Total Liab.:	$333,383,000	Indic. Yr. Divd.:	$1.400
Total Assets:	$393,058,000	Net Worth:	$59,675,000	Debt/ Equity:	NA

Cogent Communications Group Inc

1015 31st St. NW, Washington, DC, 20007; *PH:* 1-202-295-4200; *Fax:* 1-202-295-9061; *http://* www.cogentco.com; *Email:* info@cogentco.com

General - Incorporation	DE	**Stock**- Price on:12/24/2007	$28.74
Employees	377	Stock Exchange	NDQ
Auditor	Ernst & Young LLP	Ticker Symbol	CCOI
Stk Agt	Registrar & Transfer Co	Outstanding Shares	49,960,000
Counsel	NA	E.P.S	-$0.84
DUNS No.	NA	Shareholders	NA

Business: The group's principal activity is to provide Internet accesses and data communications. The group's customers are telecommunication providers, application service providers and Internet service providers located in large commercial office buildings in central business districts of major metropolitan markets. The group has its own broadband data network operating in approximately 166 office buildings and have agreements with real estate owners to operate in more than 967 office buildings. The group's network has been designed and created for the purpose of transmitting data packets using Internet protocol. The group acquired Internet service business of fiber network solutions inc, lambdanet communications France sas and lambdanet espana sa in 2003 and fmcp and majority assets of unlimited fiber optics and assets of global access in 2004.

Primary SIC and add'l.: 7375
CIK No: 0001158324
Subsidiaries: Allied Riser Communications Corporation, Allied Riser Operations Corporation, C.c.d. Cogent Communications Deutschland, Gmbh, Cogent Canada Holdings,inc., Cogent Canada,inc., Cogent Communications Belgium Sprl, Cogent Communications Espana S.a., Cogent Communications France, Sas, Cogent Communications Group,inc., Cogent Communications Netherlands B.v., Cogent Communications Of California,inc., Cogent Communications Of D.c.,inc., Cogent Communications Of Florida,inc., Cogent Communications Of Georgia,inc., Cogent Communications Of Maryland,inc. 30 Subsidiaries included in the Index
Officers: Dave Schaeffer/Chmn., Founder, CEO/$8,320,741.00, Tad Weed/CFO/$417,177.00, Reed Harrison/COO, Pres./$785,602.00, Robert N. Beury/54/Executive Officer/$411,400.00, Brad R. Kummer/59/VP, Timothy G. Oneill/52/VP - Field Engineering, Mark A. Schleifer/39/VP - IP Engineering, Jeffrey Karnes/36/VP/$328,999.00, Ried Zulager/Sec., Jeff Henriksen/Contact - Dir. - Marketing Communications
Directors: Dave Schaeffer/Chmn., Founder, CEO, Erel Margalit/Dir., Kenneth D. Peterson/Dir., Richard Liebhaber/Dir., Jean-Jacques Bertrand/Dir., Timothy Weingarten/Dir., Steven Brooks/Dir., Edward Glassmeyer/Dir., Blake Bath/Dir., Lewis H. Ferguson/Dir., Michael Carus/Dir.
Owners: Jeffrey Karnes, Insiders/5.50%, FMR Corporation/15.00%, Dave Schaeffer/2.50%, Entities Affiliated with Ziff Asset Management, L.P./6.20%, Robert Beury, Richard Liebhaber, Thaddeus Weed, Reed R. Harrison, Kenneth Peterson, Blake Bath, Edward Glassmeyer, Steven Brooks/2.50%

Financial Data: *Fiscal Year End:*12/31 *Latest Annual Data:* 12/31/2006

Year	Sales	Net Income
2006	$149,071,000	-$53,757,000
2005	$135,593,000	-$67,518,000
2004	$91,286,000	-$89,660,000

Curr. Assets:	$68,114,000	Curr. Liab.:	$36,715,000		
Plant, Equip.:	$263,268,000	Total Liab.:	$121,244,000	Indic. Yr. Divd.:	NA
Total Assets:	$336,876,000	Net Worth:	$215,632,000	Debt/ Equity:	0.3915

Cogent Inc

209 Fair Oaks Ave., South Pasadena, CA, 91030; *PH:* 1-626-799-8090; *Fax:* 1-626-799-8996; *http://* www.cogentsystems.com; *Email:* info@cogentsystems.com

General - Incorporation	DE	**Stock**- Price on:12/24/2007	$14.54
Employees	195	Stock Exchange	NDQ
Auditor	Deloitte & Touche LLP	Ticker Symbol	COGT
Stk Agt	U.S. Stock Transfer Corp	Outstanding Shares	94,660,000
Counsel	NA	E.P.S	$0.30
DUNS No.	NA	Shareholders	NA

Business: The groups principle activity is to provide automated fingerprint identification systems and other fingerprint biometrics solutions. The groups products include PMA, LiveID, WebID, WebCheck, National WebCheck and PIV Solution. The group operates from United States.

Primary SIC and add'l.: NA
CIK No: 0001289434
Subsidiaries: Cogent Systems, Inc
Officers: Ming Hsieh/Chmn., CEO, Pres., James Jasinski/58/Exec. VP - Federal, State Systems, Michael Hollowich/Exec. VP - Operations, Paul Kim/40/CFO
Directors: Ming Hsieh/Chmn., CEO, Pres., John Bolger/Dir., John P. Stenbit/Dir., Kenneth Thornton/Dir.
Owners: Paul Kim, Michael Hollowich, Ming Hsieh/53.80%, Insiders/54.20%, James Jasinski, Kenneth R. Thornton, John Bolger, T. Rowe Price Associates, Inc./9.90%, John P. Stenbit

Financial Data: *Fiscal Year End:*12/31 *Latest Annual Data:* 12/31/2006

Year	Sales	Net Income
2006	$101,657,000	$29,728,000
2005	$159,889,000	$65,286,000
2004	$87,688,000	$42,581,000

Curr. Assets:	$410,421,000	Curr. Liab.:	$45,091,000	P/E Ratio:	48.47
Plant, Equip.:	$32,874,000	Total Liab.:	$50,382,000	Indic. Yr. Divd.:	NA
Total Assets:	$540,941,000	Net Worth:	$490,559,000	Debt/ Equity:	NA

Cognex Corp

1 Vision Dr., Natick, MA, 01760; *PH:* 1-508-650-3000; *Fax:* 1-508-650-3344; *http://* www.cognex.com

General - Incorporation	MA	**Stock**- Price on:12/24/2007	$23.39
Employees	760	Stock Exchange	NDQ
Auditor	Ernst & Young LLP	Ticker Symbol	CGNX
Stk Agt	National City Bank	Outstanding Shares	44,240,000
Counsel	Goodwin, Procter & Hoar	E.P.S	$0.62
DUNS No.	05-055-9491	Shareholders	NA

Business: The group's principal activity is to design, develop, manufacture and market machine vision systems that are used to automate a wide range of manufacturing processes. The group's activities are carried out through two divisions: modular vision systems division and surface inspection systems division. Modular vision systems division designs, develops, manufactures, and markets modular vision systems that are used to control the manufacturing of discrete items, such as semiconductor chips, cellular phones, and medical instruments. Surface inspection systems division designs, develops, manufactures, and markets surface inspection vision systems that are used to inspect surfaces of materials processed in a continuous fashion, such as paper, metals, plastics, and non-wovens. It operates in United States, Japan and Ireland.

Primary SIC and add'l.: 3823
CIK No: 0000851205

Subsidiaries: Cognex Asia, Inc., Cognex Canada Technology, Inc., Cognex Canada, Inc., Cognex Distribution Corporation, Cognex Europe, b.v., Cognex Europe, Inc., Cognex Finland Oy, Cognex Foreign Sales Corporation, Cognex Germany, Inc., Cognex International, Inc., Cognex K.K., Cognex Korea, Inc., Cognex Singapore, Inc., Cognex Taiwan, Inc., Cognex Technology and Investment Corporation 20 Subsidiaries included in the Index

Officers: Robert J. Shillman/Chmn., CEO/$948,430.00, Richard A. Morin/Sr. VP - Finance, Administration, CFO, Treasurer/$627,794.00, Marilyn Matz/Sr. VP - PC Vision Products Business Group, Bill Silver/Sr. VP - Research, Development, Sr. Fellow, Eric Ceyrolle/Exec. VP - Worldwide Sales, Marketing/$762,355.00

Directors: Robert J. Shillman/Chmn., CEO, Patrick Alias/Dir., Reuben Wasserman/Dir., Jerald G. Fishman/Dir., Anthony Sun/Dir., Theodor Krantz/Dir., Edward Smith/Dir.

Owners: Eric A. Ceyrolle, OppenheimerFunds, Inc./5.40%, Wellington Management Company, LLP/9.60%, First Pacific Advisors, LLC/5.60%, Patrick A. Alias, Insiders/10.80%, James F. Hoffmaster, Anthony Sun, Richard A. Morin, The Hartford Series Fund, Inc./5.60%, Royce & Associates, LLC/10.90%, Reuben Wasserman, Jerald G. Fishman, Robert J. Shillman/8.80%

Financial Data: *Fiscal Year End:*12/31 *Latest Annual Data:* 12/31/2006

Year	Sales	Net Income
2006	$238,424,000	$39,855,000
2005	$216,875,000	$35,702,000
2004	$201,957,000	$37,744,000

Curr. Assets:	$313,081,000	**Curr. Liab.:**	$54,801,000	**P/E Ratio:**	37.73
Plant, Equip.:	$26,028,000	**Total Liab.:**	$54,801,000	**Indic. Yr. Divd.:**	$0.340
Total Assets:	$528,651,000	**Net Worth:**	$473,850,000	**Debt/ Equity:**	NA

Cognigen Networks Inc

6405 218th St. SW, Ste. 305, Mountlake Terrace, WA, 98043; *PH:* 1-425-329-2300; *Fax:* 1-425-329-2301; *http://* www.cognigen.com

General - Incorporation	CO	**Stock**- Price on:12/24/2007	$0.09
Employees	12	Stock Exchange	OTC
Auditor	KPMG LLP	Ticker Symbol	CGNW
Stk Agt	Computershare Investor Services LLC	Outstanding Shares	10,230,000
Counsel	NA	E.P.S.	-$0.144
DUNS No.	NA	Shareholders	NA

Business: The group's principle activity is to provide telecommunication product and services to worldwide markets. The group operates in three divisions. The first two divisions consist of direct and indirect sales of telecommunications and personal technology services and the third is service delivery division. The activities of the group include selling prepaid calling cards and paging, wireless communications, computers and Internet-based telecommunications products and other significant products.through a network of independent agents, the group sells directly or facilitates the sale of third party products and services to customers and subscribers worldwide. The group's total revenue for year 2007 was 5.62 millions of USD.

Primary SIC and add'l.: 4812 4822

CIK No: 0000726293

Subsidiaries: Cognigen Business Systems, Intandem Communication Corp, Lowest Cost Mall, Inc.

Officers: Gary Cook/Dir., Acting CEO, CFO, Acting Pres., Treasurer, Robert K. Bench/59/Dir., CEO, Pres.

Directors: Gary Cook/Dir., Acting CEO, CFO, Acting Pres., Treasurer, Robert K. Bench/59/Dir., CEO, Pres., Christopher R. Seelbach/Chmn., David L. Jackson/Dir., James H. Shapiro/Dir., Roy Banks/Dir., James U. Jensen/63/Dir., John M. Knab/57/Dir., John D. Thomas/36/Dir., George O. Rebensdorf/54/Dir.

Owners: David L. Jackson/1.40%, Insiders/57.20%, Robert K. Bench/47.00%, Christopher R. Seelbach/2.00%, George O. Rebensdorf/1.10%, Anderson Family Trust/5.20%, Cognigen Corporation, Peter Tilyou/5.20%, Gary L. Cook/6.40%

Financial Data: *Fiscal Year End:*06/30 *Latest Annual Data:* 6/30/2006

Year	Sales	Net Income
2006	$10,107,000	-$1,308,000
2005	$11,746,000	$1,830,000
2004	$10,735,000	-$2,879,000

Curr. Assets:	$1,320,000	**Curr. Liab.:**	$2,308,000		
Plant, Equip.:	$7,000	**Total Liab.:**	$2,308,000	**Indic. Yr. Divd.:**	NA
Total Assets:	$1,469,000	**Net Worth:**	-$839,000	**Debt/ Equity:**	NA

Cognizant Technology Solutions Corp

500 Glenpointe Ctr. W, Teaneck, NJ, 07666; *PH:* 1-201-801-0233; *Fax:* 1-201-801-0243; *http://* www.cognizant.com

General - Incorporation	DE	**Stock**- Price on:12/24/2007	$77.98
Employees	38,800	Stock Exchange	NDQ
Auditor	PricewaterhouseCoopers LLP	Ticker Symbol	CTSH
Stk Agt	American Stock Transfer & Trust Co.	Outstanding Shares	143,760,000
Counsel	Hale & Dorr LLP	E.P.S.	$1.06
DUNS No.	79-990-1301	Shareholders	NA

Business: The group's principal activities are to provide it design, development, integration and maintenance services for Fortune 1000 companies. The solutions include application development and integration, application management and re-engineering. The customers include acnielsen corporation, first data corporation, adp, incorporated, ims health incorporated (ims health), brinker international, incorporated, metropolitan life insurance group, ccc information services incorporated nielsen media research, incorporated, computer sciences corporation, pnc bank, the dun & bradstreet corporation, royal & sunalliance usa. The group operates in India, the United Kingdom, Germany, Canada and the United States. During 2003, the group acquired aces international, inc and infopulse. On 27-Feb-2004, the group acquired ygyan consulting private ltd.

Primary SIC and add'l.: 7372 7371

CIK No: 0001058290

Subsidiaries: ACES International, Inc., Cognizant (Mauritius) Development Limited, Cognizant Technology Solutions (Netherlands) B.V., Cognizant Technology Solutions (Shanghai) Co., Ltd, Cognizant Technology Solutions A.G., Cognizant Technology Solutions Asia Pacific Pte Ltd., Cognizant Technology Solutions Australia Pty Ltd., Cognizant Technology Solutions B.V., Cognizant Technology Solutions Belgium S.A., Cognizant Technology Solutions Benelux B.V., Cognizant Technology Solutions Canada, Inc., Cognizant Technology Solutions Development Corporation, Cognizant Technology Solutions France S.A., Cognizant Technology Solutions GmbH, Cognizant Technology Solutions India Pvt. Limited 25 Subsidiaries included in the Index

Officers: Francisco D'Souza/39/Dir., CEO, Pres./$1,693,882.00, Rajeev Mehta/COO - Global Client Services/$959,138.00, Chandra Sekaran/Pres., MD - Global Delivery/$671,174.00, Gordon Coburn/Chief Financial, Operating Officer/$1,586,979.00, Ramakrishnan Chandrasekaran/50/Pres., MD - Global Delivery, Kirsten Paragona/Media Relations, Corporate, Americas, Paul Hope/Media Relations, UK, David Cotterill/Media Relations, Continental Europe

Directors: Francisco D'Souza/39/Dir., CEO, Pres., Lakshmi Narayanan/55/Vice Chmn., John E. Klein/66/Chmn., Thomas M. Wendel/71/Dir., Robert W. Howe/61/Dir., Robert E. Weissman/66/Dir.

Owners: Ramakrishnan Chandrasekaran, FMR Corp./12.70%, Robert E. Weissman, Insiders/1.80%, Gordon J. Coburn, Rajeev Mehta, Lakshmi Narayanan, Robert W. Howe, Thomas M. Wendel, Francisco DSouza, John E. Klein

Financial Data: *Fiscal Year End:*12/31 *Latest Annual Data:* 12/31/2006

Year	Sales	Net Income
2006	$1,424,267,000	$232,795,000
2005	$885,830,000	$166,266,000
2004	$586,673,000	$100,243,000

Curr. Assets:	$1,040,391,000	**Curr. Liab.:**	$249,503,000	**P/E Ratio:**	45.08
Plant, Equip.:	$220,154,000	**Total Liab.:**	$252,482,000	**Indic. Yr. Divd.:**	NA
Total Assets:	$1,325,981,000	**Net Worth:**	$1,073,499,000	**Debt/ Equity:**	NA

Cognos Inc

15 Wayside Rd., Burlington, MA, 01803; *PH:* 1-781-229-6600; *Fax:* 1-781-229-2347; *http://* www.cognos.com

General - Incorporation	Canada	**Stock**- Price on:12/24/2007	NA
Employees	3,507	Stock Exchange	NDQ
Auditor	Ernst & Young, LLP	Ticker Symbol	COGN
Stk Agt	Computershare Trust Co.	Outstanding Shares	89,870,000
Counsel	Testa, Hurwitz & Thibeault	E.P.S.	$1.37
DUNS No.	20-788-6268	Shareholders	NA

Business: The group's principle activity is to provide business intelligence software solutions. The group develops, markets and supports an integrated business intelligence platform. The platform analyzes and reports data from multiple perspectives and coordinates decision-making and actions across the extended enterprise through intranets, extranets and the Internet. The software provides customers with the ability to effectively use data to make faster, more informed decisions in order to improve operational effectiveness, increase customer satisfaction and accelerate corporate response time. The services are offered through 51 sales offices in 17 countries.

Primary SIC and add'l.: 7379 7372 8243

CIK No: 0000746782

Subsidiaries: 3098000 Nova Scotia Company, Adaytum Asia Pacific Pty Limited, Adaytum KPS Limited, Adaytum Limited, APL2000 Inc., Cognos (Barbados) Limited, Cognos (Switzerland) Ltd, Cognos (UK) Limited, Cognos A/S, Cognos AB, Cognos Austria GmbH, Cognos B.V., Cognos Corporation, Cognos do Brasil Ltda., Cognos Espaa SA 50 Subsidiaries included in the Index

Officers: Rob Ashe/Dir., CEO, Pres./$4,642,713.00, Les Rechan/COO/$3,129,682.00, Rob Rose/Chief Strategy Officer, VP - Product Marketing, Ad Voogt/Pres. - Cognos Europe, Peter Griffiths/Sr. VP - Products/$2,443,406.00, Philippe Duranton/Sr. VP - Human Resources, John Jussup/Sr. VP, Chief Legal Officer, Sec., Dave Laverty/Sr. VP - Global Marketing, Chief Marketing Officer, Mel Zeledon/Sr. VP - Global Alliances, Rick Gilbody/Pres. - Cognos Americas, Phillip Beniac/Pres. - Cognos Asia Pacific, Don Campbell/CTO, Michael A. Morrison/VP, GM - Financial Performance Management, Jane Campbell/VP - Product Engineering, Barbara Cain/VP - Customer Success, Support *(20 Officers included in Index)*

Directors: Rob Ashe/Dir., CEO, Pres., Renato Zambonini/Chmn., John E. Caldwell/Dir., Paul Damp/Dir., Pierre Y. Ducros/Dir., Robert W. Korthals/Dir., Janet Perna/Dir., John Rando/Dir., Bill Russell/Corp. Dir., David Galloway/Dir., James M. Tory/Dir.

Owners: McLean Budden Ltd./5.80%, Renato Zambonini, John E. Caldwell, Pierre Y. Ducros, Insiders/2.30%, David Laverty, Paul D. Damp, Robert W. Korthals, Robert G. Ashe, James M. Tory, Tom Manley, Peter Griffiths, FMR Corp./5.00%, Barclays Global Investors NA/5.10%, John J. Rando *(17 Owners included in Index)*

Financial Data: *Fiscal Year End:*02/28 *Latest Annual Data:* 2/28/2007

Year	Sales	Net Income
2007	$979,264,000	$115,697,000
2006	$877,500,000	$124,802,000
2005	$825,531,000	$136,604,000

Curr. Assets:	$959,052,000	**Curr. Liab.:**	$470,570,000		
Plant, Equip.:	$72,256,000	**Total Liab.:**	$501,321,000	**Indic. Yr. Divd.:**	NA
Total Assets:	$1,292,761,000	**Net Worth:**	$791,440,000	**Debt/ Equity:**	NA

Coherent Inc

5100 Patrick Henry Dr., Santa Clara, CA, 95054; *PH:* 1-408-764-4000; *Fax:* 1-408-764-4800; *http://* www.coherentinc.com; *Email:* info_service@coherent.com

General - Incorporation	DE	**Stock**- Price on:12/24/2007	$30.77
Employees	2,189	Stock Exchange	NDQ
Auditor	Deloitte & Touche LLP	Ticker Symbol	COHR
Stk Agt	American Stock Transfer & Trust Co.	Outstanding Shares	31,250,000
Counsel	Wilson Sonsini Goodrich & Rosati	E.P.S.	$1.07
DUNS No.	04-371-9210	Shareholders	NA

Business: The group's principal activities are to design, manufacture and market lasers, laser-based systems, precision optics and related accessories for a diverse group of customers. It has two reportable business segments: electro-optics and lambda physik. The electro-optics segment focuses on markets such as semiconductor and related manufacturing, materials processing, OEM laser components, scientific research, biotechnology, medical OEM's, advanced packaging and graphic arts. Lambda physik focuses on markets including lasers for the production of flat panel displays, lithography, gps systems, mobile phones, ink jet printers, automotive, environmental research, refractive surgery, scientific research, medical OEM's, materials processing and micro-machining applications. The group acquired molectron detector inc & positive light inc in fiscal 2003.

Primary SIC and add'l.: 3845 3679 3827

CIK No: 0000021510

Subsidiaries: Bavarian Photonics GmbH, Coherent (Deutschland), GmbH, Coherent (U.K.) Holdings, Ltd., Coherent (U.K.) Ltd., Coherent B.V., Coherent DEOS, LLC, Coherent Europe B.V., Coherent Export Co.,Inc., Coherent Finland, Ltd., Coherent Holding Co., GmbH, Coherent International Holding,Inc., Coherent Investments,Inc., Coherent Japan,Inc., Coherent Lambda Physik GmbH, Coherent Laser Ireland, Ltd 24 Subsidiaries included in the Index

Officers: John R. Ambroseo/Dir., CEO, Pres., Ronald A. Victor/Exec. VP - Human Resources, Helene Simonet/CFO, Exec. VP, Luis Spinelli/CTO, Exec. VP, Paul L. Meissner/Exec. VP - Global Business Operations, Michael Cumbo/Exec. VP, GM - Optical Technologies, Bret Dimarco/Exec. VP, General Counsel

Directors: John R. Ambroseo/Dir., CEO, Pres., Bernard J. Couillaud/Chmn., Robert J. Quillinan/Dir., Sandeep Vij/Dir., John H. Hart/Dir., Garry Rogerson/Dir., Lawrence Tomlinson/Dir., Charles W. Cantoni/Dir.

Owners: Luis Spinelli, Charles W. Cantoni, Lawrence Tomlinson, John R. Ambroseo/2.36%, Helene Simonet, Barclays Global Investors NA./5.29%, Dimensional Fund Advisors/7.88%, Eagle Asset Management, Inc./5.55%, Insiders/4.33%, John H. Hart, Sandeep Vij, Garry W. Rogerson, Ronald A. Victor

Financial Data: Fiscal Year End:10/01 Latest Annual Data: 9/30/2005

Year	Sales	Net Income
2005	$516,252,000	$39,861,000
2004	$494,954,000	$17,360,000

Curr. Assets:	$491,721,000	Curr. Liab.:	$111,587,000	P/E Ratio:	28.76
Plant, Equip.:	$155,316,000	Total Liab.:	$162,024,000	Indic. Yr. Divd.:	NA
Total Assets:	$798,290,000	Net Worth:	$636,266,000	Debt/ Equity:	NA

Cohesant Technologies Inc

5845 W 82nd St., Ste. 102, Indianapolis, IN, 46278; PH: 1-317-871-7611; Fax: 1-317-875-5456; http:// www.cohesant.com

General		Stock	
Incorporation	DE	Price on:12/24/2007	$7.6
Employees	124	Stock Exchange	NDQ
Auditor	Ernst & Young LLP	Ticker Symbol	COHT
Stk Agt	Continental Stock Transfer & Trust Co	Outstanding Shares	3,290,000
Counsel	Kahn, Kleinman, Yonowitz & Arnson Co.	E.P.S.	$0.23
DUNS No.	87-263-9422	Shareholders	NA

Business: The group's principal activities are to design, develop, manufacture and sell specialized two component dispense equipment systems and replacement parts used in the operation of the equipment and specialty two component epoxy coating and grout products. The equipment systems are used in the construction, transportation and marine industries to apply insulation, protective coating, sealant and anti-corrosive products. These systems are also used to create packaging and fill molds. The epoxy coating and grout products protect from deterioration caused by corrosion, infiltration, atmospheric conditions and chemical attack. Major trademarks of the group are glas-craft(R), raven(R), aac(R) and aquatapoxy(r). The products of the group are sold in the United States, Canada, Asia, Pacific Rim, Europe and Middle East.

Primary SIC and add'l.: 2891 3559

CIK No: 0000928420

Subsidiaries: American Chemical Company, CIPAR Inc., CIPAR Services Inc, Cohesant Infrastructure Protection and Renewal of Canada Ltd., Cohesant Materials Inc. f/n/a Raven Lining Systems, Inc, CuraFlo of British Columbia Ltd, GlasCraft, Inc.

Officers: Morris H. Wheeler/Dir., CEO, Pres., Robert W. Pawlak/VP - Finance, CFO, Sec., Michael A. Ruby/VP - Sales, Marketing, Glascraft Inc, Brian Lemaire/Pres. - Curaflo, Joanne Hughes/Pres. - Raven Lining Systems, Sanjiv Gupta/GM - Curaflo British Columbia, Pacific Northwest Region, Stewart J. Nance/Pres. - Curaflo Spincast Services, Mike Rush/VP - Operations, Glascraft Inc

Directors: Morris H. Wheeler/Dir., CEO, Pres., Morton A. Cohen/Chmn., Dwight D. Goodman/Dir., Michael L. Boeckman/Dir., Richard L. Immerman/Dir., Terrence R. Ozan/Dir.

Owners: Michael L. Boeckman, Terrence R. Ozan, Clarion Capital Corporation/35.00%, Morton A. Cohen/37.80%, Stuart C. McNeil/4.40%, Insiders/56.20%, Richard L. Immerman/2.00%, Morris H. Wheeler/5.20%, Brian LeMaire/5.20%, Steve Goden/1.00%, Robert W. Pawlak/2.20%

Financial Data: Fiscal Year End:11/30 Latest Annual Data: 05/31/2007

Year	Sales	Net Income
2007	$7,363,000	$78,000
2006	$6,914,000	$316,000
2005	NA	NA

Curr. Assets:	$10,643,000	Curr. Liab.:	$4,061,000	P/E Ratio:	21.71
Plant, Equip.:	$2,425,000	Total Liab.:	$4,853,000	Indic. Yr. Divd.:	$0.280
Total Assets:	$22,969,000	Net Worth:	$18,116,000	Debt/ Equity:	0.0128

Cohn & Steers Inc

280 Pk. Ave., New York, NY, 10017; PH: 1-212-832-3232; Fax: 1-212-832-3622; http:// www.cohenandsteers.com; Email: investor_relations@cohenandsteers.com

General		Stock	
Incorporation	DE	Price on:12/24/2007	$46.92
Employees	178	Stock Exchange	NYSE
Auditor	Deloitte & Touche LLP	Ticker Symbol	CNS
Stk Agt	NA	Outstanding Shares	39,740,000
Counsel	NA	E.P.S.	$1.71
DUNS No.	NA	Shareholders	NA

Business: The groups principle activity is to provide investment-banking services to companies in real estate and healthcare centers. The group operates through two segments namely, asset management and investment banking. In the year 2006, the group acquired Houlihan Rovers. The group operates from the United States.

Primary SIC and add'l.: 6282

CIK No: 0001284812

Subsidiaries: Cohen& Steers Asia Limited, Cohen& Steers Capital Advisors, LLC, Cohen& Steers Houlihan Rovers, Cohen& Steers Securities, LLC, Cohen& Steers UK Limited, Cohen&SteersCapitalManagement,Inc.

Officers: Robert H. Steers/Co - Chmn., Co - CEO/$1,016,600.00, Martin Cohen/Co - Chmn., Co - Chief Executive/$1,016,600.00, Joseph M. Harvey/Pres., Chief Investment Officer, Sr. Portfolio Mgr./$2,783,034.00, James S. Corl/Exec. VP/$2,053,865.00, Thomas N. Bohjalian/Sr. VP, Gerios J.M. Rovers/MD, CIO, Derek Cheung/Sr. VP, Richard E. Helm/Sr. VP, Douglas R. Bond/Exec. VP, John J. McCombe/Exec. VP, Dir. - Sales, Marketing, Stephen W. Dunn/Sr. VP, Dir. - Institutional Marketing, William J. Frischling/Sr. VP, Dir. - Institutional Client Service, Michael Nelson/VP - Mid, Atlantic Regional Sales Dir., Mike Guetzkow/VP, Regional Sales Dir., Frank Zukowski/Sr. VP, RIA Sales Dir. *(66 Officers included in Index)*

Directors: Robert H. Steers/Co - Chmn., Co - CEO, Martin Cohen/Co - Chmn., Co - Chief Executive, Richard E. Bruce/Dir., Peter L. Rhein/Dir., Richard P. Simon/Dir., Edmond D. Villani/Dir.

Owners: Richard E. Bruce, Baron Capital Group, Inc./7.00%, Robert H. Steers/29.40%, Insiders/60.80%, Edmond D. Villani, Richard P. Simon, Peter L. Rhein, Martin Cohen/29.40%, Joseph M. Harvey/1.60%, James S. Corl, Matthew S. Stadler

Financial Data: Fiscal Year End:12/31 Latest Annual Data: 12/31/2006

Year	Sales	Net Income
2006	$191,472,000	$3,204,000
2005	$146,218,000	$31,921,000
2004	$114,113,000	$7,288,000

Curr. Assets:	$170,971,000	Curr. Liab.:	$29,581,000		
Plant, Equip.:	$10,539,000	Total Liab.:	$43,737,000	Indic. Yr. Divd.:	$0.800
Total Assets:	$285,146,000	Net Worth:	$241,409,000	Debt/ Equity:	NA

Cohu Inc

12367 Crosthwaite Cir., Poway, CA, 92064; PH: 1-858-848-8100; Fax: 1-858-848-8185; http:// www.cohu.com; Email: corp@cohu.com

General		Stock	
Incorporation	DE	Price on:12/24/2007	$21.62
Employees	1,100	Stock Exchange	NDQ
Auditor	Ernst & Young LLP	Ticker Symbol	COHU
Stk Agt	Mellon Investor Services LLC	Outstanding Shares	22,730,000
Counsel	Gray, Cary, Ware & Freidenrich	E.P.S.	$0.57
DUNS No.	00-838-1758	Shareholders	NA

Business: The group's principal activities are to design, manufacture and sell semiconductor test handling equipment to semiconductor manufacturers and semiconductor test subcontractors. The group operates through four segments: semiconductor equipment segment, television camera segment, metal detection segment and microwave communications segment. The semi-conductor equipment segment designs, manufactures and sells semi-conductor test handling equipment to manufacturers and subcontractors of semi-conductors. Television camera segment designs, manufactures and sells closed circuit television cameras and systems to original equipment manufacturers, contractors and government agencies. Metal detector segment designs, manufactures and sells metal detectors and related underground detection instruments for consumer and industrial markets. Microwave communication segment designs, manufactures and sells microwave communications equipment, antenna systems and associated equipment.

Primary SIC and add'l.: 3663 3674 3699

CIK No: 0000021535

Subsidiaries: Broadcast Microwave Services, Inc., Cohu Foreign Sales Ltd., Cohu S.A., Delta Design (Littleton), Inc., Delta Design Philippines LLC, Delta Design Singapore PTE LTD, Delta Design, Inc., Fisher Research Laboratory, Inc.

Officers: James A. Donahue/Dir., CEO, Pres./$1,581,367.00, Thomas G. Lightner/63/VP - Manufacturing/$442,744.00, John H. Allen/CFO, VP - Finance/$788,120.00, James G. McFarlane/57/Sr. VP/$501,694.00, Colin P. Scholefield/44/Sr. VP - Sales, Service/$477,901.00, Thomas L. Green/Sec.

Directors: James A. Donahue/Dir., CEO, Pres., Charles A. Schwan/Chmn., James W. Barnes/78/Dir., Harry L. Casari/71/Dir., Robert L. Ciardella/55/Dir., Harold Harrigian/73/Dir.

Owners: Harold Harrigian, Charles A. Schwan, Harry L. Casari, Barclays Global Investors Japan Limited/5.19%, John H. Allen, Nick Cedrone/5.66%, Rutabaga Capital Management/5.06%, Insiders/5.81%, James W. Barnes/1.28%, Colin P. Scholefield, James G. McFarlane, Franklin Resources, Inc./8.16%, Robert L. Ciardella, James A. Donahue/2.10%, Thomas G. Lightner

Financial Data: Fiscal Year End:12/31 Latest Annual Data: 12/30/2006

Year	Sales	Net Income
2006	$270,106,000	$17,681,000
2005	$238,902,000	$33,974,000
2004	$176,237,000	$16,703,000

Curr. Assets:	$256,617,000	Curr. Liab.:	$50,322,000	P/E Ratio:	30.89
Plant, Equip.:	$31,780,000	Total Liab.:	$56,852,000	Indic. Yr. Divd.:	$0.240
Total Assets:	$306,977,000	Net Worth:	$250,125,000	Debt/ Equity:	NA

Coinmach Corp

303 Sunnyside Blvd., Plainview, NY, 11803; PH: 1-516-349-8555; http:// www.coinmach.com

General		Stock	
Incorporation	DE	Price on:12/24/2007	$13.34
Employees	1,950	Stock Exchange	NA
Auditor	Ernst & Young LLP	Ticker Symbol	NA
Stk Agt	Bank of New York	Outstanding Shares	NA
Counsel	NA	E.P.S.	-$0.04
DUNS No.	00-193-6228	Shareholders	NA

Business: The group's principal activity is to supply outsourced laundry equipment services for multi-family housing properties in the United States. The customers of the group are landlords, property management companies and owners of rental apartment buildings, condominiums, cooperatives, university, institutional housing and other multi-family housing properties. The integrated computer systems of the group provide real-time operational and competitive data, which improves the operating efficiencies and enables the group to provide superior customer services. The complementary operations of the group include individual multi-housing units, laundromat equipment distribution and retail laundromat operations. At 31-Mar-2004, the group owned and operated 674,000 washers and dryers in 70,000 locations throughout North America. The group operates solely in domestic market.

Primary SIC and add'l.: 7359 7219 7215

CIK No: 0000091693

Subsidiaries: American Laundry Franchising Corp., Appliance Warehouse of America, Inc, Automaticos, SA de CV, Grand Wash & Dry Launderette, Inc., Macquilados Automaticos, SA de CV, Super Laundry Equipment Corp.

Officers: Stephen R. Kerrigan/Chmn., CEO, Mitchell Blatt/COO, Pres., Michael E. Stanky/Sr. VP, Ramon Norniella/Pres. - Appliance Warehouse, America, Robert M. Doyle/CFO, Raymond Loser/VP - Investor Relations

Directors: Stephen R. Kerrigan/Chmn., CEO, William M. Kelly/Dir., David A. Donnini/Dir., James N. Chapman/Dir., Woody M. McGee/Dir., Bruce V. Rauner/Dir., John R. Scheessele/Dir.

Financial Data: Fiscal Year End:03/31 Latest Annual Data: 3/31/2006

Year	Sales	Net Income
2006	$543,485,000	-$24,582,000
2005	$538,604,000	-$35,325,000
2004	$531,088,000	-$31,331,000

Curr. Assets:	$87,887,000	Curr. Liab.:	$80,414,000		
Plant, Equip.:	$252,398,000	Total Liab.:	$783,500,000	Indic. Yr. Divd.:	$0.820
Total Assets:	$922,166,000	Net Worth:	$138,666,000	Debt/ Equity:	6.0496

Coinstar Inc

1800 114th Ave. SE, Bellevue, WA, 98004; *PH:* 1-425-943-8000; *Fax:* 1-425-637-0045; *http://* www.coinstar.com; *Email:* info@coinstar.com

General - Incorporation .... DE	Stock - Price on:12/24/2007 .... $32.16
Employees 1,900	Stock Exchange .... NDQ
Auditor .... KPMG LLP	Ticker Symbol .... CSTR
Stk Agt. .... Computershare Trust Co	Outstanding Shares 27,810,000
Counsel .... Perkins Coie LLP	E.P.S. $0.58
DUNS No. 79-144-7691	Shareholders .... NA

Business: The group's principal activities are developing and operating a network of automated self service coin counting and processing machines. The consumers are provided with a convenient means to convert loose coins into cash. The group's units are located in supermarkets and financial institutions. It has its machines installed in supermarkets across the United States, Canada and the United Kingdom. The group acquired substantially all of the assets and assumed certain liabilities of prizm technologies inc on 6th feb 2003. On 15-Mar-2004, the group acquired cellcards of Illinois llc.

Primary SIC and add'l.: 7389

CIK No: 0000941604

Subsidiaries: ACMI Asia Inc, Adventure Vending Inc., Best Vendors Amusement, LLC, CellCards LLC), CellCards of Delaware, LLC, CellCards of Illinois, LLC, Coin-Op Factory Inc, Coinstar E-Payment Services Inc., Coinstar Entertainment Services, Inc., Coinstar International, Inc., Coinstar Limited, El Toro Prepaid Inc., Entertainment Vending Management, LLC, Folz Vending, Inc., Pukka, Inc. 18 Subsidiaries included in the Index

Officers: Dave Cole/CEO, Steve Verleye/Sr. VP, GM - E, Pay/$607,369.00, Peter Rowan/Corporate VP - New Ventures, John Reilly/Sr. VP - Operations, Denise Rubin/Corporate VP - Human Resources, Jim C. Blakely/Sr. VP - Sales/$590,968.00, Don Rench/General Counsel, Corp. Sec., Gretchen Marks/Corporate VP - Marketing, Mike Skinner/Sr. VP - Entertainment Services, Alex Doumani/Corporate VP - Engineering, Brian Turner/CFO/$1,393,904.00, Rich Deck/Chief Accounting Officer, Marci Maule/Contact - Corporate Public Relations, Sarah Jones/Contact - Corporate Public Relations, Alex Camara/Sr. VP, GM - Worldwide Coin *(17 Officers included in Index)*

Directors: Keith D. Grinstein/47/Chmn., Deborah L. Bevier/56/Dir., Ronald B. Woodard/Dir., Michael R. Rouleau/69/Dir., David M. Eskenazy/46/Dir., David W. Cole/60/Dir., Robert D. Sznewajs/61/Dir.

Owners: David M. Eskenazy, Brian V. Turner, Robert D. Sznewajs, David W. Cole/1.60%, Insiders/4.90%, Shamrock Partners Activist Value Fund,/7.30%, Randall J. Fagundo, Deborah L. Bevier, Frank LaGrange Johnson/5.70%, James C. Blakely, William Blair& Company, L.L.C./11.10%, Ronald B. Woodard, Stephen J. Verleye, Michael R. Rouleau, Barclays Global Investors, NA/5.20% *(17 Owners included in Index)*

*Financial Data: Fiscal Year End:*12/31 *Latest Annual Data:* 12/31/2006

Year	Sales	Net Income
2006	$534,442,000	$18,627,000
2005	$459,739,000	$22,272,000
2004	$307,100,000	$20,368,000

Curr. Assets:	$269,983,000	Curr. Liab.:	$196,849,000	P/E Ratio:	55.45
Plant, Equip.:	$160,962,000	Total Liab.:	$396,718,000	Indic. Yr. Divd.:	NA
Total Assets:	$718,083,000	Net Worth:	$321,365,000	Debt/ Equity:	0.5973

Cold Spring Capital Inc

51 Locust Ave., Ste.302, New Canaan, CT, 06840; *PH:* 1-201-972-0888; *http://* www.coldspringcapital.com

General - Incorporation .... DE	Stock - Price on:12/24/2007 .... NA
Employees .... NA	Stock Exchange .... NA
Auditor .... Goldstein Golub Kessler LLP	Ticker Symbol .... NA
Stk Agt. .... Continental Stock Transfer & Trust Co	Outstanding Shares .... NA
Counsel .... NA	E.P.S. $0.42
DUNS No. .... NA	Shareholders .... NA

Business: The group is in development stage. The group operates from the United States.

Primary SIC and add'l.: 7389

CIK No: 0001330446

Officers: Richard A. Stratton/Chmn., CEO, Sec., Joseph S. Weingarten/Dir., Pres., Treasurer

Directors: Richard A. Stratton/Chmn., CEO, Sec., Trevor I. Rozowsky/Dir., Evan E. Binder/Dir., Robert M. Chefitz/Dir., Joseph S. Weingarten/Dir., Pres., Treasurer

Owners: Insiders, Fir Tree, Inc., Richard A. Stratton, Ospraie Holding I, L.P., Millennium Management, L.L.C., The Baupost Group, L.L.C., Wellington Management Company, LLP, Jeffrey B. Larson, Satellite Asset Management, L.P., Millenco, L.L.C., Sowood Capital Management LP, Dwight Anderson, Satellite Fund Management LLC, Ospraie Management, Inc., Ospraie Management, LLC *(19 Owners included in Index)*

*Financial Data: Fiscal Year End:*12/31 *Latest Annual Data:* 12/31/2006

Year	Sales	Net Income
2006	$13,984,000	$169,000
2005	NA	-$1,293,000
2004	$534,000	-$1,327,000

Curr. Assets:	$17,313,000	Curr. Liab.:	$10,524,000		
Plant, Equip.:	$2,753,000	Total Liab.:	$14,971,000	Indic. Yr. Divd.:	NA
Total Assets:	$20,835,000	Net Worth:	$5,864,000	Debt/ Equity:	NA

Coldwater Creek Inc

1 Coldwater Creek Dr., Sandpoint, ID, 83864; *PH:* 1-208-263-2266; *Fax:* 1-208-263-1582; *http://* www.coldwater-creek.com

General - Incorporation .... DE	Stock - Price on:12/24/2007 .... $24.25
Employees 3,038	Stock Exchange .... NDQ
Auditor .... Deloitte & Touche, LLP	Ticker Symbol .... CWTR
Stk Agt. .... Mellon Investor Services LLC	Outstanding Shares 93,310,000
Counsel .... Hogan & Hartson LLP	E.P.S. $0.59
DUNS No. 11-516-8338	Shareholders .... NA

Business: The group's principal activity is the retail sale of women's apparel, jewelry, footwear, gift items and home merchandise. The group operates in two segments: direct segment and retail segment. The direct segment includes traditional catalog business and Internet-based, e-commerce business and merchandise clearance outlet stores. The retail segment operates full-line retail stores throughout the United States. Coldwater creek(R) and Spirit(R) are registered trademarks of the group. Internationally, the group sells its products primarily in Canada and Japan. As of 31-Jul-2004, the group operated 89 full-line retail stores, two resort stores and 18 merchandise clearance outlet stores in 69 markets.

Primary SIC and add'l.: 5944 5947 5961

CIK No: 0001018005

Officers: Dennis C. Pence/Founder, Chmn., CEO/$3,819,734.00, Timothy O. Martin/Sr. VP, CFO, Georgia Shonk-Simmons/Dir., Pres., Chief Merchandising Officer/$1,430,320.00, Melvin Dick/54/Exec. VP/$1,203,193.00, Brett Avner/Sr. VP - Human Resources, Tim Dilworth/VP - Marketing, Mike Carper/VP - Technology Operations, Kira Karmazin/VP - Retail Merchandising, Michael Feurer/Pres. - New Strategic Concepts Division, Daniel Griesemer/COO, Pres./$1,127,168.00, Dan Moen/CIO, Sr. VP/$592,669.00, Gerard El Chaar/Sr. VP - Operations, Ronn Hall/VP - Sourcing, Production, Peter Prandato/VP - Creative, Christine Laczai/VP - Internet Division *(22 Officers included in Index)*

Directors: Dennis C. Pence/Founder, Chmn., CEO, Georgia Shonk-Simmons/Dir., Pres., Chief Merchandising Officer, Michael Potter/Dir., Curt Hecker/Dir., James R. Alexander/Dir., Ann Pence/Dir., Kay Isaacson-Leibowitz/Dir., Frank Lesher/Dir., Robert H. McCall/Dir., Jerry Gramaglia/Dir.

Owners: Dan Moen, Dennis C. Pence/14.20%, AXA Financial, Inc./7.00%, Jerry Gramaglia, Frank M. Lesher, Daniel Griesemer, Kay Isaacson-Leibowitz, James R. Alexander, Ann E. Pence/19.50%, Georgia Shonk Simmons, Robert H. McCall, Melvin Dick, Curt Hecker, Insiders/15.50%

*Financial Data: Fiscal Year End:*01/28 *Latest Annual Data:* 2/3/2007

Year	Sales	Net Income
2007	$1,054,611,000	$55,372,000
2006	$779,663,000	$41,570,000
2005	$590,310,000	$29,130,000

Curr. Assets:	$326,648,000	Curr. Liab.:	$153,329,000	P/E Ratio:	41.10
Plant, Equip.:	$247,385,000	Total Liab.:	$263,019,000	Indic. Yr. Divd.:	NA
Total Assets:	$580,475,000	Net Worth:	$317,456,000	Debt/ Equity:	NA

Coles Myer Ltd

800 Toorak Rd. , Tooronga, Victoria, 3146; ; *http://* www.colesmyer.com; *Email:* info@colesmyer.com.au

General - Incorporation .... Australia	Stock - Price on:12/24/2007 .... NA
Employees .... NA	Stock Exchange .... NYSE
Auditor .... PricewaterhouseCoopers LLP	Ticker Symbol .... NA
Stk Agt .... Citicorp Shareholder Services	Outstanding Shares .... NA
Counsel .... Mr Hammon	E.P.S. .... NA
DUNS No. 75-317-0117	Shareholders .... NA

Business: The group's principal activities are carried out through the following business segments: food and liquor involves the retail of grocery and liquor items. General merchandise and apparel involves the retail of apparel, general merchandise and stationery items such as homewares, cosmetics, fragrances, toys, sporting goods, kitchenware, outdoor furnitures and electrical appliances. E-commerce involves the provision of e-commerce trading services to internal and external customers. Brands include bi-lo supermarkets, coles online, coles express shell service stations, harris technology, kmart, kmart tyre & auto service, liquorland, liquorland direct, megamart, myer grace bros, officeworks, shopfast, target, theo's liquor and vintage cellars. On 06-Jan-2003, the group acquired viking direct pty ltd and viking office products pty ltd and on 26-May-2003, pallas newco pty ltd and alw newco pty ltd. The group operates around 1,900 stores in Australia and New Zealand.

Primary SIC and add'l.: 5311 5411 5921 5331 5999 5699 5731

CIK No: 0000825777

Officers: John Fletcher/56/MD, CEO, Peter Merritt/MD - Supermarket Merchandise, Greg Willis/Group GM - Program Delivery, Fiona Bennett/Group GM - Assurance Services, Mick McMahon/COO - Coles Retail, Fraser MacKenzie/CFO, Larry Davis/MD - Kmart, Launa Inman/MD - Target, Tim Hammon/54/Chief Officer Corporate - Property Services, Joe Barberis/MD - Officeworks, Ian Clubb/Group GM - Human Resources, Andrew Potter/Group GM - Supply Chain, Peter Mahler/CIO, Pamela Catty/Group GM - Corporate Affairs, Richard Dammery/General Counsel, Company Sec. *(16 Officers included in Index)*

Directors: Richard H. Allert/Chmn., Sandra McPhee/Non - Exec. Dir., Patty Akopiantz/Non - Exec. Dir., Keith Barton/Non - Exec. Dir., Bill Gurry/Non - Exec. Dir., Tony Hodgson/Non - Exec. Dir., Belinda Hutchinson/Non - Exec. Dir., Ronald K. Barton/67/Non - Exec. Dir., William P. Gurry/60/Non - Exec. Dir., Michael Wemms/Non - Exec. Dir.

Owners: Tim Hammon, Rick Allert, Tony Hodgson, John Fletcher, Keith Barton, Commonwealth Bank of Australia/5.00%, Patty Akopiantz, Sandra McPhee, Bill Gurry, Belinda Hutchinson, Fraser MacKenzie, Michael Wemms, S. Lew Custodians Pty. Ltd. and its associates/5.80%

Curr. Assets:	$3,250,861,000	Curr. Liab.:	$2,990,150,000		
Plant, Equip.:	$2,682,127,000	Total Liab.:	$4,251,615,000	Indic. Yr. Divd.:	NA
Total Assets:	$6,750,623,000	Net Worth:	$2,499,008,000	Debt/ Equity:	NA

Coley Pharmaceutical Group Inc

93 Worcester St., Ste. 101, Wellesley, MA, 02481; *PH:* 1-781-431-9000; *Fax:* 1-781-431-6403; *http://* www.coleypharma.com; *Email:* corpcomm@coleypharma.com

General - Incorporation .... DE	Stock - Price on:12/24/2007 .... $8.41
Employees 150	Stock Exchange .... NDQ
Auditor .... PricewaterhouseCoopers LLP	Ticker Symbol .... COLY
Stk Agt .... Computershare Investor Services LLC	Outstanding Shares 26,500,000
Counsel .... Mintz, Levin, Glovsky & Popeo PC	E.P.S. .... -$1.34
DUNS No. .... NA	Shareholders .... NA

Business: The groups principle activities include discovering and developing a novel drug. The group operates from the United States, Germany and Canada. The group's quarterly revenue for September 2007 was 5.11 millions of USD.

Primary SIC and add'l.: 2836 2834

CIK No: 0001319197

Subsidiaries: Coley Pharmaceutical GmbH, Coley Pharmaceutical Group, Ltd., Coley Securities Corporation

Officers: Robert L. Bratzler/Dir., CEO, Pres., Arthur M. Krieg/Sr. VP - Research, Development, Chief Scientific Officer, Charles H. Abdalian/CFO, Sr. VP - Finance, Heather L. Davis/Sr. VP - Pharmacology Research & Development, MD - Coley Ltd, Ted Hibben/VP - Business Development, Alliance Management, Ferdinand E. Massari/Sr. VP - Drug Development, Chief Medical Officer, Christian Schetter/Sr. VP - European Operation MD - Coley Gmbh, Charles E. Yon/Sr. VP, General Counsel, Sue Hager/VP - Investor Relations, Corporate Communications, Corporate Development

Directors: Robert L. Bratzler/Dir., CEO, Pres., Kenneth M. Bate/Dir., Anthony B. Evnin/Dir., Robert J. Hugin/Dir., Manfred E. Karobath/Dir., Patrick J. Langlois/Dir., James E. Thomas/Dir.

Owners: Patrick Langlois, James E. Thomas/8.92%, Entities affiliated with TVM Capital/11.97%, Entities affiliated with Venrock Associates/10.96%, Anthony B. Evnin/10.96%, Arthur M. Krieg/3.31%, Charles H. Abdalian, Manfred E. Karobath/1.70%, Entities affiliated with Thomas, McNerney & Partners, L.P./8.91%, Entities affiliated with Ziff Asset Management, L.P./8.97%, Insiders/34.56%, Entities affiliated with Franklin Resources, Inc./5.16%, Robert J. Hugin, Robert L. Bratzler/4.11%, Kenneth M. Bate

Financial Data: Fiscal Year End:12/31 Latest Annual Data: 12/31/2006

Year	Sales	Net Income
2006	$20,201,000	-$29,775,000
2005	$15,884,000	-$38,064,000
2004	$14,344,000	-$33,981,000

Curr. Assets:	$111,349,000	Curr. Liab.:	$24,103,000		
Plant, Equip.:	$4,597,000	Total Liab.:	$51,633,000	Indic. Yr. Divd.:	NA
Total Assets:	$122,275,000	Net Worth:	$70,642,000	Debt/ Equity:	0.0128

Colgate Palmolive Co

300 Pk. Ave., New York, NY, 10022; **PH:** 1-212-310-2000; **Fax:** 1-212-310-2475; http:// www.colgate.com

General - Incorporation	DE	Stock- Price on:12/24/2007	$66.04
Employees	34,700	Stock Exchange	NYSE
Auditor	PricewaterhouseCoopers LLP	Ticker Symbol	CL
Stk Agt.	Bank of New York	Outstanding Shares	511,490,000
Counsel	NA	E.P.S.	$3.01
DUNS No.	00-134-4381	Shareholders	NA

Business: The group's principle activity is to manufacture and market oral and personal care products. The groups products include Palmolive(R), Murphy oil soap(R) and Ajax(R). The group operates through two segments namely oral, personal, household surface and fabric care and pet nutrition products. The group operates from North America, Latin America, Europe, Asia and Africa.

Primary SIC and add'l.: 2844 3991 2047

CIK No: 0000021665

Subsidiaries: Colgate (Guangzhou) Co. Ltd, Colgate Flavors and Fragrances, Inc., Colgate Oral Pharmaceuticals, Inc, Colgate Palmolive (Middle East Exports) Ltd, Colgate Palmolive Europe Sarl, Colgate Palmolive Industrial Unipessoal, Lda., Colgate Palmolive Peru S.A., Colgate Sanxiao Company Limited, Colgate-Palmolive (America) Inc. Moscow Representative Office, Colgate-Palmolive (America), Inc., Colgate-Palmolive (Asia) Pte. Ltd., Colgate-Palmolive (Caribbean) Inc., Colgate-Palmolive (Central America), Inc., Colgate-Palmolive (Centro America) S.A., Colgate-Palmolive (Dominican Republic), Inc. 83 Subsidiaries included in the Index

Officers: Ian M. Cook/Dir., CEO, Pres./$8,388,634.00, Robert C. Wheeler/CEO - Hill's Pet Nutrition, Thomas M. Chappell/CEO - Tom's, Maine, Fabian Garcia/Chmn., Exec. VP, Pres. - Colgate, Latin America, Global Sustainability, John J. Huston/VP - Office, Chmn., Heiko Tietke/VP, GM - Colgate, Germany, Chmn. Gaba International, Talulla R. Newsome/VP - Global Research & Development and Business Development, Peter C. Chase/VP - Global Consumer, Marketing Knowledge, Panagiotis Tsourapas/VP, GM - Colgate, Greece, Leonard D. Smith/VP - Finance, Global Sales, Advertising, Luis Gutierrez/VP, GM - Colgate, West Andean Region, Latin America, Robert C. Pierce/VP - Global Research & Development, Reuven M. Sacher/VP - Global Research & Development, Sheila A. Hopkins/VP, GM - Professional Oral Care, Hans L. Pohlschroeder/VP - Treasury (143 Officers included in Index)

Directors: Ian M. Cook/Dir., CEO, Pres., Reuben Mark/Chmn. - Colgate, Palmolive Company, R. A. Shah/Vice Chmn. - Cpil, P. K. Ghosh/Dep. Chmn. - Cpil, Fabian Garcia/Chmn., Exec. VP, Pres. - Colgate, Latin America, Global Sustainability, Stephen I. Sadove/Dir., Jill K. Conway/Dir., Elizabeth A. Monrad/Dir., Vikram Singh Mehta/Dir. - Cpil, India, J. K. Setna/Dir. - Cpil, Howard B. Wentz/Dir., Ellen M. Hancock/Dir., Pedro J. Reinhard/Dir., Delano E. Lewis/Dir., David W. Johnson/Dir. (17 Directors included in Index)

Owners: Insiders, Michael J. Tangney, Howard B. Wentz, Ian M. Cook, Michael J. Tangney, David W. Johnson, Javier G. Teruel, Ellen M. Hancock, Richard J. Kogan, Javier G. Teruel, State Street Bank and Trust Company/7.70%, Pedro J. Reinhard, John T. Cahill, Ian M. Cook, Stephen C. Patrick (22 Owners included in Index)

Financial Data: Fiscal Year End:12/31 Latest Annual Data: 12/31/2006

Year	Sales	Net Income
2006	$12,237,700,000	$1,353,400,000
2005	$11,396,900,000	$1,351,400,000
2004	$10,584,200,000	$1,327,100,000

Curr. Assets:	$3,301,000,000	Curr. Liab.:	$3,469,100,000	P/E Ratio:	23.93
Plant, Equip.:	$2,696,100,000	Total Liab.:	$7,615,300,000	Indic. Yr. Divd.:	$1.440
Total Assets:	$9,138,000,000	Net Worth:	$1,410,900,000	Debt/ Equity:	1.8765

CollaGenex Pharmaceuticals Inc

41 University Dr., Ste. 200, Newtown, PA, 18940; **PH:** 1-215-579-7388; **Fax:** 1-215-579-8577; http:// www.collagenex.com

General - Incorporation	DE	Stock- Price on:12/24/2007	$12.46
Employees	130	Stock Exchange	NDQ
Auditor	KPMG LLP	Ticker Symbol	CGPI
Stk Agt.	American Stock Transfer & Trust Co.	Outstanding Shares	21,320,000
Counsel	Hale & Dorr LLP	E.P.S.	-$0.8
DUNS No.	82-523-3844	Shareholders	NA

Business: The group's principal activity is to provide innovative medical therapies to the dental and dermatology markets. The products of the group are used for treating adult periodontitis by inhibiting the enzymes that destroy periodontal support tissues. The products marketed in the United States under the trademarks include Periostat, Metastat, Dermostat, Nephrostat, Osteostat, Arthrostat, Rheumastat, Corneostat, Gingistst, Impacs, PS20, the whole mouth treatment, Restoraderm and Dentaplex.

Primary SIC and add'l.: 2834 8731

CIK No: 0001012270

Subsidiaries: CollaGenex International, Ltd., MMP Technologies, Inc., SansRosa Pharmaceutical Development, Inc.

Officers: Colin W. Stewart/Dir., CEO, Pres./$1,533,448.00, Nancy C. Broadbent/52/CFO, Treasurer/$570,081.00, Andrew Powell/VP, General Counsel Sec./$472,480.00, Klaus Theobald/Sr. VP, Chief Medical Officer/$602,541.00, David F. Pfeiffer/Sr. VP - Sales, Marketing/$557,329.00, Gregory J. Ford/VP - Business Development, Strategic Planning

Directors: Colin W. Stewart/Dir., CEO, Pres., James E. Daverman/Chmn., Robert A. Beardsley/Dir., Robert C. Black/Dir., Robert J. Easton/Dir., Peter R. Barnett/Dir., George Lasezkay/Dir., James W. O'Shea/Dir.

Owners: Deerfield Capital, L.P./7.00%, SZ Investments, L.L.C./8.00%, Insiders/9.80%, Nancy C. Broadbent/1.20%, Andrew K.W. Powell, James W. OShea, Robert A. Beardsley, Robert J. Easton, Morgan Stanley/5.80%, Columbia Wanger Asset Management, L.P./5.30%, Colin W. Stewart/1.20%, Peter R. Barnett, George Lasezkay, David F. Pfeiffer/1.40%, Robert Black (22 Owners included in Index)

Financial Data: Fiscal Year End:12/31 Latest Annual Data: 12/31/2006

Year	Sales	Net Income
2006	$26,373,000	-$33,434,000
2005	$26,405,000	-$18,805,000
2004	$52,146,000	$6,528,000

Curr. Assets:	$76,276,000	Curr. Liab.:	$16,640,000		
Plant, Equip.:	$1,008,000	Total Liab.:	$16,905,000	Indic. Yr. Divd.:	NA
Total Assets:	$79,207,000	Net Worth:	$62,302,000	Debt/ Equity:	NA

Collectors Universe Inc

1921 E Alton Ave., Santa Ana, CA, 92705; **PH:** 1-949-567-1234; **Fax:** 1-949-833-7955; http:// www.collectors.com

General - Incorporation	DE	Stock- Price on:12/24/2007	$13.99
Employees	211	Stock Exchange	NDQ
Auditor	Grant Thornton, LLP	Ticker Symbol	CLCT
Stk Agt.	U.S. Stock Transfer Corp	Outstanding Shares	8,460,000
Counsel	Stradling Yocca Carlson & Rauth	E.P.S.	-$0.12
DUNS No.	NA	Shareholders	NA

Business: The group's principal activity is to grade, auction, market and provide content information for high-end collectibles. The authentication and grading services are provided for sportscards, rare coins, stamps and authentication-only services for sports memorabilia and autographs. The group conducts in-person, telephone and Internet auctions of rare coins and currency, sportscards and sports memorabilia, rare records and entertainment memorabilia. It also publishes magazines that provide market prices and information for certain collectibles. The group's brand names in the collectibles market include professional coin grading service (pcgs), professional sports authenticators (psa), bowers and merena and lyn knight currency auctions.

Primary SIC and add'l.: 7389

CIK No: 0001089143

Subsidiaries: Certified Asset Exchange, Inc., Collectors Finance Corporation, Gem Certification and Assurance Lab, Inc., Professional Coin Grading Services, Inc.

Officers: Michael R. Haynes/Dir., CEO, Ron Howard/Dir. - Grading, Professional Coin Grading Service, Pcgs, Bob Zafian/Consultant Authenticator -PSA, DNA Authentication Services, Brandi Piacente/Primary Investor Relations Officer, Steve Van Maanen/Assist. Dir. - Grading, Professional Sports Authenticator, PSA, Reza Tabatabai/Dir. - Grading, Professional Sports Authenticator, PSA, Bill Litle/Editor - Stamp Marketing Quarterly, SMQ, David G. Hall/Dir., Pres., Mike Sherman/Pres. - Professional Stamp Experts, PSE, Michael J. Lewis/Sr. VP, Chief Compliance Officer, Jon Bahner/Sr. Grader, Professional Sports Authenticator, PSA, Jason W. Bradford/Pres. - Pcgs Currency, William Crowe/Dir. - Research, Professional Stamp Experts, PSE, Herman Darvick/Consultant Authenticator - PSA, DNA Authentication Services, Bob Eaton/Consultant Authenticator, PSA, DNA Authentication Services (39 Officers included in Index)

Directors: Michael R. Haynes/Dir., CEO, Clinton A. Allen/Chmn., A. J. Moyer/Dir., John Dannreuther/Founder - Professional Coin Grading Service, Pcgs, Michael McConnell/Dir., David G. Hall/Dir., Pres., Deborah A. Farrington/Dir., D. Van Simmons/Dir., Bruce A. Stevens/Dir.

Owners: Michael J. Lewis, A. J. Bert Moyer, Clinton A. Allen/1.10%, Special Situations Cayman Fund, L.P./9.50%, Deborah A. Farrington, David G. Hall/9.00%, Van D. Simmons/2.80%, Insiders/17.30%, Shamrock Partner Activist Fund L.L.C./13.60%, Michael R. Haynes/3.00%, Bruce A. Stevens, Joseph J. Wallace, Sarbit Asset Management/7.00%, Royce & Associates, LLC/7.40%

Financial Data: Fiscal Year End:06/30 Latest Annual Data: 6/30/2006

Year	Sales	Net Income
2006	$36,914,000	$3,700,000
2005	$33,607,000	$4,818,000
2004	$26,420,000	$1,730,000

Curr. Assets:	$60,800,000	Curr. Liab.:	$5,913,000	P/E Ratio:	98.52
Plant, Equip.:	$1,897,000	Total Liab.:	$6,315,000	Indic. Yr. Divd.:	$1.000
Total Assets:	$78,221,000	Net Worth:	$71,906,000	Debt/ Equity:	NA

College Partnership Inc

333 S Allison Pkwy, Ste 100, Lakewood, CO, 80226; **PH:** 1-303-804-0155; http:// www.collegepartnership.com

General - Incorporation	NV	Stock- Price on:12/24/2007	$0.044
Employees	NA	Stock Exchange	OTC
Auditor	Stonefield Josephson, Inc	Ticker Symbol	CGPA
Stk Agt.	Corporate Stock Transfer, Inc.	Outstanding Shares	NA
Counsel	NA	E.P.S.	NA
DUNS No.	NA	Shareholders	NA

Business: The group's principle activity is to provide products and information services to high school students and assists parents and students with an opportunity to qualify for financial aid. It offers assistance in college major selection, college selection, college entrance test information products and services to its clients, to assist in career planning, college course selection, college selection, college entrance testing, and searches for merit awards and financial aid. The products consist of printed materials, videocassettes, and test preparation, college major and career assessment software and databases assessed through CD-ROM or the Internet. The services are offered directly to students and their parents via networking with high school coaches, direct mail, phone solicitations, Internet Website and seminar programs.

Primary SIC and add'l.: 8299

CIK No: 0001103137

Officers: Janice A. Jones/Dir., Exec. VP

Directors: John Grace/Chmn., Janice A. Jones/Dir., Exec. VP

Financial Data: **Fiscal Year End:**07/31 **Latest Annual Data:** 7/31/2004

Year	Sales	Net Income
2004	$18,472,000	-$1,234,000
2003	$17,642,000	-$561,000
2002	$12,913,000	-$398,000

Curr. Assets:	$3,459,000	**Curr. Liab.:**	$8,314,000		
Plant, Equip.:	$217,000	**Total Liab.:**	$10,358,000	**Indic. Yr. Divd.:**	NA
Total Assets:	$5,888,000	**Net Worth:**	-$4,471,000	**Debt/ Equity:**	NA

Colombia Goldfields Ltd

500-666 Burrard St. , Vancouver, BC, V6C 2X8; *PH:* 1-604-601-2040; *Fax:* 1-604-688-2419; http:// www.colombiagf.com; *Email:* Info@colombiagoldfields.com

General - Incorporation	NV	Stock - Price on:12/24/2007	$1.33
Employees	NA	Stock Exchange	OTC
Auditor	Vellmer & Chang	Ticker Symbol	CGDF
Stk Agt	Mr. Velez	Outstanding Shares	NA
Counsel	NA	E.P.S	NA
DUNS No.	NA	Shareholders	NA

Business: The groups principal activity is to exploration of minerals. In the year 2006, the group acquired Gavilan Minerales, S.A. The group operates from the United States and Canada.

Primary SIC and add'l.: 1044

CIK No: 0001223663

Subsidiaries: Compania Minera De Caldas, S.A, Gavilan Minerales S.A.

Officers: Randall J. Martin/Dir., CEO/$709,905.00, Stewart D. Redwood/VP - Exploration/$207,313.00, James Kopperson/VP - Finance, CFO/$471,051.00, Carlos Calderon/Project Mgr. - Marmato Mountain Development

Directors: Randall J. Martin/Dir., CEO, David Bikerman/Dir., Robert Van Tassell/Dir., Thomas McGrail/Dir., Jonathan Berg/Dir., Terry Lyons/Dir., James Verraster/Dir., Edward Flood/Dir.

Owners: Stewart D. Redwood, Investcol Limited/17.80%, James Kopperson, James Verraster, Jonathan Berg, Edward Flood, Randall J. Martin/1.90%, Terry Lyons, David Bikerman, Thomas Ernest McGrail, Absolute East West Master Fund/9.40%, Insiders/4.00%

Financial Data: **Fiscal Year End:**12/31 **Latest Annual Data:** 12/31/2006

Year	Sales	Net Income
2006	NA	-$6,279,000
2005	NA	-$1,491,000
2004	$5,000	-$23,000

Curr. Assets:	$1,059,000	**Curr. Liab.:**	$6,038,000		
Plant, Equip.:	$43,948,000	**Total Liab.:**	$15,797,000	**Indic. Yr. Divd.:**	NA
Total Assets:	$45,007,000	**Net Worth:**	$29,210,000	**Debt/ Equity:**	NA

Colonial Bancgroup Inc

100 Colonial Bank Blvd., Montgomery, AL, 36117; *PH:* 1-334-240-5000; *Fax:* 1-334-676-5345; http:// www.colonialbank.com

General - Incorporation	DE	Stock - Price on:12/24/2007	$24.45
Employees	4,721	Stock Exchange	NYSE
Auditor	PricewaterhouseCoopers LLP	Ticker Symbol	CNB
Stk Agt.	Computershare Investor Services LLC	Outstanding Shares	153,020,000
Counsel	Miller, Hamilton, Snider & Odom	E.P.S	$1.54
DUNS No.	03-825-7861	Shareholders	NA

Business: The groups principle activity is to provide banking and financial services. The group also provides retail and commercial banking, wealth management, mortgage banking and insurance services. The group operates from United States.

Primary SIC and add'l.: 6712 6022

CIK No: 0000092339

Subsidiaries: BP Hwy 10 San Antonio Ltd, CB Dogwood LLC, CB Habersham II LLC, CB Habersham LLC, CD Lake Deerfield LLC, CD Peachtree Corners LLC, Colonial Bank N.A., Colonial Brokerage Inc., Colonial Capital II, Colonial Capital Trust III, Colonial Capital Trust IV, Colonial Crabapple LLC, Colonial Deerfield LLC, Colonial Mead LLC, Crabapple White Columns Development LLC 23 Subsidiaries included in the Index

Officers: Robert E. Lowder/Chmn., CEO, Pres./$2,619,400.00, Sarah H. Moore/CFO, Sr. Exec. VP - Colonial Bank/$932,420.00, David B. Byrne/Exec. VP, Sec., General Counsel/$424,287.00, Lisa M. Free/Dir. - Investor Relations, Caryn D. Cope/Sr. Exec. VP, Chief Credit Officer - Colonial Bank/$921,661.00, Patti G. Hill/COO, Sr. Exec. VP - Colonial Bank/$943,153.00

Directors: Robert E. Lowder/Chmn., CEO, Pres., Clinton O. Holdbrooks/Dir. - Colonial Bank, Lewis E. Beville/Dir. - Colonial Bank, Augustus K. Clements/Dir. - Colonial Bank, Robert S. Craft/Dir. - Colonial Bank, Patrick F. Dye/Dir. - Colonial Bank, Hubert L. Harris/Dir. - Colonial Bank, John Ed Mathison/Dir., Milton E. McGregor/Dir. - Colonial Bank, John C.H. Miller/Dir. - Colonial Bank, Joe D. Mussafer/Dir., William E. Powell/Dir. - Colonial Bank, James W. Rane/Dir. - Colonial Bank, Simuel Sippial/Dir. - Colonial Bank, Edward V. Welch/Dir. - Colonial Bank *(16 Directors included in Index)*

Owners: Michael J. Crowell, Insiders/8.89%, Robert G. Stokes/3.41%, Robert L. Krieger, Donald H. Wilson, Carl J. Strang, Jack P. Brandon, Burke D. Kibler, Edward F. Koren/26.38%, Kay Harris Fields, Samuel W. Hart, George W. Harris, Bob Crawford, Insiders/11.73%, Douglas G. Small *(40 Owners included in Index)*

Financial Data: **Fiscal Year End:**12/31 **Latest Annual Data:** 12/31/2006

Year	Sales	Net Income
2006	$1,644,807,000	$265,813,000
2005	$1,374,738,000	$228,502,000
2004	$1,001,611,000	$172,877,000

Curr. Assets:	$1,379,012,000	**Curr. Liab.:**	$18,204,641,000	**P/E Ratio:**	15.88
Plant, Equip.:	$409,565,000	**Total Liab.:**	$20,726,914,000	**Indic. Yr. Divd.:**	$0.750
Total Assets:	$22,784,249,000	**Net Worth:**	$2,057,335,000	**Debt/ Equity:**	NA

Colonial Bankshares Inc

2745 S Delsea Dr., Vineland, NJ, 08360; *PH:* 1-856-205-0058; *Fax:* 1-856-205-0509; http:// www.colonialbankfsb.com

General - Incorporation	Federal	Stock - Price on:12/24/2007	$14.65
Employees	71	Stock Exchange	NDQ
Auditor	Beard Miller Company LLP	Ticker Symbol	COBK
Stk Agt	Registrar & Transfer Co	Outstanding Shares	4,430,000
Counsel	NA	E.P.S	$0.36
DUNS No.	NA	Shareholders	NA

Business: The group operates through its subsidiaries whose principle activity is to provide banking services. The groups services include family residential real estate loans, home equity loans and lines of credit, commercial real estate lending commercial loans and construction loans. The group operates from the United States.

Primary SIC and add'l.: 6035 6712

CIK No: 0001317019

Subsidiaries: CB Delaware Investments, Inc., Colonial Bank, FSB

Officers: Edward J. Geletka/Dir., CEO, Pres., Joseph L. Stella/CFO, Exec. VP, Richard Dapp/Sr. VP, Chief Credit Officer, William F. Whelan/Exec. VP, Operations Officer, Marie E. Davis/Corp. Sec., Vicki T. Cannizzaro/VP - Technology, Product Development, Wheeler Fazenbaker/VP, Compliance Officer, Tracy Holt-Jenkins/VP, Jody K. Hirata/VP, Dir. - Business Development, Leon Riggins/VP, Steven J. Sammartino/VP - Sr. Commercial Lender, Joseph Sidebotham/VP, Controller, Thomas Davies/Assist. VP, Christine Marciano/Assist. VP, Anthony Marino/Assist. VP *(18 Officers included in Index)*

Directors: Edward J. Geletka/Dir., CEO, Pres., Frank M. Hankins/Chmn., Albert A. Fralinger/Vice Chmn., Gregory J. Facemyer/Dir., James F. Quinn/Dir., Richard S. Allen/Dir., John Fitzpatrick/Dir.

Owners: Richard S. Allen, Albert A. Fralinger, James Quinn, Insiders/5.10%, Richard W. Dapp, Frank M. Hankins/1.00%, Gregory J. Facemyer, Grace and White, Inc/6.50%, Joseph L. Stella, Edward J. Geletka, Colonial Bankshares, MHC/54.00%, John Fitzpatrick, William F. Whelan

Financial Data: **Fiscal Year End:**12/31 **Latest Annual Data:** 12/31/2006

Year	Sales	Net Income
2006	$19,552,000	$1,611,000
2005	$15,662,000	$1,769,000
2004	$13,253,000	$1,847,000

Curr. Assets:	$13,974,000	**Curr. Liab.:**	$338,704,000	**P/E Ratio:**	38.55
Plant, Equip.:	$7,337,000	**Total Liab.:**	$346,934,000	**Indic. Yr. Divd.:**	NA
Total Assets:	$383,597,000	**Net Worth:**	$36,663,000	**Debt/ Equity:**	0.1825

Colonial Commercial Corp

275 Wagaraw Rd., Hawthorne, NJ, 07506; *PH:* 1-973-427-8224; *Fax:* 1-973-427-6981; http:// www.colonialcomm.com

General - Incorporation	NY	Stock - Price on:12/24/2007	$1.56
Employees	154	Stock Exchange	OTC
Auditor	Weiser LLP	Ticker Symbol	CCOM
Stk Agt	American Stock Transfer & Trust Co.	Outstanding Shares	4,640,000
Counsel	Oscar and Jeffrey Folger	E.P.S	$0.14
DUNS No.	NA	Shareholders	NA

Business: The groups principal activity activities include distributing, heating, ventilating and air conditioning equipment, parts and accessories, climate control systems, and appliances. The group operates from the United States.

Primary SIC and add'l.: 5075 1711 5039 5074 3585 3433

CIK No: 0000021828

Subsidiaries: American/Universal Supply Inc, RAL Supply Group, Inc., Universal Supply Group, Inc.

Officers: William Pagano/Dir., CEO, Pres. - Universal/$460,109.00, William Salek/CFO, Sec., VP - Universal/$150,958.00, Riannon Russo/Assist. Sec.

Directors: William Pagano/Dir., CEO, Pres. - Universal, Michael Goldman/Chmn., Bruce E. Fredrikson/Dir., Melissa Goldman-Williams/Dir., Stuart H. Lubow/Dir., Ronald Miller/Dir.

Owners: Melissa Goldman-Williams, Goldman Associates of NY, Inc./22.92%, Stuart H. Lubow, Insiders/44.19%, William Salek/1.32%, William Pagano/16.41%, Bruce E. Fredrikson, Michael Goldman/26.74%, Ronald H. Miller, Insiders, Bruce E. Fredrikson, Rita C. Folger/12.37%

Financial Data: **Fiscal Year End:**12/31 **Latest Annual Data:** 12/31/2006

Year	Sales	Net Income
2006	$71,495,000	$753,000
2005	$66,691,000	$2,116,000
2004	$61,454,000	$1,661,000

Curr. Assets:	$23,883,000	**Curr. Liab.:**	$20,448,000	**P/E Ratio:**	11.14
Plant, Equip.:	$1,513,000	**Total Liab.:**	$21,766,000	**Indic. Yr. Divd.:**	NA
Total Assets:	$28,518,000	**Net Worth:**	$6,752,000	**Debt/ Equity:**	0.2051

Colonial Properties Trust

2101 6th Ave. N, Ste. 750, Birmingham, AL, 35203; *PH:* 1-205-250-8700; *Fax:* 1-205-250-8890; http:// www.colonialprop.com

General - Incorporation	AL	Stock - Price on:12/24/2007	$39.38
Employees	1,550	Stock Exchange	NYSE
Auditor	PricewaterhouseCoopers LLP	Ticker Symbol	CLP
Stk Agt	Computershare Investor Services LLC	Outstanding Shares	46,480,000
Counsel	NA	E.P.S	$9.98
DUNS No.	NA	Shareholders	NA

Business: The groups principle activities include owning, developing and operating multifamily, office and retail properties. The group operates through three segments namely, multifamily, office and retail. In the year 2005, the group merged with Cornerstone Realty Income Trust, Inc. The group operates from the Sunbelt region of the United States. The group's quarterly revenue for September 2007 was 93.39 millions of USD.

Primary SIC and add'l.: 6798

CIK No: 0000909111

Subsidiaries: 1755 Central Park Road Condominiums, LLC, 600 Building Partners, A-Colonial 100/200 Owner, LLC, A-Colonial 300/500 Owner, LLC, A-Colonial North Development Owner, LLC, A-Colonial Retail Development Owner, LLC, A-Colonial Retail Owner, LLC, ACG-CPSI Canyon Creek LP, ACG-CRLP Crescent Matthews LLC, ACP Fitness Center LLC, APA II, LLC, Apple REIT II Limited Partnership, Apple REIT III Limited Partnership, Apple REIT IV Limited Partnership, Apple REIT Limited Partnership 263 Subsidiaries included in the Index

Officers: Reynolds C. Thompson/CEO/$1,262,119.00, Weston M. Andress/CFO, Pres./$1,318,738.00, John P. Rigrish/Chief Administrative Officer, Corp. Sec., Charles A. McGehee/Exec. VP - Mixed Use Development/$772,358.00, Paul F. Earle/Exec. VP - Multifamily Division/$665,187.00, Bo Jackson/Exec. VP - Office Division, John E. Tomlinson/Chief Accounting Officer, Jerry A. Brewer/Sr. VP - Corporate Treasury

Directors: Thomas H. Lowder/Chmn., James K. Lowder/Trustee, Herbert A. Meisler/Trustee, Claude B. Nielsen/Trustee, Carl F. Bailey/Trustee, Miller M. Gorrie/Trustee, William M. Johnson/Trustee, Glade M. Knight/Trustee, Harold W. Ripps/Trustee, John W. Spiegel/Trustee, Donald T. Senterfitt/Trustee

Owners: James K. Lowder/4.80%, Glade M. Knight/1.70%, Insiders/22.00%, Thomas H. Lowder/7.60%, Charles A. McGehee, The Vanguard Group, Inc./5.90%, Reynolds C. Thompson, Neuberger Berman, Inc/7.10%, Carl F. Bailey, Claude B. Nielsen, Herbert A. Meisler/1.30%, Donald T. Senterfitt, Robert A. Jackson, Miller M. Gorrie/1.60%, Weston M. Andress *(20 Owners included in Index)*

Financial Data: Fiscal Year End:12/31 Latest Annual Data: 12/31/2006

Year	Sales	Net Income
2006	$496,083,000	$203,480,000
2005	$495,443,000	$219,641,000
2004	$337,410,000	$54,618,000

Curr. Assets:	$129,692,000	Curr. Liab.:	$124,214,000		
Plant, Equip.:	$3,997,150,000	Total Liab.:	$2,945,209,000	Indic. Yr. Divd.:	$2.000
Total Assets:	$4,431,777,000	Net Worth:	$1,486,568,000	Debt/ Equity:	1.6130

Colonial Virginia Bank

6720 Sutton Rd., Gloucester, VA, 23061; **PH:** 1-804-695-9300; *http://* www.colonialvabank.com; **Email:** contactus@colonialvabank.com

General - Incorporation		Stock - Price on:12/24/2007	$28.5
Employees	24	Stock Exchange	OTC
Auditor	NA	Ticker Symbol	CNVB
Stk Agt.	Michelle Ammons	Outstanding Shares	NA
Counsel	NA	E.P.S.	NA
DUNS No.	NA	Shareholders	NA

Business: The groups principal activities include providing range of consumer and commercial banking services to individuals, businesses and industries. Services of the group include money market deposit accounts, time deposits, safe deposit services, credit cards, cash management, direct deposits, notary services, money orders, night depository, travelers checks, cashiers checks, domestic collections, savings bonds, bank drafts and automated teller services. The group operates from the United States.

Primary SIC and add'l.: 4833

CIK No: 0001327409

Officers: Kenneth E. Smith/CFO, Exec. VP

Colony Bankcorp Inc

115 S Grant St., Fitzgerald, GA, 31750; **PH:** 1-229-426-6000; **Fax:** 1-229-426-6039; *http://* www.colonybank.com

General - Incorporation	GA	Stock - Price on:12/24/2007	$19.56
Employees	351	Stock Exchange	NDQ
Auditor	McNair, Middlebrooks & Co. LLP	Ticker Symbol	CBAN
Stk Agt.	Suntrust Bank	Outstanding Shares	7,200,000
Counsel	NA	E.P.S.	$1.45
DUNS No.	12-093-3924	Shareholders	NA

Business: The group's principal activity is to provide retail and commercial banking services to individuals and small to medium size businesses primarily in south Georgia. The group is a multi-bank holding company located in fitzgerald, Georgia. The wholly-owned subsidiaries of the group are: the bank of fitzgerald, bank of worth, ashburn bank, colony bank southeast, the bank of dodge county, colony management services, inc. And community bank of wilcox. The group offers agricultural, financial, real estate, commercial and instalment loans. Deposits accepted include a variety of demand and saving deposits. Other services include money transfers, safe deposit services and investing in government and municipal securities.

Primary SIC and add'l.: 6712 6022

CIK No: 0000711669

Subsidiaries: Colony Bank Ashburn, Colony Bank of Dodge County, Colony Bank of Fitzgerald, Colony Bank Quitman, Colony Bank Southeast, Colony Bank Wilcox, Colony Bank Worth, Colony Management Services, Inc.

Officers: Al D. Ross/44/Dir., CEO, Pres./$322,936.00, Sam Haskell/Marketing Makers, Leonard Seawell/Marketing Makers, Terry L. Hester/53/Dir., Exec. VP, CFO, Sec./$212,674.00, Eric Lawless/Marketing Makers

Directors: Al D. Ross/44/Dir., CEO, Pres., W. B. Roberts/66/Dir., Terry L. Hester/53/Dir., Exec. VP, CFO, Sec., Charles E. Myler/65/Dir., James D. Minix/64/Dir., Morris L. Downing/65/Dir., Edward J. Harrell/63/Dir., Sidney R. Ross/66/Dir., Gene B. Waldron/48/Dir., Mark H. Massee/54/Dir.

Owners: Larry E. Stevenson/0.27%, Edward J. Harrell/0.39%, B. Gene Waldron/1.30%, R. Sidney Ross/11.67%, Insiders/25.12%, Will D. Sims/0.02%, Terry L. Hester/1.89%, James D. Minix/1.86%, W. B. Roberts, Mark H. Massee/0.69%, Terry L. Coleman/2.40%, Al D. Ross/0.39%, Walter P. Patten/0.60%, W. Mike Miller/0.04%, Morris L. Downing/3.13% *(16 Owners included in Index)*

Financial Data: Fiscal Year End:12/31 Latest Annual Data: 12/31/2006

Year	Sales	Net Income
2006	$90,630,000	$10,152,000
2005	$69,786,000	$8,977,000
2004	$58,354,000	$8,069,000

Curr. Assets:	$75,455,000	Curr. Liab.:	$1,043,516,000	P/E Ratio:	13.58
Plant, Equip.:	$28,423,000	Total Liab.:	$1,136,893,000	Indic. Yr. Divd.:	$0.370
Total Assets:	$1,213,504,000	Net Worth:	$76,611,000	Debt/ Equity:	1.0086

Colony Resorts LVH Acquisitions LLC

Las Vegas Hilton, 3000 Paradise Rd., Las Vegas, CA, 90067; **PH:** 1-702-732-5111; *http://* www.lvhilton.com

General - Incorporation	NV	Stock - Price on:12/24/2007	NA
Employees	NA	Stock Exchange	NA
Auditor	Ernst & Young LLP	Ticker Symbol	NA
Stk Agt.	NA	Outstanding Shares	NA
Counsel	NA	E.P.S.	NA
DUNS No.	NA	Shareholders	NA

Business: The group currently operates a loyalty and rewards program known as Maximum Awards. Under the Maximum Awards program, consumers earn points by purchasing products and services offered by the Company and its program partners. Accumulated points then can be redeemed in order to acquire additional desired products or services from the same list of such items offered by the Company. The Company operates its program in Australia and has done so since October 2002.

Primary SIC and add'l.: 7011

CIK No: 0001282607

Subsidiaries: Caesars Entertainment, Inc

Officers: Rodolfo Prieto/63/CEO, GM, Robert Schaffhauser/61/Exec. VP - Finance, Kenneth M. Ciancimino/46/Exec. VP - Administration

Directors: Thomas J. Barrack/60/Chmn., Nicholas L. Ribis/62/Vice Chmn., Clive S. Cummis/79/Dir.

Owners: Thomas J. Barrack, Insiders, Nicholas L. Ribis, Colony Resorts LVH Holdings, LLC, Colony Resorts LVH Co-Investment Partners, L.P.

Color Kinetics Inc

10 Milk St. , Ste. 1100, Boston, MA, 02108; **PH:** 1-617-423-9999; *http://* www.colorkinetics.com

General - Incorporation	DE	Stock - Price on:12/24/2007	$33.46
Employees	137	Stock Exchange	NA
Auditor	Deloitte & Touche, LLP	Ticker Symbol	NA
Stk Agt.	American Stock Transfer & Trust Co.	Outstanding Shares	21,330,000
Counsel	NA	E.P.S.	$1.06
DUNS No.	NA	Shareholders	NA

Business: The group's principal activities are to design, market and license intelligent solid-state lighting systems. The group's intelligent solid-state lighting systems enable the customers to achieve dramatic lighting effects, cost savings and other practical benefits not attainable using traditional lighting technology. The group has wide range of products including led lighting devices, digital controllers, software for creating and controlling lighting effects and related hardware and accessories. The group offers products for sale as individual components, or as complete, integrated lighting systems that include all the elements necessary to create and operate solid-state lighting installations for many types of interior and exterior applications.

Primary SIC and add'l.: 3648 3646

CIK No: 0001048611

Subsidiaries: Color Kinetics Europe Limited, Color Kinetics Netherlands B.V., Color Kinetics Security Corporation

Officers: William Sims/Dir., CEO, Pres./$1,228,319.00, Frederick Morgan/CTO, Frank Hillery/VP - Finance, Jeffrey Cassis/COO, Sr. VP, Gordon M. Trawick/VP - Materials Management, Kevin Dowling/VP - Innovation, Ray Letasi/VP - Apac Lighting Systems Sales, Philip Odonnell/VP - Americas - Europe, Middle East Lighting Systems Sales, John Biasi/VP - Product Development, Daniel Gaudet/Deputy General Counsel - Licensing, Paula Lapalme/VP - Human Resources, David Johnson/Sr. VP, CFO/$471,986.00, Ihor Lys/Chief Scientist/$373,970.00, John Daly/VP - Strategic Sales, Ellen Bossert/VP - Marketing *(16 Officers included in Index)*

Directors: William Sims/Dir., CEO, Pres., Elisabeth Allison/Dir., John E. Abele/Dir., Michael Hawley/Dir., George Mueller/Dir., Garo H. Armen/Dir., William K. Obrien/Dir., James F. Oconnor/Dir., Noubar B. Afeyan/Dir.

Financial Data: Fiscal Year End:12/31 Latest Annual Data: 12/31/2006

Year	Sales	Net Income
2006	$65,424,000	$3,242,000
2005	$52,907,000	$4,332,000
2004	$40,150,000	$2,383,000

Curr. Assets:	$122,008,000	Curr. Liab.:	$10,446,000	P/E Ratio:	152.09
Plant, Equip.:	$2,199,000	Total Liab.:	$10,446,000	Indic. Yr. Divd.:	NA
Total Assets:	$124,489,000	Net Worth:	$114,043,000	Debt/ Equity:	NA

Colorado Goldfields Inc

Formerly: Garpa Resources Inc
10920 W Alameda Ave., Ste. 207, Lakewood, CO, 80226; **PH:** 1-303-984-5324

General - Incorporation	NV	Stock - Price on:12/24/2007	NA
Employees	NA	Stock Exchange	OTC
Auditor	Manning Elliott LLP	Ticker Symbol	CGFI
Stk Agt.	NA	Outstanding Shares	NA
Counsel	NA	E.P.S.	NA
DUNS No.	NA	Shareholders	NA

Business: The groups principal activity is to explore gold. The group operates from the United States and Canada.

Primary SIC and add'l.: 1000

CIK No: 0001344394

Officers: Gary Schellenberg/Dir., CEO

Owners: Gary Schellenberg/44.80%, Insiders/44.80%

Financial Data: Fiscal Year End:08/31 Latest Annual Data: 08/31/2006

Year	Sales	Net Income
2006	NA	-$36,000

Curr. Assets:	$9,000	Curr. Liab.:	$8,000		
Plant, Equip.:	NA	Total Liab.:	$8,000	Indic. Yr. Divd.:	NA
Total Assets:	$9,000	Net Worth:	$1,000	Debt/ Equity:	NA

Colorado Interstate Gas Co

El Paso Bldg 1001 Louisiana St., Houston, TX, 77002; **PH:** 1-713-420-2600; **Fax:** 1-719-520-4878; *http://* www.cigco.com

General - Incorporation .... DE
Employees 5,050
Auditor .... Ernst & Young, LLP
Stk Agt..... Computershare Investor Services LLC
Counsel .... NA
DUNS No. 00-691-4865

Stock- Price on:12/24/2007 .... $17.005
Stock Exchange .... NA
Ticker Symbol .... NA
Outstanding Shares 700,240,000
E.P.S $1.02
Shareholders .... NA

Business: The group's principal activity is to operate an interstate natural gas pipeline system, natural gas processing facilities, storing and gathering systems. Pipeline segment provides natural gas transmission services and consists of approximately 4,000 miles of pipeline with a design capacity of 3,100 mmcf/d. The group has approximately 29 bcf of underground working gas storage capacity along its system. The group serve two major markets on-sytem market and off-system market. On-system market consisting of utilities and other customers located along the front range of the rocky mountains in Colorado and Wyoming, and our off-system market, consisting of the transportation of rocky mountain natural gas production from multiple supply basins to interconnections with other pipelines bound for the midwest, the southwest, California and the pacific northwest. The group discontinued field services operations.

Primary SIC and add'l.: 1311 4923

CIK No: 0000200155

Subsidiaries: El Paso Natural Gas Company, Tennessee Gas Pipeline Compa

Officers: James J. Cleary/Dir., Pres., Principal Executive Officer, Greg Ruben/Contact - Marketing, Customer Services, Julie Adams/Contact - Marketing, Customer Services, Steve Newell/Contact - Marketing, Customer Services, Liz Simonton/Contact - Business Development, Craig Coombs/Contact - Business Development, Tom Dobson/Contact - Business Development, Roland Harris/Contact - Business Development, Laine Lobban/Contact - Business Development, Ed Miller/Contact - Business Development, Audrey Lynch/Contact - Contracts, Capacity Release, Sally Turley/Contact - Contracts, Capacity Release, Kathy Royal/Contact - Scheduling, Nominations, Norm Walker/Contact - Scheduling, Nominations, Dean Makings/Contact - Gas Control *(25 Officers included in Index)*

Directors: James C. Yardley/Chmn., James J. Cleary/Dir., Pres., Principal Executive Officer, Daniel B. Martin/Dir., Sr. VP, Thomas L. Price/Dir., VP

Owners: John R. Sult, James J. Cleary, Insiders, John W. Somerhalder, Thomas L. Price, Daniel B. Martin

Financial Data: **Fiscal Year End:**12/31 **Latest Annual Data:** 12/31/2006

Year	Sales	Net Income
2006	$4,281,000,000	$475,000,000
2005	$4,017,000,000	-$606,000,000
2004	$6,543,000,000	-$947,000,000

Curr. Assets:	$7,167,000,000	**Curr. Liab.:**	$6,151,000,000	**P/E Ratio:**	16.67
Plant, Equip.:	$16,678,000,000	**Total Liab.:**	$23,044,000,000	**Indic. Yr. Divd.:**	$0.160
Total Assets:	$27,261,000,000	**Net Worth:**	$4,186,000,000	**Debt/ Equity:**	2.3979

Colorado Wyoming Reserve Company

751 Horizon Ct., Ste. 205, Grand Junciton, WY, 81506; *PH:* 1-970-255-9995

General - Incorporation .... Wy
Employees 1
Auditor .... Hein & Assoc., LLP
Stk Agt..... Computershare Investor Services LLC
Counsel .... NA
DUNS No. .... NA

Stock- Price on:12/24/2007 .... $0.08
Stock Exchange .... OTC
Ticker Symbol .... CWYR
Outstanding Shares 36,950,000
E.P.S .... NA
Shareholders .... NA

Business: The groups principal activity is focusing its exploratory efforts on its mineral interests in approximately 22,640 gross leased in the central Paradox Basin of southeastern Utah. The group operates from the United States.

Primary SIC and add'l.: 1382

CIK No: 0000318852

Subsidiaries: Shoreline Resources Company, Inc

Owners: Syed A. Daud/1.20%, Insiders/25.20%, Kim M. Fuerst/18.10%, The James E. Moore Revocable Trust,/18.40%, Kaleem A. Sayed/32.00%, Rafiq A. Sayed/6.80%, Waseem A. Sayed/1.50%

Columbia Bancorp

401 E 3rd St., Ste. 200, The Dalles, OR, 97058; *PH:* 1-541-298-6649; *Fax:* 1-541-298-3157; *http://* www.columbiariverbank.com

General - Incorporation .... MD
Employees 362
Auditor .... KPMG LLP
Stk Agt............ Wells Fargo Shareowner Services
Counsel............ Shulman, Rogers, Pordy & Ecker
DUNS No. 79-617-2674

Stock- Price on:12/24/2007 .... $21.14
Stock Exchange .... NDQ
Ticker Symbol .... CBBO
Outstanding Shares 9,990,000
E.P.S $1.46
Shareholders .... NA

Business: The group's principal activities are to provide commercial and retail banking services to individuals and small and medium-sized businesses. The group operates through its wholly owned subsidiary, the columbia bank. The services offered by the group include accepting deposits, which include checking, now accounts, savings accounts, certificate of deposits and individual retirement accounts. The lending activities include providing demand, term, time loans, loans for real estate acquisitions, development and construction and equipment, inventory and accounts receivable financing. It also provides travelers' checks, money orders, safe deposit lockers, automated teller machines and other services. The group operates through 24 branch offices located in howard county, baltimore county, baltimore city, prince george's county and montgomery county, Maryland.

Primary SIC and add'l.: 6022 6712

CIK No: 0000834105

Subsidiaries: Federal Deposit Insurance Corporation, The Columbia Bank

Officers: Roger L. Christensen/Dir., CEO, Pres.

Directors: Roger L. Christensen/Dir., CEO, Pres., Rich E. Betz/Dir., Lori R. Boyd/Dir., Terry L. Cochran/Dir., Jean S. McKinney/Dir., Charles F. Beardsley/Dir., William A. Booth/Dir., Dennis L. Carver/Dir., Jim J. Doran/Dir., Donald T. Mitchell/Dir.

Financial Data: **Fiscal Year End:**12/31 **Latest Annual Data:** 12/31/2006

Year	Sales	Net Income
2006	$80,495,000	$15,775,000
2005	$63,778,000	$13,670,000
2004	$51,026,000	$10,735,000

Curr. Assets:	$155,033,000	**Curr. Liab.:**	$868,031,000		
Plant, Equip.:	$18,089,000	**Total Liab.:**	$942,169,000	**Indic. Yr. Divd.:**	$0.400
Total Assets:	$1,033,188,000	**Net Worth:**	$91,018,000	**Debt/ Equity:**	0.8145

Columbia Bancorp OR

401 E 3rd St., Ste. 200, The Dalles, OR, 97058; *PH:* 1-541-298-6649; *Fax:* 1-541-298-3157; *http://* www.columbiariverbank.com

General - Incorporation .... OR
Employees 362
Auditor .... Moss Adams LLP
Stk Agt .... Wells Fargo Shareowner Services
Counsel .... Bennett H. Goldstein
DUNS No. 83-879-6357

Stock- Price on:12/24/2007 .... $21.14
Stock Exchange .... NDQ
Ticker Symbol .... NA
Outstanding Shares 9,990,000
E.P.S $1.46
Shareholders .... NA

Business: The group's principal activity is to accept deposits and offer loans through its principal subsidiary, columbia river bank. Deposits include checking and savings accounts, money market accounts and certificates of deposits. The group offers commercial, agricultural and real estate loans. Other financial products and services of the group include stocks, mutual funds, seps, iras, annuities and life insurance. The group also offers a visa credits and checks card program, ATMs and telephone banking service. Customers of the group include small and medium sized businesses, farmers and individuals. The group operates through 12 branch offices located in the dalles, hood river, pendleton, hermiston, mcminnville, canby, newberg, madras, redmond and bend and the communities of mcminnville, canby and newberg in the willamette valley.

Primary SIC and add'l.: 6022 6712

CIK No: 0001010002

Subsidiaries: Columbia River Bank

Officers: Roger L. Christensen/Dir., CEO, Pres./$663,409.00, Britt W. Thomas/Exec. VP, Chief Credit Officer - Columbia River Bank/$358,237.00, Greg B. Spear/CFO, Exec. VP/$443,976.00, Shane R. Correa/42/Exec. VP, Chief Banking Officer - Columbia River Bank/$387,190.00, Craig J. Ortega/Pres. - Columbia River Bank, Christine Herb/CIO - Columbia River Bank, Bob Card/Risk Management Dir. - CRB

Directors: Roger L. Christensen/Dir., CEO, Pres., Richard E. Betz/Chmn., William A. Booth/Dir., Charles F. Beardsley/Dir., Lori R. Boyd/Dir., Dennis L. Carver/Dir., Terry L. Cochran/Dir., Jim J. Doran/Dir., Jean S. McKinney/Dir., Donald T. Mitchell/Dir., James J. Doran/58/Dir.

Owners: Insiders/10.70%, Robert V. Card, Richard E. Betz, Craig J. Ortega, Greg B. Spear, Britt W. Thomas, Shane R. Correa, Donald T. Mitchell, Roger L. Christensen/1.10%, Dennis L. Carver, Lori R. Boyd, James J. Doran, Banc Fund V L.P./7.30%, Charles F. Beardsley, Jean S. McKinney *(17 Owners included in Index)*

Financial Data: **Fiscal Year End:**12/31 **Latest Annual Data:** 06/30/2007

Year	Sales	Net Income
2007	NA	NA
2006	NA	NA
2005	$63,778,000	$13,670,000

Curr. Assets:	$155,033,000	**Curr. Liab.:**	$868,031,000	**P/E Ratio:**	13.91
Plant, Equip.:	$18,089,000	**Total Liab.:**	$942,169,000	**Indic. Yr. Divd.:**	$0.400
Total Assets:	$1,033,188,000	**Net Worth:**	$91,018,000	**Debt/ Equity:**	0.2179

Columbia Banking System Inc

1301 A St., Tacoma, WA, 98402; *PH:* 1-253-305-1900; *Fax:* 1-253-305-0317; *http://* www.columbiabank.com

General - Incorporation .... WA
Employees 657
Auditor .... Deloitte & Touche LLP
Stk Agt .... Deloitte & Touche LLP
Counsel............ Gordon Thomas Honeywell Et Al
DUNS No. 03-146-5958

Stock- Price on:12/24/2007 .... $28.77
Stock Exchange .... NDQ
Ticker Symbol .... COLB
Outstanding Shares 16,160,000
E.P.S $2.00
Shareholders .... NA

Business: The group's principal activities are to provide commercial banking, retail banking and real estate lending services. Commercial banking includes origination of commercial business loans and private banking services. Retail banking includes all deposit products, with their related fee income, and all consumer loan products as well as commercial loan products offered in the branch offices. Real estate lending offers single-family residential, multi-family residential, and commercial real estate loans, and the associated loan servicing activities. The group provides a full range of banking services to small and medium sized businesses, professionals and other individuals through 34 branch offices.

Primary SIC and add'l.: 6022 6712

CIK No: 0000887343

Subsidiaries: Bank of Astoria, Columbia (WA) Statutory Trust, Columbia State Bank

Officers: Melanie J. Dressel/Dir., CEO, Pres./$567,727.00, Mark W. Nelson/Exec. VP, Chief Banking Officer - Columbia Bank/$333,212.00, Joanne Coy/VP - Columbia Bank, Clint E. Stein/Chief Accounting Officer, Sr. VP, Evans Q. Whitney/Exec. VP - Human Resources, Columbia Bank/$1,109,519.00, Andy McDonald/Exec. VP, Chief Credit Officer - Columbia Bank/$258,120.00, Frederick M. Goldberg/Dir. - Columbia Bank, Gary Schminkey/Exec. VP, CFO - Columbia Bank/$306,556.00

Directors: Melanie J. Dressel/Dir., CEO, Pres., William T. Weyerhaeuser/Chmn., Donald Rodman/Dir. - Columbia Bank, James M. Will/Dir. - Columbia Bank, Frederick M. Goldberg/Dir. - Columbia Bank, Daniel Regis/Dir. - Columbia Bank, Thomas M. Hulbert/Dir. - Columbia Bank, Thomas L. Matson/Dir. - Columbia Bank, John P. Folsom/Dir. - Columbia Bank

Owners: Frederick M. Goldberg, Andrew L. McDonald, Melanie J. Dressel, Barclays Global Investors NA/6.86%, Daniel C. Regis, Mark W. Nelson, James M. Will, Insiders/4.10%, John P. Folsom, Thomas L. Matson, Gary R. Schminkey, Thomas M. Hulbert, Donald H. Rodman, William T. Weyerhaeuser/1.40%

Financial Data: **Fiscal Year End:**12/31 **Latest Annual Data:** 12/31/2006

Year	Sales	Net Income
2006	$176,347,000	$32,103,000
2005	$146,993,000	$29,631,000
2004	$112,316,000	$22,513,000

Curr. Assets:	$116,893,000	**Curr. Liab.:**	$2,249,151,000	**P/E Ratio:**	14.39
Plant, Equip.:	$44,635,000	**Total Liab.:**	$2,300,784,000	**Indic. Yr. Divd.:**	$0.680
Total Assets:	$2,553,131,000	**Net Worth:**	$252,347,000	**Debt/ Equity:**	0.0856

Columbia Equity Trust Inc

1750 H St., NW Ste. 500, Washington, DC, 20006; *PH:* 1-202-303-3080; *Fax:* 1-202-303-3088; *http://* www.columbiareit.com; *Email:* Info@columbia.com

General - Incorporation	MD	*Stock* - Price on:12/24/2007	NA
Employees	NA	Stock Exchange	NA
Auditor	Deloitte & Touche LLP	Ticker Symbol	NA
Stk Agt.	American Stock Transfer & Trust Co.	Outstanding Shares	NA
Counsel	NA	E.P.S.	NA
DUNS No.	NA	Shareholders	NA

Business: The groups principal activities include acquiring, renovating, repositioning, developing, owning, managing and operating commercial office properties. The group operates from the Western Columbia.

Primary SIC and add'l.: 6798

CIK No: 0001316710

Subsidiaries: 1025 Vermont Avenue SPE, Inc., 1025 Vermont Avenue, LLC, 14200 Park Meadow Drive LLC, 14700 Lee Road, LLC, 15036 Conference Center Drive LLC, 15040 Conference Center Drive LLC, 1575 Eye Street Associates, 5454 Wisconsin, Inc., Atrium Building, LLC, Barlow Enterprises LLC, Barlow Holdings LLC, Carr Capital 1575 Eye, LLC, Carr Capital Atrium, LLC, Carr Capital Greenbriar, LLC, Carr Capital Madison, LLC 37 Subsidiaries included in the Index

Owners: Ramius Capital Group, L.L.C./9.09%, Insiders/4.07%, Davis Selected Advisers, L.P./7.99%, Christian H. Clifford, Rebecca L. Owen, GAMCO Investors, Inc./6.34%, Third Avenue Management LLC/8.00%, Clinton D. Fisch, John A. Schissel, Thomas A. Young, T. Rowe Price Associates, Inc./9.52%, Oliver T. Carr/11.35%, Hal A. Vasvari, Bruce M. Johnson, Robert J. McGovern (*18 Owners included in Index*)

Columbia Laboratories Inc

354 Eisenhower Pkwy., 2nd Fl., Plz. I, Livingston, NJ, 07039; *PH:* 1-973-994-3999; *Fax:* 1-973-994-3001; *http://* www.columbialabs.com; *Email:* cir@columbialabs.com

General - Incorporation	DE	*Stock* - Price on:12/24/2007	$2.11
Employees	47	Stock Exchange	NDQ
Auditor	Goldstein Golub Kessler LLP	Ticker Symbol	CBRX
Stk Agt.	American Stock Transfer & Trust Co.	Outstanding Shares	51,340,000
Counsel	NA	E.P.S.	-$0.3
DUNS No.	17-762-1224	Shareholders	NA

Business: The group's principle activity is to develop and commercialize women's health care and endocrinology products, including those used in treating infertility, dysmenorrhea, endometriosis and hormonal deficiencies and preventing pre-term birth. Its products include striant (testosterone buccal system), prochieve 8% or crinone 8% (progesterone gel) and prochieve 4% (progesterone gel). These products are delivered through its proprietary bioadhesive delivery system (bds) that enables controlled, sustained release of hormones, peptides and other difficult-to-deliver compounds. They are sold under the trademarks striant, striant sr, crinone and prochieve. The group's sales force also promotes advantage-s bioadhesive contraceptive gel, replens vaginal moisturizer and rephresh vaginal gel on behalf of lil' drug store products. Its direct customers include drug wholesalers and chain drug stores. The products are marketed in the United States and Europe. The group's quarterly revenue for September 2007 was 7.31 millions of USD.

Primary SIC and add'l.: 2834

CIK No: 0000821995

Subsidiaries: Columbia Laboratories (Bermuda) Ltd., Columbia Laboratories (France) SA, Columbia Laboratories (UK) Limited

Officers: Robert S. Mills/Dir., Pres., CEO - Columbia Laboratories, Inc/$878,390.00, Michael McGrane/Sr. VP, General Counsel, Sec./$556,486.00, David L. Weinberg/VP - Finance, Treasurer/$477,050.00, George W. Creasy/VP - Clinical Research, Development, James A. Meer/Sr. VP, CFO, Treasurer/$25,981.00, Carl Worrell/Head - Sales, Marketing

Directors: Robert S. Mills/Dir., Pres., CEO - Columbia Laboratories, Inc, Stephen G. Kasnet/Chmn., Edward Blechschmidt/Vice Chmn., Selwyn P. Oskowitz/Dir., Valerie L. Andrews/Dir., James S. Crofton/Dir., Denis M. O'Donnell/Dir.

Owners: Insiders/2.70%, Perry Partners, L.P./13.70%, Denis M. ODonnell, David M. Knott/Dorset Management/9.90%, Matterhorn Offshore Fund Ltd./13.90%, Knott Partners, L.P./11.60%, James S. Crofton, Harvest Offshore Investors, Ltd./8.90%, Perry Corp./Richard C. Perry/10.50%, Selwyn P. Oskowitz, Robert S. Mills/1.00%, Shoshone Partners, LP/7.50%, Edward Blechschmidt, Michael McGrane, James A. Meer (*19 Owners included in Index*)

Financial Data: Fiscal Year End:12/31 Latest Annual Data: 12/31/2006

Year	Sales	Net Income
2006	$17,393,000	-$12,612,000
2005	$22,041,000	-$9,307,000
2004	$17,860,000	-$25,130,000

Curr. Assets:	$30,674,000	Curr. Liab.:	$7,264,000		
Plant, Equip.:	$764,000	Total Liab.:	$47,976,000	Indic. Yr. Divd.:	NA
Total Assets:	$65,839,000	Net Worth:	$17,863,000	Debt/ Equity:	2.3412

Columbia Sportswear Co

14375 NW Science Pk. Dr., Portland, OR, 97229; *PH:* 1-503-985-4000; *Fax:* 1-503-985-5800; *http://* www.columbia.com

General - Incorporation	OR	*Stock* - Price on:12/24/2007	$68.91
Employees	2,810	Stock Exchange	NDQ
Auditor	Deloitte & Touche LLP	Ticker Symbol	COLM
Stk Agt.	Mellon Investor Services LLC	Outstanding Shares	36,300,000
Counsel	Stoel Rives LLP	E.P.S.	$3.71
DUNS No.	00-942-0159	Shareholders	NA

Business: The group's principal activities are to design, source, market and distribute active outdoor apparel. The group merchandises the products into four principal categories namely outerwear, sportswear, rugged footwear and related accessories. The outwear products include clothing accessories for outdoor activities, including skiing, snowboarding, hiking, hunting and fishing. The sportswear product line consisting primarily of hiking shorts, water sport trunks, fleece and pile products, sweaters, knit shirts, woven shirts, sweats, and jeans. The accessories include hats, caps, scarves, gloves, mittens and headbands. The group operates in North America, Europe and Asia. In Mar 2003, the group acquired mountain hardwear inc.

Primary SIC and add'l.: 5136 5137 2252

CIK No: 0001050797

Subsidiaries: Columbia Sportswear Canada Limited, Columbia Sportswear Company, Columbia Sportswear Company (Dongguan) Limited, Columbia Sportswear Company (Hong Kong) Limited, Columbia Sportswear Company Limited, Columbia Sportswear Company Windsor Ltd., Columbia

Sportswear Distribution S.A.S., Columbia Sportswear Europe S.A.S., Columbia Sportswear Finance Limited Partnership, Columbia Sportswear France S.A.S., Columbia Sportswear Germany GmbH, Columbia Sportswear Holdings Limited, Columbia Sportswear International Holdings, Columbia Sportswear International Srl, Columbia Sportswear Italy S.r.l. 29 Subsidiaries included in the Index

Officers: Timothy P. Boyle/Dir., CEO, Pres./$1,745,721.00, Grant D. Prentice/VP - Apparel Product Innovation, William Tung/VP - International Sales, Operations, Thomas B. Cusick/VP, Corporate Controller, Peter J. Bragdon/VP, General Counsel, Sec., Mark J. Sandquist/VP - Apparel, Equipment/$775,242.00, Bryan L. Timm/CFO/$917,280.00, Patrick D. Anderson/COO/$924,424.00, Daniel G. Hanson/VP - Marketing, Kerry Barnes/VP - Retail, Sherrie M. Curtin/VP - Women's Apparel, Mark N. Koppes/VP - Men's Apparel, Mark Nenow/VP - Footwear, Patrick J. Werner/VP - Global Apparel Manufacturing, Michael W. McCormick/VP - Sales (*16 Officers included in Index*)

Directors: Gertrude Boyle/Chmn., Edward S. George/Dir., Stephen E. Babson/Dir., John W. Stanton/Dir., Andy Bryant/Dir., Sarah A. Bany/Dir., Murrey R. Albers/Dir., Walter T. Klenz/Dir.

Owners: Mark J. Sandquist, Murrey R. Albers, John W. Stanton, Edward S. George, Gertrude Boyle/14.67%, Andy D. Bryant, Timothy P. Boyle/41.80%, JPMorgan Chase & Co./7.33%, Bryan L. Timm, Insiders/62.38%, Sarah A. Bany/4.60%, Stephen E. Babson, Walter T. Klenz, Patrick D. Anderson

Financial Data: Fiscal Year End:12/31 Latest Annual Data: 12/31/2006

Year	Sales	Net Income
2006	$1,287,672,000	$123,018,000
2005	$1,155,791,000	$130,736,000
2004	$1,095,307,000	$138,624,000

Curr. Assets:	$757,768,000	Curr. Liab.:	$188,740,000	P/E Ratio:	18.57
Plant, Equip.:	$199,426,000	Total Liab.:	$196,670,000	Indic. Yr. Divd.:	$0.560
Total Assets:	$1,027,373,000	Net Worth:	$830,703,000	Debt/ Equity:	NA

Columbus McKinnon Corp

140 John James Audubon Pkwy., Amherst, NY, 14228; *PH:* 1-716-689-5400; *Fax:* 1-716-689-5598; *http://* www.cmworks.com

General - Incorporation	NY	*Stock* - Price on:12/24/2007	$29.93
Employees	3,081	Stock Exchange	NDQ
Auditor	Ernst & Young LLP	Ticker Symbol	CMCO
Stk Agt.	American Stock Transfer & Trust Co.	Outstanding Shares	18,830,000
Counsel	Phillips, Lytle, Hitchcock, Blaine	E.P.S.	$2.06
DUNS No.	00-210-5534	Shareholders	NA

Business: The group's principal activity is to manufacture and market hoists, cranes, chain, conveyors, material handling systems, lift tables and component parts serving a wide variety of commercial and industrial end markets. The products of the group are used to efficiently and ergonomically move, lift, position or secure objects and loads. The brand names include budgit, chester, cm, coffing, duff-norton, little mule, shaw-box and yale. The group operates in the United States, Canada, Mexico, Germany, Denmark, France and China.

Primary SIC and add'l.: 3559 3728 3569 3536 3537 3462

CIK No: 0001005229

Subsidiaries: Asia Hoist Co., Ltd., Audubon Europe S.a.r.l., Camlok Lifting Clamps Ltd., CM Insurance Company, Inc., Columbus McKinnon de Mexico, S.A. de C.V., Columbus McKinnon de Uruguay, S.A., Columbus McKinnon do Brazil Ltda., Columbus McKinnon Limited, Crane Equipment & Service, Inc., Ejendomsselskabet Lupinvej 11, Hangzhou LILA Lifting and Lashing Co. Ltd., Larco Industrial Services, Ltd., Societe d'Exploitation des Raccords Gautier, Spreckels Consolidated Industries, Inc., Spreckels Water Company, Inc. 29 Subsidiaries included in the Index

Officers: Timothy T. Tevens/Dir., CEO, Pres./$1,090,862.00, Karen L. Howard/CFO, VP - Finance, Treasurer/$428,019.00, Joseph J. Owen/VP, Hoist Group Leader/$359,137.00, Timothy R. Harvey/General Counsel, Sec., Derwin Gilbreath/COO, VP/$788,633.00, Richard A. Steinberg/VP - Human Resources, Wolfgang Wegener/VP, Andrew M. Gates/Corporate Controller, Rakesh A. Jobanputra/Treasurer

Directors: Timothy T. Tevens/Dir., CEO, Pres., Ernest R. Verebelyi/60/Chmn., Linda A. Goodspeed/Dir., Wallace W. Creek/Dir., Carlos Pascual/Dir., Richard H. Fleming/Dir., Stephen Rabinowitz/Dir., Nicholas T. Pinchuk/Dir.

Owners: Jeffrey L. Gendell/8.00%, Derwin R. Gilbreath, Fidelity Management & Research Company/7.11%, Richard H. Fleming, Timothy T. Tevens/1.40%, Carlos Pascual, Ownership Plan/4.83%, Artisan Partners LP/9.46%, Karen L. Howard, AXA Financial, Inc./5.02%, Wallace W. Creek, Stephen Rabinowitz, Linda A. Goodspeed, Ernest R. Verebelyi, Wolfgang Wegener (*18 Owners included in Index*)

Financial Data: Fiscal Year End:03/31 Latest Annual Data: 3/31/2007

Year	Sales	Net Income
2007	$589,848,000	$34,085,000
2006	$556,007,000	$59,796,000
2005	$514,752,000	$16,710,000

Curr. Assets:	$256,182,000	Curr. Liab.:	$98,734,000	P/E Ratio:	14.97
Plant, Equip.:	$55,231,000	Total Liab.:	$324,313,000	Indic. Yr. Divd.:	NA
Total Assets:	$565,638,000	Net Worth:	$241,325,000	Debt/ Equity:	0.6719

Columbus Southern Power Co

1 Riverside Plz., Columbus, OH, 43215; *PH:* 1-614-716-1193; *http://* www.aep.com

General - Incorporation	NY	*Stock* - Price on:12/24/2007	NA
Employees	NA	Stock Exchange	NA
Auditor	Deloitte & Touche LLP	Ticker Symbol	NA
Stk Agt.	Computershare Investor Services LLC	Outstanding Shares	NA
Counsel	NA	E.P.S.	NA
DUNS No.	00-790-1739	Shareholders	NA

Business: The group's principal activity is to generate, sell, purchase, transmit and distribute electric power. The group distributes power to customers in Ohio and supplies electric power at wholesale to other electric utilities, as well as to municipally owned distribution systems within its service area. The retail customers of the group include residential, commercial, industrial and other users. The principal industries served by the group are food processing, chemicals, primary metals, electronic machinery and paper products.

Primary SIC and add'l.: 4911

CIK No: 0000022198

Subsidiaries: Colomet, Inc., Conesville Coal Preparation Company, Indiana-Kentucky Electric Corporation, Ohio Valley Electric Corporation, Simco Inc.

Officers: Michael G. Morris/61/Chmn., CEO, Pres., Kevin E. Walker/44/Pres., COO - AEP Ohio, Charles R. Patton/Pres., COO - AEP Texas, Dana E. Waldo/Pres., COO - Appalachian Power, Nicholas K. Akins/Exec. VP - Generation, Thomas M. Hagan/Exec. VP - AEP Utilities, West, Robert P. Powers/Exec. VP - AEP Utilities, East, Susan Tomasky/Exec. VP - Shared Services, Carl L. English/61/Pres. - AEP Utilities, Venita McCellon-Allen/48/Pres., COO - Southwestern Electric Power Company, Helen Murray/Pres., COO - Indiana Michigan Power, Timothy C. Mosher/Pres., COO - Kentucky Power, Stuart Solomon/Pres., COO - Public Service Company, Oklahoma, Julie Sloat/VP - Investor Relations, Strategic Initiatives, Bette Jo Rozsa/MD - Investor Relations *(23 Officers included in Index)*

Directors: Michael G. Morris/61/Chmn., CEO, Pres., Kathryn D. Sullivan/56/Dir., E. R. Brooks/71/Dir., Donald M. Carlton/71/Dir., Ralph D. Crosby/61/Dir., John P. Desbarres/69/Dir., Robert W. Fri/72/Dir., Linda A. Goodspeed/Dir., William R. Howell/72/Dir., Lester A. Hudson/69/Dir., Lionel L. Nowell/53/Dir., Richard L. Sandor/67/Dir., Donald G. Smith/73/Dir.

Com Guard Com Inc

2075 Corte del Nogal, Ste. R, Carlsbad, CA, 92009; *PH:* 1-760-431-2206; *Fax:* 1-760-431-7999; *http://* www.com-guard.com

General - Incorporation	NV	**Stock** - Price on:12/24/2007	NA
Employees	7	Stock Exchange	OTC
Auditor	Weinberg & Co. P.A	Ticker Symbol	CGUD
Stk Agt	Interwest Transfer Company, Inc.	Outstanding Shares	NA
Counsel	NA	E.P.S.	NA
DUNS No.	NA	Shareholders	NA

Business: The group's principal activity is to exploit products for the microcomputer industry. It provides enhanced system security for both individual users and network administrators. The group's primary products are com-guard(TM) and com-guard pro tm. Com-guard(TM) includes unique software that enables an authorized user to prohibit use of their computer, record events and protect and deny access to stored files. Com-guard pro tm, combines com-guard(TM) software with a patented sensor-card(TM) hardware PC board to provide the data security with expanded system level security that guards against physical tampering, theft, site access, and unauthorized use of computers.

Primary SIC and add'l.: 7372 7373

CIK No: 0001103759

Subsidiaries: PC Products, Inc.

Officers: Edward W. Savarese/Founder, Chmn., CEO, Joseph P. Sigismonti/Dir., COO, Pres.

Directors: Edward W. Savarese/Founder, Chmn., CEO, Nolan Bushnell/Member - Advisory Board, Edward H. Currie/Dir., Gerry Berg/Dir., Joseph P. Sigismonti/Dir., COO, Pres., Irwin Roth/Dir., Robert Orbach/Member - Advisory Board

Financial Data: Fiscal Year End:06/30 Latest Annual Data: 06/30/2005

Year	Sales	Net Income
2005	$6,191,000	-$1,387,000
2004	$14,000	-$2,013,000
2003	$68,000	-$1,961,000

Curr. Assets:	$882,000	**Curr. Liab.:**	$791,000		
Plant, Equip.:	NA	**Total Liab.:**	$791,000	**Indic. Yr. Divd.:**	NA
Total Assets:	$882,000	**Net Worth:**	$91,000	**Debt/ Equity:**	NA

Comarco Inc

25541 CommerCtr. Dr., Lake Forest, CA, 92630; *PH:* 1-949-599-7400; *Fax:* 1-949-599-1415; *http://* www.comarco.com; *Email:* info@comarco.com

General - Incorporation	CA	**Stock** - Price on:12/24/2007	$6.36
Employees	120	Stock Exchange	NDQ
Auditor	BDO Seidman LLP	Ticker Symbol	CMRO
Stk Agt	U.S. Stock Transfer Corp	Outstanding Shares	7,370,000
Counsel	Riordan & McKinzie	E.P.S.	-$0.5
DUNS No.	05-733-6950	Shareholders	NA

Business: The group's principal activities are to provide hardware and software products and services for the wireless industry. The group operates in two business segments: wireless test solutions and wireless applications. The wireless test solutions designs and manufactures hardware and software tools for use by wireless carriers, equipment vendors and others. These tools are used to design, deploy and optimize wireless networks and to verify the performance of the wireless networks once deployed. It also provides engineering services. The wireless applications segment designs and manufactures remote voice systems and mobile power products for notebook computers, cellular telephones and handheld devices. The group on 06-Jan-2004, sold the assets of cdx one of the reporting unit which was formerly included in the wireless test solutions segment. The group markets its products in Asia, latin and South America through its offices located in Singapore, Mexico and Brazil.

Primary SIC and add'l.: 3663 4581 8711 7363

CIK No: 0000022252

Subsidiaries: Comarco Wireless International, Inc., Comarco Wireless Technologies, Inc.

Officers: Thomas A. Franza/Dir., CEO, Pres./$692,912.00, Daniel R. Lutz/CFO, VP/$377,965.00, Peggy L. Vessell/VP - Administration, Corp. Sec., Bahram Nazardad/VP - Quality Assurance, Sebastian E. Gutierrez/46/VP, GM - Call Box Division, John McMunn/58/VP/$381,677.00, Fredrik L. Torstensson/38/VP/$297,526.00, Thomas W. Lanni/55/CTO, VP - Power Division, Mark Chapman/Sr. VP - Wireless Test Solutions

Directors: Thomas A. Franza/Dir., CEO, Pres., Don M. Bailey/62/Chmn., Jeffrey R. Hultman/Dir., Gerald D. Griffin/Dir., Erik Van Der Kaay/68/Dir.

Owners: Thomas W. Lanni, Don M. Bailey/1.90%, Daniel R. Lutz, Jeffrey R. Hultman, T. Rowe Price Associates, Inc./9.72%, John McMunn, Grueber& McBaine/8.64%, Broadwood Capital, Inc./8.90%, Insiders/10.29%, Thomas A. Franza/3.60%, Erik van der Kaay, Elkhorn Partners Limited Partnership/9.31%, Fredrik L. Torstensson, Gerald D. Griffin, Special Situations Funds/14.08%

Financial Data: Fiscal Year End:01/31 Latest Annual Data: 1/31/2007

Year	Sales	Net Income
2007	$47,776,000	$1,777,000
2006	$46,878,000	$6,331,000
2005	$29,223,000	-$10,056,000

Curr. Assets:	$44,078,000	**Curr. Liab.:**	$10,460,000	**P/E Ratio:**	26.50
Plant, Equip.:	$3,331,000	**Total Liab.:**	$13,424,000	**Indic. Yr. Divd.:**	NA
Total Assets:	$51,413,000	**Net Worth:**	$37,989,000	**Debt/ Equity:**	NA

CombinatoRx Inc

245 1st St., 16th Fl., Cambridge, MA, 02142; *PH:* 1-617-301-7000; *Fax:* 1-617-301-7010; *http://* www.combinatorx.com; *Email:* info@combinatorx.com

General - Incorporation	DE	**Stock** - Price on:12/24/2007	$6.18
Employees	144	Stock Exchange	NDQ
Auditor	Ernst & Young LLP	Ticker Symbol	CRXX
Stk Agt	Computershare Ltd.	Outstanding Shares	29,040,000
Counsel	NA	E.P.S.	-$1.4
DUNS No.	NA	Shareholders	NA

Business: The groups principle activity is to developing synergistic combinations of approved drugs. The group operates from the United States. The group's quarterly revenue for September 2007 was 3.00 millions of USD.

Primary SIC and add'l.: 2834

CIK No: 0001135906

Subsidiaries: CombinatoRx (Singapore) Pte Ltd, CombinatoRx Securities Corporation

Officers: Alexis Borisy/Founder, Dir., CEO, Pres./$1,678,325.00, Robert Forrester/CFO, Exec. VP/$1,058,778.00, Daniel Grau/COO/$1,116,365.00, Curtis T. Keith/VP, Research Founder/$854,079.00, Lynn G. Baird/Sr. VP - Regulatory, Quality, Clinical Operation, Jason F. Cole/Sr. VP, General Counsel, Gina Nugent/VP - Investor Relations, Corporate Communications, Kate Dinuovo/Assoc. Investor Relations, Corporate Communications, Gary Borisy/Scientific Advisor, Michael A. Foley/Scientific Advisor, Todd Golub/Scientific Advisor, Brent R. Stockwell/Scientific Advisor

Directors: Alexis Borisy/Founder, Dir., CEO, Pres., James W. O'Shea/Chmn., Richard Aldrich/53/Dir., Barbara Deptula/Dir., Patrick J. Fortune/Dir., Frank Haydu/Dir., Michael Kauffman/Dir., Richard Pops/Dir., Sally W. Crawford/Dir.

Owners: Richard Pops, Robert Forrester, Richard Aldrich, Funds managed by Boston Millennia Partners/5.10%, Barbara Deptula, Daniel Grau, Curtis Keith, Frank Haydu, T. Rowe Price Associates, Inc./6.90%, Alexis Borisy/2.10%, Patrick Fortune/5.10%, Insiders/9.90%, Angiotech Pharmaceuticals, Inc./6.70%

Financial Data: Fiscal Year End:12/31 Latest Annual Data: 12/31/2006

Year	Sales	Net Income
2006	$13,273,000	-$34,288,000
2005	$4,658,000	-$29,515,000
2004	$178,000	-$22,258,000

Curr. Assets:	$121,829,000	**Curr. Liab.:**	$20,873,000		
Plant, Equip.:	$12,506,000	**Total Liab.:**	$51,285,000	**Indic. Yr. Divd.:**	NA
Total Assets:	$138,335,000	**Net Worth:**	$87,050,000	**Debt/ Equity:**	0.1735

Comcast Corp

1500 Market St., Philadelphia, PA, 19102; *PH:* 1-215-665-1700; *Fax:* 1-215-981-7790; *http://* www.comcast.com; *Email:* esl_corp@cable.comcast.com

General - Incorporation	PA	**Stock** - Price on:12/24/2007	$28.18
Employees	90,000	Stock Exchange	NDQ
Auditor	Deloitte & Touche LLP	Ticker Symbol	CMCSA
Stk Agt	Computershare Investor Services LLC	Outstanding Shares	3,110,000,000
Counsel	NA	E.P.S.	$0.96
DUNS No.	NA	Shareholders	NA

Business: The group's principle activity is to provide a wide range of consumer entertainment and communication products and services. The group also provides digital services including Internet and clearer broadband phone service, and develops, and delivers innovative programming. The group operates from United States.

Primary SIC and add'l.: 4899 4841

CIK No: 0001166691

Subsidiaries: Abb Mog-wm, Inc., Abb Rfl, LLC, ABB TS Assets, LLC, Alabama T. V. Cable, Inc., American Microwave & Communications, Inc., American Televenture of Minersville, Inc., Atlantic American Cablevision of Florida, LLC, Atlantic American Cablevision, LLC, Atlantic American Holdings, Inc., Atlantic Cablevision of Florida, Inc., Beatrice Cable TV Company, Brigand Pictures, Inc., BroadNet Austria GmbH, BroadNet Czech a.s., BroadNet Czech s.r.o. 969 Subsidiaries included in the Index

Officers: Brian L. Roberts/49/Chmn., CEO - Comcast Corporation/$26,001,700.00, Ted Harbert/CEO, Pres. - Comcast Entertainment Group, David Manouglan/Pres. - Golf Channel, Joseph W. Waz/VP - External Affairs, Public Policy Counsel, Gavin Harvey/Pres. - Versus, Diane Robina/Pres. - Emerging Networks Comcast Programming Group, Rod Shanks/Pres. - AZN, Neal Tiles/Pres. - G4, Sandy Wax/Pres., GM - PBS Kids Sprout, Lawrence S. Smith/60/Exec. VP, Co - CFO/$11,452,660.00, Robert S. Pick/54/Sr. VP - Corporate Development, Gregg M. Goldstein/VP - Corporate Development, Marc A. Rockford/VP, Sr. Deputy General Counsel - Comcast Corporate Communications, Kevin M. Casey/Pres. - Northern Division, Charlie Thurston/Pres. - Comcast Spotlight, Comcast Cable *(58 Officers included in Index)*

Directors: Brian L. Roberts/49/Chmn., CEO - Comcast Corporation, Edward D. Breen/52/Dir., Sheldon M. Bonovitz/71/Dir., Michael I. Sovern/76/Dir., Ralph J. Roberts/88/Dir., Judith Rodin/63/Dir., Joseph J. Collins/64/Dir., Kenneth J. Bacon/54/Dir., Decker S. Anstrom/58/Dir., Julian A. Brodsky/75/Dir., Michael J. Cook/65/Dir., Jeffrey A. Honickman/51/Dir.

Owners: Kenneth J. Bacon, Michael J. Cook, John R. Alchin, Barclays Global Investors, N.A., Stephen B. Burke, Brian L. Roberts, Michael I. Sovern, Insiders/100.00%, Dodge& Cox, Jeffrey A. Honickman, Edward D. Breen, Marsico Capital Management, LLC, Decker S. Anstrom, Joseph J. Collins, Judith Rodin *(24 Owners included in Index)*

Financial Data: Fiscal Year End:12/31 Latest Annual Data: 12/31/2006

Year	Sales	Net Income
2006	$24,966,000,000	$2,533,000,000
2005	$22,255,000,000	$928,000,000
2004	$20,307,000,000	$970,000,000

Curr. Assets:	$5,202,000,000	**Curr. Liab.:**	$7,440,000,000	**P/E Ratio:**	30.63
Plant, Equip.:	$21,248,000,000	**Total Liab.:**	$68,997,000,000	**Indic. Yr. Divd.:**	NA
Total Assets:	$110,405,000,000	**Net Worth:**	$41,167,000,000	**Debt/ Equity:**	0.6506

Comdisco Holding Co Inc

5600 N River Rd. , Ste. 800, Rosemont, IL, 60018; *PH:* 1-847-698-3000; *http://* www.comdisco.com

General - Incorporation .... DE
Employees 3
Auditor .... KPMG LLP
Stk Agt .... Mellon Investor Services LLC
Counsel .... NA
DUNS No. 55-591-9067

Stock- Price on:12/24/2007 .... $12.75
Stock Exchange .... OTC
Ticker Symbol .... CDCO
Outstanding Shares 4,030,000
E.P.S $1.74
Shareholders .... NA

Business: The group's principal activity is selling, collecting or otherwise reducing to money in an orderly manner the remaining assets of the group. Effective 12-Aug-2002, the group reorganized by emerging from bankruptcy. Prior to bankruptcy proceedings, the group had the following operations. The us leasing and European it leasing segment sold, leased and remarked technology equipment made by manufacturers. It also leased pcs, point of sale, server, enterprise, network, telecommunications and other equipment. The venture segment invested in various stages of companies from seed stage to pre-ipo companies and offered financing products that includes leasing, subordinated debt and secured debt. The corporate asset management group is responsible for the sale of certain assets held by subsidiaries.

Primary SIC and add'l.: 7377 4899 7359 6799

CIK No: 0001179484

Subsidiaries: Comdisco Australia Pty. Ltd, Comdisco Canada Equipment Finance Limited Partnership, Comdisco Canada Ltd, Comdisco de Mexico, S.A. de C.V, Comdisco Equipment Solutions (Europe) B.V, Comdisco GmbH & Co. Leasing and Finance KG, Comdisco Holdings (U.K.) Limited, Comdisco Investment Group, Inc, Comdisco Management GmbH, Comdisco New Zealand, Comdisco United Kingdom Limited, Comdisco, Inc.

Officers: Randolph I. Thornton/Dir., CEO, Pres.

Directors: Randolph I. Thornton/Dir., CEO, Pres.

Financial Data: *Fiscal Year End:*09/30 *Latest Annual Data:* 9/30/2006

Year	Sales	Net Income
2006	$28,000,000	$15,000,000
2005	$37,000,000	$29,000,000
2004	$108,000,000	$23,000,000

Curr. Assets:	$103,000,000	**Curr. Liab.:**	$3,000,000	**P/E Ratio:**	3.43
Plant, Equip.:	NA	**Total Liab.:**	$46,000,000	**Indic. Yr. Divd.:**	$11.390
Total Assets:	$110,000,000	**Net Worth:**	$64,000,000	**Debt/ Equity:**	NA

Comerica Inc

Comerica Bank Tower, 1717 Main St., Dallas, TX, 75201; ; *http://* www.comerica.com

General - Incorporation .... DE
Employees 10,129
Auditor .... Ernst & Young LLP
Stk Agt .... Wells Fargo Shareowner Services
Counsel .... NA
DUNS No. 07-635-2947

Stock- Price on:12/24/2007 .... $61.91
Stock Exchange .... NYSE
Ticker Symbol .... CMA
Outstanding Shares 155,940,000
E.P.S $5.57
Shareholders .... NA

Business: The group's principle activity is to provide banking services. The group operates through four divisions include business bank, small business and personal financial services, wealth and institutional management and finance. Small business and personal financial services includes small business banking and personal financial services consisting of consumer lending, consumer deposits gathering and mortgage loan origination. Wealth and institutional management includes private banking, personal and institutional trust, retirement plans, and asset management. The finance division includes securities portfolio and asset and liability management activities. The group operates from United States, Canada and Mexico.

Primary SIC and add'l.: 6411 6282 6211 6712 6022

CIK No: 0000028412

Subsidiaries: CDV I Incorporated

Officers: Michael J. Fulton/CEO, Pres. - Comerica Bank, Western Marketing, Charles L. Gummer/CEO, Pres. - Comerica Bank, Texas Marketing, Ralph W. Babb/Chmn., CEO/$8,607,491.00, Joseph J. Buttigieg/Vice Chmn. - Business Bank/$4,628,586.00, Elizabeth S. Acton/CFO, Exec. VP, Comerica Management Counsel Members/$2,748,713.00, Wayne J. Mielke/Contact - Press, Paul Jaremski/Investor Relations Officer, John R. Beran/CIO, Exec. VP, Dennis J. Mooradian/Exec. VP - Wealth, Institutional Management/$3,359,851.00, Thomas D. Ogden/Pres. - Comerica Bank, Michigan Marketing, Jacquelyn H. Wolf/Exec. VP, Chief Human Resources Officer - Corporate Communications, Comerica Management Counsel Members, Connie Beck/Exec. VP - Retail Bank, Kathleen A. Pitton/Corporate Contact, Barry Holtzclaw/Contact - Northern California, San Diego, Arizona, Alfredo Padilla/Contact - Los Angeles, Orange County, California *(29 Officers included in Index)*

Directors: Ralph W. Babb/Chmn., CEO, Joseph J. Buttigieg/Vice Chmn. - Business Bank, Kenneth L. Way/Dir., William P. Vititoe/Dir., Reginald M. Turner/Dir., James F. Cordes/Dir., Robert S. Taubman/Dir., Peter D. Cummings/Dir., Alfred A. Piergallini/Dir., Lillian Bauder/Dir., Anthony F. Earley/Dir., Kevin T. Denicola/Dir., Roger A. Cregg/Dir.

Owners: Mary Constance Beck, Insiders/2.80%, Reginald M. Turner, Robert S. Taubman, Lillian Bauder, Dennis J. Mooradian, Joseph J. Buttigieg, Alfred A. Piergallini, Elizabeth S. Acton, Ralph W. Babb, Peter D. Cummings, John D. Lewis, Kenneth L. Way, James F. Cordes, William P. Vititoe *(16 Owners included in Index)*

Financial Data: *Fiscal Year End:*12/31 *Latest Annual Data:* 12/31/2006

Year	Sales	Net Income
2006	$4,290,000,000	$893,000,000
2005	$3,668,000,000	$861,000,000
2004	$3,094,000,000	$757,000,000

Curr. Assets:	$4,449,000,000	**Curr. Liab.:**	$46,899,000,000	**P/E Ratio:**	11.20
Plant, Equip.:	$568,000,000	**Total Liab.:**	$52,848,000,000	**Indic. Yr. Divd.:**	$2.560
Total Assets:	$58,001,000,000	**Net Worth:**	$5,153,000,000	**Debt/ Equity:**	1.3960

Comforce Corp

415 Crossways Pk. Dr., Woodbury, NY, 11797; *PH:* 1-516-437-3300; *Fax:* 1-516-437-3392; *http://* www.comforce.com; *Email:* investor@comforce.com

General - Incorporation .... DE
Employees 560
Auditor .... KPMG LLP
Stk Agt .... NA
Counsel .... Barnes & Thornburg
DUNS No. 00-507-1220

Stock- Price on:12/24/2007 .... $2.74
Stock Exchange .... AMEX
Ticker Symbol .... CFS
Outstanding Shares 17,390,000
E.P.S $0.15
Shareholders .... NA

Business: The group's principle activities are to provide staffing, consulting, financial and outsourcing services. The services of the group include Web-enabled solutions for the procurement, tracking and engagement of contingent or non-employee labor. The group operates through three segments: human capital management services, staff augmentation, and financial outsourcing services. Human capital management services segment provides contingent workforce management services. Staff augmentation segment provides information technology, telecom, healthcare support, technical and other staffing services. Financial outsourcing services segment provides funding and back office support services to independent consulting and staffing companies. The services of the group are primarily provided to Fortune 500 companies in the United States. Other customers include investment banking firms, computer software and hardware manufacturers, automotive industry, government agencies etc. The group's quarterly revenue for September 2007 was 150.67 millions of USD.

Primary SIC and add'l.: 8748 9999 7363 8742

CIK No: 0000006814

Subsidiaries: Brentwood of Canada, Inc., Brentwood Service Group, Inc., CIT Southeast, Inc., Clinical Labforce of America, Inc., Comforce Information Technologies, Inc., Comforce Operating, Inc., Comforce Technical Services, Inc., Comforce Technical, LLC, Comforce Telecom, Inc., CTS Global, Inc., CTS of Washington, LLC, Gerri G. Inc., Labforce Services of America, Inc., PrO Clinical Support Services, LLC, PrO Unlimited Global (HK) Limited 24 Subsidiaries included in the Index

Officers: Evan Burks/Exec. VP - Comforce Technical Services, Inc, Martha White/Regional Mgr. - Comforce Technical Services, Inc, Richard Buhl/Branch Mgr. - Comforce Technical Services, Inc, Scott Terrell/Sales Dir. - Comforce Telecom, Inc, Cyndi Thomas/VP - Coding Services, Comforce Coding Services, Inc, Pete Petix/VP - Comforce Telecom, Inc, Frank Pomeroy/Licensee, Comforce Staffing Services, Brad Turkin/Exec. VP, Gary Walton/Licensee, Comforce Staffing Services, Ellis Schultz/Licensee, Uniforce Staffing Services, Kasee Bojorquez/Administrative Dir. - Comforce Technical Services, Inc, Sandra Quintero/Branch Mgr. - Comforce Technical Services, Inc, Elizabeth Disalvo/Branch Mgr. - Comforce Technical Services, Inc, Tricia Devlin/Staffing Mgr. - Comforce Staffing Services, Bobbie Sands/Operations Mgr. - Comforce Staffing Services *(23 Officers included in Index)*

Owners: Rosemary Maniscalco, ARTRA GROUP Incorporated/8.80%, Harry V. Maccarrone/30.40%, Pierce J. Flynn, Daniel Raynor, Insiders/37.00%, Kenneth J. Daley, Linda Annicelli, Gordon Robinett, Robert F. Ende, John C. Fanning/29.80%

Financial Data: *Fiscal Year End:*12/25 *Latest Annual Data:* 12/31/2006

Year	Sales	Net Income
2006	$567,821,000	$4,078,000
2005	$539,841,000	$6,272,000
2004	$480,887,000	$1,756,000

Curr. Assets:	$136,394,000	**Curr. Liab.:**	$104,049,000	**P/E Ratio:**	18.27
Plant, Equip.:	$5,376,000	**Total Liab.:**	$193,853,000	**Indic. Yr. Divd.:**	NA
Total Assets:	$175,138,000	**Net Worth:**	-$18,715,000	**Debt/ Equity:**	NA

Comfort Systems USA Inc

777 Post Oak Blvd., Ste. 500, Houston, TX, 77056; *PH:* 1-713-830-9600; *Fax:* 1-713-830-9696; *http://* www.comfortsystemsusa.com; *Email:* hvac@comfortsystemsusa.com

General - Incorporation .... DE
Employees 6,647
Auditor .... Ernst & Young LLP
Stk Agt .... American Stock Transfer & Trust Co.
Counsel .... NA
DUNS No. 01-584-1703

Stock- Price on:12/24/2007 .... $13.87
Stock Exchange .... NYSE
Ticker Symbol .... FIX
Outstanding Shares 40,950,000
E.P.S $0.70
Shareholders .... NA

Business: The group's principal activities are to provide heating, ventilation, air conditioning (hvac) installation, maintenance, repair and replacement services. The group provides specialized applications such as process cooling, building automation control systems, fire protection, electronic monitoring and process piping. Certain locations also perform related services such as electrical and plumbing. The group operates primarily in the commercial and industrial hvac markets and perform most of its services within manufacturing plants, office buildings, retail centers, apartment complexes, healthcare, education and government facilities.

Primary SIC and add'l.: 6719 7623

CIK No: 0001035983

Subsidiaries: Accu-Temp GP,Inc., Accu-Temp LP,Inc., Accurate Air Systems, L.P., ACI Mechanical USA. Inc., ACI Mechanical,Inc., AirTemp,Inc., ARC Comfort Systems USA,Inc., Atlas Comfort Systems USA, L.P., Atlas-Accurate Holdings, LLC, Batchelors Mechanical Contractors,Inc., BCM Controls Corp., California Comfort Systems USA,Inc., Central Mechanical,Inc., Climate Control,Inc., Comfort Systems USA (Arkansas),Inc. 54 Subsidiaries included in the Index

Officers: William F. Murdy/Chmn., CEO/$1,603,543.00, Greg McKown/CIO, Sr. VP, Melissa Frazier/VP - Audit, Controls, Dean Tillison/Sr. VP - Region 2, Andrew D. Estrada/VP - Risk Management, Human Resources, Brian Lane/Sr. VP - Region 1, Julie Shaeff/Chief Accounting Officer/$349,124.00, Charles Diltz/Sr. VP - Region 3, Thomas N. Tanner/COO/$808,769.00, Trent McKenna/VP, General Counsel/$294,756.00, William George/CFO/$767,728.00

Directors: William F. Murdy/Chmn., CEO, Robert D. Wagner/Dir., Herman E. Bulls/Dir., Alfred J. Giardinelli/Dir., James H. Schultz/Dir., Franklin Myers/Dir.

Owners: Cannell Capital LLC/6.50%, William George, Robert D. Wagner, William F. Murdy/1.70%, Franklin Myers, Insiders/3.50%, Goldman Sachs Asset Management, L.P./6.80%, Dimensional Fund Advisors Inc./7.40%, Alfred J. Giardinelli, Trent T. McKenna, Thomas N. Tanner, Julie S. Shaeff, Herman E. Bulls, James H. Schultz

Financial Data: *Fiscal Year End:*12/31 *Latest Annual Data:* 12/31/2006

Year	Sales	Net Income
2006	$1,056,525,000	$28,724,000
2005	$899,531,000	-$6,226,000
2004	$819,552,000	$10,713,000

Curr. Assets:	$376,385,000	**Curr. Liab.:**	$218,160,000	**P/E Ratio:**	19.81
Plant, Equip.:	$15,504,000	**Total Liab.:**	$218,160,000	**Indic. Yr. Divd.:**	$0.140
Total Assets:	$460,874,000	**Net Worth:**	$242,714,000	**Debt/ Equity:**	NA

Comm Bancorp Inc

125 N State St., Clarks Summit, PA, 18411; *PH:* 1-570-586-0377; *Fax:* 1-570-587-4374; *http://* www.combk.com

General - Incorporation .... PA
Employees 186
Auditor .... Beard Miller Co. LLP
Stk Agt .... American Stock Transfer & Trust Co.
Counsel .... Saul, Ewing, Remick & Saul
DUNS No. 15-646-2764

Stock- Price on:12/24/2007 .... $49
Stock Exchange .... NDQ
Ticker Symbol .... CCBP
Outstanding Shares 1,760,000
E.P.S $3.61
Shareholders .... NA

Business: The group's principal activity is to provide commercial banking services in northeastern Pennsylvania. It operates through two wholly owned subsidiaries, community bank and trust company and comm realty corporation. The group's business consists primarily of the management and supervision of community bank whereas comm realty holds, manages and sells foreclosed or distressed assets on behalf of community bank. The services of the bank include accepting of time and demand deposit accounts and origination of consumer, commercial and mortgage loans and commercial leases to individuals and small- to medium-sized businesses. It provides services through 17 community banking offices located in lackawanna, susquehanna, wayne and Wyoming counties of Pennsylvania.

Primary SIC and add'l.: 6022 6712

CIK No: 0000730030

Subsidiaries: Comm Financial Services Corporation, Comm Realty Corporation, Community Bank and Trust Company, Community Leasing Corporation

Officers: William F. Farber/Chmn., CEO, Pres./$250,204.00, William R. Boyle/Sr. VP, Chief Credit Officer/$163,021.00, John P. Kameen/Dir., Sec., Scott A. Seasock/CFO, Exec. VP/$173,902.00, David L. Baker/Sr. VP - Community Bank, Trust Company, Tami L. Snyder/Information Services Officer - Community Bank, Trust Company, Harold F. Stout/Tunkhannock Branch Mgr. - Community Bank, Trust Company, Brian C. Urbas/Regional Mgr. - Clifford, Forest City, Lakewood, Community Bank, Trust Company, Ann E. Vadella/Carbondale Branch Mgr. - Community Bank, Trust Company, Louis J. Zefran/Business Development Officer - Community Bank, Trust Company, Debra A. Carr/Dickson City, Eynon Regional Mgr. - Community Bank, Trust Company, Joseph J. Muskey/Dir., Pres. - Community Leasing Corporation, Kevin J. Boylan/Commercial Loan Officer, Robin M. Bulzoni/Trust Officer, Lisa A. Hahn/Commercial Loan Officer - Community Bank, Trust Company *(43 Officers included in Index)*

Directors: William F. Farber/Chmn., CEO, Pres., Robert J. McDonnell/Vice Chmn., Eric G. Stephens/Dir., Thomas A. Chesnick/Dir., Judd B. Fitze/Dir., Dean L. Hesser/Dir., William A. Kerl/Dir., Erwin T. Kost/Dir., Susan F. Mancuso/Dir., Robert A. Mazzoni/Dir., Joseph P. Moore/Dir., Joseph P. Moore/Dir. Emeritus, Michael T. Goskowski/Dir. Emeritus, William B. Lopatofsky/Dir. Emeritus, Joseph J. Brennan/Member - Advisory Board *(41 Directors included in Index)*

Owners: William F. Farber/8.23%, Insiders/17.14%, Eric G. Stephens, Scott A. Seasock, Thomas M. Chesnick/1.45%, William A. Kerl, Dean L. Hesser, William R. Boyle, David L. Baker, Erwin T. Kost, Joseph P. Moore, John P. Kameen/1.11%, Robert A. Mazzoni, Susan F. Mancuso, Robert J. McDonnell/1.90% *(16 Owners included in Index)*

Financial Data: *Fiscal Year End:* 12/31 *Latest Annual Data:* 12/31/2006

Year	Sales	Net Income
2006	$36,448,000	$6,350,000
2005	$32,243,000	$5,210,000
2004	$29,899,000	$4,725,000

Curr. Assets:	$30,497,000	**Curr. Liab.:**	$484,548,000	**P/E Ratio:**	14.41
Plant, Equip.:	$11,370,000	**Total Liab.:**	$486,286,000	**Indic. Yr. Divd.:**	$1.040
Total Assets:	$540,404,000	**Net Worth:**	$54,118,000	**Debt/ Equity:**	NA

Command Center Inc

Formerly: Temporary Financial Services Inc
773 W Fifth Ave., Post Falls, ID, 83854; *PH:* 1-208-773-7450

General - Incorporation	WA	**Stock** - Price on:12/24/2007	$1.91
Employees	57	Stock Exchange	NA
Auditor	Decoria, Maichel & Teague, P.S	Ticker Symbol	NA
Stk Agt	Atlas Stock Transfer Corp	Outstanding Shares	23,830,000
Counsel	NA	E.P.S.	-$0.22
DUNS No.	NA	Shareholders	NA

Business: The group's principal activities are accounts receivable financing, investing in and providing business services to temporary labor businesses. The group provides the services to the operators in temporary labor industry who have experience and operational expertise and interested in starting up new operations or expanding existing operations.

Primary SIC and add'l.: 8721 6153

CIK No: 0001140102

Officers: Heddy Gudjonsson/Contact - Bellingham, WA, Nancy Williams/Contact - Everett, WA, Chuck Brewer/Contact - Peoria, AZ, Chris Frieh/Contact - Phoenix, AZ, Brenda Allen/Contact - Prescott, AZ, Melisa Lopez/Contact - Tucson, AZ, Jeff Inglis/Contact - Kent, WA, Christy Valdes/Contact - Mt. Vernon, WA, Janice Pattillo/Contact - Seattle, WA, April Wetherelt/Contact - Spokane, WA, Randy Roberts/Contact - Tacoma, WA, Laura Eppley/Contact - Vancouver, WA, Tina Posadas/Contact - Hillsboro, OR, Isabel Hernandez/Contact - Milwaukie, OR, Denise Cyr/Contact - Concord, CA *(77 Officers included in Index)*

Owners: John R. Coghlan/7.30%, Tommy R. Hancock/0.80%, Glenn Welstad/37.20%, Ronald L. Junck/12.60%, Kevin Semerad/15.30%, Insiders/78.60%, Tom Gilbert/2.40%, Todd Welstad/1.50%, Brad E. Herr/1.00%, Dwight Enget/5.40%

Financial Data: *Fiscal Year End:* 12/31 *Latest Annual Data:* 12/29/2006

Year	Sales	Net Income
2006	$71,272,000	-$2,419,000
2005	$372,000	-$200,000
2004	$292,000	$124,000

Curr. Assets:	$2,045,000	**Curr. Liab.:**	$592,000		
Plant, Equip.:	$1,589,000	**Total Liab.:**	$1,717,000	**Indic. Yr. Divd.:**	NA
Total Assets:	$5,270,000	**Net Worth:**	$3,553,000	**Debt/ Equity:**	NA

Command Security Corp

RtE 55, Lexington Pk., LaGrangeville, NY, 12540; *PH:* 1-845-454-3703; *Fax:* 1-845-454-0075;
http:// www.commandsecurity.com

General - Incorporation	NY	**Stock** - Price on:12/24/2007	NA
Employees	3,400	Stock Exchange	AMEX
Auditor	D'arcangelo & Co. LLP	Ticker Symbol	MOC
Stk Agt	Computershare Investor Services LLC	Outstanding Shares	NA
Counsel	LeBoeuf, Lamb, Greene & MacRae LLP	E.P.S.	$0.17
DUNS No.	05-298-5876	Shareholders	NA

Business: The group's principle activity is to provide uniformed security services through its twenty one operating offices to commercial, financial, industrial, aviation and governmental clients. The company provides its security services to three divisions: guard services, aviation services and support services. The guard service division includes governmental and quasi-governmental clients such as cities and statewide institutions and industrial and commercial clients such as retail chains and health care institutions. The aviation services division provides uniformed guard services to airport and airport related clients. The support services division provides a computerized scheduling and information system and programs, and accounts receivable financing. The group operates from United States.

Primary SIC and add'l.: 7381

CIK No: 0000864509

Officers: Debra M. Miller/VP - Administration, Martin C. Blake/Dir., COO/$300,000.00, Rory Wise/Mgr. - Contract Services, BWI, Pat O'Neil/GM - JFK, Sunia A. Williams/Regional VP - Aviation Services, West Region, Khalid Amjad/GM - LGA, Maria Robbins/Mgr. - Contract Services, MIA, Kathleen Denunzio/Accounting Assist., Jamie Damico/Accounting Assist., Kristin Hodor/Accounting Payable Clerk, John Tallman/Branch Mgr. - Fort Pierce, Timothy A. McDermott/Sales Coordinator, New England Region, Charles Rodriguez/Sales Exec. - South Florida Region, Tawny Gaines/Sales Coordinator, South Florida Region, Mike Fitzgibbons/Sales Exec. - Western Region *(62 Officers included in Index)*

Directors: Peter T. Kikis/Co - Chmn., Bruce R. Galloway/Chmn., Robert S. Ellin/Dir., Martin C. Blake/Dir., COO, Thomas P. Kikis/Dir., Martin R. Wade/Dir.

Owners: Peter T. Kikis/15.20%, Martin R. Wade, Trinad Capital, L.P./21.90%, Bruce Galloway/9.30%, Thomas P. Kikis/8.20%, Insiders/60.30%, Martin C. Blake/2.30%, Barry I. Regenstein/4.40%, Robert S. Ellin/22.10%

Financial Data: *Fiscal Year End:* 03/31 *Latest Annual Data:* 03/31/2007

Year	Sales	Net Income
2007	$93,823,000	$1,240,000
2006	$85,209,000	-$100,000
2005	$79,655,000	-$390,000

Curr. Assets:	$22,184,000	**Curr. Liab.:**	$15,671,000		
Plant, Equip.:	$529,000	**Total Liab.:**	$16,227,000	**Indic. Yr. Divd.:**	NA
Total Assets:	$25,330,000	**Net Worth:**	$9,104,000	**Debt/ Equity:**	NA

Commerce Bancorp Inc NJ

Commerce Atrium, 1701 Rte 70 E, Cherry Hill, NJ, 08034; *PH:* 1-856-751-9000;
http:// www.commerceonline.com

General - Incorporation	NJ	**Stock** - Price on:12/24/2007	$33.26
Employees	11,800	Stock Exchange	NYSE
Auditor	Ernst & Young LLP	Ticker Symbol	CBH
Stk Agt	Registrar & Transfer Co	Outstanding Shares	191,370,000
Counsel	Blank Rome LLP	E.P.S.	$1.52
DUNS No.	06-183-5039	Shareholders	NA

Business: The group's principle activity is to provide services including retail and commercial banking, corporate trust, insurance brokerage, investment management and business leasing services. Banking services include checking accounts and savings programs, money market accounts, negotiable orders of withdrawal accounts, certificates of deposit, safe deposit facilities, working capital loans, term loans for fixed assets, commercial loans and real estate mortgage loans. Trust services include bond trustee, paying agent and registrar for municipal bond offerings. Insurance brokerage services include commercial property and casualty insurance and employee benefit programs such as medical, life, disability, pension and risk management services. Investment management services include trading, underwriting and advisory services. The group also provides business leasing services and asset management services.

Primary SIC and add'l.: 6712 6021 6411

CIK No: 0000715096

Subsidiaries: Commerce Bank N.A., Commerce Bank/North, Commerce Capital Markets, Commerce Capital Markets, Inc, Commerce Insurance Services, Inc, Mortgage Acceptance Corp., NA Asset Management, North Asset Management, North. Commerce Commercial Leasing LLC

Officers: Vernon W. Hill/62/Chmn., CEO, Pres./$3,610,575.00, Robert D. Falese/Pres., CEO - Commerce Bank, NA/$1,727,420.00, Peter M. Musumeci/Exec. VP - Credit, Douglas J. Pauls/CFO, Exec. VP/$676,601.00, Linda Verba/Exec. VP - Retail Operations, James L. Gertie/Sr. VP, Chief Risk Officer, Edward C. Jordan/Exec. VP - Investor Relations, John J. Cunningham/Sr. VP, Chief Marketing Officer, Fred Graziano/Pres. - Regional Banking, Percival Moser/Exec. VP - Loan Operations

Directors: Vernon W. Hill/62/Chmn., CEO, Pres., Dennis M. Diflorio/Chmn. - Commerce Bank, NA, George E. Norcross/Dir., Joseph T. Tarquini/Dir., Daniel J. Ragone/Dir., Joseph S. Vassalluzzo/Dir., Nicholas A. Giordano/65/Dir., Jack R. Bershad/Dir., Steven M. Lewis/Dir., Joseph Buckelew/Dir., John K. Lloyd/Dir., Donald T. Difrancesco/Dir., Morton N. Kerr/Dir., William A. Schwartz/Dir.

Owners: Vernon W. Hill/3.17%, Capital Research and Management Company/5.46%, Robert D. Falese, George E. Norcross/1.37%, Morton N. Kerr, Donald T. DiFrancesco, Insiders/8.34%, Joseph E. Buckelew, Joseph T. Tarquini, Joseph S. Vassalluzzo, Davis Selected Advisers, LP/7.66%, The TCW Group, Inc./10.40%, Nicholas A. Giordano, Steven M. Lewis, Douglas J. Pauls *(21 Owners included in Index)*

Financial Data: *Fiscal Year End:* 12/31 *Latest Annual Data:* 12/31/2006

Year	Sales	Net Income
2006	$2,870,277,000	$299,313,000
2005	$2,122,068,000	$282,939,000
2004	$1,613,362,000	$273,418,000

Curr. Assets:	$1,322,697,000	**Curr. Liab.:**	$41,288,211,000	**P/E Ratio:**	21.60
Plant, Equip.:	$1,756,270,000	**Total Liab.:**	$42,470,718,000	**Indic. Yr. Divd.:**	NA
Total Assets:	$45,271,816,000	**Net Worth:**	$2,801,098,000	**Debt/ Equity:**	0.0425

Commerce Bancshares Inc

1000 Walnut, Kansas City, MO, 64106; *PH:* 1-816-234-2000; *Fax:* 1-816-234-2019;
http:// www.commercebank.com; *Email:* mymoney@commercebank.com

General - Incorporation	MO	**Stock** - Price on:12/24/2007	$46.5
Employees	4,478	Stock Exchange	NDQ
Auditor	KPMG LLP	Ticker Symbol	CBSH
Stk Agt	Computershare Trust Co	Outstanding Shares	69,600,000
Counsel	NA	E.P.S.	$3.09
DUNS No.	04-114-2522	Shareholders	NA

Business: The groups principle activity is to provide banking services. The group operates from United States.

Primary SIC and add'l.: 6321 6311 6021 6712 6519

CIK No: 0000022356

Subsidiaries: 21stStreet Redevelopment Company, L.C., Capital for Business, Inc., CBI Insurance Company, CBI Leasing, Inc., CBI-Kansas, Inc., CFB Partners, LLC, CFB PartnersII, LLC, CFB Venture Fund, L.P., CFB Venture FundI, Inc., CFB Venture FundII, L.P., Clayton Financial Corp., Clayton Holdings, LLC, Clayton Realty Corp., Commerce Bank, National Association, Commerce Brokerage Services, Inc. 24 Subsidiaries included in the Index

Officers: David W. Kemper/Chmn., CEO, Pres./$2,584,328.00, Jonathan M. Kemper/Vice Chmn., VP/$1,111,828.00, Seth M. Leadbeater/Vice Chmn., Member - Exec. Management/$778,561.00, Robert C. Matthews/Exec. VP, Chief Credit Officer, Risk Mgr., Daniel J. Stinnett/Sec., Sara E. Foster/Sr. VP, Jeffery D. Aberdeen/54/Controller, Bayard A. Clark/CFO, Exec. VP/$598,831.00, Robert J. Rauscher/Sr. VP, Raymond V. Stranghoener/Exec. VP, Michael J. Petrie/Sr. VP, Charles G. Kim/Exec. VP - Retail Line, Business/$679,870.00, Kevin G. Barth/Exec. VP - Commercial Line, Business/$681,169.00

Directors: David W. Kemper/Chmn., CEO, Pres., Jonathan M. Kemper/Vice Chmn., VP, Seth M. Leadbeater/Vice Chmn., Member - Exec. Management, Benjamin F. Rassieur/Dir., John R. Capps/Dir., Andrew C. Taylor/Dir., James B. Hebenstreit/Dir., Terry O. Meek/Dir., Robert H. West/Dir., Thomas A. McDonnell/Dir., Thomas W. Grant/Dir., Dan C. Simons/Dir., Kimberly G. Walker/Dir.

Owners: Thomas W. Grant, Insiders, Benjamin F. Rassieur, Thomas A. McDonnell, Robert H. West, Jonathan M. Kemper, James B. Hebenstreit, Kevin G. Barth, Terry O. Meek, Mary Ann Van Lokeren, Charles G. Kim, David W. Kemper, Bayard A. Clark, Andrew C. Taylor, Seth M. Leadbeater *(16 Owners included in Index)*

Financial Data: ***Fiscal Year End:***12/31 ***Latest Annual Data:*** 12/31/2006

Year	Sales	Net Income
2006	$1,193,927,000	$219,842,000
2005	$1,038,765,000	$223,247,000
2004	$937,021,000	$220,341,000

Curr. Assets:	$1,154,316,000	***Curr. Liab.:***	$13,516,136,000	***P/E Ratio:***	15.10
Plant, Equip.:	$386,095,000	***Total Liab.:***	$13,788,235,000	***Indic. Yr. Divd.:***	$1.000
Total Assets:	$15,230,349,000	***Net Worth:***	$1,442,114,000	***Debt/ Equity:***	0.0271

Commerce Energy Group Inc

600 Anton Blvd., Ste. 2000, Costa Mesa, CA, 92626; ***PH:*** 1-800-962-4655; ***Fax:*** 1-714-259-2501; ***http://*** www.commerceenergygroup.com; ***Email:*** contactus@commerceenergy.com

General		***Stock***	
Incorporation	DE	Price on:12/24/2007	$1.83
Employees	176	Stock Exchange	AMEX
Auditor	Hein & Assoc., LLP	Ticker Symbol	EGR
Stk Agt	Computershare Investor Services LLC	Outstanding Shares	29,750,000
Counsel	Paul,Hastings,Janofsky & Walker LLP	E.P.S	$0.134
DUNS No.	NA	Shareholders	NA

Business: The group's principle activity is the sale of retail electric power to residential and small commercial customers in California and Pennsylvania. The group also provides service to larger commercial, industrial and governmental customers. A portion of the electric power sold by the group is delivered to retail and commercial end-user customers by the incumbent utility distribution companies (udcs) and electric distribution companies (edcs). In California, the group provides customers with environmentally friendly power purchased under a contract and in Pennsylvania, it provides customers with a 50% environmentally friendly power product derived from multiple sources. The group has developed its own inside sales force to sell energy efficient and emergency preparedness products to customers by telephone. The group's total revenue for year 2007 was 371.61 millions of USD.

Primary SIC and add'l.: NA

CIK No: 0001274150

Subsidiaries: Commerce Energy, Inc., Skipping Stone Inc., UtiliHost, Inc.

Officers: Steven S. Boss/Dir., CEO, Thomas L. Ulry/Sr. VP - Sales, Marketing, Robert J. Hipps/CFO - Interim, Nick Cioll/Chief Risk Officer, Kathleen Lindner/CIO

Directors: Steven S. Boss/Dir., CEO, Robert C. Perkins/Chmn., Gary J. Hessenauer/Dir., Charles E. Bayless/Dir., Mark S. Juergensen/Dir., Dennis R. Leibel/Dir.

Owners: Thomas L. Ulry, Gary J. Hessenauer, Charles E. Bayless, Erik A. Lopez, Nick Cioll, Ian B. Carter/8.40%, Steven S. Boss/1.90%, Mark S. Juergensen, Daniel Zeff/10.50%, Dennis R. Leibel, Lawrence Clayton, Robert C. Perkins/2.30%, Insiders/6.70%

Financial Data: ***Fiscal Year End:***07/31 ***Latest Annual Data:*** 7/31/2006

Year	Sales	Net Income
2006	$247,080,000	-$2,239,000
2005	$253,853,000	-$6,114,000
2004	$210,623,000	-$21,720,000

Curr. Assets:	$64,996,000	***Curr. Liab.:***	$32,743,000	***P/E Ratio:***	10.76
Plant, Equip.:	$5,866,000	***Total Liab.:***	$32,743,000	***Indic. Yr. Divd.:***	NA
Total Assets:	$99,076,000	***Net Worth:***	$66,333,000	***Debt/ Equity:***	NA

Commerce Group Corp

6001 N 91st St., Milwaukee, WI, 53225; ***PH:*** 1-414-462-5310; ***Fax:*** 1-414-462-5312; ***http://*** www.commercegroupcorp.com; ***Email:*** info@commercegroupcorp.com

General		***Stock***	
Incorporation	WI	Price on:12/24/2007	$0.11
Employees	45	Stock Exchange	OTC
Auditor	Chisholm Bierwolf & Nilson LLC	Ticker Symbol	CGCO
Stk Agt	Nevada Agency & Trust Company	Outstanding Shares	25,730,000
Counsel	Machulak Robertson & Sodos	E.P.S	$3.50
DUNS No.	05-606-5832	Shareholders	NA

Business: The group's principal activity is to explore, exploit, and develop gold and silver mines in the republic of El Salvador, Central America. The group holds a nearly 100% interest in the joint venture which is the operator of the san sebastian gold mine (ssgm). The group is currently exploring 42-square kilometer area, which includes three formerly-operated mines and encompasses the ssgm.

Primary SIC and add'l.: 1041 1044 6519

CIK No: 0000109757

Subsidiaries: Commerce/Sanseb JointVenture, Ecomm Group Inc., Homespan Realty Co., Inc., Mineral San Sebastian, San Luis Estates, Inc., San Sebastian Gold Mines,Inc., Universal Developers, Inc.

Officers: Edward A. MacHulak/Chmn., CEO, Pres., Christine M. Wolski/Assist. Corp. Sec.

Directors: Edward A. MacHulak/Chmn., CEO, Pres., Sidney Sodos/Dir., John H. Curry/Dir.

Owners: Insiders/30.50%, John H. Curry/1.23%, Sidney Sodos/1.17%, Edward A. Machulak/3.97%, Edward L. Machulak/8.28%, General Lumber & Supply Co., Inc./11.30%, Edward L. Machulak/4.54%

Financial Data: ***Fiscal Year End:***03/31 ***Latest Annual Data:*** 03/31/2007

Year	Sales	Net Income
2007	NA	-$173,000
2006	NA	-$162,000
2005	NA	-$230,000

Curr. Assets:	$930,000	***Curr. Liab.:***	$18,852,000		
Plant, Equip.:	$4,526,000	***Total Liab.:***	$18,852,000	***Indic. Yr. Divd.:***	$1.200
Total Assets:	$39,244,000	***Net Worth:***	$20,392,000	***Debt/ Equity:***	NA

Commerce Group Inc

211 Main St., Webster, MA, 01570; ***PH:*** 1-508-943-9000; ***Fax:*** 1-508-949-4921; ***http://*** www.commerceinsurance.com; ***Email:*** Generalcomments@Commerceinsurance.com

General		***Stock***	
Incorporation	MA	Price on:12/24/2007	$34.36
Employees	2,187	Stock Exchange	NYSE
Auditor	PricewaterhouseCoopers LLP	Ticker Symbol	CGI
Stk Agt	EquiServe Trust Co N.A	Outstanding Shares	65,530,000
Counsel	NA	E.P.S	$3.44
DUNS No.	10-583-1531	Shareholders	NA

Business: The groups principle activity is to provide personal and commercial property and casualty insurance. The group product lines include personal and commercial property and casualty insurance. The group operates from United States.

Primary SIC and add'l.: 6719 6331

CIK No: 0000811612

Subsidiaries: ACIC Holding Co., Inc, American Commerce Insurance Company, Bay Finance Company, Inc, Citation Insurance Company, Clark-Prout Insurance Agency, Inc, Commerce Holdings, Inc, Commerce West Insurance Company, The Commerce Insurance Company

Officers: Gerald Fels/65/Chmn., CEO, Pres./$5,131,937.00, Debra A. Mann/48/Sr. VP - Management Information Systems, Commerce, David H. Cochrane/54/Sr. VP - Underwriting, Commerce, Citation, Randall V. Becker/CFO/$1,754,588.00, James A. Ermilio/Dir., Sr. VP, General Counsel/$3,174,419.00, Regan P. Remillard/44/Dir., Exec. VP - Policyholder Benefits, John W. Hawie/44/Chief Investment Officer, Sr. VP/$1,487,897.00, Peter J. Dignan/56/Sr. VP - Underwriting, Commerce, Citation, Cathleen M. Moynihan/52/Sr. VP - Human Resources

Directors: Gerald Fels/65/Chmn., CEO, Pres., Arthur J. Remillard/Chmn., Henry J. Camosse/Dir., Normand R. Marois/72/Dir., Suryakant M. Patel/67/Dir., Joseph A. Borski/Dir., Robert W. Harris/76/Dir., James A. Ermilio/Dir., Sr. VP, General Counsel, Regan P. Remillard/44/Dir., Exec. VP - Policyholder Benefits, Raymond J. Lauring/82/Dir., Gurbachan Singh/Dir., John W. Spillane/75/Dir., David R. Grenon/68/Dir., Eric G. Butler/80/Dir., John J. Kunkel/96/Dir.

Owners: Barclays Global Investors/5.60%, Joseph A. Borski, Gurbachan Singh, Insiders/18.90%, Arthur J. Remillard/1.50%, Normand R. Marois, Henry J. Camosse, David R. Grenon, Suryakant M. Patel/1.20%, James A. Ermilio, John J. Kunkel/3.10%, John W. Hawie, Arthur J. Remillard/1.80%, Eric G. Butler, The Commerce Group, Inc./9.30% *(21 Owners included in Index)*

Financial Data: ***Fiscal Year End:***12/31 ***Latest Annual Data:*** 12/31/2006

Year	Sales	Net Income
2006	$1,949,469,000	$241,535,000
2005	$1,884,381,000	$243,912,000
2004	$1,806,571,000	$214,431,000

Curr. Assets:	$854,088,000	***Curr. Liab.:***	$232,440,000	***P/E Ratio:***	9.99
Plant, Equip.:	$68,383,000	***Total Liab.:***	$2,600,639,000	***Indic. Yr. Divd.:***	$1.200
Total Assets:	$4,110,869,000	***Net Worth:***	$1,503,271,000	***Debt/ Equity:***	0.1971

Commerce National Bank CA

279 E Orangethorpe Ave., Fullerton, CA, 92832; ***PH:*** 1-714-451-8650; ***Fax:*** 1-714-578-6717; ***http://*** www.commercenatbank.com

General		***Stock***	
Incorporation		Price on:12/24/2007	$16.69
Employees	NA	Stock Exchange	OTC
Auditor	NA	Ticker Symbol	CNBF
Stk Agt	U.S. Stock Transfer Corp	Outstanding Shares	2,670,000
Counsel	NA	E.P.S	NA
DUNS No.	NA	Shareholders	NA

Business: The group's principle activity is to provide banking services. The group's services include commercial, construction and real estate loan. The group operates from United States.

Primary SIC and add'l.: 6021

CIK No:

Officers: Mark E. Simmons/Dir., CEO, Pres., Steven L. Hollstein/Dir., Exec. VP, Chief Credit Officer, Cheri S. George/Sr. VP, Real Estate Loan Officer, Terri Hipwell/Sr. VP, Commercial Lending Officer, Mindy Tran/VP - Business Development, J. W. Huntsberger/Sr. VP, Banking Office Mgr., Betty M. King/Sr. VP, Real Estate Lending Officer, Mary D. Miller/Sr. VP, Banking Office Mgr., Dan Palmquist/Sr. VP - Business Development, Jo Pedrojetti/Sr. VP, Real Estate Department Mgr., Herb Reynolds/Sr. VP - Financial Services Division, J. P. Swift/Sr. VP - Small Business Lending, John Broecker/VP - Business Development, Larry V. Sorensen/CFO, Exec. VP, Thomas Flannery/Sr. VP, Dir. - Operations *(19 Officers included in Index)*

Directors: Mark E. Simmons/Dir., CEO, Pres., Bernard E. Schneider/Chmn., Robert H. Smith/Vice Chmn., Steven L. Hollstein/Dir., Exec. VP, Chief Credit Officer, Allen L. Basso/Dir., Carolyn D. Beaver/Dir., Burnie H. Dunlap/Dir., William H. McAulay/Dir., Donald P. Tormey/Dir.

Commerce Union Bank TN

701 South Main St., Springfield, TN , 37172; ***PH:*** 1-615-384-3357; ***http://*** www.commerceunionbank.com; ***Email:*** customerservice@commerceunionbank.com

General		***Stock***	
Incorporation		Price on:12/24/2007	$13
Employees	NA	Stock Exchange	OTC
Auditor	NA	Ticker Symbol	CUBN
Stk Agt	NA	Outstanding Shares	NA
Counsel	NA	E.P.S	NA
DUNS No.	NA	Shareholders	NA

Business: The groups principle activity is to provide recruiting services. The groups service area includes the research and development, engineering, marketing, sales, information technology and manufacturing industries. The group operates from United States.

Primary SIC and add'l.: 6022

CIK No:

CommerceFirst Bancorp Inc

1804 W St., Ste. 200, Annapolis, MD, 21401; *PH:* 1-410-280-6695; *Fax:* 1-410-280-8565; *http://* www.commerce1st.com

General - Incorporation	MD	Stock- Price on:12/24/2007	$13.7
Employees	29	Stock Exchange	NDQ
Auditor	Trice Geary & Myers LLC	Ticker Symbol	CMFB
Stk Agt	Registrar & Transfer Co	Outstanding Shares	1,820,000
Counsel	NA	E.P.S.	$0.68
DUNS No.	NA	Shareholders	NA

Business: The group's principal activity is to provide financial services to individuals and corporate customers located in anne arundel country and surrounding areas of central Maryland, through its wholly owned subsidiary commercefirst bank. The group provides full commercial banking services to its business and professional clients. The commercial banking services are offered to sole proprietorships, small and medium-sized businesses, partnerships, corporations, non-profit organizations and associations. The group's lending activities includes commercial loans for business purposes including working capital, equipment purchases, real estate, lines of credit, and government contract financing. The group offers variety of deposits including personal checking accounts, now accounts, savings accounts and a tiered money market account.

Primary SIC and add'l.: 6022 6712

CIK No: 0001098813

Subsidiaries: CommerceFirst Bank

Officers: Richard J. Morgan/Dir., Pres., CEO - Commercefirst Bank/$209,631.00, Thomas L. Bolander/Sr. VP, Chief Lending Officer - Commercefirst Bank, George Kapusta/Sr. VP - Prince Georges County, Commercefirst Bank, Craig Engelhaupt/Sr. VP - Howard County, Commercefirst Bank, Penny L. Cantwell/Sr. VP - Anne Arundel County, Commercefirst Bank

Directors: Richard J. Morgan/Dir., Pres., CEO - Commercefirst Bank, Milton D. Jernigan/Chmn. - Commercefirst Bank, Dale R. Watson/Dir. - Commercefirst Bank, Gregory A. Gray/Dir. - Commercefirst Bank, Nicholas Marino/Dir. - Commercefirst Bank, Lamont Thomas/Dir. - Commercefirst Bank, Jerome A. Watts/Dir. - Commercefirst Bank, William F. Chesley/Dir. - Commercefirst Bank, John A. Richardson/64/Dir. - Commercefirst Bank, Robert R. Mitchell/65/Dir. - Commercefirst Bank, George C. Shenk/Dir. - Commercefirst Bank, Edward B. Howlin/Dir. - Commercefirst Bank, Charles L. Hurtt/61/Dir. - Commercefirst Bank, Wilfred T. Azar/Dir. - Commercefirst Bank, Don E. Riddle/Dir. - Commercefirst Bank *(19 Directors included in Index)*

Owners: Edward B. Howlin/9.40%, Milton D. Jernigan/2.40%, Robert R. Mitchell/1.81%, John A. Richardson/2.19%, T/R Partners/5.41%, Lamont Thomas/2.10%, Richard J. Morgan/1.35%, Charles L. Hurtt, Jerome A. Watts/1.78%, Insiders/21.75%, George G. Shenk/1.22%, Mike Rosinus/5.69%

*Financial Data: Fiscal Year End:*12/31 *Latest Annual Data:* 12/31/2006

Year	Sales	Net Income
2006	$8,839,000	$1,283,000
2005	$6,263,000	$1,033,000
2004	$3,585,000	$1,090,000

Curr. Assets:	$33,009,000	Curr. Liab.:	$121,960,000	P/E Ratio:	20.15
Plant, Equip.:	$578,000	Total Liab.:	$122,583,000	Indic. Yr. Divd.:	NA
Total Assets:	$141,270,000	Net Worth:	$18,687,000	Debt/ Equity:	NA

CommerceWest Bank CA

2111 Business Ctr. Dr., Irvine, CA, 92612; *PH:* 1-949-251-6959; *http://* www.cwbk.com

General - Incorporation		Stock - Price on:12/24/2007	$20
Employees	NA	Stock Exchange	OTC
Auditor	NA	Ticker Symbol	CWBK
Stk Agt	U.S. Stock Transfer Corp	Outstanding Shares	3,150,000
Counsel	NA	E.P.S.	NA
DUNS No.	NA	Shareholders	NA

Business: The groups principal activities include providing banking for small and mid sized businesses in Orange County and throughout surrounding areas. Services of the group include money market deposit accounts, time deposits, safe deposit services, credit cards, cash management, direct deposits, notary services, money orders, night depository, travelers checks, cashiers checks, domestic collections, savings bonds, bank drafts and automated teller services. The group operates from the United States.

Primary SIC and add'l.: 6021

CIK No:

Officers: Ivo A. Tjan/CEO

Commercial Bancshares Inc

118 S Sandusky Ave., Upper Sandusky, OH, 43351; *PH:* 1-419-294-5781; *Fax:* 1-419-294-2350; *http://* www.csbanking.com

General - Incorporation	OH	Stock- Price on:12/24/2007	$26.5
Employees	102	Stock Exchange	OTC
Auditor	Plante & Moran, PLLC	Ticker Symbol	CMOH
Stk Agt	Commercial Savings Bank	Outstanding Shares	1,140,000
Counsel	NA	E.P.S.	$0.35
DUNS No.	NA	Shareholders	NA

Business: The group's principal activity is to provide commercial and retail banking services. The deposit products include demand, savings and time accounts. The loan portfolio includes commercial, real estate, construction, consumer, credit card and home equity loans. The group operates through its branch offices located in upper sandusky, Ohio and communities in wyandot, marion, hancock, union, and franklin counties.

Primary SIC and add'l.: 6712 6022

CIK No: 0001009976

Subsidiaries: Advantage Finance, Inc., Beck Title Agency, Ltd., Commercial Financial and Insurance Agency, Ltd., The Commercial Savings Bank

Officers: Mike Shope/Dir., Interim CEO, Pres., Philip W. Kinley/48/CEO, Pres./$178,226.00, Mark D. Udin/CIO, Sr. VP/$107,300.00, Susan E. Brown/Sr. VP - Retail Banking, Bruce J. Beck/56/Sec., Treasurer/$114,121.00, Shawn P. Keller/Chief Lending Officer, Sr. VP/$111,871.00, Scott Oboy/CFO, Sr. VP/$145,292.00, Ron Wilson/Exec. VP

Directors: Mike Shope/Dir., Interim CEO, Pres., Stanley Kinnett/Vice Chmn., William Bremyer/Dir., Michael A. Mastro/Dir., Kurt Kimmel/Dir., John W. Bremyer/45/Dir., Mark E. Dillon/Dir., Richard A. Sheaffer/Dir., Dan E. Berg/Dir., Lynn R. Child/Dir., Douglas C. Smith/65/Dir., Ed Emerson/Dir., Deb J. Grafmiller/Dir.

Owners: Insiders/6.30%, Insiders/6.30%, Philip W. Kinley/1.00%, Bruce J. Beck/1.00%

*Financial Data: Fiscal Year End:*12/31 *Latest Annual Data:* 12/31/2006

Year	Sales	Net Income
2006	$21,654,000	$1,780,000
2005	$20,585,000	$1,667,000
2004	$19,090,000	$1,524,000

Curr. Assets:	$12,147,000	Curr. Liab.:	$250,063,000	P/E Ratio:	23.04
Plant, Equip.:	$9,502,000	Total Liab.:	$251,245,000	Indic. Yr. Divd.:	$0.760
Total Assets:	$273,692,000	Net Worth:	$22,447,000	Debt/ Equity:	NA

Commercial Federal Corp

13220 California St., Omaha, NE, 68154; *PH:* 1-402-554-9200; *Fax:* 1-402-554-9330; *http://* www.bankofthewest.com; *Email:* cfbinfo@commercialfed.com

General - Incorporation	NE	Stock- Price on:12/24/2007	NA
Employees	NA	Stock Exchange	AMEX
Auditor	Deloitte & Touche LLP	Ticker Symbol	CFB
Stk Agt	Wells Fargo Shareowner Services	Outstanding Shares	NA
Counsel	Stradley Ronon Stevens & Young LLP	E.P.S.	NA
DUNS No.	00-697-0073	Shareholders	NA

Business: The group's principal activity is to provide commercial, consumer, mortgage banking and treasury services. The commercial banking provides commercial demand and time deposits, cash management products and services and originates loans. These loans include commercial operating, agricultural, commercial real estate and small business loans. The mortgage banking segment originates, purchases and services residential mortgage loans. The retail banking services include credit cards, overdraft protection, electronic and telephone bill-paying and cash advances. Treasury segment manages the single-family residential mortgage loan portfolio, investment and mortgage-backed securities, wholesale deposits, advances from the fhlb and other borrowings. The group operates 192 branches located in Colorado, Iowa, Nebraska, Kansas, Oklahoma, Missouri and Arizona.

Primary SIC and add'l.: 6035 6712

CIK No: 0000744778

Subsidiaries: AmerUs Leasing Corporation, ComFed Insurance Services Company, Limited, Commercial Federal Affordable Housing, Inc., Commercial Federal Bank, Commercial Federal Capital Trust I, Commercial Federal Capital Trust II, Commercial Federal Community Development Corporation, Commercial Federal Insurance Corporation, Commercial Federal Investment Services, Inc., Commercial Federal Realty Investors Corporation, Commercial Federal Service Corporation, Community Services, Inc., First Savings Investment Corporation, Liberty Leasing Company, Mortgage REIT, Inc. 18 Subsidiaries included in the Index

Commercial Metals Co

6565 N MacArthur Blvd., Ste. 800, Irving, TX, 75039; *PH:* 1-214-689-4300; *Fax:* 1-214-689-5886; *http://* www.commercialmetals.com

General - Incorporation	DE	Stock- Price on:12/24/2007	$34.54
Employees	11,734	Stock Exchange	NYSE
Auditor	Deloitte & Touche LLP	Ticker Symbol	CMC
Stk Agt	Chase Mellon Shareholder Services	Outstanding Shares	119,220,000
Counsel	NA	E.P.S.	$2.79
DUNS No.	00-792-5845	Shareholders	NA

Business: The groups principle activities include manufacturing and marketing steel and metal products. The groups products include copper braze bronze, ferrous scrap and aluminum. In the year 2007, the group acquired Bruhler Stahlhandel GmbH steel. The group operates from United States.

Primary SIC and add'l.: 3351 5093 3341 3312 5051

CIK No: 0000022444

Subsidiaries: AHT, Inc., Centrum Zawiercie Sp.z o.o., CMC (Beijing) International Trade Company Ltd., CMC Australia Pty., Limited, CMC Centrozlom-Katowice Sp.z o.o., CMC China Guangzhou International Trade Co., Ltd., CMC Commercial Metals de Mexico S de RL de CV, CMC Europe AG, CMC Fareast Limited, CMC International AG, CMC International S.E. Asia Pte., Limited, CMC Oil Company, CMC Poland S.A., CMC Putex Sp.z o.o., CMC Receivables, Inc. 44 Subsidiaries included in the Index

Officers: Murray R. McClean/Dir., CEO, Pres., Hanns Zoellner/Exec. VP, Pres. - CMC International, William B. Larson/CFO, Sr. VP, David M. Sudbury/Sr. VP, Sec., General Counsel, Russ Rinn/Exec. VP, Pres. - CMC Americas, Louis A. Federle/Treasurer, Malinda G. Passmore/CIO, VP, Leon K. Rusch/Controller

Directors: Murray R. McClean/Dir., CEO, Pres., Stanley A. Rabin/Chmn., Ralph E. Loewenberg/Dir., Harold L. Adams/Dir., Moses Feldman/Dir., Anthony A. Massaro/Dir., Robert D. Neary/Dir., Dorothy G. Owen/Dir., David J. Smith/Dir., Robert R. Womack/Dir., Robert L. Guido/Dir.

Owners: Ralph E. Loewenberg, Hanns Zoellner, Smith J. David, Robert R. Womack, Moses Feldman, TPG-Axon Capital Management, LP/6.20%, Harold L. Adams, Goldman Sachs Asset Management, L.P./6.60%, FMR Corp./6.60%, Insiders/4.90%, Russell B. Rinn, Murray R. McClean, Anthony A. Massaro, William B. Larson, Stanley A. Rabin/1.70% *(19 Owners included in Index)*

*Financial Data: Fiscal Year End:*08/31 *Latest Annual Data:* 08/31/2007

Year	Sales	Net Income
2007	$8,329,016,000	$355,431,000
2006	$7,555,924,000	$356,347,000
2005	$6,592,697,000	$285,781,000

Curr. Assets:	$2,144,792,000	Curr. Liab.:	$1,182,305,000	P/E Ratio:	11.84
Plant, Equip.:	$588,686,000	Total Liab.:	$1,617,730,000	Indic. Yr. Divd.:	$0.360
Total Assets:	$2,898,868,000	Net Worth:	$1,220,104,000	Debt/ Equity:	0.2254

Commercial National Financial Corp

900 Ligonier St., Latrobe, PA, 15650; *PH:* 1-724-539-3501; *Fax:* 1-724-537-9966; *http://* www.cnbthebank.com

General - Incorporation....PA
Employees....112
Auditor....Beard Miller Co. LLP
Stk Agt....Commercial National Financial Corp
Counsel....NA
DUNS No....00-893-6718

Stock- Price on:12/24/2007....$19.02
Stock Exchange....NDQ
Ticker Symbol....CNAF
Outstanding Shares....3,040,000
E.P.S....$1.01
Shareholders....NA

Business: The group's principal activities are to provide general commercial banking services through its subsidiary, commercial national bank of Pennsylvania. The services include extending credit, providing deposit services, marketing non-deposit investments and offering financial counseling. The branch offices of the group are equipped with 24 hour a day automatic teller machines. It has also implemented a comprehensive electronic online banking system. By using a personal computer with Internet access, customers can access their bank accounts, perform common banking tasks and pay bills. The group operates through its branch offices located in latrobe, unity township, ligonier, west newton, greensburg, norwin and hempfield township, Pennsylvania.

Primary SIC and add'l.: 6712 6022

CIK No: 0000866054

Subsidiaries: Commercial Bank & Trust of PA, Commercial National Insurance Services, Inc.

Officers: Gregg E. Hunter/Vice Chmn., CEO, Pres., Susan R. Skoloda/VP, Assist. Sec., Treasurer, Douglas Arndt/Contact - Community Relationship Officer - Courthouse Square Office, Racquel Matijak/Contact - Community Office Assist. Mgr. - Courthouse Square Office, Molly Richards/Assist. Mgr. - Norwin Hills Office, Donna Daugherty/Contact - Pleasant Unity Office, Community Relationship Officer, Joanne Ferace/Mgr. - West Newton Office, Rose Biller/Contact - West Newton Office, Customer Service Specialist, Wendy S. Schmucker/Sr. VP, Sec., Treasurer, Thomas D. Watters/Sr. VP, CFO, Cheryl Kapelewski/Assist. - Lawson Heights Office, Thomas Sylvester/Mgr. - Ligonier Office, Linda M. Nace/Assist. - Ligonier Office, Patricia Torrance/Mgr. - Lincoln Road Office, Amy Madey/Assist. - Lincoln Road Office *(20 Officers included in Index)*

Directors: Gregg E. Hunter/Vice Chmn., CEO, Pres., George V. Welty/Chmn., Bruce A. Robinson/Dir., Richmond H. Ferguson/Dir., Steven H. Landers/Dir., George A. Conti/Dir., Dorothy S. Hunter/Dir., John T. Babilya/Dir., Frank E. Jobe/Dir., Joseph A. Mosso/Dir., Debra L. Spatola/Dir., Edward C. Wible/Dir.

Owners: T. Babilya/0.16%, George A. Conti/7.61%, George V. Welty/0.33%, Frank E. Jobe/1.00%, Debra L. Spatola/0.04%, Gregg E. Hunter/13.53%, Dorothy S. Hunter/10.99%, Richmond H. Ferguson/0.17%, Bruce A. Robinson/0.43%, Edward C. Wible, Steven H. Landers/0.17%, Joseph A. Mosso/0.84%, Insiders/24.55%

Financial Data: *Fiscal Year End:*12/31 *Latest Annual Data:* 12/31/2006

Year	Sales	Net Income
2006	$20,695,000	$2,958,000
2005	$19,143,000	$3,377,000
2004	$22,833,000	$621,000

Curr. Assets:	$11,200,000	**Curr. Liab.:**	$298,920,000	**P/E Ratio:**	18.83
Plant, Equip.:	$3,886,000	**Total Liab.:**	$300,967,000	**Indic. Yr. Divd.:**	$0.800
Total Assets:	$338,196,000	**Net Worth:**	$37,229,000	**Debt/ Equity:**	NA

Commercial Vehicle Group Inc

6530 W Campus Way, New Albany, OH, 43054; ***PH:*** 1-614-289-5360; ***Fax:*** 1-614-289-5367; ***http://*** www.cvgrp.com; ***Email:*** info@cvgrp.com

General - Incorporation....DE
Employees....5,790
Auditor....Deloitte & Touche LLP
Stk Agt....Computershare Trust Co
Counsel....NA
DUNS No....NA

Stock- Price on:12/24/2007....$19.2
Stock Exchange....NDQ
Ticker Symbol....CVGI
Outstanding Shares....21,390,000
E.P.S....NA
Shareholders....NA

Business: The group's principal activities are to provide interior systems, vision safety solutions and other cab-related products. The products include suspension seat systems, interior trim systems (including instrument panels, door panels, headliners, cabinetry and floor systems), mirrors, wiper systems, controls and switches specifically designed for applications in commercial vehicle cabs. These products are useful for the global commercial vehicle market, including the heavy-duty (class 8) truck market, the construction market and other specialized transportation markets. The group's products are marketed under the brand names: kab seating, national seating, trim systems, sprague devices, sprague controls, prutsmantm, moto mirrortm and roadwatch(r). The group's customers in the OEM market include freightliner, international, paccar, volvo/ mack, blue bird and thomas built buses.

Primary SIC and add'l.: 3711 3714

CIK No: 0001290900

Subsidiaries: A. Stokes Pressings Limited, AJ Williams Small Pressings Limited, AJW Holdings Limited, BB Seating Limited, Bostrom Europe, Bostrom International Limited, Bostrom Investments Limited, Bostrom Limited, Bostrom Specialist Engineering Limited, Bostrom Vehicle Components Limited, Cabarrus Plastics, Inc., Commercial Vehicle Systems Limited, Corvus Suspension Products Limited, CVG International Holdings Limited, CVG Logistics LLC 46 Subsidiaries included in the Index

Officers: Mervin Dunn/Dir., CEO, Pres., Chad M. Utrup/CFO, Jim F. Williams/VP - Human Resources, Gordon Boyd/Pres., Bill Haushalter/VP, GM - Electrical, Mechanical Division, Kenneth Bush/VP, GM - Interior Systems Division, Patrick Miller/VP, GM - Engineered Vehicle Structures Division, Kevin Frailey/Exec. VP - Business Development, Jerry Armstrong/Pres. - Global Truck

Directors: Mervin Dunn/Dir., CEO, Pres., Scott D. Rued/Chmn., Scott C. Arves/Dir., David R. Bovee/Dir., Robert C. Griffin/Dir., S. A. Johnson/Dir., Richard A. Snell/Dir.

Owners: Insiders/3.40%, Mervin Dunn/1.30%, Munder Capital Management/5.20%, Robert C. Griffin, Gerald L. Armstrong, Chad M. Utrup, James F. Williams, Scott C. Arves, S.A. Johnson, The Guardian Life Insurance Company of America/11.90%, Lord Abbett& Co. LLC/8.20%, Artisan Partners Limited Partnership/6.80%, Richard A. Snell, Gordon W. Boyd, David R. Bovee *(16 Owners included in Index)*

Financial Data: *Fiscal Year End:*12/31 *Latest Annual Data:* 12/31/2006

Year	Sales	Net Income
2006	NA	NA
2005	NA	NA
2004	NA	NA

Curr. Assets:	$265,106,000	**Curr. Liab.:**	$129,738,000	**P/E Ratio:**	8.73
Plant, Equip.:	$90,388,000	**Total Liab.:**	$325,917,000	**Indic. Yr. Divd.:**	NA
Total Assets:	$590,822,000	**Net Worth:**	$264,905,000	**Debt/ Equity:**	0.5906

Commodore Applied Technologies Inc

507 Knight St., Ste. B, Richland, WA, 99352; ***PH:*** 1-509-943-2565; ***Fax:*** 1-509-913-2910; ***http://*** www.commodore.com

General - Incorporation....DE
Employees....29
Auditor....Decoria, Maichel & Teague, P.s.
Stk Agt....Registrar & Transfer Co
Counsel....Greenberg Traurig Askew Et Al
DUNS No....95-898-8883

Stock- Price on:12/24/2007....$0.16
Stock Exchange....OTC
Ticker Symbol....CXIA
Outstanding Shares....8,120,000
E.P.S....-$0.317
Shareholders....NA

Business: The group's principal activities are to provide engineering, technical and environmental remediation solutions to public and private sectors. The group has two operating segments. Commodore advanced sciences provides remediating contamination in soils, liquids and other materials and disposing of or reusing certain waste by-products by utilizing solvated electron technology set to government agencies. Solutions provide services related to, environmental management for on-site and off-site identification, investigation remediation and management of hazardous, mixed and radioactive waste. The group markets its services and technologies to governmental and industrial customers throughout the United States.

Primary SIC and add'l.: 4953 7389 9511 7629 8711

CIK No: 0001013556

Subsidiaries: A.S. Environmental, Inc, Advanced Sciences Integradas S.A, Advanced Sciences Integrated Mexico, S.A. de C.V, Commodore Advanced Sciences, Inc, Commodore Government Environmental Technologies, Inc, Commodore Solution Technologies, Inc., Environmental Alternatives, Inc

Officers: Shelby T. Brewer/Chmn., CEO, Pres., James M. Deangelis/Dir., Sr. VP, Dir. - Investor Relations, Mack O. Jones/Dir., COO, Pres., Ted R. Sharp/CFO

Directors: Shelby T. Brewer/Chmn., CEO, Pres., James M. Deangelis/Dir., Sr. VP, Dir. - Investor Relations, Mack O. Jones/Dir., COO, Pres., William A. Wilson/Dir., Paul E. Hannesson/Dir., Frank E. Coffman/Dir., Michael P. Kalleres/Dir., Bentley J. Blum/Dir.

Owners: Insiders/47.54%, Frank E. Coffman, Mack O. Jones/6.88%, Shelby T. Brewer/27.28%, James M. DeAngelis/12.20%, Paul E. Hannesson/3.84%, William A. Wilson, Michael P. Kalleres, Bentley J. Blum/16.91%

Financial Data: *Fiscal Year End:*12/31 *Latest Annual Data:* 12/31/2006

Year	Sales	Net Income
2006	$7,254,000	-$1,849,000
2005	$10,275,000	-$2,714,000
2004	$738,000	-$2,404,000

Curr. Assets:	$1,067,000	**Curr. Liab.:**	$6,831,000		
Plant, Equip.:	$119,000	**Total Liab.:**	$13,340,000	**Indic. Yr. Divd.:**	NA
Total Assets:	$1,243,000	**Net Worth:**	-$12,097,000	**Debt/ Equity:**	NA

Commonwealth Bank of Australia

48 Martin Pl, Sydney, New South Wales, 1155; ; ***http://*** www.commbank.com.au

General - Incorporation....Australia
Employees....142
Auditor....Ernst & Young LLP
Stk Agt....Deutsche Bank Luxembourg S.A.
Counsel....NA
DUNS No....75-050-6131

Stock- Price on:12/24/2007....NA
Stock Exchange....NA
Ticker Symbol....NA
Outstanding Shares....NA
E.P.S....NA
Shareholders....NA

Business: The group's principle activities are the provisions of integrated financial services including retail, business and institutional banking, superannuation, life insurance, general insurance, funds management, broking services and finance company.

Primary SIC and add'l.: 6021 6311 6331 6371 6722 6733

CIK No: 0000008565

Subsidiaries: ASB Capital Limited, Colonial Group, Commonwealth Development Bank Limited, Preferred Capital Limited

Officers: Ralph Norris/MD, CEO, John O'Sullivan/General Counsel, Ross McEwan/Group Executive, Retail Banking Services, Grahame Petersen/Group Executive, Wealth Management, Garry MacKrell/Group Executive, International Financial Services, Michael Harte/Group Executive, Technology Services, Barbara Chapman/Group Executive, People, Group Services, David Craig/Group Executive, Financial, Risk Management, Stuart Grimshaw/Group Executive, Premium Business Services

Directors: John M. Schubert/Chmn., Reg J. Clairs/70/Dir.

Commonwealth Bankshares Inc

403 Boush St., Norfolk, VA, 23510; ***PH:*** 1-757-446-6900; ***Fax:*** 1-757-446-6929; ***http://*** www.bankofthecommonwealth.com

General - Incorporation....VA
Employees....184
Auditor....PKF Witt Mares, PLC
Stk Agt....Bank of the Commonwealth
Counsel....Kaufman & Canoles
DUNS No....80-479-9716

Stock- Price on:12/24/2007....$20.97
Stock Exchange....NDQ
Ticker Symbol....CWBS
Outstanding Shares....6,880,000
E.P.S....$1.71
Shareholders....NA

Business: The group's principal activity is to provide commercial banking and other financial services to individuals and corporate customers. The group is a bank holding company, which owns all of the stock of its sole subsidiary, bank of commonwealth. The group provides commercial, residential and consumer loans and a variety of deposit products to its customers in Virginia. The group operates three branches in norfolk, four branches in Virginia beach, one branch in chesapeake and one branch in portsmouth. Other services include home banking, trust, travelers' checks, safe deposit, lock box, depositor transfer, customer note payment, collections, notary public, escrow, drive-in facility and other customary banking services. On 16-Jul-2004, the group acquired community home mortgage of Virginia inc.

Primary SIC and add'l.: 6712 6022

CIK No: 0000835012

Subsidiaries: Bank of the Commonwealth, BOC Insurance Agencies of Hampton Roads, Inc, BOC Title of Hampton Roads, Inc., T/A Executive Title Center, Commonwealth Bankshares Capital Trust I, Community Home Mortgage of Virginia, Inc.

Officers: E. J. Woodard/65/Chmn., CEO, Pres./$799,761.00, Cynthia A. Sabol/Contact - Cash Sweep Representative/$320,076.00, Simon Hounslow/Contact - Business, Commercial Loan Officer/$261,067.00, Stephen G. Fields/Contact - Business, Commercial Loan Officer/$238,324.00, Richard Early/Senior Vice President, Senior Trust Officer, Alexis Peay/Assistant Vice President,

Trust Officer, Cheryl Parris/Assistant Vice President, Branch Manager, Anthony O'Connor/Branch Manager - Ocean View, David Todd/Vice President, Branch Manager - Western Branch, Avila Wimbish/Assistant Vice President, Branch Manager - London Boulevard, Deborah Hundley/Assistant Vice President, Branch Manager - Taylor Road, Sharon Snead/Assistant Vice President, Branch Manager - Greenbrier, Kevin Hirschfeld/Loan Officer - VIRGINIA BEACH, Marth Root/Loan Officer - VIRGINIA BEACH, Daryl Davies/Loan Officer - EASTERN NORTH CAROLINA *(84 Officers included in Index)*

Directors: E. J. Woodard/65/Chmn., CEO, Pres., Raju V. Uppalapati/Dir., Kenneth J. Young/57/Dir., Pres., Morton Goldmeier/84/Dir., Herbert L. Perlin/67/Dir., Pres., Thomas W. Moss/79/Dir., City Treasurer, William D. Payne/72/Dir., Richard J. Tavss/68/Dir., Sr. Counsel, Carlton E. Bowyer/74/Dir., Laurence C. Fentriss/53/Dir.

Financial Data: **Fiscal Year End:**12/31 **Latest Annual Data:** 12/31/2006

Year	Sales	Net Income
2006	$57,975,000	$10,092,000
2005	$38,181,000	$6,634,000
2004	$25,024,000	$3,101,000

Curr. Assets:	$18,399,000	**Curr. Liab.:**	$577,464,000	**P/E Ratio:**	12.12
Plant, Equip.:	$12,940,000	**Total Liab.:**	$611,980,000	**Indic. Yr. Divd.:**	$0.320
Total Assets:	$715,205,000	**Net Worth:**	$103,225,000	**Debt/ Equity:**	0.2446

Commonwealth Biotechnologies Inc

601 Biotech Dr., Richmond, VA, 23235; **PH:** 1-804-648-3820; **Fax:** 1-804-648-2641; **http://** www.cbi-biotech.com; **Email:** info@cbi-biotech.com

General - Incorporation	VA	**Stock**- Price on:12/24/2007	$3.54
Employees	45	Stock Exchange	NDQ
Auditor	BDO Seidman LLP	Ticker Symbol	CBTE
Stk Agt	American Securities T & T Inc.	Outstanding Shares	5,490,000
Counsel	Leclair Ryan	E.P.S.	-$0.51
DUNS No.	80-606-0257	Shareholders	NA

Business: The group's principal activity is to provide research and development support services on a contract basis to the biotechnology industry. The group's customers consist of private companies, academic institutions and government agencies, which uses biological processes to develop products for health care, agricultural and other purposes. The group provides macromolecular synthetic and analytical services to researches in the biotechnology industry. The group serves two types of customers namely short-term projects, where discrete set of analysis is done and long term projects in which the group enters into contract with the client for research and development.the group is accredited under the guidelines of the national forensic science technology center, (nfstc), to perform dna identity testing for submission of data into the combined dna index system (codis).

Primary SIC and add'l.: 8731

CIK No: 0001042418

Officers: Paul DSylva/Dir., CEO, Nick Hagan/CEO - Mimotopes, Richard J. Freer/Chmn., COO/$363,556.00, Julie R. Secor Mcvoy/Sr. Scientist, Joseph A. Buettner/Sr. Scientist, Tammie Crabtree/Mgr. - Laboratory, Judy Ellett/Mgr. - QA, QC, Russell L. Gross/Mgr. - DNA Reference Lab, Sarah Helber/Group Leader - Clinical Lab, Related Studies, Charles M. Kelly/Dir. - Fairfax Identity Laboratories, Doug Horejsh/Sr. Scientist, Thomas R. Reynolds/Exec. VP - Science, Technology, Sec./$285,234.00, Shelley Johnson/Sr. Scientist, Mtdna Technical Leader, Forensic Science Lab Mgr., James H. Brennan/VP - Financial Operations, Robert B. Harris/Dir., Pres./$297,214.00 *(19 Officers included in Index)*

Directors: Paul DSylva/Dir., CEO, Richard J. Freer/Chmn., COO, Robert B. Harris/Dir., Pres., Daniel O. Hayden/Dir., James Causey/Dir., Gerald P. Krueger/Dir., Donald A. McAfee/Dir., Samuel P. Sears/Dir.

Owners: Insiders/49.90%, Thomas R. Reynolds/2.30%, Daniel O. Hayden, Gerald P. Krueger, Richard J. Freer/5.80%, Donald A. McAfee, PharmAust Chemistry Ltd/39.20%, Paul DSylva/39.20%, James D. Causey, Robert B. Harris/3.50%, Samuel P. Sears/1.80%

Financial Data: **Fiscal Year End:**12/31 **Latest Annual Data:** 12/31/2006

Year	Sales	Net Income
2006	$6,532,000	-$1,153,000
2005	$7,803,000	$79,000
2004	$5,749,000	-$368,000

Curr. Assets:	$3,297,000	**Curr. Liab.:**	$587,000		
Plant, Equip.:	$5,612,000	**Total Liab.:**	$4,373,000	**Indic. Yr. Divd.:**	NA
Total Assets:	$9,502,000	**Net Worth:**	$5,129,000	**Debt/ Equity:**	0.3893

Commonwealth Business Bank

5055 Wilshire Blvd, Los Angeles, CA, 90036; **PH:** 1-323-988-3000; **http://** www.thecommonwealthbusinessbank.com

General - Incorporation		**Stock**- Price on:12/24/2007	$18.5
Employees	NA	Stock Exchange	OTC
Auditor	NA	Ticker Symbol	CWBB
Stk Agt	U.S. Stock Transfer Corp	Outstanding Shares	NA
Counsel	NA	E.P.S.	NA
DUNS No.	NA	Shareholders	NA

Business: The groups principal activity is to provide banking and financial services. Services of the group include business deposit service, personal deposits, cash management, lending, international banking, investments, loans, Retirement solution and private banking. The group operates from the United States.

Primary SIC and add'l.: 6021

CIK No:

Officers: Wun Hwa Choi/Dir., CEO, Pres., Steve Park/Exec. VP, Chief Credit Officer, Kaye Kim/CFO, Investor Relations Officer, Kate Yi/Investor Relations Contact, Cindy Kim/Executive Assist., Pres. Office, Anna Lee/Chief Marketing Officer - Banking Solution Team, Ann Choi/Relationship Mgr. - Banking Solution Team, Rachel Lee/Relationship Mgr. - Banking Solution Team, Hae Sun Kim/Operations Officer - On, Line, Telephone Banking, Joanna Lee/Relationship Mgr. - Banking Solution Team, Chris Chong/Operations Executive, On, Line, Telephone Banking, Stacy Yi/Relationship Mgr. - Banking Solution Team, Sylvester Kim/SBA Mgr. - SBA Loan Team, Young Lee/Note Mgr. - Loan Administration, Min Kang/Operations Administrator - Operations

Directors: Wun Hwa Choi/Dir., CEO, Pres., Timothy G. Haight/Chmn., Wonsook A. Chong/Dir., Jaehee C. Kim/Dir., Peter E. Lowe/Dir., David A. McCoy/Dir., Soon Han Pak/Dir., Stuart A. Whang/Dir., Choong Y. Yea/Dir.

Commonwealth Edison Co

37th Floor, 10 South Dearborn St., Chicago, IL, 60680; **PH:** 1-312-394-4321; **Fax:** 1-312-394-2231; **http://** www.exeloncorp.com

General - Incorporation	IL	**Stock**- Price on:12/24/2007	$73.82
Employees	17,200	Stock Exchange	NYSE
Auditor	PricewaterhouseCoopers LLP	Ticker Symbol	NA
Stk Agt	Computershare Investor Services LLC	Outstanding Shares	672,650,000
Counsel	NA	E.P.S.	$2.86
DUNS No.	00-692-9509	Shareholders	NA

Business: The group's principle activities include producing, purchasing, transmiting, distributing and selling electricity to residential, commercial, industrial and wholesale customers. The group operates from United States.

Primary SIC and add'l.: 4911

CIK No: 0000022606

Subsidiaries: ComEd Financing II, ComEd Financing III, ComEd Funding, LLC, ComEd Transitional Funding Trust, Commonwealth Edison Company of Indiana, Inc., Edison Development Canada Inc., Edison Finance Partnership

Officers: Frank Clark/62/Chmn., CEO, Jon D. Veurink/43/VP, Controller, Barry J. Mitchell/60/Pres., Anne R. Pramaggiore/49/Sr. VP - Regulatory, External Affairs, Robert K. McDonald/52/CFO, Chief Risk Officer, Sr. VP, Treasurer, Matthew R. Galvanoni/35/VP, Controller, John T. Costello/59/COO, Exec. VP, John T. Hooker/59/Sr. VP - Legislative, Governmental Affairs, Mitchell J. Barry/60/Pres.

Directors: Frank Clark/62/Chmn., CEO, Sue L. Gin/66/Dir., Edgar D. Jannotta/76/Dir., John W. Rogers/50/Dir., Richard L. Thomas/77/Dir., Edward J. Mooney/66/Dir., James W. Compton/70/Dir.

Financial Data: **Fiscal Year End:**12/31 **Latest Annual Data:** 12/31/2006

Year	Sales	Net Income
2006	$15,655,000,000	$1,592,000,000
2005	$15,357,000,000	$923,000,000
2004	$14,515,000,000	$1,864,000,000

Curr. Assets:	$4,992,000,000	**Curr. Liab.:**	$5,795,000,000	**P/E Ratio:**	26.55
Plant, Equip.:	$22,775,000,000	**Total Liab.:**	$34,259,000,000	**Indic. Yr. Divd.:**	$1.760
Total Assets:	$44,319,000,000	**Net Worth:**	$9,973,000,000	**Debt/ Equity:**	1.1522

CommScope Inc

1100 CommScope Pl. SE, Hickory, NC, 28602; **PH:** 1-828-324-2200; **Fax:** 1-828-328-3400; **http://** www.commscope.com

General - Incorporation	DE	**Stock**- Price on:12/24/2007	$54.95
Employees	4,550	Stock Exchange	NYSE
Auditor	Deloitte & Touche LLP	Ticker Symbol	CTV
Stk Agt	Mellon Investor Services LLC	Outstanding Shares	61,230,000
Counsel	NA	E.P.S.	NA
DUNS No.	07-062-6247	Shareholders	NA

Business: The groups principle activity is to provide cable and connectivity solutions for communications networks. The groups products include electronic, coaxial and fiber optic cable products for data networking, Internet access, wireless communication, telephony and other broadband applications. The group operates from United States.

Primary SIC and add'l.: 3357

CIK No: 0001035884

Subsidiaries: Cable Transport,Inc., CommScope International Holdings, LLC, CommScope Nevada, LLC, CommScope Optical Technologies,Inc., CommScope Solutions Holdings,Inc., CommScope Solutions Properties, LLC, CommScope Solutions,Inc., CommScope,Inc. (Registrant), CommScope,Inc. of North Carolina, Connectivity Solutions Manufacturing,Inc.

Officers: Frank M. Drendel/Chmn., CEO/$2,421,500.00, William R. Gooden/Sr. VP, Controller, Marvin S. Edwards/Exec. VP - Business Development, Jearld L. Leonhardt/CFO, Exec. VP/$920,030.00, George N. Hutton/Dir. - Private Investor, Frank B. Wyatt/Sr. VP, General Counsel, Sec., Randall W. Crenshaw/Exec. VP, GM - Enterprise/$834,343.00, Brian D. Garrett/COO, Pres./$1,256,196.00, Edward A. Hally/Exec.VP, GM - Carrier/$704,009.00, Philip M. Armstrong/VP - Investor Relations, Corporate Communications, James R. Hughes/Exec. VP - Broadband Sales, Marketing, Christopher A. Story/Exec. VP - Broadband Operations, Betsy H. Lambert/Contact - Media Relations, Beverly S. Lampe/Mgr. - Corporate Communications Commscope

Directors: Frank M. Drendel/Chmn., CEO, Katsuhiko Okubo/Dir., Richard C. Smith/Dir., James N. Whitson/Dir., George N. Hutton/Dir. - Private Investor, Boyd L. George/Dir., June E. Travis/Dir.

Curr. Assets:	$807,800,000	**Curr. Liab.:**	$183,243,000		
Plant, Equip.:	$242,012,000	**Total Liab.:**	$563,369,000	**Indic. Yr. Divd.:**	NA
Total Assets:	$1,302,473,000	**Net Worth:**	$739,104,000	**Debt/ Equity:**	0.3168

Commtouch Software Ltd

1300 Crittenden Ln., Ste. 103, Mountain View, CA, 94043; **PH:** 1-650-864-2000; **Fax:** 1-650-864-2002; **http://** www.commtouch.com; **Email:** media@commtouch.com

General - Incorporation	Israel	**Stock**- Price on:12/24/2007	$1.86
Employees	35	Stock Exchange	NDQ
Auditor	Kost Forer Gabbay & Kasierer	Ticker Symbol	CTCH
Stk Agt	Wells Fargo Bank, N.A.	Outstanding Shares	73,000,000
Counsel	Wilson Sonsini Goodrich & Rosati	E.P.S.	$0.01
DUNS No.	60-025-2340	Shareholders	NA

Business: The groups principle activity is to provides Web-based email and messaging solutions, and stand-alone email client software products for both mainframe and personal computers. The group operates from United States.

Primary SIC and add'l.: 7372 4822

CIK No: 0001084577

Subsidiaries: Commtouch Inc, Imatrix Corporation

Officers: Gideon Mantel/Co - Founder, CEO, Yossi Maslaton/VP - Network Operations, Customer Services, Ronni Zehavi/VP - International Business Development, Amir Lev/Co - Founder, CTO, Pres., Udi Trugman/VP - Research, Development, Gary Davis/General Counsel, Corp. Sec., Avner Amram/Exec. VP, Haggai Carmon/VP - Products, Ron Ela/CFO, Jay Goldin/VP - Business Development - North America, Rebecca Steinberg Herson/VP - Marketing

Directors: Gideon Mantel/Co - Founder, CEO, Gary Davis/General Counsel, Corp. Sec., Lloyd E. Shefsky/Dir., Amir Lev/Co - Founder, CTO, Pres., Nahum Sharfman/Dir., Orna Berry/Dir., Aviv Raiz/Dir., Ofer Segev/Dir.

Owners: Insiders/27.90%, Aviv Raiz/18.40%, Gideon Mantel/3.80%, Lloyd E. Shefsky/1.30%, Nahum Sharfman/3.00%, Amir Lev/2.30%

Financial Data: Fiscal Year End:12/31   Latest Annual Data: 12/31/2005

Year	Sales	Net Income
2005	$3,925,000	-$2,690,000
2004	$1,523,000	-$7,193,000
2003	$329,000	-$6,834,000

Curr. Assets:	$10,770,000	Curr. Liab.:	$3,258,000		
Plant, Equip.:	$609,000	Total Liab.:	$4,506,000	Indic. Yr. Divd.:	NA
Total Assets:	$11,999,000	Net Worth:	$7,493,000	Debt/ Equity:	NA

Communicate.com Inc

200 1st Ave. W, Ste. 400, Seattle, WA, 98119; *PH:* 1-604-697-0136; *Fax:* 1-866-898-4354; *http://* www.cmnn.com; *Email:* information@communicate.com

General - Incorporation	NV	Stock- Price on:12/24/2007	$1.6
Employees	NA	Stock Exchange	OTC
Auditor	Dale Matheson Carr-Hilton LaBonte LLP	Ticker Symbol	CMNN
Stk Agt.	Computershare Trust Co	Outstanding Shares	NA
Counsel	NA	E.P.S	NA
DUNS No.	NA	Shareholders	NA

Business: The groups principle activity is to own and operates hundreds of websites. The group operates through three segments namely domain sales, leasing and advertising, ecommerce products and ecommerce services. The group operates from the United States. The group's quarterly revenue for September 2007 was 1.77 millions of USD.

Primary SIC and add'l.: 7375 8741 8748 7379 4899 8999 4724 7389

CIK No: 0001108630

Subsidiaries: Domain Holdings Inc.

Officers: David M. Jeffs/38/Dir., CEO, Pres., Geoffrey C. Hampson/Chmn., CEO, Jonathan Ehrlich/COO, Pres., Cameron J. Pan/CFO

Directors: David M. Jeffs/38/Dir., CEO, Pres., Geoffrey C. Hampson/Chmn., CEO

Owners: Jonathan Ehrlich/1.04%, Insiders/14.27%, Cameron J. Pan/3.50%, Mark Benham, James P. Taylor, Susan Jeffs/6.99%, Klaus Schymke/4.45%, Geoffrey C. Hampson/9.58%

Financial Data: Fiscal Year End:12/31   Latest Annual Data: 12/31/2006

Year	Sales	Net Income
2006	$8,434,000	$414,000
2005	$5,768,000	$347,000
2004	$3,515,000	$498,000

Curr. Assets:	$2,388,000	Curr. Liab.:	$992,000		
Plant, Equip.:	$45,000	Total Liab.:	$992,000	Indic. Yr. Divd.:	NA
Total Assets:	$4,099,000	Net Worth:	$3,107,000	Debt/ Equity:	NA

Communication Intelligence Corp

275 Shoreline Dr., Ste. 500, Redwood Shores, CA, 94065; *PH:* 1-650-802-7888; *Fax:* 1-650-802-7777; *http://* www.cic.com; *Email:* chinasales@cic.com

General - Incorporation	DE	Stock- Price on:12/24/2007	$0.16
Employees	21	Stock Exchange	OTC
Auditor	GHP Horwath, P.C	Ticker Symbol	CICI
Stk Agt.	American Stock Transfer & Trust Co.	Outstanding Shares	107,560,000
Counsel	NA	E.P.S	-$0.031
DUNS No.	02-289-6856	Shareholders	NA

Business: The group's principle activities are to develop and market biometric signature verification and natural input software solutions and electronic signature software. The group operates in two segments: handwriting recognition software and systems integration. The handwriting recognition segment comprised of three revenue categories: original equipment manufacturers, enterprise and online sales. Systems integration represents the sale and installation of third party computer equipment and systems that use the company's software products. The products of the group include multi-lingual handwriting recognition systems and hand-writer recognition system, dynamic signature verification system and capture tools. The group's quarterly revenue for September 2007 was 0.46 millions of USD.

Primary SIC and add'l.: 7372 3577

CIK No: 0000727634

Subsidiaries: PenOp Inc

Officers: Guido Digregorio/Chmn., CEO, Pres./$294,072.00, Michael Ruden/VP - Financial Services Business Development, Russel L. Davis/CTO/$166,179.00, Chantal N. Eshghipour/VP - Investor Relations, Frank Dane/Chief Legal, Financial Officer/$160,000.00, Kathy Down-Logan/VP - Marketing, Louis P. Panetta/Dir., Management Consultant, David Welch/Dir., Independent Financial Consultant, Joe Depaola/VP - Worldwide Sales, Business Development, Michael Betts/Dir. - Financial Services Executive

Directors: Guido Digregorio/Chmn., CEO, Pres., Louis P. Panetta/Dir., Management Consultant, C. B. Sung/Dir., David Welch/Dir., Independent Financial Consultant

Owners: Francis V. Dane, Michael W. Engmann/7.46%, Insiders/4.78%, Guido DiGregorio/1.93%, David E. Welch, C. B. Sung/1.67%, Russel L. Davis, Louis P. Panetta

Financial Data: Fiscal Year End:12/31   Latest Annual Data: 12/31/2006

Year	Sales	Net Income
2006	$2,342,000	-$3,286,000
2005	$3,121,000	-$4,031,000
2004	$7,284,000	$1,620,000

Curr. Assets:	$1,319,000	Curr. Liab.:	$2,135,000		
Plant, Equip.:	$140,000	Total Liab.:	$2,469,000	Indic. Yr. Divd.:	NA
Total Assets:	$6,126,000	Net Worth:	$3,584,000	Debt/ Equity:	0.2309

Communications Systems Inc

213 S Main St., Hector, MN, 55342; *PH:* 1-320-848-6231; *Fax:* 1-320-848-2702; *http://* www.commsystems.com

General - Incorporation	MN	Stock- Price on:12/24/2007	$10.27
Employees	505	Stock Exchange	AMEX
Auditor	Deloitte & Touche LLP	Ticker Symbol	JCS
Stk Agt.	Wells Fargo Shareowner Services	Outstanding Shares	8,860,000
Counsel	NA	E.P.S	$0.78
DUNS No.	05-273-3714	Shareholders	NA

Business: The group's principal activities are to manufacture and sell modular connecting and wiring devices for voice and data communications. It operates through four segments: suttle, austin taylor, transition networks and jdl technologies inc. Suttle manufactures U.S. Standard modular connecting and wiring devices for voice and data communications. Austin taylor manufactures british standard line jacks, patch panels, wiring harness assemblies, metal boxes, distribution cabinets and central office frames. Transition networks designs and markets data transmission and computer network products and other operations. Jdl technologies inc provides telecommunications network design, specification and training services to educational institutions. It operates in the us, the UK and Costa Rica. On 24-Mar-2004, it acquired image systems corporation.

Primary SIC and add'l.: 3661 3679 4899 3678

CIK No: 0000022701

Subsidiaries: Austin Taylor Communications, Ltd., Automatic Tool & Connector Company, Inc., Image Systems Corporation, JDL Technologies, Inc., LANart Corporation, MiLAN Technology Corporation, Suttle Apparatus Corporation, Suttle Caribe, Inc., Suttle Costa Rica, S.A., Tel Products, Inc., Transition Networks, Inc.

Officers: Curtis A. Sampson/Chmn., CEO/$434,187.00, Karen J. Nesburg Bleick/Dir. - Human Resources, Jeffrey K. Berg/COO, Pres./$461,915.00, Michael J. Skucius/COO - JDL Technologies, Inc, Paul N. Hanson/CFO, VP - Finance, Treasurer, Sec./$165,474.00, Daniel G. Easter/Pres., GM - Transition Networks, Inc, David T. McGraw/Pres., GM - Suttle, Thomas J. Lapping/Pres. - JDL Technologies, Inc, Michael Griffith/Co - MD, Dir. - Finance, Paul Gaskell/Co - MD, Sales Dir. - Austin Taylor, Charles A. Braun/Controller, Janis Weikle/Contact

Directors: Curtis A. Sampson/Chmn., CEO, Edwin C. Freeman/Dir., Randall D. Sampson/Dir., Paul J. Anderson/Dir., Luella Gross Goldberg/Dir., Gerald D. Pint/Dir., Wayne E. Sampson/Dir.

Owners: Daniel G. Easter, Putnam, LLC/5.62%, Curtis A. Sampson/18.19%, Paul N. Hanson/6.32%, Insiders/26.25%, Gabelli Asset Management Inc./6.17%, John C. Ortman/6.13%, FMR Corp./7.78%, Jeffrey K. Berg, David T. McGraw, Wayne E. Sampson/5.55%

Financial Data: Fiscal Year End:12/31   Latest Annual Data: 12/31/2006

Year	Sales	Net Income
2006	$115,440,000	$4,495,000
2005	$109,709,000	$4,470,000
2004	$110,779,000	$4,763,000

Curr. Assets:	$78,410,000	Curr. Liab.:	$9,454,000	P/E Ratio:	13.51
Plant, Equip.:	$8,580,000	Total Liab.:	$10,178,000	Indic. Yr. Divd.:	$0.480
Total Assets:	$92,723,000	Net Worth:	$82,545,000	Debt/ Equity:	NA

Community 1st Bank CA

2250 Douglas Blvd., Ste. 100, Roseville, CA, 95661; *PH:* 1-916-724-2424; *http://* community1bank.com

General - Incorporation		Stock- Price on:12/24/2007	$11.5
Employees	NA	Stock Exchange	OTC
Auditor	NA	Ticker Symbol	CFBN
Stk Agt.	NA	Outstanding Shares	NA
Counsel	NA	E.P.S	NA
DUNS No.	NA	Shareholders	NA

Business: The groups principal activity is to provide community-banking services. The services of the group include originating loans, deposit, lending services, financial tools and online banking. The group operates from California in the United States.

Primary SIC and add'l.: 6029

CIK No:

Financial Data: Fiscal Year End:NA   Latest Annual Data: 12/31/2006

Year	Sales	Net Income
2006	$416,095,000	-$18,055,000
2005	$296,838,000	-$9,931,000
2004	$268,143,000	$5,178,000

Community Bancorp

400 S 4th St., Ste. 215, Las Vegas, NV, 89101; *PH:* 1-702-878-0700; *Fax:* 1-702-947-3502; *http://* www.communitybanknv.com

General - Incorporation	NV	Stock- Price on:12/24/2007	$28.98
Employees	235	Stock Exchange	NDQ
Auditor	McGladrey & Pullen LLP	Ticker Symbol	CBON
Stk Agt.	Computershare Trust Co	Outstanding Shares	10,420,000
Counsel	NA	E.P.S	$1.99
DUNS No.	01-977-1732	Shareholders	NA

Business: The group's principal activity is to provide retail banking services to individuals and businesses in northeastern Vermont. It is a holding company of community national bank and liberty savings bank. Community national bank provides a complete range of retail banking services to the residents and businesses in northeastern Vermont and liberty savings bank is inactive. The group's services include checking, savings and time deposit accounts, mortgage, consumer and commercial loans, safe deposit and night deposit services, automatic teller machine (ATM) facilities, credit card services, 24 hour telephone banking and a full line of personal fiduciary services. Its primary lending products are commercial, real estate, and consumer loans. The group operates through eight offices of which five are located in orleans county and one each in essex county, caledonia and Washington county.

Primary SIC and add'l.: 6022 6712

CIK No: 0001304366

Subsidiaries: Bank of Nevada, Community Bancorp (NV) Statutory Trust I, Community Bancorp (NV) Statutory Trust II, Connecticut statutory trust, Nevada state-chartered bank

Officers: Edward M. Jamison/Chmn., CEO, Cathy Robinson/Exec. VP, CFO - Community Bank, Nv, Don F. Bigger/Exec. VP, Credit Administrator, Bruce Ford/COO, Exec. VP, Tom McGrath/Exec. VP, Chief Risk Mgr., Joyce G. Smith/Exec. VP, Chief Retail Officer, Patrick Hartman/Exec. VP, CFO - Community Bancorp

Directors: Edward M. Jamison/Chmn., CEO, Lawrence K. Scott/Dir., Charles R. Norton/Dir., Gary W. Stewart/Dir., Jack Woodcock/Dir., Jay Bingham/Dir., Russell C. Taylor/Dir., Dan H. Stewart/Dir.

Owners: Dan H. Stewart, Barry L. Hulin, Gary W. Stewart, Jack M. Woodcock, Edward M. Jamison/3.00%, Cathy Robinson, Jacob D. Bingham, Insiders/8.40%, Bruce Ford, Lawrence K. Scott, Russell C. Taylor/2.90%

Financial Data: Fiscal Year End:12/31 Latest Annual Data: 12/31/2006

Year	Sales	Net Income
2006	$89,114,000	$15,639,000
2005	$48,612,000	$10,065,000
2004	$31,527,000	$5,421,000

Curr. Assets:	$53,784,000	Curr. Liab.:	$1,208,123,000	P/E Ratio:	14.56
Plant, Equip.:	$24,133,000	Total Liab.:	$1,351,508,000	Indic. Yr. Divd.:	NA
Total Assets:	$1,570,379,000	Net Worth:	$218,871,000	Debt/ Equity:	0.8152

Community Bank of Bergen County NJ

210 Rochelle Ave., Rochelle Park, NJ, 07662; *PH:* 1-201-843-2300; *http://* www.skyonemedical.com

General		Stock	
Incorporation		Price on:12/24/2007	$25
Employees	NA	Stock Exchange	OTC
Auditor	NA	Ticker Symbol	CMTB
Stk Agt	Registrar & Transfer Co	Outstanding Shares	NA
Counsel	NA	E.P.S	NA
DUNS No.	NA	Shareholders	NA

Business: The groups principle activity is to provide recruiting services. The groups service area includes the research and development, engineering, marketing, sales, information technology and manufacturing industries. The group operates from United States.

Primary SIC and add'l.: 6029

CIK No:

Officers: Ronald J. Meier/Chmn., CEO, Marianne Byrne/Dir., Pres., Peter A. Michelotti/Dir., Sr. VP - Assist. Cashier, Trust Officer, Maryann Chisenhall/VP - Bookkeeping, Cynthia Cisco/VP, Credit Administration Officer - Assist. Cashier, Barbara Maier/VP - Cashier, Compliance Officer, Jacqueline Waller-Sanchez/VP - Assist. Cashier, Raymond C. Zachmann/VP - Accounting, Carole Dansen/VP - Assist. Cashier, BSA Officer, Assist. Compliance Officer, Marge Buys/Assist. VP, Diona Canal/Assist. VP, Bank Security Officer, Marilyn Hogan/Assist. VP, Cecelia McMullen-James/Assist. VP, Assist. Trust Officer, Laura Lo Piccolo/Assist. VP - Assist. Cashier, Jacklyn Krall/Assist. VP - Human Resources *(18 Officers included in Index)*

Directors: Ronald J. Meier/Chmn., CEO, Carlton E. Meier/Dir., Marianne Byrne/Dir., Pres., Dominick Langeri/Dir., Jean D. Michelotti/Dir., Peter A. Michelotti/Dir., Sr. VP - Assist. Cashier, Trust Officer, Fred C. Semken/Dir.

Community Bank of Santa Maria

1421 S Broadway, Santa Maria, CA, 93454; *PH:* 1-805-922-2900; *http://* www.yourcbsm.com; *Email:* info@yourcbsm.com

General		Stock	
Incorporation		Price on:12/24/2007	$16.5
Employees	NA	Stock Exchange	OTC
Auditor	NA	Ticker Symbol	CYSM
Stk Agt	U.S. Stock Transfer Corp	Outstanding Shares	NA
Counsel	NA	E.P.S	NA
DUNS No.	NA	Shareholders	NA

Business: The group's principle activity is to provide community banking service. The group operates from United States.

Primary SIC and add'l.: 6029

CIK No:

Officers: James D. Glines/Dir., Co - Founder, CEO, Pres., Linda Small/Mortgage Officer

Directors: James D. Glines/Dir., Co - Founder, CEO, Pres., Marie Will/Co - Founder, Stephanie Ventura/Co - Founder, Robin Ventura/Co - Founder, Dean Minor/Dir., Joni Gray Wittenburg/Co - Founder, Royce R. Lewellen/Founder, Dir., Robert Torres/Co - Founder, Dir., Evelyn Teixeira/Co - Founder, Norman Teixeira/Co - Founder, Myrtle Tesene/Co - Founder, R. H. Tesene/Co - Founder, Marlene Torres/Co - Founder, Patti Van Corbach/Co - Founder, Ken Van Corbach/Co - Founder *(89 Directors included in Index)*

Community Bank of the Bay CA

1750 Broadway, Oakland, CA, 94612; *PH:* 1-510-433-5400; *Fax:* 1-510-433-5431; *http://* www.communitybankbay.com

General		Stock	
Incorporation		Price on:12/24/2007	$9
Employees	NA	Stock Exchange	OTC
Auditor	NA	Ticker Symbol	CBYAA
Stk Agt	Community Bank of the Bay	Outstanding Shares	NA
Counsel	NA	E.P.S	NA
DUNS No.	NA	Shareholders	NA

Business: The groups principal activity is to provide community-banking services. The services of the group include business checking, business loans, business investments and cash management products, checking accounts, investment products, personal loans and credit lines. The group operates from California in the United States.

Primary SIC and add'l.: 6022

CIK No:

Officers: Brian K. Garrett/CEO, Pres., Hanna Bui/AVP, Credit Services Mgr., Andy Yoo/Cash Management, Cookie Ferguson/Customer Service Mgr., Wil Hobbs/Sr. VP, Chief Credit Officer, Chaula Pandya/Sr. VP, CFO, William Smith/VP, Compliance Officer, Judy Conde/VP, Controller, Marciana Leo/Customer Service Representative, Alex De La Cruz/Loan Operations Assist., Elaine Cabilin/Customer Service Representative, Cathy Lagatuz/Customer Service Representative, Amjad Osmani/Sr. VP - Wholesale Commercial Lending, John Finan/VP, Sr. Commercial Loan Officer, Vanessa White/AVP - Client Services *(19 Officers included in Index)*

Community Bank Shares of Indiana Inc

101 W Spring St., New Albany, IN, 47150; *PH:* 1-812-944-2224; *Fax:* 1-812-949-6812; *http://* www.cbinonline.com

General		Stock	
Incorporation	IN	Price on:12/24/2007	$21.1
Employees	207	Stock Exchange	NDQ
Auditor	Crowe Chizek & Co. LLC	Ticker Symbol	CBIN
Stk Agt	Registrar & Transfer Co	Outstanding Shares	3,400,000
Counsel	Young, Lind, Endres & Kraft	E.P.S	$1.24
DUNS No.	00-700-2769	Shareholders	NA

Business: The group's principal activity is to provide a variety of banking services. It accepts deposits from the general public and uses such funds to originate loans. The group provides secured and unsecured business loans of various terms to local businesses and professional organizations, consumer loans including home equity lines of credit, automobile and recreational vehicle, construction loans and loans secured by deposit accounts and residential real estate loans. In addition, it also provides non-deposit investment products such as stocks, bonds, mutual funds and annuities. The group operates in the floyd and clark counties, Indiana, nelson county, Kentucky and surrounding areas.

Primary SIC and add'l.: 6712 6022

CIK No: 0000933590

Subsidiaries: CBSI Development Fund, Inc., CBSI Holdings, Inc., CBSI Investment Portfolio Management, LLC, CBSI Investments, Inc., Community Bank of Kentucky, Community Bank of Southern Indiana, First Community Service Corporation, Nelson Service Corporation

Officers: James D. Rickard/Dir., CEO, Pres./$397,100.00, Christopher L. Bottorff/Sr. VP/$199,300.00, Jeffrey T. Cash/Sr. VP - Audit, Risk Management, Robert J. McIlvoy/Sr. VP, Pamela P. Echols/Corp. Sec., George G. Ball/Sr. VP/$132,800.00, Paul A. Chrisco/Sr. VP, CFO/$202,100.00, Kevin J. Cecil/Sr. VP/$192,600.00, Bill Wright/48/Dir., Sr. VP, Treasurer, Carl Page/59/VP, Chief Human Resources Officer

Directors: James D. Rickard/Dir., CEO, Pres., Timothy T. Shea/Chmn., Gary L. Libs/Vice Chmn., Wayne R. Estopinal/Dir., Kerry M. Stemler/Dir., George M. Ballard/Dir., Gordon L. Huncilman/Dir., Dale Linton Orem/Dir., Steven R. Stemler/Dir., Norman Pfau/Dir., Bill Wright/48/Dir., Sr. VP, Treasurer

Owners: Gary L. Libs/2.91%, Gordon L. Huncilman, Kerry M. Stemler/1.31%, James D. Rickard, Paul A. Chrisco, Timothy T. Shea/2.92%, Kevin Cecil, George G. Ball, George M. Ballard, Insiders/11.03%, Dale L. Orem, Christopher Bottorff, Wayne R. Estopinal, Steven R. Stemler

Financial Data: Fiscal Year End:12/31 Latest Annual Data: 12/31/2006

Year	Sales	Net Income
2006	$50,827,000	$4,111,000
2005	$39,923,000	$3,749,000
2004	$31,057,000	$2,588,000

Curr. Assets:	$25,402,000	Curr. Liab.:	$729,187,000	P/E Ratio:	17.02
Plant, Equip.:	$15,025,000	Total Liab.:	$751,092,000	Indic. Yr. Divd.:	$0.700
Total Assets:	$816,633,000	Net Worth:	$65,541,000	Debt/ Equity:	0.2593

Community Bank System Inc

5790 Widewaters Pkwy., DeWitt, NY, 13214; *PH:* 1-315-445-2282; *Fax:* 1-315-445-2997; *http://* www.communitybankna.com

General		Stock	
Incorporation	DE	Price on:12/24/2007	$20.43
Employees	1,352	Stock Exchange	NYSE
Auditor	PricewaterhouseCoopers LLP	Ticker Symbol	CBU
Stk Agt	American Stock Transfer & Trust Co.	Outstanding Shares	30,090,000
Counsel	NA	E.P.S	$1.28
DUNS No.	00-697-6922	Shareholders	NA

Business: The group's principal activity is to provide commercial and retail banking services. The account services provided by the group include checking, money market, savings, time deposit and individual retirement accounts. Lending activities include residential and farm loans, business lines of credit, working capital facilities, inventory, dealer floor plans, installment, commercial, term and student loans. The other services include pension administration and consulting, asset management, corporate pension and profit sharing plans and foundations, personal trust services, estate settlement services and investment management. The group also provides mutual funds, annuities, long-term health care and selected insurance products. The group acquired first heritage bank on 06-Jan-2004.

Primary SIC and add'l.: 6712 6021

CIK No: 0000723188

Subsidiaries: Benefit Plans Administrative Services LLC, Benefit Plans Administrative Services, Inc., CBNA Preferred Funding Corp., CBNA Treasury Management Corporation, CFSI Close-Out Corp., Community Bank, N.A., Community Capital Trust I, Community Capital Trust II, Community Financial Services, Inc., Community Investment Services, Inc., Community Statutory Trust III, Elias Asset Management, Inc., First Liberty Service Corporation, First of Jermyn Realty Co., Harbridge Consulting Group LLC

Officers: Mark E. Tryniski/Dir., CEO, Pres./$616,136.00, Stephen G. Hardy/Sr. VP, Chief Credit Administrator, Nicholas S. Russell/Sr. VP, Sr. Commercial Lending Officer - Northern NY, Richard M. Heidrick/Sr. VP, Retail Banking Administrator, Timothy J. Baker/Sr. VP, Dir. - Special Projects, Bernadette R. Barber/Sr. VP, Chief Human Resources Officer, Michael J. Wilson/CTO, Sr. VP, Paul J. Ward/Sr. VP, Chief Risk Officer, David J. Clark/Sr. VP, Chief Credit Officer/$336,828.00, Scott A. Kingsley/CFO, Exec. VP/$439,171.00, Steven R. Tokach/Sr. VP, Chief Credit Administrator, Brian D. Donahue/Exec. VP, Chief Banking Officer/$449,828.00, Thomas A. McCullough/Pres. - Pennsylvania Banking/$839,497.00, Valen W. McDaniel/Sr. VP, Chief Risk Officer, Harold M. Wentworth/Sr. VP, Dir. - Sales, Marketing *(17 Officers included in Index)*

Directors: Mark E. Tryniski/Dir., CEO, Pres., Paul M. Cantwell/Chmn., Sally A. Steele/Dir., Harold S. Kaplan/Dir., Nicholas A. Dicerbo/Dir., Lee T. Hirschey/Dir., David C. Patterson/Dir., James A. Gabriel/Dir., Brian R. Ace/Dir., William M. Dempsey/Dir., Charles E. Parente/Dir.

Owners: Scott A. Kingsley/0.06%, J. David Clark/0.19%, Barclays Global Investors,/7.56%, Sally A. Steele/0.23%, Brian R. Ace/0.23%, Michael A. Patton/0.39%, Sanford A. Belden/0.26%, Dimensional Fund Advisors Inc./8.19%, David C. Patterson/0.43%, James A. Gabriel/0.56%, Thomas A. McCullough/0.03%, Mark E. Tryniski/0.14%, Brian D. Donahue/0.23%, Charles E. Parente/0.89%, Nicholas A. DiCerbo/0.98% *(19 Owners included in Index)*

Financial Data: Fiscal Year End:12/31 Latest Annual Data: 12/31/2006

Year	Sales	Net Income
2006	$283,580,000	$38,377,000
2005	$280,040,000	$50,805,000
2004	$257,240,000	$50,196,000

Curr. Assets:	$258,829,000	Curr. Liab.:	$3,230,774,000	P/E Ratio:	16.09
Plant, Equip.:	$66,199,000	Total Liab.:	$4,036,269,000	Indic. Yr. Divd.:	$0.840
Total Assets:	$4,497,797,000	Net Worth:	$461,528,000	Debt/ Equity:	1.6146

Community Bankshares Inc SC

102 Founders Ct., Orangeburg, SC, 29118; *PH:* 1-803-535-1060; *Fax:* 1-803-535-1065; *http://* www.communitybanksharesinc.com

General - Incorporation	SC	**Stock**- Price on:12/24/2007	$15.25
Employees	195	Stock Exchange	AMEX
Auditor	J. W. Hunt And Co LLP	Ticker Symbol	SCB
Stk Agt	Registrar & Transfer Co	Outstanding Shares	4,470,000
Counsel	NA	E.P.S	NA
DUNS No.	84-996-6601	Shareholders	NA

Business: The group's principal activity is to provide financial services to individuals and small businesses through its subsidiaries. Orangeburg national bank, sumter national bank and florence national bank are the group's wholly owned subsidiaries. The other services offered by the group include safe deposit boxes, night depository service, tax deposits and automated teller service. The deposits accepted by the group include business and personal checking accounts, now accounts, savings accounts, money market accounts, certificates of deposits and other deposit services. The group offers commercial, financial, agricultural, real estate and consumer loans.

Primary SIC and add'l.: 6021 6712

CIK No: 0000894508

Subsidiaries: National Bank

Officers: Samuel L. Erwin/Dir., CEO/$299,166.00, Gregory G. Burke/Chief Credit Officer/$184,515.00, Ginger S. Risher/Controller - Community Bankshares, INC, Jo H. Davies/CIO/$189,032.00, William W. Traynham/CFO, Pres./$225,812.00, Stephen M. Brakefield/Compliance, Information Security Officer, Ralph F. Faulling/COO, Cheri E. Fogle/Information Services Dir., Heyward T. Mattox/Dir., VP - Cashier, Bank, Ridgeway, Michael C. Hough/Assist. VP, Thomas W. Copeland/VP - Bank, Ridgeway, Robert D. Drake/VP - Bank, Ridgeway, Herbert C. Humphries/VP - Bank, Ridgeway, Dodd P. Buie/Deputy CFO

Directors: Samuel L. Erwin/Dir., CEO, Alvis J. Bynum/Vice Chmn., Thomas B. Edmunds/Chmn., Richard L. Havekost/Dir., E. J. Ayers/Dir., Samuel F. Reid/Dir., Reynolds Wm Williams/Dir., Martha Rose C Carson/Dir., William S. McMaster/Dir., Eleanor T. Parrish/Dir. - Bank, Ridgeway, Daniel W. Ruff/Dir. - Bank, Ridgeway, Joseph E. Sharpe/Dir. - Bank, Ridgeway, David G. Traylo/Dir. - Bank, Ridgeway, Wade A. Douroux/Dir., Heyward T. Mattox/Dir., VP - Cashier, Bank, Ridgeway *(27 Directors included in Index)*

Owners: William W. Traynham/1.46%, Charles E. Fienning, Martha Rose C. Carson/1.49%, Michael A. Wolfe/1.27%, Thomas B. Edmunds, Reynolds Williams, E. J. Ayers/1.97%, Anna O. Dantzler/2.02%, Alvis J. Bynum, Samuel L. Erwin, J. M. Guthrie/3.80%, Jo H. Davies, Insiders/19.30%, Gregory G. Burke, Charles P. Thompson *(18 Owners included in Index)*

Financial Data: **Fiscal Year End:**12/31 **Latest Annual Data:** 12/31/2006

Year	Sales	Net Income
2006	$45,360,000	$5,009,000
2005	$39,619,000	$1,011,000
2004	$32,152,000	$3,209,000

Curr. Assets:	$52,471,000	**Curr. Liab.:**	$499,705,000		
Plant, Equip.:	$10,307,000	**Total Liab.:**	$525,893,000	**Indic. Yr. Divd.:**	$0.480
Total Assets:	$578,517,000	**Net Worth:**	$52,624,000	**Debt/ Equity:**	0.4976

Community Business Bank CA

1550 Harbor Blvd., Ste. 200, West Sacramento, CA, 95691; *PH:* 1-916-830-3597; *Fax:* 1-916-376-8478; *http://* www.communitybizbank.com

General - Incorporation		**Stock**- Price on:12/24/2007	$14.7
Employees	NA	Stock Exchange	OTC
Auditor	NA	Ticker Symbol	CBBC
Stk Agt	Illinois Stock Transfer Co	Outstanding Shares	NA
Counsel	NA	E.P.S	NA
DUNS No.	NA	Shareholders	NA

Business: The group's principle activity is to provide banking service. The group's products include credit card, loans and cashmangemnt. The group operates from United States.

Primary SIC and add'l.: 6029

CIK No:

Officers: John A. Dimichele/Dir., CEO, Pres., Jeffrey Tu/Founder, Restaurant Owner, Vallejo, CA, Carl Crug/Regional Sr. VP, Jim Harris/Sr. VP, Business Development Mgr., Craig V. Walker/Founder, Ag Crop Broker, Elk Grove, CA, Michael N. Witt/Founder, Real Estate Developer, El Dorado Hills, CA, Karen Battles/VP - Construction Loan Office, Tim Clegg/VP, Business Development Officer, Chadwick B. Meyer/Dir., Sr. Exec. VP, Chief Administrative Officer, Mark Day/CFO, Exec. VP, Kelly J. Binger/Exec. VP, Chief Products Officer, Marketing Dir., Jeffrey B. Barnes/Founder, Ag Sales, Sacramento, CA, Frank J. Borges/Founder, Farmer, Modesto, CA, Michael F. Cavanagh/Founder, CPA, Vallejo, CA, Michael D. Coldani/Founder, Real Estate Sales, Lodi, CA *(21 Officers included in Index)*

Directors: John A. Dimichele/Dir., CEO, Pres., James H. Gray/Chmn., James G. Engstrom/Dir., William T. Lappas/Dir., William H. Parish/Dir., Barbara A. Vohryzek/Dir., Michael E. Rice/Dir., William T. Stokes/Dir., Chadwick B. Meyer/Dir., Sr. Exec. VP, Chief Administrative Officer, Raymond H. Coldani/Founder

Community Capital Bancshares Inc

2815 Meredyth Dr., Albany, GA, 31707; *PH:* 1-229-446-2265; *Fax:* 1-229-446-7030; *http://* www.albanybankandtrust.com

General - Incorporation	GA	**Stock**- Price on:12/24/2007	$11.16
Employees	72	Stock Exchange	NDQ
Auditor	Mauldin & Jenkins LLC	Ticker Symbol	ALBY
Stk Agt	Suntrust Bank	Outstanding Shares	3,020,000
Counsel	Powell, Goldstein, Frazer & Murphy	E.P.S	-$0.29
DUNS No.	NA	Shareholders	NA

Business: The group's principal activity is to provide a wide range of banking services through its subsidiary, albany bank and trust, n.a. The group provides a broad array of deposit services including demand deposits, regular savings accounts, money market deposits, certificates of deposit and individual retirement accounts. In addition, the group also provides cash management services, safe-deposit boxes, travelers checks, direct deposit, automatic drafts and a variety of non-deposit investment products such as trust services, stocks, mutual funds and annuities. It originates consumer loans to individuals, commercial loans to small to medium-sized businesses and professional concerns and real estate-related loans. The group provides its services to the individuals and businesses located in the dougherty county, the city of albany and parts of lee county, Georgia.

Primary SIC and add'l.: 6021 6712

CIK No: 0001074369

Subsidiaries: AB&T National Bank, Albany Bank & Trust, Community Capital Statutory Trust I, Community Capital Technology Services, Inc

Owners: Mary Helen Dykes/0.70%, Wellington Management Company, LLC/2.20%, Insiders/23.90%, John H. Monk, Phillip J. Timyan/5.90%, Mark M. Shoemaker/1.40%, John P. Ventulett, Royce & Associates, LLC/3.00%, Lawrence B. Willson/1.40%, John P. Ventulett/1.50%, David J. Baranko/0.80%, Keith G. Beckham/1.20%, Glenn A. Dowling/1.40%, Jane Anne D. Sullivan/1.70%, David C. Guillebeau/1.90% *(22 Owners included in Index)*

Financial Data: **Fiscal Year End:**12/31 **Latest Annual Data:** 12/31/2006

Year	Sales	Net Income
2006	$25,868,000	$424,000
2005	$17,078,000	$113,000
2004	$10,870,000	$856,000

Curr. Assets:	$13,808,000	**Curr. Liab.:**	$237,553,000	**P/E Ratio:**	279.00
Plant, Equip.:	$9,779,000	**Total Liab.:**	$270,144,000	**Indic. Yr. Divd.:**	$0.080
Total Assets:	$296,936,000	**Net Worth:**	$26,792,000	**Debt/ Equity:**	1.1388

Community Capital Corp

1402-C Hwy. 72 W, Greenwood, SC, 29649; *PH:* 1-864-941-8200; *Fax:* 1-864-941-8283; *http://* www.comcapcorp.com

General - Incorporation	SC	**Stock**- Price on:12/24/2007	$19.2
Employees	193	Stock Exchange	NDQ
Auditor	Elliot Davis LLC	Ticker Symbol	CPBK
Stk Agt	Registrar & Transfer Co	Outstanding Shares	3,840,000
Counsel	NA	E.P.S	$1.61
DUNS No.	19-996-0063	Shareholders	NA

Business: The group is a multi-bank holding company that operates through five of its subsidiaries, barnwell, belton, clemson, greenwood and newberry bank. The group provides financial services including accepting deposits, ira plans, selling mutual funds, trust services, origination of home mortgage loans and secured and unsecured loans for small businesses and individuals. The group has 13 branch offices located in South Carolina. On 05-Mar-2004, the group acquired abbeville capital corporation.

Primary SIC and add'l.: 6022 6712

CIK No: 0000832847

Subsidiaries: CapitalBank.

Officers: William G. Stevens/Dir., CEO, Pres./$451,803.00, Wesley R. Brewer/CFO, Exec. VP/$270,073.00

Directors: William G. Stevens/Dir., CEO, Pres., Patricia C. Hartung/Chmn., Wayne Q. Justesen/Dir., Harold Clinkscales/Dir., Marshall B. Keys/Dir., Clinton C. Lemon/Dir., Miles Loadholt/Dir., Thomas C. Lynch/Dir., Edward H. Munnerlyn/Dir., George B. Park/Dir., George D. Rodgers/Dir., Lex D. Walters/Dir.

Owners: George B. Park/2.21%, Harold Clinkscales, Clinton C. Lemon, Wesley R. Brewer, William G. Stevens/2.94%, Edward H. Munnerlyn, Lex D. Walters/1.97%, Patricia C. Hartung, George D. Rodgers, Miles Loadholt/1.25%, Thomas C. Lynch, Tontine Financial Partners, L.P/6.30%, Insiders/13.31%, Wayne Q. Justesen, Marshall B. Keys

Financial Data: **Fiscal Year End:**12/31 **Latest Annual Data:** 12/31/2006

Year	Sales	Net Income
2006	$46,707,000	$5,759,000
2005	$38,271,000	$7,094,000
2004	$31,014,000	$5,800,000

Curr. Assets:	$26,428,000	**Curr. Liab.:**	$640,549,000	**P/E Ratio:**	11.93
Plant, Equip.:	$15,429,000	**Total Liab.:**	$654,318,000	**Indic. Yr. Divd.:**	$0.600
Total Assets:	$713,244,000	**Net Worth:**	$58,926,000	**Debt/ Equity:**	1.9070

Community Central Bank Corp

120 N Main St., Mt. Clemens, MI, 48043; *PH:* 1-586-783-4500; *Fax:* 1-586-783-9471; *http://* www.communitycentralbank.com

General - Incorporation	MI	**Stock**- Price on:12/24/2007	$9.81
Employees	90	Stock Exchange	NDQ
Auditor	Plante & Moran, PLLC	Ticker Symbol	CCBD
Stk Agt	Computershare Investor Services LLC	Outstanding Shares	3,710,000
Counsel	Dickinson, Wright	E.P.S	$0.49
DUNS No.	NA	Shareholders	NA

Business: The group's principal activity is to provide banking services through its subsidiary, community central bank. The products and services of the group include accepting time, demand and savings deposits, regular checking accounts, now and money market accounts and certificates of deposit. In addition, the group originates secured and unsecured commercial, construction, mortgage and consumer loans and provides safe deposit facilities. The group also provides other financial products and services to communities located in the macomb county and metropolitan detroit area.

Primary SIC and add'l.: 6712 6022

CIK No: 0001014133

Subsidiaries: Community Central

Officers: David A. Widlak/Dir., CEO, Pres./$495,609.00, Ray T. Colonius/CFO/$299,855.00, Lisa Medlock/Corp. Sec.

Directors: David A. Widlak/Dir., CEO, Pres., Dean S. Petitpren/Chmn., Joseph F. Jeannette/Dir., John W. Stroh/Dir., Gebran S. Anton/Dir., Celestina Giles/Dir., Joseph E. Catenacci/Dir., Salvatore Cottone/Dir.

Owners: Insiders/32.85%, Joseph Catenacci/4.01%, Sam A. Locricchio, Tontine Financial Partners, L.P./9.20%, Bobby L. Hill, Celestina Giles, Dean S. Petitpren/6.13%, David E. Bonior, Charles U. Shreve, Joseph F. Jeannette/4.25%, Ronald R. Reed/2.16%, Gebran S. Anton/4.91%, David A. Widlak/3.20%, Ray T. Colonius/1.56%, John W. Stroh *(16 Owners included in Index)*

Financial Data: **Fiscal Year End:**12/31 **Latest Annual Data:** 12/31/2006

Year	Sales	Net Income
2006	$36,410,000	$2,096,000
2005	$29,039,000	$3,073,000
2004	$26,271,000	$2,207,000

Curr. Assets:	$27,325,000	**Curr. Liab.:**	$456,424,000		
Plant, Equip.:	$9,333,000	**Total Liab.:**	$468,363,000	**Indic. Yr. Divd.:**	$0.240
Total Assets:	$505,028,000	**Net Worth:**	$36,665,000	**Debt/ Equity:**	0.8014

Community Financial Corp

38 N Central Ave., Staunton, VA, 24401; *PH:* 1-540-886-0796; *Fax:* 1-540-885-0643;
http:// www.cbnk.com

General - Incorporation	VA	Stock- Price on:12/24/2007	$11.28
Employees	143	Stock Exchange	NDQ
Auditor	Yount, Hyde & Barbour, P.C	Ticker Symbol	CFFC
Stk Agt	NA	Outstanding Shares	4,300,000
Counsel	Nelson McPherson Summers Santos	E.P.S.	$0.88
DUNS No.	61-501-3349	Shareholders	NA

Business: The group's principal activity is to provide banking services to individuals and corporate customers. It accepts deposits from the general public and originates real estate loans and other types of investments. The loan products include residential real estate, commercial real estate, construction and land development, consumer and commercial loans. The deposit products include savings account, now account, money market deposit accounts and certificates of deposit. The operations of the group are conducted through offices located in staunton, waynesboro, stuart drafts, raphine and Virginia beach, Virginia.

Primary SIC and add'l.: 6712 6035
CIK No: 0000850606
Subsidiaries: Community Bank

Officers: Douglas P. Richard/64/Dir., CEO, Pres./$489,974.00, Vicki Fortner/Sr. Construction Lending Specialist - Lake Oswego, Michelle Bushnell/Construction Loan Specialist - Lake Oswego, Pat Kotz/Construction Lending Specialist - Lake Oswego, Jerry R. Giles/59/CFO/$202,556.00, John Satterberg/Property Inspector, Lake Oswego, Cynthia Grable/Treasurer, Bruce Paulson/Corporate Lending Officer - Lake Oswego, Harris M. Picoult/Corporate Lending Officer - Lake Oswego, Maureen Goeth/Corporate Lending Officer - Lake Oswego, Karen Wright/Corporate Lending Officer - Vancouver, Kevin Smith/Corporate Lending Officer - Vancouver, Bernadette Phillips/Operations Mgr. - Res, Lending, Lake Oswego, Leslie Shelton/Administrative Assist. - Lake Oswego, Norman C. Smiley/46/Chief Lending Officer, Sr. VP/$169,077.00 *(30 Officers included in Index)*

Directors: Douglas P. Richard/64/Dir., CEO, Pres., James R. Cooke/Chmn., Jane C. Hickok/71/Vice Chmn., Charles F. Andersen/66/Dir., Dale C. Smith/69/Dir., Morgan N. Trimyer/65/Dir., Charles W. Fairchilds/60/Dir.

Owners: Insiders/19.10%, R. Jerry Giles/2.00%, Benny N. Werner/1.30%, Charles F. Andersen/2.30%, Charles W. Fairchilds, Morgan N. Trimyer, Community Financial Employee Stock Ownership and 401(k) Profit Sharing Plan/5.70%, Chris P. Kyriakides/1.50%, Jane C. Hickok/3.70%, Dale C. Smith/2.50%, P. Douglas Richard/2.50%, James R. Cooke/2.00%, Norman C. Smiley/1.30%

Financial Data: *Fiscal Year End:*03/31 *Latest Annual Data:* 03/31/2007

Year	Sales	Net Income
2007	$32,605,000	$4,091,000
2006	$27,468,000	$4,268,000
2005	$22,746,000	$3,806,000

Curr. Assets:	$5,808,000	Curr. Liab.:	$380,825,000		
Plant, Equip.:	$8,335,000	Total Liab.:	$387,440,000	Indic. Yr. Divd.:	$0.260
Total Assets:	$422,606,000	Net Worth:	$35,167,000	Debt/ Equity:	NA

Community Financial Shares Inc

357 Roosevelt Rd., Glen Ellyn, IL, 60137; *PH:* 1-630-545-0900; *http://* www.commbank-wge.com

General - Incorporation	DE	Stock- Price on:12/24/2007	$23
Employees	70	Stock Exchange	OTC
Auditor	BKD LLP	Ticker Symbol	CFIS
Stk Agt	Illinois Stock Transfer Co	Outstanding Shares	1,380,000
Counsel	Mulherin Rehfeldt & Varchetto PC	E.P.S.	$1.79
DUNS No.	NA	Shareholders	NA

Business: The groups principle activity is to banking and financial services. The group operates from United States.

Primary SIC and add'l.: 6035
CIK No: 0001123735
Subsidiaries: Community Bank Wheaton/Glen Ellyn, Community Financial Shares Statutory

Owners: Insiders/15.82%, Scott W. Hamer/0.14%, Robert F. Haeger/0.17%, Penny A. Belke, Christopher P. Barton/1.44%, Donald H. Fischer/3.90%, David H. Clayton/1.84%, Mary Beth Moran/0.13%, Joseph S. Morrissey/3.41%, Raymond A. Dieter/3.11%, William F. Behrmann/0.56%, John M. Mulherin/0.64%, Kenneth S. Franklin/0.07%, William W. Mucker/0.18%

Financial Data: *Fiscal Year End:*12/31 *Latest Annual Data:* 12/31/2006

Year	Sales	Net Income
2006	$17,437,000	$2,186,000
2005	$14,810,000	$2,031,000

Curr. Assets:	$12,593,000	Curr. Liab.:	$247,531,000	P/E Ratio:	12.11
Plant, Equip.:	$13,544,000	Total Liab.:	$251,140,000	Indic. Yr. Divd.:	NA
Total Assets:	$271,741,000	Net Worth:	$20,601,000	Debt/ Equity:	0.1686

Community First BanCorp

1030 W Norton Ave., Muskegon, MI, 49441; *PH:* 1-231-780-1800; *Fax:* 1-231-780-1860;
http:// www.firstcommunitybancorp.com

General - Incorporation	SC	Stock- Price on:12/24/2007	$17.6
Employees	73	Stock Exchange	OTC
Auditor	J. W. Hunt & Co LLP	Ticker Symbol	CFOK
Stk Agt	U.S. Stock Transfer Corp	Outstanding Shares	2,970,000
Counsel	NA	E.P.S.	$0.90
DUNS No.	NA	Shareholders	NA

Business: The group's principal activity is to provide commercial banking services. The group offers deposits, loans and retail banking services in walhalla, seneca, South Carolina, anderson and williamston. The deposit services include checking accounts, now accounts, savings and money market accounts, certificates of deposit, ira accounts and other deposit services. The group offers secured and unsecured, short-to-intermediate term loans, for commercial and consumer purposes. Consumer loans include car, home equity improvement, personal expenditure, education loans and overdrafts. Commercial loans include real estate mortgage loans and loans secured by listed stocks, equipment, inventories and account receivables. Other services include residential mortgage loan origination services, safe deposit boxes, night depository service, visa and mastercard charge cards, tax deposits, travelers' checks and automated teller services operations conducts through community first bank.

Primary SIC and add'l.: 6022 6712

CIK No: 0001047446
Subsidiaries: Community First Bank

Officers: Frederick D. Shepherd/67/Dir., CEO, CFO, Pres., Treasurer/$3,386,764.00, Matthew P. Wagner/Dir., CEO, Mark Christian/Exec. VP - Operations, Systems, William M. Brown/62/Dir., Sec., Michael J. Perdue/Pres., Michael L. Thompson/Exec. VP - Human Resources, Robert M. Borgman/Exec. VP - Credit Administration, Robert G. Dyck/Exec. VP, Chief Credit Officer, Victor R. Santoro/Exec. VP, Jared M. Wolf/Exec. VP, General Counsel

Directors: Frederick D. Shepherd/67/Dir., CEO, CFO, Pres., Treasurer, Matthew P. Wagner/Dir., CEO, Larry S. Bowman/59/Vice Chmn., John M. Eggemeyer/Chmn., Gary W. Deems/Dir., Barry C. Fitzpatrick/Dir., Susan E. Lester/Dir., Arnold W. Messer/Dir., Robert A. Stine/Dir., David S. Williams/Dir., Mark N. Baker/Dir., Stephen M. Dunn/Dir., George E. Langley/Dir., Timothy B. Matz/Dir., Daniel B. Platt/Dir. *(22 Directors included in Index)*

Owners: James E. McCoy/3.70%, Larry S. Bowman/3.00%, Blake L. Griffith/4.50%, James E. Turner/6.10%, Insiders/40.60%, Robert H. Edwards/3.60%, Frederick D. Shepherd/8.80%, Charles L. Winchester/4.50%, Gary V. Thrift/3.10%, William M. Brown/3.20%, John R. Hamrick/3.60%

Financial Data: *Fiscal Year End:*12/31 *Latest Annual Data:* 12/31/2006

Year	Sales	Net Income
2006	$21,754,000	$3,018,000
2005	$18,062,000	$3,730,000
2004	$16,012,000	$3,437,000

Curr. Assets:	$33,327,000	Curr. Liab.:	$315,160,000		
Plant, Equip.:	$7,937,000	Total Liab.:	$320,694,000	Indic. Yr. Divd.:	NA
Total Assets:	$353,909,000	Net Worth:	$33,215,000	Debt/ Equity:	0.1596

Community First Bancorp Inc

240 S Main St., Madisonville, KY, 42431; *PH:* 1-270-821-7211

General - Incorporation	MD	Stock- Price on:12/24/2007	$7.4
Employees	NA	Stock Exchange	OTC
Auditor	King & Co, Psc	Ticker Symbol	CFBC
Stk Agt	U.S. Stock Transfer Corp	Outstanding Shares	NA
Counsel	NA	E.P.S.	-$2.14
DUNS No.	NA	Shareholders	NA

Business: The group's principal activity is to provide a wide range of banking services in Kentucky. The group is a holding company for community first bank. It accepts deposits and originates of loans secured by first mortgages. The group provides loans secured by mortgages on one- to four-family residences, commercial real estate and consumer loans, purchase investment and mortgage-backed securities.

Primary SIC and add'l.: 6035 6712
CIK No: 0001224499
Subsidiaries: Community First Bank

Officers: William M. Tandy/52/Chmn., CEO, Pres., Amy D. Lyons/CFO, VP, Charlotte Sellers/Sr. Lender, Sr. VP, Sec.

Directors: William M. Tandy/52/Chmn., CEO, Pres., Ralph T. Teague/Vice Chmn., Charles G. Ramsey/57/Dir., Steven E. Carson/Dir., Craig J. Riddle/83/Dir., Paul W. Arison/Dir., Charlotte E. Baldwin/Dir., Barry C. Vaughn/60/Dir.

Owners: William M. Tandy/2.10%, Insiders/16.86%, Charlotte E. Baldwin/0.71%, Ralph T. Teague/1.91%, Israel Englander/7.59%, Charles G. Ramsey/1.88%, Paul W. Arison/2.80%, Craig J. Riddle/3.95%, Gary B. Kivett/5.59%, Barry C. Vaughn/1.55%, Steven E. Carson/1.97%

Financial Data: *Fiscal Year End:*12/31 *Latest Annual Data:* 12/31/2006

Year	Sales	Net Income
2006	$4,810,000	-$675,000
2005	$3,908,000	-$439,000
2004	$2,925,000	-$1,032,000

Curr. Assets:	$2,369,000	Curr. Liab.:	$75,406,000		
Plant, Equip.:	$2,109,000	Total Liab.:	$76,640,000	Indic. Yr. Divd.:	NA
Total Assets:	$79,075,000	Net Worth:	$2,436,000	Debt/ Equity:	NA

Community First Inc

501 S James Campbell Blvd, Columbia, TN, 38401; *PH:* 1-931-380-2265; *Fax:* 1-931-388-3188;
http:// www.cfbk.com.

General - Incorporation	TN	Stock- Price on:12/24/2007	NA
Employees	716	Stock Exchange	NA
Auditor	Crowe Chizek & Co. LLC	Ticker Symbol	NA
Stk Agt	NA	Outstanding Shares	NA
Counsel	NA	E.P.S.	NA
DUNS No.	NA	Shareholders	NA

Business: The group operates through its subsidiaries whose principle activity is to provide commercial banking operations and other related financial activities. The group operates from United States.

Primary SIC and add'l.: 6712
CIK No: 0001179500
Subsidiaries: Community First Title, Inc.

Officers: Marc R. Lively/Dir., CEO, Pres./$289,488.00, Andrea Lockridge/COO, Dianne Scroggins/48/CFO/$109,416.00, Michael J. Saporito/57/COO, Sr. VP/$178,822.00, Carl B. Campbell/Sr. VP, Chief Credit Officer/$167,179.00, Roger D. Stewart/Sr. VP, Sr. Loan Officer/$159,019.00

Directors: Marc R. Lively/Dir., CEO, Pres., Eslick E. Daniel/Chmn., Bernard Childress/Dir., Vasant Hari/59/Dir., Randy A. Maxwell/Dir., Allen Pressnell/Dir., Dinah C. Vire/Dir., Stephen Walker/Dir., Fred White/Dir., Roger Witherow/Dir.

Owners: Vasant Gopal Hari, Roger D. Stewart, Dinah C. Vire/1.28%, Carl B. Campbell, Fred C. White/2.91%, Marc R. Lively/3.79%, Insiders/19.26%, Dianne Scroggins, Roger Witherow, Michael J. Saporito, H. Allen Pressnell, Stephen F. Walker, Bernard Childress, Randy Maxwell, Eslick E. Daniel/7.43%

Community Health Systems Inc

4000 Meridian Blvd., Franklin, TN, 37067; *PH:* 1-615-465-7000; *http://* www.chs.net;
Email: corporate_communications@hq.chs.net

General - Incorporation	DE	*Stock*- Price on:12/24/2007	$39.62
Employees	27,000	Stock Exchange	NYSE
Auditor	Deloitte & Touche LLP	Ticker Symbol	CYH
Stk Agt	Mellon Investor Services LLC	Outstanding Shares	95,730,000
Counsel	NA	E.P.S.	$1.82
DUNS No.	13-757-2269	Shareholders	NA

Business: The group's principle activity is to provide general hospital healthcare services. The group provides inpatient medical and surgical services, outpatient treatment and skilled nursing care. The groups services include internal medicine, general surgery, cardiology, oncology, orthopedics, diagnostic and emergency room services, outpatient surgery, laboratory, radiology, respiratory therapy, physical therapy and rehabilitation services. The group operates from United States.

Primary SIC and add'l.: 8062

CIK No: 0001108109

Subsidiaries: Ambulance Services of Dyersburg, Inc., Ambulance Services of Forrest City, LLC, Ambulance Services of Lexington, Inc., Ambulance Services of McKenzie, Inc., Ambulance Services of McNairy, Inc., Anna Hospital Corporation, Arusha LLC, Barstow Healthcare Management, Inc., Berwick Clinic Corp., Berwick Home Health Private Care, Inc., BH Trans Corporation, Big Bend Hospital Corporation, Big Spring Hospital Corporation, Brandywine Hospital Malpractice Assistance Fund, Inc., Brownsville Clinic Corp. 257 Subsidiaries included in the Index

Officers: Wayne T. Smith/Chmn., CEO, Pres./$7,317,424.00, Rachel A. Seifert/Sr. VP, Sec., General Counsel, Linda K. Parsons/VP - Human Resources, Jerry A. Weissman/VP - Medical Staff Development, Carolyn S. Lipp/Sr. VP - Quality, Resource Management, David L. Miller/Pres. - Division I Operations/$1,604,491.00, Martin G. Schweinhart/Sr. VP - Operations, William S. Hussey/Pres. - Division IV Operations, Gary J. Seay/CIO, Sr. VP, Kenneth D. Hawkins/Sr. VP - Acquisitions, Development, Robert A. Horrar/VP - Administration, Larry W. Cash/Dir., CFO/$3,745,396.00, Mark T. Buford/VP, Corporate Controller, Chief Accounting Officer, Kathie G. Thomas/VP - Home Health Group, Larry M. Carlton/VP - Revenue Management *(66 Officers included in Index)*

Directors: Wayne T. Smith/Chmn., CEO, Pres., John A. Clerico/Dir., Julia B. North/Dir., John A. Fry/Dir., Dale F. Frey/Dir., Harvey Klein/Dir., Mitchell H. Watson/Dir., Larry W. Cash/Dir., CFO

Owners: Insiders/4.60%, Michael T. Portacci/0.40%, John A. Fry, John A. Clerico, David L. Miller/0.40%, Mitchell H. Watson, Julia B. North, Larry W. Cash, T. Rowe Price Associates, Inc./5.20%, Wayne T. Smith/2.00%, Harvey Klein, Gary D. Newsome/0.30%, FMR Corp./9.70%, Dale F. Frey

Financial Data: Fiscal Year End:12/31   Latest Annual Data: 12/31/2006

Year	Sales		Net Income
2006	$4,365,576,000		$168,263,000
2005	$3,738,320,000		$167,544,000
2004	$3,332,641,000		$151,433,000
Curr. Assets:	$1,021,384,000	*Curr. Liab.:* $575,283,000	*P/E Ratio:* 22.38
Plant, Equip.:	$1,986,577,000	*Total Liab.:* $2,782,906,000	*Indic. Yr. Divd.:* NA
Total Assets:	$4,506,579,000	*Net Worth:* $1,723,673,000	*Debt/ Equity:* 1.0676

Community National BanCorp

561 E Washington Ave, Ashburn, GA, 31714; *PH:* 1-229-567-9686; *http://* www.communitynational-bank.com

General - Incorporation	GA	*Stock*- Price on:12/24/2007	$25
Employees	345	Stock Exchange	NA
Auditor	Francis & Co, CPAs	Ticker Symbol	NA
Stk Agt	Registrar & Transfer Co	Outstanding Shares	12,450,000
Counsel	NA	E.P.S.	$1.13
DUNS No.	61-305-6860	Shareholders	NA

Business: The group's principal activity is to provide commercial banking services in turner, crisp and camden counties, Georgia and pinellas county, Florida. The group provides a full range of deposit services, including checking accounts, now accounts, savings accounts and other deposits of various types, ranging from daily money market accounts to longer-term certificates of deposit and retirement accounts. Loans originated by the group include short to medium term commercial, consumer installment and real estate loans. Other services provided by the group include safe deposit boxes, travelers' checks, direct deposit of payroll and social security checks and automatic drafts for various accounts.

Primary SIC and add'l.: 6712 6021

CIK No: 0000855386

Subsidiaries: Community National Bank

Financial Data: Fiscal Year End:12/31   Latest Annual Data: 12/31/2006

Year	Sales		Net Income
2006	$73,769,000		$13,509,000
2005	$57,461,000		$11,225,000
2004	$47,018,000		$9,263,000
Curr. Assets:	$34,870,000	*Curr. Liab.:* $927,747,000	*P/E Ratio:* 22.12
Plant, Equip.:	$13,671,000	*Total Liab.:* $1,087,921,000	*Indic. Yr. Divd.:* $0.480
Total Assets:	$1,184,783,000	*Net Worth:* $96,862,000	*Debt/ Equity:* 1.5096

Community National Bank NY

200 Middle Neck Rd. , Great Neck, NY, 11021; *PH:* 1-516-498-9111; *http://* www.cnbny.com

General - Incorporation		*Stock*- Price on:12/24/2007	$13.5
Employees	NA	Stock Exchange	OTC
Auditor	NA	Ticker Symbol	CBNY
Stk Agt	Registrar & Transfer Co	Outstanding Shares	NA
Counsel	NA	E.P.S.	NA
DUNS No.	NA	Shareholders	NA

Business: The groups principal activity is to provide commercial banking services. The services of the group include originating loans, deposits, trust services, telephone banking and Internet banking services, insurance products, trust, and securities brokerage services.

Primary SIC and add'l.: 6029

CIK No:

Officers: Stuart H. Lubow/Chmn., CEO, Pres., Paul Hagan/Sr. VP, CFO, Thomas A. Morabito/Exec. VP, Sr. Commercial Loan Officer, Donna Frasco/First VP - Retail Division, Tracy Jacobs/Regional Branch Coordinator, Santo L. Gaudio/VP - Operations, Compliance, Joseph F. Lavelle/VP - Operations, Retail, Joseph Byrne/VP, Commercial Loan Officer, Michael Ogus/VP -

Small Business Lending, Brian Handler/VP - Residential Lending, Melissa Sieden/Assist. Mgr. - Great Neck Branch, Michele Staubitz/VP, Branch Mgr. - Garden City Branch, Victoria Lefayt/VP, Branch Mgr. - Woodbury Branch, Terry Dumas/VP, Branch Mgr., Maria Circosta/Assist. Mgr. - Huntington Branch

Directors: Stuart H. Lubow/Chmn., CEO, Pres.

Community National Bank of the Lakeway Area

225 W 1st N St., Morristown, TN, 37814; *PH:* 1-423-587-2345; *http://* www.cnbla.com

General - Incorporation		*Stock*- Price on:12/24/2007	$12.05
Employees	NA	Stock Exchange	NDQ
Auditor	NA	Ticker Symbol	CNLA
Stk Agt	Registrar & Transfer Co	Outstanding Shares	1,810,000
Counsel	NA	E.P.S.	NA
DUNS No.	NA	Shareholders	NA

Business: The groups principle activity is to provide banking services. The group provides personal and business services, consumer loans and mortgages services. The groups personal banking services include checking accounts, savings accounts, money market accounts, certificates of deposit and online statements. The group also provides online banking services. The group operates from United States.

Primary SIC and add'l.: 6029

CIK No:

Officers: Samuel F. Grigsby/52/Chmn., CEO, Charles A. Hughes/60/Dir., Pres., Darwin Kilday/51/Dir., Sec., Exec. VP, CFO

Directors: Samuel F. Grigsby/52/Chmn., CEO, Uriel Edde/76/Dir., Charles A. Hughes/60/Dir., Pres., Darwin Kilday/51/Dir., Sec., Exec. VP, CFO, Steven J. Adams/58/Dir., Ronald D. Ailey/49/Dir., Mary Maude Briggs/60/Dir., Jerry C. Cranford/61/Dir., Claude Leroy Royston/59/Dir., Armistead J. Smith/70/Dir., Edward Stiner/51/Dir., Eric N. Ward/47/Dir., Donald K. Watson/62/Dir.

Community National Corp

PO Box 710, 19 Natchez, Trace Dr., Drlexington, TN, 38351; *PH:* 1-901-968-6624; *http://* www.communitynatbank.com

General - Incorporation	TN	*Stock*- Price on:12/24/2007	$33.4
Employees	NA	Stock Exchange	OTC
Auditor	NA	Ticker Symbol	CMNC
Stk Agt	Corporate Transfer Agent	Outstanding Shares	NA
Counsel	NA	E.P.S.	NA
DUNS No.	NA	Shareholders	NA

Business: The groups principal activities include providing banking and financial services to the customers. Services of the group include operating checking accounts for sole proprietors, partnerships, and corporations, money market savings accounts, certificate of deposit accounts, courier deposit pick up services, cash management services and wire transfer facilities. The group operates from the United States.

Primary SIC and add'l.: 6712 6021

CIK No: 0001042726

Officers: Donald G. Burns/Chmn. - Community National Bank, Kent Libecap/Dir. - Community National Bank, Bernard Kues/Assist. VP, Compliance Officer - Community National Bank, Toni Slusher/Centerville Office, Branch Mgr. - Community National Bank, Leslie W. Earnhart/Dir. - Community National Bank, Jess Reinhardt/Sr. VP, Chief Credit Officer - Community National Bank, Robert Hoffman/Pres., Chief Loan Officer - Community National Bank, Melissa Clark/Assist. VP, Operations Officer - Community National Bank, T. C. Garland/Dir. - Community National Bank, James L. Gross/Dir. - Community National Bank, Kyle Dobbins/Carlisle Office, Branch Mgr. - Community National Bank, Marwa Staton/Branch Mgr. Middletown Office - Community National Bank, Brenda G. Harrison/Assist. VP - Cashier, Community National Bank, Paul J. Scheuermann/Dir., Pres. - Community National Bank, Stephen R. Harding/VP, Branch Mgr. - Springboro *(16 Officers included in Index)*

Financial Data: Fiscal Year End:12/31   Latest Annual Data: 12/31/2002

Year	Sales		Net Income
2002	$8,163,000		$1,163,000
2001	$8,786,000		$970,000
2000	$8,945,000		$1,088,000
Curr. Assets:	$5,753,000	*Curr. Liab.:* $103,492,000	
Plant, Equip.:	$4,820,000	*Total Liab.:* $104,140,000	*Indic. Yr. Divd.:* NA
Total Assets:	$114,670,000	*Net Worth:* $10,530,000	*Debt/ Equity:* NA

Community Partners Bancorp

1250 Hwy. 35, Middletown, NJ, 07748; *PH:* 1-732-706-9009; *http://* www.communitypartnersbancorp.com

General - Incorporation	NJ	*Stock*- Price on:12/24/2007	$9.5
Employees	113	Stock Exchange	NDQ
Auditor	Beard Miller Co. LLP	Ticker Symbol	CPBC
Stk Agt	Registrar & Transfer Co	Outstanding Shares	6,520,000
Counsel	NA	E.P.S.	$0.59
DUNS No.	NA	Shareholders	NA

Business: The groups principal activity is to provide commercial and retail banking services. The groups services include Internet banking, savings and demand deposits, and commercial, consumer and mortgage loans. The products of the group include travelers checks, money orders, treasurers checks, and direct deposit facilities. In the year 2006, the group acquired Town Bank. The group operates from Westfield, Union, County, New Jersey. The assets of the group for the year 2006 were $520,520 (thousands).

Primary SIC and add'l.: 6022

CIK No: 0001343034

Subsidiaries: The Town Bank, TRCB Investment Company*, TRCB Title Agency L.L.C*, Two River Community Bank

Officers: Barry B. Davall/Dir., CEO, Pres., Michael W. Kostelnik/Dir., Sec., Michael J. Gormley/Sr. VP, CFO, COO, William D. Moss/VP, Sr. Loan Officer, Michael Bis/Controller, Chief Accounting Officer, Robert W. Dowens/VP

Directors: Barry B. Davall/Dir., CEO, Pres., Charles T. Parton/Chmn., Joseph F.X. O'Sullivan/Vice Chmn., Michael W. Kostelnik/Dir., Sec., Robert E. Gregory/Dir., Frederick H. Kurtz/Dir., Frank J. Patock/Dir., John J. Perri/Dir.

Owners: John J. Perri/1.48%, Robert E. Gregory/1.74%, Insiders/14.39%, Barry B. Davall/2.05%, Charles T. Parton/1.64%, Robert W. Dowens/1.15%, Frank J. Patock/1.77%, Joseph F.X. OSullivan, William D. Moss/1.20%, Michael W. Kostelnik/1.42%, Michael J. Gormley/1.04%, Frederick H. Kurtz

Financial Data: *Fiscal Year End*:12/31 *Latest Annual Data:* 12/31/2006

Year	Sales	Net Income
2006	$31,285,000	$3,699,000

Curr. Assets:	$17,522,000	**Curr. Liab.:**	$450,307,000	**P/E Ratio:**	15.32
Plant, Equip.:	$5,248,000	**Total Liab.:**	$452,201,000	**Indic. Yr. Divd.:**	NA
Total Assets:	$520,520,000	**Net Worth:**	$68,319,000	**Debt/ Equity:**	NA

Community Shores Bank Corp

1030 W Norton Ave., Muskegon, MI, 49441; *PH:* 1-231-780-1800; *Fax:* 1-231-780-3006;
http:// www.communityshores.com

General - Incorporation	MI	**Stock**- Price on:12/24/2007	$11
Employees	61	Stock Exchange	NDQ
Auditor	Crowe Chizek & Co. LLC	Ticker Symbol	CSHB
Stk Agt	Mellon Investor Services LLC	Outstanding Shares	1,470,000
Counsel	NA	E.P.S.	$0.26
DUNS No.	NA	Shareholders	NA

Business: The group's principal activities are to provide a wide range of commercial and consumer banking services to individuals, businesses, governmental units and other institutions. The group operates through its subsidiary community shores bank. The services provided include checking and savings accounts, certificates of deposit, safe deposit boxes and courier services and loans for commercial, mortgage and consumer purposes. The group originates residential mortgage loans, which are generally long-term with either fixed or variable interest rates. It makes personal loans and lines of credit available to consumers for various purposes. Additionally, the group offers mutual funds and annuities, which are non-insured, through an alliance with the independent community financial services association.

Primary SIC and add'l.: 6712 6022

CIK No: 0001070523

Subsidiaries: Community Shores Bank, Community Shores Capital Trust 1, Community Shores Financial Services, Inc., Community Shores Mortgage Company

Officers: Heather D. Brolick/CEO, Pres./$219,734.00, Ralph R. Berggren/Chief Lending Officer, Sr. VP/$163,698.00, Tracey A. Welsh/Sr. VP, CFO/$151,307.00

Directors: Gary F. Bogner/Chmn., Dennis L. Cherette/Vice Chmn., Bruce C. Rice/Dir., Roger W. Spoelman/Dir., Stephen P. Moreland/Dir., Bruce J. Essex/Dir., Robert L. Chandonnet/Dir., Joy R. Nelson/Dir., Jonathan L. Smith/Dir.

Owners: Robert L. Chandonnet/4.60%, Jose A. Infante/4.70%, Tracey A. Welsh, Heather D. Brolick/2.30%, Bruce J. Essex/6.00%, Gordon H. Girod/6.80%, Joy R. Nelson, Ralph R. Berggren/2.30%, Bruce C. Rice, Roger W. Spoelman, Bruce J. Essex/1.70%, Gary F. Bogner/2.20%, Dennis L. Cherette/1.30%, Insiders/15.00%

Financial Data: *Fiscal Year End*:12/31 *Latest Annual Data:* 12/31/2006

Year	Sales	Net Income
2006	$18,007,000	$1,315,000
2005	$14,801,000	$1,213,000
2004	$11,301,000	$804,000

Curr. Assets:	$10,320,000	**Curr. Liab.:**	$225,962,000	**P/E Ratio:**	18.97
Plant, Equip.:	$10,959,000	**Total Liab.:**	$230,862,000	**Indic. Yr. Divd.:**	NA
Total Assets:	$246,981,000	**Net Worth:**	$16,119,000	**Debt/ Equity:**	0.3039

Community Trust Bancorp Inc

346 N Mayo Trl., Pikeville, KY, 41501; *PH:* 1-606-432-1414; *Fax:* 1-606-437-3366;
http:// www.ctbi.com

General - Incorporation	KY	**Stock**- Price on:12/24/2007	$33.24
Employees	1,021	Stock Exchange	NDQ
Auditor	BKD, LLP	Ticker Symbol	CTBI
Stk Agt	NA	Outstanding Shares	15,220,000
Counsel	NA	E.P.S.	$2.36
DUNS No.	10-382-8471	Shareholders	NA

Business: The group's principle activities are to accept time and demand deposits, make secured and unsecured loans to corporations, individuals and others. The other services provided by the group are cash management services to corporate and individual customers, issuing letters of credit, renting safe deposit boxes and providing funds transfer services. The group also acts as trustees of personal trusts, as executors of estates, as trustees for employee benefit trusts, as registrars, transfer agents and paying agents for bond and stock issues also as depositories for securities.

Primary SIC and add'l.: 6712 6021

CIK No: 0000350852

Subsidiaries: Community Trust and Investment Company, Community Trust Bank, Inc., CTBI Preferred Capital Trust, CTBI Preferred Capital Trust II

Officers: Jean R. Hale/Chmn., CEO, Pres./$521,324.00, Kevin J. Stumbo/Exec. VP, Treasurer, Principal Financial Officer/$236,876.00, David Wills/Winchester Marketing Pres., Earl Gene Johnson/Owner, Pres., Leonard McCoy/Pres., Jim Draughn/Exec. VP, Jim Gartner/Exec. VP, Rick Newsom/Exec. VP, Michael Wasson/Exec. VP/$267,398.00, Larry Jones/Exec. VP, Tracy Little/Exec. VP/$262,238.00, William McKenna/Mt Sterling Marketing Pres., Trippy Clark/Pres. - Flemingsburg Marketing, Mark A. Gooch/Exec. VP, Sec./$398,601.00, Steve Jameson/Exec. VP *(31 Officers included in Index)*

Directors: Jean R. Hale/Chmn., CEO, Pres., Franky Minnifield/Dir., Earl Gene Johnson/Owner, Pres., James E. McGhee/50/Dir., David E. Collins/Certified Public Accountant, Founder - Managing Partner, James R. Ramsey/59/Dir., Hobart C. Johnson/Dir., Paul E. Patton/70/Dir., Lynn M. Parrish/58/Dir., Charles J. Baird/58/Dir., Gary G. White/58/Dir., Nick A. Cooley/74/Dir., Krishna M. Malempati/Dir.

Financial Data: *Fiscal Year End*:12/31 *Latest Annual Data:* 12/31/2006

Year	Sales	Net Income
2006	$221,864,000	$39,064,000
2005	$193,629,000	$34,412,000
2004	$164,318,000	$30,950,000

Curr. Assets:	$157,538,000	**Curr. Liab.:**	$2,599,982,000	**P/E Ratio:**	13.68
Plant, Equip.:	$60,165,000	**Total Liab.:**	$2,687,386,000	**Indic. Yr. Divd.:**	NA
Total Assets:	$2,969,761,000	**Net Worth:**	$282,375,000	**Debt/ Equity:**	NA

Community Valley Bancorp

2041 Forest Ave., Chico, CA, 95928; *PH:* 1-530-899-2344; *Fax:* 1-530-891-3498;
http:// www.communityvalleybancorp.com

General - Incorporation	CA	**Stock**- Price on:12/24/2007	$12.53
Employees	191	Stock Exchange	NDQ
Auditor	Perry-Smith LLP	Ticker Symbol	CVLL
Stk Agt	U.S. Stock Transfer Corp	Outstanding Shares	7,570,000
Counsel	NA	E.P.S.	$0.87
DUNS No.	NA	Shareholders	NA

Business: The group's principal activity is the provision of community banking services in California. In its capacity as a holding company of butte community bank, the group provides its services to individuals, businesses, agricultural and real estate customers in butte, sutter and placer counties. Deposit products for the retail banking market include checking, interest bearing transaction, savings, time certificates of deposit and retirement accounts. The principal retail services consist of home equity and consumer loans. The group also offers agricultural lending and real estate financing (both construction and long term) from its agricultural credit centers in yuba city and chico. Its bank card center in chico provides credit, debit and ATM card services and eight ATMs in remote locations. Other services include traveler's checks, bank-by-mail, night depository, automated payroll services and other customary banking services.

Primary SIC and add'l.: 6022

CIK No: 0001170833

Subsidiaries: Butte Community Bank, Community Valley Bancorp Insurance Agency, LLC, Community Valley Bancorp Trust I

Officers: Keith Robbins/66/Dir., CEO, Pres., Bruce Barnett/41/CIO, Sr. VP, James S. Rickards/57/Dir., Sec., John Coger/58/Dir., CFO, COO, Exec. VP, Roger Janis/60/Sr. VP, Area Administrator, Stephen Johnson/55/Sr. VP - RE Development, Risk Management, Craig Larson/52/Chief Lending Officer, Sr. VP, Debbie Miley/54/Administrative VP - Operations, Human Resources Administrator, Gayle Lee/61/Sr. VP, Controller, Kashmir S. Gill/44/Administrative VP, Regional Mgr.

Directors: Keith Robbins/66/Dir., CEO, Pres., Gary B. Strauss/Vice Chmn., Donald W. Leforce/Chmn., James S. Rickards/57/Dir., Sec., Luther W. McLaughlin/Dir., John D. Lanam/Dir., Robert L. Morgan/Dir., Eugene B. Even/Dir., Jack B. Schmelke/Dir. Emeritus, Ellis L. Matthews/Dir., Hubert Townshed/Dir., Charles Mathews/Dir., Robert M. Ching/Dir., John Coger/58/Dir., CFO, COO, Exec. VP

Owners: Charles J. Mathews, Gary B. Strauss/4.00%, Schmelke Family Trust/5.30%, Hubert I. Townshend/2.80%, Keith C. Robbins/2.50%, Robert M. Ching/2.60%, Robert L. Morgan/3.60%, James S. Rickards/2.60%, Community Valley Bancorp ESOP/5.90%, John F. Coger/2.00%, Donald W. Leforce/2.80%, Insiders/26.90%, John D. Lanam/2.30%, Eugene B. Even/1.20%, Ellis L. Matthews/1.20% *(16 Owners included in Index)*

Financial Data: *Fiscal Year End*:12/31 *Latest Annual Data:* 12/31/2006

Year	Sales	Net Income
2006	$47,583,000	$7,151,000
2005	$39,149,000	$7,198,000
2004	$30,999,000	$5,610,000

Curr. Assets:	$69,103,000	**Curr. Liab.:**	$494,845,000	**P/E Ratio:**	14.40
Plant, Equip.:	$15,359,000	**Total Liab.:**	$504,310,000	**Indic. Yr. Divd.:**	$0.320
Total Assets:	$550,037,000	**Net Worth:**	$45,727,000	**Debt/ Equity:**	0.2010

Community West Bancshares

445 Pine Ave., Goleta, CA, 93117; *PH:* 1-805-692-5821; *Fax:* 1-805-692-5835;
http:// www.communitywest.com

General - Incorporation	CA	**Stock**- Price on:12/24/2007	$13.85
Employees	154	Stock Exchange	NDQ
Auditor	Ernst & Young LLP	Ticker Symbol	CWBC
Stk Agt	U.S. Stock Transfer Corp	Outstanding Shares	5,850,000
Counsel	NA	E.P.S.	$0.72
DUNS No.	01-663-4649	Shareholders	NA

Business: The group's principal activities are to provide commercial and retail banking services. The group is a bank holding company, which operates through goleta national bank. The banking services include the acceptance of demand, savings and time deposits, origination of real estate, construction, home improvement and other installment and term loans. The group also offers cash management, remittance processing, electronic banking, merchant credit card processing, electronic services and other customary bank services to its customers. The customer of the group consists of small to mid-sized businesses and individuals.

Primary SIC and add'l.: 6021 6712

CIK No: 0001051343

Subsidiaries: A Nationally Chartered Bank, Fka Goleta National Bank

Officers: Lynda J. Nahra/Dir., CEO, Pres., Charles G. Baltuskonis/57/CFO, Exec. VP, Cynthia M. Hooper/45/Sr. VP - SBA Lending, Bernard R. Merry/60/Sr. VP - Mortgage, William Viani/60/Exec. VP, Credit Administrator/$155,410.00

Directors: Lynda J. Nahra/Dir., CEO, Pres., William R. Peeples/65/Chmn., Jean W. Blois/Dir., Robert H. Bartlein/Dir., John D. Illgen/Dir., Richard C. Whiston/Dir., Kirk B. Stovesand/Dir., James R. Sims/Dir.

Owners: JEAN W. BLOIS/1.23%, KIRK B. STOVESAND, C. RICHARD WHISTON, Charles G. Baltuskonis, CYNTHIA M. HOOPER, ROBERT H. BARTLEIN/2.55%, WILLIAM R. PEEPLES/12.43%, LYNDA J. NAHRA/1.33%, WILLIAM VIANI, Insiders/20.01%, JOHN D. ILLGEN/1.16%, INVESTORS OF AMERICA, LIMITED PARTNERSHIP AND FIRST BANKS, INC./22.83%, JAMES R. SIMS

Financial Data: *Fiscal Year End*:12/31 *Latest Annual Data:* 12/31/2006

Year	Sales	Net Income
2006	$45,275,000	$5,328,000
2005	$37,088,000	$5,642,000
2004	$32,307,000	$3,835,000

Curr. Assets:	$11,879,000	**Curr. Liab.:**	$463,747,000	**P/E Ratio:**	17.10
Plant, Equip.:	$3,158,000	**Total Liab.:**	$469,795,000	**Indic. Yr. Divd.:**	$0.240
Total Assets:	$516,615,000	**Net Worth:**	$46,820,000	**Debt/ Equity:**	NA

Communitycorp

1100 N Jefferies Blvd, Walterboro, SC, 29488; *PH:* 1-843-549-2265;
http:// www.bankofwalterboro.com

General - Incorporation	SC	*Stock* - Price on:12/24/2007	NA
Employees	NA	Stock Exchange	NA
Auditor	Elliot Davis LLC	Ticker Symbol	NA
Stk Agt	Bank of Walterboro	Outstanding Shares	NA
Counsel	McLeod, Fraser & Cone	E.P.S	NA
DUNS No.	84-912-0936	Shareholders	NA

Business: The group's principal activity is to provide commercial banking and related services. The deposit services offered by the group include checking accounts, now accounts, savings accounts, certificate of deposits and other time deposits. The group provides commercial and personal loans. Commercial loans include secured and unsecured loans for working capital, business expansion and purchase of machinery and equipment. Consumer loans include financing automobiles, home improvements, education and personal investments. The group also provides real estate construction and acquisition loans. Other services offered by the group include cash management services, safe deposit boxes, travelers checks, direct deposit of payroll and social security checks and other banking related services.

Primary SIC and add'l.: 6712 6022
CIK No: 0001020347
Subsidiaries: Bank of Walterboro
Officers: Roger W. Crook/Dir., CEO, Pres. - Bank, Walterboro, Harry L. Hill/Dir. - Bank, Walterboro, Calvert Huffines/Dir. - Bank, Walterboro, George W. Cone/Dir. - Bank, Walterboro
Directors: Peden B. McLeod/Chmn., Harold M. Robertson/Dir., Barnwell J. Fishburne/Dir. - Bank, Walterboro, Steven D. Murdaugh/Dir. - Bank, Walterboro
Owners: Harry L. Hill/1.63%, Peden B. McLeod/11.24%, Calvert Huffines/1.08%, W. Roger Crook/1.19%, George W. Cone/2.60%, Steven D. Murdaugh/0.78%, Harold Robertson/5.05%, Barnwell Fishburne/1.36%, Insiders/25.68%

CommunitySouth Financial Corp

Formerly: CommunitySouth Bancshares Inc
6602 Calhoun Memorial Hwy., Easley, SC, 29640; *PH:* 1-864-306-2540

General - Incorporation	SC	*Stock* - Price on:12/24/2007	$14
Employees	57	Stock Exchange	OTC
Auditor	Elliott Davis, LLC	Ticker Symbol	CBSO
Stk Agt	Registrar & Transfer Co	Outstanding Shares	4,700,000
Counsel	Community Service Counsel	E.P.S	$0.23
DUNS No.	NA	Shareholders	NA

Business: The group operates through its subsidiary whose principal activity is banking operations. The group products include real estate loans, commercial real estate loans, mobile home loans, home equity lines-of-credit, construction, land loans and accepting deposits. The group operates from the United States.

Primary SIC and add'l.: 6712
CIK No: 0001295879
Subsidiaries: CommunitySouth Bank & Trust
Owners: John W. Hobbs/1.79%, Joanne M. Rogers/2.42%, Michael W. Riddle/1.73%, Dial G. DuBose/1.37%, David W. Edwards/2.46%, David A. Miller/4.30%, Neal J. Workman/2.45%, David Larry Brotherton/2.45%, Arnold J. Ramsey/1.25%, Allan C. Ducker/4.35%, Lynn B. Spencer/2.46%, Wesley R. Hammond/1.16%, Daniel E. Youngblood/2.45%, Insiders/26.73%

*Financial Data: Fiscal Year End:*12/31 *Latest Annual Data:* 12/31/2006

Year	Sales	Net Income
2006	$15,528,000	$1,157,000
Curr. Assets:	$22,219,000	Curr. Liab.:	$218,556,000	P/E Ratio:	60.87
Plant, Equip.:	$4,743,000	Total Liab.:	$218,578,000	Indic. Yr. Divd.:	NA
Total Assets:	$248,273,000	Net Worth:	$29,695,000	Debt/ Equity:	NA

CommVault Systems Inc

2 Crescent Pl., Oceanport, NJ, 07757; *PH:* 1-732-870-4000; *Fax:* 1-732-870-4525;
http:// www.commvault.com; *Email:* info@commvault.com

General - Incorporation	DE	*Stock* - Price on:12/24/2007	$17.55
Employees	NA	Stock Exchange	NDQ
Auditor	Ernst & Young LLP	Ticker Symbol	CVLT
Stk Agt	Registrar & Transfer Co	Outstanding Shares	42,190,000
Counsel	NA	E.P.S	$1.45
DUNS No.	NA	Shareholders	NA

Business: The groups principle activity is to provide data management software applications and related services. The group provides software under the brand name include QiNetix. The group operates from United States.

Primary SIC and add'l.: 7372
CIK No: 0001169561
Officers: Robert N. Hammer/Chmn., CEO, Pres./$1,853,082.00, Alan G. Bunte/COO, Exec. VP/$843,558.00, Louis F. Miceli/CFO, VP/$514,792.00, William Beattie/VP - Human Resources, Brian Carolan/VP - Finance, Chief Accounting Officer, Brian D. McAteer/VP - Sales Operations, Ron Miiller/VP - Sales, Americas/$622,816.00, Warren H. Mondschein/VP, General Counsel, Sec., Anand Prahlad/VP - Product Development, Suresh P. Reddy/VP - Worldwide Technical Services, Technical Support, Allen Shoemaker/VP - Operations, David West/VP - Marketing, Business Development, Michael Picariello/Dir. - Investor Relations
Directors: Robert N. Hammer/Chmn., CEO, Pres., Frank J. Fanzilli/Dir., Armando Geday/Dir., Keith Geeslin/Dir., Robert F. Kurimsky/Dir., Daniel Pulver/Dir., Gary B. Smith/Dir., David F. Walker/Dir.
Owners: Wells Fargo & Company, and related entities/11.00%, Steven Rose, FMR Corp/12.50%, Insiders/11.50%, Ron Miiller, Louis F. Miceli, Alan G. Bunte/1.40%

*Financial Data: Fiscal Year End:*03/31 *Latest Annual Data:* 3/31/2007

Year	Sales	Net Income
2007	$151,107,000	$64,254,000
2006	$109,472,000	$10,756,000
2005	$82,629,000	$483,000

Curr. Assets:	$100,318,000	Curr. Liab.:	$65,429,000		
Plant, Equip.:	$4,624,000	Total Liab.:	$69,717,000	Indic. Yr. Divd.:	NA
Total Assets:	$148,039,000	Net Worth:	$78,322,000	Debt/ Equity:	NA

Comp En De Mn Cemig ADS

Av. Barbacena 1.200 - 7 andar - ala B1, Bairro Santo Agostinho, Belo Horizonte;
PH: 55-3132993930; *Fax:* 55-3132993933; *http://* www.cemig.com.br; *Email:* ri@cemig.com.br

General - Incorporation	Brazil	*Stock* - Price on:12/24/2007	$21.42
Employees	NA	Stock Exchange	NYSE
Auditor	Deloitte Touche Tohmatsu CPA Ltd	Ticker Symbol	CIG
Stk Agt	NA	Outstanding Shares	NA
Counsel	NA	E.P.S	NA
DUNS No.	NA	Shareholders	NA

Business: The groups principle activity is to provide electricity. The group operates from Brazil.
Primary SIC and add'l.: 4911
CIK No: 0001157557
Subsidiaries: Cemig Distribuio S.A., Cemig Generation and Transmission
Officers: Djalma Bastos De Morais/71/Dir., CEO, Exec. VP, Fernando Henrique Schuffner Neto/Chief Generation, Transmission Officer, Jose Carlos De Mattos/62/Chief New Business Development Officer, Jose Maria De Macedo/67/Chief Distribution, Sales Officer, Luiz Fernando Rolla/CFO, Investor Relations, Marco Antonio Rodrigues Da Cunha/Alternate Dir., Chief Corporate Management Officer, Luiz Guarita Neto/53/Member - Fiscal Counsel, Aliomar Silva Lima/54/Alternate Member - Fiscal Counsel, Celene Carvalho De Jesus/53/Member - Fiscal Counsel, Leonardo Guimaraes Pinto/29/Alternate Member - Fiscal Counsel, Bernardo Afonso Salomao De Alvarenga/56/Dir., Chief Trading Officer, Luiz Otavio Nunes West/50/Member - Fiscal Counsel, Ari Barcelos Da Silva/66/Alternate Member - Fiscal Counsel, Thales De Souza Ramos Filho/68/Member - Fiscal Counsel, Marcus Eolo De Lamounier Bicalho/66/Alternate Member - Fiscal Counsel *(17 Officers included in Index)*
Directors: Djalma Bastos De Morais/71/Dir., CEO, Exec. VP, Marcio Araujo De Lacerda/62/Chmn., Francisco De Assis Soares/55/Alternate Dir., Nohad Toufic Harati/37/Alternate Dir., Franklin Moreira Goncalves/37/Alternate Dir., Lauro Sergio Vasconcelos David/40/Alternate Dir., Guilherme Horta Goncalves/57/Alternate Dir., Eduardo Leite Hoffmann/47/Alternate Dir., Maria Amalia Delfim De Melo Coutrim/Alternate Dir., Andrea Leandro Silva/33/Alternate Dir., Antonio Renato Do Nascimento/64/Alternate Dir., Bernardo Afonso Salomao De Alvarenga/56/Dir., Chief Trading Officer, Marco Antonio Rodrigues Da Cunha/Alternate Dir., Chief Corporate Management Officer, Wilson Nelio Brumer/Dir., Aecio Ferreira Da Cunha/Dir. *(27 Directors included in Index)*
Owners: State Government/50.97%, State Government/1.95%, Southern/32.96%, Insiders, Insiders

*Financial Data: Fiscal Year End:*12/31 *Latest Annual Data:* 12/31/2006

Year	Sales	Net Income
2006	$4,051,296,000	$329,168,000
2005	$4,619,918,000	$777,146,000
2004	$3,804,275,000	$654,560,000
Curr. Assets:	$2,275,572,000	Curr. Liab.:	$2,058,940,000		
Plant, Equip.:	$6,407,519,000	Total Liab.:	$7,088,830,000	Indic. Yr. Divd.:	NA
Total Assets:	$11,013,523,000	Net Worth:	$3,924,693,000	Debt/ Equity:	NA

Companhia Brasileira de Distribuicao

Av. Brigadeiro Luis Antonio, 3126, Jardim Paulista, Sao Paulo, Sao Paulo, 1402901;
PH: 55-1138860421; *Fax:* 55-1138842677; *http://* www.cbd-ri.com.br;
Email: cbd.ri@paodeacucar.com.br

General - Incorporation		*Stock* - Price on:12/24/2007	$39.06
Employees	63,607	Stock Exchange	NYSE
Auditor	NA	Ticker Symbol	CBD
Stk Agt	Bank of New York	Outstanding Shares	113,770,000
Counsel	NA	E.P.S	$316.00
DUNS No.	NA	Shareholders	NA

Business: The groups principle activity is to retail food, general merchandise, electronic goods, home appliances and other products. The group operates 556 stores in the Brazil. The groups quarterly revenue for September 2007 was 7.503.61 millions of BRL.
Primary SIC and add'l.: 3639 5411 3635 5399 3651 5064 5722 3634 3661
CIK No: 0001003972
Officers: Ramatis Rodrigues/Food Commercial Officer, Caio Racy Mattar/Investment, Construction Officer, Eneas Cesar Pestana Neto/Administrative Officer, Hugo A. Jordao Bethlem/UN Comprebem, Sendas e Hipermercados, Jose Roberto Coimbra Tambasco/Business Unit Officer, Maria Aparecida Fonseca/Human Resources Officer, Pedro Barcellos Janot Marinho/Non Food Commercial Officer, Claudia Jordao Ribeiro Pagnano/Marketing Officer
Directors: Valentim Dos Santos Diniz/Honorary Chmn., Abilio Dos Santos Diniz/Chmn., Ana Maria Falleiros Dos Santos Diniz D'Avila/Dir., Candido Botelho Bracher/Dir., Francis Andre Mauger/Dir., Gerald Dinu Reiss/Dir., Geyze Geyze Marchesi Diniz/Dir., Hakim Laurent Aouani/Dir., Henri Philippe Reichstul/Dir., Jean-Charles Henri Naouri/Dir., Joao Paulo Falleiros Dos Dos Santos Diniz/Dir., Maria Silvia Bastos Marques/Dir., Michel Alain Maurice Favre/Dir., Pedro Paulo Falleiros Dos Dos Santos Diniz/Dir., Xavier Michel Marie Jacques/Dir.

*Financial Data: Fiscal Year End:*12/31 *Latest Annual Data:* 12/31/2006

Year	Sales	Net Income
2006	$6,508,521,000	$6,798,000
2005	$4,530,905,000	$116,251,000
2004	$4,729,472,000	$184,019,000
Curr. Assets:	$2,287,489,000	Curr. Liab.:	$1,793,031,000		
Plant, Equip.:	$2,010,403,000	Total Liab.:	$3,149,136,000	Indic. Yr. Divd.:	$0.090
Total Assets:	$5,393,466,000	Net Worth:	$2,184,116,000	Debt/ Equity:	NA

Companhia de saneamento Basico Do Estado De Sao Paulo - Sabesp

Rua Costa Carvalho, 300, Sao Paulo, 5429900; *PH:* 55-33888000; *Fax:* 55-38130254;
http:// www.sabesp.com.br; *Email:* acarmignani@sabesp.com.br

General - Incorporation	Republic of Brazil	**Stock**- Price on:12/24/2007	$44.75
Employees	16,978	Stock Exchange	NYSE
Auditor	Deloitte Touche Tohmatsu CPA Ltd	Ticker Symbol	SBS
Stk Agt	Bank of New York	Outstanding Shares	NA
Counsel	NA	E.P.S	$657.75
DUNS No.	NA	Shareholders	NA

Business: The groups principle activity is to provide municipal sanitary services. The group also provides water and sewage services to residential, commercial, industrial and governmental customers. The group operates in 367 of the 645 municipalities in the states of Sao Paulo, Brazil. The groups quarterly revenue for September 2007 was 1,491.82 millions of BRL.

Primary SIC and add'l.: 4941 4959 4952

CIK No: 0001170858

Officers: Gesner Jose De Oliveira Filho/CEO, Jorge Michel Lepeltier/Fiscal Counsel Current Member, Marcio Saba Abud/Corporate Management Officer, Rui De Britto Alvares Affonso/49/CFO - Economic, Financial Officer, Investor Relations Officer, Paulo Massato Yoshimoto/Metropolitan Officer, Umberto Cidade Semeghini/Regional Systems Officer, Marcelo Salles Holanda De Freitas/Planning, Technology Officer, Maria De Fatima Alves Ferreira/Fiscal Counsel Current Member, Joao Carlos Araujo Dos Santos/Fiscal Counsel Current Member, Sandra Maria Gianella/Fiscal Counsel Current Member, Tomas Bruginski De Paula/Fiscal Counsel Alternates Members, Arthur Quartim Barbosa Araujo/Fiscal Counsel Alternates Member, Vanildo Rolando Neubauer/Fiscal Counsel Alternates Member, Ana Maria Linhares Richtman/Fiscal Counsel Alternates Member, Alexandre Luiz Oliveira De Toledo/Fiscal Counsel Alternates Member *(16 Officers included in Index)*

Directors: Dilma Seli Pena Pereira/Chmn., Humberto Rodrigues Da Silva/Vice Chmn., Ademar Magalhaes Pereira/40/Dir., Roberto Yoshikazu Yamazaki/Dir., Manuelito Pereira Magalhaes/Dir., Renilson Rehem De Souza/57/Dir., Reinaldo Guerreiro/Dir., Mario Engler Pinto/Dir., Farrer Jonathan Paul Lascelles/Dir., Alexander Bialer/Dir.

Owners: Insiders, Others/49.70%, State of So Paulo/50.30%

Financial Data: *Fiscal Year End:*12/31 *Latest Annual Data:* 12/31/2006

Year	Sales	Net Income
2006	$2,591,766,000	$291,883,000
2005	$2,127,965,000	$339,918,000
2004	$1,655,058,000	$157,158,000

Curr. Assets:	$898,732,000	**Curr. Liab.:**	$1,043,451,000		
Plant, Equip.:	$7,255,544,000	**Total Liab.:**	$5,251,930,000	**Indic. Yr. Divd.:**	NA
Total Assets:	$8,674,039,000	**Net Worth:**	$3,422,109,000	**Debt/ Equity:**	NA

Companhia Paranaense de Energia (COPEL)

800 Coronel Dulcdio St. 9th Fl., Curitiba, Paran; *PH:* 55-4133314209; *Fax:* 55-4133314376; *http://* www.copel.com; *Email:* copel@copel.com

General - Incorporation		**Stock**- Price on:12/24/2007	$17.15
Employees	8,119	Stock Exchange	NYSE
Auditor	NA	Ticker Symbol	ELP
Stk Agt	Bank of New York	Outstanding Shares	273,650,000
Counsel	NA	E.P.S	$2.25
DUNS No.	NA	Shareholders	NA

Business: The groups principle activities include generating, transmitting and distributing of electricity. The group also provides telecommunication and information technology services. The group operates from the Brazil. The groups quarterly revenue for September 2007 was 1,250.00 millions of BRL.

Primary SIC and add'l.: 5172 4924 4923 4932 4925 4899 4822 4911

CIK No: 0000924250

Officers: Rubens Ghilardi/Dir., Sec., CEO, Ronald Thadeu Ravedutti/58/Chief Distribuition Officer, Luiz Antonio Rossafa/53/Chief Corporte Management Officer, Paulo Roberto Trompczynski/63/Chief Financial, Investor Relations Officer, Zuudi Sakakihara/70/Chief Legal Officer, Raul Munhoz Neto/65/Chief Generation - Transmission, Telecommunications Officer, Antonio Rycheta Arten/Member - Fiscal Counsel, Heron Arzua/Member - Fiscal Counsel, Marcio Luciano Mancini/Member - Fiscal Counsel, Nelson Pessuti/Member - Fiscal Counsel, Moacir Jose Soares/Member - Fiscal Counsel, Maurilio Leopoldo Schmitt/Member - Fiscal Counsel, Serafim Charneski/Member - Fiscal Counsel

Directors: Rubens Ghilardi/Dir., Sec., CEO, Joao Bonifacio Cabral/Chmn., Laurita Costa Rosa/Dir., Luiz Antonio Rodrigues Elias/Dir., Nelson Fontes Siffert Filho/Dir., Jorge Michel Lepeltier/Dir., Nildo Rossato/Dir., Rogerio De Paula Quadros/Dir.

Financial Data: *Fiscal Year End:*12/31 *Latest Annual Data:* 12/31/2006

Year	Sales	Net Income
2006	$3,479,860,000	$477,948,000
2005	$2,085,079,000	$239,067,000
2004	$1,477,661,000	$70,533,000

Curr. Assets:	$1,413,093,000	**Curr. Liab.:**	$1,210,404,000		
Plant, Equip.:	$3,475,146,000	**Total Liab.:**	$2,797,655,000	**Indic. Yr. Divd.:**	$0.310
Total Assets:	$6,159,396,000	**Net Worth:**	$3,361,742,000	**Debt/ Equity:**	NA

Companhia Siderurgica Nacional S.A.

Rua Sao Jose n 20, grupo 1602, Rio De Janeiro, Guanabara; *PH:* 55-2122153021; *http://* www.csn.com.br

General - Incorporation		**Stock**- Price on:12/24/2007	$52.52
Employees	NA	Stock Exchange	NYSE
Auditor	NA	Ticker Symbol	SID
Stk Agt	Morgan ADR Service Center	Outstanding Shares	256,490,000
Counsel	NA	E.P.S	$5.55
DUNS No.	NA	Shareholders	NA

Business: The groups principal activity is to produce carbon steel and its products. The groups products include slabs, hot-rolled products, cold-rolled products, galvanized products and tin mill products. In the year 2005, the group acquired Estanho de Rondonia S.A. The group operates from the United States and Brazil.

Primary SIC and add'l.: 3479

CIK No:

Officers: Benjamin Steinbruch/Chmn., CEO, Marcos Marinho Lutz/Executive Officer - Infrastructure, Energy, Eneas Garcia Diniz/Diretor Executivo, Production, Pedro Felipe Borges Neto/Executive Officer - Supplies, Corporate Affairs, Isaac Popoutchi/Executive Officer - Institutional, Juliano De Oliveira/Executive Officer - Participations, Jose Marcos Treiger/Contact - IRO, David Salama/Mgr. - Investor Relations, Claudio Carmo Lopes Pontes/Investor Relations Specialist, Juarez Saliba De/Executive Officer - Mining, Priscila Priscila Kurata/Sr. Analyst

Directors: Benjamin Steinbruch/Chmn., CEO, Jacks Rabinovich/Vice Chmn., Mauro Molchansky/Dir., Fernando Perrone/Dir., Yoshiaki Nakano/Dir., Darc Antonio Da Luz Costa/Dir., Antonio Francisco Dos Santos/Dir., Dionisio Dias Carneiro Netto/Dir.

Financial Data: *Fiscal Year End:*NA *Latest Annual Data:* 12/31/2006

Year	Sales	Net Income
2006	$3,846,000,000	$749,000,000
2005	$3,805,000,000	$902,000,000
2004	$3,084,000,000	$759,000,000

Curr. Assets:	$3,962,000,000	**Curr. Liab.:**	$1,678,000,000	**P/E Ratio:**	13.64
Plant, Equip.:	$3,211,000,000	**Total Liab.:**	$7,501,000,000	**Indic. Yr. Divd.:**	$3.190
Total Assets:	$8,548,000,000	**Net Worth:**	$1,047,000,000	**Debt/ Equity:**	NA

Compania Anonima Nacional Telefonos de Venezuela

Avenida Libertador, Centro Nacional de Telecomunicaciones, Edificio NEA, Piso 1, Caracas, 1010; *PH:* 58-2125001831; *Fax:* 58-2125001828; *http://* www.cantv.com; *Email:* invest@cantv.com.ve

General - Incorporation	Bolivarian Republic Of Venezuela	**Stock**- Price on:12/24/2007	NA
Employees	NA	Stock Exchange	NA
Auditor	Espineira, Sheldon Y Asociados	Ticker Symbol	NA
Stk Agt	Bank of New York	Outstanding Shares	NA
Counsel	NA	E.P.S	NA
DUNS No.	NA	Shareholders	NA

Business: The groups principle activity is to provide communication services. The groups services include wireless communication, broadband internet services, data transmission, public telephone services ad modernization of analog switches. The group operates through two segments namely, wireline services and wireless services. The group operates from the United States and Canada.

Primary SIC and add'l.: 4813 7389 4812 7375 4899 4822 7379

CIK No: 0001025862

Subsidiaries: CANTV Finance, Ltd, CANTV International, Ltd, CANTV.Net, C.A., Compaa Annima Venezolana de Guas CAVEGUAS, nvercanTV, S.A., Telecomunicaciones Movilnet, C.A.

Officers: Vicente Llatas/Chmn., CEO, Pres., Armando Yanes/CFO, Compliance Officer, GM - Planning, Finance, Eloina Perez/Legal Counsel, Ramon Ramirez/GM - Enterprises, Institutions

Directors: Vicente Llatas/Chmn., CEO, Pres., German Garcia Velutini/Alternate Dir., Nicolas Vegas Chumaceiro/Alternate Dir., Edgar Hernandez Behrens/Dir., Julio Cesar Perez/Alternate Dir., Yelitza Garcia/Dir., Ricardo Armas/Alternate Dir., Daniel Petri/Dir., John Lack/Dir., Edward McQuaid/Dir., Ruth De Krivoy/Dir., Ricardo Hausmann/Dir., Christopher Bennett/Alternate Dir., Charles Fallini/Alternate Dir., Luis Esteban Palacios/Alternate Dir.

Owners: Telefnica Venezuela Holding B.V., GTE Venholdings B.V./24.95%, Ministerio del Poder Popular para la Infraestructura, Banco Mercantil, C.A., Company employees and retirees/5.72%, GTE Venholdings B.V./3.56%, Banco de Desarrollo Econmico y Social de Venezuela/6.59%, Brandes Investment Partners, LLC/14.66%, Others/44.47%

Compania de Telecomunicaciones de Chile S.A.

Avenida Providencia N111, Santiago; *PH:* 56-26912595; *Fax:* 56-26913289; *http://* www.telefonicactcchile.cl

General - Incorporation	Chile	**Stock**- Price on:12/24/2007	$9.6
Employees	NA	Stock Exchange	NYSE
Auditor	Ernst& Young LLP	Ticker Symbol	CTC
Stk Agt	Compaa de Telecomunicaciones	Outstanding Shares	239,290,000
Counsel	NA	E.P.S	$0.11
DUNS No.	NA	Shareholders	NA

Business: The groups principle activity is to provide telecommunications and other services. The group operated through four segments namely, fixed telecommunication, long distance, mobile communications, and corporate customer communication and data. The group operates from the Chile. The group's quarterly revenue for September 2007 was 459,585.00 millions of CLP.

Primary SIC and add'l.: 7379 7375 3669 7389 4813 3663 4822 4841 4812 4899 3661

CIK No: 0000863614

Subsidiaries: CTC Equipos, Globus 120, S.A., Telefnica Empresas, Telefonica Gestion de Servicios Compartidos Chile S.A., Telefnica Mundo S.A., Telemergencia

Officers: Jose Moles Valenzuela/General Dir., CEO, Juan Antonio Etcheverry/VP - Residential Communications, Cesar Valdes Morales/VP - Commercial, Administrative, Ruben Sepulveda Miranda/VP - Human Resources, Cristian Aninat Salas/General Counse, Sec., Julio Covarrubias Fernandez/CFO, VP, GM, Diego Martinez-Caro/VP - Management Control, Chief Accounting Officer, Humberto Soto Velasco/VP - Regulation, Wholesalers, Manuel Plaza Martin/VP - Technology, Operations, Rafael Zamora Sanhueza/VP - Telefonica Empresas, Luis Fernando De Godoy/VP - Small Businesses, Professional

Directors: Emilio Gilolmo Lopez/Chmn., Narcis Serra Serra/64/Dep. Chmn., Andres Concha Rodriguez/Dir., Fernando Bustamante Huerta/Dir., Patricio Rojas Ramos/Dir., Hernan Cheyre Valenzuela/Dir., Jose Maria Alvarez-Pallete/Dir., Luis Cid Alonso/Dir., Benjamin Holmes Bierwirth/Dir., Carlos Diaz Vergara/Dir., Marco Colodro Hadjes/Dir., Alfonso Ferrari Herrero/Dir.

Owners: AFP Habitat S.A/6.99%, Insiders, AFP Provida S.A/6.89%, AFP Habitat S.A/6.99%, Rafael Zamora Sanhueza, Franco Faccilongo Forno, AFP Provida S.A/5.56%, Insiders, Citibank, N.A./13.29%, Telefnica Internacional Chile/44.39%, Alfonso Ferrari Herrero, Telefnica Internacional Chile/50.19%, Marco Colodro Hadjes

Financial Data: *Fiscal Year End:*12/31 *Latest Annual Data:* 12/31/2006

Year	Sales	Net Income
2006	$1,096,687,000	$77,320,000
2005	$1,103,349,000	$86,708,000
2004	$1,265,175,000	$36,106,000

Curr. Assets:	$562,954,000	Curr. Liab.:	$369,879,000	P/E Ratio:	13.64
Plant, Equip.:	$2,361,437,000	Total Liab.:	$1,360,429,000	Indic. Yr. Divd.:	$0.450
Total Assets:	$2,874,754,000	Net Worth:	$1,514,325,000	Debt/ Equity:	NA

Compania Mina Buenaventura S.A.

Carlos Villaran 790, Santa Catalina, La Victoria, Lima; *PH:* 51-5114192500;
http:// www.buenaventura.com; *Email:* recursos@buenaventura.com.pe

General - Incorporation		**Stock**- Price on:12/24/2007	$35.35
Employees	2,487	Stock Exchange	NYSE
Auditor	NA	Ticker Symbol	BVN
Stk Agt	Mellon Trust Co	Outstanding Shares	127,220,000
Counsel	NA	E.P.S.	$1.82
DUNS No.	NA	Shareholders	NA

Business: The groups principal activities include acquiring, exploring, exploiting and mining metals. The group also produced gold. The group operates from the Peru and Latin America.
Primary SIC and add'l.: 1040
CIK No: 0001005315
Officers: Roque Benavides Ganoza/52/Dir., CEO, Pres., Luis Coleridge/70/Dir. - Financial Expert, Carlos E. Galvez Pinillos/54/CFO, VP, Raul Benavides Ganoza/51/VP - Business Development, Francois Muths/56/Operations VP, Jose Miguel Morales Dasso/61/General Counsel, Cesar E. Vidal/52/Explorations VP, Carlos Humberto Rodriguez Calle/62/Controller, Daniel Dominguez/Investor Relations Officer
Directors: Roque Benavides Ganoza/52/Dir., CEO, Pres., Alberto Benavides De La Quintana/86/Founder, Chmn., Norman Anderson/76/Dir., Luis Coleridge/70/Dir. - Financial Expert, Aubrey Laurence Paverd/68/Dir., Felipe Ortiz-De-Zevallos/59/Dir., German Suarez Chavez/65/Dir., Carlos Humberto Rodriguez Calle/62/Controller
Financial Data: Fiscal Year End: Latest Annual Data: 12/31/2006

Year	Sales	Net Income
2006	$646,872,000	$424,697,000
2005	$344,416,000	$274,259,000
2004	$336,828,000	$209,769,000

Curr. Assets:	$491,491,000	Curr. Liab.:	$176,326,000	P/E Ratio:	13.64
Plant, Equip.:	$215,643,000	Total Liab.:	$526,702,000	Indic. Yr. Divd.:	$0.350
Total Assets:	$1,732,030,000	Net Worth:	$1,205,328,000	Debt/ Equity:	NA

Compass Bancshares Inc

15 S 20th St. , Birmingham, AL, 35233; *PH:* 1-205-933-3000; *http://* www.compassweb.com

General - Incorporation	DE	**Stock**- Price on:12/24/2007	$69.39
Employees	8,400	Stock Exchange	NA
Auditor	Ernst & Young, LLP	Ticker Symbol	NA
Stk Agt	Continental Stock Transfer & Trust Co	Outstanding Shares	131,710,000
Counsel	NA	E.P.S.	$3.46
DUNS No.	05-986-4702	Shareholders	NA

Business: The groups principle activity is to provide banking services. The group also provides loan and wealth management services. The group operates from United States.
Primary SIC and add'l.: 6712 6021
CIK No: 0000018568
Subsidiaries: Central Bank of the South, Compass Bank, Compass Capital Markets, Inc., Compass Limited Partner, Inc., Compass Southwest LP, Phoenix Loan Holdings, Inc., Tucson Loan Holdings, Inc.
Officers: Paul D. Jones/Chmn., CEO - Compass Bank, Ray G. Stone/Sr. Exec. VP, Chief Credit Policy Officer - Compass Bank, Garrett R. Hegel/CFO - Compass Bank, George M. Boltwood/Sr. Exec. VP - Corporate Banking - Compass Bank, William C. Helms/Exec. VP - Wealth Management - Compass Bank, Lee E. Harris/Exec. VP - Human Resources, Compass Bank, Clayton D. Pledger/CIO, Exec. VP - Compass Bank, James D. Barri/Exec. VP - Retail Banking - Compass Bank, Gregory P. Deming/Exec. VP, Chief Risk Officer - Compass Bank, Jerry W. Powell/General Counsel, Sec. - Compass Bank, Edward J. Bilek/Dir. - Investor Relations
Directors: Paul D. Jones/Chmn., CEO - Compass Bank, James H. Click/Dir. - Compass Bank, William Eugene Davenport/Dir. - Compass Bank, Charles E. McMahen/Dir. - Compass Bank, Tranum Fitzpatrick/Dir. - Compass Bank, John S. Stein/Dir. - Compass Bank, Carl J. Gessler/Dir. - Compass Bank, Charles W. Daniel/Dir. - Compass Bank, Terry J. Strange/Dir. - Compass Bank, John C. Evins/Dir. Emeritus
Financial Data: Fiscal Year End:12/31 Latest Annual Data: 12/31/2006

Year	Sales	Net Income
2006	$2,770,700,000	$460,363,000
2005	$2,207,065,000	$401,830,000
2004	$1,902,169,000	$360,185,000

Curr. Assets:	$849,297,000	Curr. Liab.:	$27,864,020,000	P/E Ratio:	20.05
Plant, Equip.:	$589,264,000	Total Liab.:	$31,375,621,000	Indic. Yr. Divd.:	$1.720
Total Assets:	$34,199,755,000	Net Worth:	$2,824,134,000	Debt/ Equity:	1.1949

Compass Minerals International Inc

9900 W 109th St., Ste. 600, Overland Park, KS, 66210; *PH:* 1-913-344-9200; *Fax:* 1-913-338-7932; *http://* www.compassminerals.com

General - Incorporation	DE	**Stock**- Price on:12/24/2007	$35.12
Employees	1,557	Stock Exchange	NYSE
Auditor	PricewaterhouseCoopers LLP	Ticker Symbol	CMP
Stk Agt	UMB Bank, N.A.	Outstanding Shares	32,170,000
Counsel	NA	E.P.S.	$1.61
DUNS No.	NA	Shareholders	NA

Business: The group's principal activity is to produce rock, or highway deicing, salt in North America and the United Kingdom. It operates in two segments: salt and potash. Salt segment consists of mining, producing, processing and distribution of rock, evaporated and solar salt in North America and Europe. Salt is used in a variety of applications like deicer for highway and consumer use, paper bleaching, water treatment, as a flavor enhancer and preservative in food and as a nutrient in animal feeds. Potash is used as a specialty fertilizer, which provides essential potassium to high-value, chloride-sensitive crops, such as vegetables, fruits, tea, tobacco and turf grass. The markets of the group include the United States, Canada and United Kingdom.
Primary SIC and add'l.: 1479

CIK No: 0001227654
Subsidiaries: Carey Salt Company, Compass Canada Limited Partnership, Compass Minerals (Europe) Limited, Compass Minerals (UK)Limited, Compass Minerals Canada Inc., Compass Minerals Group, Inc., Compass Minerals Nova Scotia Company, Compass Resources Canada Company, Compass Resources, Inc., Direct Salt Supplies Limited, Great Salt Lake Holdings, LLC, Great Salt Lake Minerals Corporation, GSL Corporation, J.T. Lunt & Co. (Nantwich) Limited, London Salt Limited 21 Subsidiaries included in the Index
Officers: Angelo C. Brisimitzakis/Dir., CEO, Pres., Keith E. Clark/VP, GM General Trade, Peggy Landon/Dir. - Investor Relations, David J. Goadby/VP, MD Salt Union, Rodney L. Underdown/CFO, VP, John Fallis/VP, GM Highway Deicing, Ronald Bryan/VP, GM - Great Salt Lake Minerals, Salt Union
Directors: Angelo C. Brisimitzakis/Dir., CEO, Pres., David J. D'Antoni/Dir., Allan R. Rothwell/Dir., Timothy R. Snider/Dir., Bradley J. Bell/Dir., Vernon G. Baker/Dir., Perry W. Premdas/Dir., Richard S. Grant/Dir.
Owners: FMR Corp./11.50%, Timothy R. Snider, Ronald Bryan, Perry W. Premdas, Allan R. Rothwell, Insiders/1.53%, Michael E. Ducey, Neuberger Berman,Inc./14.33%, Angelo C. Brisimitzakis, Rodney Underdown, David J. Goadby, Insiders/1.53%, Insiders/1.53%, Neuberger Berman, Inc./14.33%, Bradley J. Bell (19 Owners included in Index)
Financial Data: Fiscal Year End:12/31 Latest Annual Data: 12/31/2006

Year	Sales	Net Income
2006	$660,700,000	$55,000,000
2005	$742,300,000	$30,900,000
2004	$695,100,000	$49,800,000

Curr. Assets:	$283,800,000	Curr. Liab.:	$119,000,000	P/E Ratio:	21.81
Plant, Equip.:	$374,600,000	Total Liab.:	$771,400,000	Indic. Yr. Divd.:	$1.280
Total Assets:	$706,300,000	Net Worth:	-$65,100,000	Debt/ Equity:	NA

Competitive Companies Inc

3751 Merced Dr. Ste. A, Riverside, CA, 92503; *PH:* 1-951-687-6100; *http://* www.ccius.net

General - Incorporation	NV	**Stock**- Price on:12/24/2007	$0.13
Employees	8	Stock Exchange	OTC
Auditor	Lawrence Scharfman & Co., CPA P.C.	Ticker Symbol	CCOP
Stk Agt	American Stock Transfer & Trust Co.	Outstanding Shares	54,450,000
Counsel	NA	E.P.S.	$0.00
DUNS No.	NA	Shareholders	NA

Business: The groups principle activity is to provide telephone systems and services to apartment complexes. The groups services include local, long distance telephone service, Voice-over-Internet Protocol, Internet service and cable television service. In the year 2005, the group merged with CA Networks, Inc. The group operates from the United States.
Primary SIC and add'l.: 4813
CIK No: 0001161706
Subsidiaries: CCI RESIDENTIAL SERVICES, INC., COMPETITIVE COMMUNICATIONS, INC
Officers: Jerald Woods/Dir., CEO, Principal Financial Officer, Henri R. Hornby/51/Dir., Sec., Treasurer, Principal Accounting Officer, Janice Gordon/Co - Pres.
Directors: Jerald Woods/Dir., CEO, Principal Financial Officer, Henri R. Hornby/51/Dir., Sec., Treasurer, Principal Accounting Officer, David C. Hewitt/Dir., George W. Hannah/52/Dir.
Owners: Russell Preston/12.00%, Jerald Woodsr/15.00%, Janice Gordan/1.00%, George Hannah/1.00%, David Hewitt/1.00%, David Reding/5.00%, Henri Hornby/20.00%, Insiders/55.00%
Financial Data: Fiscal Year End:12/31 Latest Annual Data: 12/31/2006

Year	Sales	Net Income
2006	$1,014,000	-$180,000
2005	$773,000	-$1,967,000

Curr. Assets:	$118,000	Curr. Liab.:	$268,000		
Plant, Equip.:	$111,000	Total Liab.:	$268,000	Indic. Yr. Divd.:	NA
Total Assets:	$231,000	Net Worth:	-$37,000	Debt/ Equity:	1.4000

Competitive Technologies Inc

777 Commerce Dr., Ste. 100, Fairfield, CT, 06825; *PH:* 1-203-368-6044; *Fax:* 1-203-368-5399; *http://* www.competitivetech.net; *Email:* ctt@competitivetech.net

General - Incorporation	DE	**Stock**- Price on:12/24/2007	$2.4601
Employees	20	Stock Exchange	AMEX
Auditor	Mahoney Cohen & Co., CPA, P.C.	Ticker Symbol	CTT
Stk Agt	American Stock Transfer & Trust Co.	Outstanding Shares	8,110,000
Counsel	D'ancona & Pflaum	E.P.S.	-$0.885
DUNS No.	04-929-4093	Shareholders	NA

Business: The group's principal activity is to provide patent and technology commercialization services. The services are provided to a broad range of digital and electronic, life sciences and physical sciences technologies. The group provides technical evaluations, patent and market assessments, patent application and prosecution, patent enforcement, licensing, license management and royalty distribution services. The digital and electronic portfolio includes telecommunications, data security, signal processing, digital entertainment, electrical circuitry, microelectronic and semiconductor technologies. The life sciences portfolio includes pharmaceuticals, biotechnology and medical devices. The physical sciences portfolio includes display, environmental and nano-technologies and smart or novel materials.
Primary SIC and add'l.: 7389
CIK No: 0000102198
Subsidiaries: CTT Trading Company, LLC, Vector Vision, Inc.
Officers: John B. Nano/Chmn., CEO, Pres., Girish Nallur/Chief Scientific Officer, Aris D. Despo/Sr. VP - Business Development, Paul A. Levitsky/VP, General Counsel, Joseph P. Ausikaitis/Sr. Business Development Executive, Ted Kutrumbos/Business Development Executive, Johnnie D. Johnson/Investor Relation Officer
Directors: John B. Nano/Chmn., CEO, Pres., Joel M. Evans/Dir., Richard D. Hornidge/Dir., Rustin Howard/Dir., William L. Reali/Dir., Ralph S. Torello/Dir.
Owners: Richard D. Hornidge/1.00%, Paul A. Levitsky, Joel M. Evans, John B. Nano/1.30%, Aris Despo, Insiders/3.00%, Rustin Howard, Ralph S. Torello, William L. Reali
Financial Data: Fiscal Year End:07/31 Latest Annual Data: 7/31/2006

Year	Sales	Net Income
2006	$5,188,000	-$2,377,000
2005	$14,174,000	$5,702,000
2004	$8,022,000	$2,955,000

Curr. Assets:	$17,484,000	**Curr. Liab.:**	$3,963,000		
Plant, Equip.:	$149,000	**Total Liab.:**	$3,963,000	**Indic. Yr. Divd.:**	NA
Total Assets:	$18,417,000	**Net Worth:**	$14,454,000	**Debt/ Equity:**	NA

Compex Technologies Inc

1811 Old Hwy 8, New Brighton, MN, 55112; *Fax:* 1-651-638-0476; *http://* www.compextechnologies.com; *Email:* info@rehabilicare.com

General - Incorporation	MN	**Stock**- Price on:12/24/2007	NA
Employees	NA	Stock Exchange	NA
Auditor	Ernst & Young LLP	Ticker Symbol	NA
Stk Agt	Registrar & Transfer Co	Outstanding Shares	NA
Counsel	NA	E.P.S.	NA
DUNS No.	05-904-0865	Shareholders	NA

Business: The group's principal activity is to design, manufacture and provide electromedical pain management and rehabilitation products and service for clinical, home healthcare and occupational medicine applications. The group also offers electrotherapy devices, which are used in rehabilitation of the injured, and provides relief from chronic and acute pain. The group's electrotherapy products consist of neuromuscular stimulators, pulsed direct current devices and interferential stimulators. The group also provides electric muscle stimulators to enhance muscle performance for sports training. Distribution of the group's products is both on a direct basis to healthcare providers and their patients and on a wholesale basis to home healthcare dealers. On 03-Jul-2003, the group acquired filsport assistance s r l.

Primary SIC and add'l.: 3845

CIK No: 0000064578

Complete Production Services Inc

11700 Old Katy Rd., Ste. 300, Houston, TX, 77079; *PH:* 1-281-372-2300; *Fax:* 1-281-372-2301; *http://* www.completeproduction.com

General - Incorporation	DE	**Stock**- Price on:12/24/2007	$26.75
Employees	6,397	Stock Exchange	NYSE
Auditor	Grant Thornton LLP	Ticker Symbol	CPX
Stk Agt	Wells Fargo Bank, N.A.	Outstanding Shares	72,560,000
Counsel	NA	E.P.S.	$2.41
DUNS No.	NA	Shareholders	NA

Business: The groups principle activity is to provide services and products on helping oil and gas companies to develop hydrocarbon. The group operates through three segments namely, completion and production services, drilling services and product sales. The group acquired Parchman Energy Group, Inc. and Big Mac group of companies in the year 2005 and J&M Rental Tool, Inc., Turner group of companies, Pinnacle Drilling Co., LLC, Femco Services, Inc., Webb Dozer Services and Pumpco in the year 2006. The group operates from the United States, Canada, Mexico and Southeast Asia. The group's quarterly revenue for September 2007 was 412.92 millions of USD.

Primary SIC and add'l.: 1389

CIK No: 0001340041

Subsidiaries: 104474 Alberta Ltd., A&W Water Service, Inc., Advanced Coiled Tubing, Inc., Bell Supply I, L.P., Big Mac Tank Trucks, LLC, Big Mac Trucking Company, Inc., BSI Holdings Management, LLC, BSI Holdings, L.P., CES Holdings LLC, CES Mid-Continent Hamm, Inc., CES Rockies, Inc., Complete Energy Services, LLC, Complete Production Services, Inc., Delaney Energy Services Corp., Femco SWD, Inc. 63 Subsidiaries included in the Index

Officers: Joseph C. Winkler/Chmn., CEO, Michael J. Mayer/Sr. VP, CFO, Jose Bayardo/VP - Corporate Development, Investor Relations, James F. Maroney/VP, Sec., General Counsel, Kenneth L. Nibling/VP - Human Resources, Administration, Robert L. Weisgarber/VP - Accounting, Controller, Ronald Boyd/Pres. - Mid, Continent Division, Lee Daniel/Pres. - Rockies Division, Brian K. Moore/COO, Pres., Thomas Burke/Pres. - Texas Division, Sherry Flato/Pres. - IE Miller Division, Bryan Supreniant/Pres. - IPS US, Mexico Division

Directors: Joseph C. Winkler/Chmn., CEO, Andrew L. Waite/Dir., Robert S. Boswell/Dir., Harold G. Hamm/Dir., Matt W. Ralls/Dir., Graham R. Whaling/Dir., James D. Woods/Dir., Marcus A. Watts/Dir.

Owners: R. Graham Whaling, Wellington Management Company, LLP/10.80%, Insiders/7.30%, Robert S. Boswell, James D. Woods, Marcus A. Watts, Robert L. Weisgarber, J. Michael Mayer, SCF-IV, L.P./34.40%, Joseph C. Winkler, Kenneth L. Nibling, James F. Maroney, Harold G. Hamm/5.80%, Andrew L. Waite, W. Matt Ralls *(16 Owners included in Index)*

Financial Data: **Fiscal Year End:**12/31 **Latest Annual Data:** 12/31/2006

Year	Sales	Net Income
2006	$1,212,424,000	$139,086,000
2005	$757,726,000	$53,862,000
2004	$320,747,000	$13,884,000

Curr. Assets:	$390,640,000	**Curr. Liab.:**	$161,405,000	**P/E Ratio:**	12.10
Plant, Equip.:	$771,703,000	**Total Liab.:**	$1,005,103,000	**Indic. Yr. Divd.:**	NA
Total Assets:	$1,740,324,000	**Net Worth:**	$735,221,000	**Debt/ Equity:**	0.9984

Composite Technology Corp

2026 Mcgaw Ave., Irvine, CA, 92614; *PH:* 1-949-428-8500; *http://* www.compositetechcorp.com

General - Incorporation	NV	**Stock**- Price on:12/24/2007	$1.18
Employees	188	Stock Exchange	OTC
Auditor	Singer Lewak Greenbaum & Goldstein	Ticker Symbol	CPTC
Stk Agt	General Securities Trnsfer Agency Inc	Outstanding Shares	179,860,000
Counsel	NA	E.P.S.	NA
DUNS No.	NA	Shareholders	NA

Business: The groups principal activity is to provide in renewable and energy electrical energy products. The group products include Aluminum Conductor Composite Core, conductors, DeWind 8.2 wind energy generators and CTC Cable Division. The group operates through two segments namely cable division and turbine division. In the year 2006, the group acquired EU Energy Ltd. The group operates from the United State and China. In the year 2006, cable division accounted for $ 3,554,436 and turbine division $ 32,137,022.

Primary SIC and add'l.: 3355

CIK No: 0000317477

Subsidiaries: EU Energy Inc.

Officers: Benton H. Wilcoxon/Chmn., CEO, James Carswell/VP - Investor Relations, Corporate Development, David C. Bryant/VP - Product Development, Dominic J. Majendie/VP - EMEA, Douglas A. Pilling/Production Mgr., Bill Ferguson/Development Mgr., Michael D. McIntosh/Dir. - Intellectual Property Strategy

Directors: Benton H. Wilcoxon/Chmn., CEO

Owners: Dean D. McCormick, Insiders/21.30%, Dominic J. Majendie, Benton H. Wilcoxon/10.40%, Michael Porter/9.74%, Michael D. McIntosh

Curr. Assets:	$39,378,000	**Curr. Liab.:**	$48,678,000	**P/E Ratio:**	29.69
Plant, Equip.:	$4,714,000	**Total Liab.:**	$54,153,000	**Indic. Yr. Divd.:**	NA
Total Assets:	$96,253,000	**Net Worth:**	$42,100,000	**Debt/ Equity:**	NA

Comprehensive Care Corp

3405 W Dr. Martin Luther King Jr. Blvd., Ste. 101, Tampa, FL, 33607; *PH:* 1-813-288-4808; *Fax:* 1-813-288-4844; *http://* www.compcare.com; *Email:* info@compcare.com

General - Incorporation	DE	**Stock**- Price on:12/24/2007	$1.1
Employees	60	Stock Exchange	OTC
Auditor	Kirkland , Russ, Murphy & Tapp P.A.	Ticker Symbol	CHCR
Stk Agt	Continental Stock Transfer & Trust Co	Outstanding Shares	7,700,000
Counsel	Greenberg Traurig	E.P.S.	-$0.45
DUNS No.	08-850-1879	Shareholders	NA

Business: The group's principal activity is to provide managed care services in the behavioral health and psychiatric fields. The group manages the delivery of a range of psychiatric and substance abuse services to commercial, medicare, and medicaid members. The group currently provides behavioral healthcare services to recipients in fourteen states, primarily through subcontracts with health plans. The customer base for its services includes both corporate and governmental entities. The group operates solely in the domestic market. The group also provides services which includes a broad spectrum of inpatient and outpatient metal health and substance abuse theraphy, counseling, and supportive interventions. The group's main objective is to provide easily accessible, high quality behavioral healthcare services and products and to manage costs through measures such as the monitoring of hospital inpatient admissions and review of authorizations for outpatient therapy.

Primary SIC and add'l.: 8741 8063

CIK No: 0000022872

Subsidiaries: CompCare of Pennsylvania, Inc., Comprehensive Behavioral Care of Connecticut, Inc., Comprehensive Behavioral Care, Inc., Comprehensive Care Integration, Inc., Comprehensive Provider Networks of Texas, Inc., Healthcare Management Services of Michigan, Inc., Healthcare Management Services, Inc.

Officers: Mary Jane Johnson/Dir., CEO, Pres., Robert J. Landis/Chmn., CFO, Treasurer, Paul Patti/VP - Clinical Operations

Directors: Mary Jane Johnson/Dir., CEO, Pres., Robert J. Landis/Chmn., CFO, Treasurer

Owners: Harry Ross/12.10%, Thomas Clay, Hythiam, Inc./50.05%, Insiders/10.70%, Robert J. Landis/5.60%, Mary Jane Johnson/4.80%, Paul Patti

Financial Data: **Fiscal Year End:**05/31 **Latest Annual Data:** 5/31/2006

Year	Sales	Net Income
2006	$23,956,000	-$181,000
2005	$24,473,000	-$268,000
2004	$27,583,000	-$777,000

Curr. Assets:	$6,682,000	**Curr. Liab.:**	$6,562,000		
Plant, Equip.:	$251,000	**Total Liab.:**	$8,925,000	**Indic. Yr. Divd.:**	NA
Total Assets:	$8,182,000	**Net Worth:**	-$743,000	**Debt/ Equity:**	NA

Comprehensive Healthcare Solutions Inc

45 Ludlow St., Ste 602, Yonkers, NY, 10705; *PH:* 1-914-375-7591; *http://* www.comprehensivehealthcaresolutions.com

General - Incorporation	DE	**Stock**- Price on:12/24/2007	NA
Employees	NA	Stock Exchange	OTC
Auditor	Jewett, Schwartz, Wolfe & Assoc.	Ticker Symbol	CMHS
Stk Agt	American Stock Transfer & Trust Co.	Outstanding Shares	NA
Counsel	NA	E.P.S.	$0.006
DUNS No.	04-618-4164	Shareholders	NA

Business: The group's principle activity is to distribute and dispense custom hearing aids. The products of the group are marketed to individual, self-pay patient, health care entities and organizations serving patient referral sources. The group currently operates three hearing sales and audiological testing facilities. The group's quarterly revenue for September 2007 was 0.94 millions of USD.

Primary SIC and add'l.: 5047

CIK No: 0000069623

Subsidiaries: Accutone Inc, Interstate Hearing Aid Service Inc

Officers: John Treglia/65/Dir., CEO, CFO, Pres.

Directors: John Treglia/65/Dir., CEO, CFO, Pres.

Owners: Insiders/7.96%, Frank J. Castanaro/5.86%, John H. Treglia/7.96%, Carlyn A. Barr/16.14%, Park Avenue Health Care Management/6.83%

Financial Data: **Fiscal Year End:**02/28 **Latest Annual Data:** 02/28/2007

Year	Sales	Net Income
2007	$108,000	$709,000
2006	$522,000	-$3,790,000
2005	$459,000	-$986,000

Curr. Assets:	$4,000	**Curr. Liab.:**	$989,000		
Plant, Equip.:	$5,000	**Total Liab.:**	$1,009,000	**Indic. Yr. Divd.:**	NA
Total Assets:	$9,000	**Net Worth:**	-$1,000,000	**Debt/ Equity:**	NA

Compton Petroleum Corp

425 - 1st St. SW, Ste. 3300, Calgary, AB, T2P 3L8; *PH:* 1-403-237-9400; *Fax:* 1-403-237-9410; *http://* www.comptonpetroleum.com; *Email:* cmt@comptonpetroleum.com

General - Incorporation	AB	Stock- Price on:12/24/2007	$10.69
Employees	NA	Stock Exchange	NYSE
Auditor	Grant Thornton LLP	Ticker Symbol	CMZ
Stk Agt	Computershare Trust Co	Outstanding Shares	129,060,000
Counsel	NA	E.P.S	$0.52
DUNS No.	NA	Shareholders	NA

Business: The groups principal activities include exploring, developing and producing natural gas, natural gas liquids and crude oil. The group operates from the Canada.

Primary SIC and add'l.: 1321 1311

CIK No: 0001043572

Officers: Ernie Sapieha/Dir., CEO, Pres., Norm Knecht/VP - Finance, CFO, B. Leonard/Mgr. - Human Resources, Administration, J. Kendrick/Mgr. - Environmental, Health, Safety, Marc Junghans/VP - Exploration, Murray Stodalka/VP - Operations - Engineering, Derek Longfield/VP - Special Projects, Tim Millar/VP, General Counsel, Corp. Sec., G. Follensbee/Mgr. - Mazeppa, T. Kosek/Controller, P. Parzen/Mgr. - Information Technology, Risk, Internal Audit, G. McCullough/Mgr. - Land, W. Mrochuk/Mgr. - Production, W. Cover/Mgr. - Drilling, Completions, R. Dion/Mgr. - Finance *(20 Officers included in Index)*

Directors: Ernie Sapieha/Dir., CEO, Pres.

Financial Data: *Fiscal Year End:*12/31 *Latest Annual Data:* 12/31/2006

Year	Sales	Net Income
2006	$351,803,000	$103,700,000
2005	$364,789,000	$71,251,000
2004	$247,631,000	$54,691,000

Curr. Assets:	$123,896,000	Curr. Liab.:	$131,560,000	P/E Ratio:	12.10
Plant, Equip.:	$1,687,999,000	Total Liab.:	$1,207,892,000	Indic. Yr. Divd.:	NA
Total Assets:	$1,829,120,000	Net Worth:	$621,228,000	Debt/ Equity:	NA

CompuCredit Corp

245 Perimeter Ctr. Pkwy., Ste. 600, Atlanta, GA, 30346; *PH:* 1-770-206-6200; *Fax:* 1-770-206-6181; *http://* www.compucredit.com; *Email:* corpinfo@compucredit.com

General - Incorporation	GA	Stock- Price on:12/24/2007	$35.56
Employees	3,600	Stock Exchange	NDQ
Auditor	BDO Seidman LLP	Ticker Symbol	CCRT
Stk Agt	Wachovia Bank N.A	Outstanding Shares	49,140,000
Counsel	Troutman Saunders LLP	E.P.S	-$1.16
DUNS No.	NA	Shareholders	NA

Business: The group's principal activities are to market credit cards and fee-based products and services including memberships, card registration, insurance products and subscription services to a specialized segment of the consumer credit market. The group purchases credit card receivables and in turn securitize all of the receivables each day by selling the receivables. The group uses analytical techniques, including sophisticated computer models to target consumer credit market that has been under served by traditional grantors of credit. Individuals in this market rely on finance companies and retail store credit cards to meet their credit. The group's database system supports decision-making functions which includes target marketing, solicitation, application processing, account management and collections activities. The group acts as an information warehouse that maintains information regarding a customer.

Primary SIC and add'l.: 6141

CIK No: 0001068199

Subsidiaries: AspireCard.com, Inc., Bluestem Holdings, LLC, C&S Intellectual Property Holdings Corp., Capacitor, LLC, CAR Financial Services, Inc., CAR Funding, Inc., Card Services, Inc., CARS Acquisition, LLC, Cash Loan Team, LLC, CCRT International Holdings, B.V., CFC, LLC, CompuCredit Acquisition Corporation, CompuCredit Acquisition Corporation II, CompuCredit Acquisition Corporation III, CompuCredit Acquisition Funding Corp. 90 Subsidiaries included in the Index

Officers: David G. Hanna/Chmn., CEO/$1,055,636.00, Richard W. Gilbert/Vice Chmn., COO/$177,574.00, Richard R. House/Dir., Pres./$19,539,610.00, Paul J. Whitehead/CFO/$919,600.00, K. K. Srinivasan/Chief Credit Officer/$1,137,098.00

Directors: David G. Hanna/Chmn., CEO, Richard W. Gilbert/Vice Chmn., COO, Deal W. Hudson/Dir., Frank J. Hanna/Dir., Richard R. House/Dir., Pres., Nicholas Paumgarten/Dir., Thomas G. Rosencrants/Dir., Mack F. Mattingly/Dir., Gregory J. Corona/Dir.

Owners: J.P. Morgan Corsair II Capital Partners, L.P./5.50%, Richard W. Gilbert/3.30%, Frank J. Hanna/26.40%, Insiders/58.20%, Gregory J. Corona, Nicholas B. Paumgarten/5.50%, Thomas K. Brown and Second Curve Capital, LLC/9.20%, Deal W. Hudson, Paul J. Whitehead, David G. Hanna/26.40%, Richard R. House/1.90%, Mack F. Mattingly, Thomas G. Rosencrants, K. K. Srinivasan

Financial Data: *Fiscal Year End:*12/31 *Latest Annual Data:* 12/31/2006

Year	Sales	Net Income
2006	$1,335,835,000	$107,475,000
2005	$948,585,000	$171,350,000
2004	$575,652,000	$100,719,000

Curr. Assets:	$912,127,000	Curr. Liab.:	$225,436,000	P/E Ratio:	50.80
Plant, Equip.:	$63,986,000	Total Liab.:	$1,189,390,000	Indic. Yr. Divd.:	NA
Total Assets:	$2,113,897,000	Net Worth:	$883,940,000	Debt/ Equity:	1.2829

CompuDyne Corp

2530 Riva Rd., Ste. 201, Annapolis, MD, 21401; *PH:* 1-410-224-4415; *http://* www.compudyne.com

General - Incorporation	NV	Stock- Price on:12/24/2007	$5.61
Employees	707	Stock Exchange	NDQ
Auditor	Aronson & Co.	Ticker Symbol	CDCY
Stk Agt	StockTrans, Inc.	Outstanding Shares	8,440,000
Counsel	Tyler Cooper & Alcorn	E.P.S	-$2.17
DUNS No.	00-226-2897	Shareholders	NA

Business: The group's principal activity is to provide products and services to public security market. The group operates in four segments: institutional security systems, attack protection, federal systems and public safety. The institutional security systems segment provides physical and electronic security products and services. The attack protection segment manufactures bullet, blast and attack resistant windows and doors designed for high-level security applications such as embassies, courthouses, federal buildings, banks, corporate headquarters and other facilities. The federal systems segment serves the federal government security needs including military, government agencies and state and local government units. The public safety segment develops, implements and supports the complex, integrated inmate management software systems that improve the efficiency of institutional security systems facility operations. On 11-Aug-2004, the group acquired 90 degrees, inc.

Primary SIC and add'l.: 7382 3812 8711

CIK No: 0000022912

Subsidiaries: CompuDyne Corp. of Maryland, CompuDyne, Inc., CompuDyne-Integrated Electronics Division, LLC, CompuDyne-Public Safety and Justice, Inc., CorrLogic, LLC, Fiber SenSys, LLC, Norment Industries S.A. (Pty) Ltd., Norment Security Group, Inc., Norshield Corporation, Xanalys Corp., Xanalys Corporation, Xanalys Limited, Xanalys Pty. Ltd.

Officers: Stuart MacKiernan/CEO, Gary A. Mangus/Contact - Institutional Security Systems, Attack Protection, William C. Rock/59/VP - Accounting, Corporate Controller, Corp. Sec., Geoffrey F. Feidelberg/CFO, Treasurer, Philip M. Blackmon/60/Exec. VP

Directors: Martin A. Roenigk/Chmn., John H. Gutfreund/Dir., David W. Clark/Dir., Wade B. Houk/Dir., Ronald J. Angelone/Dir., Albert R. Dowden/Dir.

Owners: Gary Mangus, Heartland Advisors, Inc./10.70%, David W. Clark, Martin A. Roenigk/15.10%, John H. Gutfreund, Insiders/18.74%, Dimensional Fund Advisors LP/6.29%, William C. Rock, Prescott Group Capital Management LLC/12.14%, Leviticus Partners, L.P./AMH Equity LLC/5.21%, Philip M. Blackmon, Geoffrey F. Feidelberg/1.86%, Ron Angelone, Wade B. Houk

Financial Data: *Fiscal Year End:*12/31 *Latest Annual Data:* 12/31/2006

Year	Sales	Net Income
2006	$147,462,000	-$14,993,000
2005	$141,650,000	-$8,691,000
2004	$142,782,000	-$8,198,000

Curr. Assets:	$64,164,000	Curr. Liab.:	$33,121,000		
Plant, Equip.:	$9,630,000	Total Liab.:	$77,111,000	Indic. Yr. Divd.:	NA
Total Assets:	$103,950,000	Net Worth:	$26,839,000	Debt/ Equity:	1.6978

Compugen Ltd

Compugen USA, 560 S. Winchester Blvd., Ste. 500, San Jose, CA, 95128; *PH:* 1-408-236-7336; *Fax:* 1-408-236-7334; *http://* www.compugen.co.il

General - Incorporation	Israel	Stock- Price on:12/24/2007	$2.9
Employees	80	Stock Exchange	NDQ
Auditor	Kost Forer Gabbay & Kasierer	Ticker Symbol	CGEN
Stk Agt	American Stock Transfer & Trust Co.	Outstanding Shares	28,160,000
Counsel	Yigal Arnon & Co	E.P.S	-$0.455
DUNS No.	NA	Shareholders	NA

Business: The group's principle activities are the development and marketing of platforms and tools that enhance and accelerate post-genomic research. These products also advance the study of proteins and protein pathways and support drug target discovery.

Primary SIC and add'l.: 8731 2836

CIK No: 0001119774

Subsidiaries: Compugen USA, Inc., Evogene Ltd., Keddem Bioscience Ltd.

Officers: Alex Kotzer/Dir., CEO, Pres., Nurit Benjamini/41/CFO, Yossi Cohen/VP - Research, Development, Anat Cohen-Dayag/VP - Diagnostic Biomarkers, Therapeutic Targets, Ronit Lerner/Investor Contact, Eli Zangvil/VP - Business Development, Arie Ovadia/Dir. - Consultant

Directors: Alex Kotzer/Dir., CEO, Pres., Martin S. Gerstel/Chmn., Orna Berry/58/Dir., David Schlachet/62/Dir., Nabil Hanna/Member - Scientific Advisory Board, Ronald C. Kahn/Member - Scientific Advisory Board, Joseph Schlessinger/Member - Scientific Advisory Board, Arthur Weiss/Member - Scientific Advisory Board, Yair Aharonowitz/Dir., Ruth Arnon/Dir., Arie Ovadia/Dir. - Consultant, Joshua Shemer/Dir.

Owners: AXA Assurances I.A.R.D. Mutuelle/16.51%, Clal Industries & Investments Ltd./10.85%, Martin Gerstel/6.04%

Financial Data: *Fiscal Year End:*12/31 *Latest Annual Data:* 12/31/2006

Year	Sales	Net Income
2006	$215,000	-$13,020,000
2005	$646,000	-$13,978,000
2004	$4,027,000	-$13,722,000

Curr. Assets:	$26,259,000	Curr. Liab.:	$2,950,000		
Plant, Equip.:	$2,179,000	Total Liab.:	$5,118,000	Indic. Yr. Divd.:	NA
Total Assets:	$30,856,000	Net Worth:	$25,738,000	Debt/ Equity:	NA

CompuMed Inc

5777 W Century Blvd., Ste. 1285, Los Angeles, CA, 90045; *PH:* 1-310-258-5000; *Fax:* 1-310-645-5880; *http://* www.compumed.net; *Email:* invest@compumed.net

General - Incorporation	DE	Stock- Price on:12/24/2007	$0.64
Employees	15	Stock Exchange	OTC
Auditor	Rose, Snyder & Jacobs LLP	Ticker Symbol	CMPD
Stk Agt	U.S. Stock Transfer Corp	Outstanding Shares	24,620,000
Counsel	NA	E.P.S	-$0.03
DUNS No.	08-652-2182	Shareholders	NA

Business: The group's principal activities are to provide diagnostic software solutions for the medical communities in the areas of bone mineral density measurement and the remote interpretation of electrocardiograms. The two main products are osteogram(R) and cardiogram systems. Osteogram(R) utilizes a standard X-ray of the hand to screen, diagnose and monitor osteoporosis. The cardiogram consists of computer-aided telemedicine services for cardiology that offers on-line computer interpretation of electrocardiograms (ecg's) to physicians, government and corporate healthcare providers. The group has operations in the United States, Europe, the People's Republic of China and the Middle East.

Primary SIC and add'l.: 8071 3845 8099

CIK No: 0000700998

Officers: John G. McLaughlin/CEO, Pres., Maurizio Vecchione/CEO, Pres., Manning Phillips/Dir. - Sales, Marketing, Xiaoli Bi/CTO, VP, Phuong Dang/Principal Financial Officer, Sec., Louai Al-Dayeh/Scientific Dir.

Directors: Robert Stuckelman/Chmn., John Minnick/Dir., Sydney L. Bonnick/Member - Scientific Advisory Board, Maria Greenwald/Member - Scientific Advisory Board, John Romm/Dir., Stuart L. Silverman/Dir., Member - Scientific Advisory Board, Richard Wasnich/Member - Scientific Advisory Board, Ethel S. Siris/Member - Scientific Advisory Board, Nelson B. Watts/Member - Scientific Advisory Board, Michael Kleerekoper/Member - Scientific Advisory Board, Paul Miller/Member - Scientific Advisory Board, Mark Stolper/Dir., Simon James/Dir.

Owners: Insiders/19.30%, John Minnick/4.40%, Phuong Dang, John Romm/3.80%, Maurizio Vecchione, Robert Stuckelman/6.20%, Stuart Silverman/4.90%

Financial Data: *Fiscal Year End:*09/30 *Latest Annual Data:* 9/30/2006

Year	Sales	Net Income
2006	$2,114,000	-$424,000
2005	$2,284,000	-$336,000
2004	$1,856,000	-$275,000

Curr. Assets:	$869,000	**Curr. Liab.:**	$260,000		
Plant, Equip.:	$208,000	**Total Liab.:**	$376,000	**Indic. Yr. Divd.:**	NA
Total Assets:	$1,204,000	**Net Worth:**	$828,000	**Debt/ Equity:**	0.0520

Compusonics Video Corp

33735 Enterprise Ct., Ste. 600-B, Farmington Hills, MI, 48331; *PH:* 1-248-994-0099; *Fax:* 1-248-489-9495; *http://* www.cpvd.com; *Email:* public@cpvd.com

General - Incorporation ... CO
Employees ... NA
Auditor ... UHY LLP
Stk Agt ... American Securities T & T Inc.
Counsel ... NA
DUNS No. ... 19-658-5178

Stock- Price on:12/24/2007 ... NA
Stock Exchange ... OTC
Ticker Symbol ... CPVD
Outstanding Shares ... NA
E.P.S. ... -$0.001
Shareholders ... NA

Business: The group's principle activity is to provide licensing of its patent portfolio related to audio digital recording and playback systems and parts thereof. The group develops commercial sites on the world wide Web. Delta cg product line assets represented a business line with over 600 established customers within the TV broadcast and video post production industry. Delta cg products are based upon proprietary hardware and software. Delta cg systems are capable of both analog and digital input/output support. This new business was not a successful enterprise for the group, and currently is not considered as a source of revenue. Treesoft usa inc provides leading edge cad software, erp software, crm software, software customizing and related services to small and midsize enterprises.

Primary SIC and add'l.: 7375

CIK No: 0000777844

Subsidiaries: Treesoft USA, Inc

Financial Data: **Fiscal Year End:**07/31 **Latest Annual Data:** 07/31/2005

Year	Sales	Net Income
2005	NA	-$230,000
2004	NA	-$743,000
2003	NA	-$31,000

Curr. Assets:	$3,000	**Curr. Liab.:**	$215,000		
Plant, Equip.:	$5,000	**Total Liab.:**	$215,000	**Indic. Yr. Divd.:**	NA
Total Assets:	$1,315,000	**Net Worth:**	$1,099,000	**Debt/ Equity:**	NA

Computer Horizons Corp

49 Old Bloomfield Ave., Mountain Lakes, NJ, 07046; *PH:* 1-800-322-2421; *Fax:* 1-973-402-7986; *http://* www.computerhorizons.com

General - Incorporation ... NY
Employees ... 2,890
Auditor ... Amper, Politziner & Mattia P.c
Stk Agt ... Registrar & Transfer Co
Counsel ... Sills Cummins Radin Tischman Et Al
DUNS No. ... 05-355-4382

Stock- Price on:12/24/2007 ... NA
Stock Exchange ... OTC
Ticker Symbol ... CHRZ
Outstanding Shares ... NA
E.P.S. ... $3.06
Shareholders ... NA

Business: The group's principal activities are to provide information technology services and software solutions. The group operates through three divisions: it services, solutions and chimes. The information technology services provide highly skilled software professionals to augment the internal information management staffs of major corporations. The solutions provide e-business strategy and assessment, hipaa compliance, on shore, near-shore and offshore outsourcing, enterprise network management, Web architecture designing, hosting and integration. The chimes provides workforce procurement and management services to global 2000 companies. In 2003, the group acquired it solutions operations of global business technology solutions, rgii technologies, inc and xpress software. On 01-Apr-2004, the group acquired automated information management inc.

Primary SIC and add'l.: 7373 8742 7379 7372

CIK No: 0000023019

Subsidiaries: Automated Information Management,Inc., CG Computer Services Corp., CHC Healthcare Solutions, LLC, CHC/Prince Co.,Inc., Chimes (Canada),Inc., Chimes (Puerto Rico),Inc. (Formerly: CHC Caribbean Solutions,Inc.), Chimes (UK) Limited, Chimes Netherlands B.V., Chimes Servicing Corp., CHIMES,Inc., Computer Horizons (Canada) Corp./Corporation, Computer Horizons E-Solutions (Europe) Limited, eB Networks,LLC, G. Triad Development Corp., GBS Holdings Private Limited 25 Subsidiaries included in the Index

Officers: Dennis J. Conroy/62/CEO, Pres., Barbara Moss/55/CFO, VP, David Reingold/Sr. VP - Investor Relations, Marketing, Brian A. Delle Donne/51/COO, Exec. VP, Marci Braunstein/41/Corporate Controller

Directors: Eric Rosenfeld/50/Chmn., Frank J. Tanki/67/Dir., Karl L. Meyer/69/Dir., Willem Van Rijn/58/Dir., Robert F. Walters/57/Dir.

Owners: Willem Van Rijn, Frank J. Tanki, Dennis Conroy, Karl L. Meyer, Eric Rosenfeld/7.20%, Robert F. Walters, Regan Partners L.P./11.60%, Royce & Associates, LLC/4.70%, Emancipation Capital LLC/7.90%, Marci Braunstein, Dimensional Fund Advisors, Inc/8.00%, Insiders/7.90%, Boston Avenue Capital/2.30%, Brian Delle Donne

Financial Data: **Fiscal Year End:**12/31 **Latest Annual Data:** 12/31/2006

Year	Sales	Net Income
2006	$211,990,000	-$13,438,000
2005	$268,836,000	-$46,420,000
2004	$262,527,000	-$25,172,000

Curr. Assets:	$120,595,000	**Curr. Liab.:**	$48,634,000		
Plant, Equip.:	$2,746,000	**Total Liab.:**	$49,075,000	**Indic. Yr. Divd.:**	NA
Total Assets:	$125,772,000	**Net Worth:**	$76,697,000	**Debt/ Equity:**	NA

Computer Programs and Systems Inc

6600 Wall St., Mobile, AL, 36695; *PH:* 1-251-639-8100; *Fax:* 1-251-639-8214; *http://* www.cpsinet.com

General - Incorporation ... DE
Employees ... 941
Auditor ... Grant Thornton LLP
Stk Agt ... Wachovia Bank N.A
Counsel ... Bass, Berry & Sims PLC
DUNS No. ... NA

Stock- Price on:12/24/2007 ... $31.65
Stock Exchange ... NDQ
Ticker Symbol ... CPSI
Outstanding Shares ... 10,760,000
E.P.S. ... $1.33
Shareholders ... NA

Business: The group's principle activities include designing, developing, marketing, installing and supporting computerized information technology systems. The company provided services to small and midsize hospitals. It provides comprehensive software and hardware products completed by data conversion, complete installation and extensive support. The company's fully integrated, enterprise-wide system automates the management of clinical and financial data across the primary functional areas of a hospital. In addition, the company provides outsourcing services, including electronic billing submissions, patient statement processing and business office functions, as a part of its overall information system solution. It serves more than 450 hospital customers across 45 states and the district of columbia. The group operates from United States.

Primary SIC and add'l.: 7371 7372 7375

CIK No: 0001169445

Officers: Boyd Douglas/Dir., CEO, Pres.

Directors: Boyd Douglas/Dir., CEO, Pres., David A. Dye/Chmn., John C. Johnson/Dir., Austin W. Mulherin/Dir., Charles P. Huffman/Dir., William R. Seifert/Dir., Hal L. Daugherty/Dir., John Morrissey/Dir., Ernest F. Ladd/Dir., Kenny M. Muscat/Dir.

Owners: Stephen M. Walker, Charles P. Huffman, Ernest F. Ladd, John Morrissey/3.40%, John C. Johnson, Troy D. Rosser, Kenny M. Muscat/5.10%, Palisade Capital Management, L.L.C./8.10%, Thomas W. Peterson, Boyd J. Douglas/1.20%, David A. Dye, Austin W. Mulherin, Neuberger Berman Inc./5.40%, Insiders/15.70%, Century Capital Management LLC/7.10% *(18 Owners included in Index)*

Financial Data: **Fiscal Year End:**12/31 **Latest Annual Data:** 12/31/2006

Year	Sales	Net Income
2006	$115,974,000	$15,815,000
2005	$108,826,000	$14,569,000
2004	$82,664,000	$7,064,000

Curr. Assets:	$39,253,000	**Curr. Liab.:**	$8,690,000	**P/E Ratio:**	23.80
Plant, Equip.:	$6,255,000	**Total Liab.:**	$9,198,000	**Indic. Yr. Divd.:**	$1.440
Total Assets:	$47,905,000	**Net Worth:**	$38,706,000	**Debt/ Equity:**	NA

Computer Sciences Corp

2100 E Grand Ave., El Segundo, CA, 90245; *PH:* 1-310-615-0311; *Fax:* 1-310-322-9768; *http://* www.csc.com

General - Incorporation ... NV
Employees ... 79,000
Auditor ... Deloitte & Touche LLP
Stk Agt ... Mellon Investor Services LLC
Counsel ... NA
DUNS No. ... 00-958-1091

Stock- Price on:12/24/2007 ... $57.64
Stock Exchange ... NYSE
Ticker Symbol ... CSC
Outstanding Shares ... 173,990,000
E.P.S. ... $3.08
Shareholders ... NA

Business: The group's principle activity is to provide management and information technology consulting services. The group operates in North America, Europe and Asia-pacific. The groups services include credit, hosting and legal services. In the year 2007, the group acquired Covansys Corporation. The group operates from United States.

Primary SIC and add'l.: 7372 7379 7323 7373

CIK No: 0000023082

Subsidiaries: AdvanceMed Corporation, Alliance-One Services, Inc., ASL Automated (Thailand) Ltd., ASL Automated Services (Thailand) Ltd., Automated Systems (HK) Limited, Beijing CSA Computer Sciences Technology Company Limited, Century Capital Services Corporation, Century Corporation, Century Credit Corporation, Century Leasing Corporation, Computer Sciences Canada Inc., Computer Sciences Corporation CSCEcuador S.A., Computer Sciences Corporation India Private Limited, Computer Sciences Espaa, S.A., Computer Sciences Parsons LLC 147 Subsidiaries included in the Index

Officers: Michael Shove/MD, CEO, Pres.- Csc's Australian Group, Michael W. Laphen/Chmn., CEO, Pres./$4,536,017.00, Michael E. Keane/CFO, VP/$2,249,530.00, James W. Sheaffer/North American Public Sector, Pres., Guy M. Hains/Pres. - European Group, Hayward D. Fisk/VP, General Counsel, Sec./$1,812,136.00, Mary Jo Morris/Pres. - World Sourcing Services, Paul T. Tucker/VP - Corporate Development/$2,555,202.00, Harvey N. Bernstein/61/VP - Global Legal Compliance, Assist. Sec., Irving W. Bailey/67/Dir. - Sr. Advisor, MD, Thomas R. Irvin/VP, Treasurer, Donald G. Debuck/VP, Controller, Richard Ricks/Global Infrastructure Service - Pres., George F. Bell/European Group, VP, Russ Owen/Pres. - Americas Commercial Group *(19 Officers included in Index)*

Directors: Michael W. Laphen/Chmn., CEO, Pres., B. Van Honeycutt/Chmn., Warren F. McFarlan/70/Dir., Thomas H. Patrick/64/Dir., Rodney F. Chase/65/Dir., Stephen L. Baum/67/Dir., David J. Barram/64/Dir., Irving W. Bailey/67/Dir. - Sr. Advisor, MD

Owners: David J. Barram/68.00%, Insiders/0.03%, Irving W. Bailey/68.00%, Barclays Global Investors, NA/0.10%, Goldman Sachs Asset Management, L. P./0.08%, Warren F. McFarlan/68.00%, Paul T. Tucker/56.00%, Thomas H. Patrick/68.00%, Van B. Honeycutt/0.02%, Dodge &. Cox/0.14%, Hayward D. Fisk/56.00%, Rodney F. Chase/68.00%, Michael E. Keane/56.00%, Stephen L. Baum/68.00%

Financial Data: **Fiscal Year End:**03/31 **Latest Annual Data:** 3/30/2007

Year	Sales	Net Income
2007	$14,856,600,000	$388,800,000
2006	$14,615,600,000	$634,000,000
2005	$14,058,600,000	$810,200,000

Curr. Assets:	$4,867,200,000	**Curr. Liab.:**	$3,253,200,000	**P/E Ratio:**	26.69
Plant, Equip.:	$2,178,400,000	**Total Liab.:**	$6,300,300,000	**Indic. Yr. Divd.:**	NA
Total Assets:	$11,804,000,000	**Net Worth:**	$5,503,700,000	**Debt/ Equity:**	NA

Computer Software Innovations Inc

900 E Main St., Ste. T, Easley, South Carolina, 29640; *PH:* 1-864-855-3900; *Fax:* 1-800-953-6847; *http://* www.csi-plus.com

General - Incorporation ... DE
Employees ... 107
Auditor ... Elliott Davis, LLC
Stk Agt ... Continental Stock Transfer & Trust Co
Counsel ... NA
DUNS No. ... NA

Stock- Price on:12/24/2007 ... $1.01
Stock Exchange ... OTC
Ticker Symbol ... CSWI
Outstanding Shares ... 3,500,000
E.P.S. ... $0.10
Shareholders ... NA

Business: The groups principle activities include developing software and providing hardware-based technology solutions. The group products include automated work flow, financial management software, interactive classroom, school activity accounting software. The group marketed its products under the trade names Windows(R) and Visual FoxPro(R). The groups services include consulting, network, convergence and support services. The group operates through two segments namely software applications and technology solutions. In the 2007, the group acquired McAleer. The group operates from the United States.The group's quarterly revenue for Sept 2007 was 15.35 millions of USD.

Primary SIC and add'l.: 7372

CIK No: 0001109879

Subsidiaries: CSI Technology Resources, Inc.

Officers: Nancy K. Hedrick/Dir., CEO, Pres./$190,550.00, Beverly N. Hawkins/Sec., Sr. VP - Product Development/$190,550.00, Thomas P. Clinton/Dir., Sr. VP - Strategic Relationships/$190,550.00, William J. Buchanan/Sr. VP - Delivery, Support/$190,550.00, David Dechant/CFO, Treasurer

Directors: Nancy K. Hedrick/Dir., CEO, Pres., Anthony Sobel/Chmn., Shaya Phillips/Dir., Thomas P. Clinton/Dir., Sr. VP - Strategic Relationships, Jeffery A. Bryson/Dir.

Owners: Thomas P. Clinton/14.50%, Beverly N. Hawkins/14.50%, Insiders/62.70%, Nancy K. Hedrick/14.50%, William J. Buchanan/14.50%, Jeffrey A. Bryson/0.70%, Anthony H. Sobel/2.80%, Shaya Phillips/1.40%

Financial Data: *Fiscal Year End:*12/31 *Latest Annual Data:* 12/31/2006

Year	Sales	Net Income
2006	$28,554,000	-$880,000
2005	$24,287,000	-$757,000
2004	NA	-$56,000

Curr. Assets:	$6,497,000	**Curr. Liab.:**	$9,359,000		
Plant, Equip.:	$771,000	**Total Liab.:**	$9,564,000	**Indic. Yr. Divd.:**	NA
Total Assets:	$9,460,000	**Net Worth:**	-$104,000	**Debt/ Equity:**	NA

Computer Task Group Inc

800 Delaware Ave., Buffalo, NY, 14209; *PH:* 1-716-882-8000; *Fax:* 1-716-887-7464; *http://* www.ctg.com

General - Incorporation	NY	**Stock**- Price on:12/24/2007	$4.45
Employees	3,300	Stock Exchange	NDQ
Auditor	KPMG LLP	Ticker Symbol	CTGX
Stk Agt	EquiServe Trust Co N.A	Outstanding Shares	19,920,000
Counsel	NA	E.P.S	$0.25
DUNS No.	06-364-0072	Shareholders	NA

Business: The group's principal activity is to provide information technology (IT) professional and consulting services. Services rendered include it business solution life cycle, which focuses on the planning, development, implementing, managing and maintaining the it solutions. The three primary services provided by the group are it staffing, application management outsourcing and it solutions. The group's it staffing recruits, retains and manages it talents for its clients. Application management outsourcing supports single or multiple applications and maintains a help desk. The it solutions involve selection and implementation of packaged software to design, construct, test and integrate new systems. International business machines corporation is accounted as the largest customer of the group.

Primary SIC and add'l.: 7379

CIK No: 0000023111

Subsidiaries: Computer Task Group (Holdings) Ltd, Computer Task Group (U.K.) Ltd., Computer Task Group Belgium N.V., Computer Task Group Europe B.V., Computer Task Group International, Inc., Computer Task Group of Canada, Inc., Computer Task Group of Delaware, Inc, Computer Task Group of Kansas, Inc., Computer Task Group of Luxembourg PSF, Computer Task Group of Luxembourg S.A., CTG of Buffalo, Inc., of Computer Task Group (Holdings) Ltd.), of Computer Task Group Europe B.V.), of Computer Task Group International, Inc.), of Computer Task Group, Incorporated) 16 Subsidiaries included in the Index

Officers: Tom Niehaus/Pres. - Ctghs/$510,720.00, Peter P. Radetich/Sr. VP, Sec., General Counsel

Owners: John M. Palms, Dimensional Fund Advisors LP/6.57%, George B. Beitzel/1.46%, Royce & Associates/9.94%, Thomas R.Beecher, Trustee/17.77%, Bank of America Corporation/13.76%, Randall L. Clark, Rutabaga Capital Management/5.40%, Brendan M. Harrington, Arthur W. Crumlish, Randolph A. Marks/1.99%, Thomas J. Niehaus, Daniel J. Sullivan, Filip J.L. Gyde, Thomas E. Baker *(17 Owners included in Index)*

Financial Data: *Fiscal Year End:*12/31 *Latest Annual Data:* 12/31/2006

Year	Sales	Net Income
2006	$327,253,000	$3,495,000
2005	$294,465,000	$2,423,000
2004	$237,122,000	-$1,444,000

Curr. Assets:	$62,004,000	**Curr. Liab.:**	$40,350,000	**P/E Ratio:**	19.35
Plant, Equip.:	$5,918,000	**Total Liab.:**	$50,086,000	**Indic. Yr. Divd.:**	NA
Total Assets:	$111,717,000	**Net Worth:**	$61,631,000	**Debt/ Equity:**	0.0415

Computerized Thermal Imaging Inc

1719 W 2800 S, Ogden, UT, 84401; *PH:* 1-801-776-4700; *Fax:* 1-801-459-6063; *http://* www.cti-net.com; *Email:* support@cti-net.com

General - Incorporation	NV	**Stock**- Price on:12/24/2007	NA
Employees	NA	Stock Exchange	OTC
Auditor	HJ & Assoc. LLC	Ticker Symbol	COIB
Stk Agt	Colonial Stock Transfer Co Inc	Outstanding Shares	NA
Counsel	NA	E.P.S	$0.00
DUNS No.	NA	Shareholders	NA

Business: The group's principal activities are are to design, manufacture and market thermal imaging, infrared devices and services. These are used for clinical diagnosis, pain management and non-destructive testing of industrial products and materials. The systems are configured to produce, interpret and catalogue computerized thermal images for applications in the health care industry. The group's two principal products are the breast imaging and general use systems, which are jointly referred to as medical imaging systems. Through its subsidiary, bales scientific inc, the group designs, manufactures and sells high resolution, dynamic, digital infrared imaging workstations and related products for both medical and industrial applications. The group is in the development stage.

Primary SIC and add'l.: 3841

CIK No: 0001021853

Owners: Milton R. Geilmann, Thermal Imaging, Inc./8.10%, Insiders/2.90%, Brent M. Pratley, Richard V. Secord/2.80%, Harry C. Aderholt

Financial Data: *Fiscal Year End:*06/30 *Latest Annual Data:* 06/30/2006

Year	Sales	Net Income
2006	$77,000	-$251,000
2005	$236,000	-$709,000
2004	$357,000	-$2,472,000

Curr. Assets:	$135,000	**Curr. Liab.:**	$2,321,000		
Plant, Equip.:	$6,000	**Total Liab.:**	$2,440,000	**Indic. Yr. Divd.:**	NA
Total Assets:	$151,000	**Net Worth:**	-$2,289,000	**Debt/ Equity:**	NA

Compuware Corp

1 Campus Martius, Detroit, MI, 48266; *PH:* 1-313-227-7300; *Fax:* 1-313-227-7555; *http://* www.compuware.com

General - Incorporation	MI	**Stock**- Price on:12/24/2007	$11.77
Employees	7,539	Stock Exchange	NDQ
Auditor	Deloitte & Touche LLP	Ticker Symbol	CPWR
Stk Agt	Computershare Ltd.	Outstanding Shares	301,150,000
Counsel	NA	E.P.S	$0.40
DUNS No.	07-277-3849	Shareholders	NA

Business: The group's principle activities are to develop, market and support an integrated set of systems software products. The group operates through two business segments; professional services and software products. Professional services of the group include business systems analysis, design, programming and implementation as well as software conversion and systems planning and consulting. The software products are designed to improve the productivity of data processing professionals in application development, implementation and maintenance. The group provides its services throughout North America, Europe, Asia-pacific and Brazil. The software products are sold through direct sales force in the United States, Canada, Europe, Japan, Asia-pacific, Brazil, Mexico and South Africa as well as through independent distributors in 54 other countries. The group's total revenue for 2007 was 1,213.00 millions of USD.

Primary SIC and add'l.: 7371 7372 7379

CIK No: 0000859014

Subsidiaries: Changepoint International SRL, Compuware A.B., Compuware A/S, Compuware AG, Compuware Asia Pacific Limited, Compuware Asia Pacific Pte. Ltd., Compuware Asia-Pacific Holdings Ltd., Compuware Asia-Pacific Pty. Ltd., Compuware Austria GmbH, Compuware B.V., Compuware Corporation of Canada, Compuware Covisint (Shanghai) Software Services Co. Ltd., Compuware de Mexico, Compuware do Brasil S/A, Compuware Europe B.V. 33 Subsidiaries included in the Index

Officers: Peter Karmanos/Chmn., CEO/$3,272,158.00, Donna Ventimiglia/Sr. VP - Enterprise Products Sales, Christian J. Bockhausen/Sr. VP - Technology, CIO, Lisa Elkin/VP - Corporate Communications, Investor Relations, Larry Angeli/VP - Marketing, Andrew Hittle/VP - Business Transformation, Rakesh Nagpaul/Sr. VP - Product Sales, Gery Plourde/Sr. VP - Field Technical Support, PDP, John Williams/Sr. VP - Product Solutions, Ken Baldwin/Pres., COO - Professional Services, Julie Asciutto/Sr. VP - Vertical Industry Solutions, Jamie McGuffie/Sr. VP - Partner Business Development, Tom Costello/Sr. VP, General Counsel, Sec., Denise Knobblock/Chief Administrative Officer, Laura Fournier/Sr. VP, CFO, Treasurer/$1,293,355.00 *(16 Officers included in Index)*

Directors: Peter Karmanos/Chmn., CEO, Thomas Thewes/Vice Chmn., Gurminder S. Bedi/Dir., William R. Halling/Dir., Faye Alexander Nelson/Dir., William O. Grabe/Dir., James Prowse/Dir., Scott G. Romney/Dir., Dennis W. Archer/Dir., Glenda D. Price/Dir.

Owners: Faye Alexander Nelson, Insiders/8.50%, G. Scott Romney, Massachusetts Financial Services/8.90%, Gurminder S. Bedi, Dennis W. Archer, Glenda D. Price, Henry A. Jallos/1.00%, Dodge& Cox/15.80%, William R. Halling, Robert C. Paul, Laura L. Fournier, W. James Prowse, William O. Grabe, Peter Karmanos/6.40% *(16 Owners included in Index)*

Financial Data: *Fiscal Year End:*03/31 *Latest Annual Data:* 3/31/2007

Year	Sales	Net Income
2007	$1,213,002,000	$158,092,000
2006	$1,205,361,000	$142,960,000
2005	$1,231,839,000	$76,482,000

Curr. Assets:	$921,194,000	**Curr. Liab.:**	$529,371,000		
Plant, Equip.:	$385,227,000	**Total Liab.:**	$897,264,000	**Indic. Yr. Divd.:**	NA
Total Assets:	$2,029,412,000	**Net Worth:**	$1,132,148,000	**Debt/ Equity:**	NA

CompX International Inc

5430 LBJ Fwy., Ste. 1700, Dallas, TX, 75240; *PH:* 1-972-448-1400; *Fax:* 1-972-448-1445; *http://* www.compxnet.com

General - Incorporation	DE	**Stock**- Price on:12/24/2007	$19.03
Employees	1,137	Stock Exchange	NYSE
Auditor	PricewaterhouseCoopers LLP	Ticker Symbol	CIX
Stk Agt	Computershare Investor Services LLC	Outstanding Shares	15,270,000
Counsel	NA	E.P.S	$0.69
DUNS No.	80-763-9901	Shareholders	NA

Business: The group's principal activity is to manufacture ergonomic computer support systems, precision ball bearing slides and security products for use in office furniture, computer-related applications and other industries. The group's products are principally designed for use in medium to high-end applications where product design, quality and durability are critical to the group's customer. The group has foreign operations in Canada, Netherlands and Taiwan. As of 31-Dec-2003, the group operated five manufacturing facilities in North America (two each in Illinois and Canada and one each in South Carolina and Michigan), one facility in the Netherlands and two facilities in Taiwan. The group sells its components mainly to original equipment manufacturers.

Primary SIC and add'l.: 3499 7382

CIK No: 0001049606

Officers: David A. Bowers/70/Vice Chmn., CEO, Pres., Darryl R. Halbert/43/VP, CFO - Controlle/$490,580.00, David J. Camozzi/52/VP/$402,851.00, Scott C. James/42/VP/$511,782.00, Andrew R. Louis/Sec.

Directors: David A. Bowers/70/Vice Chmn., CEO, Pres., Glenn R. Simmons/80/Chmn., Steven L. Watson/57/Dir., Norman S. Edelcup/72/Dir., Paul M. Bass/72/Dir., Ann Manix/55/Dir., Edward J. Hardin/65/Dir.

Owners: Darryl R. Halbert, TIMET Finance Management Company/100.00%, Harold C. Simmons/1.10%, Dalton, Greiner, Hartman, Maher & Co./9.20%, TIMET Finance Management Company/9.20%, Royce & Associates, LLC/5.50%, David A. Bowers/1.40%, Paul M. Bass, CompX Group, Inc./49.10%, Steven L. Watson, Annette C. Simmons, NL Industries, Inc/7.20%, Ann Manix, Insiders/4.40%, Norman S. Edelcup *(18 Owners included in Index)*

Financial Data: *Fiscal Year End:*12/31 *Latest Annual Data:* 12/31/2006

Year	Sales	Net Income
2006	$190,123,000	$11,656,000
2005	$186,349,000	$405,000
2004	$182,631,000	-$3,014,000

Curr. Assets:	$76,194,000	**Curr. Liab.:**	$17,814,000		
Plant, Equip.:	$69,688,000	**Total Liab.:**	$38,336,000	**Indic. Yr. Divd.:**	$0.500
Total Assets:	$192,026,000	**Net Worth:**	$153,690,000	**Debt/ Equity:**	NA

Comstock Homebuilding Companies Inc

11465 Sunset Hills Rd., Ste. 510, Reston, VA, 20190; *PH:* 1-703-883-1700; *Fax:* 1-703-760-1520; *http://* www.comstockhomebuilding.com

General - Incorporation .... DE
Employees 205
Auditor .... PricewaterhouseCoopers LLP
Stk Agt...... American Stock Transfer & Trust Co.
Counsel .... NA
DUNS No. .... NA

Stock- Price on:12/24/2007 .... $2.79
Stock Exchange .... NDQ
Ticker Symbol .... CHCI
Outstanding Shares 16,480,000
E.P.S. .... -$2.54
Shareholders .... NA

Business: The groups principle activity is to develop real estate services. The products of the group include single family homes, townhouses, mid rise condominiums, high rise multi-family buildings. The group operates through three segments namely Washington DC Metropolitan Area, North and South Carolina, and Georgia. In the year 2006, the group acquired Capital Homes Inc, and Parker Chandler Homes, Inc. The group operates from Washington, Raleigh, North Carolina, Atlanta and Georgia. The group's quarterly revenue for September 2007 was 51.99 millions of USD.

Primary SIC and add'l.: 1531 1521 6552 1522

CIK No: 0001299969

Subsidiaries: Buckhead Overlook, LLC, Comstock Acquisitions, L.C., Comstock Airmont, L.C., Comstock Aldie, L.C., Comstock Barrington Park, L.C., Comstock Bellemeade, L.C., Comstock Belmont Bay 5, L.C., Comstock Belmont Bay 89, L.C., Comstock Blair Mill, L.L.C., Comstock Blooms Mill II, L.C., Comstock Brandy Station, L.C., Comstock Carter Lake, L.C., Comstock Cascades, L.C., Comstock Communities, L.C., Comstock Countryside, L.C. 59 Subsidiaries included in the Index

Officers: Christopher Clemente/Chmn., CEO/$1,923,703.00, Gregory V. Benson/Dir., COO, Pres./$1,373,385.00

Directors: Christopher Clemente/Chmn., CEO, Gregory V. Benson/Dir., COO, Pres., Clayton A. Perfall/Dir., David M. Guernsey/Dir., James A. MacCutcheon/Dir., Norman D. Chirite/Dir., Robert P. Pincus/Dir., Socrates Verses/Dir.

Owners: Jason Parikh, A. Clayton Perfall, David M. Guernsey, Hayground Cove Asset Management/6.30%, Insiders/21.40%, James A. MacCuthcheon, Norman D. Chirite, Socrates Verses, Springhouse Asset Management, LLC/9.70%, Insiders/100.00%, Bruce J. Labovitz/1.10%, Gregory V. Benson/8.30%, Bonanza Capital, Ltd./7.80%, Robert P. Pincus, Royce& Associates, LLC/6.60%
(20 Owners included in Index)

Financial Data: *Fiscal Year End:*12/31 *Latest Annual Data:* 12/31/2006

Year	Sales	Net Income
2006	$245,881,000	-$39,845,000
2005	$224,305,000	$27,562,000
2004	$96,045,000	$14,303,000

Curr. Assets:	$85,431,000	**Curr. Liab.:**	$56,820,000		
Plant, Equip.:	$407,867,000	**Total Liab.:**	$393,544,000	**Indic. Yr. Divd.:**	NA
Total Assets:	$517,429,000	**Net Worth:**	$123,885,000	**Debt/ Equity:**	2.3844

Comstock Resources Inc

5300 Town and Country Blvd., Ste. 500, Frisco, TX, 75034; *PH:* 1-972-668-8800; *Fax:* 1-972-668-8812; *http://* www.comstockresources.com; *Email:* investor@comstockresources.com

General - Incorporation .... NV
Employees 130
Auditor .... Ernst & Young LLP
Stk Agt...... American Stock Transfer & Trust Co.
Counsel .... NA
DUNS No. 05-481-4132

Stock- Price on:12/24/2007 .... $30.94
Stock Exchange .... NYSE
Ticker Symbol .... CRK
Outstanding Shares 44,410,000
E.P.S. $1.27
Shareholders .... NA

Business: The group's principal activities are acquisition, development, production and exploration of oil and natural gas properties. The group's oil and natural gas operations are concentrated in the east Texas/ north Louisiana, gulf of Mexico, southeast Texas and south Texas regions. The group also has properties in the Illinois basin region in Kentucky and in the mid-continent regions located in the Texas panhandle, Oklahoma and Kansas.

Primary SIC and add'l.: 1311

CIK No: 0000023194

Subsidiaries: Comstock Offshore, LLC, Comstock Oil & Gas Louisiana, LLC, Comstock Oil & Gas GP, LLC, Comstock Oil & Gas Holdings, Inc., Comstock Oil & Gas Investments, LLC, Comstock Oil & Gas, LP

Officers: Jay M. Allison/Chmn., CEO, Pres./$6,426,446.00, Dale D. Gillette/General Counsel, VP - Land, Richard D. Singer/VP - Corporate Reporting, Daniel K. Presley/VP - Accounting, Controller/$482,621.00, Stephen E. Neukom/VP - Marketing/$496,359.00, Mack D. Good/VP - Operations/$1,057,862.00, Roland O. Burns/Sr. VP, CFO, Corp. Sec./$2,537,440.00

Directors: Jay M. Allison/Chmn., CEO, Pres., David W. Sledge/Dir., Nancy E. Underwood/Dir., Cecil E. Martin/Dir., Roland O. Burns/Sr. VP, CFO, Corp. Sec., David K. Lockett/Dir.

Owners: Richard D. Singer, Dale D. Gillette, Nancy E. Underwood, Neuberger Berman, Inc./5.10%, Cecil E. Martin, Stephen E. Neukom, David K. Lockett, Dimensional Funds Advisors, LP/5.00%, Wellington Management Company, LLP/6.30%, Third Avenue Management, LLC/7.80%, Daniel K. Presley, Insiders/6.40%, David W. Sledge, Mack D. Good

Financial Data: *Fiscal Year End:*12/31 *Latest Annual Data:* 12/31/2006

Year	Sales	Net Income
2006	$511,928,000	$70,665,000
2005	$303,336,000	$60,479,000
2004	$261,647,000	$46,867,000

Curr. Assets:	$98,828,000	**Curr. Liab.:**	$151,861,000	**P/E Ratio:**	25.36
Plant, Equip.:	$1,773,626,000	**Total Liab.:**	$975,213,000	**Indic. Yr. Divd.:**	NA
Total Assets:	$1,878,125,000	**Net Worth:**	$682,563,000	**Debt/ Equity:**	0.7320

COMSYS IT Partners Inc

4400 Post Oak Pkwy., Ste. 1800, Houston, TX, 77027; *PH:* 1-713-386-1400; *Fax:* 1-713-961-0719; *http://* www.comsys.com

General - Incorporation .... DE
Employees 4,297
Auditor .... Ernst & Young LLP
Stk Agt .... Wachovia Bank N.A
Counsel .... NA
DUNS No. .... NA

Stock- Price on:12/24/2007 .... $22.4
Stock Exchange .... NDQ
Ticker Symbol .... CITP
Outstanding Shares 19,700,000
E.P.S. $1.50
Shareholders .... NA

Business: The groups principle activity is to provide information technology services. The group provides staffing services. The groups recruiting areas include Website development and integration, application programming and development, client/server development, systems software architecture and design, systems engineering and systems integration. The group operates from United States.

Primary SIC and add'l.: 7376 8744

CIK No: 0000948850

Subsidiaries: COMSYS Information Technology Services, Inc., COMSYS Services LLC

Officers: Larry L. Enterline/Dir., CEO/$1,928,248.00, David L. Kerr/Sr. VP - Corporate Development/$796,046.00, Michael H. Barker/COO/$756,178.00, Joseph C. Tusa/Sr. VP, CFO/$850,522.00, Terry V. Bell/VP - Human Resources, Jerry Jewell/Sr. VP - Sales, Brian Westphal/VP - Customer Service, Kip Wright/Sr. VP - Managed Solutions, Ken Bramlett/Sr. VP, General Counsel, Corp. Sec./$576,795.00, Amy Bobbitt/VP - Finance

Directors: Larry L. Enterline/Dir., CEO, Robert Z. Hensley/Dir., Elias J. Sabo/Dir., Victor E. Mandel/Dir., Frederick W. Eubank/Dir., Robert Fotsch/Dir., Courtney R. McCarthy/Dir.

Owners: Insiders/10.70%, Amalgamated Gadget, L.P./10.80%, Ken R. Bramlett, Robert Fotsch, Michael H. Barker, David L. Kerr, Robert Z. Hensley, Victor E. Mandel, Larry L. Enterline/1.90%, Links Partners, L.P./5.80%, Elias J. Sabo/5.80%, Wachovia Investors, Inc./20.10%, Joseph C. Tusa/1.00%

Financial Data: *Fiscal Year End:*01/01 *Latest Annual Data:* 12/31/2006

Year	Sales	Net Income
2006	$736,645,000	$21,047,000
2005	$437,013,000	-$55,155,000

Curr. Assets:	$194,956,000	**Curr. Liab.:**	$182,899,000	**P/E Ratio:**	19.15
Plant, Equip.:	$9,214,000	**Total Liab.:**	$280,264,000	**Indic. Yr. Divd.:**	NA
Total Assets:	$375,034,000	**Net Worth:**	$94,770,000	**Debt/ Equity:**	0.9679

Comtech Group Inc

Rm. 10001, Tower C, Skyworth Bldg, High-Tech Industrial Pk., Nanshan, Shenzhen, 518057; *PH:* 86-75526743210; *http://* www.comtech.com.cn

General - Incorporation .... MD
Employees 700
Auditor .... Deloitte Touche Tohmatsu
Stk Agt ..... American Stock Transfer & Trust Co.
Counsel .... Loeb & Loeb
DUNS No. .... NA

Stock- Price on:12/24/2007 .... $16.89
Stock Exchange .... NDQ
Ticker Symbol .... COGO
Outstanding Shares 37,570,000
E.P.S. $0.54
Shareholders .... NA

Business: The groups principle activity is to provide computer and hi-tech consulting services. The group operates from United States.

Primary SIC and add'l.: 8742

CIK No: 0000028367

Subsidiaries: Alphalink Global Limited, Comtech (China) Holding Limited, Comtech (Hong Kong) Holding Limited, Comtech Group, Comtech International (Hong Kong) Limited, Comtech Software Technology Company Limited, Shanghai E&T System Company Limited, Shenzhen Comtech International Limited, United Information Technology Company Limited

Officers: Jeffrey Kang/Chmn., CEO, Pres., Henry Li/VP - Marketing, Engineering, Hope Ni/CFO, Sec., Allen Wu/Controller, Shi Yang/VP - Sales

Directors: Jeffrey Kang/Chmn., CEO, Pres., Amy Kong/Dir., Q. Y. Ma/Dir., Frank Zheng/Dir.

Owners: Fuya Zheng, Comtech Global Investment, Ltd./25.13%, Q. Y. Ma, Yi Kang/5.96%, Hope Ni, Jeffrey Kang/26.30%, Ren Investment International, Ltd./5.96%, Amy Kong, Insiders/26.88%, Nan Ji/25.13%

Financial Data: *Fiscal Year End:*12/31 *Latest Annual Data:* 12/31/2006

Year	Sales	Net Income
2006	$169,598,000	$15,796,000
2005	$107,350,000	$10,761,000
2004	$75,587,000	$7,515,000

Curr. Assets:	$105,991,000	**Curr. Liab.:**	$30,950,000	**P/E Ratio:**	33.12
Plant, Equip.:	$1,588,000	**Total Liab.:**	$31,160,000	**Indic. Yr. Divd.:**	NA
Total Assets:	$116,233,000	**Net Worth:**	$85,073,000	**Debt/ Equity:**	NA

Comtech Telecommunications Corp

68 S Service Rd., Ste. 230, Melville, NY, 11747; *PH:* 1-631-962-7000; *Fax:* 1-631-962-7001; *http://* www.comtechtel.com; *Email:* info@comtechtel.com

General - Incorporation .... DE
Employees .... NA
Auditor .... KPMG LLP
Stk Agt ..... American Stock Transfer & Trust Co.
Counsel .... Proskauer Rose
DUNS No. 04-186-8365

Stock- Price on:12/24/2007 .... $44.87
Stock Exchange .... NDQ
Ticker Symbol .... CMTL
Outstanding Shares 23,210,000
E.P.S. $2.25
Shareholders .... NA

Business: The group's principal activity is to manufacture and market sophisticated wireless telecommunications transmission products and solid state high-power broadband amplifiers for commercial and government purposes. The business of the group is carried out through three segments: telecommunications transmission, rf microwave amplifiers and mobile data communications services. The products of the group includes modems, frequency up converters and down converters, solid state high-power amplifiers, vsat transceivers and antennas and adaptive modems and microwave radios. The mobile data communications services provide secure, real time two-way location of and messaging between mobile platforms.

Primary SIC and add'l.: 4812 3663

CIK No: 0000023197

Subsidiaries: Comtech AHA Corporation, Comtech Antenna Systems, Inc., Comtech EF Data Corp., Comtech Mobile Datacom Corporation, Comtech PST Corp., Comtech Systems, Inc., Comtech Tolt Technologies, Inc., Comtech Vipersat Networks, Inc., Memotec Inc.

Officers: Fred Kornberg/Chmn., CEO, Pres., William Thomson/Pres. - Comtech AHA Corporation, Larry Konopelko/Sr. VP, Thomas Christy/Pres. - Comtech Antenna Systems, Inc, Robert Rouse/COO, Exec. VP, Michael Porcelain/Sr. VP, CFO, Robert McCollum/Sr. VP, Richard Burt/Sr. VP, Jerome Kapelus/Sr. VP - Strategy, Business Development, Daniel Wood/Sr. VP, Pres. - Comtech Mobile Datacom Corp, Patrick Ogara/Sec.

Directors: Fred Kornberg/Chmn., CEO, Pres., Edwin Kantor/Dir., Gerard R. Nocita/Dir., Ira Kaplan/Dir., Richard L. Goldberg/Dir., Robert G. Paul/Dir.

Owners: Robert L. McCollum, Robert G. Rouse, Richard L. Burt, Ira Kaplan, Gerard R. Nocita, Edwin Kantor, Barclays Global Investors NA/5.00%, Insiders/2.90%, Michael D. Porcelain, Paradigm Capital Management, Inc./PCM/6.60%, Fred Kornberg/1.10%, Lord Abbett & Co. LLC/5.90%, Richard L. Goldberg

Financial Data: ***Fiscal Year End:***07/31 ***Latest Annual Data:*** 7/31/2006

Year		Sales		Net Income
2006		$391,511,000		$45,269,000
2005		$307,890,000		$36,655,000
2004		$223,390,000		$21,827,000
Curr. Assets:	$398,449,000	**Curr. Liab.:**	$89,463,000	**P/E Ratio:** 19.94
Plant, Equip.:	$24,732,000	**Total Liab.:**	$201,024,000	**Indic. Yr. Divd.:** NA
Total Assets:	$455,266,000	**Net Worth:**	$254,242,000	**Debt/ Equity:** NA

Comtex News Network Inc

625 N Washington St., Ste. 301, Alexandria, VA, 22314; ***PH:*** 1-703-820-2000; ***Fax:*** 1-703-820-2005; ***http://*** www.comtexnews.net; ***Email:*** investor@comtex.com

General - Incorporation	DE	***Stock***- Price on:12/24/2007	$0.23
Employees	25	Stock Exchange	OTC
Auditor	Goldstein Golub Kessler LLP	Ticker Symbol	CMTX
Stk Agt	American Stock Transfer & Trust Co.	Outstanding Shares	15,290,000
Counsel	NA	E.P.S	$0.005
DUNS No.	05-261-6166	Shareholders	NA

Business: The group's principal activity is to provide real-time news content through network of news publishers. The core products of the group include a series of topic- defined real-time news products (customwires) and editorially selected top news products (comtex newsroom). The group's customers include business and consumer online services, personal investor Web sites, general information Web sites, wall street stock quote vendors, electronic clipping services and wireless information services. Customwires contain topic-relevant stories from more than 20,000 stories daily, from approximately 70 publishing providers. Comtex newsroom includes broad range of news story options includes financial markets, industries, general market and world news.

Primary SIC and add'l.: 7383

CIK No: 0000352988

Subsidiaries: nFactory Comtex, S.L

Officers: Chip Brian/CEO, Pres., Kathy Ballard/VP - Content, Amber Gordon/Corp. Sec., Executive Dir. - Communications, Investor Relations

Directors: C. W. Gilluly/Chmn., Erik Hendricks/Dir., Pieter Vanbennekom/Dir., William J. Howard/Dir., Robert J. Lynch/Dir.

Owners: Tepco Ltd./24.00%, Chip Brian/8.90%, William J. Howard, Rick McNulty, Insiders/25.20%, C. W. Gilluly/16.20%, Erik Hendricks, Pieter VanBennekom, Kathy Ballard/1.30%, Robert J. Lynch

Financial Data: ***Fiscal Year End:***06/30 ***Latest Annual Data:*** 06/30/2007

Year		Sales		Net Income
2007		$7,069,000		-$107,000
2006		$7,677,000		-$458,000
2005		$7,970,000		$729,000
Curr. Assets:	$2,753,000	**Curr. Liab.:**	$1,379,000	
Plant, Equip.:	$178,000	**Total Liab.:**	$2,238,000	**Indic. Yr. Divd.:** NA
Total Assets:	$2,969,000	**Net Worth:**	$731,000	**Debt/ Equity:** NA

Comverse Technology Inc

810 Seventh Ave., New York, NY, 10019; ***PH:*** 1-212-739-1000; ***http://*** www.cmvt.com

General - Incorporation	NY	***Stock***- Price on:12/24/2007	NA
Employees	5,050	Stock Exchange	OTC
Auditor	Deloitte & Touche LLP	Ticker Symbol	CMVT
Stk Agt	American Stock Transfer & Trust Co.	Outstanding Shares	NA
Counsel	NA	E.P.S	$0.55
DUNS No.	13-020-5297	Shareholders	NA

Business: The group's principle activity is to design, develop, manufacture, market and support computer and telecommunication systems and software for multimedia communications. The group operates through three segments: comverse network system enable telecommunications service providers to offer a variety of revenue-generating services; the service enabling signaling software provides service enabling signaling software for wireline, wireless and Internet communications.; the security and business intelligence recording products provide analytic software-based solutions for communications interception, digital video security and surveillance and enterprise business intelligence. The group operates in the United States, Germany, Japan and other European countries.

Primary SIC and add'l.: 7375 7372

CIK No: 0000803014

Subsidiaries: Amarex Technology, Inc., Boston Technology Foreign Sales Corp., Boston Technology International, Inc., Boston Technology Mexico, Inc., ComSor Investment Fund LDC, ComSor Venture Fund LDC, Comverpor Sistemas De Tlelecomunicacoes, LDA, Comverse (NZ) Limited, Comverse Argentina, S.A., Comverse Australasia Pty Ltd., Comverse Belgium SA, Comverse Chile, Inc., Comverse Denmark ApS, Comverse do Brasil Ltd., Comverse Finland OY 83 Subsidiaries included in the Index

Officers: Raz Alon/Dir., CEO

Directors: Raz Alon/Dir., CEO, Mark Terrell/Non Exec. Chmn., Andre Dahan/Dir., Susan D. Bowick/Dir., Charles J. Burdick/Dir., Richard N. Nottenburg/Dir., Joseph Odonnell/Dir., Augustus K. Oliver/Dir., Alex A. Porter/Dir., Theodore H. Schell/Dir.

Owners: Avi Aronovitz, Insiders, FMR Corporation/14.60%, Zeev Bregman, Paul Robinson, Capital Research and Management Company/10.40%, Dan Bodner, Raz Alon

Financial Data: ***Fiscal Year End:***01/31 ***Latest Annual Data:*** 01/31/2005

Year		Sales		Net Income
2005		$959,442,000		$57,330,000
2004		$765,892,000		-$5,386,000
2003		$735,889,000		-$129,478,000
Curr. Assets:	$2,627,088,000	**Curr. Liab.:**	$487,299,000	
Plant, Equip.:	$122,174,000	**Total Liab.:**	$935,432,000	**Indic. Yr. Divd.:** NA
Total Assets:	$2,925,286,000	**Net Worth:**	$1,794,029,000	**Debt/ Equity:** NA

Con-way Incorporated

Formerly: CNF Inc

2855 Campus Dr., San Mateo, CA, 94403; ***PH:*** 1-650-494-2900; ***https://*** www.con-way.com

General - Incorporation	DE	***Stock***- Price on:12/24/2007	NA
Employees	21,800	Stock Exchange	NYSE
Auditor	KPMG LLP	Ticker Symbol	NA
Stk Agt	Bank of New York	Outstanding Shares	NA
Counsel	NA	E.P.S	$4.08
DUNS No.	00-690-9519	Shareholders	NA

Business: The group's principal activity is to provide supply chain management services for commercial and industrial shipments by land, air and sea. The group operates in four segments: con-way transportation services, emery forwarding, menlo logistics and other. The con-way transportation services segment provides freight trucking in the United States, Canada and Mexico, as well as expedited transportation, air freight forwarding and truckload brokerage services. The emery forwarding segment provides domestic and international air freight and ocean forwarding services, customs brokerage and other trade services. The menlo logistics segment develops integrated contract logistics solutions, including the management of distribution networks and supply engineering and consulting. The other segment includes the operating results of road systems.

Primary SIC and add'l.: 4213 4215 4513

CIK No: 0000023675

Subsidiaries: Con-Way Transportation Services, Inc., Menlo Worldwide, LLC

Officers: Douglas W. Stotlar/Pres., CEO - Con, way Inc/$3,826,091.00, Jennifer W. Pileggi/Sr. VP, General Counsel, Corp. Sec. - Con, way Inc, Leslie P. Lundberg/VP - Human Resources, Con, way Inc, Randal C. Mullett/VP - Government Relations, Con, way Inc, Richard Lunardi/VP - Strategic Planning, Con, way Inc, Julia P. Jannausch/VP - Culture, Training, Con, way Inc, John J. Anton/Dir. - Private Investor, Mark C. Thickpenny/VP, Treasurer - Con, way Inc, Michael D. Yuenger/VP - Finance, Con, way Freight Inc, Sean M. Devine/VP - Engineering, Con, way Freight Inc, Donald C. Fegtly/VP - Sales, Con, way Truckload Services Inc, Herb Schmidt/Pres. - CFI, a Con, way Company, Gregory W. Lehmkuhl/VP - Menlo Automotive Industry Group, Menlo Worldwide, Inc, David L. Miller/COO - Con, way Freight Inc, Jacquelyn A. Barretta/CIO, VP - Con, way Inc *(41 Officers included in Index)*

Directors: Keith W. Kennedy/Chmn., Chelsea C. White/Dir., Margaret G. Gill/Dir., Robert D. Rogers/Dir., William R. Corbin/Dir., Peter W. Stott/Dir., William J. Schroeder/Dir., John J. Anton/Dir. - Private Investor, Robert Jaunich/Dir., Henry H. Mauz/Dir., Michael J. Murray/Dir., John C. Pope/Dir., Robert P. Wayman/Dir.

Owners: Douglas W. Stotlar, William R. Corbin, Chelsea C. White, W. Keith Kennedy, Insiders/1.20%, Kevin C. Schick, Robert D. Rogers, Margaret G. Gill, Robert L. Bianco, Henry H. Mauz, Michael J. Murray, Peter W. Stott, David S. McClimon, John G. Labrie, John J. Anton *(19 Owners included in Index)*

Financial Data: ***Fiscal Year End:***12/31 ***Latest Annual Data:*** 12/31/2006

Year		Sales		Net Income
2006		$4,221,478,000		$266,132,000
2005		$4,169,590,000		$223,029,000
2004		$3,712,379,000		-$115,889,000
Curr. Assets:	$1,090,484,000	**Curr. Liab.:**	$559,802,000	
Plant, Equip.:	$1,117,975,000	**Total Liab.:**	$1,561,110,000	**Indic. Yr. Divd.:** $0.400
Total Assets:	$2,301,889,000	**Net Worth:**	$740,779,000	**Debt/ Equity:** NA

ConAgra Foods Inc

1 ConAgra Dr., Omaha, NE, 68102; ***PH:*** 1-402-595-4000; ***Fax:*** 1-402-595-4707; ***http://*** www.conagra.com

General - Incorporation	DE	***Stock***- Price on:12/24/2007	$25.73
Employees	33,000	Stock Exchange	NYSE
Auditor	KPMG LLP	Ticker Symbol	CAG
Stk Agt	Wells Fargo Shareowner Services	Outstanding Shares	498,090,000
Counsel	NA	E.P.S	$1.62
DUNS No.	00-725-8908	Shareholders	NA

Business: The groups principle activities include manufacturing and marketing processed and packaged foods. The group operates through three segments namely retail, foodservice products and food ingredients. The groups products line include meals, entrees, prepared potatoes, meats, seafood, and sauces. The group operates from United States.

Primary SIC and add'l.: 2011 2099 2879 2033 2041

CIK No: 0000023217

Subsidiaries: ConAgra Foods Canada, Inc, ConAgra Foods Export Company, Inc., ConAgra Foods Food Ingredients Company, Inc, ConAgra Foods Packaged Foods Company, Inc., ConAgra Grocery Products Company, LLC, ConAgra International Fertilizer Company, ConAgra International, Inc., ConAgra Limited/ConAgra Limite, ConAgra Trade Group, Inc

Officers: Gary M. Rodkin/Chmn., CEO/$14,272,210.00, Peter M. Perez/Sr. VP - Human Resources, Douglas A. Knudsen/Pres. - Conagra Foods Sales, Al Bolles/Exec. VP - Research, Quality, Innovation, Robert F. Sharpe/Exec. VP - Legal, External Affairs/$5,141,928.00, Mark J. Warner/42/VP - Internal Audit, Andre Hawaux/CFO, Exec. VP/$2,596,792.00, Leo Knowles/Sr. VP, Chief Litigation Counsel, Scott E. Messel/49/Sr. VP, Treasurer, Assist. Corp. Sec./$1,909,473.00, Joan Chow/Exec. VP, Chief Marketing Officer, King Pouw/Exec. VP - Operations, Business Transformation, Albert D. Bolles/Exec. VP - Research, Development, Quality, Dean R. Hollis/COO, Pres. - Consumer Foods, Owen C. Johnson/Exec. VP, Chief Administrative Officer/$5,422,535.00, James H. Hardy/Exec. VP - Product Supply *(20 Officers included in Index)*

Directors: Gary M. Rodkin/Chmn., CEO, W. G. Jurgensen/Dir., Carl E. Reichardt/Dir., Mark H. Rauenhorst/Dir., Stephen G. Butler/Dir., Steven F. Goldstone/Dir., Mogens C. Bay/Dir., Kenneth E. Stinson/Dir., John T. Chain/Dir., Ruth Ann Marshall/Dir., Andrew J. Schindler/Dir., Alice B. Hayes/Dir., Ronald W. Roskens/Dir.

Owners: State Street Bank and Trust Company/5.40%, W. G. Jurgensen, Stephen G. Butler, Ronald W. Roskens, Mark H. Rauenhorst, Capital Research and Management Company/6.10%, Jacqueline McCook, Carl E. Reichardt, Andre J. Hawaux, Gary M. Rodkin, Steven F. Goldstone, Kenneth E. Stinson, Robert F. Sharpe, Alice B. Hayes, John T. Chain *(20 Owners included in Index)*

Financial Data: *Fiscal Year End:*05/28 *Latest Annual Data:* 05/27/2007

Year	Sales	Net Income
2007	$12,028,200,000	$764,600,000
2006	$11,579,400,000	$533,800,000
2005	$14,566,900,000	$641,500,000

Curr. Assets:	$5,149,300,000	**Curr. Liab.:**	$3,004,500,000	**P/E Ratio:**	20.92
Plant, Equip.:	$2,880,000,000	**Total Liab.:**	$9,428,300,000	**Indic. Yr. Divd.:**	$0.720
Total Assets:	$14,222,200,000	**Net Worth:**	$4,793,900,000	**Debt/ Equity:**	0.7363

Conceptus Inc

331 E Evelyn, Mountain View, CA, 94041; *PH:* 1-650-628-4700; *Fax:* 1-650-610-8368; *http://* www.conceptus.com; *Email:* publicrelations@conceptus.com

General		**Stock**	
Incorporation	DE	Price on:12/24/2007	$18.96
Employees	181	Stock Exchange	NDQ
Auditor	PricewaterhouseCoopers LLP	Ticker Symbol	CPTS
Stk Agt	Mellon Investor Services LLC	Outstanding Shares	29,410,000
Counsel	Latham & Watkins	E.P.S.	-$0.44
DUNS No.	79-785-6572	Shareholders	NA

Business: The group's principal activity is to develop, manufacture and market essure tm, an innovative and proprietary non-incisional permanent birth control device for women. The group's focus is to improve diagnostic and therapeutic procedures in gynecology. The products are designed to provide non-surgical approach and diagnostic procedures to treat infertility and related disorders. The group is currently focused on developing its selective tubal occlusion procedure system, which is a non-surgical approach to fallopian tube sterilization. This helps physicians to perform fallopian tube sterilization in an office setting without general anesthesia. The products of the group are marketed through distributors in Europe, Australia, Asia and Canada.

Primary SIC and add'l.: 2836

CIK No: 0000896778

Subsidiaries: Conceptus (Australia) Pty Limited, Conceptus SAS

Officers: Mark M. Sieczkarek/Dir., CEO, Pres./$2,531,291.00, Gregory E. Lichtwardt/Exec. VP, Treasurer, CFO/$1,045,961.00, Lisa Pohmajevich/VP - Marketing/$610,581.00, Ulric Cote/VP - Sales/$829,069.00, Edward J. Sinclair/VP - Clinical Research, Regulatory Affairs, Quality Assurance/$638,998.00, Darrin Uecker/VP - Research & Development and Operations, Spencer Roeck/VP - International, Kim Sutton Golodetz/Investor Relation Officer

Directors: Mark M. Sieczkarek/Dir., CEO, Pres., Kathryn A. Tunstall/Chmn., Peter L. Wilson/Dir., Rob Zurawin/Member - Medical Advisory Board, Andrew Brill/Member - Medical Advisory Board, Vivian Connor/Member - Medical Advisory Board, Barbara Levy/Member - Medical Advisory Board, Robert V. Toni/Dir., Annette Bianchi/Dir., Michael W. Baker/Dir., Thomas F. Bonadio/Dir., John E. Nichols/Member - Medical Advisory Board, Mark D. Levie/Member - Medical Advisory Board

Owners: Massachusetts Financial Services Company/4.27%, Mark Sieczkarek/2.09%, Robert Toni, Gregory Lichtwardt, Edward Sinclair, Peter Wilson, Annette Bianchi, VantagePoint Venture Partners/8.48%, Lisa Pohmajevich, Kathryn Tunstall/1.23%, Federated Investors,Inc./19.13%, Insiders/6.50%, Tom Bonadio, Michael Baker, FMR Corporation/12.45% *(18 Owners included in Index)*

Financial Data: *Fiscal Year End:*12/31 *Latest Annual Data:* 12/31/2006

Year	Sales	Net Income
2006	$41,900,000	-$18,487,000
2005	$21,169,000	-$21,801,000
2004	$11,612,000	-$26,069,000

Curr. Assets:	$34,488,000	**Curr. Liab.:**	$8,409,000		
Plant, Equip.:	$2,917,000	**Total Liab.:**	$8,737,000	**Indic. Yr. Divd.:**	NA
Total Assets:	$39,751,000	**Net Worth:**	$31,014,000	**Debt/ Equity:**	4.1065

Concha & Toro Winery Inc

Avenida Nueva Tajamar 481, Torre Norte, Piso 15, Santiago; *PH:* 56-24765000; *http://* www.conchaytoro.com

General		**Stock**	
Incorporation	Chile	Price on:12/24/2007	$49.46
Employees	1,949	Stock Exchange	NYSE
Auditor	Deloitte & Touche LLP	Ticker Symbol	NA
Stk Agt	Bank of New York	Outstanding Shares	35,960,000
Counsel	NA	E.P.S.	$1.28
DUNS No.	NA	Shareholders	NA

Business: The group's principal activities are processing and marketing of wines, champagnes, licorice and mineral water. Engages in importing, exporting, purchasing, selling, distributing, acquiring and transferring in general all types of merchandise within and outside of Chile. It also engages in rendering all types of service related to transportation and freight within and outside the country through the use of trucks and other vehicles. Major trademarks include: concha y toro, don melchor, amelia, terrunyo, marques de casas concha, trio, casillero del diablo, tocornal, cono sur, subercaseaux, clos de pirque & maipo. It exports its products in the us, UK Ireland, Norway, Denmark, Argentina, Brazil, uruguay, Colombia, Mexico, Ecuador and venezuela.

Primary SIC and add'l.: 2085 3799 2084

CIK No: 0000930543

Subsidiaries: 1338768 Ontario Inc, 1342077 Ontario Inc, African Metals Ltd, Aluminium Consortium Venezuela B.V., Angola Mining Finance Ltd, Angola Mining Services Ltd, Angola Technical Services Ltd, Atlas Steels Company Ltd, Auvernier Limited (in liquidation), Banicttor Mining (Pty) Ltd, BHP Billiton (BVI) Ltd, BHP Billiton (RA) Limited (in liquidation), BHP Billiton (UK) Limited, BHP Billiton Aluminium Ltd, UK Limited 16 Subsidiaries included in the Index

Officers: Eduardo Guilisasti Gana/GM, CEO, Alfonso Larrain Santa Maria/Chmn., Agricultural Mgr., Jose Antonio Manasevich Gavicagogeascoa/Operation Mgr., Osvaldo Solar Venegas/Administration, Finance Mgr., CFO, Tomas Larrain Leon/Corporate Export Mgr. - USA, Cristian Canevaro Jaramillo/GM - Comercial Peumo, Adolfo Hurtado Cerda/GM - Vina Cono SUR, Andres Izquierdo Bacarreza/GM - Trivento Bodegas Y Vinedos, Cristian Lopez Pascual/GM - Concha Y Toro UK, Carlos Saavedra Echeverria/Engineering, Projects Mgr., Blanca Bustamante/Head - Investor Relations, Cristian Ceppi Lewin/Corporate Export Mgr. - Souther Zone, Goetz Von Gersdorff/Technical Dir., Daniel Duran Urizar/Information Technology Mgr., Isabel Guilisasti Gana/Marketing Mgr. - Specific Origin Wines *(19 Officers included in Index)*

Directors: Alfonso Larrain Santa Maria/Chmn., Agricultural Mgr., Rafael Guilisasti Gana/Vice Chmn., Christian Skibsted-hansen Cortes/Dir., Sergio De La Cuadra Fabres/66/Dir., Pablo Guilisasti Gana/Dir., Mariano Fontecilla De Santiago Concha/Dir., Francisco Marin Estevez/Dir.

Owners: La Gloria S.A., Goetz Von Gersdorff, Citibank Chile C. Terceros Cap. XIV, Francisco Marn Estvez, Inversiones Totihue S.A., Eduardo Guilisasti Gana, Inversiones Quivolgo S.A., Osvaldo Solar Venegas, Christian Skibsted-Hansen Corts, Fundacin Cultura Nacional, Mariano Fontecilla de Santiago Concha, Domeyko C. Thomas, Insiders, AFP Habitat S.A., Pablo Guilisasti Gana *(27 Owners included in Index)*

Financial Data: *Fiscal Year End:*12/31 *Latest Annual Data:* 12/31/2005

Year	Sales	Net Income
2005	$382,597,000	$39,711,000
2004	$338,773,000	$41,238,000
2003	$260,685,000	$32,104,000

Curr. Assets:	$279,182,000	**Curr. Liab.:**	$132,431,000	**P/E Ratio:**	38.64
Plant, Equip.:	$283,229,000	**Total Liab.:**	$261,825,000	**Indic. Yr. Divd.:**	$0.180
Total Assets:	$579,935,000	**Net Worth:**	$318,093,000	**Debt/ Equity:**	NA

Concierge Technologies Inc

22048 Sherman Way, Ste. 301, Canoga Park, CA, 91303; *PH:* 1-818-610-0310

General		**Stock**	
Incorporation	NV	Price on:12/24/2007	$0.008
Employees	NA	Stock Exchange	OTC
Auditor	Kabani & Company, Inc.	Ticker Symbol	CNCG
Stk Agt	Bank One Trust Co.	Outstanding Shares	147,290,000
Counsel	Legal Concierge Inc.	E.P.S.	$0.00
DUNS No.	NA	Shareholders	NA

Business: The groups principal activity is to market the software application product known as the Personal Communications Attendant. The group operates from the United States.

Primary SIC and add'l.: 7389

CIK No: 0001005101

Subsidiaries: Planet Halo, Inc.

Owners: Polly Force Co., Ltd./6.10%, Marc Angell/5.20%, Allen E. Kahn/8.30%, Patrick F. Flaherty/1.90%, David W. Neibert, Fiori Product Development, Insiders/30.20%, James E. Kirk/1.90%, Samuel C.H. Wu/11.80%

Financial Data: *Fiscal Year End:*06/30 *Latest Annual Data:* 6/30/2006

Year	Sales	Net Income
2006	NA	-$45,000
2005	NA	-$544,000
2004	NA	-$515,000

Curr. Assets:	$4,000	**Curr. Liab.:**	$533,000		
Plant, Equip.:	NA	**Total Liab.:**	$533,000	**Indic. Yr. Divd.:**	NA
Total Assets:	$4,000	**Net Worth:**	-$529,000	**Debt/ Equity:**	NA

Concord Camera Corp

4000 Hollywood Blvd., 6th Fl., N Tower, Hollywood, FL, 33021; *PH:* 1-954-331-4200; *Fax:* 1-954-981-3055; *http://* www.concord-camera.com

General		**Stock**	
Incorporation	NJ	Price on:12/24/2007	NA
Employees	NA	Stock Exchange	NDQ
Auditor	Ernst & Young LLP, BDO Seidman LLP	Ticker Symbol	LENS
Stk Agt	Continental Stock Transfer & Trust Co	Outstanding Shares	NA
Counsel	Kronish, Lieb, Weiner & Hellman	E.P.S.	-$2.01
DUNS No.	07-773-2782	Shareholders	NA

Business: The group's principal activities are to design, develop, manufacture easy-to-use image capture products and related accessories and sell worldwide. The products of the group include digital image capture devices, 35mm and advanced photo system (aps) traditional and single use cameras and instant cameras. The digital cameras use an electronic sensor to electronically capture an image, which is then stored in a memory device. Single use cameras are sold preloaded with film and battery and are designed to be used only once. 35mm and aps cameras consist of all other non-single use cameras that use silver halide film. Instant cameras provide the advantage of instant photographs. The cameras are sold under the trademarks of concord (R), keystone (R), fun shooter (R), le clic (R), goldline (R), apex(R) and argus (r). The group also serves as a contract manufacturer of developed and co-developed products for its original equipment manufacturer customers.

Primary SIC and add'l.: 3861

CIK No: 0000831861

Subsidiaries: Concord Camera (Europe) Limited, Concord Camera (Shenzhen) Company Ltd., Concord Camera France S.A.R.L., Concord Camera GmbH, Concord Camera HK Limited, Concord Camera Illinois Corp., Concord Camera K.K. (Japan), Concord-Keystone Sales Corp., Goldline (Europe) Limited, Jenimage UK Ltd.

Officers: Ira B. Lampert/Chmn., CEO, Pres., Gerald J. Angeli/Sr. VP, Dir. - Operations, Urs W. Stampfli/Sr. VP, Dir. - Global Sales, Marketing, Blaine A. Robinson/VP - Finance, Treasurer, Assist. Sec., Scott L. Lampert/VP, General Counsel, Sec.

Directors: Ira B. Lampert/Chmn., CEO, Pres., Morris H. Gindi/Dir., Ronald S. Cooper/Dir., William J. O'Neill/Dir.

Owners: MT Trading LLC/18.70%, Urs W. Stampfli, Scott L. Lampert, Dimensional Fund Advisors Inc./5.90%, Blaine A. Robinson, Gerald J. Angeli, Morris H. Gindi, Ronald S. Cooper, MT Trading LLC, Sondra Beit, RH Trading LLC and as a gruop/23.20%, Ira B. Lampert/9.80%, William J. ONeill, Insiders/10.70%

Financial Data: *Fiscal Year End:*07/02 *Latest Annual Data:* 07/01/2006

Year	Sales	Net Income
2006	$137,529,000	-$19,611,000
2005	$174,348,000	-$44,923,000
2004	$203,132,000	-$31,222,000

Curr. Assets:	$151,271,000	**Curr. Liab.:**	$50,668,000		
Plant, Equip.:	$20,597,000	**Total Liab.:**	$62,392,000	**Indic. Yr. Divd.:**	NA
Total Assets:	$189,517,000	**Net Worth:**	$127,125,000	**Debt/ Equity:**	NA

Concrete Casting Inc

8800 N Gainey Ctr. Dr, Ste.256, Scottsdale, AZ, 85258; *PH:* 1-480-443-0851

General - Incorporation	NV	**Stock**- Price on:12/24/2007	$0.5
Employees	NA	Stock Exchange	OTC
Auditor	HJ & Associates, LLC	Ticker Symbol	CCSG
Stk Agt	NA	Outstanding Shares	NA
Counsel	Cane O'Neill Taylor, LLC	E.P.S	NA
DUNS No.	NA	Shareholders	NA

Business: The groups principal activity is to supply pre cast concrete products. The group operates from the United States.

Primary SIC and add'l.: 3272

CIK No: 0000093205

Officers: Cordell Henrie/51/Dir. CEO, Pres.

Directors: Cordell Henrie/51/Dir. CEO, Pres.

Owners: Thomas E. Hofer/12.00%, Jeff W. Holmes/14.30%, Cordell Henrie/31.90%, Insiders/31.90%

Financial Data: **Fiscal Year End:**12/31 **Latest Annual Data:** 12/31/2006

Year	Sales	Net Income
2006	$1,000	-$81,000

Curr. Assets:	$93,000	**Curr. Liab.:**	$62,000		
Plant, Equip.:	$6,000	**Total Liab.:**	$62,000	**Indic. Yr. Divd.:**	NA
Total Assets:	$100,000	**Net Worth:**	$38,000	**Debt/ Equity:**	NA

Concur Technologies Inc

18400 NE Union Hill Rd., Redmond, WA, 98052; *PH:* 1-425-702-8808; *Fax:* 1-425-702-8828; *http://* www.concur.com

General - Incorporation	WA	**Stock**- Price on:12/24/2007	$22.19
Employees	500	Stock Exchange	NDQ
Auditor	Grant Thornton, LLP	Ticker Symbol	CNQR
Stk Agt	Wells Fargo Shareowner Services	Outstanding Shares	37,760,000
Counsel	Fenwick & West LLP	E.P.S	$0.20
DUNS No.	86-726-2263	Shareholders	NA

Business: The group's principle activity is to provide Web-based corporate expense management software and services that are designed to improve business operational efficiency and reduce cost. The products are designed to suit customer business needs, technical requirements and budget objectives through flexible delivery models, including hosted license, subscription and application service provider models. The group's products include concur expense (TM) software for automating travel and entertainment expense management, concur payment (TM) software for automating employee requests for vendor payments and concur time (TM) software for automating time tracking and reporting. The customers include at&t, citigroup, delphi corporation, dupont, ford motor company, general motors and pfizer. The group's total revenue for year 2007 was 129.11 millions of USD.

Primary SIC and add'l.: 7379 7372

CIK No: 0001066026

Subsidiaries: Captura Software International, Ltd, Captura Software, Inc, Concur Technologies (Australia) Pty. Limited, Concur Technologies (UK) Ltd, Concur Technologies Pty. Limited

Officers: Steve Singh/Chmn., CEO, Rajeev Singh/COO, Pres., Michael Hilton/Dir., CTO, Kyle Sugamele/Chief Legal Officer, Michael L. Eberhard/Exec. VP - North American Sales, Michael Bowden/Exec. VP - Operations, Chief Services Officer, John Adair/CFO

Directors: Steve Singh/Chmn., CEO, Michael Hilton/Dir., CTO, Gordon Eubanks/Dir., William W. Canfield/Dir., Robert T. Abele/Dir., Jeff McCabe/Dir., Jeffrey T. Seely/Dir.

Financial Data: **Fiscal Year End:**09/30 **Latest Annual Data:** 9/30/2006

Year	Sales	Net Income
2006	$97,145,000	$34,156,000
2005	$71,831,000	$5,366,000
2004	$56,550,000	$2,035,000

Curr. Assets:	$49,078,000	**Curr. Liab.:**	$39,370,000	**P/E Ratio:**	170.69
Plant, Equip.:	$20,429,000	**Total Liab.:**	$63,925,000	**Indic. Yr. Divd.:**	NA
Total Assets:	$181,319,000	**Net Worth:**	$117,394,000	**Debt/ Equity:**	0.0958

Concurrent Computer Corp

4375 River Green Pkwy., Ste. 100, Duluth, GA, 30096; *PH:* 1-678-258-4000; *Fax:* 1-678-258-4300; *http://* www.ccur.com; *Email:* investor.relations@ccur.com

General - Incorporation	DE	**Stock**- Price on:12/24/2007	$1.8
Employees	399	Stock Exchange	NDQ
Auditor	Deloitte & Touche LLP	Ticker Symbol	CCUR
Stk Agt	American Stock Transfer & Trust Co.	Outstanding Shares	71,660,000
Counsel	NA	E.P.S	-$0.22
DUNS No.	06-351-0622	Shareholders	NA

Business: The group's principal activity is to provide computer and software systems for the video-on-demand and high-performance computing applications. The group operates through two business segments: video-on-demand and integrated solutions. The vod segment provides vod systems consisting of hardware, software and integration services to residential cable companies that have upgraded networks to support interactive, digital services. Integrated solutions segment provides high-performance, real-time computer systems used primarily for simulations and data acquisition applications for commercial and government markets. This segment focuses on strategic market areas that include hardware-in-the-loop and man-in-the-loop simulation, data acquisition, industrial systems, and software and embedded applications.

Primary SIC and add'l.: 7371 7373

CIK No: 0000749038

Subsidiaries: Concurrent Computer Asia Corporation, Concurrent Computer Canada, Inc., Concurrent Computer Corporation, Concurrent Computer Corporation Pty. Ltd., Concurrent Computer France S.A., Concurrent Computer GmbH, Concurrent Computer Hispania, S.A., Concurrent Computer Holding Corporation, Concurrent Computer Hong Kong Limited, Concurrent Computer New Zealand Limited, Concurrent Federal Systems, Inc., Concurrent Nippon Corporation, Concurrent Realisations Limited, Concurrent Securities Corporation, Concurrent UK Ltd. 18 Subsidiaries included in the Index

Officers: Gary Trimm/Dir., CEO, Pres./$694,336.00, Emory Berry/CFO/$137,857.00, James Brickmeier/VP - Products, Programs, On Demand, Tim Dodge/VP - Sales, Marketing, North America, On Demand, Michael W. Pasquinilli/VP - Engineering, On Demand, Kirk L. Somers/Exec. VP, General Counsel, Sec./$301,482.00, Suzanne Smith/Sr. VP - Worldwide Human Resources, Administrative Services, Dave Mooney/VP - Quality Assurance, Robert E. Chism/CTO, Gary Brust/Sr. VP - Worldwide Sales, Marketing, Kenrick R. Jackson/VP - Concurrent Special Systems, Del Kunert/VP - International On - Demand, Fred R. Langston/VP - Manufacturing

Directors: Gary Trimm/Dir., CEO, Pres., Steve G. Nussrallah/Chmn., Alex B. Best/Dir., Charles Blackmon/Dir., Larry Enterline/Dir., Shelton C. James/Dir.

Owners: Shelton C. James, S.A.C. Capital Advisors/8.17%, Insiders/1.60%, Gregory S. Wilson, Fidelity Management and Research Corp./5.93%, Steve G. Nussrallah, Warren K. Neuburger, Alex B. Best, Kirk L. Somers, Gary T. Trimm

Financial Data: **Fiscal Year End:**06/30 **Latest Annual Data:** 6/30/2006

Year	Sales	Net Income
2006	$71,612,000	-$9,345,000
2005	$78,685,000	-$7,729,000
2004	$79,235,000	-$5,725,000

Curr. Assets:	$37,276,000	**Curr. Liab.:**	$19,892,000		
Plant, Equip.:	$6,015,000	**Total Liab.:**	$24,984,000	**Indic. Yr. Divd.:**	NA
Total Assets:	$68,758,000	**Net Worth:**	$43,774,000	**Debt/ Equity:**	NA

Conectisys Corp

24730 Magic Mountain Pkwy, Ste. No. 41, Valencia, CA, 91355; *PH:* 1-661-295-6763; *Fax:* 1-661-295-5981; *http://* www.conectisys.com; *Email:* conectisys@conectisys.com

General - Incorporation	CO	**Stock**- Price on:12/24/2007	$0.0001
Employees	3	Stock Exchange	OTC
Auditor	Farber Hass Hurley & Mcewen, LLP	Ticker Symbol	CNES
Stk Agt	Signature Stock Transfer, Inc.	Outstanding Shares	20,670,000,000
Counsel	NA	E.P.S	$0.00
DUNS No.	83-732-9911	Shareholders	NA

Business: The group's principal activities are to develop automatic reading technologies and products for remote reading of electronic energy meters. The group also develops a technology called h-net that allows energy companies to have a wireless network of electric meters. The customers of the group include energy meter manufacturers, energy service providers, utility companies and end-users of energy. The group solely operates in the United States of America.

Primary SIC and add'l.: 3613 3825

CIK No: 0000790273

Subsidiaries: cEnergyServices.com, Inc., United Telemetry Company, Inc.

Financial Data: **Fiscal Year End:**09/30 **Latest Annual Data:** 9/30/2006

Year	Sales	Net Income
2006	NA	-$3,052,000
2005	NA	-$3,133,000
2004	NA	-$4,229,000

Curr. Assets:	$612,000	**Curr. Liab.:**	$4,796,000		
Plant, Equip.:	$104,000	**Total Liab.:**	$6,850,000	**Indic. Yr. Divd.:**	NA
Total Assets:	$748,000	**Net Worth:**	-$6,101,000	**Debt/ Equity:**	NA

Conexant Systems Inc

4000 MacArthur Blvd., Newport Beach, CA, 92660; *PH:* 1-949-483-4600; *http://* www.conexant.com

General - Incorporation	DE	**Stock**- Price on:12/24/2007	$1.38
Employees	3,120	Stock Exchange	NDQ
Auditor	Deloitte & Touche LLP	Ticker Symbol	CNXT
Stk Agt	Mellon Investor Services LLC	Outstanding Shares	490,490,000
Counsel	NA	E.P.S	-$0.39
DUNS No.	02-541-6025	Shareholders	NA

Business: The group's principle activities are to design, develop and sell semiconductor products and system solutions. It operates through one division: broadband communications. It designs, develops and sells semiconductor system solutions that connect personal communications access products. The group operates through nine domestic and eight international sales offices located in the Americas, Europe, Japan and the Asia-pacific region. The group's total revenue for year 2007 was 808.87 millions of USD.

Primary SIC and add'l.: 3674

CIK No: 0001069353

Subsidiaries: Amphion Semiconductor (Asia) Ltd., Amphion Semiconductor, Inc., Amphion Semiconductor, Ltd., Brooktree Broadband Holding, Inc., Brooktree International Ltd., Brooktree Technologies Ltd., Brooktree Worldwide Sales Corporation, Choice-Intersil Microsystems, Inc., Conexant Broadband Communications (Shanghai) Co., Ltd., Conexant Canada ULC, Conexant Digital Infotainment Limited, Conexant Digital TV (Chengdu) Co., Ltd., Conexant Foreign Sales Corporation, Conexant Korea Ltd., Conexant Mauritius Ltd. 47 Subsidiaries included in the Index

Officers: Daniel A. Artusi/Dir., CEO, Pres., Anil Mankar/Sr. VP - Worldwide Core Engineering, Chief Development Officer, Bruce Thomas/Investor Relations Officer, Scott D. Mercer/Private Investor, Dir., Bernd Lienhard/Sr. VP, GM - Imaging, PC Media, Christian Scherp/Sr. VP - Worldwide Sales, Karen Roscher/CFO, Sr. VP, George Chu/Sr. VP, Pres. - China Operations, Lewis C. Brewster/Exec. VP, GM - Broadband Media Processing, Michael Vishny/Sr. VP - Human Resources, Scott L. Allen/Sr. VP - Communications, Akram Atallah/Sr. VP, GM - Broadband Access, Sailesh Chittipeddi/Sr. VP - Global Operations, Shiva Gowni/Sr. VP, Pres. - India Operations, Jean Hu/Sr. VP - Strategy, Business Development *(16 Officers included in Index)*

Directors: Daniel A. Artusi/Dir., CEO, Pres., Dwight W. Decker/Chmn., Craig F. Farrill/Dir., Giuseppe P. Zocco/Dir., Donald R. Beall/Dir., Steven J. Bilodeau/Dir., Balakrishnan S. Iyer/Dir., John W. Marren/Dir., Scott D. Mercer/Private Investor, Dir., Jerre L. Stead/Dir.

Owners: Donald R. Beall, Dwight W. Decker, Balakrishnan S. Iyer, Dennis E. OReilly, Jerre L. Stead, Giuseppe Zocco, Lewis C. Brewster, F. Craig Farrill, D. Scott Mercer, John W. Marren, F. Matthew Rhodes, Insiders, Steven J. Bilodeau, J. Scott Blouin

Financial Data: **Fiscal Year End:**09/30 **Latest Annual Data:** 9/29/2006

Year	Sales	Net Income
2006	$970,787,000	-$122,591,000
2005	$722,739,000	-$175,990,000
2004	$901,854,000	-$544,649,000

Curr. Assets:	$539,280,000	**Curr. Liab.:**	$413,424,000		
Plant, Equip.:	$50,700,000	**Total Liab.:**	$1,012,431,000	**Indic. Yr. Divd.:**	NA
Total Assets:	$1,581,524,000	**Net Worth:**	$569,093,000	**Debt/ Equity:**	1.1784

Congoleum Corp

3500 Quakerbridge Rd., Mercerville, NJ, 08619; *PH:* 1-609-584-3000; *Fax:* 1-609-584-3522; *http://* www.congoleum.com

General - Incorporation	DE	Stock- Price on:12/24/2007	$0.9
Employees	823	Stock Exchange	AMEX
Auditor	Ernst & Young LLP	Ticker Symbol	CGM
Stk Agt	Registrar & Transfer Co	Outstanding Shares	8,270,000
Counsel	Skadden, Meagher & Flom LLP	E.P.S.	$0.04
DUNS No.	15-428-1158	Shareholders	NA

Business: The group's principal activities are to manufacture and market resilient sheet and tile flooring products with a wide variety of product features, designs and colors. The group also produces through-chip inlaid products for both residential and commercial markets. In residential applications, these products are used primarily in kitchens, bathrooms, laundry rooms, foyers, playrooms and basements. The group's major customers include lasalle-bristol and mohawk industries, inc. The group sells its products through approximately 17 distributors providing approximately 53 distribution points in the United States and Canada.

Primary SIC and add'l.: 3996

CIK No: 0000023341

Officers: Roger S. Marcus/62/Chmn., CEO, Pres./$11,329.00, Dennis P. Jarosz/62/VP - Sales, Marketing/$241,344.00, Thomas A. Sciortino/61/VP - Administration, Sidharth Nayar/47/VP - Finance/$211,683.00, John L. Russ/67/VP - Operations/$227,776.00, Howard N. Feist/51/CFO, Sec./$9,870.00

Directors: Roger S. Marcus/62/Chmn., CEO, Pres., Richard G. Marcus/60/Vice Chmn., Mark S. Newman/58/Dir., Adam H. Slutsky/44/Dir., William M. Marcus/70/Dir., Barnwell C. Straut/82/Dir., Jeffrey H. Coats/50/Dir., Mark N. Kaplan/78/Dir.

Owners: Richard G. Marcus/15.80%, Mark N. Kaplan, Insiders/36.80%, Roger S. Marcus/15.40%, William M. Marcus/11.00%

Financial Data: *Fiscal Year End:*12/31 *Latest Annual Data:* 12/31/2006

Year	Sales	Net Income
2006	$219,474,000	$679,000
2005	$237,626,000	-$21,575,000
2004	$229,493,000	$2,948,000

Curr. Assets:	$105,675,000	Curr. Liab.:	$94,222,000	P/E Ratio:	90.00
Plant, Equip.:	$67,757,000	Total Liab.:	$230,755,000	Indic. Yr. Divd.:	NA
Total Assets:	$184,202,000	Net Worth:	-$46,553,000	Debt/ Equity:	NA

Conmed Corp

525 French Rd., Utica, NY, 13502; *PH:* 1-315-797-8375; *Fax:* 1-315-797-0321; *http://* www.conmed.com; *Email:* info@conmed.com

General - Incorporation	NY	Stock- Price on:12/24/2007	$30.3701
Employees	3,200	Stock Exchange	NDQ
Auditor	PricewaterhouseCoopers LLP	Ticker Symbol	CNMD
Stk Agt	Registrar & Transfer Co	Outstanding Shares	28,290,000
Counsel	Daniel S. Jonas	E.P.S.	$0.04
DUNS No.	07-159-5540	Shareholders	NA

Business: The group's principal activity is to specialize in instruments, implants and video equipment for arthroscopic sports medicine and powered surgical instruments. In addition, it develops, manufactures and supplies rf electrosurgery systems used routinely to cut and cauterize tissue in all types of surgical procedures worldwide, endoscopy products such as trocars, clip appliers, scissors and surgical staplers and a full line of ecg electrodes for heart monitoring and other patient care products. The group also offers integrated operating room system and intensive care unit service managers. Its products are used in operating rooms, surgery centers, physician's offices and critical care areas.

Primary SIC and add'l.: 3845 3841

CIK No: 0000816956

Subsidiaries: Aspen Laboratories, Inc., CONMED Andover Medical, Inc., CONMED Endoscopic Technologies, Inc., CONMED Integrated Systems Canada ULC, CONMED Integrated Systems, Inc., CONMED Receivables Corporation, Envision Medical Corporation, GWH Limited Partnership, Largo Lakes I Limited Partnership, Linvatec Australia Pty. Ltd, Linvatec Austria, Linvatec Belgium S.A, Linvatec Biomaterials, Inc., Linvatec Biomaterials, Ltd., Linvatec Canada ULC 24 Subsidiaries included in the Index

Officers: Joseph J. Corasanti/43/Dir., CEO, COO, Pres./$1,088,507.00, William W. Abraham/Sr. VP, Luke A. Pomilio/VP, Tom Vassi/Mgr. - Northeastern US Corporate Sales, Daivd R. Murray/59/Pres. - Electrosurgery/$572,328.00, Dennis M. Werger/53/VP, GM - Endoscopic Technologies, Robert D. Shallish/CFO, VP - Finance/$612,777.00, Frank R. Williams/VP - Endosurgery, John J. Stotts/VP - Patient Care, Daniel S. Jonas/VP - Legal Affairs/$543,550.00, Bob Deluca/Mgr. - Southeastern US Corporate Sales, Ron Bellamy/Mgr. - Contracts Administration, Thomas M. Acey/Treasurer, Sec. - Gerald G. Woodard/Pres. - Linvatec Corporation, Jane E. Metcalf/50/VP - Corporate Regulatory Affairs

Directors: Joseph J. Corasanti/43/Dir., CEO, COO, Pres., Eugene R. Corasanti/Chmn., Bruce F. Daniels/Dir., Stuart J. Schwartz/Dir., Mark E. Tryniski/Dir., Jo Ann Golden/Dir., Stephen M. Mandia/Dir., William D. Matthews/Dir.

Owners: David R. Murray, Bruce F. Daniels, Jo Ann Golden, Stuart J. Schwartz, Robert D. Shallish, Wellington Management Company, LLP/5.78%, Insiders/6.90%, Dimensional Fund Advisors LP/7.88%, Joseph J. Corasanti/2.51%, FMR Corp./7.23%, William D. Matthews, Barclays Global Investors, N.A./10.18%, Stephen M. Mandia, Eugene R. Corasanti/1.99%, Artisan Partners Limited Partnership/7.45% (17 Owners included in Index)

Financial Data: *Fiscal Year End:*12/31 *Latest Annual Data:* 12/31/2006

Year	Sales	Net Income
2006	$646,812,000	-$12,507,000
2005	$617,305,000	$31,994,000
2004	$558,388,000	$33,465,000

Curr. Assets:	$249,883,000	Curr. Liab.:	$75,205,000	P/E Ratio:	759.25
Plant, Equip.:	$116,480,000	Total Liab.:	$421,217,000	Indic. Yr. Divd.:	NA
Total Assets:	$861,571,000	Net Worth:	$440,354,000	Debt/ Equity:	0.6010

Conmed Healthcare Management Inc

Formerly: Pace Health Mgmt Systems Inc
9375 Chesapeake St., Ste. 203, La Plata, MD, 20646; *PH:* 1-301-609-8460; *http://* www.pacesystems.com

General - Incorporation	IA	Stock- Price on:12/24/2007	NA
Employees	NA	Stock Exchange	NA
Auditor	McGladrey & Pullen LLP	Ticker Symbol	NA
Stk Agt	NA	Outstanding Shares	NA
Counsel	NA	E.P.S.	NA
DUNS No.	17-481-1786	Shareholders	NA

Business: The group is seeking a business combination with another entity before considering possible liquidation and distribution of its assets. The company used to develop and market advanced patient care management software systems, which improved clinical outcomes. All assets and liabilities of the group were sold to Minnesota mining and manufacturing company. Following the sale the company has no ongoing operations and no revenues. The group's quarterly revenue for September 2007 was 6.96 millions of USD.

Primary SIC and add'l.: 7372 7371

CIK No: 0000943324

Officers: George W. Buckley/CEO, Pres., Herbert L. Henkel/Pres., CEO - Ingersoll, Rand Company, Ltd, Richard Turner/61/Dir., CEO, Pres., Howard M. Haft/58/Chief Medical Officer, Exec. VP, John K. Woodworth/57/Sr. VP - Corporate Supply Chain Operations, Patrick D. Campbell/56/Sr. VP, CFO, Joe E. Harlan/49/Exec. VP - Electro, Communications Business, Angela S. Lalor/43/Sr. VP - Human Resources, Jean Lobey/43/Exec. VP - Safety, Security, Protection Services Business, Frederick J. Palensky/58/Exec. VP - Enterprise Services, Brad T. Sauer/49/Exec. VP - Health Care Business, Thomas W. Fry/63/CFO, Sec., Hak Cheol Shin/Exec. VP - Industrial, Transportation Business, Inge G. Thulin/55/Exec. VP - International Operations, James B. Stake/56/Exec. VP - Display, Graphics Business (18 Officers included in Index)

Directors: Richard Turner/61/Dir., CEO, Pres., John Pappajohn/79/Chmn., Edward B. Berger/78/Dir., Terry E. Branstad/62/Dir., Linda G. Alvarado/Dir., Vance D. Coffman/Dir., Michael L. Eskew/Dir., James W. Farrell/Dir., Edward M. Liddy/Dir., Robert S. Morrison/Dir., Aulana L. Peters/Dir., Rozanne L. Ridgway/Dir.

Owners: Richard P. Olson, Lehman Brothers/21.40%, Howard M. Haft/4.50%, Gainesborough, LLC/7.60%, John Pappajohn/21.30%, Pinnacle/21.40%, Edgewater Private Equity Fund, L.P./7.20%, Richard Turner, Insiders/28.60%, Ronald H. Grubman

Financial Data: *Fiscal Year End:*12/31 *Latest Annual Data:* 12/31/2006

Year	Sales	Net Income
2006	NA	-$399,000
2005	NA	-$71,000
2004	NA	-$91,000

Curr. Assets:	$1,205,000	Curr. Liab.:	$368,000		
Plant, Equip.:	NA	Total Liab.:	$368,000	Indic. Yr. Divd.:	NA
Total Assets:	$1,722,000	Net Worth:	$1,355,000	Debt/ Equity:	NA

Conn's Inc

3295 College St., Beaumont, TX, 77701; *PH:* 1-409-832-1696; *Fax:* 1-409-832-4344; *http://* www.conns.com; *Email:* investorrelations@conns.com

General - Incorporation	DE	Stock- Price on:12/24/2007	$29.02
Employees	2,850	Stock Exchange	NDQ
Auditor	Ernst & Young LLP	Ticker Symbol	CONN
Stk Agt	EquiServe Trust Co N.A	Outstanding Shares	23,430,000
Counsel	NA	E.P.S.	$1.64
DUNS No.	NA	Shareholders	NA

Business: The group's principal activity is to sell home appliances including refrigerators, freezers, washers, dryers and ranges and a variety of consumer electronics including projection, plasma and LCD televisions, camcorders, vcrs, DVD players and home theater products. The group introduced new product lines, including lawn and garden, bedding and generators. It offers over 1,100 product items representing national brands as general electric, whirlpool, frigidaire, mitsubishi, sony, panasonic, thomson consumer electronics, simmons, hewlett packard and compaq. It currently operates 47 retail stores located in Texas and Louisiana. The group operates solely in the United States.

Primary SIC and add'l.: 5731

CIK No: 0001223389

Subsidiaries: Conn Appliances, Inc.

Officers: Thomas J. Frank/Chmn., CEO, William C. Nylin/Dir., Executive Vice Chmn., COO, Pres., David L. Rogers/CFO, Walter M. Broussard/Sr. VP - Store Operations, David R. Atnip/Sr. VP, Sec., Treasurer, Reymundo De La Fuente/Sr. VP - Credit, Timothy L. Frank/COO, Pres., Robert B. Lee/Sr. VP - Service, Logistics, David W. Trahan/Exec. VP - Retail, Clinton W. Harwood/Sr. VP - Information Technology

Directors: Thomas J. Frank/Chmn., CEO, William C. Nylin/Dir., Executive Vice Chmn., COO, Pres., Marvin D. Brailsford/Dir., Jon E.M. Jacoby/Dir., William T. Trawick/Dir., Scott L. Thompson/Dir., Douglas H. Martin/Dir., Theodore M. Wright/Dir., Bob L. Martin/Dir.

Owners: Insiders, Jon E.M. Jacoby, Bess C. Stephens, Timothy L. Frank, Marvin D. Brailsford, GAM London Ltd, David L. Rogers, David W. Trahan, William C. Nylin, Warren A. Stephens, Scott L. Thompson, SF Holding Corp., Conns Voting Trust, Thomas J. Frank, Pamela Dianne Stephens Trust One (22 Owners included in Index)

Financial Data: *Fiscal Year End:*01/31 *Latest Annual Data:* 1/31/2007

Year	Sales	Net Income
2007	$760,657,000	$40,311,000
2006	$701,148,000	$41,103,000
2005	$567,092,000	$30,125,000

Curr. Assets:	$317,762,000	Curr. Liab.:	$97,022,000	P/E Ratio:	16.97
Plant, Equip.:	$59,440,000	Total Liab.:	$97,419,000	Indic. Yr. Divd.:	NA
Total Assets:	$389,947,000	Net Worth:	$292,528,000	Debt/ Equity:	0.0001

Connected Media Technologies Inc

80 Sw 8th St. Ste. 2230, Miami, FL, 33130; *PH:* 1-786-425-0028; *http://* www.connectedmedia.com; *Email:* sales@connectedmedia.com

General - Incorporation	DE	Stock- Price on:12/24/2007	$0.0008
Employees	14	Stock Exchange	OTC
Auditor	Salberg & Company, P.A.	Ticker Symbol	CNCM
Stk Agt	NA	Outstanding Shares	641,910,000
Counsel	NA	E.P.S.	-$0.037
DUNS No.	NA	Shareholders	NA

Business: The groups principal activities include creating patents, developing applications and solutions, enforcement, and licensing. The group operates from the United States.

Primary SIC and add'l.: 7311

CIK No: 0001302135

Officers: Jeffrey W. Sass/Dir., CEO, Isidro Gonzalez/Dir., Pres., Jorge Escasena/VP - Sales, Mark Mayo/Dir., CFO

Directors: Jeffrey W. Sass/Dir., CEO, Rafael J. Diaz-Balart/Chmn., Robert Rodriguez/Vice Chmn., Isidro Gonzalez/Dir., Pres., Mark Mayo/Dir., CFO

Owners: Rafael Diaz-Balart/2.45%, Robert Rodriguez/49.10%, Leigh M. Rothschild/26.70%, Insiders/88.89%, Jeffrey W. Sass/10.64%

Financial Data: Fiscal Year End:12/31 Latest Annual Data: 12/31/2006

Year	Sales	Net Income
2006	$447,000	-$17,486,000
2005	NA	-$1,567,000
2004	NA	-$120,000

Curr. Assets:	$132,000	Curr. Liab.:	$4,005,000
Plant, Equip.:	$276,000	Total Liab.:	$4,005,000	Indic. Yr. Divd.: NA
Total Assets:	$708,000	Net Worth:	-$3,297,000	Debt/ Equity: NA

Connecticut Light & Power Co

107 Selden St., NU East 2 Fl., Berlin, CT, 06037; **PH:** 1-860-947-2000; **http://** www.cl-p.com; **Email:** CLPWebmaster@nu.com

General - Incorporation	CT	Stock- Price on:12/24/2007	$28.7
Employees	5,869	Stock Exchange	NYSE
Auditor	Deloitte & Touche LLP	Ticker Symbol	NA
Stk Agt	NA	Outstanding Shares	154,550,000
Counsel	NA	E.P.S	$3.76
DUNS No.	00-691-7090	Shareholders	NA

Business: The group's principal activities are to transmit and distribute electric energy in Connecticut. The group provides retail electric service to municipalities and other utilities. It furnishes franchised retail electric service. The group is a wholly owned subsidiary of northeast utilities.

Primary SIC and add'l.: 4911

CIK No: 0000023426

Subsidiaries: CL&P Funding LLC, CL&P Receivables Corporation, E. S. Boulos Company, Holyoke Power and Electric Company, Holyoke Water Power Company, Mode 1 Communications, Inc., North Atlantic Energy Corporation, North Atlantic Energy Service Corporation, Northeast Generation Company, Northeast Generation Services Company, Northeast Nuclear Energy Company, Northeast Utilities (a Massachusetts business trust), Northeast Utilities Service Company, NU Enterprises, Inc., PSNH Funding LLC 29 Subsidiaries included in the Index

Officers: Peter J. Clarke/VP - Customer Operations, Relations, Dana L. Louth/VP - Energy Delivery Services, Raymond P. Necci/56/COO, Pres.

Owners: Gregory J. Butler, WMECO, David R. McHale, Cheryl W. Grise, Gary A. Long, Leon J. Olivier, Rodney O. Powell, PSNH, CL&P, Charles W. Shivery, Raymond P. Necci

Financial Data: Fiscal Year End:12/31 Latest Annual Data: 12/31/2006

Year	Sales	Net Income
2006	$6,884,388,000	$470,578,000
2005	$7,397,390,000	-$253,488,000
2004	$6,686,699,000	$122,147,000

Curr. Assets:	$1,731,051,000	Curr. Liab.:	$1,363,835,000	P/E Ratio: 7.97
Plant, Equip.:	$6,242,186,000	Total Liab.:	$8,388,857,000	Indic. Yr. Divd.: $0.800
Total Assets:	$11,303,236,000	Net Worth:	$2,798,179,000	Debt/ Equity: 1.5860

Connecticut Water Service Inc

93 W Main St., Clinton, CT, 06413; **PH:** 1-860-669-8636; **Fax:** 1-860-669-5579; **http://** www.ctwater.com

General - Incorporation	CT	Stock- Price on:12/24/2007	$23.88
Employees	200	Stock Exchange	NDQ
Auditor	PricewaterhouseCoopers LLP	Ticker Symbol	CTWS
Stk Agt	Registrar & Transfer Co	Outstanding Shares	8,300,000
Counsel	MurthaCullina LLP	E.P.S	$0.92
DUNS No.	04-412-0822	Shareholders	NA

Business: The group's principal activity is to supply water throughout Connecticut and Massachusetts. The group supplies water to over 86,750 customers in 42 towns through 4 regulated subsidiaries. The group also offers related services on a contract basis to other water utilities, communities, businesses and homeowner associations through a number of unregulated subsidiary companies and through a joint venture with a well pump service provider.

Primary SIC and add'l.: 4941

CIK No: 0000276209

Subsidiaries: Barlaco, Inc, Barnstable Holding Company, Barnstable Water Company, Chester Realty, Inc., Connecticut Water Company, Connecticut Water Emergency Services, Inc., Crystal Water Company of Danielson, Crystal Water Utilities Corporation, New England Water Utility Services, Inc., Unionville Water Company

Officers: Eric W. Thornburg/Dir., CEO, Pres./$615,915.00, Marshall T. Chiaraluce/64/Executive Chmn./$723,226.00, Peter J. Bancroft/Dir. - Rates, Forecasting, David C. Benoit/VP - Finance, CFO, Treasurer/$328,219.00, Thomas R. Marston/VP - Planning, Treatment/$294,889.00, Maureen P. Westbrook/VP - Administration, Government Affairs/$293,141.00, Michele G. Diacri/Assist. Sec., Terrance P. Oneill/VP - Operations, Engineering/$299,874.00, Daniel J. Meaney/Corp. Sec.

Directors: Eric W. Thornburg/Dir., CEO, Pres., Marshall T. Chiaraluce/64/Executive Chmn., David A. Lentini/62/Dir., Lisa Thibdaue/55/Dir., Mark G. Kachur/63/Dir., Mary Ann Hanley/51/Dir., Marcia L. Hincks/Dir., Donald B. Wilbur/66/Dir., Arthur C. Reeds/64/Dir., Robert F. Neal/Dir., Ronald D. Lengyel/70/Dir., Heather Hunt/42/Dir., Carol P. Wallace/53/Dir.

Owners: David C. Benoit, Robert F. Neal, David A. Lentini, Terrance P. ONeill, Marcia L. Hincks, Heather Hunt, Eric W. Thornburg, Lisa J. Thibdaue, Mark G. Kachur, Thomas R. Marston, Judith A. Peterson/13.50%, Dimensional FundAdvisors LP/7.25%, Carol P. Wallace, Insiders/3.00%, Marshall T. Chiaraluce/1.50% (20 Owners included in Index)

Financial Data: Fiscal Year End:12/31 Latest Annual Data: 12/31/2006

Year	Sales	Net Income
2006	$46,945,000	$6,951,000
2005	$47,453,000	$10,324,000
2004	$48,493,000	$9,394,000

Curr. Assets:	$14,150,000	Curr. Liab.:	$12,970,000	P/E Ratio: 25.96
Plant, Equip.:	$268,092,000	Total Liab.:	$218,483,000	Indic. Yr. Divd.: $0.860
Total Assets:	$315,193,000	Net Worth:	$96,710,000	Debt/ Equity: 1.1321

ConocoPhillips

600 N Dairy Ashford Rd., Houston, TX, 77079; **PH:** 1-281-293-1000; **Fax:** 1-281-293-2819; **http://** www.conocophillips.com

General - Incorporation	DE	Stock- Price on:12/24/2007	$79.87
Employees	38,400	Stock Exchange	NYSE
Auditor	Ernst & Young LLP	Ticker Symbol	COP
Stk Agt	Mellon Investor Services LLC	Outstanding Shares	1,630,000,000
Counsel	NA	E.P.S	$6.54
DUNS No.	NA	Shareholders	NA

Business: The group's principle activity is to provide fuels. The group's products include Philips 66(R) and Conoco(R). The group operates from United States.

Primary SIC and add'l.: 1321 2911 1311 2819 5984

CIK No: 0001163165

Subsidiaries: 2435239 Nova Scotia Limited, 3072496 Nova Scotia Company, 349910 Alberta Inc., 362084 Alberta Inc., 534404 Alberta Ltd., 625894 Alberta Inc., 66 Pipe Line Company, 758350 Alberta Inc., 942819 Alberta Ltd., Alpine Pipeline Company, Arizona-Florida Land & Cattle Company, Asamera Minerals (U.S.) Inc., Asamera Oil (U.S.) Inc., Asamera Resources Inc., Ashford Energy Capital S.A. 488 Subsidiaries included in the Index

Officers: James J. Mulva/61/Chmn., CEO, Pres./$43,444,020.00, John E. Lowe/Exec. VP - Exploration, Production, Carin S. Knickel/VP - Human Resources, Philip L. Frederickson/Exec. VP - Technology, John A. Carrig/CFO, Exec. VP - Finance/$11,682,440.00, Robert A. Ridge/VP - Health, Safety, Environment, William B. Berry/Exec. VP/$5,790,641.00, James L. Gallogly/Exec. VP - Refining, Marketing, Transportation/$4,169,688.00, Janet Langford Kelly/Sr. VP - Legal, General Counsel, Corp. Sec., Luc J. Messier/Sr. VP - Project Development, W. C.W. Chiang/Sr. VP - Commercial, Randy L. Limbacher/Pres. - Exploration, Production, Americas/$4,562,861.00, Ryan M. Lance/Sr. VP - Exploration, Production, Europe, Asia, Africa, The Middle East, Rand C. Berney/52/VP, Controller, Stephen R. Brand/Sr. VP - Technology (18 Officers included in Index)

Directors: James J. Mulva/61/Chmn., CEO, Pres., Charles C. Krulak/65/Dir., Norman R. Augustine/72/Dir., Richard H. Auchinleck/56/Dir., Richard L. Armitage/62/Dir., James E. Copeland/63/Dir., Harold McGraw/59/Dir., William K. Reilly/68/Dir., Stapleton J. Roy/72/Dir., Bobby S. Shackouls/57/Dir., William E. Wade/65/Dir., Kathryn C. Turner/60/Dir., Victoria J. Tschinkel/60/Dir., Ruth R. Harkin/63/Dir., Harald Norvik/61/Dir. (17 Directors included in Index)

Owners: Harold W. McGraw, Norman R. Augustine, William R. Rhodes, James L. Gallogly, William B. Berry, Vanguard Fiduciary Trust Company/6.66%, Charles C. Krulak, Richard H. Auchinleck, Insiders, Kathryn C. Turner, William E. Wade, Bobby S. Shackouls, Richard L. Armitage, Stapleton J. Roy, James E. Copeland (24 Owners included in Index)

Financial Data: Fiscal Year End:12/31 Latest Annual Data: 12/31/2006

Year	Sales	Net Income
2006	$188,523,000,000	$15,550,000,000
2005	$183,364,000,000	$13,529,000,000
2004	$136,916,000,000	$8,129,000,000

Curr. Assets:	$25,066,000,000	Curr. Liab.:	$26,431,000,000	P/E Ratio: 8.47
Plant, Equip.:	$86,201,000,000	Total Liab.:	$80,933,000,000	Indic. Yr. Divd.: $1.640
Total Assets:	$164,781,000,000	Net Worth:	$82,646,000,000	Debt/ Equity: 0.2590

Conolog Corp

5 Columbia Rd., Somerville, NJ, 08876; **PH:** 1-908-722-8081; **Fax:** 1-908-722-5461; **http://** www.conolog.com; **Email:** conolog@conolog.com

General - Incorporation	DE	Stock- Price on:12/24/2007	$1.91
Employees	14	Stock Exchange	NDQ
Auditor	Bagell, Josephs, Levine & Co. LLC	Ticker Symbol	CNLG
Stk Agt	Continental Stock Transfer & Trust Co	Outstanding Shares	3,870,000
Counsel	NA	E.P.S	-$4.26
DUNS No.	04-800-8205	Shareholders	NA

Business: The group's principal activity is to design, manufacture and distribute small electronic and electromagnetic components and subassemblies for use in telephone, radio and microwave transmission and reception and communication areas. The products include transducers, digital signal processing systems and electromagnetic wave filters, audio transmitters and modulators, audio receivers and demodulators, magnetic 'networks', analog transmitters and receivers and multiplexer supervisory controls. It also provides short and long term qualified engineering and technical services as well as human resource consulting. The products of the group are used for transceiving various quantities, data and protective relaying functions in industrial , utility and other markets. The group's customers include primarily industrial customers, which include power companies, and various branches of military.on 30-Apr- 2004 the group sold atlas design subsidiary.

Primary SIC and add'l.: 8999 3679

CIK No: 0000023503

Subsidiaries: Conolog Corporation, Lonogoc Corporation, Nologoc Corporation

Owners: Marc R. Benou/4.60%, Robert S. Benou/4.17%, Insiders/8.77%

Financial Data: Fiscal Year End:07/31 Latest Annual Data: 7/31/2006

Year	Sales	Net Income
2006	$548,000	-$3,330,000
2005	$549,000	-$2,987,000
2004	$963,000	-$6,498,000

Curr. Assets:	$3,837,000	Curr. Liab.:	$187,000	
Plant, Equip.:	$1,194,000	Total Liab.:	$1,045,000	Indic. Yr. Divd.: NA
Total Assets:	$5,294,000	Net Worth:	$4,249,000	Debt/ Equity: 0.1988

Conseco Inc

11825 N Pennsylvania St., Carmel, IN, 46032; **PH:** 1-317-817-6100; **Fax:** 1-317-817-2847; **http://** www.conseco.com

General - Incorporation	DE	Stock- Price on:12/24/2007	$21
Employees	4,000	Stock Exchange	NYSE
Auditor	PricewaterhouseCoopers LLP	Ticker Symbol	CNO
Stk Agt	American Stock Transfer & Trust Co.	Outstanding Shares	150,850,000
Counsel	NA	E.P.S	-$0.18
DUNS No.	05-236-0161	Shareholders	NA

Business: The group operates through its subsidiaries whose principle activity is to provide insurance products. The group offers health insurance products include medicare supplement, cancer insurance, hospital insurance, heart insurance and accidental injury insurance. The group operates from United States.

Primary SIC and add'l.: 6159 6311 6719 7374 6321 6153

CIK No: 0001224608

Subsidiaries: 40|86 Advisors, Inc, Conseco Finance Corp

Officers: James C. Prieur/57/Dir., CEO, Michael J. Dubes/66/Pres. - Conseco Insurance, John R. Kline/51/Chief Accounting Officer, Sr. VP, Russell M. Bostick/51/CIO, Exec. VP, Edward J. Bonach/54/CFO, Exec. VP, Steven M. Stecher/48/Exec. VP - Operations, William D. Fritts/58/Sr. VP - Government Relations, Daniel G. Walseth/61/Exec. VP, General Counsel, Sec., Scott R. Perry/46/Pres. - Bankers Life, Casualty, Anthony B. Zehnder/59/Exec. VP - Corporate Communications, Susan L. Menzel/43/Exec. VP - Human Resources, James E. Hohmann/52/COO, Pres., Christopher J. Nickele/51/Exec. VP - Product Management, Eugene M. Bullis/62/CFO, Exec. VP, Eric R. Johnson/48/Pres. - 40|86 Advisors, Inc *(16 Officers included in Index)*

Directors: James C. Prieur/57/Dir., CEO, Glenn R. Hilliard/65/Chmn., Neal C. Schneider/64/Dir., Michael T. Tokarz/59/Dir., Philip R. Roberts/66/Dir., Debra J. Perry/57/Dir., Doreen A. Wright/Dir., John G. Turner/69/Dir., Michael S. Shannon/50/Dir., Donna A. James/51/Dir.

Owners: Philip R. Roberts, Insiders/1.70%, Scott R. Perry, Lord, Abbett& Co., LLC/6.30%, Franklin Mutual Advisers LLC/6.20%, Eric R. Johnson, Eugene M. Bullis, Michael S. Shannon, Michael S. Shannon, SuttonBrook Capital Management, LLC/5.60%, Michael J. Dubes, Debra J. Perry, Michael T. Tokarz, R. Glenn Hilliard, John G. Turner *(19 Owners included in Index)*

Financial Data: **Fiscal Year End:**12/31 **Latest Annual Data:** 12/31/2006

Year	Sales	Net Income
2006	$4,467,400,000	$96,500,000
2005	$4,326,500,000	$324,900,000
2004	$4,330,000,000	$294,800,000

Curr. Assets:	$1,935,900,000	**Curr. Liab.:**	$832,300,000		
Plant, Equip.:	NA	**Total Liab.:**	$28,004,200,000	**Indic. Yr. Divd.:**	NA
Total Assets:	$32,717,300,000	**Net Worth:**	$4,713,100,000	**Debt/ Equity:**	0.3486

CONSOL Energy Inc

Consol Plz., 1800 Washington Rd., Pittsburgh, PA, 15241; ***PH:*** 1-412-831-4000; ***Fax:*** 1-412-831-4103; ***http://*** www.consolenergy.com

General - Incorporation	DE	**Stock**- Price on:12/24/2007	$48.05
Employees	7,253	Stock Exchange	NYSE
Auditor	PricewaterhouseCoopers LLP	Ticker Symbol	CNX
Stk Agt	EquiServe Trust Co N.A	Outstanding Shares	182,090,000
Counsel	Davis Polk & Wardwell	E.P.S.	$2.04
DUNS No.	78-842-1519	Shareholders	NA

Business: The groups principle activity is to produce coal, gas and electricity. The groups services include transportation, terminal, river and dock, and research and development services. The group operates from United States.

Primary SIC and add'l.: 1222 4924

CIK No: 0001070412

Subsidiaries: Buchanan Generation, LLC, Cardinal States Gathering Company, Cargo Dockers Ltd., Central Ohio Coal Company, CNX Funding Corporation, CNX Gas Company LLC, CNX Gas Corporation, CNX Land Resources Inc., CNX Marine Terminals Inc. (formerly Consolidation Coal Sales Company), Coalfield Pipeline Company, Conrhein Coal Company, CONSOL Docks Inc., CONSOL Energy Canada Ltd., CONSOL Energy Inc., CONSOL Energy Sales Company (formerly CONSOL Sales Company) 46 Subsidiaries included in the Index

Officers: Brett J. Harvey/56/Dir., CEO, Pres./$10,278,810.00, Peter B. Lilly/59/Pres. - Coal Group/$2,402,629.00, Dennis P. Duffy/Contact - Sales, Atlanta, Jack A. Holt/59/Sr. VP - Safety, Bart J. Hyita/49/COO - Coal, Robert P. King/55/Sr. VP - Administration, William J. Lyons/59/CFO/$2,873,226.00, Jerome P. Richey/58/General Counsel, Sec., Thomas F. Hoffman/VP - External Affairs, Robert F. Pusateri/Contact - Sales, Pittsburgh, Dewey R. McKay/Contact - Sales, Philadelphia, Vincent Gothier/Contact - Sales, Belgium

Directors: Brett J. Harvey/56/Dir., CEO, Pres., John Whitmire/66/Chmn., William P. Powell/51/Dir., Joseph T. Williams/69/Dir., William E. Davis/65/Dir., Patricia A. Hammick/60/Dir., Raj K. Gupta/64/Dir., James E. Altmeyer/68/Dir., David C. Hardesty/61/Dir., John T. Mills/59/Dir.

Owners: David C. Hardesty, Patricia A. Hammick, Ronald E. Smith, T. Rowe Price Associates, Inc./5.40%, Blackrock Inc/5.70%, Insiders, James E. Altmeyer, Brett J. Harvey, Nicholas J. Deluliis, John T. Mills, Peter B. Lilly, John Whitmire, Jay M. Allison/4.00%, William E. Davis, William P. Powell *(21 Owners included in Index)*

Financial Data: **Fiscal Year End:**12/31 **Latest Annual Data:** 12/31/2006

Year	Sales	Net Income
2006	$3,715,171,000	$408,882,000
2005	$3,810,449,000	$580,861,000
2004	$2,776,749,000	$198,582,000

Curr. Assets:	$914,496,000	**Curr. Liab.:**	$740,124,000	**P/E Ratio:**	20.62
Plant, Equip.:	$4,040,287,000	**Total Liab.:**	$4,461,522,000	**Indic. Yr. Divd.:**	$0.400
Total Assets:	$5,663,332,000	**Net Worth:**	$1,066,151,000	**Debt/ Equity:**	0.4275

CONSOL Energy Inc WY

Consol Plz., 1800 Washington Rd., Pittsburgh, PA, 15241; ***PH:*** 1-412-831-4000; ***Fax:*** 1-412-831-4103; ***http://*** www.consolenergy.com

General - Incorporation	DE	**Stock**- Price on:12/24/2007	NA
Employees	NA	Stock Exchange	OTC
Auditor	PricewaterhouseCoopers LLP	Ticker Symbol	CEIWE
Stk Agt	Pacific Stock Transfer Company	Outstanding Shares	NA
Counsel	NA	E.P.S.	NA
DUNS No.	NA	Shareholders	NA

Business: The groups principal activity is to produce coal, gas and electricity. The group operates from the United States.

Primary SIC and add'l.: 1311 1221 1241 5052 1222

CIK No: 0001070412

Subsidiaries: Buchanan Generation, LLC, Cardinal States Gathering Company, Cargo Dockers Ltd., Central Ohio Coal Company, CNX Funding Corporation, CNX Gas Company LLC, CNX Gas Corporation, CNX Land Resources Inc., CNX Marine Terminals Inc., Coalfield Pipeline Company, Conrhein Coal Company, CONSOL Docks Inc., CONSOL Energy Canada Ltd., CONSOL Energy Inc., CONSOL Energy Sales Company 48 Subsidiaries included in the Index

Officers: Brett J. Harvey/56/Dir., CEO, Thomas F. Hoffman/VP - External Affairs, Dennis P. Duffy/Contact - Sales, Atlanta, Robert F. Pusateri/Contact - Sales, Pittsburgh, William G. Rieland/Contact - Sales, Pittsburgh, Vincent Gothier/Contact - Sales, Belgium, Dewey R. Mckay/Contact - Sales, Philadelphia

Directors: Brett J. Harvey/56/Dir., CEO, John Whitmire/66/Chmn., James E. Altmeyer/68/Dir., William E. Davis/65/Dir., Raj K. Gupta/64/Dir., Patricia A. Hammick/60/Dir., David C. Hardesty/61/Dir., John T. Mills/59/Dir., William P. Powell/51/Dir., Joseph T. Williams/69/Dir.

Owners: Brett J. Harvey, David C. Hardesty, John Whitmire, Insiders, Blackrock Inc/5.70%, Nicholas J. Deluliis, Joseph T. Williams, William E. Davis, T. Rowe Price Associates, Inc./5.40%, Peter B. Lilly, Patricia A. Hammick, John T. Mills, Ronald E. Smith, James E. Altmeyer, William J. Lyons *(19 Owners included in Index)*

Consolidated Communications Holdings Inc

121 S 17th St., Mattoon, IL, 61938; ***PH:*** 1-217-235-3311; ***Fax:*** 1-217-258-7883; ***http://*** www.consolidated.com

General - Incorporation	DE	**Stock**- Price on:12/24/2007	$22.61
Employees	1,021	Stock Exchange	NDQ
Auditor	Ernst & Young LLP	Ticker Symbol	CNSL
Stk Agt	NA	Outstanding Shares	26,130,000
Counsel	NA	E.P.S.	$0.53
DUNS No.	NA	Shareholders	NA

Business: The groups principle activity is to provide communications services. The groups services include local and long distance, custom calling features, private line, dial-up and high speed Internet access, digital TV, carrier access and network capacity. The group operates through two segments namely telephone operations and other operations. The group operates from Lufkin, Conroe, Katy, Coles, Christian, Montgomery, Effingham and Shelby. The group's quarterly revenue for September 2007 was 80.32 millions of USD.

Primary SIC and add'l.: 4813

CIK No: 0001304421

Subsidiaries: Consolidated Communications Acquisition Texas, Inc., Consolidated Communications Business Systems, Inc., Consolidated Communications Market Response, Inc., Consolidated Communications Mobile Services, Inc., Consolidated Communications Network Services, Inc., Consolidated Communications of Fort Bend Company, Consolidated Communications of Texas Company, Consolidated Communications Operator Services, Inc., Consolidated Communications Public Services, Inc., Consolidated Communications Services Company, Consolidated Communications Telecom Services of Texas Company, Consolidated Communications Transport Company, Consolidated Communications Ventures Company, Consolidated Communications, Inc., East Texas Fiber Line, Incorporated (63% ownership) 16 Subsidiaries included in the Index

Officers: Robert J. Currey/Dir., CEO, Pres., Steven L. Childers/CFO, Joseph R. Dively/Sr. VP, Pres. - Illinois Telephone Operations, Robert C. Udell/Sr. VP, Pres. - Texas Telephone Operations, Steven J. Shirar/Sr. VP, Pres. - Enterprise Operations, Corp. Sec., Christopher A. Young/52/CIO

Directors: Robert J. Currey/Dir., CEO, Pres., Richard A. Lumpkin/Chmn., Jack W. Blumenstein/Dir., Roger H. Moore/Dir., Maribeth S. Rahe/Dir.

Owners: David E. Nelsen, Insiders/1.24%, Charles E. Thomas, Allen P. Kimble, Harry R. Brown, Royce & Associates, LLC/7.59%, Frank A. Macefe, Frederick J. Crowley, Stephen G. Kraskin, William N. Barthlow, Bulldog Investors/5.36%, Charles E. Cole

Financial Data: **Fiscal Year End:**12/31 **Latest Annual Data:** 12/31/2006

Year	Sales	Net Income
2006	$320,767,000	$13,267,000
2005	$321,429,000	-$4,462,000
2004	$269,608,000	-$1,143,000

Curr. Assets:	$74,217,000	**Curr. Liab.:**	$65,746,000	**P/E Ratio:**	42.66
Plant, Equip.:	$314,381,000	**Total Liab.:**	$774,621,000	**Indic. Yr. Divd.:**	$1.550
Total Assets:	$889,579,000	**Net Worth:**	$114,958,000	**Debt/ Equity:**	5.4601

Consolidated Edison Co of New York Inc

4 Irving Pl., New York, NY, 10003; ***PH:*** 1-212-460-4600; ***Fax:*** 1-212-982-7816; ***http://*** www.conedison.com; ***Email:*** corpcom@conEd.com

General - Incorporation	NY	**Stock**- Price on:12/24/2007	$46.93
Employees	14,795	Stock Exchange	NA
Auditor	PricewaterhouseCoopers LLP	Ticker Symbol	NA
Stk Agt	Bank of New York	Outstanding Shares	259,460,000
Counsel	NA	E.P.S.	$3.20
DUNS No.	00-698-2359	Shareholders	NA

Business: The group's principal activity is to provide electricity, gas and steam services. The group operates in New York city, westchester county and parts of manhattan. Its a wholly owned subsidiary of consolidated edison inc. Electricity is supplied to approximately 660 square mile service area with a population of more than 8 million. The group provides gas services in manhattan, the bronx, parts of queens and westchester. It provides steam service in manhattan.

Primary SIC and add'l.: 4961 4924 4911

CIK No: 0000023632

Subsidiaries: Con Edison, New Jersey, Orange and Rockland Utilities, Inc.

Officers: Kevin Burke/Chmn., CEO, Pres., John D. McMahon/CEO, Pres. - Orange, Rockland Utilities, Inc, Joseph P. Oates/VP, Treasurer, Jan C. Childress/Dir. - Investor Relations, James P. O'Brien/VP, General Auditor - Consolidated Edison Company, New York, Edward J. Rasmussen/VP, Controller, Chief Accounting Officer, Charles E. McTiernan/General Counsel/$1,157,651.00, Peter A. Irwin/Sec., John E. Perkins/Treasurer, Ellen Socolow/Mgr. - Investor Relations, Stephen B. Bram/Group Pres. - Competitive Energy Businesses, Saddie L. Smith/Sec., Assoc. General Counsel, Robert N. Hoglund/CFO, Sr. VP, Louis L. Rana/COO, Pres.

Directors: Kevin Burke/Chmn., CEO, Pres., Joan S. Freilich/Vice Chmn. - Consolidated Edison, Inc, Michael J. Del Giudice/Dir., Frederic V. Salerno/Dir., Trustee, Vincent A. Calarco/Dir., George Campbell/Dir., John F. Killian/Dir., Gordon J. Davis/Dir., Ellen V. Futter/Dir., Sally Hernandez/Dir., Peter W. Likins/Dir., Stephen R. Volk/Dir., Eugene R. McGrath/Dir.

Owners: Frederic V. Salerno, Joan S. Freilich, Robert N. Hoglund, John D. McMahon, Louis L. Rana, Stephen B. Bram

Financial Data: Fiscal Year End:12/31   Latest Annual Data: 12/31/2006

Year	Sales	Net Income
2006	$12,137,000,000	$737,000,000
2005	$11,690,000,000	$719,000,000
2004	$9,758,000,000	$537,000,000

Curr. Assets:	$2,937,000,000	Curr. Liab.:	$2,917,000,000	P/E Ratio:	14.67
Plant, Equip.:	$18,445,000,000	Total Liab.:	$18,441,000,000	Indic. Yr. Divd.:	$2.320
Total Assets:	$26,699,000,000	Net Worth:	$8,217,000,000	Debt/ Equity:	0.9585

Consolidated Edison Inc

4 Irving Pl., New York, NY, 10003; **PH:** 1-212-460-4600; **Fax:** 1-212-982-7816; **http://** www.conedison.com

General - Incorporation	NY	Stock- Price on:12/24/2007	$46.92
Employees	14,795	Stock Exchange	NYSE
Auditor	PricewaterhouseCoopers LLP	Ticker Symbol	ED
Stk Agt	Bank of New York	Outstanding Shares	259,460,000
Counsel	NA	E.P.S.	$3.26
DUNS No.	00-294-4531	Shareholders	NA

Business: The group operates through its subsidiaries whose principle activity is to provide energy services. The group operates through three segments namely electric, gas and steams utility. The group operates from United States.

Primary SIC and add'l.: 4911 4939 4961 6719 4924

CIK No: 0001047862

Subsidiaries: O&R, Rockland Electric Company

Officers: John D. McMahon/CEO, Pres. - Orange, Rockland Utilities, Inc/$2,129,997.00, Kevin Burke/Chmn., CEO, Pres./$4,720,560.00, Robert N. Hoglund/CFO, Sr. VP/$1,394,167.00, Luther Tai/59/Sr. VP - Enterprise Shared Services, Joseph P. Oates/VP, Treasurer, Stephen B. Bram/Group Pres. - Competitive Energy Businesses/$2,493,658.00, Charles E. McTiernan/General Counsel, Jan C. Childress/Dir. - Investor Relations, Louis L. Rana/COO, Pres. - Consolidated Edison Company, New York, Inc/$2,329,757.00, James P. O'Brien/VP, General Auditor - Consolidated Edison Company, New York, Inc, Peter A. Irwin/Sec., Joann Ryan/50/Sr. VP - Business Shared Services, Saddie L. Smith/Sec., Assoc. General Counsel, Edward J. Rasmussen/VP, Controller, Chief Accounting Officer, John F. Miksad/48/Sr. VP - Electric Operations (21 Officers included in Index)

Directors: Kevin Burke/Chmn., CEO, Pres., Joan S. Freilich/Vice Chmn., Stephen R. Volk/Dir., Peter W. Likins/Dir., Eugene R. McGrath/Dir., Frederic V. Salerno/Dir., Trustee, Frederick L. Sutherland/Dir., John F. Killian/Dir., George Campbell/Dir., Sally Hernandez/Dir., Vincent A. Calarco/Dir., Gordon J. Davis/Dir., Michael J. Del Giudice/Dir., Ellen V. Futter/Dir.

Financial Data: Fiscal Year End:12/31   Latest Annual Data: 12/31/2006

Year	Sales	Net Income
2006	$12,137,000,000	$737,000,000
2005	$11,690,000,000	$719,000,000
2004	$9,758,000,000	$537,000,000

Curr. Assets:	NA	Curr. Liab.:	NA	P/E Ratio:	14.66
Plant, Equip.:	NA	Total Liab.:	NA	Indic. Yr. Divd.:	$2.320
Total Assets:	NA	Net Worth:	NA	Debt/ Equity:	1.0248

Consolidated Envirowaste Industries Inc

27715 Huntingdon Rd., Abbotsford, BC, V4X 1B6;

General - Incorporation	Canada	Stock- Price on:12/24/2007	NA
Employees	NA	Stock Exchange	NA
Auditor	Ernst & Young LLP	Ticker Symbol	NA
Stk Agt	Computershare Trust Co	Outstanding Shares	NA
Counsel	NA	E.P.S.	NA
DUNS No.	24-881-0673	Shareholders	NA

Business: The group's principal activity is to process organic wastes into usable products, including natural organic fertilizer, soil amendments and fuel for power plants.

Primary SIC and add'l.: 2875

CIK No: 0000885986

Subsidiaries: Consolidated Resource Recovery, Inc, The Answer Garden Products Ltd.

Consolidated Graphics Inc TX

5858 Westheimer, Ste. 200, Houston, TX, 77057; **PH:** 1-713-787-0977; **Fax:** 1-713-787-5013; **http://** www.consolidatedgraphics.com; **Email:** econtaldi@cgx.com

General - Incorporation	TX	Stock- Price on:12/24/2007	$69.81
Employees	5,005	Stock Exchange	NYSE
Auditor	KPMG LLP	Ticker Symbol	CGX
Stk Agt	American Stock Transfer & Trust Co.	Outstanding Shares	13,700,000
Counsel	NA	E.P.S.	$3.64
DUNS No.	17-494-0270	Shareholders	NA

Business: The group's principal activity is to provide commercial printing services. The services include developing printable material through electronic prepress services, reproducing images on paper using printing presses and providing comprehensive finishing and delivery services. The traditional printing services include finishing, storage and delivery of high-quality, custom-designed products. The traditional printing products include multicolor product and capability brochures, shareholder communications, catalogs, training manuals, point-of-purchase marketing materials, trading cards and direct mail pieces. During the fiscal year 2004, the group operated 65 printing facilities in 25 states. The group acquired six printing businesses in fiscal 2004 & electric city printing in fiscal 2005.

Primary SIC and add'l.: 2759 2752

CIK No: 0000921500

Subsidiaries: A&A Amalgamated Printing Enterprises, Inc., AGS Custom Graphics, Inc., American Lithographers, Inc., Apple Graphics, Inc., Austin Printing Company, Inc., Automated Graphic Imaging/Copy Center, Inc., Automated Graphic Systems, LLC, bigINK Mailing & Fulfillment Company, Bridgetown Printing Co., Byrum Lithographing Co., CDS Publications, Inc., CGML General Partner, Inc., CGML, LLC, CGXmedia, Inc., Chas. P. Young Company 101 Subsidiaries included in the Index

Officers: Joe R. Davis/Chmn., CEO/$2,624,449.00, Michael B. Barton/Exec. VP, Chief Administrative Officer, Aaron T. Grohs/Exec. VP - Sales, Marketing, James H. Cohen/Exec. VP - Mergers, Acquisitions, Ric Davis/Exec. VP - Purchasing, Ryan C. Farris/Pres. - Cgxsolutions, Rachel S. Koenig/National Mgr. - Recruiting, Development, Sheila McClanahan/Investor Relations Contact

Directors: Joe R. Davis/Chmn., CEO, Larry J. Alexander/Dir., Brady F. Carruth/Dir., James H. Limmer/Dir., Gary L. Forbes/Dir., Hugh N. West/Dir.

Owners: Barclays Global Investors, NA/7.00%, James H. Limmer, Hugh N. West, Insiders/9.30%, Brady F. Carruth, Gary L. Forbes, Joe R. Davis/8.10%, Christopher G. Colville, Larry J. Alexander

Financial Data: Fiscal Year End:03/31   Latest Annual Data: 3/31/2007

Year	Sales	Net Income
2007	$1,006,186,000	$50,741,000
2006	$879,023,000	$38,498,000
2005	$779,016,000	$32,722,000

Curr. Assets:	$260,727,000	Curr. Liab.:	$160,574,000	P/E Ratio:	19.18
Plant, Equip.:	$354,156,000	Total Liab.:	$358,433,000	Indic. Yr. Divd.:	NA
Total Assets:	$723,969,000	Net Worth:	$365,536,000	Debt/ Equity:	0.3888

Consolidated Medical Management Inc

2500 City W Blvd., Ste. 300, Houston, TX, 77042; **PH:** 1-281-209-9800

General - Incorporation	MT	Stock- Price on:12/24/2007	$0.12
Employees	4	Stock Exchange	OTC
Auditor	James B. Mcelravy, Cpa, P.c.	Ticker Symbol	CMMI
Stk Agt	Standard Registrar & Transfer Co Inc.	Outstanding Shares	49,540,000
Counsel	NA	E.P.S.	NA
DUNS No.	NA	Shareholders	NA

Business: The groups principal activity is to exploration of minerals. The group operates from the United States.

Primary SIC and add'l.: 1040

CIK No: 1000700815

Owners: Timothy G. Byrd/15.14%, Insiders/34.61%, Sonny Wooley/16.60%, Peggy Behrens/2.87%

Financial Data: Fiscal Year End:12/31   Latest Annual Data: 12/31/2006

Year	Sales	Net Income
2006	$760,000	-$1,389,000
2005	NA	-$259,000
2004	$25,000	$485,000

Curr. Assets:	$152,000	Curr. Liab.:	$6,058,000		
Plant, Equip.:	$3,172,000	Total Liab.:	$7,558,000	Indic. Yr. Divd.:	NA
Total Assets:	$5,928,000	Net Worth:	-$1,630,000	Debt/ Equity:	NA

Consolidated Medical Mgmt Inc

2500 City W Blvd., Ste. 300, Houston, TX, 77042; **PH:** 1-281-209-9800

General - Incorporation	MT	Stock- Price on:12/24/2007	NA
Employees	NA	Stock Exchange	NA
Auditor	James B. Mcelravy, Cpa, P.c.	Ticker Symbol	NA
Stk Agt	Standard Registrar & Transfer Co Inc.	Outstanding Shares	NA
Counsel	NA	E.P.S.	NA
DUNS No.	11-735-1379	Shareholders	NA

Business: The group's principal activities are the exploration, production and transportation of oil and natural gas. The group's working interests include snake bite ellenberger prospect in edwards county, Texas.

Primary SIC and add'l.: 1311

CIK No: 0000700815

Officers: Timothy G. Byrd/46/Dir., CEO, CFO, Peggy Behrens/52/Dir., Sec., Steven M. Haag/Investor Relations Officer

Directors: Timothy G. Byrd/46/Dir., CEO, CFO, Sonny Wooley/69/Chmn., Peggy Behrens/52/Dir., Sec.

Owners: Peggy Behrens/2.87%, Timothy G. Byrd/15.14%, Sonny Wooley/16.60%, Insiders/34.61%

Consolidated Mercantile Inc

106 Ave. Rd., Toronto, ON, M5R 2H3; **PH:** 1-416-920-0500; **http://** www.consolidatedmercantile.com; **Email:** info@consolidatedmercantile.com

General - Incorporation	ON	Stock- Price on:12/24/2007	$1.16
Employees	NA	Stock Exchange	NDQ
Auditor	Bdo Dunwoody ,LLP	Ticker Symbol	CSLMF
Stk Agt	Computershare Investor Services LLC	Outstanding Shares	5,080,000
Counsel	NA	E.P.S.	NA
DUNS No.	20-629-7467	Shareholders	NA

Business: The group's principle activity is that of investment management with investments in operating companies. The group has subsidiaries in packaging, pool and furniture industries. The packaging products division manufactures specialized line of packaging products, including bubble mailers and bubble and reflective insulation. The pool products division manufactures a broad range of swimming pool accessories. The furniture division manufactures leather and fabric upholstered furniture. The group manufactures furniture in Canada and packaging and pool products in Canada and the United States. The group's quarterly revenue for September 2007 was 4.27 millions of CAD.

Primary SIC and add'l.: 3089 2512 6719

CIK No: 0000784012

Subsidiaries: Ontario Inc

Officers: Daniel S. Tamkin/VP, Stan Abramowitz/Dir., Sec., CFO, Fred A. Litwin/Dir., Pres.

Directors: Stan Abramowitz/Dir., Sec., CFO, Fred A. Litwin/Dir., Pres., Sol D. Nayman/Dir., Ian Dalrymple/Dir., Mark Dawber/Dir.

Owners: Mar-Risa Holdings Inc., Insiders, Fred A. Litwin, CDS& Co., CEDE & Co.

Consolidated Natural Gas Co

120 Tredegar St., Richmond, VA, 23219; *PH:* 1-804-819-2000; *http://* www.cng.com

General - Incorporation	DE	**Stock**- Price on:12/24/2007	$84.59
Employees	17,500	Stock Exchange	NA
Auditor	Deloitte & Touche LLP	Ticker Symbol	NA
Stk Agt	Bank One Trust Co., NA	Outstanding Shares	350,320,000
Counsel	NA	E.P.S.	NA
DUNS No.	00-698-2383	Shareholders	NA

Business: The group's principle activities include exploration, development, production, purchasing, gathering, transporting, storing and distribution of natural gas, together with by-product operations. The group operates from United States.

Primary SIC and add'l.: 1311 4922 4923 6719

CIK No: 0000023738

Subsidiaries: Dominion Resources, Inc.

Officers: Thomas F. Farrell/Chmn., CEO, Pres., Thomas N. Chewning/Dir., Exec. VP, CFO, Steven A. Rogers/Sr. VP, Chief Accounting

Directors: Thomas F. Farrell/Chmn., CEO, Pres., Thomas N. Chewning/Dir., Exec. VP, CFO

Financial Data: *Fiscal Year End:*12/31   *Latest Annual Data:* 12/31/2006

Year	Sales		Net Income
2006	$16,482,000,000		$1,380,000,000
2005	$18,041,000,000		$1,033,000,000
2004	$13,972,000,000		$1,249,000,000
Curr. Assets:	$8,098,000,000	**Curr. Liab.:** $11,229,000,000	**P/E Ratio:** 22.92
Plant, Equip.:	$29,382,000,000	**Total Liab.:** $36,076,000,000	**Indic. Yr. Divd.:** $2.840
Total Assets:	$49,269,000,000	**Net Worth:** $13,170,000,000	**Debt/ Equity:** 1.1047

Consolidated Oil & Gas Inc

316 E Main St. Ste. L, Humble, TX, 77338; *PH:* 1-281-446-7122; *http://* www.consolidatedoilgas.com; *Email:* info@consolidatedoilgas.com

General - Incorporation		**Stock**- Price on:12/24/2007	$0.07
Employees	17	Stock Exchange	OTC
Auditor	NA	Ticker Symbol	CSLG
Stk Agt	Standard Registrar & Transfer Co Inc.	Outstanding Shares	32,830,000
Counsel	NA	E.P.S.	-$0.036
DUNS No.	NA	Shareholders	NA

Business: The group's principle activities include producing and mining gold properties. The group operates from United States.

Primary SIC and add'l.: 1382

CIK No:

Officers: James Carl Yeatman/CEO, Karen Warfield/Admin Assist., Stephen Taylor/Contact - Invester Relations Representative, Douglas Newman/CFO, A. L. Dawsey/VP - Engineering, Carl Glenn/VP - South Texas Operations, Leslie Legrand/General Counsel

Financial Data: *Fiscal Year End:*NA   *Latest Annual Data:* 12/31/2006

Year	Sales		Net Income
2006	$1,918,000		-$949,000
Curr. Assets:	$49,000	**Curr. Liab.:** $849,000	
Plant, Equip.:	$908,000	**Total Liab.:** $1,247,000	**Indic. Yr. Divd.:** NA
Total Assets:	$957,000	**Net Worth:** -$289,000	**Debt/ Equity:** NA

Consolidated Tomoka Land Co

1530 Cornerstone Blvd., Ste. 100, Daytona Beach, FL, 32117; *PH:* 1-386-274-2202; *Fax:* 1-386-274-1223; *http://* www.consolidatedtomoka.com; *Email:* ctlc@consolidatedtomoka.com

General - Incorporation	FL	**Stock**- Price on:12/24/2007	$70.75
Employees	25	Stock Exchange	AMEX
Auditor	KPMG LLP	Ticker Symbol	CTO
Stk Agt	Registrar & Transfer Co	Outstanding Shares	5,720,000
Counsel	Holland & Knight LLP	E.P.S.	$1.47
DUNS No.	05-156-6586	Shareholders	

Business: The group's principle activities include real estate operations, income properties and golf businesses. The group's real estate operations include commercial real estate, land sales and development, residential, leasing properties for oil and mineral exploration and forestry operations. Income properties business consists of leasing triple-net lease properties. Golf operations consist of the operation of two golf courses, clubhouse facility, and food and beverage activities. These operations are located in volusia and highlands counties in Florida, with various income properties owned throughout the state of Florida.

Primary SIC and add'l.: 6519 7992 6531

CIK No: 0000023795

Subsidiaries: Indigo Development Inc, Indigo Group Inc, Indigo International Inc

Officers: William H. McMunn/61/Dir., CEO, Pres./$678,712.00, Ted Garn/Mgr. - Development, Operations, Gary Moothart/VP, Controller, Bruce W. Teeters/Sr. VP, CFO, Treasurer/$481,801.00, Gerald L. Degood/Dir. - Consultant, Tammy Girvin/Mgr. - Land Information, Gisele Found/Mgr. - Land Holdings, Linda Crisp/VP, Corp. Sec., Dir. - Administration, Robert F. Apgar/Sr. VP, General Counsel, Assist. Corp. Sec./$365,136.00

Directors: William H. McMunn/61/Dir., CEO, Pres., Bob D. Allen/73/Chmn., Gerald L. Degood/Dir. - Consultant, William J. Voges/Dir., James E. Gardner/Dir., John C. Adams/Dir., John C. Myers/Dir., James E. Jordan/Dir.

Owners: Robert F. Apgar, Barrington Capital Group, LP/6.80%, Wintergreen Advisers, LLC/17.90%, Bruce W. Teeters, Gerald L. DeGood, Insiders/2.00%, James E. Gardner, Pico Holdings, Inc/5.40%, William J. Voges, Third Avenue Management LLC/11.00%, John C. Myers, John C. Adams, William H. McMunn/1.00%, Bob D. Allen

Financial Data: *Fiscal Year End:*12/31   *Latest Annual Data:* 12/31/2006

Year	Sales		Net Income
2006	$43,589,000		$14,028,000
2005	$43,554,000		$14,818,000
2004	$41,985,000		$14,652,000
Curr. Assets:	$1,924,000	**Curr. Liab.:** $13,660,000	**P/E Ratio:** 35.55
Plant, Equip.:	$113,638,000	**Total Liab.:** $50,777,000	**Indic. Yr. Divd.:** $0.360
Total Assets:	$153,774,000	**Net Worth:** $102,997,000	**Debt/ Equity:** 0.0674

Consolidated Water Co Ltd

Regatta Office Pk., Windward Three, West Bay Rd., 4th Fl., Grand Cayman, Cayman Is.; ; *http://* www.cwco.com; *Email:* info@cwco.com

General - Incorporation	Cayman Islands	**Stock**- Price on:12/24/2007	$27.68
Employees	121	Stock Exchange	NDQ
Auditor	Rachlin Cohen & Holtz LLP	Ticker Symbol	CWCO
Stk Agt	American Stock Transfer & Trust Co.	Outstanding Shares	14,360,000
Counsel	Myers & Alberga Edwards AP & D	E.P.S.	$0.67
DUNS No.	86-393-4048	Shareholders	NA

Business: The groups principle activity is to process and supply potable water by pipeline for residential and business. The group operates from United States.

Primary SIC and add'l.: 4941

CIK No: 0000928340

Subsidiaries: Aquilex, Inc., Belize Water Limited, Cayman Water Company Limited, DesalCo (Barbados) Ltd., DesalCo Limited, Ocean Conversion (BVI)Ltd., Ocean Conversion (Cayman) Limited, Waterfields Company Limited

Officers: Frederick W. McTaggart/45/Dir., CEO, Pres., Gregory S. McTaggart/44/VP - Cayman Operations, Robert B. Morrison/54/VP - Purchasing, Information Technology, Gerard J. Pereira/37/VP - Engineering, David W. Sasnett/51/Dir., CFO, Exec. VP, Ramjeet Jerrybandan/39/VP - Overseas Operations

Directors: Frederick W. McTaggart/45/Dir., CEO, Pres., Jeffrey M. Parker/63/Chmn., Richard L. Finlay/49/Dir., Brian E. Butler/58/Dir., William T. Andrews/59/Dir., Steven A. Carr/57/Dir., Carson K. Ebanks/52/Dir., Clarence B. Flowers/52/Dir., Wilmer Pergande/68/Dir., David W. Sasnett/51/Dir., CFO, Exec. VP, Raymond Whittaker/54/Dir., Leonard J. Sokolow/51/Dir.

Owners: William T. Andrews, Brian E. Butler, Steven A. Carr, AMVESCAP PLC/9.27%, Leonard J. Sokolow, Jeffrey M. Parker/3.40%, Clarence B. Flowers, Frederick W. McTaggart/1.23%, Robert B. Morrison, Gregory S. McTaggart/1.11%, PowerShares Exchange/10.30%, Margaret Julier/8.93%, Richard L. Finlay, Elizabeth Triana/5.10%, Thomson, Horstmann, & Bryant, Inc/5.02% *(21 Owners included in Index)*

Financial Data: *Fiscal Year End:*12/31   *Latest Annual Data:* 12/31/2006

Year	Sales		Net Income
2006	$38,229,000		$7,521,000
2005	$26,187,000		$5,514,000
2004	$23,281,000		$6,197,000
Curr. Assets:	$48,173,000	**Curr. Liab.:** $7,622,000	**P/E Ratio:** 46.13
Plant, Equip.:	$63,568,000	**Total Liab.:** $33,117,000	**Indic. Yr. Divd.:** $0.260
Total Assets:	$138,961,000	**Net Worth:** $105,845,000	**Debt/ Equity:** 0.2097

Conspiracy Entertainment Holdings Inc

612 Santa Monica Blvd., Santa Monica, CA, 90401; *PH:* 1-310-260-6150; *Fax:* 1-310-260-1450; *http://* www.conspiracygames.com; *Email:* info@conspiracygames.com

General - Incorporation	UT	**Stock**- Price on:12/24/2007	$0.025
Employees	3	Stock Exchange	OTC
Auditor	Chisholm, Bierwolf & Nilson, LLC	Ticker Symbol	CPYE
Stk Agt	Madison Stock Transfer, Inc.	Outstanding Shares	NA
Counsel	NA	E.P.S.	-$0.008
DUNS No.	NA	Shareholders	NA

Business: The groups principle activities include developing, publishing and marketing interactive entertainment software. The group products include Sony's PlayStation 2, Sony's PSP, Nintendo GameCube, Nintendo's DS, and Microsoft's Xbox. The group operates from the United States.

Primary SIC and add'l.: 7372

CIK No: 0001136424

Subsidiaries: Conspiracy Entertainment Europe, Ltd

Officers: Sirus Ahmadi/Dir., CEO, Pres., Keith Tanaka/Dir., CFO, Principal Accounting Officer, Sec., Marco Husges/Exec. VP, August Permann/Producer, Paul Schreiber/Technical Development Dir. - Producer, Daniel Boutros/Producer, Jolene Spry/Contact - Public Relations, Marcus Brammertz/Contact - Graphic Arts, Design, Web

Directors: Sirus Ahmadi/Dir., CEO, Pres., Keith Tanaka/Dir., CFO, Principal Accounting Officer, Sec.

Owners: Sirus Ahmadi/28.90%, Insiders/33.10%, Keith Tanaka/4.20%

Financial Data: *Fiscal Year End:*12/31   *Latest Annual Data:* 12/31/2006

Year	Sales		Net Income
2006	$803,000		-$1,467,000
2005	$1,398,000		$1,051,000
2004	$1,426,000		-$2,539,000
Curr. Assets:	$334,000	**Curr. Liab.:** $4,463,000	
Plant, Equip.:	$6,000	**Total Liab.:** $4,650,000	**Indic. Yr. Divd.:** NA
Total Assets:	$1,278,000	**Net Worth:** -$3,373,000	**Debt/ Equity:** NA

Constar International Inc

1 Crown Way, Philadelphia, PA, 19154; *PH:* 1-215-552-3700; *Fax:* 1-215-552-3707; *http://* www.constar.net

General - Incorporation	DE	**Stock**- Price on:12/24/2007	$6.76
Employees	1,839	Stock Exchange	NDQ
Auditor	PricewaterhouseCoopers LLP	Ticker Symbol	CNST
Stk Agt	Computershare Trust Co	Outstanding Shares	12,580,000
Counsel	Dechert LLP	E.P.S.	-$1.59
DUNS No.	00-193-6079	Shareholders	NA

Business: The group's principal activities is to manufacture polyethylene terephthalate, plastic containers for food and beverages. The group manufactures pet containers for conventional pet applications in soft drinks and water and for custom pet applications. Custom pet applications are used for food, juices, teas, new age beverages, beer and flavored alcoholic beverages. The group supplies pet products for brands as pepsi, coca-cola, dr. Pepper, 7up, Canada dry, evian, gordon's, aquafina, fanta, lipton, peter pan, folger's, mike's hard lemonade, rolling rock and smirnoff ice. It operates in 17 manufacturing sites, 14 in the United States and 3 in Europe.

Primary SIC and add'l.: 3085 3089

CIK No: 0000029806

Subsidiaries: BFF Inc., Constar Ambalaj Sanayi Ve Ticaret A.S., Constar Foreign Holdings, Inc., Constar International Holland (Plastics) B.V., Constar International UK Limited, Constar Plastics of Italy S.R.L., Constar, Inc., DT, Inc.

Officers: Michael J. Hoffman/Dir., CEO, Pres./$1,229,604.00, Donald P. Deubel/VP - Corporate Technologies, James C.T. Bolton/Sr. VP - Administration, Strategic Planning/$511,071.00, Jerry A. Hatfield/VP - Operations, David J. Waksman/VP, General Counsel, Sec./$413,829.00, Frank E. Gregory/VP - European Operations/$369,878.00, Walter S. Sobon/CFO/$617,182.00, Daniel Ingram/Sr. VP - Sales, Marketing Constar, Henry J. Conicelli/48/VP, Corporate Controller

Directors: Michael J. Hoffman/Dir., CEO, Pres., John P. Neafsey/Chmn., Angus F. Smith/Dir., Frank J. Mechura/Dir., James A. Lewis/Dir., Alexander A. Taylor/Dir., Michael D. McDaniel/Dir.

Owners: Insiders/5.00%, William G. Little, Alexander A. Taylor, Crown Cork& Seal Company, Inc./10.00%, Michael J. Hoffman/1.70%, Douglas Troob and Peter Troob/9.10%, Walter S. Sobon, Frank J. Mechura, James C.T. Bolton, James A. Lewis, Frank E. Gregory, David J. Waksman, David J. Greene and Company, LLC/9.80%, Nader Tavakoli/23.60%, Wells Fargo& Company/15.20% *(17 Owners included in Index)*

Financial Data: Fiscal Year End:12/31 Latest Annual Data: 12/31/2006

Year	Sales	Net Income
2006	$926,969,000	-$12,022,000
2005	$975,017,000	-$59,990,000
2004	$844,182,000	-$6,820,000

Curr. Assets:	$189,815,000	Curr. Liab.:	$123,674,000		
Plant, Equip.:	$148,235,000	Total Liab.:	$548,801,000	Indic. Yr. Divd.:	NA
Total Assets:	$503,962,000	Net Worth:	-$44,839,000	Debt/ Equity:	NA

Constellation Brands Inc

370 Woodcliff Dr., Ste. 300, Fairport, NY, 14450; *PH:* 1-585-218-3600; *Fax:* 1-585-218-3601; *http://* www.cbrands.com

General - Incorporation	DE	Stock- Price on:12/24/2007	$24.02
Employees	9,200	Stock Exchange	NYSE
Auditor	KPMG LLP	Ticker Symbol	STZ
Stk Agt	Mellon Investor Srvcs LLC	Outstanding Shares	235,060,000
Counsel	NA	E.P.S	$1.15
DUNS No.	05-965-1117	Shareholders	NA

Business: The group's principle activities include manufacturing and marketing beverage alcohol products. The group operates through four segments include wines, beer, spirits, and other beverages. The group operates from North America, Europe, Australia, and United Kingdom.

Primary SIC and add'l.: 2084 5181 2085 5182

CIK No: 0000016918

Subsidiaries: 3112751 Nova Scotia Company, ACN 103 359 299, ACN 103 362 232, Allberry, Inc., Allied Drink Distributors Limited, Alto de Casablanca S.A.1, Avalon Cellars Limited, Barton Beers of Wisconsin, Ltd., Barton Beers, Ltd., Barton Brands of California, Inc., Barton Brands of Georgia, Inc., Barton Brands, Ltd., Barton Canada, Ltd., Barton Distillers Import Corp., Barton Financial Corporation 89 Subsidiaries included in the Index

Officers: Robert Sands/Dir., CEO, Pres./$1,973,226.00, Alexander Berk/CEO - Constellation Beers, Spirits/$1,445,823.00, Jose Fernandez/CEO - Constellation Wines North America, Robert Ryder/CFO, Exec. VP, David S. Sorce/Sec., Keith W. Wilson/Exec. VP, Chief Administrative Officer, Thomas J. Mullin/Exec. VP, General Counsel/$825,447.00, Paul F. Hetterich/Exec. VP - Business Development, Corporate Strategy, Patty Yahn-Urlaub/VP - Investor Relations, Bob Czudak/Dir. - Investor Relations

Directors: Robert Sands/Dir., CEO, Pres., Richard Sands/Chmn., Barry A. Fromberg/Dir., Mark Zupan/Dir., Thomas C. McDermott/Dir., Jeananne K. Hauswald/Dir., James A. Locke/Dir., Paul L. Smith/Dir., Peter H. Soderberg/Dir.

Owners: UBS AG/13.10%, Insiders, Robert Sands, Insiders/4.00%, Alexander L. Berk, Peter H. Soderberg, Thomas C. McDermott, CWC Partnership-I/0.20%, Jeananne K. Hauswald, Richard Sands/1.50%, CWC Partnership-I, Stockholders Group/2.60%, Paul L. Smith, Trust for the benefit of Andrew Stern, M.D., Robert Sands/1.50% *(25 Owners included in Index)*

Financial Data: Fiscal Year End:02/28 Latest Annual Data: 02/28/2007

Year	Sales	Net Income
2007	$5,216,400,000	$331,900,000
2006	$4,603,448,000	$325,262,000
2005	$4,087,638,000	$276,464,000

Curr. Assets:	$3,023,300,000	Curr. Liab.:	$1,591,100,000	P/E Ratio:	17.66
Plant, Equip.:	$1,750,200,000	Total Liab.:	$6,020,700,000	Indic. Yr. Divd.:	NA
Total Assets:	$9,438,200,000	Net Worth:	$3,417,500,000	Debt/ Equity:	1.0870

Constellation Energy Group Inc

750 E Pratt St., Baltimore, MD, 21202; *PH:* 1-410-783-2800; *Fax:* 1-410-783-3629; *http://* www.constellation.com; *Email:* investorrelations@constellation.com

General - Incorporation	MD	Stock- Price on:12/24/2007	$89.44
Employees	9,645	Stock Exchange	NYSE
Auditor	PricewaterhouseCoopers LLP	Ticker Symbol	CEG
Stk Agt	American Stock Transfer & Trust Co.	Outstanding Shares	180,310,000
Counsel	NA	E.P.S	$5.30
DUNS No.	NA	Shareholders	NA

Business: The group's principle activity is to provide customers seeking energy solutions in the complex and changing energy marketplace. The group operates through three segments namely merchant energy business, regulated electric and regulated gas. The group operates from United States.

Primary SIC and add'l.: 4911 6719 4923 4961

CIK No: 0001004440

Subsidiaries: Baltimore Gas and Electric Company., BGE Capital Trust II, BGE Home Products& Services,Inc., Calvert Cliffs Nuclear Power Plant,Inc., CEG Acquisition, LLC, Constellation Energy Commodities Group,Inc., Constellation Energy Projects and Services Group,Inc., Constellation Enterprises,Inc., Constellation Generation Group, LLC, Constellation Holdings,Inc., Constellation Investments,Inc., Constellation NewEnergy, Inc, Constellation Nuclear Services,Inc., Constellation Power Source Generation,Inc., Constellation Power Source Holdings,Inc. 20 Subsidiaries included in the Index

Officers: Felix J. Dawson/41/Co - CEO, Co - Pres. - Commodities Group Constellation Energy Constellation Energy/$9,205,607.00, George E. Persky/38/Co - CEO, Co - Pres. - Commodities Group Constellation Energy/$9,224,832.00, Mayo A. Shattuck/Chmn., CEO, Pres./$200,586,700.00, David S. /Machinery Mechanic, Elizabeth M. /Nuclear Engineer, Barbara G. /Supervisor, Coordination, Support, Glenn M. /Team Leader, Kevin Hadlock/VP - Investor Relations, Charles A. Berardesco/VP, Corp. Sec., Robert L. Gould/Contact - Media, Debra Larsson/Contact - Media, Tonya Cultice/Investor Relations Officer, Diana L. Hayden/Contact - Media, Reese F. /VP, Corporate Controller, Michael J. Wallace/Exec. VP *(27 Officers included in Index)*

Directors: Mayo A. Shattuck/Chmn., CEO, Pres., Michael D. Sullivan/Dir., Robert J. Lawless/Dir., Lynn M. Martin/Dir., Freeman A. Hrabowski/Dir., Edward A. Crooke/Dir., Yves C. De Balmann/Dir., James T. Brady/Dir., Douglas L. Becker/Dir., James R. Curtiss/Dir., Nancy Lampton/Dir.

Owners: Follin E. Smith, James R. Curtiss, Robert J. Lawless, Douglas L. Becker, Insiders, Barclays Global Investors, NA1/6.91%, James T. Brady, Felix J. Dawson, Thomas V. Brooks, Mayo A. Shattuck, Michael D. Sullivan, Lynn M. Martin, Edward A. Crooke, Freeman A. Hrabowski, Yves C. De Balmann *(17 Owners included in Index)*

Financial Data: Fiscal Year End:12/31 Latest Annual Data: 12/31/2006

Year	Sales	Net Income
2006	$19,284,900,000	$936,400,000
2005	$17,132,000,000	$623,100,000
2004	$12,549,700,000	$539,700,000

Curr. Assets:	$9,100,100,000	Curr. Liab.:	$7,122,700,000	P/E Ratio:	15.66
Plant, Equip.:	$9,222,100,000	Total Liab.:	$17,097,800,000	Indic. Yr. Divd.:	$1.740
Total Assets:	$21,801,600,000	Net Worth:	$4,609,300,000	Debt/ Equity:	0.9160

Consulier Engineering Inc

2391 Old Dixie Hwy., Riviera Beach, FL, 33404; *PH:* 1-561-842-2492; *Fax:* 1-561-845-3237; *http://* www.consulier.com; *Email:* contact@consulier.com

General - Incorporation	FL	Stock- Price on:12/24/2007	$3.79
Employees	NA	Stock Exchange	NDQ
Auditor	Goldstein Lewin & Co	Ticker Symbol	CSLR
Stk Agt	Affiliated Stock Transfer Co	Outstanding Shares	5,380,000
Counsel	NA	E.P.S	$0.28
DUNS No.	17-448-1333	Shareholders	NA

Business: The group's principle activities are the distribution of household and tool products and providing corporate services. The group operates through three segments. The household and tool products segment is engaged in sales of tool and ladder related products. The investments segment maintains investment interests in an investment limited partnership and limited liability companies. The group's corporate segment consists of management and finance activities as well as consulting, engineering, new product development and business management. During 2003, the group discontinued its automotive parts distribution segment. The group's quarterly revenue for September 2007 was 0.51 millions of USD.

Primary SIC and add'l.: 8748 5013

CIK No: 0000846718

Subsidiaries: Consulier International, Inc., majority-owned ST, LLC

Officers: Warren B. Mosler/58/Chmn., CEO, Pres., Tony Marsico/CEO, Pres. - Patient Care Technology Systems, LLC, Alan R. Simon/57/General Counsel, Sec., Treasurer - Principal Financial, Accounting Officer

Directors: Warren B. Mosler/58/Chmn., CEO, Pres., Alan R. Simon/57/General Counsel, Sec., Treasurer - Principal Financial, Accounting Officer, Skender Fani/68/Dir., Jean-Pierre Arnaud/Dir., James Combias/45/Dir.

Owners: Warren B. Mosler/79.00%, Alan R. Simon/3.50%, Burck E. Grosse/0.20%, Insiders/82.70%

Financial Data: Fiscal Year End:12/31 Latest Annual Data: 12/31/2006

Year	Sales	Net Income
2006	$1,607,000	-$1,544,000
2005	$1,017,000	-$1,161,000
2004	$49,000	-$2,635,000

Curr. Assets:	$3,546,000	Curr. Liab.:	$3,402,000		
Plant, Equip.:	$1,888,000	Total Liab.:	$6,807,000	Indic. Yr. Divd.:	NA
Total Assets:	$10,471,000	Net Worth:	$3,664,000	Debt/ Equity:	0.8430

Consumer Portfolio Services Inc

16355 Laguna Canyon Rd., Irvine, CA, 92618; *PH:* 1-949-753-6800; *Fax:* 1-949-753-6805; *http://* www.consumerportfolio.com

General - Incorporation	CA	Stock- Price on:12/24/2007	$6.57
Employees	789	Stock Exchange	NDQ
Auditor	McGladrey & Pullen LLP	Ticker Symbol	CPSS
Stk Agt	American Stock Transfer & Trust Co.	Outstanding Shares	21,570,000
Counsel	NA	E.P.S	$1.77
DUNS No.	78-132-8026	Shareholders	NA

Business: The group's principal activity is to provide consumer finance to purchase and service retail automobile purchase contracts. These contracts are originated by licensed motor vehicle dealers in the sale of new and used automobiles, light trucks and passenger vans. The group provides indirect financing to the dealer customers by purchasing installment contracts from dealers. The group serves as an alternative source of financing for dealers who generally would not qualify for automobile financing from traditional sources, such as commercial banks, credit unions and the captive finance companies affiliated with major automobile manufacturers. The group's servicing activities consist of collecting, accounting and posting of all payments received, responding to customer inquiries, investigating delinquencies and monitoring each contract and the related collateral. On 21-May-2003, the group acquired tfc enterprises inc.

Primary SIC and add'l.: 6159

CIK No: 0000889609

Subsidiaries: 71270 Corp., Canyon Receivables Corp., CPS 123 Corp., CPS Leasing, Inc., CPS Marketing, Inc., CPS Receivables Corp., CPS Receivables Two Corp., CPS Residual Corp., Gulfco Finance Company, Gulfco Investment, Inc., Mercury Finance Company LLC, Mercury Finance Company of Arizona, Mercury Finance Company of Colorado, Mercury Finance Company of Delaware, Mercury Finance Company of Florida 49 Subsidiaries included in the Index

Officers: Charles E. Bradley/Chmn., CEO, Pres./$2,336,986.00, Curtis K. Powell/Sr. VP - Originations/$646,418.00, Chris Terry/Sr. VP - Servicing/$697,390.00, Robert E. Riedl/Sr. VP, Chief Investment Officer/$688,418.00, Jeffrey P. Fritz/Sr. VP, CFO/$688,412.00, Mark A. Creatura/Sr. VP, General Counsel

Directors: Charles E. Bradley/Chmn., CEO, Pres., Bruce E. Fredrikson/Dir., John C. Warner/Dir., William B. Roberts/Dir., Daniel S. Wood/Dir., Brian Rayhill/Dir., Gregory S. Washer/Dir.

Owners: Levine Leichtman Capital Partners II, L.P/17.10%, Brian J. Rayhill, Curtis K. Powell/1.40%, Chris Terry/1.00%, Charles E. Bradley/15.00%, Robert E. Riedl/1.10%, Millennium Management, L.L.C./7.10%, John C. Warner, Insiders/27.70%, William B. Roberts/4.20%, Daniel S. Wood, Jeffrey P. Fritz, Gregory S. Washer, Bruce E. Fredrikson

Financial Data: *Fiscal Year End:* 12/31 *Latest Annual Data:* 12/31/2006

Year	Sales	Net Income
2006	$278,863,000	$39,555,000
2005	$193,697,000	$3,372,000
2004	$132,692,000	-$15,888,000

Curr. Assets:	$45,053,000	**Curr. Liab.:**	$30,887,000	**P/E Ratio:**	3.71
Plant, Equip.:	$824,000	**Total Liab.:**	$1,616,829,000	**Indic. Yr. Divd.:**	NA
Total Assets:	$1,728,341,000	**Net Worth:**	$111,512,000	**Debt/ Equity:**	15.6643

Consumers Bancorp Inc

614 E Lincoln Way, Minerva, OH, 44657; ***PH:*** 1-330-868-7701; ***Fax:*** 1-330-868-3460; ***http://*** www.consumersbank.com; ***Email:*** info@consumersbank.com

General - Incorporation	OH	Stock- Price on:12/24/2007	$11.75
Employees	97	Stock Exchange	OTC
Auditor	Crowe Chizek & Co. LLC	Ticker Symbol	CBKM
Stk Agt	NA	Outstanding Shares	2,080,000
Counsel	NA	E.P.S	NA
DUNS No.	02-064-8002	Shareholders	NA

Business: The group's principal activity is providing commercial and retail banking services to business and individual customers in stark, columbiana, carroll and contiguous counties in Ohio. The group attracts deposits from businesses and individual customers and originates commercial, mortgage and consumer loans. The group also invests in securities consisting primarily of the United States government and government agency obligations, municipal obligations, mortgage-backed securities and other securities.

Primary SIC and add'l.: 6021 6712

CIK No: 0001006830

Subsidiaries: Consumers National Bank

Officers: Steven L. Muckley/Dir., CEO, Pres./$240,720.00, Stormie Gross/VP - Risk Management, Compliance Officer, Paul B. Hugenberg/CIO/$112,264.00, Rebecca Geis/VP - Deposit Operations, Gloria Moser/Mgr., Loan Officer - Alliance Office, Teresa Firth/Customer Service Representative, New Accounting, Alliance Office, Theresa Linder/Corp. Sec., Phillip Suarez/Sr. VP, Sr. Loan Officer, Renee Wood/CFO, Treasurer/$91,981.00, Michele Catlett/AVP, District Mgr. West Division, Carrollton Branch Mgr. - Carrollton Office, Bev Newell/Sr. Customer Service, Operations Associate, Carrollton Office, Christina Hickey/Management Associate, Malvern Office, Melinda Serban/Customer Service Representative, New Accounting, Malvern Office, Bev Tucci/Mgr., Loan Officer - Waynesburg Office, Patti Gotschall/Sr. Customer Service, Operations Associate, Waynesburg Office *(23 Officers included in Index)*

Directors: Steven L. Muckley/Dir., CEO, Pres., Laurie L. McClellan/Chmn., John P. Furey/Dir., James V. Hanna/Dir., David W. Johnson/Dir., James R. Kiko/Dir., Thomas M. Kishman/Dir., Harry W. Schmuck/Dir., John Tonti/Dir.

Owners: Thomas M. Kishman, Harry W. Schmuck, John E. Tonti, James R. Kiko, Insiders/32.88%, Insiders/32.88%, James V. Hanna/7.48%, Laurie L. McClellan/20.84%, John P. Furey/1.40%, Paul B. Hugenberg, David W. Johnson, Renee K. Wood, Steven L. Muckley, Phillip M. Suarez

Financial Data: *Fiscal Year End:* 12/30 *Latest Annual Data:* 6/30/2006

Year	Sales	Net Income
2006	$13,558,000	$1,178,000
2005	$12,682,000	$1,955,000
2004	$12,365,000	$2,083,000

Curr. Assets:	$8,087,000	**Curr. Liab.:**	$184,448,000	**P/E Ratio:**	19.58
Plant, Equip.:	$5,397,000	**Total Liab.:**	$184,448,000	**Indic. Yr. Divd.:**	$0.320
Total Assets:	$203,550,000	**Net Worth:**	$19,102,000	**Debt/ Equity:**	NA

Consumers Energy Co

1280 Landmeier Rd., Elk Grove Village, IL, 60007; ***PH:*** 1-847-437-1666; ***Fax:*** 1-847-437-4969; ***http://*** www.consumersenergy.com; ***Email:*** foundation@consumersenergy.com

General - Incorporation	MI	Stock- Price on:12/24/2007	$1.95
Employees	74	Stock Exchange	OTC
Auditor	Ernst & Young LLP	Ticker Symbol	LMEC
Stk Agt	CMS Energy Corp	Outstanding Shares	53,570,000
Counsel	NA	E.P.S	-$0.3
DUNS No.	00-695-9803	Shareholders	NA

Business: The group's principal activity is to generate, transmit and distribute electricity. It is an electric and gas utility company and a subsidiary of cms energy corporation. The service areas are automotive, metal, chemical, food and wood products and a diversified group of other industries. The group provides services to customers in Michigan's lower peninsula. The customers of the group include residential, commercial and diversified industrial users. It operates through two segments: electric segment and gas segment. The electric segment consists of regulated activities associated with the generation, transmission and distribution of electricity. The gas segment consists of regulated activities associated with the transportation, storage and distribution of natural gas.

Primary SIC and add'l.: 4922 4911

CIK No: 0000201533

Subsidiaries: CMS Capital, LLC, CMS Viron Corporation, Dearborn Industrial Generation, LLC

Officers: David W. Joos/CEO, James Coddington/VP - Generation Operations, Glenn P. Barba/VP, Controller, Chief Accounting Officer, James E. Brunner/Sr. VP, General Counsel, Debra Dodd/Contact - Consumers Energy Electric, Natural Gas Service Media, Dennis Mckee/Contact - Consumers Energy Generating Plant, Hydros Media, Ronn J. Rasmussen/VP - Rates, Regulation, Jon R. Robinson/VP, Deputy General Counsel - Utility Law, Regulation, Jackson L. Hanson/VP - Generation Engineering, Services, James P. Pomaranski/VP - Generation Construction, Susan C. Swan/VP - Customer Operations, Jeff Holyfield/Dir. - News, Information, Dan Bishop/Dir. - Public Information, Tim Pietryga/Contact - Consumers Energy Electric, Natural Gas Service Media, Mary Gust/Contact - Consumers Energy Electric, Natural Gas Service Media *(23 Officers included in Index)*

Directors: Joseph F. Paquette/Dir., John B. Yasinsky/Dir., Michael T. Monahan/Dir., Jon E. Barfield/Dir., Richard M. Gabrys/Dir., Philip R. Lochner/Dir., Percy A. Pierre/Dir., Kenneth L. Way/Dir., Merribel S. Ayres/Dir.

Financial Data: *Fiscal Year End:* 12/31 *Latest Annual Data:* 12/31/2006

Year	Sales	Net Income
2006	$8,144,000	-$16,448,000
2005	$4,855,000	-$6,873,000
2004	$2,413,000	-$5,159,000

Curr. Assets:	$8,515,000	**Curr. Liab.:**	$4,909,000		
Plant, Equip.:	$1,201,000	**Total Liab.:**	$7,212,000	**Indic. Yr. Divd.:**	NA
Total Assets:	$25,397,000	**Net Worth:**	$18,185,000	**Debt/ Equity:**	0.0033

Contango Oil & Gas Co

3700 Buffalo Speedway, Ste. 960, Houston, TX, 77098; ***PH:*** 1-713-960-1901; ***Fax:*** 1-713-960-1065; ***http://*** www.contango-oandg.com; ***Email:*** kpeak@contango.com

General - Incorporation	DE	Stock- Price on:12/24/2007	$36.7
Employees	6	Stock Exchange	AMEX
Auditor	William D. Von Gonten, Jr.	Ticker Symbol	MCF
Stk Agt	U.S. Stock Transfer Corp	Outstanding Shares	15,950,000
Counsel	NA	E.P.S	NA
DUNS No.	NA	Shareholders	NA

Business: The group's principle activity is to explore, develop, produce, acquire, and sell natural gas and crude oil in the United States. The group's exploration and production efforts are currently focused onshore on the gulf coast and offshore in the gulf of Mexico. The primary source of production is currently in south Texas. The group's total revenue for year 2007 was 18.69 millions of USD.

Primary SIC and add'l.: 1382

CIK No: 0001071993

Subsidiaries: COE Offshore, LLC, Contango Energy Company, Contango Gas Solutions I, Inc., Contango Gas Solutions II, Inc., Contango Gas Solutions LP, Contango Offshore Exploration LLC, Contango Operators, Inc., Contango Pipeline Company, Contango Resources Company, Contango STEP I, Inc., Contango STEP II, Inc., Contango STEP, LP, Contango Sundance, Inc., Contango Venture Capital Corporation, Magnolia Offshore Exploration LLC 18 Subsidiaries included in the Index

Officers: Kenneth R. Peak/Chmn., CEO, CFO, Sergio Castro/VP, Treasurer, Marc Duncan/Pres., COO - Contango Operators, Inc, Lesia Bautina/Sr. VP, Controller, Artee Kumar/Executive Assist., Cherylin Plair/Mgr. - JIB, AP

Directors: Kenneth R. Peak/Chmn., CEO, CFO, Jay D. Brehmer/Dir., Darrell W. Williams/Dir., Charles M. Reimer/Dir., Steven L. Schoonover/Dir., B. A. Berilgen/60/Dir.

Owners: West Coast Asset Management, Inc./5.70%, Sergio Castro, Lesia Bautina/1.17%, Charles M. Reimer/1.50%, Steven L. Schoonover/1.55%, RCH Energy Opportunity Fund II, LP/33.00%, Marc Duncan, Palo Alto Global Energy Master Fund, LP/17.00%, The Northwestern Mutual Life Insurance Company/17.00%, Darrell W. Williams, B.A. Berilgen, Ironman Energy Capital, LP/10.00%, West Coast Opportunity Fund, LLC/17.00%, Sellers Capital Master Fund, Ltd/11.45%, Kenneth R. Peak/15.03% *(17 Owners included in Index)*

Financial Data: *Fiscal Year End:* 06/30 *Latest Annual Data:* 6/30/2006

Year	Sales	Net Income
2006	$920,000	-$207,000
2005	$4,330,000	$12,418,000
2004	$27,688,000	$7,700,000

Curr. Assets:	$34,513,000	**Curr. Liab.:**	$16,180,000		
Plant, Equip.:	$41,257,000	**Total Liab.:**	$26,845,000	**Indic. Yr. Divd.:**	NA
Total Assets:	$89,385,000	**Net Worth:**	$62,540,000	**Debt/ Equity:**	0.4801

Contax Holding Co

Rua Do Passeio, 56 16th Fl., Rio De Janeiro;

General - Incorporation	Brazil	Stock- Price on:12/24/2007	NA
Employees	NA	Stock Exchange	NA
Auditor	PricewaterhouseCoopers LLP	Ticker Symbol	NA
Stk Agt	Banco Do Brasil S.A.	Outstanding Shares	NA
Counsel	NA	E.P.S	NA
DUNS No.	NA	Shareholders	NA

Business: The group's principal activity is providing outsourced contact center services. The group specializes in the design, implementation, and operation of complex contact centers. The group serves many of Brazil's largest companies in the telecommunications, financial services, utilities and Internet sectors.

Primary SIC and add'l.: 8880

CIK No: 0001332750

Subsidiaries: TNL Contax S.A.

Officers: Rosangela Maria De Oliveira Lutti/54/Executive Officer

Directors: Sergio Bernstein/Dir., Fabio Schvartsman/54/Dir.

Owners: Asseca Participaes, AG Telecom Participaes, Insiders, BNDES Participaes, Fiago Participaes, Alutrens Participaes, Fundao Atlntico de Seguridade Social, Telemar Participaes S.A., L. F. Tel, Lexpart Participaes, Caixa de Previdncia dos Funcionrios do Banco do Brasil PREVI

Continan Communications Inc

11601 Wilshire Blvd., Ste. 2030, Los Angeles, CA, 90025; ***PH:*** 1-310-479-4714; ***Fax:*** 1-310-473-8995; ***http://*** www.vocalenvision.com; ***Email:*** info@1tc.com

General - Incorporation		Stock - Price on:12/24/2007	$0.19
Employees	2	Stock Exchange	OTC
Auditor	NA	Ticker Symbol	CNTN
Stk Agt.	NA	Outstanding Shares	25,470,000
Counsel	NA	E.P.S.	NA
DUNS No.	NA	Shareholders	NA

Business: The group's principle activity is to provide communication services. The group operates from United States.

Primary SIC and add'l.: 6799

CIK No:

Officers: Claude Buchert/CEO, Pres., Celine Coicaud/Dir. - Operations, James W. Gibson/VP - Business Development, Ross Nordin/Treasurer, CFO, Helene Legendre/CFO, Exec. VP

Directors: Marcia Rosenbaum/44/Dir.

Financial Data: Fiscal Year End:NA   **Latest Annual Data:** 03/31/2007

Year	Sales	Net Income
2007	NA	NA
2006	$5,000	-$1,846,000
2005	NA	-$1,995,000

Curr. Assets:	$11,000	Curr. Liab.:	$1,107,000		
Plant, Equip.:	$35,000	Total Liab.:	$1,112,000	Indic. Yr. Divd.:	NA
Total Assets:	$639,000	Net Worth:	-$473,000	Debt/ Equity:	NA

Continental Airlines Inc

1600 Smith St., Dept. HQSEO, Houston, TX, 77002; **PH:** 1-713-324-2950; **Fax:** 1-713-324-2687; **http://** www.continental.com

General - Incorporation	DE	Stock - Price on:12/24/2007	$32.9
Employees	43,770	Stock Exchange	NDQ
Auditor	Ernst & Young LLP	Ticker Symbol	CAL
Stk Agt.	Mellon Investor Services LLC	Outstanding Shares	97,130,000
Counsel	NA	E.P.S.	$4.24
DUNS No.	03-789-7840	Shareholders	NA

Business: The groups principle activity is to provide air transport services. The group's products include continental airline business cards and continental travel expense management products. The group operates from United States.

Primary SIC and add'l.: 4512

CIK No: 0000319687

Subsidiaries: Air Micronesia, Inc., Calair Capital Corporation, Calair LLC, Calfinco Inc., Caljet LLC, Century Casualty Company, Continental Airlines Purchasing Holdings LLC, Continental Airlines Purchasing Services LLC, Continental Micronesia, Inc., Presidents Club of Guam, Inc., Rubicon Indemnity, Ltd.

Officers: Lawrence W. Kellner/Chmn., CEO/$7,757,958.00, Jeffery A. Smisek/Dir., Pres./$5,829,068.00, Dave Hilfman/Sr. VP - Sales, Jeffrey J. Misner/CFO, Exec. VP/$3,453,674.00, Dante Marzetta/Sr. VP - Technical Operations, Purchasing, Jennifer Vogel/Sr. VP, General Counsel, Sec., Chief Compliance Officer, Mark Moran/Exec. VP - Operations/$3,349,723.00, Mike Bonds/Sr. VP - Human Resources, Labor Relations, Mark Erwin/Sr. VP - Asia, Pacific, Corporate Development, Rebecca Cox/Sr. VP - Government Affairs, Jim Compton/Exec. VP - Marketing/$3,414,573.00, Mark Bergsrud/Sr. VP - Marketing Programs, Distribution, David Grizzle/Sr. VP - Customer Experience, Nene Foxhall/Sr. VP - International, State Affairs, Bill Meehan/Sr. VP - Airport Services *(20 Officers included in Index)*

Directors: Lawrence W. Kellner/Chmn., CEO, Jeffery A. Smisek/Dir., Pres., Douglas H. McCorkindale/Dir., Oscar Munoz/Dir., Karen Hastie Williams/Dir., Charles A. Yamarone/Dir., Kirbyjon H. Caldwell/Dir., Henry L. Meyer/Dir., Ronald B. Woodard/Dir., George G.C. Parker/Dir., Thomas J. Barrack/Dir.

Owners: BlackRock, Inc./5.85%, Oscar Munoz, James E. Compton, Thomas J. Barrack, Ronald B. Woodard, Barclays Global Investors, NA/11.97%, Kirbyjon H. Caldwell, Mark J. Moran, Jeffery A. Smisek, Insiders, George G. C. Parker, Lawrence W. Kellner, Susquehanna Investment Group/7.40%, Charles A. Yamarone, Douglas H. McCorkindale *(19 Owners included in Index)*

Financial Data: Fiscal Year End:12/31   **Latest Annual Data:** 12/31/2006

Year	Sales	Net Income
2006	$13,128,000,000	$343,000,000
2005	$11,208,000,000	-$68,000,000
2004	$9,899,000,000	-$409,000,000

Curr. Assets:	$4,129,000,000	Curr. Liab.:	$3,955,000,000	P/E Ratio:	7.76
Plant, Equip.:	$6,263,000,000	Total Liab.:	$10,961,000,000	Indic. Yr. Divd.:	NA
Total Assets:	$11,308,000,000	Net Worth:	$347,000,000	Debt/ Equity:	8.2727

Continental Beverage & Nutrition Inc

100 Quentin Roosevelt Blvd., Ste. 404, Garden City, NY, 11530; **PH:** 1-516-222-0100; **http://** www.continentalbeverage.com; **Email:** info@continentalbeverage.com

General - Incorporation	DE	Stock - Price on:12/24/2007	NA
Employees	NA	Stock Exchange	OTC
Auditor	Linder & Linder	Ticker Symbol	COBN
Stk Agt.	Continental Stock Transfer & Trust Co	Outstanding Shares	NA
Counsel	NA	E.P.S.	-$0.005
DUNS No.	NA	Shareholders	NA

Business: The group's principle activity is to extract, distribute and bottle the natural mountain and spring water from a stream and spring fed natural reservoir in the northeastern United States. The company has a ground and water lease with the incorporated village of lake george, which provides exclusive rights to four water sources, as well as five acres of property to build a bottling plant. Products of the group are marketed in northern United States. The group operates from United States.

Primary SIC and add'l.: 2086 5149

CIK No: 0001074075

Subsidiaries: US Modular, LLC

Officers: David Sackler/CEO, CFO

Financial Data: Fiscal Year End:02/28   **Latest Annual Data:** 2/28/2006

Year	Sales	Net Income
2006	NA	-$751,000
2005	$65,000	-$463,000
2004	$234,000	-$491,000

Curr. Assets:	$125,000	Curr. Liab.:	$1,672,000		
Plant, Equip.:	NA	Total Liab.:	$1,672,000	Indic. Yr. Divd.:	NA
Total Assets:	$140,000	Net Worth:	-$1,532,000	Debt/ Equity:	NA

Continental Energy Corp

14001 Dallas Pkwy., Ste. 1200, Dallas, TX, 75240; **PH:** 1-972-934-6774; **Fax:** 1-972-934-6718; **http://** www.continentalenergy.com; **Email:** mail@continentalenergy.com

General - Incorporation	BC	Stock - Price on:12/24/2007	$0.69
Employees	1	Stock Exchange	OTC
Auditor	Staley, Okada & Partners	Ticker Symbol	CPPXF
Stk Agt.	Computershare Trust Co of Canada	Outstanding Shares	NA
Counsel	NA	E.P.S.	NA
DUNS No.	NA	Shareholders	NA

Business: The group's principle activities include exploring and developing natural resource properties, primarily oil and gas. The group's primary properties are in Indonesia and include 60% joint venture shares of the bengara - ii block and the yapen block, production sharing contracts with pertamina, the indonesian state oil company. The group operates from United States.

Primary SIC and add'l.: 1311 1382 1321

CIK No: 0000852747

Officers: Richard L. McAdoo/Dir., CEO, Pres., James D. Eger/Dir., CFO, R. M. Budijarto/Chief Geophysicist, Andrew Eriksson/Exploration Mgr., Jones S. Hasibuan/Financial Controller, Rita Mardalina/Geophysicist, Sendy Erty Soemardi/Office Mgr., M. Rojah/Administration

Directors: Richard L. McAdoo/Dir., CEO, Pres., James D. Eger/Dir., CFO, Paul L. Hayes/Dir., David T.W. Yu/Dir., Phillip B. Garrison/55/Dir.

Owners: Insiders/24.40%, Phillip B. Garrison/0.70%, Richard L. McAdoo/9.60%, James D. Eger/2.80%, Paul L. Hayes, David T.W. Yu/10.40%

Financial Data: Fiscal Year End:07/31   **Latest Annual Data:** 6/30/2006

Year	Sales	Net Income
2006	NA	$1,923,000
2005	NA	$2,343,000
2004	NA	-$1,111,000

Curr. Assets:	$260,000	Curr. Liab.:	$299,000		
Plant, Equip.:	$37,000	Total Liab.:	$299,000	Indic. Yr. Divd.:	NA
Total Assets:	$297,000	Net Worth:	-$2,000	Debt/ Equity:	NA

Continental Materials Corp

Continental Plz., 1614 Old York Rd., Abington, PA, 19001; **PH:** 1-215-884-4930; **Fax:** 1-215-887-4485; **http://** www.continentalmaterials.com

General - Incorporation	DE	Stock - Price on:12/24/2007	$29.5
Employees	802	Stock Exchange	AMEX
Auditor	Deloitte & Touche, LLP	Ticker Symbol	CUO
Stk Agt.	LaSalle Bank N.A	Outstanding Shares	1,600,000
Counsel	NA	E.P.S.	$0.78
DUNS No.	00-692-9624	Shareholders	NA

Business: The group's principle activities are production and sales of construction materials and heating and air conditioning equipment. The group operates in two business segments of construction materials and heating and air conditioning. The construction materials segment produces and sells ready mix concrete, construction aggregates and other building materials. The heating and air conditioning segment manufactures wall furnaces, console heaters, evaporative air coolers, fan coil and air handler product lines. In addition, the group also conducts a real estate operation and the holding cost for certain mining interests in mining operations. The group has operations in the United States. The group's quarterly revenue for September 2007 was 42.29 millions of USD.

Primary SIC and add'l.: 3273 6531 1422 3585

CIK No: 0000024104

Subsidiaries: Castle Concrete Company, Continental Catalina,Inc., Continental Copper,Inc., Edens Industrial Park,Inc., McKinney Door and Hardware,Inc., Phoenix Manufacturing,Inc., Rocky Mountain Ready Mix Concrete,Inc., Transit Mix Concrete Co., Transit Mix of Pueblo,Inc., Williams Furnace Co.

Officers: James G. Gidwitz/61/Chmn., CEO/$734,860.00, Mark S. Nichter/57/Sec., Controlle/$184,229.00, Joseph J. Sum/60/CFO, VP/$336,307.00, Peter J. Fischer/Pres., Marty Boland/VP - Sales, Marketing, Mark Brock/Controller, Dave Marden/Assist. Sales Mgr., Information Technology Dir., Joanne Notarianni/Import, Export Mgr., Dan Jones/Southwest Regional Sales Mgr., Marty Laslo/Midwest Regional Sales Mgr., Jim Potter/National Sales Mgr. - Fastening Division, Margaret West-Stephens/Customer Service, Transportation, Debby Edelson/Customer Service, Vienna Cline/Customer Service, Beverly Figueroa/Accounting Payable, Inventory *(17 Officers included in Index)*

Directors: James G. Gidwitz/61/Chmn., CEO, Darrell M. Trent/68/Dir., Thomas H. Carmody/61/Dir., Ronald J. Gidwitz/63/Dir., Ralph W. Gidwitz/72/Dir., Theodore R. Tetzlaff/64/Dir., Peter E. Thieriot/65/Dir.

Owners: William D. Andrews, Thomas H. Carmody, Franklin Advisory Services, LLC/6.80%, Gidwitz Family/54.60%, Peter E. Thieriot, Ralph W. Gidwitz, Insiders/56.80%, James G. Gidwitz/6.00%, Betsy R. Gidwitz, Warren G. Lichtenstein/20.90%, Ronald J. Gidwitz, Joseph J. Sum/1.00%, Darrell M. Trent

Financial Data: Fiscal Year End:12/31   **Latest Annual Data:** 12/30/2006

Year	Sales	Net Income
2006	$158,767,000	$2,042,000
2005	$138,999,000	$2,758,000

Curr. Assets:	$47,590,000	Curr. Liab.:	$19,808,000	P/E Ratio:	23.41
Plant, Equip.:	$28,844,000	Total Liab.:	$35,753,000	Indic. Yr. Divd.:	NA
Total Assets:	$87,060,000	Net Worth:	$51,307,000	Debt/ Equity:	0.2322

Continental Minerals Corp

800 W Pender St., Ste. 1020, Vancouver, BC, V6C 2V6; **PH:** 1-604-684-6365; **Fax:** 1-604-684-8092; **http://** www.hdgold.com; **Email:** info@hdgold.com

General - Incorporation	BC	**Stock**- Price on:12/24/2007	$1.56
Employees	NA	Stock Exchange	OTC
Auditor	KPMG LLP	Ticker Symbol	KMKCF
Stk Agt	Computershare Trust Co	Outstanding Shares	NA
Counsel	NA	E.P.S	NA
DUNS No.	NA	Shareholders	NA

Business: The groups principal activity is to explore Xietongmen Property. In December 2006, the group merged with Great China Mining, Inc. The group operates from British Columbia in Canada.

Primary SIC and add'l.: 1021 1041

CIK No: 0000782879

Subsidiaries: N7C Resources Inc, N8C Resources Inc

Officers: Gerald S. Panneton/Dir., CEO, Pres., Dickson Hall/Dir. - Corporate Development, Asia, Jeffery Mason/Dir., CFO, Sec., Laurie Gaborit/Dir. - Investor Relations

Directors: Gerald S. Panneton/Dir., CEO, Pres., Ronald Thiessen/Co - Chmn., Zhi Wang/Co - Chmn., Jeffery Mason/Dir., CFO, Sec., Rene G. Carrier/64/Dir., David J. Copeland/60/Dir., Scott D. Cousens/44/Dir., Gordon J. Fretwell/55/Dir., Robert A. Dickinson/60/Dir., Xiaojun Ma/42/Dir., Jie Yang/45/Dir.

Owners: Xiaojun Ma/0.70%, Jie Yang, Rene G. Carrier/0.10%, Insiders/11.73%, Zhi Wang/1.90%, Jeffrey R. Mason/1.70%, Scott D. Cousens/1.80%, David J. Copeland/1.90%, Ronald W. Thiessen/1.60%, Gerald Panneton/0.03%, Gordon J. Fretwell/0.10%, Robert A. Dickinson/1.40%

Financial Data: *Fiscal Year End:*12/31 *Latest Annual Data:* 12/31/2006

Year	Sales	Net Income
2006	NA	-$22,727,000
2005	NA	-$7,362,000
2004	NA	-$4,649,000

Curr. Assets:	$2,429,000	**Curr. Liab.:**	$14,325,000		
Plant, Equip.:	$97,198,000	**Total Liab.:**	$50,935,000	**Indic. Yr. Divd.:**	NA
Total Assets:	$111,223,000	**Net Worth:**	$60,288,000	**Debt/ Equity:**	NA

Continucare Corp

7200 Corporate Ctr. Dr., Ste. 600, Miami, FL, 33126; *PH:* 1-305-500-2000; *Fax:* 1-305-500-2080; *http://* www.continucare.com

General - Incorporation	FL	**Stock**- Price on:12/24/2007	$3.1
Employees	266	Stock Exchange	AMEX
Auditor	Ernst & Young LLP	Ticker Symbol	CNU
Stk Agt	American Stock Transfer & Trust Co.	Outstanding Shares	70,030,000
Counsel	NA	E.P.S	$0.10
DUNS No.	92-948-3873	Shareholders	NA

Business: The group's principal activity is to provide outpatient healthcare services in Florida, United States. The group provides healthcare services through its network of staff model clinics, independent physicians associations (ipa) and home health agencies. It provides healthcare services through fifteen staff model clinics, approximately 41 ipa associated physicians and four home health agencies. Staff model clinics are medical centers where physicians act as primary care physicians practicing in the area of general, family and internal medicine. Home health agencies provide comprehensive nursing, physical therapy, and nurse's aides to individuals in their home who are disabled, elderly or recovering from a debilitating illness, accident or surgery. On 01-Jan-2003, the group discontinued medicare and medicaid lines of business.

Primary SIC and add'l.: 8093 8082

CIK No: 0000803352

Subsidiaries: CNU Blue 1, Inc, Florida corporation, Miami Dade Health and Rehabilitation Services, Inc

Officers: Richard C. Pfenniger/Chmn., CEO, Pres., Gemma Rosello/Sr. VP - Operations, Luis H. Izquierdo/Sr. VP - Marketing, Business Development, Fernando Fernandez/CFO, Holly Lopez/VP - Support Services, Mark Stern/Chief Medical Officer - Tampa Bay Area, Martha Irabien/Regional Medical Dir., Jorge Luna/Chief Medical Officer - Broward, Jose M. Garcia/Exec. VP, Sadita Bustamante/Sr. VP - Center Operations, Alfredo Ginory/Chief Medical Officer - Miami, Dade County

Directors: Richard C. Pfenniger/Chmn., CEO, Pres., Luis Cruz/Vice Chmn.

Owners: Jacob Nudel, Insiders/46.70%, Luis H. Izquierdo, Carlos Garcia/4.80%, Fernando L. Fernandez, Marvin Strait, Luis Cruz/8.80%, Robert Cresci, Phillip Frost/34.80%, Neil Flanzraich, Jose M. Garcia/7.70%, Gemma Rosello, Pecks Management Partners Ltd./9.30%, Richard C. Pfenniger/2.20%

Financial Data: *Fiscal Year End:*06/30 *Latest Annual Data:* 6/30/2006

Year	Sales	Net Income
2006	$132,991,000	$5,338,000
2005	$112,231,000	$15,891,000
2004	$101,824,000	$4,653,000

Curr. Assets:	$18,601,000	**Curr. Liab.:**	$2,978,000	**P/E Ratio:**	38.75
Plant, Equip.:	$824,000	**Total Liab.:**	$3,090,000	**Indic. Yr. Divd.:**	NA
Total Assets:	$40,065,000	**Net Worth:**	$36,975,000	**Debt/ Equity:**	0.0011

Convera Corp

1921 Gallows Rd., Ste. 200, Vienna, VA, 22182; *PH:* 1-703-761-3700; *Fax:* 1-703-761-1990; *http://* www.convera.com; *Email:* info@convera.com

General - Incorporation	DE	**Stock**- Price on:12/24/2007	$4.35
Employees	180	Stock Exchange	NDQ
Auditor	Ernst & Young LLP	Ticker Symbol	CNVR
Stk Agt	American Stock Transfer & Trust Co.	Outstanding Shares	52,930,000
Counsel	NA	E.P.S	-$0.71
DUNS No.	NA	Shareholders	NA

Business: The group's principle activities are to design, develop, market, implement and support enterprise search and categorization solutions that enable mission critical applications within commercial enterprises and government agencies. The group provides a suite of search solutions for corporate intranets, Internet e-commerce, online publishing, application service providers and original equipment manufacturers. The applications include enterprise portals, knowledge management, intelligence gathering, profiling, corporate policy compliance, regulatory compliance and customer service. The solutions provided by the group enable individuals to quickly capture, analyze, access and share relevant information residing on an enterprise's networks, intranets, extranets and the Internet. Major products of the group are retrievalware, visual retrievalware, Internet spider and others. The products are marketed through a direct sales force, strategic partners and OEM's. The group's total revenue for year 2007 was 16.67 millions of USD.

Primary SIC and add'l.: 7372 7379

CIK No: 0001125536

Subsidiaries: Convera Canada, Inc., Convera France, Convera Technologies International, Ltd., Convera Technologies, Inc

Officers: Patrick C. Condo/Dir., CEO, Pres./$1,183,001.00, Graham Charlesworth/VP - Sales, Marketing, David Nunnerley/Sr. VP - Engineering, John Severance/Media, Press, Analysts, Public Relations, Matthew G. Jones/47/CFO, Treasurer, Sec./$215,537.00, Kerim Tumay/VP - Solutions

Directors: Patrick C. Condo/Dir., CEO, Pres., Ronald J. Whittier/Chmn., Jeffrey White/Dir., Herbert A. Allen/Dir., Eli S. Jacobs/Dir., Herbert A. Allen/Dir., John C. Botts/Dir., Donald R. Keough/Dir., Ajay Menon/Dir., Alexander F. Parker/Dir., Sydney Pollack/Dir., Carl J. Rickertson/Dir.

Owners: Ajay Menon, Ashford Capital Management, Inc./10.00%, Herbert A. Allen/32.70%, Herbert A. Allen/1.10%, Insiders/39.80%, John R. Polchin, Donald R. Keough/1.30%, Patrick C. Condo/3.10%, Allen Holding Inc./22.20%, Susan K. Allen/6.00%, Jeffrey White, Carl J. Rickertsen, Sydney Pollack, LMM LLC/10.50%, Eli S. Jacobs *(21 Owners included in Index)*

Financial Data: *Fiscal Year End:*01/31 *Latest Annual Data:* 1/31/2007

Year	Sales	Net Income
2007	$16,671,000	-$44,827,000
2006	$21,008,000	-$14,261,000
2005	$25,698,000	-$19,820,000

Curr. Assets:	$52,289,000	**Curr. Liab.:**	$7,963,000		
Plant, Equip.:	$3,928,000	**Total Liab.:**	$8,184,000	**Indic. Yr. Divd.:**	NA
Total Assets:	$59,281,000	**Net Worth:**	$51,097,000	**Debt/ Equity:**	NA

Convergence Ethanol Inc

Formerly: MEMS USA Inc

5701 Lindero Canyon Rd., Ste. 2-100, Westlake Village, CA, 91362; *PH:* 1-818-735-4750; *http://* www.memsusa.com

General - Incorporation	NV	**Stock**- Price on:12/24/2007	$0.33
Employees	NA	Stock Exchange	NA
Auditor	Kabani & Co.,Inc.	Ticker Symbol	NA
Stk Agt	Westcap Securities Inc	Outstanding Shares	20,790,000
Counsel	NA	E.P.S	-$0.891
DUNS No.	03-740-9331	Shareholders	NA

Business: The group's principal activity is to develop, manufacture and market advanced medical devices for the dental industry. It markets teeth-whitening systems and whitening gels to dentists through a nation-wide and international system of distributors. It has operations in the United States. On 18-Feb-2004, the group acquired mems usa inc in a reverse merger.

Primary SIC and add'l.: 3843

CIK No: 0000023778

Subsidiaries: Bott Equipment Company, Inc., Can-An Ethanol One, Inc., Gulfgate Equipment, Inc., Mems Usa, Inc.

Owners: Daniel K. Moscaritolo/14.08%, Charles L. Christensen/1.98%

Financial Data: *Fiscal Year End:*09/30 *Latest Annual Data:* 3/31/2007

Year	Sales	Net Income
2007	$1,507,000	-$1,659,000
2006	$9,211,000	-$10,928,000
2005	$8,828,000	-$2,425,000

Curr. Assets:	$4,083,000	**Curr. Liab.:**	$5,999,000		
Plant, Equip.:	$2,575,000	**Total Liab.:**	$6,034,000	**Indic. Yr. Divd.:**	NA
Total Assets:	$6,717,000	**Net Worth:**	$578,000	**Debt/ Equity:**	NA

Convergys Corp

201 E 4th St., Cincinnati, OH, 45202; *PH:* 1-513-723-7000; *Fax:* 1-513-421-8624; *http://* www.convergys.com

General - Incorporation	OH	**Stock**- Price on:12/24/2007	$24.34
Employees	75,000	Stock Exchange	NYSE
Auditor	Ernst & Young LLP	Ticker Symbol	CVG
Stk Agt	Fifth Third Bank	Outstanding Shares	136,900,000
Counsel	NA	E.P.S	$1.21
DUNS No.	02-575-0394	Shareholders	NA

Business: The group's principle activity is to provide integrated billing, employee and customer care software and services. The group develops long-term strategic relationships with clients in customer-intensive industries including telecommunications, cable, broadband, direct satellite broadcasting, Internet services, technology and financial services. It functions through two operating segments: customer management group and information management group. The customer management group provides outsourced marketing, customer support services and employee care services. The information management group provides outsourced billing and information services and software. The group's customers include at&t wireless, at&t, sprint pcs, directv, comcast, bristol-myers squibb, general electric and lucent. The group's quarterly revenue for September 2007 was 703.70 millions of USD.

Primary SIC and add'l.: 7389

CIK No: 0001062047

Subsidiaries: 3117091 Nova Scotia Company, Convergys CMG Utah Inc., Convergys Customer Management Delaware LLC, Convergys Customer Management Group Canada Holding Inc., Convergys Customer Management Group Inc., Convergys Information Management Group Inc.

Officers: David F. Dougherty/Internal Dir., CEO, Pres./$3,085,369.00, Karen R. Bowman/General Counsel, Corp. Sec., Earl Shanks/CFO/$2,465,966.00, William H. Hawkins/59/Sr. VP, General Counsel, Sec./$1,756,604.00, Timothy M. Wesolowski/49/Sr. VP, Controller, Clark D. Handy/Sr. VP - Human Resources

Directors: David F. Dougherty/Internal Dir., CEO, Pres., James F. Orr/Chmn., John F. Barrett/Dir., David B. Dillon/Dir., Richard L. Wallman/Dir., Steven C. Mason/Dir., Joseph E. Gibbs/Dir., Zoe Baird/Dir., Roger L. Howe/Dir., Philip A. Odeen/Dir., Eric C. Fast/58/Dir., Sidney A. Ribeau/Dir., David R. Whitwam/Dir.

Owners: John F. Barrett, Timothy M. Wesolowski, Philip A. Odeen, David F. Dougherty, David B. Dillon, Joseph E. Gibbs, Steven C. Mason, Sidney A. Ribeau, Roger L. Howe, David R. Whitwam, Steven G. Rolls, LSV Asset Management/5.25%, William H. Hawkins, Western and Southern Financial Group/5.41%, Earl C. Shanks *(18 Owners included in Index)*

Financial Data: *Fiscal Year End:*12/31 *Latest Annual Data:* 12/31/2006

Year	Sales	Net Income
2006	$2,789,800,000	$166,200,000
2005	$2,582,100,000	$122,600,000
2004	$2,487,700,000	$111,500,000

Curr. Assets:	$930,200,000	Curr. Liab.:	$595,900,000	P/E Ratio:	19.95
Plant, Equip.:	$368,600,000	Total Liab.:	$1,085,200,000	Indic. Yr. Divd.:	NA
Total Assets:	$2,540,300,000	Net Worth:	$1,455,100,000	Debt/ Equity:	0.1742

Conversion Services International Inc

100 Eagle Rock Ave., East Hanover, NJ, 07936; *PH:* 1-973-560-9400; *Fax:* 1-973-560-9500; *http://* www.csiwhq.com; *Email:* info@csiwhq.com

General - Incorporation............................DE
Employees...128
Auditor ....Friedman LLP
Stk Agt...... Olde Monmouth Stk Trnsfer Co. Inc.
Counsel..NA
DUNS No. ....NA

Stock - Price on:12/24/2007 ....$0.2167
Stock Exchange...AMEX
Ticker Symbol..CVN
Outstanding Shares 56,920,000
E.P.S..-$0.16
Shareholders..NA

Business: The group's principal activity is to provide a new category of professional services that embraces it management consulting, data warehousing, business intelligence consulting and e-business solutions. The group, as the center for data warehousing, offers an array of products and services to help companies define, develop and implement the warehousing and strategic use of both enterprise-wide and specific categories of strategic data. The customers include verizon wireless, morgan stanley, pfizer, goldman sachs, merck and standard & poor's. On 26-Feb-2004, the group acquired deleeuw associates, inc and all the assets of evoke software corporation on 29-Jun-2004.

Primary SIC and add'l.: 5091

CIK No: 0000934306

Subsidiaries: CSI Sub Corp. (DE), CSI Sub Corp. II (DE), DeLeeuw Associates, LLC, DeLeeuw International Yonetim Danismanli gi ve Ticaret Limited Sirketi, Doorways, Inc., Integrated Strategies, Inc., LEC Corporation of NJ, McKnight Associates, Inc.

Officers: Scott Newman/Chmn., CEO, Pres./$524,568.00, Glenn Peipert/Dir., Exec. VP, COO/$397,675.00, William McKnight/Sr. VP - Information Management/$312,883.00, William Hendry/CFO, VP, Treasurer/$193,805.00, Jeffrey Myhre/VP - Editorial, Bill Hendry/CFO, VP, Treasurer

Directors: Scott Newman/Chmn., CEO, Pres., Lawrence K. Reisman/Dir., Robert Deleeuw/Dir., Glenn Peipert/Dir., Exec. VP, COO, Frederick Lester/Dir., Thomas Pear/Dir., Bryan Carey/Dir.

Owners: Glenn Peipert/18.20%, Thomas Pear, Insiders/54.40%, Robert C. DeLeeuw/11.40%, William McKnight/1.50%, Lawrence K. Reisman, Scott Newman/34.70%, William Hendry, Bryan Carey

Financial Data: Fiscal Year End:12/31 **Latest Annual Data:** 12/31/2006

Year	Sales	Net Income
2006	$25,674,000	-$9,612,000
2005	$27,630,000	-$5,118,000
2004	$25,167,000	-$33,271,000

Curr. Assets:	$5,042,000	Curr. Liab.:	$11,314,000		
Plant, Equip.:	$265,000	Total Liab.:	$15,044,000	Indic. Yr. Divd.:	NA
Total Assets:	$14,531,000	Net Worth:	-$513,000	Debt/ Equity:	1.3370

CoolBrands International Inc

8300 Woodbine Ave., 5th Fl., Markham, ON, L3R 9Y7; *PH:* 1-905-479-8762; *http://* www.eskimopie.com; *Email:* info@coolbrandsinternational.com

General - Incorporation........................Canada
Employees...NA
Auditor ....Pricewaterhousecoopers LLP
Stk Agt...KPMG LLP
Counsel.................................Bank Rome
DUNS No. 25-255-0520

Stock - Price on:12/24/2007 ....NA
Stock Exchange...NA
Ticker Symbol..NA
Outstanding Shares ....NA
E.P.S..NA
Shareholders..NA

Business: The group's principle activities are the manufacturing and distribution of branded frozen dessert products. These products are supplied to supermarkets, grocery stores, club stores, convenience stores, gourmet shops and delicatessens in Canada, the United States and other foreign countries. The group also manufactures and distributes soft serve frozen yogurt and ice cream mixes. The group's quarterly revenue for September 2007 was 1.92 millions of USD.

Primary SIC and add'l.: 6794 5451 5142 5143 2024

CIK No: 0001005531

Subsidiaries: CoolBrands Dairy Inc., Eskimo Pie Frozen Distribution Inc, Integrated Brands, Sugar Creek Foods, Inc, Sugar Creek Foods, Inc.

Officers: Ken Mackenzie/52/CFO

Directors: Ronald W. Binns/51/Dir., Garry Macdonald/61/Dir.

CoolSavings Inc

360 N Michigan Ave, 19th Fl., Chicago, IL, 60601; *PH:* 1-312-224-5000; *http://* www.coolsavings.com

General - Incorporation............................DE
Employees...NA
Auditor ....PricewaterhouseCoopers LLP
Stk Agt...NA
Counsel..NA
DUNS No. ....NA

Stock - Price on:12/24/2007 ....NA
Stock Exchange...NA
Ticker Symbol..NA
Outstanding Shares ....NA
E.P.S..NA
Shareholders..NA

Business: The group's principle activity is to provide online direct marketing which helps marketers reach their target consumers by leveraging broad distribution network, sophisticated analytics and proprietary technology. It provides a comprehensive set of e-Marketing services for use by online and offline advertisers to build one-to-one customer relationships. The company supplies marketers with a single resource for accessing and engaging a dynamic group of shoppers. The company's customized, integrated direct marketing and media products enable advertisers to target incentives that include printed and electronic coupons, personalized e-mails, rebates, trial offers, samples, sales notices and gift certificates to promote sales of products or services. The company's database technology also track consumer response and shopping preferences at household and shopper level.

Primary SIC and add'l.: 7319 6794

CIK No: 0001087875

Subsidiaries: coolsavings.com inc.

Cooper Companies Inc (The)

21062 Bake Pkwy., Ste. 200, Lake Forest, CA, 92630; *PH:* 1-949-597-4700; *Fax:* 1-949-768-3688; *http://* www.coopercos.com; *Email:* ir@coopercompanies.com

General - Incorporation ....DE
Employees...7,500
Auditor ....KPMG LLP
Stk Agt..... American Stock Transfer & Trust Co.
Counsel..NA
DUNS No. 02-418-7130

Stock - Price on:12/24/2007 ....$53.87
Stock Exchange...NYSE
Ticker Symbol..COO
Outstanding Shares 44,780,000
E.P.S..NA
Shareholders..NA

Business: The group's principal activities are to develop, manufacture and market healthcare products. The group operates in two segments: coopervision and coopersurgical. Coopervision markets a range of specialty contact lenses including disposable and planned replacement toric and spherical lenses to correct visual defects. Coopersurgical markets medical devices, diagnostic products and surgical instruments and accessories used primarily by gynecologists and obstetricians. The group's products include toric lenses to correct astigmatism, cosmetic lenses to change or enhance the appearance of eyes' natural color, multifocal lenses and lenses for patients with dry eyes. The group acquired Avalon Medical Corporation on 28-Oct-2003.

Primary SIC and add'l.: 3841 3827

CIK No: 0000711404

Subsidiaries: Aspect Vision Holdings, Limited, Cooper Captive, Inc., Cooper Vision Italia s.r.l., CooperSurgical Acquisition Corp., CooperSurgical Acquisition GmbH, CooperSurgical, Inc., CooperVision Canada Corp., Coopervision do Brasil Ltda, CooperVision GmbH, CooperVision International Holding Company, L.P., CooperVision Limited, Coopervision Manufacturing Limited, Coopervision Nederland BV, CooperVision Optical Trade Kft, CooperVision S.A. (Pty) Limited 31 Subsidiaries included in the Index

Officers: Nicholas J. Pichotta/CEO - Coopersurgical, Inc, Robert S. Weiss/Exec. VP, CEO - Cooper Companies, Pres. - Coopervision, Thomas A. Bender/Chmn., Pres., Albert G. White/VP, Treasurer, Daniel G. McBride/VP, Sr. Corporate Counsel, John A. Weber/VP - Worldwide Manufacturing, Distribution, Coopervision, Inc, Gregory A. Fryling/53/COO, Pres. - Coopervision, Inc, Gene J. Midlock/VP - Finance, Rodney E. Folden/Corporate Controller, Norris B. Battin/VP - Investor Relations, Communications, John C. Calcagno/CFO, VP - Business Development, Coopervision, Inc, Steven M. Neil/CFO, Exec. VP, Eugene J. Midlock/VP - Taxes, Jeffery A. McLean/Pres. - US Operations, Coopervision, Inc, Paul L. Remmell/COO, Pres. - Coopersurgical, Inc *(18 Officers included in Index)*

Directors: Thomas A. Bender/Chmn., Pres., Allan E. Rubenstein/Dir., Donald Press/Dir., John D. Fruth/Dir., Jody S. Lindell/Dir., Michael H. Kalkstein/Dir., Moses Marx/Dir., Steven Rosenberg/Dir., Stanley Zinberg/Dir.

Owners: Gregory A. Fryling, John D. Fruth, Moses Marx, Insiders/4.40%, Nicholas J. Pichotta, Allan E. Rubenstein, Steven Rosenberg, Michael H. Kalkstein, Donald Press, Robert S. Weiss, Jody S. Lindell, Stanley Zinberg, Thomas A. Bender, Steven M. Neil

Financial Data: Fiscal Year End:10/31 **Latest Annual Data:** 10/31/2006

Year	Sales	Net Income
2006	$858,960,000	$66,234,000
2005	$806,617,000	$91,722,000
2004	$490,176,000	$92,825,000

Curr. Assets:	$456,951,000	Curr. Liab.:	$276,630,000		
Plant, Equip.:	$496,357,000	Total Liab.:	$974,092,000	Indic. Yr. Divd.:	$0.060
Total Assets:	$2,352,601,000	Net Worth:	$1,378,509,000	Debt/ Equity:	0.5828

Cooper Industries Ltd

600 Travis, Ste. 5800, Houston, TX, 77002; *PH:* 1-713-209-8400; *Fax:* 1-713-209-8996; *http://* www.cooperindustries.com

General - Incorporation..................Bermuda
Employees...30,561
Auditor ....Ernst & Young LLP
Stk Agt............................Computershare Trust Co
Counsel..NA
DUNS No. ....NA

Stock - Price on:12/24/2007 ....$56.94
Stock Exchange...NYSE
Ticker Symbol..CBE
Outstanding Shares 183,040,000
E.P.S...$3.20
Shareholders..NA

Business: The group's principal activities are to manufacture, market and sell electrical products and tools and hardware. The electrical products segment manufactures, markets and sells electrical and circuit protection products, including fittings, support systems, enclosures, wiring devices, plugs, emergency lighting, fire detection systems and security products. The tools and hardware segment manufactures, markets and sells hand tools for industrial, construction and consumer markets; automated assembly systems for industrial markets; and electric and pneumatic industrial power tools primarily for automotive and aerospace manufacturers. The group has manufacturing facilities in 21 countries. On 25-Mar-2004, the group acquired rsa lighting.

Primary SIC and add'l.: 3423 3646 3699 3429 3714

CIK No: 0001141982

Subsidiaries: Airetool and Yost Superior Realty, Inc., Alpha Lighting, Inc., Arrow-Hart, S.A. de C.V., Atlite Inc., Borden/Reaves, Inc., Broomco (1644)Limited, Bussmann do Brasil Ltda., Bussmann International, Inc., Bussmann, S. de R.L. de C.V., BZ Holdings Inc., Capri Codec S.A.S., CBE Services, Inc., CEAG Notlichtsysteme GmbH, CI Finance, Inc., CI Leasing Company 161 Subsidiaries included in the Index

Officers: Kirk S. Hachigian/Chmn., CEO, Pres., John B. Reed/VP - Taxes, James T. Pendley/Chief Marketing Officer, Stephen M. Kole/Treasurer, Terry A. Klebe/Sr. VP, CFO, Diane K. Schumacher/Sr. VP, General Counsel, Chief Compliance Officer/$1,517,173.00, Terrance V. Helz/Assoc. General Counsel, Sec., David T. Gunther/VP - Internal Audit, Robert W. Teets/VP - Environmental Affairs, Grant L. Gawronski/VP - International Operations/$1,374,673.00, Mike Stoessl/44/Group Pres. - Cooper Power Systems/$1,881,097.00, Melissa Scheppele/VP - Business Systems, James P. Williams/Sr. VP - Human Resources, Thomas C. O'Grady/Sr. VP - Business Development/$1,783,018.00, David L. Pawl/VP - Operations *(17 Officers included in Index)*

Directors: Kirk S. Hachigian/Chmn., CEO, Pres., James R. Wilson/Dep. Chmn., Ivor J. Evans/Dir., Linda A. Hill/Dir., Robert M. Devlin/Dir., Gerald B. Smith/Dir., Dan F. Smith/Dir., James J. Postl/Dir., Mark S. Thompson/Dir., Lawrence D. Kingsley/Dir., Stephen G. Butler/Dir.

Owners: Michael A. Stoessl, Terry A. Klebe, James R. Wilson, Gerald B. Smith, Dan F. Smith, Diane K. Schumacher, Insiders, Kirk S. Hachigian, Thomas C. OGrady, Ivor J. Evans, Robert M. Devlin, James J. Postl, Linda A. Hill, Stephen G. Butler, Grant L. Gawronski

Financial Data: Fiscal Year End:12/31 **Latest Annual Data:** 12/31/2006

Year	Sales	Net Income
2006	$5,184,600,000	$464,000,000
2005	$4,730,400,000	$163,900,000
2004	$4,462,900,000	$339,800,000

Curr. Assets:	$2,193,700,000	Curr. Liab.:	$1,499,300,000	P/E Ratio:	21.82
Plant, Equip.:	$665,400,000	Total Liab.:	$2,899,500,000	Indic. Yr. Divd.:	NA
Total Assets:	$5,374,800,000	Net Worth:	$2,475,300,000	Debt/ Equity:	0.2775

Cooper Tire & Rubber Co

701 Lima Ave., Findlay, OH, 45840; *PH:* 1-419-423-1321; *Fax:* 1-419-424-4212; *http://* www.coopertire.com; *Email:* cooperinfo@coopertire.com

General - Incorporation .... DE
Employees 13,361
Auditor .... Ernst & Young LLP
Stk Agt..... American Stock Transfer & Trust Co.
Counsel .... NA
DUNS No. 00-503-7601

Stock- Price on:12/24/2007 ....$26.81
Stock Exchange .... NYSE
Ticker Symbol.. CTB
Outstanding Shares 61,680,000
E.P.S. $0.66
Shareholders.. NA

Business: The groups principle activity is to manufacture replacement tires. The groups products include passenger and light truck replacement tires, and radial medium and bias light truck tires. The group operates through two business segments namely North American Tire Operations and International Tire Operations. The group operates from United States.

Primary SIC and add'l.: 3011 3052 3069

CIK No: 0000024491

Subsidiaries: Admiral Remco Inc., Alga Investments Company, Bfnz-orc Limited, Branch Office, Cooper International Holding Corporation, Cooper Kenda Global Holding Co. Ltd., Cooper Kenda Global Investment Co. Ltd., Cooper Kenda Tire Kunshan Co., Ltd., Cooper Shanghai Trading Co., Ltd., Cooper Tire & Rubber Co. Shanghai Rep Office, Cooper Tire & Rubber Company Deutschland GmbH, Cooper Tire & Rubber Company Espana S.L., Cooper Tire & Rubber Company Europe Ltd., Cooper Tire & Rubber Company France Sarl, Cooper Tire & Rubber Company International Development Limited 34 Subsidiaries included in the Index

Officers: Roy V. Armes/55/Dir., CEO, Pres., Philip G. Weaver/CFO, VP/$617,623.00, Harold C. Miller/55/VP/$386,459.00, James H. Geers/60/VP - Global Human Resources/$393,936.00, Pete Deischl/Contact - Synthetic Rubber, Process Oil, Tie Labels, Troy Williams/Contact - Tire Reinforcements, Dispersions, Kraig Niswander/Contact - Carbon Black, Rubber Chemicals, Rick Celeste/Contact - Capital Equipment, Information Technology Hardware, Software, Lynn Sylvain/Corporate Purchasing Mgr. - North America Materials Management, Linda Rennels/VP - Purchasing, Paul McCutcheon/Corporate Purchasing Mgr. - Raw Materials, Natural Gas, Lynn Maag/Corporate Purchasing Mgr. - Supplier Relationship Management, Steve Chasse/Supplier Quality Analyst, Supplier Relationship Management, James E. Kline/66/VP, General Counsel, Sec./$442,017.00, John Anders/Contact - MRO, Supplies, Advertising, R & D, Graphic Arts, North America Materials Management *(28 Officers included in Index)*

Directors: Arthur H. Aronson/72/Dir., John H. Shuey/62/Dir., Laurie J. Breininger/50/Dir., Steven M. Chapman/54/Dir., Richard L. Wambold/56/Dir., Byron O. Pond/71/Dir., John J. Holland/58/Dir., John F. Meier/60/Dir.

Owners: Richard L. Wambold, James H. Geers, Steven W. Chapman, John F. Meier, Harold C. Miller, James E. Kline, Brandes Investment Partners, Inc. etal./10.70%, Insiders/1.80%, John J. Holland, Byron O. Pond, Donald Smith& Co., Inc./8.00%, Arthur H. Aronson, John H. Shuey, Laurie J. Breininger, Philip G. Weaver *(19 Owners included in Index)*

Financial Data: Fiscal Year End:12/31 Latest Annual Data: 12/31/2006

Year	Sales	Net Income
2006	$2,676,242,000	-$78,511,000
2005	$2,155,185,000	-$9,356,000
2004	$2,081,609,000	$201,372,000

Curr. Assets:	$1,009,124,000	Curr. Liab.:	$527,252,000		
Plant, Equip.:	$991,816,000	Total Liab.:	$1,525,700,000	Indic. Yr. Divd.:	$0.420
Total Assets:	$2,235,279,000	Net Worth:	$639,891,000	Debt/ Equity:	0.7869

Cooperative Bankshares Inc

201 Market St., Wilmington, NC, 28401; *PH:* 1-910-343-0181; *Fax:* 1-910-251-1652; *http://* www.coop-bank.com; *Email:* info@coop-bank.com

General - Incorporation .... NC
Employees 209
Auditor .... Dixon Hughes PLLC
Stk Agt.............First Citizens Bank & Trust Co
Counsel... Stradley Ronon Stevens & Young LLP
DUNS No. 87-432-9162

Stock- Price on:12/24/2007 ....$16.255
Stock Exchange .... NDQ
Ticker Symbol... COOP
Outstanding Shares 6,520,000
E.P.S. $1.26
Shareholders.. NA

Business: The group's principle activities are to provide banking services namely deposits, bank cards and alternative investment products. The group offers commercial loans, consumer loans and other installment credit such as home equity loans, auto and boat loans and check reserves. The operations are conducted through 24 offices located in the coastal and inland communities of eastern North Carolina. The other services provided by the group include automated banking services through ATMs and access24 phone banking and safe deposit boxes. The investment services provided are discount brokerage services, annuity sales and mutual funds.

Primary SIC and add'l.: 6035 6712

CIK No: 0000923529

Subsidiaries: Cooperative Bank, Cooperative Bankshares Capital Trust I, CS&L Holdings, Inc., CS&L Real Estate Trust, Inc., Lumina Mortgage Company

Officers: Frederick Willetts/Chmn., CEO, Pres./$535,389.00, John P. Payne/VP, Chief Auditor - Cooperative Bank, Dickson B. Bridger/Sr. VP - Mortgage Lending, Cooperative Bank/$195,590.00, Todd L. Sammons/Sr. VP, CFO - Cooperative Bank/$195,657.00, Susie K. Register/VP - Mortgage Servicing, Processing, Cooperative Bank, Dare C. Rhodes/VP - Human Resources, Cooperative Bank, Craig L. Unwin/VP - Credit Administration, Cooperative Bank, Brenda McDonald/VP - Lumina Mortgage Company, Cooperative Bank, Virginia Boone/Assist. Sec. - Lumina Mortgage Company, Cooperative Bank, O. C. Burrell/COO, Exec. VP - Cooperative Bank/$333,323.00, Linda B. Garland/VP - Marketing, Corp. Sec. - Cooperative Bank, Bill Herring/Mortgage Loan Officer - Beaufort, Cooperative Bank, Jim McGee/Area Executive, Beaufort, Cooperative Bank, Sandra B. Carr/VP - Retail Banking Operations, Cooperative Bank, George B. Church/VP - Business Banking, Cooperative Bank *(37 Officers included in Index)*

Directors: Frederick Willetts/Chmn., CEO, Pres., Allen R. Rippy/Dir., Paul G. Burton/Dir., Richard O. Wright/Dir., Thompson H. King/Dir., Peter F. Fensel/Dir., James D. Hundley/Dir.

Owners: Cooperative Bank 401(k) Supplemental Retirement Plan/7.47%, Jeffrey L. Gendell/8.70%, Peter F. Fensel, Dickson B. Bridger/0.99%, Allen R. Rippy, Paul G. Burton/0.92%, Insiders/25.62%, Thompson H. King, James D. Hundley/1.27%, Frederick Willetts/17.53%, O. C. Burrell/1.77%, Richard O. Wright/1.74%, Todd L. Sammons/0.75%

Financial Data: Fiscal Year End:12/31 Latest Annual Data: 12/31/2006

Year	Sales	Net Income
2006	$61,611,000	$7,640,000
2005	$45,205,000	$5,502,000
2004	$32,787,000	$4,681,000

Curr. Assets:	$21,482,000	Curr. Liab.:	$693,931,000	P/E Ratio:	12.60
Plant, Equip.:	$11,090,000	Total Liab.:	$802,467,000	Indic. Yr. Divd.:	$0.200
Total Assets:	$860,090,000	Net Worth:	$57,623,000	Debt/ Equity:	1.8353

Copa Holdings S.A.

PO Box 0816-06819, Panama City, *PH:* 507-304-2677; *http://* www.copaair.com

General - Incorporation .. Republic of Panama
Employees .... NA
Auditor .... Ernst& Young LLP
Stk Agt .... Mellon Investor Services LLC
Counsel .... NA
DUNS No. .... NA

Stock- Price on:12/24/2007 ....$65.6
Stock Exchange .... NYSE
Ticker Symbol.. CPA
Outstanding Shares 42,940,000
E.P.S. $3.84
Shareholders.. NA

Business: The groups principle activity is to provide airline passenger and cargo services. In the year 2005, the group acquired AeroRepblica, S.A. The group operates from Latin America. The group's quarterly revenue for September 2007 was 264.63 millions of USD.

Primary SIC and add'l.: 4513 4512

CIK No: 0001345105

Subsidiaries: Aero Corporation One, Ltd, Aero Corporation Two, Ltd, Aerofinance Corporation, AeroRepublica S. A, Air Lease Company Ltd, Alsace Holdings Ltd, Ancon Leasing 2 LLC, Ancon Leasing 3 LLC, Ancon Leasing 4 LLC, Ancon Leasing LLC, Compania Panamena de Aviacion, S. A, Finance Leasing Holdings, Inc, International Aircraft Leasing Corporation, International Aviation Leasing Group, Ltd, Midwinter Offshore Holdings Ltd 19 Subsidiaries included in the Index

Officers: Pedro Heilbron/49/Dir., CEO, Victor Vial/49/CFO, Lawrence Ganse/Sr. VP - Operations, Jorge Isaac Garcia/VP - Commercial, Daniel Gunn/VP - Planning, Jaime Aguirre/VP - Maintenance, Vidalia De Casado/VP - Passenger Services, Alexander Gianareas/Sr. Dir. - Human Resources, Victor Varela/Sr. Dir. - Information Technology, Joseph Putaturo/Dir. - Investor Relations

Directors: Pedro Heilbron/49/Dir., CEO, Stanley Motta/61/Chmn., Osvaldo Heilbron/80/Dir., Jaime Arias/71/Dir., Ricardo Alberto Arias/67/Dir., Alberto C. Motta/60/Dir., Mark Erwin/51/Dir., George Mason/60/Dir., Roberto Artavia Loria/47/Dir., Jose Castaneda Velez/62/Dir.

Owners: Insiders/2.50%, Others/83.40%, Continental/14.10%

Financial Data: Fiscal Year End:12/31 Latest Annual Data: 12/31/2006

Year	Sales	Net Income
2006	$851,160,000	$133,839,000
2005	$608,574,000	$82,999,000
2004	$399,837,000	$68,572,000

Curr. Assets:	$290,651,000	Curr. Liab.:	$339,573,000		
Plant, Equip.:	$862,283,000	Total Liab.:	$883,346,000	Indic. Yr. Divd.:	$0.310
Total Assets:	$1,255,015,000	Net Worth:	$371,669,000	Debt/ Equity:	NA

Copano Energy LLC

2727 Allen Pkwy., Ste. 1200, Houston, TX, 77019; *PH:* 1-713-621-9547; *Fax:* 1-713-621-9545; *http://* www.copanoenergy.com; *Email:* ir@copanoenergy.com

General - Incorporation .... DE
Employees 207
Auditor .... Deloitte & Touche LLP
Stk Agt .... American Stock Transfer & Trust Co.
Counsel .... NA
DUNS No. .... NA

Stock- Price on:12/24/2007 ....$41.35
Stock Exchange .... NDQ
Ticker Symbol... CPNO
Outstanding Shares 42,270,000
E.P.S. $1.68
Shareholders.. NA

Business: The groups principle activity is to provide energy product. The groups operates through three segments namely mid continent operation, Texas gulf coast pipelines and Texas gulf coast processing. Specific customers of the group include ONEOK Energy Services, Enterprise Products Operating, L.P, ONEOK Hydrocarbons and Enogex. The group operates from the United States. The group's quarterly revenue for September 2007 was 293.08 millions of USD.

Primary SIC and add'l.: 1311 4923 4922

CIK No: 0001297067

Subsidiaries: Copano Energy Services/Texas Gulf Coast, L.P., Copano Energy Services/Upper Gulf Coast, L.P., Copano Field Services/Agua Dulce, L.P., Copano Field Services/Central Gulf Coast, L.P., Copano Field Services/Copano Bay, L.P., Copano Field Services/Karnes, L.P., Copano Field Services/Live Oak, L.P., Copano Field Services/South Texas, L.P., Copano Field Services/Upper Gulf Coast, L.P., Copano Houston Central, L.L.C., Copano NGL Services, L.P., Copano Pipelines Group, L.L.C., Copano Pipelines/Hebbronville, L.P., Copano Pipelines/South Texas, L.P., Copano Pipelines/Texas Gulf Coast, L.P. 19 Subsidiaries included in the Index

Officers: John R. Eckel/Chmn., CEO, Cameron Williams/Rocky Mountains, Treasurer, Bruce R. Northcutt/COO, Pres., Cynthia Lapp/Rocky Mountains, Controller, Matthew J. Assiff/Sr. VP, CFO, Ron W. Bopp/Sr. VP - Corporate Development, Lari Paradee/VP, Controller, Douglas L. Lawing/VP, General Counsel, Sec., Kathryn S. De Young/VP - Government, Regulatory Affairs, Wayne S. Harrison/CIO, VP, Carl A. Luna/VP - Finance, Brian D. Eckhart/Texas Gulf Coast, Sr. VP - Transportation, Supply, Terrell J. White/Texas Gulf Coast, VP - Operations, James J. Gibson/Texas Gulf Coast, VP - Processing, John A. Raber/Pres., COO - Mid, Continent *(21 Officers included in Index)*

Directors: John R. Eckel/Chmn., CEO, William T. Porter/Dir., William L. Thacker/Dir., James G. Crump/Dir., Ernie L. Danner/Dir., Scott A. Griffiths/Dir., Michael L. Johnson/Dir.

Owners: Kayne Anderson Capital Advisors, L.P./10.30%, Richard A. Kayne/10.30%, Goldman, Sachs& Co./5.10%, Copano Partners, L.P./9.70%, Tortoise Capital Advisors, L.L.C./5.20%, The Goldman Sachs Group, Inc./5.10%, Insiders/11.50%, John A. Raber, Bruce R. Northcutt, Matthew J. Assiff, Ronald W. Bopp, John R. Eckel/9.70%, Fiduciary Asset Management, L.L.C./5.30%

Financial Data: Fiscal Year End:12/31 Latest Annual Data: 12/31/2006

Year	Sales	Net Income
2006	$860,272,000	$65,114,000
2005	$747,743,000	$30,352,000
2004	$437,656,000	-$915,000

Curr. Assets:	$123,718,000	**Curr. Liab.:**	$105,722,000	**P/E Ratio:**	24.61
Plant, Equip.:	$566,927,000	**Total Liab.:**	$366,472,000	**Indic. Yr. Divd.:**	$1.680
Total Assets:	$839,058,000	**Net Worth:**	$472,586,000	**Debt/ Equity:**	0.5962

Copart Inc

4665 Business Ctr. Dr., Fairfield, CA, 94534; ***PH:*** 1-707-639-5000; ***Fax:*** 1-707-639-5196; ***http://*** www.copart.com; ***Email:*** investor.relations@copart.com

General - Incorporation .... CA
Employees 2,133
Auditor .... Ernst & Young, LLP
Stk Agt .... EquiServe Trust Co N.A
Counsel .... Wilson Sonsini Goodrich & Rosati
DUNS No. 02-957-2047

Stock- Price on:12/24/2007 .... $29.17
Stock Exchange .... NDQ
Ticker Symbol .... CPRT
Outstanding Shares 91,290,000
E.P.S $1.55
Shareholders .... NA

Business: The group's principal activity is to provide services to process and sell salvage vehicles to vehicle suppliers, primarily insurance companies. It offers on-line supplier access services through copart access, an Internet-based service that enable suppliers to assign vehicles for auction, check auction calendars, view vehicle images and history, view and reprint body shop invoices and towing receipts and view the historical performance of the vehicles sold at auctions. Copart finder is an Internet search engine, which enables users to locate used vehicle parts. The group also provides salvage estimation services and transportation services. The group's services are provided to licensed vehicle dismantlers, rebuilders, repair licensees and used vehicle dealers. The group operates in the United States. It acquired greater pittsburgh auto auction inc, ewe salvage pool auto auction inc and richmond auto auction of Virginia inc in fiscal 2003.

Primary SIC and add'l.: 7389 7549

CIK No: 0000900075

Subsidiaries: Motors Auction Group

Officers: Richard Rabak/GM - Ellwood City, Randy Heffner/GM - West Mifflin, Jeffrey Micklitsch/GM - York Haven, Ronald Setliff/GM - Chatham, Gerald Faries/GM - Charles City, Robert Fink/GM - Fort Pierce, FL, Kevin Parker/Regional Mgr. - Fort Pierce, FL, Matt Jones/GM - Courtice, ON, Stephen Powers/Regional Mgr. - Courtice, ON, Jason Walsh/GM - Conway, AR, John Vitale/GM - Waldorf, Gary Cox/Regional Mgr. - Waldorf, Finksburg, Daniel West/GM - Finksburg, Denise Johnson/GM - Fruitland, Richard Hulker/GM - China Grove *(139 Officers included in Index)*

Owners: Insiders/27.44%, James E. Meeks, Barry Rosenstein/5.02%, Neuberger Berman LLC/7.58%, William E. Franklin, Thomas W. Smith/6.13%, Daniel J. Englander, Steven D. Cohan, Wasatch Advisors, Inc./6.07%, Willis J. Johnson/13.70%, Jayson A. Adair/1.65%, Jana Partners LLC/5.02%, Vincent W. Mitz

Financial Data: **Fiscal Year End:**07/31 **Latest Annual Data:** 7/31/2006

Year	Sales	Net Income
2006	$528,571,000	$96,947,000
2005	$457,111,000	$102,116,000
2004	$400,796,000	$79,220,000

Curr. Assets:	$411,350,000	**Curr. Liab.:**	$83,333,000	**P/E Ratio:**	20.84
Plant, Equip.:	$341,943,000	**Total Liab.:**	$84,735,000	**Indic. Yr. Divd.:**	NA
Total Assets:	$894,705,000	**Net Worth:**	$809,970,000	**Debt/ Equity:**	NA

Copernic Inc

Formerly: Mamma.com Inc
388 St. Jacques St. W, 9th Fl., Montreal, QC, H2Y 1S1; ; ***http://*** www.mamma.com

General - Incorporation .... Canada
Employees 39
Auditor .... RSM Richter LLP
Stk Agt .... Equity Transfer Services Inc
Counsel .... Lippes Mathias Wexler Friedman LLP
DUNS No. .... NA

Stock- Price on:12/24/2007 .... $4.2
Stock Exchange .... NA
Ticker Symbol .... NA
Outstanding Shares 14,590,000
E.P.S .... -$0.33
Shareholders .... NA

Business: The group's principal activities are to develop, market, sell, install and maintain customer care and billing software solutions for the telecommunications and other industries. The group operates in three segments: investment management, billing systems and Internet media. The billing system develops, markets, sells, installs and maintains billing and customer care and mediation software for customers operating in the telecommunication industry. The Internet media segment is a provider of meta-search and media placement of product and services. The customers of the group include cellular operators, fixed line operators and direct customers. The subsidiaries of the group are mamma.com inc. And intasys billing technologies. The group has operations in u.k., Australia and North America. The group continues to hold minority interests in and seeks to provide strategic assistance to companies such as tece, inc., ltrim technologies inc. And tri-link technologies inc.

Primary SIC and add'l.: 7375 7372

CIK No: 0000839435

Subsidiaries: 4332890 Canada Inc, Copernic Technologies Inc., Digital Arrow LLC, High Performance Broadcasting Inc, Intasys Billing Technologies (Asia Pacific) Pty Ltd., Intasys Billing Technologies (Canada) Inc., Intasys Billing Technologies Limited, Intasys Management Systems, Intasys Management Systems Inc., Intasys Online limited, Mamma.com USA, Inc.

Officers: Martin Bouchard/Dir., CEO, Pres., David Goldman/65/Executive Chmn., Claude Forget/Dir. - Business Consultant, Daniel Bertrand/CFO, Exec. VP, Patrick Hopf/Exec. VP - Business Development, eric Bouchard/VP - Products

Directors: Martin Bouchard/Dir., CEO, Pres., David Goldman/65/Executive Chmn., Irwin Kramer/Dir., David Schwartz/Dir., Claude Forget/Dir. - Business Consultant

Owners: David Goldman/0.50%, David Schwartz, Claude E. Forget/0.30%, Irwin Kramer/0.10%, Daniel Bertrand, Martin Bouchard/0.30%, ric Bouchard/0.20%

Financial Data: **Fiscal Year End:**12/31 **Latest Annual Data:** 12/31/2006

Year	Sales	Net Income
2006	$9,596,000	-$4,269,000
2005	$9,465,000	-$5,658,000
2004	$15,809,000	$1,104,000

Curr. Assets:	$11,078,000	**Curr. Liab.:**	$2,544,000		
Plant, Equip.:	$504,000	**Total Liab.:**	$4,445,000	**Indic. Yr. Divd.:**	NA
Total Assets:	$33,339,000	**Net Worth:**	$28,895,000	**Debt/ Equity:**	NA

Copytele Inc

900 Walt Whitman Rd., Melville, NY, 11747; ***PH:*** 1-631-549-5900; ***Fax:*** 1-631-549-5974; ***http://*** www.copytele.com; ***Email:*** ir@copytele.com

General - Incorporation .... DE
Employees 21
Auditor .... Grant Thornton LLP
Stk Agt .... American Stock Transfer & Trust Co.
Counsel .... Weil, Gotshal & Manges LLP
DUNS No. 07-735-8083

Stock- Price on:12/24/2007 .... $0.61
Stock Exchange .... OTC
Ticker Symbol .... COPY
Outstanding Shares 103,720,000
E.P.S .... -$0.07
Shareholders .... NA

Business: The group's principal activities are to develop, produce and market multi-functional, hardware-based, peripheral digital encryption products. It operates in two business segments: encryption products and flat-panel display. The encryption products provide high-grade information security for domestic and international users over virtually any communications media. These products include the uss-900 (universal secure system), the dss-1000 (digital security system), the ulp-1 (ultimate laptop privacy) and the sts-1500 (secure teleconferencing system). The flat-panel display segment includes thin-film video color display (field emission display or fed) and ultra-high resolution charged particle e-paper(tm) flat-panel display.

Primary SIC and add'l.: 3679 3661 3669

CIK No: 0000715446

Officers: Anne Rotondo/Investor Relations Officer, Ron Tenio/Contact - Sales Inquiries

Owners: Denis A. Krusos/9.79%, Frank J. DiSanto/2.17%, Insiders/12.71%, Henry P. Herms, George P. Larounis

Financial Data: **Fiscal Year End:**10/31 **Latest Annual Data:** 10/31/2006

Year	Sales	Net Income
2006	$509,000	-$7,601,000
2005	$440,000	-$4,451,000
2004	$494,000	-$3,361,000

Curr. Assets:	$1,623,000	**Curr. Liab.:**	$582,000		
Plant, Equip.:	$23,000	**Total Liab.:**	$582,000	**Indic. Yr. Divd.:**	NA
Total Assets:	$1,864,000	**Net Worth:**	$1,282,000	**Debt/ Equity:**	NA

Coral Gold Resources Ltd

455 Granville St., Ste 400, Vancouver, BC, V6C 1T1; ***PH:*** 1-604-682-3701; ***http://*** www.coralgold.com; ***Email:*** ir@coralgold.com

General - Incorporation .... Canada
Employees .... NA
Auditor .... Ernst & Young LLP
Stk Agt .... Pacific Corporate Trust Co
Counsel .... Salley Bowes Harwardt LLP
DUNS No. .... NA

Stock- Price on:12/24/2007 .... $2.65
Stock Exchange .... OTC
Ticker Symbol .... CLHRF
Outstanding Shares .... NA
E.P.S .... NA
Shareholders .... NA

Business: The group's principal activity is to explore and develop precious mineral properties. The group operates in Nevada, the United States and british columbia. The group is also involved in several joint venture mining operations including cortez gold mines and mill bay ventures inc.

Primary SIC and add'l.: 1041

CIK No: 0000813639

Subsidiaries: Coral Energy Corporation of California, Coral Resources Inc., Marcus Corporation

Officers: Louis Wolfin/Dir., CEO, Chris Sampson/VP - Exploration, Dir., Matt Wayrynen/VP, Lindsay Gorrill/CFO, David Wolfin/Dir., Pres., Connie Lillico/Corp. Sec., Johnathon Smith/Contact - Investor Relations

Directors: Louis Wolfin/Dir., CEO, Lloyd Andrews/Chmn., Gary Robertson/Dir., Chris Sampson/VP - Exploration, Dir., David Wolfin/Dir., Pres., Vic Chevillon/Dir.

Owners: Robert McEwen/19.80%, Lloyd Andrews, Insiders/8.28%, Chris Sampson, Gary Robertson, David Wolfin/1.29%, Matt Wayrynen, Louis Wolfin/5.01%, Lindsay Gorrill, Connie Lillico

Financial Data: **Fiscal Year End:**01/31 **Latest Annual Data:** 01/31/2007

Year	Sales	Net Income
2007	NA	-$3,050,000
2006	NA	-$3,182,000
2005	NA	-$1,434,000

Curr. Assets:	$693,000	**Curr. Liab.:**	$661,000		
Plant, Equip.:	$908,000	**Total Liab.:**	$1,937,000	**Indic. Yr. Divd.:**	NA
Total Assets:	$2,021,000	**Net Worth:**	$75,000	**Debt/ Equity:**	NA

Corcept Therapeutics Inc

149 Commonwealth Dr., Menlo Park, CA, 94025; ***PH:*** 1-650-327-3270; ***Fax:*** 1-650-327-3218; ***http://*** www.corcept.com; ***Email:*** info@corcept.com

General - Incorporation .... DE
Employees 11
Auditor .... Ernst & Young LLP
Stk Agt .... Continental Stock Transfer & Trust Co
Counsel .... NA
DUNS No. .... NA

Stock- Price on:12/24/2007 .... $2.1805
Stock Exchange .... NDQ
Ticker Symbol .... CORT
Outstanding Shares 34,740,000
E.P.S .... -$0.874
Shareholders .... NA

Business: The groups principle activity is to develop drugs for the treatment of psychiatric and neurological diseases. The group operates from United States.

Primary SIC and add'l.: NA

CIK No: 0001088856

Officers: Joseph K. Belanoff/50/Dir., CEO/$395,200.00, Fred Kurland/CFO/$347,838.00, Robert L. Roe/Pres./$545,708.00, Anne Ledoux/VP, Controller, Chief Accounting Officer

Directors: Joseph K. Belanoff/50/Dir., CEO, Alan F. Schatzberg/Chmn. - Scientific Advisory Board, James N. Wilson/Chmn., Allen Andersson/Dir., James A. Harper/Dir., Bruce S. McEwen/Member - Scientific Advisory Board, Ned H. Kalin/Member - Scientific Advisory Board, Ranga K. Krishnan/Member - Scientific Advisory Board, Joseph C. Cook/Dir., David L. Mahoney/Dir., Florian Holsboer/Member - Scientific Advisory Board, Leonard G. Baker/Dir., Edo Ronald De Kloet/Member - Scientific Advisory Board, David B. Singer/Dir., Alix Marduel/Dir.

Owners: Joseph C. Cook, Joseph K. Belanoff, Leonard G. Baker, Robert L. Roe, Alix Marduel, Allen Andersson, Maverick Capital, Ltd., Sutter Hill Ventures and related entities, David B. Singer, Insiders, James N. Wilson, Anne M. LeDoux, James A. Harper, Paperboy Ventures, LLC, Alan F. Schatzberg, M.D. *(17 Owners included in Index)*

Financial Data: **Fiscal Year End:**12/31 **Latest Annual Data:** 12/31/2006

Year	Sales	Net Income
2006	$294,000	-$24,873,000
2005	NA	-$20,093,000
2004	NA	-$15,534,000

Curr. Assets:	$9,799,000	**Curr. Liab.:**	$3,513,000	
Plant, Equip.:	$38,000	**Total Liab.:**	$3,542,000	**Indic. Yr. Divd.:** NA
Total Assets:	$9,902,000	**Net Worth:**	$6,360,000	**Debt/ Equity:** 0.0020

Cord Blood America Inc

10940 Wilshire Blvd, Sixth Fl., Los Angeles, CA, 90024; **PH:** 1-310-443-4153;
http:// www.cordblood-america.com

General - Incorporation	FL	**Stock**- Price on:12/24/2007	$0.048
Employees	5	Stock Exchange	OTC
Auditor	Rose, Snyder & Jacobs	Ticker Symbol	CBAI
Stk Agt	Interwest Transfer Company, Inc.	Outstanding Shares	85,570,000
Counsel	Dave Shaub	E.P.S.	-$0.12
DUNS No.	NA	Shareholders	NA

Business: The group's principal activity is stem cell preservation. The company provides services to expectant parents, families with a history of disease and critically ill patients.

Primary SIC and add'l.: 8071

CIK No: 0001289496

Subsidiaries: CBA Professional Services, Inc., CBA Properties, Inc., D/B/A BodyCells, Inc., Family Marketing, Inc., Rainmakers International

Officers: Matthew L. Schissler/Chmn., CEO, Sandra D. Smith/CFO, Marion Malone/VP - Business Development

Directors: Matthew L. Schissler/Chmn., CEO, Joseph R. Vicente/Dir., Timothy McGrath/Dir., Richard Neeson/Dir.

Owners: Insiders/28.91%, Joseph R. Vicente, Stephanie A. Schissler/10.53%, Matthew L. Schissler/28.24%, Timothy McGrath

Financial Data: Fiscal Year End:12/31 **Latest Annual Data:** 12/31/2006

Year	Sales	Net Income
2006	$3,328,000	-$5,689,000
2005	$2,278,000	-$6,126,000
2004	$752,000	-$1,763,000

Curr. Assets:	$67,000	**Curr. Liab.:**	$6,945,000	
Plant, Equip.:	$15,000	**Total Liab.:**	$6,947,000	**Indic. Yr. Divd.:** NA
Total Assets:	$731,000	**Net Worth:**	-$6,216,000	**Debt/ Equity:** NA

Cordia Corp

2500 Silverstar Rd. , Ste 500, Orlando, FL, 32804; **PH:** 1-866-777-7777; **http://** www.cordiacorp.com

General - Incorporation	NV	**Stock**- Price on:12/24/2007	$0.68
Employees	142	Stock Exchange	OTC
Auditor	Lazar Levine & Felix LLP	Ticker Symbol	CORG
Stk Agt	Colonial Stock Transfer Co Inc	Outstanding Shares	5,620,000
Counsel	NA	E.P.S.	-$0.68
DUNS No.	NA	Shareholders	NA

Business: The group's principal activity is to provide Internet-enabled software systems, outsourcing solutions and services to businesses and organizations. The group also provides retail and wholesale telecommunications services through its wholly owned subsidiary cordia communications corp. In 2003, the group began providing outsourced solutions to competitive local exchange carriers operating in the telecommunications industry.

Primary SIC and add'l.: 7372 7379

CIK No: 0000837342

Subsidiaries: Cordia Communications Corp, Cordia HK Limited, Cordia International Corp, Cordia International Holdings Group, CordiaIP Corp, My Tel Co, Inc, VOzsIP Corp

Officers: Joel Dupre/Chmn., CEO/$243,125.00, Kevin Griffo/COO, Pres./$253,750.00, Gandolfo Verra/CFO/$120,000.00, Patrick Freeman/CTO/$200,000.00

Directors: Joel Dupre/Chmn., CEO, Robert Majernik/59/Dir.

Owners: Patrick Freeman/12.57%, Kevin Griffo/0.97%, Wesly Minella/2.03%, John Scagnelli/1.76%, Joel Dupr/1.03%, Geils Ventures, LLC/34.43%, Insiders/18.32%, Lorie Guerrera/1.38%, Alexander Minella/7.41%

Financial Data: Fiscal Year End:12/31 **Latest Annual Data:** 12/31/2006

Year	Sales	Net Income
2006	$37,505,000	-$3,095,000
2005	$41,951,000	$1,265,000
2004	$13,229,000	-$170,000

Curr. Assets:	$6,874,000	**Curr. Liab.:**	$9,623,000	
Plant, Equip.:	$1,780,000	**Total Liab.:**	$9,733,000	**Indic. Yr. Divd.:** NA
Total Assets:	$9,291,000	**Net Worth:**	-$445,000	**Debt/ Equity:** NA

Core Holdings Inc

600 California St. 9th Fl., San Francisco, CA, 94108; **PH:** 1-415-262-1353

General - Incorporation	DE	**Stock**- Price on:12/24/2007	NA
Employees	NA	Stock Exchange	NA
Auditor	E. Randall Gruber, CPA, P.C	Ticker Symbol	NA
Stk Agt	ComputerShare Investor Services LLC	Outstanding Shares	NA
Counsel	Mr. Fischers	E.P.S.	NA
DUNS No.	NA	Shareholders	NA

Business: The group's principal activity is making investments in small, high-margin, high-growth privately or publicly held companies (or assets of such companies) with business models and fundamentals that suggest the potential for a significant increase in value of any investment the company makes. Investors in the company's stock would benefit from features that are available to shareholders of public companies but are not, for example, available to investors in venture-capital limited partnerships. The disclosure obligations of a public company ensure that investors in our stock would have access to full details regarding the company's investments and their performance. Assuming that a public market develops for the company's shares, investors could readily liquidate their investment.

Primary SIC and add'l.: 6211

CIK No: 0001330698

Core Laboratories

6316 Windfern Rd., Houston, TX, 77040; **PH:** 1-713-328-2673; **Fax:** 1-713-328-2150;
http:// www.corelab.com

General - Incorporation	Netherlands	**Stock**- Price on:12/24/2007	$94.44
Employees	4,600	Stock Exchange	NYSE
Auditor	PricewaterhouseCoopers LLP	Ticker Symbol	CLB
Stk Agt	American Stock Transfer & Trust Co.	Outstanding Shares	23,910,000
Counsel	NA	E.P.S.	$4.01
DUNS No.	41-867-0030	Shareholders	NA

Business: The group's principle activities are to provide proprietary patented services & technology to the oil & gas industry in the field of reservoir description & management as well as production enhancement in order to increase oil & gas recovery. The group has over 70 offices in more than 50 countries. The group's quarterly revenue for September 2007 was 170.06 millions of USD.

Primary SIC and add'l.: 1389

CIK No: 0001000229

Subsidiaries: Coherence Technology Company, Inc., Core Export Sales, Inc., Core Lab de Mexico, S.A. de C.V., Core Lab Executives S.A. de C.V., Core Lab Operations S.A. de C.V., Core Lab Petroleum Services S.A. de C.V., Core Lab Services S.A. de C.V., Core Laboratories (Barbados) Ltd., Core Laboratories (H.K.) Limited, Core Laboratories (U.K.) Limited, Core Laboratories Angola Ltd., Core Laboratories Australia PTY LTD, Core Laboratories Canada Limited, Core Laboratories Corporate Holding B.V., Core Laboratories El Salvador S.A. de C.V. 115 Subsidiaries included in the Index

Officers: David M. Demshur/Chmn., CEO, Pres., Supervisory Dir., Stephen D. Weinroth/Chmn. Emeritus, Supervisory Dir., Mike Kearney/Supervisory Dir., John D. Ogren/Dir., Supervisory Dir., Joseph R. Perna/Dir., Supervisory Dir., J. L. Gresham/VP - Reservoir Management, J. T. Hampton/VP - Production Enhancement, J. W. Heinsbroek/VP - Reservoir Description, S. J. Lee/VP - Reservoir Description, Richard L. Bergmark/Dir., CFO, Exec. VP, Supervisory Dir., Jacobus Schouten/Dir., Supervisory Dir., Alexander Vriesendorp/Dir., Supervisory Dir., M. L. Davis/COO, Sr. VP, J. D. Denson/VP, Sec. - Legal Counsel, C. B. Miller/Chief Accounting Officer (18 Officers included in Index)

Directors: David M. Demshur/Chmn., CEO, Pres., Supervisory Dir., Stephen D. Weinroth/Chmn. Emeritus, Supervisory Dir., Alexander Vriesendorp/Dir., Supervisory Dir., Joseph R. Perna/Dir., Supervisory Dir., Jacobus Schouten/Dir., Supervisory Dir., Richard L. Bergmark/Dir., CFO, Exec. VP, Supervisory Dir., Rene R. Joyce/Dir., Supervisory Dir., John D. Ogren/Dir., Supervisory Dir.

Owners: Insiders/9.95%, Monty L. Davis/1.48%, John D. Ogren, Richard L. Bergmark/2.26%, Alexander Vriesendorp, Clearbridge Advisors, LLC/17.10%, David M. Demshur/4.11%, Michael C. Kearney, Rene R. Joyce, Joseph R. Perna, John D. Denson

Financial Data: Fiscal Year End:12/31 **Latest Annual Data:** 12/31/2006

Year	Sales	Net Income
2006	$575,689,000	$82,662,000
2005	$483,467,000	$31,211,000
2004	$427,427,000	$12,290,000

Curr. Assets:	$225,552,000	**Curr. Liab.:**	$88,920,000	
Plant, Equip.:	$87,734,000	**Total Liab.:**	$429,379,000	**Indic. Yr. Divd.:** NA
Total Assets:	$501,215,000	**Net Worth:**	$71,836,000	**Debt/ Equity:** 5.3738

Core Molding Technologies Inc

800 Manor Pk. Dr., Columbus, OH, 43228; **PH:** 1-614-870-5000; **Fax:** 1-614-870-5051;
http:// www.coremt.com; **Email:** info@coremt.com

General - Incorporation	DE	**Stock**- Price on:12/24/2007	$7.14
Employees	1,379	Stock Exchange	AMEX
Auditor	Deloitte & Touche LLP	Ticker Symbol	CMT
Stk Agt	American Stock Transfer & Trust Co.	Outstanding Shares	10,330,000
Counsel	NA	E.P.S.	$0.60
DUNS No.	96-550-7312	Shareholders	NA

Business: The group's principal activity is to manufacture reinforced plastics. Reinforced plastics are combinations of resins and reinforcing fibers that are molded to shapes. The group produces reinforced plastics by compression molding sheet molding compound (smc) in a closed mold process in its columbus, Ohio and gaffney, South Carolina facilities. The group also produces reinforced plastic products by spray-up and hand-lay-up open mold processes and a vacuum assisted resin infused closed mold process. The group supplies reinforced plastic products to truck manufacturers, to automotive manufacturers and to manufacturers of commercial products. The four major customers are international truck & engine corporation, yamaha motor manufacturing corporation, lear corporation and freightliner, llc. The group markets its products in the United States, Canada and Mexico.

Primary SIC and add'l.: 3089

CIK No: 0001026655

Subsidiaries: Automotive Technologies, LLC, Core Composites Cincinnati, LLC, Core Composites Corporation

Officers: Kevin L. Barnett/Dir., CEO, Pres./$478,394.00, Paul R. Boulier/VP - Marketing, Sales, Herman F. Dick/VP, Sec., Treasurer, CFO/$359,483.00, Stephen J. Klestinec/VP, COO/$448,036.00

Directors: Kevin L. Barnett/Dir., CEO, Pres., Malcolm M. Prine/Chmn., James F. Crowley/Dir., Thomas R. Cellitti/Dir., Ralph O. Hellmold/Dir.

Owners: James F. Crowley, Malcolm M. Prine/1.50%, James L. Simonton/1.80%, Ralph O. Hellmold, Herman F. Dick, Thomas R. Cellitti, Insiders/6.60%, Kevin L. Barnett, Stephen J. Klestinec

Financial Data: Fiscal Year End:12/31 **Latest Annual Data:** 12/31/2006

Year	Sales	Net Income
2006	$162,330,000	$10,411,000
2005	$130,543,000	$6,286,000
2004	$111,845,000	$5,135,000

Curr. Assets:	$50,669,000	**Curr. Liab.:**	$23,095,000	**P/E Ratio:** 9.27
Plant, Equip.:	$30,538,000	**Total Liab.:**	$46,811,000	**Indic. Yr. Divd.:** NA
Total Assets:	$89,506,000	**Net Worth:**	$42,694,000	**Debt/ Equity:** 0.1652

Core-Mark Holding Company Inc

395 Oyster Point Blvd., Ste. 415, South San Francisco, CA, 94080; **PH:** 1-650-589-9445;
Fax: 1-650-952-4284; **http://** www.core-mark.com; **Email:** info@core-mark.com

General		Stock	
Incorporation	DE	Price on:12/24/2007	$36.09
Employees	3,745	Stock Exchange	NDQ
Auditor	Deloitte & Touche, LLP	Ticker Symbol	CORE
Stk Agt	Wells Fargo Shareowner Services	Outstanding Shares	10,350,000
Counsel	NA	E.P.S	$1.90
DUNS No.	NA	Shareholders	NA

Business: The group's principle activity is to provide distribution and logistics services. The groups value added services include flexibility, on-time delivery, business hour deliveries, smaller trucks, accrual programs, full service programs, custom invoices, shelf labels, online data systems, marketing programs and monthly promotions. The group provides services to traditional convenience retailers, grocers, mass merchandisers, drug, liquor and specialty stores, and other stores. The group operates from United States.

Primary SIC and add'l.: 5194 2131 2111 5141 5149

CIK No: 0001318084

Subsidiaries: ASI Office Automation, Inc, C/M Products, Inc, Core-Mark Holdings I, Inc, Core-Mark Holdings II, Inc, Core-Mark Holdings III, Inc1, Core-Mark International, Inc, Core-Mark Interrelated Companies, Inc, Core-Mark Midcontinent, Inc, General Acceptance Corporation, Head Distributing Company, Marquise Ventures Company, Inc, Minter-Weisman Co

Officers: Michael J. Walsh/60/Dir., CEO, Pres., Basil P. Prokop/64/Pres. - Canada Distribution, Chris L. Walsh/43/Sr. VP - Sales, Marketing, Scott E. McPherson/38/VP - US Divisions, Thomas B. Perkins/49/VP - US Divisions, Gregory P. Antholzner/VP - Finance, Treasurer, Assist. Sec., Henry Hautau/66/VP - Employee, Corporate Services, Milton Gray Draper/Dir. - Investor Relations, Stacy Loretz-Congdon/48/CFO, Sr. VP, Christopher Miller/47/VP, Chief Accounting Officer

Directors: Michael J. Walsh/60/Dir., CEO, Pres., Randolph I. Thornton/Chmn., William L. Krause/Dir., Harvey F. Tepner/Dir., Robert A. Allen/58/Dir., Stuart W. Booth/Dir., Gary F. Colter/Dir.

Owners: William L. Krause, Stacy Loretz-Congdon, Stuart W. Booth, Gary F. Colter, Chris Walsh, Thomas B. Perkins, Third Point LLC/8.70%, Harvey L. Tepner, Randolph I. Thornton, Robert A. Allen, Michael J. Walsh/1.20%, River Run Management LLC/7.10%, Insiders/4.40%, The Goldman Sachs Group, Inc./7.10%, James E. Wall *(17 Owners included in Index)*

Financial Data: *Fiscal Year End:*12/31 *Latest Annual Data:* 12/31/2006

Year	Sales	Net Income
2006	$5,314,400,000	$20,600,000
2005	$4,891,100,000	$14,300,000

Curr. Assets:	$450,700,000	**Curr. Liab.:**	$211,600,000	**P/E Ratio:**	18.99
Plant, Equip.:	$55,000,000	**Total Liab.:**	$339,900,000	**Indic. Yr. Divd.:**	NA
Total Assets:	$555,600,000	**Net Worth:**	$215,700,000	**Debt/ Equity:**	0.0254

Corel Corp

Corel Minneapolis, Paint Shop Pro, 7905 Fuller Rd., Eden Prairie, MN, 55344; ***PH:*** 1-800-772-6735; ***http://*** investor.corel.com

General		Stock	
Incorporation	Canada	Price on:12/24/2007	NA
Employees	608	Stock Exchange	NDQ
Auditor	PricewaterhouseCoopers LLP	Ticker Symbol	CREL
Stk Agt	Mellon Trust Co	Outstanding Shares	24,850,000
Counsel	NA	E.P.S	-$0.28
DUNS No.	NA	Shareholders	NA

Business: The groups principle activity is to provide software services. The products of the group include WordPerfect office suite, CorelDraw graphics suite, coral paint shop pro and intervideo DVD copy. In December 2006, the group acquired InterVideo, Inc. The group operates from Americas, EMEA and Asia Pacific. The group's quarterly revenue for September 2007 was 60.37 millions of USD.

Primary SIC and add'l.: 7372

CIK No: 0000890640

Subsidiaries: Beijing Ulead Systems, Inc., Cayman Limited Holdco, Corel California Inc., Corel Corporation Limited, Corel do Brasil Ltda., Corel GmbH, Corel Holdings Corporation, Corel Holdings US, LLC, Corel Inc., Corel International Corp., Corel Japan Ltd., Corel Pty Ltd., Corel SARL, Corel Technologies Corp., Corel UK Limited 39 Subsidiaries included in the Index

Officers: David Dobson/Dir., CEO, Douglas R. McCollam/Dir., CFO, Randy D. Eisenbach/Sr. Exec., Patrick Morley/COO, Amanda Bedborough/Exec. VP - EMEA, Apac Operations, Graham Brown/Exec. VP - Software Development, Christopher Difrancesco/Sr. VP - Legal, General Counsel, Jonathan Kissane/Sr. VP - Corporate Development, Gail Oxley/52/VP - Human Resources, Shawn Cadeau/VP - Global Marketing, Jeff Hastings/Pres., GM - Digital Media, Nick Davies/VP, GM - Graphics, Productivity, Kevin Thornton/Sr. VP - Sales, Marketing, Americas, Jeremy Liang/Sr. VP - Digital Media Development, Philip C. Wilson/VP - Global Human Resources

Directors: David Dobson/Dir., CEO, Alexander Slusky/Chmn., Amish Mehta/Dir., Daniel T. Ciporin/Dir., Steven Cohen/Dir., Ian J. Giffen/Dir., Douglas R. McCollam/Dir., CFO

Owners: Steven Cohen, Vector Capital, Amanda Bedborough, Ian J. Giffen, Alexander Slusky, David Dobson, Douglas McCollam, Insiders, Amish Mehta, Randall Eisenbach

Financial Data: *Fiscal Year End:*11/30 *Latest Annual Data:* 11/30/2006

Year	Sales	Net Income
2006	$177,191,000	$9,251,000
2005	$164,044,000	-$8,753,000
2004	$111,692,000	$1,207,000

Curr. Assets:	$73,919,000	**Curr. Liab.:**	$42,767,000	**P/E Ratio:**	24.61
Plant, Equip.:	$3,651,000	**Total Liab.:**	$142,493,000	**Indic. Yr. Divd.:**	NA
Total Assets:	$130,686,000	**Net Worth:**	-$11,807,000	**Debt/ Equity:**	NA

Corgenix Medical Corp

11575 Main St., Broomfield, CO, 80020; ***PH:*** 1-303-457-4345; ***Fax:*** 1-303-457-4519; ***http://*** www.corgenix.com; ***Email:*** info@corgenix.com

General		Stock	
Incorporation	NV	Price on:12/24/2007	$0.24
Employees	47	Stock Exchange	OTC
Auditor	Hein & Assoc. LLP	Ticker Symbol	CONX
Stk Agt	Computershare Trust Co	Outstanding Shares	13,590,000
Counsel	Otten, Jhonson	E.P.S	-$0.16
DUNS No.	61-983-4542	Shareholders	NA

Business: The group's principle activities are to develop, manufacture and market diagnostic products. It is used for the serologic diagnosis of certain vascular diseases and autoimmune disorders using proprietary technology. The group's products include autoimmune disease products. The group markets its products to hospitals and free-standing laboratories worldwide through a network of sales representatives, distributors and private label agreements. The group sold its products through established diagnostic companies in Argentina, Australia, Austria, Belgium, Brazil, and Canada. It also sells in Chile, Denmark, Egypt, Finland, France, Germany, Greece, Guatemala, Hong Kong, Hungary, India, Ireland, Israel, Italy, Japan, Korea, Kuwait, Lebanon, Malaysia, Mexico, the Netherlands, Norway, Paraguay, Peru, Portugal, Saudi Arabia, Singapore, South Africa, South Korea, Spain, Sweden, Switzerland, Thailand, Turkey, the United Kingdom, and Uruguay. The group's trademark is Reaads. The group's total revenue for year 2007 was 7.37 millions of USD.

Primary SIC and add'l.: 2835

CIK No: 0001063665

Subsidiaries: Corgenix (UK) Limited, Corgenix, Inc

Officers: Douglass T. Simpson/CEO, Pres., Paul Bates/MD, William H. Critchfield/Sr. VP, CFO, Ann L. Steinbarger/Sr. VP - Operations, Taryn G. Reynolds/VP - Facilities - Technology

Directors: Luis R. Lopez/Chmn.

Owners: Luis R. Lopez/6.26%, Ann L. Steinbarger/1.13%, David Kikumoto/0.65%, Barron Partners LP/4.90%, Truk Opportunity Fund/4.99%, William H. Critchfield/2.15%, Dennis Walczewski/0.28%, Mid South Investor Fund/5.38%, Larry G. Rau/0.63%, CAMOFI Master LDC/4.99%, Robert Tutag/1.31%, Ascendiant Capital Group LLC, Ascendiant Securities LLC/4.99%, Medical & Biological Laboratories Co., Ltd./10.08%, Charles H. Scoggin, Taryn G. Reynolds/6.37% *(17 Owners included in Index)*

Financial Data: *Fiscal Year End:*06/30 *Latest Annual Data:* 6/30/2006

Year	Sales	Net Income
2006	$6,636,000	-$1,586,000
2005	$5,565,000	-$582,000
2004	$5,271,000	-$125,000

Curr. Assets:	$6,181,000	**Curr. Liab.:**	$1,976,000		
Plant, Equip.:	$267,000	**Total Liab.:**	$3,272,000	**Indic. Yr. Divd.:**	NA
Total Assets:	$8,214,000	**Net Worth:**	$4,691,000	**Debt/ Equity:**	0.6093

Corillian Corp

3400 Nw John Olsen Pl., Hillsboro, OR, 97124; ***PH:*** 1-503-627-0729; ***http://*** www.corillian.com

General		Stock	
Incorporation	OR	Price on:12/24/2007	NA
Employees	305	Stock Exchange	NA
Auditor	KPMG LLP	Ticker Symbol	NA
Stk Agt	Chase Mellon Shareholder Services LLC	Outstanding Shares	NA
Counsel	Perkins Coie LLP	E.P.S	NA
DUNS No.	NA	Shareholders	NA

Business: The group's principal activity is to license software and provides professional services to banks, brokerages, financial portals and other financial service providers. The services provided by the group include implementation services, hosting services, consulting services, support services and training services. In August 2005, the group acquired QBT Systems, Inc. and InteliData Technologies. The customers of the group include J.P Morgan Chase, Bank One, The Huntington National Bank, Charter One Bank And Sun Trust Bank.

Primary SIC and add'l.: 7372 7375 7371 7379

CIK No: 0001041403

Subsidiaries: Corillian Community Banking Solutions, LLC, Corillian International, Ltd., Corillian Payment Solutions, Inc., Corillian South Asia Sdn Bhd

Officers: Alex P. Hart/Dir., CEO, Pres., Paul K. Wilde/CFO, Erich Litch/Exec. VP - Sales, Marketing, Greg Hughes/Chief Security Exec., VP - Security, Information Technology, Brian Kissel/Sr. VP - Corporate Strategy, Product Management, Brian Bodell/Sr. VP - Corillian Community Banking Solutions, Chris Brooks/CTO, Andre Bouchard/Sr. VP - Professional Services

Directors: Alex P. Hart/Dir., CEO, Pres., Jay N. Whipple/Chmn., Eric Dunn/Dir., James R. Stojak/Dir., Ty B. Miller/Dir.

Owners: Raj Rajaratnam and affiliates/9.15%, Andre Bouchard, Royce& Associates, LLC/6.79%, Erich J. Litch, Brian Kissel, Jay N. Whipple/1.68%, Alex Hart/3.44%, Chris Brooks, James R. Stojak, Eric Dunn, Tyree B. Miller, Insiders/9.22%, Paul K. Wilde/1.31%, Dreman Value Management, LLC/5.66%

Corinthian Colleges Inc

6 Hutton Ctr. Dr., Ste. 400, Santa Ana, CA, 92707; ***PH:*** 1-714-427-3000; ***Fax:*** 1-714-427-5111; ***http://*** www.cci.edu

General		Stock	
Incorporation	DE	Price on:12/24/2007	$14.75
Employees	5,800	Stock Exchange	NDQ
Auditor	Ernst & Young LLP	Ticker Symbol	COCO
Stk Agt	U.S. Stock Transfer Corp	Outstanding Shares	86,640,000
Counsel	O'melveny & Myers	E.P.S	$0.09
DUNS No.	NA	Shareholders	NA

Business: The group's principal activity is to provide degree and diploma granting for-profit, post-secondary schools devoted to career program training primarily in the healthcare, electronics, information technology, criminal justice, automotive repair and diesel technician fields. The group offers a variety of master's, bachelor's and associate's degrees and diploma programs through three operating divisions. The group currently operates 88 colleges in 22 states, including 45 colleges and 15 corporate training centers in 7 Canadian provinces and serve the large and growing segment of the population seeking to acquire career-oriented education. The group acquired career choices inc, all of the assets of east coast aero tech llc, cdi education corporation in fiscal 2004 & all of the assets of ami international training center in fiscal 2005.

Primary SIC and add'l.: 8221 8222 8249

CIK No: 0001066134

Subsidiaries: Ashmead Education, Inc., Career Canada C.F.P. Limited, Career Choices, Inc., CDI Career Development Institutes Limited, CDI Education USA, Inc., Corinthian Property Group, Inc., Corinthian Schools, Inc., ECAT Acquisition, Inc., Eton Education, Inc., Florida Metropolitan University, Inc., Grand Rapids Educational Center, Inc., MJB Acquisition Corp., National School of Technology, Inc., Pegasus Education, Inc., Rhodes Business Group, Inc. 19 Subsidiaries included in the Index

Officers: Jack D. Massimino/Dir., CEO, Pres., Stan A. Mortensen/Sr. VP, General Counsel, Corp. Sec., William B. Buchanan/Exec. VP - Marketing, William P. Murtagh/Pres., COO - CSi Division, Carmella Cassetta/CIO, Sr. VP, Anna Marie Dunlap/Sr. VP - Investor Relations, Corporate Communications, Fardad Fateri Fateri/Sr. VP - Academic Affairs, David Poldoian/Pres., COO - Pegasus Division, Robert C. Owen/Chief Accounting Officer, Sr. VP, Jim Wade/Sr. VP - Human Resources, Steve Quattrociocchi/Pres. - CCi Online, Frank Stryjewski/Pres., COO - Wyotech Division, Kenneth S. Ord/CFO, Exec. VP, Janis Y. Schoonmaker/Pres., COO - FMU Division, Beth A. Wilson/Exec. VP - Operations *(18 Officers included in Index)*

Directors: Jack D. Massimino/Dir., CEO, Pres., Terry O. Hartshorn/Chmn., Paul S. Pierre/Vice Chmn., David G. Moore/Dir., Linda A. Skladany/Dir., Alice T. Kane/Dir., Robert Lee/Dir., Hank Adler/Dir.

Owners: Mark Pelesh, Westfield Capital Management Company, LLC/6.70%, Wells Fargo& Company/10.80%, Hank Adler, Ken Ord, Terry O. Hartshorn, Insiders/5.80%, David G. Moore/3.00%, Beth Wilson, FMR Corp./6.50%, RS Investment Management Co. LLC/10.40%, Paul R. St. Pierre, Peter Waller, Royce& Associates, LLC/8.60%, Jack D. Massimino *(17 Owners included in Index)*

Financial Data: ***Fiscal Year End:***06/30 ***Latest Annual Data:*** 06/30/2007

Year	Sales	Net Income
2007	$933,182,000	$7,232,000
2006	$966,646,000	$41,482,000
2005	$963,565,000	$58,423,000

Curr. Assets:	$215,003,000	***Curr. Liab.:***	$161,081,000	***P/E Ratio:***	52.68
Plant, Equip.:	$199,085,000	***Total Liab.:***	$270,479,000	***Indic. Yr. Divd.:***	NA
Total Assets:	$670,007,000	***Net Worth:***	$399,528,000	***Debt/ Equity:***	0.1121

Corn Products International Inc

5 Westbrook Corporate Ctr., Westchester, IL, 60154; ***PH:*** 1-708-551-2600; ***Fax:*** 1-708-551-2700; ***http://*** www.cornproducts.com; ***Email:*** corpcomm@cornproducts.com

General - Incorporation	DE	***Stock***- Price on:12/24/2007	NA
Employees	6,600	Stock Exchange	NYSE
Auditor	KPMG LLP	Ticker Symbol	CPO
Stk Agt	Bank of New York	Outstanding Shares	74,430,000
Counsel	NA	E.P.S.	$2.24
DUNS No.	00-481-1423	Shareholders	NA

Business: The groups principle activities include manufacturing and selling a number of ingredients to a variety of food and industrial customers. The groups products include dextrose, corn oil and dextrin. Customers served by the group include the pharmaceutical and personal care industry. The group operates from United States.

Primary SIC and add'l.: 2099 2046

CIK No: 0001046257

Subsidiaries: Almifin SRL de C.V., Argentina: Corn Products Southern Cone S.A., Arrendadora Gefemesa, S.A. de C.V., Barbados: Corn Products International Sales Company, Inc., Bebidas Internacionales, S.A. de C.V., Bebidas y Algo Mas, S.A. de C.V., Bedford Construction Company, Brazil: Corn Products Brasil-Ingredientes Industriais Ltda., Cali Investment Corp., Canada Starch Operating Company Inc., Canada: Canada Starch Company Inc., Casco Inc., Chile: Corn Products Chile-Inducorn S.A., Colombia Millers Ltd., Colombia: Industrias del Maiz S.A. Corn Products Andina 36 Subsidiaries included in the Index

Officers: Samuel C. Scott/Chmn., CEO, Pres., Dave Prichard/Dir. - Investor Relations, Kimberly A. Hunter/Corporate Treasurer, Jeffrey B. Hebble/VP, Pres. - Asia, Africa Division/$1,458,583.00, James W. Ripley/Sr. VP - Planning, Information Technology, Compliance, James J. Hirchak/VP - Human Resources, Robin A. Kornmeyer/VP, Controller, Cheryl K. Beebe/CFO, VP/$1,850,192.00, Jorge L. Fiamenghi/VP, Pres. - South America Division/$1,707,145.00, Jack C. Fortnum/VP, Pres. - North America Division/$1,795,819.00, Mary Ann Hynes/VP, General Counsel, Corp. Sec., John F. Saucier/VP - Global Business, Product Development, Sales, Marketing

Directors: Samuel C. Scott/Chmn., CEO, Pres., James M. Ringler/Dir., Barbara A. Klein/Dir., William S. Norman/Dir., Gregory B. Kenny/Dir., Richard J. Almeida/Dir., Paul Hanrahan/Dir., Bernard H. Kastory/Dir., Guenther E. Greiner/Dir., Karen L. Hendricks/Dir., Luis Aranguren-Trellez/Dir.

Owners: B. A. Klein, J. C. Fortnum, FMR Corp./14.86%, Insiders/3.30%, R. J. Almeida, J. L. Fiamenghi, G. E. Greiner, W. S. Norman, C. K. Beebe, J. M. Ringler, K. L. Hendricks, B. H. Kastory, P. Hanrahan, L. Aranguren, G. B. Kenny *(17 Owners included in Index)*

Financial Data: ***Fiscal Year End:***12/31 ***Latest Annual Data:*** 12/31/2006

Year	Sales	Net Income
2006	$2,621,000,000	$124,000,000
2005	$2,360,000,000	$90,000,000
2004	$2,283,000,000	$94,000,000

Curr. Assets:	$837,000,000	***Curr. Liab.:***	$517,000,000		
Plant, Equip.:	$1,356,000,000	***Total Liab.:***	$1,265,000,000	***Indic. Yr. Divd.:***	NA
Total Assets:	$2,662,000,000	***Net Worth:***	$1,330,000,000	***Debt/ Equity:***	0.3526

Cornell Cos Inc

1700 W Loop S, Ste. 1500, Houston, TX, 77027; ***PH:*** 1-713-623-0790; ***Fax:*** 1-713-623-2853; ***http://*** www.cornellcorrections.com

General - Incorporation	DE	***Stock***- Price on:12/24/2007	$23.78
Employees	4,186	Stock Exchange	NYSE
Auditor	PricewaterhouseCoopers LLP	Ticker Symbol	CRN
Stk Agt	Computershare Trust Co	Outstanding Shares	14,170,000
Counsel	NA	E.P.S.	$0.78
DUNS No.	79-747-0549	Shareholders	NA

Business: The group's principal activity is to provide correctional, treatment and educational services outsourced by federal, state and local government agencies. The group provides a diversified portfolio of services for adults and juveniles through three operating divisions: adult secure institutional services; residential and community-based juvenile justice, educational and treatment services and adult community-based corrections and treatment services. The services of the group include incarceration and detention, transition from incarceration, drug and alcohol treatment programs, behavioral rehabilitation and treatment and 3-12 education.

Primary SIC and add'l.: 8361 8744 9223

CIK No: 0001016152

Subsidiaries: CCGI Corporation, Cornell Abraxas Group,Inc., Cornell Archway,Inc., Cornell Companies Administration LLC, Cornell Companies Management Holdings LLC, Cornell Companies Management L.P., Cornell Companies Management Services L.P., Cornell Corrections Management,Inc., Cornell Corrections of Alaska,Inc., Cornell Corrections of California, Inc, Cornell Corrections of Rhode Island,Inc., Cornell Corrections of Texas,Inc., Cornell International,Inc., Cornell Interventions,Inc., Correctional Systems,Inc. 17 Subsidiaries included in the Index

Officers: James E. Hyman/Chmn., CEO, Pres./$1,489,436.00, Patrick N. Perrin/Sr. VP, Chief Administrative Officer/$567,321.00, John R. Nieser/CFO, Treasurer/$521,420.00, Benjamin E. Erwin/VP - Corporate Development, Michael L. Caltabiano/Sr. VP - Adult Secure Division, Adult Community, Based Division, Jonathan P. Swatsburg/Sr. VP - Abraxas Youth, Family Services Division, William E. Turcotte/General Counsel, Corp. Sec.

Directors: James E. Hyman/Chmn., CEO, Pres., Stephen D. Slack/Dir., Zachary R. George/Dir., Todd Goodwin/Dir., Anthony R. Chase/Dir., Alfred Jay Moran/Dir., Richard Crane/Dir., Max Batzer/64/Dir., Andrew R. Jones/45/Dir.

Owners: Andrew R. Jones/5.20%, Todd Goodwin, John R. Nieser, Anthony R. Chase, Albert Fried& Company, LLC/12.90%, William E. Turcotte, Insiders/8.30%, Sally L. Walker, Zachary R. George, James E. Hyman, Dolphin Management/5.10%, Alfred J. Moran, Patrick N. Perrin, North Star Partners, L.P./5.20%, Wynnefield Capital Inc./17.60% *(18 Owners included in Index)*

Financial Data: ***Fiscal Year End:***12/31 ***Latest Annual Data:*** 12/31/2006

Year	Sales	Net Income
2006	$360,855,000	$11,873,000
2005	$310,775,000	$306,000
2004	$291,025,000	-$7,433,000

Curr. Assets:	$145,751,000	***Curr. Liab.:***	$70,673,000		
Plant, Equip.:	$319,064,000	***Total Liab.:***	$341,969,000	***Indic. Yr. Divd.:***	NA
Total Assets:	$523,533,000	***Net Worth:***	$181,564,000	***Debt/ Equity:***	1.3924

Cornerstone Bancorp

1670 E Main St., Easley, SC, 29640; ***PH:*** 1-864-306-1444; ***Fax:*** 1-864-306-1473; ***http://*** www.cornerstonenatlbank.com

General - Incorporation	SC	***Stock***- Price on:12/24/2007	$35.2
Employees	NA	Stock Exchange	OTC
Auditor	Elliot Davis LLC	Ticker Symbol	CTOT
Stk Agt	American Stock Transfer & Trust Co.	Outstanding Shares	NA
Counsel	Haynsworth, Sinkler & Boyd	E.P.S.	NA
DUNS No.	NA	Shareholders	NA

Business: The group's principal activity is the provision of general banking services. The group offers the services in its capacity as a holding company for the cornerstone national bank. The primary market areas are in the city of easley, South Carolina and the surrounding areas of pickens county and greenville county. The group accepts savings accounts, retirement accounts including individual retirement accounts, checking accounts, money market accounts and time certificates of deposit. It makes commercial, real estate and installment loans to borrowers in the upstate of South Carolina and makes other authorized investments. Consumer services include both visa and mastercard brands of bankcards together with related lines of credit, traveler's checks, direct deposit of payroll and social security checks and automatic drafts for various accounts.

Primary SIC and add'l.: 6712 6021

CIK No: 0001087455

Subsidiaries: Cornerstone National Bank, Crescent Financial Services, Inc.

Officers: Rodger J. Anthony/62/Dir., CEO, Pres./$193,669.00, Jennifer M. Champagne/40/Dir., Sr. VP, CFO - Principal Financial, Principal Accounting Officer/$135,371.00

Directors: Rodger J. Anthony/62/Dir., CEO, Pres., Ervin S. Hendricks/65/Dir., Edward T. Childress/62/Dir., Walter L. Brooks/80/Dir., Joe E. Hooper/69/Dir., Robert R. Spearman/68/Dir., John M. Warren/58/Dir., George I. Wike/63/Dir., Jennifer M. Champagne/40/Dir., Sr. VP, CFO - Principal Financial, Principal Accounting Officer, Ben L. Garvin/63/Dir., Bruce J. Gaston/51/Dir.

Owners: Edward T. Childress/8.13%, George I. Wike/9.12%, Ervin S. Hendricks/2.95%, Jennifer M. Champagne/0.32%, Walter L. Brooks/1.25%, Ben L. Garvin/2.04%, Bruce J. Gaston/2.39%, Rodger J. Anthony/4.09%, John M. Warren/1.59%, Insiders/36.18%, Robert R. Spearman/0.78%, Joe E. Hooper/3.52%

Curr. Assets:	$18,401,000	***Curr. Liab.:***	$187,262,000	***P/E Ratio:***	16.21
Plant, Equip.:	$3,207,000	***Total Liab.:***	$189,170,000	***Indic. Yr. Divd.:***	NA
Total Assets:	$211,802,000	***Net Worth:***	$22,632,000	***Debt/ Equity:***	NA

Cornerstone Bancshares Inc

835 Georgia Ave., Chattanooga, TN, 37402; ***PH:*** 1-423-385-3000; ***Fax:*** 1-423-385-3100; ***http://*** www.cscbank.com

General - Incorporation	TN	***Stock***- Price on:12/24/2007	$14.75
Employees	98	Stock Exchange	OTC
Auditor	Hazlett, Lewis & Bister PLLC	Ticker Symbol	CSBQ
Stk Agt	Kefe, Bruyette & Woods, Inc.	Outstanding Shares	6,520,000
Counsel	NA	E.P.S.	$0.91
DUNS No.	NA	Shareholders	NA

Business: The group's principal activity is to provide banking and related services to individual and corporate customers. It provides a variety of financial services through four full services branches in chattanooga. As a holding company for cornerstone community bank, it accepts deposits from the general public and originates real estate loans, consumer loans, business loans, and residential and commercial construction loans. The deposits accepted include demand deposits, savings accounts, and certificates of deposit.

Primary SIC and add'l.: 6712 6022

CIK No: 0001038773

Subsidiaries: Cornerstone Community Bank, Eagle Financial, Inc.

Officers: Gregory B. Jones/Chmn., CEO/$324,249.00, Robert B. Watson/Sr. VP/$211,603.00, Jerry D. Lee/Dir., Exec. VP, Sr. Loan Officer - Cornerstone Community Bank/$232,530.00, Daniel W. Nichols/Sr. VP/$138,566.00, Nathaniel F. Hughes/Dir., COO, Pres./$238,148.00

Directors: Gregory B. Jones/Chmn., CEO, Nathaniel F. Hughes/Dir., COO, Pres., Kenneth B. Driver/Dir. - Cornerstone Community Bank, Karl Fillauer/Dir. - Cornerstone Community Bank, Jim Large/Dir. - Cornerstone Community Bank, Jerry D. Lee/Dir., Exec. VP, Sr. Loan Officer - Cornerstone Community Bank, Lawrence D. Levine/Dir. - Cornerstone Community Bank, Earl A. Marler/Dir. - Cornerstone Community Bank, Doyce G. Payne/Dir. - Cornerstone Community Bank, Turner G. Smith/Dir. - Cornerstone Community Bank, Billy G. Wiggins/Dir. - Cornerstone Community Bank, Marsha Yessick/Dir. - Cornerstone Community Bank, Wesley M. Welborn/Dir. - Cornerstone Community Bank, Frank S. McDonald/Dir. - Cornerstone Community Bank

Owners: Lawrence D. Levine/0.72%, Doyce G. Payne/2.45%, Turner G. Smith/1.22%, Kenneth B. Driver/1.61%, Karl Fillauer/2.12%, Nathaniel F. Hughes/3.17%, Insiders/22.35%, Billy O. Wiggins/2.23%, Frank S. McDonald/0.14%, Jerry D. Lee/3.15%, Gregory B. Jones/3.11%, Daniel W. Nichols/0.23%, Marsha Yessick/1.66%, Robert B. Watson/0.25%, Wesley M. Welborn/0.24%

Financial Data: ***Fiscal Year End:***12/31 ***Latest Annual Data:*** 12/31/2006

Year	Sales	Net Income
2006	$31,270,000	$5,812,000
2005	$22,577,000	$4,325,000
2004	$15,465,000	$2,571,000

Curr. Assets:	$19,757,000	Curr. Liab.:	$334,875,000	P/E Ratio:	16.21
Plant, Equip.:	$6,134,000	Total Liab.:	$336,759,000	Indic. Yr. Divd.:	$0.200
Total Assets:	$374,942,000	Net Worth:	$38,183,000	Debt/ Equity:	NA

Cornerstone Bank NJ

300 W Rte. 38 Ste. 101, Moorestown, NJ, 08057; *PH:* 1-856-439-0300;
http:// www.cornerstonebanknj.com; *Email:* info@cornerstonebanknj.com

General - Incorporation		**Stock**- Price on:12/24/2007	$11.6
Employees	NA	Stock Exchange	OTC
Auditor	NA	Ticker Symbol	CBKJ
Stk Agt	Registrar & Transfer Co	Outstanding Shares	NA
Counsel	NA	E.P.S.	NA
DUNS No.	NA	Shareholders	NA

Business: The group's principle activity is to provide community banking services. The group's services include peronal and online banking, and lending service. The group operates from United States.

Primary SIC and add'l.: 6029

CIK No:

Officers: George W. Matteo/Chmn., CEO, Pres., Dave Swoyer/Exec. VP, Chief Lending Officer, Rosemarie Giardiello/Assist. VP - Retail Banking - Moorestown, Daniel J. Hammer/VP, Lending Officer, James Martin/VP, Relationship Mgr., Jeffrey Leason/Assist. VP - Retail Banking - Cherry Hill, Sarah B. McMahon/Assist. VP, Lending Officer, Dave Matricciano/Sr. Portfolio Underwriter, Richard Sima/Dir. - Information Technology, Colleen Connell/Exec. VP, Chief Credit Officer, Keith Winchester/CFO, Exec. VP, Nicholas J. Ricciuti/Exec. VP, Sr. Credit Officer, Michael P. Madison/VP, Lending Officer, Richard Miller/Assist. VP, Lending Officer, Michael Dinoia/Assist. VP, Controller *(22 Officers included in Index)*

Directors: George W. Matteo/Chmn., CEO, Pres., Mark J. Baiada/Dir., Richard J. Carnall/Dir., Gaetano P. Giordano/Dir., Robert A. Kennedy/Dir., Richard P. Meehan/Dir., Ronald S. Murphy/Dir., Bruce Paparone/Dir., Kenneth H. Zekavat/Dir.

Cornerworld Corp

Formerly: Olympic Weddings International Inc
12222 Merit Dr., Ste. 120, Dallas, TX, 75251; *PH:* 1-604-506-8991

General - Incorporation	NV	**Stock**- Price on:12/24/2007	NA
Employees	NA	Stock Exchange	NA
Auditor	Miller and McCollom	Ticker Symbol	NA
Stk Agt	Continental Stock T & T Co.	Outstanding Shares	NA
Counsel	NA	E.P.S.	NA
DUNS No.	NA	Shareholders	NA

Business: The groups principal activity is consisted only of initial organizational activities and the issuance of common shares to original affiliate shareholders. The group is in the process of establishing as a company that will provide personally guided travel tour wedding packages to be held at locations where the Olympic Games have been held. The group operates from the United States.

Primary SIC and add'l.: 4700

CIK No: 0001338242

Officers: Brent Sheppard/48/Dir., CEO, Pres., Patrick Wallace/54/Dir., Sec., Treasurer, CFO

Directors: Brent Sheppard/48/Dir., CEO, Pres., Patrick Wallace/54/Dir., Sec., Treasurer, CFO, Brian Pierson/52/Dir.

Owners: Brian Pierson/7.69%, Brent Sheppard/69.23%, Patrick Wallace/7.69%, Insiders/84.61%

Financial Data: Fiscal Year End:04/30 Latest Annual Data: 04/30/2007

Year	Sales	Net Income
2007	NA	-$55,000

Curr. Assets:	$4,000	Curr. Liab.:	$6,000		
Plant, Equip.:	$11,000	Total Liab.:	$6,000	Indic. Yr. Divd.:	NA
Total Assets:	$20,000	Net Worth:	$14,000	Debt/ Equity:	NA

Corning Inc

1 Riverfront Plz., Corning, NY, 14831; *PH:* 1-607-974-9000; *Fax:* 1-800-539-3632;
http:// www.corning.com

General - Incorporation	NY	**Stock**- Price on:12/24/2007	$25.69
Employees	24,500	Stock Exchange	NYSE
Auditor	PricewaterhouseCoopers LLP	Ticker Symbol	GLW
Stk Agt	Computershare Investor Services LLC	Outstanding Shares	1,570,000,000
Counsel	NA	E.P.S.	$1.30
DUNS No.	00-130-7735	Shareholders	NA

Business: The group's principle activity is to produce optical fiber and cable products by utilizing glass. The group operates through four segments including display technologies, environmental technologies, life sciences and telecommunications. The groups products include optical fibers, cable assemblies, connectors, couplers, splice equipment, closures, subscriber demarcation and others. The group operates from United States, Canada, Germany, France, United Kingdom, Italy and Brazil.

Primary SIC and add'l.: 3357 3229

CIK No: 0000024741

Subsidiaries: Dow Corning Asia Ltd., Dow Corning Toray Silicone Co. Ltd., Toray Industries, Inc.

Officers: Wendell P. Weeks/Chmn., CEO/$11,288,890.00, Eric S. Musser/CEO - Corning Greater China, James B. Flaws/Vice Chmn., CFO/$8,265,157.00, Peter F. Volanakis/Dir., COO, Pres./$9,642,314.00, Pamela C. Schneider/Sr. VP, Operations Chief - Staff, Mark S. Rogus/48/Sr. VP, Treasurer, Katherine A. Asbeck/51/Sr. VP - Finance, Monica L. Ott/Contact - Optical Fiber, Joseph A. Miller/CTO, Exec. VP/$4,980,677.00, Daniel F. Collins/Contact - Corporate Communications, Kelli Hopp-Michlosky Kelli Hopp-Michlosky/Contact - Corporate Communications, Elizabeth M. Dann/Contact - Corporate Communications, Elijah Baity/Contact - Specialty Materials, Robert B. Brown/57/Exec. VP - Environmental Technologies, Kirk P. Gregg/Exec. VP, Chief Administrative Officer/$5,547,752.00 *(27 Officers included in Index)*

Directors: Wendell P. Weeks/Chmn., CEO, James R. Houghton/Chmn. Emeritus, James B. Flaws/Vice Chmn., CFO, Kurt M. Landgraf/Dir., Hansel E. Tookes/Dir., Robert F. Cummings/Dir., Peter F. Volanakis/Dir., COO, Pres., John Seely Brown/Dir., Eugene C. Sit/Dir., William D. Smithburg/Dir., Gordon Gund/Dir., Deborah D. Rieman/Dir., Onno H. Ruding/Dir., John M. Hennessy/Dir., Padmasree Warrior/Dir. *(17 Directors included in Index)*

Owners: Kirk P. Gregg, Joseph A. Miller, Robert F. Cummings, Onno H. Ruding, James R. Houghton, Insiders/1.80%, Jeremy R. Knowles, James B. Flaws, Wendell P. Weeks, William D. Smithburg, Peter F. Volanakis, John M. Hennessy, Hansel E. Tookes, FMR Corp./6.43%, Deborah D. Rieman *(20 Owners included in Index)*

Financial Data: Fiscal Year End:12/31 Latest Annual Data: 12/31/2006

Year	Sales	Net Income
2006	$5,174,000,000	$1,855,000,000
2005	$4,579,000,000	$585,000,000
2004	$3,854,000,000	-$2,165,000,000

Curr. Assets:	$4,798,000,000	Curr. Liab.:	$2,319,000,000		
Plant, Equip.:	$5,193,000,000	Total Liab.:	$5,774,000,000	Indic. Yr. Divd.:	$0.200
Total Assets:	$13,065,000,000	Net Worth:	$7,246,000,000	Debt/ Equity:	0.1917

Corning Natural Gas Corp

330 W William St., Corning, NY, 14830; *PH:* 1-607-936-3755; *Fax:* 1-607-962-2844;
http:// www.corninggas.com

General - Incorporation	NY	**Stock**- Price on:12/24/2007	$18.1
Employees	48	Stock Exchange	OTC
Auditor	Rotenberg & Co. LLP	Ticker Symbol	CNIG
Stk Agt	Kenneth J. Robinson	Outstanding Shares	NA
Counsel	Rich, May, Milodeau & Fiaherty	E.P.S.	$0.49
DUNS No.	00-287-7231	Shareholders	NA

Business: The group's principal activities are the distribution of gas and real estate. The group operates in five segments. The gas company purchases gas and distributes it through its own pipeline distribution and transmission systems to residential, commercial, industrial and municipal customers. The tax center provides tax preparation, accounting and payroll services to its clients. Corning realty is a residential and commercial real estate business with approximately 80 agents operating in three neighboring counties. Foodmart plaza is a retail complex consisting of eight tenants under multi-year leases anchored by a major supermarket. The group discontinued the appliance company segment in Sept 2003.

Primary SIC and add'l.: 7291 7359 4923 6512 6531 8721

CIK No: 0000024751

Subsidiaries: Appliance Corporation., Corning Mortgage, LLC, Corning Realty Associates, LLC, Rotenberg & Co. LLP

Officers: Michael German/57/Dir., CEO, Pres., Raymond Spear/Mgr. - Gas Control, Firouzeh Sarhangi/CFO, Treasurer, Stanley G. Sleve/VP - Administration, Deborah L. Beer/Mgr. - Customer Service, Robert A. Bush/Mgr. - Gas Construction, Barbara Dimick/Human Resources, Diane Haynes/Gas Procurement, Transp Accts Clerk, Albert Horning/Mgr. - Safety, Training, Joel D. Moore/VP - Operations

Directors: Michael German/57/Dir., CEO, Pres., Richard M. Osborne/Chmn., Ted W. Gibson/65/Dir., Matthew C. Benesh/52/Dir., Stephen G. Rigo/61/Dir., Thomas J. Smith/63/Dir., George J. Welch/62/Dir.

Owners: Gabelli Advisors, Inc./3.00%, Michael I. German/11.40%, Firouzeh Sarhangi, George J. Welch, Richard M. Osborne/19.60%, Insiders/31.90%, Gabelli Funds, LLC/11.60%, Stanley G. Sleve

Financial Data: Fiscal Year End:09/30 Latest Annual Data: 9/30/2006

Year	Sales	Net Income
2006	$26,921,000	-$3,616,000
2005	$22,878,000	$627,000
2004	$21,996,000	$613,000

Curr. Assets:	$3,737,000	Curr. Liab.:	$12,377,000		
Plant, Equip.:	$17,887,000	Total Liab.:	$24,693,000	Indic. Yr. Divd.:	NA
Total Assets:	$27,338,000	Net Worth:	$2,645,000	Debt/ Equity:	3.1202

Coronado First Bank

750 B St., San Diego, CA, 92101; *PH:* 1-619-437-1000; *http://* www.coronadofirst.com

General - Incorporation		**Stock**- Price on:12/24/2007	$11.5
Employees	NA	Stock Exchange	OTC
Auditor	NA	Ticker Symbol	CDFB
Stk Agt	U.S. Stock Transfer Corp	Outstanding Shares	NA
Counsel	NA	E.P.S.	NA
DUNS No.	NA	Shareholders	NA

Business: The groups principle activity is to provide personal banking, business banking and business lending services. The groups business lending services include accounts receivable and inventory financing, business lines of credit and term loans, professional loans and lines, equipment loans, commercial real estate loans, construction financing, and small business administration loans. The groups personal banking services include basic checking, standard checking, interest checking, senior checking, money market accounts, savings accounts, certificates of deposits, debit cards, online banking, check imaging, wire transfers, telephone banking, auto and vehicle loans. The group operates from United States.

Primary SIC and add'l.: 6099 6022

CIK No:

Officers: Bruce A. Ives/42/Dir., CEO, Pres., Paul Cable/59/CFO, Exec. VP, Philip A. Chapman/Exec. VP, Chief Credit Officer

Directors: Bruce A. Ives/42/Dir., CEO, Pres., Thomas C. Stickel/Chmn., Larry D. Kurmel/Vice Chmn., Todd Anson/Dir., Rudy W. Castruita/Dir., Barbara J. Demichele/Dir., William L. Huck/Dir., Kathleen A. Koop/Dir., Edward H. Martin/Dir., Gerald R. Sanders/Dir.

CorpBanca

Hurfanos 1072, Santiago; *PH:* 56-26878000; *http://* www.corpbanca.cl

General - Incorporation	Chile	**Stock**- Price on:12/24/2007	$30.29
Employees	2,159	Stock Exchange	NYSE
Auditor	Deloitte & Touche LLP	Ticker Symbol	BCA
Stk Agt	NA	Outstanding Shares	11,660,000
Counsel	NA	E.P.S.	$5.00
DUNS No.	NA	Shareholders	NA

Business: The groups principle activity is to operate a commercial bank. The group's services include loans, credit and debit cards, and savings. The group operates from United States.

Primary SIC and add'l.: 6029

CIK No: 0001276671

Subsidiaries: Corp Administradora de Fondos Mutuos S.A., Corp Asesoras Financieras S.A., Corp Corredores de Bolsa S.A., Corp Corredores de Seguros S.A.

Officers: Luis Morales Fernandez/43/Division Mgr. - Commercial Credit Risk, Enrique Perez Alarcon/35/CFO, Christian Gilchrist Correa/37/Division Mgr. - Human Resources, Administration, Patricio Leighton Zambelli/40/Division Mgr. - Corp Capital, Alberto Selman Hasbun/Division Mgr. - Companies, Pedro Silva Yrarrazaval/47/Division Mgr. - International, Treasury

Directors: Carlos Abumohor Touma/Chmn., Alvaro Saieh Bendeck/Vice Chmn., Jorge Andres Saieh Guzman/Vice Chmn., Julio Barriga Silva/Dir., Francisco Rosende Ramirez/Dir., Jorge Selume Zaror/Dir., Hernan Somerville Senn/Dir., Fernando Aguad Dagach/Dir., Arturo Valenzuela/Dir., Ignacio Gonzalez Martinez/Dir., Carlos Massad Abud/Dir., Juan Rafael Gutierrez Avila/Alternate Dir.

Owners: Corp Group Banking S.A./49.59%, Public/42.46%, Compaa Inmobiliaria y de Inversiones Saga S.A./7.95%, Insiders/50.38%

Financial Data: ***Fiscal Year End:*** 12/31 ***Latest Annual Data:*** 12/31/2005

Year	Sales	Net Income
2005	$552,505,000	$84,567,000
2004	$435,280,000	$105,547,000

Curr. Assets:	$404,153,000	***Curr. Liab.:***	$4,063,997,000	***P/E Ratio:***	18.99
Plant, Equip.:	$61,317,000	***Total Liab.:***	$5,712,892,000	***Indic. Yr. Divd.:***	$0.940
Total Assets:	$6,474,666,000	***Net Worth:***	$761,775,000	***Debt/ Equity:***	NA

Corporate Executive Board Co

2000 Pennsylvania Ave. NW, Ste. 6000, Washington, DC, 20006; ***PH:*** 1-202-777-5000; ***Fax:*** 1-202-777-5100; ***http://*** www.executiveboard.com; ***Email:*** jacobsg@advisory.com

General - Incorporation	DE	***Stock***- Price on:12/24/2007	$66.53
Employees	2,279	Stock Exchange	NDQ
Auditor	Ernst & Young LLP	Ticker Symbol	EXBD
Stk Agt	Mellon Investor Services LLC	Outstanding Shares	37,400,000
Counsel	NA	E.P.S.	$2.13
DUNS No.	79-358-0861	Shareholders	NA

Business: The group's principle activity is to provide research and quantitative analysis focusing on corporate strategy, operations and general management issues. Best practice research identifies and analyzes specific management initiatives, processes and strategies that have been determined to produce the best results in solving common business problems or challenges. These research and analysis are provided on an annual subscription basis to a membership of 1,903 of the world's largest and most prestigious corporations. For a fixed annual fee, members of each research program have access to an integrated set of services, including best practices research studies, executive education seminars, customized research briefs and Web-based access to the program's content database and decision support tools. The group offers 23 research programs in areas of human resources, information technology, marketing, finance, legal, operations and financial services. The group operates from United States.

Primary SIC and add'l.: 8742 8732

CIK No: 0001066104

Subsidiaries: CEB International Holdings, Inc., Corporate Executive Board India Private Ltd., The Corporate Executive Board Company (UK) Ltd.

Officers: Thomas L. Monahan/Dir., CEO/$2,699,438.00, Timothy R. Yost/CFO/$1,436,566.00, Melody L. Jones/Chief Human Resources Officer, Glenn Tobin/GM, Lisa Herold/Investor Relations Contact, Joni Renick/Contact - Media, Public Relations, Reshma Harilela/Contact - Media, Public Relations, London, Shaurav Sen/Contact - Media, Public Relations, India

Directors: Thomas L. Monahan/Dir., CEO, James J. McGonigle/Chmn., Robert C. Hall/Dir., Gregor S. Bailar/Dir., Stephen M. Carter/Dir., Nancy J. Karch/Dir., David W. Kenny/Dir., Daniel O. Leemon/Dir.

Owners: Oppenheimer Funds, Inc./5.30%, Glenn R. Tobin, Nancy J. Karch, Melody L. Jones, Insiders/3.00%, Thomas L. Monahan, Timothy R. Yost, Daniel O. Leemon, James J. McGonigle, Morgan Stanley/16.00%, Robert C. Hall, Michael A. Archer, David W. Kenny

Financial Data: ***Fiscal Year End:*** 12/31 ***Latest Annual Data:*** 12/31/2006

Year	Sales	Net Income
2006	$460,623,000	$79,171,000
2005	$362,226,000	$75,060,000
2004	$280,724,000	$53,656,000

Curr. Assets:	$482,158,000	***Curr. Liab.:***	$400,506,000	***P/E Ratio:***	32.30
Plant, Equip.:	$26,988,000	***Total Liab.:***	$418,190,000	***Indic. Yr. Divd.:***	$1.600
Total Assets:	$736,055,000	***Net Worth:***	$317,865,000	***Debt/ Equity:***	NA

Corporate Express N.V

Formerly: Buhrmann

Hoogoorddreef 62, Amsterdam, 1101 BE; ***PH:*** 31-206-511111; ***http://*** www.buhrmann.com

General - Incorporation	Netherlands	***Stock***- Price on:12/24/2007	NA
Employees	17,575	Stock Exchange	OTC
Auditor	PricewaterhouseCoopers LLP	Ticker Symbol	BUHRF
Stk Agt	Bank of New York	Outstanding Shares	NA
Counsel	NA	E.P.S.	NA
DUNS No.	NA	Shareholders	NA

Business: The group's principal activities are distributing of office products, paper and graphic systems to the business-to-business market. The group operates under following segments: office products: supplying of office and computers, including copiers, printers, plotters, fax machines, telecommunication equipment, office furniture, print, forms and facility management, customised corporate gifts, desktop software, call centre services; paper merchandising: supply of paper for the graphic industry and offices, including speciality products such as wood free coated paper; graphic systems: supply of graphic equipment, printing materials and services to the graphic art industry. The group has operations in Europe, North America, Australia and New Zealand.

Primary SIC and add'l.: 5084 5111 5045

CIK No: 0000948634

Subsidiaries: Corporate Express Ltd

Officers: Frans Koffrie/CEO, Pres., Grant Harrod/46/MD, CEO - Office Products Australia, Grant Logan/56/CFO - Office Products Australia, Ron Lalla/50/Exec. VP - Office Products Global Merchandising, Carl Thomas/61/Pres. - Printing Systems, Peter Ventress/48/Member Exec. Board, Pres. - Office Products Europe, Robert Vanhees/39/CFO - Office Products North America, Heidi Van Der Kooij/46/Dir., Company Sec., Chris Thrush/57/Dir. - Human Resources, Gerhard Nijhuis/59/Financial Dir. - Printing Systems, Neil Callahan/65/Dir. - Information Technology, Peter Damman/Pres. - Europe, Kees Bangma/52/Corporate Finance, Group Treasury, Cor Zwart/62/Dir. - Internal Audit, Roelof Hoving/46/Dir. - Corporate Tax, Pensions *(25 Officers included in Index)*

Directors: Jan Peelen/68/Vice Chmn., Paul C. Van Den Hoek/69/Chmn. - Supervisory Board, Frank L.V. Meysman/56/Chmn., Gilles Izeboud/66/Member - Supervisory Board, Rob F. Van Den Bergh/58/Member - Supervisory Board, Tom De Swaan/Member - Supervisory Board, George Dean/61/Exec. Dir., Ben J. Noteboom/50/Member - Supervisory Board

Corporate Office Properties Trust

6711 Columbia Gateway Dr., Ste. 300, Columbia, MD, 21046; ***PH:*** 1-443-285-5400; ***Fax:*** 1-443-285-7650; ***http://*** www.copt.com; ***Email:*** info@copt.com

General - Incorporation	MD	***Stock***- Price on:12/24/2007	$43.86
Employees	313	Stock Exchange	NYSE
Auditor	PricewaterhouseCoopers LLP	Ticker Symbol	OFC
Stk Agt	Wells Fargo Bank Minnesota N.A	Outstanding Shares	47,070,000
Counsel	NA	E.P.S.	$0.56
DUNS No.	NA	Shareholders	NA

Business: The groups principle activities include acquiring, developing, owning and leasing office properties. The group operates from the United States. The groups quarterly revenue for September 2007 was 105.52 millions of USD.

Primary SIC and add'l.: 6798

CIK No: 0000860546

Subsidiaries: 1099 Winterson, LLC, 110 Thomas Johnson, LLC, 11011 McCormick Road, LLC, 11101 McCormick Road, LLC, 11800 Tech Road, LLC, 1190 Winterson, LLC, 1199 Winterson, LLC, 134, LLC, 1460 Dorsey Road, LLC, 201 International Associates Limited Partnership, 226 Schilling Circle, LLC, 230 Schilling Circle, LLC, 2500 Riva Trust, 2691 Technology, LLC, 2900 Lord Baltimore Drive, LLC 221 Subsidiaries included in the Index

Officers: Randall M. Griffin/Dir., CEO, Pres., Trustee/$3,086,074.00, Roger A. Waesche/COO, Exec. VP/$1,083,153.00, Steven E. Riffee/CFO, Exec. VP/$320,244.00, Mary Ellen Fowler/VP, Treasurer - Investor Relations Contact, Karen M. Singer/Sr. VP, General Counsel, Sec./$533,729.00, Dwight S. Taylor/Pres. - Copt Development, Construction Services, LLC/$731,676.00, Colleen M. Crews/VP, Controller

Directors: Randall M. Griffin/Dir., CEO, Pres., Trustee, Jay H. Shidler/Chmn. - Board of Trustee, Clay W. Hamlin/Vice Chmn. - Board of Trustees, Thomas F. Brady/Trustee, Robert L. Denton/Trustee, Steven D. Kesler/Trustee, Kenneth D. Wethe/Trustee, Kenneth S. Sweet/Trustee, Douglas M. Firstenberg/Trustee

Owners: Security Capital Research & Management Inc./5.70%, ING Clarion Real Estate Securities, L.P./5.80%, Steven D. Kesler, Clay W. Hamlin/6.60%, Thomas F. Brady, Dwight S. Taylor, Douglas M. Firstenberg, Robert L. Denton, Davis Select Advisers, L.P./6.50%, Kenneth D. Wethe, Roger A. Waesche, ING Groep N.V./10.20%, Kenneth S. Sweet, Insiders/16.00%, Jay H. Shidler/6.90% *(20 Owners included in Index)*

Financial Data: ***Fiscal Year End:*** 12/31 ***Latest Annual Data:*** 12/31/2006

Year	Sales	Net Income
2006	$361,403,000	$49,227,000
2005	$329,145,000	$39,031,000
2004	$243,476,000	$37,032,000

Curr. Assets:	$105,470,000	***Curr. Liab.:***	$107,591,000	***P/E Ratio:***	78.32
Plant, Equip.:	$2,121,805,000	***Total Liab.:***	$1,629,111,000	***Indic. Yr. Divd.:***	$1.240
Total Assets:	$2,419,601,000	***Net Worth:***	$674,303,000	***Debt/ Equity:***	2.0537

Corrections Corp of America

10 Burton Hills Blvd., Nashville, TN, 37215; ***PH:*** 1-615-263-3000; ***Fax:*** 1-615-263-3140; ***http://*** www.correctionscorp.com; ***Email:*** invrelations@correctionscorp.com

General - Incorporation	MD	***Stock***- Price on:12/24/2007	$64.94
Employees	16,000	Stock Exchange	NYSE
Auditor	Ernst & Young LLP	Ticker Symbol	CXW
Stk Agt	American Stock Transfer & Trust Co.	Outstanding Shares	61,410,000
Counsel	NA	E.P.S.	$1.05
DUNS No.	NA	Shareholders	NA

Business: The group's principal activity is to operate and manage prisons, other correctional facilities and provide inmate residential and prisoner transportation services for governmental agencies. In addition, the group offers a variety of rehabilitation and educational programs, including basic education, life skills and employment training and substance abuse treatment. These services are intended to help reduce recidivism and to prepare inmates for their successful reentry into society upon their release. The group also provides health care (including medical, dental and psychiatric services), food services, work and recreational programs. The customers of the group include local, state and federal correctional and detention authorities. At 30-Jun-2004 the group owned 41 correctional, detention and juvenile facilities and operated 65 facilities, including 38 facilities with a total design capacity of approximately 66,000 beds in 20 states and district of columbia.

Primary SIC and add'l.: 8748 8299 8744

CIK No: 0001070985

Subsidiaries: Cca (uk) Ltd., CCA International, Inc., CCA of Tennessee, LLC, CCA Properties of America, LLC, CCA Properties of Arizona, LLC, CCA Properties of Tennessee, LLC, CCA Properties of Texas, L.P., CCA Western Properties, Inc., Prison Realty Management, Inc., Technical and Business Institute of America, Inc., TransCor America, LLC, TransCor Puerto Rico, Inc.

Officers: John D. Ferguson/Dir., CEO, Pres./$2,494,015.00, Sharon Johnson Rion/Pres., CEO - Transcor, Louise Grant/VP - Marketing, Communications, Brad Wiggins/Sr. Dir. - Site Aquisition, Development, Jay Hansom/Sr. Dir. - Program Management Office, Linda S. Scritchfield/Sr. Dir. - Technology, Enterprise Data Services, William Dubray/Sr. Dir. - Enterprise Operations, Steve Kennedy/MD - Operations Support, Internal Investigations, Steve Owen/Dir. - Marketing, Communications, Jimmy Turner/VP - Facility Operations, Business Unit 2, Steven Conry/VP - Facility Operations, Business Unit 3, Brian Collins/VP - Facility Operations, Business Unit I, John Pfeiffer/VP - Technology, CIO, G. A. Puryear/Exec. VP, General Counsel/$840,265.00, William K. Rusak/Chief Human Resources Officer, Exec. VP *(39 Officers included in Index)*

Directors: John D. Ferguson/Dir., CEO, Pres., William F. Andrews/Chmn., Joseph V. Russell/Dir., Donna M. Alvarado/Dir., Lucius E. Burch/Dir., John D. Correnti/Dir., Thurgood Marshall/Dir., Henri L. Wedell/Dir., John R. Horne/68/Dir., Charles L. Overby/Dir., John R. Prann/Dir., Michael C. Jacobi/66/Dir.

Financial Data: ***Fiscal Year End:*** 12/31 ***Latest Annual Data:*** 12/31/2006

Year	Sales	Net Income
2006	$1,331,088,000	$105,239,000
2005	$1,192,640,000	$50,122,000
2004	$1,148,258,000	$62,543,000

Curr. Assets:	$391,242,000	Curr. Liab.:	$164,382,000	P/E Ratio: 65.60
Plant, Equip.:	$1,805,098,000	Total Liab.:	$1,201,179,000	Indic. Yr. Divd.: NA
Total Assets:	$2,250,860,000	Net Worth:	$1,049,681,000	Debt/ Equity: 0.8974

Corriente Resources Inc

800 W Pender St., Ste. 520, Vancouver, BC, V6C 2V6; **PH:** 1-604-687-0449; **Fax:** 1-604-687-0827; *http://* www.corriente.com; **Email:** copper@corriente.com

General - Incorporation	BC	Stock - Price on:12/24/2007	$3.99
Employees	NA	Stock Exchange	AMEX
Auditor	PricewaterhouseCoopers LLP	Ticker Symbol	ETQ
Stk Agt.	Computershare Trust Co	Outstanding Shares	74,750,000
Counsel	Bull, Housser & Tupper LLP	E.P.S.	-$0.21
DUNS No.	NA	Shareholders	NA

Business: The group operates through its subsidiaries whose principal activities include developing and exploring of minerals. The group operates from Canada and the United States.

Primary SIC and add'l.: 1041 1021

CIK No: 0001345564

Subsidiaries: Corriente Argentina Inc., Corriente Argentina S.A.

Officers: Kenneth R. Shannon/Dir., CEO, Thomas E. Milner/Pres., Daniel A. Carriere/Sr. VP, Darryl F. Jones/CFO, Corp. Sec.

Directors: Kenneth R. Shannon/Dir., CEO, Anthony F. Holler/Chmn., Ross G. McDonald/Dir., Richard P. Clark/Dir., Dale C. Peniuk/Dir., David G. Unruh/Dir.

Financial Data: Fiscal Year End:12/31 Latest Annual Data: 12/31/2006

Year	Sales	Net Income
2006	NA	-$19,965,000
2005	NA	-$517,000

Curr. Assets:	$109,257,000	Curr. Liab.:	$6,230,000	
Plant, Equip.:	$9,366,000	Total Liab.:	$6,230,000	Indic. Yr. Divd.: NA
Total Assets:	$122,857,000	Net Worth:	$116,627,000	Debt/ Equity: NA

Cortelco Systems Puerto Rico Inc

Parque Industrial Caguas Oeste, Rd. 156 Km 58.2, Valle Tolima, Caguas, 00727-0137; **PH:** 787-758-0000

General - Incorporation	PR	Stock - Price on:12/24/2007	$0.85
Employees	61	Stock Exchange	OTC
Auditor	Horwath Vlez & Co, PSC	Ticker Symbol	CPROF
Stk Agt.	Computershare Investor Services LLC	Outstanding Shares	1,570,000
Counsel	NA	E.P.S.	$0.13
DUNS No.	NA	Shareholders	NA

Business: The group's principal activity is to market voice and data communications systems and cellular telephones and airtime. The group operates in two segments: communications systems and cellular airtime services segment. Communications systems segment offers communications solutions that address voice and data network switching. The cellular airtime services segment resells cellular airtime and cellular telephones in puerto. The group also provides value-added services through its distribution network and services. The group also operates in Caribbean and Latin America. On 31-Jul-2002 the company was spun-off from eon communications corporations.

Primary SIC and add'l.: 4812 7373 3661

CIK No: 0001167140

Subsidiaries: Puerto Rico corporation

Officers: Juan Carlos Ramos/39/CEO, Pres., Francisco Sanchez/61/VP - Finance, Administration, CFO - Treasury

Directors: Sergio R. Moren/63/Dir., Walter D. Duffey/Dir., Gloria Lee/Dir., Alan L. Laffoon/Dir., Robert A. Gordon/Dir.

Owners: Anthony Chiarenza/12.61%, Francisco Sanchez, Robert A. Gordon, Juan Carlos Ramos, Insiders/2.69%, Walter D. Duffey, David S. Lee/51.00%, Alan L. Laffoon, Sergio R. Moren, Gloria Lee, Cortelco Puerto Rico, Inc./19.09%

Financial Data: Fiscal Year End:07/31 Latest Annual Data: 7/31/2006

Year	Sales	Net Income
2006	$7,434,000	$201,000
2005	$7,414,000	$11,000
2004	$7,339,000	-$1,494,000

Curr. Assets:	$2,774,000	Curr. Liab.:	$1,364,000	P/E Ratio: 17.00
Plant, Equip.:	$116,000	Total Liab.:	$1,364,000	Indic. Yr. Divd.: NA
Total Assets:	$3,141,000	Net Worth:	$1,777,000	Debt/ Equity: NA

Cortex Pharmaceuticals Inc

15241 Barranca Pkwy., Irvine, CA, 92618; **PH:** 1-949-727-3157; **Fax:** 1-949-727-3657; *http://* www.cortexpharm.com; **Email:** info@cortexpharm.com

General - Incorporation	DE	Stock - Price on:12/24/2007	$2.85
Employees	25	Stock Exchange	AMEX
Auditor	Ernst & Young, LLP	Ticker Symbol	COR
Stk Agt.	American Stock Transfer & Trust Co.	Outstanding Shares	40,010,000
Counsel	NA	E.P.S.	-$0.37
DUNS No.	19-695-2196	Shareholders	NA

Business: The group's principal activities are to discover, develop and commercialize innovative pharmaceuticals for the treatment of neurodegenerative diseases and other neurological and psychiatric disorders. The group is developing family of chemical compounds known as ampakine that enhance the activity of this receptor. The group has been centered on developing products that affect the ampa-type glutamate receptor, a complex of proteins that is involved in most excitatory communication between nerve cells in the human brain.

Primary SIC and add'l.: 2834 8731

CIK No: 0000849636

Subsidiaries: Cortex UK Limited

Officers: Roger G. Stoll/Dir., CEO, Pres./$1,060,852.00, Maria S. Messinger/CFO, VP/$361,371.00, Steven A. Johnson/VP - Preclinical Development, Gary A. Rogers/Sr. VP - Pharmaceutical Research/$376,191.00, Mark Varney/COO, Chief Scientific Officer/$1,386,449.00, James H. Coleman/Sr. VP - Business Development/$394,494.00, Leslie J. Street/Sr. Dir. - Medicinal Chemistry

Directors: Roger G. Stoll/Chmn., CEO, Pres., Charles J. Casamento/Dir., Peter F. Drake/Dir., Robert F. Allnutt/Dir., Ross M. Johnson/Dir., Carl W. Cotman/Co - Founder, Dir., Gary D. Tollefson/Dir., John F. Benedik/Dir.

Owners: Carl W. Cotman, Gary D. Tollefson, Insiders/10.90%, John F. Benedik, Harry H. Mansbach, Charles J. Casamento, M. Ross Johnson, James H. Coleman/1.60%, Maria S. Messinger, Gary A. Rogers/1.50%, Robert F. Allnutt, Mark A. Varney, Peter F. Drake, Roger G. Stoll/4.30%

Financial Data: Fiscal Year End:12/31 Latest Annual Data: 12/31/2006

Year	Sales	Net Income
2006	$1,177,000	-$16,055,000
2005	$2,577,000	-$11,606,000
2004	$1,896,000	-$4,046,000

Curr. Assets:	$9,974,000	Curr. Liab.:	$2,056,000	
Plant, Equip.:	$428,000	Total Liab.:	$2,114,000	Indic. Yr. Divd.: NA
Total Assets:	$10,435,000	Net Worth:	$8,320,000	Debt/ Equity: NA

Cortland Bancorp

194 W Main St., Cortland, OH, 44410; **PH:** 1-330-637-8040; **Fax:** 1-330-638-3018; *http://* www.cortland-banks.com; **Email:** webhelp@cortland-banks.com

General - Incorporation	OH	Stock - Price on:12/24/2007	$18.05
Employees	144	Stock Exchange	OTC
Auditor	Packer Thomas	Ticker Symbol	CLDB
Stk Agt.	NA	Outstanding Shares	4,530,000
Counsel	George E. Gessner & Platt Co	E.P.S.	$1.00
DUNS No.	00-892-9051	Shareholders	NA

Business: The group's principal activities are to provide commercial and retail banking and trust services. The group operates through its wholly owned subsidiary, the cortland savings and banking company. The deposits accepted by the group include checking accounts, savings accounts and time deposit accounts. The group originates commercial, mortgage and installment loans. The other services include leasing, night depository, automated teller services, safe deposit boxes and a variety of Internet banking products as well as discount brokerage services. The services are provided through thirteen offices located at trumbull, windham, mantua, portage, williamsfield, ashtabula, boardman and mahoning county, Ohio.

Primary SIC and add'l.: 6022 6712

CIK No: 0000774569

Subsidiaries: New Resources Leasing Company, The Cortland Savings and Banking Company

Officers: Lawrence A. Fantauzzi/Dir., CEO, Pres./$296,335.00, Timothy Carney/COO, Sr. VP/$157,529.00, James M. Gasior/Sr. VP, CFO, Sec., Craig M. Phythyon/46/Sr. VP, Treasurer, Chief Investment Officer

Directors: Lawrence A. Fantauzzi/Dir., CEO, Pres., Ray K. Mahan/Chmn., Richard B. Thompson/Dir., David C. Cole/Dir., George E. Gessner/Dir., James E. Hoffman/Dir., Timothy K. Woofter/Dir., Jerry A. Carleton/Dir., Neil J. Kaback/Dir.

Owners: James E. Hoffman, Stephen A. Telego, Rodger W. Platt, Timothy K. Woofter/1.23%, Jerry A. Carleton, James M. Gasior, David C. Cole, Danny L. White, Insiders/7.81%, Lawrence A. Fantauzzi, K. Ray Mahan/2.53%, Richard B. Thompson/1.85%, Neil J. Kaback, Timothy Carney, George E. Gessner

Financial Data: Fiscal Year End:12/31 Latest Annual Data: 12/31/2006

Year	Sales	Net Income
2006	$29,379,000	$4,576,000
2005	$26,704,000	$4,334,000
2004	$26,290,000	$4,843,000

Curr. Assets:	$14,375,000	Curr. Liab.:	$417,833,000	
Plant, Equip.:	$4,780,000	Total Liab.:	$421,159,000	Indic. Yr. Divd.: $0.880
Total Assets:	$471,751,000	Net Worth:	$50,592,000	Debt/ Equity: NA

Corus Bankshares Inc

3959 N Lincoln Ave., Chicago, IL, 60613; **PH:** 1-800-555-5710; **Fax:** 1-773-832-3460; *http://* www.corusbank.com

General - Incorporation	MN	Stock - Price on:12/24/2007	$16.36
Employees	534	Stock Exchange	NDQ
Auditor	Ernst & Young LLP	Ticker Symbol	CORS
Stk Agt.	Mellon Investor Services LLC	Outstanding Shares	56,250,000
Counsel	NA	E.P.S.	$2.64
DUNS No.	05-072-2750	Shareholders	NA

Business: The group's principal activity is to provide consumer and corporate banking products and services through its subsidiaries. The group accepts money market, retail certificates of deposit, brokered certificates of deposit, demand deposits, savings and now accounts. The group lends commercial loans, real estate commercial loans, real estate construction loans, home equity loans, residential first mortgage, student loans, medical finance and consumer loans. The group also provides trust and investment management services; clearing, depository and credit services; safe deposit boxes and a variety of additional services. The group provides clearing, depository and credit services to more than 525 check cashing industry locations in the Chicago area and an additional 20 in milwaukee, Wisconsin.

Primary SIC and add'l.: 6712 6021

CIK No: 0000051939

Subsidiaries: Corus Bank, N.A.

Owners: Rodney D. Lubeznik, American Century Companies, Inc./5.30%, Putnam, LLC and its affiliated entities/6.50%, Robert J. Buford, Peter C. Roberts, Randy P. Curtis/0.10%, Kevin R. Callahan, Michael J. McClure, Edward W. Glickman/11.00%, Robert J. Glickman/22.10%, Joseph C. Glickman/8.70%, Timothy J. Stodder, Michael G. Stein/2.40%, Tim H. Taylor/0.30%, Insiders/33.30%

Financial Data: Fiscal Year End:12/31 Latest Annual Data: 12/31/2006

Year	Sales	Net Income
2006	$760,428,000	$189,444,000
2005	$474,898,000	$137,229,000
2004	$273,474,000	$97,939,000

Curr. Assets:	$489,500,000	Curr. Liab.:	$8,789,817,000	P/E Ratio: 5.47
Plant, Equip.:	$35,815,000	Total Liab.:	$9,213,264,000	Indic. Yr. Divd.: $1.000
Total Assets:	$10,057,791,000	Net Worth:	$844,527,000	Debt/ Equity: NA

Corus Entertainment Inc

181 Bay St., Ste. 1630, Toronto, ON, M5J 2T3; **PH:** 1-416-642-3770; **http://** www.corusent.com

General - Incorporation	Canada	Stock - Price on:12/24/2007	$45.78
Employees	2,093	Stock Exchange	NYSE
Auditor	Ernst & Young LLP	Ticker Symbol	CJR
Stk Agt	Ernest & Young LLP	Outstanding Shares	42,410,000
Counsel	NA	E.P.S.	$2.49
DUNS No.	NA	Shareholders	NA

Business: The group's principle activities are broadcasting and media advertising through radio and television. The group operates in three business segments; television, radio and content. The television segment includes interest in several specialty television networks, pay television, pay-per-view services, digital audio services and cable advertising services. The radio segments operates 52 radio stations. The content segment includes production and distribution of film and television programs, merchandise licensing and publishing business. The group's quarterly revenue for September 2007 was 187.20 millions of CAD.

Primary SIC and add'l.: 4833 4832

CIK No: 0001100868

Subsidiaries: 591987 B.c. Ltd., 591989 B.c. Ltd., 591991 B.c. Ltd., Canadian Broadcast Sales, CKIK-FM Limited, Corus Audio and Advertising Services Ltd, Corus Premium Television Ltd., Corus Radio Company, Country Music Television Ltd., Encore Avenue Ltd., Kids Can Press Limited, Max Trax Music Ltd., Metromedia CMR Broadcasting Inc, Movie Central Ltd., Nelvana Communications Inc 25 Subsidiaries included in the Index

Officers: John M. Cassaday/Dir., CEO, Pres., Paul Robertson/Pres. - Corus Television, Thomas Peddie/Sr. VP, CFO, Hal Blackadar/VP - Human Resources, John P. Hayes/Pres., David Spence/VP, Controller, Gary Maavara/VP, General Counsel, John R. Parraton/Corp. Sec., Scott Dyer/Exec. VP, GM - Corus Kids, Doug Murphy/Corporate Officers, Susan Ross/Exec. VP, GM - Lifestyle, Drama, Movies

Directors: John M. Cassaday/Dir., CEO, Pres., Heather Shaw/Chmn., Julie Shaw/Dir., Catherine Roozen/Dir., Dennis Erker/Dir., Pierre Beland/Dir., Cathy Roozen/Dir., Wendy Leaney/Dir., Terrance Royer/Dir., Ronald Rogers/Dir., Carolyn Hursh/Dir.

Financial Data: Fiscal Year End:08/31   Latest Annual Data: 8/31/2006

Year		Sales		Net Income
2006		$655,459,000		$32,832,000
2005		$573,436,000		$60,619,000
2004		$505,704,000		-$15,511,000
Curr. Assets:	$282,627,000	**Curr. Liab.:**	$163,323,000	
Plant, Equip.:	$70,771,000	**Total Liab.:**	$834,552,000	**Indic. Yr. Divd.:** $0.350
Total Assets:	$1,662,594,000	**Net Worth:**	$828,042,000	**Debt/ Equity:** NA

Corus Group Plc

30 Millbank, London, SW1P 4WY; ; **http://** www.corusgroup.com

General - Incorporation	UK	Stock - Price on:12/24/2007	NA
Employees	47,300	Stock Exchange	NA
Auditor	Remuneration Of Groups	Ticker Symbol	NA
Stk Agt	Bank of New York	Outstanding Shares	NA
Counsel	NA	E.P.S.	NA
DUNS No.	NA	Shareholders	NA

Business: The group's principal activities are the manufacture, processing and distribution of steel and aluminium products and the provision of design, technology and consultancy services for those products. It produces steel by the basic oxygen steelmaking method at three integrated steelworks in the United Kingdom at port talbot, scunthorpe and teesside, and at one in the Netherlands at ijmuiden. The group also produces primary aluminium in two smelters at delfzijl in the Netherlands and voerde in Germany. Aluminium rolling mills are located at koblenz in Germany, duffel in Belgium and cap-de-la-madeleine in Canada. Aluminium extrusions operations are located in Germany, Belgium and in China. On 17-Apr-2003, the group disposed corus aluminium service centers inc.

Primary SIC and add'l.: 5051 3317 3355 3312 3334

CIK No: 0000842021

Subsidiaries: Aluminium Delfzijl BV, Apollo Metals Limited, Blume Stahlservice GmbH, Cogent Power, Cogent Power Inc., Cogent Power Limited, Corus Aluminium Extrusions Tianjin Co Limited, Corus Aluminium Japan Limited, Corus Aluminium NV, Corus Aluminium Profiltechnik Bonn GmbH, Corus Aluminium Profiltechnik GmbH, Corus Aluminium Verkauf GmbH, Corus Aluminium Voerde GmbH, Corus Aluminium Walzprodukte GmbH, Corus America Inc 67 Subsidiaries included in the Index

Officers: Paul Lormor/Division Dir. - Long Products, Scott MacDonald/55/Division Dir. - Distribution, Building Systems, Annanya Sarin/Contact - Corporate Relations, Rauke Henstra/Dir., Division Dir. Strip Products, David Lloyd/Dir., Executive Dir. - Finance, Philippe Varin/Dir., Chief Executive, Richard Shoylekov/42/Dir., Company Sec., General Counsel, Tor Farquhar/Group Dir. - Human Resources

Directors: James Leng/Dep. Chmn., Ratan Tata/Chmn., B. Muthuraman/Dir., Richard Shoylekov/42/Dir., Company Sec., General Counsel, Eric Van Amerongen/Dir., Arunkumar Gandhi/Dir., Ishaat Hussain/Dir., Anwar Hasan/Dir., T. Mukherjee/Dir., Anthony Hayward/Dir., Andrew Robb/Dir., Rauke Henstra/Dir., Division Dir. Strip Products, David Lloyd/Dir., Executive Dir. - Finance, Philippe Varin/Dir., Chief Executive, Jacques Schraven/Dir.

Financial Data: Fiscal Year End:12/31   Latest Annual Data: 12/31/2005

Year		Sales		Net Income
2005		$17,448,912,000		$669,391,000
2004		$14,712,081,000		-$618,758,000
Curr. Assets:	$7,650,677,000	**Curr. Liab.:**	$4,245,214,000	
Plant, Equip.:	$5,048,827,000	**Total Liab.:**	$8,216,820,000	**Indic. Yr. Divd.:** NA
Total Assets:	$14,957,194,000	**Net Worth:**	$6,695,633,000	**Debt/ Equity:** NA

CorVel Corp

2010 Main St., Ste. 600, Irvine, CA, 92614; **PH:** 1-949-851-1473; **Fax:** 1-949-851-1469; **http://** www.corvel.com; **Email:** investor_relations@corvel.com

General - Incorporation	DE	Stock- Price on:12/24/2007	$25.26
Employees	2,623	Stock Exchange	NDQ
Auditor	Haskell & White LLP	Ticker Symbol	CRVL
Stk Agt	U.S. Stock Transfer Corp	Outstanding Shares	13,970,000
Counsel	Dorsey & Whitney LLP	E.P.S.	$1.43
DUNS No.	62-036-6708	Shareholders	NA

Business: The group's principal activities are to provide medical cost containment and managed care services designed to address the escalating medical costs of workers' compensation and other healthcare benefits. The services include automated medical fee auditing, preferred provider networks, out-of-network/line item bill negotiation and repricing, utilization review and management, medical case management, vocational rehabilitation services, medicare set-asides and life care planning. It also provides a variety of directed care services such as independent medical examinations, diagnostic imaging, transportation and translation, durable medical equipment and physical therapy. These services are provided to insurance companies, third-party administrators and self-administered employers. The group operates solely in the United States.

Primary SIC and add'l.: 6321 6324 7375 7372

CIK No: 0000874866

Subsidiaries: CorVel Health Care Organization, CorVel Healthcare Corporation

Officers: Daniel J. Starck/CEO, Pres./$617,445.00, Richard Schweppe/Sec., Scott McCloud/CFO/$190,861.00, Sharon O'Connor/Dir. - Legal Services, Tom Benson/VP - Information Systems, Don McFarlane/CIO/$257,422.00

Directors: Gordon Clemons/Chmn., Judd Jessup/Dir., Steven J. Hamerslag/Dir., Jeffrey J. Michael/Dir., Alan Hoops/Dir.

Owners: Scott R. McCloud, Gordon V. Clemons/10.50%, Daniel J. Starck, Alan R. Hoops, Jeffrey J. Michael/29.70%, Donald C. McFarlane, Corstar Holdings, Inc./29.00%, Goldman Sachs Asset Management, L.P./13.70%, Kestrel Investment Management Corporation/5.00%, Judd R. Jessup, Insiders/41.00%, FMR Corporation/6.10%, Steven J. Hamerslag

Financial Data: Fiscal Year End:03/31   Latest Annual Data: 3/31/2007

Year		Sales		Net Income
2007		$274,581,000		$18,576,000
2006		$266,504,000		$9,753,000
2005		$291,000,000		$10,157,000
Curr. Assets:	$64,287,000	**Curr. Liab.:**	$29,269,000	**P/E Ratio:** 18.44
Plant, Equip.:	$24,864,000	**Total Liab.:**	$34,571,000	**Indic. Yr. Divd.:** NA
Total Assets:	$113,768,000	**Net Worth:**	$79,197,000	**Debt/ Equity:** NA

CorVu Corp

3400 W 66th St., Ste. 445, Edina, MN, 55435; **PH:** 1-952-944-7777; **Fax:** 1-952-944-7447; **http://** www.corvu.com; **Email:** info@corvu.com

General - Incorporation	MN	Stock - Price on:12/24/2007	NA
Employees	86	Stock Exchange	OTC
Auditor	Virchow, Krause & Co. LLP	Ticker Symbol	CRVU
Stk Agt	Continental Stock Transfer & Trust Co	Outstanding Shares	NA
Counsel	NA	E.P.S.	$0.02
DUNS No.	NA	Shareholders	NA

Business: The group's principal activity is to develop and sell business performance management software products and professional services. Its product line includes corbusiness(tm), corstrategy(tm), corportfolio(tm) and hypervu(tm). The major customers of the group include ingersoll rand, jp morgan, fireman's fund insurance, bowne and company, us army, cvs pharmacy, merck, hilton hotels corporation, credit suisse, societe general, hm customs and excise, specsavers, bt ignite, robert bosch, and Australia department of veterans affairs.

Primary SIC and add'l.: 6719 7379 7372

CIK No: 0001103341

Subsidiaries: CorVu Asia Limited, CorVu Asia Pacific Pte Limited, CorVu Australasia Pty. Ltd., CorVu Latin America, Inc., CorVu North America, Inc., CorVu Plc, CorVu Software Marketing, Inc.

Officers: Ranjana Kundu/Sr. Sales Dir., Partnership Dir., Grant Christian/VP - Sales, Americas, Justin MacIntosh/MD, Founder, Troy Rollo/CTO, Deanna Ziemba/VP - Client Services, Julie Godfrey/Global Marketing Dir., Eddie O'Reilly/COO, Jas Padda/GM, Gary Wilson/Sr. Sales Mgr., Richard Whomes/Professional Services Mgr., Trevor Aikin/Services Dir. - Corvu Asia Pacific

Directors: Justin MacIntosh/MD, Founder

Owners: Robert L. Priddy, Daniel R. Fishback, James L. Mandel, Insiders, Marjorie Scott/5.50%, Joseph J. Caffarelli, Henry Gold/13.90%, Dominic K.K. Sum, Polaris Partners LP/13.90%, David C. Carlson/13.90%, The George McKay Reid Revocable Trust/13.90%, Opella Holdings Limited, Robert L. Doretti, John Scott/8.30%, ComVest Investment Partners II LLC (23 Owners included in Index)

Financial Data: Fiscal Year End:06/30   Latest Annual Data: 6/30/2006

Year		Sales		Net Income
2006		$15,392,000		$1,197,000
2005		$13,171,000		-$6,598,000
2004		$16,158,000		-$2,129,000
Curr. Assets:	$7,226,000	**Curr. Liab.:**	$9,364,000	
Plant, Equip.:	$222,000	**Total Liab.:**	$10,864,000	**Indic. Yr. Divd.:** NA
Total Assets:	$7,448,000	**Net Worth:**	-$3,417,000	**Debt/ Equity:** NA

Cosi Inc

1751 Lake Cook Rd., Ste. 600, Deerfield, IL, 60015; **PH:** 1-847-597-8800; **Fax:** 1-847-597-8884; **http://** www.getcosi.com

General - Incorporation	DE	Stock- Price on:12/24/2007	$4.59
Employees	4,100	Stock Exchange	NDQ
Auditor	BDO Seidman LLP	Ticker Symbol	COSI
Stk Agt	American Stock Transfer & Trust Co.	Outstanding Shares	40,400,000
Counsel	NA	E.P.S.	-$0.5
DUNS No.	NA	Shareholders	NA

Business: The group's principal activity is to own and operate fast casual restaurants in the district of columbia and in the United States. The group offers breakfast, lunch, afternoon coffee, dinner, and dessert menus full of creative, cravable foods and beverages. The group owns and operates 83 fast casual restaurants in 11 states and the district of columbia. The group operates restaurants in two formats: cosi and cosi downtown. The trademarks and trade names used in the business are cosi (R), cosi downtown tm, squagels (R), mocha kiss (R), wake up call to last call (R), cosi corners(TM) and warm n' cosi meltstm.

Primary SIC and add'l.: 5812

CIK No: 0001171014

Officers: James F. Hyatt/Dir., CEO, Pres., Roland Yates/VP - Construction, Facilities, Steve Scrima/VP - Purchasing, Distribution, Thomas Janus/VP - Information Technology, Vicki J. Baue/49/General Counsel, Chief Legal Officer, Chief Compliance Officer , William Koziel/CFO, Gilbert Melott/Chief People Officer, Christopher Carroll/Exec. VP, Chief Marketing Officer, Becky Iliff/VP - People, Jean Grossman/VP - Franchise Operations, Christopher Ames/COO, Edward Backus/52/Exec. VP, Chief Development Officer

Directors: James F. Hyatt/Dir., CEO, Pres., William D. Forrest/Chmn., Michael O'Donnell/Dir., Creed L. Ford/Dir., Eli Cohen/Dir., Mark Demilio/Dir., Robert S. Merritt/Dir.

Owners: Richard W. Shea/11.47%, Mellon Financial Corporation/9.40%, Creed L. Ford, William Koziel, William D. Forrest/3.76%, Gilbert Melott, ZAM Holdings, L.P./12.47%, Kevin Armstrong/2.11%, Edward Backus, Insiders/9.09%, Mark Demilio, Michael ODonnell, Robert Merritt, U.S. Bancorp/7.17%, Patrick Donnellan

Financial Data: Fiscal Year End:01/02 **Latest Annual Data:** 1/1/2007

Year	Sales	Net Income
2007	$126,888,000	-$12,328,000
2006	$117,181,000	-$13,126,000
2005	$110,631,000	-$18,373,000

Curr. Assets:	$14,870,000	Curr. Liab.:	$14,088,000		
Plant, Equip.:	$34,074,000	Total Liab.:	$21,985,000	Indic. Yr. Divd.:	NA
Total Assets:	$51,138,000	Net Worth:	$29,152,000	Debt/ Equity:	0.0017

Cosine Communications Inc

61 E Main, Los Gatos, CA, 95030; **PH:** 1-408-399-6494; **Fax:** 1-408-399-6491; **http://** www.cosinecom.com

General - Incorporation	DE	Stock- Price on:12/24/2007	$3.45
Employees	1	Stock Exchange	OTC
Auditor	Burr, Pilger & Mayer LLP	Ticker Symbol	COSN
Stk Agt	Mellon Investor Services LLC	Outstanding Shares	10,090,000
Counsel	Collette & Erickson	E.P.S.	$0.09
DUNS No.	NA	Shareholders	NA

Business: The group's principal activities are to develop, market and sell communications platform to enable the network service providers to rapidly deliver computer applications and communication services. The products of the group include virtual private networks, firewalls and secure broadband access. Virtual private networks run on the Internet and other communications networks. Firewalls are security programs that are designed to prevent unwanted network traffic and secure broadband access secure high-speed access to the Internet and other communications networks. The group's Internet protocol service delivery platform consists of hardware elements, such as chassis, service processing switches and electronic circuit boards known as ipsgs (Internet protocol service generators) and software components consisting of 'invision' for service network management and 'ingage' for customer network management.

Primary SIC and add'l.: 3577 7372

CIK No: 0001060824

Subsidiaries: CoSine Communications Ltd, CoSine Communications Sarl

Officers: Terry R. Gibson/Dir., CEO, CFO, Pres., Sec./$237,764.00

Directors: Terry R. Gibson/Dir., CEO, CFO, Pres., Sec., Donald Green/76/Chmn., Charles J. Abbe/66/Dir., Jack L. Howard/46/Dir.

Owners: Dimensional FundAdvisors Inc/6.80%, Insiders/3.00%, Donald Green, Empyrean Capital Partners, LP/7.50%, WHX CS Corp./18.80%, Jack L. Howard/1.70%, Terry R. Gibson, Charles J. Abbe, Steel Partners II, L.P/25.70%

Financial Data: Fiscal Year End:12/31 **Latest Annual Data:** 12/31/2006

Year	Sales	Net Income
2006	$1,361,000	$449,000
2005	$3,315,000	-$1,218,000
2004	$9,675,000	-$37,337,000

Curr. Assets:	$23,036,000	Curr. Liab.:	$559,000	P/E Ratio:	57.50
Plant, Equip.:	NA	Total Liab.:	$559,000	Indic. Yr. Divd.:	NA
Total Assets:	$23,036,000	Net Worth:	$22,477,000	Debt/ Equity:	NA

Cosmo Communications Corp

55 Travail Rd., Unit 2, Markham, ON, L3S-3J1; **PH:** 1-905-209-0488

General - Incorporation	FL	Stock- Price on:12/24/2007	$0.5
Employees	35	Stock Exchange	OTC
Auditor	Walker & Co.	Ticker Symbol	CSMO
Stk Agt	American Stock Transfer & Trust Co.	Outstanding Shares	29,100,000
Counsel	NA	E.P.S.	-$0.04
DUNS No.	10-193-8231	Shareholders	NA

Business: The group's principal activity is to market and distribute consumer electronic products. The group has operations in Hong Kong and Canada. The products marketed by the group include televisions, video cassette recorders, audio equipment, digital alarm clocks, quartz alarm clocks, quartz wall clocks, clock radios and combination products such as clock radio telephones. The audio equipment includes audio products comprising of personal cassette players, portable stereos and music centers with and without compact disc players. These products are marketed under the group's own label to mass merchandisers, drug store chains, specialty chain stores and other high-volume retailers. The group's products are generally manufactured by subcontractors in China. Principal customers of the group are wal-mart Canada inc and Canadian tire corporation.

Primary SIC and add'l.: 3873 5064

CIK No: 0000718096

Subsidiaries: Cosmo Communications (H.K.) Limited, Cosmo Communications Canada Inc.

Officers: Peter Horak/66/Dir., CEO, Philip Lau/60/Chmn., Pres., Carol Atkinson/59/Dir., CFO, Yu Wing Kin/56/VP - Hong Kong Operation, Jeff Horak/50/VP - Sales, Marketing, Canada Operations, E. J. Colin/National Sales Mgr. - Canada, Rick Bond/58/VP - Sales, Marketing, USA Operation

Directors: Peter Horak/66/Dir., CEO, Philip Lau/60/Chmn., Pres., Carol Atkinson/59/Dir., CFO, Jacky Lau/49/Dir.

Owners: Peter Horak, Starlight International,/93.80%, Insiders

Financial Data: Fiscal Year End:12/31 **Latest Annual Data:** 03/31/2007

Year	Sales	Net Income
2007	$57,854,000	$148,000
2006	$51,011,000	$147,000
2005	$37,306,000	$625,000

Curr. Assets:	$20,076,000	Curr. Liab.:	$15,826,000		
Plant, Equip.:	$57,000	Total Liab.:	$15,826,000	Indic. Yr. Divd.:	NA
Total Assets:	$20,133,000	Net Worth:	$4,307,000	Debt/ Equity:	NA

Cost Plus Inc

200 4th St., Oakland, CA, 94607; **PH:** 1-510-893-7300; **Fax:** 1-510-893-3681; **http://** www.costplusworldmarket.com

General - Incorporation	CA	Stock- Price on:12/24/2007	$7.93
Employees	2,704	Stock Exchange	NDQ
Auditor	Deloitte & Touche LLP	Ticker Symbol	CPWM
Stk Agt	EquiServe Trust Co N.A	Outstanding Shares	22,080,000
Counsel	Wilson Sonsini Goodrich & Rosati	E.P.S.	-$1.61
DUNS No.	02-917-4612	Shareholders	NA

Business: The group's principal activity is to retail casual home living furnishings and entertaining products. These products are designed to provide solutions to customers' casual living and home entertaining needs. The group operates in 212 stores in 26 states under the names world market, cost plus world market, cost plus and cost plus imports. The group offerings include home decorating items such as furniture and rugs, a variety of tabletop and kitchen products, gifts and decorative accessories including collectibles, cards, wrapping paper and other seasonal items. The group offers a wide selection of gourmet foods and beverages including wine, micro-brewed and imported beer, coffee and tea.

Primary SIC and add'l.: 5714 5722 5712 5719

CIK No: 0000798955

Subsidiaries: Cost Plus Management Services, Inc., Cost Plus of Idaho, Inc., Cost Plus of Texas, Inc.

Owners: Insiders/3.10%, Joan S. Fujii, Barry J. Feld, T. Rowe Price Associates, Inc./9.90%, Rutabaga Capital Management/6.80%, Thales Fund Management, LLC/6.20%, Christopher V. Dodds, Red Mountain Capital Partners LLC/9.80%, Kim D. Robbins, Franklin Resources, Inc./10.00%, Danny W. Gurr, ICM Asset Management, Inc./5.70%, Jakup a Dul Jacobsen/10.00%, Joseph H. Coulombe, Michael J. Allen **(19 Owners included in Index)**

Financial Data: Fiscal Year End:01/28 **Latest Annual Data:** 2/3/2007

Year	Sales	Net Income
2007	$1,040,309,000	-$22,536,000
2006	$970,441,000	$20,233,000
2005	$908,560,000	$30,221,000

Curr. Assets:	$287,173,000	Curr. Liab.:	$103,529,000		
Plant, Equip.:	$123,854,000	Total Liab.:	$154,889,000	Indic. Yr. Divd.:	NA
Total Assets:	$421,818,000	Net Worth:	$266,929,000	Debt/ Equity:	NA

Cost-U-Less Inc

3633 136th Pl SE, Ste 110, Bellevue, WA, 98006; **PH:** 1-425-945-0213; **http://** www.costuless.com; **Email:** marketing@costuless.com

General - Incorporation	WA	Stock- Price on:12/24/2007	$10.95
Employees	600	Stock Exchange	NDQ
Auditor	Grant Thornton LLP	Ticker Symbol	CULS
Stk Agt	Mellon Investor Services LLC	Outstanding Shares	4,030,000
Counsel	NA	E.P.S.	$0.63
DUNS No.	61-169-2013	Shareholders	NA

Business: The group's principal activity is to operate mid-size warehouse club-style stores. The store's products are categorized as food perishables, nonfood and food-non-perishables. Food-perishables include meat, produce, deli, dairy and frozen items. Nonfood includes tobacco, sundries, health and beauty, office, hardware, electronics, housewares, furniture and sporting goods. Food-non-perishables include dry grocery goods including soda, wine, beer, liquor, candy and snacks. At 28-Dec-2003, the group operates eleven island stores which are located in Hawaii, guam, st. Thomas, st. Croix, American samoa, fiji, curacao, st. Maarten and sonora, California.

Primary SIC and add'l.: 5331

CIK No: 0000851368

Subsidiaries: CUL (Aruba) N.V., CUL (Aust), CUL (Curacao) N.V., CUL (Fiji), CUL (NZ), CUL, Inc., Culguam, Inc., CULNEV, Inc., Culsamoa, Inc., Culusvi, Inc., CULVAN Limited

Officers: Jeffrey J. Meder/Dir., CEO, Pres./$434,687.00, Robert J. Cain/VP - Logistics, Martin P. Moore/CFO, VP/$189,716.00, Bob Boren/Marketing Mgr. - Sr. Buyer, Michael T. Scalzo/VP - Merchandising, Marketing/$232,211.00, William W. Lofgren/VP - Information Systems/$216,943.00, Roy W. Sorensen/VP, COO/$229,174.00, Brian Rose/VP - Operations - Pacific Region

Directors: Jeffrey J. Meder/Dir., CEO, Pres., George Textor/Chmn., Bob Donegan/Dir., David Enger/Dir., Gary Nettles/Dir., John Delafield/Dir.

Owners: Whitebox Advisors, LLC/6.80%, Robert C. Donegan, Loeb Partners Corporation/5.10%, Martin P. Moore/1.60%, Advisory Research, Inc./5.00%, George C. Textor, William W. Lofgren, Michael T. Scalzo/1.30%, John D. Delafield/5.70%, Insiders/20.10%, Chadwick Capital Management, LLC/6.60%, Gary W. Nettles/1.90%, David A. Enger, Roy W. Sorensen/1.70%, Delafield Hambrecht, Inc./5.90% **(16 Owners included in Index)**

Financial Data: Fiscal Year End:01/01 **Latest Annual Data:** 04/01/2007

Year	Sales	Net Income
2007	$55,628,000	$647,000
2006	$222,022,000	$2,668,000
2004	$209,390,000	$2,688,000

Curr. Assets:	$32,431,000	Curr. Liab.:	$22,115,000	P/E Ratio:	18.25
Plant, Equip.:	$20,881,000	Total Liab.:	$27,039,000	Indic. Yr. Divd.:	NA
Total Assets:	$54,035,000	Net Worth:	$26,996,000	Debt/ Equity:	0.1240

Costar Group Inc

2 Bethesda Metro Ctr., 10th Fl., Bethesda, MD, 20814; **PH:** 1-301-215-8300; **Fax:** 1-301-718-2444; **http://** www.costar.com; **Email:** info@costar.com

General - Incorporation	DE	Stock- Price on:12/24/2007	$52.3
Employees	1,308	Stock Exchange	NDQ
Auditor	Ernst & Young LLP	Ticker Symbol	CSGP
Stk Agt	American Stock Transfer & Trust Co.	Outstanding Shares	19,190,000
Counsel	NA	E.P.S.	$0.59
DUNS No.	18-890-8909	Shareholders	NA

Business: The group's principle activity is to provide information services to the United States commercial real estate industry. The group's suite of product offers customers access via the Internet to the most comprehensive, verified database of commercial real estate information. The strategy of the group is to provide commercial real estate professionals with critical knowledge to complete transactions, by offering the most up-to-date, consolidated and standardized information. The group delivers its content to customers through ten distinct products and services. The wide array of digital service offerings includes a leasing marketplace, a selling market place, sales comparable information, data hosting for clients' Web sites, decision support, contact management, tenant information, property data integration, property marketing and industry news. The group's quarterly revenue for September 2007 was 49.34 millions of USD.

Primary SIC and add'l.: 7372 7375

CIK No: 0001057352

Subsidiaries: CoStar Limited, CoStar Realty Information, Inc., FOCUS Information Limited, National Research Bureau, Inc.

Officers: Andrew C. Florance/Founder, Dir., CEO, Pres./$1,507,509.00, Jonathan Coleman/General Counsel, Sec., Dean Violagis/VP - Research, Costar Property, Costar Commercial MLS, Craig Farrington/VP - Comps/$455,456.00, Jim Black/VP - Electronic Media, John Bush/Sr. Dir. - Human Resources, Frank A. Carchedi/50/Treasurer, Frank Simuro/Sr. VP - Information Systems, Jonathan Bray/51/MD, Christopher R. Tully/Sr. VP - Sales, Customer Service/$958,542.00, Jennifer Kitchen/Sr. VP - Research, Paul Marples/MD - Focus Information Limited, Costars European Operations, Brian Radecki/CFO, Michael Glick/Dir. - E-Marketing Development, Thomas Witt/VP - Marketing *(16 Officers included in Index)*

Directors: Andrew C. Florance/Founder, Dir., CEO, Pres., Michael R. Klein/Chmn., Josiah O. Low/Dir., Christopher J. Nassetta/Dir., Catherine B. Reynolds/Dir., David Bonderman/Dir., Warren H. Haber/Dir.

Owners: Frank A. Carchedi, Christopher J. Nassetta, Transamerica Investment Management, LLC/5.09%, Waddell& Reed Financial, Inc/6.80%, Christopher R. Tully, Janus Capital Management LLC/10.00%, David Bonderman/1.46%, FMR Corp/11.19%, Craig S. Farrington, Morgan Stanley/8.00%, Jennifer L. Kitchen, Josiah O. Low, Andrew C. Florance/2.91%, Catherine B. Reynolds, TimesSquare Capital Management, LLC/7.30% *(20 Owners included in Index)*

Financial Data: **Fiscal Year End:** 12/31 **Latest Annual Data:** 12/31/2006

Year	Sales	Net Income
2006	$158,889,000	$12,410,000
2005	$134,338,000	$6,457,000
2004	$112,085,000	$24,985,000

Curr. Assets:	$178,751,000	**Curr. Liab.:**	$24,145,000	**P/E Ratio:**	88.64
Plant, Equip.:	$18,407,000	**Total Liab.:**	$25,327,000	**Indic. Yr. Divd.:**	NA
Total Assets:	$275,437,000	**Net Worth:**	$250,110,000	**Debt/ Equity:**	NA

Costco Wholesale Corp

999 Lake Dr., Issaquah, WA, 98027; ***PH:*** 1-425-313-8100; ***http://*** www.costco.com

General		**Stock**	
Incorporation	WA	Price on:12/24/2007	$56.19
Employees	71,000	Stock Exchange	NDQ
Auditor	KPMG LLP	Ticker Symbol	COST
Stk Agt	Mellon Investor Services LLC	Outstanding Shares	437,940,000
Counsel	Foster, Pepper & Shefelman PLLC	E.P.S.	$2.45
DUNS No.	80-896-9844	Shareholders	NA

Business: The groups principle activity is to provide membership warehouses based on the concept that offers its members very low prices on a limited selection of nationally branded and selected private-label products. The group operates from United States.

Primary SIC and add'l.: 5611 4226 5731 5995 5441 5331 5411

CIK No: 0000909832

Subsidiaries: Costco Canada Holdings Inc., Costco Wholesale Canada Ltd., Costco Wholesale Membership, Inc., NW Re Ltd.

Officers: James D. Sinegal/Dir., CEO, Pres., Bruce A. Greenwood/Sr. VP, GM - Los Angeles Region, Dennis R. Zook/COO, Exec. VP - Southwest Division, Mexico, Jeffrey R. Long/Sr. VP, GM - Northeast Region, Richard C. Chavez/Sr. VP - Costco Wholesale Industries, Business Development, Joseph P. Portera/COO, Exec. VP - Eastern, Canadian Divisions, Robert D. Hicok/Sr. VP, GM - San Diego Region, Ginnie M. Roeglin/Sr. VP - E, Commerce, Publishing, Roger A. Campbell/Sr. VP, GM - Southeast Region, David S. Petterson/Sr. VP, Corporate Controller, John B. Gaherty/Sr. VP, GM - Midwest Region, James P. Murphy/Sr. VP - International Operations, Paul G. Moulton/Exec. VP - Real Estate, Stephanie Bradley/Contact - Membership, Marketing, Jeffrey Lyons/Sr. VP - Merchandising, Fresh Foods *(42 Officers included in Index)*

Directors: James D. Sinegal/Dir., CEO, Pres., Jeffrey H. Brotman/Chmn., Richard A. Galanti/Dir., CFO, Exec. VP, Richard D. Dicerchio/Dir., COO, Sr. Exec. VP - Global Operations, Distribution, Construction, Benjamin S. Carson/Dir., Susan Decker/Dir., Daniel J. Evans/Dir., William H. Gates/Dir., Hamilton E. James/Dir., Richard M. Libenson/Dir., John W. Meisenbach/Dir., Charles T. Munger/Dir., Jill S. Ruckelshaus/Dir.

Owners: John W. Meisenbach, Benjamin S. Carson, W. Craig Jelinek, Jill S. Ruckelshaus, Susan L. Decker, Insiders/2.30%, Daniel J. Evans, Jeffrey H. Brotman, Paul G. Moulton, Richard M. Libenson, Richard D. DiCerchio, William H. Gates, Davis Selected Advisers, LP/14.20%, James D. Sinegal, Hamilton E. James *(17 Owners included in Index)*

Financial Data: **Fiscal Year End:** 08/28 **Latest Annual Data:** 9/3/2006

Year	Sales	Net Income
2006	$60,151,227,000	$1,103,215,000
2005	$52,935,228,000	$1,063,092,000
2004	$48,106,992,000	$882,393,000

Curr. Assets:	$8,232,082,000	**Curr. Liab.:**	$7,819,191,000	**P/E Ratio:**	24.43
Plant, Equip.:	$8,564,295,000	**Total Liab.:**	$8,288,273,000	**Indic. Yr. Divd.:**	$0.580
Total Assets:	$17,495,070,000	**Net Worth:**	$9,143,439,000	**Debt/ Equity:**	0.0191

CoTherix Inc

2000 Sierra Point Pk.way, Ste. 600, Brisbane, CA, 94005; ***PH:*** 1-650-808-6500; ***http://*** www.cotherix.com

General		**Stock**	
Incorporation	DE	Price on:12/24/2007	NA
Employees	NA	Stock Exchange	NA
Auditor	Ernst& Young LLP	Ticker Symbol	NA
Stk Agt	Computershare Investor Services,	Outstanding Shares	NA
Counsel	NA	E.P.S.	NA
DUNS No.	NA	Shareholders	NA

Business: The groups principle activities include licensing, developing and commercializing therapeutic products. The group products sold under the trade name REVEAL Registry. The group operates from the United States.

Primary SIC and add'l.: 2836

CIK No: 0001138812

Officers: Donald J. Santel/CEO, Christine E. Gray-Smith/CFO, Exec. VP

Cott Corp

6525 Viscount Rd., Mississauga, ON, L4V 1H6 ; ***PH:*** 1-905-672-1900; ***http://*** www.cott.com; ***Email:*** investor_relations@cott.com

General		**Stock**	
Incorporation	Canada	Price on:12/24/2007	$14.67
Employees	3,163	Stock Exchange	NYSE
Auditor	PricewaterhouseCoopers LLP	Ticker Symbol	COT
Stk Agt	Computershare Trust Company of Canada	Outstanding Shares	71,750,000
Counsel	NA	E.P.S.	-$0.36
DUNS No.	20-194-2422	Shareholders	NA

Business: The group's principal activities are producing and supplying of retailer brand carbonated soft drinks. The group's product line also includes beverages, juices and juice-based products, bottled water, organic and high-energy beverages and iced teas. The products are principally sold under customer controlled private labels and also under the group's own control brands and licensed brand names. The group operates its business in the United States, Canada and the United Kingdom. During 2002, the group acquired premium beverage packers inc.

Primary SIC and add'l.: 2086

CIK No: 0000884713

Subsidiaries: 156775 Canada Inc., 2011438 Ontario Ltd., 804340 Ontario Limited, 967979 Ontario Limited, BCB European Holdings, BCB International Holdings, CB Nevada Capital Inc., Cott Atlantic Company, Cott Beverages Inc., Cott Beverages Limited, Cott Beverages Wyomissing Inc., Cott do Brasil Industria, Comercio, Importacao e Exportacao de Bebidas e Concentrados Ltda, Cott Embotelladores de Mexico, S.A. de C. V., Cott Europe Trading Limited, Cott Holdings Inc. 34 Subsidiaries included in the Index

Officers: Brent D. Willis/47/Dir., CEO, Pres./$3,576,940.00, Juan Figuereo/CFO, Jason Nichol/Sr. VP - Wal, Mart, Wynn Willard/Pres. - International, Mark R. Halperin/50/Chief Legal, Corporate Development Officer, Corp. Sec./$1,164,752.00, Edmund P. Okeeffe/VP - Strategy, Investor Relations, John Dennehy/46/Pres. - North America/$1,082,710.00, Abilio Gonzalez/Chief People Officer/$906,597.00, Rick Dobry/Chief Manufacturing, Supply Chain Officer, Thomas Aruffo/Chief Information, Shared Services Officer, Tina Dell'Aquila/45/VP, Controller, Assist. Sec./$680,732.00

Directors: Brent D. Willis/47/Dir., CEO, Pres., George A. Burnett/52/Dir., David T. Gibbons/64/Dir., Stephen H. Halperin/58/Dir., Christine A. Magee/48/Dir., Frank E. Weise/63/Dir., Donald G. Watt/72/Dir., Philip B. Livingston/50/Dir., Betty Jane Hess/59/Dir., Andrew Prozes/62/Dir., Serge Gouin/65/Dir.

Owners: Dodge& Cox/5.30%, FMR Corp./13.00%, T. Rowe Price Associates, Inc./8.00%, UBS AmericasInc./7.00%, PRIMECAP Management Company/5.90%, UBS AG/7.80%, AMVESCAPPLC/18.00%, LMMLLC/6.70%

Financial Data: **Fiscal Year End:** 12/31 **Latest Annual Data:** 12/30/2006

Year	Sales	Net Income
2006	$1,771,800,000	-$17,500,000
2005	$1,755,300,000	$24,600,000

Curr. Assets:	$366,500,000	**Curr. Liab.:**	$341,200,000		
Plant, Equip.:	$394,200,000	**Total Liab.:**	$689,500,000	**Indic. Yr. Divd.:**	NA
Total Assets:	$1,171,400,000	**Net Worth:**	$481,900,000	**Debt/ Equity:**	0.5666

Cougar Biotechnology Inc

210 S Federal Hwy., Ste 205, Deerfield Beach, FL, 33441; ***PH:*** 1-310-203-2902; ***http://*** www.cougarbiotechnology.com; ***Email:*** info@cougarbiotechnology.com

General		**Stock**	
Incorporation	DE	Price on:12/24/2007	NA
Employees	NA	Stock Exchange	NDQ
Auditor	J.H. Cohn, LLP	Ticker Symbol	CGRB
Stk Agt	NA	Outstanding Shares	NA
Counsel	NA	E.P.S.	NA
DUNS No.	NA	Shareholders	NA

Business: The group's principle activity is to engage in organizational efforts and obtaining initial financing. The group was formed as a vehicle to pursue a business combination and has made no efforts to identify a possible business combination. The Company has not conducted negotiations or entered into a letter of intent concerning any target business. The business purpose of the Company is to seek the acquisition of, or merger with, an existing company. The group operates from United States.

Primary SIC and add'l.: 6770

CIK No: 0001335102

Officers: Alan H. Auerbach/Dir., CEO, Pres., Gloria T. Lee/VP - Clinical Research, Development, Charles R. Eyler/VP - Finance, Arturo Molina/Sr. VP - Clinical Research, Development, Richard B. Phillips/VP - Regulatory Affairs, Quality Assurance

Directors: Alan H. Auerbach/Dir., CEO, Pres., Arie Belldegrun/Vice Chmn., Chmn. - Scientific Advisory Board, Eric J. Small/Chmn. - Scientific Advisory Board, John P. Leonard/Member - Scientific Advisory Board, Russell H. Ellison/Dir., Harold J. Meyers/Dir., Lindsay A. Rosenwald/53/Dir., Michael S. Richman/Dir., Michael A. Carducci/Member - Scientific Advisory Board, Celestia S. Higano/Member - Scientific Advisory Board, Philip Kantoff/Member - Scientific Advisory Board, Howard I. Scher/Member - Scientific Advisory Board, Matthew R. Smith/Member - Scientific Advisory Board, Nicholas J. Vogelzang/Member - Scientific Advisory Board, Thomas R. Malley/Dir. *(16 Directors included in Index)*

Owners: Gloria T. Lee, Insiders/31.41%, Alan H. Auerbach/5.41%, Arie Belldegrun/5.12%, Lindsay A. Rosenwald/22.65%, Harold J. Meyers, Millenco, LLC/5.18%, Visium Capital Management, LLC/7.79%, Charles R. Eyler, Adage Capital Partners, L.P./9.34%, Horizon BioMedical Ventures, LLC/21.28%, Brookside Capital Partners Fund, L.P./9.34%, T. Rowe Price Associates, Inc./9.34%

Cougar Holdings Inc

P.O. Box 97555, Office 1304, The Fairmont Dubai, Dubai; ***PH:*** 971-4 332-0345; ***http://*** cougarholdings.net

General - Incorporation	NV
Employees	NA
Auditor	PKF Witt Mares, PLC
Stk Agt	Madison Stock Transfer, Inc.
Counsel	NA
DUNS No.	NA

Stock - Price on:12/24/2007	$0.65
Stock Exchange	OTC
Ticker Symbol	CGRH
Outstanding Shares	NA
E.P.S	$4.40
Shareholders	NA

Business: The groups principle activity activities include manufacturing and distributing of organic chemical products. The group products include epichlorohydrin rubber, glutaradehyde and acrolein, sodium benzoate and benzyl chloride. The group operates through two segments namely local and exports. The group operates from China, Japan, Europe and the United Kingdom.

Primary SIC and add'l.: 1481

CIK No: 0001165780

Subsidiaries: Wuhan Youji Import and Export Co. Limited, Wuhan Youji Industries Co., Limited

Officers: Zitong Li/46/Dir., CEO, Paul Tarry/Business Development Dir., Fenggang Wu/42/Dir., CFO, Ian Simm/Founder, Pres., Yuankun Gao/49/Dir., Pres., Limin Chen/51/Dir., COO, Guangyuan Hu/52/Sec.

Directors: Zitong Li/46/Dir., CEO, Xingwen Diao/43/Chmn., Fenggang Wu/42/Dir., CFO, Ian Simm/Founder, Pres., Yuankun Gao/49/Dir., Pres., Hongdun Zhou/59/Dir., Limin Chen/51/Dir., COO

Owners: Zitong Li, Insiders/33.40%, Yuankun Gao/29.20%, Wuhan Youji Employee Trust/29.30%, Wuhan Linuo Investment Co. Limited/29.20%, Limin Chen, Hongdun Zhou/3.60%

Financial Data: Fiscal Year End:12/31 Latest Annual Data: 12/31/2006

Year	Sales	Net Income
2006	$83,350,000	$1,928,000
2005	$13,000	-$26,000

Curr. Assets:	$76,000	Curr. Liab.:	$8,000		
Plant, Equip.:	NA	Total Liab.:	$8,000	Indic. Yr. Divd.:	NA
Total Assets:	$76,000	Net Worth:	$68,000	Debt/ Equity:	NA

Counterpath Corp

Formerly: Xten Networks Inc
300-505 Burrard St., Vancouver, BC, V7X 1M3; **PH:** 1-604-320-3344; **http://** www.xten.com

General - Incorporation	NV
Employees	NA
Auditor	Amisano Hanson
Stk Agt	Pacific Stock Transfer Company
Counsel	NA
DUNS No.	NA

Stock - Price on:12/24/2007	$0.37
Stock Exchange	NA
Ticker Symbol	NA
Outstanding Shares	NA
E.P.S	NA
Shareholders	NA

Business: The group's principal activity is to design, develop and market software used to make or receive phone calls from a computer. The group also provides high-quality software for ip telephony (Internet protocol telephony), which is a general term for the technologies that use the Internet protocol's packet-switched connections to exchange voice, fax, and other forms of information.

Primary SIC and add'l.: 7379

CIK No: 0001236997

Subsidiaries: Broad Scope Entertainment, Inc., CounterPath Solutions R&D Inc., CounterPath Solutions, Inc., Ineen, Inc.

Officers: Mark Bruk/Chmn., CEO/$246,776.00, David Karp/CFO, Treasurer, Sec., Jason Fischl/CTO/$255,743.00, Donovan Jones/Dir., COO, Pres./$354,773.00, Andrew Fischer/Exec. VP - Business Developement, Scott Wilson/Investor Relations Officer, Sarah Stover/Contact - Media Relation

Directors: Mark Bruk/Chmn., CEO, Owen Matthews/Vice Chmn., Robert Sparks/Member - Advisory Board, Donovan Jones/Dir., COO, Pres., Larry Timlick/Dir., Chris R. Cooper/Dir., Graeme Dollar/Member - Advisory Board, Alan Duric/Member - Advisory Board, Rohan Mahy/Member - Advisory Board, Klaus Schulz/Member - Advisory Board

Owners: Larry Timlick, Mark Bruk/15.90%, Donovan Jones/1.80%, Insiders/19.80%, David Karp, Chris Cooper, Jason Fischl/1.80%, Steven Bruk/33.00%

Financial Data: Fiscal Year End:04/30 Latest Annual Data: 4/30/2006

Year	Sales	Net Income
2006	$4,619,000	-$1,282,000
2005	$3,123,000	-$780,000
2004	$565,000	-$174,000

Curr. Assets:	$2,952,000	Curr. Liab.:	$976,000		
Plant, Equip.:	$300,000	Total Liab.:	$2,864,000	Indic. Yr. Divd.:	NA
Total Assets:	$3,260,000	Net Worth:	$397,000	Debt/ Equity:	NA

Countrywide Financial Corp

4500 Pk. Granada, Calabasas, CA, 91302; **PH:** 1-818-225-3000; **Fax:** 1-818-225-4051; **http://** www.countrywide.com

General - Incorporation	DE
Employees	54,655
Auditor	KPMG LLP
Stk Agt	American Stock Transfer & Trust Co.
Counsel	NA
DUNS No.	04-768-9971

Stock - Price on:12/24/2007	$39.34
Stock Exchange	NYSE
Ticker Symbol	CFC
Outstanding Shares	593,390,000
E.P.S	$3.59
Shareholders	NA

Business: The groups principle activity is to provide mortgage lending and other real estate finance-related businesses. The group operates from United States.

Primary SIC and add'l.: 6211 6321 6162 6311 6719

CIK No: 0000025191

Subsidiaries: Balboa Insurance Company, Balboa Insurance Group, Inc., Balboa Life & Casualty LLC, Balboa Life Insurance Company, Balboa Life Insurance Company of New York, Balboa Reinsurance Company, Balboa Reinsurance Company of South Carolina, Balboa Texas Institutional Group, Inc., Balboa Warranty Services Corporation, CAI Management Inc., CB Securities Holdings 1, Inc., CB Securities Holdings 2, Inc., CCM International Limited, CFC India Services Private Limited, CFC International Mauritius Limited 108 Subsidiaries included in the Index

Officers: Angelo R. Mozilo/Chmn., CEO/$48,133,160.00, Leora I. Goren/Sr. MD, Chief Human Resources Officer, Jack Schakett/Exec. MD, COO, Sandor E. Samuels/Exec. MD, Chief Legal Officer, Assist. Sec., Carlos M. Garcia/Exec. MD - Banking, Insurance/$4,846,391.00, Richard B. Wentz/Sr. MD, General Counsel - Mortgage Banking, Litigation, Chief Ethics Officer, Eric P. Sieracki/Exec. MD, CFO/$2,606,045.00, Susan E. Bow/Sr. MD, General Counsel, Corp. Sec.,

Andrew Gissinger/Exec. MD - Residential Lending, Walter Smiechewicz/Sr. MD - Enterprise Risk Assessment, David Sambol/Dir., COO, Pres./$11,965,710.00, Todd A. Dal Porto/Sr. MD - Wholesale Lending Division, Jennifer Sandefur/Sr. MD, Treasurer, Chris Oltmann/Sr. VP - Fixed Income Investor Relations, Sam Ourfalian/Sr. MD - Application Technologies *(35 Officers included in Index)*

Directors: Angelo R. Mozilo/Chmn., CEO, Harley W. Snyder/Dir., Henry G. Cisneros/60/Dir., Oscar P. Robertson/Dir., Keith P. Russell/Dir., Robert J. Donato/Dir., Jeffrey M. Cunningham/Dir., David Sambol/Dir., COO, Pres., Robert T. Parry/Dir., Martin R. Melone/Dir.

Owners: David Sambol, Angelo R. Mozilo/1.50%, Ranjit M. Kripalani, The TCW Group, Inc./5.35%, Michael E. Dougherty, Harley W. Snyder, Henry G. Cisneros, Barclays Global Investors, NA/10.34%, Legg Mason Capital Management, Inc./8.25%, Jeffrey M. Cunningham, Oscar P. Robertson, Stanford L. Kurland, Robert J. Donato, Robert T. Parry, Keith P. Russell *(19 Owners included in Index)*

Financial Data: Fiscal Year End:12/31 Latest Annual Data: 12/31/2006

Year	Sales	Net Income
2006	$24,876,793,000	$2,674,846,000
2005	$15,633,133,000	$2,528,090,000
2004	$11,246,740,000	$2,197,574,000

Curr. Assets:	$56,146,079,000	Curr. Liab.:	$114,140,800,000	P/E Ratio:	10.01
Plant, Equip.:	$1,625,456,000	Total Liab.:	$185,628,384,000	Indic. Yr. Divd.:	$0.600
Total Assets:	$199,946,230,000	Net Worth:	$14,317,846,000	Debt/ Equity:	5.0155

County Bank Corp

83 W Nepessing St. , Lapeer, MI, 48446; **PH:** 1-810-664-2977; **http://** www.lcbt.com

General - Incorporation	MI
Employees	NA
Auditor	Plante & Moran, PLLC
Stk Agt	NA
Counsel	NA
DUNS No.	04-941-1101

Stock - Price on:12/24/2007	$36.5
Stock Exchange	OTC
Ticker Symbol	CBNC
Outstanding Shares	NA
E.P.S	NA
Shareholders	NA

Business: The group's principle activities are to accept deposits and provide real estate, commercial and consumer loans to businesses and individuals through eight locations. The group accepts deposits, which include commercial and personal checking, savings and time deposit. The group provides commercial and industrial loans, real estate mortgages, and consumer loans to individuals, retail businesses, farming operations and industrial plants. The trust department offers employee benefit plans, estate planning services and complete trust services. The operations of the group are carried through 6 branches in Michigan.

Primary SIC and add'l.: 6712 6022

CIK No: 0000830480

Subsidiaries: Lapeer County Bank & Trust Co

Financial Data: Fiscal Year End:12/31 Latest Annual Data: 12/31/2004

Year	Sales	Net Income
2004	$15,429,000	$3,622,000
2003	$15,509,000	$3,651,000
2002	$16,462,000	$3,816,000

Curr. Assets:	$17,415,000	Curr. Liab.:	$219,701,000		
Plant, Equip.:	$6,067,000	Total Liab.:	$222,761,000	Indic. Yr. Divd.:	NA
Total Assets:	$253,261,000	Net Worth:	$30,500,000	Debt/ Equity:	0.0813

County Commerce Bank

2400 E Gonzales Rd., Oxnard, CA, 93036; **PH:** 1-805-485-7600; **Fax:** 1-805-485-7299; **http://** www.countycommercebank.com; **Email:** info@CountyCommerceBank.com

General - Incorporation	NA
Employees	NA
Auditor	NA
Stk Agt	NA
Counsel	NA
DUNS No.	NA

Stock - Price on:12/24/2007	$24.55
Stock Exchange	OTC
Ticker Symbol	CNYB
Outstanding Shares	NA
E.P.S	NA
Shareholders	NA

Business: The groups principal activities include providing banking and financial services to the customers. Services of the group include operating checking accounts for sole proprietors, partnerships, and corporations, money market savings accounts, certificate of deposit accounts, courier deposit pick up services, cash management services and wire transfer facilities. The group operates from the United States.

Primary SIC and add'l.: 6029

CIK No:

Officers: Joseph D. Kreutz/Chmn., CEO, Pres., David Brubaker/CFO, Exec. VP

Directors: Joseph D. Kreutz/Chmn., CEO, Pres., Roger J. Myers/67/Dir., Randall H. Kinsling/Dir., Martin J. Marietta/Dir., Robert M. O'Halleran/57/Dir., Jeffrey R. Becker/Dir., Gary M. Horgan/Dir.

County First Bank MD

202 Centennial St., La Plata, MD, 20646; **PH:** 1-301-934-2265; **http://** www.countyfirstbank.com; **Email:** info@countyfirstbank.com

General - Incorporation	NA
Employees	NA
Auditor	NA
Stk Agt	American Stock Transfer & Trust Co.
Counsel	NA
DUNS No.	NA

Stock - Price on:12/24/2007	$37
Stock Exchange	OTC
Ticker Symbol	CUMD
Outstanding Shares	NA
E.P.S	NA
Shareholders	NA

Business: The groups principal activities include providing banking and financial services to the customers.. Services of the group include community banking, free checking, savings account, Loans and Mortgages and financial calculations, credit cards, debit cards, housing loan, personal loans and Retirement Solutions. The group operates from the United States.

Primary SIC and add'l.: 6021

CIK No:

Courier Corp

15 Wellman Ave., N. Chelmsford, MA, 01863; *PH:* 1-978-251-6000; *Fax:* 1-978-251-8228;
http:// www.courier.com; *Email:* marketing@courier.com

General - Incorporation	MA	**Stock**- Price on:12/24/2007	$40.37
Employees	1,724	Stock Exchange	NDQ
Auditor	Deloitte & Touche LLP	Ticker Symbol	CRRC
Stk Agt	Computershare Trust Co	Outstanding Shares	12,530,000
Counsel	Goodwin, Procter & Hoar	E.P.S	NA
DUNS No.	00-104-2555	Shareholders	NA

Business: The group's principal activities are book manufacturing and specialty publishing. The group operates in two segments: full-service book manufacturing and specialty publishing. Book manufacturing segment focuses on streamlining and enhancing the process of bringing books from the point of creation to the point of use. The principal markets are religious, educational and specialty trade books with products including bibles, educational texts and consumer books. Specialty publishing segment publishes over 8,000 titles in more than 30 specialty categories ranging from literature and poetry classics to paper dolls, and from musical scores to typographical fonts. In fiscal 2003, courier sold all of the assets of courier custom publishing, inc. Which comprised all of the remaining activities of the customized education segment. On 06-Jan-2004, the group acquired research and education association.

Primary SIC and add'l.: 2731 2732

CIK No: 0000025212

Subsidiaries: Book-mart Press,Inc., Courier Companies,Inc., Courier Foreign Sales Corporation Ltd., Courier Kendallville,Inc., Courier New Media,Inc., Courier Properties,Inc., Dover Publications,Inc., National Publishing Company, Research& Education Association,Inc.

Officers: James F. Conway/Chmn., CEO, Pres., Anthony F. Caruso/VP, David J. La Fauci/VP, Diana L. Sawyer/VP, Peter D. Tobin/VP, Nicholas W. Thorndike/Corp. Dir., Trustee, Beirne F. Lovely/Clerk, Sec., Peter A. Clifford/VP, Gary S. Gluckow/VP, Peter R. Conway/VP, Robert P. Story/Dir., COO, Sr. VP, Ronald L. Skates/Corp. Dir., Trustee, Peter M. Folger/Sr. VP, CFO, George Q. Nichols/Dir., Sr. VP, Eric J. Zimmerman/VP *(18 Officers included in Index)*

Directors: James F. Conway/Chmn., CEO, Pres., George Q. Nichols/Dir., Sr. VP, Susan L. Wagner/Dir., Edward J. Hoff/Dir., Arnold S. Lerner/Dir., Peter K. Markell/Dir., Robert P. Story/Dir., COO, Sr. VP, Ronald L. Skates/Corp. Dir., Trustee, Richard K. Donahue/Dir., Kathleen Foley Curley/Dir., Nicholas W. Thorndike/Corp. Dir., Trustee

Owners: Edward J. Hoff/3.00%, George Q. Nichols/0.20%, Eric J. Zimmerman/0.50%, Richard K. Donahue/0.90%, Kathleen Foley Curley/0.40%, Peter M. Folger/0.50%, Arnold S. Lerner/0.60%, Peter K. Markell/0.10%, Insiders/17.10%, Susan L. Wagner/0.10%, Nicholas W. Thorndike/0.40%, Wasatch Advisors, Inc./5.10%, Robert P. Story/2.50%, James F. Conway/7.60%, T. Rowe Price Associates, Inc./9.40% *(18 Owners included in Index)*

Financial Data: *Fiscal Year End:*09/24 *Latest Annual Data:* 9/30/2006

Year	Sales	Net Income
2006	$269,051,000	$28,380,000
2005	$227,039,000	$22,134,000
2004	$211,179,000	$20,540,000

Curr. Assets:	$81,863,000	**Curr. Liab.:**	$35,690,000	**P/E Ratio:**	17.55
Plant, Equip.:	$85,248,000	**Total Liab.:**	$64,862,000	**Indic. Yr. Divd.:**	$0.800
Total Assets:	$247,188,000	**Net Worth:**	$182,326,000	**Debt/ Equity:**	0.1280

Cousins Properties Inc

2500 Windy Ridge Pkwy., Ste. 1600, Atlanta, GA, 30339; *PH:* 1-770-955-2200;
Fax: 1-770-857-2360; *http://* www.cousinsproperties.com

General - Incorporation	GA	**Stock**- Price on:12/24/2007	$30.52
Employees	488	Stock Exchange	NYSE
Auditor	Deloitte & Touche LLP	Ticker Symbol	CUZ
Stk Agt	American Stock Transfer & Trust Co.	Outstanding Shares	52,030,000
Counsel	NA	E.P.S	NA
DUNS No.	NA	Shareholders	NA

Business: The groups principle activities include owning, developing, redeveloping and manages its own real estate portfolio and performs real estate related services. The group operates from the United States. The groups quarterly revenue for September 2007 was 46.19 millions of USD.

Primary SIC and add'l.: 6798

CIK No: 0000025232

Subsidiaries: 3280 Peachtreel, LLC, 3280 Peachtreell, LLC, 50 Biscayne Venture, LLC*, 615 Peachtree LLC, 905 Juniper Venture, LLC, Avenue Webb Gin, LLC, Blalock Lakes, LLC, C-H Associates, Ltd., C/W Jefferson Milll, LLC, C/W King Milll, LLC, Carriage Avenue, LLC*, CCD Juniper LLC, Cedar Grove Lakes, LLC, Cousins 191 Investor LLC, Cousins Aircraft Associates, LLC 55 Subsidiaries included in the Index

Officers: Thomas D. Bell/Chmn., CEO/$2,727,304.00, James A. Fleming/CFO, Exec. VP/$755,000.00, Bruce E. Smith/Pres. - Land Division, Larry L. Gellerstedt/Pres. - Office, Multi, Family Division/$1,193,490.00, Jack A. Lahue/Sr. VP - Office Division, Daniel M. Dupree/COO, Pres./$2,595,904.00, Craig B. Jones/Exec. VP, Chief Investment Officer, Joel T. Murphy/Pres. - Retail Division/$1,668,219.00, Forrest Robinson/Pres. - Industrial Division, John McColl/Sr. VP - Office Division, Lawrence L. Gellerstedt/51/Sr. VP, Pres. - Office, Multi, Family Division, Bob Currie/Sr. VP - Leasing, Earle Yancey/VP - Development

Directors: Thomas D. Bell/Chmn., CEO, Dary R. Stone/Vice Chmn., James D. Edwards/Dir., William Porter Payne/Dir., Lillian C. Giornelli/Dir., Taylor S. Glover/Dir., James H. Hance/Dir., Boone A. Knox/Dir., William B. Harrison/Dir., Erskine B. Bowles/Dir., Thomas G. Cousins/Dir., Henry C. Goodrich/Dir. Emeritus

Owners: Larry L. Gellerstedt, Lillian C. Giornelli, Erskine B. Bowles, William Porter Payne, Boone A. Knox, Joel T. Murphy, Taylor S. Glover, CF Foundation Incorporated, Thomas G. Cousins, Daniel M. DuPree, James A. Fleming, Thomas D. Bell, James H. Hance, Richard W. Courts, William B. Harrison *(17 Owners included in Index)*

Financial Data: *Fiscal Year End:*12/31 *Latest Annual Data:* 12/31/2006

Year	Sales	Net Income
2006	$169,861,000	$232,691,000
2005	$155,736,000	$49,741,000
2004	$136,807,000	$407,784,000

Curr. Assets:	$14,362,000	**Curr. Liab.:**	$57,600,000		
Plant, Equip.:	$911,906,000	**Total Liab.:**	$526,853,000	**Indic. Yr. Divd.:**	$1.480
Total Assets:	$1,196,753,000	**Net Worth:**	$625,915,000	**Debt/ Equity:**	0.5860

Covad Communications Group Inc

110 Rio Robles, San Jose, CA, 95134; *PH:* 1-408-952-6400; *Fax:* 1-408-952-7687;
http:// www.covad.com

General - Incorporation	DE	**Stock**- Price on:12/24/2007	$0.8701
Employees	967	Stock Exchange	AMEX
Auditor	PricewaterhouseCoopers LLP	Ticker Symbol	DVW
Stk Agt	Mellon Investor Services LLC	Outstanding Shares	296,960,000
Counsel	NA	E.P.S	-$0.146
DUNS No.	03-054-2161	Shareholders	NA

Business: The group's principle activity is to provide high-speed Internet connectivity and related communication services to business and consumer end users. The group's services include a range of high-speed, high-capacity, or broadband, Internet access connectivity and related services using digital subscriber line ("Dsl"), t-1, virtual private network ("Vpn") and firewall technologies. The group operates through two divisions: covad strategic partnerships ("Csp") and covad broadband solutions ("Cbs"). The csp segment delivers services to enterprise, corporate, small business, small office/home office ("Soho") and consumer customers primarily through wholesale relationships with large Internet service providers ("Isps"), telecommunications carriers and other large resellers. The cbs segment provides services directly to end-users, through independent authorized sales agents, small isps and resellers. The group's quarterly revenue for September 2007 was 121.88 millions of USD.

Primary SIC and add'l.: 4813

CIK No: 0001043769

Subsidiaries: Covad Communications Company, DIECA Communications, Inc., Laser Link.net, Inc., NextWeb, Inc.

Officers: Charles E. Hoffman/Dir., CEO, Pres./$1,405,729.00, Deborah M. Perry/Sr. VP - Organizational Transformation, Justin Spencer/CFO, Claude Tolbert/Sr. VP - Planning, Priorities Management, Patrick J. Bennett/Exec. VP - Covad Wireless, David McMorrow/Exec. VP - Corporate Development, Sales/$491,705.00, Eric Weiss/Sr. VP, Chief Marketing Officer, Brett Flinchum/Sr. VP - Customer Operations, Lisa Graham/Sr. VP - Sales, Doug Carlen/Sr. VP, General Counsel, Ron Marquardt/CTO, Cornelia Pool/CIO

Directors: Charles E. Hoffman/Dir., CEO, Pres., Charles McMinn/Chmn., Dale L. Crandall/Dir., Larry Irving/Dir., Richard A. Jalkut/Dir., Dan Lynch/Dir., Robert M. Neumeister/Dir., Diana Einterz Leonard/Dir.

Owners: James Kirkland, Diana Leonard, Daniel Lynch, Robert Neumeister, Eric Weiss, Insiders/3.60%, Dale L. Crandall, Charles E. Hoffman/1.60%, Larry Irving, Charles McMinn/1.30%, Richard A. Jalkut, David McMorrow, EarthLink Inc./10.20%, Chris Dunn, FMR Corp./7.00% *(16 Owners included in Index)*

Financial Data: *Fiscal Year End:*12/31 *Latest Annual Data:* 12/31/2006

Year	Sales	Net Income
2006	$474,304,000	-$13,949,000
2005	$443,179,000	-$15,722,000
2004	$429,197,000	-$60,761,000

Curr. Assets:	$123,949,000	**Curr. Liab.:**	$101,670,000		
Plant, Equip.:	$87,586,000	**Total Liab.:**	$310,954,000	**Indic. Yr. Divd.:**	NA
Total Assets:	$313,308,000	**Net Worth:**	$2,354,000	**Debt/ Equity:**	NA

Covalent Group Inc

1275 Drummers Ln., Ste. 100, Wayne, PA, 19087; *PH:* 1-610-975-9533;
http:// www.covalentgroup.com

General - Incorporation	DE	**Stock**- Price on:12/24/2007	$3
Employees	248	Stock Exchange	NA
Auditor	Consent Of Deloitte & Touche LLP	Ticker Symbol	NA
Stk Agt	American Stock Transfer & Trust Co.	Outstanding Shares	18,050,000
Counsel	Pepper Hamilton LLP	E.P.S	-$0.07
DUNS No.	61-896-8960	Shareholders	NA

Business: The group's principal activity is to provide clinical research and development services to pharmaceutical, biotechnology, medical services and managed care organizations. The group designs and monitors clinical trails, manage and analyze clinical trails and clinical data and offer other related services and products. The services offered include study protocol design, clinical trials management, global data management services, biostatistics, teletrial(R) system access, medical and regulatory affairs, and quality assurance and compliance. The clinical trial services are provided through independent contract personnel having experience in pharmaceutical, biotech and managed care industries. The data management professionals of the group offer services consisting of case report form review and tracking, data entry, clinical/ statistical report and manuscripts for publication.

Primary SIC and add'l.: 8731

CIK No: 0000856569

Subsidiaries: Covalent 2000, Limited, Covalent 2001, Limited, Covalent Group, Limited

Officers: Kenneth M. Borow/60/Dir., CEO, Pres./$644,958.00, Lawrence R. Hoffman/53/Exec. VP, General Counsel, Sec., CFO/$397,307.00, Alison O'Neill/43/Sr. VP - Clinical Operations/$231,966.00, Kai Lindevall/55/Pres. - European, Asian Operations

Directors: Kenneth M. Borow/60/Dir., CEO, Pres., Scott M. Jenkins/54/Dir., Christopher F. Meshginpoosh/40/Dir., Petri Manninen/37/Dir., Jyrki Mattila/52/Dir., Paul J. Schmitt/56/Dir.

Owners: Wells Fargo & Company/11.64%, Insiders/16.02%, Kai Lindevall/7.75%, Kenneth M. Borow/5.61%, Hassan Nemazee/5.23%, Petri Mikael Manninen/1.63%, Christopher F. Meshginpoosh, Sven-Erik Nilsson/5.87%, Lawrence R. Hoffman, Jan Lilja/5.21%, Houston Ventures, Inc./5.06%, Scott M. Jenkins, Alison ONeill

Financial Data: *Fiscal Year End:*12/31 *Latest Annual Data:* 12/31/2006

Year	Sales	Net Income
2006	$17,685,000	-$494,000
2005	$12,727,000	-$1,485,000
2004	$18,977,000	-$4,223,000

Curr. Assets:	$15,412,000	**Curr. Liab.:**	$19,319,000	**P/E Ratio:**	100.00
Plant, Equip.:	$1,048,000	**Total Liab.:**	$20,995,000	**Indic. Yr. Divd.:**	NA
Total Assets:	$38,297,000	**Net Worth:**	$17,302,000	**Debt/ Equity:**	NA

Covance Inc

210 Carnegie Ctr., Princeton, NJ, 08540; *PH:* 1-609-452-4440; *Fax:* 1-609-452-9375;
http:// www.covance.com

General - Incorporation: DE	**Stock**- Price on:12/24/2007: $67.19
Employees: 7,300	Stock Exchange: NYSE
Auditor: Ernst & Young LLP	Ticker Symbol: CVD
Stk Agt: Computershare Investor Services LLC	Outstanding Shares: 63,550,000
Counsel: NA	E.P.S: $2.52
DUNS No.: 93-753-3768	Shareholders: NA

Business: The group's principal activity is to provide a wide range of product development services, on a worldwide basis, primarily to the pharmaceutical, biotechnology and medical device industries. The group also provides laboratory-testing services to the chemical, agrochemical and food industries. The operations of the group are carried out through two segments. The early development services segment includes preclinical and phase i clinical service capabilities. This involves evaluating a new compound for safety and early effectiveness as well as evaluating the absorption, distribution, metabolism and excretion of the compound in the human body. The late-stage development services segment includes central laboratory, clinical development, commercialization and other clinical support services.

Primary SIC and add'l.: 8099 8731

CIK No: 0001023131

Subsidiaries: CJBInc, Covance (Argentina) SA, Covance (Asia) Pte Ltd., Covance (Canada)Inc, Covance (Polska) SpZo, Covance AG, Covance Antibody ServicesInc, Covance Asia-PacificInc, Covance Bioanalytical Services LLC, Covance Cardiac Safety ServicesInc, Covance Central Laboratory Services Limited Partnership, Covance Central Laboratory Services SA, Covance Central Laboratory ServicesInc, Covance Clinical and Periapproval Services AG Switzerland, Covance Clinical and Periapproval Services GmbH 34 Subsidiaries included in the Index

Officers: Joseph Herring/Chmn., CEO/$5,115,406.00, Donald Kraft/Sr. VP - Human Resources, William E. Klitgaard/Corporate Sr. VP, CFO/$1,702,682.00

Directors: Joseph Herring/Chmn., CEO, Kathleen G. Bang/Dir., Randall J. MacDonald/Dir., Irwin Lerner/Dir., Sandra L. Helton/Dir., William C. Ughetta/Dir., Robert Barchi/Dir.

Owners: William E. Klitgaard, Randall J. MacDonald, Kathleen G. Bang, Robert Barchi, Irwin Lerner, Insiders/1.90%, Anthony Cork, Joseph L. Herring, William C. Ughetta, James W. Lovett, Sandra L. Helton, Robert M. Baylis, Wendell Barr

Financial Data: ***Fiscal Year End:***12/31 ***Latest Annual Data:*** 12/31/2006

Year	Sales	Net Income
2006	$1,406,058,000	$144,998,000
2005	$1,250,454,000	$119,619,000
2004	$1,056,397,000	$97,947,000

Curr. Assets:	$639,566,000	***Curr. Liab.:***	$289,704,000		
Plant, Equip.:	$500,057,000	***Total Liab.:***	$374,383,000	***Indic. Yr. Divd.:***	NA
Total Assets:	$1,297,678,000	***Net Worth:***	$923,295,000	***Debt/ Equity:***	NA

Covansys Corp

32605 W Twelve Mile Rd. , Ste. 250, Farmington Hills, MI, 48334; ***PH:*** 1-248-488-2088; ***http://*** www.covansys.com

General - Incorporation: MI	**Stock**- Price on:12/24/2007: $33.95
Employees: 8,400	Stock Exchange: NA
Auditor: BDO Seidman LLP	Ticker Symbol: NA
Stk Agt: Computershare Investor Services LLC	Outstanding Shares: 36,490,000
Counsel: NA	E.P.S: $0.95
DUNS No.: 14-869-3484	Shareholders: NA

Business: The group's principal activities are to provide information technology services worldwide to large and mid-size organizations. The group offers its clients technology services specializing in systems integration services and strategic outsourcing. The services provided by the group includes application maintenance and development outsourcing, custom application development, packaged software implementation and document management. The group's technology service also include electronic commerce solutions, including Web-to-enterprise integration services, data warehousing solutions and services to support enterprise-wide applications such as Internet/intranet development. In 2003, the group provided services to over 500 clients in North America, Europe and Asia.

Primary SIC and add'l.: 7372 7379

CIK No: 0001028461

Subsidiaries: BPR Belgium, BPR Management S.A., CBSI Belgium N.V., CBSI Financial Services Corporation, Claremont Retirement Technologies, Inc., Covansys Consulting Services Corporation, Covansys (India) Private Limited, Covansys (Mauritius) Limited, Covansys (Singapore) Pte Ltd, Covansys Canada, Inc., Covansys Deutschland GmbH, Covansys Luxembourg, Covansys Netherlands B.V., Covansys S.A., Covansys S.L. 23 Subsidiaries included in the Index

Officers: Rajendra B. Vattikuti/55/Chmn., CEO, Pres., Krishnaswamy Subrahmaniam/CEO, Pres. - Covansys India, Ravindran Ganapathy/Sr. VP, Head - Global Human Resources, Rajesh Narasimhan/Sr. VP - Asia Pacific, Middle East, Singapore, Jim Trouba/Primary Investor Relations Officer, Paul Laporte/VP - Professional Services, Canada, Joel Grenon/VP - Software Development Center, Canada, Cyrus Vaid/Sr. Mgr. - Business Development, Operations, Canada, David J. Rocco/47/Sr. VP, Head - Global PMO, James S. Trouba/CFO, Sr. VP, Siva Velu/Exec. VP - East, Stephen Nicholas/Sr. VP - Automotive, Manufacturing, Telecommunications, Jon Umstead/Sr. VP, Head - Global Business Process Outsourcing, BPO, Tom Lindsey/Accountant, Brett Pynnonen/Contact - Legal *(33 Officers included in Index)*

Directors: Rajendra B. Vattikuti/55/Chmn., CEO, Pres., David H. Wasserman/38/Dir., William C. Brooks/72/Dir., Frank D. Stella/69/Dir. Emeritus, John A. Stanley/68/Dir., Gary C. Wendt/63/Dir., Hugh R. Harris/54/Dir., Brian Hershkowitz/Dir., James E. Barlett/63/Dir., Douglas S. Land/48/Dir., Ronald K. MacHtley/58/Dir.

Owners: Insiders/18.50%, John A. Stanley, Gary C. Wendt, Frank D. Stella, Fidelity National Financial, Inc./30.10%, Rajendra B. Vattikuti/17.30%, Muralee Bhaskaran, Douglas S. Land, Siva Velu, Brian Herskowitz, CDR-Cookie Acquisition, L.L.C./5.50%

Financial Data: ***Fiscal Year End:***12/31 ***Latest Annual Data:*** 12/31/2006

Year	Sales	Net Income
2006	$455,471,000	$35,920,000
2005	$434,120,000	$37,538,000
2004	$374,373,000	$17,504,000

Curr. Assets:	$231,808,000	***Curr. Liab.:***	$58,003,000	***P/E Ratio:***	35.74
Plant, Equip.:	$33,464,000	***Total Liab.:***	$65,698,000	***Indic. Yr. Divd.:***	NA
Total Assets:	$297,328,000	***Net Worth:***	$231,630,000	***Debt/ Equity:***	NA

Covanta Holding Corp

40 Ln. Rd., Fairfield, NJ, 07004; ***PH:*** 1-973-882-9000; ***Fax:*** 1-973-882-7076; ***http://*** www.covantaholding.com

General - Incorporation: DE	**Stock**- Price on:12/24/2007: $25.82
Employees: 3,300	Stock Exchange: NYSE
Auditor: Ernst & Young LLP	Ticker Symbol: CVA
Stk Agt: American Stock Transfer & Trust Co.	Outstanding Shares: 153,790,000
Counsel: Hogan & Hartson LLP	E.P.S: $0.42
DUNS No.: 00-195-0773	Shareholders: NA

Business: The group's principal activities are to develop, construct, own and operate energy generating facilities and water and wastewater facilities. The group also provides insurance services. It is a holding company and operates through a number of diverse business activities. Through covanta energy corporation the group owns and operates infrastructure for the conversion of waste to energy, independent power production and the treatment of water and waste water in the United States and other countries. The group also has investments in subsidiaries engaged in the insurance operations in the western United States, primarily California and in American commercial lines llc, an integrated marine transportation and service company. On 10-Mar-2004, the group acquired covanta energy corporation.

Primary SIC and add'l.: 6719 6331 4491

CIK No: 0000225648

Subsidiaries: Danielson Holding Corporation

Officers: Anthony J. Orlando/Dir., CEO, Pres./$2,036,274.00, Thomas Bucks/VP, Chief Accounting Officer/$420,068.00, Timothy J. Simpson/Sr. VP, General Counsel, Sec./$809,392.00, Mark A. Pytosh/Sr. VP, CFO/$642,559.00, John M. Klett/COO, Sr. VP/$1,004,860.00

Directors: Anthony J. Orlando/Dir., CEO, Pres., Samuel Zell/Chmn., Clayton Yeutter/Dir., William C. Pate/Dir., Jean Smith/Dir., Ronald J. Broglio/Dir., Peter C.B. Bynoe/Dir., Richard L. Huber/Dir., Robert S. Silberman/Dir., David M. Barse/Dir.

Owners: SZ Investments LLC/15.10%, D. E. Shaw Laminar Portfolios, L.L.C./8.70%, Craig D. Abolt, Third Avenue Management LLC/5.70%, Samuel Zell/15.10%, Insiders/22.10%, Clayton Yeutter, Richard L. Huber, Timothy J. Simpson, William C. Pate, Ronald J. Broglio, Peter C. B. Bynoe, David M. Barse/6.10%, Jean Smith, Thomas E. Bucks *(19 Owners included in Index)*

Financial Data: ***Fiscal Year End:***12/31 ***Latest Annual Data:*** 12/31/2006

Year	Sales	Net Income
2006	$1,268,536,000	$105,789,000
2005	$978,763,000	$59,326,000
2004	$578,555,000	$34,094,000

Curr. Assets:	$803,586,000	***Curr. Liab.:***	$460,752,000	***P/E Ratio:***	61.48
Plant, Equip.:	$2,637,923,000	***Total Liab.:***	$3,655,987,000	***Indic. Yr. Divd.:***	NA
Total Assets:	$4,437,820,000	***Net Worth:***	$739,152,000	***Debt/ Equity:***	2.5933

Covenant Transport Inc

400 Birmingham Hwy., Chattanooga, TN, 37419; ***PH:*** 1-423-821-1212; ***http://*** www.covenanttransport.com

General - Incorporation: NV	**Stock**- Price on:12/24/2007: $11.31
Employees: 5,926	Stock Exchange: NDQ
Auditor: KPMG LLP	Ticker Symbol: CVTI
Stk Agt: NY Drop-United MI Trust Co of NY	Outstanding Shares: NA
Counsel: Scudder Law Firm	E.P.S: -$1.27
DUNS No.: 14-760-7360	Shareholders: NA

Business: The group's principal activity is to provide transportation services such as team and refrigerated services. The group offers just-in-time, transcontinental express and other premium services to shippers with exacting transportation requirements. The group is also a major carrier for traditional truckload customers such as manufacturers and retailers. In addition, it also provides services to transportation companies such as freight forwarders, less-than-truckload carriers and third party logistics providers that require high level of service to support their business. The group operates throughout the United States and in parts of Canada and Mexico. The group operates through its wholly owned subsidiaries covenant transport inc, harold ives trucking co, terminal truck broker inc, southern refrigerated transport inc and cvti receivables corp.

Primary SIC and add'l.: 4213 6719

CIK No: 0000928658

Subsidiaries: CIP, Inc., Covenant Asset Management, Inc., Covenant Transport, Inc., Covenant.com, Inc., CVTI Receivables Corp., Harold Ives Trucking Co., Southern Refrigerated Transport, Inc., Volunteer Insurance Limited

Officers: David R. Parker/Chmn., CEO, Pres./$680,325.00, Randy Dorn/VP - Sales, Air Freight, Joey B. Hogan/46/CFO, Exec. VP/$249,599.00, R. H. Lovin/56/Sr. VP - Administration, Corp. Sec., Jeff Taylor/41/VP, GM - Refrigerated Service, Jeff Paulsen/42/Sr. VP, GM - Regional Service, L. D. Miller/Exec. VP - Sales - Marketing/$245,300.00, Roger Dotson/VP - Corporate Accounting, Brent Bass/VP - Accounting Sales, Jeffery Acuff/45/VP, GM, Michael W. Miller/50/Exec. VP - Procurement, Corporate Operations Mgr./$330,612.00, Tony Smith/Pres. - Southern Refrigerated Transport, Inc/$326,639.00, Charles Eddy/54/VP, GM - Covenant Dedicated Service, Matt Long/Business Development Mgr., James Brower/51/Pres. - Star Transportation, Inc

Directors: David R. Parker/Chmn., CEO, Pres., William T. Alt/71/Dir., Robert E. Bosworth/60/Dir., Hugh O. MacLellan/68/Dir., Bradley A. Moline/41/Dir., Niel B. Nielson/54/Dir., Mark A. Scudder/45/Dir.

Owners: Mark A. Scudder, Bradley A. Moline, Barrow, Hanley, Mewhinney & Strauss, Inc./6.50%, Niel B. Nielson, Michael W. Miller/1.60%, Wells Fargo & Company/10.50%, Dimensional Fund Advisors Inc./8.80%, Hugh O. Maclellan, Joey B. Hogan/1.60%, Tony Smith, David R. Parker/24.90%, William T. Alt, L. D. "Micky" Miller, Insiders/41.80%, Robert E. Bosworth

Financial Data: ***Fiscal Year End:***12/31 ***Latest Annual Data:*** 12/31/2006

Year	Sales	Net Income
2006	$683,828,000	-$1,381,000
2005	$643,054,000	$5,186,000
2004	$603,622,000	$3,376,000

Curr. Assets:	$143,367,000	***Curr. Liab.:***	$110,212,000		
Plant, Equip.:	$274,974,000	***Total Liab.:***	$286,250,000	***Indic. Yr. Divd.:***	NA
Total Assets:	$475,094,000	***Net Worth:***	$188,844,000	***Debt/ Equity:***	0.6136

Coventry Health Care Inc

6705 Rockledge Dr., Ste. 900, Bethesda, MD, 20817; ***PH:*** 1-301-581-0600; ***Fax:*** 1-301-493-0731; ***http://*** www.cvty.com

General - Incorporation	DE	**Stock**- Price on:12/24/2007	$59.32
Employees	10,250	Stock Exchange	NYSE
Auditor	Ernst & Young LLP	Ticker Symbol	CVH
Stk Agt	Mellon Investor Services LLC	Outstanding Shares	156,330,000
Counsel	Bass, Berry & Sims PLC	E.P.S.	$3.61
DUNS No.	17-518-1999	Shareholders	NA

Business: The groups principle activity is to provide health care services. The groups services include physician, hospitalization, pharmacy, dental, optical, mental health and therapeutic services. The group operates from United States.

Primary SIC and add'l.: 7389 8099

CIK No: 0001054833

Subsidiaries: Altius Health Administrators Inc., Altius Health Plans Inc., American Life and Health Insurance Company, Cambridge Life Insurance Company, Carelink Health Plans, Inc., CCN Managed Care, Inc., CHC Casualty Risk Retention Group, Inc., Claims Administration Corp., Coventry Financial Management Services, Inc., Coventry Health and Life Insurance Company, Coventry Health Care Investment Corporation, Coventry Health Care of Delaware, Inc., Coventry Health Care of Georgia, Inc., Coventry Health Care of Iowa, Inc., Coventry Health Care of Kansas, Inc. 51 Subsidiaries included in the Index

Officers: Dale B. Wolf/Dir., CEO/$12,937,000.00, Thomas P. McDonough/Pres./$9,432,787.00, Harvey C. Demovick/61/Exec. VP - Customer Service Operations, CIO/$4,670,942.00, Francis S. Soistman/Exec. VP - Health Plan Operations/$4,119,697.00, Shawn M. Guertin/CFO, Exec. VP, Treasurer/$3,402,288.00, John J. Ruhlmann/45/Sr. VP, Corporate Controller, Patrisha L. Davis/52/VP, Chief Human Resources Officer, Thomas C. Zielinski/56/Sr. VP, General Counsel, Harry Creasey/53/Sr. VP, Bernard J. Mansheim/61/Sr. VP, Chief Medical Officer

Directors: Dale B. Wolf/Dir., CEO, Allen F. Wise/Chmn., Timothy T. Weglicki/Dir., John H. Austin/Dir., Joel Ackerman/Dir., Dale L. Crandall/Dir., Emerson D. Farley/Dir., Lawrence N. Kugelman/Dir., Daniel N. Mendelson/Dir., Rodman W. Moorhead/Dir., Elizabeth E. Tallett/Dir.

Owners: Lawrence N. Kugelman, Francis S. Soistman, Timothy T. Weglicki, Emerson D. Farley, Dale L. Crandall, Allen F. Wise, Shawn M. Guertin, Joel Ackerman, Harvey C. DeMovick, Dale B. Wolf, Thomas P. McDonough, Daniel N. Mendelson, Robert W. Morey, Elizabeth E. Tallett, Insiders/2.43% *(18 Owners included in Index)*

Financial Data: *Fiscal Year End:*12/31 *Latest Annual Data:* 12/31/2006

Year	Sales	Net Income
2006	$7,733,756,000	$560,045,000
2005	$6,611,246,000	$501,639,000
2004	$5,311,969,000	$337,117,000

Curr. Assets:	$2,134,382,000	**Curr. Liab.:**	$1,651,989,000	**P/E Ratio:**	16.43
Plant, Equip.:	$315,105,000	**Total Liab.:**	$2,712,105,000	**Indic. Yr. Divd.:**	NA
Total Assets:	$5,665,107,000	**Net Worth:**	$2,953,002,000	**Debt/ Equity:**	0.3376

Cover All Technologies Inc

55 Ln. Rd., Ste. 300, Fairfield, NJ, 07004; *PH:* 1-973-461-5200; *Fax:* 1-973-461-5257; *http://* www.cover-all.com; *Email:* info@cover-all.com

General - Incorporation	DE	**Stock**- Price on:12/24/2007	$1.1
Employees	45	Stock Exchange	OTC
Auditor	Moore Stephens P.C.	Ticker Symbol	COVR
Stk Agt	Wachovia Bank N.A	Outstanding Shares	23,010,000
Counsel	Piper Rudnick LLP	E.P.S.	-$0.01
DUNS No.	06-251-3460	Shareholders	NA

Business: The group's principal activity is to provide state of the art software products for property and casualty insurance industry through its wholly owned subsidiary, cover-all systems, inc. The group provides standard and customized software applications with support systems. The classic product line of the group is a self-contained rating, issuance and transaction management application system used in property and casualty insurance industry. The administrative services product line comprises off architecture and suite of application development tools for property and casualty insurers designed to enable a client-driven re-engineering of an insurer's business process. The group sells its products through its own distribution network and through its participation in trade shows organized by trade industry groups.

Primary SIC and add'l.: 7372 7374

CIK No: 0000737300

Subsidiaries: Cover-All Systems, Inc.

Owners: Mark D. Johnston/11.10%, Russell G. Cleveland, Manish D. Shah, Maryanne Z. Gallagher/1.20%, John W. Roblin/5.20%, Atlantic Employers Insurance Company/5.40%, Renaissance US Growth Investment Trust PLC/16.60%, Insiders/19.20%, Ann F. Massey, US Special Opportunities Trust PLC/16.60%, Earl Gallegos/2.20%

Financial Data: *Fiscal Year End:*12/31 *Latest Annual Data:* 12/31/2006

Year	Sales	Net Income
2006	$7,288,000	-$1,000,000
2005	$7,255,000	-$1,434,000
2004	$9,274,000	$767,000

Curr. Assets:	$1,810,000	**Curr. Liab.:**	$2,708,000		
Plant, Equip.:	$198,000	**Total Liab.:**	$4,580,000	**Indic. Yr. Divd.:**	NA
Total Assets:	$3,556,000	**Net Worth:**	-$1,024,000	**Debt/ Equity:**	NA

Cowen Group Inc

211 E 43rd St., Ste. 1606, New York, NY, 10017; *PH:* 1-212-661-0025; *Fax:* 1-646-562-1861; *http://* www.cowen.com

General - Incorporation	DE	**Stock**- Price on:12/24/2007	$18.17
Employees	537	Stock Exchange	NDQ
Auditor	Ernst & Young, LLP	Ticker Symbol	COWN
Stk Agt	Computershare Trust Co	Outstanding Shares	15,800,000
Counsel	NA	E.P.S.	$0.51
DUNS No.	NA	Shareholders	NA

Business: The groups principle activities include researching, selling and trading and investing banking services. The financial products of the group include loans, deposit taking and insurance. Customers served by the group include healthcare, technology, media and telecommunications, alternative energy and consumer sectors. The group operates from the United States, England and Europe. The group's quarterly revenue for September 2007 was 57.51 millions of USD.

Primary SIC and add'l.: 6282 6799 6289 6211

CIK No: 0001355007

Subsidiaries: Cowen and Company, LLC, Cowen International Limited

Officers: Kim S. Fennebresque/58/Chmn., CEO, Thomas K. Conner/CFO, Treasurer, David Cowen/Pres., Jared Coseglia/Contact, Christopher A. White/VP, Chief Administrative Officer

Directors: Kim S. Fennebresque/58/Chmn., CEO, Philip B. Pool/54/Dir., Charles W.B. Wardell/62/Dir., Jeffrey Kurzweil/58/Dir., John E. Toffolon/57/Dir., Thomas L. Richards/38/Dir.

Owners: Christopher A. White, Insiders/7.37%, Kim S. Fennebresque/6.63%, Charles W.B. Wardell, John E. Toffolon, Jeffrey Kurzweil, Thomas K. Conner, Mark A. Egert, Eagle Asset Management, Inc./5.62%, Steven Kotler, Philip B. Pool, Thomas L. Richards, Skyline Asset Management, LP/6.53%, SG Americas Securities Holdings, Inc./8.74%, Jean Orlowski *(16 Owners included in Index)*

Financial Data: *Fiscal Year End:*12/31 *Latest Annual Data:* 12/31/2006

Year	Sales	Net Income
2006	$344,967,000	$37,911,000
2005	$294,291,000	$12,081,000
2004	$293,061,000	$55,112,000

Curr. Assets:	$581,993,000	**Curr. Liab.:**	$466,310,000		
Plant, Equip.:	$12,629,000	**Total Liab.:**	$466,310,000	**Indic. Yr. Divd.:**	NA
Total Assets:	$684,438,000	**Net Worth:**	$218,128,000	**Debt/ Equity:**	NA

Cowlitz BanCorp

927 Commerce Ave., Longview, WA, 98632; *PH:* 1-360-423-9800; *Fax:* 1-360-423-3562; *http://* www.cowlitzbancorp.com; *Email:* info@cowlitzbank.com

General - Incorporation	WA	**Stock**- Price on:12/24/2007	$16.56
Employees	135	Stock Exchange	NDQ
Auditor	Moss Adams LLP	Ticker Symbol	CWLZ
Stk Agt	Mellon Investor Services LLC	Outstanding Shares	4,940,000
Counsel	Heller Ehrman White & McAuliffe LLP	E.P.S.	$0.88
DUNS No.	96-631-5574	Shareholders	NA

Business: The group's principal activity is to provide a broad range of financial services to small and medium-sized businesses, professionals and retail customers. It provides non-interest-bearing checking accounts, interest-bearing checking and savings accounts, money market accounts and certificates of deposit. The commercial and personal banking services include commercial and real estate lending, consumer lending and trust services. The group operates in three segments: community banking, mortgage banking and holding company. The principal executive offices are located in longview, Washington. It operates four branches in cowlitz county in southwest Washington. Outside of cowlitz county, the group operates under the name bay bank with branches in bellevue, Washington and portland, Oregon, a loan production office in vancouver, Washington and a limited service branch in a retirement center in wilsonville, Oregon.

Primary SIC and add'l.: 6712 6022

CIK No: 0000894267

Subsidiaries: Cowlitz Statutory Trust I

Officers: Richard J. Fitzpatrick/58/Dir., CEO, Pres./$490,429.00, Sue Rodgers/49/VP, Gerald L. Brickey/55/CFO, VP/$224,902.00, Donna P. Gardner/59/VP/$148,804.00, Lynda Larrabee/VP, Administrative Officer, Sec.

Directors: Richard J. Fitzpatrick/58/Dir., CEO, Pres., Phillip S. Rowley/61/Chmn., Linda M. Tubbs/60/Dir., Ernie D. Ballou/59/Dir., Brian E. Magnuson/51/Dir., John S. Maring/72/Dir., John M. Petersen/57/Dir.

Owners: Hot Creek Capital, LLC/6.07%, John S. Maring/2.26%, Brian E. Magnuson, Gerald L. Brickey, Ernie D. Ballou/1.87%, Benjamin Namatinia/14.66%, John M. Petersen, Sue Rodgers, Phillip S. Rowley, Insiders/11.71%, Donna P. Gardner/1.72%, Linda M. Tubbs, Lynda Larrabee, Richard J. Fitzpatrick/3.72%

Financial Data: *Fiscal Year End:*12/31 *Latest Annual Data:* 12/31/2006

Year	Sales	Net Income
2006	$34,852,000	$4,759,000
2005	$22,381,000	$2,957,000
2004	$18,081,000	$1,940,000

Curr. Assets:	$34,231,000	**Curr. Liab.:**	$405,298,000	**P/E Ratio:**	18.82
Plant, Equip.:	$5,891,000	**Total Liab.:**	$417,670,000	**Indic. Yr. Divd.:**	NA
Total Assets:	$468,395,000	**Net Worth:**	$50,725,000	**Debt/ Equity:**	0.2330

Cox Radio Inc

6205 Peachtree Dunwoody Rd., Atlanta, GA, 30328; *PH:* 1-678-645-0000; *Fax:* 1-678-645-5294; *http://* www.coxradio.com; *Email:* cxr.info@cox.com

General - Incorporation	DE	**Stock**- Price on:12/24/2007	$14.16
Employees	1,443	Stock Exchange	NYSE
Auditor	Deloitte & Touche LLP	Ticker Symbol	CXR
Stk Agt	American Stock Transfer & Trust Co.	Outstanding Shares	95,820,000
Counsel	NA	E.P.S.	-$0.36
DUNS No.	95-957-1399	Shareholders	NA

Business: The group's principle activities are to acquire, develop and operate radio stations. The group is an indirect majority-owned subsidiary of cox enterprises inc. It's radio stations promote local activities, advertise on local television and print media. Participate in telemarketing, direct mailing, sponsor contests, concerts and events. The group owns or operates, or provide sales or marketing services for 78 radio stations clustered in 18 markets. The group's quarterly revenue for September 2007 was 111.77 millions of USD.

Primary SIC and add'l.: 4832

CIK No: 0001018522

Subsidiaries: Cox Radio Miami, LLC, Cox Radio Texas, LLC, Cox Radio Trust I, Cox Radio Trust II, CXR Holdings, LLC.

Officers: Robert F. Neil/Dir., CEO, Pres./$1,448,867.00, Jarrett A. O'Connor/Regional VP, Gregg A. Lindahl/VP - Interactive, New Technologies, Roxann L. Miller/VP - Research, Kimberly A. Guthrie/Regional VP, Robert B. Reed/Regional VP, Richard A. Reis/Group VP/$660,301.00, Caroline J. Devine/Regional VP, Neil O. Johnston/CFO, VP/$542,271.00, Marc W. Morgan/Dir., Exec. VP, COO/$1,194,542.00, Dot Rhyne/Contact - Advertising Information

Directors: Robert F. Neil/Dir., CEO, Pres., James C. Kennedy/Chmn., Juanita P. Baranco/Dir., Paul M. Hughes/Dir., Dennis G. Berry/Dir., Jimmy W. Hayes/Dir., Marc W. Morgan/Dir., Exec. VP, COO, Nicholas D. Trigony/Dir.

Owners: Jimmy W. Hayes, James C. Kennedy, Insiders, James C. Kennedy, T. Rowe Price Associates, Inc/5.41%, Richard A. Ferguson, Cox Enterprises, Inc/9.75%, Cox Enterprises, Inc/100.00%, Dennis G. Berry, Robert F. Neil, Juanita P. Baranco, Richard A. Reis, Marc W. Morgan, Robert F. Neil, Neil O. Johnston *(22 Owners included in Index)*

Financial Data: *Fiscal Year End:* 12/31 *Latest Annual Data:* 12/31/2006

Year	Sales	Net Income
2006	$440,468,000	-$24,447,000
2005	$437,930,000	$61,273,000
2004	$438,213,000	$67,966,000

Curr. Assets:	$97,275,000	**Curr. Liab.:**	$37,418,000		
Plant, Equip.:	$74,334,000	**Total Liab.:**	$899,878,000	**Indic. Yr. Divd.:**	NA
Total Assets:	$2,117,917,000	**Net Worth:**	$1,218,039,000	**Debt/ Equity:**	0.2759

CPAC Inc

2364 Leicester Rd. , Leicester, NY, 14481; *PH:* 1-585-382-3223; *http://* www.cpac-fuller.com

General - Incorporation	NY	**Stock**- Price on: 12/24/2007	NA
Employees	473	Stock Exchange	NDQ
Auditor	PricewaterhouseCoopers LLP	Ticker Symbol	CPAK
Stk Agt	Continental Stock Transfer & Trust Co	Outstanding Shares	NA
Counsel	Chamberlain D'amanda Oppenheimer	E.P.S.	NA
DUNS No.	04-560-5615	Shareholders	NA

Business: The group's principal activities are carried out through two business segments: fuller brands and cpac imaging. The fuller brands segment develops, manufactures, distributes and markets over 2,700 branded and private-label products for consumer and commercial cleaning and personal care applications. The cpac imaging segment focuses on chemicals and equipment for color photographic, health care and graphic arts imaging applications. The products of the group include home cleaning products, brooms, brushes and mops for industrial use, commercial floor care chemicals and personal care products such as hair and skin care, fragrances, cosmetics, vitamins, nutritional supplements. The group operates in the United States, Belgium, Italy, South Africa and Thailand.

Primary SIC and add'l.: 3861 2842 2844

CIK No: 0000351717

Subsidiaries: Allied Diagnostic Imaging Resources, Inc., CPAC Africa (Pty) LTD, CPAC Asia Imaging Products Limited, CPAC Equipment, Inc., CPAC Europe, N.V., CPAC Italia, S.r.l., CPAC Taishan Chemical Products Ltd, The Fuller Brush Company, Inc.

Officers: Thomas N. Hendrickson/Dir., CEO, Pres., James W. Pembroke/Chief Accounting Officer, Thomas J. Weldgen/Dir., VP - Finance, CFO, Steven E. Baune/Segment Management, Wendy F. Clay/VP - Administration, Brady Gros/Segment Management

Directors: Thomas N. Hendrickson/Dir., CEO, Pres., William M. Carpenter/Dir., Thomas J. Weldgen/Dir., VP - Finance, CFO, Robert Oppenheimer/Dir., Jerold L. Zimmerman/Dir., Jose J. Coronas/Dir., Ronald L. Bittner/Dir., Stephen J. Carl/Dir., William E. Simon/Dir.

Owners: William M. Carpenter, Stephen J. Carl, James W. Pembroke, Thomas J. Weldgen/1.82%, Jos J. Coronas, Wendy F. Clay, Thomas N. Hendrickson/7.76%, Jerold L. Zimmerman, Robert Oppenheimer/1.83%, FMR Corporation/11.67%, Aegis Financial Corp./8.22%, Insiders/13.96%, Advisory Research, Inc./8.45%, Dimensional Fund Advisors, Inc./7.03%

CPC of America Inc

6336 17th St. Cir. E, Sarasota, FL, 34243; *PH:* 1-941-727-4370; *Fax:* 1-941-727-4371; *http://* www.cpca2000.com; *Email:* info@cpca2000.com

General - Incorporation	NV	**Stock**- Price on: 12/24/2007	$18.9
Employees	1	Stock Exchange	OTC
Auditor	Cacciamatta Accountancy Corp	Ticker Symbol	CPCF
Stk Agt	Computershare Investor Services LLC	Outstanding Shares	8,590,000
Counsel	NA	E.P.S.	-$0.4
DUNS No.	NA	Shareholders	NA

Business: The group's principal activity is to develop and acquire cardiology medical devices, therapeutic devices and disposable products. The group has completed the development of an external counterpulsation device for the treatment of coronary artery disease known as the cpca 2000. The cpca 2000 counterpulsation unit is a non-invasive, atraumatic and non-toxic method of treating certain coronary disease states. Medclose is an internal puncture closure device and technique that utilizes a human glue deployment to close puncture wounds following surgery. Medclose is in the development stage.

Primary SIC and add'l.: 8731 3841

CIK No: 0001042728

Subsidiaries: Cpca 2000 Inc., HeartMed Inc., Med Close Corp, Med Enclosure LLC

Officers: Rod A. Shipman/Chmn., CEO, Pres.

Directors: Rod A. Shipman/Chmn., CEO, Pres., Rafe Cohen/Dir., William C. Lievense/Dir.

Owners: Rafe Cohen/1.30%, Rod A. Shipman/22.10%, Insiders/24.80%, William C. Lievense/1.30%, CTM Group, Inc/29.90%

Financial Data: *Fiscal Year End:* 12/31 *Latest Annual Data:* 12/31/2006

Year	Sales	Net Income
2006	NA	-$2,812,000
2005	NA	-$1,626,000
2004	NA	-$8,314,000

Curr. Assets:	$674,000	**Curr. Liab.:**	$2,001,000		
Plant, Equip.:	NA	**Total Liab.:**	$2,001,000	**Indic. Yr. Divd.:**	NA
Total Assets:	$1,742,000	**Net Worth:**	-$259,000	**Debt/ Equity:**	NA

CPFL Energy Inc

RUA RAMOS BATISTA, 444, 13 ANDAR, Sao Paulo, D5; *PH:* 55-1138418513; *http://* www.cpfl.com.br

General - Incorporation	Brazil	**Stock**- Price on: 12/24/2007	$58.7
Employees	5,836	Stock Exchange	NYSE
Auditor	Deloitte Touche Tohmatsu	Ticker Symbol	CPL
Stk Agt	Bank of New York	Outstanding Shares	159,920,000
Counsel	NA	E.P.S.	$5.16
DUNS No.	NA	Shareholders	NA

Business: The groups principle activity is to provide energy services, power supply. The group operates from United States.

Primary SIC and add'l.: NA

CIK No: 0001300482

Subsidiaries: CPFL

Officers: Wilson Ferreira Junior/49/CEO, Reni Antonio Da Silva/58/VP - Strategy, Regulation, Miguel Normando Abdalla Saad/58/VP - Generation, Paulo Cezar Coelho Tavares/55/VP - Energy Management, Jose Antonio De Almeida Filippo/48/CFO, Head - Investor Relations, Helio Viana Pereira/54/VP - Distribution, Cecilia Mendes Garcez Siqueira/51/Dir., VP

Directors: Luiz Anibal De Lima Fernandes/66/Chmn., Francisco Caprino Neto/48/Dir., Martin Roberto Glogowsky/55/Dir., Ana Dolores Moura Carneiro De Novaes/46/Dir., Milton Luciano Dos Santos/55/Dir., Cecilia Mendes Garcez Siqueira/51/Dir., VP, Otavio Carneiro De Rezende/54/Dir.

Owners: Insiders/0.01%, Bonaire Participaes S.A./12.65%, Bradespar S.A/8.97%, 521 Participaes S.A./31.11%, BNDES Participaes S.A./5.17%, VBC Energia S.A./28.97%

Financial Data: *Fiscal Year End:* 12/31 *Latest Annual Data:* 12/31/2005

Year	Sales	Net Income
2005	$3,324,637,000	$476,753,000
2004	$2,535,526,000	$146,282,000

Curr. Assets:	$1,732,927,000	**Curr. Liab.:**	$1,774,915,000	**P/E Ratio:**	17.00
Plant, Equip.:	$2,464,688,000	**Total Liab.:**	$4,185,973,000	**Indic. Yr. Divd.:**	$5.090
Total Assets:	$7,365,750,000	**Net Worth:**	$3,179,777,000	**Debt/ Equity:**	NA

CPI Aerostructures Inc

60 Heartland Blvd., Edgewood, NY, 11717; *PH:* 1-631-586-5200; *Fax:* 1-631-586-5814; *http://* www.cpiaero.com

General - Incorporation	NY	**Stock**- Price on: 12/24/2007	$8.2844
Employees	61	Stock Exchange	AMEX
Auditor	J.H. Cohn, LLP	Ticker Symbol	CVU
Stk Agt	American Stock Transfer & Trust Co.	Outstanding Shares	5,730,000
Counsel	Goldstein Golub Kessler & Co	E.P.S.	$0.238
DUNS No.	05-484-0228	Shareholders	NA

Business: The group's principal activity is to design and produce complex aerospace structural subassemblies under United States government and commercial contracts. It provides engineering, technical and program management services to its customers. The group produces structural aircraft parts and sub-assemblies for the commercial and military sectors of the aircraft industry. Its products include aprons and engine mounts used to attach jet engine housings to aircraft. It also assembles structural replacement parts for military aircraft, including spoilers, flaps, ducts, skins and doors. The group has discontinued the operations of its wholly owned subsidiary, kolar machine inc, a precision machine parts manufacturer.

Primary SIC and add'l.: 3724

CIK No: 0000889348

Officers: Edward J. Fred/CEO, Pres./$280,083.00, Vincent Palazzolo/CFO/$214,491.00, Douglas McCrosson/45/VP - Operations

Directors: Eric S. Rosenfeld/Non Exec. Chmn., Harvey J. Bazaar/67/Dir.

Owners: Kenneth McSweeney/1.00%, Walter Paulick/1.00%, Midwood Capital Management, LLC/8.60%, Harvey J. Bazaar, Arthur August/6.30%, Edward J. Fred/6.60%, Eric Rosenfeld/17.90%, Vincent Palazzolo, Insiders/25.70%, Royce & Associates, LLC/7.80%

Financial Data: *Fiscal Year End:* 12/31 *Latest Annual Data:* 12/31/2006

Year	Sales	Net Income
2006	$17,908,000	-$1,265,000
2005	$25,526,000	$1,519,000
2004	$30,269,000	$5,076,000

Curr. Assets:	$31,006,000	**Curr. Liab.:**	$5,884,000	**P/E Ratio:**	55.98
Plant, Equip.:	$856,000	**Total Liab.:**	$5,983,000	**Indic. Yr. Divd.:**	NA
Total Assets:	$32,160,000	**Net Worth:**	$26,178,000	**Debt/ Equity:**	NA

CPI Corp

1706 Washington Ave., St. Louis, MO, 63103; *PH:* 1-314-231-1575; *Fax:* 1-314-231-8150; *http://* www.cpicorp.com

General - Incorporation	DE	**Stock**- Price on: 12/24/2007	$70
Employees	2,500	Stock Exchange	NYSE
Auditor	KPMG LLP	Ticker Symbol	CPY
Stk Agt	Computershare Investor Services LLC	Outstanding Shares	6,390,000
Counsel	NA	E.P.S.	$0.43
DUNS No.	09-671-3342	Shareholders	NA

Business: The group's principal activity is to provide portrait photography of young children and families. The group operates through portrait studios. This segment functions as the exclusive operator of sears portrait studios and has 1,023 permanent portrait studio locations in the United States, Canada and Puerto Rico. The group also provides photo accessories, such as picture frames and photo albums and services that include the smile savers plan(r).

Primary SIC and add'l.: 7384 2759 7221 6719

CIK No: 0000025354

Subsidiaries: Centrics Technology, Inc., Consumer Programs Incorporated, Consumer Programs Partner, Inc, CPI Canadian Holdings, Inc., CPI Corp., CPI Images, LLC, CPI International Holdings, Inc., CPI Portrait Studios de Mexico S. de R.L. de C.V., CPI Portrait Studios of Canada Corp., CPI Prints Plus, Inc., CPI Research and Development. Inc., CPI Technology Corp., LBP Partnership, myportraits.com, Inc., P & W/lbp Partnership 17 Subsidiaries included in the Index

Officers: Renato Cataldo/COO, CEO, Pres./$581,501.00, Gary W. Douglass/CFO, Exec. VP - Finance/$489,219.00, Jane E. Nelson/58/General Counsel, Corp. Sec./$273,138.00, Richard L. Tarpley/62/Exec. VP - Manufacturing/$298,427.00, Ervin W. Schmitz/66/CIO, Thomas P. Gallahue/58/Exec. VP - Operations/$402,816.00, Dale Heins/45/VP, Corporate Controller, Principal Accounting Officer, Keith Laakko/42/Chief Marketing Officer

Directors: David M. Meyer/Chmn., John T. White/Dir., James J. Abel/Dir., Mark R. Mitchell/Dir., Turner White/59/Dir., Michael S. Koeneke/Dir.

Owners: James Abel, Knightspoint Group, Thomas Gallahue, Renaissance Technologies Corp, Barclays Global Investors, NA., Bear Stearns Asset Management Inc., Gary Douglass, Jane Nelson, Turner White, Renato Cataldo, Insiders, Paul Rasmussen, David Meyer, Michael Koeneke, Goldman Sachs Asset Management, L.P. *(17 Owners included in Index)*

Financial Data: *Fiscal Year End:* 02/04 *Latest Annual Data:* 2/3/2007

Year	Sales	Net Income
2007	$293,803,000	$16,327,000
2006	$291,984,000	$6,389,000
2005	$281,865,000	-$18,508,000

Curr. Assets:	$73,949,000	**Curr. Liab.:**	$71,761,000	**P/E Ratio:**	26.22
Plant, Equip.:	$41,658,000	**Total Liab.:**	$112,214,000	**Indic. Yr. Divd.:**	$0.640
Total Assets:	$135,100,000	**Net Worth:**	$22,886,000	**Debt/ Equity:**	0.6445

CPI International Inc

607 Hansen Way, Palo Alto, CA, 94303; ***PH:*** 1-650-846-2900; ***Fax:*** 1-650-846-3276; ***http://*** www.cpii.com; ***Email:*** investor.relations@cpii.com

General - Incorporation ... DE
Employees ... 1,610
Auditor ... KPMG LLP
Stk Agt ... BNY Mellon Shareowner Services
Counsel ... Irell & Manella LLP
DUNS No. ... NA

Stock- Price on:12/24/2007 ... $19.87
Stock Exchange ... NDQ
Ticker Symbol ... CPII
Outstanding Shares ... 16,310,000
E.P.S. ... $1.27
Shareholders ... NA

Business: The groups principle activities include developing, manufacturing and distributing microwave and radio frequency, power and control products. The products of the group include satellite communications amplifier subsystems, radar and electronic warfare, solid state integrated microwave assemblies and medical x-ray generators and control system. The groups operates through two segments namely vacuum electron device and satcom equipment. Specific customer of the group is United State Government. The group operates from the United States and Canada. The group's quarterly revenue for September 2007 was 91.61 millions of USD.

Primary SIC and add'l.: 3663 9711 3728 3669 3844 3679

CIK No: 0001279176

Subsidiaries: Communications & Power Industries, Communications & Power Industries Asia Inc., Communications & Power Industries Australia Pty Limited, Communications & Power Industries Canada Inc., Communications & Power Industries Europe Limited, Communications & Power Industries International Inc., Communications & Power Industries Italia S.r.L., CPI Subsidiary Holdings Inc., Econco Broadcast Service, Inc.

Officers: Joe O. Caldarelli/Dir., CEO, Robert A. Fickett/COO, Pres., Pres. - Microwave Power Products, Joel A. Littman/CFO, John R. Beighley/VP - Sales, Don C. Coleman/VP, Pres. - Beverly Microwave Division, Andrew E. Tafler/VP, Pres. - Satcom Division, Amanda Mogin/Dir. - Investor Relations

Directors: Joe O. Caldarelli/Dir., CEO, Michael Targoff/Chmn., Michael F. Finley/Dir., Jeffrey P. Hughes/Dir., Stephen R. Larson/Dir., William P. Rutledge/Dir.

Owners: William P. Rutledge, Cypress Side-by-Side LLC, Jeffrey P. Hughes, Insiders, Chris Toffales, Joel A. Littman, Joe O. Caldarelli, Michael Targoff, Cypress Associates II LLC, Cypress Merchant B II C.V., Andrew E. Tafler, Michael F. Finley, Cypress Merchant Banking Partners II L.P., 55th Street Partners II L.P.

Financial Data: ***Fiscal Year End:***09/29 ***Latest Annual Data:*** 9/29/2006

Year	Sales	Net Income
2006	$339,717,000	$17,219,000
2005	$320,732,000	$13,672,000
2004	$202,266,000	$2,648,000

Curr. Assets:	$135,378,000	**Curr. Liab.:**	$69,978,000	**P/E Ratio:**	15.40
Plant, Equip.:	$83,624,000	**Total Liab.:**	$403,215,000	**Indic. Yr. Divd.:**	NA
Total Assets:	$455,882,000	**Net Worth:**	$52,667,000	**Debt/ Equity:**	2.1410

CPS Technologies Corp DE

Formerly: Ceramics Process Systems Corp
111 S Worcester St., Norton, MA, 02766; ***PH:*** 1-508-222-0614; ***http://*** www.alsic.com

General - Incorporation ... DE
Employees ... 93
Auditor ... Wolf & Co. P.C
Stk Agt ... NA
Counsel ... NA
DUNS No. ... 12-099-8661

Stock- Price on:12/24/2007 ... NA
Stock Exchange ... OTC
Ticker Symbol ... CPSH
Outstanding Shares ... NA
E.P.S. ... NA
Shareholders ... NA

Business: The group's principal activity is to develop, manufacture and market advanced metal-matrix composite components to house, interconnect and thermally manage microelectronic devices. The products serve the wireless communications infrastructure, microprocessor, satellite communications, motor controller and other microelectronic markets. The products are in the form of housings, packages, lids, substrates, thermal planes and are used in applications where thermal management is an important consideration. The group has customers in Japan and Europe.

Primary SIC and add'l.: 3679

CIK No: 0000814676

Subsidiaries: Ceramics Process Systems Corporation, CPS Superconductor Corporation

Officers: Grant Bennett/Dir., CEO, Pres., Treasurer, Principal Financial Officer, Anand Nagarajan/Sales Representative - India, Richard Adams/VP - Operations, Engineering, Dot Camara/Customer Service Representative, Mark Occhionero/VP - Marketing,Technical Sales, Research & Development, Sr. Scientist, Cheryl Oliveira/VP - Sales, Bruce Brown/Mgr. - Engineering Design, Kim Richardson/Mgr. - Production, Cheng Bang Zhang/Consultant - China Shanghai Liason, Bo Sullivan/Exec. Sales Mgr., Michael Staab/Dir. - Corp QA, HPB Operations Mgr., Jennifer Yee/Regional Sales Representative - New England, John Sandifer/Coast Sales Representative - US West, Gio Schouten/European Sales Representative

Directors: Grant Bennett/Dir., CEO, Pres., Treasurer, Principal Financial Officer, Kent H. Bowen/66/Dir., Francis J. Hughes/57/Dir.

Financial Data: ***Fiscal Year End:***12/31 ***Latest Annual Data:*** 12/30/2006

Year	Sales	Net Income
2006	$11,908,000	$1,778,000
2005	$7,156,000	$287,000
2004	$6,843,000	$1,040,000

Curr. Assets:	$2,779,000	**Curr. Liab.:**	$807,000		
Plant, Equip.:	$891,000	**Total Liab.:**	$1,119,000	**Indic. Yr. Divd.:**	NA
Total Assets:	$3,670,000	**Net Worth:**	$2,551,000	**Debt/ Equity:**	NA

Craftmade International Inc

650 S Royal Ln., Ste. 100, Coppell, TX, 75019; ***PH:*** 1-972-393-3800; ***Fax:*** 1-972-304-3753; ***http://*** www.craftmade.com; ***Email:*** investorrelations@craftmade.com

General - Incorporation ... DE
Employees ... 131
Auditor ... BDO Seidman LLP
Stk Agt ... Computershare Investor Services LLC
Counsel ... Haynes & Boone
DUNS No. ... 00-791-8592

Stock- Price on:12/24/2007 ... $17.82
Stock Exchange ... NDQ
Ticker Symbol ... CRFT
Outstanding Shares ... 5,200,000
E.P.S. ... $0.89
Shareholders ... NA

Business: The group's principal activities are carried out through two segments: craftmade and tsi. The activities are carried out through its wholly owned subsidiaries craftmade international inc and trade source international inc. Craftmade is principally engaged in the design, distribution and marketing of ceiling fans, light kits, outdoor lighting, bath-strip lighting and related accessories. Trade source international inc is principally engaged in the design, distribution and marketing of outdoor and indoor lighting, selected ceiling fans and various fan accessories to mass merchandisers. Trade source international inc's outdoor lighting consists of over one-hundred designs in different decorative finishes. The indoor lighting product line includes ceiling mount lighting fixtures and bath-strip lighting.

Primary SIC and add'l.: 5072 5084 5023 5064 5074

CIK No: 0000856250

Subsidiaries: C/D/R Incorporated, Design Trends, LLC, Durocraft International, Inc., Elitex Development Limited, Prime/Home Impressions, LLC, Teiber Lighting Products, Inc., Trade Source International, Inc., TSI Prime Asia Limited

Officers: James R. Ridings/57/Chmn., CEO, Ric Decastro/Investor Relations Officer, Marcus Scrudder/CFO, John S. Deblois/54/Inside Dir., Exec. VP - TSI, Brad D. Heimann/COO, Pres., Clifford F. Crimmings/Dir., VP - Marketing

Directors: James R. Ridings/57/Chmn., CEO, Don R. Morris/68/Dir., Lary C. Snodgrass/58/Dir., Clifford F. Crimmings/Dir., VP - Marketing, William E. Bucek/69/Dir., Dale L. Griggs/74/Dir., Paul A. Knuckley/58/Dir., John S. Deblois/54/Inside Dir., Exec. VP - TSI, Richard T. Walsh/Dir.

Owners: Schwartz Investment Counsel, Inc./2.50%, Brad Dale Heimann, Marcus J. Scrudder, William E. Bucek, John P. Pecora/7.30%, Lary C. Snodgrass, Don R. Morris, Wellington Management Company, LLP/11.20%, Schwartz Investment Trust, Inc./8.80%, Insiders/14.90%, Paul A. Knuckley, Dale L. Griggs, Richard T. Walsh, John S. DeBlois/1.00%, Clifford F. Crimmings *(17 Owners included in Index)*

Financial Data: ***Fiscal Year End:***06/30 ***Latest Annual Data:*** 06/30/2007

Year	Sales	Net Income
2007	$103,350,000	$5,911,000
2006	$118,054,000	$7,100,000
2005	$116,756,000	$6,427,000

Curr. Assets:	$45,291,000	**Curr. Liab.:**	$15,020,000	**P/E Ratio:**	15.36
Plant, Equip.:	$8,098,000	**Total Liab.:**	$32,362,000	**Indic. Yr. Divd.:**	$0.480
Total Assets:	$65,061,000	**Net Worth:**	$29,037,000	**Debt/ Equity:**	0.5592

Crafty Admiral Enterprises Ltd

1055 West Hastings St., Ste. 300, Vancouver, BC, V6E 2E9; ***PH:*** 1-604-612-4847

General - Incorporation ... NV
Employees ... NA
Auditor ... James Stafford
Stk Agt ... Transfer Online, Inc.
Counsel ... NA
DUNS No. ... NA

Stock- Price on:12/24/2007 ... NA
Stock Exchange ... NA
Ticker Symbol ... NA
Outstanding Shares ... NA
E.P.S. ... NA
Shareholders ... NA

Business: The groups principal activity is to sell classic auto parts to classic auto owners through an Internet site. The group operates from Canada and the United States.

Primary SIC and add'l.: 7389

CIK No: 0001168938

Officers: James D. MacKenzie/51/Dir., CEO, Pres., John W. Jardine/55/CFO, Sec., Treasurer, Gary J. Artmont/58/VP - Exploration

Directors: James D. MacKenzie/51/Dir., CEO, Pres., Lawrence Siccia/40/Dir.

Owners: Insiders/21.20%, James D. MacKenzie/10.30%, Lawrence Siccia/10.90%

Curr. Assets:	$27,000	**Curr. Liab.:**	$747,000		
Plant, Equip.:	$514,000	**Total Liab.:**	$747,000	**Indic. Yr. Divd.:**	NA
Total Assets:	$541,000	**Net Worth:**	-$206,000	**Debt/ Equity:**	NA

Crane Co

100 First Stamford Pl., Stamford, CT, 06902; ***PH:*** 1-203-363-7300; ***Fax:*** 1-203-363-7295; ***http://*** www.craneco.com; ***Email:*** investors@craneco.com

General - Incorporation ... DE
Employees ... 11,520
Auditor ... Deloitte & Touche LLP
Stk Agt ... EquiServe Trust Co N.A
Counsel ... NA
DUNS No. ... 00-128-0726

Stock- Price on:12/24/2007 ... $45.21
Stock Exchange ... NYSE
Ticker Symbol ... CR
Outstanding Shares ... 59,780,000
E.P.S. ... -$1.16
Shareholders ... NA

Business: The groups principle activity is to manufacture engineered products. The groups products include battery systems, inverters, fuel boost, transfer and jettison pumps, wireless microsensor networks and air suspension valves. Customers served by the group include the electronics and aerospace industries. The group operates from United States.

Primary SIC and add'l.: 3492 3594 3083 3823 3581

CIK No: 0000025445

Subsidiaries: Azonix Corporation, Barksdale Control Products GmbH, Barksdale, Inc., CR Holdings C.V., Crane (Asia Pacific) Pte. Ltd., Crane Aerospace, Inc., Crane Australia Pty. Ltd., Crane Canada Co., Crane Composites, Inc., Crane Controls, Inc., Crane Environmental Inc., Crane Europe Ltd., Crane Fengqiu (Zhejiang) Pump Co. Ltd., Crane Global Holdings S.L., Crane GmbH 66 Subsidiaries included in the Index

Officers: Eric C. Fast/Dir., CEO, Pres./$6,755,378.00, Max H. Mitchell/Group Pres. - Fluid Handling/$1,550,398.00, Anthony D. Pantaleoni/VP - Environment, Health, Safety, Gregory A. Wardpresident/Pres. - Aerospace Group/$1,546,365.00, Richard A. Maue/VP, Controller, David E. Bender/Group Pres. - Electronics, Thomas J. Craney/Group Pres. - Engineered Materials, Bradley L. Ellis/Group Pres. - Merchandising Systems, Thomas M. Noonan/VP - Taxes, Joan Atkinson Nano/52/VP, Controller, Curtis P. Robb/VP - Strategic Planning, Business Development, Thomas J. Perlitz/VP - Operational Excellence, Elise M. Kopczick/VP - Human Resources, Robert J. Vipond/CFO, VP - Finance/$1,257,728.00, Andrew L. Krawitt/VP, Treasurer *(19 Officers included in Index)*

Directors: Eric C. Fast/Dir., CEO, Pres., Robert S. Evans/Chmn., William E. Lipner/Dir., Donald G. Cook/Dir., Richard S. Forte/Dir., Thayer E. Bigelow/Dir., Ronald F. McKenna/Dir., Philip R. Lochner/Dir., Dorsey R. Gardner/Dir., Jean Gaulin/Dir., Charles J. Queenan/Dir., Karen E. Dykstra/Dir., James L.L. Tullis/Dir.

Owners: The Crane Fund/12.90%, G. A. Ward, J.P. Morgan Chase & Co./6.20%, GAMCO Investors, Inc/7.60%, J. Gaulin, R. F. McKenna, D. R. Gardner, Insiders/1.35%, K. E. Dykstra, E. C. Fast/2.66%, C. J. Queenan, A. I. duPont, R. S. Fort, J. L. L. Tullis, E. T. Bigelow *(21 Owners included in Index)*

Financial Data: ***Fiscal Year End:***12/31 ***Latest Annual Data:*** 12/31/2006

Year	Sales	Net Income
2006	$2,256,889,000	$165,887,000
2005	$2,061,249,000	$136,037,000
2004	$1,890,335,000	-$105,421,000

Curr. Assets:	$880,409,000	**Curr. Liab.:**	$461,926,000	**P/E Ratio:**	16.26
Plant, Equip.:	$289,555,000	**Total Liab.:**	$1,503,848,000	**Indic. Yr. Divd.:**	$0.720
Total Assets:	$2,430,484,000	**Net Worth:**	$918,603,000	**Debt/ Equity:**	0.4264

Crawford & Co

5620 Glenridge Dr. NE, Atlanta, GA, 30342; ***PH:*** 1-404-256-0830; ***Fax:*** 1-404-847-4028; ***http://*** www.crawfordandcompany.com; ***Email:*** info@us.crawco.com

General - Incorporation	GA	***Stock***- Price on:12/24/2007	$6.33
Employees	NA	Stock Exchange	NYSE
Auditor	Ernst & Young LLP	Ticker Symbol	CRD-A
Stk Agt	Suntrust Bank	Outstanding Shares	NA
Counsel	NA	E.P.S	-$1.156
DUNS No.	04-100-7717	Shareholders	NA

Business: The group's principal activities are providing diversified services to insurance companies and self-insured entities. The services include workers compensation claims administration, healthcare management services, property and casualty claims management, class action services and risk management information services. The claims management services include investigation and evaluation of property and casualty insurance claims. In addition to the field investigation and evaluation of their claims, the group also provides initial loss reporting services, loss mitigation services and risk management information services. The group also performs administrative services for class actions settlements for product liability, bankruptcy noticing and distribution, and other legal settlements. The services are provided with a global network of more than 700 offices in 67 countries. On 30-Sep-2003, the group acquired robco claims management pty ltd.

Primary SIC and add'l.: 6411 8331

CIK No: 0000025475

Subsidiaries: Crawford & Company (Bermuda) Limited, Crawford & Company Adjusters Limited, Crawford & Company Employment Services, Inc., Crawford & Company HealthCare Management, Inc., Crawford & Company International, Inc., Crawford & Company of California, Crawford & Company of Florida, Crawford & Company of Illinois, Crawford & Company of New York, Inc., Crawford & Company Subrogation and Recovery, Inc., Crawford Adjusters Canada Incorporated, Crawford Healthcare Management of Norfolk and Baltimore, Inc., Crawford Investigation Services, Inc., Risk Sciences Group, Inc., The Garden City Group, Inc. 16 Subsidiaries included in the Index

Officers: Thomas W. Crawford/Dir., CEO, Pres./$1,476,173.00, Glenn T. Gibson/CEO - Crawford, Company International, Americas Region, Ian V. Muress/CEO - Europe, Middle East, Africa, Jonathan M.W. Clark/Sr. VP - Quality, Compliance, Mark Harman/Sr. VP - Crawford, Company International Inc Commercial Dir. - Europe, Middle East, Africa, Robert R. Kulbick/Pres. - Integrated Services, Michael F. Reeves/Regional MD - Global Risks, Technical Services UK, Jeffrey T. Bowman/COO - Global Property, Casualty Services/$988,512.00, Robert J. Cormican/Sr. VP - Compliance, Quality, Training, Mauricio S. Alonso/Sr. VP - Crawford, Company International Inc, Regional MD - Latin America, Richard J. Martin/Sr. VP, Regional MD - Asia Pacific, Philip G. Porter/Sr. VP - US Property, Casualty Services, Kevin B. Frawley/Exec. VP - Global Business Development/$779,101.00, Thomas W. Dawson/VP - Crawford - Company International Inc, Bruce W. Swain/CFO, Exec. VP *(27 Officers included in Index)*

Directors: Thomas W. Crawford/Dir., CEO, Pres., Jesse C. Crawford/Chmn., Richard J. Martin/Sr. VP, Regional MD - Asia Pacific, James D. Edwards/Dir., Robert T. Johnson/Dir., Hicks J. Lanier/Dir., Larry L. Prince/Dir., Jenner E. Wood/Dir., Clarence H. Ridley/Dir., George P. Benson/Dir.

Owners: Jeffrey T. Bowman, James D. Edwards, George P. Benson, Thomas W. Crawford, J. Hicks Lanier, Thomas W. Crawford/1.10%, Bruce W. Swain, Clarence H. Ridley, David A. Isaac, Clarence H. Ridley, Insiders/50.60%, Kevin B. Frawley, E. Jenner Wood, Jesse C. Crawford/51.80%, David A. Isaac *(24 Owners included in Index)*

Financial Data: ***Fiscal Year End:***12/31 ***Latest Annual Data:*** 12/31/2006

Year	Sales	Net Income
2006	$900,380,000	$15,011,000
2005	$854,767,000	$12,881,000
2004	$811,662,000	$25,172,000

Curr. Assets:	$382,143,000	**Curr. Liab.:**	$282,284,000		
Plant, Equip.:	$40,884,000	**Total Liab.:**	$677,293,000	**Indic. Yr. Divd.:**	NA
Total Assets:	$892,988,000	**Net Worth:**	$211,151,000	**Debt/ Equity:**	0.9055

Cray Inc

411 1st Ave. S, Ste. 600, Seattle, WA, 98104; ***PH:*** 1-206-701-2000; ***Fax:*** 1-206-701-2500; ***http://*** www.cray.com; ***Email:*** crayinfo@cray.com

General - Incorporation	WA	***Stock***- Price on:12/24/2007	$7.7
Employees	768	Stock Exchange	NDQ
Auditor	Peterson Sullivan, PLLC	Ticker Symbol	CRAY
Stk Agt	Mellon Investor Services LLC	Outstanding Shares	32,460,000
Counsel	Stoel Rives LLP	E.P.S	$0.22
DUNS No.	19-369-4577	Shareholders	NA

Business: The group's principal activities are to design, develop, market and service high performance computer systems, commonly known as supercomputers. It presently markets four computer models: the cray sv1ex system, the cray t3e system, cluster systems and the nec sx-6 system. The group provides maintenance services to the installed base of cray computers. It is also developing enhancements to the cray sv1 and three new computer systems, the mta-2, the sv2 and t3e computers. Cray sv1 is based on group's multithreaded architecture system, the supercluster, a highly parallel system using leading commercial off the shelf components. The sv2 computer system will combine elements of the sv1. The registered trademarks are cray, cray-1, unicos and unicos/mk. In Oct 2003 the group announced to develop a product line based on the red storm system. On 02-Apr-2004, the group acquired octigabay systems corporation.

Primary SIC and add'l.: 7373

CIK No: 0000949158

Subsidiaries: 3084316 Nova Scotia Limited, 3084317 Nova Scotia Limited, Cray Australia Pty Ltd., Cray Brazil, Inc., Cray Canada (Washington), Inc., Cray Canada Corp./Societe Cray Canada, Cray Canada Inc., Cray China Limited, Cray Computadores do Brasil Ltda., Cray Computer Deutschland GmbH, Cray Computer Finland Oy, Cray Computer GmbH, Cray Computer SAS, Cray Computer South Africa (Proprietary) Limited, Cray Computer Spain, S.L. 28 Subsidiaries included in the Index

Officers: Peter J. Ungaro/Dir., CEO, Pres./$2,345,489.00, Kenneth W. Johnson/Sr. VP, General Counsel, Corp. Sec., Brian C. Henry/CFO, Exec. VP/$1,387,949.00, Christopher Jehn/VP - Government Programs, Margaret Williams/Sr. VP - Research, Development/$1,307,936.00, Steve Scott/CTO, Sr. VP/$475,048.00, Paul Ciernia/VP - Sales Operations, Linda Howitson/VP - Human Resources, Wayne J. Kugel/VP - Operations, Chuck Morreale/VP - Customer Support, Jan C. Silverman/Sr. VP - Corporate Strategy, Business Development/$472,875.00, Vic Chynoweth/Contact - Investor Relations, Erin McGhee/Contact - Public Relations, John Henderson/Contact - Sales, Australia

Directors: Peter J. Ungaro/Dir., CEO, Pres., Stephen C. Kiely/Chmn., William C. Blake/Dir., Daniel C. Regis/Dir., John B. Jones/Dir., Sally G. Narodick/Dir., Frank L. Lederman/Dir., Stephen C. Richards/Dir.

Owners: Daniel C. Regis, William C. Blake, Insiders/5.09%, Margaret A. Williams, Jan C. Silverman, Frank L. Lederman, John B. Jones, Peter J. Ungaro/1.90%, Wells Fargo& Company/13.94%, Stephen C. Richards, Brian C. Henry, Steven L. Scott, Sally G. Narodick, Stephen C. Kiely

Financial Data: ***Fiscal Year End:***12/31 ***Latest Annual Data:*** 12/31/2006

Year	Sales	Net Income
2006	$221,017,000	-$12,070,000
2005	$201,051,000	-$64,308,000
2004	$149,184,000	-$204,023,000

Curr. Assets:	$246,072,000	**Curr. Liab.:**	$109,748,000		
Plant, Equip.:	$25,856,000	**Total Liab.:**	$196,129,000	**Indic. Yr. Divd.:**	NA
Total Assets:	$337,503,000	**Net Worth:**	$141,374,000	**Debt/ Equity:**	0.5589

Crdentia Corp

5001 LBJ Fwy., Ste. 850, Dallas, TX, 75244; ***PH:*** 1-214-866-0500; ***Fax:*** 1-214-866-0415; ***http://*** www.crdentia.com

General - Incorporation	DE	***Stock***- Price on:12/24/2007	$0.34
Employees	436	Stock Exchange	OTC
Auditor	KBA Group LLP	Ticker Symbol	CRDT
Stk Agt	Continental Stock Transfer & Trust Co	Outstanding Shares	25,890,000
Counsel	NA	E.P.S	-$1.28
DUNS No.	NA	Shareholders	NA

Business: The group provide healthcare staffing services, focusing on the areas of travel nursing, per diem staffing, contractual clinical services, and private duty home care. The travel nurses are recruited domestically as well as internationally and placed on temporary assignments at healthcare facilities across the United States. The per diem nurses are local nurses placed at healthcare facilities on short-term assignments. The contractual clinical services group provides complete clinical management and staffing for healthcare facilities and the private duty home care group provides nursing case management and staffing for skilled and non-skilled care in the home. In 2003 the group acquired baker anderson christie inc, new age nurses inc, nurses network, inc, and psr nurse recruiting inc and psr nurses holdings corp. On 07-Sep-2004 the group acquired care pros staffing inc and Arizona home & healthcare.

Primary SIC and add'l.: 7361

CIK No: 0001073857

Subsidiaries: Arizona Home Health Care/Private Duty, Inc., Baker Anderson Christie, Inc., Care Pros Staffing, Inc., CRDE Corp., Health Industry Professionals, LLC, HIP Holding, Inc., New Age Staffing, Inc., Nurses Network, Inc., PSR Nurse Recruiting, Inc., PSR Nurses Holdings Corp., PSR Nurses, Ltd., Travmed USA, Inc.

Officers: John B. Kaiser/Dir., CEO, James J. Terbeest/CFO, Christina Hogan/VP - Marketing, Cheri Johnson/VP - Phoenix, Tucson, Arizona, International Recruiting, Delilah Headrick/Hub Mgr. - Phoenix, Arizona, Ko Goubeaux/VP - Birmingham, Alabama, Mavis Dedmon/Corp. Dir. - Locum Tenens, Michael Yao/National Dir. - Travel Services, Terry Brown/Area Mgr. - Odessa, Lubbock, Temple, Texas, Tiffani Mays/Hub Mgr. - San Antonio, Texas, Jackie Currence/Housing Coordinator, Jaye Alexander/Recruiter, Rachelle Bollinger/Credentialing Coordinator, Tiffani Barber/Mgr. - Accounting, Roshanda Johnson-Page/Locum Tenens Recruiter, Accounting Mgr. *(38 Officers included in Index)*

Directors: John B. Kaiser/Dir., CEO, Fred C. Toney/Chmn., William J. Nydam/Dir., Thomas F. Herman/Dir., Robert J. Kenneth/Dir.

Owners: Fred C. Toney, James J. TerBeest, William J. Nydam, John Kaiser, James D. Durham, Robert J. Kenneth, MedCap Partners, L.P., Insiders, AudioStocks, Inc., Thomas F. Herman

Financial Data: ***Fiscal Year End:***12/31 ***Latest Annual Data:*** 12/31/2006

Year	Sales	Net Income
2006	$40,138,000	-$16,073,000
2005	$32,714,000	-$6,269,000
2004	$23,018,000	-$33,703,000

Curr. Assets:	$6,675,000	**Curr. Liab.:**	$14,744,000		
Plant, Equip.:	$469,000	**Total Liab.:**	$16,405,000	**Indic. Yr. Divd.:**	NA
Total Assets:	$23,888,000	**Net Worth:**	$7,483,000	**Debt/ Equity:**	0.1206

Cream Minerals Ltd

570 Granville St., Ste. 1400, Vancouver, BC, V6C 3P1; ***PH:*** 1-604-687-4622; ***Fax:*** 1-604-687-4212; ***http://*** www.creamminerals.com; ***Email:*** info@creamminerals.com

General - Incorporation	Canada	***Stock***- Price on:12/24/2007	$0.51
Employees	NA	Stock Exchange	OTC
Auditor	Morgan & Co	Ticker Symbol	CRMXF
Stk Agt	Computershare Trust Co	Outstanding Shares	NA
Counsel	DuMoulin Black	E.P.S	NA
DUNS No.	25-408-6044	Shareholders	NA

Business: The group's principal activities are to explore and develop mineral properties. Over the past five years, the group has primarily focused its efforts in the province of british columbia and in Mexico. The group has mineral property interests in kaslo silver, raven and nuevo milenio.

Primary SIC and add'l.: 1044 1041

CIK No: 0001066130

Subsidiaries: Cream Minerals de Mexico, S.A. de C.V.

Officers: Frank A. Lang/Chmn., CEO, Pres., Arthur G. Troup/Dir., VP - Exploration, Shannon Ross/CFO, Corp. Sec., Ferdinand Holcapek/Dir., General Administrator - Cream Minerals de Mexico, SA de CV

Directors: Frank A. Lang/Chmn., CEO, Pres., Arthur G. Troup/Dir., VP - Exploration, Sargent H. Berner/Dir., Robin Merrifield/Dir., Ferdinand Holcapek/Dir., General Administrator - Cream Minerals de Mexico, SA de CV, Douglas C. Lang/Dir.

Owners: Insiders/37.78%, Sargent H. Berner/1.33%, Robin Merrifield/0.67%, Shannon M. Ross/1.08%, Frank A. Lang/27.01%, C. Douglas Lang/0.44%, Arthur G. Troup/1.67%, Ferdinand Holcapek/5.58%

Financial Data: *Fiscal Year End:*03/31   *Latest Annual Data:* 03/31/2007

Year	Sales	Net Income
2007	NA	-$2,492,000
2006	NA	-$1,179,000
2005	NA	-$1,590,000

Curr. Assets:	$971,000	**Curr. Liab.:**	$165,000		
Plant, Equip.:	$1,071,000	**Total Liab.:**	$1,088,000	**Indic. Yr. Divd.:**	NA
Total Assets:	$2,118,000	**Net Worth:**	$1,030,000	**Debt/ Equity:**	NA

Creative Beauty Supply of New Jersey Corp

380 Totowa Rd., Totowa, NJ, 07512; *PH:* 1-973-904-0004

General - Incorporation	NJ	Stock- Price on:12/24/2007	$0.3
Employees		Stock Exchange	OTC
Auditor	Rotenberg Meril Solomon	Ticker Symbol	CBSJ
Stk Agt	Continental Stock Transfer & Trust Co	Outstanding Shares	10,530,000
Counsel	NA	E.P.S.	-$0.01
DUNS No.	NA	Shareholders	NA

Business: The groups principle activity is to operate a cosmetic and beauty supply distributor at both the retail and wholesale levels. The group operates from United States.

Primary SIC and add'l.: 5122

CIK No: 0001290658

Subsidiaries: Creative Beauty Supply Inc

Officers: Carmine Catizone/56/Dir., CEO, Pres., Daniel Generelli/38/Sec., Treasurer, VP, Dir.

Directors: Carmine Catizone/56/Dir., CEO, Pres., Daniel Generelli/38/Sec., Treasurer, VP, Dir.

Owners: Insiders/33.21%, Ram Venture Holdings Corp./5.65%, Pasquale Catizone/51.15%, Daniel T. Generelli, Cede & Co./5.77%, Carmine Catizone/32.83%

Financial Data: *Fiscal Year End:*12/31   *Latest Annual Data:* 12/31/2006

Year	Sales	Net Income
2006	$134,000	-$92,000

Curr. Assets:	$432,000	**Curr. Liab.:**	$28,000		
Plant, Equip.:	$3,000	**Total Liab.:**	$28,000	**Indic. Yr. Divd.:**	NA
Total Assets:	$434,000	**Net Worth:**	$406,000	**Debt/ Equity:**	NA

Creative Technology Ltd

1901 McCarthy Blvd., Milpitas, CA, 95035; *PH:* 1-408-428-6600; *Fax:* 1-408-428-6611; *http://* www.creative.com

General - Incorporation	Singapore	Stock- Price on:12/24/2007	$4.93
Employees	6,600	Stock Exchange	OTC
Auditor	PricewaterhouseCoopers LLP	Ticker Symbol	CREAF
Stk Agt	Mellon Investor Services LLC	Outstanding Shares	83,480,000
Counsel	Morrison & Foerster LLP	E.P.S.	NA
DUNS No.	59-514-3157	Shareholders	NA

Business: The group's principle activities are the design, manufacture and distribution of digitised sound and video boards, computers and related multimedia and personal digital entertainment products. Other activities include property investment holding, sales and marketing agent and research and development. The group has manufacturing plants in Singapore and Malaysia with the European distribution center located in dublin, Ireland and the Americas distribution center located in milpitas, California. The group focuses its worldwide sales and marketing efforts predominantly through sales offices in North America, Europe and the Asia-Pacific region. The group's quarterly revenue for September 2007 was 184.56 millions of USD.

Primary SIC and add'l.: 6719 7819 8742 5734 5045 7389 8732

CIK No: 0000888295

Subsidiaries: Broadxent Pte Ltd, Cambridge SoundWorks, Inc., CL Direct, Inc., Creative Labs Ireland, Creative Labs Pty Ltd, Creative Labs, Inc., Creative Media Kabashiki Kaisha, Creative Technology (Qingdao) Co. Ltd, Creative Technology Centre Pte Ltd, CTI II Limited, CTI Limited, Cubic Electronics Sdn Bhd

Officers: Phil O'Shaughnessy/Investor Contact, Elizabeth Loo/Investor Relations Officer - Asia Inquiries

Owners: Tan Lip-Bu, Tang Chun Choy, Insiders/33.70%, Ng Kai Wa/2.90%, Sim Wong Hoo/28.70%, Lee Kheng Nam

Financial Data: *Fiscal Year End:*06/30   *Latest Annual Data:* 06/30/2007

Year	Sales	Net Income
2007	$914,906,000	$28,189,000
2006	$1,127,531,000	-$118,159,000
2005	$1,224,411,000	$588,000

Curr. Assets:	$635,187,000	**Curr. Liab.:**	$229,280,000	**P/E Ratio:**	17.00
Plant, Equip.:	$109,174,000	**Total Liab.:**	$435,873,000	**Indic. Yr. Divd.:**	$0.250
Total Assets:	$830,613,000	**Net Worth:**	$393,153,000	**Debt/ Equity:**	NA

Creative Vistas Inc

2100 Forbes St., Unit 8-10, Whitby, ON, L1N 9T3; *PH:* 1-905-666-8676; *http://* www.creativevistasinc.com

General - Incorporation	AZ	Stock- Price on:12/24/2007	$1.95
Employees	NA	Stock Exchange	OTC
Auditor	Stark Winter Schenkein & Co., LLP	Ticker Symbol	CVAS
Stk Agt	Stalt, Inc.	Outstanding Shares	NA
Counsel	NA	E.P.S.	NA
DUNS No.	NA	Shareholders	NA

Business: The groups principle activity is to provide security, surveillance products and solutions. Customers of the group include government, school boards, retail outlets, banks, and hospitals. The groups services include security and surveillance products and services, and broadband deployment and provisioning services. The group operates through three segments namely Cancable, AC Technical, and Iview DSI. In the year 2006, the group In the year 2006, the group acquired Cancable. Specific customers of the group include World Wide Electric, Phazer Electric and belMC Realty Corporation. The group operates from Canada and the United State.

Primary SIC and add'l.: 6770

CIK No: 0001113524

Subsidiaries: A.C. Technical Acquisition Corp, AC Technical Systems Ltd., Cancable Holding Corp, Cancable Inc., Iview Digital Video Solutions Inc., Iview Holding Corp

Officers: Sayan Navaratnam/33/Dir., Chmn., CEO, Dominic Burns/47/Dir., Pres., Heung Hung Lee/38/CFO, Sec., Christopher Pay/VP - Corporate Development

Directors: Sayan Navaratnam/33/Dir., Chmn., CEO, Dominic Burns/47/Dir., Pres.

Owners: Dominic Burns/34.00%, Insiders/86.00%, Heung Hung Lee/0.20%, Sayan Navaratnam/51.80%

Financial Data: *Fiscal Year End:*12/31   *Latest Annual Data:* 12/31/2006

Year	Sales	Net Income
2006	$30,457,000	-$5,542,000
2005	$8,718,000	$828,000
2004	$2,406,000	-$3,249,000

Curr. Assets:	$8,776,000	**Curr. Liab.:**	$7,927,000		
Plant, Equip.:	$3,825,000	**Total Liab.:**	$25,846,000	**Indic. Yr. Divd.:**	NA
Total Assets:	$18,270,000	**Net Worth:**	-$7,576,000	**Debt/ Equity:**	NA

Creator Capital Ltd

Canons Ct, 22 Victoria St., Hamilton; ; *http://* www.creatorcapital.com; *Email:* info@creatorcapital.com

General - Incorporation	Bermuda	Stock- Price on:12/24/2007	NA
Employees	NA	Stock Exchange	OTC
Auditor	Amisano Hanson	Ticker Symbol	CTORF
Stk Agt	Escrow	Outstanding Shares	NA
Counsel	NA	E.P.S.	NA
DUNS No.	94-294-2186	Shareholders	NA

Business: The groups principle activities include development, implementing and managing of computerized, remote gaming software for use by passengers on international airline flights. The group operates from United States.

Primary SIC and add'l.: 7999 7373

CIK No: 0000882537

Subsidiaries: Creator Island Equities Inc., Inflight Interactive Ltd., Interactive Entertainment Limited, SGI Holding Corporation Limited

Officers: Deborah Fortescue-Merrin/Chmn., CEO, Pres., Anastasia Kostoff-Mann/Dir., VP, Betty Anne Loy/Corporate Administrator

Directors: Deborah Fortescue-Merrin/Chmn., CEO, Pres., Anthony P. Clements/Dir., Anastasia Kostoff-Mann/Dir., VP

Owners: Anastasia Kostoff-Mann, CEDE & CO United States/12.41%, HARRAHS INTERACTIVE INVESTMENT COMPANY/7.82%

Financial Data: *Fiscal Year End:*12/31   *Latest Annual Data:* 12/31/2006

Year	Sales	Net Income
2006	$53,000	-$124,000
2005	$79,000	-$102,000
2004	$136,000	-$38,000

Curr. Assets:	$23,000	**Curr. Liab.:**	$1,850,000		
Plant, Equip.:	NA	**Total Liab.:**	$1,850,000	**Indic. Yr. Divd.:**	NA
Total Assets:	$23,000	**Net Worth:**	-$1,827,000	**Debt/ Equity:**	NA

Credence Systems Corp

1421 California Cir., Milpitas, CA, 95035; *PH:* 1-408-635-4300; *Fax:* 1-408-635-4985; *http://* www.credence.com

General - Incorporation	DE	Stock- Price on:12/24/2007	$3.761
Employees	NA	Stock Exchange	NDQ
Auditor	Ernst & Young LLP	Ticker Symbol	CMOS
Stk Agt	EquiServe Trust Co N.A	Outstanding Shares	101,180,000
Counsel	Brobeck, Phleger & Harrison	E.P.S.	-$4.64
DUNS No.	05-886-2236	Shareholders	NA

Business: The group's principal activities are to design, manufacture, sell and service engineering validation test and automatic test equipment, or ate, used for testing semiconductor integrated circuits, or ics. The group also develops, licenses and distributes related software products and serves a broad spectrum of the semiconductor industry's testing needs through a wide range of products that test digital logic, mixed-signal, system-on-a-chip, radio frequency, volatile and static and non-volatile memory semiconductors. The customers of the group include major semiconductor manufacturers, fabless design houses, foundries and assembly and test services companies. The group sells its products in the United States, Asia-Pacific and Europe. In 2003, the group acquired assets of sz testsystems ag, sz testsystems gmbh and sz testsysteme Japan limited, or collectively sz and optonics inc and on 28-May-2004, acquired nptest holding corporation.

Primary SIC and add'l.: 7372 3825

CIK No: 0000893162

Subsidiaries: Credence Capital Corporation, Credence Europa Limited, Credence France SAS, Credence International Limited,Inc., Credence Italia SRL, Credence Korea Ltd., Credence Systems (Philippines) Inc., Credence Systems (UK) Limited, Credence Systems GmbH, Credence Systems KK, Credence Systems Pte Ltd., Credence Systems(Malaysia) Sdn BhD, NPTest (Philippines) Inc., NPTest International Ltd., NPTest UK Ltd.

Officers: Lavi A. Lev/Dir., CEO, Pres., Byron W. Milstead/VP, General Counsel, Ping Yang/Dir., Independent Consultant, Joy E. Leo/Sr. VP, CFO, Patrick J. Brady/Sr. VP - Engineering, Rance Hale/Sr. VP - Manufacturing, Operations, Amir Aghdaei/Sr. VP - Field Operations, Marketing, Laura Owen/VP - Human Resources, John C. Batty/Sr. VP, Sec., Lori Holland/Dir., Independent Consultant

Directors: David L. House/Chmn., Richard M. Beyer/Dir., Lori Holland/Dir., Independent Consultant, Bruce R. Wright/Dir., Henk J. Evenhuis/Dir., Jon D. Tompkins/Dir., Ping Yang/Dir., Independent Consultant

Owners: Henk J. Evenhuis, Jon D. Tompkins, Barclays Global Investors, NA/6.17%, Insiders/2.27%, Renaissance Technologies Corp./6.15%, Dimensional Fund Advisors LP/5.01%, Bruce R. Wright, Byron W. Milstead, CitiGroup Global Markets/8.00%, Brett L. Hooper, Richard M. Beyer, Wells Fargo& Co./5.72%, William G. Howard, David A. Ranhoff, Lori Holland (19 Owners included in Index)

Financial Data: Fiscal Year End:10/31   Latest Annual Data: 10/31/2006

Year	Sales	Net Income
2006	$474,424,000	-$481,585,000
2005	$429,320,000	-$119,932,000
2004	$439,803,000	-$64,478,000

Curr. Assets:	$297,469,000	Curr. Liab.:	$143,709,000		
Plant, Equip.:	$120,993,000	Total Liab.:	$304,868,000	Indic. Yr. Divd.:	NA
Total Assets:	$517,594,000	Net Worth:	$212,726,000	Debt/ Equity:	0.8787

Credicorp Ltd

121 Alhambra Plz., Ste. 1200, Coral Gables, FL, 33134; PH: 1-305-448-0971; Fax: 1-305-448-0981; http:// www.credicorpnet.com

General - Incorporation	Bermuda	Stock- Price on:12/24/2007	$61.63
Employees	9,054	Stock Exchange	NYSE
Auditor	Medina, Zaldvar, Paredes & Asociados	Ticker Symbol	BAP
Stk Agt	Bank of new York	Outstanding Shares	79,760,000
Counsel	NA	E.P.S.	$4.01
DUNS No.	NA	Shareholders	NA

Business: The group's principal activity is the provision of commercial banking services including financing of foreign business and financial leasing; capital market activities including corporate finances, brokerage services and securities negotiation, asset management and trust custody, and investment in securities through own account; and insurance which include commercial property, transportation and marine hull, automobile, life, health, and pension fund underwriting. Banking accounted for 80% of 2001 revs; insurance, 15% and brokerage and others, 5%.

Primary SIC and add'l.: 6411 6021 6211

CIK No: 0001001290

Subsidiaries: ASHC, Atlantic Security Bank, BCB, BCP, PPSs

Officers: Dionisio Romero/Chmn., CEO, Jose Luis Gagliardi/Sr. VP - Administration, Human Resources, Walter Bayly/Chief Financial, Accounting Officer, Raimundo Morales/COO, Carlos Munoz/Exec. VP, Arturo Rodrigo/Sr. VP - Insurance, David Saettone/Sr. VP - Insurance, Aida Kleffmann/Investor Relations Officer, Guillermo Castillo/Investor Relations Officer, Antonella Monteverde/Investor Relations Officer

Directors: Dionisio Romero/Chmn., CEO, Luis Nicolini/Dep. Chmn., Fernando Fort/Dir., Luis Enrique Yarur/Dir., Felipe Ortiz De Zevallos/Dir., Reynaldo Llosa/Dir., Juan Carlos Verme/Dir., German Suarez/Dir.

Owners: AFP Horizonte/6.98%, AFP Integra/10.00%, AFP Prima/9.33%, Romero family/16.01%, Atlantic Security Holding Corporation/15.49%

Financial Data: Fiscal Year End:12/31   Latest Annual Data: 12/31/2006

Year	Sales	Net Income
2006	$1,372,157,000	$175,024,000
2005	$1,097,372,000	$181,885,000
2004	$825,068,000	$135,600,000

Curr. Assets:	$2,923,268,000	Curr. Liab.:	$9,559,282,000	P/E Ratio:	17.00
Plant, Equip.:	$314,657,000	Total Liab.:	$11,489,694,000	Indic. Yr. Divd.:	$1.300
Total Assets:	$12,893,638,000	Net Worth:	$1,403,944,000	Debt/ Equity:	NA

Credit Acceptance Corp

25505 W 12 Mile Rd., Ste. 3000, Southfield, MI, 48034; PH: 1-248-353-2700; Fax: 1-248-827-8553; http:// www.creditacceptance.com; Email: esupport@creditacceptance.com

General - Incorporation	MI	Stock - Price on:12/24/2007	NA
Employees	788	Stock Exchange	NDQ
Auditor	Grant Thornton LLP	Ticker Symbol	CACC
Stk Agt	Computershare Investor Services LLC	Outstanding Shares	30,290,000
Counsel	NA	E.P.S.	$1.62
DUNS No.	NA	Shareholders	NA

Business: The groups principal activity is to provide automobile financing. The groups services include consumer loan and Insurance. The groups operates through two segments namely the United States and Other. The group operates from Texas, Alabama, Michigan, Mississippi and New York. Of the assets in the year 2006, the United States accounted for $724,008 and other $1,205 (thousands).

Primary SIC and add'l.: 6141 6159

CIK No: 0000885550

Subsidiaries: Arlington Investment Company, Auto Funding America of Nevada, Inc., Auto Funding America, Inc., Auto Lease Services, LLC, Automotive Payment Services, Inc., AutoNet Finance Company.com, Inc., Buyers Vehicle Protection Plan, Inc., CAC (TCI)Ltd., CAC Funding Corp., CAC International Holdings, LLC, CAC Leasing, Inc., CAC Luxembourg, S.a.r.l, CAC of Canada Company, CAC Reinsurance, Ltd., CAC Scotland 32 Subsidiaries included in the Index

Officers: Brett A. Roberts/41/Dir., CEO/$1,239,923.00, Thomas N. Tryfores/47/Private Investor, Michael W. Knoblauch/44/COO/$463,555.00, Kenneth S. Booth/40/CFO/$338,922.00, Charles A. Pearce/43/Chief Legal Officer, Steven M. Jones/43/Pres./$483,846.00, Steve M. Dion/39/Chief Human Resources Officer, Michael P. Miotto/47/CIO, Douglas W. Busk/46/Treasurer

Directors: Brett A. Roberts/41/Dir., CEO, Donald A. Foss/63/Chmn., Glenda J. Chamberlain/54/Dir., Scott J. Vassalluzzo/36/Dir.

Owners: Prescott Associates L.P., Thomas N. Tryforos, Idoya Partners L.P., Brett A. Roberts, Donald A. Foss, Thomas W. Smith, Steven M. Jones, Scott J. Vassalluzzo, Michael W. Knoblauch, Kenneth S. Booth, Glenda J. Chamberlain, Insiders

Financial Data: Fiscal Year End:12/31   Latest Annual Data: 12/31/2006

Year	Sales	Net Income
2006	$219,332,000	$58,640,000
2005	$201,268,000	$72,601,000
2004	$176,715,000	$57,325,000

Curr. Assets:	$65,871,000	Curr. Liab.:	$78,294,000		
Plant, Equip.:	$16,203,000	Total Liab.:	$514,866,000	Indic. Yr. Divd.:	NA
Total Assets:	$725,213,000	Net Worth:	$210,347,000	Debt/ Equity:	1.9703

Credit and Asset Repackaging Vehicle Corp

One New York Plz., 37th Fl., New York, NY, 10004; PH: 1-212-902-8812

General - Incorporation	NA	Stock- Price on:12/24/2007	NA
Employees	NA	Stock Exchange	NA
Auditor	NA	Ticker Symbol	NA
Stk Agt	NA	Outstanding Shares	NA
Counsel	NA	E.P.S.	NA
DUNS No.	NA	Shareholders	NA

Business: The groups principal activity is to provide vehicles for transportation. The group operates from the United States

Primary SIC and add'l.: 6189

CIK No: 0001143886

Credit One Financial Inc

PO Box 261713, Plano, TX, 75026; ; http:// www.creditonefinancial.com; Email: customerservice@CreditOneFinancial.com

General - Incorporation	FL	Stock- Price on:12/24/2007	$0.2
Employees	NA	Stock Exchange	OTC
Auditor	Berman Hopkins Wright & Laham, LLP	Ticker Symbol	COFI
Stk Agt	Island Stock Transfer	Outstanding Shares	7,780,000
Counsel	NA	E.P.S.	-$0.01
DUNS No.	NA	Shareholders	NA

Business: The groups principal activity is to market research regarding the cost and availability of non-performing credit card debt portfolios. The group operates from the United States.

Primary SIC and add'l.: 6153

CIK No: 0001201135

Officers: Guy Wolf/Dir., CEO, Arnon Epstein/Dir., CFO, Sec.

Directors: Guy Wolf/Dir., CEO, Arnon Epstein/Dir., CFO, Sec.

Owners: Guy Wolf, Arnon Epstein, Insiders, STM 1, LLC

Financial Data: Fiscal Year End:12/31   Latest Annual Data: 12/31/2006

Year	Sales	Net Income
2006	$0	-$108,000
2005	NA	-$17,000
2004	NA	-$15,000

Curr. Assets:	$16,000	Curr. Liab.:	$9,000		
Plant, Equip.:	NA	Total Liab.:	$9,000	Indic. Yr. Divd.:	NA
Total Assets:	$16,000	Net Worth:	$7,000	Debt/ Equity:	NA

Credit Suisse First Boston USA Inc

Eleven Madison Ave., New York, NY, 10010; PH: 1-212-325-2000; Fax: 1-212-325-8057; http:// www.csfb.com

General - Incorporation	DE	Stock- Price on:12/24/2007	NA
Employees	NA	Stock Exchange	NA
Auditor	KPMG LLP	Ticker Symbol	NA
Stk Agt	First Chicago Trust Co of New York	Outstanding Shares	NA
Counsel	Davis Polk & Wardwell	E.P.S.	NA
DUNS No.	00-698-2995	Shareholders	NA

Business: The group's principal activity is to operate under two divisions: institutional securities and financial services division. The institutional securities segment includes the investment banking, equity and fixed income divisions. The investment banking division raises and invests capital and provides financial advice to companies throughout the United States and abroad. The equity division trades, originates and distributes equity securities and equity-related derivatives. The fixed income division trades, originates and distributes fixed income securities and fixed income-related derivatives, and places private debt instruments. The financial services segment provides investment advisory services to high-net-worth individual investors and the financial intermediaries that represent them.

Primary SIC and add'l.: 6211 6282 6719

CIK No: 0000029646

Subsidiaries: Credit Suisse Asset Management, LLC, Credit Suisse Capital LLC, Credit Suisse Securities (USA) LLC, CS Holdings, DLJ International Group Limited, SPS Holding Corp.

Credit Suisse Group

11 Madison Ave., New York, NY, 10010; PH: 1-212-325-2000; Fax: 1-212-325-6665; http:// www.credit-suisse.com

General - Incorporation	Switzerland	Stock- Price on:12/24/2007	$74.04
Employees	63,523	Stock Exchange	NYSE
Auditor	KPMG Klynveld Peat Marwick Goerdeler	Ticker Symbol	CS
Stk Agt	Credit Suisse First Boston LLC	Outstanding Shares	NA
Counsel	NA	E.P.S.	$9.14
DUNS No.	NA	Shareholders	NA

Business: The group's principal activity is to provide financial services including banking and insurance services. Financial services include private banking, corporate and retail banking, life and pensions, non-life insurance, institutional securities, and wealth and asset management. In May 2005, the Group merged its two Swiss banks, Credit Suisse and Credit Suisse First Boston, into one legal entity encompassing the combined operations of both banks under the name Credit Suisse. The group acquired Donaldson, Lufkin & Jenrette Inc. and Winterthur in December 2005.

Primary SIC and add'l.: 6021 6035

CIK No: 0001159510

Subsidiaries: AJP Cayman Ltd., Banco Credit Suisse (Mexico) S.A., Banco Credit Suisse First Boston (Mexico), S.A., Banco de Investimentos Credit Suisse (Brasil) S.A., Banco de Investimentos Credit Suisse First Boston S.A., Bank Hofmann AG, Bank Leu AG, BGP Banca di Gestione Patrimoniale S.A., Boston RE Ltd., City Bank, Clariden Holding AG, Column Canada Financial Corp., Column Financial, Inc., Column Guaranteed LLC, Credit Suisse 145 Subsidiaries included in the Index

Officers: Walter Berchtold/46/CEO - Private Banking, David J. Blumer/CEO - Asset Management, Paul Calello/47/CEO - Investment Bank, Michael G. Philipp/55/Chmn., CEO - Credit Suisse Europe, Middle East, Africa, Ulrich Korner/46/CEO - Credit Suisse Switzerland, Member Of The Exec. Board Of Credit Suisse, Brady W. Dougan/49/CEO - Credit Suisse Group, Credit Suisse, Richard Isarin/CEO - Credit Suisse Private Advisors, Robert Shafir/CEO - Credit Suisse Americas, Oswald J. Grubel/65/CEO, Beatrice Fischer/Corp. Sec., Tobias Guldimann/47/Chief Risk Officer, Ivo Kaufmann/Chief Investment Officer - Credit Suisse Private Advisors, Giuseppe Mazzeo/Head - Global Strategy, Credit Suisse Private Advisors, Marc Buchheister/Deputy Head - Investor Relations, Stephen Gardner/Investor Relations Officer - UK, Ireland *(27 Officers included in Index)*

Directors: Michael G. Philipp/55/Chmn., CEO - Credit Suisse Europe, Middle East, Africa, Rainer E. Gut/76/Honorary Chmn., Walter B. Kielholz/57/Chmn., Andreas N. Koopmann/Vice Chmn. - Advisory Board, Flavio Cotti/Chmn. - Advisory Board, Hans-Ulrich Doerig/68/Vice Chmn., Jean Lanier/62/Dir., Brigitta M. Gadient/Member - Advisory Board, Susy Bruschweiler/Member - Advisory Board, Felix Gutzwiller/Member - Advisory Board, Richard E. Thornburgh/56/Dir., Franz Albers/Member - Advisory Board, Michael Hilti/Member - Advisory Board, Thomas W. Bechtler/59/Dir., Andreas W. Keller/Member - Advisory Board *(30 Directors included in Index)*

Financial Data: Fiscal Year End:12/31 Latest Annual Data: 12/31/2006

Year	Sales	Net Income
2006	$67,532,073,000	$9,293,804,000
2005	$68,392,913,000	$4,447,170,000
2004	$64,543,262,000	$4,974,589,000

Curr. Assets:	$722,001,437,000	Curr. Liab.:	$626,689,695,000	P/E Ratio:	17.00
Plant, Equip.:	$5,052,639,000	Total Liab.:	$994,749,585,000	Indic. Yr. Divd.:	$1.560
Total Assets:	$1,030,511,898,000	Net Worth:	$35,762,313,000	Debt/ Equity:	NA

Creditriskmonitor.com Inc

704 Executive Blvd., Ste. A, Valley Cottage, NY, 10989; *PH:* 1-845-230-3000; *Fax:* 1-845-267-4110; *http://* www.creditriskmonitor.com; *Email:* info@creditriskmonitor.com

General - Incorporation	NV	Stock- Price on:12/24/2007	$2.32
Employees	37	Stock Exchange	OTC
Auditor	J. H. Cohn LLP	Ticker Symbol	CRMZ
Stk Agt	American Stock Transfer & Trust Co.	Outstanding Shares	7,690,000
Counsel	Meltzer Lippe Goldstein Schlissel	E.P.S.	$0.03
DUNS No.	08-603-1069	Shareholders	NA

Business: The groups' principal activity is to provide interactive Internet-based financial information and news service. These services are designed specially for corporate credit professionals. The services of the group analyzes the commercial credit risk as contrasted to the credit risk of individuals. The group monitors credit evaluation of approximately 10,000 us public corporations and through its affiliations with third parties, approximately 20 million foreign public and private companies. The group designs its product for corporate credit managers who must decide whether or not to ship to their customers before payment is received. In addition, the group is a re-distributor of international credit reports in the United States. Covers of approximately 16,200 U.S. And Canadian public companies with full financial analysis and up-to-date financial news coverage for purposes of credit evaluation.

Primary SIC and add'l.: 7375

CIK No: 0000315958

Officers: Jerry Flum/Chmn., CEO, Pres., Michael Broos/CTO, William B. Danner/Pres., Al Carmenini/Head - Product Development, Larry Fensterstock/Sr. VP, CFO

Directors: Jerry Flum/Chmn., CEO, Pres., Jeff Geisenheimer/Dir., Andrew Melnick/Dir., Richard James/Dir.

Owners: Jerome S. Flum, William B. Danner, Flum Partners, Jeffrey S. Geisenheimer, Insiders, Richard J. James, Andrew J. Melnick, Lawrence Fensterstock

Financial Data: Fiscal Year End:12/31 Latest Annual Data: 12/31/2006

Year	Sales	Net Income
2006	$4,323,000	$15,000
2005	$3,842,000	$1,046,000
2004	$3,347,000	-$139,000

Curr. Assets:	$3,412,000	Curr. Liab.:	$3,621,000	P/E Ratio:	77.33
Plant, Equip.:	$131,000	Total Liab.:	$3,981,000	Indic. Yr. Divd.:	NA
Total Assets:	$5,526,000	Net Worth:	$1,544,000	Debt/ Equity:	0.1612

Credo Petroleum Corp

1801 Broadway, Ste. 900, Denver, CO, 80202; *PH:* 1-303-297-2200; *Fax:* 1-303-297-2204; *http://* www.credopetroleum.com

General - Incorporation	CO	Stock- Price on:12/24/2007	$13.46
Employees	12	Stock Exchange	NDQ
Auditor	Hein & Assoc. LLP	Ticker Symbol	CRED
Stk Agt	Computershare Trust Co	Outstanding Shares	9,260,000
Counsel	Davis Graham & Stubbs LLP	E.P.S.	$0.65
DUNS No.	09-515-6253	Shareholders	NA

Business: The group's principal activities are acquisition, exploration, development and production of oil and gas. The group conducts its operations primarily in the mid-continent and rocky mountain regions of the United States. In addition, the group applies its patented calliope(TM) gas recovery system to low pressure gas wells and operates oil and gas properties for the group's interest and for the interests of third parties. The group operates in eight states. Currently, the group operates 94 wells and owns working and royalty interests in approximately 122 wells that are operated by outside parties.

Primary SIC and add'l.: 1311 6792 2911

CIK No: 0000277924

Subsidiaries: SECO Energy Corporation, United Oil Corporation

Officers: James T. Huffman/Chmn., CEO, Pres., Treasurer, David E. Dennis/CFO, Sec., Alford B. Neely/Mgr. - Regulatory Compliance, Kenneth J. Defehr/58/Mgr. - Petroleum Engineering, Torie A. Vandeven/53/Mgr. - Geology, Exploration

Directors: James T. Huffman/Chmn., CEO, Pres., Treasurer, Oakley Hall/Dir., Richard B. Stevens/Dir., William F. Skewes/Dir., Clarence H. Brown/Dir.

Owners: James T. Huffman/13.60%, William F. Skewes/1.50%, Clarence H. Brown/1.00%, Insiders/21.40%, Oakley Hall/1.20%, Richard B. Stevens/4.10%

Financial Data: Fiscal Year End:10/31 Latest Annual Data: 10/31/2006

Year	Sales	Net Income
2006	$16,491,000	$5,880,000
2005	$13,957,000	$5,229,000
2004	$10,314,000	$3,650,000

Curr. Assets:	$13,909,000	Curr. Liab.:	$3,836,000	P/E Ratio:	20.71
Plant, Equip.:	$33,385,000	Total Liab.:	$12,992,000	Indic. Yr. Divd.:	NA
Total Assets:	$47,759,000	Net Worth:	$34,767,000	Debt/ Equity:	NA

Cree Inc

4600 Silicon Dr., Durham, NC, 27703; *PH:* 1-919-313-5300; *Fax:* 1-919-313-5558; *http://* www.cree.com; *Email:* investorrelations@cree.com

General - Incorporation	NC	Stock- Price on:12/24/2007	$25.95
Employees	1,364	Stock Exchange	NDQ
Auditor	Ernst & Young LLP	Ticker Symbol	CREE
Stk Agt	American Stock Transfer & Trust Co.	Outstanding Shares	84,260,000
Counsel	NA	E.P.S.	$0.82
DUNS No.	18-325-2501	Shareholders	NA

Business: The group's principal activities are to develop and manufacture compound semiconductor materials and electronic devices from silicon carbide ('sic') and optoelectronic and electronic devices from gallium nitride ('gan'). The group operates in two segments: the cree segment and the cree microwave segment. The cree segment manufactures wide bandgap compound semiconductors using sic and gan. Products from this segment are used in cellular handsets, automotive backlighting, indicator lamps, full color led displays and microwave and power applications. The cree microwave segment designs, manufactures and markets silicon-based laterally diffused metal oxide semiconductors and bipolar radio frequency power semiconductors and modules for use in power amplifiers for wireless infrastructure applications. The group has operations in Europe, Malaysia and other Asian countries. On 06-Apr-2004, the group acquired gallium nitride and advanced technology materials inc.

Primary SIC and add'l.: 3674 8731 5065

CIK No: 0000895419

Subsidiaries: CI Holdings, Limited, Cree Asia-Pacific Limited, Cree Asia-Pacific, Inc., Cree Employee Services Corporation, Cree Europe GmbH, Cree International GmbH, Cree Japan, Inc, Cree Microwave, LLC, Echo Acquisition Corporation

Officers: Charles M. Swoboda/Chmn., CEO, Pres./$1,041,903.00, Michael E. McDevitt/Dir. - Financial Planning/$418,363.00, Robert C. Glass/VP - Technology, Materials, Optoelectronics/$450,970.00, John T. Kurtzweil/52/CFO, Exec. VP - Finance, Treasurer/$645,270.00, Adam H. Broome/Sec.

Directors: Charles M. Swoboda/Chmn., CEO, Pres., Dolph W. Von Arx/Dir., James E. Dykes/Dir., John W. Palmour/Founder, Dir., Harvey A. Wagner/Dir., Robert J. Potter/Dir., Clyde R. Hosein/Dir., Thomas H. Werner/Dir.

Owners: John T. Kurtzweil, Michael E. McDevitt, Robert J. Potter, Insiders/4.30%, Harvey A. Wagner, Robert C. Glass, ClearBridge Advisors, LLC/12.40%, Charles M. Swoboda/1.20%, John W. Palmour/1.50%, COTCO Holdings Limited/8.90%, Clyde R. Hosein, OppenheimerFunds, Inc./11.80%, Thomas H. Werner, James E. Dykes, FMR Corp./11.70% *(16 Owners included in Index)*

Financial Data: Fiscal Year End:06/26 Latest Annual Data: 6/25/2006

Year	Sales	Net Income
2006	$422,952,000	$76,673,000
2005	$389,064,000	$91,143,000
2004	$306,870,000	$57,960,000

Curr. Assets:	$234,893,000	Curr. Liab.:	$44,982,000	P/E Ratio:	36.04
Plant, Equip.:	$273,342,000	Total Liab.:	$48,868,000	Indic. Yr. Divd.:	NA
Total Assets:	$628,000,000	Net Worth:	$579,132,000	Debt/ Equity:	NA

Crescendo Acquisition Corp

Ratikonstr. 33, Postfach 443, Vaduz, FL, 09490; *PH:* 1-423-233-3188

General - Incorporation	DE	Stock- Price on:12/24/2007	NA
Employees	NA	Stock Exchange	NA
Auditor	NA	Ticker Symbol	NA
Stk Agt	NA	Outstanding Shares	NA
Counsel	NA	E.P.S.	NA
DUNS No.	NA	Shareholders	NA

Business: The group's principle activity involves acquisitions and mergers. The company intends to develop operating opportunities through business combinations or mergers. To date, the company has not conducted any significant operations, and its activities have focused primarily on organizational efforts, corporate compliance matters and locating potential merger candidates. Since the company has not yet commenced any principal operations, and has not yet earned significant revenues, the company is considered to be a development stage enterprise as of September 30, 2005.

Primary SIC and add'l.: 6770

CIK No: 0001289813

Crescent Banking Co

7 Caring Way, Jasper, GA, 30143; *PH:* 1-678-454-2266; *Fax:* 1-678-454-2282; *http://* www.crescentbank.com; *Email:* btrivedi@crescentbank.com

General - Incorporation	GA	Stock- Price on:12/24/2007	$43.95
Employees	182	Stock Exchange	NDQ
Auditor	Dixon Hughes PLLC	Ticker Symbol	CSNT
Stk Agt	NA	Outstanding Shares	2,610,000
Counsel	NA	E.P.S.	$2.77
DUNS No.	84-846-7668	Shareholders	NA

General - Incorporation GA
Employees 182
Auditor Dixon Hughes PLLC
Stk Agt NA
Counsel NA
DUNS No. 84-846-7668

Stock- Price on:12/24/2007 $43.95
Stock Exchange NDQ
Ticker Symbol CSNT
Outstanding Shares 2,610,000
E.P.S $2.77
Shareholders NA

Business: The group's principal activity is to provide a broad range of banking services to individual and corporate customers. The group operates through its two subsidiaries crescent bank and crescent mortgage services inc. The group's commercial banking segment provides traditional banking services offered through the bank. Banking operations are primarily retail-oriented and aimed at individuals and small to medium sized businesses in Georgia. During the year 2003, the group discontinued the mortgage banking segment.

Primary SIC and add'l.: 6712 6022

CIK No: 0000883476

Subsidiaries: Crescent Capital Trust I, Crescent Capital Trust II, Crescent Mortgage Services, Inc.

Officers: Donald J. Boggus/Dir., CEO, Pres./$401,136.00, Bradley A. Rutledge/44/Exec. VP/$330,310.00, Parke C. Day/Dir. - Crescent Bank, Dave Denton/Forsyth County Pres. - Cumming, Leland W. Brantley/36/Exec. VP/$292,781.00, Bonnie Ellis/Branch Mgr. - East Woodstock, Angie Jones/Branch Mgr. - Jasper, Lorrie Shaw/Pickens County Pres. - Jasper, Bonnie B. Boling/53/Exec. VP, Retail Administrator/$194,145.00, Richard M. Zorn/Dir. - Crescent Bank, John Agnew/Branch Mgr. - Adairsville, Tony Stancil/Contact - Riverstone, Kathy Carlson/Branch Mgr. - Cartersville, Brian Edwards/Bartow County Pres., Bobbie Warren/Branch Mgr. - Cartersville West *(23 Officers included in Index)*

Directors: Donald J. Boggus/Dir., CEO, Pres., John S. Dean/Dir., Chmn., Charles R. Fendley/Dir., John H. Bennett/Dir. - Crescent Bank, Charles A. Gehrmann/Dir., Alan J. Harris/Dir., Michael W. Lowe/Dir., Cecil Pruett/Dir., Janie F. Whitfield/Dir.

Owners: John S. Dean/1.90%, Bonnie B. Boling/0.96%, Charles Gehrmann/1.32%, Michael W. Lowe/22.84%, Leland W. Brantley/0.52%, Charles R. Fendley/0.76%, Cecil Pruett/0.46%, Donald Boggus/8.83%, Bradley A. Rutledge/0.95%, Janie Whitfield/2.50%, Anthony N. Stancil/1.02%, Insiders/40.24%

Financial Data: *Fiscal Year End:*12/31 *Latest Annual Data:* 12/31/2006

Year	Sales	Net Income
2006	$59,380,000	$7,314,000
2005	$43,174,000	$4,101,000
2004	$27,089,000	-$811,000

Curr. Assets:	$20,862,000	**Curr. Liab.:**	$679,717,000	**P/E Ratio:**	15.87
Plant, Equip.:	$21,389,000	**Total Liab.:**	$717,893,000	**Indic. Yr. Divd.:**	$0.640
Total Assets:	$779,671,000	**Net Worth:**	$61,778,000	**Debt/ Equity:**	0.5207

Crescent Communications Inc

701 N Post Oak Rd., Ste. 600, Houston, TX, 77024; *PH:* 1-713-686-1100; *http://* www.bluegate.com

General - Incorporation NV
Employees 33
Auditor Malone & Bailey, P.C
Stk Agt American Stock Transfer & Trust Co.
Counsel NA
DUNS No. NA

Stock- Price on:12/24/2007 $0.55
Stock Exchange NA
Ticker Symbol NA
Outstanding Shares 13,590,000
E.P.S -$0.91
Shareholders NA

Business: The group's principal activities are to provide co-location hosting and connectivity systems to small to mid-size businesses in Texas. The group is a network provider that develops and deploys specific technological Internet related solutions for businesses. It provides hosting and co-location services to application service providers. As a component of connectivity solutions, the group sells, installs and maintains network management components such as routers, ethernet switches and load-balancing devices from vendors like dell, cisco, radware, etc. As a part of complete solution, the group offers high-end network services such as monitoring and maintenance of sophisticated vpns and security implementations. The group also sells and configures hardware components for corporate firewalls and provides standard Web hosting as an additional service offering with options based on usage, storage requirements and bandwidth.

Primary SIC and add'l.: 7375

CIK No: 0000768216

Subsidiaries: Trilliant Technology Group, Inc.

Officers: Manfred Sternberg/48/Dir., CEO, William Koehler/42/Dir., Pres., Charles Leibold/58/CFO, Richard Yee/57/Sr. VP - Operations, Stephen Sperco/54/COO

Directors: Manfred Sternberg/48/Dir., CEO, William Koehler/42/Dir., Pres., Gilbert Gertner/83/Dir.

Owners: Stephen Sperco, Richard Yee, William Koehler, Greg J. Micek, Robert Davis, Insiders, The Chase Family Trust, Charles Leibold, Gilbert Gertner, Manfred Sternberg

Financial Data: *Fiscal Year End:*12/31 *Latest Annual Data:* 12/31/2006

Year	Sales	Net Income
2006	$3,708,000	-$9,192,000
2005	$2,493,000	-$4,165,000
2004	$1,110,000	-$640,000

Curr. Assets:	$585,000	**Curr. Liab.:**	$1,751,000		
Plant, Equip.:	$92,000	**Total Liab.:**	$1,751,000	**Indic. Yr. Divd.:**	NA
Total Assets:	$690,000	**Net Worth:**	-$1,061,000	**Debt/ Equity:**	NA

Crescent Financial Corp

1005 High House Rd., Cary, NC, 27513; *PH:* 1-919-460-7770; *Fax:* 1-919-460-2512; *http://* www.crescentstatebank.com; *Email:* virtualbanker@crescentstatebank.com

General - Incorporation NC
Employees 113
Auditor Dixon Hughes PLLC
Stk Agt Corporate Trust Dept.
Counsel NA
DUNS No. NA

Stock- Price on:12/24/2007 $11.25
Stock Exchange NDQ
Ticker Symbol CRFN
Outstanding Shares 8,350,000
E.P.S $0.65
Shareholders NA

Business: The group's principal activity is to provide banking services to individuals and small to medium-sized businesses in the United States. The banking services include checking and savings accounts, commercial, consumer and personal loans, mortgage services and other associated financial services. The group operates through its main office and three full service branch offices in cary, apex and clayton, North Carolina. On 02-Sep-2003, the group acquired centennial bank.

Primary SIC and add'l.: 6712 6022

CIK No: 0001143921

Subsidiaries: Crescent Financial Capital Trust I, Crescent State Bank

Officers: Michael G. Carlton/46/Dir., CEO, Pres./$413,683.00, Thomas E. Holder/48/Sr. Credit Officer/$202,724.00, Keith W. Betts/Marketing Pres./$122,793.00, William V. Leaming/Dir. - Operations, Ray D. Vaughn/55/COO, Sr. VP - Bank/$223,527.00, Bruce W. Elder/45/CFO/$206,335.00

Directors: Michael G. Carlton/46/Dir., CEO, Pres., Bruce I. Howell/65/Chmn., James A. Lucas/56/Dir., Brent D. Barringer/48/Dir., Sheila Hale Ogle/68/Dir., Francis R. Quis/58/Dir., Jon S. Rufty/53/Dir., Stephen K. Zaytoun/50/Dir., William H. Cameron/Dir., Jon T. Vincent/Dir., Charles A. Paul/Dir., Kenneth A. Lucas/53/Dir.

Owners: Insiders/18.55%, William H. Cameron/0.58%, Bruce W. Elder/0.29%, Sheila Hale Ogle/0.26%, Francis R. Quis, Ray D. Vaughn/0.10%, Kenneth A. Lucas/3.66%, Bruce I. Howell/1.06%, James A. Lucas/4.78%, Stephen K. Zaytoun/0.38%, Charles A. Paul/1.25%, Thomas E. Holder, Brent D. Barringer/0.93%, Michael G. Carlton/1.62%, Keith W. Betts/1.80% *(17 Owners included in Index)*

Financial Data: *Fiscal Year End:*12/31 *Latest Annual Data:* 12/31/2006

Year	Sales	Net Income
2006	$39,318,000	$4,904,000
2005	$25,244,000	$3,144,000
2004	$18,238,000	$2,333,000

Curr. Assets:	$18,196,000	**Curr. Liab.:**	$569,628,000	**P/E Ratio:**	17.58
Plant, Equip.:	$5,908,000	**Total Liab.:**	$614,876,000	**Indic. Yr. Divd.:**	NA
Total Assets:	$697,909,000	**Net Worth:**	$83,034,000	**Debt/ Equity:**	0.6496

Crescent Real Estate Equities Company

777 Main St., Ste. 2100, Fort Worth, TX, 76102; *PH:* 1-817-321-2100; *Fax:* 1-817-321-2000; *http://* www.crescent.com

General - Incorporation TX
Employees 748
Auditor Ernst& Young LLP
Stk Agt Bank of Boston
Counsel NA
DUNS No. NA

Stock- Price on:12/24/2007 $22.3
Stock Exchange NYSE
Ticker Symbol CEI
Outstanding Shares 102,830,000
E.P.S -$0.02
Shareholders NA

Business: The groups principle activity is to invest in real estate property. The group operates through four segments namely, office, resort residential development, resort/hotel and temperature-controlled logistics. In the year 2005, the group acquired Buckhead Plaza. The group operates from the United States.

Primary SIC and add'l.: 6798

CIK No: 0000918958

Subsidiaries: 1717 Main Street SM, Inc., 301 Congress Avenue, L.P., 301 Congress PT TRS, Inc., 325 HCD LLC, 335 HCD LLC, 355 HCD LLC, 3753/3763 HHP LLC, 3770 HHP, LLC, 3770 Hughes Parkway Associates, Limited Partnership, 3770 Surface Parking LLC, 3773 HHP LLC, 3790 HHP LLC, 3800 HHP LLC, 3883 HHP LLC, 3893 HHP LLC 252 Subsidiaries included in the Index

Officers: John C. Goff/Trust Mgr., CEO, Principal Executive Officer, Richard E. Rainwater/Chmn., Trust Mgr., Dennis H. Alberts/Dir., COO, Pres., Connie Angelot/VP, Assist. Controller, Bruce M. Basham/VP - Leasing, Terri Black/VP - Tax, Robert L. Carlen/VP - Property Management, Greenway Plaza, Anthony B. Click/VP - Leasing, James D. Dockal/VP, Assist. Controller, Dana B. Donahoe/VP - Investments, Jeanette I. Rice/VP - Marketing Research, Clifford M. Rudolph/VP - Investments, Thomas Shaw/VP - Human Resources, Administration, Eric S. Siegrist/VP - Leasing, Brent R. Somers/VP - Asset Management Counsel *(49 Officers included in Index)*

Directors: Richard E. Rainwater/Chmn., Trust Mgr., Dennis H. Alberts/Dir., COO, Pres., Anthony M. Frank/Dir., Trust Mgr., William F. Quinn/Dir., Trust Mgr., Paul E. Rowsey/Dir., Robert W. Stallings/Dir., Terry N. Worrell/Dir.

Owners: Insiders/20.00%, Dennis H. Alberts, Robert W. Stallings, The Vanguard Group, Inc./5.60%, John C. Goff/4.60%, Jerry R. Crenshaw, John L. Zogg, Jane E. Mody, Richard E. Rainwater/14.50%, BlackRock, Inc./6.10%, Paul E. Rowsey, Anthony M. Frank, Capital Research and Management Company/6.10%, William F. Quinn, Terry N. Worrell

Financial Data: *Fiscal Year End:*12/31 *Latest Annual Data:* 12/31/2006

Year	Sales	Net Income
2006	$928,696,000	$33,433,000
2005	$1,023,523,000	$95,307,000
2004	$978,761,000	$172,936,000

Curr. Assets:	$235,017,000	**Curr. Liab.:**	$502,624,000		
Plant, Equip.:	$2,905,819,000	**Total Liab.:**	$2,798,982,000	**Indic. Yr. Divd.:**	$1.500
Total Assets:	$4,046,971,000	**Net Worth:**	$1,122,286,000	**Debt/ Equity:**	1.9471

Crested Corp

877 N 8th W, Riverton, WY, 82501; *PH:* 1-307-856-9271; *Fax:* 1-307-857-3050; *http://* www.useg.com

General - Incorporation CO
Employees NA
Auditor Moss Adams LLP
Stk Agt Computershare Trust Co
Counsel Daniel P. Svliar
DUNS No. 08-950-3171

Stock- Price on:12/24/2007 $2.71
Stock Exchange NA
Ticker Symbol NA
Outstanding Shares 17,180,000
E.P.S $0.21
Shareholders NA

Business: The group's principle activity is to acquire, explore, develop, sell and lease mineral property and mines. The company operates in three business segments: minerals, commercial and contracts. Minerals segment consists of sales and leases of mineral-bearing properties and the production and/or marketing of uranium, gold, molybdenum and advance royalties on molybdenum property. Commercial segment consists of operation of a motel and rental of real estate and operation of an aircraft fixed real base operation. Contract segment consists of drilling/construction contract drilling of coalbed methane gas wells. Interest are held in other mineral properties, but are either non-operating interests or undeveloped claims. Crested and use also carry on small oil and gas operations in Montana and Wyoming. Other business segments include commercial operations, primarily real estate activities and general aviation.

Primary SIC and add'l.: 1041 1094 8748 5172

CIK No: 0000025657

Subsidiaries: Energx, Ltd., Rocky Mountain Gas, Inc., Sheep Mountain Partners, Sutter Gold Mining Company, USECC Gold Limited Liability Company, USECC Joint Venture, Western Executive Air, Inc., Yellow Stone Fuels, Inc.

Officers: Harold F. Herron/Co - Chmn., Pres., Robert Scott Lorimer/Dir., Principal Financial Officer, Chief Accounting Officer

Directors: Harold F. Herron/Co - Chmn., Pres., Keith G. Larsen/Dir., Robert Scott Lorimer/Dir., Principal Financial Officer, Chief Accounting Officer, Michael D. Zwickl/Dir., Kathleen R. Martin/Dir.

Owners: Michael H. Feinstein, Steven R. Youngbauer, Mark J. Larsen, Allen S. Winters, Mike Anderson, Russell H. Fraser, Keith G. Larsen, Robert Scott Lorimer, Kathleen M. Martin, Michael D. Zwickl, Harold F. Herron, Insiders

Financial Data: *Fiscal Year End:*12/31 *Latest Annual Data:* 12/31/2006

Year	Sales	Net Income
2006	NA	$3,851,000
2005	NA	$4,541,000
2004	NA	-$1,768,000

Curr. Assets:	$10,751,000	**Curr. Liab.:**	$14,482,000	**P/E Ratio:**	12.90
Plant, Equip.:	NA	**Total Liab.:**	$14,759,000	**Indic. Yr. Divd.:**	NA
Total Assets:	$15,123,000	**Net Worth:**	$364,000	**Debt/ Equity:**	1.7142

Cresud Inc

Edificio Intercontinental Plz., Calle Moreno N 877, Piso 23, Buenos Aires; *PH:* 54-1143444600; *http://* www.cresud.com.ar

General - Incorporation	AR	**Stock**- Price on:12/24/2007	$20.88
Employees	NA	Stock Exchange	NDQ
Auditor	Price Waterhouse & Co. S.R.L.	Ticker Symbol	CRESY
Stk Agt	Bank of New York	Outstanding Shares	30,850,000
Counsel	Zang Bergel & Vines	E.P.S.	$0.35
DUNS No.	97-026-6029	Shareholders	NA

Business: The group's principal activities are the acquisition and lease of fields. Production of grains, meat and milk. Products include wheat, corn, soybean, sunflower, peanuts, cotton, beans, meat and milk.

Primary SIC and add'l.: 0212 0110 0139 0219 0111 0179 0116

CIK No: 0001034957

Officers: Alejandro G. Elsztain/Vice Chmn., CEO, David A. Perednik/Chief Administrative Officer, Gabriel Blasi/CFO, Alejandro Bartolome/Chief Production Officer, Jose Luis Rinaldini/45/Chief Subsidiaries Supervisor, Alejandro Casaretto/Chief Real Estate Officer, Carlos Blousson/Chief Sales Officer

Directors: Alejandro G. Elsztain/Vice Chmn., CEO, Saul Zang/Vice Chmn., Eduardo S. Elsztain/Chmn., Salvador D. Bergel/Alternate Dir., Juan C. Quintana Teran/71/Alternate Dir., Gaston Armando Lernoud/Alternate Dir., Gabriel A.G. Reznik/Dir., Jorge Oscar Fernandez/Dir., Pedro Damaso Labaqui Palacio/Dir.

Owners: Insiders, IFISA, Eduardo S. Elsztain, Sal Zang, Argentine pension funds in the aggregate, D.E. Shaw Oculus Portfolios, L.L.C, Alejandro Casaretto, Fidelity Management & Research Co, Clarisa Lifsic, Alejandro Bartolom, Jorge Oscar Fernndez

Financial Data: *Fiscal Year End:*06/30 *Latest Annual Data:* 6/30/2006

Year	Sales	Net Income
2006	$36,432,000	$8,915,000
2005	$27,024,000	$29,970,000
2004	$21,035,000	$1,110,000

Curr. Assets:	$30,803,000	**Curr. Liab.:**	$33,049,000	**P/E Ratio:**	17.00
Plant, Equip.:	$81,440,000	**Total Liab.:**	$79,204,000	**Indic. Yr. Divd.:**	NA
Total Assets:	$271,656,000	**Net Worth:**	$191,901,000	**Debt/ Equity:**	NA

Crew Gold Corp

Abbey House Business Ctr., Wellington Way, Weybridge, KT13 OTT; *PH:* 44-1932268755; *http://* www.crewgroup.com

General - Incorporation	Canada	**Stock**- Price on:12/24/2007	$2.06
Employees	NA	Stock Exchange	OTC
Auditor	Deloitte & Touche LLP	Ticker Symbol	CRUGF
Stk Agt	Pacific Corporate Trust Co	Outstanding Shares	NA
Counsel	NA	E.P.S.	NA
DUNS No.	NA	Shareholders	NA

Business: The group's principle activity is to explore and develop mineral properties. Mineral properites of the group include gold, copper, zinc and other precious metal. The group is based in Canada with operations in Africa, Canada, greenland, Norway and the Philippines and controls seven producing mines.

Primary SIC and add'l.: 1041 1031 1021 1061 1231 1221 1222

CIK No: 0000885540

Subsidiaries: Core & Strategic Assets, Crew and Minelco AB, Crew Minerals AS, Crew Minerals Philippines Inc, Hwini-Butre Minerals Ltd, Nalunaq Gold Mine, new UK based management company

Officers: Jan Vestrum/Dir., CEO, Pres., William Leclair/CFO, Exec. VP, Jon Steen Petersen/Sr. VP - Exploration, Simon Booth/COO, Exec. VP

Directors: Jan Vestrum/Dir., CEO, Pres., Cameron Belsher/Chmn., Simon Russell/Dir., Brian Hosking/Dir., Hans Christian Qvist/Dir.

Financial Data: *Fiscal Year End:*06/30 *Latest Annual Data:* 6/30/2004

Year	Sales	Net Income
2004	NA	-$4,825,000

Curr. Assets:	$8,594,000	**Curr. Liab.:**	$7,655,000	**P/E Ratio:**	17.00
Plant, Equip.:	$40,038,000	**Total Liab.:**	$22,839,000	**Indic. Yr. Divd.:**	NA
Total Assets:	$58,853,000	**Net Worth:**	$35,777,000	**Debt/ Equity:**	NA

CRG Liquidation Co

Formerly: Cronos Group

5, Rue Guillaume Kroll, L-1855; *PH:* 352-264-83688; *http://* www.cronos.com

General - Incorporation	Luxembourg	**Stock**- Price on:12/24/2007	$15.93
Employees	74	Stock Exchange	NA
Auditor	Deloitte & Touche LLP	Ticker Symbol	NA
Stk Agt	Computershare Trust Co	Outstanding Shares	7,650,000
Counsel	Greene, Radovsky, Maloney & Share	E.P.S.	$1.17
DUNS No.	NA	Shareholders	NA

Business: The group's principle activity is to operate lessor of intermodal marine containers. The group also manages a fleet of dry cargo, refrigerated, tank and other specialized containers. The group operates from United States.

Primary SIC and add'l.: 3537

CIK No: 0000919869

Subsidiaries: C G Finance B.V., CF Leasing Limited, Cronos Capital Corp., Cronos Container Leasing GmbH, Cronos Containers (Cayman) Ltd., Cronos Containers (Hong Kong), Cronos Containers Inc., Cronos Containers Limited, Cronos Containers N.V., Cronos Containers PTE Limited, Cronos Containers Pty Limited, Cronos Containers S.R.L., Cronos Containers Scandinavia, Cronos Equipment (Bermuda) Ltd, Cronos Finance (Bermuda) Ltd 20 Subsidiaries included in the Index

Owners: Frank P. Vaughan, Steel Partners II, L.P./18.90%, Robert M. Melzer/1.60%, John C. Kirby/1.30%, Dennis J. Tietz/4.40%, John M. Foy/1.30%, Insiders/30.00%, Maurice Taylor/1.60%, S. Nicholas Walker/19.00%, Peter J. Younger, GM Investment & Co Limited/9.60%, Blavin Parties/20.00%

Financial Data: *Fiscal Year End:*12/31 *Latest Annual Data:* 12/31/2006

Year	Sales	Net Income
2006	$151,842,000	$9,227,000
2005	$148,290,000	$7,802,000
2004	$140,508,000	$8,865,000

Curr. Assets:	$77,825,000	**Curr. Liab.:**	$84,650,000	**P/E Ratio:**	14.48
Plant, Equip.:	$113,713,000	**Total Liab.:**	$177,712,000	**Indic. Yr. Divd.:**	$0.320
Total Assets:	$263,199,000	**Net Worth:**	$85,487,000	**Debt/ Equity:**	1.0694

CRH Plc

CRH plc, Belgard Castle, Clondalkin, Dublin, 22; *PH:* 353-14041000; *Fax:* 353-14041007; *http://* www.crh.com; *Email:* mail@crh.com

General - Incorporation	Ireland	**Stock**- Price on:12/24/2007	$51.3
Employees	79,560	Stock Exchange	NYSE
Auditor	Ernst & Young LLP	Ticker Symbol	CRH
Stk Agt	Citibank N.A	Outstanding Shares	542,790,000
Counsel	NA	E.P.S.	$3.00
DUNS No.	21-950-9155	Shareholders	NA

Business: The group's principal activities are in three divisions namely primary materials, value-added building products, and specialist building materials distribution. Materials division involves production of cement, aggregates, asphalt and ready-mixed concrete. Products division involves production of concrete products and a range of construction related products and services. Distribution division is engaged in the marketing and sale of builders' supplies to the construction industry and of materials and products to the diy market. During 2003, the group made 29 acquisitions for the products division and 13 for materials division including cementbouw handel and industrie.

Primary SIC and add'l.: 5033 5032 3270 3241 3271

CIK No: 0000849395

Subsidiaries: Irish public companies, Cement Limited, Roadstone, Limited

Officers: W. I. O'Mahony/61/Dir., CEO, D. W. Doyle/61/MD, Myles Lee/54/Dir., Dir. - Finance, M. Lee/54/Dir., Dir. - Finance, Tom W. Hill/51/Exec. Dir., Divisional Dir., W. P. Egan/62/Non - Exec. Dir., Albert Manifold/Divisional Dir., Maírtin Clarke/Divisional Dir.

Directors: W. I. O'Mahony/61/Dir., CEO, P. J. Molloy/70/Chmn., Tom W. Hill/51/Exec. Dir., Divisional Dir., M. Lee/54/Dir., Dir. - Finance, Nicky Hartery/56/Non - Exec. Dir., Jan Maarten De Jong/62/Dir., Myles Lee/54/Dir., Dir. - Finance, Kieran McGowan/64/Dir., David M. Kennedy/69/Non - Exec. Dir., Terry V. Neill/62/Non - Exec. Dir., Joyce M.C O'Connor/60/Non - Exec. Dir., Dan N. O'Connor/48/Non - Exec. Dir., Utz-Hellmuth Felcht/61/Non - Exec. Dir.

Owners: UBS AG/4.85%, Bank of Ireland Asset Management Limited/6.97%, The Capital Group Companies, Inc. and its affiliates/4.84%

Financial Data: *Fiscal Year End:*12/31 *Latest Annual Data:* 12/31/2006

Year	Sales	Net Income
2006	$36,708,440,000	$2,078,017,000
2005	$17,113,751,000	$1,077,449,000
2004	$16,754,968,000	$1,064,368,000

Curr. Assets:	$13,097,563,000	**Curr. Liab.:**	$7,500,218,000	**P/E Ratio:**	17.00
Plant, Equip.:	$14,600,976,000	**Total Liab.:**	$22,103,546,000	**Indic. Yr. Divd.:**	$1.040
Total Assets:	$36,490,980,000	**Net Worth:**	$14,387,434,000	**Debt/ Equity:**	NA

Crimson Exploration Inc

717 Texas Ave., Ste. 2900, Houston, TX, 77002; *PH:* 1-713-236-7400; *Fax:* 1-713-236-4424; *http://* www.crimsonexploration.com

General - Incorporation	DE	**Stock**- Price on:12/24/2007	$7.15
Employees	33	Stock Exchange	OTC
Auditor	Grant Thornton LLP	Ticker Symbol	CXPO
Stk Agt	Fidelity Transfer Co	Outstanding Shares	4,090,000
Counsel	NA	E.P.S.	$0.74
DUNS No.	NA	Shareholders	NA

Business: The group's principle activities are to acquire, develop, explore and produce crude oil and natural gas. The properties of the group are located in Texas, Colorado, Louisiana and Oklahoma. The sources of revenues are: oil and gas sales and operating overhead and other income. It operates through its nine subsidiaries namely gulfwest oil and gas company, setex oil and gas company, ltw pipeline co, rigwest well service inc, southeast Texas oil and gas company, llc, dutchwest oil company, gulfwest development company, gulfwest Texas company and gulfwest oil and gas company (Louisiana) llc. The group's quarterly revenue for Sep'07 was 38.01 millions of USD.

Primary SIC and add'l.: 1382 6719

CIK No: 0000813779

Subsidiaries: DutchWest Oil Company, GulfWest Development Company, GulfWest Oil and Gas Company, GulfWest Oil and Gas Company (Louisiana) LLC, RigWest Well Service, Inc, SETEX Oil and Gas Company

Officers: Allan D. Keel/Dir., CEO, Pres./$312,000.00, Thomas H. Atkins/Sr. VP - Exploration/$255,000.00, Joseph E. Grady/CFO, Sr. VP/$313,441.00, Tracy Price/Sr. VP - Land, Business Development/$241,000.00, Jay S. Mengle/Sr. VP - Operations, Engineering/$254,000.00, Richard L. Creel/VP - Finance

Directors: Allan D. Keel/Dir., CEO, Pres., Lee B. Backsen/Dir., Skardon F. Baker/Dir., James B. Ford/Dir., Lon McCain/Dir.

Owners: Lee B. Backsen, Virgil J. Waggoner/57.58%, Oaktree Capital Management, LLC/38.39%, Tracy Price, Gregory P. Pipkin, Insiders, Oaktree Capital Management, LLC/94.70%, Virgil J. Waggoner, Joseph E. Grady, Allan D. Keel, Allan D. Keel, Insiders, Lon McCain, Oaktree Capital Management, LLC, Jay S. Mengle (18 Owners included in Index)

Financial Data: Fiscal Year End:12/31 Latest Annual Data: 12/31/2006

Year	Sales	Net Income
2006	$21,659,000	$1,859,000
2005	$17,683,000	-$3,543,000
2004	$11,208,000	$8,072,000

Curr. Assets:	$4,232,000	Curr. Liab.:	$10,932,000		
Plant, Equip.:	$76,547,000	Total Liab.:	$23,377,000	Indic. Yr. Divd.:	NA
Total Assets:	$84,703,000	Net Worth:	$61,326,000	Debt/ Equity:	0.3032

Critical Care Inc

6646 Indian School Rd. NE, Albuquerque, NM, 87110; **PH:** 1-505-837-2020; **http://** www.criticalcareinc.com; **Email:** info@lasikamerica.org

General - Incorporation	NV	**Stock**- Price on:12/24/2007	NA
Employees	5	Stock Exchange	NA
Auditor	Weinberg & Co. P.A	Ticker Symbol	NA
Stk Agt	First American Stock Transfer, Inc.	Outstanding Shares	NA
Counsel	NA	E.P.S	NA
DUNS No.	NA	Shareholders	NA

Business: The groups principle activities include discovering, developing and commercializing products designed to treat respiratory, inflammatory and critical care diseases. The group operates from United States.

Primary SIC and add'l.: NA

CIK No: 0001157814

Subsidiaries: Lasik Acquisition Corp.

Officers: Sharli Maree Hayter/Executive Dir.

Financial Data: Fiscal Year End:07/31 Latest Annual Data: 07/31/2005

Year	Sales	Net Income
2005	$856,000	-$1,846,000
2004	$927,000	-$172,000

Curr. Assets:	$15,000	Curr. Liab.:	$1,142,000		
Plant, Equip.:	$197,000	Total Liab.:	$1,429,000	Indic. Yr. Divd.:	NA
Total Assets:	$212,000	Net Worth:	-$1,217,000	Debt/ Equity:	NA

Critical Path Inc

2 Harrison St., 2nd Fl., San Francisco, CA, 94105; **PH:** 1-415-541-2500; **Fax:** 1-415-541-2300; **http://** www.criticalpath.net

General - Incorporation	CA	**Stock**- Price on:12/24/2007	$0.1
Employees	246	Stock Exchange	OTC
Auditor	Burr, Pilger & Mayer, LLP	Ticker Symbol	CPTH
Stk Agt	Computershare Trust Co	Outstanding Shares	37,200,000
Counsel	Wilson Sonsini Goodrich & Rosati	E.P.S	-$0.723
DUNS No.	NA	Shareholders	NA

Business: The group's principal activity is to provide digital communications software and services. The software products and services enable enterprises, government agencies, wireless carriers and service providers to rapidly deploy highly scalable solutions for messaging and identity management. The group's messaging solutions are available both as licensed software and as hosted services. In addition, the solutions provide integrated access to a broad range of communication and collaboration applications from wireless devices, Web browsers, desktop clients and voice systems. The group's customers are corporate enterprises, carriers and service providers, postal authorities and government agencies. It operates in the United States, Brazil, Denmark, Canada, France, Germany, India, Ireland, Italy, Japan, Malaysia, the Netherlands, Spain, Sweden, Switzerland and the United Kingdom.

Primary SIC and add'l.: 7389 6794 7372 7375 4822

CIK No: 0001060801

Subsidiaries: 3034996 Nova Scotia Company, 3034997 Nova Scotia Company, Amplitude Software Ltd., Compass Holdings Corp., CP Datacenter Ltd., CP International (Ireland), Critical Path B.V., Critical Path Data Center AG, Critical Path Japan KK, Critical Path Sweden, DotOne Acquisition Corp., FaxNet Acquisition Corp., Netmosphere Corporation, PeerLogic, Inc., Remarq Communities, Inc.

Officers: Mark Palomba/CEO, James Clark/CFO, Exec. VP, Donald Dew/CTO, Barry Twohig/Exec. VP - Engineering

Directors: Mark Ferrer/Chmn., Ross M. Dove/Dir., Gerald Ma Lai Chee/Dir., Frost R.R. Prioleau/Dir., Mario Bobba/Dir., Tom Tinsley/Dir., Michael J. Shannahan/Dir.

Owners: Insiders, Cheung Kong Holdings Limited and affiliates, Entities affiliated with General Atlantic LLC, Zaxis Equity Neutral and affiliates, Permal U.S. Opportunities Limited, James A. Clark, Entities affiliated with General Atlantic LLC, Insiders, Frost R.R. Prioleau, Mario Bobba, Ross Dove, Tom Tinsley, Cheung Kong Holdings Limited and affiliates, Michael J. Shannahan, Crosslink Crossover Fund IV, L.P. (36 Owners included in Index)

Financial Data: Fiscal Year End:12/31 Latest Annual Data: 12/31/2006

Year	Sales	Net Income
2006	$46,430,000	-$10,966,000
2005	$66,832,000	-$13,652,000
2004	$71,072,000	-$51,997,000

Curr. Assets:	$27,252,000	Curr. Liab.:	$27,704,000		
Plant, Equip.:	$2,612,000	Total Liab.:	$50,941,000	Indic. Yr. Divd.:	NA
Total Assets:	$38,003,000	Net Worth:	-$147,344,000	Debt/ Equity:	NA

Critical Therapeutics Inc

60 Westview St., Lexington, MA, 02421; **PH:** 1-781-402-5700; **Fax:** 1-781-402-5729; **http://** www.criticaltherapeutics.com; **Email:** investor.relations@crtx.com

General - Incorporation	DE	**Stock**- Price on:12/24/2007	$2.31
Employees	61	Stock Exchange	NDQ
Auditor	Deloitte & Touche LLP	Ticker Symbol	CRTX
Stk Agt	Mellon Investor Services LLC	Outstanding Shares	43,140,000
Counsel	Wilmer Cutler Pickering H & D LLP	E.P.S	-$0.82
DUNS No.	NA	Shareholders	NA

Business: The group's principal activity is the discovery, development and commercialization of products designed to treat asthma and critical care diseases linked to body's inflammatory response. The group currently has one fda-approved product, zyflo (R), a tablet formulation for asthma. In addition, the group has three programs directed at developing products to regulate the excessive inflammatory response that can damage vital internal organs and, in the most severe cases, result in multiple organ failure and death.

Primary SIC and add'l.: 2834 8731

CIK No: 0001145404

Subsidiaries: CTI Securities Corp

Officers: Frank E. Thomas/Dir., CEO, Pres./$962,478.00, Jeffrey E. Young/VP - Finance, Chief Accounting Officer, Treasurer, Thomas P. Kelly/CFO, Sr. VP - Finance Corporate Development, Roberta Tucker/Sr. VP - Regulatory Affairs, Roger Heerman/VP - Sales, Marketing, Tucker Kelly/CFO, Sr. VP - Finance, Corporate Development, Trevor Phillips/COO, Sr. VP - Operations/$984,963.00, Scott Townsend/Sr. VP - Legal Affairs, General Counsel/$443,604.00, Linda S. Lennox/VP - Investor, Media Relations

Directors: Frank E. Thomas/Dir., CEO, Pres., Robert H. Zeiger/64/Dir., Cory M. Zwerling/Dir., Jean George/Dir., Nicholas Galakatos/Dir., Richard W. Dugan/Dir., Christopher Mirabelli/Dir., James B. Tananbaum/44/Dir., Christopher Walsh/64/Dir.

Owners: Robert H. Zeiger, Funds managed by Advanced Technology Ventures/8.34%, Funds managed by MPM Asset Management II LLC/9.33%, Paul D. Rubin, MedImmune Ventures, Inc./6.63%, Funds managed by Healthcare Ventures/12.74%, Dana Hilt, Frederick Finnegan, Trevor Phillips, Cory M. Zwerling, Sectoral Asset Management/6.04%, James B. Tananbaum/7.06%, Scott B. Townsend, Christopher Mirabelli/12.74%, Jean George/8.37% (22 Owners included in Index)

Financial Data: Fiscal Year End:12/31 Latest Annual Data: 12/31/2006

Year	Sales	Net Income
2006	$13,078,000	-$48,782,000
2005	$6,224,000	-$47,090,000
2004	$4,436,000	-$31,094,000

Curr. Assets:	$55,593,000	Curr. Liab.:	$7,855,000		
Plant, Equip.:	$2,421,000	Total Liab.:	$8,276,000	Indic. Yr. Divd.:	NA
Total Assets:	$58,182,000	Net Worth:	$49,906,000	Debt/ Equity:	0.0049

Criticare Systems Inc

20925 Crossroads Cir., Ste. 100, Waukesha, WI, 53186; **PH:** 1-262-798-8282; **Fax:** 1-262-798-8290; **http://** www.csiusa.com; **Email:** customerserv@csiusa.com

General - Incorporation	DE	**Stock**- Price on:12/24/2007	$3.39
Employees	108	Stock Exchange	AMEX
Auditor	BDO Seidman LLP	Ticker Symbol	CMD
Stk Agt	LaSalle Bank N.A	Outstanding Shares	12,300,000
Counsel	Reinhart, Boerner, Van Deuren sc	E.P.S	$0.053
DUNS No.	13-978-0712	Shareholders	NA

Business: The group's principal activity is to design, manufacture and market vital signs and gas monitoring instruments and related noninvasive sensors which are used to monitor patients. The monitors provide the clinician with information both graphically and numerically. The monitoring equipment of the group improves patient safety by delivering accurate, comprehensive and instantaneous patient information to the clinician. The products of the group are monitor oxygen saturation, carbon dioxide and anesthetic agents, temperature, heart rate and respiration rate. These instruments are sold primarily to the hospitals in seventy five countries through seventy five independent dealers.

Primary SIC and add'l.: 3845 3841

CIK No: 0000812121

Subsidiaries: Criticare Biomedical, Inc., Criticare Integration, Inc., Criticare International GmbH Marketing Services, Criticare Service GmbH, Criticare Systems Limited, CSI Trading, Inc., Sleep Care, Inc.

Officers: Emil H. Soika/70/Dir., CEO, Pres., Deborah A. Zane/54/VP - Marketing, Business Development, Joel D. Knudson/43/VP - Finance, Sec., Joseph P. Lester/58/VP, GM, Michael T. Larsen/49/VP - Quality, Regulatory Affairs VP - Quality, Regulatory Affairs, Drew M. Diaz/45/VP - Worldwide Sales

Directors: Emil H. Soika/70/Dir., CEO, Pres., Joseph N.C. Lai/66/Dir., Jeffrey T. Barnes/54/Dir., William M. Moore/60/Dir., Robert E. Munzenrider/63/Dir.

Owners: Joseph P. Lester, Emil H. Soika/1.10%, Insiders/6.00%, Joel D. Knudson, Heartland Advisors, Inc./11.60%, BlueLine Partners, L.L.C./11.10%, Higgins D. Bailey, Joseph N.C. Lai/2.90%, William M. Moore, White Pine Capital, LLC/5.40%, Deborah A. Zane, Drew M. Diaz

Financial Data: Fiscal Year End:06/30 Latest Annual Data: 06/30/2007

Year	Sales	Net Income
2007	$31,432,000	$348,000
2006	$31,351,000	$212,000
2005	$26,782,000	-$422,000

Curr. Assets:	$20,314,000	Curr. Liab.:	$6,992,000		
Plant, Equip.:	$2,452,000	Total Liab.:	$7,127,000	Indic. Yr. Divd.:	NA
Total Assets:	$22,979,000	Net Worth:	$15,853,000	Debt/ Equity:	0.0047

CRM Holdings Ltd

112 Delafield St., Poughkeepsie, NY, 12601; **PH:** 1-845-452-4100; **Fax:** 1-845-473-6154; **http://** www.trustcrm.com

General - Incorporation	Bermuda	**Stock**- Price on:12/24/2007	$7.83
Employees	245	Stock Exchange	NDQ
Auditor	Johnson Lambert & Co. LLP	Ticker Symbol	CRMH
Stk Agt	NA	Outstanding Shares	16,280,000
Counsel	NA	E.P.S	$1.19
DUNS No.	NA	Shareholders	NA

Business: The groups principle activity is to provide workers compensation insurance products. The groups services include formation, underwriting, risk assessment, safety and loss control services, medical bill review and case management, general management, and record keeping. The groups operates through four segments namely fee-based management services, primary workers compensation insurance, excess workers compensation reinsurance, and corporate and other. Customers served by the group include healthcare, transportation, contractors, banks and wholesale and retail. In November 2006, the group acquired Embarcadero Insurance Holdings, Inc. The group operates from Alaska, Arizona, Nevada, Oregon and Washington.

Primary SIC and add'l.: 8741

CIK No: 0001338949

Subsidiaries: Compensation Risk Managers of California, LLC, Compensation Risk Managers, LLC, CRM USA Holdings, Inc., EIMAR, L.L.C., Embarcedero Insurance Holdings, Inc., Majestic Insurance Company, Twin Bridges (Bermuda) Ltd.

Officers: Daniel G. Hickey/Chmn., CEO/$1,108,988.00, James J. Scardino/CFO/$412,856.00, Chester J. Walczyk/COO/$239,893.00, Louis J. Viglotti/General Counsel/$422,807.00, Thomas J. Spendley/Sr. VP - Underwriting, Joseph F. Taylor/Sr. VP - Compliance, John R. Dubois/Mgr. - Financial Reporting, Lauren Gottwald/Sr. Claims Mgr., Charlie Scott/Claims Service Mgr., Lenore Pearson-Vouitsis/Trust Analyst, Robert V. Polansky/42/Sr. VP - Sales, Product Development, Learle Brahs-Jackson/VP - Claims, Michele Cross/VP - Client Services, Alan Digiovanni/VP - Sales, Eric J. Egeland/VP - Specialty Risk, Research, Development *(25 Officers included in Index)*

Directors: Daniel G. Hickey/Chmn., CEO, Keith S. Hynes/55/Dir., Salvatore A. Patafio/63/Dir., Louis Rosner/59/Dir., Charles I. Johnston/53/Dir., David M. Birsner/40/Dir., Philip J. Magnarella/70/Dir.

Owners: Millennium Management, L.L.C./6.20%, Keith S. Hynes, Daniel G. Hickey/9.70%, Philip J. Magnarella, David M. Birsner/2.60%, Insiders/24.90%, Mendon Capital Advisors Corp./6.60%, James J. Scardino, Louis J. Viglotti/1.20%, Wells Fargo/9.90%, Salvatore A. Patafio, Daniel G. Hickey/11.40%, Chester J. Walczyk, The TCW Group, Inc./7.30%, Louis Rosner

Financial Data: **Fiscal Year End:**12/31 **Latest Annual Data:** 12/31/2006

Year	Sales	Net Income
2006	$75,048,000	$14,256,000
2005	$45,067,000	$7,275,000

Curr. Assets:	$84,932,000	**Curr. Liab.:**	$16,279,000		
Plant, Equip.:	NA	**Total Liab.:**	$222,709,000	**Indic. Yr. Divd.:**	NA
Total Assets:	$306,353,000	**Net Worth:**	$83,644,000	**Debt/ Equity:**	0.5051

Crocs Inc

6328 Monarch Pk. Pl., Niwot, CO, 80503; ***PH:*** 1-303-848-7000; ***Fax:*** 1-303-468-4266; ***http://*** www.crocs.com

General - Incorporation	DE	**Stock**- Price on:12/24/2007	$46.09
Employees	2,900	Stock Exchange	NDQ
Auditor	Deloitte & Touche LLP	Ticker Symbol	CROX
Stk Agt	Computershare Trust Co	Outstanding Shares	79,930,000
Counsel	NA	E.P.S.	$1.02
DUNS No.	NA	Shareholders	NA

Business: The groups principle activities include designing, manufacturing and marketing footwear product. The products of the group include Footwear, Apparel and Accessories and Foam. The group products sold under the trade name Crocs. The group acquired Ocean Minded, LLC for September 2007 and Fury and EXO, Jibbitz LLC in the year 2006. The group operates from the United States, Canada, Mexico, Asia and Europe. The group's quarterly revenue for September 2007 was 256.27 millions of USD.

Primary SIC and add'l.: 3021 2389 5139 3131

CIK No: 0001334036

Subsidiaries: 3179454 Nova Scotia Company, 4246519 Canada Inc., 55 Hockey Products, Inc., Crocs Asia Pte. Ltd., Crocs Australia Pty. Ltd., Crocs Brasil Comercio de Calcados Ltda., Crocs Europe B.V., Crocs Finland Oy, Crocs Footware C.V., Crocs Hong Kong Ltd., Crocs India Pvt Ltd., Crocs Industrial (Hong Kong) Co. Ltd., Crocs Industrial (Shenzhen) Co. Ltd., Crocs International Holding Limited, Crocs Marine, Ltd. 31 Subsidiaries included in the Index

Officers: Ronald R. Snyder/Dir., CEO, Pres., Peter S. Case/CFO, Sr. VP - Finance, Treasurer, John P. McCarvel/COO, Exec. VP, Michael C. Margolis/VP - Sales, Marketing

Directors: Ronald R. Snyder/Dir., CEO, Pres., Richard L. Sharp/Chmn., Michael E. Marks/Dir., Raymond D. Croghan/Dir., Thomas J. Smach/Dir., Ronald L. Frasch/58/Dir., Marie Holman-Rao/Dir.

Owners: Mazama Capital Management,Inc./11.50%, George B. Boedecker/5.70%, Michael E. Marks/3.40%, Thomas J. Smach, OppenheimerFunds,Inc/8.60%, Caryn D. Ellison, Raymond D. Croghan, John P. McCarvel, Peter S. Case, Richard L. Sharp/2.50%, Ronald R. Snyder/4.20%, Michael C. Margolis, Insiders/11.70%, Oppenheimer Global Opportunities Fund/7.50%

Financial Data: **Fiscal Year End:**12/31 **Latest Annual Data:** 12/31/2006

Year	Sales	Net Income
2006	$354,728,000	$64,417,000
2005	$108,581,000	$16,972,000
2004	$13,520,000	-$1,494,000

Curr. Assets:	$237,691,000	**Curr. Liab.:**	$87,909,000		
Plant, Equip.:	$34,849,000	**Total Liab.:**	$91,199,000	**Indic. Yr. Divd.:**	NA
Total Assets:	$299,457,000	**Net Worth:**	$208,258,000	**Debt/ Equity:**	NA

Croff Enterprises Inc

3773 Cherry Creek Dr. N, Ste 1025, Denver, CO, 80209; ***PH:*** 1-303-383-1555; ***Fax:*** 1-303-383-5018; ***http://*** www.croff.com; ***Email:*** jerry@croff.com

General - Incorporation	UT	**Stock**- Price on:12/24/2007	$2.5
Employees	1	Stock Exchange	OTC
Auditor	Ronald R. Chadwick,p.c.	Ticker Symbol	COFF
Stk Agt	Computershare Investor Services LLC	Outstanding Shares	NA
Counsel	Duffin & Dibb LLP	E.P.S.	$0.01
DUNS No.	07-299-8685	Shareholders	NA

Business: The group's principle activities include exploring and producing oil and gas, primarily through ownership of perpetual mineral interests and acquisition of oil and gas leases. The company acquires, owns, and produces, producing and non-producing leases and perpetual mineral interests in Alabama, Colorado, Michigan, Montana, New Mexico, North Dakota, Oklahoma, Texas, Utah and Wyoming. The major customers of the company include burlington resources oil and gas company, el paso production, energetics ltd and jenex petroleum corp. The group operates from United States.

Primary SIC and add'l.: 6792 6221

CIK No: 0000025743

Officers: Gerald L. Jensen/Chmn., CEO, Pres., Laura Cotton/Administrator - Investor Relations, Jennifer A. Miller/Chief Accounting Officer

Directors: Gerald L. Jensen/Chmn., CEO, Pres., Richard H. Mandel/78/Dir., Julian D. Jensen/60/Dir., Harvey Fenster/67/Dir.

Owners: Gerald L. Jensen/47.00%, Gerald L. Jensen/67.20%, Insiders/68.70%, Insiders/5.60%, Richard H. Mandel/3.20%, Julian D. Jensen/5.70%, Richard H. Mandel/1.50%

Financial Data: **Fiscal Year End:**12/31 **Latest Annual Data:** 12/31/2006

Year	Sales	Net Income
2006	$843,000	$373,000
2005	$968,000	$290,000
2004	$622,000	$142,000

Curr. Assets:	$1,111,000	**Curr. Liab.:**	$115,000	**P/E Ratio:**	16.67
Plant, Equip.:	$757,000	**Total Liab.:**	$180,000	**Indic. Yr. Divd.:**	NA
Total Assets:	$1,867,000	**Net Worth:**	$1,687,000	**Debt/ Equity:**	0.0378

Croghan Bancshares Inc

323 Croghan St., Fremont, OH, 43420; ***PH:*** 1-419-332-7301; ***Fax:*** 1-419-355-2266; ***http://*** www.croghan.com

General - Incorporation	OH	**Stock**- Price on:12/24/2007	$39.1
Employees	143	Stock Exchange	OTC
Auditor	Clifton Gunderson LLP	Ticker Symbol	CHBH
Stk Agt	Croghan Bancshares Inc	Outstanding Shares	1,770,000
Counsel	NA	E.P.S.	$3.10
DUNS No.	78-713-4048	Shareholders	NA

Business: The group's principal activity is to provide commercial, retail and savings banking services through its wholly owned subsidiary, the croghan colonial bank. These services include time, savings, money market and demand deposits; commercial, industrial, agricultural, real estate, consumer installment and credit card lending; safe deposit box rental; automatic teller machines, trust department services and other services. The group originates a variety of residential, industrial, commercial and agricultural loans secured by real estate, including interim construction financing and offers services to individuals, firms and corporations. Its investment products bearing no FDIC insurance are offered through the trust and investment services division. The group operates through its eight Ohio branch offices located in bellevue, clyde, fremont, green springs, monroeville and port clinton.

Primary SIC and add'l.: 6712 6022

CIK No: 0000887149

Subsidiaries: The Croghan Colonial Bank

Officers: Steven C. Futrell/62/CEO, Pres., Amy Lejeune/Investor Relations, Kendall W. Rieman/Treasurer, Principal Financial Officer

Directors: Allan E. Mehlow/Dir., Michael D. Allen/Dir., Stephen A. Kemper/68/Dir., James E. Bowlus/Dir., Daniel W. Lease/Dir., Terrence J. Wolfe/Dir., Gary L. Zimmerman/Dir., Thomas W. McLaughlin/Dir.

Owners: Thomas J. Elder, Claire F. Johansen, Gary L. Zimmerman, Thomas W. McLaughlin, Terrence J. Wolfe/1.70%, Allan E. Mehlow, Daniel W. Lease, Steven C. Futrell, Insiders/5.60%, Stephen A. Kemper, Michael D. Allen, James R. Faist, John P. Keller, James E. Bowlus/1.70%

Financial Data: **Fiscal Year End:**12/31 **Latest Annual Data:** 12/31/2006

Year	Sales	Net Income
2006	$29,948,000	$5,489,000
2005	$28,287,000	$5,721,000
2004	$24,640,000	$5,118,000

Curr. Assets:	$14,114,000	**Curr. Liab.:**	$387,118,000	**P/E Ratio:**	13.21
Plant, Equip.:	$7,904,000	**Total Liab.:**	$407,695,000	**Indic. Yr. Divd.:**	$1.240
Total Assets:	$458,858,000	**Net Worth:**	$51,163,000	**Debt/ Equity:**	0.3338

Crompton Corp

Benson Rd., Middlebury, CT, 06749; ***PH:*** 1-203-573-2000; ***http://*** www.chemtura.com

General - Incorporation	DE	**Stock**- Price on:12/24/2007	$11.12
Employees	6,200	Stock Exchange	NYSE
Auditor	KPMG LLP	Ticker Symbol	CEM
Stk Agt	Mellon Investor Services LLC	Outstanding Shares	241,220,000
Counsel	NA	E.P.S.	-$0.96
DUNS No.	NA	Shareholders	NA

Business: The group's principle actiivty is to produce specialty chemicals and polymer products. The group also provides home pool and spa chemicals. Customers served by the group include the automotive, transportation, construction, packaging and agriculture industries. The group operates from United States.

Primary SIC and add'l.: 2879 2819 3559 3089 2899

CIK No: 0001091862

Subsidiaries: 1167201 Ontario Limited, 9056-0921 Quebec Inc., A & M Cleaning Products, LLC, Antimony Products (Proprietary) Ltd., Aqua Clear Industries, LLC, ASCK, Inc., Asepsis, Inc., ASIA Stabilizers Co., Ltd., Assured Insurance Company, Baxenden Chemicals Limited, Baxenden Scandinavia A.S., BAYROL Deutschland GmbH, BAYROL France S.A.S., BAYROL Iberica S.A., Bio-Lab Canada, Inc. 161 Subsidiaries included in the Index

Officers: Robert L. Wood/53/Chmn., CEO, Pres./$4,078,128.00, Barry J. Shainman/64/VP, Sec., Lynn A. Schefsky/59/Sr. VP, General Counsel/$848,647.00, Marcus Meadows-Smtih/46/Exec. VP - Crop Protection, Consumer Products, Plastic Additives/$950,800.00, Eric C. Wisnefskyq/37/VP, Treasurer, Gregory E. McDaniel/56/Exec. VP - Strategy, New Business Development, Technology/$833,295.00, Gary P. Yeaw/50/Exec. VP - Human Resources, Communications, Kevin V. Mahoney/53/Sr. VP, Corporate Controller

Directors: Robert L. Wood/53/Chmn., CEO, Pres., Nigel D.T. Andrews/60/Dir., James W. Crownover/64/Dir., Robert A. Fox/70/Dir., Martin M. Hale/67/Dir., Roger L. Headrick/71/Dir., Mack G. Nichols/69/Dir., C. A. Piccolo/67/Dir., Bruce F. Wesson/65/Dir., Edward P. Garden/46/Dir.

Owners: FMR Corp./14.70%, Wellington Management Company, LLP/6.50%, Brandes Investment Partners, L.P./5.40%, Lord, Abbett & Co. LLC/8.40%, T. Rowe Price Associates, Inc./5.00%

Financial Data: **Fiscal Year End:**12/31 **Latest Annual Data:** 12/31/2006

Year	Sales	Net Income
2006	$3,722,707,000	-$205,517,000
2005	$2,986,608,000	-$186,640,000
2004	$2,549,762,000	-$34,590,000

Curr. Assets:	$1,385,790,000	Curr. Liab.:	$887,976,000	
Plant, Equip.:	$1,147,233,000	Total Liab.:	$2,720,502,000	Indic. Yr. Divd.: $0.200
Total Assets:	$4,399,406,000	Net Worth:	$1,678,904,000	Debt/ Equity: 0.7790

Cross Atlantic Commodities Inc

2800 Glades Cir Ste. 124, Weston, FL, 33327; PH: 1-754-245-6453; http:// www.crossac.com;
Email: info@crossac.com

General - Incorporation	NV	Stock- Price on:12/24/2007	$0.22
Employees	2	Stock Exchange	OTC
Auditor	Stark Winter Schenkein & Co., LLP	Ticker Symbol	CXAC
Stk Agt	NA	Outstanding Shares	23,080,000
Counsel	NA	E.P.S	-$0.5
DUNS No.	NA	Shareholders	NA

Business: The groups principle activities include importing and delivering coffee and coffee related products. The group operates from the United States.
Primary SIC and add'l.: 2024
CIK No: 0001311294
Officers: Michael Enemaerke/32/Dir., CEO, Pres., Kim Beck Nielsen/41/Dir., CFO, Controller, Jesse Starkman/79/Dir., Sec.
Directors: Michael Enemaerke/32/Dir., CEO, Pres., Kim Beck Nielsen/41/Dir., CFO, Controller, Jesse Starkman/79/Dir., Sec.
Owners: Kim Beck-Nielsen/34.32%, Insiders/67.85%, Michael Enemaerke/33.52%
Financial Data: Fiscal Year End:12/31 Latest Annual Data: 12/31/2006

Year		Sales		Net Income
2006		$342,000		-$4,934,000
Curr. Assets:	$770,000	Curr. Liab.:	$343,000	
Plant, Equip.:	$3,000	Total Liab.:	$3,811,000	Indic. Yr. Divd.: NA
Total Assets:	$773,000	Net Worth:	-$3,038,000	Debt/ Equity: NA

Cross Country Healthcare Inc

6551 Pk. of Commerce Blvd. NW, Boca Raton, FL, 33487; PH: 1-800-347-2264;
Fax: 1-561-998-8533; http:// www.crosscountry.com; Email: corpinfo@crosscountry.com

General - Incorporation	DE	Stock - Price on:12/24/2007	$17.32
Employees	6,616	Stock Exchange	NDQ
Auditor	Ernst & Young LLP	Ticker Symbol	CCRN
Stk Agt	LaSalle Bank N.A	Outstanding Shares	32,060,000
Counsel	NA	E.P.S	$0.55
DUNS No.	NA	Shareholders	NA

Business: The group's principal activity is to provide the provision of healthcare staffing services in United States and New Zealand. The services include travel nurse staffing services and placement of clinical research professionals and allied healthcare professionals. Under the cross country travcorps brand, the group provides nurses on a fixed-term contract basis. The group recruits credential nurses and other healthcare professionals and place them on assignments away from their homes. The group also provides other human capital management services including search and recruitment, consulting, education and training and resource management services. The active client base of the group includes over 3,000 hospitals, pharmaceutical companies and other healthcare providers across all 50 states. In 2003, the group acquired med-staff.
Primary SIC and add'l.: 7363
CIK No: 0001141103
Subsidiaries: Assignment America, Inc., CC Staffing, Inc., Cejka Search, Inc., ClinForce, LLC(f/k/a ClinForce, Inc.), Cross Country Capital, Inc., Cross Country Education, LLC(f/k/a Cross Country Education, Inc.), Cross Country Seminars, Inc., and CCS /Heritage Acquisition Corp.), Cross Country Infotech, Pvt, Ltd., Cross Country Local, Inc. (f/k/a Flex Staff, Inc.), Cross Country TravCorps, Inc., Cross Country TravCorps, Inc. Ltd. (NZ) (a), HealthStaffers, Inc., MCVT, Inc., Med-Staff, Inc. (f/k/a Cross Country Nurses, Inc.), NovaPro, Inc., TVCM, Inc.
Officers: Joseph A. Boshart/Dir., CEo, Pres./$546,600.00, Emil Hensel/Dir., CFO/$396,600.00, Susan E. Ball/44/General Counsel, Franklin A. Shaffer/Pres. - Education, Training Division, Vickie Anenberg/Exec. VP - Cross Country Staffing, Gregory Greene/Pres. - Cross Country Education, Daniel J. Lewis/Principal Accounting Officer, Victor Kalafa/VP - Corporate Development, Strategy, Tony Sims/Pres. - Clinical Trials Staffing Division, Jonathan W. Ward/Pres. - Cross Country Staffing/$311,150.00, Carol D. Westfall/Pres. - Search, Recruitment Division/$418,600.00, Anthony Sims/48/Pres. - Clinforce/$329,630.00
Directors: Joseph A. Boshart/Dir., CEo, Pres., Emil Hensel/Dir., CFO, Larry W. Cash/Dir., Taylor C. Cole/Dir., Thomas C. Dircks/Dir., Joseph Trunfio/Dir., Joseph Swedish/Dir., Gale Fitzgerald/Dir.
Owners: Jonathan W. Ward, Joseph A. Boshart/2.40%, Artisan Partners Limited Partnership/11.30%, Charterhouse Equity Partners III, L.P./7.70%, Larry W. Cash, FMR Corp./10.90%, Dimensional Fund Advisors LP/8.30%, Third Avenue Management LLC/5.50%, Anthony Sims, Carol D. Westfall, Joseph Trunfio, Emil Hensel/1.50%, Dawson Herman Capital Management Inc./5.10%, Insiders/6.30%
Financial Data: Fiscal Year End:12/31 Latest Annual Data: 12/31/2006

Year		Sales		Net Income
2006		$655,152,000		$16,636,000
2005		$645,393,000		$14,752,000
2004		$654,111,000		$20,659,000
Curr. Assets:	$146,225,000	Curr. Liab.:	$66,120,000	P/E Ratio: 33.96
Plant, Equip.:	$20,562,000	Total Liab.:	$129,177,000	Indic. Yr. Divd.: NA
Total Assets:	$504,032,000	Net Worth:	$374,856,000	Debt/ Equity: 0.0645

Cross Timbers Royalty Trust

901 Main St., 17th Fl., Dallas, TX, 75283; PH: 1-214-209-2400; Fax: 1-214-209-2431;
http:// www.crosstimberstrust.com; Email: trustee@crosstimberstrust.com

General - Incorporation	TX	Stock- Price on:12/24/2007	$43.04
Employees	NA	Stock Exchange	NYSE
Auditor	KPMG LLP	Ticker Symbol	CRT
Stk Agt	Mellon Investor Services LLC	Outstanding Shares	6,000,000
Counsel	NA	E.P.S	$3.632
DUNS No.	NA	Shareholders	NA

Business: The groups principal activity is to produce oil and gas. The group operates from the United States.
Primary SIC and add'l.: 6792
CIK No: 0000881787
Officers: Nancy G. Willis/VP, Louis G. Baldwin/CFO, Exec. VP
Financial Data: Fiscal Year End:12/31 Latest Annual Data: 12/31/2006

Year		Sales		Net Income
2006		$25,825,000		$25,448,000
2005		$20,631,000		$20,267,000
2004		$15,228,000		$14,924,000
Curr. Assets:	$1,976,000	Curr. Liab.:	$1,976,000	P/E Ratio: 11.26
Plant, Equip.:	NA	Total Liab.:	$1,976,000	Indic. Yr. Divd.: $3.390
Total Assets:	$21,655,000	Net Worth:	$19,680,000	Debt/ Equity: NA

CrossPoint Energy Company

2801 Network Blvd., Ste. 810, Frisco, TX, 75034; PH: 1-972-818-1100; Fax: 1-972-818-1122;
http:// www.crosspointenergy.com; Email: info@cxpe.com

General - Incorporation	NV	Stock - Price on:12/24/2007	$0.75
Employees	NA	Stock Exchange	OTC
Auditor	Cacciamatta Accountancy Corporation	Ticker Symbol	CXPE
Stk Agt	Pacific Stock Transfer Company	Outstanding Shares	18,310,000
Counsel	NA	E.P.S	NA
DUNS No.	NA	Shareholders	NA

Business: The groups principle activity is to explore minerals. In the year 2005, the group acquired the Zach Abney Unit. In the year 2006, the group merged with CrossPoint, LLC. The group operates from Canada.
Primary SIC and add'l.: 1040
CIK No: 0001309499
Subsidiaries: CrossPoint Acquisition, LLC, CrossPoint Energy Holdings, LLC, Dallas Operating Corp.
Officers: Daniel F. Collins/Dir., CEO, Pres., Jeffrey A. Krakos/Dir., Exec. VP, Margaret R. Coughlin/Controller, Corp. Sec., Michael S. Willey/Geologist, Exploration Mgr., Robert J. Wolf/Land Mgr.
Directors: Daniel F. Collins/Dir., CEO, Pres., Jeffrey A. Krakos/Dir., Exec. VP, John A. Bailey/Dir., David C. Bradshaw/Dir., J. W. Brown/Dir., Steven R. Shaw/Dir., Ross Welgehausen/Dir.
Owners: DB Zwirn Special Opportunities Fund L.P., Grove CrossPoint Investments, LLC, WSV Management, L.L.C., Insiders, Daniel F. Collins, Hoak Public Equities, L.P., John A. Bailey, David C. Bradshaw, WS Capital, L.L.C., Bonanza Master Fund LTD, Perugia Energy L.P., Jeffrey A. Krakos, Drawbridge Special Opportunities Fund LP

Curr. Assets:	$3,000	Curr. Liab.:	$18,000	
Plant, Equip.:	NA	Total Liab.:	$18,000	Indic. Yr. Divd.: NA
Total Assets:	$3,000	Net Worth:	-$15,000	Debt/ Equity: NA

Crossroads Systems Inc

11000 N Mopac Expwy., Austin, TX, 78759; PH: 1-512-349-0300; Fax: 1-512-349-0304;
http:// www.crossroads.com; Email: info@crossroads.com

General - Incorporation	DE	Stock - Price on:12/24/2007	$1.4
Employees	NA	Stock Exchange	OTC
Auditor	KPMG LLP	Ticker Symbol	CRDS
Stk Agt	American Stock Transfer & Trust Co.	Outstanding Shares	28,150,000
Counsel	Gray, Cary, Ware & Freidenrich	E.P.S	-$0.33
DUNS No.	NA	Shareholders	NA

Business: The group's principal activity is to provide enterprise data routing solutions for open system storage area networks (sans). The storage routers serve as interconnect between sans and the other devices in a computer network and allow organizations to store, manage and ensure the integrity and availability of their data. The group has developed and acquired expertise in several different input-output (i/o) and networking protocols. It provides these products in a variety of configurations including both stand-alone box and library-embedded router form factors with varying port counts. The products and services of the group are sold primarily to leading storage system and server original equipment manufacturers, distributors, vars, system integrators and storage service providers.
Primary SIC and add'l.: 3577
CIK No: 0001093207
Subsidiaries: Crossroads Systems (Texas), Inc
Officers: Robert C. Sims/Dir., CEO, Pres., David Cerf/Exec. VP - Business, Corporate Development, Brian Bianchi/COO, Greg Reny/Sr. VP - Sales, Rhonda MacLean/Members, Strategic Member - Advisory Board
Directors: Robert C. Sims/Dir., CEO, Pres., David L. Riegel/Chmn., Richard D. Eyestone/Dir., Alan B. Howe/Dir., Ann Cohen/Member - Strategic Advisory Board, Andrew Heller/Member - Strategic Advisory Board, Carolyn Purcell/Member - Strategic Advisory Board, John Stenbit/Member - Strategic Advisory Board
Financial Data: Fiscal Year End:10/31 Latest Annual Data: 10/31/2004

Year		Sales		Net Income
2004		$26,029,000		-$6,360,000
2003		$33,143,000		-$6,447,000
2002		$33,988,000		-$25,489,000
Curr. Assets:	$32,947,000	Curr. Liab.:	$7,103,000	
Plant, Equip.:	$2,909,000	Total Liab.:	$7,103,000	Indic. Yr. Divd.: NA
Total Assets:	$36,769,000	Net Worth:	$29,666,000	Debt/ Equity: NA

Crosstex Energy Inc

2501 Cedar Springs Rd., Ste. 100, Dallas, TX, 75201; PH: 1-214-953-9500; Fax: 1-214-953-9501;
http:// www.crosstexenergy.com

General - Incorporation	DE	Stock - Price on:12/24/2007	$28.99
Employees	610	Stock Exchange	NDQ
Auditor	KPMG LLP	Ticker Symbol	XTXI
Stk Agt	American Stock Transfer & Trust Co.	Outstanding Shares	45,980,000
Counsel	NA	E.P.S	$0.09
DUNS No.	NA	Shareholders	NA

Business: The groups principle activities include gathering, transmitting, treating, processing and marketing of natural gas. The group operates through two business segments namely Midstream and Treating. The group operates from United States.

Primary SIC and add'l.: NA

CIK No: 0001209821

Subsidiaries: Crosstex Acquisition Management, L.P., Crosstex Alabama Gathering System, L.P., Crosstex CCNG Gathering, Ltd., Crosstex CCNG Processing, Ltd., Crosstex CCNG Transmission, Ltd., Crosstex DC Gathering Company, J.V., Crosstex Energy Services GP, LLC, Crosstex Energy Services, L.P., Crosstex Gulf Coast Marketing Ltd., Crosstex Gulf Coast Transmission Ltd., Crosstex LIG Liquids, Crosstex LIG, LLC, Crosstex Louisiana Energy, L.P., Crosstex Mississippi Industrial Gas Sales, L.P., Crosstex Mississippi Pipeline, L.P. 30 Subsidiaries included in the Index

Officers: Barry E. Davis/Dir., CEO, Pres./$1,779,505.00, Chris A. Aulds/46/Exec. VP - Public, Governmental Affairs, Joe A. Davis/Exec. VP, General Counsel, William W. Davis/CFO, Exec. VP/$1,218,987.00, Jack M. Lafield/Exec. VP - Corporate Development/$1,218,987.00, James R. Wales/Exec. VP - Commercial Division/$963,941.00, Robert S. Purgason/COO, Exec. VP/$1,775,177.00, Danny L. Thompson/Sr. VP - Engineering, Operations, Jennifer K. Johnson/VP - Human Resources, Organizational Development, James T. Reynolds/Sr. VP - Treating

Directors: Barry E. Davis/Dir., CEO, Pres., Bryan H. Lawrence/Chmn., Frank M. Burke/Dir., Rhys J. Best/Dir. - Crosstex Energy GP, LLC, Robert F. Murchison/Dir., Sheldon B. Lubar/Dir., Cecil E. Martin/Dir., James C. Crain/Dir., Kyle D. Vann/Dir. - Crosstex Energy GP, LLC

Owners: Yorktown Energy Partners IV, L.P./3.79%, Bryan H. Lawrence/3.35%, Insiders/11.36%, Jack M. Lafield, Yorktown Energy PartnersV, L.P./1.19%, James A. Crain, Lubar Nominees/4.55%, James R. Wales/1.56%, William W. Davis, Barry E. Davis/3.32%, Robert S. Purgason, Frank M. Burke, Robert F. Murchison, Chieftain Capital Management, Inc./18.25%

Financial Data: Fiscal Year End:12/31   Latest Annual Data: 12/31/2006

Year	Sales		Net Income
2006	$3,141,804,000		$16,455,000
2005	$3,033,048,000		$49,136,000
2004	$1,978,776,000		$8,700,000
Curr. Assets:	$420,229,000	Curr. Liab.:	$490,320,000	P/E Ratio:	362.38
Plant, Equip.:	$1,107,242,000	Total Liab.:	$1,536,182,000	Indic. Yr. Divd.:	$0.920
Total Assets:	$2,206,698,000	Net Worth:	$279,413,000	Debt/ Equity:	3.8890

Crow Technologies 1977 Ltd

12 Kineret St., Airport City, 70100; ; *http://* www.thecrowgroup.com

General - Incorporation	Israel	Stock - Price on:12/24/2007	$6.5
Employees	NA	Stock Exchange	OTC
Auditor	Kost Forer Gabbay & Kasierer	Ticker Symbol	CRWTF
Stk Agt	American Stock Transfer & Trust Co.	Outstanding Shares	NA
Counsel	NA	E.P.S.	NA
DUNS No.	NA	Shareholders	NA

Business: The group operate through its subsidiary whose principal activities include designing, developing, manufacturing, selling and distributing security detection and alarm systems The group products include wireless control panels, several lines of indoor and outdoor sensors, wired and wireless sensors, access controls, communication systems for use in commercial and industrial facilities. The group operates from the United States and Israel.

Primary SIC and add'l.: 7385

CIK No: 0000770320

Subsidiaries: Actech Access Technologies Ltd., ArrowHead Alarm Products Ltd., Crow Australia Pty Ltd., Crow Electronic Engineering Ltd., Freelink Ltd., ScanVision Technologies Ltd., Secucell Ltd., Video Domain Technologies Ltd.

Officers: Shmuel Melman/Founder, Dir., CEO, Noel E. Jennings/CEO - Arrowhead Alarm Products Ltd, Yaacov Hirsh/VP - Operations, Sergai Bursakov/Factory Mgr., Monique Bennoun/Dir. - Sales, Marketing Mgr., Jacob Batchon/CFO, Moris Elkayam/Technical Support Mgr., Shuki Segal/CTO

Directors: Shmuel Melman/Founder, Dir., CEO, Meir Jacobson/Chmn., Abram J. Silver/Dir., Monique Bennoun/Dir. - Sales, Marketing Mgr., Alexander Werber/Dir., Uri Bar-Ner/Dir., Zeev Avraham Slavin/Dir., Avi Zigelman/52/External Dir.

Owners: Abram Silver, Meir Jacobson, Shmuel Melman

Financial Data: Fiscal Year End:12/31   Latest Annual Data: 12/31/2006

Year	Sales		Net Income
2006	$34,677,000		$1,144,000
2005	$26,609,000		$1,549,000
2004	$26,270,000		$448,000
Curr. Assets:	$19,529,000	Curr. Liab.:	$15,523,000		
Plant, Equip.:	$7,457,000	Total Liab.:	$18,694,000	Indic. Yr. Divd.:	NA
Total Assets:	$27,195,000	Net Worth:	$8,199,000	Debt/ Equity:	NA

Crown Castle International Corp

510 Bering Dr., Ste. 600, Houston, TX, 77057; *PH:* 1-713-570-3000; *Fax:* 1-713-570-3100; *http://* www.crowncomm.net

General - Incorporation	DE	Stock - Price on:12/24/2007	$35.03
Employees	1,160	Stock Exchange	NYSE
Auditor	KPMG LLP	Ticker Symbol	CCI
Stk Agt	Mellon Investor Services LLC	Outstanding Shares	284,450,000
Counsel	NA	E.P.S.	-$0.49
DUNS No.	96-914-8220	Shareholders	NA

Business: The group's principal activities are to own, operate and manage wireless communications sites and broadcast transmission networks. The group also provides complementary services to its customers, including network design, radio frequency engineering, site acquisition, site development and construction, antenna installation and network management and maintenance. The group's communications sites are located throughout the United States, in Puerto Rico, in the United Kingdom and in Australia. In the United States, Puerto Rico and Australia, the group's primary business is the leasing of antenna space to wireless operators under long-term contracts. In the United Kingdom, the group's primary businesses are the operation of television and radio broadcast transmission networks and the leasing of antenna space to wireless operators in the United Kingdom.

Primary SIC and add'l.: 4833 4899 4832 1799

CIK No: 0001051470

Subsidiaries: CC Castle International LLC, CC Towers Guarantor LLC, CC Towers Holding LLC, Crown Castle Australia Holdings Pty Limited, Crown Castle Australia Pty Ltd (f/k/a CCAL Towers Pty Ltd.), Crown Castle CA Corp, Crown Castle GT Corp, Crown Castle Investment Corp, Crown Castle Operating Company (f/k/a Crown Castle USA Holdings Company, Crown Castle PT Inc, Crown Castle South LLC, Crown Castle Towers 05 LLC, Crown Castle USA Inc. (f/k/a Crown Network Systems, Inc.), Crown Communication Inc

Officers: John P. Kelly/50/Dir., CEO, Pres./$3,722,014.00, Patrick Slowey/Sr. VP - Sales, Customer Relations, Benjamin W. Moreland/44/CFO, Exec. VP/$2,186,962.00, Blake E. Hawk/Exec. VP, General Counsel/$1,621,720.00, James D. Young/Pres. - US Tower Operations/$1,830,122.00, Jay Brown/Treasurer - Contact - Investor Relations Officer, Donald J. Reid/Corp. Sec., Lisa Davidson/Sr. VP - Human Resources

Directors: John P. Kelly/50/Dir., CEO, Pres., Landis J. Martin/62/Chmn., Ari Q. Fitzgerald/45/Dir., Robert E. Garrison/66/Dir., Edward C. Hutcheson/62/Dir., Robert F. McKenzie/64/Dir., Randall A. Hack/60/Dir., Lee W. Hogan/63/Dir., Dale N. Hatfield/70/Dir.

Financial Data: Fiscal Year End:12/31   Latest Annual Data: 12/31/2006

Year	Sales		Net Income
2006	$788,221,000		-$41,893,000
2005	$676,759,000		-$401,537,000
2004	$603,865,000		$235,110,000
Curr. Assets:	$800,027,000	Curr. Liab.:	$200,795,000		
Plant, Equip.:	$3,246,446,000	Total Liab.:	$3,907,964,000	Indic. Yr. Divd.:	NA
Total Assets:	$5,006,168,000	Net Worth:	$756,281,000	Debt/ Equity:	1.7161

Crown Crafts Inc

916 S Burnside Ave., Gonzales, LA, 70737; *PH:* 1-225-647-9100; *Fax:* 1-225-647-8331; *http://* www.crowncrafts.com

General - Incorporation	DE	Stock - Price on:12/24/2007	NA
Employees	202	Stock Exchange	NDQ
Auditor	Deloitte & Touche LLP	Ticker Symbol	CRWS
Stk Agt	NA	Outstanding Shares	NA
Counsel	NA	E.P.S.	$0.28
DUNS No.	00-332-7616	Shareholders	NA

Business: The group's principal activities are to design, manufacture, market and distribute infant products. The group operates in two segments: infant and juvenile products and adult home furnishing products. Infant and juvenile products consists of infant bedding, bibs, infant soft goods and accessories and juvenile products. Adult home furnishing products consists of bedroom and bath products like adult comforters, sheets and towels and throws. The group sells these products directly to retailers, primarily mass merchants, large chain stores, department stores, specialty home furnishings stores, wholesale clubs and gift stores. The group operates in the United States of America.

Primary SIC and add'l.: 5023 2273 2392 2385 3069

CIK No: 0000025895

Subsidiaries: Churchill Weavers, Inc., Crown Crafts Infant Products, Inc., Hamco, Inc.

Officers: Randall E. Chestnut/Chmn., CEO, Pres., Olivia Elliott/Sec., Treasurer - Investor Relations, Amy Vidrine Samson/CFO, VP

Directors: Randall E. Chestnut/Chmn., CEO, Pres.

Owners: Nelson Obus/14.60%, Wynnefield Partners I/6.00%, Wynnefield Partners LP/5.20%, Channel/0.10%, Wynnefield Offshore/3.40%

Financial Data: Fiscal Year End:04/02   Latest Annual Data: 4/1/2007

Year	Sales		Net Income
2007	$71,988,000		$7,601,000
2006	$72,629,000		$7,967,000
2005	$83,908,000		$2,438,000
Curr. Assets:	$29,317,000	Curr. Liab.:	$8,164,000		
Plant, Equip.:	$1,586,000	Total Liab.:	$33,249,000	Indic. Yr. Divd.:	NA
Total Assets:	$54,124,000	Net Worth:	$20,875,000	Debt/ Equity:	NA

Crown Equity Holdings Inc

One Crown Way, Philadelphia, PA, 19154; *PH:* 1-215-698-5100; *http://* www.crowncork.com; *Email:* ir@crowncork.com

General - Incorporation	PA	Stock - Price on:12/24/2007	$0.34
Employees	NA	Stock Exchange	OTC
Auditor	PricewaterhouseCoopers LLP	Ticker Symbol	CRWE
Stk Agt	Wells Fargo Bank Minnesota N.A	Outstanding Shares	5,320,000
Counsel	NA	E.P.S.	$0.00
DUNS No.	NA	Shareholders	NA

Business: The groups principal activity is to manufacture packaging products. The group operates from the United States.

Primary SIC and add'l.: 3411

CIK No: 0001219601

Subsidiaries: Crown Cork & Seal Company, Inc

Owners: Hans J. Lliger, Harold A. Sorgenti, Alan W. Rutherford/1.00%, William R. Apted, William H. Voss, Iridian Asset Management LLC and its affiliates/6.80%, Insiders/3.80%, John W. Conway/1.50%, Hugues du Rouret, Jenne K. Britell, Frank J. Mechura, Marie L. Garibaldi, William S. Urkiel, Jim L. Turner, Arnold W. Donald (17 Owners included in Index)

Financial Data: Fiscal Year End:12/31   Latest Annual Data: 12/31/2006

Year	Sales		Net Income
2006	NA		-$139,000
2005	NA		-$46,000
2004	NA		-$1,528,000
Curr. Assets:	$0	Curr. Liab.:	$152,000		
Plant, Equip.:	NA	Total Liab.:	$152,000	Indic. Yr. Divd.:	NA
Total Assets:	$0	Net Worth:	-$152,000	Debt/ Equity:	NA

Crown Holdings Inc

1 Crown Way, Philadelphia, PA, 19154; *PH:* 1-215-698-5100; *Fax:* 1-215-676-7245; *http://* www.crowncork.com; *Email:* ir@crowncork.com

General - Incorporation: PA
Employees: 21,749
Auditor: PricewaterhouseCoopers LLP
Stk Agt: Wells Fargo Bank Minnesota N.A
Counsel: NA
DUNS No.: NA

Stock- Price on:12/24/2007: $24.97
Stock Exchange: NYSE
Ticker Symbol: CCK
Outstanding Shares: 163,510,000
E.P.S: $1.87
Shareholders: NA

Business: The groups principle activities include designing, manufacturing and selling of packaging products for consumer goods. The groups products include steel and aluminum cans for food, beverage, brewing, plastic containers for beverage, processed food, household, personal care and various products. The group operates from United States.

Primary SIC and add'l.: 3565 3085 3411

CIK No: 0001219601

Subsidiaries: Carnaud Maroc, CarnaudMetalbox Engineering PLC, CarnaudMetalbox Food South Africa (Pty) Ltd., CarnaudMetalbox Group UK Limited, CarnaudMetalbox Overseas Limited, CROWN Aerosols Italia Srl, CROWN Aerosols Nederland BV, CROWN Aerosols UK Limited, CROWN Americas Capital Corp., CROWN Americas LLC, CROWN Arabia Can Company Ltd., CROWN Asia Pacific Investments (T) Limited, CROWN Asia-Pacific Holdings Limited, CROWN Bevcan and Closures (Thailand) Company Limited, CROWN Bevcan Espana S.L. 85 Subsidiaries included in the Index

Officers: John W. Conway/Chmn., CEO, Pres., Alan W. Rutherford/Vice Chmn., CFO, Exec. VP, Karen E. Berigan/VP - Corporate Risk Management, Thomas A. Kelly/VP, Corporate Controller, Timothy J. Donahue/Sr. VP - Finance, Brad Dahlgren/VP - Sales, Marketing, Aerosol Packaging, United States, Sheila M. Heath/Dir. - Marketing, Bob Bourque/Contact - Sales, Marketing, Metal Crowns, Christopher Robinson/Contact - Sales, Marketing, Speciality Packaging, Ricardo Sills/Sales Mgr. - Food Packaging, Argentina, Clarence Sammy/Regional Marketing Mgr. - Food Packaging, Caribbean, Ramiro Barney/GM - Mexico, Frank J. Mechura/65/Pres. - Americas Division, William H. Voss/Exec. VP, Patrick Lee/VP - Food Packaging, Thailand, Asia, Pacific *(60 Officers included in Index)*

Directors: John W. Conway/Chmn., CEO, Pres., Alan W. Rutherford/Vice Chmn., CFO, Exec. VP, Jenne K. Britell/Dir., Marie L. Garibaldi/Dir., Harold A. Sorgenti/Dir., Jim L. Turner/Dir., William S. Urkiel/Dir., Arnold W. Donald/Dir., William G. Little/Dir., Hugues Du Rouret/Dir., Thomas A. Ralph/Dir., Thomas R. Ralph/67/Dir., Hans J. Loliger/Dir.

Owners: William R. Apted, Harold A. Sorgenti, Thomas A. Ralph, William G. Little, Hans J. Lliger, Jim L. Turner, Frank J. Mechura, Jenne K. Britell, Insiders/3.80%, Alan W. Rutherford/1.00%, John W. Conway/1.50%, Iridian Asset Management LLC and its affiliates/6.80%, Hugues du Rouret, Arnold W. Donald, William S. Urkiel *(17 Owners included in Index)*

Financial Data: *Fiscal Year End:*12/31 *Latest Annual Data:* 12/31/2006

Year	Sales	Net Income
2006	$6,982,000,000	$309,000,000
2005	$6,908,000,000	-$362,000,000
2004	$7,199,000,000	$51,000,000

Curr. Assets:	$2,062,000,000	**Curr. Liab.:**	$1,956,000,000	**P/E Ratio:**	13.35
Plant, Equip.:	$1,608,000,000	**Total Liab.:**	$6,624,000,000	**Indic. Yr. Divd.:**	NA
Total Assets:	$6,358,000,000	**Net Worth:**	-$545,000,000	**Debt/ Equity:**	NA

Crown Media Holdings Inc

12700 Ventura Blvd., Ste. 200, Studio City, CA, 91604; ***PH:*** 1-818-755-2400; ***Fax:*** 1-818-755-2564; ***http://*** www.hallmarkchannel.com

General - Incorporation: DE
Employees: 158
Auditor: KPMG LLP
Stk Agt: Mellon Investor Services LLC
Counsel: Weil, Gotshal & Manges LLP
DUNS No.: NA

Stock- Price on:12/24/2007: $7.13
Stock Exchange: NDQ
Ticker Symbol: CRWN
Outstanding Shares: 104,790,000
E.P.S: -$1.45
Shareholders: NA

Business: The group's principal activities are the ownership and operation of pay television channels, known as the hallmark channel. The hallmark channel is dedicated to entertainment programming for adults, which is also appealing to children. Internationally, the hallmark channel is operated and distributed in approximately 116 countries by crown media international and in the United Kingdom by crown entertainment. Domestically, the hallmark channel is operated and distributed by crown media United States. The group recently purchased more than 700 titles from the hallmark entertainment distribution, llc library. The group markets its channel in the United States, Latin America, Asia-Pacific, central Europe, scandinavia, benelux, Spain, Africa, czech republic, Australia, Russia, Middle East, the United Kingdom, Israel and turkey.

Primary SIC and add'l.: 4841 7313 6719

CIK No: 0001103837

Subsidiaries: Citi TeeVee, LLC, CM Intermediary, LLC, Crown Media Distribution, LLC, Crown Media United States, LLC, Doone City Pictures, LLC, Waygoose Concerts Services B.V.

Officers: Henry Schleiff/59/Dir., CEO, Pres./$811,267.00, David Johnson/Dir. - Network Program Publicity, Jaime Saberito/Sr. Dir. - Media, Pam Slay/Sr. VP - Network Program Publicity, Davina Snyder/Assist. - Network Program Publicity, Laura Masse/44/Exec. VP, Nancy Carr/Sr. VP - Media, Jennifer Geisser/VP - Media, William J. Abbott/45/Exec. VP - Advertising Sales/$696,408.00, Charles L. Stanford/61/Exec. VP - Legal, Business Affairs, General Counsel/$510,392.00, Brian C. Stewart/43/CFO, Exec. VP - Finance/$377,723.00, Sheri Goldberg/Sr. Publicist, Network Program Publicity, Sheri Helmers/Sr. Publicist, Network Program Publicity, Andrea Cimini/Photo Mgr. - Network Program Publicity, Sara McFarlane/Photo Technician, Network Program Publicity *(17 Officers included in Index)*

Directors: Henry Schleiff/59/Dir., CEO, Pres., Herbert A. Granath/79/Co - Chmn., Donald J. Hall/52/Co - Chmn., Wilford V. Bane/69/Dir., Glenn Curtis/48/Dir., David E. Hall/45/Dir., Deanne R. Stedem/46/Dir., Anil Jagtiani/47/Dir., Brian E. Gardner/55/Dir., Irvine O. Hockaday/71/Dir., Drue A. Jennings/60/Dir., Peter A. Lund/66/Dir., Fred M. Dressler/66/Dir.

Owners: Liberty Media Corporation, Insiders, Anil Jagtiani, J.P. Morgan Partners (BHCA), L.P., Brian C. Stewart, David E. Hall, Irvine O. Hockaday, Peter A. Lund, Donald J. Hall, J.P. Morgan Partners (BHCA), L.P., Donald J. Hall, David Kenin, Deanne R. Stedem, Hallmark Entertainment Investments Co., Insiders *(22 Owners included in Index)*

Financial Data: *Fiscal Year End:*12/31 *Latest Annual Data:* 12/31/2006

Year	Sales	Net Income
2006	$201,179,000	-$388,972,000
2005	$197,384,000	-$232,758,000
2004	$241,287,000	-$316,806,000

Curr. Assets:	$197,565,000	**Curr. Liab.:**	$149,519,000		
Plant, Equip.:	$16,313,000	**Total Liab.:**	$1,246,727,000	**Indic. Yr. Divd.:**	NA
Total Assets:	$767,783,000	**Net Worth:**	-$478,944,000	**Debt/ Equity:**	NA

Crown Northcorp Inc

PO Box 613, Cheyenne, WY, 82001; ***PH:*** 1-614-488-1169; ***Fax:*** 1-614-488-9780; ***http://*** www.crownnorthcorp.com; ***Email:*** inquiries@crownnorthcorp.com

General - Incorporation: DE
Employees: 210
Auditor: Schoonover Boyer
Stk Agt: Registrar & Transfer Co
Counsel: Stephen W. Brown
DUNS No.: 62-049-5705

Stock- Price on:12/24/2007: $0.0001
Stock Exchange: OTC
Ticker Symbol: ASET
Outstanding Shares: 29,280,000
E.P.S: -$0.098
Shareholders: NA

Business: The group's principal activity is to provide mortgage banking, financial advisory services, third-party asset management and loan servicing. The group manages commercial and multifamily real estate and loan assets; services individual loans, loan portfolios and assets in securitized transactions; performs risk management services and administers various corporate, partnership and trust interests. The customers of the group include the holders of interests in commercial and multi-family real estate. The group solely operates in the United States of America. On 31-Dec-2003, the group acquired royal investments corp.

Primary SIC and add'l.: 6162 6531

CIK No: 0000915338

Subsidiaries: Crown European Holding Limited

Officers: Ronald E. Roark/Dir., CEO, Clarence Dixon/MD - Crown Mortgage Management Gmbh, Germany, Head - Business Development in Europe, Julien Holmes/Co - MD, Hakan Larsson/MD - Crown Asset Management AB, Sweden, Rick Lewis/CFO, Robyn C. Stern/Exec. VP, Corp. Sec., Member - Supervisory Board - Crown Westfalen Bank , Joachim Paulus/Dir. - Crown Westfalen Bank, Christian Von Villiez/Dir. - Crown Westfalen Bank, Lena Ellertsson Freedman/Communications Advisor, Thomas Vail/41/MD - Crown Westfalen Credit Services, Luther Ziller/62/MD - Crown Westfalen Credit Services

Directors: Ronald E. Roark/Dir., CEO, Stefan Lennhammer/Chmn., Roy Owen/Dir., John Harrison/Dir., Grace Jenkins/Dir., Jack Koczela/Dir., Peter Walker/Dir., Gordon V. Smith/Dir.

Owners: Stephen W. Brown, Peter Walker/1.10%, Insiders/61.00%, David K. Conrad/2.30%, Grace Jenkins/2.00%, Rick Lewis, Gordon V. Smith/14.40%, John S. Koczela, Ronald E. Roark/41.10%

Financial Data: *Fiscal Year End:*12/31 *Latest Annual Data:* 12/31/2006

Year	Sales	Net Income
2006	$24,223,000	-$410,000
2005	$11,216,000	-$2,164,000
2004	$10,376,000	$975,000

Curr. Assets:	$71,654,000	**Curr. Liab.:**	$34,150,000		
Plant, Equip.:	$2,362,000	**Total Liab.:**	$97,526,000	**Indic. Yr. Divd.:**	NA
Total Assets:	$110,221,000	**Net Worth:**	$12,694,000	**Debt/ Equity:**	6.0107

Crown Partners Inc

7750 Paragoan Rd., Dayton, OH, 45459; ***PH:*** 1-937-723-2300; ***Fax:*** 1-937-439-7949; ***http://*** www.crownpartners.com; ***Email:*** info@crownpartners.com

General - Incorporation: NV
Employees: NA
Auditor: LBB & Assoc. Ltd., LLP
Stk Agt: Corporate Stock Transfer, Inc.
Counsel: NA
DUNS No.: NA

Stock- Price on:12/24/2007: $0.045
Stock Exchange: OTC
Ticker Symbol: CRWP
Outstanding Shares: 23,590,000
E.P.S: -$0.051
Shareholders: NA

Business: The groups principal activity is to provide software and services for content-enabled applications. The group operates from the United States.

Primary SIC and add'l.: 6799

CIK No: 0000811036

Subsidiaries: Micro Bio-Medical Waste Systems, Sanitec Services of Hawaii, Inc., Universal Services & Acquisitions, Inc

Officers: Claudia Zaman/Dir., CEO, CFO, Rick MacArtney/Dir. - Stategic Services, Richard Hearn/Co - Founder, MD, Mark Kennedy/Co - Founder, Dir. Sales - Marketing, Elaine Price/Partner, Dir. Stategic Marketing - Channels, Barry Besecker/Partner, Dir. Emerging Marketing Products, John Garvin/Partner, Dir. Professional Services, Malcolm Bliss/Partner, Dir. Software

Directors: Claudia Zaman/Dir., CEO, CFO, Richard Hearn/Co - Founder, MD, Mark Kennedy/Co - Founder, Dir. Sales - Marketing, Elaine Price/Partner, Dir. Stategic Marketing - Channels, Barry Besecker/Partner, Dir. Emerging Marketing Products, John Garvin/Partner, Dir. Professional Services, Malcolm Bliss/Partner, Dir. Software, Sadegh Salmassi/Dir., Steven Onoue/Dir.

Owners: Cede & Co/35.56%, Tisa Capital Corp./24.04%, Sadegh Salmassi, Zaman & Company/5.30%, Claudia Zaman/8.93%, Insiders/18.13%, Steven Onoue/9.17%, Phoenix Consulting Services/15.83%

Financial Data: *Fiscal Year End:*12/31 *Latest Annual Data:* 12/31/2006

Year	Sales	Net Income
2006	NA	-$1,033,000
2005	$51,000	$241,000
2004	$85,000	-$3,811,000

Curr. Assets:	$468,000	**Curr. Liab.:**	$421,000		
Plant, Equip.:	NA	**Total Liab.:**	$421,000	**Indic. Yr. Divd.:**	NA
Total Assets:	$468,000	**Net Worth:**	$46,000	**Debt/ Equity:**	NA

Crucell

Archimedesweg 4, Leiden; ; ***http://*** www.crucell.com; ***Email:*** info@crucell.com

General - Incorporation: Netherlands
Employees: NA
Auditor: Ernst & Young Accountants
Stk Agt: NA
Counsel: NA
DUNS No.: NA

Stock- Price on:12/24/2007: $21.88
Stock Exchange: NDQ
Ticker Symbol: CRXL
Outstanding Shares: 64,910,000
E.P.S: -$1.53
Shareholders: NA

Business: The group's principal activity is to develop and produce biopharmaceuticals for the prevention and treatment of infectious diseases.

Primary SIC and add'l.: 8071

CIK No: 0001126136

Subsidiaries: Chromagenics B.V., Crucell Holland B.V., U-Bisys B.V.

Officers: Ronald Brus/45/CEO, Pres., Rene Beukema/44/General Counsel, Corp. Sec., Leonard Kruimer/50/CFO, Bjorn Sjostrand/Head - Vaccines Business Unit, Oya Yavuz/Dir. - Investor Relations, Frauke Groenevelt/Coordinator Investor Relations, Jaap Goudsmit/57/Chief Scientific Officer, Arthur Lahr/Chief Strategy Officer, Exec. VP - Sales - Business Development, Kuno Sommer/52/Chief Business Officer, Simon Rothen/46/COO

Directors: Jan Pieter Oosterveld/Chmn. - Supervisory Board, Phillip M. Satow/67/Member - Supervisory Board, Sean P. Lance/61/Member - Supervisory Board, Claes E. Wilhelmsson/69/Member - Medical Scientific Advisory Board, Arnold Hoevenaars/59/Member - Supervisory Board, Dominik S. Koechlin/49/Member - Supervisory Board

Owners: A. van Herk B.V./11.80%, Global Opportunities (GO) Capital Asset Management B.V./8.00%, Insiders/0.65%, Aviva plc/5.90%

Financial Data: *Fiscal Year End:*12/31 *Latest Annual Data:* 12/31/2006

Year	Sales	Net Income
2006	$173,708,000	-$182,736,000
2005	$44,497,000	-$18,388,000
2004	$30,865,000	-$29,104,000

Curr. Assets:	$418,629,000	**Curr. Liab.:**	$119,160,000	**P/E Ratio:**	14.48
Plant, Equip.:	$115,442,000	**Total Liab.:**	$205,855,000	**Indic. Yr. Divd.:**	NA
Total Assets:	$830,952,000	**Net Worth:**	$625,097,000	**Debt/ Equity:**	NA

Crum & Forster Holdings Corp

305 Madison Ave., Morristown, NJ, 07962; ***PH:*** 1-973-490-6600; ***Fax:*** 1-973-490-6940; ***http://*** www.cfins.com; ***Email:*** information@cfins.com

General - Incorporation	DE	**Stock**- Price on:12/24/2007	$198.17
Employees	8,258	Stock Exchange	NA
Auditor	PricewaterhouseCoopers LLP	Ticker Symbol	NA
Stk Agt	Bank of New York	Outstanding Shares	17,730,000
Counsel	NA	E.P.S.	$6.91
DUNS No.	NA	Shareholders	NA

Business: The group's principle activity is to provide commercial property and casualty insurance services. The groups insurance industrial areas include workers compensation, property, general liability, commercial automobile, commercial multi-peril and other lines of business. The group operates from United States.

Primary SIC and add'l.: NA

CIK No: 0001168338

Subsidiaries: Crum & Forster Holding Inc., Crum & Forster Indemnity Company, Crum & Forster Specialty Insurance Company, Crum and Forster Insurance Company, Seneca Insurance Company, Inc., Seneca Specialty Insurance Company, The North River Insurance Company, United States Fire Insurance Company

Officers: Nikolas Antonopoulos/CEO, Pres., Carl W. Berntsen/Sr. VP - Specialty Brokerage, E, S Casualty, John J. French/Sr. VP - Property, Donald R. Fischer/Sr. VP - Management Protection, Maurizia Reeser/Marketing Contact - New Jersey, Don Osuna/Marketing Contact - Alaska, Michelle Tripp/Marketing Contact - Arkansas, Anne Bordwell/Marketing Contact - Arizona, Mary Jane Robertson/Exec. VP, CFO, Treasurer, Kim E. Piersol/Sr. VP - Actuarial, Joseph F. Braunstein/Pres., Christopher J. Barr/VP - Crime, Financial Institutions, Robert H. Dowe/VP - Special Accounting, Robert G. Himmer/Sr. VP - Primary Casualty, Eugene E. Pittelli/VP - Loss Control *(33 Officers included in Index)*

Directors: Prem V. Watsa/57/Chmn., Paul Murray/76/Dir., Frank B. Bennett/51/Dir., Anthony F. Griffiths/77/Dir.

Financial Data: *Fiscal Year End:*12/31 *Latest Annual Data:* 12/31/2006

Year	Sales	Net Income
2006	$6,803,700,000	$654,400,000
2005	$5,900,500,000	-$313,400,000
2004	$5,792,600,000	$8,100,000

Curr. Assets:	$4,602,700,000	**Curr. Liab.:**	$2,133,200,000		
Plant, Equip.:	NA	**Total Liab.:**	$22,559,300,000	**Indic. Yr. Divd.:**	$2.750
Total Assets:	$26,776,000,000	**Net Worth:**	$2,744,600,000	**Debt/ Equity:**	NA

Cruzan International' Inc

222 Lakeview Ave., Esperante Ste. 1500, West Palm Beach, FL, 33401; ***PH:*** 1-561-655-8977; ***http://*** www.todhunter.com

General - Incorporation	DE	**Stock**- Price on:12/24/2007	NA
Employees	NA	Stock Exchange	NA
Auditor	McGladrey & Pullen LLP	Ticker Symbol	NA
Stk Agt	Southtrust Bank	Outstanding Shares	NA
Counsel	NA	E.P.S.	NA
DUNS No.	05-614-0122	Shareholders	NA

Business: The group's principal activities are to produce and supply brandy, rum, wine and spirits to other beverage alcohol manufacturers. In addition, the group produces, imports and markets premium branded spirits and bottles beverage alcohol and other beverages on a contract basis and under its own labels. Further, it produces vinegar and cooking wine. The group operates through four production facilities in the United States and one in st. Croix, United States virgin islands. The group purchases distilled products for resale, including grain alcohol, which is denatured, packaged and sold as industrial alcohol to hospitals, universities, fragrance producers and other manufacturers.

Primary SIC and add'l.: 9999 2085 2099 2084 5182

CIK No: 0000098544

Subsidiaries: ASCI, and Cruzan Acquisition, Inc, The Absolut Spirits Company, Inc, Virgin Islands

Cryo-Cell International

700 Brooker Creek Blvd., Ste. 1800, Oldsmar, FL, 34677; ***PH:*** 1-813-749-2100; ***Fax:*** 1-813-855-4745; ***http://*** www.cryo-cell.com

General - Incorporation	DE	**Stock**- Price on:12/24/2007	$2.25
Employees	60	Stock Exchange	OTC
Auditor	Grant Thornton LLP	Ticker Symbol	CCEL
Stk Agt	Continental Stock Transfer & Trust Co	Outstanding Shares	11,670,000
Counsel	Mark Richard	E.P.S.	-$0.36
DUNS No.	62-613-2575	Shareholders	NA

Business: The group's principal activities are providing storage for cryogenic cells and designing and developing cellular storage devices used for storage programs. The group preserves newborn babies' cord blood (u-cord) stem cell at the company's state-of-the-art laboratory in clearwater, Florida. The group markets its preservation services to expectant parents and distributes information to obstetricians, pediatricians, lamaze instructors and other childbirth educators, certified nurse-midwifes and other related healthcare professionals. On 29-Jan-2004, the group discontinued stem cell preservation technologies inc

Primary SIC and add'l.: 3841

CIK No: 0000862692

Subsidiaries: CCEL Bio-Therapies, Inc, CCEL Immune System Technologies, Inc, CCEL Immune Technologies, Inc, Safti-Cell, Inc., Saneron CCEL Therapeutics, Inc., Stem Cell Preservation Technologies, Inc, Stem Cell Preservation, Inc., Tumor Tissue Technology, Inc

Officers: Mercedes Walton/Chmn., CEO, Bruce M. Zafran/Member - Medical Scientific Advisory Board, Rob Doll/VP - Corporate Marketing, Sales, Services, Alphonso V. Everett/Dir. - Quality Assurance, Regulatory Affairs, Julie G. Allickson/Member - Medical & Scientific Advisory Board, VP - Laboratory Operations, R & D, Gerald F. Maass/54/Exec. VP, Buff Mair/Dir. - Medical, Jill M. Taymans/CFO, VP - Finance

Directors: Mercedes Walton/Chmn., CEO, Stephen J. Noga/Chmn. - Medical Scientific Advisory Board, Michael Boeckh/Member - Medical Scientific Advisory Board, Anthony P. Finch/Dir., Gaby W. Goubran/Dir., Scott Christian/Dir., Julie G. Allickson/Member - Medical & Scientific Advisory Board, VP - Laboratory Operations, R & D, Jagdish Sheth/Dir., Gerald Elfenbein/Member - Medical Scientific Advisory Board, Richard Kahn/Member - Medical Scientific Advisory Board, Naynesh Kamani/Member - Medical Scientific Advisory Board, Merri Buff Mair/Member - Medical Scientific Advisory Board

Owners: Insiders/16.14%, Scott Christian, Andrew J. Filipowski/5.75%, Lewis Asset Management/7.09%, Portnoy Group/13.26%, Anthony Finch, Mercedes Walton/6.93%, Jagdish Sheth, Gerald F. Maass, Gaby Goubran, Julie G. Allickson, Jill M. Taymans

Financial Data: *Fiscal Year End:*11/30 *Latest Annual Data:* 11/30/2006

Year	Sales	Net Income
2006	$17,180,000	-$2,811,000
2005	$14,451,000	$1,033,000
2004	$12,210,000	$2,840,000

Curr. Assets:	$10,512,000	**Curr. Liab.:**	$6,506,000		
Plant, Equip.:	$3,189,000	**Total Liab.:**	$16,733,000	**Indic. Yr. Divd.:**	NA
Total Assets:	$14,640,000	**Net Worth:**	-$2,092,000	**Debt/ Equity:**	NA

CryoCor Inc

9717 Pacific Hts. Blvd., San Diego, CA, 92121; ***PH:*** 1-858-909-2200; ***Fax:*** 1-858-909-2300; ***http://*** www.cryocor.com

General - Incorporation	DE	**Stock**- Price on:12/24/2007	$4.39
Employees	36	Stock Exchange	NDQ
Auditor	Ernst& Young LLP	Ticker Symbol	CRYO
Stk Agt	American Stock Transfer & Trust Co.	Outstanding Shares	12,120,000
Counsel	NA	E.P.S.	-$1.32
DUNS No.	NA	Shareholders	NA

Business: The groups principal activities include developing and manufacturing a minimally invasive system. The groups services include Medicare and Medicaid. The products of the group include cryoablation system and sterile. The group products sold under the trade name CryoCor. The group operates from the United States, the United Kingdom and Italy and Canada. The sale of the group for the year 2006 was $540 (thousands).

Primary SIC and add'l.: 3841

CIK No: 0001125294

Subsidiaries: CryoCor GmbH

Officers: Edward F. Brennan/Dir., CEO, Pres./$1,226,916.00, Gregory J. Tibbitts/CFO, VP - Finance/$368,132.00, Helen S. Barold/Chief Medical Officer/$106,128.00, Mark Adams/VP - Sales, Marketing

Directors: Edward F. Brennan/Dir., CEO, Pres., Kurt C. Wheeler/Chmn., Arda M. Minocherhomjee/Dir., Jerry C. Griffin/Dir., Mark J. Hattendorf/Dir., Hung Fat Tse/Member - Advisory Board, Robert Adelman/45/Dir., David Cooney/Dir., John A. Camm/Member - Scientific Advisory Board, Gregory K. Feld/Member - Scientific Advisory Board, Andrew A. Gage/Member - Scientific Advisory Board, Helmut U. Klein/Member - Scientific Advisory Board, Albert L. Waldo/Member - Advisory Board, Hein J.J. Wellens/Member - Advisory Board, Christoph Geller/Member - European Advisory Board *(20 Directors included in Index)*

Owners: Healthcare Equity QP Partners, L.P, Arda M. Minocherhomjee, Kurt C. Wheeler, Edward F. Brennan, Insiders, David J. Cooney, Robert Adelman, OrbiMed Associates, LLC, Gregory J. Tibbitts, Helen S. Barold, William Blair Capital Partners VII, QP, Gregory M. Ayers, Jerry C. Griffin, MPM Capital LLC, Mark J. Hattendorf

Financial Data: *Fiscal Year End:*12/31 *Latest Annual Data:* 12/31/2006

Year	Sales	Net Income
2006	$540,000	-$15,052,000
2005	$843,000	-$17,096,000
2004	$493,000	-$15,766,000

Curr. Assets:	$20,435,000	**Curr. Liab.:**	$9,520,000		
Plant, Equip.:	$610,000	**Total Liab.:**	$9,520,000	**Indic. Yr. Divd.:**	NA
Total Assets:	$21,342,000	**Net Worth:**	$11,822,000	**Debt/ Equity:**	NA

CryoLife Inc

1655 Roberts Blvd. NW, Kennesaw, GA, 30144; ***PH:*** 1-770-419-3355; ***Fax:*** 1-770-426-0031; ***http://*** www.cryolife.com; ***Email:*** info@cryolife.com

General - Incorporation	FL	**Stock**- Price on:12/24/2007	$13.62
Employees	388	Stock Exchange	NYSE
Auditor	Deloitte & Touche LLP	Ticker Symbol	CRY
Stk Agt	American Stock Transfer & Trust Co.	Outstanding Shares	25,110,000
Counsel	Arnall Golden Gregory	E.P.S.	$0.15
DUNS No.	11-925-3177	Shareholders	NA

Business: The group's principle activities are preservation of human tissues for cardiovascular, vascular and orthopaedic transplant applications. The group operates in two segments namely human tissue preservation services and implantable medical devices. Human tissue preservation services include preservation of cardiovascular, vascular and orthopaedic human tissue. Implantable medical devices segment includes product sales of bioglue surgical adhesive and bioprosthetic devices, including stentless

porcine heart valves, synergraft treated porcine heart valves and synergraft treated bovine vascular grafts. The group's human tissue cryopreservation services are marketed in North America, Europe, the Middle East, Canada, South America, Australia, and Asia. The group's quarterly revenue for September 2007 was 22.16 millions of USD.

Primary SIC and add'l.: 3842 3841 8099 8731

CIK No: 0000784199

Subsidiaries: AuraZyme Pharmaceuticals, Inc., CryoLife Acquisition Corp., CryoLife Europa, LTD., CryoLife International, Inc., CryoLife Technology, Inc.

Officers: Steven G. Anderson/Chmn., CEO, Pres./$1,718,478.00, Gerald B. Seery/Sr. VP - Sales, Marketing/$532,998.00, Suzanne K. Gabbert/Sec., Albert E. Heacox/Sr. VP - Research, Development/$488,898.00, Scott B. Capps/Corporate Officers, David M. Fronk/VP - Regulatory Affairs, Quality Assurance/$425,265.00, Amy D. Horton/Chief Accounting Officer, David Ashley Lee/Exec. VP, CFO, COO/$826,495.00, Philip A. Theodore/VP, General Counsel

Directors: Steven G. Anderson/Chmn., CEO, Pres., Ronald D. McCall/Dir., Thomas F. Ackerman/Dir., John M. Cook/Dir., Ronald C. Elkins/Dir., Daniel J. Bevevino/Dir., James S. Benson/Dir.

Owners: O.S.S. Capital Management, L.P./8.00%, Albert E. Heacox, David Ashley Lee, Gerald B. Seery, Bruce J. Van Dyne, David M. Fronk, Insiders/13.10%, Steven G. Anderson/7.00%, Virginia C. Lacy/2.10%

Financial Data: Fiscal Year End:12/31 Latest Annual Data: 12/31/2006

Year	Sales	Net Income
2006	$81,311,000	$365,000
2005	$69,282,000	-$19,535,000
2004	$62,384,000	-$18,749,000

Curr. Assets:	$49,385,000	**Curr. Liab.:**	$22,913,000	**P/E Ratio:**	90.80
Plant, Equip.:	$21,390,000	**Total Liab.:**	$27,777,000	**Indic. Yr. Divd.:**	NA
Total Assets:	$79,865,000	**Net Worth:**	$52,088,000	**Debt/ Equity:**	0.0021

Cryptologic Ltd

Formerly: CryptoLogic Inc
55 St. Clair Ave. W, 3rd Fl., Toronto, ON, M4V 2Y7; **PH:** 1-416-545-1455; http:// www.cryptologic.com

General - Incorporation	ON	**Stock** - Price on:12/24/2007	$25.02
Employees	400	Stock Exchange	NDQ
Auditor	KPMG LLP	Ticker Symbol	CRYP
Stk Agt	Equity Transfer Services Inc	Outstanding Shares	13,900,000
Counsel	Stikeman, Graham, Keeley & Spiegel	E.P.S.	$0.22
DUNS No.	NA	Shareholders	NA

Business: The group's principle activity is to provide software development and support services for electronic commerce and online gaming, proprietary commerce-enabling technology, permitting secure, reliable, high-speed, private financial transactions over the Internet. The group operates from United States.

Primary SIC and add'l.: 7371 7379

CIK No: 0001094036

Subsidiaries: Ads Dot Com Limited, ECash Direct Limited, WagerLogic

Officers: Lewis N. Rose/Dir., CEO, Pres., Justin Thouin/VP - Casino Software Development, Marilyn Shabot/Dir., VP - Human Resources, Michael Starzynski/CTO, Stephen Taylor/Dir., CFO, Andy Goetsch/VP - Poker Software Development

Directors: Lewis N. Rose/Dir., CEO, Pres., Robert Stikeman/Chmn., Stephen Freedhoff/Dir., Stephen Taylor/Dir., CFO, Thomas Byrne/Dir., Marilyn Shabot/Dir., VP - Human Resources, Randall Abramson/Dir., Nigel Simon/Dir., Brian Hadfield/Dir., Yap Wai Ming/Dir.

Owners: Pabrai Investment Fund IV, L.P./2.40%, Mohnish Pabrai/6.00%, The Pabrai Investment Fund II, L.P./2.20%, Pabrai Investment Fund 3, Ltd./1.10%, Harina Kapoor, Dalal Street, LLC

Financial Data: Fiscal Year End:12/31 Latest Annual Data: 12/31/2006

Year	Sales	Net Income
2006	$104,022,000	$25,636,000
2005	$86,307,000	$20,530,000
2004	$63,714,000	$13,668,000

Curr. Assets:	$143,718,000	**Curr. Liab.:**	$49,931,000		
Plant, Equip.:	$18,106,000	**Total Liab.:**	$72,936,000	**Indic. Yr. Divd.:**	$0.480
Total Assets:	$184,520,000	**Net Worth:**	$111,584,000	**Debt/ Equity:**	NA

Crystal International Travel Group Inc

Formerly: Mobile Reach International Inc
641 Shunpike Rd., Ste. 333, Chatham, NJ, 07928; **PH:** 1-973-210-4966

General - Incorporation	DE	**Stock** - Price on:12/24/2007	$0.0212
Employees	NA	Stock Exchange	OTC
Auditor	Scharf Pera & Co	Ticker Symbol	CINT
Stk Agt	NA	Outstanding Shares	NA
Counsel	NA	E.P.S.	NA
DUNS No.	NA	Shareholders	NA

Business: The group develops and sells mobile technology and services for information systems and communications networks. The group sells its software products and services to clients who desire to increase the efficiency by which their employees access, utilize and exchange data using mobile networks. The product and services of the company were based on the enterprise platforms, called remedy, a service management solution.

Primary SIC and add'l.: 7373

CIK No: 0001069322

Officers: Peter Dugan/54/Dir., CEO, Pres., Peter D. Gallic/42/Dir., CFO, Fabrizzio Busso-Campana/42/Dir., COO

Directors: Peter Dugan/54/Dir., CEO, Pres., Peter D. Gallic/42/Dir., CFO, Hank Cohn/39/Dir., Frank Salerno/49/Dir., Anthony Soich/48/Dir., Fabrizzio Busso-Campana/42/Dir., COO

Owners: Frank Salerno/1.04%, Peter Gallic/4.63%, Insiders/26.33%, Fabrizzio Busso Campana/7.61%, Peter Dugan/7.19%, Crystal Capital Partners Corporation/5.85%

Financial Data: Fiscal Year End:07/31 Latest Annual Data: 7/31/2006

Year	Sales	Net Income
2006	$7,000	-$11,027,000
2005	$607,000	-$971,000
2004	$1,590,000	-$3,143,000

Curr. Assets:	$167,000	**Curr. Liab.:**	$2,718,000		
Plant, Equip.:	$16,000	**Total Liab.:**	$9,129,000	**Indic. Yr. Divd.:**	NA
Total Assets:	$183,000	**Net Worth:**	-$8,946,000	**Debt/ Equity:**	NA

Crystal River Capital Inc

3 World Financial Ctr., 200 Vesey St., 10th Fl., New York, NY, 10281; **PH:** 1-212-549-8400; **Fax:** 1-212-549-8304; http:// www.crystalriverreit.com

General - Incorporation	MD	**Stock** - Price on:12/24/2007	$27.58
Employees	NA	Stock Exchange	NYSE
Auditor	Ernst & Young LLP	Ticker Symbol	CRZ
Stk Agt	American Stock Transfer & Trust Co.	Outstanding Shares	25,000,000
Counsel	NA	E.P.S.	-$3.25
DUNS No.	NA	Shareholders	NA

Business: The groups principle activity is to invest in real estates-related securities, real estate loans and instruments and various other asset classes. The group operates from the United States. The groups quarterly revenue for September 2007 was 64.67 millions of USD.

Primary SIC and add'l.: 6798

CIK No: 0001344705

Subsidiaries: CRC Spv1, LLC, CRC Spv2, LLC, CRC Spv3, LLC, Crystal River Capital TRS Holdings, Inc., Crystal River CDO 2005-1 LLC, Crystal River CDO 2005-1, Ltd., Crystal River Preferred TrustI, Crystal River Resecuritization 2006-1 LLC, Crystal River Resecuritization 2006-1 Ltd., CRZ ABCP Financing LLC, CRZ Houston I GP LLC, CRZ Houston I LP, CRZ Phoenix I LLC

Officers: Clifford Lai/Dir., CEO, Marion Hayes/Contact - Investor Relations, Craig Laurie/CFO, Treasurer, Jon Tyras/VP, General Counsel, Sec.

Directors: Clifford Lai/Dir., CEO, Bruce Robertson/Chmn., Rodman Drake/Dir., Janet Graham/Dir., Harald Hansen/Dir., William Paulsen/Dir., Louis Salvatore/Dir.

Owners: Rodman Drake, Insiders, Louis Salvatore, Entities Affiliated with Neuberger Berman Inc./12.30%, Clifford Lai, Entities Affiliated with Deutsche Bank AG/5.30%, Janet Graham, Entities Affiliated with Brookfield Asset Management Inc./7.20%, Harald Hansen, Entities Affiliated with Leon G. Cooperman/6.00%, DePrince, Race & Zollo, Inc./5.10%, William Paulsen, Bruce Robertson, Dreman Value Management, LLC/5.60%, Barry Sunshine

Financial Data: Fiscal Year End:12/31 Latest Annual Data: 12/31/2006

Year	Sales	Net Income
2006	$201,224,000	$46,917,000

Curr. Assets:	$146,649,000	**Curr. Liab.:**	$3,012,787,000		
Plant, Equip.:	NA	**Total Liab.:**	$3,218,331,000	**Indic. Yr. Divd.:**	$2.720
Total Assets:	$3,774,645,000	**Net Worth:**	$556,314,000	**Debt/ Equity:**	1.5053

Crystalix Group International Inc

1181 Grier Dr., Ste. B, Las Vegas, NV, 89119; **PH:** 1-702-740-4616; http:// www.crystalixusa.com

General - Incorporation	NV	**Stock** - Price on:12/24/2007	$0.29
Employees	64	Stock Exchange	OTC
Auditor	Dejoya Griffith & Co LLC	Ticker Symbol	SEAI
Stk Agt	Interwest Transfer Company, Inc.	Outstanding Shares	8,020,000
Counsel	NA	E.P.S.	-$1.26
DUNS No.	NA	Shareholders	NA

Business: The group's principle activity is to provide direct Internet merchandising of American-themed collectibles, gifts and memorabilia. The group operates from United States.

Primary SIC and add'l.: 7375

CIK No: 0001091356

Subsidiaries: Crystalix Imaging, Ltd, Laser Design International, Lazer-Tek Designs

Officers: Kevin T. Ryan/57/Dir., CEO, Doug Lee/43/Pres., Patty Hill/49/Corp. Sec., VP - Finance, Administration, Interim CFO, Controller

Directors: Kevin T. Ryan/57/Dir., CEO, John S. Woodward/Dir., Robert McDermott/62/Dir., Rainer Eissing/Dir., Zvi Dinstein/81/Dir.

Owners: Zvi Dinstein/16.90%, Kevin T. Ryan/49.00%, Michael D. William, Trustee/9.20%, Insiders/63.40%, Patty Hill/0.90%, Robert McDermott/0.70%, Doug E. Lee/5.40%, John S. Woodward/15.20%

Financial Data: Fiscal Year End:12/31 Latest Annual Data: 12/31/2006

Year	Sales	Net Income
2006	$4,272,000	-$9,875,000
2005	$3,619,000	-$5,691,000
2004	$4,629,000	-$8,303,000

Curr. Assets:	$1,816,000	**Curr. Liab.:**	$4,601,000		
Plant, Equip.:	$1,125,000	**Total Liab.:**	$4,601,000	**Indic. Yr. Divd.:**	NA
Total Assets:	$6,993,000	**Net Worth:**	$2,392,000	**Debt/ Equity:**	NA

Crystallex International Corp

18 King St. E, Ste. 1210, Toronto, ON, M5C 1C4; **PH:** 1-416-203-2448; http:// www.crystallex.com; **Email:** info@crystallex.com

General - Incorporation	Canada	**Stock** - Price on:12/24/2007	$4.43
Employees	177	Stock Exchange	AMEX
Auditor	Deloitte & Touche LLP	Ticker Symbol	KRY
Stk Agt	Mellon Trust Co	Outstanding Shares	246,410,000
Counsel	Gomez Cottin & Tejera	E.P.S.	-$0.19
DUNS No.	25-218-5566	Shareholders	NA

Business: The group's principal activities are to produce gold and explore properties in uruguay, venezuela, Brazil and Canada. The group is in the business of acquiring and developing mineral properties.

Primary SIC and add'l.: 1041

CIK No: 0000912500

Officers: Gordon Thompson/Dir., CEO, Pres., Andrea Boltz/Mgr. - Investor Relations, Hemdat Sawh/CFO, William Faust/COO, Sr. VP, Richard Spencer/VP - Exploration, Richard Marshall/VP - Investor Relations, Sadek El-Alfy/VP - Operations, Robert Crombie/Sr. VP - Corporate Development

Directors: Gordon Thompson/Dir., CEO, Pres., Robert A. Fung/Chmn., William C. Longden/Dir., Johan Van't Hof/Dir., Armando F. Zullo/Dir., Michael Brown/Dir., Marc J. Oppenheimer/Dir., Harry J. Near/Dir.

Financial Data: Fiscal Year End:12/31 Latest Annual Data: 12/31/2006

Year	Sales	Net Income
2006	$28,088,000	-$44,498,000
2005	$24,990,000	-$46,937,000
2004	$20,246,000	-$55,481,000

Curr. Assets:	$38,692,000	**Curr. Liab.:**	$16,203,000	**P/E Ratio:**	21.78
Plant, Equip.:	$180,729,000	**Total Liab.:**	$101,700,000	**Indic. Yr. Divd.:**	NA
Total Assets:	$222,017,000	**Net Worth:**	$120,317,000	**Debt/ Equity:**	0.7286

CSB Bancorp Inc

91 N Clay St., Millersburg, OH, 44654; *PH:* 1-330-674-9015; *Fax:* 1-330-674-6994; *http://* www.csb1.com

General - Incorporation .... OH
Employees 112
Auditor .... S. R. Snodgrass, A.C.
Stk Agt .... Registrar & Transfer Co
Counsel .... Bricker & Eckler LLP
DUNS No. 01-976-8795

Stock- Price on:12/24/2007 .... $17.6
Stock Exchange .... OTC
Ticker Symbol .... CSBB
Outstanding Shares 2,460,000
E.P.S. $1.38
Shareholders .... NA

Business: The group's principal activity is to provide retail and commercial banking services in the state of Ohio. It is a holding company for the commercial and savings bank. It accepts checking and savings accounts and time deposits and offers personal loans, commercial loans, real estate mortgage loans and installment loans. Construction loans are secured by residential and business real estate that generally will be occupied by the borrower on completion. The commercial and savings bank is a member of the federal reserve system and its deposits are insured by the federal deposit insurance corporation. The other services offered are iras, safe deposit facilities, night depository facilities and trust services. The group provides financial services through its main office and eight branches located in millersburg, Ohio and nearby communities.

Primary SIC and add'l.: 6712 6022

CIK No: 0000880417

Subsidiaries: CSB Investment Services, LLC, The Commercial and Savings Bank

Officers: Eddie L. Steiner/CEO, Pres./$115,575.00, Paul D. Greig/62/Sr. VP, Chief Operations, Information Officer/$125,319.00, Rick L. Ginther/57/Dir., Sr. VP, Pres./$167,875.00, Paula J. Meiler/53/CFO, Sr. VP/$118,937.00

Directors: John R. Waltman/Chmn., Daniel J. Miller/68/Dir., Samuel M. Steimel/50/Dir., Thomas J. Lang/64/Dir., Robert K. Baker/53/Dir., Rick L. Ginther/57/Dir., Sr. VP, Pres., Ronald E. Holtman/65/Dir., Jeffery A. Robb/58/Dir.

Owners: Paul D. Greig, John J. Limbert, John R. Waltman, Samuel M. Steimel/1.00%, Robert K. Baker, Insiders/5.87%, Jeffery A. Robb, Paula J. Meiler, Eddie L. Steiner, Daniel J. Miller/1.58%, Richard G. Elliott/5.02%, Rick L. Ginther, Ronald E. Holtman, Thomas J. Lang

Financial Data: *Fiscal Year End:*12/31 *Latest Annual Data:* 12/31/2006

Year	Sales	Net Income
2006	$22,719,000	$3,110,000
2005	$19,938,000	$2,873,000
2004	$17,754,000	$2,526,000

Curr. Assets:	$19,784,000	**Curr. Liab.:**	$289,670,000	**P/E Ratio:**	12.75
Plant, Equip.:	$7,390,000	**Total Liab.:**	$292,169,000	**Indic. Yr. Divd.:**	$0.720
Total Assets:	$327,240,000	**Net Worth:**	$35,070,000	**Debt/ Equity:**	0.0712

CSC Holdings Inc

Formerly: CSC Holdings Inc
1111 Stewart Ave., Bethpage, NY, 11714; *PH:* 1-516-803-2300; *http://* www.cablevision.com

General - Incorporation .... DE
Employees 13,938
Auditor .... KPMG LLP
Stk Agt .... Mellon Investor Services LLC
Counsel .... Willkie Farr & Gallagher LLP
DUNS No. 13-088-4570

Stock- Price on:12/24/2007 .... $35.74
Stock Exchange .... NA
Ticker Symbol .... NA
Outstanding Shares 293,230,000
E.P.S. $0.72
Shareholders .... NA

Business: The group's principal activities are to operate in four segments. Telecommunication services consists principally of cable television, telephone and modem services operations. Rainbow media group consists principally of interests in national and regional cable television programming networks. Madison square garden, which owns and operates professional sports teams, regional cable television networks, live productions and entertainment venues. Retail electronics, which represents the operations of cablevision electronics' retail electronics stores. The group is the wholly owned subsidiary of cablevision systems corporation. The group operates solely in the United States.

Primary SIC and add'l.: 4841

CIK No: 0000784681

Subsidiaries: 1015 Tiffany Street, Corp., 1047 E 46th Street Corp., 1070 Jericho Turnpike Corp., 11 Penn Tv, LLC, 111 New South Road Corporation, 1111 Stewart Corporation, 1144 Route 109 Corp., 151 S. Fulton Street Corporation, 2234 Fulton Street Corporation, 389 Adams Street Corporation, A-r Cable Services - Ny, Inc., Amc Film Holdings LLC, Amc Movie Companion LLC, Amc New Media LLC, Amc Productions, Inc. 261 Subsidiaries included in the Index

Owners: Mary S. Dolan, GAMCO Investors, Inc./8.50%, Insiders, Insiders/2.80%, Patrick F. Dolan, Thomas V. Reifenheiser, Helen A. Dolan, Richard H. Hochman, Brian G. Sweeney, David M. Dolan, Charles F. Dolan, Frank J. Biondi, John R. Ryan, Mary S. Dolan, Kathleen M. Dolan *(42 Owners included in Index)*

Financial Data: *Fiscal Year End:*12/31 *Latest Annual Data:* 12/31/2006

Year	Sales	Net Income
2006	$5,927,462,000	-$126,465,000
2005	$5,175,911,000	$89,320,000
2004	$4,932,864,000	-$676,092,000

Curr. Assets:	$1,667,447,000	**Curr. Liab.:**	$2,430,698,000	**P/E Ratio:**	49.64
Plant, Equip.:	$3,714,842,000	**Total Liab.:**	$15,134,440,000	**Indic. Yr. Divd.:**	NA
Total Assets:	$9,844,857,000	**Net Worth:**	-$5,339,253,000	**Debt/ Equity:**	NA

CSG Systems International Inc

9555 Maroon Cir., Englewood, CO, 80112; *PH:* 1-303-796-2850; *Fax:* 1-303-804-4088; *http://* www.csgsystems.com; *Email:* info@csgsystems.com

General - Incorporation .... DE
Employees 1,685
Auditor .... KPMG LLP
Stk Agt .... EquiServe Trust Co N.A
Counsel .... Baker & McKenzie LLP
DUNS No. 93-771-6835

Stock- Price on:12/24/2007 .... $26.89
Stock Exchange .... NDQ
Ticker Symbol .... CSGS
Outstanding Shares 43,380,000
E.P.S. $1.44
Shareholders .... NA

Business: The group's principle activity is to provide customer care and billing solutions for the converging communication markets, including cable television, direct broadcast satellite, telephony, on-line services and others. The group provides processing services, software and support services, which automate customer management functions. It includes billing, sales support and order processing, invoice calculation, production, management reporting and customer analysis. Processing and related services include core service bureau customer care and billing application relating to communication control system and services. Software services include software license, maintenance fees, consulting services such as product installation and customization, business consulting, project management and training services. The group's quarterly revenue for September 2007 was 107.56 millions of USD.

Primary SIC and add'l.: 7375 7372

CIK No: 0001005757

Subsidiaries: CSG International Holdings LLC, CSG Services, Inc., CSG Systems, Inc.

Officers: Ed Nafus/Dir., CEO/$3,143,755.00, Peter Kalan/Exec. VP - Business, Corporate Development/$1,793,791.00, Will Rotch/CTO - Americas, Raghu Prasad/CTO - Asia Pacific, China, Rick Norman/Sr. VP - Strategic Business Unit, Jay McCracken/Sr. VP - National Accounting, Strategic Business Unit, Alan Michels/Pres. - Worldwide Delivery Global Software Services Division, Liz Bauer/Sr. VP - Investor Relations, Corporate Communications, Donald J. Angelico/VP - Delivery Services, Asia Pacific, China, Mike Scott/COO, Exec. VP, Charles Ydoate/Executive Dir. - Sales, Caribbean, Latin America, Chevy Vithianathan/VP - Product Delivery, Americas Region, Randy Wiese/CFO, Exec. VP/$597,984.00, Joe Ruble/Exec. VP, General Counsel, Corp. Sec./$546,772.00, Hank Bonde/Pres. - Global Software Services Division *(27 Officers included in Index)*

Directors: Ed Nafus/Dir., CEO, Bernard W. Reznicek/Chmn., Donald V. Smith/Dir., James A. Unruh/Dir., Ron Cooper/Dir., Donald B. Reed/Dir., Frank V. Sica/Dir., Janice Obuchowski/Dir.

Owners: Barclays Global Investors, NA/10.65%, Robert M. Scott, James A. Unruh, Edward C. Nafus, Donald V. Smith, Janice I. Obuchowski, Goldman Sachs Asset Management, L.P./5.79%, Randy R. Wiese, State Street Bank and Trust Company/6.08%, Joseph T. Ruble, Insiders/1.66%, Bernard W. Reznicek, Donald B. Reed, Ronald H. Cooper, Frank V. Sica *(16 Owners included in Index)*

Financial Data: *Fiscal Year End:*12/31 *Latest Annual Data:* 12/31/2006

Year	Sales	Net Income
2006	$383,106,000	$59,770,000
2005	$377,317,000	$53,229,000
2004	$529,746,000	$47,184,000

Curr. Assets:	$545,628,000	**Curr. Liab.:**	$91,511,000	**P/E Ratio:**	20.07
Plant, Equip.:	$23,680,000	**Total Liab.:**	$335,762,000	**Indic. Yr. Divd.:**	NA
Total Assets:	$653,496,000	**Net Worth:**	$317,734,000	**Debt/ Equity:**	0.9000

CSK Auto Inc

645 E Missouri Ave., Ste. 400, Phoenix, AZ, 85012; *PH:* 1-602-265-9200; *Fax:* 1-602-631-7321; *http://* www.cskauto.com

General - Incorporation .... DE
Employees 9,521
Auditor .... PricewaterhouseCoopers LLP
Stk Agt .... Mellon Investor Services LLC
Counsel .... Gibson, Dunn & Crutcher LLP
DUNS No. 04-931-7357

Stock- Price on:12/24/2007 .... $18.56
Stock Exchange .... NYSE
Ticker Symbol .... CAO
Outstanding Shares 43,950,000
E.P.S. $0.14
Shareholders .... NA

Business: The group's principal activity is the retailing of automotive parts and accessories. The group offers a selection of national brand name, private-label and generic automotive products for domestic and imported cars and light trucks. The products include new and remanufactured automotive replacement parts, maintenance items, accessories and new garage maintenance and organizational products. The group serves both the do-it-yourself (diy) and do-it-for-me (difm) markets. The diy market is comprised of consumers who typically repair and maintain vehicles themselves and the difm market is comprised of auto repair professionals, fleet owners, governments and municipalities. As of 01-Aug-2004, the group operated 1,123 stores in 19 states. The group operates under three brand names: checker auto parts, schuck's auto supply and kragen auto parts.

Primary SIC and add'l.: 5531 6719

CIK No: 0001051848

Subsidiaries: CSK Auto, Inc. (Auto), Cskauto.com, Inc.

Officers: Lawrence N. Mondry/Dir., CEO, Pres., Larry Buresh/CIO, Sr. VP/$560,428.00, Larry Ellis/Sr. VP - Logistics/$423,332.00, Dale Ward/Exec. VP/$605,846.00, Brian K. Woods/Exec. VP, Michael D. Bryk/Sr. VP - Finance, Controller, Steven L. Korby/Interim CFO, Randi V. Morrison/Sr. VP, General Counsel, Sec., John W. Saar/Sr. VP - Commercial Sales

Directors: Lawrence N. Mondry/Dir., CEO, Pres., Charles K. Marquis/Chmn., Charles J. Philippin/Dir., William A. Shutzer/Dir., Morton Godlas/Dir., James G. Bazlen/Dir., Terilyn Anne Henderson/Dir.

Owners: Blue Harbour Group/7.65%, GLG Partners LP/8.88%, William A. Shutzer, Viking Global Performance LLC/5.10%, Don Watson, Robert S. Pitts/5.01%, Dale Ward, Maynard Jenkins/1.88%, Morton Godlas, OppenheimerFunds, Inc./12.61%, James Bazlen, Karsch Capital Management LP/9.32%, Martin Frase, Charles J. Philippin, Insiders/2.36% *(21 Owners included in Index)*

Financial Data: *Fiscal Year End:*01/30 *Latest Annual Data:* 02/04/2007

Year	Sales	Net Income
2007	$1,907,776,000	$6,264,000
2006	$1,651,285,000	$57,790,000
2005	$1,577,460,000	$36,881,000

Curr. Assets:	$861,917,000	**Curr. Liab.:**	$287,055,000	**P/E Ratio:**	132.57
Plant, Equip.:	$124,813,000	**Total Liab.:**	$821,907,000	**Indic. Yr. Divd.:**	NA
Total Assets:	$1,153,465,000	**Net Worth:**	$331,558,000	**Debt/ Equity:**	NA

CSP Inc

43 Manning Rd., Billerica, MA, 01821; *PH:* 1-978-663-7598; *Fax:* 1-978-663-0150; *http://* www.cspi.com; *Email:* info@cspi.com

General - Incorporation....MA
Employees....138
Auditor....Mcgladrey & Pullen, LLP
Stk Agt....American Stock Transfer & Trust Co.
Counsel....Foley, Hoag & Eliot LLP
DUNS No....04-589-7659

Stock- Price on:12/24/2007....$9.26
Stock Exchange....NDQ
Ticker Symbol....CSPI
Outstanding Shares....3,810,000
E.P.S....$1.03
Shareholders....NA

Business: The group's principal activity is to develop and market Internet software for e-commerce solutions, image processing software, network management integration services and cluster computer systems. These computers enhance the system's ability to perform high-speed arithmetic. The group also markets Internet software solutions, real-time process control systems, systems integration and services as well as develops and markets hardware and software for scientific imaging. The products are used by industrial, commercial, scientific and defense customers worldwide. The group operates in North America, Europe and Asia.

Primary SIC and add'l.: 3571 7372 7373

CIK No: 0000356037

Subsidiaries: CSP Inc., CSP Inc. Foreign Sales Corp., Ltd., CSP Inc. Securities Corp., Modcomp, Inc

Owners: Sterling Capital Management/6.60%, Julian DeMora/5.40%, Robert M. Williams, Daniel Zeff/7.80%, Shelton C. James, Christopher J. Hall/9.10%, Eliot Rose Asset Management,/15.80%, Alexander R. Lupinetti/7.20%, Gary W. Levine, David J. Lyons, William Bent, Insiders/18.30%

Financial Data: *Fiscal Year End:*09/30 *Latest Annual Data:* 06/30/2007

Year	Sales	Net Income
2007	$25,944,000	$882,000
2006	$68,937,000	$1,975,000
2005	$57,490,000	$753,000

Curr. Assets:	$31,615,000	**Curr. Liab.:**	$12,016,000	**P/E Ratio:**	9.96
Plant, Equip.:	$1,141,000	**Total Liab.:**	$19,535,000	**Indic. Yr. Divd.:**	NA
Total Assets:	$38,450,000	**Net Worth:**	$18,915,000	**Debt/ Equity:**	NA

CSS Industries Inc

1845 Walnut St., Ste. 800, Philadelphia, PA, 19103; *PH:* 1-215-569-9900; *Fax:* 1-215-569-9979; *http://* www.cssindustries.com

General - Incorporation....DE
Employees....2,700
Auditor....KPMG LLP
Stk Agt....American Stock Transfer & Trust Co.
Counsel....NA
DUNS No....00-698-2003

Stock- Price on:12/24/2007....$39.76
Stock Exchange....NYSE
Ticker Symbol....CSS
Outstanding Shares....10,890,000
E.P.S....NA
Shareholders....NA

Business: The group's principal activities are to design, manufacture, procure and market consumer products to the retailers of seasonal and social expression products. The group's products include gift wrap, gift bags, boxed greeting cards, gift tags, tissue paper, paper and vinyl decorations, classroom exchange valentines, decorative ribbons and bows, halloween masks, costumes, make-ups and novelties, easter egg dyes and novelties and educational products. The group provides its retail customers the opportunity to use a single vendor for much of their seasonal product requirements. The products are marketed in the United States and Canada to merchandise retailers, warehouse clubs, drug and food chains, independent card shops and retail teachers' stores.

Primary SIC and add'l.: 2761 2771 2621 2679

CIK No: 0000020629

Subsidiaries: Berwick Offray LLC, Cleo Inc, Paper Magic Group, Inc.

Owners: Insiders/9.18%, Leonard E. Grossman/1.23%, Rebecca C. Matthias, Clifford E. Pietrafitta/1.41%, James E. Ksansnak, Ellen B. Kurtzman/17.58%, David J. M. Erskine, Jack Farber/2.86%, Dimensional FundAdvisors LP/8.24%, William G. Kiesling, Royce& Associates, LLC/8.97%, T. Rowe Price Associates, Inc/13.33%, Christopher J. Munyan/1.06%, James H. Bromley/1.71%, Scott A. Beaumont *(16 Owners included in Index)*

Financial Data: *Fiscal Year End:*03/31 *Latest Annual Data:* 3/31/2007

Year	Sales	Net Income
2007	$530,686,000	$23,889,000
2006	$525,494,000	$21,841,000
2005	$536,362,000	$30,692,000

Curr. Assets:	$244,272,000	**Curr. Liab.:**	$55,963,000	**P/E Ratio:**	18.16
Plant, Equip.:	$58,897,000	**Total Liab.:**	$81,960,000	**Indic. Yr. Divd.:**	$0.560
Total Assets:	$343,070,000	**Net Worth:**	$261,110,000	**Debt/ Equity:**	0.0780

CSX Corp Inc

500 Water St., 15th Fl., Jacksonville, FL, 32202; *PH:* 1-904-359-3200; *Fax:* 1-904-633-3450; *http://* www.csx.com

General - Incorporation....VA
Employees....36,000
Auditor....Ernst & Young LLP
Stk Agt....Bank of New York
Counsel....NA
DUNS No....03-977-5119

Stock- Price on:12/24/2007....$44.73
Stock Exchange....NYSE
Ticker Symbol....CSX
Outstanding Shares....437,160,000
E.P.S....$2.69
Shareholders....NA

Business: The groups principle activity is to provide freight transportation services. The group operates through three segments namely rail, intermodal and international terminals. The group operates from United States.

Primary SIC and add'l.: 4011 4412 4449 4424

CIK No: 0000277948

Subsidiaries: CSX Intermodal, Inc., CSX Transportation, Inc.

Officers: Michael J. Ward/Chmn., CEO, Pres./$13,771,480.00, Lester M. Passa/VP - Strategic Planning, Tony Ingram/COO, Exec. VP - CSX Transportation/$5,151,428.00, Clarence W. Gooden/Exec. VP - Sales, Marketing, Chief Commercial Officer/$5,168,463.00, James R. Hertwig/Pres. - CSX Intermodal Inc, Frank Lonegro/Pres. - CSX Technology Inc, Andy Fogarty/MD, Pres. - Greenbrier Resort, Club Management Company, Peter J. Shudtz/VP - Regulatory Affairs, Washington Counsel, Stephen A. Crosby/Pres. - CSX Real Property Inc, Robert J. Haulter/Sr. VP - Human Resources, Labor Relations, Michael J. Ruehling/VP - Federal Legislation, David A. Boor/VP - Tax, Treasurer, Carolyn T. Sizemore/VP, Controller, Ellen M. Fitzsimmons/Sr. VP - Law, Public Affairs, General Counsel, Corp. Sec./$3,501,466.00, Oscar Munoz/CFO, Exec. VP/$4,113,581.00

Directors: Michael J. Ward/Chmn., CEO, Pres., Donald J. Shepard/Dir., David M. Ratcliffe/Dir., Elizabeth E. Bailey/Dir., Southwood J. Morcott/Dir., Steven T. Halverson/Dir., William C. Richardson/Dir., Frank S. Royal/Dir., John B. Breaux/Dir., Edward J. Kelly/Dir., Robert D. Kunisch/Dir., Donna M. Alvarado/Dir.

Owners: Frank S. Royal, Edward J. Kelly, Ellen M. Fitzsimmons, Clarence W. Gooden, Southwood J. Morcott, David M. Ratcliffe, Steven T. Halverson, Insiders, The TCW Group, Inc./5.30%, Tony L. Ingram, Donna M. Alvarado, Donald J. Shepard, Elizabeth E. Bailey, Oscar Munoz, William C. Richardson *(18 Owners included in Index)*

Financial Data: *Fiscal Year End:*12/31 *Latest Annual Data:* 12/29/2006

Year	Sales	Net Income
2006	$9,566,000,000	$1,310,000,000
2005	$8,618,000,000	$1,145,000,000
2004	$352,000,000	$140,000,000

Curr. Assets:	$334,000,000	**Curr. Liab.:**	$242,000,000	**P/E Ratio:**	16.63
Plant, Equip.:	$560,000,000	**Total Liab.:**	$1,021,000,000	**Indic. Yr. Divd.:**	$0.600
Total Assets:	$1,414,000,000	**Net Worth:**	$361,000,000	**Debt/ Equity:**	0.5683

CT Communications Inc

1000 Progress Pl. Ne, Concord, NC, 28026; *PH:* 1-704-722-2500; *http://* www.ctc.net

General - Incorporation....NC
Employees....621
Auditor....Ernst & Young, LLP
Stk Agt....Wachovia Bank N.A
Counsel....Smith Helms Mulliss & Moore
DUNS No....84-045-1777

Stock- Price on:12/24/2007....$30.63
Stock Exchange....NA
Ticker Symbol....NA
Outstanding Shares....20,270,000
E.P.S....$0.94
Shareholders....NA

Business: The group's principal activity is to provide integrated telecommunication services to residential and business customers located primarily in North Carolina. The group provides services through five segments. The incumbent local exchange carrier (ilec) provides local telephone services. The competitive local exchange carrier (clec) provides competitive local telephone services to customers. The greenfield services unit provides full telecommunications services to new-mixed-use developments. The digital wireless provides wireless phone services with palmetto mobilenet lp. The Internet and data services company (ids) provides dial-up and high -speed Internet access, Web design, hosting and other data related services.

Primary SIC and add'l.: 6719 4813

CIK No: 0000023259

Subsidiaries: Carolina Personal Communications, Inc., CT Cellular, Inc., CT Global, LLC, CT Services, Inc., CT Wireless Cable, Inc., CTC Employment Services, LLC, CTC Exchange Services, Inc., CTC Internet Services, Inc., CTC Long Distance Services, LLC, CTC Video Services, LLC, Progress Place Realty Holding Company, LLC, The Concord Telephone Company, Wavetel TN, LLC, Wavetel, LLC, WebServe, Inc. 16 Subsidiaries included in the Index

Officers: Michael R. Coltrane/Chmn., CEO, Pres./$2,109,668.00, David H. Armistead/General Counsel, Sec./$402,181.00, Jon Tyler/VP - Residential Customer Care, Amy M. Justis/VP - Administrative Operations, Michael R. Nash/Sr. VP - Engineering, Network Operations/$720,303.00, John Klein/VP - Residential Sales, Marketing, Charlotte Walsh/CIO, VP, Randy Madge/VP - Business Sales, James E. Hausman/Sr. VP, CFO/$693,900.00, Matt Dowd/Sr. VP - Business Operations/$880,476.00, Ronald A. Marino/VP - Finance, Chief Accounting Officer

Directors: Michael R. Coltrane/Chmn., CEO, Pres., Barry W. Eveland/63/Dir., James L. Moore/65/Dir., Raymond C. Groth/61/Dir., Cynthia L. Mynatt/52/Dir., Charlie O. Chewning/72/Dir., Linda M. Farthing/60/Dir., William A. Coley/64/Dir., Tom E. Smith/66/Dir.

Owners: Raymond C. Groth, Michael R. Nash, William A. Coley, Matthew J. Dowd, David H. Armistead, James E. Hausman, Insiders/7.40%, Tom E. Smith, Barry W. Eveland, Charlie O. Chewning, James L. Moore, Cynthia L. Mynatt, Linda M. Farthing, Michael R. Coltrane/5.30%

Financial Data: *Fiscal Year End:*12/31 *Latest Annual Data:* 12/31/2006

Year	Sales	Net Income
2006	$176,871,000	$71,661,000
2005	$171,665,000	$14,549,000
2004	$163,680,000	$14,703,000

Curr. Assets:	$128,998,000	**Curr. Liab.:**	$34,885,000	**P/E Ratio:**	32.59
Plant, Equip.:	$209,908,000	**Total Liab.:**	$107,980,000	**Indic. Yr. Divd.:**	$0.480
Total Assets:	$387,358,000	**Net Worth:**	$279,378,000	**Debt/ Equity:**	0.1194

CT Holdings Inc

11150 Santa Monica Blvd., Ste. 340, Los Angeles, CA, 90025; *PH:* 1-310-484-5668; *http://* www.ct-holdings.com

General - Incorporation....DE
Employees....NA
Auditor....KBA Group LLP
Stk Agt....NA
Counsel....NA
DUNS No....80-618-8611

Stock- Price on:12/24/2007....NA
Stock Exchange....NA
Ticker Symbol....NA
Outstanding Shares....NA
E.P.S....$3.94
Shareholders....NA

Business: The group's principal activity is to provide management expertise including consulting on operations, marketing and strategic planning to early stage technology companies. It also provides financial expertise along with financial capital to early stage companies. The group develops, acquires and operates technology-based businesses with strong business models and compelling valuations.

Primary SIC and add'l.: 7372

CIK No: 0000752789

Subsidiaries: Citadel Security Software Inc

Officers: Steven B. Solomon/43/Dir., CEO, Pres., Sec., Richard Connelly/56/CFO

Directors: Steven B. Solomon/43/Dir., CEO, Pres., Sec., Chris A. Economou/52/Dir., Mark Rogers/47/Dir., Axel Sawallich/62/Dir.

Owners: Daniel S. Goldberger, Insiders/74.30%, Jay A. Wolf/2.50%, Nicholas S. Lewin, Marc G. Cummins/4.80%, Terren S. Peizer/6.70%, Victor Gura

Financial Data: *Fiscal Year End:*12/31 *Latest Annual Data:* 12/31/2006

Year	Sales	Net Income
2006	NA	$5,325,000
2005	NA	-$672,000
2004	NA	-$4,227,000

Curr. Assets:	$0	**Curr. Liab.:**	$456,000		
Plant, Equip.:	NA	**Total Liab.:**	$456,000	**Indic. Yr. Divd.:**	NA
Total Assets:	$0	**Net Worth:**	-$456,000	**Debt/ Equity:**	NA

CTC Media Inc

2711 Ctr.ville Rd., Ste. 400, Wilmington, DE, 19808; *PH:* 1-302-636-5400; *http://* www.ctcmedia.ru; *Email:* info@ctcmedia.ru

General - Incorporation	DE	Stock- Price on:12/24/2007	$27.36
Employees	1,044	Stock Exchange	NDQ
Auditor	Ernst & Young LLP	Ticker Symbol	CTCM
Stk Agt	Computershare Trust Co	Outstanding Shares	151,540,000
Counsel	NA	E.P.S.	$0.74
DUNS No.	NA	Shareholders	NA

Business: The groups principal activity is to provide network services. The groups operates through four segments namely CTC Network, Domashny Network, CTC Television Station Group and Domashny Television Station Group. The group operates from the United States. Of the total revnue in the year 2006, CTC Network accounted for $264,733, Domashny Network $20,649, CTC Television Station Group $74,765and Domashny Television Station Group $11,566.

Primary SIC and add'l.: 4833

CIK No: 0001354513

Subsidiaries: CTC-Nizhny Novgorod, ZAO CTC Network

Officers: Alexander Rodnyansky/CEO, Vladimir Khanumyan/COO, Nilesh Lakhani/CFO, John Dowdy/35/Controller, Chief Accounting Officer, Sergey Petrov/36/General Dir. - Television Station Groups, Dmitry Barsukov/Dir. - Investor Relations, Katya Ostrova/Mgr. - Investor Relations, Konstantin Vorontsov/Dir. - Public Relations, Corporate Communications

Directors: Hans-Holger Albrecht/Co - Chmn., Peter Aven/Co - Chmn., Vagan Abgaryan/Dir., Tamjid Basunia/Dir., Maria Brunell/Dir., Charles Burdick/Dir., Kaj Gradevik/Dir., Werner Klatten/Dir., Oleg Sysuev/Dir.

Owners: Nilesh Lakhani, Oleg Sysuev, ABH Holdings Corporation, Alexander Rodnyansky, Vladimir Khanumyan, Maria Brunell, Vagan Abgaryan, Hans-Holger Albrecht, Leigh Sprague, MTG Broadcasting AB, Sergey Petrov, Funds managed by Baring Vostok Capital Partners, Insiders, John Dowdy, Peter Aven

Financial Data: Fiscal Year End:12/31   *Latest Annual Data:* 12/31/2006

Year	Sales	Net Income
2006	$370,834,000	$106,325,000
2005	$237,477,000	$57,295,000
2004	$155,567,000	$47,450,000

Curr. Assets:	$278,655,000	Curr. Liab.:	$46,366,000	P/E Ratio:	38.00
Plant, Equip.:	$22,388,000	Total Liab.:	$63,780,000	Indic. Yr. Divd.:	NA
Total Assets:	$484,797,000	Net Worth:	$421,017,000	Debt/ Equity:	0.0004

CTD Holdings Inc

27317 NW 78 Ave., High Springs, FL, 32643; *PH:* 1-386-454-0887; *Fax:* 1-386-454-8134; *http://* www.cyclodex.com; *Email:* ctd@cyclodex.com

General - Incorporation	FL	Stock- Price on:12/24/2007	$0.022
Employees	3	Stock Exchange	OTC
Auditor	Baumann, Raymondo & Co. P.A	Ticker Symbol	CTDH
Stk Agt	Computershare Investor Services LLC	Outstanding Shares	15,920,000
Counsel	NA	E.P.S.	$0.01
DUNS No.	80-465-2584	Shareholders	NA

Business: The group's principal activity is to market cyclodextrins and related products to the food, pharmaceutical and other industries. Additionally, the group provides consulting services. The cyclodextrins are molecules that bring together oil and water and have potential applications wherever oil and water must be used together. The cyclodextrins can improve the solubility and stability of a wide range of drugs. The cyclodextrins are donut shaped circles of glucose molecules, these are formed naturally by the action of bacterial enzymes on starch. The cyclodextrins related products include trappsol (R), aquaplex (R), and ap(tm)-flavor.

Primary SIC and add'l.: 2899 0182

CIK No: 0000922247

Officers: Rick C.E. Strattan/Chmn., CEO, Pres., Carmen Petty-Scott/Marketing, Operations Mgr.

Directors: Rick C.E. Strattan/Chmn., CEO, Pres.

Owners: Aspatuck Holdings, Inc./20.98%, George L. Fails/5.65%, Rick C.E. Strattan/33.88%, Insiders/66.84%, Kiaran Nicole Brook/6.33%

Financial Data: Fiscal Year End:12/31   *Latest Annual Data:* 12/31/2006

Year	Sales	Net Income
2006	$542,000	-$102,000
2005	$454,000	-$172,000
2004	$465,000	-$561,000

Curr. Assets:	$322,000	Curr. Liab.:	$58,000		
Plant, Equip.:	$412,000	Total Liab.:	$200,000	Indic. Yr. Divd.:	NA
Total Assets:	$760,000	Net Worth:	$560,000	Debt/ Equity:	0.2397

CTI Group Holdings Inc

333 N Alabama St., Ste. 240, Indianapolis, IN, 46204; *PH:* 1-317-262-4666; *Fax:* 1-317-262-4849; *http://* www.ctigroup.com

General - Incorporation	DE	Stock- Price on:12/24/2007	$0.35
Employees	143	Stock Exchange	OTC
Auditor	Crowe Chizek & Co. LLC	Ticker Symbol	CTIG
Stk Agt	American Stock Transfer & Trust Co.	Outstanding Shares	29,040,000
Counsel	NA	E.P.S.	-$0.02
DUNS No.	06-436-5323	Shareholders	NA

Business: The group's principal activities are to design, develop, market and support data processing software and services for managing telecom systems. The group operates in three segments: telemanagement, billing and customer care and patent enforcement. The telemanagement segment offers telemanagement software and services for end users to manage their usage of telecommunications services and equipment. The billing and customer care segment provides billing services and billing analysis software to telephone and wireless network operators to manage customer accounts, generate bills and manage customer service operation. The products and services of the group are marketed to organizations with internal telecom systems, fax and modem equipment and to providers of telecom services. In 2003, the group discontinued the operations of xila.

Primary SIC and add'l.: 7372 6794 7379

CIK No: 0000355627

Subsidiaries: Centillion Data Systems LLC., CTI Billing Solutions Inc., CTI Billing Solutions Ltd., CTI Data Solutions (USA) Inc, CTI Data Solutions Ltd., CTI Delaware Holdings Inc., XC, LLC

Officers: John Birbeck/Chmn., CEO, Pres., Manfred Hanuschek/CFO, Sid Rao/CTO, Bill Miller/COO

Directors: John Birbeck/Chmn., CEO, Pres., Harold D. Garrison/Dir., Rupert D. Armitage/Dir., Salah N. Osseiran/Dir., Bengt A. Dahl/Dir., Thomas W. Grein/Dir.

Owners: Bengt Dahl, Thomas W. Grein, Rupert D. Armitage, Manfred Hanuschek, John Birbeck, Fairford Holdings Limited, Salah N. Osseiran, Harold D. Garrison, Insiders

Financial Data: Fiscal Year End:12/31   *Latest Annual Data:* 12/31/2006

Year	Sales	Net Income
2006	$12,811,000	-$1,088,000
2005	$15,301,000	$523,000
2004	$16,158,000	$914,000

Curr. Assets:	$6,183,000	Curr. Liab.:	$5,459,000		
Plant, Equip.:	$2,355,000	Total Liab.:	$14,601,000	Indic. Yr. Divd.:	NA
Total Assets:	$24,231,000	Net Worth:	$9,630,000	Debt/ Equity:	NA

CTI Industries Corp

22160 N Pepper Rd., Barrington, IL, 60010; *PH:* 1-847-382-1000; *Fax:* 1-800-333-1831; *http://* www.ctiindustries.com

General - Incorporation	LI	Stock- Price on:12/24/2007	$4.39
Employees	304	Stock Exchange	NDQ
Auditor	Weiser LLP	Ticker Symbol	CTIB
Stk Agt	Continental Stock Transfer & Trust Co	Outstanding Shares	2,290,000
Counsel	Mr. Merrickvanasco Genelly & Miller	E.P.S.	$0.73
DUNS No.	03-089-5387	Shareholders	NA

Business: The group's principal activities are to design, manufacture and distribute balloons and other products. The group also operates systems for the production, lamination, coating and printing of films used for food packaging and other commercial uses and for conversion of films to flexible packaging containers and other products. The products of the group include metalized balloons, latex balloons, packaging films and custom film products. The products of the group's are sold throughout the United States and in 30 foreign countries through retail outlets. The popular brands of the group include superloons, ultraloons, miniloons, card-b-loons, shape-a-loons, walk-abouts , smackers and you name it.

Primary SIC and add'l.: 3081

CIK No: 0001042187

Subsidiaries: CTF International, CTI Balloons Limited, CTI Helium, Inc, CTI Mexico Corporation, Flexo Universal, S.A. de C.V

Officers: Howard W. Schwan/53/CEO, Pres./$221,256.00, Stephen M. Merrick/CFO, Exec. VP, Sec./$97,057.00, Steven Frank/47/VP - Sales/$134,381.00, Brent Anderson/42/VP, GM - Bag Division/$142,323.00, Samuel Komar/51/VP - Marketing/$148,634.00, Rick Sherman/Mgr. - Lamination Sales, Timothy Patterson/VP - Finance, Administration/$128,434.00

Directors: John H. Schwan/64/Chmn., Stanley M. Brown/62/Dir., Bret Tayne/49/Dir., Michael Avramovich/55/Dir., John I. Collins/48/Dir.

Owners: Stephen M. Merrick/27.50%, Tim Patterson, Howard W. Schwan/9.56%, Stanley M. Brown, Michael Avramovich, John Collins, Brent Anderson/2.83%, John H. Schwan/27.36%, Bret Tayne, Steve Frank, Samuel Komar, Insiders/70.23%

Financial Data: Fiscal Year End:12/31   *Latest Annual Data:* 12/31/2006

Year	Sales	Net Income
2006	$35,428,000	$1,895,000
2005	$29,190,000	-$333,000
2004	$37,193,000	-$2,479,000

Curr. Assets:	$16,491,000	Curr. Liab.:	$14,643,000	P/E Ratio:	6.01
Plant, Equip.:	$8,592,000	Total Liab.:	$21,530,000	Indic. Yr. Divd.:	NA
Total Assets:	$26,645,000	Net Worth:	$5,102,000	Debt/ Equity:	1.0216

Ctrip.com International Ltd

3f Bldg 63, No 421 Hong Cao Rd. , Peoples Republic Of China, Shanghai, 200233; *PH:* 86-2134064880; *http://* www.ctrip.com; *Email:* partner@ctrip.com

General - Incorporation	Cayman Islands	Stock- Price on:12/24/2007	$78.01
Employees	5,500	Stock Exchange	NDQ
Auditor	PricewaterhouseCoopers Zhong Tian	Ticker Symbol	CTRP
Stk Agt	Bank of New York	Outstanding Shares	32,660,000
Counsel	NA	E.P.S.	$1.01
DUNS No.	NA	Shareholders	NA

Business: The groups principle activity is to provide information on hotels and flights and enable customers to make informed and cost-effective hotel and flight bookings. The group operates from United States.

Primary SIC and add'l.: NA

CIK No: 0001269238

Subsidiaries: Beijing Ctrip International Travel Agency Co., Ltd., C-Travel International Limited, a Cayman Islands company, Ctrip Computer Technology (Shanghai) Co., Ltd., a PRC company, Ctrip Travel Information Technology (Shanghai) Co., Ltd., a PRC company, Ctrip Travel Network Technology (Shanghai) Co., Ltd., a PRC company, Ctrip.com (Hong Kong) Limited, a Hong Kong company, Guangzhou Ctrip Travel Agency Co., Ltd., Shanghai Ctrip Charming International Travel Agency Co., Ltd., Shanghai Ctrip Commerce Co., Ltd., Shanghai Huacheng Southwest Travel Agency Co., Ltd., Shenzhen Shencheng Information Consulting Service Co., Ltd.

Officers: Min Fan/CEO, Co - Founder, Jianmin Zhu/39/VP, Jane Jie Sun/CFO, Tao Yang/32/VP, Maohua Sun/36/VP, Han Ding/40/VP, James Lan Tang/40/VP, Victor Shengli Wang/53/VP, Tracy Cui/Contact, Shaw Xiaoliang Ding/43/VP

Directors: Min Fan/CEO, Co - Founder, James Jianzhang Liang/Chmn., Co - Founder, Gabriel Li/Dir., Yoshihisa Yamada/44/Dir., Suyang Zhang/Dir., Neil Nanpeng Shen/Non - Exec. Dir., Jp Gan/Dir., Qi Ji/Dir., Robert Stein/Dir., Hideaki Yokomizo/42/Dir.

Owners: Gabriel Li/0.20%, Insiders/0.30%, Neil Nanpeng Shen/0.50%, Min Fan/0.80%, Jane Jie Sun/0.10%, James Jianzhang Liang/1.50%, FMR Corp./14.50%, Rakuten, Inc./20.30%

Financial Data: Fiscal Year End:12/31   *Latest Annual Data:* 12/31/2006

Year	Sales	Net Income
2006	$99,990,000	$30,840,000
2005	$64,632,000	$27,806,000
2004	$40,392,000	$16,108,000

Curr. Assets:	$135,055,000	**Curr. Liab.:**	$53,978,000	**P/E Ratio:**	14.48
Plant, Equip.:	$19,703,000	**Total Liab.:**	$54,377,000	**Indic. Yr. Divd.:**	NA
Total Assets:	$186,127,000	**Net Worth:**	$131,751,000	**Debt/ Equity:**	NA

CTS Corp

905 W Blvd. N, Elkhart, IN, 46514; *PH:* 1-574-293-7511; *Fax:* 1-574-293-6146;
http:// www.ctscorp.com

General - Incorporation .... IN
Employees 4,977
Auditor .... Grant Thornton LLP
Stk Agt .... National City Bank
Counsel .... NA
DUNS No. 00-506-8515

Stock- Price on:12/24/2007 .... $12.67
Stock Exchange .... NYSE
Ticker Symbol .... CTS
Outstanding Shares 35,880,000
E.P.S $0.66
Shareholders .... NA

Business: The group's principal activities are to design, manufacture, assemble and sell a broad line of components and sensors. The group also provides electronics and manufacturing services primarily for the automotive, communications and computer markets. The group operates through two segments namely: components and sensors and electronics manufacturing services. Components and sensors are products which perform specific electronic functions for a given product family for use by global OEMs, contract manufacturers and electronic distributors. Electronic manufacturing services (ems) includes the higher level assembly of electronic and mechanical components into a finished subassembly or assembly performed under a contract manufacturing agreement with OEMs or other contract manufacturers. The group operates manufacturing facilities located in North America, Asia and Europe.

Primary SIC and add'l.: 3679 3678

CIK No: 0000026058

Subsidiaries: CTS (Tianjin) Electronics Company, Ltd., CTS Components Taiwan, Ltd., CTS Corporation, CTS Corporation U.K., Ltd., CTS Electro de Matamoros, S.A, CTS Electronics Components, Inc, CTS Electronics Corporation (Thailand), Ltd., CTS Electronics Dongguan, Ltd., CTS Electronics Hong Kong, Ltd., CTS Electronics Manufacturing Solutions (Massachusetts) Inc., CTS Electronics Manufacturing Solutions (Moorpark), Inc, CTS Electronics Manufacturing Solutions (Santa Clara), Inc., CTS Electronics Manufacturing Solutions, Inc., CTS International B.V, CTS Japan, Inc. 26 Subsidiaries included in the Index

Officers: Donald K. Schwanz/64/Chmn., CEO, Pres., Vinod M. Khilnani/56/Dir., CFO, Sr. VP/$1,172,444.00, Tyler H. Buchanan/Sr. VP/$922,437.00, Donald R. Schroeder/Exec. VP/$1,199,341.00, Richard G. Cutter/VP, Sec., General Counsel/$753,022.00

Directors: Donald K. Schwanz/64/Chmn., CEO, Pres., Roger R. Hemminghaus/70/Chmn., Walter S. Catlow/63/Dir., Gerald H. Frieling/78/Dir., Robert A. Profusek/58/Dir., Patricia K. Vincent/48/Dir., Thomas G. Cody/66/Dir., Michael Henning/68/Dir., Lawrence J. Ciancia/65/Dir., Vinod M. Khilnani/56/Dir., CFO, Sr. VP

Owners: GAMCO Asset Management, Inc./8.53%, Robert A. Profusek, Donald K. Schwanz, Lawrence J. Ciancia, Michael A. Henning, Dimensional FundAdvisors LP/8.79%, Walter S. Catlow, Insiders, Patricia K. Vincent, Thomas G. Cody, Richard G. Cutter, Barclays Global Investors, N.A./6.00%, FMR/6.75%, Donald R. Schroeder, Roger R. Hemminghaus *(20 Owners included in Index)*

Financial Data: **Fiscal Year End:**12/31 **Latest Annual Data:** 12/31/2006

Year	**Sales**	**Net Income**
2006	$655,614,000	$24,197,000
2005	$617,484,000	$22,234,000
2004	$531,316,000	$19,956,000

Curr. Assets:	$227,620,000	**Curr. Liab.:**	$125,681,000	**P/E Ratio:**	21.12
Plant, Equip.:	$96,468,000	**Total Liab.:**	$208,810,000	**Indic. Yr. Divd.:**	$0.120
Total Assets:	$527,833,000	**Net Worth:**	$319,023,000	**Debt/ Equity:**	0.1854

Cubic Corp

9333 Balboa Ave., San Diego, CA, 92123; *PH:* 1-858-277-6780; *Fax:* 1-858-277-1878;
http:// www.cubic.com; *Email:* cubicinfo@cubic.com

General - Incorporation .... DE
Employees 6,000
Auditor .... Ernst & Young LLP
Stk Agt...... American Stock Transfer & Trust Co.
Counsel .... NA
DUNS No. 00-838-2293

Stock- Price on:12/24/2007 .... $29.36
Stock Exchange .... AMEX
Ticker Symbol .... CUB
Outstanding Shares 26,720,000
E.P.S $1.21
Shareholders .... NA

Business: The group's principle activities are to design, develop, manufacture, install and service electronic products. These products are used in customized military range instrumentation, training and application systems, communication and surveillance systems, transceivers and avionics systems, hf and VHF/UHF surveillance receivers, computer simulation training, distributed interactive simulation and development of training doctrine. The group also designs, produces and installs electronic and mechanical revenue collection systems for mass transit projects. The group converts corrugated paper stock into pizza-boxes, high-quality packaging and shipping containers and converts paper stocks into toilet seat covers. The group's total revenue for the year 2007 was 889.87 millions of USD.

Primary SIC and add'l.: 2679 3679 3812 3578 2653

CIK No: 0000026076

Subsidiaries: Consolidated Converting Co., Cubic (u.k.) Limited, Cubic Advanced Tactical Systems, LLC, Cubic Applications, Inc., Cubic Communications, Inc., Cubic Data Systems, Inc., Cubic De Mexico, Cubic Defense Applications, Inc., Cubic Foreign Sales, Inc., Cubic Holdings Ltd., Cubic Land, Inc., Cubic Simulation Systems, Inc., Cubic Transportation Systems (australia) Pty Limited, Cubic Transportation Systems Limited, Cubic Transportation Systems, Inc. 18 Subsidiaries included in the Index

Officers: Michael L. Kelly/CEO, Pres. - Cubic Advanced Tactical Systems, LLC, Richard A. Efland/CEO, Pres. - Cubic Transportation Systems, Gerald R. Dinkel/61/CEO, VP, Pres. - Defense Group, Walter J. Zable/Chmn., CEO, Pres., Michael W. David/Corporate VP - International Operations, Brussels, Bernard A. Kulchin/76/VP - Human Resources, Kevin J. Hayes/VP, GM - Worldwide Technical Services Division, Edward Ward/Regional Dir. - Orlando, FL, Richard L. Dickson/Regional Dir. - Shalimar, FL, David A. Williams/Regional Dir. - London, Raymond C. Barker/Sr. VP, GM, Theresa W. Kohl/VP, GM - Simulation Systems Division, David M. Lapczynski/COO - Cubic Transportation Systems, Robert A. Deiter/VP, Project Dir. - Australia Operations, Cubic Transportation Systems, Australia Pty Limited, Richard Trenery/VP - Northeast Region *(42 Officers included in Index)*

Directors: Walter J. Zable/Chmn., CEO, Pres., Walter C. Zable/61/Vice Chmn., Richard C. Atkinson/78/Dir., Robert D. Weaver/61/Dir., William W. Boyle/73/Dir., Sr. VP, Raymond L. Dekozan/71/Dir., Robert T. Monagan/87/Dir., Raymond E. Peet/86/Dir., Robert S. Sullivan/63/Dir.

Owners: Insiders, Walter C. Zable, Raymond L. deKozan, J. & W. Seligman & Co., Incorporated/5.68%, Robert D. Weaver, Walter J. Zable, Richard C. Atkinson, Raymond E. Peet, William W. Boyle, Robert S. Sullivan, Walter J. Zable/40.00%, Robert T. Monagan

Financial Data: **Fiscal Year End:**09/30 **Latest Annual Data:** 9/30/2006

Year	**Sales**	**Net Income**
2006	$821,386,000	$24,133,000
2005	$804,372,000	$11,628,000
2004	$722,012,000	$36,911,000

Curr. Assets:	$438,069,000	**Curr. Liab.:**	$160,547,000	**P/E Ratio:**	24.26
Plant, Equip.:	$54,564,000	**Total Liab.:**	$224,479,000	**Indic. Yr. Divd.:**	$0.180
Total Assets:	$548,071,000	**Net Worth:**	$323,226,000	**Debt/ Equity:**	0.0979

Cubic Energy Inc

9870 Plano Rd. , Dallas, TX, 75238; *PH:* 1-972-686-0369; *Fax:* 1-972-686-9687;
http:// www.cubicenergyinc.com; *Email:* ir@cubicenergyinc.com

General - Incorporation .... TX
Employees 2
Auditor .... Philip Vogel & Co. P.C
Stk Agt.......... Securities Transfer Corp
Counsel .... NA
DUNS No. 06-523-1227

Stock- Price on:12/24/2007 .... $1.47
Stock Exchange .... OTC
Ticker Symbol .... QBIK
Outstanding Shares 55,080,000
E.P.S .... -$0.11
Shareholders .... NA

Business: The group's principle activity is to explore and develop domestic crude oil and natural gas; and produces oil and gas properties. The group operates from United States.

Primary SIC and add'l.: 1311

CIK No: 0000319156

Officers: Calvin A. Wallen/Chmn., CEO, Pres., Jon S. Ross/Dir., Sec., Richard M. Sepulvado/Exec. VP - Exploration, Production, Scott Guffey/CFO

Directors: Calvin A. Wallen/Chmn., CEO, Pres., Herbert A. Bayer/Dir., Jon S. Ross/Dir., Sec., Bob L. Clements/Dir., Gene Howard/Dir.

Owners: Scott D. Guffey, George Karfunkel/5.90%, Calvin A. Wallen/21.40%, Jon S. Ross, Gene Howard/1.00%, Herbert Bayer, Bob Clements/1.30%, James L. Busby, Wells Fargo Energy Capital, Inc./11.80%, William Bruggeman/28.70%, Insiders/25.60%, Steven S. Bruggeman/7.30%

Financial Data: **Fiscal Year End:**06/30 **Latest Annual Data:** 6/30/2006

Year	**Sales**	**Net Income**
2006	$509,000	-$2,769,000
2005	$469,000	-$785,000
2004	$415,000	-$114,000

Curr. Assets:	$808,000	**Curr. Liab.:**	$2,165,000		
Plant, Equip.:	$11,820,000	**Total Liab.:**	$7,320,000	**Indic. Yr. Divd.:**	NA
Total Assets:	$13,373,000	**Net Worth:**	$6,053,000	**Debt/ Equity:**	NA

Cubist Pharmaceuticals Inc

65 Hayden Ave., Lexington, MA, 02421; *PH:* 1-781-860-8660; *Fax:* 1-781-861-0566;
http:// www.cubist.com

General - Incorporation .... DE
Employees 410
Auditor .... PricewaterhouseCoopers LLP
Stk Agt.......... Computershare Trust Co
Counsel .... Bingham Dana Ltd
DUNS No. 80-839-4928

Stock- Price on:12/24/2007 .... $21.56
Stock Exchange .... NDQ
Ticker Symbol .... CBST
Outstanding Shares 55,340,000
E.P.S $0.80
Shareholders .... NA

Business: The group's principle activities are to research, develop and distribute new anti-infective drugs to combat life-threatening bacterial and fungal infections. The main product being cidecin, which is used for the treatment of complicated skin and skin structure infections. The group has two additional drug candidates in pre-clinical trials. One of them is an intravenous cephalosporin, cab-175 and the other, an oral formulation of ceftriaxone. It is also focused on the identification of novel compounds with a broad spectrum of activity against a variety of infections using natural product and other technologies. Majority of the revenues is generated within the United States. The group's quarterly revenue for September 2007 was 79.80 millions of USD.

Primary SIC and add'l.: 8731 2836

CIK No: 0000912183

Subsidiaries: Chiron Healthcare Ireland Ltd

Officers: Michael W. Bonney/Dir., CEO, Pres./$1,536,435.00, Oliver S. Fetzer/Sr. VP - Corporate Development, Research, Development/$897,025.00, Thomas J. Slater/VP - Commercial Development, Gregory Stea/VP - Sales, Marketing, Barry I. Eisenstein/Sr. VP - Scientific Affairs, Gloria A. Vigliani/VP - Medical Strategy, Lindon M. Fellows/Sr. VP - Technical Operations, David S. Mantus/VP - Regulatory Affairs, Maureen H. Powers/VP - Human Resources, Anthony S. Murabito/VP - Information, Business Solutions, Robert J. Perez/COO, Exec. VP/$891,681.00, Jeffrey D. Alder/VP - Drug Discovery, Evaluation, Christopher D.T. Guiffre/Sr. VP, General Counsel, Sec./$685,007.00, David W.J. McGirr/Sr. VP, CFO/$792,797.00, William Pullman/Sr. VP, Chief Medical Officer *(17 Officers included in Index)*

Directors: Michael W. Bonney/Dir., CEO, Pres., Michael B. Wood/Dir., Matthew J. Singelton/Dir., Martin Rosenberg/Dir., Sylvie Gregoire/Dir., Martin H. Soeters/Dir., Gordon L. Archer,/64/Dir., David W. Martin/Dir., Walter R. Maupay/Dir., Kenneth M. Bate/Dir.

Owners: Michael B. Wood, Insiders/3.40%, Matthew J. Singleton, Janus Capital Management LLC/5.40%, Gordon L. Archer, Oliver S. Fetzer, Christopher D.T. Guiffre, Mazama Capital Management,Inc./14.70%, Kenneth M. Bate, Robert J. Perez, Barclays Global Investors, N.A./5.90%, Unicredito Italiano S.p.A./6.00%, OrbiMed Advisors LLC/5.20%, Walter R. Maupay, David W. Martin *(24 Owners included in Index)*

Financial Data: **Fiscal Year End:**12/31 **Latest Annual Data:** 12/31/2006

Year	**Sales**	**Net Income**
2006	$194,748,000	-$376,000
2005	$120,645,000	-$31,852,000
2004	$68,071,000	-$76,512,000

Curr. Assets:	$338,367,000	**Curr. Liab.:**	$34,885,000	**P/E Ratio:**	39.20
Plant, Equip.:	$49,584,000	**Total Liab.:**	$398,445,000	**Indic. Yr. Divd.:**	NA
Total Assets:	$439,035,000	**Net Worth:**	$40,590,000	**Debt/ Equity:**	6.8008

Cuisine Solutions Inc

85 S Bragg St., Ste. 600, Alexandria, VA, 22312; **PH:** 1-703-270-2900; **Fax:** 1-703-750-1158;
http:// www.cuisinesolutions.com

General - Incorporation	DE	Stock- Price on:12/24/2007	$6.1
Employees	302	Stock Exchange	AMEX
Auditor	BDO Seidman LLP	Ticker Symbol	FZN
Stk Agt	Continental Stock Transfer & Trust Co	Outstanding Shares	16,540,000
Counsel	NA	E.P.S.	$0.55
DUNS No.	62-624-8173	Shareholders	NA

Business: The group's principal activity is to manufacture and market prepared foods to the food service industry. It also provides ongoing management advisory services. The group sells its products to channels such as airlines, passenger trains, harbor cruise lines, retail supermarket in-store delis, national restaurants and hotel banquets. The group's products are chef-created fully cooked, fully prepared entrees and sauces. The product line consists of items like osso buco, chilean sea bass, beef wellington and stuffed pork chops and also plain and stuffed chicken breast. The trademarks of the group are microroast (TM) and microroti (TM). The group operates in the United States and Europe.

Primary SIC and add'l.: 2099 8748

CIK No: 0000737602

Subsidiaries: Cuisine Solutions, Cuisine Solutions Norway, S.A.

Officers: Felipe Hasselmann/COO, Tristan Y. Kuo/CFO, Richard Keys/Contact - Sales Team, John J. Hemmer/Contact - Sales Team, Marc Brennet/Sales Executive, VP - Product Development, Herve Chignon/Contact - Sales Team, Elizabeth Lauer/Contact - Sales Team, Gerard Bertholon/Corporate Chef, VP - Sales, Roger Mallet/Chef, Christophe Jourdin/Chef, Herve Bussiere/Chef, Vincent Mallard/Chef, Bruno Bertin/Executive Chef, Bruno Goussault/Scientist, Jean-Michel Fort/Contact - Sales Team *(21 Officers included in Index)*

Owners: Stanislas Vilgrain, Gerard Bertholon, Ronald R. Zilkowski, Food Research Corporation, Thomas L. Gregg, Hugues Prince, Insiders, Felipe Hasselmann, Jean-Louis Vilgrain, Sebastien Vilgrain, John D. Firestone, Gruber and McBaine Capital Management, LLC, Robert N. Herman, Charles C. McGettigan, Robert van Roijen

Financial Data: Fiscal Year End:06/25   Latest Annual Data: 6/24/2006

Year	Sales		Net Income
2006		$64,114,000	$3,654,000
2005		$46,246,000	$1,709,000
2004		$36,721,000	-$1,004,000
Curr. Assets:	$22,707,000	**Curr. Liab.:** $12,073,000	**P/E Ratio:** 9.84
Plant, Equip.:	$12,520,000	**Total Liab.:** $18,195,000	**Indic. Yr. Divd.:** NA
Total Assets:	$42,820,000	**Net Worth:** $24,625,000	**Debt/ Equity:** NA

Cullen Frost Bankers Inc

100 W Houston St., San Antonio, TX, 78205; **PH:** 1-210-220-4011; **Fax:** 1-210-220-4325;
http:// www.frostbank.com

General - Incorporation	TX	Stock- Price on:12/24/2007	$53.28
Employees	3,652	Stock Exchange	NYSE
Auditor	Ernst & Young LLP	Ticker Symbol	CFR
Stk Agt	Bank of New York	Outstanding Shares	60,010,000
Counsel	NA	E.P.S.	$3.46
DUNS No.	05-756-7158	Shareholders	NA

Business: The group's principle activity is to provide commercial and consumer banking services. Commercial banking services are provided to corporations and other business clients, and include a wide array of lending and cash management products. Consumer banking services include direct lending and depository services. Financial management group: provides fee-based services within private trust, retirement services, and financial management services, including personal wealth management and brokerage services. The company operates through 79 financial centers and 118 ATMs across Texas. The group operates from United States.

Primary SIC and add'l.: 6712 6022

CIK No: 0000039263

Subsidiaries: Carton Service Corporation, Cullen BLP, Inc., Cullen/Frost Capital Trust I, Cullen/Frost Capital Trust II, Daltex General Agency, Inc., Frost Brokerage Services, Inc., Frost Insurance Agency, Inc., Frost Premium Finance Corporation, Frost Securities, Inc., Main Plaza Corporation, The Frost National Bank, The New Galveston Company, Inc., Tri-Frost Corporation

Officers: Richard W. Evans/Chmn., CEO/$2,959,250.00, Phillip D. Green/Group Exec. VP, CFO/$998,322.00, Paul J. Olivier/55/Group Exec. VP - Consumer Banking, Emily A. Skillman/63/Group Exec. VP - Human Resources, Richard Kardys/61/Group Exec. VP, Executive Trust Officer/$866,836.00, David W. Beck/57/Pres., Chief Business Banking Officer/$937,756.00

Directors: Richard W. Evans/Chmn., CEO, Richard M. Kleberg/Dir., Horace Wilkins/Dir., Robert S. McClane/Dir., Patrick B. Frost/Dir., Ida Clement Steen/Dir., Denny R. Alexander/Dir., Carlos Alvarez/Dir., Royce S. Caldwell/Dir., Ruben M. Escobedo/Dir., Crawford H. Edwards/Dir., T. C. Frost/Dir., Karen Jennings/Dir.

Owners: Carlos Alvarez/0.18%, Crawford H. Edwards/0.55%, Ruben M. Escobedo/0.05%, Horace Wilkins, Richard W. Evans/1.02%, R. Denny Alexander/0.20%, Royce S. Caldwell/0.02%, Richard M. Kleberg/0.06%, Robert S. McClane/0.03%, Patrick B. Frost/1.54%, Karen E. Jennings/0.01%

Financial Data: Fiscal Year End:12/31   Latest Annual Data: 12/31/2006

Year	Sales		Net Income
2006		$924,707,000	$193,591,000
2005		$740,206,000	$165,423,000
2004		$622,031,000	$141,325,000
Curr. Assets:	$1,711,969,000	**Curr. Liab.:** $11,418,670,000	**P/E Ratio:** 15.86
Plant, Equip.:	$219,533,000	**Total Liab.:** $11,847,306,000	**Indic. Yr. Divd.:** $1.600
Total Assets:	$13,224,189,000	**Net Worth:** $1,376,883,000	**Debt/ Equity:** NA

Culp Inc

1823 Eastchester Dr., High Point, NC, 27265; **PH:** 1-336-889-5161; **Fax:** 1-336-889-7246;
http:// www.culpinc.com

General - Incorporation	NC	Stock- Price on:12/24/2007	$8.42
Employees	1,300	Stock Exchange	NYSE
Auditor	KPMG LLP	Ticker Symbol	CFI
Stk Agt	EquiServe Trust Co N.A	Outstanding Shares	12,550,000
Counsel	Robinson, Bradshaw & Hinson P.A.	E.P.S.	$0.01
DUNS No.	06-179-8369	Shareholders	NA

Business: The group's principal activities are to manufacture and market upholstery fabrics and mattress ticking. The group operates in two segments: upholstery fabrics and mattress ticking. The divisions within upholstery fabrics are culp decorative fabrics, culp velvets, prints and culp yarn. This segment's products include woven jacquards and dobbies, heat-transfer prints and woven and tufted velvets. The division within mattress ticking is culp home fashions, which manufactures products such as woven jacquards, heat-transfer prints and pigment prints and knitted ticking. The products are used in the residential and commercial furniture and bedding products, including sofas, recliners, chairs, loveseats, sectionals, sofa-beds, office seating, panel systems and mattress sets. The group has ten manufacturing facilities located in North Carolina, South Carolina and quebec, Canada.

Primary SIC and add'l.: 2211 2231 2221

CIK No: 0000723603

Subsidiaries: 3096726 Canada Inc., Culp Fabrics (Shanghai) Co., Ltd., Culp Fabrics (Shanghai) International Trading Co.,Ltd., Culp International Holdings Ltd., Rayonese Textile Inc.

Officers: Franklin N. Saxon/56/Dir., CEO, Pres./$707,160.00, Kenneth M. Ludwig/Sr. VP - Human Resources, Corp. Sec./$291,018.00, Kenneth R. Bowling/CFO, VP, Treasurer/$171,841.00, Thomas B. Gallagher/36/Corporate Controller, Assist. Treasurer

Directors: Franklin N. Saxon/56/Dir., CEO, Pres., Robert G. Culp/Chmn., Patrick B. Flavin/Dir., Jean L.P. Brunel/Dir., Kenneth W. McAllister/Dir., Kenneth R. Larson/Dir., Howard L. Dunn/Dir.

Owners: Robert G. Culp/17.90%, R. Scott Asen and related entities/10.60%, Praesidium Investment Management Company, LLC/5.80%, Atlantic Trust, Trustee/13.50%, T. Rowe Price Associates, Inc./7.80%, John B. Baum and related entities/6.20%, Dimensional Fund Advisors Inc./7.80%, Insiders/22.60%

Financial Data: Fiscal Year End:04/30   Latest Annual Data: 04/29/2007

Year	Sales		Net Income
2007		$250,533,000	-$1,316,000
2006		$261,101,000	-$11,796,000
2005		$286,498,000	-$17,852,000
Curr. Assets:	$105,222,000	**Curr. Liab.:** $35,697,000	
Plant, Equip.:	$77,770,000	**Total Liab.:** $90,337,000	**Indic. Yr. Divd.:** NA
Total Assets:	$193,728,000	**Net Worth:** $103,391,000	**Debt/ Equity:** NA

Cumberland Resources Ltd

950 - 505 Burrard St., Vancouver, BC, V7X 1M4; **PH:** 1-604-608-2557;
http:// www.cumberlandresources.com

General - Incorporation	Canada	Stock- Price on:12/24/2007	$6.9
Employees	15	Stock Exchange	NA
Auditor	Ernst & Young LLP	Ticker Symbol	NA
Stk Agt	Computershare Trust Co of Canada	Outstanding Shares	75,850,000
Counsel	Gowling, Lafleur, Henderson LLP	E.P.S.	NA
DUNS No.	NA	Shareholders	NA

Business: The groups principle activity is to provide mineral development and exploration services. The group operates from Canada.

Primary SIC and add'l.: 1041

CIK No: 0001016724

Subsidiaries: Meadowbank Mining Corporation

Officers: Kerry M. Curtis/Dir., CEO, Pres., Joyce L. Musial/Mgr. - Investor Relations, Gordon I. Davidson/Exploration Mgr. - Canada, Michael Haqpi/Community Liaison Officer - Baker Lake, Stuart D. McDonald/Corporate Controller, Principal Accounting Officer, Betty Goyette/Mgr. - Administration, Roger B. March/Sr. Project Geologist, Michael L. Carroll/Sr. VP, CFO, Corp. Sec., Craig Goodings/Mgr. - Environmental, Regulatory Affairs, Brad G. Thiele/VP - Meadowbank Project Development, Michael Rukus/Sr. Operations Accountant, Brian McGrath/Project Geologist, Jeff Kellner/Mgr. - Camp Operations, Andrew Hamilton/Project Geologist, Dave Fleming/Sr. Regional Geologist *(19 Officers included in Index)*

Directors: Kerry M. Curtis/Dir., CEO, Pres., Walter T. Segsworth/Chmn., Glen D. Dickson/Dir., Jonathan A. Rubenstein/Dir., Abraham I. Aronowicz/Dir., Richard M. Colterjohn/Dir., Michael J. Kenyon/Dir.

Financial Data: Fiscal Year End:12/31   Latest Annual Data: 12/31/2006

Year	Sales		Net Income
2006		$22,101,000	$5,934,000
2005		$2,132,000	-$8,247,000
2004		$3,158,000	-$10,372,000
Curr. Assets:	$115,945,000	**Curr. Liab.:** $15,226,000	
Plant, Equip.:	$20,096,000	**Total Liab.:** $19,625,000	**Indic. Yr. Divd.:** NA
Total Assets:	$144,931,000	**Net Worth:** $125,306,000	**Debt/ Equity:** NA

Cummins Inc

500 Jackson St., Columbus, IN, 47202; **PH:** 1-812-377-5000; **Fax:** 1-812-377-3334;
http:// www.cummins.com

General - Incorporation	IN	Stock- Price on:12/24/2007	$96.52
Employees	34,600	Stock Exchange	NYSE
Auditor	PricewaterhouseCoopers LLP	Ticker Symbol	CMI
Stk Agt	Wells Fargo Shareowner Services	Outstanding Shares	104,270,000
Counsel	NA	E.P.S.	$3.63
DUNS No.	00-641-5160	Shareholders	NA

Business: The groups principle activities include designing, manufacturing, and distributing diesel and natural gas engines. The group operates through four segments namely engine, power generation, components and distribution. The group operates from United States.

Primary SIC and add'l.: 3599 5015 3510 3592 3714 9999 3621

CIK No: 0000026172

Subsidiaries: 14-15 Corporation, 35601 Yukon, Inc., 4077652 Canada Inc., 4249739 Canada Inc., Atlas Crankshaft Corporation, Auto Diesels Power Plant Ltd., AvK Deutschland Verwaltungs GmbH, AvK SEG (India) Power Ltd., AvK SEG Holding Beteiligungs GmbH, Cal Pacific Engineering, Inc., CBM Technologies Pty. Ltd., CD Power Rent, S. de R.L. de C.V., Chongqing Cummins Engine Co. Ltd., Consolidated Diesel Company, Consolidated Diesel of N.C. Inc. 42 Subsidiaries included in the Index

Officers: Tim M. Solso/Chmn., CEO/$13,581,400.00, Steve M. Chapman/Group VP - Emerging Markets, Businesses, J. D. Kelly/Pres. - Engine Business/$3,581,911.00, Rich Freeland/Pres. - Distribution Business, Diane Coleman/Contact - Global Communications, Cummins Filtration Inquiries, Joe Loughrey/Dir., COO, Pres., Jean Blackwell/CFO, Exec. VP/$3,609,092.00, Richard E. Harris/55/VP, Treasurer, Marsha L. Hunt/44/VP, Corporate Controller, Marya Rose/45/VP, General

Counsel, Corp. Sec., Rick Mills/Pres. - Components Group, John Wall/CTO, VP, Carol Lavengood/Dir. - Marketing Communications, Ted Varner/Mgr. - Communications, Cummins Mercruiser Diesel, Steve Iverson/Contact - Cummins Power Generation Inquiries *(21 Officers included in Index)*

Directors: Tim M. Solso/Chmn., CEO, Carl Ware/Dir., Georgia R. Nelson/Dir., Joe Loughrey/Dir., COO, Pres., John M. Deutch/Dir., Alexis M. Herman/Dir., Robert J. Darnall/Dir., William I. Miller/Dir., Lawrence J. Wilson/Dir.

Owners: F. J. Loughrey, T. M. Solso, Georgia R. Nelson, Joseph F. Loughrey, Robert J. Darnall, T. Linebarger, Theodore M. Solso, State Street Bank and Trust Company/11.85%, Lawrence J. Wilson, Insiders, Alexis M. Herman, Carl Ware, William I. Miller, Barclays Global Investors, NA./13.21%, J. S. Blackwell *(17 Owners included in Index)*

Financial Data: Fiscal Year End:12/31 Latest Annual Data: 12/31/2006

Year	Sales	Net Income
2006	$11,362,000,000	$715,000,000
2005	$9,918,000,000	$550,000,000
2004	$8,438,000,000	$350,000,000

Curr. Assets:	$4,488,000,000	Curr. Liab.:	$2,399,000,000	P/E Ratio:	13.58
Plant, Equip.:	$1,574,000,000	Total Liab.:	$4,409,000,000	Indic. Yr. Divd.:	$1.000
Total Assets:	$7,465,000,000	Net Worth:	$2,802,000,000	Debt/ Equity:	0.2309

Cumulus Media Inc

3280 Peachtree Rd., NW, 3280 Peachtree Rd., NW, Atlanta, GA, 30305; *PH:* 1-404-949-0700; *Fax:* 1-404-949-0740; *http://* www.cumulus.com

General - Incorporation	DE	**Stock** - Price on:12/24/2007	$9.51
Employees	3,400	Stock Exchange	NDQ
Auditor	KPMG LLP	Ticker Symbol	CMLS
Stk Agt.	Firstar Trust Co	Outstanding Shares	43,150,000
Counsel	NA	E.P.S.	-$2.82
DUNS No.	01-966-0732	Shareholders	NA

Business: The group's principle activity is to acquire, operate and develop radio stations in mid-size radio markets in the United States and eastern Caribbean. The group also provides sales and marketing services under local marketing, management and consulting agreements. Revenue is derived primarily from the sale of commercial airtime to local and national advertisers. As of 31-Dec-2003, the group owned and operated 266 radio stations in the United States. The group's quarterly revenue for September 2007 was 84.18 millions of USD.

Primary SIC and add'l.: 4832

CIK No: 0001058623

Officers: Lewis W. Dickey/Chmn., CEO, Pres./$5,033,476.00, Martin R. Gausvik/CFO, Exec. VP, Treasurer/$853,045.00, John W. Dickey/COO/$1,510,644.00, Richard Denning/VP, General Counsel, Jonathan G. Pinch/COO, Exec. VP/$933,631.00

Directors: Lewis W. Dickey/Chmn., CEO, Pres., Ralph B. Everett/Dir., Holcombe T. Green/68/Dir., Eric Robison/Dir., Robert H. Sheridan/Dir.

Owners: Jon G. Pinch/1.40%, Insiders/100.00%, Lewis W. Dickey/7.70%, Insiders/20.30%, Insiders/20.30%, Robert H. Sheridan, Banc of America Capital Investors SBIC, L.P./2.20%, Martin R. Gausvik/3.00%, BA Capital Company, L.P./2.60%, Wallace R. Weitz & Company/12.30%, BA Capital Company, L.P./14.60%, John W. Dickey/8.20%, Eric P. Robison, Dimensional Fund Advisors Inc./9.60%, Banc of America Capital Investors SBIC, L.P./85.40% *(20 Owners included in Index)*

Financial Data: Fiscal Year End:12/31 Latest Annual Data: 12/31/2006

Year	Sales	Net Income
2006	$334,321,000	-$44,588,000
2005	$327,756,000	-$213,367,000
2004	$320,132,000	$30,369,000

Curr. Assets:	$62,882,000	Curr. Liab.:	$38,326,000		
Plant, Equip.:	$71,474,000	Total Liab.:	$996,140,000	Indic. Yr. Divd.:	NA
Total Assets:	$1,333,147,000	Net Worth:	$337,007,000	Debt/ Equity:	2.2069

Curagen Corp

322 E Main St., Branford, CT, 06405; *PH:* 1-203-481-1104; *Fax:* 1-203-483-2552; *http://* www.curagen.com; *Email:* info@curagen.com

General - Incorporation	DE	**Stock** - Price on:12/24/2007	$2.09
Employees	255	Stock Exchange	NDQ
Auditor	Deloitte & Touche LLP	Ticker Symbol	CRGN
Stk Agt.	American Stock Transfer & Trust Co.	Outstanding Shares	56,940,000
Counsel	NA	E.P.S.	$0.22
DUNS No.	80-902-6289	Shareholders	NA

Business: The group's principal activity is to apply functional genomic technologies and Internet-based bioinformatic systems to discover and develop pharmaceutical products to treat unmet medical needs. The group operates in the genomics-based pharmaceutical industry, combining engineering principles with biology and information technology to discover and develop genomics-based pharmaceutical products. The main focus is on developing protein, antibody and small molecule therapeutics to treat major unmet medical needs including obesity and diabetes, oncology, inflammation, and central nervous system disorders. The group has established internal programs to develop products to treat metabolic diseases, cancer, inflammatory diseases, and central nervous system disorders.

Primary SIC and add'l.: 8731

CIK No: 0001030653

Subsidiaries: 454 Life Sciences Corporation

Officers: Timothy M. Shannon/CEO, Pres./$985,724.00, Elizabeth A. Whayland/Corp. Sec. a, Sr. VP - Finance/$537,618.00, David M. Wurzer/Exec. VP, CFO, Treasurer, Mary Taylor/Sr. VP - Regulatory Affairs, Quality Assurance, Henri S. Lichenstein/VP - Product Development, Paul M. Finigan/Exec. VP, General Counsel, Ronit Simantov/VP - Medical Development

Directors: Robert E. Patricelli/Non Exec. Chmn., Frank M. Armstrong/Dir., John H. Forsgren/Dir., Vincent T. Devita/Dir., Patrick J. Zenner/Dir., James Noble/Dir.

Owners: Alex A. Porter/7.40%, John H. Forsgren, Dimensional Fund Advisors Inc/5.60%, Frank M. Armstrong/1.00%, David R. Ebsworth, Bayer AG/5.50%, James J. Noble, Pequot Capital Management, Inc./5.00%, Timothy M. Shannon, Robert E. Patricelli, David M. Wurzer/1.00%, Elizabeth A. Whayland, Jonathan M. Rothberg/10.60%, Insiders/16.50%, Patrick J. Zenner *(17 Owners included in Index)*

Financial Data: Fiscal Year End:12/31 Latest Annual Data: 12/31/2006

Year	Sales	Net Income
2006	$39,587,000	-$59,839,000
2005	$23,531,000	-$73,244,000
2004	$6,339,000	-$90,397,000

Curr. Assets:	$195,971,000	Curr. Liab.:	$90,349,000	P/E Ratio:	19.00
Plant, Equip.:	$16,160,000	Total Liab.:	$218,470,000	Indic. Yr. Divd.:	NA
Total Assets:	$227,199,000	Net Worth:	$8,729,000	Debt/ Equity:	NA

CuraTech Industries Inc

6337 Highland Dr., Ste. 1053, Salt City, UT, 84121; *PH:* 1-801-836-9810

General - Incorporation	UT	**Stock** - Price on:12/24/2007	$1.88
Employees		Stock Exchange	OTC
Auditor	Moore & Assoc., Chartered	Ticker Symbol	CUTC
Stk Agt.	Transfer Agent Co.	Outstanding Shares	15,910,000
Counsel	NA	E.P.S.	-$0.12
DUNS No.	NA	Shareholders	NA

Business: The group's principal activities include acquiring, developing and marketing a certain health supplement. The group operates from the United States.

Primary SIC and add'l.: 6799

CIK No: 0001302143

Officers: Lincoln Dastrup/53/Dir., CEO, CFO, Jarom Dastrup/28/Dir., Exec. VP, Sec., Linda L. Dastrup/49/Dir., Treasurer

Directors: Lincoln Dastrup/53/Dir., CEO, CFO, Jarom Dastrup/28/Dir., Exec. VP, Sec., Linda L. Dastrup/49/Dir., Treasurer

Owners: Vastmann Investment Partners, LLC/5.30%, Insiders/58.00%, The Dastrup Family Trust/47.20%, Jarom Dastrup/11.70%

Financial Data: Fiscal Year End:12/31 Latest Annual Data: 12/31/2006

Year	Sales	Net Income
2006	NA	-$581,000
2005	NA	-$33,000

Curr. Assets:	$47,000	Curr. Liab.:	$7,000		
Plant, Equip.:	$7,000	Total Liab.:	$7,000	Indic. Yr. Divd.:	NA
Total Assets:	$54,000	Net Worth:	$47,000	Debt/ Equity:	NA

Curis Inc

45 Moulton St., Cambridge, MA, 02138; *PH:* 1-617-503-6500; *Fax:* 1-617-503-6501; *http://* www.curis.com; *Email:* info@curis.com

General - Incorporation	DE	**Stock** - Price on:12/24/2007	$1.22
Employees	51	Stock Exchange	NDQ
Auditor	PricewaterhouseCoopers LLP	Ticker Symbol	CRIS
Stk Agt.	Chase Mellon Shareholder Services LLC	Outstanding Shares	49,380,000
Counsel	Hale & Dorr LLP	E.P.S.	-$0.21
DUNS No.	NA	Shareholders	NA

Business: The group's principal activity is to discover and develop therapeutic drug regulatory pathways that control repair and regeneration of human tissues and organs. The group's product development involves using proteins or small molecules to modulate these pathways, so as to increase the pathway signals when they are insufficient or decrease them when they are excessive. The group has used this technology and product development strategy to produce several drug product candidates in the fields of kidney disease, neurological disorders, cancer, cardiovascular disease and hair growth regulation.

Primary SIC and add'l.: 8731 2836

CIK No: 0001108205

Subsidiaries: Curis Securities Corporation

Officers: Daniel R. Passeri/Dir., CEO, Pres./$1,045,309.00, Mark Noel/VP - Technology Management, Business Development/$355,185.00, Michael P. Gray/CFO, COO/$674,495.00, Changgeng Qian/VP - Discovery, Preclinical Development

Directors: Daniel R. Passeri/Dir., CEO, Pres., James R. McNab/Chmn., Kenneth I. Kaitin/Dir., Susan B. Bayh/Dir., Stuart A. Aaronson/Member - Scientific Advisory Board, James R. Tobin/Dir., Joseph M. Davie/Dir., Member - Scientific Advisory Board, Martyn D. Greenacre/Dir., Kenneth J. Pienta/Member - Scientific Advisory Board, George F. Vande Woude/Member - Scientific Advisory Board

Owners: Martyn D. Greenacre, Kenneth I. Kaitin, Joseph M. Davie, Biotechnology Value Fund, L.P./5.21%, Douglas A. Melton/1.22%, James R. Tobin, Susan B. Bayh, Daniel R. Passeri/2.92%, Stephens Investment Management, LLC/8.68%, Mary Elizabeth Potthoff, Lee L. Rubin, Mark W. Noel, Michael P. Gray, James R. McNab/2.57%, Insiders/10.28%

Financial Data: Fiscal Year End:12/31 Latest Annual Data: 06/30/2007

Year	Sales	Net Income
2007	$1,229,000	-$3,998,000
2006	$16,663,000	-$8,829,000
2005	$6,002,000	-$14,855,000

Curr. Assets:	$38,513,000	Curr. Liab.:	$5,992,000		
Plant, Equip.:	$4,394,000	Total Liab.:	$16,371,000	Indic. Yr. Divd.:	NA
Total Assets:	$52,268,000	Net Worth:	$35,897,000	Debt/ Equity:	0.0066

Current Technology Corp

800 W Pender St., Ste. 1430, Vancouver, BC, V6C 2V6; *PH:* 1-604-684-2727; *Fax:* 1-604-684-0526; *http://* www.ctc.com; *Email:* usa@current-technology.com

General - Incorporation	Canada	**Stock** - Price on:12/24/2007	$0.12
Employees	NA	Stock Exchange	OTC
Auditor	Cinnamon, Jang, Willoughby & Co	Ticker Symbol	CRTCF
Stk Agt.	Computershare Investor Services LLC	Outstanding Shares	NA
Counsel	NA	E.P.S.	NA
DUNS No.	24-824-9336	Shareholders	NA

Business: The group's principle activities include developing, manufacturing and marketing electrotherapeutic device designed to reduce hair loss and/or stimulate hair regrowth; and operates centers which offer company's hair treatment to clients, in Canada. The group operates from United States.

Primary SIC and add'l.: 3845 8093

CIK No: 0000883907

Subsidiaries: Anchorage Capital Partners Limited, England Corporate Finance

Officers: Robert Kramer/Dir., CEO, Pres., Anne Kramer/Chmn., Sec., Anthony J. Harrison/Dir., COO, Roger W. Gunter/Contact - Fort Leonard Wood, MO, Christopher A. Brown/Contact - Greenville, SC, Larry G. Salter/Contact - Bremerton, WA, George E. McAllister/Contact - Charleston, SC, Marty W. Rogers/VP - CTcanada, Michael A. Katz/COO, Sr. VP, Melissa J. Zegarelli/Dir. Management Systems - Services, Mary T. Bevan/Mgr. - Communications Resources, Linda A. Monzo/GM - Global Systems Group, Jerry R. Hudson/VP - Strategic Programs, Janice M. Menker/CTC Ethics Officer, Edward J. Sheehan/Sr. VP, CFO *(36 Officers included in Index)*

Directors: Robert Kramer/Dir., CEO, Pres., Anne Kramer/Chmn., Sec., Anthony J. Harrison/Dir., COO, George A. Chen/Dir., Peter W. Bell/Dir., Douglas Beder/Dir.

Financial Data: Fiscal Year End:12/31 **Latest Annual Data:** 12/31/2006

Year	Sales	Net Income
2006	$327,000	-$1,619,000
2005	$427,000	-$1,557,000
2004	$278,000	-$1,461,000

Curr. Assets:	$233,000	Curr. Liab.:	$557,000		
Plant, Equip.:	NA	Total Liab.:	$1,271,000	Indic. Yr. Divd.:	NA
Total Assets:	$233,000	Net Worth:	-$1,038,000	Debt/ Equity:	NA

Curtiss-Wright Corp

4 Becker Farm Rd., 3rd Fl., Roseland, NJ, 07068; **PH:** 1-973-597-4700; **Fax:** 1-973-597-4799; *http://* www.curtisswright.com

General - Incorporation	DE	Stock- Price on:12/24/2007	$46.34
Employees	6,233	Stock Exchange	NYSE
Auditor	Deloitte & Touche LLP	Ticker Symbol	CW
Stk Agt	American Stock Transfer & Trust Co.	Outstanding Shares	44,290,000
Counsel	NA	E.P.S.	$1.97
DUNS No.	NA	Shareholders	NA

Business: The groups principle activity is to manage and evaluates operations based on the products and services. The group operates through three segments namely, flow control, motion control and metal treatment. The group operates from the United States, Canada and the United Kingdom. The group's quarterly revenue for September 2007 was 396.27 millions of USD.

Primary SIC and add'l.: 3494 3728 3479

CIK No: 0000026324

Subsidiaries: Autronics Corporation, Curtiss-Wright Antriebstechnik GmbH, Curtiss-Wright Controls, Inc., Curtiss-Wright Electro-Mechanical Corporation, Curtiss-Wright Flow Control Company Canada, Curtiss-Wright Flow Control Corporation, Dy 4, Inc., Metal Improvement Company, LLC, Novatronics, Inc., Peerless Instrument Co., Inc., Penny & Giles Controls Limited, Primagraphics (Holdings) Limited, Synergy Microsystems, Inc., Systran Corporation, Vista Controls, Inc.

Officers: Martin R. Benante/Chmn., CEO/$4,096,812.00, David C. Adams/Pres. - Motion Control Segment/$1,145,821.00, Edward Bloom/Pres. - Metal Treatment Segment/$2,148,482.00, David J. Linton/Pres. - Flow Control Segment/$1,119,199.00, Glenn E. Tynan/CFO, VP/$1,101,527.00, Michael J. Denton/VP, General Counsel, Corp. Sec., Parker B. Miller/Sr. VP - Government Relations, Kevin McClurg/Controller, Alexandra Deignan/Dir. - Investor Relation

Directors: Martin R. Benante/Chmn., CEO, James B. Busey/Dir., Marce S. Fuller/Dir., Allen A. Kozinski/Dir., Carl G. Miller/Dir., John R. Myers/Dir., William W. Sihler/Dir., Albert E. Smith/Dir., William B. Mitchell/72/Dir.

Owners: Singleton Group LLC/8.50%, David C. Adams, William S. Sihler, Marce S. Fuller, Glenn E. Tynan, Albert E. Smith, Lord, Abbett & Co. LLC/12.80%, Edward Bloom, Martin R. Benante, Barclays Global Investors, NA/5.10%, GAMCO Investors, Inc. formerly known as Gabelli Asset Management, Inc./6.90%, David J. Linton, Insiders/1.00%, James B. Busey, William B. Mitchell *(21 Owners included in Index)*

Financial Data: Fiscal Year End:12/31 **Latest Annual Data:** 12/31/2006

Year	Sales	Net Income
2006	$1,282,155,000	$80,569,000
2005	$1,130,928,000	$75,280,000
2004	$955,039,000	$65,066,000

Curr. Assets:	$622,645,000	Curr. Liab.:	$292,125,000	P/E Ratio:	23.52
Plant, Equip.:	$296,652,000	Total Liab.:	$830,082,000	Indic. Yr. Divd.:	$0.240
Total Assets:	$1,592,156,000	Net Worth:	$762,074,000	Debt/ Equity:	0.4562

Cusac Gold Mines Ltd

911 - 470 Granville St., Vancouver, BC, V6C 1V5; **PH:** 1-604-682-2421; **Fax:** 1-604-682-7576; *http://* www.cusac.com; **Email:** info@cusac.com

General - Incorporation	BC	Stock- Price on:12/24/2007	$0.1755
Employees	NA	Stock Exchange	OTC
Auditor	BDO Dunwoody LLP	Ticker Symbol	CUSIF
Stk Agt	Pacific Corporate Trust Co.	Outstanding Shares	NA
Counsel	NA	E.P.S.	NA
DUNS No.	20-510-7113	Shareholders	NA

Business: The group's principal activities are the exploration, development and mining of resource properties in Canada. The group's principal asset table mountain gold mine is located in northern british Colombia. As at 31-Dec-2001, this mine was non-producing and in a care and maintenance mode.

Primary SIC and add'l.: 1041

CIK No: 0000768374

Officers: David H. Brett/Dir., CEO, Leonora Brett/CFO, Sec., Treasurer, Lesley Hunt/VP - Exploration

Directors: David H. Brett/Dir., CEO, Pres., Guildford H. Brett/Chmn., Luard J. Manning/Dir., Michael Smyth/Member - Advisory Board, George Sanders/Dir.

Owners: George Sanders, Garth Kirkham, David H. Brett, Luard Manning, Guilford H. Brett, Insiders/1.70%, Leonora Brett

Financial Data: Fiscal Year End:12/31 **Latest Annual Data:** 12/31/2006

Year	Sales	Net Income
2006	NA	-$5,215,000
2005	NA	-$1,431,000
2004	NA	-$1,932,000

Curr. Assets:	$1,155,000	Curr. Liab.:	$2,522,000		
Plant, Equip.:	$2,575,000	Total Liab.:	$3,539,000	Indic. Yr. Divd.:	NA
Total Assets:	$4,451,000	Net Worth:	$912,000	Debt/ Equity:	NA

Custom Branded Networks Inc

8300 Greensboro Dr., Ste. 800, Mclean, VA, 22102; **PH:** 1-703-918-4904; *http://* www.thoriumpower.com

General - Incorporation	NV	Stock- Price on:12/24/2007	$0.275
Employees	5	Stock Exchange	NDQ
Auditor	Telford Sadovnick, PLLC	Ticker Symbol	NA
Stk Agt	Computershare Trust Co	Outstanding Shares	297,690,000
Counsel	NA	E.P.S.	-$0.089
DUNS No.	NA	Shareholders	NA

Business: The group's principal activity is to provide turnkey private label Internet solutions to businesses and private organizations. It also sells the individual components of its services to established Internet service providers (isp). The group has one isp relationship in place for dial-up modem service. The group also provides the customer set-up and the branded compact disc with the customer's unique content and packaging. The group provides its services throughout the United States and Canada.

Primary SIC and add'l.: 7379

CIK No: 0001084554

Subsidiaries: Aquistar Ventures Inc., Thorium Power Inc, TP Acquisition Corp.

Owners: Insiders/9.45%, Andrey Mushakov/1.08%, Seth Grae/7.03%, Victor E. Alessi/0.06%, Thomas Graham, Erik Hallstrom/0.09%, Daniel B. Magraw/0.17%, Jack D. Ladd/0.08%, Larry Goldman/0.08%, OTC Investments Ltd./5.30%

Financial Data: Fiscal Year End:06/30 **Latest Annual Data:** 6/30/2006

Year	Sales	Net Income
2006	NA	-$13,345,000
2005	NA	-$2,692,000

Curr. Assets:	$15,240,000	Curr. Liab.:	$5,274,000		
Plant, Equip.:	NA	Total Liab.:	$17,315,000	Indic. Yr. Divd.:	NA
Total Assets:	$16,590,000	Net Worth:	-$725,000	Debt/ Equity:	NA

Cutera Inc

3240 Bayshore Blvd., Brisbane, CA, 94005; **PH:** 1-415-657-5500; **Fax:** 1-415-330-2444; *http://* www.cutera.com; **Email:** info@cutera.com

General - Incorporation	DE	Stock- Price on:12/24/2007	$24.87
Employees	221	Stock Exchange	NDQ
Auditor	PricewaterhouseCoopers LLP	Ticker Symbol	CUTR
Stk Agt	Computershare Trust Co	Outstanding Shares	13,550,000
Counsel	NA	E.P.S.	$0.89
DUNS No.	04-107-1643	Shareholders	NA

Business: The groups principle activity is to designing, development, manufacturing, marketing and servicing of laser and other light-based aesthetics systems. The group products include Xeo, Solera and coolglide. The group operates from United States.

Primary SIC and add'l.: 3845

CIK No: 0001162461

Officers: Kevin P. Connors/Dir., CEO, Pres./$1,078,676.00, David A. Gollnick/Dir., VP - Research, Development/$592,537.00, Ronald J. Santilli/CFO, VP - Finance, Administration/$667,498.00, John J. Connors/VP - North American Sales/$653,841.00, Robert J. Shine/39/VP - International/$312,692.00, John Mills/Contact - Integrated Corporate Relations

Directors: Kevin P. Connors/Dir., CEO, Pres., David A. Gollnick/Dir., VP - Research, Development, Annette J. Campbell-White/Dir., David B. Apfelberg/Dir., Jerry P. Widman/Dir., Mark Lortz/Dir., Timothy J. O'Shea/Dir.

Owners: David B. Apfelberg, Insiders/10.10%, Kevin P. Connors, Mark W. Lortz/2.30%, John J. Connors, Robert J. Shine, David A. Gollnick/5.30%, Annette J. Campbell-White, Ronald J. Santilli

Financial Data: Fiscal Year End:12/31 **Latest Annual Data:** 12/31/2006

Year	Sales	Net Income
2006	$100,692,000	$2,123,000
2005	$75,620,000	$13,801,000
2004	$52,641,000	$3,760,000

Curr. Assets:	$131,400,000	Curr. Liab.:	$19,401,000	P/E Ratio:	130.90
Plant, Equip.:	$1,029,000	Total Liab.:	$24,143,000	Indic. Yr. Divd.:	NA
Total Assets:	$133,875,000	Net Worth:	$109,732,000	Debt/ Equity:	NA

Cutter & Buck Inc

701 N 34th St., Ste. 400, Seattle, WA, 98103; **PH:** 1-206-622-4191; *http://* www.cutterbuck.com

General - Incorporation	WA	Stock- Price on:12/24/2007	NA
Employees	359	Stock Exchange	NDQ
Auditor	Ernst & Young LLP	Ticker Symbol	CBUK
Stk Agt	Mellon Investor Services LLC	Outstanding Shares	NA
Counsel	Lane Powell Spears Lubersky	E.P.S.	NA
DUNS No.	60-913-1081	Shareholders	NA

Business: The group's principal activity is to design, source, market and distribute men's and women's sportswear, fashion and outerwear apparel. The men's line offers sportswear for golf, business casual, family activities, active lifestyle and casually-elegant situations. It also offers knit and woven shirts, pants, shorts, sweaters, vests, wind and rain apparel, jackets and accessories. The women's line provides clothing for golf, active lifestyle and casual weekend use. These products are marketed under the cutter & buck brand. The group's products are sold primarily through golf pro shops and resorts, corporate accounts and specialty retail stores and international distributors and licensees. The group's products are marketed in Australia, New Zealand, the Philippines, the united arab emirates, saudi arabia, bahrain, qatar, kuwait, oman, South Africa, Singapore, Malaysia, Japan, Korea, Hong Kong, China and Canada.

Primary SIC and add'l.: 2331 2339 5651 5137 5136 2329 5611

CIK No: 0000948069

Subsidiaries: Cutter & Buck (Europe) B.V., Cutter & Buck Direct LLC.

Officers: Ernest R. Johnson/Dir., CEO, Brian C. Thompson/VP, GM - Golf, Corporate, International, Domestic Licensing, Timothy C. Cronin/Pres., Nancy Pethick/Executive Assist., Michael Gats/CFO, VP, Sec., Jon P. Runkel/VP - Global Sourcing, Distribution, Julie Snow/VP - Design, Global Marketing

Directors: Ernest R. Johnson/Dir., CEO, Torsten Jansson/Chmn., Goran Harstedt/Dir., Jens Petersson/Dir., Jack Repetto/Dir.

Owners: Jon P. Runkel, Henry L. Kotkins, Michael Gats, Thomas F. ORiordan, Douglas G. Southern, Royce & Associates LLC/12.40%, Insiders/6.00%, Julie Snow, Whitney R. Tilson/1.60%, Dimensional Fund Advisors Inc./8.00%, Ernest R. Johnson, Pirate Capital LLC/12.50%, Kaia Akre, T. Rowe Price Associates, Inc./10.20%, Larry C. Mounger/1.00% *(18 Owners included in Index)*

CV Therapeutics Inc

3172 Porter Dr., Palo Alto, CA, 94304; ***PH:*** 1-650-384-8500; ***Fax:*** 1-650-858-0390; ***http://*** www.cvt.com

General - Incorporation	DE	***Stock***- Price on:12/24/2007	$13.37
Employees	746	Stock Exchange	NDQ
Auditor	Ernst & Young LLP	Ticker Symbol	CVTX
Stk Agt	Wells Fargo Bank Minnesota N.A	Outstanding Shares	59,370,000
Counsel	Latham & Watkins LLP	E.P.S	-$3.65
DUNS No.	79-624-8110	Shareholders	NA

Business: The group's principal activity is to focus on applying molecular cardiology to the discovery, development and markets of novel, small molecule drugs for the treatment of cardiovascular diseases. The group currently has four compounds in clinical trials. Ranolazine, the first in a new class of compounds known as partial fatty acid oxidation inhibitors. Cvt-510 (tecadenoson), an a1 adenosine receptor agonist, is being developed for the potential reduction of rapid heart rate during atrial arrhythmias. Cvt-3146, an a2a adenosine receptor agonist, is being developed for the potential use as a pharmacologic agent in cardiac perfusion imaging studies. Adentri (TM), an a1 adenosine receptor antagonist, is being developed by the group's partner biogen, inc., for the potential treatment of acute and chronic congestive heart failure.

Primary SIC and add'l.: 8731 2834

CIK No: 0000921506

Officers: Louis G. Lange/Chmn., CEO, Chief Science Officer/$4,328,052.00, Richard M. Lawn/VP - Discovery Research, Member - Scientific Advisory Board, Anders Waas/VP - Business Development, Luiz Belardinelli/Sr. VP - Pharmacological, Translational Biomedical Research CVT Distinguished Fellow, Cardiovascular Science, Lewis J. Stuart/Sr. VP - Commercial Operations, David Banks/Sr. VP - Operations, Lorenz Muller/VP - Marketing, Carol D. Karp/VP - Regulatory Affairs, Daniel K. Spiegelman/CFO, Sr. VP/$1,239,177.00, Brent K. Blackburn/Sr. VP - Drug Discovery, Development/$1,259,177.00, David C. McCaleb/54/Sr. VP - Commercial Operations/$1,096,018.00, Diane L. Liguori/Sr. VP - Human Resources, Tricia Borga Suvari/Sr. VP, General Counsel, Sec./$1,124,421.00

Directors: Louis G. Lange/Chmn., CEO, Chief Science Officer, Richard M. Lawn/VP - Discovery Research, Member - Scientific Advisory Board, Burton E. Sobel/Member - Scientific Advisory Board, Barbara J. McNeil/Dir., Kenneth B. Lee/Dir., Peter Barton Hutt/Dir., Joseph M. Davie/Dir., Richard Havel/Member - Scientific Advisory Board, Stuart A. Aaronson/Member - Scientific Advisory Board, Garret Fitzgerald/Member - Scientific Advisory Board, Thomas E. Shenk/Dir., Santo J. Costa/Dir., Christopher J. Fielding/Member - Scientific Advisory Board, Andrew A. Wolff/Member - Scientific Advisory Board, Victor J. Dzau/Member - Scientific Advisory Board *(18 Directors included in Index)*

Owners: Peter Barton Hutt, Ross Financial Corporation/6.40%, Sectoral Asset Management Inc./6.89%, Citigroup, Inc./8.18%, Thomas L. Gutshall, FMR Corp/9.76%, David McCaleb, Thomas E. Shenk, Kenneth B. Lee, Joseph M. Davie, Insiders/4.50%, Morgan Stanley/5.14%, Delaware Management Holdings/5.48%, Barbara J. McNeil, Louis G. Lange/1.64% *(22 Owners included in Index)*

Financial Data: ***Fiscal Year End:***12/31 ***Latest Annual Data:*** 12/31/2006

Year	Sales	Net Income
2006	$36,785,000	-$274,320,000
2005	$18,951,000	-$227,995,000
2004	$20,428,000	-$155,083,000

Curr. Assets:	$365,495,000	***Curr. Liab.:***	$62,247,000		
Plant, Equip.:	$23,919,000	***Total Liab.:***	$467,254,000	***Indic. Yr. Divd.:***	NA
Total Assets:	$421,456,000	***Net Worth:***	-$45,798,000	***Debt/ Equity:***	NA

CVB Financial Corp

701 N HAve.n Ave., Ste. 350, Ontario, CA, 91764; ***PH:*** 1-909-980-4030; ***Fax:*** 1-909-481-2131; ***http://*** www.cbbank.com

General - Incorporation	CA	***Stock***- Price on:12/24/2007	$11.07
Employees	522	Stock Exchange	NDQ
Auditor	McGladrey & Pullen LLP, D & T LLP	Ticker Symbol	CVBF
Stk Agt	U.S. Stock Transfer Corp	Outstanding Shares	83,210,000
Counsel	Manatt, Phelps & Phillips LLP	E.P.S	$0.76
DUNS No.	60-589-7123	Shareholders	NA

Business: The group's principal activity is to provide deposit instruments, lending products and investment services. The group is a bank holding company that operates through its subsidiaries, citizens business bank, community trust deed services and cvb ventures, inc. The services provided by the group include checking, savings, money market and time deposits. The group's products include commercial, agribusiness, instalment and real estate loans. Other services include cash management systems, financial services and trust services. The banking services are offered through 37 branch offices located in san bernardino, riverside, eastern portion of los angeles, orange, and kern counties. On 19-Sep-2003, the group acquired kaweah national bank.

Primary SIC and add'l.: 6712 6022

CIK No: 0000354647

Subsidiaries: Chino Valley Bancorp., Citizens Business Bank, Community Trust Deed Services, CVB is also the indirect holding company for Golden West Enterprises, Inc, CVB Ventures, Inc, Orange National Bancorp

Officers: Christopher D. Myers/46/Dir., CEO, Pres./$834,250.00, Edward J. Mylett/59/Exec. VP/$405,533.00, Edward J. Biebrich/64/CFO/$465,653.00, Jay W. Coleman/65/Exec. VP/$469,008.00

Directors: Christopher D. Myers/46/Dir., CEO, Pres., Linn D. Wiley/69/Vice Chmn., George A. Borba/75/Chmn., Ronald O. Kruse/69/Vice Chmn., Robert M. Jacoby/66/Dir., John A. Borba/80/Dir., James C. Seley/66/Dir., San E. Vaccaro/75/Dir.

Owners: Jay W. Coleman, Robert M. Jacoby, Insiders/21.50%, San E. Vaccaro, Ronald O. Kruse/2.25%, Edward J. Biebrich, John Vander Schaaf/5.22%, George A. Borba/13.81%, James C. Seley, Christopher D. Myers, John A. Borba/2.64%, Edward J. Mylett, Linn D. Wiley, Scott R. Racusin

Financial Data: ***Fiscal Year End:***12/31 ***Latest Annual Data:*** 12/31/2006

Year	Sales	Net Income
2006	$349,918,000	$71,906,000
2005	$278,309,000	$70,618,000
2004	$231,909,000	$61,486,000

Curr. Assets:	$176,636,000	***Curr. Liab.:***	$4,612,214,000	***P/E Ratio:***	13.67
Plant, Equip.:	$44,963,000	***Total Liab.:***	$5,704,923,000	***Indic. Yr. Divd.:***	$0.340
Total Assets:	$6,094,262,000	***Net Worth:***	$389,339,000	***Debt/ Equity:***	NA

CVD Equipment Corp

1860 Smithtown Ave., Ronkonkoma, NY, 11779; ***PH:*** 1-631-981-7081; ***Fax:*** 1-631-981-7095; ***http://*** www.cvdequipment.com; ***Email:*** info@cvdequipment.com

General - Incorporation	NY	***Stock***- Price on:12/24/2007	$5.82
Employees	106	Stock Exchange	NDQ
Auditor	Moore Stephens, P.C	Ticker Symbol	CVV
Stk Agt	Continental Stock Transfer & Trust Co	Outstanding Shares	3,300,000
Counsel	Kelly, Drye & Warren	E.P.S	$0.22
DUNS No.	08-138-0198	Shareholders	NA

Business: The group's principal activity is to design, develop, manufacture, market, install and service equipment for the semiconductor industry. The products include chemical vapor deposition (cvd) equipment, customized gas control systems and hydrogen annealing and brazing furnaces. These products are used primarily to produce semiconductors and other electronic components. Cvd is a process that passes a gaseous compound over a target material surface that is heated to such a degree that the compound decomposes and deposits a desired layer onto substrate material. The group also provides semiconductor equipment consulting and refurbishing services. The customers include semiconductor, telecommunications and computer companies. The products are sold in the United States and Asia.

Primary SIC and add'l.: 3559 3679

CIK No: 0000766792

Subsidiaries: CVD Materials Corporation

Officers: Leonard A. Rosenbaum/Dir., CEO, Pres., Glen Charles/CFO, Sec.

Directors: Leonard A. Rosenbaum/Dir., CEO, Pres., Bruce T. Swan/Dir., Conrad Gunther/Dir., Alan H. Temple/Dir., Martin J. Teitelbaum/Dir.

Owners: Bruce T. Swan, Martin J. Teitelbaum/1.40%, Insiders/35.80%, Brian J. Stark/8.50%, Glen R. Charles, Leonard A. Rosenbaum/28.60%, Alan H. Temple/3.80%, Conrad J. Gunther, Michael A. Roth/8.50%

Financial Data: ***Fiscal Year End:***12/31 ***Latest Annual Data:*** 12/31/2006

Year	Sales	Net Income
2006	$13,356,000	$604,000
2005	$11,225,000	$391,000
2004	$9,874,000	$71,000

Curr. Assets:	$6,425,000	***Curr. Liab.:***	$2,274,000	***P/E Ratio:***	32.51
Plant, Equip.:	$4,779,000	***Total Liab.:***	$5,718,000	***Indic. Yr. Divd.:***	NA
Total Assets:	$12,918,000	***Net Worth:***	$7,200,000	***Debt/ Equity:***	NA

CVF Technologies Corp

8604 Main St., Ste. 1, Williamsville, NY, 14221; ***PH:*** 1-716-565-4711; ***Fax:*** 1-716-565-4717; ***http://*** www.cvfcorp.com; ***Email:*** cvf@cvftechnologies.com

General - Incorporation	NV	***Stock***- Price on:12/24/2007	$0.225
Employees	11	Stock Exchange	OTC
Auditor	Sherb & Co. LLP	Ticker Symbol	CNVT
Stk Agt	Mellon Trust Co	Outstanding Shares	12,640,000
Counsel	Hodgson Russ	E.P.S	-$0.15
DUNS No.	NA	Shareholders	NA

Business: The group's principal activity is to develop and manage start-up and early stage companies in the information and environmental technologies sectors. The group operates five business segments: bioremediation, machine controls, identification systems, natural fertilizer and corporate. The bioremediation segment is involved in bioconversion and biotransformation of industrial contamination of soil or groundwater. The machine controls division designs, manufactures and markets electric motor controls to machine manufacturers. The identification segment develops identification and database systems for precious gem business. The natural fertilizer segment develops, manufactures and markets natural fertilizers, insecticides and herbicides. The group's general corporate segment provides funding and management overview services to the holdings. The group has its operations in the United States and Canada.

Primary SIC and add'l.: 6719 7379 4952 3669 2873 3625

CIK No: 0001032997

Subsidiaries: Biorem Inc, Ecoval Corporation, G.P. Royalty Distribution Corporation, Petrozyme Technologies Inc

Officers: Jeffrey I. Dreben/62/Chmn., CEO, Pres., Robert Nally/60/Dir., COO, CTO, Sec., Treasurer, Robert Miller/56/CFO

Directors: Jeffrey I. Dreben/62/Chmn., CEO, Pres., Robert Nally/60/Dir., COO, CTO, Sec., Treasurer, Robert Glazier/59/Dir.

Owners: Bounty Equity Fund 2, LLC/6.10%, Robert L. Miller/1.60%, Jeffrey I. Dreben/11.10%, Insiders/24.00%, Robert H. Glazier/1.50%, Robert B. Nally/9.80%, The Shaar Fund Ltd./8.70%

Financial Data: ***Fiscal Year End:***12/31 ***Latest Annual Data:*** 12/31/2006

Year	Sales	Net Income
2006	$1,512,000	-$1,845,000
2005	$457,000	$5,300,000
2004	$7,958,000	-$1,863,000

Curr. Assets:	$2,834,000	***Curr. Liab.:***	$2,323,000		
Plant, Equip.:	$12,000	***Total Liab.:***	$2,999,000	***Indic. Yr. Divd.:***	NA
Total Assets:	$3,902,000	***Net Worth:***	$42,000	***Debt/ Equity:***	NA

Cyanotech Corp

73-4460 Queen Kaahumanu Hwy., Ste. 102, Kailua-Kona, HI, 96740; ***PH:*** 1-808-326-1353; ***Fax:*** 1-808-329-4533; ***http://*** www.cyanotech.com; ***Email:*** info@cyanotech.com

General - Incorporation	NV
Employees	62
Auditor	KPMG LLP
Stk Agt	Computershare Investor Services LLC
Counsel	Goodsill Anderson Quinn & Stifel
DUNS No.	11-419-2610

Stock - Price on:12/24/2007	$1.47
Stock Exchange	NDQ
Ticker Symbol	CYAN
Outstanding Shares	5,230,000
E.P.S.	-$1.38
Shareholders	NA

Business: The group's principal activities are to develop and produce natural products from microalgae. Microalgae are a diverse group of microscopic plants that have a wide range of physiological and biochemical characteristics and contain high levels of natural protein, amino acids, vitamins, pigments and enzymes. The products of the group include spirulina pacifica, natural astaxanthin and phycobiliproteins. Spirulina pacifica provides a vegetable-based, highly absorbable source of protein, natural beta-carotene, mixed carotenoids, b vitamins, gamma linolenic acid, essential amino acids and other phytonutrients. Natural astaxanthin is used in the aquaculture market primarily to impart a pink to red color to the flesh of commercially raised fish and shrimp. Phycobiliprotein products are used in medical and biotechnology research industries.

Primary SIC and add'l.: 2835 2833

CIK No: 0000768408

Subsidiaries: Cyanotech Japan YK, Nutrex Hawaii, Inc.

Officers: Gerald R. Cysewski/Chmn., CEO, Pres./$130,000.00, Glenn D. Jensen/VP - Operations, Robert J. Capelli/VP - Sales/$101,738.00, William R. Maris/CFO, VP - Finance, Administration/$104,616.00

Directors: Gerald R. Cysewski/Chmn., CEO, Pres., David I. Rosenthal/Dir., John T. Waldron/Dir., Michael A. Davis/Dir., Paul C. Yuen/Dir.

Owners: Michael A. Davis/16.60%, Paul C. Yuen, Robert J. Capelli, William R. Maris, Gerald R. Cysewski/2.30%, John T. Waldron, David I. Rosenthal, Insiders/19.70%, Gregg W. Robertson

Financial Data: Fiscal Year End:03/31   Latest Annual Data: 3/31/2006

Year	Sales	Net Income
2006	$11,131,000	-$391,000
2005	$11,445,000	$486,000
2004	$11,582,000	$399,000

Curr. Assets:	$6,916,000	Curr. Liab.:	$1,269,000		
Plant, Equip.:	$10,164,000	Total Liab.:	$2,656,000	Indic. Yr. Divd.:	NA
Total Assets:	$17,595,000	Net Worth:	$14,939,000	Debt/ Equity:	0.0872

Cyber Defense Systems Inc

10901 Roosevelt Blvd. N, Saint Petersburg, FL, 33716; *PH:* 1-727-577-0878; *Fax:* 1-727-577-0873; *http://* www.cyberdefensesystems.com

General - Incorporation	FL
Employees	12
Auditor	HANSEN, BARNETT & MAXWELL, P.C.
Stk Agt	Pacific Stock Transfer Company
Counsel	NA
DUNS No.	NA

Stock - Price on:12/24/2007	$0.031
Stock Exchange	OTC
Ticker Symbol	CYDF
Outstanding Shares	NA
E.P.S.	-$0.333
Shareholders	NA

Business: The group's principal activity is to develop and market computer-mapping products in CD-ROM format and on the Internet. The computer mapping technology allows users to interact with the maps in limited ways, allowing them to zoom in closer or farther away from a particular object or section of the map using functions contained on the computer map. The group has produced a style of computer mapping which includes drawings of buildings, features and landscapes on to the computer map of streets and cities. The products are developed in a semi-custom fashion using the specifications of individual customers with whom the group has software development contracts. The group has produced the computer maps for eight major us cities, 4 Canadian cities as well as Munich, Germany.

Primary SIC and add'l.: NA

CIK No: 0001118480

Subsidiaries: Cyber Aero, Cyber Aerospace, Cyber Aerospace Corp

Officers: William C. Robinson/Founder, Chmn., CEO, Pres. - Techsphere Systems International, Inc, Mike Lawson/Dir., CMO - Techsphere Systems International, Inc, Keith Vierela/Dir., COO - Techsphere Systems International, Inc, Frank Lively/Dir., Sec., Treasure, Ryan Robinson/Government UAV Sales, Jim Gardiner/Composite Production Technical Advisor, John Youngbeck/Exec. VP, Dir. - CMO, Techsphere Systems International, Inc, Ed Pickett/Sales Consultant, Government Applications, Hokan Colting/Airship Technology Advisor, Mayo Hadden/Military Technical Advisor

Directors: William C. Robinson/Founder, Chmn., CEO, Pres. - Techsphere Systems International, Inc, Stephen I. Johnson/Dir., Marinko Vekovic/Dir., Joseph A. Grace/Founder, Dir., Mike Lawson/Dir., CMO - Techsphere Systems International, Inc, Keith Vierela/Dir., COO - Techsphere Systems International, Inc, Frank Lively/Dir., Sec., Treasure

Owners: Insiders, James Alman, Marinko Vekovic, Frank Lively, Joseph A. Grace, David M. Barnes, Cherokee Raiders, L.P., John M. Youngbeck, Michael Lawson, Edward W. Pickett, William C. Robinson, Stephen I. Johnson, Keith Vierela, Proxity Digital Networks, Inc.

Financial Data: Fiscal Year End:12/31   Latest Annual Data: 12/31/2006

Year	Sales	Net Income
2006	$494,000	-$22,040,000
2005	$461,000	-$15,579,000
2004	$3,026,000	-$421,000

Curr. Assets:	$1,353,000	Curr. Liab.:	$20,355,000		
Plant, Equip.:	$66,000	Total Liab.:	$22,434,000	Indic. Yr. Divd.:	NA
Total Assets:	$4,358,000	Net Worth:	-$18,076,000	Debt/ Equity:	NA

Cyber Digital Inc

400 Oser Ave., Ste. 1650, Hauppauge, NY, 11788; *PH:* 1-631-231-1200; *Fax:* 1-631-231-1446; *http://* www.cyberdigitalinc.com

General - Incorporation	NY
Employees	5
Auditor	Blanchfield, Kober & Co. P.C
Stk Agt	Continental Stock Transfer & Trust Co
Counsel	NA
DUNS No.	10-361-1760

Stock - Price on:12/24/2007	$0.46
Stock Exchange	OTC
Ticker Symbol	CYBD
Outstanding Shares	33,500,000
E.P.S.	-$0.03
Shareholders	NA

Business: The group's principal activity is to design, develop, manufacture and market a range of unique distributed digital voice switching infrastructure equipment for public switched voice network operators worldwide. It also manufactures and markets high performance Internet infrastructure systems such as soft-switches, routers, gateways, firewalls and servers. The Internet service providers use these systems to create next-generation digital broadband services, voice-over Internet protocol services and virtual private networks services. The group's Internet systems include cyber business Internet gateway (cbig), cyber Internet access network (cian) distribution router, cyber firewall (cfw) ipsec based firewall appliance and cyber Web server (cweb).

Primary SIC and add'l.: 3661 7372

CIK No: 0000721295

Subsidiaries: Cyber Digital (India) Private Limited, Cyber Digital (Nigeria) Ltd.

Officers: Jawahar C. Chatpar/Chmn., Founder, CEO, Pres.

Directors: Jawahar C. Chatpar/Chmn., Founder, CEO, Pres., Jack P. Dorfman/Dir., Terry L. Jones/Dir.

Owners: Prem Chatpar, Insiders, J. C. Chatpar, Jack P. Dorfman, Laurus Master Fund, Ltd., Terry L. Jones

Financial Data: Fiscal Year End:03/31   Latest Annual Data: 03/31/2007

Year	Sales	Net Income
2007	NA	-$933,000
2006	NA	-$563,000
2005	NA	-$417,000

Curr. Assets:	$292,000	Curr. Liab.:	$2,337,000		
Plant, Equip.:	$29,000	Total Liab.:	$2,352,000	Indic. Yr. Divd.:	NA
Total Assets:	$355,000	Net Worth:	-$1,998,000	Debt/ Equity:	NA

Cyberads Inc

1191 Ctr. Point Dr., Henderson, NV, 89704; *PH:* 1-800-288-3099; *http://* www.cyberadsinc.com

General - Incorporation	FL
Employees	2
Auditor	Williams & Webster, P.S
Stk Agt	Florida Atlantic Stock Transfer, Inc.
Counsel	NA
DUNS No.	NA

Stock - Price on:12/24/2007	NA
Stock Exchange	NA
Ticker Symbol	NA
Outstanding Shares	NA
E.P.S.	NA
Shareholders	NA

Business: The group's principal activities are to develop land and real estate projects and offer new consumer products and services. The land and real estate division of the group invests in real estate development projects, thereby building a diverse portfolio of properties. The consumer products and services division offers cellular products and services, financial services and Internet marketing opportunities. The group utilizes an affiliate-driven, Internet-based marketing platform to secure new customers, and has formed promotional affiliations with hundreds of companies and websites. On 06-Jan-2004, the group acquired the vineyards country club.

Primary SIC and add'l.: 4812 7375 7389

CIK No: 0001121520

Subsidiaries: IDS Cellular, Inc.

Officers: Howard Pearl/58/Dir., CEO, Pres.

Directors: Howard Pearl/58/Dir., CEO, Pres.

Owners: Walter Tatum/17.00%, August A. DeAngelo, Insiders/25.00%, Howard Pearl/8.00%

Curr. Assets:	$142,000	Curr. Liab.:	$4,711,000		
Plant, Equip.:	$108,000	Total Liab.:	$4,771,000	Indic. Yr. Divd.:	NA
Total Assets:	$3,263,000	Net Worth:	-$1,507,000	Debt/ Equity:	NA

Cyberkinetics Neurotechnology Systems Inc

100 Foxborough Blvd., Ste. 240, Foxborough, MA, 02035; *PH:* 1-508-549-9981; *Fax:* 1-508-549-9985; *http://* www.cyberkineticsinc.com; *Email:* info@cyberkineticsinc.com

General - Incorporation	DE
Employees	38
Auditor	Vitale, Caturano & Co., Ltd.
Stk Agt	Computershare Limited
Counsel	NA
DUNS No.	NA

Stock - Price on:12/24/2007	$0.41
Stock Exchange	OTC
Ticker Symbol	CYKN
Outstanding Shares	37,560,000
E.P.S.	-$0.3
Shareholders	NA

Business: The groups principle activity is to develop products to treat neurological diseases, The group products include Andara (TM), OFS(TM), BrainGate System, and NeuroPort(TM) System. In the year 2006, the group acquired Andara (TM) Life Science, Inc. The group operates from the United States.

Primary SIC and add'l.: 3845 3826 3841

CIK No: 0001180253

Subsidiaries: Andara Life Science, Inc., Cyberkinetics, Inc., CYBK, Inc.

Officers: Timothy R. Surgenor/Dir., CEO, Pres., Elizabeth A. Razee/Mgr. - Corporate Communications, Christopher J. Flaherty/Exec. VP - Technology, Intellectual Property, Kurt H. Kruger/CFO, John P. Donoghue/Founder, Chief Scientific Officer, Dir., Mark A. Carney/Dir., Exec. VP

Directors: Timothy R. Surgenor/Dir., CEO, Pres., Mark P. Carthy/Chmn., Daniel E. Geffken/Dir., George N. Hatsopoulos/Dir., Nicholas G. Hatsopoulos/Dir., Theo Melas-Kyriazi/Dir., John P. Donoghue/Founder, Chief Scientific Officer, Dir., Mark A. Carney/Dir., Exec. VP

Owners: Theo Melas-Kyriazi, Daniel E. Geffken, Oxford Bioscience Partners and affiliated entities/31.30%, Mark P. Carthy/31.30%, Insiders/42.68%, Timothy R. Surgenor/3.28%, Kurt H. Kruger, Medica Venture Partners and affiliated entities/15.76%, John P. Donoghue/2.15%, George N. Hatsopoulos/3.52%, Hunter World Markets, Inc/5.25%, Mark A. Carney/2.82%, Nicholas G. Hatsopoulos/1.32%, Christopher J. Flaherty

Financial Data: Fiscal Year End:12/31   Latest Annual Data: 12/31/2006

Year	Sales	Net Income
2006	$1,680,000	-$12,278,000
2005	$1,059,000	-$9,326,000
2004	$1,537,000	-$7,091,000

Curr. Assets:	$13,429,000	Curr. Liab.:	$3,889,000		
Plant, Equip.:	$569,000	Total Liab.:	$6,004,000	Indic. Yr. Divd.:	NA
Total Assets:	$16,104,000	Net Worth:	$10,100,000	Debt/ Equity:	NA

Cyberlux Corp

4625 Creekstone Dr., Durham, NC, 27703; *PH:* 1-919-474-9700; *http://* www.cyberlux.com;
Email: contact_us@cyberlux.com

General - Incorporation	NV	**Stock**- Price on:12/24/2007	$0.0068
Employees	11	Stock Exchange	OTC
Auditor .. Russell Bedford Stefanou Mirchandani		Ticker Symbol	CYBL
Stk Agt.	Pacific Stock Transfer Company	Outstanding Shares	276,840,000
Counsel	NA	E.P.S	-$0.261
DUNS No.	NA	Shareholders	NA

Business: The groups principle activities include designing, manufacturing and selling of light-emitted diode lighting solutions. The group products include RELIABRIGHT(TM), EVERON(TM), and KEON(TM). The group operates from the United States. The group's quarterly revenue for September 2007 was 1.90 millions of USD.

Primary SIC and add'l.: 3648

CIK No: 0001138169

Officers: Donald F. Evans/Chmn., CEO, Mark D. Schmidt/Dir., COO, Pres., John W. Ringo/Dir., General Counsel, Sec., David D. Downing/CFO, Treasurer, Alan H. Ninneman/Dir., Sr. VP, Patricia Ryan/Investor Information

Directors: Donald F. Evans/Chmn., CEO, Mark D. Schmidt/Dir., COO, Pres., John W. Ringo/Dir., General Counsel, Sec., Alan H. Ninneman/Dir., Sr. VP

Owners: Insiders/70.71%, Alan H. Ninneman/10.50%, Mark D. Schmidt/19.43%, John W. Ringo/13.99%, David D. Downing/6.61%, Donald F. Evans/20.18%

Financial Data: *Fiscal Year End:*12/31 *Latest Annual Data:* 12/31/2006

Year	Sales	Net Income
2006	$485,000	-$6,775,000
2005	$55,000	-$9,411,000
2004	$24,000	-$6,026,000

Curr. Assets:	$793,000	Curr. Liab.:	$3,365,000		
Plant, Equip.:	$58,000	Total Liab.:	$16,296,000	Indic. Yr. Divd.:	NA
Total Assets:	$3,169,000	Net Worth:	-$13,127,000	Debt/ Equity:	NA

Cyberonics Inc

The Cyberonics Building , 100 Cyberonics Blvd., Houston, TX, 77058; *PH:* 1-281-228-7262 ; *Fax:* 1-281-218-9332 ; *http://* www.cyberonics.com; *Email:* ir@cyberonics.com

General - Incorporation	DE	**Stock**- Price on:12/24/2007	$16.83
Employees	NA	Stock Exchange	NDQ
Auditor	KPMG LLP	Ticker Symbol	CYBX
Stk Agt.	EquiServe Trust Co N.A	Outstanding Shares	25,710,000
Counsel	NA	E.P.S	-$1.63
DUNS No.	19-456-8978	Shareholders	NA

Business: The group's principal activities are to design, develop, manufacture and market medical device for the treatment of epilepsy and other debilitating neurological, psychiatric diseases and other disorders. The product of the group is the cyberonics vns therapy system. The vns therapy system delivers an electrical signal through an implantable lead to the left cervical vagus nerve in the patient's neck on a chronic, intermittent basis. It markets its products in the United States, Germany, France, Austria, Switzerland, Belgium, Norway, Sweden, Denmark and the United Kingdom.

Primary SIC and add'l.: 3845 5047

CIK No: 0000864683

Subsidiaries: Cyberonics of Europe, S.A.

Officers: Daniel J. Moore/Dir., CEO, Pres., Gregory H. Browne/Pres. - Finance, CFO/$336,208.00, Reese S. Terry/Dir. - Business Consultant, Cyberonics Founder/$345,604.00, Michael J. Strauss/Dir. - Business Consultant, George E. Parker/VP - Human Resources, Depression GM/$981,945.00, David S. Wise/VP, General Counsel, Sec./$1,149,178.00, Richard L. Rudolph/VP - Clinical, Regulatory, Medical Affairs, Chief Medical Officer/$1,047,781.00, Randal L. Simpson/VP - Quality, Operations and Research & Development, James A. Reinstein/VP - Sales, Marketing, International GM

Directors: Daniel J. Moore/Dir., CEO, Pres., Hugh M. Morrison/61/Non - Exec. Chmn., Alfred J. Novak/Dir., Arthur L. Rosenthal/Dir., Alan J. Olsen/Dir., Reese S. Terry/Dir. - Business Consultant, Cyberonics Founder, Guy C. Jackson/Dir., Michael J. Strauss/Dir. - Business Consultant, Jeffrey E. Schwarz/Dir.

Owners: Hugh M. Morrison, Joshua Ruch and affiliates/5.20%, Insiders/10.80%, Boston Scientific Corporation/13.30%, Granahan Investment Management, Inc./5.30%, Jeffrey E. Schwarz/7.20%, FMR Corp./9.60%, Carl C. Icahn and affiliates/9.30%, Daniel J. Moore, Guy C. Jackson, Alan J. Olsen, Michael J. Strauss

Financial Data: *Fiscal Year End:*04/29 *Latest Annual Data:* 04/27/2007

Year	Sales	Net Income
2007	$130,968,000	-$51,180,000
2006	$123,442,000	-$59,069,000
2005	$103,443,000	-$12,218,000

Curr. Assets:	$85,772,000	Curr. Liab.:	$25,316,000		
Plant, Equip.:	$8,349,000	Total Liab.:	$25,316,000	Indic. Yr. Divd.:	NA
Total Assets:	$94,297,000	Net Worth:	$68,980,000	Debt/ Equity:	NA

Cyberoptics Corp

5900 Golden Hills Dr., Minneapolis, MN, 55416; *PH:* 1-763-542-5000; *Fax:* 1-763-542-5100; *http://* www.cyberoptics.com; *Email:* info@cyberoptics.com

General - Incorporation	MN	**Stock**- Price on:12/24/2007	$14.217
Employees	175	Stock Exchange	NDQ
Auditor	PricewaterhouseCoopers LLP	Ticker Symbol	CYBE
Stk Agt.	Wells Fargo Shareowner Services	Outstanding Shares	8,900,000
Counsel	Dorsey & Whitney LLP	E.P.S	$0.672
DUNS No.	14-466-3069	Shareholders	NA

Business: The group's principal activity is to supply optical process control sensors and inspection systems. These products are supplied to the surface mount technology (smt) electronic circuit board assembly equipment and semiconductor fabrication equipment markets. The group's products enable the global smt and semiconductor industries to meet the demands for printed circuit board assembly and semiconductor wafer transport. The products include smt electronic assembly sensors, laseralign sensors, laser lead locator, drs (TM) range sensors, wafer mapping and alignment, frame grabber products and machine vision subsystems. The group's products are sold in Europe, Asia, Canada, Mexico and Latin America.

Primary SIC and add'l.: 3827 3826

CIK No: 0000768411

Subsidiaries: CyberOptics (China) Co., Ltd., CyberOptics (Singapore) Pte. Ltd, CyberOptics Holdings UK, Ltd., CyberOptics Semiconductor, Inc., CyberOptics UK, Ltd.

Officers: Kathleen P. Iverson/52/Dir., CEO, Pres./$452,144.00, Thomas Martin/Sec., Jeffrey A. Bertelsen/45/VP - Finance, CFO/$231,836.00, Michael Proulx/VP - Operations/$209,767.00

Directors: Kathleen P. Iverson/52/Dir., CEO, Pres., Steven K. Case/59/Chmn., Alex B. Cimochowski/68/Dir., Michael M. Selzer/55/Dir., Irene M. Qualters/58/Dir., Erwin A. Kelen/72/Dir.

Owners: Erwin A. Kelen, Jeffrey Bertelsen, Rutabaga Capital Management/10.10%, Irene M. Qualters, Steven K. Case/6.40%, Michael M. Selzer, Michael Proulx, Kathleen P. Iverson/1.20%, Insiders/9.30%, Alex B. Cimochowski, Steven J. DiMarco, T. Rowe Price Associates, Inc./8.90%

Financial Data: *Fiscal Year End:*12/31 *Latest Annual Data:* 12/31/2006

Year	Sales	Net Income
2006	$57,089,000	$6,390,000
2005	$42,179,000	$7,150,000
2004	$58,037,000	$10,626,000

Curr. Assets:	$64,652,000	Curr. Liab.:	$8,990,000		
Plant, Equip.:	$1,814,000	Total Liab.:	$8,990,000	Indic. Yr. Divd.:	NA
Total Assets:	$82,010,000	Net Worth:	$73,020,000	Debt/ Equity:	NA

Cybersource Corp

1295 Charleston Rd., Mountain View, CA, 94043; *PH:* 1-650-965-6000; *Fax:* 1-650-625-9145; *http://* www.cybersource.com; *Email:* sales@cybersource.com

General - Incorporation	DE	**Stock**- Price on:12/24/2007	$12.78
Employees	247	Stock Exchange	NDQ
Auditor	Ernst & Young LLP	Ticker Symbol	CYBS
Stk Agt.	American Stock Transfer & Trust Co.	Outstanding Shares	35,120,000
Counsel	Morrison & Foerster LLP	E.P.S	$0.37
DUNS No.	NA	Shareholders	NA

Business: The group's principle activities are to develop and provide online commerce transaction processing services, software and consulting expertise. The group operates through three segments: e-commerce transaction services and support, professional services and enterprise software. E-commerce transaction provides services to online merchants and consumers for global payment processing, fraud prevention, tax calculation, export compliance, territory management, delivery address verification and fulfillment management. Professional services support enterprise process analysis and commerce infrastructure integration. Enterprise software processes high-volumes of secure payment transactions for multiple sales channel enterprises. The group's quarterly revenue for September 2007 was 26.55 millions of USD.

Primary SIC and add'l.: 7374 7371 7372 7375

CIK No: 0000934280

Officers: William S. McKiernan/Chmn., CEO/$609,794.00, Perry Dembner/VP - Marketing, Trish Martin/VP - Customer Support, David J. Kim/VP, General Counsel, Steven D. Pellizzer/Sr. VP - Finance, CFO/$442,568.00, George Barby/VP - Worldwide Operations, Carolyn Brackett/VP - Channels, Alliances, Scott R. Cruickshank/COO, Pres./$1,311,013.00, Robert Ford/CTO, Exec. VP - Product Development/$513,274.00, Kirsten Fry-Sanchez/VP - Product Management, David A. Glaser/VP - Professional Services, David Hansen/Pres., Michael Walsh/Sr. VP - Worldwide Sales/$596,525.00, Bruce Frymire/Pres, Analyst Contact, Michael Orlando/VP - Strategic Markets

Directors: William S. McKiernan/Chmn., CEO, Scott R. Cruickshank/COO, Pres.

Owners: FMR Corporation/14.00%, John J. McDonnell/1.00%, Michael A. Walsh, Robert J. Ford/1.00%, Steven P. Novak, Richard Scudellari, Steven D. Pellizzer, Insiders/16.00%, Kenneth R. Thornton, William S. McKiernan/10.00%

Financial Data: *Fiscal Year End:*12/31 *Latest Annual Data:* 12/31/2006

Year	Sales	Net Income
2006	$70,250,000	$14,411,000
2005	$50,511,000	$9,246,000
2004	$36,709,000	$4,461,000

Curr. Assets:	$68,701,000	Curr. Liab.:	$8,415,000	P/E Ratio:	34.54
Plant, Equip.:	$3,618,000	Total Liab.:	$8,415,000	Indic. Yr. Divd.:	NA
Total Assets:	$87,043,000	Net Worth:	$78,628,000	Debt/ Equity:	NA

Cybertel Capital Corp

4603 NE St. Johns Rd., Ste. B, Vancouver, WA, 98661; *PH:* 1-858-646-7410; *Fax:* 1-858-646-7414; *http://* www.cybertelcapital.com

General - Incorporation	NV	**Stock**- Price on:12/24/2007	NA
Employees	NA	Stock Exchange	OTC
Auditor	Gruber & Co., LLC	Ticker Symbol	CBEL
Stk Agt.	Pacific Stock Transfer Company	Outstanding Shares	NA
Counsel	NA	E.P.S	NA
DUNS No.	NA	Shareholders	NA

Business: The groups principle activity is to provide technology consulting and management services. The groups services include business planning, transaction advisory services, engineering, furnishing, installation services, Internet infrastructure protocol and IMS application. The groups markets include wireless, telecommunication and broadband industries. The group operates from United States.

Primary SIC and add'l.: 4813

CIK No: 0001036148

Subsidiaries: Cybertel Broadband, Inc., Cybertel Financial International, Cybertel Holdings, CYTP Holdings, Pro Tel Communications

Officers: James A. Wheeler/47/Dir., CEO, Pres.

Directors: James A. Wheeler/47/Dir., CEO, Pres., David Brunscheon/52/Dir.

Owners: Insiders/99.89%, James Wheeler/99.89%

Financial Data: *Fiscal Year End:*12/31 *Latest Annual Data:* 12/31/2006

Year	Sales	Net Income
2006	$154,000	-$910,000
2005	$60,000	-$1,047,000
2004	$218,000	-$5,008,000

Curr. Assets:	$55,000	*Curr. Liab.:*	$348,000		
Plant, Equip.:	$38,000	*Total Liab.:*	$643,000	*Indic. Yr. Divd.:*	NA
Total Assets:	$643,000	*Net Worth:*	$0	*Debt/ Equity:*	NA

Cybex International Inc

10 Trotter Dr., Medway, MA, 02053; *PH:* 1-508-533-4300; *Fax:* 1-508-533-5500;
http:// www.ecybex.com; *Email:* info@cybexintl.com

General - Incorporation	NY	*Stock*- Price on:12/24/2007	$6.95
Employees	547	Stock Exchange	NDQ
Auditor	KPMG LLP	Ticker Symbol	CYBI
Stk Agt	Registrar & Transfer Co	Outstanding Shares	17,320,000
Counsel	Archer & Greiner	E.P.S.	$0.53
DUNS No.	00-203-6606	Shareholders	NA

Business: The group's principal activities are to develop, manufacture and market strength and cardiovascular fitness equipment products. The products of the group can generally be grouped into two major categories: cardiovascular products and strength systems. Cardiovascular equipment is designed to provide aerobic conditioning by elevating the heart rate, increasing lung capacity, endurance and circulation, and burning body fat. The group's cardiovascular products include treadmills, bikes and steppers. Strength training equipment provides a physical workout by exercising the musculo-skeletal system. Product lines of this segment include selectorized single station equipment, modular multi-station units, mg500 multi-gym, pg400 personal gym, the fi360, plate-loaded equipment and free-weight equipment. The group has international operations in Canada, Germany and the United Kingdom.

Primary SIC and add'l.: 3842 3845

CIK No: 0000060876

Subsidiaries: CIC Leasing Company (O), LLC, CIC Leasing Company, LLC, Cybex Capital Corporation, Cybex Fitness Gerate Vertriebs, GmbH, Cybex Hong Kong Limited, Cybex International UK Ltd., Tectrix Fitness Equipment, Inc.

Officers: John Aglialoro/Chmn., CEO/$513,370.00, Arthur W. Hicks/49/Dir., CFO, COO/$312,771.00, Joan Carter/Dir., Sec., Edward Kurzontkowski/Sr. VP - Manufacturing/$241,859.00, Paul Trammell/Government, Sales Representative, Raymond Giannelli/Sr. VP - Research, Development/$773,363.00, Edward J. Pryts/Sr. VP - North America Sales/$193,488.00, John P. Young/Sr. VP - International Sales, James M. A'Hearn/Treasurer, Chief Accounting Officer

Directors: John Aglialoro/Chmn., CEO, Arthur W. Hicks/49/Dir., CFO, COO, Milton Leontiades/Dir., John McCarthy/Dir., Joan Carter/Dir., Sec., James H. Carll/Dir., Harvey Morgan/Dir., Jerry Lee/Dir.

Owners: Joan Carter, John McCarthy, Grace & White, Inc., Harvey Morgan, James H. Carll, John Aglialoro, Insiders, Brightleaf Capital LLC, Jerry Lee, Edward Kurzontkowski, Pequot Capital Management, Inc., Ray Giannelli, Milton Leontiades, UM Holdings Ltd., Ed Pryts

*Financial Data: Fiscal Year End:*12/31 *Latest Annual Data:* 12/31/2006

Year		Sales	Net Income
2006		$126,924,000	$20,054,000
2005		$114,646,000	$61,000
2004		$103,023,000	$3,225,000
Curr. Assets:	$39,020,000	*Curr. Liab.:* $24,959,000	*P/E Ratio:* 5.94
Plant, Equip.:	$13,055,000	*Total Liab.:* $27,710,000	*Indic. Yr. Divd.:* NA
Total Assets:	$73,377,000	*Net Worth:* $45,667,000	*Debt/ Equity:* 0.0014

Cybrdi Inc

Formerly: Certron Corp
401 Rosemont Ave., Frederick, MD, 21701; *PH:* 1-301-644-3901

General - Incorporation	CA	*Stock*- Price on:12/24/2007	$0.65
Employees	NA	Stock Exchange	OTC
Auditor	Ms. Group CPA LLC	Ticker Symbol	CRTNE
Stk Agt	American Stock Transfer & Trust Co.	Outstanding Shares	NA
Counsel	Reed, Smith, Crosby, Heafey LLP	E.P.S.	NA
DUNS No.	04-115-8627	Shareholders	NA

Business: The group's principal activity is the distribution of magnetic media products. The magnetic media products primarily include blank audio in several cassette configurations of various sizes and playing times, as well as vhs video cassettes. The group also distributes magnetic media accessories for computers. The group's products are marketed and sold primarily in the United States to wholesale distributors, original equipment manufacturers, mail order companies and retail outlets. In addition, standard sized and miniaturized cassettes for dictation purposes and cassettes for telephone answering devices are also sold to office supply outlets and distributors. These products are distributed under own its labels, as well as under different customer labels.

Primary SIC and add'l.: 3695

CIK No: 0000019002

Subsidiaries: Certron Acquisition Corp., Certron Corporation

Owners: Lei Liu/12.36%, Insiders/30.50%, YanBiao Bai/18.15%

Cycle Country Accessories Corp

1701 38th Ave. W, Spencer, IA, 51301; *PH:* 1-712-262-4191; *Fax:* 1-712-262-0248;
http:// www.cyclecountry.com; *Email:* ccac@cyclecountry.com

General - Incorporation	NV	*Stock*- Price on:12/24/2007	$1.85
Employees	102	Stock Exchange	AMEX
Auditor	Henjes, Conner & Williams P.C	Ticker Symbol	ATC
Stk Agt	Atlas Stk Trnsfer of Salt Lake City	Outstanding Shares	7,350,000
Counsel	NA	E.P.S.	-$0.01
DUNS No.	NA	Shareholders	NA

Business: The group's principal activity is to manufacture accessories for all terrain vehicles. It operates through three segments: atv accessories, plastic wheel covers and lawn and garden. All terrain vehicles accessories designs, assembles and distributes atv accessories such as snowplow blades, lawnmowers, oil filters, spreaders, sprayers, tillage equipment, winch mounts and utility boxes. Plastic wheel covers manufactures and distributes injection-molded plastic wheel covers for vehicles such as golf carts and light-duty trailers. Lawn and garden designs, assembles and distributes lawn and garden accessories. These lawn and garden accessories include lawnmowers, spreaders, sprayers, and tillage equipment. The group has 19 international distributors distributing the products in 35 countries.

Primary SIC and add'l.: 3089 3545

CIK No: 0001157758

Subsidiaries: Corp (Cycle Country Sub)

Officers: Randy J. Kempf/54/Dir., CEO, Pres./$28,596.00, Mark Gilbert/Mgr. - Investor Relations, Lisa Bailey/48/VP - Operations, Ronald Hickman/Pres./$181,015.00, Alan Bailey/50/Dir., Sr. VP/$138,743.00, John Gault/65/Interim Pres./$101,000.00, David Davis/42/CFO, VP - Finance, Bradley Danbom/31/VP - Sales, Marketing

Directors: Randy J. Kempf/54/Dir., CEO, Pres., Alan Bailey/50/Dir., Sr. VP, Rod Simonson/51/Dir., F. L. Miller/66/Dir., Jim Danbom/64/Dir., L. G. Hancher/54/Dir.

Owners: Randy Kempf/0.58%, Commerce Street Venture Group/6.08%, David Davis/0.14%, F. L. Miller, David Bailey/7.60%, Alan Bailey/8.50%, Lisa Bailey/5.44%, L. G. Hancher/2.77%, Joan Bailey/9.98%, Insiders/18.71%, Rod Simonson/0.64%

*Financial Data: Fiscal Year End:*09/30 *Latest Annual Data:* 9/30/2006

Year		Sales	Net Income
2006		$16,464,000	$612,000
2005		$17,181,000	$812,000
2004		$20,666,000	$1,618,000
Curr. Assets:	$7,935,000	*Curr. Liab.:* $1,516,000	*P/E Ratio:* 30.83
Plant, Equip.:	$13,456,000	*Total Liab.:* $8,739,000	*Indic. Yr. Divd.:* NA
Total Assets:	$26,479,000	*Net Worth:* $17,740,000	*Debt/ Equity:* 0.2438

Cygne Designs Inc

1410 Broadway Way, New York, NY, 10019; *PH:* 1-212-489-3900

General - Incorporation	DE	*Stock*- Price on:12/24/2007	$1.94
Employees	700	Stock Exchange	NDQ
Auditor	Ernst & Young LLP	Ticker Symbol	CYDS
Stk Agt	American Stock Transfer & Trust Co.	Outstanding Shares	26,460,000
Counsel	Fulbright & Jaworski LLP	E.P.S.	-$0.04
DUNS No.	04-007-6887	Shareholders	NA

Business: The group's principal activity is to manufacture private label women's career and casual apparel. The products manufactured by the group include woven jackets, skirts and pants. The group produces apparel upon orders from its customers for sale under the customer's own labels. It also sources and manufactures garments for its customers, which have been designed and developed by the customer. The group sells its products primarily to lerner New York.

Primary SIC and add'l.: 2337 2339

CIK No: 0000906782

Subsidiaries: Cygne Guatemala, S.A., MBS Internacional, S.A.

Owners: Michel Collet, Hubert Guez/49.00%, Hubert Guez, Insiders/19.07%, Insiders, Diversified Apparel Resources, LLC, Bernard M. Manuel/18.69%, Michel Collet, Guy Kinberg, Bernard M. Manuel, James G. Groninger, Diversified Apparel Resources, LLC/16.74%, James G. Groninger, Guy Kinberg, Guez Living Trust/11.15% *(17 Owners included in Index)*

*Financial Data: Fiscal Year End:*01/31 *Latest Annual Data:* 1/31/2007

Year		Sales	Net Income
2007		$118,816,000	-$158,000
2006		$58,453,000	-$6,166,000
2005		$28,960,000	$313,000
Curr. Assets:	$15,452,000	*Curr. Liab.:* $16,462,000	
Plant, Equip.:	$619,000	*Total Liab.:* $44,135,000	*Indic. Yr. Divd.:* NA
Total Assets:	$93,553,000	*Net Worth:* $49,418,000	*Debt/ Equity:* 0.5099

Cygnus Inc

PO Box 321195, Los Gatos, CA, 95032; *PH:* 1-650-369-4300; *http://* www.cygnusaero.com

General - Incorporation	DE	*Stock*- Price on:12/24/2007	$24.49
Employees	NA	Stock Exchange	NA
Auditor	Ernst & Young LLP	Ticker Symbol	NA
Stk Agt	Chemical Trust Bank of California	Outstanding Shares	NA
Counsel	NA	E.P.S.	NA
DUNS No.	15-083-7318	Shareholders	NA

Business: The group's principal activity is to develop and manufacture diagnostic medical devices, utilizing proprietary technologies to satisfy unmet medical needs cost-effectively. The glucowatch biographer product provides frequent, automatic and non-invasive glucose measurements and is intended for detecting trends and tracking patterns of glucose levels in adults, 18 years and older, who have diabetes. The device is intended for use at home and in health care facilities to supplement, not replace, information obtained from standard home blood glucose monitoring devices. The group's glucowatch trademark is registered in the United States, the European community and other foreign countries. It operates mainly in the United States and in the United Kingdom.

Primary SIC and add'l.: 3829 2835

CIK No: 0000870755

Subsidiaries: Cygnus, Inc., Medtronic, Inc

Cymer Inc

17075 Thornmint Ct., San Diego, CA, 92127; *PH:* 1-858-385-7300; *Fax:* 1-858-385-7100;
http:// www.cymer.com

General - Incorporation	NV	*Stock*- Price on:12/24/2007	$41.66
Employees	975	Stock Exchange	NDQ
Auditor	KPMG LLP	Ticker Symbol	CYMI
Stk Agt	American Stock Transfer & Trust Co.	Outstanding Shares	36,070,000
Counsel	Cooley Godward	E.P.S.	$2.40
DUNS No.	NA	Shareholders	NA

Business: The groups principle activity is to supply excimer light sources. The products of the group include Photolithography Light Sources, ArF and KrF light sources and 248 nm KrF Light Sources. The group products sold under the trade name CYMER and INSIST ON CYMER. Specific customers of the group include Canon, Nikon, Fujitsu, Hynix, IBM, Infineon, Qimonda, Intel, Matsushita, Micron and Inotera. The groups operates through two segments namely Cymer and TCZ. The group operates from the United States, Japan, Asia and Europe. The group's quarterly revenue for September 2007 was 132.12 millions of USD.

Primary SIC and add'l.: 7372 3559 3827

CIK No: 0000897067

Subsidiaries: Cymer B.V., Cymer Japan, Inc., Cymer Korea, Inc., Cymer Semiconductor Equipment (Shanghai) Co., Ltd., Cymer Singapore Pte. Ltd., Cymer Southeast Asia, Ltd., TCZ Pte. Ltd.

Officers: Robert P. Akins/Chmn., CEO/$1,910,259.00, Edward J. Brown/COO, Pres./$3,147,310.00, Richard L. Sandstrom/Co - Founder, Sr. VP, Chief Technical Advisor, Nancy J. Baker/Sr. VP, CFO/$844,613.00, William Partlo/CTO, Sr. VP, Christopher W. Smith/Sr. VP - Worldwide Business Operations, Stephan D. Spiva/Sr. VP - Corporate Operations, Rae Ann Werner/VP, Controller, Chief Accounting Officer/$494,495.00

Directors: Robert P. Akins/Chmn., CEO, Charles J. Abbe/Dir., Ed Braun/Dir., Michael R. Gaulke/Dir., William G. Oldham/Dir., Peter J. Simone/Dir., Young K. Sohn/Dir., Richard L. Sandstrom/Co - Founder, Sr. VP, Chief Technical Advisor, Jon D. Tompkins/Dir.

Owners: Charles J. Abbe, Michael R. Gaulke, Rae Ann Werner, William G. Oldham, FMR Corporation/13.11%, Takeshi Watanabe, Peter J. Simone, Robert P. Akins, Insiders/2.37%, Edward J. Brown, Edward H. Braun, Nancy J. Baker, Young K. Sohn, Jon D. Tompkins, J&W Seligman & Co./10.15% *(16 Owners included in Index)*

Financial Data: **Fiscal Year End:**12/31 **Latest Annual Data:** 12/31/2006

Year	Sales	Net Income
2006	$543,855,000	$95,648,000
2005	$383,648,000	$46,552,000
2004	$418,079,000	$43,154,000

Curr. Assets:	$785,766,000	**Curr. Liab.:**	$99,064,000	**P/E Ratio:**	17.36
Plant, Equip.:	$112,074,000	**Total Liab.:**	$261,200,000	**Indic. Yr. Divd.:**	NA
Total Assets:	$949,094,000	**Net Worth:**	$687,894,000	**Debt/ Equity:**	0.2203

Cynosure Inc

5 Carlisle Rd., Westford, MA, 01886; ***PH:*** 1-978-256-4200; ***Fax:*** 1-978-256-6556; ***http://*** www.cynosurelaser.com

General - Incorporation	DE	**Stock**- Price on:12/24/2007	$38.38
Employees	213	Stock Exchange	NDQ
Auditor	Ernst & Young LLP	Ticker Symbol	CYNO
Stk Agt	American Stock Transfer & Trust Co.	Outstanding Shares	11,680,000
Counsel	Wilmer Cutler Pickering H & D LLP	E.P.S	$0.88
DUNS No.	NA	Shareholders	NA

Business: The groups principle activities include developing and marketing aesthetic treatment systems. The products of the group include Apogee Elite, Cynergy, Affirm, Smartlipo, Affinity and Apogee 9300. In August 31, 2006 the group acquired Suzhou Cynosure Medical Devices Company, Ltd. The group operates from the United States, Europe, Asia Pacific and other. The group's quarterly revenue for September 2007 was 31.53 millions of USD.

Primary SIC and add'l.: 3845

CIK No: 0000885306

Subsidiaries: Cynosure France, Cynosure GmbH, Cynosure K.K., Cynosure U.K. Ltd. Sucursal Espana, Cynosure UK Ltd., Suzhou Cynosure Medical Devices Company Ltd.

Officers: Michael R. Davin/Chmn., CEO, Pres./$1,220,983.00, Timothy W. Baker/Exec. VP, CFO, Treasurer/$563,550.00, Douglas J. Delaney/Exec. VP - Sales/$638,299.00, David MacKie/VP - Operations, Kenji Shimizu/Exec. VP - International, Rafael Sierra/CTO, John Lenihan/VP - International Distribution

Directors: Michael R. Davin/Chmn., CEO, Pres., Ettore V. Biagioni/Dir., Andrea Cangioli/Dir., Paul F. Kelleher/Dir., Leonardo Masotti/Dir., Thomas H. Robinson/Dir., George J. Vojta/Dir.

Owners: Timothy W. Baker, Andrea Cangioli, Michael R. Davin, George J. Vojta, Thomas H. Robinson, Paul F. Kelleher, Next Century Growth Investors, LLC, Ettore V. Biagioni, El.En. S.p.A., Insiders, Leonardo Masotti, Douglas J. Delaney, Peninsula Capital Management, LP

Financial Data: **Fiscal Year End:**12/31 **Latest Annual Data:** 12/31/2006

Year	Sales	Net Income
2006	$78,401,000	-$650,000
2005	$56,262,000	$4,160,000
2004	$41,633,000	$5,296,000

Curr. Assets:	$102,657,000	**Curr. Liab.:**	$22,197,000	**P/E Ratio:**	479.75
Plant, Equip.:	$5,662,000	**Total Liab.:**	$23,696,000	**Indic. Yr. Divd.:**	NA
Total Assets:	$109,566,000	**Net Worth:**	$85,870,000	**Debt/ Equity:**	0.0111

CYOP Systems International Inc

Unit A 149 S Reeves Dr., Beverly Hills, CA, 90212; ***PH:*** 1-310-248-4860; ***http://*** www.cyop.org; ***Email:*** ir@cyopgaming.com

General - Incorporation	NV	**Stock**- Price on:12/24/2007	NA
Employees	NA	Stock Exchange	OTC
Auditor	De Leon & Co. P.A	Ticker Symbol	CYOS
Stk Agt	Nevada Agency & Trust Company	Outstanding Shares	NA
Counsel	NA	E.P.S	NA
DUNS No.	NA	Shareholders	NA

Business: The group's principle activities include developing and providing multimedia transactional technology solutions and services for the entertainment industry. Its products and services include financial transaction platforms for on-line video games and integrated e-commerce transaction technology for on-line merchants. The group operates from United States.

Primary SIC and add'l.: 7379 7373 7375

CIK No: 0001111698

Subsidiaries: Red Felt Software Ltd, SINA Corporation

Officers: Patrick Smyth/40/CEO, Canon Bryan/34/CFO, Sec., Treasurer

Directors: Patrick Smyth/40/CEO, Randy Peterson/55/Dir., Jorge Andrade/63/Dir.

Owners: Patrick Smyth, Mitch White/18.80%, Insiders

Financial Data: **Fiscal Year End:**12/31 **Latest Annual Data:** 12/31/2006

Year	Sales	Net Income
2006	NA	-$3,574,000
2005	$8,000	-$2,012,000
2004	$25,000	-$1,050,000

Curr. Assets:	$22,000	**Curr. Liab.:**	$4,298,000		
Plant, Equip.:	NA	**Total Liab.:**	$4,298,000	**Indic. Yr. Divd.:**	NA
Total Assets:	$241,000	**Net Worth:**	-$4,057,000	**Debt/ Equity:**	NA

Cypress Bioscience Inc

4350 Executive Dr., Ste. 325, San Diego, CA, 92121; ***PH:*** 1-858-452-2323; ***Fax:*** 1-858-452-1222; ***http://*** www.cypressbio.com; ***Email:*** ir-info@cypressbio.com

General - Incorporation	DE	**Stock**- Price on:12/24/2007	$13.92
Employees	15	Stock Exchange	NDQ
Auditor	Ernst & Young LLP	Ticker Symbol	CYPB
Stk Agt	Mellon Investor Services LLC	Outstanding Shares	32,300,000
Counsel	Cooley Godward LLP	E.P.S	-$0.05
DUNS No.	06-279-0209	Shareholders	NA

Business: The group's principal activity is to sell medical devices for the treatment of certain immune system disorders. The group develops a novel therapeutic agent for the treatment of blood platelet disorders. The group's first product, the prosorba(R) column, a medical device, treats a patients defective immune system so that it can more effectively respond to certain diseases. The prosorba column is a plastic cylinder measuring three inches in diameter and three and one half inches in height. The cylinder contains a solid binding matrix composed of protein a bound to dry silica granules.

Primary SIC and add'l.: 3841 8731 2836

CIK No: 0000716054

Officers: Jay D. Kranzler/Chmn., CEO/$3,015,293.00, Frank Porreca/Member - Pain Advisory Board, Srinivas G. Rao/Chief Scientific Officer, William Maixner/Member - Pain Advisory Board, Sabrina M. Johnson/CFO, Exec. VP, Chief Business Officer/$527,013.00, Michael R. Gendreau/VP - Clinical Development, Chief Medical Officer/$555,077.00, Denise L. Wheeler/General Counsel/$549,362.00

Directors: Jay D. Kranzler/Chmn., CEO, Daniel J. Clauw/Chmn. - Scientific Advisory Board, Randall Carpenter/Chmn. - Pain Advisory Board, Charles Nemeroff/Chmn. - Psychopharmacology Advisory Board, David Dunner/Member - Psychopharmacology Advisory Board, Martin Keller/Member - Psychopharmacology Advisory Board, Lorrin M. Koran/Member - Psychopharmacology Advisory Board, Philip Mease/Member - FMS Advisory Board, Samuel D. Anderson/Dir., Jean-Pierre Millon/Dir., Ranga K. Krishnan/Member - Psychopharmacology Advisory Board, Stephen Stahl/Member - Psychopharmacology Advisory Board, Roger L. Hawley/55/Dir., Amir Kalali/Dir., Tina S. Nova/54/Dir. *(21 Directors included in Index)*

Owners: Michael R. Gendreau, Insiders/8.10%, Roger L. Hawley, Wellington Management Co. LLP/9.50%, Jean-Pierre Millon, Daniel H. Petree, Goldman Sachs & Co./5.50%, Denise Wheeler, Jay D. Kranzler/5.60%, Perry Molinoff, Sabrina Martucci Johnson, Jon W. McGarity, Samuel D. Anderson, Maverick Capital Ltd./6.60%, Tina S. Nova *(17 Owners included in Index)*

Financial Data: **Fiscal Year End:**12/31 **Latest Annual Data:** 12/31/2006

Year	Sales	Net Income
2006	$4,322,000	-$8,247,000
2005	$8,385,000	-$8,627,000
2004	$14,415,000	-$11,215,000

Curr. Assets:	$103,728,000	**Curr. Liab.:**	$4,219,000		
Plant, Equip.:	$66,000	**Total Liab.:**	$16,727,000	**Indic. Yr. Divd.:**	NA
Total Assets:	$103,825,000	**Net Worth:**	$87,097,000	**Debt/ Equity:**	NA

Cypress Semiconductor Corp

198 Champion Ct., San Jose, CA, 95134; ***PH:*** 1-408-943-2600; ***Fax:*** 1-408-943-4730; ***http://*** www.cypress.com

General - Incorporation	DE	**Stock**- Price on:12/24/2007	$23.01
Employees	5,800	Stock Exchange	NYSE
Auditor	PricewaterhouseCoopers LLP	Ticker Symbol	CY
Stk Agt	Computershare Trust Co	Outstanding Shares	151,190,000
Counsel	Victoria Tidwell	E.P.S	$2.115
DUNS No.	10-210-8446	Shareholders	NA

Business: The group's principal activities are to design, develop, manufacture and market a broad line of high-performance digital and mixed-signal integrated circuits for a broad range of markets. The group operates in two segments: memory products and non-memory products. The memory segment designs and produces static random access memories. The non-memory segment targets networking, wireless infrastructure and handsets, computation, consumer, automotive, industrial and other markets. The principal customers of the group are cisco systems inc, emc corp, epson, logitech international sa, motorola inc, primax electronics ltd, sony corp. And st microelectronics nv. The group operates in the United States, Europe, Japan and other foreign countries. On 06-Jan-2004, the group acquired cascade semiconductor corporation. On 04-Aug-2004, the group acquired fillfactory nv.

Primary SIC and add'l.: 3674

CIK No: 0000791915

Subsidiaries: Cyland Corporation, Cypress Manufacturing, Ltd., Cypress Semiconductor (Minnesota), Inc, Cypress Semiconductor (Scandinavia) AB, Cypress Semiconductor (Shanghai) Design Co., Ltd, Cypress Semiconductor (Switzerland) Sarl, Cypress Semiconductor (Texas) , Inc., Cypress Semiconductor Canada, Cypress Semiconductor Corporation (Belgium) BVBA, Cypress Semiconductor Corporation (Luxembourg) Sprl, Cypress Semiconductor GmbH, Cypress Semiconductor International (Hong Kong) Limited, Cypress Semiconductor International Inc., Cypress Semiconductor International Sales B.V., Cypress Semiconductor Italia S.r.l. 39 Subsidiaries included in the Index

Officers: Hal Zarem/CEO - Silicon Light Machines, T. J. Rodgers/Founder, Dir., CEO, Pres./$5,165,249.00, Tom Werner/CEO - Sunpower Corporation, Harry Sim/CEO - Cypress Systems, Marcus Kramer/VP - Engineering, Cypress Systems, Brad W. Buss/CFO, Exec. VP/$1,406,340.00, Steve Kim/VP, GM - Products, Cypress Systems, Ramesh Songukrishnasamy/VP, GM - Service, Cypress Systems, Bob Booton/VP - Operations, Cypress Systems, Mike Verdon/VP - Sales, Cypress Systems, Sabbas Daniel/Exec. VP - Quality, Dinesh Ramanathan/Exec. VP - Data Communications Division, Chris Seams/Exec. VP - Sales, Marketing, Norm Taffe/Exec. VP - Consumer, Computation Division/$902,679.00, Ahmad Chatila/Exec. VP - Memory, Imaging Division *(22 Officers included in Index)*

Directors: T. J. Rodgers/Founder, Dir., CEO, Pres., Eric A. Benhamou/Chmn., Lloyd Carney/Dir., Evert P. Van De Ven/Dir., Steve W. Albrecht/Dir., Daniel J. McCranie/Dir., James R. Long/Dir.

Owners: Christopher Seams, T. J. Rodgers/2.40%, Evert van de Ven, Steve W. Albrecht, Eric A. Benhamou, James R. Long, Insiders/3.70%, FMR Corp./15.00%, Daniel J. McCranie, Janus Capital Management LLC/5.70%, Paul Keswick, Brad W. Buss, Norman Taffe, Lloyd Carney

Financial Data: **Fiscal Year End:**01/01 **Latest Annual Data:** 12/31/2006

Year	Sales	Net Income
2006	$1,091,553,000	$39,482,000

Curr. Assets:	$952,628,000	**Curr. Liab.:**	$275,839,000	**P/E Ratio:**	115.05
Plant, Equip.:	$572,018,000	**Total Liab.:**	$954,494,000	**Indic. Yr. Divd.:**	NA
Total Assets:	$2,123,525,000	**Net Worth:**	$1,045,559,000	**Debt/ Equity:**	0.8180

Cytation Corp

4218 W Linebaugh Ave., Tampa, FL, 33624; ***PH:*** 1-813-885-5998

General - Incorporation	DE	**Stock**- Price on:12/24/2007	$1.15
Employees	420	Stock Exchange	NA
Auditor	Herman, Lagor, Hopkins & Meeks, P.A.	Ticker Symbol	NA
Stk Agt	Computershare Trust Co	Outstanding Shares	8,610,000
Counsel	NA	E.P.S.	-$0.938
DUNS No.	04-561-0664	Shareholders	NA

Business: The group's principal activities are provision of solutions for admission process, financial aid and scholarship applications through its Web site. The presentation programs of the group include 'making high school count', 'making your college search count' and 'making college count'.

Primary SIC and add'l.: 8748 7375

CIK No: 0000095047

Subsidiaries: Deer Valley Acquisitions Corp, Deer Valley Homebuilders, Inc.

Officers: Charles G. Masters/68/Dir., CEO, Pres., Misty King/Regional Service Coordinator, Joel Logan/GM, Pres., Steve Lawler/Dir. - Finance, Sec., Treasurer, Aaron Humphries/Regional Service Coordinator, Elvis Bailey/Regional Service Coordinator, Ben Langley/Human Resources, Safety Mgr., Max Frye/Dir. - Engineering, Quality Assurance, Chet Murphree/Sales Mgr., VP, Ray Cooper/Dir. - Service, David Shaw/Regional Sales Dir., Joey Aycock/Regional Sales Dir. - AL, Terry Holcombe/Regional Sales Dir. - MO, TX, IL, Eddie Wilson/Regional Sales Dir. - TN, KY, IN, WV, Scott Strickland/Regional Sales Dir. - LA *(22 Officers included in Index)*

Directors: Charles G. Masters/68/Dir., CEO, Pres., Hans Beyer/42/Dir., John Giordano/50/Dir., Dale Phillips/60/Dir., Charles L. Murphree/46/Dir., John Steven Lawler/39/Dir.

Owners: John Steven Lawler, Joel Stephen Logan/2.52%, Hans Beyer/2.78%, Charles G. Masters/8.90%, Charles L. Murphree/1.68%, Insiders/16.72%, Christopher Phillips/26.26%

Financial Data: ***Fiscal Year End:***12/31 ***Latest Annual Data:*** 12/31/2006

Year	Sales	Net Income
2006	$65,461,000	$2,799,000
2005	$59,000	-$174,000
2004	$240,000	-$697,000

Curr. Assets:	$11,767,000	**Curr. Liab.:**	$7,265,000		
Plant, Equip.:	$3,207,000	**Total Liab.:**	$10,386,000	**Indic. Yr. Divd.:**	NA
Total Assets:	$20,836,000	**Net Worth:**	$10,450,000	**Debt/ Equity:**	0.2986

Cytec Industries Inc

5 Garret Mountain Plz., West Paterson, NJ, 07424; ***PH:*** 1-973-357-3100; ***Fax:*** 1-973-357-3065; ***http://*** www.cytec.com; ***Email:*** custinfo@cytec.com

General - Incorporation	DE	**Stock**- Price on:12/24/2007	$61.88
Employees	6,700	Stock Exchange	NYSE
Auditor	KPMG LLP	Ticker Symbol	CYT
Stk Agt	Mellon Investor Services LLC	Outstanding Shares	NA
Counsel	NA	E.P.S.	$4.92
DUNS No.	80-974-9948	Shareholders	NA

Business: The groups principle activities include developing, manufacturing and selling specialty chemicals and materials. The groups products include building block chemicals, liquid coating resins and additives, and specialty urethanes. Customers served by the group include the aerospace, adhesives, automotive and industrial coatings, chemical intermediates, inks, mining and plastics industries. The group operates from United States.

Primary SIC and add'l.: 2869 2824 2819 2821

CIK No: 0000912513

Subsidiaries: American Materials & Technologies Corporation (The), Avondale Ammonia Company, C.I.I. Luxembourg, S.a.r.l, Carteret Development LLC, Coquimbo, SGPS LDA, Cyquim de Colombia S.A., Cytec Acrylic Fibers Inc., Cytec Aerospace Far East Corp., Cytec Ammonia Inc., Cytec Asia/Pacific Holding Pty Limited, Cytec Australia Holdings Pty Limited, Cytec Australia Limited, Cytec Brewster Phosphates Inc., Cytec Canada Inc., Cytec Carbon Fibers LLC 92 Subsidiaries included in the Index

Officers: David Lilley/Chmn., CEO, Pres./$5,068,438.00, David M. Drillock/CFO, VP, Steven C. Speak/Pres. - Cytec Engineered Materials/$1,032,785.00, Roy Smith/VP, General Counsel, Sec., Joseph E. Marosits/VP - Human Resources, Jaswant S. Gill/Pres. - Building Block Chemicals, William N. Avrin/VP - Corporate, Business Development, Thomas P. Wozniak/Treasurer, Karen E. Koster/VP - Safety, Health and Environment, James P. Cronin/54/Exec. VP/$1,651,066.00, Shane D. Fleming/Pres. - Cytec Specialty Chemicals/$1,571,957.00, Richard T. Ferguson/VP - Taxes, Jeffrey C. Futterman/VP - Information Technology

Directors: David Lilley/Chmn., CEO, Pres., Barry C. Johnson/Dir., William P. Powell/Dir., Chris A. Davis/Dir., Louis L. Hoynes/Dir., James R. Stanley/Dir., Raymond P. Sharpe/Dir., Jerry R. Satrum/Dir., Anthony G. Fernandes/Dir., Thomas W. Rabaut/Dir.

Owners: W. P. Powell/1.00%, UCB, S.A./12.10%, Insiders/5.90%, FMR Corp./9.10%, Wellington Management Company, LLP/6.90%, C. A. Davis/1.00%, J. R. Satrum/1.00%, S. D. Fleming/2.00%, A. G. Fernandes, R. P. Sharpe, J. R. Stanley, J. P. Cronin/1.10%, S. C. Speak, L. L. Hoynes, B. C. Johnson *(17 Owners included in Index)*

Financial Data: ***Fiscal Year End:***12/31 ***Latest Annual Data:*** 12/31/2006

Year	Sales	Net Income
2006	$3,329,500,000	$194,900,000
2005	$2,925,700,000	$59,100,000
2004	$1,721,300,000	$126,100,000

Curr. Assets:	$1,153,400,000	**Curr. Liab.:**	$611,900,000	**P/E Ratio:**	14.13
Plant, Equip.:	$998,500,000	**Total Liab.:**	$2,261,400,000	**Indic. Yr. Divd.:**	$0.400
Total Assets:	$3,831,500,000	**Net Worth:**	$1,570,100,000	**Debt/ Equity:**	0.5165

CytoCore Inc

414 N Orleans St. Ste. 502, Chicago, IL, 60610; ***PH:*** 1-312-222-9550; ***http://*** www.cytocoreinc.com; ***Email:*** info@cytocoreinc.com

General - Incorporation	DE	**Stock**- Price on:12/24/2007	$0.38
Employees	5	Stock Exchange	OTC
Auditor	Amper, Politziner & Mattia P.c	Ticker Symbol	CYOE
Stk Agt	LaSalle Bank N.A	Outstanding Shares	342,840,000
Counsel	NA	E.P.S.	NA
DUNS No.	NA	Shareholders	NA

Business: The groups principal activities include designing, developing and commercializing of screening systems to assist in the early detection of cancer. The group products include Cocktail-CVX(TM), Cocktail-GCI(TM), AcCell(TM) and AIPS(TM). The group marketed its products under the trade names InPath e2 Collector and Cocktail-CVX. The group operates from the United States.

Primary SIC and add'l.: 3841

CIK No: 0000075439

Subsidiaries: AccuMed International, Inc., Bell National Corporation, Inpath, LLC, Oncometrics Imaging Corp., PFI National Corporation

Officers: Robert F. McCullough/CEO, CFO, Floyd E. Taub/CEO, Richard Domanik/COO, Pres., George Gorodeski/Lead Research Scientist

Directors: Steven Waggoner/Member - Advisory Board, Stephen Raab/Member - Advisory Board, John H. Abeles/Dir., Alexander M. Milley/Dir., Clint Severson/Dir.

Owners: Augusto Ocana, Alexander M. Milley/2.80%, Standard General Holdings, LLC/7.20%, Insiders/6.90%, Robert F. McCullough/3.20%, David J. Weissberg, M.D/5.60%, Floyd E. Taub, David J. Weissberg/5.60%, Richard A. Domanik, Edward G. Renner, John H. Abeles, Monsun, AS/10.00%, BSI Multihelvetia/5.30%

Financial Data: ***Fiscal Year End:***12/31 ***Latest Annual Data:*** 12/31/2006

Year	Sales	Net Income
2006	$94,000	-$6,566,000
2005	$117,000	-$4,326,000
2004	$243,000	-$13,567,000

Curr. Assets:	$1,020,000	**Curr. Liab.:**	$4,130,000		
Plant, Equip.:	$242,000	**Total Liab.:**	$4,697,000	**Indic. Yr. Divd.:**	NA
Total Assets:	$1,282,000	**Net Worth:**	-$3,415,000	**Debt/ Equity:**	NA

Cytogen Corp

650 College Rd. E, Ste. 3100, Princeton, NJ, 08540; ***PH:*** 1-609-750-8200; ***Fax:*** 1-609-452-2476; ***http://*** www.cytogen.com; ***Email:*** investorrelations@cytogen.com

General - Incorporation	DE	**Stock**- Price on:12/24/2007	$1.93
Employees	94	Stock Exchange	NDQ
Auditor	KPMG LLP	Ticker Symbol	CYTO
Stk Agt	American Stock Transfer & Trust Co.	Outstanding Shares	29,640,000
Counsel	Hale & Dorr LLP	E.P.S.	-$1.1
DUNS No.	03-859-6862	Shareholders	NA

Business: The group's principal activity is to license, develop and commercialize both therapeutic and molecular imaging/diagnostic products. The group develops and improves diagnosis and treatment of prostate cancer and other areas of oncology. The group also conducts research in cell signaling through its subsidiary, axcell biosciences. The products include quadramet, prostascint, and nmp22 bladderchek. The group operates in United States.

Primary SIC and add'l.: 8731 2835

CIK No: 0000725058

Subsidiaries: AxCell Biosciences Corporation, Cytogen Acquisition Corporation, Prostagen, Inc

Officers: Michael D. Becker/Dir., CEO, Pres./$995,952.00, William J. Thomas/Sr. VP, General Counsel/$424,295.00, William F. Goeckeler/Sr. VP - Operations/$492,253.00, Susan M. Mesco/Dir. - Investor Relations, Kevin J. Bratton/Sr. VP - Finance, CFO/$64,781.00, Stephen A. Ross/Sr. VP - Sales, Marketing

Directors: Michael D. Becker/Dir., CEO, Pres., James A. Grigsby/Chmn., Stephen K. Carter/Dir., John E. Bagalay/Dir., Dennis H. Langer/Dir., Allen Bloom/Dir., Kevin G. Lokay/Dir., Robert F. Hendrickson/Dir., Joseph A. Mollica/Dir.

Owners: William F. Goeckeler, Stephen K. Carter, John E. Bagalay, Michael D. Becker, Dennis H. Langer, Allen Bloom, Robert F. Hendrickson, Orbimed Advisors/11.00%, Proquest Investments/6.40%, Insiders/2.10%, James A. Grigsby, William J. Thomas, Joseph A. Mollica, Kevin G. Lokay

Financial Data: ***Fiscal Year End:***12/31 ***Latest Annual Data:*** 12/31/2006

Year	Sales	Net Income
2006	$17,307,000	-$15,103,000
2005	$15,946,000	-$26,289,000
2004	$14,619,000	-$20,540,000

Curr. Assets:	$39,985,000	**Curr. Liab.:**	$10,168,000		
Plant, Equip.:	$691,000	**Total Liab.:**	$16,691,000	**Indic. Yr. Divd.:**	NA
Total Assets:	$54,353,000	**Net Worth:**	$37,662,000	**Debt/ Equity:**	NA

Cytogenix Inc

3100 Wilcrest Dr., Houston, TX, 77042; ***PH:*** 1-713-789-0070; ***Fax:*** 1-713-789-0702; ***http://*** www.cytogenix.com

General - Incorporation	NV	**Stock**- Price on:12/24/2007	$0.4
Employees	11	Stock Exchange	OTC
Auditor	Lopez, Blevins, Bork & Assoc. LLP	Ticker Symbol	CYGX
Stk Agt	Nevada Agency & Trust Company	Outstanding Shares	140,660,000
Counsel	NA	E.P.S.	-$0.06
DUNS No.	NA	Shareholders	NA

Business: The group's principle activity is to develop and commercialize proprietary technology applicable to implement the final stage delivery of therapeutic single stranded dna molecules in cells. The technology of the company prevents genetically diseased cells from manufacturing harmful proteins, thereby preventing disease. It owns patented intracellular expression system technology (cygxes) to produce any desired sequence-specific, ssdna molecules (odn) in individual cells for the purpose of triplex, antisense, catalytic dna, and aptamer applications. It seeks to market and license its technology to biotechnology companies owning dna sequences in the human genome and to assist in their determination of the function and purpose of these sequences. The company primarily operates in the United States of America. The group is in its development stage. The group operates from United States.

Primary SIC and add'l.: 8071 8731

CIK No: 0001005302

Officers: Malcolm Skolnick/Chmn., CEO, Pres./$390,000.00, Xin-Xing Tan/Sr. Research Scientist, Frederic Kendirgi/Sr. Scientist, Pam Schertz/Controller/$74,791.00, Yin Chen/Chief Scientific Officer, VP - Research, Development/$125,104.00, Cindee Ewell/In House Counsel, Frank Vazquez/COO, Exec. VP/$262,529.00, Harilyn W. McMicken/Sr. Laboratory Dir., Greg S. Taylor/VP - Finance, Administration, CFO, Maury Fogle/Dir. - Business Development

Directors: Malcolm Skolnick/Chmn., CEO, Pres., Peter Glazer/Member - Scientific Advisory Board, Madeleine Duvic/Member - Scientific Advisory Board, Cy A. Stein/Dir., Member - Scientific Advisory Board, Scott E. Parazynski/Dir., John J. Rossi/Dir., Raymond L. Ocampo/Dir., Samuel

Kaplan/Member - Scientific Advisory Board, Richard Willson/Member - Scientific Advisory Board, Alan Gewirtz/Member - Scientific Advisory Board, Charles A. Conrad/Member - Scientific Advisory Board, Mark R. Emmett/Member - Scientific Advisory Board, Stephen M. Hewitt/Member - Scientific Advisory Board, Michael Walters/Dir.

Owners: Roland L. Violette/7.40%, Raymond L. Ocampo, Yin Chen, Scott E. Parazynski, Cy Stein, Malcolm H. Skolnick/3.10%, Insiders/12.40%

Financial Data: Fiscal Year End:12/31 Latest Annual Data: 12/31/2006

Year	Sales	Net Income
2006	$77,000	-$4,096,000
2005	NA	-$3,533,000
2004	NA	-$2,365,000

Curr. Assets:	$3,293,000	Curr. Liab.:	$1,263,000		
Plant, Equip.:	$262,000	Total Liab.:	$1,308,000	Indic. Yr. Divd.:	NA
Total Assets:	$4,210,000	Net Worth:	$2,902,000	Debt/ Equity:	0.0155

Cytokinetics Inc

280 E Grand Ave., South San Francisco, CA, 94080; *PH:* 1-650-624-3000; *Fax:* 1-650-624-3010; *http://* www.cytokinetics.com; *Email:* investors@cytokinetics.com

General - Incorporation	DE	Stock- Price on:12/24/2007	$6.13
Employees	150	Stock Exchange	NDQ
Auditor	PricewaterhouseCoopers LLP	Ticker Symbol	CYTK
Stk Agt	Mellon Investor Services LLC	Outstanding Shares	46,810,000
Counsel	NA	E.P.S	-$1.15
DUNS No.	NA	Shareholders	NA

Business: The group's principal activities are to discover, develop and commercialize novel small molecule drugs that specifically target the cytoskeleton. The cytoskeleton is a complex biological infrastructure that plays a fundamental role within every human cell. The group has developed a cell biology driven approach and proprietary technologies to evaluate the function of many interacting proteins in the complex environment of the intact human cell. The group has produced novel and potentially safer and more effective classes of drugs directed at treatments for cancer, cardiovascular diseases, fungal diseases, inflammatory diseases, high blood pressure and asthma.

Primary SIC and add'l.: 2834

CIK No: 0001061983

Officers: Robert I. Blum/Dir., CEO, Pres./$958,348.00, James H. Sabry/Co - Founder, Executive Chmn./$1,118,044.00, David W. Cragg/VP - Human Resources, David J. Morgans/Sr. VP - Preclinical Research, Development/$695,995.00, Jay K. Trautman/VP - Discovery Research, Technology, Andrew A. Wolff/Chief Medical Officer, Sr. VP - Clinical Research, Development/$665,548.00, Sharon A. Surrey-Barbari/Sr. VP - Finance, CFO/$639,736.00

Directors: Robert I. Blum/Dir., CEO, Pres., James H. Sabry/Co - Founder, Executive Chmn., Mark McDade/Dir., Stephen Dow/Dir., John C. Chabala/Member - Scientific Advisory Board, Lawrence S.B. Goldstein/Member - Scientific Advisory Board, Eric M. Gordon/Member - Scientific Advisory Board, Marc W. Kirschner/Member - Scientific Advisory Board, Charles Homcy/Dir., David G. Drubin/Member - Scientific Advisory Board, Ronald D. Vale/Member - Scientific Advisory Board, James A. Spudich/Dir., Member - Scientific Advisory Board, Larry E. Overman/Member - Scientific Advisory Board, Michael Schmertzler/Dir., Grant A. Heidrich/Dir. (17 Directors included in Index)

Owners: Andrew A. Wolff, David J. Morgans, Entities affiliated with Credit Suisse First Boston/6.70%, Wellington Management Company, LLP/10.80%, Federated Investors, Inc./10.30%, Grant A. Heidrich/4.40%, James A. Spudich, Entities affiliated with Sevin Rosen Funds/6.80%, Mark McDade, Amgen, Inc./7.40%, Sharon A. Surrey-Barbari, Michael Schmertzler/6.70%, Charles Homcy, Robert I. Blum/0.90%, Stephen Dow/7.10% (17 Owners included in Index)

Financial Data: Fiscal Year End:12/31 Latest Annual Data: 12/31/2006

Year	Sales	Net Income
2006	$3,127,000	-$57,115,000
2005	$8,912,000	-$42,252,000
2004	$13,442,000	-$37,198,000

Curr. Assets:	$153,621,000	Curr. Liab.:	$26,393,000		
Plant, Equip.:	$9,202,000	Total Liab.:	$63,203,000	Indic. Yr. Divd.:	NA
Total Assets:	$169,516,000	Net Worth:	$106,313,000	Debt/ Equity:	0.0627

Cytomedix Inc

416 Hungerford Dr., Ste. 330, Rockville, MD, 20850; *PH:* 1-240-499-2680; *Fax:* 1-240-499-2690; *http://* www.cytomedix.com; *Email:* info@cytomedix.com

General - Incorporation	DE	Stock - Price on:12/24/2007	$0.79
Employees	12	Stock Exchange	AMEX
Auditor	L J Soldinger Assoc. LLC	Ticker Symbol	GTF
Stk Agt	StockTrans, Inc.	Outstanding Shares	29,000,000
Counsel	NA	E.P.S	-$0.08
DUNS No.	NA	Shareholders	NA

Business: The group's principle activity is to develop, produce, license and distribute autologous cellular therapies for the treatment of chronic non-healing wounds. The company's proprietary wound care product line is based on its branded product, autologel. This product contains autologous multiple growth factors, platelet membranes, fibrin matrix scaffold and acts as a bioactive sealant. The entire process is called autologeltm system, which begins with drawing one to six small tubes (5-30 cc) of the patient's blood through a standard blood-draw procedure. Platelet rich plasma is separated from the whole blood through centrifugation using a specially calibrated tabletop-sized centrifuge. The separated platelet rich plasma is then mixed with reagents, which, upon agitation, process the liquid into a gel. The company markets autologel into the chronic wound care market through the sale of disposable kits that provide single treatment for wound application. The group operates from United States.

Primary SIC and add'l.: 2834

CIK No: 0001091596

Officers: Kshitij Mohan/Chmn., CEO/$810,671.00, Carelyn Fylling/VP - Professional Services/$151,728.00, Lawrence A. Lavery/Member - Scientific Advisory Board, Andrew S. Maslan/CFO/$337,348.00, Eduardo March/Dir. - Quality Assurance, Regulatory Affairs, David A. Hotchkiss/VP - Sales, Marketing

Directors: Kshitij Mohan/Chmn., CEO, Arun K. Deva/Dir., James Benson/Dir., Mark T. McLoughlin/Dir., David F. Drohan/Dir., Linda G. Phillips/Member - Scientific Advisory Board, Kelman Cohen/Member - Scientific Advisory Board, David Crews/Dir.

Owners: Mark T. McLoughlin, Andrew S. Maslan, Carelyn P. Fylling, David P. Crews/3.50%, David E. Jorden/8.50%, Group consisting of Jim Benson, David Crews/9.90%, David F. Drohan, Kshitij Mohan/4.00%, James S. Benson, Arun K. Deva

---

Financial Data: Fiscal Year End:12/31 Latest Annual Data: 12/31/2006

Year	Sales	Net Income
2006	$1,948,000	-$2,263,000
2005	$1,514,000	-$6,503,000
2004	$1,146,000	-$8,139,000

Curr. Assets:	$5,803,000	Curr. Liab.:	$1,326,000		
Plant, Equip.:	$12,000	Total Liab.:	$1,702,000	Indic. Yr. Divd.:	NA
Total Assets:	$10,234,000	Net Worth:	$8,531,000	Debt/ Equity:	NA

Cytori Therapeutics Inc

3020 Callan Rd., San Diego, CA, 92121; *PH:* 1-858-458-0900; *Fax:* 1-858-458-0994; *http://* www.cytoritx.com

General - Incorporation	DE	Stock - Price on:12/24/2007	$5.74
Employees	133	Stock Exchange	NDQ
Auditor	KPMG LLP	Ticker Symbol	CYTX
Stk Agt	Computershare Investor Services LLC	Outstanding Shares	23,580,000
Counsel	NA	E.P.S	-$0.92
DUNS No.	NA	Shareholders	NA

Business: The group's principal activities are to develop, manufacture and market biodegradable surgical implants that aid in the reconstruction, repair and regeneration of bones. The group is also developing additional products for use in spinal fusion procedures, neurosurgery plating, long-bone repair, healing of non-union fractures and cyst or tumor removal site repair, among other things. The products of the group are marketed in the United States and in Europe.

Primary SIC and add'l.: 3842

CIK No: 0001095981

Officers: Christopher J. Calhoun/Vice Chmn., CEO/$786,342.00, John T. Ransom/53/VP - Research, Regenerative Cell Technology/$426,256.00, Mark E. Saad/CFO/$635,878.00, Douglas Arm/VP - Development - Regenerative Cell Technology, Bruce Reuter/Sr. VP - Business Development, Seijiro Shirahama/Sr. VP - Asia Pacific/$480,958.00, Alexander M. Milstein/VP - Clinical Development, Marc H. Hedrick/Dir., Pres./$601,062.00, Tom Baker/Investor Relations Officer

Directors: Christopher J. Calhoun/Vice Chmn., CEO, Marshall G. Cox/Interim Chmn., Ronald D. Henriksen/Interim Chmn., David Rickey/Dir., Marc H. Hedrick/Dir., Pres., Paul W. Hawran/Dir., Carmack E. Holmes/Dir.

Owners: John Ransom, Mark E. Saad/1.10%, Marc H. Hedrick/2.90%, Olympus Corporation/12.80%, Insiders/14.30%, Christopher J. Calhoun/4.20%, Marshall G. Cox/3.30%, Carmack E. Holmes, David M. Rickey, Paul W. Hawran, Neil Gagnon/9.70%, Seijiro N. Shirahama, Ronald D. Henriksen

Financial Data: Fiscal Year End:12/31 Latest Annual Data: 12/31/2006

Year	Sales	Net Income
2006	$7,927,000	-$25,447,000
2005	$5,634,000	-$26,538,000
2004	$6,818,000	-$2,090,000

Curr. Assets:	$13,978,000	Curr. Liab.:	$6,586,000		
Plant, Equip.:	$4,699,000	Total Liab.:	$35,681,000	Indic. Yr. Divd.:	NA
Total Assets:	$24,868,000	Net Worth:	-$10,813,000	Debt/ Equity:	NA

CytRx Corp

11726 San Vicente Blvd., Ste. 650, Los Angeles, CA, 90049; *PH:* 1-310-826-5648; *Fax:* 1-310-826-6139; *http://* www.cytrx.com

General - Incorporation	DE	Stock - Price on:12/24/2007	$3.72
Employees	25	Stock Exchange	NDQ
Auditor	BDO Seidman LLP	Ticker Symbol	CYTR
Stk Agt	American Stock Transfer & Trust Co.	Outstanding Shares	86,810,000
Counsel	Troy & Gould Professional Corp	E.P.S	-$0.24
DUNS No.	14-847-6302	Shareholders	NA

Business: The group's principal activity is the development and commercialisation of pharmaceutical products. The products include human therapeutics focused on high value critical care therapies. The product flocor, is an intravenous agent used to treat acute sickle cell crisis and other vascular diseases. The group operates solely in the domestic market.

Primary SIC and add'l.: 2833 2836

CIK No: 0000799698

Subsidiaries: CytRx Laboratories, Inc

Officers: Steven A. Kriegsman/Dir., CEO, Pres./$1,157,601.00, Jack R. Barber/Chief Scientific Officer/$421,044.00, Mark A. Tepper/50/Sr. VP - Drug Discovery/$454,870.00, Edward L. Umali/Dir. - Operations, Benjamin S. Levin/General Counsel, VP - Legal Affairs, Corp. Sec./$397,470.00, David J. Haen/Dir. - Business Development, Matthew Natalizio/53/Treasurer/$325,587.00, Thomas Sticht/Contact - Investor Relations, Mitchell Fogelman/CFO, Shi Chung Ng/Sr. VP - Research, Development

Directors: Steven A. Kriegsman/Dir., CEO, Pres., Geoffrey Burnstock/Member - Scientific Advisory Board, Craig C. Mello/Member - Scientific Advisory Board, Robert H. Brown/Member - Scientific Advisory Board, Joseph Rubinfeld/Dir., Member - Scientific Advisory Board, Michael R. Hayden/Member - Scientific Advisory Board, Louis Ignarro/Dir., Member - Scientific Advisory Board, Michael P. Czech/Member - Scientific Advisory Board, Tariq Rana/Member - Scientific Advisory Board, Max Link/Dir., Marvin Selter/Dir., Richard Wennekamp/Dir., Ronald C. Kahn/Member - Scientific Advisory Board, Bruce Spiegelman/Member - Scientific Advisory Board

Owners: Jack R. Barber, Marvin R. Selter, Max Link, Benjamin S. Levin, Matthew Natalizio, Insiders/8.10%, Mark A. Tepper, Richard Wennekamp, Louis Ignarro, Steven A. Kriegsman/6.00%, Joseph Rubinfeld

Financial Data: Fiscal Year End:12/31 Latest Annual Data: 12/31/2006

Year	Sales	Net Income
2006	$2,066,000	-$16,752,000
2005	$184,000	-$15,093,000
2004	$428,000	-$16,392,000

Curr. Assets:	$30,721,000	Curr. Liab.:	$10,411,000		
Plant, Equip.:	$253,000	Total Liab.:	$26,486,000	Indic. Yr. Divd.:	NA
Total Assets:	$31,636,000	Net Worth:	$5,150,000	Debt/ Equity:	NA

Cytyc Corp

250 Campus Dr., Malborough, MA, 01752; *PH:* 1-508-263-8495; *http://* www.cytyc.com

General - Incorporation DE | **Stock** - Price on:12/24/2007 $42.62
Employees 1,500 | Stock Exchange NDQ
Auditor Deloitte & Touche LLP | Ticker Symbol CYTC
Stk Agt Computershare Investor Services LLC | Outstanding Shares 115,230,000
Counsel Testa, Hurwitz & Thibeault | E.P.S $0.53
DUNS No. 60-123-1475 | Shareholders NA

Business: The group's principal activity is to design, develop, manufacture and market thinprep(R) system and thinprep imaging system for use in medical diagnostic applications. The group's thinprep(R) systems used for cervical cancer screening and non-gynaecologic cytology. The thinprep system consists of the thinprep pap test, thinprep 2000 processor and thinprep 3000 processor. The thinprep also consist of related reagents, filters and other disposable supplies. The thinprep imaging system is a device that uses computer-imaging technology to assist in primary cervical cancer screening of thinprep pap test slides. The group has operations in North America, Europe, Australia and Asia. On 24-Mar-2004, the group acquired novasure(R) system.

Primary SIC and add'l.: 3826

CIK No: 0000849778

Subsidiaries: Cruiser, Inc., Cytyc (Australia) PTY LTD, Cytyc (UK) Limited, Cytyc Canada, Limited, Cytyc Europe, S.A., Cytyc Germany GmbH, Cytyc Healthcare Ventures, LLC, Cytyc Hong Kong Limited, Cytyc Iberia, S.L., Cytyc Interim, Inc., Cytyc International, Inc., Cytyc Limited Liability Company, Cytyc Limited Partnership, Cytyc S.a.r.l., Cytyc Securities Corporation 18 Subsidiaries included in the Index

Officers: Patrick J. Sullivan/Chmn., CEO, Pres., Daniel J. Levangie/Dir., Pres. - Surgical Products Division, Exec. VP, Timothy M. Adams/Sr. VP, CFO, Treasurer, David P. Harding/Pres. - Cytyc International, Sr. VP
, Tony Kingsley/Pres. - Diagnostic Products Division, Sr. VP
, John P. McDonough/Pres. - Cytyc Development Corporation, Sr. VP - Corporate Development, Suzanne A. Meszner-Eltrich/Sr. VP, General Counsel, Sec., Ellen Sheets/Sr. VP, Chief Medical Officer

Directors: Patrick J. Sullivan/Chmn., CEO, Pres., William McDaniel/Vice Chmn., Monroe Trout/Honorary Chmn. Emeritus, Marla S. Persky/Dir., Daniel J. Levangie/Dir., Pres. - Surgical Products Division, Exec. VP, Brock Hattox/Dir., John Thomas Repke/Member - Advisory Board, Jonathan Zenilman/Member - Advisory Board, Thomas F. Purdon/Member - Advisory Board, Lawrence N. Shulman/Member - Advisory Board, Elizabeth A. Stewart/Member - Advisory Board, Jeff Boyd/Member - Advisory Board, Philip D. Darney/Member - Advisory Board, Walter E. Boomer/Dir., Sally W. Crawford/Dir. *(17 Directors included in Index)*

Financial Data: *Fiscal Year End:*12/31 *Latest Annual Data:* 12/31/2006

Year	Sales	Net Income
2006	$608,250,000	$139,537,000
2005	$508,251,000	$113,486,000
2004	$393,593,000	$73,588,000

Curr. Assets:	$437,153,000	**Curr. Liab.:**	$74,137,000	**P/E Ratio:**	80.42
Plant, Equip.:	$149,007,000	**Total Liab.:**	$405,741,000	**Indic. Yr. Divd.:**	NA
Total Assets:	$1,164,714,000	**Net Worth:**	$758,973,000	**Debt/ Equity:**	0.3479

D&E Communications Inc

124 E Main St., Ephrata, PA, 17522; *PH:* 1-717-733-4101; *Fax:* 1-717-859-4803; *http://* www.decommunications.com

General - Incorporation PA | **Stock** - Price on:12/24/2007 $17.39
Employees 569 | Stock Exchange NDQ
Auditor PricewaterhouseCoopers LLP | Ticker Symbol DECC
Stk Agt Mellon Investor Services LLC | Outstanding Shares 14,410,000
Counsel NA | E.P.S $0.53
DUNS No. NA | Shareholders NA

Business: The groups principle activity is to provide communications services. The groups services include local and long distance telephone, broadband, Internet access and video. The groups operates through four segments namely rural local exchange carrier, competitive local exchange carrier, Internet services and systems integration. The group operates from Lancaster, Berks, Lebanon, Chester, Montgomery, Lehigh, Union and Northumberland. The group's quarterly revenue for September 2007 was 38.21 millions of USD.

Primary SIC and add'l.: 4813 7379 4899 7373 7389 4822

CIK No: 0001011737

Subsidiaries: Buffalo Valley Management Services, Inc., Buffalo Valley Telephone Company, Conestoga Enterprises, Inc., Conestoga Management Services, Inc., Conestoga Telephone and Telegraph company, Conestoga Wireless Company, D&E Investments, Inc., D&E Management Services, Inc., D&E Networks, Inc., D&E Systems, Inc., D&E Wireless, Inc., Denver and Ephrata Telephone and Telegraph Company, EuroTel, L.L.C., Infocore, Inc., PCS Licenses, Inc. 16 Subsidiaries included in the Index

Officers: James W. Morozzi/Presiden, Dir., CEO/$487,510.00, Garth W. Sprecher/Dir., Sr. VP, Sec./$387,374.00, Thomas E. Morell/Sr. VP, CFO, Treasurer/$397,381.00, Albert H. Kramer/53/Sr. VP - Operations/$367,104.00, Stuart L. Kirkwood/VP - Engineering Operations/$231,151.00

Directors: James W. Morozzi/Presiden, Dir., CEO, Mark D. Thomas/Chmn., William G. Ruhl/Vice Chmn., Garth W. Sprecher/Dir., Sr. VP, Sec., John Amos/Dir., Paul W. Brubaker/Dir., Frank Coughlin/Dir., Hugh G. Courtney/Dir., Ronald E. Frisbie/Dir., John C. Long/Dir., Steven B. Silverman/Dir., Richard G. Weidner/Dir.

Owners: John C. Long, John Amos, William G. Ruhl, James W. Morozzi, Insiders/3.84%, Garth W. Sprecher/1.78%, Frank M. Coughlin, Hugh G. Courtney, Richard G. Weidner, Stuart L. Kirkwood, Ronald E. Frisbie, Albert H. Kramer, Steven B. Silverman, Paul W. Brubaker, Mark D. Thomas *(16 Owners included in Index)*

Financial Data: *Fiscal Year End:*12/31 *Latest Annual Data:* 12/31/2006

Year	Sales	Net Income
2006	$162,068,000	$6,742,000
2005	$176,247,000	$13,711,000
2004	$176,271,000	-$2,739,000

Curr. Assets:	$34,048,000	**Curr. Liab.:**	$26,944,000	**P/E Ratio:**	32.81
Plant, Equip.:	$171,412,000	**Total Liab.:**	$324,995,000	**Indic. Yr. Divd.:**	$0.500
Total Assets:	$510,574,000	**Net Worth:**	$185,579,000	**Debt/ Equity:**	1.0513

D.R. Horton Inc

301 Commerce St., Ste. 500, Fort Worth, TX, 76102; *PH:* 1-817-390-8200; *Fax:* 1-817-390-1704; *http://* www.drhorton.com

General - Incorporation DE | **Stock** - Price on:12/24/2007 $21.1
Employees 8,772 | Stock Exchange NYSE
Auditor Ernst & Young LLP | Ticker Symbol DHI
Stk Agt American Stock Transfer & Trust Co. | Outstanding Shares 314,110,000
Counsel NA | E.P.S NA
DUNS No. NA | Shareholders NA

Business: The groups principle activity is to provide financial banking services. The group operates through 7 segments namely, northeast, southeast, south central, southwest, California, west and financial services. The group operates from the United States. The group's total revenue in the year 2007 was 11,296.50 millions of USD.

Primary SIC and add'l.: 6162 6361 1521 6552 1522

CIK No: 0000882184

Subsidiaries: 2 C Development Company LLC, 3030 Management, Inc., 91st Avenue & Happy Valley, L.L.C., Austin Data, Inc., C. Richard Dobson Builders, Inc., CH Funding, LLC, CH Investments of Texas, Inc., CHI Construction Company, CHM Partners, L.P., CHTEX of Texas, Inc., Continental Homes of Texas, L.P., Continental Homes, Inc., Continental Residential, Inc., Continental Traditions, LLC, CP Water Company 199 Subsidiaries included in the Index

Officers: Donald J. Tomnitz/Vice Chmn., CEO, Pres., Bill W. Wheat/Dir., CFO, Exec. VP, Samuel R. Fuller/Sr. Exec. VP, Stacey H. Dwyer/Exec. VP, Treasurer, Ted I. Harbour/Chief Legal Officer, Chris Chambers/Pres. - California Region, Rick Horton/Pres. - South Central Region, George Seagraves/Pres. - Midwest Region, Brian Gardner/Pres. - Northeast Region, David Auld/Pres. - Southeast Region, Gordon Jones/Pres. - Southwest Region, James K. Schuler/Pres. - West Region, Randy Present/Pres. - Financial Services, Mary Horton/Investor Relations Officer, Jessica Hansen/Investor Relations Officer *(16 Officers included in Index)*

Directors: Donald J. Tomnitz/Vice Chmn., CEO, Pres., Donald R. Horton/Chmn., Bill W. Wheat/Dir., CFO, Exec. VP, Bradley S. Anderson/Dir., Michael R. Buchanan/Dir., Richard I. Galland/Dir., Michael W. Hewatt/Dir.

Owners: Donald R. Horton/8.60%, Michael R. Buchanan, Michael W. Hewatt, George W. Seagraves, Bill W. Wheat, Richard I. Galland, Bradley S. Anderson, FMR Corp/15.00%, Samuel R. Fuller, Donald J. Tomnitz, Stacey H. Dwyer, Gordon D. Jones, Insiders/9.36%

Financial Data: *Fiscal Year End:*09/30 *Latest Annual Data:* 9/30/2006

Year	Sales	Net Income
2006	$15,051,300,000	$1,233,300,000
2005	$13,863,700,000	$1,470,500,000
2004	$10,840,800,000	$975,100,000

Curr. Assets:	$12,179,000,000	**Curr. Liab.:**	$2,184,100,000	**P/E Ratio:**	9.09
Plant, Equip.:	$131,400,000	**Total Liab.:**	$8,262,700,000	**Indic. Yr. Divd.:**	$0.600
Total Assets:	$14,820,700,000	**Net Worth:**	$6,452,900,000	**Debt/ Equity:**	0.7799

D2Fusion Corp

Formerly: Enwin Resources Inc
2610-1066 West Hastings St., Vancouver, BC, V6E 3X2; *PH:* 1-604-602-1717

General - Incorporation NV | **Stock** - Price on:12/24/2007 NA
Employees NA | Stock Exchange OTC
Auditor LBB & Associates Ltd., LLP | Ticker Symbol ENWN
Stk Agt NA | Outstanding Shares NA
Counsel NA | E.P.S NA
DUNS No. NA | Shareholders NA

Business: The groups principal activity is to explore minerals properties of silver, copper and zinc. The group has acquired property consisting of five mining claims in Lac La Hache, British Columbia. The group operates from British Columbia in Canada.

Primary SIC and add'l.: 1400

CIK No: 0001195584

Officers: Nora Coccaro/51/Dir., CEO, CFO, Principal Accounting Officer, Michael Bebek/31/Dir., Pres., Sec., Treasurer

Directors: Nora Coccaro/51/Dir., CEO, CFO, Principal Accounting Officer, Michael Bebek/31/Dir., Pres., Sec., Treasurer, Derrick Strickland/40/Dir.

Owners: Michael Bebek/68.00%

Financial Data: *Fiscal Year End:*08/31 *Latest Annual Data:* 08/31/2007

Year	Sales	Net Income
2007	NA	-$182,000
2006	NA	-$66,000

Curr. Assets:	$10,000	**Curr. Liab.:**	$410,000		
Plant, Equip.:	NA	**Total Liab.:**	$410,000	**Indic. Yr. Divd.:**	NA
Total Assets:	$247,000	**Net Worth:**	-$164,000	**Debt/ Equity:**	NA

DAC Technologies Group International Inc

1601 W Pk. Dr., Ste. 4-C, Little Rock, AR, 72204; *PH:* 1-501-661-9100; *Fax:* 1-501-661-9108; *http://* www.dactec.com; *Email:* info@dactec.com

General - Incorporation FL | **Stock** - Price on:12/24/2007 $1.3
Employees 11 | Stock Exchange OTC
Auditor Moore Stephens Frost | Ticker Symbol DAAT
Stk Agt Florida Atlantic Stock Transfer, Inc. | Outstanding Shares 6,320,000
Counsel NA | E.P.S $0.07
DUNS No. NA | Shareholders NA

Business: The group's principal activities are to develop, manufacture and market various consumer products, patented and unpatented, which are designed to enhance and provide security for the consumer and their property. The group has also developed a wide range of security and non-security products for the home, automobile and individual. It primarily sells to mass market retailers such as wal-Mart, walgreens and k-Mart. The majority of the groups products are manufactured and imported from mainland China and shipped to a central location in little rock, Arkansas for distribution. The products are plastic trigger lock, lever hammer lock, steel gun lock, metal trigger lock, cable lock, body alarm, key alert, pepper spray, patient alert, tear gas, clampit cupholder, clampit plateholder and horizontal phone case.

Primary SIC and add'l.: 3429 3499 3089

CIK No: 0001102750

Subsidiaries: Summit Training International

Officers: David A. Collins/62/Chmn., CEO, Pres., Robert C. Goodwin/51/Dir., CFO

Directors: David A. Collins/62/Chmn., CEO, Pres., Robert C. Goodwin/51/Dir., CFO

Owners: Bruce M. Stachenfeld/5.30%, Praetorian Capital Management LLC/17.90%, Robert C. Goodwin, David A. Collins/8.20%

Financial Data: *Fiscal Year End:*12/31   *Latest Annual Data:* 12/31/2006

Year	Sales		Net Income
2006		$15,476,000	$753,000
2005		$13,351,000	$1,181,000
2004		$9,352,000	$1,012,000
Curr. Assets:	$5,800,000	**Curr. Liab.:** $1,906,000	**P/E Ratio:** 14.44
Plant, Equip.:	$212,000	**Total Liab.:** $1,939,000	**Indic. Yr. Divd.:** NA
Total Assets:	$6,418,000	**Net Worth:** $4,479,000	**Debt/ Equity:** NA

Dade Behring Holdings Inc

1717 Deerfield Rd., Deerfield, IL, 60015; *PH:* 1-847-267-5300; *Fax:* 1-847-267-1066; *http://* www.dadebehring.com

General - Incorporation	DE	Stock- Price on:12/24/2007	$52.86
Employees	6,400	Stock Exchange	NDQ
Auditor	KPMG LLP	Ticker Symbol	DADE
Stk Agt	Mellon Investor Services LLC	Outstanding Shares	82,160,000
Counsel	NA	E.P.S.	$1.63
DUNS No.	NA	Shareholders	NA

Business: The group operates through its subsidiary whose principle activities include manufacturing and distributing diagnostic products and services to clinical laboratories. The groups products include medical diagnostic instruments, and reagents and consumables. The group operates from United States.

Primary SIC and add'l.: 3826 2835

CIK No: 0001183920

Subsidiaries: Dade Behring A/S, Dade Behring AB, Dade Behring AS, Dade Behring Asia Pte.Ltd., Dade Behring Austria GmbH, Dade Behring B.V., Dade Behring Beteiligungs GmbH, Dade Behring CanadaInc., Dade Behring de VenezuelaC.A., Dade Behring Diagnostic Co. Ltd., Dade Behring Diagnostick TicaretLtd., Dade Behring Diagnostics India Private Limited, Dade Behring Diagnostics Malaysia SDN BHD, Dade Behring Diagnostics Philippines,Inc., Dade Behring Diagnostics Pty.,Ltd. 50 Subsidiaries included in the Index

Officers: Jim Reid-Anderson/Chmn., CEO, Pres./$5,700,526.00, Nancy A. Krejsa/VP - Corporate Communications, Investor Relations, John M. Duffey/CFO, Sr. VP/$1,814,213.00, Dominick M. Quinn/52/Exec. VP/$2,381,935.00, Mark Wolsey-Paige/Chief Strategy Officer, Techology Officer/$1,839,342.00, Louise S. Pearson/VP, Corp. Sec., Lance C. Balk/Sr. VP, General Counsel, Randy Daniel/Pres. - Global Customer Management, David G. Edelstein/Sr. VP - RA, QA, HSE, CIO, Kathy Kennedy/Sr. VP - Human Resources, Donal Quinn/COO, Connie Dubois/Dir. - Public Relations, Customer Communication

Directors: Jim Reid-Anderson/Chmn., CEO, Pres., Beverly A. Huss/Dir., Leigh N. Anderson/Dir., Samuel K. Skinner/Dir., Jeffrey D. Benjamin/Dir., Alan S. Cooper/Dir., Richard W. Roedel/Dir., James G. Andress/Dir.

Financial Data: *Fiscal Year End:*12/31   *Latest Annual Data:* 12/31/2006

Year	Sales		Net Income
2006		$1,739,200,000	$120,000,000
2005		$1,658,100,000	$124,900,000
2004		$1,559,800,000	$79,900,000
Curr. Assets:	$712,700,000	**Curr. Liab.:** $367,300,000	**P/E Ratio:** 36.21
Plant, Equip.:	$488,500,000	**Total Liab.:** $1,066,200,000	**Indic. Yr. Divd.:** $0.200
Total Assets:	$1,875,400,000	**Net Worth:** $809,200,000	**Debt/ Equity:** 0.6255

Dag Media Inc

192 Lexington Ave., New York, NY, 10016; *PH:* 1-212-489-6800; *Fax:* 1-212-779-2947; *http://* www.newyellow.com

General - Incorporation	NY	Stock- Price on:12/24/2007	$1.67
Employees	6	Stock Exchange	NDQ
Auditor	Goldstein Golub Kessler LLP	Ticker Symbol	DAGM
Stk Agt	American Stock Transfer & Trust Co.	Outstanding Shares	3,240,000
Counsel	Morse Zelnick Rose & Lander LLP	E.P.S.	-$0.15
DUNS No.	NA	Shareholders	NA

Business: The group's principal activity is to publish and distribute business directories in print and online. The group operates three Internet portals, namely Jewishyellow.com, targeting worldwide Jewish communities: Jewishmasterguide.com, targeting the ultra-orthodox and Hasidic communities; and a mainstream general portal Newyellow.com, targeting the general population. The group also sells yellow page advertisements as part of an overall media package that includes print advertising, on-line advertising and other added value services. The value added services include referral services and consumer discounts.

Primary SIC and add'l.: 2741 7375

CIK No: 0001080340

Subsidiaries: Blackbook Photography Inc, DAG Interactive, Inc, Modern Holdings Incorporated

Officers: Assaf Ran/42/Chmn., CEO, Pres./$322,760.00, Inbar Evron-Yogev/35/CFO, Treasurer, Sec./$68,328.00, Hagit Evenhaim/General Counsel

Directors: Assaf Ran/42/Chmn., CEO, Pres., Eran Goldshmid/Dir., Phillip Michals/Dir., Michael J. Jackson/Dir., Mark Alhadeff/45/Dir.

Owners: Inbar Evron-Yogev, Phillip Michals, Insiders/49.76%, Michael J. Jackson, Mark Alhadeff/2.31%, Assaf Ran/44.90%, Eran Goldshmid

Financial Data: *Fiscal Year End:*12/31   *Latest Annual Data:* 12/31/2006

Year	Sales		Net Income
2006		$232,000	-$174,000
2005		$4,447,000	-$511,000
2004		$5,949,000	$1,035,000
Curr. Assets:	$7,427,000	**Curr. Liab.:** $899,000	
Plant, Equip.:	$16,000	**Total Liab.:** $1,119,000	**Indic. Yr. Divd.:** NA
Total Assets:	$8,261,000	**Net Worth:** $7,077,000	**Debt/ Equity:** 0.0078

Dai'ei Inc

1 2 Nakatsu Hondori, Oyodo Ku, Osaka, 531 J M0;

General - Incorporation		Stock- Price on:12/24/2007	$21.38
Employees	NA	Stock Exchange	NDQ
Auditor	NA	Ticker Symbol	DAIEY
Stk Agt	Bank of New York	Outstanding Shares	NA
Counsel	NA	E.P.S.	NA
DUNS No.	NA	Shareholders	NA

Business: The groups principal activity is to provide information and related Grocery Retail facts online services. The group operates from the United States.

Primary SIC and add'l.: 5331 5411 5499 5311 5399

CIK No: 0000800167

Financial Data: *Fiscal Year End:*08/31   *Latest Annual Data:* 2/28/2006

Year	Sales		Net Income
2006		$14,440,750,000	$3,561,724,000
2005		$17,464,933,000	-$4,868,552,000
2004		$18,123,809,000	$164,982,000
Curr. Assets:	$7,533,564,000	**Curr. Liab.:** $14,738,700,000	**P/E Ratio:** 53.58
Plant, Equip.:	$8,346,155,000	**Total Liab.:** $19,547,155,000	**Indic. Yr. Divd.:** NA
Total Assets:	$20,552,564,000	**Net Worth:** $804,773,000	**Debt/ Equity:** NA

Daily Journal Corp

915 E 1st St., Los Angeles, CA, 90012; *PH:* 1-213-229-5300; *Fax:* 1-213-229-5481; *http://* www.dailyjournal.com

General - Incorporation	SC	Stock- Price on:12/24/2007	$40.59
Employees	260	Stock Exchange	NDQ
Auditor	Ernst & Young LLP	Ticker Symbol	DJCO
Stk Agt	Mellon Investor Services LLC	Outstanding Shares	1,500,000
Counsel	NA	E.P.S.	$1.67
DUNS No.	00-825-1449	Shareholders	NA

Business: The group's principal activity is the publishing of newspapers and Web sites covering California, Washington, Arizona, Colorado and Nevada. The group also publishes the California lawyer, the code of Colorado regulations and other corporate counsel magazines. The group serves as a newspaper representative specializing in public notice advertising and produces several specialized information services. The products of the group also include technologies and applications to enable justice agencies to automate their operations. The group publishes 14 newspapers of general circulation that covers news of interest to the general public.

Primary SIC and add'l.: 2721 5192 7375 7319

CIK No: 0000783412

Subsidiaries: Sustain Technologies, Inc.

Officers: Martin Berg/Editor - Los Angeles, John Roemer/Staff Writer, s, San Francisco Daily Journal, Linda S. Rapattoni/Staff Writer, Sacramento, Los Angeles Daily Journal, Michael Gottlieb/Executive Editor, Daily Commerce Group, Ron McNees/Production Editor, CA Real Estate Journal, Julie Nakashima/Staff Writer, s, CA Real Estate Journal, Keeley Webster/Staff Writer, s, CA Real Estate Journal, Mandy Jackson/Staff Writer, San Diego, CA Real Estate Journal, Jason Armstrong/Staff Writer, Riverside, Jack Briggs/Copy Editor, s, CA Real Estate Journal, Barbara Kate Repa/Legal Editor, California Lawyer, Sandra Rosenzweig/Technology Editor, Thomas K. Brom/Sr. Editor, s, California Lawyer, Martin Lasden/Editor - California Lawyer, Chuleenan Svetvilas/Sr. Editor, s, California Lawyer (74 Officers included in Index)

Directors: Peter D. Kaufman/53/Dir.

Financial Data: *Fiscal Year End:*09/30   *Latest Annual Data:* 9/30/2006

Year	Sales		Net Income
2006		$32,369,000	$2,438,000
2005		$34,350,000	$4,287,000
2004		$34,822,000	$3,731,000
Curr. Assets:	$15,948,000	**Curr. Liab.:** $13,687,000	
Plant, Equip.:	$11,917,000	**Total Liab.:** $18,728,000	**Indic. Yr. Divd.:** NA
Total Assets:	$35,703,000	**Net Worth:** $16,975,000	**Debt/ Equity:** 0.2169

DaimlerChrysler AG

Formerly: DaimlerChrysler
Mercedesstrasse 137, Stuttgart, 70327; *PH:* 011-49-711-170; *http://* www.daimlerchrysler.com

General - Incorporation	Germany	Stock- Price on:12/24/2007	$92.52
Employees	360,385	Stock Exchange	NA
Auditor	KPMG Deutsche Treuhand Gesellschaft	Ticker Symbol	NA
Stk Agt	Deutsche Bank Ag, Bank of New York	Outstanding Shares	1,030,000,000
Counsel	NA	E.P.S.	$5.72
DUNS No.	49-899-9044	Shareholders	NA

Business: The group's principle activity is the manufacture and distribution of automobiles and trucks. The company offers a wide range of products and brands including: mercedes-benz, chrysler, smart, dodge, plymouth, sterling, freightliner, setra and jeep (registered trademarks). Additionally to its core business, the company manufactures diesel engines, aircraft, helicopters, space and defense systems and offers vehicle financing services, electric and electronic engineering solutions and insurance brokerage. The company has worldwide subsidiaries.

Primary SIC and add'l.: 3728 3612 6331 6141 3711 3713 3721

CIK No: 0001067318

Subsidiaries: Chrysler International Corporation, DaimlerChrysler Corporation, DaimlerChrysler Motors Company LLC, DaimlerChrysler North, DaimlerChrysler North America Holding Corporation, DaimlerChrysler Services AG, McLaren Group Ltd, Mercedes-Benz Manhattan, Inc., Mercedes-Benz USA, LLC, Mitsubishi Fuso Truck and Bus Corporation

Officers: Thomas Weber/54/Dir., Head - Group Research, Development Mercedes, Benz Cars, Dieter Zetsche/55/Head - Mercedes, Benz Cars, Lutz Deus/Sr. Mgr. - Institutional Investors, Analysts, Bjorn Scheib/Sr. Mgr. - Institutional Investors, Analysts, Rolf Bassermann/Sr. Mgr. - Private Investors, Internet Investor Relations, Katja Wolf/Event Mgr. - Investor Relations, Treasury, Katja Sandmann/Team Leader - Mercedes Car Group, Hartmut Schick/Head - Global Communications, Thomas Frohlich/Head - Corporate Communcations, Han Tjan/Dir. - Corporate Communications North America, Silke Walters/Financial Media Relations, Marina Raptis/Contact - Human Resources, Ursula Mertzig-Stein/Contact - Social, Political Affairs, Susann Rohr/Contact - Social, Political Affairs, Andreas Renschler/50/Dir., Head - Daimler Trucks Division (19 Officers included in Index)

Directors: Hilmar Kopper/72/Chmn. - Supervisory Board, Eric Ridenour/49/Dir., Peter A. Magowan/66/Member - Supervisory Board, Rudiger Grube/57/Dir., Manfred Bischoff/66/Member - Supervisory Board, Heinrich Flegel/Member - Supervisory Board, Ron Gettelfinger/63/Dir., Earl G. Graves/73/Member - Supervisory Board, Arnaud Legardere/47/Member - Supervisory Board, William A. Owens/68/Member - Supervisory Board, Manfred Schneider/70/Member - Supervisory Board, Lynton R. Wilson/68/Member - Supervisory Board, Clemens Borsig/59/Member - Supervisory Board, Uwe Werner/56/Member - Supervisory Board, Bodo Uebber/49/Dir. *(30 Directors included in Index)*

Owners: Kuwait Investment Authority/7.10%

Financial Data: *Fiscal Year End:*12/31 *Latest Annual Data:* 12/31/2006

Year	Sales	Net Income
2006	$200,142,957,000	$4,260,608,000
2005	$177,394,694,000	$3,370,802,000
2004	$192,319,000,000	$3,338,000,000

Curr. Assets:	$111,669,654,000	**Curr. Liab.:**	$61,078,398,000	**P/E Ratio:**	14.48
Plant, Equip.:	$93,713,574,000	**Total Liab.:**	$204,915,841,000	**Indic. Yr. Divd.:**	$1.500
Total Assets:	$250,886,047,000	**Net Worth:**	$45,094,847,000	**Debt/ Equity:**	NA

Dairy Fresh Farms Inc

413 Churchill Ave. N, Ottawa, ON, K1Z 5C7; *PH:* 1-613-724-2484; *Fax:* 1-613-722-6342; *http://* www.dairyfresh.ca; *Email:* info@dairyfresh.ca

General - Incorporation	NV	Stock - Price on:12/24/2007	$0.06
Employees	NA	Stock Exchange	OTC
Auditor ... Raymond Chabot Grant Thornton LLP		Ticker Symbol	DYFR
Stk Agt.	Interwest Transfer Co. Inc.	Outstanding Shares	NA
Counsel	NA	E.P.S.	NA
DUNS No.	NA	Shareholders	NA

Business: The groups principal activity is to develop milk-based product. The group products include regular milk beverage, lactose reduced milk beverage, and field trials for premium ice cream with omega-3s. The group marketed its product under the trade name Dairy Fresh Farms(TM). The group operates from the United States and Canada.

Primary SIC and add'l.: 5143

CIK No: 0001274001

Subsidiaries: 6351492 Canada Inc., Dairy Fresh Technologies Ltd.,

Officers: Robert C. Harrison/CEO, Pres., Ian Morrice/Exec. VP, Donald Paterson/CFO, Joseph I. Emas/Contact - Securities Counsel, Tom Tomson/Contact - Transfer Agent

Directors: Nicolas Matossian/Chmn.

Owners: Nicolas Matossian/7.70%, Ian Morrice/6.90%, Don Paterson/7.20%, Robert C. Harrison/5.20%

Financial Data: *Fiscal Year End:*12/31 *Latest Annual Data:* 12/31/2006

Year	Sales	Net Income
2006	NA	-$1,143,000
2005	$151,000	-$1,662,000

Curr. Assets:	$454,000	**Curr. Liab.:**	$758,000	**P/E Ratio:**	3.75
Plant, Equip.:	$10,000	**Total Liab.:**	$758,000	**Indic. Yr. Divd.:**	NA
Total Assets:	$464,000	**Net Worth:**	-$295,000	**Debt/ Equity:**	NA

Daktronics Inc SD

331 32nd Ave., Brookings, SD, 57006; *PH:* 1-605-697-4000; *Fax:* 1-605-697-4700; *http://* www.daktronics.com; *Email:* sales@daktronics.com

General - Incorporation	SD	Stock - Price on:12/24/2007	$21.34
Employees	1,400	Stock Exchange	NDQ
Auditor	Ernst & Young LLP	Ticker Symbol	DAKT
Stk Agt.	Wells Fargo Bank Minnesota N.A	Outstanding Shares	39,340,000
Counsel	Popham Haik Schnobrich & Kaufman	E.P.S.	$0.62
DUNS No.	04-952-1511	Shareholders	NA

Business: The group's principal activities are to design, market, manufacture, install and service complete integrated systems that display real- time data, graphics, animation and video. The products of the group are classified under the following product groups: sport products, video products, business products and transportation products. The sport products include both indoor and outdoor scoreboards, controllers and timing systems. The video products consist of displays with various levels of graphic and animation. The business products are of text-based message displays with limited graphic capability. The transportation products consist of electronic displays installed over roadside to direct traffic. The group also provides related services such as on-site installation support, on-site event support, display content creation, product maintenance, marketing assistance and large screen video display rentals.

Primary SIC and add'l.: 3993

CIK No: 0000915779

Subsidiaries: Daktronics Canada, Inc., Daktronics France SARL, Daktronics Hong Kong Ltd., Daktronics Media Holdings, Inc., Daktronics Shanghai Ltd, Daktronics UK, Ltd, Daktronics, GmbH, MSC Technologies, Inc., Star Circuits, Inc.

Officers: James B. Morgan/Dir., CEO/$488,631.00, Frank J. Kurtenbach/Dir., VP - Sales, William R. Retterath/CFO, Treasurer/$298,326.00

Directors: James B. Morgan/Dir., CEO, Aelred J. Kurtenbach/Chmn., Frank J. Kurtenbach/Dir., VP - Sales, Byron J. Anderson/Dir., Robert G. Dutcher/Dir., Nancy D. Frame/Dir., John L. Mulligan/Dir., Duane E. Sander/Dir., James A. Vellenga/Dir.

Owners: Byron J. Anderson, James A. Vellenga, Bradley T. Wiemann, Aelred J. Kurtenbach/7.00%, Frank J. Kurtenbach/2.20%, John L. Mulligan, Robert G. Dutcher, William R. Retterath, Nancy D. Frame, Reece A. Kurtenbach, Insiders/18.00%, James B. Morgan/4.20%, Duane E. Sander/2.60%

Financial Data: *Fiscal Year End:*04/29 *Latest Annual Data:* 04/28/2007

Year	Sales	Net Income
2007	$433,201,000	$24,427,000
2006	$309,370,000	$20,961,000
2005	$230,346,000	$15,660,000

Curr. Assets:	$84,421,000	**Curr. Liab.:**	$35,297,000	**P/E Ratio:**	33.34
Plant, Equip.:	$27,802,000	**Total Liab.:**	$39,972,000	**Indic. Yr. Divd.:**	$0.070
Total Assets:	$126,236,000	**Net Worth:**	$86,264,000	**Debt/ Equity:**	0.0069

Dale Jarrett Racing Adventure Inc

120A N Main Ave., Newton, NC, 28658; *PH:* 1-828-466-8837; *Fax:* 1-828-465-5088; *http://* www.racingadventure.com

General - Incorporation	FL	Stock - Price on:12/24/2007	$0.2
Employees	7	Stock Exchange	OTC
Auditor	Stark Winter Schenkein & Co. LLP	Ticker Symbol	DJRT
Stk Agt.	Florida Atlantic Stock Transfer, Inc.	Outstanding Shares	19,990,000
Counsel	NA	E.P.S.	$0.01
DUNS No.	NA	Shareholders	NA

Business: The group's principle activity is to offer entertainment based oval driving schools and events. The classes are conducted at various racetracks throughout the country. The company currently owns thirteen race cars, these race cars are classified as stock cars and are equipped for oval or round tracks only. The company offers five types of drive programs namely qualifier, season opener, twin ten, happy hour and advanced stock car adventure. The group operates from United States.

Primary SIC and add'l.: 3949 5092 3944 7389

CIK No: 0001094032

Officers: Timothy B. Shannon/45/Dir., CEO, CFO, Pres., Glenn Jarrett/56/Dir., VP

Directors: Timothy B. Shannon/45/Dir., CEO, CFO, Pres., Glenn Jarrett/56/Dir., VP, Kenneth J. Scott/Dir.

Owners: Glenn Jarrett/5.13%, Insiders/14.75%, Dale Jarrett/7.70%, Brett Favre/7.70%, Ned Jarrett/9.78%, Timothy Shannon/9.62%, Brian Rosenbloom/11.31%

Financial Data: *Fiscal Year End:*12/31 *Latest Annual Data:* 12/31/2006

Year	Sales	Net Income
2006	$2,144,000	$88,000
2005	$1,785,000	-$323,000
2004	$1,201,000	-$354,000

Curr. Assets:	$576,000	**Curr. Liab.:**	$1,443,000	**P/E Ratio:**	20.00
Plant, Equip.:	$229,000	**Total Liab.:**	$1,458,000	**Indic. Yr. Divd.:**	NA
Total Assets:	$804,000	**Net Worth:**	-$654,000	**Debt/ Equity:**	NA

Daleco Resources Corp

120 N Church St., West Chester, PA, 19380; *PH:* 1-610-429-0181; *http://* www.dalecoresources.com

General - Incorporation	NV	Stock - Price on:12/24/2007	$0.35
Employees	7	Stock Exchange	OTC
Auditor	Vasquez & Co. LLP	Ticker Symbol	DLOV
Stk Agt.	StockTrans, Inc.	Outstanding Shares	42,350,000
Counsel	Ehmann, Van Denbergh & Trainer	E.P.S.	-$0.16
DUNS No.	07-227-6710	Shareholders	NA

Business: The group's principal activities are to explore, develop and produce oil and gas properties. It sells forest products and develops and sells naturally occurring minerals and patented products. As of 30-Sept-2003, the group had interests in 112 wells in the states of Texas, west Virginia, Oklahoma, Kansas and the commonwealth of Pennsylvania. The group owns titles and claims to proven non-metallic minerals, which are located in the states of Texas, New Mexico and Utah. The group mines its calcium carbonate, kaolin and zeolite deposits through the use of contract miners. The group owns two timber rights in guyana covering approximately 6,000 acres. All of its production is sold to a variety of customers, which include pipelines, oil and gas gathering firms and other purchasers, pursuant to written agreements.

Primary SIC and add'l.: 6719 0811 6792 1311

CIK No: 0000746967

Subsidiaries: CA Properties, Inc., Clean Age Minerals, Inc., Deerlick Royalty Partners, L.P., Deven Resources, Inc., DRI Operating Company, Sustainable Forest Industries, Inc., The Natural Resources Exchange, Inc., Tri-Coastal Energy, Inc., Tri-Coastal Energy, L.P., Westlands Resources Corporation

Officers: Stephan V. Benediktson/73/Chmn., CEO, Gary J. Novinskie/57/CFO, Pres., Nathan K. Trynin/76/Dir., Exec. VP, R. A. Thibault/VP - Minerals, Pres. - Clean Age Minerals, CA Properties, David Matz/VP - Operations, Mgr. O - G, Richard Blackstone/Controller, Sec.

Directors: Stephan V. Benediktson/73/Chmn., CEO, Dov Amir/82/Dir., Nathan K. Trynin/76/Dir., Exec. VP, Lord Gilbert/80/Dir., William Pipkin/53/Dir., Charles T. Maxwell/76/Dir.

Owners: Charles T. Maxwell/0.35%, Nathan K. Trynin/2.42%, Stephan V. Benediktson/2.76%, Richard A. Thibault/0.95%, Insiders/15.73%, David L. Matz/0.52%, William Pipkin/0.35%, Richard W. Blackstone/0.35%, Lord Gilbert/0.95%, Dov Amir/3.96%, Terra Silex Holdings, LLC/7.01%, Gary J. Novinskie/3.15%

Financial Data: *Fiscal Year End:*09/30 *Latest Annual Data:* 9/30/2006

Year	Sales	Net Income
2006	$2,018,000	-$6,169,000
2005	$1,572,000	-$2,341,000
2004	$7,292,000	$3,556,000

Curr. Assets:	$867,000	**Curr. Liab.:**	$5,308,000		
Plant, Equip.:	$16,328,000	**Total Liab.:**	$5,805,000	**Indic. Yr. Divd.:**	NA
Total Assets:	$18,601,000	**Net Worth:**	$12,797,000	**Debt/ Equity:**	0.0346

Dalrada Financial Corp

9449 Balboa Ave., Ste 210, San Diego, CA, 92123; *PH:* 1-858-427-8700; *Fax:* 1-858-277-3448; *http://* www.dalrada.com; *Email:* inquiries@dalrada.com

General - Incorporation	DE	Stock - Price on:12/24/2007	$0.4
Employees	75	Stock Exchange	OTC
Auditor	Pohl, McNabola, Berg & Co LLP	Ticker Symbol	DFCO
Stk Agt.	Atlas Stock Transfer Corp	Outstanding Shares	5,140,000
Counsel	NA	E.P.S.	NA
DUNS No.	03-228-2550	Shareholders	NA

Business: The group's principal activities are to design, develop and sell digital imaging solutions and color management software products the group sells a range of imaging products for use in graphics and publishing, digital photography, and other business and technical markets. The group's core technologies are related to the design and development of software products that improve the accuracy of color reproduction. The group provides personnel management services including benefits and payroll administration, health and workers' compensation insurance programs, personnel records management, and employer liability management to small and medium sized businesses. The group acquired sourceone group inc on 12-Nov-2001, enstructure inc on 08-Mar-2002, prosportshr on 14-Jul-2003 and m&m nursing services on 20-Jul-2004.

Primary SIC and add'l.: 3572 8741 7372 3577 3571

CIK No: 0000725394
Subsidiaries: DFCO and Employment Systems, Inc, SourceOne Group
Officers: Brian Bonar/Chmn., CEO, Jay Partin/Exec. VP, Chief Administrative Officer
Directors: Brian Bonar/Chmn., CEO
Owners: Brian Bonar, Richard Green, LONGVIEW INT'L EQUITY FUND, L.P., BALMORE S.A., ALPHA Capital AG, LONGVIEW FUND, L.P., David Lieberman, Eric Gaer, LONGVIEW EQUITY FUND, L.P., Stanley Hirschman
Financial Data: *Fiscal Year End:*06/30 *Latest Annual Data:* 6/30/2006

Year	Sales	Net Income
2006	$70,380,000	$2,624,000
2005	$19,476,000	-$4,218,000
2004	$13,526,000	$102,000

Curr. Assets:	$7,871,000	Curr. Liab.:	$32,787,000		
Plant, Equip.:	$355,000	Total Liab.:	$36,318,000	Indic. Yr. Divd.:	NA
Total Assets:	$14,698,000	Net Worth:	-$21,620,000	Debt/ Equity:	NA

Dana Corp

PO Box 1000, Toledo, OH, 43697; *PH:* 1-419-535-4500; *http://* www.dana.com

General - Incorporation .... VA
Employees 45,000
Auditor .... PricewaterhouseCoopers LLP
Stk Agt .... Bank of New York
Counsel .... NA
DUNS No. 00-504-0555

Stock- Price on:12/24/2007 .... $1.95
Stock Exchange .... OTC
Ticker Symbol .... DCNAQ
Outstanding Shares 150,200,000
E.P.S. .... -$3.487
Shareholders .... NA

Business: The groups principle activity is to provide modules, systems and components for light, commercial and off-highway vehicle original equipment manufacturers and service customers. The group operates through three segments namely automotive systems group, engine and fluid management group and heavy vehicle technologies and systems group. The group operates from United States.
Primary SIC and add'l.: 3594 3714 3592 3593 3053 6141 7515
CIK No: 0000026780
Subsidiaries: Access Investments I, LLC, Access Investments II, LLC, AMP Industrial e Comercio de Pecas Automotivas Ltda., Automotive Motion Technology Limited, Britannia Properties, BWDAC, Inc., C.A. Danaven, CCD Air Eleven, Inc., CCD Air Twelve, Inc., CCD Water Three, Inc., Cerro de los Medanos S.A., Coupled Products, Inc., D.E.H. Holdings SARL, Dana (Deutschland) Grundstucksverwaltung GmbH, Dana (Wuxi) Technology Co. Ltd. 227 Subsidiaries included in the Index
Officers: Michael J. Burns/Chmn., CEO, Pres., Gilberto Ceratti/Pres. - Structural Solutions Group, Automotive Systems Group, Heinz-Ubbo Eilks/Pres. - Thermal Products Group, Automotive Systems Group, Ralf Goettel/Pres. - Engine Products Group, Dana Europe, Kenneth A. Hiltz/CFO, Kevin P. Moyer/Pres. - Fluid Products Group, Automotive Systems Group, Nick L. Stanage/Pres. - Heavy Vehicle Products, Heavy Vehicle Technologies, Systems Group, Richard W. Spriggle/VP - Human Resources, Michael L. Debacker/61/VP, General Counsel, Sec., Bruce C. Carver/CIO, VP, Paul E. Miller/VP - Purchasing, Chuck Hartlage/Contact - Corporate Media Relations, Ted Stenger/Chief Restructuring Officer, Thomas R. Stone/Pres. - Traction Products Group, Automotive Systems Group, Margot Hoffman/Pres. - Torque Products Group, Automotive Systems Group *(21 Officers included in Index)*
Directors: Michael J. Burns/Chmn., CEO, Pres., Charles A. Baillie/66/Dir., Edmund M. Carpenter/64/Dir., Marilyn R. Marks/53/Dir., Richard B. Priory/59/Dir., Samir G. Gibara/66/Dir., David E. Berges/56/Dir., Cheryl W. Grise/53/Dir., Richard M. Gabrys/64/Dir., James P. Kelly/62/Dir.
Owners: James P. Kelly, Insiders, Richard B. Priory, David E. Berges, Edmund M. Carpenter, Richard M. Gabrys, Marilyn R. Marks, Paul E. Miller, Michael J. Burns, Appaloosa Investment Limited Partnership/14.80%, Cheryl W. Grise, Harbinger Capital Partners Master FundI, Ltd./5.80%, Charles A. Baillie, Brandes Investment Partners, L.P./7.35%, Nick L. Stanage *(16 Owners included in Index)*
Financial Data: *Fiscal Year End:*12/31 *Latest Annual Data:* 12/31/2006

Year	Sales	Net Income
2006	$8,504,000,000	-$739,000,000
2005	$8,699,000,000	-$1,605,000,000
2004	$8,972,000,000	$62,000,000

Curr. Assets:	$3,324,000,000	Curr. Liab.:	$2,086,000,000		
Plant, Equip.:	$1,776,000,000	Total Liab.:	$7,487,000,000	Indic. Yr. Divd.:	NA
Total Assets:	$6,734,000,000	Net Worth:	-$834,000,000	Debt/ Equity:	NA

Danaher Corp

2099 Pennsylvania Ave. NW, 12th Fl., Washington, DC, 20006; *PH:* 1-202-828-0850; *Fax:* 1-202-828-0860; *http://* www.danaher.com

General - Incorporation .... DE
Employees 45,000
Auditor .... Ernst & Young LLP
Stk Agt .... Sun Trust Stock Transfer Department
Counsel .... NA
DUNS No. 02-474-4476

Stock- Price on:12/24/2007 .... $74.64
Stock Exchange .... NYSE
Ticker Symbol .... DHR
Outstanding Shares 309,200,000
E.P.S. $3.57
Shareholders .... NA

Business: The groups principle activities include designing, manufacturing and marketing industrial and consumer products. The groups operates through wo segments process and environmental control, and tools and components. The group operates from United States.
Primary SIC and add'l.: 3545 3714 3559 3469 3625 3825 3423
CIK No: 0000313616
Subsidiaries: AB Qualitrol AKM, ABEK LLC, AC Intermediate Co., ACC Motion GmbH, ACCU-Sort Asia Pacific PTE.LTD, Accu-sort Europe Gmbh, Accu-sort Systems Australia Pty.ltd, Accu-sort Systems, Inc., ACME-Cleveland Corporation, Advanced Motion Controls AB, Aeronautique Systems BIP SAS, Alltec Angewandte Laserlicht Technologie GmbH, Alltec Italia S.r.l., Alltec UK Ltd., American Precision Industries, Inc. 572 Subsidiaries included in the Index
Officers: Lawrence H. Culp/Dir., CEO, Pres./$19,608,130.00, James A. Lico/Exec. VP/$2,702,412.00, Philip W. Knisely/Exec. VP/$3,779,259.00, Daniel A. Raskas/VP - Corporate Development, Steven E. Simms/Exec. VP/$3,711,525.00, Daniel L. Comas/CFO, Exec. VP/$2,958,089.00, Robert S. Lutz/VP, Chief Accounting Officer, James H. Ditkoff/VP - Finance, Tax, Thomas P. Joyce/Exec. VP, Jonathan P. Graham/Sr. VP, General Counsel, James F. OReilly/Sec.
Directors: Lawrence H. Culp/Dir., CEO, Pres., Steven M. Rales/Chmn., John T. Schwieters/Dir., Mitchell P. Rales/Dir., Mortimer M. Caplin/Dir., Donald J. Ehrlich/Dir., Alan G. Spoon/Dir., Walter G. Lohr/Dir., Emmet A. Stephenson/Dir., Linda P. Hefner/Dir.
Owners: Lawrence H. Culp, Walter G. Lohr, Emmet A. Stephenson, Daniel L. Comas, Linda P. Hefner, Alan G. Spoon, T. Rowe Price Associates, Inc./5.70%, Mortimer M. Caplin, James A. Lico, Steven E. Simms, Steven M. Rales/13.90%, John T. Schwieters, Donald J. Ehrlich, Mitchell P. Rales/13.70%, FMR Corp./5.90% *(17 Owners included in Index)*
Financial Data: *Fiscal Year End:*12/31 *Latest Annual Data:* 12/31/2006

Year	Sales	Net Income
2006	$9,596,404,000	$1,122,029,000
2005	$7,984,704,000	$897,800,000
2004	$6,889,301,000	$746,000,000

Curr. Assets:	$3,394,902,000	Curr. Liab.:	$2,459,556,000	P/E Ratio:	20.91
Plant, Equip.:	$874,368,000	Total Liab.:	$6,219,491,000	Indic. Yr. Divd.:	$0.120
Total Assets:	$12,864,151,000	Net Worth:	$6,644,660,000	Debt/ Equity:	0.3256

Danaos Corp

5201 Blue Lagoon Dr., Penthouse, Miami, FL, 33126; *PH:* 1-305-716-4170; *Fax:* 1-305-716-4100; *http://* www.danaos.com; *Email:* cfo@danaos.com

General - Incorporation .... Marshall Islands
Employees .... NA
Auditor .... NA
Stk Agt ..... American Stock Transfer & Trust Co.
Counsel .... NA
DUNS No. .... NA

Stock- Price on:12/24/2007 .... $31.31
Stock Exchange .... NYSE
Ticker Symbol .... DAC
Outstanding Shares 54,560,000
E.P.S. $3.70
Shareholders .... NA

Business: The groups principle activity is to provide vessels. The groups specific customers are Maersk, COSCO, Hyundai and China Shipping. The group operates from the United States and China. The groups quarterly revenue for September 2007 was 62.64 millions of USD.
Primary SIC and add'l.: 4412
CIK No: 0001369241
Subsidiaries: Alexandra Navigation Inc., Appleton Navigation S.A., Auckland Marine Inc., Baker International S.A., Balticsea Marine Inc., Bayard Maritime Ltd., Bayview Shipping Inc., Blacksea Marine Inc., Bounty Investment Inc., Boxcarrier (No.1) Corp., Boxcarrier (No.2) Corp., Boxcarrier (No.3) Corp., Boxcarrier (No.4) Corp., Boxcarrier (No.5) Corp., Channelview Marine Inc. 62 Subsidiaries included in the Index
Officers: John Coustas/Dir., CEO, Pres., Iraklis Prokopakis/Dir., COO, VP, Dimitri J. Andritsoyiannis/Dir., CFO, VP
Directors: John Coustas/Dir., CEO, Pres., Iraklis Prokopakis/Dir., COO, VP, Dimitri J. Andritsoyiannis/Dir., CFO, VP, Andrew B. Fogarty/Dir., Myles R. Itkin/Dir., Miklos Konkoly-Thege/Dir., Robert A. Mundell/Dir.
Owners: Dimitri J. Andritsoyiannis, Iraklis Prokopakis, Mikls Konkoly-Thege, Insiders, John Coustas, Danaos Investments Limited as Trustee of the 883 Trust
Financial Data: *Fiscal Year End:*12/31 *Latest Annual Data:* 12/31/2006

Year	Sales	Net Income
2006	$245,588,000	$101,082,000
2005	$241,381,000	$122,850,000
2004	$208,268,000	$116,459,000

Curr. Assets:	$59,700,000	Curr. Liab.:	$45,714,000	P/E Ratio:	9.09
Plant, Equip.:	$1,221,974,000	Total Liab.:	$731,338,000	Indic. Yr. Divd.:	$1.860
Total Assets:	$1,297,190,000	Net Worth:	$565,852,000	Debt/ Equity:	NA

Danka Business Systems Plc

11101 Roosevelt Blvd. N., St. Petersburg, FL, 33716; *PH:* 1-727-622-2100; *http://* www.danka.com

General - Incorporation .... UK
Employees .... NA
Auditor .... Ernst & Young LLP
Stk Agt .... Computershare Investor Services LLC
Counsel .... NA
DUNS No. 86-765-7611

Stock- Price on:12/24/2007 .... $0.27
Stock Exchange .... OTC
Ticker Symbol .... DANKF
Outstanding Shares .... NA
E.P.S. .... NA
Shareholders .... NA

Business: The group's principle activities are the provision of office imaging equipment, document solutions and related services in the United States and in Europe. The group's office imaging products, services, supplies and solutions include digital and colour copiers, digital and colour multifunction peripherals, facsimile machines and software. It also provides contract services, including professional and consulting services, maintenance, supplies, leasing arrangements, technical support and training, on the installed base of equipment created primarily by retail equipment and related sales.
Primary SIC and add'l.: 7629 5045 7359 5044
CIK No: 0000894010
Subsidiaries: American Business Credit Corporation, Christine Ventures Ltd. (UK), Corporate Consulting Group, Inc., D.A. Co. SrL, D.I. Investment Management, Inc., Danka Australasia Pty Ltd., Danka Australia Pty Ltd., Danka Austria GmbH, Danka Belgium NV/SA, Danka Business Finance Ltd., Danka Danmark A/S, Danka Danmark Holding A/S, Danka Datakey Pty Ltd., Danka Deutschland Holding GmbH, Danka Deutschland Leasing GmbH 79 Subsidiaries included in the Index
Officers: A. D. Frazier/Chmn., CEO/$989,895.00, Edward K. Quibell/CFO/$790,325.00, Jacqueline Gayle-Kelly/Corporate Counsel - EEO, Diversity Compliance, Training, Rod Denzer/Pres. - West Regional Business Unit/$291,685.00
Directors: A. D. Frazier/Chmn., CEO, Andrew W. McKenna/Dir., Jaime W. Ellertson/Dir., Erik Vonk/Dir., Kevin C. Daly/Non Exec. Dir., David Downes/Dir., Ernest J. Riddle/Dir., Christopher B. Harned/Dir., Joseph E. Parzick/Dir.
Owners: Cypress Associates II LLC/28.10%, Donald Thurman, Jaime W. Ellertson, A.D. Frazier, Andrew W. McKenna, William Troxil, Edward K. Quibell, Erik Vonk, David J. Downes, Rod Denzer, Ernest J. Riddle, Kevin C. Daly, Christopher B. Harned/28.10%, James Hawkins, Jean Dinovo-Johnson *(17 Owners included in Index)*

Darden Restaurants Inc

5900 Lake Ellenor Dr., Orlando, FL, 32809; *PH:* 1-407-245-4000; *Fax:* 1-407-245-5389; *http://* www.dardenrestaurants.com

General - Incorporation	FL	Stock- Price on:12/24/2007	$43.4
Employees	157,300	Stock Exchange	NYSE
Auditor	KPMG LLP	Ticker Symbol	DRI
Stk Agt	Wells Fargo Shareowner Services	Outstanding Shares	141,380,000
Counsel	Dorsey & Whitney LLP	E.P.S	$1.37
DUNS No.	88-370-4959	Shareholders	NA

Business: The group's principle activity is to operate casual dining restaurants. The groups operating restaurants include Red Lobster, Olive Garden, LongHorn Steakhouse, The Capital Grille, Bahama Breeze and Seasons 52. The group operates from United States and Canada. In the year 2007, the group acquired Rare Hospitality International, Inc.

Primary SIC and add'l.: 5812

CIK No: 0000940944

Subsidiaries: GMRI Florida, Inc., GMRI Texas, L.P., GMRI, Inc.

Officers: Clarence Otis/Chmn., CEO/$3,855,766.00, Suk Singh/Sr. VP - Development, David T. Pickens/Sr. VP, Pres. - Olive Garden/$1,756,082.00, Patty Deyoung/Exec. Administrator, Ron Bojalad/Sr. VP - Group Human Resources, Stephen Judge/Sr. VP, Pres. - Seasons 52, Ian Baines/Sr. VP, Pres. - Smokey Bones, Bob McAdam/Sr. VP - Government, Community Affairs, Barry B. Moullet/Sr. VP - Supply Chain, Development, Laurie B. Burns/Sr. VP, Pres. - Bahama Breeze, Valerie K. Collins/Sr. VP, Corporate Controller, CIO, Paula J. Shives/Sr. VP, General Counsel, Sec., Kim A. Lopdrup/Sr. VP, Pres. - Red Lobster, J. J. Buettgen/Sr. VP - Business Development, Brad Richmond/CFO, Sr. VP/$1,039,722.00 *(18 Officers included in Index)*

Directors: Clarence Otis/Chmn., CEO, David H. Hughes/Dir., Leonard L. Berry/Dir., Rita P. Wilson/Dir., Andrew H. Madsen/Dir., COO, Pres., William M. Lewis/Dir., Odie C. Donald/Dir., Jack A. Smith/Dir., Connie Mack/Dir., Maria A. Sastre/Dir., Charles A. Ledsinger/Dir., Michael D. Rose/Dir., Cornelius McGillicuddy/Dir.

Owners: Insiders/3.99%, Jack A. Smith, William M. Lewis, Odie C. Donald, Senator Connie Mack, Rita P. Wilson, Michael D. Rose, Blaine Sweatt, David H. Hughes, Leonard L. Berry, Charles A. Ledsinger, Clarence Otis, Maria A. Sastre, David T. Pickens, Bradford C. Richmond *(17 Owners included in Index)*

Financial Data: Fiscal Year End:05/28 Latest Annual Data: 05/27/2007

Year	Sales	Net Income
2007	$5,567,100,000	$201,400,000
2006	$5,720,640,000	$338,194,000
2005	$5,278,110,000	$290,606,000

Curr. Assets:	$346,307,000	Curr. Liab.:	$683,481,000		
Plant, Equip.:	$2,250,616,000	Total Liab.:	$1,605,060,000	Indic. Yr. Divd.:	$0.720
Total Assets:	$2,780,348,000	Net Worth:	$1,175,288,000	Debt/ Equity:	0.3991

Dark Dynamite Inc

Pang Gong Site, 44 Hong Guang Rd., Xi An, 710068; *PH:* 80746-3435;
http:// www.darkdynamite.com

General - Incorporation	NV	Stock- Price on:12/24/2007	$0.07
Employees	NA	Stock Exchange	NA
Auditor	Lake & Assoc. CPA's LLC	Ticker Symbol	NA
Stk Agt	Florida Atlantic Stock Transfer, Inc.	Outstanding Shares	NA
Counsel	NA	E.P.S	NA
DUNS No.	05-888-8694	Shareholders	NA

Business: The group's principal activity is the wholesale distribution of food products through its subsidiary, bestfoodonline.com, inc in the United States and the Caribbean. The products include caviar, foie gras, exotic meats, wild mushrooms, truffle products, imported spices, pastas, cheeses, chocolates, olives, olive oils and other specialty food products including Asian, Indian and jamaican ethnic specialties. The group also sells and distributes food products over the Internet. The products of the group are provided to hospitality industries including airlines, hotels, restaurants and resorts. On 19-Apr-2004, the group acquired black chandelier inc.

Primary SIC and add'l.: 5143 5141 5147

CIK No: 0000830664

Subsidiaries: Black Chandelier Inc., Shanxi Kai Da Tourism Company, Ltd.

Officers: Lei Ming/42/Dir., CEO, Pres., Xiao Jun Wang/42/Dir., CFO

Directors: Lei Ming/42/Dir., CEO, Pres., Xiao Jun Wang/42/Dir., CFO

Owners: Insiders/0.00%, Diversified Holdings X, Inc./0.01%, Hudson Consulting Group, Inc./0.01%, Diversified Holdings X, Inc./25.20%, Diversified Holdings I, Inc./12.40%, Richard Surber/74.90%, Jared Gold/0.00%

Financial Data: Fiscal Year End:12/31 Latest Annual Data: 12/31/2006

Year	Sales	Net Income
2006	$835,000	-$329,000
2005	$426,000	-$2,929,000
2004	$20,000	-$1,006,000

Curr. Assets:	$124,000	Curr. Liab.:	$226,000		
Plant, Equip.:	$503,000	Total Liab.:	$226,000	Indic. Yr. Divd.:	NA
Total Assets:	$627,000	Net Worth:	$368,000	Debt/ Equity:	NA

Darling International Inc

251 O'Connor Ridge Blvd., Ste. 300, Irving, TX, 75038; *PH:* 1-972-717-0300; *Fax:* 1-972-717-1588;
http:// www.darlingii.com

General - Incorporation	DE	Stock- Price on:12/24/2007	$8.91
Employees	1,830	Stock Exchange	NYSE
Auditor	KPMG LLP	Ticker Symbol	DAR
Stk Agt	EquiServe Trust Co N.A	Outstanding Shares	80,860,000
Counsel	Dechert, Price & Rhoads	E.P.S	$0.45
DUNS No.	00-509-2358	Shareholders	NA

Business: The group's principal activity is to collect and recycle animal processing by-products and used cooking oil from food service establishments. The group operates through two segments: rendering and restaurant services. Rendering consists of the collection and processing of animal by-products from butcher shops, grocery stores and independent meat and poultry processors, converting these wastes into useable oils and proteins utilized by the agricultural and oleochemical industries. Restaurant services consists of the collection of used cooking oils from food service establishments and recycling them into high-energy animal feed ingredients and industrial oils. Restaurant services also provides grease trap servicing. The products of the group are sold in the United States, Korea, Spain, Mexico, Japan, northern Europe, Pacific Rim, Taiwan, Canada and South America.

Primary SIC and add'l.: 2048 2899 2015

CIK No: 0000916540

Subsidiaries: National By-Products, LLC

Officers: John Bohannon/VP - Grease Trap Business, Ruth Jondle/Contact - National Service Center Mgr., Mitch Kilanowski/Contact - Exec. VP - Commodities, Ernie Diliberto/VP - International Commodities, Nick Borrelli/Contact - Chain Accounting Mgr.

Directors: Dean C. Carlson/70/Dir., Marlyn Jorgensen/68/Dir.

Owners: Charles Macaluso, Michael Urbut, SouthernSun Asset Management, Inc./8.90%, Neil Katchen, Thomas O. Albrecht, Jeffrey L. Gendell/9.70%, Marlyn Jorgensen, Insiders/4.01%, Robert H. Seemann, Nader Tavakoli/8.60%, Gates Capital Management, Inc./5.20%, Dean C. Carlson/1.90%, Fredric J. Klink, EagleRock Capital Management, LLC/8.00%, Randall C. Stuewe/1.20% *(17 Owners included in Index)*

Financial Data: Fiscal Year End:12/31 Latest Annual Data: 12/30/2006

Year	Sales	Net Income
2006	$406,990,000	$5,107,000
2005	$308,867,000	$7,741,000

Curr. Assets:	$83,075,000	Curr. Liab.:	$42,668,000	P/E Ratio:	27.00
Plant, Equip.:	$85,178,000	Total Liab.:	$117,092,000	Indic. Yr. Divd.:	NA
Total Assets:	$190,772,000	Net Worth:	$73,680,000	Debt/ Equity:	0.4102

Dassault Systemes

9, Quai Marcel Dassault, B.P. 310, Suresnes Cedex, 92156; *PH:* 33-140994099;
http:// www.3ds.com; *Email:* 3ds@ds-fr.com

General - Incorporation	France	Stock- Price on:12/24/2007	$62.06
Employees	6,840	Stock Exchange	NDQ
Auditor	PricewaterhouseCoopers LLP	Ticker Symbol	DASTY
Stk Agt	NA	Outstanding Shares	115,600,000
Counsel	NA	E.P.S	$2.22
DUNS No.	26-991-3802	Shareholders	NA

Business: The group's principle activities are the development, sale and services of software products for computer-aided design, computer-aided manufacturing and computer-aided engineering. The group also obtains revenues from its support of IBM marketing and distribution efforts, direct support to customers, technological consulting services and hardware resale activities. The group has operations in 21 countries.

Primary SIC and add'l.: 7372 7379 5045 7371

CIK No: 0001016118

Subsidiaries: ABAQUS Inc, Dassault Data Services, Dassault Systmes KK, Dassault Systmes Services LLC, Delmia Corp, Enovia Corp., SmarTeam Corporation Ltd., SolidWorks Corporation, Spatial Corp.

Officers: Joel Lemke/CEO - Enovia, John McEleney/CEO - Solidworks, Bernard Charles/CEO, Pres., Philippe Forestier/Exec. VP - Network Selling, Pres. Americas, Bruno Latchague/51/Exec. VP - PLM Business Transformation, Etienne Droit/Exec. VP - PLM Value Channel, Thibault De Tersant/Sr. Exec. VP, CFO, Muriel Penicaud/Exec. VP, Chief People Officer, Dominique Florack/Sr. Exec. VP - Research, Development, Nathalie Irvine/CIO, Pascal Daloz/Exec. VP - Strategy, Marketing

Directors: Charles Edelstenne/70/Chmn., Bernard Dufau/65/Dir., Andre Kudelski/46/Dir., Arnoud De Meyer/53/Dir., Jean-Pierre Chahid-Nourai/68/Dir., Paul R. Brown/57/Dir., Laurent Dassault/54/Dir.

Owners: Insiders/0.01%, Charles Edelstenne/6.60%, Groupe Industriel Marcel Dassault/44.44%, SW Securities L.L.C./0.23%, Public/48.72%

Financial Data: Fiscal Year End:12/31 Latest Annual Data: 12/31/2006

Year	Sales	Net Income
2006	$1,528,641,000	$237,393,000
2005	$1,106,837,000	$207,817,000
2004	$1,086,816,000	$196,988,000

Curr. Assets:	$1,158,606,000	Curr. Liab.:	$542,903,000	P/E Ratio:	14.48
Plant, Equip.:	$84,330,000	Total Liab.:	$983,642,000	Indic. Yr. Divd.:	NA
Total Assets:	$2,450,528,000	Net Worth:	$1,465,592,000	Debt/ Equity:	NA

Data I/O Corp

6464 185th Ave. NE, Redmond, WA, 98052; *PH:* 1-425-881-6444; *Fax:* 1-425-869-7423;
http:// www.dataio.com

General - Incorporation	WA	Stock- Price on:12/24/2007	$3.35
Employees	129	Stock Exchange	NDQ
Auditor	Grant Thornton LLP	Ticker Symbol	DAIO
Stk Agt	Mellon Investor Services LLC	Outstanding Shares	8,520,000
Counsel	Dorsey & Whitney LLP	E.P.S	-$0.11
DUNS No.	06-715-6240	Shareholders	NA

Business: The group's principal activities are to design, manufacture and sell programming systems, which are used by designers and manufacturers of electronic products. The group's products are used to program integrated circuits (ics), which is used by electronics industry. The group's line of programming systems includes a broad range of products, systems, modules, and accessories, which the group divides into two general categories: automated programming systems and non-automated programming systems. The major trademarks include tasklink(R), infinity(tm), flashcore(tm), proline-roadrunner and flashpak. The customers of the group are companies which design and/or manufacture electronic products that incorporate programmable devices or provide device programming services. The group operates in the United States, Germany, China and Canada.

Primary SIC and add'l.: 7373

CIK No: 0000351998

Subsidiaries: Data I/O Canada Corporation, Data I/O China, Ltd, Data I/O Electronics (Shanghai) Co. Ltd, Data I/O FSC International, Inc., Data I/O GmbH, Data I/O Programacao de Sistemas Ltda, International, Inc., RTD, Inc. (formerly Reel-Tech, Inc.)

Officers: Frederick R. Hume/Dir., CEO, Pres./$298,106.00, Joel S. Hatlen/VP, CFO, Sec., Treasurer/$168,437.00, Harald A. Weigelt/VP - Worldwide Sales, Service/$204,408.00

Directors: Frederick R. Hume/Dir., CEO, Pres., Steven M. Quist/Dir., Edward D. Lazowska/Dir., Paul A. Gary/Dir., Daniel A. Dileo/Dir., William R. Walker/Dir.

Owners: William R. Walker, Daniel A. DiLeo, John W. Stanton/6.43%, Harald A. Weigelt, Joel S. Hatlen/2.15%, Edward D. Lazowska, Royce & Associates LLC/5.79%, Steven M. Quist, Paul A. Gary/1.63%, Insiders/9.38%, Frederick R. Hume/3.01%, Leviticus Partners, L.P./9.28%

Financial Data: Fiscal Year End:12/31 Latest Annual Data: 12/31/2006

Year	Sales	Net Income
2006	$28,793,000	$46,000
2005	$28,321,000	$582,000
2004	$27,310,000	-$92,000

Curr. Assets:	$16,517,000	Curr. Liab.:	$5,762,000	
Plant, Equip.:	$2,852,000	Total Liab.:	$6,208,000	Indic. Yr. Divd.: NA
Total Assets:	$19,491,000	Net Worth:	$13,283,000	Debt/ Equity: NA

DataDirect Technologies

14100 Sw Fwy., Ste. 500, Sugarland, TX, 77478; *PH:* 1-800-505-6366; *http://* www.datadirect.com

General - Incorporation	DE	Stock - Price on:12/24/2007	NA
Employees	NA	Stock Exchange	NDQ
Auditor	KPMG LLP	Ticker Symbol	NEST
Stk Agt	Chase Mellon Shareholder Services LLC	Outstanding Shares	NA
Counsel	Locke Liddell & Sapp LLP	E.P.S	NA
DUNS No.	NA	Shareholders	NA

Business: The group's principal activity is to provide enterprise-class mainframe integration software. It develops, markets and supports a unified mainframe integration platform that supports a range of requirements for modern service-oriented architectures and emerging event-driven architectures. The group's primary product, shadow technology provides flexible, industry standard interfaces to enable highly secure and scalable mainframe integration allowing organizations to reduce total cost of ownership and risk associated with mainframe integration while streamlining the number of incumbent technologies needed for such integration. The group has international operations in the United Kingdom, Germany and Australia. On 15-Jul-2004, the group acquired inneraccess technologies inc.

Primary SIC and add'l.: 7372 7371

CIK No: 0001072978

Subsidiaries: NEON Beyond Acquisition Corp., NEON Systems Canada Inc., NEON Systems GmbH, NEON Systems Quebec Inc., NEON Systems UK Ltd

Officers: Richard D. Reidy/Pres., Robert Evelyn/VP - Strategy, GM - XML Products Group, John Goodson/VP - Product Operations, Marketing, Eric Egertson/VP - North American Sales, Terence Cooke/VP - International Sales, Carol Esau/VP - Datadirect Global Support, Custom Engineering, Sue Purkis/Sr. Mgr. - Major Accounting, Solution Engineering, Data Management, Ellen Batens/Sr. Mgr. - EMEA Supportlink, John Hight/Dir. - Global Technical Support, Greg Jesensky/Sr. Mgr - Shadow Supportlink

Datajungle Software Inc

1038 Redwood Hwy., Ste. 100a, Mill Valley, NV, 94941; *PH:* 1-415-389-1625; *http://* www.datajungle.com

General - Incorporation	NV	Stock - Price on:12/24/2007	$0.16
Employees	NA	Stock Exchange	NA
Auditor	KPMG LLP	Ticker Symbol	NA
Stk Agt	Computershare Trust Co	Outstanding Shares	NA
Counsel	Findlaw Corporate CounseL	E.P.S	NA
DUNS No.	NA	Shareholders	NA

Business: The groups principle activity is to develop enterprise business intelligence front-end applications. The group product includes Matrix(TM). The group operates from Canada and the United States.

Primary SIC and add'l.: 7372

CIK No: 0000081350

Subsidiaries: DataJungle Ltd.

Officers: Edward Munden/57/Chmn., CEO, Pres., David L. Morris/CEO, Pres., Larry Bruce/CFO, Craig Harper/CTO, Robert Lendvai/Chief Marketing Officer, Robert Poole/45/Sr. VP - Business Development, Sales, Denes Bartakovich/52/Dir., COO, Exec. VP, Don Carter/57/Dir., VP, Paul Gariboldi/Exec. VP - Global Field Operations, Mark Budgell/News Contact

Directors: Edward Munden/57/Chmn., CEO, Pres., Denes Bartakovich/52/Dir., COO, Exec. VP, Don Carter/57/Dir., VP

Owners: Pierce Diversified Strategy Master Fund LLC, ena/4.99%, Insiders/4.99%, Enable Opportunity Partners LP/4.99%, Enable Growth Partners LP/4.99%

Financial Data: *Fiscal Year End:*12/31 *Latest Annual Data:* 12/31/2006

Year	Sales	Net Income
2006	$501,000	-$3,144,000
2005	$588,000	-$1,106,000
2004	$601,000	-$881,000

Curr. Assets:	$493,000	Curr. Liab.:	$1,044,000	
Plant, Equip.:	$5,000	Total Liab.:	$1,044,000	Indic. Yr. Divd.: NA
Total Assets:	$498,000	Net Worth:	-$546,000	Debt/ Equity: NA

Datalink Corp

8170 Upland Cir., Chanhassen, MN, 55317; *PH:* 1-952-944-3462; *Fax:* 1-952-944-7869; *http://* www.datalink.com

General - Incorporation	MN	Stock - Price on:12/24/2007	$6.78
Employees	160	Stock Exchange	NDQ
Auditor	McGladrey & Pullen LLP	Ticker Symbol	DTLK
Stk Agt	Wells Fargo Shareowner Services	Outstanding Shares	12,410,000
Counsel	Messerli & Kramer P.A.	E.P.S	$0.61
DUNS No.	04-539-0531	Shareholders	NA

Business: The group's principle activities designing, integrating or assembles, installs and supports high-end open systems data storage solutions for end-users, value-added resellers and original equipment manufacturers. The group operates from United States.

Primary SIC and add'l.: 7373

CIK No: 0001056923

Officers: Charles Westling/Dir., CEO, Pres./$534,183.00, Greg Meland/Chmn., VP - Sales, Engineering/$263,490.00, Gregory T. Barnum/VP - Finance, CFO/$293,366.00, Mary West/VP - Human Resources, Administration/$242,300.00, Rob Beyer/VP - Field Operations, Denise M. Westenfield/Corporate Controller, Principal Accounting Officer

Directors: Charles Westling/Dir., CEO, Pres., Greg Meland/Chmn., VP - Sales, Engineering, Paul Lidsky/Dir., Brent G. Blackey/Dir., Patrick O'Halloran/Dir., Margaret Loftus/Dir., Robert Price/Dir., James Ousley/Dir.

Owners: Greg R. Meland/26.10%, Robert M. Price, Mary E. West, Insiders/30.10%, Bjurman, Barry& Associates/5.60%, Charles B. Westling/2.70%, James E. Ousley, Patrick J. OHalloran, Paul F. Lidsky, Brent G. Blackey, Margaret A. Loftus, Lodi Vercelli/5.80%, Gregory T. Barnum

Financial Data: *Fiscal Year End:*12/31 *Latest Annual Data:* 03/31/2007

Year	Sales	Net Income
2007	NA	NA
2006	NA	NA
2005	$117,113,000	-$2,915,000

Curr. Assets:	$77,733,000	Curr. Liab.:	$58,079,000	P/E Ratio: 11.11
Plant, Equip.:	$1,942,000	Total Liab.:	$59,527,000	Indic. Yr. Divd.: NA
Total Assets:	$86,849,000	Net Worth:	$27,322,000	Debt/ Equity: NA

Datalogic International Inc

18301 Von Karman Ave., Ste 250, Irvine, CA, 92612; *PH:* 1-949-260-0120; *Fax:* 1-949-260-0130; *http://* www.dlgi.com; *Email:* sales@dlgi.com

General - Incorporation	DE	Stock - Price on:12/24/2007	NA
Employees	150	Stock Exchange	OTC
Auditor	Corbin & Co LLP	Ticker Symbol	DLGI
Stk Agt	Signature Stock Transfer, Inc.	Outstanding Shares	NA
Counsel	NA	E.P.S	-$0.104
DUNS No.	NA	Shareholders	NA

Business: The group's principal activity is to provide information technology consulting services. The group provides information technology and healthcare related services. The group provides full life cycle it consulting services that include project management, system analysis, design, implementation, testing and maintenance. The services are provided at the clients' locations or off-site at the group's us or affiliated offshore facilities. The group also provides short and long term staff augmentation solutions to it clients, healthcare providers and to miscellaneous businesses. The group provides its services to industries of communications, energy, financial, government, healthcare, manufacturing, retail and transportation. The group's operations are primarily located in the United States.

Primary SIC and add'l.: 7379 7372 7375

CIK No: 0001083273

Subsidiaries: DataLogic Consulting International Inc., DataLogic Consulting, Inc, DataLogic New Mexico, Inc., IPN Communications, Inc.

Officers: Keith Moore/Chmn., CEO, CFO

Directors: Keith Moore/Chmn., CEO, CFO, Keith Nguyen/Dir., Alex Kreger/Dir.

Financial Data: *Fiscal Year End:*12/31 *Latest Annual Data:* 12/31/2005

Year	Sales	Net Income
2005	$17,523,000	-$420,000
2004	$14,255,000	-$1,404,000
2003	$10,703,000	-$912,000

Curr. Assets:	$3,530,000	Curr. Liab.:	$4,194,000	
Plant, Equip.:	$195,000	Total Liab.:	$4,864,000	Indic. Yr. Divd.: NA
Total Assets:	$5,591,000	Net Worth:	$727,000	Debt/ Equity: NA

DataMeg Corp

2150 S 1300 E Ste. 500, Salt Lake City, UT, 84106; *PH:* 1-866-739-3945; *Fax:* 1-941-575-4336; *http://* www.datameg.com

General - Incorporation	DE	Stock - Price on:12/24/2007	$0.032
Employees	4	Stock Exchange	OTC
Auditor Child, Van Wagoner & Bradshaw, PLLC		Ticker Symbol	DTMG
Stk Agt	Fidelity Transfer Co	Outstanding Shares	361,510,000
Counsel	NA	E.P.S	-$0.005
DUNS No.	NA	Shareholders	NA

Business: The groups principle activity is to provide service assurance systems products and services for the network operators in the telecommunications industry. The group products include Network Assurance System. In the year 2006, the group acquired D and O Insurance. The group operates from and the United States.

Primary SIC and add'l.: 7371

CIK No: 0000716749

Subsidiaries: CASCommunications, Inc, QoVox Corporation

Officers: Jim Murphy/Chmn., CEO, Pres.

Directors: Jim Murphy/Chmn., CEO, Pres.

Owners: Neil Gordon/0.20%, James Murphy/5.10%, Insiders/7.70%, Dan Ference/2.40%

Financial Data: *Fiscal Year End:*12/31 *Latest Annual Data:* 12/31/2006

Year	Sales	Net Income
2006	$43,000	-$1,508,000
2005	$46,000	-$6,540,000
2004	$46,000	-$9,303,000

Curr. Assets:	$235,000	Curr. Liab.:	$3,931,000	P/E Ratio: 0.00
Plant, Equip.:	NA	Total Liab.:	$3,963,000	Indic. Yr. Divd.: NA
Total Assets:	$458,000	Net Worth:	-$3,505,000	Debt/ Equity: NA

DataMetrics Corp

1717 Diplomacy Row, Orlando, FL, 32809; *PH:* 1-407-251-4577; *Fax:* 1-407-251-4588; *http://* www.datametricscorp.com; *Email:* info@datametrics.com

General - Incorporation	DE	Stock - Price on:12/24/2007	$0.21
Employees	28	Stock Exchange	OTC
Auditor	Davis, Monk & Company	Ticker Symbol	DMCP
Stk Agt	Continental Stock Transfer & Trust Co	Outstanding Shares	11,530,000
Counsel	NA	E.P.S	-$0.06
DUNS No.	NA	Shareholders	NA

Business: The groups principal activities include designing and manufacturing of application products for defense applications and programs. The group operates from the United States. The groups sale in the year 2006 was $3,204,000.

Primary SIC and add'l.: 3577 3679 3575 3571

CIK No: 0000027082

Subsidiaries: Peripheral Equipment Corporation

Officers: Daniel Bertram/47/Dir., CEO, Edward Kroning/Corp. Sec., Interim CFO, John Marceca/Pres., Rose Meyer/VP - Engineering

Directors: Daniel Bertram/47/Dir., CEO, Gary L. Herman/Chmn., Thomas F. Leonardis/Dir., Michael Rapisand/Dir., Seth Lukash/Dir.

Owners: Michael Rapisand/0.38%, Gary Herman/1.92%, Ed Kroning/0.71%, Thomas Leonardis/0.38%, Daniel Bertram/2.43%, Insiders/6.20%, Seth Lukash/0.38%

Financial Data: ***Fiscal Year End:***10/31 ***Latest Annual Data:*** 10/31/2006

Year	Sales	Net Income
2006	$3,204,000	-$2,900,000
2005	$3,029,000	-$583,000
2004	$4,443,000	-$623,000

Curr. Assets:	$1,147,000	***Curr. Liab.:***	$820,000		
Plant, Equip.:	$7,000	***Total Liab.:***	$1,320,000	***Indic. Yr. Divd.:***	NA
Total Assets:	$1,154,000	***Net Worth:***	-$166,000	***Debt/ Equity:***	NA

Dataram Corp

186 Princeton Rd., West Windsor, NJ, 08550; ***PH:*** 1-609-799-0071; ***Fax:*** 1-609-799-6734; ***http://*** www.dataram.com; ***Email:*** usasales@dataram.com

General - Incorporation	NJ	***Stock***- Price on:12/24/2007	$4.237
Employees	102	Stock Exchange	NDQ
Auditor	J. H. Cohn LLP	Ticker Symbol	DRAM
Stk Agt	First Union Nat'l Bank	Outstanding Shares	8,600,000
Counsel	Dillon, Bitar & Luther LLC	E.P.S	$0.04
DUNS No.	04-225-5927	Shareholders	NA

Business: The group's principal activity is to manufacture computer memory products. The group also manufactures a line of memory products for intel motherboard, original equipment manufacturers and channel assemblers. The memory products are used in workstations, network servers, desktop computers, notebooks and non-computer applications. The group's products expand the capacity and extend the economic useful life of computers manufactured by various companies like sun microsystems inc, hewlett-packard, silicon graphics, international business machines corporation and dell corporation. The group's customers are distributors, value added resellers and large end-users. The group markets its products in the United States and Europe.

Primary SIC and add'l.: 3679

CIK No: 0000027093

Officers: Robert V. Tarantino/Chmn., CEO/$323,348.00, Mark E. Maddocks/56/CFO, VP/$225,906.00, Lars Marcher/COO, Pres., Hugh F. Tucker/VP - Sales, Jeffrey H. Duncan/VP - Manufacturing - Engineering/$223,371.00, Jay Litus/VP - Business Development, Jerry R. Bresky/VP - Corporate Development

Directors: Robert V. Tarantino/Chmn., CEO, Richard Holzman/Dir., Thomas A. Majewski/56/Dir., Beranrd L. Riley/78/Dir., Roger Cady/70/Dir.

Owners: Robert V. Tarantino/10.20%, Thomas A. Majewski/1.10%, Bernard L. Riley, Mark E. Maddocks/1.60%, Jeffrey H. Duncan/2.30%, Anthony Pawlik, Roger C. Cady/1.30%, Insiders/17.30%, Al Frank Management Inc./6.10%, Rose Ann Giordano, Anthony M. Lougee, John H. Freeman, Fidelity Low Priced Stock Fund/9.60%

Financial Data: ***Fiscal Year End:***04/30 ***Latest Annual Data:*** 04/30/2007

Year	Sales	Net Income
2007	$38,404,000	$770,000
2006	$41,795,000	$2,772,000
2005	$65,684,000	$6,715,000

Curr. Assets:	$24,108,000	***Curr. Liab.:***	$2,710,000	***P/E Ratio:***	32.10
Plant, Equip.:	$847,000	***Total Liab.:***	$2,710,000	***Indic. Yr. Divd.:***	$0.240
Total Assets:	$26,236,000	***Net Worth:***	$23,526,000	***Debt/ Equity:***	NA

Datascension Inc

407 W Imperial Hwy., Ste. H314, Brea, CA, 92821; ***PH:*** 1-888-996-9238; ***Fax:*** 1-714-276-9080; ***http://*** www.datascension.com; ***Email:*** information@datascension.com

General - Incorporation	NV	***Stock***- Price on:12/24/2007	$0.65
Employees	7	Stock Exchange	OTC
Auditor	Larry O'donnell, CPA, P.C	Ticker Symbol	DSEN
Stk Agt	Transfer Online, Inc.	Outstanding Shares	23,170,000
Counsel	NA	E.P.S	$0.04
DUNS No.	NA	Shareholders	NA

Business: The group's principal activities are to provide data entry services, design and market women's resort wear clothing, produce plastic wall clocks and rail coverings. The group conducts telephone market research and provides data entry services for third parties; owns the rights to oil leases in Texas. In addition, the group also provides other consumer and industrial products. These include patented safety product that replaces standard light switch cover plates that automatically provides illumination in the event of a power failure and a patented plastic buffet plate that allows the user to hold both a plate and cup in one hand. The group acquired sin fronteras in 2002. The group is pursuing the sale of the women's resort wear business, the plastic wall clocks and plastic rail covering business.

Primary SIC and add'l.: 5621 1382 7371 7375

CIK No: 0000795824

Subsidiaries: Century Innovations, Inc., Datascension International, Inc., Kristi and Co, Inc., Nutek Oil, Inc., SRC International, Inc.

Officers: Scott Kincer/41/Chmn., CEO, Pres., Ryan Kincer/CTO, Joey Harmon/Dir., COO, Tracy Sanders/Mgr. - Sales, James Stock/Investor Relations Officer

Directors: Scott Kincer/41/Chmn., CEO, Pres., Joey Harmon/Dir., COO, Robert Sandelman/63/Dir., David Lieberman/63/Dir.

Owners: Murray Conradie/3.89%, David Scott Kincer/2.97%, Longview Fund, LP/21.96%, Robert Sandelman/0.74%, David Scott Kincer/7.83%, Joseph Harmon/0.81%, David Lieberman/0.09%, Joseph Harmon/1.14%, Longview Fund, LP/16.58%, Alpha Capital Anstalt/3.21%, Murray Conradie/1.54%, Alpha Capital Anstalt/6.44%, Insiders/13.58%

Financial Data: ***Fiscal Year End:***12/31 ***Latest Annual Data:*** 12/31/2006

Year	Sales	Net Income
2006	$14,781,000	-$232,000
2005	$9,753,000	$1,822,000
2004	$8,471,000	-$6,052,000

Curr. Assets:	$3,298,000	***Curr. Liab.:***	$2,206,000	***P/E Ratio:***	16.25
Plant, Equip.:	$3,136,000	***Total Liab.:***	$6,042,000	***Indic. Yr. Divd.:***	NA
Total Assets:	$8,172,000	***Net Worth:***	$2,130,000	***Debt/ Equity:***	2.0798

Datascope Corp

14 Philips Pkwy., Montvale, NJ, 07645; ***PH:*** 1-201-391-8100; ***Fax:*** 1-201-307-5400; ***http://*** www.datascope.com

General - Incorporation	DE	***Stock***- Price on:12/24/2007	$37.62
Employees	1,300	Stock Exchange	NDQ
Auditor	Deloitte & Touche LLP	Ticker Symbol	DSCP
Stk Agt	Continental Stock Transfer & Trust Co	Outstanding Shares	15,300,000
Counsel	Dechert LLP	E.P.S	$1.61
DUNS No.	00-166-0786	Shareholders	NA

Business: The group's principal activities are to develop, manufacture and sell medical devices for the clinical health care markets. The products are sold principally in the cardiology and radiology, cardiovascular and vascular surgery, anesthesiology, emergency medicine and critical care markets. The group operates in two segments: cardiac assist / monitoring products and interventional products / vascular grafts. The cardiac assist / monitoring products segment includes electronic intra-aortic balloon pumps and catheters that are used in the treatment of vascular disease and electronic physiological monitors that provide for patient safety and management of patient care. The interventional products / vascular grafts segment includes extravascular hemostasis devices.

Primary SIC and add'l.: 3845 3841

CIK No: 0000027096

Subsidiaries: Bioplex Corp., Bioplex Medical B.V., Datascope B.V., Datascope Biomaterials Research B.V., Datascope GmbH, Datascope Interventional GmbH, Datascope Investment Corp., Datascope Italia S.r.l., Datascope Medical Co. Ltd., Datascope S.A.R.L., Datascope SL, Datascope SPRL, Datascope Trademark Corp., Genisphere, Inc., InterVascular C, Inc. 20 Subsidiaries included in the Index

Officers: Lawrence Saper/Chmn., CEO, David A. Gibson/VP, Pres. - Patient Monitoring Division, Antonino Laudani/VP, Robert O. Cathcart/VP, Pres. - Interventional Products Division, James L. Cooper/VP - Human Resources, Nicholas E. Barker/VP - Corporate Design, Fred Adelman/VP, Chief Accounting Officer, Susan E. Chapman/Assist. Sec., Henry M. Scaramelli/CFO, VP, Timothy J. Krauskopf/VP - Regulatory, Clinical Affairs, Boris Leschinsky/VP - Technology, Frank L. Gutworth/Assist. Treasurer

Directors: Lawrence Saper/Chmn., CEO

Owners: Robert O. Cathcart, Robert E. Klatell, William L. Asmundson, Henry M. Scaramelli, Antonino Laudani, Lawrence Saper/18.10%, David Altschiller, Alan B. Abramson, Private Capital Management, L.P./6.70%, Barclays Global Investors, NA/6.40%, William W. Wyman, Insiders/20.60%, James J. Loughlin, AXA/7.90%, David A. Gibson

Financial Data: ***Fiscal Year End:***06/30 ***Latest Annual Data:*** 06/30/2007

Year	Sales	Net Income
2007	$378,800,000	$17,465,000
2006	$373,000,000	$25,843,000
2005	$352,700,000	$14,646,000

Curr. Assets:	$213,180,000	***Curr. Liab.:***	$55,633,000	***P/E Ratio:***	26.49
Plant, Equip.:	$85,460,000	***Total Liab.:***	$81,942,000	***Indic. Yr. Divd.:***	NA
Total Assets:	$375,680,000	***Net Worth:***	$293,738,000	***Debt/ Equity:***	NA

Datastream Systems Inc

50 Datastream Plaza, Greenville, SC, 29605; ***PH:*** 1-864-422-5001; ***http://*** www.dstm.com

General - Incorporation	DE	***Stock***- Price on:12/24/2007	NA
Employees	NA	Stock Exchange	NA
Auditor	BDO Seidman LLP	Ticker Symbol	NA
Stk Agt	Wachovia Bank N.A	Outstanding Shares	NA
Counsel	Alston & Bird LLP	E.P.S	NA
DUNS No.	15-187-8097	Shareholders	NA

Business: The group's principle activity is to provide asset performance management software, automated procurement and supporting services to organizations worldwide. Its product, datastream 7i, combines Internet architecture with enterprise asset management (eam) functionality and integrates with the group's iprocure industrial procurement network to provide customers with a complete eam solution. Customers of the group include American airlines, chevron, dunlop tire corporation, energizer battery corporation, fmc airport services, glaxosmithkline, holly corporation, kaiser permanente, lear corporation and sony. The group operates in the United States and has direct sales offices in Argentina, Brazil, Canada, Chile, China, France, Germany, Japan, Mexico, the Netherlands, Singapore, and the United Kingdom.

Primary SIC and add'l.: 7372 7371

CIK No: 0000938481

Subsidiaries: Asystum Participations BV, Datastream FSC, Inc., Datastream Servicios Mexicanos, S. de R.L. de C.V., Datastream Systems (Shanghai) Co., Ltd., Datastream Systems (UK), Ltd., Datastream Systems de Argentina S.A., Datastream Systems de Chile Ltd., Datastream Systems de Mexico S.A. de C.V., Datastream Systems do Brasil Ltda., Datastream Systems International, Inc., Datastream Systems Japan Kabushiki Kaisha., Datastream Systems Latinamerica SRL, Datastream Systems Pte Ltd., Datastream Systems Pty Ltd., Datastream Systems Sdn Bhd 24 Subsidiaries included in the Index

Officers: Larry G. Blackwell/Chmn., CEO, Founder, John M. Sterling/46/Exec. VP - Worldwide Sales, Bradley T. Stevens/45/Sr. VP - International Operations, Alex C. Estevez/CFO, Pres., Sec.

Directors: Larry G. Blackwell/Chmn., CEO, Founder

Datatrak International Inc

6150 Pk.land Blvd., Ste. 100, Mayfield Heights, OH, 44124; ***PH:*** 1-440-443-0082; ***Fax:*** 1-440-442-3482; ***http://*** www.datatraknet.com; ***Email:*** company@datatraknet.com

General - Incorporation	OH	***Stock***- Price on:12/24/2007	$4.43
Employees	122	Stock Exchange	NDQ
Auditor	Ernst & Young LLP	Ticker Symbol	DATA
Stk Agt	National City Bank	Outstanding Shares	13,560,000
Counsel	Calfee, Halter & Griswold	E.P.S	-$0.71
DUNS No.	80-715-5692	Shareholders	NA

Business: The group's principal activity is to provide a suite of software products. It is a worldwide application service provider (asp) for the electronic data capture (edc) industry. These products support the use of datatrak edc(TM) software and related services to the pharmaceuticals, biotechnology and medical device industries. Datatrak edc was developed in order to deliver clinical research data from investigative sites to clinical trial sponsors faster and more efficiently than conventional, manual methods. Datatrak edc can be deployed worldwide in either a distributed platform using laptop computers or in a centralized environment using the Internet.

Primary SIC and add'l.: 8731 8099

CIK No: 0000886530

Subsidiaries: CF Merger Sub, Inc., Datatrak Deutschland, Datatrak, Inc.

Officers: Jeffrey A. Green/Dir., CEO, Pres./$270,890.00, Marc J. Shlaes/53/VP - Product Strategy/$179,872.00, Wolfgang Summa/VP - Strategic Business Relationships/$237,350.00, Terry C. Black/COO, VP - Finance, Jim Bob Ward/VP - Clinical Development/$121,000.00, Ray Merk/CFO

Directors: Jeffrey A. Green/Dir., CEO, Pres., Seth B. Harris/Dir., Mark J. Ratain/Dir., Timothy G. Biro/Dir., Jerome H. Kaiser/Dir., Robert M. Stote/Dir.

Owners: Robert M. Stote/1.20%, Timothy G. Biro, Jim Bob Ward/5.00%, Mark J. Ratain, Seth B. Harris/3.10%, Wolfgang Summa, Marc J. Shlaes, Jerome H. Kaiser, Insiders/16.60%, Jeffrey A. Green/4.30%, Terry C. Black

Financial Data: Fiscal Year End:12/31   **Latest Annual Data:** 12/31/2006

Year	Sales	Net Income
2006	$17,690,000	-$4,490,000
2005	$15,735,000	$2,538,000
2004	$11,305,000	$817,000

Curr. Assets:	$7,843,000	Curr. Liab.:	$3,709,000		
Plant, Equip.:	$4,736,000	Total Liab.:	$9,156,000	Indic. Yr. Divd.:	NA
Total Assets:	$27,220,000	Net Worth:	$18,064,000	Debt/ Equity:	0.1326

Datawatch Corp

271 Mill Rd., Chelmsford, MA, 01824; **PH:** 1-978-441-2200; **Fax:** 1-978-441-1114; **http://** www.datawatch.com; **Email:** sales@datawatch.com

General - Incorporation	DE	**Stock** - Price on:12/24/2007	$5.9
Employees	131	Stock Exchange	NDQ
Auditor	Deloitte & Touche LLP	Ticker Symbol	DWCH
Stk Agt	American Stock Transfer & Trust Co.	Outstanding Shares	5,570,000
Counsel	Choate, Hall & Stewart LLP	E.P.S.	-$0.07
DUNS No.	15-724-8204	Shareholders	NA

Business: The group's principal activity is to design, develop, manufacture, market & distribute commercial software products. The products address the enterprise reporting, business intelligence, data replication & help desk markets. The group's principal products are monarch, monarch/es, monarch data pump & vortexml. The monarch includes a report mining application, letting the users extract & manipulate data from ascii report files. The monarch/es is a configurable enterprise reporting solution, which allows quick deliver business intelligence. The monarch data pump is a data replication & migration tool that offers a shortcut for populating & refreshing data marts & data warehouses. The vortexml, a desktop software converts existing, structured ascii/ansi text documents into valid xml. The group's desktop products are sold under single & multi-user license. On 16-Oct-2002, the group acquired auxilor inc. On 11-Aug-2004, the group acquired mergence technologies corp.

Primary SIC and add'l.: 7371 7372

CIK No: 0000792130

Subsidiaries: Auxilor, Inc., Datawatch Europe Limited, Datawatch France SARL, Datawatch GmbH, Datawatch International Limited, Datawatch Pty Ltd., Datawatch Technologies Corporation, Personics Corporation

Officers: Robert W. Hagger/Dir., CEO, Pres., John H. Kitchen/Chief Marketing Officer, Sr. VP, Ken Bero/COO, Sr. VP - Sales, Business Operations, Harvey Gross/VP - Product Management - Development, Murray P. Fish/CFO, VP - Finance

Directors: Robert W. Hagger/Dir., CEO, Pres., James Wood/Vice Chmn., Richard J. Osborne/Chmn., Thomas H. Kelly/Dir., William B. Simmons/Dir., Terry W. Potter/Dir., David T. Riddiford/Dir.

Owners: John J. Hulburt, Robert W. Hagger/5.29%, David T. Riddiford, Christopher Cox/12.50%, Daniel Zeff/5.22%, John H. Kitchen/2.93%, Kevin C. Howe/5.38%, Terry W. Potter, Insiders/29.88%, Richard de J. Osborne/5.41%, WC Capital, LLC/12.50%, James Wood/16.73%, Thomas H. Kelly

Financial Data: Fiscal Year End:09/30   **Latest Annual Data:** 9/30/2006

Year	Sales	Net Income
2006	$20,811,000	-$555,000
2005	$21,512,000	$800,000
2004	$19,335,000	$1,085,000

Curr. Assets:	$6,338,000	Curr. Liab.:	$8,804,000	P/E Ratio:	111.32
Plant, Equip.:	$1,129,000	Total Liab.:	$9,069,000	Indic. Yr. Divd.:	NA
Total Assets:	$16,025,000	Net Worth:	$6,955,000	Debt/ Equity:	NA

DataWave Systems Inc

145 Rte. 46 W, 3rd Fl., Wayne, NJ, 07470; **PH:** 1-973-774-5000; **http://** www.datawave.com

General - Incorporation	DE	**Stock** - Price on:12/24/2007	NA
Employees	89	Stock Exchange	NA
Auditor	Deloitte & Touche LLP	Ticker Symbol	NA
Stk Agt	Computershare Investor Services LLC	Outstanding Shares	NA
Counsel	Clark, Wilson	E.P.S.	NA
DUNS No.	24-996-8728	Shareholders	NA

Business: The group's principal activity is to design, develop, produce, own and manage an automated direct merchandising network, data wave system used to distribute prepaid calling cards. The data wave system comprises of datawave telecard merchandisers (dtms) and over-the-counter units (otcs). The datawave telecard merchandisers are free-standing machines capable of dispensing multiple prepaid product offerings and over-the-counter units for prepaid retailing which is connected to the group's proprietary server software and databases through a wireless and/or land line wide area network. In addition to this the group markets prepaid calling cards on a wholesale basis to certain retail operators and other customers. The group's major customers include airports, hotel chains, shopping malls and casinos. On 13-Jul-2001, the group acquired at&t prepaid card company.

Primary SIC and add'l.: 3581 3669

CIK No: 0001000157

Subsidiaries: CXP Canada Inc., DataWave Services (Canada) Inc., DataWave Services (U.S.) Inc., DataWave Systems (U.S.) Inc., Nextwave Card Corp.

Officers: Joshua Emanuel/Chmn., CEO, William Turner/46/VP - Business Development, Bill Turner/VP - Business Development, Corporate, John Gunn/CFO, GM, David Linton/VP - Sales, Marketing, Canada, Ardeshir Darabi/41/General Counsel, Sec., David Knox/COO, VP, Larry Wetzel/VP - Sales, US

Directors: Joshua Emanuel/Chmn., CEO, Thom Waye/Dir., John X. Adiletta/Dir., Vijay Fozdar/Dir.

Dataworld Solutions Inc

275k Marcus Blvd., Hauppauge, NY, 11788; **PH:** 1-631-951-4000

General - Incorporation	DE	**Stock** - Price on:12/24/2007	$0.0055
Employees	NA	Stock Exchange	NA
Auditor	BP Audit Group PLLC	Ticker Symbol	NA
Stk Agt	American Stock Transfer & Trust Co.	Outstanding Shares	NA
Counsel	NA	E.P.S.	NA
DUNS No.	NA	Shareholders	NA

Business: The group's principle activity is to manufacture multi-regional custom-made electronic cable assemblies used in providing connectivity solutions. The group's business strategy is to develop value added distribution network through internal growth with a focus on connectivity solutions for data and tele-communications. The product and services of the group consist principally the design and manufacture of custom-made electronic cable assemblies and harnesses used as solutions for connectivity requirements in data communications. The group operates from United States.

Primary SIC and add'l.: 3669

CIK No: 0000798438

Financial Data: Fiscal Year End:06/30   **Latest Annual Data:** 6/30/2004

Year	Sales	Net Income
2004	$695,000	-$2,201,000
2000	$13,368,000	-$628,000
1999	$5,912,000	-$1,051,000

Curr. Assets:	$93,000	Curr. Liab.:	$4,486,000		
Plant, Equip.:	$15,000	Total Liab.:	$4,929,000	Indic. Yr. Divd.:	NA
Total Assets:	$120,000	Net Worth:	-$4,809,000	Debt/ Equity:	NA

Dave & Busters Inc

2481 Manana Dr., Dallas, TX, 75220; **PH:** 1-214-357-9588; **http://** www.daveandbusters.com

General - Incorporation	MO	**Stock** - Price on:12/24/2007	NA
Employees	NA	Stock Exchange	NA
Auditor	Ernst & Young LLP	Ticker Symbol	NA
Stk Agt	Mellon Investor Services LLC	Outstanding Shares	NA
Counsel	NA	E.P.S.	NA
DUNS No.	17-909-5211	Shareholders	NA

Business: The group's principal activity is to operate restaurant and entertainment complexes. The group offers a full menu of quality food and beverage item combined with an extensive array of entertainment attractions such as pocket billiards, shuffleboard, state-of-the-art interactive simulators and virtual reality systems and traditional carnival-style games of skill. It serves well-rounded meals including gourmet pastas, steaks, seafood, chicken, sandwiches, salads and a selection of desserts. As on 01-Feb-2004, the group operated 33 entertainment complexes across the United States and in Canada. It has licensees in Korea, Mexico, certain countries in the Middle East, Canada and the Pacific Rim. It has entertainment complexes in toronto, Canada, Taipei, Taiwan and Mexico city, Mexico. On 08-Oct-2003 the group acquired funtime hospitality corp.

Primary SIC and add'l.: 5812 7999

CIK No: 0000943823

Subsidiaries: 6131646 Canada Inc, D&B Leasing, Inc., D&B Realty Holding, Inc., DANB Texas, Inc., Dave & Busters I, L.P., Dave & Busters Management Corporation, Dave & Busters of California, Inc, Dave & Busters of Colorado, Inc., Dave & Busters of Florida, Inc., Dave & Busters of Georgia, Inc., Dave & Busters of Hawaii, Inc, Dave & Busters of Illinois, Inc., Dave & Busters of Maryland, Inc., Dave & Busters of New York, Inc, Dave & Busters of Pennsylvania, Inc 29 Subsidiaries included in the Index

Officers: Stephen M. King/50/Dir., CEO, Margo Manning/43/Sr. VP - Training, Special Events, Brian A. Jenkins/46/CFO, Sr. VP, Starlette Johnson/45/Dir., COO, Pres., Michael Metzinger/51/VP - Accounting, Controller, Jeffrey C. Wood/45/Chief Development Officer, Sr. VP, Maria M. Miller/51/Sr. VP, Chief Marketing Officer, Mike Flesch/44/Sr. VP - Operations, Michael J. Plunkett/57/Sr. VP - Purchasing, International Operations, Jay L. Tobin/50/Sr. VP, General Counsel

Directors: Stephen M. King/50/Dir., CEO, Greg S. Feldman/51/Chmn., Daniel Y. Ham/30/Dir., Carl M. Stanton/40/Dir., Starlette Johnson/45/Dir., COO, Pres.

Davey Tree Expert Co (The)

1500 N Mantua St., Kent, OH, 44240; **PH:** 1-330-673-9511; **http://** www.davey.com

General - Incorporation	OH	**Stock** - Price on:12/24/2007	NA
Employees	NA	Stock Exchange	NA
Auditor	Ernst & Young LLP	Ticker Symbol	NA
Stk Agt	NA	Outstanding Shares	NA
Counsel	NA	E.P.S.	NA
DUNS No.	00-790-3180	Shareholders	NA

Business: The group's principal activity is to provide a wide range of horticultural services to residential, commercial, utility and institutional customers. The group operates in two segments: residential and commercial services and utility services. Residential and commercial services provide services for the treatment, preservation, maintenance, cultivation, planting and removal of trees, shrubs and other plant life and also include services like landscaping, tree surgery, tree feeding and tree spraying, application of fertilizers, herbicides and insecticides. Utility services provides line clearing for public utilities, including the clearing of tree growth from power lines. The group also engages in natural resource management solutions, urban and utility forestry research and development, natural resources consulting and environmental planning.

Primary SIC and add'l.: 0783 0781 8748 0782

CIK No: 0000277638

Subsidiaries: Davey Tree Expert Co. of Canada, Limited, Davey Tree Surgery Company, Standing Rock Insurance Company

Officers: Karl J. Warnke/56/Dir., CEO, Pres./$973,742.00, David E. Adante/CFO, Exec. VP/$540,390.00, Mike Binkley/Research, Development Analyst, Jerry Bond/Research, Development Analyst, Urban Forestry, Shawn William Bruzda/Sr. Urban Forester, Biologist, Elizabeth L. Buchanan/Sr. Scientist, Leonard F. Burkhart/Technical Advisor, Lianghu Tian/Research, Development Analyst, Information Technology, Greg Ina/GM, Kenneth Joehlin/Business Development Leader, Robert J. Laverne/Mgr. - Education, Training, Douglas Wade/Project Developer, Project Mgr., Karen Wise/Mgr. - Natural Resource Consulting, Keith Cottle/Field Production Mgr. - Asset Management Services, Ray Hannebique/Regional Operations Mgr. - Davey Resource *(83 Officers included in Index)*

Directors: Karl J. Warnke/56/Dir., CEO, Pres., Douglas R. Cowan/Chmn., Dawson J. Cunningham/61/Dir., William L. Phipps/57/Dir., Robert A. Stefanko/65/Dir., Douglas K. Hall/56/Dir., Carol A. Cartwright/66/Dir.

Owners: Carol A. Cartwright, Insiders/22.12%, Douglas K. Hall, Howard D. Bowles/1.97%, Dawson Cunningham, David E. Adante/2.16%, Kenneth C. Celmer/1.65%, Cary R. Blair, Douglas R. Cowan/3.08%, Robert A. Stefanko, William L. Phipps, Karl J. Warnke/2.94%

Davi Skin Inc

301 N Canon Dr., Ste 328, Beverly Hills, CA, 90210; ***PH:*** 1-310-205-9907; ***http://*** www.daviskin.com; ***Email:*** info@daviskin.com

General - Incorporation	NV	**Stock**- Price on:12/24/2007	$0.22
Employees	4	Stock Exchange	OTC
Auditor	Child, Van Wagoner & Bradshaw, LLC	Ticker Symbol	DAVN
Stk Agt	National Stock Transfer, Inc.	Outstanding Shares	12,320,000
Counsel	Cane Clark LLP	E.P.S	-$0.22
DUNS No.	NA	Shareholders	NA

Business: The group's principal activity is to develop natural grape based skin care line.

Primary SIC and add'l.: 2834

CIK No: 0001059577

Officers: Joseph Spellman/Dir., CEO, Pres., Josh Levine/Dir., Sec., Treasurer, Munjit Johal/CFO

Directors: Joseph Spellman/Dir., CEO, Pres., Carlo Mondavi/Chmn., Josh Levine/Dir., Sec., Treasurer, Elliot Smith/Dir.

Owners: Parrish Medley/6.40%, Josh LeVine/7.80%, Carlo Mondavi/34.70%, Joseph Spellman/3.30%, Insiders/44.40%

Financial Data: ***Fiscal Year End:***12/31 ***Latest Annual Data:*** 12/31/2006

Year	Sales	Net Income
2006	$23,000	-$3,779,000
2005	NA	-$3,398,000
2004	NA	-$1,569,000

Curr. Assets:	$1,539,000	**Curr. Liab.:**	$561,000		
Plant, Equip.:	$32,000	**Total Liab.:**	$561,000	**Indic. Yr. Divd.:**	NA
Total Assets:	$1,615,000	**Net Worth:**	$1,054,000	**Debt/ Equity:**	NA

Davita Inc

601 Hawaii St., El Segundo, CA, 90245; ***PH:*** 1-310-536-2400; ***Fax:*** 1-310-536-2675; ***http://*** www.davita.com

General - Incorporation	DE	**Stock**- Price on:12/24/2007	$53.2
Employees	28,900	Stock Exchange	NYSE
Auditor	KPMG LLP	Ticker Symbol	DVA
Stk Agt	Bank of New York	Outstanding Shares	105,300,000
Counsel	Riordan & McKinzie	E.P.S	$3.46
DUNS No.	03-971-1569	Shareholders	NA

Business: The group's principle activities include dialysis and related services. The group also provides ancillary services include epo and other pharmaceuticals, esrd laboratory services and esrd clinical research programs. The group also operates 566 outpatient dialysis centers. The group also provides acute inpatient dialysis services. The group operates from United States.

Primary SIC and add'l.: 8092

CIK No: 0000927066

Subsidiaries: Astro, Hobby, West Mt. Renal Care Limited Partnership, Austin Dialysis Centers, L.P., Bay Area Dialysis Partnership, Beverly Hills Dialysis Partnership, Brighton Dialysis Center, LLC, Capital Dialysis Partnership, Carroll County Dialysis Facility Limited Partnership, Carroll County Dialysis Facility, Inc., Central Carolina Dialysis Centers, LLC, Central Georgia Dialysis, LLC, Central Iowa Dialysis Partners, LLC, Central Kentucky Dialysis Centers, LLC, Chicago Heights Dialysis, LLC, Continental Dialysis Center of Springfield-Fairfax, Inc., Continental Dialysis Center, Inc. 161 Subsidiaries included in the Index

Officers: Kent J. Thiry/Chmn., CEO/$8,402,306.00, Joseph Schohl/VP, General Counsel, Corp. Sec./$957,463.00, Mark G. Harrison/CFO/$646,854.00, Charlie McAllister/60/Chief Medical Officer, Thomas O. Usilton/Sr. VP/$1,266,738.00, James K. Hilger/46/VP, Controller, Mary R. Kowenhoven/38/VP - Strategy, Georgina Randolph/60/Sr. VP, Christopher J. Riopelle/38/Chief Compliance Officer, Joseph C. Mello/COO/$4,227,484.00, Leanne Zumwalt/VP - Investor Relations

Directors: Kent J. Thiry/Chmn., CEO, Roger J. Valine/Dir., Richard C. Vaughan/Dir., Peter T. Grauer/Dir., Charles G. Berg/Dir., Willard W. Brittain/Dir., Paul J. Diaz/Dir., Nancy-Ann Deparle/Dir., William L. Roper/Dir., Charles G. Charles/50/Dir., John M. Nehra/Dir.

Owners: John M. Nehra, Kent J. Thiry/1.40%, Thomas O. Usilton, Christopher J. Riopelle, Richard B. Fontaine, Richard C. Vaughan, Peter T. Grauer, T. Rowe Price Associates, Inc./5.20%, James K. Hilger, Thomas L. Kelly, Joseph C. Mello, William L. Roper, Charles J. McAllister, Peninsula Investment Partners, L.P./5.70%, Joseph Schohl *(21 Owners included in Index)*

Financial Data: ***Fiscal Year End:***12/31 ***Latest Annual Data:*** 12/31/2006

Year	Sales	Net Income
2006	$4,880,662,000	$289,691,000
2005	$2,973,918,000	$228,643,000
2004	$2,298,595,000	$222,254,000

Curr. Assets:	$1,709,496,000	**Curr. Liab.:**	$1,112,172,000	**P/E Ratio:**	15.29
Plant, Equip.:	$849,966,000	**Total Liab.:**	$5,123,533,000	**Indic. Yr. Divd.:**	NA
Total Assets:	$6,491,816,000	**Net Worth:**	$1,245,924,000	**Debt/ Equity:**	2.7481

Dawson Geophysical Co

508 W Wall, Ste. 800, Midland, TX, 79701; ***PH:*** 1-432-684-3000; ***Fax:*** 1-432-684-3030; ***http://*** www.dawson3d.com; ***Email:*** Info@dawson3d.com

General - Incorporation	TX	**Stock**- Price on:12/24/2007	$56.39
Employees	1,023	Stock Exchange	NDQ
Auditor	KPMG LLP	Ticker Symbol	DWSN
Stk Agt	Bank of New York	Outstanding Shares	7,620,000
Counsel	Stubbeman McRae Sealy Et Al	E.P.S	$3.54
DUNS No.	00-586-0721	Shareholders	NA

Business: The group's principle activity is to acquire and process 2-d, 3-D, 4-d and seismic data used in the exploration, development and field management of oil and natural gas reserves. The operations consist of six 3-D seismic data acquisition crews and a seismic data processing center. The 3-D seismic data are used in the exploration for new reserves. It also enables oil and gas companies to better delineate existing fields and to augment their reservoir management techniques. The clients of the company range from major oil companies to small independent oil and gas operators. The company operates six input or output system, two recording systems, two with rsr radio capability and four mrx cable recording systems. The group operates from United States.

Primary SIC and add'l.: 1389

CIK No: 0000351231

Officers: Stephen C. Jumper/Dir., CEO, Pres., Christina W. Hagan/CFO, Exec. VP, Sec., Treasurer, K. S. Forsdick/VP, Howell W. Pardue/Exec. VP, Mark A. Nelson/VP, Olga Smoot/Contact - Human Resources, Ray C. Tobias/COO, Exec. VP

Directors: Stephen C. Jumper/Dir., CEO, Pres., Decker L. Dawson/Chmn., Paul H. Brown/Dir., Gary M. Hoover/Dir., Tim C. Thompson/Dir.

Owners: Stephen C. Jumper, L. Decker Dawson/1.40%, Paul H. Brown, Howell W. Pardue, Christina W. Hagan, C. Ray Tobias, Tim C. Thompson, Gary M. Hoover, K.S. Forsdick, Insiders/3.69%

Financial Data: ***Fiscal Year End:***09/30 ***Latest Annual Data:*** 9/30/2006

Year	Sales	Net Income
2006	$168,550,000	$15,855,000
2005	$116,663,000	$10,016,000
2004	$69,346,000	$8,618,000

Curr. Assets:	$62,884,000	**Curr. Liab.:**	$23,296,000	**P/E Ratio:**	18.49
Plant, Equip.:	$86,534,000	**Total Liab.:**	$30,210,000	**Indic. Yr. Divd.:**	NA
Total Assets:	$149,418,000	**Net Worth:**	$119,208,000	**Debt/ Equity:**	NA

Daxor Corp

350 5th Ave., Ste. 7120, New York, NY, 10118; ***PH:*** 1-212-330-8500; ***Fax:*** 1-212-244-0806; ***http://*** www.daxor.com; ***Email:*** info@daxor.com

General - Incorporation	NY	**Stock**- Price on:12/24/2007	$14.85
Employees	NA	Stock Exchange	AMEX
Auditor	Rotenberg Meril Solomon	Ticker Symbol	DXR
Stk Agt	Continental Stock Transfer & Trust Co	Outstanding Shares	4,600,000
Counsel	NA	E.P.S	$1.61
DUNS No.	05-666-7975	Shareholders	NA

Business: The group's principal activities are to operate human sperm and blood bank, to develop and market medical instrument, which measures human blood volume. The medical instrument is known as blood volume analyzer (bva-100). The instrument is useful in situations like hemorrhage or surgery wherein it is essential to know the blood volume in the human body. The blood banking services include autologous blood banking services, in which donors deposit their own blood up to ten years. This process eliminates donor transmitted diseases as the donors can receive their own blood at any point of emergency. The sperm banks provide frozen semen services, which target men undergoing procedures that may impair fertility.

Primary SIC and add'l.: 8099 3841

CIK No: 0000027367

Subsidiaries: Scientific Medical Systems

Officers: Joseph Feldschuh/Chmn., CEO, Pres./$264,915.00, Ronald Baldry/VP - Engineering, David Frankel/CFO/$97,500.00, Philip Frost/Member - Medical Advisory Board, Diane M. Meegan/Corp. Sec., John Reyes-Guerra/VP - Sales, Marketing/$156,000.00, Stephen Feldschuh/COO/$192,923.00, Gary Fischman/VP - Research & Development, Robert L. Rosenthal/Member - Medical Advisory Board, Eliezer Rachmilewitz/Member - Medical Advisory Board, Fred Gilbert/Member - Medical Advisory Board, James H. Brassel/Member - Medical Advisory Board, Everis Engstrom/VP - Engineering/$80,649.00, Deanna O'Brien/VP - Quality Systems, Regulatory Affairs

Directors: Joseph Feldschuh/Chmn., CEO, Pres., Philip N. Hudson/57/Dir., Robert G. Moussa/Dir., James A. Lombard/Dir., Martin S. Wolpoff/Dir., Stephen Valentine/Dir., Robert Willens/Dir.

Owners: Joseph Feldschuh/67.40%, Insiders/70.50%, Robert Willens, Philip Hudson, Martin S. Wolpoff, Stephen Valentine, James A. Lombard

Financial Data: ***Fiscal Year End:***12/31 ***Latest Annual Data:*** 12/31/2006

Year	Sales	Net Income
2006	$1,486,000	-$786,000
2005	$1,344,000	-$1,336,000
2004	$1,218,000	-$580,000

Curr. Assets:	$77,370,000	**Curr. Liab.:**	$32,529,000	**P/E Ratio:**	15.15
Plant, Equip.:	$764,000	**Total Liab.:**	$32,529,000	**Indic. Yr. Divd.:**	NA
Total Assets:	$78,166,000	**Net Worth:**	$45,638,000	**Debt/ Equity:**	NA

Day International Group Inc

130 W Second St. , Dayton, OH, 45402; ***PH:*** 1-937-224-4000; ***http://*** www.dayintl.com

General - Incorporation	DE	**Stock**- Price on:12/24/2007	NA
Employees	NA	Stock Exchange	NA
Auditor	Ernst & Young LLP	Ticker Symbol	NA
Stk Agt	NA	Outstanding Shares	NA
Counsel	NA	E.P.S	NA
DUNS No.	62-333-9066	Shareholders	NA

Business: The group's principle activity is to produce precision-engineered products, specializing in the design and customization of consumable image-transfer products. The group consists of two segments: the image transfer segment and the textile products segment. The image transfer segment consists of the transfer media division and the pressroom chemicals division. The transfer media division designs, manufacturers and markets printing blankets and sleeves for use in offset printing. The textile products segment manufacturers and marketers of precision engineered rubber cots, aprons and other fabricated rubber fiber handling components sold to textile yarn spinners. On 24-Nov-2003, the group acquired Network Distribution International. The group operates from United States.

Primary SIC and add'l.: 3069

CIK No: 0000946991

Subsidiaries: ATPG Textile Products Group GmbH, Day Germany Holdings GmbH, Day International (BRD)GmbH, Day International (U.K.) Holdings Limited, Day International (U.K.), Ltd., Day International de Mexico S.A. de C.V., Day International Finance, Inc., Day International France S.A.R.L, Day International Group GmbH, Day International, Inc., Network Distribution International, Network Distribution International, Inc., R T C do Brasil Ltda., Rotec Czech s.r.o., Rotec Hulsensysteme GmbH & Co. KG 22 Subsidiaries included in the Index

Officers: Dennis R. Wolters/CEO, Pres.

Directors: Duncan P. Varty/63/Dir.

Owners: Duncan P. Varty, Thomas J. Koenig/0.40%, Cowen Investments I, LLC/14.50%, Dennis R. Wolters/3.00%, David B. Freimuth/1.00%, Stephen P. Noe/0.50%, Unione Italiana/0.70%, Towerbrook/3.00%, Dermot J. Healy/0.30%, William C. Ferguson/0.60%, Insiders/6.40%, Carl J. Crosetto/0.30%, Greenwich IV, LLC/72.00%

Daybreak Oil & Gas Inc

601 W Main Ave. Ste. 1017, Spokane, WA, 99201; **PH:** 1-509-232-7674; **http://** www.daybreakoilandgas.com; **Email:** info@daybreakoilandgas.com

General - Incorporation	WA	Stock - Price on:12/24/2007	NA
Employees	NA	Stock Exchange	OTC
Auditor	Malone & Bailey, P.C	Ticker Symbol	DBRM
Stk Agt	Columbia Stock Transfer Co	Outstanding Shares	NA
Counsel	Greg Lipsker, PS	E.P.S.	NA
DUNS No.	NA	Shareholders	NA

Business: The groups principal activity is to explore minerals. The group operates from Canada and the United States.

Primary SIC and add'l.: 1382

CIK No: 0001164256

Officers: Eric Moe/Dir., CEO, Mike McIntyre/Contact - Corporate Relations, Ben Anderson/COO, Ronald D. Lavinge/Dir., VP, Terrence J. Dunne/Dir., CFO, Tom Kilbourne/Dir., Treasurer, Jeffrey R. Dworkin/Dir., Corp. Sec., Robert N. Martin/Dir., Pres.

Directors: Eric Moe/Dir., CEO, Dale B. Lavigne/76/Chmn., Jeffrey R. Dworkin/Dir., Corp. Sec., Ronald D. Lavinge/Dir., VP, Tim R. Lindsey/Dir., Robert N. Martin/Dir., Pres., Terrence J. Dunne/Dir., CFO, Tom Kilbourne/Dir., Treasurer, Michael Curtis/Dir.

Owners: Robert N. Martin/3.35%, Bennett W. Anderson/0.73%, Dale B. Lavigne/2.00%, Jeffrey R. Dworkin/0.07%, Keith A. Hooper/7.71%, Ronald D. Lavigne/1.67%, Eric L. Moe/2.68%, Tim R. Lindsey/0.49%, Michael Curtis/0.07%, Thomas C. Kilbourne/2.26%, Robert O' Brien/6.99%, Terrence J. Dunne/9.24%

Daystar Technologies Inc

13 Corporate Dr., Halfmoon, NY, 12065; **PH:** 1-518-383-4600; **Fax:** 1-518-383-4900; **http://** www.daystartech.com; **Email:** info@daystartech.com

General - Incorporation	DE	Stock - Price on:12/24/2007	$4.65
Employees	82	Stock Exchange	NDQ
Auditor	Hein & Assoc. LLP	Ticker Symbol	DSTI
Stk Agt	Registrar & Transfer Co	Outstanding Shares	14,900,000
Counsel	NA	E.P.S.	-$4.21
DUNS No.	NA	Shareholders	NA

Business: The group's principal activity is to develop thin-film, copper-indium-gallium-selenide solar cell, known as a cigs solar cell, for the direct conversion of sunlight into electricity. It is also developing a high-volume manufacturing process that could reduce the cost of solar cell production and reduce the cost of solar electricity. Prototypes of cigs cells, produced in batches in the laboratory, have been used on a test basis by the United States air force research laboratory and dutch space b.v. The group operates in the domestic market.

Primary SIC and add'l.: 3674 4931

CIK No: 0001262200

Subsidiaries: DayStar Solar LLC

Officers: Stephan Deluca/Dir., CEO, John J. McCaffrey/VP - Manufacturing, Steven Aragon/46/VP - Engineering, Terence Schuyler/VP - Sales, Marketing, Robert Weiss/CTO, Erica Dart/Contact - Media Relations, Raja H. Venkatesh/CFO, Christopher T. Lail/Controller, Acting Chief Accounting Officer

Directors: Stephan Deluca/Dir., CEO, Randolph A. Graves/Chmn., Robert G. Aldrich/Dir., Kelly A. Lovell/Dir., Scott M. Schecter/Dir., Steven C. Argabright/65/Dir., Kevin S. Flannery/Dir.

Owners: Robert G. Aldrich, John R. Tuttle/1.40%, Terence W. Schuyler, Scott M. Schecter, Raja H. Venkatesh, Robert E. Weiss, John J. McCaffrey, Stephan J. DeLuca, Kelly A. Waters, Richard Nevins, Steven C. Argabright, Randolph A. Graves, Quercus Trust/12.40%, Steven Aragon, Insiders/2.70% (18 Owners included in Index)

Financial Data: Fiscal Year End:12/31   **Latest Annual Data:** 12/31/2006

Year	Sales	Net Income
2006	$184,000	-$20,441,000
2005	$625,000	-$6,763,000
2004	$157,000	-$4,666,000

Curr. Assets:	$3,905,000	Curr. Liab.:	$9,105,000		
Plant, Equip.:	$11,245,000	Total Liab.:	$12,092,000	Indic. Yr. Divd.:	NA
Total Assets:	$18,062,000	Net Worth:	$5,969,000	Debt/ Equity:	0.0325

Dayton Power & Light Co (The)

1065 Woodman Dr., Dayton, OH, 45432; **PH:** 1-937-224-6000; **http://** www.dplinc.com

General - Incorporation	OH	Stock - Price on:12/24/2007	$69
Employees	NA	Stock Exchange	OTC
Auditor	KPMG LLP	Ticker Symbol	DAYTL
Stk Agt	Bank of New York	Outstanding Shares	NA
Counsel	NA	E.P.S.	NA
DUNS No.	78-086-8139	Shareholders	NA

Business: The group's principal activity is to generate and market electricity to residential, commercial, industrial, and governmental customers in a 6,000 square mile area of west central Ohio. The electricity is distributed to company's 24 county service areas. The electricity is generated at eight power plants and is distributed to more than 500,000 retail customers. Principal industries served include automotive, food processing, paper, technology, and defense.

Primary SIC and add'l.: 4911

CIK No: 0000027430

Subsidiaries: DPL Finance Company, Inc

Officers: Paul M. Barbas/Dir., Pres., CEO - DPL Inc, DP, L, Dayton, Ohio, Arthur G. Meyer/58/Sr. VP - Corporate, Regulatory Affairs, Frederick J. Boyle/VP, Chief Accounting Officer, John J. Gillen/Sr. VP, CFO, Kevin W. Crawford/VP - Power Production, Gary Stephenson/Sr. VP -

Generation, Marketing, Scott J. Kelly/Sr. VP - Service Operations, Dennis A. Lantzy/VP - Power Production Engineering, Construction, Teresa F. Marrinan/VP - Commercial Operations, Daniel J. McCabe/Sr. VP - Human Resources, Bryce W. Nickel/VP - Transmission, Distribution Operations, Timothy G. Rice/Interim Sr. VP, General Counsel, Corp. Sec., Joseph R. Boni/VP, Treasurer

Directors: Paul M. Barbas/Dir., Pres., CEO - DPL Inc, DP, L, Dayton, Ohio, Glenn E. Harder/Chmn. - DPL Inc, Robert D. Biggs/Dir., Paul R. Bishop/Dir., Barbara S. Graham/Dir., Ned J. Sifferlen/Dir., August W. Hillenbrand/Dir., Lester L. Lyles/Dir., Frank F. Gallaher/Dir.

Dayton Superior Corp

7777 Washington Village Dr., Ste. 130, Dayton, OH, 45459; **PH:** 1-937-428-6360; **Fax:** 1-937-428-9560; **http://** www.daytonsuperior.com; **Email:** info@daytonsuperior.com

General - Incorporation	OH	Stock - Price on:12/24/2007	NA
Employees	NA	Stock Exchange	NDQ
Auditor	Deloitte & Touche LLP	Ticker Symbol	DSUP
Stk Agt	American Stock Transfer & Trust Co.	Outstanding Shares	NA
Counsel	NA	E.P.S.	NA
DUNS No.	04-160-4463	Shareholders	NA

Business: The group operates through its subsidiaries whose principle activities include producing and distributing concrete modular forms, concrete form-tying devices, concrete lifting and handling systems, metal and plastic concrete accessories and masonry accessories; and supplies chemical, cementitious and epoxy products for the construction industry. The group operates from United States.

Primary SIC and add'l.: 6719 3499 3272 3315

CIK No: 0000854709

Subsidiaries: Dayton Superior Canada Ltd, Dayton Superior Corporation, Safway Services, Inc

Officers: Eric R. Zimmerman/CEO, Pres./$1,913,218.00, Edward J. Puisis/CFO, Exec. VP/$1,151,334.00, Fred Slack/VP - International

Directors: Steven M. Berzin/57/Dir., Sidney J. Nurkin/66/Dir.

Owners: Odyssey Investment Partners Fund, LP, Douglas W. Rotator, Morgan Stanley, Stephen Berger, Mark K. Kale, Edward J. Puisis, William F. Hopkins, Raymond E. Bartholomae, Peter J. Astrauskas, Eric R. Zimmerman, AXA Financial, Inc., Insiders

DCAP Group Inc

1158 Broadway, Hewlett, NY, 11557; **PH:** 1-516-374-7600; **Fax:** 1-516-295-7216; **http://** www.dcapgroup.com

General - Incorporation	DE	Stock - Price on:12/24/2007	$2.68
Employees	87	Stock Exchange	NDQ
Auditor	Holtz Rubenstein Reminick LLP	Ticker Symbol	DCAP
Stk Agt	American Stock Transfer & Trust Co.	Outstanding Shares	2,960,000
Counsel	Certilman Balin Adler & Hyman LLP	E.P.S.	$0.10
DUNS No.	61-420-4253	Shareholders	NA

Business: The group's principal activity is to provide information about insurance and financing to individual customers. The group operates under two segments insurance and premium finance. Insurance segment deals with the insurance needs of individual customers providing insurance assistance to automobile, motorcycle and homeowners. Premium financing provides loan to pay insurance premium. The group also offers automobile club services for roadside emergencies. The group owns 44 franchised locations, 24 wholly-owned offices and one joint venture office for the sale of retail auto, motorcycle, boat, business, and home owner's insurance, and provide premium financing of insurance policies for customers of their offices as well as customers of non-affiliated entities. In Jan 2003, our subsidiary, iah, inc., discontinued the operations of the international airport hotel in san juan, Puerto Rico. On 28-May-2003, the group acquired aia acquisition corp.

Primary SIC and add'l.: 6159 6411

CIK No: 0000033992

Subsidiaries: AA DCAP Greenbrook Inc., Aard-vark Agency, Ltd., Aia-dcap Corp., Baron Cycle, Inc., Barry Scott Acquisition Corp., Barry Scott Agency Inc., Barry Scott Companies, Inc., Blast Acquisition Corp., DCAP Management Corp., Dealers Choice Automotive Planning Inc., Drive Insurance Agency, Inc., IAH, Inc., Intandem Corp., Payments Inc.

Officers: Barry B. Goldstein/55/Chmn., CEO, CFO, Pres., Barry G. Lefkowitz/VP - Marketing, Product Development, Jeffrey C. Schwartz/VP - Payments, Kathleen Farrell/VP - Franchise Operations

Directors: Barry B. Goldstein/55/Chmn., CEO, CFO, Pres., Jay M. Haft/72/Vice Chmn., Jack D. Seibald/Dir., Morton Certilman/Dir., David A. Lyons/Dir.

Owners: AIA Acquisition Corp/10.90%, Barry B. Goldstein/13.20%, David A. Lyons, Jay M. Haft/5.30%, Infinity Capital Partners, L.P./14.00%, Jack D. Seibald/9.10%, Insiders/33.70%, Morton L. Certilman/5.70%, Eagle Insurance Company/10.00%

Financial Data: Fiscal Year End:12/31   **Latest Annual Data:** 12/31/2006

Year	Sales	Net Income
2006	$11,082,000	$508,000
2005	$13,921,000	$496,000
2004	$15,088,000	$1,374,000

Curr. Assets:	$17,856,000	Curr. Liab.:	$15,824,000	P/E Ratio:	16.75
Plant, Equip.:	$356,000	Total Liab.:	$18,628,000	Indic. Yr. Divd.:	NA
Total Assets:	$25,403,000	Net Worth:	$5,994,000	Debt/ Equity:	NA

DCB Financial Corp

110 Riverbend Ave., Lewis Center, OH, 43035; **PH:** 1-740-657-7000; **Fax:** 1-740-657-7901; **http://** www.dcbfinancialcorp.com; **Email:** relations@dcbfinancialcorp.com

General - Incorporation	OH	Stock - Price on:12/24/2007	$23
Employees	183	Stock Exchange	OTC
Auditor	Grant Thornton LLP	Ticker Symbol	DCBF
Stk Agt	DCB Financial Corp	Outstanding Shares	3,740,000
Counsel	NA	E.P.S.	$1.44
DUNS No.	NA	Shareholders	NA

Business: The group's principal activities are to provide retail and commercial banking services to its customers. The operations of the group are carried out through sixteen banking locations in Delaware, franklin and union counties, Ohio. The deposit products include checking and savings accounts, time deposits, iras, safe deposit facilities. The loan portfolio includes personal loans, commercial loans, real estate mortgage loans and installment loans. The other services provided include cash management, bond registrar and paying services and data processing services to other financial institutions.

Primary SIC and add'l.: 6712 6022

CIK No: 0001025877

Subsidiaries: The Delaware County Bank and Trust Company

Officers: Jeffrey T. Benton/Dir., CEO, Pres., John A. Ustaszewski/Sr. VP, CFO/$134,984.00, Thomas R. Whitney/Sr. VP - Wealth Management/$167,590.00, Barbara S. Walters/Sr. VP - Retail Banking/$141,352.00, Jay D. Wolf/VP - Marketing, Customer Relations, Brian E. Stanfill/Sr. VP - Operations, Human Resources/$138,547.00, Jerry S. Whittington/Sr. VP - Lending/$156,392.00

Directors: Jeffrey T. Benton/Dir., CEO, Pres., Terry M. Kramer/Chmn., William R. Oberfield/Dir., Edward Powers/Dir., Adam Stevenson/Dir., Jerome J. Harmeyer/Dir., Vicki J. Lewis/Dir., Gary M. Skinner/Dir., Donald J. Wolf/Dir., Phillip F. Connolly/Dir.

Owners: Donald J. Wolf, Gary M. Skinner, Adam Stevenson, Barbara Walters, Jeffrey T. Benton, Vicki J. Lewis, Terry M. Kramer/1.34%, Edward Powers, Jerry Whittington, Insiders/6.12%, Phillip Connolly, John D. Wolf, Thomas R. Whitney, Brian Stanfill, John A. Ustaszewski (17 Owners included in Index)

Financial Data: Fiscal Year End:12/31 **Latest Annual Data:** 12/31/2006

Year	Sales	Net Income
2006	$50,033,000	$7,353,000
2005	$42,255,000	$7,556,000
2004	$35,575,000	$6,975,000

Curr. Assets:	$21,889,000	**Curr. Liab.:**	$620,473,000	**P/E Ratio:**	13.86
Plant, Equip.:	$9,468,000	**Total Liab.:**	$620,473,000	**Indic. Yr. Divd.:**	$0.640
Total Assets:	$681,872,000	**Net Worth:**	$61,399,000	**Debt/ Equity:**	NA

DCI USA Inc

20 W 64th St., New York, NY, 10023; **PH:** 1-718-383-5255; http://www.dci-usa.com

General - Incorporation	DE	**Stock**- Price on:12/24/2007	$0.07
Employees	NA	Stock Exchange	OTC
Auditor	Seligson & Giannattasio LLP	Ticker Symbol	DCIU
Stk Agt	American Stock Transfer & Trust Co.	Outstanding Shares	53,290,000
Counsel	NA	E.P.S.	-$0.02
DUNS No.	NA	Shareholders	NA

Business: The group's principal activity is to own and operate income producing real estate. The group operates through its wholly owned subsidiary spring village holdings, inc. Which owns 31% controlling interest in svg properties, lp. The partnership owns 124 unit apartment complex. The spring village apartment complex owned by the group is a garden-type apartment complex, which consists of seven buildings containing 60 one-bedroom units, 49 two-bedroom units, 15 studio units and two garages. This is located in sharon hill, Delaware county, Pennsylvania. The customers of the group are moderate-income people. The group operates solely in the United States.

Primary SIC and add'l.: 6513

CIK No: 0001120210

Subsidiaries: Bartram Holdings, Inc., Spring Village Holdings, Inc.

Officers: Jonathan Ilan Ofir/44/Chmn., CEO, Karen Pitts/Administrative Assist., Stephen Solch/Pres., Michael Gibbs/70/CFO, Steve Barno/Dir. - Business Development, Cathy Manker/Human Resources Administrator, David Martin/Operations Mgr.

Directors: Jonathan Ilan Ofir/44/Chmn., CEO, Gregory Bitterman/46/Dir., Marc Narboni/49/Dir., Seth Yakatan/36/Dir.

Owners: Jonathan Ilan Ofir/52.00%, Jonathan Rigbi/10.00%, Paget Worldwide Holdings/6.70%, DCI Ltd./5.30%

Financial Data: Fiscal Year End:12/31 **Latest Annual Data:** 12/31/2006

Year	Sales	Net Income
2006	$160,000	-$535,000
2005	$200,000	-$479,000
2004	$85,000	-$56,000

Curr. Assets:	$919,000	**Curr. Liab.:**	$1,631,000		
Plant, Equip.:	$3,000	**Total Liab.:**	$1,662,000	**Indic. Yr. Divd.:**	NA
Total Assets:	$2,348,000	**Net Worth:**	$687,000	**Debt/ Equity:**	NA

DCP Midstream Partners LP

370 17th St., Ste. 2775, Denver, CO, 80202; **PH:** 1-303-633-2900; **Fax:** 1-303-605-2225; http://www.dcppartners.com

General - Incorporation	DE	**Stock**- Price on:12/24/2007	$45.8
Employees	NA	Stock Exchange	NYSE
Auditor	Deloitte & Touche LLP	Ticker Symbol	DPM
Stk Agt	American Stock Transfer & Trust Co.	Outstanding Shares	17,700,000
Counsel	NA	E.P.S.	$1.53
DUNS No.	NA	Shareholders	NA

Business: The groups principle activities include gathering, compressing, treating, processing, transporting and selling natural gas and natural gas liquids. The group operates through three segments namely, natural gas services, wholesale propane logistics and NGL logistics. The group operates from the United States. The group's quarterly revenue for September 2007 was 188.60 millions of USD.

Primary SIC and add'l.: 4613 4922

CIK No: 0001338065

Subsidiaries: Associated Louisiana Intrastate Pipe Line, LLC, DCP Assets Holding, LP, DCP Assets Holdings GP, LLC, DCP Black Lake Holding, LP, DCP Intrastate Pipeline, LLC, DCP Midstream Operating, LLC, DCP Midstream Operating, LP, Gas Supply Resources LLC, GSRI Transportation LLC, Pelico Pipeline, LLC, Pine Tree Propane Limited Liability Company, Wilbreeze Pipeline, LP

Officers: Mark A. Borer/Dir., CEO, Pres., Thomas E. Long/CFO, VP, Michael S. Richards/VP, General Counsel, Sec., Greg K. Smith/VP - Business Development, Karen Taylor/Investor Relations Contact

Directors: Mark A. Borer/Dir., CEO, Pres., Jim W. Mogg/59/Chmn., Fred J. Fowler/Chmn., Stephen R. Springer/Dir., Derrill Cody/Dir., William H. Easter/Dir., Paul F. Ferguson/Dir., John E. Lowe/Dir., Frank A. McPherson/Dir., Thomas C. Morris/Dir.

Owners: Michael S. Richards, Mark A. Borer, Derrill Cody, John E. Lowe, DCP LP Holdings, LP, Thomas C. Morris, Fiduciary Asset Management, L.L.C./9.40%, Thomas E. Long, Insiders, Greg K. Smith, Williams, Jones & Associates, LLC/9.40%, Paul F. Ferguson, William H. Easter, Frank A. McPherson, DCP Midstream, LLC (16 Owners included in Index)

Financial Data: Fiscal Year End:12/31 **Latest Annual Data:** 12/31/2006

Year	Sales	Net Income
2006	$795,800,000	$33,000,000
2005	$784,500,000	$38,000,000

Curr. Assets:	$159,600,000	**Curr. Liab.:**	$126,500,000	**P/E Ratio:**	21.01
Plant, Equip.:	$194,700,000	**Total Liab.:**	$398,200,000	**Indic. Yr. Divd.:**	$2.200
Total Assets:	$501,600,000	**Net Worth:**	$103,400,000	**Debt/ Equity:**	2.6804

DDi Corp

1220 Simon Cir., Anaheim, CA, 92806; **PH:** 1-714-688-7200; **Fax:** 1-714-688-7400 ; http://www.ddiglobal.com

General - Incorporation	DE	**Stock**- Price on:12/24/2007	$7.75
Employees	1,300	Stock Exchange	NDQ
Auditor	PricewaterhouseCoopers LLP	Ticker Symbol	DDIC
Stk Agt	Mellon Investor Services LLC	Outstanding Shares	22,610,000
Counsel	Skadden, Meagher & Flom LLP	E.P.S.	-$0.45
DUNS No.	NA	Shareholders	NA

Business: The group's principal activities are to provide design, development and manufacturing services to original equipment manufacturers and other providers of electronics manufacturing services. The group specializes in providing technologically advanced services to its customers on a short turnaround basis and focuses on this segment of the electronics manufacturing services industry. It offers integrated services in support of its customers' new development. The services provided enable the customers to develop and produce a wide variety of end products, including communications, switching and transmission equipment, wireless base stations, work stations, high-end computing equipment and data networking equipment. Its customers include intel, marconi communications, motorola, bae systems rotork and thales.

Primary SIC and add'l.: 3672

CIK No: 0001104252

Subsidiaries: DDi Capital Corp, DDi Europe Limited, Dynamic Details, Incorporated (Dynamic Details), Toppan Electronics Ltd

Officers: Mikel Williams/Dir., CEO/$2,239,923.00, Sally Goff/CFO/$386,791.00, Rajesh Kumar/VP - Research, Development, Robert Houghton/CIO, VP, Michael Mathews/Sr. VP - Manufacturing Operations/$565,929.00, Kurt E. Scheuerman/VP, General Counsel, Jerry Barnes/Sr. VP - Sales, Gerald P. Barnes/49/Sr. VP - Sales

Directors: Mikel Williams/Dir., CEO, Jay B. Hunt/Chmn., Carl Vertuca/Dir., Steven Schlepp/Dir., Robert Amman/Dir., Andrew Lietz/Dir., Bryant Riley/Dir.

Financial Data: Fiscal Year End:12/31 **Latest Annual Data:** 12/31/2006

Year	Sales	Net Income
2006	$198,115,000	-$7,233,000
2005	$184,625,000	-$63,974,000
2004	$189,007,000	-$45,865,000

Curr. Assets:	$56,218,000	**Curr. Liab.:**	$24,988,000		
Plant, Equip.:	$31,162,000	**Total Liab.:**	$30,044,000	**Indic. Yr. Divd.:**	NA
Total Assets:	$139,611,000	**Net Worth:**	$109,567,000	**Debt/ Equity:**	0.0158

DDS Technologies USA Inc

150 E Palmetto Pk. Rd. , Ste. 510, Boca Raton, FL, 33432; **PH:** 1-561-750-4450; **Fax:** 1-561-750-4310; http://www.ddstechusa.com; **Email:** info@ddstechusa.com

General - Incorporation	NV	**Stock**- Price on:12/24/2007	NA
Employees	NA	Stock Exchange	OTC
Auditor	Weinberg & Company, P.A.	Ticker Symbol	DDSU
Stk Agt	Corporate Stock Transfer, Inc.	Outstanding Shares	NA
Counsel	NA	E.P.S.	-$0.133
DUNS No.	NA	Shareholders	NA

Business: The groups principal activity is to develop Disaggregation Dry System. The group operates from Canada and the United State.

Primary SIC and add'l.: 2499

CIK No: 0001099217

Subsidiaries: DDS Holdings, Inc.

Officers: Spencer L. Sterling/Interim Chmn., CEO, Pres., Kerin Franklin/CTO, Sr. VP, Randall Bachtel/VP - Design, Manufacturing, Joseph N. Fasciglione/Sec., Treasurer, CFO

Directors: Spencer L. Sterling/Interim Chmn., CEO, Pres., Robert L. Devereux/Dir., Dennis Duitch/Dir., Marc Jeffrey Mallis/Dir.

Owners: Insiders/19.20%, Joseph Fasciglione, Dennis Duitch/1.00%, Craig L. Farlie, Kerin Franklin/2.80%, Marc J. Mallis/4.99%, Spencer L. Sterling/4.60%, Lee Rosen/5.70%, Robert L. Devereux/4.70%

Financial Data: Fiscal Year End:12/31 **Latest Annual Data:** 12/31/2005

Year	Sales	Net Income
2005	NA	-$4,644,000
2004	NA	-$6,991,000
2003	NA	-$4,670,000

Curr. Assets:	$2,137,000	**Curr. Liab.:**	$5,336,000		
Plant, Equip.:	$16,000	**Total Liab.:**	$5,336,000	**Indic. Yr. Divd.:**	NA
Total Assets:	$7,099,000	**Net Worth:**	$992,000	**Debt/ Equity:**	NA

De Beira Goldfields Inc

16801 Addison Rd., Ste. 310, Addison, TX, 75001; **PH:** 1-214-866-0606; **Fax:** 1-214-866-0460; http://www.dealeradvance.com; **Email:** support@dealeradvance.com

General - Incorporation	NV	**Stock**- Price on:12/24/2007	NA
Employees	NA	Stock Exchange	OTC
Auditor	GHP Horwath, P.C.	Ticker Symbol	DBGF
Stk Agt	Empire Stock Transfer Inc.	Outstanding Shares	NA
Counsel	R.H. Daignault Law Corp	E.P.S.	NA
DUNS No.	NA	Shareholders	NA

Business: The groups principal activity is to explore minerals. The group operates from Canada and the United State.

Primary SIC and add'l.: 1000

CIK No: 0001345756

Officers: Steven Humphries/CEO, Pres., Raj Sharma/CIO, Dave Scaturro/VP - Sales, David Wange/CFO, Jen Roberts/Dir. - Sales

Owners: Insiders/15.20%, Klaus Eckhof/1.60%, Reg Gillard/13.60%

Financial Data: Fiscal Year End:08/31 Latest Annual Data: 11/30/2006

Year	Sales	Net Income
2006	NA	-$1,411,000

Curr. Assets:	$1,337,000	**Curr. Liab.:**	$39,000		
Plant, Equip.:	NA	**Total Liab.:**	$39,000	**Indic. Yr. Divd.:**	NA
Total Assets:	$3,737,000	**Net Worth:**	$3,698,000	**Debt/ Equity:**	NA

De Rigo SpA

Zona Industriale Villanova, 12, Longarone Bl, 32012; **PH:** 39-04377777; **http://** www.derigo.com; **Email:** info@derigo.com

General - Incorporation	Italy	**Stock** - Price on:12/24/2007	NA
Employees	NA	Stock Exchange	NA
Auditor	Ernst & Young LLP	Ticker Symbol	NA
Stk Agt	NA	Outstanding Shares	NA
Counsel	NA	E.P.S.	NA
DUNS No.	42-954-9488	Shareholders	NA

Business: The group's principal activities are to design, manufacture and distribute prescription spectacles frames and sunglasses. The group offers a wide range of high quality models manufactured under owned brands (police, sting, rolling & lozza) as well as under licensed designer names (fendi, celine, loewe, prada, etc) and licensed trademarks (fila eyes, etro). Designed in Italy, the group's products are distributed in about 80 countries worldwide, primarily in Europe, Asia and the Americas.

Primary SIC and add'l.: 3851 5048

CIK No: 0001001462

Subsidiaries: De Rigo France S.a., De Rigo Hellas A.E.E., De Rigo Hong Kong Ltd, De Rigo Japan Ltd Co, De Rigo UK Ltd, De Rigo Vision S.p.A, Vogart Line Espaa S.A

Dealeradvance Inc

16801 Addison Rd., Ste. 310, Addison, TX, 75001; **PH:** 1-214-866-0606; **Fax:** 1-214-866-0460; **http://** www.dealeradvance.com; **Email:** support@dealeradvance.com

General - Incorporation		**Stock** - Price on:12/24/2007	$0.0013
Employees	7	Stock Exchange	OTC
Auditor	Paritz & Co., P.A.	Ticker Symbol	DLAV
Stk Agt	Continental Stock Transfer & Trust Co	Outstanding Shares	50,570,000
Counsel	NA	E.P.S.	-$0.109
DUNS No.	NA	Shareholders	NA

Business: The groups principle activity is to provide enterprise software solutions for the automotive industry. The groups support services include telephone help line, equipment repair and replacement, and remote diagnostics services. The group operates from United States.

Primary SIC and add'l.: 3571 7372

CIK No: 0001133598

Officers: Steven Humphries/55/Chmn., CEO, Pres., Raj Sharma/CIO, Dave Scaturro/VP - Sales, David Wange/CFO, Jen Roberts/Dir. - Sales

Directors: Steven Humphries/55/Chmn., CEO, Pres.

Owners: Christopher J. Carey/50.87%, Stanford Venture Capital Holdings/20.54%

Financial Data: Fiscal Year End:12/31 Latest Annual Data: 12/31/2006

Year	Sales	Net Income
2006	$479,000	-$4,444,000
2005	$944,000	-$3,632,000
2004	$2,490,000	-$3,090,000

Curr. Assets:	$234,000	**Curr. Liab.:**	$8,132,000		
Plant, Equip.:	$3,000	**Total Liab.:**	$12,551,000	**Indic. Yr. Divd.:**	NA
Total Assets:	$247,000	**Net Worth:**	-$12,304,000	**Debt/ Equity:**	NA

DealerTrack Holdings Inc

1111 Marcus Ave., Ste. M04, Lake Success, NY, 11042; **PH:** 1-516-734-3600; **Fax:** 1-516-734-3809; **http://** www.dealertrack.com

General - Incorporation	DE	**Stock** - Price on:12/24/2007	$36.77
Employees	670	Stock Exchange	NDQ
Auditor	PricewaterhouseCoopers LLP	Ticker Symbol	TRAK
Stk Agt	NA	Outstanding Shares	39,650,000
Counsel	NA	E.P.S.	$0.54
DUNS No.	NA	Shareholders	NA

Business: The groups principle activity is to provide software, network and data solutions. The groups services include dealers, aftermarket providers, financing sources. The group products sold under the trade names Chrome Carbook(R), PC Carbook(R) WebsitePlus(TM), SalesMaker(TM), ExactID(TM) and DealTransfer(TM). The group acquired DealerWare L.L.C, Global Fax L.L.C and WiredLogic, Inc in the year 2006and Automotive Lease Guide LLC, North American Advanced Technology, Inc and Chrome Systems Corporation in the year 2005. The group operates from the United States and Canada.

Primary SIC and add'l.: 7372 7372 7373

CIK No: 0001333513

Subsidiaries: Automotive Lease Guide (alg), Inc., Chrome Systems, Inc., Credit Online, Inc., Curomax Canada Inc., Curomax Limited, DealerAccess Canada Inc., DealerAccess, Inc., DealerTrack Aftermarket Services, Inc., DealerTrack Data Services, Inc., DealerTrack Digital Services, Inc., DealerTrack Services Corp., DealerTrack, Inc., webalg, inc.

Officers: Mark F. O'Neil/Chmn., CEO, John A. Blair/Pres. - ALG, Chrome Systems, Robert J. Cox/CFO, Sr. VP, Treasurer, Charles J. Giglia/CIO, Sr. VP - Dealertrack, Inc, Ana M. Herrera/Sr. VP - Human Resources, Dealertrack, Inc, Eric D. Jacobs/Sr. VP, General Counsel, Sec., Richard McLeer/Sr. VP - Strategy, Development, Rajesh Sundaram/Sr. VP - Dealer Solutions, Rick G. Von Push/Sr. VP - Customer Development, Vincent Passione/Pres. - Dealertrack, Inc, David P. Trinder/Sr. VP - Network Solutions

Directors: Mark F. O'Neil/Chmn., CEO, Mary Cirillo-Goldberg/Dir., Steven J. Dietz/Dir., Thomas R. Gibson/Dir., Thomas F. Gilman/57/Dir., John J. McDonnell/Dir., James David Power/Dir., Howard L. Tischler/Dir., Ann B. Lane/53/Dir., Barry Zwarenstein/Dir.

Owners: Steven J. Dietz, Robert J. Cox, Mark F. ONeil/3.25%, Thomas R. Gibson, Raj Sundaram, John A. Blair, Insiders/21.10%, Mary Cirillo-Goldberg, Howard L. Tischler/13.79%, John J. McDonnell, FMR Corp./7.87%, First Advantage Corporation/13.69%, Fred Alger Management, Inc./5.12%, James David Power, Eric D. Jacobs *(16 Owners included in Index)*

Financial Data: Fiscal Year End:12/31 Latest Annual Data: 12/31/2006

Year	Sales	Net Income
2006	$173,272,000	$19,336,000
2005	$120,219,000	$4,468,000
2004	$70,044,000	$11,253,000

Curr. Assets:	$198,330,000	**Curr. Liab.:**	$29,513,000	**P/E Ratio:**	68.09
Plant, Equip.:	$6,157,000	**Total Liab.:**	$37,176,000	**Indic. Yr. Divd.:**	NA
Total Assets:	$321,513,000	**Net Worth:**	$284,337,000	**Debt/ Equity:**	0.0102

Dean Foods Co

2515 Mckinney Ave. Lb 30, Ste. 1200, Dallas, TX, 75201; **PH:** 1-214-303-3400; **http://** www.deanfoods.com

General - Incorporation	DE	**Stock** - Price on:12/24/2007	$32.09
Employees	26,348	Stock Exchange	NYSE
Auditor	Deloitte & Touche LLP	Ticker Symbol	DF
Stk Agt	Bank of New York	Outstanding Shares	130,000,000
Counsel	NA	E.P.S.	$1.25
DUNS No.	92-918-2210	Shareholders	NA

Business: The groups principle activities include processing and distributing fresh milk and other dairy products. The group operates through two segments namely dairy group and whitewave foods. The group operates from United States.

Primary SIC and add'l.: 2024 2020 2026 5142 5149

CIK No: 0000931336

Subsidiaries: 31 Logistics, Inc., Abastecimientos Lacteos Gallegos S.L., Alta-Dena Certified Dairy, Inc., Barber Ice Cream, LLC, Barber Milk, Inc., Berkeley Farms, Inc., Broughton Foods, LLC, Colorado ES LLC, Country Delite Farms, LLC, Country Fresh, LLC, Creamland Dairies, Inc., Curan, LLC, Dairy Fresh, LLC, Dairy Group Receivables GP II, LLC, Dairy Group Receivables GP, LLC 127 Subsidiaries included in the Index

Officers: Gregg L. Engles/Chmn., CEO/$11,025,490.00, Joseph E. Scalzo/CEO, Pres. - Whitewave Foods Company, Ronald H. Klein/42/Sr. VP - Corporate Development, Jack F. Callahan/CFO, Exec. VP/$1,640,387.00, Steven J. Kemps/Sr. VP, Deputy General Counsel, Corp. Sec., Scott Stevens/VP, GM - Silk, Robert Dunn/Sr. VP - Human Resources, Dean Dairy Group, Arthur F. Fino/CIO, Sr. VP, Michelle P. Goolsby/Exec. VP, Chief Administrative Officer, General Counsel, Corp. Sec./$2,577,087.00, Mike Keown/Pres. - Indulgent Brands, Roger Theodoredis/Sr. VP, Division General Counsel, Scott J. Toth/Sr. VP - Operations, Greg McKelvey/Sr. VP - Strategic Planning, Bill Tinklepaugh/Sr. VP - Government, Industry Relations, Ronald L. McCrummen/Chief Accounting Officer, Sr. VP *(28 Officers included in Index)*

Directors: Gregg L. Engles/Chmn., CEO, Pete Schenkel/Vice Chmn., Alan J. Bernon/Dir., Lewis M. Collens/Dir., Stephen L. Green/Dir., Tom Davis/Dir., Janet Hill/Dir., Joseph S. Hardin/Dir., Ronald Kirk/Dir., John R. Muse/Dir., Hector M. Nevares/Dir., Jim L. Turner/Dir., John S. Llewellyn/73/Dir.

Owners: Iridian Asset Management LLC/5.60%, Joseph E. Scalzo, Stephen L. Green, Barclays Global Investors, NA/6.35%, Jim L. Turner, Joseph S. Hardin, John S. Llewellyn, Lewis M. Collens, John R. Muse, Jack F. Callahan, Ronald L. McCrummen, Gregg L. Engles/3.93%, Hector M. Nevares, Barry A. Fromberg, Michelle P. Goolsby *(22 Owners included in Index)*

Financial Data: Fiscal Year End:12/31 Latest Annual Data: 12/31/2006

Year	Sales	Net Income
2006	$10,098,555,000	$225,414,000
2005	$10,505,560,000	$327,531,000
2004	$10,822,285,000	$285,374,000

Curr. Assets:	$1,379,290,000	**Curr. Liab.:**	$1,336,556,000	**P/E Ratio:**	18.66
Plant, Equip.:	$1,786,907,000	**Total Liab.:**	$4,960,774,000	**Indic. Yr. Divd.:**	NA
Total Assets:	$6,770,173,000	**Net Worth:**	$1,809,399,000	**Debt/ Equity:**	1.5229

Dearborn Bancorp Inc

1360 Porter St., Dearborn, MI, 48124; **PH:** 1-313-565-5700; **Fax:** 1-313-561-2291; **http://** www.fidbank.com

General - Incorporation	MI	**Stock** - Price on:12/24/2007	$17.36
Employees	157	Stock Exchange	NDQ
Auditor	Crowe Chizek & Co. LLC	Ticker Symbol	DEAR
Stk Agt	Computershare Investor Services LLC	Outstanding Shares	8,650,000
Counsel	NA	E.P.S.	-$1.89
DUNS No.	80-590-0115	Shareholders	NA

Business: The group's principal activity is to provide financial products and services. The group is a one-bank holding company, which operates through its banking subsidiary community bank of dearborn. Services provided by the group include checking accounts, savings accounts, money market accounts, certificates of deposit, business checking and direct deposits. The group also provides commercial, consumer and real estate mortgage loans. Other services include travelers' checks, cashiers' checks, wire transfers, safety deposit boxes, collection services and night depository services. The group conducts its business through six branch offices in western wayne county and one office in macomb county.

Primary SIC and add'l.: 6022 6712

CIK No: 0000895541

Officers: Michael J. Ross/Dir., CEO, Pres./$515,654.00, Stephen C. Tarczy/Northeast Regional Pres./$292,925.00, Warren R. Musson/Sr. VP, Head - Lending/$274,234.00, Jeffrey L. Karafa/Sr. VP, CFO/$236,343.00, Jeffrey J. Wolber/Sr. VP, Head - Retail/$221,731.00, John A. Lindsey/Oakland Regional Pres.

Directors: Michael J. Ross/Dir., CEO, Pres., John E. Demmer/Chmn., Donald G. Karcher/Dir., Michael V. Dorian/Dir., Margaret I. Campbell/Dir., Jeffrey G. Longstreth/Dir., William J. Demmer/Dir., Robert C. Schwyn/Dir., Bradley F. Keller/Dir., David Himick/Dir.

Owners: Ronnie J. Story, Jeffrey L. Karafa, John E. Demmer/3.50%, Michael V. Dorian, Warren R. Musson/1.05%, Margaret I. Campbell, Donald G. Karcher, Jeffrey J. Wolber, Stephen C. Tarczy, William J. Demmer, Insiders/17.52%, David Himick/3.82%, Robert C. Schwyn, Jeffrey G. Longstreth, Michael J. Ross/1.69% *(16 Owners included in Index)*

Financial Data: Fiscal Year End:12/31 Latest Annual Data: 06/30/2007

Year	Sales	Net Income
2007	NA	NA
2006	$54,914,000	$7,819,000
2005	$45,317,000	$7,510,000

Curr. Assets:	$73,367,000	Curr. Liab.:	$700,430,000	P/E Ratio:	18.87
Plant, Equip.:	$14,345,000	Total Liab.:	$710,946,000	Indic. Yr. Divd.:	NA
Total Assets:	$855,931,000	Net Worth:	$144,985,000	Debt/ Equity:	0.0689

Debt Resolve Inc

707 Westchester Ave., Ste. L7, White Plains, NY, 10604; *PH:* 1-914-949-5500;
Fax: 1-914-428-3044; *http://* www.debtresolve.com; *Email:* info@debtresolve.com

General - Incorporation	DE	**Stock** - Price on:12/24/2007	$3.55
Employees	NA	Stock Exchange	AMEX
Auditor	Marcum & Kliegman LLP	Ticker Symbol	DRV
Stk Agt	American Stock Transfer & Trust Co.	Outstanding Shares	7,210,000
Counsel	NA	E.P.S.	-$4.13
DUNS No.	NA	Shareholders	NA

Business: The groups principle activity is to provide software solutions. The groups products marketed under the brand name DebtResolve(R). The group is in development stage. The group operates from the United States. The groups quarterly revenue for September 2007 was 0.53 millions of USD.

Primary SIC and add'l.: 7372 7374

CIK No: 0001106645

Officers: James D. Burchetta/Co - Chmn., CEO, Richard Rosa/CTO, Pres., Sandra Styer/Sr. VP, Dir. - Client Services, Katherine Dering/60/CFO, Sec., Treasurer, Howard Knauer/Pres. - DRV Capital, Dan Casey/Mgr. - Operations, Denis Dirin/Sr. Systems Developer, Tony Sakovsky/Dir. - Technical Operations, Rene Samson/Mgr. - Application Development, John Grimm/VP - Sales, Ehmonie Hainey/Public Relations Coordinator, Greg Rando/Dir., Project Mgr. - DRV Capital, Nancy Hutter/Human Resources, John Baldissera/Investor Relations Officer, Frank Pocock/Contact - UK, Europe

Directors: James D. Burchetta/Co - Chmn., CEO, Charles S. Brofman/Co - Chmn., Don Whittaker/Chmn. - Advisory Board, Alan M. Silberstein/Dir., Lawrence Dwyer/Dir., William Mooney/Dir., Michael G. Carey/Dir., Jeffrey S. Bernstein/Dir., Jamie T. Buckley/Member - Advisory Board, Robert Dunham/Member - Advisory Board, Richard Singer/Member - Advisory Board

Owners: Insiders/49.80%, Katherine A. Dering/2.30%, Michael G. Carey, Charles S. Brofman/25.10%, Alan M. Silberstein/4.50%, Lawrence E. Dwyer/2.00%, Richard Rosa/5.60%, Jeffrey S. Bernstein, James D. Burchetta/20.30%, William H. Mooney/6.90%

Financial Data: Fiscal Year End:12/31 Latest Annual Data: 12/31/2006

Year	Sales	Net Income
2006	$98,000	-$21,696,000
2005	$24,000	-$5,404,000
2004	$3,000	-$2,669,000

Curr. Assets:	$5,025,000	Curr. Liab.:	$490,000		
Plant, Equip.:	$180,000	Total Liab.:	$490,000	Indic. Yr. Divd.:	NA
Total Assets:	$5,300,000	Net Worth:	$4,810,000	Debt/ Equity:	NA

Deckers Outdoor Corp

495-A S Fairview Ave., Goleta, CA, 93117; *PH:* 1-805-967-7611; *Fax:* 1-805-967-7862;
http:// www.deckers.com

General - Incorporation	DE	**Stock** - Price on:12/24/2007	$95.89
Employees	276	Stock Exchange	NDQ
Auditor	KPMG LLP	Ticker Symbol	DECK
Stk Agt	Mellon Investor Services LLC	Outstanding Shares	12,790,000
Counsel	Sheppard Mullin Richter & Hampton LLP	E.P.S.	$3.30
DUNS No.	07-292-9078	Shareholders	NA

Business: The group's principal activity is to design and market innovative, functional and fashion-oriented footwear developed for both high performance outdoor activities and everyday casual lifestyle use. The group currently offers three primary product lines marketed under the following brand names: teva (r): sports sandals and rugged outdoor and casual footwear; simple(r): shoes that combine the comfort elements of athletic footwear with casual styling and ugg (r): sheepskin boots and other footwear. The group's principal domestic customers include specialty retailers, upscale department stores, outdoor retailers, sporting goods retailers and shoe stores.

Primary SIC and add'l.: 7379 3149 9999 3021

CIK No: 0000910521

Subsidiaries: Deckers Asia Pacific Limited, Deckers Consumer Direct Corporation, Deckers Europe B.V., Deckers Europe Limited, Deckers International Limited, Holbrook Limited, Phillipsburg Limited

Officers: Angel R. Martinez/Dir., CEO, Pres., Peter Worley/Pres. - Teva Brand, Zohar Ziv/CFO, Exec. VP - Finance, Administration, Colin Clark/Sr. VP - International, Constance X. Rishwain/Pres. - Simple, Ugg Divisions, John A. Kalinich/VP - Consumer, Patrick C. Devaney/Sr. VP, VP - Global Sourcing, Production, Development, Janice M. Howell/VP - Operations, Chad Jacobs/Integrated Corporate Relations, Primary Investor Relations Officer, Brenden Frey/Integrated Corporate Relations, Primary Investor Relations Officer

Directors: Angel R. Martinez/Dir., CEO, Pres., Douglas B. Otto/Chmn., Danie Rheggen/Dir., Gene E. Burleson/Dir., John M. Gibbons/Dir., Rex A. Licklider/Dir., John Perenchio/Dir., Daniel L. Terheggen/Dir., Tore Steen/Dir., Maureen Conners/Dir.

Owners: Daniel L. Terheggen, Patrick C. Devaney, Insiders/6.90%, Rex A. Licklider/1.70%, John G. Perenchio, FMR Corp./14.90%, John M. Gibbons, Maureen Conners, Douglas B. Otto/4.20%, Zohar Ziv, Barclays Global Investors Japan Limited/5.80%, Angel R. Martinez, Gene E. Burleson

Financial Data: Fiscal Year End:12/31 Latest Annual Data: 12/31/2006

Year	Sales	Net Income
2006	$304,423,000	$30,609,000
2005	$264,760,000	$31,845,000
2004	$214,787,000	$25,539,000

Curr. Assets:	$187,423,000	Curr. Liab.:	$39,563,000	P/E Ratio:	35.12
Plant, Equip.:	$7,770,000	Total Liab.:	$39,563,000	Indic. Yr. Divd.:	NA
Total Assets:	$249,973,000	Net Worth:	$210,410,000	Debt/ Equity:	NA

deCODE Genetics Inc

1000 Winter St., Ste. 3100, Waltham, MA, 02451; *PH:* 1-781-464-0905; *Fax:* 1-781-466-8686;
http:// www.decode.com; *Email:* info@decode.is

General - Incorporation	DE	**Stock** - Price on:12/24/2007	$3.9
Employees	429	Stock Exchange	NDQ
Auditor	Deloitte & Touche LLP	Ticker Symbol	DCGN
Stk Agt	Bank of New York	Outstanding Shares	61,700,000
Counsel	Stevens & Lee PC	E.P.S.	-$1.42
DUNS No.	NA	Shareholders	NA

Business: The group's principal activity is to develop products such as drugs,genetic diagnostic tests designed to identify genetic markers associated with elevated risk of developing a disease and services for the healthcare industry. The group uses comprehensive population data and proprietary data mining tools to identify and analyze the genetic factors involved in common diseases. The group uses this information in the development of new drugs, dna-based diagnostics and bioinformatics systems and tools. The group develops and applies modern informatics technology to discover new knowledge about health and disease through data mining. The group also develops and markets the clinical genome miner, a computer based discovery system that allows users to perform real-time analysis to study the association between variation in human genes and human disease.

Primary SIC and add'l.: 8731

CIK No: 0001022974

Subsidiaries: Stellent AB, Stellent Asia Pty. Limited, Stellent B.V., Stellent Canada Ltd, Stellent Chicago Sales, Inc, Stellent Chicago, Inc, Stellent Colorado Springs, Inc, Stellent GmbH, Stellent Holding B.V. Company, Stellent Information Systems Company Limited, Stellent Japan K.K., Stellent Limited, Stellent Sales, Inc, Stellent, S.A. De C.V.

Officers: Kari Stefansson/Chmn., CEO/$1,676,658.00, Hakon Gudbjartsson/VP - Informatics, Jeffrey Gulcher/Chief Scientific Officer, Mark Gurney/Sr. VP - Drug Discovery, Development/$779,616.00, Augustine C. Kong/VP - Statistics, Joy Bessenger/IR Contact, Lance Thibault/CFO, Treasurer/$421,354.00, Daniel L. Hartman/Sr. VP - Product Development/$982,613.00, Jakob Sigurdsson/Sr. VP - Corporate Development, Axel Nielsen/COO

Directors: Kari Stefansson/Chmn., CEO, Terrance G. McGuire/Dir., James Beery/Dir., Neal J. Armstrong/Dir., Linda Buck/Dir., Birgit Norinder/Dir., Earl M. Collier/Dir., Peter Goodfellow/Dir.

Owners: SAPAC Corporation Ltd/5.20%, James Beery, Lance Thibault, Linda Buck, Insiders/6.50%, Mark Gurney, Daniel Hartman, Tomas Sigurdsson, AXA Financial, Inc. and affiliates/7.30%, Terrance G. McGuire, Kari Stefansson/5.10%, Neal J. Armstrong, T. Rowe Price Associates, Inc./15.10%, Columbia Wanger Asset Management, L.P./6.30%

Financial Data: Fiscal Year End:12/31 Latest Annual Data: 12/31/2006

Year	Sales	Net Income
2006	$40,510,000	-$85,473,000
2005	$43,955,000	-$62,750,000
2004	$42,127,000	-$57,255,000

Curr. Assets:	$169,711,000	Curr. Liab.:	$23,498,000		
Plant, Equip.:	$24,382,000	Total Liab.:	$270,988,000	Indic. Yr. Divd.:	NA
Total Assets:	$215,609,000	Net Worth:	-$55,379,000	Debt/ Equity:	NA

Decorator Industries Inc

10011 Pines Blvd., Ste. 201, Pembroke Pines, FL, 33024; *PH:* 1-954-436-8909;
Fax: 1-954-436-1778; *http://* www.decoratorindustries.com; *Email:* investor.relations@decind.com

General - Incorporation	PA	**Stock** - Price on:12/24/2007	$7.45
Employees	650	Stock Exchange	AMEX
Auditor	Louis Plung & Co. LLP	Ticker Symbol	DII
Stk Agt	American Stock Transfer & Trust Co.	Outstanding Shares	3,000,000
Counsel	Klett Rooney Lieber & Schorling	E.P.S.	-$0.14
DUNS No.	00-450-0492	Shareholders	NA

Business: The group's principal activities are designing, manufacturing and selling of interior furnishings, which includes draperies, curtains, shades, blinds, bedspreads, valance boards, comforters, pillows and cushions. The products of the group are sold to original equipment manufacturers of recreational vehicles and manufactured housing and to the hospitality industry (motels/hotels) either through distributors or directly to the customers. The customers of the group include fleetwood enterprises and champion enterprises. The group conducts its operations throughout the United States. The group acquired fleetwood enterprises's drapery operations.

Primary SIC and add'l.: 2391 2392

CIK No: 0000027613

Officers: William A. Bassett/Chmn., CEO/$414,572.00, Michael K. Solomon/VP, CFO, Treasurer, Sec./$172,700.00, Diana Hinton/Contact - Human Resources

Directors: William A. Bassett/Chmn., CEO, William C. Dixon/Dir., Ellen Downey/Dir., Thomas L. Dusthimer/Dir., Joseph N. Ellis/Dir., Terry Murphy/Dir.

Owners: Ellen Downey, Joseph N. Ellis, William A. Bassett, as Trustee for the Trust/2.37%, Thomas L. Dusthimer, William A. Bassett/11.17%, William C. Dixon

Financial Data: Fiscal Year End:12/31 Latest Annual Data: 12/30/2006

Year	Sales	Net Income
2006	$52,238,000	$405,000
2005	$50,525,000	$1,365,000

Curr. Assets:	$11,177,000	Curr. Liab.:	$5,085,000	P/E Ratio:	57.31
Plant, Equip.:	$7,432,000	Total Liab.:	$7,207,000	Indic. Yr. Divd.:	$0.120
Total Assets:	$24,294,000	Net Worth:	$17,088,000	Debt/ Equity:	0.0993

Decorize Inc

1938 E Phelps, Springfield, MO, 65802; *PH:* 1-417-879-3326; *Fax:* 1-417-879-3330;
http:// www.decorize.com

General - Incorporation	DE	**Stock** - Price on:12/24/2007	NA
Employees	324	Stock Exchange	OTC
Auditor	BKD LLP	Ticker Symbol	NA
Stk Agt	American Registrar & Transfer Co	Outstanding Shares	NA
Counsel	Hallett & Perrin PC	E.P.S.	NA
DUNS No.	NA	Shareholders	NA

Business: The group's principal activities are to manufacture and sell imported home furnishings and home accent items. The products of the group are sourced from a network of manufacturing partners in the Far East, principally from China, the Philippines, Thailand and vietnam. The group has two state-of-the-art warehouses situated in the Far East that directly ships to retail customers in the United

States. The group does business under the names 'decorize.com', 'guildmaster' and 'faith walk'. Faith walk focuses on designing hand-painted furniture and accessories; guildmaster focuses on designing wall art and special designer collections; and decorize.com focuses on designing and customizing furniture, accent pieces and accessories to meet the design needs of large retailers.

Primary SIC and add'l.: 5023 5021

CIK No: 0001095471

Subsidiaries: Faith Walk Designs, Inc., GuildMaster, Inc., P.T. Niaga Merapi, WestWay Enterprises, Ltd.

Officers: Steve Crowder/Dir., CEO, Pres., Gaylen Ball/Corp. Sec., Billie J. Montle/36/Interim VP - Finance, Corporate Controller

Directors: Steve Crowder/Dir., CEO, Pres., Steve Fox/Dir., Marwan Atalla/Dir., Rick Chalker/Dir.

Owners: Nest USA, Inc., SRC Holdings Corporation/100.00%, Stephen R. Crowder, Marwan M. Atalla, Richard Chalker, Robert M. Allison, Jon T. Baker, Insiders, James K. Parsons, Steven W. Fox, Quest Capital Alliance, L.L.C., Michael J. Sandel, SRC Holdings Corporation

Dectron Internationale Inc

10935 Crabapple Rd., Ste. 202-A, Roswell, GA, 30075; *PH:* 1-514-336-3330; *Fax:* 1-514-337-3336; *http://* www.dectron.com; *Email:* info@dectron.com

General		Stock	
Incorporation	Canada	Price on:12/24/2007	NA
Employees	400	Stock Exchange	OTC
Auditor	Schwartz Levitsky Feldman LLP	Ticker Symbol	NA
Stk Agt	Continental Stock Transfer & Trust Co	Outstanding Shares	NA
Counsel	Gersten, Savage & Kaplowitz	E.P.S.	NA
DUNS No.	24-294-8594	Shareholders	NA

Business: The group's principal activities are to manufacture and supply products for the dehumidification, refrigeration, air conditioning and indoor air quality (iaq) markets. The group operates through its subsidiaries namely dectron inc, refplus, thermoplus, klaasco, circul-aire and ipac. The products include mechanical dehumidifiers, energy recovery systems, refrigeration, air conditioning systems, air filtration products, precision cooling products, compressed air products, iaq and heat recovery and air, gas, dust and fume filtration. The major customers of the group include celebration city, walt disney world in Florida and the goodwill games.

Primary SIC and add'l.: 3564 3585

CIK No: 0001066042

Subsidiaries: Dectron Inc, Liberty Driver Property Inc., Thermoplus. Dectron, Inc.

Officers: Ness Lakdawala/Chmn., CEO, Pres., Roshan Katrak/Dir., VP - Human Resources, Mauro Parissi/42/Dir., Sec., COO, Tina Cameron/Contact, Glenn La Rusic/47/CFO, Michel Lecompte/58/Pres. - Refplus Inc, Leena Lakdawala/40/GM - Circul, Aire Inc, Harry Topikian/VP, GM - Dectron Inc, Henri Perron/Contact

Directors: Ness Lakdawala/Chmn., CEO, Pres., Mauro Parissi/42/Dir., Sec., COO, Dick Driggs/Dir., Serge Beaudet/61/Dir., Roshan Katrak/Dir., VP - Human Resources, Gilles J. Nolet/Dir.

Deere & Co

1 John Deere Pl., Moline, IL, 61265; *PH:* 1-309-765-8000; *Fax:* 1-309-765-5671; *http://* www.deere.com

General		Stock	
Incorporation	DE	Price on:12/24/2007	$122.02
Employees	46,500	Stock Exchange	NYSE
Auditor	Deloitte & Touche LLP	Ticker Symbol	DE
Stk Agt	Bank of New York	Outstanding Shares	224,980,000
Counsel	NA	E.P.S.	$4.00
DUNS No.	00-526-7471	Shareholders	NA

Business: The group principle activity is to provide farm residential, commerical and construction equipment. The group operates through four segments namely world agriculture, world wide commercial and consumer, world wide construction and John deere credt world wide. The group's products include GreenStar(TM) 2 System, round and square balers. The group operates from United States.

Primary SIC and add'l.: 3531 6159 3523 3524

CIK No: 0000315189

Subsidiaries: AGRIS Corporation, Arrendadora John Deere S.A. de C.V. (99.9% owned), Banco John Deere S.A., Cameco Do Brasil Comercial LTDA, Cameco Industries, Inc., Chamberlain Holdings Limited, Deere Capital, Inc., Deere Credit Services, Inc., Deere Credit, Inc., Deere Receivables Corporation, Farm Plan Corporation, FPC Financial f.s.b., FPC Receivables, Inc., Industrias John Deere Argentina S.A., John Deere Agricultural Holdings, Inc. 65 Subsidiaries included in the Index

Officers: Robert W. Lane/58/Chmn., CEO, James R. Jenkins/Sr. VP, General Counsel, Klaus G. Hoehn/VP - Advanced Technology, Engineering, Ganesh Jayaram/VP - Corporate Business Development, Lawrence W. Sidwell/Sr. VP - Agricultural Financial Services, Mertroe B. Hornbuckle/VP - Human Resources, Kenneth C. Huhn/VP - Industrial Relations, Frances B. Emerson/VP - Corporate Communications, Global Brand Management, Gary L. Medd/VP - Internal Audit, Linda E. Newborn/VP, Chief Compliance Officer, Dennis R. Schwartz/VP - Pension Fund, Investments, Charles R. Stamp/VP - Public Affairs Worldwide, Martin L. Wilkinson/Sr. VP - Renewable Energy, Marie Z. Ziegler/VP - Investor Relations, Marc A. Howze/Corp. Sec., Assoc. General Counsel Counsel *(46 Officers included in Index)*

Directors: Robert W. Lane/58/Chmn., CEO, Kevin T. Dunnigan/69/Dir., Vance D. Coffman/Dir., Aulana L. Peters/Dir., Richard B. Myers/Dir., Thomas H. Patrick/64/Dir., Antonio B. Madero/Dir., Charles O. Holliday/Dir., Clayton M. Jones/Dir., Joachim Milberg/64/Dir., Crandall C. Bowles/Dir., Dipak C. Jain/Dir., Arthur L. Kelly/70/Dir.

Owners: Vance D. Coffman, Samuel R. Allen, H. J. Markley, Charles O. Holliday, Nathan J. Jones, Wellington Management Company, LLP/7.60%, Capital Research and Management Company/9.20%, Richard B. Myers, FMR Corp./6.50%, Dipak C. Jain, Joachim Milberg, Arthur L. Kelly, David C. Everitt, Clayton M. Jones, Aulana L. Peters *(21 Owners included in Index)*

Financial Data: *Fiscal Year End:*10/31 *Latest Annual Data:* 10/31/2006

Year	Sales	Net Income
2006	$22,147,800,000	$1,693,800,000
2005	$21,930,500,000	$1,446,800,000
2004	$19,986,100,000	$1,406,100,000

Curr. Assets:	$7,152,900,000	**Curr. Liab.:**	$12,787,500,000	**P/E Ratio:**	16.67
Plant, Equip.:	$4,257,500,000	**Total Liab.:**	$27,229,200,000	**Indic. Yr. Divd.:**	$2.000
Total Assets:	$34,720,400,000	**Net Worth:**	$7,491,200,000	**Debt/ Equity:**	1.4166

Deerfield Triarc Capital Corp

6250 N River Rd., Rosemont, IL, 60018; *PH:* 1-773-380-1600; *Fax:* 1-773-380-1601; *http://* www.deerfieldtriarc.com

General		Stock	
Incorporation	MD	Price on:12/24/2007	$15.29
Employees	NA	Stock Exchange	NYSE
Auditor	Deloitte & Touche LLP	Ticker Symbol	DFR
Stk Agt	American Stock Transfer & Trust Co.	Outstanding Shares	51,720,000
Counsel	NA	E.P.S.	$1.45
DUNS No.	NA	Shareholders	NA

Business: The groups principle activity is to invest in corporate loans, commercial real estate loans and residential mortgage loans. The group operates from the United States. The groups quarterly revenue for September 2007 was 125.77 millions of USD.

Primary SIC and add'l.: 6798

CIK No: 0001313918

Subsidiaries: Deerfield Triarc Capital LLC, Deerfield Triarc TRS (Bahamas) Ltd., Deerfield Triarc TRS Holdings, Inc., Deerfield Triarc TRS Holdings, LLC, DWFC, LLC, Market Square CLO Ltd., Pinetree CDO Ltd.

Officers: Jonathan W. Trutter/CEO, Robert C. Grien/Pres., Richard Smith/Sr. VP, CFO - Investor Relations, Frederick White/Sr. VP, General Counsel, Sec., Aaron D. Peck/Sr. Portfolio Mgr., MD, Michael R. Apfel/MD - Direct Corporate Lending Team, James M. Wiant/VP - Direct Corporate Lending Team, Spencer J. Mash/Assoc. - Direct Corporate Lending Team, Lauren P. Thomas/Assoc. - Direct Corporate Lending Team, David Sliwicki/MD - Direct Real Estate Lending Team, Brian R. Orr/Assoc., Direct Real Estate Lending Team, James Snyder/MD - Mortgage Investments Team, Eric Muehlhauser/Portfolio Mgr. - Mortgage Investments Team, Justin Thom/Portfolio Mgr. - Mortgage Investments

Directors: Peter Rothschild/Interim Chmn., Robert B. MacHinist/Dir., Nelson Peltz/Dir., Robert E. Fischer/Dir., Howard Rubin/Dir., Gregory H. Sachs/Dir.

Owners: Robert B. Machinist, Jonathan W. Trutter, Robert E. Fischer, Richard G. Smith, Insiders/4.97%, Howard Rubin, Robert C. Grien, Peter H. Rothschild, Nelson Peltz/4.29%, Gregory H. Sachs/2.62%

Financial Data: *Fiscal Year End:*12/31 *Latest Annual Data:* 12/31/2006

Year	Sales	Net Income
2006	$469,934,000	$71,575,000
2005	$68,157,000	$45,921,000

Curr. Assets:	$521,592,000	**Curr. Liab.:**	$7,591,090,000	**P/E Ratio:**	10.54
Plant, Equip.:	NA	**Total Liab.:**	$8,561,038,000	**Indic. Yr. Divd.:**	$1.680
Total Assets:	$9,249,991,000	**Net Worth:**	$688,953,000	**Debt/ Equity:**	1.4478

Default Proof Credit Card System Inc

1545 Miller Rd. , Coral Gables, FL, 33146; *PH:* 1-305-666-1460; *Fax:* 1-305-665-3462; *http://* www.dpccsystem.com; *Email:* dpccsystem@aol.com

General		Stock	
Incorporation	FL	Price on:12/24/2007	NA
Employees	NA	Stock Exchange	OTC
Auditor	Baum & Company, P.A.	Ticker Symbol	DPRS
Stk Agt	Registrar & Transfer Co	Outstanding Shares	NA
Counsel	NA	E.P.S.	-$0.02
DUNS No.	NA	Shareholders	NA

Business: The groups principle activity is to provide intellectual property services through licensing rights of its patents and its intellectual property to customers, retailers, stores, employers, banks and financial institutions. The group operates from United States.

Primary SIC and add'l.: 7389

CIK No: 0000803260

Financial Data: *Fiscal Year End:*12/31 *Latest Annual Data:* 12/31/2005

Year	Sales	Net Income
2005	NA	-$29,000
2004	NA	-$198,000
2003	NA	-$146,000

Curr. Assets:	$0	**Curr. Liab.:**	$195,000		
Plant, Equip.:	$0	**Total Liab.:**	$195,000	**Indic. Yr. Divd.:**	NA
Total Assets:	$0	**Net Worth:**	-$195,000	**Debt/ Equity:**	NA

Defense Industries International Inc

Industrial Zone Erez, PO Box 779, Ashkelton, 87711; *PH:* 972-76891611; *Fax:* 972-8-6899287; *http://* www.defense-industries.com; *Email:* exportez@zahav.net.il

General		Stock	
Incorporation	NV	Price on:12/24/2007	$0.6
Employees	NA	Stock Exchange	OTC
Auditor	Weinberg & Co. P.A	Ticker Symbol	DFNS
Stk Agt	OTC Corporate Transfer Service Co	Outstanding Shares	NA
Counsel	Carter Ledyard & Milburn LLP	E.P.S.	NA
DUNS No.	NA	Shareholders	NA

Business: The group's principal activity is to produce and market personal military and civilian protective equipment and supplies such as body armor, bomb disposal suits, bullet proof vests, and associated heavy fabric products, such as battle pouch and combat harness units, tents and other camping equipment. The group is also engaged in weaving, improving processing, dyeing cutting and sewing of fabrics.

Primary SIC and add'l.: 3482

CIK No: 0001069563

Subsidiaries: Achidatex Nazareth Elite Ltd, Dragonwear Trading Ltd, Export Erez USA, Inc, Mayotex, Ltd, Nevada corporation, Rizzo Inc

Officers: Josef Fostbinder/Chmn., CEO, Baruch Tosh/Pres., Avraham Hatzor/63/Dir., COO, Dan Zarchin/Mgr. - Marketing, International Business Development, Dir., Meira Postbinder/61/Dir., VP - Finance, Sec., Treasurer, Tsippy Moldovan/51/Dir., CFO

Directors: Josef Fostbinder/Chmn., CEO, Avraham Hatzor/63/Dir., COO, Dan Zarchin/Mgr. - Marketing, International Business Development, Dir., Meira Postbinder/61/Dir., VP - Finance, Sec., Treasurer, Tsippy Moldovan/51/Dir., CFO, Motti Hassan/57/Dir.

Owners: Joseph Postbinder/67.50%, Insiders/69.00%, Meira Postbinder, Tsippy Moldovan, Gov Financial Holdings Ltd./11.64%, Avraham Hatzor

Financial Data: *Fiscal Year End:*12/31 *Latest Annual Data:* 12/31/2006

Year	Sales	Net Income
2006	$10,602,000	-$331,000
2005	$11,448,000	-$27,000
2004	$12,036,000	$381,000

Curr. Assets:	$9,169,000	Curr. Liab.:	$4,366,000		
Plant, Equip.:	$2,195,000	Total Liab.:	$6,611,000	Indic. Yr. Divd.:	NA
Total Assets:	$11,923,000	Net Worth:	$5,312,000	Debt/ Equity:	0.1307

Dejour Enterprises Ltd

1100-808 W Hastings St., Vancouver, BC, V6C 2X4; *PH:* 1-604-638-5050; *http://* www.dejour.com;
Email: investor@dejour.com

General - Incorporation......................Canada	Stock - Price on:12/24/2007 ....NA
Employees ....NA	Stock Exchange...AMEX
Auditor ....Dale Matheson Carr-Hilton Labonte	Ticker Symbol..DEJ
Stk Agt.........Computershare Trust Co of Canada	Outstanding Shares ....NA
Counsel.............................DuMoulin Black	E.P.S...NA
DUNS No. ....NA	Shareholders..NA

Business: The groups principle activity is to exploration and development of uranium, oil and gas reserves. The group operates from United States.
Primary SIC and add'l.: 1400
CIK No: 0001323838
Subsidiaries: Dejour.com Investment Corp.
Officers: Robert L. Hodgkinson/58/Chmn., CEO, Mathew H. Wong/Officer, CFO, Douglas W. Cannaday/COO, Pres., David Fry/Office, Investor Relations, Lori Kozub/Dir. - Marketing, Ricardo Salazar/Operations Mgr., Phil Bretzloff/VP, General Counsel, Charles W.E. Dove/Pres. - Dejour Energy, Alberta
Directors: Robert L. Hodgkinson/58/Chmn., CEO, Marc R. Bustin/Dir., Llloyd A. Clark/Dir., Archibald J. Nesbitt/Dir., Craig Sturrock/Dir., Robert E. McNair/Member - Advisory Board, Michael A. Berry/Member - Advisory Board
Owners: Steve Gose/8.03%, Douglas W. Cannaday/2.12%, Craig Sturrock, Archibald J. Nesbitt, Marc Bustin, Insiders/11.70%, Mathew H. Wong/1.05%, Robert L. Hodgkinson/6.80%, Lloyd A. Clark

Del Global Technologies Corp

11550 W King St., Franklin Park, IL, 60131; *PH:* 1-847-288-7000; *Fax:* 1-847-288-7011;
http:// www.delglobal.com

General - Incorporation.............................NY	Stock - Price on:12/24/2007 ....NA
Employees 314	Stock Exchange...OTC
Auditor ....BDO Seidman LLP	Ticker Symbol..DGTC
Stk Agt........................Continental Stock T & T Co.	Outstanding Shares ....NA
Counsel............Olshan Grundman Frome R & W	E.P.S...$0.27
DUNS No. 00-121-0186	Shareholders..NA

Business: The group's principal activities are to develop, manufacture and market medical imaging equipment and power conversion subsystems and components worldwide. The group operates in two segments: medical systems group and power conversion group. The medical systems group designs, manufactures, markets and sells medical imaging and diagnostic systems consisting of stationary and portable imaging systems, radiographic/fluoroscopic systems, dental imaging systems and mammography systems. The power conversion group designs, manufactures, markets and sells high voltage power conversion systems and electronic noise suppression components for a variety of applications. The brand names include del high voltage, bertan high voltage, dynarad, rfi, filtron, sprague and stanley. The customers of the group include hospitals, veterinary clinics, medical clinics, military, security, medical and industrial applications.
Primary SIC and add'l.: 3845 3674 3844 3677
CIK No: 0000027748
Subsidiaries: RFI, Villa
Officers: James Risher/CEO, Pres., Mark Zorko/CFO, Susan Ferber/Contact - Customer Service
Directors: James R. Henderson/Chmn., Merrill A. McPeak/Dir., Gerald M. Czarnecki/Dir.
Owners: Walter F. Schneider/1.10%, Warren G. Lichtenstein/15.50%, Royce & Associates LLC/4.10%, James R. Henderson, Merrill McPeak, Benson Associates LLC/9.60%, Samuel P. Sporn/9.70%, Wells Fargo & Company/8.90%, Insiders/2.60%, Wellington Management Co./8.10%, Francis Capital/6.40%, Edgar J. Smith, Mark A. Koch, James A. Risher

Financial Data: Fiscal Year End:07/30 Latest Annual Data: 07/28/2007

Year	Sales	Net Income
2007	$104,167,000	$3,816,000
2006	$83,014,000	$94,000
2005	$84,872,000	$392,000

Curr. Assets:	$31,260,000	Curr. Liab.:	$21,138,000		
Plant, Equip.:	$6,485,000	Total Liab.:	$30,275,000	Indic. Yr. Divd.:	$0.400
Total Assets:	$40,776,000	Net Worth:	$9,228,000	Debt/ Equity:	NA

Del Monte Foods Co

1 Market @ The Landmark, San Francisco, CA, 94105; *PH:* 1-415-247-3000; *Fax:* 1-415-247-3565;
http:// www.delmonte.com

General - Incorporation.............................DE	Stock - Price on:12/24/2007 ....$12.33
Employees 7,500	Stock Exchange...NYSE
Auditor ....KPMG LLP	Ticker Symbol..DLM
Stk Agt.............................Bank of New York	Outstanding Shares 201,910,000
Counsel......................................Kpmg LLP	E.P.S...$0.55
DUNS No. 60-917-0790	Shareholders..NA

Business: The groups principle activities include distributing and marketing branded food and pet products. The groups products include tomato, broth, tuna products, dry and wet pet food, and pet snacks. The group operates through two business segments namely Consumer Products segment and The Pet Products segment. The groups products are sold under the brand names StarKist, Contadina, 9Lives, Kibbles 'n Bits and Pup-Peroni. The group operates from United States.
Primary SIC and add'l.: 2047 2034 2033
CIK No: 0000866873

Subsidiaries: College Inn Foods, Contadina Foods, Inc., Del Monte Andina, Del Monte Argentina, Del Monte Colombiana, S.A., Del Monte Ecuador DME C.A., Del Monte Peru, S.A., DLM Foods Canada Corp., Galapesca, S.A., Hi Continental Corporation, Industrias Citrcolas de Montemorelos, S.A. de C.V., Marine Trading (Pacific), Inc., Meow Mix Decatur Production I LLC, Meow Mix Holdings, Inc., Panapesca Fishing, Inc. 20 Subsidiaries included in the Index
Officers: Richard G. Wolford/Chmn., CEO, Pres./$7,441,081.00, David L. Meyers/Exec. VP - Administration, CFO/$2,337,966.00, Richard L. French/Sr. VP, Chief Accounting Officer, Controller, James G. Potter/Sr. VP, General Counsel, Sec., Nils Lommerin/Exec. VP - Operations/$1,866,320.00, Tim A. Cole/Exec. VP - Sales/$1,187,091.00, David W. Allen/Sr. VP - Supply Chain Operations/$979,513.00, Apurva S. Mody/Sr. VP - Consumer Products, Jeffrey M. Watters/Sr. VP - Pet Products, Jeff M. Berry/VP, Treasurer, Jennifer D. Garrison/Dir. - Investor Relations
Directors: Richard G. Wolford/Chmn., CEO, Pres., David R. Williams/Dir., Mary R. Henderson/Dir., Victor L. Lund/Dir., Joe L. Morgan/Dir., Timothy G. Bruer/Dir., Terence D. Martin/Dir., Samuel H. Armacost/Dir.
Owners: Insiders/2.80%, Wells Fargo & Company/6.20%, Mary R. Henderson, Atlantic Investment Management/7.10%, Timothy G. Bruer, David R. Williams, David L. Meyers, Timothy A. Cole, Terence D. Martin, Joe L. Morgan, Samuel H. Armacost, Nils Lommerin, Victor L. Lund, David W. Allen, Richard G. Wolford/1.50%

Financial Data: Fiscal Year End:04/30 Latest Annual Data: 04/29/2007

Year	Sales	Net Income
2007	NA	NA
2006	$2,998,600,000	$169,900,000
2005	$3,180,900,000	$117,900,000

Curr. Assets:	$1,225,700,000	Curr. Liab.:	$434,300,000		
Plant, Equip.:	$820,900,000	Total Liab.:	$2,330,800,000	Indic. Yr. Divd.:	$0.160
Total Assets:	$3,459,700,000	Net Worth:	$1,128,900,000	Debt/ Equity:	NA

Delcath Systems Inc

Rockefeller Ctr. 600 Fifth Ave., 23rd Fl., New York, NY, 10020; *PH:* 1-212-489-2100;
Fax: 1-212-489-2102; *http://* www.delcath.com; *Email:* info@delcath.com

General - Incorporation .... DE	Stock - Price on:12/24/2007 ....$4.3101
Employees 4	Stock Exchange...NDQ
Auditor ....Carlin, Charron & Rosen LLP	Ticker Symbol..DCTH
Stk Agt......American Stock Transfer & Trust Co.	Outstanding Shares 21,360,000
Counsel...NA	E.P.S...-$0.56
DUNS No. ....NA	Shareholders..NA

Business: The group's principal activity is to develop and market a proprietary drug delivery system. This system is capable of introducing and removing high dose chemotherapy agents to a diseased organ system while greatly inhibiting their entry into the general circulation system. The group has developed a system, the delcath system, to isolate the liver from the general circulatory system and to administer chemotherapy and other therapeutic agents directly to the liver. The group is in the development stage and conducts clinical trials designed to secure marketing approval for the system in the United States. The delcath system kit includes the following disposable components: infusion catheter, double balloon catheter, extracorporeal filtration circuit, filters and return catheter.
Primary SIC and add'l.: 3841
CIK No: 0000872912
Officers: Richard Taney/Dir., CEO, Pres./$62,400.00, Jonathan A. Foltz/Exec. VP, Jason A. Rifkin/VP - Business Development, Paul M. Feinstein/CFO, Treasurer/$120,000.00, Samuel Herschkowitz/58/Dir., COO, Lara S. Corrente/Dir. - Regulatory Affairs, Seymour Fein/Chief Scientific Officer
Directors: Richard Taney/Dir., CEO, Pres., Harold S. Koplewicz/Chmn., Robert B. Ladd/Dir., Jonathan J. Lewis/Dir., Laura A. Philips/Dir.
Owners: Robert Ladd/11.40%, Insiders/13.40%, M. S. Koly/7.00%, Paul M. Feinstein/0.10%, Venkol Trust/3.20%, Richard Taney/0.20%, Harold S. Koplewicz/0.20%, Samuel Herschkowitz/1.70%

Financial Data: Fiscal Year End:12/31 Latest Annual Data: 12/31/2006

Year	Sales	Net Income
2006	NA	-$10,952,000
2005	NA	-$2,865,000
2004	NA	-$3,266,000

Curr. Assets:	$8,760,000	Curr. Liab.:	$670,000		
Plant, Equip.:	$4,000	Total Liab.:	$670,000	Indic. Yr. Divd.:	NA
Total Assets:	$8,764,000	Net Worth:	$8,093,000	Debt/ Equity:	NA

Delek Resources Inc

1224 Washington Ave., Miami Beach, FL, 33139; *PH:* 1-305-531-1174

General - Incorporation .... FL	Stock - Price on:12/24/2007 ....$0.06
Employees 1	Stock Exchange...OTC
Auditor ....Jewett, Schwartz, & Assoc.	Ticker Symbol..DLKR
Stk Agt................................Liberty Transfer Co	Outstanding Shares 52,880,000
Counsel...NA	E.P.S...-$0.094
DUNS No. ....NA	Shareholders..NA

Business: The group's principal activity is to own and operate cigar emporiums devoted to the sale of premium cigars and cigar related merchandise. The operations are carried under three emporiums, which are located in the las olas river front in fort lauderdale, downtown south miami Florida and in the desert passage at the aladdin resort in las vegas, Nevada. The premium cigars are marketed under the brand name of havana republic. The group also sells cigars and accessories over the Internet. On 25-Sep-2003 the group entered into an asset purchase agreement whereby an entity formed by a former director and shareholder and officer of the group would acquire all of the operating assets of the group's cigar business in exchange for the assumption of all of the group's liabilities.
Primary SIC and add'l.: 9999 5993
CIK No: 0001049660
Officers: John T. Ruddy/CEO
Owners: Mark A. Bush/11.34%, Joseph I. Emas/5.67%, Insiders/28.87%, Leonard Sternheim/28.87%

Financial Data: Fiscal Year End:06/30 Latest Annual Data: 6/30/2006

Year	Sales	Net Income
2006	NA	-$142,000
2005	NA	-$4,105,000
2004	NA	-$1,995,000

Curr. Assets:	$0	***Curr. Liab.:***	$1,540,000		
Plant, Equip.:	NA	***Total Liab.:***	$1,540,000	***Indic. Yr. Divd.:***	NA
Total Assets:	$0	***Net Worth:***	-$1,540,000	***Debt/ Equity:***	NA

Delek US Holdings Inc

830 Crescent Ctr. Dr., Ste. 300, Franklin, TN, 37067; ***PH:*** 1-615-771-6701; ***Fax:*** 1-615-224-1185; ***http://*** www.delekus.com

General - Incorporation	DE	***Stock*** - Price on:12/24/2007	$24.37
Employees	3,064	Stock Exchange	NYSE
Auditor	Ernst & Young, LLP	Ticker Symbol	DK
Stk Agt	American Stock Transfer & Trust Co.	Outstanding Shares	51,140,000
Counsel	NA	E.P.S.	$1.98
DUNS No.	NA	Shareholders	NA

Business: The groups principle activities include refining, wholesaling and marketing of petroleum products. The group operates through three segments namely, refining, marketing and retail. The group operates from the United States. The group's quarterly revenue for September 2007 was 1,064.90 millions of USD.

Primary SIC and add'l.: 5499 4925 5411 5172 5541 5999 5399

CIK No: 0001351541

Subsidiaries: Delek Finance, Inc., Delek Land Texas, Inc., Delek Marketing GP, LLC, Delek Marketing& Supply, Inc., Delek Marketing& Supply, LP, Delek Pipeline Texas, Inc., Delek Refining, Inc., Delek Refining, Ltd., Delek U.S.Refining GP, LLC, Gasoline Associated Services, Inc., Liberty Wholesale Co., Inc, MAPCO Express, Inc., MAPCO Fleet, Inc., MPC Land Acquisition, Inc., MPC Pipeline Acquisition, Inc. 16 Subsidiaries included in the Index

Officers: Ezra Uzi Yemin/Dir., CEO, Pres., Lynwood Gregory/Sr. VP, Frederec Green/COO, VP - Delek Refining, Inc, Edward Morgan/CFO, VP, Assi Ginzburg/VP - Strategic Planning, John P. Colling/VP, Treasurer, Kent Thomas/General Counsel, Sec., Joane Walker/VP, Chief Accounting Officer, Paul Pierce/VP - Marketing, Mapco Express, Inc, Charles J. Williams/VP - Trading, Supply, Delek Refining, Inc, Pete Daily/COO, VP - Delek Marketing, Supply, Inc, Mike Norman/VP - Regulatory, Environmental Affairs, Delek Refining, Inc, Kathy Roadarmel/VP - Human Resources

Directors: Ezra Uzi Yemin/Dir., CEO, Pres., Gabriel Last/Dir., Asaf Bartfeld/Dir., Zvi Greenfeld/Dir., Carlos E. Jorda/Dir., Charles H. Leonard/Dir., Philip L. Maslowe/Dir., Alan H. Gelman/Dir.

Owners: Insiders, Delek Group Ltd., Charles H. Leonard, Philip L. Maslowe, Gabriel Last, Delek Petroleum Ltd., Edward Morgan, Zvi Greenfeld, Assi Ginzburg, Carlos E. Jord, Ezra Uzi Yemin, Lynwood Gregory, Itshak Sharon, Frederec Green, Delek Hungary Holding Limited Liability Company *(16 Owners included in Index)*

Financial Data: ***Fiscal Year End:***NA ***Latest Annual Data:*** 12/31/2006

Year	***Sales***	***Net Income***
2006	$3,207,700,000	$93,000,000
2005	$2,031,869,000	$64,116,000
2004	$857,899,000	$7,333,000

Curr. Assets:	$410,600,000	***Curr. Liab.:***	$230,900,000	***P/E Ratio:***	10.54
Plant, Equip.:	$424,700,000	***Total Liab.:***	$567,200,000	***Indic. Yr. Divd.:***	$0.150
Total Assets:	$949,400,000	***Net Worth:***	$382,200,000	***Debt/ Equity:***	NA

Delhaize America Inc

2110 Executive Dr., Salisbury, NC, 28145; ***PH:*** 1-704-633-8250; ***Fax:*** 1-704-636-5024; ***http://*** www.delhaizegroup.com

General - Incorporation	NC	***Stock*** - Price on:12/24/2007	$98.21
Employees	64,726	Stock Exchange	NA
Auditor	Deloitte & Touche LLP	Ticker Symbol	NA
Stk Agt	Bank of New York	Outstanding Shares	95,810,000
Counsel	NA	E.P.S.	$4.75
DUNS No.	00-344-8560	Shareholders	NA

Business: The group operates through its subsidiaries whose principle activity is to operate a retail food supermarkets in the eastern United States, that sells a wide variety of groceries, produce, meats, dairy products, seafood, frozen food, deli/bakery and non-food items such as health and beauty care, prescriptions, and other household and personal products; and offers nationally and regionally advertised brand name merchandise as well as products manufactured and packged under the private labels of food lion, hannaford and kash n' karry. The group operates from United States.

Primary SIC and add'l.: 6719 5411

CIK No: 0000037912

Subsidiaries: Delhaize Group, Delhaize Insurance Co, Delhaize the Lion America, Inc.

Officers: Pierre-Olivier Beckers/Chmn., CEO, Michael Waller/55/VP, General Counsel, Sec., Carol M. Herndon/Exec. VP - Accounting, Chief Accounting Officer

Directors: Pierre-Olivier Beckers/Chmn., CEO

Financial Data: ***Fiscal Year End:***12/31 ***Latest Annual Data:*** 12/31/2006

Year	***Sales***	***Net Income***
2006	$25,290,743,000	$494,980,000
2005	$21,996,440,000	$430,766,000
2004	$24,330,843,000	$420,973,000

Curr. Assets:	$3,204,764,000	***Curr. Liab.:***	$3,235,263,000		
Plant, Equip.:	$4,535,891,000	***Total Liab.:***	$7,653,779,000	***Indic. Yr. Divd.:***	$1.330
Total Assets:	$12,469,705,000	***Net Worth:***	$4,766,547,000	***Debt/ Equity:***	NA

Delhaize Group

2110 Executive Dr., Salisbury, NC, 28145; ***PH:*** 1-704-633-8250; ***Fax:*** 1-704-636-5024; ***http://*** www.delhaizegroup.com

General - Incorporation	Belgium	***Stock*** - Price on:12/24/2007	$98.21
Employees	64,726	Stock Exchange	NYSE
Auditor	Philip Maeyaert	Ticker Symbol	DEG
Stk Agt	Bank of New York	Outstanding Shares	95,810,000
Counsel	NA	E.P.S.	$6.01
DUNS No.	NA	Shareholders	NA

Business: The group's principle activity is to operate stores including self-service sale of food products and daily items. The group operates from United States, Thailand, Indonesia and Singapore.

Primary SIC and add'l.: 5411 5149 5912 5999 5961

CIK No: 0000930309

Subsidiaries: 7 Seasons NV, Aidi Center SPRL, Alfa-Beta Vassilopoulos S.A., Aniserco SA, Athenian Real Estate Development, Inc., Atlas A.S., ATTM Consulting and Commercial, Ltd., Backambacht NV, Bevermart NV, Bonney Wilson& Sons, Inc., Bucharest, Romania, Bugmart NV, Delhaize America, Inc., Delhaize Deutschland GmbH, Delhaize Finance B.V. 97 Subsidiaries included in the Index

Officers: Pierre-Olivier Beckers/48/Dir., CEO, Pres., Renaud Cogels/59/Exec. VP, Craig B. Owens/54/CFO, Exec. VP, Rick Anicetti/51/Exec. VP, Michel Eeckhout/59/CIO, Exec. VP, Ronald C. Hodge/60/Exec. VP, Michael Waller/55/Exec. VP, General Counsel, Guy Elewaut/VP, Nicolas Hollanders/46/Exec. VP - Human Resources, Organizational Development

Directors: Pierre-Olivier Beckers/48/Dir., CEO, Pres., Georges Jacobs/Chmn., Claire Babrowski/51/Dir., Arnoud De Pret Roose De Calesberg/Dir., Jacques De Vaucleroy/47/Dir., Hugh Farrington/63/Dir., Richard Goblet D'Alviella/Dir., Robert J. Murray/67/Dir., William Roper/60/Dir., Didier Smits/46/Dir., Luc Vansteenkiste/Dir.

Owners: Axa/12.30%, Axa IM/0.20%, Axa Rosenberg/1.10%, Ardenne Prevoyante - Axa/0.02%, Including:Alliance Capital Management L.P./10.90%, Rebelco SA/3.80%

Financial Data: ***Fiscal Year End:***12/31 ***Latest Annual Data:*** 12/31/2006

Year	***Sales***	***Net Income***
2006	$25,290,743,000	$494,980,000
2005	$21,996,440,000	$430,766,000
2004	$24,330,843,000	$420,973,000

Curr. Assets:	$3,204,764,000	***Curr. Liab.:***	$3,235,263,000		
Plant, Equip.:	$4,535,891,000	***Total Liab.:***	$7,703,158,000	***Indic. Yr. Divd.:***	$1.330
Total Assets:	$12,469,705,000	***Net Worth:***	$4,766,547,000	***Debt/ Equity:***	NA

Delia's Inc

435 Hudson St., New York, NY, 10014; ***PH:*** 1-212-807-9060; ***Fax:*** 1-212-590-6300; ***http://*** www.delias.com

General - Incorporation	DE	***Stock*** - Price on:12/24/2007	$7.75
Employees	737	Stock Exchange	NDQ
Auditor	BDO Seidman, LLP	Ticker Symbol	DLIA
Stk Agt	NA	Outstanding Shares	30,840,000
Counsel	NA	E.P.S.	-$0.05
DUNS No.	NA	Shareholders	NA

Business: The groups principle activity is to retailing apparel, action sports equipment and accessories. The products of the group include roomware, swimwear, footwear, outerwear and junior apparel. The group products sold under the trade name dELiA*s, Alloy and CCS. The groups operates through two segments namely direct marketing and retail stores. The group operates from the United States. The group's quarterly revenue for September 2007 was 71.23 millions of USD.

Primary SIC and add'l.: 5999 2331 5699 5621 3171 5139 5961 3144 2335 5137 2389 5131 3961

CIK No: 0001333513

Subsidiaries: Alloy Merchandise, LLC, AMG Direct, LLC, DC Restructuring, LLC, dELiA*s Assets Corp., dELiA*s Brand LLC, dELiA*s Delaware Company, Inc., dELiA*s Distribution Company, Inc., dELiA*s Foreign Sales Corp., dELiA*s Group Inc., dELiA*s Japan Company, dELiA*s Operating Company, dELiA*s Properties Inc., dELiA*s Retail Company, Droog, Inc., GFLA, Inc. 26 Subsidiaries included in the Index

Officers: Robert Bernard/Dir., CEO, Walter Killough/Dir., COO, David Desjardins/Chief Stores Officer, Steve Feldman/CFO

Directors: Robert Bernard/Dir., CEO, Matthew L. Feshbach/Chmn., Scott Rosen/Dir., Walter Killough/Dir., COO, Peter Goodson/65/Dir., Carter S. Evans/Dir., Gene Washington/Dir.

Owners: Matthew L. Feshbach/17.90%, John Holowko, Peter D. Goodson, Insiders/21.20%, David Desjardins, Gene Washington, Steadfast Capital Management LLC/5.60%, Gilder, Gagnon, Howe & Co. LLC/5.80%, Walter Killough, Carter S. Evans, Robert E. Bernard/2.70%, Scott M. Rosen

Financial Data: ***Fiscal Year End:***01/28 ***Latest Annual Data:*** 2/3/2007

Year	***Sales***	***Net Income***
2007	$257,618,000	$5,754,000
2006	$226,730,000	-$10,312,000

Curr. Assets:	$70,470,000	***Curr. Liab.:***	$45,509,000	***P/E Ratio:***	70.45
Plant, Equip.:	$39,543,000	***Total Liab.:***	$55,638,000	***Indic. Yr. Divd.:***	NA
Total Assets:	$153,505,000	***Net Worth:***	$97,867,000	***Debt/ Equity:***	0.0249

Dell Inc

1 Dell Way, Round Rock, TX, 78682; ***PH:*** 1-512-338-4400; ***Fax:*** 1-512-283-6161; ***http://*** www.dell.com; ***Email:*** investor_relations@dell.com

General - Incorporation	DE	***Stock*** - Price on:12/24/2007	$27.82
Employees	65,200	Stock Exchange	NDQ
Auditor	PricewaterhouseCoopers LLP	Ticker Symbol	DELL
Stk Agt	American Stock Transfer & Trust Co.	Outstanding Shares	NA
Counsel	NA	E.P.S.	NA
DUNS No.	NA	Shareholders	NA

Business: The group's principle activity is to provide a wide range of product categories including desktop computer systems, storage, servers and networking products, mobility products, software and peripherals, and enhanced services. Customers served by the group include large corporate, government, healthcare, small-to-medium business and individual customers. In November 2007, Dell acquired ASAP Software. The group operates from United States.

Primary SIC and add'l.: 7371 3572 3571

CIK No: 0000826083

Subsidiaries: Bracknell Boulevard (Block C) LLC, Bracknell Boulevard (Block D) LLC, Bracknell Boulevard Management Company Limited, CPS Channel Partner Solutions L.P., DCC Executive Security Inc., Dell (China) Company Limited, Dell (China) Company Limited, Beijing Liaison Office, Dell (China) Company Limited, Chengdu Liaison Office, Dell (China) Company Limited, Dalian Branch, Dell (China) Company Limited, Guangzhou Liaison Office, Dell (China) Company Limited, Hangzhou Liaison Office, Dell (China) Company Limited, Nanjing Liaison Office, Dell (China) Company Limited, Shanghai Branch, Dell (China) Company Limited, Shanghai Liaison Office, Dell (China) Company Limited, Shenzhen Liaison Office 178 Subsidiaries included in the Index

Officers: Michael Dell/Chmn., CEO, Donald J. Carty/Vice Chmn., CFO, Lawrence P. Tu/Sr. VP, General Counsel, Lynn A. Tyson/VP - Investor Relations - Global Corporate Communications, Brad R. Anderson/Sr. VP - Business Product Group, Thomas W. Sweet/VP - Corporate Finance, Principal

Accounting Officer, Paul D. Bell/Sr. VP, Pres. - Americas, Stephen J. Felice/Sr. VP, Pres. - Asia, Pacific, Japan, Paul D. McKinnon/Sr. VP - Human Resources, John K. Medica/Sr. VP - Product Group, John S. Hamlin/Sr. VP - Global Online Business, Global Brand Marketing, Jeff W. Clarke/Sr. VP - Product Group, Alex Gruzen/Sr. VP - Product Group, Michael R. Cannon/Pres. - Global Operations, Jeffrey R. Clarke/Sr. VP - Business Product Group *(22 Officers included in Index)*

Directors: Michael Dell/Chmn., CEO, Donald J. Carty/Vice Chmn., CFO, Michael A. Miles/Dir., William H. Gray/67/Dir., Klaus S. Luft/Dir., Samuel A. Nunn/Dir., Judy C. Lewent/Dir., Alex J. Mandl/Dir., Alan A.G. Lafley/61/Dir., Thomas W. Luce/Dir., Sallie L. Krawcheck/43/Dir.

Owners: Kevin B. Rollins, Stephen J. Felice, Alex J. Mandl, Sallie L. Krawcheck, Donald J. Carty, Paul D. Bell, Sam Nunn, Rosendo G. Parraf, Michael S. Dell/10.14%, Southeastern Asset Management, Inc./5.50%, William H. Gray, Alan Lafley, Insiders/10.70%, Klaus S. Luft, Judy C. Lewent *(18 Owners included in Index)*

Financial Data: *Fiscal Year End:*02/03 *Latest Annual Data:* 2/3/2006

Year	Sales	Net Income
2006	$55,908,000,000	$3,572,000,000
2005	$49,205,000,000	$3,043,000,000
2004	$41,444,000,000	$2,645,000,000

Curr. Assets:	$17,706,000,000	**Curr. Liab.:**	$15,927,000,000		
Plant, Equip.:	$2,005,000,000	**Total Liab.:**	$18,980,000,000	**Indic. Yr. Divd.:**	NA
Total Assets:	$23,109,000,000	**Net Worth:**	$4,129,000,000	**Debt/ Equity:**	0.1220

Delmar Bancorp

12 E State St., Delmar, MD, 21875; ***PH:*** 1-410-896-9041; ***Fax:*** 1-410-896-3404;
http:// www.bankofdelmar.com

General - Incorporation		**Stock**- Price on:12/24/2007	$34.43
Employees	NA	Stock Exchange	OTC
Auditor	NA	Ticker Symbol	DBCP
Stk Agt	NA	Outstanding Shares	NA
Counsel	NA	E.P.S	NA
DUNS No.	NA	Shareholders	NA

Business: The groups principle activity is to provide banking services. The groups products include loans, deluxe check re-order and checking accounts. The group also provides online banking services. The group operates from United States.

Primary SIC and add'l.: 6712 6022

CIK No:

Officers: Edward M. Thomas/Dir., CEO, Pres., Carol J. Adams/Assist. VP, Customer Service Mgr., Robert D. Core/VP, Business Development Officer, Roy J. Lewis/VP - MIS, Charles S. Gallo/Internal Auditor, Matthew P. Shaffer/Assist. VP - Bank Security, Secrecy Officer, Jeanne S. Robertson/Assist. VP - Credit Analyst, John Craig/VP, Business Development Officer, Carl L. Cottingham/Exec. VP, Lawrence L. Dernule/Sr. VP, Kimberly T. Thomas/Sr. VP, CFO, Cheryl K. Robbins/Assist. VP, Collections Mgr., Assistant Loan Department Mgr., Angela A. Hill/VP, Human Resources Mgr., Jeanette S. Smith/Assist. VP, Operations Mgr. and Deposit Compliance Officer, John Aukward/Assist. VP, Branch Mgr. - Eastern Shore Drive Office *(27 Officers included in Index)*

Directors: Edward M. Thomas/Dir., CEO, Pres., Edward J. Kremer/Chmn., Wade H. Insley/Dir., Robert L. Conaway/Dir., Mark L. Granger/Dir., Norris L. Niblett/Dir., Robert M. Lawrence/Dir., Paul H. Mylander/Dir., Robert C. Wheatley/Dir., Phillips J. Wright/Dir., Francis M. Young/Dir.

Delmarva Power & Light Co

Delmarva Power, Washington, DC, 19886; ***PH:*** 1-202-872-2000; ***Fax:*** 1-202-331-6750;
http:// www.delmarva.com

General - Incorporation	DE	**Stock**- Price on:12/24/2007	$28.34
Employees	5,156	Stock Exchange	NA
Auditor	PricewaterhouseCoopers LLP	Ticker Symbol	NA
Stk Agt	NA	Outstanding Shares	193,080,000
Counsel	NA	E.P.S	$1.29
DUNS No.	00-691-8882	Shareholders	NA

Business: The group's principle activities include producing, purchasing, delivering and selling electricity; purchases, transports and sells natural gas; and sells other non-regulated/non-utility products and services, including local and long distance telephone service, heating, ventilation and air conditioning products and installation, and power plant and landfil operating services. The group operates from United States.

Primary SIC and add'l.: 4931 4923

CIK No: 0000027879

Subsidiaries: Ace Reit, Inc, Aircraft International Management Company, American Energy Corporation, AMP Funding, LLC, ATE Investments, Inc., Atlantic City Electric Company, Atlantic City Electric Company Transition Funding LLC, Atlantic Generation, Inc., Atlantic Jersey Thermal Systems, Inc., Atlantic Southern Properties, Inc., ATS Operating Services, Inc., Bethlehem Renewable Energy LLC, Binghamton General, Inc., Binghamton Limited, Inc., Black Light Power, Inc. 110 Subsidiaries included in the Index

Officers: Thomas S. Shaw/CEO, Joseph M. Rigby/Sr. VP, CFO, Matt Likovich/Media Contact

Financial Data: *Fiscal Year End:*12/31 *Latest Annual Data:* 12/31/2006

Year	Sales	Net Income
2006	$8,362,900,000	$248,300,000
2005	$8,065,500,000	$371,200,000
2004	$7,221,800,000	$258,700,000

Curr. Assets:	$1,981,400,000	**Curr. Liab.:**	$2,526,900,000	**P/E Ratio:**	21.80
Plant, Equip.:	$7,576,600,000	**Total Liab.:**	$10,606,900,000	**Indic. Yr. Divd.:**	$1.040
Total Assets:	$14,243,500,000	**Net Worth:**	$3,612,200,000	**Debt/ Equity:**	1.2090

Delphax Technologies Inc

6100 W 110th St., Bloomington, MN, 55438; ***PH:*** 1-952-939-9000; ***Fax:*** 1-952-939-1151;
http:// www.delphax.com

General - Incorporation	MN	**Stock**- Price on:12/24/2007	$1.15
Employees	285	Stock Exchange	NDQ
Auditor	Grant Thornton LLP	Ticker Symbol	DLPX
Stk Agt	Wells Fargo Shareowner Services	Outstanding Shares	6,470,000
Counsel	NA	E.P.S	-$1.43
DUNS No.	05-139-8436	Shareholders	NA

Business: The group's principal activities are to design, manufacture, sell and service advanced print-production systems based on its exclusive electron beam imaging technology. The group is also indulged in the sale of maintenance contracts, spare parts, supplies and consumable items that are used with this equipment. The group products includes digital printing equipment. This equipment is classified as cut-sheet or roll-fed printers. These equipment are used for the following applications: folio production, insurance claims, fulfillments, disbursements, publishing, direct mail and transaction processing. The group's competitors are heidelberg, nipson, oce, IBM, hitachi, kodak and xerox.

Primary SIC and add'l.: 7373 7378

CIK No: 0000350692

Subsidiaries: Check Technology Pty Limited, Delphax Technologies Canada Ltd., Delphax Technologies Limited, Delphax Technologies S.A.S., GTI Holdings, GTI Ventures

Officers: Dieter P. Schilling/Dir., Executive Officer, CEO, Pres., M. H. Kuhn/Executive Officer, Gregory S. Furness/Executive Officer, VP - Finance, CFO, Michael A. Pasco/Executive Officer, Earl W. Rogers/Dir., Sec.

Directors: Dieter P. Schilling/Dir., Executive Officer, CEO, Pres., Kenneth E. Overstreet/Dir., Earl W. Rogers/Dir., Sec., Stephen R. Armstrong/Dir., Gary R. Holland/Dir.

Owners: Gregory S. Furness, Michael A. Pasco, Nichols Investment Management/7.90%, Gary R. Holland, Kenneth E. Overstreet, Stephen R. Armstrong, Dieter P. Schilling/2.30%, Earl W. Rogers, Fred H. Brenner/17.80%, Insiders/4.90%, M. H. Kuhn/1.30%

Financial Data: *Fiscal Year End:*09/30 *Latest Annual Data:* 9/30/2006

Year	Sales	Net Income
2006	$48,726,000	-$9,621,000
2005	$51,627,000	$306,000
2004	$53,622,000	-$389,000

Curr. Assets:	$24,246,000	**Curr. Liab.:**	$10,324,000		
Plant, Equip.:	$1,838,000	**Total Liab.:**	$18,380,000	**Indic. Yr. Divd.:**	NA
Total Assets:	$26,216,000	**Net Worth:**	$7,836,000	**Debt/ Equity:**	NA

Delphi Corp

5725 Delphi Dr., Troy, MI, 48098; ***PH:*** 1-248-813-2000; ***Fax:*** 1-248-813-2673;
http:// www.delphi.com

General - Incorporation	DE	**Stock**- Price on:12/24/2007	$2.635
Employees	171,400	Stock Exchange	OTC
Auditor	Deloitte & Touche LLP	Ticker Symbol	DPHIQ
Stk Agt	Computershare Shareholder Services	Outstanding Shares	561,780,000
Counsel	Logan Robinson	E.P.S	-$6.01
DUNS No.	04-389-8092	Shareholders	NA

Business: The group's principle activity is to supply mobile electronics and transportation systems including powertrain, safety, steering, thermal, and controls and security systems, electrical/electronic architecture, and in-car entertainment technologies. The group's products include fuel cells, body controls, connectors, microelectronics, telematics and powertrain systems. Customers served by the group include automotive, medical and commercial vehicle industry, and contract manufacturing. The group operates from United States.

Primary SIC and add'l.: 3714 3651

CIK No: 0001072342

Subsidiaries: Alambrados y Circuitos Eletricos, S.A. de C.V., AS Catalizadores Ambientales S.A. de C.V., ASEC Manfacturing (Thailand) Ltd., ASEC Manufacturing General Partnership, ASEC Private Limited, ASEC Sales General Partnership, Aspire, Inc., Beijing Delphi Technology Development Company, Ltd., Beijing Delphi Wan Yuan Engine Management Systems Company, Ltd., BlueStar Battery Systems International Corp., Bujias Mexicanas, S.A. de C.V., Calsonic Harrison Co., Ltd., Centro Tenico Herramental, S.A. de C.V., Closed Joint Stock Company PES/SCC, Condura, S. de R.L. 180 Subsidiaries included in the Index

Officers: Rodney ONeal/55/Dir., CEO, Pres., Robert S. Miller/66/Exec. Chmn., Guy C. Hachey/53/VP - Delphi Corporation, Pres. - Delphi Powertrain Systems, Pres. - Delphi Europe, Middle East, Africa, F. Timothy Richards/54/VP - Electronics Group, James P. Whitson/63/Chief Tax Officer, Jeffrey J. Owens/53/VP - Delphi Corporation, Pres. - Delphi Electronics, Safety, Pres. - Asia Pacific, David M. Sherbin/49/Chief Compliance Officer, VP, General Counsel - Delphi Corporation, Bette Walker/65/CIO, VP, Robert J. Remenar/52/VP - Delphi Corporation, Pres. - Delphi Steering, Mark R. Weber/60/Exec. VP - Global Business Services, John P. Arle/60/VP, Treasurer - Delphi Corporation, Ronald M. Pirtle/54/VP, Pres. - Delphi Thermal Systems, Robert J. Dellinger/48/CFO, Exec. VP, James A. Bertrand/51/VP - Delphi Corporation, Pres. - Delphi Automotive Holdings Group, Choon T. Chon/62/VP - Delphi Corporation, Pres. - Delphi Asia Pacific *(27 Officers included in Index)*

Directors: Rodney ONeal/55/Dir., CEO, Pres., Robert S. Miller/66/Exec. Chmn., John D. Opie/70/Dir., Robert H. Brust/65/Dir., John D. Englar/61/Dir., David N. Farr/53/Dir., Raymond J. Milchovich/58/Dir., Craig G. Naylor/59/Dir., John H. Walker/51/Dir., Martin E. Welch/60/Dir., Oscar De Paula Bernardes Neto/62/Dir., Paula Bernardes Neto/62/Dir.

Owners: Highland Capital Management, L.P./8.80%, UBS Securities LLC, Appaloosa Management L P/15.00%, David B. Wohleen, Mark R. Weber, Insiders, Harbinger Capital Partners Master Fundl, Ltd./4.70%, Rodney ONeal, Merrill Lynch, Pierce, Fenner& Smith Inc., John D. Opie, Guy C. Hachey

Financial Data: *Fiscal Year End:*12/31 *Latest Annual Data:* 12/31/2006

Year	Sales	Net Income
2006	$26,392,000,000	-$5,464,000,000
2005	$26,947,000,000	-$2,357,000,000
2004	$28,622,000,000	-$4,753,000,000

Curr. Assets:	$9,215,000,000	**Curr. Liab.:**	$8,370,000,000		
Plant, Equip.:	$4,695,000,000	**Total Liab.:**	$27,244,000,000	**Indic. Yr. Divd.:**	NA
Total Assets:	$15,392,000,000	**Net Worth:**	-$12,055,000,000	**Debt/ Equity:**	NA

Delphi Financial Group Inc

1105 N Market St., Ste. 1230, Wilmington, DE, 19899; ***PH:*** 1-302-478-5142; ***Fax:*** 1-302-427-7663;
http:// www.delphifin.com

General - Incorporation	DE	**Stock**- Price on:12/24/2007	$41.45
Employees	1,410	Stock Exchange	NYSE
Auditor	Ernst & Young LLP	Ticker Symbol	DFG
Stk Agt	American Stock Transfer & Trust Co.	Outstanding Shares	49,410,000
Counsel	NA	E.P.S	$3.09
DUNS No.	18-857-4214	Shareholders	NA

Business: The group's principle activity is to provide integrated employee benefit services. It manages all aspects of employee absence to enhance the productivity of its clients and provides the related insurance coverage: short-term and long-term disability, primary and excess workers' compensation, group life and travel accident. The group's two reportable segments are group employee benefit products and asset accumulation products. The group emphasizes the origination of specialty insurance products directed to the employee benefits market, primarily group life, disability, workers' compensation and travel accident insurance. The asset accumulation products consist primarily of single premium deferred annuities and flexible premium annuities. The group's quarterly revenue for September 2007 was 387.23 millions of USD.

Primary SIC and add'l.: 6331 6321 6311

CIK No: 0000859139

Subsidiaries: Chestnut Investors II, Inc., Chestnut Investors III, Inc., Chestnut Investors IV, Inc., Delphi Brokerage Company, Delphi Capital Management, Inc., Delphi Finance Trust I, Delphi Funding LLC, DFG Corporation, DFG II Corporation, First Reliance Standard Life Insurance Company, Greenbrook LLC, Matrix Absence Management, Inc., Matrix Payroll Services, Inc., Reliance Standard Life Insurance Company, Reliance Standard Life Insurance Company of Texas 22 Subsidiaries included in the Index

Officers: Robert Rosenkranz/Chmn., CEO/$7,313,140.00, Bernard J. Kilkelly/VP - Investor Relations, Robert M. Smith/Dir., Exec. VP/$1,665,130.00, Thomas W. Burghart/VP, Treasurer/$800,390.00, Chad W. Coulter/Sr. VP, Sec., General Counsel, Donald A. Sherman/57/Dir., COO, Pres./$2,247,557.00

Directors: Robert Rosenkranz/Chmn., CEO, James N. Meehan/Dir., Lawrence E. Daurelle/Dir., Phillip R. O'Connor/59/Dir., Robert M. Smith/Dir., Exec. VP, Harold F. Ilg/60/Dir., Robert F. Wright/Dir., Kevin R. Brine/57/Dir., Steven A. Hirsh/68/Dir., Edward A. Fox/Dir., James M. Litvack/66/Dir., Donald A. Sherman/57/Dir., COO, Pres.

Owners: EARNEST Partners, LLC./8.30%, Philip R. O'Connor, Robert Rosenkranz, Robert Rosenkranz, Robert M. Smith, Robert F. Wright, Rosenkranz & Company, L.P, Harold F. Ilg, Kevin R. Brine, James N. Meehan, Lawrence E. Daurelle, Dimensional Fund Advisors, L.P/6.90%, Thomas W. Burghart, Insiders, Insiders/2.40% (19 Owners included in Index)

Financial Data: Fiscal Year End:12/31 Latest Annual Data: 12/31/2006

Year	Sales	Net Income
2006	$1,411,591,000	$142,068,000
2005	$1,222,783,000	$113,334,000
2004	$1,055,831,000	$123,543,000

Curr. Assets:	$859,036,000	Curr. Liab.:	$55,342,000	P/E Ratio:	14.24
Plant, Equip.:	$267,920,000	Total Liab.:	$4,495,667,000	Indic. Yr. Divd.:	$0.360
Total Assets:	$5,670,475,000	Net Worth:	$1,174,808,000	Debt/ Equity:	0.3673

Delta & Pine Land Co

One Cotton Row, Scott, MS, 38772; **PH:** 1-601-742-3351; *http://* www.deltaandpine.com

General - Incorporation	DE	**Stock** - Price on:12/24/2007	NA
Employees	533	Stock Exchange	NA
Auditor	KPMG LLP	Ticker Symbol	NA
Stk Agt	Computershare Investor Services LLC	Outstanding Shares	NA
Counsel	NA	E.P.S.	NA
DUNS No.	00-696-4845	Shareholders	NA

Business: The group's principle activities is to breed, produce, condition and market proprietary varieties of cotton planting seeds in the United States and other cotton producing nations. The group also breeds, produces, conditions and distributes soybean planting seeds in the United States. The proprietary seed products are developed through research and development efforts. The products are sold in foreign countries through export sales, joint ventures and distributors.

Primary SIC and add'l.: 0131 5191 0116

CIK No: 0000902277

Officers: Kenny Avery/Regional Business Dir. - East, Ken Ferreira/Regional Tech Development Mgr. - East, Barry Knight/Regional Business Dir. - West, Kent Croon/Regional Tech Development Mgr. - West, Brad Meyer/Technical Service Agronomist, Dru Rush/Technical Service Agronomist, Brewton AL, Ken Lege/Regional Technical Services Dir. - Piedmont AL, Dave Albers/Regional Technical Services Dir. - Lubbock, TX, Autumn Atwill/Technical Service Agronomist, Marion, AR, Quentin Zaunbrecher/Technical Service Agronomist, Lecompte, LA, Stacey Bruff/District Technical Service Mgr. - Jonesboro, AR, Randy Wegener/Technical Service Agronomist, Visalia, CA, Ty Fowler/Technical Service Agronomist, Tifton, GA, Shannon Crawley/Technical Service Agronomist, Eric Best/Technical Service Agronomist, Lubbock, TX (21 Officers included in Index)

Owners: Alson Capital Partners LLC/5.80%, Insiders/5.90%, Nam-Hai Chua/0.30%, Murray F. Robinson, Jon E. M. Jacoby/0.50%, Joseph M. Murphy/0.30%, R. D. Greene, James H. Willeke/0.10%, Stanley P. Roth/0.50%, Charles R. Dismuke/0.60%, William V. Hugie/0.20%, W. T. Jagodinski/1.40%, Rudi E. Scheidt/0.40%

Delta Air Lines Inc

1030 Delta Blvd., Atlanta, GA, 30320; **PH:** 1-404-715-2600; **Fax:** 1-404-715-5042; *http://* www.delta.com; **Email:** investorrelations@delta.com

General - Incorporation	DE	**Stock** - Price on:12/24/2007	$0.018
Employees	55,700	Stock Exchange	OTC
Auditor	Deloitte & Touche LLP	Ticker Symbol	DALRQ
Stk Agt	Wells Fargo Shareowner Services	Outstanding Shares	NA
Counsel	NA	E.P.S.	NA
DUNS No.	00-692-4872	Shareholders	NA

Business: The group's principle activity is to provide scheduled air transportation for passengers and cargo worldwide. The group operates from United States.

Primary SIC and add'l.: 4512

CIK No: 0000027904

Subsidiaries: Aero Assurance Ltd., American World Airways, Inc., ASA Holdings, Inc., Comair Holdings, LLC, Comair Services, Inc., Comair, Inc., Crown Rooms, Inc., DAL Aircraft Trading, Inc., DAL Global Services, LLC, DAL Moscow, Inc., Delta Air Lines Dublin Limited, Delta Air Lines Private Limited, Delta Air Lines, Inc. and Pan, Delta AirElite Business Jets, Inc., Delta Benefits Management, Inc. 25 Subsidiaries included in the Index

Officers: Richard Anderson/53/Dir., CEO, Meridith Eakin/Contact - Business Solutions, James M. Whitehurst/39/COO, Jill S. Greer/Dir. - Investor Relations, Shirley Bridges/50/CIO, Beth Johnston/Sr. VP - Human Resources, Joanne Smith/Sr. VP - In, Flight Service, Global Product Development, Wayne Aaron/VP - Corporate Strategy, Business Development, Jeff Battcher/VP - Corporate

Communications, Doug Blissit/VP - Public Affairs, John Boatright/57/VP - Corporate Real Estate, Sourcing Strategy, Joe Kolshak/Exec. VP - Operations, Glen W. Hauenstein/Exec. VP, Chief - Network, Revenue Management, Lee MacEnczak/Exec. VP - Sales, Marketing, Edward Bastian/CFO, Pres. (17 Officers included in Index)

Directors: Richard Anderson/53/Dir., CEO, Edward H. Budd/72/Dir., Gerald Grinstein/73/Dir., Domenico De Sole/Dir., Eugene I. Davis/Dir., Richard K. Goeltz/Dir., Victor L. Lund/Dir., Walter Massey/Dir., Arthur E. Johnson/59/Dir., Karl J. Krapek/59/Dir., Paula Rosput Reynolds/50/Dir., John F. Smith/68/Dir., Kenneth B. Woodrow/62/Dir., Joan E. Spero/62/Dir., John S. Brinzo/Dir. (18 Directors included in Index)

Delta Apparel Inc

2750 Premiere Pkwy., Ste. 100, Duluth, GA, 30097; **PH:** 1-678-775-6900; **Fax:** 1-678-775-6992; *http://* www.deltaapparel.com; **Email:** info@deltaapparel.com

General - Incorporation	GA	**Stock** - Price on:12/24/2007	$17.55
Employees	4,000	Stock Exchange	AMEX
Auditor	Ernst & Young LLP	Ticker Symbol	DLA
Stk Agt	American Stock Transfer & Trust Co.	Outstanding Shares	8,450,000
Counsel	NA	E.P.S.	$0.296
DUNS No.	NA	Shareholders	NA

Business: The group's principal activity is to manufacture and market knit apparel garments that includes t-shirts, golf shirts and activewear tops and fabrics. The group's customers include the distributors, screen printers and private label accounts. The products of the group are marketed under the delta pro weight, delta magnum weight and quail hollow(R) sportswear brand names, as well as under private labels for both retail and branded apparel programs. The group operates manufacturing and distribution facilities in the southeastern United States and California and has manufacturing facilities in Mexico and Central America. On 03-Oct-2003, the group acquired m. J. Soffe co.

Primary SIC and add'l.: 2321

CIK No: 0001101396

Subsidiaries: Delta Apparel Honduras, S.A., Delta Campeche, S.A. de C.V, Delta Cortes, S.A., Junkfood Clothing Company, M. J. Soffe Co, SAIM, LLC

Officers: Robert W. Humphreys/Dir., CEO, Pres./$1,543,025.00, David S. Fraser/Dir. - Business Consultant, Max Lennon/Dir., Pres. - Education, Research Services, ERS, Philip J. Mazzilli/Dir. - Business Consultant, Gina Pepe/Sales Representative, CA, Emily Weng/Sales Representative, CO, Mary Lee Hewitt/Sales Representative, WA, Ray Prevost/Sales Representative, TN, Terry Butz/Sales Representative, AL, William T. McGhee/Pres. - Delta Activewear, Harvey Spector/Sales Representative, NY, Deborah H. Merrill/CFO, VP, Treasurer/$572,444.00, Martha M. Watson/VP, Sec./$425,156.00, Bill Zima/Contact - Integrated Corporate Relations, Elliot Floren/Sales Representative, NY (26 Officers included in Index)

Directors: Robert W. Humphreys/Dir., CEO, Pres., Elizabeth J. Gatewood/Dir., David S. Fraser/Dir. - Business Consultant, William F. Garrett/Dir., Max Lennon/Dir., Pres. - Education, Research Services, ERS, Erwin E. Maddrey/Dir., Philip J. Mazzilli/Dir. - Business Consultant, Buck A. Mickel/Dir., David Peterson/Dir.

Owners: Insiders/28.20%, Dimensional Fund Advisors LP/8.50%, FMR Corporation/11.00%, David S. Fraser, Kenneth D. Spires/1.40%, David Peterson, Minor M. Shaw/7.50%, Charles C. Mickel/7.50%, Elizabeth J. Gatewood, Buck A. Mickel/8.00%, Erwin E. Maddrey/9.20%, David R. Palmer, Deborah H. Merrill, Max Lennon, Royce & Associates/7.00% (20 Owners included in Index)

Financial Data: Fiscal Year End:07/02 Latest Annual Data: 06/30/2007

Year	Sales	Net Income
2007	$312,438,000	$6,343,000
2006	$270,108,000	$14,844,000
2005	$228,065,000	$11,243,000

Curr. Assets:	$147,522,000	Curr. Liab.:	$53,114,000	P/E Ratio:	12.72
Plant, Equip.:	$19,529,000	Total Liab.:	$93,887,000	Indic. Yr. Divd.:	$0.200
Total Assets:	$169,379,000	Net Worth:	$75,492,000	Debt/ Equity:	0.7211

Delta Financial Corp

1000 Woodbury Rd., Woodbury, NY, 11797; ; *http://* www.deltafinancial.com; **Email:** custserv@deltafunding.com

General - Incorporation	DE	**Stock** - Price on:12/24/2007	$12.47
Employees	1,395	Stock Exchange	NDQ
Auditor	BDO Seidman, LLP	Ticker Symbol	DFC
Stk Agt	Mellon Investor Services LLC	Outstanding Shares	23,580,000
Counsel	Stroock & Stroock & Lavan	E.P.S.	-$1.12
DUNS No.	96-665-4543	Shareholders	NA

Business: The group's principal activity is to originate, securitize and sell non-conforming mortgage loans that are secured by first mortgages on one- to four-family residential properties. The group provides mortgage loans through two distribution channels - wholesale and retail. The group originates wholesale mortgage loans indirectly through independent mortgage brokers and other real estate professionals who submit loan applications on behalf of borrowers. It originates most of its wholesale mortgage loans through a network of approximately 1,700 brokers in 26 states. The group develops retail loan leads primarily through telemarketing, Internet leads, direct mail, radio advertising, origination centers and retail offices. The group primarily conducts its broker lending operations out of its woodbury, New York headquarters. Retail operations are carried out through four call centers, seven retail offices and a telemarketing hub, located in nine states.

Primary SIC and add'l.: 6162

CIK No: 0001021848

Subsidiaries: Continental Property Management Corp., Delta Funding Corporation, DF Special Holdings Corporation, Dfc 1999-a Corp., Dfc 2000-b Corp., Dfc 2003-a Corp., Dfc 2005-a Company, LLC, DFC Acceptance Corporation, DFC Financial Corporation, DFC Financial of Canada Limited, DFC Funding Corporation, DFC Funding of Canada Limited, DFC Holding-A Corp., DFC Receivables Company, LLC, DFC Servicing Receivables Company, LLC 23 Subsidiaries included in the Index

Officers: Hugh Miller/Dir., CEO, Pres./$1,769,733.00, Lee Miller/Exec. VP, Chief Credit Officer, Treasurer/$668,470.00, Richard Blass/Dir., Exec. VP, CFO/$1,244,858.00, Randall F. Michaels/Exec. VP - Sales, Marketing/$1,029,449.00, Drew Biondo/Dir. - Corporate Communications

Directors: Hugh Miller/Dir., CEO, Pres., Sidney A. Miller/Founder, Chmn., Martin D. Payson/Dir., John Adamovich/Dir., William Addas/Dir., Margaret A. Williams/Dir., Arnold B. Pollard/Dir., Richard Blass/Dir., Exec. VP, CFO

Owners: Richard Blass, William J. Horan, Arnold B. Pollard, T. Rowe Price Associates, Inc., William Addas, Margaret A. Williams, John Adamovich, Angelo Gordon & Co., L.P., Sidney A. Miller, Hugh Miller, Randall F. Michaels, Marc E. Miller, Martin D. Payson, Flagg Street Capital, LLC, Insiders *(17 Owners included in Index)*

Financial Data: Fiscal Year End:12/31 **Latest Annual Data:** 12/31/2006

Year	Sales	Net Income
2006	$512,102,000	$29,765,000
2005	$332,696,000	$17,955,000
2004	$117,884,000	-$9,349,000

Curr. Assets:	$125,658,000	**Curr. Liab.:**	$78,212,000	**P/E Ratio:**	13.86
Plant, Equip.:	$8,287,000	**Total Liab.:**	$6,439,551,000	**Indic. Yr. Divd.:**	$0.200
Total Assets:	$6,589,127,000	**Net Worth:**	$149,576,000	**Debt/ Equity:**	46.0508

Delta Galil Industries Ltd

2 Kaufman St., Tel Aviv, 68012; **PH:** 972-35193744; *http://* www.deltagalil.com

General - Incorporation	Israel	**Stock**- Price on:12/24/2007	$6.38
Employees	11,000	Stock Exchange	NDQ
Auditor	Kesselman & Kesselman	Ticker Symbol	DELT
Stk Agt	NA	Outstanding Shares	18,740,000
Counsel	NA	E.P.S.	-$0.71
DUNS No.	NA	Shareholders	NA

Business: The group's principle activities include manufacturing and marketing of private label women's intimate apparel, men's underwear, socks, shirts, babywear, bras, leisurewear and nightwear, knitted fabrics, dyeing, trimmings and elastic ribbons. The group also sells its products to leading retailers including marks and spencers, gap, victoria's secret, kmart, jc penney, hema, wal-Mart and target. The group's products are sold under the brand names hugo boss, calvin klein, donna karan and nike. The group operates from United States.

Primary SIC and add'l.: 2251 2254 2322 2341

CIK No: 0001081022

Subsidiaries: Century Wear Corporation, Delta Galil USA Inc.

Officers: Aviram Lahav/49/CEO, Pres., Esti Maoz/60/Sr. VP, Chief Marketing Officer, Yossi Hajaj/40/CFO, Sr. VP, Imad Telhami/49/COO, Sr. VP

Directors: Dov Lautman/72/Chmn., Isaac Dabah/50/Vice Chmn., Noam Lautman/39/Dir., Giora Morag/63/Dir., Israel Baum/69/Dir., Gideon Chitayat/68/Dir., Aharon Dovrat/77/Dir., Harvey M. Krueger/79/Dir., Amnon Neubach/63/Dir., Dan Propper/67/Dir., Arnon Tiberg/64/Dir., Leah Perez/58/Dir.

Owners: Menorah Holdings Ltd./5.80%, Dov Lautman/24.80%, Aharon Dovrat/0.16%, Arnon Tiberg/3.50%, GMM Capital, LLC/28.40%, Insiders/62.68%, Harvey Krueger/0.03%

Financial Data: Fiscal Year End:12/31 **Latest Annual Data:** 12/31/2006

Year	Sales	Net Income
2006	$706,699,000	$3,148,000
2005	$684,481,000	-$36,347,000
2004	$654,269,000	$12,685,000

Curr. Assets:	$272,434,000	**Curr. Liab.:**	$217,581,000		
Plant, Equip.:	$99,263,000	**Total Liab.:**	$262,645,000	**Indic. Yr. Divd.:**	NA
Total Assets:	$450,862,000	**Net Worth:**	$188,217,000	**Debt/ Equity:**	NA

Delta Mutual Inc New

111 N Branch St., Sellersville, PA, 18960; **PH:** 1-215-258-2800; **Fax:** 1-215-258-2870; *http://* www.deltamutual.com; **Email:** martinchilek@deltamutual.com

General - Incorporation	DE	**Stock**- Price on:12/24/2007	$0.07
Employees	4	Stock Exchange	OTC
Auditor	Wiener, Goodman & Company, P.C.	Ticker Symbol	DLTM
Stk Agt	Standard Registrar & Transfer Co Inc.	Outstanding Shares	62,270,000
Counsel	NA	E.P.S.	-$0.05
DUNS No.	NA	Shareholders	NA

Business: The groups principle activity is to specialize in energy recovery services and construction. The groups service includes Energy Efficient Building Material System. In the year 2005, the group acquired Delta Technologies, Inc. The group operates from Middle East, Far East and Puerto Rico.

Primary SIC and add'l.: 4955 4953 7699 4959 8711 5093

CIK No: 0001112985

Subsidiaries: Delta Developers Corp., Delta Technologies, Inc.

Officers: Peter F. Russo/65/Dir., CEO, Pres., Assist. Sec./$129,266.00, Martin G. Chilek/57/CFO, Sr. VP, Treasurer, Sec./$115,466.00, John M. Latza/Pres. - Delta Technologies, Judy Dallas/Dir. - Administration, David M. Razmara/Pres.

Directors: Peter F. Russo/65/Dir., CEO, Pres., Assist. Sec.

Owners: Mesacmech Lev Company/6.42%, GZSZ/7.43%, Robyn Berman/8.91%, Martin G. Chilek/1.52%, Peter F. Russo/1.60%, Insiders/3.12%, Ben Eluzer Company/8.03%, Neil Berman/16.88%, Congregation Azrial Yehuda/7.87%

Financial Data: Fiscal Year End:12/31 **Latest Annual Data:** 3/31/2007

Year	Sales	Net Income
2007	NA	NA
2006	NA	NA
2005	$20,000	-$2,580,000

Curr. Assets:	$461,000	**Curr. Liab.:**	$1,669,000		
Plant, Equip.:	$449,000	**Total Liab.:**	$1,911,000	**Indic. Yr. Divd.:**	NA
Total Assets:	$1,045,000	**Net Worth:**	-$866,000	**Debt/ Equity:**	NA

Delta Natural Gas Co Inc

3617 Lexington Rd., Winchester, KY, 40391; **PH:** 1-859-744-6171; **Fax:** 1-859-744-6552; *http://* www.deltagas.com; **Email:** delta@mis.net

General - Incorporation	KY	**Stock**- Price on:12/24/2007	$25.77
Employees	156	Stock Exchange	NDQ
Auditor	Deloitte & Touche LLP	Ticker Symbol	DGAS
Stk Agt	Computershare Investor Services LLC	Outstanding Shares	3,270,000
Counsel	NA	E.P.S.	$1.54
DUNS No.	00-777-9408	Shareholders	NA

Business: The group's principle activities is distribution of natural gas to retail customers. The group also provides gas transportation services to industrial customers and interconnected pipelines. The group operates through two segments namely, regulated and non-regulated. The group provides services in Nicholasville, Corbin and Berea, Kentucky areas. The group's quarterly revenue for September 2007 was 12.40 millions of USD.

Primary SIC and add'l.: 4923

CIK No: 0000277375

Subsidiaries: Delgasco, Inc., Delta Resources, Inc., Enpro, Inc.

Officers: Glenn R. Jennings/59/Chmn., CEO, Pres./$714,620.00, John B. Brown/41/VP, Controller, CFO, Treasurer, Sec./$220,762.00, Brian Ramsey/Mgr. - Gas Supply, Emily P. Bennett/Dir. - Corporate Services, Johnny L. Caudill/59/VP - Administration, Customer Service/$283,766.00, John F. Hall/65/VP - Finance, Sec., Treasure/$259,100.00, Alan L. Heath/61/VP - Operations, Engineering/$316,887.00, Michael C. Downs/Dist Cust Serv Supervisor, Charles W. Gardner/Dist Cust Serv Supervisor, Robert C. Hazelrigg/Mgr. - External Affairs, Connie H. King/Mgr. - Corp, Employee Serv, Edward T. Lundy/Construction Supervisor, Sawyer J. Messer/Construction Supervisor, Gerald L. Powell/Corrosion Control Supv, Michael B. Robinson/DIV Mgr. - Cust Service *(34 Officers included in Index)*

Directors: Glenn R. Jennings/59/Chmn., CEO, Pres., Lanny D. Greer/57/Dir., Michael R. Whitley/65/Dir., Linda K. Breathitt/57/Dir., Donald R. Crowe/74/Dir., Michael J. Kistner/65/Dir., Lewis N. Melton/68/Dir., Arthur E. Walker/63/Dir., Billy Joe Hall/71/Dir.

Owners: Arthur E. Walker, Johnny L. Caudill, Michael R. Whitley, Michael J. Kistner, Billy Joe Hall, Lanny D. Greer, John B. Brown, Insiders/2.10%, Glenn R. Jennings, Alan L. Heath, Lewis N. Melton

Financial Data: Fiscal Year End:06/30 **Latest Annual Data:** 6/30/2006

Year	Sales	Net Income
2006	$117,247,000	$5,025,000
2005	$84,181,000	$4,999,000
2004	$79,194,000	$3,838,000

Curr. Assets:	$23,466,000	**Curr. Liab.:**	$18,895,000	**P/E Ratio:**	17.18
Plant, Equip.:	$120,389,000	**Total Liab.:**	$102,945,000	**Indic. Yr. Divd.:**	$1.240
Total Assets:	$155,554,000	**Net Worth:**	$52,610,000	**Debt/ Equity:**	NA

Delta Oil & Gas Inc

1122 6th Ave. N, Seattle, WA, 98109; **PH:** 1-866-355-3644; *http://* www.deltaoilandgas.com; **Email:** ir@deltaoilandgas.com

General - Incorporation	CO	**Stock**- Price on:12/24/2007	$0.65
Employees	1	Stock Exchange	OTC
Auditor	Telford Sadovnick, PLLC	Ticker Symbol	DOIG
Stk Agt	Pacific Stock Transfer Company	Outstanding Shares	NA
Counsel	NA	E.P.S.	NA
DUNS No.	NA	Shareholders	NA

Business: The group is a development stage, independent natural gas and oil company engaged in the exploration, development and acquisition of natural gas and oil properties in the United States.

Primary SIC and add'l.: 1382

CIK No: 0001166847

Subsidiaries: Delta Oil & Gas (Canada) Inc.

Officers: Douglas N. Bolen/Dir., CEO, Principal Executive Officer, Pres., Kulwant Sandher/CFO

Directors: Douglas N. Bolen/Dir., CEO, Principal Executive Officer, Pres.

Owners: Douglas N. Bolen/2.10%, Insiders/2.30%, Kulwant Sandher/0.20%

Financial Data: Fiscal Year End:12/31 **Latest Annual Data:** 12/31/2006

Year	Sales	Net Income
2006	$1,578,000	-$275,000
2005	$7,000	-$570,000
2004	$9,000	-$32,000

Curr. Assets:	$1,759,000	**Curr. Liab.:**	$40,000		
Plant, Equip.:	$2,630,000	**Total Liab.:**	$81,000	**Indic. Yr. Divd.:**	NA
Total Assets:	$4,388,000	**Net Worth:**	$4,308,000	**Debt/ Equity:**	NA

Delta Petroleum Corp

370 17th St., Ste. 4300, Denver, CO, 80202; **PH:** 1-303-293-9133; **Fax:** 1-303-298-8251; *http://* www.deltapetro.com; **Email:** investorrelations@deltapetro.com

General - Incorporation	DE	**Stock**- Price on:12/24/2007	$21.7
Employees	122	Stock Exchange	NDQ
Auditor	KPMG LLP	Ticker Symbol	DPTR
Stk Agt	Corporate Stock Transfer, Inc.	Outstanding Shares	65,690,000
Counsel	NA	E.P.S.	-$2.36
DUNS No.	18-650-8057	Shareholders	NA

Business: The group's principal activity is to acquire, explore, develop and produce oil and gas properties. As of 30-Jun-2003, the group had varying interests in 488 gross (260 net) productive wells located in 14 states and offshore California. In addition, the group owns interests in five federal units and one lease offshore California near santa barbara. The products of the group include crude oil and natural gas. The group markets its products to refineries and transmission companies located near its producing properties. On 30-Jun-2003, the group acquired producing oil and gas interests and related undeveloped acreage in Kansas. The group also acquired certain producing and drilling prospects in Colorado and Wyoming on 19-Sep-2003, as well as, certain production and acreage located primarily in eland and stadium fields in stark county, North Dakota on 10-Dec-2003. On 29-Jun-2004, the group acquired alpine resources, inc.

Primary SIC and add'l.: 1311

CIK No: 0000821483

Subsidiaries: Amber Resources Company of Colorado, Castle Texas Exploration Limited Partnership, Chapman Trucking Company, CRB Partners, LLC, Delta Exploration Company, Inc., DHS Drilling Company, PGR, LLC, Piper Petroleum Company

Officers: Roger A. Parker/Chmn., CEO/$1,717,889.00, Ted Freedman/Exec. VP, General Counsel, Sec., John R. Wallace/COO, Pres./$1,122,703.00, Kevin K. Nanke/Treasurer, CFO/$902,972.00, Broc Richardson/VP - Corporate Development, Investor Relations

Directors: Roger A. Parker/Chmn., CEO, Russell S. Lewis/Dir., Jordan R. Smith/Dir., Aleron H. Larson/Dir., Jerrie F. Eckelberger/Dir., James B. Wallace/Dir., Neal A. Stanley/Dir., Kevin R. Collins/Dir., Hank Brown/Dir.

Owners: Steinberg Asset Management, LLC/6.80%, Roger A. Parker/3.21%, Kevin K. Nanke/1.24%, James B. Wallace, Capital Research and Management Company and SMALLCAP World Fund, Inc./8.80%, Jerrie F. Eckelberger, Vega Petroleum Limited/5.10%, Capital Group International, Inc./11.60%, Kevin R. Collins, Aleron H. Larson, Russell S. Lewis, Stanley F. Freedman, Neal A. Stanley, Sprott Asset Management, Inc./13.80%, GLG North American Opportunity Fund/5.50% *(19 Owners included in Index)*

Financial Data: *Fiscal Year End:*06/30 *Latest Annual Data:* 12/31/2006

Year	Sales	Net Income
2006	$181,361,000	$435,000
2005	$94,707,000	$15,050,000

Curr. Assets:	$27,034,000	**Curr. Liab.:**	$54,150,000		
Plant, Equip.:	$473,550,000	**Total Liab.:**	$276,746,000	**Indic. Yr. Divd.:**	NA
Total Assets:	$512,983,000	**Net Worth:**	$221,623,000	**Debt/ Equity:**	0.7055

Deltathree Inc

75 Broad St., 31st Fl., New York, NY, 10004; *PH:* 1-212-500-4850; *Fax:* 1-212-500-4888; *http://* corp.deltathree.com; *Email:* ir@deltathree.com

General - Incorporation	DE	**Stock**- Price on:12/24/2007	$1.3031
Employees	115	Stock Exchange	NDQ
Auditor	Brightman Almagor & Co	Ticker Symbol	DDDC
Stk Agt	American Stock Transfer & Trust Co.	Outstanding Shares	32,770,000
Counsel	Kadden, Arps, Slate, Meagher & Flom	E.P.S	-$0.135
DUNS No.	NA	Shareholders	NA

Business: The group's principal activity is to provide integrated voice over Internet protocol (voip) telephony services. Internet protocol telephony is the real time transmission of voice communications in the form of digitized packets of information over the public Internet or a private network, similar to the way in which e-mail and other data is transmitted. The group's business includes: the transmission of voice and data traffic for communications carriers; the provision of enhanced Web-based and other communications services to individual consumers, under the iconnecthere brand name; the provision of a total hosted communications solution and the transmission of voice and data traffic for communications carriers. The operations are carried on in the United States, Europe, Argentina, the Far East and other countries.

Primary SIC and add'l.: 4813

CIK No: 0001086740

Subsidiaries: Deltathree, Ltd.

Officers: Shimmy Zimels/Dir., CEO, Pres./$296,991.00, Richard B. Grant/Sr. VP - Finance/$201,425.00, Effi Baruch/Sr. VP - Operations, Technology, Sagi Schiller/VP - Sales, Neta Issacof/Dir. - Marketing, Shely Sussman/VP - Human Resources, Tomer Treves/MD - Consumer Group, Yaron Globus/VP - Operations

Directors: Shimmy Zimels/Dir., CEO, Pres., Noam Bardin/Chmn., Lior Samuelson/Dir., Benjamin Broder/Dir., Ilan Biran/Dir.

Owners: Noam Bardin/1.70%, Insiders/4.00%, Atarey Hasharon Chevra Lepituach Vehashkaot Benadlan (1991) Ltd./36.00%, Guy Gussarsky, Benjamin Broder, Ilan Biran, Lior Samuelson, Paul C. White, Richard Grant, Shimmy Zimels/1.60%

Financial Data: *Fiscal Year End:*12/31 *Latest Annual Data:* 12/31/2006

Year	Sales	Net Income
2006	$37,953,000	$507,000
2005	$29,714,000	-$854,000
2004	$21,069,000	-$3,249,000

Curr. Assets:	$17,742,000	**Curr. Liab.:**	$5,560,000		
Plant, Equip.:	$3,458,000	**Total Liab.:**	$5,777,000	**Indic. Yr. Divd.:**	NA
Total Assets:	$22,395,000	**Net Worth:**	$16,618,000	**Debt/ Equity:**	NA

Deltic Timber Corp

210 E Elm St., El Dorado, AR, 71731; *PH:* 1-870-881-9400; *Fax:* 1-870-881-6454; *http://* www.deltic.com; *Email:* ir@deltic.com

General - Incorporation	DE	**Stock**- Price on:12/24/2007	$58.03
Employees	464	Stock Exchange	NYSE
Auditor	KPMG LLP	Ticker Symbol	DEL
Stk Agt	Computershare Investor Services LLC	Outstanding Shares	12,480,000
Counsel	NA	E.P.S	$0.58
DUNS No.	19-510-7677	Shareholders	NA

Business: The group's principle activities are to grow and harvest timber and manufacture and market lumber. The group operates under three segments: mills, woodlands and real estate. Mills: produces dimension lumber, boards, timbers, decking and finger-jointed studs. The lumber is sold to wholesalers and treaters in the south and midwest, which are used in residential construction, roof trusses and laminated beams. Woodlands: manages 434,000 acres of timberland in Arkansas and north Louisiana. Real estate: operates and develops property in stages, and real estate sales consists of residential lots sold to builders or individuals and commercial tracts. The group has been developing Chenal Valley a 4,800-acre upscale planned community, centered on two golf courses. The group's quarterly revenue for September 2007 was 25.53 millions of USD.

Primary SIC and add'l.: 2411 6531 2491 2431

CIK No: 0001022469

Subsidiaries: Chenal Country Club, Inc., Chenal Properties, Inc., Deltic Real Estate Investment Company, Deltic Southwest Timber Company, Deltic Timber Purchasers, Inc.

Officers: Ray C. Dillon/Dir., CEO, Pres./$1,089,225.00, Bayless W. Rowe/VP, General Counsel, Sec./$551,886.00, Phillip A. Pesek/VP, General Counsel, Sec., Byrom L. Walker/Controller, Kent L. Streeter/VP - Operations/$448,350.00, Clefton D. Vaughan/VP, Treasurer/$675,291.00, Kenneth D. Mann/CFO, VP, Treasurer, David V. Meghreblian/VP - Real Estate/$413,542.00

Directors: Ray C. Dillon/Dir., CEO, Pres., Robert C. Nolan/Chmn., O. H. Darling/Dir., Canon Christoph Keller/Dir., John C. Shealy/Dir., Thurston J. Roach/Dir., Madison R. Murphy/Dir., Hunter R. Pierson/Dir., Christoph Keller/53/Dir., Randolph C. Coley/Dir., David L. Lemmon/Dir., Robert Tudor/Dir.

Owners: Randy C. Coley, Insiders, David L. Lemmon, David V. Meghreblian, Advisory Research, Inc., Keely Asset Management Corporation, Christoph Keller, T. Rowe Price Associates, Inc., Robert C. Nolan, Kent L. Streeter, Hunter R. Pierson, Thurston J. Roach, John C. Shealy, Clefton D. Vaughan, Robert B. Tudor *(20 Owners included in Index)*

Financial Data: *Fiscal Year End:*12/31 *Latest Annual Data:* 12/31/2006

Year	Sales	Net Income
2006	$153,112,000	$11,323,000
2005	$168,350,000	$14,518,000
2004	$142,017,000	$11,093,000

Curr. Assets:	$23,799,000	**Curr. Liab.:**	$11,089,000	**P/E Ratio:**	54.23
Plant, Equip.:	$248,562,000	**Total Liab.:**	$116,785,000	**Indic. Yr. Divd.:**	$0.300
Total Assets:	$324,266,000	**Net Worth:**	$207,481,000	**Debt/ Equity:**	0.3334

Deluxe Corp

3680 Victoria St. N, Shoreview, MN, 55126; *PH:* 1-651-483-7111; *Fax:* 1-651-481-4163; *http://* www.deluxe.com; *Email:* feedback@deluxe.com

General - Incorporation	MN	**Stock**- Price on:12/24/2007	$42.63
Employees	8,813	Stock Exchange	NYSE
Auditor	PricewaterhouseCoopers LLP	Ticker Symbol	DLX
Stk Agt	Wells Fargo Bank Minnesota N.A	Outstanding Shares	51,900,000
Counsel	NA	E.P.S	$2.91
DUNS No.	15-006-5779	Shareholders	NA

Business: The groups principle activity is to provide customized products and services to small businesses and financial institutions. The groups products include checks, forms, business cards, stationery, greeting cards, labels and retail packaging supplies, promotional products and merchandising materials. The group operates from United States.

Primary SIC and add'l.: 2759 2761 2782 7389 2754

CIK No: 0000027996

Subsidiaries: Chiswick, Inc., Deluxe Enterprise Operations, Inc., Deluxe Financial Services Texas, L.P., Deluxe Financial Services, Inc., Deluxe Manufacturing Operations, Inc., Deluxe Small Business Sales, Inc., Dgbs (uk) Forms Limited, Dgbs (uk) Holdings Limited, Direct Checks Unlimited Sales, Inc, Direct Checks Unlimited, LLC, DLX Check Printers, Inc., DLX Check Texas, Inc, McBee Systems Ohio, Inc., McBee Systems, Inc., NEBS Business Products Limited 30 Subsidiaries included in the Index

Officers: Lee J. Schram/Dir., CEO/$1,931,391.00, Terry D. Peterson/VP - Investor Relations, Chief Accounting Officer/$419,508.00, Mike Degeneffe/CIO, Sr. VP, Lynn R. Koldenhoven/VP - Sales, Marketing Direct to Consumer Segment, Richard S. Greene/CFO, Sr. VP/$116,135.00, Jeff Stoner/Sr. VP - Human Resources/$304,590.00, Luann E. Widener/Sr. VP, Chief Sales, Marketing Officer Financial Institutions - Small Business Segments, Pres. - Financial Services/$667,078.00, Anthony C. Scarfone/Sr. VP, General Counsel, Sec./$652,664.00, Leanne E. Branham/VP - Fulfillment, Jennifer A. Anderson/Dir. - Foundations, Community Affairs

Directors: Lee J. Schram/Dir., CEO, Stephen P. Nachtsheim/Non - Exec. Chmn., Isaiah Harris/Dir., Charles A. Haggerty/Dir., Michael T. Glenn/Dir., Mary Ann ODwyer/Dir., Ronald C. Baldwin/Dir., Don J. McGrath/Dir., Neil Metviner/Dir., Cheryl E. McKissack/Dir., Martyn R. Redgrave/Dir., William A. Hawkins/54/Dir.

Owners: Ronald E. Eilers, Cheryl E. Mayberry McKissack, Jeffrey D. Stoner, Anthony C. Scarfone, Mary Ann O'Dwyer, Charles A. Haggerty, Lee J. Schram, Luann E. Widener, Richard S. Greene, Stephen P. Nachtsheim, William A. Hawkins, Michael T. Glenn, Douglas J. Treff, Insiders/1.58%, Isaiah Harris *(18 Owners included in Index)*

Financial Data: *Fiscal Year End:*12/31 *Latest Annual Data:* 12/31/2006

Year	Sales	Net Income
2006	$1,639,654,000	$100,954,000
2005	$1,716,294,000	$157,521,000
2004	$1,567,015,000	$197,991,000

Curr. Assets:	$202,117,000	**Curr. Liab.:**	$664,503,000	**P/E Ratio:**	19.65
Plant, Equip.:	$142,247,000	**Total Liab.:**	$1,332,805,000	**Indic. Yr. Divd.:**	$1.000
Total Assets:	$1,267,132,000	**Net Worth:**	-$65,673,000	**Debt/ Equity:**	NA

Denbury Resources Inc

5100 Tennyson Pkwy., Ste. 1200, Plano, TX, 75024; *PH:* 1-972-673-2000; *Fax:* 1-972-673-2150; *http://* www.denbury.com

General - Incorporation	DE	**Stock**- Price on:12/24/2007	$37.42
Employees	596	Stock Exchange	NYSE
Auditor	PricewaterhouseCoopers LLP	Ticker Symbol	DNR
Stk Agt	American Stock Transfer & Trust Co.	Outstanding Shares	121,090,000
Counsel	Jenkens & Gilchrist	E.P.S	$0.81
DUNS No.	62-447-3104	Shareholders	NA

Business: The group's principal activity is to acquire, develop, operate and explore oil and gas properties in the gulf coast region of the United States. The group holds significant reserves and production in Mississippi, where it produces oil and natural gas, onshore in Louisiana and in the offshore gulf of Mexico. The group acquired Genesis Energy, LLC on 14-May-2002.

Primary SIC and add'l.: 1311

CIK No: 0000945764

Subsidiaries: Denbury Gathering & Marketing, Inc., Denbury Marine, LLC, Denbury Onshore, LLC, Denbury Operating Company, Genesis Energy, Inc., Tuscaloosa Royalty Fund LLC

Officers: Gareth Roberts/CEO, Pres./$1,589,522.00, Phil Rykhoek/Sr. VP, CFO, Sec., Treasurer/$1,115,668.00, Mark C. Allen/VP, Chief Accounting Officer, Barry Schneider/VP - Production, Operations, Ray Dubuisson/VP - Land/$697,783.00, Sandy Sandusky/Human Resources Mgr., Tracy Evans/Sr. VP - Reservoir Engineering, Brad Cox/VP - Business Development, Charlie Gibson/VP - Reservoir Engineering, Dan Cole/VP - Marketing, Robert Cornelius/Sr. VP - Operations, Ronald T. Evans/Sr. VP - Reservoir Engineering/$1,082,255.00, Randy Stein/55/Dir., Independent Consultant, Greg McMichael/59/Dir., Independent Consultant, Cynthia Rodriguez/Contact - Data Requests *(17 Officers included in Index)*

Directors: Ronald G. Greene/59/Chmn., Donald D. Wolf/Dir., David I. Heather/Dir., Randy Stein/55/Dir., Independent Consultant, Greg McMichael/59/Dir., Independent Consultant, Wieland F. Wettstein/Dir.

Owners: Wieland F. Wettstein, David I. Heather, Phil Rykhoek, Mark C. Allen, Ronald G. Greene/1.70%, Dan Cole, Ray Dubuisson, Gareth Roberts/1.30%, Robert Cornelius, Neuberger & Berman Inc/17.90%, Brad Cox, Barry Schneider, Charlie Gibson, Randy Stein, Ronald T. Evans *(18 Owners included in Index)*

Financial Data: *Fiscal Year End:*12/31 *Latest Annual Data:* 12/31/2006

Year	Sales	Net Income
2006	$731,536,000	$202,457,000
2005	$560,392,000	$166,471,000
2004	$382,972,000	$82,448,000

Curr. Assets:	$183,269,000	*Curr. Liab.:*	$200,398,000	*P/E Ratio:*	24.14
Plant, Equip.:	$1,879,768,000	*Total Liab.:*	$1,033,778,000	*Indic. Yr. Divd.:*	NA
Total Assets:	$2,139,837,000	*Net Worth:*	$1,106,059,000	*Debt/ Equity:*	0.5445

Dendreon Corp

3005 1st Ave., Seattle, WA, 98121; *PH:* 1-206-256-4545; *Fax:* 1-206-256-0571;
http:// www.dendreon.com; *Email:* ir@dendreon.com

General - Incorporation	DE	*Stock* - Price on:12/24/2007	$7.38
Employees	232	Stock Exchange	NDQ
Auditor	Ernst & Young LLP	Ticker Symbol	DNDN
Stk Agt	Mellon Investor Services LLC	Outstanding Shares	83,510,000
Counsel	Cooley Godward LLP	E.P.S	-$1.16
DUNS No.	NA	Shareholders	NA

Business: The group's principal activities are to discover and develop novel products for the treatment of diseases through innovative manipulation of the immune system. The group's product pipeline is focused on treatment of cancer and includes therapeutic vaccines, monoclonal antibodies, small molecules and pro-drugs. It's product provenge, a therapeutic vaccine is used for the treatment of prostate cancer and apc8024 is used for the treatment of breast, ovarian and other solid tumors. On 30-Jul-2003, the group acquired corvas international, inc.

Primary SIC and add'l.: 2834 8731

CIK No: 0001107332

Subsidiaries: Dendreon San Diego LLC.

Officers: Mitchell H. Gold/Dir., CEO, Pres., James V. Caggiano/VP - Sales, Marketing, David L. Urdal/Dir., Sr. VP, Chief Scientific Officer, Rick Hamm/Sr. VP - Corporate Development, General Counsel, Sec., Gregory T. Schiffman/Sr. VP, CFO

Directors: Mitchell H. Gold/Dir., CEO, Pres., Richard B. Brewer/Chmn., David L. Urdal/Dir., Sr. VP, Chief Scientific Officer, Bogdan Dziurzynski/Dir., Ruth B. Kunath/54/Dir., Douglas Watson/Dir., Susan B. Bayh/Dir., Gerardo Canet/Dir., Blake M. Ingle/Dir.

Owners: Insiders/3.20%, Mitchell H. Gold, Douglas G. Watson, Richard F. Hamm, Robert M. Hershberg, Bogdan Dziurzynski, Blake M. Ingle, Richard B. Brewer, Susan B. Bayh, Gregory T. Schiffman, David L. Urdal/1.10%, Ruth B. Kunath, Gerardo Canet

Financial Data: Fiscal Year End:12/31   Latest Annual Data: 12/31/2006

Year	Sales	Net Income
2006	$273,000	-$91,642,000
2005	$210,000	-$81,547,000
2004	$5,035,000	-$75,240,000

Curr. Assets:	$109,978,000	*Curr. Liab.:*	$20,421,000		
Plant, Equip.:	$30,530,000	*Total Liab.:*	$37,926,000	*Indic. Yr. Divd.:*	NA
Total Assets:	$163,643,000	*Net Worth:*	$125,717,000	*Debt/ Equity:*	0.1594

Denia Enterprises Inc

1802 N Carson St., Carson City, NV, 89701; *PH:* 1-506-872-4033

General - Incorporation	NV	*Stock* - Price on:12/24/2007	NA
Employees	NA	Stock Exchange	OTC
Auditor	Dale Matheson Carr-hilton Labonte LLP	Ticker Symbol	DNIAE
Stk Agt	Integrity Stock Transfer	Outstanding Shares	NA
Counsel	NA	E.P.S	NA
DUNS No.	NA	Shareholders	NA

Business: The groups principle activity is to provide recruiting services. The groups service area includes the research and development, engineering, marketing, sales, information technology and manufacturing industries. The group operates from United States.

Primary SIC and add'l.: 1000

CIK No: 0001284802

Officers: Norm Dority/Dir., CFO, Pres.

Directors: Norm Dority/Dir., CFO, Pres.

Owners: Zoran Pudar/29.00%, Elena Ilina/29.00%, Insiders/58.00%

Denison Mines Corp

Formerly: International Uranium Corp
1050 17th St., Ste. 950, Denver, CO, 80265; *PH:* 1-303-628-7798; *http://* www.intluranium.com

General - Incorporation	ON	*Stock* - Price on:12/24/2007	$43.09
Employees	585	Stock Exchange	NYSE
Auditor	PricewaterhouseCoopers LLP	Ticker Symbol	NA
Stk Agt	Computershare Trust Co of Canada	Outstanding Shares	63,050,000
Counsel	David C. Frydenlund	E.P.S	$2.93
DUNS No.	NA	Shareholders	NA

Business: The group's principle activities include producing and selling uranium concentrates and vanadium for the international fuel market. The group operates from United States.

Primary SIC and add'l.: 1094

CIK No: 0001063259

Subsidiaries: International Uranium (Bermuda I) Ltd., International Uranium (USA) Corporation, International Uranium Company (Mongolia) Ltd., International Uranium Holdings, Urizon Recovery Systems, LLC.

Officers: Peter E. Farmer/Dir., CEO, Ron Hochstein/Dir., COO, Pres., James R. Anderson/CFO, Exec. VP

Directors: Peter E. Farmer/Dir., CEO, Lukas H. Lundin/Chmn., William A. Rand/Dir., John H. Craig/Dir., Brian D. Edgar/Dir., Ron Hochstein/Dir., COO, Pres., Robert W. Dengler/Dir., Paul F. Little/Dir., Roy J. Romanow/Dir., Catherine J.G. Stefan/Dir.

Financial Data: Fiscal Year End:09/30   Latest Annual Data: 12/31/2006

Year	Sales	Net Income
2006	$819,992,000	$168,502,000
2005	$1,072,045,000	$151,568,000
2004	$912,898,000	$122,551,000

Curr. Assets:	$261,000,000	*Curr. Liab.:*	$263,941,000	*P/E Ratio:*	14.71
Plant, Equip.:	$2,789,926,000	*Total Liab.:*	$1,755,066,000	*Indic. Yr. Divd.:*	NA
Total Assets:	$3,189,072,000	*Net Worth:*	$1,434,006,000	*Debt/ Equity:*	0.8653

Denmark Bancshares Inc

103 E Main St., Denmark, WI, 54208; *PH:* 1-920-863-2161; *Fax:* 1-920-863-6159;
http:// www.denmarkstate.com; *Email:* info@denmarkstate.com

General - Incorporation	WI	*Stock* - Price on:12/24/2007	NA
Employees	NA	Stock Exchange	OTC
Auditor	Wipfli LLP	Ticker Symbol	DMKB
Stk Agt	NA	Outstanding Shares	NA
Counsel	NA	E.P.S	NA
DUNS No.	00-895-9959	Shareholders	NA

Business: The group's principal activity is to provide retail-banking services. The group accepts various checking and time deposits and originates real estate and personal loans. The group is a holding company, which operates through its subsidiary, Denmark state bank. It operates five offices primarily in kewaunee, brown and manitowoc counties. It also has eight automated teller machines at various locations throughout its market area. The group also provides services to the villages of Denmark, maribel, reedsville and whitelaw and the town of bellevue.

Primary SIC and add'l.: 6022 6712

CIK No: 0000885531

Subsidiaries: Denmark Agricultural Credit Corporation, Denmark Investments, Inc., Denmark State Bank, McDonald-Zeamer Insurance Agency, Inc.

Officers: David Radue/Dir. - Denmark State Bank, John P. Olsen/57/Pres., Principal Executive Officer/$158,490.00, Dennis J. Heim/48/Dir., VP, Treasurer - Principal Financial, Accounting Officer/$153,869.00, Lonnie A. Loritz/Mortgage Specialist, Terese M. Deprey/44/Dir., Sec., Mark E. Looker/59/Dir., VP, Carol Behringer/Mortgage Specialist, Bev Evenson/Mortgage Specialist, Jeff Van Rens/Mortgage Specialist

Directors: Thomas F. Wall/67/Dir., Allen Peters/Dir., Thomas N. Hartman/Dir., Darrell Lemmens/Dir., Roger Lemmens/Dir., James Renier/Dir., Bernard Mleziva/Dir., Norman Tauber/Dir., Edward Q. Opichka/Dir., Terese M. Deprey/44/Dir., Sec., Mark E. Looker/59/Dir., VP, Michael L. Heim/49/Dir.

Owners: Edward Q. Optichka, Dennis J. Heim, Darrell R. Lemmens/2.10%, Allen M. Peters, Terese M. Deprey/2.80%, Mark E. Looker/2.50%, Thomas N. Hartman, Glenn J. Whipp, Insiders/12.20%, Thomas F. Wall/1.80%, John P. Olsen, Michael L. Heim

Denny's Corp

203 E Main St., Spartanburg, SC, 29319; *PH:* 1-864-597-8000; *Fax:* 1-864-597-8780;
http:// www.dennys.com

General - Incorporation	DE	*Stock* - Price on:12/24/2007	$4.45
Employees	27,000	Stock Exchange	NDQ
Auditor	KPMG LLP	Ticker Symbol	DENN
Stk Agt	Continental Stock Transfer & Trust Co	Outstanding Shares	93,680,000
Counsel	NA	E.P.S	$0.41
DUNS No.	NA	Shareholders	NA

Business: The groups principle activity is to provide restaurant services.. The groups services include breakfast, lunch and dinner. The products of the group include appetizers, sandwiches, dinner entrees and desserts. The group products sold under the trade names Denny's and Grand Slam Breakfast The group operates from the United States. The group's quarterly revenue for September 2007 was 241.41 millions of USD.

Primary SIC and add'l.: 5812

CIK No: 0000852772

Subsidiaries: Dennys Holdings, Inc, Dennys Inc, Dennys Realty, LLC, DFO, LLC

Officers: Nelson J. Marchioli/Dir., CEO, Pres./$2,896,607.00, Louis M. Laguardia/Sr. VP - Human Resources, Diversity, Alex S. Lewis/VP - Investor Relations, Treasurer, Scott J. Melton/Assist. General Counsel, Corporate Governance Officer, Assist. Sec., David J. Kahre/Divisional VP - Company Operations, Division 1, Mark E. Chmiel/Sr. VP - Concept Innovation, Gerald M. Groc/VP - Human Resources, Business Consulting, Organizational Development, Jill Van Pelt/VP - Total Rewards, John K. Sanfacon/VP - Strategic Marketing, Enrique Mayor-Mora/VP - Planning, Analysis, Mark C. Smith/VP - Procurement, Distribution, Thomas M. Starnes/VP - Food Safety, Quality Assurance, Brand Standards, Susan L. Mirdamadi/VP - Information Technology, CIO, Ross B. Nell/VP - Tax, Rhonda J. Parish/Exec. VP, Chief Legal Officer, Sec./$1,118,931.00 *(24 Officers included in Index)*

Directors: Nelson J. Marchioli/Dir., CEO, Pres., Debra Smithart-Oglesby/Chmn., Vera K. Farris/Dir., Brenda J. Lauderback/Dir., Robert E. Marks/Dir., Michael Montelongo/Dir., Henry J. Nasella/Dir., Donald R. Shepherd/Dir.

Owners: Janis S. Emplit, Morgan Stanley/6.90%, Nelson J. Marchioli/3.70%, Rhonda J. Parish, Capital Research and Management Company/6.10%, Bear Stearns Asset Management, Inc./6.20%, Debra Smithart-Oglesby, Insiders/6.20%, Robert E. Marks, Henry J. Nasella, Michael Montelongo, Mellon Financial Corporation/6.50%, Donald R. Shepherd, Ore Hill Hub Fund Ltd./5.20%, Wellington Management Company, LLP/5.80% *(20 Owners included in Index)*

Financial Data: Fiscal Year End:12/27   Latest Annual Data: 12/27/2006

Year	Sales	Net Income
2006	$994,044,000	$30,338,000
2005	$978,725,000	-$7,328,000
2004	$960,006,000	-$37,675,000

Curr. Assets:	$43,555,000	*Curr. Liab.:*	$136,244,000	*P/E Ratio:*	13.91
Plant, Equip.:	$285,401,000	*Total Liab.:*	$765,923,000	*Indic. Yr. Divd.:*	NA
Total Assets:	$500,493,000	*Net Worth:*	-$265,430,000	*Debt/ Equity:*	NA

Dental Patient Care America Inc

75 S 500 W, Bountiful, UT, 84010; *PH:* 1-801-292-0100; *Fax:* 1-801-299-8365;
http:// www.usdentistdirect.com

General - Incorporation	UT	*Stock* - Price on:12/24/2007	$0.18
Employees	3	Stock Exchange	OTC
Auditor	HJ & Assoc. LLC	Ticker Symbol	DPAT
Stk Agt	Interwest Transfer Company, Inc.	Outstanding Shares	23,410,000
Counsel	NA	E.P.S	-$0.01
DUNS No.	NA	Shareholders	NA

Business: The group's principle activity is to organize dentists into a cooperative model of contractually networked practices. The benefits include programs to purchase supplies, laboratory and other operating services, insurance and employee benefits programs, and opportunities for profit sharing through the cooperative model. The group also provides dental patient marketing programs, such as the organization of its member dentists into a network, which offers dental care plans to employers and other groups under the trade names "Intermountain Dental Plans" and "Dentist Direct".

Primary SIC and add'l.: 1382

CIK No: 0001103017

Subsidiaries: Dental Cooperative, Inc., Dental Practice Transition, Inc, U.S. DentistDirect, Inc

Owners: Insiders/33.70%, LK Anderson Family/8.60%, Brad Berrett, Marlon Berrett/10.10%, Michael Silva/11.90%, Harry L. Peterson/6.20%, Andrew Eberhardt/4.60%, Jack Rasmussen/6.50%

Financial Data: Fiscal Year End:12/31   Latest Annual Data: 12/31/2006

Year	Sales	Net Income
2006	$310,000	-$498,000
2005	$447,000	-$275,000
2004	$515,000	-$221,000

Curr. Assets:	$191,000	Curr. Liab.:	$370,000		
Plant, Equip.:	$2,000	Total Liab.:	$645,000	Indic. Yr. Divd.:	NA
Total Assets:	$314,000	Net Worth:	-$331,000	Debt/ Equity:	NA

Dentsply International Inc

221 W Philadelphia St., York, PA, 17405; **PH:** 1-717-845-7511; **Fax:** 1-717-849-4762; **http://** www.dentsply.com

General - Incorporation	DE	Stock - Price on:12/24/2007	$36.63
Employees	8,500	Stock Exchange	NDQ
Auditor	PricewaterhouseCoopers LLP	Ticker Symbol	XRAY
Stk Agt	Wachovia Bank N.A	Outstanding Shares	151,910,000
Counsel	NA	E.P.S.	$1.53
DUNS No.	10-222-1942	Shareholders	NA

Business: The groups principle activities include designing, developing, manufacturing and marketing products for the dental market. The groups products include aesthesia and x-ray products, removable prosthetics and disposables. The group operates from United States.

Primary SIC and add'l.: 3843 3844

CIK No: 0000818479

Subsidiaries: AD Engineering Limited, Amalco Holdings Ltd, Ceramco Europe Limited, Ceramco Inc., Ceramco Manufacturing Co., Ceramco UK Limited, CeraMed Dental, LLC, Cicero Dental Systems B.V., Degpar Participacoes e Empreendimentos S.A., DeguDent Austria Handels GmbH, DeguDent Benelux B.V., DeguDent da Amazonia Industria e Comercio Ltda., DeguDent GmbH, DeguDent Industria e Comercio Ltda., Dental Trust B.V. 85 Subsidiaries included in the Index

Officers: Bret W. Wise/Chmn., CEO, Pres./$2,403,089.00, Robert J. Size/49/Sr. VP, James G. Mosch/Sr. VP, Rachel P. McKinney/50/Sr. VP, Brian M. Addison/VP, Sec., General Counsel/$729,479.00, Christopher T. Clark/COO, Exec. VP/$1,133,739.00, William E. Reardon/VP, Treasurer, Timothy S. Warady/VP, Corporate Controller, William R. Jellison/CFO, Sr. VP/$947,875.00, Bob Size/Sr. VP, Linda C. Niessen/VP, Chief Clinical Officer

Directors: Bret W. Wise/Chmn., CEO, Pres., William F. Hecht/Dir., John C. Miles/Dir., Keith W. Smith/Dir., Michael J. Coleman/Dir., Michael C. Alfano/Dir., Eric K. Brandt/Dir., Leslie A. Jones/Dir., Francis J. Lunger/Dir., Wendy L. Dixon/Dir., Paula H. Cholmondeley/Dir.

Owners: Paula H. Cholmondeley, Gerald K. Kunkle, Michael J. Coleman, Eric K. Brandt, Francis J. Lunger, Leslie A. Jones, Bret W. Wise, John C. Miles, Insiders/2.20%, Keith W. Smith, Michael C. Alfano, Brian M. Addison, William R. Jellison, Wendy L. Dixon, Christopher T. Clark (16 Owners included in Index)

Financial Data: Fiscal Year End:12/31   Latest Annual Data: 06/30/2007

Year	Sales	Net Income
2007	NA	NA
2006	NA	NA
2005	$1,715,135,000	$45,413,000

Curr. Assets:	$718,191,000	Curr. Liab.:	$311,434,000	P/E Ratio:	24.75
Plant, Equip.:	$329,616,000	Total Liab.:	$907,293,000	Indic. Yr. Divd.:	NA
Total Assets:	$2,181,350,000	Net Worth:	$1,273,835,000	Debt/ Equity:	0.3089

Denver Resources Inc

115 Garfield St. No.3855, Sumas, WA, 98295; **PH:** 1-604-205-0992

General - Incorporation	NV	Stock - Price on:12/24/2007	NA
Employees	NA	Stock Exchange	NA
Auditor	Dale Matheson Carr-Hilton Labonte	Ticker Symbol	NA
Stk Agt	Corporate Stock Transfer, Inc.	Outstanding Shares	NA
Counsel	NA	E.P.S.	NA
DUNS No.	NA	Shareholders	NA

Business: The group's principal activity is of exploration of two mining properties.

Primary SIC and add'l.: 1000

CIK No: 0001338650

Department 56 Inc

One Village Pl., 6436 City W Pkwy., Eden Prairie, MN, 55344; **PH:** 1-952-944-5600; **http://** www.d56.com

General - Incorporation	DE	Stock - Price on:12/24/2007	$7.53
Employees	1,566	Stock Exchange	NYSE
Auditor	Deloitte & Touche LLP	Ticker Symbol	NA
Stk Agt	Mellon Investor Services LLC	Outstanding Shares	13,990,000
Counsel	NA	E.P.S.	-$1.926
DUNS No.	79-878-1837	Shareholders	NA

Business: The group's principle activity is to design and distribute fine quality collectibles and other giftware products. The products are sold through gift, home accessory, specialty retailers, department stores and mid-tier general merchandise chains. The group also sells through its own stores and consumer-direct home show sales business. The group's village series consists of collectible, handcrafted, lit ceramic and porcelain houses and related accessories. The group's village accessory consists of figurines, vehicles, landscaping, lighting and other decorative items. The products also include general giftware consisting of decorative giftware and home accessory items. The group operates in the United States and Canada. The group's wholesale operations serves 13,000 independent gift retailers across the United States and Canada and under retail operations, the group have 5 retail stores that sells products directly to its customers. The group's quarterly revenue for September 2007 was 137.78 millions of USD.

Primary SIC and add'l.: 3269 5999 5947

CIK No: 0000902270

Subsidiaries: Axis Holdings Corporation, CAN 56, Inc., D 56, Inc., Department 56 Retail, Inc., Department 56 Sales, Inc., Lenox, Incorporated, Time to Celebrate, Inc.

Officers: Marc L. Pfefferle/CEO, Stephen J. Ruelle/Pres. - Department, Branka Hannon/50/Sr. VP - Human Resources/$589,616.00, Lesa Chittenden Lim/49/Pres. - Lenox Brands/$445,236.00, Louis A. Fantin/57/Sr. VP, General Counsel, Sec./$628,076.00, Timothy J. Schugel/49/CFO, COO/$384,802.00, Gregg A. Peters/VP - Finance, Principal Accounting Officer, Joel D. Anderson/43/Pres. - Consumer Direct

Directors: Stewart M. Kasen/68/Chmn., Reatha Clark King/69/Dir., James E. Bloom/65/Dir., Charles N. Hayssen/57/Dir., John Vincent Weber/55/Dir., Glenda B. Glover/Dir., Dolores A. Kunda/Dir.

Owners: Branka Hannon, Lesa Chittenden Lim, Barclays Global Investor/13.60%, Clinton Group, Inc./11.60%, Dimensional Fund Advisors/8.00%, Susan E. Engel/3.80%, Ramius Capital Group, L.L.C./5.10%, Glenda B. Glover, F&C Asset Management plc/5.30%, Dolores A. Kunda, Fidelity Management & Research/11.80%, Wells Fargo & Company/7.60%, James G. Berwick, Timothy J. Schugel/1.30%, James E. Bloom (21 Owners included in Index)

Financial Data: Fiscal Year End:12/31   Latest Annual Data: 12/30/2006

Year	Sales	Net Income
2006	$502,506,000	-$49,268,000
2005	$330,915,000	$15,170,000

Curr. Assets:	$172,979,000	Curr. Liab.:	$93,653,000		
Plant, Equip.:	$88,446,000	Total Liab.:	$308,179,000	Indic. Yr. Divd.:	NA
Total Assets:	$469,928,000	Net Worth:	$161,749,000	Debt/ Equity:	0.6952

Depomed Inc

1360 O'Brien Dr., Menlo Park, CA, 94025; **PH:** 1-650-462-5900; **Fax:** 1-650-462-9993; **http://** www.depomedinc.com; **Email:** investor@depomedinc.com

General - Incorporation	CA	Stock - Price on:12/24/2007	$4.92
Employees	105	Stock Exchange	NDQ
Auditor	Ernst & Young LLP	Ticker Symbol	DEPO
Stk Agt	Continental Stock Transfer & Trust Co	Outstanding Shares	47,470,000
Counsel	Heller Ehrman White & McAuliffe LLP	E.P.S.	$0.32
DUNS No.	93-756-2890	Shareholders	NA

Business: The group's principal activity is to develop pharmaceutical products for the biopharmaceutical industry based on new and proprietary oral drug delivery technologies. The primary oral drug delivery system of the company is the patented gastric retention system. The group also develops the reduced irritation system, which is designed to provide for significant reduction in local upper gastrointestinal irritation from the effects of certain drugs. The group develops proprietary products utilizing internal technology as well as in collaboration with pharmaceutical and biotechnology companies.the group operates solely in the domestic market.

Primary SIC and add'l.: 2834 8731

CIK No: 0001005201

Subsidiaries: DDL

Officers: John W. Fara/Chmn., CEO, Pres./$901,120.00, Carl A. Pelzel/COO, Exec. VP/$579,761.00, John N. Shell/VP - Operations/$385,695.00, John F. Hamilton/CFO, VP - Finance/$466,412.00, Thadd Vargas/VP - Business Development, Matthew Gosling/VP - Legal, General Counsel/$229,026.00, John W. Shell/Dir., VP - Operations

Directors: John W. Fara/Chmn., CEO, Pres., Peter D. Staple/Dir., Steven G. Burrill/Dir., Julian N. Stern/Dir., John W. Shell/Dir., VP - Operations, Craig R. Smith/Dir., David B. Zenoff/Dir.

Owners: Baron Capital Group,Inc./6.20%, Craig R. Smith, John N. Shell/1.80%, Steven G. Burrill, Mazama Capital Management,Inc./9.10%, Biovail LaboratoriesInc./10.90%, John F. Hamilton, John W. Shell/2.70%, Bret Berner, Julian N. Stern, Insiders/9.40%, David B. Zenoff, Peter D. Staple, John W. Fara/2.60%, Polygon Global Opportunities Master Fund/6.10% (16 Owners included in Index)

Financial Data: Fiscal Year End:12/31   Latest Annual Data: 12/31/2006

Year	Sales	Net Income
2006	$9,551,000	-$39,659,000
2005	$4,405,000	-$24,467,000
2004	$203,000	-$26,874,000

Curr. Assets:	$47,880,000	Curr. Liab.:	$22,339,000		
Plant, Equip.:	$2,541,000	Total Liab.:	$79,906,000	Indic. Yr. Divd.:	NA
Total Assets:	$52,617,000	Net Worth:	-$27,288,000	Debt/ Equity:	NA

Derby Resources Inc

PO Box 110310, Naples, FL, 34108; **PH:** 1-239-598-2300

General - Incorporation	NV	Stock - Price on:12/24/2007	NA
Employees	NA	Stock Exchange	OTC
Auditor	Child, Sullivan & Co	Ticker Symbol	NA
Stk Agt	Corporate Stock Transfer, Inc.	Outstanding Shares	NA
Counsel	NA	E.P.S.	NA
DUNS No.	NA	Shareholders	NA

Business: The group's principle activities include development organizational ones, directed at developing its business plan and raising its initial capital. The Company has not commenced any commercial operations. It has no full-time employees and owns no real estate.

Primary SIC and add'l.: 9995

CIK No: 0001311546

Derek Oil & Gas Corp

32 Tub Town Rd., Newcastle, WY, 82701; ; **http://** www.derekresources.com; **Email:** info@derekoilandgas.com

General - Incorporation: BC
Employees: NA
Auditor: PricewaterhouseCoopers LLP
Stk Agt: Computershare Trust Co
Counsel: NA
DUNS No.: NA

Stock - Price on:12/24/2007: $0.37
Stock Exchange: OTC
Ticker Symbol: DRKOF
Outstanding Shares: NA
E.P.S: NA
Shareholders: NA

Business: The group's principal activities is the exploration of oil and gas properties with working interests in oil wells incanada and the United States. The group is in the development stage.

Primary SIC and add'l.: 1311 1382

CIK No: 0001087072

Subsidiaries: Derek Resources (U.S.A.) Inc

Officers: Barry C.J. Ehrl/Dir., CEO, Pres., Edward G. Byrd/70/Dir., CFO, Alan H. Stevens/VP - Operations, Dir., Brent C. Ehrl/48/Corp. Sec., Doug Symonds/GM, Erica Bearss/29/VP - Corporate Communications, Greg Amor/CFO, Robert Hurkmans/COO

Directors: Barry C.J. Ehrl/Dir., CEO, Pres., Edward G. Byrd/70/Dir., CFO, Alan H. Stevens/VP - Operations, Dir., John Lush/Dir., George Eynon/Dir., Charles B. Crowell/Dir., Eike Hamer/Dir.

Owners: Edward G. Byrd, Barry C.J. Ehrl, John Lush, Brent C. Ehrl, Doug Symonds

Financial Data: *Fiscal Year End:*04/30 *Latest Annual Data:* 4/30/2006

Year	Sales	Net Income
2006	NA	-$952,000
2005	NA	-$1,093,000
2004	NA	-$1,141,000

Curr. Assets:	$1,578,000	Curr. Liab.:	$114,000		
Plant, Equip.:	$12,931,000	Total Liab.:	$114,000	Indic. Yr. Divd.:	NA
Total Assets:	$14,544,000	Net Worth:	$14,430,000	Debt/ Equity:	NA

Derma Sciences Inc

214 Carnegie Ctr., Ste. 100, Princeton, NJ, 08540; *PH:* 1-609-514-4744; *Fax:* 1-609-514-0502; *http://* www.dermasciences.com

General - Incorporation: PA
Employees: 137
Auditor: J. H. Cohn LLP, Ernst & Young LLP
Stk Agt: StockTrans, Inc.
Counsel: Hedger & Hedger
DUNS No.: 14-428-0088

Stock - Price on:12/24/2007: $0.81
Stock Exchange: OTC
Ticker Symbol: DSCI
Outstanding Shares: 25,260,000
E.P.S: -$0.01
Shareholders: NA

Business: The group's principal activities are to provide advanced wound and skin care products. The group operates in three product lines; chronic wound care, wound closure and fasteners and personal skin care. Chronic wound care involves cleaning the wound, controlling infection with antibiotics and protecting the wound. Wound closures strips and fasteners eliminate the need for sutures on the surface of many surgical wounds, decrease the incidence of scarring and infection, promote wound healing, reduce traction blisters at wound site and also provide excellent adherence, optimum surgical wound security and protection from irritation and skin shearing. Personal skin care products are designed to enable customers implement and maintain successful skin care/hygiene programs.

Primary SIC and add'l.: 2834

CIK No: 0000892160

Subsidiaries: Dumex Medical Canada Inc., Sunshine Products, Inc.

Officers: Edward J. Quilty/55/Chmn., CEO/$554,195.00, John E. Yetter/CFO, VP/$313,393.00, Frederic Eigner/Exec. VP - Operations/$262,288.00, Robert C. Cole/Exec. VP - Sales/$295,235.00, Lester Rosenkrantz/Investor Relations, Barry J. Wolfenson/41/VP - Marketing, Business Development/$248,674.00, John McNamara/Investor Contact, Barbara Benchoff/Contact, Bob Cole/Contact - Sales, Diane Maydick/Contact - Clinical Affairs, Donna Andretta/Customer Service

Directors: Edward J. Quilty/55/Chmn., CEO, Srini Conjeevaram/47/Dir., Richard C. Stafford/70/Dir., Bruce F. Wesson/65/Dir., Richard J. Keim/70/Dir., Stephen T. Wills/51/Dir., James T. O'Brien/69/Dir., Robert G. Moussa/60/Dir., Robert S. Kirsner/Member - Advisory Board, William J. Ennis/Member - Advisory Board, Thomas E. Serena/Member - Advisory Board, William A. Marston/Member - Advisory Board, Vickie R. Driver/Member - Advisory Board, Allen Holloway/Member - Advisory Board, Cathy Thomas Hess/Member - Advisory Board *(16 Directors included in Index)*

Owners: Richard C. Stafford/1.15%, Stephen T. Wills/1.58%, Frederic Eigner/0.71%, Comvita New Zealand Limited/11.92%, John E. Yetter/1.23%, James T. O'Brien/1.38%, Srini Conjeevaram/1.16%, Robert C. Cole/1.10%, Insiders/24.66%, Edward J. Quilty/3.31%, Barry J. Wolfenson/0.53%, Robert G. Moussa/0.38%, Panacea Fund, LLC/6.33%, LB I Group Inc./19.00%, Galen III Partnerships/12.13%

Financial Data: *Fiscal Year End:*12/31 *Latest Annual Data:* 12/31/2006

Year	Sales	Net Income
2006	$27,887,000	$669,000
2005	$23,545,000	-$909,000
2004	$19,887,000	-$2,339,000

Curr. Assets:	$8,514,000	Curr. Liab.:	$2,746,000	P/E Ratio:	40.50
Plant, Equip.:	$4,134,000	Total Liab.:	$3,527,000	Indic. Yr. Divd.:	NA
Total Assets:	$18,506,000	Net Worth:	$14,978,000	Debt/ Equity:	0.0356

Dermisonics Inc

2 Pk. Plz., Ste. 450, Irvine, CA, 92614; *PH:* 1-949-733-1101; *Fax:* 1-949-266-8426; *http://* www.dermisonics.com; *Email:* info@dermisonics.com

General - Incorporation: NV
Employees: 1
Auditor: Macias Gini & Oconnell LLP
Stk Agt: NA
Counsel: Mr. Haglund
DUNS No.: NA

Stock - Price on:12/24/2007: $0.08
Stock Exchange: OTC
Ticker Symbol: DMSI
Outstanding Shares: 49,220,000
E.P.S: -$0.49
Shareholders: NA

Business: The group's principal activity is to market easy trivia Website to several Internet users. The group also seeks to market products & services to the users of the Website. The group focuses on promotion and licensing of software to other companies and Web site operators who may be interested in adding entertainment software and trivia capability to their Web site operations. The group is developing easytrivia game show through its subsidiary, easytrivia.com inc. The group is a development stage company.

Primary SIC and add'l.: 7372 7373 7375 7379 5045 6719

CIK No: 0001127470

Subsidiaries: Dermisonics, Inc, EasyTrivia, Echo RX, Inc., Valeor Resources, Inc

Officers: Bruce H. Haglund/Chmn., CEO

Directors: Bruce H. Haglund/Chmn., CEO, Bruce K. Redding/Dir., Grant Atkins/Member - Board Of Advisor

Owners: Newport Capital Corp./18.60%, Insiders/27.80%, Bruce H. Haglund/0.40%, Encapsulation Systems, Inc./26.80%

Financial Data: *Fiscal Year End:*09/30 *Latest Annual Data:* 9/30/2006

Year	Sales	Net Income
2006	NA	-$5,084,000
2005	NA	-$6,959,000
2004	NA	-$3,993,000

Curr. Assets:	$533,000	Curr. Liab.:	$3,900,000		
Plant, Equip.:	$3,000	Total Liab.:	$4,467,000	Indic. Yr. Divd.:	NA
Total Assets:	$20,084,000	Net Worth:	$15,617,000	Debt/ Equity:	NA

Descartes Systems Group Inc

120 Randall Dr., Waterloo, ON, N2V 1C6; *PH:* 1-519-746-8110; *Fax:* 1-519-747-0082; *http://* www.descartes.com

General - Incorporation: Canada
Employees: 306
Auditor: Deloitte & Touche LLP
Stk Agt: Computershare Trust Co
Counsel: NA
DUNS No.: NA

Stock - Price on:12/24/2007: $4.29
Stock Exchange: NDQ
Ticker Symbol: DSGX
Outstanding Shares: 52,340,000
E.P.S: $0.11
Shareholders: NA

Business: The group's principle activity is to provide collaborative logistics solutions, including integrated software applications and network services. The electronic logistics process enables enterprises and their trading partners, transportation carriers and other service providers to manage the flow of goods and information collaboratively with real time visibility from one end of the supply chain to the other. The group also offers consulting, training, support and hosting services to the users of its logistics software products.

Primary SIC and add'l.: 5734 7371 7372 7379

CIK No: 0001050140

Subsidiaries: Descartes Systems (USA) LLC, Descartes Systems AB, Descartes U.S. Holdings, Inc.

Officers: Arthur Mesher/Dir., CEO, Scott J. Pagan/Exec. VP - Corporate Development, General Counsel, Chris Jones/Exec. VP - Solutions, Services, Edward J. Ryan/Exec. VP - Global Field Operations, Stephanie Ratza/CFO

Directors: Arthur Mesher/Dir., CEO, Ian J. Giffen/Chmn., Chris Hewat/Dir., Stephen M. Watt/Dir., Olivier Sermet/Dir., David I. Beatson/Dir., Michael Cardiff/Dir.

Financial Data: *Fiscal Year End:*01/31 *Latest Annual Data:* 1/31/2007

Year	Sales	Net Income
2007	$51,990,000	$3,987,000
2006	$45,729,000	$2,989,000
2005	$46,395,000	-$55,331,000

Curr. Assets:	$32,356,000	Curr. Liab.:	$8,585,000		
Plant, Equip.:	$6,766,000	Total Liab.:	$8,585,000	Indic. Yr. Divd.:	NA
Total Assets:	$71,334,000	Net Worth:	$62,749,000	Debt/ Equity:	NA

Desert Commercial Bank

44801 Village Ct, Palm Desert, CA, 92260; *PH:* 1-760-340-7595; *https://* www.desertbanking.com; *Email:* customerservice@desertbanking.com

General - Incorporation:
Employees: NA
Auditor: NA
Stk Agt: NA
Counsel: NA
DUNS No.: NA

Stock - Price on:12/24/2007: $21.75
Stock Exchange: OTC
Ticker Symbol: DCBC
Outstanding Shares: NA
E.P.S: NA
Shareholders: NA

Business: The groups principal activity is to provide banking services. The groups service is Internet banking. The products of the group include easy checking account, senior interest checking, agriculture production loans, commercial real estate loans and business loans. The group operates from the United States.

Primary SIC and add'l.: 6029

CIK No:

Officers: Albert R. Roensch/Dir., CEO, Pres., Chuck Lanzrath/CFO, Exec. VP, Brian Johnston/Sr. VP, Chief Production Officer, Robert A. Koch/Exec. VP, Chief Credit Officer, Roberta Cull/Exec. VP, Operations Administrator

Directors: Albert R. Roensch/Dir., CEO, Pres., Michael Shepherd/Dir., David A. Neil/Dir., Ronald A. Pedersen/Dir., Stanley B. Sklar/Dir., Max A. Briggs/Dir., Matthew S. Costello/Dir., Michael A. Criste/Dir., Richard D. Foss/Dir., Gary N. Gardner/Dir., Wayne L. Harvey/Dir., Phillip P. Heald/Dir., Robert W. Murphy/Dir.

Desert Community Bank

12530 Hesperia Rd., Victorville, CA, 92393; *PH:* 1-760-243-2140; *http://* www.dcbk.org

General - Incorporation:
Employees: 188
Auditor: NA
Stk Agt: U.S. Stock Transfer Corp
Counsel: NA
DUNS No.: NA

Stock - Price on:12/24/2007: $23.05
Stock Exchange: NA
Ticker Symbol: NA
Outstanding Shares: 5,940,000
E.P.S: $1.02
Shareholders: NA

Business: The groups principal activity is to provide banking services. The products of the group include home loans, business loans and mortgage loans. The groups services include Internet banking and visa debit card. The group operates from the United States.

Primary SIC and add'l.: 6022

CIK No:

Financial Data: *Fiscal Year End:*NA *Latest Annual Data:* 12/31/2004

Year	Sales	Net Income
2004	$32,298,000	$4,944,000
2003	$29,202,000	$4,241,000
2002	$28,176,000	$3,746,000

Curr. Assets:	$75,541,000	Curr. Liab.:	$427,084,000	P/E Ratio:	22.60
Plant, Equip.:	$21,600,000	Total Liab.:	$427,784,000	Indic. Yr. Divd.:	$0.160
Total Assets:	$470,367,000	Net Worth:	$42,583,000	Debt/ Equity:	0.0164

Desert Mining Inc

4328 State Hwy. 66, Longmont, CO, 80504; *PH:* 1-970-535-6213; *http://* www.desertmining.com;
Email: Information@DesertMining.com

General - Incorporation	NV	Stock - Price on:12/24/2007	$0.15
Employees	NA	Stock Exchange	OTC
Auditor	Madsen & Associates, CPA's Inc.	Ticker Symbol	DSRM
Stk Agt.	NA	Outstanding Shares	14,160,000
Counsel	NA	E.P.S.	-$0.03
DUNS No.	NA	Shareholders	NA

Business: The groups principle activity is to explore minerals and natural oil. The group operates from Canada and the United States.
Primary SIC and add'l.: 1382
CIK No: 0001129916
Subsidiaries: 44 Mag Production, Inc
Officers: Randall B. Anderson/57/Dir., CEO, Peter K. Nelson/64/Dir., CFO, Pres., Sec., Treasurer
Directors: Randall B. Anderson/57/Dir., CEO, Peter K. Nelson/64/Dir., CFO, Pres., Sec., Treasurer, Gabriel Holt/31/Dir., Craig E. Gunter/73/Dir.
Owners: Craig E. Gunter/2.19%, Insiders/16.38%, Ted Cooper/7.89%, Gabriel Holt/2.19%, Randall B. Anderson/3.53%, Peter K. Nelson/8.47%

Financial Data: Fiscal Year End:12/31   Latest Annual Data: 12/31/2006

Year	Sales	Net Income
2006	$114,000	-$249,000
2005	NA	-$1,616,000
2004	NA	-$860,000

Curr. Assets:	$145,000	Curr. Liab.:	$858,000		
Plant, Equip.:	$1,100,000	Total Liab.:	$858,000	Indic. Yr. Divd.:	NA
Total Assets:	$2,045,000	Net Worth:	$1,187,000	Debt/ Equity:	NA

Desert Sun Mining Corp

65 Queen St. W, Ste. 810, Toronto, ON, M5H 2M5; *PH:* 1-416-861-0341

General - Incorporation	Canada	Stock - Price on:12/24/2007	$10.07
Employees	NA	Stock Exchange	NA
Auditor	McGovern, Hurley, Cunningham LLP	Ticker Symbol	NA
Stk Agt	Equity Transfer Services Inc	Outstanding Shares	NA
Counsel	NA	E.P.S	NA
DUNS No.	NA	Shareholders	NA

Business: The group's principle activities include acquiring and exploring mineral properties, primarily gold properties. The group operates from United States.
Primary SIC and add'l.: 6719 1041
CIK No: 0001056086
Subsidiaries: Jacobina Minerao E Comrcio Ltda.

Design Source Inc

221 N 1st St., Richmond, VA, 23219; *PH:* 1-804-644-3424; *Fax:* 1-804-644-3425;
http:// www.designsourceinteriors.com

General - Incorporation	NV	Stock - Price on:12/24/2007	NA
Employees	NA	Stock Exchange	OTC
Auditor	Williams & Webster, P.S.	Ticker Symbol	DSGS
Stk Agt	Pacific Stock Transfer Company	Outstanding Shares	NA
Counsel	NA	E.P.S	NA
DUNS No.	NA	Shareholders	NA

Business: The groups principal activity is to develop website that will offer commercial upholstery, drapery, bedspread, panel, and wall covering fabrics to interior designers. The groups services include disk space, bandwidth, 155 mbit backbone, pop mailboxes, e-mail forwarding, e-mailing aliasing, auto responder, front page support, unlimited FTP access, and java chat script. The group operates from the United States.
Primary SIC and add'l.: 5712
CIK No: 0001292519
Officers: Peter A. Reichard/51/Dir., CEO, Pres., Treasurer, Peter L. Coker/65/Dir., Sec., Jim King/Pres., Ken Ogren/VP, Jim Nicholson/VP - HH Hunt Properties, Ginger Knight/Exec. Dir., David Murlette/VP - Operations
Directors: Peter A. Reichard/51/Dir., CEO, Pres., Treasurer, Peter L. Coker/65/Dir., Sec., Ginger Knight/Exec. Dir.
Owners: Peter A. Reichard/32.97%, Insiders/65.94%, Peter L. Coker/32.97%

Design Within Reach Inc

225 Bush St., 20th Fl., San Francisco, CA, 94104; *PH:* 1-415-676-6500; *Fax:* 1-415-676-6871;
http:// www.dwr.com

General - Incorporation	DE	Stock - Price on:12/24/2007	$6.03
Employees	407	Stock Exchange	NDQ
Auditor	Grant Thornton LLP	Ticker Symbol	DWRI
Stk Agt	American Stock Transfer & Trust Co.	Outstanding Shares	14,420,000
Counsel	NA	E.P.S.	-$0.27
DUNS No.	05-360-6534	Shareholders	NA

Business: The group's principle activity is to provide distinctive modern design furnishings and accessories. The group's products include chairs, tables, workspace and outdoor furniture, lighting, floor coverings, beds and related accessories, bathroom fixtures, fans and other home and office accessories. The group's products are sold to both residential and commercial customers through four integrated sales channels, consisting of our catalog, studios, Website and direct sales force. The group's quarterly revenue for September 2007 was 49.03 millions of USD.
Primary SIC and add'l.: 5712

CIK No: 0001116755
Officers: Ray Brunner/CEO, Pres./$959,137.00, Karen John/38/VP - Design, Merchandising/$210,977.00, John Hellmann/58/CFO, Sec./$211,684.00, Andrew Greenbaum/Primary Investor Relations Officer, Christine Lumpkins/Primary Investor Relations Officer
Directors: John Hansen/Chmn., Terry Lee/Dir., Lawrence Wilkinson/Dir., Peter Lynch/Dir., James Peters/46/Dir., Hilary Billings/Dir., William McDonagh/Dir.
Owners: William McDonagh, BC Advisors LLC and affiliates/5.70%, James Peters, Insiders/8.70%, Ken La Honta, John Hellmann, Tara Poseley, Terry Lee, Glenn J. Krevlin/14.70%, Karen John, LaGrange Capital Partners, L.P./6.00%, William Harris Investors, Inc./5.90%, Peter Lynch, Ray Brunner/2.30%, John Hansen/4.50% (18 Owners included in Index)

Financial Data: Fiscal Year End:12/31   Latest Annual Data: 12/30/2006

Year	Sales	Net Income
2006	$178,142,000	-$8,289,000
2005	$158,236,000	-$2,069,000

Curr. Assets:	$53,818,000	Curr. Liab.:	$28,172,000		
Plant, Equip.:	$25,474,000	Total Liab.:	$33,791,000	Indic. Yr. Divd.:	NA
Total Assets:	$87,333,000	Net Worth:	$53,542,000	Debt/ Equity:	0.0112

Destination Television Inc

Formerly: Magic Media Networks Inc
530 N Federal Hwy., Fort Lauderdale, FL, 33301; *PH:* 1-954-764-0579; *http://* www.magicinc.com

General - Incorporation	DE	Stock - Price on:12/24/2007	NA
Employees	5	Stock Exchange	NA
Auditor	Michael F. Cronin	Ticker Symbol	NA
Stk Agt	NA	Outstanding Shares	NA
Counsel	NA	E.P.S	-$0.024
DUNS No.	NA	Shareholders	NA

Business: The group's principal activities are production of commercials and sale of advertising to bars, taverns and nightclubs. The major trademark of the group is bartv. The group has currently 36 locations installed and broadcasting bartv on a daily basis in fort lauderdale, west palm beach and south beach. The group operates in United States.
Primary SIC and add'l.: 7311
CIK No: 0001109067
Subsidiaries: Bar TV, Inc, Destination Television, Inc., Hotel TV, Inc, National Hotel Television Network, Inc.
Officers: Gordon Scott Venters/Dir., CEO, Acting CFO, Pres.
Directors: Gordon Scott Venters/Dir., CEO, Acting CFO, Pres., Todd Waddell Nugent/49/Dir.
Owners: Harold K. Terry/27.00%, Todd Nugent/0.20%, Insiders/3.40%, Gordon Scott Venters/100.00%, Gordon Scott Venters/3.20%, Insiders/100.00%

Financial Data: Fiscal Year End:10/31   Latest Annual Data: 10/31/2006

Year	Sales	Net Income
2006	$15,000	-$1,315,000
2005	$71,000	-$1,330,000
2004	$56,000	-$1,466,000

Curr. Assets:	$112,000	Curr. Liab.:	$1,086,000		
Plant, Equip.:	$107,000	Total Liab.:	$1,086,000	Indic. Yr. Divd.:	NA
Total Assets:	$221,000	Net Worth:	-$865,000	Debt/ Equity:	NA

Destiny Media Technologies Inc

800 - 570 Granville St., Vancouver, BC, V6C3P1; *PH:* 1-604-609-7736; *Fax:* 1-604-609-0611;
http:// dsny.com

General - Incorporation	CO	Stock - Price on:12/24/2007	$0.58
Employees	NA	Stock Exchange	OTC
Auditor	Ernst& Young LLP	Ticker Symbol	DSNY
Stk Agt	Transfer Online, Inc.	Outstanding Shares	NA
Counsel	NA	E.P.S.	NA
DUNS No.	NA	Shareholders	NA

Business: The groups principle activities include developing and marketing digital software tools. The group products include Clipstream(TM), MPE(TM), Clipstream (TM) and Video Clipstream(TM). The group operates from the United States and Canada. The group's quarterly revenue for September 2007 was 0.88millions of USD.
Primary SIC and add'l.: 7372
CIK No: 0001099369
Subsidiaries: Destiny Software Productions, Inc
Officers: Steve Vestergaard/CEO, John Gammack/VP - Operations - Sales, Frederick Vandenberg/40/CFO, Corp. Sec.
Owners: Sabre Value Fund LP/5.20%, Frederick Vandenberg/1.20%, Wayne Koshman/0.70%, Lawrence J. Langs/0.60%, Steven Vestergaard/20.90%, Edward Kolic/0.90%, Insiders/25.20%, Yoshitaro Kumagai/0.80%

Financial Data: Fiscal Year End:08/31   Latest Annual Data: 8/31/2006

Year	Sales	Net Income
2006	$884,000	-$485,000
2005	$769,000	-$547,000
2004	$752,000	-$419,000

Curr. Assets:	$297,000	Curr. Liab.:	$356,000		
Plant, Equip.:	$61,000	Total Liab.:	$490,000	Indic. Yr. Divd.:	NA
Total Assets:	$389,000	Net Worth:	-$101,000	Debt/ Equity:	NA

Deswell Industries Inc

17b, Edificio Comercial RoDr.igues, 599 Avenida Da Praia Grande; ; *http://* www.deswell.com

General - Incorporation British Virgin Islands		Stock - Price on:12/24/2007	$12.55
Employees	5,028	Stock Exchange	NDQ
Auditor	BDO McCabe Lo Ltd	Ticker Symbol	DSWL
Stk Agt	Computershare Trust CO.	Outstanding Shares	15,010,000
Counsel	Kirkpatrick & Lockhart	E.P.S.	$0.66
DUNS No.	66-226-6667	Shareholders	NA

Business: The group's principle activities are the manufacturing of injection-molded plastic parts and components, electronic products and metallic products. Injection-molded plastic parts include cases and key tops for calculators and personal organizers; cases for flashlights, telephones, paging machines, projectors and alarm clocks; grips and rods for fishing tackle; and toner cartridges and cases for photocopy machines. Electronic products include complex printed circuit board assemblies, telecommunication products, telephone answering machines and sophisticated professional answering machines. Metallic products include metallic molds and accessory parts used in audio equipment, telephones and copying machines. The group's operations are carried out in Hong Kong, China, North America, Europe and other. Injection molded plastic parts accounted for 55% of fiscal 2002 gross revenues; electronic products, 39% and metallic parts, 6%.

Primary SIC and add'l.: 3672 3544 2821 3699

CIK No: 0000946936

Subsidiaries: Blue Collar Holdings Ltd., Donggual Kwan Hong Electonics Co. Ltd., Ideakilop Holding Ltd., Integrated International Ltd., Jetcrown Industrial (Dongguan) Limited, Jetcrown Industrial(Macao Commerial Offshore) Limited, Jetcrown Industrial(Shenzhen) Limited, Joint Harvest Industries Ltd., Kwanssia Electronics (macao Commercial Offshore) Ltd., Rainbow Hill Ltd., Shenzhen Kwan wing Trading (Company) Ltd., Spring Fountain Investments Ltd., Star Poaco Ltd.

Officers: Richard Lau/Chmn., CEO, M. C. Tam/Dir. - Engineering, Manufacturing Electronic Operations, Dickson Lam/Dir. - Marketing Plastic, Electronics Operations, C. W. Leung/Dir., Executive Dir. - Engineering, S. K. Lee/Dir. - Administration, Marketing Electronic Operations, C. P. Li/Dir., CFO, Sec., Eliza Y.P. Pang/Financial Controller, John G. Nesbett/Investor Relations

Directors: Richard Lau/Chmn., CEO, Allen Yau-Nam Cham/Dir., C. W. Leung/Dir., Executive Dir. - Engineering, Hung-Hum Leung/Dir.

Owners: Richard Lau, Royce & Associates, Inc., FMR Corp, C. W. Leung, Wellington Management Company, LLP, C. P. Li, Leesha Holdings Ltd., Micropower Enterprises Limited

Financial Data: *Fiscal Year End:*03/31 *Latest Annual Data:* 03/31/2007

Year	Sales	Net Income
2007	$136,779,000	$12,167,000
2006	$115,276,000	$8,779,000
2005	$125,590,000	$15,183,000

Curr. Assets:	$71,380,000	**Curr. Liab.:**	$16,266,000		
Plant, Equip.:	$58,286,000	**Total Liab.:**	$16,266,000	**Indic. Yr. Divd.:**	$0.680
Total Assets:	$130,670,000	**Net Worth:**	$106,768,000	**Debt/ Equity:**	NA

Detroit Edison Co (The)

2000 2nd Ave., Detroit, MI, 48226; *PH:* 1-313-235-4000; *http://* www.dteenergy.com

General - Incorporation	MI	**Stock**- Price on:12/24/2007	$50.76
Employees	10,527	Stock Exchange	NA
Auditor	Deloitte & Touche LLP	Ticker Symbol	NA
Stk Agt	Bank of New York	Outstanding Shares	176,060,000
Counsel	NA	E.P.S	$4.80
DUNS No.	00-695-7872	Shareholders	NA

Business: The group's principle activities include generating, purchasing, transmiting, distributing and selling electricity. The group operates from United States.

Primary SIC and add'l.: 4911

CIK No: 0000028385

Subsidiaries: DTE Energy Company, The Detroit Edison Company

Officers: Sandra Kay Ennis/Dir., Corp. Sec., Douglas R. Gipson/60/Exec. VP, Chief Nuclear Officer - Detroit Edison, Peter B. Oleksiak/VP, Controller, Chief Accounting Officer

Directors: Peter B. Oleksiak/VP, Controller, Chief Accounting Officer, Sandra Kay Ennis/Dir., Corp. Sec.

Financial Data: *Fiscal Year End:*12/31 *Latest Annual Data:* 12/31/2006

Year	Sales	Net Income
2006	$9,022,000,000	$433,000,000
2005	$9,022,000,000	$537,000,000
2004	$7,114,000,000	$431,000,000

Curr. Assets:	$3,961,000,000	**Curr. Liab.:**	$4,164,000,000	**P/E Ratio:**	10.58
Plant, Equip.:	$11,451,000,000	**Total Liab.:**	$17,894,000,000	**Indic. Yr. Divd.:**	$2.120
Total Assets:	$23,785,000,000	**Net Worth:**	$5,849,000,000	**Debt/ Equity:**	1.2895

Deutsche Bank AG

60 Wall St., New York, NY, 10005; *PH:* 1-212-250-2500; *Fax:* 1-212-797-0291; *http://* www.db.com

General - Incorporation		**Stock**- Price on:12/24/2007	$149.72
Employees	NA	Stock Exchange	NYSE
Auditor	NA	Ticker Symbol	DB
Stk Agt	NA	Outstanding Shares	503,100,000
Counsel	NA	E.P.S	$21.58
DUNS No.	NA	Shareholders	NA

Business: The groups principal activity is to offer investment, financial and related products and services to private individuals, corporate entities. In the year 2007, the group acquired MortgageIT Holdings, Inc. The group operates from the United States. The groups total assts in the year 2006 was $1,814 (millions).

Primary SIC and add'l.: 6221 6289 6722 6162 6029 6282 6159 6211

CIK No: 0000948046

Officers: Hugo Banziger/Dir., Chief Risk Officer, Anthony Di Iorio/Dir., CFO, Hermann-Josef Lamberti/Dir., COO, Michael Cohrs/Head - Global Banking, Jurgen Fitschen/Global Head - Regional Management, Anshu Jain/Head - Global Markets, Rainer Neske/Head - Private, Business Clients, Kevin Parker/Head - Asset Management, Pierre De Weck/Head - Private Wealth Management, Suzanne Rice/Investor Relations Officer - New York, Wolfram Schmitt/Investor Relations Officer - Frankfurt, Wolfgang Schnorr/Investor Relations Officer - Frankfurt, Jasmin Braun/Investor Relations Officer - Frankfurt, Bernt Gade/Investor Relations Officer - Frankfurt, Gunther Jordan/Investor Relations Officer - Frankfurt *(21 Officers included in Index)*

Directors: Josef Ackermann/Chmn. - Management Board, Leo Wunderlich/Member - Supervisory Board, Tilman Todenhofer/Member - Supervisory Board, Jurgen Weber/Member - Supervisory Board, Hugo Banziger/Dir., Chief Risk Officer, Anthony Di Iorio/Dir., CFO, Hermann-Josef Lamberti/Dir., COO, Karl-Gerhard Eick/Member - Supervisory Board, Clemens Borsig/Member - Supervisory Board, Heidrun Forster/Member - Supervisory Board, Ulrich Hartmann/Member - Supervisory Board, Gerd Herzberg/Member - Supervisory Board, Sabine Horn/Member - Supervisory Board, Rolf Hunck/Member - Supervisory Board, Peter Job/Member - Supervisory Board *(24 Directors included in Index)*

Financial Data: *Fiscal Year End:*NA *Latest Annual Data:* 12/31/2006

Year	Sales	Net Income
2006	$101,182,511,000	$7,903,316,000
2005	$72,659,387,000	$4,179,748,000
2004	$61,069,180,000	$3,372,797,000

Curr. Assets:	$900,551,544,000	**Curr. Liab.:**	$1,101,866,928,000	**P/E Ratio:**	10.54
Plant, Equip.:	$5,477,925,000	**Total Liab.:**	$1,443,645,067,000	**Indic. Yr. Divd.:**	$6.760
Total Assets:	$1,486,961,469,000	**Net Worth:**	$43,316,402,000	**Debt/ Equity:**	NA

Deutsche Bank Cap Fdg Tr VIII

60 Wall St., Mail Stop Nyc60-4008, New York, NY, 10005; *PH:* 1-212-250-2077

General - Incorporation		**Stock**- Price on:12/24/2007	$24.66
Employees	NA	Stock Exchange	NYSE
Auditor	NA	Ticker Symbol	DUA
Stk Agt	NA	Outstanding Shares	NA
Counsel	NA	E.P.S	NA
DUNS No.	NA	Shareholders	NA

Business: The groups principal activity is to provide banking services. The group operates from the Germany.

Primary SIC and add'l.: 6189

CIK No: 0001377594

Officers: Detlef Bindert/Group Treasurer, Mathias Otto/Deputy General Counsel - to The Management Board, Richard Ferguson/Regular Trustee, Joseph J. Rice/Regular Trustee, Jean Devlin/VP, Helmut Mannhardt/VP

Deutsche Telekom

600 Lexington Ave., 17th Fl., New York, NY, 10022; *PH:* 1-212-424-2900; *Fax:* 1-212-424-2989; *http://* www.telekom.de; *Email:* investor.relations@telekom.de

General - Incorporation	Germany	**Stock**- Price on:12/24/2007	$18.58
Employees	248,800	Stock Exchange	NYSE
Auditor	PricewaterhouseCoopers	Ticker Symbol	DT
Stk Agt	Adeus Aktienregister	Outstanding Shares	4,360,000,000
Counsel	NA	E.P.S	$0.14
DUNS No.	32-736-653	Shareholders	NA

Business: The group's principal activity is the provision integrated telecommunication services. The group operates under four divisions t-com, t-mobile, t-systems and t-online. T-com: offers fixed network operations for residential customers and small and medium sized business customers; t-mobile: offers transatlantic gsm mobile communication network; t-systems: offers comprehensive services from the field of information technology (IT), and telecommunications (tc) as well as e-business solutions from the it/tc sectors; t-online: offers combined business model comprising access and non-access activities. The group has operations in Europe, North America and Latin America.

Primary SIC and add'l.: 4822 3663 4812 4813 2741 5999 4841

CIK No: 0000946770

Subsidiaries: EuroTel Bratislava, Finance B.V, Scout24 group, Slovak Telekom, T-Mobile Czech Republic, T-Online International AG, Telekom Montenegro

Officers: Karl-Gerhard Eick/54/Finance, CFO, Dep. Chmn.

Directors: Karl-Gerhard Eick/54/Finance, CFO, Dep. Chmn., Hubertus Von Grunberg/Member - Supervisory Board, Monika Brandl/Member - Supervisory Board, Waltraud Litzenberger/Member - Supervisory Board, Michael Loeffler/Member - Supervisory Board, Michael Sommer/Member - Supervisory Board, Josef Falbisoner/Member - Supervisory Board, Bernhard Walter/Member - Supervisory Board, Klaus G. Schlede/Member - Supervisory Board Of Deutsche Telekom AG, Lothar Holzwarth/Member - Supervisory Board, Klaus Zumwinkel/Member - Supervisory Board, Guffey H. Lawrence/Member - Supervisory Board, Hocker Ulrich/Member - Supervisory Board, Ingrid Matthaus-Maier/Member - Supervisory Board, Thomas Mirow/Member - Supervisory Board *(20 Directors included in Index)*

Owners: Ursula Steinke, Lothar Holzwarth, Josef Falbisoner, Federal Republic/14.83%, Wilhelm Wegner, Karl-Gerhard Eick, Waltraud Litzenberger, KfW/16.87%, Michael Lffler, Monika Brandl, Wolfgang Schmitt, Ren Obermann

Financial Data: *Fiscal Year End:*12/31 *Latest Annual Data:* 12/31/2006

Year	Sales	Net Income
2006	$80,996,444,000	$4,250,046,000
2005	$70,594,978,000	$6,306,930,000
2004	$78,971,472,000	$3,157,222,000

Curr. Assets:	$21,060,105,000	**Curr. Liab.:**	$29,162,786,000		
Plant, Equip.:	$64,083,401,000	**Total Liab.:**	$108,350,420,000	**Indic. Yr. Divd.:**	$0.770
Total Assets:	$177,992,284,000	**Net Worth:**	$69,641,864,000	**Debt/ Equity:**	NA

Devcon International Corp

3880 N 28th Ter., Hollywood, FL, 33020; *PH:* 1-954-926-5200; *Fax:* 1-954-926-1809; *http://* www.devc.com

General - Incorporation	FL	**Stock**- Price on:12/24/2007	$3.03
Employees	703	Stock Exchange	NDQ
Auditor	Berenfeld, Spritzer, Shechter & Sheer	Ticker Symbol	DEVC
Stk Agt	Registrar & Transfer Co	Outstanding Shares	6,220,000
Counsel	Greenberg Traurig	E.P.S	-$4.84
DUNS No.	87-318-8601	Shareholders	NA

Business: The group's principal activity is the production and distribution of ready-mix concrete, crushed stone, concrete block, asphalt and distribution of bulk and bagged cement. The group operates in two segments: materials division and construction division. The materials division includes manufacturing and distribution of ready-mix concrete, block, crushed aggregate and cement. The construction division consists of land development construction projects. The construction division also performs earthmoving, excavating, and filling operations, builds golf courses, roads, and utility infrastructures, dredges waterways and constructs deep-water piers and marinas in the Caribbean. The group acquired security equipment company inc in 2004.

Primary SIC and add'l.: 1611 3271 3272 3273 5032

CIK No: 0000028452

Subsidiaries: Antigua Heavy Constructors, Ltd., Bahamas Construction and Development, Ltd., Bouwbedrijf Boven Winden, N.V., Central One, Inc., Coastal Security Company, Coastal Security Systems, Inc., Devcon (TCI), Ltd., Devcon Caribbean Purchasing Corp., Devcon Construction& Materials Corp., Devcon Management Corp., Devcon Security Holdings, Inc., Devcon Security Services Corp., Devcon/Matrix Utility Resources, LLC., DevMat Bahamas Ltd., Guardian International, Inc. 26 Subsidiaries included in the Index

Officers: Richard C. Rochon/Chmn., Acting CEO, Ron G. Lakey/Pres. - Devcon Construction, Materials Corp, Devcon, Matrix Utility Resources, LLC, VP - Business Development/$460,955.00, Robert C. Farenhem/Pres., Sec., Manuel Mayor/Island Mgr. - Puerto Rico, Donald L. Smith/Co - Founder, VP - Construction Division/$185,385.00, Richard L. Hornsby/Dir., Consultant, Alex McCarthy/Island Mgr. - St. Martin, Keith J. Godsey/Pres., Raymond Williams/GM - Miami, Broward, Edward Warminski/GM - Bonita Springs, Ray A. McDonald/GM - Tampa, Orlando, Gary Schofield/GM - Boca Raton, Timothy Melvin/GM - Panama City, Pensacola, John Motzer/Controller, Ziad Ghossaini/Dir. - Technical Services (24 Officers included in Index)

Directors: Richard C. Rochon/Chmn., Acting CEO, Douglas W. Pitts/Dir., Donald L. Smith/Co - Founder, VP - Construction Division, Gustavo R. Benejam/Dir., Mario B. Ferrari/Dir., Richard L. Hornsby/Dir., Consultant, Donald K. Karnes/Dir., Per-Olof Loof/Dir., Rodney P. Cunningham/Dir.

Owners: Per-Olof Loof, Douglas W. Pitts, Mario B. Ferrari, Donald K. Karnes, Rodney P. Cunningham, Coconut Palm Capital Investors I, Ltd., Richard C. Rochon, Richard L. Hornsby, HBK Investments L.P., RPCP Investments, LLLP, Stephen J. Ruzika, CSS Group, Inc., Donald L. Smith, Patricia L. Armstrong Trust, Robert C. Farenhem (19 Owners included in Index)

Financial Data: Fiscal Year End: 12/31 **Latest Annual Data:** 12/31/2006

Year	Sales	Net Income
2006	$105,623,000	-$28,714,000
2005	$84,868,000	-$14,316,000
2004	$69,158,000	$10,637,000

Curr. Assets:	$40,513,000	Curr. Liab.:	$36,706,000		
Plant, Equip.:	$11,282,000	Total Liab.:	$176,771,000	Indic. Yr. Divd.:	NA
Total Assets:	$212,897,000	Net Worth:	$36,126,000	Debt/ Equity:	3.2330

Develocap Inc

180 Pineridge Dr, Bainbridge, GA, 39817; **PH:** 1-229-246-6060

General - Incorporation	NV	Stock - Price on:12/24/2007	NA
Employees	NA	Stock Exchange	NA
Auditor	Li & Co., P.C	Ticker Symbol	NA
Stk Agt	Corporate Stock Transfer, Inc.	Outstanding Shares	NA
Counsel	NA	E.P.S.	NA
DUNS No.	NA	Shareholders	NA

Business: The group is in development stage company. The group planning to be a business development company.

CIK No: 0001279740

Owners: Stephen B. Schneer/5.20%, Doyle S. Elliott/12.90%, Jody Walker/7.70%, Bret R. Jenkins/7.70%, Insiders/5.20%, Gary B. Wolff/15.50%, Jimmy B. Holton/14.20%, GCND, Inc./36.10%

Developers Diversified Realty Corp

3300 Enterprise Pkwy., Beachwood, OH, 44122; **PH:** 1-216-755-5500; **Fax:** 1-216-755-1500; **http://** www.ddrc.com; **Email:** mergerinfo@ddr.com

General - Incorporation	OH	Stock - Price on:12/24/2007	$55.85
Employees	641	Stock Exchange	NYSE
Auditor	PricewaterhouseCoopers LLP	Ticker Symbol	DDR
Stk Agt	National City Bank	Outstanding Shares	124,950,000
Counsel	NA	E.P.S.	$2.03
DUNS No.	NA	Shareholders	NA

Business: The groups principle activities include acquiring, developing, owning, leasing and managing shopping centers. The group acquired 20 properties in the year 2006 and 52 properties in the year 2005. The group operates from the United States. The groups quarterly revenue for September 2007 was 234.06 millions of USD.

Primary SIC and add'l.: 6798

CIK No: 0000894315

Subsidiaries: 1000 Van Ness Owners Association, 93-1 CORTLAND ASSOCIATES LLC, AIP OFFICE FLEX II LLC, AIP PROPERTIES #1 LP, AIP PROPERTIES #2LP, AIP PROPERTIES #3 GP INC, AIP PROPERTIES #3 LP, AIP TAMARAC INC, AIP WARD PARKWAY INC, AIP-ALFRED INC, AIP-SWAG GP INC, AIP-SWAG OPERATING PARTNERSHIP LP, AIP/GREENBRIER GP INC, AIP/POST OFFICE GP INC, AMERICAN INDUSTRIAL PROPERTIES REIT 706 Subsidiaries included in the Index

Officers: Scott A. Wolstein/54/Chmn., CEO/$6,140,477.00, Daniel B. Hurwitz/COO, Pres./$2,202,318.00, Joan U. Allgood/Exec. VP - Corporate Transactions, Governance/$809,220.00, Richard E. Brown/Exec. VP - International, Timothy J. Bruce/Exec. VP - Development, David J. /Exec. VP - Finance, Chief Investment Officer, William H. Schafer/CFO, Exec. VP/$748,196.00, Robin R. Walker - Gibbons/Exec. VP - Leasing, David Dieterle/Sr. VP - Leasing, Southeast Region, Steven M. Dorsky/Sr. VP - Leasing, Northern Region, Marc Hays/Sr. VP - Leasing, Specialty Centers, Daniel M. Herman/Sr. VP - Development, John S. Kokinchak/Sr. VP - Property Management, Joseph G. Padanilam/Sr. VP - Acquisitions, Dispositions, Christa A. Vesy/Chief Accounting Officer, Sr. VP (18 Officers included in Index)

Directors: Scott A. Wolstein/54/Chmn., CEO, Scott D. Roulston/49/Dir., Barry A. Sholem/51/Dir., William B. Summers/56/Dir., Bert L. Wolstein/Dir., Terrance R. Ahern/51/Dir., Dean S. Adler/50/Dir., Robert H. Gidel/55/Dir., Victor B. MacFarlane/55/Dir., Craig MacNab/51/Dir.

Owners: Terrance R. Ahern, Victor B. MacFarlane, Barclays Global Investors, NA/5.10%, Scott A. Wolstein/1.70%, Barry A. Sholem, Dean S. Adler, David M. Jacobstein, Scott D. Roulston, Joan U. Allgood, William H. Schafer, Daniel B. Hurwitz, Craig Macnab, Robert H. Gidel, William B. Summers, FMR Corp./11.20% (16 Owners included in Index)

Financial Data: Fiscal Year End: 12/31 **Latest Annual Data:** 12/31/2006

Year	Sales	Net Income
2006	$818,098,000	$253,264,000
2005	$727,176,000	$282,643,000
2004	$598,933,000	$269,762,000

Curr. Assets:	$198,700,000	Curr. Liab.:	$206,050,000		
Plant, Equip.:	$6,586,193,000	Total Liab.:	$4,683,570,000	Indic. Yr. Divd.:	$2.640
Total Assets:	$7,179,753,000	Net Worth:	$2,496,183,000	Debt/ Equity:	1.7021

Devine Entertainment Corp

2 Berkeley St., Ste. 504, Toronto, ON, M5A 2W3; **PH:** 1-416-364-2282; **Fax:** 1-416-364-1440; **http://** www.devine-ent.com; **Email:** info@devine-ent.com

General - Incorporation	Canada	Stock - Price on:12/24/2007	$0.09
Employees	NA	Stock Exchange	OTC
Auditor	Mintz & Partners LLP	Ticker Symbol	DVNNF
Stk Agt	Transfer Services Inc.	Outstanding Shares	NA
Counsel	NA	E.P.S.	NA
DUNS No.	NA	Shareholders	NA

Business: The group's principal activity is to produce and distribute high-quality children's and family films for the worldwide television and cablemarkets, and the international home video markets. The Company's intention is toproduce positive and meaningful films that emphasize human values and focus onart, inspiration and personal expression and simultaneously entertain andeducate its principal market of children aged six to fourteen years. TheCompany's productions are designed to make viewing films a compelling familyactivity that encourages intellectual interaction.

Primary SIC and add'l.: 7812

CIK No: 0001317035

Officers: David Devine/Chmn., CEO, Pres., Richard Mozer/Vice Chmn., CFO, Treasurer, Sec., Sharon Hicks/Controller, Arnold Tenney/Financial Consultant, Samantha Case/Marketing Mgr., Jesse Cohoon/Business Affairs, Production Supervisor

Directors: David Devine/Chmn., CEO, Pres., Richard Mozer/Vice Chmn., CFO, Treasurer, Sec., Kenneth D. Taylor/72/Dir., Bryson Farrill/78/Dir., Ron Feddersen/63/Dir.

Owners: Bryson Farrill, Ron Feddersen, David Devine/17.60%, Kenneth D. Taylor, Insiders/35.70%, Richard Mozer/16.40%, Forvest Trust S.A./9.10%

Financial Data: Fiscal Year End: 12/31 **Latest Annual Data:** 12/31/2006

Year	Sales	Net Income
2006	$364,000	-$2,196,000

Curr. Assets:	$2,363,000	Curr. Liab.:	$8,132,000		
Plant, Equip.:	$18,000	Total Liab.:	$8,789,000	Indic. Yr. Divd.:	NA
Total Assets:	$11,099,000	Net Worth:	$2,310,000	Debt/ Equity:	NA

Devon Energy Corp

20 N Broadway, Oklahoma City, OK, 73102; **PH:** 1-405-235-3611; **Fax:** 1-405-552-4550; **http://** www.devonenergy.com

General - Incorporation	DE	Stock - Price on:12/24/2007	$83.35
Employees	4,600	Stock Exchange	NYSE
Auditor	KPMG LLP	Ticker Symbol	DVN
Stk Agt	Computershare Trust CO.	Outstanding Shares	444,810,000
Counsel	NA	E.P.S.	$6.36
DUNS No.	NA	Shareholders	NA

Business: The groups principle activities include producing, exploring and developing natural gas and oil. In the year 2006, the group acquired oil and gas assets of Chief Holdings LLC. The group operates from United States.

Primary SIC and add'l.: 1311 1321 1382 5172

CIK No: 0001090012

Subsidiaries: Devon ARL Corporation, Devon AXL, Devon Canada Corporation, Devon Canadaz, Devon Energy Corporation (Oklahoma), Devon Energy Production Company, L.P., Devon Gas Services, L.P., Devon OEI Operating, Inc., Devon Operating Company Ltd., Northstar Energy Corporation

Officers: Larry J. Nichols/66/Chmn., CEO/$12,971,850.00, Darryl G. Smette/61/Sr. VP - Marketing, Midstream/$4,067,377.00, Tony D. Vaughn/51/VP, GM - Gulf Division, Alan R. Marcum/41/VP, Corporate Controller, Bradley A. Foster/50/VP, GM - Central Division, Marian J. Moon/58/Sr. VP - Administration, Earl K. Reynolds/47/VP - Strategic Planning, Lyndon C. Taylor/50/Deputy General Counsel, Danny J. Heatly/VP - Accounting/$1,423,115.00, Janice A. Dobbs/60/Corp. Sec., Mgr. - Corporate Governance, William A. Van Wie/63/VP, GM - Exploration, Don D. Decarlo/51/VP, GM - Western Division, Jerome Beaudoin/47/CIO, VP, Chris Seasons/47/VP, GM - Canadian Division, Pres. - Devon Canada, Paul R. Poley/55/VP - Human Resources (31 Officers included in Index)

Directors: Larry J. Nichols/66/Chmn., CEO, John W. Nichols/Chmn. Emeritus, Thomas F. Ferguson/72/Dir., William J. Johnson/74/Dir., David M. Gavrin/74/Dir., Michael M. Kanovsky/59/Dir., John Richels/57/Dir., Pres., John A. Hill/66/Dir., Todd J. Mitchell/49/Dir., David A. Hager/51/Dir., Robert L. Howard/72/Dir.

Owners: Peter J. Fluor, Todd J. Mitchell, Darryl G. Smette, Insiders/1.43%, Brian J. Jennings, George P. Mitchell/5.33%, Robert L. Howard, John A. Hill, Capital Research and Management Company/6.67%, Robert A. Myers, Larry J. Nichols, Danny J. Heatly, William J. Johnson, Thomas F. Ferguson, Davis Selected Advisors, L.P./6.46% (19 Owners included in Index)

Financial Data: Fiscal Year End: 12/31 **Latest Annual Data:** 12/31/2006

Year	Sales	Net Income
2006	$10,578,000,000	$2,846,000,000
2005	$10,741,000,000	$2,930,000,000
2004	$9,189,000,000	$2,186,000,000

Curr. Assets:	$3,212,000,000	Curr. Liab.:	$4,645,000,000	P/E Ratio:	13.23
Plant, Equip.:	$24,780,000,000	Total Liab.:	$17,621,000,000	Indic. Yr. Divd.:	$0.560
Total Assets:	$35,063,000,000	Net Worth:	$17,442,000,000	Debt/ Equity:	0.3238

DeVry Inc

One Tower Ln., Oakbrook Terrace, IL, 60181; **PH:** 1-630-571-7700; **Fax:** 1-630-571-0317; **http://** www.devry.com; **Email:** inquiries@devry.com

General - Incorporation	DE	Stock - Price on:12/24/2007	$35.18
Employees	4,800	Stock Exchange	NYSE
Auditor	PricewaterhouseCoopers LLP	Ticker Symbol	DV
Stk Agt	Computershare Investor Services LLC	Outstanding Shares	70,940,000
Counsel	NA	E.P.S.	$1.01
DUNS No.	02-510-2203	Shareholders	NA

Business: The group's principal activity is the operation of international system of degree-granting, career-oriented higher-education schools and international training firm. The group's institutes are located on 23 campuses in the United States and Canada. The undergraduate segment provides career-oriented technology-based education to high school graduates in the United States and Canada. The graduate and professional segment offers practitioner-based graduate management programs leading to a master's

degree. The new programs were biomedical engineering technology ("Bmet"), biomedical informatics ("Bmi") and health information technology ("Hit"). The group conducts its educational operations in the United States, Canada, the Caribbean countries of dominica and st. Kitts/nevis, Europe, the Middle East and the Pacific Rim. In Oct 2003, the group acquired the assets of person wolinsky cpa review.

Primary SIC and add'l.: 8244 8221 8249

CIK No: 0000730464

Subsidiaries: Becker CD, LLC, Becker CPA Review Corp., Becker CPA Review Limited(4), an Israeli Corporation, Becker CPA Review, Inc., Chamberlain College of Nursing and Health Science, Inc., Chamberlain College of Nursing, LLC(5), DeVry Canada, LLC, Delaware, DeVry Colorado, LLC, DeVry Educational Development Corp., a Delaware Corporation, DeVry Educational Products, Inc., DeVry Florida, LLC, DeVry Institute of Technology, Inc., a Delaware Corporation, DeVry International Holdings LLC, DeVry Leasing Corp., DeVry New York, Inc. 30 Subsidiaries included in the Index

Officers: Daniel Hamburger/COO, CEO, Pres., Julie A. McGee/Dir., Pres., CEO - Harcourt Supplemental Professional, Trade Publishing, Joan Bates/Dir. - Investor Relations, Gregory S. Davis/VP, General Counsel, Sec., Donna M. Jennings/VP - Human Resources, David J. Pauldine/Exec. VP, Pres. - Devry University, Richard M. Gunst/Sr. VP, CFO, Treasurer, Harvey A. Leffring/CIO, VP, John P. Roselli/VP - Corporate Development, Planning, Sharon Thomas Parrott/Sr. VP - Government, Regulatory Affairs, Chief Compliance Officer, Ronald L. Taylor/Dir. - Sr. Advisor, Steven P. Riehs/VP, GM - Devry University Online, Lyle Logan/48/Exec. VP, MD, Thomas J. Vucinic/Pres. - Becker Professional Review, Donna M. Loraine/VP - Academic Affairs, Dean, Keller Graduate School, Management *(16 Officers included in Index)*

Directors: Julie A. McGee/Dir., Pres., CEO - Harcourt Supplemental Professional, Trade Publishing, Dennis J. Keller/Chmn., Daniel L. Woehrer/Member - National Advisory Board, Ronald L. Taylor/Dir. - Sr. Advisor, David S. Brown/Dir., Fredrick A. Krehbiel/Dir., Robert Smith/Member - National Advisory Board, Gary S. Snodgrass/Member - National Advisory Board, Zandt Van Williams/Member - National Advisory Board, Fernando Ruiz/Dir., Harold T. Shapiro/Dir., Peter Anderson/Member - National Advisory Board, Charles A. Bowsher/Dir., Connie R. Curran/Dir., William T. Keevan/Dir. *(21 Directors included in Index)*

Owners: Baron Capital Management, Inc./9.20%, Norman M. Levine, Robert C. McCormack, Connie R. Curran, William T. Keevan, Daniel Hamburger, David S. Brown, Frederick A. Krehbiel, Dennis J. Keller/12.00%, Julia A. McGee, David J. Pauldine, Westport Asset Management Inc./7.10%, Thomas Shepherd, Harold T. Shapiro, Fidelity Management& Research/14.80% *(20 Owners included in Index)*

Financial Data: *Fiscal Year End:*06/30 *Latest Annual Data:* 6/30/2006

Year	Sales	Net Income
2006	$843,298,000	$43,053,000
2005	$781,304,000	$28,544,000
2004	$784,885,000	$58,061,000

Curr. Assets:	$218,985,000	**Curr. Liab.:**	$165,875,000	**P/E Ratio:**	34.83
Plant, Equip.:	$259,327,000	**Total Liab.:**	$202,147,000	**Indic. Yr. Divd.:**	$0.100
Total Assets:	$844,113,000	**Net Worth:**	$641,966,000	**Debt/ Equity:**	NA

Dewey Electronics Corp

27 Muller Rd., Oakland, NJ, 07436; ***PH:*** 1-201-337-4700; ***Fax:*** 1-201-337-3976; ***http://*** www.deweyelectronics.com; ***Email:*** dewey@deweyelectronics.com

General		**Stock**	
Incorporation	NY	Price on:12/24/2007	$2.8
Employees	36	Stock Exchange	OTC
Auditor	Amper, Politziner & Mattia P.C	Ticker Symbol	DEWY
Stk Agt	Registrar & Transfer Co	Outstanding Shares	1,360,000
Counsel	NA	E.P.S.	-$1.09
DUNS No.	00-194-7357	Shareholders	NA

Business: The group's principal activities are to develop, design and manufacture systems oriented military electronics. The group operates in two segments on the basis of the type of products offered. The electronics segment produces sophisticated electronic and electromechanical systems for the armed forces of the United States as a prime contractor and subcontractor. The group's pitometer log division is a long-established manufacturer of ship speed and distance measuring instrumentation. Its primary customers are the U.S. Navy and other prime contractors such as shipbuilders. The leisure and recreation segment manufactures and markets advanced, sophisticated snowmaking equipment. It also supplies replacement parts for items no longer covered under warranty.

Primary SIC and add'l.: 5561 5065

CIK No: 0000028561

Officers: John H.D. Dewey/43/Dir., CEO, Pres., Frances D. Dewey/Sec., Ronald Tassello/51/Dir., CFO, Stephen P. Krill/56/Treasurer, Edward L. Proskey/52/Sr. VP - Operations, Dana P. Hollis/57/VP - Business Development, Program Management

Directors: John H.D. Dewey/43/Dir., CEO, Pres., James M. Link/66/Dir., Nathaniel Roberts/41/Dir., John B. Rhodes/52/Dir., Ronald Tassello/51/Dir., CFO

Owners: Nathaniel Roberts/1.68%, Insiders/40.18%, John H.D. Dewey/6.59%, James M. Link, Frances D. Dewey/31.17%, Edward L. Proskey/1.10%, Hummingbird Management, LLC/8.07%

Financial Data: *Fiscal Year End:*06/30 *Latest Annual Data:* 06/30/2007

Year	Sales	Net Income
2007	$5,427,000	-$1,682,000
2006	$7,335,000	-$563,000
2005	$6,199,000	-$31,000

Curr. Assets:	$3,817,000	**Curr. Liab.:**	$871,000		
Plant, Equip.:	$1,166,000	**Total Liab.:**	$1,114,000	**Indic. Yr. Divd.:**	NA
Total Assets:	$5,761,000	**Net Worth:**	$4,646,000	**Debt/ Equity:**	NA

Dewpoint Environmental Inc

Formerly: 51148 Inc

100 Congress Ave., Ste.2000, Austin, TX, 78701; ***PH:*** 1-512-649-5550

General		**Stock**	
Incorporation	DE	Price on:12/24/2007	NA
Employees	NA	Stock Exchange	NA
Auditor	Gately & Assoc. LLC	Ticker Symbol	NA
Stk Agt	NA	Outstanding Shares	NA
Counsel	NA	E.P.S.	NA
DUNS No.	NA	Shareholders	NA

Business: The groups principle activity is to provide the highest level of solid waste expertise and customer service, improving communities, customers, partners, and employees. The group operates from United States.

Primary SIC and add'l.: 6770

CIK No: 0001317840

Officers: Jon R. Hall/61/Dir., CEO, CFO, Pres., Sec.

Directors: Jon R. Hall/61/Dir., CEO, CFO, Pres., Sec.

Owners: Jon R. Hall/100.00%

Dex Media Inc

198 Inverness Dr. W, Englewood, CO, 80112;

General		**Stock**	
Incorporation	DE	Price on:12/24/2007	$73.05
Employees	4,400	Stock Exchange	NYSE
Auditor	KPMG LLP	Ticker Symbol	NA
Stk Agt	Wachovia Bank N.A	Outstanding Shares	71,000,000
Counsel	NA	E.P.S.	-$2.14
DUNS No.	13-735-1727	Shareholders	NA

Business: The group's principal activity is to publish yellow pages and white pages directories for qwest. Qwest is the primary incumbent local exchange carrier in Arizona, Colorado, Idaho, Iowa, Minnesota, Montana, Nebraska, New Mexico, North Dakota, Oregon, South Dakota, Utah, Washington and Wyoming, or collectively known as dex states. During 2003, the group published 259 directories and distributed approximately 43 million copies of these directories to business and residential customers throughout the dex states. The group's Internet-based directory, dexonline.com, provides an integrated complement to print directories. This includes more than 15 million business listings and 200 million residential listings from across the United States. The group's trademark is dex (r).

Primary SIC and add'l.: 2741

CIK No: 0001284529

Subsidiaries: Dex Media East LLC, Dex Media West LLC

Financial Data: *Fiscal Year End:*12/31 *Latest Annual Data:* 12/31/2006

Year	Sales	Net Income
2006	$1,895,921,000	-$237,704,000
2005	$956,631,000	$67,533,000
2004	$681,083,000	$70,312,000

Curr. Assets:	$1,532,225,000	**Curr. Liab.:**	$2,009,218,000		
Plant, Equip.:	$159,362,000	**Total Liab.:**	$14,326,712,000	**Indic. Yr. Divd.:**	NA
Total Assets:	$16,147,468,000	**Net Worth:**	$1,820,756,000	**Debt/ Equity:**	5.2901

DexCom Inc

5555 Oberlin Dr., San Diego, CA, 92121; ***PH:*** 1-858-200-0200; ***Fax:*** 1-858-200-0201; ***http://*** www.dexcom.com; ***Email:*** info@dexcom.com

General		**Stock**	
Incorporation	DE	Price on:12/24/2007	$7.45
Employees	NA	Stock Exchange	NDQ
Auditor	Ernst& Young LLP	Ticker Symbol	DXCM
Stk Agt	American Stock Transfer & Trust Co.	Outstanding Shares	28,330,000
Counsel	NA	E.P.S.	-$1.58
DUNS No.	NA	Shareholders	NA

Business: The groups principle activities include designing, developing and commercializing continuous glucose monitoring systems. The groups services include Medicare & Medicaid. The groups product is Short-Term Continuous Glucose Monitoring System.

Primary SIC and add'l.: 3829 3829 3841 3841

CIK No: 0001093557

Officers: Terrance H. Gregg/Dir., CEO, Pres., Andrew P. Rasdal/49/Dir., CEO, Pres./$1,016,516.00, Andrew K. Balo/VP - Clinical, Regulatory Affairs, Quality Systems, Steven J. Kemper/53/CFO/$425,588.00, Mark Brister/VP - Short Term Research, Development, Operations/$466,881.00, Rodney Kellogg/VP - Sales/$623,910.00, Steven R. Pacelli/Sr. VP - Corporate Affairs, Jorge A. Valdes/Sr. VP - Operations/$596,360.00, John Riolo/VP - Quality Assurance, Jess Roper/Interim CFO

Directors: Terrance H. Gregg/Dir., CEO, Pres., Andrew P. Rasdal/49/Dir., CEO, Pres., Donald L. Lucas/Chmn., Jay Skyler/Dir., Glen D. Nelson/Dir., Donald A. Lucas/Dir., Kim Blickenstaff/55/Dir., Sean Carney/Dir.

Owners: Kim Blickenstaff, Entities affiliated with AIM Advisors/5.30%, Mark Brister, Rodney Kellogg, Sean Carney/8.20%, Glen D. Nelson, Entities affiliated with The Travelers Companies,Inc./5.80%, Terrance Gregg, Steven J. Kemper, Entities affiliated with Wells Fargo& Company/6.50%, Entities affiliated with Warburg Pincus Private Equity VIII, L.P./8.10%, Jay S. Skyler, Donald L. Lucas/1.40%, Michael A. Roth and Brian J. Stark, as joint filers/6.60%, Entities affiliated with Frontier Capital Management Co., LLC/5.70% *(19 Owners included in Index)*

Financial Data: *Fiscal Year End:*12/31 *Latest Annual Data:* 12/31/2006

Year	Sales	Net Income
2006	$2,170,000	-$46,599,000
2005	NA	-$30,767,000
2004	NA	-$13,946,000

Curr. Assets:	$57,356,000	**Curr. Liab.:**	$5,229,000		
Plant, Equip.:	$6,118,000	**Total Liab.:**	$7,724,000	**Indic. Yr. Divd.:**	NA
Total Assets:	$64,553,000	**Net Worth:**	$56,828,000	**Debt/ Equity:**	1.7072

DGSE Companies Inc

2817 Forest Ln., Dallas, TX, 75234; ***PH:*** 1-972-484-3662; ***Fax:*** 1-972-241-0646; ***http://*** www.dgse.com

General		**Stock**	
Incorporation	NV	Price on:12/24/2007	$8.26
Employees	50	Stock Exchange	AMEX
Auditor	Bkr Cornwell Jackson	Ticker Symbol	DGC
Stk Agt	Nevada Agency & Trust Company	Outstanding Shares	4,910,000
Counsel	NA	E.P.S.	$0.13
DUNS No.	17-357-1092	Shareholders	NA

Business: The group's principle activity is to sell jewelry and bullion products to both retail and wholesale customers throughout the United States. It also makes collateralized loans to individuals. The group has two major segments: jewelry and consulting and liquidation. The jewelry segment consists of sales to both wholesale and retail customers. This segment also includes pawn operations and bullion sale. The consulting and liquidation services segment includes consulting services related to insolvency advisory services primarily to business enterprises that are involved in or have been involved in

proceedings under chapter 11 of the U.S. The products are marketed through its facilities in Dallas, carrollton, Texas and mt. Pleasant South Carolina. It also operates four Internet sites on the world wide Web. The group discontinued the operations of dls financial services inc and eye media inc in 2003. The group's quarterly revenue for September 2007 was 16.86 millions of USD.

Primary SIC and add'l.: 7389 5094 8742

CIK No: 0000701719

Subsidiaries: American Pay Day Centers, Inc., National Jewelry Exchange, Inc

Officers: L. S. Smith/61/Chmn., CEO, Sec./$310,000.00, William H. Oyster/55/Dir., COO, Pres./$225,000.00, John Benson/62/CFO/$132,308.00, Scott S. Williamson/50/Exec. VP - Consumer Finance/$108,500.00

Directors: L. S. Smith/61/Chmn., CEO, Sec., William H. Oyster/55/Dir., COO, Pres., William P. Cordeiro/64/Dir., Craig Allan-Lee/51/Dir., Richard M. Gozia/63/Dir., David Rector/61/Dir., Mitchell T. Stoltz/54/Dir.

Financial Data: ***Fiscal Year End:***12/31 ***Latest Annual Data:*** 12/31/2006

Year	Sales	Net Income
2006	$44,083,000	$611,000
2005	$35,640,000	$485,000
2004	$28,642,000	$351,000

Curr. Assets:	$10,350,000	**Curr. Liab.:**	$2,165,000	**P/E Ratio:**	63.54
Plant, Equip.:	$1,024,000	**Total Liab.:**	$6,469,000	**Indic. Yr. Divd.:**	NA
Total Assets:	$13,146,000	**Net Worth:**	$6,677,000	**Debt/ Equity:**	NA

Dhanoa Minerals Ltd

1330 Martin Grove Rd. , Toronto, ON, M9W 4X4; ***PH:*** 1-416-838-4348;
http:// www.dhanoaminerals.com

General - Incorporation	NV	**Stock**- Price on:12/24/2007	$0.719
Employees	NA	Stock Exchange	OTC
Auditor	Webb & Company, P. A.	Ticker Symbol	DHNA
Stk Agt	Empire Stock Transfer Inc.	Outstanding Shares	NA
Counsel	NA	E.P.S.	NA
DUNS No.	NA	Shareholders	NA

Business: The groups principal activity is to explore minerals. The group operates from Canada and the United States.

Primary SIC and add'l.: 1481

CIK No: 0001343845

Officers: William E. McNerney/Dir. - Secretory, Treasurer, Thomas Daniel Kuhn/VP

Directors: Lee Andrew Balak/Dir., William E. McNerney/Dir. - Secretory, Treasurer

Owners: Darhan Mundi/16.00%, Balwant Grewal/26.00%, Insiders/42.00%

Financial Data: ***Fiscal Year End:***09/30 ***Latest Annual Data:*** 09/30/2006

Year	Sales	Net Income
2006	NA	-$65,000

Curr. Assets:	$10,000	**Curr. Liab.:**	$23,000		
Plant, Equip.:	NA	**Total Liab.:**	$23,000	**Indic. Yr. Divd.:**	NA
Total Assets:	$10,000	**Net Worth:**	-$13,000	**Debt/ Equity:**	NA

Diabetic Treatment Centers of America Inc

975 E 5400 S, Ste 100, Salt Lake City, UT, 84117; ***PH:*** 1-800-207-1816; ***Fax:*** 1-800-207-1856;
http:// www.dtcofamerica.com; ***Email:*** info@dtcofamerica.com

General - Incorporation	DE	**Stock**- Price on:12/24/2007	$0.022
Employees	2	Stock Exchange	OTC
Auditor	Tedder, James, Worden & Assoc. P.A	Ticker Symbol	DBTC
Stk Agt	Madison Stock Transfer, Inc.	Outstanding Shares	44,340,000
Counsel	NA	E.P.S.	-$0.01
DUNS No.	NA	Shareholders	NA

Business: The group's principal activity is to provide golf-related equipment, accessories and apparel on a wholesale basis. The group offers shoes, accessories and a variety of other products. The products are obtained from manufacturers and an extensive network of suppliers. It offers a majority of the brands in the golf industry such as cobra, yonex, tommy armour, nike, ping, spalding and titleist. The group operates solely in the United States.

Primary SIC and add'l.: 5091

CIK No: 0001165320

Subsidiaries: A & Z Golf Corp

Officers: Scott E. Allen/40/Dir., CEO, Pres., Steven Weldon/Dir., CFO

Directors: Scott E. Allen/40/Dir., CEO, Pres., Steven Weldon/Dir., CFO

Owners: American Medical Technologies Management, LLC/10.13%, Insiders/34.91%, Jeff Jones/19.32%, Steven Weldon/8.81%, Scott Allen/26.10%, Darren Cassels/8.81%

Financial Data: ***Fiscal Year End:***03/31 ***Latest Annual Data:*** 03/31/2007

Year	Sales	Net Income
2007	$2,036,000	-$558,000
2006	$55,000	-$445,000
2005	NA	-$376,000

Curr. Assets:	$113,000	**Curr. Liab.:**	$244,000		
Plant, Equip.:	$26,000	**Total Liab.:**	$244,000	**Indic. Yr. Divd.:**	NA
Total Assets:	$140,000	**Net Worth:**	-$103,000	**Debt/ Equity:**	NA

Diageo Plc

801 Main Ave., Norwalk, CT, 06851; ***PH:*** 1-203-229-2100; ***Fax:*** 1-203-229-8901;
http:// www.diageo.com; ***Email:*** global.general.information@diageo.com

General - Incorporation	UK	**Stock**- Price on:12/24/2007	$85.76
Employees	21,972	Stock Exchange	NYSE
Auditor	KPMG LLP	Ticker Symbol	DEO
Stk Agt	Bank of New York	Outstanding Shares	674,450,000
Counsel	NA	E.P.S.	$4.67
DUNS No.	21-077-2047	Shareholders	NA

Business: The group's principal activity is the manufacture and distribution of spirits, wines and beer. Some of the group's premium drinks includes smirnoff vodka, johnnie walker soctch whiskies, guiness stout, baileys original irish cream liquer, j&b scoth whisky, captain morgan rum and tanqueray gin. In addition the group also owns the distribution rights for the jose cuervo tequila brands in the United States and other countries.

Primary SIC and add'l.: 5182 5181 2085 2084 5812 2082

CIK No: 0000835403

Subsidiaries: Diageo Brands BV, Diageo Capital BV, Diageo Capital plc, Diageo Finance BV, Diageo Finance plc, Diageo Great Britain Limited, Diageo Investment Corporation, Diageo Ireland, Diageo North America, Inc, Diageo Scotland Limited

Officers: Paul S. Walsh/Dir., CEO, Tim Proctor/General Counsel, Isabelle Thomas/Media Contact - Head - Corporate Media Relations, Clare Fleerackers/Media Contact - Head - Brand Communications, Gary Galanis/VP - Media, Communications, Grainne MacKin/Media Contact - Head - Corporate Communications, John Pollaers/Pres. - Diageo Asia Pacific, Stuart Fletcher/Pres. - Diageo International, Andrew Morgan/Pres. - Europe, Ivan Menezes/Pres. - Diageo North America, Gareth Williams/Dir. - Human Resources, Rob Malcolm/Pres. - Global Marketing, Sales, Innovation, Nick Rose/Dir., CFO, Jim Grover/Dir. - Global Business Support

Directors: Paul S. Walsh/Dir., CEO, Lord Blyth/Chmn., Lord Hollick/Sr. Non Exec. Dir., Paul Walker/Non Exec. Dir., Maria Lilja/Non Exec. Dir., Philip Scott/Non Exec. Dir., Todd H. Stitzer/Non Exec. Dir., William Shanahan/Non Exec. Dir., Laurence Danon/Non Exec. Dir., Franz Humer/Non Exec. Dir., Nick Rose/Dir., CFO

Owners: Lord Blyth, Lord Hollick, WS Shanahan, M. Lilja, PA Walker, NC Rose, H. T. Stitzer, Insiders, JR Symonds, PS Walsh, FB Humer, LM Danon

Financial Data: ***Fiscal Year End:***06/30 ***Latest Annual Data:*** 6/30/2006

Year	Sales	Net Income
2006	$13,186,338,000	$3,569,030,000
2005	$16,308,173,000	$2,653,056,000
2004	$15,863,550,000	$3,072,580,000

Curr. Assets:	$8,785,443,000	**Curr. Liab.:**	$6,057,361,000		
Plant, Equip.:	$3,569,030,000	**Total Liab.:**	$16,793,510,000	**Indic. Yr. Divd.:**	$1.980
Total Assets:	$25,295,610,000	**Net Worth:**	$8,176,983,000	**Debt/ Equity:**	NA

Diagnostic Products Corp

5210 Pacific Concourse Dr., Los Angeles, CA, 90045; ***PH:*** 1-310-645-8200; ***http://*** www.dpcweb.com

General - Incorporation	CA	**Stock**- Price on:12/24/2007	$142.19
Employees	475,000	Stock Exchange	NA
Auditor	Deloitte & Touche LLP	Ticker Symbol	NA
Stk Agt	Mellon Investor Services LLC	Outstanding Shares	896,220,000
Counsel	NA	E.P.S.	NA
DUNS No.	06-460-8573	Shareholders	NA

Business: The group's principal activity is to develop, manufacture and market immunodiagnostic systems and immunochemistry kits. The group's products are used by hospital, veterinary, research and forensic laboratories and doctors' offices to obtain precise rapid identification and measurement of hormones, drugs, viruses, bacteria and other substances present in body fluids and tissues. The immulite products uses patented solid-phase wash technology and chemiluminescent detection method, which together are capable of measuring at exceptionally low concentrations, tsh and psa - key tests related to thyroid disorders and prostate cancer, respectively. Radioimmunoassay products are used for allergy testing, which uses liquid-allergen technology in tube and microplate formats. The group has manufacturing facilities in the United States, the United Kingdom, Germany and China.

Primary SIC and add'l.: 3842 2835

CIK No: 0000702259

Subsidiaries: Bio-Mediq DPC Pty. Ltd., Diagnostic Products International Inc., DPC Analytic, DPC Belgium b.v.b.A./s.p.r.l., DPC Benelux B.V., DPC Biermann GmbH, DPC Cirrus, Inc., DPC Czech s.r.o., DPC d.o.o. Zagreb, DPC Dipesa S.A., DPC Finland OY, DPC France SAS, DPC Holding GmbH, DPC Nederland B.V., DPC Polska sp.z.o.o. 18 Subsidiaries included in the Index

Officers: Jeffrey P. Fox/VP - Investment Accounting

Financial Data: ***Fiscal Year End:***12/31 ***Latest Annual Data:*** 9/30/2006

Year	Sales	Net Income
2006	$110,797,960,000	$3,848,270,000
2005	$90,896,136,000	$2,708,390,000
2004	$92,688,428,000	$4,198,706,000

Curr. Assets:	$65,484,037,000	**Curr. Liab.:**	$49,428,642,000	**P/E Ratio:**	25.57
Plant, Equip.:	$15,316,954,000	**Total Liab.:**	$77,352,392,000	**Indic. Yr. Divd.:**	NA
Total Assets:	$115,426,542,000	**Net Worth:**	$37,183,453,000	**Debt/ Equity:**	NA

Dialog Group Inc

257 Pk. Ave. S, 12th Fl., New York, NY, 10010; ***PH:*** 1-212-254-1917;
http:// www.thedialoggroup.com; ***Email:*** invrel@dialoggroup.com

General - Incorporation	DE	**Stock**- Price on:12/24/2007	$0.08
Employees	3	Stock Exchange	OTC
Auditor	Berenfeld Spritzer Shechter & Sheer	Ticker Symbol	DLGO
Stk Agt	Interwest Transfer Company, Inc.	Outstanding Shares	3,770,000
Counsel	NA	E.P.S.	$0.59
DUNS No.	NA	Shareholders	NA

Business: The group's principal activity is to provide a combination of traditional advertising and marketing services. It also provides a broad spectrum of proprietary and exclusive databases for healthcare, pharmaceutical, consumer and business-to-business market clients. The group operates through two divisions, data dialog and healthcare dialog. It has exclusive licensing rights to 75 Web sites, 9 databases, and 5 products. The healthcare dialog division markets it products and services through nfusion, +media, and idata. The data dialog division markets through data dialog marketing, data dialog digital and mail mogul. The group maintains exclusive contracts with leading multi-national pharmaceutical companies to operate, maintain and provide content for their consumer-directed Web sites. On 01-Mar-2003, the group acquired healthcare dialog inc and ip2m inc.

Primary SIC and add'l.: 7319 8099

CIK No: 0001051059

Subsidiaries: AdValiant USA, Inc., Data Dialog, Inc., Mail Mogul, Inc.

Owners: Cede & Co./6.77%, Peter DeCrescenzo/24.09%, Adrian Stecyk/1.56%, Vincent DeCrescenzo/7.49%, Pearl Street Holdings plc/23.09%, Peter V. DeCrescenzo/24.09%, Vincent DeCrescenzo/7.49%, Richard P. Kundrat/1.16%, Insiders/34.30%

Financial Data: ***Fiscal Year End:***12/31 ***Latest Annual Data:*** 12/31/2006

Year	Sales	Net Income
2006	NA	$1,546,000
2005	$6,723,000	-$1,782,000
2004	$7,904,000	-$1,418,000

Curr. Assets:	$841,000	Curr. Liab.:	$3,486,000	P/E Ratio:	0.14
Plant, Equip.:	NA	Total Liab.:	$3,486,000	Indic. Yr. Divd.:	NA
Total Assets:	$953,000	Net Worth:	-$2,533,000	Debt/ Equity:	NA

Dialog Semiconductor Plc

Neue Strasse 95, Kirchheim/teck-nabern; *PH:* 49-70218050; *http://* www.diasemi.com;
Email: dialog.nabern@diasemi.com

General - Incorporation	UK	Stock - Price on:12/24/2007	NA
Employees	279	Stock Exchange	NA
Auditor	KPMG LLP	Ticker Symbol	NA
Stk Agt		Outstanding Shares	NA
Counsel	Reynolds Porter Chamberlain	E.P.S.	NA
DUNS No.	NA	Shareholders	NA

Business: The group's principal activities are the design and development of mixed signal and system level integrated circuit solutions, with chip designs for power management, audio processing and imaging. The group designs and develops application specific integrated circuits (asics) and standard chip solutions with key products such as: audio and multimedia codecs, handles both speech and multimedia functions. Power management, designs electronic circuits to manage the power requirements of the various subsystems. Camera modules, includes cmos camera sensor modules complete with processor and lens for embedding a camera-on-a-chip into portable consumer electronics and automotive applications. Sensors, produces sensor signal conditioning ics that enable better and safer end-user experiences.

Primary SIC and add'l.: 3674

CIK No: 0001116581

Subsidiaries: Daimler-Benz AG, DaimlerChrysler AG

Officers: Jalal Bagherli/CEO, Gary Duncan/VP - Engineering, Jean-Michel Richard/Finance Department, Birgit Hummel/Investor Relations, Peter Hall/VP - Operations, Quality, Toshihiro Watanabe/Pres., Richard Schmitz/VP - Advanced Technology

Owners: Peter Hall, Martin Kloeble, Michael Risman, JanOlof Ingemar Tufvesson, Michael John Glover, Jalal Bagherli, Gregorio Reyes, Timothy Richard Black Anderson, Roland Pudelko, Richard Schmitz, Gary Duncan

Dialysis Corp of America

1302 Concourse Dr., Ste. 204, Linthicum, MD, 21090; *PH:* 1-410-694-0500; *Fax:* 1-410-694-0596;
http:// www.dialysiscorporation.com; *Email:* info@dialysiscorporation.com

General - Incorporation	FL	Stock - Price on:12/24/2007	$10.93
Employees	429	Stock Exchange	NDQ
Auditor	Moore Stephens, P.C	Ticker Symbol	DCAI
Stk Agt	Continental Stock Transfer & Trust Co	Outstanding Shares	9,570,000
Counsel	NA	E.P.S.	$0.32
DUNS No.	08-735-4478	Shareholders	NA

Business: The group's principle activities are to develop and operate outpatient kidney dialysis centers that provide dialysis and ancillary services to patients suffering from chronic kidney failure. The group also offers acute inpatient dialysis treatments in hospitals and provides homecare services through its wholly owned subsidiary, dca medical services inc. The services are also provided through contractual relationships with seven hospitals, medical centers and homecare services. The group operates nineteen outpatient dialysis facilities in Pennsylvania, New Jersey, Georgia, Ohio and Maryland. The medical service revenues are derived from outpatient hemodialysis services, home peritoneal dialysis services, inpatient hemodialysis services and ancillary services. The group operates solely in the United States. The group's quarterly revenue for September 2007 was 19.17 millions of USD.

Primary SIC and add'l.: 8092

CIK No: 0000201653

Subsidiaries: DCA of Adel, LLC, DCA of Aiken, LLC, DCA of Ashland, LLC, DCA of Carlisle, Inc., DCA of Central Valdosta, LLC, DCA of Chambersburg, Inc., DCA of Chesapeake, DCA of Chevy Chase, LLC, DCA of Cincinnati, LLC, DCA of Edgefield, LLC, DCA of Fitzgerald, LLC, DCA of Kilmarnock, LLC, DCA of Lemoyne, Inc., DCA of Manahawkin, Inc., DCA of Mechanicsburg, LLC 26 Subsidiaries included in the Index

Officers: Stephen W. Everett/51/Dir., CEO, Pres./$43,600.00, Joanne Zimmerman/VP - Clinical Services, Daniel R. Ouzts/61/VP - Finance, CFO, Chief Accounting Officer, Treasurer, Lawrence E. Jaffe/Counsel, Corp. Sec., Thomas P. Carey/VP - Operations

Directors: Thomas K. Langbein/Chmn., Robert W. Trause/65/Dir., Alexander Bienenstock/70/Dir., Peter D. Fischbein/68/Dir.

Owners: Schroeder Investment Management North America Inc./5.60%, Don Waite, Stephen W. Everett/3.80%, Daniel R. Ouzts/1.40%, Peter D. Fischbein/1.70%, Thomas K. Langbein/15.30%, Joanne Zimmerman, Alexander Bienenstock, Robert W. Trause, Insiders/23.00%

Financial Data: Fiscal Year End:12/31 Latest Annual Data: 12/31/2006

Year	Sales	Net Income
2006	$62,460,000	$3,049,000
2005	$45,392,000	$1,900,000
2004	$40,986,000	$2,214,000

Curr. Assets:	$25,630,000	Curr. Liab.:	$8,533,000	P/E Ratio:	34.16
Plant, Equip.:	$16,353,000	Total Liab.:	$17,151,000	Indic. Yr. Divd.:	NA
Total Assets:	$49,856,000	Net Worth:	$29,061,000	Debt/ Equity:	0.3350

Diamant Art Corp

7100 Warden Ave., Unit 5, Markham, ON, L3R 8B5; *PH:* 1-905-477-0252;
http:// www.diamantfilm.com; *Email:* info@diamantfilm.com

General - Incorporation	ON	Stock - Price on:12/24/2007	$0.0008
Employees	8	Stock Exchange	OTC
Auditor	Armstrong, Szewczyk & Tobias	Ticker Symbol	DIAAF
Stk Agt	Equity Transfer Services Inc	Outstanding Shares	2,960,000,000
Counsel	NA	E.P.S.	$0.001
DUNS No.	NA	Shareholders	NA

Business: The group's principle activities include producing, distributing and marketing oil paintings. The group operates from United States.

Primary SIC and add'l.: 7336

CIK No: 0000810269

Subsidiaries: Bio-Plastics Inc, Diamant Film Inc

Owners: Simon Meredith, Roger Kirby, Michel van Herreweghe, Insiders

Financial Data: Fiscal Year End:11/30 Latest Annual Data: 11/30/2006

Year	Sales	Net Income
2006	$11,000	-$490,000
2005	$27,000	-$443,000
2004	$52,000	-$336,000

Curr. Assets:	$96,000	Curr. Liab.:	$1,050,000		
Plant, Equip.:	$5,000	Total Liab.:	$1,050,000	Indic. Yr. Divd.:	NA
Total Assets:	$101,000	Net Worth:	-$949,000	Debt/ Equity:	NA

Diametrics Medical Inc

6033 W Century Blvd, Ste. 850, Los Angeles, CA, 90045; *PH:* 1-310-670-2093;
http:// www.diametrics.com

General - Incorporation	MN	Stock - Price on:12/24/2007	$1.85
Employees	14	Stock Exchange	NA
Auditor	Mckennon Wilson & Morgan LLP	Ticker Symbol	NA
Stk Agt	American Stock Transfer & Trust Co.	Outstanding Shares	19,580,000
Counsel	NA	E.P.S.	-$1.89
DUNS No.	62-140-8228	Shareholders	NA

Business: The group's principal activities are to develop, manufacture and commercialize critical care blood and tissue analysis systems. This provides immediate or continuous diagnostic result at the point-of-patient care. The group has two primary product platforms namely intermittent blood testing products and monitoring products. Intermittent blood testing products based primarily on electrochemical technology, which performs the tests for critical care patients. Continuous monitoring products based upon fiber optic technology, which provides direct continuous monitoring of blood gases and temperature for pediatric patients. The system also includes neurotrend cerebral tissue monitoring system which measures oxygen, carbon dioxide, acidity and temperature in brain tissue and fluids. The group's principal products are irma sl series 2000 blood analysis system, irma sl analyzer idms, capillary collection device and trendcare continuous blood gas monitoring system.

Primary SIC and add'l.: 3841 3845

CIK No: 0000895380

Subsidiaries: TGC Research Limited (United Kingdom)

Officers: Bruce W. Comer/42/Dir., CEO, Heng Chuk/28/Dir., CFO, Sec., Tim Collins/42/Dir., Exec. VP - Business Development, Darrell Dubroc/46/Dir., COO, Pres.

Directors: Bruce W. Comer/42/Dir., CEO, Heng Chuk/28/Dir., CFO, Sec., Paul A. Galleberg/47/Dir., Jeffrey Lawton/32/Dir., Tim Collins/42/Dir., Exec. VP - Business Development, Darrell Dubroc/46/Dir., COO, Pres.

Owners: Mercator Momentum Fund, Paul A. Galleberg, Monarch Pointe Fund, Ltd., Tim Collins, Mercator Momentum Fund III, Erasmus Louisiana Growth Fund, Darrell Dubroc, Asset Managers International Limited, M.A.G. Capital, LLC, W. Bruce Comer, Pentagon Dollar Satellite Fund, Ltd., Heng Chuk, Insiders, Ocean Park Advisors, LLC, St. Cloud Capital Partners (17 Owners included in Index)

Financial Data: Fiscal Year End:12/31 Latest Annual Data: 12/31/2006

Year	Sales	Net Income
2006	$1,803,000	-$75,250,000
2005	NA	-$10,032,000
2004	NA	-$10,979,000

Curr. Assets:	$6,951,000	Curr. Liab.:	$2,451,000		
Plant, Equip.:	$4,737,000	Total Liab.:	$5,468,000	Indic. Yr. Divd.:	NA
Total Assets:	$36,356,000	Net Worth:	$30,887,000	Debt/ Equity:	0.1005

Diamond Discoveries International Corp

45 Rockefeller Plz., Ste. 2000, New York, NY, 10111; *PH:* 1-212-332-8136; *Fax:* 1-212-332-3401;
http:// www.conceptvc.com

General - Incorporation	DE	Stock - Price on:12/24/2007	$0.005
Employees	NA	Stock Exchange	OTC
Auditor	Rodefer Moss & Co, PLLC	Ticker Symbol	DMDD
Stk Agt	Continental Stock Transfer & Trust Co	Outstanding Shares	305,220,000
Counsel	NA	E.P.S.	-$0.005
DUNS No.	NA	Shareholders	NA

Business: The groups principal activity is to explore minerals. The group operates from Canada and the United States.

Primary SIC and add'l.: 1499

CIK No: 0001123836

Subsidiaries: Diamond Discoveries (Canada) Inc.

Officers: Edward C. Williams/Chmn., CEO, CFO, Pres., Sec., Harrison O. Cookenboo/Consultant, Peter Ferderber/Founder, Consultant, Remo Niceforo/Pres., Joe B. Hinzer/Consultant, P. Geo/Pres.

Directors: Edward C. Williams/Chmn., CEO, CFO, Pres., Sec., Peter Ferderber/Founder, Consultant, Antonio Sciacca/Dir.

Owners: Insiders/4.20%, Edward C. Williams, Antonio Sciacca/3.90%, Teodosio V. Pangia/24.10%, Epwort Trading Ltd./20.70%

Financial Data: Fiscal Year End:12/31 Latest Annual Data: 12/31/2006

Year	Sales	Net Income
2006	NA	-$3,053,000
2005	NA	-$3,420,000
2004	$838,000	-$3,724,000

Curr. Assets:	$24,000	Curr. Liab.:	$1,600,000		
Plant, Equip.:	$161,000	Total Liab.:	$1,600,000	Indic. Yr. Divd.:	NA
Total Assets:	$218,000	Net Worth:	-$1,382,000	Debt/ Equity:	NA

Diamond Energy Partners Inc

Formerly: AAB National Co
1016 Clemons St., Ste. 302, Jupiter, FL, 33477; *PH:* 1-561-745-6789

General - Incorporation	FL	**Stock**- Price on:12/24/2007	NA
Employees	NA	Stock Exchange	NA
Auditor	Wieseneck, Andres & Co P.A	Ticker Symbol	NA
Stk Agt	Florida Atlantic Stock Transfer, Inc.	Outstanding Shares	NA
Counsel	NA	E.P.S	NA
DUNS No.	NA	Shareholders	NA

Business: The groups principle activities include acquiring, operating and developing gold properties. The group operates from United States.

Primary SIC and add'l.: 9995

CIK No: 0001321506

Subsidiaries: eCom eCom.com, Inc.

Officers: Barney A. Richmond/56/Chmn., CEO, Pres., Sec., Richard C. Turner/48/Dir., CFO, Treasurer

Directors: Barney A. Richmond/56/Chmn., CEO, Pres., Sec., Richard C. Turner/48/Dir., CFO, Treasurer

Owners: Insiders/21.90%, American Capital Holdings, Inc./28.50%, Barney A. Richmond/20.40%, United States Financial Group, Inc./9.10%, Richard C. Turner/1.50%

Diamond Entertainment Corp

800 Tucker Ln., Walnut, CA, 91789; *PH:* 1-909-839-1989; *Fax:* 1-909-869-1990; *http://* www.e-dmec.com

General - Incorporation	NJ	**Stock**- Price on:12/24/2007	NA
Employees	22	Stock Exchange	NA
Auditor	Pohl, McNabola, Berg & Co LLP	Ticker Symbol	NA
Stk Agt	Continental Stock Transfer & Trust Co	Outstanding Shares	NA
Counsel	NA	E.P.S	NA
DUNS No.	04-232-5472	Shareholders	NA

Business: The group's principle actiivties include marketing and distributing video tapes and other video products, including children's educational programs, motion picture, television programs and instructional computer videos; and purchase and distribute general merchandise including children's toy products, furniture and personal computers. The group operates from United States.

Primary SIC and add'l.: 6719 5092 7822

CIK No: 0000847420

Subsidiaries: e-DMEC Corporation, Galaxy Net International, Inc., Jewel Products International, Inc., Salesdirect123.com

Officers: Mulugetta Bezzabeh/65/Dir., CEO, Fred U. Odaka/71/CFO

Directors: Mulugetta Bezzabeh/65/Dir., CEO, James K.T. Lu/60/Dir., Howard Becker/49/Dir.

Owners: Fred U. Odaka/0.06%, James K. T. Lu/0.62%, Mulugetta Bezzabeh/44.76%, Insiders/45.44%, Insiders/45.45%, James K. T. Lu/0.63%, Margie Chassman/30.62%

Curr. Assets:	$2,184,000	**Curr. Liab.:**	$12,090,000		
Plant, Equip.:	$108,000	**Total Liab.:**	$12,090,000	**Indic. Yr. Divd.:**	NA
Total Assets:	$2,479,000	**Net Worth:**	-$9,611,000	**Debt/ Equity:**	NA

Diamond Foods Inc

1050 S Diamond St., Stockton, CA, 95205; *PH:* 1-209-467-6000; *Fax:* 1-209-461-7309; *http://* www.diamondnuts.com

General - Incorporation	DE	**Stock**- Price on:12/24/2007	$17.4
Employees	768	Stock Exchange	NDQ
Auditor	Deloitte & Touche LLP	Ticker Symbol	DMND
Stk Agt	EquiServe Trust Co N.A	Outstanding Shares	NA
Counsel	NA	E.P.S	$0.45
DUNS No.	NA	Shareholders	NA

Business: The groups principle activities include processing, marketing and distributing culinary, in shell and ingredient nuts and snack products. The products of the group include shelled nuts, glazed nuts, roasted nuts, glazed nuts and mixed nuts. In July2005, the group merged with Diamond Walnut Growers, Inc. The group operates from the California, Florida, Georgia, Illinois, Indiana, Massachusetts, New Jersey, Pennsylvania, Texas and Wisconsin. The group's total revenue for September 2007 was 522.59 millions of USD.

Primary SIC and add'l.: 0173 2096 2032 2099 2068

CIK No: 0001320947

Subsidiaries: Diamond Nut Company of California, Inc., Diamond of Europe, Diamond Walnut Capital Trust

Officers: Michael J. Mendes/Dir., CEO, Pres., Samuel J. Keiper/VP - Corporate Affairs, Human Resources, Sec., Gary K. Ford/COO, Exec. VP, Andrew Burke/Sr. VP - Marketing, Seth Halio/CFO, Exec. VP, Mike Cooke/Sr. VP - North American Retail Sales, Stephen Kim/VP, General Counsel, Robert Philipps/Treasurer, VP - Investor Relations, Bob Philipps/Investor Contact, David Conner/Contact - Press

Directors: Michael J. Mendes/Dir., CEO, Pres., John J. Gilbert/Chmn., Robert M. Lea/Dir., Laurence M. Baer/Dir., Dennis Mussell/Dir., Steven M. Neil/Dir., Joseph P. Silveira/Dir., Glen C. Warren/Dir., Robert J. Zollars/Dir.

Owners: Robert J. Zollars, Seth Halio/1.00%, Joseph P. Silveira, Laurence M. Baer, Michael J. Mendes/4.00%, Insiders/8.80%, FMR Corp./11.40%, Samuel J. Keiper, Massachusetts Financial Services Company/5.90%, Dennis Mussell, Vardon Capital Management, LLC/6.90%, Steven M. Neil, Andrew Burke, Glen C. Warren, Robert M. Lea *(18 Owners included in Index)*

Financial Data: **Fiscal Year End:**07/31 **Latest Annual Data:** 07/31/2007

Year	Sales	Net Income
2007	$522,585,000	$8,433,000
2006	$477,205,000	$7,336,000
2005	$428,297,000	$182,796,000

Curr. Assets:	$197,962,000	**Curr. Liab.:**	$110,273,000		
Plant, Equip.:	$34,291,000	**Total Liab.:**	$142,206,000	**Indic. Yr. Divd.:**	$0.120
Total Assets:	$253,032,000	**Net Worth:**	$110,826,000	**Debt/ Equity:**	0.1643

Diamond Hill Investment Group Inc

325 John H. McConnell Blvd., Ste. 200, Columbus, OH, 43215; *PH:* 1-614-255-3333; *Fax:* 1-614-255-3363; *http://* www.diamond-hill.com; *Email:* info@diamond-hill.com

General - Incorporation	OH	**Stock**- Price on:12/24/2007	$82.1201
Employees	32	Stock Exchange	NDQ
Auditor	Plante & Moran, PLLC	Ticker Symbol	DHIL
Stk Agt	Continental Stock Transfer & Trust Co	Outstanding Shares	2,140,000
Counsel	Carlile Patchen & Murphy	E.P.S	$4.94
DUNS No.	80-988-9652	Shareholders	NA

Business: The group's principal activity is to provide investment advisory services for the securities in the financial services sector. The group also offers advisory accounts and invests and trades in securities. The customers include institutional, individual investors, individuals, estates and bank trust departments. The group maintains margin accounts with broker-dealers. The group operates solely in the United States.

Primary SIC and add'l.: 6221 6211 6282

CIK No: 0000909108

Subsidiaries: Diamond Hill Capital Management, Inc.

Officers: R. H. Dillon/Dir., Chief Investment Officer, Corporate CEO/$3,836,400.00, Christopher A. Welch/Portfolio Mgr. - Equities, Samuel J. Hooper/Equity Trader - Trading & Investment Support Team, Matthew P. Swager/Head - Equity Trader - Trading & Investment Support Team, Jason R. Job/Business Analyst, Brian D. Risinger/Dir. - Administration, Compliance, Laurie Fullerton/Mgr. - Investment Operations, Client Service, Stacey L. Madison/Mgr. - Portfolio Administration, Client Service, Suken D. Patel/Research Analyst, Equities, James M. Bishop/Dir. - National, Institutional Sales, Tamala S. Gourley/Dir. - Key Accounting, James F. Laird/Pres. - Diamond Hill Funds, Corporate CFO/$921,600.00, Gary R. Young/Chief Compliance Officer - Diamond Hill Funds, Corporate Controller, Randall J. Demyan/MD - Planning, Operations, Patricia L. Schindler/Dir. - Marketing *(38 Officers included in Index)*

Directors: R. H. Dillon/Dir., Chief Investment Officer, Corporate CEO, David R. Meuse/Chmn., David P. Lauer/Dir., James G. Mathias/Dir., Diane D. Reynolds/Dir., Donald B. Shackelford/Dir.

Owners: James F. Laird/3.30%, David P. Lauer, Donald B. Shackelford, David R. Meuse/2.50%, Insiders/14.70%, James G. Mathias/1.90%, R. H. Dillon/6.80%, Diane D. Reynolds

Financial Data: **Fiscal Year End:**12/31 **Latest Annual Data:** 12/31/2006

Year	Sales	Net Income
2006	$31,904,000	$8,065,000
2005	$9,183,000	$3,651,000
2004	$2,468,000	-$177,000

Curr. Assets:	$16,761,000	**Curr. Liab.:**	$14,854,000	**P/E Ratio:**	20.74
Plant, Equip.:	$497,000	**Total Liab.:**	$16,753,000	**Indic. Yr. Divd.:**	NA
Total Assets:	$37,236,000	**Net Worth:**	$20,483,000	**Debt/ Equity:**	NA

Diamond Offshore Drilling Inc

15415 Katy Fwy., Ste. 100, Houston, TX, 77094; *PH:* 1-281-492-5300; *Fax:* 1-281-492-5316; *http://* www.diamondoffshore.com

General - Incorporation	DE	**Stock**- Price on:12/24/2007	$100.79
Employees	4,800	Stock Exchange	NYSE
Auditor	Deloitte & Touche LLP	Ticker Symbol	DO
Stk Agt	Mellon Investor Services LLC	Outstanding Shares	138,350,000
Counsel	NA	E.P.S	$6.53
DUNS No.	00-810-4846	Shareholders	NA

Business: The group's principal activity is contract drilling of offshore oil and gas wells. The group provides deep water drilling with a fleet of 45 offshore rigs. The fleet is comprised of 30 semisubmersible, 14 jack-up rigs and 1 drillship. The customers include independent oil and gas companies and government-owned oil companies. The major customers of the group are petroleo brasileiro s a, bp and murphy exploration and production company. The group markets its services in the gulf of Mexico, Europe, principally the United Kingdom, sector of the north sea, South America, Africa, Australia and southeast Asia.

Primary SIC and add'l.: 1381

CIK No: 0000949039

Subsidiaries: Afcons Arethusa Off-Shore Services Ltd., Arethusa Off-Shore Company, Arethusa/Zapata Off-Shore Brasil Ltda., Brasdril-Sociedade de Perfuracoes Ltda., Diamond Hungary Leasing, LLC, Diamond M Corporation, Diamond M Servicios , S.A., Diamond Offshore (Australia) LLC, Diamond Offshore (Bermuda) Limited, Diamond Offshore (Brazil) LLC, Diamond Offshore (Singapore) Pte. Ltd., Diamond Offshore (Trinidad) LLC, Diamond Offshore (USA)L.L.C., Diamond Offshore Company, Diamond Offshore Contract Services, S.A. 44 Subsidiaries included in the Index

Officers: James S. Tisch/Chmn., CEO/$836,509.00, Lyndol Dew/Sr. VP - Worldwide Operations, Robert N. Blank/VP - Operations Support, Robert G. Blair/VP - Contracts, Marketing, Herbert C. Hofmann/Dir., Sr. VP, Duncan C. Weir/VP - Contracts, Marketing International, Raymond S. Troubh/Dir., Financial Consultant, Paul G. Gaffney/Dir., Pres., Mark F. Baudoin/Sr. VP - Administration, Operations Support, Arthur L. Rebell/Dir., Sr. VP, Lawrence R. Dickerson/Dir., COO, Pres./$1,521,853.00, John L. Gabriel/Sr. VP - Contracts, Marketing/$788,757.00, R. L. Charles/VP - Human Resources, Bodley P. Thornton/VP - Marketing, Morrison R. Plaisance/VP - International Operations *(25 Officers included in Index)*

Directors: James S. Tisch/Chmn., CEO, Alan R. Batkin/Vice Chmn., Arthur L. Rebell/Dir., Sr. VP, John R. Bolton/Dir., Lawrence R. Dickerson/Dir., COO, Pres., Charles L. Fabrikant/Dir., Herbert C. Hofmann/Dir., Sr. VP, Raymond S. Troubh/Dir., Financial Consultant, Paul G. Gaffney/Dir., Pres.

Owners: Gary T. Krenek, FMR Corp./6.70%, Insiders/2.40%, Lawrence R. Dickerson, Herbert C. Hofmann, Arthur L. Rebell, James S. Tisch/2.40%, Charles L. Fabrikant, Raymond S. Troubh, John M. Vecchio, Loews Corporation/50.70%, Paul G. Gaffney, John L. Gabriel, Alan R. Batkin

Financial Data: **Fiscal Year End:**12/31 **Latest Annual Data:** 06/30/2007

Year	Sales	Net Income
2007	$648,875,000	$251,927,000
2006	$2,052,572,000	$706,847,000
2005	$1,221,002,000	$260,337,000

Curr. Assets:	$1,481,547,000	**Curr. Liab.:**	$333,509,000	**P/E Ratio:**	16.13
Plant, Equip.:	$2,628,453,000	**Total Liab.:**	$1,813,331,000	**Indic. Yr. Divd.:**	$0.500
Total Assets:	$4,132,839,000	**Net Worth:**	$2,319,508,000	**Debt/ Equity:**	0.2145

Diamond Powersports Inc

3771 NW 126th Ave. , Coral springs, FL, 33065; *PH:* 1-954-749-8606; *Fax:* 1-954-749-9750; *http://* www.diamondpowersports.com; *Email:* sales@diamondpowersports.com

General - Incorporation	FL
Employees	10
Auditor	Perrella & Assoc. P. A
Stk Agt	Florida Atlantic Stock Transfer, Inc.
Counsel	NA
DUNS No.	NA

Stock - Price on:12/24/2007	$0.04
Stock Exchange	OTC
Ticker Symbol	DPWS
Outstanding Shares	16,280,000
E.P.S.	-$0.02
Shareholders	NA

Business: The group's principle activities include manufacturing and distributing motorcycle accessories and apparel, specializing in brand names and after-Market products. The group operates in the powersports market, which consists primarily of street and off-road motorcycles, atvs, and small watercrafts such as jet skis and powered kayaks. It also offers services like international shipping and a fifteen-day refund policy. The group's main customers are motorcycle dealers and wholesale buyers. The group also manufactures and assembles frame sliders, lowering links, adjustable kick stands, top clamps and 180 other motorcycle parts. The group operates from United States.

Primary SIC and add'l.: 3714 3751

CIK No: 0001098865

Officers: Pierre Elliott/Dir., CEO, Pres., David Lewis/Dir., Dir. - Marketing, Sales, Mike Tober/Dir. - Inventory Control, Lisa Elliott/Dir., COO, VP

Directors: Pierre Elliott/Dir., CEO, Pres., Joe McGhee/Dir., Dir. - Marketing, Sales, Lisa Elliott/Dir., COO, VP, Margaret Hurley/Dir.

Financial Data: Fiscal Year End:12/31 Latest Annual Data: 12/31/2006

Year	Sales	Net Income
2006	$16,482,000,000	$1,380,000,000
2005	$1,265,000	-$312,000
2004	$1,492,000	-$680,000

Curr. Assets:	$252,000	**Curr. Liab.:**	$484,000		
Plant, Equip.:	$222,000	**Total Liab.:**	$492,000	**Indic. Yr. Divd.:**	NA
Total Assets	$482,000	**Net Worth:**	-$10,000	**Debt/ Equity:**	NA

Diamond Ranch Foods Ltd (New)

555 W St., New York, NY, 10014; *PH:* 1-212-807-7600; *http://* www.diamondranchfoods.com; *Email:* info@diamondranchfoods.com

General - Incorporation	NV
Employees	NA
Auditor	Gruber & Co., LLC
Stk Agt	Signature Stock Transfer, Inc.
Counsel	NA
DUNS No.	NA

Stock - Price on:12/24/2007	$0.07
Stock Exchange	OTC
Ticker Symbol	DFDR
Outstanding Shares	68,650,000
E.P.S.	-$0.01
Shareholders	NA

Business: The groups principle activity is to provide custom-cut and portion-controlled meats to foodservice institutions, restaurants, and supermarkets. The group also provides a full menu of HACCP certified meats and meat products including All American Hamburger, McCleod Brand, Hebrew National delicacies including hot dogs, seasoned pastramis, tender corned beef; fresh meats like beef, including steaks, roasts, and ribs, farm-fresh poultry, pork, veal cutlets, lamb in a variety of cuts, provisions to complement like quality gourmet cheeses, oils, and other food items. The groups services include custom cuts, butchering and processing meats. The group operates from United States.

Primary SIC and add'l.: 2011

CIK No: 0001317880

Officers: Joseph Maggio/Chmn., CEO, Louis Vucci/Dir., Pres., William Demarzo/CFO

Directors: Joseph Maggio/Chmn., CEO, Louis Vucci/Dir., Pres.

Owners: Joseph Maggio/16.25%, Insiders/39.19%, Louis Vucci/20.03%, Philip Serlin/1.45%, William DeMarzo/1.46%

Financial Data: Fiscal Year End:03/31 Latest Annual Data: 3/31/2006

Year	Sales	Net Income
2006	$12,815,000	-$597,000
2005	$10,040,000	-$1,519,000

Curr. Assets:	$1,964,000	**Curr. Liab.:**	$3,495,000		
Plant, Equip.:	$309,000	**Total Liab.:**	$4,543,000	**Indic. Yr. Divd.:**	NA
Total Assets	$2,291,000	**Net Worth:**	-$2,252,000	**Debt/ Equity:**	NA

Diamondcluster International Inc

875 N Michigan Ave., Ste. 3000, Chicago, IL, 60611; *PH:* 1-312-255-5000; *Fax:* 1-312-255-6000; *http://* www.diamondcluster.com; *Email:* investor.relations@diamondcluster.com

General - Incorporation	DE
Employees	507
Auditor	KPMG LLP
Stk Agt	Mellon Investor Services LLC
Counsel	Nancy K. Bellis
DUNS No.	NA

Stock - Price on:12/24/2007	$13.36
Stock Exchange	NDQ
Ticker Symbol	DTPI
Outstanding Shares	31,570,000
E.P.S.	$0.92
Shareholders	NA

Business: The group's principal activity is to provide management consulting services. The group helps organizations worldwide to leverage technology to develop and implement growth strategies, improve operations and capitalize on technology. The group serves clients in five vertical industries: financial services, insurance, telecommunications, healthcare and the public sector. It operates globally with offices in North America, Europe and Latin America. The group has strategic alliances with IBM, microsoft and sun microsystems.

Primary SIC and add'l.: 7379 8742

CIK No: 0000924940

Subsidiaries: Diamond Partners Limited, DiamondCluster India Private Limited, DiamondCluster International B.V., DiamondCluster International Finance S.L., DiamondCluster International FZ-LLC (Dubai), DiamondCluster International IC LLC, DiamondCluster International Limited, DiamondCluster International Ltda, DiamondCluster International Managementberatung GmbH, DiamondCluster International North America, Inc., DiamondCluster International S.L., DiamondCluster International SARL

Officers: Adam J. Gutstein/Dir., CEO, Pres., Bill McClayton/Chief Administrative Officer, William R. McClayton/Chief Administrative Officer, Sec./$972,653.00, Karl E. Bupp/CFO, Treasurer

Directors: Adam J. Gutstein/Dir., CEO, Pres., Mel Bergstein/Chmn., Don Caldwell/Dir., Samuel K. Skinner/Dir., Alan Kay/Dir., Pauline Schneider/Dir., John J. Sviokla/Dir., Javier Rubio/Dir., Arnold R. Weber/Dir., Mike Mikolajczyk/Dir., Ed Anderson/Dir.

Owners: Javier Rubio/4.10%, Arnold R. Weber, Samuel K. Skinner, Edward R. Anderson, Jay D. Norman, William M. McClayton/1.00%, Pauline A. Schneider, Karl E. Bupp/1.70%, Melvyn E. Bergstein/3.90%, BlackRock, Inc./9.50%, FMR Corp./10.10%, John J. Sviokla, Luther King Capital Management Corporation/5.00%, Michael E. Mikolajczyk, Insiders/15.20% *(19 Owners included in Index)*

Financial Data: Fiscal Year End:03/31 Latest Annual Data: 3/31/2007

Year	Sales	Net Income
2007	$190,273,000	$31,401,000
2006	$163,668,000	-$10,584,000
2005	$219,775,000	$33,038,000

Curr. Assets:	$112,959,000	**Curr. Liab.:**	$32,256,000	**P/E Ratio:**	13.21
Plant, Equip.:	$1,431,000	**Total Liab.:**	$36,599,000	**Indic. Yr. Divd:**	$0.300
Total Assets	$128,487,000	**Net Worth:**	$91,888,000	**Debt/ Equity:**	NA

Diamondhead Casino Corp

150 153rd Ave. Ste. 202, Madeira Beach, FL, 33708; *PH:* 1-727-393-2885

General - Incorporation	DE
Employees	4
Auditor	Friedman LLP
Stk Agt	Continental Stock Transfer & Trust Co
Counsel	NA
DUNS No.	60-312-2128

Stock - Price on:12/24/2007	$2.5
Stock Exchange	OTC
Ticker Symbol	DHCC
Outstanding Shares	33,410,000
E.P.S.	-$0.04
Shareholders	NA

Business: The group's principal activity is to own, operate and promote cruise vessels and offer day and evening cruise services in the state of Florida. The group owns a total of 404.5 acres of unimproved land in diamondhead, Mississippi, on which it plans to develop a casino resort. The group intends to develop its diamondhead property as a destination casino resort and to eventually operate its casino resort, with an operator, through its subsidiaries, Mississippi gaming corporation and casino world, inc. The group currently has no operations.

Primary SIC and add'l.: 7999 5812 4489

CIK No: 0000844887

Subsidiaries: Casino World, Inc, Mississippi Gaming Corporation

Owners: Frank E. Williams/1.12%, Ernst G. Walter/3.15%, Serco International Limited, Carl D. Stevens/1.52%, Serco International Limited/3.15%, Austroinvest International Limited, Austroinvest International Limited, Serco International Limited, Gregory Harrison/3.64%, Insiders/22.73%, Ernst G. Walter, H. Steven Norton/0.63%, Ernst G. Walter, Benjamin J. Harrell/1.64%, Deborah A. Vitale/14.04% *(17 Owners included in Index)*

Financial Data: Fiscal Year End:12/31 Latest Annual Data: 12/31/2006

Year	Sales	Net Income
2006	NA	-$1,650,000
2005	NA	-$642,000
2004	$168,000	-$640,000

Curr. Assets:	$1,436,000	**Curr. Liab.:**	$200,000		
Plant, Equip.:	$5,411,000	**Total Liab.:**	$200,000	**Indic. Yr. Divd.:**	NA
Total Assets	$6,874,000	**Net Worth:**	$6,674,000	**Debt/ Equity:**	NA

Diamondrock Hospitality Company

6903 Rockledge Dr., Ste. 800, Bethesda, MD, 20817; *PH:* 1-240-744-1150; *Fax:* 1-718-236-4588; *http://* www.drhc.com

General - Incorporation	MD
Employees	17
Auditor	KPMG LLP
Stk Agt	American Stock Transfer & Trust Co.
Counsel	NA
DUNS No.	NA

Stock - Price on:12/24/2007	$18.25
Stock Exchange	NYSE
Ticker Symbol	DRH
Outstanding Shares	94,530,000
E.P.S.	$0.59
Shareholders	NA

Business: The groups principle activity is to acquire premium hotels and resorts. The group acquired Oak Brook Hills Resort & Conference Center and Torrance Marriott in the year 2005 and Westin Boston Waterfront Hotel in the year 2007. The group operates from the North America. The group's quarterly revenue for September 2007 was 168.01 millions of USD.

Primary SIC and add'l.: 6798 7011

CIK No: 0001298946

Subsidiaries: Bloodstone TRS,Inc., DiamondRock Alpharetta Owner, LLC, DiamondRock Alpharetta Tenant, LLC, DiamondRock Bethesda General, LLC, DiamondRock Bethesda Limited, LLC, DiamondRock Bethesda Tenant, LLC, DiamondRock Boston Expansion Owner, LLC, DiamondRock Boston Owner, LLC, DiamondRock Boston Retail Owner, LLC, DiamondRock Boston Tenant, LLC, DiamondRock Buckhead Owner, LLC, DiamondRock Buckhead Tenant, LLC, DiamondRock Cayman Islands,Inc., DiamondRock Chicago Conrad Owner, LLC, DiamondRock Chicago Conrad Tenant, LLC 60 Subsidiaries included in the Index

Officers: William W. McCarten/Chmn., CEO/$2,228,464.00, John L. Williams/Dir., COO, Pres./$1,730,290.00, Mark W. Brugger/Exec. VP, CFO, Treasurer/$1,272,428.00, Sean M. Mahoney/Sr. VP, Corporate Controller, Chief Accounting Officer/$366,976.00, Michael D. Schecter/Exec. VP, General Counsel, Corp. Sec./$792,956.00

Directors: William W. McCarten/Chmn., CEO, Daniel J. Altobello/Dir., Robert W. Grafton/Dir., Maureen L. McAvey/Dir., Gilbert T. Ray/Dir., John L. Williams/Dir., COO, Pres.

Owners: Sean M. Mahoney, Columbia Wanger Asset Management, L.P./5.60%, Maureen L. McAvey, Insiders/1.10%, Daniel J. Altobello, Robert W. Grafton, Michael D. Schecter, Gilbert T. Ray, John L. Williams, Mark W. Brugger, William W. McCarten

Financial Data: Fiscal Year End:12/31 Latest Annual Data: 12/31/2006

Year	Sales	Net Income
2006	$491,890,000	$35,211,000
2005	$229,450,000	-$7,336,000

Curr. Assets:	$106,039,000	**Curr. Liab.:**	$77,057,000		
Plant, Equip.:	$1,686,426,000	**Total Liab.:**	$1,034,037,000	**Indic. Yr. Divd.:**	$0.960
Total Assets	$1,818,965,000	**Net Worth:**	$784,928,000	**Debt/ Equity:**	0.7949

Diana Shipping Inc

Pendelis 16, 175 64 Palaio Faliro, Athens; *PH:* 30-2109470100; *http://* www.dianashippinginc.com; *Email:* ir@dianashippinginc.com

General - Incorporation .... Marshall Islands	Stock - Price on:12/24/2007 ....$20.98
Employees..365	Stock Exchange...................................NYSE
Auditor .... Ernst & Young	Ticker Symbol..DSX
Stk Agt..... Computershare Investor Services LLC	Outstanding Shares 62,900,000
Counsel..NA	E.P.S..$2.01
DUNS No...NA	Shareholders...NA

Business: The groups principle activity is to transport iron ore, coal, grain and other dry cargoes. In the year 2005, the group acquired Pantelis SP, Erato and Thetis vessels. The group operates from Greece, the United States, China and India. The groups quarterly revenue is September 2007 was 49.09 millions of USD.

Primary SIC and add'l.: 4449 4499 4412 4491 4424

CIK No: 0001318885

Subsidiaries: Buenos Aires Compania Armadora S.A., Cerada International S.A., Changame Compania Armadora S.A., Chorrera Compania Armadora S.A., Cypres Enterprises Corp., Darien Compania Armadora S.A., Eaton Marine S.A., Husky Trading S.A., Panama Compania Armadora S.A., Skyvan Shipping Company S.A., Texford Maritime S.A., Urbina Bay Trading S.A., Vesta Commercial S.A.

Officers: Simeon P. Palios/Chmn., CEO, Anastassis C. Margaronis/Dir., Pres., Ioannis G. Zafirakis/Dir., VP, Sec., Andreas Michalopoulos/CFO, Maria Dede/Chief Accounting Officer

Directors: Simeon P. Palios/Chmn., CEO, Anastassis C. Margaronis/Dir., Pres., Ioannis G. Zafirakis/Dir., VP, Sec., William Lawes/Dir., Apostolos Kontoyannis/Dir., Boris Nachamkin/Dir., Konstantinos Psaltis/Dir.

Owners: Insiders/39.06%, Simeon Palios/39.06%, Fortis Bank/9.50%

Financial Data: Fiscal Year End:12/31 Latest Annual Data: 12/31/2006

Year	Sales	Net Income
2006	$116,101,000	$61,063,000
2005	$103,104,000	$64,990,000
2004	$63,839,000	$60,083,000

Curr. Assets:	$19,062,000	Curr. Liab.:	$7,636,000		
Plant, Equip.:	$489,683,000	Total Liab.:	$147,572,000	Indic. Yr. Divd.:	$2.320
Total Assets:	$510,675,000	Net Worth:	$363,103,000	Debt/ Equity:	NA

Diapulse Corp of America

475 Northern Blvd., Great Neck, NY, 11021; **PH:** 1-516-466-3030 ; **Fax:** 1-516-829-8069; **http://** www.diapulse.com; **Email:** diapulse@aol.com

General - Incorporation ....DE	Stock - Price on:12/24/2007 ....NA
Employees..36	Stock Exchange....................................OTC
Auditor ....Granick & Gendler	Ticker Symbol..DIAC
Stk Agt.................. Affiliated Stock Transfer Co.	Outstanding Shares ....NA
Counsel..NA	E.P.S..NA
DUNS No.......................................00-128-0593	Shareholders...NA

Business: The group's principal activities are to develop, manufacture and market a proprietary medical system to treat post-operative edema and pain in acute and chronic wounds. The grooup markets its product under the trademark diapulse, that produces non-thermal pulsed high-frequency and high-peak power electromagnetic energy to treat patients. The group's product is marketed and rented to hospitals, nursing facilities, outpatient clinics, physicians' practices and prescribed for use in patients' homes throughout the United States.

Primary SIC and add'l.: 3845 7352

CIK No: 0000028742

Officers: David M. Ross/61/Chmn., Pres.

Directors: David M. Ross/61/Chmn., Pres.

Owners: David M. Ross/40.13%

Curr. Assets:	$875,000	Curr. Liab.:	$223,000		
Plant, Equip.:	$6,000	Total Liab.:	$3,691,000	Indic. Yr. Divd.:	NA
Total Assets:	$1,019,000	Net Worth:	-$2,672,000	Debt/ Equity:	NA

Diasense Inc

211 W Wall St., Midland, TX, 79701; **PH:** 1-432-682-1761

General - Incorporation ....PA	Stock - Price on:12/24/2007 ....$0.04
Employees..NA	Stock Exchange....................................OTC
Auditor ....S. W. Hatfield, CPA	Ticker Symbol..DSNE
Stk Agt........................ Securities Transfer Corp	Outstanding Shares 22,110,000
Counsel..NA	E.P.S..-$0.002
DUNS No...NA	Shareholders...NA

Business: The groups principal activity is to research and development of noninvasive glucose sensor. The group operates from the United States.

Primary SIC and add'l.: 6799

CIK No: 0000895650

Officers: Glenn A. Little/55/Dir., CEO, CFO, Pres.

Directors: Glenn A. Little/55/Dir., CEO, CFO, Pres.

Owners: Glenn A. Little/50.20%, Insiders/50.20%

Financial Data: Fiscal Year End:09/30 Latest Annual Data: 12/31/2006

Year	Sales	Net Income
2006	NA	-$13,000

Curr. Assets:	$25,000	Curr. Liab.:	$0		
Plant, Equip.:	NA	Total Liab.:	$20,000	Indic. Yr. Divd.:	NA
Total Assets:	$25,000	Net Worth:	$5,000	Debt/ Equity:	NA

Diasys Corp

21, W Main St., Waterbury, CT, 06702; **PH:** 1-203-755-5083; **Fax:** 1-203-755-5105; **http://** www.diasys.com; **Email:** sales@diasys.com

General - Incorporation ....DE	Stock - Price on:12/24/2007 ....$0.13
Employees..12	Stock Exchange....................................OTC
Auditor ......Fiondella, Milone & Lasaracina LLP	Ticker Symbol..DYXC
Stk Agt............. American Stock Transfer & Trust Co.	Outstanding Shares 23,610,000
Counsel............... Moskowitz, Altman & Hughes	E.P.S..-$0.032
DUNS No.......................................78-588-3018	Shareholders...NA

Business: The group's principal activities are to design, develop, manufacture and distribute proprietary workstation and consumable products for medical and clinical laboratory applications. The products include workstation-systems and consumable diagnostic products, reagents and test kits. The workstation-system increases the accuracy and reduces the cost to perform routine laboratory analysis of various body fluids. The consumable diagnostic products, reagents and test kits facilitate accurate diagnosis of certain medical conditions. The group has been granted 20 patents on its r/s, fe, parasep and uriprep technologies and trade name protection for "Diasys" under the following product names (both domestically and abroad): urizyme, diasys, uriprep, parasep, urisep. The group markets its products through distributors in North America, Europe, Middle East, Africa, China and pacific Asia.

Primary SIC and add'l.: 3841

CIK No: 0000916380

Subsidiaries: DiaSys Europe Limited

Officers: Fredric H. Neikrug/63/CEO, Pres.

Directors: Sherman Lazrus/75/Dir.

Owners: Howard M. Bloom/1.17%, Insiders/48.25%, Sherwin Gilbert/0.85%, John V. Winfield/11.59%, Morris Silverman/50.47%, Robert M. Wigoda/0.80%

Financial Data: Fiscal Year End:06/30 Latest Annual Data: 06/30/2007

Year	Sales	Net Income
2007	$1,678,000	-$785,000
2006	$1,688,000	-$1,048,000
2005	$1,914,000	-$2,029,000

Curr. Assets:	$545,000	Curr. Liab.:	$1,410,000		
Plant, Equip.:	$139,000	Total Liab.:	$1,410,000	Indic. Yr. Divd.:	NA
Total Assets:	$2,468,000	Net Worth:	$1,058,000	Debt/ Equity:	NA

Diatect International Corp

875 S Industrial Pkwy, Heber, UT, 84032; **PH:** 1-435-654-4370; **Fax:** 1-435-657-9794; **http://** www.diatect.com; **Email:** info@diatect.com

General - Incorporation ....CA	Stock - Price on:12/24/2007 ....$0.035
Employees..NA	Stock Exchange....................................OTC
Auditor ....Hansen, Barnett & Maxwell	Ticker Symbol..DTCT
Stk Agt ....Interwest Transfer Company, Inc.	Outstanding Shares ....NA
Counsel..NA	E.P.S..NA
DUNS No................................. 82-468-1258	Shareholders...NA

Business: The group's principle activities include developing and producing insecticides which utilize so called "Natural-Kiling Agents" which are non-toxic to the environment as well as humans and other warm-blooded animal life; and own five fully registered epa labels and have the technical expertise, manufacturing facilities and experienced management to successfully produce and brand insect control products. The group operates from United States.

Primary SIC and add'l.: 2879

CIK No: 0000319124

Officers: Dave Andrus/42/Chmn., Pres., Principal Executive Officer, Principal Financial Officer

Directors: Dave Andrus/42/Chmn., Pres., Principal Executive Officer, Principal Financial Officer, Javvis Jacobson/35/Dir.

Owners: David H. Andrus/5.40%, Javvis Jacobson, Aspen Capital Partners/8.55%

Financial Data: Fiscal Year End:12/31 Latest Annual Data: 12/31/2004

Year	Sales	Net Income
2004	$666,000	-$2,819,000
2003	$742,000	$7,524,000
2002	$770,000	-$1,976,000

Curr. Assets:	$752,000	Curr. Liab.:	$3,854,000		
Plant, Equip.:	$1,009,000	Total Liab.:	$5,640,000	Indic. Yr. Divd.:	NA
Total Assets:	$3,002,000	Net Worth:	-$2,638,000	Debt/ Equity:	NA

Dick S Sporting Goods Inc

300 Industry Dr., RIDC Pk. W, Pittsburgh, PA, 15275; **PH:** 1-724-273-3400; **Fax:** 1-724-227-1904; **http://** www.dickssportinggoods.com

General - Incorporation .... DE	Stock - Price on:12/24/2007 ....$55.72
Employees..8,359	Stock Exchange...................................NYSE
Auditor ....Deloitte & Touche LLP	Ticker Symbol..DKS
Stk Agt ..... American Stock Transfer & Trust Co.	Outstanding Shares 54,040,000
Counsel..NA	E.P.S..$2.19
DUNS No...NA	Shareholders...NA

Business: The groups principle activity is to provide sporting goods equipment, apparel and footwear. The groups services include golf club grip replacement, bicycle repair and maintenance, and home delivery and assembly of fitness equipment services. The group operates from United States.

Primary SIC and add'l.: 5941

CIK No: 0001089063

Subsidiaries: American Sports Licensing, Inc, DSG of Virginia, LLC, Galyans Nevada, Inc, Galyans of Virginia, Inc, Galyans Trading Company, Inc

Officers: Edward W. Stack/Chmn., CEO/$11,145,110.00, William J. Colombo/Dir., COO, Pres./$2,495,067.00, Michael F. Hines/51/CFO, Exec. VP/$2,065,887.00, Gwen Manto/Exec. VP, Chief Merchandising Officer/$2,753,508.00, William R. Newlin/67/Exec. VP, Chief Administrative Officer/$1,637,150.00, Lee Belitsky/Sr. VP - Distribution, Transportation, Jeffrey R. Hennion/Sr. VP, Chief Marketing Officer, Joseph H. Schmidt/Exec. VP - Operations, Douglas Walrod/Sr. VP - Real Estate, Development, Timothy E. Kullman/CFO, Sr. VP, Matthew J. Lynch/CIO, Sr. VP, Kathy Sutter/Sr. VP - Human Resources

Directors: Edward W. Stack/Chmn., CEO, Lawrence J. Schorr/Dir., Emanuel Chirico/Dir., David I. Fuente/Dir., William J. Colombo/Dir., COO, Pres., Walter Rossi/Dir., Brian J. Dunn/Dir., Larry D. Stone/Dir.

Owners: BlackRock, Inc./6.25%, William R. Newlin/1.31%, Edward W. Stack/87.71%, Emanuel Chirico, Gwen K. Manto, David I. Fuente, Insiders/87.71%, Lawrence J. Schorr, William J. Colombo/1.72%, Walter Rossi, Frederick C. Heichemer/5.19%, Edward W. Stack/25.94%, Baron Capital Group, Inc./11.30%, Michael F. Hines, Insiders/30.81% (18 Owners included in Index)

Financial Data: Fiscal Year End:01/28 Latest Annual Data: 2/3/2007

Year	Sales	Net Income
2007	$3,114,162,000	$112,611,000
2006	$2,624,987,000	$72,980,000
2005	$2,109,399,000	$68,905,000

Curr. Assets:	$869,779,000	Curr. Liab.:	$564,983,000	P/E Ratio:	25.44
Plant, Equip.:	$446,158,000	Total Liab.:	$903,715,000	Indic. Yr. Divd.:	NA
Total Assets:	$1,524,265,000	Net Worth:	$620,550,000	Debt/ Equity:	0.2914

Dickie Walker Marine Inc

C/o American Union Securities, 100 Wall St., 15th Fl., New York, NY, 10005; *PH:* 1-212-232-0120; *http://* www.dickiewalker.com

General - Incorporation	DE	Stock - Price on:12/24/2007	$0.4999
Employees	NA	Stock Exchange	NDQ
Auditor	Patrizio & Zhao, LLC	Ticker Symbol	DWMAC
Stk Agt	Corporate Stock Transfer, Inc.	Outstanding Shares	NA
Counsel	NA	E.P.S.	NA
DUNS No.	NA	Shareholders	NA

Business: The group's principle activity is to design, source, manufacture, market and distribute authentic lines of nautically-inspired apparel, gifts and decorative items. The group also provides private label west marine(R) branded apparel and accessories for west marine products, inc., referred to as west marine. The group has operations in the United States through wholesale and retail dealers. The gift and decorative items consist of domestic soft goods, such as towels, linens, rugs, pillows, bags, placemats, napkins, potholder mitts, and aprons; cocktail coasters; storage containers; wine bags; blankets; candles; and stationery items, such as log books, photo albums, journals, guest books, and decorative note pads. The west marine apparel line is designed featuring knit and woven shirts, shorts, swim trunks, windshirts, pullovers, hats, pants, jackets, and carry bags. The group operates from United States.

Primary SIC and add'l.: 5699

CIK No: 0001138724

Officers: Wei Chenghui/46/Chmn., CEO, CFO, Hu Jufen/44/Dir., VP, Wei Chengzhao/41/Dir., VP

Directors: Wei Chenghui/46/Chmn., CEO, CFO, Hu Jufen/44/Dir., VP, Wei Chengzhao/41/Dir., VP

Owners: Wei Chenghui/56.70%, Insiders/56.70%, Huaqin Zhou/9.10%

Diebold Inc

5995 Mayfair Rd., North Canton, OH, 44720; *PH:* 1-330-490-4000; *Fax:* 1-330-490-3794; *http://* www.diebold.com

General - Incorporation	OH	Stock - Price on:12/24/2007	$51.14
Employees	15,451	Stock Exchange	NYSE
Auditor	KPMG LLP	Ticker Symbol	DBD
Stk Agt	Bank of New York	Outstanding Shares	65,790,000
Counsel	NA	E.P.S.	NA
DUNS No.	00-446-9300	Shareholders	NA

Business: The groups principle activities include selling, manufacturing, installing and servicing of automated self-service transaction systems, electronic and physical security products, election systems and software. The groups products include ImageWay(R), Opteva(R) ATMs and self-service terminals, and express delivery XT(TM) teller assist systems. The group operates from United States.

Primary SIC and add'l.: 7378 3669 3578 7382

CIK No: 0000028823

Subsidiaries: ATM Finance, Inc., Cable Print N.V., Cardinal Brothers Consulting Pty. Ltd., Cardinal Brothers Manufacturing & Operations, Pty. Ltd., Caribbean Self Service and Security Ltd., Central de Alarmas Adler, S.A. de C.V., Central Security Systems, Inc., Comercializadora Diebold Chile Limitada, Data Information Management Systems, Inc., DBD Investment Management Company, Dchc, S.a., Diebold (Romania) S.R.L., Diebold (Thailand) Company Limited, Diebold Corp Systems Sdn. Bhd., Diebold Argentina, S.A. 127 Subsidiaries included in the Index

Officers: Thomas W. Swidarski/49/Dir., CEO, Pres./$2,329,156.00, Scott M. Hunter/VP, Chief Tax Officer, John D. Kristoff/VP, Chief Communications Officer, Michael R. Moore/VP, Corporate Controller, Leslie A. Pierce/VP, Corporate Controller, Timothy J. McDannold/VP, Treasurer, William E. Rosenberg/57/VP - Corporate Development, Kevin J. Krakora/CFO, Exec. VP/$1,087,347.00, Sheila M. Rutt/VP, Chief Human Resources Officer, Dennis M. Moriarty/Sr. VP - Global Security Division/$829,521.00, Michael J. Hillock/Pres. - International/$1,718,498.00, Robert J. Warren/VP - Corporate Development, Finance, Charles E. Ducey/Sr. VP - Global Development, Services, George S. Mayes/Sr. VP - Global Manufacturing, Supply Chain, John M. Crowther/CIO, VP *(18 Officers included in Index)*

Directors: Thomas W. Swidarski/49/Dir., CEO, Pres., John N. Lauer/69/Dir., Henry D.G. Wallace/62/Dir., Alan J. Weber/59/Dir., Louis V. Bockius/72/Dir., Phillip R. Cox/60/Dir., Gale S. Fitzgerald/57/Dir., Eric J. Roorda/57/Dir., Phillip B. Lassiter/65/Dir., Richard L. Crandall/63/Dir., William F. Massy/Dir.

Owners: Alan J. Weber/0.01%, Kevin J. Krakora/0.09%, Dennis M. Moriarty/0.11%, Thomas W. Swidarski/0.21%, Insiders/2.54%, Phillip B. Lassiter/0.04%, Gale S. Fitzgerald/0.03%, Louis V. Bockius, Michael J. Hillock/0.19%, Eric J. Roorda/0.51%, Richard L. Crandall/0.04%, David Bucci/0.31%, Henry D. G. Wallace/0.02%, John N. Lauer/0.05%, Phillip R. Cox

Financial Data: *Fiscal Year End:* 12/31   *Latest Annual Data:* 12/31/2006

Year	Sales	Net Income
2006	$2,906,232,000	$86,547,000
2005	$2,587,049,000	$96,746,000
2004	$2,380,910,000	$183,797,000

Curr. Assets:	$1,595,681,000	Curr. Liab.:	$598,736,000	P/E Ratio:	49.65
Plant, Equip.:	$202,535,000	Total Liab.:	$1,395,527,000	Indic. Yr. Divd.:	$0.940
Total Assets:	$2,514,279,000	Net Worth:	$1,091,401,000	Debt/ Equity:	NA

Diedrich Coffee Inc

28 Executive Pk., Ste. 200, Irvine, CA, 92614; *PH:* 1-949-260-1600; *Fax:* 1-949-260-1610; *http://* www.diedrich.com; *Email:* info@diedrich.com

General - Incorporation	DE	Stock - Price on:12/24/2007	$4.83
Employees	570	Stock Exchange	NDQ
Auditor	BDO Seidman LLP, KPMG LLP	Ticker Symbol	DDRX
Stk Agt	U.S. Stock Transfer Corp	Outstanding Shares	5,440,000
Counsel	NA	E.P.S.	-$0.07
DUNS No.	13-184-6198	Shareholders	NA

Business: The group's principal activity is to sell brewed, espresso-based and blended beverages, light food items, whole bean coffee and accessories. It also sells whole bean and ground coffees on a wholesale basis through a network of distributors in the office coffee service market and to other wholesale customers including restaurant chains, a grocery store chain, and other retailers. The group's brands include diedrich coffee, gloria jean's coffees and coffee people. It owns and operates 56 retail locations and franchised 426 other retail locations under these brands throughout 34 states and 13 foreign countries. In addition, it also operates a large coffee roasting facility in central California that supplies freshly roasted coffee to its retail locations and wholesale accounts. The group conducts its operations through three segments: retail operations, wholesale operations and franchise operations.

Primary SIC and add'l.: 5149 5499

CIK No: 0000947661

Subsidiaries: Diedrich Coffee, Inc, Green Mountain Coffee

Officers: Patti Graves/Contact - Customer Service

Directors: Greg D. Palmer/52/Dir., Russell J. Phillips/59/Dir.

Owners: Insiders, Timothy J. Ryan, Sean M. McCarthy, Pamela J. Britton, D.C.H., L.P., Steven G. Heyman, Greg D. Palmer, Stephen W. Leach, Paul C. Heeschen, Sequoia Enterprises, LP, Clarus Capital Group Management LP, Russell J. Phillips

Financial Data: *Fiscal Year End:* 06/29   *Latest Annual Data:* 06/27/2007

Year	Sales	Net Income
2007	$36,607,000	-$1,765,000
2006	$59,447,000	-$7,796,000
2005	$52,538,000	$14,623,000

Curr. Assets:	$7,743,000	Curr. Liab.:	$7,102,000		
Plant, Equip.:	$6,687,000	Total Liab.:	$8,743,000	Indic. Yr. Divd.:	NA
Total Assets:	$25,218,000	Net Worth:	$16,475,000	Debt/ Equity:	NA

Digene Corp

1201 Clopper Rd., Gaithersburg, MD, 20878; *PH:* 1-301-944-7000; *http://* www.digene.com

General - Incorporation	DE	Stock - Price on:12/24/2007	$59.05
Employees	490	Stock Exchange	NA
Auditor	Ernst & Young LLP	Ticker Symbol	NA
Stk Agt	StockTrans, Inc.	Outstanding Shares	24,400,000
Counsel	Ballard Spahr Andrews & Ingersoll LLP	E.P.S.	$0.81
DUNS No.	13-025-0723	Shareholders	NA

Business: The group's principal activities are to develop, manufacture and market proprietary dna and rna testing systems for the screening, monitoring and diagnosis of human diseases. The group's products and proposed products include dna and rna probe-based tests, hardware, and accessories incorporating the proprietary hybrid capture(R) technology. The primary focus is on women's cancer and infectious diseases. In addition to the hpv test, the product portfolio also includes gene-based tests for the detection of chlamydia, gonorrhea, hepatitis b virus, or hbv, and cytomegalovirus, or cmv. The group has established relationships with clinical laboratories, physicians and other healthcare professionals, developed primarily through the hpv test marketing efforts.

Primary SIC and add'l.: 8731 5047 2835 3845

CIK No: 0001011582

Subsidiaries: Digene (France) S.A.S., Digene (Italia) s.r.l., Digene (Switzerland) Sarl, Digene (UK)Limited, Digene Deutschland GmbH, Digene Diagnostics S.L., Digene do Brasil LTDA, Digene Europe, Inc., Digene UK (Holdings) Limited

Officers: Daryl J. Faulkner/Dir., CEO, Pres., Belinda O. Patrick/Sr. VP - Manufacturing Operations, Donna M. Seyfried/VP - Business Development, Joseph M. Migliara/Dir. - Private Investor, Joseph P. Slattery/CFO, Sr. VP, Attila T. Lorincz/Chief Scientific Office, Douglas C. White/Sr. VP - Sales, Marketing, Americas, Asia, Robert Mcg. Lilley/Sr. VP - Global Sales, Marketing, James H. Godsey/Sr. VP - Research, Development

Directors: Daryl J. Faulkner/Dir., CEO, Pres., Evan Jones/Chmn., Joseph M. Migliara/Dir. - Private Investor, John H. Landon/Dir., Cynthia L. Sullivan/Dir., Frank J. Ryan/Dir., Kenneth R. Weisshaar/Dir.

Financial Data: *Fiscal Year End:* 06/30   *Latest Annual Data:* 6/30/2006

Year	Sales	Net Income
2006	$152,888,000	$8,439,000
2005	$115,142,000	-$8,167,000
2004	$90,161,000	$21,542,000

Curr. Assets:	$181,222,000	Curr. Liab.:	$34,381,000	P/E Ratio:	72.90
Plant, Equip.:	$33,935,000	Total Liab.:	$54,400,000	Indic. Yr. Divd.:	NA
Total Assets:	$231,886,000	Net Worth:	$177,046,000	Debt/ Equity:	0.0961

Digi International Inc

11001 Bren Rd. E, Minnetonka, MN, 55343; *PH:* 1-952-912-3444; *Fax:* 1-952-912-4952; *http://* www.digi.com

General - Incorporation	DE	Stock - Price on:12/24/2007	$14.75
Employees	549	Stock Exchange	NDQ
Auditor	PricewaterhouseCoopers LLP	Ticker Symbol	DGII
Stk Agt	Wells Fargo Bank, N.A.	Outstanding Shares	25,250,000
Counsel	Faegre & Benson LLP	E.P.S.	$0.55
DUNS No.	14-465-5669	Shareholders	NA

Business: The group's principal activities are to provide wired and wireless hardware and software connectivity solutions. The group operates in two segments: connectivity solutions & embedded networking solutions. Connectivity solutions are used by businesses to create, customize, and control retail operations, industrial automation, and other applications. The primary product lines include multi-port serial adapters, device servers, terminal servers and universal serial bus connectivity. Embedded networking solutions are integrated hardware and software solutions for manufacturers who want to build network-ready products. The primary product lines include integrated semiconductor and controller products. The group operates in the United States, Japan and Europe.

Primary SIC and add'l.: 7371 3577 7373

CIK No: 0000854775

Subsidiaries: Digi International (HK) Ltd., Digi International GmbH, Digi International Limited, Digi International SARL, Digi Services Limited, FS Forth-Systeme GmbH, ITK International, Inc., NetSilicon, Inc., Rabbit Semiconductor Inc.

Officers: Joseph T. Dunsmore/Chmn., CEO, Pres., Jan McBride/Press, Analysts, Jon A. Nyland/37/VP - Manufacturing Operations, Subramanian Krishnan/46/Sr. VP, CFO, Treasurer, Tracy Roberts/VP - Human Resources, Information Technology, Joel Young/VP - Engineering, Larry Kraft/VP - Americas Sales - Marketing, Stephen E. Popovich/VP - Business Development, Matt Serra/Press, Analysts, Mullberry Marketing Communications Chicago, Dian Griesel/Investor Relations Group, Tom Caden/Investor Relations Group, James E. Nicholson/Sec.

Directors: Joseph T. Dunsmore/Chmn., CEO, Pres., Bradley J. Williams/Dir., Kenneth E. Millard/Dir., William N. Priesmeyer/Dir., Guy C. Jackson/Dir., Ahmed Nawaz/Dir.

Owners: Bradley J. Williams, William N. Priesmeyer, Joseph T. Dunsmore/1.99%, Insiders/5.25%, Guy C. Jackson, Royce& Associates, LLC/11.49%, Ahmed Nawaz, Munder Capital Management/7.49%, John P. Schinas/5.36%, Dimensional FundAdvisors LP/6.01%, Lawrence A. Kraft, Kenneth E. Millard, Subramanian Krishnan/1.26%, Barclays Global Investors, NA./7.10%, Joel K. Young

Financial Data: *Fiscal Year End:*09/30 *Latest Annual Data:* 9/30/2006

Year	Sales	Net Income
2006	$144,663,000	$11,113,000
2005	$125,198,000	$17,665,000
2004	$111,226,000	$8,663,000

Curr. Assets:	$106,625,000	**Curr. Liab.:**	$23,284,000	**P/E Ratio:**	22.01
Plant, Equip.:	$19,488,000	**Total Liab.:**	$31,491,000	**Indic. Yr. Divd.:**	NA
Total Assets:	$225,321,000	**Net Worth:**	$193,830,000	**Debt/ Equity:**	0.0025

Digimarc Corp

9405 SW Gemini Dr., Beaverton, OR, 97008; *PH:* 1-503-469-4800; *Fax:* 1-503-469-4777; *http://* www.digimarc.com

General - Incorporation	DE	**Stock**- Price on:12/24/2007	$8.98
Employees	422	Stock Exchange	NDQ
Auditor	Grant Thornton LLP	Ticker Symbol	DMRC
Stk Agt	Computershare Ltd.	Outstanding Shares	21,550,000
Counsel	Morrison & Foerster LLP	E.P.S	-$0.32
DUNS No.	NA	Shareholders	NA

Business: The group's principal activity is to provide patented digital watermarking technologies. This technology allows imperceptible digital code to be embedded in all forms of media content, including photographs, movies, music, financial instruments, personal identification documents and product packages. The embedded codes within various types of media content can be detected and read by software or hardware detectors in personal computers and other digital processing devices. The group also supplies secure personal identification systems and issuance systems for the majority of driver licenses produced in the United States. In addition, it provides all or part of the issuance systems for national identifications, voter identifications and driver licenses in more than twenty countries outside the United States.

Primary SIC and add'l.: 7372 3825

CIK No: 0001089443

Subsidiaries: Digimarc ID Systems (UK) Limited, Digimarc ID Systems Brasil, Ltda., Digimarc ID Systems Canada Co., Digimarc ID Systems Colombia, LTDA, Digimarc ID Systems II, LLC, Digimarc ID Systems International, Digimarc ID Systems S.A. de C.V., Digimarc ID Systems, LLC, SIA Digimarc ID Systems Latvia

Officers: Bruce Davis/Chmn., CEO/$1,100,805.00, Leslie Constans/Media Inquiries, Anna Hughes/Infotech Strategies, Robert P. Chamness/Chief Legal Officer, Sec./$487,241.00, Michael McConnell/CFO, Treasurer/$541,484.00, Reed Stager/Exec. VP/$440,166.00, Robert Eckel/Pres. - Government Programs/$864,055.00

Directors: Bruce Davis/Chmn., CEO, Bern Whitney/Dir., Lloyd G. Waterhouse/Dir., Peter W. Smith/Dir., Philip J. Monego/Dir., Bill Miller/Dir., Jim Roth/Dir., Brian J. Grossi/Dir., James T. Richardson/Dir.

Owners: James T. Richardson, Reed Stager/1.83%, Koninklijke Philips Electronics N. V./9.04%, Jim Roth, Bruce Davis/6.62%, Robert Eckel/1.17%, Michael McConnell/1.53%, Dimensional Fund Advisors LP/6.51%, William Miller, Peter W. Smith, Bernard Whitney, Macrovision Corporation/9.42%, Brian J. Grossi, Philip Monego/1.87%, Robert Chamness/1.21% *(17 Owners included in Index)*

Financial Data: *Fiscal Year End:*12/31 *Latest Annual Data:* 12/31/2006

Year	Sales	Net Income
2006	$104,247,000	-$11,740,000
2005	$101,053,000	-$23,097,000
2004	$92,947,000	-$9,022,000

Curr. Assets:	$46,789,000	**Curr. Liab.:**	$16,910,000		
Plant, Equip.:	$61,898,000	**Total Liab.:**	$23,140,000	**Indic. Yr. Divd.:**	NA
Total Assets:	$134,631,000	**Net Worth:**	$111,491,000	**Debt/ Equity:**	NA

Digirad Corp

13950 Stowe Dr., Poway, CA, 92064; *PH:* 1-858-726-1600; *Fax:* 1-858-726-1700; *http://* www.digirad.com; *Email:* info@digirad.com

General - Incorporation	DE	**Stock**- Price on:12/24/2007	$4.27
Employees	371	Stock Exchange	NDQ
Auditor	Ernst & Young LLP	Ticker Symbol	DRAD
Stk Agt	NA	Outstanding Shares	18,820,000
Counsel	Brobeck, Phleger & Harrison	E.P.S	-$0.02
DUNS No.	14-854-8738	Shareholders	NA

Business: The group's principal activity is to develop, manufacture and distribution solid-state medical imaging products and services for the detection of cardiovascular diseases and other medical conditions. The group has designed and commercialised the solid state gamma cameras for physicians, outpatient clinics and hospitals. Through its wholly owned subsidiaries digirad imaging systems and digirad imaging solutions inc, provides comprehensive and mobile imaging leasing and services for physicians who perform nuclear cardiology imaging procedures. The group also provides nuclear imaging diagnostic tool for depiction of the internal anatomy or physiology, which are primarily through non-invasive means. The trade marks include imager (R), cardiussst (R), digirad (R), digirad logo(R), digirad imaging solutions(R), fleximaging(R) and spect (r). The group operates solely in the domestic market.

Primary SIC and add'l.: 3842 3845

CIK No: 0000707388

Subsidiaries: Digirad Imaging Solutions, Inc., Digirad Imaging Systems, Inc.

Officers: Mark L. Casner/Dir., CEO, Pres./$897,247.00, Richard L. Conwell/Sr. VP - Technology, Paul J. Early/VP, Corporate Radiation Safety Officer, Todd P. Clyde/CFO, Sr. VP - Finance/$432,443.00, Randy L. Weatherhead/Sr. VP - Sales, Marketing/$507,613.00, Michael J. Keenan/Pres. - Digirad Imaging Solutions/$294,885.00, Marc E. Shapiro/VP - Human Resources, James M. Portwood/VP - Operations, Virgil J. Lott/VP - Customer Service

Directors: Mark L. Casner/Dir., CEO, Pres., Timothy J. Wollaeger/Chmn., Kenneth E. Olson/Dir., Gerhard F. Burbach/Dir., Douglas Reed/Dir., Raymond V. Dittamore/Dir., King R. Nelson/Dir.

Owners: Mark L. Casner, Kenneth E. Olson, Insiders/20.60%, Timothy J. Wollaeger, Entities affiliated with HCA, Inc./6.70%, Wentworth, Hauser, Violich, Inc./5.40%, Entities affiliated with Vector Fund Management/11.40%, R. King Nelson, Michael J. Keenan, Randy L. Weatherhead, Todd P. Clyde, Royce& Associates, LLC/7.30%, Douglas Reed/11.40%, Raymond V. Dittamore, Gerhard F. Burbach *(17 Owners included in Index)*

Financial Data: *Fiscal Year End:*12/31 *Latest Annual Data:* 12/31/2006

Year	Sales	Net Income
2006	$71,926,000	-$6,290,000
2005	$68,186,000	-$9,619,000
2004	$68,137,000	$245,000

Curr. Assets:	$59,219,000	**Curr. Liab.:**	$13,431,000		
Plant, Equip.:	$9,570,000	**Total Liab.:**	$13,832,000	**Indic. Yr. Divd.:**	NA
Total Assets:	$69,277,000	**Net Worth:**	$55,445,000	**Debt/ Equity:**	0.0007

Digital Angel Corp

490 Villaume Ave., S, St. Paul, MN, 55075; *PH:* 1-651-455-1621; *Fax:* 1-651-455-0413; *http://* www.digitalangelcorp.com; *Email:* customerservice@digitalangelcorp.com

General - Incorporation	DE	**Stock**- Price on:12/24/2007	$1.7048
Employees	314	Stock Exchange	AMEX
Auditor	Eisner LLP	Ticker Symbol	DOC
Stk Agt	Wells Fargo Shareowner Services	Outstanding Shares	44,530,000
Counsel	NA	E.P.S	-$0.23
DUNS No.	00-502-0912	Shareholders	NA

Business: The group's principal activities are development and commercialization of proprietary technologies. The group operates in three segments: animal applications: segment develops, manufactures and markets radio, electronic and visual identification devices for the companion animal, livestock, laboratory animal, fish and wildlife markets worldwide. Wireless and monitoring: segment develops and markets advanced technology to gather location and local sensory data and to communicate that data to an operations center. Gps and radio communications: segment designs, manufacture and distributes intrinsically safe sounders (horn alarms) for industrial use and other electronic components. On 22-Jan-2004, the group acquired outerlink corporation. On 19-Apr-2004 the group discontinued medical systems segment.

Primary SIC and add'l.: 8099 5122 4812 3829

CIK No: 0000771252

Subsidiaries: DA International, Inc, Digital Angel Holdings, LLC, Digital Angel Technology Corporation, DSD Holding A/S, Fearing Manufacturing Co., Inc., OuterLink Corporation, Signature Industries Limited, Timely Technology Corporation

Officers: Kevin N. McGrath/Dir., CEO, Pres., Barry M. Edelstein/Dir., CEO, Interim Pres., Patricia Petersen/VP, General Counsel, Carlos Botero/VP - Human Resources, Michael May/VP - Government Affairs - Latin America, Zeke Mejia/CTO, David M. Cairnie/MD - Signature Industries, Lasse Nordfjeld/Pres. - Animal Applications, Lorraine Breece/VP, Acting CFO, Allison Tomek/Media Contact, Thomas J. Hoyer/VP, Treasurer

Directors: Kevin N. McGrath/Dir., CEO, Pres., Barry M. Edelstein/Dir., CEO, Interim Pres., Scott R. Silverman/Chmn., John R. Block/Dir., Howard S. Weintraub/Dir., Michael S. Zarriello/Dir.

Owners: Howard S. Weintraub/1.20%, Barry M. Edelstein, David Cairnie, Applied Digital Solutions, Inc./55.20%, Insiders/14.20%, Michael S. Zarriello/1.20%, James P. Santelli/1.30%, John R. Block/1.10%, Lasse Nordfjeld, Scott R. Silverman/3.30%, Kevin N. McGrath/5.10%

Financial Data: *Fiscal Year End:*12/31 *Latest Annual Data:* 12/31/2006

Year	Sales	Net Income
2006	$56,980,000	-$6,803,000
2005	$56,826,000	-$9,476,000
2004	$46,302,000	-$4,957,000

Curr. Assets:	$25,884,000	**Curr. Liab.:**	$15,403,000		
Plant, Equip.:	$10,259,000	**Total Liab.:**	$20,885,000	**Indic. Yr. Divd.:**	NA
Total Assets:	$89,896,000	**Net Worth:**	$68,546,000	**Debt/ Equity:**	0.1310

Digital Fusion Inc

5030 Bradford Dr. NW, Ste. 210, Huntsville, AL, 35805; *PH:* 1-256-327-0000; *Fax:* 1-256-327-8120; *http://* www.digitalfusion.com

General - Incorporation	DE	**Stock**- Price on:12/24/2007	$1.8
Employees	166	Stock Exchange	OTC
Auditor	Pender Newkirk & Co	Ticker Symbol	DIGF
Stk Agt	StockTrans, Inc.	Outstanding Shares	11,460,000
Counsel	NA	E.P.S	$0.13
DUNS No.	93-850-9817	Shareholders	NA

Business: The group's principal activity is to provide information technology (IT) services to businesses, organizations and public sector institutions. The group's main service lines include it consulting services, enterprise application solutions, it support and integration and government services. It specializes in helping businesses thoroughly define project requirements and processes before they invest money, time and people. The group's major customer is aetna. The group provides these services primarily in the eastern United States.

Primary SIC and add'l.: 7372 7373 7375 8243 7376

CIK No: 0001057257

Subsidiaries: Digital Fusion Solutions, Inc., Summit Research Corporation

Officers: Frank Libutti/Chmn., CEO, Management Dir., Gary S. Ryan/Dir., Pres., Edward G. Rawlinson/COO, Christopher L. Brunhoeber/CFO, Michael W. Wicks/Exec. VP - Research, Engineering Services, Maria A. Sepulveda/Exec. VP - Northeast Region, Otis Ferguson/VP - Southwest Region, Stephen O. Brown/VP - Acquisition, Business Support, James Debroux/VP - Washington DC Business Unit, Eugene Edward Lyons/VP - Information Technology Services, Stacey G. Rock/VP - Advanced Technology, Joseph L. Summers/VP - Strategic Planning, Steven L. Thornton/VP - Engineering Development, Mitford H. Merritt/VP - Contracts, Jamie Brabston/VP - Human Relations

Directors: Frank Libutti/Chmn., CEO, Management Dir., Jay M. Garner/Dir., Gary S. Ryan/Dir., Pres., Charles F. Lofty/Dir., Ronald V. Hite/Dir., Daniel E. Moore/Dir., Gilbert F. Decker/Dir., Stewart G. Hall/Dir.

Financial Data: *Fiscal Year End:*12/31 *Latest Annual Data:* 12/31/2005

Year	Sales	Net Income
2005	$20,927,000	$7,000
2004	$6,766,000	-$1,044,000
2003	$6,420,000	-$395,000

Curr. Assets:	$5,670,000	Curr. Liab.:	$5,916,000		
Plant, Equip.:	$492,000	Total Liab.:	$7,942,000	Indic. Yr. Divd.:	NA
Total Assets:	$13,675,000	Net Worth:	$5,733,000	Debt/ Equity:	0.2273

Digital Imaging Resources Inc

355 Madison Ave., Morristown, NJ, 07960; *PH:* 1-973-538-4177; *Fax:* 1-312-243-1590;
http:// www.dirinc.com; *Email:* info@dirinc.com

General - Incorporation............... DE	Stock - Price on:12/24/2007 .... $0.05
Employees 1	Stock Exchange.............................OTC
Auditor ....Liebman Goldberg & Drogin LLP	Ticker Symbol...............................DGIR
Stk Agt.................. M. H. Meyerson & Co	Outstanding Shares 9,590,000
Counsel.......................................NA	E.P.S ....-$0.22
DUNS No. 10-758-8980	Shareholders.....................................NA

Business: The group's principle activity is to sold membership interests for resort condominums; has no current operations. The group operates from United States.

Primary SIC and add'l.: 6531 6719

CIK No: 0000314712

Subsidiaries: Diamond Leasing and Management Corp., Diamond World Funding Corp., Dominion Cellular, Inc., Dominion Golf, Inc.

Officers: Joseph R. Bellantoni/45/Dir., CEO, CFO, Pres.

Directors: Joseph R. Bellantoni/45/Dir., CEO, CFO, Pres., Paul J. Donahue/72/Dir.

Owners: Paul J. Donahue, Julia Mulvihill, Howard Rittberg, Stan Checketts Properties, L.C., Christopher Mulvihill, Deerfield Place Associates, LLC, Ken Stokes, Venturetek, LP, Stanley J. Checketts, Steven Koffman, Public Loan Company, The K-6 Family Ltd. Partnership, IA-545 Madison Associates, Burton I. Koffman, Milton Koffman *(21 Owners included in Index)*

Financial Data: Fiscal Year End:09/30 Latest Annual Data: 9/30/2006

Year	Sales	Net Income
2006	$34,000	-$373,000
2005	$59,000	-$834,000
2004	NA	$92,000

Curr. Assets:	$17,000	Curr. Liab.:	$747,000		
Plant, Equip.:	$11,000	Total Liab.:	$747,000	Indic. Yr. Divd.:	NA
Total Assets:	$28,000	Net Worth:	-$718,000	Debt/ Equity:	NA

Digital Insight Corp

26025 Mureau Rd. , Calabasas, CA, 91302; *PH:* 1-818-871-0000; *http://* www.digitalinsight.com

General - Incorporation............... DE	Stock - Price on:12/24/2007 ....NA
Employees 781	Stock Exchange...................................NA
Auditor ....Deloitte & Touche LLP	Ticker Symbol.......................................NA
Stk Agt..................Computershare Ltd.	Outstanding Shares ....NA
Counsel..................O'melveny & Myers	E.P.S ....NA
DUNS No. ....NA	Shareholders.......................................NA

Business: The group's principal activity is to provide Internet banking services to banks, credit unions and savings and loans associations. The group operates through two divisions namely, Internet banking division and lending division. The primary products offered by the group include, Internet retail and business and automated lending applications. Internet banking application is an Internet based system through which financial institutions are able to provide Internet banking to their retail customers. The group also offers additional tools such as target marketing, check imaging, wireless capability, online statements and portal websites and with implementation and Web site services. The group currently serving more than 1,700 client financial institutions. On 25-Nov-2003, the group acquired magnet communications inc thereby the group also offers online cash management products to large financial institutions.

Primary SIC and add'l.: 7375 9651 7379 7371

CIK No: 0001037275

Subsidiaries: Magnet, Mureau Acquisitions LLC

Owners: Greg J. Santora, Joseph M. McDoniel, Jeffrey E. Stiefler/1.30%, James H. McGuire, Robert R. Surridge, Insiders/4.00%, John C. Dorman, Michael R. Hallman, Henry T. DeNero, Paul J. Pucino, Robert L. North, Robert J. Meagher, Barclays Global Investors, N.A./5.30%

Digital Lightwave Inc

5775 Rio Vista Dr., Clearwater, FL, 33760; *PH:* 1-727-442-6677; *Fax:* 1-727-536-3541;
http:// www.lightwave.com

General - Incorporation............... DE	Stock - Price on:12/24/2007 .... $0.16
Employees 35	Stock Exchange.............................OTC
Auditor ....Grant Thornton LLP	Ticker Symbol...............................DIGL
Stk Agt..... American Stock Transfer & Trust Co.	Outstanding Shares 255,470,000
Counsel.......................Baker & McKenzie LLP	E.P.S ....-$0.024
DUNS No. 79-137-9696	Shareholders.....................................NA

Business: The group's principal activities are to design, develop and market a portfolio of portable and network products for monitoring, maintaining and installing fiber-optic circuits and networks. The products of the group are portable network information computers and network access agents. Network information computers enable users to verify, qualify and monitor the performance of telecommunication networks and transmission equipment. Network access agents are unattended, software controlled performance monitoring and diagnostic equipment used for analyzing and managing telecommunication network from a centralized location. The customers of the group include incumbent local exchange carriers, inter-exchange carriers, competitive local exchange carriers, Internet service providers, communications equipment manufacturers, carriers' carriers, utility companies, equipment rental and leasing companies, wireless service providers and enterprise network operators.

Primary SIC and add'l.: 3663

CIK No: 0001016100

Subsidiaries: Digital Lightwave (UK) Limited, Digital Lightwave Asia Pacific Pty, Ltd., Digital Lightwave Latino Americana Ltda, Digital Lightwave, Inc. (a Delaware corporation

Officers: Ted Myers/CEO

Directors: Bryan J. Zwan/Chmn., Robert Moreyra/Dir., Robert F. Hussey/Dir., Gerald A. Fallon/Dir., Peter H. Collins/Dir.

Owners: Insiders/91.60%, Gerald A. Fallon, Bryan J. Zwan/91.10%, Robert Moreyra, Peter H. Collins, Robert F. Hussey, Kenneth T. Myers

Financial Data: Fiscal Year End:12/31 Latest Annual Data: 03/31/2007

Year	Sales	Net Income
2007	$2,491,000	-$603,000
2006	$10,481,000	-$14,488,000
2005	$12,882,000	-$21,093,000

Curr. Assets:	$5,813,000	Curr. Liab.:	$68,670,000		
Plant, Equip.:	NA	Total Liab.:	$68,909,000	Indic. Yr. Divd.:	NA
Total Assets:	$6,031,000	Net Worth:	-$62,878,000	Debt/ Equity:	NA

Digital Music Group Inc

2151 River Plz. Dr., Ste. 200, Sacramento, CA, 95833; *PH:* 1-916-239-6010; *Fax:* 1-916-239-6018;
http:// www.theorchard.com; *Email:* info@dmgi.com

General - Incorporation .... DE	Stock- Price on:12/24/2007 .... $3.91
Employees 35	Stock Exchange.................................NDQ
Auditor ....Perry-Smith LLP	Ticker Symbol.................................DMGI
Stk Agt.......................U.S. Stock Transfer Corp	Outstanding Shares 9,060,000
Counsel.......................................NA	E.P.S ....-$0.39
DUNS No. ....NA	Shareholders.....................................NA

Business: The groups principle activities include recordings and distributing music and other sound. The groups service is digital entertainment. Customers served by the group include a digital music retailer, record labels, artists, television and film production companies. In the year 2006, the group acquired Digital Musicworks International, Inc and Rio Bravo Entertainment LLC. The group operates from the United States. The group's quarterly revenue for September 2007 was 3.08 millions of USD.

Primary SIC and add'l.: 8999 7375 7379

CIK No: 0001339729

Subsidiaries: Digital Rights Agency, LLC

Officers: Karen Davis/Interim CEO

Directors: Clayton Trier/Chmn., David Altschul/Dir., Roger Biscay/Dir., Peter Csathy/Dir., Terry Hatchett/Dir., John Kilcullen/Dir., Mitchell Koulouris/Dir., Tuhin Roy/Dir.

Owners: Peter Koulouris/4.10%, Cliff Haigler/3.10%, John Kilcullen, Peter Csathy, Tuhin Roy/3.30%, Roger Biscay, Richard Rees/4.30%, David Altschul, Clayton Trier/1.40%, Mitchell Koulouris/6.20%, Karen Davis, Insiders/26.80%, Anders Brown/2.70%, Terry Hatchett

Financial Data: Fiscal Year End:12/31 Latest Annual Data: 12/31/2006

Year	Sales	Net Income
2006	$5,565,000	-$2,622,000
2005	NA	-$85,000

Curr. Assets:	$24,012,000	Curr. Liab.:	$2,820,000		
Plant, Equip.:	$803,000	Total Liab.:	$2,922,000	Indic. Yr. Divd.:	NA
Total Assets:	$38,326,000	Net Worth:	$35,404,000	Debt/ Equity:	0.0001

Digital Power Corp

41324 Christy St., Fremont, CA, 94538; *PH:* 1-510-657-2635; *Fax:* 1-510-353-4023;
http:// www.digipwr.com; *Email:* sales@digipwr.com

General - Incorporation ....CA	Stock- Price on:12/24/2007 .... $1.3599
Employees 33	Stock Exchange.................................AMEX
Auditor .... Kost Forer Gabbay & Kasierer	Ticker Symbol....................................DPW
Stk Agt................ Computershare Trust Co	Outstanding Shares 6,610,000
Counsel.......................................NA	E.P.S ....-$0.017
DUNS No. 05-051-6533	Shareholders.....................................NA

Business: The group's principal activities are the developing, manufacturing, marketing and selling switching power supplies to telecommunications, data communications, test and measurement equipment, office and factory automation and instrumentation equipment manufacturers. In addition to the products offered, the group also provides services like incorporation of OEM's selected electronic components, enclosures and cable assemblies with the its power supply products. The group's products are sold throughout the United States and Europe. .

Primary SIC and add'l.: 3613

CIK No: 0000896493

Subsidiaries: Digital Power Limited

Officers: Jonathan Wax/Dir., CEO, Pres., Leo Yen/CFO, Ita Geva/Controller

Directors: Jonathan Wax/Dir., CEO, Pres., Ben-Zion Diamant/Chmn., Amos Kohn/Dir., Yhezkel Manea/Dir., Benjamin Kiryati/Dir.

Owners: Yeheskel Manea, Digital Power ESOP, Benjamin Kiryati, Jonathan Wax, Insiders, Telkoor Power Ltd., Amos Kohn, Ben-Zion Diamant, Barry W. Blank

Financial Data: Fiscal Year End:12/31 Latest Annual Data: 12/31/2006

Year	Sales	Net Income
2006	$12,631,000	$131,000
2005	$10,856,000	$26,000
2004	$8,713,000	-$1,175,000

Curr. Assets:	$5,542,000	Curr. Liab.:	$2,233,000	P/E Ratio:	68.00
Plant, Equip.:	$162,000	Total Liab.:	$2,233,000	Indic. Yr. Divd.:	NA
Total Assets:	$5,704,000	Net Worth:	$3,471,000	Debt/ Equity:	NA

Digital Realty Trust Inc

560 Mission St., Ste. 2900, San Francisco, CA, 94105; *PH:* 1-415-738-6500; *Fax:* 1-415-738-6501;
http:// www.digitalrealtytrust.com

General - Incorporation .... MD	Stock- Price on:12/24/2007 .... $38.98
Employees 109	Stock Exchange.................................NYSE
Auditor ....KPMG LLP	Ticker Symbol....................................DLR
Stk Agt...... American Stock Transfer & Trust Co.	Outstanding Shares 60,690,000
Counsel.......................................NA	E.P.S $0.68
DUNS No. ....NA	Shareholders.....................................NA

Business: The groups principle activity is to operate real estate investment trust. In the year 2006, the group acquired 114 Rue Ambroise Croizat, 2001 Sixth Avenue and 2055 E. Technology Drive. The group operates from the United States. The group's quarterly revenue for September 2007 was 104.79 millions of USD.

Primary SIC and add'l.: 6798 4226

CIK No: 0001297996

Subsidiaries: 1100 Space Park Holding Company, LLC, 1100 Space Park, LLC, 150 South First Street, LLC, 200 Paul Holding Company, LLC, 200 Paul, LLC, 2045-2055 LaFayette Street, LLC, 2334 Lundy Holding Company, LLC, 2334 Lundy, LLC, 34551 Ardenwood Holding Company, LLC, 34551 Ardenwood, LLC, 4650 Old Ironsides, LLC, Asbury Park Holdings Limited, Digital Bryan Street Partnership, L.P., Digital Bryan Street, LLC, Digital 113 N. Myers, LLC 119 Subsidiaries included in the Index

Officers: Michael F. Foust/Dir., CEO/$1,410,586.00, William A. Stein/CFO, Chief Investment Officer, Sec./$826,328.00, Scott E. Peterson/Sr. VP - Acquisition Activities/$818,296.00, Chris J. Crosby/Sr. VP - Sales, Technical Services/$768,156.00, James R. Trout/Sr. VP - Portfolio, Technical Operations, Pamela A. Matthews/Dir. - Investor Relations

Directors: Michael F. Foust/Dir., CEO, Rick Magnuson/Chmn., Laurence A. Chapman/Dir., Ruann F. Ernst/Dir., Kathleen Earley/Dir., Dennis E. Singleton/Dir.

Owners: Laurence A. Chapman, Deutsche Bank AG/10.80%, Kathleen Earley, Richard A. Magnuson/1.70%, Christopher J. Crosby, Michael F. Foust, Dennis E. Singleton, Scott E. Peterson, William A. Stein, Cambay Tele.com, LLC/6.90%, Insiders/2.80%, Ruann F. Ernst

Financial Data: Fiscal Year End:12/31 Latest Annual Data: 12/31/2006

Year	Sales		Net Income
2006	$281,903,000		$31,392,000
2005	$208,809,000		$16,101,000
2004	$107,121,000		$4,557,000
Curr. Assets:	$53,554,000	Curr. Liab.: $127,906,000	P/E Ratio: 49.97
Plant, Equip.:	$1,706,847,000	Total Liab.: $1,338,031,000	Indic. Yr. Divd.: $1.150
Total Assets:	$2,186,219,000	Net Worth: $709,772,000	Debt/ Equity: 1.6339

Digital Recorders Inc

5949 Sherry Ln., Ste. 1050, Dallas, TX, 75225; **PH:** 1-214-378-8992; **Fax:** 1-214-378-8437; **http://** www.digrec.com; **Email:** ir@digrec.com

General - Incorporation	NC	Stock - Price on:12/24/2007	$2.5
Employees	198	Stock Exchange	NDQ
Auditor	PricewaterhouseCoopers LLP	Ticker Symbol	TBUS
Stk Agt	American Stock Transfer & Trust Co.	Outstanding Shares	10,390,000
Counsel	NA	E.P.S.	-$0.33
DUNS No.	10-586-9218	Shareholders	NA

Business: The group's principal activities are to design, manufacture, sell and service information technology products. The group operates through two segments: transportation products segment and the law enforcement and surveillance segment. The transportation products segment produces automated announcement and passenger information systems and electronic sign products for municipalities, transportation districts, and transportation department and bus manufacturers. The law enforcement and surveillance segment of the group focuses on digital audio filter systems and tape transcribers used to improve quality of both live and recorded voices.

Primary SIC and add'l.: 3663

CIK No: 0000853695

Subsidiaries: Digital Audio Corporation, DRI-Europa AB, Mobitec AB, Mobitec Brasil Ltda, Mobitec GmbH, Mobitec Pty Ltd., RTI, Inc., TwinVision of North America, Inc.

Officers: David L. Turney/Chmn., CEO, Pres./$283,425.00, Agne I. Axelsson/Deputy MD - Mobitec AB, Roberto Demore/Executive Mgr. - Mobitec Brasil Ltda, William F. Fay/VP, GM - Twinvision na, Inc/$214,940.00, Lawrence A. Hagemann/64/CTO, Exec. VP/$207,500.00, Tanya L. Johnson/VP, GM, Digital Recorders Division Interim Operations Manager/$166,703.00, James Kennedy/VP - Engineering, Veronica B. Marks/Mgr. - Corporate Communications, Rob Taylor/50/VP, COO - North Carolina Operations, Oliver Wels/MD - Mobitec AB, Stephen P. Slay/45/VP, CFO, Treasurer, Sec.

Directors: David L. Turney/Chmn., CEO, Pres., James C. Meese/Dir., Juliann Tenney/Dir., John D. Higgins/Dir., John K. Pirotte/Dir., Stephanie L. Pinson/Dir.

Owners: William F. Fay, John K. Pirotte, Dolphin Offshore Partners, L.P./9.90%, Lawrence A. Hagemann/1.50%, Kathleen B. Oher, Tanya L. Johnson, Riverview Group, LLC/11.40%, Juliann Tenney, Insiders/11.60%, John D. Higgins/4.40%, Barclays Global Investors, N.A./5.90%, James C. Meese, Laurus Master Fund, Ltd./7.80%, Stephanie L. Pinson, David L. Turney/3.50%

Financial Data: Fiscal Year End:12/31 Latest Annual Data: 12/31/2006

Year	Sales		Net Income
2006	$51,338,000		-$3,894,000
2005	$45,345,000		-$5,924,000
2004	$47,773,000		-$3,192,000
Curr. Assets:	$20,879,000	Curr. Liab.: $18,417,000	
Plant, Equip.:	$3,131,000	Total Liab.: $19,929,000	Indic. Yr. Divd.: NA
Total Assets:	$37,358,000	Net Worth: $17,195,000	Debt/ Equity: 0.0021

Digital River Inc

9625 W 76th St., Ste. 150, Eden Prairie, MN, 55344; **PH:** 1-952-253-1234; **Fax:** 1-952-253-8497; **http://** www.digitalriver.com

General - Incorporation	DE	Stock - Price on:12/24/2007	$50.82
Employees	1,086	Stock Exchange	NDQ
Auditor	Ernst & Young LLP	Ticker Symbol	DRIV
Stk Agt	Wells Fargo Shareowner Services	Outstanding Shares	41,350,000
Counsel	Howard Rice Nemerovski Canady F & R	E.P.S.	$1.49
DUNS No.	NA	Shareholders	NA

Business: The group's principle activity is to provide comprehensive electronic commerce outsourcing solutions. The group has two operating segments: software and digital commerce services and e-business services. The group has developed a technology platform to provide a suite of electronic commerce services, including Web commerce development and hosting, transaction processing, fraud screening, digital delivery, integration to physical fulfillment and customer service. Analytical marketing and merchandising services are provided to assist clients in increasing Web page view traffic to, and sales through, their Web commerce systems. The group's quarterly revenue for September 2007 was 82.54 millions of USD.

Primary SIC and add'l.: 7375 7373 5045 7379

CIK No: 0001062530

Subsidiaries: BlueHornet Networks, Inc., CCNow, Inc., Commerce5, Inc., Digibuy, Inc., Digital River E-Business Services, Inc., Digital River Ireland Limited, Digital River Japan K.K., Digital River Korea YH, Digital River oneNetwork Corporation, Digital River Technology Limited, Digital River UK Limited, Digital River, Inc., DR Acquisition 03-F, Inc., DR Acquisition Corp 04-E, Dr Apac, Inc. 33 Subsidiaries included in the Index

Officers: Joel Ronning/Founder, Chmn., CEO, Thomas Donnelly/CFO/$1,062,313.00, Gerri Dyrek/Assoc. Dir. - Public Relations, Kristin Mattson/Sr. Public Relations Specialist

Directors: Joel Ronning/Founder, Chmn., CEO, Paul J. Thorin/Dir., Will Lansing/Dir., Thomas F. Madison/Dir., Frederic M. Seegal/Dir., Perry Steiner/Dir.

Owners: Paul J. Thorin, Thomas F. Madison, T. Rowe Price Associates, Inc./4.00%, Joel A. Ronning/3.70%, MSD Capital, L.P./6.00%, American Century Investment Management, Inc./7.20%, Goldman Sachs Asset Management, L.P./6.00%, Insiders/5.00%, Perry W. Steiner, Thomas M. Donnelly, William J. Lansing, J&W Seligman& Co. Incorporated/5.60%, Frederic M. Seegal

Financial Data: Fiscal Year End:12/31 Latest Annual Data: 12/31/2006

Year	Sales		Net Income
2006	$307,632,000		$60,810,000
2005	$220,408,000		$54,343,000
2004	$154,130,000		$35,324,000
Curr. Assets:	$704,046,000	Curr. Liab.: $206,159,000	P/E Ratio: 34.57
Plant, Equip.:	$24,079,000	Total Liab.: $402,504,000	Indic. Yr. Divd.: NA
Total Assets:	$1,006,263,000	Net Worth: $603,759,000	Debt/ Equity: 0.3063

Digital Video Systems Inc

430 Cambridge Ave., Ste 110, Palo Alto, CA, 94306; **PH:** 1-650-322-8108; **Fax:** 1-650-938-8829; **http://** www.dvsystems.com; **Email:** ir@dvsystems.com

General - Incorporation	DE	Stock - Price on:12/24/2007	$0.12
Employees	NA	Stock Exchange	OTC
Auditor	Stonefield Josephson, Inc	Ticker Symbol	DVID
Stk Agt	American Stock Transfer & Trust Co.	Outstanding Shares	NA
Counsel	Wilson Sonsini Goodrich & Rosati	E.P.S.	NA
DUNS No.	84-870-1397	Shareholders	NA

Business: The group's principal activities are to develop, manufacture and market digital video compression and decompression hardware and software. These are used for entertainment, commercial and educational applications. The group markets and develops products and technologies in the digital video arena. The group's products primarily include digital versatile disc products, such as DVD loaders, DVD sub-systems and components. The group also markets and develops video CD players, networked video servers that provide near video-on-demand, digital ad-insertion systems that automatically insert digital video commercials into broadcasting programs and video players for commercial kiosk applications.

Primary SIC and add'l.: 3679 3651 7629

CIK No: 0001009395

Subsidiaries: DVS Electronics Pvt. Ltd., DVS Electronics, Inc, DVS Korea Co., Ltd, Shanghai Fangyuan Digital Technology Ltd.

Officers: Mali Kuo/54/Chairwoman, CEO, Douglas T. Watson/54/Dir., COO, Alok Sen/Contact - DVSE

Directors: Mali Kuo/54/Chairwoman, CEO, Jeff Bumb/59/Dir., Douglas T. Watson/54/Dir., COO, Thomas J. Parilla/Dir., John M. Fuller/Dir.

Financial Data: Fiscal Year End:12/31 Latest Annual Data: 12/31/2004

Year	Sales		Net Income
2004	$87,200,000		-$13,070,000
2003	$89,133,000		-$8,345,000
2002	$157,214,000		-$2,991,000
Curr. Assets:	$27,519,000	Curr. Liab.: $34,690,000	
Plant, Equip.:	$10,877,000	Total Liab.: $34,928,000	Indic. Yr. Divd.: NA
Total Assets:	$39,283,000	Net Worth: -$311,000	Debt/ Equity: NA

Digital Youth Network Corp

880-916 W Broadway, Vancouver, BC, V5Z 1K7; **PH:** 1-604-408-7480; **Fax:** 1-604-408-9480; **http://** www.digitalyouth.ca; **Email:** info@digitalyouth.ca

General - Incorporation	Canada	Stock - Price on:12/24/2007	NA
Employees	NA	Stock Exchange	OTC
Auditor	Amisano Hanson	Ticker Symbol	DYOUF
Stk Agt	Computershare Investor Services LLC	Outstanding Shares	NA
Counsel	NA	E.P.S.	NA
DUNS No.	NA	Shareholders	NA

Business: The groups principle activity is to provide web hosting and domain and certs services. The group operates from United States.

Primary SIC and add'l.: NA

CIK No: 0001137764

Subsidiaries: Digital Youth Network Inc

Curr. Assets:	NA	Curr. Liab.:	NA	
Plant, Equip.:	NA	Total Liab.:	NA	Indic. Yr. Divd.: NA
Total Assets:	NA	Net Worth:	NA	Debt/ Equity: NA

DigitalFX International Inc

3035 E Patrick Ln., Ste. No. 9, Las Vegas, NV, 89120; **PH:** 1-702-506-0779; **http://** www.digitalfx.com; **Email:** lorne@digitalfx.com

General - Incorporation	FL	Stock - Price on:12/24/2007	$4
Employees	55	Stock Exchange	OTC
Auditor	Weinberg & Co., P.A	Ticker Symbol	DFXN
Stk Agt	Florida Atlantic Stock Transfer, Inc.	Outstanding Shares	23,690,000
Counsel	NA	E.P.S.	$0.02
DUNS No.	NA	Shareholders	NA

Business: The groups principle activity is to develop social networking software application. The group products include vedeio e-mail, video IM, live web casting, and podcasting. The groups services include professional and support services. The group operates from the United States.

Primary SIC and add'l.: 4813

CIK No: 0001095691

Subsidiaries: DigitalFX Networks, LLC, VMdirect, L.L.C

Officers: Craig Ellins/Chmn., CEO, Pres., Lorne Walker/CFO, Sec., Amy Black/Pres. - VMdirect

Directors: Craig Ellins/Chmn., CEO, Pres., Jerry Haleva/62/Dir., Kevin R. Keating/68/Dir.

Owners: Lorne Walker, VM Investors, LLC, Craig Ellins, Richard Kall, Amy Black, Insiders, Kevin R. Keating

Financial Data: Fiscal Year End:12/31 Latest Annual Data: 12/31/2006

Year	Sales	Net Income
2006	$22,800,000	$480,000
2005	NA	-$61,000
2004	NA	$134,000

Curr. Assets:	$6,439,000	Curr. Liab.:	$2,789,000		
Plant, Equip.:	$277,000	Total Liab.:	$2,789,000	Indic. Yr. Divd.:	NA
Total Assets:	$7,873,000	Net Worth:	$5,084,000	Debt/ Equity:	NA

DigitalTown Inc

Formerly: BDC Capital Inc
11974 Portland Ave., Burnsville, MN, 55337; PH: 1-952-890-2362; http:// www.enetpc.com

General - Incorporation	MN	Stock- Price on:12/24/2007	NA
Employees	2	Stock Exchange	OTC
Auditor	Carver Moquist & O'connor LLC	Ticker Symbol	DGTW
Stk Agt	Signature Stock Transfer, Inc.	Outstanding Shares	NA
Counsel	NA	E.P.S	-$0.3
DUNS No.	NA	Shareholders	NA

Business: The group's principle activities include designing and manufacturing computer systems and products, including desktops, midtowers, minitowers, notebooks, workstations and file servers. The group operates from United States.

Primary SIC and add'l.: 3571 3575

CIK No: 0001065598

Subsidiaries: BDC Partners, Inc

Officers: Richard A. Pomije/52/Chmn., CEO

Directors: Richard A. Pomije/52/Chmn., CEO, Jeff Mills/49/Dir., Peirce McNally/Dir.

Owners: Insiders/67.60%, Dan Janisch/0.78%, Jeff Mills/1.57%, Richard A. Pomije/65.25%

Financial Data: Fiscal Year End:02/28 Latest Annual Data: 02/28/2007

Year	Sales	Net Income
2007	NA	-$5,742,000
2006	$1,000	-$1,059,000
2005	$111,000	$219,000

Curr. Assets:	$10,000	Curr. Liab.:	$284,000		
Plant, Equip.:	$2,000	Total Liab.:	$284,000	Indic. Yr. Divd.:	NA
Total Assets:	$453,000	Net Worth:	$169,000	Debt/ Equity:	NA

Digitas Inc

800 Boylston St., Prudential Tower, Boston, MA, 02199; PH: 1-617-867-1000; http:// www.digitas.com

General - Incorporation	DE	Stock- Price on:12/24/2007	NA
Employees	1,740	Stock Exchange	NA
Auditor	Ernst & Young LLP	Ticker Symbol	NA
Stk Agt	American Stock Transfer & Trust Co.	Outstanding Shares	NA
Counsel	NA	E.P.S	NA
DUNS No.	NA	Shareholders	NA

Business: The group's principal activities are to provide strategy consulting, marketing agency and marketing technology infrastructure services. The group provides marketing programs, customer strategy, technology platforms and channel operations support that enable clients to achieve measurable, lasting improvement in their marketing productivity. The clients of the group include allstate, American express, at&t, delta air lines and general motors. The group has offices in New York, san francisco, Chicago and london.

Primary SIC and add'l.: 7375 8742

CIK No: 0001100885

Subsidiaries: Bronner Slosberg Humphrey Inc., BSH Holding LLC, Digitas (Europe) LLC, Digitas Cayman Island, Digitas International Inc., Digitas Netherlands Holding Inc., Digitas Security Corp., DM Europe Limited, Modem Media UK Limited, Modem Media, Inc.

Officers: Alan Rutherford/CEO - Digitas Global, David Kenny/Chmn., CEO, Laura Lang/CEO - Digitas USA, Mark Beeching/Chief Creative Officer, Torrence Boone/Pres. - Digitas Boston, Joe Tomasulo/CFO, Jim Rossman/COO, Joanne Zaiac/Pres. - Digitas New York

Directors: David Kenny/Chmn., CEO

Diguang International Development Company Ltd

8th Fl., Bldg. 64, Jinlong Industry District Majialong, Nanshan, SH, 518052; PH: 86-755-2655-3580

General - Incorporation	NV	Stock- Price on:12/24/2007	$1.6
Employees	NA	Stock Exchange	OTC
Auditor	Bdo Reanda	Ticker Symbol	DGNG
Stk Agt	Signature Stock Transfer, Inc.	Outstanding Shares	NA
Counsel	NA	E.P.S	NA
DUNS No.	NA	Shareholders	NA

Business: The groups principle activities include designing, manufacturing, selling and distributing small to medium-sized Light Emitting Diode and Cold Cathode Fluorescent. The group products include backlights for Liquid Crystal Displays and LED/CCFL backlight products. Specific customers of the group include PVI, ALCO, HOT TRACKS, IZTECHNOLOGY, Gree, Tianma, Seiko, Midea, Affitronics, Samsung, CCT, LG, and Ellipse. The group operates from China and the United States.

Primary SIC and add'l.: 3670

CIK No: 0001158722

Subsidiaries: Diguang International Holdings Limited, Diguang Science & Technology (HK) Limited, Shenzhen Diguang Electronics Co. Ltd., Well Planner Limited

Officers: Yi Song/50/Chmn., CEO, Pres., Keith Hor/43/CFO

Directors: Yi Song/50/Chmn., CEO, Pres., Hong Song/45/Dir., Tuen-Ping Yang/62/Dir., Dexter Fong/49/Dir., Hoi S. Kwok/57/Dir.

Owners: Insiders, Yi Song, Sino Olympics Industrial Limited, Tuen-Ping Yang, Hong Song

Financial Data: Fiscal Year End:12/31 Latest Annual Data: 12/31/2006

Year	Sales	Net Income
2006	$31,858,000	$1,667,000
2005	NA	-$1,664,000
2004	NA	-$24,000

Curr. Assets:	$31,558,000	Curr. Liab.:	$8,117,000		
Plant, Equip.:	$2,672,000	Total Liab.:	$8,117,000	Indic. Yr. Divd.:	NA
Total Assets:	$37,699,000	Net Worth:	$29,582,000	Debt/ Equity:	NA

Dillard's Inc

1600 Cantrell Rd., Little Rock, AR, 72201; PH: 1-501-376-5200; Fax: 1-501-399-7831; http:// www.dillards.com

General - Incorporation	DE	Stock- Price on:12/24/2007	$34.9
Employees	51,385	Stock Exchange	NYSE
Auditor	Deloitte & Touche LLP	Ticker Symbol	DDS
Stk Agt	Deloitte & Touche LLP	Outstanding Shares	80,330,000
Counsel	NA	E.P.S	$2.81
DUNS No.	00-486-7198	Shareholders	NA

Business: The groups principle activity is to operate retail department stores. The groups products include women clothing, children's clothing, shoes, accessories and other home articles. The group operates from United States.

Primary SIC and add'l.: 5311

CIK No: 0000028917

Subsidiaries: Brownsville Shopping Center, Inc., Condev Mission, Inc., Condev Nevada, Inc., Construction Developers, Inc., Dillard Credit Corp., Dillard Dollars, Inc., Dillard International, Inc., Dillard Investment Co., Inc., Dillard Store Services, Inc., Dillards Nevada, Inc., Dillards Travel, Inc., Dillards Utah, Inc., Dillards Wyoming, Inc., Dillards, Inc., Gayfer Montgomery Fair Co. 22 Subsidiaries included in the Index

Officers: William Dillard/63/Dir., CEO, Rhonda D. Roberts/Store Mgr. - Rimrock Mall, Terry M. Myhre/Store Mgr. - Capital Hill Mall, Mitch O. Guinn/Store Mgr. - Southgate Mall, Melody Walker/Store Mgr. - Galleria At Sunset, Patricia P. Alvillar/Store Mgr. - Fashion Show Mall, Robert E. Gore/Store Mgr. - Fashion Place Mall, Robert S. Sagers/Store Mgr. - Newgate Mall, Kathleen A. Evans/Store Mgr. - Provo Towne Centre, Lisa A. Mc Millan/Store Mgr. - South Towne Center, Jeremy A. Fry/Store Mgr. - Red Cliffs Mall, Wayne H. Rooks/Store Mgr. - Imperial Valley Mall, Drue Corbusier/61/Dir., Exec. VP/$2,364,867.00, Sid Sanders/VP - Internal Audit, Raymond S. Hicks/Store Mgr. - Governor's Square (254 Officers included in Index)

Directors: William Dillard/63/Dir., CEO, J. C. Watts/50/Dir., John Paul Hammerschmidt/85/Dir., Alex Dillard/58/Dir., Pres., Mike Dillard/56/Dir., Exec. VP, Drue Corbusier/61/Dir., Exec. VP, Robert C. Connor/66/Dir., Will D. Davis/78/Dir., Peter R. Johnson/60/Dir., Warren A. Stephens/51/Dir., William H. Sutton/77/Dir.

Owners: William Dillard, Insiders/9.50%, Insiders, Goldman Sachs Asset Management, L.P./13.50%, Alex Dillard, Alex Dillard/2.70%, Donald Smith& Co., Inc./9.40%, Warren A. Stephens, Drue Corbusier/1.10%, Peter R. Johnson, Robert C. Connor/0.10%, W.D. Company, Inc., Mike Dillard, James I. Freeman/0.90%, W.D. Company, Inc./0.10% (23 Owners included in Index)

Financial Data: Fiscal Year End:01/28 Latest Annual Data: 2/3/2007

Year	Sales	Net Income
2007	$7,810,067,000	$245,646,000
2006	NA	NA
2005	$7,816,271,000	$117,666,000

Curr. Assets:	$2,047,846,000	Curr. Liab.:	$977,115,000	P/E Ratio:	12.42
Plant, Equip.:	$3,157,906,000	Total Liab.:	$2,821,062,000	Indic. Yr. Divd.:	$0.160
Total Assets:	$5,408,015,000	Net Worth:	$2,586,953,000	Debt/ Equity:	0.4136

Dime Community Bancshares Inc

209 HAve.meyer St., Brooklyn, NY, 11211; PH: 1-718-782-6200; Fax: 1-718-486-7535; http:// www.dsbwdirect.com

General - Incorporation	DE	Stock- Price on:12/24/2007	$13.52
Employees	327	Stock Exchange	NDQ
Auditor	Deloitte & Touche LLP	Ticker Symbol	DCOM
Stk Agt	American Stock Transfer & Trust CO.	Outstanding Shares	35,960,000
Counsel	Conway Farrell Curtin & Kelly	E.P.S	$0.67
DUNS No.	94-937-6792	Shareholders	NA

Business: The group's principal activity is to accept deposits from customers, invest the deposits in loans. The various loans include multi-family residential mortgage loans, commercial real estate loans, one-to four-family residential mortgage loans, consumer loans, mortgage-backed securities and obligation of the United States government and government sponsored entities. The mortgage loans include multi-family and one-to four-family residential mortgage loans. The subsidiaries are: havemeyer equities corp, boulevard funding corp, havemeyer brokerage corp, havemeyer investments inc. And dsbw residential preferred funding corp. The group operates twenty full-service retail banking offices located in the New York city boroughs of brooklyn, queens and the bronx and in nassau county, New York. On 29-Jan-2004 the group acquired the kimbrell company, inc., the kimbrell company, inc/Florida, preferred markets, inc, preferred markets, inc/Florida and Atlantic acceptance corporation.

Primary SIC and add'l.: 6035 6712

CIK No: 0001005409

Subsidiaries: 842 Manhattan Avenue Corporation, Dime Community Capital Trust I, DSBW Preferred Funding Corporation, DSBW Residential Preferred Funding Corporation, Havemeyer Equities, Inc., Havemeyer Investments, Inc., The Dime Savings Bank of Williamsburgh

Officers: Vincent F. Palagiano/Chmn., CEO, Kenneth Ceonzo/Investor Relations Contact, Michael P. Devine/Dir., COO, Pres., Kenneth J. Mahon/Dir., Exec. VP, CFO, Timothy B. King/Sr. VP, Chief Investment Officer, Michael Pucella/Chief Accounting Officer, Sr. VP, Christopher D. Maher/Exec. VP - Retail Banking/$422,980.00

Directors: Vincent F. Palagiano/Chmn., CEO, George L. Clark/Dir., Fred P. Fehrenbach/Dir., Steven D. Cohn/Dir., Joseph J. Perry/Dir., Patrick E. Curtin/Dir., John J. Flynn/Dir., Anthony Bergamo/Dir., Michael P. Devine/Dir., COO, Pres., Kenneth J. Mahon/Dir., Exec. VP, CFO, Donald E. Walsh/Dir., Omer S.J. Williams/Dir.

Owners: John J. Flynn, Patrick E. Curtin, Timothy B. King, Michael P. Devine/2.30%, Steven D. Cohn, George L. Clark, Anthony Bergamo, Insiders/18.50%, Joseph H. Farrell, Christopher D. Maher, Joseph J. Perry, Stanley Meisels, Donald E. Walsh, Fred P. Fehrenbach, Kenneth J. Mahon/1.40% (18 Owners included in Index)

Financial Data: Fiscal Year End:12/31 Latest Annual Data: 12/31/2006

Year	Sales	Net Income
2006	$183,200,000	$30,592,000
2005	$180,039,000	$36,210,000
2004	$184,134,000	$46,222,000

Curr. Assets:	$105,016,000	Curr. Liab.:	$2,700,267,000	P/E Ratio:	19.04
Plant, Equip.:	$22,886,000	Total Liab.:	$2,882,746,000	Indic. Yr. Divd.:	$0.560
Total Assets:	$3,173,377,000	Net Worth:	$290,631,000	Debt/ Equity:	0.6213

Dimeco Inc

820 Church St., Honesdale, PA, 18431; PH: 1-570-253-1970; Fax: 1-570-253-5845; http:// www.thedimebank.com

General - Incorporation	PA	Stock - Price on:12/24/2007	$48
Employees	96	Stock Exchange	OTC
Auditor	S R Snodgrass, A.C	Ticker Symbol	DIMC
Stk Agt	Registrar & Transfer Co	Outstanding Shares	1,530,000
Counsel	NA	E.P.S.	$4.11
DUNS No.	82-895-8785	Shareholders	NA

Business: The group's principal activity is to provide commercial banking services including accepting time, demand and savings deposits and originating commercial, real estate and consumer loans. The group provides services to individuals and small to medium sized businesses in wayne and pike counties, Pennsylvania and sullivan county, New York. The operations of the group are conducted through four branch offices located in honesdale hawley, damascus and greentown, Pennsylvania. The group also provides ATM services to its customers. The group operates in non-banking activities such as acquiring and servicing of loans, operating as a trust and also as a financial advisor.

Primary SIC and add'l.: 6022 6712

CIK No: 0000898037

Subsidiaries: TDB Insurance Services, LLC, The Dime Bank

Officers: Gary C. Beilman/Dir., CEO, Pres./$224,979.00, Amy Burke/Mgr. - Community Office, Dingmans Ferry Office, Jan Hoadley/Mgr. - Community Office, Damascus Office, Melanie F. Seagraves/Mgr. - Community Office, Greentown Office, Maureen H. Beilman/52/CFO, Treasurer, Assist. Sec./$144,512.00, Peter Bochnovich/46/Sr. VP, Assist. Sec./$139,699.00, Mary Carol Cicco/Community Banking Officer - Honesdale, Tom Onions/Mgr. - Community Office, Hawley Office

Directors: Gary C. Beilman/Dir., CEO, Pres., William E. Schwarz/Chmn., John S. Kiesendahl/Vice Chmn., Henry M. Skier/Dir., John F. Spall/Dir., Barbara J. Genzlinger/Dir., Thomas A. Peifer/Dir., Robert E. Genirs/72/Dir.

Owners: Robert E. Genirs, William E. Schwarz/1.40%, Peter Bochnovich, Barbara J. Genzlinger, Maureen H. Beilman/1.20%, Henry M. Skier/5.80%, Gary C. Beilman/1.90%, Insiders/18.30%, John F. Spall/2.40%, Thomas A. Peifer/1.80%, John S. Kiesendahl/2.40%

Financial Data: Fiscal Year End:12/31　Latest Annual Data: 12/31/2006

Year	Sales	Net Income
2006	$27,802,000	$5,585,000
2005	$22,003,000	$4,455,000
2004	$18,741,000	$3,906,000

Curr. Assets:	$20,769,000	Curr. Liab.:	$352,250,000	P/E Ratio:	12.40
Plant, Equip.:	$5,731,000	Total Liab.:	$368,240,000	Indic. Yr. Divd.:	$1.160
Total Assets:	$403,577,000	Net Worth:	$35,337,000	Debt/ Equity:	0.3894

Dimensional Visions Inc

2301 W Dunlap, Ste. 207, Phoenix, AZ, 85021; PH: 1-480-861-1183; http:// www.dimensionalvisions.com

General - Incorporation	DE	Stock - Price on:12/24/2007	$6.5
Employees	1	Stock Exchange	OTC
Auditor	Moore & Assoc., Chartered	Ticker Symbol	SOMD
Stk Agt	American Stock Transfer & Trust Co.	Outstanding Shares	3,640,000
Counsel	NA	E.P.S.	-$0.43
DUNS No.	19-796-5668	Shareholders	NA

Business: The group's principal activity is to produce and market lithographically printed stereoscopic and animation print products. The group's wholly owned subsidiary, infopak, inc., is no longer an operating entity. Infopak, inc., developed a data delivery system that provided end users with specific industry printed materials by way of a portable hand-held reader. Data is acquired electronically from the data provided by mainframe systems and distributed through a computer network to all subscribers. The group is currently not actively conducting any operations.

Primary SIC and add'l.: 7373 2752

CIK No: 0000836809

Subsidiaries: InfoPak, Inc.

Officers: Shelly Yakus/62/VP, Matthew Long/42/VP

Owners: Perry D. Logan/11.98%, Paul D. Fisher/0.87%, Preston J. Shea/0.52%, Andrea Dworshak/6.09%, Matthew Long/0.22%, Insiders/46.70%, Barry M. Goldwater, Shelly Yakus/0.44%, Lawrence G. Ryckman/44.65%

Financial Data: Fiscal Year End:06/30　Latest Annual Data: 6/30/2006

Year	Sales	Net Income
2006	NA	-$108,000
2005	NA	-$107,000
2004	NA	-$108,000

Curr. Assets:	$582,000	Curr. Liab.:	$1,079,000		
Plant, Equip.:	NA	Total Liab.:	$1,079,000	Indic. Yr. Divd.:	NA
Total Assets:	$588,000	Net Worth:	-$490,000	Debt/ Equity:	NA

DineWise Inc

500 Bi-County Blvd., Ste. 400, Farmingdale, NY, 11735; PH: 1-631-694-1111; Fax: 1-631-694-4064; http:// www.coloradoprimefoods.com; Email: info@dinewise.com

General - Incorporation	NV	Stock - Price on:12/24/2007	$0.29
Employees	26	Stock Exchange	OTC
Auditor	BDO Seidman, LLP	Ticker Symbol	DWIS
Stk Agt	Fidelity Transfer Co.	Outstanding Shares	30,060,000
Counsel	NA	E.P.S.	-$0.041
DUNS No.	NA	Shareholders	NA

Business: The groups principle activity is to provide in-home restaurant quality beef shopping services. The group products include filet mignon, rack of lamb, rib roast, chicken cordon bleu, jumbo shrimp, tuna steaks and lobster tails. The group operates from the United States.

Primary SIC and add'l.: 5499 5411 5963

CIK No: 0001192323

Subsidiaries: Craig Laughlin ("Laughlin"), Simplagene USA, Inc, New Colorado Prime Holdings, Inc, SMPG Merco Co., Inc.

Officers: Paul A. Roman/Chmn., CEO, Pres., Thomas McNeill/Dir., VP, CFO

Directors: Chef Dana McCauley/Member - Advisory Board, Debbie Judd/Member - Advisory Board, Thomas McNeill/Dir., VP, CFO, Richard F. Gray/Dir., Amy Snider/Member - Advisory Board, Chef Craig Noche/Member - Advisory Board

Owners: Paul A. Roman, Insiders, AIG Global Investment, Dutchess Private Equities Fund, Ltd., Crusader Securities, LLC, MacKay Shields, LLC, Trust Company of the West, Golden Tree Asset Management, LP

Financial Data: Fiscal Year End:12/31　Latest Annual Data: 12/31/2006

Year	Sales	Net Income
2006	$10,944,000	-$3,509,000
2005	NA	-$14,000
2004	NA	-$24,000

Curr. Assets:	$1,184,000	Curr. Liab.:	$2,694,000	P/E Ratio:	3.75
Plant, Equip.:	$318,000	Total Liab.:	$5,591,000	Indic. Yr. Divd.:	NA
Total Assets:	$1,882,000	Net Worth:	-$3,709,000	Debt/ Equity:	NA

Diodes Inc

15660 N Dallas Pkwy., Ste. 850, Dallas, TX, 75248; PH: 1-805-446-4800; Fax: 1-805-446-4850; http:// www.diodes.com

General - Incorporation	DE	Stock - Price on:12/24/2007	$40.93
Employees	2,268	Stock Exchange	NDQ
Auditor	Moss Adams LLP	Ticker Symbol	DIOD
Stk Agt	Continental Stock Transfer & Trust Co	Outstanding Shares	26,200,000
Counsel	Sheppard Mullin Richter & Hampton LLP	E.P.S.	$1.35
DUNS No.	04-935-0432	Shareholders	NA

Business: The group's principal activity is to manufacture, market and distribute semiconductor devices. The products are distributed to manufacturers in the communications, computing, industrial, consumer electronics and automotive markets. The product line includes high-density diode and transistor arrays in ultra-miniature surface-mount packages, as well as silicon wafers. The group's products also include small signal transistors and mosfets, transient voltage suppressers (tvss), zeners, schottkys, diodes, rectifiers, bridges and silicon wafers. The products are marketed primarily throughout North America, Far East, Europe and Asia.

Primary SIC and add'l.: 3674

CIK No: 0000029002

Subsidiaries: Diodes Taiwan Company, Limited, Diodes-Hong Kong Limited, FabTech Incorporated, Shanghai KaiHong Electronics Company, Limited (Diodes-China, Shanghai KaiHong Technology Company, Limited (Diodes-Shanghai)

Officers: Keh-Shew Lu/Dir., CEO, Pres./$3,333,764.00, Rick White/Sr. VP - Finance, Francis Tang/VP - Product Development, Ed Tang/VP - Corporate Administration, Carl C. Wertz/CFO, Sec., Treasurer/$707,066.00, Mark A. King/Sr. VP - Sales, Marketing/$926,446.00, Steven Ho/Asia Pres., VP - Asia Sales, Marketing/$588,655.00, Joseph Liu/Sr. VP - Operations/$1,026,013.00, Kim McDonald/Mgr. - National Distribution Sales

Directors: Keh-Shew Lu/Dir., CEO, Pres., Raymond Soong/Chmn., C. H. Chen/Vice Chmn., Michael R. Giordano/Dir., Shing Mao/Dir., John M. Stich/Dir., L. P. Hsu/Dir.

Owners: Shing Mao, John M. Stich, C.H. Chen/1.50%, Joseph Liu/1.40%, Steven Ho, Insiders/8.80%, Mark A. King, Carl C. Wertz, Francis Tang, Keh-Shew Lu/1.90%, Michael R. Giordano

Financial Data: Fiscal Year End:12/31　Latest Annual Data: 12/31/2006

Year	Sales	Net Income
2006	$343,308,000	$48,143,000
2005	$214,765,000	$33,329,000
2004	$185,703,000	$25,551,000

Curr. Assets:	$478,846,000	Curr. Liab.:	$83,492,000	P/E Ratio:	21.89
Plant, Equip.:	$95,469,000	Total Liab.:	$323,185,000	Indic. Yr. Divd.:	NA
Total Assets:	$622,139,000	Net Worth:	$294,167,000	Debt/ Equity:	0.7701

Diomed Holdings Inc

1 Dundee Pk., Ste.S 4-6, Andover, MA, 01810; PH: 1-978-475-7771; Fax: 1-978-475-8488; http:// www.diomedinc.com

General - Incorporation	DE	Stock - Price on:12/24/2007	$1.22
Employees	100	Stock Exchange	AMEX
Auditor	BDO Seidman LLP	Ticker Symbol	DIO
Stk Agt	Continental Stock Transfer & Trust Co	Outstanding Shares	29,850,000
Counsel	McGuireWoods LLP	E.P.S.	-$0.77
DUNS No.	NA	Shareholders	NA

Business: The group's principal activity is to develop and commercialize laser and related disposable product technologies used in minimal and micro-invasive medical procedures. The products are used for general surgical applications. The products are sold to hospitals and office-based physicians, including specialists in vascular surgery, oncology, interventional-radiology, phlebology and dermatology. The products and services are provided through a network of distributors in Europe, the Middle East, South America, Central America and Asia.

Primary SIC and add'l.: 3841

CIK No: 0001074874

Subsidiaries: Diomed, Inc., Diomed, Ltd

Officers: James A. Wylie/Dir., CEO, Pres./$657,123.00, John J. Welch/VP - North American Marketing/$240,558.00, David Swank/Dir., CFO/$343,854.00, Christopher Geberth/VP - Finance/$210,367.00, Cary Paulette/VP - North American Sales/$309,049.00, Kevin Stearn/GM - Diomed, Ltd/$201,004.00

Directors: James A. Wylie/Dir., CEO, Pres., Geoffrey Jenkins/Chmn., Sidney Braginsky/Dir., David Swank/Dir., CFO, Gary Brooks/Dir., Kim A. Campbell/Dir., Joseph Harris/Dir., Peter Klein/Dir., Edwin Snape/Dir.

Owners: Edwin Snape/0.18%, David Swank/0.63%, Peter Klein/0.19%, Samuel Belzberg/5.90%, Cary Paulette/0.36%, William D. Allan/0.05%, Geoffrey Jenkins/0.39%, Joseph Harris/0.15%, Gary Brooks/0.17%, John J. Welch/0.31%, James A. Wylie/2.59%, ProMed Partners, L.P. and affiliates/7.30%, Sowood Capital Management, L.P./5.30%, Sidney Braginsky/0.15%, Kim A. Campbell *(17 Owners included in Index)*

Financial Data: *Fiscal Year End:*12/31 *Latest Annual Data:* 12/31/2006

Year	Sales	Net Income
2006	$22,382,000	-$10,269,000
2005	$19,049,000	-$11,438,000
2004	$13,385,000	-$10,077,000

Curr. Assets:	$17,367,000	**Curr. Liab.:**	$5,628,000		
Plant, Equip.:	$1,261,000	**Total Liab.:**	$6,781,000	**Indic. Yr. Divd.:**	NA
Total Assets:	$23,839,000	**Net Worth:**	$17,058,000	**Debt/ Equity:**	0.0611

Dionex Corp

1228 Titan Way, Sunnyvale, CA, 94085; *PH:* 1-408-737-0700; *Fax:* 1-408-730-9403; *http://* www1.dionex.com

General - Incorporation	DE	**Stock**- Price on:12/24/2007	$71.73
Employees	1,135	Stock Exchange	NDQ
Auditor	Deloitte & Touche LLP	Ticker Symbol	DNEX
Stk Agt	Computershare Ltd.	Outstanding Shares	19,020,000
Counsel	Cooley Godward LLP	E.P.S	$2.40
DUNS No.	05-539-5487	Shareholders	NA

Business: The group's principle activity is to design, manufacture, market and service liquid chromatography systems, sample preparation devices and related products. The products include ion chromatography, high-performance liquid chromatography including capillary- and nano lc and accelerated solvent extract systems, chromeleon chromatography software and consumables. These products are used in environmental analysis, life science, biotechnology, chemical, petrochemical, power generation, food and beverage and electronics industries. The group also provides maintenance contracts, spare part sales, customer training and sale of other products and value-added services. It operates in the United States, the United Kingdom, Germany, Italy, France, the Netherlands, Belgium, Switzerland, Austria, Denmark, Japan, China and Canada. The group's total revenue for year 2007 was 82.42 millions of USD.

Primary SIC and add'l.: 7378 3826 7389 3823

CIK No: 0000708850

Subsidiaries: Dionex (India) Pvt. Ltd., Dionex (Switzerland) AG, Dionex (U.K.) Limited, Dionex Austria GmbH, Dionex Benelux B.V., Dionex Canada Ltd. /Ltee., Dionex China Ltd., Dionex Denmark A/S, Dionex Export Corporation, Dionex GmbH Federal Republic of, Dionex Holding GmbH, Dionex Korea Ltd., Dionex Pty Ltd. (AU), Dionex Pty Ltd. (NZ), Dionex S.A. 19 Subsidiaries included in the Index

Officers: Lukas Braunschweiler/Dir., CEO, Pres./$1,718,098.00, Bruce Barton/VP - Asia, Pacific Sales, Service, Kevin Chance/Exec. VP/$923,512.00, David Bow/VP - North American Sales, Service, Dietrich Hauffe/VP - Corporate Marketing, Business Development, Peter Jochum/VP - Life Sciences Business Unit/$930,286.00, Craig A. McCollam/CFO, VP/$835,238.00, Christopher A. Pohl/VP - Research, Development, Chief Science Officer/$835,228.00, Christopher A. Westover/Sec., David Fairbanks/VP - Information Technology, John Plohetski/VP - Chemical Analysis Business Unit

Directors: Lukas Braunschweiler/Dir., CEO, Pres., Roderick C. McGeary/Dir., David L. Anderson/Dir., Blaine A. Bowman/Dir., Riccardo Pigliucci/Dir., Michael W. Pope/Dir.

Owners: Neuberger Berman, LLC./14.80%, Aster Investment Management Company, Inc./5.80%, Christopher Pohl, Lukas Braunschweiler/1.50%, Barclays Global Investors, NA/5.20%, Westfield Capital Management Company, LLC/5.20%, Riccardo Pigliucci, Kevin Chance, Michael W. Pope, David L. Anderson, Royce & Associates, LLC/8.40%, Blaine A. Bowman, Insiders/5.10%, Pictet Asset Management/7.50%, Craig A. McCollam *(16 Owners included in Index)*

Financial Data: *Fiscal Year End:*06/30 *Latest Annual Data:* 6/30/2006

Year	Sales	Net Income
2006	$291,300,000	$35,693,000
2005	$279,317,000	$45,490,000
2004	$258,834,000	$41,375,000

Curr. Assets:	$170,774,000	**Curr. Liab.:**	$77,413,000	**P/E Ratio:**	36.60
Plant, Equip.:	$62,366,000	**Total Liab.:**	$86,061,000	**Indic. Yr. Divd.:**	NA
Total Assets:	$271,769,000	**Net Worth:**	$185,708,000	**Debt/ Equity:**	NA

Direct Equity International Inc

Formerly: Triad Industries Inc

122 E Grand Ave., Escondido, CA, 92025; *PH:* 1-760-741-1128; *http://* www.triadindustries.com

General - Incorporation	NV	**Stock**- Price on:12/24/2007	NA
Employees	3	Stock Exchange	NA
Auditor	Armando C. Ibarra CPA	Ticker Symbol	NA
Stk Agt	Signature Stock Transfer, Inc.	Outstanding Shares	NA
Counsel	NA	E.P.S	-$0.14
DUNS No.	NA	Shareholders	NA

Business: The group's principal activities are to provide merger and acquisition consulting business which includes corporate filing and capital reorganization services for small emerging private and public corporations. The group is formed through a recapitalization of rb capital and equities inc with healthcare resource management. After the recapitalization rb capital and equities inc is termed as the acquiring entity for accounting purposes and healthcare resource management is the surviving entity for legal purposes.

Primary SIC and add'l.: 7389 8099 6719

CIK No: 0001092105

Subsidiaries: Corporate Capital Formation, Inc, Healthcare Resource Management, Inc, RB Capital and Equities, Inc

Officers: Jeffrey Heintz/GM

Financial Data: *Fiscal Year End:*12/31 *Latest Annual Data:* 12/31/2005

Year	Sales	Net Income
2005	$28,000	-$243,000
2004	$93,000	-$184,000

Curr. Assets:	$206,000	**Curr. Liab.:**	$52,000		
Plant, Equip.:	$27,000	**Total Liab.:**	$52,000	**Indic. Yr. Divd.:**	NA
Total Assets:	$354,000	**Net Worth:**	$302,000	**Debt/ Equity:**	NA

Direct Insite Corp

80 Orville Dr., Bohemia, NY, 11716; *PH:* 1-631-873-2900; *Fax:* 1-631-563-8085; *http://* www.directinsite.com; *Email:* investor@directinsite.com

General - Incorporation	DE	**Stock**- Price on:12/24/2007	$2.25
Employees	39	Stock Exchange	OTC
Auditor	Marcum & Kliegman LLP	Ticker Symbol	DIRI
Stk Agt	Manhattan Transfer Registrar Co	Outstanding Shares	5,250,000
Counsel	NA	E.P.S	$0.13
DUNS No.	60-692-3159	Shareholders	NA

Business: The group's principal activity is to provide high volume processing of transactional data. The group processes transactional data for billing purposes, electronic bill presentation and payment as well as visual data analysis and reporting tools delivered via the Internet for the customers. The group's products and services include application service provider (asp) services, account management systems (ams) services and custom engineering fees. The group has two federally registered trademarks, d.b.express and dbaccel. The group operates fully redundant data centers located at its main office in bohemia, New York, newark and New Jersey.

Primary SIC and add'l.: 7371 7372 3571

CIK No: 0000879703

Subsidiaries: Unique Ventures, Inc

Officers: James A. Cannavino/Chmn., CEO, Arnold P. Leap/CTO, Exec. VP, Michael J. Beecher/CFO, Sec., Christopher Cauley/Exec. VP - Sales, Marketing, Matthew E. Oakes/COO, Exec. VP, Debra Epstein/Media Contact

Directors: James A. Cannavino/Chmn., CEO, Bernard Puckett/Dir., Michael Levin/Dir., Dennis J. Murray/Dir.

Owners: Tall Oaks Group, LLC, Dennis Murray, Robert Carberry, James Cannavino, Michael Levin, Metropolitan Venture Partners II, L.P., Christopher Cauley, Carla Steckline, Bernard Puckett, Insiders, Michael Beecher, Matthew Oakes, Arnold Leap, Sigma Opportunity Fund, LLP

Financial Data: *Fiscal Year End:*12/31 *Latest Annual Data:* 12/31/2006

Year	Sales	Net Income
2006	$8,889,000	$269,000
2005	$8,870,000	-$991,000
2004	$7,558,000	-$1,283,000

Curr. Assets:	$2,433,000	**Curr. Liab.:**	$6,898,000	**P/E Ratio:**	17.31
Plant, Equip.:	$450,000	**Total Liab.:**	$7,062,000	**Indic. Yr. Divd.:**	NA
Total Assets:	$3,163,000	**Net Worth:**	-$3,899,000	**Debt/ Equity:**	NA

Direct Response Financial Services Inc

2899 Agoura Rd. , Ste 115, Westlake Village, CA, 91361; *PH:* 1-818-735-3726; *http://* www.drfs.net; *Email:* info@directcardservices.net

General - Incorporation	CO	**Stock**- Price on:12/24/2007	NA
Employees	NA	Stock Exchange	NA
Auditor	Miller & McCollom	Ticker Symbol	NA
Stk Agt	First American Stock Transfer, Inc.	Outstanding Shares	NA
Counsel	NA	E.P.S	NA
DUNS No.	NA	Shareholders	NA

Business: The group's principal activity is to deliver proprietary technology and service support to its customers and clients in the financial industry. Services include payment gateway system, merchant banking services, transmitter business/cash cards, wireless payment solutions, debit cards, ATM cards, development of card loading stations and networks. The group is in the development stage and has had no significant operations. Its primary customers are banks, credit and debit card issuers and users of such cards, third party marketing companies in need of financial products, media companies, the direct response industry and any company or group in need of deploying electronic or digital payment acceptance technologies.

Primary SIC and add'l.: 7375

CIK No: 0001121076

Subsidiaries: Direct Card Services, LLC

Officers: Travis W. Huff/VP, Portfolio Mgr.

Financial Data: *Fiscal Year End:*01/31 *Latest Annual Data:* 01/31/2006

Year	Sales	Net Income
2006	$35,000	-$853,000
2005	$12,000	-$1,509,000
2004	$2,000	-$1,377,000

Curr. Assets:	$149,000	**Curr. Liab.:**	$1,701,000		
Plant, Equip.:	$1,000	**Total Liab.:**	$1,701,000	**Indic. Yr. Divd.:**	NA
Total Assets:	$150,000	**Net Worth:**	-$1,551,000	**Debt/ Equity:**	NA

Directed Electronics Inc

1 Viper Way, Vista, CA, 92081; *PH:* 1-760-598-6200; *Fax:* 1-760-598-6400; *http://* www.directed.com

General - Incorporation	FL	**Stock**- Price on:12/24/2007	$8.84
Employees	513	Stock Exchange	NDQ
Auditor	PricewaterhouseCoopers LLP	Ticker Symbol	DEIX
Stk Agt	American Stock Transfer & Trust Co.	Outstanding Shares	25,220,000
Counsel	NA	E.P.S	$0.26
DUNS No.	NA	Shareholders	NA

Business: The groups principal activities include designing and marketing home theater loudspeakers, consumer vehicle security, and vehicle remote start systems. The products of the group include speakers, subwoofers, car amplifiers, and mobile video units, hybrid systems, GPS tracking, and navigation systems. The group products sold under the trade name Polk Audio(R), Polk MOMO(R), Orion(R), Precision Power(R), Directed Audio(R), Xtreme(R) Directed(R) and Automate(R). Customers served by the group include electronics chains, mass merchants, automotive parts retailers, car dealers, and international distributors. In the year 2006, the group acquired Polk Holding Corp, Astroflex, Inc, M&P Directed Electronics and Autostart, Inc. Specific customers of the group include Wal-Mart, Sams Club, COSTCO, Sears, Target, and Staples. The group operates from the United Sates. The net sale of the group for the year 2006 was $437,778 (thousands).

Primary SIC and add'l.: 5063 3999 5013 3699 5065 3699 5063 3999 5065 3651 5013

CIK No: 0001323630

Subsidiaries: 4366778 Canada Inc., 4366859 Canada Inc., Britannia Investment Corporation, DEI Headquarters, Inc., DEI International, Inc., DEI Sales, Inc., Directed Electronics Hong Kong Limited, Directed Electronics, Canada Inc, Polk Audio, Inc., Polk Holding Corp.

Officers: James E. Minarik/Dir., CEO, Pres., Ron Dutt/CFO, Exec. VP, Glenn R. Busse/Sr. VP - Sales, Mark E. Rutledge/Sr. VP - Engineering, Product Development, Kevin P. Duffy/Sr. VP - Corporate Development, Marketing, Michael N. Smith/VP - Operations, K. C. Bean/VP, General Counsel, Richard J. Hirshberg/Treasurer, VP - Information Technology, John Mills/MD - Integrated Corporate Relations

Directors: James E. Minarik/Dir., CEO, Pres., Troy D. Templeton/Chmn., Jon E. Elias/Dir., Darrell E. Issa/Dir., Andrew D. Robertson/Dir., Victor J. Orler/Dir., James S. Spierer/Dir., Kevin B. McColgan/Dir., Edmond S. Thomas/Dir., Seth R. Johnson/Dir.

Owners: Glenn R. Busse, Troy D. Templeton, Victor J. Orler, James S. Spierer, Insiders, James E. Minarik, Jon E. Elias, Edmond S. Thomas, Massachusetts Mutual Life Insurance Company, Putnam Funds, Andrew D. Robertson, FMR Corp., Richard J. Hirshberg, Darrell E. Issa, Trivest Funds *(18 Owners included in Index)*

Financial Data: *Fiscal Year End:*12/31 *Latest Annual Data:* 12/31/2006

Year	Sales	Net Income
2006	$437,778,000	$21,009,000
2005	$304,558,000	-$5,137,000
2004	$189,869,000	$13,962,000

Curr. Assets:	$321,326,000	**Curr. Liab.:**	$160,388,000	**P/E Ratio:**	16.07
Plant, Equip.:	$7,068,000	**Total Liab.:**	$554,316,000	**Indic. Yr. Divd.:**	NA
Total Assets:	$678,707,000	**Net Worth:**	$124,391,000	**Debt/ Equity:**	2.6453

DIRECTV Group Inc (The)

2250 E Imperial Hwy, El Segundo, CA, 90245; *PH:* 1-310-964-5000; *http://* www.directtv.com; *Email:* politicalfileinfo@directv.com

General - Incorporation	DE	**Stock**- Price on:12/24/2007	$24.21
Employees	9,900	Stock Exchange	NYSE
Auditor	Deloitte & Touche LLP	Ticker Symbol	DTV
Stk Agt	Computershare Investor Services LLC	Outstanding Shares	1,220,000,000
Counsel	NA	E.P.S.	$1.19
DUNS No.	82-501-6934	Shareholders	NA

Business: The group's principle activity is to provide digital television entertainment. The group operates through two segments namely DIRECTV U.S. and DIRECTV Latin America. The group operates from United States.

Primary SIC and add'l.: 4899 3663

CIK No: 0000944868

Subsidiaries: California Broadcast Center, LLC, DIRECTV Argentina, S.A., DIRECTV Caribbean LLC, DIRECTV Customer Services, Inc., DIRECTV de Uruguay, Ltda, DIRECTV Enterprises, LLC, DIRECTV Financing Co., Inc., DIRECTV Holdings LLC, DIRECTV Home Services, LLC, DIRECTV International, Inc., DIRECTV Latin America Holdings, Inc., DIRECTV Latin America, LLC, DIRECTV Merchandising, Inc., DIRECTV Mexico Holdings, LLC, DIRECTV Operations, LLC 76 Subsidiaries included in the Index

Officers: Chase Carey/Dir., CEO, Pres./$12,470,900.00, Larry D. Hunter/Exec. VP, General Counsel, Sec./$2,392,273.00, Neil R. Austrian/Dir. - Private Investor, Patrick T. Doyle/CFO, Sr. VP, Michael W. Palkovic/Exec. VP/$2,154,113.00, Bruce B. Churchill/Exec. VP/$3,427,854.00, Romulo G. Pontual/CTO, Exec. VP/$2,016,497.00, William J. Little/Sr. VP, Treasurer, John F. Murphy/Sr. VP, Controller, Chief Accounting Officer

Directors: Chase Carey/Dir., CEO, Pres., Rupert Murdoch/Chmn., Ralph F. Boyd/Dir., Peter A. Lund/Dir., Charles R. Lee/Dir., James M. Cornelius/Dir., Neil R. Austrian/Dir. - Private Investor, Haim Saban/Dir., Peter Chernin/Dir., David F. Devoe/Dir., Nancy S. Newcomb/Dir.

Owners: Chase Carey, Insiders, Charles R. Lee, Peter A. Lund, Neil R. Austrian, Larry D. Hunter, Nancy S. Newcomb, Ralph F. Boyd, Bruce B. Churchill, Michael W. Palkovic, Haim Saban, Rupert K. Murdoch, James M. Cornelius, Romulo Pontual

Financial Data: *Fiscal Year End:*12/31 *Latest Annual Data:* 12/31/2006

Year	Sales	Net Income
2006	$14,755,500,000	$1,420,100,000
2005	$13,164,500,000	$335,900,000
2004	$11,360,000,000	-$1,949,200,000

Curr. Assets:	$4,555,600,000	**Curr. Liab.:**	$3,322,500,000	**P/E Ratio:**	19.68
Plant, Equip.:	$4,453,200,000	**Total Liab.:**	$8,398,100,000	**Indic. Yr. Divd.:**	NA
Total Assets:	$15,141,100,000	**Net Worth:**	$6,680,800,000	**Debt/ Equity:**	0.4879

DirectView Inc

10-18 Pk. St., 2nd Fl., Gouverneur, NY, 13642; *PH:* 1-315-287-1122; *http://* www.directviewinc.com

General - Incorporation	NV	**Stock**- Price on:12/24/2007	$0.0007
Employees	NA	Stock Exchange	NA
Auditor	Rosenberg Rich Baker Berman & Co.	Ticker Symbol	NA
Stk Agt	Atlas Stock Transfer Corp	Outstanding Shares	421,580,000
Counsel	NA	E.P.S.	-$0.005
DUNS No.	NA	Shareholders	NA

Business: The group's principal activity is to provide video conferencing services and products. The services of the group include multipoint video conferencing, network integration services, custom room design, staffing, document conferencing and ip/Web conferencing services. The group also distribute video conference products and peripherals to organizations such as professional service firms, investment banks, high tech companies, law firms, state and local government agencies, investor relations firms, and other domestic and multi-national companies. The group offers convenience of single-vendor sourcing for most aspects of their communications needs to their customers.on 23-Feb-2004, group acquired meeting technologies, inc.

Primary SIC and add'l.: 3577

CIK No: 0000884380

Subsidiaries: Meeting Technologies, Inc, Ralston Communications, Inc

Owners: Kevin Kreisler/80.00%, Kevin Kreisler/100.00%

Financial Data: *Fiscal Year End:*12/31 *Latest Annual Data:* 12/31/2006

Year	Sales	Net Income
2006	NA	$222,000
2005	$690,000	-$2,927,000
2004	$733,000	-$1,180,000

Curr. Assets:	$0	**Curr. Liab.:**	$1,040,000		
Plant, Equip.:	$147,000	**Total Liab.:**	$2,814,000	**Indic. Yr. Divd.:**	NA
Total Assets:	$2,629,000	**Net Worth:**	-$185,000	**Debt/ Equity:**	NA

Dirt Motor Sports Inc

7575-D W Winds Blvd, Concord, NC, 28027; *PH:* 1-405-360-0858; *http://* www.dirtmotorsports.com

General - Incorporation	DE	**Stock**- Price on:12/24/2007	$1.4
Employees	50	Stock Exchange	OTC
Auditor	Murrell, Hall, McIntosh & Co., PLLP	Ticker Symbol	DMSP
Stk Agt	Mountain Share Transfer	Outstanding Shares	14,570,000
Counsel	NA	E.P.S.	-$0.93
DUNS No.	NA	Shareholders	NA

Business: The groups principle activities include marketing and promoting motor sports entertainment in the United States. In the year 2005, the group acquired Volusia Speedway Park, Inc. The group operates from the United States. The groups quarterly revenue for September 2007 was 4.39 millions of USD.

Primary SIC and add'l.: 7948

CIK No: 0000793041

Subsidiaries: Boundless Racing, Inc

Officers: Tom W. Deery/53/Pres., Interim CEO, Pres., Robert L. Butcher/35/Exec. VP, Chief Marketing Officer, Benjaman L. Geisler/31/Exec. VP - Operations

Directors: Harvey W. Schiller/68/Chmn., Cary J. Agajanian/66/Dir., Robert F. Hussey/58/Dir.

Owners: Daniel W. Rumsey, Insiders/10.90%, Benjamin L. Geisler/2.10%, Cary J. Agajanian, Harvey Schiller, Brian M. Carter/3.60%, Tom W. Deery/1.70%, Robert L. Butcher/2.10%, Robert F. Hussey

Financial Data: *Fiscal Year End:*12/31 *Latest Annual Data:* 12/31/2006

Year	Sales	Net Income
2006	$15,144,000	-$22,809,000
2005	$1,963,000	-$3,792,000

Curr. Assets:	$1,196,000	**Curr. Liab.:**	$2,465,000		
Plant, Equip.:	$10,448,000	**Total Liab.:**	$6,467,000	**Indic. Yr. Divd.:**	NA
Total Assets:	$12,051,000	**Net Worth:**	$5,584,000	**Debt/ Equity:**	0.7166

Discovery Bancorp CA

338 Via Vera Cruz, San Marcos, CA, 92078; *PH:* 1-760-736-8900; *Fax:* 1-760-410-9018; *http://* www.discovery-bank.com

General - Incorporation	CA	**Stock**- Price on:12/24/2007	$16.39
Employees	43	Stock Exchange	OTC
Auditor	Hutchinson And Bloodgood LLP	Ticker Symbol	DVBC
Stk Agt	U.S. Stock Transfer Corp	Outstanding Shares	1,930,000
Counsel	NA	E.P.S.	$0.50
DUNS No.	NA	Shareholders	NA

Business: The group operates through its subsidiaries whose principal activity is banking operations. The group financial products include acceptance of savings, demand and term deposits, trust services, cash management and electronic fund transfer, on line internet banking, commercial loans. The group operates from the United States. In the year 2005, the group acquired Celtic Merger Corp.

Primary SIC and add'l.: 6022

CIK No: 0001313868

Subsidiaries: Celtic Capital Corporation, Discovery Bank, San Marcos Building, LLC

Officers: James P. Kelley/Dir., CEO, Pres., Joseph C. Carona/Exec. VP, Chief Administrative Officer, Alineh Moradian/Assist. VP, Accounting Relationship Officer - Discovery Bank, Los Angeles, Martin McNabb/CFO, Exec. VP, Robert Cairns/Sec., Anthony Desalvo/Exec. VP, Chief Credit Officer - Discovery Bank, Stephen Friedman/Sr. VP - Business Banking Group, Discovery Bank, San Marcos, Brenda Shelly/Sr. VP - Commercial Real Estate Land, Construction Lending, Discovery Bank, San Marcos, Marcia Schaefer/VP, San Marcos Branch Mgr., Sheree Keller/VP, Business Development Officer - San Marcos, Margaret Oppliger/VP, Relationship Mgr. - Discovery Bank, San Marcos, Sara Leposke/Assist. VP, Relationship Mgr. - Discovery Bank, San Marcos, Wanda Allen/Sr. VP, Poway Branch Mgr. - Discovery Bank, Pamela Carson/Assist. VP, Business Development Officer - Discovery Bank, Poway, Rebecca Pollastrini/VP, Business Development Officer - Discovery Bank, Poway *(17 Officers included in Index)*

Directors: James P. Kelley/Dir., CEO, Pres., John Plavan/Chmn., Gabriel Castano/Vice Chmn., Albert Boyajian/Dir., Walter F. Cobb/Dir., Anthony Pitale/Dir., Stuart Rubin/Dir., Bron Hafner/Dir.

Owners: James P. Kelley/3.34%, Insiders/20.59%, Walter F. Cobb/1.25%, Mark A. Hafner/1.19%, Gabriel P. Castano/2.36%, Stuart Rubin/2.87%, Robert Cairns/2.99%, Joseph C. Carona/0.73%, Stanley M. Cruse/0.23%, John R. Plavan/2.07%, Mark W. Santar/2.17%, Anthony J. Pitale/0.92%, Bron Hafner/1.67%

Financial Data: *Fiscal Year End:*12/31 *Latest Annual Data:* 12/31/2006

Year	Sales	Net Income
2006	$18,173,000	$1,356,000
2005	$10,871,000	$553,000
2002	$1,939,000	-$728,000

Curr. Assets:	$27,820,000	**Curr. Liab.:**	$131,951,000	**P/E Ratio:**	26.02
Plant, Equip.:	$5,960,000	**Total Liab.:**	$172,155,000	**Indic. Yr. Divd.:**	NA
Total Assets:	$197,346,000	**Net Worth:**	$25,191,000	**Debt/ Equity:**	NA

Discovery Holding Co

12300 Liberty Blvd., Englewood, CO, 80112; *PH:* 1-720-875-4000; *Fax:* 1-720-875-7469; *http://* www.discoveryholding.com

General - Incorporation	DE	**Stock**- Price on:12/24/2007	$23.41
Employees	4,000	Stock Exchange	NDQ
Auditor	KPMG LLP	Ticker Symbol	DISCA
Stk Agt	Computershare Investor Services LLC	Outstanding Shares	280,270,000
Counsel	NA	E.P.S.	-$0.13
DUNS No.	NA	Shareholders	NA

Business: The group's principal activities are services for the entertainment media & retail sale & licensing of products. The services provided by the group include production, acquisition, and distribution of entertainment, educational and information programming and software, retail sale and licensing of branded and other specialty products, creative and media management, and networking services to the

media and entertainment industries. Their subsidiaries and affiliates operate in the United States, Europe, Latin America and Asia. The group is awaiting a spin off from LMC- their holding company, following which it will be an independent publicly traded company and still continue to serve the business interests of the existing wholly owned subsidiary, Ascent Media and 50% owned equity affiliate, Discovery of the LMC holding company.

Primary SIC and add'l.: 7812

CIK No: 0001320482

Subsidiaries: AFA Products Group, Inc., Animal Planet LLC, Ascent Media Cancom, Inc., Ascent Media Creative Services, Inc. , Ascent Media Creative Sound Services, Inc., Ascent Media Group Limited, Ascent Media Group, LLC, Ascent Media Holdings Limited, Ascent Media Holdings Ltd., Ascent Media Holdings, Inc., Ascent Media Limited, Ascent Media Management Services, Inc. , Ascent Media Network Services Europe Limited, Ascent Media Network Services, LLC, Ascent Media Pte. Ltd. 35 Subsidiaries included in the Index

Officers: John C. Malone/Chmn., CEO, Robert R. Bennett/Dir., Pres.

Directors: John C. Malone/Chmn., CEO, Lavoy M. Robison/Dir., Robert R. Bennett/Dir., Pres., Paul A. Gould/Dir., David J. Wargo/Dir.

Owners: Christopher W. Shean, John C. Malone/1.40%, Robert R. Bennett, T. Rowe Price Associates, Inc./6.00%, Capital Research and Management Company/6.70%, Paul A. Gould, Insiders, LaVoy M. Robison, Robert R. Bennett, David J. Wargo, Harris Associates L.P./10.00%, Paul A. Gould, John C. Malone, Southeastern Asset Management, Inc./10.40%, Insiders/1.90% *(18 Owners included in Index)*

Financial Data: *Fiscal Year End:*12/31 *Latest Annual Data:* 12/31/2006

Year	Sales	Net Income
2006	$688,087,000	-$46,010,000
2005	$694,509,000	$33,276,000

Curr. Assets:	$317,362,000	**Curr. Liab.:**	$121,887,000		
Plant, Equip.:	$280,775,000	**Total Liab.:**	$1,321,718,000	**Indic. Yr. Divd.:**	NA
Total Assets:	$5,870,982,000	**Net Worth:**	$4,549,264,000	**Debt/ Equity:**	NA

Discovery Laboratories Inc

2600 Kelly Rd., Ste. 100, Warrington, PA, 18976; ***PH:*** 1-215-488-9300; ***Fax:*** 1-215-488-9301; ***http://*** www.discoverylabs.com; ***Email:*** ir@discoverylabs.com

General - Incorporation	DE	**Stock**- Price on:12/24/2007	$3.27
Employees	100	Stock Exchange	NDQ
Auditor	Ernst & Young LLP	Ticker Symbol	DSCO
Stk Agt	Continental Stock Transfer & Trust Co	Outstanding Shares	84,590,000
Counsel	Roberts Sheridan & Kotel	E.P.S	-$0.47
DUNS No.	80-885-6116	Shareholders	NA

Business: The group's principal activity is to develop respiratory therapies and pulmonary drug delivery products. The group also performs research and development of aerosolized formulations of its humanized surfactant technology to treat respiratory conditions such as asthma. The group's product, surfaxin(R), is an engineered humanized surfactant. Surfaxin(R) is currently in two phase 3 clinical trials for respiratory distress syndrome in premature infants (rds), a phase 3 clinical trial for meconium aspiration syndrome in full-term infants (mas), and a phase 2 clinical trial for acute lung injury/acute respiratory distress syndrome in adults (ali/ards).

Primary SIC and add'l.: 8731 2834

CIK No: 0000946486

Subsidiaries: Ortho Pharmaceutical Corporation

Officers: Robert J. Capetola/Dir., Pres., CEO - Discovery Laboratories, Inc/$1,740,511.00, David L. Lopez/Exec. VP, General Counsel/$947,022.00, Fernando R. Moya/Scientific Advisors, Thomas F. Miller/Sr. VP - Commercialization, Corporate Development/$542,206.00, Robert Segal/Sr. VP - Medical, Scientific Affairs, Chief Medical Officer/$572,916.00, Kathryn Cole/Sr. VP - Human Resources, Charles F. Katzer/Sr. VP - Manufacturing Operations, Russell G. Clayton/VP - Worldwide Clinical Research, Development, Cynthia Davis/VP - Special Business Projects, Thomas Hofmann/VP - New Product Development, Marjorie Hurley/VP - Regulatory Affairs, Mark E. Johnson/VP - Pharmaceutical Development, Gerald J. Orehostky/VP - Quality Operations, Duncan R. Hite/Scientific Advisor, Allen T. Merritt/Scientific Advisors *(19 Officers included in Index)*

Directors: Robert J. Capetola/Dir., Pres., CEO - Discovery Laboratories, Inc, Thomas W. Amick/Chmn., Max Link/Dir., Antonio Esteve/Dir., Herbert H. McDade/Dir., Marvin E. Rosenthale/Dir.

Owners: Antonio Esteve/3.84%, Herbert H. McDade, Robert Segal, Thomas F. Miller, Insiders/10.23%, Heartland Advisors Inc./7.27%, Marvin E. Rosenthale, Morgan Stanley/7.59%, Robert J. Capetola/2.53%, Thomas W. Amick, John G. Cooper/1.13%, Max E. Link, David L. Lopez

Financial Data: *Fiscal Year End:*12/31 *Latest Annual Data:* 12/31/2006

Year	Sales	Net Income
2006	NA	-$46,333,000
2005	$134,000	-$58,904,000
2004	$1,209,000	-$46,203,000

Curr. Assets:	$27,567,000	**Curr. Liab.:**	$7,968,000		
Plant, Equip.:	$4,794,000	**Total Liab.:**	$20,078,000	**Indic. Yr. Divd.:**	NA
Total Assets:	$34,400,000	**Net Worth:**	$14,322,000	**Debt/ Equity:**	1.2915

Discovery Oil Ltd

6127 Ramierez Canyon Rd., Malibu, DE, 90265; ***PH:*** 1-310-457-1967

General - Incorporation	DE	**Stock**- Price on:12/24/2007	$0.021
Employees	NA	Stock Exchange	OTC
Auditor	Williams & Webster, P.S.	Ticker Symbol	DSCY
Stk Agt	NA	Outstanding Shares	25,250,000
Counsel	NA	E.P.S	$0.00
DUNS No.	NA	Shareholders	NA

Business: The groups principle activity is to provide recruiting services. The groups service area includes the research and development, engineering, marketing, sales, information technology and manufacturing industries. The group operates from United States.

Primary SIC and add'l.: 6799

CIK No: 0000029071

Officers: Andrew V. Ippolito/73/Chmn., CFO, Pres., Jeanette M. Ippolito/63/Sec.

Directors: Andrew V. Ippolito/73/Chmn., CFO, Pres.

Owners: M. Jeanett Ippolito/9.90%, Andrew V. Ippolito/17.80%, Jeanett Ippolito/39.80%, CEDE & CO/11.40%, Insiders/67.50%

Financial Data: *Fiscal Year End:*12/31 *Latest Annual Data:* 12/31/2006

Year	Sales	Net Income
2006	NA	-$65,000
2005	NA	-$375,000
2004	$17,000	$3,000

Curr. Assets:	$1,000	**Curr. Liab.:**	$182,000		
Plant, Equip.:	$1,000	**Total Liab.:**	$182,000	**Indic. Yr. Divd.:**	NA
Total Assets:	$2,000	**Net Worth:**	-$180,000	**Debt/ Equity:**	NA

Dispatch Auto Parts Inc

4th/fl, Block A, 12 Xiang Zi Miao St., Bei Lin Qu, Xian, 50000; ***PH:*** 86-585-586-5573

General - Incorporation	FL	**Stock**- Price on:12/24/2007	$0.51
Employees	NA	Stock Exchange	NA
Auditor	Zhong Yi (hong Kong) C.P.A. Co. Ltd.	Ticker Symbol	NA
Stk Agt	Guardian Registrar and Transfer, Inc	Outstanding Shares	NA
Counsel	NA	E.P.S	NA
DUNS No.	NA	Shareholders	NA

Business: The groups principle activity is to market automotive parts and accessories. The group products include clutches, batteries and accessories, shoes, pads, carburetors , alternators and mufflers. The group operates from the United States.

Primary SIC and add'l.: 5013

CIK No: 0001352419

Subsidiaries: Dispatch Auto Parts II, Inc

Officers: Sheng Li Liu/40/Chmn., CEO, Pres., Shun Cheng Ma/45/Dir., CFO

Directors: Sheng Li Liu/40/Chmn., CEO, Pres., Shun Cheng Ma/45/Dir., CFO, Wei Sheng Lu/34/Dir., Hong Mei Ding/36/Dir., Wei Tian/35/Dir.

Owners: Insiders/34.43%, Liu Sheng Li/100.00%, Xie Qing/8.16%, Liu Sheng Li/29.93%, Cai Xiao Ying/8.16%, Insiders/34.43%, Insiders/100.00%, Ding Hong Mei/4.50%

Financial Data: *Fiscal Year End:*06/30 *Latest Annual Data:* 6/30/2006

Year	Sales	Net Income
2006	$149,000	-$207,000

Curr. Assets:	$50,000	**Curr. Liab.:**	$4,000		
Plant, Equip.:	NA	**Total Liab.:**	$4,000	**Indic. Yr. Divd.:**	NA
Total Assets:	$50,000	**Net Worth:**	$46,000	**Debt/ Equity:**	NA

Distributed Energy Systems Corp

10 Technology Dr., Wallingford, CT, 06492; ***PH:*** 1-203-678-2000; ***Fax:*** 1-203-949-8016; ***http://*** www.distributed-energy.com

General - Incorporation	DE	**Stock**- Price on:12/24/2007	$0.89
Employees	226	Stock Exchange	NDQ
Auditor	PricewaterhouseCoopers LLP	Ticker Symbol	DESC
Stk Agt	American Stock Transfer & Trust Co.	Outstanding Shares	39,770,000
Counsel	Hale & Dorr LLP	E.P.S	-$1.63
DUNS No.	NA	Shareholders	NA

Business: The group's principal activities are to design, develop and manufacture proton exchange membrane (pem) electrochemical products for commercial applications. The pem technology is incorporated in two families of products namely, hydrogen generators and regenerative fuel cell systems. The hydrogen generators convert water and electricity into high purity, pressurized hydrogen gas using pem electrolysis. The regenerative fuel cell systems integrates pem hydrogen generation technology with pem fuel cell technology to create a power quality device that produces hydrogen from water and electricity, stores the hydrogen, and uses the hydrogen as fuel for the production of electricity. The products of the group function as power generating and energy storage devices.the registered trademarks include proton(R), hogen(R), unigen(R), fuelgen(tm), hipress(tm) and transforming energy(tm). On 10-Dec-2003, the group acquired northern power systems inc.

Primary SIC and add'l.: 3629

CIK No: 0001261482

Subsidiaries: Northern Power Systems, Inc., Proton Energy Systems, Inc., Technology Drive LLC

Officers: Ambrose L. Schwallie/CEO/$2,851,679.00, Walter W. Schroeder/Dir., Pres./$431,807.00, Robert J. Friedland/Sr. VP - Hydrogen Generation/$203,942.00, Peter J. Tallian/CFO/$30,210.00, Erika Schramm/Dir. - Human Resources, Betsy Anderson/Sr. VP - Operations, John Speranza/Hydrogen Generation Sales Group, Robert Melusky/Hydrogen Generation Sales Group, Scott Knapp/Hydrogen Generation Sales Group, Frank Vonesh/Hydrogen Generation Sales Group, David Wolff/Hydrogen Generation Sales Group, Jim Brannen/Power Generation Sales Group, Ron Puryear/Power Generation Sales Group, Marc McMenamin/Power Generation Sales Group, North Hefley/Power Generation Sales Group

Directors: Ambrose L. Schwallie/CEO, Theodore Stern/78/Dir., Richard S. Grant,/62/Dir., Bernard H. Cherry,/68/Dir., James H. Ozanne/64/Dir., Walter W. Schroeder/Dir., Pres.

Owners: Richard S. Grant, Paul F. Koeppe, Perseus Partners VII, L.P./16.66%, John A. Glidden, Gerald B. Ostroski, Bernard H. Cherry, James H. Ozanne, Mark E. Murray, Theodore Stern, Robert B. Nieszczezewski, Walter W. Schroeder/2.70%, Robert J. Friedland/1.35%, Insiders/6.51%, Morgan Stanley Wind LLC/10.26%, Ambrose L. Schwallie *(16 Owners included in Index)*

Financial Data: *Fiscal Year End:*12/31 *Latest Annual Data:* 12/31/2006

Year	Sales	Net Income
2006	$45,093,000	-$53,355,000
2005	$44,980,000	-$16,244,000
2004	$22,460,000	-$22,437,000

Curr. Assets:	$37,679,000	**Curr. Liab.:**	$14,814,000		
Plant, Equip.:	$22,740,000	**Total Liab.:**	$23,149,000	**Indic. Yr. Divd.:**	NA
Total Assets:	$69,890,000	**Net Worth:**	$46,740,000	**Debt/ Equity:**	0.2073

Distribution & Service D&S

Av Presidente Eduardo Frei Montalva, 8301 Quilicura, Santiago; ***PH:*** 56-22005000; ***http://*** www.dys.cl; ***Email:*** info@dys.cl

General - Incorporation .... Chile
Employees 30,124
Auditor .... Deloitte & Touche LLP
Stk Agt .... Morgan ADR Service Center
Counsel .... Cristobal Lira
DUNS No. .... NA

Stock- Price on:12/24/2007 .... $32.5
Stock Exchange .... NYSE
Ticker Symbol .... DYS
Outstanding Shares 108,670,000
E.P.S. $0.95
Shareholders .... NA

Business: The group's principal activities are carried out through four main divisions: retail division includes three different formats under the lider brand: hypermarkets,vecino compact hypermarkets and express supermarkets; and the farmlider pharmacy stores. Logistics division corresponds to the 72,000 square meter distribution center located in santiago, where the its merchandise is centralized and distributed to stores. Financial services division are provided through its presto credit card and real estate division manages rental operations in its six shopping malls and commercial locations in the company stores. Additionally, this division maintains a land bank to secure locations for its future projects. In Dec 2003, it has 68 stores - 23 lider hypermarkets, 19 lider vecino compact hypermarkets and 23 lider express supermarkets in addition to 40 pharmacy stores.

Primary SIC and add'l.: 5399 5023 5411 2099

CIK No: 0001046247

Subsidiaries: Administradora de Concesiones Comerciales de Hipermercados S.A., Administradora de Concesiones Comerciales de Supermercados S.A., Administradora de Crditos Comerciales Presto S.A., Comercial Divisin Productos Lider Limitada, Comercial Outlet y Pajaritos Limitada, Comercializadora de Vestuario S.A., Corredores de Seguros Presto Limitada, Distribuidora y Comercializadora Farmalider S.A., Escatec Limitada, Escuela de capacitacin tcnica, Grupo de Restaurantes Chile S.A., Hipermercado Alameda Limitada, Hipermercado Antofagasta Limitada, Hipermercado Bo Bio Limitada, Hipermercado Calama Limitada 102 Subsidiaries included in the Index

Officers: Enrique Cambiaso Ostale/CEO, Sebastian Heuser Rozas/GM - Saitec Real Estate Division, Marcelo Saldias Galvez/Mgr. - Corporate Develepment, Gonzalo Ferrer Smith/General Counsel, Juan Pablo Vega Walker/40/Mgr. - Development, Loreto V. Bradford/Investor Relations Officer, Roberto Vergara/Investor Relations Officer, Alejandro Droste/CFO, Silvio Hayes Rostagno/COO, Tina K. Rosenfeld/Corporate Controller, Claudio Barrientos Hohmann/Mgr. - Corporate Affairs, Manuel Barranco Lopez/Mgr. - Hypermarkets, Andres Donoso Fernandez/Mgr. - Supermarkets, Alfonso Mujica Sierra/Corporate Mgr. - Logistic Division, Paulo Escobar Gajardo/Financial Mgr. - Saitec Real Estate Division *(18 Officers included in Index)*

Directors: Hans Eben Oyanedel/Dep. Chmn., Felipe Ibanez Scott/52/Chmn., Nicolas Ibanez Scott/50/Dir., Veronica Edwards Guzman/48/Dir., Felipe Larrain Bascunan/Dir., Jonny Kulka Fraenkel/Dir., Gonzalo Eguiguren Correa/Dir., Rene Cortazar Sanz/Dir., Gerardo Jofre Miranda/Dir., Francisco Gana Eguiguren/Dir., Fernando Larrain Cruzat/47/Dir.

Owners: Manuel Lopez Barranco/0.00%, Insiders/0.04%, Nicols Ibez Scott/0.03%, Servicios Profesionales y de Comercializacin S.A./35.37%, Jonny Kulka Fraenkel/0.01%, Empresas Almac S.A./9.20%, Inversiones Triplesis Limitada/0.12%, Inversiones Triplevis Limitada/0.17%, Future Investments S.A./8.06%, Servicios e Inversiones Trucha S.A./7.36%, International Supermarket Holdings S.A./3.27%

Financial Data: ***Fiscal Year End:***12/31 ***Latest Annual Data:*** 12/31/2006

Year	Sales	Net Income
2006	$3,223,663,000	$72,845,000
2005	$3,037,657,000	$88,165,000
2004	$2,592,831,000	$17,240,000

Curr. Assets:	$649,749,000	**Curr. Liab.:**	$781,290,000		
Plant, Equip.:	$1,226,717,000	**Total Liab.:**	$1,306,248,000	**Indic. Yr. Divd.:**	$0.310
Total Assets:	$2,294,561,000	**Net Worth:**	$988,314,000	**Debt/ Equity:**	NA

Ditech Communications Corp

825 E Middlefield Rd. , Mountain View, CA, 94043; ***PH:*** 1-650-623-1300; ***http://*** www.ditechnetworks.com

General - Incorporation .... DE
Employees 216
Auditor .... PricewaterhouseCoopers LLP
Stk Agt .... Wells Fargo Bank Minnesota N.A
Counsel .... Cooley Godward LLP
DUNS No. .... NA

Stock- Price on:12/24/2007 .... $8.16
Stock Exchange .... NDQ
Ticker Symbol .... NA
Outstanding Shares 32,750,000
E.P.S. $0.16
Shareholders .... NA

Business: The group's principal activities are to design, develop and market stand-alone and system-based voice quality enhancement and echo cancellation products. Echo cancellation products are used for wireline, wireless, satellite, and voice-over-packet networks throughout the world. The voice processing products include echo cancellers, which are used to effectively eliminate echo. The echo cancellation product family includes a mixture of both single and multi-port, stand-alone echo cancellers as well as several broadband, system-based products. The customers of the group include the United States, Asia-Pacific, Canada, Latin America and Europe. During the year, the group discontinued optical subsystem communications business.

Primary SIC and add'l.: 3663 3679 3669

CIK No: 0001080667

Subsidiaries: Ditech Communications Canada,Inc., Ditech Communications Europe Limited, Ditech Communications International,Inc., Ditech India Private Limited, Jasomi Networks,Inc.

Officers: Lowell Trangsrud/COO, Exec. VP/$748,860.00, Lee H. House/VP - Platform Engineering, Sandeep Pombra/CTO Voice Communications - Echo Cancellation Products, William Tamblyn/CFO, Exec. VP/$747,149.00, Gary Testa/VP - Worldwide Sales/$1,106,483.00

Directors: William A. Hasler/Dir., David M. Sugishita/Dir., Gregory M. Avis/Dir., Andrei M. Manoliu/Dir., Edwin L. Harper/Dir.

Owners: David M. Sugishita, Gary D. Testa, Caglan M. Aras, Barclays Global Investors, NA./7.19%, Dimensional Fund Advisors LP/7.46%, Lloyd I. Miller/5.03%, Timothy K. Montgomery/4.47%, Lowell B. Trangsrud/1.74%, William J. Tamblyn/2.48%, Edwin L. Harper, Lee H. House, William A. Hasler, Insiders/10.81%, CCM Master Qualified Fund, Ltd./5.02%, Riley Investment Management LLC/6.76% *(19 Owners included in Index)*

Financial Data: ***Fiscal Year End:***04/30 ***Latest Annual Data:*** 4/30/2006

Year	Sales	Net Income
2006	$54,905,000	-$883,000
2005	$94,055,000	$71,105,000
2004	$69,590,000	$8,195,000

Curr. Assets:	$155,213,000	**Curr. Liab.:**	$20,088,000	**P/E Ratio:**	102.00
Plant, Equip.:	$4,740,000	**Total Liab.:**	$20,732,000	**Indic. Yr. Divd.:**	NA
Total Assets:	$219,313,000	**Net Worth:**	$198,581,000	**Debt/ Equity:**	NA

Dittybase Technologies Inc

31 Bastion Sq., Ste 102, Victoria, BC, V8W 1J1; ***PH:*** 1-250-381-8780; ***Fax:*** 1-250-384-6761; ***http://*** www.dittybase.com; ***Email:*** investor@dittybase.com

General - Incorporation .... AB
Employees .... NA
Auditor .... Amisano Hanson
Stk Agt .... Pacific Corporate Trust Co
Counsel .... NA
DUNS No. .... NA

Stock- Price on:12/24/2007 .... NA
Stock Exchange .... OTC
Ticker Symbol .... DTTY
Outstanding Shares .... NA
E.P.S. .... NA
Shareholders .... NA

Business: The group's activity is to maintain an online music library. The services provided by the group includes enabling enterprises to acquire digitized production music, managing music rights, encoding, archiving, searching, retrieving and enabling the delivery, merchandising, selling and reuse of digitized production music. The group expects to automate the process of licensing music for broadcast. The Company's music licensing application allows the user to complete the process of search, audition, download, license and cue sheet reporting for royalty reporting purposes in one sitting, all within its automated application. The group serves the entertainment and corporate media industries.

Primary SIC and add'l.: 7389

CIK No: 0001311170

Subsidiaries: Dittybase America Inc., Dittybase Inc. (Dittybase) and The Decibel Collective Inc

Officers: Tim Daniels/Dir., Pres., Lance Landiak/Dir., VP - Business Development, Mike Knutsen/VP - Product Management, Blake Fallis/VP - Investor Relations, Duane Miller/VP - Operations, Amisano Hanson/Auditor

Directors: Tim Daniels/Dir., Pres., Lance Landiak/Dir., VP - Business Development, Bruce Urquhart/Dir.

Owners: Tim Daniels/4.10%, Duane Miller/2.80%, Lance Landiak/6.60%, Jason Stevenson/4.70%, Blake Fallis/8.10%, Bruce Urquhart, Blake Fallis/7.20%, Mike Knutsen/6.60%

Curr. Assets:	$85,000	**Curr. Liab.:**	$1,214,000		
Plant, Equip.:	$16,000	**Total Liab.:**	$1,214,000	**Indic. Yr. Divd.:**	NA
Total Assets:	$126,000	**Net Worth:**	-$1,089,000	**Debt/ Equity:**	NA

Diversified Corporate Resources Inc

12801 N Central Expressway, Ste 600, Dallas, TX, 75231; ***PH:*** 1-972-458-8500; ***Fax:*** 1-866-280-8911; ***http://*** www.dcri.net; ***Email:*** investors@dcri.net

General - Incorporation .... TX
Employees 149
Auditor .... Pender Newkirk & Co
Stk Agt .... Computershare Trust Co
Counsel .... Jenkens & Gilchrist
DUNS No. 08-931-7648

Stock- Price on:12/24/2007 .... $0.035
Stock Exchange .... OTC
Ticker Symbol .... HIRD
Outstanding Shares 5,270,000
E.P.S. .... -$0.987
Shareholders .... NA

Business: The group's principle activities are to provide professional and technical personnel on a permanent, temporary and contract placement basis to high and niche employment markets. The group's revenues are generated primarily from placements made in the information technology and telecommunication markets. The group also fills other high value-added employment positions in the engineering or technical, accounting or finance, professional or technical and administrative or human resources sales disciplines. The group provides professional and technical personnel to several Fortune 500 companies. Provides staffing solutions in specific professional and technical skill area.

Primary SIC and add'l.: 7361 7363

CIK No: 0000779226

Subsidiaries: Alpine Overland & Wireless Company, Alpine Overland & Wireless Ltd., Datatek Group Corporation, Geier Assessment and Performance Systems, Inc., Information Systems Consulting Corporation, MAGIC Northeast, Inc., Management Alliance Corporation, Management Alliance Group of Independent Consultants, Inc., Mountain Services, Inc., Preferred Funding Corporation, Searchnet International, Inc., Texcel Services, Inc., Train International, Inc.

Financial Data: ***Fiscal Year End:***12/31 ***Latest Annual Data:*** 12/31/2005

Year	Sales	Net Income
2005	$36,648,000	-$4,954,000
2004	$23,264,000	-$6,462,000
2002	$51,828,000	-$5,971,000

Curr. Assets:	$4,371,000	**Curr. Liab.:**	$17,748,000		
Plant, Equip.:	$178,000	**Total Liab.:**	$18,245,000	**Indic. Yr. Divd.:**	NA
Total Assets:	$12,336,000	**Net Worth:**	-$5,909,000	**Debt/ Equity:**	NA

Diversified Financial Resources Corp

Fu Xi Technology Industry Pk., Nan Feng County, Jiang Xi Province; ***PH:*** 86-9549-759601; ***http://*** www.dfrcorp.com

General - Incorporation .... DE
Employees .... NA
Auditor ... Zhong Yi (hong Kong) C.P.A. Co. Ltd.
Stk Agt ..... American Stock Transfer & Trust Co.
Counsel .... NA
DUNS No. 80-620-9011

Stock- Price on:12/24/2007 .... $0.22
Stock Exchange .... NA
Ticker Symbol .... NA
Outstanding Shares .... NA
E.P.S. .... NA
Shareholders .... NA

Business: The group's principal activities are to acquire, manage, lease and sale of real estate through its subsidiaries. On 08-Jul-2003, acquired 100% controlling interest in wichita development corp. During the year the group acquired mt&c and impact beverages inc in 2004.

Primary SIC and add'l.: 7319 6552 7372 7375

CIK No: 0001029802

Subsidiaries: Coal Slurry Impoundment, Diversified Holdings XIX, Inc, eLocity, Inc, International Natural Resources Corp, mining operation holding company, MT&C Diversified Land, Natural Resources Corp., real-estate holding company, Value Plus Marketing, Wichita Development Corporation, Wichita Properties Corporation

Officers: Xiao Yun Huang/38/CFO

Directors: Li Li Zhao/35/Dir.

Owners: Huang Xiao Yun, Chen Quan Long/100.00%, Insiders/100.00%, Chen Quan Long/2.00%, Insiders/2.00%, Chen Quan Long/100.00%, Zhao Li Li, Insiders/100.00%

Financial Data: ***Fiscal Year End:***12/31 ***Latest Annual Data:*** 12/31/2006

Year	Sales	Net Income
2006	$1,243,000	-$792,000
2005	NA	-$374,000
2004	$61,000	-$5,928,000

Curr. Assets:	$912,000	Curr. Liab.:	$196,000		
Plant, Equip.:	$518,000	Total Liab.:	$1,191,000	Indic. Yr. Divd.:	NA
Total Assets:	$1,429,000	Net Worth:	$238,000	Debt/ Equity:	NA

Diversified Product Inspections Inc

1059 E Tri-County Blvd, Oliver Springs, TN, 37840; *PH:* 1-865-482-8480; *Fax:* 1-865-482-8477; *http://* www.dpi-inc.com; *Email:* marketing@dpi-inc.com

General - Incorporation..............................FL	Stock - Price on:12/24/2007 ....$0.041
Employees 30	Stock Exchange..OTC
Auditor ....Coulter & Justus, P.C	Ticker Symbol...DPRI
Stk Agt..........Interwest Transfer Company, Inc.	Outstanding Shares 20,180,000
Counsel...NA	E.P.S...$0.00
DUNS No. ....NA	Shareholders...NA

Business: The group's principle activity is to conduct investigations and laboratory analysis for various products to determine the cause and origin of product failures. Its primary customers consist of national insurance companies that are interested in subrogating claims to recover losses. The group has a large database of known defective products that includes photos and other documentation that are used in investigations. Additionally, the group provides for the storage of evidence and derives revenue from the secure storage of materials. For consumers, the group provides a service called homechecksafety.com. This helps the consumer to identify and remove recalled products from their home. The group also publishes a monthly newsletter that appears on its Website. Each newsletter features a particular hazard or defective product reports or official product recall notices.

Primary SIC and add'l.: 4226 8734 7375

CIK No: 0001079297

Subsidiaries: Diversified Product Investigations, Inc.

Owners: John Van Zyll, EIG Venture Capital Ltd., Insiders, EIG Capital, Ltd., Marvin Stacy, Ann M. Furlong, Warren Wankelman, Jan Telander, Matt Walters

Financial Data: *Fiscal Year End:*12/31   *Latest Annual Data:* 12/31/2006

Year	Sales	Net Income
2006	$2,288,000	$67,000
2005	$1,928,000	-$95,000
2004	$2,094,000	$28,000

Curr. Assets:	$691,000	Curr. Liab.:	$263,000		
Plant, Equip.:	$989,000	Total Liab.:	$1,009,000	Indic. Yr. Divd.:	NA
Total Assets:	$2,018,000	Net Worth:	$1,009,000	Debt/ Equity:	0.6989

Diversified Thermal Solutions Inc

4126 Delp St., Ste. 200, Memphis, TN, 38118; *PH:* 1-901-365-6632 ; *Fax:* 1-901-365-9617; *http://* www.dthermal.com; *Email:* productdata@ris-group.com

General - Incorporation................................NV	Stock - Price on:12/24/2007 ....$0.11
Employees 80	Stock Exchange..OTC
Auditor ....Coulter & Justus, P.C	Ticker Symbol..DVTS
Stk Agt..........................Alexis Stock Transfer	Outstanding Shares 18,830,000
Counsel...NA	E.P.S...$0.09
DUNS No. ....NA	Shareholders...NA

Business: The group's principal activity is to acquire businesses related to the manufacturing and distribution of materials used in the refractory industry. The group intends to operate as a manufacturer of specialized brick in the refractory industry.

Primary SIC and add'l.: 3251

CIK No: 0001096835

Subsidiaries: Mt. Savage Firebrick Company, Refractory & Industrial Supply Group, Inc.

Officers: Grant B. Hunter/44/Dir., CEO, John F. Curry/Dir., Sec. Treasurer, VP - Operations, Terry J. Medovitch/56/CFO

Directors: Grant B. Hunter/44/Dir., CEO, Jerry W. Hunter/Dir., Ed H. Gatlin/Dir., Burley W. Shedd/Dir., John F. Curry/Dir., Sec. Treasurer, VP - Operations, D. Michael Hartley/70/Dir.

Owners: Jerry W. Hunter/4.00%, Grant B. Hunter/39.00%, Insiders/63.00%, Terry J. Medovitch, Ed Gatlin, John F. Curry/20.00%

Financial Data: *Fiscal Year End:*12/31   *Latest Annual Data:* 12/31/2006

Year	Sales	Net Income
2006	$10,309,000	$1,328,000
2005	$8,734,000	-$176,000
2004	$107,000	-$554,000

Curr. Assets:	$3,979,000	Curr. Liab.:	$2,998,000	P/E Ratio:	1.83
Plant, Equip.:	$1,768,000	Total Liab.:	$5,104,000	Indic. Yr. Divd.:	NA
Total Assets:	$5,747,000	Net Worth:	$644,000	Debt/ Equity:	3.3509

Diversinet Corp

2235 Sheppard Ave. E., Ste. 1700, Toronto, ON, M2J 5B5; *PH:* 1-416-756-2324; *http://* www.dvnet.com; *Email:* info@diversinet.com

General - Incorporation......................Canada	Stock - Price on:12/24/2007 ....$0.83
Employees ....NA	Stock Exchange..OTC
Auditor ....KPMG LLP	Ticker Symbol..DVNTF
Stk Agt.....Computershare Investor Services LLC	Outstanding Shares ....NA
Counsel..........................McCarthy Ttrault LLP	E.P.S...$0.85
DUNS No. 25-220-9929	Shareholders...NA

Business: The group's principal activity is to develop, market and distribute public key infrastructure security solutions for the secure transmission of data over wireless networks and devices. The group's digital certificates provide a secure electronic link between an individual and an organization. Security infrastructure solutions enable mobile e-commerce services, delivering end-to-end wireless security to wireless device makers, asp's and operators, application software developers and network infrastructure providers. On 18-Dec-2002, the group acquired dss software technologies.

Primary SIC and add'l.: 7372

CIK No: 0000918387

Subsidiaries: Caradas, Inc.

Officers: Nagy Moustafa/45/Dir., CEO, Jay Couse/Sr. VP - Business Development, Stuart Vaeth/Chief Security Officer, David B. Annan/CTO, David Hackett/43/CFO

Directors: Nagy Moustafa/45/Dir., CEO, Albert Wahbe/Chmn., Khalil E. Barsoum/Chmn. - Advisory Board, William Reed/Dir., Mark Steinman/61/Dir., Ravi Chiruvolu/Dir., James B. Wigdale/Dir., Taher Elgamal/Member - Advisory Board, Gregory Milavsky/Dir., Philippe Tardif/Dir.

Owners: Insiders/41.60%, David Hackett/1.40%, Albert Wahbe/24.20%, Mark Steinman/1.00%, Lakefront Partners, LLC/16.10%, Nagy Moustafa/3.20%

Financial Data: *Fiscal Year End:*12/31   *Latest Annual Data:* 12/31/2006

Year	Sales	Net Income
2006	$1,667,000	-$3,451,000
2005	$1,101,000	-$6,670,000
2004	$7,045,000	-$6,939,000

Curr. Assets:	$5,442,000	Curr. Liab.:	$1,745,000		
Plant, Equip.:	$389,000	Total Liab.:	$1,745,000	Indic. Yr. Divd.:	NA
Total Assets:	$5,855,000	Net Worth:	$4,111,000	Debt/ Equity:	NA

DivX Inc

4780 Eastgate Mall, San Diego, CA, 92121; *PH:* 1-858-882-0600; *Fax:* 1-858-882-0601; *http://* www.divx.com

General - Incorporation .... DE	Stock - Price on:12/24/2007 ....$15.69
Employees 258	Stock Exchange..NDQ
Auditor ....Ernst & Young, LLP	Ticker Symbol..DIVX
Stk Agt......American Stock Transfer & Trust Co.	Outstanding Shares 33,950,000
Counsel...NA	E.P.S...$0.37
DUNS No. ....NA	Shareholders...NA

Business: The groups principle activity is to provide products and services designed to media. The products of the group include DivX community codec, DivX Player, DivX for Windows bundle and DivX Pro video codec. The group products sold under the trade name DivX. In March 2006 the group acquired Corporate Green. Customers served by the group include content consumers, advertisers, digital media software vendors and content creators. The group operates from North America, Europe and Asia. The group's quarterly revenue for September 2007 was 21.89 millions of USD.

Primary SIC and add'l.: 7819 7372

CIK No: 0001342960

Subsidiaries: DivX International, Inc., DivXNetworks (Europe) GmbH

Officers: Kevin Hell/CEO, John Tanner/CFO - Finance, Administration, David Richter/Exec. VP - Corporate Development, Legal, Chris Russell/CTO, Tay Nguyen/Co - Founder, Dir. - Product Development, John Villasenor/Advisor, James Lee/Advisor, Dan Halvorson/CFO, Exec. VP, Johnny Chen/General Counsel, Trevor Renfield/Treasurer, Sr. Dir. - Finance, Patrice Lagrange/VP, Group Business Mgr. - Media Languages, Pamela Thompson Johnston/Sr. VP - Sales, Marketing, Karen Fisher/VP - Investor Relations, Compliance, Jerome Rota/VP, Group Business Mgr. - Media Experience

Directors: Jordan Greenhall/Co - Founder, Chmn., Darrius Thompson/Co - Founder, Joe Bezdek/Co - Founder, Jerome Vashisht-Rota/Co - Founder, Dir., Tay Nguyen/Co - Founder, Dir. - Product Development, Frank M. Creer/Dir., Fred Gerson/Dir., Jerry Murdock/Dir., Christopher McGurk/Dir.

Owners: Chris Russell, Zone Venture Fund and its affiliates/20.70%, John A. Tanner, David J. Richter, Jordan R. Greenhall/8.40%, Insiders/32.80%, Christopher McGurk, Kevin Hell/1.40%, Insight Holdings and its affiliates/6.80%, Jrme J-P. Vashisht-Rota/1.00%, Frank Creer/13.10%, WI Harper Group and its affiliates/8.60%, Fred Gerson, Jerry Murdock/6.80%

Financial Data: *Fiscal Year End:*12/31   *Latest Annual Data:* 12/31/2006

Year	Sales	Net Income
2006	$59,325,000	$16,440,000
2005	$33,047,000	$2,295,000
2004	$16,351,000	-$4,343,000

Curr. Assets:	$158,821,000	Curr. Liab.:	$11,802,000		
Plant, Equip.:	$3,488,000	Total Liab.:	$13,475,000	Indic. Yr. Divd.:	NA
Total Assets:	$164,386,000	Net Worth:	$150,911,000	Debt/ Equity:	0.0004

Dixie Group Inc

104 Nowlin Ln., Ste. 101, Chattanooga, TN, 37421; *PH:* 1-423-510-7000; *Fax:* 1-706-876-5896; *http://* www.thedixiegroup.com; *Email:* info@thedixiegroup.com

General - Incorporation .... TN	Stock - Price on:12/24/2007 ....$12.69
Employees 1,500	Stock Exchange..NDQ
Auditor ....Ernst & Young LLP	Ticker Symbol..DXYN
Stk Agt....Computershare Investor Services LLC	Outstanding Shares 13,090,000
Counsel.....Shumacker, Witt, Gaither & Whitaker	E.P.S...$0.66
DUNS No. 00-333-0016	Shareholders...NA

Business: The group's principal activities are to manufacture, sell and distribute products to the soft floorcovering industry. The group operates through two segments: carpet manufacturing (floorcovering products) and floorcovering base materials (carpet yarns). Floorcovering products operations supply carpet and rugs to high-end residential and high-end commercial customers through fabrica international, masland carpets and dixie home brands. The carpet yarn operations produce a variety of filament and spun yarns for internal needs and external customers through candlewick yarns. The group operates only in the United States.the group sold a spun yarn production facility on jan-2004.

Primary SIC and add'l.: 2273

CIK No: 0000029332

Subsidiaries: Bretlin, Inc., C-knit Apparel, Inc., Candlewick Yarns, Inc., Dixie Group Logistics, Inc., Fabrica International, Masland Carpets, LLC

Officers: Daniel K. Frierson/Chmn., CEO/$965,319.00, Eugene D. Lasater/Controller, David E. Polley/VP - Marketing, Pres. - Dixie Home/$336,168.00, Craig S. Lapeere/VP, Pres. - Fabrica International/$382,010.00, Gary A. Harmon/CFO, VP/$352,428.00, Jon A. Faulkner/VP - Planning, Development, Starr T. Klein/Sec., Derek W. Davis/VP - Human Resources, Kenneth L. Dempsey/VP, Pres. - Masland Commercial/$339,340.00, Kennedy D. Frierson/VP, Pres. - Masland Residential, Wayne D. Pattillo/VP - Manufacturing

Directors: Daniel K. Frierson/Chmn., CEO, Paul K. Frierson/Dir., Don J. Brock/Dir., Lowry F. Kline/Dir., John W. Murrey/Dir., Walter W. Hubbard/Dir.

Owners: Wachovia Corporation/6.57%, Daniel K. Frierson, Don J. Brock, Van Den Berg Management/15.34%, RGM Capital, LLC/7.78%, Insiders, John W. Murrey, Kenneth L. Dempsey, Paul K. Frierson, Daniel K. Frierson/6.67%, Dimensional Fund Advisors, L.P./8.45%, Wellington Management Company, LLP/5.17%, T. Rowe Price Associates, Inc/9.68%, Walter W. Hubbard, Insiders/13.24% (20 Owners included in Index)

Financial Data: Fiscal Year End:12/31 **Latest Annual Data:** 12/30/2006

Year	Sales	Net Income
2006	$331,100,000	$7,703,000
2005	$318,526,000	$10,136,000
2004	$291,971,000	$12,315,000

Curr. Assets:	$115,081,000	Curr. Liab.:	$39,565,000	P/E Ratio:	23.50
Plant, Equip.:	$92,948,000	Total Liab.:	$153,519,000	Indic. Yr. Divd.:	NA
Total Assets:	$277,003,000	Net Worth:	$123,484,000	Debt/ Equity:	0.6079

DJO Incorporated

Formerly: dj Orthopedics Inc
1430 Decision St., Vista, CA, 92081; **PH:** 1-800-336-5690; **http://** www.djortho.com

General - Incorporation	DE	Stock- Price on:12/24/2007	$39.73
Employees	3,000	Stock Exchange	NA
Auditor	Ernst& Young LLP	Ticker Symbol	NA
Stk Agt	American Stock Transfer & Trust Co.	Outstanding Shares	23,560,000
Counsel	NA	E.P.S.	$0.54
DUNS No.	NA	Shareholders	NA

Business: The groups principle activity is to provide solutions for muschuloskeletal and vascular health. In the year 2006, the group acquired Aircast Incorporated. The group operates from the United States.

Primary SIC and add'l.: 3845 3842

CIK No: 0001157972

Subsidiaries: Aircast Asia-Pacific Ltd., Aircast Belgium SPRL, Aircast Europe GmbH, Aircast France SARL, Aircast Handels GmbH, Aircast Holding Company LLC, Aircast Incorporated, Aircast Italia S.r.l., Aircast LLC, Aircast Productos Medicos SL, Aircast Scandinavia, AB, Aircast UK Limited, DJ Orthopedics Capital Corporation, DJ Orthopedics de Mexico S.A. de C.V., DJ Orthopedics Development Corporation 25 Subsidiaries included in the Index

Officers: Leslie H. Cross/Dir., CEO, Pres./$1,407,890.00, Vickie L. Capps/CFO, Exec. VP/$830,007.00, Luke T. Faulstick/COO/$774,653.00, Donald M. Roberts/Sr. VP, General Counsel, Sec./$724,496.00, Louis T. Ruggiero/Chief Sales, Marketing Officer/$753,751.00

Directors: Leslie H. Cross/Dir., CEO, Pres., Jack R. Blair/Chmn., Mitchell J. Blutt/Dir., Kirby L. Cramer/Dir., Lesley H. Howe/Dir., Charles T. Orsatti/Dir., Lewis Parker/Dir., Thomas W. Mitchell/Dir.

Owners: FMR Corp./14.70%, Charles T. Orsatti, Luke T. Faulstick, Vickie L. Capps, BlackRock,Inc./7.80%, Leslie H. Cross, Kirby L. Cramer, Lewis Parker, Mitchell J. Blutt, Lesley H. Howe, Jack R. Blair, Thomas W. Mitchell, Donald M. Roberts, Louis T. Ruggiero, Insiders/3.50% (16 Owners included in Index)

Financial Data: Fiscal Year End:12/31 **Latest Annual Data:** 12/31/2006

Year	Sales	Net Income
2006	$413,058,000	$12,641,000
2005	$286,167,000	$29,198,000
2004	$255,999,000	$14,015,000

Curr. Assets:	$169,774,000	Curr. Liab.:	$67,162,000	P/E Ratio:	49.97
Plant, Equip.:	$32,699,000	Total Liab.:	$398,065,000	Indic. Yr. Divd.:	NA
Total Assets:	$668,334,000	Net Worth:	$270,269,000	Debt/ Equity:	NA

DNAPrint Genomics Inc

1621 W University Pkwy., Sarasota, FL, 34243; **PH:** 1-941-366-3400; **Fax:** 1-941-952-9770; **http://** www.dnaprint.com; **Email:** info@dnaprint.com

General - Incorporation	UT	Stock- Price on:12/24/2007	$0.0072
Employees	24	Stock Exchange	OTC
Auditor	Pender Newkirk & Company LLP	Ticker Symbol	DNAG
Stk Agt	Standard Registrar & Transfer Co Inc.	Outstanding Shares	537,930,000
Counsel	NA	E.P.S.	-$0.009
DUNS No.	NA	Shareholders	NA

Business: The groups principle activities include developing and marketing of innovative genetic testing products and services. The group products include AncestryByDNA (TM), DNAWitness (TM) 2.5, Retinome (TM), and DNAWitness-Y(TM). The group operates from the United States.

Primary SIC and add'l.: 7374 8731 2835 8734

CIK No: 0001127354

Subsidiaries: DNAPrint Genomics, Inc., DNAPrint Pharmaceuticals, Inc., Ellipsis Biotherapeutics Corporation, Kenna Technologies, Inc., Trace Genetics, Inc.

Officers: Richard Gabriel/Dir., CEO, Pres./$265,202.00, Hector J. Gomez/Chmn., Chief Medical Officer/$270,064.00, Tony Frudakis/Dir., Founder, Chief Scientific Officer/$212,203.00, Karen Surplus/CFO/$76,822.00, Mark Shriver/Scientific Advisor

Directors: Richard Gabriel/Dir., CEO, Pres., Hector J. Gomez/Chmn., Chief Medical Officer, Tony Frudakis/Dir., Founder, Chief Scientific Officer

Owners: Hector Gomez/3.63%, Insiders/10.97%, Tony Frudakis/3.93%, Richard Gabriel/4.18%

Financial Data: Fiscal Year End:12/31 **Latest Annual Data:** 12/31/2006

Year	Sales	Net Income
2006	$2,433,000	-$12,348,000
2005	$1,276,000	-$8,716,000
2004	$786,000	-$3,735,000

Curr. Assets:	$8,783,000	Curr. Liab.:	$13,774,000		
Plant, Equip.:	$1,238,000	Total Liab.:	$13,980,000	Indic. Yr. Divd.:	NA
Total Assets:	$10,270,000	Net Worth:	-$3,711,000	Debt/ Equity:	NA

DNB Financial Corp

4 Brandywine Ave., Downingtown, PA, 19335; **PH:** 1-610-269-1040; **Fax:** 1-610-873-5298; **http://** www.dnb4you.com

General - Incorporation	PA	Stock- Price on:12/24/2007	$19.75
Employees	121	Stock Exchange	OTC
Auditor	KPMG LLP	Ticker Symbol	DNBF
Stk Agt	Registrar & Transfer Co	Outstanding Shares	2,500,000
Counsel...	Stradley Ronon Stevens & Young LLP	E.P.S.	$0.72
DUNS No.	00-791-0516	Shareholders	NA

Business: The group's principal activity is to provide various banking services to individual customers and small to medium sized businesses. The group accepts interest and non-interest bearing deposits, money market, savings, certificate of deposits and ira deposits. The group also provides residential mortgage, commercial mortgage, commercial and consumer loans. The group provides various insurance and trust services to its customers. The group has nine full service branches in chester county and Pennsylvania.

Primary SIC and add'l.: 6021 6712

CIK No: 0000713671

Subsidiaries: DNB Capital Trust I, DNB Capital Trust II, DNB Financial Services, DNB First, National Association, DOWNCO, Inc.

Officers: William S. Latoff/Chmn., CEO/$508,912.00, William Hieb/COO, Pres./$225,136.00, Thomas Cozza/Sr. VP - Commercial Lending, Gerald F. Sopp/CFO, Exec. VP, Tomlinson C. Kline/Sr. VP, Sr. Credit Officer/$138,158.00, R. M. Mincarelli/Sr. VP - Commercial Real Estate, Albert J. Melfi/Exec. VP, Chief Lending Officer/$45,099.00, Charles S. Moore/Sr. VP - Commercial Lending, Ronald K. Dankanich/Exec. VP - Operations, Information Technology, Human Resources/$159,722.00, Bruce E. Moroney/Exec. VP/$151,612.00, Richard J. Hartmann/Exec. VP - Retail Banking, Marketing/$133,958.00

Directors: William S. Latoff/Chmn., CEO, James H. Thornton/Vice Chmn., Mildred C. Joyner/Dir., James J. Koegel/Dir., Eli Silberman/Dir., Thomas A. Fillippo/Dir., Ellis Y. Brown/Dir. Emeritus, Robert J. Charles/Dir. Emeritus, Newton I. Evans/Dir. Emeritus, Vernon J. Jameson/Dir. Emeritus, Ilario S. Polite/Dir. Emeritus, Thomas R. Greenleaf/Dir. Emeritus, Henry Thorne/Dir. Emeritus

Owners: William J. Hieb/1.19%, Albert J. Melfi/0.01%, James J. Koegel/1.33%, Thomas A. Fillippo/0.52%, Tomlinson C. Kline, Insiders/14.80%, Richard J. Hartmann/0.07%, DNB First 401(k) Plan/1.42%, Mildred C. Joyner/0.28%, James H. Thornton/0.99%, Ronald K. Dankanich/1.18%, William S. Latoff/6.32%, Eli Silberman/0.51%, Bruce E. Moroney/1.08%, Thomas M. Miller/1.01% (16 Owners included in Index)

Financial Data: Fiscal Year End:12/31 **Latest Annual Data:** 12/31/2006

Year	Sales	Net Income
2006	$31,663,000	$1,747,000
2005	$26,445,000	$2,148,000
2004	$23,189,000	$298,000

Curr. Assets:	$26,647,000	Curr. Liab.:	$482,658,000	P/E Ratio:	27.43
Plant, Equip.:	$7,699,000	Total Liab.:	$493,831,000	Indic. Yr. Divd.:	$0.520
Total Assets:	$525,242,000	Net Worth:	$31,411,000	Debt/ Equity:	NA

DND Technologies Inc

375 E Elliot Rd., Bldg. 6, Chandler, AZ, 85225; **PH:** 1-480-892-7020; **Fax:** 1-480-892-8044; **http://** www.aspectsys.com

General - Incorporation	NV	Stock- Price on:12/24/2007	NA
Employees	62	Stock Exchange	OTC
Auditor	Farber Hass Hurley & Mcewen LLP	Ticker Symbol	DNDT
Stk Agt	Interwest Transfer Company, Inc.	Outstanding Shares	NA
Counsel	NA	E.P.S.	-$0.062
DUNS No.	NA	Shareholders	NA

Business: The group's principal activity is to operate as a holding company for aspect systems inc. The group's subsidiary manufactures, assembles, markets and services semiconductor wafer fabrication equipment for the worldwide semiconductor industry. The group's products include semiconductor wafer manufacturers and semiconductor integrated circuit or chip manufacturers, which either use the chips they manufacture in their own products or sell them to other companies for use in advanced electronic components. The group's nitrogen clean system provides cleaning of wafer fabrication equipment. The group's customers include intel, Texas instruments, st micro, motorola, national semiconductor, and on-semi.

Primary SIC and add'l.: 2834 8099

CIK No: 0001118344

Subsidiaries: ASI Team Asia Ltd., Aspect Semiquip International, Inc.

Officers: Douglas N. Dixon/65/Chmn., CEO, Pres., Ronny Baker/62/Controller, Dennis G. Key/65/Dir., CFO, Sec., Aki Nagatoishi/Dir. - Aspect Systems inc

Directors: Douglas N. Dixon/65/Chmn., CEO, Pres., Ernie L. Recsetar/Dir., Dennis G. Key/65/Dir., CFO, Sec., Lowell Giffhorn/61/Dir.

Owners: Lowell Giffhorn/2.50%, Insiders/62.30%, Douglas Dixon/54.60%, Ronny Baker, G. Dennis Key/22.70%

Financial Data: Fiscal Year End:12/31 **Latest Annual Data:** 12/31/2006

Year	Sales	Net Income
2006	$7,091,000	-$1,893,000
2005	$13,754,000	-$4,560,000
2004	$15,800,000	$1,235,000

Curr. Assets:	-$684,000	Curr. Liab.:	$158,000		
Plant, Equip.:	$0	Total Liab.:	$169,000	Indic. Yr. Divd.:	NA
Total Assets:	-$394,000	Net Worth:	$1,584,164,000	Debt/ Equity:	NA

Doane Pet Care Co

210 Westwood Pl S, Brentwood, TN, 37027; **PH:** 1-615-373-7774; **Fax:** 1-615-309-1189; **http://** www.doanepetcare.com

General - Incorporation	DE	Stock- Price on:12/24/2007	NA
Employees	NA	Stock Exchange	NA
Auditor	KPMG LLP	Ticker Symbol	NA
Stk Agt	NA	Outstanding Shares	NA
Counsel	Vinson & Elkins LLP	E.P.S.	NA
DUNS No.	00-713-4919	Shareholders	NA

Business: The group's principal activity is to manufacture pet food products for dogs and cats. Products of the group include dry, wet, semi-moist, soft dry, soft treats and biscuits. The group also operates a machine shop and a structural steel fabrication plant that sells to third parties and supports the group's facilities. The products are manufactured for store brands owned by retail customers, also known as private labels. The products are also manufactured under contract for national branded pet food

companies and produced and sold under regional brands owned by the group. The group's customers include store brand customers such as mass merchandisers, pet specialty stores, grocery chains and farm and feed stores. The group has over 600 customers including wal-Mart and costco and operates in the United States, Spain, Denmark and the United Kingdom.

Primary SIC and add'l.: 8711 2047

CIK No: 0001002211

Subsidiaries: A/S Arovit Pet Food, Arovit Petfood Benelux B.V., Arovit Petfood Deutschland G.m.b.H., Arovit Petfood Italia S.R.L., Arovit Petfood UK Ltd., Carat Tiernahrungsgesellschaft m.b.H., Doane International Pet Products LLC, Doane Management Corp., Doane Pet Care (Europe) ApS, Doane Pet Care (UK)Limited, Doane/Windy Hill Joint Venture LLC, DPC International Limited, DPC Investment Corp, Effeffe S.p.A., Ipes Iberica, S.A. 16 Subsidiaries included in the Index

Officers: Douglas J. Cahill/Dir., CEO, Pres., Joseph J. Meyers/VP - Supply Chain, Philip K. Woodlief/VP - Finance, CFO, Richard A. Hannasch/VP - Co - Manufacturing - Specialty, David L. Horton/VP, GM - North American Operations

Directors: Douglas J. Cahill/Dir., CEO, Pres., George B. Kelly/Chmn., Stephen C. Sherrill/Dir., Paul E. Suckow/Dir., Lawrence S. Benjamin/Dir., Jerry W. Finney/Dir., Terry R. Peets/Dir., Mathew J. Lori/Dir., Edward H. D'Alelio/Dir., Jeffrey C. Walker/Dir.

Dobson Communications Corp

14201 Wireless Way, Oklahoma City, OK, 73134; ***PH:*** 1-405-529-8500; ***Fax:*** 1-405-529-8515; ***http://*** www.netidentity.com

General - Incorporation	OK	***Stock***- Price on:12/24/2007	$10.16
Employees	2,500	Stock Exchange	NDQ
Auditor	KPMG LLP	Ticker Symbol	DCEL
Stk Agt	Countersigned and Registered UMB Bank	Outstanding Shares	171,340,000
Counsel	McAfee & Taft	E.P.S	$0.06
DUNS No.	NA	Shareholders	NA

Business: The group's principal activity is to provide wireless communication service to rural and suburban in the United States. The group offers digital voice and digital feature services to customers through time division multiple access (tdma) and digital network. The group is in the process of updating digital network to global system for mobile communications (gsm), general packet radio service (gprs) and enhanced data for gsm evolution (edge) technology for subscribers and roaming partners. The group provides services in Alaska, Arizona, Illinois, Kentucky, Kansas, Maryland, Michigan, Minnesota, Missouri, New York, Ohio, Oklahoma, Pennsylvania, Texas, west Virginia and Wisconsin. During the year 2003, the group acquired assets of npi-omnipoint wireless llc, acc escrow corp and American cellular corporation.

Primary SIC and add'l.: 4812 4813

CIK No: 0001035985

Subsidiaries: American Cellular Corporation, Cellular One Properties, LLC, Dec Pcs, Inc., Dobson Cellular Systems Inc., Dobson Jv Company, Dobson Operating Co., LLC, Wireless Investments, Inc.

Officers: Steven P. Dussek/Dir., CEO, Pres./$1,691,000.00, Stephen T. Dobson/Dir., Sec., Bruce R. Knooihuizen/Exec. VP, Chife Financial Officer/$1,073,147.00, Timothy J. Duffy/CTO, Sr. VP/$670,499.00, Thomas R. Morgan/CIO, Sr. VP, Ronald L. Ripley/Sr. VP - Genral Counsel, Frank Franzese/Sr. VP - Sales/$1,043,888.00, Thomas A. Coates/VP - Corporate Development, Trent W. Leforce/Controller, Assist. Sec., Thomas K. Roberts/Chief Marketing Officer, Lori Engel/VP - Human Resources, Brian W. Boone/Sr. VP, Chief Service Officer

Directors: Steven P. Dussek/Dir., CEO, Pres., Everett R. Dobson/Chmn., Stephen T. Dobson/Dir., Sec., Fred J. Hall/Dir., Justin I. Jashke/Dir., Albert H. Pharis/Dir., Mark S. Feighner/Dir., Robert Schriesheim/47/Dir.

Owners: Insiders, Robert A. Schriesheim, Highbridge Capital Management, LLC/5.20%, Jennison Associates LLC/9.90%, Dobson CC Limited Partnership, Dobson CC Limited Partnership, Everett R. Dobson, Bruce R. Knooihuizen, Fred J. Hall, Steven P. Dussek, Stephen T. Dobson, Albert H. Pharis, Mark S. Feighner, TCS Capital GP, LLC/9.60%, Timothy J. Duffy *(23 Owners included in Index)*

Financial Data: ***Fiscal Year End:***12/31 ***Latest Annual Data:*** 12/31/2006

Year		***Sales***			***Net Income***
2006		$1,271,096,000			$12,781,000
2005		$1,179,462,000			-$121,610,000
2004		$1,023,482,000			-$51,621,000
Curr. Assets:	$285,681,000	***Curr. Liab.:***	$252,091,000	***P/E Ratio:***	203.20
Plant, Equip.:	$512,202,000	***Total Liab.:***	$3,296,701,000	***Indic. Yr. Divd.:***	NA
Total Assets:	$3,494,752,000	***Net Worth:***	$191,586,000	***Debt/ Equity:***	16.4617

Document Sciences Corp

5958 Priestly Dr., Carlsbad, CA, 92008; ***PH:*** 1-760-602-1400; ***Fax:*** 1-760-602-1450; ***http://*** www.docscience.com; ***Email:*** info@docscience.com

General - Incorporation	DE	***Stock***- Price on:12/24/2007	$6.5
Employees	392	Stock Exchange	NDQ
Auditor	Ernst & Young LLP	Ticker Symbol	DOCX
Stk Agt	U.S. Stock Transfer Corp	Outstanding Shares	4,420,000
Counsel	Gibson, Dunn & Crutcher LLP	E.P.S	-$0.43
DUNS No.	78-540-3411	Shareholders	NA

Business: The group's principle activity is to develop, market and support a family of document automation software used in high-volume print and transactional electronic publishing applications. The group's document automation software, the document sciences autograph family of products, enables personalized publishing solutions for many industries, including insurance, managed healthcare, financial services, commercial print outsourcing, government, telecommunications and manufacturing. The products of the group facilitate an important form of communication between organizations and their customers by employing enterprise database assets to produce high-quality, personalized documents that are ready to print on demand, e-mail or distribute over the Web using html or adobe systems' pdf technology. On 23-Jul-2004 the group acquired objectiva software solutions inc. The group operates from United States.

Primary SIC and add'l.: 7371 7372

CIK No: 0001016831

Subsidiaries: Objectiva Software Solutions, Inc.

Officers: John L. McGannon/Dir., CEO, Pres./$335,791.00, Todd Schmidt/CFO/$187,962.00, Edward Calnan/Sr. VP - Sales, Daniel J. Fregeau/Exec. VP, Tao Ye/GM - Asian Operations/$338,578.00, Douglas J. Winter/COO/$315,755.00, Nasser Barghouti/CTO/$308,357.00

Directors: John L. McGannon/Dir., CEO, Pres., Thomas L. Ringer/Chmn., Colin J. Obrien/Dir., Ronald S. Beard/Dir., Barton L. Faber/Dir., Marge Breya/Dir.

Owners: Tao Ye, Kevin C. Howe, Insiders, Todd W. Schmidt, John L. McGannon, Wedbush, Inc., Barton L. Faber, Thomas Satterfield, E. Jeffrey Peierls, Thomas L. Ringer, Margaret A. Breya, Nasser S. Barghouti, E. M. Palandri, Ronald S. Beard, Daniel Zeff *(17 Owners included in Index)*

Financial Data: ***Fiscal Year End:***12/31 ***Latest Annual Data:*** 12/31/2006

Year		***Sales***			***Net Income***
2006		$33,411,000			-$1,479,000
2005		$29,574,000			$19,000
2004		$23,346,000			$719,000
Curr. Assets:	$20,148,000	***Curr. Liab.:***	$19,912,000		
Plant, Equip.:	$725,000	***Total Liab.:***	$19,919,000	***Indic. Yr. Divd.:***	NA
Total Assets:	$26,114,000	***Net Worth:***	$6,196,000	***Debt/ Equity:***	0.0011

Document Security Systems Inc

28 E Main St., Ste. 1525, Rochester, NY, 14614; ***PH:*** 1-585-325-3610; ***Fax:*** 1-585-325-2977; ***http://*** www.documentsecurity.com

General - Incorporation	NY	***Stock***- Price on:12/24/2007	$12.25
Employees	53	Stock Exchange	AMEX
Auditor	Freed Maxick & Battaglia	Ticker Symbol	DMC
Stk Agt	American Stock Transfer & Trust Co.	Outstanding Shares	13,680,000
Counsel	NA	E.P.S	-$0.42
DUNS No.	15-149-2170	Shareholders	NA

Business: The group's principal activity is to develop, license and sell anti-counterfeiting technology and products. Its products and services are safety paper, block-out product, laser moire, software verification system and security consulting services. Safety paper product reveals hidden words, bar codes, logos and images. Block-out product prevents color copiers and photo processors from replicating any image, laser moire product which prevents desktop scanners from imaging into computers and software. Software verification system verifies the authenticity of currency and critical documents. Security consulting services which provides services like designing, labeling and packaging critical documents. Its new trading symbol on the over-the-counter bulletin board is dcss.

Primary SIC and add'l.: 2759 7812

CIK No: 0000771999

Subsidiaries: Document Security Consultants, Inc, Lester Levin, Inc., Plastic Printing Professionals, Inc., Secured Document Systems, Inc, Thomas M. Wicker Enterprises, Inc

Officers: Patrick White/Chmn., CEO/$204,891.00, Michael S. Caton/VP - Research, Development, Emerging Technologies, Lori Frederick/International Business Development Dir., Thomas Wicker/Dir., CTO, Philip Jones/VP - Finance, Treasurer/$101,840.00, David M. Wicker/VP - Operations, Technology, Cherrie Mahon/Investor Relations, Earle L. Ingalls/VP - Marketing, Sales, Philip Sinopoli/Exec. VP - Sales, Peter Ettinger/Pres./$283,228.00, Michael T. Hughes/Sr. VP - Business Development, General Counsel, Terry Carlisano/VP - Sales, Ken Wicker/VP - Emerging Technology, Robin Pedace/Dir. - Marketing, Public Relations

Directors: Patrick White/Chmn., CEO, Alan Harrison/Dir., Timothy Ashman/Dir., Thomas Wicker/Dir., CTO, Robert B. Fagenson/Dir., Ira A. Greenstein/Dir.

Owners: Ira A. Greenstein/1.00%, Philip Jones/1.00%, Vera Neuman/7.30%, Timothy Ashman/1.00%, Insiders/18.10%, Charles M. LaLoggia/11.40%, Patrick White/6.00%, Peter Ettinger/2.80%, Martin Vegh/7.30%, Alan E. Harrison/1.00%, Thomas M. Wicker/1.50%, Robert B. Fagenson/7.40%

Financial Data: ***Fiscal Year End:***12/31 ***Latest Annual Data:*** 12/31/2006

Year		***Sales***			***Net Income***
2006		$4,834,000			-$4,832,000
2005		$1,750,000			-$2,843,000
2004		$1,595,000			-$1,704,000
Curr. Assets:	$6,885,000	***Curr. Liab.:***	$2,760,000		
Plant, Equip.:	$638,000	***Total Liab.:***	$3,277,000	***Indic. Yr. Divd.:***	NA
Total Assets:	$14,466,000	***Net Worth:***	$11,189,000	***Debt/ Equity:***	0.0038

Dolby Laboratories Inc

100 Potrero Ave., San Francisco, CA, 94103; ***PH:*** 1-415-558-0200; ***Fax:*** 1-415-863-1373; ***http://*** www.dolby.com

General - Incorporation	DE	***Stock***- Price on:12/24/2007	$31.37
Employees	864	Stock Exchange	NYSE
Auditor	KPMG LLP	Ticker Symbol	DLB
Stk Agt	EquiServe Trust Co N.A	Outstanding Shares	109,560,000
Counsel	NA	E.P.S	$1.26
DUNS No.	NA	Shareholders	NA

Business: The groups principle activities include designing manufacturing, developing and delivering audio products and technologies, music, video game and motion pictures. The groups products include DVD players, set top boxes and TV. The group operates through two segments namely, technology licensing, and products and production services. The group operates from the United States, Japan, China, Taiwan and Europe.

Primary SIC and add'l.: 3663

CIK No: 0001308547

Subsidiaries: Dolby Laboratories Licensing Corporation, Dolby Laboratories, Inc.

Officers: N. W. Jasper/Dir., CEO, Pres., Ray Dolby/Chmn., Founder, Masaaki Fushiki/VP - Japan, David Gray/VP - Worldwide Production Services, Jeff Griffith/VP - Manufacturing, US, John Iles/VP - Cinema, Steve Jacobs/VP - Engineering, Professional Products, Francois Modarresse/VP - Marketing, Bruce Nottage/VP - Finance UK, Robert Schumann/GM, Peter Seagger/VP - International Sales, Cinema, Tony Spath/VP - International Sales, Broadcast, Craig Todd/CTO, Sr. VP, Sherie Berger/VP - Human Resources, John Carey/VP - Marketing *(29 Officers included in Index)*

Directors: N. W. Jasper/Dir., CEO, Pres., Ray Dolby/Chmn., Founder, Peter Gotcher/Dir., Ted W. Hall/Dir., Sanford R. Robertson/Dir., Roger S. Siboni/Dir.

Owners: Roger Siboni, Ray Dolby, Insiders, Tim Partridge, Kevin Yeaman, Roger Siboni, David Watts, Peter Gotcher, Peter Gotcher, Bill Jasper, T. Rowe Price Associates, Inc./8.70%, Ray Dolby, Mark Anderson, Ray Dolby Trust, Ray Dolby 2002 Trust A dated April19, 2002 *(26 Owners included in Index)*

Financial Data: ***Fiscal Year End:***09/29 ***Latest Annual Data:*** 9/29/2006

Year	***Sales***	***Net Income***
2006	$391,542,000	$89,549,000
2005	$327,967,000	$52,293,000
2004	$289,041,000	$39,842,000

Curr. Assets:	$454,188,000	***Curr. Liab.:***	$72,794,000		
Plant, Equip.:	$76,462,000	***Total Liab.:***	$125,138,000	***Indic. Yr. Divd.:***	NA
Total Assets:	$586,277,000	***Net Worth:***	$461,139,000	***Debt/ Equity:***	0.0165

Dole Food Co Inc

One Dole Dr., Westlake Village, CA, 91362; ***PH:*** 1-718-921-8124; ***http://*** www.dole.com; ***Email:*** info@amstock.com

General - Incorporation	DE	***Stock***- Price on:12/24/2007	$67.77
Employees	NA	Stock Exchange	NA
Auditor	Deloitte & Touche LLP	Ticker Symbol	NA
Stk Agt	American Stock Transfer & Trust Co.	Outstanding Shares	NA
Counsel	NA	E.P.S	NA
DUNS No.	00-896-5428	Shareholders	NA

Business: The group's principle activities are to source, grow, process, distribute and market quality fresh produce, packaged foods and fresh-cut flowers. The group sources, distributes and markets fresh fruit products, including bananas, pineapples, table grapes, apples, pears, stone fruit, oranges, grapefruit, lemons, mangoes, kiwi, tangelos, melons, cherries, strawberries, raspberries, cranberries and other tropical, deciduous and citrus fruits. Packaged food products of the group include sliced, chunk, tidbit and crushed pineapple, tropical fruit salad, Mandarin oranges and pineapple juice in cans. The group markets its products through 50 direct selling offices in North America, 50 in Europe and 12 in Asia.

Primary SIC and add'l.: 2099 0170 5193 5148 2030

CIK No: 0000018169

Subsidiaries: Ag 1972, Inc., Agricola Santa Ines, S.A., Agroindustrial Pinas del Bosque S.A., Agropecuaria El Provenir, S.A. de C.V., Ashford Company Limited, Bananapuerto Puerto Bananero S.A., Bananera La Paz, S.A, Bud Antle, Inc., C.I. Tecnicas Baltime de Colombia, S.A., Cartones San Fernando S.A., Castle & Cooke Worldwide Limited, Cerulean, Inc., Coastal Berry Company, LLC, Dole Chile S.A., Dole Comercializacion, S.A. 50 Subsidiaries included in the Index

Officers: David H. Murdock/Chmn., CEO, Joseph S. Tesoriero/54/CFO, VP, Roberta Wieman/Dir., Exec. VP, Chief - Staff, Scott A. Griswold/Dir., Exec. VP - Corporate Development, Richard J. Dahl/Dir., COO, Pres., Sue Hagen/Sr. VP - Human Resources, Javier H. Idrovo/Sr. VP, Jeffrey B. Conner/VP, Assoc. General Counsel, Assist. Corp. Sec., Remedios Rivera/Dole Sr. Scientist, Martha Rodriguez/Dole Sr. Scientist, Jose Ruiz/Dole Sr. Scientist, Leonor Travina-Balito/Dole Sr. Scientist, Reynato Umali/Dole Sr. Scientist, John Washington/Dole Sr. Scientist, Ligia Zuniga/Dole Sr. Scientist *(66 Officers included in Index)*

Directors: David H. Murdock/Chmn., CEO, Scott A. Griswold/Dir., Exec. VP - Corporate Development, Edward C. Roohan/Dir., David A. Delorenzo/Dir., Michael C. Carter/Dir., Exec. VP, General Counsel, Corp. Sec., Justin M. Murdock/Dir., Andrew J. Conrad/Dir., Roberta Wieman/Dir., Exec. VP, Chief - Staff, Richard J. Dahl/Dir., COO, Pres., Richard M. Ferry/Dir.

Owners: David H. Murdock/100.00%

Dollar Financial Corp

1436 Lancaster Ave., Ste. 300, Berwyn, PA, 19312; ***PH:*** 1-610-296-3400; ***Fax:*** 1-610-296-7844; ***http://*** www.dfg.com; ***Email:*** info@dfg.com

General - Incorporation	DE	***Stock***- Price on:12/24/2007	$30.66
Employees	4,226	Stock Exchange	NDQ
Auditor	Ernst & Young LLP	Ticker Symbol	DLLR
Stk Agt	American Stock Transfer & Trust Co.	Outstanding Shares	23,850,000
Counsel	NA	E.P.S	NA
DUNS No.	NA	Shareholders	NA

Business: The groups principle activity is to provide financial services. The groups services include Western Union money order and money transfer products, electronic tax filing, bill payment, foreign currency exchange, photo ID and prepaid local. The products of the group include check cashing, short-term consumer loans, money orders, money transfers and legal document preparation. The group products sold under the trade name Money Mart(R), Loan Mart(R), Cash Til Payday(R), CustomCash(R) and We The People(R). The groups operates through three segments namely United States, Canada and United Kingdom. In the year 2006, International Paper Converters Limited, Alexandria Financial Services, L.L.C and Tenant Financial Enterprises, Inc. The group operates from the United States, Canada and the United Kingdom. The group's quarterly revenue for September 2007 was 116.05 millions of USD.

Primary SIC and add'l.: 4822 6163 6099 7389 6141 8111

CIK No: 0001271625

Subsidiaries: A.E. Osborne & Sons Limited, Any Kind Check Cashing Centers, Inc., C.C. Financial Services Limited, Cash A Cheque (GB)Limited, Cash A Cheque (South) Limited, Cash A Cheque Great Britain Limited, Cash A Cheque Holdings Great Britain Limited, Cash Centres Corporation Limited, Cash Centres International Limited, Cash Centres Limited, Cash Centres Retail Limited, Cash Centres Scotland Limited, Cash Unlimited of Arizona, Inc., Check Mart of Louisiana, Inc., Check Mart of New Mexico, Inc. 46 Subsidiaries included in the Index

Officers: Jeffrey Weiss/Chmn., CEO, Sydney Franchuk/Exec. VP, Chmn. - National Money Mart, Paul Mildenstein/Sr. VP, MD - United Kingdom Operations, Donald Gayhardt/Dir., Pres., Peter Sokolowski/Sr. VP, Chief Credit Officer, Melissa Soper/VP, GM - We The People Division, William Athas/Sr. VP - Finance, Corporate Controller, Roy W. Hibberd/Sr. VP, General Counsel, Julie Prozeller/Primary Investor Relations Officer, Randy Underwood/CFO, Exec. VP, Norm Miller/COO, Exec. VP, Patti Smith/Sr. VP - North American Operations

Directors: Jeffrey Weiss/Chmn., CEO, Donald Gayhardt/Dir., Pres., David Jessick/Dir., David Golub/Dir., Kenneth Schwenke/Dir., John Gavin/Dir., Clive Kahn/Dir.

Owners: John Gavin, Kenneth Schwenke, David Jessick, Randy Underwood, Donald Gayhardt/1.46%, Jeffrey A. Weiss/3.85%, Clive Kahn, Wellington Management Company, LLP/12.32%, Sydney Franchuk, Paul Mildenstein, All directors and executive officers as a group/6.30%

Curr. Assets:	$305,869,000	***Curr. Liab.:***	$98,013,000		
Plant, Equip.:	$55,031,000	***Total Liab.:***	$687,636,000	***Indic. Yr. Divd.:***	NA
Total Assets:	$833,619,000	***Net Worth:***	$145,983,000	***Debt/ Equity:***	NA

Dollar General Corp

100 Mission Ridge, Goodlettsville, TN, 37072; ***PH:*** 1-615-855-4000; ***http://*** www.dollargeneral.com

General - Incorporation	TN	***Stock***- Price on:12/24/2007	$21.79
Employees	69,500	Stock Exchange	NA
Auditor	Ernst & Young LLP	Ticker Symbol	NA
Stk Agt	Registrar & Transfer Co	Outstanding Shares	314,880,000
Counsel	NA	E.P.S	$0.40
DUNS No.	00-694-6172	Shareholders	NA

Business: The groups principle activity is to operate retail general merchandise stores. The group operates from United States.

Primary SIC and add'l.: 5331

CIK No: 0000029534

Subsidiaries: Ashley River Insurance Company, Inc., DG Logistics, LLC, DG Promotions, Inc., DG Retail, LLC, DG Transportation, Inc., DGC Holdings, LLC, DGC Properties of Kentucky, LLC, DGC Properties, LLC, Dolgencorp of New York, Inc., Dolgencorp of Texas, Inc., Dolgencorp, Inc., Dollar General Global Sourcing Limited, Dollar General Investment, Inc., Dollar General Literacy Foundation, Dollar General Merchandising, Inc. 16 Subsidiaries included in the Index

Officers: David L. Bere/Interim Chmn., CEO, David A. Perdue/58/Chmn., CEO, Beryl J. Buley/Division Pres. - Merchandising, Marketing, Supply Chain, Challis M. Lowe/Exec. VP - Human Resources, Anita C. Elliott/43/Sr. VP, Controller, Kathleen R. Guion/Division Pres. - Store Operations, Store Development, David M. Tehle/CFO, Exec. VP, Susan S. Lanigan/Exec. VP, General Counsel, Wayne Gibson/49/Sr. VP - Dollar General Marketing

Directors: David L. Bere/Interim Chmn., CEO, David A. Perdue/58/Chmn., CEO, David M. Wilds/Dir., James D. Robbins/Dir., Dennis C. Bottorff/Dir., Richard E. Thornburgh/Dir., Reginald D. Dickson/Dir., Barbara M. Knuckles/Dir., Barbara L. Bowles/Dir., Gordon E. Gee/Dir., Neal J. Purcell/Dir.

Owners: KKR, Citigroup Capital Partners, Challis M. Lowe, CPP Investment Board (USRE II) Inc., Adrian Jones, Raj Agrawal, David L. Ber, David M. Tehle, Kathleen R. Guion, Michael M. Calbert, Insiders, GS Capital Partners, Beryl J. Buley, Wellington Management Company, LLP

Financial Data: ***Fiscal Year End:***02/03 ***Latest Annual Data:*** 2/2/2007

Year	***Sales***	***Net Income***
2007	$9,169,822,000	$137,943,000
2006	$8,582,237,000	$350,155,000
2005	$7,660,927,000	$344,190,000

Curr. Assets:	$1,762,925,000	***Curr. Liab.:***	$933,797,000	***P/E Ratio:***	54.48
Plant, Equip.:	$1,192,172,000	***Total Liab.:***	$1,271,392,000	***Indic. Yr. Divd.:***	$0.200
Total Assets:	$2,992,187,000	***Net Worth:***	$1,720,795,000	***Debt/ Equity:***	0.1449

Dollar Thrifty Automotive Group Inc

5330 E 31st St., Tulsa, OK, 74135; ***PH:*** 1-918-660-7700; ***Fax:*** 1-918-669-2934; ***http://*** www.dtag.com

General - Incorporation	DE	***Stock***- Price on:12/24/2007	$43.2
Employees	8,500	Stock Exchange	NYSE
Auditor	Deloitte & Touche LLP	Ticker Symbol	DTG
Stk Agt	Computershare Investor Services LLC	Outstanding Shares	23,700,000
Counsel	Mall Estill	E.P.S	$1.20
DUNS No.	61-123-9542	Shareholders	NA

Business: The groups principle activity is to provide daily rental of vehicles to business and leisure customers. The groups products are sold under the brand names dollar and thrifty. The group also provides vehicle leasing services. The group operates from United States.

Primary SIC and add'l.: 7514 6794

CIK No: 0001049108

Subsidiaries: Dollar Rent A Car, Inc., DTG Operations, Inc., Rental Car Finance Corp., Thrifty Rent-A-Car System, Inc., Thrifty, Inc.

Officers: Gary L. Paxton/61/Dir., CEO, Pres./$4,254,567.00, Stephen W. Ray/Sec., Yves Boyer/Exec. VP - International/$1,018,005.00, John J. Foley/Sr. Exec. VP - Corporate Operations/$1,448,199.00, Richard Halbrook/Exec. VP - Administration, Steven B. Hildebrand/CFO, Sr. Exec. VP/$1,669,008.00, Vicki Vaniman/Exec. VP, General Counsel, Scott Anderson/Sr. Exec. VP - Corporate Operations/$1,455,180.00

Directors: Gary L. Paxton/61/Dir., CEO, Pres., Thomas P. Capo/54/Chmn., Molly Shi Boren/64/Dir., Edward L. Wax/71/Dir., Maryann N. Keller/64/Dir., Edward C. Lumley/68/Dir., Richard W. Neu/52/Dir., John C. Pope/59/Dir.

Owners: T. Rowe Price Associates, Inc./8.80%, Edward C. Lumley, Franklin Resources, Inc./9.20%, Maryann N. Keller, Scott R. Anderson, Donald M. Himelfarb, MSD Capital, L.P./8.60%, John P. Tierney, Steven B. Hildebrand, Gary L. Paxton, Dimensional Fund Advisors LP/8.80%, Insiders/4.10%, Richard W. Neu, Thomas P. Capo, Peter B. Cannell & Co., Inc./5.40% *(21 Owners included in Index)*

Financial Data: ***Fiscal Year End:***12/31 ***Latest Annual Data:*** 06/30/2007

Year	***Sales***	***Net Income***
2007	NA	NA
2006	NA	NA
2005	$1,507,554,000	$76,355,000

Curr. Assets:	$924,729,000	***Curr. Liab.:***	$249,138,000		
Plant, Equip.:	$2,740,506,000	***Total Liab.:***	$3,363,798,000	***Indic. Yr. Divd.:***	NA
Total Assets:	$4,011,498,000	***Net Worth:***	$647,700,000	***Debt/ Equity:***	4.2369

Dollar Tree Stores Inc

500 Volvo Pkwy., Chesapeake, VA, 23320; ***PH:*** 1-757-321-5000; ***Fax:*** 1-757-321-5111; ***http://*** www.dollartree.com

General - Incorporation	VA	***Stock***- Price on:12/24/2007	$42.66
Employees	12,700	Stock Exchange	NDQ
Auditor	KPMG LLP	Ticker Symbol	DLTR
Stk Agt	National City Stock	Outstanding Shares	98,340,000
Counsel	Hofheimer, Nusbaum	E.P.S	$2.06
DUNS No.	18-895-5553	Shareholders	NA

Business: The group's principle activity is to operate discount variety retail stores. The groups selling products include candy and food, health and beauty care, housewares, paper and plastics. The grous other products include toys, durable housewares, gifts, hardware, and other items. The group operates their stores under the brand name Dollar Tree, Dollar Express, Dollar Bills, Only One Dollar and Only $one. The group operates from United States.

Primary SIC and add'l.: 5331

CIK No: 0000935703

Subsidiaries: Dollar Tree Distribution, Inc., Dollar Tree Management, Inc., Greenbrier International, Inc

Officers: Bob Sasser/Dir., CEO, Pres./$1,628,294.00, Gary M. Philbin/51/COO/$756,114.00, Arvil L. Priode/Sr. VP - Merchandise Planning, Control, James E. Fothergill/Chief People Officer, Stephen W. White/Chief Logistics Officer, Raymond K. Hamilton/CIO, Kent A. Kleeberger/CFO/$886,792.00, Robert H. Rudman/Chief Merchandising Officer, James A. Gorry/General Counsel, Corp. Sec., Michael A. Saltzer/Sr. VP - New Business Development, Bob Rudman/Chief Merchandising Officer/$645,732.00

Directors: Bob Sasser/Dir., CEO, Pres., Macon F. Brock/Chmn., Douglas J. Perry/Chmn. Emeritus, Mary Anne Citrino/Dir., Ray H. Compton/Dir., Eileen R. Scott/Dir., Richard G. Lesser/Dir., Thomas E. Whiddon/Dir., Thomas A. Saunders/Dir., John F. Megrue/Dir., Alan L. Wurtzel/Dir.

Owners: Eileen R. Scott, Gary M. Philbin, Cramer Rosenthal McGlynn, LLC/6.50%, Douglas J. Perry/1.20%, Macon F. Brock/2.00%, Richard G. Lesser, FMR Corp./10.50%, Robert H. Rudman, John F. Megrue, Alan L. Wurtzel, Kent A. Kleeberger, Barclays Group./6.10%, Thomas E. Whiddon, Thomas A. Saunders/1.10%, Insiders/4.90% *(18 Owners included in Index)*

Financial Data: Fiscal Year End:01/28   Latest Annual Data: 2/3/2007

Year	Sales	Net Income
2007	$3,969,400,000	$192,000,000
2006	$3,393,924,000	$173,918,000
2005	$3,126,009,000	$180,250,000

Curr. Assets:	$959,000,000	**Curr. Liab.:**	$383,300,000	**P/E Ratio:**	22.10
Plant, Equip.:	$715,300,000	**Total Liab.:**	$705,600,000	**Indic. Yr. Divd.:**	NA
Total Assets:	$1,873,300,000	**Net Worth:**	$1,167,700,000	**Debt/ Equity:**	0.2277

Dome Holding Corp

3928 S Sheridan Rd., Tulsa, OK, 74145; *PH:* 1-918-622-0696

General - Incorporation	OK	**Stock**- Price on:12/24/2007 ....NA
Employees	NA	Stock Exchange ....NA
Auditor	NA	Ticker Symbol ....NA
Stk Agt	US Transfer Agent	Outstanding Shares ....NA
Counsel	NA	E.P.S ....NA
DUNS No.	NA	Shareholders ....NA

Business: The groups principle activity is to voluntary basis in order to make the company's financial information equally available to all parties, including potential investors, and to meet certain listing requirements for publicly traded securities. The group operates from United States.

Primary SIC and add'l.: 6770
CIK No: 0001308695

Dominion Homes Inc

5000 Tuttle Crossing Blvd., Dublin, OH, 43016; *PH:* 1-614-356-5000; *Fax:* 1-614-356-6010; *http://* www.dominionhomes.com

General - Incorporation	OH	**Stock**- Price on:12/24/2007 ....$4.95
Employees	283	Stock Exchange ....NDQ
Auditor	PricewaterhouseCoopers LLP	Ticker Symbol ....DHOM
Stk Agt	Registrar & Transfer Co	Outstanding Shares 8,520,000
Counsel	Vorys, Sater, Seymour & Pease	E.P.S ....-$8.995
DUNS No.	00-428-6399	Shareholders ....NA

Business: The group's principle activity is to build single family homes. The group offers three series of single-family homes namely independence series, century series, celebrity series and tradition series. Size, price, standard features and available options differentiate the products. Products of the group are marketed under the trade name dominion homes(r). The group has introduced a new Web-site to provide potential homebuyers to take virtual tours of models and search the group's home inventory by specifying size, location, amenities and price. The group conducts home sales from over 50 furnished model home sales offices in central Ohio, louisville, Kentucky and homestore(R) in central, Ohio. The group's quarterly revenue for September 2007 was 38.12 millions of USD.

Primary SIC and add'l.: 1521 1531
CIK No: 0000917857
Subsidiaries: Alliance Title Agency of Kentucky, LLC, Dominion Homes Financial Services, Ltd., Dominion Homes of Kentucky GP, LLC, Dominion Homes of Kentucky, Ltd. (d/b/a Dominion Homes), Dominion Homes Realty, LLC, Dominion Structural Warranty Company, LLC, Resolution Property Company, LLC

Officers: Douglas G. Borror/Chmn., CEO/$906,630.00, Jeffrey A. Croft/COO, Pres./$587,104.00, Lori M. Steiner/Sr. VP, Chief Marketing Officer, Terry E. George/Sr. VP, Treasurer, William G. Cornely/CFO, Exec. VP - Finance/$320,119.00, Michael A. Archer/Sr. VP - Sales Operations, Ohio Division, Christine A. Murry/Sec.

Directors: Douglas G. Borror/Chmn., CEO, David S. Borror/Vice Chmn., Carl A. Nelson/Dir., Zuheir Sofia/Dir., David P. Blom/Dir., Andrew R. Johnson/Dir., Robert R. McMaster/Dir., Betty D. Montgomery/Dir.

Owners: Edward A. Mule, Insiders, Robert R. McMaster, BRC Properties Inc., Carl A. Nelson, David S. Borror, Dimensional Funds Advisors Inc., Jeffrey A. Croft, Scott L. Barbee, Angelo, Gordon & Co., L.P., Terry E. George, William S. Berno, William G. Cornely, Douglas G. Borror, Andrew R. Johnson *(20 Owners included in Index)*

Financial Data: Fiscal Year End:12/31   Latest Annual Data: 12/31/2006

Year	Sales	Net Income
2006	$256,760,000	-$34,009,000
2005	$415,700,000	$5,326,000
2004	$541,970,000	$20,202,000

Curr. Assets:	$23,204,000	**Curr. Liab.:**	$25,427,000		
Plant, Equip.:	$375,609,000	**Total Liab.:**	$235,752,000	**Indic. Yr. Divd.:**	NA
Total Assets:	$404,216,000	**Net Worth:**	$168,464,000	**Debt/ Equity:**	1.2569

Dominion Resources Black Warrior Trust

901 Main St., Ste. 1700, Dallas, TX, 75202; *PH:* 1-214-209-2400; *Fax:* 1-214-209-2431; *http://* www.dom-dominionblackwarriortrust.com; *Email:* trustee@dom-dominionblackwarriortrust.com

General - Incorporation	DE	**Stock**- Price on:12/24/2007 ....$24.5
Employees	NA	Stock Exchange ....NYSE
Auditor	Deloitte & Touche LLP	Ticker Symbol ....DOM
Stk Agt	Mellon Investor Services LLC	Outstanding Shares 7,850,000
Counsel	Thompson & Knight, LLC	E.P.S $3.06
DUNS No.	NA	Shareholders ....NA

Business: The groups principal activity is to acquire oil and gas properties. The group operates from the United States.

Primary SIC and add'l.: 6792
CIK No: 0000923680
Officers: Ron E. Hooper/Sr. VP, Administrator

Financial Data: Fiscal Year End:12/31   Latest Annual Data: 12/31/2006

Year	Sales	Net Income
2006	$31,496,000	$30,467,000
2005	$31,983,000	$31,029,000
2004	$24,358,000	$23,450,000

Curr. Assets:	$203,000	**Curr. Liab.:**	$248,000		
Plant, Equip.:	NA	**Total Liab.:**	$248,000	**Indic. Yr. Divd.:**	$2.590
Total Assets:	$30,693,000	**Net Worth:**	$30,445,000	**Debt/ Equity:**	NA

Dominion Resources Inc VA

120 Tredegar St., Richmond, VA, 23219; *PH:* 1-804-819-2000; *http://* www.domres.com

General - Incorporation	VA	**Stock**- Price on:12/24/2007 ....$84.59
Employees	17,500	Stock Exchange ....NYSE
Auditor	Deloitte & Touche LLP	Ticker Symbol ....D
Stk Agt	Continental Stock Transfer & Trust Co	Outstanding Shares 350,320,000
Counsel	NA	E.P.S $1.73
DUNS No.	10-171-5035	Shareholders ....NA

Business: The group operates through its subsidiary whose principle activity is to provide gas and electric energy. The group operates from United States.

Primary SIC and add'l.: 4911 4923 1382
CIK No: 0000715957
Subsidiaries: Armstrong Energy Limited Partnership, LLLP, Carthage Energy Services, Inc., CNG Coal Company, CNG International Corporation, CNG Kauai, Inc., CNG Main Pass Gas Gathering Corporation, CNG Oil Gathering Corporation, CNG Power Services Corporation, Consolidated Natural Gas Company, DEPI Texas Holdings, LLC, DFV Capital Corporation, Domcan Boundary Corp., Domcan NS1ULC, Dominion Alliance Holding, Inc., Dominion Appalachian Development Properties, LLC 134 Subsidiaries included in the Index

Officers: Thomas F. Farrell/53/Dir., CEO, Pres./$7,304,530.00, Duane C. Radtke/59/Exec. VP/$3,486,100.00, Mark F. McGettrick/50/Exec. VP/$2,421,365.00, Thomas N. Chewning/62/CFO, Exec. VP/$2,879,679.00, Jay L. Johnson/61/Exec. VP/$1,793,171.00, Mary C. Doswell/49/Sr. VP - CAO, Eva S. Hardy/63/Exec. VP - External Affairs, Corporate Communications, James L. Sanderlin/66/Sr. VP - Law, Scott G. Hetzer/51/Sr. VP, Treasurer, Steven A. Rogers/46/Chief Accounting Officer, Sr. VP, Paul D. Koonce/48/Exec. VP, David A. Christian/53/Sr. VP - Nuclear Operations, James F. Stutts/63/Sr. VP, General Counsel

Directors: Thomas F. Farrell/53/Dir., CEO, Pres., Thos E. Capps/Chmn., Peter W. Brown/65/Dir., Ronald J. Calise/Dir., John W. Harris/60/Dir., Robert S. Jepson/65/Dir., Mark J. Kington/48/Dir., Benjamin J. Lambert/Dir., Richard L. Leatherwood/Dir., Margaret A. McKenna/62/Dir., Frank S. Royal/68/Dir., Dallas S. Simmons/Dir., David A. Wollard/70/Dir., George A. Davidson/69/Dir.

Owners: Mark F. McGettrick, David A. Wollard, Margaret A. McKenna, Capital Research and Management Company, Richard L. Leatherwood, Thomas F. Farrell, Duane C. Radtke, George A. Davidson, Robert S. Jepson, Dallas S. Simmons, Mark J. Kington, Thomas N. Chewning, Ronald J. Calise, Benjamin J. Lambert, John W. Harris *(20 Owners included in Index)*

Financial Data: Fiscal Year End:12/31   Latest Annual Data: 12/31/2006

Year	Sales	Net Income
2006	$16,482,000,000	$1,380,000,000
2005	$18,041,000,000	$1,033,000,000
2004	$13,972,000,000	$1,249,000,000

Curr. Assets:	$8,098,000,000	**Curr. Liab.:**	$11,229,000,000	**P/E Ratio:**	22.92
Plant, Equip.:	$29,382,000,000	**Total Liab.:**	$36,076,000,000	**Indic. Yr. Divd.:**	$2.840
Total Assets:	$49,269,000,000	**Net Worth:**	$13,170,000,000	**Debt/ Equity:**	1.1747

Domino's Pizza Inc

30 Frank Lloyd Wright Dr., Ann Arbor, MI, 48106; *PH:* 1-734-930-3030; *Fax:* 1-734-747-6210; *http://* www.dominos.com

General - Incorporation	DE	**Stock**- Price on:12/24/2007 ....$18.74
Employees	13,300	Stock Exchange ....NYSE
Auditor	PricewaterhouseCoopers LLP	Ticker Symbol ....DPZ
Stk Agt	electronic funds transfer	Outstanding Shares 62,680,000
Counsel	NA	E.P.S $0.82
DUNS No.	NA	Shareholders ....NA

Business: The group's principal activity is to own and operate pizza delivery stores. The group operates in three segments: domestic stores, domestic distribution and international. The domestic stores segment consists of domestic franchise operations and domestic company owned stores that operate a network of 4,344 franchise stores and 576 company owned stores. The domestic distribution segment operates 18 regional dough manufacturing and food distribution centers and one distribution center providing equipment and supplies to domestic and international stores. The international segment oversees a network of 2,534 international franchise stores in more than 50 countries, operates 17 company owned stores in the Netherlands and two company owned store in France. It also distributes food to a limited number of markets from eight dough manufacturing and distribution centers in Alaska, Hawaii, Canada (four), the Netherlands and France.

Primary SIC and add'l.: 6794 5812
CIK No: 0001079458
Subsidiaries: Dominos National Advertising Fund Inc., Dominos Pizza International, Inc., Dominos Pizza LLC, Dominos Pizza PMC, Inc., Dominos, Inc.

Officers: David A. Brandon/Chmn., CEO, Patrick J. Doyle/Exec. VP - Team USA, David L. Mounts/CFO, Exec. VP - Finance, Lynn M. Liddle/Exec. VP - Communications, Investor Relations, Patricia A. Wilmot/Exec. VP - Peoplefirst, Ken C. Calwell/Exec. VP - Build The Brand, Michael D. Soignet/Exec. VP - Maintain High Standards, Distribution, Michael Lawton/Exec. VP - International, James G. Stansik/Exec. VP - Franchise Development

Directors: David A. Brandon/Chmn., CEO, Vernon O. Hamilton/Dir., Diana F. Cantor/Dir., Robert M. Rosenberg/Dir., Andrew B. Balson/Dir., Dennis F. Hightower/Dir., Mark E. Nunnelly/Dir.

Financial Data: Fiscal Year End:01/01 Latest Annual Data: 12/31/2006

Year	Sales	Net Income
2006	$1,437,319,000	$106,227,000
2005	$1,446,497,000	$62,287,000

Curr. Assets:	$166,305,000	Curr. Liab.:	$155,201,000	P/E Ratio:	18.19
Plant, Equip.:	$117,144,000	Total Liab.:	$945,096,000	Indic. Yr. Divd.:	$0.480
Total Assets:	$380,203,000	Net Worth:	-$564,893,000	Debt/ Equity:	NA

Domtar Inc

100 Kingsley Pk. Dr., Fort Mill, SC, 29715; PH: 1-803-802-7500; Fax: 1-800-923-2205; http:// www.domtar.com; Email: information@domtar.com

General		Stock	
Incorporation	Canada	Price on:12/24/2007	NA
Employees	9,800	Stock Exchange	NYSE
Auditor	PricewaterhouseCoopers LLP	Ticker Symbol	NA
Stk Agt	Computershare Trust Co of Canada	Outstanding Shares	NA
Counsel	NA	E.P.S.	NA
DUNS No.	24-460-1712	Shareholders	NA

Business: The group operates in three reportable segments: papers represents the aggregation of the manufacturing and distribution of communication and specialty papers as well as pulp; wood includes forest resources, saw mill operations and remanufacturing facilities; and packaging, manufactures and distributes container board and corrugated products.

Primary SIC and add'l.: 3275 2421 2653 2652 2621 2499

CIK No: 0000819817

Subsidiaries: Norampac Inc.

Officers: Raymond Royer/Dir., CEO, Pres., Michel Dagenais/Sr. VP - Human Resources, Roger H. Brear/Sr. VP - Southern Region Mills, Steven A. Barker/Sr. VP - Marketing, James F. Lenhoff/Sr. VP - Distribution, Gilles Pharand/Sr. VP - Law, Corporate Affairs, Richard Garneau/Exec. VP - Operations, Daniel Buron/Sr. VP, CFO, Razvan L. Theodoru/VP, Sec. - Corporate Governance, Ethics, Marvin D. Cooper/Dir., Exec. VP, COO, Ghislain Dinel/Sr. VP - Northern Region Mills, Michael Edwards/Group Sr. VP - Pulp, Paper Manufacturing, Patrick Loulou/Sr. VP - Corporate Development, Jean-Francois Merette/Sr. VP - Forest Products, Bart Nicholson/Sr. VP - Specialty Mills, Converting Operations *(19 Officers included in Index)*

Directors: Raymond Royer/Dir., CEO, Pres., Brian M. Levitt/Chmn., Louis P. Gignac/Dir., Jack C. Bingleman/Dir., Raymond Chretien/Dir., Claude R. Lamoureux/Dir., Gene R. Tyndall/Dir., Robert J. Steacy/Dir., Marvin D. Cooper/Dir., Exec. VP, COO, Harold H. MacKay/Dir., Henson Moore/Dir., Michael R. Onustock/Dir., William C. Stivers/Dir., Pamela B. Strobel/Dir., Richard Tan/Dir. *(19 Directors included in Index)*

Donaldson Co Inc

1400 W 94th St., Minneapolis, MN, 55431; PH: 1-952-887-3131; Fax: 1-952-887-3155; http:// www.donaldson.com; Email: filterinfo@mail.donaldson.com

General		Stock	
Incorporation	DE	Price on:12/24/2007	$34.36
Employees	11,500	Stock Exchange	NYSE
Auditor	PricewaterhouseCoopers LLP	Ticker Symbol	DCI
Stk Agt	Wells Fargo Shareowner Services	Outstanding Shares	79,920,000
Counsel	NA	E.P.S.	$1.93
DUNS No.	00-647-7301	Shareholders	NA

Business: The group's principle activity is to manufacture filtration systems and replacement parts. The group's product includes air and liquid filters, and exhaust and emission control products for mobile equipment. On March 1, 2007, the group acquired Aerospace Filtration Systems, Inc. The group operates from United States.

Primary SIC and add'l.: 3599 3564 3569

CIK No: 0000029644

Subsidiaries: Almere, Netherlands, ASHC, Inc., DCE Donaldson Ltd., DCE Group Ltd., DFCH Ltd., Donaldson (Thailand) Ltd., Donaldson (Wuxi) Filters Co., Ltd., Donaldson Australasia Pty. Ltd., Donaldson Belgie., Donaldson Canada, Inc., Donaldson Capital, Inc., Donaldson Company Inc. (Luxembourg) SCS, Donaldson Coordination Center, Donaldson Deutschland Holding GmbH, Donaldson Far East Ltd. 59 Subsidiaries included in the Index

Officers: William M. Cook/Chmn., CEO, Pres./$4,672,553.00, Charles J. McMurray/Sr. VP - Industrial Products, South Africa/$905,371.00, Lowell F. Schwab/Sr. VP - Engine Systems, Parts/$1,445,108.00, William I. Vann/VP - Nafta Operations, Mexico, Norman C. Linnell/VP, General Counsel, Sec., Jay L. Ward/VP - Europe, Middle East, Debra L. Wilfong/CTO, VP, Thomas R. Verhage/CFO, VP/$1,536,310.00, Sandra N. Joppa/VP - Human Resources, Communications, James F. Shaw/Controller, Tod E. Carpenter/VP - Global Industrial Filtration Solutions, Peggy A. Herrmann/VP - Global Disk Drive, Microelectronic, Adsorbant Products, Dennis D. Jandik/VP - Global Engine OEM Sales, Joseph E. Lehman/VP - Global Engine Aftermarket Sales, Mary Lynne Perushek/CIO, VP *(16 Officers included in Index)*

Directors: William M. Cook/Chmn., CEO, Pres., Guillaume F. Bastiaens/Dir., Janet Dolan/Dir., Jack Eugster/Dir., John Wiehoff/Dir., Paul David Miller/Dir., Jeffrey Noddle/Dir., John Grundhofer/Dir., Michael Hoffman/Dir., Willard Oberton/Dir.

Owners: Paul D. Miller, John P. Wiehoff, Guillaume F. Bastiaens, Charles J. McMurray, Columbia Wanger Asset Management, L.P/5.60%, Geert Henk Touw, Jack W. Eugster, Insiders/3.50%, William M. Cook/1.10%, Michael J. Hoffman, Thomas R. VerHage, Janet M. Dolan, Willard D. Oberton, Lowell F. Schwab, Jeffrey Noddle *(16 Owners included in Index)*

Financial Data: Fiscal Year End:07/31 Latest Annual Data: 07/31/2007

Year	Sales	Net Income
2007	$1,918,828,000	$150,717,000
2006	$1,694,327,000	$132,307,000
2005	$1,595,733,000	$110,554,000

Curr. Assets:	$561,405,000	Curr. Liab.:	$359,869,000	P/E Ratio:	20.45
Plant, Equip.:	$317,364,000	Total Liab.:	$577,265,000	Indic. Yr. Divd.:	$0.360
Total Assets:	$1,124,067,000	Net Worth:	$546,802,000	Debt/ Equity:	NA

Donar Enterprises Inc

Concertgebouwplein 13, 1071 LL, Amsterdam, P7 XXXXX; PH: 011-31-20-676-0304; http:// www.donarenterprises.com

General		Stock	
Incorporation	DE	Price on:12/24/2007	NA
Employees	NA	Stock Exchange	OTC
Auditor	Cordovano & Honeck LLP	Ticker Symbol	PLGC
Stk Agt	Securities Transfer Corp	Outstanding Shares	NA
Counsel	NA	E.P.S.	NA
DUNS No.	NA	Shareholders	NA

Business: The group's principle activity is to provide document formatting and electronic filing services to public corporations and individuals. It provides edgar filing services to small public corporations traded on the over-the-counter market and individuals by marketing the services to the companies directly or through legal and accounting firms. The group is in the development stage. The group operates from United States.

Primary SIC and add'l.: 7389

CIK No: 0001141590

Subsidiaries: Playlogic Game Factory B.V., Playlogic International N.V.

Officers: Willem M. Smit/Dir., CEO, Pres., Dominique Morel/CTO - French, Rogier W. Smit/Exec. VP - Dutch, Stefan Layer/Chief Marketing, Sales Officer, VP - German, Maarten Minderhoud/General Counsel, Sec., Beco Mulderij/Marketing Mgr., Russell Beadle/Sales Mgr., Wilbert Knol/CFO, Jeroen Zandt/Legal Counsel

Directors: Willem M. Smit/Dir., CEO, Pres., Willy J. Simon/Chmn., Erik L.A. Van Emden/Dir., George M. Calhoun/Dir.

Owners: Sloterhof Investments N.V./30.36%, Insiders/38.00%, Castilla Investments B.V./7.39%, Willem Smit/30.36%, Rogier Smit/7.39%, Wind Worth Luxembourg Holding S.A.H/8.89%, George M. Calhoun, Stefan Layer/1.52%, Sophia International Holding S.A.H./6.70%, Willy J. Simon

Financial Data: Fiscal Year End:12/31 Latest Annual Data: 12/31/2006

Year	Sales	Net Income
2006	$5,043,000	-$12,548,000
2005	$1,824,000	-$9,674,000
2004	$4,000	-$106,000

Curr. Assets:	$4,688,000	Curr. Liab.:	$17,727,000		
Plant, Equip.:	$884,000	Total Liab.:	$17,964,000	Indic. Yr. Divd.:	NA
Total Assets:	$7,074,000	Net Worth:	-$10,890,000	Debt/ Equity:	NA

Donegal Group Inc

1195 River Rd., Marietta, PA, 17547; PH: 1-717-426-1931; Fax: 1-717-426-7009; http:// www.donegalgroup.com

General		Stock	
Incorporation	DE	Price on:12/24/2007	$14.95
Employees	NA	Stock Exchange	NDQ
Auditor	KPMG LLP	Ticker Symbol	DGICA
Stk Agt	Computershare Investor Services LLC	Outstanding Shares	NA
Counsel	NA	E.P.S.	NA
DUNS No.	15-214-3913	Shareholders	NA

Business: The group's principal activity is to provide property and casualty insurance in 14 mid-Atlantic and southeastern states through its subsidiaries. The group operates in three segments: the investment function, personal lines of insurance and commercial lines of insurance. Products offered in the personal lines of insurance consist primarily of homeowners and private passenger automobile policies. Products offered in the commercial lines of insurance consist primarily of commercial automobile, commercial multiple peril and workers' compensation policies. The group operates in the domestic market. In Jan 2004, the group acquired le mars mutual insurance company and the peninsula insurance company and peninsula indemnity company.

Primary SIC and add'l.: 6331

CIK No: 0000800457

Subsidiaries: Atlantic States Insurance Company, Le Mars Insurance Company, Peninsula Indemnity Company, Southern Insurance Company of Virginia, The Peninsula Insurance Company

Officers: Donald H. Nikolaus/CEO, Pres./$1,850,238.00, Jeffrey D. Miller/CFO, Sr. VP/$359,251.00, Eric G. Crouchley/Pres. - Peninsula Insurance Group, Salisbury, Maryland, Kenneth P. Kirchner/VP - Information Technology, Peninsula Insurance Group, Salisbury, Maryland, Joseph J. O'Donnell/VP - Claims, Peninsula Insurance Group, Salisbury, Maryland, Eric W. Pippen/VP - Commercial Underwriting, Peninsula Insurance Group, Salisbury, Maryland, William K. Ryan/VP, Treasurer - Peninsula Insurance Group, Salisbury, Maryland, Rebecca V. Simowitz/Sec. - Peninsula Insurance Group, Salisbury, Maryland, Sheri O. Smith/Sec., Daniel J. Wagner/Sr. VP, Treasurer/$352,251.00, William H. Shupert/Sr. VP - Underwriting, Kevin G. Burke/Sr. VP - Human Resources, Cyril J. Greenya/Sr. VP, Chief Underwriting Officer/$359,867.00, Charles M. Ferraro/CIO, Sr. VP, Richard G. Kelley/Sr. VP - Sales, Business Development *(32 Officers included in Index)*

Directors: Robert S. Bolinger/Dir., Patricia A. Gilmartin/Dir., John J. Lyons/Dir., Richard D. Wampler/Dir., Philip H. Glatfelter/Dir., Richard R. Sherbahn/Dir., Jon M. Mahan/Dir.

Financial Data: Fiscal Year End:12/31 Latest Annual Data: 12/31/2006

Year	Sales	Net Income
2006	NA	NA
2005	NA	NA
2004	NA	NA

Curr. Assets:	$235,281,000	Curr. Liab.:	$18,563,000		
Plant, Equip.:	$5,146,000	Total Liab.:	$510,895,000	Indic. Yr. Divd.:	NA
Total Assets:	$831,698,000	Net Worth:	$320,802,000	Debt/ Equity:	0.0945

Donini Inc

4555 Blvd. des Grandes Prairies, Ste. 30, Saint-Lonard, PQ, H1R 1A5; PH: 1-514-327-6006; http:// www.pizzadonini.com; Email: info@pizzadonini.com

General		Stock	
Incorporation	NJ	Price on:12/24/2007	$0.045
Employees	NA	Stock Exchange	OTC
Auditor	Rotenberg Meril Solomon	Ticker Symbol	DNNI
Stk Agt	NA	Outstanding Shares	NA
Counsel	NA	E.P.S.	NA
DUNS No.	NA	Shareholders	NA

Business: The group's principal activities are franchising, manufacturing and distributing frozen ready-made pizza, frozen and refrigerated sauces and pizza dough. The group's products are sold to franchisees, retail grocery outlets including mass merchandise stores and supermarkets and wholesalers. It provides one number central telephone system to process customers' orders and thus provide home delivery through its wholly owned subsidiary pizza donini inc. It has also embarked on an Internet-based

order taking and processing program. In addition to the pizza delivery services, the group has also introduced full service restaurants and supports over 26 franchised pizza outlets. The group's franchise outlets operate under the trade name pizza donini which is also used for the distribution of its frozen pizza to the food service industry.

Primary SIC and add'l.: 2038

CIK No: 0001129900

Subsidiaries: People Ridesharing Systems, Inc., Pizza Donini.Com Inc.

Financial Data: Fiscal Year End:05/31 **Latest Annual Data:** 5/31/2005

Year		Sales			Net Income
2005		$1,038,000			-$2,314,000
2004		$1,467,000			-$246,000
2003		$1,496,000			-$363,000
Curr. Assets:	$528,000	Curr. Liab.:		$2,035,000	
Plant, Equip.:	$240,000	Total Liab.:		$3,305,000	Indic. Yr. Divd.: NA
Total Assets:	$910,000	Net Worth:		-$2,395,000	Debt/ Equity: NA

Dor Biopharma Inc

1101 Brickell Ave., Ste. 701 S, Miami, FL, 33131; *PH:* 1-786-425-3848 ; *Fax:* 1-786-425-3853; *http://* www.dorbiopharma.com; *Email:* info@dorbiopharma.com

General - Incorporation	DE	**Stock**- Price on:12/24/2007	$0.325
Employees	8	Stock Exchange	OTC
Auditor	Sweeney, Gates & Co	Ticker Symbol	DORB
Stk Agt	American Stock Transfer & Trust Co.	Outstanding Shares	92,690,000
Counsel	NA	E.P.S	-$0.12
DUNS No.	15-388-0778	Shareholders	NA

Business: The group's principal activity is to specialize in the development of oral and nasal delivery of vaccines and drugs. The group develops a proprietary oral and nasal vaccine delivery technology called the microvax(tm) system. This system is used in biodefense vaccines, including nasal vaccines against ricin toxins and anthrax and an oral delivered vaccine against botulinum toxin. The group also develops orbec(R), an oral therapeutic product, for the treatment of intestinal graft-vs-host. The group develops oral drug delivery systems, named the lpm(tm), plp(tm) and lpe(tm) systems, for the delivery of proteins and water insoluble drugs. The group has preclinical animal data demonstrating the oral delivery of the drug leuprolide and paclitaxel.

Primary SIC and add'l.: 2834

CIK No: 0000812796

Subsidiaries: Corporate Technology Development Inc., DOR BioDefense Inc., Endorex Newco LTD, Enteron Pharmaceuticals Inc., Formulation Technologies Inc., Innovaccines Corp., Intero Corp., Magyer Pharmaceuticals, Oral Solutions Inc., Orasomal Technologies Inc., Rx Eyes Inc., Wisconsin Genetics Inc.

Officers: Christopher J. Schaber/Dir., CEO, Pres./$340,331.00, Evan Myrianthopoulos/Dir., CFO/$403,045.00, James Clavijo/Controller, Treasurer, Corp. Sec./$227,835.00, Robert N. Brey/Chief Scientific Officer

Directors: Christopher J. Schaber/Dir., CEO, Pres., James S. Kuo/Chmn., Steve Kanzer/Dir., Evan Myrianthopoulos/Dir., CFO, Cyrille Buhrman/Dir.

Owners: James Clavijo, James S. Kuo, Christopher J. Schaber/1.80%, Evan Myrianthopoulos/1.50%, Sigma-Tau Pharmaceuticals, Inc./4.40%, Cyrill F. Buhrman/5.40%, Insiders/8.90%

Financial Data: Fiscal Year End:12/31 **Latest Annual Data:** 12/31/2006

Year		Sales			Net Income
2006		$2,313,000			-$8,163,000
2005		$3,076,000			-$4,720,000
2004		$997,000			-$5,872,000
Curr. Assets:	$304,000	Curr. Liab.:		$2,515,000	
Plant, Equip.:	$30,000	Total Liab.:		$2,515,000	Indic. Yr. Divd.: NA
Total Assets:	$1,407,000	Net Worth:		-$1,108,000	Debt/ Equity: NA

Doral Financial Corp

1451 Franklin D. Roosevelt Ave., San Juan, PR, 00920; *PH:* 1-787-474-6700; *http://* www.doralfinancial.com

General - Incorporation	PR	**Stock**- Price on:12/24/2007	$1.66
Employees	2,317	Stock Exchange	NYSE
Auditor	PricewaterhouseCoopers LLP	Ticker Symbol	DRL
Stk Agt	Mellon Investor Services LLC	Outstanding Shares	107,950,000
Counsel	Pietrantoni, Mendez & Alvarez	E.P.S	-$2.76
DUNS No.	09-043-7831	Shareholders	NA

Business: The group's principal activities are to provide mortgage banking, banking, institutional securities operations and insurance agency activities. It is a financial holding company with the commercial banking activities conducted through its wholly owned subsidiaries, doral bank pr and doral bank, fsb. The mortgage banking activities are conducted through its hf mortgage bankers division, and through its subsidiaries, doral mortgage corporation, centro hipotecario de Puerto Rico inc and sana investment mortgage bankers inc. It operates 56 mortgage banking offices in Puerto Rico and one branch office in the United States. The primary business of the group includes origination, purchase, sale and servicing of mortgage loans. The group also issues and sells various types of mortgage-backed securities and other investment securities.

Primary SIC and add'l.: 6712 6022

CIK No: 0000840889

Subsidiaries: CB, LLC, Centro Hipotecario de Puerto Rico, Inc., Doral Bank, Doral Bank, FSB, Doral Insurance Agency, Inc., Doral International, Inc., Doral Money, Inc., Doral Mortgage Corporation, Doral Properties, Inc., Doral Securities, Inc., SANA Mortgage Corporation

Officers: Glen R. Wakeman/Dir., CEO, Pres./$3,409,538.00, Lesbia Blanco-Diaz/Exec. VP, Chief Talent Officer, Administration Officer/$442,414.00, Marangal I. Domingo/CFO, Exec. VP/$751,834.00, Calixto Garcia-Velez/41/Exec. VP/$1,353,041.00, Olga Mayoral-Wilson/Exec. VP, Chief Communications Officer/$363,405.00, Enrique R. Ubarri-Baragano/Exec. VP, General Counsel/$482,426.00, Christopher Poulton/Exec. VP, Chief Business Development Officer, Gerardo Leiva/COO, Exec. VP, Paul Makowski/Exec. VP, Chief Risk Officer

Directors: Glen R. Wakeman/Dir., CEO, Pres., Dennis G. Buchert/Chmn., Adolfo Marzol/47/Dir., Manuel Pena-Morros/62/Dir., Frank W. Baier/Dir., John L. Ernst/67/Dir., Peter A. Hoffman/68/Dir., Efraim Kier/78/Dir., Howard M. Levkowitz/Dir., Ori Uziel/Dir., David Edward King/Dir., Michael J. O'Hanlon/Dir., Frederick C. Teed/50/Dir., John B. Hughes/52/Dir., Harold D. Vicente/62/Dir. *(16 Directors included in Index)*

Financial Data: Fiscal Year End:12/31 **Latest Annual Data:** 12/31/2006

Year		Sales			Net Income
2006		$866,177,000			-$223,901,000
2005		$1,054,531,000			$13,192,000
2004		$846,629,000			$214,794,000
Curr. Assets:	$1,210,224,000	Curr. Liab.:		$9,369,621,000	
Plant, Equip.:	$172,002,000	Total Liab.:		$10,953,020,000	Indic. Yr. Divd.: NA
Total Assets:	$11,856,424,000	Net Worth:		$903,404,000	Debt/ Equity: 1.5604

Dorchester Minerals LP

3838 Oak Lawn, Ste. 300, Dallas, TX, 75219; *PH:* 1-214-559-0300

General - Incorporation	DE	**Stock**- Price on:12/24/2007	$22.5
Employees	28	Stock Exchange	NDQ
Auditor	Grant Thornton LLP	Ticker Symbol	DMLP
Stk Agt	American Stock Transfer & Trust Co.	Outstanding Shares	28,240,000
Counsel	NA	E.P.S	$1.40
DUNS No.	NA	Shareholders	NA

Business: The groups principle activity is to acquire oil and gas properties. Specific customer of the group is Williams Power Company, Inc. The group operates from Alabama, Arkansas, California, Colorado, Florida, Georgia, Kansas, Illinois and Indiana. The group's quarterly revenue for September 2007 was 14.72 millions of USD.

Primary SIC and add'l.: 1311 4922 4923 1321

CIK No: 0001172358

Subsidiaries: Dorchester Minerals Acquisition GP Inc, Dorchester Minerals Acquisition LP, Dorchester Minerals Oklahoma GP Inc, Dorchester Minerals Oklahoma LP

Officers: William Casey McManemin/CEO/$110,400.00, H. C. Allen/CFO, Mgr./$110,400.00, James E. Raley/COO, Mgr./$110,400.00, Preston A. Peak/Mgr., Robert C. Vaughn/Mgr., Buford P. Berry/Mgr., Rawles Fulgham/Mgr., C. W. Russell/Mgr.

Directors: C. W. Russell/Mgr.

Owners: Insiders/12.10%, Rawles Fulgham, Robert C. Vaughn/1.80%, Preston A. Peak/5.60%, C. W. Russell, H. C. Allen, William Casey McManemin/4.20%, Energy Trust LLC/27.20%, James E. Raley

Financial Data: Fiscal Year End:12/31 **Latest Annual Data:** 12/31/2006

Year		Sales			Net Income
2006		$74,927,000			$50,210,000
2005		$79,765,000			$52,775,000
2004		$56,767,000			$30,076,000
Curr. Assets:	$24,191,000	Curr. Liab.:		$342,000	P/E Ratio: 14.15
Plant, Equip.:	$144,214,000	Total Liab.:		$629,000	Indic. Yr. Divd.: $2.240
Total Assets:	$168,429,000	Net Worth:		$167,800,000	Debt/ Equity: NA

Dorel Industries Inc

1255 Greene Ave., Ste. 300, Montreal, PQ, H3Z 2A4; *PH:* 1-514-934-3034; *http://* www.dorel.com; *Email:* info@dorel.com

General - Incorporation	QC	**Stock**- Price on:12/24/2007	$25.55
Employees	4,500	Stock Exchange	NDQ
Auditor	KPMG LLP	Ticker Symbol	DIIB
Stk Agt	Computershare Investor Services LLC	Outstanding Shares	NA
Counsel	NA	E.P.S	NA
DUNS No.	20-217-0288	Shareholders	NA

Business: The groups principle activities include designing, manufacturing and marketing consumer brands, sold through its juvenile, home furnishings, and recreational and leisure segments. The groups products are sold under the brand names Cosco, Safety 1st, Maxi-Cosi, and Quinny. The group operates from Canada.

Primary SIC and add'l.: 2517 2512 2511

CIK No: 0000843405

Subsidiaries: Leadra Design Inc., Ridgewood Industries Ltd.

Officers: Martin Schwartz/Dir., CEO, Pres., Jeffrey Schwartz/Dir., CFO, Exec. VP, Sec., Frank Rana/VP - Finance, Assist., Sec., Camillo Lisio/VP, COO, Jeff Segel/Dir., Exec. VP - Sales, Marketing, Ed Wyse/VP - Global Procurement, Alan Schwartz/Exec. VP - Operations

Directors: Martin Schwartz/Dir., CEO, Pres., Jeffrey Schwartz/Dir., CFO, Exec. VP, Sec., Maurice Tousson/Dir., Dian Cohen/Corp. Dir., Robert P. Baird/Dir., Harold P. Gordon/Dir., Alain Benedetti/Corp. Dir., Jeff Segel/Dir., Exec. VP - Sales, Marketing

Dorman Products Inc

3400 E Walnut St., Colmar, PA, 18915; *PH:* 1-215-997-1800; *Fax:* 1-215-997-8577; *http://* www.rbinc.com; *Email:* generalinquiry@dormanproducts.com

General - Incorporation	PA	**Stock**- Price on:12/24/2007	$14.04
Employees	942	Stock Exchange	NDQ
Auditor	KPMG LLP	Ticker Symbol	DORM
Stk Agt	StockTrans, Inc.	Outstanding Shares	17,690,000
Counsel	NA	E.P.S	$1.07
DUNS No.	NA	Shareholders	NA

Business: The groups principal activity is to supply automotive replacement parts, and fasteners and service line products. The products of the group include window handles, and switches, door hardware, interior trim parts, headlamp aiming screws and retainer rings and radiator parts. The group products sold under the trade names OE Solutions(TM), HELP!(R), AutoGrade(TM), First Stop(TM), Conduct-Tite(R), Pik-A-Nut(R), and Scan-Tech(TM). In June 2005, the group acquired The Automotive Edge Hermoff. The group operates from the United States, Canada, Sweden, China and Korea. The net sale of the group for the year 2006 was $295,825 (thousands).

Primary SIC and add'l.: 3714

CIK No: 0000868780

Subsidiaries: 1664403 Ontario Inc.(Hermoff), Allparts, Inc., Dorman Products of America, Ltd., Motor Power Industries, Inc., RB Distribution, Inc., RB Management, Inc., Scan-Tech USA/Sweden, A.B.

Officers: Richard N. Berman/Chmn., CEO, Pres., Joseph M. Beretta/Sr. VP - Product, Don Barry/Sr. VP - Sales, Mathias J. Barton/CFO, Sr. VP, Steven L. Berman/Dir., Exec. VP, Sec., Treasurer, Fred Frigo/Sr. VP - Operations

Directors: Richard N. Berman/Chmn., CEO, Pres., Steven L. Berman/Dir., Exec. VP, Sec., Treasurer, George L. Bernstein/Dir., John F. Creamer/Dir., Paul R. Lederer/Dir., Edgar W. Levin/Dir.

Owners: Jordan S. Berman/7.70%, Steven L. Berman/15.20%, Insiders/32.00%, George L. Bernstein, Richard N. Berman/14.20%, Paul R. Lederer, Columbia Management Advisors, LLC/7.20%, Mathias J. Barton, Edgar W. Levin, Donald J. Barry, Joseph M. Beretta, T Rowe Price Small-Cap Value Fund, Inc/6.20%, Royce & Associates, LLC/10.30%, John F. Creamer, Dimensional Fund Advisors LP/6.80%

Financial Data: Fiscal Year End:12/30 **Latest Annual Data:** 12/30/2006

Year	Sales	Net Income
2006	$295,825,000	$13,799,000
2005	$278,117,000	$17,077,000
2004	$249,526,000	$17,081,000

Curr. Assets:	$154,362,000	**Curr. Liab.:**	$38,550,000	**P/E Ratio:**	17.55
Plant, Equip.:	$27,473,000	**Total Liab.:**	$73,614,000	**Indic. Yr. Divd.:**	NA
Total Assets:	$212,156,000	**Net Worth:**	$138,542,000	**Debt/ Equity:**	0.1243

Dot Hill Systems Corp

2200 Faraday Ave., Ste. 100, Carlsbad, CA, 92008; **PH:** 1-760-931-5500; **Fax:** 1-760-931-5527; *http://* www.dothill.com

General - Incorporation	DE	**Stock** - Price on:12/24/2007	$3.4
Employees	269	Stock Exchange	NDQ
Auditor	Deloitte & Touche LLP	Ticker Symbol	HILL
Stk Agt	American Stock Transfer & Trust Co.	Outstanding Shares	45,580,000
Counsel	NA	E.P.S.	-$0.51
DUNS No.	19-616-9437	Shareholders	NA

Business: The group's principle activity is to design, manufacture, market and support high-performance data storage and networking solutions. The group also provides backup solutions, which consist of tape libraries and backup management software. The other services provided by the group include design consulting, installation, integration, training, 24-hour post-sales service and technical support and software-based management tools. The products and services are marketed to data-intensive industries such as telecommunications, enterprise Internet applications, financial services, health care, government/defense and academia. The group sells directly to end-users and through local distributors in eighteen countries including the United Kingdom, the Netherlands, Japan, Germany, Singapore and Israel. The group's quarterly revenue for September 2007 was 45.69 millions of USD.

Primary SIC and add'l.: 7372 7379 3572 7373

CIK No: 0001042783

Subsidiaries: National Life Finance Corporation, Tokyo Mitsubishi Bank

Officers: Dana W. Kammersgard/Dir., CEO, Pres./$832,808.00, Philip A. Davis/Exec. VP - Worldwide Field Operations/$541,651.00, Hanif I. Jamal/Sr. VP, CFO/$201,581.00, James E. Kuenzel/Sr. VP - Engineering, Kirsten Garvin/Dir. - Investor Relations, Robert Finley/58/VP - Manufacturing

Directors: Dana W. Kammersgard/Dir., CEO, Pres., Charles Christ/Chmn., W. R. Sauey/Dir., Joseph D. Markee/Dir., Kimberly Alexy/Dir., Roderick M. Sherwood/Dir.

Owners: Joseph D. Markee, Charles F. Christ, W.R. Sauey/4.10%, Shad L. Burke, TCW Asset Management Co./8.60%, ICM Asset Management, Inc./9.10%, James L. Lambert/3.70%, Philip A. Davis, Becker Capital Management, Inc./5.10%, Goldman Capital Management, Inc./5.20%, Dana W. Kammersgard/1.90%, Insiders/7.40%, Kimberly E. Alexy, Roderick M. Sherwood, Wellington Management Co. LLP/7.70% (17 Owners included in Index)

Financial Data: Fiscal Year End:12/31 **Latest Annual Data:** 12/31/2006

Year	Sales	Net Income
2006	$239,217,000	-$80,772,000
2005	$233,799,000	$26,597,000
2004	$239,376,000	$11,597,000

Curr. Assets:	$146,670,000	**Curr. Liab.:**	$43,729,000		
Plant, Equip.:	$9,738,000	**Total Liab.:**	$45,739,000	**Indic. Yr. Divd.:**	NA
Total Assets:	$201,651,000	**Net Worth:**	$155,912,000	**Debt/ Equity:**	NA

Double Eagle Petroleum Co

777 Overland Trl., Ste. 208, Casper, WY, 82602; **PH:** 1-307-237-9330; **Fax:** 1-307-266-1823; *http://* www.dble.us

General - Incorporation	MD	**Stock** - Price on:12/24/2007	$19.35
Employees	17	Stock Exchange	NDQ
Auditor	Hein & Assoc. LLP	Ticker Symbol	DBLE
Stk Agt	Computershare Investor Services LLC	Outstanding Shares	9,140,000
Counsel	Patton Boggs LLP	E.P.S.	$0.08
DUNS No.	06-407-4271	Shareholders	NA

Business: The group's principle activities include exploring, developing, producing and marketing crude oil and natural gas. The operations of the group are concentrated in green river basin in southwestern Wyoming, the powder river basin in northeastern Wyoming. The group has operations in the washakie basin in south central Wyoming, the wind river basin in central Wyoming and the christmas meadows area in northeastern Utah. As of 31-Dec-2003, the group owned interests in a total of 421 producing wells with oil constituting 7 percent and natural gas constituting approximately 33 percent. The group operates from United States.

Primary SIC and add'l.: 1311

CIK No: 0000029834

Officers: Stephen H. Hollis/57/Chmn., CEO, Pres./$240,003.00, Lonnie Brock/57/CFO/$128,849.00, Steven D. Degenfelder/51/VP - Land/$187,594.00, Carol A. Osborne/56/Corp. Sec., John Campbell/Investor Relations Officer

Directors: Stephen H. Hollis/57/Chmn., CEO, Pres., Sigmund Balaban/66/Dir., Roy G. Cohee/58/Dir., Richard Dole/62/Dir.

Owners: C.K. Adams, D. Steven Degenfelder/1.20%, Insiders/11.20%, Stephen H. Hollis/8.50%, Carol Osborne, Lonnie R. Brock, Richard Dole, Sigmund Balaban, Roy G. Cohee

Financial Data: Fiscal Year End:12/31 **Latest Annual Data:** 12/31/2006

Year	Sales	Net Income
2006	$19,032,000	$2,109,000
2005	$20,502,000	$3,965,000
2004	$13,267,000	$4,028,000

Curr. Assets:	$7,174,000	**Curr. Liab.:**	$14,180,000	**P/E Ratio:**	113.82
Plant, Equip.:	$57,186,000	**Total Liab.:**	$31,364,000	**Indic. Yr. Divd.:**	NA
Total Assets:	$64,406,000	**Net Worth:**	$33,042,000	**Debt/ Equity:**	0.2051

Double Hull Tankers Inc

26 New St., St. Helier, JE4 8PP; **PH:** 44-1534639759; **Fax:** 44-1534878427; *http://* www.dhtankers.com; **Email:** info@dhtankers.com

General - Incorporation	Jersey	**Stock** - Price on:12/24/2007	NA
Employees	2	Stock Exchange	NYSE
Auditor	Ernst& Young LLP	Ticker Symbol	DHT
Stk Agt	Mellon Investor Services LLC	Outstanding Shares	30,010,000
Counsel	NA	E.P.S.	$1.02
DUNS No.	NA	Shareholders	NA

Business: The groups principle activity is to acquire vessel properties. The group operates from the Canada. The groups quarterly revenue for September 2007 was 20.15 millions of USD.

Primary SIC and add'l.: 4412

CIK No: 0001331284

Subsidiaries: Ania Aframax Corporation, Ann Tanker Corporation, Cathy Tanker Corporation, Chris Tanker Corporation, Rebecca Corporation, Regal Unity Tanker Corporation, Sophie Corporation

Officers: Ole Jacob Diesen/CEO, Eirik Uboe/CFO, Tom R. Kjeldsberg/Sr. VP - Business Development

Directors: Erik Lind/Chmn., Randee Day/Dir., Rolf Wikborg/Dir.

Owners: Ole Jacob Diesen, Randee Day, Tom R. Kjeldsberg, Rolf A. Wikborg, Scott A. Bommer/5.68%, Erik A. Lind, Eirik Ube, FMR Corp./12.55%, Insiders

Financial Data: Fiscal Year End:12/31 **Latest Annual Data:** 12/31/2006

Year	Sales	Net Income
2006	$86,793,000	$35,750,000
2005	$104,307,000	$53,110,000

Curr. Assets:	$25,056,000	**Curr. Liab.:**	$9,625,000		
Plant, Equip.:	$322,577,000	**Total Liab.:**	$245,625,000	**Indic. Yr. Divd.:**	$1.560
Total Assets:	$349,040,000	**Net Worth:**	$103,415,000	**Debt/ Equity:**	NA

Douglas Emmett Inc

808 Wilshire Blvd., Ste. 200, Santa Monica, CA, 90401; **PH:** 1-310-255-7700; **Fax:** 1-310-255-7701; *http://* www.douglasemmett.com

General - Incorporation	MD	**Stock** - Price on:12/24/2007	$27.09
Employees	400	Stock Exchange	NYSE
Auditor	Ernst & Young, LLP	Ticker Symbol	DEI
Stk Agt	Computershare Trust Co	Outstanding Shares	115,010,000
Counsel	NA	E.P.S.	-$0.18
DUNS No.	NA	Shareholders	NA

Business: The groups principle activities include owning and acquiring office properties. The group operates from the United States. The group's quarterly revenue for September 2007 was 130.93 millions of USD.

Primary SIC and add'l.: 6512 6798 6513

CIK No: 0001364250

Subsidiaries: Barrington Pacific, LLC, Barrington/Kiowa Properties, Barry Properties, Ltd., Brentwood Court, Brentwood Plaza, Brentwood-San Vicente Medical, Ltd., DECO Acquisition, LLC, DEG Residential, LLC, DEG, LLC, DEGA, LLC, DERA Acquisition, LLC, DERF 2005 Acquisition, LLC, Douglas Emmett 1993, LLC, Douglas Emmett 1995, LLC, Douglas Emmett 1996, LLC 40 Subsidiaries included in the Index

Officers: Jordan L. Kaplan/Dir., CEO, Pres., Kenneth M. Panzer/Dir., COO, William Kamer/CFO, Andres R. Gavinet/Exec. VP - Finance, Allan B. Golad/Sr. VP - Property Management, Michael J. Means/Sr. VP - Commercial Leasing, Mary Jensen/VP - Investor Relations, Greg Hambly/Chief Accounting Officer

Directors: Jordan L. Kaplan/Dir., CEO, Pres., Dan A. Emmett/68/Chmn., Leslie E. Bider/Dir., Kenneth M. Panzer/Dir., COO, Victor J. Coleman/Dir., Ghebre Selassie Mehreteab/Dir., Thomas E. Ohern/Dir., Andrea L. Rich/Dir., William Wilson/Dir.

Owners: Andrea Rich, Thomas E. OHern, Victor J. Coleman, Ghebre Selassie Mehreteab, Wellington Management Company, LLP/5.79%, Dan A. Emmett/4.94%, William Wilson, Insiders/13.87%, Jordan L. Kaplan/4.48%, William Kamer, Yale University Investments Office/10.28%, Kenneth M. Panzer/4.48%, Leslie E. Bider, FMR Corp/5.48%, Andres Gavinet

Financial Data: Fiscal Year End:NA **Latest Annual Data:** 12/31/2006

Year	Sales	Net Income
2006	$433,663,000	-$36,953,000

Curr. Assets:	$11,711,000	**Curr. Liab.:**	$59,480,000		
Plant, Equip.:	$6,056,096,000	**Total Liab.:**	$4,088,345,000	**Indic. Yr. Divd.:**	$0.700
Total Assets:	$6,200,118,000	**Net Worth:**	$2,111,773,000	**Debt/ Equity:**	1.3381

Douglas Lake Minerals Inc

602 W Hastings St., Ste. 500, Vancouver, BC, V6B 1P2; **PH:** 1-604-230-4930; **Fax:** 1-604-899-1240; *http://* www.douglaslakeminerals.com

General - Incorporation	NV	**Stock** - Price on:12/24/2007	$0.5
Employees	NA	Stock Exchange	OTC
Auditor	Manning Elliott LLP	Ticker Symbol	DLKM
Stk Agt	NA	Outstanding Shares	NA
Counsel	NA	E.P.S.	NA
DUNS No.	NA	Shareholders	NA

Business: The groups principal activity is to explore minerals. The group operates from Canada and the United States.

Primary SIC and add'l.: 1000

CIK No: 0001297223

Officers: Harpreet Singh Sangha/Dir., CEO, Pres., Antonia Bold-De-Haughton/Dir., CFO, Manning Elliott/Auditor

Directors: Harpreet Singh Sangha/Dir., CEO, Pres., Joseph Rugumyamheto/Chmn., Richard Radez/Chmn. - Advisory Board, Andrew Lee Smith/Member - Advisory Board, David W. Moore/Member - Advisory Board, Joanne Freeze/Member - Advisory Board, Gurpreet Singh Sangha/Dir., David Groves/Dir., Thomas J. Deutsch/Partner, Antonia Bold-De-Haughton/Dir., CFO

Owners: The M-B Trust/10.30%, Insiders/10.30%, Gurpreet Sangha/1.00%, Muganyizi Lutagwaba/6.90%, Joseph Rugumyamheto/2.80%, Harpreet Sangha/5.80%, Antonia Bold-de-Haughton, Charanjit Brar/3.40%

Financial Data: Fiscal Year End:05/31 **Latest Annual Data:** 5/31/2006

Year	Sales	Net Income
2006	NA	-$5,985,000
2005	NA	-$430,000

Curr. Assets:	$2,000	**Curr. Liab.:**	$397,000		
Plant, Equip.:	$350,000	**Total Liab.:**	$397,000	**Indic. Yr. Divd.:**	NA
Total Assets:	$352,000	**Net Worth:**	-$45,000	**Debt/ Equity:**	NA

Dov Pharmaceutical Inc

150 Pierce St., Somerset, NJ, 08873; ***PH:*** 1-732-907-3600; ***Fax:*** 1-732-907-3799; ***http://*** www.dovpharm.com; ***Email:*** ir@dovpharm.com

General - Incorporation ... DE
Employees ... 41
Auditor ... PricewaterhouseCoopers LLP
Stk Agt ... Continental Stock Transfer & Trust Co
Counsel ... Goodwin Procter LLP
DUNS No. ... NA

Stock- Price on:12/24/2007 ... $0.315
Stock Exchange ... OTC
Ticker Symbol ... DOVP
Outstanding Shares ... 26,710,000
E.P.S ... $0.26
Shareholders ... NA

Business: The group's principal activities are to discover, in-license, develop and commercialize novel drug candidates for central nervous system, cardiovascular and urological disorders. The group has six product candidates in clinical trails. The products of the group include indiplon, ocinaplon, bicifadine, dov 216,303, dov 21,947 and dov diltiazem. These products will be used for the treatment of insomnia, anxiety disorders, pain, depression and angina and hypertension. The group also has two compounds in preclinical development namely, dov 102,677 and dov 51,892, for the potential treatment of Parkinson's disease, restless leg syndrome, attention deficit disorder and anxiety disorders including panic.

Primary SIC and add'l.: 2834 8731

CIK No: 0001066833

Subsidiaries: DOV Pharmaceutical Luxembourg S.a.r.l., Nascime Limited

Officers: Barbara G. Duncan/Dir., CEO/$1,236,077.00, Arnold S. Lippa/Co - Founder, Exec. Chmn., Advisor/$768,399.00, Robert Guillemin/Dir., Advisor, Phil Skolnick/Pres., Chief Scientific Officer/$734,866.00, Warren Stern/Sr. VP - Drug Development/$1,694,064.00, Arvid Carlsson/Dir., Advisor, John W. Daly/Dir., Advisor, David H. Farb/Dir., Advisor, Robert Horton/Exec. Officer/$2,095,078.00, William Kaltnecker/Chief Accounting Officer, Controller

Directors: Barbara G. Duncan/Dir., CEO, Arnold S. Lippa/Co - Founder, Exec. Chmn., Advisor, Robert Cancro/Co - Founder, Chmn. - Scientific Advisory Board, Zola Horovitz/Dir., Morton E. Goldberg/Member - Dovs Scientific Advisory Board, Arvid Carlsson/Dir., Advisor, Robert Guillemin/Dir., Advisor, Theresa A. Bischoff/Dir., Patrick Ashe/Dir., John W. Daly/Dir., Advisor, David H. Farb/Dir., Advisor, Daniel S. Van Riper/Dir., Dennis G. Podlesak/Dir.

Owners: Dennis Podlesak, Daniel S. Van Riper, Insiders/3.30%, Warren Stern, Arnold S. Lippa/1.20%, Patrick Ashe, Barbara G. Duncan, Zola Horovitz, Phil Skolnick, Theresa A. Bischoff, Polygon Global Opportunities Master Fund/10.70%

Financial Data: ***Fiscal Year End:***12/31 ***Latest Annual Data:*** 12/31/2006

Year	Sales	Net Income
2006	$25,951,000	-$38,368,000
2005	$8,647,000	-$52,968,000
2004	$2,542,000	-$32,921,000

Curr. Assets:	$44,936,000	**Curr. Liab.:**	$23,799,000		
Plant, Equip.:	$1,214,000	**Total Liab.:**	$79,995,000	**Indic. Yr. Divd.:**	NA
Total Assets:	$50,361,000	**Net Worth:**	-$29,634,000	**Debt/ Equity:**	NA

Dover Corp

280 Pk. Ave., Fl. 34W, New York, NY, 10017; ***PH:*** 1-212-922-1640; ***Fax:*** 1-212-922-1656; ***http://*** www.dovercorporation.com

General - Incorporation ... DE
Employees ... 33,000
Auditor ... PricewaterhouseCoopers LLP
Stk Agt ... Mellon Investor Services LLC
Counsel ... NA
DUNS No. ... 00-324-5271

Stock- Price on:12/24/2007 ... $52.44
Stock Exchange ... NYSE
Ticker Symbol ... DOV
Outstanding Shares ... 204,420,000
E.P.S ... $2.90
Shareholders ... NA

Business: The groups principle activity is to manufacture industrial products and innovative equipment. The group operates through four segments namely industrial products, engineered systems, fluid management and electronic technologies. The group operates from United States.

Primary SIC and add'l.: 3541 3589 3429 3679 3530 3559 3565

CIK No: 0000029905

Subsidiaries: Acumen Technology (M) Sdn. Bhd., ALMATEC Maschinenbau GmbH, Alphasem (Shenzhen) Co., Ltd., Alphasem (Suzhou) Co., Ltd., Alphasem AG, Alphasem Asia Ltd., Alphasem Asia Pte. Ltd., Alphasem Corporation, Alphasem Far East (L) Ltd., Alphasem Holding GmbH, Alphasem Korea Ltd., Alphasem Philippines, atg test systems asia Ltd., atg test systems GmbH & Co KG, Avborne Accessory Group, Inc. 329 Subsidiaries included in the Index

Officers: Ronald L. Hoffman/Dir., CEO, Pres./$9,074,562.00, Robert A. Livingston/CEO, VP, Pres. - Dover Engineered Systems, William W. Spurgeon/CEO, VP, Pres. - Dover Fluid Management, Paul E. Goldberg/Treasure, Dir. - Investor Relations, David J. Ropp/VP/$5,502,322.00, George Pompetzki/VP - Taxes, David R. Van Loan/VP/$3,881,064.00, Joseph W. Schmidt/VP, General Counsel, Sec., Raymond T. McKay/VP, Controller, Ralph S. Coppola/63/VP, Timothy J. Sandker/59/VP/$4,883,346.00, Robert G. Kuhbach/CFO, VP - Finance/$2,866,999.00, Robert A. Tyre/VP - Corporate Development

Directors: Ronald L. Hoffman/Dir., CEO, Pres., Thomas L. Reece/Chmn., Thomas J. Derosa/Dir., Peter T. Francis/Dir., Jean-Pierre M. Ergas/Dir., Michael B. Stubbs/Dir., Richard K. Lochridge/Dir., Bernard G. Rethore/Dir., Kristiane C. Graham/Dir., David H. Benson/Dir., James L. Koley/Dir., Mary A. Winston/Dir., Robert W. Cremin/Dir.

Owners: Timothy J. Sandker, David H. Benson, Jean-Pierre M. Ergas, Michael B. Stubbs, Bernard G. Rethore, Richard K. Lochridge, Robert G. Kuhbach, Kristiane C. Graham, Robert W. Cremin, GE Asset Management Incorporated/6.47%, Insiders/2.13%, David R. Van Loan, James L. Koley, David J. Ropp, Thomas L. Reece *(17 Owners included in Index)*

Financial Data: ***Fiscal Year End:***12/31 ***Latest Annual Data:*** 12/31/2006

Year	Sales	Net Income
2006	$6,511,623,000	$561,782,000
2005	$6,078,380,000	$510,142,000
2004	$5,488,112,000	$412,755,000

Curr. Assets:	$2,271,506,000	**Curr. Liab.:**	$1,433,980,000	**P/E Ratio:**	22.13
Plant, Equip.:	$856,799,000	**Total Liab.:**	$3,815,636,000	**Indic. Yr. Divd.:**	$0.800
Total Assets:	$7,626,658,000	**Net Worth:**	$3,811,022,000	**Debt/ Equity:**	NA

Dover Downs Gaming & Entertainment Inc

1131 N DuPont Hwy., Dover, DE, 19901; ***PH:*** 1-302-674-4600; ***Fax:*** 1-302-857-3253; ***http://*** www.doverdowns.com

General - Incorporation ... DE
Employees ... 772
Auditor ... KPMG LLP
Stk Agt ... Mellon Investor Services LLC
Counsel ... NA
DUNS No. ... NA

Stock- Price on:12/24/2007 ... $14.52
Stock Exchange ... NYSE
Ticker Symbol ... DDE
Outstanding Shares ... 32,640,000
E.P.S ... $0.82
Shareholders ... NA

Business: The group's principal activity is to operate a casino, a hotel with a conference center and a harness racing track. All these facilities are located adjacent to each other at the group's property in dover, Delaware. The casino is named as dover downs slots, which is an 80,000 square feet las vegas style and features 2,000 video lottery (slot) machines. The hotel with a conference center is known as dover downs hotel and conference center. This hotel features accommodations with conference center, banquet, dining, ballroom and concert hall facilities. The harness racing track is called as dover downs raceway, which is a 5/8-mile horse racetrack with a state-of-the-art simulcasting parlor. The facility is located in close proximity to the metropolitan areas of philadelphia, baltimore and Washington D.C.

Primary SIC and add'l.: 7999 7948

CIK No: 0001162556

Subsidiaries: Dover Downs Inc., Dover Downs Management Corp.

Officers: Edward J. Sutor/CEO, Pres./$421,963.00, Timothy R. Horne/41/Sr. VP - Finance, Treasurer, CFO/$332,089.00, Klaus M. Belohoubek/Sr. VP, General Counsel/$286,132.00

Directors: Henry B. Tippie/81/Chmn., Randall R. Rollins/76/Dir., Patrick J. Bagley/60/Dir., John W. Rollins/65/Dir., Denis McGlynn/62/Dir., Jeffrey W. Rollins/43/Dir., Kenneth K. Chalmers/78/Dir.

Owners: Michele M. Rollins, Henry B. Tippie/1.10%, Jeffrey W. Rollins, Patrick J. Bagley, Gabelli Asset Management,Inc./5.00%, John W. Rollins/2.30%, Henry B. Tippie, Timothy R. Horne, Gates Capital Management,Inc./5.30%, Eugene W. Weaver, Randall R. Rollins, Michele M. Rollins, Insiders/7.70%, Edward J. Sutor/1.00%, Kenneth K. Chalmers *(26 Owners included in Index)*

Financial Data: ***Fiscal Year End:***12/31 ***Latest Annual Data:*** 12/31/2006

Year	Sales	Net Income
2006	$236,451,000	$25,328,000
2005	$216,852,000	$26,040,000
2004	$227,717,000	$16,381,000

Curr. Assets:	$40,295,000	**Curr. Liab.:**	$28,316,000	**P/E Ratio:**	18.15
Plant, Equip.:	$132,732,000	**Total Liab.:**	$95,768,000	**Indic. Yr. Divd.:**	$0.200
Total Assets:	$173,027,000	**Net Worth:**	$77,259,000	**Debt/ Equity:**	0.6320

Dover Motorsports Inc

1131 N DuPont Hwy., Dover, DE, 19903; ***PH:*** 1-302-883-6500 ; ***Fax:*** 1-302-672-0100; ***http://*** www.dovermotorsportsinc.com; ***Email:*** info@dovermotorsports.com

General - Incorporation ... DE
Employees ... 131
Auditor ... KPMG LLP
Stk Agt ... Mellon Investor Services LLC
Counsel ... NA
DUNS No. ... 07-552-5410

Stock- Price on:12/24/2007 ... $6.12
Stock Exchange ... NYSE
Ticker Symbol ... DVD
Outstanding Shares ... 36,240,000
E.P.S ... $0.07
Shareholders ... NA

Business: The group's principal activity is to market and promote motorsports entertainment in the United States. The group operates four permanent motorsports tracks and one temporary circuit in four states. The group promotes its events in four premier sanctioning bodies in motorsports. The four sanctioning bodies in motorsports include the national association for stock car auto racing (nascar), championship auto racing teams (cart), the indy racing league (irl) and the national hot rod association (nhra). The group also organizes and promotes the toyota grand prix of long beach in long beach, California and the grand prix of denver in denver, Colorado.

Primary SIC and add'l.: 7948

CIK No: 0001017673

Subsidiaries: Dover International Speedway, Inc., Gateway International Motorsports Corporation, Gateway International Services Corporation, M & N Services Corp, Memphis International Motorsports Corporation, Midwest Racing, Inc., Nashville Speedway, USA, Inc.

Officers: Klaus M. Belohoubek/Sr. VP, General Counsel/$236,714.00, Patrick J. Bagley/Sr. VP - Finance/$300,988.00

Owners: Eugene W. Weaver/0.20%, Gary W. Rollins/1.80%, Henry B. Tippie, Michele M. Rollins/2.00%, Denis McGlynn, Insiders, Denis McGlynn/1.20%, Thomas G. Wintermantel/0.30%, Gabelli Asset Management, Inc./7.50%, Gary W. Rollins, Randall R. Rollins, Jeffrey W. Rollins, Randall R. Rollins/1.80%, Dimensional Fund Advisors Inc./7.90%, Kenneth K. Chalmers/0.10% *(24 Owners included in Index)*

Financial Data: ***Fiscal Year End:***12/31 ***Latest Annual Data:*** 12/31/2006

Year	Sales	Net Income
2006	$91,274,000	-$35,345,000
2005	$90,999,000	$4,576,000
2004	$93,617,000	$2,440,000

Curr. Assets:	$5,487,000	**Curr. Liab.:**	$16,519,000		
Plant, Equip.:	$152,502,000	**Total Liab.:**	$88,674,000	**Indic. Yr. Divd.:**	$0.060
Total Assets:	$162,934,000	**Net Worth:**	$74,260,000	**Debt/ Equity:**	0.7750

Dover Saddlery Inc

525 Great Rd., Littleton, MA, 01460; ***PH:*** 1-978-952-8062; ***Fax:*** 1-978-952-8065; ***http://*** www.doversaddlery.com; ***Email:*** customerservice@doversaddlery.com

General - Incorporation ... DE
Employees ... NA
Auditor ... Ernst & Young LLP
Stk Agt ... NA
Counsel ... NA
DUNS No. ... NA

Stock- Price on:12/24/2007 ... NA
Stock Exchange ... NDQ
Ticker Symbol ... DOVR
Outstanding Shares ... NA
E.P.S ... NA
Shareholders ... NA

Business: The groups principal activities include retailing and marketing equestrian products. The products of the group include saddles and tack, specialized apparel, and horse care and stable. The group products sold under the trade names Hermes, Ariat, Grand Prix, Mountain Horse, Passier and Prestige. In June 2006, the group acquired Dominion Saddlery. The group operates from the United States. The net sale of the group for the year 2006 was $73,046,123.

Primary SIC and add'l.: 5961 5941

CIK No: 0001071625

Subsidiaries: Dover Saddlery Direct, Inc., Dover Saddlery Retail, Inc., Old Dominion Enterprises, Inc., Smith Brother, Inc.

Officers: Stephen L. Day/62/Chmn., CEO, Pres., Treasurer/$393,987.00, Jonathan A.R. Grylls/43/Dir., COO, VP, Sec./$282,738.00, William Schmidt/59/VP - Operations/$254,398.00, Michael W. Bruns/52/CFO/$186,445.00

Directors: Stephen L. Day/62/Chmn., CEO, Pres., Treasurer, Jonathan A.R. Grylls/43/Dir., COO, VP, Sec., David J. Powers/Dir., James F. Powers/58/Dir., John Mitchell/Dir., Gregory F. Mulligan/55/Dir., William F. Meagher/69/Dir.

Owners: Gregory F. Mulligan, Glenhill Capital, Austin W. Marxe, James F. Powers, Stephen L. Day, Jonathan A.R. Grylls, William G. Schmidt, Gruber and McBaine Capital Management, LLC, William F. Meagher, Michele R. Powers, Michael W. Bruns, Insiders, David J. Powers, Wellington Management

Financial Data: Fiscal Year End:12/31 Latest Annual Data: 12/31/2006

Year	Sales			Net Income
2006		$73,046,000		$1,392,000
2005		$62,650,000		$826,000
2004		$58,698,000		$1,366,000
Curr. Assets:	$18,828,000	Curr. Liab.:	$9,119,000	P/E Ratio: 33.38
Plant, Equip.:	$2,832,000	Total Liab.:	$18,136,000	Indic. Yr. Divd.: NA
Total Assets:	$36,866,000	Net Worth:	$18,730,000	Debt/ Equity: NA

Dow Chemical Co

2030 Dow Ctr., Midland, MI, 48674; **PH:** 1-989-636-1000; **Fax:** 1-989-832-1556;
http:// www.dow.com

General - Incorporation	DE	**Stock**- Price on:12/24/2007	$45.06
Employees	42,578	Stock Exchange	NYSE
Auditor	Deloitte & Touche LLP	Ticker Symbol	DOW
Stk Agt	Bank of New York	Outstanding Shares	953,240,000
Counsel	NA	E.P.S.	$3.60
DUNS No.	00-138-1581	Shareholders	NA

Business: The group's principle activity is to provide chemical, plastic and agricultural products and services to various consumer markets. The group's products include adhesives and sealants, medical, paper, textiles, paints, coatings and inks, and plastic and rubber products, copolymers, and saran resins and films. The group operates from United States.

Primary SIC and add'l.: 2812 2861 2869 2821 2891 2873 3089

CIK No: 0000029915

Subsidiaries: Advanced Design Concepts GmbH, Agrigenetics Molokai LLC, Agrigenetics, Inc., AgroPartners Corporation, Alsan Research, Ambito DAS S.A., Amerchol Corporation, American Mortell Corporation, Anabond Essex India Private Limited, ANGUS Chemical Company, ANGUS Chemie GmbH, Arabian Chemical Company (Latex) Ltd., Arabian Chemical Company (Polystyrene) Limited, Arakawa Europe GmbH, Ascot Chemicals Limited 414 Subsidiaries included in the Index

Officers: Andrew N. Liveris/52/Chmn., CEO, Pres./$16,821,540.00, Jerome A. Peribere/CEO, Pres. - Dow Agrosciences, Theo Walthie/Business Group Pres. - Hydrocarbons, Energy, David E. Kepler/Sr. VP, Chief Sustainability Officer, CIO - Shared Services/$4,289,395.00, Fernando Ruiz/Corporate VP, Treasurer, Thomas E. Moran/Assist. Sec., William H. Weideman/VP, Controller, Frank H. Brod/Corporate VP, Controller, William F. Banholzer/CTO, Group VP, Luciano Respini/Corporate VP - Geography, Responsibility Dow Europe, The Global Geographic Counsel, Marketing, Sales/$6,216,135.00, Gary R. Veurink/Corporate VP - Manufacturing, Engineering, Lawrence J. Washington/Corporate VP, William L. Curry/Chief Tax Officer, Assist. Sec., Michael W. McGuire/Assist. Sec., Douglas J. Anderson/Corporate Auditor (37 Officers included in Index)

Directors: Andrew N. Liveris/52/Chmn., CEO, Pres., Arnold A. Allemang/Dir. - Sr. Advisor, Ruth G. Shaw/Dir., James M. Ringler/Dir., Jeff M. Fettig/Dir., Barbara Hackman Franklin/66/Dir., Jacqueline K. Barton/Dir., James A. Bell/58/Dir., Geoffery E. Merszei/55/Dir., CFO, Exec. VP, Michael J. Cook/Dir., Pedro J. Reinhard/62/Dir., John B. Hess/Dir., Dennis H. Reilley/Dir.

Owners: A. A. Allemang, B. H. Franklin, D. E. Kepler, J. M. Ringler, A. N. Liveris, Dodge & Cox/6.06%, R. Kreinberg, L. Respini, J. B. Hess, P. G. Stern, J. K. Barton, J. A. Bell, G. E. Merszei, Insiders/0.41%, J. M. Fettig (18 Owners included in Index)

Financial Data: Fiscal Year End:12/31 Latest Annual Data: 12/31/2006

Year	Sales			Net Income
2006		$49,124,000,000		$3,724,000,000
2005		$46,307,000,000		$4,515,000,000
2004		$40,161,000,000		$2,797,000,000
Curr. Assets:	$17,209,000,000	Curr. Liab.:	$10,601,000,000	P/E Ratio: 12.59
Plant, Equip.:	$13,722,000,000	Total Liab.:	$27,151,000,000	Indic. Yr. Divd.: $1.680
Total Assets:	$45,581,000,000	Net Worth:	$17,065,000,000	Debt/ Equity: 0.4603

Dow Jones & Co Inc

200 Liberty St., New York, NY, 10281; **PH:** 1-212-416-2000; **Fax:** 1-212-416-4348;
http:// www.dowjones.com; **Email:** djcom@dowjones.com

General - Incorporation	DE	**Stock**- Price on:12/24/2007	$59.71
Employees	7,400	Stock Exchange	NYSE
Auditor	PricewaterhouseCoopers LLP	Ticker Symbol	DJ
Stk Agt	Mellon Investor Services LLC	Outstanding Shares	83,790,000
Counsel	NA	E.P.S.	$4.03
DUNS No.	00-131-6702	Shareholders	NA

Business: The groups principle activity is to provide accessible business and related content and information services across all consumer and enterprise media channels. The groups services include Dow Jones integrated solutions and Dow Jones conferences. The group operates from United States.

Primary SIC and add'l.: 2721 6289 7383 2711 7375

CIK No: 0000029924

Subsidiaries: Davill, Inc., DJBI, LLC, Dow Jones & Company (Australia) Pty Limited, Dow Jones & Company (Schweiz) GmbH, Dow Jones & Company (Singapore) Pte Limited, Dow Jones Advertising (Shanghai) Co., Limited, Dow Jones AER Company, Inc., Dow Jones BD Services, Inc., Dow Jones Broadcasting (Asia), Inc., Dow Jones Broadcasting (Europe), Inc., Dow Jones Canada, Inc., Dow Jones Cash Management, Inc., Dow Jones Consulting (Shanghai) Limited, Dow Jones Distribution Co. (Asia), Inc., Dow Jones Distribution Malaysia 51 Subsidiaries included in the Index

Officers: Richard F. Zannino/Dir., CEO/$4,159,012.00, Edwin A. Finn/Chmn., Editorial Dir. - Smartmoney, Pres. - Editor, Barron's, Consumer Media Group, John N. Wilcox/Sr. VP, Joseph A. Stern/Dir., Exec. VP, General Counsel, Corp. Sec./$1,270,800.00, Clare Hart/Exec. VP, Pres. - Dow Jones Enterprise Media Group/$1,716,211.00, Paul A. Gigot/Editorial Page Editor, The Wall Street Journal, Consumer Media Group, Todd H. Larsen/COO - Consumer Media Group, Ann Marks/Chief Marketing Officer, Michael A. Petronella/Pres. - Dow Jones Indexes, Reprints, Scott D. Schulman/Pres. - Dow Jones Financial Information Services, Andrew Langhoff/Sr. VP, General Counsel, Catherine D. Paffenroth/VP - Human Resources, William A. Zurilla/CFO, VP - Ottaway Newspapers, Local Media Group, Joseph J. Cantamessa/VP - Corporate Security, Thomas W. McGuirl/VP - Tax (33 Officers included in Index)

Directors: Richard F. Zannino/Dir., CEO, Peter R. Kann/Chmn., Peter M. McPherson/Chmn., Frank N. Newman/Dir., Christopher Bancroft/Dir., John M. Engler/Dir., Leslie Hill/54/Dir., John Brock/Dir., Paul Sagan/Dir., Michael B. Elefante/Dir., Lewis B. Campbell/Dir., Joseph A. Stern/Dir., Exec. VP, General Counsel, Corp. Sec., Harvey Golub/Dir., William C. Steere/Dir., Elizabeth Steele/Dir. (20 Directors included in Index)

Financial Data: Fiscal Year End:12/31 Latest Annual Data: 12/31/2006

Year	Sales			Net Income
2006		$1,783,870,000		$386,564,000
2005		$1,769,690,000		$60,395,000
2004		$1,671,458,000		$99,548,000
Curr. Assets:	$313,648,000	Curr. Liab.:	$828,114,000	P/E Ratio: 14.39
Plant, Equip.:	$638,772,000	Total Liab.:	$1,456,589,000	Indic. Yr. Divd.: $1.000
Total Assets:	$1,955,562,000	Net Worth:	$498,973,000	Debt/ Equity: NA

Downey Financial Corp

3501 Jamboree Rd., Newport Beach, CA, 92660; **PH:** 1-949-854-0300;
https:// www.downeysavings.com

General - Incorporation	DE	**Stock**- Price on:12/24/2007	$69.98
Employees	1,974	Stock Exchange	NYSE
Auditor	KPMG LLP	Ticker Symbol	DSL
Stk Agt	American Stock Transfer & Trust Co.	Outstanding Shares	27,850,000
Counsel	NA	E.P.S.	$7.33
DUNS No.	NA	Shareholders	NA

Business: The groups principal activity is to invest in real estate property. The group operated from the United States.

Primary SIC and add'l.: 6552 6035 6512 6712

CIK No: 0000935063

Subsidiaries: Butterfield Services, Inc., Downey Affiliated Insurance Agency, Downey Savings and Loan Association, F.A., DSL Service Company

Officers: Daniel D. Rosenthal/Dir., CEO/$1,552,496.00, Edward J. Adams/Exec. VP, Dir. - Residential Lending, Bank, Thomas E. Prince/Exec. VP, COO - Downey, The Bank/$1,089,660.00, Jon A. MacDonald/Exec. VP, General Counsel, Corp. Sec. - Downey, The Bank/$599,603.00, Brian E. Cote/Exec. VP, CFO - Downey, The Bank/$369,631.00, Lillian E. Gavin/Exec. VP, Dir. - Operational, Compliance Risk, Bank, Jeffrey D. Pratt/47/Sr. VP, Chief Risk Officer - Bank, Francisco De Cordova/61/Dir., Exec. VP, Edward A. Luther/Sr. VP, Dir. - Major Loans, Bank, Hugh C. Chewning/Sr. VP, Dir. - Marketing, Bank, Kent J. Smith/Sr. VP, Controller - Bank, Stanley M. Tarbell/Sr. VP, Tax Dir. - Downey, The Bank, David A. Casty/Sr. VP, Mgr. - DSL Service Company, Rick McGill/Pres. - Downey, The Bank, Robert Suarez/CIO, Exec. VP - Bank (20 Officers included in Index)

Directors: Daniel D. Rosenthal/Dir., CEO, Maurice L. McAlister/Chmn., Cheryl E. Olson/Vice Chmn., Michael B. Abrahams/Dir., Michael D. Bozarth/Dir., Brent G. McQuarrie/Dir., Gerald E. Finnell/Dir., James H. Hunter/Dir., Lester C. Smull/Dir., Jane Wolfe/Dir., Gary W. Brummett/Dir.

Owners: Goldman Sachs Asset Management, L.P./6.60%, Cheryl E. Olson/2.50%, Gerald E. Finnell, Brent McQuarrie/1.20%, Thomas E. Prince, Jeffrey L. Gendell/9.60%, James H. Hunter, Michael B. Abrahams, Maurice L. McAlister/20.20%, Jane Wolfe, Cliff Piscitelli, Insiders/23.90%, McAlister Family Trust/20.20%, Gerald H. McQuarrie Family Trusts/5.50%, Lester C. Smull (16 Owners included in Index)

Financial Data: Fiscal Year End:12/31 Latest Annual Data: 12/31/2006

Year	Sales			Net Income
2006		$1,227,542,000		$205,174,000
2005		$1,032,781,000		$217,434,000
2004		$698,534,000		$107,662,000
Curr. Assets:	$216,058,000	Curr. Liab.:	$14,505,422,000	P/E Ratio: 9.55
Plant, Equip.:	$122,576,000	Total Liab.:	$14,806,932,000	Indic. Yr. Divd.: NA
Total Assets:	$16,209,389,000	Net Worth:	$1,402,457,000	Debt/ Equity: 0.1377

DPAC Technologies Corp

5675 Hudson Industrial Pk., Hudson, OH, 44236; **PH:** 1-330-655-9000; **Fax:** 1-330-655-9070;
http:// www.dpactech.com; **Email:** ir@dpactech.com

General - Incorporation	CA	**Stock**- Price on:12/24/2007	NA
Employees	NA	Stock Exchange	OTC
Auditor	Hausser & Taylor, LLC	Ticker Symbol	DPAC
Stk Agt	NA	Outstanding Shares	NA
Counsel	NA	E.P.S.	-$0.015
DUNS No.	01-860-1930	Shareholders	NA

Business: The group's principal activities are to design and manufacture high-density electronic components. The group designs and manufactures ceramic and plastic high-density, high-reliability memory modules. The products include static random access memories, electrically erasable programmable read-only memories, including flash technology and dynamic random access memories. These products are used in applications such as network servers, computer storage devices, guidance systems, medical instrumentation and communication electronics. The group operates mainly in the United States of America.

Primary SIC and add'l.: 3674

CIK No: 0000784770

Subsidiaries: QuaTech

Officers: Steve Runkel/CEO, Kevin Kline/VP - Sales, Marketing, Stewart Guy/VP - Operations, David Purtill/Sales, Dpac Regional Sales Mgr., Mo Kapila/Regional Sales Mgr. - Eastern, Central US, Stephen J. Vukadinovich/CFO, Sec. - Principal Financial, Accounting Officer

Directors: Creighton Kim Early/Chmn., Samuel W. Tishler/Dir., William Roberts/Dir., Mark Chapman/Dir., Dennis R. Leibel/Dir., Jim Bole/Dir.

Financial Data: **Fiscal Year End:**02/28 **Latest Annual Data:** 12/31/2006

Year	Sales	Net Income
2006	$13,740,000	-$1,002,000
2005	$1,426,000	-$10,465,000
2004	$19,567,000	-$13,924,000

Curr. Assets:	$6,615,000	**Curr. Liab.:**	$2,338,000		
Plant, Equip.:	$1,538,000	**Total Liab.:**	$3,027,000	**Indic. Yr. Divd.:**	NA
Total Assets:	$13,088,000	**Net Worth:**	$10,061,000	**Debt/ Equity:**	NA

DPL Inc

1065 Woodman Dr., Dayton, OH, 45432; ***PH:*** 1-937-224-6000; ***Fax:*** 1-937-259-7147; ***http://*** www.dplinc.com

General - Incorporation	OH	**Stock**- Price on:12/24/2007	$28.65
Employees	1,203	Stock Exchange	NYSE
Auditor	KPMG LLP	Ticker Symbol	DPL
Stk Agt	Computershare Investor Services LLC	Outstanding Shares	113,340,000
Counsel	NA	E.P.S	$1.46
DUNS No.	14-721-2336	Shareholders	NA

Business: The group's principal activity is to provide electricity to residential, commercial and governmental customers. It operates in a diversified regional energy segment. The principal subsidiaries of the group are the dayton power & light company (dp&l) and dpl energy. Dp&l provides electric services to over 500,000 retail customers in west central Ohio. Dpl energy operates over 4,600 megawatts of generation capacity and markets wholesale energy throughout the eastern United States of America.

Primary SIC and add'l.: 4911 4924 6719

CIK No: 0000787250

Subsidiaries: DPL Energy Resources,Inc., DPL Energy, LLC, DPL Finance Company,Inc., Miami Valley Insurance Company, MVE,Inc., The Dayton Power and Light Company

Officers: Paul M. Barbas/Dir., CEO, Pres./$544,739.00, Robert D. Biggs/Exec. Chmn./$1,170,996.00, Miggie E. Cramblit/VP, General Counsel, Frederick J. Boyle/VP, Chief Accounting Officer, Gary G. Stephenson/43/Sr. VP - Generation, Marketing/$908,597.00, Steven W. Wolff/54/Pres. - Power Production/$902,124.00, Arthur G. Meyer/58/Sr. VP - Corporate, Regulatory Affairs, John J. Gillen/54/CFO, Sr. VP/$1,365,684.00, Joseph R. Boni/VP, Treasurer, Scott J. Kelly/Sr. VP - Service Operations, Dennis A. Lantzy/VP - Power Production Engineering, Construction, Teresa F. Marrinan/VP - Commercial Operations, Daniel J. McCabe/Sr. VP - Human Resources, Bryce W. Nickel/VP - Transmission, Distribution Operations, Timothy G. Rice/Interim Sr. VP, General Counsel, Corp. Sec. *(19 Officers included in Index)*

Directors: Paul M. Barbas/Dir., CEO, Pres., August W. Hillenbrand/67/Non - Exec. Vice Chmn., Robert D. Biggs/Exec. Chmn., Ned J. Sifferlen/Dir., Paul R. Bishop/Dir., Barbara S. Graham/Dir., Ernie Green/69/Dir., Lester L. Lyles/Dir., Frank F. Gallaher/Dir.

Owners: August W. Hillenbrand, Ned J. Sifferlen, Lester L. Lyles, Patricia K. Swanke, Ernie Green, Fifth Third Bancorp/5.16%, Goldman Sachs Group, Inc./6.54%, Paul R. Bishop, Seneca Capital Management/5.87%, Barbara S. Graham, Steven W. Wolff, Lehman Brothers Inc./9.60%, Glenn E. Harder, Robert D. Biggs, James V. Mahoney *(18 Owners included in Index)*

Financial Data: **Fiscal Year End:**12/31 **Latest Annual Data:** 12/31/2006

Year	Sales	Net Income
2006	$1,393,500,000	$139,600,000
2005	$1,284,900,000	$174,400,000
2004	$1,199,900,000	$217,300,000

Curr. Assets:	$668,400,000	**Curr. Liab.:**	$624,000,000	**P/E Ratio:**	19.62
Plant, Equip.:	$2,710,500,000	**Total Liab.:**	$2,877,200,000	**Indic. Yr. Divd.:**	$1.040
Total Assets:	$3,612,200,000	**Net Worth:**	$712,100,000	**Debt/ Equity:**	2.0226

Dr Reddy's Laboratories Ltd

200 Somerset Corp. Blvd., Bridgewater, NJ, 08807; ***PH:*** 1-908-203-4984; ***Fax:*** 1-908-203-4970; ***http://*** www.drreddys.com

General - Incorporation	India	**Stock**- Price on:12/24/2007	$15.49
Employees	7,525	Stock Exchange	NYSE
Auditor	KPMG LLP	Ticker Symbol	RDY
Stk Agt	Big Share Services Pvt. Ltd	Outstanding Shares	170,000,000
Counsel	NA	E.P.S	$1.47
DUNS No.	NA	Shareholders	NA

Business: The group's principal activities are to manufacture and market pharmaceutical products. The group's business segments include research, generic formulations, branded formulations, bulk actives, custom chemical synthesis, critical care, biotechnology and diagnostics. The operations span 65 countries, including the United States, Europe and Japan. The group has 6 multi-ton manufacturing facilities. In fiscal 2004, the group acquired trigenesis therapeutics inc.

Primary SIC and add'l.: 2834 2835 3841 2836

CIK No: 0001135951

Subsidiaries: Aurigene Discovery Technologies Limited, Aurigene Discovery Technologies, Inc., beta Healthcare GmbH & Co. KG, beta Healthcare Solutions GmbH, beta Healthcare Verwaltungs GmbH, beta Holding GmbH, beta institut fur sozialmedizinische Forschung und Entwicklung GmbH, betapharm Arzneimittel GmbH, Cheminor Investments Limited, Dr.Reddys Bio-sciences Limited, Dr.Reddys Farmaceutica do Brasil Ltda, Dr.Reddys Laboratories (EU)Limited, Dr.Reddys Laboratories (Proprietary) Limited, Dr.Reddys Laboratories (U.K.) Limited, Dr.Reddys Laboratories, Inc. 29 Subsidiaries included in the Index

Officers: G. V. Prasad/Vice Chmn., CEO, Amit Patel/VP - Corporate Development, Strategic Planning, Satish Reddy/MD, COO, V. S Vasudevan/Pres., Europe Geography Head, Cartikeya Reddy/VP, Head - Biologics, Prabir Jha/Sr. VP, Global Chief - Human Resources, Rajinder Kumar/Pres. - Research, Development, Commercialization, Nikhil Shah/Investor Relation Officer, V. Viswanath/Contact - Company Sec., Abhijit Mukherjee/Pres. - Chemical Technical Operations, Raghu Cidambi/Advisor, Legal, Strategy, Jaspal S. Bajwa/Pres. - Branded Formulations, RoW, Arun Sawhney/Pres. - Active Pharmaceutical Ingredients, Mark Hartman/Pres. - NA Generics, Saumen Chakraborty/CFO, Pres. *(19 Officers included in Index)*

Directors: G. V. Prasad/Vice Chmn., CEO, Anji Reddy/Chmn., Satish Reddy/MD, COO, P. N. Devarajan/72/Dir., Krishna G. Palepu/55/Dir., J. P. Moreau/Dir., Daniel Rader/Member - Scientific Advisory Board, Janardhan K. Reddy/Member - Scientific Advisory Board, Henry Ginsberg/Member - Scientific Advisory Board, Ira J. Goldberg/Member - Scientific Advisory Board, Ravi Bhoothalingam/61/Dir., Anupam Puri/62/Dir., Omkar Goswami/51/Dir.

Owners: Satish Reddy/0.72%, G. V. Prasad, Insiders/25.18%, Anji K. Reddy/22.99%

Financial Data: **Fiscal Year End:**03/31 **Latest Annual Data:** 3/31/2006

Year	Sales	Net Income
2006	$546,009,000	$36,649,000
2005	$446,399,000	$4,843,000
2004	$462,702,000	$57,008,000

Curr. Assets:	$452,025,000	**Curr. Liab.:**	$421,759,000		
Plant, Equip.:	$204,442,000	**Total Liab.:**	$1,046,168,000	**Indic. Yr. Divd.:**	$0.090
Total Assets:	$1,547,282,000	**Net Worth:**	$501,114,000	**Debt/ Equity:**	NA

Dragon International Group Corp

742 Buckskin Trl, Arlington, TX, 76015; ***PH:*** 1-817-419-9711; ***http://*** www.drgg.net

General - Incorporation	NV	**Stock**- Price on:12/24/2007	$0.08
Employees	NA	Stock Exchange	OTC
Auditor	Sherb & Co., LLP	Ticker Symbol	DRGG
Stk Agt	NA	Outstanding Shares	NA
Counsel	NA	E.P.S	NA
DUNS No.	NA	Shareholders	NA

Business: The groups principle activities include manufacturing and distributing assorted industrial paper and packaging products. The group products include waterproof art paper. transfer paper, and Zhong Hua SBS. The group acquired Hangzhou Yongxin Paper Company, Limited in July 2005 and JinKui Packaging Material Co., Ltd. in 2006.The group operates from the United States and China.

Primary SIC and add'l.: 5812

CIK No: 0001050691

Subsidiaries: Dragon International Group Corp, Hangzhou Yongxin Paper Company, Limited, Ningbo City Jiangdong Yonglongxin Special Paper Company, Limited, Ningbo Dragon International Trade Company, Limited, Ningbo Dragon Packaging Technology Company, Limited, Shanghai JinKui Packaging Material Company, Limited

Officers: David Wu/37/Chmn., CEO, Pres., Xuejun Chen/37/Dir., VP, Xiali Gan/41/Dir., CFO, Orson Zhang/40/VP, Sec.

Directors: David Wu/37/Chmn., CEO, Pres., Xuejun Chen/37/Dir., VP, Xiali Gan/41/Dir., CFO

Owners: Capital One Resource Co., Ltd./5.10%, David Wu/12.70%, Insiders/12.70%

Financial Data: **Fiscal Year End:**06/30 **Latest Annual Data:** 06/30/2006

Year	Sales	Net Income
2006	$18,434,000	-$2,594,000
2005	$11,282,000	-$267,000
2004	NA	-$24,000

Curr. Assets:	$15,214,000	**Curr. Liab.:**	$12,407,000		
Plant, Equip.:	$2,852,000	**Total Liab.:**	$13,011,000	**Indic. Yr. Divd.:**	NA
Total Assets:	$21,232,000	**Net Worth:**	$8,221,000	**Debt/ Equity:**	NA

Dragon Pharmaceuticals Inc

650 W Georgia St., Ste. 310, Vancouver, BC, V6B 4N9; ***PH:*** 1-604-669-8817; ***Fax:*** 1-604-669-4243; ***http://*** www.dragonpharma.com; ***Email:*** info@dragonpharma.com

General - Incorporation	FL	**Stock**- Price on:12/24/2007	$0.451
Employees	NA	Stock Exchange	OTC
Auditor	Ernst& Young LLP	Ticker Symbol	DRUG
Stk Agt	Computershare Trust Co	Outstanding Shares	NA
Counsel	NA	E.P.S	NA
DUNS No.	NA	Shareholders	NA

Business: The groups principle activity is to manufacture formulated generic drugs. The group products include -ACA, Avecil and Clavulanate Potassium, Amoxicillin Clavulanate Potassium (5:1), Ceftriaxone for Injection, Amoxicillin Clavulanate Potassium (2:1), EPO, clavulanic acid, Mezlocillin, and Amoxicillin Sulbactam. The group operates through three segments namely chemical, pharma, and biotech division. The group operates from the United States. The groups quarterly revenue for September 2007 was 23.10 millions of USD.

Primary SIC and add'l.: 2836 2834

CIK No: 0001075206

Subsidiaries: Allwin Biotrade, Inc., Allwin Newtech Ltd, Dragon Pharmaceuticals (Canada) Ltd, Nanjing Huaxin Bio-Pharmaceutical Co., Ltd., Oriental Wave Holding, Ltd.,, Sanhe Kailong Bio-pharmaceutical Co. Ltd, Shanxi Weiqida Pharmaceutical Ltd., Weixiang Bio-pharmaceutical Co., Ltd.

Officers: Yanlin Han/Chmn., CEO/$172,065.00, Garry Wong/CFO/$114,710.00, Maggie Deng/40/COO/$114,710.00, Lang Michener/Legal Counsel - Canada, Xiaochun Zhang/GM - Chinese Operation, Ernst /Independent Auditor, Young /Independent Auditor

Directors: Yanlin Han/Chmn., CEO, Alexander Wick/69/Dir., Yiu Kwong Sun/Dir., Zhanguo Weng/52/Dir., Xuemei Liu/Dir., Peter Mak/45/Dir., Heinz Frey/68/Dir., Jin Li/39/Dir.

Owners: Alexander Wick/2.40%, Heinz Frey/0.90%, Zhanguo Weng/14.20%, Xuemei Liu/7.40%, Peter Mak/1.00%, Insiders/71.60%, Yanlin Han/48.00%, Jin Li/0.90%, Maggie Deng/1.00%, Yiu Kwong Sun/2.10%, Garry Wong/1.00%, Bright Faith Overseas Limited/5.30%

Financial Data: **Fiscal Year End:**12/31 **Latest Annual Data:** 12/31/2006

Year	Sales	Net Income
2006	$54,866,000	$4,535,000
2005	$56,245,000	$183,000
2004	$3,705,000	-$943,000

Curr. Assets:	$17,734,000	**Curr. Liab.:**	$33,954,000		
Plant, Equip.:	$62,681,000	**Total Liab.:**	$45,039,000	**Indic. Yr. Divd.:**	NA
Total Assets:	$83,972,000	**Net Worth:**	$38,933,000	**Debt/ Equity:**	NA

Dravco Mining Inc

580 Hornby St., Ste. 210, Vancouver, BC, V6C 3B6; ***PH:*** 1-604 687-6991

General - Incorporation	NV
Employees	NA
Auditor	Manning Elliott LLP
Stk Agt	Pacific Stock Transfer Co.
Counsel	NA
DUNS No.	NA

Stock - Price on:12/24/2007	$1.2
Stock Exchange	OTC
Ticker Symbol	DVCO
Outstanding Shares	NA
E.P.S.	NA
Shareholders	NA

Business: The groups principal activity is to explore minerals and natural oil. The group operates from Canada and the United States.

Primary SIC and add'l.: 1000

CIK No: 0001130808

Officers: Rodney Lozinski/53/Dir., CEO, CFO, Pres., Sec.

Directors: Rodney Lozinski/53/Dir., CEO, CFO, Pres., Sec.

Owners: Rodney Lozinski/55.55%, Insiders/55.55%

Financial Data: Fiscal Year End: 12/31　**Latest Annual Data:** 12/31/2006

Year	Sales	Net Income
2006	NA	-$29,000
2005	NA	-$26,000
2004	NA	-$17,000

Curr. Assets:	$130,000	Curr. Liab.:	$48,000	P/E Ratio:	26.02
Plant, Equip.:	NA	Total Liab.:	$48,000	Indic. Yr. Divd.:	NA
Total Assets:	$130,000	Net Worth:	$82,000	Debt/ Equity:	NA

DRAXIS Health Inc

6870 Goreway Dr. , Ste. 200, Mississauga, ON, L4V 1P1; **PH:** 1-905-677-5500; **Fax:** 1-905-677-5494; **http://** www.draxis.com; **Email:** requestforinfo@draxis.com

General - Incorporation	Canada
Employees	504
Auditor	Deloitte & Touche LLP
Stk Agt	Computershare Trust Co of Canada
Counsel	NA
DUNS No.	24-844-1495

Stock - Price on:12/24/2007	$5.909
Stock Exchange	NDQ
Ticker Symbol	DRAX
Outstanding Shares	42,020,000
E.P.S.	NA
Shareholders	NA

Business: The group's principle activity is the preparation of integrated pharmaceuticals. The group operates in two business segments: manufacturing and radiopharmaceuticals. The manufacturing segment provides contract pharmaceutical manufacturing services through its subsidiary draxis pharma inc. The radiopharmaceutical segment produces and distributes specialized radiopharmaceutical products for both diagnostic and therapeutic applications. The operations of group are carried out in the United States and other countries.

Primary SIC and add'l.: 2834

CIK No: 0000845802

Subsidiaries: 4271513 Canada Inc., DAHI Animal Health (New Zealand) Pty Limited, DAHI Animal Health (UK) Limited, DAHI LLC, DAHI Nevada Inc., Deprenyl Animal Health, Inc., Draximage (u.k.) Limited, Draximage LLC, DRAXIS Specialty Pharmaceuticals Inc., Draxis U.s. Inc.

Officers: Martin Barkin/Dir., CEO, Pres., Dan Brazier/COO, Jerry Ormiston/Executive Dir. - Investor Relations, Jack A. Carter/VP - Administration, Shared Services, Jean-Pierre Robert/Pres. - Draxis Specialty Pharmaceuticals Inc, Mark Oleksiw/CFO, Chien Huang/VP - Finance, Alida Gualtieri/General Counsel, Sec., John Durham/Pres. - Draxis Pharma, Kendall McAlister/Mgr. - Investor Relations

Directors: Martin Barkin/Dir., CEO, Pres., Brian M. King/Chmn., Leslie L. Dan/Dir., George M. Darnell/Dir., John A. Vivash/Dir., Rolf H. Henel/Dir., Samuel W. Sarick/Dir., Bruce W. Simpson/Dir.

Owners: Beutel, Goodman & Company Ltd/8.20%, Neil Gagnon/7.00%, Mackenzie Financial Corporation/10.90%, Natcan Investment Management Inc./8.90%

Financial Data: Fiscal Year End: 12/31　**Latest Annual Data:** 12/31/2006

Year	Sales	Net Income
2006	$88,967,000	$11,547,000
2005	$79,433,000	$7,784,000
2004	$69,320,000	$7,916,000

Curr. Assets:	$53,633,000	Curr. Liab.:	$11,845,000		
Plant, Equip.:	$46,292,000	Total Liab.:	$13,547,000	Indic. Yr. Divd.:	NA
Total Assets:	$105,962,000	Net Worth:	$92,415,000	Debt/ Equity:	NA

DRDGold Ltd

299 Pendoring Ave., Blackheath, Randburg, Gauteng, 2195; **PH:** 27-0112198700; **Fax:** 27-114762637; **http://** www.drd.co.za

General - Incorporation	Republic of South Africa
Employees	12,554
Auditor	KPMG LLP
Stk Agt	Citibank N.A
Counsel	NA
DUNS No.	NA

Stock - Price on:12/24/2007	$0.7337
Stock Exchange	NDQ
Ticker Symbol	DROOY
Outstanding Shares	324,340,000
E.P.S.	NA
Shareholders	NA

Business: The groups principal activities include mining, exploration, extraction, processing and smelting underground and surface gold. The group operates from South Africa and Australia. OF the total revneue in the year 2006, South Africa accounted for $148,785 and Australia $96,516 (thousands).

Primary SIC and add'l.: 1040

CIK No: 0001023512

Subsidiaries: Blyvooruitzicht Gold Mining Company Limited, Crown Consolidated Gold Recoveries Limited, Crown Gold Recoveries (Pty) Limited, DRD (Offshore) Limited, DRD (Porgera) Limited, DRD Australasia (Pty) Limited, DRD Australasia Services Company (Pty) Limited, DRD Australia APS, DRD International Aps (Pty) Limited, DRDGOLD South African Operations (Pty) Limited, DRR (Isle of Man) Limited, East Rand Proprietary Mines Limited, Emperor Mines Limited, Fortis (Pty) Limited, Net-Gold Services Limited 17 Subsidiaries included in the Index

Officers: Mark Munroe/38/CEO - Drdgold Capital, Niel Pretorius/40/CEO - Drdgold SA, Louis Lamsley/59/COO - Drdgold SA, Amanda Hoosen/29/Mgr. - Internal Audit, Compliance, Collie Russouw/49/GM - Blyvoor, Themba Gwebu/43/Company Sec. - Group Legal Counsel, Andrew Weir/43/Group Strategic Mgr. - Human Resources, Craig Barnes/37/CFO - Drdgold SA, Manny Da Silva/37/GM - Erpm, Kevin Kruger/39/Regional Engineering Mgr., Environmental Mgr. - Drdgold SA, Kobus Dissel/49/Alternate Dir., Group Financial Mgr., Wayne Swanepoel/44/Regional Human Resources Mgr. - Drdgold SA, Charles Symons/53/Regional GM - Crown, Erpm, Phillip Watters/51/GM - Projects, Drdgold SA, David Whittaker/Regional Geologist, Drdgold SA *(18 Officers included in Index)*

Directors: Geoffrey Campbell/46/Non Exec. Chmn., Robert Hume/67/Non Exec. Dir., Kobus Dissel/49/Alternate Dir., Group Financial Mgr., John Sayers/61/Executive Dir., Douglas Blackmur/63/Sr. Non Exec. Dir., James Turk/60/Dir.

Owners: Bank of New York ADRs/70.20%, Soges Fiducem SA/6.30%

Dreamworks Animation SKG Inc

1000 Flower St., Glendale, CA, 91201; **PH:** 1-818-695-5000; **Fax:** 1-818-695-9944; **http://** www.dreamworksanimation.com; **Email:** ir@dreamworksanimation.com

General - Incorporation	DE
Employees	1,300
Auditor	Ernst& Young LLP
Stk Agt	Bank of New York
Counsel	NA
DUNS No.	NA

Stock - Price on:12/24/2007	$28.53
Stock Exchange	NYSE
Ticker Symbol	DWA
Outstanding Shares	104,790,000
E.P.S.	$0.64
Shareholders	NA

Business: The groups principle activities include developing and producing computer generated and animates feature films. In the year 2006, the group acquired Pacific Data Images, Inc. The group operates from the United States. The groups quarterly revenue for September 2007 was 160.75 millions of USD.

Primary SIC and add'l.: 7812

CIK No: 0001297401

Subsidiaries: DreamWorks Animation Home Entertainment, Inc., DreamWorks Animation Home Entertainment, L.L.C., DreamWorks Animation L.L.C., DreamWorks Animation Live Theatrical Productions, L.L.C., DreamWorks Post-Production L.L.C., DreamWorks, Inc., DWA Finance I L.L.C., Pacific Data Images L.L.C., Pacific Data Images, Inc.California, Pacific Productions LLC

Officers: Jeffrey Katzenberg/Dir., CEO/$5,199,615.00

Directors: Jeffrey Katzenberg/Dir., CEO, Roger A. Enrico/Chmn., Lew Coleman/Dir., David Geffen/Dir., Mellody Hobson/Dir., Nathan Myhrvold/Dir., Howard Schultz/Dir., Meg Whitman/Dir., Karl M. Von Der Heyden/Dir., Judson C. Green/Dir., Michael J. Montgomery/Dir.

Owners: Margaret C. Whitman, Insiders, Karl M. von der Heyden, Jeffrey Katzenberg/22.90%, Katherine Kendrick, Ann Daly, Wellington Management Company, LLP/7.10%, Roger A. Enrico, David Geffen, Lewis W. Coleman, Paul G. Allen/22.90%, Judson Green, Steven Spielberg/8.00%, Jeffrey Katzenberg, Insiders/23.70% *(23 Owners included in Index)*

Financial Data: Fiscal Year End: 12/31　**Latest Annual Data:** 12/31/2006

Year	Sales	Net Income
2006	$394,842,000	$15,125,000
2005	$462,316,000	$104,585,000
2004	$1,078,160,000	$333,000,000

Curr. Assets:	$1,133,217,000	Curr. Liab.:	$67,146,000	P/E Ratio:	158.50
Plant, Equip.:	$83,416,000	Total Liab.:	$247,201,000	Indic. Yr. Divd.:	NA
Total Assets:	$1,280,469,000	Net Worth:	$1,033,268,000	Debt/ Equity:	0.1174

Dress Barn Inc

30 Dunnigan Dr., Suffern, NY, 10901; **PH:** 1-845-369-4500; **Fax:** 1-845-369-4829; **http://** www.dress-barn.com

General - Incorporation	CT
Employees	5,000
Auditor	Deloitte & Touche LLP
Stk Agt	American Stock Transfer & Trust Co.
Counsel	Proskauer Rose
DUNS No.	01-881-6942

Stock - Price on:12/24/2007	$21.93
Stock Exchange	NDQ
Ticker Symbol	DBRN
Outstanding Shares	62,520,000
E.P.S.	$1.35
Shareholders	NA

Business: The group's principal activity is to operate a chain of women's apparels specialty stores. It offers in-season, moderate to better quality career and casual fashion apparels to the working women. The stores are operated under the name 'dress barn' and 'dress barn woman'. Combo stores offer a combination of dress barn and dress barn woman merchandise. The group also offers other wardrobe items, which include accessories, hosiery, handbags and shoes. As of 26-Jul-2003, the group operated 772 stores in 44 states and the district of columbia, consisting of 521 combo stores, 194 dress barn stores and 57 dress barn woman stores.

Primary SIC and add'l.: 5621 5632

CIK No: 0000717724

Subsidiaries: D.B.R., Inc., DBX Inc., Dress Barn Credit Management, LLC, Dunnigan Realty, LLC, Maurices Credit Management, Inc., Maurices Incorporated

Officers: David R. Jaffe/CEO, Pres., Vivian Behrens/Sr. VP, Chief Marketing Officer, Eric Hawn/Sr. VP - Store Operations, Armand Correia/Sr. VP, CFO, Roslyn S. Jaffe/Dir. Emeritus, Sec., Treasurer, Co - Founder, Keith Fulsher/Exec. VP, Chief Merchandising Officer, Burt Steinberg/Executive Dir., Elise Jaffe/Sr. VP - Real Estate, Gene Wexler/Sr. VP, General Counsel, Assist. Sec., Jeff Gerstel/Sr. VP - Operations, Jamie Paster/Contact - Media Representative

Directors: Elliot S. Jaffe/Co - Founder, Chmn., Roslyn S. Jaffe/Dir. Emeritus, Sec., Treasurer, Co - Founder, Burt Steinberg/Executive Dir., Kate Buggeln/Dir., Klaus Eppler/Dir., Randy Pearce/Dir., John Usdan/Dir.

Owners: Klaus Eppler, Elise Jaffe/8.27%, Insiders/11.66%, Vivian Behrens, Burt Steinberg, Gene Wexler, Kate Buggeln, Elliot S. Jaffe/1.65%, Randy L. Pearce, PRIMECAP Management Company/7.82%, John Usdan, Vanguard Horizon Funds/7.32%, David R. Jaffe/9.52%, Richard Jaffe/7.77%, Armand Correia

Financial Data: Fiscal Year End: 07/30　**Latest Annual Data:** 7/29/2006

Year	Sales	Net Income
2006	$1,300,277,000	$78,954,000
2005	$1,000,264,000	$52,560,000
2004	$754,903,000	$30,932,000

Curr. Assets:	$317,157,000	Curr. Liab.:	$164,051,000	P/E Ratio:	16.74
Plant, Equip.:	$163,204,000	Total Liab.:	$236,358,000	Indic. Yr. Divd.:	NA
Total Assets:	$489,316,000	Net Worth:	$252,958,000	Debt/ Equity:	NA

Dresser-Rand Group Inc

1200 W Sam Houston Pkwy N, Houston, TX, 77043; **PH:** 1-713-467-2221; **Fax:** 1-713-935-3490; **http://** www.dresser-rand.com

General - Incorporation	DE	**Stock** - Price on:12/24/2007	NA
Employees	5,612	Stock Exchange	NYSE
Auditor	PricewaterhouseCoopers LLP	Ticker Symbol	DRC
Stk Agt	Bank of New York	Outstanding Shares	85,830,000
Counsel	NA	E.P.S	$1.12
DUNS No.	NA	Shareholders	NA

Business: The groups principle activities include supplying and manufacturing rotating equipment solutions, refinery processes, natural gas processing, pipelines and petrochemical production. The groups products include compressors, gas and power turbines, hot gas expanders, control systems and steam turbines. The group operates through two segments namely, new units, and aftermarket parts and services. In the year 2005, the group acquired Tuthill Corporation. The group operates from the United States, France, Germany, Norway and India. The group's quarterly revenue for September 2007 was 389.30 millions of USD.

Primary SIC and add'l.: 3511 3533 3563 3491 3332

CIK No: 0001316656

Subsidiaries: D-R Central Service GmbH& Co. KG, D-R Holdings (France) S.A.S., D-R Holdings (Germany) GmbH, D-R Holdings (Netherlands) B.V., D-R Holdings (U.K.) Ltd., D-R Holdings Norway AS, D-R International Sales LLC, D-R Management GmbH, D-R Nadrowski Holdings GmbH, D-R Steam LLC, Dresser-Rand (Nigeria) Ltd., Dresser-Rand (SEA) Pte. Ltd., Dresser-Rand (U.K.) Ltd., Dresser-Rand AS, Dresser-Rand Asia Pacific Sdn. Bhd. 46 Subsidiaries included in the Index

Officers: Vincent R. Volpe/49/CEO, Pres., Leonard M. Anthony/53/CFO, Exec. VP, Mark E. Baldwin/CFO, Exec. VP, Jesus Pacheco/Exec. VP - New Equipment Worldwide, Dick Heusinkveld/VP, GM - Asia Pacific Operations, Kuala Lumpur, Malaysia, Mark F. Mai/VP, General Counsel, Sec., Elizabeth C. Powers/VP, Chief Administrative Officer, Christopher Rossi/Exec. VP - Product Services Worldwide, Executive Vice Preside, Jean-Francois Chevrier/VP, GM - North American Operations, Peter Salvatore/VP, GM - Worldwide Field Operations, Bradford W. Dickson/VP, Chief Marketing Officer, Walter J. Nye/VP, GM - European Operations, James Heid/VP - Business Solutions, Houston, Texas, Honor Guiney/VP - Global Singular Processes, CIO, Kenneth Marcia/VP - Supply Chain Management - Process Innovation *(19 Officers included in Index)*

Directors: Vincent R. Volpe/49/CEO, Pres., William E. MacAulay/Chmn., Mark A. McComiskey/35/Dir., Kenneth W. Moore/38/Dir., Michael L. Underwood/Dir., Jean-Paul Vettier/Dir., Rita V. Foley/54/Dir., Joseph C. Winkler/56/Dir., Louis A. Raspino/Dir., Philip R. Roth/Dir.

Owners: Vincent R. Volpe, Kenneth W. Moore, Insiders, Neuberger Berman, Inc/7.60%, BlackRock, Inc/4.98%, Mark A. McComiskey, Jean-Paul Vettier, Federated Investors, Inc./12.03%, Iridian Asset Management LLC/5.00%, Louis A. Raspino, Walter J. Nye, Philip R. Roth, William E. Macaulay, Michael L. Underwood

Financial Data: **Fiscal Year End:**12/31 **Latest Annual Data:** 12/31/2006

Year	Sales	Net Income
2006	$1,501,527,000	$78,759,000
2005	$1,208,203,000	$37,095,000

Curr. Assets:	$669,032,000	**Curr. Liab.:**	$471,500,000		
Plant, Equip.:	$223,085,000	**Total Liab.:**	$1,139,458,000	**Indic. Yr. Divd.:**	NA
Total Assets:	$1,771,329,000	**Net Worth:**	$631,871,000	**Debt/ Equity:**	NA

Drew Industries Inc

200 Mamaroneck Ave., Ste. 301, White Plains, NY, 10601; ***PH:*** 1-914-428-9098; ***Fax:*** 1-914-428-4581; ***http://*** www.drewindustries.com

General - Incorporation	DE	**Stock** - Price on:12/24/2007	$34.03
Employees	3,690	Stock Exchange	NYSE
Auditor	KPMG LLP	Ticker Symbol	DW
Stk Agt	American Stock Transfer & Trust Co.	Outstanding Shares	21,760,000
Counsel	Phillips Nizer LLP	E.P.S	$1.49
DUNS No.	00-787-1643	Shareholders	NA

Business: The group's principal activity is to manufacture and market aluminum and vinyl windows, thermo-formed bath and shower units for manufactured homes and aluminum windows and doors for recreational vehicles. The group has two reportable segments: manufactured housing products segment and recreational vehicle products segment. Recreational vehicle products segment manufactures and markets a number of components for recreational vehicles, including aluminum windows, a variety of doors, steel chassis and steel chassis parts. The group operates through its subsidiaries, kinro inc and lippert components inc. Manufactured housing product segment manufactures and markets aluminum and vinyl windows and screens, thermo-formed bath and shower units, steel chassis and steel chassis parts, galvanized roofing and new axles. The group discontinued the axle and tire refurbishing operations in 2003. On 04-May-2004, the group acquired zieman manufacturing company.

Primary SIC and add'l.: 3714 3444 3446

CIK No: 0000763744

Subsidiaries: BBD Realty Texas Limited Partnership, Coil Clip, Inc., Kinro Holding, Inc., Kinro Manufacturing, Inc., Kinro Tennessee Limited Partnership, Kinro Texas Limited Partnership, Kinro, Inc., LD Realty, Inc., Lippert Components Holding, Inc., Lippert Components Manufacturing, Inc., Lippert Components of Canada, Inc., Lippert Components Texas Limited Partnership, Lippert Components, Inc., Lippert Tire & Axle Holding, Inc., Lippert Tire & Axle Texas Limited Partnership 18 Subsidiaries included in the Index

Officers: Leigh J. Abrams/Dir., CEO, Pres./$1,299,929.00, Harvey F. Milman/VP, Chief Legal Officer, Fredric M. Zinn/CFO, Exec. VP/$570,377.00, John F. Cupak/Dir. - Internal Audit, Joseph S. Giordano/Corporate Controller, Treasurer

Directors: Leigh J. Abrams/Dir., CEO, Pres., Edward W. Rose/Chmn., David L. Webster/Dir., Douglas L. Lippert/60/Dir., John B. Lowe/Dir., Frederick B. Hegi/Dir., Jason D. Lippert/Dir., David A. Reed/Dir., James F. Gero/Dir.

Owners: David L. Webster/1.10%, Edward W. Rose/6.70%, Douglas L. Lippert/5.00%, Leigh J. Abrams/1.20%, David A. Reed/0.10%, Frederick B. Hegi, FMR Corp./8.30%, James F. Gero/0.60%, Royce & Associates, LLC/9.00%, Insiders/16.70%, John B. Lowe, Jason D. Lippert/0.60%, Columbia Wanger Asset Management, LP/6.50%

Financial Data: **Fiscal Year End:**12/31 **Latest Annual Data:** 12/31/2006

Year	Sales	Net Income
2006	$729,232,000	$31,023,000
2005	$669,147,000	$33,602,000
2004	$530,870,000	$25,108,000

Curr. Assets:	$121,040,000	**Curr. Liab.:**	$59,061,000	**P/E Ratio:**	22.84
Plant, Equip.:	$124,558,000	**Total Liab.:**	$106,388,000	**Indic. Yr. Divd.:**	NA
Total Assets:	$311,276,000	**Net Worth:**	$204,888,000	**Debt/ Equity:**	0.1967

Dril-Quip Inc

13550 Hempstead Hwy., Houston, TX, 77040; ***PH:*** 1-713-939-7711; ***Fax:*** 1-713-939-8063; ***http://*** www.dril-quip.com; ***Email:*** information@dril-quip.com

General - Incorporation	DE	**Stock** - Price on:12/24/2007	$48.06
Employees	1,709	Stock Exchange	NYSE
Auditor	BDO Seidman, LLP	Ticker Symbol	DRQ
Stk Agt	Mellon Investor Services LLC	Outstanding Shares	40,440,000
Counsel	Baker & Botts LLP	E.P.S	$2.45
DUNS No.	01-687-4125	Shareholders	NA

Business: The group's principal activities are to manufacturing and marketing of offshore drilling and production equipment. The group designs and manufactures subsea equipment, surface equipment and offshore rig equipment for oil and gas companies. The group's products are subsea, surface wellheads, dual-bore, single-bore subsea production trees, mudline hanger systems, specialty connectors, spar and tension leg platform production risers, wellhead connectors and diverters. The group provides installation and reconditioning services. The group's trademarks are quik-thread(R), quik-stab(R) specialty connectors, ms-15(R) mudline hanger systems, ss-10(R) and ss-15(R) subsea wellheads. The group manufactures its products in Texas, Scotland and Singapore and maintains facilities for fabrication and reconditioning in Brazil, Norway, Denmark and Australia.

Primary SIC and add'l.: 3533

CIK No: 0001042893

Subsidiaries: Dril-Quip (Europe) Limited, Dril-Quip (Nigeria) Ltd, Dril-Quip Asia Pacific PTE Ltd, Dril-Quip do Brasil LTDA

Officers: Gary D. Smith/Co - Chmn., Co - CEO/$1,526,730.00, Larry E. Reimert/Co - Chmn., Co - CEO/$1,526,730.00, Mike J. Walker/Co - Chmn., Co - CEO/$1,526,730.00, Jerry M. Brooks/CFO/$290,047.00

Directors: Gary D. Smith/Co - Chmn., Co - CEO, Larry E. Reimert/Co - Chmn., Co - CEO, Mike J. Walker/Co - Chmn., Co - CEO, Dick L.H. Robertson/Dir., John V. Lovoi/Dir., Gary L. Stone/Dir., Alexander P. Shukis/Dir.

Owners: Mike J. Walker/14.00%, Jerry M. Brooks, Gary D. Smith/10.10%, Larry E. Reimert/10.40%, Gary L. Stone, Insiders/34.10%

Financial Data: **Fiscal Year End:**12/31 **Latest Annual Data:** 06/30/2007

Year	Sales	Net Income
2007	$114,701,000	$24,109,000
2006	$442,742,000	$86,891,000
2005	$340,829,000	$32,567,000

Curr. Assets:	$465,055,000	**Curr. Liab.:**	$117,805,000	**P/E Ratio:**	20.81
Plant, Equip.:	$129,340,000	**Total Liab.:**	$127,438,000	**Indic. Yr. Divd.:**	NA
Total Assets:	$594,935,000	**Net Worth:**	$467,497,000	**Debt/ Equity:**	0.0054

Drinks Americas Holdings Ltd

372 Danbury Rd., Ste. 163, Wilton, CT, 06897; ***PH:*** 1-203-762-7000; ***Fax:*** 1-203-762-8992; ***http://*** www.drinksamericas.com; ***Email:*** info@drinksamericas.com

General - Incorporation	DE	**Stock** - Price on:12/24/2007	$1.25
Employees	8	Stock Exchange	OTC
Auditor	Bernstein & Pinchuk, LLP	Ticker Symbol	DKAM
Stk Agt	National Stock Transfer, Inc.	Outstanding Shares	79,530,000
Counsel	NA	E.P.S	-$0.14
DUNS No.	NA	Shareholders	NA

Business: The groups principal activities include developing, producing, marketing and distributing alcoholic and non-alcoholic beverages. The group products include Swiss T, Old Whiskey River Bourbon and R, Y Sake. The group operates through three segments namely beer, wine and distilled spirits. In the year 2005, the group acquired Rheingold Brewing Company. The group operates from the United States. The groups net sale in the year 2006 was $1,607,606.

Primary SIC and add'l.: 2080

CIK No: 0000873540

Subsidiaries: D.T. Drinks, LLC, Drinks Americas, Inc., Drinks Global Imports, LLC, Maxmillian Mixers, LLC

Officers: Patrick J. Kenny/CEO, Pres., Jason Lazo/COO, Frederick Schulman/Dir., General Counsel, Stanley Altschuler/Investor Relations Officer, Jeffrey Daub/CFO

Directors: Bruce K. Klein/Chmn., Marvin Traub/Dir., Thomas Schwalm/Dir., Frederick Schulman/Dir., General Counsel, Hubert Millet/Dir.

Owners: Hubert Millet/0.10%, Marvin Traub/2.10%, J. Patrick Kenny/18.00%, Richard Shickman/0.10%, Jason Lazo/1.40%, Fredrick Schulman/1.20%, Brian Kenny/0.30%, Kenneth Close/11.80%, Fabio Berkowicz/2.10%, Thomas Schwalm/4.70%, Insiders/43.50%, Bruce Klein/13.90%

Financial Data: **Fiscal Year End:**04/30 **Latest Annual Data:** 4/30/2006

Year	Sales	Net Income
2006	$1,608,000	-$4,391,000
2005	$2,072,000	-$4,328,000
2001	$8,571,000	-$632,000

Curr. Assets:	$2,045,000	**Curr. Liab.:**	$5,192,000		
Plant, Equip.:	$1,679,000	**Total Liab.:**	$5,252,000	**Indic. Yr. Divd.:**	NA
Total Assets:	$6,801,000	**Net Worth:**	$1,549,000	**Debt/ Equity:**	NA

Driver Passport Inc

1168 12th St. Ne, Grand Forks, ND, 58201; ***PH:*** 1-800-743-1824; ***Fax:*** 1-701-775-9587; ***http://*** www.driverpassport.com; ***Email:*** customerservice@driverpassport.com

General - Incorporation	ND	**Stock** - Price on:12/24/2007	$0.1
Employees	3	Stock Exchange	OTC
Auditor	Michael Pollack, CPA	Ticker Symbol	DPSS
Stk Agt	NA	Outstanding Shares	29,850,000
Counsel	NA	E.P.S	NA
DUNS No.	NA	Shareholders	NA

Business: The groups principal activity is to provide an online system with photo, driver license and transport equipment verifications. The group operates from the United States.

Primary SIC and add'l.: 7382

CIK No: 0001362388

Officers: Randy Brown/Dir., CEO, Pres., Principal Financial Officer, Principal Accounting Officer, Kyle Reierson/Technical Lead, Chris Dunnigan/Contact, Alan Mulhern/Marketing Mgr.

Directors: Randy Brown/Dir., CEO, Pres., Principal Financial Officer, Principal Accounting Officer

Owners: Randy Brown/94.00%

Financial Data: *Fiscal Year End:*12/31   *Latest Annual Data:* 12/31/2006

Year	Sales	Net Income
2006	NA	-$214,000

Curr. Assets:	NA	Curr. Liab.:	$287,000		
Plant, Equip.:	$1,000	Total Liab.:	$287,000	Indic. Yr. Divd.:	NA
Total Assets:	$12,000	Net Worth:	-$275,000	Debt/ Equity:	NA

DRS Technologies Inc

5 Sylvan Way, Parsippany, NJ, 07054; *PH:* 1-973-898-1500; *Fax:* 1-973-898-4730; *http://* www.drs.com; *Email:* info@drs.com

General - Incorporation	DE	Stock - Price on:12/24/2007	$55.82
Employees	9,700	Stock Exchange	NYSE
Auditor	KPMG LLP	Ticker Symbol	DRS
Stk Agt	Mellon Investor Services LLC	Outstanding Shares	40,720,000
Counsel	Skadden, Arps	E.P.S.	$3.12
DUNS No.	06-134-5351	Shareholders	NA

Business: The groups principle activity is to supply defense electronic products and systems. The groups products include thermal imaging devices, combat display workstations, electronic sensor systems, power systems, battlefield digitization systems and air combat training systems. The group operates from United States.

Primary SIC and add'l.: 3812 3827 3679

CIK No: 0000028630

Subsidiaries: 3083683 Novia Scotia Limited, Air Eagle Holdings,Inc., Canopy Technologies, LLC, DRS Codem Systems,Inc., DRS Communications Company LLC, DRS Data& Imaging Systems Limited, DRS Data& Imaging Systems, Inc., DRS Electric Power Technologies, Inc., DRS Electronic Systems, Inc., DRS Engineering Development Labs, Inc., DRS EW& Network Systems (Canada) Limited, DRS EW& Network Systems, Inc., Drs Fpa, Inc., DRS Hadland Ltd., DRS Infrared Technologies, LP 63 Subsidiaries included in the Index

Officers: Mark S. Newman/58/Chmn., CEO, Pres./$6,196,046.00, Robert F. Mehmel/COO, Exec. VP/$1,588,188.00, Michael L. Bowman/Exec. VP - Washington Operations/$957,379.00, Steven T. Schorer/Pres. - C4I Group, Louis J. Belsito/CIO, Sr. VP, Lawrence K. Brewer/Sr. VP - Government Relations, Thomas P. Crimmins/Sr. VP, Corporate Controller, Alan R. Gross/Sr. VP - Contracts, Compliance, Andrea J. Mandel/Sr. VP - Human Resources, Jason W. Rinsky/Sr. VP - Corporate Taxation, Robert Russo/Sr. VP - Operations, David W. Stapley/Sr. VP - International Business Development, Government Relations, Thomas F. Daley/VP, Corporate Counsel, Mark A. Dorfman/VP, Corporate Counsel, Christopher W. Durborow/VP, Assist. Controller *(32 Officers included in Index)*

Directors: Mark S. Newman/58/Chmn., CEO, Pres., Ira Albom/79/Dir., Donald C. Fraser/67/Dir., Dennis J. Reimer/68/Dir., William F. Heitmann/59/Dir., Steven S. Honigman/60/Dir., Shelton C. James/68/Dir., Stuart F. Platt/74/Dir., Eric J. Rosen/47/Dir., Charles G. Boyd/70/Dir., Mark N. Kaplan/58/Dir.

Owners: Steven S. Honigman, FMR Corp./12.07%, Richard A. Schneider, Robert F. Mehmel, William F. Heitmann, Dennis J. Reimer, Neuberger Berman, LLC/7.56%, Ira Albom, Marsico Capital Management, LLC/12.29%, Stuart F. Platt, Mark N. Kaplan, Eric J. Rosen, Insiders/3.50%, Mark S. Newman/2.00%, Michael L. Bowman *(19 Owners included in Index)*

Financial Data: *Fiscal Year End:*03/31   *Latest Annual Data:* 3/31/2007

Year	Sales	Net Income
2007	$2,821,113,000	$127,060,000
2006	$1,735,532,000	$81,494,000
2005	$1,308,600,000	$60,677,000

Curr. Assets:	$1,125,662,000	Curr. Liab.:	$770,532,000	P/E Ratio:	17.89
Plant, Equip.:	$231,206,000	Total Liab.:	$2,712,260,000	Indic. Yr. Divd.:	$0.120
Total Assets:	$4,214,710,000	Net Worth:	$1,502,450,000	Debt/ Equity:	1.1867

Drugstore.com Inc

411 108th Ave. NE, Ste. 1400, Bellevue, WA, 98004; *PH:* 1-425-372-3200; *Fax:* 1-425-372-3800; *http://* www.drugstore.com

General - Incorporation	DE	Stock - Price on:12/24/2007	$2.66
Employees	732	Stock Exchange	NDQ
Auditor	Ernst & Young LLP	Ticker Symbol	DSCM
Stk Agt	Mellon Investor Services LLC	Outstanding Shares	95,040,000
Counsel	Wilson Sonsini Goodrich & Rosati	E.P.S.	-$0.13
DUNS No.	NA	Shareholders	NA

Business: The group's principal activity is to provide an online retail drugstore and information site for health, beauty, wellness, personal care, pharmacy products and health related information. The group's products are categorized into health, beauty, wellness, personal care and pharmacy. Health products include first aid, medical devices for home healthcare and other related health products. Beauty products include cosmetics, fragrances and a variety of skin care products. Wellness products include vitamins, nutritional supplements and other natural products. Personal care products include products related to hair, body and eye care, shaving, oral hygiene and feminine needs. Pharmacy products consist of prescription and medication for chronic illnesses, such as blood pressure, osteoporosis and depression. During 2003, the group acquired international vision direct corporation, acumins inc and concept development llc.

Primary SIC and add'l.: 7375 5912 5961

CIK No: 0001086467

Subsidiaries: Beauty.com, Inc1, Custom Nutrition Services, Inc, Drugstore.com Foundation, DS Distribution, Inc, DS Non-Pharmaceutical Sales, Inc, DS Pharmacy, Inc., DSGC Idaho, Inc., International Vision Direct Corp

Officers: Dawn G. Lepore/Chmn., CEO, Pres./$3,497,940.00, Ronald E. Kelly/VP - Customer, Pharmacy Services, William D. Savoy/Dir., Consultant, Luke Friang/CIO, VP/$1,135,493.00, There Du Pont/Sr. VP - Operations, CFO, Robert Hargadon/VP - Human Resources, Julie Johnston/VP - OTC Merchandising, David Lonczak/VP, Chief Marketing Officer, Kathleen McNeill/VP - Beauty, Yukio Morikubo/General Counsel, VP - Strategy, Robert Potter/VP, Chief Accountant, Tracy Wright/VP - Financial Planning, Analysis

Directors: Dawn G. Lepore/Chmn., CEO, Pres., Jeffrey M. Killeen/Dir., Richard W. Bennet/Dir., Geoffrey R. Entress/Dir., Gregory S. Stanger/Dir., William D. Savoy/Dir., Consultant

Owners: Amazon.com, Inc./13.70%, William D. Savoy, Yukio Morikubo, Richard W. Bennet, Geoffrey R. Entress, Robert Hargadon, Ziff Asset Management LP/10.60%, Gregory S. Stanger, Robert A. Barton, Insiders/2.70%, Carlo J. Cannell/6.30%, Jeffrey M. Killeen, Dawn G. Lepore/1.40%, Kleiner Perkins Caufield& Byers/11.70%

Financial Data: *Fiscal Year End:*12/31   *Latest Annual Data:* 07/01/2007

Year	Sales	Net Income
2007	$110,412,000	-$3,015,000
2006	$108,598,000	-$2,947,000
2005	$360,099,000	-$47,735,000

Curr. Assets:	$108,701,000	Curr. Liab.:	$71,250,000		
Plant, Equip.:	$18,293,000	Total Liab.:	$75,644,000	Indic. Yr. Divd.:	NA
Total Assets:	$168,322,000	Net Worth:	$92,678,000	Debt/ Equity:	0.0177

Dryclean USA Inc

7492 SW 117th Ave., Miami, FL, 33183; *PH:* 1-305-412-7444 ; *Fax:* 1-305-412-7400; *http://* www.dryclean-usa.com

General - Incorporation	DE	Stock - Price on:12/24/2007	$2.05
Employees	35	Stock Exchange	AMEX
Auditor	Berkovits & Co., LLP	Ticker Symbol	DCU
Stk Agt	Registrar & Transfer Co	Outstanding Shares	7,030,000
Counsel	Parker Chapin Flattau & Klimpl	E.P.S.	$0.12
DUNS No.	00-205-2314	Shareholders	NA

Business: The group's principal activities are to supply laundry equipment, boilers and replacement parts to commercial and industrial consumers. The laundry products include washers, coin-operated machines, garment presses, finishing equipment and distributing conveyors. The group sells spare parts for these product lines and provides repair services. The products are exported to Latin America, the Caribbean and other countries. The trademarks of the group include aero-tech(R), logitrol(R), petro-star(R), aqua star(R) and enviro-star(r). In Jul 2002, the group sold substantially all of the operating assets of its metro-tel telecommunications segment.

Primary SIC and add'l.: 5087

CIK No: 0000065312

Subsidiaries: Dryclean Usa Development Corp., Dryclean Usa License Corp., Steiner-Atlantic Brokerage Corp., Steiner-Atlantic Corp.

Owners: Stuart Wagner, Michael S. Steiner, Alan M. Grunspan, David Blyer, Cindy B. Greenstein, Insiders, William K. Steiner, Lloyd Frank, Venerando J. Indelicato

Financial Data: *Fiscal Year End:*06/30   *Latest Annual Data:* 6/30/2006

Year	Sales	Net Income
2006	$20,415,000	$804,000
2005	$18,389,000	$706,000
2004	$14,672,000	$536,000

Curr. Assets:	$8,926,000	Curr. Liab.:	$3,171,000	P/E Ratio:	17.08
Plant, Equip.:	$262,000	Total Liab.:	$3,171,000	Indic. Yr. Divd.:	$0.080
Total Assets:	$9,444,000	Net Worth:	$6,272,000	Debt/ Equity:	NA

DryShips Inc

80 Kifissias Ave., Marousi, Athens, 15125; *PH:* 30-2108090570; *http://* www.dryships.com; *Email:* finance@dryships.com

General - Incorporation	Marshall Islands	Stock - Price on:12/24/2007	NA
Employees	NA	Stock Exchange	NDQ
Auditor	Ernst & Young LLP	Ticker Symbol	DRYS
Stk Agt	American Stock Transfer & Trust Co.	Outstanding Shares	35,490,000
Counsel	NA	E.P.S.	$8.91
DUNS No.	NA	Shareholders	NA

Business: The groups principle activity is to provide shipping transportation services. The products of the group include bauxite, phosphate, fertilizers and steel. Specific customers of the group include Baumarine AS and Oldendorff Carriers Gmbh. The group operates from the United States. The group's quarterly revenue for September 2007 was 150.01 millions of USD.

Primary SIC and add'l.: 4412

CIK No: 0001308858

Subsidiaries: Alma Shipholding Inc., Amara Shipping Company, Anemone Marine Co., Annapolis Shipping Company Limited, Araldo Marine Ltd., Argante Navigation Corp., Ariadne Marine S.A., Ariana Marine Ltd., Arleta Navigation Company Limited, Armanno Marine Co., Ashby Shipmanagement Corp., Astarte Maritime S.A., Blueberry Shipping Company Limited, Borsari Shipping Company Limited, Celine Shipping Company Limited 79 Subsidiaries included in the Index

Officers: George Economou/Chmn., CEO, Pres., Olga Lambrianidou/Corporate Secreary, Nicolas Bornozis/Investor Relations

Directors: George Economou/Chmn., CEO, Pres., Angelos Papoulias/Dir., George Demathas/Dir., George Xiradakis/Dir., Aristidis Ioannidis/Dir.

Owners: Magic Management Inc./5.30%, Advice Investment S.A./7.90%, George Economou/34.30%, Elios Investments Inc/30.80%

Financial Data: *Fiscal Year End:*12/31   *Latest Annual Data:* 12/31/2006

Year	Sales	Net Income
2006	$248,431,000	$56,731,000
2005	$228,913,000	$111,017,000
2004	$15,699,000	$10,856,000

Curr. Assets:	$26,821,000	Curr. Liab.:	$129,344,000	P/E Ratio:	17.55
Plant, Equip.:	$1,112,304,000	Total Liab.:	$717,281,000	Indic. Yr. Divd.:	$0.800
Total Assets:	$1,168,173,000	Net Worth:	$450,892,000	Debt/ Equity:	NA

DSA Financial Corp

118 Walnut St., Lawrenceburg, IN, 47025; *PH:* 1-812-537-0940; *Fax:* 1-812-537-3576; *http://* www.dearbornsavings.com

General - Incorporation	DE	Stock - Price on:12/24/2007	$12.65
Employees	17	Stock Exchange	OTC
Auditor	Grant Thornton LLP	Ticker Symbol	DSFN
Stk Agt	Registrar & Transfer Co	Outstanding Shares	1,670,000
Counsel	NA	E.P.S.	$0.40
DUNS No.	NA	Shareholders	NA

Business: The group's principle activity is to provide financial services to individuals, families and businesses. The primary services provided by the group are savings bank services. The services of the group include accepting deposits from general public and investing those deposits, together with funds generated from operations and borrowings, in one- to four-family residential, multi-family residential, construction and non-residential real estate and land loans, home equity and consumer loans and in agency securities and mortgage-backed securities. The group operates from United States.

Primary SIC and add'l.: 6035 6712

CIK No: 0001282852

Subsidiaries: Dearborn Savings Association, F.A.

Officers: Delmar C. Schiferl/46/Contact - Loan Information, Thomas J. Sicking/67/Contact - Loan Information, Yavone Seymour/Contact - Deposit Information, Juanita Sutton/Contact - Deposit Information, Susan Buehler/Contact - Loan Information

Owners: Dennis Richter/6.40%, David P. Lorey/6.30%

Financial Data: *Fiscal Year End:*06/30 *Latest Annual Data:* 6/30/2006

Year	Sales	Net Income
2006	$6,063,000	$873,000
2005	$4,884,000	$836,000
2004	$4,659,000	$825,000

Curr. Assets:	$2,842,000	**Curr. Liab.:**	$76,493,000	**P/E Ratio:**	31.63
Plant, Equip.:	$2,092,000	**Total Liab.:**	$85,829,000	**Indic. Yr. Divd.:**	$0.420
Total Assets:	$103,074,000	**Net Worth:**	$17,245,000	**Debt/ Equity:**	NA

DSG International Ltd

17/f Watson Ctr., 16-22 Kung Yip St, Kwai Chun; *PH:* 86-4276951; *http://* www.dsgil.com

General - Incorporation	British Virgin Islands	**Stock**- Price on:12/24/2007	$3.2
Employees	NA	Stock Exchange	OTC
Auditor	Delotte & Touche LLP	Ticker Symbol	DSITF
Stk Agt	Mellon Investor Services LLC	Outstanding Shares	NA
Counsel	NA	E.P.S	NA
DUNS No.	66-218-8606	Shareholders	NA

Business: The groups principle activity is to manufacture and market disposable diapers, adult incontinence, feminine hygiene and training pants products. The group operates from United States.

Primary SIC and add'l.: 2676

CIK No: 0000883230

Subsidiaries: Advance Medical Supply Company Limited, Associated Hygienic Products Inc., Associated Hygienic Products LLC, Disposable Soft Goods (Malaysia) Sdn. Bhd., Disposable Soft Goods (S) Pte Limited, Disposable Soft Goods (UK) Plc., Disposable Soft Goods (Zhongshan) Limited, Disposable Soft Goods Limited, DSG (Malaysia) Sdn. Bhd., DSG (Shanghai) Manufacturing Limited, DSG International (Thailand) Public Company Limited, PT DSG Surya Mas Indonesia, Shanghai DSG MegaThin Company Limited, Shuiling Holding Company Limited

DSL.net Inc

545 Long Wharf Dr, New Haven, CT, 06511; *PH:* 1-203-772-1000; *http://* www.dsl.net

General - Incorporation	DE	**Stock**- Price on:12/24/2007	NA
Employees	98	Stock Exchange	NA
Auditor	Carlin, Charron & Rosen, LLP	Ticker Symbol	NA
Stk Agt	American Stock Transfer & Trust Co.	Outstanding Shares	NA
Counsel	Brobeck, Phleger & Harrison	E.P.S	NA
DUNS No.	NA	Shareholders	NA

Business: The group's principal activities are to provide high-speed data communications, Internet access and related services to small and medium sized businesses. The group provides high-speed digital connections and related services using its digital subscriber line (DSL) technology. The services provided by the group include Internet access, enhanced e-mail, domain name or Internet address registration for customers, firewalls, nationwide dial-up services, hosting customers' Web sites, virtual private networks that connect customers' various offices and other services such as collocation of customer equipment and limited alternative access solutions. The group acquired network access solutions corporation and talkingnets inc in 2003.

Primary SIC and add'l.: 4813 7375 7371

CIK No: 0001085866

Subsidiaries: DSLnet Atlantic, LLC, DSLnet Communications VA, Inc., DSLnet Communications, LLC

Officers: David F. Struwas/Dir., CEO, Pres., Marc R. Esterman/Sr. VP - Corporate Affairs, General Counsel, Sec., Walter R. Keisch/CFO, Treasurer

Directors: David F. Struwas/Dir., CEO, Pres., Paul Milley/Dir., Robert B. Hartnett/Dir., Paul J. Keeler/Dir., Emerson Walters/Dir., Steven B. Chisholm/Dir., J. Brooke Mastin/Dir.

Owners: Robert B. Hartnett, Insiders, Alan E. Salzman, Marc R. Esterman, Paul J. Keeler, Walter R. Keisch, James D. Marver, MegaPath Inc., David F. Struwas

DSP Group Inc

2580 N First St., Ste. 460, San Jose, CA, 95131; *PH:* 1-408-986-4300; *Fax:* 1-408-986-4323; *http://* www.dspg.com

General - Incorporation	DE	**Stock**- Price on:12/24/2007	$21.57
Employees	319	Stock Exchange	NDQ
Auditor	Kost Forer Gabbay & Kasierer	Ticker Symbol	DSPG
Stk Agt	American Stock Transfer & Trust Co.	Outstanding Shares	28,490,000
Counsel	Morrison & Foerster LLP	E.P.S	-$0.06
DUNS No.	18-190-7312	Shareholders	NA

Business: The group's principal activity is to develop, design and market integrated circuit ('ic') products and technologies. The group's system-on-a-chip solution includes applications for digital 900mhz, 2.4ghz and 5.8ghz telephony, European digital enhanced cordless telecommunications telephony and bluetooth systems for voice, data and video communication. In addition, it offers ic products that are used in hand-held digital voice recorders, mp3 players, voice over Internet protocols (voip) phones, residential gateways and integrated access devices. These products are marketed to OEMs for use in consumer products for the residential wireless telecommunication market worldwide. Customers include Panasonic, Sony, Uniden, CCT Telecom, Motorola, Samsung, Philips, Alcatel, Thomson, General Electric, Deutsche Telecom and others. The group has international operations in Europe and Asia, including Japan and Israel.

Primary SIC and add'l.: 3674 7372 3663

CIK No: 0000915778

Subsidiaries: DSP Group Ltd., DSP R&D Ireland Ltd., DSP Video Korea Ltd, DSPG Edinburgh Ltd, Nihon DSP K.K., RF Integrated Systems, Inc.

Officers: Eliyahu Ayalon/Chmn., CEO, Pres./$991,961.00, Boaz Edan/COO, Exec. VP/$557,417.00, Eli Fogel/CTO, Sr. VP/$429,516.00, Tal Simchony/52/Pres./$975,247.00, Dror Levy/VP - Finance, CFO/$283,009.00, Ofer Shneyour/Corporate VP, Broadband Division Mgr., Avi Barel/Corporate VP - Sales, Orit Menkes/Corporate VP - Human Resources, Danny Hacohen/Corporate VP - Business Operation

Directors: Eliyahu Ayalon/Chmn., CEO, Pres., Zvi Limon/Dir., Yair Seroussi/Dir., Louis Silver/Dir., Yair Shamir/Dir., Patrick Tanguy/Dir.

Owners: FMR Corporation/6.93%, Patrick Tanguy, Yair Seroussi, Eliyahu Ayalon, ClearBridge Advisors, LLC/5.89%, Artisan Partners Limited Partnership/7.65%, Zvi Limon, Tal Simchony, Yair Shamir, Insiders/4.01%, Moshe Zelnik, Boaz Edan, Louis Silver, Eli Fogel, Dror Levy

Financial Data: *Fiscal Year End:*12/31 *Latest Annual Data:* 12/31/2006

Year	Sales	Net Income
2006	$216,948,000	$22,379,000
2005	$187,225,000	$29,473,000
2004	$157,511,000	$51,094,000

Curr. Assets:	$210,934,000	**Curr. Liab.:**	$41,174,000	**P/E Ratio:**	44.94
Plant, Equip.:	$12,644,000	**Total Liab.:**	$47,239,000	**Indic. Yr. Divd.:**	NA
Total Assets:	$413,988,000	**Net Worth:**	$366,749,000	**Debt/ Equity:**	NA

DST Systems Inc

333 W 11th St., Kansas City, MO, 64105; *PH:* 1-816-435-1000; *Fax:* 1-816-435-8618; *http://* www.dstsystems.com; *Email:* ir@dstsystems.com

General - Incorporation	DE	**Stock**- Price on:12/24/2007	$79.53
Employees	10,500	Stock Exchange	NYSE
Auditor	PricewaterhouseCoopers LLP	Ticker Symbol	DST
Stk Agt	EquiServe Trust Co N.A	Outstanding Shares	64,460,000
Counsel	NA	E.P.S	$3.82
DUNS No.	07-303-1197	Shareholders	NA

Business: The groups principle activity is to provide information processing and computer software services and products. Customers served by the group include the financial services, telecommunications, healthcare and other service industries. The group operates from United States.

Primary SIC and add'l.: 7372 6799 7371

CIK No: 0000714603

Subsidiaries: DST lock\line, Inc, DST Output, LLC, DSTI Luxembourg Sarl, West Side Holdings, Inc

Officers: Steven J. Towle/50/CEO, Pres. - DST Output, Thomas A. McDonnell/62/Dir., CEO, Pres./$5,953,492.00, Thomas R. Abraham/56/CEO - DST International, Michael J. Winn/61/Non - Exec. Chmn. - DST International, Randall D. Young/51/VP, General Counsel, Sec., Robert L. Tritt/52/Group VP - Mutual Funds Remote/$1,474,889.00, Kenneth V. Hager/57/CFO, VP/$1,291,580.00, Jonathan J. Boehm/47/Group VP - Mutual Funds/$1,448,909.00, Gregg Wm. Givens/47/Chief Accounting Officer

Directors: Thomas A. McDonnell/62/Dir., CEO, Pres., George L. Argyros/Dir., Jeannine M. Strandjord/Dir., Thomas A. McCullough/65/Dir., William C. Nelson/Dir., Travis E. Reed/Dir., Edward A. Allinson/73/Dir.

Owners: Neil H. Nguyen, Insiders/20.70%, Travis E. Reed, Kinderhook Partners, LP/8.70%, Marshall& Ilsley Corporation/5.60%, CrossPoint Venture Partners/5.30%, Costa Brava Partnership III, LP/6.30%, Iridian Asset Management, LLC,/8.10%, David M. Kantor, Thomas A. McCullough/1.50%, Omar A. Choucair, Lisa C. Gallagher, Pamela Maythenyi, Jeannine M. Strandjord, William C. Nelson *(30 Owners included in Index)*

Financial Data: *Fiscal Year End:*12/31 *Latest Annual Data:* 12/31/2006

Year	Sales	Net Income
2006	$2,235,800,000	$272,900,000
2005	$2,515,100,000	$424,600,000
2004	$2,428,600,000	$222,800,000

Curr. Assets:	$652,500,000	**Curr. Liab.:**	$1,596,300,000	**P/E Ratio:**	22.28
Plant, Equip.:	$542,800,000	**Total Liab.:**	$2,546,800,000	**Indic. Yr. Divd.:**	NA
Total Assets:	$3,119,100,000	**Net Worth:**	$572,300,000	**Debt/ Equity:**	NA

DSW Inc

4150 E 5th Ave., Columbus, OH, 43219; *PH:* 1-614-237-7100; *Fax:* 1-614-238-4200; *http://* www.dswshoe.com

General - Incorporation	OH	**Stock**- Price on:12/24/2007	$34.89
Employees	5,800	Stock Exchange	NYSE
Auditor	Deloitte & Touche LLP	Ticker Symbol	DSW
Stk Agt	National City Bank	Outstanding Shares	43,950,000
Counsel	Vorys, Sater, Seymour and Pease LLP	E.P.S	$1.48
DUNS No.	NA	Shareholders	NA

Business: The groups principle activity is to retail footwear, designer dress, casual and athletic footwear for women and men. The group operates through two segments namely, DSW stores and leased departments. The group operates from the United States. The group's total revenue in the year 2007 was 1,279.06 millions of USD.

Primary SIC and add'l.: 5661

CIK No: 0001319947

Subsidiaries: DSW Shoe Warehouse, Inc.

Officers: Jay L. Schottenstein/Chmn., CEO, Deborah L. Ferree/Vice Chmn., Chief Merchandising Officer, Peter Z. Horvath/Pres., Kevin M. Lonergan/COO, Exec. VP, Harris Mustafa/Exec. VP - Supply Chain, Merchandise Planning, Allocation, Douglas J. Probst/Exec. VP, CFO, Treasurer, Jon J. Ricker/Exec. VP - Strategic Business Development, CTO, Derek Ungless/Exec. VP, Chief Marketing Officer, Richard J. Golden/Sr. VP - Real Estate, Kathleen C. Maurer/Sr. VP - Human Resources, Steven E. Miller/Sr. VP, Controller, William L. Jordan/VP, General Counsel

Directors: Jay L. Schottenstein/Chmn., CEO, Deborah L. Ferree/Vice Chmn., Chief Merchandising Officer, Heywood Wilansky/Dir., Carolee Friedlander/Dir., Philip B. Miller/Dir., James D. Robbins/Dir., Harvey L. Sonnenberg/Dir., Allan J. Tanenbaum/Dir.

Owners: AMVESCAP PLC/14.50%, Retail Ventures, Inc./100.00%, Baron Capital Management, Inc./18.70%, Schottenstein Stores Corporation/12.40%, Wellington Management Company, LLP/11.30%, Jay L. Schottenstein/14.30%, Delaware Management Holdings/7.20%

Financial Data: *Fiscal Year End:*01/28 *Latest Annual Data:* 2/3/2007

Year	Sales	Net Income
2007	$1,279,060,000	$65,464,000
2006	$1,144,061,000	$37,181,000
2005	$961,089,000	$34,955,000

Curr. Assets:	$457,971,000	**Curr. Liab.:**	$159,267,000		
Plant, Equip.:	$116,872,000	**Total Liab.:**	$233,724,000	**Indic. Yr. Divd.:**	NA
Total Assets:	$608,303,000	**Net Worth:**	$374,579,000	**Debt/ Equity:**	NA

DTE Energy Co

2000 2nd Ave., Detroit, MI, 48226; ***PH:*** 1-313-235-4000; ***Fax:*** 1-313-235-8055; ***http://*** www.dteenergy.com

General - Incorporation	MI	**Stock**- Price on:12/24/2007	$49.48
Employees	10,527	Stock Exchange	NYSE
Auditor	Deloitte & Touche LLP	Ticker Symbol	DTE
Stk Agt	Bank of New York	Outstanding Shares	176,060,000
Counsel	NA	E.P.S	$4.80
DUNS No.	83-932-9158	Shareholders	NA

Business: The groups principle activity is to provide oilfield products and services. The group operates from United States.

Primary SIC and add'l.: 4932 6719 4961 4911

CIK No: 0000936340

Subsidiaries: DTE Energy Resources, Inc., DTE Enterprises, Inc., Michigan Consolidated Gas Company, The Detroit Edison Company

Officers: Anthony F. Earley/58/Chmn., CEO/$7,330,805.00, David E. Meador/50/CFO, Exec. VP/$1,795,821.00, Gerard M. Anderson/49/COO, Pres./$3,152,312.00, Bruce D. Peterson/Sr. VP, General Counsel, Michael C. Porter/VP - Corporate Communications, Ron A. May/56/Sr. VP, Paul C. Hillegonds/Sr. VP - Corporate Affairs, Larry E. Steward/VP - Human Resources Strategy, Karla Hall/VP, Sec., Mgr. - Corporate Contributions, Community Involvement, DTE Energy Foundation, John Wilkinson/Dir. - Operations, Engineering, Lisa Muschong/Dir. - Investor Relations, Gerardo Norcia/45/Exec. VP - Michcon, Peter B. Oleksiak/41/VP, Controller, Sandra K. Ennis/51/Corp. Sec., Nick A. Khouri/VP, Treasurer - Corporate Finance *(23 Officers included in Index)*

Directors: Anthony F. Earley/58/Chmn., CEO, Alfred R. Glancy/69/Dir., Josue Robles/62/Dir., Frank M. Hennessey/Dir., Allan D. Gilmour/73/Dir., Frank W. Fountain/64/Dir., John E. Lobbia/66/Dir., Charles W. Pryor/63/Dir., Lillian Bauder/68/Dir., Gail J. McGovern/56/Dir., Eugene A. Miller/70/Dir., James H. Vandenberghe/58/Dir., Stephen E. Ewing/Dir., COO, Pres. - DTE Energy Gas

Owners: Insiders, Robert J. Buckler, Allan D. Gilmour, James H. Vandenberghe, Charles W. Pryor, John E. Lobbia, Howard F. Sims, Lillian Bauder, Josue Robles, Barclays Global Investors, NA/5.92%, Franklin Resources, Inc./8.40%, Alfred R. Glancy, Gerard M. Anderson, Stephen E. Ewing, Gail J. McGovern *(19 Owners included in Index)*

Financial Data: ***Fiscal Year End:***12/31 ***Latest Annual Data:*** 12/31/2006

Year	Sales	Net Income
2006	$9,022,000,000	$433,000,000
2005	$9,022,000,000	$537,000,000
2004	$7,114,000,000	$431,000,000

Curr. Assets:	$3,961,000,000	**Curr. Liab.:**	$4,164,000,000	**P/E Ratio:**	10.31
Plant, Equip.:	$11,451,000,000	**Total Liab.:**	$17,894,000,000	**Indic. Yr. Divd.:**	$2.120
Total Assets:	$23,785,000,000	**Net Worth:**	$5,849,000,000	**Debt/ Equity:**	1.2895

DTS Inc

Formerly: Digital Theater Systems Inc

5171 Clareton Dr., Agoura Hills, CA, 91301; ***PH:*** 1-818-735-4287; ***http://*** www.dtsonline.com

General - Incorporation	DE	**Stock**- Price on:12/24/2007	$22
Employees	325	Stock Exchange	NDQ
Auditor	PricewaterhouseCoopers LLP	Ticker Symbol	NA
Stk Agt	Computershare Investor Services LLC	Outstanding Shares	18,190,000
Counsel	NA	E.P.S	-$0.41
DUNS No.	NA	Shareholders	NA

Business: The group's principal activities are to provide digital multi-channel audio technology, products and services for entertainment markets. The group operates through two segments: theatrical business segment and consumer business segment. The theatrical business segment provides digital playback systems and cinema processor equipment to movie theaters and provides film licensing services to film studios and production companies. The consumer business segment licenses audio technology, trademarks and know-how to consumer electronics, personal computer, broadcast and professional audio companies and sells multi-channel audio content and products to consumers. It sells its products in the United States and in other foreign countries.

Primary SIC and add'l.: 7812 3651 3652 6794

CIK No: 0001226308

Subsidiaries: Digital Theater Systems (UK) Limited, Dts (asia) Limited, Dts (bvi) Az Research Limited, Dts (bvi) Limited, DTS AZ Research, LLC, DTS Canada Holdings, Inc., DTS Canada ULC, DTS China Holding Limited, DTS China Licensing (Hong Kong) Limited, DTS Digital Images, Inc., DTS France S.A.R.L., DTS Italia Sr.l., dts Japan KK, Guangzhou DTS Digital Theater System, Co. Ltd., International Cinema Services, Inc.

Officers: Jon Kirchner/CEO, Pres., Patrick Watson/Sr. VP - Strategy, Business Development, Bill Neighbors/Pres., Paul Smith/Sr. VP - Research, Development, DTS Northern Ireland, John Lowry/Chief Technologist - DTS Digital Cinema Division, William Elswick/Chief Technologist - Digital Cinema, DTS Digital Cinema Division, Sharon Kong Faltemier/Sr. VP - Human Resources, Nicholas Clay/Sr. VP - Technology, Strategy, Digital Cinema, DTS Digital Cinema Division, Gina Deboutez/Contact, William Neighbors/48/Sr. VP - DTS Digital Images, Brian D. Towne/Sr. VP - Consumer, Pro Division, Don Bird/Sr. VP - Corporate Strategy, Business Development, DTS Digital Cinema Division, Blake A. Welcher/Exec. VP, Legal General Counsel, Corp. Sec., Nao Ohtake/Dir. - Operations, DTS Japan, Tony Nowak/MD - Europe, DTS Digital Cinema Division *(19 Officers included in Index)*

Directors: Dan Slusser/Chmn., Joerg Agin/Dir., Joseph Fischer/Dir., James B. McElwee/Dir., Ron Stone/Dir., Ann C. Busby/52/Dir.

Owners: Andrea M. Nee, Insiders/5.68%, Blake A. Welcher, Ronald N. Stone, Burgundy Asset Management Ltd./7.11%, Melvin L. Flanigan, Daniel E. Slusser, Brown Capital Management,Inc./10.62%, William Neighbors, Baron Capital Group,Inc./9.12%, Joseph A. Fischer, T. Rowe Price Associates, Inc./5.18%, William Blair& Company, LLC/5.07%, Ann C. Busby, Joerg D. Agin *(18 Owners included in Index)*

Financial Data: ***Fiscal Year End:***12/31 ***Latest Annual Data:*** 12/31/2006

Year	Sales	Net Income
2006	$78,314,000	$3,024,000
2005	$75,252,000	$7,908,000
2004	$61,431,000	$9,976,000

Curr. Assets:	$133,428,000	**Curr. Liab.:**	$12,918,000		
Plant, Equip.:	$11,338,000	**Total Liab.:**	$14,384,000	**Indic. Yr. Divd.:**	NA
Total Assets:	$168,200,000	**Net Worth:**	$153,816,000	**Debt/ Equity:**	NA

Ducati Motor Holding SPA

Via Cavalieri Ducati 3, Bologna, 40132; ***PH:*** 39-0516413111; ***http://*** www.ducati.com; ***Email:*** info@ducatiuk.com

General - Incorporation	Italy	**Stock**- Price on:12/24/2007	NA
Employees	1,134	Stock Exchange	OTC
Auditor	KPMG Spa	Ticker Symbol	DMHYY
Stk Agt	Bank of New York	Outstanding Shares	NA
Counsel	NA	E.P.S	NA
DUNS No.	NA	Shareholders	NA

Business: The group's principal activities are the manufacturing and distribution of motorcycles, spare parts, technical riding gear and related clothing. The group also issues licenses for the production of replica models. The group is closely associated with motorcycle racing both through its own teams and by supplying others. The group has 8 subsidiaries, located in Europe, North America and Japan.

Primary SIC and add'l.: 2329 3751 5012 7948

CIK No: 0001080063

Subsidiaries: Ducati, Ducati Motor

Officers: Paolo Poma/Dir. - Investor Relations, Jennifer O'Brien/Assist. Investor Relations Officer, Livio Lodi/Contact - Museum

Financial Data: ***Fiscal Year End:***12/31 ***Latest Annual Data:*** 12/31/2005

Year	Sales	Net Income
2005	$380,011,000	-$88,599,000
2004	$522,240,000	-$2,826,000
2003	$495,349,000	-$766,000

Curr. Assets:	$291,180,000	**Curr. Liab.:**	$229,431,000		
Plant, Equip.:	$62,637,000	**Total Liab.:**	$407,958,000	**Indic. Yr. Divd.:**	NA
Total Assets:	$412,728,000	**Net Worth:**	$4,770,000	**Debt/ Equity:**	NA

Duckwall-ALCO Stores Inc

1903 N Buckeye St., Abilene, KS, 67410; ***PH:*** 1-785-263-1268; ***Fax:*** 1-785-263-7531; ***http://*** www.duckwall.com

General - Incorporation	KS	**Stock**- Price on:12/24/2007	$37.62
Employees	4,800	Stock Exchange	NDQ
Auditor	KPMG LLP	Ticker Symbol	DUCK
Stk Agt	UMB Bank, N.A.	Outstanding Shares	3,800,000
Counsel	NA	E.P.S	$1.49
DUNS No.	00-694-2353	Shareholders	NA

Business: The group's principal activity is the retail of general merchandise throughout the central portion of the United States of America. The retailing is carried through discount department and variety store outlets. The group operates 265 stores in 21 states and targets smaller markets that are not served by other regional or national full-line retail discount chains. The group's alco discount stores offer a full line of merchandise consisting of approximately 35,000 items. These items include automotive, candy, crafts, electronics, fabrics, furniture, hardware, health and beauty aids, housewares, jewelry, apparel and shoes, pre-recorded music and video, sporting goods, seasonal items, stationery and toys. The smaller duckwall variety stores offer a more limited selection of similar merchandise. The group operates 185 alco discount stores and 80 duckwall variety stores.

Primary SIC and add'l.: 5399 5311

CIK No: 0000030302

Subsidiaries: SPD Truck Line, Inc.

Officers: Bruce C. Dale/CEO, Pres./$630,628.00, Charles E. Bogan/VP, Corp. Sec., James E. Schoenbeck/Sr. VP - Real Estate/$222,334.00, John R. Sturdivant/Sr. VP - Stores/$242,088.00, Tom L. Canfield/Sr. VP - Administration, Logistics/$190,856.00, Virginia A. Meyer/VP - Marketing, Brent A. Streit/VP - Supply Chain Management, John R. Wagner/VP - Logistics, Michael S. Marcus/53/VP - Finance, Treasurer/$150,925.00, Tony C. Corradi/Sr. VP - Technology, Supply Chain Management, Michael J. Gawin/VP, Divisional Merchandise Mgr. - Softlines, Robert E. Swartz/VP, Divisional Merchandise Mgr. - Hardlines, Anthony C. Corradi/47/CTO, Sr. VP/$188,970.00, Donny R. Johnson/CFO, Sr. VP, Ronald V. Mapp/Sr. VP - Merchandising *(18 Officers included in Index)*

Directors: Warren H. Gfeller/Chmn., Dennis E. Logue/Dir., Lolan C. MacKey/Dir., Patrick G. Doherty/Dir., Jeffrey J. MacKe/39/Dir., Dennis A. Mullin/Dir., Robert L. Ring/Dir.

Owners: Franklin Resources, Inc./5.98%, Bruce C. Dale/1.85%, Lolan C. Mackey, Warren H. Gfeller, Michael S. Marcus, Kansas Public Employees Retirement System/6.31%, Dimensional Fund Advisors, Inc./9.26%, Jeffrey J. Macke/1.22%, James E. Schoenbeck, Strongbow Capital Management, Ltd./14.29%, Dennis E. Logue, Dennis A. Mullin/1.82%, Insiders/12.87%, John R. Sturdivant, William Blair & Company, L.L.C./12.11% *(19 Owners included in Index)*

Financial Data: ***Fiscal Year End:***01/29 ***Latest Annual Data:*** 1/28/2007

Year	Sales	Net Income
2007	$475,255,000	$5,704,000
2006	$435,015,000	$1,949,000
2005	$433,854,000	$3,923,000

Curr. Assets:	$135,064,000	**Curr. Liab.:**	$39,633,000	**P/E Ratio:**	25.25
Plant, Equip.:	$27,034,000	**Total Liab.:**	$48,861,000	**Indic. Yr. Divd.:**	NA
Total Assets:	$163,537,000	**Net Worth:**	$114,676,000	**Debt/ Equity:**	0.3877

Ducommun Inc

23301 Wilmington Ave., Carson, CA, 90745; ***PH:*** 1-310-513-7280; ***Fax:*** 1-310-513-7279; ***http://*** www.ducommun.com

General - Incorporation	DE	**Stock**- Price on:12/24/2007	$25.83
Employees	1,740	Stock Exchange	NYSE
Auditor	PricewaterhouseCoopers LLP	Ticker Symbol	DCO
Stk Agt	Mellon Investor Services LLC	Outstanding Shares	10,320,000
Counsel	NA	E.P.S	$1.61
DUNS No.	00-690-7042	Shareholders	NA

Business: The group's principal activity is to design, engineer and manufacture aerostructure and electromechanical components. It operates in two segments: ducommun aerostructures and ducummum technologies. Ducommun aerostructures engineers and manufactures aerospace structural components and subassemblies. Ducummum technologies designs, engineers and manufactures electromechanical components and subsystems principally for the aerospace and military markets. They also design and manufacture illuminated push button switches and panels, microwave switches and filters, fractional horsepower motors and resolvers and mechanical and electromechanical subassemblies. The other operations include the testing of complex components using stretch forming and thermal forming processes and computer-controlled machining. The group's major customers are boeing, raytheon and lockheed martin.

Primary SIC and add'l.: 3769 3728

CIK No: 0000030305

Subsidiaries: Composite Structures, LLC, Ducommun AeroStructures, Inc., Ducommun Technologies (Thailand) Ltd., Ducommun Technologies, Inc.

Officers: Joseph C. Berenato/Chmn., CEO, Pres./$900,240.00, Joseph Adams/VP - Operational Excellence - Ducommun Technologies, Inc, Anthony J. Reardon/Pres. - Ducommun Aerostructures, Inc, Gregory A. Hann/53/CFO, VP, Treasurer/$218,478.00, Don Devore/Vp - Finance, Information Technology, Ducommun Aerostructures, Michael Pollack/VP - Sales, Marketing, Programs, Ducommun Aerostructures, Michael Smith/VP - Material - Ducommun Aerostructures, Don Bach/VP - Lean Manufacturing - Ducommun Aerostructures, Don Miller/Pres. - Miltec, Ducommun Technologies, Inc, Todd Kawai/VP - Finance - Ducommun Technologies, Inc, Robert Sepulveda/VP - Operations - Phoenix, Ducommun Technologies, Inc, Jess Jimenez/VP - Human Resources - Ducommun Technologies, Inc, Rick Placido/VP - Supply Chain - Information Technology, Ducommun Technologies, Inc, Todd Rosin/VP - Product - Business Management, Ducommun Technologies, Inc, Terri Robbins/VP - Operations - Carson, Ducommun Technologies, Inc *(22 Officers included in Index)*

Directors: Joseph C. Berenato/Chmn., CEO, Pres., Thomas P. Mullaney/74/Dir., Frederick H. Christie/74/Dir., Robert C. Ducommun/56/Dir., Eric K. Shinseki/65/Dir., Ralph D. Crosby/60/Dir., Robert D. Paulson/62/Dir., Eugene P. Conese/48/Dir.

Owners: FMR Corp./9.90%, Royce& Associates, LLC/10.90%, Dimensional Fund Advisors, Inc./7.90%, The Clark Estates, Inc./8.90%, Joseph C. Berenato/1.30%, Robert C. Ducommun/6.10%, Robert D. Paulson, Anthony J. Reardon, John J. Walsh, Insiders/9.00%, Eugene P. Conese, Frederick H. Christie, Samuel D. Williams, Ralph D. Crosby, Thomas P. Mullaney *(16 Owners included in Index)*

Financial Data: **Fiscal Year End:**12/31 **Latest Annual Data:** 12/31/2006

Year	Sales	Net Income
2006	$319,021,000	$14,297,000
2005	$249,696,000	$15,993,000
2004	$224,876,000	$11,172,000

Curr. Assets:	$122,742,000	**Curr. Liab.:**	$67,387,000	**P/E Ratio:**	17.41
Plant, Equip.:	$52,987,000	**Total Liab.:**	$110,008,000	**Indic. Yr. Divd.:**	NA
Total Assets:	$297,033,000	**Net Worth:**	$187,025,000	**Debt/ Equity:**	0.2264

Duke Energy Corp

526 S Church St., Ec03t, Charlotte, NC, 28202; ***PH:*** 1-704-594-6200; ***http://*** www.duke-energy.com

General - Incorporation	NC	**Stock**- Price on:12/24/2007	$18.69
Employees	25,600	Stock Exchange	NYSE
Auditor	KPMG LLP	Ticker Symbol	DUK
Stk Agt	NA	Outstanding Shares	1,260,000,000
Counsel	NA	E.P.S	$1.42
DUNS No.	00-699-6052	Shareholders	NA

Business: The groups principle activity is to provide electric power and gas. The group also provide real estate and telecommunication services. The group operates from United States.

Primary SIC and add'l.: 4923 4922 4911 6519

CIK No: 0000030371

Subsidiaries: 1780, LLC, 280464 Ontario Limited, Advance SC LLC, Aguaytia Energy del Peru S.R. Ltda, Algonquin Gas Transmission, LLC, American Natural Gas Corporation, Associated Louisiana Intrastate Pipe Line, LLC, Ballantyne Properties, LLC, Bartram Lakes, LLC, Beaver Gas Services LLC, Belfort 36, LLC, Belfort Developers, LLC, Bison Insurance Company Limited, Black Forest on Lake James, LLC, Bridgeport Energy LLC 520 Subsidiaries included in the Index

Officers: James E. Rogers/Chmn., CEO, Pres., Keith B. Trent/Group Exec., Chief Strategy - Policy, Regulatory Officer, David L. Hauser/Group Exec., CFO, Marc E. Manly/Group Exec., Chief Legal Officer, Christopher C. Rolfe/Group Exec., Chief Administrative Officer, James L. Turner/Group Exec., COO, Pres. - US Franchised Electric, Gas, Steven K. Young/49/Sr. VP, Controller, Henry B. Barron/Group Exec., Chief Nuclear Officer, Lynn J. Good/Sr. VP, Treasurer, Julia S. Janson/Sr. VP - Ethics, Compliance, Corp. Sec., Sandra P. Meyer/Pres. - Duke Energy Ohio, Duke Energy Kentucky, Tom Shiel/Contact - Corporate Media Relations, Tom Williams/Contact - Policy, Energy Efficiency, Environmental Media Relations, Joseph P. Crapster/Mgr. - Shareholder Communications, Pilar Davila/Contact - Peru, Ecuador *(32 Officers included in Index)*

Directors: James E. Rogers/Chmn., CEO, Pres., William Barnet/Dir., Daniel R. Dimicco/Dir., Philip R. Sharp/Dir., Alex G. Bernhardt/Dir., Michael G. Browning/Dir., Phillip R. Cox/Dir., Ann Maynard Gray/Dir., James H. Hance/Dir., James T. Rhodes/Dir., Mary L. Schapiro/Dir., Dudley S. Taft/Dir.

Financial Data: **Fiscal Year End:**12/31 **Latest Annual Data:** 12/31/2006

Year	Sales	Net Income
2006	$15,184,000,000	$1,863,000,000
2005	$16,746,000,000	$1,824,000,000
2004	$22,503,000,000	$1,490,000,000

Curr. Assets:	$6,940,000,000	**Curr. Liab.:**	$6,613,000,000	**P/E Ratio:**	11.90
Plant, Equip.:	$41,581,000,000	**Total Liab.:**	$41,793,000,000	**Indic. Yr. Divd.:**	$0.880
Total Assets:	$68,700,000,000	**Net Worth:**	$26,102,000,000	**Debt/ Equity:**	0.4664

Duke Realty Corp

600 E 96th St., Ste. 100, Indianapolis, IN, 46240; ***PH:*** 1-317-808-6000; ***Fax:*** 1-317-808-6770; ***http://*** www.dukerealty.com

General - Incorporation	IN	**Stock**- Price on:12/24/2007	$37.06
Employees	1,250	Stock Exchange	NYSE
Auditor	KPMG LLP	Ticker Symbol	DRE
Stk Agt	American Stock Transfer & Trust Co.	Outstanding Shares	136,920,000
Counsel	NA	E.P.S	$1.53
DUNS No.	NA	Shareholders	NA

Business: The groups principal activity is to provide leasing property and asset management, development, construction, build-to-suit and other tenant-related services. The group also acquires real estate properties. The group operates through two segments namely, office and industrial. In the year 2006, the group acquired 50 new properties and placed 27 development projects in-service. The group operates from the United States. Of the total rental income in the year 2006, the office segment accounted for $562,903 and industrial $203,259 (thousands).

Primary SIC and add'l.: 4225 6798

CIK No: 0000783280

Subsidiaries: AD Pembroke Gardens, LLC, ADS Place Phase I, LLC, B/D Limited Partnership, BD Adena Development LLC, BD Clermont Development, LLC, BD Evansville Development, LLC, BD Greenwood Development, LLC, BD Kendall, LLC, BD Miamisburg Development, LLC, BD Overlook Development, LLC, BD Plainfield Development, LLC, BD Richmond Development, LLC, BD SMMC Development, LLC, BD St. Louis Development, LLC, Browning/Duke, LLC 57 Subsidiaries included in the Index

Officers: Dennis D. Oklak/Chmn., CEO/$2,631,532.00, Robert M. Chapman/COO/$1,356,117.00, Jeffrey D. Turner/Exec. VP - South Region, Joel Reuter/VP - Communications, Public Relations, Shona Bedwell/Assist. VP - Investor Relations, Matthew A. Cohoat/CFO, Exec. VP/$1,066,802.00, Howard L. Feinsand/Exec. VP, General Counsel, Corp. Sec., Andrew H. Kelton/Exec. VP - East Region, Donald J. Hunter/Exec. VP - Mid, East Region, Steve R. Kennedy/Exec. VP - Construction, Sam O'Briant/Exec. VP - Southeast Region, Kevin T. Rogus/Exec. VP - West Region/$1,427,188.00, Chris L. Seger/Exec. VP - National Group, James B. Connor/Exec. VP - Central Region/$984,398.00, William J. Deboer/Exec. VP - Redevelopment, Logistics

Directors: Dennis D. Oklak/Chmn., CEO, Barrington H. Branch/Dir., Geoffrey Button/Dir., William Cavanaugh/Dir., Ngaire E. Cuneo/Dir., Glenn R. Hubbard/Dir., Martin C. Jischke/Dir., Ben L. Lytle/Dir., William O. McCoy/Dir., Jack Shaw/Dir., Robert J. Woodward/Dir., Charles R. Eitel/Dir.

Owners: Geoffrey Button, Managed Accounts LLC/5.00%, Robert J. Woodward, Insiders/1.13%, Dennis D. Oklak, Glenn R. Hubbard, Martin C. Jischke, Matthew A. Cohoat, James B. Connor, Kevin T. Rogus, Ben L. Lytle, FMR Corp./12.47%, Barrington H. Branch, Jack R. Shaw, Charles R. Eitel *(20 Owners included in Index)*

Financial Data: **Fiscal Year End:**12/31 **Latest Annual Data:** 12/31/2006

Year	Sales	Net Income
2006	$1,193,433,000	$204,147,000
2005	$1,136,387,000	$355,662,000
2004	$1,165,999,000	$188,701,000

Curr. Assets:	$262,688,000	**Curr. Liab.:**	$342,228,000		
Plant, Equip.:	$6,427,379,000	**Total Liab.:**	$4,735,012,000	**Indic. Yr. Divd.:**	$1.920
Total Assets:	$7,238,595,000	**Net Worth:**	$2,503,583,000	**Debt/ Equity:**	NA

Dun & Bradstreet Corp

103 JFK Pkwy., Short Hills, NJ, 07078; ***PH:*** 1-973-921-5500; ***Fax:*** 1-973-921-6056; ***http://*** www.dnb.com; ***Email:*** custserv@dnb.com

General - Incorporation	DE	**Stock**- Price on:12/24/2007	$101.09
Employees	4,400	Stock Exchange	NYSE
Auditor	PricewaterhouseCoopers LLP	Ticker Symbol	DNB
Stk Agt	Computershare Trust CO.	Outstanding Shares	59,400,000
Counsel	NA	E.P.S	$4.73
DUNS No.	09-29 -	Shareholders	NA

Business: The group's principle activity is to provide business-to-business information to public and private business entities. The product lines include risk management solutions, sales & marketing solutions, supply management solutions and e-business solutions. Risk management solutions provide information related to commercial credit, evaluate clients, mitigate fraud risk etc. Sales and marketing solutions help customers to conduct market segmentation, client profiling etc. Supply management solutions provides a comprehensive system that offers enterprise-wide supplies base management. E-business solutions provides information on public and private companies. The group operates in the United States, Canada, Europe, Africa, Middle East, Asia-Pacific and Latin America. The group's quarterly revenue for Sep'07 was 389.90 millions of USD.

Primary SIC and add'l.: 7375

CIK No: 0001115222

Subsidiaries: Corinthian Holdings, Inc., Corinthian Leasing Corporation, D & B Group Ltd., D&B Acquisition Corporation, D&B Europe Ltd., D&B Holdings (UK), D&B Holdings (UK)Limited, D&B Iberia Holding BV, D&B Information Services (M)Sdn. Bhd., D&B International Consultant (Shanghai) Co. Ltd., D&B Investors L.P., D&B Property Holdings, Inc., DataHouse S.p.A., DBS Medium Systems Ireland, DBS Moyens Systems S.A. 72 Subsidiaries included in the Index

Officers: Steven W. Alesio/Chmn., CEO - D&B/$8,300,374.00, James P. Burke/Chief Marketing Officer, Sr. VP - Global Solutions/$1,391,495.00, Stacy Cashman/Sr. VP - Middle Marketing Customer Group, Patricia A. Clifford/Sr. VP - Human Resources, Jim Delaney/Sr. VP - Global Sales, Marketing Solutions, David J. Emery/Sr. VP - Asia Pacific, International Business Development, John Lawler/Sr. VP - Customer Transformation, David J. Lewinter/Sr. VP - Global Reengineering/$1,582,883.00, Sara Mathew/COO, Pres./$3,885,130.00, Tim McChristian/Sr. VP - Enterprise Customer Group, David Palmieri/Sr. VP - Global Risk Management Solutions, Michael Pepe/Pres. - US, Lee A. Spirer/Sr. VP - Strategy, Business Development, Reengineering, Byron C. Vielehr/CIO, Sr. VP - Technology/$1,633,033.00, Rich Veldran/Leader - Investor Relations, Treasury *(21 Officers included in Index)*

Directors: Steven W. Alesio/Chmn., CEO - D&B, John W. Alden/Dir., Christopher J. Coughlin/Dir., James N. Fernandez/Dir., Ronald L. Kuehn/Dir., Victor A. Pelson/Dir., Sandra E. Peterson/Dir., Michael R. Quinlan/Dir., Naomi O. Seligman/Dir., Michael J. Winkler/Dir., Austin A. Adams/Dir.

Owners: Steven W. Alesio/1.34%, Naomi O. Seligman, James P. Burke, Harris Associates Investment Trust/5.16%, Harris Associates L.P./5.64%, David J. Lewinter, Victor A. Pelson, Michael R. Quinlan, Sandra E. Peterson, Ronald L. Kuehn, James N. Fernandez, Byron C. Vielehr, Christopher J. Coughlin, Davis Selected Advisers, L.P./15.80%, John W. Alden *(19 Owners included in Index)*

Financial Data: **Fiscal Year End:**12/31 **Latest Annual Data:** 12/31/2006

Year	Sales	Net Income
2006	$1,531,300,000	$240,700,000
2005	$1,443,600,000	$221,200,000
2004	$1,414,000,000	$211,800,000

Curr. Assets:	$645,000,000	**Curr. Liab.:**	$805,500,000	**P/E Ratio:**	26.39
Plant, Equip.:	$50,700,000	**Total Liab.:**	$1,756,600,000	**Indic. Yr. Divd.:**	$1.000
Total Assets:	$1,360,100,000	**Net Worth:**	-$399,100,000	**Debt/ Equity:**	NA

Dundee Corp

Formerly: Dundee Bancorp Inc
28th Floor 1 Adelaide St. E, 40 King St W, Toronto, ON, M5C 2V9; *PH:* 1-416-863-6990;
Fax: 1-416-363-4536; *http://* www.dundeebancorp.com; *Email:* investor@dundeebancorp.com

General - Incorporation	ON	*Stock*- Price on:12/24/2007	NA
Employees	NA	Stock Exchange	NA
Auditor	Ernst & Young, LLP	Ticker Symbol	NA
Stk Agt	Computershare Trust Co	Outstanding Shares	NA
Counsel	Goodman & Co	E.P.S.	NA
DUNS No.	24-947-2978	Shareholders	NA

Business: The group's principle activities are to provide investment management and administrative services to dynamic mutual funds, closed end funds, pension funds, institutional accounts and private individuals, securities brokerage, corporate finance, financial planning and advisory services to corporations and individuals and merchant banking.

Primary SIC and add'l.: 6799 6282 6722

CIK No: 0000897455

Subsidiaries: DCC Equities Limited, Dundee Capital Corporation, Dundee Realty Corporation, Dundee Wealth Bank, Dundee Wealth Management Inc, The Dundee Bank

Officers: Ned Goodman/CEO, Pres., Joanne Ferstman/Exec. VP, CFO, Corp. Sec.

Directors: Harold P. Gordon/Chmn., Harry R. Steele/Dir., Barry K. Sparks/Dir., Robert McLeish/Dir., Garth MacRae/Dir., Jonathan Goodman/Dir., Frederick H. Lowy/Dir., Normand Beauchamp/Dir.

Dune Energy Inc

Two Shell Plz., 777 Walker St., Ste. 2450, Houston, TX, 77002; *PH:* 1-713-229-6300;
Fax: 1-713-229-6388; *http://* www.duneenergy.com

General - Incorporation	DE	*Stock*- Price on:12/24/2007	$2.38
Employees	10	Stock Exchange	AMEX
Auditor	Malone & Bailey, PC	Ticker Symbol	DNE
Stk Agt	American Stock Transfer & Trust Co.	Outstanding Shares	60,810,000
Counsel	NA	E.P.S.	-$1.3
DUNS No.	NA	Shareholders	NA

Business: The groups principle activities include exploring, developing and acquiring natural gas and crude oil properties. The group operates from the Texas and Louisiana. The groups quarterly revenue for September 2007 was 27.51 millions of USD.

Primary SIC and add'l.: 1311

CIK No: 0001092839

Subsidiaries: Dune Operating Company, Vaquero Partners LLC

Officers: James A. Watt/58/Dir., CEO, Pres., Steven J. Craig/VP - Investor Relations - Administration, Amiel David/COO, Pres./$333,615.00, Richard M. Cohen/Dir., Sec., Frank T. Smith/61/CFO

Directors: James A. Watt/58/Dir., CEO, Pres., Alan Gaines/52/Chmn., Richard M. Cohen/Dir., Sec., Steven Barrenechea/Dir., Steven M. Sisselman/Dir., Alan D. Bell/Dir., Marshall Lynn Bass/38/Dir., Raissa S. Frenkel/46/Dir., William E. Greenwood/Dir.

Owners: Natural Gas Partners VII, L.P./12.90%, Steven Barrenechea, Steven M. Sisselman, Itera Holdings BV/45.50%, Richard M. Cohen, Frank T. Smith, Insiders/6.30%, Alan Gaines/5.50%, Alan D. Bell

Financial Data: Fiscal Year End:12/31 *Latest Annual Data:* 12/31/2006

Year		Sales		Net Income
2006		$7,580,000		-$53,636,000
2005		$3,724,000		-$1,585,000
Curr. Assets:	$7,557,000	*Curr. Liab.:*	$9,471,000	
Plant, Equip.:	$41,120,000	*Total Liab.:*	$66,108,000	*Indic. Yr. Divd.:* NA
Total Assets:	$50,859,000	*Net Worth:*	-$15,250,000	*Debt/ Equity:* NA

Dupont Direct Financial Holdings Inc

42 Broadway Way, Ste. 1100-26, New York, NY, 10004; *PH:* 1-917-320-4800

General - Incorporation	GA	*Stock*- Price on:12/24/2007	$0.0095
Employees	NA	Stock Exchange	NA
Auditor	Bernstein Pinchuk & Kaminsky LLP	Ticker Symbol	NA
Stk Agt	American Stock Transfer & Trust Co.	Outstanding Shares	NA
Counsel	NA	E.P.S.	NA
DUNS No.	NA	Shareholders	NA

Business: The group's principle activity is to provide wide range of innovative products and services for markets including agriculture, nutrition and electronics. The group's products include fluropolymer additives and polymer modefiers. The group operartes from United States.

Primary SIC and add'l.: 6211

CIK No: 0000807904

Financial Data: Fiscal Year End:03/31 *Latest Annual Data:* 3/31/2003

Year		Sales		Net Income
2003		$5,275,000		-$343,000
2002		$5,336,000		-$758,000
2001		$3,306,000		-$149,000
Curr. Assets:	$1,652,000	*Curr. Liab.:*	$726,000	
Plant, Equip.:	$35,000	*Total Liab.:*	$837,000	*Indic. Yr. Divd.:* NA
Total Assets:	$3,868,000	*Net Worth:*	$3,031,000	*Debt/ Equity:* NA

Duquesne Light Co

411 Seventh Ave. (16-4), Pittsburgh, PA, 15219; *PH:* 1-412-393-6000;
http:// www.duquesnelight.com

General - Incorporation	PA	*Stock*- Price on:12/24/2007	NA
Employees	NA	Stock Exchange	NA
Auditor	Deloitte & Touche LLP	Ticker Symbol	NA
Stk Agt.	NA	Outstanding Shares	NA
Counsel	NA	E.P.S.	NA
DUNS No.	00-791-5606	Shareholders	NA

Business: The group's principal activity is transmission and distribution of electric energy. The electric utility operations provide service to approximately 587,000 direct customers in southwestern Pennsylvania, a territory of approximately 800 square miles. The group is a wholly owned subsidiary of dqe, inc.

Primary SIC and add'l.: 4911

CIK No: 0000030573

Subsidiaries: Alkmaar, LLC, Apollo Energy III, LLC, BodyMedia, Inc., Chautauqua LFG, LLC, Cherrington Insurance, Ltd., Cop Lfg, LLC, CRMC Bethlehem LLC, Dade County LGP, LLC, DataCom Information Systems, LLC, DES Corporate Services, Inc., DES Operating Services, Inc., DES Synfuel Operating Services, Inc., DH Canada, Inc., DH Energy, L.P., DH Energy, LLC 61 Subsidiaries included in the Index

Officers: Morgan K. Obrien/47/Dir., CEO, Pres., Mark E. Kaplan/46/Sr. VP, CFO, Susan S. Betta/Controller, Stevan R. Schott/44/VP - Finan, William F. Fields/57/VP, Treasurer, Maureen L. Hogel/47/Sr. VP, Chief Legal, Administrative Officer, James E. Wilson/42/VP - Corporate Development

Directors: Morgan K. Obrien/47/Dir., CEO, Pres., Pritam Advani/Dir., Doreen E. Boyce/Dir., Robert P. Bozzone/Dir., Charles C. Cohen/Dir., Sigo Falk/Dir., Joseph C. Guyaux/Dir., David M. Kelly/Dir., John D. Turner/Dir.

Dura Automotive Systems Inc

2791 Research Dr., Rochester Hills, MI, 48309; *PH:* 1-248-299-7500; *Fax:* 1-248-299-7501;
http:// www.duraauto.com; *Email:* investors@duraauto.com

General - Incorporation	DE	*Stock*- Price on:12/24/2007	NA
Employees	NA	Stock Exchange	OTC
Auditor	Moss Adams LLP	Ticker Symbol	DRRAQ
Stk Agt	Wachovia Bank N.A	Outstanding Shares	NA
Counsel	Dickinson, Wright	E.P.S.	-$48.267
DUNS No.	78-152-0275	Shareholders	NA

Business: The groups principle activity is to manufacture driver control systems. The group also supplies modules, glass systems, seat mechanisms and structures, and engineered assemblies. The group operates through two business segments namely automotive and atwood mobile products. The group operates from United States.

Primary SIC and add'l.: 6719 3714

CIK No: 0001016177

Subsidiaries: ACK Controls, Inc, Adwest Electronics, Inc., Atwood Automotive, Inc., Atwood Mobile Products, Inc., Automotive Aviation Partners LLC, Autopartes Excel de Mexico, S.A. de C.V., Creation Group Holdings, Inc., Creation Group Transportation, Inc, Creation Group, Inc., Creation Windows, Inc, Creation Windows, LLC., Dura Aircraft Operating Company, LLC, Dura Auto Holding Spain, S.L, Dura Automotive Body & Glass Systems Components, S.R.O, Dura Automotive Body & Glass Systems GmbH & Co 86 Subsidiaries included in the Index

Officers: Lawrence A. Denton/Chmn., CEO, Pres., Theresa L. Skotak/VP, Chief Administrative Officer, John J. Knappenberger/61/VP, Timothy C. Stephens/47/VP, Pres. - Atwood Mobile Products Division, David T. Szczupak/COO - Automotive Group, Timothy C. Trenary/CFO, VP, David L. Harbert/65/CFO, VP, Treasurer

Directors: Lawrence A. Denton/Chmn., CEO, Pres., Yousif B. Ghafari/55/Dir., Richard J. Jones/65/Dir., Ralph R. Whitney/73/Dir., Jack K. Edwards/63/Dir., James O. Futterknecht/61/Dir., Nick G. Preda/62/Dir., Walter P. Czarnecki/64/Dir.

Owners: Insiders/12.20%, Keith R. Marchiando, Dimensional Fund Advisors/6.60%, Theresa L. Skotak/1.00%, John J. Knappenberger/1.80%, Richard J. Jones, Jack K. Edwards, Yousif B. Ghafari, Jurgen Heyden/1.20%, James O. Futterknecht, Nick G. Preda, Lawrence A. Denton/3.30%, Timothy C. Stephens, Walter P. Czarnecki, Milton D. Kniss/1.90% *(16 Owners included in Index)*

Financial Data: Fiscal Year End:12/31 *Latest Annual Data:* 12/31/2005

Year		Sales		Net Income
2005		$2,344,139,000		$1,814,000
2004		$2,492,543,000		$11,723,000
2003		$2,380,794,000		$22,338,000
Curr. Assets:	$682,048,000	*Curr. Liab.:*	$499,339,000	
Plant, Equip.:	$465,475,000	*Total Liab.:*	$1,952,709,000	*Indic. Yr. Divd.:* NA
Total Assets:	$1,454,841,000	*Net Worth:*	-$503,327,000	*Debt/ Equity:* NA

Duraswitch Industries Inc

234 S Ext. Rd., Mesa, AZ, 85210; *PH:* 1-480-586-3300; *http://* www.duraswitch.com

General - Incorporation	NV	*Stock*- Price on:12/24/2007	$1.97
Employees	21	Stock Exchange	NDQ
Auditor	Deloitte & Touche LLP	Ticker Symbol	NA
Stk Agt	Computershare Investor Services LLC	Outstanding Shares	11,500,000
Counsel	Greenberg Traurig LLP	E.P.S.	$0.31
DUNS No.	NA	Shareholders	NA

Business: The group's principal activities are marketing and licensing electronic switches and integrated control panels. The products are used in computers, consumer electronics, mobile phones, consumer appliances, automobiles, fitness equipment, trains, ships, airplanes, generators, tractors, medical devises and commercial food preparation equipment. The group licenses electronic switch technology used to operate or control products in a variety of commercial and consumer applications. The products of the group include duraswitch pushgate, duraswitch thincoder rotor & duraswitch magnamouse. The trademarks and service marks of the group include duraswitch(R), pushgate(R) and thincoder(r).

Primary SIC and add'l.: 3674 6794

CIK No: 0001054070

Subsidiaries: Aztec Industries, Inc., FinePoint Innovations, Inc., Total Switch, Inc.

Officers: Bob Brilon/Dir., CEO, CFO, Pres., Robert J. Brilon/47/Dir., CEO, CFO, Pres./$378,970.00, Tim Kuhn/VP - Business Development, Tony Van Zeeland/CTO, Co - Founder,, Heather Beshears/VP - Corporate Communications, Bill Rowland/Dir. - Commercial Technology, Deborah Moore/VP - Finance - Administration

Directors: Bob Brilon/Dir., CEO, CFO, Pres., Robert J. Brilon/47/Dir., CEO, CFO, Pres., Steven P. Hanson/Chmn., John W. Hail/Dir., William E. Peelle/Dir., Tony Van Zeeland/CTO, Co - Founder,, Robert P. Moya/Dir., Michael A. Van Zeeland/Dir.

Owners: Anthony J. Van Zeeland/8.10%, Zeke L.P./6.00%, Robert J. Brilon/5.10%, Insiders/7.30%, Gruber & McBaine Capital Management/10.80%, Delphi Corp/14.40%, Jon D. Gruber/12.70%, John W. Hail, Potomac Capital Management/7.50%, AIGH Investment Partners LLC/5.90%, Steven P. Hanson, Robert P. Moya, William E. Peelle, Patterson J. McBaine/14.10%

Financial Data: Fiscal Year End:12/31 *Latest Annual Data:* 12/31/2006

Year	Sales	Net Income
2006	$9,492,000	-$3,215,000
2005	$6,456,000	$668,000
2004	$1,757,000	-$1,272,000

Curr. Assets:	$3,321,000	**Curr. Liab.:**	$1,871,000	**P/E Ratio:**	6.35
Plant, Equip.:	$510,000	**Total Liab.:**	$1,872,000	**Indic. Yr. Divd.:**	NA
Total Assets:	$6,468,000	**Net Worth:**	$4,596,000	**Debt/ Equity:**	NA

Durect Corp

2 Results Way, Cupertino, CA, 95014; *PH:* 1-408-777-1417; *Fax:* 1-408-777-3577; *http://* www.durect.com

General - Incorporation .... DE
Employees 170
Auditor .... Ernst & Young LLP
Stk Agt. .... Computershare Trust Co
Counsel. Heller Ehrman White & McAuliffe LLP
DUNS No. .... NA

Stock- Price on:12/24/2007 .... $3.79
Stock Exchange .... NDQ
Ticker Symbol .... DRRX
Outstanding Shares 69,400,000
E.P.S .... -$0.4
Shareholders .... NA

Business: The group's principal activities are pioneering the treatment of chronic diseases and conditions by developing and commercializing pharmaceutical systems. The group's pharmaceutical systems combine engineering innovations and delivery technology from the medical device and drug delivery industries. The group's products include chronogesic pain therapy system, alzet osmotic pumps, intracar catheters and biodegradable polymers. The group enables new drug therapies and optimizes existing therapies based on a broad range of compounds, including small molecule pharmaceuticals as well as biotechnology molecules such as proteins, peptides and genes. The group has entered into a development and commercialization agreement with alza corporation for certain product development rights, patent rights and other know-how relating to the duros system.

Primary SIC and add'l.: 8731 2834

CIK No: 0001082038

Subsidiaries: Absorbable Polymers International Corporation (API),

Officers: James E. Brown/Dir., CEO, Pres./$998,119.00, Felix Theeuwes/Chmn., Chief Scientific Officer/$1,010,431.00, Thomas P. McCracken/VP, Chief Patent Counsel, Su-il Yum/Exec. VP - Pharmaceutical Systems Research & Development, Principal Engineer/$570,299.00, Jean I. Liu/Sr. VP, General Counsel, Sec./$534,227.00, Jian Li/VP - Finance, Corporate Controller/$452,769.00, Steven C. Halladay/VP - Clinical, Regulatory Affairs, Paula Mendenhall/Exec. VP - Operations, Administration, Matthew J. Hogan/CFO/$146,402.00, Peter J. Langecker/Chief Medical Officer, Harry Guy/VP - Engineering, Safety, Schond L. Greenway/VP - Investor Relations, Strategic Planning, Andrew R. Miksztal/VP - Pharmaceutical Research, Development, Nacer E. Dean Abrouk/VP - Biostatistics

Directors: James E. Brown/Dir., CEO, Pres., Felix Theeuwes/Chmn., Chief Scientific Officer, Jon S. Saxe/Dir., Simon X. Benito/Dir., Terrence F. Blaschke/Dir., Michael D. Casey/Dir., David R. Hoffmann/Dir., Armand P. Neukermans/Dir.

Owners: Felix Theeuwes/3.50%, Zazove Associates, LLC/7.40%, Michael D. Casey, David R. Hoffmann, Matthew J. Hogan, James E. Brown/4.20%, Insiders/9.60%, Zesiger Capital Group LLC/7.20%, Su Il Yum, ALZA Corporation/9.50%, Armand P. Neukermans, Simon X. Benito, Jon S. Saxe, Jean I. Liu, Jian Li

Financial Data: *Fiscal Year End:*12/31 *Latest Annual Data:* 12/31/2006

Year	Sales	Net Income
2006	$21,894,000	-$33,327,000
2005	$28,571,000	-$18,128,000
2004	$13,853,000	-$27,637,000

Curr. Assets:	$75,799,000	**Curr. Liab.:**	$12,699,000		
Plant, Equip.:	$7,451,000	**Total Liab.:**	$65,453,000	**Indic. Yr. Divd.:**	NA
Total Assets:	$102,485,000	**Net Worth:**	$37,032,000	**Debt/ Equity:**	1.2532

Dusa Pharmaceuticals Inc

25 Upton Dr., Wilmington, MA, 01887; *PH:* 1-978-657-7500; *Fax:* 1-978-657-9193; *http://* www.dusapharma.com

General - Incorporation .... NJ
Employees 83
Auditor .... Deloitte & Touche LLP
Stk Agt...... American Stock Transfer & Trust Co.
Counsel .... Reed Smith LLP
DUNS No. 25-276-0483

Stock- Price on:12/24/2007 .... $3.11
Stock Exchange .... NDQ
Ticker Symbol .... DUSA
Outstanding Shares 19,480,000
E.P.S .... -$1.43
Shareholders .... NA

Business: The group's principal activity is to conduct research and develop drugs in combination with light devices to treat or detect a variety of conditions in processes known as photodynamic therapy or photodetection. The group develops Levulan(R), which is used to treatment actinic keratoses of the face or scalp. Several additional dermatological and internal indications are under development. Apart from this, the group also has continued funding the development of Levulan(R) PDT to treat warts and onychomycosis commonly known as nail fungus and also the development on broader labeling for the actinic keratoses indication. The group's trademarks include Levulan(R), Kerastick(R) and Blu-U(R).

Primary SIC and add'l.: 2834 8731

CIK No: 0000879993

Subsidiaries: DUSA Acquisition Corp., DUSA Pharmaceuticals New York, Inc.

Officers: Robert F. Doman/Dir., CEO, COO, Pres./$767,703.00, Geoffrey D. Shulman/Chmn., Chief Strategic Officer/$1,553,783.00, Nanette W. Mantell/Sec., Richard Christopher/CFO, VP - Finance/$348,460.00, Stuart Marcus/VP - Scientific Affairs, Chief Medical Officer/$450,320.00, Mark Carota/VP - Operations, William F. O'Dell/Exec. VP - Sales, Marketing/$401,497.00, Scott Lundahl/VP - Regulatory Affairs, Intellectual Property, Michael J. Todisco/VP, Controller, Shari Lovell/Dir. - Shareholder Services

Directors: Robert F. Doman/Dir., CEO, COO, Pres., Geoffrey D. Shulman/Chmn., Chief Strategic Officer, David M. Bartash/Dir., Richard C. Lufkin/Dir., Jay M. Haft/Dir., Magnus Moliteus/Dir., John H. Abeles/Dir.

Owners: Richard C. Christopher, Magnus Moliteus, Robert F. Doman, State of Wisconsin Investment Board/9.70%, Stuart L. Marcus, Cooper Hill Partners, LLC/14.30%, Jay M. Haft, Insiders/9.55%, FMR Corp. Edward C. Johnson, III/10.00%, Geoffrey D. Shulman/5.40%, Richard C. Lufkin, John H. Abeles, David M. Bartash, JPMorgan Chase & Co./5.70%, Royce & Associates, LLC/7.35%

Financial Data: *Fiscal Year End:*12/31 *Latest Annual Data:* 12/31/2006

Year	Sales	Net Income
2006	$25,583,000	-$31,350,000
2005	$11,337,000	-$14,999,000
2004	$7,988,000	-$15,629,000

Curr. Assets:	$24,308,000	**Curr. Liab.:**	$6,223,000		
Plant, Equip.:	$2,567,000	**Total Liab.:**	$7,422,000	**Indic. Yr. Divd.:**	NA
Total Assets:	$33,756,000	**Net Worth:**	$26,334,000	**Debt/ Equity:**	NA

Duska Therapeutics Inc

Two Bala Plz., Ste 300, Bala Cynwyd, PA, 19004; *PH:* 1-610-660-6690; *Fax:* 1-610-660-0966; *http://* www.duskatherapeutics.com; *Email:* info@duskascientific.com

General - Incorporation .... NV
Employees 2
Auditor .... Stonefield Josephson, Inc
Stk Agt. .... U.S. Stock Transfer Corp
Counsel .... Troy & Gould
DUNS No. .... NA

Stock- Price on:12/24/2007 .... NA
Stock Exchange .... OTC
Ticker Symbol .... DSKA
Outstanding Shares .... NA
E.P.S .... -$1.03
Shareholders .... NA

Business: The group's principle activity is to provide installation of landscaping for new homes in the metropolitan area of phoenix and Arizona. It includes installation of irrigation systems for new homes as well as the repair of previously installed sprinkler systems. The customers of the group include new homebuyers and longer term homeowners. The group operates from United States.

Primary SIC and add'l.: 7699 1522

CIK No: 0001127842

Subsidiaries: Duska Scientific Co.

Officers: James S. Kuo/Chmn., CEO, Wayne Lorgus/CFO/$36,780.00, Amir Pelleg/Dir., Pres., Chief Scientific Officer, Investor Contact/$175,000.00, Stephen P. Kutalek/Medical Dir.

Directors: James S. Kuo/Chmn., CEO, Kathryn Szabat/Member - Scientific Advisory Board, Pasquale Patrizio/Member - Scientific Advisory Board, Edward S. Schulman/Member - Scientific Advisory Board, Manuel F. Graiwer/Dir., Philip A. Sobol/Dir., Jane Kinsel/Member - Scientific Advisory Board, Amir Pelleg/Dir., Pres., Chief Scientific Officer, Investor Contact, David Benditt/Member - Scientific Advisory Board, Donald A. McAfee/Member - Scientific Advisory Board, Geoffrey Burnstock/Member - Scientific Advisory Board, Peter J. Barnes/Member - Scientific Advisory Board, Francesco Divirgilio/Member - Scientific Advisory Board, Daniel Flammang/Member - Scientific Advisory Board

Owners: Philip Sobol, Wayne Lorgus, Insiders, Livorno Latin American Promotions BV,, Gary Kaplan, James S. Kuo, Manuel Graiwer, Alexander Angerman and Judith Angerman Family Trust,, Amir Pelleg

Financial Data: *Fiscal Year End:*12/31 *Latest Annual Data:* 12/31/2006

Year	Sales	Net Income
2006	NA	-$2,000,000
2005	NA	-$2,760,000
2004	NA	-$1,561,000

Curr. Assets:	$356,000	**Curr. Liab.:**	$1,254,000		
Plant, Equip.:	$3,000	**Total Liab.:**	$1,254,000	**Indic. Yr. Divd.:**	NA
Total Assets:	$361,000	**Net Worth:**	-$894,000	**Debt/ Equity:**	NA

DVL Inc

70 E 55th St., 7th Fl., New York, NY, 10022; *PH:* 1-212-350-9900; *Fax:* 1-212-350-9911; *http://* www.dvlnet.com; *Email:* info@dvlnet.com

General - Incorporation .... DE
Employees .... NA
Auditor .... Imowitz Koenig & Co., LLP
Stk Agt. .... NA
Counsel .... NA
DUNS No. .... NA

Stock- Price on:12/24/2007 .... $0.15
Stock Exchange .... OTC
Ticker Symbol .... DVLN
Outstanding Shares 32,910,000
E.P.S $0.04
Shareholders .... NA

Business: The groups principle activity is to provide loans. The group financial products include real estate, residual and mortgage loans. The group operates from the United States. The groups anuual revenue for September 2007 was millions of USD.

Primary SIC and add'l.: 6159 1541 7389 6162 6726 6799 6519

CIK No: 0000215639

Subsidiaries: Del Toch, LLC, Delborne Land Company, LLC, Delbrook Holdings, LLC, DVL Mortgage Holdings, LLC, Professional Service Corporation, Receivables II-A, LLC, Receivables II-B, LLC, S2 Holdings, Inc.

Officers: Michael P. Murphy/CEO, Alan E. Casnoff/64/Dir., CEO, Pres., Lissa Dimitri/Parts Sales Mgr., Keith B. Stein/50/Special Purpose Dir., Gary Halliwell/Sales Mgr. - Pennsylvania, John Yacina/Sales Mgr. - Bucks County, PA, Southern NJ, Luis Davila/Sales Mgr. - New Jersey, Pennsylvani, Sanja Dolezar-Motz/DVL Services Sales Mgr., Rex Thompson/Mgr. - Power Services, John A. Deflores/VP - Power Systems - Sales Management, UPS Power, Michael G. Beck/Pres. - Sales Management, Precision Air, Joe Everman/Sales Mgr. - New Jersey, Delaware, Bob Gusciora/VP - Services, Sales Mgr. - Delaware, Gary Hill/Sales Mgr. - Pennsylvania, Bob Debski/Sales Mgr. - Greater Philadelphia *(17 Officers included in Index)*

Directors: Alan E. Casnoff/64/Dir., CEO, Pres., Gary Flicker/49/Chmn., Ira Akselrad/53/Dir.

Owners: Jay Chazanoff, Ron Jacobs, Jan Sirota, Milton Neustadter, Adam Frieman, Robert W. Barron, Peter Offerman, The SIII Associates Limited, Neal Polan, Lawrence J. Cohen, Michael Zarriello, Keith B. Stein, Joseph Huston, J.G. Wentworth, Stephen Simms *(16 Owners included in Index)*

Financial Data: *Fiscal Year End:*12/31 *Latest Annual Data:* 12/31/2006

Year	Sales	Net Income
2006	$9,417,000	$1,759,000
2005	$9,282,000	$1,730,000
2004	$8,926,000	$1,478,000

Curr. Assets:	$46,209,000	**Curr. Liab.:**	$242,000	**P/E Ratio:**	3.75
Plant, Equip.:	$7,488,000	**Total Liab.:**	$60,577,000	**Indic. Yr. Divd.:**	NA
Total Assets:	$80,486,000	**Net Worth:**	$19,909,000	**Debt/ Equity:**	NA

Dwango North America Corp

2211 Elliot Ave., Ste. 601, Seattle, WA, 98121; *PH:* 1-206-832-0600

General - Incorporation ... NV
Employees ... 33
Auditor ... Eisner LLP
Stk Agt ... Interwest Transfer Company, Inc.
Counsel ... NA
DUNS No. ... NA

Stock- Price on:12/24/2007 ... $0.015
Stock Exchange ... NA
Ticker Symbol ... NA
Outstanding Shares ... 9,570,000
E.P.S. ... -$0.289
Shareholders ... NA

Business: The groups' principal activities are to develop and distribute wireless applications for users of next generation wireless devices. The group currently distributes games that can be played on cell phones through agreements with wireless carriers and handset manufacturers. It distributes content through agreements with wireless carriers and handsets manufactures. It also publishes licensed content from third parties for distribution through our channels. On 04-Feb-2004, the group acquired over-the-air wireless inc.

Primary SIC and add'l.: 7372 0921

CIK No: 0001158134

Subsidiaries: OTA Acquisition Corp

Owners: Rick J. Hennessey/3.10%, Meruelo Capital Partners/7.80%, Van L. Brady/9.70%, David Adams/3.10%, Trafelet & Company, LLC/9.90%, Weiss, Peck & Greer Investments, a division of Robeco U.S.A., LLC/9.90%, James Scoroposki/5.00%, Paul J. Quinn/1.20%, Vishal Bhutani, James Scibelli/7.80%, Paul Eibeler/4.90%, Derrick L. Ashcroft/1.50%, Alexandra Global Master Fund Ltd./9.90%, RG Securities, LLC/5.20%, Silverman Partners/5.60% *(20 Owners included in Index)*

Financial Data: **Fiscal Year End:**12/31 **Latest Annual Data:** 12/31/2005

Year	Sales	Net Income
2005	$3,499,000	$2,185,000
2004	$1,645,000	-$9,683,000
2003	$22,000	-$4,650,000

Curr. Assets:	$6,321,000	**Curr. Liab.:**	$3,665,000		
Plant, Equip.:	$548,000	**Total Liab.:**	$7,658,000	**Indic. Yr. Divd.:**	NA
Total Assets:	$7,448,000	**Net Worth:**	-$15,373,000	**Debt/ Equity:**	NA

DXP Enterprises Inc

7272 Pinemont, Houston, TX, 77040; ***PH:*** 1-713-996-4700; ***Fax:*** 1-713-996-4701; ***http://*** www.dxpe.com; ***Email:*** info@dxpe.com

General - Incorporation ... TX
Employees ... 763
Auditor ... Hein & Assoc. LLP
Stk Agt ... American Stock Transfer & Trust Co.
Counsel ... NA
DUNS No. ... 96-729-6120

Stock- Price on:12/24/2007 ... $45.36
Stock Exchange ... NDQ
Ticker Symbol ... DXPE
Outstanding Shares ... 5,310,000
E.P.S. ... $2.33
Shareholders ... NA

Business: The group's principal activity is to distribute, maintain, repair and operate products, equipment and service to industrial customers. The group operates through two segments: maintenance, repair and operating and electrical contractor. The group offers fluid handling equipment, bearings and power transmission equipment, general mill and safety supplies and electrical products in its distribution activities. The fluid handling equipment consists of centrifugal pumps for transfer and process service applications such as petrochemicals refining and crude oil production. The bearings and power transmission equipment consists of mounted and unmounted bearings for a variety of applications. The general mill and safety supply consists of abrasives, tapes and adhesive products. The group also offers electrical products such as wire conduit, electrical fittings, boxes and batteries.

Primary SIC and add'l.: 5085 5084 5063

CIK No: 0001020710

Subsidiaries: American MRO, Inc., DXP Acquisition, Inc., Global Pump Service and Supply, LLC, Pelican States Supply Company, Inc., PMI Operating Company, Ltd., Pump - PMI LLC, R. A. Mueller, Inc., SEPCO Industries, Inc.

Officers: David R. Little/56/Chmn., CEO, Pres., Mac McConnell/54/Sr. VP - Finance, CFO, Sec., Michael J. Wappler/55/Sr. VP, David C. Vinson/57/Sr. VP, John J. Jeffery/40/Sr. VP - Sales, Marketing, Gregory Oliver/48/Sr. VP - Service Centers

Directors: David R. Little/56/Chmn., CEO, Pres., Cletus Davis/78/Dir., Kenneth H. Miller/69/Dir., Timothy P. Halter/42/Dir., Charles R. Strader/58/Dir.

Owners: Cletus Davis, Norman O. Schenk/33.30%, Ernest E. Herbert/16.70%, Insiders/1.00%, Timothy P. Halter, Donald E. Tefertiller/33.30%, Charles R. Strader, Insiders/40.60%, Kenneth H. Miller, Mac McConnell/1.40%, John Jeffery, Greg Oliver, David R. Little/13.80%, David C. Vinson/24.70%, David C. Vinson/1.00% *(16 Owners included in Index)*

Financial Data: **Fiscal Year End:**12/31 **Latest Annual Data:** 12/31/2006

Year	Sales	Net Income
2006	$279,820,000	$11,922,000
2005	$185,364,000	$5,467,000
2004	$160,585,000	$2,780,000

Curr. Assets:	$83,130,000	**Curr. Liab.:**	$43,661,000	**P/E Ratio:**	19.47
Plant, Equip.:	$9,944,000	**Total Liab.:**	$81,077,000	**Indic. Yr. Divd.:**	NA
Total Assets:	$116,807,000	**Net Worth:**	$35,718,000	**Debt/ Equity:**	NA

Dyadic International Inc

140 Intracoastal Pointe Dr., Ste. 404, Jupiter, FL, 33477; ***PH:*** 1-561-743-8333; ***Fax:*** 1-561-743-8343; ***http://*** www.dyadic-group.com

General - Incorporation ... DE
Employees ... 125
Auditor ... Ernst & Young, LLP
Stk Agt ... Continental Stock Transfer & Trust Co
Counsel ... NA
DUNS No. ... NA

Stock- Price on:12/24/2007 ... $5.3
Stock Exchange ... AMEX
Ticker Symbol ... DIL
Outstanding Shares ... 29,920,000
E.P.S. ... -$0.45
Shareholders ... NA

Business: The groups principle activities include research, developing and manufacturing biotechnology products. The groups services include high throughput robotic screening, gene overexpression and optimization, strain improvement and process development. The group operates from United States.

Primary SIC and add'l.: NA

CIK No: 0001213809

Subsidiaries: Dongguan Puridet Softener Company Limited, Dyadic International (USA), Inc., Dyadic International, Spo ka z orgraniczon odpwiedzialno ci, Dyadic Nederland BV, Dyadic Real Estate Holdings, Inc., Geneva International Holdings Limited, Puridet (Asia) Limited

Officers: Mark A. Emalfarb/52/Chmn., CEO, Pres., Wayne Moor/CFO, VP, Ratnesh Chandra/60/Sr. VP - Marketing, Biotechnology Systems, Charles W. Kling/VP - Sales, Enzymes, Alexander Bondar/Exec. VP, Chief Business Officer, Kent Sproat/Exec. VP - Manufacturing, Glenn Nedwin/52/Dir., Pres., Chief Scientific Officer - Biosciences Business, Daniel Michalopoulos/VP - Marketing, Enzymes

Directors: Mark A. Emalfarb/52/Chmn., CEO, Pres., Richard A. Learner/Chmn., Dyadic Scientific Advisory Board, Carlos Barbas/Member - Scientific Advisory Board, Stephen J. Warner/Dir., Glenn Nedwin/52/Dir., Pres., Chief Scientific Officer - Biosciences Business, Richard Berman/Dir., Harry Z. Rosengart/58/Dir., Robert Shapiro/69/Dir., Arnold Demain/Member - Scientific Advisory Board, Gerald R. Fink/Member - Scientific Advisory Board, Peter J. Punt/Member - Scientific Advisory Board, Arkady P. Sinitsyn/Member - Scientific Advisory Board, Cees Van Den Hondel/Member - Scientific Advisory Board, Joseph Villafranca/Member - Scientific Advisory Board

Owners: Stephen J. Warner/1.00%, Mark A. Emalfarb/22.70%, The Francisco Trust U/A/D February 28, 1996 ./15.90%, Glenn E. Nedwin, The Pinnacle Fund, L.P. Barry M. Kitt/8.30%, Insiders/40.00%, Richard J. Berman, Wayne Moor, Abengoa Bioenergy R&D, Inc./7.10%, Harry Z. Rosengart, Robert B. Shapiro

Financial Data: **Fiscal Year End:**12/31 **Latest Annual Data:** 12/31/2006

Year	Sales	Net Income
2006	$15,384,000	-$10,882,000
2005	$15,883,000	-$10,515,000
2004	$16,741,000	-$6,080,000

Curr. Assets:	$41,071,000	**Curr. Liab.:**	$4,411,000		
Plant, Equip.:	$1,813,000	**Total Liab.:**	$16,949,000	**Indic. Yr. Divd.:**	NA
Total Assets:	$45,137,000	**Net Worth:**	$28,189,000	**Debt/ Equity:**	NA

Dyax Corp

300 Technology Sq., Cambridge, MA, 02139; ***PH:*** 1-617-225-2500; ***Fax:*** 1-617-225-2501; ***http://*** www.dyax.com

General - Incorporation ... DE
Employees ... 161
Auditor ... PricewaterhouseCoopers LLP
Stk Agt ... American Stock Transfer & Trust Co.
Counsel ... Palmer & Dodge LLP
DUNS No. ... 60-986-9318

Stock- Price on:12/24/2007 ... $4.5
Stock Exchange ... NDQ
Ticker Symbol ... DYAX
Outstanding Shares ... 48,250,000
E.P.S. ... -$1.54
Shareholders ... NA

Business: The group's principal activity are to discover, develop and commercialize antibody, protein and peptide based therapeutic products for unmet medical conditions, particularly in the areas of inflammation and oncology. The two product candidates in clinical trials are dx-88 and dx-890. The group has collaborative agreements for the development of both of these product candidates. Dx-88 is in phase ii trials for the potential treatment of hereditary angioedema in collaboration with genzyme corporation. The group's second clinical compound, dx-890, is in phase ii clinical trials for the potential treatment of cystic fibrosis. The group uses its proprietary, patented technology, known as phage display, to identify human monoclonal antibodies, small proteins and peptides as potential therapeutics for the treatment of various conditions and diseases. On 29-Oct-2003, the group discontinued its operations of biotage llc.

Primary SIC and add'l.: 2834 8731

CIK No: 0000907562

Subsidiaries: Dyax B.V., Dyax Holdings B.V., Dyax S.A.

Officers: Henry E. Blair/Chmn., CEO, Pres./$9,087,162.00, Stephen S. Galliker/Exec. VP - Finance, Administration, CFO/$518,345.00, Clive R. Wood/Exec. VP - Discovery Research, Chief Scientific Officer/$541,513.00, Ivana Magovcevic-Liebisch/General Counsel, Exec. VP - Administration/$497,415.00, Nicole Jones/Assoc. Dir. - Investor Relations, Corporate Communications, Gustav A. Christensen/Exec. VP, Chief Business Officer, Ellen Flipse/Assoc. Investor Relations, Corporate Communications

Directors: Henry E. Blair/Chmn., CEO, Pres., Susan B. Bayh/Dir., James W. Fordyce/Dir., Mary Ann Gray/Dir., Henry R. Lewis/Dir., Constantine E. Anagnostopoulos/Dir., Thomas L. Kempner/Dir., David J. McLachlan/Dir.

Owners: Constantine E. Anagnostopoulos, Mary Ann Gray, Federated Investors,Inc. and certain related entities/12.59%, Clive R. Wood, Genzyme Corporation/10.32%, David J. McLachlan, James W. Fordyce, Thomas R. Beck, Susan B. Bayh, Royce& Associates, LLC/7.58%, Insiders/8.73%, Thomas L. Kempner/2.59%, Ivana Magovcevic-Liebisch, Stephen S. Galliker/1.06%, Henry R. Lewis *(16 Owners included in Index)*

Financial Data: **Fiscal Year End:**12/31 **Latest Annual Data:** 12/31/2006

Year	Sales	Net Income
2006	$12,776,000	-$50,323,000
2005	$19,859,000	-$30,944,000
2004	$16,590,000	-$33,114,000

Curr. Assets:	$63,765,000	**Curr. Liab.:**	$17,396,000		
Plant, Equip.:	$8,960,000	**Total Liab.:**	$64,712,000	**Indic. Yr. Divd.:**	NA
Total Assets:	$88,173,000	**Net Worth:**	$23,461,000	**Debt/ Equity:**	1.8867

Dycom Industries Inc

11770 US Hwy. 1, Ste. 101, Palm Beach Gardens, FL, 33408; ***PH:*** 1-561-627-7171; ***Fax:*** 1-561-627-7709; ***http://*** www.dycomind.com; ***Email:*** info@dycominc.com

General - Incorporation ... FL
Employees ... 9,352
Auditor ... Deloitte & Touche LLP
Stk Agt ... American Stock Transfer & Trust Co.
Counsel ... Shearman & Sterling LLP
DUNS No. ... 05-376-3637

Stock- Price on:12/24/2007 ... $30.18
Stock Exchange ... NYSE
Ticker Symbol ... DY
Outstanding Shares ... 40,820,000
E.P.S. ... $0.93
Shareholders ... NA

Business: The group's principal activity is to provide contracting services to telecommunications providers. Telecommunications infrastructure services provided by the group include engineering, placement and maintenance of aerial, underground and buried fiber-optic, coaxial and copper cable systems owned by local and long distance communications carriers and cable television multiple system operators. It also provides similar services related to the installation of integrated voice, data and video local and wide area networks within buildings. Other services include electrical and other construction and maintenance services for electric utilities. The services of the group are provided to customers in the United States. Customers include bellsouth, qwest, sprint, alltel corporation, verizon, adelphia, comcast, directv, charter, cablevision, insight communications, mediacom and time warner. On 03-Dec-2003, the group acquired utiliquest holdings corp.

Primary SIC and add'l.: 4911 1623 4931 1731 8711

CIK No: 0000067215

Subsidiaries: Ansco& Associates, LLC, Apex Digital, LLC, C-2 Utility Contractors, LLC, Cable Connectors, LLC, Cablecom of California, Inc., Cablecom, LLC, Can-Am Communications, Inc., Communications Construction Group of California, Inc., Communications Construction Group, LLC, Crystal Clear Satellite Sales& Service, LLC, Dycom Aviation, LLC, Dycom Capital Management, Inc., Dycom Corporate Identity, Inc., Dycom Identity, LLC, Dycom Investments, Inc. 47 Subsidiaries included in the Index

Officers: Steven E. Nielsen/Chmn., CEO, Pres., Timothy R. Estes/COO, Exec. VP, Richard B. Vilsoet/VP, General Counsel, Sec., Richard L. Dunn/Sr. VP, CFO, Andrew H. Deferrari/VP, Chief Accounting Officer, Patricia M. Chang/Dir. - Internal Audit

Directors: Steven E. Nielsen/Chmn., CEO, Pres., Stephen C. Coley/Dir., Charles M. Brennan/Dir., Charles B. Coe/Dir., Jack H. Smith/Dir., Thomas G. Baxter/Dir., Joseph M. Schell/Dir., James A. Chiddix/63/Dir.

Owners: Insiders/3.67%, FMR Corp./15.57%, Joseph M. Schell, Thomas G. Baxter, Steven E. Nielsen/2.14%, Jack H. Smith, Andrew H. DeFerrari, Charles B. Coe, Tontine Overseas Associates, L.L.C./9.10%, Richard B. Vilsoet, Barclays Global Investors, N.A/5.54%, Timothy R. Estes, Charles M. Brennan, Richard L. Dunn, Stephen C. Coley *(16 Owners included in Index)*

Financial Data: *Fiscal Year End:*07/30 *Latest Annual Data:* 7/29/2006

Year	Sales	Net Income
2006	$1,023,673,000	$18,180,000
2005	$986,627,000	$24,314,000
2004	$872,716,000	$58,633,000

Curr. Assets:	$276,033,000	**Curr. Liab.:**	$102,478,000	**P/E Ratio:**	32.45
Plant, Equip.:	$100,353,000	**Total Liab.:**	$132,874,000	**Indic. Yr. Divd.:**	NA
Total Assets:	$651,835,000	**Net Worth:**	$518,961,000	**Debt/ Equity:**	NA

Dynacq Healthcare Inc

10304 Interstate 10 E, Ste. 369, Houston, TX, 77029; *PH:* 1-713-378-2000; *Fax:* 1-713-673-6416; *http://* www.dynacq.com; *Email:* info@dynacq.com

General - Incorporation	DE	**Stock**- Price on:12/24/2007	$2.43
Employees	267	Stock Exchange	NDQ
Auditor	Killman, Murrell & Co. P.C	Ticker Symbol	DYII
Stk Agt	American Stock Transfer & Trust Co.	Outstanding Shares	15,740,000
Counsel	NA	E.P.S	$0.26
DUNS No.	NA	Shareholders	NA

Business: The group's principal activities are to develop and operate general acute hospitals that provide specialized general surgeries which include bariatric, orthopedic and neuro spine surgeries. The surgeries are covered by workers compensation insurance or by commercial insurers on an out-of-network health plan basis. The group's hospitals are equiped with operating rooms, pre- and post-operative space, intensive care units, nursing units and modern diagnostic facilities. It provides its services to physicians and other healthcare professionals. The group acquired the assets of vista diagnostic center and remaining interests in pasadena facility and baton rouge facility in fiscal 2004.

Primary SIC and add'l.: 8062

CIK No: 0000890908

Subsidiaries: Ambulatory Infusion Therapy Specialist, Inc., Dallas Nevada, Inc., DeAn Joint Venture, Doctors Practice Management, Inc., DPM II, Inc., Pasadena Nevada, Inc., Surgi+ Group, Inc., Vista Community Medical Center, LLP d/b/a Vista Medical Center Hospital, Vista Dallas, LLC, Vista Healthcare, Inc., Vista Holdings, LLC, Vista Hospital of Baton Rouge, LLCd/b/a Vista Surgical Hospital of Baton Rouge, Vista Hospital of Dallas, LLP d/b/a Vista Hospital of Dallas, Vista Land and Equipment, LLC, Vista Medical Management, LLC 16 Subsidiaries included in the Index

Officers: Chiu M. Chan/55/Dir., Founder, Chmn., CEO, Philip S. Chan/56/Dir., VP, CFO, Ringo Cheng/Dir. - Information Technology, Hemant Khemka/Corporate Controller, Alan A. Beauchamp/COO, Exec. VP

Directors: Chiu M. Chan/55/Dir., Founder, Chmn., CEO, Philip S. Chan/56/Dir., VP, CFO, James G. Gerace/70/Dir., Stephen L. Huber/57/Dir., Earl R. Votaw/80/Dir., Ping S. Chu/56/Dir.

Owners: Philip S. Chan/3.25%, Chiu M. Chan/54.30%, James G. Gerace, Ping S. Chu/1.69%, Insiders/59.17%, Earl R. Votaw, Alan A. Beauchamp

Financial Data: *Fiscal Year End:*08/31 *Latest Annual Data:* 08/31/2007

Year	Sales	Net Income
2007	$42,846,000	$4,155,000
2006	$35,989,000	-$5,936,000
2005	$55,275,000	-$5,137,000

Curr. Assets:	$19,303,000	**Curr. Liab.:**	$16,397,000		
Plant, Equip.:	$34,811,000	**Total Liab.:**	$16,397,000	**Indic. Yr. Divd.:**	NA
Total Assets:	$71,273,000	**Net Worth:**	$54,219,000	**Debt/ Equity:**	NA

Dynamex Inc

5429 LBJ Fwy., Ste. 1000, Dallas, TX, 75240; *PH:* 1-214-560-9000; *Fax:* 1-214-560-9349; *http://* www.dynamex.com; *Email:* help@dxnow.com

General - Incorporation	DE	**Stock**- Price on:12/24/2007	$25.61
Employees	2,000	Stock Exchange	NDQ
Auditor	BDO Seidman LLP	Ticker Symbol	DDMX
Stk Agt	Computershare Investor Services LLC	Outstanding Shares	10,620,000
Counsel	NA	E.P.S	$1.33
DUNS No.	79-900-9410	Shareholders	NA

Business: The group's principal activity is to provide delivery and logistics services in the United States and Canada. The group through its branches provides same-day, door-to-door delivery services through its ground couriers. In addition to traditional on-demand delivery services, the group offers scheduled distribution services, which encompass recurring, point-to-point deliveries or multiple destination deliveries that require intermediate handling. The group also offers outsourcing services, which include fleet management and mailroom or other facilities management, such as maintenance of call centers for inventory tracking and delivery. The group operates in two U.S. Regions and one Canadian region, with each of its approximately 44 branches assigned to the appropriate region.

Primary SIC and add'l.: 4215

CIK No: 0001015483

Subsidiaries: Dynamex Canada Holdings, Inc., Dynamex Fleet Services, Inc., Dynamex Franchise Holdings, Inc., Dynamex Operations East Inc., Dynamex Operations West Inc., Dynamex Provincial Couriers, Inc.

Officers: Richard K. McClelland/Dir., CEO, Pres., Ray E. Schmitz/VP, CFO, Assist. Sec., Wayne Kern/Dir., Sec., Samuel T. Hicks/65/Corporate Controller, Pam Henderson/Investor Contact, James R. Aitken/48/Pres. - Dynamex Canada, Catherine J. Taylor/53/Pres. - Dynamex USA

Directors: Richard K. McClelland/Dir., CEO, Pres., Stephen P. Smiley/Dir., Kenneth H. Bishop/Dir., Brian J. Hughes/Dir., Bruce E. Ranck/Dir., Wayne Kern/Dir., Sec.

Owners: Richard K. McClelland, Insiders/2.18%, Wells Capital Management Inc./7.57%, Brian J. Hughes, Thomas F. Frist/10.06%, Dalton, Greiner, Hartman, Maher & Co., LLC/5.92%, Timothy E. Moriarty/6.49%, James R. Aitken, Catherine J. Taylor, Pequot Capital Management Inc./6.06%, Bruce E. Ranck, AMVESCAP PLC/9.07%, Ray E. Schmitz, Akre Capital Management, LLC/5.73%, Stephen P. Smiley *(18 Owners included in Index)*

Financial Data: *Fiscal Year End:*07/31 *Latest Annual Data:* 7/31/2006

Year	Sales	Net Income
2006	$358,374,000	$12,392,000
2005	$321,103,000	$11,185,000
2004	$287,856,000	$12,833,000

Curr. Assets:	$49,071,000	**Curr. Liab.:**	$30,182,000	**P/E Ratio:**	19.26
Plant, Equip.:	$5,967,000	**Total Liab.:**	$31,087,000	**Indic. Yr. Divd.:**	NA
Total Assets:	$110,299,000	**Net Worth:**	$79,212,000	**Debt/ Equity:**	NA

Dynamic Health Products Inc

12399 Belcher Rd. S, Ste. 140, Largo, FL, 33773; *PH:* 1-727-683-0670; *http://* www.dynamiclifeinc.com

General - Incorporation	FL	**Stock**- Price on:12/24/2007	$0.6
Employees	89	Stock Exchange	NA
Auditor	Brimmer, Burek & Keelan LLP	Ticker Symbol	NA
Stk Agt	Registrar & Transfer Co	Outstanding Shares	17,120,000
Counsel	NA	E.P.S	-$0.35
DUNS No.	NA	Shareholders	NA

Business: The group's principle activities are to create, manufacture, pack and distribute dietary supplements, over-the-counter drugs and health and beauty care products and to provide prescription services. The segments include distribution and prescription services. Through it's wholly owned subsidiaries, the group markets and distributes dietary supplements, and over-the-counter drugs and health and beauty care products. The group's in-house salespeople market products of the group directly to its wholesale customers. The group markets and distributes approximately 40 products packaged into approximately 76 skus throughout the United States

Primary SIC and add'l.: 5122 2844

CIK No: 0000949925

Subsidiaries: Bob OLeary Health Food Distributor Co., Inc, Bryan Capital Limited Partnership, DYHP Acquisitions, Inc., Dynamic Financial Consultants, LLC, Dynamic Life Products, Inc., Dynamic Marketing I, Inc., Florida limited liability company, Herbal Health Products, Inc, Online Meds Rx, Inc, Pharma Labs Rx, Inc, Pharma Labs Rx, Inc.

Officers: Mandeep K. Taneja/Dir., CEO, Pres., Cani I. Shuman/51/Dir., CFO, Joseph A. Mies/COO - Bob Oleary Health Food Distributor Co, Inc, Gregg A. Madsen/COO - Dynamic Marketing I, Inc

Directors: Mandeep K. Taneja/Dir., CEO, Pres., Jugal K. Taneja/Chmn., Kotha S. Sekharam/Dir., Cani I. Shuman/51/Dir., CFO, Rakesh K. Sharma/Dir., Morton L. Stone/77/Dir.

Owners: Insiders/48.10%, Mihir K. Taneja/9.10%, Manju Taneja/13.10%, Rakesh K. Sharma, Mandeep K. Taneja/11.30%, Cani I. Shuman, Morton L. Stone/1.40%, Jugal K. Taneja/30.00%, William L. LaGamba/9.50%, Laurus Master Fund, Ltd./9.90%, Kotha S. Sekharam/3.60%, Michele LaGamba/9.50%

Financial Data: *Fiscal Year End:*03/31 *Latest Annual Data:* 03/31/2007

Year	Sales	Net Income
2007	$56,810,000	-$3,815,000
2006	$50,142,000	$5,904,000
2005	$16,080,000	$136,000

Curr. Assets:	$10,426,000	**Curr. Liab.:**	$11,115,000		
Plant, Equip.:	$744,000	**Total Liab.:**	$11,363,000	**Indic. Yr. Divd.:**	NA
Total Assets:	$16,255,000	**Net Worth:**	$4,892,000	**Debt/ Equity:**	0.0092

Dynamic Leisure Corp

5680-A W Cypress St., Tampa, FL, 33607; *PH:* 1-813-877-6300; *Fax:* 1-813-877-6333; *http://* www.dylicorp.com; *Email:* InvestorRelations@dylicorp.com

General - Incorporation	MN	**Stock**- Price on:12/24/2007	$5.98
Employees	44	Stock Exchange	OTC
Auditor	Salberg & Company, P.A.	Ticker Symbol	DYLI
Stk Agt	Computershare Investor Services LLC	Outstanding Shares	13,650,000
Counsel	NA	E.P.S	-$0.589
DUNS No.	NA	Shareholders	NA

Business: The groups principle activities include marketing, selling and distributing travel products. The group products include vacation packages, cruises, domestic and international airline tickets, car rental services and accommodation products and services on a wholesale basis.In the year 2006, the group acquired Changes in L'Attitudes, Inc., L'Attitudes, Inc., Island Resort Tours, Inc. and International Travel and Resorts, Inc., The group operates from the United States.

Primary SIC and add'l.: 4700

CIK No: 0000934873

Subsidiaries: Changes in L Attitudes, Inc., Dynamic Leisure Group North America, Inc.,, DynEco International, Inc., International Travel and Resorts, Inc., Island Resort Tours, Inc.

Officers: Daniel G. Brandano/Chmn., CEO, Dan Gallogly/Counsulting CFO, Nigel P. Osborne/COO, Exec. VP, Mark Lightsey/VP - Finance, Stephen A. Hicks/Sr. VP, Chief Business Development Officer, Cynthia Bentley-Denight/Sr. VP, Chief Marketing Officer, Marianne B. Williams/VP - Product, Planning, James Dryer/Investor Contact, Mark E. Crone/43/Sec.

Directors: Daniel G. Brandano/Chmn., CEO, Ben J. Dyer/59/Dir., Eric H. Winston/Dir., David Shapiro/Dir., John E. Vahl/Dir.

Owners: Thomas W. Busch, MMA Capital, LLC, Raymon Valdes, Stephen A. Hicks, Ben J. Dyer, AJW Partners, LLC, Daniel G. Brandano, Diversified Acquisition Trust, LLC, Insiders, Trafalgar Capital Specialized Investment Fund, Eric H. Winston, David Shapiro

Financial Data: *Fiscal Year End:*12/31 *Latest Annual Data:* 12/31/2006

Year	Sales	Net Income
2006	$5,817,000	-$11,009,000
2005	NA	-$604,000
2004	$287,000	-$435,000

Curr. Assets:	$1,064,000	**Curr. Liab.:**	$13,160,000	**P/E Ratio:**	3.75
Plant, Equip.:	$1,077,000	**Total Liab.:**	$15,809,000	**Indic. Yr. Divd.:**	NA
Total Assets:	$9,544,000	**Net Worth:**	-$6,265,000	**Debt/ Equity:**	NA

Dynamic Materials Corp

5405 Spine Rd., Boulder, CO, 80301; ***PH:*** 1-303-665-5700; ***Fax:*** 1-303-604-1897;
http:// www.dynamicmaterials.com; ***Email:*** info@dynamicmaterials.com

General - Incorporation .... DE
Employees 210
Auditor .... Ernst & Young LLP
Stk Agt..... Computershare Investor Services LLC
Counsel LeBoeuf, Lamb, Greene & MacRae LLP
DUNS No. 00-709-4105

Stock- Price on:12/24/2007 .... $36.9
Stock Exchange .... NDQ
Ticker Symbol .... BOOM
Outstanding Shares 12,100,000
E.P.S. $1.70
Shareholders .... NA

Business: The group's principal activity is to provide products and services requiring explosive metalworking. The group operates through the following two segments: the explosive metalworking group and the aerospace group. Explosive manufacturing uses explosives to perform metal cladding and shock synthesis. The most significant product of this group is clad metal which is used in the fabrication of pressure vessels, heat exchangers and transition joints used in the hydrocarbon processing, chemical processing, power generation, petrochemical, pulp and paper, mining, shipbuilding and heat, ventilation and air conditioning industries. Aerospace group includes aerospace machines, forms and welds parts for the commercial aircraft, aerospace and defense industries. The group discontinued spin forge division during the year.

Primary SIC and add'l.: 3728 2892

CIK No: 0000034067

Subsidiaries: Nitro Metall Aktiebolag, Nobelclad Europe S.A.

Officers: Yvon Pierre Cariou/CEO, Pres./$1,026,375.00, Richard A. Santa/VP, CFO, Sec./$507,276.00, Philippe Roquette/Dir. - Finance, Human Resources, John G. Banker/VP - Marketing, Sales, Clad Metal Division/$500,895.00, S. Raghu/Sales Mgr., Cladue Fernandez/Dir. - Sales, Antoine Mion/Sales, Xavier Poly/Sales, Jan Denney/Accounting Payable, Don Rittenhouse/Controller, Elaine Braught/Accounting Receivable, Human Resources, George A. Young/Dir. - Marketing, Preston Fenn/Marketing Consultant, Jose Olivas/Sales Mgr., James Gray/Clad Metal Sales *(29 Officers included in Index)*

Directors: Dean K. Allen/Chmn., Bernard Hueber/Dir., Richard P. Graff/Dir., Gerard Munera/Dir.

Owners: FMR Corp./7.44%, Delaware Management/10.41%, Wellington Management Co LLP/5.89%, Dean K. Allen, Bernard Hueber, John G. Banker, Insiders/2.57%, Gerard Munera, Richard A. Santa, Next Century Growth Investors LLC/9.84%

Financial Data: ***Fiscal Year End:***12/31 ***Latest Annual Data:*** 12/31/2006

Year	Sales	Net Income
2006	$113,472,000	$20,764,000
2005	$79,291,000	$10,372,000
2004	$54,165,000	$2,833,000

Curr. Assets:	$63,847,000	**Curr. Liab.:**	$25,297,000	**P/E Ratio:**	22.36
Plant, Equip.:	$20,260,000	**Total Liab.:**	$27,393,000	**Indic. Yr. Divd.:**	$0.150
Total Assets:	$84,973,000	**Net Worth:**	$57,580,000	**Debt/ Equity:**	NA

Dynamics Research Corp

60 Frontage Rd., Andover, MA, 01810; ***PH:*** 1-978-475-9090; ***Fax:*** 1-978-474-9204;
http:// www.drc.com

General - Incorporation .... MA
Employees 1,500
Auditor .... Grant Thornton LLP
Stk Agt...... American Stock Transfer & Trust Co.
Counsel .... Nixon Peabody
DUNS No. 00-101-4182

Stock- Price on:12/24/2007 .... $12.74
Stock Exchange .... NDQ
Ticker Symbol .... DRCO
Outstanding Shares 9,460,000
E.P.S. $0.53
Shareholders .... NA

Business: The group's principal activity is to provide information technology, engineering, logistics and other consulting services. The services of the group enhance performance and cost effectiveness of mission critical systems. The group operates in two segments: systems and services and metrigraphics. Systems and services segment provides specialized technical services to the dod, federal agencies, state governments and other customers. Metrigraphics uses photolithographic and material deposition processes to manufacture optical discs, scales and reticles that are used for precision measurement. In may 2, 2003, the group completed the sale of its encoder division assets to gsi lumonics inc in billerica, Massachusetts.

Primary SIC and add'l.: 3577 7372 7379

CIK No: 0000030822

Subsidiaries: DRC International Corporation, H.J. Ford Associates, Inc.

Officers: James P. Regan/Chmn., CEO, Pres./$1,007,092.00, James Hatch/VP, GM - Engineering, Sustainment, Irv Zaks/VP, GM - C4isr, Randy Sablich/VP, GM - Metrigraphics Precision Components, Robert L. Smith/Sr. VP, GM - Acquisition Management, Engineering Group, Richard A. Covel/CIO, VP/$341,942.00, Lawrence H. Obrien/Sr. VP, GM - Business Development, Business Solutions/$365,747.00, Jeanne D. Lefevre/Sr. VP, GM - Federal Solutions Group, Bob Patterson/VP, GM - Defense Systems Support, Steven P. Wentzell/Sr. VP, GM - Human Resources/$372,075.00, David Keleher/Sr. VP, CFO/$483,580.00, Frank Grosso/VP, GM - Aviation Systems, Bob Alford/VP, GM - Secure Programs, David E. Kistler/CIO, VP, Thomas J. Kelly/Sr. VP, GM - Systems Engineering, Information Technology Group *(20 Officers included in Index)*

Directors: James P. Regan/Chmn., CEO, Pres., Charles P. McCausland/Dir., George T. Babbitt/Dir., Kenneth F. Kames/Dir., John S. Anderegg/Dir., Nickolas Stavropoulos/Dir., Francis J. Aguilar/Dir.

Owners: Nickolas Stavropoulos, Kenneth F. Kames, Kennedy Capital Management, Inc./6.20%, Richard A. Covel, David Keleher, James P. Regan/3.30%, Steven P. Wentzell, George T. Babbitt, Heartland Advisors, Inc./14.30%, Charles P. McCausland, Lawrence H. OBrien, Francis J. Aguilar, John S. Anderegg/7.90%, Insiders/14.00%

Financial Data: ***Fiscal Year End:***12/31 ***Latest Annual Data:*** 12/31/2006

Year	Sales	Net Income
2006	$258,987,000	$4,072,000
2005	$300,440,000	$11,433,000
2004	$275,706,000	$9,373,000

Curr. Assets:	$74,611,000	**Curr. Liab.:**	$48,282,000	**P/E Ratio:**	32.67
Plant, Equip.:	$11,509,000	**Total Liab.:**	$76,087,000	**Indic. Yr. Divd.:**	NA
Total Assets:	$159,852,000	**Net Worth:**	$83,765,000	**Debt/ Equity:**	NA

Dynamotive Energy Systems Corp

1700 W 75th Ave., Ste.105, Vancouver, BC, V6P 6G2; ***PH:*** 1-604-267-6000; ***Fax:*** 1-604-267-6005;
http:// www.dynamotive.com; ***Email:*** info@dynamotive.com

General - Incorporation .... BC
Employees .... NA
Auditor .... Ernst & Young LLP
Stk Agt .... Computershare Trust Co
Counsel .... NA
DUNS No. .... NA

Stock- Price on:12/24/2007 .... $1.2
Stock Exchange .... OTC
Ticker Symbol .... DYMTF
Outstanding Shares .... NA
E.P.S. .... NA
Shareholders .... NA

Business: The groups principal activities include developing and marketing biofuel technology products. The group products include bio-oil, char, and international bio-oil. The group operates from the United States and Canada.

Primary SIC and add'l.: 2869 1321

CIK No: 0000941625

Officers: Robert Andrew Kingston/Dir., CEO, Pres., Andrew R. Kingston/48/Dir., CEO, Pres., Richard Lin/Chmn., VP - Asian Affairs, Laura Santos/Corp. Sec., Anton Kuipers/VP - Strategic Initiatives, Brian Richardson/CFO, Jan Barynin/VP - Engineering, James Acheson/COO - Dynamotive US, Jeffrey Lin/VP - Business Development, Raul Parisi/VP - Dynamotive Latinoamericana SA, Diego Parisi/GM - Dynamotive Latinoamericana SA

Directors: Robert Andrew Kingston/Dir., CEO, Pres., Andrew R. Kingston/48/Dir., CEO, Pres., Richard Lin/Chmn., VP - Asian Affairs, Curtin Winsor/Dir., Desmond Radlein/Dir., George Terwilliger/Dir., Shing-Cheng Hong/Dir., Chih Lin Chu/Dir.

Owners: Desmond Radlein/0.03%, George J. Terwilliger, Richard Chen-Hsing Lin/1.21%, Laura Santos/0.00%, Shing-Cheng Hong/0.07%, Robert Andrew Kingston/0.49%, Chih-Lin Chu/0.01%, Brian Richardson/0.08%

Financial Data: ***Fiscal Year End:***12/31 ***Latest Annual Data:*** 12/31/2006

Year	Sales	Net Income
2006	NA	-$14,670,000
2005	NA	-$13,125,000
2004	NA	-$8,405,000

Curr. Assets:	$11,377,000	**Curr. Liab.:**	$6,438,000		
Plant, Equip.:	$26,362,000	**Total Liab.:**	$8,313,000	**Indic. Yr. Divd.:**	NA
Total Assets:	$37,993,000	**Net Worth:**	$29,680,000	**Debt/ Equity:**	NA

Dynasil Corp of America

385 Cooper Rd., West Berlin, NJ, 08091; ***PH:*** 1-856-767-4600; ***Fax:*** 1-856-767-6813;
http:// www.dynasil.com; ***Email:*** info@dynasil.com

General - Incorporation .... NJ
Employees 75
Auditor .... Haefele,flanagan & Co. P.C
Stk Agt .... Continental Stock Transfer & Trust Co
Counsel .... NA
DUNS No. 00-235-5774

Stock- Price on:12/24/2007 .... $1.9
Stock Exchange .... OTC
Ticker Symbol .... DYSL
Outstanding Shares 6,110,000
E.P.S. $0.07
Shareholders .... NA

Business: The group's principal activities are to manufacture and market customized synthetic fused silica products. The products are used in the optical lens and laser manufacturing industries and in the medical industry. The products of the group are also used in the manufacturing of analytical instruments and semi-conductors. The products and services are sold throughout the United States and internationally.

Primary SIC and add'l.: 3220 3827

CIK No: 0000030831

Subsidiaries: Optometrics Corporation

Officers: Craig T. Dunham/CEO, Pres., Laura Lunardo/CFO, Bruce Leonetti/VP - Sales, Marketing, Michael A. Orlando/Marketing, Inside Sales Mgr.

Directors: Cecil Ursprung/63/Dir.

Owners: James Saltzman/5.30%, Saltzman Partners/4.00%, Insiders/53.40%, Craig Dunham/44.50%, Bruce Leonetti, Laura Lunardo/2.50%, Cecil Ursprung/1.30%, Megan Shay/1.30%

Financial Data: ***Fiscal Year End:***09/30 ***Latest Annual Data:*** 9/30/2006

Year	Sales	Net Income
2006	$6,937,000	$460,000
2005	$5,078,000	$173,000
2004	$2,296,000	-$176,000

Curr. Assets:	$2,761,000	**Curr. Liab.:**	$1,022,000	**P/E Ratio:**	27.14
Plant, Equip.:	$627,000	**Total Liab.:**	$1,616,000	**Indic. Yr. Divd.:**	NA
Total Assets:	$3,466,000	**Net Worth:**	$1,851,000	**Debt/ Equity:**	NA

Dynatem Inc

23263 Madero St., Ste. C, Mission Viejo, CA, 92691; ***PH:*** 1-949-855-3235; ***Fax:*** 1-949-770-3481;
http:// www.dynatem.com; ***Email:*** sales@dynatem.com

General - Incorporation .... CA
Employees 19
Auditor .... Squar, Milner, Raehl & Williamson
Stk Agt .... Continental Stock Transfer & Trust Co
Counsel .... Higham, McConnell & Dunning
DUNS No. 05-256-7443

Stock- Price on:12/24/2007 .... $1.25
Stock Exchange .... OTC
Ticker Symbol .... DYTM
Outstanding Shares 1,460,000
E.P.S. .... -$0.17
Shareholders .... NA

Business: The group's principal activities are to design, manufacture and market modular single board microcomputers and microcomputer-based systems and software. The products of the group consist of modular single board microcomputers known as central processing unit boards, peripheral systems and software. The manufacturing companies use these products for factory automation, sensor monitoring, process control and other electronic implementations. The military services use these products for a number of applications including navigation, control of systems and rapid handling of data. The group exports its products to United Kingdom, Germany, Japan and Mexico.

Primary SIC and add'l.: 3571 3674 7371

CIK No: 0000795424

Financial Data: ***Fiscal Year End:***05/31 ***Latest Annual Data:*** 5/31/2006

Year	Sales	Net Income
2006	$3,703,000	$69,000
2005	$2,487,000	-$745,000
2004	$4,477,000	$404,000

Curr. Assets:	$1,810,000	Curr. Liab.:	$408,000		
Plant, Equip.:	$68,000	Total Liab.:	$408,000	Indic. Yr. Divd.:	NA
Total Assets:	$1,889,000	Net Worth:	$1,482,000	Debt/ Equity:	NA

Dynatronics Corp

7030 Pk. Ctr. Dr., Salt Lake City, UT, 84121; *PH:* 1-801-568-7000; *Fax:* 1-801-568-7711; *http://* www.dynatronics.com; *Email:* info@dynatron.com

General - Incorporation	UT	Stock- Price on:12/24/2007	NA
Employees	141	Stock Exchange	NDQ
Auditor	Tanner LC	Ticker Symbol	DYNT
Stk Agt	Interwest Transfer Company, Inc.	Outstanding Shares	8,800,000
Counsel	NA	E.P.S	-$0.06
DUNS No.	11-339-9125	Shareholders	NA

Business: The group's principal activities are to design, manufacture, market and distribute physical medicine products and aesthetic products. Products of the group include, therapy devices, medical supplies and soft goods, treatment tables, rehabilitation equipment, aesthetic massage and microdermabrasion devices, skin care products. Physical therapists, chiropractors, sports medicine practitioners, podiatrists, plastic surgeons, dermatologists, estheticians and other aesthetic service providers use the products of the group.

Primary SIC and add'l.: 3845 3842 3829

CIK No: 0000720875

Officers: Kelvyn H. Cullimore/Chmn., CEO, Pres., Ronald J. Hatch/VP - Research & Development, Larry K. Beardall/Dir., Exec. VP - Sales, Marketing, Robert J. Cardon/Sec., Treasurer, Terry M. Atkinson/55/CFO, James E. Woods/Dir. - Manufacturing

Directors: Kelvyn H. Cullimore/Chmn., CEO, Pres., Kelvyn H. Cullimore/73/Vice Chmn., Keith E. Hansen/Dir., Val J. Christensen/Dir., Joseph H. Barton/Dir., Larry K. Beardall/Dir., Exec. VP - Sales, Marketing, Howard L. Edwards/Dir.

Owners: Terry M. Atkinson, Keith E. Hansen/1.70%, Donald G. Whittington/6.10%, Howard L. Edwards, Insiders/11.90%, Val J. Christensen, Ronald J. Hatch, Anthony Trolio/5.10%, Larry K. Beardall/1.70%, Kelvyn H. Cullimore/1.40%, John Rajala/9.60%, Joseph H. Barton, Kelvyn H. Cullimore/5.00%, Stephen Cyman/5.50%

Financial Data: Fiscal Year End:06/30 Latest Annual Data: 6/30/2006

Year	Sales	Net Income
2006	$19,513,000	$194,000
2005	$20,404,000	$729,000
2004	$20,587,000	$883,000

Curr. Assets:	$11,652,000	Curr. Liab.:	$3,536,000		
Plant, Equip.:	$3,453,000	Total Liab.:	$7,498,000	Indic. Yr. Divd.:	NA
Total Assets:	$18,568,000	Net Worth:	$11,071,000	Debt/ Equity:	NA

Dynavax Technologies Corp

2929 7th St., Ste. 100, Berkeley, CA, 94710; *PH:* 1-510-848-5100; *Fax:* 1-510-848-1327; *http://* www.dynavax.com; *Email:* contact@dvax.com

General - Incorporation	DE	Stock- Price on:12/24/2007	$4.32
Employees	153	Stock Exchange	NDQ
Auditor	Ernst & Young LLP	Ticker Symbol	DVAX
Stk Agt	ComputerShare Trust Co	Outstanding Shares	39,740,000
Counsel	NA	E.P.S	-$1.64
DUNS No.	NA	Shareholders	NA

Business: The group's principal activity is to develop and intend to commercialize innovative products to treat and prevent allergies, infectious diseases and chronic inflammatory diseases using versatile, proprietary approaches that alter immune system responses in highly specific ways. The clinical development programs are based on immunostimulatory sequences, which are short dna, which are short dna sequences that enhance the ability of the immune system to fight disease and control chronic inflammation. As on 24-Feb-2004, the group completed initial public offering.

Primary SIC and add'l.: 2834

CIK No: 0001029142

Subsidiaries: Dynavax Asia Pte. Ltd., Ryden Therapeutics KK

Officers: Zbigniew Janowicz/CEO - Dynavax Europe, Dino Dina/Dir., CEO, Pres./$1,324,425.00, Gary A. Van Nest/VP - Preclinical Research/$480,604.00, Deborah A. Smeltzer/VP - Operations, CFO/$640,504.00, Eduardo B. Martins/VP - Clinical Development, William D. Turner/VP - Regulatory Affairs, Shari Annes/Contact - Investor Relations, Petra Zimmer/CFO - Dynavax Europe, Michael S. Ostrach/VP, Chief Business Officer, General Counsel, Cecilia Vitug/VP - Human Resources, Robert L. Coffman/VP, Chief Scientific Officer/$585,915.00, Timothy G. Henn/50/VP - Finance, Administration, Chief Accounting Officer, Stephen F. Tuck/VP - Biopharmaceutical Development/$533,266.00

Directors: Dino Dina/Dir., CEO, Pres., Arnold L. Oronsky/Chmn., Stanley A. Plotkin/Dir., Nancy L. Buc/Dir., Denise M. Gilbert/Dir., Eyal Raz/Founder, David M. Lawrence/Dir., Dennis A. Carson/Founder, Dir., Peggy V. Phillips/Dir., Lawrence M. Lichtenstein/Founder

Owners: Dennis Carson, Arnold L. Oronsky/2.00%, Denise M. Gilbert, Pictet Funds (LUX) Biotech/5.00%, Dino Dina/2.00%, Sectoral Asset Management, Inc/11.00%, Stanley A. Plotkin, Nancy L. Buc, Stephen F. Tuck, Federated Investors Tower Inc/22.00%, Deborah A. Smeltzer, Robert L. Coffman, Insiders/6.00%, Gary A. Van Nest, Entities Affiliated with Deerfield Management Company, L.P./12.00% *(16 Owners included in Index)*

Financial Data: Fiscal Year End:12/31 Latest Annual Data: 12/31/2006

Year	Sales	Net Income
2006	$4,847,000	-$52,052,000
2005	$14,655,000	-$20,555,000
2004	$14,812,000	-$15,971,000

Curr. Assets:	$89,686,000	Curr. Liab.:	$13,701,000		
Plant, Equip.:	$5,200,000	Total Liab.:	$23,818,000	Indic. Yr. Divd.:	NA
Total Assets:	$102,890,000	Net Worth:	$77,056,000	Debt/ Equity:	NA

Dyncorp International Inc

3190 Fairview Pk. Dr., Ste. 700, Falls Church, VA, 22042; *PH:* 1-571-722-0210; *Fax:* 1-571-722-0252; *http://* www.dyn-intl.com; *Email:* inquiry@dyn-intl.com

General - Incorporation	DE	Stock- Price on:12/24/2007	$20.72
Employees	NA	Stock Exchange	NYSE
Auditor	Deloitte & Touche LLP	Ticker Symbol	DCP
Stk Agt	Bank of New York	Outstanding Shares	57,000,000
Counsel	NA	E.P.S	$1.00
DUNS No.	NA	Shareholders	NA

Business: The groups principle activity is to provide specialized mission critical outsourced technical services, training and support, security services, base operations, and aviation services and operations. The group operates through two segments namely, international technical services and field technical services. In the year 2005, the group acquired DynCorp International LLC. The group operates from the United States, Middle East and Europe. The group's total revenue in year 2007 was 2,082.27 millions of USD.

Primary SIC and add'l.: 7379 3732 3731 3724 8331 3489 8734 7381 4731 8711 8744 3728

CIK No: 0001338916

Subsidiaries: Computer Sciences Corporation, DynCorp, DynCorp International LLC

Officers: Herbert J. Lanese/63/Dir., CEO, Pres., Robert B. Rosenkranz/68/Pres. - Operating Company's Government Services Division, Natale S. Digesualdo/68/Pres. - Operating Company's Maintenance, Technical Support Services Division, Henry S. Miller/Pres. - CRS, Mgr. - Program, Curtis L. Schehr/49/Sr. VP, General Counsel, Sec., William D. Cavanaugh/54/Sr. VP - Business Development, Michael J. Thorne/51/CFO, Sr. VP, Treasurer

Directors: Herbert J. Lanese/63/Dir., CEO, Pres., Robert B. McKeon/53/Chmn., Mark H. Ronald/66/Dir., Anthony C. Zinni/64/Dir., Michael J. Bayer/60/Dir., Richard E. Hawley/66/Dir., Barry R. McCaffrey/65/Dir., Ramzi M. Musallam/39/Dir., Joseph W. Prueher/65/Dir., Charles S. Ream/64/Dir., Leighton W. Smith/68/Dir., William G. Tobin/70/Dir.

Owners: Robert B. McKeon/56.50%, Charles S. Ream, Michael J. Thorne, Natale S. DiGesualdo, Insiders/56.60%, Richard E. Hawley, Robert B. Rosenkranz, Leighton W. Smith, William G. Tobin, Joseph W. Prueher, Herbert J. Lanese

Financial Data: Fiscal Year End:03/31 Latest Annual Data: 3/31/2006

Year	Sales	Net Income
2006	$1,966,993,000	$7,243,000

Curr. Assets:	$505,296,000	Curr. Liab.:	$253,967,000		
Plant, Equip.:	$8,769,000	Total Liab.:	$912,930,000	Indic. Yr. Divd.:	NA
Total Assets:	$1,239,089,000	Net Worth:	$106,338,000	Debt/ Equity:	1.7491

Dynegy Inc

1000 Louisiana St., Ste. 5800, Houston, TX, 77002; *PH:* 1-713-507-6400; *Fax:* 1-713-507-6808; *http://* www.dynegy.com; *Email:* ir@dynegy.com

General - Incorporation	IL	Stock- Price on:12/24/2007	$9.33
Employees	1,339	Stock Exchange	NYSE
Auditor	PricewaterhouseCoopers LLP	Ticker Symbol	DYN
Stk Agt	Mellon Investor Services LLC	Outstanding Shares	839,230,000
Counsel	Lerach Coughlin Stoia & Robbins	E.P.S	NA
DUNS No.	NA	Shareholders	NA

Business: The groups principle activity is to provide wholesale power, capacity and ancillary services to utilities, cooperatives, municipalities and other energy companies. The group operates from United States.

Primary SIC and add'l.: 4911 1321 6719 1311

CIK No: 0000879215

Subsidiaries: Dynegy Administrative Services Company, Dynegy Catlin Member, Dynegy Holdings Inc., Dynegy Midwest Generation, Inc., Dynegy Northeast Generation, Inc., Dynegy Power Marketing, Inc., Illinova Corporation

Officers: Bruce A. Williamson/Chmn., CEO, Holli C. Nichols/CFO, Exec. VP, Norelle Lundy/VP - Investor, Public Relations, Nir Grossman/Sr. Dir. - Investor Relations, Jason A. Hochberg/Exec. VP - Strategic Planning, Corporate Business Development, David W. Byford/Dir. - Public Relations, Carolyn J. Stone/Sr. VP, Controller, Stephen A. Furbacher/COO, Pres., Kevin J. Blodgett/General Counsel, Exec. VP - Administration, Lynn A. Lednicky/Exec. VP - Commercial, Development

Directors: Bruce A. Williamson/Chmn., CEO, Mike Segal/Dir., James T. Bartlett/Dir., Frank E. Hardenbergh/Dir., George L. Mazanec/Dir., David W. Biegler/Dir., Robert C. Oelkers/Dir., William L. Trubeck/Dir., Thomas D. Clark/Dir., Howard B. Sheppard/Dir., Patricia A. Hammick/Dir., Victor E. Grijalva/Dir., Rebecca B. Roberts/Dir.

Owners: Mikhail Segal, Kevin J. Blodgett, Insiders/1.10%, Insiders, Thomas D. Clark, David W. Biegler, Victor E. Grijalva, LS Power Equity Partners, L.P., Bruce A. Williamson, Patricia A. Hammick, William L. Trubeck, LS Power Partners, L.P., Lynn Lednicky, Chevron Corporation/19.50%, George L. Mazanec *(23 Owners included in Index)*

Dynex Capital Inc

4551 Cox Rd., Ste. 300, Glen Allen, VA, 23060; *PH:* 1-804-217-5800; *Fax:* 1-804-217-5860; *http://* www.dynexcapital.com; *Email:* askdx@dynexcapital.com

General - Incorporation	VA	Stock- Price on:12/24/2007	$8.21
Employees	17	Stock Exchange	NYSE
Auditor	BDO Seidman, LLP	Ticker Symbol	DX
Stk Agt	American Stock Transfer & Trust Co.	Outstanding Shares	12,140,000
Counsel	NA	E.P.S	$0.13
DUNS No.	NA	Shareholders	NA

Business: The groups principle activity is to provide mortgage loans in real estate properties. The group also provides single-family residential and commercial mortgage loans. The group operates from the United States. The groups quarterly revenue for September 2007 was 7.47 millions of USD.

Primary SIC and add'l.: 6798

CIK No: 0000826675

Subsidiaries: Allegheny Commercial Properties I, LLC, Allegheny Income Properties I, LLC, Allegheny Special Properties, LLC, Commercial Capital Access One, Inc., Dynex Commercial Services, Inc., Dynex Securities, Inc., Financial Asset Securitization, Inc., GLS Capital Services - Marlborough, Inc., GLS Capital Services, Inc., GLS Capital, Inc., GLS Development, Inc., GLS Properties, LLC, Issued Holdings Capital Corporation, MERIT Securities Corporation, MSC I L.P. 20 Subsidiaries included in the Index

Officers: Stephen J. Benedetti/COO, Exec. VP, Sec., Treasurer/$440,780.00, Wayne E. Brockwell/VP - Portfolio, Jeffrey L. Childress/Controller, John L. Goodhue/VP - Information Systems, Alison G. Griffin/Assist. VP - Investor Relations, Human Resources, Robert M. Nilson/VP - Risk Management

Directors: Thomas B. Akin/Chmn., Daniel K. Osborne/Dir., Eric P. Von Der Porten/Dir., Leon A. Felman/Dir., Barry Igdaloff/Dir., Sidney J. Davenport/Dir.

Owners: Leon A. Felman/1.25%, Wellington Management/5.53%, Eric P. Von der Porten, Daniel K. Osborne, Thomas B. Akin/13.97%, Barry Igdaloff/9.86%, Thomas B. Akin/14.65%, Rockwood Partners, L.P./7.50%, Insiders/21.00%, Stephen J. Benedetti, Eric P. Von der Porten/1.36%, Barry Igdaloff/4.44%, Daniel K. Osborne, Insiders/25.82%, Arthur D. Lipson/4.84% *(18 Owners included in Index)*

Financial Data: *Fiscal Year End:*12/31 *Latest Annual Data:* 12/31/2006

Year	Sales	Net Income
2006	$50,449,000	$4,909,000
2005	$74,395,000	$9,585,000
2004	$136,713,000	-$3,375,000

Curr. Assets:	$56,880,000	**Curr. Liab.:**	$95,978,000	**P/E Ratio:**	63.15
Plant, Equip.:	NA	**Total Liab.:**	$330,019,000	**Indic. Yr. Divd.:**	NA
Total Assets:	$466,557,000	**Net Worth:**	$136,538,000	**Debt/ Equity:**	1.6137

Dyntek Inc

19700 Fairchild Rd., Ste. 230, Irvine, CA, 92612; *PH:* 1-949-271-6700; *Fax:* 1-949-271-6799; *http://* www.dyntek.com; *Email:* info@dyntek.com

General		Stock	
Incorporation	DE	Price on:12/24/2007	$0.12
Employees	155	Stock Exchange	OTC
Auditor	Marcum & Kliegman LLP	Ticker Symbol	DYNK
Stk Agt	American Stock Transfer & Trust Co.	Outstanding Shares	58,230,000
Counsel	Stradling Yocca Carlson & Rauth	E.P.S	-$0.2
DUNS No.	18-290-2627	Shareholders	NA

Business: The group's principal activity is to provide information technology solutions and business process outsource services for state and local government agencies. The group operates through its subsidiary dyntek services inc. The group operates through two segments: information technology services and business process outsourcing. Information technology services provides it infrastructure services such as architectural design, legacy systems integration, network engineering, applications development, network security services, help desk support and operational support. The business process outsourcing segment contracts outsourced program operations such as privatization of child support enforcement services, the arrangement of non-emergency medical transportation for eligible medicaid, general relief and welfare recipients and other consulting expertise to state and local governments. The group acquired mormar technology inc and alex woda & associates in fiscal 2004.

Primary SIC and add'l.: 7371

CIK No: 0000879465

Subsidiaries: BugSolver.Com,Inc., DynTek Canada,Inc., DynTek Services,Inc., TekInsight e-Government,Inc., TekInsight Research,Inc.

Officers: Casper Zublin/Dir., CEO, Alex Woda/Dir. - Security Architecture, Wade Stevenson/VP - Finance, Bill Tomlinson/VP - Emerging Technologies, Bob Deschamps/Area VP - West, David W. Berry/CFO, Steve Struthers/CTO, Ron Ben-Yishay/Area VP - East, June Hazzard/VP - Human Resources, Organizational Development, Linda Ford/VP - Sales Operations, Frank W. Lyons/International Dir. - Application Security, Training

Directors: Casper Zublin/Dir., CEO, Michael J. Gullard/Chmn., Alan B. Howe/Dir.

Owners: Glen Ackerman, Bryant R. Riley, Alan B. Howe, Insiders, Michael J. Gullard, Wade Stevenson, Casper Zublin, Lloyd I. Miller

Financial Data: *Fiscal Year End:*06/30 *Latest Annual Data:* 6/30/2006

Year	Sales	Net Income
2006	$80,831,000	-$28,262,000
2005	$76,559,000	-$22,591,000
2004	$49,947,000	-$18,999,000

Curr. Assets:	$6,300,000	**Curr. Liab.:**	$6,257,000		
Plant, Equip.:	$763,000	**Total Liab.:**	$8,807,000	**Indic. Yr. Divd.:**	NA
Total Assets:	$29,688,000	**Net Worth:**	$20,881,000	**Debt/ Equity:**	0.4886

E Com Ventures Inc

251 International Pkwy., Sunrise, FL, 33325; *PH:* 1-954-335-9100; *Fax:* 1-954-335-9026; *http://* www.perfumania.com; *Email:* info@ecomv.com

General		Stock	
Incorporation	FL	Price on:12/24/2007	$21.99
Employees	1,599	Stock Exchange	NDQ
Auditor	Deloitte & Touche LLP	Ticker Symbol	ECMV
Stk Agt	Continental Stock Transfer & Trust Co	Outstanding Shares	3,060,000
Counsel	NA	E.P.S	$1.29
DUNS No.	18-638-8500	Shareholders	NA

Business: The group is a specialty retailer and wholesaler of fragrances and related products. The products of the group are sold through Internet as well. Through the wholesale division the group distributes the products throughout North America and abroad. Retail stores of the group are located in regional malls, manufacturers' outlet malls, airports and on a stand-alone basis in suburban strip shopping centers. The operations of the group are conducted in the United States and Puerto Rico. The group operates through its wholly owned subsidiaries perfumania inc and perfumania.com inc.

Primary SIC and add'l.: 5999 5122

CIK No: 0000880460

Subsidiaries: Magnifique Parfumes and Cosmetics, Inc., Perfumania International Franchising, Inc., Perfumania Puerto Rico, Inc., Perfumania, Inc., perfumania.com, inc., Ten Kesef II, Inc.

Owners: Stephen Nussdorf/44.50%, Michael W. Katz/3.20%, Donovan Chin, Paul Garfinkle, Insiders/46.60%, Slater Capital Management, L.L.C./5.10%, Carole A. Taylor, Joseph Bouhadana, Jeffrey L. Feinberg/19.30%

Financial Data: *Fiscal Year End:*01/28 *Latest Annual Data:* 02/03/2007

Year	Sales	Net Income
2007	$243,609,000	$4,522,000
2006	$233,694,000	$14,265,000
2005	$225,003,000	$3,151,000

Curr. Assets:	$86,955,000	**Curr. Liab.:**	$75,625,000	**P/E Ratio:**	18.02
Plant, Equip.:	$30,213,000	**Total Liab.:**	$88,178,000	**Indic. Yr. Divd.:**	NA
Total Assets:	$125,749,000	**Net Worth:**	$37,571,000	**Debt/ Equity:**	0.3341

E I Du Pont De Nemours & Co

1007 Market St., Wilmington, DE, 19898; *PH:* 1-302-774-1000; *Fax:* 1-302-999-4399; *http://* www.dupont.com

General		Stock	
Incorporation	DE	Price on:12/24/2007	$52.25
Employees	59,000	Stock Exchange	NYSE
Auditor	PricewaterhouseCoopers LLP	Ticker Symbol	DD
Stk Agt	Computershare Trust Co	Outstanding Shares	923,670,000
Counsel	NA	E.P.S	$3.51
DUNS No.	00-131-5704	Shareholders	NA

Business: The group's principal activity is to manufacture and sell materials, synthetic fibers, agriculture and biotechnology products. It operates in six segments: agriculture and nutrition segment leverages biotechnology and food chain knowledge. The coatings and color technologies segment develops and markets coating ingredients. The electronic and communication technologies segment provides materials for flexible printing and color proofing system. The performance materials segment provides polymer materials. The safety and protection segment delivers solutions to protect people, property, operations and the environment. The textiles and interiors segment provides flooring systems, industrial fibers, polyester fibers, elastane and textiles. The group operates in 75 countries in North America, South America, Europe, Middle East, Africa and Asia-Pacific. The group acquired griffin llc on 06-Nov-2003 and dupont Canada inc on 17-Apr-2003.

Primary SIC and add'l.: 2824 2834 3479 2869 2879 2822 2851

CIK No: 0000030554

Subsidiaries: Agar Cross S.A., Antec International Ltd., Building Media, Inc., ChemFirst Inc., Christiana Insurance, LLC, Destination Realty Inc., DPC (Luxembourg) SARL, DPC S/A Brazil, DPC South America, DSRB Ltda., DuPont (Australia) Ltd., DuPont (China) Research & Development Company Limited, DuPont (Korea) Inc., DuPont (New Zealand) Limited, DuPont (Shanghai) Sourcing Center Company,Ltd. 187 Subsidiaries included in the Index

Officers: Charles O. Holliday/Chmn., CEO/$10,691,860.00, Francine C. Shaw/CEO, Pres. - Dupont Performance Elastomers, Craig F. Binetti/Pres. - Dupont Nutrition, Health, Chmn. - Solae Company, Steve Chen/Chmn., Pres. - Dupont Taiwan, Sales Excellence Leader - Dupont Titanium Technologies, Asia Pacific, John C. Groves/Vice Chmn. - DTF JV, COO, Dean C. Oestreich/Chmn. - Pioneer Hi-Bred, VP - Dupont, Ferdinand Bauerdick/VP, GM - Dupont Advanced Coatings Systems, Dupont Performance Coatings Europe, Douglas W. Muzyka/Pres. - Dupont Greater China, Dupont China Holding Co Ltd, William S. Niebur/VP - Dupont Crop Genetics Research, Development, Mark P. Vergnano/Group VP - Dupont Safety, Protection, Mathieu Vrijsen/Sr. VP - Dupont Operations, Engineering, John Bedbrook/VP - Research, Development, Dupont Agriculture, Nutrition, James C. Collins/VP, GM - Dupont Crop Protection, James C. Borel/Sr. VP - Dupont Human Resources, Terry Caloghiris/Group VP - Dupont Coatings, Color Technologies *(75 Officers included in Index)*

Directors: Charles O. Holliday/Chmn., CEO, Donald W. Johnson/Chmn. - Dupont KK, Japan, John C. Groves/Vice Chmn. - DTF JV, COO, Steve Chen/Chmn., Pres. - Dupont Taiwan, Sales Excellence Leader - Dupont Titanium Technologies, Asia Pacific, Dean C. Oestreich/Chmn. - Pioneer Hi-Bred, VP - Dupont, Robert A. Brown/Dir., Bertrand P. Collomb/Dir., Marillyn Hewson/Dir., Sean O'Keefe/Dir., Alain J.P. Belda/Dir., William K. Reilly/Dir., John T. Dillon/Dir., Richard H. Brown/Dir., Masahisa Naitoh/Dir., Curtis J. Crawford/Dir. *(17 Directors included in Index)*

Owners: C. J. Crawford, Insiders/1.20%, Capital Research and Management Company/5.90%, M. Naitoh, W. K. Reilly, R. R. Goodmanson, A. J.P. Belda, J. T. Dillon, G. M. Pfeiffer, E. I. du Pont, R. H. Brown, C. O. Holliday, J. L. Keefer, T. M. Connelly, E. J. Kullman *(17 Owners included in Index)*

Financial Data: *Fiscal Year End:*12/31 *Latest Annual Data:* 12/31/2006

Year	Sales	Net Income
2006	$28,982,000,000	$3,148,000,000
2005	$28,491,000,000	$2,053,000,000
2004	$27,995,000,000	$1,780,000,000

Curr. Assets:	$12,870,000,000	**Curr. Liab.:**	$7,940,000,000	**P/E Ratio:**	14.89
Plant, Equip.:	$10,498,000,000	**Total Liab.:**	$21,914,000,000	**Indic. Yr. Divd.:**	$1.480
Total Assets:	$31,777,000,000	**Net Worth:**	$9,422,000,000	**Debt/ Equity:**	NA

E Med Future Inc

794 Morrison Rd. , Ste 911, Columbus, OH, 43230; *PH:* 1-877-855-1319; *http://* www.needlezap.com; *Email:* info@needlezap.com

General		Stock	
Incorporation	NV	Price on:12/24/2007	$0.008
Employees	2	Stock Exchange	OTC
Auditor	Meyler & Co. LLC	Ticker Symbol	EMDF
Stk Agt	National Stock Transfer, Inc.	Outstanding Shares	42,510,000
Counsel	NA	E.P.S	-$0.01
DUNS No.	NA	Shareholders	NA

Business: The group's principal activitiy is to manufacture and market products designed to reduce accidental hypodermic needlestick injuries. Its primary product, needlezap(R), completely disintegrates the sharp portion of the needle. It is designed to work within the parameters of recent osha needlestick mandates which require employers to take advantage of new technologies to prevent needlesticks in the workplace. The product of the group is marketed under the trademark needlezap. On 04-Apr-2003, the group acquired e med future inc and on 30-Dec-2003, it acquired medical safety technologies inc.

Primary SIC and add'l.: 3841

CIK No: 0000894552

Officers: Donald Sullivan/65/Dir., CFO, Interim CEO

Directors: Donald Sullivan/65/Dir., CFO, Interim CEO, Ronald L. Alexander/58/Dir.

Owners: Robert J. Ochsendorf/7.00%, Ronald L. Alexander/10.00%, Insiders/19.40%, Donald Sullivan/9.40%, PR Market Research Company/5.90%

Financial Data: *Fiscal Year End:*12/31 *Latest Annual Data:* 12/31/2006

Year	Sales	Net Income
2006	$82,000	-$320,000
2005	$121,000	-$2,098,000
2004	$119,000	-$1,118,000

Curr. Assets:	$97,000	**Curr. Liab.:**	$825,000		
Plant, Equip.:	$11,000	**Total Liab.:**	$1,373,000	**Indic. Yr. Divd.:**	NA
Total Assets:	$108,000	**Net Worth:**	-$1,265,000	**Debt/ Equity:**	NA

E On AG

E.ON-Platz 1, Dusseldorf, 40479; *PH:* 49-21145790; *http://* www.eon.com; *Email:* info@eon.com

General - Incorporation	Germany	**Stock**- Price on:12/24/2007	$54.44
Employees	80,612	Stock Exchange	OTC
Auditor	PricewaterhouseCoopers	Ticker Symbol	EONGY
Stk Agt	JP Morgan Chase Bank, N.A.	Outstanding Shares	2,000,000,000
Counsel	NA	E.P.S.	$4.10
DUNS No.	31-501-5040	Shareholders	NA

Business: The group's principal activity is the provision of energy services. The group also imports natural gas and supplies specialty chemicals. The operations of the group are carried on in 17 European countries that include scandinavia, the Netherlands, hungary, the slovak republic, the czech republic, Switzerland, Austria, Italy, Russia, Poland, the United Kingdom and the usa. The main customers of the group include regional and municipal energy utilities, industrial enterprises and power stations. Additionally, the group also provides residential real estate services with approximately 165,000 housing units, in addition to developing office and apartment buildings. The group also provides mobile communications services.

Primary SIC and add'l.: 4731 2911 4813 4931 6531 2899 2999

CIK No: 0001136808

Subsidiaries: CRC-Evans International Inc., E.ON Energie, E.ON Nordic AB (energy), E.ON Ruhrgas, E.ON Ruhrgas AG (energy), E.ON U.S.LLC (energy), Hungarian oil and gas company, ON Energie AG (energy), OOO Gazexport

Officers: Wulf H. Bernotat/60/Dir., CEO, Johannes Teyssen/49/Dir., COO, Sabine Palm/Exec. Assist. - Investor Relations, Peter Blau/Contact - Corporate Communications, Kiran Bhojani/Investor Relations Officer, Peter Blankenhorn/Mgr. - Investor Relations, Francois Poullet/Mgr. - Investor Relations, Sigrid Fielenbach/Assist. Mgr. - Investor Relations, Carmen Schneider/Assist. Mgr. - Investor Relations, Nina Wetzmuller/Assist. - Investor Relations, Jens Schreiber/Contact - External Communications, Volker Laudien/Sr. Management - Human Resources Corporate Center, Sandra Deimel/Contact - Human Resources Development, Josef Nelles/Head - Communication Department, Dirk Hachmann/Head - Corporate Communications Dep *(20 Officers included in Index)*

Directors: Wulf H. Bernotat/60/Dir., CEO, Gunter Vogelsang/Honorary Chmn., Member - Supervisory Board, Ulrich Hartmann/69/Chmn. - Supervisory Board, Karl-Hermann Baumann/Member - Supervisory Board, Gerhard Skupke/Member - Supervisory Board, Eva Kirchhof/Member - Supervisory Board, Ulrich Hocker/Member - Supervisory Board, Hans Michael Gaul/65/Dir., Burckhard Bergmann/65/Dir., Johannes Teyssen/49/Dir., COO, Klaus Dieter Raschke/Member - Supervisory Board, Ulrich Otte/58/Member - Supervisory Board, Seppel Kraus/54/Member - Supervisory Board, Wolf-Rudiger Hinrichsen/Member - Supervisory Board, Klaus Liesen/Member - Supervisory Board *(31 Directors included in Index)*

Financial Data: Fiscal Year End:12/31 **Latest Annual Data:** 12/31/2006

Year	Sales	Net Income
2006	$89,422,000,000	$6,674,000,000
2005	$66,788,000,000	$8,771,000,000
2004	$60,576,000,000	$5,874,000,000

Curr. Assets:	$40,763,000,000	**Curr. Liab.:**	$35,891,000,000		
Plant, Equip.:	$56,367,000,000	**Total Liab.:**	$98,278,000,000	**Indic. Yr. Divd.:**	$1.190
Total Assets:	$167,908,000,000	**Net Worth:**	$63,141,000,000	**Debt/ Equity:**	NA

E Trade Financial Corp

135 E 57th St., Newyork, NY, 10022; **PH:** 1-800-783-3388; **Fax:** 1-866-650-0003; **http://** www.etrade.com; **Email:** salesinfo@etrade.com

General - Incorporation	DE	**Stock**- Price on:12/24/2007	NA
Employees	3,439	Stock Exchange	NDQ
Auditor	Deloitte & Touche LLP	Ticker Symbol	ET
Stk Agt	American Stock Transfer & Trust Co.	Outstanding Shares	NA
Counsel	NA	E.P.S.	NA
DUNS No.	NA	Shareholders	NA

Business: The group's principle activity is to provide online brokerage, banking, lending and planning and advisory services to retail, corporate and institutional clients. The group also provides consumer banking products, FDIC-insured time deposit, savings and transactional products. The groups lending services include first and second mortgage, refinance of existing mortgage and home equity loan. The group operates from United States.

Primary SIC and add'l.: 7376 6211 6712

CIK No: 0001015780

Subsidiaries: 3045175 Nova Scotia Company, 3744221 Canada Inc., Affiliate Company, BRE Holdings, LLC, BrownCo, LLC, BWL Aviation, LLC, Canopy Acquisition Corp., Capitol View, LLC, ClearStation, Inc., Confluent, Inc., Converging Arrows, Inc. (Delaware), Converging Arrows, Inc. (Nevada), E TRADE Nordic AB, E TRADE Sverige AB, E TRADE Systems India Private Limited 125 Subsidiaries included in the Index

Officers: Mitchell H. Caplan/Dir., CEO/$9,945,506.00, Jarrett Robert Lilien/Dir., COO, Pres./$7,766,937.00, Arlen W. Gelbard/Chief Administrative Officer, General Counsel/$3,150,555.00, Connie M. Dotson/Chief Communications Officer, Dennis E. Webb/Pres. - E*trade Capital Markets/$3,993,101.00, Robert J. Simmons/CFO/$3,157,605.00, Nicholas A. Utton/Chief Marketing Officer, Russell S. Elmer/General Counsel, Corp. Sec., Celie Niehaus/Sr. VP, Head - Global Bank Compliance E*trade Bank, Kelvin James/Dir. - Community Investment E*trade Bank, Gina M. Angelo/Community Development Mgr. - E*trade Bank, Kathleen R. Sanchez/Compliance Analyst E*trade Bank

Directors: Mitchell H. Caplan/Dir., CEO, George A. Hayter/Chmn., Cathleen C. Raffaeli/Dir., Donna L. Weaver/Dir., Lewis E. Randall/Dir., Jarrett Robert Lilien/Dir., COO, Pres., Michael K. Parks/48/Dir., Stephen H. Willard/Dir., Daryl G. Brewster/50/Dir., Ronald D. Fisher/60/Dir.

Owners: Jarrett R. Lilien, Dennis Webb, Lewis E. Randall, Wellington Management Company, LLP/9.83%, Cathleen C. Raffaeli, Donna L. Weaver, Ronald D. Fisher, Insiders/3.61%, Daryl G. Brewster, Michael K. Parks, George A. Hayter, Stephen H. Willard, Robert J. Simmons, T. Rowe Price Associates, Inc./8.33%, Arlen W. Gelbard *(16 Owners included in Index)*

Curr. Assets:	$9,308,808,000	**Curr. Liab.:**	$42,376,802,000		
Plant, Equip.:	$318,389,000	**Total Liab.:**	$49,542,933,000	**Indic. Yr. Divd.:**	NA
Total Assets:	$53,739,303,000	**Net Worth:**	$4,196,370,000	**Debt/ Equity:**	2.2464

E-centives Inc

6901 Rockledge Dr., 6th Fl., Bethesda, MD, 20817; **PH:** 1-240-333-6100; **http://** www.e-centives.com

General - Incorporation	DE	**Stock**- Price on:12/24/2007	NA
Employees	NA	Stock Exchange	NA
Auditor	BDO Seidman LLP	Ticker Symbol	NA
Stk Agt	American Stock Transfer & Trust Co.	Outstanding Shares	NA
Counsel	NA	E.P.S.	NA
DUNS No.	NA	Shareholders	NA

Business: The group's principal activities are to provide interactive marketing technologies and services. The group has two reportable operating segments: e-centives and consumerreview.com. E-centives includes the services of the interactive database marketing system, e-mail marketing system, performone network, the commerce engine and the commerce network. Consumerreview.com sells advertising and e-commerce services that are provided through its network of Web communities. The group provides online marketing and commerce capabilities and solutions to retail, banking, insurance and telecommunications industries. The solutions offered by the group include promotions network, member services, commerce network, commerce engine, outsourced e-mail marketing and online promotions system.

Primary SIC and add'l.: 7379 7372

CIK No: 0001092283

Officers: Kamran Amjadi/Chmn., CEO, Co - Founder/$250,000.00, Dadi Akhavan/Co - Founder, Pres. - CMO, John Hoffman/VP - Network, Operations/$161,250.00, Tracy Slavin/CFO/$194,707.00, Amori Langstaff/VP - Client Services/$186,375.00

Directors: Kamran Amjadi/Chmn., CEO, Co - Founder, Dadi Akhavan/Co - Founder, Pres. - CMO, Peter Friedli/Dir., David Jodoin/Dir.

Owners: Amori Langstaff, Peter Friedli, Tracy Slavin, Kamran Amjadi, Mehrdad Akhavan, US Venture 05, Inc., Venturetec, Inc., John Hoffman, New Venturetec AG, David Jodoin, InVenture, Inc., Insiders

E-Future Information Technology Inc

Building No. 10, No.1. Disheng North St., Beijing, 100176; **PH:** 86-861051650998; **http://** www.e-future.com.cn; **Email:** Info@E-Future.com.cn

General - Incorporation	Cayman Islands	**Stock**- Price on:12/24/2007	$14.8
Employees	NA	Stock Exchange	NDQ
Auditor	Hansen, Barnett & Maxwell P.C.	Ticker Symbol	EFUT
Stk Agt	NA	Outstanding Shares	2,630,000
Counsel	NA	E.P.S.	NA
DUNS No.	NA	Shareholders	NA

Business: The groups principle activity is to provide software and professional services. The products of the group include -Future ONE SCM CRM and e-Future ESCM e-Market Place. Customers served by the group include Chinese retail, distribution and logistics industries. Specific customers of the group include Procter & Gamble, Haier Group, Shijiazhuang Belren Group, Wuhan Zhongbai Group, Co., Ltd, Hongkong Lane Crawford group and Changsha Youyi Apolo Group. The group operates from China and the United States. The group's quarterly revenue for September 2007 was 35.56 millions of CNY.

Primary SIC and add'l.: 7372

CIK No: 0001329365

Subsidiaries: e-Future (Beijing) Tornado Information Technology Inc.

Officers: Adam Yan/Chmn., CEO, Qicheng Yang/CTO, Founder, Hongjun Zou/COO, Founder, Johnson Li/VP, Founder, Kefu Zhou/Chief Architecture Officer

Directors: Adam Yan/Chmn., CEO, Qicheng Yang/CTO, Founder, Hongjun Zou/COO, Founder, Johnson Li/VP, Founder, Ming Zhu/Dir., Dong Cheng/Dir., Ping Yu/Dir., Dennis O. Laing/Dir., Brian Lin/Dir., John Dai/Dir.

Owners: Zhou Kefu, Johnson Li/7.10%, Hongjun Zou/8.20%, Yu Ping, C Tech Fund/11.60%, Adam Yan/14.70%, Insiders/34.80%, Chaoyong Wang, Qicheng Yang/4.40%, Dong Cheng

Curr. Assets:	$9,598,000	**Curr. Liab.:**	$2,367,000	**P/E Ratio:**	17.55
Plant, Equip.:	$130,000	**Total Liab.:**	$2,367,000	**Indic. Yr. Divd.:**	NA
Total Assets:	$10,639,000	**Net Worth:**	$8,271,000	**Debt/ Equity:**	NA

E-Z-EM Inc

1111 Marcus Ave., Ste. LL26, Lake Success, NY, 11042; **PH:** 1-516-333-8230; **Fax:** 1-516-333-8278; **http://** www.ezem.com

General - Incorporation	DE	**Stock**- Price on:12/24/2007	$15.94
Employees	611	Stock Exchange	NDQ
Auditor	Grant Thornton LLP	Ticker Symbol	EZEM
Stk Agt	NA	Outstanding Shares	10,970,000
Counsel	NA	E.P.S.	$0.64
DUNS No.	00-204-1226	Shareholders	NA

Business: The group's principal activities are to develop, manufacture and market medical diagnostic products and therapeutic products. The group's operations are carried out through two business segments: e-z-em and angiodynamics. The diagnostic products are designed to facilitate the detection of physical abnormalities and gastrointestinal diseases. E-z-em segment supplies medical products used by radiologists, gastroenterologists and speech language pathologists for diagnostic imaging of diseases and disorders of the gi tract. The diagnosis also includes testing for swallowing disorders and colorectal cancers. The angiodynamics segment supplies medical products used by interventional radiologists and other physicians for the minimally invasive diagnosis and therapeutic treatment of peripheral vascular disease. It operates in the United States, Canada, the United Kingdom, Holland, Belgium and Japan.

Primary SIC and add'l.: 3841 2835

CIK No: 0000727008

Subsidiaries: E-Z-EM Canada Inc., E-Z-EM Ltd., E-Z-EM Nederland B.V., Toho Kagaku Kenkyusho Co., Ltd.

Officers: Anthony A. Lombardo/CEO, Pres./$405,313.00, Joseph A. Cacchioli/52/VP, Controller, Acting CFO/$225,684.00, Jeffrey S. Peacock/51/Sr. VP - Global Scientific, Technical, Manufacturing Operations/$263,609.00, Brad S. Schreck/51/Sr. VP - Global Sales, Marketing, Engineering/$259,210.00, Peter J. Graham/42/Sr. VP, Chief Legal Officer - Global Human Resources, Sec./$234,217.00, Robert J. Beckman/Dir., Sec.

Directors: Paul S. Echenberg/Chmn., George P. Ward/Dir., Robert J. Beckman/Dir., Sec., James H. Thrall/Dir., James L. Katz/Dir., John T. Preston/Dir., David P. Meyers/Dir., Adel Michael/64/Dir.

Owners: Jeffrey S. Peacock, Paul S. Echenberg/1.20%, Joseph A. Cacchioli, David P. Meyers/4.90%, Robert J. Beckman, George P. Ward, Anthony A. Lombardo/3.70%, James L. Katz, Wellington Management Company, LLP/8.20%, Brad S. Schreck, Peter J. Graham/4.40%, Insiders/16.60%, Linda B. Stern/17.20%, James H. Thrall, Ira Albert/7.30% *(16 Owners included in Index)*

Financial Data: Fiscal Year End:06/03 **Latest Annual Data:** 6/3/2006

Year	Sales	Net Income
2006	$138,369,000	$9,766,000
2005	$113,075,000	$6,936,000
2004	$148,771,000	$6,726,000

Curr. Assets:	$95,381,000	**Curr. Liab.:**	$18,320,000	**P/E Ratio:**	24.91
Plant, Equip.:	$13,048,000	**Total Liab.:**	$21,950,000	**Indic. Yr. Divd.:**	NA
Total Assets:	$123,792,000	**Net Worth:**	$101,842,000	**Debt/ Equity:**	NA

E.W. Scripps Co (The)

125 E Ct. St., Cincinnati, OH, 45202; ***PH:*** 1-513-352-2000; ***http://*** www.scripps.com; ***Email:*** corpcomm@scripps.com

General - Incorporation	OH	**Stock**- Price on:12/24/2007	$44.95
Employees	9,000	Stock Exchange	NYSE
Auditor	Deloitte & Touche LLP	Ticker Symbol	SSP
Stk Agt	Fifth Third Bank	Outstanding Shares	163,450,000
Counsel	NA	E.P.S	$2.27
DUNS No.	19-601-3718	Shareholders	NA

Business: The group's principle activities are newspaper circulation, cable television and broadcasting. The group operates in five segments. The newspaper segment operates 21 daily newspapers in the United States and revenues are derived from advertising and circulation. The scripps networks includes four national television networks: home and garden television, food network, do it yourself and fine living. The broadcast televisions include ten television stations and rely on local sales operations. The shop at home sells a range of consumer goods directly to television viewers and visitors to its Website. The licensing and other media aggregates operating segments that are too small to report separately, and primarily includes syndication and licensing of news features and comics. Under the trade name united media, the group distributes news columns, comics and other features for the newspaper industry. The group's quarterly revenue for Sep'07 was 2,498.08 millions of USD.

Primary SIC and add'l.: 4841 7622 4833 2711 6794

CIK No: 0000832428

Subsidiaries: Boulder Publishing Company, BRV, Inc., Channel 7 of Detroit, Inc., Collier County Publishing Company, D.I.Y. Insurance Company, Denver Publishing Company, Evansville Courier Company, Inc., Fine Living Network, LLC, Great American Country, Inc., Independent Publishing Company, Knoxville News-Sentinel Company, Memphis Publishing Company, New Mexico State Tribune Company, Scripps Howard Broadcasting Company, Scripps Howard Publishing Co. 25 Subsidiaries included in the Index

Officers: Judith G. Clabes/63/CEO, Pres. - Scripps Howard Foundation, Sharon Hite/CEO, Pres. - Media Procurement Services, Inc, Pres. - Scripps Howard Supply, Kenneth W. Lowe/58/Dir., CEO, Pres./$1,931,432.00, John Lansing/51/Sr. VP, Pres. - Scripps Networks/$1,705,221.00, Timothy E. Stautberg/45/VP - Communications, Investor Relations, Lori A. Hickok/45/VP, Controller, William B. Peterson/65/Sr. VP - Television, A. B. Cruz/50/Exec. VP, General Counsel, Mark G. Contreras/47/Sr. VP - Newspapers/$1,140,329.00, Jennifer L. Weber/41/Sr. VP - Human Resources, Mark Hale/Sr. VP - Technology Operations, The E W Scripps Company, Exec. VP - Operations, Scripps Networks, Mark F. Schuermann/36/Assist. Treasurer, Mary Denise Kuprionis/VP, Corp. Sec., Dir. - Legal Affairs, John E. Viterisi/50/VP - Tax, Tim A. Peterman/41/Sr. VP - Corporate Development *(18 Officers included in Index)*

Directors: Kenneth W. Lowe/58/Dir., CEO, Pres., William R. Burleigh/72/Chmn., Julie A. Wrigley/59/Dir., John H. Burlingame/74/Dir., David Galloway/64/Dir., Nicholas B. Paumgarten/62/Dir., David M. Moffett/56/Dir., Paul K. Scripps/62/Dir., Ronald W. Tysoe/55/Dir., Jeff Sagansky/56/Dir., Edward W. Scripps/49/Dir., Nackey E. Scagliotti/62/Dir.

Owners: Jeffrey Sagansky, Joseph G. NeCastro, Nicholas B. Paumgarten, Jarl Mohn, David A. Galloway, Julie A. Wrigley, Paul K. Scripps and John P. Scripps Trust, William R. Burleigh, Mark G. Contreras, The Edward W. Scripps Trust/87.73%, Ronald W. Tysoe, The Edward W. Scripps Trust/29.41%, John F. Lansing, Paul K. Scripps and John P. Scripps Trust/8.84%, Nackey E. Scagliotti *(24 Owners included in Index)*

Financial Data: ***Fiscal Year End:***12/31 ***Latest Annual Data:*** 12/31/2006

Year	Sales	Net Income
2006	$2,498,077,000	$353,220,000
2005	$2,513,890,000	$249,153,000
2004	$2,167,503,000	$303,811,000

Curr. Assets:	$875,319,000	**Curr. Liab.:**	$399,268,000	**P/E Ratio:**	19.80
Plant, Equip.:	$511,738,000	**Total Liab.:**	$1,640,470,000	**Indic. Yr. Divd.:**	$0.560
Total Assets:	$4,344,334,000	**Net Worth:**	$2,581,435,000	**Debt/ Equity:**	0.2867

eAcceleration Corp

1050 NE Hostmark St., Ste. 100B, Poulsbo, WA, 98370; ***PH:*** 1-360-779-6301; ***Fax:*** 1-360-598-2450; ***http://*** www.eacceleration.com; ***Email:*** support@eacceleration.com

General - Incorporation	DE	**Stock**- Price on:12/24/2007	NA
Employees	NA	Stock Exchange	NA
Auditor	Peterson Sullivan PLLC	Ticker Symbol	NA
Stk Agt	American Stock Transfer & Trust Co.	Outstanding Shares	NA
Counsel	Kaufman & Moomjian	E.P.S	NA
DUNS No.	NA	Shareholders	NA

Business: The group provides online direct marketing services, advertising solutions and pre-packaged software through their websites, homepageware, downloadsales, clicksales and signupsales. Online direct marketing media include banner advertisements, targeted email and Website sponsorships. The products of the company include webcelerator, superfast, mp3creator, net butler, d-time and phantom CD. During the year the company acquired acceleration software international corporation. The company became publicly held in Aug 2000.

Primary SIC and add'l.: 7372

CIK No: 0001098862

Subsidiaries: Acceleration Software International Corporation

Eaco Corp

1500 N Lakeview Ave., Anaheim, CA, 92807; ***PH:*** 1-714-876-2490; ***Fax:*** 1-714-876-2410; ***http://*** www.eacocorp.com

General - Incorporation	FL	**Stock**- Price on:12/24/2007	$0.72
Employees	4	Stock Exchange	OTC
Auditor	Reehl And Williamson LLP	Ticker Symbol	EACO
Stk Agt	Mellon Investor Services LLC	Outstanding Shares	3,910,000
Counsel	NA	E.P.S	-$2.09
DUNS No.	NA	Shareholders	NA

Business: The group is the sole franchisee of ryan's family steak house restaurants in the state of Florida. The group presently operates 18 ryan's restaurants in Florida. The restaurant serves lunch and dinner and offers a variety of charbroiled entrees, including various cuts of beef, chicken and seafood. Each restaurant features a diverse selection of items from scatter bars and a separate fresh bakery and dessert bar. The scatter bars offer hot meats, pre-made salads, soups, baked potatoes with toppings, cheeses and a variety of vegetables. The proprietary trademarks of the group include ryan's family steak house and mega bar.

Primary SIC and add'l.: 5812

CIK No: 0000784539

Officers: Glen F. Ceiley/Chmn., CEO, Principal Financial Officer/$12,000.00

Directors: Glen F. Ceiley/Chmn., CEO, Principal Financial Officer, Jay Conzen/Dir., Steve Catanzaro/Dir., William L. Means/Dir.

Owners: Stephen Catanzaro, Insiders/64.30%, Glen F. Ceiley/63.30%, William L. Means, Edward B. Alexander, Jay Conzen

Financial Data: ***Fiscal Year End:***12/28 ***Latest Annual Data:*** 12/27/2006

Year	Sales	Net Income
2006	$832,000	-$6,769,000
2005	$216,000	$9,354,000
2004	$37,800,000	-$2,032,000

Curr. Assets:	$894,000	**Curr. Liab.:**	$4,421,000		
Plant, Equip.:	$25,868,000	**Total Liab.:**	$25,037,000	**Indic. Yr. Divd.:**	NA
Total Assets:	$27,789,000	**Net Worth:**	$2,752,000	**Debt/ Equity:**	1.0856

Eagle Bancorp Inc

7815 Woodmont Ave., Bethesda, MD, 20814; ***PH:*** 1-301-986-1800; ***Fax:*** 1-301-986-8529; ***http://*** www.eaglebankmd.com

General - Incorporation	MD	**Stock**- Price on:12/24/2007	$16.65
Employees	171	Stock Exchange	NDQ
Auditor	Stegman & Co	Ticker Symbol	EGBN
Stk Agt	Computershare Shareholder Ser Inc	Outstanding Shares	9,520,000
Counsel	NA	E.P.S	$0.77
DUNS No.	NA	Shareholders	NA

Business: The group's principal activity is to provide commercial banking services to the business and professional clients, and to individuals living in the service area. The group's customers include sole proprietors, small and medium-sized businesses, partnerships, corporations, and non-profit organizations. The group is an active originator of SBA loans and sells the insured portion of these loans at a premium. The group is headquartered in Bethesda, Maryland and has five offices serving Montgomery County and three offices in the District of Columbia.

Primary SIC and add'l.: 6022 6712

CIK No: 0001050441

Subsidiaries: Bethesda Leasing, LLC, Eagle Land Title, LLC, EagleBank

Officers: Ronald D. Paul/Dir., CEO, Pres./$222,235.00, Leonard L. Abel/Chmn. - Financial Consultant, James H. Langmead/Sr. VP, CFO, Zandra D. Nichols/Corp. Sec.

Directors: Ronald D. Paul/Dir., CEO, Pres., Leonard L. Abel/Chmn. - Financial Consultant, Leland M. Weinstein/Dir., Benson Klein/Dir., Philip N. Margolius/Dir., Arthur H. Blitz/Dir., Eric H. West/Dir., Thomas D. Murphy/Dir., Donald R. Rogers/Dir., Leslie M. Alperstein/Dir., Dudley C. Dworken/Dir., Benjamin M. Soto/Dir., Kim Natovitz/Dir., Neal R. Gross/Dir., Harvey M. Goodman/Dir. *(20 Directors included in Index)*

Owners: Insiders/19.74%, Leonard L. Abel/3.14%, Leland M. Weinstein/1.11%, Susan G. Riel, Martha Foulon-Tonat, Ronald D. Paul/6.76%, Dudley C. Dworken/1.96%, Donald R. Rogers, James H. Langmead, Harvey M. Goodman, Michael T. Flynn, Thomas D. Murphy, Eugene F. Ford/1.17%, Philip N. Margolius/2.00%, Leslie M. Alperstein

Financial Data: ***Fiscal Year End:***12/31 ***Latest Annual Data:*** 06/30/2007

Year	Sales	Net Income
2007	$15,303,000	$1,978,000
2006	$54,164,000	$8,025,000
2005	$40,724,000	$7,544,000

Curr. Assets:	$51,522,000	**Curr. Liab.:**	$674,579,000	**P/E Ratio:**	21.35
Plant, Equip.:	$6,954,000	**Total Liab.:**	$700,535,000	**Indic. Yr. Divd.:**	$0.240
Total Assets:	$773,451,000	**Net Worth:**	$72,916,000	**Debt/ Equity:**	0.2954

Eagle Broadband Inc

101 Courageous Dr., League City, TX, 77573; ***PH:*** 1-281-538-6000; ***Fax:*** 1-281-334-5302; ***http://*** www.eaglebroadband.com; ***Email:*** info@eaglebroadband.com

General - Incorporation	TX	**Stock**- Price on:12/24/2007	NA
Employees	44	Stock Exchange	OTC
Auditor	Lopez, Blevins, Bork & Assoc. LLP	Ticker Symbol	EAGBE
Stk Agt	Registrar & Transfer Co	Outstanding Shares	NA
Counsel	NA	E.P.S	-$1.789
DUNS No.	87-841-2998	Shareholders	NA

Business: The group's principal activity is to provide broadband, communications, project management and enterprise management products and services. Its four-play suite of high-speed Internet, cable-style television, voice and security monitoring bundled digital services, high-definition television-ready multimedia set-top boxes and turnkey suite of financing, design, deployment and operational services enable municipalities, real estate developers, hotels, multi-tenant owners and service providers to deliver entertainment and communications choices and single-bill convenience to their residential and business customers. The products manufactured include transmitters, receivers, controllers, software, convergent set-top boxes and other equipment used in personal communications and radio and telephone systems. Other services provided include information technology business integration, structured wiring/cabling, 24/7 customer service, technical support and network monitoring.

Primary SIC and add'l.: 7382 3661 7389 3663 7373 7372 3669

CIK No: 0001023139

Subsidiaries: Eagle Broadband Services, Inc, EBI Funding Corp

Officers: David Micek/CEO, Pres., Tony Cordaro/VP, GM - Information Technology Services, Brian Morrow/COO, GM - Iptv Solutions, Richard Sanger/63/VP - Administration, Jeff Adams/Corporate Counsel, Mark Mann/Corporate Controller

Owners: Anthony R. Cordaro, Mark Mann, The Tail Wind Fund Ltd./8.90%, Insiders, YA Global Investments, L.P./8.60%, Glenn Goerke, Robert Bach, C. J. Reinhartsen, Richard Sanger, Brian Morrow, Lorne Persons, Charlton Conine/9.30%, David Micek

Financial Data: Fiscal Year End:08/31 **Latest Annual Data:** 8/31/2006

Year	Sales		Net Income
2006	$3,941,000		-$26,933,000
2005	$8,592,000		-$57,010,000
2004	$12,490,000		-$39,005,000
Curr. Assets:	$5,610,000	Curr. Liab.:	$16,223,000		
Plant, Equip.:	$11,344,000	Total Liab.:	$19,901,000	Indic. Yr. Divd.:	NA
Total Assets:	$21,764,000	Net Worth:	$1,863,000	Debt/ Equity:	NA

Eagle Bulk Shipping Inc

477 Madison Ave., Ste. 1405, New York, NY, 10022; *PH:* 1-212-785-2500; *Fax:* 1-212-785-3311; http:// www.eagleships.com

General - Incorporation .... Marshall Islands	**Stock** - Price on:12/24/2007 ....$21.94
Employees ....NA	Stock Exchange..NDQ
Auditor .... Ernst & Young LLP	Ticker Symbol..EGLE
Stk Agt.......................Computershare Trust Co	Outstanding Shares 41,710,000
Counsel ....NA	E.P.S..$1.03
DUNS No. ....NA	Shareholders...NA

Business: The groups principle activity is to provide ocean transportation. The groups product is bulk cargo, including iron ore, coal, grain, cement and fertilizer, along worldwide shipping routes. In the year 2005, the group acquired CARDINAL, CONDOR, FALCON, HARRIER, HAWK SHIKRA, GRIFFON and PEREGRINE vessels. Specific customers of the group include Korea Line, Ltd., Western Bulk ASA, Daeyang Shipping Ltd., Armada Bulk Shipping Ltd and Strategic Bulk Carriers. The group operates from the United States. The group's quarterly revenue for September 2007 was 33.96 millions of USD.

Primary SIC and add'l.: 4412

CIK No: 0001322439

Subsidiaries: Cardinal Shipping LLC, Condor Shipping LLC, Crested Eagle Shipping LLC, Crowned Eagle Shipping LLC, Eagle Bulk (Delaware) LLC, Eagle Shipping International (USA) LLC, Falcon Shipping LLC, Griffon Shipping LLC, Harrier Shipping LLC, Hawk Shipping LLC, Heron Shipping LLC, Jaeger Shipping LLC, Kestrel Shipping LLC, Kite Shipping LLC, Kittiwake Shipping LLC 25 Subsidiaries included in the Index

Officers: Sophocles N. Zoullas/Chmn., CEO, Alan S. Ginsberg/CFO, Claude G. Thouret/COO, Edward H. James/Chartering Mgr.

Directors: Sophocles N. Zoullas/Chmn., CEO, Joseph M. Cianciolo/Dir., Douglas P. Haensel/Dir., David B. Hiley/Dir., Jon Tomasson/Dir., Alexis P. Zoullas/Dir., Forrest E. Wylie/45/Dir.

Owners: Michael W. Mitchell, Douglas P. Haensel, Insiders, Joseph M. Cianciolo, Sophocles N. Zoullas, David B. Hiley, Alan S. Ginsberg

Financial Data: Fiscal Year End:12/31 **Latest Annual Data:** 12/31/2006

Year	Sales		Net Income
2006	$104,648,000		$33,802,000
2005	$56,066,000		$6,653,000
Curr. Assets:	$27,653,000	Curr. Liab.:	$6,881,000		
Plant, Equip.:	$502,142,000	Total Liab.:	$247,215,000	Indic. Yr. Divd.:	$2.000
Total Assets:	$568,791,000	Net Worth:	-$321,576,000	Debt/ Equity:	0.7462

Eagle Exploration Company (COLO)

1775 Sherman St. Ste. 2995, Denver, CO, 80203; *PH:* 1-303-863-0800

General - Incorporation ....CO	**Stock** - Price on:12/24/2007 ....$0.17
Employees 2	Stock Exchange..OTC
Auditor ....Ehrhardt Keefe Steiner & Hottman PC	Ticker Symbol...EGXP
Stk Agt.....Computershare Investor Services LLC	Outstanding Shares 3,070,000
Counsel ....NA	E.P.S...$0.063
DUNS No. ....NA	Shareholders...NA

Business: The groups principle activity is to explore minerals and natural oil. The group operates from Canada and the United. The groups annual revenue for September 2007 was 0.05 millions of USD.

Primary SIC and add'l.: 6519

CIK No: 0000030906

Subsidiaries: Eagle Development Company

Officers: Raymond N. Joeckel/82/Dir., CEO, Pres., Paul M. Joeckel/56/Dir., CFO, Sec.

Directors: Raymond N. Joeckel/82/Dir., CEO, Pres., Paul M. Joeckel/56/Dir., CFO, Sec., M. D. Young/84/Dir.

Owners: Raymond N. Joeckel/3.26%, M. D. Young, Norman K. Brown/11.22%, Paul M. Joeckel/14.31%, Paul M. Joeckel/43.82%, Insiders/61.39%

Financial Data: Fiscal Year End:03/31 **Latest Annual Data:** 03/31/2007

Year	Sales		Net Income
2007	$49,000		$195,000
2006	$53,000		-$156,000
2005	$39,000		-$159,000
Curr. Assets:	$857,000	Curr. Liab.:	$12,000	P/E Ratio:	2.70
Plant, Equip.:	$44,000	Total Liab.:	$12,000	Indic. Yr. Divd.:	NA
Total Assets:	$1,190,000	Net Worth:	$1,178,000	Debt/ Equity:	NA

Eagle Financial Services Inc

PO Box 391, Berryville, VA, 22611; *PH:* 1-540-955-2510; *Fax:* 1-540-955-2521; http:// www.bankofclarke.com; *Email:* customerservice@bankofclarke.com

General - Incorporation ....VA	**Stock** - Price on:12/24/2007 ....$29.45
Employees 151	Stock Exchange..OTC
Auditor ....Smith Elliott Kearns & Co. LLC	Ticker Symbol..EFSI
Stk Agt..... American Stock Transfer & Trust Co.	Outstanding Shares 3,110,000
Counsel ....NA	E.P.S..$1.78
DUNS No. 85-849-1483	Shareholders...NA

Business: The group's principal activities are to provide retail and commercial banking services through its wholly owned subsidiary, bank of clarke county. The deposit products include demand deposits, savings accounts and time deposits. The lending products offered by the group primarily consist of real estate loans secured by one-to-four family residential properties, consumer loans, commercial real estate loans, commercial and industrial loans not secured by real estate, agricultural production loans and construction loans. The group also offers a wide variety of trust services to customers. The group operates through its office located in berryville, clarke county, Virginia and its branch offices located in boyce, jubal early drive in winchester, piccadilly street in winchester, senseny road in frederick county and in stephens city.

Primary SIC and add'l.: 6022 6712

CIK No: 0000880641

Subsidiaries: Bank of Clarke County, Eagle Financial Statutory Trust I

Officers: John R. Milleson/51/Dir., CEO, Pres./$290,382.00, Barbara Clark/Loan Officer, Sherri Ambrogi/Loan Officer, Kay Anderson/Loan Officer, Harry Leipfert/Loan Officer, Jim Locke/Loan Officer, Janet Luttrell/Loan Officer, Carol McVeigh/Loan Officer, Roger Crosen/Loan Officer, Angie Edwards/Loan Officer, Debbie Edwards/Loan Officer, Dale Fritts/Loan Officer, James W. McCarty/CFO, VP/$183,847.00, Jeffrey S. Boppe/Loan Officer/$208,905.00, Libba Pendleton/Sr. VP, Trust Officer *(28 Officers included in Index)*

Directors: John R. Milleson/51/Dir., CEO, Pres., Thomas T. Gilpin/55/Chmn., Randall G. Vinson/61/Dir., James R. Wilkins/62/Dir., Robert W. Smalley/56/Dir., James T. Vickers/55/Dir., Thomas T. Byrd/62/Dir., Lewis M. Ewing/73/Dir., Douglas C. Rinker/48/Dir., John D. Stokely/55/Dir., Mary Bruce Glaize/52/Dir.

Owners: James W. McCarty, John D. Stokely, Jeffrey S. Boppe, John R. Milleson/1.89%, Thomas T. Gilpin/3.52%, James R. Wilkins/5.45%, Douglas C. Rinker, Mary Bruce Glaize, James T. Vickers, Elizabeth M. Pendleton, Lewis M. Ewing, John E. Hudson, Thomas T. Byrd, Insiders/15.87%, Robert W. Smalley *(16 Owners included in Index)*

Financial Data: Fiscal Year End:12/31 **Latest Annual Data:** 12/31/2006

Year	Sales		Net Income
2006	$34,656,000		$5,858,000
2005	$28,970,000		$5,612,000
2004	$24,054,000		$4,610,000
Curr. Assets:	$15,962,000	Curr. Liab.:	$462,816,000	P/E Ratio:	16.54
Plant, Equip.:	$15,425,000	Total Liab.:	$472,059,000	Indic. Yr. Divd.:	$0.640
Total Assets:	$512,996,000	Net Worth:	$40,937,000	Debt/ Equity:	0.1716

Eagle Hospitality Properties Trust Inc

100 E River Ctr. Blvd., Ste. 480, Covington, KY, 41011; *PH:* 1-859-581-5900; http:// www.eaglehospitality.com

General - Incorporation ....MD	**Stock**- Price on:12/24/2007 ....$13.4
Employees 12	Stock Exchange..NA
Auditor ....Meagher & Flom LLP	Ticker Symbol..NA
Stk Agt ....LaSalle Bank N.A	Outstanding Shares 17,690,000
Counsel ....NA	E.P.S...NA
DUNS No. ....NA	Shareholders...NA

Business: The groups principle activity is to acquire real estate properties. The group acquired Embassy Suites Hotel and Casino San Juan, Embassy Suited Boston, Embassy Hotel Phoenix-Scottsdale and Hilton Glendale in the year 2005. The group operates from the United States.

Primary SIC and add'l.: 7011 6798

CIK No: 0001289169

Subsidiaries: Boston Suites TRS, Inc., Burr Ridge TRS, Inc., CVG Airport TRS, Inc., DIA Suites TRS, Inc., Dublin Suites TRS, Inc., Eagle San Juan Suites, LLC, EHP Boston Suites, LLC, EHP Burr Ridge, LLC, EHP CVG Airport, LLC, EHP DIA Suites, LLC, EHP Dublin Suites, LLC, EHP Glendale, LLC, EHP Independence Suites, LLC, EHP Operating Partnership, L.P., EHP Phoenix Suites, LLC 29 Subsidiaries included in the Index

Officers: William J. Blackham/Dir., CEO, Raymond D. Martz/CFO, Brian Guernier/Sr. VP - Acquisitions, Cheryl Barnes/Contact - Investor Relations

Directors: William J. Blackham/Dir., CEO, William P. Butler/Chmn., Paul S. Fisher/Dir., Robert J. Kohlhepp/64/Dir., Frank C. McDowell/Dir., Louis D. George/Dir., Thomas R. Engel/Dir., Thomas E. Costello/Dir., Thomas E. Banta/Dir.

Owners: Deutsche Bank AG/8.30%, Insiders/20.30%, Morgan Stanley Investment Management Inc./6.30%, Brian Guernier, Frank C. McDowell, Thomas E. Costello, Thomas E. Banta, William P. Butler/17.70%, Robert J. Kohlhepp, Paul F. Fisher, Louis D. George, William J. Blackham, Raymond D. Martz, Hotchkis and Wiley Capital Management, LLC/6.00%, Franklin Resources, Inc./5.30% *(19 Owners included in Index)*

Financial Data: Fiscal Year End:12/31 **Latest Annual Data:** 12/31/2006

Year	Sales		Net Income
2006	$150,983,000		$11,336,000
2005	$116,425,000		$7,493,000
2004	$82,298,000		$2,637,000

Eagle Materials Inc

3811 Turtle Creek Blvd., Ste. 1100, Dallas, TX, 75219; *PH:* 1-214-432-2000; *Fax:* 1-214-432-2100; http:// www.eaglematerials.com; *Email:* info@eaglematerials.com

General - Incorporation ....DE	**Stock**- Price on:12/24/2007 ....$48.09
Employees 1,600	Stock Exchange...NYSE
Auditor .... Ernst & Young LLP	Ticker Symbol..EXP
Stk Agt .... Mellon Investor Services LLC	Outstanding Shares 47,980,000
Counsel ....NA	E.P.S..$4.07
DUNS No. 04-331-3394	Shareholders...NA

Business: The group's principal activity is the production of basic construction products used in residential, industrial, commercial and infrastructure applications. It produces and sells cement, gypsum wallboard, recycled paperboard, aggregates and readymix concrete. The group also mines limestone and manufactures, produces, distributes and sells portland cement. The cement production facilities of the group are located in or near buda, Texas; lasalle, Illinois; laramie, Wyoming; and fernley, Nevada. The group operates in four business segments: cement, gypsum wallboard, recycled paperboard, and concrete and aggregates. It operates solely in the domestic market.

Primary SIC and add'l.: 9999 3241 3275 2631 3273

CIK No: 0000918646

Subsidiaries: Ag South Carolina LLC, American Gypsum Company, American Gypsum Marketing Company, Ccp Cement Company, Ccp Concrete/aggregates LLC, Ccp Gypsum Company, Centex Materials LLC, Illinois Cement Company LLC, Mathews Readymix LLC, Mountain Cement Company, Nevada Cement Company, Republic Paperboard Company LLC, Texas Cement Company, Texas Lehigh Cement Company Lp, Tlcc Gp LLC 17 Subsidiaries included in the Index

Officers: Steven R. Rowley/55/Dir., CEO, Pres./$3,220,980.00, Keith Metcalf/49/VP - Gypsum Sales, Arthur R. Zunker/65/Sr. VP, CFO/$1,280,310.00, Craig Kesler/32/VP - Investor Relations, Corporate Development, James H. Graass/51/Exec. VP, General Counsel, Sec./$1,304,573.00, Kerry Gannaway/49/VP - Gypsum Manufacturing, Dave Powers/58/Exec. VP - Gypsum/$1,480,210.00, Gerald J. Essl/59/Exec. VP - Cement, Concrete, Aggregates/$1,121,647.00, William R. Devlin/42/VP, Controller, Franklin Green/39/VP - Engineering, Technology

Directors: Steven R. Rowley/55/Dir., CEO, Pres., Laurence E. Hirsch/62/Chmn., O. G. Dagnan/68/Dir., David W. Quinn/66/Dir., Frank W. Maresh/69/Dir., Michael R. Nicolais/50/Dir., William F. Barnett/61/Dir.

Owners: Insiders/4.90%, Gerald J. Essl, D.E. Shaw & Co., L.P./5.11%, Richard R. Stewart, Arthur R. Zunker, Laurence E. Hirsch/2.30%, Frank W. Maresh, David W. Quinn, Robert L. Clarke, Barclays Global Investors, NA/12.62%, Michael R. Nicolais, Stephen F. Mandell/5.97%, David B. Powers, James H. Graass, O.G. Dagnan (17 Owners included in Index)

Financial Data: Fiscal Year End:03/31   Latest Annual Data: 3/31/2007

Year	Sales	Net Income
2007	$922,401,000	$202,664,000
2006	$859,702,000	$160,984,000
2005	$616,541,000	$106,687,000

Curr. Assets:	$216,626,000	Curr. Liab.:	$104,699,000	P/E Ratio:	12.96
Plant, Equip.:	$557,562,000	Total Liab.:	$424,178,000	Indic. Yr. Divd.:	$0.700
Total Assets:	$888,916,000	Net Worth:	$464,738,000	Debt/ Equity:	0.3662

Eagle Rock Energy Partners LP

16701 Greenspoint Pk. Dr., Ste. 200, Houston, TX, 77060; *PH:* 1-281-408-1200; *Fax:* 1-281-408-1399; *http://* www.eaglerockenergy.com; *Email:* info@eaglerockenergy.com

General - Incorporation	DE	Stock- Price on:12/24/2007	$23.96
Employees	163	Stock Exchange	NDQ
Auditor	NA	Ticker Symbol	EROC
Stk Agt	American Stock Transfer & Trust Co.	Outstanding Shares	35,420,000
Counsel	NA	E.P.S.	-$0.77
DUNS No.	NA	Shareholders	NA

Business: The groups principle activities include gathering, compressing, treating, processing, transporting, selling, and fractionating natural gas. The group operates through two geographical segments namely Panhandle and Southeast Texas and Louisiana. In December 1, 2005, the group acquired ONEOK Texas Field Services, L.P. The group operates from the United States. The group's quarterly revenue for September 2007 was 276.86 millions of USD.

Primary SIC and add'l.: 4925 4923 4922

CIK No: 0001364541

Subsidiaries: Eagle Rock Energy Services, L.P., Eagle Rock Field Services, L.P., Eagle Rock Gas Gathering & Processing, Ltd., Eagle Rock Operating, L.P., Eagle Rock Pipeline GP, LLC, Eagle Rock Pipeline, L.P., Midstream Gas Services, L.P.

Officers: Alex A. Bucher/Founder, Dir., CEO, Pres., Joseph A. Mills/Chmn., CEO, Charles C. Boettcher/Sr. VP, General Counsel, Sec., Stacy J. Horn/VP - Commercial Development, Stephen O. McNair/VP - Operations, Technical Services, Richard W. Fitzgerald/Sr. VP, CFO, Treasurer, Alfredo Garcia/Sr. VP - Corporate Development, William E. Puckett/Sr. VP - Commercial Operations, Steven G. Hendrickson/Sr. VP - E, P Technical Evaluation, Joseph E. Schimelpfening/Sr. VP - E, P Operations, Development, Bob Boyd/VP - Operations

Directors: Alex A. Bucher/Founder, Dir., CEO, Pres., Joseph A. Mills/Chmn., CEO, William J. Quinn/Chmn., Philip B. Smith/Dir., Kenneth A. Hersh/Dir., Joan A.W. Schnepp/Founder, John A. Weinzierl/Dir., William K. White/Dir., William A. Smith/Dir.

Owners: John A. Weinzierl, William A. Smith, NGP 2004 Co-Investment Income, L.P./6.80%, William J. Quinn, Alfredo Garcia, Lehman Brothers Holdings, Inc/14.90%, Philip B. Smith, Kenneth A. Hersh/23.70%, Montierra Minerals& Production, L.P./5.50%, William E. Puckett, Stacy J. Horn, Joseph A. Mills, Steven G. Hendrickson, Joseph E. Schimelpfening, William K. White (21 Owners included in Index)

Financial Data: Fiscal Year End:12/31   Latest Annual Data: 12/31/2006

Year	Sales	Net Income
2006	$502,394,000	-$23,314,000

Curr. Assets:	$70,664,000	Curr. Liab.:	$58,559,000		
Plant, Equip.:	$554,063,000	Total Liab.:	$487,914,000	Indic. Yr. Divd.:	$1.450
Total Assets:	$779,901,000	Net Worth:	$291,987,000	Debt/ Equity:	1.5234

Eagle Test Systems Inc

2200 Millbrook Dr., Buffalo Grove, IL, 60089; *PH:* 1-847-367-8282; *Fax:* 1-847-367-8640; *http://* www.eagletest.com

General - Incorporation	DE	Stock- Price on:12/24/2007	$16.5
Employees	302	Stock Exchange	NDQ
Auditor	Ernst & Young LLP	Ticker Symbol	EGLT
Stk Agt	American Stock Transfer & Trust Co.	Outstanding Shares	22,960,000
Counsel	Goodwin Procter LLP	E.P.S.	NA
DUNS No.	NA	Shareholders	NA

Business: The groups principle activities include designing, manufacturing, selling and servicing automated test equipment. The products of the group include analog channels, digital pins, RF ports, multi-site capability and video processing. The group products sold under the trade name SmartPin(TM), Chameleon(TM) and Pattern-Based Testing(TM). Customers served by the group include analog, mixed signal and RF semiconductor manufacturers. Specific customers of the group include Agape Packaging Mfg. Co. Ltd, Allegro MicroSystems, Inc, Microchip Technology Incorporated, PDF Solutions, Inc and STATS ChipPAC Ltd. The group operates from the United States, Malaysia and other. The group's quarterly revenue for September 2007 was 20.78 millions of USD.

Primary SIC and add'l.: 3559 3825

CIK No: 0001290096

Subsidiaries: Eagle Test Systems Malaysia, Inc., Eagle Test Systems (Philippines) LLC, Eagle Test Systems (Suzhou) Co., Ltd, Eagle Test Systems (Taiwan) LLC, Eagle Test Systems GmbH, Eagle Test Systems Italy S.r.l., Eagle Test Systems PTE Ltd., Eagle Test Systems, YH

Officers: Leonard A. Foxman/Dir., CEO, Pres., Theodore D. Foxman/Dir., COO, Exec. VP, Stephen J. Hawrysz/CFO, Jack E. Weimer/CTO, VP - Technical Solutions, James M. Bolotin/Controller, Chief Accounting Officer, Dale R. Buxton/VP - Asia, Adam B. Plummer/VP - Information Technology, Rene J. Verhaegen/VP - Europe, Daniel A. Faia/VP - Sales, North America

Directors: Leonard A. Foxman/Dir., CEO, Pres., Theodore D. Foxman/Dir., COO, Exec. VP, William H. Gibbs/Dir., David B. Mullen/Dir., Ross W. Manire/Dir., Michael C. Child/Dir.

Owners: Leonard A. Foxman/17.20%, Michael C. Child/28.90%, Foxman Family LLC/10.30%, Jack E. Weimer, David B. Mullen, Insiders/47.10%, Theodore D. Foxman, Stephen J. Hawrysz, TA Associates Funds/28.90%, Eagle Test Systems, Inc. Employee Stock Ownership Plan/3.70%, William H. Gibbs, Ross W. Manire

Financial Data: Fiscal Year End:09/30   Latest Annual Data: 9/30/2006

Year	Sales	Net Income
2006	$124,738,000	$22,573,000
2005	$63,477,000	$7,419,000
2004	$111,210,000	$22,053,000

Curr. Assets:	$153,502,000	Curr. Liab.:	$27,764,000		
Plant, Equip.:	$11,745,000	Total Liab.:	$29,472,000	Indic. Yr. Divd.:	NA
Total Assets:	$165,886,000	Net Worth:	$136,414,000	Debt/ Equity:	0.0017

EaglePicher Holdings Inc

11201 N Tatum Blvd., Ste. 110, Phoenix, AZ, 85028; *PH:* 1-602-652-9600; *http://* www.epcorp.com

General - Incorporation	DE	Stock- Price on:12/24/2007	NA
Employees	NA	Stock Exchange	NA
Auditor	Deloitte & Touche LLP	Ticker Symbol	NA
Stk Agt	Bank of New York	Outstanding Shares	NA
Counsel	NA	E.P.S.	NA
DUNS No.	NA	Shareholders	NA

Business: The group's principle activity is to manufacture industrial products for the automotive, aerospace, defense, telecommunications, food and beverage and construction industries. The group operates from United States.

Primary SIC and add'l.: 3479 3069 3724 3714

CIK No: 0001059364

Subsidiaries: CarpenterEnterprisesLimited, CincinnatiIndustrialMachinerySalesCompany, DaisyParts,Inc., Eagle-Picher,Inc., Eagle-PicherAcceptanceCorporation, Eagle-PicherAutomotiveGmbH, Eagle-PicherDevelopmentCompany,Inc., Eagle-PicherEnergyProductsCorp., Eagle-PicherFarEast,Inc., Eagle-PicherHillsdaleLimited, Eagle-PicherIndustriesEuropeB.V., Eagle-PicherIndustriesofCanadaLimited, Eagle-PicherMineralsEuropeGmbH&Co.KG, Eagle-PicherMineralsEuropeVerwaltungs-undBeteiligungsGmbH, Eagle-PicherMineralsInternationalS.A.R.L. 29 Subsidiaries included in the Index

Officers: David L. Treadwell/Dir., CEO, Pres., Scott Koepke/Pres. - Wolverine Advanced Materials, Patrick S. Aubry/CFO, Benjamin A. Depompei/VP - Human Resources, John Hrit/Member - Leadership, David Keselica/Member - Leadership, Steven Westfall/Member - Leadership

Directors: David L. Treadwell/Dir., CEO, Pres., Donald L. Runkle/Chmn., Todd Arden/Dir., Richard Bermingham/Dir., James Gaffney/Dir., Mark Holdsworth/Dir., Edward Horowitz/Dir., General Ronald Yates/Dir.

EAPI Entertainment Inc

210 Brd.way, Unit 208, Orangeville, ON, L9W5G4; *PH:* 1-888-419-0430; *http://* www.ortechteam.com

General - Incorporation	NV	Stock- Price on:12/24/2007	$0.53
Employees	NA	Stock Exchange	NA
Auditor	Weinberg & Co. P.A	Ticker Symbol	NA
Stk Agt	Silverado Stock Transfer, Inc.,	Outstanding Shares	NA
Counsel	NA	E.P.S.	NA
DUNS No.	NA	Shareholders	NA

Business: The group's principal activity is to currently seek new areas of business. Previously, the group's principal activity was to manufacture unique, stable and natural enzymes and specialty end products through its licenses and research. The enzyme products are used in processes and commercial products in a variety of industries including pharmaceuticals, biofuels, bioremediation, food, beverages, textiles, leather, pulp and paper, health, animal feeds and diagnostics.

Primary SIC and add'l.: 9999 2819

CIK No: 0001040227

Subsidiaries: Duro Enzyme Solutions Inc., EAPI Center Inc., EASI Education Inc., EASI Games Inc., EASI Movies, Music TV Inc., EASI Studio Inc., Home.web Sub. Inc., SuperNet Computing Inc.

Officers: Edwin Kroeker/59/Dir., CEO, Pres., Dean Branconnier/39/Dir., CFO, Treasurer, Peter Gardner/Dir., Pres., Chad Burback/Dir., Officer

Directors: Edwin Kroeker/59/Dir., CEO, Pres., Peter Gardner/Dir., Pres., Micheal D. Brown/Dir., Chad Burback/Dir., Officer, Dean Branconnier/39/Dir., CFO, Treasurer

Owners: Dean Branconnier/1.50%, Insiders/3.00%, Chad Burback/1.50%, Rene Branconnier/12.60%

Financial Data: Fiscal Year End:09/30   Latest Annual Data: 09/30/2006

Year	Sales	Net Income
2006	NA	-$3,319,000
2004	NA	-$1,085,000
2002	NA	-$5,162,000

Curr. Assets:	$0	Curr. Liab.:	$2,987,000		
Plant, Equip.:	NA	Total Liab.:	$2,987,000	Indic. Yr. Divd.:	NA
Total Assets:	$0	Net Worth:	-$2,986,000	Debt/ Equity:	NA

Earth Biofuels Inc

3001 Knox St., Ste. 303, Dallas, TX, 75205; *PH:* 1-866-765-4940; *Fax:* 1-214-520-0507; *http://* www.earthbiofuels.com; *Email:* investors@earthbiofuels.net

General - Incorporation	DE
Employees	76
Auditor	Malone & Bailey, PC
Stk Agt	Colonial Stock Transfer Co Inc
Counsel	NA
DUNS No.	NA

Stock- Price on:12/24/2007	$0.2
Stock Exchange	OTC
Ticker Symbol	EBOF
Outstanding Shares	246,020,000
E.P.S.	-$0.5
Shareholders	NA

Business: The groups principle activities include production and the distributing of petroleum, and biodiesel blended fuels. In the year 2005, the group acquired Earth Biofuels, Inc and Resources International, Inc. The group operates from the United States. The groups annual revenue for September 2007 was 41.55 millions of USD.

Primary SIC and add'l.: 2860

CIK No: 0001268471

Subsidiaries: Distribution Drive, Durant Biofuels, LLC, Earth Biofuels Operating Inc

Officers: Dennis G. McLaughlin/Chmn., CEO, Christopher Chambers/Exec. VP, Sec., Darren L. Miles/CFO, Randy Hepler/Sr. VP - Sales, Operations, Kristin Herring/VP - Marketing, Public Relations, Linda Berndt/VP - Government Affairs, Miguel Dabdoub/Pres., Robert D. Dubek/COO, Shawne Horn/Media Relations, Doug Jones/Business Development, Jim Horton/Distribution, Sales

Directors: Dennis G. McLaughlin/Chmn., CEO, Bruce Blackwell/Dir., Morgan Freeman/Dir., Bill Luckett/Dir., Herbert E. Meyer/Dir.

Owners: Colonel Robert Dubek, Dennis McLaughlin, Tommy Johnson, Bill Luckett/1.20%, Kit Chambers, Apollo Resources International, Inc./54.00%, Darren Miles, Morgan Freeman/2.40%, Bruce Blackwell, Willie Nelson/2.60%, Herbert E. Meyer, CEDE& Co/8.80%, Insiders/7.70%, Lance Bakrow/8.80%, Mammoth Corporation/8.50%

Financial Data: Fiscal Year End: 12/31 **Latest Annual Data:** 12/31/2006

Year	Sales	Net Income
2006	$41,545,000	-$67,482,000
2005	$1,944,000	-$10,454,000

Curr. Assets:	$6,708,000	Curr. Liab.:	$48,548,000	P/E Ratio:	16.13
Plant, Equip.:	$27,015,000	Total Liab.:	$48,548,000	Indic. Yr. Divd.:	NA
Total Assets:	$113,731,000	Net Worth:	$65,183,000	Debt/ Equity:	NA

Earth Energy Reserves Inc

Formerly: Asian American Business Development Co
671 Heinz Pkwy., Estes Park, CO, 80517; *PH:* 1-970-577-8325

General - Incorporation	NV
Employees	NA
Auditor	Killman, Murrell & Co. P.C
Stk Agt	NA
Counsel	NA
DUNS No.	NA

Stock - Price on:12/24/2007	NA
Stock Exchange	NA
Ticker Symbol	NA
Outstanding Shares	NA
E.P.S.	NA
Shareholders	NA

Business: The group's principal activities include providing investors with the opportunity to participate with a modest amount in venture capital investments that are generally not available to the public and that typically require substantially larger financial commitments. Major lines of business include providing professional management and administration that might otherwise be unavailable to investors if they were to engage directly in venture capital investing. The group is regulated as a business development company and operates as a non-diversified company.

Primary SIC and add'l.: 8742

CIK No: 0001327557

Subsidiaries: Wiltex A, Inc

Officers: James E. Hogue/69/Chmn., CEO, Pres., James Phillips/58/Dir., VP, Sec., Treasurer, John Malone/58/Dir., CFO, Chief Marketing Officer

Directors: James E. Hogue/69/Chmn., CEO, Pres., James Phillips/58/Dir., VP, Sec., Treasurer, John Malone/58/Dir., CFO, Chief Marketing Officer

Owners: Insiders/59.39%, John Malone/4.64%, James Phillips/8.35%, James E. Hogue/46.40%

Earth Search Sciences Inc

306 Stoner Loop Rd., Ste. 6, Lakeside, MT, 59922; *PH:* 1-406-751-5200; *Fax:* 1-406-752-7433;
http:// www.earthsearch.com

General - Incorporation	UT
Employees	4
Auditor	Malone & Bailey, P.C
Stk Agt	Atlas Stock Transfer Corp
Counsel	NA
DUNS No.	60-180-8272

Stock - Price on:12/24/2007	$0.2
Stock Exchange	OTC
Ticker Symbol	ESSE
Outstanding Shares	81,290,000
E.P.S.	$0.04
Shareholders	NA

Business: The group's principal activity is to collect high value imagery of the earth's surface utilizing the proprietary hyperspectral imaging sensors. This imagery is sold to end users via contracts to collect the information for own exploration purposes. This is also sold to third parties through the group's Web based e-commerce site. The group also performs imagery processing services. Information collected by the sensor has applications in natural resources development, environmental monitoring and remediation. The information also has applications in wildlife habitat monitoring, hydrocarbon exploration and development, agricultural assessment and planning, including weed species identification, land use planning, forestry monitoring and planning and defence surveillance. The group operates solely in the domestic market.

Primary SIC and add'l.: 7374 7375 1382 4899

CIK No: 0000752634

Subsidiaries: Earth Search Resources, Inc., ESSI Probe 1 LC, Petro Probe, Inc., Polyspectrum Imaging, Inc., Quasar Resource Inc., Skywatch Exploration Inc., Space Technology Development Corporation, Terranet, Inc.

Officers: Larry F. Vance/Chmn., CEO, Joe Zamudio/VP - Technical Operations, Tami J. Story/Corp. Sec., Treasurer, Laurel Gordner/Image Processing

Directors: Larry F. Vance/Chmn., CEO

Owners: Insiders/90.00%, Larry Vance/74.00%, Tami Story/16.00%

Financial Data: Fiscal Year End: 03/31 **Latest Annual Data:** 03/31/2007

Year	Sales	Net Income
2007	$91,000	$3,649,000
2006	$400,000	-$2,189,000
2005	$416,000	-$5,186,000

Curr. Assets:	$224,000	Curr. Liab.:	$18,799,000	P/E Ratio:	4.00
Plant, Equip.:	$414,000	Total Liab.:	$19,148,000	Indic. Yr. Divd.:	NA
Total Assets:	$638,000	Net Worth:	-$18,510,000	Debt/ Equity:	NA

Earthblock Technologies Inc

2637 Erie Ave., Ste. 207, Cincinnati, OH, 45208; *PH:* 1-513-533-1220; *Fax:* 1-513-533-1990;
http:// www.eblk.com

General - Incorporation	NV
Employees	2
Auditor	Pollard-Kelley Auditing Services, Inc
Stk Agt	Interwest Transfer Company, Inc.
Counsel	NA
DUNS No.	NA

Stock - Price on:12/24/2007	$0.004
Stock Exchange	OTC
Ticker Symbol	EBLC
Outstanding Shares	96,970,000
E.P.S.	-$0.002
Shareholders	NA

Business: The group's principal activity is to manufacture, distribute and apply technologically advanced building products through a licensing agreement with its subsidiary terra block, inc. The group has the exclusive right to make, use and sell the terra block, inc. Products anywhere in the world. The license agreement provides the group with the rights to all intellectual property. The terra block system of the group features a machine developed, perfected and patented by terra block, inc. That manufactures building blocks using common soil as the raw material. The terra block system has been used all over the world to construct houses, schools, churches and commercial facilities.

Primary SIC and add'l.: 5039 3271

CIK No: 0001103719

Officers: Gregory A. Pitner/Chmn., CEO, Pres., James E. Hines/Dir., CFO, VP

Directors: Gregory A. Pitner/Chmn., CEO, Pres., Gary S. Barker/Dir., James E. Hines/Dir., CFO, VP

Owners: Insiders/6.00%, Prendiville Revocable Trust/13.90%, Gregory A. Pitner/3.00%, Capital Consortium Anstalt/7.20%, James E. Hines/3.00%, C & M Capital, Ltd./6.20%

Financial Data: Fiscal Year End: 12/31 **Latest Annual Data:** 12/31/2006

Year	Sales	Net Income
2006	NA	-$1,448,000
2005	$27,000	-$283,000
2004	NA	-$629,000

Curr. Assets:	$180,000	Curr. Liab.:	$1,425,000		
Plant, Equip.:	$5,000	Total Liab.:	$1,425,000	Indic. Yr. Divd.:	NA
Total Assets:	$185,000	Net Worth:	-$1,240,000	Debt/ Equity:	NA

EarthFirst Technologies Inc

2515 E Hanna Ave., Tampa, FL, 33610; *PH:* 1-813-238-5010; *Fax:* 1-813-238-8490;
http:// www.earthfirsttech.com

General - Incorporation	FL
Employees	253
Auditor	Aidman, Piser & Company, P.A.
Stk Agt	Continental Stock Transfer & Trust Co
Counsel	NA
DUNS No.	NA

Stock - Price on:12/24/2007	$0.08
Stock Exchange	OTC
Ticker Symbol	EFTI
Outstanding Shares	604,260,000
E.P.S.	NA
Shareholders	NA

Business: The groups principle activities include researching, developing and commercializing technologies for the production of alternative fuel sources. The group operates through three segments namely waste disposal, contracting, and biofuels. The group operates from the United States. The group's annual revenue for Sept 2007 was 45.37 millions of USD.

Primary SIC and add'l.: 3990

CIK No: 0001056748

Subsidiaries: Electric Machinery Enterprises, Inc, Prime Power Residential, Inc

Officers: John D. Stanton/Chmn., CEO, Pres., Frank W. Barker/CFO

Directors: John D. Stanton/Chmn., CEO, Pres., Jaime Jurado/Vice Chmn., Nicholas R. Tomassetti/Dir., David Edward Crow/Dir.

Owners: Sic Semper Tyrannis, Incorporated/19.86%, Ralph W. Hughes Revocable Family Trust/5.30%, Stone Enclosure, Inc./8.40%, Wade, Inc. of Tampa Bay/8.40%, Bunker Positioning, Inc./6.79%, Barry Markowitz/0.08%, Denoument Strategies, Inc./13.27%, Frank W. Barker/0.25%, Insiders/72.12%, Nicholas R. Tomassetti/0.17%, David E. Crow/0.10%

Financial Data: Fiscal Year End: 12/31 **Latest Annual Data:** 12/31/2006

Year	Sales	Net Income
2006	$45,372,000	-$19,872,000
2005	$41,743,000	-$17,685,000
2004	$15,315,000	-$2,267,000

Curr. Assets:	$13,304,000	Curr. Liab.:	$18,336,000		
Plant, Equip.:	$4,746,000	Total Liab.:	$24,219,000	Indic. Yr. Divd.:	NA
Total Assets:	$24,667,000	Net Worth:	$330,000	Debt/ Equity:	NA

Earthlink Inc

1375 Peachtree St., Level A, Atlanta, GA, 30309; *PH:* 1-404-815-0770; *Fax:* 1-404-892-7616;
http:// www.earthlink.net

General - Incorporation	DE
Employees	2,210
Auditor	Ernst & Young LLP
Stk Agt	American Stock Transfer & Trust Co.
Counsel	Hunton & Williams LLP
DUNS No.	NA

Stock- Price on:12/24/2007	$7.33
Stock Exchange	NDQ
Ticker Symbol	ELNK
Outstanding Shares	123,320,000
E.P.S.	-$1.23
Shareholders	NA

Business: The group's principal activity is to provide nationwide Internet access and related value-added services. The group's activities are divided into four operating segments: narrowband access, broadband or high speed access, Web hosting and content and commerce and advertising. The narrowband access segment provides dial up Internet access. The broadband access segment provides high-speed, high-capacity access services including DSL, cable, satellite, fixed wireless and dedicated circuit services. The Web hosting segment rents server space and provides Web hosting services to companies and individuals. The content, commerce and advertising segment provides and sells banners, content space and other online ads.

Primary SIC and add'l.: 7375 7379

CIK No: 0001102541

Subsidiaries: Cidco Incorporated, EarthLink/OneMain, Inc., PeoplePC Inc.

Officers: Rolla P. Huff/Dir., CEO, Pres., Stacie Hagan/Chief People Officer, Linda Beck/Pres. - New Edge Networks/$752,056.00, Donald B. Berryman/Pres. - Earthlink Municipal Networks/$928,074.00, Ken Uhlig/Exec. VP, Chief People Officer, Kevin M. Dotts/CFO/$867,681.00, Christopher Putala/Exec. VP - Public Policy, Samuel R. Desimone/Exec. VP, General Counsel, Mike Lunsford/Exec. VP/$946,462.00, Craig Forman/Exec. VP, Pres. - Access, Audience

Directors: Rolla P. Huff/Dir., CEO, Pres., Robert M. Kavner/64/Chmn., Marce Fuller/47/Dir., Thomas E. Wheeler/61/Dir., Terrell Jones/60/Dir., Linwood A. Lacy/62/Dir., Sky Dayton/Dir., Bill Harris/52/Dir., William H. Harris/52/Dir.

Owners: Linda W. Beck, Robert M. Kavner, Linwood A. Lacy, William S. Heys, William H. Harris, Steel Partners II, LLC/6.10%, Donald B. Berryman, Insiders/4.40%, Artisan Partners Limited Partnership/5.50%, Thomas E. Wheeler, Coghill Capital Management, L.L.C./5.70%, Terrell B. Jones, Sky D. Dayton/1.90%, Kevin M. Dotts, Marce Fuller (18 Owners included in Index)

Financial Data: Fiscal Year End:12/31   Latest Annual Data: 12/31/2006

Year	Sales	Net Income
2006	$1,301,267,000	$4,987,000
2005	$1,290,072,000	$142,780,000
2004	$1,382,202,000	$111,009,000

Curr. Assets:	$456,750,000	Curr. Liab.:	$230,770,000		
Plant, Equip.:	$96,620,000	Total Liab.:	$509,375,000	Indic. Yr. Divd.:	NA
Total Assets:	$968,039,000	Net Worth:	$458,664,000	Debt/ Equity:	0.5985

Earthworks Entertainment Inc

105 S Narcissus Ave., West Palm Beach, FL, 33401; *PH:* 1-561-791-1380 ;
http:// www.etntwebsite.com

General - Incorporation	DE	Stock - Price on:12/24/2007	NA
Employees	3	Stock Exchange	OTC
Auditor	Rosenberg Rich Baker Berman & Co	Ticker Symbol	EWKE
Stk Agt	Computershare Investor Services LLC	Outstanding Shares	NA
Counsel	NA	E.P.S.	-$0.029
DUNS No.	NA	Shareholders	NA

Business: The group's principal activity is to create, produce, market and distribute children and family oriented entertainment properties. The properties of the group are marketed in all multi-platform areas of commercial exposition ranging from television to home video to merchandise licensing to electronic and video games to book and music publishing. The group operates solely in the United States of America. On 10-Feb-2003, it acquired econtent inc.

Primary SIC and add'l.: 7999

CIK No: 0000820789

Subsidiaries: Z-Force Enterprises, LLC., Z-Force property

Owners: Peter Keefe/19.60%, William Campbell/6.70%, Catherine Malatesta/0.40%

Financial Data: Fiscal Year End:09/30   Latest Annual Data: 09/30/2005

Year	Sales	Net Income
2005	NA	-$2,363,000
2004	NA	-$1,846,000
2003	NA	-$850,000

Curr. Assets:	$311,000	Curr. Liab.:	$1,637,000		
Plant, Equip.:	$1,000	Total Liab.:	$1,637,000	Indic. Yr. Divd.:	NA
Total Assets:	$1,934,000	Net Worth:	-$287,000	Debt/ Equity:	NA

East Delta Resources Corp

447 St. Francois-Xavier St., Ste. 600, Montreal, Quebec, H2Y 2T1; *PH:* 1-514-845-6448;
Fax: 1-514-844-0272; *http://* www.eastdelta.ca; *Email:* vic2@videotron.ca

General - Incorporation	DE	Stock - Price on:12/24/2007	$0.27
Employees	NA	Stock Exchange	OTC
Auditor	Malone & Bailey, PC	Ticker Symbol	EDLT
Stk Agt	l'Continental Registry & Stk Trnsfer	Outstanding Shares	NA
Counsel	NA	E.P.S.	NA
DUNS No.	NA	Shareholders	NA

Business: The groups principal activity is to explore minerals and natural oil. The group operates from Canada and the United States.

Primary SIC and add'l.: 1081

CIK No: 0001093933

Subsidiaries: Amingo Resources Inc., Guizhou Amingo Resources Ltd, Sino-Canadian Metals Inc.

Officers: Victor I.H. Sun/Dir., CEO, David Bikerman/48/Dir., Pres., Lu Huan-Zhang/Chief Geologist, Pres. - Amingo Resources

Directors: Victor I.H. Sun/Dir., CEO, David Bikerman/48/Dir., Pres., Felix J. Furst/61/Dir., Louis H. Ladouceur/Dir.

Owners: David Bikerman, Victor Sun/4.10%, Louis Ladouceur/3.20%, Felix Furst/8.30%, Insiders/15.60%

Financial Data: Fiscal Year End:12/31   Latest Annual Data: 12/31/2006

Year	Sales	Net Income
2006	NA	-$2,992,000
2005	NA	-$10,245,000

Curr. Assets:	$835,000	Curr. Liab.:	$71,000		
Plant, Equip.:	NA	Total Liab.:	$71,000	Indic. Yr. Divd.:	NA
Total Assets:	$835,000	Net Worth:	$765,000	Debt/ Equity:	NA

East Penn Financial Corp

731 Chestnut St., Emmaus, PA, 18049; *PH:* 1-610-965-5959; *Fax:* 1-610-967-3940;
http:// www.eastpennbank.com

General - Incorporation	PA	Stock - Price on:12/24/2007	$13.9
Employees	118	Stock Exchange	NDQ
Auditor	Beard Miller Co. LLP	Ticker Symbol	EPEN
Stk Agt	Registrar & Transfer Co	Outstanding Shares	6,310,000
Counsel	NA	E.P.S.	$0.57
DUNS No.	NA	Shareholders	NA

Business: The group's principal activity is to provide a variety of financial services to individuals, small businesses and municipalities through its seven branches located principally in lehigh county, Pennsylvania. The group operates through its wholly owned subsidiary east penn bank. The deposit services offered by the group include checking accounts, savings accounts, business accounts and individual retirement accounts. The lending services include business loans, home equity loans, residential mortgage loans, commercial mortgage loans, automobile loans and student loans. The group also provides banking services through mail. It also provides safe deposit boxes, travellers checks, wire transfers, merchant credit card, visa debit card and other banking related services.

Primary SIC and add'l.: 6712 6022

CIK No: 0001220483

Subsidiaries: East Penn Bank

Officers: Brent L. Peters/Chmn., CEO, Pres., Theresa M. Wasko/CFO - Finance Department, Exec. VP, Treasurer, Investor Relations Officer, Steve Peters/Web Developer, Technology Department, Kelly Pfleiger/Information Systems Officer - Technology Department, Debra K. Peters/VP, Exec. VP - Deposit Funding, Anthony Betz/Commercial Loan Officer - Bethlehem Branch, Scott Cave/Teller - Bethlehem Branch, Audrey Grube/Teller - Bethlehem Branch, Pamela Kohler/Loan Operations Mgr. - Loan Operations Department, Bethany Love/Loan Operations Clerk - Loan Operations Department, Doloris Schapitl/Loan Operations Clerk - Loan Operations Department, Carole Lipics/Mortgage Officer - Mortgage Department, Kara Morrison/Mortage Processor, Mortgage Department, Kenneth Pavkovic/Private Banking Officer - Private Banking Department, Rahul Dekhtawala/Systems Support Specialist - Technology Department (135 Officers included in Index)

Directors: Brent L. Peters/Chmn., CEO, Pres., Forrest A. Rohrbach/Vice Chmn., Donald R. Schneck/Vice Chmn., Geoffrey F. Toonder/Dir., Thomas R. Gulla/Dir., Peter L. Shaffer/Dir., Dale A. Dries/Dir., Gordon K. Schantz/Dir., Donald S. Young/Dir., Allen E. Kiefer/Dir., Konstantinos A. Tantaros/Dir., Linn H. Schantz/Dir.

Owners: Konstantinos A. Tantaros/4.56%, Debra K. Peters/2.24%, Linn H. Schantz/3.36%, Peter L. Shaffer/0.31%, Thomas R. Gulla/2.54%, Allen E. Kiefer/0.07%, Donald S. Young/2.33%, Theresa M. Wasko/0.10%, Dale A. Dries/1.75%, Gordon K. Schantz/1.29%, Forrest A. Rohrbach/3.14%, Brent L. Peters/2.24%, Geoffrey F. Toonder/2.13%, Donald R. Schneck/2.34%, Insiders/26.27%

Financial Data: Fiscal Year End:12/31   Latest Annual Data: 12/31/2006

Year	Sales	Net Income
2006	$26,515,000	$3,611,000
2005	$22,537,000	$3,503,000
2004	$18,978,000	$3,250,000

Curr. Assets:	$29,307,000	Curr. Liab.:	$382,043,000	P/E Ratio:	23.97
Plant, Equip.:	$9,820,000	Total Liab.:	$414,291,000	Indic. Yr. Divd.:	$0.240
Total Assets:	$439,452,000	Net Worth:	$25,161,000	Debt/ Equity:	1.2680

East Texas Financial Services Inc

1200 S Beckham Ave, Tyler, TX, 75701; *PH:* 1-903-593-1767

General - Incorporation		Stock - Price on:12/24/2007	$16.75
Employees	NA	Stock Exchange	OTC
Auditor	NA	Ticker Symbol	ETFS
Stk Agt	Registrar & Transfer Co.	Outstanding Shares	NA
Counsel	Nelson Mullins serves	E.P.S.	NA
DUNS No.	NA	Shareholders	NA

Business: The groups principle activity is to provide recruiting services. The groups service area includes the research and development, engineering, marketing, sales, information technology and manufacturing industries. The group operates from United States.

Primary SIC and add'l.: 6035 6712 6022

CIK No: 0000929646

Financial Data: Fiscal Year End:09/30   Latest Annual Data: 9/30/2002

Year	Sales	Net Income
2002	$14,798,000	$2,069,000
2001	$15,046,000	$700,000
2000	$12,022,000	$296,000

Curr. Assets:	$7,669,000	Curr. Liab.:	$196,900,000		
Plant, Equip.:	$3,263,000	Total Liab.:	$198,428,000	Indic. Yr. Divd.:	NA
Total Assets:	$217,710,000	Net Worth:	$19,282,000	Debt/ Equity:	NA

East West Bancorp Inc

135 N Los Robles Ave., Pasadena, CA, 91101; *PH:* 1-626-768-6000; *Fax:* 1-626-799-3167;
http:// www.eastwestbank.com; *Email:* info@eastwestbank.com

General - Incorporation	DE	Stock - Price on:12/24/2007	$40.46
Employees	1,257	Stock Exchange	NDQ
Auditor	Deloitte & Touche LLP	Ticker Symbol	EWBC
Stk Agt	U.S. Stock Transfer Corp	Outstanding Shares	61,060,000
Counsel	NA	E.P.S.	$2.64
DUNS No.	NA	Shareholders	NA

Business: The group's principal activities are to provide a wide range of personal and commercial banking services through its network of 39 branches located in California. The services are mainly provided to small and medium-sized businesses, business executives, professionals and other individuals. It also provides multilingual services to all of its customers in English, Cantonese, Mandarin and Spanish. The banking services include financing international trade, commercial, construction and residential real estate projects, lending for accounts receivables, small business administration, inventory and working capital loans. On 09-Aug-2004, the group acquired trust bank.

Primary SIC and add'l.: 6022 6712

CIK No: 0001069157

Subsidiaries: East West Bank, East West Capital Statutory Trust III, East West Capital Trust I, East West Capital Trust II, East West Capital Trust IV, East West Capital Trust V, East West Capital Trust VI, East West Insurance Services, Inc.

Officers: Dominic Ng/Dir., CEO, Pres./$4,611,716.00, William J. Lewis/Exec. VP/$502,976.00, Wellington Chen/Exec. VP/$563,036.00, Donald S. Chow/Exec. VP, David Spigner/Exec. VP/$530,034.00, Julia S. Gouw/Exec. VP, CFO, Investor Relations Officer/$1,261,980.00, Douglas P. Krause/Exec. VP, Michael W. Lai/Exec. VP

Directors: Dominic Ng/Dir., CEO, Pres., John Lee/Vice Chmn., Peggy Cherng/Dir., Keith W. Renken/Dir., Julia S. Gouw/Dir., Exec. VP, CFO, Investor Relations Officer, Jack C. Liu/Dir., Herman Y. Li/Dir., John D. Kooken/Dir., Rudolph I. Estrada/Dir., Peggy Tsiang Cherng/Dir., Steven P. Erwin/Dir.

Owners: Rudolph I. Estrada, David L. Spigner, Tseng Yun Tsai/5.15%, John Kooken, Jack C. Liu, William J. Lewis, Neuberger Berman Inc./5.90%, Herman Y. Li, Julia S. Gouw, Wellington Chen, John Lee, Peggy Cherng, Keith W. Renken, FMR Corporation/8.47%, Insiders/3.88% *(16 Owners included in Index)*

Financial Data: *Fiscal Year End:*12/31   *Latest Annual Data:* 12/31/2006

Year	Sales	Net Income
2006	$694,408,000	$143,369,000
2005	$441,048,000	$108,380,000
2004	$283,896,000	$78,022,000

Curr. Assets:	$321,957,000	*Curr. Liab.:*	$9,608,919,000	*P/E Ratio:*	16.31
Plant, Equip.:	$46,708,000	*Total Liab.:*	$9,804,321,000	*Indic. Yr. Divd:*	$0.400
Total Assets:	$10,823,711,000	*Net Worth:*	$1,019,390,000	*Debt/ Equity:*	0.2104

East West Distributors Inc

10105 E Via Linda, No.103, Scottsdale, AZ, 85258; *PH:* 1-480-614-2874

General - Incorporation	NV	*Stock*- Price on:12/24/2007	$0.0001
Employees	NA	Stock Exchange	NDQ
Auditor	NA	Ticker Symbol	NA
Stk Agt.	NA	Outstanding Shares	NA
Counsel	NA	E.P.S.	NA
DUNS No.	NA	Shareholders	NA

Business: The group's principle activities include researching, developing, and marketing in the biomedical products. The group operates from United States.

Primary SIC and add'l.: 2836

CIK No: 0001330718

Eastern American Natural Gas Trust

919 Congress Ave., Ste. 500, Austin, TX, 78701; *PH:* 1-800-852-1422

General - Incorporation	DE	*Stock*- Price on:12/24/2007	$25.11
Employees	NA	Stock Exchange	NYSE
Auditor	PricewaterhouseCoopers LLP	Ticker Symbol	NA
Stk Agt.	JP Morgan Chase Bank, N.A.	Outstanding Shares	5,900,000
Counsel	NA	E.P.S.	$2.40
DUNS No.	NA	Shareholders	NA

Business: The groups principal activities include developing and acquiring natural gas properties. The group operates from the United States.

Primary SIC and add'l.: 6792

CIK No: 0000895474

Officers: Mike Ulrich/VP, Larry T. Nelms/Managing Sr. VP

Financial Data: *Fiscal Year End:*12/31   *Latest Annual Data:* 12/31/2006

Year	Sales	Net Income
2006	$17,664,000	$14,159,000
2005	$18,179,000	$14,597,000
2004	$14,449,000	$12,020,000

Curr. Assets:	$3,605,000	*Curr. Liab.:*	$2,905,000	*P/E Ratio:*	10.46
Plant, Equip.:	NA	*Total Liab.:*	$2,905,000	*Indic. Yr. Divd:*	$2.120
Total Assets:	$28,166,000	*Net Worth:*	$25,261,000	*Debt/ Equity:*	NA

Eastern Co

112 Bridge St., Naugatuck, CT, 06770; *PH:* 1-203-729-2255; *Fax:* 1-203-723-8653; *http://* www.easterncompany.com

General - Incorporation	CT	*Stock*- Price on:12/24/2007	$30.94
Employees	695	Stock Exchange	AMEX
Auditor	UHY LLP	Ticker Symbol	EML
Stk Agt.	American Stock Transfer & Trust Co.	Outstanding Shares	5,580,000
Counsel	NA	E.P.S.	$2.62
DUNS No.	00-116-5679	Shareholders	NA

Business: The group's principal activities are carried out through three segments; security products, industrial hardware and metal products. The security products division manufactures and markets electronic and mechanical locking devices, including keyed and keyless devices, for the computers, electronics and vending and gaming industries. The industrial hardware division produces latching devices for industrial equipment, instruments and vehicular type equipment. The products include latches, hinges, handles, fasteners and other closing devices. The metal products division produces anchoring devices used in supporting the roofs of underground coal mines. This segment also manufactures specialty products, which serve the construction, automotive and electrical industries. The group has operations in Canada, Hong Kong and Mexico.

Primary SIC and add'l.: 3499 7382 3429

CIK No: 0000031107

Subsidiaries: Canadian Commercial Vehicles Corporation, Eastern Industrial Ltd., Eberhard Hardware Manufacturing, Ltd., Sesamee Mexicana, World Lock Co. Ltd.

Officers: Leonard F. Leganza/Chmn., CEO, Pres. - Eastern Company/$876,931.00, David C. Robinson/Dir. - Business Consultant, John L. Sullivan/CFO, VP/$479,284.00

Directors: Leonard F. Leganza/Chmn., CEO, Pres. - Eastern Company, Russell G. McMillen/Dir. Emeritus, David C. Robinson/Dir. - Business Consultant, John W. Everets/Dir., Donald S. Tuttle/Dir., Charles W. Henry/Dir.

Owners: Leonard F. Leganza/5.70%, Russell Trust Co. as trustee under the Salaried/5.60%, John W. Everets/2.10%, Insiders/19.30%, Russell G. McMillen/4.60%, Brown Advisory Holdings Incorporated/10.40%, Charles W. Henry/2.50%, David C. Robinson/2.60%, Donald S. Tuttle/2.40%, John L. Sullivan/1.80%

Financial Data: *Fiscal Year End:*12/31   *Latest Annual Data:* 12/30/2006

Year	Sales	Net Income
2006	$138,465,000	$9,659,000
2005	$109,107,000	$4,367,000

Curr. Assets:	$45,045,000	*Curr. Liab.:*	$13,823,000		
Plant, Equip.:	$22,397,000	*Total Liab.:*	$35,450,000	*Indic. Yr. Divd:*	$0.320
Total Assets:	$81,622,000	*Net Worth:*	$46,172,000	*Debt/ Equity:*	0.2734

Eastern Environment Solutions Corp

Formerly: USIP.Com Inc

Harbin Dongdazhi St. 165, Harbin, 150001; *PH:* 86-451-53948666

General - Incorporation	NV	*Stock*- Price on:12/24/2007	NA
Employees	3	Stock Exchange	NA
Auditor	Bagell, Josephs, Levine & Co., L.l.c.	Ticker Symbol	NA
Stk Agt	Colonial Stock Transfer Co Inc	Outstanding Shares	NA
Counsel	NA	E.P.S.	NA
DUNS No.	NA	Shareholders	NA

Business: The group's principle activities are to own, operate and manage privately owned public payphones in New York, Pennsylvania and Massachusetts. The group derives its revenue from coin-calls, non-coin calls, sales and service of payphones and prepaid phone cards. The majority of the payphones are located at convenience stores, truck stops, service stations, grocery stores, colleges and hospitals. Approximately 70% of the customers of the group are a result of acquisitions from (itoc's) independent telephone operating companies.

Primary SIC and add'l.: 4813

CIK No: 0001119721

Subsidiaries: Datone, Inc, NB Payphones, Ltd, The Platinum Funding Corporation

Officers: Yun Wang/53/Chmn., CEO, Shibin Jiang/51/Dir., COO, Jianhua Sun/32/Dir., CFO

Directors: Yun Wang/53/Chmn., CEO, Shibin Jiang/51/Dir., COO, Jianhua Sun/32/Dir., CFO

Owners: Insiders/92.00%, Bin Feng/16.56%, Yun Wang/63.48%, Shibin Jiang/11.96%

Financial Data: *Fiscal Year End:*12/31   *Latest Annual Data:* 12/31/2006

Year	Sales	Net Income
2006	$3,201,000	$2,651,000
2005	$281,000	-$522,000
2004	$452,000	-$403,000

Curr. Assets:	$2,376,000	*Curr. Liab.:*	$1,148,000		
Plant, Equip.:	$5,026,000	*Total Liab.:*	$3,360,000	*Indic. Yr. Divd.:*	NA
Total Assets:	$10,714,000	*Net Worth:*	$7,354,000	*Debt/ Equity:*	NA

Eastern Insurance Holdings Inc

25 Race Ave., Lancaster, PA, 17603; *PH:* 1-717-396-7095; *Fax:* 1-717-399-3781; *http://* www.easterninsuranceholdings.com

General - Incorporation	PA	*Stock*- Price on:12/24/2007	$14.97
Employees	136	Stock Exchange	NDQ
Auditor	NA	Ticker Symbol	EIHI
Stk Agt	NA	Outstanding Shares	11,520,000
Counsel	NA	E.P.S.	$1.44
DUNS No.	NA	Shareholders	NA

Business: The groups principle activity is to provide workers compensation and group insurance products and reinsurance products. The products of the group include guaranteed cost policies, policyholder dividend policies dental insurance and term life insurance. The group operates through five segments namely workers compensation insurance, segregated portfolio cell reinsurance, group benefits insurance, specialty reinsurance, and corporate. In June 2006 the group acquired Eastern Holding Company, Ltd. The group operates from the United States. The group's quarterly revenue for September 2007 was 38.91 millions of USD.

Primary SIC and add'l.: 6321 6311 6399 6331

CIK No: 0001321268

Subsidiaries: Allied Eastern Indemnity Company, Eastern Alliance Insurance Company, Eastern Holding Company, Ltd., Eastern Life and Health Insurance Company, Eastern Re Ltd., S.P.C., Eastern Services Corporation, Employers Alliance, Inc., Global Alliance Holdings, Ltd., Global Alliance Statutory Trust I

Officers: Bruce M. Eckert/Dir., CEO, Michael L. Boguski/COO, Pres., Kevin M. Shook/Treasurer, CFO, Robert A. Gilpin/Sr. VP - Marketing

Directors: Robert M. McAlaine/Chmn., Lawrence W. Bitner/Dir., Paul R. Burke/Dir., Ronald L. King/Dir., Scott C. Penwell/Dir., John O. Shirk/Dir., William Lloyd Snyder/Dir., Richard Stevens/Dir., Charles H. Vetterlein/Dir., James L. Zech/Dir.

Owners: Sterling Financial Trust Company, as trustee of the/6.40%, Robert M. McAlaine/1.00%, Richard Stevens, Insiders/27.10%, OZ Management, L.L.C./5.40%, James L. Zech/7.50%, Suzanne M. Emmet, John O. Shirk, Robert A. Gilpin, Kevin M. Shook, Michael L. Boguski/1.00%, Bruce M. Eckert/1.70%, Steven J. Tynan/7.50%, Scott C. Penwell, Northaven Management, Inc. and its affiliates/8.80% *(20 Owners included in Index)*

Financial Data: *Fiscal Year End:*12/31   *Latest Annual Data:* 12/31/2006

Year	Sales	Net Income
2006	$86,981,000	$8,278,000

Curr. Assets:	$101,453,000	*Curr. Liab.:*	$25,767,000	*P/E Ratio:*	11.43
Plant, Equip.:	NA	*Total Liab.:*	$194,462,000	*Indic. Yr. Divd:*	$0.200
Total Assets:	$368,206,000	*Net Worth:*	$173,744,000	*Debt/ Equity:*	0.0455

Eastern Services Holdings Inc

269 S Beverly Dr., Ste. 732, Beverly Hills, CA, 90212; *PH:* 1-310-587-0029

General - Incorporation	DE	*Stock*- Price on:12/24/2007	$1.2
Employees	2	Stock Exchange	OTC
Auditor	Gately & Associates, LLC	Ticker Symbol	ESVH
Stk Agt	stock transfer services	Outstanding Shares	1,400,000
Counsel	NA	E.P.S.	-$0.03
DUNS No.	NA	Shareholders	NA

Business: The groups principle activity is to provide tax consultation and analysis. The group operates from the United States. The groups annual revenue for September 2007 was 86.98 millions of USD.

Primary SIC and add'l.: 8742

CIK No: 0001335795

Subsidiaries: Eastern Services Group, Inc.

Officers: Akhee Rahman/36/Chmn., CEO, CFO, Pres., Sec., Treasurer

Directors: Akhee Rahman/36/Chmn., CEO, CFO, Pres., Sec., Treasurer, Richard Carrigan/41/Dir.

Owners: Ahkee Rahman/26.30%, Insiders/79.20%, Richard Carrigan/71.90%

Financial Data: *Fiscal Year End:*12/31   *Latest Annual Data:* 12/31/2006

Year		Sales		Net Income	
2006		$81,000		-$90,000	
Curr. Assets:	$48,000	Curr. Liab.:	$112,000		
Plant, Equip.:	$3,000	Total Liab.:	$112,000	Indic. Yr. Divd.:	NA
Total Assets:	$51,000	Net Worth:	-$60,000	Debt/ Equity:	NA

Eastern Virginia Bankshares Inc

330 Hospital Rd., Tappahannock, VA, 22560; *PH:* 1-804-443-8400; *Fax:* 1-804-445-1047; *http://* www.evb.org; *Email:* info@rtco.com

General - Incorporation .... VA
Employees 296
Auditor .... Yount, Hyde & Barbour, P.C
Stk Agt .... Registrar & Transfer Co
Counsel .... NA
DUNS No. .... NA

Stock- Price on:12/24/2007 .... $22
Stock Exchange .... NDQ
Ticker Symbol .... EVBS
Outstanding Shares 6,090,000
E.P.S $1.49
Shareholders .... NA

Business: The group's principal activity is to provide banking services. The services include originating loans and accepting deposits. The group lends loans for commercial, real estate, construction and consumer loans. The group's services include accepting demand and time deposits, visa and mastercard revolving credit, drive-in banking services and automated teller machine transactions, Internet banking and wire transfer services. The group operates through 20 branch offices in counties of essex, northumberland, king and queen, king william, richmond, lancaster, hanover, gloucester, middlesex and caroline.

Primary SIC and add'l.: 6712 6022

CIK No: 0001047170

Subsidiaries: Bank of Northumberland, Inc., Hanover Bank, Southside Bank

Officers: Joe A. Shearin/Dir., CEO, Pres./$392,723.00, Ronald L. Blevins/CFO, VP/$198,765.00, Joseph H. James/COO, Patricia H. Gallagher/Dir. - Strategic Planning, Corp. Sec., Robin M. Jett/Dir. - Human Resources, Lloyd J. Railey/Chief Risk Officer/$164,316.00

Directors: Joe A. Shearin/Dir., CEO, Pres., F. L. Garrett/Vice Chmn., Rand W. Cook/Chmn., Ira C. Harris/Dir., Warren F. Haynie/Dir., Charles R. Revere/Dir., Leslie E. Taylor/Dir., J. T. Thompson/Dir., Howard R. Straughan/Dir., William L. Lewis/Dir.

Owners: Leslie E. Taylor, James S. Thomas, Ronald L. Blevins, Rand W. Cook, Jay T. Thompson, Lewis R. Reynolds, Lloyd J. Railey, F. L. Garrett, William L. Lewis, Warren F. Haynie, Joseph H. James, Insiders/3.47%, Howard R. Straughan/1.57%, Joe A. Shearin, Ira C. Harris *(17 Owners included in Index)*

Financial Data: *Fiscal Year End:*12/31 *Latest Annual Data:* 12/31/2006

Year		Sales		Net Income	
2006		$56,181,000		$7,237,000	
2005		$47,956,000		$6,726,000	
2004		$44,328,000		$7,240,000	
Curr. Assets:	$40,547,000	Curr. Liab.:	$746,757,000	P/E Ratio:	14.77
Plant, Equip.:	$16,906,000	Total Liab.:	$763,591,000	Indic. Yr. Divd.:	$0.640
Total Assets:	$851,398,000	Net Worth:	$87,807,000	Debt/ Equity:	0.1144

EastGroup Properties Inc

300 One Jackson Pl., 188 East Capitol St., Jackson, MS, 39201; *PH:* 1-601-354-3555; *Fax:* 1-601-352-1441; *http://* www.eastgroup.net; *Email:* investor@eastgroup.net

General - Incorporation .... MD
Employees 63
Auditor .... KPMG LLP
Stk Agt .... Wells Fargo Shareowner Services
Counsel .... NA
DUNS No. .... NA

Stock- Price on:12/24/2007 .... $45.81
Stock Exchange .... NYSE
Ticker Symbol .... EGP
Outstanding Shares 23,750,000
E.P.S $1.17
Shareholders .... NA

Business: The groups principle activities include developing, acquiring and operating industrial properties. The group operates from the United States. The groups quarterly revenue for September 2007 was 39.24 millions of USD.

Primary SIC and add'l.: 6798

CIK No: 0000049600

Subsidiaries: 55 Castilian, LLC, EastGroup Jacksonville, LLC, EastGroup Kearn Creek, LLC, EastGroup Properties General Partners, Inc., EastGroup Properties Holdings, Inc., EastGroup Properties, LP, EastGroup Property Services of Florida, LLC, EastGroup Property Services, LLC, EastGroup TRS, Inc., Sample I-95 Associates, University Business Center Associates

Officers: David H. Hoster/Dir., CEO, Pres./$1,643,717.00, Keith N. Mckey/Exec. VP, CFO, Treasurer, Sec./$1,058,706.00, Bruce Corkern/Chief Accounting Officer, Sr. VP, Controller, William D. Petsas/Sr. VP/$744,436.00, John F. Coleman/Sr. VP/$758,010.00, Brent Wood/Sr. VP/$570,656.00, Jann W. Puckett/VP, Anthony A. Rufrano/VP, William D. Gray/VP, Chris Segrest/VP, Mary L. McNair/VP, Assist. Controller, John E. Travis/VP, Michael P. Sacco/VP

Directors: David H. Hoster/Dir., CEO, Pres., Leland R. Speed/Chmn., Pike D. Aloian/Dir., H. C. Bailey/Dir., Hayden C. Eaves/Dir., Frederic Gould/Dir., David M. Osnos/Dir., Mary Beth Beth McCormick/Dir.

Owners: Pike D. Aloian, Barclays Global Investors, NA/6.00%, David M. Osnos, Keith N. McKey, Hayden C. Eaves, William D. Petsas, Neuberger Berman, Inc./5.00%, H. C. Bailey, John F. Coleman, Mary E. McCormick, T. Rowe Price Associates, Inc./11.40%, The Vanguard Group, Inc./6.00%, Fredric H. Gould, Brent W. Wood, Heitman Real Estate Securities LLC/5.40% *(20 Owners included in Index)*

Financial Data: *Fiscal Year End:*12/31 *Latest Annual Data:* 12/31/2006

Year		Sales		Net Income	
2006		$133,613,000		$29,234,000	
2005		$126,505,000		$22,191,000	
2004		$114,684,000		$23,327,000	
Curr. Assets:	$19,659,000	Curr. Liab.:	$32,589,000	P/E Ratio:	39.15
Plant, Equip.:	$857,790,000	Total Liab.:	$492,990,000	Indic. Yr. Divd.:	$2.000
Total Assets:	$911,787,000	Net Worth:	$418,797,000	Debt/ Equity:	1.2543

Eastman Chemical Co

PO Box 431, Kingsport, TN, 37662; *PH:* 1-423-229-2000; *Fax:* 1-423-229-2145; *http://* www.eastman.com

General - Incorporation .... DE
Employees 11,000
Auditor .... PricewaterhouseCoopers LLP
Stk Agt .... American Stock Transfer & Trust Co.
Counsel .... NA
DUNS No. 80-889-8381

Stock- Price on:12/24/2007 .... $66.2
Stock Exchange .... NYSE
Ticker Symbol .... EMN
Outstanding Shares 84,100,000
E.P.S $4.40
Shareholders .... NA

Business: The groups principle activities include manufacturing and selling chemicals, plastics and fibers. The groups products include inks and graphic arts, adhesives, and textile sizes. The group operates from United States, Canada, Europe, and the Middle East.

Primary SIC and add'l.: 2819 2821

CIK No: 0000915389

Subsidiaries: Altovar Ltd., Cendian Argentina, S.R.L., Cendian Asia Pacific Pte Ltd, Cendian Corporation, Cendian de Mexico, S. DE. R.L. DE C.V., Cendian do Brasil Ltda, Cendian holding, B.V., Cendian International, Inc., Cendian Servicious, S. DE R.L. DE C.V., Cendian, B.V., Centrus International Canada Company, Centrus International, Inc., Eastman (Shanghai) Chemical Commercial Co., Ltd., Eastman (Shanghai) Chemical Trading Co., Ltd., Eastman Belgium B.V.B.A. 87 Subsidiaries included in the Index

Officers: Brian J. Ferguson/54/Chmn., CEO/$9,449,415.00, Gregory O. Nelson/Exec. VP, Head - Polymers Business Group/$1,808,948.00, Mark J. Costa/Sr. VP - Corporate Strategy, Marketing, Ronald C. Lindsay/CTO, Sr. VP, Theresa K. Lee/Sr. VP, Chief Legal Officer, Corp. Sec./$1,716,877.00, Richard A. Lorraine/CFO, Sr. VP/$1,944,985.00, James P. Rogers/57/Pres., Head - Chemicals, Fibers Business Group/$2,616,557.00, Norris P. Sneed/Sr. VP - Human Resources, Communications, Public Affairs, Greg Riddle/Dir. - Investor Relations, Jennifer Bogni/Mgr. - Investor Relations, Curtis E. Espeland/43/VP, Chief Accounting Officer

Directors: Brian J. Ferguson/54/Chmn., CEO, Peter M. Wood/Dir., Renee J. Hornbaker/Dir., Thomas H. McLain/Dir., Donald W. Griffin/Dir., Stephen R. Demeritt/Dir., Robert M. Hernandez/Dir., David W. Raisbeck/Dir., Michael P. Connors/Dir., Howard L. Lance/Dir., Gary E. Anderson/Dir., Lewis M. Kling/Dir.

Owners: Peter M. Wood, Robert M. Hernandez, James P. Rogers, Theresa K. Lee, Insiders, Richard A. Lorraine, Thomas H. McLain, David W. Raisbeck, Michael P. Connors, Stephen R. Demeritt, Lewis M. Kling, Gregory O. Nelson, Renee J. Hornbaker, Howard L. Lance, Donald W. Griffin *(16 Owners included in Index)*

Financial Data: *Fiscal Year End:*12/31 *Latest Annual Data:* 12/31/2006

Year		Sales		Net Income	
2006		$7,450,000,000		$409,000,000	
2005		$7,059,000,000		$557,000,000	
2004		$6,580,000,000		$170,000,000	
Curr. Assets:	$2,422,000,000	Curr. Liab.:	$1,059,000,000	P/E Ratio:	14.58
Plant, Equip.:	$3,069,000,000	Total Liab.:	$4,144,000,000	Indic. Yr. Divd.:	$1.760
Total Assets:	$6,173,000,000	Net Worth:	$2,029,000,000	Debt/ Equity:	0.7577

Eastman Kodak Co

343 State St., Rochester, NY, 14650; *PH:* 1-800-698-3324; *Fax:* 1-585-724-1089; *http://* www.kodak.com

General - Incorporation .... NJ
Employees 40,900
Auditor .... PricewaterhouseCoopers LLP
Stk Agt .... Computershare Trust Co
Counsel .... NA
DUNS No. 00-220-6183

Stock- Price on:12/24/2007 .... $29.87
Stock Exchange .... NYSE
Ticker Symbol .... EK
Outstanding Shares 287,690,000
E.P.S .... NA
Shareholders .... NA

Business: The groups principle activities include developing, manufacturing and marketing consumer, professional, health and other imaging products and services. The group operates from United States.

Primary SIC and add'l.: 7384 3861

CIK No: 0000031235

Subsidiaries: Algotec Systems Ltd., Cinesite (Europe) Limited, Cinesite, Inc., Eastman Canada Company, Eastman Gelatine Corporation, Eastman Kodak Company, Eastman Kodak Holdings B.V., Eastman Kodak International Capital Company, Inc., Eastman Kodak SA, ENCAD, Inc., FPC, Inc., K.K. Kodak Information Systems, Kodak (Australasia) Pty. Ltd., Kodak (China) Company Limited, Kodak (China) Investment Company Ltd. 79 Subsidiaries included in the Index

Officers: Antonio M. Perez/Chmn., CEO/$8,374,300.00, Ying Yeh/Chmn., Pres. - North Asia Region, GM - External Affairs, Asia, VP, John O'Grady/Chmn. - Eastman Kodak SA, GM - Europe, Africa, Middle East, Consumer Digital Imaging Group, Film Products Group, VP, Gerard K. Meuchner/Dir. - Communications, Public Affairs, VP, Nicoletta A. Zongrone/GM - Worldwide Kiosk Systems, Services, Consumer Digital Imaging Group, VP, Antoinette McCorvey/Dir. - Investor Relations, Douglas J. Edwards/GM, VP - Prepress Consumables Graphic Communications Group, VP, Jeffrey W. Hayzlett/Chief Business Development Officer, VP, Judi Hess/GM - Enterprise Solutions, Graphic Communications Group, MD - Kodak Canada, VP, Dolores K. Kruchten/GM - Document Imaging, Graphic Communications Group, VP, Paul Walrath/Dir., COO - Worldwide Operations Film Products Group, VP, William G. Tompkins/GM - Motion Picture Film Group, Entertainment Imaging, VP, Frank S. Sklarsky/CFO, Exec. VP/$340,942.00, Mary Jane Hellyar/Pres. - Film, Photofinishing Systems Group, Sr. VP/$2,219,312.00, Michael Marsh/GM - Digital Capture Solutions, Kodak Health Group *(69 Officers included in Index)*

Directors: Antonio M. Perez/Chmn., CEO, John O'Grady/Chmn. - Eastman Kodak SA, GM - Europe, Africa, Middle East, Consumer Digital Imaging Group, Film Products Group, VP, Paul Walrath/Dir., COO - Worldwide Operations Film Products Group, VP, Martha Layne Collins/Dir., Michael J. Hawley/46/Dir., Delano E. Lewis/69/Dir., Richard S. Braddock/66/Dir., Timothy M. Donahue/59/Dir., Laura DAndrea Tyson/60/Dir., William H. Hernandez/59/Dir., Hector De J. Ruiz/62/Dir., Durk I. Jager/Dir., Debra L. Lee/53/Dir.

Owners: Paul H. O'Neil/0.00%, Robert H. Brust/0.15%, Private Capital Management, Inc./10.20%, James T. Langley/0.02%, Delano E. Lewis/0.00%, Legg Mason Capital Management, Inc./21.18%, Frank S. Sklarsky/0.02%, Debra L. Lee/0.01%, LLM LLC/2.85%, Insiders/0.84%, Philip J. Faraci/0.02%, Hector J. de Ruiz, FMR Corp./5.31%, Michael J. Hawley/0.00%, Martha Layne Collins/0.01% *(25 Owners included in Index)*

Financial Data: *Fiscal Year End:*12/31 *Latest Annual Data:* 12/31/2006

Year		Sales		Net Income	
2006		$13,274,000,000		-$601,000,000	
2005		$14,268,000,000		-$1,362,000,000	
2004		$13,517,000,000		$556,000,000	
Curr. Assets:	$5,557,000,000	Curr. Liab.:	$4,971,000,000		
Plant, Equip.:	$2,842,000,000	Total Liab.:	$12,911,000,000	Indic. Yr. Divd.:	NA
Total Assets:	$14,320,000,000	Net Worth:	$1,388,000,000	Debt/ Equity:	1.7044

EasyLink Services Corp

Formerly: Internet Commerce Corp
6025 The Corners Pkwy., Ste. 100, Norcross, GA, 30092; *PH:* 1-678-533-8000; *http://* www.icc.net

General - Incorporation	DE	**Stock**- Price on:12/24/2007	$3.46
Employees	134	Stock Exchange	NA
Auditor	Tauber & Balser, P.C	Ticker Symbol	NA
Stk Agt	American Stock Transfer & Trust Co.	Outstanding Shares	23,110,000
Counsel	Kramer, Levin, Naftalis & Frankel	E.P.S	$0.12
DUNS No.	79-111-0810	Shareholders	NA

Business: The group's principle activities are offering Internet based services for the e-commerce business-to-business communication services market. The operations of the group are conducted through three segments: icc.net: it delivers customers documents and data files using Internet and proprietary technology; service bureau: it manages and translates data of small and mid-sized companies and professional services: it facilitates development of operations of comprehensive business-to-business e-commerce solutions. Its trade marks are icc.net, infosafe, commercesense, edi mapping factory, ez-edi and upc. The customers of the group include pharmaceutical, publishing, office supplies, e-tailing, manufacturing and retail industries. The group markets products directly through sales force, indirectly through hub companies, seminars and trade shows.

Primary SIC and add'l.: 7379 7372 7375

CIK No: 0000894738

Subsidiaries: Enable Corp., The Kodiak Group, Inc.

Officers: Thomas J. Stallings/Dir., CEO, Glen E. Shipley/CFO, Arthur R. Medici/Dir., COO, Terri Deuel/Sr. VP - Customer Communications, Support, Service, Chief Marketing Officer, Jim Walsh/VP - Sales, Marketing, Rick Gooding/VP - Operations, John Mecke/VP - Global Product Management, Les Russell/VP - International

Directors: Thomas J. Stallings/Dir., CEO, Kim D. Cooke/Chmn., Donald R. Harkleroad/Dir., Paul D. Lapides/Dir., Joseph W. Zalewski/Dir., Richard J. Berman/Dir., John S. Simon/Dir., Arthur R. Medici/Dir., COO

Owners: Thomas J. Stallings/3.10%, Insiders/12.10%, Blue Water Venture Fund II, L.L.C/5.60%, Arthur R. Medici/2.40%, Donald R. Harkleroad/2.20%, Paul D. Lapides, James J. Walsh, Richard J. Berman/1.60%, John S. Simon, Teresa A. Deuel, Glen E. Shipley/1.10%, Kim D. Cooke, Joseph W. Zalewski

Financial Data: **Fiscal Year End:**07/31 **Latest Annual Data:** 7/31/2006

Year	Sales	Net Income
2006	$19,771,000	$2,976,000
2005	$16,705,000	$234,000
2004	$11,705,000	-$4,087,000

Curr. Assets:	$11,082,000	**Curr. Liab.:**	$2,097,000	**P/E Ratio:**	28.83
Plant, Equip.:	$1,114,000	**Total Liab.:**	$3,064,000	**Indic. Yr. Divd.:**	NA
Total Assets:	$23,644,000	**Net Worth:**	$20,580,000	**Debt/ Equity:**	NA

Eat At Joes Ltd

670 White Plains Rd., Ste. 120, Scarsdale, NY, 10583; *PH:* 1-914-725-2700

General - Incorporation	DE	**Stock**- Price on:12/24/2007	$0.018
Employees	12	Stock Exchange	OTC
Auditor	Robison, Hill & Co.	Ticker Symbol	JOES
Stk Agt	Signature Stock Transfer, Inc.	Outstanding Shares	45,050,000
Counsel	NA	E.P.S	-$0.01
DUNS No.	NA	Shareholders	NA

Business: The groups principle activities include developing, owning and operating theme restaurants. The group operates from the United States. The group's quarterly revenue for Sep '07 was 0.37 millions of USD.

Primary SIC and add'l.: 5812

CIK No: 0000829325

Subsidiaries: 1337855 Ontario Inc, 1398926 Ontario Inc, E.A.J. Cherry Hill Inc, E.A.J. Echelon Inc, E.A.J. Market East Inc, E.A.J. MO Inc, E.A.J. Neshaminy Inc, E.A.J. Owings Inc, E.A.J. PHL Airport Inc, E.A.J. PM Inc, E.A.J. Shoppes Inc, E.A.J. Syracuse Inc, E.A.J. Walnut Street Inc

Owners: Insiders/22.00%, Joseph Fiore/19.00%

Financial Data: **Fiscal Year End:**12/31 **Latest Annual Data:** 12/31/2006

Year	Sales	Net Income
2006	$1,427,000	-$466,000
2005	$1,294,000	-$428,000
2004	$1,255,000	-$468,000

Curr. Assets:	$1,100,000	**Curr. Liab.:**	$4,643,000		
Plant, Equip.:	$38,000	**Total Liab.:**	$4,643,000	**Indic. Yr. Divd.:**	NA
Total Assets:	$1,156,000	**Net Worth:**	-$3,487,000	**Debt/ Equity:**	NA

Eaton Corp

Eaton Ctr., 1111 Superior Ave., Cleveland, OH, 44114; *PH:* 1-216-523-5000; *Fax:* 1-216-523-4787; *http://* www.eaton.com; *Email:* customer@eaton.com

General - Incorporation	OH	**Stock**- Price on:12/24/2007	$94.03
Employees	60,000	Stock Exchange	NYSE
Auditor	Ernst & Young LLP	Ticker Symbol	ETN
Stk Agt	Mellon Investor Services LLC	Outstanding Shares	146,500,000
Counsel	NA	E.P.S	$6.51
DUNS No.	00-415-5818	Shareholders	NA

Business: The group's principle activity is to manufacture fluid power systems, electrical power quality, distribution and controls, automotive engine air management, and fuel economy and intelligent truck components for fuel economy and safety. The group operates through four segments namely fluid power, electrical power distribution systems, automotive and truck. The group operates from United States.

Primary SIC and add'l.: 3714 3625 3823

CIK No: 0000031277

Subsidiaries: Aeroquip (South Africa) Pty. Ltd., Aeroquip de Mexico S.A. de C.V., Aeroquip do Brasil, Ltda., Aeroquip Iberica S.L., Aeroquip International Inc., Aeroquip Ltd., Aeroquip Servicios S.A. de C.V., Aeroquip Singapore Pte. Limited, Aeroquip-Vickers Assurance Ltd., Aeroquip-Vickers Canada, Inc., Aeroquip-Vickers International Inc., Aeroquip-Vickers, Inc., CAPCO Automotive Products Corporation, Controladora Aeroquip-Vickers de Mexico S.A. de C.V., Cutler-Hammer Company 165 Subsidiaries included in the Index

Officers: Alexander M. Cutler/56/Chmn., CEO, Pres./$14,127,950.00, Stephen M. Buente/57/Sr. VP, Pres. - Automotive/$4,298,789.00, Richard H. Fearon/Exec. VP, Chief Financial, Planning Officer/$4,647,257.00, James E. Sweetnam/Sr. VP, Pres. - Truck Group/$4,051,521.00, Randy W. Carson/Sr. VP, Pres. - Electrical Group/$4,212,806.00, William W. Blausey/CIO, VP, Susan J. Cook/VP - Human Resources, Earl R. Franklin/VP, Sec., Richard D. Holder/VP - Eaton Business System, Donald J. McGrath/VP - Communications, Mark M. McGuire/VP, General Counsel, John S. Mitchell/VP - Taxes, Billie K. Rawot/VP, Controller, Ken D. Semelsberger/VP - Corporate Development, Treasury, Yannis P. Tsavalas/CTO, VP *(38 Officers included in Index)*

Directors: Alexander M. Cutler/56/Chmn., CEO, Pres., Michael J. Critelli/59/Dir., Ernie Green/69/Dir., Christopher M. Connor/51/Dir., Ned C. Lautenbach/64/Dir., Deborah L. McCoy/53/Dir., John R. Miller/70/Dir., Gregory R. Page/56/Dir., Victor A. Pelson/70/Dir., Gary L. Tooker/68/Dir., Charles E. Golden/61/Dir.

Owners: G. R. Page, J. E. Sweetnam, M. J. Critelli, A. M. Cutler, J. R. Miller, Barclays Global Investors,NA./8.59%, AXA Financial, Inc./5.80%, R. H. Fearon, C. M. Connor, N. C. Lautenbach, G. L. Tooker, D. L. McCoy, V. A. Pelson, C. E. Golden, E. Green *(19 Owners included in Index)*

Financial Data: **Fiscal Year End:**12/31 **Latest Annual Data:** 12/31/2006

Year	Sales	Net Income
2006	$12,370,000,000	$950,000,000
2005	$11,115,000,000	$805,000,000
2004	$9,817,000,000	$648,000,000

Curr. Assets:	$4,408,000,000	**Curr. Liab.:**	$3,407,000,000	**P/E Ratio:**	14.65
Plant, Equip.:	$2,271,000,000	**Total Liab.:**	$7,311,000,000	**Indic. Yr. Divd.:**	$1.720
Total Assets:	$11,417,000,000	**Net Worth:**	$4,106,000,000	**Debt/ Equity:**	NA

Eaton Vance Corp

The Eaton Vance Bldg., 255 State St., Boston, MA, 02109; *PH:* 1-617-482-8260; *Fax:* 1-617-482-2396; *http://* www.eatonvance.com

General - Incorporation	MD	**Stock**- Price on:12/24/2007	$44.74
Employees	869	Stock Exchange	NYSE
Auditor	Deloitte & Touche LLP	Ticker Symbol	EV
Stk Agt	EquiServe Trust Co N.A	Outstanding Shares	125,740,000
Counsel	NA	E.P.S	NA
DUNS No.	04-480-9994	Shareholders	NA

Business: The group's principal activities are creating, marketing and management of mutual funds, providing investment management and counseling services to institutions and individuals. The group provides investment advisory and administration services to 195 funds and to 1,648 separately managed individual and institutional accounts. The group markets and distributes offered shares of funds through a retail network of national and regional broker/dealers, banks, insurance companies and financial planning firms. On 10-Sep-2003, the group acquired 80% capital interest in parametric portfolio associates.

Primary SIC and add'l.: 6282 6091 6531

CIK No: 0000350797

Subsidiaries: Atlanta Capital Management Company, LLC, Boston Management and Research, Eaton Vance Acquisitions, Eaton Vance Distributors,Inc., Eaton Vance Investment Counsel, Eaton Vance Management, Eaton Vance Management (International) Limited, Fox Asset Management LLC, Parametric Portfolio Associates LLC

Officers: James B. Hawkes/65/Chmn., CEO, West G. Saltonstall/Pres., CEO - Eaton Vance Investment Counsel, Jeffrey P. Beale/51/VP, Chief Administrative Officer, Laurie G. Hylton/41/VP, Chief Accounting Officer, Edward P. Bliss/VP, Robert H. Bortnick/VP, Dexter A. Dodge/Sr. Advisor, Leonard F. Dolan/VP, William M. Steul/CFO, Barclay Tittmann/VP, Jonathan B. Treat/VP, Whiting R. Willauer/VP, Thomas E. Faust/49/Dir., Chief Investment Officer, Pres., Alan R. Dynner/67/VP, Sec., Chief Legal Officer, Duncan W. Richardson/50/Exec. VP, Chief Equity Investment Officer *(25 Officers included in Index)*

Directors: James B. Hawkes/65/Chmn., CEO, Dorothy E. Puhy/55/Dir., Thomas E. Faust/49/Dir., Chief Investment Officer, Pres., Ann E. Berman/55/Dir., Winthrop H. Smith/58/Dir., John G.L. Cabot/73/Dir., Leo I. Higdon/61/Dir., Vincent M. Oreilly/70/Dir.

Owners: Lisa Jones, Scott H. Page, West G. Saltonstall, Michael R. Mach, Robert J. Whelan, Thomas M. Metzold, Alan R. Dynner, Michael W. Weilheimer, Robert B. MacIntosh, Thomas E. Faust, Matthew J. Witkos, Cynthia J. Clemson, Judith A. Saryan, William M. Steul, Payson F. Swaffield *(18 Owners included in Index)*

Financial Data: **Fiscal Year End:**10/31 **Latest Annual Data:** 10/31/2006

Year	Sales	Net Income
2006	$862,194,000	$159,377,000
2005	$753,175,000	$159,884,000
2004	$661,813,000	$138,943,000

Curr. Assets:	$329,367,000	**Curr. Liab.:**	$139,645,000	**P/E Ratio:**	56.63
Plant, Equip.:	$21,495,000	**Total Liab.:**	$162,165,000	**Indic. Yr. Divd.:**	$0.480
Total Assets:	$668,195,000	**Net Worth:**	$496,485,000	**Debt/ Equity:**	NA

EAU Technologies Inc

Formerly: Electric Aquagenics Unlimited Inc
1890 Cobb International Blvd, Ste A, Kennesaw, GA, 30152; *PH:* 1-678-388-9492; *Fax:* 1-770-424-8684; *http://* www.eau-x.com; *Email:* gaylord@eau-x.com

General - Incorporation	DE	**Stock**- Price on:12/24/2007	NA
Employees	43	Stock Exchange	NA
Auditor	HJ & Assoc. LLC	Ticker Symbol	NA
Stk Agt	NA	Outstanding Shares	NA
Counsel	NA	E.P.S	NA
DUNS No.	NA	Shareholders	NA

Business: The groups principle activity is to provide water electrolysis technology. The groups Empowered Water(TM) technology produce electrolyzed oxidative water. The groups markets include agriculture, diary, meat and poultry processing, grocery and consumer products. The group operates from United States.

Primary SIC and add'l.: NA

CIK No: 0001170816

Subsidiaries: Equilease, Inc

Officers: Wade Bradley/CEO, Pres., Randall Waters/GM, Chris Anderson/Contact - Customer Service, Brian D. Heinhold/35/CFO, Doug Kindred/Sr. VP - Manufacturing, Randy K. Johnson/Dir., Sec., Laary Earle/Sr. VP - Live Processing, Joseph A. Stapley/Sr. VP - Investor Relations, Business Development

Directors: Leo J. Montgomery/Chmn., Ted Jacoby/Dir., Karl Helman/Dir., Peter F. Ullrich/Dir., Randy K. Johnson/Dir., Sec., William J. Warwick/Dir., Jay S. Potter/Dir.

Owners: Doug Kindred, William J. Warwick, Water Science, LLC., Larry Earle, Theodore C. Jacoby, Jay S. Potter, Joseph A. Stapley, Peter F. Ullrich, Wade R. Bradley, Insiders, Leo J. Montgomery

Curr. Assets:	$3,078,000	Curr. Liab.:	$2,116,000
Plant, Equip.:	$633,000	Total Liab.:	$8,868,000	Indic. Yr. Divd.:	NA
Total Assets:	$4,930,000	Net Worth:	-$3,939,000	Debt/ Equity:	NA

eAutoclaims Inc

110 E Douglas Rd., Oldsmar, FL, 34677; **PH:** 1-813-749-1020; **http://** www.eautoclaims.com

General - Incorporation	NV	**Stock** - Price on:12/24/2007	$0.12
Employees	80	Stock Exchange	OTC
Auditor	Goldstein Golub Kessler LLP	Ticker Symbol	EACC
Stk Agt	Equity Transfer Services Inc	Outstanding Shares	85,540,000
Counsel	NA	E.P.S.	-$0.01
DUNS No.	25-405-9397	Shareholders	NA

Business: The group's principal activity is to provide Internet based collision claims services for insurance companies, third party claims administrators (tpa) and self-insured automobile fleet management companies. The group serves automobile insurance and corporate automobile fleet management companies to streamline and lower their overall costs of automotive repairs paid. The group also handles the entire collision repair function for the customers from the time of reporting of the accident. The group monitors and audits all repair work to assure that proper repair work is performed at the negotiated price. The group provides the subscriber an interface which is a claims management tool for the elink software that is used by in-house staff claims handlers.

Primary SIC and add'l.: 7379 7538

CIK No: 0001034694

Officers: Jeffrey D. Dickson/65/Dir., CEO, Pres., Larry C. Colton/59/Dir., CFO, Donald Thomas/42/CIO

Directors: Jeffrey D. Dickson/65/Dir., CEO, Pres., Eric Seidel/45/Vice Chmn., William Austin Lewis/32/Chmn., Larry C. Colton/59/Dir., CFO, John K. Pennington/53/Dir., Christopher Korge/54/Dir.

Owners: Christopher Korge/7.66%, Eric Seidel/1.93%, John K. Pennington/0.70%, Jeffrey D. Dickson/2.12%, Insiders/45.81%, Canadian Advantage Limited Partnership/3.19%, Larry Colton/0.14%, Advantage (Bermuda) Fund, Ltd./1.18%, William Lewis/28.90%

Financial Data: Fiscal Year End:07/31 Latest Annual Data: 07/31/2007

Year	Sales	Net Income
2007	$11,791,000	-$379,000
2006	$15,621,000	-$1,612,000
2005	$14,651,000	-$2,444,000

Curr. Assets:	$2,157,000	Curr. Liab.:	$4,474,000
Plant, Equip.:	$672,000	Total Liab.:	$4,496,000	Indic. Yr. Divd.:	NA
Total Assets:	$3,962,000	Net Worth:	-$533,000	Debt/ Equity:	NA

Ebank Financial Services Inc

2410 Paces Ferry Rd., Ste. 190, Atlanta, GA, 30339; **PH:** 1-770-863-9225; **Fax:** 1-770-863-9228; **http://** www.ebank.com; **Email:** customerservice@ebank.com

General - Incorporation	GA	**Stock** - Price on:12/24/2007	$0.82
Employees	25	Stock Exchange	OTC
Auditor	Porter Keadle Moore LLP	Ticker Symbol	EBDC
Stk Agt	Continental Stock Transfer & Trust Co	Outstanding Shares	7,210,000
Counsel	NA	E.P.S.	NA
DUNS No.	NA	Shareholders	NA

Business: The group's principal activity is to provide banking and other financial services to small business and retail customers via the Internet. The services are provided through the offices in atlanta, Georgia. The group provides a broad array of financial products and services including checking accounts, money markets, cds, sweep accounts, ATM cards, home equity loans, mortgage loans, commercial loans, credit cards, bill payment services and human resource services.

Primary SIC and add'l.: 6712 6035

CIK No: 0001050725

Subsidiaries: ebank, a federal savings bank

Officers: James L. Box/Dir., CEO, Pres., Wayne W. Byers/CFO

Directors: James L. Box/Dir., CEO, Pres., Richard D. Jackson/Chmn., Gary M. Bremer/Dir., Terry L. Ferrero/Dir., Edward L. Terry/Dir., Paul C. Roberts/Dir.

Financial Data: Fiscal Year End:12/31 Latest Annual Data: 09/30/2006

Year	Sales	Net Income
2006	$2,672,000	-$25,000
2005	$2,456,000	$209,000
2004	$6,978,000	-$64,000

Curr. Assets:	$7,978,000	Curr. Liab.:	$107,169,000
Plant, Equip.:	$2,200,000	Total Liab.:	$116,169,000	Indic. Yr. Divd.:	NA
Total Assets:	$127,189,000	Net Worth:	$11,020,000	Debt/ Equity:	0.8351

eBay Inc

2145 Hamilton Ave., San Jose, CA, 95125; **PH:** 1-408-376-7400; **Fax:** 1-408-376-7401; **http://** www.ebay.com

General - Incorporation	DE	**Stock** - Price on:12/24/2007	$31.51
Employees	13,200	Stock Exchange	NDQ
Auditor	PricewaterhouseCoopers LLP	Ticker Symbol	EBAY
Stk Agt	Mellon Investor Services LLC	Outstanding Shares	1,360,000,000
Counsel	Cooley Godward LLP	E.P.S.	$0.12
DUNS No.	96-382-3786	Shareholders	NA

Business: The group's principle activity is to provide online marketplaces for the sale of goods and services. In the year 2007, the group acquired ViA-Online GmbH. The group operates from United States.

Primary SIC and add'l.: 7375 7374 5961 5999

CIK No: 0001065088

Subsidiaries: 111 Potrero Partners, LLC., A1 Markt B.V., Baazee.com Private Limited, Baazee.com, Inc., Blackthorne Software, Inc., CARad Inc., Confinity, Inc., DealTime (Europe) B.V., DealTime (Germany) GmbH, EachNet, Inc., EachNet.com (Hong Kong) Limited, EachNet.com Limited, EachNet.com Network Information Services (Shanghai) Co., Ltd., eBay Asia Pacific Regional Management Services Ltd., eBay Australia and New Zealand Pty Limited 57 Subsidiaries included in the Index

Officers: Meg Whitman/CEO, Pres. - Ebay/$15,741,040.00, Niklas Zennstrom/CEO, Rajan Mehra/39/Country Mgr., William C. Cobb/Pres. - Ebay North America, Elizabeth L. Axelrod/45/Sr. VP - Human Resources, Bob Swan/CFO, Sr. VP - Finance - Ebay/$3,482,719.00, Rajiv Dutta/Pres. - Paypal, Henry Gomez/Pres. - Skype, Eskander E. Kazim/42/Head - Strategic Initiatives, Michael Jacobson/Sr. VP, General Counsel - Ebay/$4,480,326.00, Beth Axelrod/Sr. VP - Human Resources, Ebay, John Donahoe/Pres. - Ebay Marketplaces/$5,831,461.00

Directors: Pierre M. Omidyar/Chmn., Founder - Ebay, Dawn G. Lepore/54/Dir., William C. Ford/50/Dir., Fred D. Anderson/63/Dir., Edward W. Barnholt/64/Dir., Thomas J. Tierney/54/Dir., Richard T. Schlosberg/64/Dir., Robert C. Kagle/52/Dir., Scott D. Cook/55/Dir., Philippe Bourguignon/60/Dir.

Owners: Rajiv Dutta, Pierre M. Omidyar/14.00%, Scott D. Cook, Philippe Bourguignon, Richard T. Schlosberg, John J. Donahoe, Robert H. Swan, Insiders/17.30%, Michael R. Jacobson, Robert C. Kagle, Dawn G. Lepore, Fred D. Anderson, Capital Research and Management Company/6.20%, William C. Ford, Thomas J. Tierney (17 Owners included in Index)

Financial Data: Fiscal Year End:12/31 Latest Annual Data: 12/31/2006

Year	Sales	Net Income
2006	$5,969,741,000	$1,125,639,000
2005	$4,552,401,000	$1,082,043,000
2004	$3,271,309,000	$778,223,000

Curr. Assets:	$4,970,586,000	Curr. Liab.:	$2,518,395,000	P/E Ratio:	31.83
Plant, Equip.:	$998,196,000	Total Liab.:	$2,589,379,000	Indic. Yr. Divd.:	NA
Total Assets:	$13,494,011,000	Net Worth:	$10,904,632,000	Debt/ Equity:	NA

Ebix Inc

5 Concourse Pkwy., Ste. 3200, Atlanta, GA, 30328; **PH:** 1-678-281-2020; **Fax:** 1-678-281-2019; **http://** www.ebix.com

General - Incorporation	DE	**Stock** - Price on:12/24/2007	$38.1
Employees	292	Stock Exchange	NDQ
Auditor	BDO Seidman LLP	Ticker Symbol	EBIX
Stk Agt	Mellon Investor Services LLC	Outstanding Shares	2,850,000
Counsel	NA	E.P.S.	$2.15
DUNS No.	08-270-3679	Shareholders	NA

Business: The group's principle activity is to provide software and Internet-based solutions for the insurance industry. It derives revenues from two segments: licensing and sale of software and professional and support services. The licensing and sale of software consists of proprietary software and third-party software. The professional services include consulting, implementation, training and project management provided to the group's customers. The professional services also include fees for software license maintenance, initial registration and ongoing monthly subscription fees from the ebixasp product, transaction fees generated from the ebix.mall Website, and business process outsourcing revenue. It also provides agency management product line comprising of a modular, state of the art, agency management solution providing flexibility and the ability to handle unstructured data and complex risk. The group's quarterly revenue for Sep'07 was 11.81 millions of USD.

Primary SIC and add'l.: 7372

CIK No: 0000814359

Subsidiaries: Canadian Insurance Computer Systems,Inc., Ebix Australia Pty. Ltd., Ebix Australia Pty. Ltd. (VIC), Ebix Information Systems International,Inc., Ebix Insurance Agency,Inc., Ebix New Zealand, Ebix New Zealand Holdings, Ebix Singapore PTE LTD, Ebix Software India, Private Limited, EIH Holdings AB, EIH Holdings KB, Mauritius Holdco

Officers: Robin Raina/41/Chmn., CEO, Pres., Graham Prior/Sr. VP - Agency Systems, Leon Dapice/MD - Ebix Australia, Tony Wisniewski/MD - Ebix New Zealand, Andy Wakefield/MD - Ebix Singapore, Richard J. Baum/CFO, Exec. VP, Sec., Tom Gill/GM - Ebix Europe, Robert Rinderman/Investor Relations Contact, David Collins/Investor Relations Contact

Directors: Robin Raina/41/Chmn., CEO, Pres., Hans U. Benz/60/Dir., Pavan Bhalla/43/Dir., Hans Ueli Keller/55/Dir., Neil D. Eckert/44/Dir., Rolf Herter/43/Dir.

Owners: Hans U. Benz, Rolf Herter, CF Epic Insurance and General Fund/8.10%, Hans Ueli Keller, Rennes Foundation/9.50%, BRiT Insurance Holdings PLC/25.20%, Neil D. Eckert, Richard J. Baum, Luxor Capital Group, LP/15.20%, Pavan Bhalla, Robin Raina/16.80%

Financial Data: Fiscal Year End:12/31 Latest Annual Data: 12/31/2006

Year	Sales	Net Income
2006	$29,253,000	$5,965,000
2005	$24,100,000	$4,322,000
2004	$19,983,000	$2,240,000

Curr. Assets:	$13,899,000	Curr. Liab.:	$20,008,000
Plant, Equip.:	$2,183,000	Total Liab.:	$21,186,000	Indic. Yr. Divd.:	NA
Total Assets:	$47,352,000	Net Worth:	$26,166,000	Debt/ Equity:	0.0360

Ecash Inc

140 Green Dr., Avilla, IN, 46710; **PH:** 1-651-452-1606; **Fax:** 1-260-897-2246; **http://** www.ecash-atm.com

General - Incorporation	DE	**Stock** - Price on:12/24/2007	$0.8
Employees	NA	Stock Exchange	OTC
Auditor	George Brenner, CPA	Ticker Symbol	ECSI
Stk Agt	Continental Stock T & T Co.	Outstanding Shares	NA
Counsel	NA	E.P.S.	NA
DUNS No.	NA	Shareholders	NA

Business: The groups principle activity is to provide ATM products and services. The group operates from United States.

Primary SIC and add'l.: 1700

CIK No: 0001083638

Subsidiaries: The Perma Grass Corporation

Officers: Michael D. Chermak/Chmn., CEO, Pres., Sec.

Directors: Michael D. Chermak/Chmn., CEO, Pres., Sec., John Relic/54/Dir., Lynn Dixon/49/Dir.

Owners: Lynn Dixon/0.10%, Michael Chermak/5.00%, Bridgetech Holdings International, Inc./72.50%, John Relic/5.00%, Insiders/10.10%

Financial Data: *Fiscal Year End:*12/31 *Latest Annual Data:* 12/31/2005

Year	Sales	Net Income
2005	$5,000	-$384,000
2004	$125,000	-$482,000

Curr. Assets:	NA	Curr. Liab.:	$800,000	P/E Ratio:	16.13
Plant, Equip.:	NA	Total Liab.:	$800,000	Indic. Yr. Divd.:	NA
Total Assets:	NA	Net Worth:	-$800,000	Debt/ Equity:	NA

ECB Bancorp Inc

35050 US Hwy. 264, Engelhard, NC, 27824; *PH:* 1-252-925-9411; *Fax:* 1-252-925-8491; *http://* www.ecbbancorp.com; *Email:* ecbonline@ecbbancorp.com

General - Incorporation	NC	**Stock** - Price on:12/24/2007	$30
Employees	195	Stock Exchange	NDQ
Auditor	Dixon Hughes PLLC	Ticker Symbol	ECBE
Stk Agt	First Citizens Bank & Trust Co	Outstanding Shares	2,920,000
Counsel	Davis & Davis	E.P.S	$1.69
DUNS No.	NA	Shareholders	NA

Business: The group's principal activity is to provide general, community-oriented commercial and consumer banking business to its customers through 19 full-service offices in North Carolina. The group operates through its wholly owned subsidiary, east carolina bank. The group's operations are primarily retail oriented and directed toward individuals, small and medium-sized businesses and local governmental units located in its banking markets. It provides construction loans, residential, commercial real estate, consumer installment, credit card, agricultural, commercial and industrial loans. It accepts deposit accounts that include business and individual checking accounts, savings accounts, now accounts, certificates of deposit and money market checking accounts.

Primary SIC and add'l.: 6022 6712

CIK No: 0001066254

Subsidiaries: ECB Financial Services, Inc., ECB Realty, Inc., ECB Statutory Trust I, The East Carolina Bank

Officers: Arthur H. Keeney/Dir., CEO, Pres./$552,075.00, Gary M. Adams/CFO, Sr. VP/$148,313.00, Dorson J. White/COO, Exec. VP/$234,794.00, Olin T. Davis/CCO, Sr. VP

Directors: Arthur H. Keeney/Dir., CEO, Pres., George Thomas Davis/Vice Chmn., R. S. Spencer/Chmn., Joseph T. Lamb/Dir., Gregory C. Gibbs/Dir., Michael D. Weeks/Dir., John F. Hughes/Dir., Bryant J. Kittrell/Dir., Martelle B. Marshall/Dir.

Owners: Insiders, OZ Master Fund, Ltd., Caxton Associates, LLC, OZ Management, LLC, Arthur H. Keeney, John F. Hughes, Dorson J. White, Gregory C. Gibbs, George T. Davis, Joseph T. Lamb, Bryant J. Kittrell, Gary M. Adams, Charles G. Gibbs, R. S. Spencer, Martelle B. Marshall *(19 Owners included in Index)*

Financial Data: *Fiscal Year End:*12/31 *Latest Annual Data:* 12/31/2006

Year	Sales	Net Income
2006	$42,769,000	$5,582,000
2005	$34,828,000	$4,853,000
2004	$28,932,000	$3,280,000

Curr. Assets:	$44,676,000	Curr. Liab.:	$545,717,000	P/E Ratio:	16.57
Plant, Equip.:	$23,042,000	Total Liab.:	$561,277,000	Indic. Yr. Divd.:	$0.700
Total Assets:	$624,070,000	Net Worth:	$62,793,000	Debt/ Equity:	NA

Echelon Corp

550 Meridian Ave., San Jose, CA, 95126; *PH:* 1-408-938-5200; *Fax:* 1-408-790-3800; *http://* www.echelon.com; *Email:* lonworks@echelon.com

General - Incorporation	DE	**Stock** - Price on:12/24/2007	$16.99
Employees	283	Stock Exchange	NDQ
Auditor	KPMG LLP	Ticker Symbol	ELON
Stk Agt	Mellon Investor Services LLC	Outstanding Shares	39,430,000
Counsel	Wilson Sonsini Goodrich & Rosati	E.P.S	-$0.59
DUNS No.	NA	Shareholders	NA

Business: The group's principal activities are to develop, market and support a wide range of hardware and software products and services for the control network industry. The group's products and services enable original equipment manufacturers (OEMs) and systems integrators to design and implement open, interoperable, distributed control networks. The products are based on lonworks networking technology. Lonworks technology is an open standard for interoperable networked control developed by the group. The services provided to customers include technical support and training courses covering its lonworks network technology and products. The group markets its products in North America, Europe, Japan, South America and Asia-pacific.

Primary SIC and add'l.: 3679 7373 3674 7372 3677

CIK No: 0000031347

Officers: Kenneth M. Oshman/Chmn., CEO/$608,493.00, Beatrice Yormark/Presiden, COO/$531,862.00, Chris Stanfield/Investor Relation Officer, Lars Rider/Contact - Employment, Julia O'Shaughnessy/Contact - Press Information, Allen Bruskirk/Dir. - Quality, Anders Axelsson/Sr. VP - Sales, Marketing, Russell Harris/Sr. VP - Operations, Oliver Stanfield/CFO, Exec. VP/$531,862.00, Frederik Bruggink/Sr. VP, GM - Service Provider Group/$559,007.00, Kathleen Bloch/Sr. VP, General Counsel/$452,631.00

Directors: Kenneth M. Oshman/Chmn., CEO, Armas Clifford Markkula/Vice Chmn., Betsy Rafael/Dir., Robert R. Maxfield/Dir., Richard M. Moley/Dir., Larry W. Sonsini/Dir., Robert J. Finocchio/Dir.

Owners: Beatrice Yormark/2.90%, Oliver R. Stanfield/2.60%, Armas Clifford Markkula/4.70%, Betsy Rafael, Capital Research and Management Company SMALLCAP World Fund, Inc./5.10%, Robert R. Maxfield/1.10%, Frederik H. Bruggink/1.30%, Robert J. Finocchio, Richard M. Moley, ENEL Investment Holding BV/7.60%, Kathleen B. Bloch, Larry W. Sonsini, Kenneth M. Oshman/15.10%, AMVESCAP PLC/6.40%, Insiders/28.90%

Financial Data: *Fiscal Year End:*12/31 *Latest Annual Data:* 12/31/2006

Year	Sales	Net Income
2006	$57,276,000	-$24,440,000
2005	$74,428,000	-$19,719,000
2004	$109,921,000	$5,272,000

Curr. Assets:	$170,853,000	Curr. Liab.:	$38,433,000		
Plant, Equip.:	$15,188,000	Total Liab.:	$39,701,000	Indic. Yr. Divd.:	NA
Total Assets:	$196,276,000	Net Worth:	$156,575,000	Debt/ Equity:	NA

Echo Healthcare Acquisition Corp

8000 Towers Crescent Dr., Ste. 1300, Vienna, VA, 22182; *PH:* 1-703-448-7688; *http://* www.echohealthcare.com

General - Incorporation		**Stock** - Price on:12/24/2007	$7.75
Employees	3	Stock Exchange	OTC
Auditor	NA	Ticker Symbol	EHHA
Stk Agt	Corporate Stock Transfer, Inc.	Outstanding Shares	8,750,000
Counsel	NA	E.P.S	-$0.08
DUNS No.	NA	Shareholders	NA

Business: The groups principle activity is to provide recruiting services. The groups service area includes the research and development, engineering, marketing, sales, information technology and manufacturing industries. The group operates from United States.

Primary SIC and add'l.: 7389

CIK No:

Officers: Gene Burleson/Chmn., CEO, Joel Kanter/Dir., Pres., Sec., Kevin Pendergest/Dir., CFO, Treasurer

Directors: Gene Burleson/Chmn., CEO, Joel Kanter/Dir., Pres., Sec., Kevin Pendergest/Dir., CFO, Treasurer, Eugene A. Bauer/Dir., Gary A. Brukardt/Dir., Alastair Clemow/Dir., Richard O. Martin/Dir.

Financial Data: *Fiscal Year End:*NA *Latest Annual Data:* 12/31/2006

Year	Sales	Net Income
2006	NA	$526,000

Curr. Assets:	$67,000	Curr. Liab.:	$9,188,000	P/E Ratio:	2.70
Plant, Equip.:	NA	Total Liab.:	$20,451,000	Indic. Yr. Divd.:	NA
Total Assets:	$56,756,000	Net Worth:	$36,304,000	Debt/ Equity:	NA

Echo Resources Inc

500 Australian Ave. S, Ste. 619, West Palm Beach, FL, 33401; *PH:* 1-561-514-0194

General - Incorporation	DE	**Stock** - Price on:12/24/2007	$1.5
Employees	NA	Stock Exchange	OTC
Auditor	Pollard-kelley Auditing Services, Inc	Ticker Symbol	ECHR
Stk Agt	American Securities T & T Inc.	Outstanding Shares	5,540,000
Counsel	NA	E.P.S	-$0.01
DUNS No.	NA	Shareholders	NA

Business: The group's principle activity is to operate metals and minerals mining industries with an emphasis on gold mining activities. In 2003, the group has changed its business from marketing and distribution of English language learning programmes to focus on the precious metal and mineral mining industries. The group operates from United States.

Primary SIC and add'l.: 1041

CIK No: 0001084899

Officers: Pieter Durand/41/Dir., CEO, Pres., Sec., CFO

Directors: Pieter Durand/41/Dir., CEO, Pres., Sec., CFO

Owners: Insiders/54.20%, Gala Enterprises Ltd./54.20%

Financial Data: *Fiscal Year End:*12/31 *Latest Annual Data:* 12/31/2006

Year	Sales	Net Income
2006	NA	-$79,000
2005	NA	-$188,000
2004	NA	-$28,000

Curr. Assets:	$8,000	Curr. Liab.:	$173,000		
Plant, Equip.:	NA	Total Liab.:	$173,000	Indic. Yr. Divd.:	NA
Total Assets:	$58,000	Net Worth:	-$116,000	Debt/ Equity:	NA

Echo Therapeutics Inc

Formerly: Sontra Medical Corp

10 Forge Pk.way, Franklin, MA, 02038; *PH:* 1-508-553-8850; *http://* www.sontra.com

General - Incorporation	MN	**Stock** - Price on:12/24/2007	NA
Employees	21	Stock Exchange	OTC
Auditor	Wolf & Co. P.C	Ticker Symbol	SONT
Stk Agt	Wells Fargo Shareowner Services	Outstanding Shares	NA
Couns	Thomas B. Rosedale BRL Law Group LLC	E.P.S	NA
DUNS No.	60-895-3162	Shareholders	NA

Business: The group's principal activity is research and development of transdermal diagnostic and drug delivery products. The group's product sonoprep (R), a non-invasive ultrasound mediated skin permeation technology for medical and therapeutic applications including transdermal diagnostics and the enhanced delivery of drugs through the skin. Sonoprep(R) skin permeation device, makes the skin permeable for up to 24 hours by applying ultrasonic energy to skin for 5-15 seconds, to be used in conjunction with all of our product applications.

Primary SIC and add'l.: 5047 8731

CIK No: 0001031927

Subsidiaries: ChoiceTel, Sontra Medical, Inc.

Officers: Harry G. Mitchell/CEO, CFO, Treasurer/$125,670.00, Kathy Dickinson/Dir. - Clinical Research, Scott Kellogg/VP - Engineering, Barry Marston/VP - Sales, Marketing, Han Chuang/Dir. - Research, Development, Karen Cowgill/Controller, Skip Farinha/VP - Operations, Regulatory Affairs

Directors: Michael R. Wigley/Chmn., Joseph F. Amaral/Dir., Gerard E. Puorro/Dir., Gary S. Kohler/Dir., Robert S. Langer/Dir., Brian F. Sullivan/Dir., Walter Witoshkin/Dir.

Owners: Cipher 06 LLC/6.30%, Joseph F. Amaral, Robert S. Langer/4.10%, Thomas W. Davison, Michael R. Wigley/9.90%, Sean F. Moran, Brian F. Sullivan, Matthew Balk/24.30%, Gerard E. Puorro/2.80%, Walter W. Witoshkin/1.20%, Harry G. Mitchell/2.50%, Insiders/20.00%

Echostar Communications Corp

9601 S Meridian Blvd., Englewood, CO, 80112; *PH:* 1-303-723-1000; *Fax:* 1-303-723-1999; *http://* www.dishnetwork.com

General - Incorporation	NV	**Stock**- Price on:12/24/2007	$43.57
Employees	21,000	Stock Exchange	NDQ
Auditor	KPMG LLP	Ticker Symbol	DISH
Stk Agt	Computershare Trust Co	Outstanding Shares	446,770,000
Counsel	Sullivan & Cromwell	E.P.S	$1.50
DUNS No.	82-702-8143	Shareholders	NA

Business: The groups principle activity is to provide satellite digital television. In the year 2007, the group acquired Sling Media, Inc. The group operates from United States.

Primary SIC and add'l.: 4899 3663 4841

CIK No: 0001001082

Subsidiaries: Echosphere LLC, EchoStar DBS Corporation, EchoStar Orbital Corporation, EchoStar Orbital Corporation II, EchoStar Satellite LLC, EchoStar Technologies Corporation

Officers: Charles W. Ergen/Chmn., CEO, Founder/$2,821,053.00, Carl Vogel/Vice Chmn., Pres./$2,828,427.00, Steven B. Schaver/Pres. - Echostar International, Michael T. Dugan/Dir., Sr. Advisor, Michael Kelly/Exec. VP - Commercial, Business Services, James Defranco/Dir., Exec. VP - Sales, Distribution, Mark Jackson/Pres. - Echostar Technologies Corporation, David K. Moskowitz/Dir., Exec. VP, General Counsel, Sec./$1,832,587.00, Nolan O. Daines/48/Exec. VP - Strategic Initiatives/$1,615,608.00, David J. Rayner/Exec. VP - Installation, Service Network, Stephen Wood/Exec. VP - Human Resources, Bernard L. Han/CFO, Exec. VP, Stanton R. Dodge/Exec. VP, General Counsel, Sec., Thomas A. Cullen/48/Exec. VP - Corporate Development, Carol Kline/Exec. VP - Operations

Directors: Charles W. Ergen/Chmn., CEO, Founder, Carl Vogel/Vice Chmn., Pres., Michael T. Dugan/Dir., Sr. Advisor, Steven J. Goodbarn/Dir., Cantey Ergen/Dir., James Defranco/Dir., Exec. VP - Sales, Distribution, David K. Moskowitz/Dir., Exec. VP, General Counsel, Sec., Michael C. Schroeder/Dir., Gary S. Howard/Dir., Tom A. Ortolf/Dir.

Owners: Charles W. Ergen, Bernard L. Han, David J. Rayner, Michael T. Dugan, Insiders, Steven R. Goodbarn, James DeFranco, Barclays Global Investors, NA., Nolan O. Daines, Charles W. Ergen, Tom A. Ortolf, Insiders, Carl E. Vogel, Dodge & Cox, Cantey Ergen *(22 Owners included in Index)*

Financial Data: ***Fiscal Year End:***12/31 ***Latest Annual Data:*** 12/31/2006

Year	*Sales*	*Net Income*
2006	$9,818,486,000	$608,272,000
2005	$8,425,501,000	$1,514,540,000
2004	$7,151,216,000	$214,769,000

Curr. Assets:	$4,599,541,000	***Curr. Liab.:***	$3,591,474,000	***P/E Ratio:***	29.05
Plant, Equip.:	$3,765,596,000	***Total Liab.:***	$9,988,079,000	***Indic. Yr. Divd.:***	NA
Total Assets:	$9,768,696,000	***Net Worth:***	-$219,383,000	***Debt/ Equity:***	NA

Echostar Dbs Corp

9601 S Meridian Blvd, Englewood, CO, 80112; ***PH:*** 1-303-723-1000; ***http://*** www.dishnetwork.com

General - Incorporation	CO	**Stock**- Price on:12/24/2007	$44.155
Employees	21,000	Stock Exchange	NA
Auditor	KPMG LLP	Ticker Symbol	NA
Stk Agt	Computershare Trust Co	Outstanding Shares	446,770,000
Counsel	NA	E.P.S	$1.50
DUNS No.	NA	Shareholders	NA

Business: The group's principle activity is to broadcast satellite programming services in the United States. The group operates from United States.

Primary SIC and add'l.: 4841

CIK No: 0001042642

Subsidiaries: EchoStar Communications Corporation, EchoStar DBS Corporation, EchoStar International Corporation, EchoStar Orbital Corporation (EOC), EIC, EOC II, ETC, Nagra USA, Satellite Communications Operating Corporation, Transponder Encryption Services Corporation

Financial Data: ***Fiscal Year End:***12/31 ***Latest Annual Data:*** 12/31/2006

Year	*Sales*	*Net Income*
2006	$9,818,486,000	$608,272,000
2005	$8,425,501,000	$1,514,540,000
2004	$7,151,216,000	$214,769,000

Curr. Assets:	$4,599,541,000	***Curr. Liab.:***	$3,591,474,000	***P/E Ratio:***	29.44
Plant, Equip.:	$3,765,596,000	***Total Liab.:***	$9,988,079,000	***Indic. Yr. Divd.:***	NA
Total Assets:	$9,768,696,000	***Net Worth:***	-$219,383,000	***Debt/ Equity:***	NA

ECI Telecom Ltd

30 Hasivim St., Petah Tikva, 49133; ; ***http://*** www.ecitele.com

General - Incorporation	Israel	**Stock**- Price on:12/24/2007	$9.11
Employees	NA	Stock Exchange	NA
Auditor	Somekh Chaikin	Ticker Symbol	NA
Stk Agt	American Stock Transfer & Trust Co.	Outstanding Shares	119,620,000
Counsel	Goldfarb, Levy, Eran & Co	E.P.S	$0.31
DUNS No.	60-000-7900	Shareholders	NA

Business: The group's principle activities are the design, development, manufacture, marketing and support of network solutions for digital telecommunications networks. Its hardware and software products create and manage bandwidth, maximize revenues for network operators, reduce operating expenses, provide capacity expansion, improve performance and enable new revenue-producing services, such as voice, data, video and multimedia services.

Primary SIC and add'l.: 3663 3357 3661 4899 4812 4813

CIK No: 0000701544

Subsidiaries: ECI De Mexico, S.A. de C.V., ECI Network Solutions B.V., ECI Telecom (AUS) Pty Limited, ECI Telecom (HK) Limited, ECI Telecom (Philippines) Inc., ECI Telecom (UK) Limited, ECI Telecom 2005 LLC., ECI Telecom Costa Rica, S.A., ECI Telecom De Colombia Finanzas Ltda., ECI Telecom DND, Inc., ECI Telecom Do Brasil Ltda., ECI Telecom GmbH, ECI Telecom Holdings B.V., ECI Telecom India Private Limited, ECI Telecom Italy SrL 29 Subsidiaries included in the Index

Officers: Rafi Maor/CEO, Pres., Amnon Shachar/56/Corporate VP - Global Resources, Giora Bitan/53/CFO, Exec. VP, Avi Cohen/COO, Dan Eisner/46/Exec. VP, GM - Broadband Access Division, Eyal Shaked/Exec. VP, GM - Optical Networks Division, Ido Gur/Exec. VP - Global Sales, Marketing, Dror Nahumi/Exec. VP, Chief Strategy Officer, Laura Howard/Chief Marketing Officer, Tony Scarfo/Exec. VP, GM - Networking Division, Itzik Zion/Exec. VP, Dave Robison/Contact - Americas, Joop Van Aard/Contact - EMEA HQ, UK, Avi Tenenbaum/Contact - Asia Pacific HQ, Boris Mirkin/Contact - FSU HQ, Israel *(18 Officers included in Index)*

Directors: Shlomo Dovrat/Chmn., Gerd Tenzer/Dir., Yocheved Dvir/Dir., Craig Ehrlich/Dir., Colin R. Green/Dir., Michael J. Anghel/Dir., Raanan Cohen/Dir., Eyal Desheh/Dir., Niel Ransom/Dir., Casimir Skrzypczak/Dir., Jonathan B. Kolber/Dir., Avraham Fischer/Dir.

Owners: Clal Electronics Industries Ltd./12.70%, Manning & Napier Advisors, Inc./5.70%, M.A.G.M. Chemistry Holdings Ltd/27.60%, Other Entities within the IDB Group/0.20%, IDB Holding Corporation Ltd./40.60%, Ofer (Ships Holding) Ltd./5.90%

Financial Data: ***Fiscal Year End:***12/31 ***Latest Annual Data:*** 3/31/2006

Year	*Sales*	*Net Income*
2006	$656,342,000	$22,095,000
2005	$629,918,000	$39,864,000
2004	$496,712,000	$10,153,000

Curr. Assets:	$565,196,000	***Curr. Liab.:***	$203,376,000		
Plant, Equip.:	$123,892,000	***Total Liab.:***	$248,025,000	***Indic. Yr. Divd.:***	NA
Total Assets:	$895,880,000	***Net Worth:***	$643,711,000	***Debt/ Equity:***	NA

Eclipsys Corp

200 Ashford Ctr. N, Atlanta, GA, 30338; ***PH:*** 1-404-847-5000; ***Fax:*** 1-404-847-5700; ***http://*** www.eclipsys.com; ***Email:*** info@eclipsys.com

General - Incorporation	DE	**Stock**- Price on:12/24/2007	$20.5
Employees	2,220	Stock Exchange	NDQ
Auditor	PricewaterhouseCoopers LLP	Ticker Symbol	ECLP
Stk Agt	EquiServe Trust Co N.A	Outstanding Shares	53,060,000
Counsel	NA	E.P.S	$0.34
DUNS No.	03-696-8709	Shareholders	NA

Business: The group's principal activity is to provide healthcare information technology solutions. The products of the group include sunrise clinical manager, sunrise access manager, sunrise record manager, sunrise erp manager, sunrise decision support manager. The group provides services including implementation, integration, support, maintenance and training, outsourcing, remote hosting, networking technologies and other related services. The services are provided on an integrated basis in clinical management, access management, patient financial management, health information management, strategic decision support and resource planning management. In Mar 2004, the group acquired cpm resource center, which improve and enhance the care process.

Primary SIC and add'l.: 7372 7379

CIK No: 0001034088

Subsidiaries: Eclipsys International Corp, Eclipsys Solutions Corp., Eclipsys Technologies Corporation, HVision, Inc

Officers: Andrew R. Eckert/46/Dir., CEO, Pres./$2,794,733.00, John Gomez/Exec. VP, Chief Technology Strategy Officer/$1,674,150.00, Frank Stearns/Sr. VP - Professional Services/$791,054.00, Robert J. Colletti/Sr. VP, CFO/$672,536.00, Brian W. Copple/Chief Legal Officer, General Counsel, Corp. Sec., Jay Deady/Exec. VP - Customer Solutions/$2,296,690.00, Jan Smith/Sr. VP - Human Resources, Lillian Vassilatos/Primary Investor Relations Officer, Nitin Deshpande/Pres. - Eclipsys India, John McAuley/GM, Sr. VP - Outsourcing, Joe Petro/Sr. VP - Product Development

Directors: Andrew R. Eckert/46/Dir., CEO, Pres., Eugene V. Fife/65/Chmn., Dan Crippen/Dir., Braden R. Kelly/Dir., Steven A. Denning/Dir., Edward A. Kangas/Dir., Jay B. Pieper/Dir.

Owners: Braden R. Kelly, FMR Corp./5.40%, Robert J. Colletti, John P. Gomez, Eugene V. Fife, Insiders/13.80%, Thornburg Investment Management, Inc./14.90%, Edward A. Kangas, Frank E. Stearns, Andrew R. Eckert, Dan L. Crippen, Jay B. Pieper/1.70%, Investment entities affiliated with General Atlantic LLC/8.90%, Tremblant Capital Group/5.30%, John A. Adams *(17 Owners included in Index)*

Financial Data: ***Fiscal Year End:***12/31 ***Latest Annual Data:*** 12/31/2006

Year	*Sales*	*Net Income*
2006	$427,542,000	$4,093,000
2005	$383,271,000	$485,000
2004	$309,075,000	-$32,565,000

Curr. Assets:	$249,683,000	***Curr. Liab.:***	$160,086,000	***P/E Ratio:***	60.29
Plant, Equip.:	$45,806,000	***Total Liab.:***	$172,622,000	***Indic. Yr. Divd.:***	NA
Total Assets:	$363,278,000	***Net Worth:***	$190,656,000	***Debt/ Equity:***	NA

Eco Depot Inc

1326 E Sprague Ave., Spokane, WA, 99202; ***PH:*** 1-509-924-8803; ***Fax:*** 1-866-378-0344; ***http://*** www.ecodepotinc.com; ***Email:*** info@ecodepotinc.com

General - Incorporation	NV	**Stock**- Price on:12/24/2007	NA
Employees	NA	Stock Exchange	OTC
Auditor	Kyle L. Tingle, CPA, LLC	Ticker Symbol	ECDP
Stk Agt	NA	Outstanding Shares	NA
Counsel	NA	E.P.S	NA
DUNS No.	NA	Shareholders	NA

Business: The groups principal activities include developing and marketing an e-commerce enabled website. The group operates from the United States.

Primary SIC and add'l.: 5084

CIK No: 0001337261

Officers: Sheldon Gold/59/Chmn., CEO, CFO, Pres., Nadine Sullivan/Pres., Eco Product Specialist, Bruce Gage/Solar, Wind Consultant, Eco Product Specialist, Glenn Probert/Marketing, Julia McHugh/Interiors Eco Product Specialist

Directors: Sheldon Gold/59/Chmn., CEO, CFO, Pres.

Owners: Halston Capital, Ltd./65.80%

Eco2 Plastics Inc

Formerly: ITec Environmental

5300 Claus Rd., Riverbank, CA, 95367; ***PH:*** 1-209-848-3900; ***http://*** www.eco2plastics.com

General - Incorporation	DE	**Stock**- Price on:12/24/2007	NA
Employees	NA	Stock Exchange	NA
Auditor	Salberg & Co., P.A	Ticker Symbol	NA
Stk Agt	NA	Outstanding Shares	NA
Counsel	NA	E.P.S	NA
DUNS No.	NA	Shareholders	NA

Business: The groups principle activity is to develop the revolutionary patent pending process and system. The product of the group is ECO2 environmental system. The group operates from the United States.

Primary SIC and add'l.: 4955

CIK No: 0000855372

Subsidiaries: Environmental Systems, Inc

Officers: Rodney S. Rougelot/44/Dir., CEO, Interim CFO, Gary M. De Laurentiis/Dir., CTO, Mario Sandoval/COO, Paul Dittmeier/VP - Sales, Marketing, Randall Reed/VP - Engineering

Directors: Rodney S. Rougelot/44/Dir., CEO, Interim CFO, William L. Whittaker/Chmn., Ronald Domingue/Dir., Roy Herberger/Dir., Gary M. De Laurentiis/Dir., CTO, David M. Otto/Dir., Lawrence A. Krause/Dir.

Owners: Mario Sandoval/4.00%, Lawrence A. Krause/5.00%, Rodney S. Rougelot/9.00%, Gary De Laurentiis/7.00%, Jerjis T. Alajaji/4.00%, Todd Greenhalgh/4.00%, David M. Otto/6.00%, Insiders/85.00%, Excipio Group, S.A./4.00%, William Whittaker/20.00%, Frederick W. Smith, Ronald M. Domingue/20.00%, Voting Trustee/6.00%

Financial Data: **Fiscal Year End:**12/31 **Latest Annual Data:** 12/31/2006

Year	Sales	Net Income
2006	$61,000	-$20,760,000
2005	NA	-$15,325,000
2004	$2,000	-$2,238,000

Curr. Assets:	$1,616,000	**Curr. Liab.:**	$4,830,000		
Plant, Equip.:	$5,894,000	**Total Liab.:**	$7,553,000	**Indic. Yr. Divd.:**	NA
Total Assets:	$10,283,000	**Net Worth:**	$2,730,000	**Debt/ Equity:**	NA

Ecolab Inc

370 Wabasha St. N, St. Paul, MN, 55102; ***PH:*** 1-651-293-2233; ***Fax:*** 1-651-293-2092; ***http://*** www.ecolab.com

General - Incorporation	DE	**Stock**- Price on:12/24/2007	$43.82
Employees	23,130	Stock Exchange	NYSE
Auditor	PricewaterhouseCoopers LLP	Ticker Symbol	ECL
Stk Agt	Computershare Investor Services LLC	Outstanding Shares	246,860,000
Counsel	NA	E.P.S	$1.48
DUNS No.	00-615-4611	Shareholders	NA

Business: The group's principle activities include developing and marketing products and services. The group provides cleaning, sanitizing, pest elimination, maintenance and repair products, systems and services. The groups servicing areas include the hospitality, foodservice, institutional and industrial markets. The groups products sold under the brand names Kay, Airkem and Huntington. The group operates from United States.

Primary SIC and add'l.: 5087 2841 2842 3589 5169

CIK No: 0000031462

Subsidiaries: ABP SAS, AEDES SAS, Aidamort SAS, Alpha Holding SAS, Amboile Services SAS, Amperia SARL, Artois Chimie SAS, Associated Chemicals & Services, Inc., Bionagro Natureprodukte GmbH, Biophyte SARL, Centre Rgional de Dsinfectisation et de Dratisation SAS, Daydots Inc., Eclab Export Limited, Ecolab (Antigua) Ltd., Ecolab (Barbados) Limited 159 Subsidiaries included in the Index

Officers: Douglas M. Baker/Chmn., CEO, Pres./$6,558,393.00, James H. White/Sr. VP - Strategy, Marketing Development, Lawrence T. Bell/Sr. VP, General Counsel, Sec., Thomas W. Handley/Exec. VP - Industrial Sector, Daniel J. Schmechel/Sr. VP, Controller, Diana D. Lewis/Sr. VP - Human Resources, James A. Miller/Exec. VP - Institutional Sector North America, Phillip J. Mason/Exec. VP - Asia Pacific, Latin America, Steven L. Fritze/CFO, Exec. VP/$2,213,336.00, Carol McDonald/Contact - Martinsburg Plant, Lynda Lundry/Contact - San Jose Plant, Keith Kurich/Contact - South Beloit Plant, Scott Lang/Contact - South Beloit Plant, Shelley Baldridge/Contact - Warren Plant, Angela M. Busch/VP - Corporate Development *(33 Officers included in Index)*

Directors: Douglas M. Baker/Chmn., CEO, Pres., Leslie S. Biller/Dir., Robert L. Lumpkins/Dir., Joel W. Johnson/Dir., Jerry W. Levin/Dir., Jerry A. Grundhofer/Dir., Beth M. Pritchard/Dir., Stefan Hamelmann/Dir., Richard U. De Schutter/Dir., Kasper Rorsted/Dir., John J. Zillmer/Dir., Hans Van Bylen/Dir.

Owners: Richard U. De Schutter, Kasper Rorsted, Henkel Corporation/11.60%, Lawrence T. Bell, Edward C. Johnson/5.70%, Beth M. Pritchard, Jerry A. Grundhofer, John J. Zillmer, Douglas M. Baker, James A. Miller, Robert L. Lumpkins, Jerry W. Levin, Joel W. Johnson, William C. Snedeker, Stefan Hamelmann *(19 Owners included in Index)*

Financial Data: **Fiscal Year End:**12/31 **Latest Annual Data:** 12/31/2006

Year	Sales	Net Income
2006	$4,895,814,000	$368,615,000
2005	$4,534,832,000	$319,481,000
2004	$4,184,933,000	$310,488,000

Curr. Assets:	$1,853,557,000	**Curr. Liab.:**	$1,502,730,000	**P/E Ratio:**	29.61
Plant, Equip.:	$951,569,000	**Total Liab.:**	$2,739,135,000	**Indic. Yr. Divd.:**	$0.460
Total Assets:	$4,419,365,000	**Net Worth:**	$1,680,230,000	**Debt/ Equity:**	0.3480

Ecolocap Solutions Inc

Formerly: XL Generation International Inc

353, St-nicolas St., Ste. 205, Montreal, QC, H2Y 2P1; ***PH:*** 1-514-397-0575

General - Incorporation	NV	**Stock**- Price on:12/24/2007	$0.61
Employees	NA	Stock Exchange	NA
Auditor	Paritz & Company, P.A.	Ticker Symbol	NA
Stk Agt	Pacific Stock Transfer Company	Outstanding Shares	NA
Counsel	NA	E.P.S	NA
DUNS No.	NA	Shareholders	NA

Business: The groups principle activity is a manufacturer of an artificial sport surface. The groups product is designed to reduce accidents while reproducing the natural feeling of playing on grass. The group operates from the United States.

Primary SIC and add'l.: 3990

CIK No: 0001290506

Subsidiaries: XL Generation AG, XL Generation International Canada Inc.

Officers: Michel St. Pierre/45/Acting CFO

Directors: Alexander C. Gilmour/76/Chmn., Claude Pellerin/38/Dir., Albert Beerli/66/Dir., Arthur Rawl/66/Dir.

Owners: Michel St-Pierre/1.69%, DT Crystal Holdings Ltd./39.36%, Insiders/7.14%, Albert Beerli/4.50%, Arthur Rawl, Claude Pellerin, CEDE, Inc./29.57%, Capex Investments Limited/6.25%, Alexander Gilmour

Financial Data: **Fiscal Year End:**12/31 **Latest Annual Data:** 12/31/2006

Year	Sales	Net Income
2006	$4,846,000	-$17,748,000
2005	NA	-$29,000

Curr. Assets:	$79,000	**Curr. Liab.:**	$3,000		
Plant, Equip.:	NA	**Total Liab.:**	$3,000	**Indic. Yr. Divd.:**	NA
Total Assets:	$79,000	**Net Worth:**	$76,000	**Debt/ Equity:**	NA

Ecoloclean Industries Inc

2242 S Hwy 83, Crystal City, TX, 78839; ***PH:*** 1-830-374-9100; ***Fax:*** 1-830-374-0202; ***http://*** www.ecoloclean.com; ***Email:*** barry@grosscapital.com

General - Incorporation	NV	**Stock**- Price on:12/24/2007	NA
Employees	11	Stock Exchange	OTC
Auditor	Baum & Co. P.A	Ticker Symbol	ECCI
Stk Agt	Signature Stock Transfer, Inc.	Outstanding Shares	NA
Counsel	NA	E.P.S	-$0.041
DUNS No.	NA	Shareholders	NA

Business: The group's principal activity is to process the liquid waste, remove contaminants and dispose of the treated liquid waste as required by applicable regulations. Electrocoagulation process is a non-chemical additive electrochemical system used in commercial water treatment. The electrocoagulation unit places an electrical charge in the waste fluid which destabilizes suspended material electrochemically and causes the coagulation of the dissolved and suspended contaminants.

Primary SIC and add'l.: 9511

CIK No: 0001161165

Subsidiaries: Aquatronics Industries, Inc., Ecoloclean of Texas, Inc., Ecoloclean, Inc., Reliant Drilling Systems, Inc, World Environmental Technologies, Inc.

Officers: Royis Ward/Investor Relations Officer

Financial Data: **Fiscal Year End:**12/31 **Latest Annual Data:** 12/31/2005

Year	Sales	Net Income
2005	$388,000	-$2,173,000
2004	$922,000	-$2,739,000
2003	$330,000	-$794,000

Curr. Assets:	$289,000	**Curr. Liab.:**	$1,541,000		
Plant, Equip.:	$364,000	**Total Liab.:**	$2,858,000	**Indic. Yr. Divd.:**	NA
Total Assets:	$983,000	**Net Worth:**	-$1,875,000	**Debt/ Equity:**	NA

Ecology & Environment Inc

Buffalo Corporate Ctr., 368 Pleasant View Dr., Lancaster, NY, 14086; ***PH:*** 1-716-684-8060; ***Fax:*** 1-716-684-0844; ***http://*** www.ecolen.com

General - Incorporation	NY	**Stock**- Price on:12/24/2007	$13
Employees	801	Stock Exchange	AMEX
Auditor	Schneider Downs & Co., Inc	Ticker Symbol	EEI
Stk Agt	American Stock Transfer & Trust Co.	Outstanding Shares	4,030,000
Counsel	Gross, Shuman, Brizdle & Gilfillan	E.P.S	$0.74
DUNS No.	05-864-8312	Shareholders	NA

Business: The group's principal activity is to provide broad based environmental consulting and testing services. The group provides professional services worldwide to enable sustainable economic and human development with minimum negative impact on the environment. The group operates through three segments: consulting services, analytical laboratory services and aquaculture. Consulting services provides environmental audits and impact assessments; terrestrial, aquatic and marine surveys; air and water quality management, environmental engineering and infrastructure planning and other related services. Analytical laboratory provides analytical testing services to industrial and governmental clients for the analysis of waste, soil, air and sediment samples. Aquaculture produces and markets shrimp and tilapia in Costa Rica.

Primary SIC and add'l.: 0919 8734 9511

CIK No: 0000809933

Subsidiaries: American Arab Aquaculture Company, Beijing YIYI Ecology and Environment Engineering Co. Ltd., Consortium of International Consultants LLC, E & E Budapest Kft., E & E Drilling and Testing Co., Inc., E & E Umwelt-Beratung GmbH, Ecology & Environment Engineering, Inc., Ecology & Environment of Saudi Arabia Co. Ltd., Ecology and Environment de Chile S.A., Ecology and Environment de Mexico, S.A. de C.V., ecology and environment do brasil ltda., Ecology and Environment Eurasia, Ecology and Environment International Services Inc., Ecology and Environment Limited, Ecology and Environment of Kazakhstan 25 Subsidiaries included in the Index

Officers: Gerhard J. Neumaier/71/Dir., CEO, Pres., Laurence M. Brickman/64/Sr. VP, Dan Sewall/Contact - Chicago, IL, Gerald A. Strobel/68/Dir., Exec. VP - Technical Services, Jim Bolleter/Contact - Miami Lakes, FL, Joe Tessitore/Contact - Orlando, FL, Doug Heatwole/Contact - Pensacola, FL, Bob King/Contact - Arlington, VA, Ronald L. Frank/Exec. VP - Administration - Finance, Roger J. Gray/67/Sr. VP, Frank B. Silvestro/71/Dir., Exec. VP, John Caoile/Contact - Kansas City, KS, Aaron J. Tuley/Mgr. - Houston, TX, Amy Mahl/Contact - Albany, NY, Nermin Ahmad/Contact - New York, NY *(25 Officers included in Index)*

Directors: Gerhard J. Neumaier/71/Dir., CEO, Pres., Gerard A. Gallagher/77/Dir., Harvey J. Gross/80/Dir., Frank B. Silvestro/71/Dir., Exec. VP, Timothy Butler/67/Dir., Ross M. Cellino/76/Dir., Gerald A. Strobel/68/Dir., Exec. VP - Technical Services

Owners: Gerhard J. Neumaier/21.80%, Ronald L. Frank/11.50%, Gerald A. Strobel/7.90%, Gerald A. Strobel/13.10%, Gerhard J. Neumaier/12.90%, Ronald L. Frank/7.50%, Frank B. Silvestro/10.20%, Bank of New York, Inc./7.60%, Wedbush, Inc./8.60%, Frank B. Silvestro/17.40%

Financial Data: **Fiscal Year End:**07/31 **Latest Annual Data:** 7/31/2006

Year	Sales	Net Income
2006	$81,836,000	$2,583,000
2005	$74,461,000	-$1,587,000
2004	$89,501,000	$2,401,000

Curr. Assets:	$56,876,000	**Curr. Liab.:**	$29,437,000	**P/E Ratio:**	18.31
Plant, Equip.:	$7,776,000	**Total Liab.:**	$29,779,000	**Indic. Yr. Divd.:**	$0.360
Total Assets:	$69,152,000	**Net Worth:**	$37,627,000	**Debt/ Equity:**	0.0083

Ecology Coatings Inc

Formerly: OCIS Corp
35980 Woodward Ave., Ste. 200, Bloomfield Hills, MI, 48304; *PH:* 1-248-723-2223

General - Incorporation	NV	**Stock**- Price on:12/24/2007	NA
Employees	NA	Stock Exchange	NA
Auditor Child, Van Wagoner & Bradshaw, PLLC		Ticker Symbol	NA
Stk Agt	Colonial Stock Transfer Co Inc	Outstanding Shares	NA
Counsel	NA	E.P.S.	NA
DUNS No.	NA	Shareholders	NA

Business: The groups principal activities include buying and selling used warehouse storage systems, lift trucks and office components. The group operates from the United States.
Primary SIC and add'l.: 5084
CIK No: 0001173313
Officers: Kirk Blosch/53/Dir., Pres., Sec., Treasurer, Jeff W. Holmes/54/Dir., VP
Directors: Kirk Blosch/53/Dir., Pres., Sec., Treasurer, Jeff W. Holmes/54/Dir., VP, Brent W. Schlesinger/53/Dir.
Owners: Richard D. Stromback/50.38%, Douglas Stromback/9.33%, Insiders/60.15%, Deanna Stromback/9.33%, Thomas F. Krotine, Adam S. Tracy, Sally J.W. Ramsey/9.33%
Financial Data: Fiscal Year End:12/31　Latest Annual Data: 09/30/2007

Year	Sales	Net Income
2007	$42,000	-$4,651,000
2006	NA	-$25,000
2005	NA	-$27,000

Curr. Assets:	$88,000	**Curr. Liab.:**	$53,000		
Plant, Equip.:	NA	**Total Liab.:**	$53,000	**Indic. Yr. Divd.:**	NA
Total Assets:	$88,000	**Net Worth:**	$35,000	**Debt/ Equity:**	NA

Ecost Com Inc

2555 W 190th St. , Ste. 106, Torrance, CA, 90504; *PH:* 1-310-225-4044

General - Incorporation	DE	**Stock**- Price on:12/24/2007	$0.95
Employees	1,200	Stock Exchange	NA
Auditor	PricewaterhouseCoopers LLP	Ticker Symbol	NA
Stk Agt	Mellon Investor Services LLC	Outstanding Shares	46,560,000
Counsel	NA	E.P.S.	-$0.34
DUNS No.	NA	Shareholders	NA

Business: The group's principle activities are to operate a multi-category online discount retailer of new , close-out and refurbished brand-name merchandise. The company offers over 100,000 products in seven merchandise categories, including computer hardware and software, home electronics, digital imaging, watches and jewelry, housewares, DVD movies, and video games. The company appeals to a broad range of consumers and small business customers through what we believe is a unique and convenient buying experience offering two shopping formats: every day low price and our proprietary bargain countdowntm. This combination of shopping formats helps attract value-conscious customers looking for high quality products at low prices to our ecost.com Website. The company also provides rapid response customer service utilizing a strategically located distribution center and third-party fulfillment providers, as well as customer support from online and on-call sales representatives.
Primary SIC and add'l.: 6794 5961
CIK No: 0001287503
Financial Data: Fiscal Year End:12/31　Latest Annual Data: 12/31/2006

Year	Sales	Net Income
2006	$423,253,000	-$14,530,000
2005	$331,657,000	-$747,000
2004	$321,665,000	$226,000

Curr. Assets:	$128,411,000	**Curr. Liab.:**	$107,708,000		
Plant, Equip.:	$12,884,000	**Total Liab.:**	$115,312,000	**Indic. Yr. Divd.:**	NA
Total Assets:	$164,152,000	**Net Worth:**	$48,840,000	**Debt/ Equity:**	0.1265

Ecotality Inc

2940 N 67th Pl, Scottsdale, AZ, 85251; *PH:* 1-480-219-5005; *Fax:* 1-480-219-5338;
http:// www.ecotality.com; *Email:* info@ecotality.com

General - Incorporation	NV	**Stock**- Price on:12/24/2007	$0.73
Employees	5	Stock Exchange	OTC
Auditor	Beckstead and Watts, LLP	Ticker Symbol	ETLY
Stk Agt	Holladay Stock Transfer, Inc.	Outstanding Shares	107,000,000
Counsel	NA	E.P.S.	-$0.07
DUNS No.	NA	Shareholders	NA

Business: The groups principal activities include designing and licensing electric power cell for use in motorized vehicles and industrial equipment. The group operates from the United States.
Primary SIC and add'l.: 7389
CIK No: 0001301206
Officers: Jonathan R. Read/Dir., CEO, Pres., Priscilla A. Wilson/CEO, Pres. - Fuel Cell Store, Colin Read/Dir. - Marketing, Gwen Lexa/Corporate Controller, Barry S. Baer/64/CFO, Raghu Ram/VP - Finance, Brooke Lowry/Dir. - New Media
Directors: Jonathan R. Read/Dir., CEO, Pres., Jerry Y.S. Lin/Chmn., Harold Sciotto/Dir., Slade Mead/Dir., Donald B. Karner/Dir.
Owners: Edward S. Mead/0.26%, Pierce Diversified Strategy Master Fund, LLC/0.38%, Jonathan R. Read/5.93%, Jerry Y.S. Lin/0.16%, Enable Opportunity Partners, LP/0.76%, Donald Karner/3.06%, Enable Growth Partners, LP/6.46%, Harold Sciotto/29.09%, Kevin Morrow/2.00%, Insiders/42.96%, Innergy Power/2.45%
Financial Data: Fiscal Year End:12/31　Latest Annual Data: 03/31/2007

Year	Sales	Net Income
2007	NA	NA
2006	NA	-$14,498,000
2005	$1,000	-$15,000

Curr. Assets:	$7,152,000	**Curr. Liab.:**	$606,000		
Plant, Equip.:	$778,000	**Total Liab.:**	$606,000	**Indic. Yr. Divd.:**	NA
Total Assets:	$7,929,000	**Net Worth:**	$7,323,000	**Debt/ Equity:**	NA

ECtel Ltd

8211 W Broward Blvd., Ste. 460, Plantation, FL, 33324; *PH:* 1-954-465-2400; *Fax:* 1-954-351-4306;
http:// www.ectel.com; *Email:* ectel@ectel.com

General - Incorporation	Israel	**Stock**- Price on:12/24/2007	$3.09
Employees	187	Stock Exchange	NDQ
Auditor	Somekh Chaikin	Ticker Symbol	ECTX
Stk Agt	NA	Outstanding Shares	16,650,000
Counsel	NA	E.P.S.	-$0.55
DUNS No.	NA	Shareholders	NA

Business: The groups principle activities include development and marketing of products that enable telecommunications service to monitor networks, detect and prevent telecommunications fraud, such as cellular fraud, calling card fraud and premium rate services fraud. The group operates from United States.
Primary SIC and add'l.: 3661 7373 7372
CIK No: 0001096197
Subsidiaries: ECI Telecom Ltd.
Officers: Itzik Weinstein/CEO, Pres., Ron Fainaro/40/Sr. VP, CFO, Hadar Solomon/VP - Legal Counsel, David Ronen/Sr. VP - Strategy, Business Development, Benny Yehezkel/Exec. VP - Worldwide Marketing - Sales, Michael Neumann/Sr. VP, CFO, Hanun Dvey-Aharon/Sr. VP - Products - Professional Services, Yoav Geva/VP - Corporate Development
Directors: Yair Cohen/Chmn., Rami Entin/Dir., Raanan Cohen/Dir., Sami Totah/External Dir., Mali Baron/External Dir., Jonathan Kolber/46/Dir.
Owners: Insiders/1.36%, IDB Holding Corporation Ltd/29.80%, Kingdon Capital Management, LLC/5.84%, Potomoc Capital Management LLC/5.60%, FMR Corp./10.53%
Financial Data: Fiscal Year End:12/31　Latest Annual Data: 12/31/2006

Year	Sales	Net Income
2006	$28,802,000	-$2,300,000
2005	$23,151,000	-$1,367,000
2004	$12,605,000	-$13,495,000

Curr. Assets:	$38,665,000	**Curr. Liab.:**	$13,062,000		
Plant, Equip.:	$2,342,000	**Total Liab.:**	$15,567,000	**Indic. Yr. Divd.:**	NA
Total Assets:	$65,524,000	**Net Worth:**	$49,957,000	**Debt/ Equity:**	NA

Ecuity Inc

800 Bellevue Way NE, Ste 600, Bellevue, WA, 98004; *PH:* 1-425-562-2900; *Fax:* 1-425-643-0716;
http:// www.ythk.com; *Email:* feedback@ecuity.net

General - Incorporation	NV	**Stock**- Price on:12/24/2007	NA
Employees	15	Stock Exchange	OTC
Auditor	De Leon & Co. P.A	Ticker Symbol	ECUI
Stk Agt	Nevada Agency & Trust Company	Outstanding Shares	NA
Counsel	NA	E.P.S.	-$0.018
DUNS No.	NA	Shareholders	NA

Business: The group's principal activity is to provide business software designed for telecommunications, banking and government sectors. The group's product is fusionpak 3.0 - enterprise business suite, which is composed of integrated software modules that allow for instant communication, content management, electronic commerce and collaboration. The software allows Internet and traditional businesses to keep track of large amounts of data which a user may input from time to time using a personal computer. The fusionpak enterprise business suite includes instant communication systems (ics) module and fusionpak integrated suite. The ics enables companies and their customers to communicate through an Internet based real-time instant messaging system. The fusionpak integrated suite allows businesses to establish websites where they can sell their products and services using credit. The group acquired fox communications corporation on 02-Jan-2004.
Primary SIC and add'l.: 7372
CIK No: 0001082673
Subsidiaries: Ecuity Advanced Communications, Inc.
Owners: Jeffrey Haberman/4.81%, Insiders/4.84%, King Cole/0.03%
Financial Data: Fiscal Year End:06/30　Latest Annual Data: 6/30/2006

Year	Sales	Net Income
2006	$2,352,000	-$5,648,000
2005	$3,067,000	-$4,976,000
2004	$2,135,000	-$11,253,000

Curr. Assets:	$247,000	**Curr. Liab.:**	$12,702,000		
Plant, Equip.:	$319,000	**Total Liab.:**	$14,430,000	**Indic. Yr. Divd.:**	NA
Total Assets:	$1,453,000	**Net Worth:**	-$12,977,000	**Debt/ Equity:**	NA

Edac Technologies Corp

1806 New Britain Ave., Farmington, CT, 06032; *PH:* 1-860-678-8140; *Fax:* 1-860-674-2718;
http:// www.edactechnologies.com; *Email:* info@edactechnologies.com

General - Incorporation	WI	**Stock**- Price on:12/24/2007	NA
Employees	209	Stock Exchange	NDQ
Auditor	Carlin, Charron & Rosen LLP	Ticker Symbol	EDAC
Stk Agt	American Stock Transfer & Trust Co.	Outstanding Shares	NA
Counsel	Reinhart, Boerner, Van Deuren sc	E.P.S.	$0.643
DUNS No.	14-492-1780	Shareholders	NA

Business: The group's principal activities are to design and manufacture special tools, equipment and gauges. The group's products are used in the manufacture, assembly and inspection of jet engines. The group also provides specialized services for the design and repair of precision spindles. The products manufactured by the group include precision rings, and other components for jet engines, industrial spindles and specialized machinery designed by the group and other assemblies requiring close tolerances.
Primary SIC and add'l.: 3549 7699 3545 3559
CIK No: 0000772572
Subsidiaries: Apex Machine Tool Company, Inc., Gros-Ite Industries, Inc.
Officers: Dominick A. Pagano/Dir., CEO, Pres./$227,813.00, Glenn L. Purple/VP - Finance, CFO, Sec./$173,565.00, Luciano M. Melluzzo/VP, COO/$187,290.00
Directors: Dominick A. Pagano/Dir., CEO, Pres., Daniel C. Tracy/Chmn. - Edac Technologies, Stephen Raffay/Dir., Ross C. Towne/Dir., Joseph Lebel/Dir.
Owners: Luciano M. Melluzzo, John Moses/8.90%, Ross C. Towne/1.70%, Stephen J. Raffay, Dominick A. Pagano/7.50%, William B. Bayne/3.40%, Insiders/16.50%, Daniel C. Tracy/2.90%, Joseph P. Lebel/3.10%, Glenn L. Purple/1.10%

Financial Data: *Fiscal Year End:*01/02 *Latest Annual Data:* 12/30/2006

Year	Sales	Net Income
2006	$38,329,000	$1,554,000
2005	$35,045,000	$3,299,000

Curr. Assets:	$13,259,000	**Curr. Liab.:**	$6,221,000		
Plant, Equip.:	$8,968,000	**Total Liab.:**	$14,979,000	**Indic. Yr. Divd.:**	NA
Total Assets:	$23,777,000	**Net Worth:**	$8,798,000	**Debt/ Equity:**	NA

EDAP TMS

4/6, Rue Du Dauphine, Vaulx-en-velin, 69120; ***PH:*** 33-19724588000;
http:// www.edaptechnomed.com

General - Incorporation	France	**Stock**- Price on:12/24/2007	$6.2
Employees	142	Stock Exchange	NDQ
Auditor	Ernst & Young LLP	Ticker Symbol	EDAP
Stk Agt	Bank of New York	Outstanding Shares	8,940,000
Counsel	NA	E.P.S.	-$0.73
DUNS No.	39-515-3406	Shareholders	NA

Business: The group's principal activities are to develop, produce and market minimally invasive medical devices, mainly for urological diseases. The group's operations are carried out through three business divisions: uds, hifu and edap tms. The uds division's primary business is producing and marketing devices, known as lithotripters, for the treatment of urinary tract stones by means of eswl technology. Hifu division of the group develops and markets devices for the minimally invasive destruction of certain types of localized tumors using hifu technology. Edap tms s.a. Is a holding company and is responsible for providing common services to its subsidiaries

Primary SIC and add'l.: 3842 5047

CIK No: 0001041934

Subsidiaries: HeathTronics Surgical Services, Inc

Officers: Marc Oczachowski/CEO, Eric Soyer/CFO, Thierry Turbant/CFO, Blandine Confort/Investor Relations

Directors: Philippe Chauveau/Chmn., Karim Fizazi/Dir., Jean-Philippe Deschamps/Dir., Siemens France/Dir., Pierre Beysson/Dir., Hugues De Bantel/Dir., Guy Vallancien/Dir., Olivier Missoffe/Dir.

Financial Data: *Fiscal Year End:*12/31 *Latest Annual Data:* 12/31/2006

Year	Sales	Net Income
2006	$26,756,000	-$4,530,000
2005	$24,647,000	-$1,261,000
2004	$30,239,000	-$1,568,000

Curr. Assets:	$34,848,000	**Curr. Liab.:**	$14,426,000		
Plant, Equip.:	$4,239,000	**Total Liab.:**	$17,392,000	**Indic. Yr. Divd.:**	NA
Total Assets:	$42,874,000	**Net Worth:**	$25,482,000	**Debt/ Equity:**	NA

Edd Helms Group Inc

17850 NE 5th Ave., Miami, FL, 33162; ***PH:*** 1-305-653-2520; ***Fax:*** 1-305-651-5527;
http:// www.eddhelms.com

General - Incorporation	FL	**Stock**- Price on:12/24/2007	$0.41
Employees	143	Stock Exchange	OTC
Auditor	Dohan & Co	Ticker Symbol	EDDH
Stk Agt	NA	Outstanding Shares	12,570,000
Counsel	NA	E.P.S.	$0.05
DUNS No.	15-176-6631	Shareholders	NA

Business: The group's principle activity is to provide air conditioning installation, service and maintenance. The group operates from United States.

Primary SIC and add'l.: 1711

CIK No: 0000854883

Subsidiaries: DataTelcom, Inc., Edd Helms Air Conditioning Inc., Edd Helms Marine Air Conditioning and Refrigeration LLC.

Officers: Edd W. Helms/Founder, Chmn., CEO, Pres., Wade L. Helms/51/Dir., Exec. VP, Sec., Treasurer, Dean Goodson/CFO, Joe Kelly/GM - Electrical, John Garzia/Electrical Field Superintendent, Janice Jhonson/Mgr. - Electrical Service, Bob Roberts/GM - HVAC, Scott Levy/Mgr. - HVAC Installation, Joni Alonso/Mgr. - Trade Shows, Sherrie Helms/Mgr. - Westin Diplomat Events, Shawn Saunders/Mgr. - Marine HVAC, Mara Abbattista/Mgr. - HVAC South Zone, Teresa Larabee/Mgr. - HVAC North Zone

Directors: Edd W. Helms/Founder, Chmn., CEO, Pres., Edward J. McCarthy/64/Dir., Wade L. Helms/51/Dir., Exec. VP, Sec., Treasurer, Walter Revell/73/Dir., John Salvaggio/46/Dir.

Owners: Walter L. Revell/0.21%, Edd W. Helms/80.00%, Wade L. Helms/0.44%, Edward McCarthy, Insiders/89.93%, ESOP/7.07%

Financial Data: *Fiscal Year End:*05/31 *Latest Annual Data:* 05/31/2007

Year	Sales	Net Income
2007	$22,785,000	$869,000
2006	$21,205,000	$788,000
2005	$17,062,000	$181,000

Curr. Assets:	$7,485,000	**Curr. Liab.:**	$3,626,000	**P/E Ratio:**	4.10
Plant, Equip.:	$1,025,000	**Total Liab.:**	$4,044,000	**Indic. Yr. Divd.:**	NA
Total Assets:	$8,924,000	**Net Worth:**	$4,879,000	**Debt/ Equity:**	0.0403

Eddie Bauer Holdings Inc

15010 NE 36th St., Redmond, WA, 98052; ***PH:*** 1-425-755-6544; ***Fax:*** 1-425-755-7696;
http:// www.eddiebauer.com

General - Incorporation	DE	**Stock**- Price on:12/24/2007	$14.07
Employees	2,457	Stock Exchange	NDQ
Auditor	NA	Ticker Symbol	EBHI
Stk Agt	NA	Outstanding Shares	30,460,000
Counsel	NA	E.P.S.	-$0.67
DUNS No.	NA	Shareholders	NA

Business: The groups principle activity is to sells casual sportswear and accessories. The products of the group include outerwear, pants, jeans, dresses, skirts, sweaters, shirts, sleepwear, underwear, swimwear and gadgets. The group products sold under the trade name Eddie Bauer(R), EBTek(R), Eddie Bauer and Adventurer(R). The groups operates through three segments namely retail stores, outlet stores and direct. The group operates from California, Illinois, Texas and Washington. The group's quarterly revenue for September 2007 was 210.95 millions of USD.

Primary SIC and add'l.: 3144 5621 3171 5139 2252 5961 2321 3143 2384 3142 2322 2325 5699 5963 5137 3151 2339 3149 2389 2337 2331 2311 5611 2329 5136

CIK No: 0001345968

Subsidiaries: Eddie Bauer Customer Services Inc., Eddie Bauer Diversified Sales, LLC, Eddie Bauer Fulfillment Services, Inc, Eddie Bauer Information Technology LLC, Eddie Bauer International Development, LLC, Eddie Bauer of Canada, Inc., Eddie Bauer Services, LLC, Eddie Bauer, Inc., Financial Services Acceptance Corporation, Spiegel Acceptance Corporation

Officers: Howard Gross/64/Dir., Interim CEO, Neil Fiske/Dir., CEO, Pres., David Taylor/Interim CFO - Treasuer, Tom Helton/Sr. VP, Chief Human Resources Officer, Ann Perinchief/Sr. VP - Retail, Kathleen Boyer/Sr. VP, Chief Merchandising Officer, Shelley Milano/51/Sr. VP, General Counsel, Sec.

Directors: Howard Gross/64/Dir., Interim CEO, Neil Fiske/Dir., CEO, Pres., William T. End/Chmn., John C. Brouillard/Dir., Paul E. Kirincic/Dir., Kenneth M. Reiss/Dir., Laurie M. Shahon/Dir., Edward M. Straw/Dir., Stephen E. Watson/Dir., William E. Redmond/Dir.

Owners: Kathleen Boyer, Howard Gross, Fabian Mnsson, Paul E. Kirincic, Kenneth M. Reiss, Laurie M. Shahon, William T. End, Edward M. Straw, FMR Corp./11.90%, Bank of America, N.A./6.80%, John C. Brouillard, Stephen E. Watson, Insiders/1.50%, JP Morgan Chase Bank,/6.10%, Wellington Management Company, LLP/13.80% *(17 Owners included in Index)*

Financial Data: *Fiscal Year End:*12/31 *Latest Annual Data:* 12/30/2006

Year	Sales	Net Income
2006	$1,013,447,000	-$211,983,000

Curr. Assets:	$308,621,000	**Curr. Liab.:**	$203,554,000		
Plant, Equip.:	$177,344,000	**Total Liab.:**	$509,269,000	**Indic. Yr. Divd.:**	NA
Total Assets:	$855,910,000	**Net Worth:**	$346,641,000	**Debt/ Equity:**	0.7823

Eden Bioscience Corp

11816 N Creek Pkwy. N, Bothell, WA, 98011; ***PH:*** 1-425-806-7300; ***Fax:*** 1-425-806-7400;
http:// www.edenbio.com; ***Email:*** messenger@edenbio.com

General - Incorporation	WA	**Stock**- Price on:12/24/2007	$1.12
Employees	5	Stock Exchange	NDQ
Auditor	KPMG LLP	Ticker Symbol	EDEN
Stk Agt	Mellon Shareholder Services LLC	Outstanding Shares	8,150,000
Counsel	Brown & Wood LLP	E.P.S.	-$0.384
DUNS No.	NA	Shareholders	NA

Business: The group's principal activities are to develop, manufacture and market innovative natural products for agriculture to improve plant protection and crop production worldwide. The group has recently initiated marketing activities designed to promote the distribution and sale of its first product, messenger. Messenger is a water-soluble, granular powder that is topically applied either independently or in conjunction with traditional chemical pesticides. Messenger provide growers with valuable benefits by increasing crop yields, quality and shelf-life and improving the plant's ability to withstand diseases and other environmental stresses. The group is currently concentrating its efforts in the United States on high-value crops, such as citrus, grapes, tomatoes, peppers, stone fruits, tobacco, cucumbers, melons, strawberries and other horticultural and specialty crops.

Primary SIC and add'l.: 2879 7389

CIK No: 0000930095

Subsidiaries: EDEN Bioscience Corporation of New York, Inc, EDEN Bioscience Europe SARL, EDEN Bioscience Mexico, S. de R.L. de C.V.

Officers: Bradley S. Powell/47/CFO, Pres., Sec./$206,083.00

Directors: William T. Weyerhaeuser/64/Chmn., Gilberto H. Gonzalez/60/Dir., Agatha L. Maza/68/Dir., Albert A. James/76/Dir., Jon E.M. Jacoby/Dir., Rhett R. Atkins/54/Dir., Richard N. Pahre/67/Dir., Roger M. Ivesdal/63/Dir.

Owners: SF Holding Corp./16.60%, Albert A. James/2.50%, Roger Ivesdal, Bradley S. Powell/1.67%, Jon E. M. Jacoby/2.39%, Richard N. Pahre, William T. Weyerhaeuser/5.26%, Gilberto H. Gonzalez, Rhett R. Atkins/2.03%, Agatha L. Maza/2.86%, Yorktown Avenue Capital, LLC/9.76%, Insiders/16.31%

Financial Data: *Fiscal Year End:*12/31 *Latest Annual Data:* 12/31/2006

Year	Sales	Net Income
2006	$3,790,000	-$9,445,000
2005	$3,764,000	-$10,858,000
2004	$1,040,000	-$8,886,000

Curr. Assets:	$6,946,000	**Curr. Liab.:**	$808,000		
Plant, Equip.:	$740,000	**Total Liab.:**	$1,265,000	**Indic. Yr. Divd.:**	NA
Total Assets:	$7,973,000	**Net Worth:**	$6,709,000	**Debt/ Equity:**	NA

Eden Energy Corp

200 Burrard St., Ste. 1925, Vancouver, BC, V6C 3L6; ***PH:*** 1-604-693-0179; ***Fax:*** 1-604-357-1062;
http:// www.edenenergycorp.com; ***Email:*** info@edenenergycorp.com

General - Incorporation	NV	**Stock**- Price on:12/24/2007	$1.05
Employees	NA	Stock Exchange	OTC
Auditor	Dale Matheson Carr-hilton Labonte	Ticker Symbol	EDNE
Stk Agt	Pacific Stock Transfer Company	Outstanding Shares	NA
Counsel	NA	E.P.S.	NA
DUNS No.	NA	Shareholders	NA

Business: The group's has ceased operations and currently has no sales. The company is in the process of seeking new business opportunities, merger and acquisition. The company was engaged in developing e-commerce solutions, Web-based applications, performing Internet marketing and consulting services. Operated through wholly owned subsidiary e-com consultants (Canada) corp.

Primary SIC and add'l.: 7372 7375

CIK No: 0001083866

Subsidiaries: Frontier Explorations Ltd, Southern Frontier Explorations Ltd

Officers: Donald Sharpe/CEO, Pres., Drew Bonnell/Dir., CFO, Sec., Treasurer, Larry Kellison/COO

Directors: John Martin/Dir., Drew Bonnell/Dir., CFO, Sec., Treasurer, Ralph Stensaker/Dir.

Owners: Ralph Stensaker, Insiders/27.07%, John Martin, Larry Kellison, Drew Bonnell/1.63%, Donald Sharpe/24.84%

Financial Data: *Fiscal Year End:*12/31 *Latest Annual Data:* 12/31/2006

Year	Sales	Net Income
2006	NA	-$6,218,000
2005	NA	-$5,562,000
2004	$6,000	-$322,000

Curr. Assets:	$23,875,000	Curr. Liab.:	$262,000		
Plant, Equip.:	$11,867,000	Total Liab.:	$7,811,000	Indic. Yr. Divd.:	NA
Total Assets:	$36,844,000	Net Worth:	$29,033,000	Debt/ Equity:	0.2664

Edentify Inc

Formerly: Budgethotels Network Inc
74 W Brd. St., Ste. 350, Bethlehem, PA, 18018; *PH:* 1-610-814-6830; *http://* www.budgethotels.com

General - Incorporation	NV	Stock- Price on:12/24/2007	$0.52
Employees	14	Stock Exchange	NA
Auditor	Cinnamon, Jang, Willoughby & Co	Ticker Symbol	NA
Stk Agt	Computershare Trust Co	Outstanding Shares	26,900,000
Counsel	NA	E.P.S.	-$0.36
DUNS No.	NA	Shareholders	NA

Business: The group's principal activities are to install and maintain information display boards and provide innovative Internet hotel and travel reservations. The group operates in two segments: display boards and reservation system. The display boards segment installs and maintains illuminated information boards in transportation terminals, primarily bus and rail stations. The reservation system segment through its Website, www.budgethotels.com provides hotel reservations on-line on commission basis from the respective hotel for each reservation. The group currently operates 81 boards throughout the United States and Canada. During 2003, the group discontinued its Internet2u division.

Primary SIC and add'l.: 7389 7319 7312

CIK No: 0001091938

Subsidiaries: Edentify, Inc., InfoCenter, Inc., InMotion Biometrics, Inc.

Owners: Insiders/33.20%, Thomas Harkins, Kenneth Vennera, Mark Gelnaw, Face2face, Inc./29.30%, Eric Gertler, Michael Preston, Terrence DeFranco/32.70%

Financial Data: *Fiscal Year End:*12/31 *Latest Annual Data:* 12/31/2006

Year	Sales	Net Income
2006	$109,000	-$8,642,000
2005	$1,000	-$2,115,000
2004	$344,000	-$194,000

Curr. Assets:	$496,000	Curr. Liab.:	$3,004,000		
Plant, Equip.:	$1,282,000	Total Liab.:	$3,591,000	Indic. Yr. Divd.:	NA
Total Assets:	$4,324,000	Net Worth:	$733,000	Debt/ Equity:	2.5162

Edgar Online Inc

50 Washington St., 11th Fl., Norwalk, CT, 06854; *PH:* 1-203-852-5666; *Fax:* 1-203-852-5667; *http://* www.edgar-online.com

General - Incorporation	DE	Stock- Price on:12/24/2007	$2.58
Employees	85	Stock Exchange	NDQ
Auditor	BDO Seidman, LLP	Ticker Symbol	EDGR
Stk Agt	American Stock Transfer & Trust Co.	Outstanding Shares	26,040,000
Counsel	NA	E.P.S.	-$0.28
DUNS No.	NA	Shareholders	NA

Business: The groups principal activity is to provide business and financial information. The groups services include I-Metrix Professional and EDGAR Pro and EDGAR Access. The products of the group include I-Metrix Data Feeds and I-Metrix Data Solutions. Specific customers of the group include Bank of America, Citigroup, Bloomberg, Reuters, Moodys, SNL, Thomson Financial, FactSet, McGraw Hill and Standard and Poors. The group operates from the United States. The assets of the group for the year 2006 were $15,872 (thousands).

Primary SIC and add'l.: 7379 7375 4899

CIK No: 0001080224

Subsidiaries: Financial Insight Systems, Inc., Freeedgar.com, Inc.

Officers: Philip Moyer/Dir., CEO, Pres., Sue Childs/Sr. VP - Marketing, Business Development, Greg D. Adams/CFO, COO/$384,595.00, Stefan Chopin/CTO/$385,429.00, David Colgren/Contact - Public Relations

Directors: Philip Moyer/Dir., CEO, Pres., Mark Maged/Chmn., Douglas K. Mellinger/Dir., John Mutch/Dir., Marc Strausberg/72/Dir., Susan Strausberg/Dir., Elisabeth Demarse/Dir., Richard L. Feinstein/Dir., William O'Neill/Dir.

Owners: Insiders/12.10%, John Mutch, Mark Maged, Elisabeth DeMarse, Stefan Chopin/1.59%, OTRNominee Name for The State Teachers Retirement Board of Ohio/11.53%, Susan Strausberg/7.74%, Marc Strausberg/7.74%, Richard L. Feinstein, Morton Mackof, Douglas K. Mellinger, Midwood Capital/6.93%, Theodore L. Cross/6.92%, Greg D. Adams/1.93%, R.L. Renck & Co., Inc./5.78% *(16 Owners included in Index)*

Financial Data: *Fiscal Year End:*12/31 *Latest Annual Data:* 12/31/2006

Year	Sales	Net Income
2006	$16,246,000	-$5,926,000
2005	$14,235,000	-$5,578,000
2004	$12,885,000	-$2,166,000

Curr. Assets:	$5,849,000	Curr. Liab.:	$5,942,000		
Plant, Equip.:	$1,132,000	Total Liab.:	$5,942,000	Indic. Yr. Divd.:	NA
Total Assets:	$15,872,000	Net Worth:	$9,930,000	Debt/ Equity:	NA

Edge Petroleum Corp

1301 Travis, Ste. 2000, Houston, TX, 77002; *PH:* 1-713-654-8960; *Fax:* 1-713-650-6494; *http://* www.edgepet.com; *Email:* ir@edgepet.com

General - Incorporation	DE	Stock- Price on:12/24/2007	$15.01
Employees	75	Stock Exchange	NDQ
Auditor	BDO Seidman LLP	Ticker Symbol	EPEX
Stk Agt	Computershare Investor Services LLC	Outstanding Shares	28,460,000
Counsel	Baker & Botts LLP	E.P.S.	-$2.38
DUNS No.	13-025-2992	Shareholders	NA

Business: The group's principal activities are to explore, develop and produce oil and natural gas. The operations are conducted primarily along the onshore United States, gulf coast with its primary emphasis in south Texas and south central Louisiana where it controls interests in excess of 208,926 gross acres under lease or option. The group has seismic and production data and operations in over 20 specific project areas. Its exploration activities based on an integrated geologic interpretation method incorporating 3-D seismic technology and advanced visualization and data analysis techniques utilizing state-of-the-art computer hardware and software. During 2003, the group acquired miller exploration company.

Primary SIC and add'l.: 1311

CIK No: 0001021010

Subsidiaries: Edge Petroleum Exploration Company, Edge Petroleum Operating Company, Inc., Edge Petroleum Production Company, Miller Exploration Company, Miller Oil Corporation

Officers: John W. Elias/Chmn., CEO, Pres./$579,772.00, John O. Tugwell/COO, Exec. VP/$406,342.00, Michael G. Long/CFO, Exec. VP/$391,502.00, John Sfondrini/Dir. - Private Investor, Howard Creasey/VP - Exploration, Robert C. Thomas/VP, General Counsel, Corp. Sec., C. W. MacLeod/VP - Business Development, Planning, Keith Turner/VP - Land, Kurt Primeaux/VP - Production

Directors: John W. Elias/Chmn., CEO, Pres., John Sfondrini/Dir. - Private Investor, Vincent S. Andrews/Dir., Thurmon Andress/Dir., Stanley Raphael/Dir., Robert W. Shower/Dir., David F. Work/Dir., Jonathan M. Clarkson/Dir., Michael A. Creel/Dir.

Owners: John Sfondrini, Royce & Associates, LLC/11.51%, Insiders/4.33%, Vincent S. Andrews, David F. Work, Jonathan M. Clarkson, Robert W. Shower, Michael G. Long, John O. Tugwell, Thurmon Andress, Michael A. Creel, Stanley S. Raphael, John W. Elias/2.49%

Financial Data: *Fiscal Year End:*12/31 *Latest Annual Data:* 12/31/2006

Year	Sales	Net Income
2006	$129,744,000	-$41,261,000
2005	$121,183,000	$33,358,000
2004	$66,965,000	$15,129,000

Curr. Assets:	$31,940,000	Curr. Liab.:	$21,778,000		
Plant, Equip.:	$289,457,000	Total Liab.:	$165,605,000	Indic. Yr. Divd.:	NA
Total Assets:	$321,657,000	Net Worth:	$156,052,000	Debt/ Equity:	0.5724

Edgeline Holdings Inc

Formerly: Dragon Gold Resources Inc
1330 Post Oak Blvd., Ste. 1600, Houston, TX, 77056; *PH:* 1-713-621-5208; *http://* www.dragon-gold.com

General - Incorporation	NV	Stock- Price on:12/24/2007	$0.028
Employees	NA	Stock Exchange	NA
Auditor	Thomas Leger & Co. LLP	Ticker Symbol	NA
Stk Agt	NA	Outstanding Shares	NA
Counsel	NA	E.P.S.	NA
DUNS No.	NA	Shareholders	NA

Business: The groups principal activity is to explore minerals. In the year 2006, the group acquired Dragon Minerals Holdings Inc. The group operates from Canada and the United States.

Primary SIC and add'l.: 1000

CIK No: 0001229089

Subsidiaries: Dragon Minerals Holdings Inc, Dragon Minerals-Taiyu Inc, Dragon Minerals-Xunyang Inc., Dragon Minerals, Inc, Dragon Minerals-Shiquan Inc.

Officers: Leonard J. Ivins/71/Dir., CEO, Carl A. Chase/58/Dir., CFO, Sec.

Directors: Leonard J. Ivins/71/Dir., CEO, Carl A. Chase/58/Dir., CFO, Sec., Hank Vanderkam/Dir.

Owners: Jonathan Camarillo Trust/8.70%, Insiders/7.80%, Silver Star Holdings/54.30%, Leonard J. Ivins/3.90%, Trevor D. Ling/9.80%, Danny Chan/6.90%, Carl A. Chase/3.90%

Financial Data: *Fiscal Year End:*03/31 *Latest Annual Data:* 3/31/2007

Year	Sales	Net Income
2007	NA	-$1,356,000
2006	NA	-$830,000
2005	NA	-$549,000

Curr. Assets:	$11,000	Curr. Liab.:	$42,000		
Plant, Equip.:	$3,000	Total Liab.:	$42,000	Indic. Yr. Divd.:	NA
Total Assets:	$23,000	Net Worth:	-$19,000	Debt/ Equity:	NA

Edgewater Technology Inc

20 Harvard Mill Sq., Wakefield, MA, 01880; *PH:* 1-781-246-3343; *Fax:* 1-781-246-5903; *http://* www.edgewater.com; *Email:* makewaves@edgewater.com

General - Incorporation	DE	Stock- Price on:12/24/2007	$7.75
Employees	303	Stock Exchange	NDQ
Auditor	Deloitte & Touche LLP	Ticker Symbol	EDGW
Stk Agt	Computershare Trust Co	Outstanding Shares	11,950,000
Counsel	NA	E.P.S.	$0.34
DUNS No.	95-745-5132	Shareholders	NA

Business: The group's principal activity is to provide technical consulting, custom software development and system integration services. The group's strategy services include analyzing customers' business goals, business processes and existing technology infrastructure to determine which it investments provide the most value and how to apply technology to support their business. The group specializes in developing and implementing technology applications that are tailored for each client's unique business needs. The customized applications are both flexible and scalable. It also provides a spectrum of post-deployment support services, including application outsourcing and site maintenance that enables customers to focus on their core competencies. Services are provided primarily to middle-Market companies and divisions of global 2000 companies. On 02-Jun-2003, it acquired Intelix Inc.

Primary SIC and add'l.: 8742 7379

CIK No: 0001017968

Subsidiaries: Edgewater Technology (Delaware),Inc., Edgewater Technology (Europe) Limited, Edgewater Technology (Virginia),Inc., Edgewater Technology Securities Corp., Edgewater Technology-Ranzal,Inc.

Officers: Shirley Singleton/Chmn., CEO, Pres./$665,693.00, David Clancey/Exec. VP, Chief Strategy Officer, CTO/$581,223.00, Kevin Rhodes/CFO/$302,875.00, Veda Gagliardi/VP - Operations, Ranzal, Associates, Robin Ranzal/Pres. - Ranzal, Associates, Barbara Warren-Sica/VP - Corporate Communications, Eva Vinson/VP - Delivery Management, Methodology, Betsy Norris/VP

- Business Development, Lawrence Fortin/VP - Consulting Services, Northern Operations, William Hall/VP - Consulting Services, Southern Region, John Inselman/VP - Consulting Services, Steve Bailey/VP - Consulting, Kristin Zaepfel/VP - Human Resources/$228,321.00, David Gallo/COO/$503,072.00, Joseph Navetta/VP - Technology

Directors: Shirley Singleton/Chmn., CEO, Pres., Wayne Wilson/Dir., Paul Flynn/Dir., Paul Guzzi/Dir., Michael Loeb/Dir., Clete Brewer/Dir., Nancy Leaming/Dir., Barry B. White/Dir.

Owners: Paul Guzzi, Insiders/17.30%, Shirley Singleton/4.90%, Oberweis Asset Management, Inc./5.30%, Dimensional Fund Advisors Inc./7.80%, Kevin R. Rhodes, David Gallo/2.30%, Paul E. Flynn, Nancy L. Leaming, Michael R. Loeb, GAMCO Investors, Inc., et. al./13.30%, David Clancey/4.50%, Wayne Wilson, Barry B. White, AXA Financial, Inc./5.40% *(17 Owners included in Index)*

Financial Data: ***Fiscal Year End:***12/31 ***Latest Annual Data:*** 12/31/2006

Year	Sales	Net Income
2006	$60,083,000	$3,203,000
2005	$43,126,000	$1,600,000
2004	$25,322,000	-$595,000

Curr. Assets:	$46,225,000	***Curr. Liab.:***	$8,592,000	***P/E Ratio:***	22.79
Plant, Equip.:	$3,391,000	***Total Liab.:***	$9,370,000	***Indic. Yr. Divd.:***	NA
Total Assets:	$95,620,000	***Net Worth:***	$86,250,000	***Debt/ Equity:***	0.0082

eDiets.com Inc

1000 Corporate Dr., Ste. 600, Fort Lauderdale, FL, 33334; ***PH:*** 1-954-360-9022; ***Fax:*** 1-954-360-9095; ***http://*** www.ediets.com

General - Incorporation	DE	***Stock*** - Price on:12/24/2007	$3.43
Employees	108	Stock Exchange	NDQ
Auditor	Ernst & Young LLP	Ticker Symbol	DIET
Stk Agt	American Stock Transfer & Trust Co.	Outstanding Shares	24,710,000
Counsel	NA	E.P.S.	-$0.07
DUNS No.	NA	Shareholders	NA

Business: The group provides online diet and fitness programs and related products and services. The ediets program includes customized meal plans and workout schedules and related tools such as shopping lists, journals and weight and exercise tracking, self-guided education including a ten-week tutorial on a healthy lifestyle entitled 'ediets u' and animated strength exercise instruction, provides interactive online support and education and counselling services.

Primary SIC and add'l.: 7299

CIK No: 0001094058

Subsidiaries: eDiets, B.V.I., Inc., eDiets, Europe Limited, eDiets, Inc.

Officers: James A. Epstein/General Counsel, Sec./$311,213.00, Robert T. Hamilton/CFO/$494,306.00, Alison C. Tanner/Sr. VP - Corporate Development/$406,401.00, Stephen J. Rattner/Pres., Principal Executive Officer/$140,400.00, Kimberly Evenson/Sr. VP - Marketing, Sales, Patrick C. Theimer/VP - Online Subscriptions, Operations, Robert J. Drago/VP - Meal Delivery, Lynn Freek/VP - Ediets Corporate Services, Ron Tomczyk/Contact - Media

Directors: Kevin A. Richardson/Chmn., Robert Doretti/Dir., Stephen Cootey/Dir., Lee S. Isgur/Dir., Ronald Luks/Dir., Pedro N. Ortega-Dardet/Dir., Andrea Weiss/Dir.

Owners: Insiders/55.40%, James A. Epstein, Andrea M. Weiss, Alejandro Gonzalez/9.00%, Robert T. Hamilton, Pedro N. Ortega-Dardet, Alison C. Tanner, Prides Capital Partners, LLC/52.40%, Ronald Luks, Robert L. Doretti, Lee S. Isgur/1.70%

Financial Data: ***Fiscal Year End:***12/31 ***Latest Annual Data:*** 12/31/2006

Year	Sales	Net Income
2006	$48,814,000	-$4,100,000
2005	$53,679,000	$1,336,000
2004	$45,407,000	-$9,903,000

Curr. Assets:	$8,488,000	***Curr. Liab.:***	$9,127,000		
Plant, Equip.:	$1,806,000	***Total Liab.:***	$11,348,000	***Indic. Yr. Divd.:***	NA
Total Assets:	$27,544,000	***Net Worth:***	$16,196,000	***Debt/ Equity:***	0.0058

eDigital Corp

16770 W Bernardo Dr., San Diego, CA, 92127; ***PH:*** 1-866-502-8234; ***Fax:*** 1-858-304-3023; ***http://*** www.edig.com

General - Incorporation	DE	***Stock*** - Price on:12/24/2007	$0.181
Employees	15	Stock Exchange	OTC
Auditor	Singer Lewak Greenbaum & Goldstein	Ticker Symbol	EDIG
Stk Agt	Interwest Transfer Company, Inc.	Outstanding Shares	243,300,000
Counsel	NA	E.P.S.	-$0.005
DUNS No.	19-843-2437	Shareholders	NA

Business: The group's principal activity is to offer proprietary technology platforms and engineering services to leading electronic companies to create portable digital devices that can link to personal computers, the Internet and other electronic devices. The group develops and markets consumer electronics products such as digital music players, dictation equipment, consumer electronics, digital image and video and other electronic product markets. The services and technologies are marketed to original equipment manufacturers (OEMs) and original design manufacturers (odms). The group also offers custom hardware, technology platform development, product design, manufacturing services, fulfillment services, warranty services, and licensing of its patented file management systems. The customers include aircraft protective systems, bang & olufsen, softeq, tai guen enterprise group and musical.

Primary SIC and add'l.: 7372 3651 3669 7373

CIK No: 0000886328

Subsidiaries: San Diego, California

Officers: Alfred H. Falk/VP - Corporate Development, William Blakeley/Pres., CTO, Principal Executive Officer, Robert Putnam/Dir., Sr. VP

Directors: Alex Diaz/43/Chmn., Renee Warden/Dir., Robert Putnam/Dir., Sr. VP, Allen Cocumelli/55/Dir.

Owners: Jerry E. Polis Family Trust/93.40%, William Blakeley, Allen Cocumelli, Insiders, Robert Putnam, Renee Warden, Palermo Trust/6.60%, Alex Diaz

Financial Data: ***Fiscal Year End:***03/31 ***Latest Annual Data:*** 03/31/2007

Year	Sales	Net Income
2007	$1,815,000	-$3,129,000
2006	$3,250,000	-$3,107,000
2005	$4,252,000	-$2,417,000

Curr. Assets:	$1,093,000	***Curr. Liab.:***	$3,609,000		
Plant, Equip.:	$63,000	***Total Liab.:***	$3,609,000	***Indic. Yr. Divd.:***	NA
Total Assets:	$1,156,000	***Net Worth:***	-$2,454,000	***Debt/ Equity:***	NA

Edison International

2244 Walnut Grove Ave., Rosemead, CA, 91770; ***PH:*** 1-626-302-2222; ***Fax:*** 1-626-302-2517; ***http://*** www.edison.com

General - Incorporation	CA	***Stock*** - Price on:12/24/2007	$55.58
Employees	16,139	Stock Exchange	NYSE
Auditor	PricewaterhouseCoopers LLP	Ticker Symbol	EIX
Stk Agt	Wells Fargo Shareowner Services	Outstanding Shares	325,810,000
Counsel	NA	E.P.S.	$3.81
DUNS No.	19-513-8458	Shareholders	NA

Business: The group's principle activity is to provide electric services. The group operates through three segments namely electric utility operation, a non-utility power generation and financial services provider segment. The group operates from United States.

Primary SIC and add'l.: 6282 4911 6552 1623

CIK No: 0000827052

Subsidiaries: 1010 Svn Associates Lp, 1028 Howard Street Associates LP, 1101 Howard Street Associates LP, 1475 167th Avenue Associates LP, 16th and Church Street Associates LP, 1856 Wells Court Partners, LP, 2601 North Broad Street Associates LP, 2814 Fifth Street Associates LP, 5363 Dent Avenue Associates LP, 708 Pico LP, Abby Associates LP, Admiralty Heights Associates II 1995 LP, AE Associates LP, Affordable/Citrus Glenn Phase II, Ltd., Agape Housing LP 592 Subsidiaries included in the Index

Officers: John E. Bryson/64/Chmn., CEO, Pres./$12,743,940.00, Theodore F. Craver/Chmn., CEO, Pres. - Edison Mission Group/$4,704,456.00, Mahvash Yazdi/Sr. VP - Business Integration, CIO/$1,878,848.00, Cecil R. House/Sr. VP - Safety, Operations Support, Chief Procurement Officer, Linda G. Sullivan/VP, Controller, Jeff Barnett/VP - Tax, Scott Cunningham/VP - Investor Relations, Megan Scott-Kakures/VP, General Auditor, Robert C. Boada/VP, Treasurer, Gerald P. Loughman/Sr. VP - Development, Edison Mission Group, Polly Gault/Exec. VP - Public Affairs, Barbara E. Mathews/VP, Assoc. General Counsel, Chief Governance Officer, Corp. Sec., Barbara J. Parsky/Sr. VP - Corporate Communications, Kenneth S. Stewart/VP, Chief Ethics, Compliance Officer, J. A. Bouknight/Exec. VP, General Counsel *(49 Officers included in Index)*

Directors: John E. Bryson/64/Chmn., CEO, Pres., Theodore F. Craver/Chmn., CEO, Pres. - Edison Mission Group, Richard T. Schlosberg/64/Dir., Thomas C. Sutton/65/Dir., Charles B. Curtis/68/Dir., Alan J. Fohrer/Dir., Bruce Karatz/61/Dir., Ronald L. Olson/66/Dir., France A. Cordova/60/Dir., Brett White/48/Dir., Vanessa C.L. Chang/55/Dir., Bradford M. Freeman/66/Dir., Luis G. Nogales/64/Dir., James M. Rosser/69/Dir., Robert H. Smith/72/Dir.

Owners: Insiders/1.51%, Theodore F. Craver, State Street Bank and Trust Company/10.60%, Robert H. Smith, Thomas M. Noonan, Thomas C. Sutton, Ronald L. Olson, James M. Rosser, Barclays Global Investors, N.A./6.93%, John R. Fielder, Edison International/100.00%, Thomas R. McDaniel, Bradford M. Freeman, Luis G. Nogales, Charles B. Curtis *(20 Owners included in Index)*

Financial Data: ***Fiscal Year End:***12/31 ***Latest Annual Data:*** 12/31/2006

Year	Sales	Net Income
2006	$12,622,000,000	$1,181,000,000
2005	$11,852,000,000	$1,137,000,000
2004	$10,199,000,000	$916,000,000

Curr. Assets:	$5,482,000,000	***Curr. Liab.:***	$4,303,000,000		
Plant, Equip.:	$22,764,000,000	***Total Liab.:***	$27,366,000,000	***Indic. Yr. Divd.:***	$1.160
Total Assets:	$36,261,000,000	***Net Worth:***	$8,624,000,000	***Debt/ Equity:***	1.1440

Edmonds 1 Inc

4000 Bridgeway, Ste. 101, Sausalito, CA, 94965; ***PH:*** 1-415-339-4240; ***http://*** www.redmileentertainment.com

General - Incorporation	DE	***Stock*** - Price on:12/24/2007	NA
Employees	NA	Stock Exchange	NA
Auditor	Burr, Pilger & Mayer LLP	Ticker Symbol	NA
Stk Agt	Corporate Stock Transfer, Inc.	Outstanding Shares	NA
Counsel	NA	E.P.S.	-$1.56
DUNS No.	NA	Shareholders	NA

Business: The group's principal activity is to engage in any lawful corporate undertaking, including selected mergers and acquisitions. The company offers services to foreign or domestic private companies to become public company whose securities are qualified for trading in the United States secondary market.

Primary SIC and add'l.: 9995

CIK No: 0001309053

Subsidiaries: 2WG LLC, 2WG Media, Inc

Officers: Chester Aldridge/Chmn., CEO/$761,625.00, Ben Zadik/CFO/$761,625.00, Mike Fegan/Dir. - International Publishing/$1,264,167.00, Glenn Wong/COO, Pres., Henry Price/Sr. Dir. - Sales, Marketing, Simon Price/Mgr. - Financial Planning, Analysis, Yas Noguchi/Dir. - Product Development

Directors: Chester Aldridge/Chmn., CEO, R. H. Auchinleck/56/Dir., Geoff Heath/Dir., Kenny Cheung/Dir., James T. McCubbin/Dir.

Owners: Insiders/26.78%, Kenny Cheung/22.91%, James McCubbin, Ben Zadik/1.33%, Richard Auchinleck, Glenn Wong, Geoff Heath, JJJ Joseph Abrams/5.86%, Fluent Entertainment, Inc./26.32%, Chester Aldridge/2.56%

Financial Data: ***Fiscal Year End:***03/31 ***Latest Annual Data:*** 03/31/2007

Year	Sales	Net Income
2007	$1,018,000	-$8,039,000

Curr. Assets:	$8,917,000	***Curr. Liab.:***	$2,119,000		
Plant, Equip.:	$241,000	***Total Liab.:***	$10,363,000	***Indic. Yr. Divd.:***	NA
Total Assets:	$9,762,000	***Net Worth:***	-$602,000	***Debt/ Equity:***	NA

EDO Corp

60 E 42nd St., 42nd Fl., New York, NY, 10165; ***PH:*** 1-212-716-2000; ***Fax:*** 1-212-716-2049; ***http://*** www.edocorp.com; ***Email:*** ir@edocorp.com

General - Incorporation	NY	**Stock**- Price on:12/24/2007	$34.01
Employees	4,000	Stock Exchange	NYSE
Auditor	Ernst & Young LLP	Ticker Symbol	EDO
Stk Agt	American Stock Transfer & Trust Co.	Outstanding Shares	21,190,000
Counsel	NA	E.P.S	$0.93
DUNS No.	00-187-6440	Shareholders	NA

Business: The group's principal activities are designing and manufacturing advanced electronic mechanical systems and engineered materials for use in domestic and international defense and industrial markets. The group operates in three segments. The defense segment provides integrated front-line war fighting systems and components including electronic warfare systems, aircraft weapons-suspension and release systems and integrated combat systems. The products of the defense segment are sold to the us department of defense and to the us government for resale to foreign governments. The communications and space products segment includes antenna products and ultra-miniature electronics and systems. The engineered materials segment includes electro-ceramic products and advanced fiber-composite structural products. During 2003, the group acquired advanced engineering & research associates, inc, darlington, inc and emblem group ltd.

Primary SIC and add'l.: 3429 3559 3812

CIK No: 0000031617

Subsidiaries: Darlington Inc., Edo (uk) Limited, EDO Artisan Inc., EDO Communications and Countermeasures Systems Inc., EDO MBM Technology Limited, EDO MTech Inc., EDO Professional Services Inc., EDO Reconnaissance and Surveillance Systems, Inc., EDO Rugged Systems Limited, EDO Western Corporation, EVI Technology, LLC, Fiber Innovations, Inc., NexGen Communications LLC, Specialty Plastics, Inc.

Officers: James M. Smith/67/Chmn., CEO, Pres./$1,470,410.00, Lee Buchanan/VP - Advanced Concepts, Milo Hyde/VP - Systems, Analysis Group, Frank W. Otto/Sr. VP - Strategic Development/$469,950.00, Roy Byrd/VP - Usmc Relations, Greg Kudla/Corporate Controller, Michael Bechara/Dir. - Internal Audit, William Bender/VP - Corporate Contracts Management, John Vollmer/VP - C4 Sector, Jon A. Anderson/Sr. VP - Washington Operations, Effie Pavlou/Dir.y, Treasury, Lisa M. Palumbo/Sr. VP, General Counsel, Sec./$534,369.00, Gayle Lombardi/VP - Corporate Tax, Art Causin/Dir. - Corporate Compliance, Regina M. Ducati/Dir. - Staffing, Organizational Development *(26 Officers included in Index)*

Directors: James M. Smith/67/Chmn., CEO, Pres., John A. Gordon/61/Dir., Paul J. Kern/62/Dir., Robert Walmsley/67/Dir., Michael J. Hegarty/68/Dir., Robert Alvine/69/Dir., Robert S. Tyrer/50/Dir., Robert M. Hanisee/69/Dir., James Roth/71/Dir., Robert E. Allen/63/Dir., Leslie F. Kenne/60/Dir.

Owners: Paul J. Kern, Cardinal Capital Management, LLC/9.88%, Robert E. Allen, James Roth, Leslie F. Kenne, Robert S. Tyrer, Insiders/6.10%, Patricia D. Comiskey, EDO Employee Stock Ownership Plan/16.90%, Robert Alvine, Lisa M. Palumbo, Citadel Limited Partnership/5.90%, BlackRock Inc./10.93%, Frank W. Otto, Frederic B. Bassett *(21 Owners included in Index)*

Financial Data: *Fiscal Year End:*12/31 *Latest Annual Data:* 12/31/2006

Year	Sales	Net Income
2006	$715,197,000	$11,577,000
2005	$648,482,000	$26,269,000
2004	$536,173,000	$29,068,000

Curr. Assets:	$372,717,000	**Curr. Liab.:**	$375,997,000	**P/E Ratio:**	35.06
Plant, Equip.:	$59,109,000	**Total Liab.:**	$674,906,000	**Indic. Yr. Divd.:**	$0.120
Total Assets:	$949,822,000	**Net Worth:**	$274,916,000	**Debt/ Equity:**	NA

eDOORWAYS Corp

Formerly: M Power Entertainment Inc
2602 Yorktown Pl, Houston, TX, 77056; *PH:* 1-713-966-9893; *Fax:* 1-832-565-9290; *http://* www.mpe.us.com; *Email:* Info@mpe.us.com

General - Incorporation	DE	**Stock**- Price on:12/24/2007	$0.0005
Employees	1	Stock Exchange	OTC
Auditor	NA	Ticker Symbol	EDWY
Stk Agt	American Registrar & Transfer Co	Outstanding Shares	212,870,000
Counsel	NA	E.P.S	-$2.553
DUNS No.	NA	Shareholders	NA

Business: The groups principal activity is to create ubiquitous lifestyle platform named Edoorways, designed to offer interactivity and support for today's visually oriented web surfing community. Services of the group include e-commerce, distance learning, advertising, consultative and marketing. The group operates from the United States.

Primary SIC and add'l.: 7379

CIK No: 0001024095

Subsidiaries: Ascendant Texas Source Group, Inc., CoraZong Music Management B.V., R.S. Entertainment, Inc., Stellar Software Network, Inc., Texas Source Group, Inc.

Officers: Gary F. Kimmons/Chmn., CEO, Pres.

Directors: Gary F. Kimmons/Chmn., CEO, Pres.

Owners: Dick Meador, Lance Kimmons, Kathryn Kimmons/3.70%, Gary F. Kimmons/3.70%

Financial Data: *Fiscal Year End:*12/31 *Latest Annual Data:* 12/31/2006

Year	Sales	Net Income
2006	NA	-$4,465,000
2005	NA	-$13,858,000
2004	$953,000	-$4,657,000

Curr. Assets:	$743,000	**Curr. Liab.:**	$5,193,000		
Plant, Equip.:	$4,000	**Total Liab.:**	$5,323,000	**Indic. Yr. Divd.:**	NA
Total Assets:	$1,048,000	**Net Worth:**	-$4,275,000	**Debt/ Equity:**	NA

EDP Energias De Portugal SA

Formerly: EDP Electricidade de Portugal
Praa Marqus De Pombal, 12, Lisbon; ; *http://* www.edp.pt

General - Incorporation	Portugal	**Stock**- Price on:12/24/2007	NA
Employees	13,918	Stock Exchange	NA
Auditor	KPMG & Associados, Sroc, S.A	Ticker Symbol	NA
Stk Agt	NA	Outstanding Shares	NA
Counsel	Puglisi & Associates	E.P.S	NA
DUNS No.	44-921-1283	Shareholders	NA

Business: The group's principle activities include generation and distribution of electric power, telecommunications and information technologies. The group operates from United States.

Primary SIC and add'l.: 4911 4899

CIK No: 0001039610

Subsidiaries: EBE Empresa Bandeirante de Energia, S.A, EDP Distribuio Energia, S.A, EDP Energias do Brasil, S.A., EDP Gesto da Produo de Energia, S.A, EDP Comercial, S.A, Enersul Empresa Energtica do Mato Grosso do Sul S.A, Escelsa Espirito Santo Centrais Elctricas S.A, Genesa I, S.L., Hidrocantbrico Hidroelctrica del Cantbrico, S.A, Hidrocantbrico Distribuicin Elctrica, S.A.U., Naturcorp Multiservicios, S.A.U., Nuevas Energias de Occidente, SL, ONI Operadora Nacional de Interactivos, Portgs Sociedade de Produo e Distribuio de Gs

Officers: Antonio Luis Guerra Nunes Mexia/Chmn., CEO, Joao Manuel Manso Neto/Executive Dir., Ana Maria Machado Fernandes/Executive Dir., Joao Manuel Manso Neto/Executive Dir., Maria Teresa Isabel Pereira/Company Sec., Maria Virginia Bastos Dos Santos/Alternative Sec., Antonio Fernando Melo Martins Da Costa/Executive Dir., Antonio Manuel Barreto Pita De Abreu/Executive Dir., Jorge Manuel Pragana Da Cruz Morais/Member - Executive Dir., Nuno Maria Pestana De Almeida Alves/Executive Dir.

Directors: Antonio Luis Guerra Nunes Mexia/Chmn., CEO, Antonio De Almeida/Chmn. - General, Supervisory Board, Alberto Joao Coraceiro De Castro/Vice Chmn. - General, Member - Supervisory Board, Manuel Fernando De Macedo Alves Monteiro/Member - General Supervisory Board, Jose Manuel Archer Galvao Teles/Member - General Supervisory Board, Vitor Fernando Da Conceicao Goncalves/Member - General Supervisory Board, Carlos Jorge Feijoo Pereira Ribeiro/Member - Supervisory Board, Antonio Fernando Melo Martins Da Costa/Executive Dir., Antonio Manuel Barreto Pita De Abreu/Executive Dir., Joao Manuel Manso Neto/Executive Dir., Nuno Maria Pestana De Almeida Alves/Executive Dir., Manuel Fernando De Macedo Alves Monteiro/Member - General Supervisory Board, Eduardo De Almeida Catroga/Member - General Supervisory Board, Ana Maria Machado Fernandes/Executive Dir., Joao Manuel Manso Neto/Executive Dir. *(25 Directors included in Index)*

Financial Data: *Fiscal Year End:*12/31 *Latest Annual Data:* 12/31/2005

Year	Sales	Net Income
2005	$10,954,166,000	$1,313,394,000
2004	$9,853,274,000	$325,544,000
2003	$8,761,672,000	$625,347,000

Curr. Assets:	$5,123,449,000	**Curr. Liab.:**	$7,735,508,000		
Plant, Equip.:	$15,762,238,000	**Total Liab.:**	$22,973,938,000	**Indic. Yr. Divd.:**	NA
Total Assets:	$29,556,559,000	**Net Worth:**	$6,582,620,000	**Debt/ Equity:**	NA

Educate Inc

1001 Fleet St., Baltimore, MD, 21022; *PH:* 1-410-843-6848; *http://* www.educate-inc.com

General - Incorporation	DE	**Stock**- Price on:12/24/2007	NA
Employees	2,375	Stock Exchange	NA
Auditor	Ernst & Young LLP	Ticker Symbol	NA
Stk Agt	LaSalle Bank N.A	Outstanding Shares	NA
Counsel	NA	E.P.S	NA
DUNS No.	NA	Shareholders	NA

Business: The groups principle activity is to provide supplemental education services. The group provides to public and non-public schools through its school partnership business, Catapult Learning. The group operates from United States.

Primary SIC and add'l.: NA

CIK No: 0001286862

Subsidiaries: Catapult Learning, LLC, Catapult Online, LLC, Dorana Einundvierzigste Verwal tungsgesellschaft mbH, Educate Group, LLC, Educate Operating Company, LLC, Education Station, LLC, eSylvan, Inc., HOP, LLC, L&S Education, Inc., MLS Education, Inc., Progressus Therapy, Inc., Schuelerhilfe Promotion GmbH, Schulerhilfe Gesellschaft fur Nachhilfeunterricht GmbH& Co. KG, SLC California, LLC, Sylvan Canada, Inc. 21 Subsidiaries included in the Index

Officers: Christopher R. Hoehn-Saric/Chmn., CEO, Peter J. Cohen/Pres. - Sylvan Learning, Educate, Inc, Jeffrey H. Cohen/Pres. - Catapult Learning, Alan C. Schroeder/General Counsel, Sec., Kevin E. Shaffer/CFO, Chip Paucek/Pres. - Educate Products

Directors: Christopher R. Hoehn-Saric/Chmn., CEO, Douglas L. Becker/Dir., Michael Devine/Dir., Raul Yzaguirre/Dir., Cheryl Gordon Krongard/Dir., Aaron Stone/Dir., Michael Gross/Dir., David Hornbeck/Dir., Laurence Berg/Dir.

Owners: Jeffrey H. Cohen, Michael D. Weiner, Raul Yzaguirre, Aaron Stone, Peter J. Cohen, Kevin E. Shaffer, Laurence Berg, Cheryl Krongard, Apollo Advisors IV, L.P., Kornitzer Capital Management, Inc., Christopher R. Hoehn-Saric, David W. Hornbeck, Christopher J. Paucek, Michael F. Devine

Education Mgmt Corp

300 Sixth Ave., Pittsburgh, PA, 15222; *PH:* 1-412-562-0900; *http://* www.edumgt.com

General - Incorporation	PA	**Stock**- Price on:12/24/2007	NA
Employees	NA	Stock Exchange	NDQ
Auditor	Ernst & Young LLP	Ticker Symbol	EDMC
Stk Agt	Mellon Investor Services LLC	Outstanding Shares	NA
Counsel	Kirkpatrick & Lockhart	E.P.S	NA
DUNS No.	06-872-8039	Shareholders	NA

Business: The group's principal activities are to provide private post-secondary education and career-oriented education. It delivers education to its students through traditional classroom settings as well as through online instruction. As of Jun 30, 2004, the group had 67 primary campus locations in 24 states and two Canadian provinces. The group's educational systems offer a broad range of academic programs concentrated in the media arts, design, fashion, culinary arts, behavioural sciences, health sciences, education, information technology, legal studies and business fields, culminating in the award of associate's through doctoral degrees. The group offers its academic programs through the art institutes, argosy university, south university & American education centers. The group acquired south university inc, American education centers inc, dubrulle international culinary and hotel institute of Canada and bradley academy for the visual arts in fiscal 2004.

Primary SIC and add'l.: 8221 8249

CIK No: 0000880059

Subsidiaries: American Education Centers Inc., Argosy Education Group, Inc., Brown Mackie Education Corporation, Brown Mackie Holding Company, Commonwealth Business College Education Corporation, Miami International University of Art& Design, Inc., Michiana College Education Corporation, South University of Alabama, Inc., South University of Carolina, Inc., South University of Florida, Inc., South University, Inc., Southern Ohio College, LLC, Stautzenberger College Education Corporation, TAICSan Diego, Inc. d/b/a The Art Institute of CaliforniaSan Diego, TAICSan Francisco, Inc. d/b/a The Art Institute of CaliforniaSan Francisco 39 Subsidiaries included in the Index

Officers: Stacey R. Sauchuk/Sr. VP - Academic Programs, Student Affairs, Ronald W. Orgodnik/Sr. VP - Human Resources, John M. Mazzoni/43/Sr. VP, Pres. - Art Institute, Joe Charlson/Sr. VP, Chief Marketing Officer, Stephen J. Weiss/Pres., Roberta Troike/Sr. VP - Human Resources, James R. Sober/VP - Finance, Edward H. West/CFO, Exec. VP

Directors: John R. McKernan/58/Chmn., Adrian M. Jones/42/Dir., Jeffrey T. Leeds/52/Dir., Todd S. Nelson/48/Dir., Leo F. Mullin/64/Dir., Paul J. Salem/43/Dir., Peter Wilde/38/Dir.

Owners: Paul J. Salem, Peter O. Wilde, Leeds Equity Partners, Adrian M. Jones, Edward H. West, GS EDMC Investors, LP, Stephen J. Weiss, John R. McKernan, Todd S. Nelson, GS Private Equity Partners Funds, Insiders, Leo F. Mullin, John M. Mazzoni, Jeffrey T. Leeds, GS Limited Partnerships *(17 Owners included in Index)*

Education Realty Trust Inc

530 Oak Ct. Dr., Ste. 300, Memphis, TN, 38117; *PH:* 1-901-259-2500; *Fax:* 1-901-259-2594; *http://* www.educationrealty.com

General		Stock	
Incorporation	MD	Price on:12/24/2007	$14.35
Employees	1,065	Stock Exchange	NYSE
Auditor	Deloitte & Touche LLP	Ticker Symbol	EDR
Stk Agt	American Stock Transfer & Trust CO.	Outstanding Shares	27,970,000
Counsel	Bass Berry & Sims, PLC	E.P.S	-$0.45
DUNS No.	NA	Shareholders	NA

Business: The groups principle activities include owning, managing and developing of student housing. The group operates through three segments namely, student housing leasing, third party development consulting services and third party management services. The group operates from the United States. The group's quarterly revenue for September 2007 was 28.33 millions of USD.

Primary SIC and add'l.: 6798

CIK No: 0001302343

Subsidiaries: A & O/ Acedemic Privatization, Allen & OHara Development Company, LLC, Allen & OHara Education Services, Inc., AOD / Raleigh Residence Hall, LLC, AODC/CPA, LLC, APF EDR, LP, APF Food Services, LP, Cape Place (DE), LLC, Carrolton Place, LLC, Clayton Place (DE), LLC, EDR Athens I, LLC, EDR Auburn, LLC, EDR Berkeley Place GP, LLC, EDR Berkeley Place Limited Partnership, EDR C Station, LLC 111 Subsidiaries included in the Index

Officers: Paul O. Bower/Chmn., CEO, Pres. - Education Realty Trust, Randall H. Brown/Exec. VP, CFO, Treasurer, Sec. - Allen, O'hara Education Services, Inc, Craig L. Cardwell/Exec. VP, Chief Investment Officer - Allen, O'hara Education Services, Inc, William W. Harris/Sr. VP - Development, Allen, O'hara Education Services, Inc, Thomas J. Hickey/Sr. VP - Operations, Allen, O'hara Education Services, Inc, Wallace L. Wilcox/VP - Construction, Engineering, Allen, O'hara Education Services, Inc, Susan B. Arrison/VP - Human Resources, Allen, O'hara Education Services, Inc, Drew J. Koester/VP, Assist. Sec., Chief Accounting Officer, Thomas Trubiana/Sr. VP, Chief Investment Officer

Directors: Paul O. Bower/Chmn., CEO, Pres. - Education Realty Trust, Monte J. Barrow/Dir. - Allen, O'hara Education Services, Inc, William J. Cahill/Dir. - Allen, O'hara Education Services, Inc, John L. Ford/Dir. - Allen, O'hara Education Services, Inc, Wendell W. Weakley/53/Dir.

Owners: Thomas Trubiana, Monte J. Barrow, Paul O. Bower/3.10%, Randall H. Brown, Insiders/4.20%, William J. Cahill, John L. Ford, William W. Harris, Craig L. Cardwell, Randall L. Churchey

Financial Data: *Fiscal Year End:*12/31 *Latest Annual Data:* 12/31/2006

Year	Sales	Net Income
2006	$119,291,000	-$12,245,000
2005	$87,243,000	-$15,551,000
2004	NA	-$222,000

Curr. Assets:	$16,177,000	Curr. Liab.:	$10,764,000		
Plant, Equip.:	$805,511,000	Total Liab.:	$532,459,000	Indic. Yr. Divd.:	NA
Total Assets:	$835,458,000	Net Worth:	$302,999,000	Debt/ Equity:	1.5760

Educational Development Corp

10302 E 55th Pl., Tulsa, OK, 74146; *PH:* 1-918-622-4522; *Fax:* 1-918-665-7919; *http://* www.edcpub.com

General		Stock	
Incorporation	DE	Price on:12/24/2007	$8.19
Employees	78	Stock Exchange	NDQ
Auditor	Tullius Taylor Sartain & Sartain LLP	Ticker Symbol	EDUC
Stk Agt	American Stock Transfer & Trust Co.	Outstanding Shares	3,770,000
Counsel	NA	E.P.S	$0.62
DUNS No.	00-747-0578	Shareholders	NA

Business: The group's principle activity is to distribute books and publications through its publishing and usborne books at home divisions to book, toy and gift stores, libraries and home educators located throughout the United States. The group operates through two divisions: usborne books at home division and publishing division. The usborne books at home division distributes books through independent consultants who hold book showings in individual homes and through book fairs, direct sales and Internet sales. It also distributes these titles to schools and public libraries. The publishing division markets books to bookstores, toy stores, specialty stores and other retail outlets. The group operates solely in the domestic market. The group's total revenue for the year 2007 was 31.40 millions of USD.

Primary SIC and add'l.: 5192

CIK No: 0000031667

Officers: Randall W. White/Chmn., CEO, Pres.

Directors: Randall W. White/Chmn., CEO, Pres.

Owners: James F. Lewis/2.40%, FMR Corp/9.90%, Dean G. Cosgrove, Randall W. White/19.60%, Insiders/25.70%, John A. Clerico, Richard L. Scott Revocable Trust/9.30%

Financial Data: *Fiscal Year End:*02/28 *Latest Annual Data:* 2/28/2007

Year	Sales	Net Income
2007	$31,403,000	$2,407,000
2006	$31,789,000	$2,398,000
2005	$31,651,000	$2,406,000

Curr. Assets:	$16,708,000	Curr. Liab.:	$4,041,000	P/E Ratio:	13.21
Plant, Equip.:	$2,844,000	Total Liab.:	$4,041,000	Indic. Yr. Divd.:	$0.220
Total Assets:	$19,702,000	Net Worth:	$15,661,000	Debt/ Equity:	NA

Edwards LifeSciences Corp

1 Edwards Way, Irvine, CA, 92614; *PH:* 1-949-250-2500; *Fax:* 1-949-250-2525; *http://* www.edwards.com; *Email:* investor_relations@edwards.com

General		Stock	
Incorporation	DE	Price on:12/24/2007	$49.26
Employees	5,550	Stock Exchange	NYSE
Auditor	PricewaterhouseCoopers LLP	Ticker Symbol	EW
Stk Agt	Computershare Investor Services LLC	Outstanding Shares	57,630,000
Counsel	NA	E.P.S	$1.91
DUNS No.	NA	Shareholders	NA

Business: The group's principal activities are to provide products and technologies that are designed to treat advanced cardiovascular disease. The product lines are grouped into four areas: cardiac surgery, critical care, vascular and perfusion. The cardiac surgery product line manufactures cannulae and cardioplegia products used during open-heart surgery. Critical care products include hemodynamic monitoring systems used to measure patient's heart function. Vascular products include a line of angioscopy equipment and artificial implantable grafts used to treat life threatening abdominal aortic aneurysms. The perfusion products consist of a diverse line of disposable and hardware products used during cardiopulmonary bypass surgical procedures. On 27-Jan-2004, the group acquired percutaneous valve technologies inc.

Primary SIC and add'l.: 3845 2834

CIK No: 0001099800

Subsidiaries: Benchmark, Inc., Edwards Lifesciences (Canada) Inc., Edwards Lifesciences (India) Private Limited, Edwards Lifesciences (Japan) Limited, Edwards Lifesciences (Singapore) Pte Ltd, Edwards Lifesciences (Thailand) Ltd., Edwards Lifesciences (U.S.) Inc., Edwards Lifesciences A/S, Edwards Lifesciences AG, Edwards Lifesciences Asset Management Corporation, Edwards Lifesciences Austria GmbH, Edwards Lifesciences B.V., Edwards Lifesciences Comercio e Industria de Produtos Medico-Cirurgicos Ltda., Edwards Lifesciences Corporation of Puerto Rico, Edwards Lifesciences Export (Puerto Rico) Corporation 48 Subsidiaries included in the Index

Officers: Michael A. Mussallem/Chmn., CEO/$4,634,268.00, John H. Kehl/Corporate VP - Corporate Strategy, Business Development, Anita B. Bessler/Corporate VP - Global Franchise Management/$1,411,819.00, Stanton Rowe/Corporate VP - Advanced Technology, Larry Wood/Corporate VP - Transcatheter Valve Replacement, Jay P. Wertheim/VP, Assoc. General Counsel, Sec., Patrick B. Verguet/Corporate VP - Europe, Stuart L. Foster/Corporate VP - Critical Care, Vascular/$1,676,265.00, Bruce P. Garren/Corporate VP, General Counsel - Government Affairs, David K. Erickson/VP - Investor Relations, Elizabeth O'Hare/Mgr. - Investor Relations, Donald E. Bobo/Corporate VP - Heart Valve Therapy, Alex Martin/Corporate VP - North America, John P. McGrath/Corporate VP - Quality, Paul C. Redmond/Corporate VP - Vascular *(20 Officers included in Index)*

Directors: Michael A. Mussallem/Chmn., CEO, John T. Cardis/Dir., Robert A. Ingram/Dir., David E.I. Pyott/Dir., Philip M. Neal/Dir., Mike R. Bowlin/Dir., Barbara J. McNeil/Dir., Vernon R. Loucks/Dir.

Owners: T. Rowe Price Associates, Inc./9.00%, Corinne H. Lyle, Thomas M. Abate, Iridian Asset Management LLC/8.00%, Mike R. Bowlin, Stuart L. Foster, Anita B. Bessler, Michael A. Mussallem/2.00%, Insiders/5.80%, Philip M. Neal, Vernon R. Loucks, Barbara J. McNeil, Robert A. Ingram, David E.I. Pyott, John T. Cardis

Financial Data: *Fiscal Year End:*12/31 *Latest Annual Data:* 12/31/2006

Year	Sales	Net Income
2006	$1,037,000,000	$130,500,000
2005	$997,900,000	$79,300,000
2004	$931,500,000	$1,700,000

Curr. Assets:	$531,600,000	Curr. Liab.:	$226,200,000	P/E Ratio:	25.79
Plant, Equip.:	$213,000,000	Total Liab.:	$497,400,000	Indic. Yr. Divd.:	NA
Total Assets:	$1,246,800,000	Net Worth:	$749,400,000	Debt/ Equity:	0.2859

EESTech Inc

23011 Moulton Pkwy., A-10, Laguna Hills, CA, 92653; *PH:* 1-949-380-4033; *http://* eestechinc.com

General		Stock	
Incorporation	DE	Price on:12/24/2007	$0.89
Employees	1	Stock Exchange	OTC
Auditor	Vasquez & Co. LLP	Ticker Symbol	EESH
Stk Agt	Integrity Stock Transfer, Inc.	Outstanding Shares	18,280,000
Counsel	NA	E.P.S	-$0.29
DUNS No.	NA	Shareholders	NA

Business: The groups principal activity is to provide engineering advice for solution solving. In the year 2006, the group acquired Methgen Inc. The group operates from the United States.

Primary SIC and add'l.: 3589 4911 4941 3589 4911

CIK No: 0001138867

Subsidiaries: Aqua Dyne Australia Pty Ltd

Officers: Murray Bailey/Chmn., CEO, Pres./$26,200.00, Ian Hutcheson/Sec. - Fcis Company, Antony Sachs/Mgr. - Business Development, Paul Wootton/Mgr. - Engineering Services, Greg Paxton/Mgr. - Research, Development, Chris Cooper/CFO, Sec.

Directors: Murray Bailey/Chmn., CEO, Pres., Gaylord Beeson/Dir.

Owners: Murray Bailey, Insiders, Ian Hutcheson, Gaylord Beeson

Financial Data: *Fiscal Year End:*12/31 *Latest Annual Data:* 12/31/2006

Year	Sales	Net Income
2006	NA	-$1,873,000
2005	NA	-$1,738,000
2004	NA	-$5,159,000

Curr. Assets:	$53,000	Curr. Liab.:	$394,000		
Plant, Equip.:	$58,000	Total Liab.:	$394,000	Indic. Yr. Divd.:	NA
Total Assets:	$114,000	Net Worth:	-$280,000	Debt/ Equity:	NA

EFC Bancorp Inc

1695 Larkin Ave, Elgin, IL, 60123; *PH:* 1-847-741-3900; *http://* www.mafbancorp.com

General		Stock	
Incorporation	DE	Price on:12/24/2007	$34.65
Employees	NA	Stock Exchange	AMEX
Auditor	KPMG LLP	Ticker Symbol	EFC
Stk Agt	LaSalle Bank N.A	Outstanding Shares	NA
Counsel	Muldoon Murphy & Faucette	E.P.S	NA
DUNS No.	NA	Shareholders	NA

Business: The group's principal activity is to provide financial services to customers located in the United States. The group is a community-oriented financial institution that accepts deposits from the general public and invests these deposits in one-to four-family residential mortgage loans, multi-family and commercial real estate loans, construction and land loans, commercial business loans, home equity loans, and automobile and passbook savings loans. The group also invests in government insured or guaranteed mortgage-backed securities and us government obligations. The activities are conducted through four banking facilities located in elgin and four facilities located in carpentersville, west dundee, east dundee and huntley, Illinois. The group is a holding company for elgin financial savings bank.

Primary SIC and add'l.: 6162 6035 6712

CIK No: 0001047947

Subsidiaries: Computer Dynamics Group, Inc, EFS Financial Services, Inc., EFS Service Corporation

EFJ Inc

1440 Corporate Dr., Irving, TX, 75038; *PH:* 1-972-819-0700; *Fax:* 1-972-819-0639; *http://* www.efji.com

General - Incorporation	DE	**Stock**- Price on:12/24/2007	$5.66
Employees	375	Stock Exchange	NDQ
Auditor	Grant Thornton LLP	Ticker Symbol	EFJI
Stk Agt	Wells Fargo Shareowner Services	Outstanding Shares	26,030,000
Counsel	NA	E.P.S	-$0.16
DUNS No.	10-231-7096	Shareholders	NA

Business: The group's principal activities are to manufacture wireless communication products and systems and information security products. It also designs, develops, manufactures and markets: stationary land mobile radio ('lmr') transmitters/receivers (base stations or repeaters); and mobile and portable radios. It sells its lmr products and systems mainly to two broad markets: public safety and other governmental users and commercial users. The customers of the group include public safety agencies and police forces, federal government agencies, foreign governments, the military, cellular service providers, lmr manufacturers and business and corporate users in finance, manufacturing and media/entertainment and other industries. It sells its products in the United States, Europe, Asia and central and Latin America.

Primary SIC and add'l.: 3663 3660

CIK No: 0001023516

Subsidiaries: E.F. Johnson Company, Transcrypt International, Inc.

Officers: Michael E. Jalbert/Chmn., CEO, Pres./$1,132,750.00, Jana Ahlfinger Bell/Sr. VP, CFO, Massoud Safavi/COO/$123,607.00, Jenny Christensen/Dir. - Marketing, Secured Communications Division, Kevin Nolan/Marketing Communications Dir., Steven Chen/Sr. VP, Technology Officer, John Rothermel/General Counsel

Directors: Michael E. Jalbert/Chmn., CEO, Pres., Winston J. Wade/Dir., Veronica Haggart/Dir., Thomas R. Thomsen/Dir., Edward H. Bersoff/Dir., Mark S. Newman/Dir.

Owners: Insiders/2.10%, Jana Ahlfinger Bell, Winston J. Wade, Ellen OHara, Robert C. Donohoo, Thomas R. Thomsen, Edward H. Bersoff, ICM Asset Management/11.30%, Michael B. Gamble, Mark S. Newman, Wellington Management Company, LLP/13.15%, Veronica A. Haggart, Michael E. Jalbert/1.30%, Putnam Investments/7.10%

Financial Data: *Fiscal Year End:*12/31 *Latest Annual Data:* 12/31/2006

Year	Sales	Net Income
2006	$96,721,000	-$6,781,000
2005	$94,616,000	$22,549,000
2004	$80,870,000	$9,958,000

Curr. Assets:	$88,467,000	**Curr. Liab.:**	$20,525,000		
Plant, Equip.:	$6,744,000	**Total Liab.:**	$35,857,000	**Indic. Yr. Divd.:**	NA
Total Assets:	$152,563,000	**Net Worth:**	$116,706,000	**Debt/ Equity:**	0.1283

eFoodSafety.com Inc

7702 E Doubletree Ranch Rd., Ste. 300, Scottsdale, AZ, 85258; *PH:* 1-480-607-2606; *Fax:* 1-480-348-3999; *http://* www.efoodsafety.com

General - Incorporation	NV	**Stock**- Price on:12/24/2007	$0.29
Employees	4	Stock Exchange	OTC
Auditor	Gruber & Co., LLC	Ticker Symbol	EFSF
Stk Agt	Signature Stock Transfer, Inc.	Outstanding Shares	156,320,000
Counsel	NA	E.P.S	NA
DUNS No.	NA	Shareholders	NA

Business: The group operates through its subsidiary whose principle activity is to improve health conditions around the world. In the year 2005, the group acquired MedElite, Inc. The group operates from the United States. The groups annual revenue for September 2007 was 1.17 millions of USD.

Primary SIC and add'l.: 2833

CIK No: 0001157075

Subsidiaries: Knock-Out Technologies, Inc, MedElite, Inc

Officers: Patricia Ross-Gruden/Chmn., CEO, Pres., Timothy Matula/Dir., Sec., Bob Bowker/Dir., MD - Research, Development, Steven Kushner/Efoodsafetycom Nutritionist

Directors: Patricia Ross-Gruden/Chmn., CEO, Pres., Timothy Matula/Dir., Sec., Richard M. Goldfarb/Dir., Bob Bowker/Dir., MD - Research, Development

Owners: Richard Goldfarb/6.11%, Patricia Gruden/15.38%, Timothy Matula, Insiders/24.00%, Robert Bowker/1.56%

Curr. Assets:	$3,433,000	**Curr. Liab.:**	$119,000		
Plant, Equip.:	$8,000	**Total Liab.:**	$119,000	**Indic. Yr. Divd.:**	NA
Total Assets:	$4,405,000	**Net Worth:**	$4,286,000	**Debt/ Equity:**	NA

eFunds Corp

4900 N Scottsdale Rd., Ste. 1000, Scottsdale, AZ, 85251; *PH:* 1-480-629-7700; *http://* www.efunds.com

General - Incorporation	DE	**Stock**- Price on:12/24/2007	$35.41
Employees	5,300	Stock Exchange	NA
Auditor	KPMG LLP	Ticker Symbol	NA
Stk Agt	EquiServe Trust Co N.A	Outstanding Shares	47,380,000
Counsel	Simpson Thacher & Bartlett LLP	E.P.S	$1.16
DUNS No.	NA	Shareholders	NA

Business: The group's principal activities are transaction processing, ATM management, risk management and professional services to financial institutions, retailers, electronic funds transfer networks and government agencies. The group operates in four segments: electronic payments which provides electronic funds transfer, automated clearinghouse and other payment processing services; ATM management services which provides ATM deployment, management and branding services; decision support and risk management which provides risk management based data and other products that assist in detecting fraud and assessing the risk of opening a new account or accepting a check; professional services which provides business process management; it outsourcing services, maintenance and installation services. During the year 2003, the group acquired oasic technology ltd. On 21-Apr-2004, the group acquired penley inc and loss control solutions.

Primary SIC and add'l.: 8742 7375

CIK No: 0001109190

Subsidiaries: ACI-ATM Management Services, Inc., Analytic Research Technologies, Inc., Chex Systems, Inc., ClearCommerce Corporation, Deposit Payment Protection Services, Inc., eFunds (Canada) Corporation, eFunds Canada, Inc., eFunds Corporation, eFunds Corporation Payments Solutions and Services, eFunds Global Holdings Corporation, eFunds Holdings Limited, eFunds International India Private Limited, eFunds International Limited, eFunds IT Solutions Group, Inc., eFunds Overseas, Inc. 23 Subsidiaries included in the Index

Officers: Paul F. Walsh/Chmn., CEO/$3,092,572.00, Laura De Cespedes/Exec. VP - Human Resources, Clyde L. Thomas/CIO, Exec. VP - Global Technology, Operations/$876,219.00, Kay Nichols/Exec. VP - Strategy, Marketing, Product Development, Steven F. Coleman/Exec. VP, General Counsel, Sec., Helen Johnson/Investor Relations, Nelson G. Eng/Pres. - EFD US, George W. Gresham/CFO, Exec. VP - Finance/$603,940.00, Shailesh Kotwal/Pres. - EFD International

Directors: Paul F. Walsh/Chmn., CEO, Richard J. Almeida/Dir., Hatim A. Tyabi/Dir., John Boyle/Dir., Janet M. Clarke/Dir., Angel Cabrera/Dir., Richard J. Lehmann/Dir., Robert C. Nakasone/Dir.

Owners: Richard J. Lehmann, Kathleen Flanagan, Eminence Capital/7.74%, Westfield Capital Management Company, LLC/5.77%, Janet M. Clarke, John J. Boyle, George W. Gresham, Paul F. Walsh/1.45%, Gary L. Palmer, Richard J. Almeida, Insiders/3.01%, Royce & Associates, LLC/7.01%, Clyde L. Thomas, Harris Associates L.P./5.29%, Scoggin Capital Management, L.P. II/6.82% *(18 Owners included in Index)*

Financial Data: *Fiscal Year End:*12/31 *Latest Annual Data:* 12/31/2006

Year	Sales	Net Income
2006	$552,414,000	$54,546,000
2005	$501,708,000	$55,743,000
2004	$552,148,000	$40,818,000

Curr. Assets:	$341,882,000	**Curr. Liab.:**	$161,933,000	**P/E Ratio:**	31.06
Plant, Equip.:	$60,145,000	**Total Liab.:**	$290,012,000	**Indic. Yr. Divd.:**	NA
Total Assets:	$824,538,000	**Net Worth:**	$534,526,000	**Debt/ Equity:**	0.1851

eGain Communications Corp

345 E Middlefield Rd., Mountain View, CA, 94043; *PH:* 1-650-230-7500; *Fax:* 1-650-230-7600; *http://* www.egain.com

General - Incorporation	DE	**Stock**- Price on:12/24/2007	$1.06
Employees	253	Stock Exchange	OTC
Auditor	BDO Seidman LLP	Ticker Symbol	EGAN
Stk Agt	Boston EquiServe Shareholder Services	Outstanding Shares	15,320,000
Counsel	Pillsbury Madison & Sutro	E.P.S	-$0.56
DUNS No.	NA	Shareholders	NA

Business: The group's principal activity is to provide customer service and contact center enterprise software. The group's egain service (TM) includes applications for knowledge management, self-service, email management and Web collaboration. The software suite enables online customers to communicate through each of the three primary eservice channels: email, real-time and self-service. The group also provides software maintenance and support, training and system implementation consulting. The software applications are deployed either as a licensed application installed on servers at the customer location or as a hosted application service maintained and operated by the group's hosted operations.

Primary SIC and add'l.: 7372 6794 7376 7375

CIK No: 0001066194

Subsidiaries: eGain (Cayman) Ltd., eGain Communications B.V., eGain Communications GmbH, eGain Communications Ltd., eGain Communications Pacific Pte. Ltd, eGain Communications Pty Ltd., eGain Communications Pvt. Ltd., eGain Communications S.A., eGain Communications SrL, Inference Corporation

Officers: Ashutosh Roy/Co - Founder, Chmn., CEO, Eric Smit/CFO, Promod Narang/Sr. VP - Products, Technologies, Anand Subramaniam/VP - Marketing, Gunjan Sinha/Co - Founder, Dir., Ex - Pres., Stratos Davlos/VP - Professional Services, Andrew Mennie/VP, GM - Europe, Anurag Juneja/VP - Solutions, Tom Hresko/Sr. VP - Worldwide Sales, Stanley F. Pierson/Sec.

Directors: Ashutosh Roy/Co - Founder, Chmn., CEO, David Brown/Dir., Phiroz P. Darukhanavala/Dir., Mark A. Wolfson/Dir., Gunjan Sinha/Co - Founder, Dir., Ex - Pres.

Owners: Eric Smit/1.40%, Promod Narang/1.80%, Taylor J. Crandall/9.00%, Deutsche Bank A.G./6.40%, OHCP GenPar, L.P./27.90%, Mark A. Wolfson, Ashutosh Roy/10.40%, Insiders/20.70%, Granite Private Equity III, LLC/7.30%, Gunjan Sinha/7.30%, Thomas Hresko, David G. Brown, Crosslink Capital, Inc/8.80%

Financial Data: *Fiscal Year End:*06/30 *Latest Annual Data:* 6/30/2006

Year	Sales	Net Income
2006	$22,564,000	-$1,059,000
2005	$20,428,000	-$842,000
2004	$19,603,000	-$4,894,000

Curr. Assets:	$9,702,000	**Curr. Liab.:**	$9,355,000		
Plant, Equip.:	$1,169,000	**Total Liab.:**	$18,301,000	**Indic. Yr. Divd.:**	NA
Total Assets:	$16,105,000	**Net Worth:**	-$2,196,000	**Debt/ Equity:**	NA

eGene Inc

5525 S 900 E, Ste. 110, Salt City, UT, 84117; *PH:* 1-949-250-8686; *http://* www.egeneinc.com

General - Incorporation	NV	**Stock**- Price on:12/24/2007	$1.36
Employees	13	Stock Exchange	NA
Auditor	Mantyla McReynolds, LLC	Ticker Symbol	NA
Stk Agt	NA	Outstanding Shares	19,470,000
Counsel	NA	E.P.S	-$0.05
DUNS No.	NA	Shareholders	NA

Business: The groups principle activities include developing, manufacturing and marketing multi-channel bio-separation and detection tools. The group products include HDA-GT12(TM) and HLA SSP(TM). The group operates from the United States.

Primary SIC and add'l.: 1044

CIK No: 0001105409

Subsidiaries: BioCal Technology, Inc

Officers: Ming S. Liu/Chmn., CEO, Exec. VP, Varouj D. Amirkhanian/Dir., Exec. VP, Peter Sheu/CFO, David Molnar/Sales Dir.

Directors: Ming S. Liu/Chmn., CEO, Exec. VP, Varouj D. Amirkhanian/Dir., Exec. VP, Shing-Ching Lu/Dir., Andras Guttman/Member - Scientific Advisory Board, David Senitzer/Member - Scientific Advisory Board

Owners: Mark Bright Investments Ltd/9.49%, Sing-Ching Lu/4.67%, Ming S. Liu/7.16%, Varoujan Amirkhanian/4.85%

Financial Data: *Fiscal Year End:*12/31 *Latest Annual Data:* 12/31/2006

Year	Sales	Net Income
2006	$2,749,000	-$782,000
2005	$1,294,000	-$857,000
2004	$858,000	-$1,206,000

Curr. Assets:	$1,526,000	*Curr. Liab.:*	$1,102,000		
Plant, Equip.:	$255,000	*Total Liab.:*	$1,157,000	*Indic. Yr. Divd.:*	NA
Total Assets:	$2,179,000	*Net Worth:*	$1,022,000	*Debt/ Equity:*	0.0366

EGL Inc

15350 Vickery Dr., Houston, TX, 77032; *PH:* 1-281-618-3100; *Fax:* 1-281-618-3223; *http://* www.eaglegl.com; *Email:* eglinfo@eaglegl.com

General - Incorporation	TX	**Stock**- Price on:12/24/2007	$46.52
Employees	11,500	Stock Exchange	NA
Auditor	PricewaterhouseCoopers LLP	Ticker Symbol	NA
Stk Agt	Computershare Trust Co	Outstanding Shares	40,810,000
Counsel	Baker & Botts LLP	E.P.S.	$1.53
DUNS No.	11-299-8638	Shareholders	NA

Business: The group's principle activities include providing global transportation, supply chain management and information services. The group also provides air and ocean freight forwarding, customs brokerage, local pick up and delivery service, materials management, warehousing, trade facilitation, procurement, integrated logistics services. The group operates from United States.

Primary SIC and add'l.: 4212 4731

CIK No: 0001001718

Subsidiaries: Circle International Group, Inc., Circle International Holdings, Inc., Circle International, Inc., Eagle Global Logistics do Brasil, Ltda., EGL (Belgium) Holding Company, B.V.B.A., Egl (uk) Holding Company Limited, EGL Asia-Pacific Holdings Company Pte. Ltd., EGL Delaware Limited Liability Company, EGL Eagle Global Logisitcs (M) Sdn. Bhd., EGL Eagle Global Logisitcs (South Africa) (Pty) Ltd., EGL Eagle Global Logistica de Chile Ltda, EGL Eagle Global Logistics (Aust) Pty. Limited, EGL Eagle Global Logistics (Belgium) NV, EGL Eagle Global Logistics (Canada) Corp., EGL Eagle Global Logistics (Espana) SL 39 Subsidiaries included in the Index

Officers: James R. Crane/54/Chmn., CEO, Joseph E. Bento/45/Chief Marketing Officer, Pres. - North America, Vittorio Favati/49/Pres. - Asia Pacific Region, Ronald E. Talley/56/Pres. - Select Carrier Group, Dana A. Carabin/40/General Counsel, Sec., Chief Compliance Officer, Charles H. Leonard/59/CFO, Bruno Sidler/50/Pres. - Europe, Middle East, Africa Regions

Directors: James R. Crane/54/Chmn., CEO, Milton Carroll/Dir., James C. Flagg/Dir., Frank J. Hevrdejs/Dir., Paul William Hobby/Dir., Michael Jhin/Dir., Neil E. Kelley/Dir., Sherman Wolff/Dir.

Owners: James R. Crane/18.19%, Milton Carroll, Paul W. Hobby, Greg Weigel, Joseph E. Bento, Ronald E. Talley, Insiders/18.79%, Neil E. Kelley, Vittorio Favati, Bruno Sidler, Frank J. Hevrdejs, Michael K. Jhin, James C. Flagg, Sherman Wolff, Keith Winters

Financial Data: *Fiscal Year End:*12/31 *Latest Annual Data:* 12/31/2006

Year	Sales	Net Income
2006	$3,217,636,000	$56,330,000
2005	$3,096,516,000	$58,160,000
2004	$2,741,392,000	$50,878,000

Curr. Assets:	$835,550,000	*Curr. Liab.:*	$548,050,000	*P/E Ratio:*	30.41
Plant, Equip.:	$188,498,000	*Total Liab.:*	$760,624,000	*Indic. Yr. Divd.:*	NA
Total Assets:	$1,180,438,000	*Net Worth:*	$418,053,000	*Debt/ Equity:*	0.2714

EGPI Firecreek Inc

6564 Smoke Tree Ln., Scottsdale, AZ, 85253; *PH:* 1-480-948-6581; *Fax:* 1-480-443-1403; *http://* www.energyproducersinc.net; *Email:* bud@firecreek.us

General - Incorporation	NV	**Stock**- Price on:12/24/2007	$0.0055
Employees	NA	Stock Exchange	OTC
Auditor	Donahue Assoc. LLC	Ticker Symbol	EFCR
Stk Agt	U.S. Stock Transfer Corp	Outstanding Shares	399,390,000
Counsel	NA	E.P.S.	-$0.007
DUNS No.	NA	Shareholders	NA

Business: The group's principal activities are to explore, develop and produce oil and gas. It also acquire existing production facilities with proven reserves. The group through its wholly owned subsidiary producers supply, inc supplies and services oil and gas field equipment. The group acquired international group holdings inc in 2004.

Primary SIC and add'l.: 1389 1382

CIK No: 0001106848

Subsidiaries: Firecreek Petroleum, Inc., International Yacht Sales Group, Ltd., Producers Supply, Inc

Officers: Dennis R. Alexander/54/Chmn., CFO, Pres., Principal Executive Officer, Melvena Alexander/74/Dir., Co - Treasurer, Sec., Controller, Dermot McAtamney/52/Dir., Exec. VP, Co - Treasurer

Directors: Dennis R. Alexander/54/Chmn., CFO, Pres., Principal Executive Officer, Michael J. Hester/67/Member - Advisory Board, Rupert C. Johnson/58/Dir., Melvena Alexander/74/Dir., Co - Treasurer, Sec., Controller, Mousa Hawamdah/59/Dir., Dermot McAtamney/52/Dir., Exec. VP, Co - Treasurer

Owners: Insiders/39.15%, Dennis R. Alexander/7.59%, Rupert C. Johnson/22.72%, Mousa Hawamdah/2.85%, Melvena Alexande/1.34%, Dermot McAtamney/4.64%

Financial Data: *Fiscal Year End:*12/31 *Latest Annual Data:* 12/31/2006

Year	Sales	Net Income
2006	$147,000	-$4,246,000
2005	NA	-$10,868,000
2004	$21,000	-$6,026,000

Curr. Assets:	$334,000	*Curr. Liab.:*	$5,344,000		
Plant, Equip.:	$869,000	*Total Liab.:*	$5,887,000	*Indic. Yr. Divd.:*	NA
Total Assets:	$1,203,000	*Net Worth:*	-$4,683,000	*Debt/ Equity:*	NA

Ehealth Inc

440 E Middlefield Rd., Mountain View, CA, 94043; *PH:* 1-877-456-7180; *Fax:* 1-650-961-2153; *https://* www.ehealthinsurance.com; *Email:* headquarters@ehealth.com

General - Incorporation	DE	**Stock**- Price on:12/24/2007	$18
Employees	357	Stock Exchange	NDQ
Auditor	NA	Ticker Symbol	EHTH
Stk Agt	NA	Outstanding Shares	22,530,000
Counsel	NA	E.P.S.	$0.80
DUNS No.	NA	Shareholders	NA

Business: The groups principle activity is to provide online health insurance services. The groups services include online rate quoting and comprehensive plan information, plan comparison and recommendations, online application and enrollment forms and electronic processing interchange. The products of the group include health savings account, dental, vision and life insurance. The group operates from the United States and China. The group's quarterly revenue for September 2007 was 23.00 millions of USD.

Primary SIC and add'l.: 6411

CIK No: 0001333493

Subsidiaries: eHealth China (Xiamen) Technology Co., Ltd., eHealth China, Inc., eHealthInsurance Services, Inc.

Officers: Gary Lauer/Chmn., CEO, Pres., Robert L. Fahlman/Sr. VP - Carrier Relations, COO, Sam Gibbs/Sr. VP, GM - Small Business, Stuart M. Huizinga/Sr. VP, CFO, Robert S. Hurley/VP - Strategic Initiatives, Bruce Telkamp/Sr. VP - Business Development, Marketing, General Counsel, Sec., Sheldon X. Wang/CTO, Sr. VP

Directors: Gary Lauer/Chmn., CEO, Pres., Steven Cakebread/Dir., Michael D. Goldberg/Dir., Joseph S. Lacob/Dir., Kathleen D. Laporte/46/Dir., Jack L. Oliver/Dir., Sheryl Sandberg/Dir., Christopher J. Schaepe/Dir.

Owners: Sheldon X. Wang, Bruce A. Telkamp, Michael D. Goldberg, Entities affiliated with QuestMark Partners, Entities affiliated with Kleiner Perkins Caufield& Byers, Joseph S. Lacob, Robert L. Fahlman, Christopher J. Schaepe, Kathleen D. LaPorte, Vipool M. Patel, Entities affiliated with Gilder, Gagnon, Howe& Co. LLC, Stuart M. Huizinga, Gary L. Lauer, Entities affiliated with Sprout Group, Entities affiliated with Weiss, Peck& Greer Venture Partners *(19 Owners included in Index)*

Financial Data: *Fiscal Year End:*12/31 *Latest Annual Data:* 12/31/2006

Year	Sales	Net Income
2006	$61,310,000	$16,477,000
2005	$41,752,000	-$414,000
2004	$30,215,000	-$3,327,000

Curr. Assets:	$95,374,000	*Curr. Liab.:*	$8,871,000	*P/E Ratio:*	22.78
Plant, Equip.:	$3,936,000	*Total Liab.:*	$9,188,000	*Indic. Yr. Divd.:*	NA
Total Assets:	$104,928,000	*Net Worth:*	$95,740,000	*Debt/ Equity:*	NA

Eidos Plc

Wimbledon Bridge House 1 Hartfield Rd. , Wimbeledon, SW19 3RU; *PH:* 44-2086363000; *http://* www.eidos.com; *Email:* plc@eidos.co.uk

General - Incorporation	UK	**Stock**- Price on:12/24/2007	NA
Employees	NA	Stock Exchange	NA
Auditor	KPMG Audit Plc	Ticker Symbol	NA
Stk Agt	Bank of New York	Outstanding Shares	NA
Counsel	Cooley Godward LLP	E.P.S.	NA
DUNS No.	NA	Shareholders	NA

Business: The group's principal activities include the development and publishing of entertainment software. Brands include commandos, soul reaver, championship manager and tomb raider. The group develops and publishes a diverse mix of titles for the PC, playstation game console, playstation2 computer entertainment system, nintendo gamecube and the xbox video game system from microsoft. The group operates in the United Kingdom, France, Germany, rest of Europe, United States of America and rest of world.

Primary SIC and add'l.: 7812 7372

CIK No: 0001002717

Eiger Technology Inc

330 Bay St., Ste 602, Toronto, ON, M5H 2S8; *PH:* 1-416-216-8659; *http://* www.eigertechnology.com

General - Incorporation	ON	**Stock**- Price on:12/24/2007	$0.11
Employees	NA	Stock Exchange	OTC
Auditor	Monteith, Monteith & Co	Ticker Symbol	ETIFF
Stk Agt	Pacific Corporate Trust Co	Outstanding Shares	NA
Counsel	NA	E.P.S.	NA
DUNS No.	24-939-8439	Shareholders	NA

Business: The group's principle activities are to manufacture and distribute electronic/computer peripherals and electronic ballasts to OEM and consumer markets worldwide. In addition the group offers voice over Internet protocol services to the Canadian long distance markets. The group manufactures fluorescent light fixtures, data racks and metal cabinetry and distributes electronic ballasts and electronic communication products. The main products of the group include digital subscriber line modems, mp3 players and mp3 modules for notebook PC's. As on 31-Jul-2001 the group acquired onlinetel, inc. Subsequent to 31-Dec-2001 the group intends to sell 53% interest in k-tronik int'l corporation and 100% interest in vision unlimited equipment inc. And its subsidiaries.

Primary SIC and add'l.: 3612 3641 3679 3577 7379

CIK No: 0001040702

Subsidiaries: ADH Custom Metal Fabricators Inc, Energy Products, Inc, K-Tronik International Corp, Newlook Industries Corp, Onlinetel Corp

Officers: Gerry A. Racicot/Dir., CEO, Pres., John G. Simmonds/Dir., CEO, Gary Hokkanen/CFO, Jason R. Moretto/Dir., COO, Pres.

Directors: Gerry A. Racicot/Dir., CEO, Pres., John G. Simmonds/Dir., CEO, Sydney S. Harkema/Dir., Jason R. Moretto/Dir., COO, Pres., Brian M. Cato/Dir., Neal Romanchych/Dir., Stephen Dulmage/Dir.

Owners: Gerry A. Racicot, Jason R. Moretto, Insiders/8.80%, Sidney S. Harkema

Financial Data: Fiscal Year End:09/30   Latest Annual Data: 9/30/2006

Year	Sales	Net Income
2006	$3,375,000	$83,000
2005	$4,189,000	-$3,371,000
2004	$10,101,000	-$5,114,000

Curr. Assets:	$364,000	Curr. Liab.:	$2,006,000	
Plant, Equip.:	$885,000	Total Liab.:	$2,006,000	Indic. Yr. Divd.: NA
Total Assets:	$2,605,000	Net Worth:	-$25,000	Debt/ Equity: NA

El Capitan Precious Metals Inc

14301 N 87th St., Ste 216, Scottsdale, AZ, 85260; *PH:* 1-480-607-7093; *http://*www.elcapitanpmi.com; *Email:* inf@elcapitanpmi.com

General - Incorporation	NV	Stock - Price on:12/24/2007	$0.39
Employees	5	Stock Exchange	OTC
Auditor	Epstein Weber & Conover, PLC	Ticker Symbol	ECPN
Stk Agt	Interwest Transfer Company, Inc.	Outstanding Shares	79,170,000
Counsel	NA	E.P.S.	-$0.06
DUNS No.	NA	Shareholders	NA

Business: The group's principal activity is to acquire mining properties containing precious metals. It is in the development stage. The group is in the development stage. In Oct 2003, the group acquired 40% interest in certain assets of el capitan ltd.

Primary SIC and add'l.: 1099

CIK No: 0001135202

Subsidiaries: Gold, Minerals Company, Inc.

Officers: Charles C. Mottley/73/Chmn., CEO, Pres., Stephen J. Antol/64/CFO, Treasurer, Ronald L. Perkins/62/Dir., VP - Administration, Marketing, Communication, James Ricketts/69/Dir., Sec.

Directors: Charles C. Mottley/73/Chmn., CEO, Pres., Ronald L. Perkins/62/Dir., VP - Administration, Marketing, Communication, William R. Willson/Dir., James Ricketts/69/Dir., Sec., Donald W. Gentry/Dir., Marvin K. Kaiser/Dir., Kenneth P. Pavlich/Dir., Bruce F. Snyder/Dir.

Owners: Kenneth P. Pavlich, William R. Wilson, Ronald L. Perkins/1.30%, Stephen Antol/1.50%, Bruce F. Snyder, Charles C. Mottley/8.00%, James Rickets/3.90%, Insiders/15.10%

Financial Data: Fiscal Year End:09/30   Latest Annual Data: 9/30/2006

Year	Sales	Net Income
2006	NA	-$4,042,000
2005	NA	-$3,245,000
2004	NA	-$1,314,000

Curr. Assets:	$432,000	Curr. Liab.:	$1,173,000	
Plant, Equip.:	$908,000	Total Liab.:	$1,324,000	Indic. Yr. Divd.: NA
Total Assets:	$1,522,000	Net Worth:	$198,000	Debt/ Equity: NA

El Nino Ventures Inc

1166 Alberni St., Vancouver, BC, V6M3Z3; *PH:* 1-604-683-4886; *Fax:* 1-604-685-6550; *http://*www.elninoventures.com; *Email:* info@elninoventures.com

General - Incorporation	BC	Stock - Price on:12/24/2007	$0.53
Employees	NA	Stock Exchange	OTC
Auditor	Pricewaterhousecoopers LLP	Ticker Symbol	ELNOF
Stk Agt	Computershare Trust Co	Outstanding Shares	NA
Counsel	Devlin Jensen	E.P.S.	NA
DUNS No.	NA	Shareholders	NA

Business: The groups principal activity is to explore minerals and natural oil. The group operates from Canada and the United States.

Primary SIC and add'l.: 1081

CIK No: 0001136861

Officers: Jean Luc Roy/CEO, Pres., Harry Barr/Chmn., Pres., Gord Steblin/CFO, Taryn Downing/Corp. Sec.

Directors: Harry Barr/Chmn., Pres., Bernard Barlin/Dir., Michael Philpot/Dir., Spiros Cacos/Dir., John Royall/Dir., Morris Medd/Dir.

Owners: CDS & Company/63.90%, Harry Barr/12.30%, Canaccord Capital Corporation/12.90%

Financial Data: Fiscal Year End:01/31   Latest Annual Data: 01/31/2007

Year	Sales	Net Income
2007	NA	-$2,515,000
2006	NA	-$210,000
2005	NA	-$123,000

Curr. Assets:	$2,872,000	Curr. Liab.:	$116,000	P/E Ratio: 2.70
Plant, Equip.:	$38,000	Total Liab.:	$116,000	Indic. Yr. Divd.: NA
Total Assets:	$2,910,000	Net Worth:	$2,794,000	Debt/ Equity: NA

EL Paso CGP Co LLC

Formerly: El Paso CGP Co
El Paso Bldg., 1001 Louisiana St., Houston, TX, 77002; *PH:* 1-713-420-2131; *http://*www.elpaso.com

General - Incorporation	DE	Stock - Price on:12/24/2007	$17.18
Employees	5,050	Stock Exchange	NA
Auditor	PricewaterhouseCoopers LLP	Ticker Symbol	NA
Stk Agt	Computershare Trust Co	Outstanding Shares	700,240,000
Counsel	NA	E.P.S.	$1.02
DUNS No.	05-511-7741	Shareholders	NA

Business: The group's principle activity is to provide energy products and services, such as natural gas systems; refining, marketing and chemicals; exploration and production; power; and coal. The group operates from United States.

Primary SIC and add'l.: 5171 4923 2911 4613 1220

CIK No: 0000021267

Subsidiaries: Coastal Mart, Inc., El Paso Corporation, El Paso Production Holding Company, El Paso Remediation Company, Merchant Energy-Petroleum Company

Officers: Douglas L. Foshee/48/Dir., CEO, Pres., Robert W. Goldman/66/Dir. - Financial Consultant, James L. Dunlap/70/Dir. - Business Consultant, Ferrell P. McClean/61/Dir. - Business Consultant, Bill Baerg/Mgr. - Investor Relations, David Siddall/Corp. Sec., Alan Bishop/Dir. - Shareholder Relations, Steven J. Shapiro/56/Dir. - Business Consultant, Bruce Connery/VP - Investor, Public Relations, Marguerite Woung-Chapman/VP, Corp. Sec.

Directors: Douglas L. Foshee/48/Dir., CEO, Pres., Ronald L. Kuehn/73/Chmn., Robert F. Vagt/61/Dir., Paul Malter/Dir. - Health, Safety, Robert W. Goldman/66/Dir. - Financial Consultant, Anthony W. Hall/63/Dir., Michael J. Talbert/61/Dir., Thomas R. Hix/60/Dir., John L. Whitmire/67/Dir., Juan Carlos Braniff/51/Dir., James L. Dunlap/70/Dir. - Business Consultant, William H. Joyce/72/Dir., Ferrell P. McClean/61/Dir. - Business Consultant, Steven J. Shapiro/56/Dir. - Business Consultant, Thomas D. Hutchins/Dir. - Health, Safety

Financial Data: Fiscal Year End:12/31   Latest Annual Data: 12/31/2006

Year	Sales	Net Income
2006	$4,281,000,000	$475,000,000
2005	$4,017,000,000	-$606,000,000
2004	$6,543,000,000	-$947,000,000

Curr. Assets:	$7,167,000,000	Curr. Liab.:	$6,151,000,000	P/E Ratio: 17.01
Plant, Equip.:	$16,678,000,000	Total Liab.:	$23,044,000,000	Indic. Yr. Divd.: $0.160
Total Assets:	$27,261,000,000	Net Worth:	$4,186,000,000	Debt/ Equity: 2.3979

El Paso Corp

1001 Louisiana St., Houston, TX, 77002; *PH:* 1-713-420-2600; *http://*www.elpaso.com

General - Incorporation	DE	Stock - Price on:12/24/2007	$16.82
Employees	5,050	Stock Exchange	NYSE
Auditor	PricewaterhouseCoopers LLP	Ticker Symbol	EP
Stk Agt	Computershare Trust Co	Outstanding Shares	700,240,000
Counsel	NA	E.P.S.	$1.02
DUNS No.	86-101-9594	Shareholders	NA

Business: The group's principle activities include exploring, extracting, marketing and transporting natural gas and energy and energy related commodities. The group operates through four segments include merchant energy, pipelines, field services and production. The group operates in Canada, Mexico, Australia, Bolivia, Hungary and Indonesia.

Primary SIC and add'l.: 4922

CIK No: 0001066107

Subsidiaries: Acajutla (Cayman) Company, Agropecuaria Santo Antonio Ltda., Agua del Cajon (Cayman) Company, Aguaytia Energy del Peru S.R. Ltda., Aguaytia Energy, LLC, Alpheus Communications, L.P., American Natural Resources Company, Americas Generation Corp., Americas Holding Corp., Amethyst Power Holdings, LLC, ANR Advance Holdings, Inc., ANR Blue Lake Company, ANR Capital Corporation, ANR Development Corporation, ANR Eaton Company 602 Subsidiaries included in the Index

Officers: Douglas L. Foshee/48/Dir., CEO, Pres./$5,893,656.00, James L. Dunlap/70/Dir. - Business Consultant, Robert Newberry/Contact - Media Relations, Steven J. Shapiro/56/Dir. - Business Consultant, Jaye Alford/Contact - Corporate Real Estate, Sandy Siegel/Contact - Gustafson Realty, Cheryl Moeller/Contact - Corporate Real Estate, Susan A. Brown/Contact, John R. Sult/Sr. VP, Controller, Brent J. Smolik/Pres. - El Paso Exploration - Production Company/$1,066,809.00, Michael Hundley/Contact - Health, Safety, Marguerite Woung-Chapman/VP, Corp. Sec., Robert W. Goldman/66/Dir. - Financial Consultant, Ferrell P. McClean/61/Dir. - Business Consultant, Mark D. Leland/CFO, Exec. VP/$1,805,798.00 (28 Officers included in Index)

Directors: Douglas L. Foshee/48/Dir., CEO, Pres., Ronald L. Kuehn/73/Chmn., Robert F. Vagt/61/Dir., Thomas R. Hix/61/Dir., William H. Joyce/72/Dir., Michael J. Talbert/61/Dir., Juan Carlos Braniff/51/Dir., Robert W. Goldman/66/Dir. - Financial Consultant, Anthony W. Hall/63/Dir., John L. Whitmire/67/Dir., Joe B. Wyatt/72/Dir., Steven J. Shapiro/56/Dir. - Business Consultant, James L. Dunlap/70/Dir. - Business Consultant

Owners: Insiders, Franklin Resources, Inc./10.80%, J. C. Yardley, J. L. Dunlap, T. R. Hix, W. H. Joyce, R. W. Goldman, J. L. Whitmire, F. P. McClean, J. B. Wyatt, R. L. Kuehn, J. M. Talbert, D. M. Leland, B. J. Smolik, D. L. Foshee (20 Owners included in Index)

Financial Data: Fiscal Year End:12/31   Latest Annual Data: 12/31/2006

Year	Sales	Net Income
2006	$4,281,000,000	$475,000,000
2005	$4,017,000,000	-$606,000,000
2004	$6,543,000,000	-$947,000,000

Curr. Assets:	$7,167,000,000	Curr. Liab.:	$6,151,000,000	
Plant, Equip.:	$16,678,000,000	Total Liab.:	$23,044,000,000	Indic. Yr. Divd.: NA
Total Assets:	$27,261,000,000	Net Worth:	$4,186,000,000	Debt/ Equity: 2.3979

El Paso Electric Co

PO Box 982, El Paso, TX, 79960; *PH:* 1-915-543-5970; *http://* www.epelectric.com; *Email:* customerservices@epelectric.com

General - Incorporation	TX	Stock - Price on:12/24/2007	$25.03
Employees	1,000	Stock Exchange	NYSE
Auditor	KPMG LLP	Ticker Symbol	EE
Stk Agt	Bank of New York	Outstanding Shares	45,780,000
Counsel	Davis Polk & Wardwell	E.P.S.	$1.65
DUNS No.	00-792-8955	Shareholders	NA

Business: The group's principal activity is to generate, transmit and distribute electricity in an area of approximately 10,000 square miles in west Texas and southern New Mexico. It also serves wholesale customers in Texas and periodically in the republic of Mexico. It owns significant ownership interests in six electrical generating facilities providing it with a total capacity of approximately 1,500 mw. The group also serves approximately 324,000 residential, commercial, industrial and wholesale customers. It distributes electricity to retail customers mainly in el paso, Texas, las cruces and New Mexico. The principal industrial and other customers of the group include steel production, copper and oil refining and United States military installations, including the United States army air defense center at fort bliss in Texas and white sands missile range and holloman air force base in New Mexico.

Primary SIC and add'l.: 4911

CIK No: 0000031978

Subsidiaries: MiraSol Energy Services, Inc.

Officers: Ershel C. Redd/Dir., CEO, Pres., Robert Clay Doyle/VP - New Mexico Affairs, Gary R. Hedrick/Dir., Exec. VP/$2,298,926.00, Guillermo Silva/Corp. Sec., John A. Whitacre/VP - System Operations, Planning/$536,757.00, Hector R. Puente/VP - Transmission, Distribution, Steven P. Busser/VP, Treasurer, Chief Risk Officer/$390,115.00, Scott D. Wilson/CFO, Exec. VP, Chief Administrative Officer/$689,714.00, Frank J. Bates/COO, Exec. VP, Helen Knopp/VP - Public Affairs, Hector Gutierrez/Exec. VP - External Affairs, Andy Ramirez/VP - Power Generation, Gary D. Sanders/General Counsel, Rachelle Williams/Supervisor - Investor Relations, Nora Herrera/Analyst - Investor Relations (19 Officers included in Index)

Directors: Ershel C. Redd/Dir., CEO, Pres., Michael K. Parks/Vice Chmn., George W. Edwards/Chmn., Kenneth R. Heitz/Dir., Patricia Z. Holland-Branch/Dir., James W. Cicconi/Dir., Robert J. Brown/Dir., John Robert Brown/Dir., Gary R. Hedrick/Dir., Exec. VP, Eric B. Siegel/Dir., James W. Harris/Dir., Charles A. Yamarone/Dir., Ramiro Guzman/Dir., Stephen N. Wertheimer/Dir.

Owners: Stephen N. Wertheimer, Ramiro Guzmn, Insiders/2.84%, Wellington Management, Inc./5.60%, Steven P. Busser, George W. Edwards, Patricia Z. Holland-Branch, T. Rowe Price Associates, Inc./6.70%, Julius F. Bates, Charles A. Yamarone, James W. Harris, Scott D. Wilson, Barclays Global Investors, N.A./7.21%, John Robert Brown, James W. Cicconi (21 Owners included in Index)

Financial Data: Fiscal Year End:12/31 Latest Annual Data: 12/31/2006

Year	Sales	Net Income
2006	$816,455,000	$67,450,000
2005	$803,913,000	$35,522,000
2004	$708,628,000	$35,171,000

Curr. Assets:	$213,796,000	Curr. Liab.:	$111,058,000	P/E Ratio:	16.25
Plant, Equip.:	$1,332,194,000	Total Liab.:	$1,134,979,000	Indic. Yr. Divd.:	NA
Total Assets:	$1,714,654,000	Net Worth:	$579,675,000	Debt/ Equity:	1.0642

El Paso Natural Gas Co

1001 Louisiana St., Houston, TX, 77002; PH: 1-713-420-2600; http:// www.elpaso.com; Email: investorrelations@elpaso.com

General - Incorporation	DE	Stock- Price on:12/24/2007	NA
Employees	5,700	Stock Exchange	NA
Auditor	PricewaterhouseCoopers LLP	Ticker Symbol	NA
Stk Agt	Computershare Trust Co	Outstanding Shares	NA
Counsel	NA	E.P.S.	NA
DUNS No.	00-800-1703	Shareholders	NA

Business: The group's principle activity is to operate field and mainline natural gas transmission systems. The group operates from United States.

Primary SIC and add'l.: 4922

CIK No: 0000031986

Officers: Douglas L. Foshee/48/Dir., CEO, Pres., James L. Dunlap/70/Dir., Business Consultant, Steven J. Shapiro/56/Dir., Business Consultant, Marguerite Woung-Chapman/VP, Corp. Sec., James J. Cleary/Dir., Principal Executive Officer, Pres., Alan Bishop/Dir. - Shareholder Relations, John R. Sult/CFO, Sr. VP, Controller, Thomas L. Price/Dir., VP, Robert W. Goldman/66/Dir., Financial Consultant, Ferrell P. McClean/61/Dir., Business Consultant, Daniel B. Martin/Sr. VP - Operations, El Paso Pipeline Group, Bruce Connery/VP - Investor, Public Relations, Bill Baerg/Mgr. - Investor Relations

Directors: Douglas L. Foshee/48/Dir., CEO, Pres., Ronald L. Kuehn/73/Chmn., James C. Yardley/Chmn., Ferrell P. McClean/61/Dir., Business Consultant, Anthony W. Hall/63/Dir., Thomas R. Hix/60/Dir., Michael J. Talbert/61/Dir., Robert F. Vagt/61/Dir., John L. Whitmire/67/Dir., Joe B. Wyatt/73/Dir., Robert W. Goldman/66/Dir., Financial Consultant, Juan Carlos Braniff/51/Dir., James L. Dunlap/70/Dir., Business Consultant, William H. Joyce/72/Dir., James J. Cleary/Dir., Principal Executive Officer, Pres. (17 Directors included in Index)

Owners: John R. Sult, James J. Cleary, Daniel B. Martin, James C. Yardley, Insiders, Thomas L. Price, ElPaso EPNG Investments, L.L.C./100.00%

Elamex

1800 Nwestern Dr., El Paso, TX, 79912; PH: 1-915-298-3061; Fax: 1-915-298-3065; http:// www.elamex.com; Email: tomb@elamex.com

General - Incorporation	Mexico	Stock- Price on:12/24/2007	$0.73
Employees	NA	Stock Exchange	OTC
Auditor	Michael A. Bryant	Ticker Symbol	ELAMF
Stk Agt	Bank of New York	Outstanding Shares	NA
Counsel	NA	E.P.S.	-$0.06
DUNS No.	81-183-8549	Shareholders	NA

Business: The group's principle activity is to manufacture electromechanical, mechanical, appliance, avionics, medical appliance, heating, venting and air conditioning, and automotive industries. The group operates from United States.

Primary SIC and add'l.: 3679 3821 7539 3842 3639

CIK No: 0001009302

Subsidiaries: Elamex USA, Corp, Machine Company, Precision Tool

Officers: Alma D. Diaz/Contact

Financial Data: Fiscal Year End:12/31 Latest Annual Data: 12/31/2004

Year	Sales	Net Income
2004	$97,587,000	-$5,151,000
2003	$157,250,000	-$34,608,000
2002	$134,269,000	-$6,017,000

Curr. Assets:	$22,323,000	Curr. Liab.:	$24,168,000		
Plant, Equip.:	$26,956,000	Total Liab.:	$27,870,000	Indic. Yr. Divd.:	NA
Total Assets:	$54,250,000	Net Worth:	$26,380,000	Debt/ Equity:	0.1134

Elan Corp Plc

800 Gateway Blvd., South San Francisco, CA, 94080; PH: 1-650-877-0900; Fax: 1-650-877-7669; http:// www.elan.com

General - Incorporation	Ireland	Stock - Price on:12/24/2007	$21.13
Employees	1,734	Stock Exchange	NYSE
Auditor	KPMG LLP	Ticker Symbol	ELN
Stk Agt	NA	Outstanding Shares	467,490,000
Counsel	NA	E.P.S.	-$0.75
DUNS No.	98-709-5338	Shareholders	NA

Business: The group's principal activities are carried out through two business units, core elan and elan enterprises. Core elan comprises pharmaceutical commercial activities which includes the marketing of products in the therapeutic areas of neurology, pain management and infectious diseases, and biopharmaceutical research and development activities which includes the discovery and development of products in the therapeutic areas of neurology, pain management and auto immune diseases. Elan enterprises comprises drug delivery businesses which includes the development, licensing and marketing of drug delivery products, technologies and services.

Primary SIC and add'l.: 6794 5122 8734 8731

CIK No: 0000737572

Subsidiaries: Athena Neurosciences, Inc., Elan Capital Corporation, Ltd., Elan Drug Delivery, Inc., Elan Finance, plc, Elan Holdings, Inc., Elan Holdings, Ltd., Elan International Services Ltd, Elan Management, Ltd., Elan Pharma International, Ltd., Elan Pharmaceuticals, Inc., Neuralab Ltd.

Officers: Kelly Martin/Dir., CEO, Pres., Allison Hulme/Exec. VP, Head - Autoimmune, Tysabri Franchise, Ted Yednock/Sr. VP, Head - Global Research, Menghis Bairu/Sr. VP, Head - International, Nigel Clerkin/Sr. VP - Finance, Group Controller, Richard T. Collier/Exec. VP, General Counsel, Ivan Lieberburg/Chief Medical Officer, Exec. VP, Shane Cooke/Dir., CFO, Exec. VP, James Callaway/Sr. VP, Head - Immunotherapy Alzheimer's Disease Clinical Programs, David Feigal/Sr. VP, Head - Global Regulatory, Global Safety Surveillance, Johannes Roebers/Sr. VP, Head - Biologic Strategy, Planning, Operations, Chris Burns/Sr. VP - Investor Relations, Lars Ekman/Dir., Exec. VP, Pres. - Global Research & Development, Head - Neurodegeneration Franchise, Karen Kim/Exec. VP - Corporate Strategy, Alliances, Communications, Branding, Specialty Business Group, Dale Schenk/Chief Scientific Officer, Sr. VP (18 Officers included in Index)

Directors: Kelly Martin/Dir., CEO, Pres., Kyran McLaughlin/Chmn., Alan R. Gillespie/57/Non Exec. Dir., Dennis Selkoe/Dir., Giles Kerr/Dir., Lars Ekman/Dir., Exec. VP, Pres. - Global Research & Development, Head - Neurodegeneration Franchise, Laurence Crowley/Dir., Kieran McGowan/Dir., Shane Cooke/Dir., CFO, Exec. VP, Ann Maynard Gray/Dir., Gary Kennedy/Dir., William Rohn/Dir., Floyd Bloom/Dir., Jonas Frick/Dir., Jeffrey Shames/Dir.

Owners: Fidelity Management and Research Company/14.80%, Wellington Management/7.00%, Insiders/1.20%, Westfield Capital Management Co. LLC/4.20%

Financial Data: Fiscal Year End:12/31 Latest Annual Data: 12/31/2006

Year	Sales	Net Income
2006	$560,400,000	-$267,300,000
2005	$490,300,000	-$383,600,000
2004	$481,700,000	-$394,700,000

Curr. Assets:	$1,756,300,000	Curr. Liab.:	$851,500,000		
Plant, Equip.:	$349,000,000	Total Liab.:	$2,661,200,000	Indic. Yr. Divd.:	NA
Total Assets:	$2,746,300,000	Net Worth:	$85,100,000	Debt/ Equity:	NA

Elbit Imaging Ltd

Formerly: Elbit Medical Imaging Ltd
13, Noah Mozes St., Tel-aviv, 67442; PH: 972-36086010; http:// www.emitf.co.il; Email: info@emitf.co.il

General - Incorporation	Israel	Stock- Price on:12/24/2007	$45.3
Employees	87	Stock Exchange	NDQ
Auditor	Brightman Almagor & Co	Ticker Symbol	EMITF
Stk Agt	American Stock Transfer & Trust Co.	Outstanding Shares	NA
Counsel	NA	E.P.S.	NA
DUNS No.	NA	Shareholders	NA

Business: The group's principle activities are the operation of hotels and shopping malls and developing, manufacturing, marketing and providing support for medical imaging systems and equipment. In addition, the company is involved in the establishment and operation of medical centers throughout the world. The company's products include equipment for the general radiology and cardiology markets. The company operates in Israel, Europe, United States of America and other countries. The group's quarterly revenue for September 2007 was 357.86 millions of ILS.

Primary SIC and add'l.: 3845 6512 6513 8069 5047 7011

CIK No: 0001027662

Subsidiaries: BEA Hotels N.V, Elscint Bio-Medical Ltd., Plaza House Kft., Praha Plaza s.r.o.

Officers: Mordechay Zisser/53/Exec. Chmn., Shimon Yitzhaki/53/Dir., Pres., Marc Lavine/55/General Counsel, Corp. Sec., Dudi MacHluf/36/CFO

Directors: Mordechay Zisser/53/Exec. Chmn., Abraham Goren/48/Vice Chmn., Zvi Tropp/68/Dir., Rachel Lavine/43/Dir., David Rubner/68/Dir., Shimon Yitzhaki/53/Dir., Pres., Yehoshua Forer/64/Dir., Yosef Apter/53/Dir., Moshe Lion/47/Dir., Shmuel Peretz/68/Dir.

Owners: IDB Holding Corporation Ltd., Insiders, Mordechay Zisser, Ruth Manor, IDB Development Corporation Ltd., Nochi Dankner, Shelly Bergman, Clal Insurance Enterprises Holdings Ltd., Europe Israel (M.M.S.) Ltd., Avraham Livnat

Financial Data: Fiscal Year End:12/31 Latest Annual Data: 12/31/2006

Year	Sales	Net Income
2006	$375,460,000	$122,822,000
2005	$100,873,000	$21,800,000
2004	$110,544,000	-$21,459,000

Curr. Assets:	$857,443,000	Curr. Liab.:	$209,603,000		
Plant, Equip.:	$564,593,000	Total Liab.:	$1,130,684,000	Indic. Yr. Divd.:	NA
Total Assets:	$1,514,889,000	Net Worth:	$384,205,000	Debt/ Equity:	NA

Elbit Systems Ltd

EFW Inc., 4700 Marine Creek Pkwy., Fort Worth, TX, 76136; PH: 1-817-234-6600; Fax: 1-817-234-6768; http:// www.elbit.co.il

General - Incorporation	Israel	Stock- Price on:12/24/2007	$45.1
Employees	NA	Stock Exchange	NDQ
Auditor	Kost Forer Gabbay & Kasierer	Ticker Symbol	ESLT
Stk Agt	American Stock Transfer & Trust Co.	Outstanding Shares	42,030,000
Counsel	NA	E.P.S.	$1.63
DUNS No.	NA	Shareholders	NA

Business: The group's principle activities are upgrading of existing airborne, ground and naval defense platforms, development, manufacture, integration and marketing of advanced integrated defense electronics systems and subsystems. It operates through the following divisions: airborne systems - aircraft and helicopter upgrades for airborne and ground military platforms; armored vehicle systems; command, control and communication systems; electro-optical systems and other.

Primary SIC and add'l.: 5063 3812 3679 3721 3669 7381 3711

CIK No: 0001027664

Subsidiaries: AeroAstro, Inc., BAE Systems Ltd., Cyclone Aviation Products Ltd., Cyclone Aviation Products Ltd., EFW Inc., Electro-Optics Industries El-Op Ltd., Elmec Inc., Elop Electro-Optics Industries, Ltd., Elta Systems Ltd., Grumman Corporation, Raytheon Inc., Honeywell, IEI. International Enterprises, Inc., International Enterprises Inc., KMC Systems, Inc., Kollsman, Inc. 27 Subsidiaries included in the Index

Officers: Raanan Horowitz/CEO, Pres. - Elbit Systems, America, LLC, Joseph Ackerman/CEO, Pres., Yoram Shmuely/Corporate VP, Co - GM - Airborne Helmet Systems, Bezhalel MacHlis/Corporate VP, GM - Land Systems, C4I, David Block Temin/Corporate VP, General Counsel, Ran Hellerstein/Corporate VP, Co - GM - Airborne - Helmet Systems, Ehud Helft/Investor Relations Officer, Kenny Green/Investor Relations Officer, Ran Galli/Corporate VP - Strategic Initiatives, Joseph Gaspar/CFO, Corporate VP, Haim Kellerman/Corporate VP, GM - UAV Systems, Haim Rousso/Corporate VP, GM - Elop, Gideon Sheffer/Corporate VP - Strategic Planning, Itzhak Dvir/COO, Corporate VP, Ilan Pacholder/Corp. Sec., VP - Finance, Capital Markets *(20 Officers included in Index)*

Directors: Michael Federmann/Chmn., Dov Ninveh/Dir., Avraham Asheri/Dir., David Federmann/Dir., Moshe Arad/Dir., Nathan Sharony/Dir., Rina Baum/Dir., Yaacov Lifshitz/Dir., Yigal Neeman/Dir.

Owners: Insiders/0.42%, Federmann Enterprises Ltd./45.42%, Heris Aktiengesellschaft/9.12%

Financial Data: Fiscal Year End:12/31   Latest Annual Data: 12/31/2006

Year	Sales	Net Income
2006	$1,523,243,000	$72,242,000
2005	$1,069,876,000	$32,487,000
2004	$939,925,000	$52,535,000

Curr. Assets:	$928,556,000	Curr. Liab.:	$810,591,000		
Plant, Equip.:	$294,628,000	Total Liab.:	$1,276,204,000	Indic. Yr. Divd.:	$0.680
Total Assets:	$1,770,082,000	Net Worth:	$493,878,000	Debt/ Equity:	NA

Elbit Vision Systems Ltd

1 Haofe St., 1 Ha'Yasur St., Kadima, 60920,; *PH:* 1-864-288-9777; *Fax:* 1-864-288-9799; *http://* www.evs.co.il; *Email:* info@evs.co.il

General - Incorporation	Israel	Stock - Price on:12/24/2007	$0.32
Employees	NA	Stock Exchange	OTC
Auditor	Kesselman & Kesselman LLP	Ticker Symbol	EVSNF
Stk Agt.	Newbridge Securities Corp	Outstanding Shares	NA
Counsel	NA	E.P.S.	NA
DUNS No.	60-059-6753	Shareholders	NA

Business: The groups principle activities include designing, development, manufacturing, marketing and support automatic vision inspection and quality monitoring systems for the textile and other fabric industries. The group operates from United States.

Primary SIC and add'l.: 3823

CIK No: 0001011664

Subsidiaries: Elbit Data System Ltd., Elbit Vision Systems, Elbit Vision Systems B.V., Inframetrics, Inc., Panoptes, ScanMaster Inc., ScanMaster Ltd., Water Technologies Ltd.

Officers: David Gal/Chmn., CEO, Dirk Benoit/EVS Sales Representative - Dirk Benoit Elektronika Nvsa, Shmuel Cohen/Pres. - EVS, Scanmaster US, Hillel Avni/VP - Vision Technology, Sam Cohen/VP - Sales, Marketing, EVS US, John Belew/Sales Mgr., Chen Ofer/Dir. - Sales, Marketing, Hans Friedrich Packpfeifer/EVS Sales Representative - E Packpfeifer KG, Benjamin Mano/VP - Sales, Marketing, Vision, Silviu Rabinovich/VP - Marketing, Business Development, UT, Ofer Sela/VP - Research & Development, Michael Bron/Software Dir., Yaron Menashe/VP - Finance, CFO, Ron Mahler/59/VP - Sales, Marketing, UT, CTO, Roni Vardi/Dir. - Human Resources *(49 Officers included in Index)*

Directors: David Gal/Chmn., CEO, Linda Harnevo/52/Dir., David Schwartz/58/Dir., Menashe Shohat/49/Dir., Yuval Berman/41/Dir., Nir Alon/45/Dir.

Owners: Insiders/17.96%, Shavit Capital Entities/9.10%, M.S.N.D. Real Estate Holdings Ltd./7.60%, Elbit Ltd./7.95%, M.S. Master Investments (2002) Ltd./7.96%, Nir Alon/7.46%, Nir Alon Holdings GmbH/3.41%, Tamir Fishman Provident and Education Funds Ltd./4.16%

Financial Data: Fiscal Year End:12/31   Latest Annual Data: 12/31/2006

Year	Sales	Net Income
2006	$16,997,000	-$6,093,000
2005	$20,791,000	$611,000
2004	$10,960,000	-$5,905,000

Curr. Assets:	$9,517,000	Curr. Liab.:	$15,590,000		
Plant, Equip.:	$455,000	Total Liab.:	$18,389,000	Indic. Yr. Divd.:	NA
Total Assets:	$19,390,000	Net Worth:	$1,001,000	Debt/ Equity:	NA

Elcom International Inc

10 Oceana Way, Norwood, MA, 02062; *PH:* 1-781-440-3333; *Fax:* 1-781-762-1540; *http://* www.elcominternational.com

General - Incorporation	DE	Stock - Price on:12/24/2007	NA
Employees	31	Stock Exchange	OTC
Auditor	Vitale, Caturano & Co. Ltd	Ticker Symbol	ELCO
Stk Agt.	American Stock Transfer & Trust Co.	Outstanding Shares	NA
Counsel	NA	E.P.S.	-$0.02
DUNS No.	80-914-1088	Shareholders	NA

Business: The group's principal activity is the development and sale of esourcing Internet-based software solutions which automate many supply chain and financial settlement functions associated with procurement. The products include pecos.ipm, an automated procurement system and pecos.icm, that automates the online selling process from product information through financial settlement. The group also offers a dynamic trading system and asset management system from third parties. It offers various consulting and supplier services to its clients. These services range from implementation of pecos.ipm and training, to interfacing data from pecos.ipm into back-end erp systems. The group markets its solutions in the United States and the United Kingdom.

Primary SIC and add'l.: 7371 7372 5961

CIK No: 0000900096

Subsidiaries: Elcom Holdings Limited, elcom, inc.

Officers: Gregory D. King/Dir., CEO, David Elliott/Dir., Exec. VP - Finance, Paul C. Bogonis/VP - Finance

Directors: Gregory D. King/Dir., CEO, William Lock/Non Exec. Chmn., Justin Dignam/Non Exec. Dir., Elliot Bance/Non Exec. Dir., David Elliott/Dir., Exec. VP - Finance

Owners: Smith & Williamson Investment Management Limited and Smith & Williamson Nominees Limited/74.00%, Justin Dignam, Insiders/6.00%, William Lock, Elliott Bance, Gregory D. King, Sean Lewis/6.00%

Financial Data: Fiscal Year End:12/31   Latest Annual Data: 12/31/2005

Year	Sales	Net Income
2005	$2,714,000	-$5,840,000
2004	$3,807,000	-$3,272,000
2003	$3,028,000	-$5,451,000

Curr. Assets:	$7,021,000	Curr. Liab.:	$6,126,000		
Plant, Equip.:	$743,000	Total Liab.:	$6,549,000	Indic. Yr. Divd.:	NA
Total Assets:	$7,774,000	Net Worth:	$1,225,000	Debt/ Equity:	NA

Eldorado Artesian Springs Inc

1783 Dogwood St., Louisville, CO, 80027; *PH:* 1-303-499-1316; *Fax:* 1-303-499-1339; *http://* www.eldoradosprings.com; *Email:* info@eldoradosprings.com

General - Incorporation	CO	Stock - Price on:12/24/2007	$4.5
Employees	67	Stock Exchange	OTC
Auditor	Ehrhardt Keefe Steiner & Hottman P.C	Ticker Symbol	ELDO
Stk Agt.	Mr. Larson	Outstanding Shares	3,000,000
Counsel	NA	E.P.S.	-$0.02
DUNS No.	10-569-7759	Shareholders	NA

Business: The group's principle activity is to bottle, market and distribute natural spring water under the eldorado artesian spring water brand and rents water dispensers. The group owns and operates a resort on its property during the summer months and rents a single-family home. It also operates a natural artesian spring pool. The group sells spring water directly to home and business, retail grocery stores and distributors located in Colorado. It also sells water at wholesale to retail food stores packaged in smaller, more convenient sizes, which are suitable for retail distribution. The group operates solely in the domestic market. The group operates from United States.

Primary SIC and add'l.: 2086 7389 7011

CIK No: 0000796124

Officers: Douglas A. Larson/Dir., CEO, Pres./$131,308.00, Kate Janssen/VP - Sales, Customer Service, Robert E. Weidler/63/VP - Production, Cathleen M. Shoenfeld/CFO, Jeremy S. Martin/Dir., VP - Marketing/$132,000.00, Kevin M. Sipple/Dir., VP - Operations, Sec./$130,479.00

Directors: Douglas A. Larson/Dir., CEO, Pres., Jeremy S. Martin/Dir., VP - Marketing, George J. Schmitt/Dir., Kevin M. Sipple/Dir., VP - Operations, Sec., Ross J. Colbert/Dir.

Owners: Jeremy S. Martin/20.60%, Insiders/72.00%, George J. Schmitt/2.70%, Kevin M. Sipple/20.40%, Douglas A. Larson/20.30%

Financial Data: Fiscal Year End:03/31   Latest Annual Data: 03/31/2007

Year	Sales	Net Income
2007	$8,248,000	$88,000
2006	$7,910,000	-$10,000
2005	$7,634,000	-$548,000

Curr. Assets:	$1,308,000	Curr. Liab.:	$1,089,000	P/E Ratio:	150.00
Plant, Equip.:	$4,161,000	Total Liab.:	$4,674,000	Indic. Yr. Divd.:	NA
Total Assets:	$6,250,000	Net Worth:	$1,576,000	Debt/ Equity:	1.7495

Eldorado Gold Corp

550 Burrard St., Ste. 1188, Vancouver, BC, V6C 2B5; *PH:* 1-604-687-4018; *Fax:* 1-604-687-4026; *http://* www.eldoradogold.com; *Email:* info@eldoradogold.com

General - Incorporation	Canada	Stock - Price on:12/24/2007	$5.93
Employees	1,264	Stock Exchange	AMEX
Auditor	PricewaterhouseCoopers LLP	Ticker Symbol	EGO
Stk Agt.	Computershare Trust Co of Canada	Outstanding Shares	343,430,000
Counsel	Fasken Martineau Dumoulin	E.P.S.	$0.14
DUNS No.	NA	Shareholders	NA

Business: The group's principal activities are gold mining and other, including exploration, extraction, processing and reclamation. The exploration activities are carried on in South America and turkey.

Primary SIC and add'l.: 1041

CIK No: 0000918608

Officers: Paul N. Wright/Dir., CEO, Pres., Norm Pitcher/COO, Earl W. Price/CFO, Berne Jansson/VP - Operations, Dawn Moss/Corp. Sec., Stephen Juras/Mgr. - Geology

Directors: Paul N. Wright/Dir., CEO, Pres., Hugh C. Morris/Non Exec. Chmn., Robert R. Gilmore/Dir., John S. Auston/Dir., Donald Shumka/Dir., Wayne D. Lenton/Dir., Ross K. Cory/Dir., Geoffrey Handley/Dir.

Financial Data: Fiscal Year End:12/31   Latest Annual Data: 12/31/2006

Year	Sales	Net Income
2006	$84,689,000	$831,000
2005	$33,797,000	-$49,776,000
2004	$35,915,000	-$14,451,000

Curr. Assets:	$155,402,000	Curr. Liab.:	$53,238,000		
Plant, Equip.:	NA	Total Liab.:	$131,115,000	Indic. Yr. Divd.:	NA
Total Assets:	$508,302,000	Net Worth:	$377,187,000	Debt/ Equity:	NA

Elec Communications Corp

75 S Broadway, Ste. 302, White Plains, NY, 10601; *PH:* 1-914-682-0214; *Fax:* 1-914-682-0820; *http://* www.pervasip.com

General - Incorporation	NY	Stock - Price on:12/24/2007	$0.33
Employees	34	Stock Exchange	OTC
Auditor	Nussbaum Yates & Wolpow, P.C	Ticker Symbol	ELEC
Stk Agt	Registrar & Transfer Co	Outstanding Shares	22,460,000
Counsel	NA	E.P.S.	-$0.19
DUNS No.	09-383-7177	Shareholders	NA

Business: The group's principal activity is to develop integrated telecommunication services in local exchange carrier industry. The group offers an integrated set of telecommunication products and services to small businesses and residential consumers. The products and services offered include local exchange, local access, domestic and international long distance telephone, enhanced voice, data and a full suite of local features and calling plans. The group has built a scalable operating platform that can provide local phone line, read usage records, rate phone calls for billing purposes and prepare monthly invoices to customers.

Primary SIC and add'l.: 4813

CIK No: 0000090721

Subsidiaries: BiznessOnline.com, Inc., Essex Communications Inc., New Rochelle Telephone Corp., Telecarrier Services, Inc., VoX Communications Corp.

Officers: Paul H. Riss/52/Chmn., CEO, CFO, Treasurer, Michael H. Khalilian/44/Dir., CTO, Ron Harden/Exec. VP - Sales, Marketing, Mark Richards/CIO, Pres.

Directors: Paul H. Riss/52/Chmn., CEO, CFO, Treasurer, Gayle Greer/Member - Advisory Board, Michael H. Khalilian/44/Dir., CTO, Greg M. Cooper/48/Dir., Payam Maveddat/Member - Advisory Board, Farshid Mohammadi/Member - Advisory Board, Rich Tehrani/Member - Advisory Board, Mark Adolph/Member - Advisory Board, Jay Allen/Member - Advisory Board, William Glynn/Member - Advisory Board, Miller S. Williams/55/Dir.

Owners: Mark Richards/2.90%, Greg M. Cooper, Insiders/18.40%, Gayle Greer, Paul H. Riss/10.10%, Miller S. Williams/2.20%, 478 E. Altamonte Drive, Suite 108-480/3.50%

Financial Data: Fiscal Year End:11/30   Latest Annual Data: 11/30/2006

Year	Sales		Net Income
2006	$8,357,000		-$2,345,000
2005	$15,881,000		-$2,266,000
2004	$9,558,000		$170,000
Curr. Assets:	$1,661,000	Curr. Liab.:	$3,600,000
Plant, Equip.:	$192,000	Total Liab.:	$3,600,000 Indic. Yr. Divd.: NA
Total Assets:	$1,904,000	Net Worth:	-$1,696,000 Debt/ Equity: NA

Elecsys Corp

846 N Mart-Way Ct., Olathe, KS, 66061; *PH:* 1-913-647-0158; *Fax:* 1-913-647-0132; *http://* www.elecsyscorp.com; *Email:* investorrelations@elecsyscorp.com

General - Incorporation	KS	Stock - Price on:12/24/2007	$7.7
Employees	104	Stock Exchange	AMEX
Auditor	McGladrey & Pullen LLP	Ticker Symbol	ASY
Stk Agt	UMB Bank, N.A.	Outstanding Shares	3,280,000
Counsel	Blackwell Sanders Peper Martin LLP	E.P.S.	$0.24
DUNS No.	62-804-7565	Shareholders	NA

Business: The group's principal activities are to design, manufacture, integrate and test electronic interface solutions for original equipment manufacturers (OEMs). These interface solutions are used by human operators to view, extract or exchange information with electronic or electro-mechanical equipment. The products manufactured by the group include circuit boards, high-frequency electronic modules, microelectronic displays and assemblies and full turn-key products, along with custom LCD devices and modules, and custom led display arrays. The group's solutions are used in medical, aerospace, industrial, military, consumer and other applications.

Primary SIC and add'l.: 3679 8711

CIK No: 0000914398

Subsidiaries: Airport Systems International, Inc., DCI, Inc., NTG, Inc.

Officers: Karl B. Gemperli/Dir., CEO, Pres./$201,479.00, Todd A. Daniels/CFO/$128,994.00

Directors: Karl B. Gemperli/Dir., CEO, Pres., Robert D. Taylor/Chmn., Stan Gegen/Dir.

Owners: Michael D. Morgan/3.60%, Todd A. Daniels/2.40%, Insiders/35.60%, Robert D. Taylor/6.80%, Karl Gemperli/15.10%, Stan Gegen/4.80%

Financial Data: Fiscal Year End:04/30   Latest Annual Data: 04/30/2007

Year	Sales		Net Income
2007	$19,809,000		$1,046,000
2006	$14,692,000		$1,667,000
2005	$12,307,000		$699,000
Curr. Assets:	$6,978,000	Curr. Liab.:	$3,622,000 P/E Ratio: 24.84
Plant, Equip.:	$2,470,000	Total Liab.:	$3,622,000 Indic. Yr. Divd.: NA
Total Assets:	$9,811,000	Net Worth:	$6,189,000 Debt/ Equity: 0.5367

Electric & Gas Technology Inc

3233 W Kingsley Rd., Garland, TX, 75041; *PH:* 1-972-840-3223; *Fax:* 1-972-271-8925; *http://* www.elgt.com

General - Incorporation	TX	Stock - Price on:12/24/2007	$0.2
Employees	122	Stock Exchange	NA
Auditor	Turner, Stone & Co. LLP	Ticker Symbol	NA
Stk Agt	Securities Transfer Corp	Outstanding Shares	8,600,000
Counsel	Carl A. Generes	E.P.S.	-$0.24
DUNS No.	13-957-1996	Shareholders	NA

Business: The group's principal activities are carried out through three business segments: water products, utilities product and contract manufacturing (fabrication). The group owns patented technology that extracts water from the atmosphere, turning it into clean drinking water, known as the watermaker, wet air and infinite fountain of water. The group's utilities product manufactures equipment used in the natural gas industry known as "Recor" are electronic pressure, temperature and volumetric instrumentation and accessories peripheral to gas measurement. The group's contract manufacturing manufactures sheet metal fabrication for a diverse customer base, including telecom and networking cabinetry, elevator controls, and sheet metal applications. The group's operations are carried out in the United States and Canada.the group has discontinued and disposed the wholly owned subsidiary hydel enterprises inc in 2004.

Primary SIC and add'l.: 3643 3589 3823

CIK No: 0000785819

Owners: George M. Johnston/1.44%, Mort S. Zimmerman/10.71%, Daniel A. Zimmerman/27.02%, Fred M. Updegraff/0.97%, Insiders/40.15%

Financial Data: Fiscal Year End:07/31   Latest Annual Data: 7/31/2006

Year	Sales		Net Income
2006	$12,672,000		-$1,511,000
2005	$8,508,000		$148,000
2004	$6,436,000		-$2,991,000
Curr. Assets:	$4,621,000	Curr. Liab.:	$5,619,000
Plant, Equip.:	$5,467,000	Total Liab.:	$10,928,000 Indic. Yr. Divd.: NA
Total Assets:	$10,340,000	Net Worth:	-$588,000 Debt/ Equity: NA

Electro Energy Inc

30 Shelter Rock Rd., Danbury, CT, 06810; *PH:* 1-203-797-2699; *Fax:* 1-203-797-2697; *http://* www.electroenergyinc.com; *Email:* info@electroenergyinc.com

General - Incorporation	FL	Stock - Price on:12/24/2007	$1.1499
Employees	52	Stock Exchange	NDQ
Auditor	Marcum & Kliegman LLP	Ticker Symbol	EEEI
Stk Agt	NA	Outstanding Shares	23,440,000
Counsel	NA	E.P.S.	-$0.36
DUNS No.	78-766-0216	Shareholders	NA

Business: The group's principal activity is to develop products used in providing energy. The group specifically focuses upon development of bipolar nickel metal hydride batteries and other battery chemistries. The group also provides contract research and development to the United States government or its agencies.

Primary SIC and add'l.: 3499

CIK No: 0001175636

Subsidiaries: Electro Energy Mobile Products, Inc., Mobile Energy Products, Inc.

Officers: Michael E. Reed/Dir., CEO, Pres., Martin Klein/Founder, Chmn., Chief Technologist, Rolan Farmer/Mgr. - Operations, Paula Ralston/Mgr. - Operations, Audra J. Mace/Sec., Michael Eskra/COO, Pres., Robert Plivelich/Chemical Engineer, Timothy E. Coyne/53/CFO

Directors: Michael E. Reed/Dir., CEO, Pres., Martin Klein/Founder, Chmn., Chief Technologist, Joseph Engelberger/Dir., Warren Bagatelle/Dir., Farhad Assari/Dir., Robert Hamlen/Dir., William B. Wylam/Dir., Lawrence G. Schafran/Dir.

Owners: Bruce L. Lev/3.75%, KIT Financial, Inc./9.77%, Farhad Assari, Lawrence Schafran, Martin G. Klein/22.14%, Insiders/27.13%, Lithium Nickel Asset Holding Company/27.51%, Michael E. Reed/1.09%, Robert Hamlen, Timothy E. Coyne, William Wylam

Financial Data: Fiscal Year End:12/31   Latest Annual Data: 12/31/2006

Year	Sales		Net Income
2006	$4,667,000		-$5,962,000
2005	$3,862,000		-$3,291,000
2004	$6,760,000		-$1,603,000
Curr. Assets:	$7,128,000	Curr. Liab.:	$1,704,000
Plant, Equip.:	$22,671,000	Total Liab.:	$11,144,000 Indic. Yr. Divd.: NA
Total Assets:	$31,650,000	Net Worth:	$20,505,000 Debt/ Equity: 0.4881

Electro Rent Corp

6060 Sepulveda Blvd., Van Nuys, CA, 91411; *PH:* 1-818-786-2525; *Fax:* 1-818-786-4354; *http://* www.electrorent.com

General - Incorporation	CA	Stock - Price on:12/24/2007	$14.17
Employees	284	Stock Exchange	NDQ
Auditor	Deloitte & Touche LLP	Ticker Symbol	ELRC
Stk Agt	U.S. Stock Transfer Corp	Outstanding Shares	25,930,000
Counsel	Guth Christopher	E.P.S.	$0.86
DUNS No.	02-266-1383	Shareholders	NA

Business: The group's principal activities are to rent, lease and sale of electronic equipment. The group's equipment portfolio comprises of general purpose test and measurement instruments, personal computers and workstations purchased from various manufacturers. The test and measurement instruments are purchased from manufacturers including agilent technologies and tektronix. Personal computers are purchased from compaq, dell, IBM, apple and toshiba; while workstations are purchased from sun microsystems and hewlett packard. The group's customers consist of various industry segments including aerospace, defense, electronics, telecommunications and consulting and computer technology. The group provides services to its customers through a network of equipment, calibration and service centers in the United States and Canada.

Primary SIC and add'l.: 7359 6719 7377

CIK No: 0000032166

Subsidiaries: Electro Rent (Tianjin) Rental Co., Ltd, Electro Rent Asia, Inc, Electro Rent Europe NV, ER International, Inc, Genstar Rental Electronics, Inc

Officers: Daniel Greenberg/Chmn., CEO/$898,498.00, Van Nuys/Sr. RF Technician

Directors: Daniel Greenberg/Chmn., CEO

Owners: Lee S. Kling, Steven Markheim, Gerald D. Barrone, Private Capital Management/15.00%, T. Rowe Price Associates, Inc./14.90%, Nancy Y. Bekavac, Karen J. Curtin, James S. Pignatelli, Daniel Greenberg/16.50%, Dimensional FundAdvisors Inc./5.60%, Insiders/18.70%, Craig R. Jones, Phillip Greenberg/9.10%, Joseph J. Kearns

Financial Data: Fiscal Year End:05/31   Latest Annual Data: 05/31/2007

Year	Sales		Net Income
2007	$125,251,000		$21,049,000
2006	$114,806,000		$22,184,000
2005	$107,616,000		$24,265,000
Curr. Assets:	$72,749,000	Curr. Liab.:	$19,939,000 P/E Ratio: 17.94
Plant, Equip.:	$155,636,000	Total Liab.:	$37,841,000 Indic. Yr. Divd.: $0.100
Total Assets:	$259,682,000	Net Worth:	$221,841,000 Debt/ Equity: NA

Electro Scientific Industries Inc

13900 NW Science Pk. Dr., Portland, OR, 97229; *PH:* 1-503-641-4141; *Fax:* 1-503-671-5571; *http://* www.esi.com; *Email:* info@esi.com

General		Stock	
Incorporation	OR	Price on:12/24/2007	$21.04
Employees	603	Stock Exchange	NDQ
Auditor	KPMG LLP	Ticker Symbol	ESIO
Stk Agt	Mellon Investor Services LLC	Outstanding Shares	29,220,000
Counsel	NA	E.P.S	NA
DUNS No.	00-903-1485	Shareholders	NA

Business: The group's principle activities are to design and manufacture electronic products used in wireless communications, computers, automotive and other electronic products. The group provides high technology manufacturing equipment to the global electronics market. The product line includes advanced laser systems used to improve the production yield of semiconductor devices and to fine tune electronic components and circuitry; high-speed test and termination equipment used in the production of electronic components. Other products include laser drilling systems used in the production of advanced electronic packaging; inspection systems and original equipment manufacturer machine vision products. The group markets its products through direct esi sales and service offices, franchised distributors, value added resellers (vars) and independent representatives located around the world. The group's total revenue for the year 2007 was 250.82 millions of USD.

Primary SIC and add'l.: 3675 3676 3679 3674

CIK No: 0000726514

Subsidiaries: Electro Scientific Industries Europe Ltd., Electro Scientific Industries GmbH, Electro Scientific Industries Japan Co., Ltd., Electro Scientific Industries Singapore PTE Ltd., Electro Scientific Industries, SARL, ESI (Beijing) R&D Center Co., Ltd., ESI China R&D Investment, Pte. Ltd., ESI China, Inc., ESI Electronic Equipment (Shanghai) Co., Ltd., ESI International Corp., ESI Korea Co. Ltd., ESI Taiwan (Branch Office), ESI Technology Development, Pte. Ltd.

Officers: Nick Konidaris/Dir., CEO, Pres./$1,713,337.00, Ian Corr/VP - Service, Robert M. Debakker/VP - Operations/$652,411.00, Steve Harris/VP - Research, Development, Engineering, Yu-Chong Tai/SAB Members, Steve Vogt/SAB Members, Ming Wu/SAB Members, Tung H. Tom/47/VP - Worldwide Sales, Tom Wu/VP - Sales/$738,659.00, Kerry L. Mustoe/VP, Corporate Controller, Chief Accounting Officer/$442,680.00, R. A. Srinivas/VP - Marketing, Pei Hsien Fang/VP - New Wave Research Division, Chris Butterfield/Dir. - Investor Relations ESI, Thomas Baer/SAB Members, John Carruthers/SAB Members

Directors: Nick Konidaris/Dir., CEO, Pres., Jon D. Tompkins/Chmn., Gerald F. Taylor/Dir., Arthur W. Porter/Dir., Robert R. Walker/Dir., Richard J. Faubert/Dir., Barry L. Harmon/Dir., Keith L. Thomson/Dir., Frederick A. Ball/Dir.

Owners: Robert DeBakker, Richard J. Faubert, Third Avenue Management LLC/13.70%, John Metcalf, Insiders/5.00%, Tung H. Tom Wu, Robert R. Walker, Jon D. Tompkins, W. Arthur Porter, Gerald F. Taylor, Nierenberg Investment Management Company Inc./12.00%, Frederick A. Ball, Barry L. Harmon, Dimensional Fund Advisors LP/5.90%, Barclays Global Investors NA/5.10% *(19 Owners included in Index)*

Financial Data: *Fiscal Year End:*06/03 *Latest Annual Data:* 6/3/2006

Year	Sales		Net Income
2006	$207,006,000		$20,823,000
2005	$233,371,000		$19,837,000
2004	$207,242,000		$11,887,000

Curr. Assets:	$353,782,000	**Curr. Liab.:**	$49,298,000	**P/E Ratio:**	28.43
Plant, Equip.:	$51,673,000	**Total Liab.:**	$49,298,000	**Indic. Yr. Divd.:**	NA
Total Assets:	$437,465,000	**Net Worth:**	$388,167,000	**Debt/ Equity:**	NA

Electro-Optical Sciences Inc

3 W Main St., Ste. 201, Irvington, NY, 10533; ***PH:*** 1-914-591-3783; ***Fax:*** 1-914-591-3785; ***http://*** www.eo-sciences.com; ***Email:*** info@eosciences.com

General		Stock	
Incorporation	DE	Price on:12/24/2007	$6.394
Employees	28	Stock Exchange	NDQ
Auditor	Eisner LLP	Ticker Symbol	MELA
Stk Agt	American Stock Transfer & Trust Co.	Outstanding Shares	13,400,000
Counsel	NA	E.P.S	-$0.83
DUNS No.	NA	Shareholders	NA

Business: The groups principal activities include designing and developing medical device. The groups services include Medicare and Medicaid. The group products sold under the trade names MelaFind(R) and DIFOTI(R). The group operates from the United States.

Primary SIC and add'l.: 3841

CIK No: 0001051514

Officers: Joseph V. Gulfo/Dir., CEO, Pres./$296,715.00, Joanna Adrian/Dir. - Clinical Operations, Martin Raneri/Dir. - Quality Assurance, Yuri Malinkevich/Dir. - Electro, Optical Engineering, Richard I. Steinhart/VP - Finance, CFO/$463,125.00, Jon I. Klippel/VP - Marketing, Sales/$169,273.00, Chris Butler/VP - Technical Support/$253,125.00, Marek Elbaum/Founder, Chief Scientist - Technical Team, Alex Bogdan/Dir. - Melafind Algorithm Development, Technical Team, Dina Gutkowicz/Principal Scientist, Dir. - Clinical Research, Michael Greenebaum/Dir. - Data Analysis, Nick Kabelev/Melafind Project Team Leader, David Carey/Primary Investor Relations Officer

Directors: Joseph V. Gulfo/Dir., CEO, Pres., Breaux Castleman/Chmn., Martin C. Mihm/Chmn. - Scientific Advisory Board, Jeffrey P. Callen/Member - Scientific Advisory Board, Armand B. Cognetta/Member - Scientific Advisory Board, Robert Friedman/Member - Scientific Advisory Board, Harold S. Rabinovitz/Member - Scientific Advisory Board, Sidney Braginsky/Dir., Darrell S. Rigel/Member - Scientific Advisory Board, George C. Chryssis/Dir., Martin D. Cleary/Dir., Daniel W. Lufkin/Dir., Gerald Wagner/Dir.

Owners: FMR Corp./8.29%, Joseph V. Gulfo, Jon I. Klippel, Karen Krumeich, Caremi Partners, Ltd./6.37%, Insiders/8.74%, William Bronner, Richard I. Steinhart, Gerald Wagner/1.17%, George C. Chryssis, Dan W. Lufkin/3.91%, Martin Cleary, Breaux Castleman, Phronesis Partners, LLC/5.41%, Manulife Financial Corporation/8.56% *(17 Owners included in Index)*

Financial Data: *Fiscal Year End:*12/31 *Latest Annual Data:* 12/31/2006

Year	Sales		Net Income
2006	NA		-$10,591,000
2005	NA		-$6,726,000
2004	NA		-$3,619,000

Curr. Assets:	$21,771,000	**Curr. Liab.:**	$1,162,000		
Plant, Equip.:	$564,000	**Total Liab.:**	$1,162,000	**Indic. Yr. Divd.:**	NA
Total Assets:	$22,476,000	**Net Worth:**	$21,314,000	**Debt/ Equity:**	NA

Electro-Sensors Inc

6111 Blue Cir. Dr., Minnetonka, MN, 55343; ***PH:*** 1-952-930-0100; ***Fax:*** 1-952-930-0130; ***http://*** www.electro-sensors.com; ***Email:*** investorrelations@electro-sensors.com

General		Stock	
Incorporation	MN	Price on:12/24/2007	$5.85
Employees	27	Stock Exchange	NDQ
Auditor	Virchow, Krause & Co. LLP	Ticker Symbol	ELSE
Stk Agt	Mellon Investor Services LLC	Outstanding Shares	3,360,000
Counsel	Fredrikson & Byron	E.P.S	$0.312
DUNS No.	04-479-0210	Shareholders	NA

Business: The group's principal activities are to manufacture and distribute process control systems and PC-based software. The group operates in three divisions based on product lines: production monitoring systems division, character recognition systems division and investment division. The production monitoring division manufactures and markets speed monitoring and motor control systems for industrial machinery. Character recognition division designs and markets a desktop software-based system that reads hand printed characters, checkmarks and bar code information from scanned or faxed forms. The investment division holds investments in marketable and non-Marketable securities. The trademarks of the group include electro-sensors and autodata.

Primary SIC and add'l.: 6799 3823

CIK No: 0000351789

Subsidiaries: ESI Investment Company

Owners: Insiders/39.50%, Bradley D. Slye/1.50%, Peter R. Peterson/37.60%, Geoffrey W. Miller, AXA Financial, Inc./5.10%

Financial Data: *Fiscal Year End:*12/31 *Latest Annual Data:* 12/31/2006

Year	Sales		Net Income
2006	$5,756,000		$1,724,000
2005	$4,903,000		$761,000
2004	$4,799,000		$172,000

Curr. Assets:	$12,597,000	**Curr. Liab.:**	$2,717,000	**P/E Ratio:**	18.87
Plant, Equip.:	$1,273,000	**Total Liab.:**	$2,717,000	**Indic. Yr. Divd.:**	$0.160
Total Assets:	$13,870,000	**Net Worth:**	$11,153,000	**Debt/ Equity:**	NA

Electroglas Inc

5729 Fontanoso Way, San Jose, CA, 95138; ***PH:*** 1-408-528-3000; ***Fax:*** 1-408-528-3562; ***http://*** www.electroglas.com

General		Stock	
Incorporation	DE	Price on:12/24/2007	$2.11
Employees	278	Stock Exchange	NDQ
Auditor	BDO Seidman, LLP	Ticker Symbol	EGLS
Stk Agt	Bank Boston EquiServe	Outstanding Shares	26,470,000
Counsel	Morrison & Foerster LLP	E.P.S	-$0.62
DUNS No.	80-451-3778	Shareholders	NA

Business: The group's principal activities are to develop, manufacture, market and service semiconductor wafer inspection products and process management software products to the global semiconductor industry. The group also supplies wafer probers. The group's activities are divided into three divisions: prober products, inspection products and egsoft software products. The wafer prober product line consists of horizon 4000 series, the eg4/200, eg5/300, eg5/300e and eg4/200e. Inspection product line includes the quicksilver series, which are designed for automated inspection of the wafers after the completion of the manufacturing process. Egsoft's software products division provides software tools and solutions for semiconductor manufacturing.

Primary SIC and add'l.: 3825

CIK No: 0000902281

Subsidiaries: EGsoft Holdings Corporation, EGsoft, Inc., Electroglas Far East Holding Company, Electroglas Far East Technical Services (Shanghai) Ltd., Electroglas GmbH Germany, Electroglas International, Inc, Electroglas Private Limited

Officers: Thomas M. Rohrs/Chmn., CEO/$691,309.00, Wes Highfill/Exec. VP - Global Sales, Marketing/$245,344.00, Richard J. Casler/CTO/$263,616.00, Thomas E. Brunton/VP - Finance, CFO, Treasurer, Sec./$236,972.00

Directors: Thomas M. Rohrs/Chmn., CEO, John Osborne/Dir., Mel Friedman/Dir., Scott C. Gibson/Dir., Fusen E. Chen/Dir., Jack G. Wilborn/Dir.

Owners: Wesley D. Highfill, Insiders/4.91%, Scott C. Gibson, Richard J. Casler, QVT Financial GP LLC/9.97%, John F. Osborne, Peninsula Capital Management LP/17.61%, Thomas M. Rohrs, Thomas E. Brunton, Jack G. Wilborn, Westcliff Capital Management/9.67%, Mel Friedman, Fairfield Greenwich Limited/6.54%, Royce and Associates, LLC/8.04%, Dimensional Fund Advisors, Inc./5.40% *(17 Owners included in Index)*

Financial Data: *Fiscal Year End:*12/31 *Latest Annual Data:* 05/31/2007

Year	Sales		Net Income
2007	$44,624,000		-$18,783,000
2006	$44,317,000		-$34,030,000
2004	$63,004,000		-$6,372,000

Curr. Assets:	$51,450,000	**Curr. Liab.:**	$18,632,000		
Plant, Equip.:	$5,089,000	**Total Liab.:**	$28,664,000	**Indic. Yr. Divd.:**	NA
Total Assets:	$61,846,000	**Net Worth:**	$33,182,000	**Debt/ Equity:**	0.3875

Electronic Arts Inc

209 Redwood Shores Pkwy., Redwood City, CA, 94065; ***PH:*** 1-650-628-1393; ***Fax:*** 1-650-628-1422; ***http://*** www.ea.com; ***Email:*** privacy_policy@ea.com

General		Stock	
Incorporation	DE	Price on:12/24/2007	$48.01
Employees	7,200	Stock Exchange	NDQ
Auditor	KPMG LLP	Ticker Symbol	ERTS
Stk Agt	Wells Fargo Bank, N.A.	Outstanding Shares	311,470,000
Counsel	Ruth A. Kennedy	E.P.S	-$0.62
DUNS No.	07-319-9531	Shareholders	NA

Business: The groups principle activities include developing, marketing, publishing and distributing interactive software games. The group also publishes interactive software games for multiple platforms. The group operates from United States.

Primary SIC and add'l.: 7375 7371 7372

CIK No: 0000712515

Subsidiaries: Axent (emea) Limited, BindView Development Corporation, DataCenter Technologies N.V., Delrina Corporation, Ejasent, Inc., Invio Software, Inc., Jareva Technologies, Inc., Kvault Software Ltd., Precise Software Solutions, Inc., Sygate Technologies LLC, Symantec (Australia) Pty Ltd., Symantec (Canada) Corp., Symantec (Japan), Inc., Symantec Australia Holding Pty. Ltd., Symantec Cyprus Ltd. 40 Subsidiaries included in the Index

Officers: Riccitiello John/CEO, Gabrielle Toledano/41/Sr. VP - Human Resources, Frank D. Gibeau/39/Exec. VP, GM North American Publishing, Paul V. Lee/43/Pres. - Worldwide Studios/$4,102,461.00, Jenson C. Warren/50/Exec. VP, Chief Financial, Administrative Officer/$5,618,715.00, Gerhard Florin/48/Exec. VP, GM International Publishing/$3,607,442.00, Steven G. Bene/Sr. VP, General Counsel, Corp. Sec., Joel Linzner/55/Exec. VP - Business, Legal Affairs, Peter Moore/Pres. - EA Sports, Kathy Vrabeck/Pres. - EA Casual Entertainment, Warren C. Jenson/51/Exec. VP, Chief Financial, Administrative Officer, Michael Marchetti/39/Sr. VP, GM - EA Mobile, John Schappert/37/COO, Sr. VP - Worldwide Studios, Nancy L. Smith/Exec. VP, GM The Sims, William B. Gordon/57/Exec. VP, Chief Creative Officer (16 Officers included in Index)

Directors: Lawrence F. Probst/57/Chmn., Timothy Mott/59/Dir., Linda J. Srere/52/Dir., Gregory B. Maffei/48/Dir., Richard A. Simonson/49/Dir., Leonard S. Coleman/59/Dir., Vivek Paul/49/Dir., Gary M. Kusin/57/Dir.

Owners: Linda J. Srere, John S. Riccitiello, Gregory B. Maffei, Richard A. Simonson, Richard M. Asher, Lawrence F. Probst/1.50%, Insiders/3.00%, Leonard S. Coleman, FMR Corp/6.00%, Gerhard Florin, Timothy Mott, Warren C. Jenson, Gary M. Kusin, Vivek Paul, Legg Mason Capital Management, Inc/6.30% (16 Owners included in Index)

Financial Data: Fiscal Year End:03/31   Latest Annual Data: 3/31/2007

Year	Sales	Net Income
2007	$3,091,000,000	$76,000,000
2006	$2,951,000,000	$236,000,000
2005	$3,129,000,000	$504,000,000

Curr. Assets:	$3,597,000,000	**Curr. Liab.:**	$1,026,000,000	**P/E Ratio:**	200.04
Plant, Equip.:	$484,000,000	**Total Liab.:**	$1,114,000,000	**Indic. Yr. Divd.:**	NA
Total Assets:	$5,146,000,000	**Net Worth:**	$4,032,000,000	**Debt/ Equity:**	NA

Electronic Clearing House Inc

730 Paseo Camarillo, Camarillo, CA, 93010; **PH:** 1-805-419-8700; **Fax:** 1-805-419-8683; http:// www.echo-inc.com

General - Incorporation	NV	Stock - Price on:12/24/2007	$12.39
Employees	211	Stock Exchange	NDQ
Auditor	PricewaterhouseCoopers LLP	Ticker Symbol	ECHO
Stk Agt	OTR Inc	Outstanding Shares	6,860,000
Counsel	NA	E.P.S.	-$0.04
DUNS No.	10-305-4011	Shareholders	NA

Business: The group's principle activity is to provide a complete solution to the payment processing needs of merchants, banks and collection agencies. The services of the group include debit and credit card processing, check guarantee, check verification, check conversion, check re-presentment, check collection and inventory tracking. It derives revenues from two main business segments, bankcard and transaction processing services and check services. It operates under the following brands: merchantamerica, a retail provider of processing services to both the merchant and bank markets; national check network for transaction verification; xpresschex, inc for processing check guarantee, check conversion, check collection and check verification; and u-haul services, which provides credit card authorization, rental activity and tracks available inventory. The group's total revenue for the year 2007 was 76.88 millions of USD.

Primary SIC and add'l.: 6099 6719 7359 6712 7389

CIK No: 0000721773

Subsidiaries: Xpresschex, Inc.

Officers: Charles J. Harris/Dir., COO, CEO, Pres./$549,650.00, Patricia A. Williams/Sr. VP, Alice L. Cheung/CFO, Treasurer/$203,885.00, Kris Winckler/Sr. VP, Karl Asplund/Sr. VP, Todd Baum/Sales Representative/$253,405.00, Shawn Alikian/General Counsel, Sharat Shankar/Sr. VP/$184,850.00, Donna L. Rehman/Corp. Sec., Rick Slater/CTO, VP, Steve Hoofring/Sr. VP, Jack Wilson/Sr. VP/$202,832.00, William Wied/CIO

Directors: Charles J. Harris/Dir., COO, CEO, Pres., Aristides W. Georgantas/Dir., Richard D. Field/Dir., H. Eugene Lockhart/58/Dir., Herbert L. Lucas/Dir., Jerry McElhatton/Dir., Keith B. Hall/Dir., Carl R. Terzian/Dir.

Owners: Richard Field/2.97%, Insiders/15.08%, Charles Harris/0.95%, Alice L. Cheung/1.19%, Glazer Capital LLC/7.13%, Jack Wilson/0.97%, Herbert L. Lucas, Joel M. Barry/4.66%, Eugene H. Lockhart, Carl R. Terzian/0.04%, Sharat Shankar/0.86%, Aristides W. Georgantas/0.24%, Discovery Equity Partners, LP/12.95%, Melvin Laufer/7.57%

Financial Data: Fiscal Year End:09/30   Latest Annual Data: 9/30/2006

Year	Sales	Net Income
2006	$75,311,000	$2,317,000
2005	$55,551,000	$1,033,000
2004	$47,584,000	$2,849,000

Curr. Assets:	$41,893,000	**Curr. Liab.:**	$29,351,000		
Plant, Equip.:	$2,521,000	**Total Liab.:**	$32,721,000	**Indic. Yr. Divd.:**	NA
Total Assets:	$55,007,000	**Net Worth:**	$22,286,000	**Debt/ Equity:**	NA

Electronic Control Security Inc

790 Bloomfield Ave., Bldg. C-1, Clifton, NJ, 07012; **PH:** 1-973-574-8555; **Fax:** 1-973-574-8562; http:// www.anti-terrorism.com; **Email:** info@anti-terrorism.com

General - Incorporation	NJ	Stock - Price on:12/24/2007	$1.01
Employees	27	Stock Exchange	OTC
Auditor	Demetrius & Co LLC	Ticker Symbol	EKCS
Stk Agt	Continental Stock Transfer & Trust Co	Outstanding Shares	8,720,000
Counsel	NA	E.P.S.	-$0.14
DUNS No.	06-078-4014	Shareholders	NA

Business: The group's principal activities are designing, manufacturing and marketing of security detection equipment for correctional, commercial and industrial use. The group also provides consulting and advisory services for risk assessment, including threat, vulnerability and criticality analysis. The product line includes perimeter detection equipment, intrusion detection and monitoring system, computer security system, vehicle and vessel tracking devices, asset tracking devices and a personal identification and location system. The products are designed to protect a site against terrorism, theft and arson. The products are marketed to large correctional facilities, government facilities such as military bases, nuclear power stations, airports and private corporations including international oil producers and high technology companies desiring to protect trade secrets and prevent intrusion into facilities. The group operates in the United States and the Middle East.

Primary SIC and add'l.: 7382

CIK No: 0000803044

Subsidiaries: Clarion Sensing Systems Acquisition Corp, Clarion Sensing Systems, Inc

---

Officers: Arthur Barchenko/Dir., CEO, Pres., Thomas Isdanavich/VP - Project Management, Eldon Moberg/VP - Ecsi, Foids Div, Mark R. Barchenko/VP - Strategic Planning, Richard Stern/VP - Marketing, Sales Support, Jerry Dropik/VP, GM - Middle East, Africa, Jeffrey S. Holmes/Project Mgr., Ashok Saxena/VP - Advanced Systems, Richard Deyulio/Security Professional, Hamid Kaber/VP - Latin American, Robert Robinson/Corporate Accounting Mgr., Natalie Barchenko/74/Dir., Corp. Sec., Treasurer, Yaser Hassan/Project Engineer, Ronald Thomas/64/Dir., VP - Program Management

Directors: Arthur Barchenko/Dir., CEO, Pres., Natalie Barchenko/74/Dir., Corp. Sec., Treasurer, Edward Snow/69/Dir., Stephen Rossetti/58/Dir., Henry J. Schweiter/53/Dir., David J. Friedman/62/Dir., Ronald Thomas/64/Dir., VP - Program Management

Owners: Stephen Rossetti, Arthur Barchenko, David J. Friedman, Richard Stern, Ronald Thomas, Regency Resources, Inc., Henry J. Schweiter, Insiders, Mark Barchenko, Edward Snow, Eldon Moberg, Richard Lippe, Natalie Barchenko, View Far Management Ltd., John A. Gentile (18 Owners included in Index)

Financial Data: Fiscal Year End:06/30   Latest Annual Data: 6/30/2006

Year	Sales	Net Income
2006	$8,822,000	-$1,736,000
2005	$5,967,000	-$122,000
2004	$2,061,000	-$1,119,000

Curr. Assets:	$4,895,000	**Curr. Liab.:**	$2,531,000		
Plant, Equip.:	$397,000	**Total Liab.:**	$3,800,000	**Indic. Yr. Divd.:**	NA
Total Assets:	$7,674,000	**Net Worth:**	$3,874,000	**Debt/ Equity:**	0.4169

Electronic Data Systems Corp

5400 Legacy Dr., Plano, TX, 75024; **PH:** 1-972-604-6000; **Fax:** 1-972-605-6033; http:// www.eds.com; **Email:** info@eds.com

General - Incorporation	DE	Stock - Price on:12/24/2007	$27.99
Employees	131,000	Stock Exchange	NYSE
Auditor	KPMG LLP	Ticker Symbol	EDS
Stk Agt	American Stock Transfer & Trust Co.	Outstanding Shares	508,860,000
Counsel	NA	E.P.S.	$1.41
DUNS No.	04-666-7523	Shareholders	NA

Business: The group's principle activity is to provide information technology and business process outsourcing services. The group operates from United States.

Primary SIC and add'l.: 8742 7373 7379 7371

CIK No: 0001007456

Subsidiaries: Atraxis Africa (Pty) Limited, E.D.S. de Mexico, Sociedad Anonima de Capital Variable, E.D.S. International Corporation, E.D.S. International Limited, E.D.S. Spectrum Corporation, E.D.S. World Corporation (Far East), E.D.S. World Corporation (Netherlands), eBreviate UK Limited, EDS (Australia) Pty Limited, EDS (Australia) Superannuation Fund Pty Ltd, EDS (Business Process Administration) Pty Limited, EDS (China) Co., Ltd., EDS (Electronic Data Systems) France S.A.S., EDS (Korea) Ltd., EDS (New Zealand) Limited 141 Subsidiaries included in the Index

Officers: Ronald A. Rittenmeyer/Dir., CEO, Pres./$5,399,527.00, Tina M. Sivinski/Chief Administrative Officer, Sr. Exec. VP, Larry Bissinger/Industry Analyst, Joe Eazor/Exec. VP - Corporate Strategy - Business Development, Storrow Gordon/Exec. VP, General Counsel, Paul W. Currie/49/Exec. VP - Corporate Strategy, Business Development, Charlie Feld/Sr. Exec. VP - Applications Services/$6,301,762.00, Ronald P. Vargo/CFO, Exec. VP/$1,736,537.00, Thomas A. Haubenstricke/45/VP/$1,357,768.00, Michael Coomer/Exec. VP - Asia Pacific Region, Jeff Kelly/Exec. VP - Americas, Bill Thomas/Exec. VP - EDS EMEA, Dave Kost/VP - EDS Investor Relations, Roxane Barry/Sr. Analyst, Deanna Rogers/Sr. Analyst (35 Officers included in Index)

Directors: Ronald A. Rittenmeyer/Dir., CEO, Pres., Michael H. Jordan/71/Chmn., Jeffrey M. Heller/Vice Chmn., Roy W. Dunbar/Dir., Martin Faga/Dir., Ray J. Groves/Dir., David R. Yost/Dir., Malcolm S. Gillis/Dir., Ellen M. Hancock/Dir., Ray L. Hunt/Dir., Edward A. Kangas/Dir., James K. Sims/Dir., Ernesto Zedillo/Dir.

Owners: Roger A. Enrico, State Street Bank and Trust Company, Thomas A. Haubenstricker, Dodge & Cox, Charles S. Feld, Roy W. Dunbar, Ray J. Groves, Edward A. Kangas, David R. Yost, AXA Financial, Inc., James K. Sims, Jeffrey M. Heller, Ray L. Hunt, Hotchkiss and Wiley Capital Management, LLC, Robert H. Swan (23 Owners included in Index)

Financial Data: Fiscal Year End:12/31   Latest Annual Data: 12/31/2006

Year	Sales	Net Income
2006	$21,268,000,000	$470,000,000
2005	$19,757,000,000	$150,000,000
2004	$20,669,000,000	$158,000,000

Curr. Assets:	$8,257,000,000	**Curr. Liab.:**	$5,234,000,000	**P/E Ratio:**	23.13
Plant, Equip.:	$2,179,000,000	**Total Liab.:**	$9,908,000,000	**Indic. Yr. Divd.:**	$0.200
Total Assets:	$17,954,000,000	**Net Worth:**	$7,896,000,000	**Debt/ Equity:**	0.3771

Electronic Game Card Inc

712 Fifth Ave., 19th Fl., New York, NY, 10019; **PH:** 1-646-723-8936; **Fax:** 1-212-581-1922; http:// www.electronicgamecard.com; **Email:** info@electronicgamecard.com

General - Incorporation	NV	Stock - Price on:12/24/2007	$0.315
Employees	5	Stock Exchange	OTC
Auditor	Mendoza Berger & Co., LLP	Ticker Symbol	EGMI
Stk Agt	Liberty Transfer Co	Outstanding Shares	44,170,000
Counsel	NA	E.P.S.	-$0.04
DUNS No.	NA	Shareholders	NA

Business: The group's principal activity is to develop and manufacture various energy generation devices and energy efficient mechanisms. The portable electronic devices include portable laptop computers, handheld devices, cellular phones and other electronic devices. The group is in the development stage.

Primary SIC and add'l.: 3679

CIK No: 0001083036

Subsidiaries: Electronic Game Card Marketing, Inc, New Ham International, N.V., Scientific Energy, Inc

Officers: John Bentley/Chmn, CEO, Linden J. Boyne/Dir., CFO, Sec., Gordon McNally/Non Exec. Dir., Daniel Kane/VP, Yvonne L. Zappulla/MD

Directors: John Bentley/Chmn., CEO, Lee J. Cole/Dir., Linden J. Boyne/Dir., CFO, Sec.

Owners: Pequot Capital Management/6.80%, Insiders/0.70%, Linden Boyne/0.70%

Financial Data: Fiscal Year End:12/31   Latest Annual Data: 12/31/2006

Year	Sales	Net Income
2006	$997,000	-$9,714,000
2004	$80,000	-$8,617,000
2003	$8,000	-$542,000

Curr. Assets:	$4,007,000	Curr. Liab.:	$1,140,000		
Plant, Equip.:	$91,000	Total Liab.:	$1,152,000	Indic. Yr. Divd.:	NA
Total Assets:	$5,117,000	Net Worth:	-$4,443,000	Debt/ Equity:	NA

Electronic Media Central Corp

413 Ave. G, No. 1, Redondo Beach, CA, 90277; *PH:* 1-310-318-2244; *http://* www.iiemc.com

General - Incorporation	CA	**Stock** - Price on:12/24/2007	$2.5
Employees	1	Stock Exchange	NA
Auditor	Kabani & Co, Inc	Ticker Symbol	NA
Stk Agt	Cede & Co	Outstanding Shares	1,300,000
Counsel	NA	E.P.S.	-$0.04
DUNS No.	NA	Shareholders	NA

Business: The group's principle activities are to provide electronic media duplication and packaging services. The group provides duplication and packaging services for compact disks, digital videodisk and videocassette tape. The sales of electronic media duplication and packaging services of the group are primarily the duplication and packaging of a customer's pre-recorded video programs. The programs are principally used for education, promotion and documentation of the customer's products or services. The group provides services to create multiple copies of a customer's material on videotape, compact disks CD and DVD formats with related packaging. The main target markets for services are business, religious, government and other non-profit organizations.

Primary SIC and add'l.: 7334
CIK No: 0001133901
Subsidiaries: Apple Media Corporation
Officers: Roger Casas/Dir., CEO, George Morris/Chmn., CFO, Sec., VP, Shirlene Bradshaw/69/Dir., Business Mgr.
Directors: Roger Casas/Dir., CEO, George Morris/Chmn., CFO, Sec., VP
Owners: Shirlene Bradshaw, L&M Media, Inc./16.70%, Insiders/83.10%, George Morris/62.30%, Roger Casas

Financial Data: *Fiscal Year End:* 03/31 *Latest Annual Data:* 03/31/2007

Year	Sales	Net Income
2007	$157,000	-$49,000
2006	$274,000	-$26,000
2005	$236,000	-$82,000

Curr. Assets:	$148,000	Curr. Liab.:	$349,000		
Plant, Equip.:	NA	Total Liab.:	$349,000	Indic. Yr. Divd.:	NA
Total Assets:	$148,000	Net Worth:	-$201,000	Debt/ Equity:	NA

Electronic Sensor Technology Inc

1077 Business Ctr. Cir., Newbury Park, CA, 91320; *PH:* 1-805-480-1994; *Fax:* 1-805-480-1984; *http://* www.znose.com; *Email:* marketing@estcal.com

General - Incorporation	NV	**Stock** - Price on:12/24/2007	$0.21
Employees	20	Stock Exchange	OTC
Auditor	Sherb & Co., LLP	Ticker Symbol	ESNR
Stk Agt	Continental Stock Transfer & Trust Co	Outstanding Shares	54,170,000
Counsel	NA	E.P.S.	-$0.095
DUNS No.	NA	Shareholders	NA

Business: The groups principle activities include developing, manufacturing, and selling of a patented product. The group products include zNose(R). The group operates from the United States.

Primary SIC and add'l.: 3679
CIK No: 0001122860
Subsidiaries: Amerasia Technology, Inc., Electronic Sensor Technology, LP, L & G Sensor Technology, Inc.
Officers: Barry S. Howe/Dir., CEO, Pres., Michele Serpico/Contact - Sales, Marketing, John Rice/Contact - Application Support, Norman Chin-You/Salea, Support, Southeast, Phillip Yee/Sec., Treasurer, CFO/$64,750.00, Gary W. Watson/VP - Engineering/$149,527.00, Catherine F. Koeritz/Contact - Sales, Marketing, Frank Zuhde/Dir. - Marketing, Sales, David Sunday/Contact - North America Central, Ken Zeiger/Sales, Support, North America California, Mac Smith/Sales, Support, North America Northwest
Directors: Barry S. Howe/Dir., CEO, Pres., James H. Frey/Chmn., Teong C. Lim/Dir., James R. Wilburn/Dir., Francis H. Chang/Dir., Mike Krishnan/66/Dir., Michel A. Amsalem/Dir., Lewis E. Larson/Dir.
Owners: Lewis Larson, Gary Watson, Teong Lim, Barry Howe, Land & General Berhad, James Wilburn, L&G Resources (1994), Inc., Midsummer Investment Ltd., TC Lim, LLC, James Frey, Insiders, Francis Chang, 3 Springs, LLC, Islandia L.P., Philip Yee

Financial Data: *Fiscal Year End:* 12/31 *Latest Annual Data:* 12/31/2006

Year	Sales	Net Income
2006	$2,180,000	-$2,812,000
2005	$2,122,000	$2,779,000
2004	NA	-$73,000

Curr. Assets:	$3,711,000	Curr. Liab.:	$3,852,000		
Plant, Equip.:	$198,000	Total Liab.:	$6,380,000	Indic. Yr. Divd.:	NA
Total Assets:	$4,451,000	Net Worth:	-$1,929,000	Debt/ Equity:	NA

Electronic Systems Technology Inc

415 N Quay St., Bldg. B1, Kennewick, WA, 99336; *PH:* 1-509-735-9092; *Fax:* 1-509-783-5475; *http://* www.esteem.com; *Email:* support@esteem.com

General - Incorporation	WA	**Stock** - Price on:12/24/2007	$1.15
Employees	14	Stock Exchange	OTC
Auditor	Moe O'shaughnessy & Assoc. P.S	Ticker Symbol	ELST
Stk Agt	TranSecurities International, Inc	Outstanding Shares	5,150,000
Counsel	NA	E.P.S.	$0.06
DUNS No.	13-012-4928	Shareholders	NA

Business: The group's principle activities include manufacturing and developing wireless modem products. The group's products provide communication links between computers, peripherals and instrumentation controls using radio frequency waves. The products are used in process automation for commercial, industrial and government arenas. Some of the industries using the products of the group are water and waste water industry, industrial process control, power utility and public safety. The group also sells accessories that support the product line of the group like antennas and cable assemblies. In addition, the group provides professional services, site survey testing, system start-up and custom engineering services to assist in the application of wireless modems. The group operates from United States.

Primary SIC and add'l.: 5065 3661
CIK No: 0000752294
Officers: T. L. Kirchner/59/Dir., CEO, Pres., Founder/$145,987.00, Jon Correio/40/Dir., VP - Finance, Sec., Treasurer
Directors: T. L. Kirchner/59/Dir., CEO, Pres., Founder, Robert Southworth/64/Dir., Melvin H. Brown/77/Dir., Jon Correio/40/Dir., VP - Finance, Sec., Treasurer, John L. Schooley/68/Dir.
Owners: John Schooley/2.60%, EDCO Partners LLP/8.00%, Paul D. Sonkin/11.80%, T. L. Kirchner/7.80%, D. B. Strecker, Melvin H. Brown/1.50%

Financial Data: *Fiscal Year End:* 12/31 *Latest Annual Data:* 12/31/2006

Year	Sales	Net Income
2006	$2,618,000	$226,000
2005	$2,418,000	$113,000
2004	$2,298,000	$175,000

Curr. Assets:	$3,135,000	Curr. Liab.:	$310,000	P/E Ratio:	19.17
Plant, Equip.:	$153,000	Total Liab.:	$361,000	Indic. Yr. Divd.:	NA
Total Assets:	$3,320,000	Net Worth:	$2,959,000	Debt/ Equity:	NA

Electronics For Imaging Inc

303 Velocity Way, Foster City, CA, 94404; *PH:* 1-650-357-3500; *Fax:* 1-650-357-3907; *http://* www.efi.com; *Email:* investor.relations@efi.com

General - Incorporation	DE	**Stock** - Price on:12/24/2007	$28.9
Employees	1,723	Stock Exchange	NDQ
Auditor	PricewaterhouseCoopers LLP	Ticker Symbol	EFII
Stk Agt	American Stock Transfer & Trust Co.	Outstanding Shares	58,980,000
Counsel	Testa, Hurwitz & Thibeault	E.P.S.	$0.39
DUNS No.	60-232-5755	Shareholders	NA

Business: The group's principal activity is to design and market products that support color and black-and-white printing on a variety of peripheral devices. The group's products include stand-alone servers and controllers. Stand-alone servers are connected to digital copiers and other peripheral devices and controllers are embedded in digital copiers and desktop color laser printers. The group sells its products primarily to original equipment manufacturers in North America, Europe and Japan. In jan 2003, the group acquired best gmbh and printcafe and in feb 2004, automated dispatch systems inc.

Primary SIC and add'l.: 7379 7372 3577
CIK No: 0000867374
Subsidiaries: Best GmbH, Bestcolor Asia Sdn Bhd, EFI (Canada), Inc., EFI Brazil LTDA, EFI Israel Limited, EFI KK, EFI Luxembourg SARL, EFIIrelandImagingSolutionsInvestmentCompanyLtd, Electronics for Imaging (Europe) Limited, Electronics for Imaging AB, Electronics for Imaging Australia Pty Ltd, Electronics for Imaging Espaa S.L., Electronics for Imaging France SARL, Electronics for Imaging GmbH, Electronics for Imaging Holding GmbH 29 Subsidiaries included in the Index
Officers: Guy Gecht/Dir., CEO, Fred Rosenzweig/Dir., Pres., John Ritchie/CFO
Directors: Guy Gecht/Dir., CEO, Gill Cogan/Interim Chmn., James S. Greene/Dir., Jean-Louis Gassee/Dir., Dan Maydan/Dir., Fred Rosenzweig/Dir., Pres., Christopher Paisley/Dir., Thomas I. Unterberg/Dir.
Owners: Guy Gecht/1.20%, John Ritchie, Joseph Cutts, J.& W. Seligman& Co. Incorporated/7.08%, Neuberger Berman Inc./5.03%, Wellington Management Co. LLP/6.75%, Dan Maydan, Christopher B. Paisley, Blum Capital Partners/5.28%, Mellon Financial Corporation/5.86%, Thomas Unterberg, James S. Greene, Third Avenue Management LLC/6.99%, Fred Rosenzweig/1.13%, Jean-Louis Gasse *(17 Owners included in Index)*

Financial Data: *Fiscal Year End:* 12/31 *Latest Annual Data:* 12/31/2006

Year	Sales	Net Income
2006	$564,611,000	-$183,000
2005	$468,501,000	-$4,067,000
2004	$394,604,000	$38,019,000

Curr. Assets:	$654,847,000	Curr. Liab.:	$393,073,000		
Plant, Equip.:	$52,646,000	Total Liab.:	$393,073,000	Indic. Yr. Divd.:	NA
Total Assets:	$1,144,651,000	Net Worth:	$751,578,000	Debt/ Equity:	0.3218

Element 21 Golf Co

207 Queens Quay W No. 455, Toronto, ON, M5J 1A7; *PH:* 1-800-710-2021; *http://* www.e21golf.com

General - Incorporation	DE	**Stock** - Price on:12/24/2007	$0.16
Employees	NA	Stock Exchange	OTC
Auditor	Lazar Levine & Felix LLP	Ticker Symbol	EGLF
Stk Agt	Jersey Transfer & Trust Co	Outstanding Shares	NA
Counsel	NA	E.P.S.	NA
DUNS No.	NA	Shareholders	NA

Business: The group's principal activity is to develop licenses and markets biotech and therapeutic product lines. The group is a development stage company. The products of the group include erythrogentm and chondroitin sulfate. Erythrogentm is a cell culture additive, sold to research laboratories and pharmaceutical companies for incorporation into their experimental cell culture media. On 03-Oct- 2002 the group acquired element 21 golf company.

Primary SIC and add'l.: 8731 2836
CIK No: 0000797662
Subsidiaries: Advanced Conductor Technologies, Inc, I-JAM Entertainment, Inc
Officers: Nataliya Hearn/Chmn., CEO, Pres., John Grippo/CFO, Bill Dey/COO, Keith Keindel/VP - International Sales, Ken Whiting/VP - Fishing, Mark Myrhum/Production Management, Product Development, Andy Harris/PGA Tour Rep
Directors: Nataliya Hearn/Chmn., CEO, Pres., Benton Wilcoxon/Dir., Mary Bryan/Dir., Sergey Bedziouk/Dir.

Owners: Clearline Capital LLC/21.00%, Bill Dey/6.90%, Mary Bryan, Clearline Capital LLC/50.00%, BOLSHAYA POLYANKA UNIT/42.00%, John Grippo, Benton Wilcoxon, Vladimir Goryunov Alderstasse/50.00%, Nataliya Hearn/8.20%, Insiders/15.90%, Vladimir Goryunov/21.00%, Nataliya Hearn/58.00%

Financial Data: *Fiscal Year End:*06/30 *Latest Annual Data:* 6/30/2006

Year	Sales	Net Income
2006	$52,000	-$4,496,000
2005	$66,000	-$1,353,000
2004	NA	-$2,229,000

Curr. Assets:	$422,000	**Curr. Liab.:**	$3,084,000		
Plant, Equip.:	$511,000	**Total Liab.:**	$3,692,000	**Indic. Yr. Divd.:**	NA
Total Assets:	$932,000	**Net Worth:**	-$2,760,000	**Debt/ Equity:**	NA

Elephant & Castle Group Inc

1190 Hornby St., 12th Fl., Vancouver, BC, V6Z 2K5; *PH:* 1-604-684-6451; *http://* www.elephantcastle.com

General - Incorporation ....Canada
Employees ....NA
Auditor ....Pannell Kerr Forster
Stk Agt...... American Stock Transfer & Trust Co.
Counsel........................Georald Ingborg Fasken
DUNS No. 24-980-3198

Stock- Price on:12/24/2007 ....$0.82
Stock Exchange........................NA
Ticker Symbol........................NA
Outstanding Shares ....NA
E.P.S........................NA
Shareholders........................NA

Business: The group's principal activities are to own, operate and franchise casual full dinning brand name restaurants in Canada and Washington, Pennsylvania, Massachusetts, Minnesota, Texas, California and Illinois in United States. The two principal brands are elephant and castle and alamo steakhouse and grill. The group operates authentic british-style pubs in North America. These pubs and restaurants serve traditional british fare as well as all the American favorites along with an extensive line of spirits. In addition, the group owns and operates the casual, themed restaurant concept called alamo steakhouse and grill. This southwestern-style steakhouse features Texas-sized portions of steaks and ribs and southwestern specialties along with a cantina that features the alamo's famous 20 oz. Margaritas. As on 08-Jan-2001 the group closed its twin restaurant in franklin mills.

Primary SIC and add'l.: 6794 5812

CIK No: 0000899849

Subsidiaries: BC Restaurants, LLC, E & C Pub, Inc., E&C Capital, LLC, E&C San Francisco, LLC, Elephant & Castle (Chicago) Corporation, Elephant & Castle East Huron, LLC, Elephant & Castle International, Inc., Elephant & Castle, Inc., Elephant and Castle of Pennsylvania, Inc., Good Times Restaurants, LLC, Massachusetts Elephant & Castle Group, Inc., The Elephant and Castle Canada Inc.

Officers: Rick Bryant/Dir., CEO, Pres., Richard Bryant/Chmn., CEO, Principal Executive Officer, Hans Klaekken/Dir. - Culinary Services, Roger Sexton/CFO, Peter Laurie/COO, Thomas Chambers/Dir. - Sr. Partner Services, Colin Stacey/Dir. - Restaurant Consultant, John Luvison/Dir. - Operations, Eastern Region, Steve Meeker/Dir. - Operations, Western Region, Dennis O'Brien/Dir. - Operations, Midwest Region

Directors: Rick Bryant/Dir., CEO, Pres., Richard Bryant/Chmn., CEO, Principal Executive Officer, George Pitman/Dir. - Elephant, Castle, Colin Stacey/Dir. - Restaurant Consultant, Chris Anderson/Dir., Jeffrey Barnett/Founder, Dir., Thomas Chambers/Dir. - Sr. Partner Services, David Wiederecht/Dir.

Owners: Insiders/21.00%, Peter Laurie/4.50%, General Electric Investment Private Placement Partners II,/53.80%, Thomas Chambers, George W. Pitman/1.30%, Peter Laurie, Insiders, Roger Sexton, Richard H. Bryant, Jeffrey M. Barnett/4.10%, Richard H. Bryant/8.10%, Roger Sexton/2.10%, GEIPPP, Colin Stacey/0.50%

Financial Data: *Fiscal Year End:*12/25 *Latest Annual Data:* 12/31/2006

Year	Sales	Net Income
2006	$36,312,000	-$154,000
2005	$33,045,000	-$3,266,000
2004	$28,202,000	-$1,170,000

Curr. Assets:	$2,445,000	**Curr. Liab.:**	$3,974,000		
Plant, Equip.:	$10,008,000	**Total Liab.:**	$23,045,000	**Indic. Yr. Divd.:**	NA
Total Assets:	$16,797,000	**Net Worth:**	-$6,248,000	**Debt/ Equity:**	NA

Elephant Talk Communications Inc

438 E Katella Ave., Ste. 217, Orange, CA, 92867; *PH:* 1-714-288-1570; *Fax:* 1-714-288-2045; *http://* www.elephanttalk.com; *Email:* info@elephanttalk.com

General - Incorporation ....CA
Employees 8
Auditor ....Kabani & Co.,Inc.
Stk Agt........................Signature Stock Transfer, Inc.
Counsel........................NA
DUNS No. ....NA

Stock- Price on:12/24/2007 ....$0.085
Stock Exchange........................OTC
Ticker Symbol........................ETLK
Outstanding Shares 238,270,000
E.P.S........................-$0.028
Shareholders........................NA

Business: The group's principal activity is to provide international long distance services through its state-of-the-art digital switches and transmission facilities as well as through its interconnections with major international carriers. The group's operations employ advanced systems including call collection and call data storage linking to a proprietary reporting system. This permits management to determine the gross margin by destination country, by customer, as well as for overall operations on a daily basis. The international call services are provided through an integrated network infrastructure comprising both the packet-switched system and circuit switched system focusing on the Asia-Pacific region as well the United States. The services are provided to first-tier local and international telecommunications carriers, enabling those carriers and other service providers to offer voice and fax services to their end-customers.

Primary SIC and add'l.: 7389

CIK No: 0001084384

Subsidiaries: Elephant Talk Limited, Elephant Talk Middle East, Full Mark Limited, Guangdong Elephant Talk Network Consulting Limited, True Precise Technology Limited

Officers: Steven Van Der Velden/CEO, Russelle Choi/51/Dir., Pres., Manu Ohri/50/Dir., Exec. VP - Finance, Pius Lam/47/Dir., VP, COO, Martin Zuurbier/COO, CTO, Willem Ackermans/CFO

Directors: Francis Lim/47/Dir., Manu Ohri/50/Dir., Exec. VP - Finance, Pius Lam/47/Dir., VP, COO, Russelle Choi/51/Dir., Pres., James Wang/48/Dir., Erik De Jonghe/60/Dir., Johan Dejager/48/Dir., Yves R. Van Sante/47/Dir.

Owners: Russelle Choi, Calfin Trust, Rising Water Capital, A.G., Willem Ackermans, Steven Van der Velden, Johan Dejager, Lam Kwok Hung, Anarjay Concepts, Inc., Martin Zuurbier, Insiders

Financial Data: *Fiscal Year End:*12/31 *Latest Annual Data:* 12/31/2006

Year	Sales	Net Income
2006	$158,000	-$4,830,000
2005	$282,000	-$1,214,000
2004	$637,000	-$2,129,000

Curr. Assets:	$4,128,000	**Curr. Liab.:**	$7,309,000		
Plant, Equip.:	$158,000	**Total Liab.:**	$12,834,000	**Indic. Yr. Divd.:**	NA
Total Assets:	$13,695,000	**Net Worth:**	$733,000	**Debt/ Equity:**	NA

Eli Lilly & Co

Lilly Corporate Ctr., 893 S. Delaware, Indianapolis, IN, 46285; *PH:* 1-317-276-2000; *http://* www.lilly.com

General - Incorporation ....IN
Employees........................41,500
Auditor ....Ernst & Young LLP
Stk Agt .... Wells Fargo Shareowner Services
Counsel........................R. O. Goss
DUNS No. 00-642-1325

Stock- Price on:12/24/2007 ....$56.81
Stock Exchange........................NYSE
Ticker Symbol........................LLY
Outstanding Shares 1,130,000,000
E.P.S........................$2.05
Shareholders........................NA

Business: The groups principle activities include discovering, developing, manufacturing and market ing pharmaceutical products. The groups products include Alimta(R), Actos(R) and Humulin(R). In the year 2007, the group completed the acquisition of Hypnion, Inc. The group operates from United States.

Primary SIC and add'l.: 3845 2834

CIK No: 0000059478

Subsidiaries: AME Torreview LLC, Andean Technical Operations Center, Applied Molecular Evolution, Inc., Beirmirco Sociedad Anonima, Control Diabetes Services, Inc., Darilor Sociedad Anonima, Del Sol Financial Services, Inc., Dista Ilac Ticaret Ltd. Sti., Dista Italia S.r.L., Dista Mexicana, S.A. de C.V., Dista Products & Compania Venezuela S.A., Dista, Inc., Dista, S.A., Dista-Produtos Quimicos & Farmaceuticos, LDA, E L Management LLC 140 Subsidiaries included in the Index

Officers: Sidney Taurel/Chmn., CEO/$15,229,820.00, Robert W. Armstrong/VP - Discovery Chemistry Research, William W. Chin/VP - Discovery Research, Clinical Investigation, Robert A. Cole/VP - Global Engineering, Environmental Health, Safety, Newton F. Crenshaw/Pres., GM - Lilly Japan, Andrew M. Dahlem/VP - LRL Operations, Johanna Carmel Egan/VP - Project Management, Thomas W. Grein/VP, Treasurer, Anthony Murphy/Sr. VP - Human Resources, Robert A. Armitage/Sr. VP, General Counsel/$4,415,339.00, Patrick C. James/Pres. - Elanco Animal Health, Michael C. Heim/VP - Information Technology, CIO, Steven M. Paul/Exec. VP - Science - Technology, Pres. - Lilly Research Laboratories/$5,727,393.00, Richard D. Pilnik/Group VP, Chief Marketing Officer, Anne Nobles/VP - Compliance, Enterprise Risk Management, Chief Compliance Officer *(40 Officers included in Index)*

Directors: Sidney Taurel/Chmn., CEO, Franklyn G. Prendergast/Dir., Martin S. Feldstein/Dir., George M.C. Fisher/Dir., Kathi P. Seifert/Dir., Michael J. Cook/65/Dir., Winfried Bischoff/Dir., Alfred G. Gilman/Dir., Erik J. Fyrwald/Dir., Karen N. Horn/Dir., Ellen R. Marram/Dir.

Owners: Martin S. Feldstein, Ellen R. Marram, Alfred G. Gilman, John C. Lechleiter, Derica W. Rice, Sidney Taurel, Steven M. Paul, Lilly Endowment, Inc./12.40%, Winfried Bischoff, Franklyn G. Prendergast, Charles E. Golden, Erik J. Fyrwald, Insiders, Michael J. Cook, Robert A. Armitage *(20 Owners included in Index)*

Financial Data: *Fiscal Year End:*12/31 *Latest Annual Data:* 12/31/2006

Year	Sales	Net Income
2006	$15,691,000,000	$2,662,700,000
2005	$14,645,300,000	$1,979,600,000
2004	$13,857,900,000	$1,810,100,000

Curr. Assets:	$9,694,400,000	**Curr. Liab.:**	$5,085,500,000	**P/E Ratio:**	26.42
Plant, Equip.:	$8,152,300,000	**Total Liab.:**	$10,974,700,000	**Indic. Yr. Divd.:**	$1.700
Total Assets:	$21,955,400,000	**Net Worth:**	$10,980,700,000	**Debt/ Equity:**	NA

Eline Entertainment Group Inc

8905 Kingston Pike, Ste 313, Knoxville, TN, 37923; *PH:* 1-215-895-9859; *http://* www.eegi.net; *Email:* info@eegi.net

General - Incorporation ....NV
Employees........................NA
Auditor .... Baumann, Raymondo & Co. P.A
Stk Agt .... Pacific Stock Transfer Company
Counsel........................NA
DUNS No. ....NA

Stock- Price on:12/24/2007 ....$0.09
Stock Exchange........................OTC
Ticker Symbol........................EEGI
Outstanding Shares 3,270,000
E.P.S........................$0.018
Shareholders........................NA

Business: The group's principal activity is to produce music, develop film and video productions for retail, theatrical, radio, Internet, television and cable broadcasting distribution networks. During the year 2003, the group acquired industrial fabrication & repair inc (ifr). The company is in the development stage.

Primary SIC and add'l.: 7812

CIK No: 0001043150

Subsidiaries: 24/7 Mri, Inc, CTD Holdings,Inc, Industrial Holding Group, Inc

Financial Data: *Fiscal Year End:*10/31 *Latest Annual Data:* 10/31/2005

Year	Sales	Net Income
2005	$1,015,000	$47,000
2004	$4,025,000	-$1,148,000
2003	$1,404,000	-$483,000

Curr. Assets:	$2,614,000	**Curr. Liab.:**	$2,828,000	**P/E Ratio:**	5.00
Plant, Equip.:	$431,000	**Total Liab.:**	$2,977,000	**Indic. Yr. Divd.:**	NA
Total Assets:	$3,107,000	**Net Worth:**	-$105,000	**Debt/ Equity:**	3.3409

Elite Artz Inc

251 Jeanell Dr., Ste. 3, Carson City, NV, 89703; *PH:* 1-801-244-2423

General - Incorporation ....NV
Employees........................NA
Auditor .... Madsen & Associates, CPA's Inc.
Stk Agt ....Action Stock Transfer Corp.
Counsel........................James Barber Esq
DUNS No. ....NA

Stock- Price on:12/24/2007 ....NA
Stock Exchange........................OTC
Ticker Symbol........................ELRZ
Outstanding Shares ....NA
E.P.S........................NA
Shareholders........................NA

Business: The groups principle activity is direct marketing of fine-quality original paintings. The group operates from the United States.

Primary SIC and add'l.: 5990

CIK No: 0001306035

Officers: David Miles Oman/54/Dir., CFO, CEO, Treasurer, Pres.

Directors: David Miles Oman/54/Dir., CFO, CEO, Treasurer, Pres., Wong Nga Leung/29/Dir.

Owners: IPacific Asset Management Limited/38.71%, Profit Smooth Enterprises Limited/5.88%, IBroader Developments Limited/13.45%, Sze Tang Li/9.81%, Canary Global Investments Inc./9.81%

Curr. Assets:	$4,000	***Curr. Liab.:***	$53,000		
Plant, Equip.:	$1,000	***Total Liab.:***	$53,000	***Indic. Yr. Divd.:***	NA
Total Assets:	$5,000	***Net Worth:***	-$48,000	***Debt/ Equity:***	NA

Elite Flight Solutions Inc

710 Third St., Ste. 200, Roanoke, VA, 24061; ***PH:*** 1-540-345-3358; ***http://*** www.flyjets.biz

General - Incorporation	DE	***Stock***- Price on:12/24/2007	$0.0016
Employees	NA	Stock Exchange	OTC
Auditor	LL Bradford & Co	Ticker Symbol	EFLT
Stk Agt	Registrar & Transfer Co	Outstanding Shares	NA
Counsel	NA	E.P.S	NA
DUNS No.	NA	Shareholders	NA

Business: The group's principle activities are carried out through four segments: aircraft acquisitions and sales, charter and aircraft management, contracted services and maintenance fuel and part sales. The aircraft acquisitions and sales segment acts as a broker in the aircraft industry for clients wishing to sell or purchase an aircraft. The charter and aircraft management segment provides the luxury and pleasures of private jet travel. The contracted services segment solicits the business of the entertainment industry, local and regional sports teams and various governmental agencies. The maintenance fuel and part sales segment intends to acquire profitable strategic fixed based operators ("Fbo") throughout the u.s.a.

Primary SIC and add'l.: 4522

CIK No: 0001161723

Subsidiaries: Optimum Aviation Inc.

Officers: Bruce Edwards/CEO

Elite Pharmaceuticals Inc

165 Ludlow Ave., Northvale, NJ, 07647; ***PH:*** 1-201-750-2646; ***Fax:*** 1-201-750-2755; ***http://*** www.elitepharma.com; ***Email:*** eliteinfo@elitepharma.com

General - Incorporation	DE	***Stock***- Price on:12/24/2007	$2.2001
Employees	26	Stock Exchange	AMEX
Auditor	Miller, Ellin & Co. LLP	Ticker Symbol	ELI
Stk Agt	Jersey Transfer & Trust Co	Outstanding Shares	20,710,000
Counsel	NA	E.P.S	-$0.9
DUNS No.	NA	Shareholders	NA

Business: The group's principal activities are to research, develop, license, manufacture and market proprietary drug delivery systems and products. The drug delivery technology involves releasing a drug into the bloodstream or delivering it to a certain site in the body at predetermined rates or at predetermined times. The products include drugs, which provide therapeutic benefits for pain, angina, hypertension, allergy and infection. The trademarks of the group include albulite cr, nifelite cr, diltilite CD, ketolite cr, verelite cr and glucolite cr.

Primary SIC and add'l.: 8734 8731 2834 6794 8748

CIK No: 0001053369

Subsidiaries: Elite Laboratories, Inc., Elite Research, Inc

Officers: Bernard Berk/Chmn., CEO, Pres./$988,885.00, Mark Gittelman/CFO, Sec., Treasurer/$83,293.00, Chris Dick/Sr. VP - Business Development, Veerappan Subramanian/Dir., Chief Scientific Officer

Directors: Bernard Berk/Chmn., CEO, Pres., Barry Dash/Dir., Melvin Van Woert/Dir., Robert J. Levenson/Dir., Veerappan Subramanian/Dir., Chief Scientific Officer

Owners: Insiders/26.60%, Melvin Van Woert, Chad Comiteau/5.50%, Bernard Berk/6.90%, Trellus Management Company/14.80%, Mark I. Gittelman, Barry Dash, Edward Neugeboren, Charan Behl/6.00%, Veerappan Subramanian/13.00%, Chris Dick/4.10%, Davidson Kempner Healthcare International Ltd./15.20%, Mark Fain/5.80%

Financial Data: ***Fiscal Year End:***03/31 ***Latest Annual Data:*** 03/31/2007

Year	***Sales***	***Net Income***
2007	$1,144,000	-$11,804,000
2006	$551,000	-$6,884,000
2005	$301,000	-$5,907,000

Curr. Assets:	$10,564,000	***Curr. Liab.:***	$1,949,000		
Plant, Equip.:	$4,309,000	***Total Liab.:***	$5,929,000	***Indic. Yr. Divd.:***	NA
Total Assets:	$15,702,000	***Net Worth:***	$9,774,000	***Debt/ Equity:***	0.5794

Elizabeth Arden Inc

2400 SW 145th Ave., 2nd Fl., Miramar, FL, 33027; ***PH:*** 1-954-364-6900; ***Fax:*** 1-954-364-6910; ***http://*** www.elizabetharden.com

General - Incorporation	FL	***Stock***- Price on:12/24/2007	$23.79
Employees	2,100	Stock Exchange	NDQ
Auditor	PricewaterhouseCoopers LLP	Ticker Symbol	RDEN
Stk Agt	Mellon Investor Services LLC	Outstanding Shares	28,520,000
Counsel	NA	E.P.S	$1.33
DUNS No.	00-411-8873	Shareholders	NA

Business: The group's principal activities are to manufacture, distribute and market prestige fragrances, skin care and cosmetic products. The portfolio of leading fragrance brands include elizabeth arden's red door, 5th avenue, elizabeth arden green tea and sunflowers, elizabeth taylor's white diamonds and passion, white shoulders, halston z-14, ps fine cologne for men, design and wings by giorgio beverly hills. The skin care products include moisturizers, creams, lotions, cleansers and sunscreens. The cosmetics products include lipstick, mascaras, eye shadows and powder. These products are sold under the brands elizabeth arden's visible difference, ceramides and millenium. The group sells products to retailers, departmental stores and to independent fragrance, cosmetic, gift and other stores. The operations of the group are carried in the United States, geneva, Switzerland, Australia, Austria, Canada, Denmark, Italy, Korea, New Zealand, Puerto Rico and Singapore.

Primary SIC and add'l.: 2844

CIK No: 0000095052

Subsidiaries: DF Enterprises, Inc., Elizabeth Arden (Australia) Pty Ltd., Elizabeth Arden (Canada) Limited, Elizabeth Arden (Denmark) ApS, Elizabeth Arden (Export), Inc., Elizabeth Arden (Financing), Inc., Elizabeth Arden (Italy) S.r.l., Elizabeth Arden (Netherlands) Holding B.V., Elizabeth Arden (New Zealand) Limited, Elizabeth Arden (Norway) AS, Elizabeth Arden (Puerto Rico), Inc., Elizabeth Arden (Shanghai) Cosmetics& Fragrances Trading, Ltd., Elizabeth Arden (Singapore) PTE Ltd., Elizabeth Arden (South Africa)(Pty) Ltd., Elizabeth Arden (Sweden) AB 30 Subsidiaries included in the Index

Officers: Scott E. Beattie/Chmn., CEO, Pres., Hoy L. Heise/CIO, Exec. VP - Operations Planning, Stephen J. Smith/CFO, Exec. VP, Michael H. Lombardi/Exec. VP - Operations, Logisitics, Oscar E. Marina/Exec. VP, General Counsel, Sec., Ronald L. Rolleston/Exec. VP - Global Fragrance Marketing, Joel B. Ronkin/Exec. VP, GM - North America Fragrances, Jacobus A.J. Steffens/Exec. VP, GM - International, Elizabeth Park/Exec. VP, GM - Global Skincare, Color Marketing, Arden USA, Marcey Becker/Sr. VP - Finance, Treasurer - Corporate Development, Jeffrey M. Arnold/Sr. VP - Mass Selling Business Unit, Adam Booksin/Sr. VP - Global Human Resources, Smith Chih-Hsin Chen/Pres. - Elizabeth Arden, Greater China, William Dubose/Sr. VP - Global Wal, Mart, Sam's Business Gretchen Goslin, Gretchen Goslin/Exec. VP - Business Development *(20 Officers included in Index)*

Directors: Scott E. Beattie/Chmn., CEO, Pres., Paul F. West/Dir., Fred Berens/Dir., Maura J. Clark/Dir., Richard C.W. Mauran/Dir., William M. Tatham/Dir., Nevil J.W. Thomas/Dir.

Owners: Paul F. West/1.30%, Insiders/20.50%, Ronald L. Rolleston, Joel B. Ronkin, Scott E. Beattie/6.20%, William M. Tatham, Richard C. W. Mauran/6.30%, Fred Berens/3.00%, Nevil J.W. Thomas, Goldman Sachs Asset Management, L.P./5.20%, Wells Fargo & Company/6.40%, M&G Investment Funds 1/5.10%, Jacobus A. J. Steffens, Stephen J. Smith

Financial Data: ***Fiscal Year End:***06/30 ***Latest Annual Data:*** 6/30/2006

Year	***Sales***	***Net Income***
2006	$954,550,000	$32,794,000
2005	$920,538,000	$37,604,000
2004	$814,425,000	$2,036,000

Curr. Assets:	$515,920,000	***Curr. Liab.:***	$234,978,000	***P/E Ratio:***	18.30
Plant, Equip.:	$34,681,000	***Total Liab.:***	$482,056,000	***Indic. Yr. Divd.:***	NA
Total Assets:	$759,903,000	***Net Worth:***	$277,847,000	***Debt/ Equity:***	NA

ElkCorp

14911 Quorum Dr., Ste. 600, Dallas, TX, 75254; ***PH:*** 1-972-851-0500; ***http://*** www.elcor.com

General - Incorporation	DE	***Stock***- Price on:12/24/2007	NA
Employees	1,496	Stock Exchange	NA
Auditor	Grant Thornton LLP	Ticker Symbol	NA
Stk Agt	Mellon Investor Services LLC	Outstanding Shares	NA
Counsel	NA	E.P.S	NA
DUNS No.	00-840-9070	Shareholders	NA

Business: The group's principal activity is to manufacture premium laminated fiberglass asphalt shingles, coated and non-coated nonwoven fabrics and nontoxic composite wood decking, railing, marine dock and fencing products. The building products segment manufactures and sells premium laminated fiberglass asphalt shingles, accessory roofing products and coated and non-coated nonwoven performance fabric. These products are used in asphalt shingles and other applications in the building and construction, filtration, floor coverings and other industries. The other technologies segment is engaged in plating proprietary finishes for use in remanufacturing diesel engine cylinder liners, pistons and valves for the railroad and marine industries.the group discontinued the operations of cybershield on 10-Aug-2004.

Primary SIC and add'l.: 2952 8711 5033 3592

CIK No: 0000032017

Subsidiaries: Chromium Corporation, Elk Composite Building Products, Inc., Elk Corporation of Alabama, Elk Corporation of America, Elk Corporation of Arkansas, Elk Corporation of Texas, Elk Performance Nonwoven Fabrics, Inc., Elk Premium Building Products, Inc., Elk Technologies, Inc., Elk Technology Group, Inc., Elk VersaShield Building Solutions, Inc., Midland Path Forward, Inc., RGM Products, Inc., Ridgemate Manufacturing Co. Inc.

Elmira Savings Bank FSB (The)

333 E Water St., Elmira, NY, 14901; ***PH:*** 1-607-734-3374; ***Fax:*** 1-607-732-4007; ***http://*** www.elmirasavingsbank.com; ***Email:*** info@elmirasavingsbank.com

General - Incorporation		***Stock***- Price on:12/24/2007	$24.39
Employees	NA	Stock Exchange	NDQ
Auditor	NA	Ticker Symbol	ESBK
Stk Agt	Computershare Trust Co	Outstanding Shares	1,470,000
Counsel	NA	E.P.S	$1.11
DUNS No.	NA	Shareholders	NA

Business: The groups principle activity is to provide personal, business and online banking services. The groups personal services include checking, savings and certificates, ebanking, retirement accounts, home equity loans and personal loans. The group operates from United States.

Primary SIC and add'l.: 6035

CIK No:

Officers: Michael P. Hosey/Dir., CEO, Pres., Susan M. Cook/Assist., Sec., Tamara S. Pabis/Assist. VP, Marley J. Wylie/Assist. Sec., Joseph L. Walker/VP - Management Information Systems, Philip J. Collins/Assist. Treasurer - Management Information Systems, Margaret A. Phillips/Assist. VP - Operations, Karen J. Dovey/VP - Retail Services, Alfred A. Dupuis/VP - Retail Services, Deborah L. Adams/Assist. Treasurer - Retail Services, Janet M. Wells/Sr. VP - Sales, Marketing, Donna J. Tangorre/Assist. Treasurer - Sales, Marketing, Thomas M. Carr/CFO, Exec. VP, Shirley A. Weigand/Assist. Sec., Patrick J. Phillips/VP, Treasurer *(21 Officers included in Index)*

Directors: Michael P. Hosey/Dir., CEO, Pres., George L. Howell/Chmn., Cynthia A. Welliver/Dir., John R. Alexander/Dir., Thomas D. Morse/Dir., John Brand/Dir., Kristin A. Swain/Dir., Anthony J. Cooper/Dir., Scott A. Welliver/Dir., Jerry B. Gapp/Dir., Cornelius J. Milliken/Dir. Emeritus

Financial Data: ***Fiscal Year End:***NA ***Latest Annual Data:*** 12/31/2003

Year	***Sales***	***Net Income***
2003	$18,199,000	$2,443,000
2002	$19,557,000	$2,336,000
2001	$21,495,000	$2,272,000

Curr. Assets:	$7,281,000	***Curr. Liab.:***	$232,478,000	***P/E Ratio:***	21.21
Plant, Equip.:	$6,161,000	***Total Liab.:***	$262,533,000	***Indic. Yr. Divd.:***	$0.880
Total Assets:	$284,654,000	***Net Worth:***	$22,121,000	***Debt/ Equity:***	NA

Elong Inc

Block B, Xingke Plz., 10 Jiuxianqiao Middle Rd., Chaoyang District, Beijing, 100016;
PH: 86-1058602288; *http://* www.elong.net; *Email:* ir@corp.elong.com

General - Incorporation .... Cayman Islands	Stock - Price on:12/24/2007 ....$10.39
Employees .... NA	Stock Exchange..NDQ
Auditor .... KPMG LLP	Ticker Symbol.. LONG
Stk Agt.................. Morgan ADR Service Center	Outstanding Shares 25,340,000
Counsel................................ Goulston & Storrs	E.P.S...-$0.06
DUNS No. .... NA	Shareholders.. NA

Business: The groups principle activity is to provide online travel service. The group products sold under the trade name eLong. The groups services include air ticketing, vacation packages, corporate travel, vip call and hotel reservation. The group operates from China. The group's quarterly revenue for September 2007 was 83.86 millions of USD.

Primary SIC and add'l.: 4729 4725 4724

CIK No: 0001290903

Subsidiaries: Bravado Investments Limited, eLongNet Information Technology (Beijing) Co., Ltd.

Officers: Guangfu Cui/CEO, Kenneth Liao/CTO, Thomas P. Chen/VP - Marketing, Linda Guo/Dir. - Finance, Philip Yang/Dir. - Internal Audit, Chris Chan/CFO, Richard Chen/38/CTO, VP, Frank Zheng/42/VP - Operations, Hal Fiske/General Counsel, Thomas Zheng/VP - Human Resources, Armstrong Wang/44/VP - Business Development

Directors: Henrik Kjellberg/Chmn., Barney Harford/Dir., Mike Doyle/Dir., Justin Tang/Dir., Dermot Halpin/Dir., Cameron Jones/Dir., Arthur Hoffman/Dir., Thomas Gurnee/Dir., Marty Pompadur/Dir., David Goldhill/47/Dir., Johan Svanstrom/Dir., Matthew Crummack/Dir.

Owners: The Eureka Interactive Fund Limited/6.77%, Lawrence Auriana/17.63%, Richard Chen/3.22%, Frank Zheng/2.52%, Justin Tang/18.31%, Purple Mountain Holding, Ltd./17.32%, Expedia, Inc./2.95%

*Financial Data: Fiscal Year End:*12/31   *Latest Annual Data:* 12/31/2006

Year	Sales	Net Income
2006	$33,898,000	-$142,000
2005	$26,255,000	-$7,710,000
2004	$16,729,000	-$2,218,000

Curr. Assets:	$158,987,000	Curr. Liab.:	$17,225,000	P/E Ratio:	21.21
Plant, Equip.:	$4,845,000	Total Liab.:	$17,367,000	Indic. Yr. Divd.:	NA
Total Assets:	$171,105,000	Net Worth:	$153,737,000	Debt/ Equity:	NA

Eloyalty Corp

150 Field Dr., Ste. 250, Lake Forest, IL, 60045; *PH:* 1-847-582-7000; *Fax:* 1-847-582-7001;
http:// www.eloyaltyco.com; *Email:* euro@eloyalty.com

General - Incorporation .... DE	Stock - Price on:12/24/2007 ....$23.39
Employees 406	Stock Exchange..NDQ
Auditor .... PricewaterhouseCoopers LLP	Ticker Symbol.. ELOY
Stk Agt.................. Mellon Investor Services LLC	Outstanding Shares 9,350,000
Counsel....................,........................... NA	E.P.S...-$1.93
DUNS No. .... NA	Shareholders.. NA

Business: The group's principle activity is to provide management consulting and systems integration services. The group provides a broad range of customer relationship management ("Crm") related services including business strategy, technical architecture, selecting, implementing and integrating appropriate crm software applications and providing ongoing support for multi-vendor systems. The services provided by the group are referred as "Loyalty Solutions". The group's solutions align many isolated customer contact channels including the Internet, e-mail, call centers, field sales and field service. The group also licenses its trademark: Loyalty Suite(TM) software. The group operates in Canada, Germany, United Kingdom and other foreign countries. The group's quarterly revenue for Sep'07 was 26.61 millions of USD.

Primary SIC and add'l.: 7379 7372

CIK No: 0001094348

Subsidiaries: eLoyalty (Canada) Corporation, eLoyalty (Deutschland) GmbH, eLoyalty (France) S.A.R.L., eLoyalty (Netherlands) B.V., eLoyalty (UK) Limited, eLoyalty Corporation (Australia) Pty. Ltd., eLoyalty Europe Holding Corporation, eLoyalty International Holding, Inc., eLoyalty International Limited

Officers: Kelly D. Conway/Dir., CEO, Pres./$1,119,101.00, Steven C. Pollema/VP - Operations, CFO/$539,081.00, Christopher J. Danson/VP - Delivery/$535,766.00, Karen Bolton/VP - Client Services/$713,340.00, Steven H. Shapiro/VP, General Counsel, Corp. Sec./$280,734.00, Marian Lippman/Contact Person - North America

Directors: Kelly D. Conway/Dir., CEO, Pres., Tench Coxe/Chmn., Michael J. Murray/Dir., John T. Kohler/Dir., John C. Staley/Dir., Henry J. Feinberg/Dir.

Owners: Michael J. Murray/1.70%, Michael T. Tokarz/3.90%, Steven H. Shapiro, Brookside Capital Partners Fund, LP/5.00%, Steven C. Pollema/1.30%, S Squared Technology Corp/6.20%, Christopher J. Danson/1.20%, John T. Kohler, Insiders/45.10%, Henry J. Feinberg/16.50%, Peninsula Capital Management and Scott Bedford/5.50%, Kelly D. Conway/4.30%, Karen Bolton, Tench Coxe/13.50%, John A. Murphy/4.40% (*17 Owners included in Index*)

*Financial Data: Fiscal Year End:*12/31   *Latest Annual Data:* 12/30/2006

Year	Sales	Net Income
2006	$89,828,000	-$11,148,000
2005	$79,008,000	-$7,630,000

Curr. Assets:	$37,039,000	Curr. Liab.:	$11,698,000		
Plant, Equip.:	$3,131,000	Total Liab.:	$33,753,000	Indic. Yr. Divd.:	NA
Total Assets:	$45,228,000	Net Worth:	$11,475,000	Debt/ Equity:	NA

Elron Electronic Industries Ltd

3 Azrieli Ctr, 42nd Fl., Tel-aviv, 67023; *PH:* 972-36075555; *http://* www.elron.com

General - Incorporation .... Israel	Stock - Price on:12/24/2007 ....$14.9
Employees .... NA	Stock Exchange..NDQ
Auditor .... Kost Forer Gabbay & Kasierer	Ticker Symbol.. ELRN
Stk Agt..... American Stock Transfer & Trust Co.	Outstanding Shares 29,600,000
Counsel.... Kramer Levin Naftalis & Frankel LLP	E.P.S...$0.00
DUNS No. 60-004-0299	Shareholders.. NA

Business: The group's principle activities are represented by three main segments: the Internet product division, the system integration division and the holding in various companies engaged in communication, software, defense industry, medical devices, semiconductors and others. The operations of the Internet product division include development and sale of software products which enable organizations to manage the access to the Internet network and to control incoming and outgoing Internet content. The operations of the system integration division include development and sale of customized telecommunication software solutions, ranging from system analysis and design through implementation and integration. Products include integrated IP service management platform for Internet access management, call performance management products and network management systems.

Primary SIC and add'l.: 3841 3674 3829 7374 6719 3812

CIK No: 0000315126

Subsidiaries: DEP Technology Holdings Ltd., Elbit Ltd., Elron SW Inc., Rafael Development Corporation Ltd.

Officers: Avishai Friedman/CEO, Pres. - Rafael Development Corporation, Doron Birger/CEO, Pres., Yair Cohen/VP, Assaf Topaz/VP, Nava Ladin/Investor Relations Officer - Gelbert, Kahana, Paul Weinberg/General Counsel, Corp. Sec., Mira Rosenzweig/Dir. - Finance, Yaron Elad/Controller, Moshe Fourier/CTO, VP, Rinat Remler/CFO, VP

Directors: Arie Mientkavich/Chmn., Shay Livnat/Dir., Arie Ovadia/Dir., Tida Shamir/Dir., Amos Shapira/Dir., Ami Erel/Dir., Gabi Barbash/Dir., Nochi Dankner/Dir., Dori Manor/Dir., Yair Be'Ery/Dir., Avraham Asheri/Dir., Avraham Fischer/Dir., Yaacov Goldman/Dir., Ari Bronshtein/Dir.

Owners: Clal Insurance Group, Insiders, Ami Erel, Discount Investment Corporation Ltd/48.65%

*Financial Data: Fiscal Year End:*12/31   *Latest Annual Data:* 12/31/2006

Year	Sales	Net Income
2006	$12,863,000	$3,032,000
2005	NA	NA
2004	NA	NA

Curr. Assets:	$134,033,000	Curr. Liab.:	$20,535,000		
Plant, Equip.:	$7,223,000	Total Liab.:	$28,745,000	Indic. Yr. Divd.:	NA
Total Assets:	$326,249,000	Net Worth:	$297,504,000	Debt/ Equity:	NA

Eltek Ltd

PO Box 159, Petach Tikva, 49101; *PH:* 972-39395025; *http://* www.eltekdataloggers.co.uk;
Email: sales@eltekdataloggers.co.uk

General - Incorporation .... Israel	Stock - Price on:12/24/2007 ....$4.3
Employees 310	Stock Exchange..NDQ
Auditor .... Somekh Chaikin	Ticker Symbol.. ELTK
Stk Agt ..... American Stock Transfer & Trust Co.	Outstanding Shares 5,620,000
Counsel.. NA	E.P.S...$0.128
DUNS No. 60-007-2144	Shareholders.. NA

Business: The groups principle activity is to manufacture a wide range of custom designed printed circuit boards including complex rigid, double sided, multilayer and flexible circuitry boards made of glass epoxy and high-performance substrates, primarily for use in short run quick-turnaround, prototype and pre-production advanced electronics applications. The group operates from United States.

Primary SIC and add'l.: 3672

CIK No: 0001024672

Subsidiaries: Eltek Europe Ltd, En-Eltek Netherlands, Kubatronik Leiterplatten GmbH

Officers: Arieh Reichart/CEO, Pres., Moshe Leibovich/VP - Sales, Marketing, Greg Hawkins/Mgr. - European Marketing, Helmut Steinhaus/Contact - North Germany, Giorgio Pinamonti/Contact - Eltos SPA, Waldemar Bielecki/Contact - RCL, Philippe Mascaro/Contact - MSA, Srini Iyer/Contact - Irys, Dan Eshed/VP - Subsidiaries, Eli Dvora/VP - Operations, Amnon Shemer/VP - Finance, CFO, Shlomo Danino/VP - Engineering, Quality Assurance, Roberto Tulman/VP - Technologies, CTO, Vardit Dekel/VP - Human Resources, Hillel Dzigan/QA Mgr. (*18 Officers included in Index*)

Directors: Nissim Gilam/Chmn., Ophira Rosolio-Aharonson/Dir., Eliyaho Tov/Dir., Joseph Yerushalmi/Dir., Joseph Maiman/Dir., David Banitt/Dir., Jack Bigio/Dir.

Owners: Arieh Reichart/1.70%, Integral International Inc./9.10%, Vardit Dekel, Merhav M.N.F. Ltd./14.90%, Roberto Tulman, Nissim Gilam, Moshe Leibovich, Amnon Shemer, Eli Dvora, Josef Maiman/24.00%

*Financial Data: Fiscal Year End:*12/31   *Latest Annual Data:* 12/31/2006

Year	Sales	Net Income
2006	$41,294,000	$1,649,000
2005	$31,587,000	$1,150,000
2004	$28,913,000	-$1,243,000

Curr. Assets:	$13,998,000	Curr. Liab.:	$12,158,000		
Plant, Equip.:	$8,308,000	Total Liab.:	$15,775,000	Indic. Yr. Divd.:	NA
Total Assets:	$23,212,000	Net Worth:	$7,437,000	Debt/ Equity:	NA

Elva International Inc

222 Lakeview Ave., Pmb 160-415, West Palm Beach, FL, 33401; *PH:* 1-561-659-6530

General - Incorporation .... FL	Stock - Price on:12/24/2007 ....$0.07
Employees 5	Stock Exchange...OTC
Auditor .... Durland & Co. Cpas, P.A.	Ticker Symbol.. EVAI
Stk Agt .... Interwest Transfer Company, Inc.	Outstanding Shares .... NA
Counsel.. NA	E.P.S... NA
DUNS No. .... NA	Shareholders.. NA

Business: The group's principal activity is to provide secure online purchasing and customer loyalty incentives between individuals and businesses. The group issues vocalid(R) smart card to allow for payment and to promote customer loyalty. Smart card technology focuses on e-commerce environments including home banking and telecommunication services and can be used from an ordinary telephone, a magnetic stripe reader, a chip card reader or a personal computer. The customers of the group are semiconductor manufacturers like atmel and Internet service providers, telecommunication operators, banks offering home banking services and retailers.

Primary SIC and add'l.: 7375 7379 8999

CIK No: 0001103718

Subsidiaries: ELVA, SA.

*Financial Data: Fiscal Year End:*12/31   *Latest Annual Data:* 12/31/2005

Year	Sales	Net Income
2005	$598,000	-$132,000
2004	$403,000	$145,000
2003	$336,000	-$578,000

Curr. Assets:	$155,000	**Curr. Liab.:**	$425,000		
Plant, Equip.:	$46,000	**Total Liab.:**	$425,000	**Indic. Yr. Divd.:**	NA
Total Assets:	$733,000	**Net Worth:**	$308,000	**Debt/ Equity:**	NA

Emageon Inc

1200 Corporate Dr., Ste. 200, Birmingham, AL, 35242; ***PH:*** 1-205-980-9222; ***Fax:*** 1-205-980-9815; ***http://*** www.emageon.com; ***Email:*** info@emageon.com

General - Incorporation	DE	**Stock**- Price on:12/24/2007	$8.5
Employees	438	Stock Exchange	NDQ
Auditor	Ernst& Young LLP	Ticker Symbol	EMAG
Stk Agt	Wachovia Bank N.A	Outstanding Shares	21,330,000
Counsel	Kilpatrick Stockton, LLP	E.P.S	-$0.2
DUNS No.	NA	Shareholders	NA

Business: The groups principle activity is to provide enterprise level information technology solution. Customers served by the group include hospital and diagnostic imaging centers. The products of the group include radsuite advanced visualization tools, clinical workflow, heartsuite hemodynamics, vericis and cvis. The groups services include adoption success management and total solution management. In November 1, 2005 the group acquired Camtronics Medical Systems, Ltd. The group operates from the United States. The group's quarterly revenue for September 2007 was 22.73 millions of USD.

Primary SIC and add'l.: 7372

CIK No: 0001121439

Subsidiaries: Camtronics Medical Systems Canada, Inc., Camtronics Medical Systems, Ltd., Ultravisual Medical Systems Corporation

Officers: Charles A. Jett/Chmn., CEO, Pres./$1,195,225.00, Grady Floyd/COO/$369,271.00, Randall W. Pittman/CFO, Treasurer/$513,402.00, Robert W. Grubb/41/Sr. VP - Sales/$636,439.00, Wendell G.R. Brown/46/Sr. VP - Business Development /$259,608.00

Directors: Charles A. Jett/Chmn., CEO, Pres., Arthur P. Beattie/Dir., Roddy J.H. Clark/Dir., Douglas D. French/Dir., Fred C. Goad/Dir., Chris H. Horgen/Dir., Mylle H. Mangum/Dir., John W. Thompson/Dir., Hugh H. Williamson/Dir.

Owners: Fred C. Goad, Brown Advisory Holdings Incorporated/6.12%, Mylle H. Mangum, Deerfield Management Company, L.P./7.51%, Chris H. Horgen, Hugh H. Williamson, Wendell G. R. Brown, Wells Fargo& Company/7.07%, John W. Thompson, Robert W. Grubb, Charles A. Jett/2.41%, Grady O. Floyd, Insiders/5.12%, Randal lW. Pittman, Arthur Cohen/5.62% *(18 Owners included in Index)*

Financial Data: ***Fiscal Year End:***12/31 ***Latest Annual Data:*** 12/31/2006

Year	**Sales**	**Net Income**
2006	$123,505,000	-$6,032,000
2005	$73,791,000	-$4,997,000
2004	$45,802,000	-$10,473,000

Curr. Assets:	$63,648,000	**Curr. Liab.:**	$42,256,000		
Plant, Equip.:	$18,362,000	**Total Liab.:**	$48,801,000	**Indic. Yr. Divd.:**	NA
Total Assets:	$113,908,000	**Net Worth:**	$65,107,000	**Debt/ Equity:**	NA

eMagin Corp

10500 NE 8th St., Ste. 1400, Bellevue, WA, 98004; ***PH:*** 1-425-749-3600; ***Fax:*** 1-425-749-3601; ***http://*** www.emagin.com; ***Email:*** info@emagin.com

General - Incorporation	DE	**Stock**- Price on:12/24/2007	NA
Employees	98	Stock Exchange	OTC
Auditor	Eisner LLP	Ticker Symbol	EMAN
Stk Agt	Continental Stock Transfer & Trust Co	Outstanding Shares	NA
Counsel	Sichenzia Ross Friedman Ference	E.P.S	NA
DUNS No.	NA	Shareholders	NA

Business: The group's principal activity is to design, develop and market oled (organic light emitting diode)-on-silicon microdisplays and related information technology solutions. The group integrates oled technology with silicon chips to produce high-resolution microdisplays smaller than one-inch diagonally. When viewed through a magnifier, this creates a virtual image that appears comparable to that of a computer monitor or a large-screen television. These products are being applied or considered for near-eye and headset applications in products such as entertainment and gaming headsets, handheld Internet and telecommunication appliances, viewfinders and wearable computers to be manufactured by original equipment manufacturer (OEM) customers. The group's first commercial product is the svga+ (super video graphics array plus 52 added columns of data) oled microdisplay.

Primary SIC and add'l.: 8731 3674 3699

CIK No: 0001046995

Subsidiaries: Virtual Vision, Inc

Officers: K. C. Park/Dir., Interim CEO, Pres., Susan K. Jones/Chief Marketing, Strategy Officer, Exec. VP, Sec., Olivier Prache/Sr. VP - Display Operations, Design, Development, John Atherly/CFO, Treasurer

Directors: K. C. Park/Dir., Interim CEO, Pres., Paul Cronson/Dir., Stephen Seay/Dir., Claude Charles/Dir., Irwin Engleman/Dir., Thomas Paulsen/Dir., Jacob Goldman/Dir.

Owners: Insiders/6.00%, Moriah Capital, L.P./4.80%, K. C. Park, Ginola Limited/13.80%, Stephen Seay, Irwin Engelman, Jacob Goldman, Paul Cronson/1.60%, Stillwater LLC/16.50%, John Atherly, Susan K. Jones/3.60%, Rainbow Gate Corporation/6.20%, Alexandra Global Master Fund Ltd/9.90%, Claude Charles, Thomas Paulsen

Curr. Assets:	$5,635,000	**Curr. Liab.:**	$5,940,000		
Plant, Equip.:	$666,000	**Total Liab.:**	$8,169,000	**Indic. Yr. Divd.:**	NA
Total Assets:	$7,005,000	**Net Worth:**	-$1,164,000	**Debt/ Equity:**	NA

EMAK Worldwide Inc

6330 San Vicente Blvd, Los Angeles, CA, 90048; ***PH:*** 1-323-932-4300; ***http://*** www.emak.com

General - Incorporation	DE	**Stock**- Price on:12/24/2007	$2.98
Employees	342	Stock Exchange	NDQ
Auditor	PricewaterhouseCoopers LLP	Ticker Symbol	EMAK
Stk Agt	Continental Stock Transfer & Trust Co	Outstanding Shares	5,890,000
Counsel	NA	E.P.S	-$1.35
DUNS No.	NA	Shareholders	NA

Business: The group's principle activities are to design and produce custom promotional programs that build sales and brand value for retailers, restaurant chains and consumer goods companies. The group also develops and markets distinctive consumer products. The products of the group include character figurines, action vehicles, drinking vessels, watches, plush toys, play sets and a variety of other items. Programs of the promotions division of the company are utilized primarily in promotional campaigns implemented by quick service restaurant and consumer product customers. The group has operations in the United Kingdom, Germany, Spain, Sweden, Italy, turkey, Australia, the Philippines, Singapore, Korea, Mexico and throughout Latin America. The group's quarterly revenue for Sep'07 was 42.53 millions of USD.

Primary SIC and add'l.: 8742 7319 5092

CIK No: 0000911151

Subsidiaries: Corinthian Marketing, Inc., EMAK Asia Holding Company Limited, EMAK China Limited, EMAK Europe Holdings Limited, EMAK Europe Services Limited, EMAK Hong Kong Limited, EMAK Worldwide Service Corp., Equity Marketing Hong Kong, Ltd., Equity Marketing, Inc., Johnson Grossfield, Inc., Logistix Limited, Logistix, Inc., Megaprint Group Limited, Megaprint Limited, Megapromotions (U.K.) Limited 26 Subsidiaries included in the Index

Officers: Jim Holbrook/Dir., CEO, Mike Sanders/VP - Finance/$255,063.00, Tracy Tormey/Chief Administrative Officer, General Counsel, Rachel Saunders/Dir. - Communications, Juergen Dold/VP - New Business Development, Brian Kristofek/Pres. - Upshot, Kristie Ritchie/Sr. Dir. - New Business, Sharon Mord/VP - Business Development, Americas, Pat Reading/VP - Client Services, Peter Boutros/Chief Executive - Logistix Worldwide/$288,368.00

Directors: Jim Holbrook/Dir., CEO, Stephen P. Robeck/Chmn., Howard D. Bland/Dir., Jeffrey S. Deutschman/Dir., Daniel W. O'Connor/Dir., Alfred E. Osborne/Dir., Charles H. Rivkin/Dir.

Owners: Charles H. Rivkin, Crown EMAK Partners, LLC/100.00%, Peter Ackerman/100.00%, Gruber & McBaine Capital Management LLC, Stephen P. Robeck, Michael W. Sanders, Heartland Advisors, Inc., Rutabaga Capital Management, Crown EMAK Partners, LLC, Alfred E. Osborne, Peter Ackerman, James L. Holbrook, Jeffrey S. Deutschman, Teresa L. Tormey, Daniel W. O'Connor *(23 Owners included in Index)*

Financial Data: ***Fiscal Year End:***12/31 ***Latest Annual Data:*** 12/31/2006

Year	**Sales**	**Net Income**
2006	$181,397,000	-$2,265,000
2005	$223,397,000	-$39,872,000
2004	$236,661,000	-$9,684,000

Curr. Assets:	$44,441,000	**Curr. Liab.:**	$34,478,000		
Plant, Equip.:	$3,583,000	**Total Liab.:**	$36,772,000	**Indic. Yr. Divd.:**	NA
Total Assets:	$62,370,000	**Net Worth:**	$6,557,000	**Debt/ Equity:**	NA

Embarcadero Technologies Inc

100 California St., Ste. 1200, San Francisco, CA, 94111; ***PH:*** 1-415-834-3131; ***http://*** www.embarcadero.com

General - Incorporation	DE	**Stock**- Price on:12/24/2007	$7.17
Employees	222	Stock Exchange	NA
Auditor	PricewaterhouseCoopers LLP	Ticker Symbol	NA
Stk Agt	Chase Mellon Shareholder Services LLC	Outstanding Shares	26,130,000
Counsel	Heller Ehrman White & McAuliffe LLP	E.P.S	$0.67
DUNS No.	NA	Shareholders	NA

Business: The group's principal activity is to provide software products that enable organizations to manage their data base infrastructure and e-business applications. The product group includes database administration, performance management, data and application architecture and data integration. These products support database platforms including oracle, microsoft sql server, IBM db2 universal database and sybase, running on unix, windows nt and linux environments. The group also provides customer service and technical support. Customer service includes handling of product licensing inquiries, activating customer licenses and managing maintenance renewals. Technical support involves the provision of optional annual maintenance contracts to customers. The group has operations in Europe, the Middle East, Africa, Australia and Latin America.

Primary SIC and add'l.: 7370

CIK No: 0001107112

Subsidiaries: Advanced Software Technologies, Inc., Embarcadero Australia Ltd., Embarcadero Canada, Ltd, Embarcadero Europe Ltd., Embarcadero Technologies Australia PTY Ltd, Embarcadero Technologies Europe Ltd., Engineering Performance, Inc., List of Subsidiaries

Officers: Raj P. Sabhlok/CEO, Pres., Greg Keller/VP - Product Management, Lorraine C. Gnecco/VP - Human Resources, Michael Shahbazian/61/Sr. VP, CFO, Wayne D. Williams/COO, Sr. VP - Products, Greg Davoll/VP - Marketing, Nigel Brown/VP - International, Scott Schoonover/VP - Sales Americas, David T. Oro/Contact - Media Relations, Rebecca Metz/Contact - Media Relations, James Hanson/Contact - Media Relations, Michelle Chase/Media Contact, Caitlin Haberberger/Investor Relations Contact, John Sommerfield/Contact - Media Relations

Directors: Gary E. Haroian/56/Dir., Frank M. Polestra/82/Dir., Michael J. Roberts/50/Dir., Samuel T. Spadafora/65/Dir.

Owners: Gary E. Haroian, S Squared Technology, LLC/11.30%, Michael Shahbazian, Frank M. Polestra, Stephen R. Wong/20.14%, Michael J. Roberts, Insiders/4.30%, Chapman Capital L.L.C./9.27%, AMVESCAP PLC/13.43%, Samuel T. Spadafora, Raj P. Sabhlok/2.29%, Timothy C.K. Chou, Wells Fargo & Company/8.57%

Financial Data: ***Fiscal Year End:***12/31 ***Latest Annual Data:*** 12/31/2006

Year	**Sales**	**Net Income**
2006	$59,953,000	$5,833,000
2005	$57,552,000	$4,337,000
2004	$56,294,000	$1,988,000

Curr. Assets:	$83,910,000	**Curr. Liab.:**	$25,302,000	**P/E Ratio:**	37.74
Plant, Equip.:	$1,542,000	**Total Liab.:**	$26,153,000	**Indic. Yr. Divd.:**	NA
Total Assets:	$106,620,000	**Net Worth:**	$80,467,000	**Debt/ Equity:**	NA

Embarq Corp

5454 W 110th St., Overland Park, KS, 66211; ***PH:*** 1-913-323-4637; ***http://*** www.embarq.com; ***Email:*** mediarelations@embarq.com

General - Incorporation	DE	**Stock**- Price on:12/24/2007	$63.41
Employees	20,000	Stock Exchange	NYSE
Auditor	KPMG LLP	Ticker Symbol	EQ
Stk Agt	UMB Bank, N.A.	Outstanding Shares	151,060,000
Counsel	NA	E.P.S	$4.54
DUNS No.	NA	Shareholders	NA

Business: The groups principle activity is to provide communication services. The groups services include long distance voice and data services, high-speed internet access, and wireless and satellite video services. The group operates through two segments namely, telecommunication and logistics. The group operates from the United States. The group's quarterly revenue for September 2007 was 1,594.00 millions of USD.

Primary SIC and add'l.: 4899 7389 4813 4822

CIK No: 0001350031

Subsidiaries: Carolina Telephone and Telegraph Company, Centel Capital Corporation, Centel Corporation, Centel Directories LLC, Centel SPE LLC, Centel-Texas, Inc., Central Telephone Company, Central Telephone Company of Texas, Central Telephone Company of Virginia, Embarq Capital Corporation, Embarq Communications of Virginia, Inc., Embarq Communications, Inc., Embarq Directory Trademark Company, LLC, Embarq Florida Inc., Embarq Holdings Company LLC 54 Subsidiaries included in the Index

Officers: Daniel R. Hesse/Chmn., CEO/$5,913,524.00, Gene M. Betts/CFO/$1,868,087.00, William R. Blessing/Sr. VP - Corporate Strategy Development, Thomas A. Gerke/General Counsel - Law, External Affairs/$2,907,930.00, Dennis G. Huber/Sr. VP - Product Development, E. J. Holland/Sr. VP - Human Resources, William E. Cheek/Pres. - Wholesale Markets, Harrison S. Campbell/Pres. - Consumer Markets/$1,629,550.00, James A. Hansen/Sr. VP - Network Services, James C. Mayfield/Pres. - Embarq Logistics, Thomas J. McEvoy/Pres. - Business Markets, Vallerie Parrish-Porter/CIO, Daniel A. Alcazar/VP - Communications, Brand Mangement, Claudia S. Toussaint/VP, Corp. Sec., Chief Ethics Officer, Michael B. Fuller/COO/$12,410,640.00

Directors: Daniel R. Hesse/Chmn., CEO, John P. Mullen/Dir., Peter C. Brown/Dir., Steven A. Davis/Dir., William A. Owens/Dir., Dinesh C. Paliwal/Dir., Stephanie M. Shern/Dir., Laurie A. Siegel/Dir., Richard A. Gephardt/Dir.

Owners: Capital Research and Management Co./8.70%, Barclays Global Investors, NA/5.77%, Thomas A. Gerke, Thomas J. McEvoy, Daniel R. Hesse, Gene M. Betts, Harrison S. Campbell, Michael B. Fuller

Financial Data: *Fiscal Year End:*12/31 *Latest Annual Data:* 12/31/2006

Year	Sales	Net Income
2006	$6,363,000,000	$784,000,000
2005	$6,254,000,000	$878,000,000
2004	$6,139,000,000	$917,000,000

Curr. Assets:	$1,023,000,000	Curr. Liab.:	$1,264,000,000	P/E Ratio:	13.97
Plant, Equip.:	$7,988,000,000	Total Liab.:	$9,559,000,000	Indic. Yr. Divd.:	$2.500
Total Assets:	$9,091,000,000	Net Worth:	-$468,000,000	Debt/ Equity:	NA

Embotelladora Andina S.A.

Ave. El Golf 40, Piso 4, Las Condes, Santiago; *PH:* 56-23380500; *Fax:* 56-23380530; *http://* www.koandina.com

General - Incorporation		Stock - Price on:12/24/2007	$19.25
Employees	NA	Stock Exchange	NYSE
Auditor	NA	Ticker Symbol	AKO-A
Stk Agt	NA	Outstanding Shares	126,710,000
Counsel	NA	E.P.S	$1.17
DUNS No.	NA	Shareholders	NA

Business: The groups principle activities include producing, distributing and selling soft drinks. The group operates from Chile, Brazil and Argentina. The groups quarterly revenue for September 2007 was 442,229.56 millions of CLP.

Primary SIC and add'l.: 2086 2082 3721 3728 5088 5181 8711

CIK No:

Officers: Jaime Garcia/CEO, Juan Javier Negri/Vice Chmn. - Embotelladora DEL Atlantico SA, Argentina, Pedro Jullian/Chmn. - Envases CMF SA, Rodolfo Echeverria/Vice Chmn. - Envases Central SA, Washington Ponce/Chmn. - Cican SA, David Lee/Vice Chmn. - Cican SA, Raul Guerrero/Dir. - Cican SA, Ruy Campos Vieira/Dir. - Kaik Participacoes Ltda, Claudio Fuhrmann/GM - Envases Central SA, Carlos Eduardo Correa/Dir. - Kaik Participacoes Ltda, Ricardo Vontobel/Dir. - Kaik Participacoes Ltda, Francisco Miguel Alarcon/Dir. - Kaik Participacoes Ltda, Cristian Larrain/GM - Envases CMF SA, Joaquin Barros/Dir. - Envases CMF SA, Jaime Claro/Dir. - Envases CMF SA *(61 Officers included in Index)*

Financial Data: *Fiscal Year End:*NA *Latest Annual Data:* 12/31/2006

Year	Sales	Net Income
2006	$1,038,790,000	$146,021,000
2005	$909,096,000	$142,850,000
2004	$744,758,000	$92,824,000

Curr. Assets:	$311,837,000	Curr. Liab.:	$239,909,000	P/E Ratio:	13.97
Plant, Equip.:	$267,157,000	Total Liab.:	$455,824,000	Indic. Yr. Divd.:	NA
Total Assets:	$1,003,785,000	Net Worth:	$545,737,000	Debt/ Equity:	NA

Embratel Participacoes

Regente Feijo, 166, 16 Andar Sala 1687-B, Rio De Janeiro; *PH:* 55-08007032111; *http://* www.embratel.com.br

General - Incorporation	Brazil	Stock - Price on:12/24/2007	NA
Employees	12,470	Stock Exchange	NA
Auditor	Ernst & young LLP	Ticker Symbol	NA
Stk Agt	Banco Itau S.A.	Outstanding Shares	NA
Counsel	NA	E.P.S	NA
DUNS No.	NA	Shareholders	NA

Business: The group's principal activities are the management and exploration of private, public and industrial telephone services such as; leased lines, data transmission, cellular mobile telephone services, text and telex transmission and other related activities in Brazil and Argentina.

Primary SIC and add'l.: 4813

CIK No: 0001066117

Subsidiaries: Embratel, Empresa Brasileira de, Telecomunicaes S.A.

Officers: Carlos Henrique Moreira/Dir., Pres., Isaac Berensztejn/Dir., Financial Dir., Investor Relations Dir., Jose Formoso Martinez/Dir., VP, Edison Giraldo/Fiscal Counsel, Ruy Dell'Avanzi/Fiscal Counsel

Directors: Carlos Henrique Moreira/Dir., Pres., Isaac Berensztejn/Dir., Financial Dir., Investor Relations Dir., Dilio Sergio Penedo/Dir., Joel Korn/Dir., Jose Formoso Martinez/Dir., VP, Alberto De Orleans E. Braganca/Dir., Oscar Von Hauske Solis/Dir.

Embrex Inc

1040 Swabia Ct., Durham, NC, 27703; *PH:* 1-919-941-5185; *http://* www.embrex.com

General - Incorporation	NC	Stock - Price on:12/24/2007	NA
Employees	304	Stock Exchange	NA
Auditor	Ernst & Young LLP	Ticker Symbol	NA
Stk Agt	American Stock Transfer & Trust Co.	Outstanding Shares	NA
Counsel	Smith, Anderson, Blount Et Al	E.P.S	NA
DUNS No.	14-436-5046	Shareholders	NA

Business: The group's principal activity is to focus on the development of biological and mechanical products to improve bird health and to reduce production costs in the poultry industry. The products of the group include inovoject system a proprietary, automated in-the-egg injection system. This system inoculates 20,000 to 60,000 eggs per hour and eliminates the need for manual, post-hatch injection of certain vaccines. The other products of the group include vaccine saver and egg remover modules to provide additional automation benefits to the poultry hatchery. The group operates in the United States, the United Kingdom, People's Republic of China, Brazil, France and Spain.

Primary SIC and add'l.: 0254 2836 2834

CIK No: 0000878725

Subsidiaries: Embrex BioTech Trade (Shanghai) Co., Ltd., Embrex de Mexico, S. de R.L. de C.V., Embrex Europe Limited, Embrex France s.a.s., Embrex Iberica, Embrex Poultry Health, LLC, Embrex Sales, Inc., Inovoject do Brasil Ltda., Vaccination Services, S. de R.L. de C.V.

Embryo Development Corp

305 Madison Ave., Ste. 4510, New York, NY, 10165; *PH:* 1-212-808-0607

General - Incorporation	DE	Stock - Price on:12/24/2007	NA
Employees	1	Stock Exchange	OTC
Auditor	Rothstein, Kass & Co, P.C	Ticker Symbol	EMBR
Stk Agt	American Stock Transfer & Trust Co.	Outstanding Shares	NA
Counsel	NA	E.P.S	-$0.06
DUNS No.	93-785-3406	Shareholders	NA

Business: The group's principle activity is to explore several business opportunities, inclusive of the possible acquisition of a new line of business, which may or may not be related to the development of medical devices. It terminated all of its license agreements as of 30-Apr-2002. Earlier the group's principal activities were to develop, acquire, manufacture and market various bio-medical devices throughout the United States.

Primary SIC and add'l.: 3845 6794

CIK No: 0000945439

Subsidiaries: Hydrogel Design Systems, Inc, Yellow Brick Road Ventures LLC, a

Owners: Santo Petrocell/5.00%, Insiders/35.80%, Daniel Durchslag/1.30%, Startek Entertainment Corp./5.00%, Matthew L. Harriton/32.50%, Daniel Durchslag/1.30%, Karen Nazzareno/2.00%, Matthew L. Harriton/32.50%, Insiders/35.80%, Startek Entertainment Corp./5.00%, Advisor Shares/7.50%, Santo Petrocell/5.00%, Karen Nazzareno/2.00%, YBR/21.30%

Financial Data: *Fiscal Year End:*04/30 *Latest Annual Data:* 04/30/2006

Year	Sales	Net Income
2006	NA	-$657,000
2005	NA	-$504,000
2004	NA	-$629,000

Curr. Assets:	$3,000	Curr. Liab.:	$1,488,000		
Plant, Equip.:	NA	Total Liab.:	$1,488,000	Indic. Yr. Divd.:	NA
Total Assets:	$48,000	Net Worth:	-$1,440,000	Debt/ Equity:	NA

EMC Corp

176 S St., Hopkinton, MA, 01748; *PH:* 1-508-435-1000; *http://* www.emc.com

General - Incorporation	MA	Stock - Price on:12/24/2007	$17.98
Employees	26,500	Stock Exchange	NYSE
Auditor	PricewaterhouseCoopers LLP	Ticker Symbol	EMC
Stk Agt	EquiServe Trust Co N.A	Outstanding Shares	2,100,000,000
Counsel	NA	E.P.S	$0.61
DUNS No.	09-744-7148	Shareholders	NA

Business: The groups principle activities include designing, manufacturing, and marketing networked storage platforms, software and related services. The group operates through four segments namely information storage, content management and archiving, RSA information security and VMware virtual Infrastructure. In the year 2007, the group acquired Berkeley Data Systems, Inc. The group operates from United States.

Primary SIC and add'l.: 7378 7379 3572 7372

CIK No: 0000790070

Subsidiaries: 3401 Hillview Avenue LLC, 6027270 Canada, Inc., 900 West Park Drive LLC, A.c.n. 096 059862 Pty Limited, Acartus, Inc., ActionPoint GmbH, ActionPoint UK Ltd., Australian Outsourcing Pty Limited, Authentica International, Inc., Captiva Context, Inc., Captiva Software B.V., Captiva Software France EURL, Captiva Software GmbH, Captiva Software Pty. Ltd., Captiva Software SA 130 Subsidiaries included in the Index

Officers: Joseph M. Tucci/Chmn., CEO, Pres./$20,213,030.00, Thomas J. Dougherty/Sec., Balaji Yelamanchili/Sr. VP, Co - GM - Content Management, Archiving, Toshio Morohoshi/Pres., Representative Dir. - EMC Japan Emc Corporation, Mark A. Link/Chief Accounting Officer, Sr. VP, Michael C. Ruettgers/Sr. Advisor, Arthur W. Coviello/Exec. VP - EMC Corporation, Pres. - RSA, The Security Division, EMC, Louise O'Brien/Exec. VP - Corporate Strategy, Development, EMC Corporation, Hadley Weinzierl/International Public Relations, Lesley Ogrodnick/Financial, Human Resources, Public Sector, Steve Bardige/Sr. Dir. - Corporate Analyst Relations, Robert Callery/Corporate Analyst Relations, Bill Loughlin/Corporate Analyst Relations, Irene Mirageas/Corporate Analyst Relations, Deborah Thomson Filer/Corporate Analyst Relations *(40 Officers included in Index)*

Directors: Joseph M. Tucci/Chmn., CEO, Pres., William J. Teuber/Vice Chmn., Olli-Pekka Kallasvuo/Dir., Michael W. Brown/Dir., Paul W. Fitzgerald/Dir., Edmund F. Kelly/Dir., John R. Egan/Dir., David Strohm/Dir., Michael J. Cronin/Dir., Gail Deegan/Dir., Alfred M. Zeien/78/Dir., Windle B. Priem/Dir.

Owners: David Donatelli, John R. Egan, Michael J. Cronin, Gail Deegan, Insiders/1.55%, Alfred M. Zeien, Windle B. Priem, Joseph M. Tucci, Olli-Pekka Kallasvuo, Diane Greene, Michael W. Brown, Paul W. Fitzgerald, David N. Strohm, David I. Goulden, William J. Teuber *(17 Owners included in Index)*

Financial Data: *Fiscal Year End:*12/31 *Latest Annual Data:* 12/31/2006

Year	Sales	Net Income
2006	$11,155,090,000	$1,223,982,000
2005	$9,663,955,000	$1,133,165,000
2004	$8,229,488,000	$871,189,000

Curr. Assets:	$6,520,587,000	Curr. Liab.:	$3,881,104,000	P/E Ratio:	29.48
Plant, Equip.:	$2,035,559,000	Total Liab.:	$8,240,540,000	Indic. Yr. Divd.:	NA
Total Assets:	$18,566,247,000	Net Worth:	$10,325,707,000	Debt/ Equity:	0.3542

EMC Insurance Group Inc

717 Mulberry St., Des Moines, IA, 50309; *PH:* 1-515-345-2902; *Fax:* 1-515-345-2895; *http://* www.emcins.com

General - Incorporation	IA	**Stock**- Price on:12/24/2007	$24.02
Employees	NA	Stock Exchange	NDQ
Auditor	Ernst & Young LLP	Ticker Symbol	EMCI
Stk Agt	UMB Bank, N.A.	Outstanding Shares	13,760,000
Counsel	Nyemaster Goode Voigts West Et Al	E.P.S.	$3.72
DUNS No.	04-152-3598	Shareholders	NA

Business: The group's principal activities are to provide multiple-line property and casualty insurance and reinsurance services. The group is an insurance holding company and it is 80.9 percent owned by employers mutual casualty company. The group conducts its insurance business through two segments: property and casualty insurance segment that underwrites both commercial and personal lines of insurance and reinsurance segment provides reinsurance for other insurers and reinsurers. The operations are carried out through 16 branch offices and 3,150 independent agents throughout the United States. The group's subsidiaries include emcasco insurance company, Illinois emcasco insurance company, dakota fire insurance company, farm and city insurance company, emc reinsurance company and emc underwriters, llc.

Primary SIC and add'l.: 6331 6719 6321

CIK No: 0000356130

Subsidiaries: Dakota Fire Insurance Company, EMC Reinsurance Company, EMC Underwriters, LLC, EMCASCO Insurance Company, Farm and City Insurance Company, Illinois EMCASCO Insurance Company

Officers: Bruce G. Kelley/Dir., CEO, Pres./$2,006,376.00, Richard L. Gass/Sr. VP - Technology, Donald D. Klemme/Sr. VP - Administration, Sec., Mark E. Reese/CFO, Sr. VP - Accounting/$416,972.00, Richard W. Hoffmann/VP - General Counsel, Ronald W. Jean/Exec. VP - Corporate Development/$1,045,873.00, Ronald A. Paine/VP - Internal Audit, Kevin J. Hovick/Sr. VP - Business Development, Raymond W. Davis/Sr. VP - Investments, Treasurer/$662,125.00, Carla A. Prather/Assist. VP - Accounting, Controller, Richard K. Schulz/Sr. VP - Claims, William A. Murray/COO, Exec. VP/$1,682,182.00, Steven C. Peck/Sr. VP - Actuarial, Robert L. Link/Assist. VP, Assist. Sec., Anita L. Novak/Assist. Sec., Dir. - Investor Relations *(42 Officers included in Index)*

Directors: Bruce G. Kelley/Dir., CEO, Pres., Fred A. Schiek/Chmn. - Employers Mutual Casualty Company, Margaret A. Ball/Vice Chmn., George W. Kochheiser/82/Chmn., George C. Carpenter/80/Dir., Joanne L. Stockdale/Dir., David J. Fisher/Dir., Thomas W. Booth/Dir., John C. Burgeson/Dir., Gale L. Griffin/Dir., John H. Kelley/Dir., Richard Koch/Dir., David J.W. Proctor/Dir., Terrill H. Watts/Dir., Raymond A. Michel/Dir.

Owners: William A. Murray, George C. Carpenter, Bruce G. Kelley/1.00%, David J. Fisher, Insiders/3.40%, Mark E. Reese, Joanne L. Stockdale, George W. Kochheiser, Raymond A. Michel, Raymond W. Davis, Margaret A. Ball, Fredrick A. Schiek, Ronald W. Jean

Financial Data: *Fiscal Year End:*12/31 *Latest Annual Data:* 12/31/2006

Year	Sales	Net Income
2006	$443,086,000	$53,547,000
2005	$460,812,000	$43,009,000
2004	$380,359,000	$13,185,000

Curr. Assets:	$102,956,000	Curr. Liab.:	NA	P/E Ratio:	6.73
Plant, Equip.:	NA	Total Liab.:	$897,864,000	Indic. Yr. Divd.:	$0.680
Total Assets:	$1,206,159,000	Net Worth:	$308,294,000	Debt/ Equity:	NA

Emclaire Financial Corp

612 Main St., Emlenton, PA, 16373; *PH:* 1-724-867-2311; *Fax:* 1-724-867-1614; *http://* www.emclairefinancial.com

General - Incorporation	PA	**Stock**- Price on:12/24/2007	$26
Employees	101	Stock Exchange	OTC
Auditor	Beard Miller Co. LLP	Ticker Symbol	EMCF
Stk Agt	Illinois Stock Transfer Co	Outstanding Shares	1,270,000
Counsel	NA	E.P.S.	$1.61
DUNS No.	03-992-2158	Shareholders	NA

Business: The group's principal activity is to attract deposits from the general public and investing such funds in real estate loans, commercial loans, marketable securities and interest-earning deposits. The services provided by the group include accepting time and demand deposits from the general public and together with other funds, using the proceeds to originate secured and unsecured loans. In addition, funds are also used to purchase investment securities. The group operates through its subsidiary, the farmers national bank of emlenton. The group has a network of ten retail branch offices in venango, butler, clarion, clearfield, elk and jefferson counties, Pennsylvania.

Primary SIC and add'l.: 6021 6712

CIK No: 0000858800

Subsidiaries: Farmers National Bank of Emlenton

Officers: David L. Cox/Chmn., CEO, Pres./$220,299.00, Raymond M. Lawton/Sec./$129,833.00, William C. Marsh/Dir., Treasurer, CFO/$107,738.00

Directors: David L. Cox/Chmn., CEO, Pres., James M. Crooks/Dir., George W. Freeman/Dir., John B. Mason/Dir., Mark A. Freemer/Dir., Michael J. King/Dir., Ronald L. Ashbaugh/Dir., Robert L. Hunter/Dir., Brian C. McCarrier/Dir., William C. Marsh/Dir., Treasurer, CFO

Owners: Brian C. McCarrier, Ronald L. Ashbaugh, Mark A. Freemer, George W. Freeman/6.21%, Michael J. King, John B. Mason, Robert L. Hunter, David L. Cox, William C. Marsh, Insiders/11.65%, Barbara C. McElhattan/5.23%, Mary E. Dascombe/7.14%, James M. Crooks

Financial Data: *Fiscal Year End:*12/31 *Latest Annual Data:* 12/31/2006

Year	Sales	Net Income
2006	$19,193,000	$1,966,000
2005	$18,194,000	$2,573,000
2004	$16,488,000	$2,557,000

Curr. Assets:	$18,091,000	Curr. Liab.:	$246,643,000	P/E Ratio:	16.15
Plant, Equip.:	$7,958,000	Total Liab.:	$276,643,000	Indic. Yr. Divd.:	$1.160
Total Assets:	$300,560,000	Net Worth:	$23,917,000	Debt/ Equity:	1.2464

Emcor Group Inc

301 Merritt Seven Corporate Pk., Norwalk, CT, 06851; *PH:* 1-203-849-7800; *Fax:* 1-203-849-7900; *http://* www.emcorgroup.com; *Email:* emcor_info@emcorgroup.com

General - Incorporation	DE	**Stock**- Price on:12/24/2007	NA
Employees	27,000	Stock Exchange	NYSE
Auditor	Ernst & Young LLP	Ticker Symbol	EME
Stk Agt	Bank of New York	Outstanding Shares	NA
Counsel	Muldoon, Murphy & Faucette	E.P.S.	NA
DUNS No.	01-710-6386	Shareholders	NA

Business: The group's principle activities include designing, integrating, installing, testing, operating and maintaining complex mechanical and electrical systems. The products of the group include lighting, low-voltage, voice and data communication, heating and ventilation systems. The group also provides site-based operations and maintenance, mobile maintenance service and other such services. The group operates in United States, Canada, United Kingdom, Middle East, South Africa and Europe.

Primary SIC and add'l.: 1731 8744 1796 6719

CIK No: 0000105634

Subsidiaries: Dyn Specialty Contracting, Inc., Emcor (uk) Limited, EMCOR Construction Services, Inc, EMCOR Facilities Services, Inc., EMCOR Group (UK) plc, EMCOR International, Inc., EMCOR Mechanical/Electrical Services (East), Inc, Emcor-csi Holding Co., MES Holdings Corporation, Monumental Investment Corporation

Officers: Michael Parry/CEO, Pres. - Emcor Construction Services, Frank T. MacInnis/Chmn., CEO/$4,007,268.00, Rex C. Thrasher/VP - Risk Management, William E. Feher/VP, Controller, Joseph A. Serino/Treasurer, Arthur L. Strenkert/Pres. - Emcor Energy Services, Kevin R. Matz/Sr. VP - Shared Services, Mark A. Pompa/CFO, Exec. VP/$1,575,517.00, Sheldon I. Cammaker/Exec. VP, General Counsel, Sec./$1,939,171.00, Mava K. Heffler/VP - Marketing, Communications, Anthony J. Guzzi/COO, Pres./$2,791,595.00, Joseph A. Puglisi/CIO, VP, Anthony R. Triano/VP - Integrated Services

Directors: Frank T. MacInnis/Chmn., CEO, Gene Martin/Chmn. - Emcor Energy Services, Stephen W. Bershad/Dir., Richard F. Hamm/Dir., Larry J. Bump/Dir., Michael T. Yonker/Dir., David A.B. Brown/Dir., Albert Fried/Dir.

Owners: Munder Capital/5.20%, Goldman Sachs Asset Management, L.P./12.40%

Financial Data: *Fiscal Year End:*12/31 *Latest Annual Data:* 12/31/2006

Year	Sales	Net Income
2006	$5,021,036,000	$86,634,000
2005	$4,714,547,000	$60,042,000
2004	$4,747,880,000	$33,207,000

Curr. Assets:	$1,662,413,000	Curr. Liab.:	$1,208,348,000		
Plant, Equip.:	$52,780,000	Total Liab.:	$1,378,714,000	Indic. Yr. Divd.:	NA
Total Assets:	$2,089,023,000	Net Worth:	$710,309,000	Debt/ Equity:	0.0015

Emcore Corp

10420 Research Rd., SE, Albuquerque, NM, 87123; *PH:* 1-505-332-5000; *Fax:* 1-505-332-5038; *http://* www.emcore.com

General - Incorporation	NJ	**Stock**- Price on:12/24/2007	$5.18
Employees	650	Stock Exchange	NDQ
Auditor	Deloitte & Touche LLP	Ticker Symbol	EMKR
Stk Agt	American Stock Transfer & Trust Co.	Outstanding Shares	50,930,000
Counsel	NA	E.P.S.	$1.00
DUNS No.	12-224-5046	Shareholders	NA

Business: The group's principal activity is to offer versatile portfolio of compound semiconductor products for the broadband and wireless communications and solid-state lighting markets. The group operates in two business units: the systems-related business unit designs, develops and manufactures tools and manufacturing processes used to fabricate compound semiconductor wafer and devices. The materials-related business unit designs, develops and manufactures compound semiconductor materials that enable circuits and devices to operate at radio frequencies. The group's products include mocvd tools, optical devices, photodetectors, vcsel-based array transceivers and transponders, rf and electronic materials and solar cells. In fiscal 2003, the group acquired certain assets of privately held alvesta corporation, agere systems, inc.'s catv transmission systems, telecom access and satcom components business and molex inc.'s 10g ethernet transceiver business.

Primary SIC and add'l.: 3674

CIK No: 0000808326

Subsidiaries: Corona Optical Systems, Inc., Emcore Irb Company, Inc., EMCORE Optoelectronics Acquisition Corporation

Officers: Reuben F. Richards/Dir., CEO, Thomas G. Werthan/Dir. - Investor Relations Contact, Victor J. Allgeier/Investor Relations Contact, Hong Q. Hou/Dir., COO, Pres., Adam Gushard/CFO, John Iannelli/CTO, Keith J. Kosco/General Counsel, Corp. Sec., Christopher Larocca/VP, GM - Broadband Fiber Optics, Stephen Krasulick/VP, GM - Data, Telecom Fiber Optics, David Danzilio/VP, GM - Photovoltaics, Monica Van Berkel/VP - Business Management

Directors: Reuben F. Richards/Dir., CEO, Thomas J. Russell/Chmn., Robert Bogomolny/Dir., John Gillen/Dir., Thomas G. Werthan/Dir. - Investor Relations Contact, Robert Louis-Dreyfus/Dir., Charles Scott/Dir., Hong Q. Hou/Dir., COO, Pres.

Financial Data: *Fiscal Year End:*09/30 *Latest Annual Data:* 9/30/2005

Year	Sales	Net Income
2005	$127,603,000	-$13,107,000
2004	$93,069,000	-$13,426,000
2003	$113,106,000	-$38,525,000

Curr. Assets:	$89,538,000	Curr. Liab.:	$36,015,000		
Plant, Equip.:	$56,957,000	Total Liab.:	$130,724,000	Indic. Yr. Divd.:	NA
Total Assets:	$206,287,000	Net Worth:	$75,563,000	Debt/ Equity:	1.3224

Emerge Interactive Inc

10305 102nd Ter., Sebastian, FL, 32958; *PH:* 1-561-589-7331; *http://* www.emergeinteractive.com

General - Incorporation	DE	**Stock**- Price on:12/24/2007	NA
Employees	24	Stock Exchange	NA
Auditor	KPMG LLP	Ticker Symbol	NA
Stk Agt	Mellon Investor Services LLC	Outstanding Shares	NA
Counsel	NA	E.P.S.	NA
DUNS No.	NA	Shareholders	NA

Business: The group's principal activities are to provide food-safety, individual-animal tracking and supply-management services to the beef production industry. The group operates in two segments: the food safety technologies and the animal information solutions. The food safety technologies segment consists of verifeye inspection systems, a unique machine vision technology designed to instantly detect microscopic levels of organic contamination. The animal information solutions segment provides comprehensive, data-driven solutions to meet its customers' information challenges. The products consist of cattlelogtmdata collection, usda process verified program, cattlelog Web-based reports and verifeye. The customers include the cow/calf producers, the stockers and backgrounders, the feedyard operators, the packer or beef processors, various state beef quality assurance programs and branded beef alliances supporting retailers within the entire beef production chain.

Primary SIC and add'l.: 7375

CIK No: 0001092605

Emergency Filtration Products Inc

175 Cassia Way, Ste. A115, Henderson, NV, 89014; ***PH:*** 1-888-656-3697; ***Fax:*** 1-702-567-1893; ***http://*** www.emergencyfiltration.com; ***Email:*** info@emfp.com

General - Incorporation	NV	**Stock**- Price on:12/24/2007	NA
Employees	NA	Stock Exchange	NA
Auditor	Piercy Bowler Taylor & Kern	Ticker Symbol	NA
Stk Agt	American Registrar & Transfer Co	Outstanding Shares	NA
Counsel	NA	E.P.S.	$0.016
DUNS No.	NA	Shareholders	NA

Business: The groups principle activity is to design and manufacture NanoMask(R) the first protective face mask in the world to utilize nanoparticle enhanced filters to address potentially harmful airborne contaminants. The group's products include Superstat, NanoMask and ELVIS. The group operates from United States.

Primary SIC and add'l.: 3841 3842 3845

CIK No: 0001088213

Officers: Philip Dascher/CEO

Directors: Thomas Glenndahl/Dir., David Bloom/Dir., Raymond Yuan/Dir., William Dodge Rueckert/Dir.

Owners: William Rueckert/0.09%, Douglas K. Beplate/7.33%, Philip Dascher/0.66%, David Bloom/0.37%, Josiah T. Austin/18.15%, Steve M. Hanni/0.51%, Lynn Hayse/0.22%, John Masenheimer/0.22%, Raymond C.L. Yuan/0.89%, Thomas Glenndahl/0.42%

Financial Data: *Fiscal Year End:*12/31 *Latest Annual Data:* 12/31/2005

Year	Sales	Net Income
2005	$655,000	-$1,613,000
2004	$406,000	-$1,605,000
2003	$764,000	-$706,000

Curr. Assets:	$1,236,000	*Curr. Liab.:*	$382,000		
Plant, Equip.:	$302,000	*Total Liab.:*	$382,000	*Indic. Yr. Divd.:*	NA
Total Assets:	$2,439,000	*Net Worth:*	$2,057,000	*Debt/ Equity:*	NA

Emergency Medical Services Corp

6200 S Syracuse Way, Ste. 200, Greenwood Village, CO, 80111; ***PH:*** 1-303-495-1200; ***Fax:*** 1-303-495-1466; ***http://*** www.emsc.net; ***Email:*** information@emsc.net

General - Incorporation	DE	**Stock**- Price on:12/24/2007	$38.67
Employees	12,848	Stock Exchange	NYSE
Auditor	Ernst & Young LLP	Ticker Symbol	EMS
Stk Agt	American Stock Transfer & Trust Co.	Outstanding Shares	41,540,000
Counsel	NA	E.P.S.	$1.23
DUNS No.	NA	Shareholders	NA

Business: The groups principle activity is to provide emergency medical services. The group also provides ambulance services. The group operates through two segments namely, healthcare transportation services and emergency management services. The group operates from the United States. The group's quarterly revenue for September 2007 was 529.75 millions of USD.

Primary SIC and add'l.: 7363 8099 4119 8748

CIK No: 0001344154

Subsidiaries: A1 Leasing, Inc., Adam Transportation Service, Inc., Air Ambulance Specialists, Inc., Ambulance Acquisition, Inc., American Emergency Physicians Management, Inc., American Investment Enterprises, Inc., American Medical Pathways, Inc., American Medical Response Delaware Valley, LLC, American Medical Response Holdings, Inc., American Medical Response Management, Inc., American Medical Response Mid-Atlantic, Inc., American Medical Response Northwest, Inc., American Medical Response of Colorado, Inc., American Medical Response of Connecticut,, American Medical Response of Georgia, Inc. 146 Subsidiaries included in the Index

Officers: William A. Sanger/Chmn., CEO, Don S. Harvey/Dir., COO, Pres., Dighton C. Packard/Chief Medical Officer, Randel G. Owen/CFO, Exec. VP, Todd G. Zimmerman/General Counsel, Exec. VP, Steve Murphy/Sr. VP - Government, National Services, Kimberly Norman/Sr. VP - Human Resources, Steve Ratton/Sr. VP, Treasurer, Joseph Taylor/Exec. VP - National Sales, Marketing, Deborah Hileman/VP - Public Relations, Communications, William L. Jordan/Sec.

Directors: William A. Sanger/Chmn., CEO, Don S. Harvey/Dir., COO, Pres., Robert M. Le Blanc/Dir., Steven B. Epstein/Dir., Paul B. Iannini/Dir., James T. Kelly/Dir., Michael L. Smith/Dir.

Owners: FMR Corp./15.90%, Onex Partners LLC, River Road Asset Management, LLC/6.30%, Entities affiliated with Accipiter Life Sciences Fund, LP/4.10%, Onex EMSC Co-Invest LP, Onex Partners LP, Entities affiliated with Deerfield Capital, L.P./3.20%, Onex Corporation, Healthinvest Partners AB/5.30%

Financial Data: *Fiscal Year End:*12/31 *Latest Annual Data:* 12/31/2006

Year	Sales	Net Income
2006	$1,934,205,000	$39,071,000
2005	$1,655,485,000	$20,067,000

Curr. Assets:	$532,489,000	*Curr. Liab.:*	$300,962,000	*P/E Ratio:*	31.44
Plant, Equip.:	$147,162,000	*Total Liab.:*	$932,177,000	*Indic. Yr. Divd.:*	NA
Total Assets:	$1,318,217,000	*Net Worth:*	$386,040,000	*Debt/ Equity:*	1.1916

Emergent Biosolutions Inc

2273 Research Blvd., Ste. 400, Rockville, MD, 20850; ***PH:*** 1-301-795-1800; ***Fax:*** 1-301-795-1899; ***http://*** www.emergentbiosolutions.com

General - Incorporation	DE	**Stock**- Price on:12/24/2007	$9.2
Employees	494	Stock Exchange	NYSE
Auditor	Ernst& Young LLP	Ticker Symbol	EBS
Stk Agt	American Stock Transfer & Trust Co.	Outstanding Shares	28,170,000
Counsel	NA	E.P.S.	$0.73
DUNS No.	NA	Shareholders	NA

Business: The groups principle activities include developing, manufacturing and commercializing immunobiotics. The groups products include Biothrax. The group operates through two segments namely, biodefense and commercial. The group operates from the United States.

Primary SIC and add'l.: 2834 2836 2834 2836

CIK No: 0001367644

Subsidiaries: Emergent BioDefense Operations Lansing Inc., Emergent BioSolutions Inc., Emergent BioSolutions Malaysia SDN BHD, Emergent Commercial Operations Frederick Inc., Emergent Europe Inc., Emergent Frederick LLC, Emergent International Inc., Emergent Product Development Gaithersburg Inc., Emergent Product Development Germany GmbH, Emergent Product Development UK Limited, Emergent Sales and Marketing Germany GmbH, Emergent Sales and Marketing Singapore Pte. Ltd., Emergent Sales and Marketing US LLC

Officers: Fuad El-Hibri/Chmn., CEO, Pres., Daniel J. Abdun-Nabi/COO, Pres., Sec., Edward J. Arcuri/COO, Exec. VP, Steven N. Chatfield/Pres. - Emergent Product Development UK Limited, Chief Scientific Officer, Robert G. Kramer/Exec. VP - Manufacturing Operations, Michael J. Langford/Pres. - Emergent Product Development Gaithersburg Inc, Kyle W. Keese/Sr. VP - Corporate Affairs, Don R. Elsey/Sr. VP - Finance - Administration, CFO, Thomas K. Zink/Sr. VP - Medical - Clinical Development, Chief Medical Officer, Robert Burrows/Contact - Investor Relations, Kim Brennen Root/Contact - Corporate Communications, Jose Ochoa/Contact - Business Development, Tracey Schmitt/Contact - Corporate Communications, Denise Esposito/Sr. VP - Legal Affairs, General Counsel, Mauro Gibellini/Sr. VP - Corporate Development *(17 Officers included in Index)*

Directors: Fuad El-Hibri/Chmn., CEO, Pres., Joe M. Allbaugh/Dir., Zsolt Harsanyi/Dir., Jerome M. Hauer/Dir., Shahzad Malik/Dir., Ronald B. Richard/Dir., Louis W. Sullivan/Dir., Sue Bailey/Dir.

Owners: Don R. Elsey, Shahzad Malik, Mauro Gibellini, Stockholder voting group under voting agreement dated June30, 2004, Robert G. Kramer, Zsolt Harsanyi, Fuad El-Hibri, Ronald B. Richard, Jerome M. Hauer, Daniel J. Abdun-Nabi, Edward J. Arcuri, Former shareholders of Microscience Investments Limited, Insiders, Robert Myers

Financial Data: *Fiscal Year End:*12/31 *Latest Annual Data:* 12/31/2006

Year	Sales	Net Income
2006	$152,732,000	$22,793,000
2005	$130,688,000	$15,784,000
2004	$83,494,000	$11,472,000

Curr. Assets:	$147,337,000	*Curr. Liab.:*	$64,347,000	*P/E Ratio:*	11.08
Plant, Equip.:	$78,174,000	*Total Liab.:*	$99,783,000	*Indic. Yr. Divd.:*	NA
Total Assets:	$238,255,000	*Net Worth:*	$138,472,000	*Debt/ Equity:*	NA

Emergent Group Inc

932 Grand Central Ave., Glendale, CA, 91201; ***PH:*** 1-818-240-8250

General - Incorporation	NV	**Stock**- Price on:12/24/2007	$3.7
Employees	84	Stock Exchange	OTC
Auditor	Rose, Snyder & Jacobs	Ticker Symbol	EMGP
Stk Agt	American Stock Transfer & Trust Co.	Outstanding Shares	5,540,000
Counsel	NA	E.P.S.	$0.44
DUNS No.	NA	Shareholders	NA

Business: The group operates through its subsidiaries whose principle activity is to provide funding with investors' money and their own capital, financing growth or facilitating transactions for their clients; and provide medical equipment solutions in the areas of laser surgery, cryosurgery, bracbrachytherapy and other capital-i tensive medical technologies to health care facilities and physicians. The group operates from United States.

Primary SIC and add'l.: 5047 6159 6719

CIK No: 0001021097

Subsidiaries: Medical Resources Management Financial, Inc, PRI Medical Technologies, Inc.

Owners: Bruce J. Haber/22.10%, Howard Waltman/6.50%, Arie Kanofsky/9.20%, Louis Buther/11.80%, William M. McKay/3.80%, Daniel Yun/12.60%, K. Deane Reade/0.50%, Insiders/52.00%

Financial Data: *Fiscal Year End:*12/31 *Latest Annual Data:* 12/31/2006

Year	Sales	Net Income
2006	$15,929,000	$2,724,000
2005	$12,479,000	$966,000
2004	$10,967,000	$23,000

Curr. Assets:	$5,581,000	*Curr. Liab.:*	$4,434,000	*P/E Ratio:*	7.71
Plant, Equip.:	$3,919,000	*Total Liab.:*	$6,390,000	*Indic. Yr. Divd.:*	$0.200
Total Assets:	$10,930,000	*Net Worth:*	$4,083,000	*Debt/ Equity:*	0.4790

Emerging Vision Inc

100 Quentin Roosevelt Blvd., Ste. 508, Garden City, NY, 11530; ***PH:*** 1-516-390-2106; ***http://*** www.emergingvision.com; ***Email:*** investor.relations@emergingvision.com

General - Incorporation	NY	**Stock**- Price on:12/24/2007	$0.38
Employees	146	Stock Exchange	OTC
Auditor	Miller, Ellin & Co. LLP	Ticker Symbol	ISEE
Stk Agt	Mellon Investor Services LLC	Outstanding Shares	70,320,000
Counsel	NA	E.P.S.	$0.02
DUNS No.	79-065-0329	Shareholders	NA

Business: The group's principal activity is to operate retail optical stores and franchising of optical chains in the United States. The products of the group include eye care products and services such as prescription and non-prescription eyeglasses, eyeglass frames, ophthalmic lenses, contact lenses, sunglasses and a broad range of ancillary items. The group markets its products under the trade names: sterling optical, site for sore eyes, duling optical and singer specs. The group also operates a specialized health care maintenance organization. The group test-Markets various brands of sunglasses, ophthalmic lenses, contact lenses and designer frames. As on 31-Dec-2003, the group operated 172 sterling stores, consisting of 14 company -owned stores and 158 franchised stores. The group operates mainly in the United States.

Primary SIC and add'l.: 6794 5995

CIK No: 0001002554

Subsidiaries: Emerging Vision King Of Prussia, Inc., Ev Acquisition, Inc., Insight Ipa Of New York, Inc., Singer Specs Of Westmoreland, Inc., Singer Specs, Inc., Sterilng Vision Of Arnot Mall, Inc., Stering Vision Of Montgomery Mall, Inc., Stering Vision Of Myrtle Ave., Inc., Sterling Optical Of Arrowhead, Inc., Sterling Optical Of Bayshore, Inc., Sterling Optical Of Chautauqua, Inc., Sterling Optical Of Commack, Inc., Sterling Optical Of Crossgates Mall, Inc., Sterling Optical Of Flagstaff, Inc., Sterling Optical Of Jefferson Valley, Inc. 66 Subsidiaries included in the Index

Owners: Harvey Ross/6.30%, Lou Weisbach/3.30%, Alan Cohen/6.20%, Robert Cohen/5.00%, Seymour G. Siegel, Brian P. Alessi, Samuel Z. Herskowitz/1.60%, Nicholas Shashati, Joel L. Gold, Christopher G. Payan/6.40%, Insiders/25.10%, Horizons Investors Corp./40.30%, Rita Folger/0.74%

Financial Data: *Fiscal Year End:*12/31 *Latest Annual Data:* 12/31/2006

Year	Sales	Net Income
2006	$21,712,000	$1,860,000
2005	$13,979,000	$266,000
2004	$14,484,000	$884,000

Curr. Assets:	$6,893,000	**Curr. Liab.:**	$7,566,000	**P/E Ratio:**	38.00
Plant, Equip.:	$923,000	**Total Liab.:**	$9,246,000	**Indic. Yr. Divd.:**	NA
Total Assets:	$12,597,000	**Net Worth:**	$3,351,000	**Debt/ Equity:**	0.3058

Emeritus Corp

3131 Elliott Ave., Ste. 500, Seattle, WA, 98121; *PH:* 1-206-298-2909; *Fax:* 1-206-301-4500; *http://* www.emeritus.com

General - Incorporation	WA	Stock- Price on:12/24/2007	$34.65
Employees	7,700	Stock Exchange	AMEX
Auditor	KPMG LLP	Ticker Symbol	ESC
Stk Agt.	Mellon Investor Services LLC	Outstanding Shares	18,970,000
Counsel	Perkins Coie LLP	E.P.S.	$0.02
DUNS No.	84-729-5722	Shareholders	NA

Business: The group is a housing services company focused on operating residential style assisted living communities. Assisted living communities provide a residential housing alternative for senior citizens who need help with the activities of daily living, with an emphasis on assisted living and personal care services. In addition to its direct operation of residential communities, the company operates residential communities pursuant to management agreements with the property owners or the holders of property leasehold interests. The group operates 175 assisted living communities, consisting of approximately 14,845 units with a capacity for 18,208 residents, located in 33 states.

Primary SIC and add'l.: 8361

CIK No: 0001001604

Subsidiaries: Em I, LLC, EMAC, Emeritus Management I, L.P., Emeritus Management LLC, Emeritus Properties I, Inc., Emeritus Properties II, Inc., Emeritus Properties III, Inc., Emeritus Properties IV, Inc., Emeritus Properties IX, LLC, Emeritus Properties V, Inc., Emeritus Properties VI, Inc., Emeritus Properties VII, Inc., Emeritus Properties X, LLC, Emeritus Properties XI, LLC, Emeritus Properties XII, LLC 43 Subsidiaries included in the Index

Officers: Daniel R. Baty/Chmn., Co - CEO, Granger Cobb/Co - CEO, Pres., Justin Hutchens/COO, Exec. VP - Operations, Melanie Werdel/Exec. VP - Administration, Budgie Amparo/Sr. VP - Quality, Risk Management, John Cincotta/Sr. VP - Sales, Marketing, Jim L. Hanson/Sr. VP - Financial Services, Controller, Eric Mendelsohn/Sr. VP - Corporate Development, Kacy P. Kang/40/VP - Operations, Western Division, Raymond R. Brandstrom/Dir., CFO, Exec. VP - Finance, Sec., Gary S. Becker/60/Sr. VP - Operations, Suzette McCanless/59/VP - Operations, Eastern Division, Martin D. Roffe/Sr. VP - Financial Planning, Frank Ruffo/65/VP - Administration, Christopher M. Belford/46/VP - Operations, Central Division

Directors: Daniel R. Baty/Chmn., Co - CEO, Raymond R. Brandstrom/Dir., CFO, Exec. VP - Finance, Sec., Bruce L. Busby/Dir., David W. Niemiec/Dir., Robert E. Marks/Dir., Stanley L. Baty/Dir., Michael T. Young/Dir., Charles P. Durkin/Dir.

Owners: Brandon D. Baty, Gary S. Becker, B.F., Limited Partnership, Stanley L. Baty, Frank Ruffo, David W. Niemiec, Daniel R. Baty, Raymond R. Brandstrom, Christopher Belford, Charles P. Durkin, Saratoga Partners IV, L.P., FMR Corp., Robert E. Marks, Bruce L. Busby, Michael T. Young (16 Owners included in Index)

Financial Data: *Fiscal Year End:*12/31 *Latest Annual Data:* 12/31/2006

Year	Sales	Net Income
2006	$421,865,000	-$14,618,000
2005	$387,732,000	$12,302,000
2004	$317,935,000	-$40,540,000

Curr. Assets:	$51,171,000	**Curr. Liab.:**	$93,048,000		
Plant, Equip.:	$601,292,000	**Total Liab.:**	$822,092,000	**Indic. Yr. Divd.:**	NA
Total Assets:	$703,060,000	**Net Worth:**	-$119,032,000	**Debt/ Equity:**	NA

Emerson Electric Co

PO Box 4100, 8000 West Florissant Ave., St. Louis, MO, 63136; *PH:* 1-314-553-2000; *Fax:* 1-314-553-3527; *http://* www.gotoemerson.com

General - Incorporation	MO	Stock- Price on:12/24/2007	$48.1
Employees	127,800	Stock Exchange	NYSE
Auditor	KPMG LLP	Ticker Symbol	EMR
Stk Agt.	Mellon Investor Services LLC	Outstanding Shares	795,260,000
Counsel	NA	E.P.S.	$2.66
DUNS No.	00-626-9633	Shareholders	NA

Business: The groups principle activity is to provide products and services for a wide range of industries, commercial markets and end-users including consumers. The groups products include sophisticated process control and automation systems, climate control technologies, and home and work place products. The group products are sold under the brand names Emerson network power (TM) and Emerson process management(TM). The group operates from United States.

Primary SIC and add'l.: 3546 3491 3629 3640 3433 3823

CIK No: 0000032604

Subsidiaries: AIH, Inc., AIHL, LLC, Alber Corp., Alco Controls S.A. de C.V., Alco Controls Spol s.r.o., Alliance Compressors LLC, Apple JV Holding Corp., Appleton Electric LLC, Appleton Electric, S.A. de C.V., Appleton Holding Corp., Applied Concepts, Inc., Artesyn Asset Management, Inc., Artesyn Austria GmbH, Artesyn Austria GmbH& Co. KG, Artesyn Cayman LP 771 Subsidiaries included in the Index

Officers: David N. Farr/Chmn., CEO, Pres., F. L. Steeves/54/Sr. VP, Sec., General Counsel, Cindy Stork/Contact - Emerson Global Finance, C. W. Ashmore/46/Sr. VP - Planning, Development, W. W. Withers/68/Exec. VP - Special Legal Advisor, Edward L. Monser/COO, R. J. Schlueter/54/VP, Chief Accounting Officer, Mark Polzin/Contact - Media Relations, Walter J. Galvin/Dir., CFO, Sr. Exec.

VP, Charles A. Peters/Dir., Sr. Exec. VP, John Hastings/Contact - Financial Media Relations, Dave Baldridge/Contact - Division Media Relation, Brian Pelletier/General Contact - International Media Relations, Rachel Catenach/Contact - Asia, Matt Wisla/Contact - China *(17 Officers included in Index)*

Directors: David N. Farr/Chmn., CEO, Pres., Charles F. Knight/Chmn. Emeritus, Walter J. Galvin/Dir., CFO, Sr. Exec. VP, Charles A. Peters/Dir., Sr. Exec. VP, Arthur F. Golden/Dir., Robert B. Horton/Dir., Joseph W. Prueher/Dir., Carlos G. Fernandez/Dir., Vernon R. Loucks/Dir., John B. Menzer/Dir., August A. Busch/Dir., David C. Farrell/Dir., Rozanne L. Ridgway/Dir., Randall L. Stephenson/Dir.

Financial Data: *Fiscal Year End:*09/30 *Latest Annual Data:* 9/30/2006

Year	Sales	Net Income
2006	$20,133,000,000	$1,845,000,000
2005	$17,305,000,000	$1,422,000,000
2004	$15,615,000,000	$1,257,000,000

Curr. Assets:	$7,330,000,000	**Curr. Liab.:**	$5,374,000,000	**P/E Ratio:**	20.04
Plant, Equip.:	$3,220,000,000	**Total Liab.:**	$10,342,000,000	**Indic. Yr. Divd.:**	$1.050
Total Assets:	$18,672,000,000	**Net Worth:**	$8,154,000,000	**Debt/ Equity:**	NA

Emerson Radio Corp

9 Entin Rd., Parsippany, NJ, 07054; *PH:* 1-973-884-2098; *Fax:* 1-973-428-2010; *http://* www.emersonradio.com; *Email:* internet@emersonradio.com

General - Incorporation	DE	Stock- Price on:12/24/2007	$3.19
Employees	115	Stock Exchange	NDQ
Auditor	Moore Stephens, P. C.	Ticker Symbol	MSON
Stk Agt.	Computershare Investor Services LLC	Outstanding Shares	27,110,000
Counsel	Lowenstein Sandler PC	E.P.S.	-$0.14
DUNS No.	00-153-9337	Shareholders	NA

Business: The group's principal activities are carried out through two segments consumer electronics and sporting goods. Consumer electronics designs, sources, imports, markets and licenses a variety of video products, including televisions, digital video disc, video cassette recorders and set top boxes, microwave ovens, audio, home theater systems and multi-media, house ware products, various accessories and specialty products. Sporting goods manufactures and markets sports related equipment and leisure products. The group markets domestically and internationally . The group has international operations in South America, Canada, and Mexico. The group's trade names include Emerson(R) and HH Scott(R). During 2003 the group discontinued and disposed of Athletic Training Equipment Company, Inc.

Primary SIC and add'l.: 3949 5064 5139

CIK No: 0000032621

Subsidiaries: Emerson Global Limited, Emerson Radio (Hong Kong) Limited., Emerson Radio International Ltd.

Officers: Adrian Ma/Dir., CEO, John J. Raab/COO, Sr. Exec. VP, Eduard Will/65/Dir., Pres. - North American Operations, Michael A.B. Binney/47/Dir., Pres. - International Sales, Greenfield Pitts/57/Dir., CFO

Directors: Adrian Ma/Dir., CEO, Christopher Ho/57/Chmn., Jerome H. Farnum/72/Non - Exec. Dir., Peter G. Bunger/66/Non - Exec. Dir., Eduard Will/65/Dir., Pres. - North American Operations, Michael A.B. Binney/47/Dir., Pres. - International Sales, Norbert R. Wirsching/70/Non - Exec. Dir., Michael W. Driscoll/61/Non - Exec. Dir., Greenfield Pitts/57/Dir., CFO, Mirzan Mahathir/Dir., David R. Peterson/64/Dir., Kareem E. Sethi/31/Dir.

Owners: Peter G. Bunger, Michael W. Driscoll, Insiders/58.30%, Eduard Will, Jerome H. Farnum, Christopher Ho/57.60%, Norbert R. Wirsching, Michael A. B. Binney, Greenfield Pitts

Financial Data: *Fiscal Year End:*03/31 *Latest Annual Data:* 03/31/2007

Year	Sales	Net Income
2007	$284,399,000	$3,458,000
2006	$233,843,000	$16,630,000
2005	$320,704,000	$5,905,000

Curr. Assets:	$92,028,000	**Curr. Liab.:**	$24,845,000		
Plant, Equip.:	$2,492,000	**Total Liab.:**	$25,521,000	**Indic. Yr. Divd.:**	NA
Total Assets:	$99,408,000	**Net Worth:**	$73,887,000	**Debt/ Equity:**	NA

Emgold Mining Corp

570 Granville St., Ste 1400, Vancouver, BC, V6C 3P1; *PH:* 1-604-687-4622; *http://* www.emgold.com

General - Incorporation	BC	Stock- Price on:12/24/2007	$0.169
Employees	NA	Stock Exchange	OTC
Auditor	PricewaterhouseCoopers LLP	Ticker Symbol	EGMCF
Stk Agt.	Computershare Investor Services LLC	Outstanding Shares	NA
Counsel	NA	E.P.S.	NA
DUNS No.	NA	Shareholders	NA

Business: The groups principle activity is to engage in conducting research and development to commercialize the Ceramext Process, which converts mine wastes and other siliceous waste materials to stone and ceramic building products. The group operates from United States.

Primary SIC and add'l.: 1000

CIK No: 0001199392

Subsidiaries: Golden Bear, Idaho-Maryland Mining Corporation (IMMC)

Officers: William J. Witte/Dir., CEO, Pres., Michael E. O'Connor/Mgr. - Investor Relations, Shannon M. Ross/CFO, Corp. Sec.

Directors: William J. Witte/Dir., CEO, Pres., John K. Burns/Chmn., Sargent H. Berner/Co - Chmn., Kenneth R. Yurichuk/Co - Chmn., Robin A.W. Elliott/Dir., Stephen J. Wilkinson/Dir.

Owners: David Watkinson/0.18%, Robin A.W. Elliott/0.14%, Sargent H. Berner/0.42%, John King Burns/0.35%, Ian Chang/0.25%, Shannon M. Ross/0.47%, Kenneth Yurichuk/0.12%, William J. Witte/1.06%, David Sinitsin/0.12%

Emisphere Technologies Inc

765 Old Saw Mill River Rd., Tarrytown, NY, 10591; *PH:* 1-914-347-2220; *Fax:* 1-914-347-2498; *http://* www.emisphere.com

General - Incorporation	DE	Stock - Price on:12/24/2007	$4.2
Employees	111	Stock Exchange	NDQ
Auditor	PricewaterhouseCoopers LLP	Ticker Symbol	EMIS
Stk Agt	Mellon Investor Services LLC	Outstanding Shares	28,330,000
Counsel	Paul Weiss Rifkind Wharton & Garrison	E.P.S	-$1
DUNS No.	15-772-8445	Shareholders	NA

Business: The group's principal activity is to specialize in the oral delivery of therapeutic macromolecules and other compounds that are not currently deliverable by oral means. The group is focused primarily on developing a form of its anticoagulant/anti thrombotic treatment for cardiovascular disease and heparin. The group has several product candidates in pre clinical and clinical development across a broad range of therapeutic areas such as cardiovascular, osteoporosis, growth disorders, diabetes, asthma/allergies, obesity and anti-infectives. These product candidates include oral heparin solution dose, oral heparin solid dose, oral lmwh solid dose, oral lmwh solution dose, oral salmon calcitonin, oral recombinant parathyroid harmone, oral recombinant human growth harmone, oral insulin, oral cromolyn sodium, oral ciliary neutrophic growth factor and oral daptomycin.

Primary SIC and add'l.: 8731 2834

CIK No: 0000805326

Officers: Michael V. Novinski/CEO, Pres., Barbara E. Mohl/Assist. VP - Human Resources, Shepard M. Goldberg/Sr. VP - Operations/$391,035.00, Steven M. Dinh/VP - Research, Technology Development, Lewis H. Bender/CTO/$483,986.00, Richard E. Connor/Assist. VP - Quality, Facilities, Elliot M. Maza/52/CFO/$114,001.00, Ehud Arbit/VP - Medical Research, Laura Kragie/VP - Clinical Development, Chief Medical Officer, Bob Madison/Sr. Dir. - Corporate Communications

Directors: Robert J. Levenson/Dir., Michael Black/Dir., Bernard Zinman/Member - Scientific Advisory Board, Julio Rosenstock/Member - Scientific Advisory Board, Steven E. Kahn/Member - Scientific Advisory Board, Robert A. Gelfand/Member - Scientific Advisory Board, Howard M. Pack/Dir., Michael M. Goldberg/Dir., Stephen K. Carter/Dir., John D. Harkey/Dir., Mark H. Rachesky/Dir., Michael Weiser/Dir., Arthur Dubroff/Dir., Daniel J. Drucker/Member - Scientific Advisory Board, Jay S. Skyler/Member - Scientific Advisory Board

Financial Data: *Fiscal Year End:*12/31 *Latest Annual Data:* 12/31/2006

Year	Sales	Net Income
2006	$7,259,000	-$41,766,000
2005	$3,540,000	-$18,051,000
2004	$1,953,000	-$37,522,000

Curr. Assets:	$22,831,000	Curr. Liab.:	$9,454,000		
Plant, Equip.:	$2,652,000	Total Liab.:	$34,198,000	Indic. Yr. Divd.:	NA
Total Assets:	$28,092,000	Net Worth:	-$6,106,000	Debt/ Equity:	NA

Emission Differentials Ltd

101, 435- 4th Ave., Calgary, AB, T2P 3A8; *PH:* 1-403-615-7748

General - Incorporation	AB	Stock - Price on:12/24/2007	NA
Employees	NA	Stock Exchange	NA
Auditor	De Joya Griffith & Co., LLC	Ticker Symbol	NA
Stk Agt	Interwest Transfer Co., Inc.	Outstanding Shares	NA
Counsel	NA	E.P.S	NA
DUNS No.	NA	Shareholders	NA

Business: The groups principle activity is to provide recruiting services. The groups service area includes the research and development, engineering, marketing, sales, information technology and manufacturing industries. The group operates from United States.

Primary SIC and add'l.: 8900

CIK No: 0001292428

Officers: Steve Turcotte/41/Dir., CEO, Sec., James Durward/53/Dir., Pres., Andrew Brown/50/COO, Pres., David W. Crombie/66/Dir., CFO

Directors: Steve Turcotte/41/Dir., CEO, Sec., Carl Roland Jonsson/72/Dir., James Durward/53/Dir., Pres., Patrick Shannon/67/Dir., David W. Crombie/66/Dir., CFO, John R. MacMillan/66/Dir.

Owners: Steven J. Turcotte/68.21%

Financial Data: *Fiscal Year End:*12/31 *Latest Annual Data:* 04/30/2007

Year	Sales	Net Income
2007	NA	-$41,000
2006	NA	-$29,000

Curr. Assets:	$3,000	Curr. Liab.:	$2,000		
Plant, Equip.:	NA	Total Liab.:	$20,000	Indic. Yr. Divd.:	NA
Total Assets:	$3,000	Net Worth:	-$17,000	Debt/ Equity:	NA

Emmis Communications Corp

1 Emmis Plz., 40 Monument Cir., Ste. 700, Indianapolis, IN, 46204; *PH:* 1-317-266-0100; *Fax:* 1-317-631-3750; *http://* www.emmis.com; *Email:* ir@emmis.com

General - Incorporation	IN	Stock - Price on:12/24/2007	$9.55
Employees	1,500	Stock Exchange	NDQ
Auditor	Ernst & Young LLP	Ticker Symbol	EMMS
Stk Agt	Wachovia Bank N.A	Outstanding Shares	37,530,000
Counsel	NA	E.P.S	NA
DUNS No.	02-666-2379	Shareholders	NA

Business: The group's principal activities are radio broadcasting, television broadcasting and magazine publishing. The group owns and operates twenty-three FM radio stations and four AM radio stations in New York city, los angeles and Chicago, as well as phoenix, st louis, indianapolis and terre haute, Indiana. The group also owns and operates sixteen television stations in mid-sized markets in the us and in the markets of portland and orlando. It also operates a news information radio network in Indiana, publish Texas monthly, los angeles, atlanta, indianapolis monthly, cincinnati and country sampler and related magazines and operates an international radio business. During 2003, the group acquired substantially all of the assets of wbpg-TV in mobile, al-pensacola & pegasus communications corporation and has discontinued the operations of votionis that owns and operates two radio stations in buenos aires, Argentina.

Primary SIC and add'l.: 4833 4832 2721

CIK No: 0000783005

Subsidiaries: Ciudad, LLC, dExpres, a.s., Emmis Austin Radio Broadcasting Company, L.P., Emmis Belgium Broadcasting NV, Emmis Bulgarian Broadcasting EOOD, Emmis Communications Corporation, Emmis Enterprises, Inc., Emmis Indiana Broadcasting, L.P., Emmis International Broadcasting Corporation, Emmis License Corporation of New York, Emmis Meadowlands Corporation, Emmis Operating Company, Emmis Publishing Corporation, Emmis Publishing, L.P., Emmis Radio License Corporation of New York 27 Subsidiaries included in the Index

Officers: Jeffrey H. Smulyan/61/Chmn., CEO, Pres./$1,942,160.00, Richard F. Cummings/Radio Division Pres./$1,412,041.00, Mickey Levitan/Chief Human Resources Officer, Gary L. Kaseff/Dir., Exec. VP, General Counsel/$1,075,774.00, Paul W. Fiddick/Pres. - Emmis International/$651,088.00, Gary Thoe/Pres. - Emmis Publishing LP, Barbara Brill/Sr. VP - Emmis International, Paul V. Brenner/VP - Integrated Technologie, Patrick Walsh/41/CFO/$517,803.00, Scott J. Enright/Sr. VP, Assoc. General Counsel, Sec., David R. Newcomer/Sr. VP - Finance, Assist. Sec./$370,035.00, Curtis E. Taylor/Sr. VP - Information Technology, Marty Draper/VP - Engineering, Norman H. Gurwitz/VP - Administration, Assist. Sec., Ryan A. Hornaday/VP - Finance, Assist. Treasurer *(17 Officers included in Index)*

Directors: Jeffrey H. Smulyan/61/Chmn., CEO, Pres., Greg A. Nathanson/Dir., Richard A. Leventhal/Dir., Gary L. Kaseff/Dir., Exec. VP, General Counsel, Susan Bayh/Dir., Peter Lund/Dir., Lawrence Sorrel/Dir.

Financial Data: *Fiscal Year End:*02/28 *Latest Annual Data:* 2/28/2007

Year	Sales	Net Income
2007	$359,535,000	$113,581,000
2006	$387,381,000	$357,771,000
2005	$618,460,000	-$304,368,000

Curr. Assets:	$119,009,000	Curr. Liab.:	$59,981,000	P/E Ratio:	3.72
Plant, Equip.:	$61,488,000	Total Liab.:	$776,179,000	Indic. Yr. Divd.:	NA
Total Assets:	$1,207,904,000	Net Worth:	$237,195,000	Debt/ Equity:	2.0967

Empire District Electric Co (The)

602 Joplin St., Joplin, MO, 64801; *PH:* 1-417-625-5100; *Fax:* 1-417-625-5146; *http://* www.empiredistrict.com

General - Incorporation	KS	Stock - Price on:12/24/2007	$22.2
Employees	705	Stock Exchange	NYSE
Auditor	PricewaterhouseCoopers LLP	Ticker Symbol	EDE
Stk Agt	Wells Fargo Bank, N.A.	Outstanding Shares	30,360,000
Counsel	NA	E.P.S	$1.38
DUNS No.	00-696-5305	Shareholders	NA

Business: The group's principal activities are to generate, purchase, transmit, distribute and sell electricity in parts of Missouri, Kansas, Oklahoma and Arkansas. The group also provides water service to three towns in Missouri. The group provides electric service at retail to 119 incorporated communities and to various unincorporated areas and at wholesale to four municipally-owned distribution systems and two rural electric cooperatives. The group operates under franchises having original terms of twenty years or longer in virtually all of the incorporated communities. The group also offers electronic monitored security services, generators, surge suppressors, decorative lighting and other energy services. On 01-Feb-2003, the group acquired joplin.com holdings, inc.

Primary SIC and add'l.: 4911 4941

CIK No: 0000032689

Subsidiaries: Conversant, Inc., EDE Holdings, Inc., Empire District Industries, Inc., Fast Freedom, Inc., Mid-America Precision Products, LLC, The Empire District Gas Company, Utility Intelligence, Inc.

Officers: William L. Gipson/Dir., CEO, Pres./$759,906.00, Bradley P. Beecher/COO, VP - Electric/$255,090.00, Laurie A. Delano/Controller, Assist. Sec., Assist. Treasurer, Kelly S. Walters/VP - Regulatory, General Services, Ronald F. Gatz/COO, VP - Gas/$227,053.00, Gregory A. Knapp/CFO, VP - Finance/$257,054.00, Michael E. Palmer/VP - Commercial Operations/$262,506.00, Janet S. Watson/Sec., Treasurer, Amy Bass/Dir. - Corporate Communications, Julie Maus/Communications Specialist, Robin Hardin/Sr. Shareholder Relations Specialist, Harold Colgin/VP - Energy Supply, Emily Stanley/Communications Coordinator

Directors: William L. Gipson/Dir., CEO, Pres., Myron W. McKinney/63/Chmn., Allan T. Thoms/69/Dir., Mary McCleary Posner/68/Dir., Julio S. Leon/Dir., Bill D. Helton/69/Dir., Kenneth R. Allen/50/Dir., Ross C. Hartley/Dir., Thomas B. Mueller/60/Dir., Randy D. Laney/Dir.

Owners: Allan T. Thoms, Gregory A. Knapp, William L. Gipson, Bradley P. Beecher, Insiders, Randy D. Laney, Insiders, Michael E. Palmer, Bill D. Helton, Mary M. Posner, Ross C. Hartley, Myron W. McKinney, Ronald A. Gatz, Julio S. Leon, Thomas B. Mueller *(16 Owners included in Index)*

Financial Data: *Fiscal Year End:*12/31 *Latest Annual Data:* 12/31/2006

Year	Sales	Net Income
2006	$413,453,000	$39,280,000
2005	$386,160,000	$23,768,000
2004	$325,540,000	$21,848,000

Curr. Assets:	$128,100,000	Curr. Liab.:	$146,111,000	P/E Ratio:	15.31
Plant, Equip.:	$1,030,994,000	Total Liab.:	$847,279,000	Indic. Yr. Divd.:	$1.280
Total Assets:	$1,315,888,000	Net Worth:	$468,609,000	Debt/ Equity:	NA

Empire Energy Corpo International

16801 W 116th St., Ste. 100, Lenexa, KS, 66219; *PH:* 1-913-469-5615; *Fax:* 1-913-469-1662; *http://* www.empireenergy.com; *Email:* info@empireenergy.com

General - Incorporation	NV	Stock - Price on:12/24/2007	NA
Employees	NA	Stock Exchange	OTC
Auditor	Uhy Haines Norton	Ticker Symbol	EEGC
Stk Agt	Interwest Transfer Company, Inc.	Outstanding Shares	NA
Counsel	NA	E.P.S	-$0.04
DUNS No.	NA	Shareholders	NA

Business: The groups principal activities include exploring, producing and mining oil and gas. The group operates from Tasmania, Australia and the United States.

Primary SIC and add'l.: 1311

CIK No: 0000788206

Subsidiaries: Blue Mountain Resources Inc., Commonwealth Energy (USA) Inc., Cyber-Finance Limited, Great South Land Minerals Limited, Pacific Rim Foods Ltd

Officers: S. A. Sehsuvaroglu/Dir., CEO, Pres., Tara Ledbetter/Executive Assist.

Financial Data: *Fiscal Year End:*12/31 *Latest Annual Data:* 12/31/2006

Year	Sales	Net Income
2006	NA	-$9,030,000
2005	NA	-$1,898,000
2004	NA	-$1,579,000

Curr. Assets:	$6,678,000	Curr. Liab.:	$2,965,000		
Plant, Equip.:	$1,360,000	Total Liab.:	$8,891,000	Indic. Yr. Divd.:	NA
Total Assets:	$15,213,000	Net Worth:	$6,322,000	Debt/ Equity:	NA

Empire Financial Holding Co

2170 W State Rd. 434, Ste. 100, Longwood, FL, 32779; *PH:* 1-407-774-1300; *Fax:* 1-407-682-5867; *http://* www.empirefinancialgroup.com

General - Incorporation	FL	Stock- Price on:12/24/2007	$1.41
Employees	153	Stock Exchange	AMEX
Auditor	Miller, Ellin & Co. LLP	Ticker Symbol	EFH
Stk Agt	Continental Stock Transfer & Trust Co	Outstanding Shares	11,010,000
Counsel	Greenberg Traurig Askew Et Al	E.P.S	-$0.541
DUNS No.	NA	Shareholders	NA

Business: The group's principal activity is to provide financial brokerage services to institutional, retail and wholesale customers. The group operates in two business segments: retail brokerage services and advisory services and order execution and market making services. Retail brokerage services segment includes sale of equities and mutual funds and fixed income products are provided on a discount basis to retail and institutional customers through online trading. Clearing and order execution services segment fills orders to purchase or sell securities received from approximately independent broker dealers on behalf of their retail customers. Services are delivered through the Internet and traditional means. It also involves account settlement and delivery functions.

Primary SIC and add'l.: 9999 6211 6719 6282

CIK No: 0001094320

Subsidiaries: Empire Financial Group, Inc., Empire Investment Advisors, Inc.

Officers: Donald A. Wojnowski/48/Dir., CEO, Pres./$568,275.00, James Matthew/CFO/$190,791.00, John J. Wilson/Chief Compliance Officer/$292,865.00, Gerard A. Mastrianni/Dir. - Trading, Ed Cabrera/Contact

Directors: Donald A. Wojnowski/48/Dir., CEO, Pres.

Owners: Steven A. Horowitz, Stephen J. DeGroat, Kirk M. Warshaw, Donald A. Wojnowski, Insiders, The Gagne First Revocable Trust, John J. Wilson, EFH Partners, LLC, Bradley L. Gordon, John C. Rudy, Steven M. Rabinovici, William F. Moreno, James M. Matthew

Financial Data: *Fiscal Year End:*12/31 *Latest Annual Data:* 12/31/2006

Year	Sales	Net Income
2006	$35,642,000	$11,000
2005	$22,486,000	$2,462,000
2004	$21,596,000	-$1,572,000

Curr. Assets:	$5,912,000	Curr. Liab.:	$8,352,000		
Plant, Equip.:	$637,000	Total Liab.:	$15,825,000	Indic. Yr. Divd.:	NA
Total Assets:	$33,786,000	Net Worth:	$17,960,000	Debt/ Equity:	0.4160

Empire Global Corp

501 Alliance Ave., Ste. 400, Toronto, ON, M6N 2J1; *PH:* 1-416-769-8788; *http://* www.empireglobalcorp.com; *Email:* info@EmpireGlobalCorp.com

General - Incorporation	DE	Stock- Price on:12/24/2007	NA
Employees	NA	Stock Exchange	OTC
Auditor	SF Partnership LLP	Ticker Symbol	EMGL
Stk Agt	Signature Stock Transfer, Inc.	Outstanding Shares	NA
Counsel	Gary L. Blum Esq	E.P.S	NA
DUNS No.	NA	Shareholders	NA

Business: The groups principle activities include acquiring, developing and managing real estate properties. The group operates from United States.

Primary SIC and add'l.: NA

CIK No: 0001080319

Subsidiaries: 501 Canada Inc., Blazing Holdings, Inc., Brookstreet Capital Corp., Empire Global Acquisition Corp., Excel Empire Ltd., Foreign Invested Enterprise, IMM Investments Inc., IMM Investments, Inc., Montebello Developments Corp, Real Estate Development Co. Ltd.

Financial Data: *Fiscal Year End:*12/31 *Latest Annual Data:* 12/31/2005

Year	Sales	Net Income
2005	$636,000	-$631,000
2004	NA	-$140,000
2003	NA	-$6,000

Curr. Assets:	$424,000	Curr. Liab.:	$918,000		
Plant, Equip.:	$6,334,000	Total Liab.:	$8,238,000	Indic. Yr. Divd.:	NA
Total Assets:	$9,955,000	Net Worth:	$1,717,000	Debt/ Equity:	NA

Empire Petroleum Corp

15 E 5th St., Ste. 4000, Tulsa, OK, 74103; *PH:* 1-918-587-8093

General - Incorporation	DE	Stock- Price on:12/24/2007	$0.1
Employees	1	Stock Exchange	OTC
Auditor	Tullius Taylor Sartain & Sartain LLP	Ticker Symbol	EMPR
Stk Agt	Securities Transfer Corp	Outstanding Shares	50,080,000
Counsel	NA	E.P.S	-$0.03
DUNS No.	93-833-8290	Shareholders	NA

Business: The group's principal activities are exploring oil and natural gases. The group extracts oil and natural gases in the cheyenne river development project. The group has no income producing properties and its principal asset is substantially unexplored. Oil and natural gas test well were drilled on the cheyenne river development project. The test well encountered continual flows of oil and natural gas during the drilling period and was subsequently completed as an oil well.

Primary SIC and add'l.: 1041 1382 1389

CIK No: 0000887396

Officers: Albert E. Whitehead/77/Chmn., CEO

Directors: Albert E. Whitehead/77/Chmn., CEO, John C. Kinard/73/Dir., Montague H. Hackett/75/Dir.

Owners: Insiders/35.41%, George H. Plewes/6.55%, Albert E. Whitehead/26.89%, Montague H. Hackett/7.37%, John C. Kinard/1.15%

Financial Data: *Fiscal Year End:*12/31 *Latest Annual Data:* 06/30/2007

Year	Sales	Net Income
2007	$5,000	-$429,000
2006	$102,000	-$318,000
2005	$58,000	-$158,000

Curr. Assets:	$151,000	Curr. Liab.:	$492,000		
Plant, Equip.:	$1,800,000	Total Liab.:	$510,000	Indic. Yr. Divd.:	NA
Total Assets:	$1,951,000	Net Worth:	$1,440,000	Debt/ Equity:	NA

Empire Resorts Inc

701 N Green Valley Pkwy, Ste. 200, Henderson, NV, 89074; *PH:* 1-702-990-3355; *Fax:* 1-845-791-1402; *http://* www.empireresorts.com

General - Incorporation	DE	Stock- Price on:12/24/2007	$8.26
Employees	370	Stock Exchange	NDQ
Auditor	Friedman LLP	Ticker Symbol	NYNY
Stk Agt	Continental Stock Transfer & Trust Co	Outstanding Shares	29,490,000
Counsel	NA	E.P.S	-$0.56
DUNS No.	84-791-5311	Shareholders	NA

Business: The group's principal activity is to own, develop and operate gaming facilities in New York. It currently operates monticello raceway, a harness track in the catskills area of New York. The group is also working to develop the site into a multi-dimensional gaming resort, including horse racing, video gaming machines and a native American owned casino called the cayuga catskill resort. On 30-Jun-2004, the group opened the mighty m gaming racetrack at monticello raceway, featuring 1,743 video gaming machines and amenities such as a 350 seat buffet and live nightly entertainment.

Primary SIC and add'l.: 6719 7999 5812 7011

CIK No: 0000906780

Subsidiaries: Alpha Casino Management Inc., Alpha Entertainment, Inc., Alpha Florida Entertainment, LLC, Alpha Greenville Hotel, Inc., Alpha Gulf Coast, Inc., Alpha Missouri, Inc., Alpha Monticello, Inc., Alpha Peach Tree Corporation, Alpha Rising Sun, Inc., Alpha St. Regis, Inc., Empire Resorts Holdings, Inc., Empire Resorts Sub, Inc., Jubilation Lakeshore, Inc., Mohawk Management, LLC, Monticello Casino Management, LLC 18 Subsidiaries included in the Index

Officers: David P. Hanlon/Dir., CEO, Pres./$2,416,262.00, Linda Kaempf/Dir. - Corporate Development, Thomas W. Aro/COO/$312,640.00, Charles A. Degliomini/VP - Communications, Government Relations, Ronald Radcliffe/CFO/$636,069.00, Hilda A. Manuel/Sr. VP - Native American Government Relations/$321,916.00

Directors: David P. Hanlon/Dir., CEO, Pres., John Sharpe/Chmn., Paul A. Debary/Dir., Ralph J. Bernstein/Dir., Robert H. Friedman/Dir., Frank Catania/Dir.

Owners: Patricia Cohen/100.00%, Hilda Manuel, Wells Fargo & Company/5.47%, Joseph E. Bernstein/7.08%, Robert H. Friedman, Paul A. deBary, Frank Catania, Ralph J. Bernstein/7.72%, Bryanston Group, Inc./89.60%, Ronald J. Radcliffe, John Sharpe, Insiders/19.39%, Thomas W. Aro, Concord Associates, L.P./11.89%, David P. Hanlon/3.09% *(16 Owners included in Index)*

Financial Data: *Fiscal Year End:*12/31 *Latest Annual Data:* 12/31/2006

Year	Sales	Net Income
2006	$98,110,000	-$7,076,000
2005	$86,764,000	-$18,527,000
2004	$44,875,000	-$12,745,000

Curr. Assets:	$18,016,000	Curr. Liab.:	$21,287,000		
Plant, Equip.:	$31,703,000	Total Liab.:	$86,287,000	Indic. Yr. Divd.:	NA
Total Assets:	$60,564,000	Net Worth:	-$25,723,000	Debt/ Equity:	NA

Empire Resources Inc

1 Pk.er Plz., Fort Lee, NJ, 07024; *PH:* 1-201-944-2200; *Fax:* 1-201-944-2226; *http://* www.empireresources.com

General - Incorporation	DE	Stock- Price on:12/24/2007	$10.09
Employees	65	Stock Exchange	AMEX
Auditor	Eisner LLP	Ticker Symbol	ERS
Stk Agt	American Stock Transfer & Trust Co.	Outstanding Shares	9,790,000
Counsel	Goodwin, Procter & Hoar	E.P.S	$0.57
DUNS No.	80-600-8421	Shareholders	NA

Business: The group's principal activity is to distribute semi-finished aluminum products, which includes aluminum sheet, plate and foil, rod, bar and wire, extruded and cast products and aluminum powder and paste. The group also provides services to its customers such as arranging for products to be stored in warehouse facilities, information concerning market trends and product development, arranging for subsequent metal processing or finishing services required by the customer. The operations of the group are carried on in the United States, Canada, Australia and New Zealand.

Primary SIC and add'l.: 5051

CIK No: 0001019272

Subsidiaries: 6900 Quad Avenue LLC, CompuPrint Ltd., Empire Resources Extrusions LLC, Empire Resources Pacific Ltd., I.T.I. Innovative Technology, Ltd., Imbali

Officers: Nathan Kahn/53/Dir., CEO, Pres./$904,000.00, Harvey Wrubel/54/Dir., VP - Sales/$2,129,300.00, Sandra Kahn/50/Dir., CFO/$329,000.00, Peter G. Howard/72/Dir., Regional MD - Australia, Asia, David Kronfeld/Investor Relations Officer, Ross Toombs/Dir. - Information Technology, Joe Wolf/GM - Empire Resources Extrusions LLC, Ginette Raymond/Mgr. - Customer Service, Andrew Sabel/Mgr. - Marketing, Sales, Western Region, Jeff Lowy/Mgr. - Sales, Alan Papier/Mgr. - Sales, Tom Lehr/Sr. Logistics Mgr., Joseph Appel/Mgr. - Logistics, Charles Davis/Mgr. - Logistics, Jane Barnett/Marketing Administrator *(18 Officers included in Index)*

Directors: Nathan Kahn/53/Dir., CEO, Pres., William Spier/73/Non - Exec. Chmn., Nathan Mazurek/46/Dir., Sandra Kahn/50/Dir., CFO, Peter G. Howard/72/Dir., Regional MD - Australia, Asia, Harvey Wrubel/54/Dir., VP - Sales, Morris J. Smith/50/Dir., Jack Bendheim/61/Dir., L. R. Milner/62/Dir.

Owners: William Spier/0.50%, Harvey Wrubel/4.30%, Nathan Mazurek, Nathan Kahn/38.50%, Sandra Kahn/38.50%, Insiders/42.60%, Peter G. Howard

Financial Data: *Fiscal Year End:*12/31 *Latest Annual Data:* 12/31/2006

Year	Sales	Net Income
2006	$425,980,000	$8,739,000
2005	$358,476,000	$9,544,000
2004	$212,550,000	$4,810,000

Curr. Assets:	$191,738,000	Curr. Liab.:	$167,115,000	P/E Ratio:	14.01
Plant, Equip.:	$7,739,000	Total Liab.:	$169,286,000	Indic. Yr. Divd.:	$0.200
Total Assets:	$199,885,000	Net Worth:	$30,599,000	Debt/ Equity:	0.0709

Empresa Brasileira de Aeronautica S.A.

276 SW 34th St., Fort Lauderdale, FL, 33315; *PH:* 1-954-359-3700; *Fax:* 1-954-359-8170; *http://* www.embraer.com; *Email:* investor.relations@embraer.com.br

General - Incorporation.....Federative Republic of Brazil.......	Stock - Price on:12/24/2007.............................NA
Employees..19,265	Stock Exchange......................................NYSE
Auditor ....Deloitte Touche Tohmatsu CPA Ltd	Ticker Symbol...ERJ
Stk Agt.................................Bank of New York	Outstanding Shares........................184,980,000
Counsel..NA	E.P.S...$1.69
DUNS No. ....NA	Shareholders...NA

Business: The groups principle activities include assembling and selling aircraft. The group operates through three segments namely, commercial aviation, defense and government, and executive aviation. The group operates from the Brazil. The group's quarterly revenue for September 2007 was 2,728.72 millions of USD.

Primary SIC and add'l.: 3721

CIK No: 0001355444

Subsidiaries: Air Holding SGPS, S.A., Canal Investments LLC, ECC do Brasil Cia de Seguros, ECC Insurance & Financial Company Ltd., ECC Investment Switzerland AG Swin, ECC Leasing Company Ltd., ELEB-Embraer Liebherr Equipamentos do Brasil S.A., Embraer Aircraft Customer Services, Inc. (EACS), Embraer Aircraft Holding, Inc (EAH), Embraer Aircraft Maintenance Services, Inc. (EAMS), Embraer Aircraft Marketing Corp. (EMC), Embraer Australia Pty Ltd. (EAL), Embraer Aviation Europe - EAE, Embraer Aviation International (EAI), Embraer Credit Ltd. (ECL) 27 Subsidiaries included in the Index

Officers: Frederico Fleury Curado/CEO, Pres., Flavio Rimoli/Exec. VP - Legal Counsel, Luis Carlos Affonso/Exec. VP - Executive Aviation, Luiz Carlos Siqueira Aguiar/43/Exec. VP - Defense Marketing, Governments, Vitor Sarquis Hallack/Dir., Vice - Pres., Mauro Kern Junior/Exec. VP - Airline Marketing, Edson Carlos Mallaco/Sr. VP - Aviation Services, Emilio Kazunoli Matsuo/56/Sr. VP - Engineering, Satoshi Yokota/67/Exec. VP - Strategic Planning, Technology Development, Artur Aparecido Valerio Coutinho/Exec. VP - Industrial Operations, Antonio Luiz Pizarro Manso/Exec. VP - Corporate, CFO, Horacio Aragones Forjaz/56/Exec. VP - Corporate Communications, Antonio Julio Franco/VP - Organizational Development, Personnel, Henrique Rzezinski/VP - External Relations

Directors: Mauricio Novis Botelho/66/Chmn., Vitor Sarquis Hallack/Dir., Vice - Pres., Jose Reinaldo Magalhaes/Dir., Wilson Carlos Duarte Delfino/Dir., Neimar Dieguez Barreiro/Dir., Boris Tabacof/Dir., Eduardo Salomao Neto/Dir., Hermann Wever/Dir., Samir Zraick/Dir., Paulo Cesar De Souza Lucas/Dir., Claudemir Marques De Almeida/Dir.

Owners: BNDESPAR/5.00%, Unio Federal/Brazilian Government, Safran/1.10%, PREVI/13.90%, Dassault Aviation, Bozano Group/9.70%, Insiders/0.50%, SISTEL/3.00%

Financial Data: Fiscal Year End:12/31   Latest Annual Data: 12/31/2006

Year	Sales	Net Income
2006	$3,807,403,000	$390,140,000
2004	$3,440,533,000	$380,206,000
2003	$2,143,460,000	$136,044,000

Curr. Assets:	$4,759,721,000	Curr. Liab.:	$3,018,798,000	P/E Ratio:	13.97
Plant, Equip.:	$412,244,000	Total Liab.:	$5,441,420,000	Indic. Yr. Divd.:	$0.540
Total Assets:	$7,315,701,000	Net Worth:	$1,874,281,000	Debt/ Equity:	NA

Empresa Nacional de Electricidad S.A.

Santa Rosa 76, Santiago; **Fax:** 56-26354980; **http://** www.endesa.cl

General - Incorporation ....Chile	Stock - Price on:12/24/2007 ....$48.45
Employees..NA	Stock Exchange......................................NYSE
Auditor ....Deloitte & Touche LLP	Ticker Symbol..EOC
Stk Agt.................JP Morgan Chase Bank, N.A.	Outstanding Shares........................273,390,000
Counsel..NA	E.P.S..$1.20
DUNS No. ....NA	Shareholders...NA

Business: The groups principle activity is to generate electricity. The group acquired Ingendesa S.A. in the year 2005 and Inversiones Lo Venecia Ltda in the year 2006. The group operates from Argentina, Brazil, Peru, Chile and Columbia. The group's quarterly revenue for September 2007 was 529.75 millions of USD.

Primary SIC and add'l.: 4923 4924 4932 4911

CIK No: 0000926864

Subsidiaries: Cachoeira DouradaS.A., Capital de EnergaS.A., Central Hidroelctrica BetaniaS.A., Compaia Elctrica Cono SurS.A., Compaia Elctrica San IsidroS.A., Compaia Elctrica TarapacS.A., EdegelS.A., EmgesaS.A., Endesa ArgentinaS.A., Endesa Brasil Participacoes Ltda., Endesa Chile Internacional, Endesa de ColombiaS.A., Endesa EcoS.A., EndesaCostanera S.A., EnigesaS.A. 25 Subsidiaries included in the Index

Officers: Rafael Mateo Alcala/CEO, Renato Fernandez Baeza/Communications, Carlos Martin Vergara/Legal Counsel, Manuel Irarrazaval Aldunate/Administration, Finance, Juan Carlos Mundaca alvarez/Human Resources, Julio Valbuena Sanchez/Planning, Control, Jose Venegas Maluenda/Trading, Commercialization, Rafael Errazuriz Ruiz-Tagle/Energy Planning, Juan Benabarre Benaiges/Production, Transport, Claudio Iglesis Guillard/Generacion Chile, Jose Miguel Granged Brunen/Generation, Argentina, Administracion de Principales Filiales, Francisco Bugallo Sanchez/Generation, Brazil, Administracion de Principales Filiales, Lucio Rubio Diaz/Generation, Colombia, Administracion de Principales Filiales, Jose Griso Gines/Generation, Peru, Administracion de Principales Filiales

Directors: Mario Valcarce Duran/Chmn., Jose Maria Calvo-Sotelo Ibanez-Martin/Dir., Rafael Espanol Navarro/Dir., Enrique Garcia alvarez/Dir., Carlos Torres Vila/Dir., Jose Fernandez Olano/Dir., Jaime Estevez Valencia/Dir., Leonidas Vial Echeverria/Dir., Raimundo Valenzuela Lang/Dir.

Owners: Citibank, N.A/4.38%, Enersis/59.98%, Insiders

Financial Data: Fiscal Year End:12/31   Latest Annual Data: 12/31/2006

Year	Sales	Net Income
2006	$2,540,530,000	$402,598,000
2005	$2,133,774,000	$190,524,000
2004	$1,858,792,000	$116,551,000

Curr. Assets:	$794,817,000	Curr. Liab.:	$877,073,000	P/E Ratio:	11.08
Plant, Equip.:	$7,198,812,000	Total Liab.:	$6,736,286,000	Indic. Yr. Divd.:	$0.570
Total Assets:	$9,479,857,000	Net Worth:	$2,743,570,000	Debt/ Equity:	NA

Empresa Nacional De Electricidad SA

Formerly: National Electricity Co of Chile Inc
Santa Rosa 76, Santiago; **PH:** 56-263-09000

General - Incorporation ....Chile	Stock - Price on:12/24/2007 ....$49.59
Employees..NA	Stock Exchange...NA
Auditor ....Ernst & Young LTDA.	Ticker Symbol..NA
Stk Agt ....NA	Outstanding Shares........................273,390,000
Counsel..NA	E.P.S...NA
DUNS No. ....NA	Shareholders...NA

Business: The group's principal activities are the generation and supply of electric energy, together with consulting and engineering services in all expertise areas.

Primary SIC and add'l.: 4911

CIK No: 0000926864

Subsidiaries: Cachoeira DouradaS.A., Capital de EnergaS.A., Central Hidroelctrica BetaniaS.A., Compaia Elctrica Cono SurS.A., Compaia Elctrica San IsidroS.A., Compaia Elctrica TarapacS.A., EdegelS.A., EmgesaS.A., Endesa ArgentinaS.A., Endesa Brasil Participacoes Ltda., Endesa Chile Internacional, Endesa de ColombiaS.A., Endesa EcoS.A., EndesaCostanera S.A., EnigesaS.A. 25 Subsidiaries included in the Index

Officers: Rafael Mateo Alcala/CEO, Jose Venegas Maluenda/Trading, Commercialization, Renato Fernandez Baeza/Communications, Carlos Martin Vergara/Legal Counsel, Claudio Iglesis Guillard/Generacion Chile, Julio Valbuena Sanchez/Planning, Control, Rafael Errazuriz Ruiz-Tagle/Energy Planning, Juan Benabarre Benaiges/Production, Transport, Jose Miguel Granged Brunen/Generation, Argentina, Francisco Bugallo Sanchez/Generation, Brazil, Lucio Rubio Diaz/Generation, Colombia, Jose Griso Gines/Generation, Peru, Manuel Irarrazaval Aldunate/Administration, Finance, Juan Carlos Mundaca alvarez/Human Resources

Directors: Carlos Torres Vila/Vice Chmn., Mario Valcarce Duran/Chmn., Jose Fernandez Olano/Dir., Jaime Estevez Valencia/Dir., Leonidas Vial Echeverria/Dir., Raimundo Valenzuela Lang/Dir., Jose Maria Calvo-sotelo Ibanez-Martin/Dir., Rafael Espanol Navarro/Dir., Enrique Garcia alvarez/Dir.

Owners: Enersis/59.98%, Citibank, N.A./4.38%, Insiders/0.00%

Empresas Ica Soc Contrladora

Mineria No. 145, Edificio Central, Distrito Federal, 11800; **PH:** 52-2126886840;
http:// www.ica.com.mx

General - Incorporation	Stock - Price on:12/24/2007.................$58.98
Employees..NA	Stock Exchange......................................NYSE
Auditor ....NA	Ticker Symbol...ICA
Stk Agt ....Bank of New York	Outstanding Shares..........................67,540,000
Counsel..NA	E.P.S..$0.69
DUNS No. ....NA	Shareholders...NA

Business: The groups principle activity is to provide recruiting services. The groups service area includes the research and development, engineering, marketing, sales, information technology and manufacturing industries. The group operates from United States.

Primary SIC and add'l.: 1522 1521 4581 4941 1629 1541 1542 4789 6552 1623 1611 1622 1794

CIK No:

Officers: Jose Luis Guerrero/Dir., CEO, Bernardo Quintana/Dir., Pres., Sergio Montano/Dir., Exec. VP - Administration, Luis Fernando Zarate/Dir., VP - Housing, Jorge Aguirre/Dir., VP - Civil Construction

Directors: Jose Luis Guerrero/Dir., CEO, Sergio Montano/Dir., Exec. VP - Administration, Bernardo Quintana/Dir., Pres., Jorge Borja Navarrete/Dir., Emilio Carrillo/Dir., Alberto Escofet/Dir., Luis Fernando Zarate/Dir., VP - Housing, Jorge Aguirre/Dir., VP - Civil Construction, Juan Claudio Salles/Dir., Esteban Malpica/Dir., Angeles Espinoza/Dir., Elmer Franco/Dir., Alberto Mulas/Dir., Francisco Garza/Dir., Fernando Ruiz/Dir. (18 Directors included in Index)

Financial Data: Fiscal Year End:NA Latest Annual Data: 12/31/2006

Year	Sales	Net Income
2006	$1,985,523,000	$43,309,000
2005	$1,711,656,000	$43,093,000
2004	$1,174,929,000	$3,304,000

Curr. Assets:	$2,174,990,000	Curr. Liab.:	$1,291,240,000	P/E Ratio:	11.08
Plant, Equip.:	$323,251,000	Total Liab.:	$2,477,623,000	Indic. Yr. Divd.:	NA
Total Assets:	$3,299,922,000	Net Worth:	$822,298,000	Debt/ Equity:	NA

Empyrean Holdings Inc

2537 S Gessner, Ste 114, Houston, TX, 77063; **PH:** 1-713-260-7236; **Fax:** 1-713-243-8714;
http:// www.epyh.com; **Email:** info@epyh.com

General - Incorporation ....NV	Stock - Price on:12/24/2007 ....$0.05
Employees..NA	Stock Exchange......................................OTC
Auditor ....Malone & Bailey, P.C	Ticker Symbol......................................EMPY
Stk Agt ....Pacific Stock Transfer Company	Outstanding Shares............................9,860,000
Counsel..NA	E.P.S...-$0.099
DUNS No. ....NA	Shareholders...NA

Business: The group's principal activity was to provide secure and quality optical digital broadband services on both domestic and international basis. The broadband services enable to meet the voice, data and video communications needs of business on optical network which interface with private lines and private networks, coaxial cable and wireless networks. The group intends to move into the basalt fiber manufacturing and derivative products business which will produce coated mineral fiber in the form of continuous basalt glass filament.

Primary SIC and add'l.: 9999

CIK No: 0001076886

Officers: Robert L. Lee/65/Dir., CEO, Pres., Sec., Treasurer, William Melchiori/58/Dir., CFO

Directors: Robert L. Lee/65/Dir., CEO, Pres., Sec., Treasurer, William Melchiori/58/Dir., CFO

Financial Data: Fiscal Year End:12/31 Latest Annual Data: 12/31/2006

Year	Sales	Net Income
2006	$7,000	-$331,000
2005	NA	-$615,000
2004	NA	-$348,000

Curr. Assets:	$136,000	Curr. Liab.:	$32,000		
Plant, Equip.:	$387,000	Total Liab.:	$32,000	Indic. Yr. Divd.:	NA
Total Assets:	$522,000	Net Worth:	$491,000	Debt/ Equity:	NA

Emrise Corp

9485 HAve.n Ave., Ste. 100, Rancho Cucamonga, CA, 91730; *PH:* 1-909-987-9220; *Fax:* 1-909-987-9228; *http://* www.emrise.com; *Email:* info@emrise.com

General - Incorporation	DE	**Stock**- Price on:12/24/2007	$1.15
Employees	305	Stock Exchange	NYSE
Auditor	Grant Thornton LLP	Ticker Symbol	ERI
Stk Agt	Computershare Investor Services LLC	Outstanding Shares	NA
Counsel	NA	E.P.S	-$0.107
DUNS No.	NA	Shareholders	NA

Business: The group's principal activity is to manufacture defense and aerospace electronic components and subsystems, as well as communications equipment. It operates through two segments: electronic components and communications equipment. The electronic components segment, which includes the operations of xet corporation and its international subsidiaries, provides custom power conversion products, digital and rotary switches and subsystem assemblies to the electronic components global market. These products are primarily used in military, aerospace and industrial applications. The communications equipment segment, which consists of cxr telecom corporation and cxr (France) , provides transmission, network access and test equipment to the north American and European communications industry. The group operates out of facilities in the United States, France, the United Kingdom and Japan.

Primary SIC and add'l.: 7379 3679 3661 3672 6719

CIK No: 0000854852

Officers: Carmine T. Oliva/Chmn., CEO, Pres./$363,821.00, Graham Jefferies/COO, Exec. VP/$306,381.00, John Donovan/VP - Finance, Administration

Directors: Carmine T. Oliva/Chmn., CEO, Pres., Richard E. Mahmarian/Dir., Laurence P. Finnegan/Dir., Otis W. Baskin/Dir.

Owners: Randolph D. Foote, Patterson J. McBaine/6.27%, Austin W. Marxe/10.34%, Graham Jefferies, Insiders/5.27%

Financial Data: *Fiscal Year End:*12/31 *Latest Annual Data:* 12/31/2006

Year	Sales	Net Income
2006	$46,384,000	-$3,615,000
2005	$41,270,000	$1,441,000
2004	$29,861,000	$1,480,000

Curr. Assets:	$25,405,000	**Curr. Liab.:**	$15,794,000		
Plant, Equip.:	$2,245,000	**Total Liab.:**	$19,612,000	**Indic. Yr. Divd.:**	NA
Total Assets:	$44,785,000	**Net Worth:**	$25,173,000	**Debt/ Equity:**	0.0633

EMS Technologies Inc

660 Engineering Dr., Norcross, GA, 30092; *PH:* 1-770-263-9200; *Fax:* 1-770-263-9207; *http://* www.ems-t.com

General - Incorporation	GA	**Stock**- Price on:12/24/2007	$21.2
Employees	900	Stock Exchange	NDQ
Auditor	KPMG LLP	Ticker Symbol	ELMG
Stk Agt	Suntrust Bank	Outstanding Shares	15,350,000
Counsel	NA	E.P.S	$2.42
DUNS No.	04-794-9979	Shareholders	NA

Business: The group's principal activities are to design, manufacture and market products that are used in a wide range of wireless communications. It operates through five segments: space and technology, lxe, ems wireless, satcom and satnet. Space and technology division manufactures custom-designed, highly engineered hardware for use in space and satellite communications. Lxe division manufactures wireless mobile computers and wireless local area network products for logistics and other enterprise applications. Ems wireless manufactures base-station antennas and repeaters for pcs/cellular communications systems. Satcom manufactures earth-based antennas, terminals and other hardware for communications via satellite link. Satnet segment focuses on high speed, two way Internet via satellite hubs and terminals. The group has operations in the United States, Canada, France and other foreign countries. Space and technology operations were discontinued in 2003.

Primary SIC and add'l.: 3643 4899 3663 3679

CIK No: 0000032198

Subsidiaries: EMS Investment Holdings, Inc, EMS Technologies Canada, Ltd., favour of Bank of America, National Association (Canada Branch), Thrane & Thrane, Chelton, Ltd.

Officers: Paul B. Domorski/Dir., CEO, Pres./$616,832.00, Timothy C. Reis/VP, General Counsel/$287,772.00, Don T. Scartz/Exec. VP, CFO, Treasurer/$500,395.00, Gary Shell/VP - Corporate Finance, Chief Accounting Officer, Michael R. Robertson/Dir. - Human Resources, Administration, Michael Fatig/VP - Business Development, Steven R. Edgett/VP - Emergency Management Products Group, Gary M. Hebb/VP, GM, Steven J. Chambers/Dir. - Operations, William H. Roeder/Sr. VP, Deputy GM - LXE Inc, Anne Wainscott-Sargent/Corporate, EMS Defense, Space, James S. Childress/Pres., GM/$462,434.00, Perry D. Tanner/VP - Corporate Marketing, David Smith/VP, GM, Joanne Walker/VP - Business Operations *(18 Officers included in Index)*

Directors: Paul B. Domorski/Dir., CEO, Pres., John B. Mowell/Chmn., Thomas W. Oconnell/Dir., Francis J. Erbrick/Dir., Bradford W. Parkinson/Dir., John L. Woodward/Dir., Norman E. Thagard/Dir., Hermann Buerger/Dir., John R. Kreick/Dir.

Owners: Hermann Buerger, Bradford W. Parkinson, James S. Childress, Capital Group Inc./7.10%, Insiders/4.40%, Alfred G. Hansen/1.70%, Don T. Scartz, Royce& Associates, LLC/5.30%, Blackrock, Inc./5.10%, Barclays Global Investors, NA/5.20%, John L. Woodward, Paul B. Domorski, Francis J. Erbrick, John B. Mowell, AXA Financial, Inc./5.20% *(20 Owners included in Index)*

Financial Data: *Fiscal Year End:*12/31 *Latest Annual Data:* 12/31/2006

Year	Sales	Net Income
2006	$261,119,000	$33,008,000
2005	$310,033,000	-$11,443,000
2004	$260,418,000	$192,000

Curr. Assets:	$239,015,000	**Curr. Liab.:**	$62,445,000	**P/E Ratio:**	9.14
Plant, Equip.:	$31,735,000	**Total Liab.:**	$78,601,000	**Indic. Yr. Divd.:**	NA
Total Assets:	$291,684,000	**Net Worth:**	$213,083,000	**Debt/ Equity:**	NA

Emtec Inc

525 Lincoln Dr., 5 Greentree Ctr., Ste. 117, Marlton, NJ, 08053; *PH:* 1-856-552-4204; *Fax:* 1-856-552-4298; *http://* www.emtecinc.com; *Email:* investor_relations@emtecinc.com

General - Incorporation	DE	**Stock**- Price on:12/24/2007	$0.89
Employees	208	Stock Exchange	OTC
Auditor	Ernst & Young LLP	Ticker Symbol	ETEC
Stk Agt	Zions First National Bank	Outstanding Shares	14,390,000
Counsel	Goldberg, Mufson & Spar	E.P.S	-$0.16
DUNS No.	05-609-0210	Shareholders	NA

Business: The group's principal activity is to provide technology solutions enabling customers to effectively use and manage their data to grow their businesses. The it services provided by the group includes remote network monitoring, help desk, network design, enterprise backup, storage server consolidation and network security. The group's geothermal division identifies and acquires geothermal oil and gas leases in the western United States.

Primary SIC and add'l.: 7379 7379 1382 4961 7373 4961 7373

CIK No: 0000005117

Subsidiaries: Emtec Viasub LLC, Emtec, Inc. q, Westwood Computer Corporation, Westwood Solutions LLC

Officers: John P. Howlett/Vice Chmn., Corporate Development, Contact - Investor Relations, Howlett, Frank Blaul/43/Exec. VP

Directors: John P. Howlett/Vice Chmn., Corporate Development, Contact - Investor Relations, Howlett, Robert Mannarino/Dir.

Owners: Carla Seitz/2.20%, Ronald A. Seitz/3.10%, Rosemary A. Howlett/4.00%, Brian McAdams/4.60%, Keith Grabel/13.50%, Gregory Chandler/0.30%, Robert Mannarino/0.30%, Mary Margaret Grabel/14.70%, Insiders/64.10%, Stephen C. Donnelly/0.30%, Dinesh R. Desai/54.40%

Financial Data: *Fiscal Year End:*08/31 *Latest Annual Data:* 8/31/2006

Year	Sales	Net Income
2006	$224,512,000	$198,000
2005	$162,632,000	$827,000

Curr. Assets:	$33,434,000	**Curr. Liab.:**	$31,133,000		
Plant, Equip.:	$1,316,000	**Total Liab.:**	$36,482,000	**Indic. Yr. Divd.:**	NA
Total Assets:	$52,025,000	**Net Worth:**	$15,543,000	**Debt/ Equity:**	0.2714

Emulex Corp

3333 Susan St., Costa Mesa, CA, 92626; *PH:* 1-714-662-5600; *Fax:* 1-714-241-0792; *http://* www.emulex.com

General - Incorporation	DE	**Stock**- Price on:12/24/2007	$22.52
Employees	618	Stock Exchange	NYSE
Auditor	KPMG LLP	Ticker Symbol	ELX
Stk Agt	Mellon Investor Services LLC	Outstanding Shares	85,350,000
Counsel	NA	E.P.S	$0.29
DUNS No.	09-324-4218	Shareholders	NA

Business: The group's principal activity is to design, develop and supply of a broad line of storage networking host bus adapters (hbas), application specific computer chips (asics) and software products. These products provide connectivity solutions for storage area networks (sans), network attached storage (nas) and redundant array of independent disks (raid) storage. The fibre channel products manufactured by the group include centralized wiring connection, improved network reliability and a monitoring point in fibre channel arbitrated loop environment. The group provides external and embedded printer servers, which provide LAN connectivity for printers. The network access products comprise of various products that provide connectivity between computing resources across both lans and wans. On 17-Nov-2003, the group acquired vixel corporation.

Primary SIC and add'l.: 3577 7373

CIK No: 0000350917

Subsidiaries: Aarohi Communications Private Limited, Arcxel Technologies, Inc., Emulex Caribe, Inc., Emulex Communications Corporation, Emulex Corporate Services Corporation, Emulex Corporation, Emulex Design & Manufacturing Corporation, Hyland Enterprise Development, Inc.

Officers: James M. McCluney/57/CEO, Pres., Paul F. Folino/63/Exec. Chmn., Bob Whitson/Sr. VP, GM - Embedded Storage Products, Robin Austin/Dir. - Public Relations, Katherine Henry/Mgr. - Public Relations, Ameesh Divatia/Sr. VP, GM - Intelligent Network Products, Fred Gill/Exec. VP - Worldwide Sales, Mike Smith/Exec. VP - Worldwide Marketing, John Warwick/Sr. VP - Operations, Marshall D. Lee/Exec. VP - Engineering, Michael J. Rockenbach/47/CFO, Exec. VP, Randall Wick/VP, General Counsel, Sadie Herrera/Exec. VP - Human Resources, Facilities, William F. Gill/51/Exec. VP - Worldwide Sales, Stuart Berman/CTO, Sr. VP *(16 Officers included in Index)*

Directors: Paul F. Folino/63/Exec. Chmn., Bruce C. Edwards/Dir., Fred B. Cox/Dir., Michael P. Downey/Dir., Robert H. Goon/Dir., Don M. Lyle/Dir., Dean A. Yoost/Dir.

Owners: Michael P. Downey, Bruce C. Edwards, James M. McCluney/1.00%, Putnam Investment Management, LLC/6.74%, Robert H. Goon, PRIMECAP Management Company/7.47%, Paul F. Folino/2.30%, AVESCAP PLC/5.46%, Don M. Lyle, Wellington Management Company, LLP/10.87%, Insiders/7.20%, Dean A. Yoost, Fred B. Cox, Michael E. Smith, Marshall D. Lee *(17 Owners included in Index)*

Financial Data: *Fiscal Year End:*07/03 *Latest Annual Data:* 07/01/2007

Year	Sales	Net Income
2007	$470,187,000	$29,434,000
2006	$402,813,000	$40,451,000
2005	$375,653,000	$71,589,000

Curr. Assets:	$584,457,000	**Curr. Liab.:**	$76,644,000	**P/E Ratio:**	68.24
Plant, Equip.:	$65,976,000	**Total Liab.:**	$324,190,000	**Indic. Yr. Divd.:**	NA
Total Assets:	$801,781,000	**Net Worth:**	$477,591,000	**Debt/ Equity:**	NA

Emvelco Corp

Formerly: Euroweb International Corp

468 N Camden Dr., Ste. 315, Beverly Hills, CA, 90210; *PH:* 1-310-285-5350; *http://* www.euroweb.hu

General - Incorporation	DE	**Stock**- Price on:12/24/2007	NA
Employees	85	Stock Exchange	NDQ
Auditor	Robison, Hill & Co	Ticker Symbol	EMVL
Stk Agt	American Stock Transfer & Trust Co.	Outstanding Shares	NA
Counsel	Cohen & Cohen	E.P.S	NA
DUNS No.	79-275-4681	Shareholders	NA

Business: The group's principal activities are to provide complete communication solutions using Internet technologies. The group provides traditional isp services, international leased line, ip data services and voice over ip services. The traditional isp services include Internet access and design, development, hosting and maintenance of home pages and Web servers. International leased line includes single and

virtual private network ip connections. The customers of the group include businesses and professionals, telecommunication carriers and multinational corporations having cross-border bandwidth communication needs. The group operates through the subsidiaries euroweb czech republic, euroweb slovakia and euroweb romania.

Primary SIC and add'l.: 7372 7375

CIK No: 0000905428

Subsidiaries: AT&T Corp, Czech Republic, Euroweb Czech, Euroweb Slovakia, Luko Czech

Officers: Yossi Attia/Dir., CEO, Pres., Robin Ann Gorelick/Dir., Sec., Gregory Sichenzia/Legal Representative, Stephen Fleming/Legal Representative

Directors: Yossi Attia/Dir., CEO, Pres., Stewart Reich/62/Chmn., Ilan Kenig/Dir., Robin Ann Gorelick/Dir., Sec., Gerald Schaffer/84/Dir.

Owners: Graeton Holdings Limited, KPN Telecom B.V., CORCYRA d.o.o., Ilan Kenig, Stewart Reich, Yossi Attia, Insiders

Financial Data: *Fiscal Year End:*12/31 *Latest Annual Data:* 12/31/2006

Year	Sales	Net Income
2006	$23,000	$6,913,000
2005	$1,965,000	$1,680,000
2004	$36,616,000	-$734,000

Curr. Assets:	$10,309,000	**Curr. Liab.:**	$3,840,000		
Plant, Equip.:	NA	**Total Liab.:**	$6,840,000	**Indic. Yr. Divd.:**	NA
Total Assets:	$30,691,000	**Net Worth:**	$23,851,000	**Debt/ Equity:**	NA

En Pointe Technologies Inc

18701 S Figueroa St., Gardena, CA, 90248; ; *http://* www.enpointe.com

General - Incorporation	DE	**Stock**- Price on:12/24/2007	$3.95
Employees	479	Stock Exchange	NDQ
Auditor	BDO Seidman LLP	Ticker Symbol	ENPT
Stk Agt	U.S. Stock Transfer Corp	Outstanding Shares	7,150,000
Counsel	Stradling Yocca Carlson & Rauth	E.P.S.	$0.41
DUNS No.	87-765-3337	Shareholders	NA

Business: The group's principle activity is to provide information technology products and value-added services. Products offered includes desktop and laptop computers, servers, monitors, memory, peripherals and accessories, operating systems, application software, consumables and supplies. The group uses proprietary and non-proprietary software and systems to drop-ship materials, repair and operation products to its customers through an electronically linked network of suppliers that include distributors and certain manufacturers in the United States. It conducts ebusiness offering that is supported by its Internet procurement system, accesspointetm, catalog-content management, service management tools and back-office systems. The group is represented in approximately 17 sales and service markets throughout the United States, and maintains a value-added iso 9001: 2000 certified integration facility in ontario and California. The group's total revenue for the year 2007 was 347.13 millions of USD.

Primary SIC and add'l.: 5045

CIK No: 0001010305

Subsidiaries: En Pointe Gov, Inc., En Pointe Technologies Canada, Inc., En Pointe Technologies Sales, Inc., The Xyphen Corporation

Officers: Attiazaz Din/Dir., CEO, Pres., Javed Latif/CFO, Sr. VP - Contact - Investor Relations

Directors: Attiazaz Din/Dir., CEO, Pres., Mansoor S. Shah/Chmn., Edward O. Hunter/Dir., Timothy J. Lilligren/Dir., Naureen Din/Dir., Zubair Ahmed/Dir., Mark Briggs/Dir.

Owners: Mansoor Shah, Kevin Schatzle/2.90%, Insiders/40.70%, Attiazaz Din/16.70%, Javed Latif/2.40%, Richard Emil, Edward Hunter, David Mochalski, Mediha Din/6.80%, Naureen Din/16.70%, Timothy Lilligren, Zubair Ahmed/9.60%, Mark Briggs

Financial Data: *Fiscal Year End:*09/30 *Latest Annual Data:* 9/30/2006

Year	Sales	Net Income
2006	$323,733,000	$511,000
2005	$328,332,000	$145,000
2004	$279,234,000	$1,401,000

Curr. Assets:	$61,999,000	**Curr. Liab.:**	$45,502,000	**P/E Ratio:**	11.97
Plant, Equip.:	$2,765,000	**Total Liab.:**	$45,740,000	**Indic. Yr. Divd.:**	NA
Total Assets:	$66,238,000	**Net Worth:**	$19,011,000	**Debt/ Equity:**	NA

Enable IPC Corp

25520 Ave. Stnford Ste. 311, Valencia, CA, 91355; *PH:* 1-661-775-9273; *Fax:* 1-661-775-9274; *http://* www.enableipc.com; *Email:* info@enableipc.com

General - Incorporation	DE	**Stock**- Price on:12/24/2007	$0.15
Employees	1	Stock Exchange	OTC
Auditor	L.L. Bradford & Company, LLC	Ticker Symbol	EIPC
Stk Agt	U.S. Stock Transfer Corp	Outstanding Shares	12,720,000
Counsel	NA	E.P.S.	NA
DUNS No.	NA	Shareholders	NA

Business: The groups principal activities include developing and commercializing rechargeable batteries for use in low power applications. The group products include nickel metal hydride, sealed lead acid, nickel cadmium and lithium ion. The group operates from and the United States.

Primary SIC and add'l.: 3691

CIK No: 0001326068

Officers: David A. Walker/Chmn., CEO, Rich Kaiser/Investor Relations Officer, Mark A. Daugherty/CTO, Member, Dir., Anna Rhee/CFO, Sung Choi/Technical Advisor, Neil Rosso/VP - Investor Services, Dustin M. Lewis/Financial Auditor

Directors: David A. Walker/Chmn., CEO, Cathryn S. Gawne/Dir., Philip M. Verges/Dir., Mark A. Daugherty/CTO, Member, Dir., Jin Suk Kim/Dir., Timothy Lambirth/Dir., Daniel Teran/Dir.

Owners: David A. Walker/11.00%, Sung H. Choi/11.20%, Daniel Teran/1.50%, Reuven Zfat/35.40%, Philip Verges/1.50%, Anna Rhee/0.10%, Insiders/26.50%, Mark A. Daugherty/1.60%, Timothy Lambirth/1.80%, Jin Suk Kim/9.00%

Enbridge Energy LP

1100 Louisiana St., Ste. 3300, Houston, TX, 77002; *PH:* 1-713-821-2000; *Fax:* 1-713-821-2232; *http://* www.enbridgepartners.com

General - Incorporation	DE	**Stock**- Price on:12/24/2007	$55.85
Employees	NA	Stock Exchange	NYSE
Auditor	NA	Ticker Symbol	EEP
Stk Agt	Enbridge Energy Partners	Outstanding Shares	78,020,000
Counsel	NA	E.P.S.	$2.65
DUNS No.	NA	Shareholders	NA

Business: The groups principal activity is to provide crude oil and natural gas. The group operates from the Canada and the United States.

Primary SIC and add'l.: 4610

CIK No: 0001066629

Officers: Stephen J.J. Letwin/Dir., MD, Terrance L. McGill/Dir., Pres.

Directors: Martha O. Hesse/Chmn., Stephen J.J. Letwin/Dir., MD, Richard J. Bird/Dir., Jeffrey A. Connelly/Dir., Terrance L. McGill/Dir., Pres., George K. Petty/Dir., Dan Westbrook/Dir.

Financial Data: *Fiscal Year End:*12/31 *Latest Annual Data:* 12/31/2006

Year	Sales	Net Income
2006	$6,509,000,000	$284,900,000
2005	$6,476,900,000	$89,200,000
2004	$4,291,700,000	$138,200,000

Curr. Assets:	$1,009,300,000	**Curr. Liab.:**	$961,600,000	**P/E Ratio:**	21.08
Plant, Equip.:	$3,824,900,000	**Total Liab.:**	$3,180,400,000	**Indic. Yr. Divd.:**	$3.700
Total Assets:	$5,223,800,000	**Net Worth:**	$2,043,400,000	**Debt/ Equity:**	1.1104

Enbridge Energy Management LLC

1100 Louisiana, Ste. 3300, Houston, TX, 77002; *PH:* 1-713-821-2000; *Fax:* 1-713-821-2232; *http://* www.enbridgemanagement.com; *Email:* investor@enbridgemanagement.com

General - Incorporation	DE	**Stock**- Price on:12/24/2007	$55.1652
Employees	NA	Stock Exchange	NYSE
Auditor	PricewaterhouseCoopers LLP	Ticker Symbol	EEQ
Stk Agt	Enbridge Energy Management, L.L.C.	Outstanding Shares	13,110,000
Counsel	NA	E.P.S.	$1.896
DUNS No.	NA	Shareholders	NA

Business: The groups principle activity is to provide petroleum and natural gas. The group operates from the United States.

Primary SIC and add'l.: 4612 4925 4613 4923 4922

CIK No: 0001173911

Subsidiaries: Enbridge Management Services, L.L.C

Officers: Richard J. Bird/Dir., Exec. VP - Liquids Pipelines, Stephen J.J. Letwin/Dir., MD, Principal Executive Officer, Terrance L. McGill/Dir., Pres., L. A. Zupan/52/VP - Liquids Pipelines Operations, Mark A. Maki/43/VP - Finance, Principal Financial Officer, R. L. Adams/43/VP - Operations, Technologies, J. M. Gerez/51/VP - Liquids Pipelines Project Management, Engineering, J. A. Holder/50/VP - Liquids Pipelines Support Services, J. A. Loiacono/45/VP - Commercial Activities, D. V. Krenz/56/VP, V. D. Yu/41/Treasurer, J. N. Rose/40/Assist. Treasurer, S. J. Neyland/40/Controller, E. C. Kaitson/51/Assist. Sec., B. A. Stevenson/52/Corp. Sec.

Directors: Martha O. Hesse/Chmn., E. C. Hambrook/70/Dir., Richard J. Bird/Dir., Exec. VP - Liquids Pipelines, Jeffrey A. Connelly/Dir., Stephen J.J. Letwin/Dir., MD, Principal Executive Officer, Terrance L. McGill/Dir., Pres., George K. Petty/Dir., Dan Westbrook/Dir.

Owners: E. C. Hambrook, Neuberger Berman, Inc./11.60%, Goldman, Sachs & Co./6.70%, J.R. Bird, G.K. Petty, Kayne Anderson Capital Advisors, L.P./10.60%, T. L. McGill, Enbridge Energy Company, Inc./17.20%, Insiders, M.O. Hesse, Oppenheimer Funds, Inc./5.30%

Financial Data: *Fiscal Year End:*12/31 *Latest Annual Data:* 12/31/2006

Year	Sales	Net Income
2006	NA	$28,700,000
2005	NA	$12,400,000
2004	$28,800,000	$18,700,000

Curr. Assets:	NA	**Curr. Liab.:**	NA	**P/E Ratio:**	29.10
Plant, Equip.:	NA	**Total Liab.:**	$36,200,000	**Indic. Yr. Divd.:**	$3.700
Total Assets:	$428,900,000	**Net Worth:**	$392,700,000	**Debt/ Equity:**	NA

Enbridge Inc

3000 Fifth Ave. Pl., 425 - 1st St. S.W., Calgary, AB, T2P 3L8; *PH:* 1-403-231-3900; *Fax:* 1-403-231-3920; *http://* www.enbridge.com; *Email:* investor.relations@enbridge.com

General - Incorporation	Canada	**Stock**- Price on:12/24/2007	$33.95
Employees	5,193	Stock Exchange	NYSE
Auditor	PricewaterhouseCoopers LLP	Ticker Symbol	ENB
Stk Agt	Mellon Trust Co (Canada)	Outstanding Shares	349,230,000
Counsel	NA	E.P.S.	$1.77
DUNS No.	24-906-3751	Shareholders	NA

Business: The group's principle activities include transporting and distributing energy. The group operates through three operating segments: energy transportation, energy distribution and international. The group's quarterly revenue for September 2007 was 2,634.00 millions of USD. The group operates from United States.

Primary SIC and add'l.: 4931 4612 4922 1311

CIK No: 0000895728

Subsidiaries: Enbridge (U.S.) Inc., Enbridge Capital ApS, Enbridge Energy Company, Inc., Enbridge Energy Distribution Inc., Enbridge Gas Distribution Inc., Enbridge Gas Services (U.S.) Inc., Enbridge Gas Services Inc., Enbridge Income Fund2, Enbridge Pipelines (Athabasca) Inc., Enbridge Pipelines (NW)Inc., Enbridge Pipelines Inc., IPL AP Holdings (U.S.A.) Inc.1, IPL System Inc., Tidal Energy Marketing Inc.

Officers: Patrick D. Daniel/61/Dir., CEO, Pres., Mel F. Belich/Group VP - International, Corporate Law, Alison T. Love/VP, Corp. Sec., Stephen J. Wuori/CFO, Exec. VP, Anu Phatak/Mgr. - Investor Relations, Enbridge Income Fund, Larry Springer/Sr. Community Relations Advisor, News Media, Enbridge Energy Partners, LP, Jennifer Varey/Contact - News Media, Debbie Boukydis/Contact - News Media, Enbridge Gas Distribution, Jim Schultz/Sr. VP - New Ventures, Pres. - Enbridge Management Services Inc, Richard J. Bird/Exec. VP - Liquids Pipelines, Terry L. McGill/Pres. - Enbridge Energy Partners, LP, Al Monaco/Pres. - Enbridge Gas Distribution, David T. Robottom/Group VP - Corporate Law, Rick Sandahl/Sr. VP - US Marketing Development, Enbridge Pipelines, Greg Sevick/Sr. VP - Planning, Customer Services, Enbridge Pipelines *(20 Officers included in Index)*

Directors: Patrick D. Daniel/61/Dir., CEO, Pres., David A. Arledge/63/Chmn., Herb J. England/61/Dir., George K. Petty/66/Dir., Dan C. Tutcher/59/Dir., James J. Blanchard/65/Dir., Charles E. Schultz/68/Dir., Lorne J. Braithwaite/66/Dir., Robert W. Martin/71/Dir., David A. Leslie/64/Dir., Susan E. Evans/62/Dir.

Financial Data: *Fiscal Year End:*12/31 *Latest Annual Data:* 12/31/2006

Year	Sales	Net Income
2006	$9,134,045,000	$533,996,000
2005	$7,252,760,000	$468,725,000
2004	$5,430,577,000	$541,522,000

Curr. Assets:	$2,620,809,000	Curr. Liab.:	$2,766,429,000	P/E Ratio:	19.62
Plant, Equip.:	$9,666,239,000	Total Liab.:	$11,814,921,000	Indic. Yr. Divd.:	$1.280
Total Assets:	$15,771,277,000	Net Worth:	$3,956,356,000	Debt/ Equity:	NA

EnCana Corp

EnCana Corporation, 1800, 855, 2nd St. SW, Calgary, AB, T2P 2S5; *PH:* 1-403-645-2000; *Fax:* 1-403-645-3400; *http://* www.encana.com

General		Stock	
Incorporation	Canada	Price on:12/24/2007	$65.42
Employees	4,678	Stock Exchange	NYSE
Auditor	PricewaterhouseCoopers LLP	Ticker Symbol	ECA
Stk Agt	PricewaterhouseCoopers LLP	Outstanding Shares	761,300,000
Counsel	NA	E.P.S	$4.55
DUNS No.	NA	Shareholders	NA

Business: The group's principle activities of the group are to explore, develop, produce and market natural gas, crude oil and natural gas liquids. The group also generates and markets electricity. The group has encompassing interests in Canada, the United States, Mexico and the United Kingdom. The group's quarterly revenue for September 2007 was 5,596.00 millions of USD.

Primary SIC and add'l.: 4612 1311

CIK No: 0001157806

Subsidiaries: Ecuador

Officers: Randall K. Eresman/49/Dir., CEO, Pres., Gerard Protti/Exec. VP - Corporate Relations, Pres. - Offshore, International Division, Connie Heath/US New Ventures, US Region, Land Negotiations, Doug Jones/South Business Unit, US Region, Land Negotiations, Karina Berrade/Peace Country Business Unit, Land Negotiations, Kevin George/Peace Country Business Unit, Land Negotiations, Chris Clark/Peace Country Business Unit, Land Negotiations, John Eresman/Peace Country Business Unit, Land Negotiations, John Knox/Contact - Fort Nelson Business Unit, Land Negotiations, Barb Wylegly/Contact - Fort Nelson Business Unit, Land Negotiations, Brian Weston/Peace Country Business Unit, Land Negotiations, Tina Thomison/Peace Country Business Unit, Land Negotiations, Crystal Pomedli/Peace Country Business Unit, Land Negotiations, Jason Heilman/Peace Country Business Unit, Land Negotiations, Jeff Collins/Peace Country Business Unit, Land Negotiations *(88 Officers included in Index)*

Directors: Randall K. Eresman/49/Dir., CEO, Pres., Patrick D. Daniel/61/Dir., David P. Obrien/66/Dir., Ralph S. Cunningham/67/Dir., Ian W. Delaney/64/Dir., Michael A. Grandin/63/Dir., Barry W. Harrison/67/Dir., Dale A. Lucas/70/Dir., Ken F. McCready/68/Dir., Valerie A.A. Nielsen/62/Dir., Jane L. Peverett/49/Dir., Dennis A. Sharp/70/Dir., James M. Stanford/70/Dir., Allan P. Sawin/52/Dir., Wayne G. Thomson/56/Dir.

Financial Data: *Fiscal Year End:*12/31 *Latest Annual Data:* 12/31/2006

Year	Sales	Net Income
2006	$16,399,000,000	$5,652,000,000
2005	$14,049,000,000	$3,252,000,000
2004	$11,810,000,000	$3,513,000,000

Curr. Assets:	$3,702,000,000	Curr. Liab.:	$3,691,000,000		
Plant, Equip.:	$28,213,000,000	Total Liab.:	$17,640,000,000	Indic. Yr. Divd.:	$0.800
Total Assets:	$35,106,000,000	Net Worth:	$17,466,000,000	Debt/ Equity:	NA

Encision Inc

6797 Winchester Cir., Boulder, CO, 80301; *PH:* 1-303-444-2600; *Fax:* 1-303-444-2693; *http://* www.encision.com; *Email:* feedback@encision.com

General		Stock	
Incorporation	CO	Price on:12/24/2007	$3.5
Employees	35	Stock Exchange	AMEX
Auditor	Gordon Hughes & Banks LLP	Ticker Symbol	ECI
Stk Agt	Computershare Trust Co	Outstanding Shares	6,430,000
Counsel	NA	E.P.S	-$0.08
DUNS No.	61-225-0175	Shareholders	NA

Business: The group's principal activities are to design, develop, manufacture and market patented electro surgical devices and aem laparoscopic instruments. The aem laparoscopic instruments are shielded and monitored to prevent stray electrochemical burns from insulation failure and capacitive coupling. The group's product lines include a broad range of scissors, graspers and dissectors, fixed-tip electrodes and suction-irrigation electrodes. The instruments are available in a wide array of reusable and disposable options. The group also markets the aem monitor product line that is used in conjunction with the aem instruments. The aem technology provides surgeons with the desired tissue effects, while preventing stray electro surgical energy that can cause unintended and unseen tissue injury.

Primary SIC and add'l.: 3841

CIK No: 0000930775

Officers: John R. Serino/Dir., CEO, Pres., Roger C. Odell/Chmn., Co - Founder, VP - Business Development, Marcia McHaffie/Investor Relations Officer, Shirley Thompson/Principal Media Contact, Bevo Beaven/VP, GM - Media Contact, Sheila Whitman/Sr. Accounting Executive, Media Contact, Kent Cherrey/Mountain Regional Sales Mgr., John Flaiz/Central Regional Sales Mgr., Todd Theis/Southern Regional Sales Mgr., Jeff Kirchman/Western Regional Sales Mgr., Steve Koehler/Eastern Regional Sales Mgr., Janet Padgham/Dir. - Sales, Austrailia, Murray McMillan/Dir. - Sales, New Zealand

Directors: John R. Serino/Dir., CEO, Pres., Roger C. Odell/Chmn., Co - Founder, VP - Business Development, Vern D. Kornelsen/Co - Founder, Dir., David W. Newton/Co - Founder, Dir., Robert H. Fries/Dir., Bruce Arfmann/Dir., George Stewart/Dir.

Owners: George A. Stewart, John R. Serino/2.60%, Vern D. Kornelsen/18.20%, CMED Partners LLLP/17.40%, Robert H. Fries, Bruce L. Arfmann, Roger C. Odell/11.90%, Intertec Healthcare Management, L.L.C./6.00%, David W. Newton/4.50%, Insiders/38.00%, James A. Bowman/9.50%

Financial Data: *Fiscal Year End:*03/31 *Latest Annual Data:* 03/31/2007

Year	Sales	Net Income
2007	$11,010,000	-$90,000
2006	$9,127,000	-$338,000
2005	$8,054,000	-$595,000

Curr. Assets:	$3,325,000	Curr. Liab.:	$1,086,000		
Plant, Equip.:	$316,000	Total Liab.:	$1,086,000	Indic. Yr. Divd.:	NA
Total Assets:	$3,817,000	Net Worth:	$2,732,000	Debt/ Equity:	NA

Enclaves Group Inc

2550 E Trinity Mills Rd., Ste. 122, Carrollton, TX, 75006; *PH:* 1-972-416-9304; *Fax:* 1-972-416-9441; *http://* www.enclavesgroup.com; *Email:* contactus@enclavesgroup.com

General		Stock	
Incorporation	DE	Price on:12/24/2007	NA
Employees	NA	Stock Exchange	OTC
Auditor	Friedman LLP	Ticker Symbol	ECGR
Stk Agt	Continental Stock Transfer & Trust Co	Outstanding Shares	NA
Counsel	NA	E.P.S	-$0.02
DUNS No.	NA	Shareholders	NA

Business: The groups principal activity is real estate business. The group operates from the United States.

Primary SIC and add'l.: 6531

CIK No: 0001045260

Subsidiaries: Enclaves of Spring Magnolia II LLC, Enclaves of Grand Oaks LLC, Enclaves of Eagle Nest LLC, Enclaves of Live Oak LLC, Enclaves of Spring Magnolia LLC

Officers: Daniel G. Hayes/Dir., CEO, Pres., Mark D. MacFarlane/COO, Emilia Nuccio/VP - Sales, Marketing, Maria Bristol/Project Dir., Patricia Castro/Administrative Assist., Dean M. O'Neill/Acquisition Mgr.

Directors: Daniel G. Hayes/Dir., CEO, Pres., Robert A. MacFarlane/Chmn., Marlin K. Wiggins/Dir., Robert M. Kohn/Dir.

Financial Data: *Fiscal Year End:*12/31 *Latest Annual Data:* 12/31/2005

Year	Sales	Net Income
2005	NA	-$937,000
2004	$141,000	-$1,665,000

Curr. Assets:	$617,000	Curr. Liab.:	$7,644,000		
Plant, Equip.:	$9,393,000	Total Liab.:	$14,263,000	Indic. Yr. Divd.:	$2.600
Total Assets:	$13,283,000	Net Worth:	-$979,000	Debt/ Equity:	NA

Encompass Holdings Inc

Formerly: Nova Communications Ltd
1005 Terminal Way, Ste. 110, Reno, NV, 89502; *PH:* 1-775-324-8531; *http://* www.encompassholdings.com

General		Stock	
Incorporation	NV	Price on:12/24/2007	NA
Employees	NA	Stock Exchange	NA
Auditor	Timothy L. Steers, CPA LLC	Ticker Symbol	NA
Stk Agt	OTC Corporate Transfer Service Co	Outstanding Shares	NA
Counsel	NA	E.P.S	NA
DUNS No.	18-632-0388	Shareholders	NA

Business: The group's principal activity is to acquire ownership interests in developing companies and providing financial and managerial assistance to those companies. On 21-07-2003, the group discontinued kadfield, inc.

Primary SIC and add'l.: 5045

CIK No: 0000769882

Subsidiaries: Aqua Xtremes, Inc., Nacio Systems, Inc, Rotary Engine Technologies, Inc., Xtreme Engines, Inc.

Officers: Arthur N. Robins/56/Dir., CEO, Leslie I. Handler/70/Dir., Pres., James F. Abel/46/Corp. Sec., Dir.

Directors: Arthur N. Robins/56/Dir., CEO, Leslie I. Handler/70/Dir., Pres., James F. Abel/46/Corp. Sec., Dir., Greg K. Hoggatt/49/Dir., Scott J. Webber/57/Dir., Larry Cooper/59/Dir., Murray Goldenberg/68/Dir.

Owners: NovaNet Media, Inc./100.00%, Insiders, Arthur N. Robins/100.00%, Rotary Engines, Inc./73.00%, J. Scott Webber, Insiders

Encore Acquisition Co

777 Main St., Ste. 1400, Fort Worth, TX, 76102; *PH:* 1-817-877-9955; *Fax:* 1-817-877-1655; *http://* www.encoreacq.com; *Email:* info@encoreacq.com

General		Stock	
Incorporation	DE	Price on:12/24/2007	$28.61
Employees	236	Stock Exchange	NYSE
Auditor	Ernst & Young LLP	Ticker Symbol	EAC
Stk Agt	Mellon Investor Services LLC	Outstanding Shares	53,130,000
Counsel	NA	E.P.S	$0.15
DUNS No.	NA	Shareholders	NA

Business: The group's principal activities are to acquire, develop, explore and market onshore north American oil and natural gas reserve. The group operates wells in fields located in the williston basin of Montana and North Dakota, the permian basin of Texas and New Mexico, the anadarko basin of Oklahoma and the powder river basin of Montana. In 2003, the total wells included 95.7 operated wells and 7.9 non-operated well. The oil and natural gas production is principally sold to end users, marketers and refiners. On 14-Apr-2004, the group acquired cortez oil & gas, inc.

Primary SIC and add'l.: 1311

CIK No: 0001125057

Subsidiaries: EAP Energy Services, L.P., EAP Energy, Inc., EAP Operating, Inc., EAP Properties, Inc., Encore Operating Louisiana LLC, Encore Operating, L.P.

Officers: Jon S. Brumley/Dir., CEO, Pres./$2,282,425.00, Philip D. Devlin/Sr. VP, General Counsel, Corp. Sec., Andy R. Lowe/VP - Marketing, Diane Weaver/VP - Investor Relations, Kevin N. Treadway/VP - Land, Dan Lott/Dir. - Human Resources, Thomas H. Olle/VP - Mid, Continent Region/$802,390.00, Ben L. Nivens/47/COO, Sr. VP/$565,422.00, Robert C. Reeves/CFO, Sr. VP/$682,001.00, John W. Arms/Sr. VP - Acquisitions

Directors: Jon S. Brumley/Dir., CEO, Pres., Jon I. Brumley/Chmn., John A. Bailey/Dir., James A. Winne/Dir., Ted Collins/Dir., Martin C. Bowen/Dir., John V. Genova/Dir., Ted A. Gardner/Dir.

Owners: Jon S. Brumley/1.60%, T. Rowe Price Associates, Inc./9.10%, Ted A. Gardner, Martin C. Bowen, John A. Bailey, Ted Collins, Robert C. Reeves, Insiders/8.70%, Ben L. Nivens, Thomas H. Olle, Barclays Global Investors, N.A./6.30%, Neuberger Berman Inc./9.20%, Jon I. Brumley/5.90%, John V. Genova, James A. Winne *(18 Owners included in Index)*

Financial Data: *Fiscal Year End:*12/31 *Latest Annual Data:* 12/31/2006

Year	Sales	Net Income
2006	$640,862,000	$92,398,000
2005	$457,324,000	$103,425,000
2004	$298,533,000	$82,147,000

Curr. Assets:	$145,718,000	**Curr. Liab.:**	$186,463,000	**P/E Ratio:**	34.06
Plant, Equip.:	$1,727,122,000	**Total Liab.:**	$1,190,035,000	**Indic. Yr. Divd.:**	NA
Total Assets:	$2,006,900,000	**Net Worth:**	$816,865,000	**Debt/ Equity:**	1.5479

Encore Capital Group Inc

8875 Aero Dr., Ste. 200, San Diego, CA, 92123; ***PH:*** 1-858-560-2600; ***Fax:*** 1-858-309-6978; ***http://*** www.mcmcg.com

General - Incorporation	DE	**Stock**- Price on:12/24/2007	$11.88
Employees	893	Stock Exchange	NDQ
Auditor	BDO Seidman LLP	Ticker Symbol	ECPG
Stk Agt	American Stock Transfer & Trust Co.	Outstanding Shares	22,800,000
Counsel	NA	E.P.S.	$0.72
DUNS No.	NA	Shareholders	NA

Business: The group's principal activities are to include the purchase, collection, restructuring, resale and securitization of receivable portfolios acquired at deep discounts. The business of the group is of acquiring and servicing charged-off loan portfolios originated by credit card issuers and other financial institutions. The receivable portfolios managed by the group consist primarily of charged-off domestic consumer credit card receivables purchased from national financial institutions and major retail credit corporations. The purchase of receivable portfolios are financed by operations and borrowings from third parties.

Primary SIC and add'l.: 6153

CIK No: 0001084961

Subsidiaries: Ascension Capital Group, LP, Midland Acquisition Corporation, Midland Credit Management, Inc., Midland Funding 98-A Corporation, Midland Funding LLC, Midland Funding NCC-1 Corporation, Midland Funding NCC-2 Corporation, Midland Portfolio Services, Inc., Midland Receivables 98-1 Corporation, Midland Receivables 99-1 Corporation, MRC Receivables Corporation

Officers: Brandon J. Black/Dir., CEO, Pres., Olivier Baudoux/CIO, VP, Glen Freter/VP, Controller, Fritz Heirich/Sr. VP, GM - Healthcare, Anthony Riggio/Sr. VP - Business Development, Acquisitions, Jim Syran/Sr. VP, Chief Marketing Officer, Erich Ramsey/Pres., GM - Ascension Capital Group, Robin R. Pruitt/Sr. VP, General Counsel, Sec./$501,268.00, Alison James/Sr. VP - Human Resources, George Brooker/Sr. VP - Outsourcing Channels/$369,946.00, Paul Grinberg/CFO, Exec. VP/$1,496,539.00

Directors: Brandon J. Black/Dir., CEO, Pres., Carl C. Gregory/Chmn., Richard A. Mandell/Dir., Barry R. Barkley/Dir., Timothy J. Hanford/Dir., George Lund/Dir., Willem Mesdag/Dir., John J. Oros/Dir., Christopher Teets/Dir., Warren Wilcox/Dir., Alexander Lemond/Dir.

Owners: Insiders, Timothy J. Hanford, CNH Partners LLC, Carl C. Gregory, George Brooker, JCF FPK I LP, Paul Grinberg, Barry R. Barkley, Red Mountain Capital Partners LLC, Richard A. Mandell, Willem Mesdag, Second Curve Capital, LLC, Brandon J. Black, Alexander Lemond, Robin R. Pruitt

Financial Data: ***Fiscal Year End:***12/31 ***Latest Annual Data:*** 12/31/2006

Year	Sales	Net Income
2006	$255,140,000	$24,008,000
2005	$221,835,000	$31,091,000
2004	$178,475,000	$23,176,000

Curr. Assets:	$18,050,000	**Curr. Liab.:**	$30,613,000		
Plant, Equip.:	$5,249,000	**Total Liab.:**	$244,202,000	**Indic. Yr. Divd.:**	NA
Total Assets:	$395,338,000	**Net Worth:**	$151,136,000	**Debt/ Equity:**	1.3094

Encore Clean Energy Inc

Ste. 610 375 Water St., Vancouver, BC, V6B 5C6; ***PH:*** 1-604-805566; ***http://*** www.encorecleanenergy.com; ***Email:*** info@encorecleanenergy.com

General - Incorporation	DE	**Stock**- Price on:12/24/2007	$0.02
Employees	10	Stock Exchange	OTC
Auditor	Dohan & Co., Pa	Ticker Symbol	ECLN
Stk Agt	StockTrans, Inc.	Outstanding Shares	15,910,000
Counsel	NA	E.P.S.	-$0.28
DUNS No.	NA	Shareholders	NA

Business: The group's principal activity is to deliver online direct marketing and promotional and informational offers and to develop and implement integrated marketing and advertising strategies. The services include the design, delivery, tracking and analysis of targeted one-to-one e-mail campaigns, customized loyalty programs, comprehensive list management / brokerage packages and the creation, integration and execution of both online and offline advertising strategies. The products and services include: integrated marketing solutions; creative direction and production; innovative delivery technologies; multiple email deployment formats; permission-based email list access; customer profile and tracking systems; list management and brokerage; comprehensive data mining capabilities and others. On 16-Oct-2003 the group acquired cryotherm, inc.

Primary SIC and add'l.: 7331 7311

CIK No: 0001036588

Subsidiaries: Ignite Communications Inc.

Financial Data: ***Fiscal Year End:***12/31 ***Latest Annual Data:*** 12/31/2004

Year	Sales	Net Income
2004	$2,634,000	-$3,380,000
2003	$2,858,000	-$773,000
2002	$2,060,000	-$697,000

Curr. Assets:	$145,000	**Curr. Liab.:**	$3,182,000		
Plant, Equip.:	$68,000	**Total Liab.:**	$4,149,000	**Indic. Yr. Divd.:**	NA
Total Assets:	$213,000	**Net Worth:**	-$3,936,000	**Debt/ Equity:**	NA

Encore Wire Corp

1410 Millwood Rd., McKinney, TX, 75069; ***PH:*** 1-972-562-9473; ***Fax:*** 1-972-542-4744; ***http://*** www.encorewire.com

General - Incorporation	DE	**Stock**- Price on:12/24/2007	$30.97
Employees	755	Stock Exchange	NDQ
Auditor	Ernst & Young LLP	Ticker Symbol	WIRE
Stk Agt	Bank One Trust Company, N.A.	Outstanding Shares	23,350,000
Counsel	Thompson & Knight	E.P.S.	$2.88
DUNS No.	36-409-5273	Shareholders	NA

Business: The group's principal activity is to manufacture copper electrical building wire and non-metallic cable. The group supplies residential wire for interior electrical wiring in homes, apartments and manufactured housing. It also provides building wire for electrical distribution in commercial and industrial buildings. The residential wire product consists of non-metallic cable and underground feeder cable and commercial wire product consists of thhn cable. The products are sold through approximately 30 manufacturers representatives located throughout the United States and to a lesser extent through the group's own direct in-house marketing efforts. The customers of the group are wholesale electrical distributors and retail home improvement centers.

Primary SIC and add'l.: 3357

CIK No: 0000850460

Subsidiaries: Encore Wire Limited, EWC Aviation Corp., EWC GP Corp, EWC LP Corp

Officers: Daniel L. Jones/44/Dir., CEO, Pres./$948,850.00, Frank J. Bilban/51/VP - Finance, Treasurer, Sec., CFO/$399,011.00

Directors: Daniel L. Jones/44/Dir., CEO, Pres., Joseph M. Brito/Dir., John H. Wilson/Dir., Donald E. Courtney/Dir., Thomas L. Cunningham/Dir., William R. Thomas/Dir., Scott D. Weaver/Dir.

Owners: Frank J. Bilban, Joseph M. Brito, Insiders/4.17%, Goldman Sachs Asset Management, L.P./5.10%, Capital Southwest Corporation/17.58%, Daniel L. Jones/1.82%, Vincent A. Rego/6.18%, Scott D. Weaver, David K. Smith, FMR Corp/9.98%, Donald E. Courtney/1.27%, Thomas L. Cunningham, Rick R. Gottschalk

Financial Data: ***Fiscal Year End:***12/31 ***Latest Annual Data:*** 12/31/2006

Year	Sales	Net Income
2006	$1,249,330,000	$115,133,000
2005	$758,089,000	$50,078,000
2004	$603,225,000	$33,360,000

Curr. Assets:	$371,050,000	**Curr. Liab.:**	$37,185,000	**P/E Ratio:**	10.75
Plant, Equip.:	$102,987,000	**Total Liab.:**	$147,036,000	**Indic. Yr. Divd.:**	$0.080
Total Assets:	$474,157,000	**Net Worth:**	$327,121,000	**Debt/ Equity:**	0.2977

Encysive Pharmaceuticals Inc

4848 Loop Central Dr., 7th Fl., Houston, TX, 77081; ***PH:*** 1-713-796-8822; ***Fax:*** 1-713-796-8232; ***http://*** www.encysive.com; ***Email:*** encyinfo@encysive.com

General - Incorporation	DE	**Stock**- Price on:12/24/2007	$2
Employees	220	Stock Exchange	NDQ
Auditor	KPMG LLP	Ticker Symbol	ENCY
Stk Agt	Bank of New York	Outstanding Shares	70,160,000
Counsel	NA	E.P.S.	-$1.86
DUNS No.	78-627-2732	Shareholders	NA

Business: The group's principal activity is to discover, develop and market novel, synthetic and small molecule compounds for the treatment of cardiovascular, vascular and related inflammatory diseases. The research and development programs of the group are focused on the treatment and prevention of interrelated diseases of the vascular endothelium. The group presently has development programs such as thrombosis, vasospasm program, vascular inflammation program and vascular remodeling. The group operates in the United States and Germany. On 23-Apr-2003, the group acquired icos-Texas biotechnology l.p.

Primary SIC and add'l.: 5912 8731 2834 2836

CIK No: 0000887023

Subsidiaries: Encysive (UK) Limited, Encysive, L.P., Ep-et, LLC, ImmunoPharmaceutics, Inc.

Officers: Bruce D. Given/53/Dir., CEO, Pres./$1,283,380.00, George W. Cole/Dir., CEO, Pres./$855,637.00, Paul S. Manierre/VP, General Counsel, Denton Cooley/Advisory Dir., Ferid Murad/Advisory Dir., Heather Giles/VP - Strategic Planning, Derek Maetzold/VP - Marketing, Sales, Ann Tanabe/VP - Corporate Communications, Investor Relations, Richard A.F. Dixon/Dir., Sr. VP - Research, Chief Scientific Officer/$950,938.00, Pamela Mabry/Dir. - Global Human Resources, Jeffrey D. Keyser/VP - Regulatory Affairs/$598,899.00, Gordon H. Busenbark/51/CFO/$519,698.00

Directors: Bruce D. Given/53/Dir., CEO, Pres., George W. Cole/Dir., CEO, Pres., John M. Pietruski/Chmn., James T. Willerson/Dir., Chmn. - Scientific Advisory Board, Ron J. Anderson/Dir., John H. Dillon/Dir., Suzanne Oparil/Dir., James A. Thomson/Dir., Richard A.F. Dixon/Dir., Sr. VP - Research, Chief Scientific Officer, Kevin J. Buchi/Dir., Robert J. Cruikshank/Dir.

Owners: Wellington Management Company, LLP/13.60%, John H. Dillon, Kevin J. Buchi, Jeffrey D. Keyser, John M. Pietruski, George W. Cole, Insiders/4.70%, Robert J. Cruikshank, Suzanne Oparil, Gordon H. Busenbark, James T. Willerson, Richard A. F. Dixon/1.40%, Ron J. Anderson, Stephen L. Mueller, Bruce D. Given/1.60% *(17 Owners included in Index)*

Financial Data: ***Fiscal Year End:***12/31 ***Latest Annual Data:*** 12/31/2006

Year	Sales	Net Income
2006	$18,995,000	-$109,283,000
2005	$14,006,000	-$74,877,000
2004	$13,778,000	-$54,660,000

Curr. Assets:	$53,419,000	**Curr. Liab.:**	$26,854,000		
Plant, Equip.:	$5,976,000	**Total Liab.:**	$156,854,000	**Indic. Yr. Divd.:**	NA
Total Assets:	$63,137,000	**Net Worth:**	-$93,717,000	**Debt/ Equity:**	NA

Endeavor Acquisition Corp

7 Times Sq., 17th Fl., New York, NY, 10036; ***PH:*** 1-212-446-1898; ***Fax:*** 1-212-486-9094; ***http://*** www.endeavoracq.com; ***Email:*** Inquiries@endeavoracq.com

General - Incorporation	DE	**Stock**- Price on:12/24/2007	$12
Employees	NA	Stock Exchange	AMEX
Auditor	Marcum & Kliegman LLP	Ticker Symbol	EDA
Stk Agt	Continental Stock Transfer & Trust Co	Outstanding Shares	19,910,000
Counsel	NA	E.P.S.	$0.14
DUNS No.	NA	Shareholders	NA

Business: The group is in development stage. The group operates from the United States.

Primary SIC and add'l.: 6770

CIK No: 0001336545

Officers: Eric J. Watson/Chmn., Treasurer - Principal Financial, Accounting Officer, Jonathan J. Ledecky/Dir., Pres., Sec., Principal Executive Officer, Martin J. Dolfi/Consultant

Directors: Eric J. Watson/Chmn., Treasurer - Principal Financial, Accounting Officer, Jonathan J. Ledecky/Dir., Pres., Sec., Principal Executive Officer, Robert B. Hersov/Dir., Kerry Kennedy/Dir., Edward J. Mathias/Dir., Jay H. Nussbaum/Dir., Richard Y. Roberts/Dir.

Owners: Jonathan J. Ledecky, Scott A. Bommer, Prentice Capital Management, LP, Richard Y. Roberts, Weiss Multi-Strategy Advisors LLC et al, JLF Asset Management, L.L.C., Eric J. Watson, Fir Tree, Inc., Steven A. Cohen, Kerry Kennedy, Morgan Stanley, T. Rowe Price Associates, Inc., Jay H. Nussbaum, Gilder, Gagnon, Howe & Co. LLC, FMR Corp. (19 Owners included in Index)

Financial Data: Fiscal Year End:12/31 Latest Annual Data: 12/31/2006

Year	Sales	Net Income
2006	NA	$2,870,000
2005	NA	$54,000

Curr. Assets:	$125,396,000	Curr. Liab.:	$260,000	P/E Ratio:	85.71
Plant, Equip.:	$4,000	Total Liab.:	$25,282,000	Indic. Yr. Divd.:	NA
Total Assets:	$125,546,000	Net Worth:	$100,264,000	Debt/ Equity:	NA

Endeavour International Corp

1000 Main St., Ste. 3300, Houston, TX, 77002; **PH:** 1-713-307-8700; **http://** www.endeavourcorp.com; **Email:** ir@endeavourcorp.com

General - Incorporation	NV	Stock - Price on:12/24/2007	$1.4
Employees	60	Stock Exchange	AMEX
Auditor	KPMG LLP	Ticker Symbol	END
Stk Agt.	StockTrans, Inc.	Outstanding Shares	120,740,000
Counsel	NA	E.P.S.	-$0.32
DUNS No.	NA	Shareholders	NA

Business: The group's principal activity is explore and develop oil and gas. The group targets high-potential oil and gas assets in the Mississippi, Louisiana, Texas and other traditional oil producing states in the southwestern United States and Thailand. The group's operations are focused on exploration activities to find and evaluate prospective oil and gas properties and providing capital to participate in these projects. The group participates in projects directly, through consolidated subsidiaries and as equity participants in limited partnerships. On 26-Feb-2004 the group acquired nsnv inc.

Primary SIC and add'l.: 1311

CIK No: 0001112412

Subsidiaries: END Management Company, END Operating Management Company, Endeavour Energy Netherlands B.V., Endeavour Energy Norge AS, Endeavour Energy UK Limited, Endeavour International Holding B.V.

Officers: William L. Transier/Co - Founder, Chmn., CEO, Pres./$2,636,413.00, Lance G. Gilliland/40/Exec. VP/$1,864,179.00, Don H. Teague/Exec. VP - Administration, General Counsel, Sec./$1,400,922.00, Robert L. Thompson/61/VP, Chief Accounting Officer - Corporate Planning/$594,170.00, Bruce H. Stover/Exec. VP - Operations, Business Development/$1,979,377.00, Rusty Fisher/VP - Investor Relations, Tore Lybekk/CIO, Michael J. Kirksey/CFO, Exec. VP, John G. Williams/Exec. VP - Exploration

Directors: William L. Transier/Co - Founder, Chmn., CEO, Pres., John N. Seitz/Vice Chmn., John B. Connally/Dir., Nancy K. Quinn/Dir., Barry J. Galt/Dir., Thomas D. Clark/Dir., Charles Hue Williams/Dir.

Owners: Eton Park Capital Management, L.P./8.50%, John N. Seitz/5.90%, TPG-Axon GP, LLC/5.60%, John B. Connally, The Mitchell Group, Inc./10.20%, Bruce H. Stover, Nancy K. Quinn, Kings Road Investments Ltd./4.00%, HBK Investments L.P./8.50%, Thomas D. Clark, Palo Alto Investors, LLC/8.00%, Goldman, Sachs & Co./9.40%, Magnetar Master Fund, Ltd/3.30%, Lance G. Gilliland, Robert L. Thompson (21 Owners included in Index)

Financial Data: Fiscal Year End:12/31 Latest Annual Data: 12/31/2006

Year	Sales	Net Income
2006	$54,131,000	-$6,838,000
2005	$38,656,000	-$31,373,000
2004	$3,663,000	-$23,372,000

Curr. Assets:	$128,568,000	Curr. Liab.:	$81,137,000		
Plant, Equip.:	$319,315,000	Total Liab.:	$532,642,000	Indic. Yr. Divd.:	NA
Total Assets:	$774,470,000	Net Worth:	$116,828,000	Debt/ Equity:	2.4150

Endesa

410 Pk. Ave., Ste. 410, New York, NY, 10022; **PH:** 1-212-750-7200; **Fax:** 1-212-750-7433; **http://** www.endesa.es

General - Incorporation	Spain	Stock - Price on:12/24/2007	$53.81
Employees	26,758	Stock Exchange	NA
Auditor Ernst & Young, Deloitte & Co. S.R.L.		Ticker Symbol	NA
Stk Agt. Morgan ADR Service Center, Citibank		Outstanding Shares	1,060,000,000
Counsel	Francisco De Borja Acha Besga	E.P.S.	$3.14
DUNS No.	46-227-7716	Shareholders	NA

Business: The group's principal activities are the generation, transmission, marketing and distribution of electricity. The group's operation consists of six divisions: generation, diversification, international, red, engergia and servicios. The generation divisions generates electricity, nuclear power and mining. The diversification segment consists of telecommunication, gas and water supply. The international segment includes operations outside Europe. The red segment is involved in domestic distribution of energy. Energia division commercializes energy and value services to retail segment. The endesa services division provides assistance to the group's subsidiaries. The group has its operations in Spain, Europe and Latin America.

Primary SIC and add'l.: 4899 1231 4923 4911 1222 4941

CIK No: 0001046649

Subsidiaries: Ampla Energa e Servios, S.A. (Ampla), Carboex, S.A., Central Hidroelctrica de Betania, S.A., Chilectra, S.A., Codensa, S.A., Companha de Interconexao Energtica, S.A. (Cien), Companha Energtica do Cear, S.A. (Coelce), Edegel, S.A., Empresa de Distribucin Elctrica de Lima, Empresa Distribuidora Sur, S.A. (Edesur), Empresa Elctrica Pehuenche, S.A., Empresa Generadora de Energa Elctrica, S.A. (Emgesa), Endesa Brasil, S.A., Endesa Chile, Endesa Cogeneracin y Renovables, S.A. (ECyR) 31 Subsidiaries included in the Index

Officers: Rafael Miranda Robredo/Dir., CEO, angel Ferrera Martinez/Chmn. - Advisory Board, Unelco, Endesa Canary Islands, Mario Valcarce Duran/Dir., Chmn. - Endesa Chile, Bartolome Reus Beltran/Chmn. - Advisory Board Of Gesa - Endesa Balearic Islands, Jose Maria Plans Gomez/Chmn. - Advisory Board, GM at Unelco - Endesa Canary Islands, Antonio Pareja Molina/Sr. VP - Services, Jose Luis Puche Castillejo/Mgr. - Corporate Audit, Jose Maria Rovira Vilanova/GM - Fecsa, Endesa

Cataluna, Carlos Torres Vila/Sr. VP - Strategy, Rafael Lopez Rueda/GM - Chilectra, Rafael Mateo Alcala/GM - Endesa Chile, Javier Uriarte Monereo/GM - Retailing, German Medina Carrillo/Sr. VP - Human Resources, M Isabel Fernandez Lozano/Corporate Mgr., Assist. to Corporate Services Mgr., Jose Antonio Gutierrez Perez/GM - Erz, Endesa Aragon (31 Officers included in Index)

Directors: Rafael Miranda Robredo/Dir., CEO, Amado Franco Lahoz/Chmn. - Advisory Board Of Erz - Endesa Aragon, Jaime Ybarra Llosent/Chmn. - Advisory Board Of Sevillana Endesa Andalucia - Extremadura, Jose Maria Plans Gomez/Chmn. - Advisory Board, GM at Unelco - Endesa Canary Islands, Jorge Rosemblut Ratinoff/Chmn. - Chilectra, Pablo Yrarrazabal Valdes/Chmn. - Enersis, Anton Costas Comesana/Chmn. - Advisory Board Of Fecsa - Endesa Cataluna, Francisco Javier Ramos Gascon/Dir., Jose Manuel Fernandez-Norniella/Dir., Juan Ramon Quintas Seoane/Dir., Rafael Gonzalez-Gallarza Morales/Dir., Miguel Blesa De La Parra/Dir., Jose Serna Masia/Dir., Manuel Rios Navarro/Dir., Jose Maria Fernandez Cuevas/Dir. (27 Directors included in Index)

Owners: Alberto Recarte Garca-Andrade, Juan Rosell Lastortras, Rafael Gonzlez-Gallarza Morales, Francisco Javir Ramos Gascn, Juan Ramn Quints Seoane, Rafael Miranda Robredo, Miguel Blesa de la Parra, Manuel Ros Navarro, Jos Serna Masi, Manuel Pizarro Moreno

Financial Data: Fiscal Year End:12/31 Latest Annual Data: 12/31/2006

Year	Sales	Net Income
2006	$27,171,774,000	$3,849,995,000
2005	$21,590,428,000	$3,260,653,000
2004	$24,647,886,000	$2,150,294,000

Curr. Assets:	$10,176,872,000	Curr. Liab.:	$10,753,844,000		
Plant, Equip.:	$43,033,858,000	Total Liab.:	$51,882,509,000	Indic. Yr. Divd.:	NA
Total Assets:	$73,561,835,000	Net Worth:	$15,546,533,000	Debt/ Equity:	NA

Endevco Inc

2425 Fountain View, Ste 215, Houston, TX, 77057; **PH:** 1-713-977-4662; **Fax:** 1-713-628-8240; **http://** www.endevcoinc.com; **Email:** info@endevcoinc.com

General - Incorporation	TX	Stock - Price on:12/24/2007	$0.034
Employees	3	Stock Exchange	OTC
Auditor	Killman, Murrell & Co. P.C	Ticker Symbol	ENDE
Stk Agt	Superior Stock Transfer Inc	Outstanding Shares	249,280,000
Counsel	Warejacksonlee & Chambers LLP	E.P.S.	-$0.008
DUNS No.	04-948-3563	Shareholders	NA

Business: The group's principal activities are oil and gas exploration and power generation. The group has oil and gas properties in yeman and intends to generate power in future.

Primary SIC and add'l.: 1311 4911

CIK No: 0000355300

Subsidiaries: Adair Colombia Oil and Gas, S.A, Africa Energy Group, Inc, EnDevCo Minerals Inc, EnDevCo Refining Corporation, Superior Stock Transfer, Inc

Officers: Chris A. Dittmar/Chmn., CEO, Richard G. Boyce/Dir., COO, Larry Swift/CFO, Tom Cloutier/Dir. - Investor Relations

Directors: Chris A. Dittmar/Chmn., CEO, John A. Brush/Dir., Charles R. Close/Dir., Richard G. Boyce/Dir., COO

Owners: Chris A. Dittmar/14.57%, Insiders/43.10%, John A. Brush/2.26%, James C. Row/1.19%, Richard G. Boyce/15.08%, Larry Swift/7.72%, Charles R. Close/2.29%, Insiders/1.30%, Richard G. Boyce/1.30%

Financial Data: Fiscal Year End:12/31 Latest Annual Data: 12/31/2006

Year	Sales	Net Income
2006	$2,071,000	-$1,201,000
2005	$1,000	-$701,000
2004	NA	-$6,260,000

Curr. Assets:	$1,300,000	Curr. Liab.:	$5,956,000		
Plant, Equip.:	$17,799,000	Total Liab.:	$18,105,000	Indic. Yr. Divd.:	NA
Total Assets:	$19,100,000	Net Worth:	-$2,006,000	Debt/ Equity:	NA

Endo Pharmaceuticals Holdings Inc

100 Endo Blvd., Chadds Ford, PA, 19317; **PH:** 1-610-558-9800; **Fax:** 1-610-558-8979; **http://** www.endo.com

General - Incorporation	DE	Stock - Price on:12/24/2007	$34.82
Employees	1,024	Stock Exchange	NDQ
Auditor	Deloitte & Touche LLP	Ticker Symbol	ENDP
Stk Agt	American Stock Transfer & Trust Co.	Outstanding Shares	133,770,000
Counsel	Skadden, Meagher & Flom LLP	E.P.S.	$1.43
DUNS No.	NA	Shareholders	NA

Business: The group's principal activities are to conduct research, develop, sale and market branded and generic prescription pharmaceuticals used primarily to treat and manage pain. The group markets branded pharmaceutical products to doctors, drug wholesalers, pharmacies, hospitals, governmental agencies, physicians and other healthcare professionals. The group also markets its generics through customer service activities, chain and independent retail pharmacists. The group's products include percocet(R), percodan(R), zydone(R) , lidoderm(R), morphine sulfate er, morphidex(R) oxymorphone er, oxymorphone ir, hydrocodex tm, oxycodex tm, percodex(TM) and oxycodone er. The group contracts with third parties to provide certain critical services such as manufacturing, warehousing, distribution, customer service, financial functions, certain research and development activities and medical affairs.

Primary SIC and add'l.: 2834 5122

CIK No: 0001100962

Subsidiaries: BML Pharmaceuticals, Inc., Endo Pharma Canada Inc., Endo Pharmaceuticals Inc., EPI Company

Officers: Peter A. Lankau/Dir., CEO, Pres./$6,382,574.00, David A.H. Lee/Exec. VP - Research, Development, Chief Scientific Officer/$622,360.00, Caroline B. Manogue/Exec. VP, Chief Legal Officer, Sec./$7,363,233.00, Bill Newbould/VP - Corporate Communications, Primary Investor Relations Officer, Jeremy Goldberg/MD - Corporate Development, Charles A. Rowland/Exec. VP, CFO, Treasurer/$288,060.00, Joyce N. Laviscount/Chief Accounting Officer, VP - Financial Operations/$464,299.00, Nancy J. Wysenski/COO

Directors: Peter A. Lankau/Dir., CEO, Pres., Roger H. Kimmel/61/Chmn., Michael Hyatt/Dir., Clive A. Meanwell/Dir., John J. Delucca/Dir., Michel De Rosen/Dir., George F. Horner/Dir.

Owners: Insiders/2.30%, George F. Horner, Carol A. Ammon, Michael Hyatt, David A. H. Lee, Royce& Associates, LLC/5.80%, John J. Delucca, Barclays Global Investors, Ltd, Barclays Global Fund Advisors, Peter A. Lankau, Michel de Rosen, Capital Research and Management Co./9.20%, Roger H. Kimmel, Clive A. Meanwell, Joyce N. LaViscount (19 Owners included in Index)

Financial Data: Fiscal Year End:12/31 Latest Annual Data: 06/30/2007

Year	Sales	Net Income
2007	$257,147,000	$60,546,000
2006	$909,659,000	$137,839,000
2005	$820,164,000	$202,295,000

Curr. Assets:	$1,036,014,000	**Curr. Liab.:**	$338,099,000	**P/E Ratio:**	26.78
Plant, Equip.:	$36,565,000	**Total Liab.:**	$355,701,000	**Indic. Yr. Divd.:**	NA
Total Assets:	$1,396,689,000	**Net Worth:**	$1,040,988,000	**Debt/ Equity:**	NA

Endocare Inc

201 Technology Dr., Irvine, CA, 92618; *PH:* 1-949-450-5400; *Fax:* 1-949-450-5300;
http:// www.endocare.com; *Email:* ir@endocare.com

General - Incorporation	DE	**Stock**- Price on:12/24/2007	$2.8
Employees	123	Stock Exchange	NDQ
Auditor	Ernst & Young LLP	Ticker Symbol	ENDO
Stk Agt	U.S. Stock Transfer Corp	Outstanding Shares	31,220,000
Counsel	Brobeck, Phleger & Harrison	E.P.S.	-$0.15
DUNS No.	92-895-5509	Shareholders	NA

Business: The group's principal activities are to develop, manufacture and market urological healthcare products. It offers temperature based surgical devices and technologies to treat prostate diseases including prostate cancer and benign prostate hyperplasia (bph). It also offers vacuum therapy systems and penile implant for the treatment of erectile dysfunction. The group's timm medical technologies, inc. Offerings now include an additional product used in the treatment of bph, five products used in the diagnosis and treatment of erectile dysfunction, six products used in the diagnosis and management of urinary incontinence and one product used in the diagnosis of bladder cancer. Few of the product names include cryoprobes, fasttrac, guidewires, biopsy tool and snap gauge. The group markets and sells its products worldwide to distributors of medical devices, hospitals and other medical professional organizations.

Primary SIC and add'l.: 3841

CIK No: 0001003464

Officers: Craig T. Davenport/Chmn., CEO, Pres./$1,688,252.00, Michael R. Rodriguez/Sr. VP - Finance, CFO/$379,644.00, Clint B. Davis/Sr. VP - Legal Affairs, General Counsel, Sec./$404,120.00, Matt Clawson/Investor Relation Officer

Directors: Craig T. Davenport/Chmn., CEO, Pres., David L. Goldsmith/Dir., Eric S. Kentor/Dir., Thomas R. Testman/Dir., John R. Daniels/Dir., Terrence A. Noonan/Dir.

Owners: Craig T. Davenport/3.30%, Eric S. Kentor, Black River Asset Management LLC/6.50%, Thomas R. Testman, Insiders/5.50%, State of Wisconsin Investment Board/9.30%, Clint B. Davis, Terrence A. Noonan, Michael R. Rodriguez, John R. Daniels, William J. Nydam/2.50%, David L. Goldsmith, Midwood Capital Management LLC/5.60%

Financial Data: *Fiscal Year End:*12/31   *Latest Annual Data:* 12/31/2006

Year	Sales	Net Income
2006	$27,990,000	-$10,765,000
2005	$28,274,000	-$13,679,000
2004	$32,685,000	-$37,619,000

Curr. Assets:	$9,516,000	**Curr. Liab.:**	$9,987,000		
Plant, Equip.:	$1,040,000	**Total Liab.:**	$11,368,000	**Indic. Yr. Divd.:**	NA
Total Assets:	$16,246,000	**Net Worth:**	$4,878,000	**Debt/ Equity:**	NA

Endologix Inc

11 Studebaker, Irvine, CA, 92618; *PH:* 1-949-595-7200; *Fax:* 1-949-457-9561;
http:// www.endologix.com; *Email:* investorrelations@endologix.com

General - Incorporation	DE	**Stock**- Price on:12/24/2007	$4.42
Employees	164	Stock Exchange	NDQ
Auditor	PricewaterhouseCoopers LLP	Ticker Symbol	ELGX
Stk Agt	American Stock Transfer & Trust Co.	Outstanding Shares	42,720,000
Counsel	NA	E.P.S.	-$0.4
DUNS No.	NA	Shareholders	NA

Business: The group's principal activity is to develop, manufacture, sell and market minimally invasive therapies for the treatment of cardiovascular disease. The group's products are the powerlink system and powerweb system, which are catheter-based alternative treatments for abdominal aortic aneurysm. These products are self-expanding stainless steel stent cage is covered by eptfe, a common surgical graft material that reduce the mortality and morbidity rates associated with conventional aaa surgery and provide a clinical alternative patients who could not undergo conventional surgery. The group caters to markets in Europe, Japan and Latin America besides the domestic market.

Primary SIC and add'l.: 3841

CIK No: 0001013606

Subsidiaries: CVD/RMS Acquisition Corp, Radiance Medical Systems GmbH

Officers: Paul McCormick/Dir., CEO, Pres./$602,066.00, Stefan G. Schreck/VP - Research, Development/$385,171.00, Robert J. Krist/Sec., CFO/$382,296.00, Karen Uyesugi/VP - RA, QA, CA/$333,239.00

Directors: Paul McCormick/Dir., CEO, Pres., Franklin D. Brown/Chmn., Gregory D. Waller/Dir., Edward B. Diethrich/Dir., Ronald H. Coelyn/Dir., Roderick De Greef/Dir., Jeffrey F. Odonnell/Dir.

Owners: Paul McCormick/1.50%, Ronald H. Coelyn, Federated Investors, Inc./23.30%, Karen Uyesugi, Gregory D. Waller, Robert J. Krist, Edward B. Diethrich/1.40%, Franklin D. Brown/1.10%, Goldman, Sachs & Co./8.10%, Insiders/5.90%, Stefan D. Schreck, Elliott Associates/12.00%, Roderick de Greef, Jeffrey F. ODonnell

Financial Data: *Fiscal Year End:*12/31   *Latest Annual Data:* 12/31/2006

Year	Sales	Net Income
2006	$14,672,000	-$17,543,000
2005	$7,139,000	-$15,518,000
2004	$4,232,000	-$9,683,000

Curr. Assets:	$31,942,000	**Curr. Liab.:**	$5,009,000		
Plant, Equip.:	$4,516,000	**Total Liab.:**	$6,181,000	**Indic. Yr. Divd.:**	NA
Total Assets:	$52,686,000	**Net Worth:**	$46,505,000	**Debt/ Equity:**	NA

Endovasc Inc

550 Club Dr., Ste. 345, Montgomery, TX, 77316; *PH:* 1-936-582-5920; *Fax:* 1-936-582-5996;
http:// www.endovasc.com; *Email:* robjohnson@endovasc.com

General - Incorporation	NV	**Stock**- Price on:12/24/2007	$0.019
Employees	4	Stock Exchange	OTC
Auditor	McConnell & Jones LLP	Ticker Symbol	EVSC
Stk Agt	Integrity Stock Transfer, Inc.	Outstanding Shares	160,980,000
Counsel	NA	E.P.S.	-$0.001
DUNS No.	NA	Shareholders	NA

Business: The group's principle activities include developing, marketing and licensing biopharmaceutical products for the human healthcare industry. The products are developed using liposomal drug delivery method that helps to deliver drugs to the intended target and release them with efficiency and control. Liposomes are microscopic cell-like spheres composed of a thin, durable lipid membrane surrounding a hollow compartment. The group develops three product lines namely, liprostin, nicotine receptor agonist and stent coating. The group operates from United States.

Primary SIC and add'l.: 3841 8731

CIK No: 0001040415

Subsidiaries: Angiogenix Limited, Inc. (Angiogenix)

Officers: Diane Dottavio/CEO, Pres., Sam H. Lindsey/CFO, Chief Compliance Officer

Owners: Insiders/3.20%, Robert G. Johnson, Estate of Dwight Cantrell/2.80%, Donald Leonard, Diane Dottavio/2.30%

Financial Data: *Fiscal Year End:*06/30   *Latest Annual Data:* 6/30/2006

Year	Sales	Net Income
2006	$449,000	-$225,000
2005	$90,000	-$205,000
2004	$72,000	-$4,679,000

Curr. Assets:	$45,000	**Curr. Liab.:**	$303,000		
Plant, Equip.:	$29,000	**Total Liab.:**	$470,000	**Indic. Yr. Divd.:**	NA
Total Assets:	$1,714,000	**Net Worth:**	$1,244,000	**Debt/ Equity:**	NA

Endurance Specialty Holdings Ltd

Endurance Re, 230 Pk. Ave., New York, NY, 10169; *PH:* 1-212-471-1740; *Fax:* 1-212-471-1741;
http:// www.endurancebermuda.com

General - Incorporation	Bermuda	**Stock**- Price on:12/24/2007	$39.26
Employees	484	Stock Exchange	NYSE
Auditor	Ernst & Young LLP	Ticker Symbol	ENH
Stk Agt	Computershare Investor Services LLC	Outstanding Shares	65,940,000
Counsel	NA	E.P.S.	$7.72
DUNS No.	NA	Shareholders	NA

Business: The groups principle activity is to provide insurance and reinsurance services. The group operates from United States.

Primary SIC and add'l.: NA

CIK No: 0001179755

Subsidiaries: Baytown SurgiCare, Inc., Bellaire ASC, LP, Bellaire SurgiCare, Inc., Dennis Cain Management, LLC, Dennis Cain Physician Solutions, Ltd., Endurance Reinsurance Corporation of America, Endurance Specialty Insurance Ltd., Endurance U.S. Holding Corp., Endurance Worldwide Holdings Limited, Endurance Worldwide Insurance Limited, Integrated Physician Solutions, Inc., Medical Billing Services, Inc., San Jacinto Surgery Center, Ltd.

Officers: William M. Jewett/CEO, Pres. - Worldwide Reinsurance Operations/$2,022,687.00, Michael P. Fujii/CEO, Pres. - Worldwide Insurance Operations, Kenneth J. Lestrange/Chmn., CEO, Pres. - Endurance Specialty Holdings Ltd/$2,721,532.00, John V. Del Col/General Counsel, Sec., Exec. VP - Acquisitions/$1,610,506.00, David S. Cash/42/Chief Underwriting Officer, John L. O'Connor/COO, Pres. - Endurance Services Limited, Michael J. McGuire/CFO/$1,251,284.00, Michael Angelina/Chief Actuary, Chief Risk Officer, Thomas D. Bell/Exec. VP - Endurance US Holdings Corp, Daniel M. Izard/COO/$1,649,661.00, Mark Silverstein/45/Chief Investment Officer

Directors: Kenneth J. Lestrange/Chmn., CEO, Pres. - Endurance Specialty Holdings Ltd, Gregor S. Bailar/Dir., John T. Baily/Dir., Norman Barham/Dir., Galen R. Barnes/Dir., William H. Bolinder/Dir., Steven W. Carlsen/Dir., Brendan R. O'Neill/57/Dir., Richard C. Perry/Dir., William J. Raver/Dir., Robert A. Spass/Dir., Therese M. Vaughan/Dir., Max R. Williamson/Dir.

Owners: Performance Co-Investment Fund I, L.P, Anthony DeFelice, Texas Pacific Group, First Plaza Group Trust, Aon Corporation/5.80%, Perry Corp/10.80%, Thomas H. Lee related entities, Richard Rose, Metro Center Investment Pte Ltd, Capital Z Financial Services Fund II, LP/8.00%

Financial Data: *Fiscal Year End:*12/31   *Latest Annual Data:* 12/31/2006

Year	Sales	Net Income
2006	$1,877,071,000	$498,126,000
2005	$1,904,669,000	-$220,484,000
2004	$1,760,575,000	$355,584,000

Curr. Assets:	$1,357,644,000	**Curr. Liab.:**	$560,114,000		
Plant, Equip.:	NA	**Total Liab.:**	$4,627,680,000	**Indic. Yr. Divd.:**	$1.000
Total Assets:	$6,925,554,000	**Net Worth:**	$2,297,874,000	**Debt/ Equity:**	0.2809

Endwave Corp

130 Baytech Dr., San Jose, CA, 95134; *PH:* 1-408-522-3100; *Fax:* 1-408-522-3197;
http:// www.endwave.com

General - Incorporation	DE	**Stock**- Price on:12/24/2007	$11.01
Employees	151	Stock Exchange	NDQ
Auditor	Burr, Pilger & Mayer LLP	Ticker Symbol	ENWV
Stk Agt	Computershare Trust Co	Outstanding Shares	11,530,000
Counsel	Cooley Godward LLP	E.P.S.	-$0.45
DUNS No.	NA	Shareholders	NA

Business: The group's principal activity is to design and manufacture radio frequency subsystems that enable the transmission, reception and processing of high-speed data signals in broadband wireless access systems. Their products are used in point-to-point access, point-to-multipoint access and high capacity cellular backhaul applications. They also offers build-to-print manufacturing services for customer designed products such as multi-function modules, transceivers and outdoor units. Main products of the group include rf modules, integrated transceivers, broadband antennas, outdoor units and others. Their customers are microwave radio manufacturers and wireless system integrators that provide the broadband wireless equipment used by communications service providers. The major customers of the group include nokia, stratex networks and nera networks. In 2003, the group acquired the assets of verticom inc and arcom wireless of dover corporation.

Primary SIC and add'l.: 3663

CIK No: 0001118941

Subsidiaries: Endwave Defense Systems Inc.

Officers: Edward A. Keible/Dir., CEO, Pres./$945,266.00, Julianne M. Biagini/45/Sr. VP/$271,173.00, Daniel P. Teuthorn/Sr. VP - Technology, Arthur A. Arrington/VP - Manufacturing, Steven F. Layton/Sr. VP, GM - Telecom Products Division, John J. Mikulsky/COO, Exec. VP/$542,960.00, Mark A. Hebeisen/VP - Marketing, Business Development, James R. Crossen/VP, General Counsel, David M. Hall/Sr. VP, GM - Defense, Security Products Division, Brett W. Wallace/CFO, Exec. VP/$582,146.00, Curt P. Sacks/VP - Finance, Corporate Controller

Directors: Edward A. Keible/Dir., CEO, Pres., Edward C.V. Winn/69/Non Exec. Chmn., John F. McGrath/Dir., Wade Meyercord/Dir., Joseph J. Lazzara/56/Dir., Eric Stonestrom/Dir.

Owners: Entities affiliated with Potomac Capital Management/9.30%, Brett W. Wallace/1.40%, Entities affiliated with Wood River Management LLC/35.30%, Joseph J. Lazzara, Entities affiliated with EagleRock Capital Management/6.50%, Edward C.V. Winn, Julianne M. Biagini/1.10%, Wade Meyercord, Eric D. Stonestrom, Insiders/10.20%, John F. McGrath, John J. Mikulsky/2.10%, Pate Capital Partners, LP/6.90%, Entities Affiliated with Oak Investment Partners XI, Limited Partnership/25.10%, Entities Affiliated with Oak Investment Partners XI, Limited Partnership/100.00% *(16 Owners included in Index)*

Financial Data: *Fiscal Year End:*12/31 *Latest Annual Data:* 12/31/2006

Year	Sales	Net Income
2006	$62,226,000	-$1,344,000
2005	$48,735,000	-$874,000
2004	$33,162,000	-$4,404,000

Curr. Assets:	$94,067,000	**Curr. Liab.:**	$11,024,000		
Plant, Equip.:	$2,024,000	**Total Liab.:**	$11,255,000	**Indic. Yr. Divd.:**	NA
Total Assets:	$100,653,000	**Net Worth:**	$89,398,000	**Debt/ Equity:**	NA

Enel SpA

Viale Regina Margherita 137, Rome, 13700198; *PH:* 39-0683052129; *http://* www.enel.it

General - Incorporation	Italy	**Stock**- Price on:12/24/2007	$53.55
Employees	58,548	Stock Exchange	NYSE
Auditor	KPMG Spa	Ticker Symbol	EN
Stk Agt	Morgan ADR Service Center	Outstanding Shares	1,240,000,000
Counsel	NA	E.P.S.	-$1.41
DUNS No.	NA	Shareholders	NA

Business: The group's principal activities are the production, import and export, transmission and distribution of electricity for domestic and industrial use. The group is also active in the telecommunications sector. During 2003, the group acquired 73% of maritza east iii power company and 80% of union fenosa energia especiales. The group operates in Italy, North America, Latin America, Middle East, Africa and other countries.

Primary SIC and add'l.: 4931 4911 4812

CIK No: 0001096200

Subsidiaries: Agassiz beach LLC, Agricola Rio Sahuil Ltda, Agricola Y Constructora Rio Guanehue SA, Aiten AS, Aquenergy Systems Inc., Asotin Hydro Company Inc., Autumn Hills LLC, Avisio Energia S.p.A., Aziscohos Hydro Company Inc., Barras Electricas Galaico Asturianas SA, Barras Electricas Generacion SL, Beaver Falls Water Power Company, Beaver Valley Holdings Ltd., Beaver Valley Power Company, Boot Field LLC 188 Subsidiaries included in the Index

Officers: Fulvio Conti/60/Dir., CEO, GM, A. Cardani/Internal Audit, L. Ferraris/Adminisration Planning, Control, L. Gallo/Infrastructures, Network, M. Cioffi/Human Resources, Claudio MacHetti/49/CFO, Iin Charge - Finance, Andrea Brentan/59/Business Development, M&A Unit, International Division, S. Cardillo/Legal Affairs, S. Fontecedro/Generation, Energy Management, Claudio Sartorelli/63/Sec. - Corporate Affairs, A. Bufacchi/Information, Communication Technology, G. Comin/External Relations, C. Tamburi/Procurement, Services, A. Trebbi/Assist., J. Anzola/International Activities Assist. *(19 Officers included in Index)*

Directors: Fulvio Conti/60/Dir., CEO, GM, Piero Gnudi/69/Chmn., Franco Fontana/65/Chmn., Board Of Statutory Auditors, Alessandro Luciano/56/Dir., Fernando Napolitano/43/Dir., Carlo Conte/60/Member - Board of Statutory Auditors, Gianfranco Tosi/60/Dir., Augusto Fantozzi/68/Dir., Francesco Taranto/68/Dir., Giulio Ballio/68/Dir., Francesco Valsecchi/44/Dir., Gennaro Mariconda/65/Member - Board of Statutory Auditors, Claudio Sartorelli/63/Sec. - Corporate Affairs

Owners: Giulio Ballio, Gennaro Mariconda, Francesco Taranto, Piero Gnudi, Giancarlo Giordano, Fulvio Conti

Financial Data: *Fiscal Year End:*12/31 *Latest Annual Data:* 12/31/2005

Year	Sales	Net Income
2005	$40,333,000,000	$5,562,000,000
2004	$49,785,592,000	$1,406,696,000
2003	$39,324,757,000	$2,983,543,000

Curr. Assets:	$103,265,000	**Curr. Liab.:**	$61,858,000		
Plant, Equip.:	$8,420,000	**Total Liab.:**	$1,863,311,000	**Indic. Yr. Divd.:**	$2.830
Total Assets:	$202,989,000	**Net Worth:**	$9,414,000	**Debt/ Equity:**	NA

Ener1 Inc

500 W Cypress Creek Rd., Ste. 100, Fort Lauderdale, FL, 33309; *PH:* 1-954-556-4020; *Fax:* 1-954-556-4031; *http://* www.ener1.com; *Email:* info@ener1.com

General - Incorporation	FL	**Stock**- Price on:12/24/2007	$0.22
Employees	73	Stock Exchange	OTC
Auditor	Malone & Bailey, P.C	Ticker Symbol	ENEI
Stk Agt	Registrar & Transfer Co	Outstanding Shares	462,940,000
Counsel	NA	E.P.S.	-$0.07
DUNS No.	13-178-8879	Shareholders	NA

Business: The group's principal activities are to develop and market new technologies and products for clean, efficient energy sources, including high-energy lithium batteries, fuel cells and solar cells. The technologies and products have applications for military, industrial and consumer markets ranging from lightweight battery packs for military field use and high-end consumer applications to fuel cells and high-rate lithium-ion batteries for electric vehicles. The group's subsidiary, nanoener develops and markets its proprietary nanotechnologies and nanomaterials. The advanced nanotechnologies provide rechargeable batteries that offer high rates of discharge, giving applications more power faster. The group develops, tests and manufactures its advanced lithium batteries and other energy devices at its facility in ft.lauderdale, Florida.

Primary SIC and add'l.: 3691 3692

CIK No: 0000895642

Subsidiaries: AppsComm, Inc., Boca Global, Inc., Boca Research (UK) Limited, Boca Research Holland B.V., Boca Research International Holding, Ltd., Boca Research International, Inc., Boca Research of Delaware, Inc., Ener EL Holdings, Inc., Ener1 Battery Company, Ener1 Technologies, Inc., Ener1 Ukraine, EnerDel, Inc., EnerFuel, Inc., EnerNow Technologies, Inc., NanoEner, Inc.

Officers: Peter Novak/Dir., CEO, Pres., Gerard Herlihy/CFO, Ulrik Grape/Exec. VP - Global Sales, Marketing, Business Development, Rex Hodge/Exec. VP, Naoki Ota/COO, Anton Zingarevich/VP - Operations, Jerry Herlihy/Contact - Public, Investor Relations, Curtis Wolfe/44/General Counsel, Sec.

Directors: Peter Novak/Dir., CEO, Pres., Charles Gassenheimer/Chmn., Mike Zoi/Dir., Ludovico Manfredi/Dir., Philip Carlson/Member - Advisory Board, Karl Gruns/Dir., Wilson Greatbatch/Member - Advisory Board, Toshihiko Fujioka/Member - Advisory Board, Marshall S. Cogan/Dir., Thomas J. Snyder/Dir., Kenneth R. Baker/Dir.

Owners: Ludovico Manfredi, Ajit Habbu, Charles Gassenheimer, Bzinfin, S.A., Gerard Herlihy, Ulrik Grape, Rex Hodge, Marshall Cogan, The Quercus Trust, Mike Zoi, Karl Gruns, Ener1 Group, Inc., Insiders, Peter Novak

Financial Data: *Fiscal Year End:*12/31 *Latest Annual Data:* 12/31/2006

Year	Sales	Net Income
2006	$100,000	-$41,305,000
2005	$60,000	$28,604,000
2004	$42,000	-$35,815,000

Curr. Assets:	$691,000	**Curr. Liab.:**	$14,426,000		
Plant, Equip.:	$3,554,000	**Total Liab.:**	$35,693,000	**Indic. Yr. Divd.:**	NA
Total Assets:	$7,168,000	**Net Worth:**	-$50,263,000	**Debt/ Equity:**	NA

Enercorp Inc

37735 Ent. Ct, Ste. 600-b, Farmington Hills, MI, 48331; *PH:* 1-248-994-0099

General - Incorporation	CO	**Stock**- Price on:12/24/2007	$0.16
Employees	NA	Stock Exchange	OTC
Auditor	UHY LLP	Ticker Symbol	ENCP
Stk Agt	Computershare Trust Co	Outstanding Shares	NA
Counsel	NA	E.P.S.	NA
DUNS No.	09-991-5175	Shareholders	NA

Business: The group's principle activity is to provides managerial assistance to developing companies. The group operates from United States.

Primary SIC and add'l.: 6799

CIK No: 0000313116

Officers: Brett A. Homovec/Dir., COO, Pres.

Financial Data: *Fiscal Year End:*06/30 *Latest Annual Data:* 6/30/2005

Year	Sales	Net Income
2005	$1,000	-$578,000
2001	$1,476,000	-$795,000
2000	$514,000	-$1,802,000

Curr. Assets:	NA	**Curr. Liab.:**	$57,000		
Plant, Equip.:	NA	**Total Liab.:**	$436,000	**Indic. Yr. Divd.:**	NA
Total Assets:	$471,000	**Net Worth:**	$35,000	**Debt/ Equity:**	NA

Energas Resources Inc

800 NE 63rd St., 3rd Fl., Oklahoma City, OK, 73105; *PH:* 1-405-879-1752; *Fax:* 1-405-879-0175; *http://* www.energasresources.com; *Email:* info@energasresources.com

General - Incorporation	DE	**Stock**- Price on:12/24/2007	$0.043
Employees	10	Stock Exchange	OTC
Auditor	Murrell, Hall, McIntosh & Co., PLLP	Ticker Symbol	EGSR
Stk Agt	Pacific Corporate Trust Co	Outstanding Shares	78,670,000
Counsel	NA	E.P.S.	-$0.02
DUNS No.	NA	Shareholders	NA

Business: The group's principal activities are to explore and develop oil and gas resources. The group conducts its oil and gas exploration and production activities through its wholly-owned subsidiary, a t gas gathering systems, inc. The group principally operates in the arkoma basin in Oklahoma, the powder river basin in Wyoming and the appalachian basin of eastern Kentucky. It also owns and operates a natural gas gathering system that serves the wells operated by the group for delivery to a mainline transmission system. This system is located in atoka county, Oklahoma and consists of four miles of pipeline and is connected to four wells that supply natural gas. In Aug 2003, the group acquired 31 producing gas wells, 28 miles of pipeline, 2 compressor stations and approximately 23,000 leased and 8,500 optioned acres located in appalachian basin of eastern Kentucky.

Primary SIC and add'l.: 1382 4612 1311

CIK No: 0001029402

Subsidiaries: A.T. Gas Gathering Systems, Inc., TGC, Inc

Officers: George G. Shaw/Dir., CEO, Pres., Principal Financial Officer, Scott Shaw/Dir., VP, Andy Biddy/VP - Administration

Directors: George G. Shaw/Dir., CEO, Pres., Principal Financial Officer, Scott Shaw/Dir., VP

Owners: Scott G. Shaw/1.00%, Marguerite S. Tyson/11.00%, Insiders/25.00%, George G. Shaw/24.00%

Financial Data: *Fiscal Year End:*01/31 *Latest Annual Data:* 01/31/2007

Year	Sales	Net Income
2007	$644,000	-$1,516,000
2006	$1,197,000	-$1,584,000
2005	$668,000	-$1,164,000

Curr. Assets:	$2,134,000	**Curr. Liab.:**	$1,603,000		
Plant, Equip.:	$4,206,000	**Total Liab.:**	$1,707,000	**Indic. Yr. Divd.:**	NA
Total Assets:	$6,340,000	**Net Worth:**	$4,633,000	**Debt/ Equity:**	NA

Energen Corp

605 Richard Arrington Jr. Blvd. N, Birmingham, AL, 35203; *PH:* 1-205-326-2700; *Fax:* 1-205-326-2704; *http://* www.energen.com

General - Incorporation	AL	**Stock**- Price on:12/24/2007	$55.46
Employees	1,530	Stock Exchange	NYSE
Auditor	PricewaterhouseCoopers LLP	Ticker Symbol	EGN
Stk Agt	Computershare Investor Services LLC	Outstanding Shares	71,730,000
Counsel	Bradley, Arant, Rose & White	E.P.S.	$4.50
DUNS No.	09-570-6032	Shareholders	NA

Business: The group's principal activity is to acquire, develop, explore and produce oil, natural gas and natural gas liquids in the continental United States. It also purchases, distributes and sells natural gas in the central and north Alabama. The natural gas is purchased through interstate and intrastate marketers and suppliers. This is then distributed to residential, commercial and industrial customers and other end-users of natural gas. On 02-Aug-2004, the group acquired san juan basin coalbed methane properties from a private company.

Primary SIC and add'l.: 6719 1311 4924

CIK No: 0000277595

Subsidiaries: Alabama Gas Corporation, Energen Resources Corporation, Energen Resources TEAM, Inc., Incorporated in the State of Alabama

Officers: William M. Warren/Chmn., CEO, James T. McManus/Dir., CEO/$1,991,073.00, Grace B. Carr/VP, Controller, Marvell Bivins/VP - Audit, Compliance, Julie S. Ryland/VP - Investor Relations, Brunson L. White/CIO, VP, David J. Woodruff/General Counsel, Sec./$1,118,522.00, William K. Bibb/VP - Human Resources, Charles W. Porter/CFO, VP, Treasurer

Directors: William M. Warren/Chmn., CEO, James T. McManus/Dir., CEO, Michael Wm. Warren/61/Chmn., Michael T. Goodrich/62/Dir., Mason J. Davis/72/Dir., Kenneth W. Dewey/Dir., James S.M. French/67/Dir., David W. Wilson/64/Dir., Stephen A. Snider/60/Dir., Stephen D. Ban/67/Dir., Judy M. Merritt/64/Dir., Gary C. Youngblood/64/Dir., Julian W. Banton/67/Dir.

Owners: David W. Wilson, David J. Woodruff, JPMorgan Chase& Co./5.90%, Stephen A. Snider, Vanguard Fiduciary Trust Company/5.78%, Judy M. Merritt, Geoffrey C. Ketcham, Michael T. Goodrich, Julian W. Banton, Mason J. Davis, Dudley C. Reynolds, Michael Wm. Warren, Insiders/1.40%, James S. M. French, Stephen D. Ban (17 Owners included in Index)

Financial Data: Fiscal Year End:12/31   Latest Annual Data: 12/31/2006

Year	Sales	Net Income
2006	$1,393,986,000	$273,570,000
2005	$1,128,394,000	$173,012,000
2004	$937,384,000	$127,463,000

Curr. Assets:	$489,579,000	**Curr. Liab.:**	$570,642,000	**P/E Ratio:**	13.93
Plant, Equip.:	$2,252,414,000	**Total Liab.:**	$1,634,818,000	**Indic. Yr. Divd.:**	$0.460
Total Assets:	$2,836,887,000	**Net Worth:**	$1,202,069,000	**Debt/ Equity:**	NA

Energenx Inc

6200 East Commerce Loop, Post Falls, ID, 83854; PH: 1-208-665-5553; http:// www.energenx.com

General - Incorporation	NV	Stock - Price on:12/24/2007	NA
Employees	NA	Stock Exchange	OTC
Auditor	Williams & Webster, P.S	Ticker Symbol	EENX
Stk Agt	Nevada Agency & Trust Company	Outstanding Shares	NA
Counsel	NA	E.P.S.	NA
DUNS No.	NA	Shareholders	NA

Business: The groups principle activities include discovering, research and developing novel electromagnetic motor, generator and battery charger systems. The group also markets energy generation and technical applications. The group operates from United States.

Primary SIC and add'l.: 6770

CIK No: 0001289047

Officers: Gary A. Bedini/55/Dir., CEO, Pres./$123,214.00, Rick M. Street/50/Dir., CFO, Sec., Treasurer, John C. Bedini/58/Dir., VP - Research, Development/$127,282.00

Directors: Gary A. Bedini/55/Dir., CEO, Pres., Rick M. Street/50/Dir., CFO, Sec., Treasurer, John C. Bedini/58/Dir., VP - Research, Development, Thomas E. Bearden/79/Dir., Marvin Redenius/43/Dir., Hans Werner Huss/65/Dir.

Owners: Hans Werner Huss, Insiders/60.00%, Frank & Judith Ten Thy/5.50%, Thomas G. Walsh/6.29%, Gary A. Bedini/12.10%, John C. Bedini/19.05%, Rick M. Street, Marvin Redenius/26.27%, Thomas E. Bearden/1.08%

Energizer Holdings Inc

533 Maryville University Dr., St. Louis, MO, 63141; PH: 1-314-985-2000; Fax: 1-314-985-2205; http:// www.energizer.com

General - Incorporation	MO	Stock - Price on:12/24/2007	$99.22
Employees	14,800	Stock Exchange	NYSE
Auditor	PricewaterhouseCoopers LLP	Ticker Symbol	ENR
Stk Agt	Continental Stock Transfer & Trust Co	Outstanding Shares	56,450,000
Counsel	NA	E.P.S.	$4.72
DUNS No.	NA	Shareholders	NA

Business: The groups principle activity is to manufacture primary batteries, flashlights and mens and womens wet-shave products. On October 1, 2007, Energizer Holdings, Inc. acquired Playtex Products, Inc., manufacturer and marketer of branded consumer products. The group operates from United States.

Primary SIC and add'l.: 3421 3648 3691

CIK No: 0001096752

Subsidiaries: Berec Overseas Investments Limited, Corepile S.a., EBC (India) Company Private Limited, EBC Batteries, Inc., EBC Uruguay, S. A., ECOBAT s.r.o., Ecopilhas Lda., Energizer (China) Co., Ltd., Energizer (South Africa) Ltd., Energizer (Thailand) Limited, Energizer Argentina S.A., Energizer Asia Investments Pte. Ltd., Energizer Asia Pacific, Inc., Energizer Australia Pty. Ltd., Energizer Battery Manufacturing, Inc. 87 Subsidiaries included in the Index

Officers: Ward Klein/CEO, Joe W. McClanathan/CEO, Pres. - Energizer Battery, David P. Hatfield/CEO, Pres. - Schick, Wilkinson Sword, Peter J. Conrad/VP - Human Resources, Gayle G. Stratmann/VP, General Counsel, Timothy L. Grosch/Sec., Daniel J. Sescleifer/CFO, Exec. VP

Directors: William P. Stiritz/74/Dir., Patrick J. Mulcahy/64/Dir., David R. Hoover/63/Dir., John E. Klein/63/Dir., Richard A. Liddy/73/Dir., Patrick W. McGinnis/60/Dir., Joe R. Micheletto/72/Dir., Pamela M. Nicholson/49/Dir., John R. Roberts/67/Dir., John C. Hunter/61/Dir., Bill G. Armstrong/60/Dir.

Owners: David P. Hatfield, Patrick W. McGinnis, Goldman Sachs Asset Management/8.92%, John E. Klein, Richard A. Liddy, Ward M. Klein, Daniel J. Sescleifer, John R. Roberts, Pamela M. Nicholson, Insiders/8.34%, Joseph W. McClanathan, Joe R. Micheletto, Bill G. Armstrong, Gayle G. Stratmann, Ariel Capital Management, LLC/8.29% (18 Owners included in Index)

Financial Data: Fiscal Year End:09/30   Latest Annual Data: 9/30/2006

Year	Sales	Net Income
2006	$3,076,900,000	$260,900,000
2005	$2,989,800,000	$286,400,000
2004	$2,812,700,000	$267,400,000

Curr. Assets:	$1,635,100,000	**Curr. Liab.:**	$926,900,000	**P/E Ratio:**	21.02
Plant, Equip.:	$659,900,000	**Total Liab.:**	$2,920,200,000	**Indic. Yr. Divd.:**	NA
Total Assets:	$3,132,600,000	**Net Worth:**	$212,400,000	**Debt/ Equity:**	3.9009

Energroup Holdings Corp

Formerly: Energroup Technologies Corp
4685 S Highland Dr., Ste. 202, Salt City, UT, 84117; PH: 1-801-278-9424

General - Incorporation	UT	Stock - Price on:12/24/2007	$4.95
Employees	NA	Stock Exchange	NA
Auditor	Mantyla McReynolds, LLC	Ticker Symbol	NA
Stk Agt	NA	Outstanding Shares	NA
Counsel	NA	E.P.S.	NA
DUNS No.	NA	Shareholders	NA

Business: The group's principal activity is to manufacture interfacing devices used in microprocessors-based control systems. The group operates from the United States.

Primary SIC and add'l.: 6770

CIK No: 0000766659

Officers: Stephen R. Fry/35/Dir., Pres., Barry Richmond/55/Dir., VP, Thomas J. Howells/35/Dir., Sec.

Directors: Stephen R. Fry/35/Dir., Pres., Barry Richmond/55/Dir., VP, Thomas J. Howells/35/Dir., Sec.

Owners: James Doolin/13.00%, Barry Richmond, Alycia Anthony/14.00%, Jenson Services, Inc./68.00%

Financial Data: Fiscal Year End:12/31   Latest Annual Data: 12/31/2006

Year	Sales	Net Income
2006	NA	-$6,000
2005	NA	-$4,000
2004	NA	-$3,000

Curr. Assets:	NA	**Curr. Liab.:**	$23,000		
Plant, Equip.:	NA	**Total Liab.:**	$23,000	**Indic. Yr. Divd.:**	NA
Total Assets:	NA	**Net Worth:**	-$23,000	**Debt/ Equity:**	NA

Energtek Inc

4965 Preston Pk. Blvd., Ste. 270-E, Plano, TX, 75093; PH: 1-561-740-0103; Fax: 1-972-985-6714; http:// www.newenergytec.com; Email: energytec@energytec.com

General - Incorporation	CO	Stock - Price on:12/24/2007	NA
Employees	NA	Stock Exchange	OTC
Auditor	Madsen & Associates, CPA's Inc.	Ticker Symbol	EGTK
Stk Agt	Holladay Stock Transfer	Outstanding Shares	NA
Counsel	NA	E.P.S.	-$0.07
DUNS No.	NA	Shareholders	NA

Business: The group's principle activity is to develop clean energy related technologies. The group operates from United States.

Primary SIC and add'l.: 3714

CIK No: 0001260037

Subsidiaries: Energtek Products Ltd, GATAL (Natural Gas for Israel) Ltd, Moregastech LLC, Primecyl LLC, Ukcyl Ltd

Officers: Lev Zaidenberg/CEO, Dir., Constantine Stukalin/Treasurer, Chief Accounting Officer, Dorothea Krempein/CFO, VP - Finance, CAO, Corp. Sec., Paul Willingham/VP, Controller

Directors: Lev Zaidenberg/CEO, Dir., Wayne Hardin/Chmn., Charles Spradlin/Dir., Eric Brewster/Dir., Ben Benedum/Dir., Ed Timmons/Dir., Yishai Aizik/44/Dir.

Owners: International Executive Consulting SPRL/7.18%, Insiders/0.87%, Doron Uziel/0.87%

Financial Data: Fiscal Year End:12/31   Latest Annual Data: 12/31/2006

Year	Sales	Net Income
2006	NA	-$847,000
2005	NA	-$42,000

Curr. Assets:	$341,000	**Curr. Liab.:**	$40,000		
Plant, Equip.:	$3,000	**Total Liab.:**	$40,000	**Indic. Yr. Divd.:**	NA
Total Assets:	$343,000	**Net Worth:**	$303,000	**Debt/ Equity:**	NA

Energy & Engine Technology Corp

5308 W Plano Pkwy., Plano, TX, 75093; PH: 1-972-732-6360; Fax: 1-972-732-6440; http:// www.eent.net; Email: info@eent.net

General - Incorporation	NV	Stock - Price on:12/24/2007	$0.001
Employees	NA	Stock Exchange	OTC
Auditor	Marcum & Kliegman LLP	Ticker Symbol	EENT
Stk Agt	Holladay Stock Transfer, Inc.	Outstanding Shares	NA
Counsel	NA	E.P.S.	NA
DUNS No.	NA	Shareholders	NA

Business: The group's principal activity is to operate natural gas gathering system in the united sates. It also services general aviation aircraft in Colorado. The group operates through its wholly owned subsidiaries, gas gathering enterprises, llc and wind dancer aviation services, inc. Gas gathering system is a branch-like that winds throughout the field that have heavy concentration of wells. The wind dancer aviation services inc provides fuel, oxygen, aircraft parking, flight training and catering, ground transportation, supplies, pilots' lounge, rental cars. It is a major center for aircraft repair, maintenance and upgrades.

Primary SIC and add'l.: 1311 4581

CIK No: 0001121811

Subsidiaries: BMZ Generators Technology, Inc., Gas Gathering Enterprises, LLC, Wind Dancer Aviation Services, Inc.

Financial Data: Fiscal Year End:12/31   Latest Annual Data: 12/31/2004

Year	Sales	Net Income
2004	$207,000	-$5,849,000
2003	$383,000	-$5,042,000
2002	$99,000	-$1,681,000

Curr. Assets:	$1,094,000	**Curr. Liab.:**	$1,342,000		
Plant, Equip.:	$261,000	**Total Liab.:**	$1,342,000	**Indic. Yr. Divd.:**	NA
Total Assets:	$2,278,000	**Net Worth:**	$936,000	**Debt/ Equity:**	NA

Energy Conversion Devices Inc

2956 Waterview Dr., Rochester Hills, MI, 48309; *PH:* 1-248-293-0440; *Fax:* 1-248-844-1214;
http:// www.ovonic.com; *Email:* investor.relations@ovonic.com

General - Incorporation	DE	Stock - Price on:12/24/2007	$30.08
Employees	964	Stock Exchange	NDQ
Auditor	Grant Thornton LLP	Ticker Symbol	ENER
Stk Agt	Computershare Investor Services LLC	Outstanding Shares	39,600,000
Counsel	NA	E.P.S.	-$0.33
DUNS No.	00-652-2080	Shareholders	NA

Business: The group's principal activity is to develop and market enabling technologies for use in the fields of alternative energy and information technologies. The group develops ovonic materials such as nickel metal hydride batteries, thin-film solar cell products and phase-change optical memory media. It operates through three segments: battery technology, photovoltaic technology and energy conversion devices (ecd). The battery technology is involved in developing and commercializing battery technology. The photovoltaic technology segment develops, manufactures and commercializes photovoltaic technology. The ecd segment is involved in photovoltaics, microelectronics, hydrogen storage technologies and machine building. The products are sold through its subsidiaries and joint venture companies. The group acquired interest in texaco ovonic fuel cell in fiscal 2003. Its patent portfolio consists of 374 us patents and 737 foreign counterparts.

Primary SIC and add'l.: 3674 3692 3691

CIK No: 0000032878

Subsidiaries: Ovonic Battery Company, Inc., Ovonic Fuel Cell Company LLC, Ovonic Hydrogen Systems LLC, United Solar Ovonic Corp., United Solar Ovonic LLC

Officers: Mark D. Morelli/Dir., CEO, Pres., Tyler A. Lowrey/CEO, Pres., Dir. - Ovonyx, Inc, Subhendu Guha/Sr. VP, Chmn. - United Solar Ovonic, Ghazaleh Koefod/Corp. Sec., Dick Thompson/Dir. - Communications, Sanjeev Kumar/CFO, VP, Nancy M. Bacon/Sr. VP, Stephan W. Zumsteg/VP, CFO - United Solar Ovonic, David Strand/Contact, Ovonic Information Business, Alan R. Chan/Contact - Central Analytical Laboratory, David A. Pawlik/Contact - Central Analytical Laboratory, James R. Metzger/Exec. VP, Stanford R. Ovshinsky/Founder, Pres., Chief Scientist - Technologist, Dennis A. Corrigan/Pres., COO - Ovonic Fuel Cell Company, Jay B. Knoll/Sr. VP, General Counsel, Chief Administrative Officer (*20 Officers included in Index*)

Directors: Mark D. Morelli/Dir., CEO, Pres., Robert Stempel/75/Chmn., William J. Ketelhut/55/Dir., Stephen Rabinowitz/64/Dir., Florence I. Metz/78/Dir., Joseph A. Avila/Dir., Stanford R. Ovshinsky/Founder, Pres., Chief Scientist - Technologist, Robert I. Frey/64/Dir., George A. Schreiber/59/Dir.

Owners: FMR Corp./9.90%, Stephen Rabinowitz, Robert C. Stempel/2.00%, Sanjeev Kumar, Insiders/4.40%, William J. Ketelhut, Florence I. Metz, James R. Metzger, CCM Master Qualified Fund/7.60%, George A. Schreiber, Mark D. Morelli, Subhendu Guha, Robert I. Frey, Stanford R. Ovshinsky/2.00%, Jay B. Knoll (*16 Owners included in Index*)

*Financial Data: Fiscal Year End:*06/30 *Latest Annual Data:* 6/30/2006

Year	Sales	Net Income
2006	$102,419,000	-$18,596,000
2005	$156,570,000	$50,332,000
2004	$66,305,000	-$51,422,000

Curr. Assets:	$284,883,000	Curr. Liab.:	$42,940,000		
Plant, Equip.:	$311,369,000	Total Liab.:	$75,172,000	Indic. Yr. Divd.:	NA
Total Assets:	$600,679,000	Net Worth:	$525,507,000	Debt/ Equity:	NA

Energy Corp of America

501 56th St., Charleston, WV, 25304; *PH:* 1-304-925-6100; *Fax:* 1-304-925-3139;
http:// www.eca-eaec.com

General - Incorporation	WV	Stock - Price on:12/24/2007	NA
Employees	NA	Stock Exchange	NA
Auditor	Deloitte & Touche LLP	Ticker Symbol	NA
Stk Agt	NA	Outstanding Shares	NA
Counsel	NA	E.P.S	NA
DUNS No.	NA	Shareholders	NA

Business: The group's principle activities include developing, producing, transporting and marketing natural gas and oil in the appalachian basin. The group operates from United States.

Primary SIC and add'l.: 4924 1311

CIK No: 0000032880

Subsidiaries: A&W, LLC, Allegheny & Western Energy Corporation, Eastern American Energy Corporation, Eastern Exploration Corporation, Eastern Marketing Corporation, Eastern Pipeline Corporation, ECA Alliance, LLC, ECA Holdings, L.P., ECA Partners, LLC, Westech Energy Corporation, Westech Energy New Zealand, Westech Energy New Zealand, LLC

Energy East Corp

52 Farm View Dr., New Gloucester, ME, 04260; *PH:* 1-207-688-6300; *Fax:* 1-207-688-4354;
http:// www.energyeast.com

General - Incorporation	NY	Stock - Price on:12/24/2007	$23.13
Employees	5,884	Stock Exchange	NYSE
Auditor	PricewaterhouseCoopers LLP	Ticker Symbol	EAS
Stk Agt	Mellon Investor Services LLC	Outstanding Shares	158,030,000
Counsel	NA	E.P.S	$1.67
DUNS No.	01-318-3587	Shareholders	NA

Business: The group's principle activities include generating, distributing and transmitting electric delivery, and natural gas delivery. The group also distributes natural gas and propane air. The group also generates electricity from its share of a nuclear plant and its several hydroelectric stations. The group operates from United States.

Primary SIC and add'l.: 4932 6719 4931

CIK No: 0001046861

Subsidiaries: Central Maine Power Company, Connecticut Natural Gas Corporation, Energetix, Inc., Energy East Enterprises, Inc., Energy East Management Corporation, Maine Electric Power Co., Inc., Maine Natural Gas Corporation, New York State Electric & Gas Corporation, NORVARCO, Rochester Gas and Electric Corporation, The Berkshire Gas Company, The Energy Network, Inc., The Southern Connecticut Gas Company

Officers: Wesley W. Von Schack/Chmn., CEO, Pres./$8,655,708.00, Richard R. Benson/Sr. VP, Chief Administrative Officer, Robert D. Kump/CFO, Sr. VP/$676,135.00, Michael F. McClain/Sr. VP, Chief Development, Integration Officer/$1,041,377.00, Paul K. Connolly/VP, General

Counsel/$1,227,080.00, Steven R. Adams/VP - Regulatory Policy, Elaine T. Dubrava/Sec., Patrick Nev/VP - Information Technology, Clifton B. Olson/VP - Supply, Jessica Raines/VP - Procurement, Contracts, Angela S. Beddoe/VP - Public Affairs, Robert E. Rude/Sr. VP, Chief Regulatory Officer/$1,131,401.00

Directors: Wesley W. Von Schack/Chmn., CEO, Pres., James H. Brandi/Dir., John T. Cardis/Dir., Thomas B. Hogan/Dir., Patricia M. Nazemetz/Dir., David M. Jagger/Dir., Walter G. Rich/Dir., Peter J. Moynihan/Dir., Jean G. Howard/Dir., Ben E. Lynch/Dir., Seth A. Kaplan/Dir.

Owners: Peter J. Moynihan, Insiders/1.64%, Walter G. Rich, Robert D. Kump, Ben E. Lynch, Jean G. Howard, John T. Cardis, Robert E. Rude, Michael F. McClain, Seth A. Kaplan, Wesley W. von Schack, David M. Jagger, James H. Brandi, Paul K. Connolly

*Financial Data: Fiscal Year End:*12/31 *Latest Annual Data:* 12/31/2006

Year	Sales	Net Income
2006	$5,230,665,000	$259,832,000
2005	$5,298,543,000	$256,833,000
2004	$4,756,692,000	$229,337,000

Curr. Assets:	$1,626,809,000	Curr. Liab.:	$1,313,659,000	P/E Ratio:	13.85
Plant, Equip.:	$6,131,338,000	Total Liab.:	$8,673,462,000	Indic. Yr. Divd.:	$1.240
Total Assets:	$11,562,401,000	Net Worth:	$2,864,347,000	Debt/ Equity:	1.2339

Energy Exploration Technologies Inc

Ste. 1400, 505- 3rd St. S.W, Calgary, AB, T2P 3E6; *PH:* 1-403-264-7020;
http:// www.nxtenergy.com; *Email:* info@nxtenergy.com

General - Incorporation	Canada	Stock - Price on:12/24/2007	NA
Employees	NA	Stock Exchange	OTC
Auditor	Deloitte & Touche LLP	Ticker Symbol	ENXTF
Stk Agt	Dean Naugler Olympia Trust Co	Outstanding Shares	NA
Counsel	NA	E.P.S	NA
DUNS No.	NA	Shareholders	NA

Business: The group's principal activities are to provide a remote-sensing technology in the business of wide-area hydrocarbon reconnaissance exploration. The group uses stress field detector technology to survey or reconnoiter large exploration areas from the group's survey aircraft. The stress field detector is a recently developed technology which the group adapted for airborne survey operations and field tested for independent geologists and joint venture partners. The stress field detector is used to measure variations in energy fields which the group believes to be related to stressed subsurface structures and hydrocarbon accumulations. The group operates in the United States and Canada.

Primary SIC and add'l.: 8713 1311 1321

CIK No: 0001009922

Subsidiaries: NXT Aero Canada Inc., NXT Energy Canada Inc., NXT Energy USA, Inc.

Officers: George Liszicasz/Chmn., CEO, Scott R. Schrammar/Corp. Sec., Charles V. Selby/Dir., Consultant, Andrew Steedman/VP - Operations, Ken Rogers/VP - Finance, CFO

Directors: George Liszicasz/Chmn., CEO, Robert Van Caneghan/Dir., Brian Kohlhammer/Dir., Douglas Rowe/Dir.

Owners: Oil &Gas Ventures, LLC/5.30%, Goodman & Company, Investment Counsel Ltd./5.70%, Brian Kohlhammer/0.30%, Andrew Steedman/0.60%, Scott Schrammer/0.70%, Charles Selby/1.60%, Douglas J. Rowe/1.90%, Ken Rogers/0.40%, George Liszicasz/26.50%, Robert Van Canaghan/0.40%

*Financial Data: Fiscal Year End:*12/31 *Latest Annual Data:* 12/31/2006

Year	Sales	Net Income
2006	$1,101,000	-$3,767,000
2005	$49,000	-$7,836,000
2004	$78,000	-$3,182,000

Curr. Assets:	$2,563,000	Curr. Liab.:	$1,478,000		
Plant, Equip.:	$342,000	Total Liab.:	$1,478,000	Indic. Yr. Divd.:	NA
Total Assets:	$2,904,000	Net Worth:	$1,427,000	Debt/ Equity:	NA

Energy International Inc

1628 W First Ave., Vancouver, BC, V6J 1G1; *PH:* 1-604-659-5001; *Fax:* 1-604-659-5029;
http:// www.internationalenergyinc.com; *Email:* Investors@InternationalEnergyInc.com

General - Incorporation	NV	Stock - Price on:12/24/2007	$0.73
Employees	NA	Stock Exchange	OTC
Auditor	Peterson Sullivan PLLC	Ticker Symbol	NA
Stk Agt	Holladay Stock Transfer, Inc.	Outstanding Shares	36,930,000
Counsel	NA	E.P.S	$0.00
DUNS No.	NA	Shareholders	NA

Business: The groups principal activities include exploring petroleum and natural gas and providing online automotive information. The group operates from the United States and Canada.

Primary SIC and add'l.: 7389

CIK No: 0001081074

Subsidiaries: e.Deal Enterprises Corp., International Energy Corp.

Officers: Derek J. Cooper/Dir., CEO, Pres.

Directors: Derek J. Cooper/Dir., CEO, Pres., Harmel S. Rayat/46/Dir.

Owners: Harmel S. Rayat/69.00%, Insiders/69.00%

*Financial Data: Fiscal Year End:*03/31 *Latest Annual Data:* 03/31/2007

Year	Sales	Net Income
2007	NA	-$225,000
2006	NA	-$842,000
2005	NA	-$59,000

Curr. Assets:	$24,000	Curr. Liab.:	$320,000		
Plant, Equip.:	$0	Total Liab.:	$320,000	Indic. Yr. Divd.:	NA
Total Assets:	$24,000	Net Worth:	-$296,000	Debt/ Equity:	NA

Energy Partners Ltd

201 St. Charles Ave., Ste. 3400, New Orleans, LA, 70170; *PH:* 1-504-569-1875;
Fax: 1-504-569-1874; *http://* www.eplweb.com

General - Incorporation	DE	Stock- Price on:12/24/2007	$17.93
Employees	179	Stock Exchange	NYSE
Auditor	KPMG LLP	Ticker Symbol	EPL
Stk Agt	Chase Mellon Shareholder Services LLC	Outstanding Shares	31,680,000
Counsel	Cahill Gordon & Reindel LLP	E.P.S.	-$2.12
DUNS No.	NA	Shareholders	NA

Business: The group's principal activity is to explore and produce oil and natural gas. The operations of the group are concentrated in the shallow to moderate depth waters of the gulf of Mexico shelf. At 31-Dec-2003, the group had interests in 24 producing fields and 6 fields under development, all of which are located in the gulf of Mexico shelf region.

Primary SIC and add'l.: 8741 1382

CIK No: 0000750199

Subsidiaries: Delaware EPL of Texas, LLC, EPL International, Ltd., EPL Nicaragua, Ltd., EPL of Louisiana, LLC, EPL Pioneer Houston, Inc., EPL Pipeline, LLC, Nighthawk, LLC

Officers: Richard A. Bachmann/Chmn., CEO, Pres./$2,301,088.00, Phillip A. Gobe/COO, Exec. VP/$1,780,643.00, John H. Peper/Exec. VP, General Counsel, Corp. Sec./$815,113.00, Timothy Woodall/40/CFO, Exec. VP/$525,208.00, Rodney T. Dykes/Sr. VP - Production/$612,869.00, Keith L. Vincent/Sr. VP - Land, Business Development, T. J. Thom/Dir. - Investor Relations, Thomas D. De Brock/Sr. VP - Exploration, Dina M. Bracci/Controller, Joseph H. Leblanc/Treasurer/$366,558.00, Joseph T. Leary/CFO, Exec. VP, Steve E. Longon/Exec. VP - Drilling, Engineering, Lee J. Alcock/Assoc. General Counsel

Directors: Richard A. Bachmann/Chmn., CEO, Pres., John C. Bumgarner/66/Dir., Jerry D. Carlisle/62/Dir., Harold D. Carter/69/Dir., Enoch L. Dawkins/70/Dir., Norman C. Francis/76/Dir., Robert D. Gershen/54/Dir., William R. Herrin/73/Dir., William O. Hiltz/56/Dir., John G. Phillips/85/Dir.

Owners: John H. Peper, John C. Bumgarner, Farallon Capital Partners, L.P/7.10%, Enoch L. Dawkins, Harold D. Carter, William O. Hiltz, Timothy R. Woodall, Richard A. Bachmann/8.30%, William R. Herrin, John G. Phillips, Rodney T. Dykes, Jerry D. Carlisle, Robert D. Gershen, Insiders/10.80%, Joseph H. LeBlanc *(17 Owners included in Index)*

Financial Data: ***Fiscal Year End:***12/31 ***Latest Annual Data:*** 12/31/2006

Year	Sales	Net Income
2006	$449,550,000	-$50,400,000
2005	$402,947,000	$73,095,000
2004	$295,210,000	$46,416,000

Curr. Assets:	$140,572,000	Curr. Liab.:	$181,904,000		
Plant, Equip.:	$846,459,000	Total Liab.:	$631,575,000	Indic. Yr. Divd.:	NA
Total Assets:	$1,003,845,000	Net Worth:	$372,270,000	Debt/ Equity:	0.8343

Energy Transfer Partners LP

3738 Oak Lawn Ave., Dallas, TX, 75219; ***PH:*** 1-214-981-0700; ***Fax:*** 1-214-981-0703; ***http://*** www.energytransfer.com

General - Incorporation	DE	Stock- Price on:12/24/2007	$60.14
Employees	3,898	Stock Exchange	NYSE
Auditor	Grant Thornton LLP	Ticker Symbol	ETP
Stk Agt	American Stock Transfer & Trust Co.	Outstanding Shares	136,980,000
Counsel	NA	E.P.S.	$1.554
DUNS No.	NA	Shareholders	NA

Business: The groups principle activities include transporting and storing natural gas. The group operates through two segments namely, midstream, and the transportation and storage. The group acquired HPL Consolidation, L.P. in the year 2005, and titan Energy Partners, LP and Titan Energy, GP LLC in the year 2006. The group operates from the United States. The group's quarterly revenue for September 2007 was 1,626.33 million of USD.

Primary SIC and add'l.: 4923 4922 5984

CIK No: 0001012569

Subsidiaries: AAA Propane, Action Gas, Adobe Propane, Amogas, Apache Gas, Archibald Propane, Arrow Propane, Balgas, Ballard Gas Service, Bi-State Propane, Blue Flame Gas, Blue Flame Gas of Charleston, Blue Flame Gas of Mt. Pleasant, Blue Flame Gas of Richmond, Boland Energy 179 Subsidiaries included in the Index

Officers: Kelcy L. Warren/Chmn., CEO, R. C. Mills/Pres. - Propane Operations, Marshall S. McCrea/Pres. - Midstream Operations, Pres. - ETC OLP, Sr. VP - Commercial Development, General Partner, Karen Z. Hicks/VP - Administration, Controller, Michael J. Howard/COO, Mark A. Darr/VP - Southern Operations, William G. Powers/VP - Northern Operations, Paul Ward/VP - Northwest Operations, Curtis L. Weishahn/VP - Western Operations, Brian J. Jennings/CFO, Jerry J. Langdon/Chief Administrative, Compliance Officer, Thomas P. Mason/General Counsel, Sec., Dave Riggan/VP - Finance

Directors: Kelcy L. Warren/Chmn., CEO, Ray C. Davis/Dir., David R. Albin/Dir., Bill W. Byrne/Dir., Ted Collins/70/Dir., Paul E. Glaske/75/Dir., Michael K. Grimm/53/Dir., John D. Harkey/48/Dir., Kenneth A. Hersh/45/Dir., John W. McReynolds/57/Dir., Rick K. Turner/50/Dir.

Owners: ETE, John W. McReynolds, John D. Harkey, Kelcy L. Warren, Mackie McCrea, Ted Collins, Bill W. Byrne, FHM Investments, L.L.C, Michael K. Grimm, R. C. Mills, Heritage Holdings, Inc, Rick K. Turner, Ray C. Davis, Paul E. Glaske, Insiders

Financial Data: ***Fiscal Year End:***08/31 ***Latest Annual Data:*** 8/31/2006

Year	Sales	Net Income
2006	$7,859,096,000	$515,852,000
2005	$6,168,798,000	$349,350,000
2004	$2,482,254,000	$99,152,000

Curr. Assets:	$1,301,804,000	Curr. Liab.:	$1,016,490,000		
Plant, Equip.:	$3,313,649,000	Total Liab.:	$3,718,151,000	Indic. Yr. Divd.:	$1.560
Total Assets:	$5,455,013,000	Net Worth:	$1,736,862,000	Debt/ Equity:	1.0378

Energy West Inc

1 1st Ave. S, Great Falls, MT, 59401; ***PH:*** 1-406-791-7500; ***Fax:*** 1-406-791-7560; ***http://*** www.ewest.com; ***Email:*** info@netread.com

General - Incorporation	MT	Stock- Price on:12/24/2007	$14.93
Employees	100	Stock Exchange	NDQ
Auditor	Hein & Assoc. LLP	Ticker Symbol	EWST
Stk Agt	Computershare Trust Co	Outstanding Shares	3,000,000
Counsel	NA	E.P.S.	$2.18
DUNS No.	00-282-1890	Shareholders	NA

Business: The group's principal activity is to conduct regulated utility operations which involves the distribution and sale of natural gas and propane. The group operates through three segments: natural gas operations, propane operations, and marketing and wholesale operations. Natural gas operations involves the distribution and sale of natural gas to residential, commercial and industrial customers in and around great falls and west yellowstone, Montana and cody, Wyoming. The group's propane operations involve the distribution of propane in the payson, Arizona area and in the cascade, Montana area. This also includes the wholesale and retail distribution of bulk propane in Wyoming, Arizona and Montana. Marketing and wholesale operations involve the sale of natural gas and electricity in Montana and Wyoming.

Primary SIC and add'l.: 4923 4931

CIK No: 0000043350

Subsidiaries: Energy West Development Inc., Energy West Propane Inc., Energy West Resources Inc.

Officers: David A. Cerotzke/Vice Chmn., CEO, Pres., Wade Brooksby/CFO, Sec., Brad Samuels/Contact - Energy West Development, Pipelines, Regional Mgr. - Energy West Wyoming, Evan Mattews/Regional Manger, West Yellowstone, Mary Stanich/Contact - Energy West Resources, Steve Miller/Contact - Energy West Development, Kevin J. Degenstein/Business Unit Manger, Natural Gas, Jed D. Henthorne/Regional Mgr. - Energy West Montana, Cheryl Johnson/Contact - Contributions Information, Tony Pietrykowski/Contact - Energy West Montana, New Construction

Directors: David A. Cerotzke/Vice Chmn., CEO, Pres., Richard M. Osborne/59/Chmn., Steve A. Calabrese/48/Dir., W. E. Argo/62/Dir., Mark D. Grossi/54/Dir., Thomas J. Smith/60/Dir.

Owners: Steven A. Calabrese/4.90%, Insiders/30.00%, Thomas J. Smith, David A. Cerotzke/2.80%, Mark D. Grossi, James E. Sprague, W. E. Argo, Wade Brooksby, John C. Allen/1.80%, Kevin J. Degenstein, Jed D. Henthorne, Richard M. Osborne/21.50%, Tim A. Good

Financial Data: ***Fiscal Year End:***06/30 ***Latest Annual Data:*** 06/30/2007

Year	Sales	Net Income
2007	$59,373,000	$6,212,000
2006	$84,278,000	$2,317,000
2005	$76,709,000	$1,381,000

Curr. Assets:	$14,455,000	Curr. Liab.:	$10,143,000	P/E Ratio:	13.95
Plant, Equip.:	$39,104,000	Total Liab.:	$38,766,000	Indic. Yr. Divd.:	$0.600
Total Assets:	$57,931,000	Net Worth:	$19,165,000	Debt/ Equity:	0.7023

Energysouth Inc

2828 Dauphin St., Mobile, AL, 36606; ***PH:*** 1-251-450-4774; ***Fax:*** 1-251-478-5817; ***http://*** www.energysouth.com

General - Incorporation	AL	Stock- Price on:12/24/2007	$50.54
Employees	260	Stock Exchange	NDQ
Auditor	Deloitte & Touche LLP	Ticker Symbol	NA
Stk Agt	EquiServe Trust Co N.A	Outstanding Shares	7,980,000
Counsel	Armbrecht, Jackson, Demouy Et Al	E.P.S.	$1.99
DUNS No.	79-769-3355	Shareholders	NA

Business: The group's principal activity is to distribute and transport natural gas to residential, commercial and industrial customers in southwest Alabama. The group's operations are classified into three business segments, namely, natural gas distribution, natural gas storage and other. The natural gas distribution segment distributes and transports natural gas to residential, commercial and industrial customers in southwest Alabama through mobile gas service corporation and southern gas transmission company. The natural gas storage segment provides for the underground storage of natural gas and transportation services through the operations of bay gas and storage. The other segment includes marketing, merchandising and other energy-related services, which are provided through mgs marketing services inc, mobile gas and services.

Primary SIC and add'l.: 4922 4923 4924

CIK No: 0001051286

Subsidiaries: Bay Gas Storage Company, Ltd., EnergySouth Services, Inc., MGS Marketing Services, Inc., MGS Storage Services, Inc., Mobile Gas Service Corporation, Southern Gas Transmission Co.

Officers: C. S. Liollio/CEO, Exec. VP, Daniel T. Ford/Treasurer, Assist. Sec., Edward E. Fields/VP - Governmental Affairs, Mobile Gas Service Corporation, Labarron McClendon/Sr. VP - Administration, James M. Fine/VP - Operations, Edgar G. Downing/Sr. VP, Sec., General Counsel, Greg H. Welch/Pres., COO - Mobile Gas Service Corporation, Ben J. Reese/COO, Pres., Martha Loper/Investor Relations, Todd Brown/VP - Marketing - Sales, John Pirraglia/VP - Business Development - Operations, Charles P. Huffman/CFO, Exec. VP, Susan P. Stringer/VP, Controller

Directors: John C. Hope/Chmn., J. D. Woodward/Dir., Judy A. Marston/Dir., Felton S. Mitchell/Dir., Thomas B. Van Antwerp/Dir., Walter A. Bell/Dir., Harris V. Morrissette/Dir., Robert H. Rouse/Dir.

Owners: Insiders/10.04%, Thomas B. Van Antwerp/7.12%, Harris V. Morrissette, Charles P. Huffman, Robert H. Rouse, J.D. Woodward, Benjamin J. Reese, Judy A. Marston, Edgar G. Downing, Walter A. Bell, C. S. Liollio, Felton S. Mitchell, John C. Hope, Gregory H. Welch

Financial Data: ***Fiscal Year End:***09/30 ***Latest Annual Data:*** 09/30/2007

Year	Sales	Net Income
2007	$135,033,000	$16,033,000
2006	$135,867,000	$14,036,000
2005	$124,606,000	$13,841,000

Curr. Assets:	$27,946,000	Curr. Liab.:	$32,288,000	P/E Ratio:	28.83
Plant, Equip.:	$228,570,000	Total Liab.:	$145,796,000	Indic. Yr. Divd.:	$1.000
Total Assets:	$262,680,000	Net Worth:	$111,090,000	Debt/ Equity:	0.5792

Energytec Inc

14785 Preston Rd., Ste 550, Dallas, TX, 75254; ***PH:*** 1-972-789-5136; ***http://*** www.energytec.com

General - Incorporation	NV	Stock- Price on:12/24/2007	$0.055
Employees	85	Stock Exchange	OTC
Auditor	Turner, Stone & Co. LLP	Ticker Symbol	EYTC
Stk Agt	Atlas Stock Transfer Corp	Outstanding Shares	69,850,000
Counsel	NA	E.P.S.	-$0.158
DUNS No.	NA	Shareholders	NA

Business: The group's activity is to produce oil and gas. The group expects to acquire oil and gas properties that have previously been the object of exploration or producing activity.

Primary SIC and add'l.: 1311

CIK No: 0001202963

Subsidiaries: Comanche Rig Services Corporation, Comanche Supply Corporation, Comanche Well Service Corporation

Officers: Don L. Lambert/62/CEO, COO, Pres., Eric Brewster/62/Dir., Sec., Dorothea Krempein/CFO, VP, Paul J. Willingham/VP, Controller

Directors: Ben T. Benedum/71/Chmn., Eric Brewster/62/Dir., Sec., Charles B. Spradlin/74/Dir., Wayne Hardin/68/Dir., Ed Timmons/60/Dir.

Owners: Ed Timmons/0.40%, Insiders/2.60%, Ben T. Benedum/0.70%, Wayne Hardin, Don L. Lambert/0.30%, B. Charles Spradlin/0.30%, Eric A. Brewster/0.90%

Financial Data: **Fiscal Year End:**12/31 **Latest Annual Data:** 12/31/2006

Year	Sales	Net Income
2006	$10,071,000	-$10,761,000
2005	$15,643,000	-$404,000

Curr. Assets:	$4,677,000	**Curr. Liab.:**	$13,742,000		
Plant, Equip.:	$36,204,000	**Total Liab.:**	$19,373,000	**Indic. Yr. Divd.:**	NA
Total Assets:	$42,283,000	**Net Worth:**	$22,910,000	**Debt/ Equity:**	0.1478

EnerLume Energy Management Corp

Formerly: Host America Corp

2 Broadway Way, Hamden Ct, CT, 06518; ***PH:*** 1-203-248-4100; ***http://*** www.hostamericacorp.com

General - Incorporation	DE	**Stock**- Price on:12/24/2007	$2.13
Employees	427	Stock Exchange	OTC
Auditor	Mahoney Cohen & Co., CPA, P.C.	Ticker Symbol	ENLU
Stk Agt	Computershare Trust Co	Outstanding Shares	10,510,000
Counsel	Berenbaum Weinshenk & Easor	E.P.S	-$0.74
DUNS No.	NA	Shareholders	NA

Business: The group's principal activities are to provide food services to corporate, special event catering, vending and office coffee products to business and industry accounts. The group operates through three segments namely, business dining, unitized meals and screening services. It also provides fresh, unitized meals for governmental programs and drug screening offers criminal histories, motor vehicle reports, workers compensation records, verification of education and social security numbers and credit reports. On sep 24, 2003 the group acquired globalnet energy investors, inc.

Primary SIC and add'l.: 5812 5962 8999

CIK No: 0000809012

Subsidiaries: Lindley Food Service Corporation, RS Services, Inc.

Officers: David J. Murphy/Dir., CEO, Pres./$356,456.00, Michael C. Malota/CFO/$229,710.00

Directors: David J. Murphy/Dir., CEO, Pres., Patrick J. Healy/Dir., Gilbert Rossomando/Dir., Nicholas M. Troiano/Dir., John D'Antona/Dir.

Owners: Gilbert Rossomando, First New York Securities L.L.C./5.39%, Mark Cerreta/1.01%, Michael C. Malota/1.23%, Patrick J. Healy/2.82%, Insiders/16.22%, Nicholas M. Troiano, Ronald R. Sparks/4.50%, MidSouth Investor Fund LP/6.44%, David J. Murphy/4.56%, John DAntona

Financial Data: **Fiscal Year End:**06/30 **Latest Annual Data:** 6/30/2006

Year	Sales	Net Income
2006	$36,995,000	-$12,937,000
2005	$30,794,000	-$9,663,000
2004	$26,827,000	-$4,919,000

Curr. Assets:	$7,648,000	**Curr. Liab.:**	$9,265,000		
Plant, Equip.:	$1,352,000	**Total Liab.:**	$13,049,000	**Indic. Yr. Divd.:**	NA
Total Assets:	$9,785,000	**Net Worth:**	-$3,264,000	**Debt/ Equity:**	NA

Enerplus Resources Fund

111 8th Ave., 13th Fl., New York, NY, 10011; ***PH:*** 1-212-894-8940; ***http://*** www.enerplus.com; ***Email:*** investorrelations@enerplus.com

General - Incorporation	AB	**Stock**- Price on:12/24/2007	$47.32
Employees	NA	Stock Exchange	NYSE
Auditor	Deloitte & Touche, LLP	Ticker Symbol	ERF
Stk Agt	CIBC Mellon Trust Co.	Outstanding Shares	123,430,000
Counsel	NA	E.P.S	$2.81
DUNS No.	NA	Shareholders	NA

Business: The groups principle activity is to acquire crude oil and natural gas properties. The group acquired Lyco Energy Corporation, Sleeping Giant LLC in the year 2005 and Gross Overriding Royalty in the year 2007. The group operates from the United States. The group's quarterly revenue for September 2007 was 305.73 millions of CAD.

Primary SIC and add'l.: 1382 6726 6733 1311 6792

CIK No: 0001126874

Subsidiaries: EnerMark, Enerplus Oil & Gas, ERC

Officers: Gordon J. Kerr/Dir., CEO, Pres., Robert L. Normand/Corp. Dir., Glen D. Roane/Corp. Dir., Donald T. West/Corp. Dir., Garry A. Tanner/COO, Exec. VP, Ian C. Dundas/Sr. VP - Business Development, Robert J. Waters/CFO, Sr. VP, Jo-Anne M. Caza/VP - Investor Relations, Rodney D. Gray/VP - Finance, Larry Hammond/VP - Operations, Lyonel G. Kawa/VP - Information Services, Jennifer F. Koury/VP - Corporate Services, Eric G. Le Dain/VP - Marketing, David A. McCoy/VP, General Counsel, Corp. Sec., Daniel M. Stevens/VP - Development Services *(18 Officers included in Index)*

Directors: Gordon J. Kerr/Dir., CEO, Pres., Douglas R. Martin/Chmn., W. C. Seth/Dir., Edwin Dodge/Corp. Dir., Harry B. Wheeler/Dir., Robert L. Zorich/Dir.

Financial Data: **Fiscal Year End:**12/31 **Latest Annual Data:** 12/31/2006

Year	Sales	Net Income
2006	$1,371,063,000	$483,439,000
2005	$990,758,000	$389,245,000
2004	$956,389,000	$249,586,000

Curr. Assets:	$189,124,000	**Curr. Liab.:**	$288,329,000		
Plant, Equip.:	$2,652,854,000	**Total Liab.:**	$5,660,570,000	**Indic. Yr. Divd.:**	$5.460
Total Assets:	$3,077,983,000	**Net Worth:**	-$2,582,587,000	**Debt/ Equity:**	NA

Enersis

Avenida Santa Rosa 76, Santiago, Santiago; ***PH:*** 56-23534682; ***http://*** www.enersis.cl

General - Incorporation	Chile	**Stock**- Price on:12/24/2007	$19.98
Employees	11,653	Stock Exchange	NYSE
Auditor	Deloitte & Touche LLP	Ticker Symbol	ENI
Stk Agt	Citibank N.A	Outstanding Shares	653,020,000
Counsel	Domingo-Valdes, Prieto	E.P.S	$0.46
DUNS No.	98-000-2174	Shareholders	NA

Business: The group's principle activity is to provide electricity utility company primarily engaged, through its principal subsidiaries and related companies, in the generation, transmission and distribution of electricity in Chile, Argentina, Brazil, Columbia and Peru. Enersis is one of the largest private sector electricity companies in South America in terms of consolidated assets and operating revenues with over 10 million customers and the largest electricity company in Chile. Through Endesa-Chile, it's largest consolidated subsidiary, Enersis is one of the largest private sector electricity generation company in South America in terms of installed capactiy. Enersis also has smaller operations in other non electricity businesses.

Primary SIC and add'l.: 3612 4911 7374 8711

CIK No: 0000912505

Subsidiaries: Ampla Energa e Servios S.A., Centrais Eltricas Cachoeira Dourada S.A., Central Hidroelctrica de Betania S.A. E.S.P., CGTF - Central Geradora Termeltrica Fortaleza S.A., Chilectra S.A., Codensa S.A. E.S.P., Compaa Americana de Multiservicios Ltda., Compaa de Inteconexin Energtica, Compaa Elctrica Cono Sur S.A., Compaa Elctrica Tarapac S.A., Edegel S.A.A., Elesur S.A., Emgesa S.A. E.S.P., Empresa Distribuidora Sur S.A., Empresa Elctrica Pangue S.A. 25 Subsidiaries included in the Index

Officers: Ignacio Antonanzas Alvear/CEO, Jose L. Dominguez-Covarrubias/Communications Officer, Susana Rey/Head - Investor Relations, Doris Saba/Investor Relations Representative, Ignacio Gonzalez/Investor Relations Representative, Denisse Labarca/Investor Relations Representative, Ramiro Alfonsin Balza/Planning, Control Officer, Nicolas Billikopf Encina/Compliance, Capital Markets Officer, Alfredo Ergas Segal/CFO, Rafael Miranda Robredo/VP, Domingo Valdes Prieto/General Counsel, Francisco Herrera Fernandez/Auditing Officer, Martin Serrano Spoerer/International Finance Officer, Fernando Gardeweg Ried/National Finance Officer, Ricardo Alvial Munoz/Investor Relations, Risk Officer *(17 Officers included in Index)*

Directors: Pablo Yrarrazaval Valdes/Chmn., Eugenio Tironi Barrios/Dir., Rafael Espanol Navarro/Dir., Juan Ignacio De La Mata Gorostiaga/Dir., Patricio Claro Grez/Dir., Hernan Somerville Senn/Dir., Pedro Larrea Paguaga/Dir.

Owners: Endesa Spain/60.60%, AFP Provida/6.00%

Financial Data: **Fiscal Year End:**12/31 **Latest Annual Data:** 12/31/2006

Year	Sales	Net Income
2006	$7,394,923,000	$688,088,000
2005	$6,110,015,000	$232,462,000
2004	$4,876,066,000	$273,194,000

Curr. Assets:	$3,118,596,000	**Curr. Liab.:**	$2,659,022,000		
Plant, Equip.:	$15,329,562,000	**Total Liab.:**	$15,741,629,000	**Indic. Yr. Divd.:**	$0.110
Total Assets:	$21,506,833,000	**Net Worth:**	$5,765,204,000	**Debt/ Equity:**	NA

Enersys

2366 Bernville Rd., Reading, PA, 19605; ***PH:*** 1-610-208-1991; ***Fax:*** 1-610-372-8457; ***http://*** www.enersysinc.com

General - Incorporation	DE	**Stock**- Price on:12/24/2007	$18.88
Employees	7,500	Stock Exchange	NYSE
Auditor	Ernst & Young LLP	Ticker Symbol	ENS
Stk Agt	National City Bank	Outstanding Shares	47,120,000
Counsel	NA	E.P.S	$0.95
DUNS No.	01-946-1495	Shareholders	NA

Business: The group's principal activity is to manufacture, market and distribute industrial batteries. It also manufactures, market and distribute related products such as chargers, power equipment and battery accessories and provides related after-Market and customer-support services. The group operates through two segments: reserve power batteries and motive power batteries. Reserve power batteries are used to provide backup power for the continuous operation of critical telecommunications and uninterruptable power systems during power disruptions. It is marketed and sold principally under the powersafe, datasafe and genesis brands. Motive power batteries are used to power mobile manufacturing, warehousing and other ground handling equipment. It is marketed and sold principally under the hawker, exide and general brands. The batteries are manufactured at 19 locations across the Americas, Europe and Asia and market and sell these products in more than 100 countries.

Primary SIC and add'l.: 3625 3629

CIK No: 0001289308

Subsidiaries: Accumuladores Industriales EnerSys SA, B Trakce, EH France SARL, EnerSys (China) Huada Batteries Company Limited, EnerSys (Jiangsu) Huada Batteries Company Limited, EnerSys A/S, EnerSys AB, EnerSys Australia Pty Ltd., EnerSys Canada Inc., EnerSys Capital Inc., EnerSys Cayman L.P., EnerSys CJSC, EnerSys de Mexico, S.A. de CV, EnerSys Delaware Inc., EnerSys Delaware LLCI 51 Subsidiaries included in the Index

Officers: John D. Craig/Chmn., CEO, Pres., Michael T. Philion/CFO, Exec. VP - Finance, Richard W. Zuidema/Exec. VP - Administration, Sanjay L. Deshpande/VP - Aerospace, Defense, John A. Shea/Exec. VP - Americas, Raymond R. Kubis/Pres. - Europe, Patrick M. Steffen/Sr. VP - Asia

Directors: John D. Craig/Chmn., CEO, Pres., Dennis S. Marlo/Dir., Hwan-Yoon Chung/Dir., Kenneth F. Clifford/Dir., Howard I. Hoffen/Dir., Michael C. Hoffman/Dir., Arthur T. Katsaros/Dir., John F. Lehman/Dir.

Owners: Michael C. Hoffman, Kenneth F. Clifford, Dimensional Fund Advisors LP, Insiders, J.P. Morgan Funds, MSGEM Funds, Arthur T. Katsaros, John D. Craig, MSCP IV 892, L.P., Raymond R. Kubis, MSCI IV, L.P., John F. Lehman, Eric T. Fry, GM Stockholders, Michael T. Philion *(19 Owners included in Index)*

Financial Data: **Fiscal Year End:**03/31 **Latest Annual Data:** 3/31/2006

Year	Sales	Net Income
2006	$1,283,265,000	$30,726,000
2005	$1,083,862,000	$32,383,000
2004	$969,079,000	$4,836,000

Curr. Assets:	$674,293,000	**Curr. Liab.:**	$398,041,000	**P/E Ratio:**	19.87
Plant, Equip.:	$303,705,000	**Total Liab.:**	$864,115,000	**Indic. Yr. Divd.:**	NA
Total Assets:	$1,409,013,000	**Net Worth:**	$542,099,000	**Debt/ Equity:**	0.7003

EnerTeck Corp

10701 Corporate Dr., Ste 150, Stafford, TX, 77477; ***PH:*** 1-281-240-1787; ***Fax:*** 1-423-698-6629; ***http://*** www.enerteck.net/P/about-management.html; ***Email:*** sales@unitedenertech.com

General - Incorporation	DE	**Stock**- Price on:12/24/2007	$1.35
Employees	5	Stock Exchange	OTC
Auditor	Malone & Bailey, P.C	Ticker Symbol	ETCK
Stk Agt	Jersey Transfer & Trust Co	Outstanding Shares	16,760,000
Counsel	NA	E.P.S	-$0.06
DUNS No.	NA	Shareholders	NA

Business: The groups principle activities include manufacturing, selling and marketing fuel borne catalytic engine treatment products. The group operates from United States.

Primary SIC and add'l.: NA

CIK No: 0001128353

Subsidiaries: EnerTeck Chemical Corp.

Officers: Dwaine Reese/Chmn., CEO, Stan Crow/59/Pres., Richard B. Dicks/60/CFO

Directors: Dwaine Reese/Chmn., CEO, Gary B. Aman/Dir., Jack D. Cowles/Dir., Thomas F. Donino/Dir.

Owners: Gary B. Aman/3.70%, Thomas F. Donino/28.80%, Stan Crow/3.90%, BATL Bioenergy LLC/20.50%, Dwaine Reese/20.10%, Richard B. Dicks, Insiders/56.30%, Jack D. Cowles/2.20%

Financial Data: *Fiscal Year End:*12/31 *Latest Annual Data:* 12/31/2006

Year	Sales	Net Income
2006	$641,000	-$639,000
2005	$48,000	-$12,960,000
2004	$179,000	-$1,863,000

Curr. Assets:	$906,000	**Curr. Liab.:**	$605,000		
Plant, Equip.:	$167,000	**Total Liab.:**	$2,105,000	**Indic. Yr. Divd.:**	NA
Total Assets:	$4,073,000	**Net Worth:**	$1,968,000	**Debt/ Equity:**	0.8581

Enesco Group Inc

225 Windsor Dr., Itasca, IL, 60143; ***PH:*** 1-630-875-5300; ***http://*** www.enesco.com

General - Incorporation	IL	**Stock**- Price on:12/24/2007	NA
Employees	1,182	Stock Exchange	OTC
Auditor	KPMG LLP	Ticker Symbol	ENCZQ
Stk Agt	Mellon Investor Services LLC	Outstanding Shares	NA
Counsel	NA	E.P.S	-$3.719
DUNS No.	00-111-6854	Shareholders	NA

Business: The group's principal activities is to design and supply gift, collectibles and home and garden decorative products to retailers, department stores, mass marketers and other direct distributors. The product include diverse lines of branded porcelain bisque, cold cast and resin figurines, cottages, musicals, music boxes, ornaments, plush animals, waterballs, tableware and general home accessories. The group has approximately 40,000 customers worldwide including independent gift retail customers. The products were sold to national card and gift chains, mass merchants, military p/x's, home television shopping, jewellery and department store. The group operates mainly in the United States, Canada, Europe and Asia. On 01-Mar-2004, the group acquired gregg gift company.

Primary SIC and add'l.: 5199 5094 5099

CIK No: 0000093542

Subsidiaries: Enesco France S.A., Enesco Holdings Limited, Enesco International (H.K) Limited, Enesco International Ltd., Enesco Limited, Gregg Manufacturing, Inc., N.C. Cameron& Sons Limited

Officers: Marie Meisenbach Graul/CFO

Financial Data: *Fiscal Year End:*12/31 *Latest Annual Data:* 12/31/2005

Year	Sales	Net Income
2005	$244,434,000	-$54,025,000
2004	$268,967,000	-$45,188,000
2003	$249,059,000	$17,282,000

Curr. Assets:	$100,116,000	**Curr. Liab.:**	$76,084,000		
Plant, Equip.:	$15,504,000	**Total Liab.:**	$77,365,000	**Indic. Yr. Divd.:**	NA
Total Assets:	$130,191,000	**Net Worth:**	$52,826,000	**Debt/ Equity:**	NA

Engelhard Corp

101 Wood Ave., Iselin, NJ, 08830; ***PH:*** 1-732-205-5000; ***http://*** www.engelhard.com

General - Incorporation	DE	**Stock**- Price on:12/24/2007	$125.87
Employees	95,247	Stock Exchange	NA
Auditor	Ernst & Young LLP	Ticker Symbol	NA
Stk Agt	Mellon Investor Services LLC	Outstanding Shares	494,700,000
Counsel	NA	E.P.S	$9.21
DUNS No.	09-929-0629	Shareholders	NA

Business: The group's principal activity is to develop, manufacture and market value-adding technologies based on surface and materials science. The group operates in four segments: the environmental technologies segment markets compliance with environmental regulations, enabled by sophisticated emission-control technologies and systems. The process technologies segment supplies advanced chemical-process catalysts, additives and sorbents. The appearance and performance technologies segment provides pigments, effect materials and performance additives. The materials services segment serves the group's technology segments, their customers and others with precious and base metals and related services. The group's international operations are carried out primarily in the United States, Europe, South Africa, South Korea, China, Finland and Japan. On 30-Jul-2004, the group acquired the collaborative group ltd.

Primary SIC and add'l.: 3341 2899 2819 2816 3339

CIK No: 0000352947

Subsidiaries: Bioetica SA, CTN Assurance Company, EAP Holdings, LLC, EC Delaware, Inc., ECT Environmental Technologies AB, Engelhard (BVI) Corporation, Engelhard (France) SARL, Engelhard (Shanghai) Co. Ltd., Engelhard Aluminas, Inc., Engelhard Asia Pacific (Hong Kong) Ltd., Engelhard Asia Pacific (India) Private Limited, Engelhard Asia Pacific (Korea) Ltd., Engelhard Asia-Pacific, LLC, Engelhard Belgium BVBA, Engelhard C Cubed Corporation 84 Subsidiaries included in the Index

Financial Data: *Fiscal Year End:*12/31 *Latest Annual Data:* 12/31/2006

Year	Sales	Net Income
2006	$69,460,587,000	$4,117,884,000
2005	$50,627,060,000	$3,534,960,000
2004	$50,817,000,000	$2,521,800,000

Curr. Assets:	$24,283,618,000	**Curr. Liab.:**	$18,458,190,000		
Plant, Equip.:	$19,674,450,000	**Total Liab.:**	$35,269,041,000	**Indic. Yr. Divd.:**	$3.220
Total Assets:	$60,255,059,000	**Net Worth:**	$24,285,598,000	**Debt/ Equity:**	NA

ENGlobal Corp

654 N Sam Houston Pkwy. E, Ste. 400, Houston, TX, 77060; ***PH:*** 1-281-878-1000; ***Fax:*** 1-281-878-1010; ***http://*** www.englobal.com

General - Incorporation	NV	**Stock**- Price on:12/24/2007	$12.19
Employees	2,100	Stock Exchange	AMEX
Auditor	Hein & Assoc. LLP	Ticker Symbol	ENG
Stk Agt	Computershare Investor Services LLC	Outstanding Shares	26,850,000
Counsel	NA	E.P.S	$0.21
DUNS No.	14-716-7704	Shareholders	NA

Business: The group's principal activity is to provide engineering consulting services and engineered systems to the petroleum refining, petrochemical, pipeline and process industries throughout the United States and internationally. It operates under two segments : engineering and systems. The group develops projects from the feasibility studies during the initial planning stage through the detailed design, procurement, and construction management stages, while also supplying automation, control and uninterruptible electrical power systems to its clients worldwide. The major customers include atofina, basf, chevron phillips, exxonmobil, frontier refining, motiva enterprises, premcor refining group, enterprise products, fluor daniels, honeywell inc and yokogawa corp of America . The group acquired petro-chem engineering inc and senftleber and associates lp during 2003 and engineering design group inc on jan-2004.

Primary SIC and add'l.: 3634 3433 8711 3585 3571 3629 3564

CIK No: 0000933738

Subsidiaries: dba ENGlobal, ENGlobal Automation Group, Inc, ENGlobal Canada, ULC, ENGlobal Construction Resources, Inc., ENGlobal Corporate Services, Inc., ENGlobal Engineering, Inc, ENGlobal Systems, Inc., ENGlobal Technical Services, Inc., RPM Engineering, Inc.

Officers: William A. Coskey/55/Chmn., CEO/$269,558.00, Don A. Johnson/Mgr. - Corporate Safety, David W. Smith/Pres. - Englobal Engineering, Inc, Eastern Division, Robert J. Church/Corporate Human Resources Mgr., Natalie S. Hairston/Investor Relations Officer, Chief Governance Officer, Corp. Sec., David R. Kelley/Sr. VP - Corporate Services/$173,200.00, Michael H. Lee/Pres., COO - WRC Corporation, Shelly D. Leedy/Pres. - Englobal Automation Group, Inc, Englobal Systems, Inc, Ronald W. Winthrop/Pres. - Englobal Construction Resources, Inc, Paul H. Cohen/VP - Legal Affairs, Contracts, Alex Schroeder/Corporate Information Technology Mgr., Amanda White/Human Resources Administrator, Carrie Stansbury/Benefits Administrator, Teri Guillory/Human Resources Assist., Mandi Snell/Human Resources Assist. *(34 Officers included in Index)*

Directors: William A. Coskey/55/Chmn., CEO, David C. Roussel/59/Dir., Randall B. Hale/44/Dir., David W. Gent/54/Dir.

Owners: Michael M. Patton, David R. Kelley, Insiders/39.90%, Tontine Overseas Associates, L.L.C./10.01%, Randall B. Hale, Robert W. Raiford, David C. Roussel, William A. Coskey/33.06%, Alliance 2000, Ltd/32.95%, Michael L. Burrow/5.01%, David W. Gent

Financial Data: *Fiscal Year End:*12/31 *Latest Annual Data:* 12/31/2006

Year	Sales	Net Income
2006	$303,090,000	-$3,486,000
2005	$233,585,000	$4,782,000
2004	$148,888,000	$2,364,000

Curr. Assets:	$72,275,000	**Curr. Liab.:**	$37,088,000		
Plant, Equip.:	$8,725,000	**Total Liab.:**	$65,364,000	**Indic. Yr. Divd.:**	NA
Total Assets:	$106,227,000	**Net Worth:**	$40,862,000	**Debt/ Equity:**	0.7327

Enhance Biotech Inc

631 United Dr., Ste 200, Durham, NC, 27713; ***PH:*** 1-919-806-1806; ***Fax:*** 1-919-806-1161; ***http://*** www.enhancebiotech.com

General - Incorporation	DE	**Stock**- Price on:12/24/2007	NA
Employees	6	Stock Exchange	OTC
Auditor	Cacciamatta Accountancy Corp	Ticker Symbol	EBOI
Stk Agt	Liberty Transfer Co	Outstanding Shares	NA
Counsel	NA	E.P.S	NA
DUNS No.	NA	Shareholders	NA

Business: The group's principal activity is acquisition development and commercialization of new therapeutic drugs for the treatment of lifestyle disorders. The group's six product candidates are premature ejaculation, male fertility enhancement, psoriasis/atopic dermatitis, eczema itch, cellulite, anti-aging. On 01-May-2003, the group acquired enhance lifesciences inc.

Primary SIC and add'l.: 2834

CIK No: 0001124077

Subsidiaries: Ardent Pharmaceuticals, Inc., Enhance Life Sciences, Ltd., Enhance Lifesciences, Inc.

Enherent Corp

101 Eisenhower Pkwy., Ste. 300, Roseland, NJ, 07068; ***PH:*** 1-973-795-1290; ***Fax:*** 1-973-795-1311; ***http://*** www.enherent.com

General - Incorporation	DE	**Stock**- Price on:12/24/2007	$0.14
Employees	212	Stock Exchange	OTC
Auditor	Cornick, Garber & Sandler LLP	Ticker Symbol	ENHT
Stk Agt	Mellon Investor Services LLC	Outstanding Shares	50,660,000
Counsel	NA	E.P.S	$0.01
DUNS No.	78-140-4884	Shareholders	NA

Business: The group's principle activity is to provide information technology solutions and services internationally. The services of the group include strategic consulting, project solutions and staff augmentation to industries including insurance, financial services, banking and capital markets. The group offers full life cycle information technology solutions, beginning with the understanding of client's business issues and continuing through problem analysis, coding, testing and ongoing maintenance. The group has sales and account management offices located in Texas and Connecticut. The group's line of business includes ebusiness enablement, it solutions outsourcing and it staffing. Ebusiness enablement enables commerce-oriented dot-com companies to enter the net economy at Internet speed prepared to execute large-scale transaction. It solutions outsourcing enables clients to turn over management of an it project, function or department. The group's quarterly revenue for Sep'07 was 7.11 millions of USD.

Primary SIC and add'l.: 7379 7375

CIK No: 0001045560

Subsidiaries: enherent (Barbados) Ltd.

Officers: Pamela Fredette/Chmn., CEO, Pres./$406,250.00, Lori Stanley/General Counsel, Corp. Sec., VP - Human Resources/$188,500.00, Karl Brenza/CFO/$288,709.00, Dean Ferro/VP - Solution Sales, Bruce Morgan/VP - Sales

Directors: Pamela Fredette/Chmn., CEO, Pres., Thomas Minerva/Vice Chmn., Faith Griffin/Dir., Douglas K. Mellinger/Dir., William J. Cary/Dir., Elliot Smith/Dir.

Owners: Lori Stanley, Pamela A. Fredette/8.50%, Karl Brenza/2.51%, Roger DiPiano, Faith Griffin, Thomas Minerva, Insiders/16.33%, Douglas K. Mellinger/4.40%, William J. Cary

Financial Data: *Fiscal Year End:* 12/31 **Latest Annual Data:** 12/31/2006

Year	Sales	Net Income
2006	$30,120,000	-$298,000
2005	$27,321,000	-$744,000
2004	$12,963,000	-$933,000

Curr. Assets:	$5,087,000	**Curr. Liab.:**	$7,823,000	**P/E Ratio:**	28.00
Plant, Equip.:	$175,000	**Total Liab.:**	$11,057,000	**Indic. Yr. Divd.:**	NA
Total Assets:	$10,038,000	**Net Worth:**	-$1,019,000	**Debt/ Equity:**	NA

Eni SpA

666 Fifth Ave., New York, NY, 10103; *PH:* 1-212-887-0330; *Fax:* 1-212-246-0009; *http://* www.eni.it

General - Incorporation	Italy	Stock - Price on:12/24/2007	$72.6
Employees	73,572	Stock Exchange	NYSE
Auditor	PricewaterhouseCoopers S.P.A	Ticker Symbol	E
Stk Agt	Morgan ADR Service Center	Outstanding Shares	736,080,000
Counsel	NA	E.P.S	$17.09
DUNS No.	43-320-3270	Shareholders	NA

Business: The group's principal activities are the exploration, extraction and production of oil and natural gas; supply, transport and distribution of natural gas; refinement and distribution of oil derivative products; petrochemicals; engineering projects and related services. Other activities include involvement in real estate management, marketing ventures and information technology sectors. The group operates in 70 countries worldwide through out companies located in 5 continents.

Primary SIC and add'l.: 1311 6719 8711 3339 4925 4613 2911

CIK No: 0001002242

Subsidiaries: Agip Caspian Sea BV, Agip Deutschland GmbH, Agip Espaa SA, Agip Franaise SA, Agip Karachaganak BV, Agip Oil Ecuador BV, AgipFuel SpA, American Agip Co Inc, CEPAV (Consorzio Eni per lAlta Velocit) Uno, Distribuidora de Gas Cuyana SA, Dunastyr Polystyrene Manufacturing Co Ltd, Ecofuel, Eni Angola Exploration BV, Eni Congo SA, Eni Coordination Center SA 56 Subsidiaries included in the Index

Officers: Paolo Scaroni/62/CEO, Paolo Andrea Colombo/48/Chmn., Statutory Auditor, Claudia Carloni/Head - Investor Relations, Antonio Pinto/Mgr. - Investor Relations, Raffaella Leone/Executive Assist., R. Marino/Sr. VP - Internal Audit, Sergio Polito/Sr. VP - Procurement, S. Lucchini/Sr. VP - Public Affairs, Communication, Domenico Dispenza/62/COO - Gas, Power, S. Sardo/Sr. VP - Human Resources, Business Services, R. Ulissi/Sr. VP - Corporate Affairs, Governance, M. Mantovani/Sr. VP - Legal Affairs, Stefano Cao/57/COO - Exploration, Production, Marco Mangiagalli/CFO, Angelo Taraborrelli/60/COO Eni Refining - Marketing Division *(17 Officers included in Index)*

Directors: Roberto Poli/70/Chmn., Paolo Andrea Colombo/48/Chmn., Statutory Auditor, Edoardo Grisolia/61/Member - Board Of Statutory Auditors, Riccardo Perotta/59/Member - Board Of Statutory Auditors, Giorgio Silva/63/Member - Board Of Statutory Auditors, Francesco Bilotti/67/Member - Board Of Statutory Auditors, Massimo Gentile/45/Member - Board Of Statutory Auditors, Filippo Duodo/Member - Board Of Statutory Auditors, Marco Reboa/53/Dir., Dario Fruscio/71/Dir., Pierluigi Scibetta/49/Dir., Mario Resca/63/Dir., Marco Pinto/46/Dir., Alberto Clo/61/Dir., Renzo Costi/71/Dir.

Owners: Stefano Cao, Paolo Scaroni, Domenico Dispenza, Dario Fruscio, Cassa Depositi e Prestiti/10.00%, Renzo Costi, Angelo Taraborrelli, Ministry of Economy and Finance/20.31%

Financial Data: *Fiscal Year End:* 12/31 **Latest Annual Data:** 12/31/2006

Year	Sales	Net Income
2006	$114,718,226,000	$13,209,602,000
2005	$88,268,594,000	$8,981,305,000
2004	$81,427,392,000	$8,733,524,000

Curr. Assets:	$36,001,940,000	**Curr. Liab.:**	$28,404,934,000		
Plant, Equip.:	$58,353,299,000	**Total Liab.:**	$63,572,445,000	**Indic. Yr. Divd.:**	$2.480
Total Assets:	$113,289,662,000	**Net Worth:**	$49,717,217,000	**Debt/ Equity:**	NA

Enigma Software Group Inc

150 Sfield Ave., Ste. 100, Stamford, CT, 06902; *PH:* 1-888-360-0646; *http://* www.enigmasoftware.com

General - Incorporation	DE	Stock - Price on:12/24/2007	$0.39
Employees	8	Stock Exchange	OTC
Auditor	Bagell, Levine & Company, LLC	Ticker Symbol	ENGM
Stk Agt	Mellon Investor Services LLC	Outstanding Shares	4,190,000
Counsel	NA	E.P.S	-$3.057
DUNS No.	NA	Shareholders	NA

Business: The groups principal activity is to develop software products. The group products include Spy hunter v.2.9, spy ware help desk medic v 5.0, and medic v 4.0. The group operates from the United States. In the year 2005, the group acquired Adorons.

Primary SIC and add'l.: 7371

CIK No: 0000799511

Subsidiaries: Adorons.com, Inc., Enigma Software Group, Inc.

Officers: Alvin Estevez/36/Dir., CEO, Pres./$193,806.00, Colorado Stark/Executive Chmn./$190,652.00, Richard M. Scarlata/CFO, Treasurer/$133,570.00

Directors: Colorado Stark/Executive Chmn., Edwin McGuinn/56/Dir.

Owners: Alvin Estevez/33.90%, Insiders/68.20%, Dutchess Private Equities Fund, LP, Dutchess Private Equities Fund, II, LP/7.90%, Colorado Stark/34.30%

Financial Data: *Fiscal Year End:* 12/31 **Latest Annual Data:** 12/31/2006

Year	Sales	Net Income
2006	$1,327,000	-$1,967,000
2005	$22,023,000	$10,173,000
2004	NA	-$21,000

Curr. Assets:	$725,000	**Curr. Liab.:**	$2,708,000	**P/E Ratio:**	2.70
Plant, Equip.:	$14,000	**Total Liab.:**	$2,772,000	**Indic. Yr. Divd.:**	NA
Total Assets:	$836,000	**Net Worth:**	-$1,936,000	**Debt/ Equity:**	NA

Ennis Inc

2441 Presidential Pkwy., Midlothian, TX, 76065; *PH:* 1-972-775-9801; *Fax:* 1-972-775-9820; *http://* www.ennis.com

General - Incorporation	TX	Stock - Price on:12/24/2007	$24.81
Employees	6,383	Stock Exchange	NYSE
Auditor	Grant Thornton LLP	Ticker Symbol	EBF
Stk Agt	Computershare Investor Services LLC	Outstanding Shares	25,590,000
Counsel	NA	E.P.S	$1.60
DUNS No.	00-731-9445	Shareholders	NA

Business: The group's principal activities are carried out through three segments: forms solutions group, promotional solutions group and financial solutions group. The forms solutions group primarily manufactures and sells business forms and other printed business products. The promotional solutions group designs, manufactures and distributes printed and electronic media, presentation products, flexographic printing, advertising specialties and post-it notes. The financial solutions group designs, manufactures and markets printed forms and specialize in internal bank forms, secure and negotiable documents and custom products. The group operates 30 manufacturing locations in 12 states.

Primary SIC and add'l.: 2759 2761 3549

CIK No: 0000033002

Subsidiaries: A&G, Inc. , Adams McClure, LP, Admore, Inc., Alstyle Apparel, LLC, Alstyle Ensenada LLC, Alstyle Hermosilla LLC, Alvest, S.A. de C.V., American Forms I, LP, Cactex S.A. de C.V. (3), Calibrated Forms Co., Inc., Connolly Tool and Machine Company, Crabar/GBF, Inc., Diaco USA LLC(3), Diaco, International S.A. de C.V. (3), Ennis Acquisitions, Inc. 25 Subsidiaries included in the Index

Officers: Keith S. Walters/Chmn., CEO, Pres./$1,686,945.00, Richard L. Travis/VP - Finance, CFO/$439,902.00, Michael D. Magill/Exec. VP, Treasurer/$741,226.00, Ronald M. Graham/VP - Administration/$447,777.00, Todd Scarborough/VP - Apparel Division, Pres. - Alstyle Apparel, David T. Scarborough/VP - Apparel Division/$766,333.00

Directors: Keith S. Walters/Chmn., CEO, Pres., Alejandro Quiroz/Dir., Thomas R. Price/Dir., Kenneth G. Pritchett/Dir., Godfrey M. Long/Dir., James C. Taylor/Dir., Robert L. Mitchell/Dir., James B. Gardner/Dir., Michael J. Schaefer/Dir.

Owners: Alejandro Quiroz, Ronald M. Graham, Keith S. Walters/1.40%, James B. Gardner, Kenneth G. Pritchett, Godfrey M. Long, Richard L. Travis, Thomas R. Price, Insiders/3.10%, James C. Taylor, Harold W. Hartley, Michael D. Magill, David T. Scarborough

Financial Data: *Fiscal Year End:* 02/28 **Latest Annual Data:** 2/28/2007

Year	Sales	Net Income
2007	$584,713,000	$41,601,000
2006	$559,397,000	$40,537,000
2005	$365,353,000	$22,959,000

Curr. Assets:	$63,605,000	**Curr. Liab.:**	$25,400,000	**P/E Ratio:**	15.31
Plant, Equip.:	$46,480,000	**Total Liab.:**	$43,461,000	**Indic. Yr. Divd.:**	$0.620
Total Assets:	$154,043,000	**Net Worth:**	$110,582,000	**Debt/ Equity:**	NA

Enova Systems Inc

19850 S Magellan Dr., Torrance, CA, 90502; *PH:* 1-310-527-2800; *Fax:* 1-310-527-7888; *http://* www.enovasystems.com; *Email:* contact@enovasystems.com

General - Incorporation	CA	Stock - Price on:12/24/2007	$6.2
Employees	39	Stock Exchange	AMEX
Auditor	Singer Lewak Greenbaum & Goldstein	Ticker Symbol	ENA
Stk Agt	Computershare Investor Services LLC	Outstanding Shares	14,830,000
Counsel	NA	E.P.S	-$0.5
DUNS No.	83-876-1856	Shareholders	NA

Business: The group's principle activity is to develop and production of commercial digital power management and power conversion systems. The group produces under contract with global vehicle and technology companies, digital power processing and energy management enabling technologies for electric, hybrid electric, and fuel cell powered vehicles. These power management technologies are applied to commercialization of fuel cell power generation for stationary non-automotive applications. The group's products include both on-site distributed power and on-site telecommunications back-up power applications. During 2003, it experienced a shift to more development work, both commercial and military.the group develops and sells components in the United States, Asia, Europe, China, Italy, the United Kingdom, Malaysia and Japan.

Primary SIC and add'l.: 3714 3694 3621

CIK No: 0000922237

Officers: Mike Staran/CEO, Pres., Don C. Kang/Enova Special Projects, ITC Pres., Bill Frederiksen/Chief Engineer, Jarett Fenton/CFO, Terry Morano/Dir. - Global Sales, Marketing, Aaron Shay/Dir. - Operations, Integration, Michael Staran/51/Exec. VP

Directors: Anthony Rawlinson/Chmn., John R. Wallace/Dir., Sten Langenius/74/Dir., Edwin O. Riddell/Dir., Malcolm R. Currie/Dir., Bjorn Ahlstrom/Dir., Donald H. Dreyer/Dir.

Owners: Mike Staran, Edwin O. Riddell, Sten Langenius, Delphi Delco Electronics, Bjorn Ahlstrom, Hyundai Heavy Industries, Co./5.16%, Anthony N. Rawlinson/3.90%, Donald H. Dreyer, Malcolm Currie, Jean Schulz, Jagen, Pty., Ltd./21.75%, Insiders/4.98%, John R. Wallace

Financial Data: *Fiscal Year End:* 12/31 **Latest Annual Data:** 12/31/2006

Year	Sales	Net Income
2006	$1,666,000	-$4,836,000
2005	$6,084,000	-$2,127,000
2004	$2,554,000	-$3,382,000

Curr. Assets:	$13,382,000	**Curr. Liab.:**	$1,736,000		
Plant, Equip.:	$627,000	**Total Liab.:**	$3,766,000	**Indic. Yr. Divd.:**	NA
Total Assets:	$15,730,000	**Net Worth:**	$11,964,000	**Debt/ Equity:**	0.1696

Enpath Medical Inc

2300 Berkshire Ln. N, Plymouth, MN, 55441; *PH:* 1-763-951-8181; *http://* www.medamicus.com

General - Incorporation	MN	Stock - Price on:12/24/2007	NA
Employees	160	Stock Exchange	NA
Auditor	McGladrey & Pullen LLP	Ticker Symbol	NA
Stk Agt	Wells Fargo Bank Minnesota N.A	Outstanding Shares	NA
Counsel	Lindquist & Vennum PLLP	E.P.S	NA
DUNS No.	NA	Shareholders	NA

Business: The group's principal activities are to design, develop, manufacture and market medical devices consisting of percutaneous vessel introducers, safety needles and related vascular delivery products. The group manufactures medical devices and components for other medical product companies on a contract basis. Vessel introducers allow physicians to create a conduit through which they can insert infusion catheters, implantable ports and pacemaker leads into a blood vessel. The major customer of the group is medtronic. The group manufactures medical devices and components for other medical product companies on a contract basis.

Primary SIC and add'l.: 3829

CIK No: 0000833140

Subsidiaries: C. R. Bard, Inc, Enpath Lead Technologies, Inc. (ELT), Enpath Medical, Inc, M&I Marshall & Ilsley Bank

Officers: Mark C. Kraus/VP, GM - Introducers/$282,527.00, Michael D. Erdmann/Corporate Controller, Corp. Sec./$161,233.00, Steven D. Mogensen/VP - Sales, Marketing/$279,974.00, Mike Winegar/VP - Regulatory Affairs, Quality Assurance, Anthony F. Headley/VP, GM Stimulation Leads - Advanced Delivery Systems

Owners: Blueline Capital Partners, L.P./8.40%, Mark C. Kraus/1.40%, Albert Emola, James M. Reed, Michael D. Dale, John C. Hertig, Thomas L. Auth/1.60%, James D. Hartman/3.30%, Healthinvest Partners AB/8.10%, David A. Grenz, Richard T. Schwarz, Richard F. Sauter, Michael D. Erdmann, Wasatch Advisors, Inc./9.80%, Insiders/8.80% (16 Owners included in Index)

EnPro Industries Inc

5605 Carnegie Blvd., Charlotte, NC, 28209; **PH:** 1-704-731-1500; **Fax:** 1-704-731-1511; **http://** www.enproindustries.com

General - Incorporation	NC	Stock- Price on:12/24/2007	$42.21
Employees	4,400	Stock Exchange	NYSE
Auditor	PricewaterhouseCoopers LLP	Ticker Symbol	NPO
Stk Agt	Bank of New York	Outstanding Shares	21,460,000
Counsel	NA	E.P.S.	-$7.19
DUNS No.	NA	Shareholders	NA

Business: The group's principal activity is to design, develop, manufacture and market the engineered industrial products. The products include sealing products, bearings, air compressors and heavy-duty diesel and natural gas engines. The group operates in two segments: sealing products and engineered products. Sealing products segment designs, manufactures and sells sheet gaskets, metallic gaskets, resilient metal seals, compression packing, rotary lip seals, elastomeric seals, hydraulic components, expansion joints and ptfe products. Engineered products segment designs, manufactures and sells self-lubricating, non-rolling, metal polymer and filament wound bearing products, air compressor systems and vacuum pumps, reciprocating compressor components and heavy-duty medium-speed diesel and natural gas engines. On 01-Oct-2003, the group acquired pikotek.

Primary SIC and add'l.: 3563 3519 2891 3562

CIK No: 0001164863

Subsidiaries: Coltec do Brasil Productos Industriais Ltda., Coltec Finance Company Limited, Coltec Industrial Products LLC, Coltec Industries France SAS, Coltec Industries Inc, Coltec Industries Pacific Pte Ltd, Coltec International Services Co., Coltec Productos y Servicios S.A., Corrosion Control Corporation, EnPro Industries Trading (Shanghai) Co. Ltd., EnPro Industries, Inc., Garlock (Great Britain) Limited, Garlock de Mexico, S.A., Garlock France SAS, Garlock GmbH 49 Subsidiaries included in the Index

Officers: Ernest F. Schaub/Dir., CEO, Pres./$3,449,760.00, William Dries/Sr. VP, CFO/$1,542,826.00, Richard L. Magee/Sr. VP, General Counsel, Sec./$1,118,836.00, Milton J. Childress/VP - Strategic Planning, Business Development/$581,425.00, Don Washington/Dir. - Investor Relations, Communications, Primary Investor Relations Officer

Directors: Ernest F. Schaub/Dir., CEO, Pres., William R. Holland/Non Exec. Chmn., Peter C. Browning/Dir., David L. Hauser/Dir., Wilbur J. Prezzano/Dir., J. P. Bolduc/Dir., Joe T. Ford/Dir., Gordon D. Harnett/Dir.

Owners: David L. Hauser, William R. Holland, Keeley Asset Management Corp./7.50%, Barclays Global Investors,/10.80%, Richard L. Magee, Insiders/4.30%, J. P. Bolduc, Steel PartnersII, L.P./14.80%, Dimensional FundAdvisors Inc./8.30%, Richard C. Driscoll, William Dries, Bank of America Corporation etal/5.70%, Peter C. Browning, Gordon D. Harnett, Milton J. Childress (17 Owners included in Index)

Financial Data: Fiscal Year End:12/31 Latest Annual Data: 12/31/2006

Year	Sales	Net Income
2006	$928,400,000	-$158,900,000
2005	$838,600,000	$58,600,000
2004	$826,300,000	$33,800,000

Curr. Assets:	$472,300,000	Curr. Liab.:	$225,100,000		
Plant, Equip.:	$166,300,000	Total Liab.:	$1,002,700,000	Indic. Yr. Divd.:	NA
Total Assets:	$1,406,600,000	Net Worth:	$403,900,000	Debt/ Equity:	0.4409

ENSCO International Inc

500 N Akard St., Ste. 4300, Dallas, TX, 75201; **PH:** 1-214-397-3000; **Fax:** 1-214-397-3370; **http://** www.enscous.com; **Email:** ir.hdqrs@enscous.com

General - Incorporation	DE	Stock- Price on:12/24/2007	$62.75
Employees	3,900	Stock Exchange	NYSE
Auditor	KPMG LLP	Ticker Symbol	ESV
Stk Agt	American Stock Transfer & Trust Co.	Outstanding Shares	149,090,000
Counsel	NA	E.P.S.	NA
DUNS No.	NA	Shareholders	NA

Business: The groups principle activities include exploring, developing and production of oil and natural gas. The group operates from the United States, the United Kingdom and Qatar. The group's quarterly revenue for September 2007 was 551.90 millions of USD.

Primary SIC and add'l.: 1389 1381

CIK No: 0000314808

Subsidiaries: ENSCO (Barbados) Limited, ENSCO Arabia Limited, ENSCO Asia Company, ENSCO Asia Pacific Pte Limited, ENSCO Australia Pty Limited, ENSCO Brazil Servicos de Petroleo Limitada, ENSCO de Venezuela, CA, ENSCO Drilling (Caribbean), Inc, ENSCO Drilling Company, ENSCO Drilling Company (Nigeria) Ltd, ENSCO Drilling Venezuela, Inc, ENSCO Gerudi (M) Sdn Bhd, ENSCO Holding Company, ENSCO Holland BV, ENSCO Incorporated 30 Subsidiaries included in the Index

Officers: Daniel W. Rabun/54/Dir., CEO, Pres./$3,176,514.00, William S. Chadwick/61/COO, Exec. VP/$2,146,818.00, Jay W. Swent/58/CFO, Sr. VP/$1,548,969.00, Philip J. Saile/56/Sr. VP, Richard A. Leblanc/58/VP - Investor Relations, H. E. Malone/65/VP - Finance, Paul Mars/50/Pres. - Ensco Offshore International Company/$1,493,863.00, Charles A. Mills/59/VP - Human Resources, Security, Cary A. Moomjian/61/VP, General Counsel, Sec., David A. Armour/51/Controller, Ramon Yi/54/Treasurer, Michelle A. Anderson/Investor Relations Advisor

Directors: Daniel W. Rabun/54/Dir., CEO, Pres., Carl F. Thorne/67/Non - Exec. Chmn., Paul E. Rowsey/53/Dir., Gerald W. Haddock/61/Dir., Morton H. Meyerson/70/Dir., Joel V. Staff/64/Dir., David M. Carmichael/70/Dir., Thomas L. Kelly/49/Dir., Rita M. Rodriguez/66/Dir.

Owners: Barclays Global Investors, NA/11.36%, Daniel W. Rabun, Joel V. Staff, Morton H. Meyerson, Thomas L. Kelly, J. W. Swent, Rita M. Rodriguez, Carl F. Thorne, Paul E. Rowsey, Insiders/1.44%, Gerald W. Haddock, William S. Chadwick, David M. Carmichael, Paul Mars, UBS AG/8.71%

Financial Data: Fiscal Year End:12/31 Latest Annual Data: 12/31/2006

Year	Sales	Net Income
2006	$1,813,500,000	$769,700,000
2005	$1,046,900,000	$294,200,000
2004	$768,000,000	$102,800,000

Curr. Assets:	$987,200,000	Curr. Liab.:	$384,900,000	P/E Ratio:	10.37
Plant, Equip.:	$2,960,400,000	Total Liab.:	$1,118,400,000	Indic. Yr. Divd.:	NA
Total Assets:	$4,334,400,000	Net Worth:	$3,216,000,000	Debt/ Equity:	NA

enSurge Inc

2089 Ft. Union Blvd., Salt Lake City, UT, 84121; **PH:** 1-801-673-2953

General - Incorporation	NV	Stock- Price on:12/24/2007	$0.51
Employees	1	Stock Exchange	OTC
Auditor	Hansen, Barnett & Maxwell	Ticker Symbol	ESGI
Stk Agt	NA	Outstanding Shares	NA
Counsel	NA	E.P.S.	$0.13
DUNS No.	NA	Shareholders	NA

Business: The group's principal activity is to provide business-to-business database lists and services. These services support direct marketing to technology and Internet based companies. The group owns electronic databases and mailing lists. The group's operations are carried out through its wholly owned subsidiary nowseven.com, inc.

Primary SIC and add'l.: 6719 7372

CIK No: 0000789879

Subsidiaries: NowSeven.com, Inc.

Officers: Jeff A. Hanks/42/Dir., CEO, CFO, Pres.

Directors: Jeff A. Hanks/42/Dir., CEO, CFO, Pres.

Financial Data: Fiscal Year End:12/31 Latest Annual Data: 12/31/2006

Year	Sales	Net Income
2006	NA	NA
2005	NA	NA
2004	NA	NA

Curr. Assets:	$3,000	Curr. Liab.:	$2,539,000	P/E Ratio:	3.92
Plant, Equip.:	NA	Total Liab.:	$2,539,000	Indic. Yr. Divd.:	NA
Total Assets:	$3,000	Net Worth:	-$2,536,000	Debt/ Equity:	NA

Entegris Inc

3500 Lyman Blvd., Chaska, MN, 55318; **PH:** 1-952-556-3131; **Fax:** 1-952-556-1880; **http://** www.entegris.com; **Email:** webrequest@entegris.com

General - Incorporation	DE	Stock- Price on:12/24/2007	$11.86
Employees	3,000	Stock Exchange	NDQ
Auditor	KPMG LLP	Ticker Symbol	ENTG
Stk Agt	Wells Fargo Shareowner Services	Outstanding Shares	135,160,000
Counsel	Latham & Watkins	E.P.S.	$0.38
DUNS No.	NA	Shareholders	NA

Business: The group's principal activity is to design, develop, manufacture and market material management and handling products and services within the microelectronics industry. The group provides materials integrity management solutions that assure the integrity of materials as they are handled, stored, processed and transported throughout the semiconductor manufacturing process, from raw silicon wafers to completed integrated circuits. In the semiconductor industry, the group offers products to ship, test and store wafers before, during and after the integrated circuit manufacturing process. They also offer a complete product line to transport, process, store and ship chemicals used in the semiconductor manufacturing process. The group has international operations in Japan, Germany, Malaysia, Korea and Singapore. In fiscal 2004, the group acquired the assets of electrol specialties company and wafer and reticle carrier product lines of asyst technologies, inc.

Primary SIC and add'l.: 3531 3537 3592

CIK No: 0001101302

Subsidiaries: Atcor-JCS Pte Ltd, Electrol Specialities, Inc., Entegris Europe GmbH., Entegris Ireland Ltd., Entegris Japan Holding KK, Entegris Japan KK, Entegris Korea JuShik Hoesa, Entegris Malaysia Sdn. Bhd., Entegris Netherlands, Inc., Entegris Precision Technology Corp.(4), Entegris SAS, Entegris Singapore Pte Ltd., Entegris Taiwan, Inc., Fluoroware Jamacia Ltd., Millipore France Holding Company B.V.(3) 28 Subsidiaries included in the Index

Officers: Gideon Argov/Dir., CEO, Pres./$3,443,916.00, John Murphy/Sr. VP - Human Resources, John D. Villas/49/Sr. VP, Treasurer/$1,801,383.00, Jean-Marc Pandraud/COO, Exec. VP/$1,666,142.00, John Goodman/CTO, Sr. VP, Innovation Officer, Peter Walcott/Sr. VP, General Counsel, Corp. Sec./$1,158,724.00, Bertrand Loy/Exec. VP, Chief Administrative Officer/$1,474,544.00, Gregory B. Graves/CFO, Sr. VP

Directors: Gideon Argov/Dir., CEO, Pres., James E. Dauwalter/Chmn., Michael A. Bradley/Dir., Paul L.H. Olson/Dir., Gary F. Klingl/Dir., Brian F. Sullivan/Dir., Daniel W. Christman/Dir., Thomas O. Pyle/Dir., Roger D. McDaniel/Dir., Michael P.C. Carns/Dir.

Owners: Gerald Catanacci/5.20%, Cooke& Bieler LP/6.70%, T. Rowe Price Associates, Inc./9.90%

Financial Data: Fiscal Year End:08/27 Latest Annual Data: 12/31/2006

Year	Sales	Net Income
2006	$678,706,000	$63,466,000
2005	$367,100,000	$9,393,000
2004	$346,764,000	$24,770,000

Curr. Assets:	$264,615,000	Curr. Liab.:	$64,919,000	P/E Ratio:	25.78
Plant, Equip.:	$97,634,000	Total Liab.:	$94,861,000	Indic. Yr. Divd.:	NA
Total Assets:	$467,046,000	Net Worth:	$372,185,000	Debt/ Equity:	0.0027

Entercom Communications Corp

401 City Ave., Ste. 809, Bala Cynwyd, PA, 19004; *PH:* 1-610-660-5610; *Fax:* 1-610-660-5620; http:// www.entercom.com

General - Incorporation............................PA
Employees...1,799
Auditor ....PricewaterhouseCoopers LLP
Stk Agt...... American Stock Transfer & Trust Co.
Counsel...NA
DUNS No. ....NA

Stock- Price on:12/24/2007 ....$24.71
Stock Exchange..NYSE
Ticker Symbol...ETM
Outstanding Shares 40,460,000
E.P.S...$0.20
Shareholders...NA

Business: The group's principal activities are to acquire, develop and operate radio broadcast properties throughout the United States. The group serves the broadcasting time to local and national advertisers. The group owns and operates radio stations at Boston, seattle, portland, sacramento, Kansas city, milwaukee, norfolk, new orleans, greensboro, buffalo, memphis, rochester, greenville/spartanburg, wilkes-barre/scranton, wichita, madison, longview/kelso and in gainesville/ocala.

Primary SIC and add'l.: 4832

CIK No: 0001067837

Subsidiaries: Delaware Equipment Holdings, LLC, Entercom Boston 1 Trust, Entercom Boston License, LLC, Entercom Boston, LLC, Entercom Buffalo License, LLC, Entercom Buffalo, LLC, Entercom Capital,Inc., Entercom Denver License, LLC, Entercom Denver, LLC, Entercom Gainesville License, LLC, Entercom Gainesville, LLC, Entercom Greensboro License, LLC, Entercom Greensboro, LLC, Entercom Greenville License, LLC, Entercom Greenville, LLC 45 Subsidiaries included in the Index

Officers: John C. Donlevie/Exec. VP/$740,589.00

Owners: Dimensional Fund/6.34%, Edwin R. Boynton/6.03%, Daniel E. Gold, Stephen F. Fisher/2.48%, John C. Donlevie/1.07%, David J. Field/9.31%, Robert S. Wiesenthal, Joseph M. Field/86.96%, Eugene D. Levin, David J. Berkman, Joseph M. Field/3.44%, Wellington Management/8.93%, David J. Field/6.48%, Insiders/96.27%, Insiders/12.82% *(16 Owners included in Index)*

Financial Data: *Fiscal Year End:*12/31 *Latest Annual Data:* 12/31/2006

Year	Sales	Net Income
2006	$440,485,000	$47,981,000
2005	$432,520,000	$78,361,000
2004	$423,455,000	$75,634,000
Curr. Assets:	$118,341,000	Curr. Liab.:	$42,326,000		
Plant, Equip.:	$88,032,000	Total Liab.:	$956,166,000	Indic. Yr. Divd.:	$1.520
Total Assets:	$1,733,258,000	Net Worth:	$777,092,000	Debt/ Equity:	0.9253

Entergy Arkansas Inc

425 W Capitol Ave., 40th Fl., Little Rock, AR, 72201; *PH:* 1-501-377-4000; *Fax:* 1-501-377-4448; http:// www.entergy-arkansas.com

General - Incorporation............................AR
Employees...13,679
Auditor ....Deloitte & Touche LLP
Stk Agt.......................................Mellon Trust Co
Counsel...NA
DUNS No. 00-690-3298

Stock- Price on:12/24/2007 ....$111.3
Stock Exchange..NYSE
Ticker Symbol...EHB
Outstanding Shares 197,260,000
E.P.S...NA
Shareholders...NA

Business: The group's principal activity is to generate, transmit and distribute electricity in Arkansas. The group is a wholly owned subsidiary of entergy corporation, which is involved in the following businesses: domestic utility, power marketing and trading, global power development and domestic nuclear operations.

Primary SIC and add'l.: 4911

CIK No: 0000007323

Subsidiaries: Arkansas Power & Light Company, Bom Jardim Energetica LTDA, Damhead Finance (Netherlands Antilles) N.V., Damhead Finance LDC, EK Holding III, LLC, EKLP, LLC, EN Services II, EN Services L.P., EN Services, L.P., Entergy Arkansas, Inc., Entergy Asset Management, Inc, Entergy Asset Management, Inc., Entergy Commerce, Inc., Entergy Corporation, Entergy Enterprises, Inc. 141 Subsidiaries included in the Index

Officers: Hugh McDonald/CEO, Pres., Wayne J. Leonard/57/Chmn., CEO, Curtis L. Hebert/45/Exec. VP, Chris Marsh/Project Mgr. - Business Recruitment, Robert D. Sloan/60/Exec. VP, General Counsel, Sec., Gary J. Taylor/54/Exec. VP, Chief Nuclear Officer, William E. Madison/61/Sr. VP, Mike Maulden/Dir. - External Affairs, Becky Rogers/Sr. Sec., Flave Carpenter/Community Development Consultant, Sherry McDonnell/Community Development Consultant, Russell Harris/Project Mgr. - Business Recruitment, Tandee White/Marketing Mgr., Ashley Peterson/Community Resource Center Mgr., Nathan E. Langston/59/Chief Accounting Officer, Sr. VP *(17 Officers included in Index)*

Directors: Wayne J. Leonard/57/Chmn., CEO, Alexis Herman/Dir., Leo P. Denault/48/Dir., Mark T. Savoff/51/Dir.

Owners: Mark T. Savoff, Jay A. Lewis, Hugh T. McDonald, Richard J. Smith, Wayne J. Leonard, Leo P. Denault, Insiders

Financial Data: *Fiscal Year End:*12/31 *Latest Annual Data:* 12/31/2006

Year	Sales	Net Income
2006	$10,932,158,000	$1,132,602,000
2005	$10,106,247,000	$923,758,000
2004	$10,123,724,000	$933,049,000
Curr. Assets:	$537,912,000	Curr. Liab.:	$360,556,000		
Plant, Equip.:	$3,878,441,000	Total Liab.:	$3,990,760,000	Indic. Yr. Divd.:	$2.160
Total Assets:	$5,541,036,000	Net Worth:	$1,550,276,000	Debt/ Equity:	1.2010

Entergy Corp

639 Loyola Ave., New Orleans, LA, 70113; *PH:* 1-504-576-4000; *Fax:* 1-504-576-4428; http:// www.entergy.com

General - Incorporation .... DE
Employees...13,679
Auditor ....Deloitte & Touche LLP
Stk Agt................. Mellon Investor Services LLC
Counsel...NA
DUNS No. 05-252-4212

Stock- Price on:12/24/2007 ....$108.27
Stock Exchange..NYSE
Ticker Symbol...ETR
Outstanding Shares 197,260,000
E.P.S...$5.90
Shareholders...NA

Business: The groups principle activities include producing and distributing electricity. The group operates through three segments namely U.S. Utility, non-utility nuclear and energy commodity services. The group operates from United States.

Primary SIC and add'l.: 4931 4922 4911

CIK No: 0000065984

Subsidiaries: Arkansas Power & Light Company, Bom Jardim Energetica LTDA, Damhead Finance (Netherlands Antilles) N.V., Damhead Finance LDC, EK Holding III, LLC, EKLP, LLC, EN Services II, EN Services L.P., EN Services, L.P., Entergy Arkansas, Inc., Entergy Asset Management, Inc, Entergy Asset Management, Inc., Entergy Commerce, Inc., Entergy Corporation, Entergy Enterprises, Inc. 137 Subsidiaries included in the Index

Officers: Renae E. Conley/CEO, Pres. - Entergy Louisiana, Wayne J. Leonard/57/Chmn., CEO/$14,761,940.00, Joe Domino/CEO, Pres. - Entergy Texas, Roderick West/CEO, Pres. - Entergy New Orleans, Hugh T. McDonald/CEO, Pres. - Entergy Arkansas, Carolyn C. Shanks/CEO, Pres. - Entergy Mississippi, Micheal D. Bakewell/Sr. VP - Fossil Operations, Michael Dupre/Mgr. - Investor Relations, Reyne Beatmann/Accountant - II, Robert D. Sloan/Exec. VP, General Counsel, Sec., Gary Taylor/Group Pres. - Utility Operations/$2,969,224.00, Terry R. Seamons/Sr. VP - Human Resources, Administration, Karen Fitzsimmons/Sr. Staff Analyst, Maureen Tedrow/Exec Sec., John R. McGaha/Pres. - Entergy Nuclear Planning, Development, Oversight *(23 Officers included in Index)*

Directors: Wayne J. Leonard/57/Chmn., CEO, Steven V. Wilkinson/66/Dir., Maureen Scannell Bateman/64/Dir., Frank W. Blount/69/Dir., Simon D. Debree/70/Dir., Gary W. Edwards/66/Dir., Alexis Herman/60/Dir., Donald C. Hintz/64/Dir., Stuart L. Levenick/54/Dir., James R. Nichols/69/Dir., William A. Percy/68/Dir., W. J. Tauzin/64/Dir.

Owners: FMR Corp./5.90%, Barrow, Hanley, Mewhinney & Strauss, Inc. (2)/7.43%, AXA Assurances I.A.R.D. Mutuelle/5.00%, James R. Nichols, Insiders, Gary W. Edwards, Wayne J. Leonard, Frank W. Blount, Donald C. Hintz, Richard J. Smith, Maureen S. Bateman, William A. Percy, Steven V. Wilkinson, Mark T. Savoff, W. J. Tauzin *(20 Owners included in Index)*

Financial Data: *Fiscal Year End:*12/31 *Latest Annual Data:* 12/31/2006

Year	Sales	Net Income
2006	$10,932,158,000	$1,132,602,000
2005	$10,106,247,000	$923,758,000
2004	$10,123,724,000	$933,049,000
Curr. Assets:	$3,325,434,000	Curr. Liab.:	$2,465,130,000	P/E Ratio:	19.76
Plant, Equip.:	$19,650,803,000	Total Liab.:	$22,884,844,000	Indic. Yr. Divd.:	$3.000
Total Assets:	$31,082,731,000	Net Worth:	$8,197,887,000	Debt/ Equity:	1.2010

Entergy Gulf States Inc

350 Pine St., Beaumont, TX, 77701; *PH:* 1-409-838-6631; *Fax:* 1-504-576-4879; http:// www.entergy-louisiana.com

General - Incorporation .... TX
Employees..NA
Auditor ....Deloitte & Touche LLP
Stk Agt................. Mellon Investor Services LLC
Counsel...NA
DUNS No. 00-792-4251

Stock- Price on:12/24/2007 ....NA
Stock Exchange..NA
Ticker Symbol...NA
Outstanding Shares ....NA
E.P.S...NA
Shareholders...NA

Business: The group's principal activity is the distribution of retail electric services. The group also provides natural gas utility services in and around baton rouge and Louisiana. The group, through its wholly owned subsidiaries, owns and operates intrastate gas pipelines in Louisiana. The group owns several miles of railroad track constructed in Louisiana, primarily for the transportation of fuel and coal.

Primary SIC and add'l.: 4924 4931

CIK No: 0000044570

Subsidiaries: Arkansas Power & Light Company, Bom Jardim Energetica LTDA, Damhead Finance (Netherlands Antilles) N.V., Damhead Finance LDC, EK Holding III, LLC, EKLP, LLC, EN Services II, EN Services L.P., EN Services, L.P., Entergy Arkansas, Inc., Entergy Asset Management, Inc, Entergy Asset Management, Inc., Entergy Commerce, Inc., Entergy Corporation, Entergy Enterprises, Inc. 141 Subsidiaries included in the Index

Officers: Joseph F. Domino/59/Dir., CEO, Pres., Robert D. Sloan/60/Exec. VP, General Counsel, Sec., Nathan E. Langston/59/Chief Accounting Officer, Sr. VP, Wayne J. Leonard/COO - Entergy Gulf States, Inc, Jay A. Lewis/CFO, VP

Directors: Joseph F. Domino/59/Dir., CEO, Pres., Leo P. Denault/48/Dir., Richard J. Smith/56/Dir., Mark T. Savoff/51/Dir., Renae E. Conley/50/Dir.

Entergy Louisiana Holdings Inc

Formerly: Entergy Louisiana Inc
4809 Jefferson Hwy, Jefferson, LA, 70121; *PH:* 1-504-840-2734; *http://* www.entergy-louisiana.com

General - Incorporation .... DE
Employees..948
Auditor ....Deloitte & Touche LLP
Stk Agt................. Mellon Investor Services LLC
Counsel...NA
DUNS No. 87-751-0883

Stock- Price on:12/24/2007 ....$25.45
Stock Exchange..NYSE
Ticker Symbol...EHL
Outstanding Shares 146,970,000
E.P.S...$0.89
Shareholders...NA

Business: The group's principle activity is to generate, transmit, distribute and sell electric power to retail and wholesale customers. It also provides domestic non-utility nuclear operations. The group provides electric services to 657,000 customers. The group operates from United States.

Primary SIC and add'l.: 4911 4924 4931

CIK No: 0000060527

Subsidiaries: Arkansas Power & Light Company, Bom Jardim Energetica LTDA, Damhead Finance (Netherlands Antilles) N.V., Damhead Finance LDC, EK Holding III, LLC, EKLP, LLC, EN Services II, EN Services L.P., EN Services, L.P., Entergy Arkansas, Inc., Entergy Asset Management, Inc, Entergy Asset Management, Inc., Entergy Commerce, Inc., Entergy Corporation, Entergy Enterprises, Inc. 141 Subsidiaries included in the Index

Officers: Renae E. Conley/CEO, Pres., Pamela Webster/Assoc. Analyst, Economic Development Staff, Murphy A. Dreher/VP - Governmental Affairs, P. J. Martinez/VP - Distribution Operations, Michael T. Twomey/VP - Regulatory Affairs, Clifton Avant/Mgr. - Area Development, Economic Development Staff, Merite Cain/Sr. Administrative Assist. - Economic Development Staff, Bridget

Carter/Contact - Economic Development Staff, Bill Peperone/Community Developer, Economic Development Staff, Gesele Sabathia/Contact - Economic Development Staff, Philip Seghers/Industrial Recruiter, Economic Development Staff, Sam Richardson/Staff Accounting Executive, Economic Development Staff, Don Terry/Economic Development Staff, Community Developer, Karen K. Yates/Economic Development Staff, Community Developer, Shelley MacNary/Dir. - Economic Development Entergy Louisiana *(18 Officers included in Index)*

Financial Data: Fiscal Year End:12/31 Latest Annual Data: 12/31/2006

Year	Sales	Net Income
2006	$2,451,258,000	$137,618,000

Curr. Assets:	$392,997,000	Curr. Liab.:	$582,730,000	P/E Ratio:	28.60
Plant, Equip.:	$4,261,771,000	Total Liab.:	$4,236,534,000	Indic. Yr. Divd.:	NA
Total Assets:	$5,654,842,000	Net Worth:	$1,418,308,000	Debt/ Equity:	NA

Entergy Mississippi Inc

308 E Pearl St., Jackson, MS, 39201; *PH:* 1-601-368-5000; *Fax:* 1-601-969-2583; *http://* www.entergy-mississippi.com

General - Incorporation	MS	Stock - Price on:12/24/2007	$24.19
Employees	802	Stock Exchange	NYSE
Auditor	Deloitte & Touche LLP	Ticker Symbol	EMQ
Stk Agt	Mellon Investor Services LLC	Outstanding Shares	8,670,000
Counsel	NA	E.P.S.	NA
DUNS No.	00-696-4381	Shareholders	NA

Business: The group's principle activity is to generate, transmit and distribute electric power to retail and wholesale customers. The major industrial customers of the domestic utility companies are in chemical, petroleum refining, paper and food products industries. The group operates from United States.

Primary SIC and add'l.: 4911 4922

CIK No: 0000066901

Subsidiaries: Arkansas Power & Light Company, Bom Jardim Energetica LTDA, Damhead Finance (Netherlands Antilles) N.V., Damhead Finance LDC, EK Holding III, LLC, EKLP, LLC, EN Services II, EN Services L.P., EN Services, L.P., Entergy Arkansas, Inc., Entergy Asset Management, Inc, Entergy Asset Management, Inc., Entergy Commerce, Inc., Entergy Corporation, Entergy Enterprises, Inc. 141 Subsidiaries included in the Index

Officers: Carolyn C. Shanks/CEO, Pres., Wayne J. Leonard/Chmn., CEO, Robert D. Sloan/60/Exec. VP, General Counsel, Sec., Leo P. Denault/CFO, Exec. VP, Mark T. Savoff/51/Exec. VP, John E. Wesley/Project Mgr., Karmon Evans/Research, Marketing, Jay A. Lewis/46/VP, CFO - Utility Operations, Glenn Parker/Business Retention, Expansion Mgr., Anita Lewis/Community Development Mgr., Nathan E. Langston/59/Chief Accounting Officer, Sr. VP, William E./ Madison/61/Sr. VP - Human Resources And Administration, Steve Kelly/Community Development Mgr., Taurus Wright/Project Mgr.

Directors: Wayne J. Leonard/Chmn., CEO, Richard J. Smith/56/Dir., William A. Percy/Dir., John Turner/Dir.

Owners: Wayne J. Leonard, Mark T. Savoff, Richard J. Smith, Insiders, Jay A. Lewis, Leo P. Denault, Carolyn C. Shanks

Entergy New Orleans Inc

1600 Perdido St. , Bldg 505, New Orleans, LA, 70112; *PH:* 1-504-670-3674; *http://* www.entergy-neworleans.com

General - Incorporation	LA	Stock - Price on:12/24/2007	$108.27
Employees	13,679	Stock Exchange	NA
Auditor	Deloitte & Touche LLP	Ticker Symbol	NA
Stk Agt	Mellon Investor Services LLC	Outstanding Shares	197,260,000
Counsel	NA	E.P.S.	$5.46
DUNS No.	00-694-7824	Shareholders	NA

Business: The group's principle activity is to provide electric and gas services in new orleans. The group is a wholly owned subsidiary of entergy corporation. The group supplies retail electric services to residential, commercial, industrial, governmental and municipal customers. The group operates from United States.

Primary SIC and add'l.: 4931 4923

CIK No: 0000071508

Subsidiaries: Arkansas Power & Light Company, Bom Jardim Energetica LTDA, Damhead Finance (Netherlands Antilles) N.V., Damhead Finance LDC, EK Holding III, LLC, EKLP, LLC, EN Services II, EN Services L.P., EN Services, L.P., Entergy Arkansas, Inc., Entergy Asset Management, Inc, Entergy Asset Management, Inc., Entergy Commerce, Inc., Entergy Corporation, Entergy Enterprises, Inc. 141 Subsidiaries included in the Index

Officers: Daniel F. Packer/60/Chmn., CEO, Robert D. Sloan/60/Exec. VP, General Counsel, Sec. - Entergy Corporation, Bridget Carter/Economic Development Executive, Joan Dumes/Administrative Assist., Leo P. Denault/48/Exec. VP, CFO - Entergy Corporation, William E. Madison/61/Sr. VP - Human Resources, Gary B. Silbert/Dir. - Economic Development, Gesele Sabathia/Sr. Economic Development Executive, Mark T. Savoff/51/Exec. VP - Operations, Entergy Corporation, Richard J. Smith/56/Group Pres. - Utility Operations, Entergy Corporation, Jay A. Lewis/46/VP, CFO - Utility, Gary J. Taylor/54/Exec. VP, Chief Nuclear Officer, Curtis L. Hebert/45/Exec. VP - External Affairs, Entergy, Nathan E. Langston/59/Chief Accounting Officer, Sr. VP

Directors: Daniel F. Packer/60/Chmn., CEO, Richard J. Smith/56/Group Pres. - Utility Operations, Entergy Corporation, Tracie L. Boutte/44/Dir., Roderick K. West/39/Dir.

Owners: Jay A. Lewis, Insiders, Hugh T. McDonald, Mark T. Savoff, Leo P. Denault, Wayne J. Leonard, Richard J. Smith

Financial Data: Fiscal Year End:12/31 Latest Annual Data: 12/31/2006

Year	Sales	Net Income
2006	$10,932,158,000	$1,132,602,000
2005	$10,106,247,000	$923,758,000
2004	$10,123,724,000	$933,049,000

Curr. Assets:	$3,325,434,000	Curr. Liab.:	$2,465,130,000	P/E Ratio:	19.76
Plant, Equip.:	$19,650,803,000	Total Liab.:	$22,884,844,000	Indic. Yr. Divd.:	$3.000
Total Assets:	$31,082,731,000	Net Worth:	$8,197,887,000	Debt/ Equity:	1.2010

Enterprise Bancorp Inc

222 Merrimack St., Lowell, MA, 01852; *PH:* 1-978-459-9000; *Fax:* 1-978-934-8738; *http://* www.enterprisebankandtrust.com

General - Incorporation	MA	Stock - Price on:12/24/2007	$15.97
Employees	282	Stock Exchange	NDQ
Auditor	KPMG LLP	Ticker Symbol	EBTC
Stk Agt	Computershare Trust Co	Outstanding Shares	7,770,000
Counsel	NA	E.P.S.	$1.23
DUNS No.	61-410-6896	Shareholders	NA

Business: The group's principal activity is to offer commercial and consumer loan and deposit products. It also provides investment management, trust and insurance services with a goal to satisfy the needs of individuals, professionals, non-profit organizations. Loans include commercial mortgage loans, construction loans, revolving lines of credit, working capital loans, equipment financing and asset-based lending. Deposit accounts include personal interest checking accounts, savings accounts, money market accounts, individual retirement accounts and certificates of deposit. The operations are conducted primarily in lowell and the surrounding Massachusetts cities and towns of andover, billerica, chelmsford, dracut, tewksbury, tyngsboro, westford and in the cities of leominster and fitchburg. The group's subsidiaries are enterprise bank and trust company, enterprise insurance services llc and enterprise investment services llc.

Primary SIC and add'l.: 6022 6712

CIK No: 0001018399

Subsidiaries: Enterprise (MA) Capital Trust I, Enterprise Bank and Trust Company, Enterprise Insurance Services LLC, Enterprise Investment Services LLC, Enterprise Security Corporation

Officers: George L. Duncan/Chmn., CEO, John P. Clancy/Dir., Exec. VP, COO/$281,637.00, Richard W. Main/Dir., Pres., Chief Lending Officer/$411,500.00, Nancy Hargreaves-Pierce/VP - Branch Relationship Mgr. - Andover, Sandi Wilson/VP - Branch Relationship Mgr. - Billerica, Linda Welch/VP - Branch Relationship Mgr. - Chelmsford, Denise Marcaurelle/VP - Regional Mgr. - Chelmsford, Meredith Boumil-Flynn/VP - Branch Relationship Mgr. - Dracut, Cheryl Gaudreau/VP - Branch Relationship Mgr. - Fitchburg, Deborah Lapointe/VP - Branch Relationship Mgr. - Leominster, Frank Carvalho/VP - Branch Relationship Mgr. - Lowell, Maria Lobao/VP - Branch Relationship Mgr. - Lowell, Main Office, Joy Harmer/Branch Mgr. - North Billerica, Susan Covey/VP - Regional Mgr. - Salem NH, Heather Starr/Branch Mgr. - Tewksbury *(20 Officers included in Index)*

Directors: George L. Duncan/Chmn., CEO, Arnold S. Lerner/Vice Chmn., Kenneth S. Ansin/Dir., Eric W. Hanson/Dir., Kathleen W. Bradley/Honorary Dir., Richard W. Main/Dir., Pres., Chief Lending Officer, John R. Clementi/Dir., John P. Clancy/Dir., Exec. VP, COO, Philip S. Nyman/Dir. - Bank Counsel, James F. Conway/Dir., Michael A. Spinelli/Dir., Carol Reid/Dir., Carole A. Cowan/Dir., Gerald G. Bousquet/Honorary Dir., Charles P. Sarantos/Honorary Dir. *(20 Directors included in Index)*

Owners: Carol L. Reid, Carole A. Cowan, Eric W. Hanson/5.74%, James A. Marcotte, Robert R. Gilman, Michael A. Spinelli/3.59%, Ronald M. Ansin/9.25%, Arnold S. Lerner/6.59%, Richard W. Main/3.08%, John P. Harrington, James F. Conway, Walter L. Armstrong/1.75%, Charles P. Sarantos, John R. Clementi, Kenneth S. Ansin/1.58% *(21 Owners included in Index)*

Financial Data: Fiscal Year End:12/31 Latest Annual Data: 12/31/2006

Year	Sales	Net Income
2006	$67,531,000	$9,234,000
2005	$54,741,000	$8,414,000
2004	$46,745,000	$7,507,000

Curr. Assets:	$56,351,000	Curr. Liab.:	$876,286,000	P/E Ratio:	13.20
Plant, Equip.:	$16,015,000	Total Liab.:	$902,216,000	Indic. Yr. Divd.:	$0.320
Total Assets:	$979,259,000	Net Worth:	$77,043,000	Debt/ Equity:	0.3266

Enterprise Financial Services Corp

150 N Meramec Ave., Clayton, MO, 63105; *PH:* 1-314-725-5500; *Fax:* 1-314-812-4025; *http://* www.enterprisebank.com

General - Incorporation	DE	Stock - Price on:12/24/2007	$25.68
Employees	329	Stock Exchange	NDQ
Auditor	KPMG LLP	Ticker Symbol	EFSC
Stk Agt	UMB Bank, N.A.	Outstanding Shares	12,530,000
Counsel	NA	E.P.S.	$1.38
DUNS No.	NA	Shareholders	NA

Business: The group's principal activity is to provide commercial banking and trust services to individual and corporate customers in Missouri and Kansas. The group is a bank holding company and offers services through two segments: enterprise banking and enterprise trust. Enterprise banking provides real estate, commercial, residential and consumer loans. The depository products offered include certificates of deposits and savings, money market, commercial sweep, checking and negotiable order of withdrawal accounts and individual retirement accounts. Other banking services include treasury management and safe-deposit boxes. Enterprise trust provides fee-based personal and corporate financial consulting and trust services to the group's target market. Personal financial consulting includes estate planning, investment management, and retirement planning. It operates through three branches and an operations center located in st louis region and two branches in Kansas region.

Primary SIC and add'l.: 6022 6712

CIK No: 0001025835

Subsidiaries: Charford, Inc., EFSC Capital Trust I, EFSC Capital Trust II, EFSC Capital Trust III, EFSC Capital Trust IV, Enterprise Bank & Trust, Enterprise IHC, LLC, Enterprise Real Estate Mortgage Company, LLC, Millennium Brokerage Group, LLC, Millennium Holding Company, Inc.

Officers: Paul Vogel/CEO, Pres. - Enterprise Trust, Clayton Exec., Kevin C. Eichner/Vice Chmn., CEO, Pres./$1,287,607.00, James C. Wagner/Exec. VP/$282,726.00, Frank H. Sanfilippo/CFO, Exec. VP - Enterprise Financial, Clayton/$381,598.00, Peter F. Benoist/Dir., Exec. VP/$949,299.00, Steven Albart/VP, Mgr. - Sunset Hills Relationship, Lending, Mitchell Baris/Sr. VP, Dir. - Tax Credit Lending, Clayton Relationship Mgr., Tim Barringhaus/VP, Mgr. - Sunset Hills Relationship, Doug Bauche/Group Pres., Relationship Mgr. - St. Peters, Marti Beltrani/VP - Clayton Trust, Richard Blume/VP, Sr. Trust Administrator - Clayton Trust, Buck Brase/Assist. VP - Lending, Mgr. - St. Peters Relationship, William Bruce/VP, Dir. - Mortgage Lending, Clayton Mortgage, Ellen Cressey/VP, Mgr. - Clayton Relationship, James Defrancisco/Branch Mgr. - Overland Park Unit Operations *(95 Officers included in Index)*

Directors: Kevin C. Eichner/Vice Chmn., CEO, Pres., Robert E. Guest/Dir., Lewis A. Levey/Dir., William H. Downey/Dir., Robert E. Saur/Dir., Richard S. Masinton/Dir., Sandra A. Van Trease/47/Dir., James J. Murphy/Dir., Birch M. Mullins/Dir., Peter F. Benoist/Dir., Exec. VP, Henry D. Warshaw/Dir., Paul R. Cahn/Dir.

Owners: Sandra VanTrease, Robert E. Guest/1.60%, Lewis Levey, James Murphy/1.10%, Robert E. Saur/1.10%, Frank H. Sanfilippo, Paul R. Cahn/2.40%, Peter F. Benoist/1.70%, Richard S. Masinton, Stephen P. Marsh, Kevin C. Eichner/6.00%, Henry D. Warshaw, Birch M. Mullins, James C. Wagner, William H. Downey *(16 Owners included in Index)*

Financial Data: Fiscal Year End:12/31 Latest Annual Data: 12/31/2006

Year	Sales	Net Income
2006	$111,334,000	$15,472,000
2005	$77,566,000	$11,295,000
2004	$56,015,000	$8,215,000

Curr. Assets:	$58,288,000	Curr. Liab.:	$1,353,782,000	P/E Ratio:	19.31
Plant, Equip.:	$18,550,000	Total Liab.:	$1,402,593,000	Indic. Yr. Divd.:	$0.210
Total Assets:	$1,535,587,000	Net Worth:	$132,994,000	Debt/ Equity:	0.4385

Enterprise GP Holdings LP

1100 Louisiana, 10th Fl., Houston, TX, 77002; *PH:* 1-713-381-3500; *Fax:* 1-713-381-8200; *http://* www.enterprisegp.com

General - Incorporation	DE	Stock - Price on:12/24/2007	$38.09
Employees	NA	Stock Exchange	NYSE
Auditor	Deloitte & Touche LLP	Ticker Symbol	EPE
Stk Agt	Mellon Investor Services LLC	Outstanding Shares	88,880,000
Counsel	NA	E.P.S.	$1.27
DUNS No.	NA	Shareholders	NA

Business: The groups principle activity is to produce natural gas, natural gas liquids, crude oil and petrochemicals. The group operates through four segments namely, NGL pipelines and services, onshore natural gas pipelines and services, offshore pipelines and services, and petrochemical services. In the year 2006, the group acquired EnCana Oil and Gas. The groups quarterly revenue for September 2007 was 6,721.72 millions of USD.

Primary SIC and add'l.: 4613 4612 4925 4923 4922 1311

CIK No: 0001324592

Subsidiaries: Acadian Acquisition, LLC, Acadian Consulting LLC, Acadian Gas Pipeline System, Acadian Gas, LLC, Arizona Gas Storage, L.L.C., Atlantis Offshore, LLC, Baton Rouge Fractionators LLC, Baton Rouge Pipeline LLC, Baton Rouge Propylene Concentrator, LLC, Belle Rose NGL Pipeline, L.L.C., Belvieu Environmental Fuels GP, LLC, Belvieu Environmental Fuels L.P., Cajun Pipeline Company, LLC, Calcasieu Gas Gathering System, Cameron Highway Oil Pipeline Company 118 Subsidiaries included in the Index

Officers: Michael A. Creel/54/Dir., CEO, Pres., Ralph S. Cunningham/Dir., CEO, Pres., William Ordemann/COO, Exec. VP, Richard H. Bachmann/Dir., Exec. VP, Chief Legal Officer, Sec., Randall W. Fowler/Dir., CFO, Sr. VP, Michael J. Knesek/Sr. VP, Controller, Principal Accounting Officer

Directors: Michael A. Creel/54/Dir., CEO, Pres., Ralph S. Cunningham/Dir., CEO, Pres., Dan L. Duncan/Chmn., Richard H. Bachmann/Dir., Exec. VP, Chief Legal Officer, Sec., Randall W. Fowler/Dir., CFO, Sr. VP, Robert G. Phillips/53/Dir., O. S. Andras/Dir., Matt W. Ralls/58/Dir., Charles E. McMahen/Dir., Randa Duncan Williams/Dir., Edwin E. Smith/Dir., Thurmon Andress/Dir.

Owners: W. Randall Fowler, Edwin W. Smith, O. S. Andras, Insiders/87.20%, Michael A. Creel, Richard H. Bachmann, James H. Lytal, Charles E. McMahen, Thurmon Andress, Robert G. Phillips, Dan L. Duncan/86.80%, A. J. Teague

Financial Data: Fiscal Year End:12/31   Latest Annual Data: 12/31/2006

Year	Sales	Net Income
2006	$13,990,969,000	$99,499,000
2005	$12,256,959,000	$55,276,000

Curr. Assets:	$1,922,558,000	Curr. Liab.:	$1,986,944,000	P/E Ratio:	32.84
Plant, Equip.:	$9,832,547,000	Total Liab.:	$13,281,458,000	Indic. Yr. Divd.:	$1.520
Total Assets:	$13,990,458,000	Net Worth:	$709,000,000	Debt/ Equity:	NA

Enterprise National Bank NJ

11811 US Hwy. One, North Palm Beach, FL, 33408; *PH:* 1-561-624-4400; *http://* www.enbpb.com; *Email:* info@enbpb.com

General - Incorporation		Stock - Price on:12/24/2007	$5.9
Employees	18	Stock Exchange	OTC
Auditor	NA	Ticker Symbol	ENBN
Stk Agt	NA	Outstanding Shares	1,670,000
Counsel	NA	E.P.S.	NA
DUNS No.	NA	Shareholders	NA

Business: The groups principal activity is to provide banking services. The groups services include Internet, bill pay, and telephone banking. The products of the group include car and boat loans, home mortgages and commercial real estate loan. The group operates from the United States.

Primary SIC and add'l.: 5999

CIK No:

Officers: Timothy L. Terry/Chmn., CEO, Pres., Michele R. Glorie/CFO, Exec. VP, Patrick M. Jacks/Sr. VP - Sr. Commercial Lender, Ted A. Tetrick/Sr. VP, Chief Risk Officer, Chief Credit Officer, Sue Craig/Dir., VP - Human Resources

Directors: Timothy L. Terry/Chmn., CEO, Pres., Sue Craig/Dir., VP - Human Resources, James E. Davis/Dir., Barrie S. Godown/Dir., Mark E. Holmes/Dir., Warren B. Mosler/Dir., Jeanne K. Simon/Dir., Lawrence L. Sugarman/Dir.

Enterprise Products Partners LP

1100 Louisiana St., 10th Fl., Houston, TX, 77002; *PH:* 1-713-381-6500; *Fax:* 1-713-381-8200; *http://* www.epplp.com

General - Incorporation	DE	Stock - Price on:12/24/2007	$31.03
Employees	1,900	Stock Exchange	NYSE
Auditor	Deloitte & Touche LLP	Ticker Symbol	EPD
Stk Agt	Mellon Investor Services LLC	Outstanding Shares	433,000,000
Counsel	NA	E.P.S.	$1.13
DUNS No.	NA	Shareholders	NA

Business: The groups principle activity is to produce natural gas, natural gas liquids, crude oil and petrochemicals. The group operates through four segments namely, NGL pipelines and services, onshore natural gas pipelines and services, offshore pipelines and services, and petrochemical services. In the year 2006, the group acquired EnCana Oil and Gas. The group operates from the United States and Gulf of Mexico. The groups quarterly revenue for September 2007 was 4,112.00 millions of USD.

Primary SIC and add'l.: 1311 4612 4922 4925 4923 4613

CIK No: 0001061219

Subsidiaries: Acadian Acquisition, LLC, Acadian Consulting LLC, Acadian Gas Pipeline System, Acadian Gas, LLC, Arizona Gas Storage, L.L.C., Atlantis Offshore, LLC, Baton Rouge Fractionators LLC, Baton Rouge Pipeline LLC, Baton Rouge Propylene Concentrator, LLC, Belle Rose NGL Pipeline, L.L.C., Belvieu Environmental Fuels GP, LLC, Belvieu Environmental Fuels L.P., Cajun Pipeline Company, LLC, Calcasieu Gas Gathering System, Cameron Highway Oil Pipeline Company 116 Subsidiaries included in the Index

Officers: Ralph S. Cunningham/Dir., Exec. VP, COO, Richard H. Bachmann/Dir., Exec. VP, Chief Legal Officer, Sec., Michael A. Creel/Dir., Exec. VP, CFO, James H. Lytal/Exec. VP, A. J. Teague/Exec. VP, Lynn L. Bourdon/Sr. VP, Charles M. Brabson/Sr. VP, James A. Cisarik/Sr. VP, James M. Collingsworth/Sr. VP, Randall W. Fowler/Dir., Sr. VP, Treasurer, Terry L. Hurlburt/Sr. VP, Michael J. Knesek/Sr. VP, Controller, Principal Accounting Officer, Rudy Nix/Sr. VP, William Ordemann/Sr. VP, Gil H. Radtke/Sr. VP *(17 Officers included in Index)*

Directors: Dan L. Duncan/Chmn., Ralph S. Cunningham/Dir., Exec. VP, COO, Richard H. Bachmann/Dir., Exec. VP, Chief Legal Officer, Sec., Michael A. Creel/Dir., Exec. VP, CFO, Randall W. Fowler/Dir., Sr. VP, Treasurer, William E. Barnett/Dir., Rex Ross/Dir., Charles M. Rampacek/Dir.

Owners: Dan L. Duncan/34.00%, Ralph S. Cunningham, Richard H. Bachmann, Randall W. Fowler, James H. Lytal, Michael A. Creel, Insiders/34.20%, Robert G. Phillips, William E. Barnett, A. J. Teague, Rex C. Ross

Financial Data: Fiscal Year End:12/31   Latest Annual Data: 12/31/2006

Year	Sales	Net Income
2006	$13,990,969,000	$601,155,000
2005	$12,256,959,000	$419,508,000
2004	$8,321,202,000	$268,261,000

Curr. Assets:	$1,922,158,000	Curr. Liab.:	$1,984,921,000	P/E Ratio:	32.84
Plant, Equip.:	$9,832,547,000	Total Liab.:	$7,509,485,000	Indic. Yr. Divd.:	$1.900
Total Assets:	$13,989,718,000	Net Worth:	$6,480,233,000	Debt/ Equity:	NA

Enterra Energy Trust

Formerly: Enterra Energy Corp
4th Ave. S.w., Ste. 2700, 500, Calgary, AB, T2P 2V6; *PH:* 1-403-263-0262; *http://* www.enterraenergy.com

General - Incorporation	AB	Stock - Price on:12/24/2007	$6.19
Employees	80	Stock Exchange	NYSE
Auditor	KPMG LLP, Deloitte & Touche LLP	Ticker Symbol	ENT
Stk Agt	Olympia Trust Co	Outstanding Shares	56,330,000
Counsel	Gowling, Strathy & Henderson	E.P.S.	-$3.06
DUNS No.	NA	Shareholders	NA

Business: The group's principal activity is to explore and develop petroleum and natural gas reserves in alberta, calgary and saskatchewan.

Primary SIC and add'l.: 1382 1321

CIK No: 0001116377

Subsidiaries: Enterra Acquisition Corp., Enterra Energy Commercial Trust, Enterra Energy Corp., Enterra Energy II Partner Corp., Enterra Energy Trust, Enterra Exchangeco Ltd., Enterra US Acquisitions Inc, High Point Resources Inc., Rainee Resources Ltd. PTR Resources Ltd., Rocky Mountain Energy Corp.

Officers: James (jim) Tyndall/Sr. VP - Operations, COO - Calgary, Alberta

Directors: R. H. Joe Vidal/Dir., Chmn. - Saskatoon, Saskatchewan, Peter Carpenter/Dir. - Toronto, Ontario, Roger Giovanetto/Dir. - Calgary, Alberta, Chip W.C. Hazelrig/Dir. - Birmingham, Alabama

Financial Data: Fiscal Year End:12/31   Latest Annual Data: 12/31/2006

Year	Sales	Net Income
2006	$168,291,000	-$240,567,000
2005	$104,388,000	-$16,113,000
2004	$89,916,000	$8,584,000

Curr. Assets:	$48,576,000	Curr. Liab.:	$210,591,000		
Plant, Equip.:	$206,963,000	Total Liab.:	$700,766,000	Indic. Yr. Divd.:	$0.720
Total Assets:	$399,597,000	Net Worth:	-$301,169,000	Debt/ Equity:	NA

Entertainment Is Us Inc

Formerly: Auto-Q International Inc
11555 Heron Bay Blvd., Ste. 200, Coral Springs, FL, 33076; *PH:* 1-954-603-0494

General - Incorporation	DE	Stock - Price on:12/24/2007	NA
Employees	NA	Stock Exchange	NA
Auditor	De Joya & Co	Ticker Symbol	NA
Stk Agt	Interwest Transfer Company, Inc.	Outstanding Shares	NA
Counsel	NA	E.P.S.	NA
DUNS No.	NA	Shareholders	NA

Business: The group's principal activity is to develop, supply and install mobile data acquisition and vehicle tracking systems using global positioning systems and telematics technology. The group provides solutions for fleet and asset management including tracking, fuel monitoring, navigation, security and data acquisition. The products of the group include fleettrak standard and premium, fleettrak trailer, aic diesel flowmeter, eguard, FM series-fuel monitor systems, touchtag-intelligent data transfer key, software-transport information management systems and active risk management package. Most of its business is currently conducted in the United Kingdom. The customers of the group include walkers snack foods ltd, alco waste management limited, brian currie ltd, mercedes benz, and aea technology.

Primary SIC and add'l.: 3669

CIK No: 0001144254

Subsidiaries: Auto-Q Solutions Limited, EIU

Curr. Assets:	$8,581,000	Curr. Liab.:	$10,653,000		
Plant, Equip.:	$64,054,000	Total Liab.:	$39,754,000	Indic. Yr. Divd.:	NA
Total Assets:	$76,572,000	Net Worth:	$36,818,000	Debt/ Equity:	NA

Entertainment Properties Trust

30 Pershing Rd., Ste. 201, Kansas City, MO, 64108; *PH:* 1-816-472-1700; *Fax:* 1-816-472-5794; *http://* www.eprkc.com

General - Incorporation	MD
Employees	13
Auditor	KPMG LLP
Stk Agt	UMB Bank, N.A.
Counsel	NA
DUNS No.	NA

Stock - Price on:12/24/2007	$55.05
Stock Exchange	NYSE
Ticker Symbol	EPR
Outstanding Shares	26,650,000
E.P.S.	$2.70
Shareholders	NA

Business: The groups principle activities include developing, acquiring and financing to the entertainment properties. The groups properties include megaplex movie theatre complexes, entertainment retail centers and other destination recreational and specialty properties. In the year 2006, the group acquired two megaplex theatre properties in Garland, Texas and Columbia, Maryland. The group operates from the United States. The groups quarterly revenue for September 2007 was 61.01 millions of USD.

Primary SIC and add'l.: 6798

CIK No: 0001045450

Subsidiaries: 3 Theatres, Inc., 30 West Pershing, LLC, Burbank Village, Inc., Burbank Village, L.P., Cantera 30 Theatre, L.P., Cantera 30, Inc., EPR Canada, Inc., EPR Hialeah, Inc., EPR Metropolis Trust, EPR North II Holdings, Inc., EPR North Trust, EPR TRS Holdings, Inc., EPR TRS I, Inc., EPR TRS II, Inc., EPT Aliso Viejo, Inc. 69 Subsidiaries included in the Index

Officers: David M. Brain/CEO, Pres./$2,050,784.00, Gregory K. Silvers/VP, COO, General Counsel, Sec./$1,090,675.00, Mark A. Peterson/CFO, VP/$575,234.00, Michael Hirons/VP - Finance/$199,328.00

Directors: Robert Druten/Chmn., James A. Olson/65/Trustee, Barrett Brady/61/Trustee, Morgan G. Earnest/52/Trustee

Owners: Robert J. Druten, Michael L. Hirons, Insiders/3.80%, David M. Brain/2.70%, The Vanguard Group, Inc./5.80%, Gregory K. Silvers, Barrett Brady, Morgan G. Earnest, James A. Olson, Mark A. Peterson, Barclays Global/9.30%

Financial Data: Fiscal Year End:12/31   Latest Annual Data: 12/31/2006

Year	Sales	Net Income
2006	$195,500,000	$82,289,000
2005	$164,815,000	$69,060,000
2004	$124,980,000	$53,713,000

Curr. Assets:	$46,822,000	Curr. Liab.:	$37,794,000	P/E Ratio:	20.39
Plant, Equip.:	$1,415,175,000	Total Liab.:	$714,123,000	Indic. Yr. Divd.:	$3.040
Total Assets:	$1,571,279,000	Net Worth:	$852,682,000	Debt/ Equity:	0.8623

Entheos Technologies Inc

1628 W 1st Ave., Ste. 216, Vancouver, BC, V6J 1G1; **PH:** 1-604-659-5005

General - Incorporation	NV
Employees	NA
Auditor	Peterson Sullivan PLLC
Stk Agt	American Registrar & Transfer Co
Counsel	NA
DUNS No.	NA

Stock - Price on:12/24/2007	$0.62
Stock Exchange	OTC
Ticker Symbol	ETHT
Outstanding Shares	NA
E.P.S.	NA
Shareholders	NA

Business: The group operates as an application service provider (asp) of reliable, scalable, real time, high volume outsourced email services. The group also operates media streaming portal and Website focused on the home improvement market. The group operates solely in the domestic market.

Primary SIC and add'l.: 7372 7375

CIK No: 0001016708

Subsidiaries: Email Solutions, Inc., Entheos Technologies, Corp

Officers: Harmel S. Rayat/47/Dir., CEO, Pres., Timothy N. Luu/43/Dir., Sec., Treasurer, CTO

Directors: Harmel S. Rayat/47/Dir., CEO, Pres., Timothy N. Luu/43/Dir., Sec., Treasurer, CTO

Owners: Insiders/95.90%, Harmel S. Rayat & family/89.70%, Harmel S. Rayat/6.20%

Financial Data: Fiscal Year End:12/31   Latest Annual Data: 12/31/2006

Year	Sales	Net Income
2006	NA	-$45,000
2005	NA	-$68,000
2004	NA	-$175,000

Curr. Assets:	$0	Curr. Liab.:	$38,000		
Plant, Equip.:	NA	Total Liab.:	$38,000	Indic. Yr. Divd.:	NA
Total Assets:	$84,000	Net Worth:	$46,000	Debt/ Equity:	NA

Entourage Mining Ltd

475 Howe St. , Ste. 614, Vancouver, BC, V6C 2B3; **PH:** 1-604-669-4367; **Fax:** 1-604-669-4368; http:// www.entouragemining.com; **Email:** info@entouragemining.com

General - Incorporation	BC
Employees	NA
Auditor	Dale Matheson Carr-Hilton LaBonte LLP
Stk Agt	Computershare Trust Co
Counsel	NA
DUNS No.	NA

Stock - Price on:12/24/2007	$0.23
Stock Exchange	OTC
Ticker Symbol	ETGMF
Outstanding Shares	NA
E.P.S.	NA
Shareholders	NA

Business: The groups principal activities include exploring and developing black warrior property. The products of the group include gold and silver. The group operates from Nevada in the United States.

Primary SIC and add'l.: 1041

CIK No: 0001239672

Subsidiaries: Entourage USA Inc

Officers: Gregory Kennedy/Dir., CEO, Pres., Michael Hart/Dir., Corp. Sec., Craig Doctor/Consultant - Corporate Communications

Directors: Gregory Kennedy/Dir., CEO, Pres., Paul Shatzko/Chmn., Michael Hart/Dir., Corp. Sec., Corey Klassen/Dir.

Owners: CMKM Diamonds Inc./59.00%, 101047025 Saskatchewan Ltd/5.20%

Financial Data: Fiscal Year End:12/31   Latest Annual Data: 12/31/2006

Year	Sales	Net Income
2006	NA	-$2,551,000
2005	NA	-$8,639,000
2004	NA	-$794,000

Curr. Assets:	$163,000	Curr. Liab.:	$88,000		
Plant, Equip.:	$3,000	Total Liab.:	$88,000	Indic. Yr. Divd.:	NA
Total Assets:	$166,000	Net Worth:	$78,000	Debt/ Equity:	NA

Entrada Networks Inc

5755 Oberlin Dr., Ste 204, San Diego, CA, 92121; **PH:** 1-858-597-1102; http:// www.entradanetworks.com

General - Incorporation	DE
Employees	NA
Auditor	BDO Seidman LLP
Stk Agt	Computershare Investor Services LLC
Counsel	NA
DUNS No.	15-207-0496

Stock - Price on:12/24/2007	$0.001
Stock Exchange	OTC
Ticker Symbol	ESAN
Outstanding Shares	NA
E.P.S.	NA
Shareholders	NA

Business: The group's principal activity is to develop, market and sell products for the network connectivity industry. The group operates in three segments: rixon networks, sync research and torrey pines networks. The rixon networks segment designs, manufactures, markets and sells a line of fast and gigabit ethernet products. The ethernet products are incorporated into the remote access and other server products of original equipment manufacturers. The sync research segment designs, manufactures, markets, sells and services frame relay products for some of the major financial institutions in the United States and abroad. The torrey pines networks designs, manufactures, markets and sells storage area network transport switching products. In addition the group also provides telecommunications network services, Internet service for the purpose of providing access to and transport within their networks. On 18-May-2004, the group acquired microtek systems.

Primary SIC and add'l.: 3577 7373

CIK No: 0001000695

Subsidiaries: Entrada Networks, Inc., Sorrento Networks Corporation, Sync Research, Inc.

Financial Data: Fiscal Year End:01/31   Latest Annual Data: 4/30/2005

Year	Sales	Net Income
2005	$975,000	-$824,000
2004	$6,221,000	-$1,984,000

Curr. Assets:	$2,975,000	Curr. Liab.:	$4,682,000		
Plant, Equip.:	$420,000	Total Liab.:	$4,682,000	Indic. Yr. Divd.:	NA
Total Assets:	$4,553,000	Net Worth:	-$129,000	Debt/ Equity:	NA

Entravision Communications Corp

2425 Olympic Blvd., Ste. 6000 W, Santa Monica, CA, 90404; **PH:** 1-310-447-3870; **Fax:** 1-310-447-3899; http:// www.entravision.com

General - Incorporation	DE
Employees	1,111
Auditor	McGladrey & Pullen LLP
Stk Agt	Mellon Investor Services LLC
Counsel	O'melveny & Myers
DUNS No.	NA

Stock - Price on:12/24/2007	$10.35
Stock Exchange	NYSE
Ticker Symbol	EVC
Outstanding Shares	104,120,000
E.P.S.	$0.25
Shareholders	NA

Business: The group's principal activity is to reach hispanic community in the United States through a combination of television, radio and outdoor advertising. The group owns and operates 45 primary television stations located in the southwestern United States including the United States/Mexican border markets. The group also owns and operates 57 radio stations in 22 U.S. Markets, including Spanish language stations in los angeles, san francisco, phoenix and Dallas-ft. Worth. These radio stations consist of 42 FM and 12 AM stations. The outdoor advertising operations are located primarily in high-density hispanic communities in los angeles and New York. On 03-Jul-2003, the group sold el diario/la prensa (a newspaper division) to cpk nyc, llc.the group acquired the assets of kssc-FM, kssd-FM ,ksse-FM and assets of television stations ktsb-lp, k10og, k17gd, k28fk and k35er in 2003. The group sold radio station kzfo-FM in the fresno, California to univision.

Primary SIC and add'l.: 2711 4833 7312 4832

CIK No: 0001109116

Subsidiaries: 26 de Mexico, S. de R.L. de C.V., Arizona Radio, Inc., Aspen FM, Inc., Channel Fifty Seven, Inc., Comercializadora Frontera Norte, S. de R.L. de C.V., Diamond Radio, Inc., Entravision Communications Company, LLC, Entravision Holdings, LLC, Entravision San Diego, Inc., Entravision, LLC, Entravision-El Paso, LLC, Entravision-Texas G.P., LLC, Entravision-Texas L.P., Inc., Entravision-Texas Limited Partnership, KNVO de Mexico, S. de R.L. de C.V. 27 Subsidiaries included in the Index

Officers: Walter F. Ulloa/Chmn., CEO/$1,601,138.00, Larry E. Safir/Exec. VP, Christopher T. Young/Pres. - Outdoor Division/$293,017.00, John F. Delorenzo/Exec. VP, Treasurer, CFO/$639,811.00, Jeffery A. Liberman/Pres. - Radio Division/$617,490.00, Philip C. Wilkinson/Dir., CQO, Pres./$1,602,156.00

Directors: Walter F. Ulloa/Chmn., CEO, Jesse Casso/Dir., Gilbert R. Vasquez/Dir., Esteban E. Torres/Dir., Darryl B. Thompson/Dir., Philip C. Wilkinson/Dir., COO, Pres., Paul A. Zevnik/Dir.

Owners: Walter F. Ulloa/11.05%, Jeffery A. Liberman, Columbia Wagner Asset Management LP/5.76%, Goldman Sachs Asset Management, L.P./10.29%, Philip C. Wilkinson/1.42%, Christopher T. Young, Michael S. Rosen, Paul A. Zevnik/4.52%, Insiders/4.15%, Walter F. Ulloa/1.13%, Esteban E. Torres, Insiders/24.28%, Jesse Casso, Darryl B. Thompson, John F. DeLorenzo (17 Owners included in Index)

Financial Data: Fiscal Year End:12/31   Latest Annual Data: 12/31/2006

Year	Sales	Net Income
2006	$291,752,000	-$134,599,000
2005	$280,964,000	-$9,657,000
2004	$259,053,000	$6,164,000

Curr. Assets:	$193,205,000	Curr. Liab.:	$37,585,000		
Plant, Equip.:	$145,975,000	Total Liab.:	$666,945,000	Indic. Yr. Divd.:	NA
Total Assets:	$1,418,664,000	Net Worth:	$751,719,000	Debt/ Equity:	NA

Entree Gold Inc

1166 Alberni St., Ste. 1201, Vancouver, BC, V6E 3Z3; **PH:** 1-604-687-4777; http:// www.entreegold.com

General - Incorporation	Canada
Employees	NA
Auditor	Davidson & Co LLP
Stk Agt	Pacific Corporate Trust Co
Counsel	P. MacNeill Law Corp
DUNS No.	NA

Stock - Price on:12/24/2007	NA
Stock Exchange	AMEX
Ticker Symbol	EGI
Outstanding Shares	NA
E.P.S.	NA
Shareholders	NA

Business: The group's principal activity is to explore natural resource properties. The group operates in Mongolia.

Primary SIC and add'l.: 1040

CIK No: 0001271554

Subsidiaries: Entre LLC

Officers: Gregory G. Crowe/Dir., CEO, Pres., Lindsay R. Bottomer/Dir., VP - Corporate Development, Hamish Malkin/CFO, Robert M. Cann/VP - Exploration, Mona Forster/Corp. Sec., Monica Hamm/Investor Relations Officer, Cary Pinkowski/Advisor - Finance, Acquisitions

Directors: Gregory G. Crowe/Dir., CEO, Pres., James L. Harris/Chmn., Michael Howard/Dep. Chmn., Peter G. Meredith/Dir., Lindsay R. Bottomer/Dir., VP - Corporate Development, Mark H. Bailey/Dir.

EntreMed Inc

9640 Medical Ctr. Dr., Rockville, MD, 20850; **PH:** 1-240-864-2600; **Fax:** 1-240-864-2601; http:// www.entremed.com

General - Incorporation	DE	Stock - Price on:12/24/2007	$1.66
Employees	56	Stock Exchange	NDQ
Auditor	Ernst & Young LLP	Ticker Symbol	ENMD
Stk Agt	American Stock Transfer & Trust Co.	Outstanding Shares	84,890,000
Counsel	Kilpatrick Stockton	E.P.S.	-$0.31
DUNS No.	79-617-6915	Shareholders	NA

Business: The group's principal activity is to sponsor and conduct research and development on biopharmaceutical products. It is in the clinical-stage of developing antiangiogenesis therapeutic products. These products inhibit abnormal blood vessel growth associated with a broad range of diseases such as cancer, blindness atherosclerosis and endometriosis. The group's core technologies also include a blood cell permeation device, which is designed to enhance the ability of red blood cells to deliver oxygen to organs and tissues. This device may also be used to deliver drugs, genes or other therapeutic agents that otherwise would not readily diffuse through blood cell membranes. The antiangiogenic product candidates include endostatin, panzem and angiostatin. These products are used to inhibit the growth of tumor-feeding blood vessels.

Primary SIC and add'l.: 8731

CIK No: 0000895051

Subsidiaries: Cytokine Sciences, Inc

Officers: James S. Burns/Dir., CEO, Pres./$863,292.00, Carolyn F. Sidor/VP, Chief Medical Officer, Member - Scientific Advisory Board/$475,138.00, Dane Saglio/CFO/$384,494.00, Marc Corrado/VP - Corporate Development/$383,780.00, Cynthia Wong Hu/VP, General Counsel, Corp. Sec./$219,979.00, Ginny Dunn/Assoc. Dir. - Corporate Communications, Investor Relations, Kenneth W. Bair/Sr. VP - Research, Development

Directors: James S. Burns/Dir., CEO, Pres., Michael M. Tarnow/Chmn., Tak W. Mak/Chmn. - Scientific Advisory Board, Donald S. Brooks/Dir., Hans Wigzell/Member - Scientific Advisory Board, Michael E. Weinblatt/Member - Scientific Advisory Board, Gail S. Eckhard/Member - Scientific Advisory Board, Ronald Cape/Dir., Dwight L. Bush/Dir., Peter S. Knight/Dir., Jennie Hunter-Cevera/Dir., Mark C.M. Randall/Dir., Carolyn F. Sidor/VP, Chief Medical Officer, Member - Scientific Advisory Board

Owners: Carolyn F. Sidor, Jennie C. Hunter-Cevera, Insiders/3.27%, Peter S. Knight, Cynthia Wong Hu, Celgene Corporation/27.22%, Marc G. Corrado, Dwight L. Bush, Donald S. Brooks, James S. Burns, Dane R. Saglio, Ronald Cape, Michael M. Tarnow, Mark C.M. Randall

Financial Data: Fiscal Year End:12/31 **Latest Annual Data:** 12/31/2006

Year	Sales	Net Income
2006	$6,894,000	-$49,889,000
2005	$5,918,000	-$16,313,000
2004	$514,000	-$12,622,000

Curr. Assets:	$54,867,000	Curr. Liab.:	$8,598,000		
Plant, Equip.:	$848,000	Total Liab.:	$8,738,000	Indic. Yr. Divd.:	NA
Total Assets:	$55,720,000	Net Worth:	$46,963,000	Debt/ Equity:	NA

EntreMetrix Corp

18101 Von Karman Ave., Ste. 330, Irvine, CA, 92612; **PH:** 1-888-798-9100; http:// www.entremetrix.com; **Email:** info@entremetrix.com

General - Incorporation	NV	Stock - Price on:12/24/2007	$0.15
Employees	3	Stock Exchange	OTC
Auditor	Spector & Wong, LLP	Ticker Symbol	NA
Stk Agt	Columbia Stock Transfer Co	Outstanding Shares	56,990,000
Counsel	NA	E.P.S.	-$0.01
DUNS No.	NA	Shareholders	NA

Business: The groups principle activity is to provide early stage capital, strategic guidance and operational support. The groups services include financial guidance in areas of treasury management, general accounting oversight and capital formation, employee-related administration and regulatory compliance. The group operates from the United States.

Primary SIC and add'l.: 8742

CIK No: 0000755328

Subsidiaries: EnStruxis, Inc

Officers: Scott Absher/48/Dir., CEO, George Lefevre/41/Dir., CFO, Sec.

Directors: Scott Absher/48/Dir., CEO, George Lefevre/41/Dir., CFO, Sec., Mark Absher/45/Dir., Richard Granieri/63/Dir., Patrick Shane/56/Dir.

Owners: Insiders/66.00%, Scott Absher/31.89%, Richard Granieri, George LeFevre/31.89%

Financial Data: Fiscal Year End:12/31 **Latest Annual Data:** 12/31/2006

Year	Sales	Net Income
2006	$6,202,000	-$411,000
2005	$7,642,000	-$591,000
2004	$10,615,000	-$310,000

Curr. Assets:	$141,000	Curr. Liab.:	$616,000		
Plant, Equip.:	$2,000	Total Liab.:	$1,050,000	Indic. Yr. Divd.:	NA
Total Assets:	$148,000	Net Worth:	-$902,000	Debt/ Equity:	NA

Entropin Inc

13314 Lost Key Pl., Bradenton, FL, 34202; **PH:** 1-760-775-8333; http:// www.entropininc.com

General - Incorporation	DE	Stock - Price on:12/24/2007	NA
Employees	NA	Stock Exchange	OTC
Auditor	LL Bradford & Co	Ticker Symbol	ETOP
Stk Agt	Corporate Stock Transfer, Inc.	Outstanding Shares	NA
Counsel	NA	E.P.S.	-$0.022
DUNS No.	60-435-8515	Shareholders	NA

Business: The group's principal activity is to engage in the research and development of proprietary compounds, ent-103 for pain therapy. Ent-103 has the potential to effectively treat a number of medical conditions using various delivery systems. Ent-103 is effective in acute pain states, acute inflammatory pain, neuropathic pain and suppresses the abnormal pain to tactile stimulation that occurs after an incision. At present, the group is pursuing two delivery systems, injectable and topical, for ent-103.

Primary SIC and add'l.: 2834 8731

CIK No: 0000837600

Officers: Louis Coppage/CEO, Pres.

Financial Data: Fiscal Year End:12/31 **Latest Annual Data:** 12/31/2005

Year	Sales	Net Income
2005	NA	-$2,823,000
2004	NA	-$2,991,000
2003	NA	-$3,245,000

Curr. Assets:	$113,000	Curr. Liab.:	$589,000		
Plant, Equip.:	NA	Total Liab.:	$589,000	Indic. Yr. Divd.:	NA
Total Assets:	$113,000	Net Worth:	-$476,000	Debt/ Equity:	NA

Entrust Financial Services Inc

1270 Ave. Of The Americas, 16th Fl., New York, NY, 10020; **PH:** 1-212-356-0500; http:// www.entrustfs.com

General - Incorporation	CO	Stock - Price on:12/24/2007	NA
Employees	NA	Stock Exchange	NA
Auditor	Lazar Levine & Felix LLP	Ticker Symbol	NA
Stk Agt	NA	Outstanding Shares	NA
Counsel	NA	E.P.S.	$0.07
DUNS No.	NA	Shareholders	NA

Business: The group's principal activities are to develop and maintain business associated with wholesale mortgage banking. The group acts as a mortgage broker. The group originates residential real estate loans in thirty seven states and sells them to financial institutions. The group has a correspondent relationship with several financial institutions. The group operates through regional offices in Florida, Colorado, Nevada and California.

Primary SIC and add'l.: 6162

CIK No: 0001054303

Subsidiaries: Entrust Mortgage, Inc.

Owners: John J. Borer, Thomas Pinou, Sam Dryden, Steven A. Horowitz, Matthew Geller, Insiders, Edward Rubin, Wesley K. Clark

Financial Data: Fiscal Year End:12/31 **Latest Annual Data:** 12/31/2006

Year	Sales	Net Income
2006	NA	-$57,000
2005	NA	-$11,000
2004	$11,498,000	-$216,000

Curr. Assets:	$17,000	Curr. Liab.:	$24,000		
Plant, Equip.:	NA	Total Liab.:	$24,000	Indic. Yr. Divd.:	NA
Total Assets:	$17,000	Net Worth:	-$7,000	Debt/ Equity:	NA

Entrust Inc

1 Hanover Pk., 16633 Dallas Pkwy., Ste. 800, Addison, TX, 75001; **PH:** 1-972-713-5800; **Fax:** 1-972-713-5805; http:// www.entrust.com; **Email:** entrust@entrust.com

General - Incorporation	MD	Stock - Price on:12/24/2007	$4.15
Employees	503	Stock Exchange	NDQ
Auditor	Grant Thornton LLP	Ticker Symbol	ENTU
Stk Agt	Computershare Investor Services LLC	Outstanding Shares	60,570,000
Counsel	NA	E.P.S.	-$0.15
DUNS No.	79-945-4061	Shareholders	NA

Business: The group's principle activity is to provide Internet security solutions and services to e-businesses and other organizations. These solutions provide identification, entitlements, verification, privacy and security management capabilities. The group provides security solutions related services including managed security services, Internet security consulting services, deployment services, systems integration services and training. The customers include domestic and foreign government agencies, global 1000 enterprises such as financial, healthcare, telecommunications and large manufacturing organizations. As on 31-Dec-2003, the group licensed software to more than 1,250 customers world wide. The group markets its products through direct sales force in the North America, Europe, Middle East, Africa and in the other continents. The group's quarterly revenue for Sep'07 was 23.94 millions of USD.

Primary SIC and add'l.: 7373 7372

CIK No: 0001031283

Subsidiaries: CygnaCom Solutions, Inc., enCommerce Limited, enCommerce, Inc., Entrust (Europe) Limited, Entrust GmbH, Entrust International LLC, Entrust Japan Co. Ltd., Entrust Limited, Entrust s.a.r.l., Entrust Technologies (Switzerland) GmbH

Officers: William F. Conner/Chmn., CEO, Pres./$1,761,772.00, Sam Morcos/Sr. VP - Sales, Services Canada, Asia Pacific, Latin America/$544,834.00, Peter Bello/Sr. VP, GM US Federal Government/$431,403.00, David Rockvam/VP - Corporate Business Development, Investor Relations, Andrew Pinder/Sr. VP, GM - EMEA, David Wagner/Sr. VP, CFO/$496,229.00, Kevin Simzer/Sr. VP, Chief Marketing Officer/$514,259.00, Hans Downer/Sr. VP, GM - EMEA, Steve Holton/Sr. VP, GM - US Sales, Managed Services, Eric Skinner/CTO

Directors: William F. Conner/Chmn., CEO, Pres., Terdema Ussery/Dir., Ray W. Washburne/Dir., Michael E. McGrath/Dir., Jerry C. Jones/Dir., Michael P. Ressner/Dir., Douglas Schloss/Dir., Butler C. Derrick/Dir.

Owners: Insiders/13.96%, Hans Ydema, Peter Bello, Ray Washburne, Jerry C. Jones, Royce and Associates, LLC/7.46%, Butler C. Derrick, William F. Conner/9.70%, Douglas Schloss/1.14%, Terdema L. Ussery, Franklin Resources, Inc./7.76%, David Wagner, Michael P. Ressner, Sam Morcos, Michael McGrath (16 Owners included in Index)

Financial Data: Fiscal Year End:12/31 **Latest Annual Data:** 12/31/2006

Year	Sales	Net Income
2006	$95,183,000	-$15,417,000
2005	$98,128,000	$6,374,000
2004	$90,957,000	$1,078,000

Curr. Assets:	$46,548,000	Curr. Liab.:	$49,060,000		
Plant, Equip.:	$2,721,000	Total Liab.:	$68,592,000	Indic. Yr. Divd.:	NA
Total Assets:	$127,816,000	Net Worth:	$59,220,000	Debt/ Equity:	NA

Entrx Corp

800 Nicollet Mall, Ste. 2690, Minneapolis, MN, 55402; *PH:* 1-612-333-0614; *Fax:* 1-612-338-7332; *http://* metalclad.com

General - Incorporation	DE	Stock- Price on:12/24/2007	$0.19
Employees	127	Stock Exchange	OTC
Auditor	Virchow, Krause & Co. LLP	Ticker Symbol	ENTX
Stk Agt	American Stock Transfer & Trust Co.	Outstanding Shares	7,620,000
Counsel	NA	E.P.S.	$0.09
DUNS No.	00-839-6509	Shareholders	NA

Business: The group's principal activity is to provide insulation and asbestos abatement services, primarily on the west coast of the United States. The insulation services provided by the group include the installation of insulation on pipe, ducts, furnaces, boilers and other types of industrial equipment and commercial applications. Asbestos abatement services include the removal and disposal of asbestos-containing products in similar applications.

Primary SIC and add'l.: 1742

CIK No: 0000013547

Subsidiaries: Allstate Insurance Company, Chiral Quest, Inc., Far East National Bank, Metalclad Insulation Corporation

Owners: Peter L. Hauser/13.00%, Joseph M. Caldwell/1.60%, Wayne W. Mills/10.90%, David R. Trueblood, Insiders/18.50%, Anthony C. Dabbene/6.30%, Bradley Resources Company/6.50%, Thomas E. Welch, George W. Holbrook/7.60%, Brian D. Niebur/1.00%, Grant S. Kesler/9.70%, James R. McGoogan/6.70%

Financial Data: Fiscal Year End:12/31 Latest Annual Data: 12/31/2006

Year	Sales	Net Income
2006	$19,517,000	$2,052,000
2005	$14,711,000	-$1,743,000
2004	$12,996,000	$611,000

Curr. Assets:	$14,928,000	Curr. Liab.:	$10,628,000	P/E Ratio:	0.83
Plant, Equip.:	$331,000	Total Liab.:	$45,696,000	Indic. Yr. Divd.:	NA
Total Assets:	$51,667,000	Net Worth:	$5,971,000	Debt/ Equity:	NA

Enucleus Inc

PO Box 1649, Vancouver, WA, 98668; ; *http://* www.enucleus.com

General - Incorporation	DE	Stock- Price on:12/24/2007	$0.025
Employees	162	Stock Exchange	OTC
Auditor	Danziger & Hochman	Ticker Symbol	ENUI
Stk Agt	Illinois Stock Transfer Co	Outstanding Shares	49,860,000
Counsel	NA	E.P.S.	-$0.021
DUNS No.	16-089-8284	Shareholders	NA

Business: The group's principle activity is to distribute Internet infrastructure. The product offerings include co-location, high-speed Internet access, data storage and application delivery. These products provide clients with a scaleable and brandable platform for the development of customers' ebusiness initiatives. The customers targeted include system integrators, Web developers, software providers and telecom resellers. In Jan 2004, it acquired primewire inc. On 02-Jun-2004, the group acquired takgroup inc. On 28-Sep-2004, the group acquired frontier technologies. The group operates from United States.

Primary SIC and add'l.: 7373 5734

CIK No: 0000761034

Subsidiaries: Alliance Net, Inc., eNucleus Pte. Ltd., Financial ASPx, Inc., Supply Chain ASPx, Inc.

Officers: Randy Edgerton/CEO, Pres., Ankil Patel/MD - Asia Pacific, India

Directors: Dhru Desai/Chmn., John C. Paulsen/Dir., Frank Menon/Dir.

Financial Data: Fiscal Year End:12/31 Latest Annual Data: 12/31/2004

Year	Sales	Net Income
2004	$3,204,000	$445,000
2003	$578,000	-$3,452,000
2002	$286,000	-$5,758,000

Curr. Assets:	$1,098,000	Curr. Liab.:	$1,195,000		
Plant, Equip.:	$1,615,000	Total Liab.:	$1,893,000	Indic. Yr. Divd.:	NA
Total Assets:	$3,853,000	Net Worth:	$1,960,000	Debt/ Equity:	0.1886

Enviro Voraxial Technology Inc

821 NW 57th Pl., Fort Lauderdale, FL, 33309; *PH:* 1-954-958-9968; *Fax:* 1-954-958-8057; *http://* www.evtn.com; *Email:* info@evtn.com

General - Incorporation	ID	Stock- Price on:12/24/2007	$0.8
Employees	5	Stock Exchange	OTC
Auditor	Jewett, Schwartz, Wolfe & Associates	Ticker Symbol	EVTN
Stk Agt	Jersey Transfer & Trust Co	Outstanding Shares	22,090,000
Counsel	NA	E.P.S.	-$0.09
DUNS No.	NA	Shareholders	NA

Business: The group's principal activity is to develop voraxial separator, a technology that separates solids and liquids with distinct specific gravities. The patented technology can be employed in oil production, oil remediation services, municipal sewage treatment, bilge water purification, metal finishing, manufacturing, agricultural production and numerous other industrial production and environmental remediation processes. The group's operations are carried out through two segments: the manufacture and distribution of the voraxial separator and contract manufacturing services to the aerospace and automotive industries. The products and services are marketed in the United States, Europe, Middle East and South America.

Primary SIC and add'l.: 3812

CIK No: 0001043894

Subsidiaries: Florida Precision Aerospace, Inc

Officers: Alberto Di Bella/75/Chmn., CEO, Pres., John A. Dibella/36/Dir., Exec. VP, Dan Samela/Contact - Technical Papers, Frank J. Demicco/Consultant

Directors: Alberto Di Bella/75/Chmn., CEO, Pres., John A. Dibella/36/Dir., Exec. VP

Owners: John DiBella/17.90%, Alberto DiBella/16.60%, Insiders/34.50%, Robert Weinberg/10.30%, Peter Chiappetta/15.40%

Financial Data: Fiscal Year End:12/31 Latest Annual Data: 12/31/2006

Year	Sales	Net Income
2006	$310,000	-$834,000
2005	$128,000	-$1,091,000
2004	$19,000	-$1,742,000

Curr. Assets:	$650,000	Curr. Liab.:	$652,000		
Plant, Equip.:	$5,000	Total Liab.:	$652,000	Indic. Yr. Divd.:	NA
Total Assets:	$665,000	Net Worth:	$13,000	Debt/ Equity:	NA

Envirokare Tech Inc

641 Lexington Ave., 14th Fl., New York, NY, 10022; *PH:* 1-212-634-6333; *Fax:* 1-212-634-6339; *http://* www.envirokare.com

General - Incorporation	NV	Stock- Price on:12/24/2007	$0.55
Employees	2	Stock Exchange	OTC
Auditor	Williams & Webster, P.S	Ticker Symbol	ENVK
Stk Agt	Pacific Stock Transfer Company	Outstanding Shares	59,590,000
Counsel	NA	E.P.S.	-$0.07
DUNS No.	NA	Shareholders	NA

Business: The group's principal activity is to design, develop and manufacture, utilizing proprietary thermoplastic composite technologies including thermo plastic flowforming for tpf(tm). The end-use products of this process are fabricated using other materials including wood, metal, concrete or reinforced thermoset resins-fiber-glass. The group also focuses licenses proprietary process technology to manufacturers and converters. The group's product 'the pallet' comprises of long-fiber reinforced recycled material and is 100% recyclable.

Primary SIC and add'l.: 2542

CIK No: 0001065677

Subsidiaries: Electroship Acquisition Corp, Envirokare Composite Corp

Officers: Louis F. Savelli/Chmn., CEO, George Kazantzis/Pres., Sec., Dir.

Directors: Louis F. Savelli/Chmn., CEO, Paul Gillease/Dir., Douglas Davidian/Dir., John Sereda/Dir., Walter V. Gerasimowicz/Dir., John Verbicky/Dir., George Kazantzis/Pres., Sec., Dir., Steve Pappas/Dir.

Owners: Insiders/36.90%, John Verbicky/3.30%, Nicholas Pappas/5.10%, Steve Pappas/20.30%, Vanessa Houiris/5.30%, Walter V. Gerasimowicz/2.40%, Adrian Alexandru/6.60%, Douglas B. Davidian/1.10%, James Pappas/5.30%, Louis F. Savelli/1.80%, George E. Kazantzis/6.40%, Nova Chemicals, Inc./22.60%, Paul G. Gillease/0.50%

Financial Data: Fiscal Year End:12/31 Latest Annual Data: 12/31/2006

Year	Sales	Net Income
2006	$471,000	-$5,310,000
2005	$1,074,000	-$8,456,000
2004	NA	-$2,060,000

Curr. Assets:	$4,864,000	Curr. Liab.:	$2,838,000		
Plant, Equip.:	$4,394,000	Total Liab.:	$11,759,000	Indic. Yr. Divd.:	NA
Total Assets:	$16,100,000	Net Worth:	-$229,000	Debt/ Equity:	NA

Environmental Control Corp

605- 1525 Robson St., Vancouver, BC, V6G 1C3; *PH:* 1-604-669-3532; *Fax:* 1-604-608-9030; *http://* www.econtrolcorp.com

General - Incorporation	NV	Stock- Price on:12/24/2007	$1.28
Employees	NA	Stock Exchange	OTC
Auditor	Manning Elliott LLP	Ticker Symbol	EVCC
Stk Agt	Empire Stock Transfer Inc.	Outstanding Shares	NA
Counsel	NA	E.P.S.	NA
DUNS No.	NA	Shareholders	NA

Business: The groups principal activity is to explore minerals properties. In September 2007 the group acquired Environmental Control Corporation. The group operates from the United States.

Primary SIC and add'l.: 3714

CIK No: 0001284454

Officers: Albert E. Hickman/66/Chmn., CEO, Pres., Gary Bishop/Dir., CFO, Nils Rodeblad/Dir., VP - Business Development, Europe, Asia, Bert Hickman/VP - Business Development, North America, Michael J. Mugford/Dir., VP - Sales, Marketing, Glenn Knight/Chief Scientific Officer

Directors: Albert E. Hickman/66/Chmn., CEO, Pres., Gary Bishop/Dir., CFO, Nils Rodeblad/Dir., VP - Business Development, Europe, Asia, Michael J. Mugford/Dir., VP - Sales, Marketing, Edward P. Noonan/Dir.

Owners: Alexei Jirniaguine/30.49%, Andrei Krioukov/30.49%

Financial Data: Fiscal Year End:09/30 Latest Annual Data: 9/30/2006

Year	Sales	Net Income
2006	NA	-$300,000
2005	NA	-$32,000

Curr. Assets:	$286,000	Curr. Liab.:	$22,000		
Plant, Equip.:	NA	Total Liab.:	$22,000	Indic. Yr. Divd.:	NA
Total Assets:	$286,000	Net Worth:	$264,000	Debt/ Equity:	1.2000

Environmental Power Corp

1 Cate St., 4th Fl., Portsmouth, NH, 03801; *PH:* 1-603-431-1780; *Fax:* 1-603-431-2650; *http://* www.environmentalpower.com

General - Incorporation	DE	Stock- Price on:12/24/2007	$9.0407
Employees	47	Stock Exchange	AMEX
Auditor	Vitale, Caturano & Co., Ltd.	Ticker Symbol	EPG
Stk Agt	American Stock Transfer & Trust Co.	Outstanding Shares	9,790,000
Counsel	Dorsey & Whitney LLP	E.P.S.	-$2.34
DUNS No.	13-084-1174	Shareholders	NA

Business: The group's principal activities are the development and ownership of electrical generating facilities powered by non-commodity fuels and renewable energy sources. The group's power generating facilities use alternative fuels most of that are wastes, which are generally not subject to the same cost fluctuations as traditional fuels. The power generating facilities have also been able to exceed air quality emission standards and to assist with the clean-up of wastes that are sources of water pollution. The group operates in two business segment: scrubgrass project and microgy. The scrubgrass project is an approximate 83 megawatt waste coal-fired electric generating station located on a 600-acre site in venango county, Pennsylvania. Microgy is engaged in the development and deployment of a proprietary technology for the extraction of methane gas from animal wastes and its use to fuel generation of energy.

Primary SIC and add'l.: 4911

CIK No: 0000805012

Subsidiaries: Buzzard Power Corporation, EPC Corporation, Microgy, Inc, Mission Biogas, LLC, MST Estates LLC, Mst Gp LLC, MST Production Ltd

Officers: Richard E. Kessel/CEO, Pres./$722,242.00, Eben Kane/VP - Finance, Clay Walton/CTO, VP, Sean Breen/Sr. VP - Development , Eastern Region, Steven J. Brunner/Sr. VP - Engineering, Michael P. Newman/VP - Operations, Albert Morales/Exec. VP, Dennis Haines/VP, General Counsel, Sec./$67,469.00, Michael Thomas/CFO, Sr. VP, Mark Hall/Sr. VP, Michael J. Hvisdos/Exec. VP, Dan Eastman/Sr. VP - Development , Central Region, Brian Bzdawka/Sr. VP - Development , Meat Industry Solutions, Jeff Dasovich/Sr. VP - Development, Western Region

Directors: Joseph E. Cresci/Chmn., Kamlesh R. Tejwani/Vice Chmn., Donald Andy Livingston/Dir., Lon Hatamiya/Dir., August Schumacher/Dir., Robert I. Weisberg/Dir., Steven Kessner/Dir., Roger S. Ballentine/Dir., John R. Cooper/Dir., Jesse J. Knight/Dir.

Owners: Dennis Haines, John R. Cooper, Robert I. Weisberg/1.05%, Lon Hatamiya, John F. ONeill/1.46%, Dynamis Advisors, LLC/7.79%, Donald A. Livingston/6.58%, Insiders/21.27%, Richard E. Kessel, Joseph E. Cresci/10.60%, Black River Commodity Clean Energy Investment Fund LLC/9.99%, Kamlesh R. Tejwani/5.35%, Steven Kessner/3.44%, August Schumacher

Financial Data: *Fiscal Year End:*12/31 *Latest Annual Data:* 12/31/2006

Year	Sales	Net Income
2006	$53,878,000	-$14,115,000
2005	$55,800,000	-$11,414,000
2004	$59,790,000	-$3,958,000

Curr. Assets:	$83,928,000	**Curr. Liab.:**	$17,502,000		
Plant, Equip.:	$14,535,000	**Total Liab.:**	$157,190,000	**Indic. Yr. Divd.:**	NA
Total Assets:	$185,867,000	**Net Worth:**	$18,521,000	**Debt/ Equity:**	3.4664

Environmental Solutions Worldwide Inc

335 Connie Crescent, Concord, ON, L4K 5R2; ***PH:*** 1-905-695-4142; ***Fax:*** 1-905-695-5013; ***http://*** www.cleanerfuture.com; ***Email:*** investor-relations@cleanerfuture.com

General - Incorporation	FL	**Stock**- Price on:12/24/2007	$0.8
Employees	NA	Stock Exchange	OTC
Auditor	Goldstein & Morris CPAs P.C	Ticker Symbol	ESWW
Stk Agt	Interwest Transfer Company, Inc.	Outstanding Shares	NA
Counsel	Baratta Baratta & Aidala LLP	E.P.S	NA
DUNS No.	NA	Shareholders	NA

Business: The group's principal activities are to develop, manufacture and market catalytic converter technology and services for diesel and gasoline products. The group has also been developing spark plug/fuel injector technology. The catalytic converters' product line include clean cat(R) which is used for diesel applications, quiet cat (TM) which is launched for small engine applications and enviro cat (TM) which are used for gasoline applications. The group's markets include automobiles, trucks, garden equipment, marine vehicles, specialty vehicles, stationary generator sets and large diesel equipment. The group products are now being marketed both domestically and internationally, including China, India and Mexico. The trade names include clean cat (R), enviro cat (TM), quiet cat (TM), pro cat (TM) and air sentinel (TM).

Primary SIC and add'l.: 3714

CIK No: 0001082278

Subsidiaries: ESW America, Inc., ESW Canada, Inc., ESW Technologies, Inc.

Officers: David Johnson/Dir., CEO, Pres., Joey Schwartz/Dir., CFO

Directors: David Johnson/Dir., CEO, Pres., Nitin Amersey/Chmn., Bengt Odner/Dir., Joey Schwartz/Dir., CFO, Michael F. Albanese/Dir., John Dunlap/Dir.

Owners: Insiders/20.54%, Robert C. Fanch/10.70%, Dunlap John, Leon D. Black Trust UAD/1.42%, Albanese Michael/0.75%, Leon D. Black/12.62%, Black Family 1997 Trust/10.38%, Louis E. Edmondson/12.02%, Joey Schwartz/1.17%

Financial Data: *Fiscal Year End:*12/31 *Latest Annual Data:* 03/31/2007

Year	Sales	Net Income
2007	$3,327,000	-$385,000
2006	$3,195,000	-$4,423,000
2005	$3,072,000	-$3,347,000

Curr. Assets:	$3,683,000	**Curr. Liab.:**	$10,206,000		
Plant, Equip.:	$4,657,000	**Total Liab.:**	$10,218,000	**Indic. Yr. Divd.:**	NA
Total Assets:	$9,190,000	**Net Worth:**	-$1,028,000	**Debt/ Equity:**	NA

Environmental Tectonics Corp

125 James Way, Southampton, PA, 18966; ***PH:*** 1-215-355-9100; ***Fax:*** 1-215-357-4000; ***http://*** www.etcusa.com; ***Email:*** info@etcusa.com

General - Incorporation	PA	**Stock**- Price on:12/24/2007	$3.05
Employees	257	Stock Exchange	AMEX
Auditor	Grant Thornton LLP	Ticker Symbol	ETC
Stk Agt	American Stock Transfer & Trust Co.	Outstanding Shares	9,030,000
Counsel	NA	E.P.S	-$1.02
DUNS No.	04-964-1798	Shareholders	NA

Business: The group's principal activities are to design, manufacture and sell software driven products. The products are used to create and monitor the physiological effects of motion on humans and equipment and also control, modify, simulate and measure environmental conditions. The operations are carried on through two segments: aircrew training systems and the industrial group. Aircrew training systems include aircrew training devices, entertainment products and disaster management simulation. Industrial group product lines include sterilizers, environmental systems and other products and hyperbarics. The group also provides control upgrades, maintenance and repair services and spare parts for equipment. The customers of the group include governmental agencies from the United States and other foreign countries, commercial and governmental entities worldwide. It operates in the u.k, the Middle East, and Asia & sevices of 100 organizations in seeking foreign orders.

Primary SIC and add'l.: 3823 3841 3822

CIK No: 0000033113

Subsidiaries: Entertainment Technology Corporation, ETC-Delaware, ETC-Europe, ETC-PZL Aerospace Industries, ETL International Corporation, NASTAR Center Holdings Corporation, NASTAR Center LLC

Officers: William F. Mitchell/Chmn., CEO, Pres., Dick Leland/VP - Aircrew Training Systems, ATS, Glenn King/Applications Mgr. - Aircrew Training Systems, ATS, Ernie Lewis/Sales Dir. - ETC Tactical Flight Simulation, Mark Peterson/International Service - ILS, Coms, Marco Van Wijngaarden/Pres. - ETC Simulation, Dariusz Olowski/Regional Sales Contact - All Product Lines, Keith George/Regional Sales Contact - All Product Lines, Theresa Wagner/Business Unit Mgr. - Testing, Simulation Systems, Allan Firth/European Operations, Testing, Simulation Systems, Western Europe, Regional Sales Contact - All Product Lines, Christine Stephenson/Sales Mgr. - ETC PZL, USA, Anna Brzozwoska/Commercial, Marketing Dir. - ETC PZL, USA, Eric Sprague/Asia, Regional Sales Contact - All Product Lines, Husnu Onus/VP - International Sales - Marketing, Turkey, Middle East, North Africa, Regional Sales Contact - All Product Lines, Essam El Taib/Egypt, Regional Sales Contact - All Product Lines *(23 Officers included in Index)*

Directors: William F. Mitchell/Chmn., CEO, Pres., George K. Anderson/Dir., H. F. Lenfest/Dir., Alan Mark Gemmill/Dir., Howard W. Kelley/Dir.

Owners: William F. Mitchell/11.80%, George K. Anderson/1.00%, Todd T. Martin/22.00%, Howard W. Kelley, Pete L. Stephens/7.20%, H. F. Lenfest/35.70%, Alan M. Gemmill, Insiders/45.20%, Emerald Advisors, Inc./8.00%

Financial Data: *Fiscal Year End:*02/24 *Latest Annual Data:* 2/24/2006

Year	Sales	Net Income
2006	$25,069,000	-$6,714,000
2005	$27,814,000	-$8,113,000
2004	$25,995,000	-$793,000

Curr. Assets:	$39,845,000	**Curr. Liab.:**	$9,938,000		
Plant, Equip.:	$4,886,000	**Total Liab.:**	$23,597,000	**Indic. Yr. Divd.:**	NA
Total Assets:	$48,696,000	**Net Worth:**	$25,054,000	**Debt/ Equity:**	NA

Envoy Communications Group Inc

172 John St., Toronto, ON, M5T 1X5; ***PH:*** 1-416-593-1212; ***Fax:*** 1-416-593-4434; ***http://*** www.envoy.to; ***Email:*** info@envoy.to

General - Incorporation	Canada	**Stock**- Price on:12/24/2007	$3.07
Employees	226	Stock Exchange	NDQ
Auditor	KPMG LLP	Ticker Symbol	ECGI
Stk Agt	Computershare Trust Co	Outstanding Shares	NA
Counsel	Blake, Cassels & Graydon LLP	E.P.S	NA
DUNS No.	24-725-0996	Shareholders	NA

Business: The group's principle activities are the provision of marketing communication services. The group provides brand strategy and design consultancy services. These services include strategic brand consulting, corporate identity and communications, retail branding and store design and packaging design services. The group also provides marketing services including creative concept development, branding, print and broadcast production, media planning and buying, event marketing and public relations. The group operates in Canada, the United States, the United Kingdom and continental Europe. The group's quarterly revenue for September 2007 was 4.44 millions of CAD.

Primary SIC and add'l.: 4899 7312 7319

CIK No: 0001031516

Subsidiaries: John Street Inc, Parker Williams Design Limited, Watt Gilchrist Limited, Watt International Inc.

Officers: Geoffrey B. Genovese/Chmn., CEO, Pres., John H. Bailey/Dir., Exec. VP, Corp. Sec., Joseph J. Leeder/53/Exec. VP - Mergers, Acquisitions, CFO

Directors: Geoffrey B. Genovese/Chmn., CEO, Pres., John H. Bailey/Dir., Exec. VP, Corp. Sec., Hugh Aird/Dir., David I. Hull/51/Dir., David Parkes/61/Dir.

Owners: Geoffrey Genovese/3.50%, John H. Bailey/0.30%, Patrick Rodmell/0.10%, David Parkes/0.10%, David Hull/0.60%

Financial Data: *Fiscal Year End:*09/30 *Latest Annual Data:* 9/30/2006

Year	Sales	Net Income
2006	$8,684,000	-$506,000
2005	$36,865,000	$5,369,000
2004	$32,136,000	-$2,813,000

Curr. Assets:	$61,687,000	**Curr. Liab.:**	$5,441,000		
Plant, Equip.:	$1,847,000	**Total Liab.:**	$5,591,000	**Indic. Yr. Divd.:**	NA
Total Assets:	$70,769,000	**Net Worth:**	$65,178,000	**Debt/ Equity:**	0.1069

EnXnet Inc

11333 E Pine St., Ste. 75, Tulsa, OK, 74116; ***PH:*** 1-918-592-0015; ***Fax:*** 1-918-592-0016; ***http://*** www.enxnet.com; ***Email:*** investors@enxnet.com

General - Incorporation	OK	**Stock**- Price on:12/24/2007	$0.5
Employees	4	Stock Exchange	OTC
Auditor	Pattillo, Brown & Hill, LLP	Ticker Symbol	EXNT
Stk Agt	Pacific Stock Transfer Company	Outstanding Shares	30,010,000
Counsel	NA	E.P.S	-$0.03
DUNS No.	NA	Shareholders	NA

Business: The group's principal activities are to develop, market and license emerging technologies and innovative business strategies and practices focusing primarily on products, solutions and services, which support and enhance multimedia management. The group's products and services include disc security tag, talentmatrix and clearvideo. Disc security tag is distributed by direct licensing of the technology. Talentmatrix is marketed to artists, musicians, actors, agents and other entertainment professionals. The group distributes clearvideo by direct licenses or through downloading to users on the Internet. The group is in its development stage. On 14-Jul-2004, the group acquired 10% in castaway record company llc and 10% in onedisc distribution co llc.

Primary SIC and add'l.: 7372 3572

CIK No: 0001083706

Subsidiaries: Entertainment Corporation

Officers: Linda Howard/Sec.

Directors: Richard W. Martel/50/Dir.

Owners: Richard W. Martel, Insiders/43.88%, Ryan Corley/42.91%, Steve Hoelscher, Linda Howard

Financial Data: *Fiscal Year End:*03/31 *Latest Annual Data:* 03/31/2007

Year	Sales	Net Income
2007	$14,000	-$977,000
2005	$395,000	-$734,000
2004	$32,000	-$543,000

Curr. Assets:	$33,000	**Curr. Liab.:**	$1,222,000		
Plant, Equip.:	$5,000	**Total Liab.:**	$1,222,000	**Indic. Yr. Divd.:**	NA
Total Assets:	$409,000	**Net Worth:**	-$813,000	**Debt/ Equity:**	NA

Enzo Biochem Inc

60 Executive Blvd., Farmingdale, NY, 11735; ***PH:*** 1-631-755-5500; ***Fax:*** 1-631-755-5561; ***http://*** www.enzo.com

General - Incorporation .... NY
Employees 285
Auditor .... Ernst & Young LLP
Stk Agt...... American Stock Transfer & Trust Co.
Counsel..... Morrison, Cohen, Singer & Weinstein
DUNS No. 08-166-4328

Stock- Price on:12/24/2007 .... $15.85
Stock Exchange .... NYSE
Ticker Symbol .... ENZ
Outstanding Shares 36,700,000
E.P.S .... -$0.37
Shareholders .... NA

Business: The group's principal activities are the research, development, manufacture and marketing of diagnostic and research products based on genetic engineering, biotechnology and molecular biology. These products are designed for the diagnosis of and/or screening for infectious diseases, cancers, genetic defects and other medically pertinent diagnostic information. The group conducts research and development for the rapeutic products based on the genetic modulation and immune modulation technology platform. It also operates a clinical reference laboratory that provides diagnostic medical testing services to the health care community.

Primary SIC and add'l.: 2835 8071 8731 2836

CIK No: 0000316253

Subsidiaries: Enzo Life Sciences, Inc.

Officers: Elazar Rabbani/Chmn., CEO, Shahram K. Rabbani/Dir., COO, Treasurer, Sec., Barbara E. Thalenfeld/VP - Corporate Development, Ronald C. Fedus/Patent Counsel, Herbert B. Bass/VP - Finance, Barry W. Weiner/Dir., Pres., Natalie Bogdanos/Corporation, Patent Counsel, David C. Goldberg/VP - Business Development, Norman E. Kelker/Sr. VP, Steve Anreder/Contact - Investor, Public Relations, Carl W. Balezentis/69/Sr. VP, Andrew R. Crescenzo/52/Sr. VP - Finance

Directors: Elazar Rabbani/Chmn., CEO, Melvin F. Lazar/Dir., John J. Delucca/Dir., Stephen B.H. Kent/63/Dir., Barry W. Weiner/Dir., Pres., John B. Sias/Dir., Irwin C. Gerson/Dir., Shahram K. Rabbani/Dir., COO, Treasurer, Sec.

Owners: Elazar Rabbani/6.00%, Andrew R. Crescenzo, Stephen B.H. Kent, Insiders/17.40%, Irwin C. Gerson, Carl W. Balezentis, Melvin F. Lazar, Shahram K. Rabbani/5.60%, Clearbridge Advisors, LLC/14.89%, Barry W. Weiner/3.90%, Morton J. Davis/8.80%, John B. Sias, John J. Delucca

Financial Data: *Fiscal Year End:*07/31 *Latest Annual Data:* 7/31/2006

Year	Sales	Net Income
2006	$39,826,000	-$15,667,000
2005	$43,403,000	$3,004,000
2004	$41,644,000	-$6,232,000

Curr. Assets:	$86,098,000	**Curr. Liab.:**	$5,937,000		
Plant, Equip.:	$5,848,000	**Total Liab.:**	$5,937,000	**Indic. Yr. Divd.:**	NA
Total Assets:	$101,524,000	**Net Worth:**	$95,587,000	**Debt/ Equity:**	NA

Enzon Pharmaceuticals Inc

685 Rt E 202/206, Bridgewater, NJ, 08807; ***PH:*** 1-908-541-8600; ***Fax:*** 1-908-575-9457; ***http://*** www.enzon.com

General - Incorporation .... DE
Employees 359
Auditor .... KPMG
Stk Agt........ Continental Stock Transfer & Trust Co
Counsel........ Dorsey & Whitney LLP
DUNS No. 10-168-6731

Stock- Price on:12/24/2007 .... $8.35
Stock Exchange .... NDQ
Ticker Symbol .... ENZN
Outstanding Shares 44,060,000
E.P.S .... -$0.22
Shareholders .... NA

Business: The group's principal activity is to develop, manufacture and sell human therapeutics for life-threatening diseases. The group uses technologies, which include the polyethylene glycol technology (peg) and single-chain antibodies technology (sca), for the development of such therapeutics. The polyethylene glycol technology is used to improve the delivery, safety and efficacy of proteins and small molecules with known therapeutic efficacy. The single-chain antibody technology is used to discover and produce antibody-like molecules that offer many of the therapeutic benefits of monoclonal antibodies. The group's products include abelcet, adagen, depocyt and oncaspar.

Primary SIC and add'l.: 2834 8731 2836

CIK No: 0000727510

Subsidiaries: Fresenius Biotech GmbH, Zeneus Pharma Ltd. (Zeneus)

Officers: Jeffrey Buchalter/Chmn., CEO/$3,803,706.00, Craig Tooman/CFO, Exec. VP - Finance/$1,163,901.00, Paul Davit/Exec. VP - Human Resources/$735,716.00, Ralph D. Campo/Exec. VP - Technical Operations/$885,802.00, Ivan Horak/Exec. VP - Research, Development, Chief Scientific Officer/$1,291,573.00

Directors: Jeffrey Buchalter/Chmn., CEO, Phillip M. Renfro/Dir., Robert Lebuhn/Dir., Goran Ando/Dir., Victor Micati/Dir., Rolf Classon/Dir., Robert Salisbury/Dir.

Owners: Robert LeBuhn, Victor P. Micati, Renaissance Technologies Corp./7.82%, Ivan D. Horak, Robert C. Salisbury, The Vanguard Group, Inc./5.60%, Paul S. Davit, Ralph del Campo, Goran A. Ando, Group comprised of Barclays Global Investors, N.A./7.27%, Jeffrey H. Buchalter/5.23%, Group comprised of Citadel Limited Partnership/5.37%, Pequot Capital Management, Inc./17.04%, Phillip M. Renfro, Craig A. Tooman *(20 Owners included in Index)*

Financial Data: *Fiscal Year End:*12/31 *Latest Annual Data:* 12/31/2006

Year	Sales	Net Income
2006	$185,653,000	$21,309,000
2005	$166,250,000	-$89,606,000

Curr. Assets:	$212,053,000	**Curr. Liab.:**	$37,854,000	**P/E Ratio:**	83.50
Plant, Equip.:	$33,214,000	**Total Liab.:**	$447,359,000	**Indic. Yr. Divd.:**	NA
Total Assets:	$650,861,000	**Net Worth:**	$203,502,000	**Debt/ Equity:**	NA

EOG Resources Inc

1111 Bagby, Sky Lobby 2, Houston, TX, 77002; ***PH:*** 1-713-651-7000; ***Fax:*** 1-713-651-6995; ***http://*** www.eogresources.com; ***Email:*** ir@eogresources.com

General - Incorporation .... DE
Employees 1,570
Auditor .... Deloitte & Touche LLP
Stk Agt .... Computershare Investor Services LLC
Counsel .... NA
DUNS No. 00-685-9995

Stock- Price on:12/24/2007 .... $79.62
Stock Exchange .... NYSE
Ticker Symbol .... EOG
Outstanding Shares 244,600,000
E.P.S $4.29
Shareholders .... NA

Business: The group's principle activities include exploring, developing, producing and marketing natural gas and crude oil. The group operates from United States, Canada, Trinidad.

Primary SIC and add'l.: 1321 1311

CIK No: 0000821189

Subsidiaries: Belring Company (a Texas Limited Partnership), Big Sky Ranches, Inc., Energy Search, Incorporated, EOG - Canada, Inc., EOG Canada Company Ltd., EOG Canada Holdings I Inc., EOG Canada Holdings II Inc., EOG Company of Canada, EOG Expat Services, Inc., EOG Finance Canada Company, EOG Finance Canada Inc., EOG Resources (Nevis) Block 4 (a) Limited, EOG Resources - Callaghan, Inc., EOG Resources - Carthage, Inc., EOG Resources Acquisitions L.P. 53 Subsidiaries included in the Index

Officers: Mark G. Papa/61/Chmn., CEO/$7,966,606.00, Joseph C. Landry/Controller - Operations Accounting, Ann Janssen/Controller - Financial Reporting, Planning, William R. Thomas/Exec. VP, GM - Fort Worth, Patricia L. Edwards/VP - Human Resources, Administration, Corp. Sec., Edmund P. Segner/VP/$2,556,632.00, Gary Y. Peng/Controller - Financial Reporting, David L. Rolando/Controller - Land Administration, Steven B. Coleman/Sr. VP, GM - Fort Worth West, Barry Hunsaker/Sr. VP, General Counsel/$1,309,375.00, Timothy K. Driggers/CFO, VP, Helen Y. Lim/VP, Treasurer, Kurt D. Doerr/Sr. VP, GM - Denver, Gary L. Thomas/Exec. VP - Operations/$2,628,505.00, Tony C. Maranto/VP, GM - Oklahoma City *(34 Officers included in Index)*

Directors: Mark G. Papa/61/Chmn., CEO, Donald F. Textor/61/Dir., Charles R. Crisp/60/Dir., William D. Stevens/73/Dir., George A. Alcorn/75/Dir., Leighton H. Steward/73/Dir., Frank G. Wisner/69/Dir.

Owners: Insiders, Charles R. Crisp, Loren M. Leiker, Gary L. Thomas, Edmund P. Segner, Leighton H. Steward, Mark G. Papa, William D. Stevens, Barry Hunsaker, George A. Alcorn, Donald F. Textor, Frank G. Wisner

Financial Data: *Fiscal Year End:*12/31 *Latest Annual Data:* 12/31/2006

Year	Sales	Net Income
2006	NA	NA
2005	NA	NA
2004	NA	NA

Curr. Assets:	$1,350,080,000	**Curr. Liab.:**	$1,255,012,000	**P/E Ratio:**	18.14
Plant, Equip.:	$7,944,047,000	**Total Liab.:**	$3,802,489,000	**Indic. Yr. Divd.:**	$0.360
Total Assets:	$9,402,160,000	**Net Worth:**	$5,599,671,000	**Debt/ Equity:**	0.1402

eOn Communications Corp

185 Martinvale Ln. , San Jose, CA, 95119; ***PH:*** 1-408-694-9500; ***Fax:*** 1-408-694-9600; ***http://*** www.eonec.com; ***Email:*** info@eonec.com

General - Incorporation .... DE
Employees 79
Auditor .... GHP Horwath, P.C
Stk Agt .... Computershare Investor Services LLC
Counsel........ Cooley Godward LLP
DUNS No. .... NA

Stock- Price on:12/24/2007 .... $1.04
Stock Exchange .... NDQ
Ticker Symbol .... EONC
Outstanding Shares 13,480,000
E.P.S .... -$0.1
Shareholders .... NA

Business: The group's principal activities are to design, develop and market next generation communication server and software. The products of the group are used for integration and management of voice, e-mail and Internet communications for customer contact centers and other applications. Software consists of eon Web center for e-mail and real-time Web-based communications applications. The communications server products include the equeue, enterprise and the millennium trademarks. Software features include the eon Web center software suite. The customers of the group include retail, government, schools, service bureaus, major league sports, financial sectors and more.

Primary SIC and add'l.: 7375 7371 7372 7373

CIK No: 0001084752

Subsidiaries: Aelix Systems Inc., a California corporation with operations in Bangalore, India, Cortelco China Corporation, a California corporation, eOn Communications (Beijing) Corporation Limited

Officers: David Lee/Chmn., CEO, Pres., Mitch C. Gilstrap/COO, Stephen Bowling/CFO, Vijay Sharma/CTO

Directors: David Lee/Chmn., CEO, Pres., Frank King/Dir., Frederick Gibbs/Dir., Robert Dilworth/Dir.

Owners: David S. Lee/27.18%, Insiders/31.75%, Stephen R. Bowling, Vijay Sharma, Mitch Gilstrap, Frank W. King, Robert P. Dilworth, Frederick W. Gibbs

Financial Data: *Fiscal Year End:*07/31 *Latest Annual Data:* 07/31/2007

Year	Sales	Net Income
2007	$10,662,000	-$1,330,000
2006	$12,014,000	$1,637,000
2005	$21,372,000	-$1,951,000

Curr. Assets:	$10,895,000	**Curr. Liab.:**	$2,298,000		
Plant, Equip.:	$338,000	**Total Liab.:**	$2,298,000	**Indic. Yr. Divd.:**	NA
Total Assets:	$12,105,000	**Net Worth:**	$9,807,000	**Debt/ Equity:**	NA

EP Global Communications Inc

416 Main St., Johnstown, PA, 15901; ***PH:*** 1-814-361-3860; ***http://*** www.eparent.com; ***Email:*** ofrankfraga@eparent.com

General - Incorporation .... DE
Employees 24
Auditor .... Malin, Bergquist & Company, LLP
Stk Agt .... NA
Counsel .... NA
DUNS No. .... NA

Stock- Price on:12/24/2007 .... $0.0015
Stock Exchange .... OTC
Ticker Symbol .... EPGL
Outstanding Shares 136,540,000
E.P.S .... -$0.012
Shareholders .... NA

Business: The groups principle activity is to provide education and services to Family and Morale, Welfare and Recreation Commands, Exceptional Family Member Program, Medical Staff and families of childrens and adult. The groups services include EP Bookstore, Custom Publishing & Contract Publishing and Online Interactive Educational Seminars. The group operates from the United States. The groups annual revenue for September 2007 was 2.56 millions of USD.

Primary SIC and add'l.: 2721

CIK No: 0001113947

Subsidiaries: Psy-Ed Corporation

Officers: Joseph M. Valenzano/Dir., CEO, Pres., Matthew Valenzano/Publisher, VP - Sales, Marketing, James McGinnis/CFO, VP - Operations, Sec., Treasurer

Directors: Joseph M. Valenzano/Dir., CEO, Pres., Donald S. Chadwick/55/Dir., David Hirsch/60/Dir., William J. Bleil/65/Dir., Diane Jones/62/Dir.

Owners: William J. Bleil/1.30%, Donald Chadwick/1.20%, Raymond C. Smith/4.00%, Insiders/8.04%, Diane Jones/0.43%, David Hirsch/0.55%, Matthew J. Valenzano/0.19%, Robert Salluzzo/0.01%, Joseph M. Valenzano/3.79%

Financial Data: Fiscal Year End:12/31 Latest Annual Data: 12/31/2006

Year	Sales	Net Income
2006	$2,566,000	-$1,436,000
2005	$2,671,000	-$1,359,000
2004	$2,597,000	-$959,000

Curr. Assets:	$451,000	Curr. Liab.:	$1,550,000		
Plant, Equip.:	$118,000	Total Liab.:	$5,788,000	Indic. Yr. Divd.:	NA
Total Assets:	$889,000	Net Worth:	-$4,899,000	Debt/ Equity:	NA

EP MedSystems Inc

575 Rt E 73 N, Bldg. D, Cooper Run Executive Pk., West Berlin, NJ, 08091; **PH:** 1-856-753-8533; **Fax:** 1-856-753-8544; **http://** www.epmedsystems.com

General - Incorporation	NJ	Stock- Price on:12/24/2007	$1.73
Employees	86	Stock Exchange	NDQ
Auditor	Grant Thornton LLP	Ticker Symbol	EPMD
Stk Agt	Registrar & Transfer Co	Outstanding Shares	30,320,000
Counsel... Stradley Ronon Stevens & Young LLP		E.P.S	-$0.15
DUNS No.	83-580-8882	Shareholders	NA

Business: The group's principal activity is to develop, manufacture and market a line of products for the cardiac electrophysiology market. These products are used to diagnose, monitor and treat irregular heartbeats known as arrhythmias. The products include ep-workmate(R) electrophysiology work station, the ep-3(TM) stimulator, diagnostic electrophysiology catheters and the alert(R) system including the alert(R) companion and alert(R) internal cardioversion catheters and related disposable supplies like unique one-piece catheter. The group also develops an intracardiac ultrasound product line including the viewmate(tm) ultrasound imaging console and viewflex(tm) intracardiac imaging catheters. The products are sold to medical institutions and physicians in the United States.

Primary SIC and add'l.: 3845

CIK No: 0001012394

Subsidiaries: EP MedSystems Benelux, EP MedSystems France S.A.R.L, EP MedSystems UK Ltd, ProCath Corporation

Officers: David Bruce/CEO, Pres./$191,586.00, John Huley/VP - Sales/$271,565.00, Thomas Maguire/VP - Regulatory, Quality Assurance/$160,470.00, Bryan C. Byrd/VP - Operations, Engineering/$258,865.00, James Caruso/Information Contact, Matthew C. Hill/CFO, Sec.

Directors: David A. Jenkins/Chmn., Abhijeet Lele/Dir., Richard C. Williams/Dir., Gerard Michel/Dir.

Owners: David A. Jenkins/10.40%, Group comprised of Greenberg Healthcare Management, LLC/8.60%, Matthew C. Hill, Group comprised of S.A.C. Capital Advisors, LLC/7.20%, Richard Williams, Thomas Maguire, Bryan C. Byrd, John Huley, Gerard Michel, David I. Bruce, Michael A. Roth and Brian J. Stark as Joint Filers/7.80%, Insiders/20.50%

Financial Data: Fiscal Year End:12/31 Latest Annual Data: 12/31/2006

Year	Sales	Net Income
2006	$15,558,000	-$6,477,000
2005	$16,669,000	-$5,773,000
2004	$16,369,000	-$4,410,000

Curr. Assets:	$15,831,000	Curr. Liab.:	$3,797,000		
Plant, Equip.:	$1,937,000	Total Liab.:	$6,123,000	Indic. Yr. Divd.:	NA
Total Assets:	$18,311,000	Net Worth:	$12,189,000	Debt/ Equity:	NA

EPCOS AG

PO Box 80 17 09, Munich, 81617; **PH:** 49-8963609; **http://** www.epcos.com

General - Incorporation	Germany	Stock - Price on:12/24/2007	$21.87
Employees	17,948	Stock Exchange	NA
Auditor . KPMG Deutsche Treuhand Gesellschaft		Ticker Symbol	NA
Stk Agt	Registrar Services GmbH	Outstanding Shares	65,300,000
Counsel	NA	E.P.S	$0.93
DUNS No.	NA	Shareholders	NA

Business: The group's principal activity is to develop, manufacture and market passive electronic components. The group's activities are carried out through four divisions: capacitors, ceramic components, surface acoustic wave (saw) components and ferrites and inductors. The capacitors division includes aluminum electrolytic capacitors, tantalum capacitors, film capacitors, power capacitors and ultracapacitors. The ceramic components division includes thermistors, sensors, varistors, multilayer ceramic capacitors, surge arresters and piezo actuators. The saw components division includes saw components for TV and audio applications, saw filters for mobile phones, multimedia and automotive electronics. The ferrites and inductors division include rm/ep cores for telecommunications and industrial electronics, e/u cores for consumer electronics and information technology, toroids for electromagnetic compatibility and LAN applications and inductors ferrite components.

Primary SIC and add'l.: 3674 3675 3264

CIK No: 0001095409

Subsidiaries: Crystal Technology Inc, Crystal Technology, Inc, Czech Republic, EPCOS (China) Investment Ltd, EPCOS (Shanghai), EPCOS (Wuxi) Co, EPCOS (Xiaogan) Co, EPCOS (Zhuhai FTZ) Co, EPCOS (Zhuhai) Co, EPCOS do Brasil Ltda, EPCOS Electronic Components S, EPCOS Elektronikai Alkatrsz Kft, EPCOS Ferrites Private Ltd, EPCOS Finance B, EPCOS Inc 28 Subsidiaries included in the Index

Officers: Gerhard Pegam/46/CEO, Christoph Jehle/Contact - Trade Media, Helmut Konig/48/CFO, Heinz Kahlert/Contact - Media, Werner Faber/60/CTO

Directors: Anton Kathrein/57/Dep. Chmn. - Supervisory Board, Klaus Ziegler/74/Chmn., Peter Hoffmann/46/Dep. Chmn. - Supervisory Board, Claus Ryschawy/49/Member - Supervisory Board, Wolf-Dieter Bopst/69/Member - Supervisory Board, Andreas Strobel/55/Member - Supervisory

Board, Burkhard Ischler/45/Member - Supervisory Board, Winfried Wolff/58/Member - Supervisory Board, Jurgen Heraeus/72/Member - Supervisory Board, Michael Leppek/38/Member - Supervisory Board, Claus Weyrich/Member - Supervisory Board, Peter Geschka/59/Member - Supervisory Board, Joachim Reinhart/62/Member - Supervisory Board, Bodo Luttge/68/Member - Supervisory Board

Owners: AQR Capital Management/3.20%, AXA, S.A./5.04%, UBS AG/3.21%, Dodge& Cox International Stock Fund/5.29%, Odey Asset Management LLP/4.91%, Vauban Fund/5.24%

Financial Data: Fiscal Year End:09/30 Latest Annual Data: 9/30/2006

Year	Sales	Net Income
2006	$1,661,469,000	$26,869,000
2005	$1,490,959,000	-$143,687,000
2004	$1,679,752,000	$60,703,000

Curr. Assets:	$973,189,000	Curr. Liab.:	$520,680,000		
Plant, Equip.:	$625,998,000	Total Liab.:	$1,061,724,000	Indic. Yr. Divd.:	$0.210
Total Assets:	$1,794,772,000	Net Worth:	$730,441,000	Debt/ Equity:	NA

Ephrata National Bank PA

31 E Main St., Ephrata, PA, 17522; **PH:** 1-717-733-4181; **Fax:** 1-717-733-7034; **http://** www.ephratanationalbank.com

General - Incorporation		Stock- Price on:12/24/2007	$34.5
Employees	140	Stock Exchange	OTC
Auditor	NA	Ticker Symbol	EPNB
Stk Agt	Ephrata National Bank	Outstanding Shares	2,850,000
Counsel	NA	E.P.S	$1.73
DUNS No.	NA	Shareholders	NA

Business: The groups principal activity is to provide banking services. The products of the group include mortgage loans, home equity, personal loans, agricultural loans and auto loans. The group operates from the United States.

Primary SIC and add'l.: 6021

CIK No: 0001027602

Officers: Aaron L. Groff/Chmn., CEO, Pres., Barry W. Harting/Sr. VP - Administrative Services, Paul W. Wenger/Sr. VP - Operations, Cashier, Paul W. Brubaker/Exec. VP, Corp. Sec., Dale G. Burkholder/Sr. VP, Sr. Loan Officer, Scott E. Lied/Sr. VP, CFO, Joe Howe/CFP, Financial Advisor

Directors: Aaron L. Groff/Chmn., CEO, Pres., Paul W. Brubaker/Exec. VP, Corp. Sec., James C. Gibbel/Dir., Donald Z. Musser/Dir., Harold J. Summers/Dir., Paul M. Zimmerman/Dir., Willis R. Lefever/Dir., Bonnie R. Sharp/Dir., Walter K. Trumbauer/Dir., Thomas H. Zinn/Dir.

Financial Data: Fiscal Year End: Latest Annual Data: 12/31/2002

Year	Sales	Net Income
2002	$29,577,000	$6,244,000
2001	$29,128,000	$5,358,000
2000	$26,834,000	$4,963,000

Curr. Assets:	$17,472,000	Curr. Liab.:	$372,962,000	P/E Ratio:	26.14
Plant, Equip.:	$11,985,000	Total Liab.:	$417,780,000	Indic. Yr. Divd.:	$1.240
Total Assets:	$478,885,000	Net Worth:	$61,105,000	Debt/ Equity:	0.5678

Epic Bancorp

630 Las Gallinas Ave., San Rafael, CA, 94903; **PH:** 1-415-526-6400; **Fax:** 1-415-526-6414; **http://** www.epicbancorp.com

General - Incorporation	CA	Stock - Price on:12/24/2007	$13.29
Employees	75	Stock Exchange	NDQ
Auditor	Vavrinek, Trine, Day & Co. LLP	Ticker Symbol	EPIK
Stk Agt	U.S. Stock Transfer Corp	Outstanding Shares	3,970,000
Counsel	NA	E.P.S	$1.02
DUNS No.	NA	Shareholders	NA

Business: The groups principle activity is to provide banking services. The group operates seven full service Tamalpais Bank branches within the county and also has two loan production offices, located in Santa Rosa and Sacramento. The group operates from United States.

Primary SIC and add'l.: NA

CIK No: 0001099980

Subsidiaries: Epic Wealth Management, San Rafael Capital Trust I, Tamalpais Bank

Officers: Mark Garwood/Dir., CEO, Pres./$323,340.00, Kit M. Cole/Exec. Chmn./$416,210.00, Michael E. Moulton/CFO, Exec. VP/$174,126.00, William Jeffery Tappan/43/Dir., Sec., Karry Bryan/Chief Accounting Officer, Sr. VP, Erwin Martinez/CIO, Sr. VP, Michael Rice/Chief Lending Officer, Sr. VP, William David Osher/COO, Chief Economist, Seth Scholar/Dir. - Equity Investments, Mgr. - Portfolio

Directors: Mark Garwood/Dir., CEO, Pres., Kit M. Cole/Exec. Chmn., Richard E. Smith/Vice Chmn., Carolyn B. Horan/76/Dir., Paul David Schaeffer/57/Dir., William Jeffery Tappan/43/Dir., Sec., Allan G. Bortel/67/Dir.

Owners: Insiders/14.71%, Kit M. Cole/5.55%, Richard E. Smith/2.69%, Mark Garwood/2.03%, FMR Corp/7.36%, Carolyn B. Horan/1.99%, The Banc Funds Company, LLC/6.04%, Jeffery W. Tappan/1.10%, Allan G. Bortel/0.04%, Michael Moulton/1.22%, Wasatch Advisors Inc./6.07%, Paul Schaeffer/0.09%

Financial Data: Fiscal Year End:12/31 Latest Annual Data: 12/31/2006

Year	Sales	Net Income
2006	$37,992,000	$3,928,000
2005	$30,357,000	$4,096,000
2004	$22,459,000	$3,448,000

Curr. Assets:	$16,561,000	Curr. Liab.:	$459,231,000	P/E Ratio:	13.03
Plant, Equip.:	$5,275,000	Total Liab.:	$472,634,000	Indic. Yr. Divd.:	$0.180
Total Assets:	$503,514,000	Net Worth:	$30,881,000	Debt/ Equity:	NA

Epic Financial Corp

7545 N Del Mar Ave., Ste. 102, Fresno, CA, 93711; **PH:** 1-559-435-2767; **http://** www.epicfinancialcorp.com

General - Incorporation	NV	Stock - Price on:12/24/2007	$0.016
Employees	NA	Stock Exchange	OTC
Auditor	Kabani & Co, Inc	Ticker Symbol	EPFL
Stk Agt	Pacific Stock Transfer Company	Outstanding Shares	NA
Counsel	NA	E.P.S.	NA
DUNS No.	NA	Shareholders	NA

Business: The group principal activity is to provide financial services specifically real estate mortgage financing. The group abandoned the focus of business form of providing business and e-commerce solutions to small- and medium- sized construction companies and adopted a new business strategy, a financial services firm.

Primary SIC and add'l.: 6162

CIK No: 0001144892

Officers: Rodney R. Ray/CEO, Pres.

Financial Data: Fiscal Year End:10/31 **Latest Annual Data:** 10/31/2004

Year	Sales	Net Income
2004	$241,000	-$1,942,000
2003	$131,000	-$1,418,000
2002	NA	-$27,000

Curr. Assets:	$0	Curr. Liab.:	$5,000		
Plant, Equip.:	$11,000	Total Liab.:	$5,000	Indic. Yr. Divd.:	NA
Total Assets:	$12,000	Net Worth:	$7,000	Debt/ Equity:	NA

EpiCept Corp

777 Old Saw Mill River Rd., Tarrytown, NY, 10591; *PH:* 1-914-606-3500; *Fax:* 1-914-606-3501; *http://* www.epicept.com; *Email:* mail@epicept.com

General - Incorporation	DE	Stock - Price on:12/24/2007	$2.56
Employees	34	Stock Exchange	NDQ
Auditor	Deloitte & Touche LLP	Ticker Symbol	EPCT
Stk Agt	American Stock Transfer & Trust Co.	Outstanding Shares	32,400,000
Counsel	NA	E.P.S.	-$0.85
DUNS No.	NA	Shareholders	NA

Business: The groups principle activity is to develop pharmaceutical products. The products of the group include Ceplene and Azixa. The group products sold under the trade name Neurontin(R), Lidoderm(R) and Lyrica(R). In January 2006, the group acquired Maxim Pharmaceuticals, Inc. The group operates from the United States and Germany.

Primary SIC and add'l.: 2834 2834

CIK No: 0001208261

Subsidiaries: Cytovia, Inc., EpiCept GmbH, Maxim Pharmaceuticals Europe Ltd, Maxim Pharmaceuticals Inc.

Officers: Jack V. Talley/Dir., CEO, Pres./$3,461,970.00, Robert W. Cook/CFO, Sr. VP - Finance, Administration/$782,668.00, Ben Tseng/62/Chief Scientific Officer/$328,266.00, Oliver Wiedemann/MD - Medical Affairs, Epicept Gmbh/$221,554.00, Dileep Bhagwat/Sr. VP - Pharmaceutical Development/$490,464.00, Gavril Pasternak/Chief Advisor, Member - Scientific, Medical Advisory Board, Morton I. Hyson/Inventors, Scientific Consultants, Stephane Allard/Chief Medical Officer, Michael Chen/VP - Global Business Development, Charles Darder/Controller

Directors: Jack V. Talley/Dir., CEO, Pres., Robert G. Savage/Chmn., Gert Caspritz/Dir., Guy C. Jackson/Dir., Gerhard Waldheim/Dir., John F. Bedard/Dir., Wayne P. Yetter/Dir., Gavril Pasternak/Chief Advisor, Member - Scientific, Medical Advisory Board, Christoph Stein/Member - Scientific, Medical Advisory Board, Bruce F. MacKler/Member - Scientific, Medical Advisory Board, Howard Maibach/Member - Scientific, Medical Advisory Board

Owners: Ben Tseng, John V. Talley/3.40%, Guy C. Jackson, Robert W. Cook, TVM Capital/14.14%, Insiders/18.81%, Robert G. Savage, Stephane Allard, Wayne P. Yetter, Dileep Bhagwat, Private Equity Direct Finance/9.17%, Oliver Wiedemann, Gerhard Waldheim, Cornell Capital Partners, LP/7.40%, Gert Caspritz/14.14% *(17 Owners included in Index)*

Financial Data: Fiscal Year End:12/31 **Latest Annual Data:** 12/31/2006

Year	Sales	Net Income
2006	$2,095,000	-$65,453,000
2005	$829,000	-$7,215,000

Curr. Assets:	$15,264,000	Curr. Liab.:	$19,746,000		
Plant, Equip.:	$1,316,000	Total Liab.:	$27,799,000	Indic. Yr. Divd.:	NA
Total Assets:	$18,426,000	Net Worth:	-$9,373,000	Debt/ Equity:	NA

Epicor Software Corp

18200 Von Karman Ave., Ste. 1000, Irvine, CA, 92612; *PH:* 1-949-585-4000; *Fax:* 1-949-585-4091; *http://* www.epicor.com

General - Incorporation	DE	Stock - Price on:12/24/2007	$14.22
Employees	2,178	Stock Exchange	NDQ
Auditor	Deloitte & Touche LLP	Ticker Symbol	EPIC
Stk Agt	Mellon Shareholder Services LLC	Outstanding Shares	58,100,000
Counsel	L. George Klaus	E.P.S.	$0.44
DUNS No.	61-982-6159	Shareholders	NA

Business: The group's principle activity is to design, develop, market and support integrated enterprise business software solutions. These products integrate back office applications for manufacturing, distribution and accounting with front office applications for sales, marketing and customer service and support. The group also provides integrated e-commerce capabilities that allow companies to leverage the power of the Internet to allow their organization to further extend beyond the traditional 'four walls' of their enterprise, and further integrate their operations with their customers, suppliers and partners. It also offers consulting, training and support services to supplement the use of its software products by its customers. The group acquired ROI systems, inc. On 08-Jul-2003, quantum group, amida limited and platsoft limited on 18-Feb-2004 and scala business solutions on 18-Jun-2004. The group's quarterly revenue for Sep'07 was 103.10 millions of USD.

Primary SIC and add'l.: 7372 7379

CIK No: 0000891178

Subsidiaries: CRS Retail Technology Group, Inc., Epicor Limited, Epicor Software (Asia) PTE Ltd., Epicor Software (Aust) Pty. Ltd., Epicor Software (North Asia) Ltd., Epicor Software (Taiwan) Limited, Epicor Software (UK) Limited, Epicor Software Argentina S.A., Epicor Software Canada, Ltd., Epicor Software Mexico, S.A. de C.V., Epicor Software Nordic AB, Scala Business Solutions N.V.

Officers: George L. Klaus/Chmn., CEO, Pres./$2,789,240.00, Damon Wright/Sr. Dir. - Investor Relations

Directors: George L. Klaus/Chmn., CEO, Pres., Thomas Kelly/Dir., Harry Copperman/Dir., Robert Smith/Dir., Michael Kelly/Dir.

Owners: LeRoy C. Kopp/6.32%, Michael Kelly, Insiders/5.92%, Thomas F. Kelly, Mark Duffell, Richard H. Pickup/9.05%, Michael A. Piraino, George L. Klaus/4.29%, Royce & Associates, LLC/5.36%, Harold D. Copperman, Robert H. Smith

Financial Data: Fiscal Year End:12/31 **Latest Annual Data:** 12/31/2006

Year	Sales	Net Income
2006	$384,096,000	$23,818,000
2005	$289,413,000	$52,035,000
2004	$226,210,000	$25,313,000

Curr. Assets:	$184,524,000	Curr. Liab.:	$130,840,000	P/E Ratio:	35.55
Plant, Equip.:	$12,251,000	Total Liab.:	$233,270,000	Indic. Yr. Divd.:	NA
Total Assets:	$441,890,000	Net Worth:	$208,620,000	Debt/ Equity:	0.4581

Epicus Communications Group Inc

1750 Osceola Dr., West Palm Beach, FL, 33409; *PH:* 1-561-688-0440; *http://* www.ecg-us.com; *Email:* customercare@epicus.com

General - Incorporation	FL	Stock - Price on:12/24/2007	$0.0011
Employees	NA	Stock Exchange	OTC
Auditor	S. W. Hatfield, CPA	Ticker Symbol	EPCG
Stk Agt	Executive Registrar & Transfer, Inc.	Outstanding Shares	35,860,000
Counsel	NA	E.P.S.	-$0.234
DUNS No.	NA	Shareholders	NA

Business: The group's principal activity is to provide telecommunication services to its customers in the United States. The group develops integrated telephone service in the competitive local exchange carrier area of the telecommunications industry. The group offers small businesses and residential consumers an integrated set of telecommunications products and services, including local exchange, local access, domestic and international long distance telephone, data and dial up access to the Internet. The group is certified to offer long distance and Internet services in the 48 contiguous states. Currently, the group supplies local and long distance service to customers in 7 of the 9 states in the bellsouth system. Additionally, the group has long distance customers in 40 of the 48 states in which it is certified.

Primary SIC and add'l.: 7379 6719 4813

CIK No: 0000800401

Subsidiaries: Mic-Mac Investments, Inc., Moye & Associates

Officers: Mark Schaftlein/CEO, CFO, Ken Koller/COO, Thomas N. Donaldson/Exec. VP, VP - Corporate Operations, Contact - Public Relations, Gerard Haryman/General Consultant, Ginny Bohrer/Dir. - Finance, Administration, Rosie Johnson/Dir. - Operations, Don Casement/Dir. - Network Services, Richard Reiss/Sr. Consultant, Business Development

Owners: Mark Schaftlein/8.65%, Insiders/9.35%, Thomas Donaldson/0.01%

Financial Data: Fiscal Year End:05/31 **Latest Annual Data:** 5/31/2006

Year	Sales	Net Income
2006	$5,830,000	-$2,670,000
2005	$18,776,000	-$8,380,000
2004	$25,191,000	-$3,287,000

Curr. Assets:	$1,111,000	Curr. Liab.:	$1,486,000		
Plant, Equip.:	$87,000	Total Liab.:	$11,395,000	Indic. Yr. Divd.:	NA
Total Assets:	$9,354,000	Net Worth:	-$2,040,000	Debt/ Equity:	NA

EPIQ Systems Inc

501 Kansas Ave., Kansas City, KS, 66105; *PH:* 1-913-621-9500; *Fax:* 1-913-321-1243; *http://* www.epiqsystems.com

General - Incorporation	MO	Stock - Price on:12/24/2007	$16.23
Employees	500	Stock Exchange	NDQ
Auditor	Deloitte & Touche LLP	Ticker Symbol	EPIQ
Stk Agt	Wells Fargo Shareowner Services	Outstanding Shares	29,560,000
Counsel	Seigfreid Bingham Levy Selzer Gee	E.P.S.	$0.08
DUNS No.	06-577-0638	Shareholders	NA

Business: The group's principal activities are to develop, market and license proprietary software solutions for workflow management and data communications infrastructure for the bankruptcy trustee market and the financial services market. The group's products streamline the customers' internal business operations and external communications and enable them to minimize operating costs through automation. The group also provide a high level of coordinated support, including network integration, post-installation support and industry-specific value-added services.during 2003 the group acquired bankruptcy services llc , on 30-Jan-2004, the group acquired p-d holding corp and its wholly-owned operating subsidiary, poorman-douglas company. The group sold infrastructure software business on 30-Apr-2004.

Primary SIC and add'l.: 7372 7371

CIK No: 0001027207

Subsidiaries: Bankruptcy Services LLC, EPIQ Systems Acquisition,Inc., Financial Balloting Group LLC, Hilsoft,Inc, nMatrix Australia Pty. Ltd, nMatrix Ltd., nMatrix,Inc., Novare,Inc, Poorman-Douglas Corporation

Officers: Tom W. Olofson/Chmn., CEO/$2,169,754.00, Christopher E. Olofson/Dir., COO, Pres./$1,972,947.00, Elizabeth M. Braham/Exec. VP, CFO, Corp. Sec./$1,149,198.00, Mary Ellen Berthold/Investor Relations Officer

Directors: Tom W. Olofson/Chmn., CEO, Bryan W. Satterlee/Dir., Joel Pelofsky/Dir., Christopher E. Olofson/Dir., COO, Pres., Edward M. Connolly/Dir., James A. Byrnes/Dir.

Owners: Goodgate Holdings Limited/5.20%, Tom W. Olofson/13.60%, Elizabeth M. Braham/2.20%, James A. Byrnes, Christopher E. Olofson/5.70%, St. Denis J. Villere & Co., LLC/8.10%, FMR Corp./12.80%, Edward M. Connolly, Bryan W. Satterlee, Highbridge International LLC/8.40%, Insiders/22.20%, Lorenzo Mendizabal, Ron Jacobs, Joel Pelofsky

Financial Data: Fiscal Year End:12/31 **Latest Annual Data:** 12/31/2006

Year	Sales	Net Income
2006	$224,170,000	$35,131,000
2005	$106,330,000	-$3,842,000
2004	$125,420,000	$9,730,000

Curr. Assets:	$43,262,000	Curr. Liab.:	$89,126,000	P/E Ratio:	162.30
Plant, Equip.:	$23,153,000	Total Liab.:	$198,041,000	Indic. Yr. Divd.:	NA
Total Assets:	$382,220,000	Net Worth:	$184,179,000	Debt/ Equity:	0.7828

Epix Pharmaceuticals Inc

4 Maguire Rd., Lexington, MA, 02421; ***PH:*** 1-781-761-7600; ***Fax:*** 1-781-761-7641;
http:// www.epixpharma.com; ***Email:*** info@epixpharma.com

General - Incorporation	DE	**Stock**- Price on:12/24/2007	$5.91
Employees	89	Stock Exchange	NDQ
Auditor	Ernst & Young LLP	Ticker Symbol	EPIX
Stk Agt	Donnie Amado	Outstanding Shares	32,600,000
Counsel	NA	E.P.S	-$2.1
DUNS No.	NA	Shareholders	NA

Business: The group's principal activity is to develop targeted contrast agents to improve and expand the use of magnetic resonance imaging to diagnose human diseases. The group's principal product under development, ms-325, is an injectable intravascular contrast agent designed for multiple cardiovascular imaging applications, including peripheral vascular disease and coronary artery disease. Ms-325 is a small molecule chelate, which produces a mri signal. This molecule is designed with the group's proprietary technology to bind to albumin, the most common blood protein. Ms-325 is under human clinical trials.

Primary SIC and add'l.: 2835

CIK No: 0001027702

Officers: Michael G. Kauffman/Dir., CEO/$1,608,864.00, Andrew C.G. Uprichard/Pres., Head - Research, Development/$1,221,372.00, Sheila Dewitt/VP - Discovery, Simon S. Jones/VP - Biology, Admet, Kimberlee C. Drapkin/CFO/$518,352.00, Chen Schor/Chief Business Officer/$907,611.00, Brenda Sousa/VP - Human Resources, Sharon Shacham/VP - Drug Development

Directors: Michael G. Kauffman/Dir., CEO, Frederick Frank/Chmn., Michael Gilman/Dir., Gregory D. Phelps/Dir., Patrick J. Fortune/Dir., Mark Leuchtenberger/Dir., Robert J. Perez/Dir., Ian F. Smith/Dir.

Owners: Michael G. Kauffman/1.58%, Patrick J. Fortune, GlaxoSmithKline plc/13.09%, Silvia Noiman, Ian F. Smith, Chen Schor, OrbiMed Entities/10.23%, T. Rowe Price Associates, Inc./5.78%, Robert Pelletier, Andrew C.G. Uprichard, Insiders/3.57%, Frederick Frank, Mark Leuchtenberger, Kim C. Drapkin, Christopher F.O. Gabrieli *(18 Owners included in Index)*

Financial Data: ***Fiscal Year End:***12/31 ***Latest Annual Data:*** 12/31/2006

Year	Sales	Net Income
2006	$6,041,000	-$157,393,000
2005	$7,190,000	-$24,311,000
2004	$12,259,000	-$20,381,000

Curr. Assets:	$112,165,000	**Curr. Liab.:**	$36,983,000		
Plant, Equip.:	$3,593,000	**Total Liab.:**	$157,049,000	**Indic. Yr. Divd.:**	NA
Total Assets:	$125,027,000	**Net Worth:**	-$32,021,000	**Debt/ Equity:**	NA

Epixtar Corp

11900 Biscayne Blvd., Ste. 262, Miami, FL, 33181; ***PH:*** 1-305-503-8600; ***Fax:*** 1-305-503-8610;
http:// www.epixtar.com

General - Incorporation	FL	**Stock**- Price on:12/24/2007	$0.22
Employees	1,632	Stock Exchange	OTC
Auditor	Rachlin Cohen & Holtz LLP	Ticker Symbol	EPXR
Stk Agt	Interwest Transfer Company, Inc.	Outstanding Shares	12,470,000
Counsel	NA	E.P.S	-$1.579
DUNS No.	NA	Shareholders	NA

Business: The group's principal activity is to acquire or establish companies specialized in mass-Market communication products. Currently, the group has two operating subsidiaries, namely, national online services, inc and one world public communication corp. The group started outsourcing telemarketing programs and other services for third parties using contact center facilities. The group currently has approximately 250 contact center seats.

Primary SIC and add'l.: 4899 7375

CIK No: 0001099730

Subsidiaries: Ameripages, Inc., B2B Advantage, Inc., Centers, Ltd., Epixtar Communications Corp., Epixtar Information Technology, Epixtar International Contact, Epixtar International Contact Center, Epixtar Marketing Corp., Epixtar Philippines IT-Enabled, Epixtar Prepaid Communications Corp., Epixtar Solutions Corp., Group, Inc., IMS International, Inc., Liberty Online Services, Inc., National Online Services, Inc. 20 Subsidiaries included in the Index

Officers: Martin Miller/CEO, Rod Goins/Exec. VP, Jeff Myatt/Sr. VP - Client Services, Irv Greenman/CFO, Pres., Michelle Willey/VP - Applications Development, Robb Auber/VP - Outbound Operations, Philippines Operations, John Callaghan/VP - Inbound Operations, Raymond Lowers/VP - US Operations, Ma. Leilani Reyes/Dir. - Finance, Richard Sablon/CTO, Bradley Yeater/COO

Directors: Ken Elan/Dir., Jack Cooney/Dir., David Berman/Dir., Sheldon Goldstein/Dir.

Financial Data: ***Fiscal Year End:***12/31 ***Latest Annual Data:*** 09/30/2005

Year	Sales	Net Income
2005	$9,649,000	-$3,016,000
2004	$17,735,000	-$9,729,000
2003	$37,121,000	$4,379,000

Curr. Assets:	$6,854,000	**Curr. Liab.:**	$14,888,000		
Plant, Equip.:	$5,103,000	**Total Liab.:**	$18,781,000	**Indic. Yr. Divd.:**	NA
Total Assets:	$18,049,000	**Net Worth:**	-$733,000	**Debt/ Equity:**	NA

ePlus inc

13595 Dulles Technology Dr., Herndon, VA, 20171; ***PH:*** 1-703-984-8400; ***Fax:*** 1-703-984-8600;
http:// www.eplus.com; ***Email:*** info@eplus.com

General - Incorporation	DE	**Stock**- Price on:12/24/2007	$9.5
Employees	637	Stock Exchange	OTC
Auditor	Deloitte & Touche LLP	Ticker Symbol	PLUS
Stk Agt	National City Bank	Outstanding Shares	8,140,000
Counsel	NA	E.P.S	$1.32
DUNS No.	96-152-3214	Shareholders	NA

Business: The group's principle activities are to market, lease, finance and manage information technology assets, equipment and software. It has developed its enterprise cost management model through development and acquisition of software products and business process services. The group operates through two segments: financing business unit and technology business unit. The financing business unit consists of equipment and financing business to both commercial and government-related entities and the associated business process outsourcing services. The technology sales business unit includes all the technology sales and related services including procurement, asset management and catalog software sales and services. The customers include commercial customers, federal, state and local governments and higher education institutions.

Primary SIC and add'l.: 7377 6159 6719 7372

CIK No: 0001022408

Subsidiaries: ePlus Canada Company, ePlus Capital, inc., ePlus Content Services, inc., ePlus Document Systems, inc., ePlus Government Services, inc., ePlus Government, inc., ePlus Group, inc., ePlus Information Holdings, inc., ePlus Systems, inc., ePlus Technology, inc., MLC Leasing, SA. de CV.

Officers: Phillip G. Norton/Chmn., CEO, Pres., Steven J. Mencarini/Sr. VP, CFO, Kleyton L. Parkhurst/Sr. VP, Treasurer, Assist. Sec., Kenneth G. Farber/Pres. - Eplus Systems, Eplus Content Services, Bruce M. Bowen/Dir., Exec. VP, Pres. - Eplus Group, Inc, Mark P. Marron/Sr. VP - Sales

Directors: Phillip G. Norton/Chmn., CEO, Pres., Thomas C. Faulders/Dir., Terrence O'Donnell/Dir., Lawrence S. Herman/Dir., Bruce M. Bowen/Dir., Exec. VP, Pres. - Eplus Group, Inc, Milton E. Cooper/Dir., Eric D. Hovde/Dir., Irving R. Beimler/Dir.

Financial Data: ***Fiscal Year End:***03/31 ***Latest Annual Data:*** 03/31/2006

Year	Sales	Net Income
2006	$647,318,000	-$521,000
2005	$575,799,000	$25,288,000
2004	$330,557,000	$10,154,000

Curr. Assets:	$132,407,000	**Curr. Liab.:**	$98,015,000	**P/E Ratio:**	3.64
Plant, Equip.:	$198,234,000	**Total Liab.:**	$228,638,000	**Indic. Yr. Divd.:**	NA
Total Assets:	$360,740,000	**Net Worth:**	$132,102,000	**Debt/ Equity:**	1.0784

Epoch Holding Corp

640 5th Ave., 18th Fl., New York, NY, 10019; ***PH:*** 1-212-303-7200; ***Fax:*** 1-212-202-4948;
http:// www.eipny.com

General - Incorporation	DE	**Stock**- Price on:12/24/2007	$13.64
Employees	38	Stock Exchange	NDQ
Auditor	CF & Co. LLP	Ticker Symbol	EPHC
Stk Agt	Continental Stock Transfer & Trust Co	Outstanding Shares	19,900,000
Counsel	NA	E.P.S	$0.48
DUNS No.	05-871-4981	Shareholders	NA

Business: The group's principle activity is to operate as a technology holding company with concentrated investments in enterprise software & technology infrastructure companies. The group operates in two business segments. The e-commerce operations segment provides integrated enterprise commerce software solutions. Its products include software that addresses distributed order management, customer relationship management, supplier relationship management, sales channel management & business intelligence for companies in the retail, manufacturing, distribution, telecommunications & transportation industries. The technology-related businesses include the effect of transactions and operations of the group's non-consolidated investments. The customers of the group include ann taylor, brooks brothers, crane co., ikon office solutions, msc industrial direct, oki data Americas, verizon & walt disney Internet group. The group's total revenue for year 2007 was 23.93 millions of USD.

Primary SIC and add'l.: 6719 7372

CIK No: 0000351903

Subsidiaries: Epoch Investment Partners, Inc.

Officers: William W. Priest/CEO, CIO, Richard Watt/MD - Global Portfolio Management, Timothy T. Taussig/COO, Pres., Philip J. Clark/Exec. VP, Head - Client Relations, Janet K. Navon/MD - Portfolio Management, Sr. Analyst, Jason Root/VP - Performance, David J. Siino/Dir. - Analyst, Nishu Trivedi/VP - International Trader, David N. Pearl/Exec. VP, Head - US Equities, Joseph W. Donaldson/MD, Associate Portfolio Mgr. - Analyst, Daniel Geber/MD, Portfolio Mgr. - Sr. Analyst, John P. Reddan/MD - Sr. Analyst, Mark H. Strauss/MD, Head - US Trading, Jeff Ulness/MD, Head - Sub Advisory Relations, Jon T. Williams/MD - Client Relations *(30 Officers included in Index)*

Directors: Allan R. Tessler/Chmn., David R. Markin/Dir., Eugene M. Freedman/Dir., Jeffrey L. Berenson/Dir., Enrique Arzac/Dir., Peter A. Flaherty/Dir.

Owners: Eugene Freedman, Keeley Asset Management Corporation/8.40%, Philip J. Clark/6.80%, William W. Priest/15.40%, General American Investors Company, Inc./7.60%, Bedford Oak Advisors, LLC/7.70%, Insiders/51.30%, Enrique R. Arzac, Timothy T. Taussig/6.30%, David R. Markin/2.50%, David N. Pearl/5.50%, Allan R. Tessler/3.40%, Jeffrey L. Berenson/10.20%, Adam Borak, Peter A. Flaherty

Financial Data: ***Fiscal Year End:***06/30 ***Latest Annual Data:*** 6/30/2007

Year	Sales	Net Income
2007	$23,935,000	$7,893,000
2006	$10,231,000	-$5,722,000
2005	$4,307,000	-$6,537,000

Curr. Assets:	$35,495,000	**Curr. Liab.:**	$2,810,000	**P/E Ratio:**	104.92
Plant, Equip.:	$2,013,000	**Total Liab.:**	$3,931,000	**Indic. Yr. Divd.:**	$0.100
Total Assets:	$39,374,000	**Net Worth:**	$35,443,000	**Debt/ Equity:**	NA

EPod International Inc

2223 Hayman Rd. , Kelowna, BC, V1Z 1Z6; ***PH:*** 1-604-669-0600; ***http://*** www.epodinc.com;
Email: info@epondic.com

General - Incorporation	NV	**Stock**- Price on:12/24/2007	NA
Employees	NA	Stock Exchange	OTC
Auditor	Williams & Webster, P.S	Ticker Symbol	EPOI
Stk Agt	Signature Stock Transfer, Inc.	Outstanding Shares	NA
Counsel	NA	E.P.S	NA
DUNS No.	NA	Shareholders	NA

Business: The group's principal activity is to develop, produce, license and sell innovative energy management and electronic technology. It currently owns the worldwide rights to certain patent-pending technology that improves the efficiency of electrical power usage. The group is also developing other innovative products with synergetic technologies. On 13-Jan-2004, the group through reverse merger acquired cyokonos corporation. The group is in development stage. The group currently has operations in Canada.

Primary SIC and add'l.: 1382

CIK No: 0001079990

Subsidiaries: EPOD Industries Inc

Officers: Mark L. Roseborough/Dir., CEO, Pres., Frank Wisehart/CFO

Directors: Mark L. Roseborough/Dir., CEO, Pres., Michael Matvieshen/46/Chmn., Ljubisan Stamenic/49/Dir., Hans Schroth/Dir., Rene Dureault/Dir., Robert Stabinsky/Dir., Lou Stamenic/Dir., Larry Faulk/Dir.

Owners: Frank A. Wisehart, Peter Lacey/25.10%, Hans Schroth, Mark L. Roseborough/1.80%, Insiders/79.00%, Michael Matvieshen/51.50%

Curr. Assets:	$793,000	**Curr. Liab.:**	$2,016,000		
Plant, Equip.:	$194,000	**Total Liab.:**	$2,016,000	**Indic. Yr. Divd.:**	NA
Total Assets:	$1,510,000	**Net Worth:**	-$506,000	**Debt/ Equity:**	NA

Epolin Inc

358-364 Adams St., Newark, NJ, 07105; ***PH:*** 1-973-465-9495; ***Fax:*** 1-973-465-5353; ***http://*** www.epolin.com; ***Email:*** epolin@epolin.com

General - Incorporation	NJ	**Stock**- Price on:12/24/2007	$0.706
Employees	10	Stock Exchange	OTC
Auditor	Weismann Assoc. LLC	Ticker Symbol	EPLN
Stk Agt	Securities Transfer Corp	Outstanding Shares	11,970,000
Counsel	NA	E.P.S.	$0.052
DUNS No.	13-047-0602	Shareholders	NA

Business: The group's principal activities are to develop, manufacture and market near infrared dyes to the optical industry for laser protection and welding applications. It also develops and manufactures other dyes and specialty chemical products. These products serve as intermediates and additives used in the adhesive, plastic, aerospace, credit card security and protective documents industries to customers located in the United States and throughout the world. The group sells its dyes primarily to lens manufacturers who serve as the suppliers to the laser protection eyewear market and the welding market. Epolin holding corp, the group's wholly owned subsidiary operates as a real estate company.

Primary SIC and add'l.: 2865 6798

CIK No: 0000797079

Subsidiaries: Epolin Holding, Corp.

Officers: Greg Amato/CEO/$230,721.00, Murray Cohen/Chmn., Chief Scientist/$276,719.00, James Ivchenko/Pres., Operations Dir./$340,689.00

Directors: Murray Cohen/Chmn., Chief Scientist

Owners: Santa Monica Partners, L.P./6.90%, Sandra Lifschitz/5.10%, Claire Bluestein/8.10%, Herve A. Meillat, Murray S. Cohen/16.10%, Insiders/32.80%, James Ivchenko/12.70%, Greg Amato/1.70%, Morris Dunkel/2.30%, James R. Torpey

Financial Data: **Fiscal Year End:**02/28 **Latest Annual Data:** 2/28/2007

Year	**Sales**	**Net Income**
2007	$3,610,000	$623,000
2006	$3,701,000	$594,000
2005	$2,880,000	$504,000

Curr. Assets:	$3,040,000	**Curr. Liab.:**	$305,000	**P/E Ratio:**	15.35
Plant, Equip.:	$823,000	**Total Liab.:**	$591,000	**Indic. Yr. Divd.:**	$0.020
Total Assets:	$4,243,000	**Net Worth:**	$3,652,000	**Debt/ Equity:**	NA

Equicap Inc

12373 E Cornell Ave, Aurora, CO, 80014; ***PH:*** 1-303-478-4442

General - Incorporation	NV	**Stock**- Price on:12/24/2007	$1.3
Employees	NA	Stock Exchange	OTC
Auditor	Patrizio & Zhao, LLC	Ticker Symbol	EQPI
Stk Agt	Executive Registrar & Transfer, Inc.	Outstanding Shares	28,170,000
Counsel	NA	E.P.S.	-$0.238
DUNS No.	NA	Shareholders	NA

Business: The groups principle activities include developing and distributing diesel engine products and automotive parts. The group also provides medium-sized diesel engines, which are used in industrial equipment, including forklifts, excavators, construction equipment, power generators; agricultural equipment, including tractors, combined harvesters and water pumps. The group operates from United States.

Primary SIC and add'l.: 5010

CIK No: 0001006840

Officers: Jason Lu/52/Dir., CEO, Peter Wang/54/Chmn., Pres., David Ming He/38/CFO

Directors: Jason Lu/52/Dir., CEO, Peter Wang/54/Chmn., Pres., Haining Liu/55/Dir.

Owners: Jayhawk Private Equity Fund, L.P./7.66%, Pinnacle China Fund, L.P/13.60%, Peter Wang/9.36%, Insiders/23.79%, SIJ Holding Ltd./7.63%, Jason Zhongyuan Lu/14.43%, Sinoquest Management Ltd./19.71%, Philip Widmann/7.55%, The Pinnacle Fund, LP/6.80%

Financial Data: **Fiscal Year End:**12/31 **Latest Annual Data:** 06/30/2007

Year	**Sales**	**Net Income**
2007	$1,817,000	-$5,279,000
2006	NA	-$92,000
2005	NA	-$48,000

Curr. Assets:	NA	**Curr. Liab.:**	$105,000		
Plant, Equip.:	NA	**Total Liab.:**	$105,000	**Indic. Yr. Divd.:**	NA
Total Assets:	NA	**Net Worth:**	-$105,000	**Debt/ Equity:**	NA

Equifax Inc

1550 Peachtree St. NW, Atlanta, GA, 30309; ***PH:*** 1-404-885-8000; ***Fax:*** 1-404-885-8988; ***http://*** www.equifax.com; ***Email:*** investor@equifax.com

General - Incorporation	GA	**Stock**- Price on:12/24/2007	$44.3
Employees	4,960	Stock Exchange	NYSE
Auditor	Ernst & Young LLP	Ticker Symbol	EFX
Stk Agt	Computershare Investor Services LLC	Outstanding Shares	125,130,000
Counsel	NA	E.P.S.	$2.02
DUNS No.	04-581-2369	Shareholders	NA

Business: The group's principal activities are to provide consumer and commercial credit information. The group collects, organizes and manages various types of credit, financial, public record, demographic and marketing information regarding individuals and businesses. The group's products are classified as information services, marketing services and consumer direct services. The information services allow customers to make credit decisions about consumers and commercial enterprises. Marketing services information products and databases enable customers to identify a target audience for marketing purposes and consumer direct services provide information to consumers that enable them to reduce their exposure to identity fraud and to monitor their credit health. The group operates in 13 countries including the United States, Canada, the United Kingdom and Brazil.

Primary SIC and add'l.: 7389 7375 8999 7999 7323

CIK No: 0000033185

Subsidiaries: 3032423 Nova Scotia Company, 3651754 Canada Inc., Acrofax Inc., Alphafax Properties Limited Partnership, Appro Systems, Inc., CD Holdings, Inc., Clearing de Informes S.A., Compliance Data Center, Inc., Computer Ventures, Inc., Credit Bureau Services, Inc., Dicom S.A., Equifax (Isle of Man) Ltd, Equifax Canada Inc, Equifax Capital Management, Inc., Equifax Commercial Services Ltd. 50 Subsidiaries included in the Index

Officers: Richard F. Smith/Chmn., CEO/$7,083,869.00, Dann J. Adams/Pres. - US Information Solutions/$1,539,799.00, Paul J. Springman/Chief Marketing Officer/$1,798,366.00, Steven P. Ely/Pres. - North American Personal Solutions, Michael S. Shannon/Pres. - North American Commercial Solutions, Robert J. Webb/CTO, Kent E. Mast/Corporate VP, Chief Legal Officer/$1,836,510.00, Owen V. Flynn/Global Operations Officer, Coretha M. Rushing/Chief Human Resources Officer, Jeff Dodge/Sr. VP - Investor Relations, William W. Canfield/Pres. - Talx Corporation, Rudy Ploder/Pres. - Equifax International, Rajib Roy/Pres. - Enabling Technologies, Trey Loughran/Sr. VP - Corporate Development

Directors: Richard F. Smith/Chmn., CEO, Lee A. Kennedy/Dir., John L. Clendenin/Dir., William A. Dahlberg/Dir., Robert D. Daleo/Dir., Phillip L. Humann/Dir., Siri S. Marshall/Dir., Larry L. Prince/Dir., James E. Copeland/Dir., Jackie M. Ward/Dir.

Owners: Mark L. Feidler, Lee Adrean, Kent E. Mast, Robert D. Daleo, Larry L. Prince, Dann J. Adams, Richard F. Smith, Lee A. Kennedy, Insiders/2.10%, Paul J. Springman, Phillip L. Humann, James E. Copeland, William A. Dahlberg, Jacquelyn M. Ward, John L. Clendenin *(16 Owners included in Index)*

Financial Data: **Fiscal Year End:**12/31 **Latest Annual Data:** 12/31/2006

Year	**Sales**	**Net Income**
2006	$1,546,300,000	$274,500,000
2005	$1,443,400,000	$246,500,000
2004	$1,272,800,000	$234,700,000

Curr. Assets:	$345,200,000	**Curr. Liab.:**	$582,100,000	**P/E Ratio:**	20.23
Plant, Equip.:	$161,900,000	**Total Liab.:**	$952,500,000	**Indic. Yr. Divd.:**	$0.160
Total Assets:	$1,790,600,000	**Net Worth:**	$838,100,000	**Debt/ Equity:**	NA

Equinix Inc

301 Velocity Way, 5th Fl., Foster City, CA, 94404; ***PH:*** 1-650-513-7000; ***Fax:*** 1-650-513-7900; ***http://*** www.equinix.com; ***Email:*** support@equinix.com

General - Incorporation	DE	**Stock**- Price on:12/24/2007	$84.63
Employees	616	Stock Exchange	NDQ
Auditor	PricewaterhouseCoopers LLP	Ticker Symbol	EQIX
Stk Agt	Computershare Investor Services LLC	Outstanding Shares	31,440,000
Counsel	Gunderson Dettmer Stough Et Al	E.P.S.	$0.32
DUNS No.	NA	Shareholders	NA

Business: The group's principal activities are to network neutral colocation, interconnection and managed services to enterprises, content companies and systems integrators and networks. Through the group's 14 Internet business exchange hubs in the United States and Asia, customers can directly interconnect with each other for critical traffic exchange requirements. The group operates in New York, Virginia, los angeles, Dallas, Chicago and silicon valley.

Primary SIC and add'l.: 4899

CIK No: 0001101239

Subsidiaries: Equinix Asia Pacific Pte Ltd, Equinix Australia Pty Ltd, Equinix Cayman Islands Holdings, Equinix Dutch Holdings N.V., Equinix Europe, Inc., Equinix Germany GmbH, Equinix Hong Kong Ltd, Equinix Japan KK (in Kanji), Equinix Netherlands B.V., Equinix Operating Co., Inc., Equinix Pacific Business Recovery, Inc., Equinix Pacific Pte Ltd, Equinix Pacific, Inc., Equinix RP II LLC, Equinix RP, Inc. 21 Subsidiaries included in the Index

Officers: Stephen M. Smith/Dir., CEO, Pres., Peter F. Vancamp/52/Exec. Chmn., Doug Oates/MD - Equinix Australia, Clement Goh/MD - Equinix Singapore, Guy De Rohan Willner/Pres. - Equinix Europe, Keri Crask/VP - Human Resources, Jason Starr/Dir. - Investor Relations, Christophe De Buchet/COO - Equinix Europe, Sushil K. Kapoor/VP - IBX Operations, Marjorie Backaus/Chief Business Officer/$1,470,400.00, William Norton/Chief Technical Liaison, Lane Patterson/Chief Technologist, Keith D. Taylor/CFO/$1,704,760.00, Margie Backaus/Chief Business Officer, Samuel Lee/VP - Equinix Asia, Pacific *(27 Officers included in Index)*

Directors: Stephen M. Smith/Dir., CEO, Pres., Peter F. Vancamp/52/Exec. Chmn., Steven T. Clontz/57/Dir., Terry Clontz/Dir., Scott Kriens/Dir., Irving F. Lyons/Dir., Christopher Paisley/Dir., Gary Hromadko/Dir., Steven Eng/Dir.

Owners: Insiders/3.53%, Fidelity Management& Research/9.68%, Janus Capital Management/6.60%, Steven P. Eng, Gary F. Hromadko, Stephen M. Smith, Keith D. Taylor, Peter T. Ferris, Marjorie S. Backaus, i-STT Investments (Bermuda) Ltd./13.64%, TCS Capital Management/5.09%, Rene F. Lanam, Peter F. Van Camp/1.40%, Steven T. Clontz, Scott G. Kriens

Financial Data: **Fiscal Year End:**12/31 **Latest Annual Data:** 06/30/2007

Year	**Sales**	**Net Income**
2007	NA	NA
2006	$286,915,000	-$6,397,000
2005	$221,057,000	-$42,612,000

Curr. Assets:	$166,261,000	**Curr. Liab.:**	$78,353,000		
Plant, Equip.:	$546,395,000	**Total Liab.:**	$416,804,000	**Indic. Yr. Divd.:**	NA
Total Assets:	$771,832,000	**Net Worth:**	$355,028,000	**Debt/ Equity:**	NA

Equitable Financial Corp

250 Dunlop St. W, Barrie, ON, L4N 1B6; ***PH:*** 1-705-733-2066; ***Fax:*** 1-705-050-0512; ***http://*** www.equitableonline.com; ***Email:*** info@equitableonline.com

General - Incorporation	USA	**Stock**- Price on:12/24/2007	$10.35
Employees	69	Stock Exchange	OTC
Auditor	Crowe, Chizek and Company LLC	Ticker Symbol	EQFC
Stk Agt	NA	Outstanding Shares	3,230,000
Counsel	NA	E.P.S.	-$0.47
DUNS No.	NA	Shareholders	NA

Business: The group's principle activity is to provide banking services. The group financial products include acceptance of savings, demand and term deposits, trust services, cash management and electronic fund transfer, on line internet banking, commercial loans. The group operates from the United States. The groups asset in the year 2006 was $178,761,061.

Primary SIC and add'l.: 8742

CIK No: 0001329998

Subsidiaries: Equitable Bank

Officers: Richard L. Harbaugh/60/Chmn., CEO, Pres., Thomas E. Gdowski/47/Dir., COO, Exec. VP, Terry M. Pfeifer/45/Chief Investment Officer, Sr. VP, Cynthia L. Pope/Corp. Sec., Kim E. Marco/56/CFO, Exec. VP

Directors: Richard L. Harbaugh/60/Chmn., CEO, Pres., Gary L. Hedman/64/Dir., Jonas A. Proffitt/91/Dir., Benedict P. Wassinger/65/Dir., Douglas J. Redman/49/Dir., Pamela L. Price/63/Dir., Jack E. Rasmussen/78/Dir., Thomas E. Gdowski/47/Dir., COO, Exec. VP, Vincent J. Dugan/47/Dir.

Owners: Jonas A. Proffitt, Pamela L. Price, Vincent J. Dugan, Douglas J. Redman, Terry M. Pfeifer, Insiders/5.54%, Thomas E. Gdowski, Benedict P. Wassinger, Richard L. Harbaugh/1.17%, Gary L. Hedman, Jack E. Rasmussen

Financial Data: *Fiscal Year End:*06/30 *Latest Annual Data:* 6/30/2006

Year	Sales	Net Income
2006	$11,053,000	-$969,000

Curr. Assets:	$5,247,000	**Curr. Liab.:**	$152,773,000		
Plant, Equip.:	$6,067,000	**Total Liab.:**	$153,727,000	**Indic. Yr. Divd.:**	NA
Total Assets:	$178,761,000	**Net Worth:**	$25,034,000	**Debt/ Equity:**	NA

Equitable Resources Inc

225 N Shore Dr., Pittsburgh, PA, 15212; ***PH:*** 1-412-553-5700; ***Fax:*** 1-412-553-7781; ***http://*** www.eqt.com

General - Incorporation	PA	**Stock**- Price on:12/24/2007	$50.96
Employees	1,340	Stock Exchange	NYSE
Auditor	Ernst & Young LLP	Ticker Symbol	EQT
Stk Agt	Mellon Investor Services LLC	Outstanding Shares	121,610,000
Counsel	NA	E.P.S.	$2.19
DUNS No.	00-791-5663	Shareholders	NA

Business: The group's principal activity is to offer natural gas, natural gas liquids and crude oil products and services to wholesale and retail customers. Its operations are carried out through three segments: equitable utilities: consists of the state-regulated local distribution company, natural gas transportation, storage and marketing activities and supply and transportation services for the natural gas and electricity markets. Equitable supply: explores, develops, produces, gathers and sells natural gas and oil, extracts and sells natural gas liquids. Noresco: consists of cogeneration and power plant development, the development and implementation of energy and water efficiency programs, performance contracting and central facility plant operations. The group operates primarily in the northeastern section of the United States.

Primary SIC and add'l.: 1311 1321 4939 4922 4932

CIK No: 0000033213

Subsidiaries: Appalachian Drilling LLC, Eastern Four, LLC, Eastern Series 1997 Trusta, Eastern Seven Partners, LP, EPC Investments, Inc., EQT Capital Corporation, EQT Holdings Company, LLC, EQT Holdings Management Company, LLC, EQT International Holdings Corporation, EQT Investments, LLC, EQT IP Ventures, LLC, Equitable Energy Holdings Corporation, Equitable Energy, LLC, Equitable Gathering Equity, LLC, Equitable Gathering, Inc. 29 Subsidiaries included in the Index

Officers: Murry S. Gerber/Chmn., CEO, Pres./$8,288,624.00, David L. Porges/Vice Chmn., Exec. VP - Finance, Administration, Pres./$5,505,899.00, Johanna G. O'Loughlin/Sr. VP, General Counsel, Corp. Sec./$1,522,089.00, Philip P. Conti/Sr. VP, CFO/$1,408,511.00, John A. Bergonzi/VP - Finance, Randall L. Crawford/Pres. - Equitable Utilities, Sr. VP/$1,548,904.00, Joseph E. O'Brien/Pres. - Supply, Midstream, Sr. VP/$1,547,293.00, Charlene Petrelli/VP, Chief Human Resources Officer, Martin A. Fritz/VP, Chief Administrative Officer, James E. Crockard/Treasurer, Theresa Z. Bone/VP, Corporate Controller

Directors: Murry S. Gerber/Chmn., CEO, Pres., David L. Porges/Vice Chmn., Exec. VP - Finance, Administration, Pres., Phyllis A. Domm/Dir., Barbara S. Jeremiah/Dir., James W. Whalen/Dir., Vicky A. Bailey/Dir., Thomas A. McConomy/Dir., George L. Miles/Dir., James E. Rohr/Dir., David S. Shapira/Dir., Lee T. Todd/Dir.

Owners: George P. Sakellaris/5.30%, Philip P. Conti, Barbara S. Jeremiah, Capital Research and Management Company/6.90%, Randall L. Crawford, Murry S. Gerber/1.41%, Lee T. Todd, David L. Porges, David S. Shapira, Thomas A. McConomy, Johanna G. OLoughlin, Insiders/2.78%, Joseph E. OBrien, Phyllis A. Domm, James E. Rohr *(16 Owners included in Index)*

Financial Data: *Fiscal Year End:*12/31 *Latest Annual Data:* 12/31/2006

Year	Sales	Net Income
2006	$1,267,910,000	$220,286,000
2005	$1,253,724,000	$260,055,000
2004	$1,191,609,000	$279,854,000

Curr. Assets:	$701,450,000	**Curr. Liab.:**	$1,079,779,000	**P/E Ratio:**	30.51
Plant, Equip.:	$2,377,471,000	**Total Liab.:**	$2,310,631,000	**Indic. Yr. Divd.:**	$0.880
Total Assets:	$3,256,911,000	**Net Worth:**	$946,280,000	**Debt/ Equity:**	0.8552

Equity Inns Inc

7700 Wolf River Blvd., Germantown, TN, 38138; ***PH:*** 1-901-754-7774; ***http://*** www.equityinns.com

General - Incorporation	TN	**Stock**- Price on:12/24/2007	$19.75
Employees	20	Stock Exchange	NA
Auditor	PricewaterhouseCoopers LLP	Ticker Symbol	NA
Stk Agt	Computershare Investor Services LLC	Outstanding Shares	55,040,000
Counsel	NA	E.P.S.	NA
DUNS No.	NA	Shareholders	NA

Business: The groups principle activity is to invest in real estate properties. In the year 2006, the group acquired two hotels in Austin, Texas. The group operates from the United States.

Primary SIC and add'l.: 7011 6798

CIK No: 0000916530

Subsidiaries: E. Inns Orlando, Inc., E.I.P. Orlando, L.P., ENN Ann Arbor, L.L.C., ENN Asheville, L.L.C., ENN Athens, L.L.C., ENN Augusta, L.L.C., ENN Austin, L.L.C., ENN Carlsbad, L.L.C., ENN Chattanooga, L.L.C., ENN College Station, L.L.C., ENN Company, Inc., ENN East Lansing, L.L.C., ENN Ft. Myers L.L.C., ENN Gainesville, L.L.C., ENN Houston, L.L.C. 142 Subsidiaries included in the Index

Officers: Howard A. Silver/53/Dir., CEO, Pres./$3,403,295.00, Mitchell J. Collins/Exec. VP, CFO, Sec., Treasurer/$1,599,833.00, Phillip H. McNeill/46/Exec. VP - Development, Richard F. Mitchell/62/Sr. VP - Asset Management/$1,007,500.00, Edwin F. Ansbro/50/Sr. VP - Real Estate/$976,250.00, Brad D. Cohen/Contact - Integrated Corporate Relations

Directors: Howard A. Silver/53/Dir., CEO, Pres., Phillip H. McNeill/69/Chmn., Robert P. Bowen/66/Dir., Harry S. Hays/72/Dir., Joseph W. McLeary/68/Dir., Raymond E. Schultz/74/Dir.

Owners: Ronald J. Cooper, Mitchell J. Collins, Raymond E. Schultz, Phillip H. McNeill, Howard A. Silver, Harry S. Hays, Vanguard Group, Inc./6.17%, Richard F. Mitchell, Phillip H. McNeill/2.11%, Robert P. Bowen, Edwin F. Ansbro, Joseph W. McLeary, Insiders/4.44%

Financial Data: *Fiscal Year End:*12/31 *Latest Annual Data:* 12/31/2006

Year	Sales	Net Income
2006	$385,628,000	$21,037,000
2005	$335,364,000	$14,398,000
2004	$256,909,000	$4,083,000

Curr. Assets:	$15,251,000	**Curr. Liab.:**	$57,300,000	**P/E Ratio:**	20.39
Plant, Equip.:	$1,091,319,000	**Total Liab.:**	$692,665,000	**Indic. Yr. Divd.:**	$1.000
Total Assets:	$1,137,282,000	**Net Worth:**	$439,764,000	**Debt/ Equity:**	NA

Equity Lifestyle Properties Inc

2 N Riverside Plz., Ste. 800, Chicago, IL, 60606; ***PH:*** 1-312-279-1400; ***Fax:*** 1-312-454-0614; ***http://*** www.mhchomes.com

General - Incorporation	MD	**Stock**- Price on:12/24/2007	$50.52
Employees	1,400	Stock Exchange	NYSE
Auditor	Ernst & Young LLP	Ticker Symbol	ELS
Stk Agt	LaSalle Bank	Outstanding Shares	24,320,000
Counsel	NA	E.P.S.	$0.92
DUNS No.	NA	Shareholders	NA

Business: The group's principle activity is that of a real estate investment trust. The group has been approved as a real estate investment trust under sections 856 through 860 of the internal revenue code of 1986. It owns and operates manufactured home communities and recreational vehicle resorts. The properties are located in Florida, California, Arizona, Michigan, Colorado, Delaware, Nevada, Indiana, Oregon, Illinois, Iowa, New York, Utah, Pennsylvania, Montana, New Mexico, Texas, Virginia and Washington. The group's quarterly revenue for September 2007 was 94.20 millions of USD.

Primary SIC and add'l.: 6798

CIK No: 0000895417

Subsidiaries: MHC Encore Holdings, LLC, MHC Financing Limited Partnership, MHC Financing Limited Partnership Two, Mhc Ltra, Inc., Mhc Nac, Inc., MHC Operating Limited Partnership, MHC Stagecoach, LLC, MHC TT Leasing Company, LLC, MHC TT, Inc., MHC-DeAnza Financing Limited Partnership, Realty Systems, Inc

Officers: Thomas P. Heneghan/44/Dir., CEO, Pres./$1,251,794.00, Ellen Kelleher/47/Exec. VP, General Counsel, Sec./$803,607.00, Roger A. Maynard/50/COO, Exec. VP/$864,340.00, Michael B. Berman/50/CFO, Exec. VP/$803,607.00, Marguerite Nader/39/VP - New Business Development/$447,717.00

Directors: Thomas P. Heneghan/44/Dir., CEO, Pres., Samuel Zell/66/Chmn., Howard Walker/68/Vice Chmn., Donald S. Chisholm/73/Dir., Thomas E. Dobrowski/64/Dir., Philip C. Calian/45/Dir., Sheli Z. Rosenberg/66/Dir., Gary L. Waterman/66/Dir.

Owners: Ellen Kelleher, Gary L. Waterman, Morgan Stanley/13.70%, Insiders/19.80%, General Motors Employees Global Group Pension Trust/6.20%, Michael B. Berman, Roger A. Maynard, Sheli Z. Rosenberg, Philip C. Calian, JPMorgan Chase& Co./8.30%, Marguerite Nader, Thomas E. Dobrowski, Howard Walker, Samuel Zell/14.90%, Samuel Zell and entities affiliated with Samuel Zell/14.90% *(18 Owners included in Index)*

Financial Data: *Fiscal Year End:*12/31 *Latest Annual Data:* 12/31/2006

Year	Sales	Net Income
2006	$412,786,000	$16,632,000
2005	$386,480,000	-$2,333,000
2004	$343,132,000	$4,026,000

Curr. Assets:	$2,899,000	**Curr. Liab.:**	$78,707,000		
Plant, Equip.:	$1,971,742,000	**Total Liab.:**	$1,795,919,000	**Indic. Yr. Divd.:**	$0.600
Total Assets:	$2,055,831,000	**Net Worth:**	$47,118,000	**Debt/ Equity:**	26.7082

Equity Media Holdings Corp

Formerly: Coconut Palm Acquisition Corp

595 S Federal Hwy., Ste. 600, Boca Raton, FL, 33432; ***PH:*** 1-561-955-7300

General - Incorporation	DE	**Stock**- Price on:12/24/2007	$5.05
Employees	NA	Stock Exchange	OTC
Auditor	Eisner LLP	Ticker Symbol	CNUT
Stk Agt	Continental Stock Transfer & Trust Co	Outstanding Shares	NA
Counsel	NA	E.P.S.	NA
DUNS No.	NA	Shareholders	NA

Business: The groups principal activities include milling, extracting and processing technologies that preserve nutritional content and derive higher quality products from grains, and other biomass resources. The group operates from the United States and the United Kingdom.

Primary SIC and add'l.: 4833

CIK No: 0001327012

Owners: Michael Zimmerman/13.30%, RPCP Investments, LLLP/17.90%, Insiders/17.90%, Sapling, LLC/9.30%, Richard C. Rochon/17.90%, Prentice Capital Management, LP/13.30%, Millenco, LLC/8.50%

Equity One Inc

1600 NE Miami Gardens Dr., North Miami Beach, FL, 33179; ***PH:*** 1-305-947-1664; ***Fax:*** 1-305-947-1734; ***http://*** www.equityone.net

General - Incorporation	MD	**Stock**- Price on:12/24/2007	$26.58
Employees	217	Stock Exchange	NYSE
Auditor	Deloitte & Touche LLP	Ticker Symbol	EQY
Stk Agt	American Stock Transfer & Trust Co.	Outstanding Shares	73,820,000
Counsel	Arthur Gallagher	E.P.S.	$2.37
DUNS No.	NA	Shareholders	NA

Business: The groups principle activities include owning, managing, acquiring and developing neighborhood and community shopping centers. In the year 2006, the group acquired the Shops at Westrigde McDonough. The group operates from the United States. The groups quarterly revenue for September 2007 was 61.62 millions of USD.

Primary SIC and add'l.: 6798

CIK No: 0001042810

Subsidiaries: Boca Village Square, Inc., Boca Village Square, Ltd., Boynton Plaza Shopping Center, Inc., Cashmere Developments, Inc., CDG Park Place LLC, Centrefund (US), LLC, Centrefund Development Group LLC, Centrefund Realty (U.S.) Corporation, Dolphin Village Partners, LLC, Equity (Park Promenade) Inc., Equity One (Alafaya Village) Inc., Equity One (Andros) Inc., Equity One (Belfair) Inc., Equity One (Bridgemill) Inc., Equity One (Commonwealth) Inc. 76 Subsidiaries included in the Index

Officers: Jeffrey S. Olson/Dir., CEO, Pres./$806,654.00, Jeffrey S. Stauffer/COO, Exec. VP, Gregory R. Andrews/46/CFO, Exec. VP/$106,779.00, Arthur L. Gallagher/Sr. VP, General Counsel, Corp. Sec., Barbara Miller/VP - Human Resources, Tom McDonough/Chief Investment Officer, Deborah Cheek/VP, Chief Accounting Officer

Directors: Jeffrey S. Olson/Dir., CEO, Pres., Chaim Katzman/Chmn., Dori J. Segal/Vice Chmn., James S. Cassel/Dir., Nathan Hetz/Dir., Neil Flanzraich/Dir., Noam Ben-Ozer/Dir., Peter Linneman/Dir., Cynthia R. Cohen/Dir.

Owners: Howard M. Sipzner, Peter Linneman, Silver Maple (2001), Inc., Noam Ben-Ozer, Cynthia R. Cohen, David W. Briggs, Gazit-Globe Ltd., Insiders, Chaim Katzman, Ficus, Inc., Gregory Andrews, Neil Flanzraich, Alony Hetz Properties & Investments, Ltd., James S. Cassel, Jeffrey S. Olson *(23 Owners included in Index)*

Financial Data: *Fiscal Year End:*12/31 *Latest Annual Data:* 12/31/2006

Year	Sales	Net Income
2006	$233,421,000	$176,955,000
2005	$252,964,000	$92,741,000
2004	$229,857,000	$97,804,000

Curr. Assets:	$18,967,000	**Curr. Liab.:**	$46,187,000	**P/E Ratio:**	11.22
Plant, Equip.:	$1,888,411,000	**Total Liab.:**	$1,126,171,000	**Indic. Yr. Divd.:**	$1.200
Total Assets:	$2,051,849,000	**Net Worth:**	$925,678,000	**Debt/ Equity:**	1.2730

Equity Residential

2 N Riverside Plz., Ste. 450, Chicago, IL, 60606; ***PH:*** 1-312-474-1300; ***Fax:*** 1-312-454-8703; ***http://*** www.equityapartments.com

General - Incorporation	MD	**Stock**- Price on:12/24/2007	$47.11
Employees	5,200	Stock Exchange	NYSE
Auditor	Ernst & Young LLP	Ticker Symbol	EQR
Stk Agt	Computershare Investor Services LLC	Outstanding Shares	290,750,000
Counsel	NA	E.P.S.	$2.49
DUNS No.	NA	Shareholders	NA

Business: The groups principal activities include acquiring, developing and managing high quality apartment properties. The group operates through three geographic regions namely, Northeast, South and West. The group acquired 41 properties in the year 2005 and 35 properties in the year 2006. The group operates from the United States. Of the total income in the year 2006, the Northeast region accounted for $550,827, South $691,019 and West $653,125 (thousands).

Primary SIC and add'l.: 6798

CIK No: 0000906107

Subsidiaries: 1145 Acquisition , LLC, 1401 State, LLC, 303 Third Street Developers, LLC, 303 Third Street Venture I, LLC, 303 Third Street Venture II, LLC, 402 West 38Th Street Corp., 722 W Kennedy LLC, Alta Pacific, LLC, Amberton Apartments, LLC, ANE Associates, LLC, Argus Land Company, Inc., Artery Northampton Limited Partnership, Avon Place Associates, LLC, Balaton Condominium Association, Balaton Condominium, LLC 710 Subsidiaries included in the Index

Officers: David J. Neithercut/51/Trustee, CEO, Pres./$3,433,340.00, Donna Brandin/51/CFO, Exec. VP/$849,125.00, John Powers/59/Exec. VP - Human Resources, Bruce C. Strohm/52/Exec. VP, General Counsel, Sec., Frederick C. Tuomi/52/Pres. - Property Management/$1,785,476.00, Gerald A. Spector/60/Trustee, COO, Exec. VP/$3,785,550.00, Alan W. George/49/Exec. VP, Chief Investment Officer/$1,975,892.00, Gregory H. Smith/56/Exec. VP - Portfolio Management, Mark N. Tennison/46/Exec. VP - Development, Marty McKenna/Investor Relations Officer, Mark J. Parrell/CFO, Exec. VP, David S. Santee/Exec. VP - Operations, Yasmina Duwe/First VP, Assoc. General Counsel, Sec.

Directors: David J. Neithercut/51/Trustee, CEO, Pres., Samuel Zell/65/Chmn., Stephen O. Evans/Trustee, Gerald A. Spector/60/Trustee, COO, Exec. VP, Boone A. Knox/70/Trustee, Desiree G. Rogers/47/Trustee, Charles L. Atwood/58/Trustee, James D. Harper/74/Trustee, John E. Neal/57/Trustee, Sheli Z. Rosenberg/Trustee, Joseph B. White/59/Trustee, John W. Alexander/60/Trustee

Owners: The Vanguard Group, Inc./5.90%, FMR Corp./9.20%, Barclays Global Investors, N.A. and affiliates/5.60%, Capital Research and Management Company/5.10%

Financial Data: *Fiscal Year End:*12/31 *Latest Annual Data:* 12/31/2006

Year	Sales	Net Income
2006	$1,990,436,000	$1,072,844,000
2005	$1,954,937,000	$861,793,000
2004	$1,889,501,000	$472,329,000

Curr. Assets:	$657,592,000	**Curr. Liab.:**	$708,882,000	**P/E Ratio:**	18.92
Plant, Equip.:	$14,212,695,000	**Total Liab.:**	$9,177,997,000	**Indic. Yr. Divd.:**	NA
Total Assets:	$15,062,219,000	**Net Worth:**	$5,884,222,000	**Debt/ Equity:**	1.4878

Equity Ventures Group Inc

22154 Martella Ave., Boca Raton, FL, 33433; ; ***http://*** www.evgmortgage.com

General - Incorporation	FL	**Stock**- Price on:12/24/2007	NA
Employees	NA	Stock Exchange	NA
Auditor	Webb & Co P.A	Ticker Symbol	NA
Stk Agt	NA	Outstanding Shares	NA
Counsel	NA	E.P.S.	NA
DUNS No.	NA	Shareholders	NA

Business: The groups principle activity is to engage in any lawful corporate undertaking, including, but not limited to, selected mergers and acquisitions. They are setting up their services in the field and are in the developmental stage with shares issued to their original shareholders. The group operates from United States.

Primary SIC and add'l.: 9995

CIK No: 0001298327

Officers: Colette Kim/35/Dir., CEO, CFO, Pres., Sec.

Directors: Colette Kim/35/Dir., CEO, CFO, Pres., Sec.

Owners: Peter Goldstein/41.07%, Colette Kim/41.07%

Equus Total Return Inc

2727 Allen Pkwy Fl 13, Houston, TX, 77019; ***PH:*** 1-713-529-0900; ***Fax:*** 1-713-529-9545; ***http://*** www.equuscap.com

General - Incorporation	DE	**Stock**- Price on:12/24/2007	$8.791
Employees	NA	Stock Exchange	NYSE
Auditor	UHY Mann Frankfort Stein & Lipp CPAs	Ticker Symbol	EQS
Stk Agt	American Stock Transfer & Trust Co.	Outstanding Shares	8,220,000
Counsel	Dechert LLP	E.P.S.	-$0.35
DUNS No.	NA	Shareholders	NA

Business: The groups principal activity is to provide financing solutions. In the year 2006, the group acquired RP&C International Investments LLC. The group operates from the United States.

Primary SIC and add'l.: 6799

CIK No: 0000878932

Subsidiaries: Equus Media Development Company, LLC

Officers: Kenneth I. Denos/CEO, Exec. VP, Sec., Dawn Clark/Assist. Sec., Paula T. Douglass/VP, Gary Forbes/Sr. VP, Brett Chiles/Assist. VP, LSheryl D. Hudson/VP, CFO, Chief Compliance Officer

Directors: Anthony R. Moore/Co - Chmn., Sharon Clayton/Vice Chmn., Sam Douglass/Co - Chmn., Richard F. Bergner/Dir., Charles M. Boyd/Dir., Alan D. Feinsilver/Dir., Gregory J. Flanagan/Dir., Henry W. Hankinson/Dir., Robert L. Knauss/Dir., Francis D. Tuggle/Dir.

Owners: Robert L. Knauss, Alan D. Feinsilver, Charles M. Boyd, MCCE, MCC/17.80%, Francis D. Tuggle, Insiders/23.99%, Gregory J. Flanagan, Sam P. Douglass/5.49%

Financial Data: *Fiscal Year End:*12/31 *Latest Annual Data:* 12/31/2006

Year	Sales	Net Income
2006	$6,016,000	$14,159,000
2005	$2,530,000	$16,720,000
2004	$9,199,000	$1,236,000

Curr. Assets:	$82,453,000	**Curr. Liab.:**	$2,652,000	**P/E Ratio:**	18.92
Plant, Equip.:	NA	**Total Liab.:**	$32,630,000	**Indic. Yr. Divd.:**	$0.500
Total Assets:	$125,866,000	**Net Worth:**	$93,236,000	**Debt/ Equity:**	0.3215

eResearchTechnology Inc

30 S 17th St., Philadelphia, PA, 19103; ***PH:*** 1-215-972-0420; ***Fax:*** 1-215-972-0414; ***http://*** www.ert.com; ***Email:*** eresearch@ert.com

General - Incorporation	DE	**Stock**- Price on:12/24/2007	$9.0501
Employees	325	Stock Exchange	NDQ
Auditor	KPMG LLP	Ticker Symbol	ERES
Stk Agt	Wachovia Bank N.A	Outstanding Shares	50,410,000
Counsel	Duane, Morris LLP	E.P.S.	$0.24
DUNS No.	86-728-8557	Shareholders	NA

Business: The group's principal activities are to provide technology and services that enables the pharmaceutical, biotechnology and medical device industries to collect, interpret and distribute cardiac safety and clinical data. The group provides cardiac safety services which are utilized by clinical trial sponsors and clinical research organizations during their conduct of clinical trials. The group also offers licensing which involves hosting of proprietary clinical data management software products and the provision of maintenance and consulting services in support of our proprietary clinical data management software products. The operations of the group are carried out in the United States and the United Kingdom.

Primary SIC and add'l.: 8071 7372 7374

CIK No: 0001026650

Subsidiaries: eRT Investment Corporation, eRT Tech Corporation

Officers: Michael J. McKelvey/Dir., CEO, Pres./$410,945.00, Joel Morganroth/Chmn., Chief Scientist/$636,055.00, George Tiger/Dir., Sr. VP - Americas Sales/$370,271.00, Thomas P. Devine/Dir., Executive Sr. VP, Chief Development Officer, Robert S. Brown/Dir., Sr. VP - Outsourcing Partnerships, Jeffrey S. Litwin/Dir., Executive Sr. VP, Chief Medical Officer/$387,480.00, Amy Furlong/Dir., Exec. VP - Cardiac Safety Operations, Scott Grisanti/Sr. VP - BD, Chief Marketing Officer, Richard A. Baron/Dir., Executive Sr. VP, CFO/$219,869.00, John M. Blakeley/Dir., Sr. VP - International Operations, Sales

Directors: Michael J. McKelvey/Dir., CEO, Pres., Joel Morganroth/Chmn., Chief Scientist, George Tiger/Dir., Sr. VP - Americas Sales, Thomas P. Devine/Dir., Executive Sr. VP, Chief Development Officer, Robert S. Brown/Dir., Sr. VP - Outsourcing Partnerships, Richard A. Baron/Dir., Executive Sr. VP, CFO, Amy Furlong/Dir., Exec. VP - Cardiac Safety Operations, Jeffrey S. Litwin/Dir., Executive Sr. VP, Chief Medical Officer, John M. Blakeley/Dir., Sr. VP - International Operations, Sales

Owners: Blum Capital Partners, L.P./17.00%, Royce & Associates, LLC/12.40%, Insiders/8.90%, Sheldon M. Bonovitz, David D. Gathman, Mazama Capital Management, Inc./8.90%, Bruce Johnson, RS Investment Management Co. LLC/14.70%, Gerald A. Faich, Elam M. Hitchner, Joel Morganroth/6.40%, Jeffrey S. Litwin, George Tiger, Stephen S. Phillips, Michael J. McKelvey *(16 Owners included in Index)*

Financial Data: *Fiscal Year End:*12/31 *Latest Annual Data:* 12/31/2006

Year	Sales	Net Income
2006	$86,368,000	$8,310,000
2005	$86,847,000	$15,365,000
2004	$109,393,000	$29,724,000

Curr. Assets:	$81,271,000	**Curr. Liab.:**	$19,951,000	**P/E Ratio:**	41.14
Plant, Equip.:	$31,129,000	**Total Liab.:**	$21,442,000	**Indic. Yr. Divd.:**	NA
Total Assets:	$115,064,000	**Net Worth:**	$93,622,000	**Debt/ Equity:**	0.0079

ERF Wireless Inc

2911 S Shore Blvd. Ste. 100, League City, TX, 77573; ***PH:*** 1-281-538-2101; ***Fax:*** 1-281-538-2121; ***http://*** www.erfwireless.com; ***Email:*** info2911@erfwireless.com

General - Incorporation............NV
Employees............46
Auditor............Lopez, Bork & Associates, LLP
Stk Agt............NA
Counsel............NA
DUNS No.............NA

Stock- Price on:12/24/2007............$0.21
Stock Exchange............OTC
Ticker Symbol............ERFW
Outstanding Shares............36,230,000
E.P.S............-$0.18
Shareholders............NA

Business: The group's principle activity is to provide wireless communications products and services. The groups services include Internet, data, voice, security and limited video services. The group operates through three segments namely wireless bundled services, wireless messaging services, and network operations services. The group operates from the United States. Of the total sale in the 2006, wireless bundled services accounted for 33%, wireless messaging services 8%, and network operations services 59%.

Primary SIC and add'l.: 4813

CIK No: 0001020646

Subsidiaries: ERF Enterprise Network Services, Inc, ERF Wireless Bundled Services, Inc., ERF Wireless Messaging Services, Inc.

Officers: Dean H. Cubley/67/Chmn., CEO, Greg R. Smith/49/Dir., CFO, Bartus H. Batson/64/Dir., Advisory Dir., Sam Hartman/Advisory Dir.

Directors: Dean H. Cubley/67/Chmn., CEO, Greg R. Smith/49/Dir., CFO, Bartus H. Batson/64/Dir., Advisory Dir.

Owners: Carson Family Trust, Pauline Trust, Leopard Family Trust, Systom Trust, Insiders, Jauquine Trust, Leopard Family Trust, John Nagel, Frances Cubley, Carson Family Trust, Jauquine Trust, John Burns, Systom Trust, Arley Burns, Greg R. Smith *(23 Owners included in Index)*

Financial Data: **Fiscal Year End:**12/31 **Latest Annual Data:** 12/31/2006

Year	Sales	Net Income
2006	$1,716,000	-$5,232,000
2005	$643,000	-$3,411,000
2004	$325,000	-$719,000

Curr. Assets:	$1,118,000	**Curr. Liab.:**	$1,814,000		
Plant, Equip.:	$802,000	**Total Liab.:**	$4,758,000	**Indic. Yr. Divd.:**	NA
Total Assets:	$2,224,000	**Net Worth:**	-$2,534,000	**Debt/ Equity:**	NA

ERHC Energy Inc

5444 Westheimer Rd., Ste. 1440, Houston, TX, 77056; ***PH:*** 1-713-626-4700; ***Fax:*** 1-713-626-4704; ***http://*** www.erhc.com; ***Email:*** contact@erhc.com

General - Incorporation............CO
Employees............3
Auditor............Malone & Bailey, P.C
Stk Agt............Corporate Stock Transfer, Inc.
Counsel............Mintmire & Associates
DUNS No.............78-893-6177

Stock- Price on:12/24/2007............$0.32
Stock Exchange............OTC
Ticker Symbol............ERHE
Outstanding Shares............721,940,000
E.P.S............$0.00
Shareholders............NA

Business: The group's principal activities are to explore, develop, produce and market crude oil and natural gas properties. The group's current focus is to explore oil and gas in sao tome, off the coast of central west Africa, in a joint development zone between sao tome and the federal republic of nigeria. The group is also exploring relationships with other oil and gas companies having technical and financial capabilities to assist in leveraging its interests in sao tome and the joint development zone.

Primary SIC and add'l.: 1382

CIK No: 0000799235

Officers: Nicolae Luca/Dir., CEO, Interim Pres., Peter C. Ntephe/Corp. Sec., Dan Keeney/Contact, Sylvan Odobulu/Controller, James Ledbetter/VP - Technical

Directors: Nicolae Luca/Dir., CEO, Interim Pres., Howard F. Jeter/Dir., Clement Nwizubo/Dir., Andrew C. Uzoigwe/Dir.

Owners: Chrome Energy, LLC/14.30%, Insiders/43.10%, Andrew Uzoigwe, Nicolae Luca, Howard Jeter, Chrome Oil Services LTD/28.10%, Peter Ntephe, Emeka Offor/43.00%, Clement Nwizubo, First Atlantic Bank/8.40%

Financial Data: **Fiscal Year End:**09/30 **Latest Annual Data:** 9/30/2006

Year	Sales	Net Income
2006	NA	$23,172,000
2005	NA	-$11,270,000
2004	NA	-$3,593,000

Curr. Assets:	$42,544,000	**Curr. Liab.:**	$10,390,000		
Plant, Equip.:	$15,000	**Total Liab.:**	$10,390,000	**Indic. Yr. Divd.:**	NA
Total Assets:	$45,878,000	**Net Worth:**	$35,488,000	**Debt/ Equity:**	NA

Erie Indemnity Co

100 Erie Insurance Pl., Erie, PA, 16530; ***PH:*** 1-814-870-2000; ***Fax:*** 1-814-870-3126; ***http://*** www.erie-insurance.com

General - Incorporation............PA
Employees............4,300
Auditor............Ernst & Young LLP
Stk Agt......American Stock Transfer & Trust Co.
Counsel............NA
DUNS No.............05-909-1918

Stock- Price on:12/24/2007............$53.67
Stock Exchange............NDQ
Ticker Symbol............ERIE
Outstanding Shares............63,510,000
E.P.S............$3.58
Shareholders............NA

Business: The group's principal activities are to provide administrative and underwriting services to insurance exchanges. It has two operating segments: management operations and property insurance. In the management operation segment, the group performs the role of attorney-in-fact for the policyholders of the erie insurance exchange. Erie insurance exchange is a Pennsylvania-domiciled reciprocal insurance exchange. In the property insurance segment, the group provides property and casualty insurance services. This segment provides insurance in the personal and commercial lines, which is sold by independent agents. Personal lines are marketed to individuals and commercial lines to small and medium-sized businesses. These services are provided in Pennsylvania, Ohio, west Virginia, Maryland and Virginia.

Primary SIC and add'l.: 6331 6311

CIK No: 0000922621

Subsidiaries: EI Holding Corp., EI Service Corp., Erie Insurance Company, Erie Insurance Company of New York - Wholly owned by Erie Insurance Company, Erie Insurance Property & Casualty Company

Officers: John J. Brinling/Interim CEO, Pres., Jeffrey A. Ludrof/48/Dir., CEO, Pres./$3,310,409.00, Karen Kraus Phillips/Mgr., VP - Corporate Communications, Investor Relations, Jan R. Van Gorder/Acting Sec., General Counsel/$1,684,569.00, Michael J. Krahe/Exec. VP - Human Development, Leadership, Philip A. Garcia/CFO, Exec. VP/$1,279,980.00, Thomas B. Morgan/Exec. VP - Insurance Operations/$1,165,952.00, Vanessa Paris/Media Relations, Public Affairs Specialist - Corporate Communications, Ann Scott/VP, Mgr. - Employment, Kevin A. Marti/Exec. VP - Erie Family Life Insurance Company, James J. Tanous/Exec. VP, Sec., General Counsel, Mark Dombrowski/Supervisor - Public, Media Relations, Corporate Communications

Directors: Jeffrey A. Ludrof/48/Dir., CEO, Pres., Claude C. Lilly/Dir., Patricia A. Garrison-Corbin/Dir., Susan Hirt Hagen/Dir., John T. Baily/Dir., Kaj Ahlmann/Dir., Robert C. Wilburn/Dir., Jonathan Hirt Hagen/Dir., Ralph J. Borneman/Dir., Scott C. Hartz/Dir., William F. Hirt/82/Dir., Lucian L. Morrison/Dir., Thomas W. Palmer/Dir., Thomas B. Hagen/Dir., Elizabeth A. Vorsheck/Dir.

Owners: Jonathan Hirt Hagen, Claude C. Lilly, John T. Baily, Jan R. Van Gorder, Douglas F. Ziegler, Patricia Garrison-Corbin, Philip A. Garcia, William F. Hirt/3.24%, Ralph J. Borneman, Insiders/15.47%, John R. Graham, Thomas W. Palmer, Jan R. Van Gorder, David C. Abrams, William F. Hirt *(28 Owners included in Index)*

Financial Data: **Fiscal Year End:**12/31 **Latest Annual Data:** 12/31/2006

Year	Sales	Net Income
2006	$1,133,982,000	$204,025,000
2005	$1,124,950,000	$231,104,000
2004	$1,123,144,000	$226,413,000

Curr. Assets:	$1,538,675,000	**Curr. Liab.:**	$191,065,000	**P/E Ratio:**	15.20
Plant, Equip.:	NA	**Total Liab.:**	$1,877,513,000	**Indic. Yr. Divd.:**	$1.600
Total Assets:	$3,039,361,000	**Net Worth:**	$1,161,848,000	**Debt/ Equity:**	0.0257

eRoomSystem Technologies

6801 Koll Ctr. Pkwy., leasanton, CA, 94566; ***PH:*** 1-925-600-6800; ***Fax:*** 1-732-810-0380; ***http://*** www.eroom.com

General - Incorporation............NV
Employees............2
Auditor............Hansen, Barnett & Maxwell
Stk Agt.....Computershare Investor Services LLC
Counsel............Packer Duryee Rosoff & Haft
DUNS No.............NA

Stock- Price on:12/24/2007............$0.12
Stock Exchange............OTC
Ticker Symbol............ERMS
Outstanding Shares............23,900,000
E.P.S............$0.02
Shareholders............NA

Business: The group's principal activities are to provide in-room computer platform and communications network or the eroomsystem for the lodging industry. The group has designed processor-based eroomsystem that collects and controls data and offers eroomserv refreshment centers. The eroomserv refreshment centers provide guests with a selection of different beverages and snacks. It also offers electronic in-room safes called eroomsafes, which offers sufficient space for items such as laptop computers, video cameras and briefcases. The group designs, assembles and markets a complete line of fully automated refreshment centers and eroomsafes traditionally installed in hotels. The refreshment centers and eroomsafes use proprietary software and patented credit card technology that integrates with the data collection computer in each hotel.

Primary SIC and add'l.: 7373 7379

CIK No: 0001110361

Subsidiaries: eRoomSystem Services, Inc., a Nevada corporation, eRoomSystem SPE, Inc., a Nevada corporation

Owners: James C. Savas/16.70%, Ash Capital, LLC/16.10%, David A. Gestetner/21.60%, Lawrence K. Wein/0.40%, Herbert A. Hardt/2.50%, Insiders/40.60%

Financial Data: **Fiscal Year End:**12/31 **Latest Annual Data:** 12/31/2006

Year	Sales	Net Income
2006	$1,337,000	$162,000
2005	$1,557,000	$161,000
2004	$1,591,000	$900,000

Curr. Assets:	$1,781,000	**Curr. Liab.:**	$181,000	**P/E Ratio:**	12.00
Plant, Equip.:	$846,000	**Total Liab.:**	$181,000	**Indic. Yr. Divd.:**	NA
Total Assets:	$2,846,000	**Net Worth:**	$2,665,000	**Debt/ Equity:**	NA

ES Bancshares Inc MD

68 N Plank Rd., Newburgh, NY, 12550; ***PH:*** 1-866-646-0003

General - Incorporation............MD
Employees............NA
Auditor..........Crowe, Chizek and Company LLC
Stk Agt......American Stock Transfer & Trust Co.
Counsel............NA
DUNS No.............NA

Stock- Price on:12/24/2007............$9
Stock Exchange............OTC
Ticker Symbol............ESBS
Outstanding Shares............NA
E.P.S............-$0.38
Shareholders............NA

Business: The group's principle activity is to provide banking services. The group financial products include acceptance of savings, demand and term deposits, trust services, cash management and electronic fund transfer, on line internet banking, commercial loans. The group operates from the United States. The groups total asset in the year 2006 was $75,945.

Primary SIC and add'l.: 6712

CIK No: 0001358254

Subsidiaries: Empire State Bank, NA

Officers: Emil Mian/60/Sr. VP, Chief Credit Officer, Branca Gatto/47/Sr. VP, Joseph MacChia/56/Sr. VP - Branch Administration, Sales, Marketing

Directors: Leslie M. Apple/Dir., William Davenport/Dir., Peter Ferrante/Dir., Andrew Finklestein/Dir., Gale Foster/Dir., David Freer/Dir., Harold Kahn/Dir., David Mesches/Dir., Michael Ostrow/Dir., Albert Pagano/Dir., Richard B. Rowley/Dir., Peter Savago/Dir., Thomas D. Weddell/Dir.

Owners: Richard B. Rowley/1.96%, Leslie M. Apple/2.59%, Thomas D. Weddell, Philip Guarnieri/4.61%, David Freer/2.41%, William W. Davenport/2.50%, Arthur W. Budich, Insiders/30.79%, Albert J. Pagano/3.31%, Emil Mian, Michael P. Ostrow/1.62%, David N. Mesches/2.60%, Branca Gatto, Anthony P. Costa/3.94%, Andrew G. Finklestein/2.64% *(19 Owners included in Index)*

Financial Data: **Fiscal Year End:**12/31 **Latest Annual Data:** 12/31/2006

Year	Sales	Net Income
2006	$5,060,000	-$1,427,000

Curr. Assets:	$20,604,000	**Curr. Liab.:**	$81,604,000		
Plant, Equip.:	$741,000	**Total Liab.:**	$82,097,000	**Indic. Yr. Divd.:**	NA
Total Assets:	$93,039,000	**Net Worth:**	$10,942,000	**Debt/ Equity:**	0.0052

ESB Financial Corp

600 Lawrence Ave., Ellwood City, PA, 16117; *PH:* 1-724-758-5584; *Fax:* 1-724-758-0576; *http://* www.esbbank.com

General		Stock	
Incorporation	PA	Price on:12/24/2007	$11.05
Employees	217	Stock Exchange	NDQ
Auditor	S R Snodgrass, A.C	Ticker Symbol	ESBF
Stk Agt	Registrar & Transfer Co	Outstanding Shares	12,800,000
Counsel	Elias, Matz, Tierman & Herrick	E.P.S	$0.69
DUNS No.	78-165-9206	Shareholders	NA

Business: The group's principal activities are to provide a wide range of retail and commercial financial products and services to customers in western Pennsylvania. The loans offered include residential-single family, residential multi-family, commercial real estate, construction, consumer and commercial business loans. The deposits accepted include non-interest bearing deposits, now accounts, money market, passbook accounts and time deposits. The group operates through 17 full service banking branches in allegheny, beaver, butler and lawrence counties, Pennsylvania.

Primary SIC and add'l.: 6712 6035

CIK No: 0000872835

Subsidiaries: AMSCO, Inc, ESB Bank, ESB Capital Trust II, ESB Capital Trust IV, ESB Financial Services, Inc, ESB Statutory Trust III, PennFirst Financial Services, Inc, THF, Inc

Officers: Charlotte A. Zuschlag/56/Dir., CEO, Pres./$623,401.00, Sarah K. Anthony/Human Resources Representative, Todd F. Palkovich/53/Group Sr. VP, Sr. VP - Lending/$226,514.00, John T. Stunda/Sr. VP - Human Resources, Bonita L. Wadding/38/Sr. VP, Controller, Charles P. Evanoski/49/CFO, Group Sr. VP/$221,208.00, Thomas F. Angotti/60/Group Sr. VP - Administration/$229,670.00, Richard E. Canonge/45/Sr. VP, Treasurer, Frank D. Martz/52/Group Sr. VP, Sec., Sr. VP - Operations/$219,236.00

Directors: Charlotte A. Zuschlag/56/Dir., CEO, Pres., William B. Salsgiver/74/Chmn., Herbert S. Skuba/69/Vice Chmn., Lloyd L. Kildoo/68/Dir., Mario J. Manna/72/Dir., James P. Wetzel/63/Dir., Charles Delman/82/Dir.

Owners: James P. Wetzel/1.20%, ESB Financial Corporation/12.50%, Thomas F. Angotti/1.00%, Todd F. Palkovich, Charles Delman, Charlotte A. Zuschlag/3.50%, Frank D. Martz/1.60%, Lloyd L. Kildoo/2.50%, Herbert S. Skuba/1.30%, Charles P. Evanoski, William B. Salsgiver/2.90%, Mario J. Manna, Insiders/17.00%

Financial Data: Fiscal Year End:12/31 Latest Annual Data: 12/31/2006

Year	Sales	Net Income
2006	$102,257,000	$10,616,000
2005	$86,404,000	$9,179,000
2004	$67,758,000	$9,990,000

Curr. Assets:	$32,572,000	Curr. Liab.:	$1,725,839,000	P/E Ratio:	16.01
Plant, Equip.:	$32,214,000	Total Liab.:	$1,794,187,000	Indic. Yr. Divd.:	$0.400
Total Assets:	$1,922,722,000	Net Worth:	$128,535,000	Debt/ Equity:	0.5009

Escala Group Inc

5 Frances J. Clarke Blvd., Bethel, CT, 06801; *PH:* 1-203-702-8480; *http://* www.escalagroup.com; *Email:* info@escalagroup.com

General		Stock	
Incorporation	NY	Price on:12/24/2007	NA
Employees	168	Stock Exchange	OTC
Auditor	BDO Seidman, LLP	Ticker Symbol	ESCL
Stk Agt	American Stock Transfer & Trust Co.	Outstanding Shares	NA
Counsel	Kramer Levin Naftalis & Frankel LLP	E.P.S	$0.52
DUNS No.	80-666-6475	Shareholders	NA

Business: The group's principle activity is to conduct auctions and private sales of collectibles, including rare stamps, rare documents, sports trading cards and sports memorabilia. The business is conducted through its subsidiaries, Ivy and Mader Philatelic Auctions Inc, Greg Manning Galleries Inc, Teletrade Inc, Greg Manning Direct Inc, Spectrum Numismatics International Inc and Kensington Associates, LLC. The group organizes its business in three categories, collectibles auctioneer, merchant/dealer and wholesale coins. Rare stamps and stamp collection auctions are the core business of the group. The group conducts live auctions, mail and absentee auctions and telephone auctions.

Primary SIC and add'l.: 7389

CIK No: 0000895516

Subsidiaries: A-Mark Precious Metals, Inc., Auctentia Deutschland, GmbH, Auctentia Subastas, S.L., Bowers & Merena Galleries, LLC, Corinphila Auktionen AG, GMAI Auctentia Central de Compras, S.L.U., GMAI-Auctentia Europe, S.L., Greg Manning Auctions Real Estate, LLC, Greg Manning Galleries, Inc., Greg Manning Nutmeg Auctions, Inc., H.R. Harmer, Inc., Heinrich Kohler Auktionshaus, GmbH & Co.KG, Heinrich Kohler Berliner Briefmarken-Auktionen GmbH, Heinrich Kohler Briefmarkenhandel, GmbH & Co. KG, Heinrich Kohler Verwaltungs, GmbH 25 Subsidiaries included in the Index

Officers: Matthew Walsh/Acting CEO, CFO, Pres., Carol Meltzer/Exec. VP, General Counsel, Laurence Gibson/COO - North American, Asian Philatelic Auction Division, Gregory N. Roberts/Dir., Pres. - North America Coin Division, Greg Martin/Pres. - Greg Martin Auctions, Arts, Antiques Division, Dieter Michelson/MD - European Philatelic Division

Directors: Antonio Arenas/Chmn., Jay Moorhead/Dir., Christopher W. Nolan/Dir., Gregory N. Roberts/Dir., Pres. - North America Coin Division, James M. Davin/Dir., Irving Kagan/Dir., George Lumby/Dir.

Financial Data: Fiscal Year End:06/30 Latest Annual Data: 06/30/2005

Year	Sales	Net Income
2005	$240,314,000	$38,275,000
2004	$212,890,000	$29,366,000
2003	$101,191,000	$2,823,000

Curr. Assets:	$132,507,000	Curr. Liab.:	$37,930,000		
Plant, Equip.:	$9,461,000	Total Liab.:	$47,111,000	Indic. Yr. Divd.:	NA
Total Assets:	$158,450,000	Net Worth:	$111,339,000	Debt/ Equity:	0.0551

Escalade Inc

817 Maxwell Ave., Evansville, IN, 47711; *PH:* 1-812-467-4449; *Fax:* 1-812-467-1303; *http://* www.escaladeinc.com

General		Stock	
Incorporation	IN	Price on:12/24/2007	$9.45
Employees	891	Stock Exchange	NDQ
Auditor	BKD LLP	Ticker Symbol	ESCA
Stk Agt	American Stock Transfer & Trust Co.	Outstanding Shares	12,970,000
Counsel	Graydon, Head & Ritchey	E.P.S	$0.71
DUNS No.	05-831-2877	Shareholders	NA

Business: The group's principal activities are to manufacture and sell sporting goods and office and graphic art products. Sporting goods include table tennis tables and accessories, archery equipment, home pool tables and accessories, combination bumper pool and card tables, basketball backboards and goals. The brand names under which the group sells sporting goods include Indian archery(R), harvard(R), xi(R), ping pong(R), stiga(R), goalrilla(tm) and goalith(r). The group's office and graphic art products include paper trimmers, folding machines, shredders, joggers and drills, collators, de collators and bursting machines and letter openers. These products are sold under the martin yale(tm), premier(R), master(tm) and mead hatcher(tm) brand names. During the year 2003 the group acquired 97% interest of schleicher and co international ag and assets of north American archery group.

Primary SIC and add'l.: 3949 3579

CIK No: 0000033488

Subsidiaries: ChildLife, Inc, Lemont Industries, Inc., Schleicher & Co. International

Officers: Robert Keller/CEO, Pres., Terry D. Frandsen/CFO, VP, Treasurer, Sec./$517,113.00

Directors: Robert Griffin/Chmn., Daniel A. Messmer/54/Dir., Richard D. White/Dir., George Savitsky/Dir., Blaine E. Matthews/Dir., Edward E. Williams/Dir., Richard F. Baalmann/Dir.

Owners: Robert E. Griffin/25.50%, Daniel A. Messmer/1.50%, Terry D. Frandsen/0.90%, Royce & Associates, LLC/6.10%, Charmenz Guagenti/8.40%

Financial Data: Fiscal Year End:12/31 Latest Annual Data: 12/30/2006

Year	Sales	Net Income
2006	$191,465,000	$8,495,000
2005	$185,617,000	$12,916,000
2004	$220,709,000	$8,180,000

Curr. Assets:	$70,751,000	Curr. Liab.:	$28,401,000	P/E Ratio:	15.75
Plant, Equip.:	$20,307,000	Total Liab.:	$48,237,000	Indic. Yr. Divd.:	$0.200
Total Assets:	$124,860,000	Net Worth:	$76,623,000	Debt/ Equity:	0.3814

Escalon Medical Corp

565 E Swedesford Rd., Ste. 200, Wayne, PA, 19087; *PH:* 1-610-688-6830; *Fax:* 1-610-688-3641; *http://* www.escalonmed.com; *Email:* info@escalonmed.com

General		Stock	
Incorporation	PA	Price on:12/24/2007	$3.95
Employees	174	Stock Exchange	NDQ
Auditor	Mayer Hoffman Mccann, P.C	Ticker Symbol	ESMC
Stk Agt	American Stock Transfer & Trust Co.	Outstanding Shares	6,370,000
Counsel	Duane, Morris LLP	E.P.S	NA
DUNS No.	61-300-5404	Shareholders	NA

Business: The group's principal activities are to develop, manufacture, market and distribute ophthalmic medical devices, pharmaceutical, vascular access products and digital cameras. The group operates through four segments: sonomed,vascular, medical/trek and digital. Sonomed develops, manufactures and markets ultrasound systems used for diagnostic or biometric applications in ophthalmology. Vascular develops, manufactures and markets vascular access products presently focusing on selling to cardiac catheterization laboratories. Medical/trek develops, manufactures and distributes ophthalmic surgical products. Vitreoretinal ophthalmic surgeons primarily utilize these products. Digital markets its high-end digital camera system for ophthalmologists known as the cfa digital imaging system. The camera back is being marketed to medical institutions, educational institutions and ophthalmologists for the purpose of diagnosis of retinal disorders.

Primary SIC and add'l.: 3841 3851

CIK No: 0000862668

Subsidiaries: Drew Scientific Group, Inc., Drew Scientific Group, Plc, Escalon Digital Vision, Inc., Escalon Holdings, Inc., Escalon Medical Europe GmbH, Escalon Pharmaceutical, Inc., Escalon Vascular Access, Inc., Sonomed, Inc.

Officers: Richard J. Depiano/67/Chmn., CEO, Robert M. O'Connor/CFO, Richard J. Depiano/42/COO, General Counsel

Directors: Richard J. Depiano/67/Chmn., CEO, Lisa A. Napolitano/Dir., Jay L. Federman/Dir., Anthony J. Coppola/Dir., William L.G. Kwan/Dir., Fred G. Choate/62/Dir.

Owners: Richard J. DePiano, Fidelity Management& Research Co./9.20%, Insiders/2.30%, Jay L. Federman, Barclays Global Investors, N.A./6.00%

Financial Data: Fiscal Year End:06/30 Latest Annual Data: 06/30/2007

Year	Sales	Net Income
2007	$38,838,000	$5,915,000
2006	$29,791,000	-$1,986,000
2005	$26,925,000	$2,448,000

Curr. Assets:	$14,911,000	Curr. Liab.:	$4,295,000	P/E Ratio:	4.25
Plant, Equip.:	$970,000	Total Liab.:	$5,545,000	Indic. Yr. Divd.:	NA
Total Assets:	$38,645,000	Net Worth:	$33,100,000	Debt/ Equity:	0.0003

Eschelon Telecom Inc

730 Second Ave S., Ste. 12001, Minneapolis, MN, 55402; *PH:* 1-612-376-4400; *http://* www.eschelon.com

General		Stock	
Incorporation	DE	Price on:12/24/2007	$29.65
Employees	1,390	Stock Exchange	NA
Auditor	Ernst & Young LLP	Ticker Symbol	NA
Stk Agt	Wells Fargo Shareowner Services	Outstanding Shares	18,070,000
Counsel	NA	E.P.S	$0.03
DUNS No.	NA	Shareholders	NA

Business: The group's principal activity is to provide integrated voice and data communications services to small and medium-sized businesses in 19 markets in the western United States. Voice and data services, also referred to as network services, include local dial tone, long distance, enhanced voice features and dedicated Internet access services. Capabilities include selling, installing and maintaining business telephone and data systems and equipment, referred to as BTS. Products and services are provided individually or in customized packages to address customers' need for a fully-outsourced voice and data network solution.

Primary SIC and add'l.: 4813

CIK No: 0001110507

Subsidiaries: Advanced TelCom, Inc., Business Productivity Solutions,Inc., Eschelon Telecom of Arizona, Inc., Eschelon Telecom of California,Inc., Eschelon Telecom of Colorado, Inc., Eschelon Telecom of Minnesota, Inc., Eschelon Telecom of Nevada, Inc., Eschelon Telecom of Oregon, Inc., Eschelon Telecom of Utah, Inc., Eschelon Telecom of Washington, Inc., Shared Communications Services, Inc.

Officers: Richard A. Smith/57/Dir., CEO, Pres./$938,843.00, Arlin B. Goldberg/52/Exec. VP - Information Technology, Robert E. Pickens/47/COO, Jeffery J. Oxley/53/Exec. VP - Law, Policy, Geoffrey M. Boyd/40/CFO/$520,616.00, David A. Kunde/48/Exec. VP - Engineering, Network Operations/$313,149.00, William D. Markert/43/Exec. VP - Network Financial Management, Steven K. Wachter/46/Exec. VP - Sales/$341,757.00

Directors: Richard A. Smith/57/Dir., CEO, Pres., Clifford D. Williams/60/Founder, Chmn., Ian K. Loring/41/Dir., Marvin C. Moses/63/Dir., Mark E. Nunnelly/49/Dir., James P. Tenbroek/47/Dir., Louis L. Massaro/61/Dir.

Owners: Wells Fargo & Company, Richard A. Smith, Bain Capital Fund VI, L.P., Geoffrey M. Boyd, Mark E. Nunnelly, Insiders, Clifford D. Williams, David A. Kunde, Steven K. Wachter, Schroder Investment Management North America, Inc., James P. TenBroek, Marvin C. Moses, Louis L. Massaro, Ian K. Loring, Wind Point Partners IV, L.P.

Financial Data: Fiscal Year End:12/31   Latest Annual Data: 12/31/2006

Year	Sales	Net Income
2006	$274,526,000	-$2,780,000
2005	$227,743,000	-$30,991,000
2004	$158,096,000	$1,111,000

Curr. Assets:	$76,950,000	Curr. Liab.:	$54,568,000		
Plant, Equip.:	$145,785,000	Total Liab.:	$199,071,000	Indic. Yr. Divd.:	NA
Total Assets:	$330,521,000	Net Worth:	$131,450,000	Debt/ Equity:	1.0901

ESCO Technologies Inc

9900A Clayton Rd., Ste. 200, St. Louis, MO, 63124; *PH:* 1-314-213-7200; *Fax:* 1-314-213-7250; *http://* www.escotechnologies.com

General - Incorporation	MO	Stock- Price on:12/24/2007	$36.77
Employees	2,685	Stock Exchange	NYSE
Auditor	KPMG LLP	Ticker Symbol	ESE
Stk Agt	Registrar & Transfer Co	Outstanding Shares	25,940,000
Counsel	NA	E.P.S.	$1.13
DUNS No.	61-895-7153	Shareholders	NA

Business: The group's principal activities are to design, manufacture, sell and support engineered products for industrial and commercial applications. The group operates through three segments: filtration/fluid flow, communications and test. The filtration/fluid flow segment develops and manufactures a wide range of filtration products and supplies filters to the commercial aerospace and microfiltration market. The communications segment provides two-way power line communication systems for the utility industry. The test segment designs and manufactures electromagnetic compatibility test equipment, test chambers, electromagnetic absorption materials, radio frequency shielding products and components.

Primary SIC and add'l.: 3569 3795 3669 3679 3812 6719 3823

CIK No: 0000866706

Subsidiaries: Beijing Lindgren ElectronMagnetic Technology Co., Ltd., Comtrak Technologies, LLC, Distribution Control Systems Caribe, Inc., Distribution Control Systems, Inc., ESCO Electronica De Mexico,S.A. de C.V., ESCO Technologies Holding Inc., ETS-Lindgren Japan, Inc., ETS-Lindgren, L.P., Euroshield OY, Filtertek BV, Filtertek do Brasil Industria E Commercio LTDA, Filtertek Inc., Filtertek SA, Lindgren R.F. Enclosures, Inc., PTI Technologies Inc. 17 Subsidiaries included in the Index

Officers: Victor L. Richey/Chmn., CEO, Pres., Gary E. Muenster/Sr. VP, CFO, Alyson Schlinger Barclay/VP, Sec., General Counsel

Directors: Victor L. Richey/Chmn., CEO, Pres., L. W. Solley/Dir., W. S. Antle/Dir., J. M. McConnell/Dir., J. M. Stolze/Dir., D. C. Trauscht/Dir., J. D. Woods/Dir.

Owners: Insiders/3.00%, Columbia Wanger Asset Management, L.P./14.70%, T. Rowe Price Associates, Inc./10.00%, J. M. Stolze, L. W. Solley, V. L. Richey/1.30%, Jeffrey L. Gendell/9.50%, A. S. Barclay, J. D. Woods, D. C. Trauscht, Waddell & Reed Investment Management Company/9.90%, J. M. McConnell, G. E. Muenster

Financial Data: Fiscal Year End:09/30   Latest Annual Data: 9/30/2006

Year	Sales	Net Income
2006	$458,865,000	$31,280,000
2005	$429,115,000	$43,544,000
2004	$422,085,000	$35,671,000

Curr. Assets:	$207,257,000	Curr. Liab.:	$75,895,000	P/E Ratio:	35.02
Plant, Equip.:	$68,754,000	Total Liab.:	$112,260,000	Indic. Yr. Divd.:	NA
Total Assets:	$488,694,000	Net Worth:	$376,434,000	Debt/ Equity:	NA

eSecureSoft CO

1016 Clemons St., Ste. 302, Jupiter, FL, 33477; *PH:* 1-561-880-0004

General - Incorporation	FL	Stock- Price on:12/24/2007	NA
Employees	NA	Stock Exchange	NA
Auditor	Wieseneck, Andres & Co P.A	Ticker Symbol	NA
Stk Agt	Florida Atlantic Stock Transfer	Outstanding Shares	NA
Counsel	NA	E.P.S.	NA
DUNS No.	NA	Shareholders	NA

Business: The groups principle activity is to provide distribution services for digital encryption software products. The group operates from United States.

Primary SIC and add'l.: 9995

CIK No: 0001321511

Officers: Barney A. Richmond/56/Chmn., Pres., Sec., Richard C. Turner/48/Dir., Treasurer, CFO

Directors: Barney A. Richmond/56/Chmn., Pres., Sec., Richard C. Turner/48/Dir., Treasurer, CFO

Owners: American Capital Holdings Inc./36.00%, Richard C. Turner/1.50%, United States Financial Group Inc./7.70%, Insiders/19.10%, Barney A. Richmond/17.60%

Curr. Assets:	$67,000	Curr. Liab.:	$155,000		
Plant, Equip.:	$0	Total Liab.:	$876,000	Indic. Yr. Divd.:	NA
Total Assets:	$67,000	Net Worth:	-$809,000	Debt/ Equity:	NA

eSpeed Inc

110 E 59th St., New York, NY, 10022; *PH:* 1-212-610-2200; *Fax:* 1-212-829-4866; *http://* www.espeed.com

General - Incorporation	DE	Stock- Price on:12/24/2007	$8.87
Employees	400	Stock Exchange	NDQ
Auditor	Deloitte & Touche LLP	Ticker Symbol	ESPD
Stk Agt	American Stock Transfer & Trust Co.	Outstanding Shares	50,440,000
Counsel	NA	E.P.S.	-$0.16
DUNS No.	NA	Shareholders	NA

Business: The group's principal activity is the development and deployment of interactive vertical electronic marketplaces and related technology. The suite of marketplace tools provides end-to-end transaction solutions for the purchase and sale of financial and non-financial products through Internet or its global private network. The group's customer base includes companies, industries, global non-equity capital marketplace involving multiple buyers and multiple sellers, government bond markets and other fixed income and equities marketplaces. The group has operations in the United States, Europe and Asia.

Primary SIC and add'l.: 7375

CIK No: 0001094831

Subsidiaries: AMEEFI Services, Inc., EC Consulting Limited, Ecco LLC, EccoWare Limited, eSpeed (Australia) Pty Limited, eSpeed (Canada), Inc., eSpeed (Hong Kong) Holdings I, Inc., eSpeed (Hong Kong) Holdings II, Inc., eSpeed (Hong Kong) Limited, eSpeed (Japan) Limited, eSpeed Government Securities, Inc., eSpeed International Limited, eSpeed Markets, Inc., eSpeed Securities, Inc., eSpeed, LLC 18 Subsidiaries included in the Index

Officers: Howard W. Lutnick/Chmn., CEO, Stephen M. Merkel/Exec. VP, General Counsel, Sec., Paul Saltzman/COO, Joseph C. Noviello/Exec. VP, Chief Product Architect, Matthew Claus/CTO, Sr. VP, Adrian Thomas/Contact - Media Relations, UK, Frank V. Saracino/41/Interim Chief Accounting Officer

Directors: Howard W. Lutnick/Chmn., CEO, John H. Dalton/Dir., Albert M. Weis/Dir., Barry M. Gosin/Dir., Barry R. Sloane/Dir.

Owners: Lee M. Amaitis/4.20%, Howard W. Lutnick/52.10%, Barry R. Sloane, Insiders/1.00%, Stephen M. Merkel/2.10%, Frank V. Saracino, Albert M. Weis, John H. Dalton, Paul Saltzman/1.20%, Howard W. Lutnick/1.00%, Insiders/54.30%

Financial Data: Fiscal Year End:12/31   Latest Annual Data: 12/31/2006

Year	Sales	Net Income
2006	$164,683,000	$4,652,000
2005	$152,943,000	$2,044,000
2004	$166,509,000	$25,850,000

Curr. Assets:	$203,149,000	Curr. Liab.:	$31,880,000	P/E Ratio:	147.83
Plant, Equip.:	$57,443,000	Total Liab.:	$39,994,000	Indic. Yr. Divd.:	NA
Total Assets:	$293,073,000	Net Worth:	$253,079,000	Debt/ Equity:	NA

Esperanza Silver Corp

570 Granville St., 9th Fl., Vancouver, BC, V6C 3P1; *PH:* 1-604-685-2242; *http://* www.esperanzasilver.com; *Email:* info@esperanzasilver.com

General - Incorporation	Canada	Stock- Price on:12/24/2007	NA
Employees	NA	Stock Exchange	NA
Auditor	De Visser Gray	Ticker Symbol	NA
Stk Agt	Computershare Investor Services LLC	Outstanding Shares	NA
Counsel	Northwest Law Group	E.P.S.	NA
DUNS No.	NA	Shareholders	NA

Business: The groups principle activity is to discover new precious-metal deposits, leveraging off the track record of its management and field exploration teams. The group operates from United States.

Primary SIC and add'l.: 1400

CIK No: 0001261252

Officers: William Pincus/55/Dir., CEO, William Bond/VP - Exploration, Kim Casswell/51/Corp. Sec., David L. Miles/57/CFO, Stevens J. Zuker/Sr. VP, Julio Mendoza/Mgr. - Peruvian Exploration, Paul Bartos/VP, Chief Geologist, Bill Pincus/Contact - Investor Relations

Directors: William Pincus/55/Dir., CEO, Michael Halvorson/Dir., Joseph Ovsenek/Dir., Steve Ristorcelli/Dir., Brian E. Bayley/Dir.

Owners: Kim Casswell, William Bond/0.63%, Steve Ristorcelli/0.78%, Joseph Ovsenek/0.56%, Stevens J. Zuker, Insiders/10.70%, Silver Standard Resources Inc./14.46%, William Pincus/3.73%, Brian Bayley/1.05%, David Miles/0.27%, Paul Bartos/0.42%, Michael Halvorson/2.89%

Espey Mfg & Electronics Corp

233 Ballston Ave., Saratoga Springs, NY, 12866; *PH:* 1-518-245-4400; *Fax:* 1-518-245-4421; *http://* www.espey.com

General - Incorporation	NY	Stock- Price on:12/24/2007	$24.1
Employees	169	Stock Exchange	AMEX
Auditor	Rotenberg & Co., LLP	Ticker Symbol	ESP
Stk Agt	Registrar & Transfer Co	Outstanding Shares	2,320,000
Counsel	Honen & Wood	E.P.S.	$1.24
DUNS No.	00-126-5396	Shareholders	NA

Business: The group's principle activity is to develop, design, produce and sell specialized electronic supplies, transformers and other types of iron-core components and electronic system components. The electronic power supplies and components are used in shipboard and land based radar, locomotives, aircraft, short, medium range and global communication systems, navigation systems for aircraft, nuclear submarine control systems, missile guidance and control systems and land-based military vehicles. The iron-core components include transformers of the audio, power and pulse types, magnetic amplifiers and audio filters. The electronic system components include antenna systems and high power radar transmitters. The products are marketed through own direct sales organization. The customers of the group are companies that provide electronic support to both military and industrial applications. The group's total revenue for the year 2007 was 27.66 millions of USD.

Primary SIC and add'l.: 3677

CIK No: 0000033533

Officers: Howard Pinsley/68/Dir., CEO, Pres., Bruce Dietrich/Dir. - Quality, Peggy Murphy/Corp. Sec., Dir. - Human Resources, James Clemens/VP - Sales, Marketing, Dave O'Neil/Treasurer, Principal Financial Officer, Alan Winslow/VP - Engineering, Bob Walton/Dir. - Information Technology, Webmaster, Cynthia Cook/Saratoga Electro, Finishing, Art Schrum/Dir. - Supply Chain, Katrina L. Sparano/37/Assist. Treasurer, Principal Accounting Officer

Directors: Howard Pinsley/68/Dir., CEO, Pres., Alvin O. Sabo/65/Dir., Carl Helmetag/60/Dir., Barry Pinsley/67/Dir., Seymour Saslow/87/Dir., Paul J. Corr/64/Dir., Michael W. Wool/62/Dir.

Owners: Advisory Research, Inc./9.50%, Howard Pinsley/5.40%, Espey Mfg. & Electronics Corp./29.50%, Franklin Resources, Inc./6.70%

Financial Data: Fiscal Year End: 06/30 **Latest Annual Data:** 6/30/2006

Year	Sales	Net Income
2006	$20,852,000	$1,558,000
2005	$18,829,000	$979,000
2004	$22,507,000	$961,000

Curr. Assets:	$30,315,000	**Curr. Liab.:**	$2,014,000	**P/E Ratio:**	20.42
Plant, Equip.:	$2,935,000	**Total Liab.:**	$2,193,000	**Indic. Yr. Divd.:**	$0.600
Total Assets:	$33,250,000	**Net Worth:**	$31,057,000	**Debt/ Equity:**	NA

Espirito Santo Financial Group

320 Pk. Ave., 29th Fl., New York, NY, 10022; **PH:** 1-212-702-3400; **Fax:** 1-212-750-3888; *http://* www.esfg.com

General - Incorporation	Luxembourg	**Stock** - Price on:12/24/2007	$39.563
Employees	NA	Stock Exchange	OTC
Auditor	KPMG & Associados, Sroc, S.A	Ticker Symbol	ESFHF
Stk Agt	NA	Outstanding Shares	NA
Counsel	NA,	E.P.S.	NA
DUNS No.	40-042-1418	Shareholders	NA

Business: The group's principle activity is to provides a global and diversified range of financial products to its clients, including commercial banking, insurance, merchant banking, brokerage and asset management, both in Portugal and internationally.

Primary SIC and add'l.: 6321 6211 6021

CIK No: 0000906522

Subsidiaries: Advancecare Gesto de Servios de Sade, SA, Banco Esprito Santo de Angola, SARL, Banco Esprito Santo de Investimento, SA, Banco Esprito Santo do Oriente, SA, Banco Esprito Santo dos Aores, SA, Banco Esprito Santo North American Capital Corp., Banco Esprito Santo, SA, Banco Esprito Santo, SA (Spanish subsidiary), Banco Internacional de Crdito, SA, Bank Esprito Santo International Ltd, Banque Esprito Santo et de la Vntie, SA, BES Finance Ltd., BES Investimento Brasil SA, BES Overseas Ltd., BES Securities SA 103 Subsidiaries included in the Index

Officers: Jim Prout/MD, Teresa De Souza/Company Sec., Erich Dahler/Sr. VP

Directors: Ricardo Espirito Santo Silva Salgado/Chmn., Jose Pedro Torres Garcia Caldeira Da Silva/Dir., Manuel Antonio Ribeiro Serzelo De Almeida/Dir., Pedro Guilherme Beauvillain De Brito E Cunha/Dir., Carlos Augusto Machado De Almeida Freitas/Dir., Patrick Monteiro De Barros/Dir., Anibal Da Costa Reis Oliveira/Dir., Mario Mosqueira Do Amaral/Dir., Othman Benjelloun/Dir., Jackson Behr Gilbert/Dir., Yves Alain Marie Morvan/Dir., Alexandre Da Paixao Coelho/Dir., Fernando Pedro Braga Pereira Coutinho/Dir., Horacio Lisboa Afonso/Dir., Juan Villalonga Navarro/Dir. (23 Directors included in Index)

Financial Data: Fiscal Year End: 12/31 **Latest Annual Data:** 12/31/2004

Year	Sales	Net Income
2004	$5,490,346,000	$52,529,000
2003	$4,968,177,000	$61,278,000
2002	$3,506,983,000	-$284,613,000

Curr. Assets:	$11,437,356,000	**Curr. Liab.:**	$36,511,480,000		
Plant, Equip.:	$510,695,000	**Total Liab.:**	$68,446,900,000	**Indic. Yr. Divd.:**	NA
Total Assets:	$69,086,121,000	**Net Worth:**	$639,221,000	**Debt/ Equity:**	NA

ESS Technology Inc

48401 Fremont Blvd., Fremont, CA, 94538; **PH:** 1-510-492-1088; **Fax:** 1-510-492-1098; *http://* www.esstech.com

General - Incorporation	CA	**Stock** - Price on:12/24/2007	$1.52
Employees	260	Stock Exchange	NDQ
Auditor	PricewaterhouseCoopers LLP	Ticker Symbol	ESST
Stk Agt	Mellon Investor Services LLC	Outstanding Shares	35,530,000
Counsel	Orrick, Herrington & Sutcliffe LLP	E.P.S.	-$0.18
DUNS No.	03-885-4584	Shareholders	NA

Business: The group's principal activity is to design, develop, support, manufacture and market highly integrated digital system processor chips. The product line includes DVD chips, video CD chips, communication chips and PC audio chips. Dvd chips can be used to play DVD, CD and other audio and video formats through the home entertainment system. Video CD products consist of both the standard vcd chips and the enhanced version known as svcd chips. Communication products enable PC manufacturers to provide fax, modem, network capabilities to add-on cards and directly to the motherboards of desktops. Pc audio chips enable PC manufacturers to provide audio capabilities on add-in sound cards and directly to the motherboards of desktop and notebook computers. The group sells its products to distributors and original equipment manufacturers. On 09-Jun-2003, it acquired pictos technologies inc and on 18-Aug-2003, it acquired divio inc.

Primary SIC and add'l.: 7373 3674

CIK No: 0000907410

Subsidiaries: Divio, Inc, ESS (Far East) Ltd., ESS British Columbia Holdings, Inc(formerly known as Silicon Analog Systems Corporation), ESS Electronics Technology (Shenzhen) Co., Ltd., ESS KK, ESS Technology Holdings, Inc, ESS Technology International (Korea) Ltd., ESS Technology International, Inc, Pictos Technologies, Inc, Zing Network, Inc, Zing Networks Ltd. (formerly known as Pix.com, Ltd.)

Officers: Robert L. Blair/CEO, Pres., James B. Boyd/CFO

Owners: Bruce J. Alexander, Gary L. Fischer, Insiders/15.30%, Peter T. Mok, Robert L. Blair/2.60%, Annie M.H. Chan/12.10%, Dimensional FundAdvisors, Inc./5.70%, James B. Boyd/0.60%, Alfred Stein, Renaissance Technologies Corp./6.10%

Financial Data: Fiscal Year End: 12/31 **Latest Annual Data:** 12/31/2006

Year	Sales	Net Income
2006	$100,465,000	-$44,094,000
2005	$181,921,000	-$99,553,000
2004	$257,278,000	-$35,550,000

Curr. Assets:	$64,380,000	**Curr. Liab.:**	$43,405,000		
Plant, Equip.:	$16,996,000	**Total Liab.:**	$43,405,000	**Indic. Yr. Divd.:**	NA
Total Assets:	$90,428,000	**Net Worth:**	$47,023,000	**Debt/ Equity:**	NA

Essential Group Inc

1325 Tri-State Pkwy., Ste. 300, Gurnee, IL, 60031; **PH:** 1-847-855-7676; **Fax:** 1-847-855-9676; *http://* www.essentialgroupinc.com; **Email:** sales@essentialgroupinc.com

General - Incorporation	DE	**Stock** - Price on:12/24/2007	NA
Employees	NA	Stock Exchange	NA
Auditor	Grant Thornton LLP	Ticker Symbol	NA
Stk Agt	NA	Outstanding Shares	NA
Counsel	NA	E.P.S.	NA
DUNS No.	NA	Shareholders	NA

Business: The group's principal activity is to facilitate and coordinate independent clinical research trials on drugs for pharmaceutical, biotechnology, nutritional and device companies and contract research organizations. It performs various services for the site through central office or management service company including patient recruitment, source documentation, regulatory services, quality assurance and other consultation services. The group provides study management services to sponsors of clinical research, experienced investigators, study coordinators, patients and centralized management of clinical research studies. As on 30-Jun-2004, it offered clinical research services through 110 independently owned investigative sites encompassing approximately 300 principal investigators, with over 1,000 total physicians, operating in 32 states in the United States and the district of columbia.

Primary SIC and add'l.: 8731 2834

CIK No: 0001088000

Subsidiaries: AmericasDoctor.com Coordinator Services, Inc(Delaware)

Officers: Lee C. Jones/Dir., CEO, Pres., Dennis N. Cavender/Dir., CFO, Exec. VP, Julie A. Ross/Exec. VP

Directors: Lee C. Jones/Dir., CEO, Pres., Joan Neuscheler/Dir., Dennis N. Cavender/Dir., CFO, Exec. VP, Bruce Wesson/Dir., Sam B. Nickerson/Dir.

Owners: Tullis-Dickerson Capital Focus II, L.P, Lee C. Jones, Jane Taylor, Tullis-Dickerson Capital Focus II, L.P, Geoffrey T. Freeman, Premier Research Worldwide Ltd., Delphi Ventures, Julie A. Ross, Delphi Ventures, Insiders, Geoffrey T. Freeman, Protostar Equity Partners, L.P., Joan P. Neuscheler, Premier Research Worldwide Ltd., Insiders (29 Owners included in Index)

Essential Innovations Technology Corp

114 W Magnolia St., Ste. 400-142, Bellingham, WA, 98225; **PH:** 1-360-392-3902; **Fax:** 1-360-733-3941; *http://* www.eitechcorp.com; **Email:** info@eitechcorp.com

General - Incorporation	NV	**Stock** - Price on:12/24/2007	$0.052
Employees	30	Stock Exchange	OTC
Auditor	Peterson Sullivan PLLC	Ticker Symbol	ESIV
Stk Agt	NA	Outstanding Shares	31,860,000
Counsel	NA	E.P.S.	-$0.19
DUNS No.	NA	Shareholders	NA

Business: The groups principle activities include manufacturing and distributing Geoexchange systems. The group operates through two segments namely manufacturing and geo exchange design and installation. In the year 2006, the group acquired Pacific Geo Exchange Inc. The group operates from the United States.

Primary SIC and add'l.: 3443

CIK No: 0001250897

Subsidiaries: Earth Source Energy Inc., Essential Innovations Asia Ltd., Essential Innovations Corp., Pacfic Geoexchange Inc.

Officers: Jason McDiarmid/Dir., CEO, Pres., Kenneth G.C. Telford/Dir., CFO, Sec., Treasurer, Steve Wuschke/Dir., CTO, Peter Bond/Dir., COO

Directors: Jason McDiarmid/Dir., CEO, Pres., Kenneth G.C. Telford/Dir., CFO, Sec., Treasurer, Steve Wuschke/Dir., CTO, Peter Bond/Dir., COO, Salvador Diaz-Verson/Dir., James Paterson/Member - Advisory Board, William Yang/Member - Advisory Board, Diana M. Allen/Member - Advisory Board, William W. Carr/Member - Advisory Board, Russell White/Member - Advisory Board

Owners: Kenneth G.C. Telford/10.90%, Ecogenics Limited/6.30%, Peter Bond/9.90%, Insiders/43.40%, Jason McDiarmid/12.70%, Steve Wuschke/10.10%, Morpheus Financial Corp./5.80%, Laurus Master Fund/8.40%, Stevan Perry/9.40%, Salvador Diaz-Verson/1.30%

Financial Data: Fiscal Year End: 10/31 **Latest Annual Data:** 10/31/2006

Year	Sales	Net Income
2006	$2,335,000	-$7,689,000
2005	$227,000	-$2,608,000
2004	NA	-$2,089,000

Curr. Assets:	$1,241,000	**Curr. Liab.:**	$2,760,000		
Plant, Equip.:	$164,000	**Total Liab.:**	$3,531,000	**Indic. Yr. Divd.:**	NA
Total Assets:	$3,957,000	**Net Worth:**	$426,000	**Debt/ Equity:**	NA

Essex Corp

6708 Alexander Bell Dr., Columbia, MD, 21046; **PH:** 1-301-939-7000; *http://* www.essexcorp.com

General - Incorporation	VA	**Stock** - Price on:12/24/2007	NA
Employees	761	Stock Exchange	NA
Auditor	Stegman & Co	Ticker Symbol	NA
Stk Agt	Registrar & Transfer Co	Outstanding Shares	NA
Counsel	NA	E.P.S.	NA
DUNS No.	05-736-3939	Shareholders	NA

Business: The group's principal activities are to develop and commercialize optoelectronic devices for industry and government. The group provides optoelectronic and signal processing expertise to government customers under classified advanced and next generation research and development (r&d) contracts, supports the intelligence community mission critical voice and video systems infrastructure, and provides classified systems engineering to government customers. The group also builds optical communications and networking system elements and components. On 01-Mar-2003, the group acquired sensys development laboratories inc. In 2004, the group acquired computer science innovations and performance group inc.

Primary SIC and add'l.: 7371 3669 8711

CIK No: 0000355199

Subsidiaries: Computer Science Innovations, Inc., The Windermere Group, LLC

Essex Property Trust Inc

925 E Meadow Dr., Palo Alto, CA, 94303; *PH:* 1-650-494-3700; *Fax:* 1-650-494-8743; *http://* www.essexproperties.com; *Email:* investors@essexpropertytrust.com

General - Incorporation: MD; Employees: NA; Auditor: KPMG LLP; Stk Agt: Computershare Investor Services LLC; Counsel: NA; DUNS No.: NA

Stock - Price on:12/24/2007: $120.14; Stock Exchange: NYSE; Ticker Symbol: ESS; Outstanding Shares: 24,420,000; E.P.S: $2.84; Shareholders: NA

Business: The groups principle activities include owning, managing, acquiring, developing and redeveloping of real estate. In the year 2006, the group acquired two apartment communities, Belmont Terrace, Camino Ruix Square and Hillsdale Garden. The group operates from the United States. The groups quarterly revenue for September 2007 was 101.25 millions of USD.

Primary SIC and add'l.: 6798

CIK No: 0000920522

Subsidiaries: ESG Property I LLC, Essex Alamo, LLC, Essex Alderwood Park Apartments, L.P., Essex Anaheim, LLC, Essex Apartment Value Fund II, L.P., Essex Apartment Value Fund L.P., Essex Bluffs, L.P., Essex Bridle Trails, L.P., Essex Brighton Ridge, L.P., Essex Broadway, LLC, Essex Bunker Hill Corporation, Essex Bunker Hill, L.P., Essex CAL-WA, L.P., Essex Camarillo Corporation, Essex Camarillo L.P. 131 Subsidiaries included in the Index

Officers: Keith R. Guericke/Vice Chmn., CEO, Pres./$1,335,716.00, Michael J. Schall/Dir., Sr. Exec. VP, COO/$1,132,034.00, Jamie Williams/VP - Information Technology, Lisa Burton/Dir. - Finance, Les Filler/VP - Development, Redevelopment Accounting, Michael T. Dance/CFO, Exec. VP/$557,663.00, John D. Eudy/Exec. VP - Development/$785,591.00, Craig K. Zimmerman/Exec. VP - Acquisitions/$760,308.00, John F. Burkart/Sr. VP, Fund Mgr. - Essex Apartment Value Fund, Mark J. Mikl/Sr. VP - Asset Management, Jordan E. Ritter/Sr. VP, General Counsel, Michael J. Vanderley/Sr. VP - Structured Finance, Erik J. Alexander/First VP, Division Mgr. - Southern California, Gerald E. Kelly/First VP - Research, Due Diligence, Bruce Knoblock/First VP - Development *(22 Officers included in Index)*

Directors: Keith R. Guericke/Vice Chmn., CEO, Pres., George M. Marcus/Chmn., William A. Millichap/Dir., Michael J. Schall/Dir., Sr. Exec. VP, COO, David W. Brady/Dir., Robert E. Larson/Dir., Gary P. Martin/Dir., Issie N. Rabinovitch/Dir., Thomas E. Randlett/Dir., Willard H. Smith/Dir.

Owners: Michael T. Dance, Insiders/9.40%, Michael J. Schall, Morgan Stanley/9.40%, RREEF America, L.L.C./7.90%, Vanguard Group, Inc./6.30%, Willard H. Smith, AMVESCAP, PLC/6.70%, Barclays Global Investors, NA/5.70%, George M. Marcus/7.10%, David W. Brady, Robert E. Larson, Cohen & Steers, Inc./7.30%, John D. Eudy, Keith R. Guericke *(21 Owners included in Index)*

Financial Data: Fiscal Year End:12/31 Latest Annual Data: 12/31/2006

Year	Sales	Net Income
2006	$348,074,000	$62,748,000
2005	$327,291,000	$79,716,000
2004	$283,483,000	$79,693,000

Curr. Assets:	$23,610,000	Curr. Liab.:	$63,524,000	P/E Ratio:	18.92
Plant, Equip.:	$2,348,880,000	Total Liab.:	$1,873,631,000	Indic. Yr. Divd.:	$3.720
Total Assets:	$2,485,840,000	Net Worth:	$612,209,000	Debt/ Equity:	NA

Estee Lauder Cos Inc

767 5th Ave., New York, NY, 10153; *PH:* 1-212-572-4200; *Fax:* 1-212-572-3941; *http://* www.elcompanies.com; *Email:* asampogn@estee.com

General - Incorporation: DE; Employees: 26,200; Auditor: KPMG LLP; Stk Agt: Mellon Investor Services LLC; Counsel: NA; DUNS No.: 00-591-4387

Stock - Price on:12/24/2007: $45.9; Stock Exchange: NYSE; Ticker Symbol: EL; Outstanding Shares: 193,410,000; E.P.S: $2.11; Shareholders: NA

Business: The groups principle activities include manufacturing, marketing and selling skin care, makeup, fragrance and hair care products. The group's products include moisturizers, lotions, sunscreens and self-tanning products. The group operates from United States.

Primary SIC and add'l.: 2844 6794

CIK No: 0001001250

Subsidiaries: Aramis Inc., Clinique Laboratories, LLC, ELCA Cosmeticos LDA, Estee Lauder Cosmetics Limited, Estee Lauder Europe, Inc., Estee Lauder Inc., Estee Lauder International, Inc., Estee Lauder Nova Scotia Co.

Officers: William P. Lauder/Dir., CEO, Pres., Evelyn H. Lauder/Sr. Corporate VP, Amy Digeso/Exec. VP - Human Resources, Sara E. Moss/Exec. VP, General Counsel, Sec., Cedric Prouve/Group Pres. - International, Patrick Bousquet-Chavanne/Group Pres., Philip Shearer/Group Pres., Sally Susman/Exec. VP - Global Communications, Malcolm Bond/Exec. VP - Global Operations, Daniel J. Brestle/COO, Jennifer Mann/Contact - Corporate Global Communications, Janet Bartucci/Contact - Corporate Global Communications, Melissa Bedolis Cattanach/Contact - Corporate Global Communications, Adair Sampogna/Contact - Global Consumer Communications, Spencer G. Smul/VP, Deputy General Counsel, Sec. *(17 Officers included in Index)*

Directors: William P. Lauder/Dir., CEO, Pres., Leonard A. Lauder/Chmn., Barry S. Sternlicht/46/Dir., Ronald S. Lauder/63/Dir., Paul Fribourg/Dir., Irvine O. Hockaday/70/Dir., Charlene Barshefsky/56/Dir., Rose Marie Bravo/55/Dir., Aerin Lauder/37/Dir., Richard D. Parsons/59/Dir., Mellody Hobson/37/Dir., Lynn Forester De Rothschild/53/Dir.

Owners: Richard D. Parsons, individually and as trustee, Insiders, Mellody Hobson, Philip Shearer/0.20%, Daniel J. Brestle/0.60%, Irvine O. Hockaday, Leonard A. Lauder/8.80%, Charlene Barshefsky, Lynn Forester de Rothschild, Paul J. Fribourg, Richard D. Parsons, individually and as trustee, Ira T. Wender, as trustee, Barry S. Sternlicht/0.10%, Gary M. Lauder, Leonard A. Lauder *(30 Owners included in Index)*

Financial Data: Fiscal Year End:06/30 Latest Annual Data: 06/30/2007

Year	Sales	Net Income
2007	$7,037,500,000	$449,200,000
2006	$6,463,800,000	$244,200,000
2005	$6,336,300,000	$406,100,000

Curr. Assets:	$2,176,900,000	Curr. Liab.:	$1,438,200,000	P/E Ratio:	21.25
Plant, Equip.:	$758,000,000	Total Liab.:	$2,136,400,000	Indic. Yr. Divd.:	$0.500
Total Assets:	$3,784,100,000	Net Worth:	$1,622,300,000	Debt/ Equity:	0.9700

Esterline Technologies Corp

City Ctr. Bellevue, 500 108th Ave. NE, Ste. 1500, Bellevue, WA, 98004; *PH:* 1-425-453-9400; *Fax:* 1-425-453-2916; *http://* www.esterline.com; *Email:* info@esterline.com

General - Incorporation: DE; Employees: 8,150; Auditor: Ernst & Young LLP; Stk Agt: Mellon Investor Services LLC; Counsel: NA; DUNS No.: 04-319-0826

Stock - Price on:12/24/2007: $48.4; Stock Exchange: NYSE; Ticker Symbol: ESL; Outstanding Shares: 25,630,000; E.P.S: $3.52; Shareholders: NA

Business: The group's principal activities are to design, manufacture and market highly engineered products and systems for applications in aerospace, defense and electronic equipment manufacturing industries. Avionics and controls focuses on technology interface systems for commercial and military aircraft and similar devices for military vehicles, secure communications systems and other industrial applications. Sensors and systems develop and manufacture sensors and controls. Advanced materials focuses on process related technology including high-performance elastomer products used in commercial aerospace and military applications. In addition the group manufactures molded fiber cartridge cases, igniter tubes and other combustible ammunition components. On 11-Jun-2003, it acquired the weston group, on 1-Dec-2003, acquired avista, incorporated and on 30-Aug-2004, acquired leach holding corporation.

Primary SIC and add'l.: 3679 3647 3829

CIK No: 0000033619

Subsidiaries: Advanced Input Devices (UK) Ltd., Advanced Input Devices, Inc., Armtec Countermeasures Co., Armtec Defense Products Co., Auxitrol Co., Auxitrol S.A., Auxitrol Technologies S.A., AVISTA Incorporated, BVR Technologies Co., Esterline Input Devices (Shanghai) Ltd., Hytek Finishes Co., Kirkhill - TA Co., Korry Electronics Co., Leach International Corporation, Leach International Europe S.A. 23 Subsidiaries included in the Index

Officers: Robert W. Cremin/Chmn., CEO, Pres., Frank Houston/Group VP, Marcia J.M. Greenberg/VP - Human Resources, Larry A. Kring/Group VP, Richard Wood/Group VP, Robert D. George/VP, CFO, Sec., Treasurer, Stephen R. Larson/VP - Strategy, Technology, Brian D. Keogh/Dir. - Corporate Communications, Gary Posner/Corporate Controlle, Chief Accounting Officer, Brad Lawrence/Group VP

Directors: Robert W. Cremin/Chmn., CEO, Pres., Robert S. Cline/Dir., James L. Pierce/Dir., Lewis E. Burns/Dir., Charles R. Larson/Dir., John F. Clearman/Dir., Anthony P. Franceschini/Dir., Paul V. Haack/Dir., Jerry D. Leitman/Dir.

Owners: Robert W. Cremin/1.30%, Robert D. George, Robert S. Cline, James L. Pierce, Friess Associates LLC/5.00%, John F. Clearman, Dimensional Fund Advisors Inc./7.50%, Anthony P. Franceschini, Lewis E. Burns, Charles R. Larson, M&G Investment Management Limited/10.10%, Insiders/3.10%, Larry A. Kring, Jerry D. Leitman, Stephen R. Larson *(16 Owners included in Index)*

Financial Data: Fiscal Year End:10/28 Latest Annual Data: 10/27/2006

Year	Sales	Net Income
2006	$972,275,000	$55,615,000
2005	$835,403,000	$58,026,000
2004	$628,169,000	$39,583,000

Curr. Assets:	$322,625,000	Curr. Liab.:	$149,591,000	P/E Ratio:	20.17
Plant, Equip.:	$145,135,000	Total Liab.:	$471,942,000	Indic. Yr. Divd.:	NA
Total Assets:	$935,348,000	Net Worth:	$461,028,000	Debt/ Equity:	NA

eTelcharge.com Inc

1636 N Hampton Rd. Ste. 270, Desoto, TX, 75115; *PH:* 1-972-298-3800; *Fax:* 1-972-298-3802; *http://* www.macreport.net; *Email:* info@etelcharge.com

General - Incorporation: NV; Employees: NA; Auditor: Malone & Bailey, PC; Stk Agt: Securities Transfer Corp; Counsel: NA; DUNS No.: NA

Stock - Price on:12/24/2007: NA; Stock Exchange: OTC; Ticker Symbol: ETLC; Outstanding Shares: NA; E.P.S: -$0.012; Shareholders: NA

Business: The groups principal activity is to provide services in the online payment field. Services of the group include providing online customers the option to charge for approved goods or services purchased over the internet directly to their phone bill and receive payment from their consumers including VISA, Master Card, American Express, Discover, Diners Card, Loyalty cards, EBT, Check authorization and guarantee. The group operates from the United States.

Primary SIC and add'l.: 7389

CIK No: 0001112682

Officers: Carl O. Sherman/41/CEO, Rob Howe/CEO, Robyn Priest/CFO, John Todd/Sr. VP - Business Development, Toby Wilson/CTO, Laurinda Johnson/Provisioning Mgr., Michelle Sherman/38/Dir., Sec., Cynthia Demonte/Allegro Business Development, Investor Relations

Directors: Michelle Sherman/38/Dir., Sec., Thomas Jackson/37/Dir.

Owners: Thomas Jackson, Carl O. Sherman/30.80%, Insiders/30.90%, Michelle R. Sherman/30.80%

Financial Data: Fiscal Year End:12/31 Latest Annual Data: 12/31/2006

Year	Sales	Net Income
2006	$35,000	-$440,000
2005	$19,000	-$2,108,000
2004	NA	-$773,000

Curr. Assets:	$2,000	Curr. Liab.:	$867,000		
Plant, Equip.:	$4,000	Total Liab.:	$867,000	Indic. Yr. Divd.:	NA
Total Assets:	$7,000	Net Worth:	-$859,000	Debt/ Equity:	NA

Eternal Energy Corp

2549 W Main St., Ste. 202, Littleton, CO, 80120; *PH:* 1-303-385-1230; *Fax:* 1-303-798-5767; *http://* www.eternalenergy.com; *Email:* ir@eternalenergy.com

General - Incorporation: NV; Employees: 1; Auditor: Kelly & Company; Stk Agt: Holladay Stock Transfer, Inc.; Counsel: NA; DUNS No.: NA

Stock - Price on:12/24/2007: $0.2; Stock Exchange: OTC; Ticker Symbol: EERG; Outstanding Shares: 42,550,000; E.P.S: -$0.11; Shareholders: NA

Business: The groups principal activity is to explore minerals and natural oil. The group acquired Eden Energy Corp. in the year 2005 and Pebble Petroleum, Inc. in the year 2006. The group operates from Canada and the United States.

Primary SIC and add'l.: 1000

CIK No: 0001282613

Officers: Brad Colby/51/Dir., CEO, Pres., Treasurer, CFO, Sec., Craig Phelps/VP - Engineering, Jamie Kelley/Contact

Directors: Brad Colby/51/Dir., CEO, Pres., Treasurer, CFO, Sec., John Anderson/Dir., Paul Rumler/Dir.

Owners: Insiders/9.60%, Dennis Eldjarnson/6.60%, Bradley M. Colby/9.20%, RAB Special Situations (Master) Fund Ltd./7.10%, John Anderson/0.50%

Financial Data: Fiscal Year End:12/31 Latest Annual Data: 12/31/2006

Year	Sales	Net Income
2006	NA	$3,135,000
2005	NA	-$230,000
2004	NA	-$34,000

Curr. Assets:	$2,380,000	Curr. Liab.:	$2,293,000		
Plant, Equip.:	$1,262,000	Total Liab.:	$2,293,000	Indic. Yr. Divd.:	NA
Total Assets:	$6,646,000	Net Worth:	$4,353,000	Debt/ Equity:	NA

Eternal Technologies Group Inc

Ste. D 5/f, Block A, Innotec Tower, 235 Nanjing Rd., Heping District, Tianjin, 300052; PH: 86-2227217020; http:// www.eternaltechs.com

General - Incorporation	NV	Stock- Price on:12/24/2007	$0.615
Employees	NA	Stock Exchange	OTC
Auditor	Ham, Langston & Brezina LLP	Ticker Symbol	NA
Stk Agt	OTC Stock Transfer, Inc.	Outstanding Shares	NA
Counsel	NA	E.P.S.	$0.36
DUNS No.	NA	Shareholders	NA

Business: The group's principal activity is to market technologies based on animal genetics and gene engineering, through its acquisition of eternal technology group. The group is an agricultural genetics and bio-pharmaceutical company operating in China and focused on the development and application of advanced animal husbandry and pharmaceutical techniques to produce improved and novel food and pharmaceutical products. In the fourth quarter of 2003, expanded our embryo transfer and breeding services to include, in addition to sheep, high-yielding pure-bread dairy cattle and also commenced the production and sale of mutton.

Primary SIC and add'l.: 8731 0214 0139

CIK No: 0001096662

Subsidiaries: British Virgin Islands company, E-Sea Biomedical Engineering Co. International Ltd, Eternal Technology Group Ltd

Officers: Jijun Wu/Chmn., Pres., Jiansheng Wei/Dir., COO, Rui Zhai/40/Sec., Zheng Shen/CFO

Directors: Jijun Wu/Chmn., Pres., Xingjian Ma/Dir., Jiansheng Wei/Dir., COO, Genchang Li/Dir., Shien Zhu/Dir., Shicheng Fu/Dir., Yuguo Chang/40/Dir., Mika Zhang/33/Dir.

Owners: Mike Zhang, Zheng Shen, Insiders/6.54%, Jijun Wu/3.78%, Zhai Rui, Jiansheng Wei/1.45%, Shien Zhu, Shicheng Fu, Yugo Cheng, Genchang Li

Financial Data: Fiscal Year End:12/31 Latest Annual Data: 12/31/2006

Year	Sales	Net Income
2006	$28,718,000	$4,882,000
2005	$23,033,000	$4,051,000
2004	$16,835,000	$4,233,000

Curr. Assets:	$43,724,000	Curr. Liab.:	$1,860,000		
Plant, Equip.:	$6,882,000	Total Liab.:	$1,860,000	Indic. Yr. Divd.:	$0.210
Total Assets:	$58,066,000	Net Worth:	$56,206,000	Debt/ Equity:	NA

Ethan Allen Interiors Inc

Ethan Allen Dr., Danbury, CT, 06813; PH: 1-203-743-8000; http:// www.ethanallen.com; Email: accents@ethanalleninc.com

General - Incorporation	DE	Stock - Price on:12/24/2007	$35.18
Employees	6,400	Stock Exchange	NYSE
Auditor	KPMG LLP	Ticker Symbol	ETH
Stk Agt	Computershare Investor Services LLC	Outstanding Shares	31,290,000
Counsel	NA	E.P.S.	$2.47
DUNS No.	00-121-3545	Shareholders	NA

Business: The group's principal activity is to manufacture and provide wholesale and retail distribution of home furnishings. It operates in two business segments: wholesale and retail. The wholesale segment manufactures, markets and distributes home furnishing product to a network of independently-owned and group-owned stores. The retail segment markets home furnishing products through a network of group-owned stores to consumers. Home furnishing product lines consist of case goods, upholstered products and home accessories and other. Case goods include bedroom and dining room furniture, wall units and tables. Upholstered products consist of sofas, loveseats, chairs and recliners. Home accessories and other products include carpeting and area rugs, lighting, clocks, wall decor, bedding ensembles, draperies, decorative accessories, home and garden furnishings.

Primary SIC and add'l.: 5719 5712 2512 5021

CIK No: 0000896156

Subsidiaries: Ethan Allen Global, Inc.

Officers: M. F. Kathwari/Chmn., CEO, Pres., Farooq E. Kathwari/60/Chmn., CEO, Pres., Margaret W. Lupton/Dir. - Investor Relations, Assist. Sec., Corey Whitely/VP - Operations, Kenneth Musante/Manufacturing Controller, Peggy McLinden/VP - Store Planning, Max A. Sneed/VP - Southeast Case Goods Manufacturing, Nora Murphy/VP - Style, Paula Mandeville/Dir. - Retail Services, Pamela A. Banks/VP, General Counsel, Sec., Craig Stout/VP - Design, Product Development, Ann M. Zaccaria/VP - Business Development, Kelly A. Bean/VP - Advertising, Don Garrett/VP, GM - Case Goods Manufacturing, Jack Dekorne/VP - Retailer Relations *(24 Officers included in Index)*

Directors: M. F. Kathwari/Chmn., CEO, Pres., Farooq E. Kathwari/60/Chmn., CEO, Pres., Clinton A. Clark/62/Dir., Richard A. Sandberg/62/Dir., Horace G. McDonell/75/Dir., Margaret W. Lupton/Dir. - Investor Relations, Assist. Sec., Kristin Gamble/59/Dir., Edward H. Meyer/77/Dir., Frank G. Wisner/66/Dir.

Owners: Kristin Gamble, Corey Whitely, Frank G. Wisner, Lord, Abbett & Co., LLC/8.72%, Insiders/13.62%, Farooq M. Kathwari/12.83%, Nora Murphy, Edward Teplitz, Horace G. McDonell, Richard A. Sandberg, AMVESCAP PLC/8.77%, FMR Corp./10.79%, Clinton A. Clark, Royce & Associates, LLC/10.70%, Jeffrey Hoyt *(18 Owners included in Index)*

Financial Data: Fiscal Year End:06/30 Latest Annual Data: 06/30/2007

Year	Sales	Net Income
2007	$1,005,312,000	$69,227,000
2006	$1,066,390,000	$85,682,000
2005	$949,012,000	$79,338,000

Curr. Assets:	$423,756,000	Curr. Liab.:	$145,718,000	P/E Ratio:	16.36
Plant, Equip.:	$294,170,000	Total Liab.:	$394,799,000	Indic. Yr. Divd.:	$0.800
Total Assets:	$812,241,000	Net Worth:	$417,442,000	Debt/ Equity:	0.4932

Ethanex Energy Inc

14500 Parallel Rd. Ste. A, Basehor, KS, 66007; PH: 1-913-724-4106; Fax: 1-913-721-5801; http:// www.ethanexenergy.com; Email: info@ethanexenergy.com

General - Incorporation	NV	Stock- Price on:12/24/2007	$0.66
Employees	11	Stock Exchange	OTC
Auditor	Bagell, Levine & Company, LLC	Ticker Symbol	EHNX
Stk Agt	Island Stock Transfer	Outstanding Shares	82,740,000
Counsel	NA	E.P.S.	-$0.302
DUNS No.	NA	Shareholders	NA

Business: The groups principal activity is to produce fuel ethanol through the ownership and operation of ethanol plants. In the year 2006, the group acquired Ethanex Energy North America. The group operates from and the United States.

Primary SIC and add'l.: 2869

CIK No: 0001343611

Subsidiaries: Ethanex Energy North America, Inc., Ethanex Southern Illinois, LLC, IPT Ethanol, Inc.

Officers: Albert W. Knapp/Dir., CEO, Pres., Robert C. Walther/Executive Chmn., Randall L. Rahm/Dir., Co - COO, Bryan Sherbacow/Dir., Co - COO, David McKittrick/CFO, Exec. VP, Alan H. Belcher/Exec. VP - Technology, Leslie Turner/Investor Relation Officer

Directors: Albert W. Knapp/Dir., CEO, Pres., Robert C. Walther/Executive Chmn., Randall L. Rahm/Dir., Co - COO, Bryan Sherbacow/Dir., Co - COO, Johnny F. Norris/Dir., Thomas Kraemer/Dir., William A. Nitze/Dir., Robert E. Dowling/Dir.

Owners: Bryan J. Sherbacow/9.38%, Insiders/39.22%, WellingtonTrust Company, NA/6.80%, Wellington Management Company, LLP/21.87%, Randall L. Rahm/9.38%, Albert W. Knapp/9.38%, Robert C. Walther/9.38%

Financial Data: Fiscal Year End:12/31 Latest Annual Data: 12/31/2006

Year	Sales	Net Income
2006	NA	-$6,564,000

Curr. Assets:	$12,978,000	Curr. Liab.:	$1,066,000	P/E Ratio:	2.70
Plant, Equip.:	$1,201,000	Total Liab.:	$1,598,000	Indic. Yr. Divd.:	NA
Total Assets:	$17,911,000	Net Worth:	$16,313,000	Debt/ Equity:	NA

Ethos Environmental Inc

Formerly: Victor Industries Inc
6800 Gateway Pk. Dr., San Diego, CA, 92154; PH: 1-619-575-6800; http:// www.victorindustries.com

General - Incorporation	ID	Stock- Price on:12/24/2007	$2.4
Employees	25	Stock Exchange	NA
Auditor	Peterson Sullivan PLLC	Ticker Symbol	NA
Stk Agt	Action Stock Transfer Corp	Outstanding Shares	23,810,000
Counsel	NA	E.P.S.	-$2.84
DUNS No.	NA	Shareholders	NA

Business: The group's principal activities are the sale and distribution of zeolite products. The group extracts zeolite by utilizing independent contractors at a property in owhyee county, Idaho. The private contractors do the milling, manufacturing and packaging. The group markets the packaged and bulk ordered zeolite through distributors and under distributor's private labels. Zeolite is ammonia absorbent, air purifier, hazardous waste absorbent and a negatively charged mineral. The proprietary compound solutions are marketed to the golf course and horticulture industries. Zeolites are useful for metal and toxic chemical absorbents, water softeners, gas absorbents, radiation absorbents and soil and fertilizer amendments. The group acquired new wave media inc in 2003. The group holds four mining claims, two of which are located in pershing county, Nevada. The group discontinued radio station operations in 2003.

Primary SIC and add'l.: 1099

CIK No: 0001056598

Subsidiaries: New Wave Media

Officers: Enrique De Vilmorin/56/Dir., CEO, Pres., Thomas W. Maher/CFO

Directors: Enrique De Vilmorin/56/Dir., CEO, Pres., Jose Manuel Escobedo/67/Dir., Luis Willars/Dir.

Owners: Jose Manuel Escobedo/1.08%, Enrique de Vilmorin/45.44%, Insiders/46.52%

Financial Data: Fiscal Year End:12/31 Latest Annual Data: 09/30/2007

Year	Sales	Net Income
2007	$2,299,000	-$898,000
2006	$4,768,000	-$6,490,000
2005	$4,000	-$654,000

Curr. Assets:	$1,123,000	Curr. Liab.:	$5,823,000		
Plant, Equip.:	$6,391,000	Total Liab.:	$5,823,000	Indic. Yr. Divd.:	NA
Total Assets:	$7,519,000	Net Worth:	$1,696,000	Debt/ Equity:	NA

Etotalsource Inc

1510 Poole Blvd., Yuba City, CA, 95993; PH: 1-530-759-6615; Fax: 1-530-674-4624; http:// www.etotalsource.com; Email: info@etotalsource.com

General - Incorporation	CO	Stock- Price on:12/24/2007	NA
Employees	3	Stock Exchange	OTC
Auditor	Gordon Hughes & Banks LLP	Ticker Symbol	ETLS
Stk Agt	Executive Registrar & Transfer, Inc.	Outstanding Shares	NA
Counsel	NA	E.P.S.	-$0.006
DUNS No.	NA	Shareholders	NA

Business: The group's principal activity is to develop and supply proprietary multimedia software technology. It also publishes multimedia training content. The products of the group include presenta pro (TM) which is used in back-end development of multi-panel time synchronized presentations and course work, as well as testing, feedback and performance monitoring. The customers of the group include U.S. Department of defense, boeing, steven spielberg online film school, pacific bell/sbc, grant school district, California state university, logistics management institute and first American title company.

Primary SIC and add'l.: 8243 7372

CIK No: 0000822998

Officers: Frank J. Orlando/Dir., Principal Executive Officer, CFO

Directors: David Marks/Dir., Frank J. Orlando/Dir., Principal Executive Officer, CFO

Owners: Fred Berens/3.00%, Joel B. Ronkin, Ronald L. Rolleston, William M. Tatham, M&G Investment Funds 1/5.10%, Jacobus A. J. Steffens, Insiders/20.50%, Richard C. W. Mauran/6.30%, Wells Fargo & Company/6.40%, Goldman Sachs Asset Management, L.P./5.20%, Stephen J. Smith, Paul F. West/1.30%, Scott E. Beattie/6.20%, Nevil J.W. Thomas

Financial Data: Fiscal Year End:12/31 Latest Annual Data: 12/31/2006

Year	Sales	Net Income
2006	$26,000	-$945,000
2005	$55,000	-$1,285,000
2004	$209,000	-$2,373,000

Curr. Assets:	$1,000	Curr. Liab.:	$3,344,000		
Plant, Equip.:	NA	Total Liab.:	$4,106,000	Indic. Yr. Divd.:	NA
Total Assets:	$1,000	Net Worth:	-$4,105,000	Debt/ Equity:	NA

Etrials Worldwide Inc

4000 Aerial Ctr. Pkwy., Morrisville, NC, 27560; *PH:* 1-919-653-3400; *Fax:* 1-919-653-3620; *http://* www.etrials.com

General - Incorporation	DE	Stock - Price on:12/24/2007	$4.49
Employees	124	Stock Exchange	NDQ
Auditor	BDO Seidman, LLP	Ticker Symbol	ETWC
Stk Agt	NA	Outstanding Shares	12,300,000
Counsel	NA	E.P.S.	-$0.05
DUNS No.	NA	Shareholders	NA

Business: The groups principle activity is to provide eClinical software technology and services. Customers served by the group include pharmaceutical, biotechnology, medical device, and contract research organizations. In February 9, 2006 the group merged with etrials Acquisition, Inc. Specific customers of the group include Wyeth, The Medicines Company, Genzyme Corporation and Pfizer, Inc. The group operates from the United States and the United Kingdom.

Primary SIC and add'l.: 7372 7372

CIK No: 0001268904

Subsidiaries: Etrials Inc

Officers: John Cline/Dir., CEO, Pres., James W. Clark/CFO, David Levin/38/VP - Marketing, Michael Harte/Sr. VP - Global Sales, Marketing, Mark Jewett/42/VP - Finance, Chief Accounting Officer, Robert Sammis/VP - Client Services, Richard Piazza/VP - Research, Development, Arthur D. Campbell/47/Dir. - Information Technology, Global Services, Chip Jennings/Sr. Corporate VP, Peter Benton/Interim COO, Art Campbell/CIO, VP, Marc K. Leighton/VP - Human Resources, Chuck Piccirillo/VP - Product Development

Directors: John Cline/Dir., CEO, Pres., Hans Lindroth/Chmn., Peter Coker/Dir., Robert Brill/Dir., Donald Russell/Dir., Peter Collins/Dir., Harold D. Ewen/Dir., Kenneth Jennings/53/Dir., Eugene Jennings/55/Dir.

Owners: Fred F. Nazem, Richard Piazza, John Cline, MiniDoc AB, Kenneth Jennings, Michael Harte, Robert Moreyra, Hans Lindroth, Insiders, Eugene Jennings, Robert Sammis, Peninsular Capital Management, L.P., Donald Russell, Robert Brill, Peter Collins (22 Owners included in Index)

Financial Data: Fiscal Year End:12/31 Latest Annual Data: 12/31/2006

Year	Sales	Net Income
2006	$19,180,000	-$641,000
2005	NA	$196,000
2004	NA	-$182,000

Curr. Assets:	$25,378,000	Curr. Liab.:	$5,515,000		
Plant, Equip.:	$1,857,000	Total Liab.:	$5,582,000	Indic. Yr. Divd.:	NA
Total Assets:	$35,378,000	Net Worth:	$29,796,000	Debt/ Equity:	0.0015

eTwine Holdings Inc

366 N Broadway Ste. 41042, Jericho, NY, 11753; *PH:* 1-516-942-2030; *http://* www.etwine.com; *Email:* info@etwine.com

General - Incorporation		Stock - Price on:12/24/2007	$0.43
Employees	1	Stock Exchange	NA
Auditor	NA	Ticker Symbol	NA
Stk Agt	NA	Outstanding Shares	9,250,000
Counsel	NA	E.P.S.	-$0.08
DUNS No.	NA	Shareholders	NA

Business: The groups principal activity is to provide the next generation online dating services. The group operates from the United States.

Primary SIC and add'l.: 7299

CIK No: 0001355839

Subsidiaries: Etwine, Inc.

Owners: Insiders/77.70%, Clifford Lerner/77.70%

Financial Data: Fiscal Year End:NA Latest Annual Data: 12/31/2006

Year	Sales	Net Income
2006	$0	-$587,000

Curr. Assets:	$216,000	Curr. Liab.:	$24,000		
Plant, Equip.:	NA	Total Liab.:	$109,000	Indic. Yr. Divd.:	NA
Total Assets:	$237,000	Net Worth:	$128,000	Debt/ Equity:	1.0227

Eugene Science Inc

16-7 Samjung-dong, Ojung-ku, Pucheon, Kyonggi-do; *PH:* 82-326766283; *Fax:* 82-326766373; *http://* www.eugene21.com; *Email:* eugene@eugene21.com

General - Incorporation	DE	Stock- Price on:12/24/2007	$0.46
Employees	NA	Stock Exchange	OTC
Auditor	Russell Bedford Stefanou Mirchandani	Ticker Symbol	EUSI
Stk Agt	Signature Stock Transfer, Inc.	Outstanding Shares	NA
Counsel	NA	E.P.S.	NA
DUNS No.	NA	Shareholders	NA

Business: The groups principle activities include developing, manufacturing and marketing nutraceuticals, or functional foods. Products of the group include CZTM Series of food additives and CholZeroTM beverages and capsules. The specific customer of the group is Amway Korea. The group operates from the United States, Korea and Japan.

Primary SIC and add'l.: 2834

CIK No: 0001107685

Subsidiaries: Eugene Science Korea, Ucole Bio Co., Ltd.

Officers: Seung-Kwon Noh/47/Chmn., CEO, Pres., Tae-Hwan Lee/45/Dir., Sr. VP - Sales, Marketing, Jang Hyun Cho/Chief Reseach Scentist, Chang Gon Kim/Principle Research Scientist, Erika Lee/Principal Research Scientist, Jae Hong Yoo/40/CFO, Se Cheon Ahn/47/Dir., Sr. VP - Plant, Manufacturing

Directors: Seung-Kwon Noh/47/Chmn., CEO, Pres., Tae-Hwan Lee/45/Dir., Sr. VP - Sales, Marketing, Tony Kim/35/Dir., Se Cheon Ahn/47/Dir., Sr. VP - Plant, Manufacturing

Owners: Tony Kim/6.42%, Telos, LLC/6.46%, Se Cheon Ahn, Insiders/34.25%, H&Q Asia Pacific/6.86%, Tae Hwan Lee, Seung Kwon Noh/26.64%

Financial Data: Fiscal Year End:12/31 Latest Annual Data: 12/31/2006

Year	Sales	Net Income
2006	$669,000	-$2,007,000
2005	$886,000	-$6,344,000

Curr. Assets:	$2,501,000	Curr. Liab.:	$16,320,000		
Plant, Equip.:	$1,169,000	Total Liab.:	$17,254,000	Indic. Yr. Divd.:	NA
Total Assets:	$4,275,000	Net Worth:	-$12,979,000	Debt/ Equity:	NA

Euoko Inc

Formerly: Vita Equity Inc
837 W Hastings St., Ste. 314, Vancouver, BC, V6C 3N6; *PH:* 1-604-684-6412

General - Incorporation	NV	Stock- Price on:12/24/2007	NA
Employees	NA	Stock Exchange	NA
Auditor	Weinberg & Company, P.A.	Ticker Symbol	NA
Stk Agt	Holladay Stock Transfer, Inc.	Outstanding Shares	NA
Counsel	NA	E.P.S.	NA
DUNS No.	NA	Shareholders	NA

Business: The groups principle activities include manufacturing custom pieces of jewellery on a piece by piece basis for customers. The group operates from the United States.

Primary SIC and add'l.: 3911

CIK No: 0001125918

Subsidiaries: Vita Equity Inc. (Canada).

Officers: Dwight Webb/57/Chmn., CEO, Pres., Principal Financial Officer, Mauro Baessato/54/Sec., Treasurer

Directors: Dwight Webb/57/Chmn., CEO, Pres., Principal Financial Officer

Owners: Dwight Webb/11.16%, Insiders/11.16%

Financial Data: Fiscal Year End:12/31 Latest Annual Data: 12/31/2006

Year	Sales	Net Income
2006	NA	$1,000
2005	$1,293,000	$45,000

Curr. Assets:	$709,000	Curr. Liab.:	$699,000		
Plant, Equip.:	NA	Total Liab.:	$699,000	Indic. Yr. Divd.:	NA
Total Assets:	$709,000	Net Worth:	$9,000	Debt/ Equity:	NA

EUPA International Corp

2995 El Camino Rd., Las Vegas, NV, 84146; *PH:* 1-702-768-2133

General - Incorporation	NV	Stock- Price on:12/24/2007	NA
Employees	7	Stock Exchange	OTC
Auditor	Lichter, Yu & Assoc.	Ticker Symbol	EUPI
Stk Agt	Stalt, Inc.	Outstanding Shares	NA
Counsel	NA	E.P.S.	NA
DUNS No.	NA	Shareholders	NA

Business: The group's principle activities are to market, research and design home appliances and consumer electronic products manufactured by tsann kuen enterprise co ltd. The group operates in two segments namely sales services and research and development. The sales services segment assists with the product sales of home appliances in the United States. The research and development segment designs and develops products in the home appliance market. The products marketed by the group include coffee makers, electric grills, irons, pop-up toaster, toaster ovens, motor-driven products rice cookers and vacuum cleaners. These products are sold to numerous brand name companies. The group markets these products in the United States through an internal sales force. The products are sold in over 80 countries throughout the world.

Primary SIC and add'l.: 7389 5199 5065

CIK No: 0001084382

Subsidiaries: Tsann Kuen U.S.A., Union Channel Limited

Curr. Assets:	$1,130,000	Curr. Liab.:	$144,000		
Plant, Equip.:	$779,000	Total Liab.:	$148,000	Indic. Yr. Divd.:	NA
Total Assets:	$2,191,000	Net Worth:	$2,043,000	Debt/ Equity:	NA

Euramax International Inc

5445 Triangle Pkwy., Ste. 350, Norcross, GA, 30092; *PH:* 1-770-449-7066; *http://* www.euramax.com

General - Incorporation	DE	Stock- Price on:12/24/2007	NA
Employees	NA	Stock Exchange	NA
Auditor	Ernst & Young LLP	Ticker Symbol	NA
Stk Agt	Wachovia Bank N.A	Outstanding Shares	NA
Counsel	NA	E.P.S.	NA
DUNS No.	NA	Shareholders	NA

Business: The groups principle activities include manufacturing, distributing and contracting aluminum, steel, vinyl, copper and fiberglass products. The group also provides steel roofing, siding and trim for commercial and architectural building construction. The groups core products include coated coils, metal wall and roof systems, metal and vinyl rain carrying systems, fascia systems, roofing accessories, aluminum and vinyl windows and doors, patio products, aluminum recreational vehicle doors, windows and sidewalls, and aluminum bath and shower enclosures. The group operates from United States, North America and Western Europe.

Primary SIC and add'l.: 3442

CIK No: 0001026743

Subsidiaries: Amerimax Building Products,Inc., Amerimax Diversified Products,Inc., Amerimax Fabricated Products,Inc., Amerimax Finance Company,Inc., Amerimax Home Products,Inc., Amerimax Richmond Company,Inc., Amerimax UK,Inc., Berger Bros Company, Berger Holdings, Ltd., Ellbee Limited, Euramax Coated Products B.V., Euramax Coated Products Limited, Euramax Continental Limited, Euramax Europe B.V., Euramax Europe Limited 25 Subsidiaries included in the Index

Owners: Paul E. Drack, David J. Smith, Joseph M. Silvestri, Insiders, Mitchell B. Lewis, Scott R. Vansant, Citigroup Venture Capital Equity Partners, L.P., Stuart M. Wallis, Richard E. Mayberry, Thomas F. McWilliams

Eurasia Energy Ltd

409 Granville St., Ste. 1003, Vancouver, V6C 1T2; **PH:** 1-250-807-2970; **Fax:** 1-604-681-4760; *http://* www.eurasiaenergy.com; **Email:** info@eurasiaenergy.com

General - Incorporation	NV	Stock- Price on:12/24/2007	$0.35
Employees	NA	Stock Exchange	OTC
Auditor	Peterson Sullivan PLLC	Ticker Symbol	EUEN
Stk Agt	Nevada Agency & Trust Company	Outstanding Shares	NA
Counsel	NA	E.P.S.	NA
DUNS No.	NA	Shareholders	NA

Business: The groups principal activity is to design marketing and advertising campaigns for corporate clients to increase awareness of their products, services, corporate image and general corporate branding. The group operates from Phoenix, Arizona in the United States.

Primary SIC and add'l.: 7311

CIK No: 0001278465

Officers: Nicholas W. Baxter/Dir., CEO, Pres., Gerald R. Tuskey/Dir., CFO, Corp. Sec.

Directors: Nicholas W. Baxter/Dir., CEO, Pres., Gerald R. Tuskey/Dir., CFO, Corp. Sec., Roger Thomas/Dir.

Owners: Graham Crabtree/7.20%, Lloyd Blackmore/6.16%, Insiders/21.48%, Roger Thomas/0.61%, CEDE & Co./24.01%, Kevin Bell/6.16%, Nicholas W. Baxter/14.69%, Gerald R. Tuskey/6.17%, Lynwood S. Bell/6.99%

Financial Data: Fiscal Year End:12/31   **Latest Annual Data:** 12/31/2006

Year	Sales	Net Income
2006	NA	-$4,099,000
2005	NA	-$36,000
2004	$34,000	-$18,000

Curr. Assets:	$519,000	Curr. Liab.:	$57,000		
Plant, Equip.:	$66,000	Total Liab.:	$57,000	Indic. Yr. Divd.:	NA
Total Assets:	$585,000	Net Worth:	$528,000	Debt/ Equity:	NA

Eureka Financial Corp

3455 Forbes Ave., Pittsburgh, PA, 15213; **PH:** 1-412-681-8400; **Fax:** 1-412-681-6625; *http://* www.eurekabancorp.com

General - Incorporation		Stock- Price on:12/24/2007	$27.5
Employees	NA	Stock Exchange	OTC
Auditor	NA	Ticker Symbol	EKFC
Stk Agt	Illinois Stock Transfer Co	Outstanding Shares	NA
Counsel	NA	E.P.S.	NA
DUNS No.	NA	Shareholders	NA

Business: The group's principle activity is to provide banking services. The group also provides personal and business banking services. The group's products include deposit accounts and loans. The group operates from United States.

Primary SIC and add'l.: 6712 6035

CIK No: 0001224549

Officers: Edward F. Seserko/CEO, Pres., Gary B. Pepper/CFO, Exec. VP, Kevin A. Butler/VP - Lending, Operations, Michael P. Abriola/VP - Business Development, Marketing

Financial Data: Fiscal Year End:09/30   **Latest Annual Data:** 09/30/2003

Year	Sales	Net Income
2003	$4,805,000	$795,000
2002	$4,909,000	$834,000
2001	$4,828,000	$721,000

Curr. Assets:	$8,837,000	Curr. Liab.:	$62,840,000	P/E Ratio:	2.70
Plant, Equip.:	$1,241,000	Total Liab.:	$64,250,000	Indic. Yr. Divd.:	$1.400
Total Assets:	$83,321,000	Net Worth:	$19,071,000	Debt/ Equity:	NA

Euro Disney SCA

Immeubles Administratifs, Route National 34, Chessy, 77700; **PH:** 33-164744000; *http://* www.eurodisney.com

General - Incorporation	France	Stock- Price on:12/24/2007	NA
Employees	NA	Stock Exchange	NA
Auditor	PricewaterhouseCoopers LLP	Ticker Symbol	NA
Stk Agt	NA	Outstanding Shares	NA
Counsel	NA	E.P.S.	NA
DUNS No.	38-151-7754	Shareholders	NA

Business: The group's principle activity is to provide operation of the disneyland Paris resort. This resort features the disneyland Paris theme park, seven themed hotels, conference facilities, the disney village entertainment centre including 15 screen cinema and 3D adventure honey, i shrunk the audience, and a 27-hole golf course at marne-la-vallee. In addition, the group manages the real estate development and expansion of the related infrastructure of the property.

Primary SIC and add'l.: 7832 7996 5812 7011 7999 7922

CIK No: 0000924284

Officers: Karl L. Holz/Chmn., CEO, Neil Corbett/VP - Business Insight, Improvement, Daniel Dreux/VP - Human Resources, Federico J. Gonzalez/VP - Marketing, Antoine Jeancourt-Galignani/Pres., Member - Supervisory Board, Dominique Cocquet/Sr. VP - Development - External Affairs, Francois Pinon/VP, General Counsel, Norbert Stiekema/VP - Sale, Distribution, Andrew D. Csillery/VP - Strategic Planning, Integration, George Kalogridis/COO, Ignace Lahoud/Sr. VP, CFO, Jeff Archambault/VP - Corporate Communication, Patrick Avice/VP - Operations

Directors: Karl L. Holz/Chmn., CEO, Michel Corbiere/Member - Supervisory Board, Gerard Bouche/Member - Advisory Board, Philippe Geslin/Member - Advisory Board, Thomas O. Staggs/Member - Supervisory Board, Antoine Jeancourt-Galignani/Pres., Member - Supervisory Board, Philippe Labro/Member - Supervisory Board, James A. Rasulo/Member - Supervisory Board, Martin Robinson/Member - Supervisory Board, Jens Odewald/Member - Supervisory Board

Owners: Kingdom 5-KR-135 Ltd./10.00%, EDL Holding Company/39.78%

Euro Group of Companies Inc

Formerly: ICT Technologies Inc
181 Westchester Ave., Ste. 303-c, Port Chester, NY, 10573; **PH:** 1-914-937-3900; *http://* www.icttechnologies.com

General - Incorporation	DE	Stock- Price on:12/24/2007	$0.12
Employees	2	Stock Exchange	OTC
Auditor	Drakeford & Drakeford LLC	Ticker Symbol	ICTTE
Stk Agt	The Bank of New York	Outstanding Shares	96,430,000
Counsel	NA	E.P.S.	-$0.01
DUNS No.	NA	Shareholders	NA

Business: The group's principal activity is to distribute products and services in the telecommunications and consumer durable sectors. The group operates through three divisions namely: prepaid telephone cards, durable goods and long distance telephone. The products and services include prepaid telephone cards, mobile telephone, Internet services, airconditioners and motorcycles.

Primary SIC and add'l.: 4813

CIK No: 0001005663

Subsidiaries: Eurokool, Inc., Europhone USA LLC, Europhone USA, Inc., Europhone, Inc., Eurospeed, Inc.

Officers: Vassilios Koutosbinas/Chmn., CEO, Andrew Eracleous/79/Dir., CFO, Aris Constandinidies/Dir., Pres., George G. Cheng/Pres.

Directors: Vassilios Koutosbinas/Chmn., CEO, Andrew Eracleous/79/Dir., CFO, Paul Kotrotsios/53/Dir., Georgia Dumas/39/Dir., Aris Constandinidies/Dir., Pres.

Owners: Insiders/75.70%, Vasilios Koutsobinas/74.60%, Andrew Eracleous, Cheng G. Cheng

Financial Data: Fiscal Year End:12/31   **Latest Annual Data:** 12/31/2006

Year	Sales	Net Income
2006	$161,000	-$414,000
2005	NA	-$94,000
2004	$99,000	-$980,000

Curr. Assets:	$369,000	Curr. Liab.:	$2,882,000		
Plant, Equip.:	$41,000	Total Liab.:	$2,882,000	Indic. Yr. Divd.:	NA
Total Assets:	$409,000	Net Worth:	-$2,472,000	Debt/ Equity:	NA

Euro Tech Holdings Co Ltd

18/f Gee Chang Hong Ctr., 65 Wong Chuk Hong Rd, Hong Kong; **PH:** 852-28140311; *http://* www.euro-tech.com; **Email:** euro-tech@euro-tech.com

General - Incorporation British Virgin Islands		Stock - Price on:12/24/2007	$2.9
Employees	180	Stock Exchange	NDQ
Auditor	Pricewaterhousecoopers LLP	Ticker Symbol	CLWT
Stk Agt	American Stock Transfer & Trust Co.	Outstanding Shares	8,200,000
Counsel	NA	E.P.S.	$0.041
DUNS No.	NA	Shareholders	NA

Business: The group operates through its subsidiaries whose principle activity is to distribute water and waste waterr treatment equipment, including chlorination equipment, laboratory instruments, disinfection equipment, analyzers, test kits and related supplies such as analytical re-agents and chemicals, for laboratory, scientific and industrial purposes. The group operates from United States, Hong Kong and China.

Primary SIC and add'l.: 5049 5169 5084 6719

CIK No: 0001026662

Subsidiaries: ChinaH2O.com Limited, Euro Tech (Far East) Limited, Pact Asia Pacific Limited, Yixing Pact Environmental Technology

Owners: Xu Hong Wang, Nancy Wong, Alex Sham, Pearl Venture Ltd., T. C. Leung, Insiders, C. P. Kwan, Jerry Wong

Financial Data: Fiscal Year End:12/31   **Latest Annual Data:** 12/31/2006

Year	Sales	Net Income
2006	$27,161,000	$361,000
2005	$31,250,000	$1,051,000
2004	$32,282,000	$594,000

Curr. Assets:	$17,252,000	Curr. Liab.:	$6,985,000		
Plant, Equip.:	$1,628,000	Total Liab.:	$8,052,000	Indic. Yr. Divd.:	NA
Total Assets:	$19,975,000	Net Worth:	$11,923,000	Debt/ Equity:	NA

EuroBancshares Inc

270 Muoz Rivera Ave., San Juan, PR, 00918; **PH:** 1-787-751-7340; **Fax:** 1-787-758-5611; *http://* www.eurobankpr.com

General - Incorporation	PR	**Stock**- Price on:12/24/2007	$9.04
Employees	509	Stock Exchange	NDQ
Auditor	KPMG LLP	Ticker Symbol	EUBK
Stk Agt	American Stock Transfer & Trust Co.	Outstanding Shares	19,370,000
Counsel	NA	E.P.S	$0.24
DUNS No.	NA	Shareholders	NA

Business: The group operates through its subsidiary whose principle activity is to provide financial services. The groups services include cuentas de cheques and cuentas de ahorro. The group operates from United States.

Primary SIC and add'l.: NA

CIK No: 0001164554

Subsidiaries: Eurobank, Eurobank Statutory Trust, EuroSeguros

Officers: Rafael Arrillaga-Torrens/Chmn., CEO, Pres., Jorge Sepulveda-Estrada/53/Sr. VP, Treasurer, Felix Leon/Exec. VP - Operations, Noel Aponte/VP - Information Systems, Miguel Mendez/Branch Mgr. - Caguas II, Eurobank, Roberto Carreras Sosa/Sr. VP - Eastern Region, Yadira R. Mercado Pineiro/CFO, Exec. VP, Corp. Sec., Luis S. Suau Hernandez/Sr. VP - San Juan, Metropolitan Region, Fausto Pena Villegas/Sr. VP - Northern Region, Luis Berrios Lopez/Exec. VP, Chief Lending Officer, Jose R. Munoz/VP - Business, Luis S. Suau/Sr. VP - Metropolitan Area, Angel F. Cotto/Assist. VP - Administrative Services, Nixida Bermudez/Branch Mgr. - Ponce Marvesa, Eurobank, Tomas R. Capestany/Branch Mgr. - Ponce Hostos, Eurobank *(37 Officers included in Index)*

Directors: Rafael Arrillaga-Torrens/Chmn., CEO, Pres., Pedro Feliciano Benitez/Vice Chmn., Ricardo Levy Echeandia/Dir., Juan Ramon Gomez-Cuetara Aguilar/Dir., William Torres Torres/Dir., Luis Hernandez Santana/Dir., Juan Ramon Gomez-Cuetara Aguilar/Dir., Antonio R. Pavia Bibiloni/Dir., Placido Gonzalez Cordova/Dir., Diana Lopez-Feliciano/Dir.

Owners: FMR Corp./5.54%, Pedro Feliciano Bentez/27.25%, Juan Gmez-Cutara Fernndez/5.72%, Luis F. Hernandez, William Torres Torres/2.78%, Plcido Gonzlez Crdova/10.30%, Yadira R. Mercado, Rafael Arrillaga-Torrens/3.23%, Flix M. Len, Insiders/49.51%, Juan Ramon Gomez-Cuetara Aguilar, Diana Lpez-Feliciano, Ricardo Levy Echeanda/4.19%, Antonio R. Pavia Bibiloni, James I. Thomson *(16 Owners included in Index)*

Financial Data: *Fiscal Year End:*12/31 *Latest Annual Data:* 12/31/2006

Year	Sales	Net Income
2006	$171,039,000	$8,012,000
2005	$143,247,000	$16,530,000
2004	$112,928,000	$22,720,000

Curr. Assets:	$146,102,000	**Curr. Liab.:**	$2,310,424,000	**P/E Ratio:**	33.48
Plant, Equip.:	$27,937,000	**Total Liab.:**	$2,331,042,000	**Indic. Yr. Divd.:**	NA
Total Assets:	$2,500,920,000	**Net Worth:**	$169,878,000	**Debt/ Equity:**	0.1179

EuroGas Inc

1006-100 Pk. Royal S, West Vancouver, BC, V7T 1A2; *PH:* 1-212-785-2626; *http://* www.eugs.de; *Email:* eurogas@eunet.at

General - Incorporation	UT	**Stock**- Price on:12/24/2007	$0.044
Employees	NA	Stock Exchange	OTC
Auditor	NA	Ticker Symbol	EUGS
Stk Agt	Computershare Trust Co	Outstanding Shares	NA
Counsel	NA	E.P.S	NA
DUNS No.	86-101-6236	Shareholders	NA

Business: The group's principal activities are to acquire, explore and dispose oil, natural gas, coal bed methane gas, crude oil, talc and other minerals. The group also has business in co-generation and mineral reclamation projects. The group has mineral properties in eastern Europe, Canada, Poland, slovakia and eastern Russia.

Primary SIC and add'l.: 1311

CIK No: 0000783209

Subsidiaries: Beaver River Resources Ltd, Dissolution of Energy Global A.G., Energy Global A.G., EuroGas GmbH Austria, EuroGas Polska Sp. zo.o., GlobeGas B.V, McKenzie Methane Jastrzebie Sp. zo.o., Pol-Tex Methane, Sp. zo.o., Rozmin s.r.o, Wolfgang Rauball and Reinhard Rauball

Officers: Wolfgang Rauball/62/Chmn., CEO, Hank Blankenstein/66/Dir., CFO, Michael Slater/58/Pres.

Directors: Wolfgang Rauball/62/Chmn., CEO, Andreas Danicek/30/Dir., Hank Blankenstein/66/Dir., CFO

Owners: Insiders/26.00%, Wolfgang Rauball/26.00%

Financial Data: *Fiscal Year End:*12/31 *Latest Annual Data:* 12/31/2006

Year	Sales	Net Income
2006	NA	-$11,000
2003	NA	-$2,631,000
2002	$5,000	-$18,552,000

Curr. Assets:	-$4,000	**Curr. Liab.:**	$29,891,000		
Plant, Equip.:	$0	**Total Liab.:**	$46,571,000	**Indic. Yr. Divd.:**	NA
Total Assets:	$3,094,000	**Net Worth:**	-$43,477,000	**Debt/ Equity:**	NA

Euronet Worldwide Inc

4601 College Blvd., Ste. 300, Leawood, KS, 66211; *PH:* 1-913-327-4200; *Fax:* 1-913-327-1921; *http://* www.euronetworldwide.com; *Email:* investor@euronetworldwide.com

General - Incorporation	DE	**Stock**- Price on:12/24/2007	$30.01
Employees	1,098	Stock Exchange	NDQ
Auditor	KPMG LLP	Ticker Symbol	EEFT
Stk Agt	EquiServe Trust Co N.A	Outstanding Shares	48,260,000
Counsel	Sonnenschein Nath & Rosenthal LLP	E.P.S	$1.10
DUNS No.	NA	Shareholders	NA

Business: The group's principal activity is to provide secure electronic financial transactions. It offers outsourcing and consulting services, integrated electronic funds transfer software, network gateways and electronic prepaid top-up services. It also provides electronic payment solutions consisting of ATM network participation, outsourced ATM management solutions and electronic recharge services for prepaid mobile airtime. The customers of the group include banks, mobile phone operators and retailers that require electronic financial transaction processing services. The solutions of the group are used in more than 60 countries. As of 31-Dec-2003, the group had 10 offices in Europe, four in the Asia-pacific region, two in the U.S. And one in egypt. The group acquired transact elektronische zahlungssysteme gmbh, austin international marketing and investments, inc. And e-pay limited in 2003 and prepaid concepts, inc. In 2004.

Primary SIC and add'l.: 6099 7371 7389

CIK No: 0001029199

Subsidiaries: ATX, Ltd. (ATX), Bankomat 24/Euronet Sp. z o.o. (Bankomat), Call Processing, Inc., Cashnet Holding B.V., CashNet Telecommunications Egypt SAE (CashNet), Delta Euronet GmbH, e-pay Australia Holdings Pty Ltd, e-pay Australia Pty Ltd, e-pay Holdings Limited, e-pay Limited, e-pay Malaysia Sdn Bhd, e-pay New Zealand Pty Ltd, EFT Services Hellas EPE, EFT Services Holding B.V., EFT-Usluge d o.o. 37 Subsidiaries included in the Index

Officers: Michael J. Brown/Chmn., CEO, Pres. - Euronet Worldwide/$1,271,466.00, Rick L. Weller/CFO, Exec. VP, John Romney/Exec. VP - Euronet Worldwide, MD - EMEA EFT Processing Segment, Europe, Middle East, Africa Region/$778,685.00, Anthony Grandidge/Sr. VP - Euronet Worldwide, MD - Asia Pacific EFT Processing Segment, Roger Heinz/Sr. VP - Euronet Worldwide, MD - Western Europe, EFT Processing Segment, Cindy Ashcraft/VP - Euronet Worldwide, MD - Euronet Software Segment, Tom Cregan/Pres. - Payspot Inc, Gareth Gumbley/MD - e-pay Australia, New Zealand, Jeffrey B. Newman/Exec. VP, General Counsel, David Morgan/VP - Global Business Development - Software Segment, Tony Westlake/MD - e-pay UK, Kevin Caponecchi/Pres. - Euronet Worldwide, Juan C. Bianchi/MD - Euronet Worldwide Money Transfer Segment, Karyn Clewes Zaborny/Sr. VP - Human Resources, Euronet Worldwide, Miro I. Bergman/Exec. VP, COO - Prepaid Processing Segment/$848,800.00 *(18 Officers included in Index)*

Directors: Michael J. Brown/Chmn., CEO, Pres. - Euronet Worldwide, Thomas A. McDonnell/Dir., Daniel R. Henry/Dir., Paul S. Althasen/Dir., Exec. VP - Euronet Worldwide, Andrzej Olechowski/Dir., Eriberto R. Scocimara/Dir., Jeannine M. Strandjord/62/Dir., Andrew B. Schmitt/Dir.

Owners: DST Systems, Inc./5.00%, Miro I. Bergman, Eriberto R. Scocimara, Andrzej Olechowski, John M. Romney, Paul S. Althasen, Rick L. Weller, Michael J. Brown/7.10%, William Blair& Company L.L.C./14.00%, Jeannine M. Strandjord, Daniel R. Henry, Andrew B. Schmitt, Insiders/8.30%, Waddell& Reed Investment Management Company/10.00%, Thomas A. McDonnell

Financial Data: *Fiscal Year End:*12/31 *Latest Annual Data:* 12/31/2006

Year	Sales	Net Income
2006	$629,181,000	$46,307,000
2005	$531,159,000	$27,375,000
2004	$381,080,000	$18,427,000

Curr. Assets:	$688,471,000	**Curr. Liab.:**	$404,110,000	**P/E Ratio:**	28.86
Plant, Equip.:	$55,174,000	**Total Liab.:**	$811,474,000	**Indic. Yr. Divd.:**	NA
Total Assets:	$1,108,139,000	**Net Worth:**	$288,315,000	**Debt/ Equity:**	0.7412

EuroTrust

Poppelgaardvej 11-13, Soeborg, 2860; *PH:* 45-39540000; *http://* www.eurotrust.dk; *Email:* info@eurotrust.dk

General - Incorporation	Denmark	**Stock**- Price on:12/24/2007	NA
Employees	NA	Stock Exchange	NA
Auditor	Gregory & Assoc. LLC	Ticker Symbol	NA
Stk Agt	NA	Outstanding Shares	NA
Counsel	NA	E.P.S	NA
DUNS No.	30-529-4944	Shareholders	NA

Business: The group' s principal activities are in the Internet services and broadcast media sectors. The Internet segment includes business operations related to Web site hosting, security consultancy, Internet access and e-mail services; the broadcast media segment includes the operations of the company's cable TV (dk4) and a production company (primevision a/s).

Primary SIC and add'l.: 6719 7379 7375

CIK No: 0001041457

Subsidiaries: Arhustudiet A/S, Ciac A/S, Europe-Visions A/S, Formedia A/S, Mobile Broadcasting A/S, Prime Vision A/S, Publishing & Management ApS, TV Akademiet A/S

Officers: Robert Skjoedt/40/CEO, Kim Simonsen/38/CFO

Directors: Bo Kristensen/Non Exec. Chmn., Jan Berger/Dir., Erik Damgaard/Non Exec. Dir., Peter Juul/46/Dir., Christian F. Rovsing/Dir., Brian Birkenhead/Non Exec. Dir., Ernst Hoffmann/Non Exec. Dir.

Owners: Invesco Perpetual/8.00%, Insiders/23.50%, Volleshave Holding ApS/7.74%, J,L,Invest Holding ApS/6.20%, Bo Kristensen/9.28%, Erik Damgaard/7.74%, Peter Juul/5.58%, Dansk Anlaegsinvest ApS/9.28%, A,O, Holding ApS/10.55%, Vind Energi Invest A/S/6.71%, Erik Damgaard/5.58%, Peter Forchhammer/6.84%

Financial Data: *Fiscal Year End:*12/31 *Latest Annual Data:* 12/31/2005

Year	Sales	Net Income
2005	$14,967,000	-$1,252,000
2004	$16,650,000	$10,691,000

Curr. Assets:	$7,752,000	**Curr. Liab.:**	$6,935,000		
Plant, Equip.:	$10,613,000	**Total Liab.:**	$8,168,000	**Indic. Yr. Divd.:**	NA
Total Assets:	$25,451,000	**Net Worth:**	$17,271,000	**Debt/ Equity:**	NA

EV Energy Partners LP

1001 Fannin St., Ste. 800, Houston, TX, 77002; *PH:* 1-713-651-1144; *Fax:* 1-713-651-1260; *http://* www.evenergypartners.com

General - Incorporation	DE	**Stock**- Price on:12/24/2007	$37.06
Employees	NA	Stock Exchange	NDQ
Auditor	Deloitte & Touche, LLP	Ticker Symbol	EVEP
Stk Agt	Computershare Shareholder Ser Inc	Outstanding Shares	8,430,000
Counsel	NA	E.P.S	-$0.69
DUNS No.	NA	Shareholders	NA

Business: The groups principle activities include acquiring, producing and developing oil and natural gas properties. In December 2006, the group acquired Five States Energy Company. The group operates from the United States. The group's quarterly revenue for September 2007 was 29.43 millions of USD.

Primary SIC and add'l.: 1311

CIK No: 0001361937

Subsidiaries: CGAS Properties, L.P., EnerVest Cargas, Ltd., EnerVest Production Partners, Ltd., EV Properties GP, LLC, EV Properties, L.P., EVCG GP, LLC, EVPP GP, LLC, Lower Cargas Operating Company, LLC

Officers: John B. Walker/Chmn., CEO, Mark A. Houser/Dir., COO, Pres., Michael E. Mercer/Sr. VP, CFO, Kathryn S. MacAskie/Sr. VP - Acquisitions, Divestitures, Frederick Dwyer/48/Controller

Directors: John B. Walker/Chmn., CEO, Mark A. Houser/Dir., COO, Pres., Victor Burk/Dir., James R. Larson/Dir., George Lindahl/Dir., Gary R. Petersen/Dir.

Owners: ZLP Fund, L.P./6.70%, Insiders/2.20%, John B. Walker/2.20%, Frederick Dwyer, Kathryn S. MacAskie, Mark A. Houser, Gary R. Petersen, James R. Larson

Financial Data: *Fiscal Year End:* 12/31 *Latest Annual Data:* 12/31/2006

Year	Sales	Net Income
2006	$47,909,000	$19,941,000

Curr. Assets:	$15,254,000	**Curr. Liab.:**	$3,248,000	**P/E Ratio:**	308.83
Plant, Equip.:	$114,684,000	**Total Liab.:**	$36,436,000	**Indic. Yr. Divd.:**	$1.840
Total Assets:	$132,689,000	**Net Worth:**	$96,253,000	**Debt/ Equity:**	0.5212

Evans & Sutherland Computer Corp

770 Komas Dr., Salt Lake City, UT, 84108; *PH:* 1-801-588-1000; *Fax:* 1-801-588-4500; *http://* www.es.com; *Email:* info@es.com

General - Incorporation	UT	***Stock***- Price on:12/24/2007	$2.59
Employees	118	Stock Exchange	NDQ
Auditor	KPMG LLP	Ticker Symbol	ESCC
Stk Agt	American Stock Transfer & Trust Co.	Outstanding Shares	11,090,000
Counsel	Snell & Wilmer	E.P.S.	-$0.99
DUNS No.	04-526-3035	Shareholders	NA

Business: The group's principal activity is to design, manufacture, market and support visual systems used to display images of the real world rapidly and accurately. The product is designed for simulation for use in military and commercial applications. The group also provides visual system technology to planetariums, science centers and entertainment venues. The group develops and delivers a complete line of image generators, displays, databases, services and support products that match technology to customer requirements. The group has operations in the United States, Europe and Asia.

Primary SIC and add'l.: 7372 5045 7371

CIK No: 0000276283

Subsidiaries: Evans & Sutherland Computer Limited, Evans & Sutherland Graphics Corporation, REALimage, Inc., Xionix Simulation, Inc.

Officers: David H. Bateman/Dir., CEO, Pres./$345,244.00, Allen H. Tanner/GM - Advanced Displays/$241,480.00, Luann Jensen/Mgr. - Corporate Marketing, Kirk Johnson/GM - Digital Theater/$217,833.00, Bob Morishita/VP - Human Resources/$397,303.00, Jeri Panek/Contact - Digital Theater, Planetarium Sales, Scott Niskach/Contact - Digital Theater, Planetarium Sales, Lance Sessions/Acting CFO/$113,678.00, Paul L. Dailey/CFO, Corp. Sec./$192,486.00

Directors: David H. Bateman/Dir., CEO, Pres., David J. Coghlan/Chmn., William Schneider/65/Dir., James P. McCarthy/Dir.

Owners: Royce & Associates, LLC/12.40%, Dimensional Fund Advisers Inc./5.70%, Bob Morishita, State of Wisconsin Investment Board/18.40%, James R. Oyler, Kirk D. Johnson, David H. Bateman, Allen H. Tanner, James P. McCarthy, Insiders/7.80%, William Schneider, Wells Fargo & Company/15.10%, Paul L. Dailey, David J. Coghlan, Peter R. Kellogg/14.80%

Financial Data: *Fiscal Year End:* 12/31 *Latest Annual Data:* 12/31/2006

Year	Sales	Net Income
2006	$15,048,000	$21,985,000
2005	$73,567,000	-$1,134,000
2004	$69,159,000	-$8,867,000

Curr. Assets:	$31,603,000	**Curr. Liab.:**	$15,367,000		
Plant, Equip.:	$12,689,000	**Total Liab.:**	$32,999,000	**Indic. Yr. Divd.:**	NA
Total Assets:	$55,381,000	**Net Worth:**	$22,382,000	**Debt/ Equity:**	0.1434

Evans Bancorp Inc

1 Grimsby Dr., Hamburg, NY, 14075; *PH:* 1-716-926-2000; *Fax:* 1-716-926-2005; *http://* www.evansbancorp.com

General - Incorporation	NY	***Stock***- Price on:12/24/2007	$19.5
Employees	174	Stock Exchange	NDQ
Auditor	KPMG LLP	Ticker Symbol	EVBN
Stk Agt	Computershare Investor Services LLC	Outstanding Shares	2,750,000
Counsel	NA	E.P.S.	$1.31
DUNS No.	00-213-5333	Shareholders	NA

Business: The group's principal activity is to provide commercial banking services. It originates loans to customers that include secured and unsecured commercial loans, mortgage loans and consumer loans, property and casualty insurance agency services, mutual funds and annuities. The group operates through its subsidiary, evans national bank. The group operates through nine banking offices located in amherst, angola, derby, evans, forestville, hamburg, lancaster, north Boston and west seneca, New York.

Primary SIC and add'l.: 6022 6712

CIK No: 0000842518

Subsidiaries: ENB Insurance Agency, Inc, Evans National Bank, Evans National Financial Services, Inc., Evans National Leasing, Inc

Officers: David J. Nasca/Dir., CEO, Pres., William R. Glass/Assist. Sec./$303,455.00, James Tilley/Dir., Sr. VP/$432,655.00, James E. Biddle/Dir., Sec., Gary A. Kajtoch/CFO

Directors: David J. Nasca/Dir., CEO, Pres., Phillip Brothman/Chmn., Thomas H. Waring/Vice Chmn., Kenneth C. Kirst/Dir., Robert G. Miller/Dir., John O'Brien/Dir., Mary Catherine Militello/Dir., James Tilley/Dir., Sr. VP, James E. Biddle/Dir., Sec., Laverne G. Hall/Dir., David M. Taylor/Dir., William F. Barrett/Dir., Nancy W. Ware/Dir.

Owners: Thomas H. Waring, William R. Glass, Phillip Brothman/1.40%, Robert G. Miller/2.60%, Mark DeBacker, Mary Catherine Militello, James Tilley, Kenneth C. Kirst, Nancy W. Ware, William F. Barrett/8.80%, Insiders/17.80%, Mark A. Kasperczyk, John R. OBrien, James E. Biddle, David J. Nasca *(17 Owners included in Index)*

Financial Data: *Fiscal Year End:* 12/31 *Latest Annual Data:* 12/31/2006

Year	Sales	Net Income
2006	$37,317,000	$4,921,000
2005	$33,322,000	$4,819,000
2004	$26,280,000	$4,509,000

Curr. Assets:	$14,644,000	**Curr. Liab.:**	$389,456,000	**P/E Ratio:**	14.89
Plant, Equip.:	$8,743,000	**Total Liab.:**	$434,351,000	**Indic. Yr. Divd.:**	$0.680
Total Assets:	$473,894,000	**Net Worth:**	$39,543,000	**Debt/ Equity:**	0.8374

EVCI Career Colleges Holding Corp

1 Van Der Donck St., 2nd Fl., Yonkers, NY, 10701; *PH:* 1-914-623-0700; *Fax:* 1-914-964-8222; *http://* www.evcinc.com

General - Incorporation	DE	***Stock***- Price on:12/24/2007	$0.925
Employees	465	Stock Exchange	NDQ
Auditor	Goldstein Golub Kessler LLP	Ticker Symbol	EVCID
Stk Agt	Continental Stock Transfer & Trust Co	Outstanding Shares	12,690,000
Counsel	NA	E.P.S.	-$2.28
DUNS No.	NA	Shareholders	NA

Business: The group's principle activity is to provide instructor-led education and training through traditional post-secondary schools and non-degree granting professional certification schools. It owns and operates the interboro institute and icts inc. Interboro is a two year college that offers degree programs leading to the associate of occupational studies degree and has a main campus in manhattan and an extension center in flushing, queens. It plans for expansion includes an additional admissions office in corona, queens to service flushing campus and additional campuses in Washington heights (manhattan) and yonkers, New York. Icts operates five professional certification schools through its college partners in three states. The certification schools are located in atlanta, baltimore, alexandria, hampton and Virginia beach. The group's quarterly revenue for Sep'07 was 12.89 millions of USD.

Primary SIC and add'l.: 7389 8299

CIK No: 0001065591

Subsidiaries: Interboro Holding, Inc., Interboro Institute, Inc., Pennsylvania School of Business, Inc., Technical Career Institutes, Inc.

Owners: Com Vest Investment Partners III, L.P./17.40%, Joseph D. Alperin/1.77%, Philip M. Getter, Arol I. Buntzman/9.27%, John J. McGrath/4.66%, Robert F. Kennedy/1.62%, Stephen Schwartz, Insiders/16.57%, Donald Grunewald

Financial Data: *Fiscal Year End:* 12/31 *Latest Annual Data:* 12/31/2006

Year	Sales	Net Income
2006	$65,446,000	-$13,542,000
2005	$50,742,000	$361,000
2004	$33,070,000	$6,254,000

Curr. Assets:	$10,010,000	**Curr. Liab.:**	$15,659,000		
Plant, Equip.:	$6,062,000	**Total Liab.:**	$28,215,000	**Indic. Yr. Divd.:**	NA
Total Assets:	$41,684,000	**Net Worth:**	$13,468,000	**Debt/ Equity:**	0.6798

Ever-Glory International Group Inc

9175 Mainwaring Rd., Sidney, BC, V8L 1J9; *PH:* 1-250-656-8860; *http://* www.everglorygroup.com; *Email:* info@everglorygroup.com

General - Incorporation	FL	***Stock***- Price on:12/24/2007	$0.29
Employees	600	Stock Exchange	OTC
Auditor	Godwin, Longley & Ronquillo, LLP	Ticker Symbol	EVGY
Stk Agt	Holladay Stock Transfer, Inc.	Outstanding Shares	19,970,000
Counsel	NA	E.P.S.	$0.03
DUNS No.	96-819-9455	Shareholders	NA

Business: The group's principal activities are to provide engineering and project management services for water and energy related private and public works. The group operates through two major segments: engineering and development of energy and education software, hardware and communications. The energy segment designs, coordinates, project management and quality assurance of tunnels, material handling, civil works and power islands for thermal and hydroelectric power plants. The water and sewage segment designs, constructs and manages installations to produce drinkable water, treat sewage, industrial and chemical refuse and sewage, desalt sea water for industrial and human use. The educational software, hardware and communications segment focuses on designing, production and installation of a communication system that will provide high-speed connection to the Internet and to television in remote rural regions. The group has decided to divest itself and cease operations.

Primary SIC and add'l.: 1623 8711

CIK No: 0000943184

Subsidiaries: Goldenway Nanjing Garments Co. Ltd.

Officers: Kang Yi Hua/45/Dir., CEO, Pres., Sun Jia Jun/35/Dir., COO, Guo Yan/31/CFO, Jin Qiu/34/Sec.

Directors: Kang Yi Hua/45/Dir., CEO, Pres., Sun Jia Jun/35/Dir., COO, Yan Xiao Dong/45/Dir., Wei Ru Qin/54/Dir., Li Ning/45/Dir.

Owners: Jia Jun Sun/2.90%, Ru Qin Wei/1.50%, Ning Li/4.90%, Yi Hua Kang/79.10%, Insiders/88.40%, Insiders/3.10%, Yi Hua Kang/3.10%

Financial Data: *Fiscal Year End:* 12/31 *Latest Annual Data:* 12/31/2006

Year	Sales	Net Income
2006	$31,975,000	$2,471,000
2005	$10,814,000	$1,044,000
2004	NA	-$1,000

Curr. Assets:	$10,234,000	**Curr. Liab.:**	$12,979,000	**P/E Ratio:**	9.67
Plant, Equip.:	$12,159,000	**Total Liab.:**	$17,218,000	**Indic. Yr. Divd.:**	NA
Total Assets:	$24,914,000	**Net Worth:**	$7,696,000	**Debt/ Equity:**	NA

Evercore Partners Inc

55 E 52nd St., 43rd Fl., New York, NY, 10055; *PH:* 1-212-857-3100; *Fax:* 1-212-857-3101; *http://* www.evercore.com

General - Incorporation	DE	***Stock***- Price on:12/24/2007	$29.31
Employees	247	Stock Exchange	NYSE
Auditor	Thacher & Bartlett LLP	Ticker Symbol	EVR
Stk Agt	Bank of New York	Outstanding Shares	10,560,000
Counsel	NA	E.P.S.	-$12.81
DUNS No.	NA	Shareholders	NA

Business: The groups principle activity is to provide advisory services to prominent multinational corporations on significant mergers, acquisitions, divestitures, restructurings and other strategic corporate transactions. The group operates through two segments namely, advisory and investment management. In the year 2006, the group acquired Braveheart Financial Services Limited. The group operates from the United States. The group's quarterly revenue for September 2007 was 78.11 millions of USD.

Primary SIC and add'l.: 6289 6211 6726 8742

CIK No: 0001360901

Subsidiaries: BD Protego S. de R.L., Evercore Advisors I L.L.C., Evercore Advisors L.L.C., Evercore Financial Advisors L.L.C., Evercore GP Holdings L.L.C., Evercore Group Holdings L.L.C., Evercore Group Holdings L.P., Evercore Group L.L.C., Evercore LP, Evercore Partners Limited, Evercore Partners Services East L.L.C., Evercore Properties L.L.C., Evercore Restructuring L.L.C., Evercore Venture Advisors L.L.C., Protego Administradores, S. de R.L. 22 Subsidiaries included in the Index

Officers: Roger C. Altman/Chmn., Co - CEO, Austin M. Beutner/Pres., Co - CEO, Chief Investment Officer, Dir., Pedro Aspe/Chmn., Sr. MD, Bernard Taylor/51/Co - Vice Chmn., Michael P. Riordan/Dir. - Taxation, Sharon M. Lewellen/Sr. MD, Gary Swiman/Chief Compliance Officer, Jorge Marcos/Dir. - Protegos Mergers, Acquisitions Group, Sergio Sanchez/Dir. - Protegos Asset Management Business, Antonio Souza/Dir. - Protegos Energy Group, Gail S. Landis/Sr. MD, Sangam Pant/Sr. MD, Kathleen G. Reiland/Sr. MD, Ashim Gulati/Dir. - Finance, Administration, Puneet Gulati/Dir. - Finance, Administration *(72 Officers included in Index)*

Directors: Roger C. Altman/Chmn., Co - CEO, Austin M. Beutner/Pres., Co - CEO, Chief Investment Officer, Dir., Pedro Aspe/Chmn., Sr. MD, Eduardo Mestre/Vice Chmn., Adam B. Frankel/Sr. MD, General Counsel, Gail Block Harris/55/Dir., Curt Hessler/64/Dir., Francois De St. Phalle/62/Dir., Anthony N. Pritzker/47/Dir., Roger A. Enrico/Member - Advisory Board, Michael W. Blumenthal/Member - Advisory Board, Irvine O. Hockaday/Member - Advisory Board, Juan Gallardo/Member - Advisory Board

Owners: Capital Group International, Inc/5.50%, Baron Capital Group, Inc/9.10%, Curt Hessler, Marisco Capital Management, LLC/5.70%, Gail Block Harris, Insiders/27.10%, Anthony N. Pritzker/2.60%, Francois de Saint Phalle, Bernard J. Taylor/23.30%

Financial Data: ***Fiscal Year End:***12/31 ***Latest Annual Data:*** 12/31/2006

Year	Sales	Net Income
2006	$216,497,000	$69,737,000

Curr. Assets:	$215,759,000	***Curr. Liab.:***	$151,907,000		
Plant, Equip.:	$4,373,000	***Total Liab.:***	$189,026,000	***Indic. Yr. Divd.:***	$0.480
Total Assets:	$301,503,000	***Net Worth:***	$112,477,000	***Debt/ Equity:***	0.0005

Everest Re Group Ltd

477 Martinsville Rd., Liberty Corner, NJ, 07938; ***PH:*** 1-908-604-3000; ***Fax:*** 1-908-604-3322; ***http://*** www.everestre.com

General - Incorporation	Bermuda	***Stock***- Price on:12/24/2007	$105.54
Employees	736	Stock Exchange	NYSE
Auditor	PricewaterhouseCoopers LLP	Ticker Symbol	RE
Stk Agt	Computershare Trust Co	Outstanding Shares	63,180,000
Counsel	NA	E.P.S	$16.10
DUNS No.	NA	Shareholders	NA

Business: The group's principal activity is underwriting of property and casualty reinsurance and insurance. The activities of the group are carried out through five segments: U.S. Reinsurance: underwrites property and casualty reinsurance through brokers and directly with ceding companies. The U.S. Reinsurance segment underwrites property and casualty reinsurance through brokers and directly with ceding companies. The specialty underwriting division underwrites accident, health, marine, aviation and surety business through brokers and directly with ceding companies. The international division underwrites property and casualty reinsurance through the group's branches in london, Canada and Singapore. The Bermuda segment underwrites property, casualty, life and annuity business through brokers and directly with ceding companies.

Primary SIC and add'l.: 6331 6311 6719

CIK No: 0001095073

Subsidiaries: Everest Advisors (Ireland) Limited, Everest Global Services, Inc., Everest Indemnity Insurance Company, Everest Insurance Company of Canada, Everest International Reinsurance, Ltd., Everest National Insurance Company, Everest Re Advisors, Ltd. - Bermuda, Everest Re Capital Trust, Everest Re Capital Trust II, Everest Re Holdings, Ltd., Everest Reinsurance (Bermuda), Ltd., Everest Reinsurance Company, Everest Reinsurance Holdings, Inc., Everest Security Insurance Company, Mt. McKinley Insurance Company 18 Subsidiaries included in the Index

Officers: Mark S. De Saram/52/Sr. VP - Group, MD, CEO - Everest Reinsurance, Bermuda, Ltd/$1,213,978.00, Joseph V. Taranto/Chmn., CEO/$8,817,386.00, Barry H. Smith/Exec. VP, Chief Administrative Officer, Frank N. Lopapa/Sr. VP, Treasurer, Scott P. Callahan/Exec. VP, Stephen L. Limauro/56/Dir., Exec. VP/$1,886,257.00, Daryl Bradley/Pres. - US Insurance Operations, Robert E. Capicchioni/Sr. VP, Sanjoy Mukherjee/Sr. VP, General Counsel, Sec., James H. Foster/Sr. VP, Craig E. Eisenacher/CFO, Exec. VP/$282,692.00, Luis E. Monteagudo/Sr. VP, Thomas J. Gallagher/Dir., COO, Pres./$2,095,654.00, Steven A. Mestman/Exec. VP, Keith Shoemaker/VP, Controller/$445,189.00 *(16 Officers included in Index)*

Directors: Joseph V. Taranto/Chmn., CEO, Thomas J. Gallagher/Dir., COO, Pres., William F. Galtney/Dir., John A. Weber/Dir., Stephen L. Limauro/56/Dir., Exec. VP, Martin Abrahams/Dir., Kenneth J. Duffy/Dir., John R. Dunne/Dir.

Owners: Craig Eisenacher, Keith T. Shoemaker, John R. Dunne, Martin Abrahams, William F. Galtney, Kenneth J. Duffy, John A. Weber, Insiders/1.84%, FMR Corp./8.28%, Oppenheimer Funds, Inc/10.44%, Thomas J. Gallagher, Stephen L. Limauro, Joseph V. Taranto, Putnam, LLC/5.30%, Southeastern Asset Management Inc/5.40% *(16 Owners included in Index)*

Financial Data: ***Fiscal Year End:***12/31 ***Latest Annual Data:*** 12/31/2006

Year	Sales	Net Income
2006	$4,517,300,000	$840,828,000
2005	$4,576,210,000	-$218,667,000
2004	$5,008,685,000	$494,858,000

Curr. Assets:	$3,818,532,000	***Curr. Liab.:***	$100,526,000	***P/E Ratio:***	7.09
Plant, Equip.:	NA	***Total Liab.:***	$11,999,883,000	***Indic. Yr. Divd.:***	$1.920
Total Assets:	$17,107,570,000	***Net Worth:***	$5,107,687,000	***Debt/ Equity:***	NA

Evergreen Energy Inc

Formerly: KFx Inc
55 Madison St., Ste. 500, Denver, CO, 80206; ***PH:*** 1-303-293-2992; ***http://*** www.kfx.com

General - Incorporation	DE	***Stock***- Price on:12/24/2007	$5.9692
Employees	216	Stock Exchange	NYSE
Auditor	Deloitte & Touche LLP	Ticker Symbol	EEE
Stk Agt	Chemical Mellon Shareholder Srvcs	Outstanding Shares	NA
Counsel	Bangs, McCullen, Butler, Foye	E.P.S	-$1
DUNS No.	18-549-6601	Shareholders	NA

Business: The group's principal activities are to develop and deliver various technology and service solutions to the electric power generation industry. The group facilitates in the various air quality emission standards and to lower the cost of producing electricity. The technology solutions enhance the output of coal, gas and oil-fired electric utility boilers. The group develops patented technology, that uses heat and pressure to physically and chemically transform high-moisture, low-energy value coal and other organic feedstock into a low-moisture, high-energy solid clean fuel.

Primary SIC and add'l.: 8711 7372

CIK No: 0000912365

Subsidiaries: KFx Plant, LLC

Officers: Mark S. Sexton/52/Chmn., CEO Pres./$2,033,255.00, William G. Laughlin/Sr. VP, General Counsel, Sec./$910,523.00, Robert I. Hanfling/70/COO, Pres./$2,062,084.00, Theodore Venners/60/Founder, Chief Strategy Officer, Dir./$2,916,141.00, Dennis W. Coolidge/Sr. VP - Engineering, Operations, Diana Kubik/CFO, VP/$181,876.00, Karli Anderson/Dir. - Investor Relations

Directors: Mark S. Sexton/52/Chmn., CEO Pres., Robert J. Clark/Chmn., Stanford M. Adelstein/Dir., John V. Lovoi/46/Dir., Kevin R. Collins/51/Dir., James S. Pignatelli/Dir., James R. Schlesinger/Dir., Manuel H. Johnson/Dir., Jack C. Pester/Dir., Grady W. Rosier/Dir., Robert S. Kaplan/Dir., Theodore Venners/60/Founder, Chief Strategy Officer, Dir.

Owners: Westcliff Capital Management, LLC/9.50%, Theodore Venners/5.40%, Robert J. Clark, William G. Laughlin, Insiders/8.70%, Robert S. Kaplan, Diana L. Kubik, Security Management Company, LLC/12.10%, John V. Lovoi, James R. Schlesinger, James S. Pignatelli, Grady W. Rosier, Kevin R. Collins, Manuel H. Johnson, Mark S. Sexton/1.40% *(18 Owners included in Index)*

Financial Data: ***Fiscal Year End:***12/31 ***Latest Annual Data:*** 12/31/2006

Year	Sales	Net Income
2006	$36,710,000	-$51,527,000
2005	$984,000	-$23,313,000
2004	$28,000	-$10,555,000

Curr. Assets:	$93,898,000	***Curr. Liab.:***	$14,742,000		
Plant, Equip.:	$129,940,000	***Total Liab.:***	$27,335,000	***Indic. Yr. Divd.:***	NA
Total Assets:	$252,319,000	***Net Worth:***	$224,984,000	***Debt/ Equity:***	NA

Evergreen Solar Inc

138 Bartlett St., Marlboro, MA, 01752; ***PH:*** 1-508-357-2221; ***Fax:*** 1-508-357-0747; ***http://*** www.evergreensolar.com

General - Incorporation	DE	***Stock***- Price on:12/24/2007	$9.15
Employees	330	Stock Exchange	NDQ
Auditor	PricewaterhouseCoopers LLP	Ticker Symbol	ESLR
Stk Agt	American Stock Transfer & Trust Co.	Outstanding Shares	77,200,000
Counsel	Wilson Sonsini Goodrich & Rosati	E.P.S	-$0.29
DUNS No.	NA	Shareholders	NA

Business: The group's principle activities are to develop, manufacture and market solar power products that are capable of providing reliable and environmentally clean electric power. The solar power products include solar cells, panels and systems, with solar panel sales being the major one. Solar panels are used to generate electricity for on-grid and off-grid applications. The group's research revenues consist of revenues from various state and federal government agencies to fund the ongoing research, development, testing and enhancement of products and manufacturing technology. The group's quarterly revenue for Sep'07 was 18.19 millions of USD.

Primary SIC and add'l.: 3674

CIK No: 0000947397

Subsidiaries: Evergreen Solar GmbH, Evergreen Solar Securities, Inc, EverQ

Officers: Richard M. Feldt/Chmn., CEO, Pres./$2,002,349.00, Gary T. Pollard/VP - Human Resources, Richard G. Chleboski/VP - Worldwide Expansion/$595,268.00, Michael El-Hillow/CFO, Terry Bailey/Sr. VP - Marketing, Sales/$558,870.00, Donald M. Muir/VP, Sec., Treasurer/$310,696.00, Brown F. Williams/VP - Science, Engineering/$834,537.00, Rodolfo Archbold/VP - Operations

Directors: Richard M. Feldt/Chmn., CEO, Pres., Allan H. Cohen/Dir., Edward C. Grady/Dir., Gerald L. Wilson/Dir., Tom L. Cadwell/Dir., Peter W. Cowden/Dir.

Owners: Wellington Management Company, LLP/9.47%, Richard G. Chleboski, Edward C. Grady, Gary T. Pollard, Peter W. Cowden, FMR Corp Entities/10.26%, Brown F. Williams, Gerald L. Wilson, Michael El-Hillow, Tom L. Cadwell, Insiders/4.00%, Allan H. Cohen, Terry J. Bailey, Richard M. Feldt/2.05%, DC Chemical Co., Ltd/15.08%

Financial Data: ***Fiscal Year End:***12/31 ***Latest Annual Data:*** 12/31/2006

Year	Sales	Net Income
2006	$103,146,000	-$26,669,000
2005	$44,032,000	-$17,316,000
2004	$23,536,000	-$19,363,000

Curr. Assets:	$81,994,000	***Curr. Liab.:***	$24,404,000		
Plant, Equip.:	$50,516,000	***Total Liab.:***	$114,404,000	***Indic. Yr. Divd.:***	NA
Total Assets:	$207,251,000	***Net Worth:***	$92,847,000	***Debt/ Equity:***	1.0132

EvergreenBancorp Inc

301 Eastlake Ave. E, Seattle, WA, 98109; ***PH:*** 1-206-628-4250; ***Fax:*** 1-206-628-4022; ***https://*** www.evergreenbank.com

General - Incorporation	WA	***Stock***- Price on:12/24/2007	$15.25
Employees	68	Stock Exchange	OTC
Auditor	Crowe Chizek & Co. LLC	Ticker Symbol	EVGG
Stk Agt	Computershare Trust Co	Outstanding Shares	2,360,000
Counsel	NA	E.P.S	$1.20
DUNS No.	NA	Shareholders	NA

Business: The group's principal activities are to offer commercial, real estate, consumer loans and provide savings, checking and certificate of deposit accounts. The other services provided are financial planning, investment services and merchant credit card processing services. The operations are conducted through three offices located in northeast of downtown seattle, north of seattle and bellevue. The group is a holding company for evergreenbank, which is a Washington state chartered bank.

Primary SIC and add'l.: 6022 6712

CIK No: 0001143566

Subsidiaries: EvergreenBancorp Capital Trust I, EvergreenBank

Officers: Gerald O. Hatler/Vice Chmn., CEO, Pres., Gordon D. Browning/CFO, Exec. VP

Directors: Gerald O. Hatler/Vice Chmn., CEO, Pres., Stanley William McNaughton/Chmn., Carole J. Grisham/Dir., Don C. Filer/Dir., Joseph M. Phillips/Dir., Richard William Baldwin/Dir., Russel E. Olson/Dir., Robert J. Grossman/Dir., Craig O. Dawson/Dir.

Owners: Carole J. Grisham, Michael H. Tibbits, Russel E. Olson, Gordon D. Browning/1.17%, Gerald O. Hatler/2.80%, Robert J. Grossman, Insiders/13.31%, Richard W. Baldwin, Stan W. McNaughton/5.13%, Michelle P. Worden, Don C. Filer/1.74%

Financial Data: ***Fiscal Year End:***12/31 ***Latest Annual Data:*** 12/31/2006

Year	Sales	Net Income
2006	$22,614,000	$1,819,000
2005	$15,405,000	$966,000
2004	$13,072,000	$1,282,000

Curr. Assets:	$15,930,000	Curr. Liab.:	$307,484,000	P/E Ratio:	15.25
Plant, Equip.:	$3,078,000	Total Liab.:	$319,701,000	Indic. Yr. Divd.:	$0.280
Total Assets:	$343,520,000	Net Worth:	$23,819,000	Debt/ Equity:	0.5010

Everlast Worldwide Inc

1350 Broadway Way, Fl. 23, New York, NY, 10018; *PH:* 1-212-239-0990; *http://* www.everlast.com

General - Incorporation	DE	Stock - Price on:12/24/2007	$26.09
Employees	140	Stock Exchange	NA
Auditor	Berenson LLP	Ticker Symbol	NA
Stk Agt	Continental Stock Transfer & Trust Co	Outstanding Shares	4,070,000
Counsel	NA	E.P.S.	$0.17
DUNS No.	79-108-6143	Shareholders	NA

Business: The group's principal activities are to design, manufacture, market and sell apparel products. The products include women's activewear, sportswear, swimwear and coverups and men's activewear, sportswear and outerwear under the everlast(R) trademark. Sports products manufactured by the group include a line of boxing related sporting goods such as boxing gloves, heavy bags, speed bags, boxing trunks, and miscellaneous gym equipment. The group has the exclusive right to use and distribute these apparel products in the United States and Canada. The group licenses the everlast(R) trademark to numerous companies that source and manufacture products such as men's, women's and children's apparel, sleepwear, underwear, hosiery, footwear, leatherwear, cardiovascular equipment, eyewear, sports bags, hats and other accessories.

Primary SIC and add'l.: 2329 2331 2369

CIK No: 0000934795

Subsidiaries: Active Apparel New Corp., American Fitness Products, Inc., Everlast Fitness Mfg. Corp., Everlast Sports International, Inc., Everlast Sports Mfg. Corp., Everlast World Boxing Headquarters Corp.

Officers: Seth A. Horowitz/31/Chmn., CEO, Pres./$1,336,439.00, Hal G. Worsham/Sr. VP - Global Licensing/$336,395.00, Gary J. Dailey/40/CFO/$485,167.00, Angelo Giusti/57/Sr. VP - Sales, Sec./$290,958.00, Thomas K. Higgerson/59/Sr. VP - Manufacturing, Distribution/$86,645.00, Gerard J. Delisser/49/Chief Merchandising Officer, Mark R. MacKay/47/Sr. VP - Global Licensing

Directors: Seth A. Horowitz/31/Chmn., CEO, Pres., James K. Anderson/71/Dir., Larry A. Kring/67/Dir., Jeffrey M. Schwartz/48/Dir., James McGuire/72/Dir., Theodore A. Atlas/51/Dir., Edward R. Epstein/68/Dir., Mark Ackereizen/63/Dir.

Owners: James K. Anderson/2.80%, Gary J. Dailey, Larry A. Kring/1.20%, Angelo V. Giusti, James J. McGuire, Theodore A. Atlas, Burlingame Equity Investors, LP/14.30%, Seth A. Horowitz/21.40%, The Estate of Ben Nadorf/11.20%, The Estate of George Q. Horowitz/15.10%, Insiders/26.60%, Edward R. Epstein, Mark Ackereizen, Jeffrey M. Schwartz

Financial Data: *Fiscal Year End:*12/31 *Latest Annual Data:* 12/31/2006

Year	Sales	Net Income
2006	$51,887,000	$4,724,000
2005	$43,253,000	-$948,000
2004	$44,999,000	-$1,027,000

Curr. Assets:	$25,729,000	Curr. Liab.:	$22,785,000	P/E Ratio:	153.47
Plant, Equip.:	$6,235,000	Total Liab.:	$42,613,000	Indic. Yr. Divd.:	NA
Total Assets:	$65,276,000	Net Worth:	$22,663,000	Debt/ Equity:	0.8171

Evolution Petroleum Corp Inc

820 Gessner, Ste. 1340, Houston, TX, 77024; *PH:* 1-713-935-0122; *Fax:* 1-713-935-0199; *http://* www.evolutionpetroleum.com

General - Incorporation	NV	Stock - Price on:12/24/2007	$3.05
Employees	NA	Stock Exchange	AMEX
Auditor	Hein & Associates LLP	Ticker Symbol	EPM
Stk Agt	Continental Stock Transfer & Trust Co	Outstanding Shares	26,760,000
Counsel	NA	E.P.S	NA
DUNS No.	NA	Shareholders	NA

Business: The groups principle activities include operating, developing, acquiring and financing oil and gas properties. The group operates from the United States. The group's quarterly revenue for September 2007 was 0.50 millions of USD.

Primary SIC and add'l.: 1321 1311

CIK No: 0001006655

Subsidiaries: ARKLA Petroleum, LLC, Four Star Development Corporation, Natural Gas Systems, Inc., NGS Sub Corp., NGS Technology

Officers: Robert S. Herlin/CEO, Pres. & Dir., Sterling McDonald/CFO, Daryl Mazzanti/VP - Operations, David Joe/Controller

Directors: Robert S. Herlin/CEO, Pres. & Dir., Laird Q. Cagan/Chmn., E. J. Dipaolo/Dir., Gene Stoever/Dir., Bill Dozier/Dir.

Owners: Robert S. Herlin/7.60%, Sterling H. McDonald/2.40%, E. J. DiPaolo, Gene Stoever, William Dozier, Laird Q. Cagan/28.60%, Daryl V. Mazzanti/1.50%, Insiders/38.40%, Eric A. McAfee, P2 Capital LLC and McAfee Capital LLC/19.40%

Curr. Assets:	$28,922,000	Curr. Liab.:	$1,597,000	P/E Ratio:	3.24
Plant, Equip.:	$5,614,000	Total Liab.:	$2,123,000	Indic. Yr. Divd.:	NA
Total Assets:	$34,906,000	Net Worth:	$32,783,000	Debt/ Equity:	NA

Evolving Gold Corp

1188 W Georgia St., Ste. 1200, Vancouver, BC, V6E 4A2; *PH:* 1-604-685-6375; *http://* www.evolvinggold.com; *Email:* info@evolvinggold.com

General - Incorporation	Canada	Stock - Price on:12/24/2007	NA
Employees	NA	Stock Exchange	OTC
Auditor	Amisano Hanson	Ticker Symbol	EVOGF
Stk Agt	Pacific Corporate Trust of Canada	Outstanding Shares	NA
Counsel	Mr. Bruce Bragagnolo	E.P.S	NA
DUNS No.	NA	Shareholders	NA

Business: The groups principle activity is to acquire and explore mineral properties. The group also focuses on setting up advanced stage acquisition and exploration methods in the mineral properties. The group operates from United States.

Primary SIC and add'l.: 1040

CIK No: 0001303202

Officers: Robert Bick/Dir., CEO, Quinton Hennigh/VP - Exploration, Chief Geologist, Chris Osterman/Consulting Geologist, Lawrence A. Dick/Dir., Pres., Donald Gee/Dir., CFO, Bill Gillies/EVG Investor Relations

Directors: Robert Bick/Dir., CEO, Lawrence A. Dick/Dir., Pres., Donald Gee/Dir., CFO, Gildar J. Arseneau/52/Dir., William Majcher/Dir.

Owners: Pinetree Resource Partnership/11.66%, Robert F. Bick, Passport Materials Master Fund, LP/11.43%, Lawrence A. Dick

Financial Data: *Fiscal Year End:*03/31 *Latest Annual Data:* 03/31/2006

Year	Sales	Net Income
2006	NA	-$953,000
2005	NA	-$486,000

Curr. Assets:	$96,000	Curr. Liab.:	$250,000		
Plant, Equip.:	$29,000	Total Liab.:	$250,000	Indic. Yr. Divd.:	NA
Total Assets:	$126,000	Net Worth:	-$124,000	Debt/ Equity:	NA

Evolving Systems Inc

9777 Pyramid Ct., Ste. 100, Englewood, CO, 80112; *PH:* 1-303-802-1000; *Fax:* 1-303-802-1420; *http://* www.evolving.com

General - Incorporation	DE	Stock - Price on:12/24/2007	$2.29
Employees	227	Stock Exchange	NDQ
Auditor	KPMG LLP	Ticker Symbol	EVOL
Stk Agt	American Stock Transfer & Trust Co.	Outstanding Shares	17,660,000
Counsel	NA	E.P.S.	$0.07
DUNS No.	14-856-7266	Shareholders	NA

Business: The group's principal activity is to provide innovative and cost-effective software solutions to tier one telecommunication companies in relation to their operational support systems(oss) and network elements(ne) applications. The group's operations include custom programming, systems integration, annual maintenance contracts, training services, packaged software products and related services. The group's prime product, local number portability (lnp) software helps the carriers to accommodate customer requests to change service providers while retaining the same phone number. The group provides a wide range of custom solutions to incumbent local exchange carriers and competitive local exchange carriers for providing and fulfilling of customer orders. On 03-Nov-2003, the group acquired cms communications inc.

Primary SIC and add'l.: 7379 7372 7373

CIK No: 0001052054

Subsidiaries: Evolving Systems Holdings Limited, Evolving Systems Holdings,Inc., Evolving Systems Networks India Private Limited, Telecom Software Enterprises, LLC.

Officers: Thaddeus Dupper/Dir., CEO, Pres., Anita T. Moseley/Sr. VP, General Counsel, Sec./$297,127.00, Stuart Cochran/CTO/$345,349.00, Madhu Reddy/GM - Evolving Systems India, Brian R. Ervine/46/Exec. VP, Chief Financial, Administrative Officer, Treasurer, Assist. Sec./$320,459.00, Steve Farnsworth/VP - Pre, Sales Engineering, Andy Ross/VP - Worldwide Professional Services, James King/VP - Worldwide Sales, Marketing, Grant Thornton/Auditor

Directors: Thaddeus Dupper/Dir., CEO, Pres., Stephen K. Gartside/Chmn., Steve B. Warnecke/Dir., Philip M. Neches/Dir., David J. Nicol/Dir., George A. Hallenbeck/Dir., Bruce W. Armstrong/Dir.

Owners: Apax Europe IV GP Co. Limited/7.30%, Steve B. Warnecke, Anita T. Moseley/2.20%, Philip M. Neches, Stuart Cochran, Disciplined Growth Investors,Inc./5.10%, Thaddeus Dupper/1.60%, George A. Hallenbeck/8.00%, Brian R. Ervine/1.90%, Apax Europe IV GP Co. Limited/88.00%, Insiders/19.30%, David J. Nicol, Stephen K. Gartside/3.60%

Financial Data: *Fiscal Year End:*12/31 *Latest Annual Data:* 12/31/2006

Year	Sales	Net Income
2006	$33,833,000	-$16,783,000
2005	$39,452,000	-$2,905,000
2004	$26,342,000	$424,000

Curr. Assets:	$17,347,000	Curr. Liab.:	$16,544,000	P/E Ratio:	57.25
Plant, Equip.:	$1,349,000	Total Liab.:	$29,899,000	Indic. Yr. Divd.:	NA
Total Assets:	$51,338,000	Net Worth:	$10,158,000	Debt/ Equity:	0.6907

Exact Sciences Corp

100 Campus Dr., Marlborough, MA, 01752; *PH:* 1-508-683-1200; *Fax:* 1-508-683-1201; *http://* www.exactlabs.com; *Email:* customerservice@exactsciences.com

General - Incorporation	DE	Stock - Price on:12/24/2007	$2.94
Employees	22	Stock Exchange	NDQ
Auditor	Ernst & Young LLP	Ticker Symbol	EXAS
Stk Agt	American Stock Transfer & Trust Co.	Outstanding Shares	26,840,000
Counsel	Testa, Hurwitz & Thibeault	E.P.S.	-$0.39
DUNS No.	NA	Shareholders	NA

Business: The group's principal activity is application of proprietary genomics technologies in the early detection of colorectal cancer and other types of common cancers. Pregen-plus utilizes pregen technologies to isolate the minute amounts of human dna shed from the colon into stool and then identifies mutations in dna shed from abnormal cells indicative of colorectal cancer and pre-cancerous lesions. The group's technology platform consists of the proprietary cancer detection methods such as multiple mutation detection (mumu (r)), deletion technology, dna integrity assay (dia) and enumerated loss of heterozygosity (e-loh).

Primary SIC and add'l.: 8071 8731

CIK No: 0001124140

Subsidiaries: EXACT Sciences Securities Corporation

Officers: Don M. Hardison/57/Dir., CEO, Pres./$738,058.00, Patrick J. Zenner/Exec. Chmn., Interim CEO, Charles R. Carelli/VP - Finance/$247,304.00, Jeffrey R. Luber/Pres./$537,276.00, Barry M. Berger/Chief Medical Officer

Directors: Don M. Hardison/57/Dir., CEO, Pres., Patrick J. Zenner/Exec. Chmn., Interim CEO, Lance Willsey/Dir., Connie Mack/67/Dir., Edwin M. Kania/Dir., Sally W. Crawford/Dir., Senator Connie Mack/Dir.

Owners: Sally W. Crawford, Connie Mack, Lance Willsey, Charles R. Carelli, Patrick J. Zenner, Edwin M. Kania/5.08%, Intrinsic Value Asset Management/8.74%, Insiders/10.85%, Harry W. Wilcox, Don M. Hardison/3.76%, The TCW Group,Inc./10.12%, Paloma International L.P./8.35%, One Liberty Fund Entities/4.48%, Jeffrey R. Luber

Financial Data: *Fiscal Year End:* 12/31 *Latest Annual Data:* 12/31/2006

Year	Sales	Net Income
2006	$4,750,000	-$12,915,000
2005	$4,250,000	-$14,520,000
2004	$4,935,000	-$18,523,000

Curr. Assets:	$21,461,000	**Curr. Liab.:**	$6,365,000		
Plant, Equip.:	$844,000	**Total Liab.:**	$8,910,000	**Indic. Yr. Divd.:**	NA
Total Assets:	$23,868,000	**Net Worth:**	$14,958,000	**Debt/ Equity:**	NA

Exactech Inc

2320 NW 66th Ct., Gainesville, FL, 32653; *PH:* 1-352-377-1140; *Fax:* 1-352-378-2617; *http://* www.exac.com; *Email:* investor.relations@exac.com

General - Incorporation .... FL
Employees 215
Auditor .... Deloitte & Touche LLP
Stk Agt...... American Stock Transfer & Trust Co.
Counsel .... Greenberg Traurig
DUNS No. 15-756-5946

Stock- Price on:12/24/2007 .... $14.37
Stock Exchange .... NDQ
Ticker Symbol .... EXAC
Outstanding Shares 11,560,000
E.P.S $0.68
Shareholders .... NA

Business: The group's principal activities are to develop, manufacture, market and sell orthopaedic implant devices and related surgical instrumentation to hospitals and physicians in the United States and overseas. These devices are used in replacing joints that have deteriorated as a result of injury or diseases, such as arthritis. The customers for the group's products are hospitals, surgeons, physicians and clinics. The group currently offers its products in twenty-five countries in addition to the United States: Argentina, Australia, Austria, Belgium, Brazil, China, Colombia, cyprus, Germany, Greece, Japan, Italy, lebanon, luxembourg, Mexico, the Netherlands, Portugal, Spain, turkey, and the United Kingdom.

Primary SIC and add'l.: 3842

CIK No: 0000913165

Subsidiaries: Exactech (UK), Ltd., Exactech Medical (Shanghai), Ltd., d/b/a Exactech Asia

Officers: William Petty/65/Chmn., CEO, Pres./$593,326.00, Bruce Thompson/50/Sr. VP, GM - Biologics Division/$345,618.00, Gary J. Miller/60/Exec. VP - Research, Development/$409,985.00, Joel C. Phillips/40/CFO, Treasurer/$298,814.00, David W. Petty/41/Exec. VP - Sales, Marketing/$296,636.00, Betty Petty/65/VP - Administration, Human Resources, Corp. Sec.

Directors: William Petty/65/Chmn., CEO, Pres., William B. Locander/64/Dir., Wynn R. Kearney/64/Dir., Albert Burstein/70/Dir., Paul E. Metts/65/Dir., James G. Binch/60/Dir.

Owners: Millerworks, Limited Partnership/3.60%, Bruce Thompson, Gary J. Miller/5.00%, William Petty/34.00%, Joel C. Phillips/1.30%, Insiders/44.00%, Albert H. Burstein, Wynn R. Kearney/3.20%, GAMCO Investors, Inc/8.10%, Prima Investments, Limited Partnership/31.80%, William B. Locander, Paul Metts, David W. Petty/1.20%, FMR Corp./9.80%

Financial Data: *Fiscal Year End:*12/31 **Latest Annual Data:** 12/31/2006

Year	Sales	Net Income
2006	$102,430,000	$7,752,000
2005	$91,016,000	$6,604,000
2004	$81,815,000	$7,304,000

Curr. Assets:	$60,087,000	**Curr. Liab.:**	$11,940,000	**P/E Ratio:**	22.81
Plant, Equip.:	$43,907,000	**Total Liab.:**	$36,351,000	**Indic. Yr. Divd.:**	NA
Total Assets:	$113,274,000	**Net Worth:**	$76,923,000	**Debt/ Equity:**	0.2831

Exar Corp

48720 Kato Rd., Fremont, CA, 94538; *PH:* 1-510-668-7000; *Fax:* 1-510-668-7001; *http://* www.exar.com

General - Incorporation .... DE
Employees 234
Auditor .... PricewaterhouseCoopers LLP
Stk Agt .... Computershare Trust Co
Counsel .... Wilson Sonsini Goodrich & Rosati
DUNS No. 05-949-5325

Stock- Price on:12/24/2007 .... $13.88
Stock Exchange .... NDQ
Ticker Symbol .... EXAR
Outstanding Shares 35,930,000
E.P.S $0.22
Shareholders .... NA

Business: The group's principal activity is to design, develop and market high-performance, high-bandwidth physical interface and access control solutions for the worldwide communications infrastructure. The group provides original equipment manufacturers with innovative, highly integrated circuits that facilitate the transport and aggregation of signals in access, metro and wide area networks. The group's physical layer silicon solutions address transmission standards such as t/e carrier, ATM and sonet/sdh. In addition, the group designs, develops and markets ic products that address select applications for the video and imaging markets. The major customers of the group include alcatel, cisco, nokia, hewlett-packard, lucent and tellabs. The group operates in North America, South America, Europe and the Asia/pacific.

Primary SIC and add'l.: 3674

CIK No: 0000753568

Subsidiaries: Exar, Exar Japan Corporation, Exar Ltd, Exar SARL, Micro Power Systems, Inc.

Officers: Ralph H. Schmitt/47/Dir., CEO, Pres., Scott J. Kamsler/Sr. VP, CFO/$80,053.00, Lee Cleveland/Sr. VP - Engineering, Interface, Power, Edward M. Lam/47/Sr. VP - Product Lines, Thomas R. Melendrez/General Counsel, Sec., Exec. VP - Business Development/$356,014.00, Al Gharakhanian/VP - Marketing, Networking, Transmission Products, John Herzing/VP - World Wide Sales, Levent Ozcolak/Dir. - Engineering, Video, Imaging Division, Hung P. Le/VP - Engineering, Vlsi, Gene L. Schaeffer/44/Sr. VP - Sales, Trong Vu/CIO, VP - Information Technology, Greg Kaufman/Media Contact - Marketing Communications, Stephen W. Michael/Sr. VP - Operations, Reliability, Quality Assurance/$246,849.00, Bahram Ghaderi/Dir. - Engineering, Startech Division, Roubik Gregorian/Pres. - Startech Division/$1,425,961.00

Directors: Ralph H. Schmitt/47/Dir., CEO, Pres., Richard L. Leza/Chmn., Guy W. Adams/Dir., Frank P. Carrubba/Dir., John S. McFarlane/Dir., Oscar J. Rodriguez/Dir., Pierre G. Guilbault/54/Dir., Brian Hilton/65/Dir., Pete Rodriguez/Dir.

Owners: John S. McFarlane, Scott J. Kamsler, Trivium Capital Management, LLC/8.00%, Brian Hilton, Insiders/2.40%, Ralph Schmitt, Guy W. Adams, Roubik Gregorian/1.60%, Alonim Investments Inc./14.60%, Stephen W. Michael, Richard L. Leza, Dimensional Fund Advisors LP/8.30%, Pierre Guilbault, Pete Rodriguez, Thomas R. Melendrez *(18 Owners included in Index)*

Financial Data: *Fiscal Year End:*03/31 **Latest Annual Data:** 3/31/2007

Year	Sales	Net Income
2007	$68,502,000	$8,024,000
2006	$67,024,000	$7,786,000
2005	$57,369,000	$5,319,000

Curr. Assets:	$371,295,000	**Curr. Liab.:**	$14,227,000	**P/E Ratio:**	63.09
Plant, Equip.:	$25,404,000	**Total Liab.:**	$14,418,000	**Indic. Yr. Divd.:**	NA
Total Assets:	$421,174,000	**Net Worth:**	$406,756,000	**Debt/ Equity:**	0.0004

Excel Maritime Carriers Ltd

Par La Ville Pl, 14 Par La Ville Rd., Hamilton; ; *http://* www.excelmaritime.com; *Email:* info@excelmaritime.com

General - Incorporation .... Liberia
Employees 487
Auditor .... Ernst & Young LLP
Stk Agt...... American Stock Transfer & Trust Co.
Counsel .... NA
DUNS No. .... NA

Stock- Price on:12/24/2007 .... $24.93
Stock Exchange .... NYSE
Ticker Symbol .... EXM
Outstanding Shares 19,650,000
E.P.S $3.04
Shareholders .... NA

Business: The groups principle activity is to provide seaborne transportation services for crude oil and dry cargo. The group operates from United States.

Primary SIC and add'l.: 4412

CIK No: 0000842294

Subsidiaries: Amanda Enterprises Ltd., Barland Holdings Inc., Becalm Shipping Co. Ltd., Candy Enterprises Inc., Castalia Services Ltd., Centel Shipping Co. Ltd, Fianna Navigation S.A., Fountain Services Ltd., Harvey Development Corp., Ingram Limited, Liegh Jane Navigation S.A., Madlex Shipping Co. Ltd., Magalie Investments Corp., Marias Trading Inc., Maryville Maritime Inc. 28 Subsidiaries included in the Index

Officers: Christopher J. Georgakis/43/Dir., CEO, Pres., George Agadakis/53/VP, COO, Dir., Georgina E. Sousa/Dir., Sec., Eleftherios A. Papatrifon/37/CFO

Directors: Christopher J. Georgakis/43/Dir., CEO, Pres., Gabriel Panayotides/52/Chmn., Apostolos Kontoyannis/56/Non Exec. Dir., Trevor J. Williams/63/Dir., Georgina E. Sousa/Dir., Sec., Evangelos MacRis/56/Non Exec. Dir., George Agadakis/53/VP, COO, Dir., Frithjof Platou/70/Non Exec. Dir.

Owners: Insiders/15.52%, Gabriel Panayotides/15.06%, Argon S.A./25.60%, George Agadakis/0.46%, Boston Industries S.A./41.14%

Financial Data: *Fiscal Year End:*12/31 **Latest Annual Data:** 12/31/2006

Year	Sales	Net Income
2006	$124,109,000	$31,106,000
2005	$118,604,000	$67,759,000
2004	$52,603,000	$32,050,000

Curr. Assets:	$95,788,000	**Curr. Liab.:**	$43,719,000	**P/E Ratio:**	7.09
Plant, Equip.:	$438,401,000	**Total Liab.:**	$229,190,000	**Indic. Yr. Divd.:**	$0.800
Total Assets:	$549,351,000	**Net Worth:**	$320,161,000	**Debt/ Equity:**	NA

Excel Technology Inc

41 Research Way, East Setauket, NY, 11733; *PH:* 1-631-784-6175; *Fax:* 1-631-784-6195; *http://* www.exceltechinc.com

General - Incorporation .... DE
Employees 704
Auditor .... KPMG LLP
Stk Agt...... American Stock Transfer & Trust Co.
Counsel .... Breslow & Walker LLP
DUNS No. 14-803-9415

Stock- Price on:12/24/2007 .... $27.1
Stock Exchange .... NDQ
Ticker Symbol .... XLTC
Outstanding Shares 12,160,000
E.P.S $1.36
Shareholders .... NA

Business: The group's principal activities are to design, develop, manufacture and market laser systems and electro-optical components. The products include computer controlled industrial laser marking systems, 3D engraving machines for coining dies, bottles and tire molds, sealed co2 laser for cutting, marking, drilling and galvanometer based optical scanners. The customers of the group are the electronic, semiconductor, scientific and other industrial markets. The products are marketed under the brand names insignia, icon, aurora and concorde. The group operates in the United States, Europe and Asia.

Primary SIC and add'l.: 3699 3827 3845

CIK No: 0000873603

Subsidiaries: Baublys GmbH, Cambridge Technology, Inc., Continuum Electro-Optics, Inc., Control Laser Corporation, Control Systemation, Inc., D Green (Electronics) Limited, Excel Laser Technology Private Limited, Excel Technology Asia Sdn. Bhd., Excel Technology Europe GmbH, Excel Technology France S.A.S., Excel Technology Italy Srl., Excel Technology Japan Holding Co., Ltd., Excel Technology Lanka (Private) Limited, Excel Technology Services Company, Photo Research, Inc. 18 Subsidiaries included in the Index

Officers: Antoine Dominic/Dir., CEO, COO, Pres., Alice Varisano/CFO, Sec.

Directors: Antoine Dominic/Dir., CEO, COO, Pres., Donald J. Hill/Chmn., Donald E. Weeden/Dir., Steven Georgiev/Dir., Ira J. Lamel/Dir.

Owners: Antoine Dominic/4.60%, Alice Varisano, Insiders/9.00%, Columbia Wanger Asset Management, L.P/6.30%, Donald E. Weeden, Steven Georgiev, Ira Lamel, ClearBridge Advisors, LLC./14.00%, Donald J. Hill/3.30%

Financial Data: *Fiscal Year End:*12/31 **Latest Annual Data:** 12/31/2006

Year	Sales	Net Income
2006	$154,496,000	$14,019,000
2005	$137,717,000	$15,208,000
2004	$136,631,000	$14,762,000

Curr. Assets:	$124,190,000	**Curr. Liab.:**	$13,642,000	**P/E Ratio:**	22.03
Plant, Equip.:	$25,503,000	**Total Liab.:**	$18,188,000	**Indic. Yr. Divd.:**	NA
Total Assets:	$181,979,000	**Net Worth:**	$163,725,000	**Debt/ Equity:**	NA

Excellency Investment Realty Trust Inc

Formerly: Gift Liquidators Inc
270 Laurel St., First Fl. Office, Hartford, CT, 06105; *PH:* 1-860-246-7672; *http://* www.giftliquidators.com

General - Incorporation .... OK
Employees 1
Auditor .... Carlin, Charron & Rosen LLP
Stk Agt .... Fidelity Transfer Co.
Counsel .... NA
DUNS No. .... NA

Stock- Price on:12/24/2007 .... $1.01
Stock Exchange .... NA
Ticker Symbol .... NA
Outstanding Shares 43,760,000
E.P.S .... -$0.36
Shareholders .... NA

Business: The group is a wholesale distributor of a diverse line of gift and novelty products that are acquired in closeout from other gift developers, distributors and wholesalers. To date, all of the products have been acquired from Laid Back Enterprises, a private company affiliated with the Company and

owned by the Company's executive officers, but the Company is looking for additional sources of products and to develop additional sales through an internet presence. The Company normally operates a seasonal retail business for its products during the Christmas holiday season, however, in 2004 the Company did not operate a retail store.

Primary SIC and add'l.: 5099

CIK No: 0001286218

Officers: David Mladen/52/Dir., CEO, Pres., Daniel Norensberg/CFO

Directors: David Mladen/52/Dir., CEO, Pres.

Owners: Insiders/99.80%, David Mladen/99.80%

Financial Data: Fiscal Year End:12/31 **Latest Annual Data:** 12/31/2006

Year	Sales	Net Income
2006	$1,550,000	-$2,395,000
2005	$1,617,000	-$1,661,000
2004	$278,000	-$110,000

Curr. Assets:	$1,084,000	Curr. Liab.:	$431,000		
Plant, Equip.:	$4,859,000	Total Liab.:	$12,406,000	Indic. Yr. Divd.:	NA
Total Assets:	$6,514,000	Net Worth:	-$5,893,000	Debt/ Equity:	NA

Excelligence Learning Corp

2 Lower Ragsdale Dr., Ste. 200, Monterey, CA, 93940; **PH:** 1-831-333-2000; **http://** www.excelligencelearning.com

General - Incorporation	DE	Stock - Price on:12/24/2007	NA
Employees	NA	Stock Exchange	NA
Auditor	KPMG LLP	Ticker Symbol	NA
Stk Agt	Mellon Investor Services LLC	Outstanding Shares	NA
Counsel	NA	E.P.S.	NA
DUNS No.	NA	Shareholders	NA

Business: The groups' principal activity is to provide educational products, services and information to schools, educational professionals and consumers. The group operates in two segments: early childhood and elementary school. The early childhood segment includes the brand names discount school supply, earlychildhood news and smarterkids.com. It develops, manufactures and sells educational products through multiple distribution channels to early childhood professionals and parents and also provides information to teachers and other education professional regarding the development of children from infancy through age eight. The elementary school segment sells school supplies and other products targeted for use by children in kindergarten through sixth grade to elementary schools, teachers and other education organizations for fundraising activities.

Primary SIC and add'l.: 5961

CIK No: 0001130950

Subsidiaries: Earlychildhood LLC, Educational Products, Inc., Marketing Logistics, Inc., SmarterKids.com, Inc.

Exco Resources Inc

12377 Merit Dr., Ste. 1700, Dallas, TX, 75251; **PH:** 1-214-368-2084; **Fax:** 1-214-368-2087; **http://** www.excoresources.com

General - Incorporation	TX	Stock - Price on:12/24/2007	$19.48
Employees	471	Stock Exchange	NYSE
Auditor	PricewaterhouseCoopers LLP	Ticker Symbol	XCO
Stk Agt	Continental Stock Transfer & Trust Co	Outstanding Shares	104,310,000
Counsel	Gilbert & Tobin	E.P.S.	$0.13
DUNS No.	07-855-0639	Shareholders	NA

Business: The group's principal activities are to acquire, develop and exploit interest in oil and gas properties located in the continental United States and Canada. It also acts as an operator on certain of these properties and receives overhead reimbursement fees. The group's operations are primarily located in Texas,Louisiana, Colorado, Mississippi and alberta, Canada the major customers of the group include plains all American, inc. And affiliates and engage energy America, llc . It sells majority of the oil and natural gas produced, under short-term contracts. In 2002, the group acquired medicine river properties in Canada and dj basin properties in Colorado.

Primary SIC and add'l.: 1382 1311

CIK No: 0000316300

Subsidiaries: EXCO Investment I, LLC, EXCO Investment II, LLC, EXCO Operating, LP, North Coast Energy Eastern, Inc., North Coast Energy, Inc., Pinestone Resources, LLC, ROJO Pipeline, Inc., TXOK Acquisition, Inc., TXOK Energy Resources Company, TXOK Energy Resources Holdings, LLC, TXOK Texas Energy Holdings, LLC, TXOK Texas Energy Resources, L.P.

Officers: Douglas H. Miller/Chmn., CEO/$1,795,116.00, Stephen F. Smith/Vice Chmn., Pres., Sec./$797,234.00, Harold L. Hickey/VP, COO/$512,783.00, Douglas J. Ramsey/VP, CFO, Chief Accounting Officer, Treasurer/$511,783.00, Mark E. Wilson/VP, Controller, William L. Boeing/VP, General Counsel/$1,225,827.00, Charles R. Evans/VP - Marketing, Outside Operations, Richard L. Hodges/VP, John D. Jacobi/VP, Daniel A. Johnson/VP

Directors: Douglas H. Miller/Chmn., CEO, Stephen F. Smith/Vice Chmn., Pres., Sec., Boone Pickens/Dir., Robert L. Stillwell/Dir., Jeffrey S. Serota/42/Dir., Robert H. Niehaus/Dir., Jeffrey D. Benjamin/Dir., Earl E. Ellis/Dir., Rajath Shourie/34/Dir.

Owners: Cyrus Capital Partners, LP/5.00%, Ares Corporate Opportunities Fund, L.P./6.30%, American International Group, Inc/5.00%, Cyrus Capital Partners, LP/5.00%, Oaktree Capital Group HoldingsGP,LLC/30.00%, Oaktree Capital Group HoldingsGP,LLC/3.10%, Steven A. Cohen/5.10%, FMR Corp./5.00%, Ares Corporate Opportunities Fund, L.P./7.50%, Ares Corporate Opportunities Fund, L.P./7.50%, FMR Corp./8.00%, American International Group, Inc/5.00%, FMR Corp./5.00%, Oaktree Capital Group HoldingsGP,LLC/30.00%, Thomas Boone Pickens/10.20%

Financial Data: Fiscal Year End:12/31 **Latest Annual Data:** 12/31/2006

Year	Sales	Net Income
2006	NA	NA
2005	NA	NA
2004	NA	NA

Curr. Assets:	$236,710,000	Curr. Liab.:	$190,924,000	P/E Ratio:	149.85
Plant, Equip.:	$2,862,352,000	Total Liab.:	$2,527,207,000	Indic. Yr. Divd.:	NA
Total Assets:	$3,707,057,000	Net Worth:	$1,179,850,000	Debt/ Equity:	1.5333

Execute Sports Inc

21143 HawthorneBL No. 333, Torrence, CA, 90503; **PH:** 1-310-515-8902; **Fax:** 1-949-498-6122; **http://** www.executesports.com; **Email:** info@executesports.com

General - Incorporation	NV	Stock - Price on:12/24/2007	$0.019
Employees	NA	Stock Exchange	OTC
Auditor	Bedinger & Company	Ticker Symbol	EXCS
Stk Agt	American Stock Transfer & Trust Co.	Outstanding Shares	53,860,000
Counsel	NA	E.P.S.	NA
DUNS No.	NA	Shareholders	NA

Business: The groups principle activity is to manufacture sports apparel. Products of the group include wetsuits, vests, rash guards, wake skates, shoes, snowboards, related accessories and apparel. The group markets its products under the brandnames Execute Sports, Kampus, Academy and EagleRider. In December 28, 2005 the group acquired Pacific Sports Group, Inc. The group operates from the United States, Europe, Australia, South Africa and Asia.

Primary SIC and add'l.: 2320

CIK No: 0001330292

Officers: Donald Dallape/48/Chmn., CEO, Sheryl Gardner/44/CFO, Geno Apicella/41/VP - Water Sports, Celeste Berouty/Pres., Todd M. Pitcher/38/Dir., Pres., Sec., Duane Pacha/37/Brand Mgr., Jeff Baughn/36/Dir. - Marketing

Directors: Donald Dallape/48/Chmn., CEO, Craig Washington/43/Dir., Todd M. Pitcher/38/Dir., Pres., Sec., Benedict Amendolara/47/Dir.

Owners: Celeste Berouty/5.00%, Sheryl Gardner/2.70%, Insiders/27.40%, Geno Apicella/12.60%, Leon Monfort/6.40%, Benedict Amendolar/3.40%, Craig Washington/3.60%

Financial Data: Fiscal Year End:10/31 **Latest Annual Data:** 12/31/2006

Year	Sales	Net Income
2006	$2,018,000	-$5,609,000
2005	$1,389,000	-$3,567,000

Curr. Assets:	$656,000	Curr. Liab.:	$1,896,000		
Plant, Equip.:	$98,000	Total Liab.:	$1,896,000	Indic. Yr. Divd.:	NA
Total Assets:	$754,000	Net Worth:	-$1,143,000	Debt/ Equity:	NA

Exelixis Inc

210 E Grand Ave., South San Francisco, CA, 94083; **PH:** 1-650-837-7000; **Fax:** 1-650-837-8300; **http://** www.exelixis.com

General - Incorporation	DE	Stock - Price on:12/24/2007	$12.03
Employees	651	Stock Exchange	NDQ
Auditor	Ernst & Young LLP	Ticker Symbol	EXEL
Stk Agt	Mellon Investor Services LLC	Outstanding Shares	96,790,000
Counsel	Cooley Godward LLP	E.P.S.	-$0.95
DUNS No.	NA	Shareholders	NA

Business: The group's principal activity is to develop therapeutically and commerically valuable pharmaceutical products by leveraging its integrated discovery platform. This platform increases the speed, efficiency and quality of pharmaceutical product discovery and development. The platform includes model system genetics and comparative genomics, libraries of modified model organisms, specialized reagents, assay biology, informatics databases and software, mechanism of action technology, automated high-throughput screening. The group designs its research to identify novel genes and protiens that specify disease pathway in a therapeutically relevant manner. The technologies of the group are applicable to all industries such as pharmaceutical, diagnostic, agrochemical and agricultural industries.

Primary SIC and add'l.: 8731

CIK No: 0000939767

Subsidiaries: Artemis Pharmaceuticals GmbH, Exelixis Plant Sciences, Inc., X-Ceptor Therapeutics, Inc.

Officers: George A. Scangos/Dir., CEO, Pres./$3,664,867.00, Lupe M. Rivera/Sr. VP - Operations, D. Ry Wagner/VP - Research, Exelixis Plant Sciences, Peter Lamb/Sr. VP - Discovery Research, Chief Scientific Officer, Frank L. Karbe/CFO, Exec. VP/$1,177,130.00, Jeffrey R. Latts/Exec. VP - Development/$1,353,558.00, Pamela A. Simonton/Sr. VP - Patents, Licensing/$1,006,619.00, Michael Morrissey/Pres. - Research, Development/$1,408,807.00, Gisela M. Schwab/Sr. VP, Chief Medical Officer

Directors: George A. Scangos/Dir., CEO, Pres., Stelios Papadopoulos/Co - Founder, Chmn., Ronald M. Evans/Member - Scientific Advisory Board, Charles Sawyers/Member - Scientific Advisory Board, Carl B. Feldbaum/Dir., Jose Baselga/Member - Scientific Advisory Board, Frank L. Karbe/CFO, Exec. VP, Lance Willsey/Dir., Vincent Marchesi/Dir., Charles Cohen/Dir., George Poste/Dir., Frank McCormick/Dir., Member - Scientific Advisory Board, Jack L. Wyszomierski/Dir., Alan M. Garber/Dir.

Owners: Entities Associated with OrbiMed Advisors LLC/5.70%, Lance Willsey, Jack Wyszomierski, Wellington Management Company LLP/6.80%, Persons Associated with FMR Corp./15.00%, T. Rowe Price Associates, Inc./9.20%, Insiders/6.60%, Stelios Papadopoulos, Michael M. Morrissey, Entities Associated with Barclays Global Investors, NA/5.60%, Frank McCormick, Vincent T. Marchesi, George A. Scangos/3.20%, Jeffrey R. Latts, Pamela A. Simonton (19 Owners included in Index)

Financial Data: Fiscal Year End:12/31 **Latest Annual Data:** 12/29/2006

Year	Sales	Net Income
2006	$98,670,000	-$101,492,000
2005	$75,961,000	-$84,404,000
2004	$52,857,000	-$137,245,000

Curr. Assets:	$210,361,000	Curr. Liab.:	$108,755,000		
Plant, Equip.:	$35,577,000	Total Liab.:	$275,417,000	Indic. Yr. Divd.:	NA
Total Assets:	$332,712,000	Net Worth:	$33,543,000	Debt/ Equity:	2.7806

Exelon Corp

10 S Dearborn St., 37th Fl., Chicago, IL, 60680; **PH:** 1-312-394-7398; **Fax:** 1-312-394-7945; **http://** www.exeloncorp.com

General - Incorporation	PA	Stock - Price on:12/24/2007	$73.82
Employees	17,200	Stock Exchange	NYSE
Auditor	PricewaterhouseCoopers LLP	Ticker Symbol	EXC
Stk Agt	Computershare Investor Services LLC	Outstanding Shares	672,650,000
Counsel	NA	E.P.S.	$4.08
DUNS No.	NA	Shareholders	NA

Business: The group operates through its subsidiaries whose principle activities include enacting the energy and power marketing. The group operates from United States.

Primary SIC and add'l.: 4931 4911 4939 4922

CIK No: 0001109357

Subsidiaries: Adwin (Schuylkill) Cogeneration, Inc., Adwin Realty Company, AllEnergy Gas & Electric Marketing Company, LLC, Ambassador II Joint Venture, AmerGen Clinton NQF, LLC, AmerGen Consolidation, LLC, AmerGen Energy Company, LLC, AmerGen Oyster Creek NQF, LLC, AmerGen TMI NQF, LLC, ATNP Finance Company, Bradford Associates, Braidwood 1 NQF, LLC, Braidwood 2 NQF, LLC, Byron 1 NQF, LLC, Byron 2 NQF, LLC 171 Subsidiaries included in the Index

Officers: John W. Rowe/63/Chmn., CEO, Pres./$16,427,070.00, Frank M. Clark/63/Chmn., CEO - Comed/$3,920,291.00, Denis P. O'Brien/48/Exec. VP - Exelon Corporation, CEO, Pres. - Peco Energy, Katherine K. Combs/Sr. VP - Corporate Governance, Corp. Sec., Deputy General Counsel, John L. Skolds/57/Exec. VP - Exelon, Pres. - Exelon Energy Delivery, Pres. - Exelon Generation, Gary S. Snodgrass/56/Chief Human Resources Officer, Exec. VP, Mark Schiavoni/52/Sr. VP - Exelon Generation, Pres. - Exelon Power, Christopher M. Crane/49/Exec. VP - Exelon Corporation, COO - Exelon Generation, Randall E. Mehrberg/52/Exec. VP, Chief Administrative Officer, Chief Legal Officer/$5,136,583.00, John F. Young/51/Exec. VP - Finance, Markets, CFO/$3,767,077.00, Elizabeth Anne Moler/59/Exec. VP - Government, Environmental Affairs, Public Policy, Ruth Ann M. Gillis/54/Sr. VP - Exelon Corporation, Pres. - Exelon Business Services Company, Beth Rapczynski/Mgr. - Communications, Exelon Nuclear Mid, Atlantic Regional Operating Group, Andrea L. Zopp/51/Sr. VP, Chief Human Resources Officer, Matthew F. Hilzinger/44/Sr. VP, Corporate Controller *(42 Officers included in Index)*

Directors: John W. Rowe/63/Chmn., CEO, Pres., Frank M. Clark/63/Chmn., CEO - Comed, Edgar D. Jannotta/76/Dir. - Commonwealth Edison Company, Edward A. Brennan/74/Dir., Richard L. Thomas/Dir., Walter M. Dalessio/74/Dir., Thomas J. Ridge/62/Dir., Nelson A. Diaz/60/Dir., Bruce Demars/72/Dir., Rosemarie B. Greco/61/Dir., Ronald Rubin/Dir., Nicholas Debenedictis/62/Dir., Sue Ling Gin/66/Dir., John W. Rogers/50/Dir., John M. Palms/72/Dir. *(19 Directors included in Index)*

Owners: Insiders, John F. Young, Wellington Management Company, Capital Research and Management Company, Nelson A. Diaz, Sue L. Gin, Walter M. D'Alessio, John M. Palms, Nicholas DeBenedictis, William C. Richardson, Ronald Rubin, Edgar D. Jannotta, Edward A. Brennan, John W. Rogers, Thomas J. Ridge *(20 Owners included in Index)*

Financial Data: Fiscal Year End:12/31 **Latest Annual Data:** 12/31/2006

Year	Sales	Net Income
2006	$15,655,000,000	$1,592,000,000
2005	$15,357,000,000	$923,000,000
2004	$14,515,000,000	$1,864,000,000

Curr. Assets:	$4,992,000,000	**Curr. Liab.:**	$5,795,000,000	**P/E Ratio:**	26.55
Plant, Equip.:	$22,775,000,000	**Total Liab.:**	$34,259,000,000	**Indic. Yr. Divd.:**	$1.760
Total Assets:	$44,319,000,000	**Net Worth:**	$9,973,000,000	**Debt/ Equity:**	1.1522

Exeter Resource Corp

PO Box 41, Vancouver, BC, V6C 3L9; **PH:** 1-604-688-9592; **http://** www.exeterresource.com; **Email:** exeter@exeterresource.com

General - Incorporation	BC	**Stock** - Price on:12/24/2007	NA
Employees	NA	Stock Exchange	AMEX
Auditor	MacKay LLP	Ticker Symbol	XRA
Stk Agt	Computershare Investor Services LLC	Outstanding Shares	NA
Counsel	NA	E.P.S.	NA
DUNS No.	NA	Shareholders	NA

Business: The groups principle activity is to explore of mineral properties and discover epithermal gold or silver and porphyry copper or gold projects. The group also conducts the examination and acquisition of mineral exploration opportunities and secures capital for the implementation of its exploration programs., and developmental studies and carries out progressive environmental and engineering studies along with exploration. The group's properties include an advanced stage project at La Cabeza in Argentina, with an inferred resource containing 891, 000 ounces of gold based on 18.3 million tonnes grading 1.5 g/t gold. The group operates from United States.

Primary SIC and add'l.: 1400

CIK No: 0001306900

Officers: Bryce Roxburgh/Dir., CEO, Pres., Jerry Perkins/VP - Development, Operations, Matthew Williams/Exploration Mgr., Glen Van Kerkvoort/Chief Geologist, Cecil Bond/CFO, Rob Grey/VP - Investor Communications, Patricia Inzirillo/Argentina, Mgr. - Admin, Legal, Paul Cholakos/COO, Patrick Esnouf/Dir. - Chilean Subsidiary, Gustavo Delendatti/Don Sixto Site Mgr., Gonzalo Damond/Commercial Mgr. - Argentina, Mafalda Arias/Administration Mgr.

Directors: Bryce Roxburgh/Dir., CEO, Pres., Yale Simpson/Chmn., Michael McPhie/Dir., Paul MacNeill/Dir., Douglas Scheving/Dir., William McCartney/51/Dir., Robert G. Reynolds/Dir.

Owners: Bryce Roxburgh/12.00%, Cecil Bond/1.10%, Douglas Scheving, Michael McPhie, Yale Simpson/5.85%, Jerry Perkins, Insiders/24.12%, William McCartney, Paul MacNeill/3.20%

EXFO Electro-Optical Engineering Inc

400 Godin Ave., Vanier, PQ, G1M 2K2; **PH:** 1-418-683-0211; **Fax:** 1-418-683-2170; **http://** www.exfo.com; **Email:** order.management@exfo.com

General - Incorporation	Canada	**Stock** - Price on:12/24/2007	$6.74
Employees	NA	Stock Exchange	NDQ
Auditor	PricewaterhouseCoopers LLP	Ticker Symbol	EXFO
Stk Agt	CIBC Mellon Trust CO.	Outstanding Shares	68,840,000
Counsel	NA	E.P.S.	$0.61
DUNS No.	NA	Shareholders	NA

Business: The group's principal activities are to design, manufacture and market fiber-optic test, measurement and automation solutions for the global telecommunications industry. The customers of the group include telecommunications carriers, optical component and system manufacturers and research and development laboratories. The products are marketed in the United States, Canada, Europe, Asia and South America.

Primary SIC and add'l.: 3669 3661

CIK No: 0001116284

Subsidiaries: Vanguard Technical Solutions, Inc

Officers: Germain Lamonde/Chmn., CEO, Pres., Stephen Bull/VP - Research, Development, Allan Firhoj/VP, GM - Life Sciences, Industrial Division, Luc Gagnon/VP - Telecom Manufacturing Operations, Customer Service, Benoit Ringuette/General Counsel, Corp. Sec., Normand Durocher/VP

- Human Resources, Pierre Plamondon/VP - Finance, CFO, Etienne Gagnon/VP - Optical, Layer Product Management, Customer Service, Vance Oliver/Mgr. - Investor Relations, Dana Yearian/VP - Telecom Sales - North America, Jon Bradley/VP - International Telecom Sales, Robert Fitts/VP - Corporate Development

Directors: Germain Lamonde/Chmn., CEO, Pres., Michael Unger/Dir., Guy Marier/Corp. Dir., Pierre Marcouiller/Dir., David A. Thompson/Dir., Andre Tremblay/Dir.

Owners: Jon Bradley, Pierre Plamondon, Insiders, David A. Thompson, Germain Lamonde, Pyramis Global Advisors, LLC/11.05%, Germain Lamonde/100.00%, Fiducie Germain Lamonde, Kern Capital Management, LLC/5.73%, Allan Firhoj, G. Lamonde Investissements Financiers inc, Michael Unger, Insiders/100.00%, Pierre Marcouiller, Germain Lamonde *(17 Owners included in Index)*

Financial Data: Fiscal Year End:08/31 **Latest Annual Data:** 08/31/2007

Year	Sales	Net Income
2007	$152,934,000	$42,257,000
2006	$128,253,000	$8,135,000
2005	$97,216,000	-$2,920,000

Curr. Assets:	$163,201,000	**Curr. Liab.:**	$19,216,000		
Plant, Equip.:	$17,392,000	**Total Liab.:**	$22,925,000	**Indic. Yr. Divd.:**	NA
Total Assets:	$212,702,000	**Net Worth:**	$189,777,000	**Debt/ Equity:**	NA

Exide Technologies

13000 Deerfield Pkwy., Bldg. 200, Alpharetta, GA, 30004; **PH:** 1-678-566-9000; **Fax:** 1-678-566-9188; **http://** www.exide.com

General - Incorporation	DE	**Stock** - Price on:12/24/2007	$9.22
Employees	13,862	Stock Exchange	NDQ
Auditor	PricewaterhouseCoopers LLP	Ticker Symbol	XIDE
Stk Agt	American Stock Transfer & Trust Co.	Outstanding Shares	60,690,000
Counsel	NA	E.P.S.	-$1.95
DUNS No.	60-657-8904	Shareholders	NA

Business: The groups principle activity is to provide stored electrical energy solutions. The group also manufactures lead acid batteries used in transportation, motive power, network power and military applications. The groups products are sold under the brand names Centra, Champion, DETA and Exide. The group operates from United States.

Primary SIC and add'l.: 3691 3694

CIK No: 0000813781

Subsidiaries: Ac Technibat S.l., Aim Munchen Gmbh, All Batteries Limited, Anker Defense A/s, Ceac Immobilier Sas, Ceac, Compagnie Europeene Daccumulateurs, Sas (ceac), Centra Spolka Akcyjna (centra Sa), Centra Trading Sp Zoo, Chloride Motive Power Iberica, S.l., Cmp Batterier Ab, Cmp Batteries Ltd., Cmp Batteries Pensions Limited, Cooperatie Exide Europe U.a., Deta Batterijen Bv, Deta Polska Spolka Akcyjna 74 Subsidiaries included in the Index

Officers: Gordon A. Ulsh/Dir., CEO, Pres./$3,284,846.00, Rodolphe Reverchon/Pres. - Transportation Europe, George S. Jones/Exec. VP - Human Resources, Communications, Mitchell S. Bregman/Pres. - Industrial Energy Americas/$766,337.00, Joel Campbell/Pres. - Industrial Energy Europe, Bruce A. Cole/Pres. - Transportation Americas, Douglas Gillespie/VP - Global Procurement, James R. Kautz/Primary Investor Relations Officer, Edward E.J. O'Leary/COO/$1,227,057.00, Francis M. Corby/CFO, Exec. VP/$1,030,321.00, Barbara A. Hatcher/Exec. VP, General Counsel, Mark W. Cummings/VP - Global Environment, Health, Safety, Todd Atenhan/Primary Investor Relations Officer, Brad S. Kalter/Deputy General Counsel, Corp. Sec., Phillip A. Damaska/Sr. VP, Corporate Controller/$854,833.00

Directors: Gordon A. Ulsh/Dir., CEO, Pres., John P. Reilly/Chmn., Michael R. Dappolonia/Dir., Michael P. Ressner/Dir., Carroll R. Wetzel/Dir., Joseph V. Lash/Dir., David S. Ferguson/Dir., Paul W. Jennings/Dir., Herbert F. Aspbury/Dir.

Owners: Michael R. DAppolonia, Phillip A. Damaska, John P. Reilly, Paul W. Jennings, Michael P. Ressner, Francis M. Corby, David S. Ferguson, Edward J. OLeary, Gordon A. Ulsh/1.30%, Jeffrey L. Gendell/28.10%, Insiders/2.30%, Legg Mason/13.80%, Carroll R. Wetzel, Herbert F. Aspbury, Mitchell S. Bregman

Financial Data: Fiscal Year End:03/31 **Latest Annual Data:** 3/31/2007

Year	Sales	Net Income
2007	$2,939,785,000	-$105,879,000
2006	$2,819,876,000	-$172,732,000
2005	$2,476,259,000	-$466,923,000

Curr. Assets:	$1,109,820,000	**Curr. Liab.:**	$678,250,000		
Plant, Equip.:	$685,842,000	**Total Liab.:**	$1,845,504,000	**Indic. Yr. Divd.:**	NA
Total Assets:	$2,082,909,000	**Net Worth:**	$224,739,000	**Debt/ Equity:**	2.0165

ExlService Holdings Inc

350 Pk. Ave., 10th Fl., New York, NY, 10022; **PH:** 1-212-277-7100; **Fax:** 1-212-277-7111; **http://** www.exlservice.com; **Email:** marketing@exlservice.com

General - Incorporation	DE	**Stock** - Price on:12/24/2007	$19.8
Employees	8,200	Stock Exchange	NDQ
Auditor	Ernst & Young, LLP	Ticker Symbol	EXLS
Stk Agt	Registrar & Transfer Co	Outstanding Shares	28,460,000
Counsel	NA	E.P.S.	$0.82
DUNS No.	NA	Shareholders	NA

Business: The groups principle activities include offshore solutions services. The groups services include business process outsourcing, research and analytics and advisory. The group products sold under the trade names MOST, ECS, ProMPT and SOFT. Customers served by the group include industry sectors, banking, financial services and insurance sector. In July 2006, the group acquired Inductis Inc. The group operates from the United States, the United Kingdom, Rest of World and India. The group's quarterly revenue for September 2007 was 46.63 millions of USD.

Primary SIC and add'l.: 8742 8748 7379 7389

CIK No: 0001297989

Subsidiaries: Exl Support Service Private Limited, ExlService (UK) Limited,, ExlService.com India Private Limited,, ExlService.com, Inc.,, Inductis (Singapore) PTE Ltd., Inductis India Private Limited, Inductis LLC, Inductis, Inc., Noida Customer Operations Private Limited,

Officers: Vikram Talwar/CEO, Vice Chmn., Rohit Kapoor/Dir., COO, Pres., Raju Taneja/VP - Information Security, Business Continuity Management, Krishna Nacha/VP, Chief Sales, Marketing Officer, Kal Bittianda/VP, Head - Strategic Accounting Management, North America, Sridhar Kadaba/VP, Head - Value Added Services, Lalit Wangikar/Principal, Head - Analytics Services, Matt

Appel/CFO, VP, Pavan Bagai/VP, Head - Operations, EXL India, Deepak Dhawan/VP, Global Head - Human Resources, Sandeep Tyagi/VP, Head - Knowledge Services, Amit Shashank/VP, General Counsel, Corp. Sec., Narasimha Kini/VP, Business Leader - Risk Advisory, Vikas Bhalla/VP, Business Leader, Madhavi Dahanukar/VP, Business Leader *(21 Officers included in Index)*

Directors: Vikram Talwar/CEO, Vice Chmn., Steven Gruber/Chmn., Garen K. Staglin/Dir., Rohit Kapoor/Dir., COO, Pres., Edward Dardani/Dir., Mohanbir Sawhney/Dir., David B. Kelso/Dir., Dennis R. Sheehan/Member - Advisory Board, Allen J. Gula/Member - Advisory Board, John Ainley/Member - Advisory Board

Owners: Vikram Talwar/7.50%, Pavan Bagai/1.40%, Oak Hill Partnerships/37.50%, Mohanbir Sawhney, David B. Kelso, Garen K. Staglin, Insiders/21.00%, FTVentures/12.30%, Narasimha Kini, Amit Shashank, Rohit Kapoor/7.50%

Financial Data: ***Fiscal Year End:***12/31 ***Latest Annual Data:*** 12/31/2006

Year	Sales	Net Income
2006	$121,769,000	$14,058,000
2005	$73,954,000	$7,060,000
2004	$60,467,000	$5,380,000

Curr. Assets:	$122,721,000	**Curr. Liab.:**	$37,699,000	**P/E Ratio:**	29.12
Plant, Equip.:	$21,545,000	**Total Liab.:**	$38,412,000	**Indic. Yr. Divd.:**	NA
Total Assets:	$165,609,000	**Net Worth:**	$127,196,000	**Debt/ Equity:**	0.0013

Expedia Inc

3150 139th Ave. SE, Bellevue, WA, 98005; ***PH:*** 1-425-679-7200; ***Fax:*** 1-425-679-7240; ***http://*** www.expediainc.com; ***Email:*** ir@expedia.com

General		***Stock***	
Incorporation	DE	Price on:12/24/2007	$29.21
Employees	6,600	Stock Exchange	NDQ
Auditor	Ernst & Young LLP	Ticker Symbol	EXPE
Stk Agt	Bank of New York	Outstanding Shares	303,130,000
Counsel	NA	E.P.S.	$0.92
DUNS No.	NA	Shareholders	NA

Business: The groups principle activity is to provide online travel services. The groups services include destination services, air ticketing and hotel reservation. The group products sold under the trade name Expedia(R), eLong(TM) Hotels.com(R) and Hotwire.com(TM). In the year 2005, the group acquired TripAdvisor. The group operates from North America, Europe and other. The group's quarterly revenue for September 2007 was 759.60 millions of USD.

Primary SIC and add'l.: 4481 7375 4481 4724 4724 7375 4729 4700 4729

CIK No: 0001324424

Subsidiaries: AceNet Travel Network, LLC, Activity Information Center, Inc., Bravado Investments Limited, C.A. ID SA, Canadian Holdings, LLC, Classic Vacations, LLC, DigitalAdvisor LLC, DN Holdings LLC, EIGAC Holdings, Inc., EL 2003 Holdings, Inc., eLong, Inc., eLongNet Information Technology (Beijing) Co., Ltd., Expedia Alpha Y.K., Expedia Asia Pacific Limited, Expedia Asia Pacific-Alpha Limited 79 Subsidiaries included in the Index

Officers: Dara Khosrowshahi/Dir., CEO, Pres., Stephen Kaufer/CEO, Pres. - Tripadvisorcom, Barry Diller/Chmn., Sr. Exec., Tim MacDonald/Pres. - Classic Vacations, Michael Adler/CFO, Paul Brown/Pres. - Expedia, Inc Partner Services Group Pres., Expedia North America, Bill Holtz/CIO, Kathy Dellplain/Exec. VP - Human Resources, Burke Norton/Exec. VP, General Counsel, Corp. Sec., Sean D. Kell/Sr. VP, GM - Hotelscom, Jean-Pierre Remy/Pres. - Expedia Corporate Travel, Eric Grosse/Sr. VP, GM - Hotwirecom, Dhiren Fonseca/Sr. VP - Corporate Development, Gary Fritz/Sr. VP - Corporate Development, Dermot Halpin/Pres. - Europe, Middle East, Africa *(18 Officers included in Index)*

Directors: Dara Khosrowshahi/Dir., CEO, Pres., Barry Diller/Chmn., Sr. Exec., Victor A. Kaufman/Vice Chmn., Simon Breakwell/Dir., Peter Kern/Dir., John C. Malone/Dir., William R. Fitzgerald/Dir., David Goldhill/Dir., George A. Battle/Dir., Jonathan Dolgen/Dir.

Owners: Capital Research and Management Company, Victor A. Kaufman, Liberty Media Corporation, Legg Mason Capital Management, Inc., LMM LCC and Legg Mason Value Trust,Inc, Jonathan L. Dolgen, David Goldhill, George A. Battle, Simon J. Breakwell, Michael B. Adler, Peter M. Kern, Kathleen K. Dellplain, UBS AG, Franklin Resources, Inc, Barry Diller, Insiders *(17 Owners included in Index)*

Financial Data: ***Fiscal Year End:***12/31 ***Latest Annual Data:*** 12/31/2006

Year	Sales	Net Income
2006	$2,237,586,000	$244,934,000
2005	$2,119,455,000	$228,730,000

Curr. Assets:	$1,182,685,000	**Curr. Liab.:**	$1,400,125,000	**P/E Ratio:**	38.95
Plant, Equip.:	$137,144,000	**Total Liab.:**	$2,364,894,000	**Indic. Yr. Divd.:**	NA
Total Assets:	$8,269,184,000	**Net Worth:**	$5,904,290,000	**Debt/ Equity:**	0.0993

Expeditors International of Washington Inc

1015 3rd Ave., 12th Fl., Seattle, WA, 98104; ***PH:*** 1-206-674-3400; ***Fax:*** 1-206-674-3459; ***http://*** www.expeditors.com

General		***Stock***	
Incorporation	WA	Price on:12/24/2007	$41.07
Employees	11,600	Stock Exchange	NDQ
Auditor	KPMG LLP	Ticker Symbol	EXPD
Stk Agt	EquiServe Trust Co N.A	Outstanding Shares	213,140,000
Counsel	NA	E.P.S.	$1.14
DUNS No.	03-523-9425	Shareholders	NA

Business: The group's principle activity is to provide global logistic services, which include consolidation or forwarding of air and ocean freight. It also provides additional services including distribution management, vendor consolidation, cargo insurance, purchase order management and customized logistics information. The group derives revenues from three segments: airfreight, ocean freight and ocean services and customs brokerage and import services. The customers of the group include retailing and wholesaling, electronics and manufacturing companies around the world. The group has operations in the United States, North America, Far East, Europe, Australia, Latin America and the Middle Eastern countries. The group's quarterly revenue for Sep'07 was 1,411.03 millions of USD.

Primary SIC and add'l.: 4491 6399 4449 4731

CIK No: 0000746515

Subsidiaries: 1015 Third Avenue Parking Corporation, ECI Taiwan Co., Ltd., ECMS Ltd., EI Freight (Micronesia),Inc., EI Freight (Taiwan) Ltd., EI Freight (U.S.A.),Inc., EI Freight Forwarding Co. Ltd. (12), EI Holdings, Ltd. (6), EI Logistics Ltd., Eif Sdn. Bhd. (7), Expeditors (Asia) Holding Co. Pte. Ltd., Expeditors (Bangladesh), Ltd., Expeditors (China) Investment Co. Pte. Ltd. (9), Expeditors (Malaysia) Sdn. Bhd. (5), Expeditors (Portugal)Transitarios Internacionais Lda. 71 Subsidiaries included in the Index

Officers: Peter J. Rose/Chmn., CEO/$5,220,789.00, Daniel R. Wall/Sr. VP - Ocean, Cargo Management Services, Rommel C. Saber/Pres., Pres. - Europe, Middle East, Africa, Indian Subcontinent, Charles J. Lynch/Sr. VP, Corporate Controller, Jordan R. Gates/Dir., CFO, Exec. VP/$3,305,708.00, Jean.claude Carcaillet/Sr. VP - Australasia, Rosanne Esposito/Exec. VP - Global Customs, Robert L. Villanueva/Pres. - Americas/$3,636,125.00, Roger A. Idiart/Sr. VP - Air Cargo, Sandy K.Y. Liu/COO - Asia, Manfred L. Amberger/Sr. VP - Continental Europe, Timothy C. Barber/Exec. VP - Global Sales, James L.K. Wang/Dir., Pres. - Asia/$4,829,438.00, Glenn M. Alger/COO, Pres./$4,538,322.00, Philip M. Coughlin/Sr. VP - North America *(18 Officers included in Index)*

Directors: Peter J. Rose/Chmn., CEO, James J. Casey/Dir., John W. Meisenbach/Dir., Dan P. Kourkoumelis/Dir., James L.K. Wang/Dir., Pres. - Asia, Michael J. Malone/Dir., Jordan R. Gates/Dir., CFO, Exec. VP

Owners: James J. Casey, James L.K. Wang, Neuberger Berman Inc./5.15%, Dan P. Kourkoumelis, Peter J. Rose/1.16%, Michael J. Malone, Delaware Management Holdings/5.64%, Jordan R. Gates, John W. Meisenbach, Glenn M. Alger, Insiders/4.30%, Ruane, Cunniff & Goldfarb Inc./6.16%, Robert L. Villanueva

Financial Data: ***Fiscal Year End:***12/31 ***Latest Annual Data:*** 12/31/2006

Year	Sales	Net Income
2006	$4,625,966,000	$235,094,000
2005	$3,901,781,000	$218,634,000
2004	$3,317,499,000	$156,126,000

Curr. Assets:	$1,341,837,000	**Curr. Liab.:**	$709,145,000	**P/E Ratio:**	36.03
Plant, Equip.:	$450,856,000	**Total Liab.:**	$735,888,000	**Indic. Yr. Divd.:**	$0.280
Total Assets:	$1,822,338,000	**Net Worth:**	$1,069,935,000	**Debt/ Equity:**	NA

Expleo Solutions Inc

Formerly: Kohler Capital I Corp

1415 W 22nd St., Tower Fl., Oak Brook, IL, 60523; ***PH:*** 1-630-684-2250

General		***Stock***	
Incorporation	FL	Price on:12/24/2007	NA
Employees	1,667	Stock Exchange	NA
Auditor	Stark Winter Schenkein & Co. LLP	Ticker Symbol	NA
Stk Agt	NA	Outstanding Shares	NA
Counsel	NA	E.P.S.	-$1.35
DUNS No.	NA	Shareholders	NA

Business: The group was incorporated under the laws of the State of Florida on 7-May-2001, and is in the early developmental and promotional stages. To date the Company's only activities have been organizational ones, directed at developing its business plan and raising its initial capital. The Company has not commenced any commercial operations. The Company has no full-time employees and owns no real estate.

Primary SIC and add'l.: 7372

CIK No: 0001231072

Officers: Kenneth C. Pavichevich/Dir., CEO, Gerard Werner/Attorney, Kerry R. Labant/53/Dir., Pres.

Directors: Kerry R. Labant/53/Dir., Pres., Corey Ferengul/36/Dir., Mary Warmus/46/Dir.

Owners: Kenneth Pavichevich/19.90%, Corey Ferengul/10.20%, Insiders/87.30%, Kerry LaBant/56.90%, Mary Warmus/0.26%

Financial Data: ***Fiscal Year End:***12/31 ***Latest Annual Data:*** 12/31/2006

Year	Sales	Net Income
2006	$259,716,000	-$134,642,000
2005	$343,448,000	-$64,124,000
2004	$191,447,000	$28,276,000

Curr. Assets:	$73,200,000	**Curr. Liab.:**	$70,097,000		
Plant, Equip.:	$33,197,000	**Total Liab.:**	$3,652,023,000	**Indic. Yr. Divd.:**	NA
Total Assets:	$3,779,994,000	**Net Worth:**	$127,971,000	**Debt/ Equity:**	NA

Exploration Drilling Corp

Goethestrae 61, Haltern am See, Deutschland, 45721; ***PH:*** 49-2364604428; ***Fax:*** 49-2364604429; ***http://*** www.edipower.com; ***Email:*** info@edipower.com

General		***Stock***	
Incorporation	NV	Price on:12/24/2007	$0.3
Employees	6	Stock Exchange	OTC
Auditor	Cordovano and Honeck, LLP	Ticker Symbol	EXDL
Stk Agt	Pacific Stock Transfer Company	Outstanding Shares	106,320,000
Counsel	NA	E.P.S.	-$0.05
DUNS No.	NA	Shareholders	NA

Business: The groups principal activity is to provide products for customer oriented solutions in water well construction. EDI technologies enable water to be found in regions where this was once considered impossible. The group operates from Nevada in the United States.

Primary SIC and add'l.: 1040

CIK No: 0001219606

Officers: Rainer Rotthauser/51/MD, CEO - Responsible for, Sales, Corporate Strategy, Organization, key Functions, Strategic Corporate Planning, Peter Scherer/Chmn. - Advisory Counsel, Attila Gal/Member - Technical - Commercial Advisory Counsel, Gunter Thiemann/51/GM, CFO, Christian Runge/GM

Owners: Rainer Rotthaeuser/1.50%, Guenter Thiemann, Insiders/2.20%, EDI Exploration Drilling International Holding/65.80%, John Boschert

Financial Data: ***Fiscal Year End:***07/31 ***Latest Annual Data:*** 12/31/2006

Year	Sales	Net Income
2006	NA	-$4,109,000
2005	NA	-$12,000

Curr. Assets:	$2,000	**Curr. Liab.:**	$6,000		
Plant, Equip.:	NA	**Total Liab.:**	$6,000	**Indic. Yr. Divd.:**	NA
Total Assets:	$2,000	**Net Worth:**	-$4,000	**Debt/ Equity:**	NA

Explortex Energy Inc

650 West Georgia St. , Ste. 2410, Vancouver, BC, V6B 4N7; *PH:* 1-604-689-8336

General - Incorporation	NV	Stock - Price on:12/24/2007	$0.1
Employees	NA	Stock Exchange	OTC
Auditor	Peterson Sullivan, PLLC	Ticker Symbol	EXPX
Stk Agt	Energy Transfer Partners, L.P.	Outstanding Shares	NA
Counsel	NA	E.P.S.	NA
DUNS No.	NA	Shareholders	NA

Business: The groups principal activities include acquiring, exploring and developing oil and natural gas reserves. The group operates from the United States and Canada.

Primary SIC and add'l.: 1311

CIK No: 0001364255

Owners: Insiders/64.50%, Chris Cooper/64.50%

Financial Data: *Fiscal Year End:* NA   *Latest Annual Data:* 04/30/2007

Year	Sales		Net Income
2007	NA		-$36,000
Curr. Assets:	$9,000	**Curr. Liab.:**	$10,000
Plant, Equip.:	$42,000	**Total Liab.:**	$10,000 **Indic. Yr. Divd.:** NA
Total Assets:	$51,000	**Net Worth:**	$41,000 **Debt/ Equity:** NA

Exponent Inc

149 Commonwealth Dr., Menlo Park, CA, 94025; *PH:* 1-650-326-9400; *Fax:* 1-650-326-8072; *http://* www.exponent.com; *Email:* info@exponent.com

General - Incorporation	DE	Stock - Price on:12/24/2007	$22.75
Employees	835	Stock Exchange	NDQ
Auditor	KPMG LLP	Ticker Symbol	EXPO
Stk Agt	Mellon Investor Services LLC	Outstanding Shares	14,840,000
Counsel. Heller Ehrman White & McAuliffe LLP		E.P.S.	$1.10
DUNS No.	60-406-1267	Shareholders	NA

Business: The group's principal activity is to provide consulting services relating to science, engineering, environment and health. The group's team of scientists, physicians, engineers and business consultants perform scientific research and analysis in over 70 technical disciplines to solve complicated issues facing industry and business. These operations are conducted through two segments: environmental and health segment and scientific and engineering segment. The environmental and health segment provides a wide range of services in the area of environmental hazards and risks and the impact on both human health and the environment. The scientific and engineering segment provides technical consulting in different practices and primarily in the areas of impending litigation and technology development. The group serves clients in automotive, aviation, chemical, construction, energy, government, health, insurance, manufacturing, technology and other sectors of the economy.

Primary SIC and add'l.: 8711 7389 8099

CIK No: 0000851520

Subsidiaries: Exponent International Ltd., Exponent Realty LLC, Exponent Science and Technology Consulting (Hangzhou) Co., Ltd., Failure Analysis Associates B.V., Failure Analysis Associates, Spolka z o.o.

Officers: Michael R. Gaulke/Dir., CEO, Pres./$1,803,097.00, Bernard Ross/Chmn. Emeritus, Principal Engineer, Larry W. Anderson/Corporate VP, Principal Engineer, John E. Moalli/Group VP, Principal Engineer, Gregory P. Klein/Corporate VP, Paul D. Boehm/Group VP - Principal Scientist - Ecosciences, Richard L. Schlenker/CFO, Corp. Sec./$625,033.00, Paul R. Johnston/COO, Pres./$969,469.00, Subbaiah V. Malladi/CTO, Ron Joseph/Sr. Managing Engineer - Materials, Metallurgy, Seymour W. Linovitz/Managing Engineer - Vehicle Engineering, Steave H. Su/Managing Scientist - Center Exposure, Dose Reconstruction, Steven Zebich/Managing Engineer - Civil, Structural Engineering, Walter R. Bak/Sr. Managing Engineer - Mechanical Engineering, Wei Wei/Managing Engineer - Electrical, Semiconductors Practice *(301 Officers included in Index)*

Directors: Michael R. Gaulke/Dir., CEO, Pres., Bernard Ross/Chmn. Emeritus, Principal Engineer, Leslie G. Denend/Chmn., Jon R. Katzenbach/74/Dir., Stephen C. Riggins/62/Dir., Barbara M. Barrett/56/Dir., Roger L. McCarthy/Dir., John B. Shoven/61/Dir., Samuel H. Armacost/68/Dir.

Owners: Richard L. Schlenker/2.00%, Royce & Associates, LLC/13.60%, Roger L. McCarthy, Heartland Advisors, Inc/6.20%, Barbara M. Barrett, Samuel H. Armacost/1.00%, Paul R. Johnston/1.60%, Mesirow Financial Investment Management/5.90%, Leslie G. Denend, Stephen C. Riggins, Jon R. Katzenbach, Robert D. Caligiuri/1.10%, Michael R. Gaulke/6.60%, Insiders/13.10%

Financial Data: *Fiscal Year End:* 12/30   *Latest Annual Data:* 12/29/2006

Year	Sales		Net Income
2006	$168,496,000		$14,194,000
2005	$155,196,000		$14,186,000
2004	$151,509,000		$12,040,000
Curr. Assets:	$103,460,000	**Curr. Liab.:**	$24,539,000
Plant, Equip.:	$30,211,000	**Total Liab.:**	$27,097,000 **Indic. Yr. Divd.:** NA
Total Assets:	$144,081,000	**Net Worth:**	$116,984,000 **Debt/ Equity:** NA

Express Scripts Inc

1 Express Way, St. Louis, MO, 63121; *PH:* 1-314-996-0900; *Fax:* 1-866-254-2313; *http://* www.express-scripts.com

General - Incorporation	DE	Stock - Price on:12/24/2007	$99.71
Employees	11,300	Stock Exchange	NDQ
Auditor	PricewaterhouseCoopers LLP	Ticker Symbol	ESRX
Stk Agt	American Stock Transfer & Trust Co.	Outstanding Shares	136,210,000
Counsel	NA	E.P.S.	$2.01
DUNS No.	17-349-0459	Shareholders	NA

Business: The group's principle activity is to provide pharmacy benefit and health care management services. In the year 2007, the group acquired ConnectYourCare, L.L.C. The group operates from United States and Canada.

Primary SIC and add'l.: 5961 8742 5122 8082 6411

CIK No: 0000885721

Subsidiaries: Acuity Health Solutions, Inc., Airport Holdings, LLC, Byfield Drug, Inc., Central Fill, Inc., CFI New Jersey, Inc., Chesapeake Infusion, Inc., Comprehensive Renal Care of Dunwoody, Inc., Comprehensive Renal Care, Inc., CuraScript PBM Services, Inc., CuraScript, Inc., Custom Medical Products, Inc., Diversified NY IPA, Inc., Diversified Pharmaceutical Services (Puerto Rico), Inc., Diversified Pharmaceutical Services, Inc., ESI Canada 63 Subsidiaries included in the Index

Officers: George Paz/Chmn., CEO, Pres./$5,092,120.00, Kelley Elliott/35/VP, Chief Accounting Officer, Controller, Thomas M. Boudreau/56/Sr. VP, General Counsel, Corp. Sec./$1,750,481.00, Edward Stiften/53/CFO, Sr. VP/$2,418,301.00, Michael Holmes/49/Sr. VP, Chief Human Resources Officer, Edward Ignaczak/42/Sr. VP - Sales, Accounting Management/$1,257,877.00, Patrick McNamee/48/CIO, Sr. VP, Brenda Motheral/38/Sr. VP - Product Management, Douglas Porter/49/Sr. VP - Client, Patient Services, Agnes Rey-Giraud/43/Sr. VP - Supply Chain Management

Directors: George Paz/Chmn., CEO, Pres., Barrett A. Toan/Dir., Tom MacMahon/Dir., Samuel Skinner/Dir., Howard L. Waltman/Dir., Gary G. Benanav/Dir., Woodrow A. Myers/Dir., Seymour Sternberg/Dir., John O. Parker/Dir., Nicholas J. Lahowchic/Dir., Maura C. Breen/Dir., Frank J. Borelli/Dir., Nick Lahowchic/Dir.

Owners: Thomas P. Mac Mahon, Barrett A. Toan, Nicholas J. LaHowchic, George Paz, Samuel K. Skinner, Thomas M. Boudreau, Maura C. Breen, NYLIFE, LLC/14.72%, Gary G. Benanav, Howard L. Waltman, Insiders/1.86%, Edward Stiften, Frank J. Borelli, Edward Ignaczak, David A. Lowenberg *(17 Owners included in Index)*

Financial Data: *Fiscal Year End:* 12/31   *Latest Annual Data:* 12/31/2006

Year	Sales		Net Income
2006	$17,660,000,000		$474,400,000
2005	$16,266,000,000		$400,000,000
2004	$15,114,728,000		$278,207,000
Curr. Assets:	$1,772,100,000	**Curr. Liab.:**	$2,429,400,000 **P/E Ratio:** 49.61
Plant, Equip.:	$201,400,000	**Total Liab.:**	$3,983,200,000 **Indic. Yr. Divd.:** NA
Total Assets:	$5,108,100,000	**Net Worth:**	$1,124,900,000 **Debt/ Equity:** 0.9009

Express Systems Corp

Bahnhofstr. 9, Baar, V8 6341; *PH:* 41-44-718-10-32

General - Incorporation	NV	Stock - Price on:12/24/2007	NA
Employees	NA	Stock Exchange	OTC
Auditor	Staley, Okada & Partners	Ticker Symbol	EXPY
Stk Agt	Island Stock Transfer	Outstanding Shares	NA
Counsel	NA	E.P.S.	NA
DUNS No.	NA	Shareholders	NA

Business: The groups principle activities include generating and selling e-mail leads. The group operates from Nevada in the United States.

Primary SIC and add'l.: 1311

CIK No: 0001074447

Subsidiaries: Masterlist International, Inc

Officers: Alexander Becker/49/Dir., CEO, Peter-mark Vogel/Dir., CFO, Yaroslav Bandurak/37/CTO

Directors: Alexander Becker/49/Dir., CEO, Heinz Scholz/66/Chmn., Peter-mark Vogel/Dir., CFO, Michael Velletta/Dir.

Owners: Steven Sanders, Insiders/57.40%, Erik Herlyn, Neil Maedel/1.00%, Heinz J. Scholz/20.60%, Michael Velletta/2.00%, Peter-Mark Vogel/16.20%, Yaroslav Bandurak/1.80%, Alexander Becker/16.40%

Financial Data: *Fiscal Year End:* 03/31   *Latest Annual Data:* 03/31/2007

Year	Sales		Net Income
2007	NA		-$534,000
2006	$36,000		-$192,000
Curr. Assets:	$63,000	**Curr. Liab.:**	$38,000
Plant, Equip.:	$1,000	**Total Liab.:**	$38,000 **Indic. Yr. Divd.:** NA
Total Assets:	$64,000	**Net Worth:**	$26,000 **Debt/ Equity:** NA

Express-1 Expedited Solutions Inc

Formerly: Segmentz Inc

429 Post Rd. , Buchanan, MI, 49107; *PH:* 1-269-695-4947; *http://* www.express-1.com

General - Incorporation	DE	Stock - Price on:12/24/2007	$1.33
Employees	129	Stock Exchange	NA
Auditor	Pender Newkirk & Co	Ticker Symbol	NA
Stk Agt	Pender Newkirk & Co	Outstanding Shares	26,920,000
Counsel	NA	E.P.S.	$0.14
DUNS No.	NA	Shareholders	NA

Business: The group's principal activity is to provide transportation and logistics management services to its target client base, ranging from mid-sized to fortune 100 companies. The services of the group include regional outsourced trucking, time definite transportation, dedicated delivery and other services. It operates a network of terminals in the southeast and midwest United States. It offers a 24 hour, seven day a week call center allowing the customer immediate status of shipments in transit. Shipment tracking is available for customers via a custom designed Web site and carrier links and also provides tracking and service failure reports. In 2003, it acquired bullet freight systems of miami inc, bullet freight systems of palm beach inc, bullet freight system inc, bullet courier service inc, bullet freight systems of orlando inc, b.c.s. Transportation inc, dasher express inc and in 2004, it acquired frontline freight and express-1.

Primary SIC and add'l.: 4214 8748 4225

CIK No: 0001166003

Officers: Michael R. Welch/45/Dir., CEO, Pres., Mark K. Patterson/45/Dir., CFO, Jeff Curry/47/Pres., VP - Investor Relations, John Welch/Controller, Jim Welch/51/VP - Internal Sales, Marketing, Dennis McCaffrey/VP - Sales, Keith Avery/Dir. - Carrier Relations, Joe Campbell/VP - Information Technology, Robert Tracey/Dir. - Safety, Brian Glaser/GM - Dedicated Operations

Directors: Michael R. Welch/45/Dir., CEO, Pres., James J. Martell/53/Chmn., John F. Affleck-Graves/57/Dir., Jennifer H. Dorris/40/Dir., Mark K. Patterson/45/Dir., CFO, Jay N. Taylor/60/Dir., Calvin Whitehead/60/Dir.

Owners: Insiders/18.00%, John F. Affleck-Graves, Calvin R. Whitehead/1.00%, Mark K. Patterson/1.00%, James M. Welch/2.00%, James J. Martell/1.00%, Michael R. Welch/7.00%, Jennifer H. Dorris/1.00%, Jay N. Taylor/1.00%, Dennis M. McCaffrey/1.00%, John D. Welch/2.00%

Financial Data: *Fiscal Year End:* 12/31   *Latest Annual Data:* 12/31/2006

Year	Sales		Net Income
2006	$42,191,000		$3,904,000
2005	$39,848,000		-$5,815,000
2004	$42,481,000		-$3,238,000
Curr. Assets:	$6,948,000	**Curr. Liab.:**	$4,870,000 **P/E Ratio:** 9.50
Plant, Equip.:	$2,488,000	**Total Liab.:**	$6,271,000 **Indic. Yr. Divd.:** NA
Total Assets:	$21,609,000	**Net Worth:**	$15,338,000 **Debt/ Equity:** 0.1635

Expressjet Holdings Inc

700 N Sam Houston Pkwy. W, Ste. 200, Houston, TX, 77067; *PH:* 1-832-353-1000; *Fax:* 1-832-353-1008; *http://* www.expressjet.com

General - Incorporation	DE	**Stock**- Price on:12/24/2007	$5.88
Employees	7,300	Stock Exchange	NYSE
Auditor	Ernst & Young LLP	Ticker Symbol	XJT
Stk Agt	Mellon Investor Services LLC	Outstanding Shares	54,210,000
Counsel	Vinson & Elkins LLP	E.P.S	$0.54
DUNS No.	NA	Shareholders	NA

Business: The groups principle activity is to provide investments services to the air transportation industry. The group operates from United States.

Primary SIC and add'l.: 4581 4512

CIK No: 0001144331

Subsidiaries: ExpressJet Airlines, Inc., XJT Holdings, Inc.

Officers: James B. Ream/Dir., CEO, Pres./$1,010,074.00, Scott Peterson/VP, General Counsel, Sec./$638,864.00, Jon Weaver/Staff VP - System Operations, Chuck Coble/VP - Field Services, Karen Miles/VP - Human Resources, Administration, Fred Cromer/CFO, VP/$771,071.00, Jay Perez/Staff VP - Material Services, Jim Nides/VP - Flight Operations, Maintenance, Fred Junck/VP - Safety, Regulatory Compliance, Phung Ngo-Burns/Staff VP - Finance, Controller, Dale Darcy/Staff VP - Maintenance, Trish Winebrenner/VP - Marketing, Rob Austin/Staff VP - Treasury, Planning, Bob McConnell/Staff VP - Expressjet Services, LLC

Directors: James B. Ream/Dir., CEO, Pres., George R. Bravante/Chmn., Salvatore J. Badalamenti/Dir., Patrick Kelly/Dir., Kim A. Fadel/Dir., Janet M. Clarke/Dir., Judith R. Haberkorn/Dir., Bonnie S. Reitz/Dir., Richard F. Wallman/56/Dir.

Owners: Richard F. Wallman, FMR Corp./10.10%, Dimensional Fund Advisors LP/7.30%, Jerry E. Losness, James B. Ream, Insiders/1.98%, Janet M. Clarke, LSV Asset Management/5.00%, Frederick S. Cromer, George R. Bravante, Vardon Capital Management, LLC/8.80%, Judith R. Haberkorn, Salvatore J. Badalamenti, Scott R. Peterson, Barclays Global Investors, NA/6.10% *(18 Owners included in Index)*

Financial Data: *Fiscal Year End:*12/31 *Latest Annual Data:* 12/31/2006

Year	Sales	Net Income
2006	$1,679,637,000	$92,565,000
2005	$1,562,818,000	$97,993,000
2004	$1,507,524,000	$122,771,000

Curr. Assets:	$348,794,000	**Curr. Liab.:**	$135,092,000	**P/E Ratio:**	10.89
Plant, Equip.:	$245,083,000	**Total Liab.:**	$332,715,000	**Indic. Yr. Divd.:**	NA
Total Assets:	$637,029,000	**Net Worth:**	$304,314,000	**Debt/ Equity:**	0.4737

Extendicare Canada Inc

3000 Steeles Ave E, Markham, ON, L3R 9W2; *PH:* 1-905-470-4000; *http://* www.extendicare.com

General - Incorporation	Canada	**Stock**- Price on:12/24/2007	NA
Employees	NA	Stock Exchange	NDQ
Auditor	KPMG LLP	Ticker Symbol	NADX
Stk Agt	Computershare Investor Services LLC	Outstanding Shares	NA
Counsel	Fasken Campbell Godfrey	E.P.S	NA
DUNS No.	24-666-5509	Shareholders	NA

Business: The group's principal activities are to operate long-term care facilities and services. It provides medical specialty services in the United States, including subacute care and rehabilitative therapy services. It also provides home health care and rehabilitative therapy services in Canada. The group operates as follows: nursing and assisted living centres, outpatient therapy and medical supplies, home health and other. Nursing and assisted living centres provide skilled nursing and rehabilitative therapy to support patients recovering from acute illness and injury. Outpatient therapy and medical supplies provides services requiring physical, occupational and speech-language therapy, pulmonary rehabilitation and nursing services. Home health is a private home health care services company that provides all levels of nursing care, home support and physiotherapy.

Primary SIC and add'l.: 6311 8052 8069 6321 8059

CIK No: 0001012881

Subsidiaries: 159524 Canada Inc., Arbors at Toledo, Inc., Assisted Living Concepts, Inc., Extendicare (Canada) Inc., Extendicare Health Facilities Holdings, Inc., Extendicare Health Services, Inc., Extendicare Homes, Inc., Extendicare of Indiana, Inc., Fir Lane Terrace Convalescent Center, Inc., Laurier Indemnity Company, Laurier Indemnity Company, Ltd., New Orchard Lodge Limited, Northern Health Facilities, Inc.

Officers: Philip W. Small/Chmn., CEO, Pres., Jillian E. Fountain/Corp. Sec., Elaine E. Everson/VP, Controller, Christina L. Mckey/VP - Human Resources, Paul Tuttle/Pres., Susan C. Cullen/VP - Eastern Operations, Len G. Koroneos/VP - Taxation, Privacy Officer, Paul Rushforth/VP - Western Operations, Douglas J. Harris/CFO, Deborah Bakti/VP - Paramed Home Health Care, Dennis Boschetto/VP - Managed Contracts, Business Development, Hamilton Jukes/Dir. - Purchasing, LTC Group Purchasing

Extra Space Storage Inc

2795 E Cottonwood Pkwy., Ste. 400, Salt Lake City, UT, 84121; *PH:* 1-801-562-5556; *Fax:* 1-801-365-4801; *http://* www.extraspace.com; *Email:* helpmarketing@extraspace.com

General - Incorporation	MD	**Stock**- Price on:12/24/2007	$16.84
Employees	1,835	Stock Exchange	NYSE
Auditor	Ernst & Young LLP	Ticker Symbol	EXR
Stk Agt	American Stock Transfer & Trust Co.	Outstanding Shares	64,380,000
Counsel	NA	E.P.S	$0.49
DUNS No.	NA	Shareholders	NA

Business: The groups principal activities include owning, acquiring, developing and redeveloping professionally managed self-storage facilities. The group operates through two segments namely, property management and development, and rental operations. In the year 2006, the group acquired 25 properties. The group operates from the United States. In the year 2006, the property management and development segment accounted for $26,271, and rental operations $170,993

Primary SIC and add'l.: 4225 6798

CIK No: 0001289490

Subsidiaries: Extra Space Properties Eleven LLC, Extra Space Properties Four LLC, Extra Space Properties One LLC, Extra Space Properties Seven LP, Extra Space Storage LLC

Officers: Kenneth M. Woolley/Chmn., CEO, Charles L. Allen/Exec. VP, Chief Legal Officer, Kent W. Christensen/CFO, Exec. VP, Karl Haas/COO, Exec. VP, David L. Rasmussen/VP, General Counsel, Assist. Sec., Richard S. Tanner/Sr. VP - Development

Directors: Kenneth M. Woolley/Chmn., CEO, Hugh W. Horne/Dir., Spencer F. Kirk/Dir., Roger B. Porter/Dir., Fred K. Skousen/Dir., Joseph D. Margolis/Dir., Anthony Fanticola/Dir.

Owners: Hugh W. Horne, Anthony Fanticola, Roger B. Porter, Fred K. Skousen, Charles L. Allen, Vanguard Group, Inc./5.84%, Cohen & Steers Capital Management Inc./11.66%, RREEF Real Estate Securities Advisors, L.P./5.60%, Karl Haas, ING Clarion Real Estate Securities/8.09%, Insiders/7.50%, Spencer F. Kirk/3.72%, Kent W. Christensen, Joseph D. Margolis, Kenneth M. Woolley/2.11% *(16 Owners included in Index)*

Financial Data: *Fiscal Year End:*12/31 *Latest Annual Data:* 12/31/2006

Year	Sales	Net Income
2006	$197,264,000	$14,876,000
2005	$134,728,000	-$4,966,000
2004	$65,971,000	-$18,462,000

Curr. Assets:	$140,336,000	**Curr. Liab.:**	$20,800,000		
Plant, Equip.:	$1,421,910,000	**Total Liab.:**	$1,026,270,000	**Indic. Yr. Divd.:**	$1.000
Total Assets:	$1,669,825,000	**Net Worth:**	$643,555,000	**Debt/ Equity:**	NA

Extreme Networks Inc

3585 Monroe St., Santa Clara, CA, 95051; *PH:* 1-408-579-2800; *Fax:* 1-408-579-3000; *http://* www.extremenetworks.com; *Email:* info@extremenetworks.com

General - Incorporation	DE	**Stock**- Price on:12/24/2007	$3.79
Employees	847	Stock Exchange	NDQ
Auditor	Ernst & Young LLP	Ticker Symbol	EXTR
Stk Agt	Mellon Investor Services LLC	Outstanding Shares	117,300,000
Counsel	Gray, Cary, Ware & Freidenrich	E.P.S	-$0.05
DUNS No.	NA	Shareholders	NA

Business: The group's principal activity is to provide ethernet networking solutions and infrastructure equipment for business applications and services. The products share a common hardware, software and network management architecture. The group's hardware and software products are categorised into the summit stackable product family, blackdiamond modular chassis and alpine modular chassis. The principal products include summit1i , layer 3 summit, the summit 400 series, the extremeware(R) xos, the summit 300-48/altitude 300 and extremeware(r). The customers include corporate, government, education and health care enterprises and metropolitan service providers. It markets its products and services in the United States, western Europe, Japan and People's Republic of China as well as in the other countries throughout the Asia-pacific region.

Primary SIC and add'l.: 3577

CIK No: 0001078271

Subsidiaries: Extreme Networks Argentina, SRL, Extreme Networks Australia PTE, Ltd., Extreme Networks B.V., Extreme Networks Brasil, Ltda., Extreme Networks Canada, Inc., Extreme Networks Chile, Ltda., Extreme Networks China Ltd., Extreme Networks EMEA, Extreme Networks GmbH, Extreme Networks Hong Kong Limited, Extreme Networks IHC, Inc., Extreme Networks India Private Limited, Extreme Networks International, Extreme Networks Japan K.K., Extreme Networks Korea, Ltd. 24 Subsidiaries included in the Index

Officers: Mark Canepa/Dir., CEO, Pres., Frank Blohm/VP - Operations, Suresh Gopalakrishnan/VP - Marketing, Product Management, Alexander J. Gray/VP, GM - Scalable Products, Paul Hooper/CIO, Heidi Mosher/Sales Representative, Rebecca Guerra/VP - Human Resources, Alicia Jayne Moore/VP, General Counsel, Sec., Michael Gray/VP - Corporate Quality, Reliability, Douglas Murray/VP, GM - Volume Products, Helmut Wilke/Sr. VP - Worldwide Sales, Sandra Raygoza/Sales Representative, Bill Shelton/Regional Dir. - Federal, Mid, Atlantic, Jo Zack/Mgr. - Federal, Mid, Atlantic Operations, FSO

Directors: Mark Canepa/Dir., CEO, Pres., Gordon L. Stitt/Co - Founder, Chmn., Robert Corey/Dir., Mike West/Dir., John C. Shoemaker/Dir., Kenneth Levy/Dir., Charles Carinalli/Dir., Harry Silverglide/Dir.

Owners: Insiders/8.00%, Gordon Stitt/3.60%, Kenneth Levy, Charles Carinalli, Harry Silverglide, Mark Canepa, Bob L. Corey, Merrill Lynch& Co., Inc./6.70%, Alexander J. Gray, Michael W. West, Wells Fargo& Company/7.60%, William Slakey, BlackRock, Inc./6.10%, Michael Palu, Herb Schneider/1.70%

Financial Data: *Fiscal Year End:*07/03 *Latest Annual Data:* 07/02/2006

Year	Sales	Net Income
2006	$358,601,000	$8,509,000
2005	$383,347,000	$12,942,000
2004	$351,848,000	-$1,748,000

Curr. Assets:	$324,490,000	**Curr. Liab.:**	$104,904,000		
Plant, Equip.:	$50,438,000	**Total Liab.:**	$335,602,000	**Indic. Yr. Divd.:**	NA
Total Assets:	$583,614,000	**Net Worth:**	$248,012,000	**Debt/ Equity:**	NA

EXX Inc

6330 San Vigente Blvd, Ste. 689, Los Angeles, CA, 90048; *PH:* 1-323-932-4300; *http://* www.emak.com

General - Incorporation	NV	**Stock**- Price on:12/24/2007	$3.05
Employees	825	Stock Exchange	AMEX
Auditor	Rothstein, Kass & Co, P.C	Ticker Symbol	EXX-A
Stk Agt	Continental Stock Transfer & Trust Co	Outstanding Shares	11,250,000
Counsel	NA	E.P.S	$0.151
DUNS No.	83-553-6699	Shareholders	NA

Business: The group's principal activities are to design, assemble and market capital and consumer goods. The group operates through two segments: mechanical equipment and toy industries. The mechanical equipment segment designs, assembles and sells capital goods, such as electric motors and cable pressurization equipment. The toy segment business designs, assembles and distributes consumer goods in the form of toys and kites, which are primarily imported from the Far East.

Primary SIC and add'l.: 3944 3621

CIK No: 0000089261

Subsidiaries: Blackhawk Engineering, Inc., Boramco, Inc., Deco Engineering, Inc., Handi-Pac, Inc., Henry Gordy International Inc., Hi-Flier Inc., Machine Tool& Gear, Inc., Newcor, Inc., Plastronics Plus, Inc., Rochester Gear, Inc., Sellers& Josephson Inc., SFM CORP., TX Systems Inc., TX Technology Corp.

Owners: Insiders/56.37%, David A. Segal/46.12%, Laura L. Bradley/8.39%, Lisa M. Bethune/10.43%, Lisa M. Bethune/8.39%, APG Capital, LP/5.39%, Werner Moehring/7.17%, Insiders/46.19%, Laura L. Bradley/10.43%, David A. Segal/56.33%

Financial Data: *Fiscal Year End:*12/31 *Latest Annual Data:* 12/31/2006

Year	Sales	Net Income
2006	$158,916,000	$5,706,000
2005	$147,337,000	$881,000
2004	$143,548,000	$1,504,000

Curr. Assets:	$53,051,000	**Curr. Liab.:**	$16,718,000	**P/E Ratio:**	9.24
Plant, Equip.:	$20,879,000	**Total Liab.:**	$54,402,000	**Indic. Yr. Divd.:**	NA
Total Assets:	$79,797,000	**Net Worth:**	$25,395,000	**Debt/ Equity:**	0.5108

Exxon Mobil Corp

5959 Las Colinas Blvd., Irving, TX, 75039; *PH:* 1-972-444-1000; *Fax:* 1-972-444-1350; *http://* www.exxon.mobil.com

General - Incorporation: NJ; Employees: 106,400; Auditor: PricewaterhouseCoopers LLP; Stk Agt: ExxonMobil Shareholder Services; Counsel: NA; DUNS No.: 00-121-3214

Stock- Price on:12/24/2007: $84.3; Stock Exchange: NYSE; Ticker Symbol: XOM; Outstanding Shares: 5,630,000,000; E.P.S: $6.915; Shareholders: NA

Business: The groups principle activity is to provide energy and gas services. The group operates from United States.

Primary SIC and add'l.: 1311 5169 2911 1321

CIK No: 0000034088

Subsidiaries: Abu Dhabi Petroleum Company Limited, Aera Energy LLC, Al-Jubail Petrochemical Company, Ampolex (CEPU) Pte Ltd, Ancon Insurance Company, Inc., BEB Erdgas und Erdoel GmbH , Cameroon Oil Transportation Company S.A. (5), Caspian Pipeline Consortium (5), Castle Peak Power Company Limited (5), Chalmette Refining, LLC(4)(5), Esso (Thailand) Public Company Limited, Esso Australia Resources Pty Ltd, Esso Austria GmbH, Esso Brasileira de Petroleo Limitada, Esso Chile Petrolera Limitada 146 Subsidiaries included in the Index

Officers: Rex W. Tillerson/Chmn., CEO/$13,009,500.00, P. T. Mulva/VP, Controller, S. R. McGill/65/Sr. VP/$9,214,816.00, M. J. Dolan/VP, A. T. Cejka/Functional, Service Organizations, L. J. Cavanaugh/VP - Human Resources, S. R. Lasala/VP - General Tax Counsel, R. A. Luxbacher/GM - Corporate Planning, J. S. Simon/Sr. VP/$8,580,148.00, G. L. Kohlenberger/VP, H. H. Hubble/VP - Investor Relations, Sec., C. W. Matthews/VP, General Counsel, P. E. Sullivan/64/VP - General Tax Counsel, M. E. Foster/VP, Donald D. Humphreys/Sr. VP, Treasurer/$7,150,378.00 *(28 Officers included in Index)*

Directors: Rex W. Tillerson/Chmn., CEO, James R. Houghton/72/Dir., Walter V. Shipley/72/Dir., Marilyn Carlson Nelson/68/Dir., Michael J. Boskin/62/Dir., Reatha Clark King/70/Dir., Philip E. Lippincott/Dir., William R. Howell/72/Dir., William W. George/65/Dir., Samuel J. Palmisano/56/Dir., Stephen J. Simon/65/Dir., Sr. VP, Steven S. Reinemund/60/Dir.

Owners: S. S. Reinemund, R. C. King, J. R. Houghton, S. R. McGill, H. R. Cramer, W. R. Howell, W. V. Shipley, W. W. George, M. J. Boskin, S. J. Palmisano, E. G. Galante, H. A. McKinnell, D. D. Humphreys, J. S. Simon, P. E. Lippincott *(17 Owners included in Index)*

Financial Data: *Fiscal Year End:*12/31 *Latest Annual Data:* 12/31/2006

Year	Sales	Net Income
2006	$377,635,000,000	$39,500,000,000
2005	$370,680,000,000	$36,130,000,000
2004	$298,035,000,000	$25,330,000,000

Curr. Assets:	$75,777,000,000	**Curr. Liab.:**	$48,817,000,000	**P/E Ratio:**	12.25
Plant, Equip.:	$113,687,000,000	**Total Liab.:**	$101,367,000,000	**Indic. Yr. Divd.:**	$1.400
Total Assets:	$219,015,000,000	**Net Worth:**	$113,844,000,000	**Debt/ Equity:**	0.0592

EYI Industries Inc

7865 Edmonds St., Burnaby, BC, V3N 1B9; *PH:* 1-604-759-5000; *Fax:* 1-604-759-5001; *http://* www.eyicom.com

General - Incorporation: NV; Employees: NA; Auditor: Williams & Webster, P.S.; Stk Agt: Corporate Stock Transfer, Inc.; Counsel: NA; DUNS No.: NA

Stock- Price on:12/24/2007: $0.0036; Stock Exchange: OTC; Ticker Symbol: EYII; Outstanding Shares: NA; E.P.S: NA; Shareholders: NA

Business: The groups principle activities include selling, marketing, and distributing dietary supplements, personal care, water filtration systems and a fuel additive product. The group operates through five segments namely administration fees, binary sales, direct sales, affiliate sales and sales aids. The group's quarterly revenue for September 2007 was 1.06 millions of USD.

Primary SIC and add'l.: 2833

CIK No: 0001104120

Subsidiaries: 642706 B.C. Ltd., Essentially Yours Industries (Canada), Inc., Essentially Yours Industries (Hong Kong) Limited, Essentially Yours Industries (International) Limited, Essentially Yours Industries, Inc., Halo Distribution LLC, RGM International, Inc., World Wide Buyers' Club Inc.

Officers: Jay Sargeant/Dir., CEO, Pres., Dori ONeill/48/Dir., COO, Exec. VP, Sec., Donna Keay/CFO, Janet Carpenter/VP - Product Development, Jay Paterson/Dir. - Channel Marketing, Lisa Baldwin/Mgr. - Operations, Jennifer Moreland/Supervisor, Investor Relations, Marketing

Directors: Jay Sargeant/Dir., CEO, Pres., Dori ONeill/48/Dir., COO, Exec. VP, Sec.

Owners: Rajesh Raniga, Jay Sargeant/47.53%, Insiders/71.51%, Donna Keay/1.68%, Dori ONeill/23.91%

Financial Data: *Fiscal Year End:*12/31 *Latest Annual Data:* 12/31/2006

Year	Sales	Net Income
2006	$1,063,000	-$1,009,000
2005	$4,980,000	-$4,262,000
2004	$6,229,000	-$4,463,000

Curr. Assets:	$1,904,000	**Curr. Liab.:**	$5,929,000		
Plant, Equip.:	$77,000	**Total Liab.:**	$6,425,000	**Indic. Yr. Divd.:**	NA
Total Assets:	$2,041,000	**Net Worth:**	-$4,384,000	**Debt/ Equity:**	NA

Ezcomm Inc

16-7 Smjung-dong, Ojung-gu Bucheon, Kyonggi-do; *PH:* 82-326-766283; *http://* www.eugene21.com

General - Incorporation: DE; Employees: NA; Auditor: SF Partnership LLP; Stk Agt: Signature Stock Transfer, Inc.; Counsel: NA; DUNS No.: NA

Stock- Price on:12/24/2007: NA; Stock Exchange: NA; Ticker Symbol: NA; Outstanding Shares: NA; E.P.S: NA; Shareholders: NA

Business: The groups principle activity is to develop hardware and software that allows retailers to establish and administer customer incentive and loyalty programs. The group operates from United States.

Primary SIC and add'l.: 7990

CIK No: 0001107685

Subsidiaries: Eugene Science Korea, Ucole Bio Co., Ltd.

Officers: Seung-Kwon Noh/47/Chmn., CEO, Pres., Tae-Hwan Lee/VP - Domestic Marketing, Se-Choen Ahn/VP - Research & Development, Jang-Hyun Cho/Chief Research Scientist, Erika Lee/Principle Research Scientist, Jae Hong Yoo/40/CFO

Directors: Seung-Kwon Noh/47/Chmn., CEO, Pres., Tony Kim/35/Dir.

Owners: Telos, LLC/6.46%, Insiders/34.25%, Se Cheon Ahn, H&Q Asia Pacific/6.86%, Seung Kwon Noh/26.64%, Tae Hwan Lee, Tony Kim/6.42%

EZcorp Inc

1901 Capital Pkwy., Austin, TX, 78746; *PH:* 1-512-314-3400; *Fax:* 1-512-314-3404; *http://* www.ezcorp.com; *Email:* investorrelations@ezcorp.com

General - Incorporation: DE; Employees: 3,100; Auditor: BDO Seidman LLP; Stk Agt: American Stock Transfer & Trust Co.; Counsel: Jenkens & Gilchrist; DUNS No.: 60-284-2502

Stock- Price on:12/24/2007: $13.33; Stock Exchange: NDQ; Ticker Symbol: EZPW; Outstanding Shares: 41,250,000; E.P.S: $0.88; Shareholders: NA

Business: The group's principle activity is to provide small non-recourse loans secured by pledging of tangible personal property known as pawn loans. The pawn shop functions as convenient source of consumer credit and as value-oriented specialty retailers of previously owned merchandise. The group acquires inventory for its retail sales primarily through pawn loan forfeitures and, to a lesser extent, through purchases from customers and wholesale distributors. The pawnshops are located in 280 locations: 181 in Texas, 24 in Colorado, 20 in Oklahoma, 18 in Florida, 15 in Indiana, 8 in Alabama, 4 in Nevada, 3 in Tennessee, 3 in Louisiana, 3 in Mississippi and 1 in Arkansas. The group operates all of its pawnshops under the trade name ez pawn. The group also operates under the trade names ezmoney payroll advance payroll advance express and ezcorp collection center. The group's total revenue of the year 2007 was 372.21 millions of USD.

Primary SIC and add'l.: 5932

CIK No: 0000876523

Subsidiaries: EZCORP International, Inc, EZMONEY Colorado, Inc., EZMONEY Holdings, Inc., EZMONEY Management, Inc., EZMONEY Utah, Inc., EZMONEY Wisconsin, Inc., EZPAWN Alabama, Inc., EZPAWN Arkansas, Inc., EZPAWN Colorado, Inc., EZPAWN Florida, Inc., EZPAWN Holdings, Inc., EZPAWN Indiana, Inc., EZPAWN Louisiana, Inc., EZPAWN Nevada, Inc., EZPAWN Oklahoma, Inc. 18 Subsidiaries included in the Index

Officers: Joseph L. Rotunda/Dir., CEO, Pres., Eric Fosse/VP - Ezmoney Operations, Daniel N. Tonissen/Dir., Sr. VP, CFO, Assist. Sec., Robert Jackson/CIO, VP, Danny M. Chism/Controller, Assist. Sec., Connie L. Kondik/VP, Sec., General Counsel, Mike Volpe/VP - Ezpawn Operations, John Kissick/VP - Strategic Development, Bob Kasenter/Sr. VP - Administration

Directors: Joseph L. Rotunda/Dir., CEO, Pres., Sterling B. Brinkley/Chmn., Thomas C. Roberts/Dir., Gary C. Matzner/Dir., Daniel N. Tonissen/Dir., Sr. VP, CFO, Assist. Sec., Richard D. Sage/Dir., Richard M. Edwards/Dir.

Owners: Dan N. Tonissen, Joseph L. Rotunda/1.37%, Sterling B. Brinkley/1.07%, Gary C. Matzner, Richard D. Sage, Eric Fosse, Robert A. Kasenter, MS Pawn Limited Partnership/7.25%, Insiders/4.06%, MS Pawn Limited Partnership/100.00%, Thomas C. Roberts

Financial Data: *Fiscal Year End:*09/30 *Latest Annual Data:* 9/30/2006

Year	Sales	Net Income
2006	$315,852,000	$29,259,000
2005	$254,159,000	$14,752,000
2004	$227,797,000	$9,123,000

Curr. Assets:	$142,008,000	**Curr. Liab.:**	$24,469,000	**P/E Ratio:**	16.66
Plant, Equip.:	$29,447,000	**Total Liab.:**	$27,718,000	**Indic. Yr. Divd.:**	NA
Total Assets:	$197,858,000	**Net Worth:**	$170,140,000	**Debt/ Equity:**	NA

Ezenia Inc

14 Celina Ave., Ste. 17-18, Nashua, NH, 03063; *PH:* 1-781-505-2100; *https://* www.ezenia.com; *Email:* customersupport@ezenia.com

General - Incorporation: DE; Employees: 47; Auditor: Brown & Brown LLP; Stk Agt: Computershare Investor Services LLC; Counsel: Bingham, Dana & Gould LLP; DUNS No.: 78-040-4067

Stock- Price on:12/24/2007: $1.23; Stock Exchange: OTC; Ticker Symbol: EZEN; Outstanding Shares: 14,670,000; E.P.S: $0.09; Shareholders: NA

Business: The group's principal activities are to design, develop, manufacture, market and sell real-time collaboration solutions for corporate networks and ebusiness. The group develops and markets products that enable organizations to provide group communication and collaboration capabilities to commercial, consumer and institutional users. The group's products enable connectivity across a range of networks including lans, intranet, isdn, ATM and frame relay. The isdn videoconferencing products, ip-based encounter and infoworkspace products enable videoconferencing, voice communication, instant messaging, whiteboarding and virtual workspaces. It sells its products worldwide through resellers, integrators and remarketers of collaboration, videoconferencing and networking solutions, including tandberg, sony, general dynamics and ntt-me.

Primary SIC and add'l.: 3669 7373

CIK No: 0000943894

Subsidiaries: Ezenia International, Inc., Ezenia Latin America, Inc.

Officers: Khoa D. Nguyen/Chmn., CEO/$563,192.00

Directors: Khoa D. Nguyen/Chmn., CEO, Robert N. McFarland/63/Dir.

Owners: Robert N. McFarland, Kenneth E. Garofano, Michael A. Bass, Thomas G. McInerney, Ronald L. Breland, John A. McMullen, Khoa D. Nguyen/11.35%, Roger N. Tuttle, John F. Stewart, Insiders/12.91%, Gerald P. Carmen

Financial Data: *Fiscal Year End:*12/31 *Latest Annual Data:* 12/31/2006

Year	Sales	Net Income
2006	$13,192,000	$3,918,000
2005	$13,175,000	$3,803,000
2004	$10,391,000	$3,184,000

Curr. Assets:	$20,058,000	**Curr. Liab.:**	$8,548,000	**P/E Ratio:**	7.24
Plant, Equip.:	$304,000	**Total Liab.:**	$8,548,000	**Indic. Yr. Divd.:**	NA
Total Assets:	$20,449,000	**Net Worth:**	$11,901,000	**Debt/ Equity:**	NA

F & M Bank Corp

205 S Main St., Timberville, VA, 22853; ***PH:*** 1-540-896-8941; ***Fax:*** 1-540-896-2840; ***http://*** www.farmersandmerchants.biz

General - Incorporation....VA
Employees....133
Auditor....S. B. Hoover & Co. LLP
Stk Agt....Farmers & Merchants Bank
Counsel....NA
DUNS No....03-583-8382

Stock- Price on:12/24/2007....$32.1
Stock Exchange....OTC
Ticker Symbol....FMBM
Outstanding Shares....2,370,000
E.P.S....$1.91
Shareholders....NA

Business: The group's principal activity is to provide commercial banking services to individuals and businesses. The banking services include accepting commercial and individual demand and time deposits, repurchase agreements of commercial customers, commercial and individual loans and trust services. The group operates through its wholly owned subsidiary, farmers and merchants bank. In addition it also provides insurance and financial services through its subsidiaries, teb life insurance and farmers and merchants financial services, inc. The group provides the banking services through its eight branches to customers located primarily in the rockingham county, Virginia and the adjacent counties of page, shenandoah and augusta.

Primary SIC and add'l.: 6022 6712

CIK No: 0000740806

Subsidiaries: Farmers & Merchants Bank, Farmers & Merchants Financial Services, TEB Life Insurance Company

Officers: Dean W. Withers/Dir., CEO, Pres./$265,915.00, Judy Shumaker/Teller, Woodstock Branch, Farmers, Merchants Bank, Sarah Voigt/Lender, Business Development Officer - Timberville Branch, Farmers, Merchants Bank, Mary P. Miller/Customer Service, Investment Associate, Woodstock Branch, Farmers, Merchants Bank, Tom Campbell/Lender, Timberville Branch, Farmers, Merchants Bank, Janeea Garber/Teller, Timberville Branch, Farmers, Merchants Bank, Joann Runion/Teller, Timberville Branch, Farmers, Merchants Bank, Serena Sherman/Customer Service - Timberville Branch, Farmers, Merchants Bank, Natalie Shifflett/Teller, Elkton Branch, Farmers, Merchants Bank, Beth Lucas/Branch Mgr. - Luray Branch, Farmers, Merchants Bank, Cynthia Lyles/Teller, Luray Branch, Farmers, Merchants Bank, Yvette McCoy/Head Teller - Luray Branch, Farmers, Merchants Bank, Cassandra Mauck/Teller, Luray Branch, Farmers, Merchants Bank, Ashley Huffman/Teller, Port Road Branch, Harrisonburg, Farmers, Merchants Bank, Judy Lyles/Teller, Port Road Branch, Harrisonburg, Farmers, Merchants Bank *(129 Officers included in Index)*

Directors: Dean W. Withers/Dir., CEO, Pres., Julian D. Fisher/Chmn., Ellen R. Fitzwater/Dir., Thomas L. Cline/Dir., John N. Crist/Dir., Daniel J. Harshman/Dir., Richard S. Myers/Dir., Michael W. Pugh/Dir., Ronald E. Wampler/Dir.

Owners: Neil W. Hayslett/4.99%, Ellen R. Fitzwater/0.15%, Daniel J. Harshman/0.02%, John N. Crist/0.72%, Dean W. Withers/0.39%, Julian D. Fisher/1.07%, Michael W. Pugh/0.07%, Thomas L. Cline/0.36%, Richard S. Myers/0.56%, Larry A. Caplinger/5.30%, Ronald E. Wampler/0.45%, Insiders/9.10%

Financial Data: ***Fiscal Year End:***12/31 ***Latest Annual Data:*** 12/31/2006

Year	Sales	Net Income
2006	$25,472,000	$4,529,000
2005	$22,592,000	$4,780,000
2004	$19,590,000	$4,350,000

Curr. Assets:	$10,129,000	**Curr. Liab.:**	$308,571,000	**P/E Ratio:**	16.81
Plant, Equip.:	$7,710,000	**Total Liab.:**	$337,818,000	**Indic. Yr. Divd.:**	$0.840
Total Assets:	$375,924,000	**Net Worth:**	$38,105,000	**Debt/ Equity:**	0.7253

F5 Networks Inc

401 Elliott Ave. W, Seattle, WA, 98119; ***PH:*** 1-206-272-5555; ***Fax:*** 1-206-272-5556; ***http://*** www.f5.com; ***Email:*** info@f5.com

General - Incorporation....WA
Employees....1,068
Auditor....PricewaterhouseCoopers LLP
Stk Agt....American Stock Transfer & Trust Co.
Counsel....Gunderson Dettmer Stough Et Al
DUNS No....NA

Stock- Price on:12/24/2007....$84.15
Stock Exchange....NDQ
Ticker Symbol....FFIV
Outstanding Shares....41,740,000
E.P.S....$0.90
Shareholders....NA

Business: The group's principal activity is to provide integrated products and services to manage, control and optimize Internet traffic. The core products include the big-ip, ip application witch and controller, 3-dns controller, icontrol tm. These solutions are designed to improve the availability and performance of Internet-based servers and applications. The group operates in the United States, Asia-Pacific and Europe. During the year 2003, the group acquired uroam inc. On 01-Jun-2004, the group acquired magnifire websystems inc.

Primary SIC and add'l.: 7375 7379 7372

CIK No: 0001048695

Subsidiaries: AESR, LLC, Cereales Partners Latin America LLC, Colombo, Inc., Croissant King Pty Limited, D.h. Austral (uruguay) Sociedad Anonima, Elysees Consult S.a., FYL CORP., GARDETTOS BAKERY, INC., Gcf Servicios De Mexico S. De R.l. De C.v., General Mills (suisse) Sve Sarl

Officers: John McAdam/Dir., CEO, Pres., Edward J. Eames/Sr. VP - Business Operations, Karl Triebes/Sr. VP - Product Development, CTO, Tom Hull/Sr. VP - Worldwide Sales, Dan Matte/Sr. VP - Marketing, Andy Reinland/Sr. VP, CFO, John Rodriguez/Chief Accounting Officer, Sr. VP, Christopher P. Lynch/Sr. VP - Data Solutions, Jeff Christianson/Sr. VP, General Counsel

Directors: John McAdam/Dir., CEO, Pres., Alan J. Higginson/Chmn., Rich Malone/Dir., Deborah Bevier/Dir., Karl D. Guelich/Dir., Keith D. Grinstein/Dir., Gary Ames/Dir.

Owners: Insiders/1.10%, Rich Malone, Karl D. Guelich, Dan Matte, Gary A. Ames, Karl Triebes, John McAdam, Keith D. Grinstein, Wellington Management Company, LLP/5.80%, Alan J. Higginson, FMR Corp. and its affiliates/14.30%, Edward J. Eames, Tom Hull

Financial Data: ***Fiscal Year End:***09/30 ***Latest Annual Data:*** 09/30/2007

Year	Sales	Net Income
2007	$525,667,000	$77,000,000
2006	$394,049,000	$66,005,000
2005	$281,410,000	$46,902,000

Curr. Assets:	$462,975,000	**Curr. Liab.:**	$99,637,000	**P/E Ratio:**	45.98
Plant, Equip.:	$29,951,000	**Total Liab.:**	$113,053,000	**Indic. Yr. Divd.:**	NA
Total Assets:	$729,511,000	**Net Worth:**	$616,458,000	**Debt/ Equity:**	NA

Faceprint Global Solutions Inc

1111 E Herndon Ave., Ste.115, Fresno, CA, 93720; ***PH:*** 1-559-436-1060; ***Fax:*** 1-559-436-1061; ***http://*** www.faceprint.tv; ***Email:*** customerservice@faceprint.tv

General - Incorporation....WY
Employees....3
Auditor....Pritchett, Siler & Hardy, P.C.
Stk Agt....Colonial Stock Transfer Co Inc
Counsel....NA
DUNS No....NA

Stock- Price on:12/24/2007....$0.003
Stock Exchange....OTC
Ticker Symbol....FPRNE
Outstanding Shares....122,340,000
E.P.S....-$0.073
Shareholders....NA

Business: The groups principle activity is to develop software in the field of facial recognition and facial imagery. Products of the group include EZ-Face and EZ-Match. The group operates from California in the United States.

Primary SIC and add'l.: 7372

CIK No: 0001263764

Subsidiaries: Apometrix Technologies, Inc, FacePrint Global Solutions, Inc.

Officers: Pierre Cote/Chmn., CEO, CFO, Pres., Sylvie Lariviere Traub/Member - Advisory Board, Consultant

Directors: Pierre Cote/Chmn., CEO, CFO, Pres., Jean Houle/Dir., Allan J. Balchi/Dir., Lois Gibson/Member - Advisory Board, Gary Rosenfeldt/Member - Advisory Board, Stanley Friedman/Member - Advisory Board, Sylvie Lariviere Traub/Member - Advisory Board, Consultant

Owners: Jean Houle/2.30%, Allan J. Balchi, Pierre Cote/27.10%, Insiders/29.70%

Financial Data: ***Fiscal Year End:***03/31 ***Latest Annual Data:*** 3/31/2006

Year	Sales	Net Income
2006	$0	-$9,505,000
2005	$13,000	-$7,013,000

Curr. Assets:	$1,000	**Curr. Liab.:**	$1,650,000		
Plant, Equip.:	$8,000	**Total Liab.:**	$2,004,000	**Indic. Yr. Divd.:**	NA
Total Assets:	$9,000	**Net Worth:**	-$1,996,000	**Debt/ Equity:**	NA

Fact Corp

1530 9th Ave.nye SE, Calgary, AB, T2G 0T7; ***PH:*** 1-732-922-0911; ***Fax:*** 1-732-922-0912; ***http://*** www.factfoods.com; ***Email:*** info@factfoods.com

General - Incorporation....CO
Employees....NA
Auditor....Miller & McCollom
Stk Agt....Computershare Investor Services LLC
Counsel....NA
DUNS No....16-048-1057

Stock- Price on:12/24/2007....$0.47
Stock Exchange....OTC
Ticker Symbol....FCTOA
Outstanding Shares....NA
E.P.S....NA
Shareholders....NA

Business: The group's principal activities are commercial food industry operations, real estate operations and oil and gas operations. The group operates in the functional food industry through its wholly owned subsidiary, food and culinary technology group inc. It develops, licenses and supplies functional premixes to customers who manufacture, distribute, and market bakery and pasta products. The group owns two real estate properties located in the city of calgary which generates rental income. The group owns interests in a producing oil and gas property in Washington county, Colorado and oil and gas leases in Montana though its wholly owned subsidiary, capital Canada.

Primary SIC and add'l.: 6519 2099 1382

CIK No: 0000707674

Subsidiaries: FACT Group, FACT Products Inc, Food and Culinary Technology Group Inc, Wall Street Investment Corp, Wall Street Real Estate Ltd

Officers: Brian Raines/Dir., Scientific Advisor, Scott W. Lawler/Dir., General Counsel, Caroline Winsor/Contact - Investment Inquiries, Jacqueline Danforth/Pres. - Principal Exec., Financial, Accounting Officer, Paul Litwack/Dir., Advisor

Directors: Paul Litwack/Dir., Advisor, Brian Raines/Dir., Scientific Advisor, Scott W. Lawler/Dir., General Counsel

Owners: Paul Litwack/2.09%, Scott W. Lawler/29.16%, Insiders/9.26%, Thomas Ringoir/5.82%, Daniel Koyich/5.82%, Jacqueline R. Danforth/2.44%, Brian Raines/5.58%

Financial Data: ***Fiscal Year End:***12/31 ***Latest Annual Data:*** 12/31/2006

Year	Sales	Net Income
2006	$1,804,000	-$841,000
2005	$800,000	-$626,000
2004	$1,418,000	-$595,000

Curr. Assets:	$771,000	**Curr. Liab.:**	$2,256,000		
Plant, Equip.:	$1,000	**Total Liab.:**	$3,992,000	**Indic. Yr. Divd.:**	NA
Total Assets:	$2,289,000	**Net Worth:**	-$1,703,000	**Debt/ Equity:**	NA

Factory Card & Party Outlet Corp

2727 Diehl Rd., Naperville, IL, 60563; ***PH:*** 1-630-579-2000; ***Fax:*** 1-630-579-2400; ***http://*** www.factorycard.com

General - Incorporation....DE
Employees....950
Auditor....Deloitte & Touche LLP
Stk Agt....Wells Fargo Shareowner Services
Counsel....NA
DUNS No....15-120-1852

Stock- Price on:12/24/2007....$10.97
Stock Exchange....NDQ
Ticker Symbol....FCPO
Outstanding Shares....3,350,000
E.P.S....$0.67
Shareholders....NA

Business: The group's principal activity is to operate a chain of stores offering a variety of greeting cards, giftwrap, balloons, everyday and seasonal party supplies and other special occasion merchandise. The stores offer product selection for all major holidays and seasonal events such as valentine's day, st. Patrick's day, mother's day, father's day, thanksgiving, christmas, new year's; celebratory events, such as birthdays, graduations, weddings and other family, religious, special occasions and many such other occasions. The group's registered trademarks include factory card outlet(R) and partymania(r). As on

20-Mar-2002, the group operated 172 stores. The stores are located in around 20 states including Delaware, Florida, Illinois, Indiana, Iowa, Kentucky, Maryland, Michigan, Minnesota, Missouri, Nebraska, North Carolina, Ohio, Pennsylvania, South Carolina, Tennessee, Virginia, west Virginia and Wisconsin. The group closed 3 stores during the ye

Primary SIC and add'l.: 5947

CIK No: 0001024441

Subsidiaries: Factory Card Outlet of America, Ltd

Owners: Richard E. George/1.40%, Timothy J. Benson, Timothy F. Gower/2.90%, Ben Evans/1.00%, CR Intrinsic Investors, LLC/5.20%, Gary W. Rada/5.70%, Jarrett A. Misch, Insiders/15.40%, Michael Perri/1.40%, Robert S. Sandler/1.00%, Midwood Capital Management, LLC/7.70%, Skylands Capital, LLC/5.60%, Martin G. Mand/1.00%, Patrick W. OBrien, Peter M. Holmes/1.00% *(16 Owners included in Index)*

Financial Data: *Fiscal Year End:*01/28 *Latest Annual Data:* 2/3/2007

Year	Sales	Net Income
2007	$244,232,000	$2,283,000
2006	$233,131,000	-$1,003,000
2005	$230,148,000	-$200,000

Curr. Assets:	$55,572,000	**Curr. Liab.:**	$37,235,000	**P/E Ratio:**	16.37
Plant, Equip.:	$9,400,000	**Total Liab.:**	$39,148,000	**Indic. Yr. Divd.:**	NA
Total Assets:	$71,032,000	**Net Worth:**	$31,884,000	**Debt/ Equity:**	NA

Factory Point Bancorp Inc VT

4928 Main St., Manchester Center, Vermont, 05255; ; ***http://*** www.factorypoint.com

General - Incorporation		**Stock**- Price on:12/24/2007	$19
Employees	NA	Stock Exchange	NA
Auditor	NA	Ticker Symbol	NA
Stk Agt	NA	Outstanding Shares	NA
Counsel	NA	E.P.S	NA
DUNS No.	NA	Shareholders	NA

Business: The groups principal activity is to provide banking services. The services of the group include lending, small business loan, deposit consumer banking, mortgage, trust and investment, ATM facilities and online brokerage services. The group operates from the United States.

Primary SIC and add'l.: 7379

CIK No:

Factset Research Systems Inc

601 Merritt 7, Norwalk, CT, 06851; ***PH:*** 1-203-810-1000; ***Fax:*** 1-203-810-1001; ***http://*** www.factset.com

General - Incorporation	DE	**Stock**- Price on:12/24/2007	$70.56
Employees	1,368	Stock Exchange	NYSE
Auditor	PricewaterhouseCoopers LLP	Ticker Symbol	FDS
Stk Agt	Mellon Investor Services LLC	Outstanding Shares	48,850,000
Counsel	Cravath, Swaine & Moore LLP	E.P.S	$2.25
DUNS No.	18-974-0558	Shareholders	NA

Business: The group's principal activity is to provide online integrated database services to the global investment community. It combines more than 200 databases, including data from thousands of companies as well as multiple stock markets, research firms and governments, into a single online source of information and analytics. The group's product includes the portfolio returns product named as spar (style, performance and risk). Spar allows portfolio managers to analyze the style, performance and risk of selected portfolios, benchmarks and competitor funds. On 07-May-2004, the group acquired callstreet llc. On 01-Sep-2004, the group acquired jcf group of companies.

Primary SIC and add'l.: 7374 7375 7371

CIK No: 0001013237

Subsidiaries: Decision Data System B.V., Derivative Solutions,Inc., FactSet CallStreet, LLC, FactSet Data Systems,Inc., FactSet Europe Limited, FactSet Europe S..r.l, FactSet France S..r.l, FactSet France,Inc., FactSet Global Filings Limited, FactSet GmbH, FactSet Holdings UK Limited, FactSet Italia S.r.l., FactSet JCF S.A.S., FactSet Limited, FactSet Mergerstat, LLC 25 Subsidiaries included in the Index

Officers: Philip A. Hadley/Chmn., CEO, Michael D. Frankenfield/Sr. VP, Dir. - US Investment Management Services, Peter Walsh/Sr. VP, CFO, Treasurer, Michael F. Dichristina/Dir., COO, Pres., Kieran Kennedy/Sr. VP, Dir. - Investment Banking, Brokerage Services

Directors: Philip A. Hadley/Chmn., CEO, Charles J. Snyder/64/Vice Chmn., Walter F. Siebecker/65/Dir., James J. McGonigle/43/Dir., Joseph E. Laird/61/Dir., Scott A. Billeadeau/Dir., Michael F. Dichristina/Dir., COO, Pres., Joseph Zimmel/54/Dir.

Owners: T. Rowe Price Associates, Inc./7.60%, Michael D. Frankenfield, Kieran M. Kennedy, Peter G. Walsh, Scott A. Billeadeau, Michael F. DiChristina, Insiders/10.60%, Joseph E. Laird, Walter F. Siebecker, James J. McGonigle, Philip A. Hadley/2.70%, Charles J. Snyder/6.40%

Financial Data: *Fiscal Year End:*08/31 *Latest Annual Data:* 08/31/2007

Year	Sales	Net Income
2007	$475,801,000	$109,567,000
2006	$387,350,000	$82,916,000
2005	$312,644,000	$71,765,000

Curr. Assets:	$206,980,000	**Curr. Liab.:**	$79,301,000		
Plant, Equip.:	$59,812,000	**Total Liab.:**	$98,540,000	**Indic. Yr. Divd.:**	$0.480
Total Assets:	$457,228,000	**Net Worth:**	$358,688,000	**Debt/ Equity:**	NA

FAGE Dairy Industry

35, Hermou St., Metamorfossi, Athens; ***PH:*** 30-12892555; ***http://*** www.fage.gr; ***Email:*** info@fage.gr

General - Incorporation	Prefecture Of Athens Attica, Hellenic Republic	**Stock**- Price on:12/24/2007	NA
Employees	NA	Stock Exchange	NA
Auditor	Ernst & Young LLP	Ticker Symbol	NA
Stk Agt	NA	Outstanding Shares	NA
Counsel	NA	E.P.S	NA
DUNS No.	NA	Shareholders	NA

Business: The group's principal activity is to sell branded dairy products, fruit juices and refrigerated snacks. Dairy products include yogurt and dairy desserts, milk and milk cream, and cheese. The group's products are sold under the trademarks FAGE and Total. In 2005, the group acquired of the U.K. distributor for yogurt. The group operates in Greece, U.S., U.K. and Italy.

Primary SIC and add'l.: 2026 2023 2022 5142

CIK No: 0001037601

Subsidiaries: Evga Holdings S.A

Fair Isaac Corp

901 Marquette Ave., Ste. 3200, Minneapolis, MN, 55402; ***PH:*** 1-612-758-5200; ***Fax:*** 1-612-758-5201; ***http://*** www.fairisaac.com; ***Email:*** info@fairisaac.com

General - Incorporation	DE	**Stock**- Price on:12/24/2007	$37.01
Employees	2,737	Stock Exchange	NYSE
Auditor	Deloitte & Touche LLP	Ticker Symbol	FIC
Stk Agt	Mellon Investor Services LLC	Outstanding Shares	57,360,000
Counsel	NA	E.P.S	$1.66
DUNS No.	07-466-4715	Shareholders	NA

Business: The group's principle activity is to provide analytic, software and data management products and services to automate and improve decisions. It operates through four segments: scoring solutions segment includes the scoring services distributed through major credit reporting agencies. The strategy machine solutions segment includes industry-tailored applications designed for specific processes in customer acquisition, origination and account management. The analytic software tools segment includes tools sold to businesses for use in building their own applications. The professional services segment includes revenues from custom projects and consulting services, as well as, services associated with implementing and delivering the products. The group's total revenue for the year 2007 was 822.24 millions of USD.

Primary SIC and add'l.: 7372 7379 7371 7323

CIK No: 0000814547

Subsidiaries: Data Research Technologies, Inc., Diversified Healthcare Services, Inc., Fair Isaac (ASPAC)Pte. Ltd., Fair Isaac Asia Pacific Corp., Fair Isaac Credit Services, Inc., Fair Isaac Europe Limited, Fair Isaac India Software Private Limited, Fair Isaac International Limited, Fair Isaac Network, Inc., Fair Isaac SA Limited, Fair Isaac Services Limited, Fair Isaac Software, Inc., Fair Isaac UK Group Limited, Fair Isaac UK Holdings, Inc., Fair Isaac UK IP Limited 32 Subsidiaries included in the Index

Officers: Mark N. Greene/CEO, Bernhard Nann/CTO, Sr. VP, Tracey Stout/Sr. VP, Chief Marketing Officer, Greg Corgan/VP - Global Sales, Andrew N. Jennings/Sr. VP, Chief Research Officer, Mark R. Scadina/Sr. VP, General Counsel, Corp. Sec., Richard A. Stewart/VP - Professional Services, John D. Emerick/VP - Corporate Development, Treasurer, Michael J. Pung/VP - Finance, Michael H. Campbell/COO, Exec. VP, Larry E. Rosenberger/VP - Analytic Research Fellow, Richard S. Deal/Sr. VP, Chief Human Resources Officer, Charles M. Osborne/CFO, Exec. VP

Directors: George A. Battle/Chmn., Margaret L. Taylor/Dir., James Kirsner/Dir., Tony J. Christianson/Dir., Alex W. Hart/Dir., Guy R. Henshaw/Dir., William J. Lansing/Dir.

Owners: Insiders/3.50%, James Kirsner, Southeastern Asset Management, Inc./7.50%, Tony Christianson, Charles Osborne, FMR Corp./17.20%, Margaret Taylor, Bernhard Nann, Thomas Grudnowski/1.40%, Michael Campbell, Neuberger Berman, LLC/6.20%, Sandell Asset Management Corp./5.80%, Alex Hart, William Lansing, Guy Henshaw *(18 Owners included in Index)*

Financial Data: *Fiscal Year End:*09/30 *Latest Annual Data:* 9/30/2006

Year	Sales	Net Income
2006	$825,365,000	$103,486,000
2005	$798,671,000	$134,548,000
2004	$706,206,000	$102,788,000

Curr. Assets:	$413,310,000	**Curr. Liab.:**	$537,029,000	**P/E Ratio:**	22.30
Plant, Equip.:	$56,611,000	**Total Liab.:**	$551,177,000	**Indic. Yr. Divd.:**	$0.080
Total Assets:	$1,321,205,000	**Net Worth:**	$770,028,000	**Debt/ Equity:**	NA

Fairchild Corp

48720 Kato Rd., Fremont, CA, 94538; ***PH:*** 1-510-668-7000; ***Fax:*** 1-703-478-5775; ***http://*** www.fairchild.com

General - Incorporation	DE	**Stock**- Price on:12/24/2007	$1.89
Employees	550	Stock Exchange	NYSE
Auditor	KPMG LLP	Ticker Symbol	FA
Stk Agt	Mellon Investor Services LLC	Outstanding Shares	25,230,000
Counsel	Cahill Gordon & Reindel LLP	E.P.S	-$0.28
DUNS No.	00-306-2544	Shareholders	NA

Business: The group's principal activities are to manufacture and distribute airframe components for commercial and military aircraft. It operates in three business segments: the aerospace distribution segment stocks and distributes a wide variety of aircraft parts and related support services to commercial airlines, air cargo carriers, fixed-base operators, corporate aircraft operators and other aerospace companies. Its products are flight data recorders, radar and navigation systems, instruments, hydraulic and electrical components and space components. Aerospace manufacturing segment manufactures airframe components used in the construction and maintenance of commercial and military aircraft. The real estate operations segment owns and leases a shopping center located in New York, and owns and rents a building in chatsworth and a manufacturing facility located in fullerton. In mar 2003, the group acquired c-line automation ltd. On 02-Jan-2004, it acquired poloexpress.

Primary SIC and add'l.: 5088 3452 3728 6512

CIK No: 0000009779

Subsidiaries: Banner Aerospace Holding Company I, Inc., Fairchild Holding Corp., Hein Gericke UK Ltd, PoloExpress, Republic Thunderbolt, LLC

Officers: Jeffrey J. Steiner/Chmn., CEO, Eric I. Steiner/Dir., COO, Pres., Donald E. Miller/Exec. VP, General Counsel, Sec., Michael L. McDonald/Sr. VP, CFO, Warren D. Persavich/Pres. - Aerospace Segment, Klaus Esser/MD - Polo Express

Directors: Jeffrey J. Steiner/Chmn., CEO, Eric I. Steiner/Dir., COO, Pres., Daniel Lebard/Dir., Robert E. Edwards/Dir., Michael J. Vantusko/Dir., Didier Choix/Dir., Glenn Myles/Dir.

Owners: GAMCO Investors, Inc., Insiders, Didier Choix, Dimensional Fund Advisors, Inc., Jeffrey J. Steiner, Natalia Hercot, Daniel Lebard, The Steiner Group LLC, Michael J. Vantusko, Natalia Hercot, Jeffrey J. Steiner, Eric Steiner, Glenn Myles, Donald E. Miller, Eric Steiner *(17 Owners included in Index)*

Financial Data: *Fiscal Year End:*09/30 *Latest Annual Data:* 9/30/2005

Year	Sales	Net Income
2005	$352,417,000	-$21,284,000
2004	$338,346,000	$3,361,000
2003	$77,519,000	-$53,192,000

Curr. Assets:	$199,493,000	Curr. Liab.:	$101,708,000		
Plant, Equip.:	$58,698,000	Total Liab.:	$326,111,000	Indic. Yr. Divd.:	NA
Total Assets:	$415,129,000	Net Worth:	$89,018,000	Debt/ Equity:	NA

Fairchild International Corp

78 Belleville Ave., Spruce Grove, AB, T7A 1H8; PH: 1-780-980-0028;
http://www.syngasinternational.com

General - Incorporation.............................NV	Stock- Price on:12/24/2007 ....NA
Employees...NA	Stock Exchange.......................................OTC
Auditor ....Morgan & Co	Ticker Symbol...FCS
Stk Agt..........American Registrar & Transfer Co	Outstanding Shares.................................NA
Counsel...NA	E.P.S..-$7.28
DUNS No...NA	Shareholders...NA

Business: The group's principle activity is to seek and identify a suitable business opportunity or enter into a suitable business combination. Till then the company will operate as a blank check company. Previously the company was focused on the identification and acquisition of mineral resource properties in Australia. The group operates from United States.

Primary SIC and add'l.: 9999

CIK No: 0001096550

Subsidiaries: Syngas Energy Corp.

Officers: Wilf Ouellette/Dir., CEO, Pres./$39,054.00, Margaret Hunt/60/Dir., Sec., Treasurer, Richard Sadowski/Inventor, Technical, Scientific Advisor, Steve Eilers/Dir., Sec., Treasurer

Directors: Wilf Ouellette/Dir., CEO, Pres., Margaret Hunt/60/Dir., Sec., Treasurer, Robert Klein/59/Dir., Steve Eilers/Dir., Sec., Treasurer, Jim Clark/Dir.

Owners: Wilf Ouellette/23.00%, Insiders/23.00%, Carolyn Foster/17.00%

Financial Data: Fiscal Year End:12/31 Latest Annual Data: 12/31/2006

Year	Sales	Net Income
2006	NA	-$1,696,000
2005	NA	-$1,095,000
2004	$40,000	-$589,000

Curr. Assets:	$13,000	Curr. Liab.:	$312,000		
Plant, Equip.:	NA	Total Liab.:	$312,000	Indic. Yr. Divd.:	NA
Total Assets:	$39,000	Net Worth:	-$273,000	Debt/ Equity:	NA

Fairchild Semiconductor International Inc

82 Running Hill Rd., South Portland, ME, 04106; PH: 1-207-775-8100; Fax: 1-207-761-6020;
http:// www.fairchildsemi.com; Email: investor@fairchildsemi.com

General - Incorporation.............................DE	Stock- Price on:12/24/2007 ....$19.5
Employees...9,344	Stock Exchange.....................................NYSE
Auditor ....KPMG LLP	Ticker Symbol...FCS
Stk Agt..................Computershare Trust Co	Outstanding Shares.....................123,730,000
Counsel...NA	E.P.S..$0.31
DUNS No...NA	Shareholders...NA

Business: The groups principle activity is to provide power analog, power discrete, and optoelectronic components that optimize system power. The groups product The Power Franchise(R) provides industrys components for todays leading electronic applications in the computing, communications, consumer, industrial, and automotive segments. The group operates through three business segments namely analog products, functional power and standard products. The group operates from United States.

Primary SIC and add'l.: 3674

CIK No: 0001036960

Subsidiaries: Fairchild Energy LLC, Fairchild Korea Semiconductor Ltd., Fairchild Korea Trading Company, Fairchild Semiconductor (Bermuda) Ltd., Fairchild Semiconductor (Malaysia) Sdn. Bhd., Fairchild Semiconductor (Optoelectronics) Pte. Ltd., Fairchild Semiconductor (Optoelectronics) Sdn. Bhd., Fairchild Semiconductor (Philippines), Inc., Fairchild Semiconductor (Shanghai) Co., Ltd, Fairchild Semiconductor (Suzhou) Co., Ltd., Fairchild Semiconductor (Wuxi) Co. Ltd., Fairchild Semiconductor Asia Pacific Pte. Ltd., Fairchild Semiconductor Corporation, Fairchild Semiconductor Corporation of California, Fairchild Semiconductor GmbH 30 Subsidiaries included in the Index

Officers: Mark S. Thompson/Dir., CEO, Pres./$6,925,674.00, Paul D. Delva/Sr. VP, General Counsel, Corp. Sec., Laurenz Schmidt/Exec. VP - Global Operations/$1,349,975.00, Robin A. Sawyer/VP, Corporate Controller, Kevin B. London/Sr. VP - Human Resources, Administration, Izak Bencuya/Exec. VP, GM - Functional Power Group, Chief Strategy Officer/$1,630,577.00, Andrea M. Mirenda/VP - Marketing, Mark Norman/VP - Worldwide Distribution, C. G. Park/VP - Korea Sales, Marketing, Eric Kuo/Pres. - Asia Pacific, Paul S. Lones/VP - Information Technology, K. T. Tan/Sr. VP - Asian Operations, Dan Janson/VP - Investor Relations, Ole-Petter Brusdal/VP - Europe Sales, Marketing, Mark S. Frey/CFO, Exec. VP/$1,410,609.00 (22 Officers included in Index)

Directors: Mark S. Thompson/Dir., CEO, Pres., William N. Stout/Chmn., Charles P. Carinalli/Dir., Richard A. Aurelio/Dir., Kevin J. McGarity/Dir., Ronald W. Shelly/Dir., Bryan R. Roub/Dir., Robert F. Friel/Dir., Thomas L. Magnanti/Dir.

Owners: Capital Group International, Inc/6.60%, Kevin J. McGarity, Kirk P. Pond/2.80%, T. Rowe Price Associates, Inc./5.60%, Charles M. Clough, Charles P. Carinalli, Laurenz Schmidt, Mark S. Frey, Richard A. Aurelio, Robert F. Friel, Insiders/4.20%, Bryan R. Roub, Mark S. Thompson, Thomas A. Beaver, Thomas L. Magnanti (21 Owners included in Index)

Financial Data: Fiscal Year End:12/25 Latest Annual Data: 07/01/2007

Year	Sales	Net Income
2007	$408,900,000	$3,400,000
2006	$1,651,100,000	$83,400,000
2005	$1,425,100,000	-$241,200,000

Curr. Assets:	$1,028,500,000	Curr. Liab.:	$262,500,000	P/E Ratio:	38.24
Plant, Equip.:	$646,400,000	Total Liab.:	$913,400,000	Indic. Yr. Divd.:	NA
Total Assets:	$2,045,600,000	Net Worth:	$1,132,200,000	Debt/ Equity:	0.5208

Fairfax Financial Holdings Ltd

95 Wellington St. W, Ste. 800, Toronto, ON, M5J 2N7; PH: 1-416-367-4941; http:// www.fairfax.ca

General - Incorporation ....Canada	Stock- Price on:12/24/2007 ....$193.48
Employees...8,258	Stock Exchange.....................................NYSE
Auditor ....PricewaterhouseCoopers LLP	Ticker Symbol...FFH
Stk Agt.............................. Mellon Trust Co	Outstanding Shares.........................17,730,000
Counsel....................................... Torys LLP	E.P.S..$35.37
DUNS No.............................. 20-785-4969	Shareholders...NA

Business: The group's principle activities are the provision of insurance and reinsurance for commercial and personal property, casualty, oil and gas and life risks. The group is a holding company which provides financial services through its subsidiaries. Other activities include investment management services and claims adjusting, appraisal and loss management services. The operations of the group are conducted in Canada, the United States and Europe and Far East countries. The group's quarterly revenue for September 2007 was 1,871.20 millions of USD.

Primary SIC and add'l.: 6411 6399 6311 6331 6321 6719

CIK No: 0000915191

Subsidiaries: Clearwater Insurance Company, Commonwealth Insurance Company, CRC (Bermuda) Reinsurance Limited, Crum & Forster Holdings Corp., Fairmont Insurance Company, Falcon Insurance Company, Federated Holdings of Canada Limited, First Capital Insurance Limited, Guild Napa Insurance Services, Hamblin Watsa Investment Counsel Ltd., Hong Kong Ltd., Lindsey Morden Group Inc., Lombard General Insurance Company of Canada, Markel Insurance Company of Canada, MFXchange Holdings Inc. 27 Subsidiaries included in the Index

Officers: Prem V. Watsa/Chmn., CEO, James F. Dowd/Chmn., CEO - Fairfax Asia, Dennis C. Gibbs/Chmn. - TRG Holding Corporation, Jan Christiansen/Pres. - Cunningham Lindsey Group Inc, David Bonham/VP - Financial Reporting, Richard Patina/Pres. - Lombard General Insurance Company, Canada, Silvy Wright/Pres. - Markel Insurance Company, Canada, Andrew A. Barnard/Pres. - Odyssey Re Holdings Corp, Bradley P. Martin/VP, COO, Corp. Sec., Trevor J. Ambridge/VP, Sammy Y. Chan/Pres. - Fairfax Asia, Ronald Schokking/VP, Treasurer, Ray Roy/Pres. - Mfxchange Holdings Inc, Roger D. Lace/Pres. - Hamblin Watsa Investment Counsel Ltd, Craig Hurford/Pres. - Commonwealth Insurance Company (29 Officers included in Index)

Directors: Prem V. Watsa/Chmn., CEO, James F. Dowd/Chmn., CEO - Fairfax Asia, Robert J. Gunn/Corp. Dir., David L. Johnston/Dir., Anthony F. Griffiths/Corp. Dir., Frank B. Bennett/Dir., Paul L. Murray/Dir., Brandon W. Sweitzer/Dir.

Financial Data: Fiscal Year End:12/31 Latest Annual Data: 12/31/2006

Year	Sales	Net Income
2006	$6,803,700,000	$654,400,000
2005	$5,900,500,000	-$313,400,000
2004	$5,792,600,000	$8,100,000

Curr. Assets:	$4,602,700,000	Curr. Liab.:	$2,133,200,000		
Plant, Equip.:	NA	Total Liab.:	$23,852,200,000	Indic. Yr. Divd.:	$2.750
Total Assets:	$26,776,000,000	Net Worth:	$2,744,600,000	Debt/ Equity:	NA

Fairmont Hotels & Resorts Inc

100 Wellington St., W, Ste. 1600, TD Ctr., Toronto, ON, M5K 1B7; PH: 1-416-874-2600;
http:// www.fairmont.com

General - Incorporation ....Canada	Stock- Price on:12/24/2007 ....NA
Employees...NA	Stock Exchange.......................................NA
Auditor ....PricewaterhouseCoopers LLP	Ticker Symbol...NA
Stk Agt..................Computershare Trust Co	Outstanding Shares.................................NA
Counsel...NA	E.P.S..NA
DUNS No.............................. 25-388-3805	Shareholders...NA

Business: The group's principle activity is to operate luxury hotels and resorts. The portfolio consists of 77 luxury and first class properties with more than 31,000 rooms in Canada, the United States, Mexico, Bermuda, barbados and the united arab emirates. It manages 37 luxury properties in major city centers and destination resorts. In addition to hotel management, the group holds real estate interests in 21 properties, two undeveloped land blocks and 35 per cent investment interest in legacy hotels real estate investment trust, which owns 22 properties.

Primary SIC and add'l.: 7011 8741

CIK No: 0001030561

Subsidiaries: Delta Hotels Limited, Fairmont, FHR Holdings Inc., FHR Properties Inc, FHR Real Estate Corporation

FairPoint Communications Inc

521 E Morehead St., Ste. 250, Charlotte, NC, 28202; PH: 1-704-344-8150; Fax: 1-704-344-8121;
http:// www.fairpoint.com; Email: mediarelations@fairpoint.com

General - Incorporation ....DE	Stock- Price on:12/24/2007 ....$18.17
Employees...952	Stock Exchange.....................................NYSE
Auditor ....KPMG LLP	Ticker Symbol...FRP
Stk Agt.......................... Bank of New York	Outstanding Shares.........................35,240,000
Counsel...NA	E.P.S..$0.86
DUNS No...NA	Shareholders...NA

Business: The group's principal activity is to provide telecommunications services to customers in rural communities, offering an array of services that include local voice, long distance, data and Internet. The group provides wholesale long distance service and support to rural local exchange carriers subsidiaries and other independent local exchange companies. These services allow such companies to operate their own long distance communication services and sell such services to their respective customers. Rural local exchange carriers network consists of central office hosts and remote sites with advanced digital switches, primarily manufactured by nortel and siemens, operating with the most current software. The group's business customers are predominantly agriculture, light manufacturing and service industries. On 01-Dec-2003, the group acquired the community service telephone co. & commtel communications inc.

Primary SIC and add'l.: 4813

CIK No: 0001062613

Subsidiaries: BE Mobile Communications, Incorporated, Bentleyville Communications Corporation, Berkshire Cable Corp., Berkshire Cellular,Inc., Berkshire Net,Inc., Berkshire New York Access,Inc., Berkshire Telephone Corporation, Big Sandy Telecom,Inc., Bluestem Telephone Company, C-R Communications,Inc., C-R Long Distance,Inc., C-R Telephone Company, C& E Communications, Ltd., Chautauqua and Erie Telephone Corporation, Chautauqua& Erie Communications,Inc. 73 Subsidiaries included in the Index

Officers: Eugene B. Johnson/Chmn., CEO, John Crowley/CFO, Exec. VP, Peter G. Nixon/Pres., Walter E. Leach/Exec. VP - Corporate Development, Shirley J. Linn/Exec. VP, General Counsel, Lisa R. Hood/COO - Telecom Group, Jennifer Sharpe/Dir. - Corporate Communications

Directors: Eugene B. Johnson/Chmn., CEO, Patricia Garrison-Corbin/Dir., David L. Hauser/Dir., Claude C. Lilly/Dir., Robert S. Lilien/Dir., Jane E. Newman/Dir.

Owners: Insiders/2.70%, David L. Hauser, Eugene B. Johnson/1.30%, Walter E. Leach, Claude C. Lilly, Wellington Management Company LLP/9.30%, Patricia Garrison-Corbin, Peter G. Nixon/0.20%, Shirley J. Linn/0.30%, John P. Crowley/0.40%

Financial Data: *Fiscal Year End:*12/31 *Latest Annual Data:* 12/31/2006

Year	Sales	Net Income
2006	$270,069,000	$31,090,000
2005	$262,843,000	$28,930,000
2004	$252,645,000	-$23,682,000

Curr. Assets:	$79,170,000	*Curr. Liab.:*	$46,334,000		
Plant, Equip.:	$246,264,000	*Total Liab.:*	$660,503,000	*Indic. Yr. Divd.:*	$1.590
Total Assets:	$885,230,000	*Net Worth:*	$224,719,000	*Debt/ Equity:*	2.9423

Falcon Natural Gas Corp

2500 Citywest Blvd, Ste. 300, Houston, TX, 77042; *PH:* 1-713-267-2240; *Fax:* 1-713-456-2581; *http://* www.falcongas.com

General - Incorporation	NV	**Stock**- Price on:12/24/2007	NA
Employees	NA	Stock Exchange	OTC
Auditor	Williams & Webster, P.S	Ticker Symbol	FNGCE
Stk Agt	Pacific Stock Transfer Company	Outstanding Shares	NA
Counsel	NA	E.P.S	NA
DUNS No.	NA	Shareholders	NA

Business: The groups principal activity is to explore natural gas. The group operates from Louisiana and Texas in the United States.

Primary SIC and add'l.: 1321

CIK No: 0001167764

Subsidiaries: Falcon Natural Gas Corporation

Officers: Saul S. Deutsch/CFO

Falcon Ridge Development Inc

Formerly: Pocketspec Technologies Inc

5111 Juan Tabo Blvd. N.e., Albuquerque, NM, 87111; *PH:* 1-505-856-6043; *http://* www.pocketspec.com

General - Incorporation	CO	**Stock**- Price on:12/24/2007	$0.92
Employees	NA	Stock Exchange	OTC
Auditor	Epstein, Weber & Conover, Plc	Ticker Symbol	FCNR
Stk Agt	Corporate Stock Transfer, Inc.	Outstanding Shares	14,620,000
Counsel	NA	E.P.S	-$0.13
DUNS No.	NA	Shareholders	NA

Business: The group's principle activities are to develop, produce and market color comparison devices, ultra-violet measurement devices and related software products. The group's products include colorqatm and bronzchecktm. The measuring device can be suited to fit any color matching needs, whether solid, liquid or powder. The products are used mainly for plastic injection molding, textile production and sales, cosmetics manufacturing, sign painting, automotive-commercial-residential paint industry and for decorations. The group operates in United States and other foreign countries.

Primary SIC and add'l.: 3829

CIK No: 0001065659

Subsidiaries: Sierra Norte, LLC, Spanish Trails, LLC

Officers: Fred M. Montano/55/Chmn., CEO, Pres., Jack Gordon/Consultant, Product Designer, R & D Specialist, Chris Wrigley/Consultant, Electrical Engineer, Gregg Wagner/Consultant, Product Designer, Karen Y. Duran/65/CFO, Sec., Treasurer

Directors: Fred M. Montano/55/Chmn., CEO, Pres., Sebastian Ramirez/53/Dir., Troy Duran/42/Dir.

Owners: Karen Y. Duran/41.10%, Fred M. Montano/48.00%, Insiders/80.00%

Financial Data: *Fiscal Year End:*01/31 *Latest Annual Data:* 9/30/2006

Year	Sales	Net Income
2006	NA	-$418,000
2005	$7,457,000	-$119,000

Curr. Assets:	$4,000	*Curr. Liab.:*	$482,000		
Plant, Equip.:	$2,879,000	*Total Liab.:*	$1,834,000	*Indic. Yr. Divd.:*	NA
Total Assets:	$2,884,000	*Net Worth:*	$565,000	*Debt/ Equity:*	6.8455

Falconbridge Ltd

Bce Pl. 181 Bay St., Ste. 200, Toronto, ON, M5J 2T3; *PH:* 1-416-982-7111; *http://* www.noranda.com

General - Incorporation	Canada	**Stock**- Price on:12/24/2007	NA
Employees	NA	Stock Exchange	NA
Auditor	Ernst & Young LLP	Ticker Symbol	NA
Stk Agt	Noranda Inc	Outstanding Shares	NA
Counsel	NA	E.P.S	NA
DUNS No.	20-171-8269	Shareholders	NA

Business: The group's principle activity is the production of copper, nickel, aluminum, lead, silver, gold, sulfuric acid and recycling and complex materials.

Primary SIC and add'l.: 1099 3399 1031 1021 1061

CIK No: 0000889211

FalconStor Software Inc

2 Huntington Quadrangle, Ste. 2S01, Melville, NY, 11747; *PH:* 1-631-777-5188; *Fax:* 1-631-501-7633; *http://* www.falconstor.com

General - Incorporation	DE	**Stock**- Price on:12/24/2007	$11.05
Employees	340	Stock Exchange	NDQ
Auditor	KPMG LLP	Ticker Symbol	FALC
Stk Agt	Computershare Investor Services LLC	Outstanding Shares	49,230,000
Counsel	NA	E.P.S	$0.19
DUNS No.	60-448-7975	Shareholders	NA

Business: The group's principal activity is to develop, manufacture and market storage networking infrastructure software. In addition, the group also provides related maintenance, implementation and engineering services. The group's product line includes a software solution namely ipstor(tm). This software combines industry-standard connectivity with next-generation network storage services that offer large, distributed enterprises, a complete storage management solution. The products are marketed through value-added resellers and distributors. The products of the group are primarily sold in the United States and Asia.

Primary SIC and add'l.: 7373 3678 5045 7371 3577

CIK No: 0000922521

Subsidiaries: FalconStor AC, Inc., FalconStor Software (Korea), Inc., FalconStor, Inc.

Officers: Reijane Huai/Chmn., CEO/$384,723.00, Wai Lam/CTO, VP - Engineering, John Lallier/VP - Technology, Jimmy Wu/VP, Chief Technologist, Wendy Petty/VP - North American Sales, Alex Jiang/VP - Worldwide Marketing, Joanne Ferrara/Investor Relations Contact, Bernie Wu/VP - Business Development/$357,600.00, Alan Chen/VP - Technical Services, Ipstor Development, Guillaume Imberti/VP, GM - EMEA Operations, Wayne Lam/Co - Founder, VP/$352,600.00, James Weber/CFO, VP, Treasurer/$357,600.00, Prakash Babu/VP - Data Protection, Eric Chen/VP, GM - Asia Pacific Operations, Seth Horowitz/VP, General Counsel, Sec.

Directors: Reijane Huai/Chmn., CEO, Alan W. Kaufman/Dir., Patrick B. Carney/Dir., Lawrence S. Dolin/Dir., Steven R. Fischer/Dir., Wayne Lam/Co - Founder, VP, Steven L. Bock/Dir.

Owners: Insiders/24.00%, Bernard Wu, Irwin Lieber/9.30%, ReiJane Huai/21.30%, Steven R. Fischer, Lawrence S. Dolin, Barry Fingerhut/6.40%, Wayne Lam/1.20%, Alan W. Kaufman, Seth Lieber/6.20%, Marilyn Rubenstein/5.00%, Patrick B. Carney, Eli Oxenhorn/5.50%, Steven L. Bock, Jonathan Lieber/6.00% *(17 Owners included in Index)*

Financial Data: *Fiscal Year End:*12/31 *Latest Annual Data:* 12/31/2006

Year	Sales	Net Income
2006	$55,066,000	-$3,375,000
2005	$40,964,000	$2,293,000
2004	$28,709,000	-$5,889,000

Curr. Assets:	$66,339,000	*Curr. Liab.:*	$19,405,000	*P/E Ratio:*	221.00
Plant, Equip.:	$5,960,000	*Total Liab.:*	$23,187,000	*Indic. Yr. Divd.:*	NA
Total Assets:	$78,231,000	*Net Worth:*	$55,043,000	*Debt/ Equity:*	NA

Falcontarget Inc

4201 Massachusetts Ave Nw 8037c, Washington, DC, 20016; *PH:* 1-202-364-8395

General - Incorporation	DE	**Stock**- Price on:12/24/2007	NA
Employees	NA	Stock Exchange	NA
Auditor	Pollard-Kelley Auditing Services, Inc	Ticker Symbol	NA
Stk Agt	Fidelity Transfer Co.	Outstanding Shares	NA
Counsel	NA	E.P.S	NA
DUNS No.	NA	Shareholders	NA

Business: The groups principal activity is to engage in a reverse merger transaction with a private company, acquire assets or engage into other yet unspecified business or businesses (a "Business Transaction"). The term "reverse merger" refers to a transaction where a private company seeks public listing and becomes a publicly traded company.The company is currently a development stage company, whose activities to date have been limited to the organization of the company, the filing of this registration statement and activities incidental thereto. The company has not conducted any research, development or other business, and has not been involved in any bankruptcy, receivership or similar proceeding, or any material reclassification, merger, consolidation, or purchase or sale of assets. The company has offered no products or services, and has never owned any patents, trademarks, licenses, franchises, concessions, royalty agreements, labor contracts or other intellectual or intangible property. There is no assurance that the company will be able to identify a profitable opportunity and consummate a business transaction.

Primary SIC and add'l.: 6770

CIK No: 0001295130

Subsidiaries: Atlantic Republic Investment Company, Atlantic Republic Securities Corp

Officers: Thomas Kirchner/39/Dir., CEO

Directors: Thomas Kirchner/39/Dir., CEO, Serge Atlan/50/Chmn.

Owners: Thomas Kirchner/50.00%, Serge Atlan/50.00%, Insiders/100.00%

Family Dollar Stores Inc

PO Box 1017, Matthews, NC, 28201; *PH:* 1-704-847-6961; *Fax:* 1-704-847-0189; *http://* www.familydollar.com

General - Incorporation	DE	**Stock**- Price on:12/24/2007	$34.71
Employees	24,000	Stock Exchange	NYSE
Auditor	PricewaterhouseCoopers LLP	Ticker Symbol	FDO
Stk Agt	Mellon Investor Services LLC	Outstanding Shares	150,810,000
Counsel	NA	E.P.S	$1.62
DUNS No.	02-447-2631	Shareholders	NA

Business: The group's principle activity is to operate a chain of self-service retail discount stores. The groups products include health and beauty aids, candy, snack and other food, electronics, housewares, giftware and various products. The group operates from United States.

Primary SIC and add'l.: 5331 5251 5441 5136 5399 5137

CIK No: 0000034408

Subsidiaries: Family Dollar Distribution, L.P., Family Dollar Holdings, Inc., Family Dollar Merchandising, L.P., Family Dollar Operations, Inc., Family Dollar Services, Inc., Family Dollar Stores of Alabama, Inc., Family Dollar Stores of Arkansas, Inc., Family Dollar Stores of Colorado, Inc., Family Dollar Stores of Connecticut, Inc., Family Dollar Stores of D.C., Inc., Family Dollar Stores of Delaware, Inc., Family Dollar Stores of Florida, Inc., Family Dollar Stores of Georgia, Inc., Family Dollar Stores of Indiana, L.P., Family Dollar Stores of Iowa, Inc. 41 Subsidiaries included in the Index

Officers: Howard R. Levine/Chmn., CEO/$3,117,263.00, David Jose/Real Estate Mgr., Regional VP - Midwest Territories, Richard Hillesheim/Real Estate Mgr. - Expansions, Relocations, Allan Neibart/Real Estate Mgr., Regional VP - Northeastern Territories, John Wexler/Real Estate Mgr., Regional VP - Northeastern Territories, Kent Davick/Real Estate Mgr., Regional VP, Brad Rogers/Real Estate Mgr., Regional VP, Gerald Martin/Real Estate Mgr., Regional VP, Dorlisa K. Flur/Sr. VP - Strategy, Business Development, Janet G. Kelley/Sr. VP, General Counsel, Sec./$695,380.00, Nick Stratigakes/Real Estate Mgr. - Major Urban Metro, Carolinas, Eastern Virginia, Barry Sullivan/Sr. VP - Store Operations, Keith M. Gehl/Sr. VP - Construction, Facilities Management, John J. Scanlon/Sr. VP - Hardlines, Marketing, Joshua R. Jewett/CIO, Sr. VP *(49 Officers included in Index)*

Directors: Howard R. Levine/Chmn., CEO, Edward C. Dolby/Dir., James G. Martin/Dir., Dale C. Pond/Dir., George R. Mahoney/Dir., Mark R. Bernstein/Dir., Glenn A. Eisenberg/Dir., Sharon Allred Decker/Dir.

Owners: Charles S. Gibson, George R. Mahoney, Robert A. George, James R. Kelly, Harvey Morgan, Bank of America Corporation/6.20%, FMR Corp/9.60%, Mark R. Bernstein, Howard R. Levine/7.20%, Barclays Global Investors, NA/10.40%, Franklin Resources, Inc./5.50%, Kenneth T. Smith, Insiders/8.20%, James G. Martin, Edward C. Dolby *(18 Owners included in Index)*

Financial Data: ***Fiscal Year End:***08/27 ***Latest Annual Data:*** 09/01/2007

Year	Sales	Net Income
2007	$6,834,305,000	$242,854,000
2006	$6,394,772,000	$195,111,000
2005	$5,824,808,000	$217,509,000

Curr. Assets:	$1,290,312,000	***Curr. Liab.:***	$800,585,000	***P/E Ratio:***	22.54
Plant, Equip.:	$918,449,000	***Total Liab.:***	$887,279,000	***Indic. Yr. Divd.:***	$0.460
Total Assets:	$2,224,361,000	***Net Worth:***	$1,337,082,000	***Debt/ Equity:***	0.1865

Family Room Entertainment Corp

8530 Wilshire Blvd., Ste. 420, Beverly Hills, CA, 90211; ***PH:*** 1-310-659-9411; ***Fax:*** 1-310-659-9412; ***http://*** www.fmlyroom.com; ***Email:*** ir@fmlyroom.com

General - Incorporation	NM	***Stock***- Price on:12/24/2007	$0.0005
Employees	7	Stock Exchange	OTC
Auditor	Ham, Langston & Brezina, L.L.P	Ticker Symbol	FMLY
Stk Agt	Securities Transfer Corp	Outstanding Shares	1,080,000,000
Counsel	NA	E.P.S	NA
DUNS No.	NA	Shareholders	NA

Business: The group's principle activities include developing and producing motion pictures. The group also provides production related services. The group operates from United States.

Primary SIC and add'l.: 7812

CIK No: 0000049444

Officers: George Furla/Co - Chmn., CEO, Randall Emmett/Co - Chmn., COO, Stanley Tepper/CFO, Dal M. Walton/VP - Development, Business Affairs, Investor Relations

Directors: George Furla/Co - Chmn., CEO, Randall Emmett/Co - Chmn., COO

Owners: Longview Fund, LP, Alpha Capital Aktiengesellschaft, George Furla, Standard Resources Limited, Longview Equity Fund, LP, Arthur Lieberman, Ron Smith, Insiders

Familymeds Group Inc

Formerly: Drugmax Inc

312 Farmington Ave., Farmington, CT, 06032; ***PH:*** 1-860-676-1222; ***http://*** www.drugmax.com

General - Incorporation	NV	***Stock***- Price on:12/24/2007	NA
Employees	535	Stock Exchange	NA
Auditor	Deloitte & Touche LLP	Ticker Symbol	NA
Stk Agt	Computershare Investor Services LLC	Outstanding Shares	NA
Counsel	Robinson & Cole LLP	E.P.S	NA
DUNS No.	87-661-9701	Shareholders	NA

Business: The group's principal activity is to provide wholesale distribution of pharmaceuticals, over-the-counter products, health and beauty care products, nutritional supplements and related products. The group distributes its products primarily to independent pharmacies in the continental United States, and secondarily to small and medium-sized pharmacy chains, alternative care facilities and other wholesalers and retailers. The group's headquarter is in clearwater, Florida and maintains distribution centers in Pennsylvania, Ohio, and Louisiana. The group trademark and service mark is drugmax(R) and drugmax.com (r). The group maintains inventory in excess of 20,000 stock keeping units from leading manufacturers and holds licenses to ship to all 50 states and Puerto Rico.

Primary SIC and add'l.: 5122

CIK No: 0000921878

Owners: Mark T. Majeske, James E. Flynn, Allison D. Kiene, Insiders, Peter J. Grua, Jugal K. Taneja, DEERFIELD INTERNATIONAL LIMITED, Philip P. Gerbino, James E. Searson, Laura L. Witt, Fred C. Toney, James S. Beaumariage, James A. Bologa, DEERFIELD MANAGEMENT COMPANY, L.P., KELLOG CAPITAL GROUP, LLC *(22 Owners included in Index)*

Famous Dave's of America Inc

12701 Whitewater Dr., Ste. 200, Minnetonka, MN, 55343; ***PH:*** 1-952-294-1300; ***Fax:*** 1-952-294-1301; ***http://*** www.famousdaves.com

General - Incorporation	MN	***Stock***- Price on:12/24/2007	$23.2
Employees	270	Stock Exchange	NDQ
Auditor	Grant Thornton LLP	Ticker Symbol	DAVE
Stk Agt	Wells Fargo Shareowner Services	Outstanding Shares	10,130,000
Counsel	NA	E.P.S	$0.52
DUNS No.	93-260-6262	Shareholders	NA

Business: The group's principal activity is to develop, operate and franchise casual dining restaurants. The group operates restaurants under the name famous dave's. The group's restaurant strives to emphasize value and speed of service by employing a streamlined operating system based on a focused menu and simplified food preparation techniques. The menu focuses on a number of popular smoked meat barbecue entree items and delicious side dishes which are prepared using easy-to-operate kitchen equipment and processes that use prepared seasonings, sauces and mixes. The group operates solely in the United States. As of 28-Dec-2003, the group operates 92 restaurants through 38 owned restaurants and 54 franchises.

Primary SIC and add'l.: 5812

CIK No: 0001021270

Subsidiaries: D&D of Minnesota, Inc., Famous Daves of America, Inc., Famous Daves Properties of Texas, Inc., Famous Daves Ribs of Maryland, Inc., Famous Daves Ribs of Texas, Inc., Famous Daves Ribs of Texas, LP, Famous Daves Ribs, Inc., Famous Daves Ribs-U, Inc., FDA Properties of Texas, LP, FDA Properties, Inc., Lake & Hennepin BBQ and Blues, Inc., Minwood Partners, Inc.

Officers: David Goronkin/CEO/$1,167,053.00, Diana Garvis Purcel/CFO/$384,626.00, Christopher O'Donnell/COO/$339,400.00

Owners: David Goronkin/2.75%, Diana G. Purcel, Christopher ODonnell, Lane F. Cardwell, Jeffrey K. Dahlberg/3.44%, Mary L. Jeffries, Richard L. Monfort, Dean A. Riesen/1.21%, FMR Corporation (Fidelity Management Research Corp)./10.47%, Vicuna Advisors, L.L.C./8.46%, Insiders/9.84%

Financial Data: ***Fiscal Year End:***01/01 ***Latest Annual Data:*** 12/31/2006

Year	Sales	Net Income
2006	$116,621,000	$4,924,000
2005	$99,325,000	$3,498,000

Curr. Assets:	$12,930,000	***Curr. Liab.:***	$12,807,000	***P/E Ratio:***	40.70
Plant, Equip.:	$50,037,000	***Total Liab.:***	$29,807,000	***Indic. Yr. Divd.:***	NA
Total Assets:	$65,642,000	***Net Worth:***	$35,835,000	***Debt/ Equity:***	0.3175

Far East Energy Corp

400 N Sam Houston Pkwy E, Ste. 205, Houston, TX, 77060; ***PH:*** 1-832-598-0470; ***Fax:*** 1-832-598-0479; ***http://*** www.fareastenergy.com; ***Email:*** contactus@fareastenergy.com

General - Incorporation	NV	***Stock***- Price on:12/24/2007	$1.66
Employees	31	Stock Exchange	OTC
Auditor	Payne Smith & Jones, P.C.	Ticker Symbol	FEEC
Stk Agt	Corporate Stock Transfer, Inc.	Outstanding Shares	124,590,000
Counsel	NA	E.P.S	-$0.09
DUNS No.	NA	Shareholders	NA

Business: The groups principal activities include exploring, developing, producing and selling coalbed methane gas. The group has acquired 25 kilometers of 2D seismic information in the Qinnan Block. The group has entered into three production sharing contracts (PSCs) that enable it to explore for, develop, produce and sell CBM on over 1.3 million acres located in the Yunnan and Shanxi provinces of the PRC. The group operates from the United States.

Primary SIC and add'l.: 1311

CIK No: 0001124024

Subsidiaries: Far East Energy (Bermuda), Ltd, Far East Energy (BVI), Inc., Newark Valley Oil & Gas, Inc, Yunnan Huayi Eco-tech Consulting Co., Ltd

Officers: Michael R. McElwrath/Dir., CEO, Pres., Garry Ward/Sr. VP - Engineering, Alex Yang/VP - Exploration, Randall D. Keys/CFO, Dir., Don Gunther/Technical Advisors, David Nahmias/Investor Relations Officer, Andrew Lai/Dir., Sec., Zhendong Yang/Sr. VP - Exploration

Directors: Michael R. McElwrath/Dir., CEO, Pres., Thomas E. Williams/Chmn., Randall D. Keys/CFO, Dir., John C. Mihm/Dir., C. P. Chiang/Dir., Donald A. Juckett/Dir., Andrew Lai/Dir., Sec., William A. Anderson/69/Dir.

Owners: Randall D. Keys, Zhendong Alex Yang, Citco Trustees (Cayman) Limited on behalf of the Sofaer Capital Global Hedge Fund/8.60%, C. P. Chiang, Persistency/8.00%, Citco Trustees (Cayman) Limited on behalf of the Sofaer Capital Natural Resources Hedge Fund/8.60%, Insiders/7.10%, Thomas E. Williams, Sofaer Capital Inc./8.60%, John C. Mihm, International Finance Corporation/13.90%, Michael R. McElwrath/2.70%, Donald A. Juckett, William A. Anderson, Heartland Advisors, Inc./5.50% *(17 Owners included in Index)*

Financial Data: ***Fiscal Year End:***12/31 ***Latest Annual Data:*** 06/30/2007

Year	Sales	Net Income
2007	NA	-$3,348,000
2006	NA	-$10,343,000
2005	NA	-$8,292,000

Curr. Assets:	$21,147,000	***Curr. Liab.:***	$3,943,000		
Plant, Equip.:	$24,507,000	***Total Liab.:***	$3,943,000	***Indic. Yr. Divd.:***	NA
Total Assets:	$45,654,000	***Net Worth:***	$41,711,000	***Debt/ Equity:***	NA

Fargo Electronics Inc

6533 Flying Cloud Dr., Eden Prairie, MN, 55344; ***PH:*** 1-952-941-9470; ***Fax:*** 1-952-941-7836; ***http://*** www.fargo.com; ***Email:*** sales@fargo.com

General - Incorporation	DE	***Stock***- Price on:12/24/2007	NA
Employees	NA	Stock Exchange	NA
Auditor	PricewaterhouseCoopers LLP	Ticker Symbol	NA
Stk Agt	NA	Outstanding Shares	NA
Counsel	Oppenheimer Wolff & Donnelly LLP	E.P.S	NA
DUNS No.	NA	Shareholders	NA

Business: The group's principle activities include designing, manufacturing and supplying of printers used for plastic card personalization and data encoding. The group also sells consumable supplies including ink ribbons, printheads and blank cards that are used with the group's product. The group's products are used in corporate, education, commerce, government, healthcare, transportation, entertainment and hospitality sectors. The group's products are sold in the global market through the distributors and resellers in more then 80 countries including Europe, Asia, Africa, Latin America and Australia.

Primary SIC and add'l.: 3577 3571

CIK No: 0001098834

Subsidiaries: Sony Chemical Corporation, Sony Corporation

Farmer Bros Co

20333 S Normandie Ave., Torrance, CA, 90502; ***PH:*** 1-310-787-5200; ***Fax:*** 1-310-787-5302; ***http://*** www.farmerbroscousa.com

General - Incorporation	DE	***Stock***- Price on:12/24/2007	$20.95
Employees	1,091	Stock Exchange	NDQ
Auditor	Ernst & Young LLP	Ticker Symbol	FARM
Stk Agt	Wells Fargo Bank Minnesota N.A	Outstanding Shares	16,080,000
Counsel	Walker, Wright, Tyler & Ward	E.P.S	$0.34
DUNS No.	00-828-8979	Shareholders	NA

Business: The group's principal activities are to manufacture and distribute roasted coffee and coffee related products. The products include teas, cocoa, spices, soup and beverage bases. The group also distributes coffee related products that include coffee filters, stir sticks, sugar and creamers. As on 30-Jun-2003, the product line included over 300 items. The products are sold to restaurants and other institutional establishments that prepare food, including hotels, hospitals, convenience stores and fast food outlets. The group owns approximately 38 registered U.S. Trademarks. The products are distributed from branches located in most cities throughout the western United States.

Primary SIC and add'l.: 3556 2095

CIK No: 0000034563

Subsidiaries: FBC Finance Co., a California corporation

Officers: Guenter W. Berger/Chmn., CEO, Roger M. Laverty/COO, Pres., George Zaikowski/Mgr. - Seattle, Randy Skeie/Mgr. - Spokane, Mark Cannon/Mgr. - Tacoma, Barry Mote/Mgr. - Yakima, Al Eisele/Mgr. - Boise, Travis Pierce/Mgr. - Twin Falls, Steve Smith/Mgr. - Flagstaff, Erik Stanley/Mgr. - Phoenix, Richard Meadows/Mgr. - Yuma, Lake Havasu/Mgr. - Lake Havasu, Dennis Sisk/Mgr. - Tucson, Michael J. King/VP - Restaurant, Institutional Sales Division, John E. Simmons/Treasurer, CFO *(97 Officers included in Index)*

Directors: Guenter W. Berger/Chmn., CEO, John H. Merrell/Dir., Thomas A. Maloof/Dir., Carol Farmer Waite/Dir., Lewis A. Coffman/Dir., John Samore/Dir., Independent Consultant, CPA, Martin A. Lynch/71/Dir., James M. McGarry/55/Dir., Kenneth R. Carson/Dir.

Owners: John H. Merrell, John Samore, Insiders, Thomas A. Maloof, Richard F. Farmer, Employee Stock Ownership Plan, Carol Farmer Waite, John E. Simmons, Farmer Group, Jeanne Farmer Grossman, Franklin Mutual Advisers, LLC, Michael J. King, Farmer Equities, LP, Guenter W. Berger, Trust A

Financial Data: Fiscal Year End:06/30 Latest Annual Data: 06/30/2007

Year	Sales		Net Income
2007	$216,259,000		$6,815,000
2006	$207,453,000		$4,756,000
2005	$198,420,000		-$5,427,000
Curr. Assets:	$246,808,000	**Curr. Liab.:** $16,578,000	**P/E Ratio:** 63.48
Plant, Equip.:	$46,385,000	**Total Liab.:** $48,014,000	**Indic. Yr. Divd.:** $0.440
Total Assets	$317,237,000	**Net Worth:** $269,223,000	**Debt/ Equity:** NA

Farmers & Merch Bank

2601 Wilma Rudolph Blvd, Clarksville, TN, 37040; **PH:** 1-931-905-7925; **http://** www.fmb.com

General - Incorporation		**Stock**- Price on:12/24/2007	$6786
Employees	550	Stock Exchange	OTC
Auditor	NA	Ticker Symbol	FMBL
Stk Agt	NA	Outstanding Shares	NA
Counsel	NA	E.P.S.	$378.81
DUNS No.	NA	Shareholders	NA

Business: The groups principal activity is to provide banking services. Services of the group include savings money market, time certificates of deposit, individual retirement accounts, online banking, commercial, real estate construction, agribusiness, installment, credit card and real estate loans. The groups commercial and financial products include lines of credit, capital financing, letters of credit automobile financing, residential real estate, and home improvement and home equity lines of credit. The group operates from California in the United States.

Primary SIC and add'l.: 6029

CIK No:

Financial Data: Fiscal Year End:NA Latest Annual Data: 12/31/2002

Year	Sales		Net Income
2002	$148,900,000		$49,381,000
2001	$144,382,000		$43,560,000
2000	$137,476,000		$40,607,000
Curr. Assets:	$153,460,000	**Curr. Liab.:** $1,922,494,000	**P/E Ratio:** 17.91
Plant, Equip.:	$20,430,000	**Total Liab.:** $1,926,318,000	**Indic. Yr. Divd.:** $80.000
Total Assets	$2,449,268,000	**Net Worth:** $522,950,000	**Debt/ Equity:** NA

Farmers & Merchants Bancorp

121 W Pine St., Lodi, CA, 95241; **PH:** 1-209-367-2300; **http://** www.fmbonline.com

General - Incorporation	DE	**Stock**- Price on:12/24/2007	$22.35
Employees	252	Stock Exchange	OTC
Auditor	Perry-Smith LLP	Ticker Symbol	FMCB
Stk Agt	Corporate Stock Transfer, Inc.	Outstanding Shares	5,080,000
Counsel	NA	E.P.S.	$27.46
DUNS No.	NA	Shareholders	NA

Business: The group operates through its subsidiary whose principle activity is to perform commercial banking operations and other related financial activities. New registrant. The group operates from United States.

Primary SIC and add'l.: 6712 6022

CIK No: 0001085913

Subsidiaries: F & M Bancorp, Inc., Farmers & Merchants Bank of Central California, Farmers & Merchants Investment Corporation, Farmers/Merchants Corp., FMCB Statutory Trust I

Officers: Kent A. Steinwert/Dir., Pres., CEO - F, M Bank/$2,388,897.00, Stephen W. Haley/Exec. VP, CFO - F, M Bank/$651,413.00, Deborah E. Hodkin/Exec. VP, Chief Administrative Officer - F, M Bank/$615,193.00, Richard S. Erichson/Exec. VP, Sr. Credit Officer - F, M Bank/$653,239.00, Kenneth W. Smith/Exec. VP, Dir. - Business, Retail Markets, F, M Bank, Susan Clark/Assist. VP - F, M Bank

Directors: Kent A. Steinwert/Dir., Pres., CEO - F, M Bank, Ole R. Mettler/Chmn. - F, M Bank, Calvin Suess/Dir. - F, M Bank, Stewart C. Adams/Dir. - F, M Bank, Ralph Burlington/Dir. - F, M Bank, Kevin Sanguinetti/Dir. - F, M Bank, Edward Corum/Dir. - F, M Bank, James E. Podesta/Dir. - F, M Bank, C. A. Wishek/Dir. - F, M Bank

Owners: Richard S. Erichson, Kevin Sanguinetti, Kent A. Steinwert, Stewart C. Adams, Stephen W. Haley, Joan Rider/5.30%, Bruce Mettler/5.54%, Robert F. Hunnell, Ralph Burlington, Sheila M. Wishek/5.52%, Ole R. Mettler/3.33%, Deborah E. Hodkin, Calvin Suess, James R. Podesta, Edward Corum *(18 Owners included in Index)*

Financial Data: Fiscal Year End:12/31 Latest Annual Data: 12/31/2006

Year	Sales		Net Income
2006	$102,627,000		$20,629,000
2005	$84,685,000		$18,428,000
2004	$73,567,000		$16,450,000
Curr. Assets:	$66,411,000	**Curr. Liab.:** $1,268,583,000	**P/E Ratio:** 14.15
Plant, Equip.:	$20,496,000	**Total Liab.:** $1,278,893,000	**Indic. Yr. Divd.:** $8.700
Total Assets	$1,411,233,000	**Net Worth:** $132,340,000	**Debt/ Equity:** 0.2593

Farmers & Merchants Bancorp Inc

PO Box 216, Archbold, OH, 43502; **PH:** 1-419-446-2501; **http://** www.fm-bank.com;
Email: fmsb@fm-bank.com

General - Incorporation	OH	**Stock**- Price on:12/24/2007	$22.35
Employees	252	Stock Exchange	OTC
Auditor	Plante & Moran, PLLC	Ticker Symbol	FMAO
Stk Agt	Registrar & Transfer Co	Outstanding Shares	5,080,000
Counsel	NA	E.P.S.	$1.59
DUNS No.	01-976-6385	Shareholders	NA

Business: The group's principal activity is to provide general commercial and savings banking services. The group also provides checking account services, as well as, savings and other time deposit services such as certificates of deposits. The general commercial and savings banking services activities include commercial and residential mortgage, consumer and credit card lending activities. The group also provides checking account services as well as savings and other time deposit services. The group's substantial amount of the loan portfolio is composed of loans made to agricultural industry. The group provides direct lease financing and has invested in leveraged type leases.

Primary SIC and add'l.: 6712 6021

CIK No: 0000792966

Subsidiaries: Farmers & Merchants Life Insurance Company, Farmers & Merchants State Bank

Officers: Paul S. Siebenmorgen/Dir., CEO, Pres./$313,283.00, David A. Kowalski/Auditor, Norma J. Kauffman/Assist. Corp. Sec., Barbara J. Britenriker/CFO/$200,007.00, David P. Rupp/Dir., VP, Lydia A. Huber/Corp. Sec.

Directors: Paul S. Siebenmorgen/Dir., CEO, Pres., Joe E. Crossgrove/Chmn., Robert G. Frey/Dir., Jack C. Johnson/Dir., Merle J. Short/Dir., David P. Rupp/Dir., VP, Dean E. Miller/Dir., Steven A. Everhart/Dir., James C. Saneholtz/Dir., Kevin J. Sauder/Dir., Anthony J. Rupp/Dir., Betty Young/Dir., Dexter L. Benecke/Dir., Steven J. Wyse/Dir.

Owners: Dean E. Miller/0.71%, James C. Saneholtz/0.04%, Jack C. Johnson/0.02%, Anthony J. Rupp/0.23%, Dexter L. Benecke/0.14%, Betty K. Young/0.01%, Steven A. Everhart/0.08%, Merle J. Short/0.43%, Paul S. Siebenmorgen/0.26%, Steven J. Wyse/2.02%, Robert G. Frey/0.38%, Insiders/6.27%, Edward A. Leininger/0.10%, Barbara J. Britenriker/0.03%, David P. Rupp/1.47% *(18 Owners included in Index)*

Financial Data: Fiscal Year End:12/31 Latest Annual Data: 12/31/2006

Year	Sales		Net Income
2006	$48,712,000		$8,136,000
2005	$44,541,000		$8,576,000
2004	$42,777,000		$8,230,000
Curr. Assets:	$37,247,000	**Curr. Liab.:** $626,131,000	**P/E Ratio:** 14.06
Plant, Equip.:	$14,189,000	**Total Liab.:** $649,364,000	**Indic. Yr. Divd.:** $0.600
Total Assets	$737,096,000	**Net Worth:** $87,732,000	**Debt/ Equity:** 0.2593

Farmers & Merchants Bank F

116 E Ladiga St., Piedmont, AL , 36272; **PH:** 1-256-447-9041; **Fax:** 1-256-447-9143;
http:// www.f-mbank.com

General - Incorporation		**Stock**- Price on:12/24/2007	$32.45
Employees	NA	Stock Exchange	OTC
Auditor	NA	Ticker Symbol	FMFG
Stk Agt	American Stock Transfer & Trust Co.	Outstanding Shares	NA
Counsel	NA	E.P.S.	NA
DUNS No.	NA	Shareholders	NA

Business: The groups principle activity is to provide recruiting services. The groups service area includes the research and development, engineering, marketing, sales, information technology and manufacturing industries. The group operates from United States.

Primary SIC and add'l.: 6022

CIK No:

Farmers Capital Bank Corp

PO Box 309, Frankfort, KY, 40602; **PH:** 1-502-227-1668; **Fax:** 1-502-227-1692;
http:// www.farmerscapital.com; **Email:** info@farmerscapital.com

General - Incorporation	KY	**Stock**- Price on:12/24/2007	$28.98
Employees	585	Stock Exchange	NDQ
Auditor	Crowe Chizek & Co. LLC	Ticker Symbol	FFKT
Stk Agt	American Stock Transfer & Trust Co.	Outstanding Shares	7,880,000
Counsel	NA	E.P.S.	$2.86
DUNS No.	11-596-7135	Shareholders	NA

Business: The group's principal activity is to provide a wide range of banking and bank-related services through its 23 banking locations throughout central Kentucky. The services primarily include the activities of lending and leasing, receiving deposits, providing cash management services, safe deposit box rental and trust activities. The types of deposits accepted by the group include savings, time and demand deposits. The loans provided include commercial, construction, mortgage, personal loans and lines of credit to corporations, individuals and others. The other services include issuing letters of credit; providing funds transfer services and serving as an agent in providing credit card loans. On 01-Jul-2004, the group acquired citizens bank inc.

Primary SIC and add'l.: 6712 6022

CIK No: 0000713095

Subsidiaries: Austin Park Apartments, LTD, Citizens Acquisition Subsidiary Corporation, Citizens Bank of Northern Kentucky, Inc., Citizens Financial Services, Community Development of Kentucky, Inc, EG Properties, Inc, EH Properties, Inc, EV Properties, Inc, Farmers Bank & Capital Trust Co., Farmers Bank and Trust Company, Farmers Bank Realty Co, Farmers Capital Bank Trust I, Farmers Capital Bank Trust II, Farmers Capital Insurance Corporation, Farmers Fidelity Insurance Agency, LLP 28 Subsidiaries included in the Index

Officers: Anthony G. Busseni/Dir., CEO, Pres./$320,804.00, Bruce E. Dungan/Advisory Dir., Teresa Tipton/Assist. VP - Human Resources, Charles T. Mitchell/Advisory Dir., Douglas C. Carpenter/CFO, Sr. VP, Sec./$116,467.00, Allison B. Gordon/Sr. VP, Linda L. Faulconer/VP, Dir. - Human Resources, Kaye Hall/VP - Finance, Mark A. Hampton/VP - Finance, Jean T. Harrod/VP, General Counsel, Sec., Janelda R. Mitchell/VP, Dir. - Marketing, Jason Purcell/VP - Internal Audit, James Barsotti/Assist. VP - Internal Audit, Sue Coles/Assist. VP - Compliance, Carol Raskin/Assist. VP, Dir. - Training

Directors: Anthony G. Busseni/Dir., CEO, Pres., Frank W. Sower/Chmn., Shelley S. Sweeney/Dir., Lloyd C. Hillard/Dir., Barry J. Banker/Dir., John D. Sutterlin/Dir., Robert Roach/Dir., John P. Stewart/Dir., Cecil D. Bell/Dir., Donald J. Mullineaux/Dir., Harold G. Mays/Dir., Frank R. Hamilton/Dir., Michael M. Sullivan/Dir., Terry R. Bennett/Dir., Donald A. Saelinger/Dir.

Owners: Farmers Bank & Capital Trust Co., as Fiduciary/7.20%, Donald J. Mullineaux, Bruce E. Dungan, Charles T. Mitchell, Shelley S. Sweeney/2.45%, John P. Steward, Frank W. Sower, Michael M. Sullivan/2.14%, Barry J. Banker, John D. Sutterlin, Insiders/9.42%, Terry R. Bennett, Anthony G. Busseni, Harold G. Mays, Douglas C. Carpenter *(22 Owners included in Index)*

Financial Data: Fiscal Year End:12/31 Latest Annual Data: 12/31/2006

Year	Sales	Net Income
2006	$112,994,000	$21,372,000
2005	$94,469,000	$15,772,000
2004	$79,653,000	$13,392,000

Curr. Assets:	$156,828,000	Curr. Liab.:	$1,535,010,000	P/E Ratio:	10.28
Plant, Equip.:	$37,775,000	Total Liab.:	$1,645,925,000	Indic. Yr. Divd.:	NA
Total Assets:	$1,824,366,000	Net Worth:	$178,441,000	Debt/ Equity:	0.4862

Farmers National Banc Corp

20 S Broad St., Canfield, OH, 44406; *PH:* 1-330-533-3341; *Fax:* 1-330-533-0451; *http://* www.fnbcanfield.com

General - Incorporation	OH	Stock- Price on:12/24/2007	$10.55
Employees	284	Stock Exchange	OTC
Auditor	Crowe Chizek & Co. LLC	Ticker Symbol	FMNB
Stk Agt	Farmers National Bank of Canfield	Outstanding Shares	13,070,000
Counsel	NA	E.P.S	$0.51
DUNS No.	00-892-6644	Shareholders	NA

Business: The group's principal activity is to provide commercial and retail banking services in mahoning, columbiana and trumbull counties in Ohio. The group accepts checking accounts, savings accounts and time deposit accounts. The group lends commercial loans, mortgage loans, installment loans, home equity loans and home equity lines of credit. In addition, the group also provides night depository, safe deposit boxes, money orders, bank checks, travelers checks, e bond transactions, utility bill payments, mastercard and visa credit cards, brokerage services and other miscellaneous services.

Primary SIC and add'l.: 6712 6021

CIK No: 0000709337

Subsidiaries: Farmers National Bank of Canfield

Officers: Frank L. Paden/Dir., CEO, Pres., Sec./$246,289.00, Carl D. Culp/CFO, Exec. VP, Treasurer/$134,364.00, Mark L. Graham/Sr. VP, Sr. Loan Officer - Farmers National Bank/$107,842.00, Donald F. Lukas/Sr. VP/$140,677.00

Directors: Frank L. Paden/Dir., CEO, Pres., Sec., Anne Frederick-Crawford/Dir., Ronald V. Wertz/Dir., Benjamin R. Brown/Dir., Earl R. Scott/Dir., Joseph D. Lane/Dir., Ralph D. MacAli/Dir., James R. Fisher/Dir.

Owners: Carl D. Culp, Donald F. Lukas, Benjamin R. Brown, Insiders/5.02%, Frank L. Paden, Ronald V. Wertz, Anne Frederick Crawford, Ralph D. Macali, James R. Fisher, Joseph D. Lane/2.01%, Earl R. Scott, Mark L. Graham

Financial Data: Fiscal Year End:12/31 Latest Annual Data: 12/31/2006

Year	Sales	Net Income
2006	$49,232,000	$7,215,000
2005	$46,867,000	$8,060,000
2004	$45,534,000	$7,181,000

Curr. Assets:	$34,038,000	Curr. Liab.:	$697,539,000	P/E Ratio:	19.54
Plant, Equip.:	$14,744,000	Total Liab.:	$745,361,000	Indic. Yr. Divd.:	$0.640
Total Assets:	$821,584,000	Net Worth:	$76,223,000	Debt/ Equity:	0.6138

FARO Technologies Inc

125 Technology Pk., Lake Mary, FL, 32746; *PH:* 1-407-333-9911; *Fax:* 1-407-333-4181; *http://* www.faro.com

General - Incorporation	FL	Stock- Price on:12/24/2007	$33.47
Employees	641	Stock Exchange	NDQ
Auditor	Grant Thornton LLP	Ticker Symbol	FARO
Stk Agt	Firstar Trust Co	Outstanding Shares	14,680,000
Counsel	Foley & Lardner LLP	E.P.S	$0.88
DUNS No.	61-730-8929	Shareholders	NA

Business: The group's principal activity is to develop, manufacture, market and support computer aided design products and inspection and statistical process control software. The product's of the group are the faroarm and faro gage articulated measuring devices. The product integrates the measurement and quality inspection function with cad and cam technology to improve productivity, enhance product quality and decrease rework and scrap in the manufacturing process. The operations of the group are carried in the United States, Germany, United Kingdom, France, Japan,Spain and Italy.

Primary SIC and add'l.: 3823

CIK No: 0000917491

Subsidiaries: BRE Holdings, LLC, BrownCo, LLC, BWL Aviation, LLC, Canopy Acquisition Corp., Capitol View, LLC, ClearStation, Inc., Confluent, Inc., Converging Arrows, Inc. (Delaware), Converging Arrows, Inc. (Nevada), E TRADE Nordic AB, E TRADE Sverige AB, E TRADE Systems India Private Limited, ETRADE Access, Inc., ETRADE Advisory Services, Inc., ETRADE Archipelago Holdings, LLC 23 Subsidiaries included in the Index

Officers: Jay Freeland/Dir., CEO, Pres./$484,962.00, Keith Bair/Sr. VP, CFO/$137,595.00, Jim West/Sr. VP - Integrated Engineering, John Townsley/Sr. VP - Human Resources, David Morse/Sr. VP, MD The Americas, Siggi Buss/Sr. VP, MD Europe, Bob Large/Sr. VP, MD Asia - Pacific

Directors: Jay Freeland/Dir., CEO, Pres., Simon Raab/Chmn., Co - Founder, John Caldwell/Dir., Andre Julien/Dir., Stephen Cole/Dir., Hubert D'Amours/Dir., Norman H. Schipper/Dir.

Owners: Barbara R. Smith, Jay W. Freeland, Ronald J. Juvonen/8.40%, Franklin Resources, Inc./6.90%, Stephen R. Cole, Hubert dAmours, Gregory Fraser, Royce & Associates, LLC/6.47%, Manulife Financial Corp./5.20%, John Caldwell, Andre Julien, Norman H. Schipper, Simon Raab/8.50%, Insiders/9.70%

Financial Data: Fiscal Year End:12/31 Latest Annual Data: 12/31/2006

Year	Sales	Net Income
2006	$152,405,000	$8,196,000
2005	$125,590,000	$8,179,000
2004	$97,020,000	$14,931,000

Curr. Assets:	$102,681,000	Curr. Liab.:	$28,989,000	P/E Ratio:	31.28
Plant, Equip.:	$14,123,000	Total Liab.:	$33,221,000	Indic. Yr. Divd.:	NA
Total Assets:	$144,276,000	Net Worth:	$111,055,000	Debt/ Equity:	0.0009

Fashion Tech International Inc

311 S State, Ste. 460, Saltcity, UT, 84111; *PH:* 1-801-364-9262

General - Incorporation	NV	Stock- Price on:12/24/2007	$0.65
Employees	NA	Stock Exchange	OTC
Auditor	Pritchett, Siler & Hardy, P.C.	Ticker Symbol	FTEC
Stk Agt	American Registrar & Transfer Co	Outstanding Shares	3,590,000
Counsel	NA	E.P.S	$0.00
DUNS No.	NA	Shareholders	NA

Business: The groups principle activity is to provide recruiting services. The groups service area includes the research and development, engineering, marketing, sales, information technology and manufacturing industries. The group operates from United States.

Primary SIC and add'l.: 6770

CIK No: 0000753224

Officers: Richard Crimmins/Dir., CEO, CFO, Pres., Pam Jowett/53/Dir., Pres., Sec., Treasurer

Directors: Richard Crimmins/Dir., CEO, CFO, Pres., Pam Jowett/53/Dir., Pres., Sec., Treasurer

Owners: Insiders/0.70%, Pam Jowett/0.70%, Lynn Dixon/54.99%, Thomas G. Kimble/29.50%

Financial Data: Fiscal Year End:03/31 Latest Annual Data: 03/31/2007

Year	Sales	Net Income
2007	NA	-$10,000
2006	NA	-$10,000
2005	NA	-$6,000

Curr. Assets:	NA	Curr. Liab.:	$27,000		
Plant, Equip.:	NA	Total Liab.:	$27,000	Indic. Yr. Divd.:	NA
Total Assets:	NA	Net Worth:	-$27,000	Debt/ Equity:	NA

Fastenal Co

2001 Theurer Blvd., Winona, MN, 55987; *PH:* 1-507-454-5374; *Fax:* 1-507-453-8049; *http://* www.fastenal.com; *Email:* support@fastenal.com

General - Incorporation	MN	Stock- Price on:12/24/2007	$41.5
Employees	10,415	Stock Exchange	NDQ
Auditor	KPMG LLP	Ticker Symbol	FAST
Stk Agt	Wells Fargo Bank, N.A.	Outstanding Shares	151,110,000
Counsel	Faegre & Benson LLP	E.P.S	$1.47
DUNS No.	04-265-3634	Shareholders	NA

Business: The groups principle activity is to provide industrial and construction supplies. The groups product lines include fasteners, tools and equipment, cutting tools and abrasives, hydraulics, and pneumatics. The groups services include bandsaw welding, hose crimping and engineering services. The group operates from United States.

Primary SIC and add'l.: 5085 5072

CIK No: 0000815556

Subsidiaries: FASTCO (Shanghai) Trading Co., Ltd., Fastenal Asia Pacific, Limited., Fastenal Canada Company, Fastenal Company Leasing, Fastenal Company Purchasing1, Fastenal Europe, B.V., Fastenal IP Company, Fastenal Mexico S. de R.L. de C.V., Fastenal Mexico Services S. de R.L. de C.V., Fastenal Singapore P.T.E. Ltd.

Officers: Willard D. Oberton/Dir., CEO, Pres./$791,967.00, Daniel L. Florness/CFO, Exec. VP/$777,202.00, Nicholas J. Lundquist/COO, Exec. VP/$668,706.00, Steven L. Appelwick/VP - Product Procurement, Marketing, Logistics/$382,347.00

Directors: Willard D. Oberton/Dir., CEO, Pres., Robert A. Kierlin/Chmn., John D. Remick/Dir., Stephen M. Slaggie/Dir., Robert A. Hansen/Dir., Reyne K. Wisecup/Dir., Michael M. Gostomski/Dir., Michael J. Dolan/Dir., Henry K. McConnon/Dir.

Owners: Michael J. Dolan, Stephen M. Slaggie/4.36%, Steven L. Appelwick, William Blair& Company LLC/5.81%, Insiders/16.32%, Hugh L. Miller, John D. Remick/2.67%, Michael M. Gostomski, Daniel L. Florness, Henry K. McConnon/1.69%, Ruane, Cunniff& Goldfarb Inc./7.57%, Robert A. Hansen, Robert A. Kierlin/6.71%, Reyne K. Wisecup, Willard D. Oberton *(16 Owners included in Index)*

Financial Data: Fiscal Year End:12/31 Latest Annual Data: 06/30/2007

Year	Sales	Net Income
2007	NA	NA
2006	$1,809,337,000	$199,038,000
2005	$1,523,333,000	$166,814,000

Curr. Assets:	$767,776,000	Curr. Liab.:	$103,896,000	P/E Ratio:	29.23
Plant, Equip.:	$264,030,000	Total Liab.:	$116,923,000	Indic. Yr. Divd.:	$0.460
Total Assets:	$1,039,016,000	Net Worth:	$922,093,000	Debt/ Equity:	NA

Fastfunds Financial Corp

11100 Wayzata Blvd, Ste 111, Minnetonka, MN, 55305; *PH:* 1-952-540-4455; *Fax:* 1-952-417-1996; *http://* www.equitex.net

General - Incorporation	NV	Stock- Price on:12/24/2007	$0.72
Employees	9	Stock Exchange	OTC
Auditor	GHP Horwath, P.C	Ticker Symbol	FFFC
Stk Agt	Corporate Stock Transfer, Inc.	Outstanding Shares	7,250,000
Counsel	NA	E.P.S	-$0.19
DUNS No.	NA	Shareholders	NA

Business: The group's principal activities are to provide financial services, primarily check cashing, automated teller machine (ATM) access, and credit card advances to customers. The group operates at forty-four establishments. The group operates in gaming establishments located in Arizona, Michigan, Minnesota, Nebraska, New Mexico, North Dakota and Wisconsin.

Primary SIC and add'l.: 1011

CIK No: 0000779956

Subsidiaries: Chex Services, Inc., FastFunds International, Inc.

Officers: Barry Hollander/Acting CEO, Principal Executive Officer, Principal Accounting Officer, Thomas B. Olson/41/Sec.

Directors: Henry Fong/71/Chmn., Aaron A. Grunfeld/61/Dir.

Owners: Insiders/16.60%, Hydrogen Power, Inc./49.30%, James Welbourn/2.40%, Thomas Olson, Henry Fong/12.50%, Aaron A. Grunfeld/1.90%

Financial Data: **Fiscal Year End:**12/31 **Latest Annual Data:** 12/31/2006

Year	Sales	Net Income
2006	$2,192,000	-$1,410,000
2005	$18,531,000	-$5,906,000
2004	$15,234,000	-$4,788,000

Curr. Assets:	$206,000	**Curr. Liab.:**	$5,771,000		
Plant, Equip.:	$14,000	**Total Liab.:**	$5,771,000	**Indic. Yr. Divd.:**	NA
Total Assets:	$220,000	**Net Worth:**	-$5,550,000	**Debt/ Equity:**	NA

Fauquier Bankshares Inc

10 Courthouse Sq., Warrenton, VA, 20186; ***PH:*** 1-540-347-2700; ***Fax:*** 1-540-349-9533; ***http://*** www.fauquierbank.com

General - Incorporation .... VA
Employees 121
Auditor .... Smith Elliott Kearns & Co. LLC
Stk Agt...... American Stock Transfer & Trust Co.
Counsel .... NA
DUNS No. .... NA

Stock- Price on:12/24/2007 .... $24
Stock Exchange .... NDQ
Ticker Symbol .... FBSS
Outstanding Shares 3,550,000
E.P.S $1.50
Shareholders .... NA

Business: The group's principal activities are to provide consumer and commercial banking services to individuals, businesses and industries. The group operates through seven branch offices located in warrenton, catlett, the plains, sudley road-manassas old town-manassas and new baltimore. The services offered include interest and non-interest bearing deposits, safe deposit services, credit cards, cash management, notary services, money orders, night depository, traveler's checks, domestic collections, automated teller services and banking by mail. Lending activities include secured and unsecured commercial and real estate loans, stand-by letters of credit and grants available credit for installment, secured and unsecured personal loans, residential mortgages, home equity loans, automobile and other consumer financing.

Primary SIC and add'l.: 6712 6022

CIK No: 0001083643

Subsidiaries: Fauquier Bank Services, Inc, Fauquier Statutory Trust I

Officers: Randy Kent Ferrell/Dir., CEO, Pres./$498,446.00, Eric Peter Graap/CFO, Exec. VP/$243,542.00, Jessica Wilson/Assist. VP - Personal Banker - Bealeton, Traci Lambert/Office Mgr. - Bealeton, Darcy Menefee/Office Mgr. - Catlett, Krista Tucker/Personal Banker, Warrenton, Vickie Dingus/Hub Mgr. - Main Office, Andrea Robertson/Office Mgr. - Telephone Center, Denise Roach/Hub Mgr. - New Baltimore, Carol Morgan/Hub Mgr. - Old Town Manassas, Ellen Winston/Personal Banker, Sudley Road, Melissa Gill/Office Mgr. - Plains, Alice Brown/Office Mgr. - View Tree, Gregory Frederick/COO, Exec. VP, Mark Debes/Sr. VP - Retail - Marketing *(29 Officers included in Index)*

Directors: Randy Kent Ferrell/Dir., CEO, Pres., John B. Adams/Vice Chmn., Claude H. Lawrence/Chmn., Pat H. Nevill/Dir., Helen Frances Stringfellow/Dir., Harold Paul Neale/Dir., Kurt P. Rodgers/Dir., Sterling T. Strange/Dir., Alexander G. Green/Dir., Hunton C. Tiffany/Dir., John J. Norman/Dir., Stanley C. Haworth/Dir., Douglas Clower Larson/Dir., Brian S. Montgomery/Dir., Randolph T. Minter/Dir.

Owners: Stanley C. Haworth/2.77%, Sterling T. Strange, Randy K. Ferrell/1.26%, Douglas C. Larson, Brian S. Montgomery, C. H. Lawrence/1.43%, Alexander G. Green/4.44%, Kurt P. Rodgers, John J. Norman, Eric P. Graap, Royce & Associates, LLC/8.18%, Randolph T. Minter, Insiders/15.97%, Pat H. Nevill, John B. Adams *(17 Owners included in Index)*

Financial Data: **Fiscal Year End:**12/31 **Latest Annual Data:** 12/31/2006

Year	Sales	Net Income
2006	$36,060,000	$5,604,000
2005	$30,684,000	$5,702,000
2004	$27,064,000	$4,978,000

Curr. Assets:	$43,482,000	**Curr. Liab.:**	$471,071,000	**P/E Ratio:**	15.89
Plant, Equip.:	$7,584,000	**Total Liab.:**	$474,802,000	**Indic. Yr. Divd.:**	$0.800
Total Assets:	$521,762,000	**Net Worth:**	$38,712,000	**Debt/ Equity:**	0.1036

Favrille Inc

10445 Pacific Ctr. Ct., San Diego, CA, 92121; ***PH:*** 1-858-526-8000; ***Fax:*** 1-858-597-7040; ***http://*** www.favrille.com; ***Email:*** hr@favrille.com

General - Incorporation .... DE
Employees 151
Auditor .... Ernst & Young LLP
Stk Agt........ Mellon Investor Services LLC
Counsel .... NA
DUNS No. .... NA

Stock- Price on:12/24/2007 .... $3.72
Stock Exchange .... NDQ
Ticker Symbol .... FVRL
Outstanding Shares 32,500,000
E.P.S .... -$1.37
Shareholders .... NA

Business: The groups principal activities include developing and commercializing immune system. The group products sold under the trade name FavId(R) and Rituxan(R). The group operates from the United States.

Primary SIC and add'l.: 2836 2834

CIK No: 0001285701

Officers: John P. Longenecker/Dir. CEO, Pres., David L. Guy/Chief Commercial Officer, Daniel P. Gold/Founder, Chief Scientific Officer, Tamara A. Seymour/CFO, VP - Finance, Administration, Richard Murawski/Sr. VP - Operations, John F. Bender/Sr. VP - Clinical Research, Alice M. Wei/VP - Regulatory Affairs, Quality, Pete De Spain/Dir. - Investor Relations, Corporate Communications, Richard Ghalie/Chief Medical Officer

Directors: John P. Longenecker/Dir. CEO, Pres., Michael L. Eagle/Chmn., Cam L. Garner/Dir., Antonio J. Grillo-Lopez/Dir., Peter B. Hutt/Dir., Fred Middleton/Dir., Arda M. Minocherhomjee/54/Dir., David Molowa/Dir., Wayne I. Roe/Dir., Ivor Royston/Dir.

Owners: John Bender, Sanderling Venture Partners V L.P., Fred Middleton, William Blair Capital Partners VII QP, L.P., Peter Barton Hutt, Michael Eagle, Tamara A. Seymour, Antonio Grillo-Lopez, Wayne Roe, Arda Minocherhomjee, David Molowa, Daniel P. Gold, Alloy Corporate 2000, L.P., David L. Guy, John P. Longenecker *(20 Owners included in Index)*

Financial Data: **Fiscal Year End:**12/31 **Latest Annual Data:** 12/31/2006

Year	Sales	Net Income
2006	NA	-$40,511,000
2005	NA	-$35,875,000
2004	NA	-$26,036,000

Curr. Assets:	$43,259,000	**Curr. Liab.:**	$11,755,000		
Plant, Equip.:	$25,071,000	**Total Liab.:**	$27,654,000	**Indic. Yr. Divd.:**	NA
Total Assets:	$72,289,000	**Net Worth:**	$44,635,000	**Debt/ Equity:**	0.1784

FBL Financial Group Inc

5400 University Ave., West Des Moines, IA, 50266; ***PH:*** 1-515-225-5400; ***Fax:*** 1-515-226-6053; ***http://*** www.fblfinancial.com

General - Incorporation .... IA
Employees 1,858
Auditor .... Ernst & Young LLP
Stk Agt .... Mellon Investor Services LLC
Counsel .... NA
DUNS No. 84-743-6052

Stock- Price on:12/24/2007 .... $39.72
Stock Exchange .... NYSE
Ticker Symbol .... FFG
Outstanding Shares 29,910,000
E.P.S $3.25
Shareholders .... NA

Business: The group's principal activities are to market universal life, variable universal life, traditional life insurance and variable and traditional annuity products. The group's other activities include non-insurance services such as investment advisory, leasing, marketing and distribution services. The traditional and universal life insurance products consist of whole life, term life and universal life policies. The variable universal life insurance and variable annuity products allow the customer to direct the cash value of the policy to a wide range of investment sub-accounts. The offices are located mainly in Arizona, Iowa, Minnesota, New Mexico, South Dakota, Utah, Colorado, Idaho, Kansas, Montana, Nebraska, North Dakota, Oklahoma, Wisconsin and Wyoming.

Primary SIC and add'l.: 6321 6311 9999

CIK No: 0001012771

Subsidiaries: EquiTrust Assigned Benefit Company, EquiTrust Financial Group, EquiTrust Investment Management Services, Inc., EquiTrust Life Insurance Company, EquiTrust Marketing Services, LLC, Farm Bureau Life Insurance Company, FBL Financial Group Capital Trust, FBL Financial Services, Inc., FBL Leasing Services, Inc.

Officers: James W. Noyce/Dir., CEO/$1,492,371.00, Lou Ann Sandburg/VP - Investments, Assist. Treasurer, Bruce A. Trost/Exec. VP - Property Casualty Companies/$1,042,544.00, Douglas W. Gumm/VP - Information Technology, David Thompson Sebastian/VP - Sales, Marketing, John M. Paule/Exec. VP - Equitrust Life Insurance Company, Stephen M. Morain/62/Sr. VP, Sec., General Counsel/$1,197,464.00, James P. Brannen/CFO, Chief Administrative Officer, Treasurer, Joann W. Rumelhart/Exec. VP - Farm Bureau Life, Donald J. Seibel/VP - Finance, Richard J. Kypta/Sr. VP, General Counsel, Sec.

Directors: James W. Noyce/Dir., CEO, Craig A. Lang/Chmn., Steven G. Kouplen/Dir., Jerry L. Chicoine/Dir., Robert H. Hanson/Dir., Kim M. Robak/Dir., John E. Walker/Dir., Craig D. Hill/Dir., Keith R. Olsen/Dir., Steve L. Baccus/Dir., Tim H. Gill/Dir., Paul E. Larson/Dir., Edward W. Mehrer/Dir., Frank S. Priestley/Dir.

Owners: Steven G. Kouplen, Jerry L. Chicoine, JoAnn W. Rumelhart, Bruce A. Trost, Edward W. Mehrer, James W. Noyce, Kim M. Robak, Tim H. Gill, Keith R. Olsen, Insiders, James P. Brannen, Craig A. Lang, Steve L. Baccus, Craig D. Hill, Paul E. Larson *(19 Owners included in Index)*

Financial Data: **Fiscal Year End:**12/31 **Latest Annual Data:** 12/31/2006

Year	Sales	Net Income
2006	$887,353,000	$90,129,000
2005	$728,148,000	$72,842,000
2004	$682,602,000	$66,076,000

Curr. Assets:	$321,043,000	**Curr. Liab.:**	$187,790,000		
Plant, Equip.:	$46,030,000	**Total Liab.:**	$11,273,154,000	**Indic. Yr. Divd.:**	$0.480
Total Assets:	$12,154,012,000	**Net Worth:**	$880,720,000	**Debt/ Equity:**	0.3480

FC Banc Corp

PO Box 567, Bucyrus, OH, 44820; ***PH:*** 1-419-562-7040; ***Fax:*** 1-419-562-8322; ***http://*** www.farmerscitizensbank.com; ***Email:*** generalinfo@farmerscitizensbank.com

General - Incorporation .... OH
Employees .... NA
Auditor .... S. R. Snodgrass, A.C.
Stk Agt .... NA
Counsel........ Kennedy Purdy Hoeffel & Gernert
DUNS No. 00-892-6628

Stock- Price on:12/24/2007 .... $28
Stock Exchange .... OTC
Ticker Symbol .... FCBZ
Outstanding Shares .... NA
E.P.S .... NA
Shareholders .... NA

Business: The group's principal activity is to provide commercial and retail banking services in the United States through its wholly owned subsidiary the farmers citizens bank. The deposits accepted include time, savings, money market and demand deposits accounts. The group offers commercial, industrial, agricultural, real estate and consumer instalment loans. The group also provides safe deposit box rental, automated teller machines and other services tailored to individual customers. The group operates through three of its branches. The customers of the group are primarily located in crawford, morrow and knox counties and the surrounding areas.

Primary SIC and add'l.: 6712 6022

CIK No: 0000893539

Subsidiaries: The Farmers Citizens Bank

Officers: Coleman J. Clougherty/Dir., Pres.

Directors: Robert D. Hord/Chmn., Patrick J. Drouhard/Dir., Lawrence A. Morrison/Dir., Randy Asmo/Dir., Samuel J. Harvey/Dir., Coleman J. Clougherty/Dir., Pres., Charles W. Kimerline/Dir., David G. Dostal/Dir.

Financial Data: **Fiscal Year End:**12/31 **Latest Annual Data:** 12/31/2004

Year	Sales	Net Income
2004	$8,267,000	$683,000
2003	$8,789,000	$1,205,000
2002	$7,890,000	$1,052,000

Curr. Assets:	$6,154,000	**Curr. Liab.:**	$114,136,000		
Plant, Equip.:	$6,698,000	**Total Liab.:**	$135,023,000	**Indic. Yr. Divd.:**	NA
Total Assets:	$148,291,000	**Net Worth:**	$13,268,000	**Debt/ Equity:**	2.6231

FCB Bancorp CA

1100 Paseo Camarillo, Camarillo, CA, 93010; ***PH:*** 1-805-484-0534; ***http://*** www.fcbank.com

General - Incorporation	CA	Stock- Price on:12/24/2007	NA
Employees	NA	Stock Exchange	NA
Auditor	Moss Adams LLP	Ticker Symbol	NA
Stk Agt	U.S. Stock Transfer Corp	Outstanding Shares	NA
Counsel	NA	E.P.S.	NA
DUNS No.	NA	Shareholders	NA

Business: The groups principal activity is to provide banking services. Services of the group include credit, deposit and cash management. In December 2005, the group acquired South Coast Commercial Bank. The group operates from Anaheim Hills, Camarillo, Irvine, Oxnard, Simi Valley, Thousand Oaks, Ventura and Westlake Village in the United States. The groups total assets in the year 2006, was $510,016,000.

Primary SIC and add'l.: 6035

CIK No: 0001331825

Subsidiaries: FCB Statutory Trust I, First California Bank, SC Financial

Officers: C. G. Kum/Pres., CEO - First California Bank, Thomas E. Anthony/Mgr. - Commercial Banking, Northern Region, First California Bank, Romolo Santarosa/CFO - First California Bank, Robert W. Bartlett/Chief Credit Officer - First California Bank, Cheryl L. Knight/Chief Risk Officer - First California Bank

Directors: John W. Birchfield/56/Chmn., Richard D. Aldridge/60/Vice Chmn., Tenisha M. Fitzgerald/33/Dir., Syble R. Roberts/71/Dir., Thomas Tignino/60/Dir.

FCCC Inc

200 Connecticut Ave., Norwalk, CT, 06854; *PH:* 1-203-855-7700; *http://* www.fccc.edu

General - Incorporation	CT	Stock- Price on:12/24/2007	$1.1
Employees	NA	Stock Exchange	OTC
Auditor	Mahoney Sabol & Co LLP	Ticker Symbol	FCIC
Stk Agt	Registrar & Transfer Co	Outstanding Shares	1,420,000
Counsel	NA	E.P.S.	-$0.01
DUNS No.	00-691-6654	Shareholders	NA

Business: The group's principal activities are to provide mortgage banking services and servicing of its own loan portfolio. The mortgage banking services include the origination, purchase, sale and servicing of mortgage loans secured by residential or commercial real estate. The mortgage services of own portfolio loan program involve the processing and administration of mortgage loan payments and remitting of principal and interest to purchasers. The group also monitors delinquencies, collects late fees, manages foreclosures, processes prepayments and loan assumption fees, provides purchasers with required reports and answers borrowers' inquiries.

Primary SIC and add'l.: 6159 6162

CIK No: 0000730669

Officers: Bernard Zimmerman/75/Dir., CEO, Pres., Principal Financial Officer, Jay J. Miller/75/Dir., Sec.

Directors: Bernard Zimmerman/75/Dir., CEO, Pres., Principal Financial Officer, Jay J. Miller/75/Dir., Sec., Lawrence R. Yurdin/67/Dir., Martin Cohen/73/Dir., Michael L. Goldman/47/Dir.

Owners: Bernard Zimmerman/18.42%, Jay J. Miller/0.64%, Lawrence R. Yurdin/3.85%, Robert E. Humphreys/8.07%, Insiders/44.07%, Walter P. Carucci/9.80%, Martin Cohen/18.42%, Michael L. Goldman/2.74%, John C. Boland/3.90%

Financial Data: Fiscal Year End:03/31   Latest Annual Data: 3/31/2007

Year	Sales	Net Income
2007	$77,000	-$25,000
2006	$57,000	-$45,000
2005	$273,000	$119,000

Curr. Assets:	$1,611,000	Curr. Liab.:	$11,000		
Plant, Equip.:	NA	Total Liab.:	$11,000	Indic. Yr. Divd.:	NA
Total Assets:	$1,612,000	Net Worth:	$1,601,000	Debt/ Equity:	NA

Featherlite Inc

Hwy. 63 9, Cresco, IA, 52136; *PH:* 1-319-547-6000; *http://* www.featherliteinc.com

General - Incorporation	MN	Stock- Price on:12/24/2007	NA
Employees	NA	Stock Exchange	NA
Auditor	Grant Thornton LLP	Ticker Symbol	NA
Stk Agt	Firstar Trust Co	Outstanding Shares	NA
Counsel	Fredrikson & Byron	E.P.S.	NA
DUNS No.	19-439-4789	Shareholders	NA

Business: The group's principal activity is to manufacture and sell various types of specialty trailers and luxury motorcoaches. The group markets its trailers under the featherlite(R) brand name. Trailers are primarily sold through a network of over 240 full-line dealers throughout the United States and Canada. The types of trailers include horse, livestock, utility and cargo, snowmobile and car trailers as well as racecar transporters. The group markets its motorcoaches under the featherlite vantare (R), featherlite vogue(R), featherlite luxury coaches(R) and foretravel(R) brand names. The motorcoaches are made from a bus shell for conversions that is purchased and completed to provide an interior area designed according to the customers specifications, which are the most luxurious of all recreational vehicles.

Primary SIC and add'l.: 3713 3715

CIK No: 0000928064

Subsidiaries: Featherlite Aviation Company, Featherlite Chemicials Holdings, LLC

Fedders Corp

Westgate Corporate Ctr., 505 Martinsville Rd., Liberty Corner, NJ, 07938; *PH:* 1-908-604-8686; *Fax:* 1-908-604-0715; *http://* www.fedders.com; *Email:* investorrelations@fedders.com

General - Incorporation	DE	Stock- Price on:12/24/2007	$0.22
Employees	1,664	Stock Exchange	OTC
Auditor	UHY LLP	Ticker Symbol	FJCC
Stk Agt	American Stock Transfer & Trust Co.	Outstanding Shares	34,510,000
Counsel	NA	E.P.S.	-$4.31
DUNS No.	13-048-8604	Shareholders	NA

Business: The group's principal activities are to manufacture and market air treatment products, which include air conditioners, air cleaners, gas furnaces, humidifiers and dehumidifiers. The operations are carried out under two segments: heating, ventilation, air conditioning and refrigeration (hvacr) and engineered products. The hvacr segment designs, manufactures and distributes portable and vertical packaged unit air conditioners and dehumidifiers. These products are distributed through national retailers, regional retailers, wholesale distributors, catalog supply houses and private label/original equipment manufacturers. The engineered products segment designs, manufactures and distributes media filters, electronic filters and solid-state thermoelectric heat pump modules. The group operates in the United States, China, India, Germany, the United Kingdom and Philippines.

Primary SIC and add'l.: 3585

CIK No: 0000744106

Subsidiaries: Changzhou Fedders Xingrong Air Conditioner Components Co., Co., Ltd., Emerson Quiet Kool Corporation, Envirco Corporation, Fedders (Suzhou) Indoor Air Quality Co. Ltd, Fedders Addison Company, Inc, Fedders Air Treatment Research and Development, Fedders Eubank Company, Inc, Fedders International Air Conditioning Pvt., Ltd., Fedders International, Inc., Fedders Investment Corporation, Fedders Islandaire, Inc, Fedders Koppel, Inc., Fedders North America, Inc., Fedders Shanghai Co., Ltd 23 Subsidiaries included in the Index

Officers: Warren Emley/53/VP, Pres. - Fedders Asia Pacific, Mark Mishler/49/Corporate Controller

Owners: Herbert A. Morey, Howard S. Modlin/2.20%, Robert L. Laurent/1.40%, Peter Gasiewicz, Michael L. Ducker, Insiders/30.90%, Michael Giordano/1.80%, David C. Chang, Jitendra V. Singh, Anthony E. Puleo, Sal Giordano/22.80%, Joseph Giordano/10.50%, William J. Brennan, S.A. Muscarnera

Financial Data: Fiscal Year End:12/31   Latest Annual Data: 12/31/2006

Year	Sales	Net Income
2006	$279,255,000	-$124,624,000
2005	$297,716,000	-$62,081,000
2004	$413,016,000	-$26,107,000

Curr. Assets:	$86,216,000	Curr. Liab.:	$102,145,000		
Plant, Equip.:	$39,342,000	Total Liab.:	$297,875,000	Indic. Yr. Divd.:	NA
Total Assets:	$181,360,000	Net Worth:	-$121,366,000	Debt/ Equity:	NA

Federal Agricultural Mortgage Corp

1133 21st St., NW, Ste. 600, Washington, DC, 20036; *PH:* 1-202-872-7700; *Fax:* 1-202-872-7713; *http://* www.farmermac.com

General - Incorporation	US	Stock- Price on:12/24/2007	$34.14
Employees	45	Stock Exchange	NYSE
Auditor	Deloitte & Touche LLP	Ticker Symbol	AGM
Stk Agt	American Stock Transfer & Trust Co.	Outstanding Shares	10,320,000
Counsel	Shearman & Sterling LLP	E.P.S.	NA
DUNS No.	61-296-1276	Shareholders	NA

Business: The group's principal activity is to provide a secondary market for agricultural real estate and rural housing mortgage loans and to increase the availability of long-term credit at stable interest rates to farmers, ranchers and rural homeowners. The group's secondary market for agricultural mortgage loans provides liquidity and lending capacity to agricultural mortgage lenders. The services provided by the group also includes purchasing qualified loans directly from lenders; exchanging qualified loans for securities; issuing long-term standby purchase commitments for newly originated and seasoned eligible mortgage loans and purchasing and guaranteeing mortgage-backed bonds secured by eligible mortgage loans known as agvantage bonds.

Primary SIC and add'l.: 6159

CIK No: 0000845877

Subsidiaries: Farmer Mac Securities Corporation

Officers: Henry D. Edelman/CEO, Pres./$1,794,138.00, Jerome G. Oslick/VP, General Counsel, Corp. Sec./$365,119.00, Paul N. Peiffer/VP - Agricultural Credit, Tom D. Stenson/Exec. VP - Agricultural Finance, COO/$757,085.00, Timothy L. Buzby/VP, Controller/$539,376.00, Nancy E. Corsiglia/CFO, Exec. VP - Finance/$963,859.00, Mary K. Waters/VP - Corporate Relations

Directors: Fred L. Dailey/Chmn., Glen O. Klippenstein/Dir., Paul A. Debriyn/Dir., Dennis L. Brack/Dir., Charles E. Kruse/Dir., John Dan Raines/Dir., Dennis A. Everson/Dir., Timothy F. Kenny/Dir., Ernest M. Hodges/Dir., Lowell L. Junkins/Dir., Grace Trujillo Daniel/Dir., Ralph W. Cortese/Dir., Julia Bartling/Dir., Mitchell A. Johnson/Dir., Michael A. Gerber/Dir.

Owners: Tom D. Stenson/2.14%, Lowell L. Junkins, John G. Nelson, Charles E. Kruse, Jerome G. Oslick, Ralph W. Cortese, Grace T. Daniel, Paul N. Peiffer, Mary K. Waters, Dennis L. Brack, Timothy L. Buzby/1.02%, Fred L. Dailey, Insiders/18.74%, Dennis A. Everson, Paul A. DeBriyn *(22 Owners included in Index)*

Federal Express Corp

3610 Hacks Cross Rd., Bldg. A, First Fl., Memphis, TN, 38125; *PH:* 1-901-369-3600; *Fax:* 1-901-395-2000; *http://* fedex.com; *Email:* ir@fedex.com

General - Incorporation	DE	Stock- Price on:12/24/2007	NA
Employees	NA	Stock Exchange	NA
Auditor	Ernst & Young LLP	Ticker Symbol	NA
Stk Agt	Computershare Investor Services LLC	Outstanding Shares	NA
Counsel	NA	E.P.S.	NA
DUNS No.	05-807-0459	Shareholders	NA

Business: The group's principle activity is to provide transportation, e-commerce and supply chain management services through over 214,000 employees and contractors. The services offered by the group include worldwide express delivery, ground small-parcel delivery, less-than-truckload freight delivery, supply chain management, customs brokerage, trade facilitation and electronic commerce solutions. The group offers various international packages and document delivery services to 212 countries, as well as international freight services and also offers commercial and military charter services.

Primary SIC and add'l.: 4213 4513 4215

CIK No: 0000230211

Subsidiaries: FedEx Corporate Services, Inc, FedEx Express, FedEx Ground Package System, Inc

Officers: David J. Bronczek/CEO, Pres., Juan N. Cento/Pres. - Latin America, Caribbean Region, LAC, David Binks/Pres. - Canada Region, William J. Logue/Exec. VP - Operations, Systems Support, Worldwide Customer Operations, Robert W. Elliott/Pres. - Europe, Middle East, Africa Region, David L. Cunningham/Pres. - Asia Pacific Region, Apac, Michael L. Ducker/Pres. - International

Federal Home Loan Bank of Boston

111 Huntington Ave., 24th Fl., Boston, MA, 02199; *PH:* 1-617-292-9600; *Fax:* 1-617-292-9645; *http://* www.fhlbboston.com; *Email:* info@fhlbboston.com

General		Stock	
Incorporation	Federally Chartered Corporation	Price on:12/24/2007	NA
Employees	NA	Stock Exchange	NA
Auditor	PricewaterhouseCoopers LLP	Ticker Symbol	NA
Stk Agt	NA	Outstanding Shares	NA
Counsel	NA	E.P.S	NA
DUNS No.	NA	Shareholders	NA

Business: The group's principle activity is to serve the residential-mortgage and community-development lending activities of member financial institutions located in the New England region. Altogether, there are 12 district Federal Home Loan Banks (FHLBanks) located across the United States (U.S.), each supporting the lending activities of member financial institutions within their specific regions. Each FHLBank is a separate entity with its own board of directors, management, and employees. It is a federally chartered corporation organized by Congress in 1932 and is a GSE.

Primary SIC and add'l.: 6111

CIK No: 0001331463

Officers: Michael A. Jessee/CEO, Pres., Susan M. Elliott/Exec. VP, Member Services, William P. Hamilton/Sr. VP - Public Affairs, Ellen McLaughlin/Sr. VP, General Counsel, Frank Nitkiewicz/CFO, Exec. VP, William L. Oakley/CIO, Sr. VP, Janelle K. Authur/Sr. VP, Executive Dir. - Human Resources, Earl W. Baucom/Chief Accounting Officer, Sr. VP, George H. Collins/Sr. VP, Chief Risk Officer, Martin Corona/Contact - Community Investment Mgr., Christine Gimbel/Contact - Community Investment Mgr., Tobi Goldberg/Contact - Community Investment Mgr., Kathy Naczas/Contact - Community Investment Mgr., Paul Peduto/Mgr. - Relationship, Loughlin Cleary/Mgr. - Relationship *(20 Officers included in Index)*

Directors: Robert F. Verdonck/Chmn., Joyce H. Errecart/Vice Chmn., Jan A. Miller/Dir., William P. Morrissey/Dir., Stephen F. Christy/Dir., Steven A. Closson/Dir., Mark E. MacOmber/Dir., Kevin M. McCarthy/Dir., James L. Taft/Dir., David R. Rosato/Dir., Andrew J. Calamare/Dir., Patrick E. Clancy/Dir., John Goldsmith/Dir., Cornelius K. Hurley/Dir., Jay F. Malcynsky/Dir. *(19 Directors included in Index)*

Owners: Bank of Newport, Newport Federal Savings Bank, Citizens Bank of Connecticut/1.10%, Androscoggin Savings Bank, The Savings Bank Life Insurance Company of Massachusetts, Citizens Bank of Rhode Island/3.60%, Insiders/2.94%, Citizens Bank of New Hampshire/2.50%, Litchfield Bancorp, Bank of America Rhode Island, N.A./14.80%, South Shore Savings Bank, Mascoma Savings Bank, FSB, Passumpsic Savings Bank, Citizens Bank of Massachusetts/7.80%, East Boston Savings Bank *(18 Owners included in Index)*

Federal Home Loan Bank of Cincinnati

221 E 4th St., 1000 Atrium Two, Cincinnati, OH, 45202; ***PH:*** 1-513-852-7500; ***https://*** www.fhlbcin.com

General		Stock	
Incorporation	Federal	Price on:12/24/2007	NA
Employees	NA	Stock Exchange	NA
Auditor	PricewaterhouseCoopers LLP	Ticker Symbol	NA
Stk Agt	NA	Outstanding Shares	NA
Counsel	NA	E.P.S	NA
DUNS No.	NA	Shareholders	NA

Business: The group's activity is to provide banking services. The primary services provided by the group include providing loans, purchasing mortgages from, and providing other financial services to its member financial institutions, facilitate and expand the availability of finance for housing and community lending, and making fully collateralized loans (Advances) to their members. The secondary services provided by the group includes purchasing qualifying residential mortgages through the Mortgage Purchase Program.

Primary SIC and add'l.: 6111

CIK No: 0001326771

Officers: David H. Hehman/CEO, Pres., Stephen J. Sponaugle/Sr. VP, Chief Risk Officer, Andrew S. Howell/Sr. VP, Carole L. Cosse/Sr. VP, CFO, Carol Mount Peterson/Sr. VP - Housing, Community Investment, Thomas F. Schlager/Sr. VP - Bank Operations, Kyle R. Lawler/Sr. VP - Credit Services, Paul J. Imwalle/Sr. VP, Member Services, Jamie M. Helmes/Marketing Coordinator, Joe Castlen/Assist. Dir., Scott D. Alsip/Sr. Production Specialist, Peg M. Bruggeman/Operations Supervisor, Pat A. Cope/Operations Assist., Heike M. Scott/Operations Assist., Connie M. Kolita/Projects Mgr. *(73 Officers included in Index)*

Directors: Richard C. Baylor/Vice Chmn., Carl F. Wick/Chmn., Stan R. Puckett/Dir., Stephen B. Smith/Dir., James R. Powell/Dir., William Y. Carroll/Dir., Proctor B. Caudill/Dir., Stephen D. Hailer/Dir., Michael R. Melvin/Dir., Grady P. Appleton/Dir., Donald R. Ball/Dir., Leslie Dolin Dunn/Dir., Charles J. Ruma/Dir., William J. Small/Dir., Billie W. Wade/Dir. *(16 Directors included in Index)*

Owners: Charter One Bank, N.A./15.40%, U.S. Bank, N.A./13.90%, Ohio Savings Bank/5.70%, Fifth Third Bank/9.90%

Federal Home Loan Bank of Indianapolis

8250 Woodfield Crossing Blvd, Indianapolis, IN, 46240; ***PH:*** 1-317-465-0200; ***http://*** www.fhlbi.com

General		Stock	
Incorporation	Federally Chartered Corporation	Price on:12/24/2007	NA
Employees	NA	Stock Exchange	NA
Auditor	PricewaterhouseCoopers LLP	Ticker Symbol	NA
Stk Agt	NA	Outstanding Shares	NA
Counsel	NA	E.P.S	NA
DUNS No.	NA	Shareholders	NA

Business: The groups principle activity is to provide a readily available, low-cost source of funds to our members. The group operates from United States.

Primary SIC and add'l.: 6111

CIK No: 0001331754

Officers: Brian K. Fike/49/Interim CEO, Pres., Jane Clingman-Scott/Chmn. - Advisory Counsel, Mark Lindenlaub/Vice Chmn. - Advisory Counsel, Meg Haller/Member - Advisory Counsel, Harold Mast/Member - Advisory Counsel, Ted Rozeboom/Member - Advisory Counsel, Linda Smith/Member - Advisory Counsel, William Taft/Member - Advisory Counsel, William McDowell/Dir. - Sales, Brian McCoy/Contact - Advances Information, Jonathan R. West/51/Sr. VP, General Counsel, Corp. Sec., Ethics Officer, Michael R. Barker/46/Sr. VP, General Counsel, Corp. Sec., Ethics Officer, Douglas J. Iverson/58/Acting COO, Sr. VP, Paul J. Weaver/47/Sr. VP, Acting Chief Accounting Officer, Jacquelyn Dodyk/Member - Advisory Counsel *(18 Officers included in Index)*

Directors: Paul C. Clabuesch/Chmn., Charles L. Crow/Vice Chmn., Ronald G. Seals/69/Dir., Thomas R. Sullivan/Dir., Timothy P. Gaylord/Dir., Vincent J. Otto/48/Dir., Michael H. Price/Dir., Valde Garcia/Dir., Teresa S. Lubbers/Dir., Ray D. Tooker/Dir., Gregory F. Ehlinger/Dir., Jeffrey A. Poxon/Dir., Jonathan P. Bradford/Dir., Robert F. Fix/Dir., Michael J. Hannigan/Dir. *(18 Directors included in Index)*

Owners: Gregory F. Ehlinger/2.20%, Ronald G. Seals/0.10%, Fifth Third Bank/7.42%, Thomas R. Sullivan/0.07%, Flagstar Bank, FSB/16.24%, Thomas R. Sullivan/0.04%, Thomas R. Sullivan/0.07%, Gregory F. Ehlinger/0.08%, Thomas R. Sullivan/0.03%, LaSalle Bank Midwest National Association/16.49%, Timothy P. Gaylord/0.12%, Thomas R. Sullivan/0.08%, Charles L. Crow/0.02%, Thomas R. Sullivan/0.01%, Michael H. Price/0.37% *(22 Owners included in Index)*

Federal Home Loan Bank of Pittsburgh

601 Grant St., Pittsburgh, PA, 15219; ***PH:*** 1-412-288-3400; ***Fax:*** 1-412-288-2861; ***http://*** www.fhlb-pgh.com

General		Stock	
Incorporation	Federally Chartered Corporation	Price on:12/24/2007	NA
Employees	NA	Stock Exchange	NA
Auditor	PricewaterhouseCoopers LLP	Ticker Symbol	NA
Stk Agt	NA	Outstanding Shares	NA
Counsel	NA	E.P.S	NA
DUNS No.	NA	Shareholders	NA

Business: The groups principle activity is to provide low-cost funding and opportunities for affordable housing and community development to approximately 340 member financial institutions. The group operates from United States.

Primary SIC and add'l.: 6111

CIK No: 0001330399

Owners: ING Bank, FSB, Wilmington, DE/9.20%, Penn Liberty Bank, Wayne, PA, Citizens Bank, Wilmington, DE/0.10%, Willow Financial, Ambler, PA/0.40%, Sovereign Bank, Reading, PA/26.40%, First Commonwealth Bank, Indiana, PA/0.90%, Harleysville Savings Bank, Harleysville, PA/0.50%, Wilmington Savings Fund Society, FSB, Wilmington, DE/1.10%, Summit Community Bank, Charleston, WV/0.30%, GMAC Bank, Midvale, UT/12.10%, Columbia County Farmers National Bank, Bloomsburg, PA, Wilmington Trust Company, Wilmington, DE/0.20%, Citicorp Trust Bank, FSB, Newark, DE/10.90%

Federal Home Loan Bank of San Francisco

600 California St., San Francisco, CA, 94108; ***PH:*** 1-415-616-1000; ***Fax:*** 1-415-616-2626; ***http://*** www.fhlbsf.com

General		Stock	
Incorporation	CA	Price on:12/24/2007	NA
Employees	NA	Stock Exchange	NA
Auditor	PricewaterhouseCoopers LLP	Ticker Symbol	NA
Stk Agt	NA	Outstanding Shares	NA
Counsel	NA	E.P.S	NA
DUNS No.	NA	Shareholders	NA

Business: The group's principle activity is regional home loan banking services. The San Franciscoare branch of the group is a separate entity with its own Board of Directors, management, and employees. The branch operates under a federal charter and is a government-sponsored enterprise. The branch is regulated by the Federal Housing Finance Board and is not a government agency and does not receive financial support from taxpayers. The U.S. government does not guarantee, directly or indirectly, the debt securities or other obligations of the branch.

Primary SIC and add'l.: 6111

CIK No: 0001316944

Subsidiaries: Affordable Housing Program

Officers: Dean Schultz/CEO, Pres., Roger A. Chembot/VP, Curtis Tung/VP, Amy E. Stewart/VP, Anne C.W Yee/VP, Michael Yeh/VP, Julia L. Young/VP, James Zabel/VP, John Manuel Ramirez/Advisory Counsel, Susan M. Reynolds/Advisory Counsel, Ann Sewill/Advisory Counsel, Mary Ellen Shay/Advisory Counsel, Lisa B. MacMillen/COO, Exec. VP, David H. Martens/Sr. VP - Enterprise Risk Management, Vera Maytum/Sr. VP, Controller *(70 Officers included in Index)*

Directors: Timothy R. Chrisman/Chmn., James P. Giraldin/Vice Chmn., Tad D. Lowrey/Dir., Craig G. Blunden/Dir., David A. Funk/Dir., Robert F. Nielsen/Dir. - Advisory Counsel, James F. Burr/Dir., Reginald Chen/Dir., Melinda Guzman/Dir., Kenneth R. Harder/Dir., John T. Wasley/Dir., Rick McGill/Dir., Monte L. Miller/Dir., John F. Robinson/Dir., Michael Roster/Dir. *(18 Directors included in Index)*

Federal Home Loan Bank of Seattle

1501 4th Ave., Ste. 1800, Seattle, WA, 98101; ***PH:*** 1-206-340-2300; ***http://*** www.fhlbsea.com

General		Stock	
Incorporation	Federally Chartered Corporation	Price on:12/24/2007	NA
Employees	NA	Stock Exchange	NA
Auditor	PricewaterhouseCoopers LLP	Ticker Symbol	NA
Stk Agt	NA	Outstanding Shares	NA
Counsel	NA	E.P.S	NA
DUNS No.	NA	Shareholders	NA

Business: The groups principle activity is to build financial partnerships that enhance the success of our members and make our communities better places to work and live. The group is divided into two business segments namely traditional member finance and Mortgage Purchase Program, or MPP. The group operates from United States.

Primary SIC and add'l.: 6111

CIK No: 0001329701

Officers: Richard M. Riccobono/CEO, Pres., Carol Gore/Chmn. - Advisory Counsel, John Berdes/Vice Chmn.- Advisory Counsel, Ty C. Tippets/Member - Advisory Counsel, Ren Essene/Member - Advisory Counsel, Peter Hainley/Member - Advisory Counsel, Michael Stanfield/Member - Advisory Counsel, John Biestman/Business Development Team, Lisa A. Grove/VP, Dir. - Auditing, Kelly Lindner/Collateral Operations Analyst, Denise Dougan/MPP Compliance Analyst, Debra Davis/Business Development Team, Charlie Eiseman/Business Development Team, Brett Manning/Business Development Team, Jim Mochizuki/Business Development Team *(22 Officers included in Index)*

Directors: Mike C. Daly/Chmn., Craig E. Dahl/Vice Chmn., Russell J. Lau/Dir., Harold B. Gilkey/Dir., Jack T. Riggs/Dir., William A. Longbrake/Dir., Daniel R. Fauske/Dir., Michael A. Devico/47/Dir., Park Price/Dir., William V. Humphreys/Dir., Donald V. Rhodes/Dir., David F. Wilson/Dir., Michael W. McGowan/Dir., Gordon Zimmerman/Dir., Les Aucoin/Dir. *(17 Directors included in Index)*

Owners: Washington Federal Savings and Loan/5.86%, Merrill Lynch Bank, U.S.A./5.50%, Bank of America Oregon, N.A./11.28%, Washington Mutual Bank, F.S.B./26.70%

Federal Home Loan Banks

8500 Freeport Pkwy. S, Ste 600, Irving, TX, 75063; ***PH:*** 1-214-441-8500; ***http://*** www.fhlb.com; ***Email:*** fhlb@fhlb.com

General - Incorporation	Federally Chartered Corporation	**Stock**- Price on:12/24/2007	$10.57
Employees	17	Stock Exchange	NA
Auditor	PricewaterhouseCoopers LLP	Ticker Symbol	NA
Stk Agt	John Hancock Signature Services, Inc	Outstanding Shares	3,450,000
Counsel	NA	E.P.S	$0.19
DUNS No.	NA	Shareholders	NA

Business: The group's activities are to provide banking services. The group serves commercial banks, savings institutions, credit unions and insurance companies. The primary services provided by the group include serving as a financial intermediary between the capital markets and its members. Other services provided by the group include promoting housing, jobs and general prosperity through products and services. The area of operations include Arkansas, Louisiana, Mississippi, New Mexico, and Texas.

Primary SIC and add'l.: 6111

CIK No: 0001331757

Officers: Terry Smith/CEO, Pres., Mary E. Ceverha/Vice Chmn. - Community Development Representative, Dallas, TX, Robert Oberg/Sr. VP, Chief Risk Officer, Tom Lewis/Chief Accounting Officer, Sr. VP, Nancy Parker/CIO, Sr. VP, Paul Joiner/Sr. VP, Chief Strategy Officer, Michael Sims/CFO, Sr. VP, Treasurer, Earl Willey/59/VP, Dir. - Internal Audit, Karen Krug/Sr. VP, Chief Administrative Officer, Corp. Sec.

Directors: Lee R. Gibson/Chmn., Mary E. Ceverha/Vice Chmn. - Community Development Representative, Dallas, TX, Sarah S. Agee/Dir., Bobby L. Chain/Dir., Charles G. Morgan/Dir., Robert Wertheim/Dir., Anthony S. Sciortino/Dir., Howard R. Hackney/Dir., Melvin H. Johnson/65/Dir., Tyson T. Abston/Dir., Gary Blankenship/Dir., Kent Conine/Dir., Willard Jackson/Dir., James Pate/Dir., Margo Sneller Scholin/Dir. *(19 Directors included in Index)*

Owners: Texas Bank and Trust Company, World Savings Bank, FSB Texas/25.12%, Citizens National Bank of Bossier City, Charter Bank/1.07%, Capital One, National Association/5.88%, First-Lockhart National Bank, Washington Mutual Bank/6.14%, Southside Bank/1.07%, Insiders/2.50%, Pine Bluff National Bank, State-Investors Bank, Guaranty Bond Bank, Bank of the West, First National Bankers Bank, Planters Bank and Trust Company *(17 Owners included in Index)*

Financial Data: ***Fiscal Year End:*** 12/31 ***Latest Annual Data:*** 6/30/2006

Year	Sales	Net Income
2006	$5,808,000	$634,000
2005	$5,451,000	$850,000

Curr. Assets:	$5,395,000	**Curr. Liab.:**	$85,242,000	**P/E Ratio:**	55.63
Plant, Equip.:	$948,000	**Total Liab.:**	$85,461,000	**Indic. Yr. Divd.:**	$0.240
Total Assets:	$114,000,000	**Net Worth:**	$28,539,000	**Debt/ Equity:**	NA

Federal Mogul Corp

26555 NW Hwy., Southfield, MI, 48033; ***PH:*** 1-248-354-7700; ***Fax:*** 1-248-354-8950; ***http://*** www.Federal-Mogul.com

General - Incorporation	MI	**Stock**- Price on:12/24/2007	$1.11
Employees	43,100	Stock Exchange	OTC
Auditor	Ernst & Young LLP	Ticker Symbol	FDMLQ
Stk Agt	American Stock Transfer & Trust Co.	Outstanding Shares	89,610,000
Counsel	NA	E.P.S	-$4.96
DUNS No.	00-655-7045	Shareholders	NA

Business: The group's principle activity is to manufacture automotive parts. The groups products include bearings, pistons, piston pins, rings, cylinder liners, camshafts, sintered products and connecting rods. The group operates from United States.

Primary SIC and add'l.: 3714 3562

CIK No: 0000034879

Subsidiaries: AE International Ltd., AE Limited, Antwerp Branch, Champion Pensions Limited, Coventry Assurance, Ltd., Curzon Insurance Ltd., F-M UK Holding Ltd., Federal Mogul Aftermarket France SAS, Federal Mogul Argentina SA, Federal Mogul do Brazil Ltda., Federal Mogul Electrical do Brazil Ltda., Federal Mogul Ignition Company, Federal Mogul K.K., Federal Mogul Materiais de Friccao Ltda, Federal Mogul of South Africa (Pty) Ltd 126 Subsidiaries included in the Index

Officers: Josu Maria Alapont/Chmn., CEO, Pres., Renu L.F. Dalleur/Sr. VP - Vehicle Safety, Protection, Mario Leone/Sr. VP, Chief Information Systems Officer, Rainer Jueckstock/Sr. VP - Powertrain Energy, Jean Brunol/Sr. VP - Business, Operations Strategy, Marie Remboulis/VP - Corporate Communications, James Burkhart/Sr. VP - Global Aftermarket, Robert L. Katz/Sr. VP, General Counsel, Ramzi Hermiz/Sr. VP - Worldwide Aftermarket Products, Services, Jeff Kaminiski/Sr. VP - Global Purchasing, Charles B. Grant/Sr. VP - Corporate Development, Strategic Planning, David Bozynski/VP, Treasurer, Joseph P. Felicelli/61/Exec. VP - Aftermarket Products, Services, Alan Haughie/VP, Controller, William Bowers/Sr. VP - Sales, Marketing *(19 Officers included in Index)*

Directors: Josu Maria Alapont/Chmn., CEO, Pres., Paul S. Lewis/Dir., John J. Fannon/Dir., Geoffrey Whalen/Dir., John C. Pope/Dir., Shirley D. Peterson/Dir.

Owners: Insiders/6.00%, Joseph P. Felicelli, Geoffrey H. Whalen, Michael G. Lynch, John C. Pope, Paul S. Lewis, John J. Fannon

Financial Data: ***Fiscal Year End:*** 12/31 ***Latest Annual Data:*** 12/31/2006

Year	Sales	Net Income
2006	$6,326,400,000	-$549,600,000
2005	$6,286,000,000	-$334,200,000
2004	$6,174,100,000	-$334,000,000

Curr. Assets:	$2,492,700,000	**Curr. Liab.:**	$1,654,700,000		
Plant, Equip.:	$2,078,600,000	**Total Liab.:**	$8,872,800,000	**Indic. Yr. Divd.:**	NA
Total Assets:	$7,179,100,000	**Net Worth:**	-$1,747,900,000	**Debt/ Equity:**	NA

Federal Mortgage Corp of Puerto Rico

444 Pk. Forest Way, Wellington, FL, 33414; ***PH:*** 1-561-798-4294

General - Incorporation	DE	**Stock**- Price on:12/24/2007	NA
Employees	NA	Stock Exchange	NA
Auditor	Miller & McCollom	Ticker Symbol	NA
Stk Agt	Bank of New York	Outstanding Shares	NA
Counsel	NA	E.P.S	NA
DUNS No.	NA	Shareholders	NA

Business: The group's principal activity is to acquire interests in natural gas projects located in the US waters of the Gulf of Mexico. The fund's investment objective is to generate cash flow from the acquiring, drilling, developing and completing of natural gas prospects in the offshore waters of Texas and Louisiana in the Gulf of Mexico. The company will make decisions as to the management, business and affairs of the fund in its sole discretion and judgment. The company intends to have the fund acquire interests in as many projects as is possible, given the dollars raised, the size of the interest acquired, and the risk factors. The group's existing projects are located in the offshore waters of the Gulf of Mexico and it anticipates future projects will likewise be located in the Gulf of Mexico.

Primary SIC and add'l.: 6770

CIK No: 0000034884

Subsidiaries: Pride Lending, Inc.

Federal Realty Investment Trust

1626 E Jefferson St., Rockville, MD, 20852; ***PH:*** 1-301-998-8100; ***Fax:*** 1-301-998-3700; ***http://*** www.federalrealty.com; ***Email:*** ir@federalrealty.com

General - Incorporation	MD	**Stock**- Price on:12/24/2007	$82.29
Employees	221	Stock Exchange	NYSE
Auditor	Grant Thornton LLP	Ticker Symbol	FRT
Stk Agt	American Stock Transfer & Trust Co.	Outstanding Shares	56,350,000
Counsel	NA	E.P.S	$1.62
DUNS No.	NA	Shareholders	NA

Business: The groups principle activities include owning, managing, developing and redeveloping high quality retail and mixed use properties. The group operates through two operating regions namely, east and west. In the year 2007, the group acquired 1020 Revere Beach Parkway. The group operates from the United States. The groups quarterly revenue for September 2007 was 129.34 millions of USD.

Primary SIC and add'l.: 6798

CIK No: 0000034903

Subsidiaries: FRIT San Jose Town and Country Village, LLC, Street Retail, Inc

Officers: Donald C. Wood/47/CEO, Pres., Trustee, Bob Walsh/VP - Development, Northeast Region, Jan Sweetnam/VP, Dir. - Asset Management, West Coast, John Tschiderer/VP - Development, Larry Finger/Exec. VP, CFO, Treasurer/$1,173,964.00, Gretchen Boyd/Mgr., Assist. Marketing, Joe Squeri/Exec. VP, Dawn Becker/Exec. VP, General Counsel, Sec./$989,711.00, Jeffrey S. Berkes/44/Exec. VP, Chief Investment Officer/$1,102,064.00, Andrew Blocher/Sr. VP - Capital Markets, Investor Relations, Don Briggs/Sr. VP - Development, Debbie Colson/Sr. VP - Legal Operations, Chris Weilminster/Sr. VP - Leasing, Philip Altschuler/VP - Human Resources, Wayne Christmann/VP - Human Resources *(20 Officers included in Index)*

Directors: Donald C. Wood/47/CEO, Pres., Trustee, Joseph S. Vassalluzzo/Chmn., Gail P. Steinel/Trustee, Kristin Gamble/Trustee, Walter F. Loeb/83/Trustee, Warren M. Thompson/Trustee, Jon E. Bortz/Trustee, David W. Faeder/Trustee

Owners: Larry E. Finger, Jeffrey S. Berkes, Insiders/1.60%, Jon E. Bortz, The Vanguard Group, Inc./5.90%, David W. Faeder, Stichting Pensioenfonds ABP/5.20%, Walter F. Loeb, Donald C. Wood/1.00%, Deutsche Bank AG/5.70%, Gail P. Steinel, Joseph S. Vassalluzzo, Cohen & Steers, Inc./5.50%, Kristin Gamble, ING Groep N.V./7.70% *(17 Owners included in Index)*

Financial Data: ***Fiscal Year End:*** 12/31 ***Latest Annual Data:*** 12/31/2006

Year	Sales	Net Income
2006	$451,022,000	$118,712,000
2005	$410,330,000	$114,612,000
2004	$394,274,000	$84,156,000

Curr. Assets:	$58,988,000	**Curr. Liab.:**	$129,536,000	**P/E Ratio:**	50.80
Plant, Equip.:	$2,463,751,000	**Total Liab.:**	$1,904,528,000	**Indic. Yr. Divd.:**	$2.440
Total Assets:	$2,688,606,000	**Net Worth:**	$784,078,000	**Debt/ Equity:**	NA

Federal Signal Corp

1415 W 22nd St., Ste. 1100, Oak Brook, IL, 60523; ***PH:*** 1-630-954-2000; ***Fax:*** 1-630-954-2030; ***http://*** www.federalsignal.com; ***Email:*** info@federalsignal.com

General - Incorporation	DE	**Stock**- Price on:12/24/2007	$15.8
Employees	5,400	Stock Exchange	NYSE
Auditor	Ernst & Young LLP	Ticker Symbol	FSS
Stk Agt	EquiServe Trust Co N.A	Outstanding Shares	47,940,000
Counsel	NA	E.P.S	$1.39
DUNS No.	04-525-6666	Shareholders	NA

Business: The group's principal activities are to manufacture and supply safety, signaling and communications equipment, hazardous area lighting, fire rescue vehicles, vehicle-mounted aerial access platforms, street sweeping and vacuum loader vehicles. The group operates in four business segments. The environmental products segment manufactures and markets a full range of street and parking lot sweeping and high performance waterblasting equipment. The safety products segment markets a broad range of safety related products, serving public and industry safety. The fire rescue segment manufactures fire/emergency apparatus, rescue vehicles and aerial access platforms. The tools segment manufactures high precision and consumable tools for metal stamping, metal cutting and plastic injection mold industries. On 30-Apr-2003, the group discontinued its sign group segment.

Primary SIC and add'l.: 6159 3544 3545 3993 3669 3711

CIK No: 0000277509

Subsidiaries: Bronto Skylift Oy Ab, ClappDico Corporation, Dayton Progress (U.K.), Ltd., Dayton Progress Perfuradores, LDA, Dayton Progress Canada, Ltd., Dayton Progress Corporation, Dayton Progress GmbH, Dayton Progress International Corporation, Dayton Progress, S.A.S., E-ONE Canada, Ltd., E-One, Inc, Elgin Sweeper Company, Federal APD do Brasil, Federal APD, Inc., Federal Signal Credit Corporation 36 Subsidiaries included in the Index

Officers: Robert D. Welding/Dir., CEO, Pres./$2,759,686.00, David E. Janek/VP, Treasurer, David R. McConnaughey/Pres. - Safety, Security Systems Group/$1,225,732.00, Peter Guile/Pres. - E, ONE, Fred H. Lietz/VP, Chief Procurement Officer, Esa Peltola/Pres. - Bronto Skylift, Michael K.

Wons/CIO, VP, Stephanie K. Kushner/Sr. VP, CFO/$989,696.00, John A. Gruber/VP - Corporate Development, Alan L. Shaffer/Pres. - Tool Group, Mark D. Weber/Pres. - Environmental Solutions Group/$805,304.00, Kimberly L. Dickens/VP - Human Resources, Jennifer L. Sherman/VP, General Counsel, Sec., John A. Deleonardis/VP - Taxes, Paul Brown/VP, Controller

Directors: Robert D. Welding/Dir., CEO, Pres., James C. Janning/Chmn., Robert S. Hamada/Dir., Charles R. Campbell/Dir., Robert M. Gerrity/Dir., James E. Goodwin/Dir., Paul W. Jones/Dir., John McCartney/Dir., Brenda L. Reichelderfer/Dir.

Owners: Stephanie K. Kushner, Robert D. Welding/1.10%, Insiders/3.20%, Franklin Mutual Advisers, LLC/9.07%, James C. Janning, James E. Goodwin, Dimensional FundAdvisors L.P./5.27%, Robert M. Gerrity, Stephen C. Buck, Charles R. Campbell, Paul W. Jones, David R. McConnaughey, Robert S. Hamada, Brenda L. Reichelderfer, John F. McCartney (17 Owners included in Index)

Financial Data: Fiscal Year End:12/31   Latest Annual Data: 12/31/2006

Year	Sales	Net Income
2006	$1,211,600,000	$22,700,000
2005	$1,156,900,000	-$4,600,000
2004	$1,139,000,000	-$2,300,000

Curr. Assets:	$418,800,000	Curr. Liab.:	$273,900,000	P/E Ratio:	11.37
Plant, Equip.:	$85,700,000	Total Liab.:	$663,000,000	Indic. Yr. Divd.:	$0.240
Total Assets:	$1,049,400,000	Net Worth:	$386,400,000	Debt/ Equity:	0.7496

Federal Trust Corp

312 W 1st St., Sanford, FL, 32771; **PH:** 1-407-323-1833; **Fax:** 1-407-645-1501; **http://** www.federaltrust.com

General - Incorporation	FL	**Stock**- Price on:12/24/2007	$8.56
Employees	100	Stock Exchange	AMEX
Auditor	Hacker, Johnson & Smith P.A.	Ticker Symbol	FDT
Stk Agt	Registrar & Transfer Co	Outstanding Shares	9,390,000
Counsel	Igler & Dougherty	E.P.S.	-$0.22
DUNS No.	61-416-5157	Shareholders	NA

Business: The group's principal activity is to provide savings bank services through its subsidiary, federal trust bank. The group obtains funds in the form of deposits and federal home loan bank advances and invests such funds in permanent loans on residential and to a lesser extent commercial real estate. The group conducts its operations primarily in Florida. The lending products of the group include residential real estate loans, commercial real estate, commercial business, United States small business administration guaranteed business loans, home equity and other consumer loans. The group has offices in sanford, winter park, new smyrna beach and casselberry.

Primary SIC and add'l.: 6035 6712
CIK No: 0000842640

Subsidiaries: Federal Trust Bank, Federal Trust Mortgage Company, FTB Financial, Inc

Officers: James V. Suskiewich/Chmn., CEO, Pres./$775,847.00, Stephen C. Green/Exec. VP, COO - Federal Trust Bank/$203,423.00, Marcia Zdanys/Corp. Sec., Daniel C. Roberts/Sr. VP, Chief Credit Officer - Federal Trust Bank/$139,484.00, Jennifer B. Brodnax/Assist. Corp. Sec./$134,166.00, Thomas J. Punzak/Treasurer - Federal Trust Bank, Gregory E. Smith/CFO, Exec. VP/$202,447.00

Directors: James V. Suskiewich/Chmn., CEO, Pres., Stephen H. Coover/Dir. - Federal Trust Bank, Kenneth W. Hill/Dir., George A. Igler/Dir., Stuart A. Hall/Dir. - Federal Trust Bank, George W. Foster/Dir., Samuel C. Certo/Dir., Dennis J. Harward/Dir. - Federal Trust Bank, Robert G. Cox/67/Dir., Charles R. Webb/66/Dir., Eric J. Reinhold/43/Dir.

Owners: Keefe Managers, LLC/8.90%, James V. Suskiewich/8.68%, Estate of Einar Paul Robsham/5.20%, Benjamin Partners/5.41%

Financial Data: Fiscal Year End:12/31   Latest Annual Data: 12/31/2006

Year	Sales	Net Income
2006	$46,068,000	$3,410,000
2005	$36,510,000	$4,436,000
2004	$27,000,000	$3,089,000

Curr. Assets:	$13,512,000	Curr. Liab.:	$655,933,000		
Plant, Equip.:	$17,414,000	Total Liab.:	$668,344,000	Indic. Yr. Divd.:	$0.160
Total Assets:	$722,964,000	Net Worth:	$54,620,000	Debt/ Equity:	0.0957

Federated Investors Inc

Federated Investors Tower, 1001 Liberty Ave., Pittsburgh, PA, 15222; **PH:** 1-412-288-1900; **Fax:** 1-412-288-1171; **http://** www.federatedinvestors.com; **Email:** investors@federatedinv.com

General - Incorporation	PA	**Stock**- Price on:12/24/2007	$40.93
Employees	1,243	Stock Exchange	NYSE
Auditor	Ernst & Young LLP	Ticker Symbol	FII
Stk Agt	Computershare Investor Services LLC	Outstanding Shares	102,990,000
Counsel	NA	E.P.S.	$2.11
DUNS No.	NA	Shareholders	NA

Business: The groups principal activity is to provide investment management products and related financial services. In the year 2006, the group acquired MDTA LLC. The group operates from the United States.

Primary SIC and add'l.: 6289 6722 6282
CIK No: 0001056288

Subsidiaries: Edgewood Services Inc, Federated Administrative Services, Federated Administrative Services Inc., Federated Advisory Services Company, Federated Asset Management GmbH, Federated Equity Management Company of Pennsylvania, Federated Funding 1997-1, Inc, Federated Global Investment Management Corp., Federated International Europe GmbH, Federated International Holdings B.V., Federated International Management Limited, Federated Investment Counseling, Federated Investment Management Company, Federated Investors (UK) Ltd., Federated Investors Management Company 27 Subsidiaries included in the Index

Officers: Christopher J. Donahue/Dir., CEO, Pres./$3,641,184.00, John B. Fisher/Pres., CEO - Federated Advisory Companies/$2,768,598.00, Eugene F. Maloney/Exec. VP - Federated Investors Management Company, Thomas R. Donahue/Pres. - FII Holdings, Inc. CFO, Treasurer/$2,526,804.00, Thomas E. Territ/Pres. - Federated Securities Corp, Denis McAuley/VP, Principal Accounting Officer, Pres. - Federated Shareholder Services Company, Brian P. Bouda/VP, Chief Compliance Officer

Directors: Christopher J. Donahue/Dir., CEO, Pres., John F. Donahue/Chmn., Richard B. Fisher/Co - Founder, Vice Chmn., Michael J. Farrell/Dir., David M. Kelly/Dir., John W. McGonigle/Dir., James L. Murdy/Dir., Edward G. O'Connor/Dir.

Owners: Michael J. Farrell, John F. Donahue/2.10%, John B. Fisher, Christopher J. Donahue/6.40%, Insiders/15.37%, Voting Shares Irrevocable Trust/100.00%, James L. Murdy, Edward G. OConnor, John W. McGonigle/3.90%, Thomas R. Donahue/2.40%, David M. Kelly

Financial Data: Fiscal Year End:12/31   Latest Annual Data: 12/31/2006

Year	Sales	Net Income
2006	$978,858,000	$197,729,000
2005	$909,216,000	$160,283,000
2004	$846,964,000	$181,179,000

Curr. Assets:	$182,051,000	Curr. Liab.:	$131,907,000	P/E Ratio:	20.67
Plant, Equip.:	$24,168,000	Total Liab.:	$280,919,000	Indic. Yr. Divd.:	$0.840
Total Assets:	$810,294,000	Net Worth:	$529,375,000	Debt/ Equity:	0.1947

Fedex Corp

942 S Shady Grove Rd., Memphis, TN, 38120; **PH:** 1-901-818-7600; **Fax:** 1-901-395-2000; **http://** www.fedex.com

General - Incorporation	DE	**Stock**- Price on:12/24/2007	$108.06
Employees	189,150	Stock Exchange	NYSE
Auditor	Ernst & Young LLP	Ticker Symbol	FDX
Stk Agt	Computershare Investor Services LLC	Outstanding Shares	307,800,000
Counsel	NA	E.P.S.	$6.43
DUNS No.	00-314-1970	Shareholders	NA

Business: The group's principle activity is to access growing global marketplace through a network of supply chain, transportation, business and related information services. The group operates from United States.

Primary SIC and add'l.: 4213 4215 4513
CIK No: 0001048911

Subsidiaries: American Freightways,Inc., AutoQuik,Inc., Bay Cities Diesel Engine Rebuilders Inc., Beijing Stone Kinkos Electronic Office Technology Co., Ltd., Caliber Logistics de Mexico, S.A. de C.V., Caliber Logistics Healthcare,Inc., Caliber System (Canada),Inc., Caribbean Transportation Services,Inc., CEDC,Inc., Dencom Freight Holdings Limited, Dencom Investments Limited, F.e.d.s. (ireland) Limited, Federal Express (Antigua) Limited, Federal Express (Antilles Francaises) S.A.R.L., Federal Express (Aruba) N.V. 142 Subsidiaries included in the Index

Officers: Kenneth A. May/CEO, Pres. - Fedex Kinko's, Tom Schmitt/CEO, Pres. - Fedex Services, Fedex Global Supply Chain Services, David F. Rebholz/CEO, Pres. - Fedex Ground, David J. Bronczek/CEO, Pres. - Fedex Express/$8,560,024.00, Frederick W. Smith/64/Chmn., CEO, Pres./$17,015,350.00, Douglas G. Duncan/CEO, Pres. - Fedex Freight, Christine P. Richards/Exec. VP, General Counsel, Sec., Alan B. Graf/CFO, Exec. VP/$7,130,772.00, Michael L. Ducker/Pres. - International, Fedex Express, Gene Huang/Chief Economist - Fedex Services, Michael T. Glenn/Exec. VP - Marketing Development, Corporate Communications/$6,251,419.00, David L. Cunningham/Pres. - Asia Pacific Region, Apac, Fedex Express, David Binks/Pres. - Canada Region, Fedex Express, Robert W. Elliott/Pres. - Europe, Middle East, Africa Region, Fedex Express, Juan N. Cento/Pres. - Latin America, Caribbean Region, Fedex Express (21 Officers included in Index)

Directors: Frederick W. Smith/64/Chmn., CEO, Pres., James L. Barksdale/Dir., Philip Greer/Dir., Charles T. Manatt/Dir., Judith L. Estrin/Dir., Peter S. Willmott/Dir., Shirley A. Jackson/Dir., Paul S. Walsh/Dir., August A. Busch/Dir., John A. Edwardson/Dir., J. R. Hyde/Dir., Steven R. Loranger/Dir., Joshua I. Smith/Dir.

Owners: J. R. Hyde, Frederick W. Smith/7.07%, Philip Greer, Daniel J. Sullivan, Charles T. Manatt, Peter S. Willmott, Judith L. Estrin, Shirley A. Jackson, Dodge & Cox/7.08%, Paul S. Walsh, David J. Bronczek, PRIMECAP Management Company/6.74%, Alan B. Graf, August A. Busch, Marsico Capital Management, LLC/6.65% (23 Owners included in Index)

Financial Data: Fiscal Year End:05/31   Latest Annual Data: 05/31/2007

Year	Sales	Net Income
2007	$35,214,000,000	$2,016,000,000
2006	$32,294,000,000	$1,806,000,000
2005	$29,363,000,000	$1,449,000,000

Curr. Assets:	$6,464,000,000	Curr. Liab.:	$5,473,000,000		
Plant, Equip.:	$10,770,000,000	Total Liab.:	$11,179,000,000	Indic. Yr. Divd.:	$0.360
Total Assets:	$22,690,000,000	Net Worth:	$11,511,000,000	Debt/ Equity:	0.1541

FedFirst Financial Corp

Donner at 6th St., Monessen, PA, 15062; **PH:** 1-724-684-6800; **Fax:** 1-724-684-4851; **http://** www.firstfederal-savings.com; **Email:** info@firstfederal-savings.com

General - Incorporation	USA	**Stock**- Price on:12/24/2007	$9.15
Employees	79	Stock Exchange	NDQ
Auditor	Edwards Saues & Owens, P.C.	Ticker Symbol	FFCO
Stk Agt	Registrar & Transfer Co	Outstanding Shares	6,660,000
Counsel	NA	E.P.S.	-$0.23
DUNS No.	NA	Shareholders	NA

Business: The group operates through its subsidiaries whose principle activity is to provide financial services. The groups services include deposit and loan. The products of the group include residential, multi family and commercial mortgages, consumer loan's and commercial business loans, and deposit accounts. Customers served by the group include brokerage firms, credit unions and insurance companies. The group operates from the United States. The assets of the group for the year 2006 were $283,517 (thousands).

Primary SIC and add'l.: 6712 6035
CIK No: 0001308017

Subsidiaries: FedFirst Exchange Corporation, First Federal Savings Bank

Officers: John G. Robinson/57/Dir., CEO, Pres., Robert C. Barry/CFO, Sr. VP, Dacosta Smith/VP, Jamie Prah/VP

Directors: John G. Robinson/57/Dir., CEO, Pres., Jack M. McGinley/52/Dir., David L. Wohleber/Dir., John J. Lacarte/41/Dir., John M. Kish/62/Dir., Joseph U. Frye/66/Dir., Richard Boyer/49/Dir.

Owners: FedFirst Financial Mutual Holding Company/54.20%, John J. LaCarte, John G. Robinson, Richard B. Boyer, Jack M. McGinley, Insiders, John M. Kish, Patrick G. OBrien, Joseph U. Frye

Financial Data: Fiscal Year End:12/31   Latest Annual Data: 12/31/2006

Year	Sales	Net Income
2006	$16,109,000	$344,000
2005	$15,646,000	-$102,000
2004	$16,019,000	-$883,000

Curr. Assets:	$6,024,000	Curr. Liab.:	$234,317,000		
Plant, Equip.:	$2,731,000	Total Liab.:	$237,171,000	Indic. Yr. Divd.:	NA
Total Assets:	$283,517,000	Net Worth:	$46,346,000	Debt/ Equity:	NA

FEI Co

5350 NE Dawson Creek Dr., Hillsboro, OR, 97124; *PH:* 1-503-726-7500; *Fax:* 1-503-726-7509; *http://* www.feic.com; *Email:* cust-info@feico.com

General - Incorporation	OR	**Stock** - Price on:12/24/2007	$35.08
Employees	1,624	Stock Exchange	NDQ
Auditor	Deloitte & Touche LLP	Ticker Symbol	FEIC
Stk Agt	Mellon Investor Services LLC	Outstanding Shares	35,460,000
Counsel	Stoel Rives LLP	E.P.S	$1.37
DUNS No.	09-914-1541	Shareholders	NA

Business: The group's principal activity is to design, manufacture, market and support products based on focused charged particle beam technology. These products include transmission electron microscopes, scanning electron microscopes and focused ion beam systems. The group also manufactures products that incorporate an electron beam and an ion beam into a single system. All of these products are sold to semiconductor manufacturers, thin film head manufacturers in the data storage industry and to industrial and institutional organizations in the life science industries. The group's products are marketed in the North America, Europe and in the Asia-pacific region.

Primary SIC and add'l.: 3699 3674 7389 3825

CIK No: 0000914329

Subsidiaries: Charged Particle Beam Technology Latin America S.A. de C.V., FEI Company Japan Ltd., FEI Company of U.S.A. (SE Asia P.t.e. Ltd.), FEI Czech Republic s.r.o., FEI Deutschland GmbH, FEI Electron Optics B.V., FEI Electron Optics International B.V., FEI Europe B.V., FEI Europe Ltd., FEI France SAS, FEI FSC Ltd., FEI Hong Kong Co., Ltd., FEI Italia S.r.l., FEI Particle Beam Systems Oesterreich GmbH, FEI Software (India) Private Limited 21 Subsidiaries included in the Index

Officers: Don R. Kania/Dir., CEO, Pres./$2,052,539.00, Dirk Lanens/VP - Sales, Service, Europe, Stephen F. Loughlin/VP - Finance, Paul J. O'Mara/Sr. VP - Worldwide Service, Rob H.J. Fastenau/Exec. VP - Marketing, Technology, Sr. Exec. - Europe/$723,354.00, Robert S. Gregg/Exec. VP - Global Strategic Relations/$598,778.00, Steven D. Berger/Sr. VP, Tony Edwards/VP, GM - Nanoelectronics, Dominique Hubert/VP, GM - Nanoresearch, Jan Hulsmann/VP - Manufacturing, Benjamin Loh/Exec. VP - Global Sales, Service, Brian E. Pierson/VP - Worldwide Operations, Jim Pouquette/VP - Sales, Asia, Paul Scagnetti/VP, GM - Nanoindustry, Michael R. Scheinfein/CTO, VP - Research *(21 Officers included in Index)*

Directors: Don R. Kania/Dir., CEO, Pres., James T. Richardson/Chmn., Gerhard Parker/Dir., Jan C. Lobbezoo/Dir., Donald R. Vanluvanee/Dir., Thomas F. Kelly/Dir., Wilfred J. Corrigan/Dir., William W. Lattin/Dir., Lawrence A. Bock/Dir., Michael J. Attardo/Dir.

Owners: Third Point LLC/6.20%, Raymond A. Link, Donald R. VanLuvanee, FMR Corp./5.80%, John A. Doherty, Vah A. Sarkissian/2.40%, Wilfred J. Corrigan, Lawrence A. Bock, Insiders/2.00%, Kern Capital Management, LLC/5.40%, William W. Lattin, Jan C. Lobbezoo, Michael J. Attardo, Robert S. Gregg, T. Rowe Price Associates, Inc./12.30% *(19 Owners included in Index)*

Financial Data: *Fiscal Year End:*12/31 *Latest Annual Data:* 12/31/2006

Year	Sales		Net Income
2006		$479,491,000	$20,040,000
2005		$427,229,000	-$78,158,000
2004		$465,705,000	$16,573,000
Curr. Assets:	$645,315,000	**Curr. Liab.:** $167,655,000	**P/E Ratio:** 29.98
Plant, Equip.:	$98,314,000	**Total Liab.:** $488,171,000	**Indic. Yr. Divd.:** NA
Total Assets:	$838,079,000	**Net Worth:** $349,908,000	**Debt/ Equity:** 0.8884

FelCor Lodging Trust Inc

545 E John Carpenter Fwy., Ste. 1300, Irving, TX, 75062; *PH:* 1-972-444-4900; *Fax:* 1-972-444-4949; *http://* www.felcor.com; *Email:* information@felcor.com

General - Incorporation	MD	**Stock** - Price on:12/24/2007	$24.18
Employees	74	Stock Exchange	NYSE
Auditor	PricewaterhouseCoopers LLP	Ticker Symbol	FCH
Stk Agt	Computershare Investor Services LLC	Outstanding Shares	62,390,000
Counsel	NA	E.P.S	$1.05
DUNS No.	NA	Shareholders	NA

Business: The groups principle activities include owning, acquiring and operating hotels. The group operates from the United States. The groups quarterly revenue for September 2007 was 257.16 millions of USD.

Primary SIC and add'l.: 6798 7011

CIK No: 0000923603

Subsidiaries: BHR Canada Tenant Company, BHR Lodging Tenant Company, BHR Operations, L.L.C., Brighton at Kingston Plantation, L.L.C., Center City Hotel Associates, DJONT Leasing, L.L.C., DJONT Operations, L.L.C., DJONT/Charlotte Leasing, L.L.C., DJONT/CMB Buckhead Leasing, L.L.C., DJONT/CMB Corpus Leasing, L.L.C., DJONT/CMB Deerfield Leasing, L.L.C., DJONT/CMB FCOAM, L.L.C., DJONT/CMB New Orleans Leasing, L.L.C., DJONT/CMB Orsouth Leasing, L.L.C., DJONT/CMB Piscataway Leasing, L.L.C. 132 Subsidiaries included in the Index

Officers: Richard A. Smith/45/Dir., CEO, Pres./$1,722,697.00, Robert P. Carl/48/Sr. VP, Dir. - Design, Construction, Michael A. Denicola/46/Exec. VP, Chief Investment Officer/$865,161.00, Troy A. Pentecost/46/Exec. VP, Dir. - Asset Management/$472,125.00, Andrew J. Welch/45/CFO, Exec. VP/$715,134.00, Jonathan H. Yellen/40/Exec. VP, General Counsel, Sec./$503,015.00, Lester C. Johnson/Sr. VP, Controller

Directors: Richard A. Smith/45/Dir., CEO, Pres., Thomas J. Corcoran/Chmn., Melinda J. Bush/Dir., Robert F. Cotter/Dir., Richard S. Ellwood/Dir., Thomas C. Hendrick/Dir., David C. Kloeppel/Dir., Charles A. Ledsinger/Dir., Robert H. Lutz/Dir., Robert A. Mathewson/Dir.

Owners: Insiders, AXA Financial, Inc./5.90%, Robert F. Cotter, Barclays Global Investors, NA/7.25%, Lawrence D. Robinson, Charles A. Ledsinger, Robert A. Mathewson, Franklin Resources, Inc./5.28%, Thomas J. Corcoran, Thomas J. Corcoran, Insiders/3.85%, Michael A. DeNicola, Deutsche Bank AG/7.27%, David C. Kloeppel, Thomas J. Corcoran *(25 Owners included in Index)*

Financial Data: *Fiscal Year End:*12/31 *Latest Annual Data:* 12/31/2006

Year	Sales		Net Income
2006		$991,038,000	$51,045,000
2005		$1,212,179,000	-$251,615,000
2004		$1,191,584,000	-$100,127,000
Curr. Assets:	$180,327,000	**Curr. Liab.:** $163,355,000	**P/E Ratio:** 20.67
Plant, Equip.:	$2,248,747,000	**Total Liab.:** $1,572,318,000	**Indic. Yr. Divd.:** $1.200
Total Assets:	$2,583,249,000	**Net Worth:** $1,010,931,000	**Debt/ Equity:** NA

Feldman Mall Properties Inc

1010 Nern Blvd., Ste. 314, Great Neck, NY, 11021; *PH:* 1-516-684-1239; *Fax:* 1-516-684-1059; *http://* www.feldmanmall.com; *Email:* ir@feldmanmall.com

General - Incorporation	MD	**Stock** - Price on:12/24/2007	$11.47
Employees	NA	Stock Exchange	NYSE
Auditor	KPMG LLP	Ticker Symbol	FMP
Stk Agt	American Stock Transfer & Trust Co.	Outstanding Shares	13,110,000
Counsel	NA	E.P.S	-$0.81
DUNS No.	NA	Shareholders	NA

Business: The groups principle activities include acquiring, renovating and repositioning retail shopping malls. The group acquired Colonie Center Mall, Tallahassee Mall and Northgate Mall in the year 2005. The group operates from the United States.

Primary SIC and add'l.: 6798 6798

CIK No: 0001299901

Subsidiaries: Feldman Equities General Partner Inc., Feldman Equities Management, Inc., Feldman Equities Management, LLC, Feldman Equities of Arizona, LLC, Feldman Equities Operating Partnership, LP, Feldman Foothills Mall, LP, Feldman Foothills Pads, LP, Feldman Harrisburg General Partner Inc., Feldman Holdings Business Trust I, Feldman Holdings Business Trust II, Feldman Mall Investors, LLC, Feldman Mall Partner, Inc., Feldman Pads Partner, Inc., FMP Colonie Center LLC, FMP Northgate LLC 19 Subsidiaries included in the Index

Officers: Lawrence H. Feldman/Chmn., CEO, Thomas E. Wirth/CFO, Exec. VP, James C. Bourg/Dir., Exec. VP, COO, Lloyd Miller/Exec. VP - Leasing, Marketing

Directors: Lawrence H. Feldman/Chmn., CEO, James C. Bourg/Dir., Exec. VP, COO, Lawrence S. Kaplan/Dir., Bruce E. Moore/Dir., Paul H. McDowell/Dir.

Owners: Insiders/2.10%, Thomas Wirth, Kensington Investment Group, Inc./9.10%, James C. Bourg, Lawrence S. Kaplan, Wells Fargo Capital Management Incorporated/9.80%, Paul H. McDowell, Bruce E. Moore, Larry Feldman/1.30%, Inland American Real Estate Trust, Inc./9.80%

Financial Data: *Fiscal Year End:*12/31 *Latest Annual Data:* 12/31/2006

Year	Sales		Net Income
2006		$65,305,000	$20,181,000
2005		$55,195,000	-$2,633,000
2004		$12,261,000	-$3,497,000
Curr. Assets:	$26,913,000	**Curr. Liab.:** $33,038,000	**P/E Ratio:** 7.45
Plant, Equip.:	$318,440,000	**Total Liab.:** $300,306,000	**Indic. Yr. Divd.:** $0.910
Total Assets:	$413,851,000	**Net Worth:** $113,545,000	**Debt/ Equity:** 2.1210

Fellows Energy Ltd

370 Interlocken Blvd, Ste. 400, Boulder, CO, 80021; *PH:* 1-303-926-4415; *Fax:* 1-866-845-2884; *http://* www.fellowsenergy.com; *Email:* info@fellowsenergy.com

General - Incorporation	NV	**Stock** - Price on:12/24/2007	$0.041
Employees	8	Stock Exchange	OTC
Auditor	Mendoza Berger & Co LLP	Ticker Symbol	FLWE
Stk Agt	Pacific Stock Transfer Company	Outstanding Shares	100,000,000
Counsel	NA	E.P.S	-$0.146
DUNS No.	NA	Shareholders	NA

Business: The group's principle activity is to acquire coal bed methane, tight sands gas and conventional oil and gas projects. It has acquired interests in the 10,678 acre carter creek project, a low risk hyrocarbon project and the 19,290 acre weston county project in Wyoming. It has also acquired the 5,200 acre gordon creek project, a coal bed methane project in Utah. The group is actively negotiating on a number of additional projects in the western United States. On 05-Jan-2004, the group acquired the exploration and drilling interests in certain oil and gas leases in Utah and additional rights in Wyoming and Montana from diamond oil & gas corporation. The group operates from United States.

Primary SIC and add'l.: 7389 1311 8742

CIK No: 0001144439

Subsidiaries: Fuel Centers, Inc.

Officers: George S. Young/56/Chmn., CEO, Pres./$122,000.00, Steven L. Prince/Dir., VP - Operations/$110,000.00, Robert Lamarre/Employee, Consultant, David T. Terry/Employee, Consultant, Art Jacobs/Employee, Consultant, Harry Terbest/Employee, Consultant, Brooke E. Horspoool/CFO

Directors: George S. Young/56/Chmn., CEO, Pres., Steven L. Prince/Dir., VP - Operations

Owners: George S. Young/3.80%, Steven L. Prince, Insiders/4.10%

Financial Data: *Fiscal Year End:*12/31 *Latest Annual Data:* 12/31/2006

Year	Sales		Net Income
2006		$424,000	-$8,591,000
2005		NA	-$3,592,000
2004		NA	-$3,760,000
Curr. Assets:	$496,000	**Curr. Liab.:** $3,866,000	
Plant, Equip.:	$8,979,000	**Total Liab.:** $7,567,000	**Indic. Yr. Divd.:** NA
Total Assets:	$9,864,000	**Net Worth:** $2,297,000	**Debt/ Equity:** 0.7770

Female Health Co

515 N State St., Ste. 2225, Chicago, IL, 60610; *PH:* 1-312-595-9123; *Fax:* 1-312-595-9122; *http://* www.femalehealth.com; *Email:* info@femalehealth.com

General - Incorporation	WI	**Stock** - Price on:12/24/2007	$2.15
Employees	159	Stock Exchange	AMEX
Auditor	McGladrey & Pullen LLP	Ticker Symbol	FHC
Stk Agt	Firstar Trust Co	Outstanding Shares	24,530,000
Counsel	Reinhart, Boerner, Van Deuren sc	E.P.S	$0.00
DUNS No.	05-530-0578	Shareholders	NA

Business: The group's principal activities are to manufacture, market and sell the female condom, which can prevent unintended pregnancy and sexually transmitted diseases, including HIV/aids. This product is currently sold or available in various venues including commercial (private sector) and public sector clinics in over 100 countries. It is commercially marketed in 21 countries by various country specific partners, including the United States, the United Kingdom, Japan, Canada, Holland, France, venezuela, and Brazil. In the United States, the product is marketed to city and state public health clinics, as well as not-for-profit organizations. The group currently holds product and technology patents in the United States, Japan, the United Kingdom, France, Italy, Germany, Spain and Canada. The group has trademarks on the name femidom and femy in certain foreign countries.

Primary SIC and add'l.: 3069

CIK No: 0000863894
Subsidiaries: Female Health Company - UK, NutraSweet Company, Pulse Nutrition Solutions, Inc, WPC Holdings, Inc. (Holdings)
Officers: O. B. Parrish/74/Chmn., CEO, Denese Shervington/Special Advisor, Carol Rogers/Special Advisor, Pramilla Senanayake/Special Advisor, Michael Pope/50/VP, GM - Female Health Company, Donna Felch/60/CFO, VP, Erica L. Gollub/Consultant, Member - Advisory Board, Robert R. Zic/44/VP - Finance, William R. Gargiulo/79/Assist. Sec., Patrick Friel/RH, HIV, Aids Consultant, Member - Advisory Board, Jack Weissman/60/VP - Sales, Virginia Gonzales/Special Advisor, Marilyn John/Special Advisor, Sharon Marshall/Special Advisor
Directors: O. B. Parrish/74/Chmn., CEO, Mitchell Warren/Member - Advisory Board, Patrick Friel/RH, HIV, Aids Consultant, Member - Advisory Board, Erica L. Gollub/Consultant, Member - Advisory Board, Mary Latka/Member - Advisory Board, Martha Brady/Member - Advisory Board, Pamela P. French/Member - Advisory Board
Owners: Michael Pope/1.50%, O. B. Parrish/5.00%, William R. Gargiulo, Gary Benson/4.70%, Donna Felch, Mary Ann Leeper/3.50%, Michael R. Walton/3.20%, Richard E. Wenninger/11.50%, James R. Kerber/2.00%, David R. Bethune, Red Oak Partners/5.80%, Stephen M. Dearholt/13.80%, Mary Margaret Frank, Insiders/37.90%
Financial Data: *Fiscal Year End:*09/30 *Latest Annual Data:* 9/30/2006

Year	Sales	Net Income
2006	$14,824,000	$282,000
2005	$11,162,000	-$1,356,000
2004	$8,829,000	-$2,019,000

Curr. Assets:	$6,651,000	**Curr. Liab.:**	$1,581,000		
Plant, Equip.:	$607,000	**Total Liab.:**	$2,674,000	**Indic. Yr. Divd.:**	NA
Total Assets:	$7,446,000	**Net Worth:**	$4,772,000	**Debt/ Equity:**	NA

Fentura Financial Inc

175 N Leroy St., Fenton, MI, 48430; *PH:* 1-810-750-8725; *Fax:* 1-810-629-3892; *http://* www.fentura.com

General		**Stock**	
Incorporation	MI	Price on:12/24/2007	$29.8
Employees	188	Stock Exchange	OTC
Auditor	Crowe Chizek & Co. LLC	Ticker Symbol	FETM
Stk Agt	NA	Outstanding Shares	2,170,000
Counsel	Varnum Riddering S & H LLP	E.P.S	$0.55
DUNS No.	60-264-5673	Shareholders	NA

Business: The group's principal activities are to provide banking and trust services to individuals, small businesses and government entities in southeastern Michigan. The services are provided through nine community banking offices in genesee, livingston and oakland counties in southeastern Michigan. The group also provides other additional services like safe deposit boxes, credit card services, transmitting funds and other services through its nine branch offices. The deposit products of the group are checking, savings and term certificate accounts. The lending products are residential mortgage, commercial and installment loans. On 15-Mar-2004, the group acquired west Michigan financial corporation.
Primary SIC and add'l.: 6712 6022
CIK No: 0000919865
Subsidiaries: Community Bank Services, Inc., Community Insurance Services, Inc., Davison State Bank, Fentura Mortgage Company, The State Bank, West Michigan Community Bank, West Michigan Mortgage, LLC
Owners: Kenneth R. Elston, Mary Alice Heaton/5.26%, Donald E. Johnson/10.22%, Douglas J. Kelley, David J. Karr, Forrest A. Shook/1.41%, Robert E. Sewick, Ian W. Schonsheck, Linda J. Lemieux/5.17%, Brian P. Petty, Dennis E. Leyder, Holly J. Pingatore, Ronald L. Justice, Thomas P. McKenney, Insiders/4.16% *(17 Owners included in Index)*
Financial Data: *Fiscal Year End:*12/31 *Latest Annual Data:* 12/31/2006

Year	Sales	Net Income
2006	$47,561,000	$5,308,000
2005	$40,909,000	$5,054,000
2004	$33,386,000	$4,034,000

Curr. Assets:	$32,431,000	**Curr. Liab.:**	$556,980,000	**P/E Ratio:**	13.93
Plant, Equip.:	$16,854,000	**Total Liab.:**	$570,980,000	**Indic. Yr. Divd.:**	$1.000
Total Assets:	$622,298,000	**Net Worth:**	$51,318,000	**Debt/ Equity:**	0.2676

Fermavir Pharmaceuticals Inc

420 Lexington Ave. Rm 445, New York, NY, 10170; *PH:* 1-212-413-0802; *http://* www.fermavir.com

General		**Stock**	
Incorporation	FL	Price on:12/24/2007	$1.26
Employees	NA	Stock Exchange	NA
Auditor	J.H. Cohn LLP	Ticker Symbol	NA
Stk Agt	NA	Outstanding Shares	20,850,000
Counsel	NA	E.P.S	-$0.33
DUNS No.	NA	Shareholders	NA

Business: The groups principal activity is to provide services in the biotechnology field. In August 2005, the group acquired FermaVir Research, Inc. The group operates from the United States.
Primary SIC and add'l.: 2834
CIK No: 0001283383
Subsidiaries: FermaVir Research, Inc.
Officers: Geoffrey W. Henson/Dir., CEO, Pres., Sec., Frederick Larcombe/CFO
Directors: Geoffrey W. Henson/Dir., CEO, Pres., Sec., Gabriele M. Cerrone/Chmn., Richard J. Whitley/Dir., Chris McGuigan/Dir., John P. Brancaccio/59/Dir., Erik De Clercq/Dir.
Owners: Insiders/32.90%, Goldeneye Biocapital Limited/15.40%, Chris McGuigan/5.30%, Early Bird Bioinvestments, Ltd./7.30%, Gabriele M. Cerrone/24.50%, Erik DeClercq/2.80%, RAB Special Situations (Master) FundLimited/7.60%, Richard J. Whitley, John P. Brancaccio, Geoffrey W. Henson/1.90%, Eureka Science Incubator S.A.R.L/11.20%, Panetta Partners, Ltd./14.60%, Frederick Larcombe
Financial Data: *Fiscal Year End:*04/30 *Latest Annual Data:* 4/30/2006

Year	Sales	Net Income
2006	NA	-$5,558,000
2005	NA	-$24,000

Curr. Assets:	$145,000	**Curr. Liab.:**	$402,000		
Plant, Equip.:	$22,000	**Total Liab.:**	$414,000	**Indic. Yr. Divd.:**	NA
Total Assets:	$211,000	**Net Worth:**	-$203,000	**Debt/ Equity:**	NA

Ferrellgas Partners LP

7500 College Blvd., Ste. 1000, Overland Park, KS, 66210; *PH:* 1-913-661-1500; *http://* www.ferrellgas.com

General		**Stock**	
Incorporation	DE	Price on:12/24/2007	$24.1399
Employees	NA	Stock Exchange	NYSE
Auditor	Deloitte & Touche LLP	Ticker Symbol	FGP
Stk Agt	Computershare Trust Co	Outstanding Shares	62,960,000
Counsel	NA	E.P.S	$0.651
DUNS No.	NA	Shareholders	NA

Business: The groups principle activity is to distribute propane and related equipment. The group acquired Eastern Fuels, Inc. and Petro Star, Corp. in the year 2005 and United Energy, Inc. and Gaines Propane, Inc. in the year 2006. The group operates from the United States. The groups total revenue in the year 2007 was 1,992.44 millions of USD.
Primary SIC and add'l.: 5984
CIK No: 0000922358
Subsidiaries: Blue Rhino Canada, Inc., Blue Rhino Global Sourcing, LLC, bluebuzz, Inc., Ferrellgas Finance Corp, Ferrellgas Partners Finance Corp., Ferrellgas Receivables, LLC, Ferrellgas, L.P., Quick Ship, Inc., R-4 Technical Center-NC, LLC, Uni Asia, Ltd
Officers: James E. Ferrell/Chmn., CEO, Stephen L. Wambold/COO, Pres., Tod D. Brown/VP - Blue Rhino, Gene D. Caresia/VP - Human Resources, Kevin T. Kelly/CFO, Sr. VP, Brian J. Kline/VP - Corporate Development, George L. Koloroutis/VP - Ferrell North America, James Campbell/VP - South Division, Steve Faacks/VP - North Division, Micah Redman/VP - East Division, Randy V. Schott/VP - West Division, Patrick J. Walsh/VP - Midwest Division, Eugene D. Caresia/44/VP - Human Resources
Directors: James E. Ferrell/Chmn., CEO, William K. Hoskins/Dir., Andrew A. Levison/Dir., John R. Lowden/Dir., Michael F. Morrissey/Dir., Billy D. Prim/Dir., Elizabeth T. Solberg/Dir.
Owners: William K. Hoskins, Ferrell Companies Inc. Employee Stock Ownership Trust/32.30%, Insiders/7.60%, Billy D. Prim, Michael F. Morrissey, Kevin T. Kelly, James E. Ferrell/6.80%, A. Andrew Levison, Elizabeth T. Solberg
Financial Data: *Fiscal Year End:*07/31 *Latest Annual Data:* 7/31/2006

Year	Sales	Net Income
2006	$1,895,470,000	$25,009,000
2005	$1,754,114,000	$88,814,000
2004	$1,379,381,000	$28,550,000

Curr. Assets:	$269,584,000	**Curr. Liab.:**	$227,081,000	**P/E Ratio:**	43.11
Plant, Equip.:	$720,190,000	**Total Liab.:**	$1,266,746,000	**Indic. Yr. Divd.:**	$2.000
Total Assets:	$1,503,403,000	**Net Worth:**	$236,657,000	**Debt/ Equity:**	3.5253

Ferro Corp

1000 Lakeside Ave., Cleveland, OH, 44114; *PH:* 1-216-641-8580; *Fax:* 1-216-875-7205; *http://* www.ferro.com; *Email:* investor@ferro.com

General		**Stock**	
Incorporation	OH	Price on:12/24/2007	$24.72
Employees	6,660	Stock Exchange	NYSE
Auditor	Deloitte & Touche LLP	Ticker Symbol	FOE
Stk Agt	National City Bank	Outstanding Shares	43,390,000
Counsel	Venable LLP	E.P.S	NA
DUNS No.	NA	Shareholders	NA

Business: The groups principle activity is to manufacture inorganic, organic and electronic products. The groups products include enamels, pigments, dinnerware, polymer, plastic compounds, metal powders and polishing materials. The group operates through six segments namely, tile coating systems, porcelain enamel, color and glass performance materials, polymer additives, specialty plastics, pharmaceuticals, and fine chemicals. The group operates from the United States.
Primary SIC and add'l.: 2816 2816 2851 2851 2821 2821 3255 2899 5198 5198 3255 2899
CIK No: 0000035214
Subsidiaries: DC-Ferro Co., Ltd, ESFEL SA, FC France Acquisition Sarl, Ferro (Belgium) Sprl, Ferro (Great Britain) Ltd, Ferro (Holland) BV, Ferro (Italia) SrL, Ferro (Suzhou) Performance Materials Co. Ltd, Ferro (Thailand) Co. Ltd, Ferro Argentina SA, Ferro Arnsberg GmbH iL, Ferro B.V., Ferro Cerdec (Thailand) Co. Ltd, Ferro Chemicals SA, Ferro China Holdings Inc. 49 Subsidiaries included in the Index
Officers: James F. Kirsch/Chmn., CEO, Pres./$2,241,681.00, Sallie B. Bailey/CFO, Corporate VP, James C. Bays/Corporate VP, General Counsel/$944,008.00, Ann E. Killian/VP - Human Resources, Celeste Beeks Mastin/39/VP - Growth, Development, Michael J. Murry/VP - Inorganic Specialties/$819,478.00, Barry D. Russell/VP - Electronic Material Systems/$669,250.00, Peter T. Thomas/VP - Organic Specialties, Thomas W. Austin/VP - Operations
Directors: James F. Kirsch/Chmn., CEO, Pres., Sandra Austin Crayton/57/Dir., Michael H. Bulkin/66/Dir., William B. Lawrence/60/Dir., Michael F. Mee/62/Dir., William J. Sharp/63/Dir., Dennis W. Sullivan/66/Dir., Alberto Weisser/52/Dir., Perry W. Premdas/Dir., Jennie S. Hwang/Dir., Richard J. Hipple/55/Dir.
Owners: Wellington Management Company, LLP/8.90%, Barry D. Russell, Michael H. Bulkin, Dimensional Fund Advisors LP/5.10%, Insiders, William B. Lawrence, Michael J. Murry, Sandra Austin Crayton, Mario J. Gabelli/13.80%, James C. Bays, Alberto Weisser, Jeffrey L. Gendell/6.80%, James F. Kirsch, Jennie S. Hwang, Perry W. Premdas *(19 Owners included in Index)*
Financial Data: *Fiscal Year End:*12/31 *Latest Annual Data:* 12/31/2006

Year	Sales	Net Income
2006	$2,041,525,000	$20,090,000
2005	$1,882,305,000	$16,276,000
2004	$1,843,721,000	$24,925,000

Curr. Assets:	$622,605,000	**Curr. Liab.:**	$382,884,000	**P/E Ratio:**	63.38
Plant, Equip.:	$526,802,000	**Total Liab.:**	$1,208,388,000	**Indic. Yr. Divd.:**	$0.580
Total Assets:	$1,732,937,000	**Net Worth:**	$524,549,000	**Debt/ Equity:**	0.9952

FFD Financial Corp

321 N Wooster Ave., Dover, OH, 44622; *PH:* 1-330-364-7777; *Fax:* 1-330-364-7779; *http://* www.onlinefirstfed.com

General - Incorporation	OH	Stock- Price on:12/24/2007	$15.93
Employees	44	Stock Exchange	NDQ
Auditor	Grant Thornton LLP	Ticker Symbol	FFDF
Stk Agt	Registrar & Transfer Co	Outstanding Shares	1,110,000
Counsel	NA	E.P.S.	$1.44
DUNS No.	03-041-9477	Shareholders	NA

Business: The group's principal activity is to provide fixed-rate and adjustable-rate first mortgage loans, secured by one- to four-family residential real estate located in tuscarawas county, Ohio. It also originates loans for the construction of residential real estate, loans secured by multifamily real estate, loans for commercial business purposes and nonresidential real estate loans. The consumer loans provided by the group include unsecured loans, passbook loans, loans secured by motor vehicles and home improvement loans. The categories of deposits include now, money market accounts, passbook accounts and certificates of deposits. In addition, the group also invests in U.S. Government and agency obligations, interest-bearing deposits in other financial institutions and mortgage-backed securities. The group operates through its wholly owned subsidiary first federal community bank.

Primary SIC and add'l.: 6035 6712

CIK No: 0001006177

Officers: Trent B. Troyer/CEO, Pres./$186,147.00, Michele L. Larkin/VP - Mortgage Lending, Melissa Johnson/Commercial Credit Analyst, Kayla Alsept/Financial Service Rep, New Philadelphia Office, Leslie Riker/Branch Mgr. - Dover Office, Sally K. O'Donnell/Sr. VP, Corp. Sec., Scott C. Finnell/Exec. VP, Commercial Loan Officer/$136,786.00, Robert R. Gerber/CFO, VP, Treasurer, Mary M. Mitchell/Compliance, Systems Administrator, Perriann McCoy/Branch Mgr. - Boulevard Office, Stephenie Wilson/Human Resources, Marketing Dir., Nick G. McMillen/Commercial Lending, Kristopher Kreinbihl/Commercial Lending, Kerry Egler-Whytsell/Mortgage Loan Originator, Boulevard Office, Angie L. Liggett/Financial Service Rep, Dover Office (20 Officers included in Index)

Directors: Enos L. Loader/Chmn., David W. Kaufman/Dir., Stephen G. Clinton/Dir., Robert D. Sensel/Dir., Richard A. Brinkman/Dir., Leonard L. Gundy/Dir.

Owners: David W. Kaufman/0.09%, Insiders/17.23%, Stephen G. Clinton/3.47%, Enos L. Loader/2.49%, Scott C. Finnell/1.11%, Leonard L. Gundy/0.99%, FFD Financial Corporation/11.03%, Bulldog Investors, et al./6.20%, Robert D. Sensel/2.95%, Richard A. Brinkman, Trent B. Troyer/3.37%

Financial Data: Fiscal Year End:06/30   Latest Annual Data: 06/30/2007

Year	Sales	Net Income
2007	$12,052,000	$1,623,000
2006	$10,074,000	$1,352,000
2005	$7,990,000	$1,086,000

Curr. Assets:	$8,263,000	Curr. Liab.:	$141,057,000	P/E Ratio:	11.22
Plant, Equip.:	$1,970,000	Total Liab.:	$142,870,000	Indic. Yr. Divd.:	$0.560
Total Assets:	$161,233,000	Net Worth:	$18,363,000	Debt/ Equity:	NA

FFW Corp

1205 N Cass St., Wabash, IN, 46992; *PH:* 1-260-563-3185; *Fax:* 1-260-563-4841; *http://* www.ffsbwabash.com

General - Incorporation	DE	Stock- Price on:12/24/2007	$26
Employees	NA	Stock Exchange	OTC
Auditor	NA	Ticker Symbol	FFWC
Stk Agt	New York Drop-Depository Trust Co.	Outstanding Shares	NA
Counsel	NA	E.P.S.	$2.33
DUNS No.	NA	Shareholders	NA

Business: The group's principle activity is to provide banking services. The group also provides personal and business banking services. The group's products include deposit accounts and loans. The group operates from United States.

Primary SIC and add'l.: 6712 6035

CIK No: 0000895401

Officers: Roger K. Cromer/Pres., Jack Vineyard/Branch Mgr. - North Manchester, Debbie Bauer/New Accounting, North Manchester, Marvin Goble/Branch Mgr. - South Whitley, Brenda Heagy/New Accounting, South Whitley, Deb Roy/Branch Mgr. - Columbia City, Jane Davisson/New Accounting, Columbia City, Peggy Genshaw/Branch Mgr. - Syracuse, A. J. Eubank/New Accounting, Syracuse

Financial Data: Fiscal Year End:06/30   Latest Annual Data: 6/30/2004

Year	Sales	Net Income
2004	$14,735,000	$2,437,000
2003	$16,451,000	$2,358,000
2002	$18,326,000	$2,048,000

Curr. Assets:	$7,897,000	Curr. Liab.:	$161,552,000	P/E Ratio:	11.16
Plant, Equip.:	$3,966,000	Total Liab.:	$217,285,000	Indic. Yr. Divd.:	NA
Total Assets:	$239,910,000	Net Worth:	$22,624,000	Debt/ Equity:	NA

Fiat SpA

Via Nizza 250, Turino, 10126; *PH:* 39-0110063796; *http://* www.fiatgroup.com; *Email:* investor.relations@fiatgroup.com

General - Incorporation	Italy	Stock- Price on:12/24/2007	$28.96
Employees	NA	Stock Exchange	NA
Auditor	Deloitte & Touche LLP	Ticker Symbol	NA
Stk Agt	Morgan ADR Service Center	Outstanding Shares	NA
Counsel	NA	E.P.S.	NA
DUNS No.	42-800-3065	Shareholders	NA

Business: The group's principle activities include production and marketing of cars, commercial vehicles, tractors, combine harvesters and other agricultural machinery. The group also manufactures cast-iron, aluminum and magnesium components for the automotive industry; instrument panels, petrol injection systems and headlights for its own vehicles and for other car makers; components and systems for airplanes and helicopters engines as well as turbines for marine propulsion. The group also supply industrial automation system processes for the motor vehicle industries, including installation and maintenance of production lines, logistics and manufacturing programs. The groups services include publishing and communications, insurance, financial and business services. The group operates from United States. In may 2003 the group sold tora assicurazioni group.

Primary SIC and add'l.: 2711 3713 3711 5012 3531 3724 6411

CIK No: 0000842317

Subsidiaries: Fiat Finance and Trade Ltd., Magneti Marelli Holding S.p.A.

Officers: Harold Boyanovsky/63/CEO, Pres. - Agricultural, Construction Equipment, Riccardo Tarantini/CEO - Metallurgical Products, Sergio Marchionne/Dir., CEO, Eugenio Razelli/57/CEO - Magneti Marelli, Ferruccio Luppi/58/CEO - Business Solutions, Paolo Monferino/61/CEO, Pres. - Iveco, Gianni Coda/61/Chmn. Fiat Purchasing Italia, Group Purchasing Coordination, Fiat Group Automobiles, Carlo Pasteris/Chmn., Statutory Auditor, Giuseppe Camosci/Statutory Auditor, Francesco Paolo Mattioli/Dir. - Publishing, Communications, Lodovico Passerin D'Entreves/Dir. - Publishing, Communications, Maurizio Francescatti/45/Group Treasurer, Ernesto Auci/Dir. - Publishing, Communications, Mauro Di Gennaro/46/Chief Audit Exec., Compliance Officer, Paolo Rebaudengo/60/Sr. VP - Industrial Relations (24 Officers included in Index)

Directors: Sergio Marchionne/Dir., CEO, Luca Cordero Di Montezemolo/Chmn., John Elkann/Vice Chmn., Gian Maria Gros-Pietro/Dir., Mario Zibetti/Dir., Tiberto Brandolini Dadda/Dir., Andrea Agnelli/Dir., Rene Carron/Dir., Vittorio Mincato/Dir., Roland Berger/Dir., Luca Garavoglia/Dir., Hermann-Josef Lamberti/52/Dir., Virgilio Marrone/Dir., Pasquale Pistorio/Dir., Carlo Sant'Albano/Dir. (16 Directors included in Index)

Financial Data: Fiscal Year End:12/31   Latest Annual Data: 12/31/2006

Year	Sales	Net Income
2006	$68,433,790,000	$719,564,000
2005	$55,126,714,000	$148,050,000
2004	$66,618,194,000	-$2,865,240,000

Curr. Assets:	$48,313,738,000	Curr. Liab.:	$25,156,996,000	P/E Ratio:	7.09
Plant, Equip.:	$14,763,595,000	Total Liab.:	$63,948,730,000	Indic. Yr. Divd.:	NA
Total Assets:	$74,000,174,000	Net Worth:	$8,719,261,000	Debt/ Equity:	NA

FiberMark Inc

161 Wellington Rd. , Brattleboro, VT, 05302; *PH:* 1-802-257-5974; *http://* www.fibermark.com

General - Incorporation	DE	Stock- Price on:12/24/2007	NA
Employees	NA	Stock Exchange	NA
Auditor	KPMG LLP	Ticker Symbol	NA
Stk Agt	American Stock Transfer & Trust Co.	Outstanding Shares	NA
Counsel	Hale & Dorr LLP	E.P.S.	NA
DUNS No.	60-237-4688	Shareholders	NA

Business: The group's principal activity is to produce specialty fiber-based materials to meet its industrial and consumer needs. Its versatile manufacturing capabilities comprising papermaking, synthetic or nonwoven Web technology, saturating, coating and other finishing processes generate products sold in roll or sheet form. The product line of the group are specialty papers, high-density pressboards, treated cloth, nonwoven materials that may offer the performance or appearance of cloth or advanced fiber-based materials. It includes latex-saturated papers with the feel of leather or other durable materials and composite materials. The group operates with 12 production facilities in the u.s and Europe.

Primary SIC and add'l.: 3069 3569 2631

CIK No: 0000887591

Subsidiaries: FiberMark International Holdings LLC, FiberMark North America, Inc

Officers: Anthony MacLaurin/CEO, Pres., Ed Slepski/VP - Research, Development, Susan Hurt/VP - Marketing, Product Management, New Business Development, John E. Hanley/CFO, VP, Stephen F. Pfistner/Sr. VP - Human Resources - Organizational Development, Mike Wright/Sr. VP - Finishing Operations, John Pucul/Sr. VP - Sales, Les Eustace/VP - Sales, Kevin Archbald/VP - Sales, Jeff Hopkins/VP - International Sales

Directors: Thomas Weld/Chmn.

Fibernet Telecom Group Inc

570 Lexington Ave., 3rd Fl., New York, NY, 10022; *PH:* 1-212-405-6200; *http://* www.ftgx.com; *Email:* investor.relations@ftgx.com

General - Incorporation	DE	Stock- Price on:12/24/2007	$8.64
Employees	67	Stock Exchange	NDQ
Auditor	Deloitte & Touche LLP	Ticker Symbol	FTGX
Stk Agt	American Stock Transfer & Trust Co.	Outstanding Shares	7,340,000
Counsel	Mintz Levin Cohn Ferris Et Al	E.P.S.	-$0.88
DUNS No.	80-659-0923	Shareholders	NA

Business: The group's principal activity is to provide wholesale broadband connectivity for data, voice and video transmission on its state-of-the art fiber optic networks. It offers an advanced high-bandwidth, fiber-optic solution to support the demand for network capacity in the local loop. The group provides three general types of services: transport services provide broadband circuits on the group's metropolitan transport networks and in-building networks. Colocation facility services provide customers with the ability to locate their communications and networking equipment at its carrier point facilities. Communication access management services provide customers with the non-exclusive rights. These rights enable the customers to market and provide their services to tenants in the on-net and off-net buildings. On 30-Jan 2004, the group acquired operating assets of gateway colocation.

Primary SIC and add'l.: 4899 4813

CIK No: 0001001868

Subsidiaries: Consolidated Edison Communications Holding Company, Inc, Desert Native Designs, Inc.

Officers: Jon A. Deluca/Dir., CEO, Pres./$1,054,383.00, Arthur Valhuerdi/VP - Infrastructure, Michael Hubner/VP, General Counsel, Ernest Hoffmann/Sr. VP - Network Services, John Ennis/VP - Operations, Information Technology, John P. Dowd/VP - Business Development, Thomas Brown/Sr. VP - Sales, Marketing/$535,520.00, Charles Wiesenhart/CFO, VP - Finance/$320,500.00

Directors: Jon A. Deluca/Dir., CEO, Pres., Michael S. Liss/Chmn., Richard E. Sayers/Vice Chmn., Roy Farmer/Dir., Oskar Brecher/Dir., Robert E. La Blanc/Dir., Charles J. Mahoney/Dir., Timothy P. Bradley/Dir., Adam M. Brodsky/Dir.

Owners: Michael S. Liss/3.30%, Robert E. La Blanc, Insiders/15.00%, Adam M. Brodsky/4.00%, Oskar Brecher, Charles Wiesenhart, Timothy P. Bradley, Jon A. DeLuca/4.00%, Thomas Brown/1.40%, Charles J. Mahoney, Deutsche Bank AG/9.10%, Roy D. Farmer, Kamran Hakim/8.30%, Richard E. Sayers

Financial Data: Fiscal Year End:12/31   Latest Annual Data: 12/31/2006

Year	Sales	Net Income
2006	$40,080,000	-$6,925,000
2005	$33,824,000	-$13,935,000
2004	$34,579,000	-$18,394,000

Curr. Assets:	$10,666,000	Curr. Liab.:	$9,947,000		
Plant, Equip.:	$59,534,000	Total Liab.:	$28,712,000	Indic. Yr. Divd.:	NA
Total Assets:	$71,732,000	Net Worth:	$43,020,000	Debt/ Equity:	0.3380

Fiberstars Inc

32000 Aurora Rd., Solon, OH, 44139; *PH:* 1-440-715-1300; *http://* www.fiberstars.com

General - Incorporation	CA	*Stock*- Price on:12/24/2007	$22.29
Employees	NA	Stock Exchange	NDQ
Auditor	Grant Thornton LLP	Ticker Symbol	FBST
Stk Agt	Mellon Investor Services LLC	Outstanding Shares	NA
Counsel	NA	E.P.S.	NA
DUNS No.	NA	Shareholders	NA

Business: The groups principle activities include designing, developing, manufacturing and marketing fiber optic lighting systems. The products of the group include pool and spa lighting and commercial lighting. The group products sold under the trade names Fiberstars(R), BritePak(R), OptiCore(TM), Lightly Expressed(R), Jazz Light(TM), FX Light(TM), FX Spa Light(TM), EFO ICE(TM), EnergyFocus(TM), and Fiberstars EFO(R). The group operates from the United States, North America and Europe.

Primary SIC and add'l.: 3640

CIK No: 0000924168

Subsidiaries: Crescent Lighting, Ltd, Lichtberatung Mann Gmbh

Officers: John M. Davenport/62/Dir., CEO, Pres./$544,812.00, Robert A. Connors/59/CFO, VP - Finance/$244,511.00, Roger Buelow/35/CTO, VP - Engineering/$188,861.00, Ted Des Enfants/36/VP, GM - Fiberstars EFO/$245,576.00, Barry R. Greenwald/61/Pres., GM - Pool Division/$237,901.00, Eric Hilliard/40/COO

Directors: John M. Davenport/62/Dir., CEO, Pres., John B. Stuppin/74/Dir., Ronald A. Casentini/69/Dir., Michael Kasper/58/Dir., Paul Von Paumgartten/61/Dir., David N. Ruckert/70/Dir., Philip E. Wolfson/64/Dir.

Owners: Ronald A. Casentini, Philip Wolfson, Insiders/8.80%, Michael Kasper, David N. Ruckert/2.40%, Welch & Forbes LLC/8.80%, Roger Buelow, Barry R. Greenwald, Jeffrey H. Brite, John M. Davenport/2.40%, Robert Connors, Paul von Paumgartten, New York, New York 10151/6.90%, John B. Stuppin/2.00%, Ted des Enfants

FiberTower Corp

Formerly: First Avenue Networks Inc
185 Berry St., Ste. 4800, San Francisco, CA, 94107; *PH:* 1-415-659-1350; *http://* www.firstavenet.com

General - Incorporation	DE	*Stock*- Price on:12/24/2007	$4.16
Employees	219	Stock Exchange	NA
Auditor	KBA Group LLP	Ticker Symbol	NA
Stk Agt	Computershare Investor Services LLC	Outstanding Shares	145,680,000
Counsel	NA	E.P.S.	-$1.19
DUNS No.	92-932-3277	Shareholders	NA

Business: The group's principal activity is to provide wireless, high-speed, point-to-point, broadband telecommunication services. It provides wireless backbone networks for Internet service providers (isps) and competitive local exchange carriers (clecs), short-range oc-3 links to fiber optic data and telephony carriers. Point to point links are provided between buildings for organizations with metropolitan areas and campus environments and connect remote cellular tower sites to the telephone network. The group owns over 750 wireless telecommunications licenses granted by the federal communications commission. This license portfolio represents over 1billion channel pops. It has 9 fixed transmission links, which is incorporate into their telecommunication networks.

Primary SIC and add'l.: 7379 4812

CIK No: 0001010286

Subsidiaries: ART Leasing Corp., ART Licensing Corp., Big Creek Systems LLC., DCT Communications Inc., First Avenue Licenses, LLC, First Avenue Networks Enterprise Solutions, Inc., First Avenue Networks Government Solutions, Inc., First Avenue Networks Solutions, Inc., First Avenue Spectrum Labs, Inc., Teligent Services Acquisition, Inc.

Officers: Michael Gallagher/Dir., CEO, Pres./$7,418,318.00, Joseph M. Sandri/Sr. VP - Regulatory, Government Affairs/$635,492.00, Michael Finlayson/Sr. VP - Technology/$1,508,281.00, Gus Okwu/Investor Contact, David Leeds/39/Sr. VP - Sales, Sales Operations, Ravi Potharlanka/Sr. VP - Operations, Ferdi Schell/Sr. VP - Systems, Ornella Napolitano/Contact - Investor, Company, Thomas Scott/Sr. VP, CFO/$1,165,611.00

Directors: Michael Gallagher/Dir., CEO, Pres., John Beletic/Chmn., Neil Subin/Dir., John Muleta/Dir., Bandel Carano/Dir., Randall A. Hack/Dir., John Kelly/Dir., Darryl Schall/Dir., Steven Scheiwe/Dir.

Owners: Steven D. Schiewe, Michael Finlayson, John B. Muleta, Louis Olsen, Aspen Advisors LLC/15.40%, Michael K. Gallagher, TCS Capital and affiliates/8.10%, John P. Kelly/18.10%, Thomas A. Scott, Bandel Carano/8.30%, OZ Management, L.L.C. and affiliates/7.60%, Michael Casey, Insiders/29.40%, Oak Investment Partners and affiliates/8.30%, Tudor Investment Corporation and affiliates/9.80% (20 Owners included in Index)

Financial Data: Fiscal Year End:12/31 Latest Annual Data: 06/30/2007

Year	Sales	Net Income
2007	NA	NA
2006	$13,763,000	-$57,278,000
2005	$1,325,000	-$11,326,000

Curr. Assets:	$406,571,000	*Curr. Liab.:*	$31,146,000	
Plant, Equip.:	$171,612,000	*Total Liab.:*	$542,656,000	*Indic. Yr. Divd.:* NA
Total Assets:	$1,216,478,000	*Net Worth:*	$673,822,000	*Debt/ Equity:* 0.6237

Fidelis Energy Inc

9595 Wilshire Blvd, Ste. 900, Beverly Hills, CA, 90212; *PH:* 1-310-300-4062; *http://* www.fidelisenergy.com; *Email:* ir@fidelisenergy.com

General - Incorporation	NV	*Stock*- Price on:12/24/2007	NA
Employees	NA	Stock Exchange	NA
Auditor	Robison, Hill & Co.	Ticker Symbol	NA
Stk Agt	Holladay Stock Transfer, Inc.	Outstanding Shares	112,830,000
Counsel	Dieterich & Associates	E.P.S.	NA
DUNS No.	NA	Shareholders	NA

Business: The groups principle activities include identifying, acquiring and developing working interest percentages in smaller, underdeveloped oil and gas projects. The group operates from the United States and Canada. The group's quarterly revenue for September 2007 was 0.53 millions of USD.

Primary SIC and add'l.: 1382

CIK No: 0001157723

Officers: William Marshall/48/Chmn., CEO, Pres., Sterling Klein/43/Dir., CFO, Sec., Treasurer, Brent Davies/Independent Auditor, Brian Wildes/Advisory, Independent Operations, Engineering Consultant

Directors: William Marshall/48/Chmn., CEO, Pres., Sterling Klein/43/Dir., CFO, Sec., Treasurer, Thomas Herdman/Dir.

Owners: SNK Capital Trust/12.34%, TMC Capital Trust/12.34%, Insiders/12.77%, Sterling Klein/0.43%

Financial Data: Fiscal Year End:12/31 Latest Annual Data: 12/31/2006

Year	Sales	Net Income
2006	$1,971,000	-$2,297,000
2005	$1,396,000	-$2,843,000
2004	$49,000	-$833,000

Curr. Assets:	NA	*Curr. Liab.:*	NA	
Plant, Equip.:	NA	*Total Liab.:*	NA	*Indic. Yr. Divd.:* NA
Total Assets:	NA	*Net Worth:*	NA	*Debt/ Equity:* NA

Fidelity Bancorp Inc

1009 Perry Hwy., Pittsburgh, PA, 15237; *PH:* 1-412-367-3300; *Fax:* 1-412-364-6504; *http://* www.fidelitybancorp-pa.com; *Email:* customerservice@fidelitybank-pa.com

General - Incorporation	PA	*Stock*- Price on:12/24/2007	$17.35
Employees	132	Stock Exchange	NDQ
Auditor	Beard Miller Co. LLP	Ticker Symbol	FSBI
Stk Agt	Registrar & Transfer Co	Outstanding Shares	2,990,000
Counsel	NA	E.P.S.	$1.35
DUNS No.	06-684-4796	Shareholders	NA

Business: The group's principal activity is to provide banking services. It operates through eleven full-service offices in allegheny and butler counties. The subsidiaries of the group are fidelity bank, pasb and fb capital trust and fb statutory capital trust ii. The group accepts demand deposits, now accounts, passbook accounts and money market deposits. The types of loans offered by the group are first mortgage, home equity, consumer, commercial, credit cards and other loans.

Primary SIC and add'l.: 6712 6035

CIK No: 0000769207

Subsidiaries: FB Statutory Trust II, FBIC, Inc., Fidelity Bank, PaSB

Officers: Richard G. Spencer/Dir., CEO, Pres., Richard L. Barron/Assist. Sec., Michael A. Mooney/Exec. VP, Lisa L. Griffith/Sr. VP, CFO, Treasurer

Directors: Richard G. Spencer/Dir., CEO, Pres., William L. Windisch/Chmn., Robert J. Gales/Dir., Joanne Ross Wilder/Dir., Robert F. Kastelic/Dir., Christopher S. Green/Dir., Charles E. Nettrour/Dir., Oliver D. Keefer/Dir., Donald J. Huber/Dir.

Owners: Banc Fund V L.P./5.50%, Fidelity Bancorp, Inc./9.10%

Financial Data: Fiscal Year End:09/30 Latest Annual Data: 9/30/2006

Year	Sales	Net Income
2006	$41,206,000	$4,184,000
2005	$35,495,000	$3,876,000
2004	$33,092,000	$4,321,000

Curr. Assets:	$12,026,000	*Curr. Liab.:*	$576,445,000	*P/E Ratio:* 12.57
Plant, Equip.:	$6,288,000	*Total Liab.:*	$686,537,000	*Indic. Yr. Divd.:* $0.560
Total Assets:	$730,732,000	*Net Worth:*	$44,195,000	*Debt/ Equity:* 2.7662

Fidelity Capital Concepts Ltd

1800 Boulder St., Ste. 400, Denver, CO, 80211; *PH:* 1-303-458-5727; *http://* www.id-confirm.com

General - Incorporation	NV	*Stock*- Price on:12/24/2007	$0.025
Employees	6	Stock Exchange	NA
Auditor	Gordon, Hughes & Banks LLP	Ticker Symbol	NA
Stk Agt	The Nevada Agency and Trust Co.	Outstanding Shares	71,010,000
Counsel	NA	E.P.S.	NA
DUNS No.	NA	Shareholders	NA

Business: The group's principle activity is to seek potential business opportunities. The group operates from United States.

Primary SIC and add'l.: 6799

CIK No: 0001111696

Officers: David A. Grasch/43/Dir., CEO, Thomas A. Breen/51/Dir., Pres., Sec., Principal Financial Officer, Robert A. Morrison/Dir., CTO, Kevin Brady/Dir. - Network Administration

Directors: David A. Grasch/43/Dir., CEO, Thomas A. Breen/51/Dir., Pres., Sec., Principal Financial Officer, Robert A. Morrison/Dir., CTO

Owners: Ronald Nelson Baird/7.60%, David Grasch/7.12%, S&G Holdings/6.25%, Insiders/11.35%, Robert A. Morrison/10.77%, Thomas Breen/4.22%

Financial Data: Fiscal Year End:06/30 Latest Annual Data: 6/30/2006

Year	Sales	Net Income
2006	$51,000	-$1,138,000
2005	NA	-$1,603,000
2004	$87,000	-$27,000

Curr. Assets:	$154,000	*Curr. Liab.:*	$58,000	
Plant, Equip.:	$1,000	*Total Liab.:*	$58,000	*Indic. Yr. Divd.:* NA
Total Assets:	$156,000	*Net Worth:*	$98,000	*Debt/ Equity:* NA

Fidelity D & D Bancorp Inc

Blakely and Drinker StS, Dunmore, PA, 18512; *PH:* 1-570-342-8281; *Fax:* 1-570-346-5724; *http://* www.the-fidelity.com; *Email:* admin@fidelitybank-pa.com

General - Incorporation	PA	*Stock*- Price on:12/24/2007	$33.25
Employees	188	Stock Exchange	OTC
Auditor	Parente Randolph LLC	Ticker Symbol	FDBC
Stk Agt	Registrar & Transfer Co	Outstanding Shares	2,060,000
Counsel	NA	E.P.S.	$2.19
DUNS No.	NA	Shareholders	NA

Business: The group's principal activity is the provision of a variety of financial services in Pennsylvania. A holding company of the fidelity deposit and discount bank, the group accepts deposits like savings accounts, now accounts, money market deposit accounts, and certificates of deposit and checking accounts. The primary lending products are single-family residential loans, secured consumer

loans, and secured loans to businesses. The group also offered discounts on home equity loan fees and first year free safe deposit box rentals for customers who had their payments directly charged to a demand deposit account. In addition, it also provides annuities, mutual funds and trust services. The services are provided through twelve offices to individuals and corporate customers in lackawanna and luzerne counties of Pennsylvania.

Primary SIC and add'l.: 6712 6022

CIK No: 0001098151

Subsidiaries: The Fidelity Deposit and Discount Bank

Officers: Steven C. Ackmann/Dir., CEO, Pres./$258,550.00, John T. Cognetti/58/Dir., Assist. Sec., Barbara Shimkus/Investor Relations Officer, Paul A. Barrett/Dir., Sec., Daniel J. Santaniello/COO, VP/$147,642.00, Salvatore R. Defrancesco/CFO, Treasurer/$121,531.00, James T. Gorman/Sr. Lending Officer/$184,355.00

Directors: Steven C. Ackmann/Dir., CEO, Pres., Patrick J. Dempsey/Chmn., Samuel C. Cali/91/Chmn. Emeritus, Michael J. McDonald/Vice Chmn., John T. Cognetti/58/Dir., Assist. Sec., Paul A. Barrett/Dir., Sec., Mary E. McDonald/Dir., David L. Tressler/Dir., Brian J. Cali/Dir.

Owners: Mary E. McDonald/4.17%, David L. Tressler, Samuel C. Cali/3.02%, Insiders/19.74%, Paul A. Barrett/2.03%, Patrick J. Dempsey/1.47%, Michael J. McDonald/3.32%, John T. Cognetti, Brian J. Cali/4.02%

Financial Data: *Fiscal Year End:* 12/31 *Latest Annual Data:* 12/31/2006

Year	Sales	Net Income
2006	$38,075,000	$4,125,000
2005	$33,520,000	$4,592,000
2004	$31,863,000	$3,364,000

Curr. Assets:	$16,304,000	**Curr. Liab.:**	$448,170,000	**P/E Ratio:**	16.46
Plant, Equip.:	$11,522,000	**Total Liab.:**	$510,706,000	**Indic. Yr. Divd.:**	$1.000
Total Assets:	$562,318,000	**Net Worth:**	$51,612,000	**Debt/ Equity:**	1.1842

Fidelity National Financial Inc

601 Riverside Ave., Jacksonville, FL, 32204; **PH:** 1-904-854-8100; *http://* www.fnf.com

General - Incorporation	DE	**Stock** - Price on:12/24/2007	$24.97
Employees	17,800	Stock Exchange	NYSE
Auditor	KPMG LLP	Ticker Symbol	FNF
Stk Agt	Continental Stock Transfer & Trust Co	Outstanding Shares	221,590,000
Counsel	NA	E.P.S.	$1.12
DUNS No.	12-146-3335	Shareholders	NA

Business: The groups principle activity is to provide insurance services. The groups services include flood, personal lines and home warranty insurance. In the year 2007, the group acquired ATM Holdings. The group operates from United States.

Primary SIC and add'l.: 6719 6541 6361 6159

CIK No: 0000809398

Subsidiaries: 2027267 Ontario Inc., A.s.a.p. Legal Publication Services, Inc., Adnoram Settlement Agency of Ohio, LLC, Aero Records & Title Co., AIS Alamo Insurance Services, Inc., Alamo Title Company, Alamo Title Company of Brazoria County, Inc., Alamo Title Company of Harris County, Inc., Alamo Title Company of Tarrant County, Inc., Alamo Title Holding Company, Alamo Title Insurance, Alamo Title of Guadalupe County, Inc., Alamo Title of Travis County, Inc., Alexander Title Agency, Incorporated, All Counties Courier, Inc 375 Subsidiaries included in the Index

Officers: Alan L. Stinson/CEO, Daniel Kennedy Murphy/Sr. VP, Peter T. Sadowski/General Counsel, Brent B. Bickett/Co - Pres., Raymond R. Quirk/Co - Pres., Anthony J. Park/CFO

Directors: William P. Foley/Chmn., Frank P. Willey/Vice Chmn., Douglas K. Ammerman/Dir., John F. Farrell/Dir., Thomas M. Hagerty/Dir., Daniel D. Lane/Dir., Richard N. Massey/Dir., Cary H. Thompson/Dir., Willie D. Davis/Dir., Philip G. Heasley/Dir., William Lyon/Dir., Peter O. Shea/Dir.

Financial Data: *Fiscal Year End:* 12/31 *Latest Annual Data:* 09/30/2006

Year	Sales	Net Income
2006	NA	$5,518,000
2005	$6,315,861,000	$538,981,000

Curr. Assets:	$1,318,926,000	**Curr. Liab.:**	$790,598,000	**P/E Ratio:**	11.72
Plant, Equip.:	$156,952,000	**Total Liab.:**	$3,416,158,000	**Indic. Yr. Divd.:**	$1.200
Total Assets:	$5,900,533,000	**Net Worth:**	$2,480,037,000	**Debt/ Equity:**	NA

Fidelity National Information Services Inc

Formerly: Certegy Inc
601 Riverside Ave., Jacksonville, FL, 32204; **PH:** 1-904-854-8547; *http://* www.certegy.com

General - Incorporation	GA	**Stock** - Price on:12/24/2007	$54.97
Employees	24,871	Stock Exchange	NA
Auditor	KPMG LLP	Ticker Symbol	NA
Stk Agt	Fidelity National Information Srvs	Outstanding Shares	192,460,000
Counsel	NA	E.P.S.	$2.69
DUNS No.	NA	Shareholders	NA

Business: The group's principal activities are to provide credit and debit card processing and check risk management services to financial institutions and merchants. The group operates through 2 segments: card services and check services. Card services provides credit and debit card issuer services that enable institutions and retailers to issue visa, American express, mastercard credit, debit cards and other electronic payment cards for consumers. It also provides merchant processing, e-banking services, card issuer software and support services. Check services provides check risk management services and related processing services to businesses accepting or cashing checks at the point-of-sale. The group provides these services in the U.S., the u.k., Canada, Brazil, Chile, Thailand, France, Ireland, Australia, New Zealand and the Dominican Republic. In 2004, it acquired crittson financial services llc, game financial corporation and Caribbean caricard services inc.

Primary SIC and add'l.: 7322 7323

CIK No: 0001136893

Subsidiaries: A.s.a.p. Legal Publication Services, Inc., AGES Participacoes Ltda, Aircrown Ltd., ALLTEL Servicios de Informacion (Costa Rica) S.A., APTItude Solutions, Inc., Arizona Sales and Posting, Inc., Aurum Technology Inc., BenchMark Consulting International Europe GmbH, BenchMark Consulting International N.A., Inc., Card Brazil Holdings, Inc., Card Brazil LLC, Central Credit Services, Ltd., Certegy (Cayman Islands) Limited, Certegy Asia Pacific Holdings, LLC, Certegy Asset Management, Inc. 170 Subsidiaries included in the Index

Officers: Lee A. Kennedy/CEO, Pres./$12,828,230.00, William P. Foley/63/Exec. Chmn./$16,147,630.00, Walter M. Korchun/Exec. VP, General Counsel, Sec., Francis K. Chan/38/Chief Accounting Officer, Sr. VP, Ronald G. Cook/Sr. VP, General Counsel, Kelly D. Feese/Sr. VP - Human Resources, Gary A. Norcross/42/Exec. VP - Integrated Financial Solutions, Frederick C. Parvey/56/CIO, Exec. VP, Francis R. Sanchez/51/Exec. VP - Enterprise Solutions, Michael A. Sanchez/50/Exec. VP - International, Daniel T. Scheuble/49/Exec. VP - Mortgage Processing Services, Eric Swenson/48/Exec. VP - Mortgage Information Services, Alan L. Stinson/62/Exec. VP - Finance/$2,788,294.00, Brent B. Bickett/43/Exec. VP - Strategic Planning/$2,805,043.00, Gerard Ballard/CTO, Corporate VP (17 Officers included in Index)

Directors: William P. Foley/63/Exec. Chmn., Robert M. Clements/45/Dir., Thomas M. Hagerty/45/Dir., Marshall Haines/40/Dir., Keith W. Hughes/Dir., David K. Hunt/Dir., James K. Hunt/56/Dir., Daniel D. Lane/73/Dir., Cary H. Thompson/Dir., Charles T. Doyle/72/Dir., Richard N. Child/50/Dir., Phillip B. Lassiter/63/Dir., Kathy Brittain White/Dir., Richard N. Massey/52/Dir.

Owners: Thomas H. Lee Advisors, LLC/6.13%, Lee A. Kennedy, Alan L. Stinson, William P. Foley/2.90%, Thomas M. Hagerty, TPG Advisors III, Inc./6.13%, Richard N. Massey, Insiders/4.62%, Cary H. Thompson, Brent B. Bickett, Daniel D. Lane, Jeffrey S. Carbiener, Keith W. Hughes, David K. Hunt

Financial Data: *Fiscal Year End:* 12/31 *Latest Annual Data:* 12/31/2006

Year	Sales	Net Income
2006	$4,132,602,000	$259,087,000
2005	$1,117,141,000	$130,319,000
2004	$1,039,506,000	$111,810,000

Curr. Assets:	$1,300,539,000	**Curr. Liab.:**	$880,515,000	**P/E Ratio:**	38.36
Plant, Equip.:	$345,799,000	**Total Liab.:**	$4,474,846,000	**Indic. Yr. Divd.:**	$0.200
Total Assets:	$7,630,560,000	**Net Worth:**	$3,142,744,000	**Debt/ Equity:**	0.9026

Fidelity Southern Corp

3490 Piedmont Rd. NE, Ste. 1550, Atlanta, GA, 30305; **PH:** 1-404-639-6500; **Fax:** 1-404-814-8060; *http://* www.lionbank.com

General - Incorporation	GA	**Stock** - Price on:12/24/2007	$17.64
Employees	374	Stock Exchange	NDQ
Auditor	Ernst & Young LLP	Ticker Symbol	LION
Stk Agt	Bank of New York	Outstanding Shares	9,320,000
Counsel	Ernst & Young LLP	E.P.S.	$0.99
DUNS No.	10-202-7687	Shareholders	NA

Business: The group's principal activity is to provide deposit, lending, mortgage, securities brokerage and international trade services to commercial and retail customers. The origination of loans include direct and indirect automobile and home equity lending, secured and unsecured installment loans, credit card loans, construction and residential real estate loans and commercial loans. Deposit products include demand, savings and time deposits. The group conducts service banking and residential mortgage lending through 19 branches in fulton, dekalb, cobb, clayton and gwinnett counties, Georgia.

Primary SIC and add'l.: 6021 6712

CIK No: 0000822662

Subsidiaries: Fidelity Bank, Fidelity National Capital Trust I, Fidelity Southern Statutory Trust I, Fidelity Southern Statutory Trust II, FNC Capital Trust I, LionMark Insurance Company

Officers: James B. Miller/67/Chmn., CEO, Pres./$538,511.00, Rodrick B. Marlow/65/CFO, Principal Accounting Officer/$181,257.00, Palmer H. Proctor/40/Dir., Pres./$360,184.00, David Buchanan/50/VP/$274,622.00

Directors: James B. Miller/67/Chmn., CEO, Pres., David R. Bockel/63/Dir., James H. Miller/58/Dir., Robert J. Rutland/66/Dir., Edward G. Bowen/72/Dir., Palmer H. Proctor/40/Dir., Pres., Kevin S. King/60/Dir., Rankin M. Smith/60/Dir., Clyde W. Shepherd/47/Dir.

Owners: Tontine Partners, LP/9.58%, David R. Bockel, Clyde W. Shepherd, Edward G. Bowen, Kevin S. King, Rankin M. Smith, The Banc Funds Co., LLC/5.99%, Palmer H. Proctor, Rodrick B. Marlow, Howard M. Griffith, Robert J. Rutland/1.60%, Dalton, Greiner, Hartman, Maher & Co, LLC/5.12%, James H. Miller, David Buchanan, Insiders/34.94% (16 Owners included in Index)

Financial Data: *Fiscal Year End:* 12/31 *Latest Annual Data:* 12/31/2006

Year	Sales	Net Income
2006	$113,503,000	$10,374,000
2005	$88,355,000	$10,326,000
2004	$74,250,000	$7,632,000

Curr. Assets:	$68,287,000	**Curr. Liab.:**	$1,465,644,000		
Plant, Equip.:	$18,803,000	**Total Liab.:**	$1,554,532,000	**Indic. Yr. Divd.:**	NA
Total Assets:	$1,649,179,000	**Net Worth:**	$94,647,000	**Debt/ Equity:**	0.8663

FieldPoint Petroleum Corp

1703 Edelweiss Dr., Ste. 301, Cedar Park, TX, 78613; **PH:** 1-512-250-8692; **Fax:** 1-512-335-1294; *http://* www.fppcorp.com; **Email:** fppc@ix.netcom.com

General - Incorporation	CO	**Stock** - Price on:12/24/2007	$1.82
Employees	4	Stock Exchange	AMEX
Auditor	Hein & Assoc. LLP	Ticker Symbol	FPP
Stk Agt	Computershare Investor Services LLC	Outstanding Shares	8,610,000
Counsel	NA	E.P.S.	$0.09
DUNS No.	14-942-4095	Shareholders	NA

Business: The group's principal activities are to acquire and develop oil and gas properties located in Oklahoma, Texas and Wyoming. The group collects and analyses geological and geophysical data for exploration areas. The group is also into drilling oil and natural gas wells, using independent contractors for drilling operations. As of dec-31-2003, the group operates 59 wells on their own and 279 wells through independent contractors.

Primary SIC and add'l.: 2911 1381 1311

CIK No: 0000316736

Subsidiaries: Bass Petroleum, Inc, Raya Energy Corp.

Officers: Ray D. Reaves/Chmn., CEO, CFO, Pres./$192,000.00

Directors: Ray D. Reaves/Chmn., CEO, CFO, Pres., Debra Funderburg/Dir., Mel Slater/Dir., Dan Robinson/Dir., Roger D. Bryant/Dir., Karl Reimers/Dir.

Owners: Roger D. Bryant, Ray D. Reaves/0.35%, Mel Slater/0.05%, Dan Robinson/0.01%, Karl Reimer, Debbie Funderburg

Financial Data: *Fiscal Year End:* 12/31 *Latest Annual Data:* 12/31/2006

Year	Sales	Net Income
2006	$4,054,000	$1,182,000
2005	$3,979,000	$1,041,000
2004	$3,017,000	$519,000

Curr. Assets:	$2,212,000	Curr. Liab.:	$166,000	P/E Ratio:	20.22
Plant, Equip.:	$8,196,000	Total Liab.:	$2,400,000	Indic. Yr. Divd.:	NA
Total Assets:	$10,477,000	Net Worth:	$8,077,000	Debt/ Equity:	0.1238

Fieldstone Investment Corp

11000 Brokenland Pkwy, Columbia, MD, 21044; *PH:* 1-410-772-7200;
http:// www.fieldstoneinvestment.com; *Email:* investors@fieldstoneinvestment.com

General - Incorporation	MD	Stock- Price on:12/24/2007	$3.88
Employees	1,000	Stock Exchange	NA
Auditor	Deloitte & Touche LLP	Ticker Symbol	NA
Stk Agt	American Stock Transfer & Trust Co.	Outstanding Shares	46,870,000
Counsel	NA	E.P.S.	-$3.2
DUNS No.	NA	Shareholders	NA

Business: The groups principle activity is to provide banking services. The products of the group include residential mortgage loans, conventional loan, va loans, credit score and jumbo loans. The groups operates through four segments namely wholesale, retail, Investment Portfolio and Corporate. The group operates from California, Texas, Illinois, Washington, Florida, Arizona, Colorado, Missouri, Georgia and Nevada.

Primary SIC and add'l.: 6163

CIK No: 0001271831

Subsidiaries: Fieldstone Mortgage Company, Fieldstone Mortgage Investment Corporation, Fieldstone Mortgage Ownership Corp., Fieldstone Servicing Corp.

Officers: Michael J. Sonnenfeld/Dir., CEO, Pres., Nayan V. Kisnadwala/CFO, Exec. VP, Walter P. Buczynski/Exec. VP - Secondary, John C. Kendall/Exec. VP - Investment Portfolio, John C. Camp/CIO, Sr. VP, George D. Colclough/Sr. VP, Dir. - Portfolio Analytics, Timothy B. Ferriter/Sr. VP - Decision Support, Thomas M. Gillen/Sr. VP - Secondary Marketing, Andrew C. Goresh/Sr. VP - Human Resources, Mark C. Krebs/Sr. VP, Treasurer, Teresa A. McDermott/Sr. VP, Controller, Gary K. Uchino/Sr. VP, Chief Credit Officer, James T. Hagan/Exec. VP - Production, J. D. Abts/Sr. VP - Retail, John M. Camarena/41/Sr. VP - Southwest Region *(19 Officers included in Index)*

Directors: Michael J. Sonnenfeld/Dir., CEO, Pres., Thomas D. Eckert/Chmn., David S. Engelman/Dir., Celia V. Martin/Dir., Jonathan E. Michael/Dir., David A. Schoenholz/Dir., Jeffrey R. Springer/Dir.

Owners: John C. Camp, Insiders/3.90%, Thomas D. Eckert, David S. Engelman, Teresa A. McDermott, Michael J. Sonnenfeld/2.50%, Jeffrey R. Springer, David A. Schoenholz, Celia V. Martin, Walter P. Buczynski, Jonathan E. Michael, Massachusetts Mutual Life Insurance Company/9.80%, James T. Hagan, Gary K. Uchino, Nayan V. Kisnadwala

Financial Data: Fiscal Year End:12/31   Latest Annual Data: 12/31/2006

Year	Sales	Net Income
2006	$471,985,000	-$68,385,000
2005	$483,816,000	$99,390,000
2004	$296,426,000	$65,564,000

Curr. Assets:	$197,635,000	Curr. Liab.:	$45,348,000		
Plant, Equip.:	$67,555,000	Total Liab.:	$6,009,456,000	Indic. Yr. Divd.:	$0.200
Total Assets:	$6,390,785,000	Net Worth:	$381,329,000	Debt/ Equity:	17.5053

Fifth Third Bancorp

38 Fountain Sq. Plz., Fifth Third Ctr., Cincinnati, OH, 45263; *PH:* 1-513-579-5300;
Fax: 1-513-534-0629; *http://* www.53.com

General - Incorporation	OH	Stock- Price on:12/24/2007	$42.28
Employees	21,362	Stock Exchange	NDQ
Auditor	Deloitte & Touche LLP	Ticker Symbol	FITB
Stk Agt	Computershare Investor Services LLC	Outstanding Shares	550,080,000
Counsel	NA	E.P.S.	$2.13
DUNS No.	00-699-9403	Shareholders	NA

Business: The groups principle activity is to provide financial services. The groups services include commercial, retail banking and investment advisory services. The group operates through four segments namely retail banking, commercial banking, Investment advisory and electronic payment processing. The group operates from United States.

Primary SIC and add'l.: 6712 8999 6282 6022

CIK No: 0000035527

Subsidiaries: Community Financial Services, Inc., Fifth Third Asset Management, Inc., Fifth Third Auto Funding, LLC, Fifth Third Bank, Fifth Third Bank (Michigan), Fifth Third Bank, National Association, Fifth Third Capital Trust I, Fifth Third Community Development Corporation, Fifth Third Financial Corporation, Fifth Third Foreign Lease Management, LLC, Fifth Third Funding, LLC, Fifth Third Holdings, LLC, Fifth Third Insurance Agency, Inc., Fifth Third International Company, Fifth Third Investment Company 37 Subsidiaries included in the Index

Officers: George A. Schaefer/Chmn., CEO/$6,105,173.00, Kevin T. Kabat/Dir., CEO, Pres./$2,900,253.00, Philip R. McHugh/CEO, Affiliate Pres., Louisville, Raymond J. Webb/CEO, Affiliate Pres., Western Ohio, Gregory L. Kosch/CEO, Affiliate Pres., Eastern Michigan, Robert W. Laclair/CEO, Affiliate Pres., Northwestern Ohio, Brian P. Keenan/CEO, Affiliate Pres., Tampa Bay, Samuel G. Barnes/CEO, Affiliate Pres., Central Kentucky, Dan W. Hogan/CEO, Affiliate Pres., Tennessee, Robert M. Eversole/CEO, Affiliate Pres., Central Ohio, Todd F. Clossin/CEO, Affiliate Pres., Northeastern Ohio, John N. Daniel/CEO, Affiliate Pres., Southern Indiana, Mark Eckhoff/CEO, Affiliate Pres., Northern Michigan, Michelle L. Vandyke/CEO, Affiliate Pres., Western Michigan, John E. Pelizzari/CEO, Affiliate Pres., Central Indiana *(32 Officers included in Index)*

Directors: George A. Schaefer/Chmn., CEO, Kevin T. Kabat/Dir., CEO, Pres., Gordon E. Inman/Affiliate Chmn. - Tennessee, Daniel R. Sadlier/Affiliate Chmn. - Western Ohio, John S. Szuch/Affiliate Chmn. - Northwestern Ohio, Charlie W. Brinkley/Affiliate Chmn. - Central Florida, John Condon/Affiliate Chmn. - Ohio Valley, Lee H. Cooper/Affiliate Chmn. - Southern Indiana, Alton C. Wendzel/Dir. Emeriti, Ulysses L. Bridgeman/Dir., Gary R. Heminger/Dir., Joan R. Herschede/Dir., David E. Reese/Dir. Emeriti, Brian H. Rowe/Dir. Emeriti, Wesley C. Rowles/Dir. Emeriti *(52 Directors included in the Index)*

Owners: Cecil O. Smith, Richard A. Manley, Ellen L. Messinger, Insiders/4.86%, Hugh H. Morrison, L. D. Warlick, William R. Black, Scott J. Ensor, Charles A. James, Michael R. Coltrane, Robert E. James, Jewell D. Hoover, John J. Godbold, Walter H. Jones, John S. Poelker *(22 Owners included in Index)*

Financial Data: Fiscal Year End:12/31   Latest Annual Data: 12/31/2006

Year	Sales	Net Income
2006	$8,472,000,000	$1,188,000,000
2005	$7,495,000,000	$1,549,000,000
2004	$6,616,000,000	$1,525,000,000

Curr. Assets:	$5,712,000,000	Curr. Liab.:	$75,880,000,000	P/E Ratio:	19.85
Plant, Equip.:	$2,232,000,000	Total Liab.:	$90,647,000,000	Indic. Yr. Divd.:	$1.680
Total Assets:	$100,669,000,000	Net Worth:	$10,022,000,000	Debt/ Equity:	1.2872

FIIC Holdings

Formerly: Nicklebys Com Inc
1585 Bethel Rd., First Fl., Columbus, OH, 43220; *PH:* 1-614-451-5030

General - Incorporation	DE	Stock- Price on:12/24/2007	$0.3
Employees	NA	Stock Exchange	OTC
Auditor	Russell Bedford Stefanou Mirchandani	Ticker Symbol	NBYSE
Stk Agt	Corporate Stock Transfer, Inc.	Outstanding Shares	15,370,000
Counsel	Scott Thornock	E.P.S.	-$0.14
DUNS No.	NA	Shareholders	NA

Business: The group's principal activity is to conduct interactive auctions of the group's own inventory of fine art, antiques and collectibles over the Internet. These products include antique maps, Italian oil paintings, contemporary artworks, modern masters, original paintings, antique art, southwest art and art books, jewelry, sculpture and wholesale items. The group operates through its subsidiaries nickleby's auction gallery ltd and art exchange inc.

Primary SIC and add'l.: 5999 5961

CIK No: 0001077720

Subsidiaries: Federated Group Agency, Inc, FIIC, Inc.

Officers: Scott M. Thornock/47/Dir., CEO, Pres., Sec., Treasurer, James W. France/60/Dir., CEO, Pres., James E. Bowser/61/COO, Exec. VP, Wade Estep/60/CFO, Robert V.R. Ostrander/62/Dir., VP, Sec., Hubert T. McDonald/76/VP - Administration, Thomas M. O'Leary/63/VP - Underwriting, Scott Smith/40/VP - Information Technology

Directors: Scott M. Thornock/47/Dir., CEO, Pres., Sec., Treasurer, James W. France/60/Dir., CEO, Pres., Robert V.R. Ostrander/62/Dir., VP, Sec., Kevin Loychik/41/Dir., Brent Peterson/52/Dir., Bruce A. Capra/53/Dir., Paul J. Zueger/69/Dir., Wayne F.J. Yakes/53/Dir., Dean Barrett/63/Dir.

Owners: Insiders/16.03%, Oceanus Value Fund, L.P./6.62%, Robert V. R. Ostrander, Bridge Finance Partners LLC/5.93%, Dean Barrett/7.71%, John P. Schinas Trust/16.35%, Kevin Loychik/2.02%, Accelerate-Financial, Inc./5.95%, James W. France/4.82%, Robert Hernandez/6.25%, James E. Bowser, Corporate Management Solutions, LLC/6.23%

Financial Data: Fiscal Year End:12/31   Latest Annual Data: 12/31/2006

Year	Sales	Net Income
2006	NA	-$3,514,000
2005	NA	-$53,000
2004	$38,000	-$89,000

Curr. Assets:	$5,000	Curr. Liab.:	$2,185,000		
Plant, Equip.:	$8,000	Total Liab.:	$2,185,000	Indic. Yr. Divd.:	NA
Total Assets:	$330,000	Net Worth:	-$1,855,000	Debt/ Equity:	NA

Film & Music Entertainment Inc

25 Noel St., London, W1F 8GX; *PH:* 44-2074346655; *http://* www.fame.uk.com;
Email: info@fame.uk.com

General - Incorporation	NV	Stock- Price on:12/24/2007	$0.03
Employees	NA	Stock Exchange	OTC
Auditor	Kabani & Co, Inc	Ticker Symbol	FLME
Stk Agt	Equity Transfer Services Inc	Outstanding Shares	NA
Counsel	NA	E.P.S.	NA
DUNS No.	NA	Shareholders	NA

Business: The group is trying to revive its principal activity of independent film and television production and distribution. The group has the capability to develop a steady stream of good quality product and an opportunity to achieve some major success. The group believes that it can increase the value of the Company's products for hareholders and filmmaking partners by producing and distributing quality, cost effective films and associated entertainment at a reduced cost. The group intends to develop a film library for ongoing residual revenue.

Primary SIC and add'l.: 7812

CIK No: 0001309152

Officers: Zorana Piggott/Head - Production

Directors: Sam Taylor/Dir., Joint Owner, Stephen Daldry/Member - Advisory Board, Johanna Baldwin/Member - Advisory Board, James Markwick/Member - Advisory Board

Filtering Associates Inc

1495 Belleau Rd., Glendale, CA, 91206; *PH:* 1-818-632-5853

General - Incorporation	NV	Stock- Price on:12/24/2007	NA
Employees	NA	Stock Exchange	OTC
Auditor	Jonathon P. Reuben, CPA	Ticker Symbol	FLTG
Stk Agt	NA	Outstanding Shares	NA
Counsel	NA	E.P.S.	NA
DUNS No.	NA	Shareholders	NA

Business: The groups principal activities include purchasing, developing and reselling direct and indirect interests in the rights to construct FM radio broadcast facilities. The group operates from the United States.

Primary SIC and add'l.: 5734

CIK No: 0001163882

Officers: David Y. Choi/41/Dir., Pres., Sec., Treasurer

Directors: David Y. Choi/41/Dir., Pres., Sec., Treasurer

Owners: David Choi, Edward Wiggins/17.40%, Kevin Frost/41.10%, Insiders

Financial Federal Corp

733 3rd Ave., New York, NY, 10017; *PH:* 1-212-599-8000; *Fax:* 1-212-286-5885;
http:// www.financialfederal.com

General - Incorporation	NV	Stock - Price on:12/24/2007	$29.81
Employees	247	Stock Exchange	NYSE
Auditor	KPMG LLP	Ticker Symbol	FIF
Stk Agt	National City Bank	Outstanding Shares	25,780,000
Counsel	Orrick, Herrington & Sutcliffe LLP	E.P.S.	$1.90
DUNS No.	60-685-9924	Shareholders	NA

Business: The group's principle activity is to provide collateralized lending, financing and leasing services nationwide. These services are provided primarily to the middle-Market enterprises representing diverse industries such as general construction, road and infrastructure construction and repair, road transport, manufacturing and waste disposal. The group lends against, finances and leases a wide range of revenue-producing equipment such as cranes, earthmovers, machine tools, personnel lifts, trailers and trucks. It operates through five service operations centers that perform credit analysis and approval, collection and marketing activities. These offices are located in houston, Texas; lisle (Chicago), Illinois; teaneck (New York metropolitan area), New Jersey; charlotte, North Carolina, irvine (los angeles) and California. The group's total revenue for the year 2007 was 49.60 millions of USD.

Primary SIC and add'l.: 6159 7359

CIK No: 0000854711

Subsidiaries: Financial Federal Credit Inc.

Officers: Paul R. Sinsheimer/61/Chmn., CEO, Pres., John Golio/Exec. VP, Mike Gallagher/Sr. VP, Chief Credit Officer, Steven F. Groth/CFO, Sr. VP, Troy Geisser/Sr. VP, Sec., James Mayes/Exec. VP

Directors: Paul R. Sinsheimer/61/Chmn., CEO, Pres., H. E. Timanus/Dir., Michael C. Palitz/Dir., Michael J. Zimmerman/Dir., Lawrence B. Fisher/Dir., Leopold Swergold/Dir.

Owners: Waddell & Reed Financial, Inc./9.00%, John V. Golio, Barclays Global Investors UK Holdings Ltd/5.90%, Troy H. Geisser, Michael C. Palitz/1.40%, Steven F. Groth, Paul R. Sinsheimer/3.00%, Kayne Anderson Rudnick Investment Management, LLC/8.30%, Goldman Sachs Group Inc/5.20%, H. E. Timanus, Leopold Swergold, Michael J. Zimmerman, M. A. Weatherbie & Co., Inc/5.90%, James H. Mayes, Insiders/8.80% *(16 Owners included in Index)*

Financial Data: Fiscal Year End:07/31   Latest Annual Data: 07/31/2007

Year	Sales		Net Income
2007	$191,254,000		$50,050,000
2006	$162,475,000		$43,619,000
2005	$126,643,000		$36,652,000

Curr. Assets:	$8,143,000	Curr. Liab.:	$325,904,000	P/E Ratio:	16.31
Plant, Equip.:	NA	Total Liab.:	$1,597,965,000	Indic. Yr. Divd.:	$0.600
Total Assets:	$1,988,344,000	Net Worth:	$390,379,000	Debt/ Equity:	3.0165

Financial Industries Corp

6500 River Pl. Blvd., Bldg. 1, Austin, TX, 78730; *PH:* 1-512-404-5000; *Fax:* 1-512-404-5210; *http://* www.ficgroup.com; *Email:* hr@ficgroup.com

General - Incorporation	TX	Stock - Price on:12/24/2007	$6.1
Employees	98	Stock Exchange	OTC
Auditor	PricewaterhouseCoopers LLP	Ticker Symbol	FNIN
Stk Agt	Financial Industries Corp	Outstanding Shares	10,210,000
Counsel	NA	E.P.S.	-$2.35
DUNS No.	04-964-6862	Shareholders	NA

Business: The group's principal activity is to acquire and administer existing portfolios of individual life insurance and annuity products. The group provides insurance products that include annuity, a variety of life insurance products, universal life insurance, life insurance and mortgage protection business through term and universal life. It also provides mortgage protection life insurance to borrowers of financial institution. The products are marketed and sold through investors life distribution system and family life distribution system. The group operates in 49 states, the district of columbia and the u s virgin islands. On 05-Jun-2003, the group acquired total consulting group inc, paragon and jnt group inc.

Primary SIC and add'l.: 6719 6311

CIK No: 0000035733

Subsidiaries: AZERTY de MEXICO, S.A. de C.V., Lagasse, Inc. (f/k/a/ Lagasse Bros., Inc.), United Stationers Financial Services, LLC, United Stationers Hong Kong Limited, United Stationers Supply Co., United Stationers Technology Services LLC, United Worldwide Limited, Uss Receivables Company, Ltd.

Officers: William B. Prouty/CEO, William J. McCarthy/Sr. VP, Chief Actuary, Michael P. Hydanus/COO, Exec. VP/$300,499.00, Vincent L. Kasch/CFO/$199,008.00, Sylvia T. McDaniel/Assoc. Counsel, Corp. Sec.

Directors: Keith R. Long/Chmn., Robert Nikels/Dir., Kenneth S. Shifrin/Dir., Patrick E. Falconio/Dir., Richard H. Gudeman/Dir., John D. Barnett/Dir., Eugene J. Woznicki/Dir., Lonnie Steffen/Dir.

Owners: Eugene J. Woznicki, Lonnie L. Steffen, Vincent L. Kasch, John D. Barnett, Financial & Investment Management Group, Ltd./8.70%, Fidelity Management & Research Company/12.68%, Investors Life Insurance Company of North America/12.26%, RoyF. and Joann Cole Mitte Foundation/9.49%, Wellington Management Company, LLP/5.95%, Robert A. Nikels, Patrick E. Falconio, Keith R. Long/3.73%, Kenneth J. Shifrin, Insiders/4.11%, Richard H. Gudeman *(16 Owners included in Index)*

Financial Data: Fiscal Year End:12/31   Latest Annual Data: 12/31/2006

Year	Sales		Net Income
2006	$72,413,000		-$24,782,000
2005	$106,415,000		-$165,000
2004	$102,612,000		-$14,338,000

Curr. Assets:	$93,303,000	Curr. Liab.:	$6,907,000		
Plant, Equip.:	$550,000	Total Liab.:	$977,630,000	Indic. Yr. Divd.:	NA
Total Assets:	$1,038,311,000	Net Worth:	$60,681,000	Debt/ Equity:	0.1858

Financial Institutions Inc

220 Liberty St., Warsaw, NY, 14569; *PH:* 1-585-786-1100; *Fax:* 1-585-786-5254; *http://* www.fiiwarsaw.com; *Email:* info@fiiwarsaw.com

General - Incorporation	NY	Stock - Price on:12/24/2007	$20.42
Employees	640	Stock Exchange	NDQ
Auditor	KPMG LLP	Ticker Symbol	FISI
Stk Agt	American Stock Transfer & Trust Co.	Outstanding Shares	11,200,000
Counsel	Gibson, Dunn & Crutcher LLP	E.P.S.	$1.22
DUNS No.	NA	Shareholders	NA

Business: The group's principal activities are providing deposits, lending and other financial services. The group serves individuals, small and medium sized businesses and municipalities. The group operates through 48 branches and 69 ATMs in 15 counties in central and western New York state. The categories of loans offered by the group include commercial, real estate, agricultural, consumer and home equity loans. The kinds of deposits accepted consist of demand, savings, money market and certificates of deposits.

Primary SIC and add'l.: 6712 6022

CIK No: 0000862831

Subsidiaries: FISI Statutory Trust, Five Star Bank, The FI Group, Inc.

Owners: Kevin B. Klotzbach, Susan R. Holliday, John E. Benjamin, James H. Wyckoff/3.15%, Erland E. Kailbourne, Insiders/7.55%, John R. Tyler, Ronald A. Miller, James L. Robinson, Canandaigua National Bank& Trust Company/12.18%, Barton P. Dambra, James T. Rudgers, Thomas P. Connolly, Samuel M. Gullo, JPMorgan Chase Bank/5.10% *(19 Owners included in Index)*

Financial Data: Fiscal Year End:12/31   Latest Annual Data: 12/31/2006

Year	Sales		Net Income
2006	$124,984,000		$17,362,000
2005	$133,271,000		$2,166,000
2004	$131,546,000		$12,493,000

Curr. Assets:	$109,772,000	Curr. Liab.:	$1,650,005,000	P/E Ratio:	16.74
Plant, Equip.:	$34,562,000	Total Liab.:	$1,725,164,000	Indic. Yr. Divd.:	$0.440
Total Assets:	$1,907,552,000	Net Worth:	$182,388,000	Debt/ Equity:	0.2973

Financial Media Group Inc

Formerly: Giant Jr Investments Corp
2355 Main St., Ste. 120, Irvine, CA, 92614; *PH:* 1-949-486-3990; *http://* www.giantjr.com

General - Incorporation	NV	Stock - Price on:12/24/2007	$0.7
Employees	30	Stock Exchange	NA
Auditor	Kabani & Co, Inc	Ticker Symbol	NA
Stk Agt	U.S. Stock Transfer Corp	Outstanding Shares	26,770,000
Counsel	NA	E.P.S.	-$0.21
DUNS No.	NA	Shareholders	NA

Business: The group's principle activities are to design, develop, manufacture and market athletic equipment for adults and children under the essxsport(tm) brand name and private label for other suppliers. The group's products include sports equipment for various sports, track and field, baseball, volleyball, football, and soccer. The group assembles most of its essxsport products sold at its manufacturing facilities located in sun valley, California. The group contracts with manufacturers for the production of shoes, team apparel, pole vaults and landing systems, and various other lines, primarily targeting the track and field market, marketing directly to end users via the Internet, catalog sales and trade shows.

Primary SIC and add'l.: 3949

CIK No: 0001107998

Officers: Albert Aimers/45/Chmn., CEO, Javan Khazali/44/Dir., COO, Tyson Le/27/Sec., Manu Ohri/53/CFO

Directors: Albert Aimers/45/Chmn., CEO, Nick Iyer/28/Dir., Javan Khazali/44/Dir., COO, Tom Hemingway/51/Dir., Wendy Borow-Johnson/55/Dir.

Owners: Javan Khazali/4.10%, Albert Aimers/44.70%, Nick Iyer/2.60%, Insiders/53.00%, Tom Hemingway

Financial Data: Fiscal Year End:08/31   Latest Annual Data: 8/31/2006

Year	Sales		Net Income
2006	$6,632,000		-$1,608,000
2005	NA		-$309,000
2004	NA		-$4,903,000

Curr. Assets:	$5,745,000	Curr. Liab.:	$6,545,000		
Plant, Equip.:	$95,000	Total Liab.:	$8,045,000	Indic. Yr. Divd.:	NA
Total Assets:	$5,870,000	Net Worth:	-$2,175,000	Debt/ Equity:	NA

Financial Security Assurance Holdings Ltd

31 W 52nd St., New York, NY, 10019; *PH:* 1-212-826-0100; *Fax:* 1-212-688-3101; *http://* www.fsa.com

General - Incorporation	NY	Stock - Price on:12/24/2007	$21.75
Employees	375	Stock Exchange	NYSE
Auditor	PricewaterhouseCoopers LLP	Ticker Symbol	FSF
Stk Agt	NA	Outstanding Shares	33,280,000
Counsel	NA	E.P.S.	NA
DUNS No.	13-136-4994	Shareholders	NA

Business: The group's principle activity is to provide financial guaranty insurance on asset-backed and municipal obligations. The group operates from United States.

Primary SIC and add'l.: 6399 6719

CIK No: 0000913357

Subsidiaries: Financial Security Assurance (U.K.) Limited, Financial Security Assurance Inc, Financial Security Assurance International Ltd., FSA Asset Management Services LLC, FSA Capital Management Services LLC, FSA Capital Markets Services LLC, FSA Global Funding Limited, FSA Insurance Company, FSA Portfolio Management Inc., Transaction Services Corp.

Officers: Robert P. Cochran/Chmn., CEO, Joseph W. Simon/MD, CFO, Russell B. Brewer/MD, Chief Risk Management Officer, Richard G. Holzinger/MD, Head - Corporate Finance, Sean W. McCarthy/Dir., COO, Pres., Bruce E. Stern/MD, General Counsel, Sec., Dennis H. Kim/MD, Treasurer, Laura A. Bieling/MD, Controller, Scott C. Richbourg/MD - Municipal Finance, Philippe Z. Tromp/MD - Europe, Glenn Tso/MD - Financial Products

Directors: Robert P. Cochran/Chmn., CEO, Xavier De Walque/Dir., James H. Ozanne/Dir., Rembert Von Lowis/Dir., Axel Miller/Dir., Roger K. Taylor/Dir., Michele Colin/Dir., John W. Everets/Dir., Sean W. McCarthy/Dir., COO, Pres., Robert N. Downey/Dir., Jacques Guerber/Dir., Bruno Deletre/46/Dir., George U. Wyper/52/Dir.

Owners: George U. Wyper, Robert P. Cochran, Robert N. Downey, Dexia S.A./99.70%, Insiders

Financial Telecom Ltd (Usa) Inc

1507 Greenland Commercial Ctr., 1258 Yuyan Rd., Shanghai, 200050; *PH:* 8621-6335-4111

General - Incorporation ....NV
Employees ....NA
Auditor .... Kabani & Co.,Inc.
Stk Agt ....NA
Counsel ....NA
DUNS No. ....NA

Stock- Price on:12/24/2007 ....NA
Stock Exchange ....NA
Ticker Symbol ....NA
Outstanding Shares ....NA
E.P.S ....NA
Shareholders ....NA

Business: The group is a private company limited by shares incorporated in Hong Kong in 1983. FTLHK is principally engaged in the business of providing financial information to institutional and retail investors. FTLHK was the first company in Hong Kong to provide real-time financial information services using a wireless network for the dissemination of data. FTLHK generates revenue through the provision of financial information services and the sale of technical analysis software. In return, FTLHK receives re-current commissions.

Primary SIC and add'l.: 7839

CIK No: 0001288195

Subsidiaries: MK Aviation SA

Officers: Klaus Shen/34/CFO

Directors: Jimmy Yiu/49/Dir.

Owners: Yiu Lo Chung, Jack Chen, Chen Guanliang, David Chen

Financial Data: *Fiscal Year End:*12/31 *Latest Annual Data:* 12/31/2006

Year	Sales	Net Income
2006	$3,447,000	$18,000
2005	$3,181,000	$542,000
2004	$288,000	-$688,000

Curr. Assets:	$584,000	**Curr. Liab.:**	$872,000		
Plant, Equip.:	$270,000	**Total Liab.:**	$925,000	**Indic. Yr. Divd.:**	NA
Total Assets:	$854,000	**Net Worth:**	-$71,000	**Debt/ Equity:**	NA

FinancialContent Inc

101 Lincoln Ctr. Dr., Ste. 410, Foster City, CA, 94404; *PH:* 1-650-286-9702; *Fax:* 1-650-745-2677; *http://* www.financialcontent.com; *Email:* info@financialcontent.com

General - Incorporation ....DE
Employees 13
Auditor ....PMB Helin Donovan, LLP
Stk Agt.... American Stock Transfer & Trust Co.
Counsel ....NA
DUNS No. ....NA

Stock- Price on:12/24/2007 ....$0.51
Stock Exchange ....OTC
Ticker Symbol ....FCON
Outstanding Shares 10,980,000
E.P.S ....-$0.04
Shareholders ....NA

Business: The group's principal activity is to offer financial-related services through the world wide Web. It offers a network of branded, technology and community-driven websites focussed on personal finance and investing; search and directory; commerce and games. The other services of the group include providing incubation services, strategic consulting, business services and seed capital to emerging companies that were developing Internet Website or Web-enabling technologies. The principal businesses of the group are financialcontent and streetiq. Financialcontent provides on-line financial data and information, streetiq provides online financial information targeted to women and published 'whisper numbers'.

Primary SIC and add'l.: 7375 8999 8748

CIK No: 0001100360

Subsidiaries: FinancialContent Services, Inc.

Officers: Wing Yu/CEO, Dave Neville/CFO, Pres., George Katsch/VP - Sales, Mark Dierolf/VP - Technology, Brian Deweese/Dir. - Operations

Owners: Jade Special Strategy, LLC/15.92%, Gregg Fidan/7.64%, Times Square International/5.63%, Wilfred Shaw/20.30%, Brian Deweese/1.71%, Dave Neville/2.53%, Wing Yu/5.69%, Mark Dierolf/5.69%, Asia Pacific Ventures/10.25%, CNET Networks, Inc./16.94%, Insiders/51.52%

Financial Data: *Fiscal Year End:*06/30 *Latest Annual Data:* 6/30/2006

Year	Sales	Net Income
2006	$1,833,000	-$455,000
2005	$1,276,000	-$866,000
2004	$985,000	-$1,636,000

Curr. Assets:	$535,000	**Curr. Liab.:**	$2,319,000		
Plant, Equip.:	$74,000	**Total Liab.:**	$2,319,000	**Indic. Yr. Divd.:**	NA
Total Assets:	$856,000	**Net Worth:**	-$1,464,000	**Debt/ Equity:**	NA

Findex.com Inc

620 N 129th, Omaha, NE, 68154; *PH:* 1-402-333-1900; *Fax:* 1-402-778-5763; *http://* www.quickverse.com; *Email:* sales@quickverse.com

General - Incorporation ....NV
Employees 23
Auditor .... Brimmer, Burek & Keelan LLP
Stk Agt.... Continental Stock Transfer & Trust Co
Counsel ....NA
DUNS No. ....NA

Stock- Price on:12/24/2007 ....$0.032
Stock Exchange ....OTC
Ticker Symbol ....FIND
Outstanding Shares 49,790,000
E.P.S $0.031
Shareholders ....NA

Business: The group's principal activities are to develop, publish and distribute christian faith-based software products to individuals and religious organizations including schools, churches and other faith-based ministries. The group provides bible study and related software products and content to the domestic and international markets. The religious software titles are divided among six categories: quickverse/bible study, financial/office management products for churches and other christian faith-based ministries, print & graphic products, pastoral products, children's products and language tutorial products. The products are sold to distributors in Canada, New Zealand, Australia, Malaysia, South Africa, South Korea, Germany, the United Kingdom, Singapore and the United States.

Primary SIC and add'l.: 7372

CIK No: 0001089061

Subsidiaries: Findex.com, Inc., Reagan Holdings, Inc.

Officers: Steven Malone/41/Chmn., CEO, Pres., William Terrill/51/CTO, Brittian Edwards/45/VP - CBA Sales, Licensing, Kirk R. Rowland/Dir., CFO

Directors: Steven Malone/41/Chmn., CEO, Pres., John A. Kuehne/50/Dir., Kirk R. Rowland/Dir., CFO

Owners: William Terrill/2.40%, Insiders/11.30%, Kirk R. Rowland/2.50%, John A. Kuehne/3.40%, Steven Malone/3.00%, Barron Partners, LP/60.10%

Financial Data: *Fiscal Year End:*12/31 *Latest Annual Data:* 12/31/2006

Year	Sales	Net Income
2006	$3,743,000	$654,000
2005	$5,337,000	-$1,581,000
2004	$5,422,000	$964,000

Curr. Assets:	$725,000	**Curr. Liab.:**	$2,431,000	**P/E Ratio:**	1.03
Plant, Equip.:	$87,000	**Total Liab.:**	$2,511,000	**Indic. Yr. Divd.:**	NA
Total Assets:	$3,056,000	**Net Worth:**	$544,000	**Debt/ Equity:**	0.0408

Finisar Corp

1389 Moffett Pk. Dr., Sunnyvale, CA, 94089; *PH:* 1-408-548-1000; *Fax:* 1-408-745-6097; *http://* www.finisar.com; *Email:* sales@finisar.com

General - Incorporation ....DE
Employees 3,688
Auditor .... Ernst & Young LLP
Stk Agt .... American Stock Transfer & Trust Co.
Counsel.... Gray, Cary, Ware & Freidenrich
DUNS No. ....NA

Stock- Price on:12/24/2007 ....$3.95
Stock Exchange ....NDQ
Ticker Symbol ....FNSR
Outstanding Shares 307,740,000
E.P.S ....-$0.02
Shareholders ....NA

Business: The group's principal activities are to design, develop, manufacture and market optical subsystems, components and test and monitoring systems for high-speed data communications. The group operates through two segments: optical subsystems and components and network test and monitoring systems. The optical subsystems and components segment consists primarily of transmitters, receivers and transceivers that convert electrical signals into optical signals. The network test and monitoring systems segment includes products designed to test the reliability and performance of equipment for fibre channel, gigabit ethernet and the infiniband protocols. The group's major customers include brocade, cisco systems, emc, emulex, hewlett-packard company and qlogic. It operates in the United States, China, Malaysia, Singapore and Germany.

Primary SIC and add'l.: 3661 3663 3674

CIK No: 0001094739

Subsidiaries: Finisar Hong Kong Ltd., Finisar Japan Ltd. (KK), Finisar Malaysia Sdn Bhd, Finisar Sales Inc., Finisar Shanghai, Inc., Finisar Singapore Pte. Ltd., InterSAN, Inc.

Officers: Jerry S. Rawls/Chmn., CEO, Pres., Stephen K. Workman/Sr. VP - Finance, CFO, Sec., Anders Olsson/Sr. VP - Engineering, Joseph Young/Sr. VP, GM - Optics Group, David Buse/Sr. VP, GM - Network Tools Group

Directors: Jerry S. Rawls/Chmn., CEO, Pres., Larry D. Mitchell/Dir., Robert N. Stephens/Dir., Frank H. Levinson/Dir., Roger C. Ferguson/Dir., Dominique Trempont/Dir., David Fries/Dir.

Owners: David Buse, T. Rowe Price Associates, Inc./6.00%, Roger C. Ferguson, Insiders/9.10%, Stephen K. Workman, Larry D. Mitchell, Robert N. Stephens, David C. Fries, Jerry S. Rawls/2.30%, Joseph A. Young, Frank H. Levinson/5.80%, FMR Corp./13.20%, Oppenheimer Funds, Inc./6.50%, Dominique Trempont, Anders Olsson

Financial Data: *Fiscal Year End:*04/30 *Latest Annual Data:* 4/30/2006

Year	Sales	Net Income
2006	$364,293,000	-$24,919,000
2005	$280,823,000	-$114,107,000
2004	$185,618,000	-$113,833,000

Curr. Assets:	$224,010,000	**Curr. Liab.:**	$65,338,000		
Plant, Equip.:	$82,225,000	**Total Liab.:**	$328,919,000	**Indic. Yr. Divd.:**	NA
Total Assets:	$505,874,000	**Net Worth:**	$176,955,000	**Debt/ Equity:**	NA

Finish Line Inc

3308 N Mitthoeffer Rd., Indianapolis, IN, 46235; *PH:* 1-317-899-1022; *Fax:* 1-317-899-0237; *http://* www.thefinishline.com; *Email:* generalcounsel@finishline.com

General - Incorporation ....IN
Employees 3,900
Auditor .... Ernst & Young LLP
Stk Agt .... American Stock Transfer & Trust Co.
Counsel ....NA
DUNS No. 04-515-5652

Stock- Price on:12/24/2007 ....$10.15
Stock Exchange ....NDQ
Ticker Symbol ....FINL
Outstanding Shares 47,720,000
E.P.S $0.68
Shareholders ....NA

Business: The group's principal activity is the retail distribution of brand name athletic and lifestyle footwear, activewear and accessories in the United States. The group's retail stores generally provide a large selection of men's, women's, and children's athletic and lifestyle shoes, as well as a broad assortment of activewear and accessories. The group operates its stores in two formats: traditional format concept consisting of 507 stores which are less than 10,000 square feet in size stocked with 600-800 footwear styles and 10,000+ pairs of shoes. The larger format concept consists of 38 large stores, which are more than 10,000 square feet in size stocked with 1,000-1,300 footwear styles and 20,000-30,000+ pairs of shoes. Brand names offered include nike, adidas, reebok, new balance, k-swiss, and 1, timberland, asics, saucony, converse and skechers. As of 16-Apr-2004, the group operated 545 stores in 46 states.

Primary SIC and add'l.: 5699 5661

CIK No: 0000886137

Subsidiaries: Finish Line Transportation Co., Inc, Paiva, Inc., Spikes Holding, LLC, The Finish Line Distribution, Inc, The Finish Line Man Alive, Inc, The Finish Line USA, Inc

Officers: Alan H. Cohen/Chmn., CEO/$977,605.00, George S. Sanders/Exec. VP - Real Estate, Store Development, Gary D. Cohen/Exec. VP, General Counsel, Sec./$612,084.00, Michael L. Marchetti/Exec. VP - Store Operations, Donald E. Courtney/CIO, Exec. VP, Assist. Sec., Steven J. Schneider/COO, Sr. Exec. VP/$759,896.00, David I. Klapper/Dir., Sr. Exec. VP, Michael J. Smith/Sr. VP - Loss Prevention, Kevin G. Flynn/Sr. VP - Marketing, Kevin S. Wampler/Exec. VP, CFO, Assist. Sec./$544,224.00, Larry J. Sablosky/Dir., Sr. Exec. VP, Roger C. Underwood/Sr. VP - Information Systems, Robert A. Edwards/Sr. VP - Distribution, Glenn S. Lyon/Pres./$1,023,662.00, Samuel M. Sato/Exec. VP, Chief Merchandising Officer

Directors: Alan H. Cohen/Chmn., CEO, David I. Klapper/Dir., Sr. Exec. VP, Stephen Goldsmith/Dir., Jeffrey H. Smulyan/Dir., William P. Carmichael/Dir., Larry J. Sablosky/Dir., Sr. Exec. VP, Bill Kirkendall/Dir., Catherine Langham/Dir.

Owners: Larry J. Sablosky, Alan H. Cohen, Insiders/100.00%, Samuel M. Sato, George S. Sanders, Steven J. Schneider, David I. Klapper/35.50%, Insiders/3.32%, William P. Carmichael, SCSF Equities, LLC/5.70%, Larry J. Sablosky/22.30%, Donald E. Courtney, Michael L. Marchetti, First Pacific Advisors, LLC/8.50%, Royce & Associates, LLC/11.15% *(20 Owners included in Index)*

Financial Data: *Fiscal Year End:*02/25 *Latest Annual Data:* 3/3/2007

Year	Sales	Net Income
2007	$1,338,207,000	$32,364,000
2006	$1,306,045,000	$60,533,000
2005	$1,166,767,000	$61,263,000

Curr. Assets:	$380,376,000	***Curr. Liab.:***	$142,886,000	***P/E Ratio:***	19.90
Plant, Equip.:	$247,468,000	***Total Liab.:***	$207,358,000	***Indic. Yr. Divd.:***	$0.100
Total Assets:	$656,636,000	***Net Worth:***	$449,278,000	***Debt/ Equity:***	NA

Finlay Enterprises Inc

529 5th Ave., New York, NY, 10017; ***PH:*** 1-212-808-2800; ***Fax:*** 1-212-557-3848; ***http://*** www.finlayenterprises.com

General - Incorporation	DE	**Stock**- Price on:12/24/2007	$5.32
Employees	2,500	Stock Exchange	NDQ
Auditor	Deloitte & Touche LLP	Ticker Symbol	FNLY
Stk Agt	HSBC Bank U.S.	Outstanding Shares	9,220,000
Counsel	Blank Rome Tenzer Greenblatt	E.P.S	-$0.85
DUNS No.	19-614-6716	Shareholders	NA

Business: The group's principal activities are the retailing of fine jewelry products and operating leased fine jewelry department stores throughout the United States and France. The operations are conducted through its wholly owned subsidiary, finlay fine jewelry corporation. The products include a selection of moderately priced fine jewelry, including necklaces, earrings, bracelets, rings and watches. The group operated 967 locations in 17 host store groups, in 46 states and the district of columbia as of 31-Jul-2004.

Primary SIC and add'l.: 3911 5094 5944

CIK No: 0000878731

Subsidiaries: Carlyle & Co. Jewelers, Carlyle & Co. of Montgomery, eFinlay, Inc., Finlay Fine Jewelry Corporation, Finlay Jewelry, Inc., Finlay Merchandising & Buying, Inc., J.E. Caldwell & Co., Park Promenade, Inc., Societe Nouvelle D'Achat de Bijouterie - S.O.N.A.B., Sonab Holdings, Inc., Sonab International, Inc.

Officers: Arthur E. Reiner/Chmn., CEO, Pres./$2,832,320.00, Thomas M. Murnane/Dir. - Business Advisor, Bonni G. Davis/VP, Sec., General Counsel - Finlay Fine Jewelry, Joseph M. Melvin/COO, Pres./$867,439.00, Bruce E. Zurlnick/Sr. VP, Treasurer, CFO - Finlay Fine Jewelry/$585,165.00, Joan Durkin/VP, Corporate Controller - Finlay Fine Jewelry, Norman S. Matthews/Dir. - Retail Consultant, Leslie A. Philip/Exec. VP, Chief Merchandising Officer - Finlay Fine Jewelry/$904,143.00, Joyce Manning Magrini/Exec. VP - Administration, Finlay Fine Jewelry, Edward J. Stein/Sr. VP, Dir. - Stores, Finlay Fine Jewelry, Louis Lipschitz/Dir., Consultant, James Giantomenico/Sr. VP, CIO - Finlay Fine Jewelry

Directors: Arthur E. Reiner/Chmn., CEO, Pres., Thomas M. Murnane/Dir. - Business Advisor, Ellen R. Levine/Dir., David B. Cornstein/Dir., Rohit M. Desai/Dir., Norman S. Matthews/Dir. - Retail Consultant, Louis Lipschitz/Dir., Consultant, Charles E. McCarthy/Dir.

Owners: Edward J. Stein, David B. Cornstein/4.40%, Bruce E. Zurlnick, Insiders/30.50%, Arthur E. Reiner/5.50%, Barclays Global Investors, N.A./3.90%, Wells Fargo & Company/14.90%, Dimensional Fund Advisors LLC/7.70%, Prides Capital Partners, L.L.C/17.10%, Charles E. McCarthy/17.10%, Rohit M. Desai, Joseph M. Melvin/1.10%, Ellen R. Levine, Thomas M. Murnane, Leslie A. Philip/1.40% *(18 Owners included in Index)*

Financial Data: Fiscal Year End:01/28 ***Latest Annual Data:*** 2/3/2007

Year	***Sales***	***Net Income***
2007	$761,795,000	$4,408,000
2006	$990,134,000	-$55,736,000
2005	$923,606,000	$16,025,000

Curr. Assets:	$465,835,000	***Curr. Liab.:***	$206,362,000		
Plant, Equip.:	$54,993,000	***Total Liab.:***	$415,125,000	***Indic. Yr. Divd.:***	NA
Total Assets:	$537,354,000	***Net Worth:***	$122,229,000	***Debt/ Equity:***	1.7428

Finlay Fine Jewelry Corp

529 Fifth Ave., New York, NY, 10017; ***PH:*** 1-212-808-2800; ***http://*** www.finlayenterprises.com; ***Email:*** humanresources@fnly.com

General - Incorporation	DE	**Stock**- Price on:12/24/2007	NA
Employees	NA	Stock Exchange	NA
Auditor	Deloitte & Touche LLP	Ticker Symbol	NA
Stk Agt	HSBC Bank U.S.	Outstanding Shares	NA
Counsel	NA	E.P.S	NA
DUNS No.	19-657-4909	Shareholders	NA

Business: The group's principal activity is the retail sale of jewelry products in the United States. It operates leased jewelry departments in department stores for retailers such as the may department stores company, federated department stores, belk, and the carson pirie scott division of saks incorporated, marshall field's and dilliard's. The products of the group include necklaces, earrings, bracelets, rings and watches. On 31-Jan-2004, the group had 972 locations in 20 host store groups located in 45 states and the district of columbia. During the year, the group opened 32 departments and closed 71 departments. The group has added marshall field's, parisian, dillard's and bloomingdale's to its host store relationships.

Primary SIC and add'l.: 5944

CIK No: 0000898684

Subsidiaries: Carlyle & Co. Jewelers, Carlyle & Co. of Montgomery, eFinlay, Inc., Finlay Jewelry, Inc., Finlay Merchandising & Buying, Inc., J.E. Caldwell & Co., Park Promenade, Inc., Societe Nouvelle DAchat de Bijouterie - S.O.N.A.B., Sonab Holdings, Inc., Sonab International, Inc.

Officers: Arthur E. Reiner/Chmn., CEO, Pres., Leslie A. Philip/Exec. VP, Chief Merchandising Officer, Joseph M. Melvin/COO, Pres., Bruce E. Zurlnick/CFO, Sr. VP, Treasurer, Bonni G. Davis/VP, Sec., General Counsel, Joan Durkin/VP, Corporate Controller, Edward J. Stein/Sr. VP, Dir. - Stores, Joyce Manning Magrini/Exec. VP - Administration, James Giantomenico/CIO, Sr. VP

Directors: Arthur E. Reiner/Chmn., CEO, Pres., David B. Cornstein/Dir., Rohit M. Desai/Dir., Ellen R. Levine/Dir., Norman S. Matthews/Dir., Thomas M. Murnane/Dir., Louis Lipschitz/Dir., Charles E. McCarthy/Dir.

Owners: Insiders/30.20%, Ellen R. Levine, Edward J. Stein, Prides Capital Partners, L.L.C./17.10%, Dimensional Fund Advisors LLC/7.80%, Barclays Global Investors, N.A./3.90%, Bruce E. Zurlnick, FMR Corp./10.80%, Norman S. Matthews, Louis Lipschitz, Charles McCarthy/17.10%, Thomas M. Murnane, Joseph M. Melvin/1.50%, Rohit M. Desai, Wells Fargo & Company/14.90% *(18 Owners included in Index)*

Finmetal Mining Ltd

Formerly: Gondwana Energy Ltd

666 Burrard St., Ste. 500, Vancouver, BC, V6C 2X8; ***PH:*** 1-604-601-2040

General - Incorporation	NV	**Stock**- Price on:12/24/2007	NA
Employees	NA	Stock Exchange	OTC
Auditor	Vellmer & Chang	Ticker Symbol	FNMM
Stk Agt	Fidelity Transfer Co.	Outstanding Shares	NA
Counsel	NA	E.P.S	NA
DUNS No.	NA	Shareholders	NA

Business: The group's principal activity is to engage in the assessment , acquisition, exploration and development of oil and gas properties that meet the following general investment criteria: onshore shallow targets, adjacent to and/or on trend with previous discoveries, at least twelve months before any cash outlays are required, maintaining 10-15% ownership interest, and with total cash commitments of $250,000 to $300,000 per well.

Primary SIC and add'l.: 1382

CIK No: 0001045929

Officers: Daniel Hunter/48/Chmn., CEO, Kenneth Phillippe/56/Sec., Treasurer, CFO, Principal Accounting Officer, Peter Lofberg/Dir., Pres., Nico Civelli/30/VP - Finance

Directors: Daniel Hunter/48/Chmn., CEO, Peter Lofberg/Dir., Pres., Robert A. Horn/65/Dir.

Owners: Peter Lfberg/3.06%, Kenneth Phillippe/1.38%, Daniel Hunter/4.60%, Insiders/9.04%

Financial Data: Fiscal Year End:12/31 ***Latest Annual Data:*** 12/31/2006

Year	***Sales***	***Net Income***
2006	NA	-$2,507,000
2005	NA	-$41,000

Curr. Assets:	$1,727,000	***Curr. Liab.:***	$150,000		
Plant, Equip.:	$7,000	***Total Liab.:***	$150,000	***Indic. Yr. Divd.:***	NA
Total Assets:	$1,743,000	***Net Worth:***	$1,593,000	***Debt/ Equity:***	NA

Finova Group Inc

8300 N Hayden Rd., Ste. 207, Scottsdale, AZ, 85258; ***PH:*** 1-480-624-4988; ***Fax:*** 1-480-624-4989; ***http://*** www.finova.com

General - Incorporation	DE	**Stock**- Price on:12/24/2007	$0.045
Employees	32	Stock Exchange	OTC
Auditor	Ernst & Young LLP	Ticker Symbol	FNVG
Stk Agt	Computershare Investor Services LLC	Outstanding Shares	122,040,000
Counsel	William Hallinan	E.P.S	-$0.5
DUNS No.	78-598-5441	Shareholders	NA

Business: The group's principal activity is to provide capital and collateralized financing products to commercial enterprises. The group provides a wide range of financial products. These products include commercial equipment financing, term financing for the communications industry, corporate financing, franchise, healthcare, investment alliance, mezzanine capital, resort, specialty real estate and transportation related finances. In addition, the group also provides public-tax-exempt term financing and revolving credit facilities. The group provides these services to various mid-sized businesses.

Primary SIC and add'l.: 7359 6159 6719

CIK No: 0000883701

Subsidiaries: Aircraft 48008/48009 LLC, Aircraft Lease Finance V, Inc., Aquis Communications Group, Inc., Cactus Resort Properties II, Inc., Cactus Resort Properties III, LLC, Cactus Resort Properties, Inc., Commonwealth Avenue Warehouse, LLC, Desert Communications I, LLC, Desert Communications V, LLC, Desert Communications VII, Inc., Desert Healthcare New York, LLC, Desert Healthcare, LLC, Desert Island Capital Corporation, FCC Resort LLC, Fcs 525, Inc. 54 Subsidiaries included in the Index

Officers: Thomas E. Mara/62/Dir., CEO, Phil Donnelly/Sr. VP - General Counsel, Sec., Richard A. Ross/Sr. VP, CFO, Treasurer, Joseph S. Steinberg/64/Dir., Pres., Michele Minetto/VP, Corporate Controller, Lisa Wethor/VP - Tax, Lori Kochert/Executive Sec., James M. Wifler/48/Sr. VP, Transportation Group Mgr.

Directors: Thomas E. Mara/62/Dir., CEO, Ian M. Cumming/67/Chmn., Thomas F. Boland/64/Dir., Robert G. Durham/79/Dir., Gregory R. Morgan/54/Dir., Kenneth R. Smith/65/Dir., Joseph S. Steinberg/64/Dir., Pres.

Owners: Leucadia National Corporation/25.00%, Berkshire Hathaway Inc./25.00%

Financial Data: Fiscal Year End:12/31 ***Latest Annual Data:*** 12/31/2005

Year	***Sales***	***Net Income***
2005	$183,928,000	-$94,447,000
2004	$472,681,000	$132,013,000
2003	$365,661,000	$256,113,000

Curr. Assets:	$279,486,000	***Curr. Liab.:***	$68,870,000		
Plant, Equip.:	$77,356,000	***Total Liab.:***	$1,222,882,000	***Indic. Yr. Divd.:***	NA
Total Assets:	$611,151,000	***Net Worth:***	-$611,731,000	***Debt/ Equity:***	NA

Firearms Training Systems Inc

7340 Mcginnis Ferry Rd. , Suwanee, GA, 30024; ***PH:*** 1-770-813-0180; ***http://*** www.fatsinc.com

General - Incorporation	DE	**Stock**- Price on:12/24/2007	NA
Employees	NA	Stock Exchange	NA
Auditor	PricewaterhouseCoopers LLP	Ticker Symbol	NA
Stk Agt	EquiServe Trust Co N.A	Outstanding Shares	NA
Counsel	NA	E.P.S	NA
DUNS No.	12-094-4665	Shareholders	NA

Business: The group's principal activities are to develop, manufacture and sell supporting arms training simulators and simulated firearms. The products offered include simulators for the military, law enforcement, sport shooting and hunter education. It offers an entire spectrum of products to meet the training needs of its customers, ranging from small handguns to light armored vehicles and missile system weaponry. The products of the group include small arms simulation system and strives, stimulated training weapons, video authoring station, hostile fire return stimulator, military and law enforcement equipments and various training softwares. The customers of the group include military and law enforcement agencies primarily throughout the United States, Canada, Europe, Australia and Asia.

Primary SIC and add'l.: 3484 3699 3483 7372

CIK No: 0001021770

Subsidiaries: F.a.t.s. Singapore Pte, Ltd., FATS Canada, Inc., FATS, Inc., Firearms Training Systems Australia Pty Ltd., Firearms Training Systems Limited, Firearms Training Systems Netherlands, B.V.

Officers: Ron Mohling/CEO, Greg Ton/CFO, David McGrane/COO, Peter Stammers/VP - Customer Support, Training, Fats Corporate, Ed Gerot/ILS Program Mgr. - Fats Corporate, Gina Bartlett/Customer Relations Mgr. - Fats Corporate, Don Durfee/Corporate Service Engineer - Fats Corporate, Steve Shiffman/Dir. - Customer Support, Fats USA, Scott Kruszka/CLS Service Contracts

Mgr. - Fats USA, Eric Perez/Latin America Service Mgr. - Fats USA, Tayeb Ghilane/Customer Support Mgr. - Fats Canada, Rejean Calille/GM - Fats Canada, Chris Jordan/GM - Fats Australia, Greg Cosgrove/Customer Support Mgr. - Fats Australia, Max Clarke/Technical Supervisor, Fats Australia *(20 Officers included in Index)*

Firepond Inc

Formerly: FP Technology Inc
181 Wells Ave., Ste. 100, Newton, MA, 02459; ***PH:*** 1-617-928-6001; ***http://*** www.fptech.com

General - Incorporation	DE	**Stock**- Price on:12/24/2007	$6.75
Employees	48	Stock Exchange	NA
Auditor	Causey Demgen and Moore Inc	Ticker Symbol	NA
Stk Agt	NA	Outstanding Shares	8,160,000
Counsel	NA	E.P.S	NA
DUNS No.	NA	Shareholders	NA

Business: The groups principle activity is to provide the software that automates and simplifies product pricing and configuration for companies. Products of the group include data maintenance tools, shared libraries and application program interfaces. The group markets its products under the tradenames Firepond OnDemand and Interactive Configurator Suite. for September 2005, the group acquired Firepond, Inc. The group operates from the United States, Europe and Japan.

Primary SIC and add'l.: 5084

CIK No: 0001012316

Owners: Benchmark Equity Group, Inc/6.10%, William Santo/7.40%, Jonathan M. Glaser/5.90%, Stephen Peary/6.20%, JP Morgan Securities Inc/9.90%, Douglas Croxall/31.10%, Mark Campion, Mark Tunney, Jaguar Technology Holdings, LLC/23.10%, Cheyne Capital/6.70%, Insiders/46.10%

Financial Data: *Fiscal Year End:*06/30 *Latest Annual Data:* 06/30/2007

Year	Sales	Net Income
2007	$4,625,000	-$23,270,000
2006	$3,762,000	-$4,783,000
2005	NA	-$309,000

Curr. Assets:	$50,682,000	**Curr. Liab.:**	$56,812,000		
Plant, Equip.:	$191,000	**Total Liab.:**	$56,812,000	**Indic. Yr. Divd.:**	NA
Total Assets:	$55,701,000	**Net Worth:**	-$1,111,000	**Debt/ Equity:**	0.1835

First Acceptance Corp

3813 Green Hills Village Dr., Nashville, TN, 37215; ***PH:*** 1-615-327-4888; ***Fax:*** 1-615-844-2835; ***http://*** www.firstacceptancecorp.com

General - Incorporation	DE	**Stock**- Price on:12/24/2007	$10.11
Employees	1,225	Stock Exchange	NYSE
Auditor	KPMG LLP	Ticker Symbol	FAC
Stk Agt	Bank of New York	Outstanding Shares	47,600,000
Counsel	NA	E.P.S	-$0.34
DUNS No.	07-138-8508	Shareholders	NA

Business: The group's principal activity is to invest in notes receivable, primarily first mortgage construction notes and first mortgage acquisition and development notes. It also invests in other secured or guaranteed notes related directly or indirectly to real estate. The group operates solely in the domestic market. On 20-Apr-2004, the group acquired usauto holdings inc.

Primary SIC and add'l.: 6799

CIK No: 0001017907

Subsidiaries: Acceptance Insurance Agency of Illinois, Inc., Acceptance Insurance Agency of Tennessee, Inc., Acceptance Insurance Agency of Texas, Inc., Acceptance Insurance Agency, Inc., Alabama Acceptance Insurance Agency, Inc., First Acceptance Insurance Company of Georgia, Inc., First Acceptance Insurance Company, Inc., First Acceptance Services, Inc., LNC Holdings, Inc., Transit Automobile Club Inc., USAuto Holdings, Inc.

Officers: Stephen J. Harrison/Dir., CEO, Pres., Randy L. Reed/Sr. VP - Sales, Marketing, Thomas M. Harrison/Dir., Exec. VP, Michael J. Bodayle/CFO - Insurance Company Operations, Edward L. Pierce/CFO, Exec. VP, Kevin P. Cohn/Chief Accounting Officer, Corporate Controller, William R. Pentecost/CIO, William R. Wilkins/Sr. VP, Chief Actuary

Directors: Stephen J. Harrison/Dir., CEO, Pres., Gerald J. Ford/Chmn., Thomas M. Harrison/Dir., Exec. VP, William A. Shipp/Dir., Lyndon L. Olson/Dir., Donald J. Edwards/Dir., Harvey B. Cash/Dir., Rhodes Bobbitt/Dir., Tom C. Nichols/Dir.

Owners: William R. Pentecost, Stephen J. Harrison/14.80%, Insiders/66.90%, Thomas M. Harrison/14.80%, William A. Shipp, Lyndon L. Olson, Tom C. Nichols, Rhodes R. Bobbitt, Donald J. Edwards/8.30%, Gerald J. Ford/32.90%, Edward L. Pierce, Harvey B. Cash

Financial Data: *Fiscal Year End:*06/30 *Latest Annual Data:* 06/30/2007

Year	Sales	Net Income
2007	$347,637,000	-$16,670,000
2006	$249,002,000	$28,068,000
2005	$166,795,000	$26,156,000

Curr. Assets:	$98,483,000	**Curr. Liab.:**	$4,914,000	**P/E Ratio:**	22.98
Plant, Equip.:	$3,463,000	**Total Liab.:**	$180,883,000	**Indic. Yr. Divd.:**	NA
Total Assets:	$434,306,000	**Net Worth:**	$253,423,000	**Debt/ Equity:**	0.0937

First Advantage Corp

100 Carillon Pkwy., St. Petersburg, FL, 33716; ***PH:*** 1-727-214-3411; ***Fax:*** 1-727-214-3410; ***http://*** www.fadv.com; ***Email:*** communications@fadv.com

General - Incorporation	DE	**Stock**- Price on:12/24/2007	$23.01
Employees	4,400	Stock Exchange	NDQ
Auditor	PricewaterhouseCoopers LLP	Ticker Symbol	FADV
Stk Agt	Wells Fargo Bank Minnesota N.A	Outstanding Shares	58,970,000
Counsel	White & Case LLP	E.P.S	$1.13
DUNS No.	NA	Shareholders	NA

Business: The groups principle activity is to provide risk mitigation and business solutions and services. The group provide services include employer services, tax consulting services, litigation consulting services, investigative services, supply chain security, transportation services, multifamily services, data recovery services, credit and related services and lead generation services. The groups transportation services include credit reporting and services, driver screening, motor vehicle record services and fleet management. The group operates from United States.

Primary SIC and add'l.: NA

CIK No: 0001210677

Subsidiaries: American Driving, Bar None, Inc., CIG Investments, LLC, CMSI Credit Services, Inc., CreditReportsPlus LLC, First Advantage Background Services Corp, First Advantage Canada, Inc., First Advantage Credco, LLC, First Advantage Enterprise Screening Corporation, First Advantage Government Services, LLC, First Advantage Litigation Consulting, LLC, First Advantage Occupational Health Services Corp, First Advantage Philippines, Inc., First Advantage Public Records, LLC, First Advantage Quest Research (Beijing) Co., Ltd. 47 Subsidiaries included in the Index

Officers: Anand Nallathambi/CEO, Pres., Julie Waters/General Counsel, VP, Akshaya Mehta/Exec. VP - Operations/$1,445,874.00, Thomas Milligan/VP, Treasurer, Isabelle Theisen/Chief Security Officer, Todd Mavis/Exec. VP - Operations, Alan Missen/CIO, John Lamson/CFO, Exec. VP/$1,310,491.00, Anita Tefft/VP - Human Resources, Lisa Steinbach/VP, Controller

Directors: Parker Kennedy/Chmn., Donald Nickelson/Dir., Barry Connelly/Dir., Frank V. McMahon/Dir., D. Van Skilling/Dir., Jill Kanin-Lovers/Dir., Donald Robert/Dir., David Walker/Dir., David J. Chatham/Dir.

Owners: Barry Connelly, FADV Holdings LLC/100.00%, FADV Holdings LLC, David J. Chatham, John Long, Magnetar Capital Partners LP, Parker Kennedy, Lawrence Lenihan, Insiders, Maverick Capital, Ltd., John Lamson, Evan Barnett, David Walker, Donald Robert, Baron Capital Group, Inc. *(21 Owners included in Index)*

Financial Data: *Fiscal Year End:*12/31 *Latest Annual Data:* 12/31/2006

Year	Sales	Net Income
2006	$817,564,000	$66,161,000
2005	$643,749,000	$58,426,000
2004	$266,537,000	$9,933,000

Curr. Assets:	$198,892,000	**Curr. Liab.:**	$136,898,000	**P/E Ratio:**	20.73
Plant, Equip.:	$68,931,000	**Total Liab.:**	$366,569,000	**Indic. Yr. Divd.:**	NA
Total Assets:	$1,089,923,000	**Net Worth:**	$674,941,000	**Debt/ Equity:**	0.2760

First American Corp

1 First American Way, Santa Ana, CA, 92707; ***PH:*** 1-714-800-3000; ***Fax:*** 1-714-800-3135; ***http://*** www.firstam.com; ***Email:*** dwarren@firstam.com

General - Incorporation	CA	**Stock**- Price on:12/24/2007	$51.01
Employees	39,670	Stock Exchange	NYSE
Auditor	PricewaterhouseCoopers LLP	Ticker Symbol	FAF
Stk Agt	First American Trust	Outstanding Shares	96,620,000
Counsel	Mark R Arnesen	E.P.S	$1.72
DUNS No.	00-931-1572	Shareholders	NA

Business: The groups principle activity is to provide business information and related products and services. The group operates from United States.

Primary SIC and add'l.: 6361 6282 6351 6331 6022 7389

CIK No: 0000036047

Subsidiaries: 1031 Corp., 1031 Facilitators, Inc., 1031 Usa, LLC, A+ Escrow Company, Abstracters` Information Service, Inc., Accounting Services, LLC, Accu-Search, Inc., Advanced Collateral Solutions, LLC, Albany County Title, Inc., All American Title Agency, LLC, All New York Title Agency, Corp., Allegiance Title Company, Alliance Home Warranty, Inc., Alliance Title Agency, LLC, Allied Trustee Services, Inc. 527 Subsidiaries included in the Index

Officers: Parker S. Kennedy/60/Chmn., CEO/$4,306,782.00, Anand K. Nallathambi/47/CEO, Pres. - First Advantage Corporation, Frank V. McMahon/48/Vice Chmn., CFO/$2,179,485.00, Barry M. Sando/49/Pres. - Mortgage Information Group/$2,549,947.00, David S. Schulz/Corporate Communications, Jo Etta Bandy/VP - Corporate Communications, Curt A. Caspersen/52/Exec. VP, Dennis J. Gilmore/50/COO/$3,077,560.00, Gary L. Kermott/55/Exec. VP/$3,577,445.00, Kenneth D. Degiorgio/37/Sr. VP, General Counsel, Max O. Valdes/53/VP, Chief Accounting Officer/$1,031,975.00, Craig I. Deroy/56/Pres., Carrie Gaska/Media, Public Relations, Mark Seaton/Investor Relations Officer, John M. Hollenbeck/46/Exec. VP - Technology

Directors: Parker S. Kennedy/60/Chmn., CEO, Frank V. McMahon/48/Vice Chmn., CFO, Donald P. Kennedy/90/Dir., Lewis W. Douglas/84/Dir., George L. Argyros/71/Dir., Herbert B. Tasker/72/Dir., Mary Lee Widener/70/Dir., Virginia M. Ueberroth/68/Dir., Gary J. Beban/62/Dir., David J. Chatham/57/Dir., Frank E. OBryan/75/Dir., William G. Davis/79/Dir., D. Van Skilling/75/Dir., James L. Doti/62/Dir., Roslyn B. Payne/62/Dir.

Owners: Lewis W. Douglas, George L. Argyros/1.10%, Dennis J. Gilmore, James L. Doti, Frank V. McMahon, Fidelity Management Trust Company/9.90%, Herbert B. Tasker, Glenview Capital Management, LLC/5.50%, William G. Davis, Thomas A. Klemens, Virginia M. Ueberroth, Parker S. Kennedy/3.60%, D. P. Kennedy, Max O. Valdes, Roslyn B. Payne *(24 Owners included in Index)*

Financial Data: *Fiscal Year End:*12/31 *Latest Annual Data:* 12/31/2006

Year	Sales	Net Income
2006	$8,499,066,000	$287,676,000
2005	$8,061,758,000	$485,266,000
2004	$6,722,326,000	$349,099,000

Curr. Assets:	$1,962,841,000	**Curr. Liab.:**	$1,871,737,000	**P/E Ratio:**	16.56
Plant, Equip.:	$741,691,000	**Total Liab.:**	$4,510,183,000	**Indic. Yr. Divd.:**	$0.880
Total Assets:	$8,224,285,000	**Net Worth:**	$3,202,053,000	**Debt/ Equity:**	0.3188

First American Scientific Corp

100 Pk. Royal S., Ste. 811, West Vancouver, BC, V2A 1A8; ***PH:*** 1-604-913-9035; ***http://*** www.fasc.net; ***Email:*** help@fasc.net

General - Incorporation	NV	**Stock**- Price on:12/24/2007	$0.02
Employees	NA	Stock Exchange	OTC
Auditor	Williams & Webster, P.S	Ticker Symbol	FASC
Stk Agt	Pacific Stock Transfer Company	Outstanding Shares	NA
Counsel	NA	E.P.S	NA
DUNS No.	25-384-6307	Shareholders	NA

Business: The group's principle activity is to produce extremely fine powders, comparable to talcum powder from a wide variety of recycled and raw materials. The group operates from United States.

Primary SIC and add'l.: 4959

CIK No: 0001002822

Subsidiaries: VMH VideoMovieHouse.com Inc.

Officers: John Brian Nichols/71/Dir., CEO, Pres., Calvin L. Kantonen/57/Chmn., Treasurer, CFO, David Gibson/66/Dir., Sec.

Directors: John Brian Nichols/71/Dir., CEO, Pres., Calvin L. Kantonen/57/Chmn., Treasurer, CFO, David Gibson/66/Dir., Sec.

Owners: Brian Nichols/3.90%, Cal Kantonen/4.90%, Insiders/9.00%, David Gibson/0.20%

Financial Data: *Fiscal Year End:*06/30 *Latest Annual Data:* 06/30/2007

Year	Sales	Net Income
2007	$324,000	-$1,087,000
2006	NA	NA
2005	$852,000	-$430,000

Curr. Assets:	$505,000	**Curr. Liab.:**	$286,000		
Plant, Equip.:	$151,000	**Total Liab.:**	$766,000	**Indic. Yr. Divd.:**	NA
Total Assets:	$1,816,000	**Net Worth:**	$1,049,000	**Debt/ Equity:**	1.3023

First Aviation Services Inc

15 Riverside Ave., Westport, CT, 06880; *PH:* 1-203-291-3300; *Fax:* 1-203-291-3330; *http://* www.favs.com; *Email:* first@firstaviation.com

General - Incorporation DE
Employees 212
Auditor Ernst & Young LLP
Stk Agt American Stock Transfer & Trust Co.
Counsel NA
DUNS No. 88-377-4077

Stock- Price on:12/24/2007 $2.46
Stock Exchange OTC
Ticker Symbol FAVS
Outstanding Shares 7,380,000
E.P.S -$1.38
Shareholders NA

Business: The group's principle activities are to supply aircraft parts and components to the aviation industry. The group acquires parts and components from small, specialized manufacturers as well as major original equipment manufacturers. The group also provides supply chain management services, including third party logistics and inventory management services, to the aerospace industry. In providing these services the group uses its internal resources and warehouse to manage and control its customers' product in a seamless method to the end customer. The group uses regional sales managers, salespersons, outbound telephone salespersons, independent contract representatives, and associated distributors in its sales and marketing efforts. The group's total revenue for the year 2007 was 30.88 millions of USD.

Primary SIC and add'l.: 7389 5088 4581 3724

CIK No: 0001025743

Subsidiaries: Aerospace Products International Inc., Aircraft Parts International Ltd., API (China) Inc., API Asia Pacific Inc.

Officers: Aaron P. Hollander/51/Chmn., CEO/$197,115.00, Robert Costantini/Investor Relations Officer, Dir. - Financial Reporting, Sec./$149,923.00, Bill Reznicek/48/CFO, VP/$26,358.00, Robert Malachowski/Sec./$97,015.00

Directors: Aaron P. Hollander/51/Chmn., CEO, Michael C. Culver/Dir., Robert L. Kirk/79/Dir., Joseph J. Lhota/53/Dir., Stanley J. Hill/66/Dir.

Owners: Robert L. Kirk, Aaron P. Hollander, Michael C. Culver, First Equity Group Inc., The Wynnefield Group, Joseph J. Lhota, Insiders, Stanley J. Hill

Financial Data: *Fiscal Year End:*01/31 *Latest Annual Data:* 1/31/2007

Year	Sales	Net Income
2007	$119,361,000	-$14,494,000
2006	$131,525,000	$1,024,000
2005	$124,249,000	-$2,229,000

Curr. Assets:	$57,140,000	**Curr. Liab.:**	$39,234,000		
Plant, Equip.:	$5,095,000	**Total Liab.:**	$40,190,000	**Indic. Yr. Divd.:**	NA
Total Assets:	$62,235,000	**Net Worth:**	$22,045,000	**Debt/ Equity:**	0.0433

First Bancorp

341 N Main St., Troy, NC, 27371; *PH:* 1-910-576-6171; *Fax:* 1-910-576-1070; *http://* www.firstbancorp.com

General - Incorporation NC
Employees 579
Auditor Elliott Davis, PLLC
Stk Agt Registrar & Transfer Co
Counsel Robinson, Bradshaw & Hinson P.A.
DUNS No. 03-583-3284

Stock- Price on:12/24/2007 $19.41
Stock Exchange NDQ
Ticker Symbol FBNC
Outstanding Shares 14,380,000
E.P.S $1.46
Shareholders NA

Business: The group's principal activity is to provide banking services through two wholly-owned subsidiaries, First Bank Insurance Services Inc and First Montgomery Financial Services Corporation. The services include acceptance of checking, saving, now and money market accounts and provision of loans for business, agriculture, real estate and automobiles. Other services of the group include credit cards, debit cards, letters of credit, safe deposit box rentals, bank money orders, electronic funds transfer services, including wire transfers and automated teller machines. It also provides insured investment and insurance products, including mutual funds, annuities, long-term care insurance, life insurance, and company retirement plans, as well as financial planning services. The operations of the group are carried out through 58 branches in North & South Carolina. During jan-2003 the group acquired Uwharrie Insurance Group and Carolina Community Bancshares Inc.

Primary SIC and add'l.: 6712 6022

CIK No: 0000811589

Subsidiaries: First Bancorp Capital Trust I, First Bancorp Financial, First Bank Insurance Services, Inc. (First Bank Insurance), First Montgomery, First Troy Realty Corporation (First Troy)

Officers: Jerry L. Ocheltree/Dir., CEO, Pres./$419,550.00, John F. Burns/Dir., Exec. VP, Kevin Fish/Contact - Angier Branch, Kim O'Quinn/Contact - Apex Branch, Steve Foley/Contact - Archdale Branch, Brooks Hedrick/Contact - Asheboro Branch, Lauren Rivers/Contact - Public Relations, Timothy S. Maples/Sr. VP - First Bank, Frederick H. Taylor/Dir. - Troy, NC, Chuck Boyer/Contact - Aberdeen Branch, Angela Krol/Contact - Albemarle Eastgate Branch, Richard Clayton/Contact - Albemarle Highway 52 Branch, Dean Martin/Contact - Albemarle Highway 52 Branch, Kristy Patton/Contact - Anderson Creek Branch, Susie Jones/Contact - Lumberton Branch *(94 Officers included in Index)*

Directors: Jerry L. Ocheltree/Dir., CEO, Pres., David L. Burns/Chmn., David H. Bruton/Dir., Jack D. Briggs/Dir., Walton R. Brown/Dir., Exec. VP, John F. Burns/Dir., Exec. VP, Mary Clara Capel/Dir., Goldie H. Wallace-Gainey/Dir., James H. Garner/Dir., James G. Hudson/Dir., George R. Perkins/Dir., Thomas F. Phillips/Dir., Edward T. Taws/Dir., Frederick L. Taylor/Dir., Virginia C. Thomasson/Dir. *(23 Directors included in Index)*

Owners: Virginia C. Thomasson/0.18%, Lee C. McLaurin/0.12%, Anna G. Hollers/0.67%, Eric P. Credle/0.20%, David L. Burns/0.54%, Dennis A. Wicker/0.14%, John F. Burns/0.56%, Thomas F. Phillips/0.59%, James H. Garner/0.37%, Goldie H. Wallace/1.75%, Jack D. Briggs/0.79%, Mary Clara Capel/0.05%, Jerry L. Ocheltree/0.11%, David H. Bruton, Timothy S. Maples/0.17% *(25 Owners included in Index)*

Financial Data: *Fiscal Year End:*12/31 *Latest Annual Data:* 12/31/2006

Year	Sales	Net Income
2006	$145,616,000	$19,302,000
2005	$116,696,000	$16,090,000
2004	$97,457,000	$20,114,000

Curr. Assets:	$158,826,000	**Curr. Liab.:**	$1,744,604,000	**P/E Ratio:**	14.17
Plant, Equip.:	$43,540,000	**Total Liab.:**	$1,973,919,000	**Indic. Yr. Divd.:**	$0.760
Total Assets:	$2,136,624,000	**Net Worth:**	$162,705,000	**Debt/ Equity:**	1.2907

First BanCorp (Puerto Rico)

1519 Ponce de Len Ave., Stop 23, Santurce, PR, 00908; *PH:* 1-787-729-8200; *Fax:* 1-787-729-8205; *http://* www.firstbancorp.com

General - Incorporation PR
Employees NA
Auditor PricewaterhouseCoopers LLP
Stk Agt Bank of New York
Counsel Fiddler, Gonzalez & Rodriguez
DUNS No. NA

Stock- Price on:12/24/2007 $12.41
Stock Exchange NYSE
Ticker Symbol FBP
Outstanding Shares NA
E.P.S $0.51
Shareholders NA

Business: The group's principal activity is to provide a wide range of banking services through its main office located in san juan, Puerto Rico. The group provides commercial loans, consumer loans, mortgage loans and investment securities. Commercial loan primarily includes commercial real estate loans and construction loans. Consumer loan consists of auto loans, personal loans and credit card loans. It has forty-two full-service branches located in Puerto Rico, twelve branches in the United States virgin islands of st. Thomas and st. Croix and a wide network of ATM all over the world. In addition, the group has eleven loan originating offices focusing on mortgage loans and two focusing on auto loans. As on 30-Jun-2004, the group has 55 full service branches.

Primary SIC and add'l.: 6712 6022

CIK No: 0001057706

Subsidiaries: IntranetSolutions International Limited, Stellent AB, Stellent Asia Pty. Limited, Stellent B.V., Stellent Canada Ltd, Stellent Chicago Sales, Inc, Stellent Chicago, Inc, Stellent Colorado Springs, Inc, Stellent GmbH, Stellent Holding B.V. Company, Stellent Iberica, S.L., Stellent Information Systems Company Limited, Stellent Japan K.K, Stellent Limited, Stellent S.A.R.L 19 Subsidiaries included in the Index

Officers: Luis M. Beauchamp/65/Chmn., CEO, Pres./$3,525,216.00, Emilio Martino/58/Exec. VP, Chief Lending Officer, Miguel A. Babilonia/43/Sr. VP, Chief Credit Risk Officer, Pedro Romero/35/Chief Accounting Officer, Sr. VP, Aurelio Aleman/49/Dir., COO, Sr. Exec. VP/$2,072,885.00, Fernando Scherrer/40/CFO, Exec. VP/$803,149.00, Dacio A. Pasarell/59/Exec. VP, Exec. - Banking Operations, Lawrence Odell/60/Dir., Exec. VP, General Counsel, Sec./$1,499,805.00, Victor M. Barreras-Pellegrini/40/Sr. VP, Treasurer, Nayda Rivera-Batista/35/Sr. VP, Chief Risk Officer, Assist. Sec., Randolfo Rivera/54/Exec. VP, Exec. - Wholesale Banking/$1,325,787.00, Cassan A. Pancham/48/Exec. VP, Exec. - Eastern Caribbean Region

Directors: Luis M. Beauchamp/65/Chmn., CEO, Pres., Fernando Rodriguez-Amaro/60/Dir., Jorge L. Diaz/53/Dir., Frank Kolodziej/65/Dir., Hector M. Nevares/57/Dir., Jose F. Rodriguez/58/Dir., Jose Menendez-Cortada/60/Dir., Jose Luis Ferrer-Canals/49/Dir., Jose Teixidor/54/Dir., Aurelio Aleman/49/Dir., COO, Sr. Exec. VP, Sharee Ann Umpierre-Catinchi/49/Dir., Lawrence Odell/60/Dir., Exec. VP, General Counsel, Sec.

Owners: Aurelio Alemn, Victor Barreras, Sharee Ann Umpierre-Catinchi, Jorge L. Daz, Fernando Rodrguez-Amaro, Pedro Romero, Luis M. Beauchamp/2.41%, Lawrence Odell, The Bank of Nova Scotia/10.00%, FMR Corp./8.69%, Insiders/12.41%, Dacio Pasarell, Frank Kolodziej/2.90%, Miguel Babilonia, Jos Teixidor *(25 Owners included in Index)*

Financial Data: *Fiscal Year End:*12/31 *Latest Annual Data:* 12/31/2006

Year	Sales	Net Income
2006	$1,338,983,000	$84,634,000
2005	$1,130,667,000	$114,604,000
2004	$749,958,000	$177,325,000

Curr. Assets:	$681,466,000	**Curr. Liab.:**	$15,746,156,000		
Plant, Equip.:	$158,531,000	**Total Liab.:**	$16,160,703,000	**Indic. Yr. Divd.:**	$0.280
Total Assets:	$17,390,256,000	**Net Worth:**	$1,229,553,000	**Debt/ Equity:**	0.8326

First Bancorp of Indiana Inc

5001 Davis Lant Dr., Evansville, IN, 47715; *PH:* 1-812-492-8100; *http://* www.firstfedevansville.com

General - Incorporation IN
Employees 75
Auditor BKD LLP
Stk Agt Registrar & Transfer Co
Counsel Johnson, Carroll & Griffith
DUNS No. NA

Stock- Price on:12/24/2007 $16.1
Stock Exchange NDQ
Ticker Symbol FBEI
Outstanding Shares 1,840,000
E.P.S $0.30
Shareholders NA

Business: The group is a federally chartered savings bank operating through its wholly owned subsidiary, first federal savings bank. The bank operates through 7 offices in evansville and Indiana. The loans provided by the bank include residential real estate, construction, commercial mortgage, consumer line of credit, saving loan account, commercial and automobiles loan. The deposits accepted by the bank include demand, savings, now checking accounts, money market deposit accounts and certificate of deposits.

Primary SIC and add'l.: 6035 6712

CIK No: 0001074543

Subsidiaries: FFSB Financial Corporation, FFSL Service Corporation, Inc., First Federal Savings Bank

Officers: Michael H. Head/Dir., CEO, Pres., Kirby W. King/COO, Exec. VP, Jeffrey Smith/Exec. VP, CFO, Treasurer, Ruthanne Orth/VP, Corp. Sec., Monica Stinchfield/Sr. VP - Mortgage Lending, Richard S. Witte/Sr. VP - Information Technology, Burt King/Sr. VP - Commercial Lending, Dale Holt/Sr. VP - Consumer Lending

Directors: Michael H. Head/Dir., CEO, Pres., Harold Duncan/Chmn., Jerome A. Ziemer/Dir., Timothy A. Flesch/Dir., David E. Gunn/Dir., Daniel L. Schenk/Dir., Harvey E. Seaman/Dir., Gregory L. Haag/Dir.

Owners: First Federal Savings Bank/8.57%, David E. Gunn, Daniel L. Schenk, Kirby W. King/1.95%, George J. Smith, Gregory L. Haag/1.67%, Harold Duncan/3.06%, Timothy A. Flesch, Michael H. Head/6.08%, Jerome A. Ziemer/1.68%, Insiders/18.95%

Financial Data: *Fiscal Year End:*06/30 *Latest Annual Data:* 06/30/2007

Year	Sales	Net Income
2007	$21,303,000	$518,000
2006	$16,880,000	$1,340,000
2005	$15,124,000	$1,532,000

Curr. Assets:	$13,262,000	Curr. Liab.:	$191,844,000	P/E Ratio:	53.67
Plant, Equip.:	$8,543,000	Total Liab.:	$266,345,000	Indic. Yr. Divd.:	$0.600
Total Assets:	$294,551,000	Net Worth:	$28,206,000	Debt/ Equity:	2.2581

First Bancshares Inc/MO

142 E 1st St., Mountain Grove, MO, 65711; *PH:* 1-417-926-5151; *Fax:* 1-417-926-4362; *http://* www.firsthomesavingsbank.com; *Email:* tabbyh@firsthomesavingsbank.com

General - Incorporation	MO	Stock - Price on:12/24/2007	$16.37
Employees	100	Stock Exchange	NDQ
Auditor	Mcgladrey & Pullen, LLP	Ticker Symbol	FBSI
Stk Agt	Registrar & Transfer Co	Outstanding Shares	1,550,000
Counsel	Harold F. Glass	E.P.S.	$0.275
DUNS No.	04-012-5510	Shareholders	NA

Business: The group's principal activities are to provide community banking services to the customers. The group's operations are conducted primarily through its subsidiary first home savings bank. The group's lending activities include one-to-four family residential mortgage loans, multi-family residential, consumer and commercial mortgage loans, including home equity loans. The group offers a variety of deposits consisting of now accounts, money market accounts, regular savings accounts, certificates of deposit and retirement savings plans. The savings bank conducts business in mountain grove and nine full service branch facilities in marshfield, ava, gainesville, sparta, theodosia, crane, galena, kissee mills and rockaway beach, Missouri. The other subsidiaries of the group are south central Missouri title, inc. Which provides real estate closing services and sells title insurance.

Primary SIC and add'l.: 6712 6035

CIK No: 0000912967

Subsidiaries: First Home Savings Bank

Officers: R. J. Breidenthal/Advisory Dir. - First Home Savings Bank, Ronald J. Walters/58/CFO, Sr. VP, Treasurer, Dale W. Keenan/45/Exec. VP - Sr. Lender, Adrian C. Rushing/39/COO

Directors: Thomas M. Sutherland/Chmn. - First Home Savings Bank, Billy E. Hixon/Dir., Harold F. Glass/Dir. - First Home Savings Bank, John G. Moody/Dir., Daniel P. Katzfey/Dir. - First Home Savings Bank, Mitch D. Ashlock/Dir. - First Home Savings Bank

Owners: Tontine Financial Partners, L.P./7.01%, Thomas M. Sutherland/1.64%, Susan J. Uchtman/0.99%, First Home Savings Bank Employee/9.33%, Harold F. Glass/2.94%, James W. Duncan/0.50%, Insiders/8.20%, John G. Moody/0.57%, James F. Moore/1.11%, Stephen H. Romines/0.29%

Financial Data: Fiscal Year End:06/30 Latest Annual Data: 06/30/2007

Year	Sales	Net Income
2007	$16,299,000	$272,000
2006	$15,195,000	-$173,000
2005	$16,218,000	$1,317,000
Curr. Assets:	$28,795,000	Curr. Liab.:	$202,104,000	P/E Ratio:	90.94
Plant, Equip.:	$8,525,000	Total Liab.:	$202,104,000	Indic. Yr. Divd.:	$0.160
Total Assets:	$228,395,000	Net Worth:	$26,291,000	Debt/ Equity:	NA

First Bancshares Inc/MS

6480 US Hwy. 98 W, Hattiesburg, MS, 39402; *PH:* 1-601-268-8998; *Fax:* 1-601-268-8904; *http://* www.thefirstbank.com

General - Incorporation	MS	Stock - Price on:12/24/2007	$24.94
Employees	150	Stock Exchange	NDQ
Auditor	T. E. Lott & Co	Ticker Symbol	FBMS
Stk Agt	Registrar & Transfer Co	Outstanding Shares	2,980,000
Counsel	Nelson Mullins Riley & Scarborough	E.P.S.	$1.32
DUNS No.	95-767-1340	Shareholders	NA

Business: The group's principal activity is to provide general, commercial and retail banking business through the first national bank of south Mississippi and the first national bank of the pine belt. The deposit services offered by the group include checking accounts, now accounts, savings accounts and other time deposits. Commercial loans include both secured and unsecured loans for working capital loans secured by inventory and accounts, business expansion and purchase of equipment and machinery. Consumer loans include equity lines of credit and secured and unsecured loans for financing automobiles, home improvements, education, and personal investments. The banks also make real estate construction and acquisition loans. In addition, the group offers certain retirement account services, such as individual retirement accounts.

Primary SIC and add'l.: 6712 6021

CIK No: 0000947559

Subsidiaries: First National Bank of South Mississippi, First National Bank of the Pine Belt

Officers: David E. Johnson/CEO, Chmn. - First, A National Banking Association, Dottie Benz/Mortgage Originator, The First A National Banking Association, Bay St. Louis, Eric Waldron/Sr. VP - First, A National Banking Association, Hattiesburg Main, Deedee Lowery/Exec. VP, CFO - First, A National Banking Association/$125,248.70, Becky Smith/Branch Mgr. - First A National Banking Association, Purvis, Tina Barnes/Retail Lending Officer - First A National Banking Association, Purvis, Ken Kennedy/VP - First A National Banking Association, Laurel, Lori Freeman/Customer Service, Loan Representative, The First A National Banking Association, Laurel, Chandra Kidd/VP, Corp. Sec. - First, A National Banking Association, John Shappley/Pres. - Northern Region, First, A National Banking Association, Hattiesburg Main, Trish King/VP - First A National Banking Association, Chris Hester/Sr. VP - First A National Banking Association, Lincon Road, Lori Porche/Customer Service Representative, The First, A National Banking Association, Hattiesburg Main, Jeff Lacher/Branch Mgr. - First A National Banking Association, University, Sharon Carpenter/Customer Service Representative, The First A National Banking Association, Pascagoula *(79 Officers included in Index)*

Directors: Michael W. Chancellor/40/Dir.

Owners: Ray M. Cole, Charles R. Lightsey/1.05%, Ricky E. Gibson/1.74%, Ted E. Parker/1.28%, Insiders/27.83%, Donna T. Lowery, David W. Bomboy/2.32%, A. L. Smith/1.00%, David E. Johnson/5.05%, Andrew D. Stetelman/1.02%, Douglas J. Seidenburg/1.74%, Perry E. Parker/3.58%, Fred A. McMurry/1.71%, Michael W. Chancellor

Financial Data: Fiscal Year End:12/31 Latest Annual Data: 12/31/2006

Year	Sales	Net Income
2006	$26,039,000	$3,315,000
2005	$17,440,000	$1,909,000
2004	$13,063,000	$1,243,000
Curr. Assets:	$22,092,000	Curr. Liab.:	$352,743,000	P/E Ratio:	21.14
Plant, Equip.:	$9,953,000	Total Liab.:	$385,404,000	Indic. Yr. Divd.:	$0.300
Total Assets:	$417,769,000	Net Worth:	$32,365,000	Debt/ Equity:	0.7299

First Banctrust Corp

101 S Central Ave., Paris, IL, 61944; *PH:* 1-217-465-6381; *Fax:* 1-217-465-0201; *http://* www.firstbanktrust.com

General - Incorporation	DE	Stock - Price on:12/24/2007	$11.65
Employees	90	Stock Exchange	NDQ
Auditor	BKD LLP	Ticker Symbol	FBTC
Stk Agt	Illinois Stock Transfer Co	Outstanding Shares	2,290,000
Counsel	Elias, Matz, Tierman & Herrick	E.P.S.	$0.46
DUNS No.	NA	Shareholders	NA

Business: The group's principal activity is to provide a full range of banking and mortgage services to individual and corporate customers in east central Illinois. The operations of the group are conducted through its subsidiary, first bank and trust savings bank. The group generates commercial, mortgage and consumer loans and accepts deposits from customers located primarily in edgar and clark counties and surrounding communities. The loans offered are generally secured by specific items of collateral including real property, consumer assets and business assets.

Primary SIC and add'l.: 6035 6712

CIK No: 0001129847

Subsidiaries: ECS Service Corporation, FBTC Statutory Trust I

Officers: Larry W. Strohm/Contact/$105,697.00, Sarah Aguirre/Corp. Sec., Phyllis Webster/Contact, Diane Sullivan/Contact, Madonna Imel/Contact, Deb Morgan/Contact

Owners: John P. Graham/0.13%, James D. Motley/1.03%, David W. Dick/2.36%, John W. Welborn/1.72%, Joseph R. Schroeder/2.12%, Insiders/19.90%, David F. Sullivan/1.17%, Terry T. Hutchison/1.53%, Terry J. Howard/4.47%, Vick N. Bowyer/1.05%, Larry W. Strohm/2.36%, Ellen M. Litteral/1.67%, Jack R. Franklin/2.02%

Financial Data: Fiscal Year End:12/31 Latest Annual Data: 12/31/2006

Year	Sales	Net Income
2006	$19,754,000	$1,116,000
2005	$16,336,000	$1,248,000
2004	$15,243,000	$1,228,000
Curr. Assets:	$31,710,000	Curr. Liab.:	$276,332,000	P/E Ratio:	25.33
Plant, Equip.:	$11,383,000	Total Liab.:	$284,401,000	Indic. Yr. Divd.:	$0.240
Total Assets:	$311,058,000	Net Worth:	$26,656,000	Debt/ Equity:	NA

First Bank Of DE

1000 Rocky Run Pkwy., Wilmington, DE, 19803; *PH:* 1-302-529-5984; *Fax:* 1-302-529-5987; *http://* www.fbdel.com; *Email:* invrelations@fbdel.com

General - Incorporation		Stock - Price on:12/24/2007	NA
Employees	NA	Stock Exchange	OTC
Auditor	NA	Ticker Symbol	FBOD
Stk Agt	Registrar & Transfer Co	Outstanding Shares	11,360,000
Counsel	NA	E.P.S.	NA
DUNS No.	NA	Shareholders	NA

Business: The groups principal activity is to provide banking services. The services of the group include personal banking, business banking and customer services. The group operates from Delaware in the United States.

Primary SIC and add'l.: 6712

CIK No:

First Banking Center Inc

400 Milwaukee Ave., Burlington, WI, 53105; *PH:* 1-262-763-3581; *Fax:* 1-262-763-5314; *http://* www.firstbankingctr.com

General - Incorporation		Stock - Price on:12/24/2007	$83
Employees	NA	Stock Exchange	OTC
Auditor	NA	Ticker Symbol	FBCI
Stk Agt	Registrar & Transfer Co	Outstanding Shares	NA
Counsel	NA	E.P.S.	NA
DUNS No.	NA	Shareholders	NA

Business: The groups principal activity is to provide banking services. The services of the group include providing loans, credit and deposit, brokerage services, investment and trust services, and online banking. The group operates from the United States.

Primary SIC and add'l.: 6022 6712

CIK No: 0000356858

Officers: Brantly Chappell/Dir., CEO, John Smith/Dir., Pres., Jim Schuster/Dir., CFO

Directors: Brantly Chappell/Dir., CEO, Richard Torhorst/Dir., Frank Cannella/Dir., James Scherrer/Dir., John Smith/Dir., Pres., Jim Schuster/Dir., CFO, David Boilini/Dir., John M. Ernster/Dir., Keith Blumer/Dir., Daniel T. Jacobson/Dir., Thomas Laken/Dir., Robert Fait/Dir., Charles Wellington/Dir., Thomas Beere/Dir.

First Banks Inc

Formerly: First Banks Inc
135 N Meramec, St Louis, MO, 63105; *PH:* 1-314-854-4600; *http://* www.firstbanks.com

General - Incorporation	MO	Stock - Price on:12/24/2007	NA
Employees	NA	Stock Exchange	OTC
Auditor	KPMG LLP	Ticker Symbol	FRBA
Stk Agt	Computershare Investor Services LLC	Outstanding Shares	NA
Counsel	NA	E.P.S.	NA
DUNS No.	07-198-7895	Shareholders	NA

Business: The group's principal activity is to provide commercial and personal banking services. It provides commercial and personal deposit products including demand, savings, money market and time deposit accounts. The group originates real estate, home equity, installment loans, commercial, financial and agricultural loans. Other financial services of the group include mortgage banking, credit and debit cards, brokerage services, credit related insurance, automatic teller machines, telephone banking, safe deposit boxes, trust and private banking services and cash management services. The group operates through 147 banking offices located in eastern Missouri and Illinois, Texas and California. On 30-Jul-2004, the group acquired continental mortgage corporation and continental community bank and trust company (ccb).

Primary SIC and add'l.: 6712 6021

CIK No: 0000710507

Subsidiaries: Bank of San Francisco Realty Investors, Inc., First Bank, First Land Trustee Corp., Missouri Valley Partners, Inc., Small Business Loan Source Funding Corporation, Small Business Loan Source LLC, The San Francisco Company

Officers: Terrance M. McCarthy/Dir., CEO, Pres., Steven F. Schepman/Dir., Exec. VP, Dir. - Corporate Development, Business Segments, Russell L. Goldammer/CIO, Exec. VP, Daniel W. Jasper/Exec. VP, Chief Credit Officer, John G. Kitson/Sr. VP, Chief Human Resources Officer, Christopher F. McLaughlin/Exec. VP, Dir. - Retail, Mary P. Sherrill/Exec. VP, Dir. - Operations, Mark T. Turkcan/Pres. - Mortgage Banking, Lisa K. Vansickle/Sr. VP, CFO, Peter D. Wimmer/Sr. VP, General Counsel, Corp. Sec., Robert S. Holmes/Exec. VP, Laura Schumacher/Sr. VP, Dir. - Risk Management, Audit

Directors: Terrance M. McCarthy/Dir., CEO, Pres., James F. Dierberg/Chmn., Gordon A. Gundaker/Dir., Steven F. Schepman/Dir., Exec. VP, Dir. - Corporate Development, Business Segments, David L. Steward/Dir., Douglas H. Yaeger/Dir.

Owners: Michael J Dierberg Family Trust/17.99%, Michael J Dierberg Irrevocable Trust/14.62%, James F Dierberg II Family Trust/32.61%, Ellen C Dierberg Family Trust/32.61%, First Trust/2.18%

First Busey Corp

201 W Main St., Urbana, IL, 61801; **PH:** 1-217-384-4513; *http://* www.busey.com

General - Incorporation	NV	Stock- Price on:12/24/2007	$20.41
Employees	640	Stock Exchange	NDQ
Auditor	McGladrey & Pullen LLP	Ticker Symbol	BUSE
Stk Agt	First Busey Corp	Outstanding Shares	21,460,000
Counsel	NA	E.P.S.	NA
DUNS No.	03-532-0720	Shareholders	NA

Business: The group's principal activity is to provide a range of banking services, including security broker or dealer services, investment management and fiduciary services. It is a financial holding company, which conducts its operation through its subsidiaries, busey bank and busey bank Florida. The banking services include commercial, financial, agricultural and real estate loans. The retail banking services include accepting customary types of demand and savings deposits, making individual, consumer, installment, first mortgage and second mortgage loans, offering money transfers, safe deposit services, ira, keogh and other fiduciary services, automated banking and automated fund transfers. The non-banking services provide a full range of trust and investment management services, investment advice and offers a variety of insurance products.

Primary SIC and add'l.: 6712 6022

CIK No: 0000314489

Subsidiaries: Busey Bank, Busey Bank, N.A., Busey Capital Management, Busey Insurance Services, Inc., Busey Investment Group, Inc., First Busey Capital Trust I, First Busey Resources, Inc., First Busey Securities, Inc., First Busey Statutory Trust II, First Busey Statutory Trust III, First Busey Trust & Investment Co., Tarpon Coast Financial Services, Inc.

Officers: Lee H. Oneill/CEO, Pres. - Busey Bank/$277,990.00, A. Van Dukeman/Dir., CEO, Pres., David D. Mills/Exec. VP, Chmn. - Busey Bank, NA, Barbara J. Harrington/CFO, Exec. VP, David B. White/COO, Exec. VP, Susan E. Abbott/Exec. VP, Chief Retail Officer, Thomas M. Good/Exec. VP, Chief Risk Officer

Directors: A. Van Dukeman/Dir., CEO, Pres., Gregory B. Lykins/Vice Chmn., Douglas C. Mills/Chmn., Edwin A. Scharlau/Vice Chmn. - First Busey Corp, David L. Ikenberry/Dir., Joseph M. Ambrose/Dir., Arthur R. Wyatt/Dir., V. B. Leister/Dir., Phillips E. Knox/Dir., Joseph Edward O'Brien/Dir., David J. Downey/Dir., Paul David Kuhl/Dir., August C. Meyer/Dir., George T. Shapland/Dir.

Owners: V. B. Leister, Douglas C. Mills/13.00%, David J. Downey/1.20%, Barbara J. Harrington, Lee H. ONeill, Insiders/28.90%, David B. White, David L. Ikenberry, Van A. Dukeman, August C. Meyer, Phillips E. Knox, David D. Mills/1.20%, George T. Shapland/1.60%, Gregory B. Lykins/9.10%, Joseph M. Ambrose

Financial Data: Fiscal Year End:12/31 **Latest Annual Data:** 12/31/2006

Year	Sales	Net Income
2006	$174,827,000	$28,888,000
2005	$139,895,000	$26,934,000
2004	$109,709,000	$22,454,000

Curr. Assets:	$63,316,000	**Curr. Liab.:**	$2,094,609,000		
Plant, Equip.:	$41,001,000	**Total Liab.:**	$2,324,240,000	**Indic. Yr. Divd.:**	$0.720
Total Assets:	$2,509,514,000	**Net Worth:**	$185,274,000	**Debt/ Equity:**	1.0855

First Business Bank N.A

Formerly: Ramona National Bank CA
1315 Main St., Ramona, CA, 92065; **PH:** 1-760-788-8788; **Fax:** 1-760-789-5576; *http://* www.ramonanationalbank.com

General - Incorporation		Stock- Price on:12/24/2007	$10.7
Employees	NA	Stock Exchange	OTC
Auditor	NA	Ticker Symbol	RNBK
Stk Agt	NA	Outstanding Shares	2,640,000
Counsel	NA	E.P.S.	NA
DUNS No.	NA	Shareholders	NA

Business: The groups principal activity is to provide serving the needs of individual, professional and business clients in San Diego County. The group delivers a complete line of deposit and loan products designed to grow.

Primary SIC and add'l.: 6036

CIK No:

Officers: John McGrath/Dir., CEO, Pres., Nathan L. Rogge/Dir., Exec. VP, COO, Paula J. Berggren/Exec. VP, Chief Credit Officer, William T. Roche/CFO, Exec. VP, Brett Pivoriunas/Business Banking Associate, David Veit/Business Banking Associate, Hassan Khan/Business Banking Associate, Jason Willman/Business Banking Associate, Rick Martinez/Business Banking Associate, Gabriele Distler/VP, SBA Loan Officer, Aracely Scott/AVP, Branch Mgr. - La Mesa, Melanie Hamilton/VP, Branch Mgr.

Directors: John McGrath/Dir., CEO, Pres., John Farkash/Chmn., William V. Ehlen/Dir., Nathan L. Rogge/Dir., Exec. VP, COO, Lester MacHado/Dir.

Curr. Assets:	$41,438,000	**Curr. Liab.:**	$3,339,000		
Plant, Equip.:	$764,000	**Total Liab.:**	$3,409,000	**Indic. Yr. Divd.:**	NA
Total Assets:	$42,729,000	**Net Worth:**	$39,320,000	**Debt/ Equity:**	NA

First Business Financial Services Inc

401 Charmany Dr., Madison, WI, 53719; **PH:** 1-608-238-8008; **Fax:** 1-608-232-5920; *http://* www.fbfinancial.net

General - Incorporation	WI	Stock- Price on:12/24/2007	$19.9
Employees	112	Stock Exchange	NDQ
Auditor	KPMG LLP	Ticker Symbol	FBIZ
Stk Agt	NA	Outstanding Shares	2,500,000
Counsel	NA	E.P.S.	$1.40
DUNS No.	NA	Shareholders	NA

Business: The group's principle activity is to provide commercial banking products and services in the greater Madison, Wisconsin area, specifically designed to meet the financial needs of businesses, business owners, executives and professionals. The group is a wholly-owned subsidiary of FBB operating as an asset-based commercial finance company specializing in providing secured lines of credit as well as term loans on equipment and real estate assets primarily to manufacturers and wholesale distribution. The group operates from United States.

Primary SIC and add'l.: 6022

CIK No: 0001305399

Subsidiaries: First Business Bank, First Business Bank Milwaukee

Officers: Corey A. Chambas/Dir., CEO, Pres./$454,896.00, Mark J. Meloy/CEO, Pres. - First Business Bank, Madison/$248,384.00, Margaret M. Bomber/Corp. Sec., James F. Ropella/CFO, Sr. VP/$247,946.00, Joan A. Burke/Pres. - First Business Trust, Investments, Michael J. Losenegger/COO/$278,590.00

Directors: Corey A. Chambas/Dir., CEO, Pres., Jerome J. Smith/Chmn., Leland C. Bruce/Dir., Jan A. Eddy/58/Dir., Loren D. Mortenson/Dir., Dean W. Voeks/65/Dir., Gary E. Zimmerman/65/Dir., Mark D. Bugher/59/Dir., John M. Silseth/Dir.

Owners: Loren D. Mortenson, Jan A. Eddy, Gary E. Zimmerman/3.70%, Charles H. Batson, Dean W. Voeks, Michael J. Losenegger, John M. Silseth, Corey A. Chambas/2.50%, Jerome J. Smith/2.30%, Sam Jacobsen/12.90%, Leland C. Bruce/3.00%, James F. Ropella/1.00%, Insiders/15.80%, Mark D. Bugher

Financial Data: Fiscal Year End:12/31 **Latest Annual Data:** 12/31/2006

Year	Sales	Net Income
2006	$51,617,000	$3,747,000
2005	$40,867,000	$4,757,000

Curr. Assets:	$29,087,000	**Curr. Liab.:**	$742,567,000	**P/E Ratio:**	14.21
Plant, Equip.:	$1,051,000	**Total Liab.:**	$742,567,000	**Indic. Yr. Divd.:**	$0.260
Total Assets:	$788,323,000	**Net Worth:**	$45,756,000	**Debt/ Equity:**	NA

First Capital Inc

220 Federal Dr. NW, Corydon, IN, 47112; **PH:** 1-812-738-2198; **Fax:** 1-812-738-2202; *http://* www.firstharrison.com

General - Incorporation	IN	Stock- Price on:12/24/2007	$17.75
Employees	121	Stock Exchange	NDQ
Auditor	Monroe Shine & Co. Inc	Ticker Symbol	FCAP
Stk Agt	Registrar & Transfer Co	Outstanding Shares	2,840,000
Counsel	Simpson & Thompson	E.P.S.	$1.23
DUNS No.		Shareholders	NA

Business: The group's principal activity is to offer variety of banking services to individuals and business customers. The group is a federally chartered bank operating in corydon, Indiana. The deposit products include now accounts, money market accounts, regular savings accounts, certificates of deposits and retirement savings plans. The group's principal lending activity is the origination of residential mortgage loans, consumer, commercial businesses, commercial real estate including farm properties and residential construction loans. The group operates through its wholly owned subsidiary, first federal bank. The group operates through its branch offices located in harrison, floyd and Washington counties in Indiana. In 2003, the group acquired hometown bancshares inc.

Primary SIC and add'l.: 6712 6035

CIK No: 0001070296

Subsidiaries: A Federal Savings Bank, First Federal Bank

Officers: William W. Harrod/Dir., CEO, Pres./$172,166.00, Michael C. Frederick/Sr. VP, Treasurer/$104,482.00, Chris M. Frederick/40/CFO, Sr. VP, Treasurer, Joel E. Voyles/55/Sr. VP - Retail, Corp. Sec., Dennis L. Thomas/51/Sr. VP - Lending/$108,731.00, Samuel E. Uhl/Dir., COO/$173,714.00

Directors: William W. Harrod/Dir., CEO, Pres., Gordon J. Pendleton/74/Chmn., Kathryn W. Ernstberger/Dir., John W. Buschemeyer/Dir., James E. Nett/Dir., James S. Burden/Dir., Michael L. Shireman/Dir., Kenneth R. Saulman/Dir., Samuel E. Uhl/Dir., COO, Dennis L. Huber/Dir., Gerald L. Uhl/Dir., Mark D. Shireman/Dir.

Owners: Kathryn W. Ernstberger, Michael L. Shireman, James S. Burden, Kenneth R. Saulman, John W. Buschemeyer, Dennis L. Huber, James E. Nett, Samuel E. Uhl/1.70%, Insiders/9.80%, Gordon J. Pendleton/1.00%, Mark D. Shireman/1.40%, Gerald L. Uhl/1.40%, William W. Harrod

Financial Data: Fiscal Year End:12/31 **Latest Annual Data:** 12/31/2006

Year	Sales	Net Income
2006	$29,641,000	$3,708,000
2005	$26,620,000	$3,688,000
2004	$24,775,000	$3,431,000

Curr. Assets:	$26,965,000	**Curr. Liab.:**	$413,016,000	**P/E Ratio:**	14.62
Plant, Equip.:	$10,165,000	**Total Liab.:**	$413,016,000	**Indic. Yr. Divd.:**	$0.680
Total Assets:	$457,105,000	**Net Worth:**	$44,089,000	**Debt/ Equity:**	NA

First Capital International Inc

5120 Woodway Dr., Ste 9000, Houston, TX, 77056; **PH:** 1-713-629-4866; **Fax:** 1-713-629-5913; *http://* www.firstcap.net

General - Incorporation	DE	Stock- Price on:12/24/2007	$0.18
Employees	12	Stock Exchange	OTC
Auditor	McConnell & Jones, LLP	Ticker Symbol	FCPN
Stk Agt	OTC Stock Transfer, Inc.	Outstanding Shares	32,900,000
Counsel	NA	E.P.S.	-$0.02
DUNS No.	NA	Shareholders	NA

Business: The groups principle activities include developing, producing and selling home automation and video surveillance systems. The group operates from the United States.

Primary SIC and add'l.: 3571

CIK No: 0001072842

Subsidiaries: VIP Systems, Inc

Officers: Alex Gennin/56/Chmn., CEO, CFO, Pres., James Gooch/VP - Technology, Advisory Members, Edward Genin/VP - VIP Systems, Advisory Member, Richard MacNamee/Advisory Members - Maritime Response

Directors: Alex Gennin/56/Chmn., CEO, CFO, Pres., James Gooch/VP - Technology, Advisory Members, Sergey Tomillan/Member - Advisory Board, Roger Klotz/Member - Advisory Board, Merrill P. O'Neal/79/Dir., Andrew H. Grebe/52/Dir., Edward Genin/VP - VIP Systems, Advisory Member, Richard MacNamee/Advisory Members - Maritime Response, Cathy K. George/57/Dir.

Owners: Insiders/64.70%, Alex Genin/63.80%, Merrill P. O'Neal/0.10%, Cathy K. George/0.60%, Andrew H. Grebe

Financial Data: Fiscal Year End:12/31 Latest Annual Data: 12/31/2006

Year	Sales	Net Income
2006	$199,000	-$990,000
2005	$146,000	-$563,000
2004	$363,000	-$841,000

Curr. Assets:	$173,000	Curr. Liab.:	$1,293,000		
Plant, Equip.:	NA	Total Liab.:	$1,568,000	Indic. Yr. Divd.:	NA
Total Assets:	$173,000	Net Worth:	-$1,395,000	Debt/ Equity:	NA

First Carolina Investors Inc

9347a Founders St., Fort Mill, SC, 29708; **PH:** 1-803-802-0890

General - Incorporation	DE	**Stock** - Price on:12/24/2007	$30
Employees	NA	Stock Exchange	OTC
Auditor	KPMG LLP	Ticker Symbol	FCAR
Stk Agt	Stock Transfer & Trust Co.	Outstanding Shares	NA
Counsel	NA	E.P.S.	$2.93
DUNS No.	NA	Shareholders	NA

Business: The groups principle activity is to provide investment services. The group operates from the United States.

Primary SIC and add'l.: 6029

CIK No: 0000811040

Officers: Bruce C. Baird/62/VP, Sec., Dir., Brent D. Baird/69/Pres., Cynthia J. Raby/Assist. Sec.

Directors: Thomas H. Webb/60/Chmn., Bruce C. Baird/62/VP, Sec., Dir., Theodore E. Dann/54/Dir., Patrick W.E. Hodgson/67/Dir., James E. Traynor/58/Dir.

Owners: Insiders, Bruce C. Baird, James E. Traynor, Thomas H. Webb, Patrick W.E. Hodgson, Brent D. Baird, Theodore E. Dann

Financial Data: Fiscal Year End:12/31 Latest Annual Data: 12/31/2006

Year	Sales	Net Income
2006	$11,933,000	$4,457,000
2005	$9,609,000	$4,823,000
2004	$7,223,000	$4,091,000

Curr. Assets:	$8,618,000	Curr. Liab.:	$6,582,000	P/E Ratio:	18.96
Plant, Equip.:	NA	Total Liab.:	$10,049,000	Indic. Yr. Divd.:	$2.000
Total Assets:	$40,114,000	Net Worth:	$30,066,000	Debt/ Equity:	NA

First Cash Financial Services Inc

690 E Lamar Blvd., Ste. 400, Arlington, TX, 76011; **PH:** 1-817-460-3947; **Fax:** 1-817-461-7019; **http://** www.firstcash.com

General - Incorporation	DE	**Stock** - Price on:12/24/2007	$24.46
Employees	2,900	Stock Exchange	NDQ
Auditor	Hein & Assoc. LLP	Ticker Symbol	FCFS
Stk Agt	Registrar & Transfer Co	Outstanding Shares	32,420,000
Counsel	NA	E.P.S.	$1.19
DUNS No.	62-613-6535	Shareholders	NA

Business: The group's principal activity is to lend money on the collateral of pledged personal property and retail previously-owned merchandise acquired through pawn forfeitures. It also operates check cashing and short-term advance stores that provide short-term advances, check cashing services, and other related financial services. As on 8-Mar-2004 the group owns 167 pawn stores and 76 check cashing and short-term advance stores . The group has operations in the United States and Mexico.

Primary SIC and add'l.: 5932 6162

CIK No: 0000840489

Subsidiaries: American Loan and Jewelry, Inc., American Loan Employee Services, Capital Pawnbrokers, Inc., Cash & Go Management, LLC, Cash & Go, Inc., Cash & Go, Ltd., Elegant Floors, Inc., Famous Pawn, Inc., Fcfs Mi, Inc., Fcfs Mo, Inc., Fcfs Ok, Inc., Fcfs Sc, Inc., First Cash Corp., First Cash Credit Management, LLC, First Cash Credit, Ltd. 24 Subsidiaries included in the Index

Officers: Rick L. Wessel/Vice Chmn., CEO, Sec., Treasurer/$1,238,326.00, Douglas R. Orr/CFO, Exec. VP/$440,478.00, John C. Powell/Sr. VP, Dir. - Information Technology/$236,624.00

Directors: Rick L. Wessel/Vice Chmn., CEO, Sec., Treasurer, Phillip E. Powell/Chmn., Tara U. MacMahon/Dir., Richard T. Burke/Dir., Neil Irwin/Dir.

Owners: Neil R. Irwin/0.04%, Phillip E. Powell/1.88%, Richard T. Burke/11.15%, Douglas R. Orr/1.43%, John C. Powell/0.66%, Insiders/18.96%, Rick L. Wessel/4.68%, Tara U. MacMahon/0.43%

Financial Data: Fiscal Year End:12/31 Latest Annual Data: 12/31/2006

Year	Sales	Net Income
2006	$269,722,000	$31,744,000
2005	$207,775,000	$25,383,000
2004	$179,813,000	$20,706,000

Curr. Assets:	$115,414,000	Curr. Liab.:	$21,761,000		
Plant, Equip.:	$30,643,000	Total Liab.:	$45,246,000	Indic. Yr. Divd.:	NA
Total Assets:	$233,842,000	Net Worth:	$188,596,000	Debt/ Equity:	0.0576

First Century Bankshares Inc

500 Federal St., Bluefield, WV, 24701; **PH:** 1-304-325-8181; **http://** www.firstcentury.com; **Email:** online@firstcentury.com

General - Incorporation	WV	**Stock** - Price on:12/24/2007	$26
Employees	166	Stock Exchange	OTC
Auditor	PricewaterhouseCoopers LLP	Ticker Symbol	FCBS
Stk Agt	PricewaterhouseCoopers LLP	Outstanding Shares	1,960,000
Counsel	NA	E.P.S.	$2.32
DUNS No.	11-445-7088	Shareholders	NA

Business: The group's principal activities are to provide commercial banking services to individuals and businesses. The group is a financial holding company, which operates through its wholly owned subsidiaries, first century bank, n.a. And first century financial services, llc. The services provided by the group include commercial, real estate, installment and other loans, interest bearing and non-interest bearing deposits, savings and time deposit accounts. The operations are conducted through eleven branch offices and 14 ATM locations throughout southern west Virginia and southwestern Virginia.

Primary SIC and add'l.: 6021 6712

CIK No: 0000723594

Subsidiaries: First Century Financial Services, LLC

Officers: R. W. Wilkinson/Dir., CEO, Pres./$190,392.00, Ronald J. Hypes/CFO, Sr. VP, Investor Relations Officer/$153,029.00, Frank W. Wilkinson/Dir., COO, Pres., John P. Beckett/Sr. VP, Trust Officer/$186,969.00, Jeffrey L. Forlines/Sr. VP, Chief Credit Officer/$173,178.00, William E. Albert/Sr. VP - Cashier

Directors: R. W. Wilkinson/Dir., CEO, Pres., B. L. Jackson/Chmn., Robert M. Jones/Vice Chmn., Paul W. Cole/Dir., John H. Shott/Dir., Marshall S. Miller/Dir., Eustace Frederick/Dir., Brookins J. Taylor/Dir., Frank W. Wilkinson/Dir., COO, Pres., Charles A. Peters/Dir., Walter L. Sowers/Dir., William Chandler Swope/Dir., J. J. Booker/Dir., Samuel V. Jones/Dir.

Owners: Eustace Frederick, Charles A. Peters, Ronald J. Hypes, Walter L. Sowers, Brookins J. Taylor/1.85%, R. W. Wilkinson/10.92%, The Ethel N. Bowen Foundation/6.62%, Scott H. Shott/1.38%, Robert M. Jones/4.20%, Sam Jones, Paul Cole/1.10%, B. L. Jackson, John P. Beckett, John H. Shott, J. J. Booker (19 Owners included in Index)

Financial Data: Fiscal Year End:12/31 Latest Annual Data: 12/31/2006

Year	Sales	Net Income
2006	$28,943,000	$4,489,000
2005	$24,815,000	$4,004,000
2004	$21,621,000	$3,055,000

Curr. Assets:	$10,212,000	Curr. Liab.:	$370,029,000	P/E Ratio:	11.40
Plant, Equip.:	$12,719,000	Total Liab.:	$372,516,000	Indic. Yr. Divd.:	$1.040
Total Assets:	$410,948,000	Net Worth:	$38,432,000	Debt/ Equity:	NA

First Charter Corp

10200 David Taylor Dr., Charlotte, NC, 28262; **PH:** 1-704-688-4300; **http://** www.firstcharter.com

General - Incorporation	NC	**Stock** - Price on:12/24/2007	$20.18
Employees	1,099	Stock Exchange	NDQ
Auditor	KPMG LLP	Ticker Symbol	FCTR
Stk Agt	Registrar & Transfer Co	Outstanding Shares	35,150,000
Counsel	Helms Mulliss & Wicker	E.P.S.	$1.36
DUNS No.	13-141-1753	Shareholders	NA

Business: The group's principle activities are to provide financial services, which include banking products, comprehensive financial planning and annuity sales. The group operates its banking services principally through first charter bank and other subsidiaries. The banking products includes interest bearing and non-interest bearing checking accounts, certificate of deposits, individual retirement accounts, overdraft protection and commercial, consumer, agriculture and other loans. In addition, the group provides discount brokerage services, annuity sales and financial planning services. The group operates fifty-four financial centers, five insurance offices and one mortgage origination office in addition to its main office, as well as 93 ATMs. The group's quarterly income for Sep'07 was 11.07 millions of USD.

Primary SIC and add'l.: 6712 6022

CIK No: 0000717306

Subsidiaries: FCB Real Estate, Inc., First Charter Bank, First Charter Insurance Services, Inc., First Charter Leasing and Investments, Inc., First Charter of Virginia Realty Investments, Inc., First Charter Real Estate Holdings, LLC, First Charter Realty Investments, Inc., Lincoln Center at Mallard Creek, LLC

Officers: Robert E. James/Dir., Pres., CEO - First Charter Corporation, First Charter Bank/$651,645.00, Jane Vallaire/Investor Relations Officer, Scott J. Ensor/Exec. VP, Chief Risk Officer/$304,997.00, Sheila A. Stoke/Sr. VP, Interim Principal Financial Officer, Cecil O. Smith/CIO, Exec. VP/$350,953.00, Stephen M. Rownd/Exec. VP, Chief Banking Officer/$442,847.00

Directors: Robert E. James/Dir., Pres., CEO - First Charter Corporation, First Charter Bank, Michael R. Coltrane/Vice Chmn., James E. Burt/Chmn., Lawrence D. Warlick/Dir., Samuel C. King/Dir., Charles A. James/Dir., Hugh H. Morrison/Dir., John J. Godbold/Dir., Ellen L. Messinger/Dir., Jerry E. McGee/Dir., John S. Poelker/Dir., William W. Waters/Dir., William R. Black/Dir., Jewell D. Hoover/Dir., Richard F. Combs/Dir. (16 Directors included in Index)

Owners: Insiders/4.78%, Walter H. Jones, Richard F. Combs, Samuel C. King, Stephen M. Rownd, Robert E. James, Charles A. Caswell, L. D. Warlick, Jerry E. McGee, Hugh H. Morrison, John S. Poelker, Scott J. Ensor, Richard A. Manley, Cecil O. Smith, Thomas R. Revels (23 Owners included in Index)

Financial Data: Fiscal Year End:12/31 Latest Annual Data: 12/31/2006

Year	Sales	Net Income
2006	$338,435,000	$47,395,000
2005	$291,779,000	$25,311,000
2004	$248,548,000	$42,442,000

Curr. Assets:	$102,827,000	Curr. Liab.:	$3,921,561,000	P/E Ratio:	14.84
Plant, Equip.:	$111,588,000	Total Liab.:	$4,409,355,000	Indic. Yr. Divd.:	$0.780
Total Assets:	$4,856,717,000	Net Worth:	$447,362,000	Debt/ Equity:	1.1590

First Chester County Corp

PO Box 523, West Chester, PA, 19381; **PH:** 1-484-881-4000; **Fax:** 1-484-881-4775; **http://** www.fnbchestercounty.com

General - Incorporation	PA	**Stock** - Price on:12/24/2007	$20
Employees	258	Stock Exchange	OTC
Auditor	Grant Thornton LLP	Ticker Symbol	FCEC
Stk Agt	Registrar & Transfer Co	Outstanding Shares	5,160,000
Counsel	NA	E.P.S.	$1.25
DUNS No.	15-728-8457	Shareholders	NA

Business: The group's principle activities are to provide retail banking, commercial banking, Internet banking, trust and financial management services to individuals and businesses. Retail services include checking accounts, savings programs, money-Market accounts, certificates of deposit, safe deposit facilities, consumer loan programs, residential mortgages, overdraft checking, automated tellers and extended banking hours. Commercial services include revolving lines of credit, commercial mortgages, equipment leasing and letter of credit services. In addition, it also provides investment management services for estates, trusts, agency accounts and employee benefit plans. The group's customers primarily include consumers and small to mid-sized companies. The group's quarterly income for Sep'07 was 2.78 millions of USD.

Primary SIC and add'l.: 6021 6712

CIK No: 0000744126

Subsidiaries: First National Bank of Chester County, FNB Properties, LLC

Officers: John A. Featherman/Chmn., CEO/$493,558.00, Anthony J. Poluch/Exec. VP - Business Development, First National Bank, Michael Steinberger/Sr. VP - Commercial Mortgage Lending, First National Bank, Chester County, Kevin C. Quinn/Dir., Pres./$375,259.00, Clay Henry/Exec. VP - Wealth Management, First National Bank, Chester County, Karen D. Walter/Exec. VP - Retail Banking, First National Bank, Chester County, Lynn Mander/Sr. VP, Chief Investment Officer - First National Bank, Chester County, Rick McMullen/Sr. VP - Retail Lending, First National Bank, Chester County, Deborah Pierce/Exec. VP - Human Resources, First National Bank, Chester County/$217,298.00, John E. Balzarini/CFO, Exec. VP - Financial Support Services/$259,359.00, Thomas A. Imler/Sr. VP - Financial Advisory Services, First National Bank, Chester County, Richard W. Kaufmann/Sr. VP - Credit Administration, First National Bank, Chester County, Donna J. Steigerwalt/Sr. VP, Branch Administrator - First National Bank, Chester County, Andrew Stump/Sr. VP - Commercial Lending, First National Bank, Chester County, Patricia A. Travaglini/Sr. VP - Residential Mortgage Department, First National Bank, Chester County *(20 Officers included in Index)*

Directors: John A. Featherman/Chmn., CEO, Clifford E. Debaptiste/83/Dir., David L. Peirce/79/Dir., John J. Ciccarone/79/Dir., Brian K. Campbell/Dir., Matthew S. Naylor/Dir., Kevin C. Quinn/Dir., Pres., John S. Halsted/74/Dir., John B. Waldron/77/Dir., Sec., Edward A. Leo/60/Dir., Carol J. Hanson/60/Dir., Robert M. Clarke/61/Dir., Lynn Marie Johnson-Porter/46/Dir.

Owners: Deborah R. Pierce, Lawrence E. MacElree/5.61%, Brian K. Campbell, Edward A. Leo, Banc Fund V, L.P., et al./8.98%, John S. Halsted, Insiders/13.29%, Kevin C. Quinn, Clifford E. DeBaptiste/2.96%, David L. Peirce, John A. Featherman/1.47%, John B. Waldron, Carol J. Hanson, Robert M. Clarke, Matthew S. Naylor *(19 Owners included in Index)*

Financial Data: *Fiscal Year End:*12/31 *Latest Annual Data:* 12/31/2006

Year	Sales	Net Income
2006	$61,493,000	$7,335,000
2005	$53,935,000	$6,511,000
2004	$46,831,000	$6,161,000

Curr. Assets:	$72,341,000	Curr. Liab.:	$786,264,000	P/E Ratio:	16.00
Plant, Equip.:	$13,988,000	Total Liab.:	$808,832,000	Indic. Yr. Divd.:	$0.540
Total Assets:	$872,094,000	Net Worth:	$63,262,000	Debt/ Equity:	0.2420

First Choice Health Network Inc

600 University St., Ste. 1400, Seattle, WA, 98101; *PH:* 1-800-467-5281; *Fax:* 1-206-667-8062; *http://* www.fchn.com

General		Stock	
Incorporation	WA	Price on:12/24/2007	NA
Employees	NA	Stock Exchange	NDQ
Auditor	Moss Adams LLP	Ticker Symbol	PDF
Stk Agt	NA	Outstanding Shares	NA
Counsel	NA	E.P.S	NA
DUNS No.	14-834-3775	Shareholders	NA

Business: The group's principle activity is to operate a preferred provider organization which provides health care services through its network of physicians, hospitals and other health care providers. The group operates from United States.

Primary SIC and add'l.: 6324

CIK No: 0000922622

Subsidiaries: First Choice Health Plan, Incorporated

Officers: Ken Hamm/CEO, Pres., Zeev Young/Chief Medical Officer, Tom Maschhoff/VP - First Choice Health EAP Services, Beth Johnson/VP - Network Development, David Burn/Dir. - Employee Assistance Programs, George Harper/Network Contract Mgr., Greg Palmberg/VP - Information Technology

First Citizens Banc Corp

100 E Water St. , Sandusky, OH, 44870; *PH:* 1-419-625-4121; *http://* www.fcza.com

General		Stock	
Incorporation	OH	Price on:12/24/2007	$19.02
Employees	250	Stock Exchange	NDQ
Auditor	Crowe Chizek & Co. LLC	Ticker Symbol	FCZA
Stk Agt	Illinois Stock Transfer Co	Outstanding Shares	5,430,000
Counsel	NA	E.P.S	$1.12
DUNS No.	00-790-4097	Shareholders	NA

Business: The group's principal activity is to provide general banking business, which include collecting customer deposits, making loans and purchasing securities. The group's primary deposit products are checking, savings and term certificate accounts. Its primary lending products are residential mortgage, commercial and installment loans. The group operates through three banking subsidiaries: the citizens banking company, the farmers state bank and the castalia banking company located in erie, crawford, huron, union, marion, richland, and ottawa counties, Ohio. The group through its subsidiaries, scc resources, inc. And r. A. Reynolds appraisal service, inc. Provides data processing and real estate appraisal services, for lending purposes, to the banks and to other financial institutions and it also provides insurance and security related services. On 01-Apr-2002, the group completed the merger of independent community banc corp.

Primary SIC and add'l.: 6021 6712

CIK No: 0000944745

Subsidiaries: First Citizens Insurance Agency, First Citizens Title Insurance Agency, Mr. Money Finance Co., SCC Resources, Inc., The Citizens Banking Company, Water Street Properties, Inc.

Officers: James O. Miller/Dir., Pres., CEO - Citizens Banking Company/$237,734.00, William Patrick Murray/Dir. - Citizens Banking Company, Carolyn M. Armstrong/VP - Commercial Lender, Brian R. Benes/VP - Consumer Lending, Phyllis L. Bransky/VP - Select Banking, Scott M. Donnenwirth/VP - Commercial Lender, Richard C. Finneran/VP - Commercial Lender, Robin J. Grathwol/VP - Commercial Lender, Jackie A. Griggs/VP, Trust Officer - Citizens Banking Company, Jeffery C. Huber/VP - Commercial Lender, Citizens Banking Company, Lee A. Jordan/VP - Business Development, Citizens Banking Company, Brenda R. Leal/VP - Deposit Operations, Melissa L. McDougal/VP - Commercial Lender, Michael Milchen/VP - Credit Control Administration, Jack D. Ulrich/VP - Commercial Lender, Citizens Banking Company *(47 Officers included in Index)*

Directors: David A. Voight/Chmn., Blythe Anne Friedley/Dir. - Citizens Banking Company, Laurence A. Bettcher/Dir., George J. Williams/Dir. - Citizens Banking Company, John O. Bacon/Dir. - Citizens Banking Company, Patrick W. Murray/67/Dir. - Citizens Banking Company, George L. Mylander/Dir. Emeritus, Allen R. Nickles/Dir. - Citizens Banking Company

Owners: Richard A. Weidrick, Michael J. Lamping, Barry W. Boerger, Robert J. Gantzer, Insiders/6.00%, Jerry L. Gecowets/1.40%, David A. Shiffer, Lilli A. Johnson/1.30%, Allen R. Maurice/1.10%, Gregg N. Bedell

Financial Data: *Fiscal Year End:*12/31 *Latest Annual Data:* 12/31/2006

Year	Sales	Net Income
2006	$53,209,000	$6,160,000
2005	$50,289,000	$6,659,000
2004	$41,066,000	$4,813,000

Curr. Assets:	$23,005,000	Curr. Liab.:	$635,079,000	P/E Ratio:	16.98
Plant, Equip.:	$12,184,000	Total Liab.:	$669,514,000	Indic. Yr. Divd.:	NA
Total Assets:	$748,986,000	Net Worth:	$79,472,000	Debt/ Equity:	0.4239

First Citizens BanCorp Inc

PO Box 29, 1225 Lady St., Columbia, SC, 29202; *PH:* 1-803-253-6028; *http://* www.firstcitizensonline.com

General		Stock	
Incorporation	SC	Price on:12/24/2007	$690
Employees	NA	Stock Exchange	OTC
Auditor	PricewaterhouseCoopers LLP	Ticker Symbol	FCBN
Stk Agt	NA	Outstanding Shares	NA
Counsel	NA	E.P.S	$64.02
DUNS No.	00-791-9392	Shareholders	NA

Business: The group's principal activity is to provide commercial and retail banking services through 147 offices in 101 communities in South Carolina. The group is a three-bank holding company that operates through subsidiaries: first citizens bank and trust company of South Carolina, the exchange bank of South Carolina inc and citizens bank. The group provides banking and financial services to individuals, small and medium-sized businesses and governmental units located in banking markets. The financial services provided includes accepting deposits, corporate cash management, discount brokerage, ira plans, trust services and secured and unsecured loans. The trust services provide estate planning, estate and trust administration, ira trust and personal investment and pension and profit sharing administration. The group also originates and services mortgage loans. On 01-Apr-2003 the group acquired first banks inc.

Primary SIC and add'l.: 6712 6022

CIK No: 0000708848

Subsidiaries: Congaree 1, LLC, Daniel Island HPR, LLC, FCB/SC Capital Trust I, FCB/SC Capital Trust II, First Citizens Bank and Trust Company, Inc., First Citizens Housing Development, LLC, First Citizens Mortgage Corporation (Inactive), The Exchange Bank of South Carolina, Inc., Wateree Enterprises, Inc.

Financial Data: *Fiscal Year End:*12/31 *Latest Annual Data:* 12/31/2004

Year	Sales	Net Income
2004	$256,612,000	$36,709,000
2003	$257,342,000	$39,883,000
2002	$261,243,000	$39,048,000

Curr. Assets:	$290,634,000	Curr. Liab.:	$4,012,920,000	P/E Ratio:	10.78
Plant, Equip.:	$154,823,000	Total Liab.:	$4,164,195,000	Indic. Yr. Divd.:	$1.400
Total Assets:	$4,533,651,000	Net Worth:	$369,456,000	Debt/ Equity:	NA

First Citizens Bancshares Inc/DE

3128 Smoketree Ct, Raleigh, NC, 27604; *PH:* 1-919-716-7000; *http://* www.firstcitizens.com; *Email:* fcbdirectors@firstcitizens.com

General		Stock	
Incorporation	DE	Price on:12/24/2007	$195.08
Employees	3,942	Stock Exchange	NA
Auditor	Dixon Hughes PLLC	Ticker Symbol	NA
Stk Agt	Suntrust Bank	Outstanding Shares	10,430,000
Counsel	NA	E.P.S	$12.07
DUNS No.	11-972-3906	Shareholders	NA

Business: The group's principal activity is to provide banking services to retail and commercial customers. The services offered include commercial and consumer lending; transaction and savings deposits; a full service trust department; a full service securities broker-dealer; insurance services and other activities. It operates through two subsidiaries: first citizens bank and trust company and Atlantic states bank. The group accepts deposits and provides numerous checking and savings plan, commercial, small business and consumer lending and other activities to its customers. The group also offers investment products including annuities, discount brokerage services and third-party mutual funds to customers. The operations are conducted through 330 branches located in North Carolina, Virginia and west Virginia.

Primary SIC and add'l.: 6712 6022

CIK No: 0000798941

Subsidiaries: American Guaranty Insurance Company, FCB/NC Capital Trust I, FCB/NC Capital Trust II, First-Citizens Bank & Trust Company, IronStone Bank, Neuse, Incorporated

Officers: Lewis R. Holding/Chmn., CEO/$1,135,300.00, James B. Hyler/60/Vice Chmn., COO/$829,751.00, Frank B. Holding/Exec. Vice Chmn., Pres./$942,009.00, Hope Holding Connell/45/Dir., Exec. VP, Mgr. - Business Banking Segment, Joseph A. Cooper/54/Exec. VP, Exec. - Technology, Operations, James M. Parker/COO, Exec. VP - Ironstone Bank, Carol B. Yochem/48/Exec. VP, Mgr. - Wealth Management/$775,012.00, James E. Creekman/60/Sec., Allen J. Woodward/57/Exec. VP, Mgr. - Compliance, Credit Risk Management, Lou Jones Davis/55/Chief Human Resources Officer, Exec. VP, William C. Orr/65/Exec. VP, Chief Credit Officer, Kenneth A. Black/55/CFO, VP, Treasurer/$378,627.00, Donald P. Geaslen/50/Exec. VP, General Auditor

Directors: Lewis R. Holding/Chmn., CEO, James B. Hyler/60/Vice Chmn., COO, Frank B. Holding/Exec. Vice Chmn., Pres., Lewis M. Fetterman/86/Dir., H. M. Craig/52/Dir., Lee H. Durham/60/Dir., Charles B.C. Holt/75/Dir., Lewis T. Nunnelee/82/Dir., R. C. Soles/Dir., Robert T. Newcomb/47/Dir., David L. Ward/Dir., Ralph K. Shelton/Dir., Lucius S. Jones/65/Dir., Carmen Holding Ames/39/Dir., Victor E. Bell/52/Dir. *(19 Directors included in Index)*

Owners: Carson H. Brice, Charles B. C. Holt, Lewis T. Nunnelee, Ralph K. Shelton, Robert T. Newcomb, Kenneth A. Black, David L. Ward, Olivia B. Holding, Claire H. Bristow, Lee H. Durham, George H. Broadrick, Lucius S. Jones, Hope Holding Connell, John M. Alexander, Hope Holding Connell *(51 Owners included in Index)*

Financial Data: *Fiscal Year End:*12/31 *Latest Annual Data:* 12/31/2006

Year	Sales	Net Income
2006	$1,105,255,000	$126,491,000
2005	$929,778,000	$112,862,000
2004	$772,073,000	$74,843,000

Curr. Assets:	$1,431,143,000	**Curr. Liab.:**	$13,894,171,000	**P/E Ratio:**	16.16
Plant, Equip.:	$702,926,000	**Total Liab.:**	$14,418,878,000	**Indic. Yr. Divd.:**	$1.100
Total Assets:	$15,729,697,000	**Net Worth:**	$1,310,819,000	**Debt/ Equity:**	0.3019

First Citizens Bancshares Inc/TN

4300 Six Forks Rd., Raleigh, NC, 27609; *PH:* 1-919-716-7000; *Fax:* 1-919-716-7074; *http://* www.firstcitizens.com

General - Incorporation	TN	**Stock**- Price on:12/24/2007	$193.06
Employees	3,942	Stock Exchange	NDQ
Auditor	Alexander Thompson Arnold PLLC	Ticker Symbol	FCNCA
Stk Agt	First Citizens Bank	Outstanding Shares	10,430,000
Counsel	NA	E.P.S.	$12.07
DUNS No.	00-792-1059	Shareholders	NA

Business: The group's principal activity is to provide commercial banking services to individuals and corporate customers in the mid-southern United States. The group's primary products are checking and savings deposits including residential, commercial and consumer lending. The customary services of the bank include checking and savings accounts, negotiable order of withdrawal accounts, personal and business checking accounts, various types of time deposits and financing commercial, residential and consumer loans. In addition, the group provides agricultural services that include operating loans as well as financing for the purchase of equipment and farmland. The consumer lending department makes direct loans to individuals for personal, automobile, real estate, home improvement, business and collateral needs.

Primary SIC and add'l.: 6021 6712

CIK No: 0000719264

Subsidiaries: First Citizens Capital Assets, Inc, First Citizens Financial Plus, Inc., First Citizens Holdings, Inc., First Citizens Investments, Inc., First Citizens National Bank, First Citizens Properties, Inc., White and Associates/First Citizens Insurance, LLC

Officers: Katie S. Winchester/67/Chmn., CEO, Pres./$403,334.00, Jeffrey D. Agee/47/Dir., Pres./$262,684.00, Ralph E. Henson/66/Dir., Chief Credit Officer/$256,895.00, Laura Beth Butler/32/CFO, Sr. VP/$112,602.00, Barry T. Ladd/67/Dir., Chief Administrative Officer/$229,338.00

Directors: Katie S. Winchester/67/Chmn., CEO, Pres., John M. Lannom/54/Dir., Allen G. Searcy/66/Dir., Joseph S. Yates/45/Dir., Eddie Eugene Anderson/60/Dir., Bentley F. Edwards/50/Dir., William C. Cloar/71/Dir., Jeffrey D. Agee/47/Dir., Pres., Ralph E. Henson/66/Dir., Chief Credit Officer, Daniel L. Heavner/60/Dir., Robert E. Mason/49/Dir., James M. Parker/65/Dir., Christian E. Heckler/40/Dir., P. H. White/76/Dir., G. W. Smitheal/52/Dir. *(45 Directors included in Index)*

Owners: Christian E. Heckler, Milton E. Magee/1.38%, Jeffrey D. Agee, Ralph E. Henson/1.44%, First Citizens National Bank Employee Stock Ownership Plan & Trust/20.10%, Barry T. Ladd, Joseph S. Yates, Insiders/13.37%, Bentley F. Edwards, Eddie Eugene Anderson, P. H. White, Stallings Lipford/1.47%, G. W. Smitheal, David R. Taylor, Dwight Steven Williams *(24 Owners included in Index)*

Financial Data: *Fiscal Year End:*12/31 *Latest Annual Data:* 12/31/2006

Year	Sales	Net Income
2006	$1,105,255,000	$126,491,000
2005	$929,778,000	$112,862,000
2004	$772,073,000	$74,843,000

Curr. Assets:	$1,431,143,000	**Curr. Liab.:**	$13,894,171,000	**P/E Ratio:**	15.89
Plant, Equip.:	$702,926,000	**Total Liab.:**	$14,418,878,000	**Indic. Yr. Divd.:**	$1.100
Total Assets:	$15,729,697,000	**Net Worth:**	$1,310,819,000	**Debt/ Equity:**	0.3019

First Clover Leaf Financial Corp

Formerly: First Federal Financial Services Inc

300 St. . Louis St. , Edwardsville, IL, 62025; *PH:* 1-618-656-6200; *http://* www.1stfedsavings.com

General - Incorporation	Federal	**Stock**- Price on:12/24/2007	$10.85
Employees	44	Stock Exchange	NDQ
Auditor	McGladrey & Pullen LLP	Ticker Symbol	FCLF
Stk Agt	Mcgladrey & Pullen LLP	Outstanding Shares	9,070,000
Counsel	Luse Gorman Pomerenk & Schick PC	E.P.S.	NA
DUNS No.	NA	Shareholders	NA

Business: The groups principle activity is to provide personal, and business banking services. The groups personal services include personal deposit accounts, HAS accounts, loans, and ATM. The groups business banking services include small business checking, corporate checking accounts, corporate sweep accounts, business NOW accounts, Business Money Market, and consumer loans The groups other services include check recorder, ELAN credit card, financial calculators, SEC fillings and CreditGUARD Coach(TM). The group operates from United States.

Primary SIC and add'l.: NA

CIK No: 0001283582

Subsidiaries: First Federal Savings & Loan Association of Edwardsville

Officers: Dennis M. Terry/Dir., CEO, Pres., Don Engelke/44/Dir., Sr. VP - Residential Lending, Darlene F. McDonald/CFO, Sr. VP, Lisa R. Fowler/Chief Lending Officer, Sr. VP, Chad Abernathy/Assist. VP - First Clover Leaf Bank, Melanie Nolen/Loan Operations Officer - First Clover Leaf Bank, Kelly Wagner/Business Banking Officer, Assist. VP - First Clover Leaf Bank, Mary Kokorudz/Loan Officer - First Clover Leaf Bank, Donna Scherff/Operations Officer - First Clover Leaf Bank, Shannon Bond/Business Development Officer, Assist. VP - First Clover Leaf Bank, Karen Kirkover/Compliance Officer, VP - First Clover Leaf Bank, Ann Schmidt/Assist. VP - First Clover Leaf Bank, Grant Swan/Electronic Banking Officer - First Clover Leaf Bank, Nathan Ballard/Assist. VP - First Clover Leaf Bank, Tim Mitchell/Commercial Loan Officer, Assist. VP - First Clover Leaf Bank *(18 Officers included in Index)*

Directors: Dennis M. Terry/Dir., CEO, Pres., Joe Helms/70/Chmn., Ken Highlander/Dir. - First Clover Leaf Bank, Larry W. Mosby/66/Dir., Nina Baird/80/Dir., Robert Richards/83/Dir., Don Engelke/44/Dir., Sr. VP - Residential Lending, Dennis E. Ulrich/54/Dir., Gary Niebur/Dir. - First Clover Leaf Bank, Bob Richards/Dir. - First Clover Leaf Bank, Gerry Schuetzenhofer/Dir. - First Clover Leaf Bank, Robert Schwartz/69/Dir., Joseph Stevens/61/Dir.

Owners: Gary D. Niebur, Joseph J. Gugger/5.60%, Investors of America, Limited/9.60%, Harry Gallatin, Kenneth P. Highlander, Larry W. Mosby, Darlene F. McDonald, Donald Engelke, Dennis M. Terry, Dean Pletcher, Insiders/15.50%, Dennis E. Ulrich, Nina Baird, Gerard A. Schuetzenhofer/1.00%, Robert W. Schwartz/2.40% *(20 Owners included in Index)*

Financial Data: *Fiscal Year End:*12/31 *Latest Annual Data:* 12/31/2006

Year	Sales	Net Income
2006	$14,167,000	$1,837,000
2005	$7,762,000	$1,863,000
2004	$7,276,000	$1,945,000

Curr. Assets:	$94,507,000	**Curr. Liab.:**	$311,280,000		
Plant, Equip.:	$6,893,000	**Total Liab.:**	$316,964,000	**Indic. Yr. Divd.:**	$0.240
Total Assets:	$410,292,000	**Net Worth:**	$93,329,000	**Debt/ Equity:**	0.3062

First Commerce Community Bankshares Inc

9001 Hospital Dr., Douglasville, GA, 30134; *PH:* 1-770-489-3222; *http://* www.firstccbank.com

General - Incorporation		**Stock**- Price on:12/24/2007	NA
Employees	NA	Stock Exchange	OTC
Auditor	NA	Ticker Symbol	FCGA
Stk Agt	NA	Outstanding Shares	NA
Counsel	NA	E.P.S.	NA
DUNS No.	NA	Shareholders	NA

Business: The groups principle activity is to provide recruiting services. The groups service area includes the research and development, engineering, marketing, sales, information technology and manufacturing industries. The group operates from United States.

Primary SIC and add'l.: 6712

CIK No: 0001178933

Financial Data: *Fiscal Year End:*NA *Latest Annual Data:* 12/31/2003

Year	Sales	Net Income
2003	$1,628,000	-$656,000

Curr. Assets:	$5,475,000	**Curr. Liab.:**	$48,537,000		
Plant, Equip.:	$1,294,000	**Total Liab.:**	$48,598,000	**Indic. Yr. Divd.:**	NA
Total Assets:	$58,636,000	**Net Worth:**	$10,039,000	**Debt/ Equity:**	NA

First Commonwealth Financial Corp

601 Philadelphia St., Indiana, PA, 15701; *PH:* 1-724-349-7220; *Fax:* 1-800-711-2265; *http://* www.fcbanking.com

General - Incorporation	PA	**Stock**- Price on:12/24/2007	$11.34
Employees	1,579	Stock Exchange	NYSE
Auditor	KPMG LLP	Ticker Symbol	FCF
Stk Agt	Bank of New York	Outstanding Shares	74,010,000
Counsel	NA	E.P.S.	$0.69
DUNS No.	10-732-3057	Shareholders	NA

Business: The group's principal activities are to provide general retail banking services through its 91 community banking offices. The group provides a wide range of loan, deposit, trust and insurance services. The deposits include demand, savings and time deposits. The loan portfolio includes mortgage, consumer installment and commercial loans. In addition, it provides personal financial planning and other financial services. The group has a network of 91 automated teller machines. The community banking offices are located in the counties of allegheny, armstrong, beaver, bedford, blair, cambria, centre, clearfield, elk, franklin, huntingdon, Indiana, jefferson, lawrence, somerset, Washington and westmoreland. On 05-Dec-2003, the group acquired pittsburgh financial corp and on 24-May-2004, the group acquired ga financial inc.

Primary SIC and add'l.: 6021 6712

CIK No: 0000712537

Subsidiaries: Commonwealth Trust Credit Life Insurance Company, First Commonwealth Bank, First Commonwealth Capital Trust I, First Commonwealth Capital Trust II, First Commonwealth Capital Trust III, First Commonwealth Financial Advisors Incorporated, First Commonwealth Professional Resources Incorporated, First Commonwealth Systems Corporation, First Commonwealth Trust Company, FraMal Holdings Corporation

Officers: John J. Dolan/Dir., CEO, Pres./$382,976.00, Edward J. Lipkus/Exec. VP, CFO, Controller, Thaddeus J. Clements/Sr. VP - Strategic Resources, John R. Previte/Sr. VP - Investments, William R. Jarrett/Exec. VP, Chief Audit Executive, David R. Tomb/Dir., Sr. VP, Sec., Treasurer/$356,576.00, Sue A. McMurdy/CIO, Exec. VP/$351,076.00, Gerard M. Thomchick/COO, Sr. Exec. VP/$492,119.00

Directors: John J. Dolan/Dir., CEO, Pres., David S. Dahlmann/Chmn., John A. Robertshaw/Dir., Julia E. Trimarchi Cuccaro/Dir., Julie A. Caponi/Dir., Dale P. Latimer/Dir., Edward T. Cote/Dir., James W. Newill/Dir., David R. Tomb/Dir., Sr. VP, Sec., Treasurer, Laurie Stern Singer/Dir., Ray T. Charley/Dir., Johnston A. Glass/Dir., Robert J. Ventura/Dir.

Owners: Ray T. Charley, John J. Dolan, David S. Dahlmann, Julia E. Trimarchi Cuccaro, Julie A. Caponi, Robert J. Ventura, Edward T. Cote, Gerard M. Thomchick, David R. Tomb/1.00%, Joseph E. ODell, John A. Robertshaw, James W. Newill, Johnston A. Glass, Sue A. McMurdy, Laurie S. Singer *(17 Owners included in Index)*

Financial Data: *Fiscal Year End:*12/31 *Latest Annual Data:* 12/31/2006

Year	Sales	Net Income
2006	$377,317,000	$52,954,000
2005	$369,966,000	$57,836,000
2004	$325,674,000	$38,652,000

Curr. Assets:	$96,119,000	**Curr. Liab.:**	$4,826,454,000	**P/E Ratio:**	16.43
Plant, Equip.:	$70,408,000	**Total Liab.:**	$5,472,555,000	**Indic. Yr. Divd.:**	$0.680
Total Assets:	$6,043,916,000	**Net Worth:**	$571,361,000	**Debt/ Equity:**	1.0103

First Community Bancorp

401 W "A" St., San Diego, CA, 92101; *PH:* 1-619-233-5588; *Fax:* 1-619-235-1268; *http://* www.firstcommunitybancorp.com

General - Incorporation	CA	**Stock**- Price on:12/24/2007	$55.71
Employees	1,010	Stock Exchange	NDQ
Auditor	KPMG LLP	Ticker Symbol	FCBP
Stk Agt	U.S. Stock Transfer Corp	Outstanding Shares	28,850,000
Counsel	NA	E.P.S.	$3.35
DUNS No.	NA	Shareholders	NA

Business: The group's principle activity is to provide banking and financial services. Acting as a holding company of first national bank and pacific western national bank, the group operates in southern California. The group offers the services to small and medium-sized businesses, their owners and the employees. The services consist of accepting time and demand deposits, originating commercial, real estate and construction loans, small business administration guaranteed loans, consumer loans, mortgage loans, international loans for trade finance and other business-oriented products. The operations are conducted through thirty four banking offices in los angeles, orange, riverside, and san bernardino counties. The group's quarterly income for Sep'07 was 22.20 millions of USD.

Primary SIC and add'l.: 6021 6712

CIK No: 0001102112

Subsidiaries: First Community Financial Corp., First Community Statutory Trust III, First Community Statutory Trust VII, First Community/CA Statutory Trust, First Community/CA Statutory Trust II, First Community/CA Statutory Trust IV, First Community/CA Statutory Trust V, First Community/CA Statutory Trust VI, First National Bank, Pacific Western National Bank

Officers: Matthew P. Wagner/Dir., CEO/$2,197,990.00, William T. Powers/67/Pres. - Desert Region, Pacific Western Bank, Robert G. Dyck/Exec. VP, Chief Credit Officer, Christopher D. Blake/48/Pres. - Eastern Region, Pacific Western Bank, Lynn M. Hopkins/40/Exec. VP, Victor R. Santoro/CFO, Exec. VP/$1,098,872.00, Michael L. Thompson/Exec. VP - Human Resources/$521,138.00, Jared M. Wolff/Exec. VP, General Counsel, Corp. Sec./$610,870.00, Mark Christian/Exec. VP - Operations, Systems, Robert M. Borgman/Exec. VP - Credit Administration, Michael J. Perdue/Pres.

Directors: Matthew P. Wagner/Dir., CEO, John M. Eggemeyer/Chmn., Stephen M. Dunn/Dir., Barry C. Fitzpatrick/Dir., George E. Langley/Dir., Susan E. Lester/Dir., Timothy B. Matz/Dir., Arnold W. Messer/Dir., Daniel B. Platt/Dir., Robert A. Stine/Dir., David S. Williams/Dir., Mark N. Baker/Dir., Gary W. Deems/Dir.

Owners: Insiders/10.80%, Mark N. Baker, Stephen M. Dunn, Arnold W. Messer, Daniel B. Platt, Robert A. Stine, Jared M. Wolff, Michael L. Thompson, Barry C. Fitzpatrick, John M. Eggemeyer/6.30%, Timothy B. Matz, David S. Williams, Victor R. Santoro, Susan E. Lester, Gary W. Deems *(20 Owners included in Index)*

Financial Data: Fiscal Year End:12/31   Latest Annual Data: 12/31/2006

Year	Sales	Net Income
2006	$320,395,000	$75,998,000
2005	$197,287,000	$50,366,000
2004	$157,067,000	$36,363,000

Curr. Assets:	$172,799,000	Curr. Liab.:	$3,736,776,000		
Plant, Equip.:	$37,102,000	Total Liab.:	$4,384,995,000	Indic. Yr. Divd.:	$1.280
Total Assets:	$5,553,323,000	Net Worth:	$1,168,328,000	Debt/ Equity:	NA

First Community Bancshares Inc

1 Community Pl., Bluefield, VA, 24605; *PH:* 1-276-326-9000; *Fax:* 1-276-326-9010; *http://* www.fcbinc.com; *Email:* marketing@fcbinc.com

General - Incorporation	NV	**Stock**- Price on:12/24/2007	$31.97
Employees	602	Stock Exchange	NDQ
Auditor	Dixon Hughes PLLC	Ticker Symbol	FCBC
Stk Agt	Mellon Investor Services LLC	Outstanding Shares	11,270,000
Counsel	NA	E.P.S.	$2.61
DUNS No.	00-794-4291	Shareholders	NA

Business: The group's principal activity is to provide financial and trust services to individuals and commercial customers through 47 full-service banking locations in west Virginia, Virginia and North Carolina. The group provides commercial, financial, agricultural, real estate mortgage, real estate construction and consumer loans. The group also offers asset management and estate administration services through its trust and financial services division. In 2003, the group acquired monroe financial inc, stone capital management inc and the commonwealth bank. On 01-Apr-2004, the group acquired pcb bancorp inc.

Primary SIC and add'l.: 6021 6712

CIK No: 0000859070

Subsidiaries: United First Mortgage, Inc.

Officers: John M. Mendez/Dir., CEO, Pres./$557,037.00, Robert L. Buzzo/VP, Sec./$312,800.00, Stephen E. Lilly/COO/$321,644.00, David D. Brown/CFO/$124,988.00

Directors: John M. Mendez/Dir., CEO, Pres., William P. Stafford/Chmn., Aldo A. Modena/Dir., Allen T. Hamner/Dir., Norris I. Kantor/Dir., Billy W. Harvey/Dir., Robert E. Perkinson/Dir., Harold V. Groome/Dir., William P. Stafford/Dir., Franklin P. Hall/Dir.

Owners: A. A. Modena, B. W. Harvey, Robert E. Perkinson, William P. Stafford/2.20%, John M. Mendez, David D. Brown, Stephen E. Lilly, Samuel L. Elmore, Harold V. Groome, Robert L. Buzzo, William P. Stafford/1.36%, Insiders/6.75%, The H. P.& Anne S. Hunnicutt Foundation/10.85%, Norris I. Kantor, Allen T. Hamner

Financial Data: Fiscal Year End:12/31   Latest Annual Data: 12/31/2006

Year	Sales	Net Income
2006	$141,349,000	$28,948,000
2005	$131,813,000	$26,303,000
2004	$113,465,000	$22,364,000

Curr. Assets:	$69,900,000	Curr. Liab.:	$1,801,327,000	P/E Ratio:	12.30
Plant, Equip.:	$37,147,000	Total Liab.:	$1,820,968,000	Indic. Yr. Divd.:	$1.080
Total Assets:	$2,033,698,000	Net Worth:	$212,730,000	Debt/ Equity:	NA

First Community Bank Corp of America

9001 Belcher Rd., Pinellas Park, FL, 33782; *PH:* 1-727-520-0987; *Fax:* 1-727-471-0010; *http://* www.efirstcommbank.com

General - Incorporation	FL	**Stock**- Price on:12/24/2007	$16.45
Employees	103	Stock Exchange	NDQ
Auditor	Hacker, Johnson & Smith P.A, P.C	Ticker Symbol	FCFL
Stk Agt	Registrar & Transfer Co	Outstanding Shares	4,070,000
Counsel	NA	E.P.S.	$1.46
DUNS No.	NA	Shareholders	NA

Business: The group's principal activity is to provide a variety of banking services. The group's services are provided to small and middle market businesses and individuals, including service companies, manufacturing companies, commercial real estate developers, entrepreneurs and professionals. The group operates through three full-service branch locations in pinellas county and one full-service branch location in charlotte county.

Primary SIC and add'l.: 6035 6712

CIK No: 0001082564

Subsidiaries: First Community Bank of America, First Community Lender Services, Inc.

Officers: Kenneth P. Cherven/48/Dir., CEO, Pres./$332,134.00, Sam S. Ferlita/Dir. - First Community Bank, America, Hillsborough Region, David S. Cox/Dir. - First Community Bank, America, Pinellas Region, Carol K. Reid/Sr. VP, Branch Administrator - First Community Bank, America, Pinellas Region, Gar Lippincott/Dir. - First Community Bank, America, Hillsborough Region, Robert L. Stahl/Dir. - First Community Bank, America, Pinellas Region, John C. Burket/Dir. - First Community Bank, America, Pinellas Region, Craig Beggins/Dir. - First Community Bank, America, Hillsborough Region, David S. Felman/Dir. - First Community Bank, America, Hillsborough Region, Scott C. Boyle/Dir. - First Community Bank, America, Pinellas Region/$237,372.00, Catherine A. Anderson/Dir. - First Community Bank, America, Hillsborough Region, Clifton E. Tufts/Exec. VP - First Community Bank, America/$185,901.00, Thomas P. Croom/Exec. VP, Sr. Credit Officer - First Community Bank, America, S. T. Kamide/Dir., Pres. - First Community Bank, America, Hillsborough Region, Michael J. Bullerdick/Dir. - First Community Bank, America, Charlotte Region *(38 Officers included in Index)*

Directors: Kenneth P. Cherven/48/Dir., CEO, Pres., Robert M. Menke/74/Chmn., James MacAluso/64/Dir., Brad Bishop/65/Dir., Edwin C. Hussemann/61/Dir., David K. Meehan/60/Dir., Kenneth Delarbre/65/Dir., Robert G. Menke/45/Dir.

Owners: Kenneth Delarbre/1.63%, Robert G. Menke, David K. Meehan/1.09%, Clifton E. Tufts/1.55%, Sue A. Gilman, James Macaluso/4.77%, Siede T. Kamide, Edwin C. Hussemann, Michael J. Bullerdick, Ralph W. Cumbee, Insiders/50.68%, Kenneth P. Cherven/4.64%, Scott C. Boyle/2.10%, Robert M. Menke/37.13%, Brad Bishop/1.04%

Financial Data: Fiscal Year End:12/31   Latest Annual Data: 12/31/2006

Year	Sales	Net Income
2006	$26,045,000	$3,652,000
2005	$17,930,000	$2,863,000
2004	$12,643,000	$2,023,000

Curr. Assets:	$13,678,000	Curr. Liab.:	$350,928,000	P/E Ratio:	19.82
Plant, Equip.:	$7,462,000	Total Liab.:	$357,217,000	Indic. Yr. Divd.:	NA
Total Assets:	$390,899,000	Net Worth:	$33,682,000	Debt/ Equity:	0.1965

First Community Corp/SC

5455 Sunset Blvd, Lexington, SC, 29072; *PH:* 1-803-951-2265; *http://* www.forstcommunitysc.com

General - Incorporation	SC	**Stock**- Price on:12/24/2007	$16.69
Employees	137	Stock Exchange	NDQ
Auditor	Clifton D. Bodiford	Ticker Symbol	FCCO
Stk Agt	Registrar & Transfer Co	Outstanding Shares	3,220,000
Counsel	NA	E.P.S.	$1.10
DUNS No.	94-392-2393	Shareholders	NA

Business: The group's principal activity is to offer general commercial and retail banking business to small-to-medium sized businesses, professional concerns and individuals. The deposit services offered by the group include checking accounts, now accounts, and savings accounts. The services also include other time deposit ranging from daily money market accounts to long-term certificate of deposits. The origination of loans includes residential mortgage, commercial, home equity, installment and credit card loans. Other bank services include cash management services, safe deposit boxes, travelers checks and direct deposit of payroll and social security checks and automatic drafts for various accounts. The group operates through the main office located in the city of lexington and five branch offices in richland and lexington counties of South Carolina.

Primary SIC and add'l.: 6021 6712

CIK No: 0000932781

Subsidiaries: First Community Bank, N.A.

Officers: Michael C. Crapps/Dir., CEO, Pres./$238,494.00, Jeff Branum/Mortgage Loan Originator, Rachelle L. Paquette/Product Sales Specialist, Susie Hartsell/Mortgage Loan Officer, Joseph G. Sawyer/CFO/$136,670.00, David K. Proctor/Sr. Credit Officer/$123,483.00, Ted J. Nissen/Exec. - Group Banking/$122,789.00, Robin D. Brown/Dir. - Human Resources, Marketing, Harry A. Deith/Commercial Lender, Joseph A. Painter/Commercial Banker - Northeast, Kevin T. Adams/Commercial Banker - Irmo, Von G. Wessinger/Commercial Banker - Chapin, Clarence Dickerson/Commercial Banker - Cayce, West Columbia, Edward J. Pearce/Commercial Banker - Cayce, West Columbia, Alan J. George/Commercial Banker - Forest Acres *(32 Officers included in Index)*

Directors: Michael C. Crapps/Dir., CEO, Pres., James C. Leventis/Chmn., Thomas J. Johnson/Vice Chmn., Richard K. Bogan/Dir., O. A. Ethridge/Dir., Hinton G. Davis/Dir., James W. Kitchens/Dir., Alex Snipe/Dir., Roderick M. Todd/Dir., Chimin J. Chao/Dir., George H. Fann/Dir., Thomas C. Brown/Dir., Mitchell M. Willoughby/Dir., Anita B. Easter/Dir., Loretta R. Whitehead/Dir.

Owners: Alexander Snipe, Michael C. Crapps/1.31%, Richard K. Bogan, Thomas C. Brown, Chimin J. Chao, O. A. Ethridge, Joseph G. Sawyer, David K. Proctor, Loretta R. Whitehead, George H. Fann/1.87%, Roderick M. Todd, Insiders/14.73%, Thomas J. Johnson/2.61%, James W. Kitchens, Anita B. Easter *(19 Owners included in Index)*

Financial Data: Fiscal Year End:12/31   Latest Annual Data: 12/31/2006

Year	Sales	Net Income
2006	$31,715,000	$3,501,000
2005	$24,642,000	$3,093,000
2004	$14,818,000	$2,185,000

Curr. Assets:	$27,815,000	Curr. Liab.:	$464,171,000	P/E Ratio:	16.36
Plant, Equip.:	$20,960,000	Total Liab.:	$484,848,000	Indic. Yr. Divd.:	$0.280
Total Assets:	$548,056,000	Net Worth:	$63,208,000	Debt/ Equity:	0.2470

First Community Corp/TN

PO Box 820, 1104 East Main St., Rogersville, TN, 37857; *PH:* 1-423-272-5800; *Fax:* 1-423-272-6607; *http://* www.fcbanktn.com; *Email:* internetbanking@fcbanktn.com

General - Incorporation	TN	**Stock**- Price on:12/24/2007	$16.69
Employees	137	Stock Exchange	NDQ
Auditor	Pugh & Co, P.C	Ticker Symbol	NA
Stk Agt	NA	Outstanding Shares	3,220,000
Counsel	NA	E.P.S.	$1.02
DUNS No.	80-181-3429	Shareholders	NA

Business: The group's principal activity is to provide a range of customary services in Tennessee. The group is a state chartered commercial bank and operates through its subsidiary, first community bank of east Tennessee. The services provided include checking, now accounts, money market and savings accounts, certificates of deposit, individual retirement accounts, money transfers and safe deposit

facilities. Lending services include loans for business, agriculture, real estate, personal use, home improvements and automobiles. Other services provided include various uninsured, non-deposit products including annuities and mutual funds, brokerage services and secondary market mortgage processing services. The group conducts its operations through five offices located in rogersville and church hill.

Primary SIC and add'l.: 6712 6022

CIK No: 0000924960

Subsidiaries: First Community Bank Of East Tennessee, Rogersville Statutory Trust I, Rogersville Statutory Trust Ii

Officers: Mark A. Gamble/53/Dir., CEO, Pres., Tommy W. Young/72/Dir., Sec., Alan D. Baker/Sr. VP, Information Technology Officer - First Community Bank, Matthew V. Branham/Sr. VP, Collections Mgr., BSA Officer, Security Officer - First Community Bank, Betsy A. Newton/VP, Controller - First Community Bank, Tyler Clinch/44/CFO, Sr. VP - First Community Bank, Mary E. Boehms/Banking Officer, Exec. Assist., Assist. Sec. - Board, First Community Bank, Jerry C. Greene/43/Dir., VP, Steven M. Waller/VP, Mgr. - Church Hill Office, First Community Bank, Kaye M. Stewart/Sr. VP - Sr. Retail Lender, First Community Bank, Miranda Ferguson/VP - Retail Sales, Marketing Mgr. - Http, Wwwfcbanktncom, Pg_viewaspxpageid=216, Tammy L. Clevinger/VP, Mgr. - West Main Street Office, Rogersville, First Community Bank, Dana Parkinson/Banking Officer, Loan Administration Officer - First Community Bank, Steve Swinney/VP - Commercial Lender, First Community Bank, Brandy Wolfe/Baking Officer, Mgr. - Center Street Office, Kingsport, First Community Bank *(18 Officers included in Index)*

Directors: Mark A. Gamble/53/Dir., CEO, Pres., William J. Krickbaum/Chmn., Sidney K. Lawson/64/Dir., Kenneth E. Jenkins/82/Dir., David R. Johnson/57/Dir., Max A. Richardson/54/Dir., Jerry C. Greene/43/Dir., VP, Tommy W. Young/72/Dir., Sec., Leland A. Davis/85/Dir.

Owners: Mark A. Gamble/5.69%, Leland A. Davis/1.41%, Max A. Richardson, Kenneth E. Jenkins/7.50%, Insiders/35.79%, Tyler K. Clinch/0.61%, Sidney K. Lawson/4.93%, Tommy W. Young/3.38%, David R. Johnson/2.14%, Jerry C. Greene/2.51%, William J. Krickbaum/7.10%

Financial Data: *Fiscal Year End:* 12/31 *Latest Annual Data:* 12/31/2006

Year	Sales	Net Income
2006	$31,715,000	$3,501,000
2005	$24,642,000	$3,093,000
2004	$14,818,000	$2,185,000

Curr. Assets:	$27,815,000	Curr. Liab.:	$464,171,000	P/E Ratio:	16.36
Plant, Equip.:	$20,960,000	Total Liab.:	$484,848,000	Indic. Yr. Divd.:	$0.280
Total Assets:	$548,056,000	Net Worth:	$63,208,000	Debt/ Equity:	0.2470

First Community Financial Corp

4000 N Central Ave., Ste.100, Phoenix, AZ, 85012; *PH:* 1-717-789-4500; *http://* www.fcfinancial.com

General - Incorporation	PA	Stock - Price on:12/24/2007	NA
Employees	NA	Stock Exchange	OTC
Auditor	Beard Miller Co. LLP	Ticker Symbol	FCMP
Stk Agt	NA	Outstanding Shares	NA
Counsel	NA	E.P.S	NA
DUNS No.	NA	Shareholders	NA

Business: The group operates through its subsidiary whose principle activity is to provide banking services. Services of the group include residential real estate, commercial real estate, commercial loans, agricultural loans and consumer installment loans. The group operates from Mifflintown, Pennsylvania in the United States.

Primary SIC and add'l.: 6021

CIK No: 0000763293

Subsidiaries: First Community Financial Capital Trust I, The First National Bank of Mifflintown

Officers: Jim Adamany/Founder, Pres., Jody D. Graybill/43/Dir., Pres., Principal Executive Officer/$143,003.00, Lowell M. Shearer/61/Dir., Sec., Richard R. Leitzel/CFO, VP/$118,683.00, Timothy P. Stayer/55/VP, Community Services Division Mgr. - Bank, Lee K. Hopkins/65/VP, Credit Services Division Mgr. - Bank

Directors: Roger Shallenberger/60/Vice Chmn., Lowell M. Shearer/61/Dir., Sec., Samuel G. Kint/68/Dir., Clair E. McMillen/73/Dir., Jim Adamany/Founder, Pres., John P. Henry/54/Dir., James R. McLaughlin/67/Dir., Frank L. Wright/67/Dir., Jody D. Graybill/43/Dir., Pres., Principal Executive Officer, Joseph E. Barnes/71/Dir., Nancy S. Bratton/66/Dir., Charles C. Saner/63/Dir.

Owners: Frank L. Wright/7.14%, Insiders/19.95%, James R. McLaughlin/1.43%, Samuel G. Kint/1.81%, The First National Bank of Mifflintown Trust Department/7.25%, Jody D. Graybill, Clair E. McMillen, Marcie A. Barber, Lowell M. Shearer/3.18%, Charles C. Saner, Richard R. Leitzel, Joseph E. Barnes, Nancy S. Bratton, John P. Henry, Roger Shallenberger/3.57% *(16 Owners included in Index)*

First Consulting Group Inc

111 W Ocean Blvd., 4th Fl., Long Beach, CA, 90802; *PH:* 1-562-624-5200; *Fax:* 1-562-432-5774; *http://* www.fcg.com

General - Incorporation	DE	Stock - Price on:12/24/2007	$8.73
Employees	2,716	Stock Exchange	NDQ
Auditor	Grant Thornton LLP	Ticker Symbol	FCGI
Stk Agt	American Stock Transfer & Trust Co.	Outstanding Shares	26,880,000
Counsel	NA	E.P.S	$1.19
DUNS No.	03-190-3834	Shareholders	NA

Business: The group's principal activity is to provide information based consulting, integration and management services for healthcare, pharmaceutical and life sciences industries. The group operates through three segments: healthcare, which provides health delivery, health plans, government healthcare and technology services. Life sciences designs and develops the information systems used by pharmaceutical companies worldwide throughout their drug development life cycle. The group also provides information technology outsourcing services, hiring of the information technology staff of clients and running a part or all of the information technology operations at the client site. The group provides services throughout North America, Europe and Asia. The group acquired paragon solutions, inc. On 12-Feb-2003, phyve corporation on 20-Feb-2003 and coactive systems corporation on 30-May-2003.

Primary SIC and add'l.: 8742 8099 7379

CIK No: 0001049758

Subsidiaries: Fcg Csi, Inc., FCG Investment Company, Inc., FCG Software Services, FCG Ventures, Inc., First Consulting Group (UK) Limited, First Consulting Group GmbH, First Consulting Group, B.V., First Consulting Group, Inc., HPA Acquisition Corporation

Officers: Larry R. Ferguson/Dir., CEO/$669,368.00, Scot McConkey/Sr. VP, GM - Health Plan Business Unit, Josh Lieberman/Pres., GM - FCG Software Services, Jan L. Blue/Sr. VP - Corporate, Joseph M. Casper/57/Sr. VP, GM - Software Products/$438,702.00, Thomas D. Underwood/49/Sr. VP - FCG, Pres. - Global Shared Services Business Unit/$498,889.00, David C. Classen/Chief Medical Officer, Donald L. Driscoll/Pres., GM - Health Delivery Services Business Unit, Robert J. Smith/Pres., GM - Health Delivery Outsourcing Business Unit, Nigel Whitehead/Pres., GM - Life Sciences Business Unit, John T. Guda/CTO, Pres. - FCG Global Services, Thomas A. Watford/CFO, COO/$510,878.00, Michael A. Zuercher/Sr. VP - Corporate Affairs, General Counsel, Corp. Sec./$363,188.00, Philip Ockelmann/VP - Finance, Chief Accounting Officer

Directors: Larry R. Ferguson/Dir., CEO, Douglas G. Bergeron/45/Chmn., Cora M. Tellez/57/Dir., Fatima J. Reep/57/Dir., Steven Heck/58/Dir., Richard F. Nichol/64/Dir., Michael P. Downey/59/Dir., Robert G. Funari/59/Dir., Stephen E. Olson/64/Dir., Ronald V. Aprahamian/60/Dir.

Owners: Richard F. Nichol, Insiders/6.00%, Thomas A. Watford, Michael A. Zuercher, Michael P. Downey, Great Point Partners, LLC/6.00%, Robert G. Funari, Cora M. Tellez, Ronald V. Aprahamian/2.30%, Larry R. Ferguson, Douglas G. Bergeron, Bear Stearns Asset Management Inc./5.20%

Financial Data: *Fiscal Year End:* 12/30 *Latest Annual Data:* 12/29/2006

Year	Sales	Net Income
2006	$277,842,000	$20,860,000
2005	$293,152,000	-$18,609,000
2004	$287,289,000	$3,827,000

Curr. Assets:	$88,471,000	Curr. Liab.:	$31,770,000	P/E Ratio:	13.03
Plant, Equip.:	$11,829,000	Total Liab.:	$44,084,000	Indic. Yr. Divd.:	NA
Total Assets:	$140,399,000	Net Worth:	$96,315,000	Debt/ Equity:	NA

First Coweta Bank

61 Bullsboro Dr., Newnan, GA, 30263; *PH:* 1-770-251-4311; *http://* www.firstcowetabank.com

General - Incorporation		Stock - Price on:12/24/2007	$9.1
Employees	NA	Stock Exchange	OTC
Auditor	NA	Ticker Symbol	FCWT
Stk Agt	Registrar & Transfer Co	Outstanding Shares	NA
Counsel	NA	E.P.S	NA
DUNS No.	NA	Shareholders	NA

Business: The groups principal activity is to provide banking services. The services of the group include personal and business services, credit cards, merchant services, safe deposit boxes and telephone and online banking. The group operates from Georgia in the United States. The total assets of the group in the year 2006, was $121(million).

Primary SIC and add'l.: 6035

CIK No:

Officers: Mike Barber/Dir., CEO, Pres., James B. Ashurst/Investor Relations Officer, Mike Justice/Exec. VP - SLO, Dave Scogin/Sr. VP, CFO, Cindy D. Gosdin/COO, Sr. VP, Harold M. McCoy/VP, Stacy Roberts/Loan Operations Officer, Elizabeth Hodgson/Deposit Operations Officer, Heidi Roemer/Banking Officer - Relationship Banker, Jennie Freeman/Retail Loan Officer, Branch Mgr. - Summergrove, Rhonda Thornhill/Banking Officer, Branch Mgr. - Whitesburg, Kayla Hawthorne/Branch Mgr. - Main Office, Leonard Seawell/Investor Relations Officer

Directors: Mike Barber/Dir., CEO, Pres., Mayo H. Royal/Chmn., Walter W. Arnall/Dir., Keith Brooking/Dir., John E. Daviston/Dir., Dwight D. Ellison/Dir., Tommy Hardy/Dir., Tony Owens/Dir., Bernie Parks/Dir., Monte R. Sharp/Dir., Lynn Smith/Dir., John M. Stuckey/Dir.

First Data Corp

6200 S Quebec St., Greenwood Village, CO, 80111; *PH:* 1-402-951-7008; *http://* www.firstdatacorp.com

General - Incorporation	DE	Stock - Price on:12/24/2007	$32.81
Employees	26,100	Stock Exchange	NA
Auditor	Ernst & Young LLP	Ticker Symbol	NA
Stk Agt	Transfer Agent & Registrar	Outstanding Shares	754,410,000
Counsel	NA	E.P.S	$1.34
DUNS No.	60-436-0081	Shareholders	NA

Business: The groups principle activity is to provide innovative payment solutions for merchants and financial institutions. The groups solutions include payment, card issuing and loyalty solutions. The group operates from United States.

Primary SIC and add'l.: 7322 6153 7323

CIK No: 0000883980

Subsidiaries: Achex, Inc., Acn 095 393 338 Pty. Limited, ACT (Computer Services) Limited, Active Business Services Limited, Active Computer Services Limited, Active Software Projects Limited, American Rapid Corporation, Angelo Costa International, Ltd., Angelo Costa Srl, Atlantic Bankcard Properties Corporation, Atlantic States Bankcard Association, Inc., Autocash Pty. Limited, B1 PTI Services, Inc., Banc One Payment Services, LLC, Bankcard Investigative Group Inc. 354 Subsidiaries included in the Index

Officers: Michael D. Capellas/Chmn., CEO, Henry C. Duques/64/Chmn., CEO/$2,150,369.00, David Dibble/CTO, Exec. VP, David P. Bailis/52/Sr. Exec., VP/$2,150,266.00, Peter W. Boucher/Exec. VP - Human Resources, David Treinen/51/Exec. VP, Colin Wheeler/Contact - Media Relations, Nancy Etheredge/Contact - Media Relations, First Data Government Solutions, Thomas R. Bell/Chief Strategy Officer, Exec. VP, David R. Money/Exec. VP, General Counsel, Assist. Sec., Grace Chen Trent/Exec. VP - Marketing, Communications, Lee-Anne Porter/Contact - Sales Enquiries, First Data, Africa, Marianna Kollitiri/Media Enquiries, First Data in Africa, Suzi West/Media Enquiries, Africa, David Yates/Pres. - First Data International *(23 Officers included in Index)*

Directors: Michael D. Capellas/Chmn., CEO, Henry C. Duques/64/Chmn., CEO, David A. Coulter/60/Dir., Joan E. Spero/63/Dir., Arthur F. Weinbach/64/Dir., Peter B. Ellwood/64/Dir., Courtney F. Jones/67/Dir., Daniel P. Burnham/61/Dir., Charles T. Russell/78/Dir., James D. Robinson/72/Dir., Alison Davis/46/Dir., Richard P. Kiphart/66/Dir.

Owners: Pamela H. Patsley, David P. Bailis, David A. Coulter, Wellington Management Company/6.02%, Charles T. Russell, Daniel P. Burnham, Edward A. Labry, Peter B. Ellwood, Michael T. Whealy, James D. Robinson, Joan E. Spero, Guy A. Battista, Alison Davis, Richard P. Kiphart, Henry C. Duques *(20 Owners included in Index)*

Financial Data: *Fiscal Year End:* 12/31 *Latest Annual Data:* 12/31/2006

Year	Sales	Net Income
2006	$7,076,400,000	$1,513,400,000
2005	$10,568,200,000	$1,717,400,000
2004	$10,013,200,000	$1,875,200,000

Curr. Assets:	$3,331,900,000	Curr. Liab.:	$1,108,400,000	P/E Ratio:	24.49
Plant, Equip.:	$882,400,000	Total Liab.:	$24,207,600,000	Indic. Yr. Divd.:	$0.120
Total Assets:	$34,460,700,000	Net Worth:	$10,141,200,000	Debt/ Equity:	1.9243

First Defiance Financial Corp

601 Clinton St., Defiance, OH, 43512; *PH:* 1-419-782-5015; *Fax:* 1-419-782-5145; *http://* www.fdef.com

General - Incorporation	OH	**Stock** - Price on:12/24/2007	$28.57
Employees	476	Stock Exchange	NDQ
Auditor	Crowe Chizek & Co. LLC	Ticker Symbol	FDEF
Stk Agt	Registrar & Transfer Co	Outstanding Shares	7,200,000
Counsel	Vorys, Sater, Seymour & Pease	E.P.S.	$2.09
DUNS No.	92-853-8941	Shareholders	NA

Business: The group's principal activity is to provide banking services through its subsidiaries: first federal bank of the midwest and first insurance & investments. It operates in two lines of business: retail banking and insurance products. Retail banking consists of the operations of first federal, a federally chartered stock savings bank, which includes direct and indirect lending, deposit-gathering, small business services, commercial lending and consumer finance. First federal bank operates with 19 full service bank offices and 25 ATM locations in northwest Ohio counties. First insurance and investments is an insurance agency, which offers property and casualty insurance, life insurance, group health insurance and investment products.

Primary SIC and add'l.: 6712 6035 6411

CIK No: 0000946647

Subsidiaries: First Defiance Loan Servicing Company, First Defiance Service Company, First Federal Bank of the Midwest, First Insurance & Investments, Inc.

Officers: William J. Small/Chmn., CEO, Pres./$406,485.00, Rachel L. Ulrich/Exec. VP - Human Resources, John C. Wahl/Investor Relations Contact/$246,668.00, Gregory R. Allen/Exec. VP, Pres. - Southern Marketing, First Federal Bank/$271,859.00, Dennis E. Rose/Exec. VP - Operations, First Federal Bank, Jeffery D. Vereecke/Exec. VP - Retail Banking, First Federal Bank

Directors: William J. Small/Chmn., CEO, Pres., Thomas A. Voigt/Dir., Dwain I. Metzger/Dir., Douglas A. Burgei/Dir., James L. Rohrs/Dir., Peter A. Diehl/Dir., John U. Fauster/Dir., Gerald W. Monnin/Dir., Stephen L. Boomer/Dir., John L. Bookmyer/Dir., Samuel S. Strausbaugh/Dir.

Owners: Gregory R. Allen, Samuel S. Strausbaugh, Stephen L. Boomer, Private Capital Management/9.54%, John U. Fauster, Insiders/8.28%, Douglas A. Burgei, Dimensional Fund Advisors, Inc./7.32%, John C. Wahl/1.22%, James L. Rohrs/1.43%, John L. Bookmyer, Peter A. Diehl, Gerald W. Monnin, Dwain I. Metzger, First Defiance Financial Corp./7.78% (17 Owners included in Index)

Financial Data: Fiscal Year End:12/31 Latest Annual Data: 12/31/2006

Year	Sales		Net Income
2006	$112,691,000		$15,600,000
2005	$92,099,000		$11,970,000
2004	$69,432,000		$10,796,000
Curr. Assets:	$57,007,000	**Curr. Liab.:** $1,331,097,000	**P/E Ratio:** 13.67
Plant, Equip.:	$37,291,000	**Total Liab.:** $1,368,054,000	**Indic. Yr. Divd.:** $1.000
Total Assets:	$1,527,879,000	**Net Worth:** $159,825,000	**Debt/ Equity:** 0.2192

First Empire Entertainment Corp Inc

3400 One First Canadian Pl., Toronto, ON, M5X 1A4; *PH:* 1-416-622-2299

General - Incorporation	Canada	**Stock** - Price on:12/24/2007	NA
Employees	NA	Stock Exchange	NA
Auditor	Schwartz Levitsky Feldman LLP	Ticker Symbol	NA
Stk Agt	Equity Transfer Services Inc	Outstanding Shares	NA
Counsel	NA	E.P.S.	NA
DUNS No.	NA	Shareholders	NA

Business: The group's principle activity is to provide critical intelligence for the business, investor, and legal communities. The group operates from United States.

Primary SIC and add'l.: 7900

CIK No: 0001168981

Subsidiaries: Noble House Film and Television Inc.

Officers: Gregg Goldstein/Chmn., CEO, Stephen Wilson/Dir., CFO, Corp. Sec.

Directors: Gregg Goldstein/Chmn., CEO, Stephen Wilson/Dir., CFO, Corp. Sec., Joanne Butterfield Douglas/Dir., Steve Dabbah/Dir.

Curr. Assets:	$2,337,000	**Curr. Liab.:**	$104,000		
Plant, Equip.:	NA	**Total Liab.:**	$104,000	**Indic. Yr. Divd.:**	NA
Total Assets:	$2,359,000	**Net Worth:**	$2,255,000	**Debt/ Equity:**	NA

First Farmers & Merchants Corp

816 S Garden St., Columbia, TN, 38402; *PH:* 1-800-882-8378; *Fax:* 1-931-380-8359; *http://* www.fandmbank.com

General - Incorporation	TN	**Stock** - Price on:12/24/2007	$42
Employees	301	Stock Exchange	OTC
Auditor	KraftCPAs PLLC	Ticker Symbol	FIME
Stk Agt	NA	Outstanding Shares	NA
Counsel	NA	E.P.S.	NA
DUNS No.	00-894-2591	Shareholders	NA

Business: The group's principal activity is to provide commercial and mortgage banking services through twenty-one offices. The group also provides automatic teller machine services. The group accepts deposits and lends various loans along with investment activities. The deposit services provided by the group includes demand deposits, now and money market accounts, savings deposits and time deposits. The loan products offered are commercial, financial, agricultural, consumer and real estate loans.

Primary SIC and add'l.: 6021 6712

CIK No: 0000703329

Subsidiaries: First Farmers and Merchants Bank

Officers: Randy T. Stevens/Chmn., CEO/$330,144.00, Martha M. McKennon/63/Sec., Michael L. Ayer/Sr. Banking Exec. - Commercial Banking, Berry Brooks/Exec. VP - Commercial Sales Manger, Carol Messer/Contact - Columbia, Judy Musgrave/Contact - Spring Hill, John P. Tomlinson/Chief Administrative Officer/$218,681.00, Jody Claiborne/Contact - Campbell Station, Tim Pettus/Pres./$197,896.00, Patricia P. Moody/45/Assist. Treasurer/$96,562.00, Patricia P. Bearden/CFO, Harvey M. Church/Sr. Exec. - Private Banking, Maury County, Lynda Prosser/Contact - Columbia, Brian Williams/Chief Credit Officer, Timothy E. Pettus/56/Pres. (30 Officers included in Index)

Directors: Randy T. Stevens/Chmn., CEO, Dan C. Wheeler/65/Dir., Darlene M. Baxter/61/Dir., W. Lacy Upchurch/61/Dir., Kenneth A. Abercrombie/65/Dir., James L. Bailey/65/Dir., Hulet M. Chaney/63/Dir., Terry H. Cook/67/Dir., Thomas Napier Gordon/56/Dir., Rebecca O. Hawkins/67/Dir., Joseph W. Remke/57/Dir., William R. Walter/66/Dir., Daniel C. Wheeler/65/Dir., David S. Williams/61/Dir., Donald W. Wright/68/Dir. (16 Directors included in Index)

Owners: Hulet M. Chaney, James L. Bailey, Lacy W. Upchurch, David S. Williams, Martha M. McKennon, Houston N. Parks, Joseph W. Remke, Donald W. Wright, First Farmers and Merchants Bank/13.92%, Darlene M.Baxter, Randy T. Stevens/1.25%, Thomas Napier Gordon/2.37%, John P. Tomlinson, James E. York/1.38%, Patricia P. Moody (22 Owners included in Index)

First Federal Bancshares of Arkansas Inc

1401 Hwy. , 62-65 North, Harrison, AR, 72601; *PH:* 1-870-741-7641; *Fax:* 1-870-365-8369; *http://* www.ffbh.com; *Email:* info@ffbh.com

General - Incorporation	TX	**Stock** - Price on:12/24/2007	$23.5001
Employees	279	Stock Exchange	NDQ
Auditor	Deloitte & Touche LLP	Ticker Symbol	FFBH
Stk Agt	Registrar & Transfer Co	Outstanding Shares	4,870,000
Counsel	NA	E.P.S.	$0.97
DUNS No.	96-521-2632	Shareholders	NA

Business: The group's principal activities are to provide conventional first mortgage loans collateralized by one-to-four family residential property. The group is a unitary holding company of the first federal bank of Arkansas. The bank provides multi-family residential loans, commercial real estate loans, construction loans, commercial loans and consumer loans. The group operates through its main office and thirteen full service branch offices located in northcentral and northwest Arkansas. The group provides services mainly to individuals and small and medium-sized businesses.

Primary SIC and add'l.: 6712 6035

CIK No: 0001006424

Subsidiaries: First Federal Bank of Arkansas, FA, First Harrison Service Corporation

Officers: Larry J. Brandt/59/Chmn., CEO/$487,070.00, Tommy Richardson/COO, Pres., Sec./$314,885.00, Sherri R. Billings/50/CFO, Exec. VP/$299,951.00, Ross Mallioux/45/Pres. - Western Division, Chief Lending Officer/$278,320.00

Directors: Larry J. Brandt/59/Chmn., CEO, John P. Hammerschmidt/85/Chmn., Frank Conner/58/Dir., Jeffrey L. Brandt/37/Dir., Kenneth C. Savells/55/Dir.

Owners: John P. Hammerschmidt/1.10%, Kenneth C. Savells, Frank Conner, Sherri R. Billings/1.50%, First Manhattan Co./8.40%, Insiders/14.20%, Ross Mallioux/1.20%, Larry J. Brandt/7.30%, First Federal Bancshares of Arkansas, Inc./13.10%, Dimensional Fund Advisors, Inc./7.40%, Jeffrey L. Brandt/2.50%, Tommy W. Richardson/1.70%

Financial Data: Fiscal Year End:12/31 Latest Annual Data: 06/30/2007

Year	Sales		Net Income
2007	NA		NA
2006	NA		NA
2005	$53,046,000		$7,850,000
Curr. Assets:	$45,517,000	**Curr. Liab.:** $772,570,000	**P/E Ratio:** 16.27
Plant, Equip.:	$24,242,000	**Total Liab.:** $776,902,000	**Indic. Yr. Divd.:** $0.640
Total Assets:	$852,475,000	**Net Worth:** $75,573,000	**Debt/ Equity:** NA

First Federal Bankshares Inc

329 Pierce St., Sioux City, IA, 51101; *PH:* 1-712-277-0200; *Fax:* 1-712-277-0213; *http://* www.firstfederalbank.com

General - Incorporation	DE	**Stock** - Price on:12/24/2007	$18.5
Employees	198	Stock Exchange	NDQ
Auditor	McGladrey & Pullen LLP	Ticker Symbol	FFSX
Stk Agt	Registrar & Transfer Co	Outstanding Shares	3,400,000
Counsel	NA	E.P.S.	$0.76
DUNS No.	NA	Shareholders	NA

Business: The group's principal activities are to provide retail and commercial banking services and related financial services. The group provides traditional banking products and services through accepting deposits and offering mortgage, consumer and commercial loans. The group's primary lending activity involves the origination of fixed rate and adjustable rate mortgage loans secured by single-family residential, multi-family residential and non-residential real estate. The group conducts operations through its main office in sioux city, Iowa, and its 15 branch offices in northwest and central Iowa and northeast Nebraska.

Primary SIC and add'l.: 6035 6712

CIK No: 0001075348

Subsidiaries: Equity Services, Inc., First Federal Bank

Officers: Michael W. Dosland/Dir., CEO, Pres./$297,418.00, Scott Sehnert/Exec. VP/$181,025.00, Suzette F. Hoevet/Corp. Sec., Michael S. Moderski/Sr. VP, CFO, Treasurer/$147,287.00, B. J. Schneiderman/Sr. VP/$194,302.00, Peggy Smith/Sr. VP/$140,059.00, Amy Anderson-Vali/Sr. VP

Directors: Michael W. Dosland/Dir., CEO, Pres., Arlene T. Curry/Chmn., Ronald A. Jorgensen/Dir., Barry E. Backhaus/Dir., Gary L. Evans/Dir., Charles D. Terlouw/Dir., Jon G. Cleghorn/Dir., Allen J. Johnson/Dir., David M. Roederer/Dir.

Owners: David M. Roederer, Insiders/3.90%, Michael W. Dosland, Ronald A. Jorgensen, Allen J. Johnson, Michael S. Moderski, Katherine A. Bousquet, Jon G. Cleghorn/1.30%, Barry E. Backhaus/2.70%, Charles D. Terlouw, Amy Anderson-Vali, B. J. Schneiderman, Vantus Bank Employee Stock Ownership Plan/6.10%, Peggy E. Smith, Gary L. Evans (18 Owners included in Index)

Financial Data: Fiscal Year End:12/31 Latest Annual Data: 06/30/2007

Year	Sales		Net Income
2007	$41,571,000		$3,069,000
2006	$39,059,000		$3,332,000
2005	$38,626,000		$4,213,000
Curr. Assets:	$42,533,000	**Curr. Liab.:** $543,235,000	**P/E Ratio:** 20.11
Plant, Equip.:	$12,545,000	**Total Liab.:** $544,212,000	**Indic. Yr. Divd.:** $0.420
Total Assets:	$612,535,000	**Net Worth:** $68,324,000	**Debt/ Equity:** NA

First Federal of Northern Michigan Bancorp Inc

100 S 2nd Ave., Alpena, MI, 49707; ***PH:*** 1-989-356-9041; ***Fax:*** 1-989-354-8671; ***http://*** www.first-federal.com

General - Incorporation	MD	**Stock**- Price on:12/24/2007	$9.1899
Employees	105	Stock Exchange	NDQ
Auditor	Plante & Moran, PLLC	Ticker Symbol	FFNM
Stk Agt	Registrar & Transfer Co	Outstanding Shares	2,880,000
Counsel	NA	E.P.S	-$0.04
DUNS No.	NA	Shareholders	NA

Business: The group's principal activity is to attract deposits from the general public and lend loans. The deposit instruments include now accounts, regular savings, money market deposit, term certificate accounts and individual retirement accounts. The loan portfolio includes real estate loans and non-real estate loans including commercial loans, consumer installment loans, credit card advances and loans secured by savings accounts, automobiles, mobile homes, boats, recreational vehicles and other personal property. The group's operations are carried out through eight full-service facilities located in cheboygan, alpena, iosco, otsego, montmorency and oscoda counties, Michigan.

Primary SIC and add'l.: 6712 6035

CIK No: 0001128227

Subsidiaries: Financial Services and Mortgage Corporation, First Federal of Northern Michigan, InsuranCenter of Alpena

Officers: Martin Thomson/Dir., CEO/$202,099.00, Michael Mahler/Dir., Exec. VP, COO, Jerry Tracey/Exec. VP, Chief Lending Officer, Amy Essex/CFO, Corp. Sec., Treasurer/$117,329.00, Joseph Gentry/VP - Human - Resources, Kathy Brown/VP - Compliance, Jerome W. Tracey/48/Exec. VP, Chief Lending Officer/$122,063.00, Linda Sansom/Sr. VP - Mortgage, Consumer Lending/$169,340.00, Shauna McLean/Internal Auditor

Directors: Martin Thomson/Dir., CEO, James Rapin/Chmn., Gary Vanmassenhove/Dir., Keith Wallace/Dir., Tom R. Townsend/Dir.

Owners: Thomas R. Townsend, Thomson Horstmann & Bryant, Inc./6.01%, First Federal of Northern Michigan Employee Stock Ownership Plan/5.74%, Tontine Associates, LLC/8.43%, Michael W. Mahler, James C. Rapin, Jerome W. Tracey, Keith D. Wallace, Gary C. VanMassenhove, Insiders/6.49%, Amy E. Essex, Martin A. Thomson/2.09%

Financial Data: ***Fiscal Year End:*** 12/31 ***Latest Annual Data:*** 12/31/2006

Year	Sales	Net Income
2006	$21,568,000	$463,000
2005	$19,534,000	$442,000
2004	$18,036,000	$404,000

Curr. Assets:	$7,132,000	**Curr. Liab.:**	$244,314,000	**P/E Ratio:**	102.11
Plant, Equip.:	$8,075,000	**Total Liab.:**	$245,506,000	**Indic. Yr. Divd.:**	$0.200
Total Assets:	$280,959,000	**Net Worth:**	$35,453,000	**Debt/ Equity:**	0.2963

First Financial Bancorp

300 High St., Hamilton, OH, 45011; ***PH:*** 1-513-867-4700; ***Fax:*** 1-513-867-3111; ***http://*** bankatfirst.com

General - Incorporation	OH	**Stock**- Price on:12/24/2007	$14.88
Employees	1,283	Stock Exchange	NDQ
Auditor	Ernst & Young LLP	Ticker Symbol	FFBC
Stk Agt	Registrar & Transfer Co	Outstanding Shares	38,920,000
Counsel	NA	E.P.S	$0.75
DUNS No.	10-148-8302	Shareholders	NA

Business: The group's principal activity is to provide a wide range of banking services to individuals and business concerns. The operations of the group are conducted through its subsidiaries. The banking services include commercial lending, residential mortgage, real estate lending, consumer credit, credit card and other personal loan financing. The group provides various deposits including savings and transaction accounts, checking accounts, regular savings accounts, money market deposit accounts and time deposits. In addition, it provides trust and asset management services and insurance services. The group and its subsidiaries operate from 108 banking offices and one service center. The service center and 56 banking offices are located in Ohio, 47 offices are located in Indiana, three in Kentucky and two in Michigan. During 2003, the group acquired statutory trust ii.

Primary SIC and add'l.: 6021 6035

CIK No: 0000708955

Subsidiaries: First Financial Bank, National Association

Officers: Claude E. Davis/Dir., CEO, Pres./$1,118,925.00, Jill L. Wyman/Sr. VP - Sales, Marketing, Franklin J. Hall/Sr. VP, CFO/$349,866.00, John C. Hoying/Sr. VP - Retail Credit, Product Mgmt, Douglas C. Lefferson/COO, Exec. VP/$493,077.00, Samuel J. Munafo/Exec. VP - Banking Markets/$470,740.00, Richard Barbercheck/Sr. VP, Chief Credit Officer, Margaret Stratman/Contact - Agent, Anthony M. Stollings/Chief Accounting Officer, Sr. VP, Gregory A. Gehlmann/Sr. VP, General Counsel/$341,871.00, Terri J. Ziepfel/VP - Shareholder Relations

Directors: Claude E. Davis/Dir., CEO, Pres., Bruce E. Leep/Chmn., Susan L. Knust/Dir., Richard E. Olszewski/Dir., Wickliffe J. Ach/Dir., Corinne R. Finnerty/Dir., Barry S. Porter/Dir., Steven C. Posey/Dir., William J. Kramer/Dir., Murph Knapke/Dir., Donald M. Cisle/Dir.

Owners: First Financial Bank, National Association/14.72%, Franklin J.Hall, Richard E. Olszewski, Murph Knapke, Barry S. Porter, Samuel J. Munafo, Donald M. Cisle, Steven C. Posey, Barclays Global Investors Japan Trust and/5.06%, Susan L. Knust, Wickliffe J. Ach, Insiders, Bruce E. Leep, Gregory A. Gehlmann, Douglas C. Lefferson *(18 Owners included in Index)*

Financial Data: ***Fiscal Year End:*** 12/31 ***Latest Annual Data:*** 12/31/2006

Year	Sales	Net Income
2006	$281,854,000	$21,271,000
2005	$260,478,000	$37,933,000
2004	$263,019,000	$41,118,000

Curr. Assets:	$360,392,000	**Curr. Liab.:**	$2,921,428,000	**P/E Ratio:**	22.89
Plant, Equip.:	$79,609,000	**Total Liab.:**	$3,016,120,000	**Indic. Yr. Divd.:**	$0.640
Total Assets:	$3,301,599,000	**Net Worth:**	$285,479,000	**Debt/ Equity:**	0.3208

First Financial Bankshares Inc

400 Pine St., Abilene, TX, 79601; ***PH:*** 1-325-627-7155; ***Fax:*** 1-325-627-7393; ***http://*** www.ffin.com; ***Email:*** investorrelations@ffin.com

General - Incorporation	TX	**Stock**- Price on:12/24/2007	$38.18
Employees	975	Stock Exchange	NDQ
Auditor	Ernst & Young LLP	Ticker Symbol	FFIN
Stk Agt	Bank of New York	Outstanding Shares	20,750,000
Counsel	NA	E.P.S	$2.33
DUNS No.	02-033-1286	Shareholders	NA

Business: The group's principle activity is to provide banking services to consumers and commercial customers in north central and west Texas. A holding company for ten banks, the group accepts holding checking, savings and time deposits, makes loans and offers automated teller machines, drive-in and night deposit services, safe deposit facilities, funds transmit and other customary banking services. Its trust department administers estates, testamentary trusts, living trusts and agency accounts. Some of the subsidiaries also administer pension plans, profit sharing plans and other employee benefit plans and provide securities brokerage services. The deposits of all the banks are insured by the federal deposit insurance corporation upto $100,000 per depositor. The group's quarterly income for Sep'07 was 12.25 millions of USD.

Primary SIC and add'l.: 6021 6712

CIK No: 0000036029

Subsidiaries: City National Bank, First Financial Bank, National Association, First Financial Bankshares of Delaware, Inc., First Financial Insurance Agency, Inc., First Financial Investments, Inc., First Financial Trust & Asset Management, First National Bank, Sweetwater, First Technology Services, Inc., Hereford State Bank, San Angelo National Bank, Weatherford National Bank

Officers: Scott F. Dueser/CEO, Pres./$489,831.00, J. V. Martin/Chmn., CEO - First National Bank, Doyle Lee/Chmn., CEO - Weatherford National Bank, Ron Butler/Pres., CEO - First Financial Bank, Michael Boyd/Pres., CEO - San Angelo National Bank, Marelyn Shedd/Sr. VP - First Financial Bank, Dave Hogan/Dir. - Investor Relations, Corporate Communications, William Mills/Loan Review Officer, Daniel A. Ortiz/VP - Multicultural Development, Bill Rowe/VP, Gary S. Gragg/Exec. VP/$172,772.00, Kirk Thaxton/Exec. VP, Trust Officer - Abilenes First National Bank, Michelle Stevens/Sr. VP, Bruce J. Hildebrand/Exec. VP, CFO, Treasurer, Sec./$291,019.00, Gaila Kilpatrick/Assist. Sec. *(19 Officers included in Index)*

Directors: Kenneth T. Murphy/Chmn., F. L. Stephens/Dir., Johnny Trotter/Dir., Joseph E. Canon/Dir., Raymond A. McDaniel/Dir., Jack D. Ramsey/Dir., Kade L. Matthews/Dir., Bynum Miers/Dir., Mac A. Coalson/Dir., Derrell E. Johnson/Dir., David Copeland/Dir., James M. Parker/Dir., Dian Graves Stai/Dir.

Owners: F. L. Stephens/0.34%, Bruce J. Hildebrand, Robert S. Patterson/0.07%, Scott F. Dueser/1.11%, Kade L. Matthews/0.91%, Kenneth T. Murphy/0.76%, Bynum Miers/0.28%, Gary Gragg/0.04%, Murray Edwards/0.21%, Gary L. Webb/0.01%, Insiders/6.78%, Johnny E. Trotter/0.44%, Dian Graves Stai/0.35%, Derrell E. Johnson/0.19%

Financial Data: ***Fiscal Year End:*** 12/31 ***Latest Annual Data:*** 12/31/2006

Year	Sales	Net Income
2006	$199,172,000	$46,029,000
2005	$168,124,000	$44,023,000
2004	$138,797,000	$39,171,000

Curr. Assets:	$192,977,000	**Curr. Liab.:**	$2,532,682,000	**P/E Ratio:**	17.28
Plant, Equip.:	$60,963,000	**Total Liab.:**	$2,549,263,000	**Indic. Yr. Divd.:**	$1.280
Total Assets:	$2,850,165,000	**Net Worth:**	$300,901,000	**Debt/ Equity:**	NA

First Financial Corp/IN

1 First Financial Plz., Terre Haute, IN, 47807; ***PH:*** 1-812-398-4100; ***Fax:*** 1-812-398-4101; ***http://*** www.first-online.com

General - Incorporation	IN	**Stock**- Price on:12/24/2007	$28.59
Employees	798	Stock Exchange	NDQ
Auditor	Crowe Chizek & Co. LLC	Ticker Symbol	NA
Stk Agt	NA	Outstanding Shares	13,200,000
Counsel	NA	E.P.S	$1.85
DUNS No.	11-733-1447	Shareholders	NA

Business: The group's principle activities are to provide wide variety of financial services, including commercial and consumer loans, trust account services, lease financing and depository services. It is a multi-bank holding company, which operates through its 9 subsidiaries and has 46 branches in west-central Indiana and east-central Illinois. The primary source of the group's revenue is derived through loans to middle-income individuals and investment activities. The group's quarterly income for Sep'07 was 6.36 millions of USD.

Primary SIC and add'l.: 6021 6712

CIK No: 0000714562

Subsidiaries: First Financial Bank N.A., Forrest Sherer, Inc., The Morris Plan Company of Terre Haute, Inc.

Officers: Norman L. Lowery/61/Vice Chmn., CEO/$1,066,504.00, Donald E. Smith/81/Chmn., Pres./$1,165,897.00, Michael A. Carty/CFO, Sec.,Treasurer/$287,675.00, Jeff Nickels/Contact - Commercial Sale, First Financial Bank

Directors: Norman L. Lowery/61/Vice Chmn., CEO, Donald E. Smith/81/Chmn., Pres., Curtis W. Brighton/54/Dir., Guille B. Cox/62/Dir., Anton H. George/48/Dir., Thomas T. Dinkel/57/Dir., Patrick O'Leary/71/Dir., Ronald K. Rich/70/Dir., Gregory L. Gibson/45/Dir., Virginia L. Smith/59/Dir.

Owners: Guille B. Cox, Ronald K. Rich, Patrick OLeary, T. Rigasco Trust Co-Trustees:/7.26%, Anton H. George, Donald E. Smith/1.21%, Michael A. Carty, Princeton Mining Company/9.94%, First Financial Corporation/6.47%, Curtis W. Brighton, Thomas T. Dinkel, Richard O. White, Norman L. Lowery, Dimension Fund Advisors LP/6.22%, Insiders/3.45% *(18 Owners included in Index)*

Financial Data: ***Fiscal Year End:*** 12/31 ***Latest Annual Data:*** 12/31/2006

Year	Sales	Net Income
2006	$159,658,000	$23,539,000
2005	$153,672,000	$23,054,000
2004	$152,807,000	$28,009,000

Curr. Assets:	$113,091,000	**Curr. Liab.:**	$1,518,885,000	**P/E Ratio:**	15.45
Plant, Equip.:	$36,461,000	**Total Liab.:**	$1,904,738,000	**Indic. Yr. Divd.:**	$0.860
Total Assets:	$2,175,998,000	**Net Worth:**	$271,260,000	**Debt/ Equity:**	1.2329

First Financial Corp/TX

800 Washington Ave., Waco, TX, 76701; ***PH:*** 1-254-772-5432; ***http://*** www.first-online.com

General - Incorporation	TX	**Stock**- Price on:12/24/2007	$28.08
Employees	798	Stock Exchange	NDQ
Auditor	Pattillo, Brown & Hill LLP	Ticker Symbol	THFF
Stk Agt	Mellon Investor Services LLC	Outstanding Shares	13,200,000
Counsel	NA	E.P.S	$1.92
DUNS No.	07-934-2861	Shareholders	NA

Business: The group's principal activities are to provide various financial services through its wholly-owned subsidiaries. The services provided by the group include servicing of manufactured home loans, originating and servicing residential mortgage loans, insurance activities, consulting and data processing services to related companies. The loan servicing activity includes the collection of payments from borrowers and remitting the proceeds to investors, accounting for loan principal and interest, investor reporting and holding escrow funds. Under the insurance services, the company sells hazard insurance policies relating to manufactured home loans.

Primary SIC and add'l.: 6162 7374 6159 6331

CIK No: 0000036315

Subsidiaries: First Advisory Services, Inc., First Financial Information Services, First Preference Mortgage Corp, First Preference Properties, Inc., Shelter Resources, Inc., Tri-Triangle Insurance Agency, Inc.

Officers: Cary W. Sparks/Sr. VP, Trust Officer, Chris E. Fenimore/VP, Trust Officer, Carol D. Myers/Assist. VP, Trust Officer, Amanda Henry/Trust Officer, Christine Hollowell/Trust Officer, Richard Hudson/VP, Trust Officer, Stephen M. Browning/Employee Benefits Officer, Tammy S. Evinger/Corporate Trust Officer, Beverly A. Christopher/Trust Tax Officer, Jennifer L. Hanley/Assist. VP, Trust Operations Officer - Trust Operations Department, Dan Callahan/VP, Trust Investment Officer

Owners: David W. Mann, First Financial Holdings, Ltd, Insiders, Harold E. Allison, III, JRPM Investments, Ltd.

Financial Data: *Fiscal Year End:*12/31 *Latest Annual Data:* 12/31/2006

Year	Sales	Net Income
2006	$159,658,000	$23,539,000
2005	$153,672,000	$23,054,000
2004	$152,807,000	$28,009,000

Curr. Assets:	$113,091,000	**Curr. Liab.:**	$1,518,885,000	**P/E Ratio:**	15.26
Plant, Equip.:	$36,461,000	**Total Liab.:**	$1,904,738,000	**Indic. Yr. Divd.:**	$0.880
Total Assets:	$2,175,998,000	**Net Worth:**	$271,260,000	**Debt/ Equity:**	1.2600

First Financial Holdings Inc

34 Broad St., Charleston, SC, 29401; ***PH:*** 1-843-529-5931; ***Fax:*** 1-843-529-5929; ***http://*** www.firstfinancialholdings.com; ***Email:*** investorrelations@firstfinancialholdings.com

General - Incorporation	DE	**Stock**- Price on:12/24/2007	$33.95
Employees	847	Stock Exchange	NDQ
Auditor	KPMG LLP	Ticker Symbol	FFCH
Stk Agt	Registrar & Transfer Co	Outstanding Shares	11,930,000
Counsel	Breyer & Associate PC	E.P.S	$2.25
DUNS No.	36-230-5120	Shareholders	NA

Business: The group's principal activity is to provide a wide range of financial services including acceptance of deposits, origination of loans and insurance services. It provides a number of deposit accounts including noninterest-bearing and interest-bearing checking accounts, savings accounts, money market account, individual retirement accounts and certificate accounts. The group's loan portfolio includes first mortgage loans on residential properties, non-residential mortgage loans, construction, consumer and commercial business loans. In addition, it provides brokerages services, property and casualty insurance, trust and fiduciary services, reinsurance of private mortgage insurance and certain passive investment activities. During the fiscal year 2003, it acquired woodruff and company inc and certain assets of mca administrators inc. On 29-Jan-2004, the group acquired the kimbrell company inc, preferred markets inc & Atlantic acceptance corporation.

Primary SIC and add'l.: 6712 6035

CIK No: 0000787075

Subsidiaries: Atlantic Acceptance Corporation, Benefit Administrators, Inc., Broad Street Holdings, Inc., Broad Street Investments, Inc., Edisto Corporation of Oristo, First Federal Savings and Loan Association of Charleston, First Reinsurance Holdings, Inc., First Southeast Fiduciary and Trust Services, Inc., First Southeast Insurance Services, Inc., First Southeast Investor Services, Inc., First Southeast Reinsurance Co., Inc., Great Atlantic Mortgage, Johnson Insurance Associates, Inc., Kimbrell Insurance Group, Inc., Kinghorn Insurance Services, Inc 22 Subsidiaries included in the Index

Officers: Thomas A. Hood/62/CEO, Pres., John L. Ott/60/Exec. VP, Exec. VP - Retail Banking Division, Charles F. Baarcke/61/Exec. VP, Exec. VP - Lending Division, Susan E. Baham/58/COO, Exec. VP, Dee Bee Wright/VP - Investor Relations, Wayne R. Hall/58/CFO, Exec. VP

Directors: Thomas A. Hood/62/CEO, Pres., James C. Murray/Chmn., James L. Rowe/Dir., Paula Harper Bethea/Dir., Ronnie M. Givens/Dir., Kent D. Sharples/Dir., Thomas J. Johnson/Dir.

Owners: Thomas J. Johnson, Charles F. Baarcke, Wayne R. Hall, Susan E. Baham, Kent D. Sharples, James L. Rowe, Private Capital Management, L. P./8.11%, John L. Ott/1.20%, Thomas A. Hood/1.96%, Ronnie M. Givens, Paula Harper Bethea, Paul G. Campbell, James C. Murray, Barclays Global Investors, NA/7.00%, Insiders/6.61% *(16 Owners included in Index)*

Financial Data: *Fiscal Year End:*09/30 *Latest Annual Data:* 9/30/2006

Year	Sales	Net Income
2006	$205,504,000	$27,629,000
2005	$180,076,000	$26,225,000
2004	$168,768,000	$24,554,000

Curr. Assets:	$135,572,000	**Curr. Liab.:**	$2,422,230,000	**P/E Ratio:**	15.43
Plant, Equip.:	$58,000,000	**Total Liab.:**	$2,474,363,000	**Indic. Yr. Divd.:**	$1.000
Total Assets:	$2,658,128,000	**Net Worth:**	$183,765,000	**Debt/ Equity:**	0.2450

First Financial Service Corp

2323 Ring Rd., Elizabethtown, KY, 42701; ***PH:*** 1-270-765-2131; ***Fax:*** 1-270-765-2135; ***http://*** www.ffsbky.com

General - Incorporation	KY	**Stock**- Price on:12/24/2007	$28.5
Employees	262	Stock Exchange	NDQ
Auditor	Crowe Chizek & Co. LLC	Ticker Symbol	FFKY
Stk Agt	Illinois Stock Transfer Co	Outstanding Shares	4,330,000
Counsel	NA	E.P.S	$2.01
DUNS No.	NA	Shareholders	NA

Business: The group's principal activity is to provide bank services to retail and commercial customers. It is a holding company for first federal savings bank of elizabethtown and operations in 13 full-service banking centers in six contiguous counties in Kentucky along the interstate 65 corridor. The bank attracting deposits from the general public and origination of mortgage loans on single-family residences, multi-family housing and commercial property. The bank also makes home improvement loans, consumer loans and commercial business loans. The principal sources of funds for the bank's lending and investment activities are deposits, repayment of loans and federal home loan bank advances. The bank's principal source of income is interest on loans. In addition, other income is derived from loan origination fees, service charges, returns on investment securities, gain on sale of mortgage loans, and brokerage and insurance commissions.

Primary SIC and add'l.: 6035 6712

CIK No: 0000854395

Subsidiaries: First Federal Office Park, LLC, First Federal Savings Bank of Elizabethtown, First Heartland Mortgage of Elizabethtown, First Service Corporation of Elizabethtown

Officers: Keith B. Johnson/Dir., CEO, Pres./$414,456.00, Shelia Johnson/VP - Business Lending, Jim McFerran/Sr. VP - Business Lending, Miller Boley/Business Development Officer - Business Lending, Donna Bernard/Mgr. - Shepherdsville Banking Center, Mary Willis/Mgr. - Hillview Banking Center, Walter Brown/Mgr. - Stony Brook Banking Center, David G. Bush/VP, Mgr. - Collections, James Thomas/Mgr. - Assist. Collection, Alan Howell/Sr. VP - Business Lending, Cathy England/VP - Business Lending, Dwight Brown/Sr. VP - Business Lending, Jeremy Janes/Assist. VP - Business Lending, Larry Hawkins/Exec. VP, Chief Lending Officer - Business Lending/$177,247.00, Anne Moran/55/Chief Retail Officer, Exec. VP/$181,525.00 *(29 Officers included in Index)*

Directors: Keith B. Johnson/Dir., CEO, Pres., Stephen Mouser/Dir., Donald Scheer/Dir., Alton J. Rider/Dir., Michael Thomas/Dir., Robert M. Brown/Dir., Diane Logsdon/Dir., Bob Brown/Dir., Gail Schomp/Dir., Walter D. Huddleston/Dir., Wreno M. Hall/Dir., John L. Newcomb/Dir.

Owners: Donald Scheer, Keith B. Johnson/1.62%, Gregory Schreacke, Diane E. Logsdon, Larry Hawkins, Wreno M. Hall/2.47%, Walter D. Huddleston/2.26%, Alton J. Rider/2.44%, Anne Moran, Gail L. Schomp/5.21%, Robert M. Brown, Stephen J. Mouser, Michael L. Thomas, Insiders/17.79%, Charles Chaney *(16 Owners included in Index)*

Financial Data: *Fiscal Year End:*12/31 *Latest Annual Data:* 12/31/2006

Year	Sales	Net Income
2006	$61,571,000	$10,337,000
2005	$53,435,000	$9,144,000
2004	$47,247,000	$7,790,000

Curr. Assets:	$23,176,000	**Curr. Liab.:**	$739,355,000	**P/E Ratio:**	12.23
Plant, Equip.:	$23,837,000	**Total Liab.:**	$750,728,000	**Indic. Yr. Divd.:**	$0.760
Total Assets:	$822,826,000	**Net Worth:**	$72,098,000	**Debt/ Equity:**	0.1390

First Fortis Life Insurance Co

308 Maltbie St., Ste. 200, Syracuse, NY, 13204; ***PH:*** 1-315-451-0066

General - Incorporation	NY	**Stock**- Price on:12/24/2007	$58.94
Employees	13,400	Stock Exchange	NYSE
Auditor	PricewaterhouseCoopers LLP	Ticker Symbol	NA
Stk Agt	NA	Outstanding Shares	121,010,000
Counsel	NA	E.P.S	$6.00
DUNS No.	62-181-6750	Shareholders	NA

Business: The group's principle activity is to offer and market insurance products. The products offered by the group include fixed and variable annuity contracts and group life, accident and health insurance policies. The products of the group are marketed to small business and individuals through independent agents, brokers and financial institutions. The group operates solely in the domestic market. The group operates from United States.

Primary SIC and add'l.: 6321 6311

CIK No: 0000914804

Officers: Bruce P. Camacho/CEO, Pres., Peter A. Walker/CFO, Treasurer

Directors: Terry Kryshak/Dir., Melissa J.T. Hall/Dir., Allen R. Freedman/Dir., Carroll H. MacKin/Dir., Dale Edward Gardner/Dir., Lesley G. Silvester/Dir., Esther L. Nelson/Dir.

Financial Data: *Fiscal Year End:*12/31 *Latest Annual Data:* 12/31/2006

Year	Sales	Net Income
2006	$8,070,584,000	$717,418,000
2005	$7,497,675,000	$479,355,000
2004	$7,403,464,000	$350,560,000

Curr. Assets:	$5,828,769,000	**Curr. Liab.:**	$5,120,832,000	**P/E Ratio:**	9.82
Plant, Equip.:	$275,201,000	**Total Liab.:**	$21,310,391,000	**Indic. Yr. Divd.:**	$0.480
Total Assets:	$25,165,148,000	**Net Worth:**	$3,832,597,000	**Debt/ Equity:**	0.3490

First Franklin Corp

4750 Ashwood Dr., Cincinnati, OH, 45241; ***PH:*** 1-513-469-8000; ***Fax:*** 1-513-469-5360; ***http://*** www.franklinsavings.com

General - Incorporation	DE	**Stock**- Price on:12/24/2007	$16
Employees	49	Stock Exchange	NDQ
Auditor	Clark, Schaefer, Hackett & Co	Ticker Symbol	FFHS
Stk Agt	National City Bank	Outstanding Shares	1,680,000
Counsel	Vorys, Sater, Seymour & Pease	E.P.S	$0.77
DUNS No.	18-854-5289	Shareholders	NA

Business: The group's principal activity is to accept savings deposits from the general public and originate mortgage loans for the purpose of financing, refinancing or constructing one-to-four family owner occupied residential real estate. The group is a state chartered savings and loan association operating through seven banking offices in hamilton county, Ohio. The deposits accepted by the group include regular passbook accounts, checking accounts, various money market accounts, fixed interest rate certificates, individual retirement accounts and keogh accounts. The group's wholly owned subsidiary, madison service corporation offers mutual funds and brokerage services to customers.

Primary SIC and add'l.: 6035 6712

CIK No: 0000742161

Subsidiaries: DirectTeller systems, Inc., Madison Service Corporation, The Franklin Savings and Loan company

Officers: Thomas H. Siemers/Dir., CEO, Pres./$222,553.00, Gretchen J. Schmidt/Sec., Treasurer, Daniel T. Voelpe/CFO, VP/$165,908.00

Directors: Thomas H. Siemers/Dir., CEO, Pres., John J. Kuntz/Dir., Mary W. Sullivan/Dir., Richard H. Finan/Dir., John L. Nolting/Dir.

Owners: John L. Nolting/0.49%, Thomas H. Siemers/23.73%, Mary W. Sullivan/0.42%, Daniel T. Voelpel/4.34%, Jeffrey L. Gendell/6.85%, Richard H. Finan/5.09%, John J. Kuntz/0.13%, The Franklin Savings and Loan Company/12.76%, Tontine Management, L.L.C./6.31%, Gretchen J. Schmidt/5.25%, Insiders/39.66%

Financial Data: Fiscal Year End:12/31   Latest Annual Data: 12/31/2006

Year	Sales		Net Income
2006	$19,934,000		$1,357,000
2005	$16,016,000		$1,240,000
2004	$14,830,000		$673,000

Curr. Assets:	$8,949,000	Curr. Liab.:	$231,179,000	P/E Ratio:	20.78
Plant, Equip.:	$4,492,000	Total Liab.:	$305,888,000	Indic. Yr. Divd.:	$0.360
Total Assets:	$332,039,000	Net Worth:	$25,746,000	Debt/ Equity:	2.7266

First Georgia Community Corp

150 Covington St., Jackson, GA, 30233; *PH:* 1-770-504-1090; *http://* www.firstga.com

General - Incorporation	GA	Stock - Price on:12/24/2007	NA
Employees	NA	Stock Exchange	OTC
Auditor	Mauldin & Jenkins LLC	Ticker Symbol	FGCC
Stk Agt	NA	Outstanding Shares	NA
Counsel	NA	E.P.S.	NA
DUNS No.	96-362-3913	Shareholders	NA

Business: The group's principal activity is to conduct general commercial banking business through its wholly owned subsidiary, first Georgia community bank. The deposit services offered by the group are personal and business checking accounts, interest-bearing checking accounts, savings accounts, money market funds and various types of certificates of deposit. The loan products offered include installment loans, real estate loans, second mortgage loans, commercial loans and home equity lines of credit. The other services offered by the group are official bank checks and money orders, mastercard and visa credit cards, safe deposit boxes, travelers' checks, bank by mail, direct deposit of payroll and social security checks and U.S. Savings bonds. The services are provided in and around butts county, Georgia and adjacent counties.

Primary SIC and add'l.: 6712 6022

CIK No: 0001024132

Subsidiaries: First Georgia Community Bank

Officers: Emory B. Lewis/71/Dir., CEO, Pres./$205,846.00, Arthur H. Hammond/CEO, Exec. VP - Henry, Spalding, Hudson Wade/CEO, Sr. VP - Newton County, Kent Berry/Sr. VP, Sr. Credit Officer, Harry Lewis/55/Dir., Sec., Treasurer, Larry Morgan/Exec. VP, Sr. Loan Officer, Elaine Kendrick/CFO, Sr. VP/$114,977.00

Directors: Emory B. Lewis/71/Dir., CEO, Pres., George Weaver/Chmn., James H. Warren/69/Dir., Harry Lewis/55/Dir., Sec., Treasurer, Joey McClelland/61/Dir., Charles Carter/Dir., Alfred D. Fears/Dir., William Jones/Dir., Harold G. Lewis/Dir., Joseph McClelland/Dir., Alexander Pollack/Dir., Herbert J. Warren/Dir.

Owners: James H. Warren/2.55%, George L. Weaver/6.33%, Emory B. Lewis, William B. Jones/13.01%, Alfred D. Fears/6.02%, Charles W. Carter/5.35%, Joey McClelland/4.45%, Alexander Pollack/8.11%, Harry Lewis/3.82%, Insiders/50.17%

First Growth Investors Inc

2508 S, 1300 E, Saltlake, UT, 84106; *PH:* 1-801-466-7808

General - Incorporation	NV	Stock - Price on:12/24/2007	$0.8
Employees	NA	Stock Exchange	OTC
Auditor	Pritchett, Siler & Hardy, P.C.	Ticker Symbol	FGIV
Stk Agt	Interwest Transfer Company, Inc.	Outstanding Shares	2,000,000
Counsel	NA	E.P.S.	-$0.01
DUNS No.	NA	Shareholders	NA

Business: The groups principle activity is to provide recruiting services. The groups service area includes the research and development, engineering, marketing, sales, information technology and manufacturing industries. The group operates from United States.

Primary SIC and add'l.: 7389

CIK No: 0001047857

Officers: Pam Jowett/54/Dir., CEO, CFO, Pres., Sec., Treasurer

Directors: Pam Jowett/54/Dir., CEO, CFO, Pres., Sec., Treasurer

Owners: Insiders/0.02%, Lynn Dixon/28.40%, Laszlo Schwartz/8.40%, Pam Jowett/0.02%, Devonshire Partners, LLC/28.40%, Real Path, Inc/20.00%

Financial Data: Fiscal Year End:12/31   Latest Annual Data: 03/31/2007

Year	Sales		Net Income
2007	NA		NA
2006	NA		-$10,000
2005	NA		-$8,000

Curr. Assets:	NA	Curr. Liab.:	$1,000		
Plant, Equip.:	NA	Total Liab.:	$1,000	Indic. Yr. Divd.:	NA
Total Assets:	NA	Net Worth:	-$1,000	Debt/ Equity:	NA

First Hartford Corp

149 Colonial Rd., Manchester, CT, 06045; *PH:* 1-860-646-6555; *Fax:* 1-860-646-8572; *http://* firsthartford.com; *Email:* gpitruzzello@firsthartford.com

General - Incorporation	ME	Stock - Price on:12/24/2007	$2.32
Employees	32	Stock Exchange	OTC
Auditor	Carlin, Charron & Rosen LLP	Ticker Symbol	FHRT
Stk Agt	Continental Stock Transfer & Trust Co	Outstanding Shares	3,050,000
Counsel	NA	E.P.S.	-$0.38
DUNS No.	00-691-7447	Shareholders	NA

Business: The group's principal activities are to purchase, develop, own, manage and distribute real estate. The group owns and operates real estate through its subsidiaries located in Connecticut, New Jersey, Texas and Rhode Island. It obtains tenants through brokers and employed representatives, by means of newspaper advertisements, inquiries by potential tenants at its on-site offices and direct contacts with retail stores, banks and other potential commercial tenants. The group also extends credit to companies and tenants throughout the United States.

Primary SIC and add'l.: 6512

CIK No: 0000036369

Subsidiaries: Lead Tech, Inc

Officers: Neil H. Ellis/Chmn., CEO, Pres., Mary-Ann Condon/Controller, David B. Harding/Dir., VP, Stuart Greenwald/Dir., Sec., Treasurer, Jeffrey M. Carlson/General Counsel, John Toic/VP, Dir. - Project Development, Herbert Byk/Dir. - Engineering, Michael Sweeney/Pres., Dir. - Environmental Services, Lead Tech, Inc, Jay Shaw/Sr. VP, Dir. - Leasing, Stamford, CT, First Hartford Realty Corporation, Alice Zimmerman Seale/First Hartford Realty Corporation, Leasing, Dallas, TX, Ellis Mayer/Sr. Regional Property Mgr., Malcolm Davis/Property Mgr., Tony Gallinari/VP, Dir. - Acquisitions, First Hartford Realty Corporation, Margaret Jacques/Internal Auditor - First Hartford Realty Corporation, Peter J. Higgins/VP, Dir. - Leasing, Stamford, CT, First Hartford Realty Corporation *(16 Officers included in Index)*

Directors: Neil H. Ellis/Chmn., CEO, Pres., David B. Harding/Dir., VP, Stuart Greenwald/Dir., Sec., Treasurer

Owners: Insiders/47.07%, Richard Kaplan/19.41%, John Filippelli/8.32%, Joel Lehrer/6.05%, Stuart I. Greenwald/1.64%, Neil H. Ellis/43.79%, David B. Harding/1.64%, David Kaplan/16.47%

Financial Data: Fiscal Year End:04/30   Latest Annual Data: 04/30/2007

Year	Sales		Net Income
2007	$12,225,000		$11,000
2006	$33,876,000		$684,000
2005	$6,465,000		-$167,000

Curr. Assets:	$6,027,000	Curr. Liab.:	$3,243,000	P/E Ratio:	1.49
Plant, Equip.:	$33,920,000	Total Liab.:	$50,223,000	Indic. Yr. Divd.:	NA
Total Assets:	$49,348,000	Net Worth:	-$875,000	Debt/ Equity:	NA

First Horizon National Corp

165 Madison Ave., Memphis, TN, 38103; *PH:* 1-901-523-4444; *Fax:* 1-901-523-4266; *http://* www.fhnc.com

General - Incorporation	TN	Stock - Price on:12/24/2007	$39.38
Employees	12,398	Stock Exchange	NYSE
Auditor	KPMG LLP	Ticker Symbol	FHN
Stk Agt	Wells Fargo Shareowner Services	Outstanding Shares	125,750,000
Counsel	NA	E.P.S.	$1.21
DUNS No.	05-023-9599	Shareholders	NA

Business: The group operates through its subsidiary whose principle activity is to provide financial services. The group operates through four business segments namely retail/commercial banking, mortgage banking, capital markets and corporate. The group operates from United States.

Primary SIC and add'l.: 6021 6712

CIK No: 0000036966

Subsidiaries: CC Community Development Holdings, Inc., Employers Risk Services, Inc., Federal Flood Certification Corporation, FH-FF Mortgage Services, L.P., FHEL, Inc., FHMSH, Inc., FHR Holding, Inc., FHREC, Inc., FHRF, Inc., Fhriii, LLC, Fhriv, LLC, FHRV, LLC, Fhrvi, LLC, FHTRS, Inc., First Express Remittance Processing, Inc. 58 Subsidiaries included in the Index

Officers: Gerald L. Baker/Dir., CEO, Pres/$1,296,468.00, Elbert L. Thomas/Exec. VP, Herbert H. Hilliard/60/Exec. VP - Risk Management, Kim Cherry/Mgr. - Media Relations, Clyde A. Billings/Sr. VP, Assist. General Counsel, Corp. Sec., Charles G. Burkett/Pres. - Tennessee, National Banking/$1,627,623.00, Jimmie L. Hughes/Exec. VP/$5,854,591.00, Peter F. Makowiecki/48/Pres. - Mortgage Banking/$691,084.00, Marlin L. Mosby/CFO, Sarah L. Meyerrose/Exec. VP, James F. Keen/57/Exec. VP, Harry A. Johnson/Exec. VP, John P. O'Connor/Exec. VP

Directors: Gerald L. Baker/Dir., CEO, Pres., Michael D. Rose/Chmn., Jonathan P. Ward/Dir., James A. Haslam/Dir., Brad R. Martin/Dir., Luke Yancy/Dir., Robert B. Carter/Dir., William B. Sansom/Dir., Mary F. Sammons/Dir., Vicki R. Palmer/Dir., Colin V. Reed/Dir., Robert C. Blattberg/Dir., Simon F. Cooper/Dir.

Owners: Peter F. Makowiecki, Luke Yancy, T. Rowe Price Associates, Inc., Mary F. Sammons, Jim L. Hughes, Simon F. Cooper, Kenneth J. Glass, James A. Haslam, Colin V. Reed, Gerald L. Baker, Brad R. Martin, Marlin L. Mosby, Charles G. Burkett, Vicki R. Palmer, Larry B. Martin *(21 Owners included in Index)*

Financial Data: Fiscal Year End:12/31   Latest Annual Data: 12/31/2006

Year	Sales		Net Income
2006	$3,571,904,000		$462,914,000
2005	$3,240,509,000		$438,000,000
2004	$2,529,988,000		$454,408,000

Curr. Assets:	$5,160,220,000	Curr. Liab.:	$25,974,520,000	P/E Ratio:	15.82
Plant, Equip.:	$515,227,000	Total Liab.:	$35,160,599,000	Indic. Yr. Divd.:	$1.800
Total Assets:	$37,918,259,000	Net Worth:	$2,462,390,000	Debt/ Equity:	2.5959

First Independence Corp

Myrtle and 6th, Independence, KS, 67301; *PH:* 1-620-331-1660; *Fax:* 1-620-331-1600; *http://* www.firstfederalsl.com

General - Incorporation		Stock - Price on:12/24/2007	$18.75
Employees	NA	Stock Exchange	OTC
Auditor	NA	Ticker Symbol	FFSL
Stk Agt	Registrar & Transfer Co	Outstanding Shares	NA
Counsel	NA	E.P.S.	NA
DUNS No.	NA	Shareholders	NA

Business: The groups principal activity is to provide community-banking services. The services of the group include providing loans, personal and business banking services, lending, investment, treasury management and online banking. The group operates from Detroit in the United States.

Primary SIC and add'l.: 6712 6035

CIK No:

Officers: Phyllis Johnson/Branch Mgr. - Coffeyville Branch, Jeri Farmer/Branch Mgr. - Neodesha Branch, James Teats/Branch Mgr. - Pittsburg Branch, Alan Hoggatt/Branch Mgr. - Lawrence Loan Origination Branch

Financial Data: Fiscal Year End:NA   Latest Annual Data: 9/30/2002

Year	Sales		Net Income
2002	$11,155,000		$2,032,000
2001	$12,409,000		$1,541,000
2000	$11,637,000		$1,376,000

Curr. Assets:	$13,107,000	Curr. Liab.:	$140,673,000	P/E Ratio:	13.49
Plant, Equip.:	$2,241,000	Total Liab.:	$141,473,000	Indic. Yr. Divd.:	$0.700
Total Assets:	$156,050,000	Net Worth:	$14,577,000	Debt/ Equity:	NA

First Indiana Corp

135 N Pennsylvania St., Ste. 2800, Indianapolis, IN, 46204; *PH:* 1-317-269-1200; *Fax:* 1-317-269-1341; *http://* www.FirstIndiana.com

General		Stock	
Incorporation	IN	Price on:12/24/2007	$21.7
Employees	514	Stock Exchange	NDQ
Auditor	KPMG LLP	Ticker Symbol	FINB
Stk Agt	National City Corp	Outstanding Shares	16,520,000
Counsel	NA	E.P.S	$1.29
DUNS No.	00-605-1106	Shareholders	NA

Business: The group's principal activity is to provide a wide range of banking services through 26 offices located in central Indiana. The group accepts deposits from the general public and originates commercial, consumer and construction loans. It also originates home equity loans in 46 states through a national independent agent network. In addition, the group provides tax planning and preparation services, accounting services, retirement and estate planning, investment advisory and trust services. It operates 26 banking centers located throughout metropolitan indianapolis, franklin, mooresville, pendleton, rushville and westfield, Indiana. On 13-Jan-2003, the group acquired metrobancorp.

Primary SIC and add'l.: 6021 6712

CIK No: 0000789670

Subsidiaries: First Indiana Bank, National Association, First Indiana Capital Statutory Trust II, First Indiana Capital Trust I, First Indiana Financial Services, LLC, First Indiana Investor Services, Inc., MB Realty Company, One Investment Company, LLC, One Investment Partners, LLC, One Mortgage Corporation, Pioneer Service Corporation

Officers: Robert H. Warrington/Dir., CEO, Pres./$1,444,015.00, William J. Brunner/CFO, Exec. VP/$506,782.00

Directors: Robert H. Warrington/Dir., CEO, Pres., Marni McKinney/Chmn., Gerald L. Bepko/Dir., Robert H. McKinney/Dir., Phyllis W. Minott/Dir., Pedro P. Granadillo/Dir., Anat Bird/Dir., William G. Mays/Dir., Michael W. Wells/Dir.

Owners: Insiders/24.20%, Pedro P. Granadillo, Reagan K. Rick, Marni McKinney/20.70%, William J. Brunner, Michael W. Wells, Robert H. McKinney/20.70%, Robert H. Warrington/1.50%, Anat Bird, David L. Maraman, Gerald L. Bepko, Marvin C. Schwartz/6.00%, William G. Mays, Phyllis W. Minott

Financial Data: *Fiscal Year End:*12/31 *Latest Annual Data:* 12/31/2006

Year	Sales	Net Income
2006	$159,603,000	$32,949,000
2005	$138,960,000	$25,271,000
2004	$142,334,000	$14,678,000

Curr. Assets:	$113,038,000	**Curr. Liab.:**	$1,911,221,000	**P/E Ratio:**	16.82
Plant, Equip.:	$27,218,000	**Total Liab.:**	$1,980,019,000	**Indic. Yr. Divd.:**	$0.840
Total Assets:	$2,162,113,000	**Net Worth:**	$182,094,000	**Debt/ Equity:**	0.2575

First Industrial Realty Trust Inc

311 S Wacker Dr., Ste. 4000, Chicago, IL, 60606; *PH:* 1-312-344-4300; *Fax:* 1-312-922-6320; *http://* www.firstindustrial.com; *Email:* info@firstindustrial.com

General		Stock	
Incorporation	MD	Price on:12/24/2007	$41.82
Employees	500	Stock Exchange	NYSE
Auditor	PricewaterhouseCoopers LLP	Ticker Symbol	FR
Stk Agt	Computershare Trust Co	Outstanding Shares	NA
Counsel	NA	E.P.S	$2.48
DUNS No.	NA	Shareholders	NA

Business: The groups principle activities include owning, managing, selling, developing, redeveloping and acquiring industrial real estate. In the year 2006, the group acquired 107 industrial properties. The group operates from the United States. The groups quarterly revenue for September 2007 was 108.92 millions of USD.

Primary SIC and add'l.: 6798

CIK No: 0000921825

Subsidiaries: FI Development Services Corporation, FI Development Services Group, L.P., FI Development Services, L.P., First Industrial Finance Corporation, First Industrial Financing Partnership, L.P., First Industrial Harrisburg, Corporation, First Industrial Harrisburg, L.P., First Industrial Indianapolis Corporation, First Industrial Indianapolis, L.P., First Industrial Investment, Inc., First Industrial Mortgage Corporation, First Industrial Mortgage Partnership, L.P., First Industrial Pennsylvania Corporation, First Industrial Pennsylvania, L.P., First Industrial Securities Corporation 31 Subsidiaries included in the Index

Officers: Michael W. Brennan/Dir., CEO, Pres./$2,742,529.00, Michael J. Havala/CFO/$1,658,701.00, Brady Scott/Sr. Investment Officer, David O'Reilly/Investment Officer, Scott A. McGregor/Sr. Investment Officer, Kyle Rockey/Sr. Investment Officer, Andrew Zgutowicz/Investment Officer, Michael Schack/Investment Officer, James Redland/Investment Officer - West Region, Art Harmon/Sr. Mgr. - Investor Relations, Mike Murphy/Dir. - Government Solutions, John Atwell/Dir. - Development, West Region, Joseph H. Mikes/Dir. - Development, Central Region, Tom Trocheck/Dir. - Development, East Region, Richard A. Astheimer/Sr. VP - Development *(97 Officers included in Index)*

Directors: Michael W. Brennan/Dir., CEO, Pres., Jay H. Shidler/Chmn., Michael G. Damone/Dir., Dir. - Strategic Planning, John Brenninkmeijer/Dir., Kevin W. Lynch/Dir., Robert D. Newman/Dir., John Rau/Dir., Robert J. Slater/Dir., Ed W. Tyler/Dir., Steven J. Wilson/Dir.

Owners: ADI Alternative Investments c/o Casam ADI CB Arbitrage, CQS Convertible and Quantitative Strategies Master Fund Limited, JMG Triton Offshore Fund, Ltd, Xavex Convertible Arbitrage 10 Fund, Credit Agricole Structured Asset Management, ADI Alternative Investments c/o Axix Pan, Vicis Capital Master Fund, LDG Limited, Tamarack International, Ltd, Merced Partners Limited Partnership, PNC Equity Securities LLC, Zurich Institutional Benchmarks Master Fund Ltd, Royal Bank of Canada, TQA Master Plus Fund, Ltd, ADI Alternative Investments *(30 Owners included in Index)*

Financial Data: *Fiscal Year End:*12/31 *Latest Annual Data:* 12/31/2006

Year	Sales	Net Income
2006	$396,036,000	$112,082,000
2005	$367,129,000	$87,104,000
2004	$319,732,000	$110,606,000

Curr. Assets:	$68,958,000	**Curr. Liab.:**	$161,575,000	**P/E Ratio:**	63.38
Plant, Equip.:	$2,870,271,000	**Total Liab.:**	$2,201,420,000	**Indic. Yr. Divd.:**	$2.840
Total Assets:	$3,224,399,000	**Net Worth:**	$1,022,979,000	**Debt/ Equity:**	NA

First Internet Bancorp

7820 Innovation Blvd., Ste. 210, Indianapolis, IN, 46278; *PH:* 1-317-532-7900; *http://* www.firstinternetbancorp.com; *Email:* investors@firstib.com

General		Stock	
Incorporation		Price on:12/24/2007	$14
Employees	NA	Stock Exchange	OTC
Auditor	NA	Ticker Symbol	FIBP
Stk Agt	NA	Outstanding Shares	NA
Counsel	NA	E.P.S	NA
DUNS No.	NA	Shareholders	NA

Business: The groups principal activity is to provide banking services through Internet. The services of the group include installment loans, credit cards, certificates of deposits, lines of credit, IRAs, mortgages, saving and checking services and money market savings. The group operates from the United States.

Primary SIC and add'l.: 6022 6712

CIK No:

Officers: David B. Becker/Chmn., CEO

Directors: David B. Becker/Chmn., CEO

First Interstate BancSystem Inc

401 N 31st St., Billings, MT, 59116; *PH:* 1-406-255-5390; *Fax:* 1-406-255-5160; *http://* www.firstinterstatebank.com

General		Stock	
Incorporation	MT	Price on:12/24/2007	NA
Employees	NA	Stock Exchange	NA
Auditor	McGladrey & Pullen LLP	Ticker Symbol	NA
Stk Agt	NA	Outstanding Shares	NA
Counsel	NA	E.P.S	NA
DUNS No.	09-330-0853	Shareholders	NA

Business: The group's principal activities are to provide commercial banking services to individual and corporate customers. The group operates a wholly-owned bank subsidiary, first interstate bank with 59 banking offices in 31 Montana and Wyoming communities. The services of the group include personal and business checking and savings accounts, time deposits, individual retirement accounts, cash management, trust and brokerage services and commercial, consumer, real estate, agricultural and other loans. The group conducts various other financial-related business activities such as data processing services and technology services through wholly owned non-bank subsidiaries. On 01-Jan-2003, the group acquired silver run bancorporation inc.

Primary SIC and add'l.: 6022 6712

CIK No: 0000860413

Subsidiaries: Commerce Financial, Inc., FI Reinsurance, Ltd., FIB, LLC, Fibet, LLC, First Interstate Bank, First Interstate Insurance Agency, Inc., First Interstate Statutory Trust, i_Tech Corporation

Officers: Lyle R. Knight/Dir., CEO, Pres./$966,568.00, Terrill R. Moore/CFO, Exec. VP/$379,971.00

Directors: Lyle R. Knight/Dir., CEO, Pres., Thomas W. Scott/Chmn., James R. Scott/Vice Chmn., Jonathan R. Scott/Dir., Richard A. Dorn/Dir., Charles M. Heyneman/Dir., Julie A. Scott/Dir., James W. Haugh/Dir., Robert L. Nance/Dir., David H. Crum/Dir., William B. Ebzery/Dir., Sandra A. Scott Suzor/Dir., Michael J. Sullivan/Dir., Terry W. Payne/Dir., Randall I. Scott/Dir. *(17 Directors included in Index)*

Owners: Richard A. Dorn, Randall I. Scott/13.54%, Homer A. Scott/8.69%, Terry W. Payne, Sandra A. Scott Suzor/1.02%, Terry Moore, Ralph K. Cook, Julie A. Scott/3.01%, John M. Heyneman/5.24%, Thomas W. Scott/8.99%, First Interstate Bank/16.46%, Martin A. White, Elouise C. Cobell, William B. Ebzery, Robert A. Jones *(25 Owners included in Index)*

First Investors Financial Svcs Group Inc

675 Bering Dr., Houston, TX, 30339; *PH:* 1-800-603-4484; *Fax:* 1-800-528-2384; *http://* www.fifsg.com

General		Stock	
Incorporation	TX	Price on:12/24/2007	$7.1
Employees	193	Stock Exchange	OTC
Auditor	Grant Thornton LLP	Ticker Symbol	FIFS
Stk Agt	Mellon Investor Services LLC	Outstanding Shares	4,480,000
Counsel	NA	E.P.S	$0.67
DUNS No.	36-075-9344	Shareholders	NA

Business: The group's principal activity is to purchase receivables and to originate loans to consumers. The group is a consumer finance company that operates through first investors financial services, inc. And its subsidiaries. The group acquires automobile loans from dealers and originates loans directly to consumers. It also originates loans directly to consumers in connection with the sale of new and late model used vehicles. The group operates in 28 states.

Primary SIC and add'l.: 6153 6719

CIK No: 0000948034

Subsidiaries: First Investors Auto Owner Trust 2006-A, First Investors Residual Funding LP

Officers: Tommy A. Moore/Chmn., CEO, Pres., Bennie H. Duck/Exec. VP, Sec., Treasurer, CFO, Blaise Rodon/COO, Sr. VP

Directors: Tommy A. Moore/Chmn., CEO, Pres., Robert L. Clarke/Dir., Roberto Marchesini/Dir., John H. Buck/Dir., Seymour M. Jacobs/Dir., Walter A. Stockard/Dir., Daniel M. Theriault/Dir.

Owners: Walter A. Stockard/9.70%, John H. Buck/1.80%, Dimensional Fund Advisors/7.70%, Hot Creek Ventures I, LP/10.30%, Tommy A. Moore/10.00%, Kristene S. Moore/7.90%, Blaise G. Rodon, Daniel M. Theriault/7.60%, Robert L. Clarke/3.30%, JAM Partners, LP/10.80%, Insiders/45.20%, Bennie H. Duck/1.50%, Seymour M. Jacobs/15.00%, Roberto Marchesini

Financial Data: *Fiscal Year End:*04/30 *Latest Annual Data:* 04/30/2007

Year	Sales	Net Income
2007	$62,540,000	$3,192,000
2006	$46,740,000	$2,445,000
2005	$36,600,000	$684,000

Curr. Assets:	$32,716,000	**Curr. Liab.:**	$7,783,000	**P/E Ratio:**	10.60
Plant, Equip.:	$1,332,000	**Total Liab.:**	$391,168,000	**Indic. Yr. Divd.:**	NA
Total Assets:	$419,288,000	**Net Worth:**	$28,120,000	**Debt/ Equity:**	15.8110

First Keystone Corp

111 W Front St., Berwick, PA, 18603; *PH:* 1-570-752-3671; *http://* www.fnbbwk.com

General		**Stock**	
Incorporation	PA	Price on:12/24/2007	$18.5
Employees	117	Stock Exchange	OTC
Auditor	J. H. Williams & Co. LLP	Ticker Symbol	FKYS
Stk Agt	First National Bank of Berwick	Outstanding Shares	4,520,000
Counsel	NA	E.P.S	$1.31
DUNS No.	15-262-6792	Shareholders	NA

Business: The group's principal activities are to provide a wide range of banking, trust and related services to individuals and businesses in northeastern and central Pennsylvania. The group provides personal financial services such as accepting deposits, making loans, personal and corporate trust management services. The loans extended by the group include secured and unsecured commercial, real estate and consumer loans. The group also provides personal, corporate, pension and fiduciary services through its trust department. The group has 5 branches within columbia county, 4 branches within luzerne county and 1 branch in montour county, Pennsylvania.

Primary SIC and add'l.: 6021 6712

CIK No: 0000737875

Subsidiaries: The First National Bank of Berwick

Officers: Gerald J. Bazewicz/Dir., Pres., CEO - Contact - Investor Relation/$293,606.00, Matthew P. Prosseda/Treasurer/$154,350.00, Diane C.A. Rosler/CFO/$51,944.00

Directors: Gerald J. Bazewicz/Dir., Pres., CEO - Contact - Investor Relation, Robert J. Wise/Vice Chmn., Robert E. Bull/Chmn., David R. Saracino/63/Dir., Jerome F. Fabian/Dir., Dudley P. Cooley/Dir., John G. Gerlach/Dir., John E. Arndt/Dir., Robert A. Bull/55/Dir., Peter W. Ahnert/Dir., Don E. Bower/Dir.

Owners: Robert E. Bull/5.04%, Don E. Bower, David R. Saracino, Jerome F. Fabian, Diane C. Rosler, Insiders/14.27%, Matthew P. Prosseda, Robert J. Wise/4.51%, Dudley P. Cooley, John E. Arndt, Gerald J. Bazewicz, Berbank/12.22%, Robert A. Bull/1.40%

Financial Data: **Fiscal Year End:**12/31 **Latest Annual Data:** 12/31/2006

Year	Sales	Net Income
2006	$32,365,000	$6,190,000
2005	$30,164,000	$6,847,000
2004	$29,632,000	$6,787,000

Curr. Assets:	$12,874,000	**Curr. Liab.:**	$414,780,000	**P/E Ratio:**	13.91
Plant, Equip.:	$5,016,000	**Total Liab.:**	$472,533,000	**Indic. Yr. Divd.:**	$0.880
Total Assets:	$525,920,000	**Net Worth:**	$53,387,000	**Debt/ Equity:**	1.0573

First Keystone Financial Inc

22 W State St., Media, PA, 19063; *PH:* 1-610-565-6210; *Fax:* 1-610-892-5150; *http://* www.firstkeystone.com; *Email:* loanoriginations@firstkeystone.com

General		**Stock**	
Incorporation	PA	Price on:12/24/2007	$18.9
Employees	104	Stock Exchange	NDQ
Auditor	Deloitte & Touche LLP	Ticker Symbol	FKFS
Stk Agt	Registrar & Transfer Co	Outstanding Shares	2,430,000
Counsel	Elias, Matz, Tierman & Herrick	E.P.S	$0.41
DUNS No.	00-249-6438	Shareholders	NA

Business: The group's principal activities are to attract deposits from the general public and invest such deposits along with other sources of funds, in loans secured by one-to four family residential real estate. The group's operations are conducted primarily through its subsidiary first keystone federal savings bank. The services are conducted in Delaware and chester counties, Pennsylvania and to a lesser degree, montgomery county, Pennsylvania and new castle county, Delaware. The group originates loans secured by first and second lines on single-family residences. The lending activities of the group include origination of loans secured by commercial and multi-family residential real estate properties as well as residential and commercial construction loans secured by properties. The group offers a variety of deposits consisting of now, passbook accounts, money market and certificates of deposits. As at 30-Sep-2003, the group operated 8 full-service offices.

Primary SIC and add'l.: 6035 6712

CIK No: 0000856751

Subsidiaries: First Keystone Bank, First Keystone Capital Trust I, First Keystone Capital Trust II, First Keystone Insurance Services, LLC, FKF Management Corp., Inc, State Street Services Corp.

Officers: Thomas M. Kelly/51/Dir., CEO, Pres., Carol Walsh/Corp. Sec.

Directors: Thomas M. Kelly/51/Dir., CEO, Pres., William J. O'Donnell/40/Dir., Edmund Jones/89/Dir., Bruce C. Hendrixson/63/Dir., Jerry A. Naessens/71/Dir., Donald S. Guthrie/72/Dir., Donald G. Hosier/52/Dir., Marshall J. Soss/61/Dir.

Owners: Nedret E. Vidinli/9.10%, Insiders/2.70%, Employee Stock Ownership Plan Trust/13.90%, Lawrence Garshofsky and Company, LLC/6.40%, Financial Stocks Capital Partners IV L.P./9.10%, Robin G. Otto, Donald S. Guthrie/4.40%, Donald G. Hosier, Bruce C. Hendrixson, Tontine Financial Partners, L.P./7.00%, Jerry A. Naessens, Edmund Jones/1.80%, William J. O'Donnell, Marshall J. Soss, Thomas M. Kelly/2.50% *(17 Owners included in Index)*

Financial Data: **Fiscal Year End:**09/30 **Latest Annual Data:** 9/30/2006

Year	Sales	Net Income
2006	$31,005,000	$1,035,000
2005	$30,665,000	$610,000
2004	$30,042,000	$2,203,000

Curr. Assets:	$15,454,000	**Curr. Liab.:**	$471,952,000	**P/E Ratio:**	46.67
Plant, Equip.:	$7,093,000	**Total Liab.:**	$494,301,000	**Indic. Yr. Divd.:**	$0.330
Total Assets:	$522,960,000	**Net Worth:**	$28,659,000	**Debt/ Equity:**	0.6181

First Litchfield Financial Corp

13 N St., Litchfield, CT, 06759; *PH:* 1-860-567-8752; *Fax:* 1-860-567-9326; *http://* www.fnbl.com; *Email:* banking@fnbl.com

General		**Stock**	
Incorporation	DE	Price on:12/24/2007	$19.4
Employees	116	Stock Exchange	OTC
Auditor	McGladrey & Pullen, LLP	Ticker Symbol	FLFL
Stk Agt	Registrar & Transfer Co	Outstanding Shares	2,260,000
Counsel	NA	E.P.S	NA
DUNS No.	NA	Shareholders	NA

Business: The groups operates through its subsidiaries whose principal activity is to provide commercial and personal banking services. Services of the group include accepting demand deposits, accepting savings and time deposit accounts, making secured and unsecured loans issuing letters of credit, originating mortgage loans, and providing personal and corporate trust services. The group operates from Delaware in the United States.

Primary SIC and add'l.: 6021 6712

CIK No: 0000840886

Subsidiaries: First Litchfield Leasing Corporation, First Litchfield Statutory Trust I, First Litchfield Statutory Trust II, Lincoln Corporation, Litchfield Mortgage Service Corporation, The First National Bank of Litchfield

Officers: Joseph J. Greco/Dir., Pres., CEO - First National Bank, Litchfield/$386,765.00, George M. Madsen/Dir., Sec. - First National Bank, Litchfield, Mark A. Ronaldes/VP, Commercial Lending Officer - First National Bank, Litchfield, Kathleen M. Stockalis/Assist. VP, Accountant - First National Bank, Litchfield, Cynthia H. Harmon/VP - Branch Administration, BSA, Privacy Act Officer - First National Bank, Litchfield, Dale Leifert/Assist. VP - Goshen, The First National Bank, Litchfield, Linda Parady/VP - First Litchfield Leasing Corporation, Kara Perrin/Banking Officer - Goshen, The First National Bank, Litchfield, Frederick F. Judd/Sr. VP - Trust, Wealth Management, First National Bank, Litchfield/$152,577.00, Carroll A. Pereira/Sr. VP, CFO - First National Bank, Litchfield/$200,370.00, Joelene E. Smith/Sr. VP - Bank Operations, First National Bank, Litchfield, Robert E. Teittinen/Sr. VP, Sr. Loan Officer, CRA Officer - First National Bank, Litchfield/$149,360.00, Edgar S. Auchincloss/VP, Sr. Banking Officer - First National Bank, Litchfield, Belinda L. Dipietro/VP, Loan Operations Mgr. - First National Bank, Litchfield, Celeste F. Echlin/VP, Commercial Lending Officer - First National Bank, Litchfield *(54 Officers included in Index)*

Directors: Joseph J. Greco/Dir., Pres., CEO - First National Bank, Litchfield, Charles E. Orr/Chmn. - First National Bank, Litchfield, William J. Sweetman/Dir. - First National Bank, Litchfield, Alan B. Magary/Dir. - First National Bank, Litchfield, Gregory S. Oneglia/Dir. - First National Bank, Litchfield, Patricia D. Werner/Dir. - First National Bank, Litchfield, Clayton L. Blick/Dir. Emeritus - First National Bank, Litchfield, Perley H. Grimes/Dir. - First National Bank, Litchfield, Kathleen A. Kelley/Dir. - First National Bank, Litchfield, George M. Madsen/Dir., Sec. - First National Bank, Litchfield, Patrick J. Boland/Dir. - First National Bank, Litchfield, Ray H. Underwood/Dir. - First National Bank, Litchfield, Richard E. Pugh/Dir. - First National Bank, Litchfield, John A. Brighenti/Dir. - First National Bank, Litchfield

Owners: Joseph J. Greco/0.08%, Alan B. Magary/0.01%, John A. Brighenti/0.01%, Gregory S. Oneglia/0.75%, William J. Sweetman/5.13%, Robert E. Teittinen, Insiders/9.10%, Kathleen A. Kelley/0.05%, Carroll A. Pereira/0.48%, Joelene E. Smith/0.01%, Charles E. Orr/0.75%, Patricia D. Werner/0.21%, Perley H. Grimes, Ray H. Underwood/0.17%, Richard E. Pugh *(17 Owners included in Index)*

Financial Data: **Fiscal Year End:**12/31 **Latest Annual Data:** 12/31/2006

Year	Sales	Net Income
2006	$28,745,000	$1,409,000
2005	$24,565,000	$4,036,000
2004	$22,241,000	$3,916,000

Curr. Assets:	$31,797,000	**Curr. Liab.:**	$463,772,000	**P/E Ratio:**	9.85
Plant, Equip.:	$7,440,000	**Total Liab.:**	$475,026,000	**Indic. Yr. Divd.:**	NA
Total Assets:	$501,232,000	**Net Worth:**	$26,206,000	**Debt/ Equity:**	NA

First M & F Corp

134 W Washington St., Kosciusko, MS, 39090; *PH:* 1-662-289-5121; *Fax:* 1-662-289-8084; *http://* www.mfbank.com

General		**Stock**	
Incorporation	MS	Price on:12/24/2007	NA
Employees	NA	Stock Exchange	NYSE
Auditor	Shearer, Taylor & Co	Ticker Symbol	HWD
Stk Agt	Registrar & Transfer Co	Outstanding Shares	NA
Counsel	NA	E.P.S	NA
DUNS No.	03-908-7705	Shareholders	NA

Business: The group's principal activity is to provide commercial and consumer banking services through its main office and 2 branches in kosciusko within central Mississippi. The group offers a variety of deposit, investment and credit products to customers. These services are provided to middle market and professional businesses ranging from payroll checking, business checking, corporate savings and secured and unsecured lines of credit. The group also provides services such as direct deposit payroll, sweep accounts and letters of credit, and offers credit card services to its customers to include check debit cards and automated teller machine card through several networks. Trust services are also offered in the kosciusko main office.

Primary SIC and add'l.: 6022 6712

CIK No: 0000320387

Subsidiaries: First M & F Insurance Company, Inc., M & F Business Credit, Inc., M & F Insurance Agency, Inc., M & F Insurance Group, Inc., Merchants and Farmers Bank, Merchants and Farmers Bank Securities Corporation, Merchants Financial Services Group, LLC, MS Statewide Title, LLC

Officers: Hugh S. Potts/Chmn., CEO, Jeffrey A. Camp/48/Dir., Exec. VP, Sr. Credit Officer, Scott M. Wiggers/63/Dir., Pres., Robert K. Autry/Exec. VP - Administration, Michael E. Crandall/Exec. VP - Retail Administration, Kin Kinney/Sr. VP - Retail Administration, John G. Copeland/CFO

Directors: Hugh S. Potts/Chmn., CEO, Charles W. Ritter/Dir., Marlin J. Ivey/Dir., Charles T. England/Dir., Jeffrey A. Camp/48/Dir., Exec. VP, Sr. Credit Officer, Susan McCaffery/68/Dir., Larry Terrell/Dir., James I. Tims/Dir., Charles V. Imbler/Dir., Dale R. McBride/69/Dir., Michael L. Nelson/Dir., W. C. Shoemaker/Dir., Scott M. Wiggers/63/Dir., Pres., Hollis C. Cheek/Dir., Jon A. Crocker/Dir. *(21 Directors included in Index)*

Owners: L. F. Sams, Michael W. Sanders/0.16%, Marlin J. Ivey/2.69%, Hollis C. Cheek/0.05%, Hugh S. Potts/7.37%, Charles V. Imbler, Otho E. Pettit, Susan McCaffery/2.59%, James I. Tims/1.97%, Jon A. Crocker/1.14%, Larry Terrell/0.03%, Charles W. Ritter/3.70%, Insiders/24.42%, Samuel B. Potts/1.63%, Barbara K. Hammond/0.31% *(21 Owners included in Index)*

First Marblehead Corp

The Prudential Tower, 800 Boylston St., 34th Fl., Boston, MA, 02199; *PH:* 1-617-638-2000; *Fax:* 1-617-638-2100; *http://* www.firstmarblehead.com; *Email:* info@firstmarblehead.com

General - Incorporation	DE	Stock- Price on:12/24/2007	$38.57
Employees	917	Stock Exchange	NYSE
Auditor	KPMG LLP	Ticker Symbol	FMD
Stk Agt	EquiServe Trust Co N.A	Outstanding Shares	93,680,000
Counsel	NA	E.P.S.	$3.83
DUNS No.	NA	Shareholders	NA

Business: The group's principal activity is to provide outsourcing services for private education lending in the United States. It helps to meet the demand for private education loans by providing financial and educational institutions with an integrated suite of services for student loan programs. It provide its clients with a continuum of services, from the initial phases of program design through application processing and support to the ultimate disposition of the loans through securitization transactions that they structure and administer. The group receives fees for the services they provide in connection with processing and securitizing their clients' loans. First marblehead, guaranteed access to education and the national collegiate trust are the trademarks of the group.

Primary SIC and add'l.: 7374 8999

CIK No: 0001262279

Subsidiaries: First Marblehead Data Services, Inc, First Marblehead Education Resources, Inc., GATE Holdings, Inc., The National Collegiate Funding LLC

Officers: Jack L. Kopnisky/Dir., CEO, COO, Pres., Peter B. Tarr/Chmn., General Counsel, John A. Hupalo/Sr. Exec. VP, CFO, Andrew J. Hawley/Exec. VP - Client Services, Pres. - First Marblehead Educational Resources, Anne Bowen/Exec. VP, Chief Administrative Officer, Sandra M. Stark/Exec. VP - Business Development, William Baumer/Exec. VP, Chief Risk Officer, Kenneth S. Klipper/Sr. VP, Treasurer, Chief Accounting Officer, Greg D. Johnson/Exec. VP, Chief Marketing Officer, Richard E. Ross/CIO, Exec. VP, Stein I. Skaane/Exec. VP - Product Strategy, Lee Jacobson/VP - Investor Relations, Gregory M. Woods/Sec.

Directors: Jack L. Kopnisky/Dir., CEO, COO, Pres., Peter B. Tarr/Chmn., General Counsel, Stephen E. Anbinder/Vice Chmn., Leslie L. Alexander/Dir., Dort A. Cameron/Dir., George G. Daly/Dir., Peter S. Drotch/Dir., William D. Hansen/Dir., William R. Berkley/Dir.

Owners: Dort A. Cameron/1.00%, Second Curve Capital, LLC/6.20%, William R. Berkley/6.30%, Leslie L. Alexander/22.50%, Delta Partners LLC/5.30%, Peter B. Tarr, John A. Hupalo, Peter S. Drotch, George G. Daly, Daniel Maxwell Meyers/8.60%, William D. Hansen, Baron Capital Group,Inc/10.00%, Daniel Maxwell Meyers/8.60%, Artisan Partners Limited Partnership/6.90%, Insiders/34.70% *(17 Owners included in Index)*

Financial Data: Fiscal Year End:06/30 **Latest Annual Data:** 6/30/2006

Year	Sales	Net Income
2006	$563,572,000	$235,960,000
2005	$417,977,000	$159,665,000
2004	$199,260,000	$75,271,000

Curr. Assets:	$694,528,000	**Curr. Liab.:**	$34,430,000		
Plant, Equip.:	$36,743,000	**Total Liab.:**	$194,177,000	**Indic. Yr. Divd.:**	$1.000
Total Assets:	$770,346,000	**Net Worth:**	$576,169,000	**Debt/ Equity:**	0.0122

First Mariner Bancorp

1501 S Clinton St., Baltimore, MD, 21224; **PH:** 1-410-342-2600; **Fax:** 1-410-563-1594; http:// www.1stmarinerbank.com

General - Incorporation	MD	Stock- Price on:12/24/2007	$13.48
Employees	1,000	Stock Exchange	NDQ
Auditor	Stegman & Co	Ticker Symbol	FMAR
Stk Agt	American Stock Transfer & Trust Co.	Outstanding Shares	6,430,000
Counsel	NA	E.P.S.	-$1.76
DUNS No.	88-418-7196	Shareholders	NA

Business: The group's principle activities are to provide commercial and consumer banking, mortgage banking and consumer financial services. It is a holding company and conducts its business through its wholly owned subsidiaries, first mariner bank and finance Maryland llc. Commercial and consumer banking is conducted through the bank and involves delivering a broad range of financial products and services, including lending and deposit taking to individuals and commercial enterprises. Mortgage banking is conducted through first mariner mortgage, a division of the bank, and involves originating residential single-family mortgages for sale in the secondary market and to the bank. Consumer finance is conducted through finance Maryland, and involves making small direct consumer loans and the purchase of retail installment sales contracts. As on 31-Dec-2003 it had 23 full service bank branches, 14 mortgage loan offices, 13 consumer finance offices and 201 ATMs.

Primary SIC and add'l.: 6712 6022

CIK No: 0000946090

Subsidiaries: Canton Borrowing, LLC, Canton Crossing II, LLC, Compass Properties, Inc., Finance Maryland, LLC, First Mariner Bank, First Mariner Financial Services, Inc., First Mariner Mortgage Corporation, FM Appraisals, LLC, FMB Holdings, Inc., Hale Canton, LLC, Mariner Capital Trust II, Mariner Capital Trust III, Mariner Capital Trust IV, Mariner Capital Trust V, Mariner Capital Trust VI 17 Subsidiaries included in the Index

Officers: Edwin F. Hale/Chmn., CEO/$721,181.00, Cindi Joynes/VP - Reporting, Joseph A. Cicero/Dir., COO, Pres./$289,035.00, George H. Mantakos/Dir., Exec. VP/$276,748.00

Directors: Edwin F. Hale/Chmn., CEO, John Brown/Dir., Hector Torres/Dir., John J. Oliver/Dir., John Perry McDaniel/Dir., Robert Caret/Dir., William Donald Schaefer/Dir. Emeritus, Marvin Mandel/Dir. Emeritus, Joseph A. Cicero/Dir., COO, Pres., George H. Mantakos/Dir., Exec. VP, Howard Friedman/Dir., Barry B. Bondroff/Dir., Patricia L. Schmoke/Dir., Michael R. Watson/Dir., Melvin S. Kabick/Dir. *(16 Directors included in Index)*

Owners: Banc Fund V L.P./5.90%, Edwin F. Hale/21.21%, John Brown, John J. Oliver, Hector Torres, Jeffrey L. Gendell/7.91%, Joseph A. Cicero/1.99%, Wellington Management Company, LLP/9.03%, George H. Mantakos/1.78%, Insiders/27.06%, Robert Caret, Edith B. Brown, Howard Friedman, Mark A. Keidel/1.25%, Michael R. Watson *(19 Owners included in Index)*

Financial Data: Fiscal Year End:12/31 **Latest Annual Data:** 12/31/2006

Year	Sales	Net Income
2006	$122,552,000	$1,924,000
2005	$105,075,000	$7,822,000
2004	$84,460,000	$6,101,000

Curr. Assets:	$53,548,000	**Curr. Liab.:**	$978,380,000		
Plant, Equip.:	$51,502,000	**Total Liab.:**	$1,184,661,000	**Indic. Yr. Divd.:**	NA
Total Assets:	$1,263,290,000	**Net Worth:**	$78,629,000	**Debt/ Equity:**	2.8081

First McMinnville Corp

200 E Main St., Mcminnville, TN, 37110; **PH:** 1-615-473-4402

General - Incorporation	TN	Stock- Price on:12/24/2007	NA
Employees	NA	Stock Exchange	NA
Auditor	Maggart & Assoc., P.C	Ticker Symbol	NA
Stk Agt	NA	Outstanding Shares	NA
Counsel	NA	E.P.S.	NA
DUNS No.	15-650-7006	Shareholders	NA

Business: The group's principal activity is to provide commercial banking products and services to small and medium-sized businesses, including those in to nursery business, the real estate development business, local industry, professionals, business executives, and other individuals. The products and services offered by the group includes, regular and money market checking accounts, money market savings accounts, certificates of deposit, individual retirement accounts and safe deposit facilities. Additionally, the group provides consumer and other installment loans and credit services. The group operates throughout warren county, Tennessee, with five offices located in mcmiinnville, morrison and viola.

Primary SIC and add'l.: 6712 6021

CIK No: 0000743397

Subsidiaries: First Community Title & Escrow Company, First National Bank

Officers: Thomas D. Vance/54/Dir., CEO, Pres., C. P. Whisenhunt/64/Sr. VP, David W. Marttala/46/Sr. VP, Kenny D. Neal/57/CFO, Sr. VP/$96,404.00, Cindy Swann/56/Corp. Sec. - Transfer Agent, Mgr. - Human Resources, Larry B. Foster/48/Sr. VP, P. D. Bogle/61/Sr. VP, Dwayne Woods/45/Sr. VP, Kenneth D. Woods/46/Sr. VP

Directors: Thomas D. Vance/54/Dir., CEO, Pres., Levoy C. Knowles/54/Chmn., Douglas J. Milner/60/Dir., Carl M. Stanley/73/Dir., John Gregory Brock/53/Dir., Rufus W. Gonder/53/Dir., Charles C. Jacobs/Dir., G. B. Greene/69/Dir., Robert W. Jones/79/Dir., Arthur J. Dyer/56/Dir., Mark A. Pirtle/56/Dir.

Owners: Thomas D. Vance, C. M. Stanley/1.23%, Mark A. Pirtle/7.87%, Douglas J. Milner, Rufus W. Gonder, G. B. Greene/1.76%, Insiders/16.52%, Arthur J. Dyer, Robert W. Jones/1.85%, Levoy C. Knowles, J. G. Brock

First Merchants Corp

200 E Jackson St., Muncie, IN, 47305; **PH:** 1-765-747-1500; **Fax:** 1-765-747-1473; http:// www.firstmerchants.com; **Email:** customerservice@firstmerchants.com

General - Incorporation	IN	Stock- Price on:12/24/2007	$24.5
Employees	1,131	Stock Exchange	NDQ
Auditor	BKD LLP	Ticker Symbol	FRME
Stk Agt	American Stock Transfer & Trust Co.	Outstanding Shares	18,320,000
Counsel	NA	E.P.S.	$1.59
DUNS No.	00-693-9417	Shareholders	NA

Business: The group's principal activity is to provide a wide range of financial services through 70 locations. The group accepts time, savings and demand deposits and provides consumer, commercial, agri-business and real estate mortgage loans. The group also rents safe deposit facilities; provides personal and corporate trust services; brokerage services and other corporate services, letters of credit and repurchase agreements and provides personal and commercial lines of insurance and the reinsurance of credit life, accident, and health insurance. The banking centers are located in adams, boone, carroll, Delaware, fayette, hamilton, henry, howard, jasper, jay, madison, miami, tippecanoe, wabash, wayne, white, randolph, and union counties in Indiana and butler and franklin counties in Ohio. The group acquired commerce national bank on 01-Mar-2003.

Primary SIC and add'l.: 6021 6712

CIK No: 0000712534

Subsidiaries: Commerce National Bank, Decatur Bank & Trust Company, National Association, First Merchants Bank, National Association, First United Bank, National Association, Frances Slocum Bank & Trust Company, National Association, Lafayette Bank and Trust Company, National Association, The First National Bank of Portland, The Madison Community Bank, National Association, United Communities National Bank

Officers: Michael C. Rechin/Dir., CEO, Pres./$472,184.00, Brian Edwards/Investor Relations Officer, Kelly Smith/Contact - Website Coordinator, Kimberly J. Ellington/48/Sr. VP, Dir. - Human Resources, David W. Spade/55/Sr. VP, Chief Credit Officer/$198,100.00, Cynthia G. Holaday/Sec., Robert R. Connors/Sr. VP - Operations, Technology/$240,434.00, Mark K. Hardwick/CFO, Sr. VP/$265,555.00

Directors: Michael C. Rechin/Dir., CEO, Pres., Charles E. Schalliol/Chmn., Roderick English/Dir., Thomas B. Clark/Dir., Richard A. Boehning/Dir., Jo Ann M. Gora/Dir., Barry J. Hudson/Dir., Terry L. Walker/Dir., William L. Hoy/Dir., Michael L. Cox/Dir., Jean L. Wojtowicz/Dir.

Owners: Charles E. Schalliol, Dimensional Fund Advisors LP/8.35%, Mark K. Hardwick, Thomas D. McAuliffe, David W. Spade, Barry J. Hudson/2.45%, Robert M. Smitson, Roderick English, Michael L. Cox, Thomas B. Clark, Jean L. Wojtowicz, Terry L. Walker, Jo Ann M. Gora, Michael C. Rechin, First Merchants Trust Company, N A/5.95% *(18 Owners included in Index)*

Financial Data: Fiscal Year End:12/31 **Latest Annual Data:** 12/31/2006

Year	Sales	Net Income
2006	$243,223,000	$30,198,000
2005	$211,928,000	$30,239,000
2004	$191,528,000	$29,411,000

Curr. Assets:	$125,586,000	**Curr. Liab.:**	$2,759,864,000	**P/E Ratio:**	14.85
Plant, Equip.:	$42,393,000	**Total Liab.:**	$3,227,545,000	**Indic. Yr. Divd.:**	$0.920
Total Assets:	$3,554,870,000	**Net Worth:**	$327,325,000	**Debt/ Equity:**	0.2980

First Mercury Financial Corp

29621 Nwestern Hwy., Southfield, MI, 48034; **PH:** 1-248-358-4010; **Fax:** 1-248-358-2459; http:// www.firstmercury.com

General - Incorporation	DE	Stock- Price on:12/24/2007	$19.7
Employees	142	Stock Exchange	NYSE
Auditor	BDO Seidman, LLP	Ticker Symbol	FMR
Stk Agt	TBD	Outstanding Shares	17,340,000
Counsel	NA	E.P.S.	$1.91
DUNS No.	NA	Shareholders	NA

Business: The groups principle activity is to provide insurance products and services. In the year 2006, the group acquired First Mercury Financial Corporation. The group operates from the United States. The groups quarterly revenue in october 2007 was 51.69 millions of USD.

Primary SIC and add'l.: 6411 6331

CIK No: 0000929186

Subsidiaries: All Nation Insurance Company, American Risk Pooling Consultants, Inc., ARPCO Holdings, Inc., CoverX Corporation, First Mercury Capital Trust I, First Mercury Capital Trust II, First Mercury Insurance Company, Integrated Risk Management, Inc., PERSI, LLC, Public Entity Risk Services of Illinois, LLC, Public Entity Risk Services of Ohio, Inc., Quantum Direct Service Corporation, Quantum Insurance Agency, Inc., Questt Agency, Inc., Van American Insurance Services, Inc.

Officers: Richard H. Smith/Chmn., CEO, Pres./$2,258,339.00, John A. Marazza/CFO, Exec. VP, Treasurer, Corp. Sec./$747,031.00, Jeffrey R. Wawok/Exec. VP/$592,152.00, William S. Weaver/Sr. VP/$1,591,188.00

Directors: Richard H. Smith/Chmn., CEO, Pres., Jerome Shaw/Dir., William C. Tyler/Dir., Thomas Kearney/Dir., Louis J. Manetti/Dir., Hollis W. Rademacher/Dir., Steven A. Shapiro/Dir.

Owners: Hollis W. Rademacher, Steven A. Shapiro, Insiders/27.50%, John A. Marazza, The Guardian Life Insurance Company of America/5.00%, Jeffrey R. Wawok, Louis J. Manetti, William C. Tyler, Thomas Kearney, William S. Weaver/1.20%, Jerome M. Shaw/21.90%, Richard H. Smith/5.20%

Financial Data: Fiscal Year End:12/31   Latest Annual Data: 12/31/2006

Year	Sales	Net Income
2006	$137,492,000	$21,869,000

Curr. Assets:	$182,370,000	Curr. Liab.:	$9,343,000	P/E Ratio:	63.38
Plant, Equip.:	NA	Total Liab.:	$340,195,000	Indic. Yr. Divd.:	NA
Total Assets:	$512,933,000	Net Worth:	$172,738,000	Debt/ Equity:	NA

First Mid-Illinois Bancshares Inc

1515 Charleston Ave., Mattoon, IL, 61938; **PH:** 1-217-234-7454; **Fax:** 1-217-268-5705; http:// www.firstmid.com

General - Incorporation	DE	Stock - Price on:12/24/2007	$41.7
Employees	347	Stock Exchange	OTC
Auditor	BKD LLP	Ticker Symbol	FMBH
Stk Agt	American Stock Transfer & Trust Co.	Outstanding Shares	4,250,000
Counsel	NA	E.P.S.	$1.54
DUNS No.	07-912-9748	Shareholders	NA

Business: The group's principal activities are to provide general banking business services to consumer and commercial sector. The group operates through its wholly owned subsidiaries first mid-Illinois bank & trust, n.a., mid-Illinois data services, inc. And the checkley agency, inc. The group provides banking business services through first mid-Illinois bank & trust n.a. These services include the acceptance of demand, savings and time accounts and the servicing of such accounts. The lending activities include commercial, industrial, agricultural, consumer and real estate lending, including installment, credit card, personal lines of credit and overdraft protection. The other services include the provision of safe deposit box operations, traveler's checks and cashiers' checks, foreign currency and other special services. Through the subsidiary, mid-Illinois data services, the group provides data processing services to affiliates and the checkley agency, inc subsidiary.

Primary SIC and add'l.: 6712 6021

CIK No: 0000700565

Subsidiaries: First Mid-Illinois Bank & Trust, N.A., First Mid-Illinois Statutory Trust I, Mid-Illinois Data Services, Inc., The Checkley Agency, Inc.

Owners: Ray Anthony Sparks/4.40%, John W. Hedges, Michael L. Taylor, Insiders/31.60%, Stanley E. Gilliland/1.10%, Gary W. Melvin/4.60%, Kenneth R. Diepholz/1.00%, Richard Anthony Lumpkin/9.60%, Steven L. Grissom/6.80%, Daniel E. Marvin/1.80%, Robert J. Swift, Sara Jane Preston, Laurel G. Allenbaugh, David R. Hodgman/6.00%, William S. Rowland/2.40% *(17 Owners included in Index)*

Financial Data: Fiscal Year End:12/31   Latest Annual Data: 12/31/2006

Year	Sales	Net Income
2006	$68,936,000	$10,009,000
2005	$57,098,000	$9,807,000
2004	$51,663,000	$9,751,000

Curr. Assets:	$30,253,000	Curr. Liab.:	$839,733,000	P/E Ratio:	17.90
Plant, Equip.:	$16,293,000	Total Liab.:	$904,773,000	Indic. Yr. Divd.:	$0.370
Total Assets:	$980,559,000	Net Worth:	$75,786,000	Debt/ Equity:	0.8514

First Midwest Bancorp Inc

1 Pierce Pl., Ste. 1500, Itasca, IL, 60143; **PH:** 1-630-875-7450; **Fax:** 1-630-875-7369; http:// www.firstmidwest.com

General - Incorporation	DE	Stock - Price on:12/24/2007	$36.4266
Employees	1,892	Stock Exchange	NDQ
Auditor	Ernst & Young LLP	Ticker Symbol	FMBI
Stk Agt	Mellon Investor Services LLC	Outstanding Shares	49,720,000
Counsel	NA	E.P.S.	$2.41
DUNS No.	88-420-1401	Shareholders	NA

Business: The group's principal activities are to provide commercial and retail banking services. The group operates through 66 branch offices in suburban metropolitan Chicago. The loans offered by the group include commercial and industrial, mortgage loans and consumer loans. It offers a broad array of lending, depository, investment management, mortgage banking, insurance and related financial services tailored for individual, commercial, industrial and governmental customers. The group also operates four affiliates, which offer trust, investment advisory and credit insurance and mortgage banking-related services. It maintains branch operations in vermilion and champaign counties of Illinois. On 31-Dec-2003, the group acquired covest bancshares, inc.

Primary SIC and add'l.: 6712 6022

CIK No: 0000702325

Subsidiaries: First Midwest Bank, First Midwest Capital Trust I, First Midwest Insurance Company

Officers: John M. Omeara/62/Dir., CEO, Pres./$2,602,205.00, Kent S. Belasco/56/CIO, Exec. VP - Bank, Mark M. Dietrich/Group COO, Exec. VP/$554,152.00, Michael L. Scudder/CFO, Exec. VP/$746,005.00, Stephanie R. Wise/40/Exec. VP - Business, Institutional Services, Michael J. Kozak/Exec. VP, Chief Credit Officer, Janet M. Viano/52/Group Pres. - Retail Banking, Bank/$455,871.00, Thomas J. Schwartz/Group Pres. - Commercial Banking, First Midwest Bank/$997,173.00, Cynthia A. Lance/Exec. VP, Corp. Sec., Paul F. Clemens/CFO, Exec. VP, Barbara E. Briick/Sr. VP, Corp. Sec.

Directors: John M. Omeara/62/Dir., CEO, Pres., Robert P. OMeara/70/Chmn., John E. Rooney/65/Dir., Ellen A. Rudnick/57/Dir., Vernon A. Brunner/Dir., John F. Chlebowski/Dir. - First Midwest Bank, Thomas M. Garvin/Dir., John L. Sterling/Dir., Patrick J. McDonnell/64/Dir., Joseph W. England/67/Dir., Stephen J. Vanderwoude/Dir., Bruce S. Chelberg/73/Dir., Brother James Gaffney/Dir.

Owners: Robert P. OMeara/1.30%, Barclays Global Investors, N.A./5.13%, Insiders/4.50%, Mark M. Dietrich, Vernon A. Brunner, James Gaffney, Bruce S. Chelberg, BlackRock, Inc./8.95%, John E. Rooney, Ellen A. Rudnick, Patrick J. McDonnell, Thomas M. Garvin, John M. OMeara/1.30%, Joseph W. England, John L. Sterling *(19 Owners included in Index)*

Financial Data: Fiscal Year End:12/31   Latest Annual Data: 12/31/2006

Year	Sales	Net Income
2006	$579,692,000	$117,246,000
2005	$444,627,000	$101,377,000
2004	$397,376,000	$99,136,000

Curr. Assets:	$284,799,000	Curr. Liab.:	$6,189,139,000	P/E Ratio:	15.22
Plant, Equip.:	$126,677,000	Total Liab.:	$7,690,512,000	Indic. Yr. Divd.:	$1.180
Total Assets:	$8,441,526,000	Net Worth:	$751,014,000	Debt/ Equity:	1.9442

First Montauk Financial Corp

Pkwy. 109 Office Ctr., 328 Newman Springs Rd., Red Bank, NJ, 07701; **PH:** 1-732-842-4700; **Fax:** 1-732-842-9047; http:// www.montaukfinancial.com; **Email:** info@montaukfinancial.com

General - Incorporation	NJ	Stock - Price on:12/24/2007	$0.38
Employees	100	Stock Exchange	OTC
Auditor	Lazar Levine & Felix LLP	Ticker Symbol	FMFK
Stk Agt	North American Transfer Co	Outstanding Shares	18,530,000
Counsel	Goldstein & Digioia	E.P.S.	-$0.03
DUNS No.	08-762-4466	Shareholders	NA

Business: The group's principle activity is to provide securities brokerage and investment banking services of listed and unlisted securities. The listed and unlisted securities include equity and fixed-income securities, sales of government and corporate securities and other market securities. The group also provides insurance services and sells insurance products, private and public security offerings and investment advisory services. The customers of the group include finance and investment banks, corporations and businesses. The group's quarterly revenue for Sep'07 was 9.52 millions of USD.

Primary SIC and add'l.: 6282 6211 6719

CIK No: 0000083125

Subsidiaries: First Montauk Securities Corp., Montauk Insurance Services, Inc.

Officers: Victor K. Kurylak/CEO, Pres./$500,000.00, Fred M. Haas/Sr. VP - Business Development, William J. Kurinsky/CFO, Exec. VP, Robert I. Rabinowitz/50/Exec. VP, General Counsel, Sec./$400,000.00, Mindy A. Horowitz/Acting CFO/$187,000.00, Phillip D'Ambrisi/50/Dir., COO/$450,000.00

Directors: Ward R. Jones/76/Dir., Barry D. Shapiro/66/Dir., David I. Portman/66/Dir., Phillip D'Ambrisi/50/Dir., COO, Celeste M. Leonard/51/Dir.

Owners: David I. Portman, Mindy A. Horowitz/1.47%, Insiders/9.49%, Barry D. Shapiro, Edward H. Okun/52.80%, Ward R. Jones, Victor K. Kurylak/7.99%

Financial Data: Fiscal Year End:12/31   Latest Annual Data: 12/31/2006

Year	Sales	Net Income
2006	NA	NA
2005	$58,084,000	$2,424,000
2004	$59,187,000	$731,000

Curr. Assets:	$6,904,000	Curr. Liab.:	$3,892,000		
Plant, Equip.:	$239,000	Total Liab.:	$3,985,000	Indic. Yr. Divd.:	NA
Total Assets:	$7,799,000	Net Worth:	$3,813,000	Debt/ Equity:	0.0068

First Morris Bank NJ

250 Madison Ave., Morristown, NJ, 07960; **PH:** 1-973-267-0900; **Fax:** 1-973-267-1079; http:// www.firstmorrisbank.com

General - Incorporation	NA	Stock - Price on:12/24/2007	NA
Employees	NA	Stock Exchange	NA
Auditor	NA	Ticker Symbol	NA
Stk Agt	NA	Outstanding Shares	NA
Counsel	NA	E.P.S.	NA
DUNS No.	NA	Shareholders	NA

Business: The groups principle activity is to provide banking services. The group operates from the United States.

Primary SIC and add'l.: 6029

CIK No:

First Mutual Bancshares Inc

400 108th Ave. NE, Bellevue, WA, 98004; **PH:** 1-425-455-7300; **Fax:** 1-425-453-5302; http:// www.firstmutual.com

General - Incorporation	WA	Stock - Price on:12/24/2007	$22
Employees	226	Stock Exchange	NDQ
Auditor	Moss Adams LLP	Ticker Symbol	FMSB
Stk Agt	Mellon Investor Services LLC	Outstanding Shares	6,690,000
Counsel	Preston Gates & Ellis	E.P.S.	$1.29
DUNS No.	NA	Shareholders	NA

Business: The group's principal activity is to provide banking services to retail customers and offers housing and commercial real estate loans. The principal business of the group consists of attracting deposits from the general public as well as wholesale funding sources and investing those funds in real estate loans, small to mid-sized business loans secured by savings accounts and consumer loans. The group conducts business through 10 full service office facilities located in bellevue, kirkland, redmond, seattle, issaquah, and monroe and a loan production office at bellingham and tacoma, Washington, and a consumer loan office located in jacksonville, Florida.

Primary SIC and add'l.: 6712 6036

CIK No: 0001098337

Subsidiaries: First Mutual Bank, First Mutual Services

Officers: John R. Valaas/Dir., CEO, Pres./$477,628.00, Kari A. Stenslie/Sr. VP, Controller, Janine M. Berryman/Corp. Sec.

Directors: John R. Valaas/Dir., CEO, Pres., James J. Doud/Vice Chmn., Kemper F. Freeman/Chmn., Robert J. Herbold/Dir., Victor E. Parker/Dir., Mary Case Dunnam/Dir., Robert C. Wallace/Dir., George W. Rowley/Dir., Janine A. Florence/Dir., Richard S. Sprague/Dir.

Owners: James J. Doud, Robert J. Herbold, Roger A. Mandery/1.11%, George W. Rowley/2.09%, Employee Stock Ownership Plan/7.14%, Joseph P. Zavaglia, Robert C. Wallace/1.92%, Mary Case Dunnam, John R. Valaas/5.08%, Janine Florence/4.71%, Richard S. Sprague/1.32%, Victor E. Parker/1.79%, 237 Park Avenue, Suite 801/6.83%, Kemper F. Freeman/9.36%, Scott B. Harlan *(19 Owners included in Index)*

Financial Data: ***Fiscal Year End:***12/31 ***Latest Annual Data:*** 12/31/2006

Year	Sales	Net Income
2006	$88,293,000	$10,980,000
2005	$72,718,000	$10,319,000
2004	$59,379,000	$9,288,000

Curr. Assets:	$30,896,000	**Curr. Liab.:**	$986,058,000	**P/E Ratio:**	13.84
Plant, Equip.:	$35,566,000	**Total Liab.:**	$1,009,241,000	**Indic. Yr. Divd.:**	$0.360
Total Assets:	$1,079,263,000	**Net Worth:**	$70,022,000	**Debt/ Equity:**	NA

First National Bancshares Inc/FL

5817 Manatee Ave. W, Bradenton, FL, 34209; ***PH:*** 1-941-794-6969;
http:// www.firstnational-online.com

General - Incorporation	FL	***Stock***- Price on:12/24/2007	$16.802
Employees	87	Stock Exchange	NA
Auditor	Christopher, Smith, Bristow & Stanell	Ticker Symbol	NA
Stk Agt	First Citizens Bank & Trust Co	Outstanding Shares	3,700,000
Counsel	NA	E.P.S	$0.96
DUNS No.	NA	Shareholders	NA

Business: The group's principal activity is to provide a wide range of banking services in manatee county, Florida. It provides various deposit accounts such as personal and commercial checking accounts, negotiable order of withdrawals, certificates of deposit, money market accounts, savings accounts, individual retirement accounts and automatic transfers. The depository services are complemented by direct deposit capabilities, night depository services and bank by mail. The group originates various loans including consumer, commercial and real estate loans. It also provides various trust and investment products. The services are provided to individuals, professionals and small and medium size businesses located in manatee county, Florida. On 15-Mar-2004 the group acquired the trust company of Florida.

Primary SIC and add'l.: 6021 6712

CIK No: 0001067077

Subsidiaries: 1ST National Bank & Trust

Officers: Jerry L. Calvert/Vice Chmn., CEO, Pres., Dana Tinsley/Banking Officer, Loan Administration Specialist, Robert W. Murdoch/Exec. VP, Retail Banking Mgr., Kitty B. Payne/CFO, Exec. VP, David H. Zabriskie/Exec. VP - Sr. Lender, Louie W. Blanton/Sr. VP - Commercial Banking, Business Development, Peter A. Seitz/Sr. VP, John S. Higdon/Sr. VP, Dir. - Wholesale Mortgage, Mark Johnston/Greenville Regional Dir., Nick Legrand/Greenville Regional Dir., Foster McKissick/Greenville Regional Dir., Emile Sarmiento/Greenville Regional Dir., Lindsay Smith/Greenville Regional Dir., Ronnie Strange/Greenville Regional Dir., Billy Weaver/Greenville Regional Dir. *(67 Officers included in Index)*

Directors: Jerry L. Calvert/Vice Chmn., CEO, Pres., Gaines W. Hammond/Chmn., Benjamin R. Hines/Dir., Russel W. Floyd/Dir., Tyrone C. Gilmore/Dir., Martha C. Chapman/Dir., Dan C. Adams/Dir., Mellnee G. Buchheit/Dir., William A. Hudson/Dir., Norman F. Pulliam/Dir., Peter E. Weisman/Dir., Donald B. Wildman/Dir., Coleman L. Young/Dir.

Financial Data: ***Fiscal Year End:***12/31 ***Latest Annual Data:*** 12/31/2006

Year	Sales	Net Income
2006	$30,965,000	$4,052,000
2005	$19,196,000	$2,835,000
2004	$12,195,000	$1,815,000

Curr. Assets:	$8,205,000	**Curr. Liab.:**	$424,989,000	**P/E Ratio:**	17.50
Plant, Equip.:	$6,906,000	**Total Liab.:**	$438,392,000	**Indic. Yr. Divd.:**	NA
Total Assets:	$465,382,000	**Net Worth:**	$26,990,000	**Debt/ Equity:**	0.4822

First National Bancshares Inc/SC

215 N Pine St., Spartanburg, SC, 29302; ***PH:*** 1-864-948-9001; ***Fax:*** 1-864-948-0001;
http:// www.firstnational-online.com; ***Email:*** info@firstnbt.com

General - Incorporation	SC	***Stock***- Price on:12/24/2007	$16.802
Employees	87	Stock Exchange	NDQ
Auditor	Elliot Davis LLC	Ticker Symbol	FNSC
Stk Agt	First Citizens Bank & Trust Co	Outstanding Shares	3,700,000
Counsel	NA	E.P.S	$0.93
DUNS No.	NA	Shareholders	NA

Business: The group's principal activities are to accept deposits and provide commercial, consumer and mortgage loans to the general public in spartanburg county. The other services offered by the group include safe deposit boxes, traveler's checks, direct deposits, us savings bond, drive-up ATM's and banking by telephone. The group is associated with the cirrus and pulse ATM networks. The group provides a full range of deposit services that are typically available in most banks and savings and loan associations, including checking accounts, commercial accounts, savings accounts and time deposits. The group's wholly owned subsidiary is first national bank of spartanburg.

Primary SIC and add'l.: 6712 6021

CIK No: 0001095274

Subsidiaries: First National Bank of the South, FNSC Capital Trust I, FNSC Capital Trust II, FNSC Capital Trust III

Officers: Jerry L. Calvert/Vice Chmn., CEO, Pres./$423,018.00, Renee Cothran/VP, Commercial Banking Officer, Pamela Gilliam/VP, Loan Operations Mgr., Shany Ezell/AVP, Mortgage Loan Officer, Susan Gustafson/AVP, Business Banking Officer, Peter A. Seitz/Sr. VP, Barry Starling/Sr. VP, Regional Executive Officer - Western Region, Sandy Meister/VP, Dir. - Finance, Mary Jane Davidson/VP - City Executive Spartanburg, Carrie Wallace/AVP, Branch Mgr. East Bay Street, David H. Zabriskie/Exec. VP - Sr. Lender/$230,784.00, David Bowdish/VP, Operations Mgr., Robert W. Murdoch/Exec. VP, Retail Banking Mgr./$191,676.00, Marilyn Smith/VP, Branch Operations Mgr., Foster Alexander/AVP, Commercial Banking Officer *(66 Officers included in Index)*

Directors: Jerry L. Calvert/Vice Chmn., CEO, Pres., Gaines W. Hammond/Chmn., Russel W. Floyd/Dir., Dan C. Adams/Dir., Norman F. Pulliam/Dir., Tyrone C. Gilmore/Dir., Mellnee G. Buchheit/Dir., Donald B. Wildman/Dir., Peter E. Weisman/Dir., Coleman L. Young/Dir., Martha C. Chapman/Dir., Benjamin R. Hines/Dir., William A. Hudson/Dir.

Owners: Jerry L. Calvert/7.26%, Norman F. Pulliam/7.35%, Donald B. Wildman/2.50%, William A. Hudson/6.90%, Mellnee G. Buchheit/3.62%, David H. Zabriskie, Russel W. Floyd/3.93%, Dan C. Adams/6.09%, Benjamin R. Hines/4.93%, Coleman L. Young/3.03%, Insiders/51.93%, Peter E. Weisman/3.83%, Tyrone C. Gilmore/1.15%, Robert W. Murdoch, Martha C. Chapman/2.27% *(17 Owners included in Index)*

Financial Data: ***Fiscal Year End:***12/31 ***Latest Annual Data:*** 12/31/2006

Year	Sales	Net Income
2006	$30,965,000	$4,052,000
2005	$19,196,000	$2,835,000
2004	$12,195,000	$1,815,000

Curr. Assets:	$8,205,000	**Curr. Liab.:**	$424,989,000	**P/E Ratio:**	17.29
Plant, Equip.:	$6,906,000	**Total Liab.:**	$438,392,000	**Indic. Yr. Divd.:**	NA
Total Assets:	$465,382,000	**Net Worth:**	$26,990,000	**Debt/ Equity:**	NA

First National Bank Alaska

PO Box 100720, Anchorage, AK, 99510; ***PH:*** 1-907-777-4362; ***Fax:*** 1-907-777-4569;
http:// www.fnbalaska.com

General - Incorporation		***Stock***- Price on:12/24/2007	$2200
Employees	NA	Stock Exchange	OTC
Auditor	NA	Ticker Symbol	FBAK
Stk Agt	Continental Stock Transfer & Trust Co	Outstanding Shares	NA
Counsel	NA	E.P.S	$116.01
DUNS No.	NA	Shareholders	NA

Business: The groups principal activity is to provide commercial banking services. Services of the group include providing home, consumer and business loans, safe deposit, trust and investment, ATM facilities and online brokerage services. The group operates from Alaska in the United States. The total assets of the group in the year 2006, was $2,310,499.

Primary SIC and add'l.: 6021

CIK No: 0000838874

Officers: D. H. Cuddy/Chmn., Pres., Betsy Lawer/Vice Chmn., COO, Doug Longacre/Sr. VP, Sue Foley/Sr. VP, Bill Renfrew/Sr. VP, Regional Mgr. Interior Alaska, David Lawer/Sr. VP, Jason Roth/Sr. VP, David Stringer/Sr. VP, Charles Weimer/Sr. VP, Regional Mgr., Debra Wilson/Sr. VP, Bill Inscho/Sr. VP, Craig Thorn/Sr. VP, Jill Reitz/Trust Officer

Directors: D. H. Cuddy/Chmn., Pres., Betsy Lawer/Vice Chmn., COO, Maurice Coyle/Dir., George E. Gordon/Dir., Loren H. Lounsbury/Dir., Margy Johnson/Dir., John T. Kelsey/Dir., Jane Klopfer/Dir., Morton V. Plumb/Dir.

Financial Data: ***Fiscal Year End:***NA ***Latest Annual Data:*** 12/31/2002

Year	Sales	Net Income
2002	$149,465,000	$42,775,000
2001	$150,491,000	$38,772,000
2000	$143,134,000	$31,251,000

Curr. Assets:	$98,164,000	**Curr. Liab.:**	$1,557,795,000	**P/E Ratio:**	18.96
Plant, Equip.:	$42,652,000	**Total Liab.:**	$1,617,317,000	**Indic. Yr. Divd.:**	$100.000
Total Assets:	$2,050,443,000	**Net Worth:**	$433,126,000	**Debt/ Equity:**	NA

First National Community Bancorp Inc

102 E Drinker St., Dunmore, PA, 18512; ***PH:*** 1-570-346-7667; ***Fax:*** 1-570-348-6426;
http:// www.fncb.com; ***Email:*** fncb@fncb.com

General - Incorporation	PA	***Stock***- Price on:12/24/2007	NA
Employees	NA	Stock Exchange	OTC
Auditor	Demetrius & Co LLC	Ticker Symbol	FNCB
Stk Agt	Registrar & Transfer Co	Outstanding Shares	NA
Counsel	Shumaker Williams	E.P.S	$0.95
DUNS No.	NA	Shareholders	NA

Business: The group's principal activity is to provide a wide range of commercial banking services to individuals and businesses. It provides deposit products including demand, checking and interest-bearing deposit accounts. The loans originated by the group include secured and unsecured installment loans, fixed and variable rate mortgages, home equity term loans, lines of credit and instant money overdraft protection loans. It provides other services such as mastercard and visa personal credit cards, working capital loans, letters of credit, accounts receivable, inventory or equipment financing loans, demand and term loans and commercial mortgages. In addition, the group provides 24-hour banking services, telephone banking, loan by phone and mortgage link to customers. The operations are conducted through offices located in lackawanna and luzerne counties, Pennsylvania. As of 30-Jun-2004, the group has 16 branch offices.

Primary SIC and add'l.: 6021 6712

CIK No: 0001035976

Subsidiaries: First National Community Bank

Officers: David J. Lombardi/CEO, Pres./$922,708.00, William S. Lance/First Sr. VP, Finance Control Division Mgr./$216,753.00, Sara Matusinski/Community Office Mgr. - Pittston, PA, Stephen J. Kavulich/First Sr. VP - Loan Administration, Compliance Division Mgr./$192,979.00, Linda A. D'Amario/VP, Controller, Jason A. Bohenek/Assist. Cashier, Accounting Supervisor, Jerry A. Champi/Exec. VP, Retail Sales Division Mgr., Anthony J. Gabello/Sr. VP - Credit, Branch Administrator, Thomas P. Tulaney/Exec. VP, Commercial Sales Division Mgr./$347,056.00, Cynthia T. Hennan/Community Office Mgr. - Back Mountain Office, Bernice A. Shipp/Community Office Mgr. - Nanticoke Office, Christine A. Gresh/Community Office Mgr., Assist. VP - Hazleton, Richard D. Padula/Assist. VP - Mortgage Loan Consultant, Leslie Conserette/Administrative Assist., Executive Sec., Ellen Ward/Community Office Mgr. - Stroudsburg *(52 Officers included in Index)*

Directors: David J. Lombardi/CEO, Pres.

Owners: Joseph J. Gentile/2.95%, John P. Moses/0.48%, Michael J. Cestone/1.30%, Michael T. Conahan/0.35%, Joseph O. Haggerty/0.21%, David J. Lombardi, Dominick L. DeNaples/8.41%, Joseph Coccia/1.01%, John R. Thomas/1.11%, Louis A. DeNaples/9.94%, William P. Conaboy/0.08%, Michael G. Cestone/0.44%, Insiders/28.51%

Financial Data: ***Fiscal Year End:***12/31 ***Latest Annual Data:*** 12/31/2006

Year	Sales	Net Income
2006	$73,769,000	$13,509,000
2005	$57,461,000	$11,225,000
2004	$47,018,000	$9,263,000

Curr. Assets:	$34,870,000	**Curr. Liab.:**	$927,747,000		
Plant, Equip.:	$13,671,000	**Total Liab.:**	$1,087,921,000	**Indic. Yr. Divd.:**	$0.510
Total Assets:	$1,184,783,000	**Net Worth:**	$96,862,000	**Debt/ Equity:**	NA

First National Corp

112 W King St., Strasburg, VA, 22657; *PH:* 1-540-465-9121; *Fax:* 1-540-465-5946;
http:// www.firstbank-va.com; *Email:* info@firstbank-va.com

General		Stock	
Incorporation	VA	Price on:12/24/2007	$25.9
Employees	151	Stock Exchange	OTC
Auditor	Yount, Hyde & Barbour, P.C	Ticker Symbol	FXNC
Stk Agt	Registrar & Transfer Co	Outstanding Shares	2,920,000
Counsel	NA	E.P.S	$1.89
DUNS No.	19-045-2532	Shareholders	NA

Business: The group's principal activities are to provide banking services. These services include a wide range of deposits, loans and other banking services to individuals, businesses, institutions and government entities. The group's operations are carried out in the areas of frederick, shenandoah, warren and clarke counties and the city of winchester in Virginia. The group's deposit services include checking, statement savings, now accounts, money market accounts, ira deposits, certificates of deposit, christmas club accounts, direct deposit programs, life-line checking accounts and investment savings accounts. The group also offers commercial, financial, agricultural, residential and consumer loans. The group also offers consumers other general banking services, such as safe deposit facilities, travelers checks and collections and acts as an agent for the purchase and redemption of United States savings bonds.

Primary SIC and add'l.: 6022 6712

CIK No: 0000719402

Subsidiaries: First Bank Financial Services, Inc., First Bank, Inc, First National (VA) Statutory Trust I, First National (VA) Statutory Trust II

Officers: Harry S. Smith/Dir. - First Bank, CEO, Pres./$315,544.00, Byron A. Brill/Vice Chmn. - First Bank, Douglas C. Arthur/Chmn. - First Bank, Marshall J. Beverley/Exec. VP, Sr. Trust Officer/$159,099.00, Dennis A. Dysart/Exec. VP, Chief Administrative Officer/$174,487.00, Christopher T. Martin/Exec. VP - Operations, Henry L. Shirkey/Dir. - First Bank, Elizabeth H. Cottrell/Dir. - First Bank, James R. Wilkins/Dir. - First Bank, Charles E. Maddox/Dir. - First Bank, John K. Marlow/Dir. - First Bank, Christopher E. French/Dir. - First Bank, Shane M. Bell/CFO, Exec. VP/$148,252.00, Allen W. Nicholls/Dir. - First Bank, Andrew J. Hershey/Exec. VP - Loan Administration/$180,289.00 *(17 Officers included in Index)*

Owners: Christopher E. French, Byron A. Brill/2.01%, James R. Wilkins/6.16%, Andrew J. Hershey, Charles E. Maddox, James A. Davis, Henry L. Shirkey, Harry S. Smith/1.66%, Marshall J. Beverley, Allen W. Nicholls, Elizabeth H. Cottrell/1.67%, Dennis A. Dysart, John K. Marlow/2.03%, Shane M. Bell, Insiders/13.40% *(16 Owners included in Index)*

Financial Data: *Fiscal Year End:*12/31 *Latest Annual Data:* 12/31/2006

Year	Sales	Net Income
2006	$38,117,000	$5,798,000
2005	$30,534,000	$5,389,000
2004	$24,951,000	$4,206,000

Curr. Assets:	$22,595,000	Curr. Liab.:	$437,267,000	P/E Ratio:	13.28
Plant, Equip.:	$17,603,000	Total Liab.:	$495,389,000	Indic. Yr. Divd.:	$0.520
Total Assets:	$527,944,000	Net Worth:	$32,555,000	Debt/ Equity:	1.5769

First National Lincoln Corp

223 Main St., Damariscotta, ME, 04543; *PH:* 1-207-563-3195; *Fax:* 1-207-563-6853;
http:// www.the1st.com

General		Stock	
Incorporation	ME	Price on:12/24/2007	$16.05
Employees	208	Stock Exchange	NDQ
Auditor	Berry, Dunn, Mcneil & Parker	Ticker Symbol	FNLC
Stk Agt	Shareholder Services Group	Outstanding Shares	9,780,000
Counsel	NA	E.P.S	$1.259
DUNS No.	15-089-9557	Shareholders	NA

Business: The group's principal activity is to provide commercial banking services to individual and corporate customers through six branch offices located in mid-coast Maine. The group offers checking, savings and investment accounts, consumer, commercial and mortgage loans and credit cards. It also provides investment management and trust services. The customers of the group are primarily small businesses and individuals.

Primary SIC and add'l.: 6021 6712

CIK No: 0000765207

Subsidiaries: The First, N.A.

Officers: Daniel R. Daigneault/Dir., CEO, Pres./$417,908.00, Charles A. Wootton/Exec. VP, Clerk/$166,214.00, Stephen F. Ward/CFO/$203,304.00

Directors: Daniel R. Daigneault/Dir., CEO, Pres., Bruce B. Tindal/Dir., Tony C. Mckim/Dir., Stuart G. Smith/Dir., Katherine M. Boyd/Dir., Randy A. Nelson/Dir., David B. Soule/Dir., Robert B. Gregory/Dir., Carl S. Poole/Dir., Mark N. Rosborough/Dir.

Owners: Bruce B. Tindal, Stephen F. Ward, Randy A. Nelson, Daniel R. Daigneault/2.12%, Charles A. Wootton, Mark N. Rosborough/1.37%, David B. Soule, Carl S. Poole/2.83%, Katherine M. Boyd, Tony C. McKim, Stuart G. Smith, Ronald J. Wrobel, Robert B. Gregory

Financial Data: *Fiscal Year End:*12/31 *Latest Annual Data:* 12/31/2006

Year	Sales	Net Income
2006	$74,510,000	$12,295,000
2005	$59,465,000	$12,843,000
2004	$35,195,000	$8,509,000

Curr. Assets:	$30,328,000	Curr. Liab.:	$805,235,000	P/E Ratio:	12.75
Plant, Equip.:	$16,989,000	Total Liab.:	$997,542,000	Indic. Yr. Divd.:	$0.680
Total Assets:	$1,104,869,000	Net Worth:	$107,327,000	Debt/ Equity:	1.4936

First National Power Corp

No. 219 - 227 Bellevue Way NE, Bellevue, WA, 98004; *PH:* 1-416-918-6987;
http:// www.firstnationalpower.com

General		Stock	
Incorporation	DE	Price on:12/24/2007	$0.05
Employees	NA	Stock Exchange	OTC
Auditor	Schwartz Levitsky Feldman LLP	Ticker Symbol	FNPR
Stk Agt	Interwest Transfer Company, Inc.	Outstanding Shares	76,280,000
Counsel	NA	E.P.S	-$0.001
DUNS No.	NA	Shareholders	NA

Business: The groups principal activity is to create business based on Green Energy Power Generation business model. This model is designed to develop and implement cutting edge technology not formerly utilized in the electrical power generation industry and current technology configurations in new and exciting commercial applications. The group operates from Delaware in the United States.

Primary SIC and add'l.: 4911

CIK No: 0001142129

Officers: Peter Wanner/54/Dir., Treasurer, CFO

Directors: Peter Wanner/54/Dir., Treasurer, CFO

Owners: Peter Wanner/0.00%, Insiders/0.00%

Financial Data: *Fiscal Year End:*12/31 *Latest Annual Data:* 12/31/2006

Year	Sales	Net Income
2006	NA	-$33,000
2004	NA	-$75,000
2003	NA	-$107,000

Curr. Assets:	$203,000	Curr. Liab.:	$281,000		
Plant, Equip.:	NA	Total Liab.:	$281,000	Indic. Yr. Divd.:	NA
Total Assets:	$203,000	Net Worth:	-$78,000	Debt/ Equity:	NA

First Niagara Financial Group Inc

6950 S Transit Rd., Lockport, NY, 14095; *PH:* 1-716-625-7500; *Fax:* 1-716-625-8405;
http:// www.fnfg.com

General		Stock	
Incorporation	DE	Price on:12/24/2007	$13.52
Employees	1,922	Stock Exchange	NDQ
Auditor	KPMG LLP	Ticker Symbol	FNFG
Stk Agt	Mellon Investor Services LLC	Outstanding Shares	107,710,000
Counsel	NA	E.P.S	$0.74
DUNS No.	NA	Shareholders	NA

Business: The group's principal activity is to provide a wide range of financial services to individuals, families and businesses located in western and central New York. It provides various deposit account products including savings accounts, negotiable order of withdrawal ("Now") accounts, checking accounts, money market accounts, certificates of deposit, individual retirement accounts ("Iras") and other qualified plan accounts. The group also provides insurance, trust and investment services. The operations are conducted through 47 full-service banking offices, a loan production office and 70 ATM locations. On 17-Jan-2003, the group acquired finger lakes bancorp, inc, on 01-Jul-2003, costello, dreher, kaiser insurance agency and loomis & co inc. On 18-Feb-2003, the group sold nova healthcare administrators inc. During the year 2004, the group acquired troy financial corporation and troy commercial bank and savannah bank.

Primary SIC and add'l.: 6712 6036 6311

CIK No: 0001051741

Subsidiaries: Hatch Leonard Naples, Inc

Officers: John R. Koelmel/Dir., CEO, Pres./$688,233.00, Gerard J. Wenzke/CEO - First Niagara Risk Management, Daniel A. Dintino/Sr. VP - Residential, Specialized Lending, Michael W. Harrington/CFO, Treasurer/$284,272.00, Thomas L. Amell/Regional Pres. - Eastern New York, Area Retail Marketing Leader, Linda Mussen/Investor Relations Officer, Anthony Leo/Financial Consultant - Amherst, Clarence, Crosspoint, Main, Transit, Walker Center, West Amherst, Williamsville, Diana Sparks/Financial Consultant - City, Lockport, Newfane, Mike Macy/Regional Mgr. - Syracuse, Diane Benson/Regional Mgr., Krista Bailey/Regional Mgr., Robyn Lapenta/Regional Mgr., Diane Ronald/Regional Mgr., Thomas Russell/Financial Consultant - Lewiston, Niagara Falls, Ransomville, Jeff Forgie/Commercial Leasing Coordinator *(48 Officers included in Index)*

Directors: John R. Koelmel/Dir., CEO, Pres., William H. Jones/Vice Chmn., David M. Zebro/Vice Chmn., Thomas G. Bowers/Chmn., Paul J. Kolkmeyer/Dir., Pres. - Financial Consultants, Depew, Hamburg, Orchard Park, West Seneca, George M. Philip/Dir., Thomas E. Baker/Dir., Daniel J. Hogarty/Dir., Louise Woerner/Dir., Sharon D. Randaccio/Dir., Daniel W. Judge/Dir., John J. Bisgrove/Dir.

Owners: Michael J. Rogers, Insiders/16.30%, Peter B. Babiarz, William A. Evans/2.60%, Charles G. Cooper, Barry M. Snyder/5.20%, Robert McKnight, James A. Smith/1.60%, John P. McGrath, John W. Rose, Andrew W. Dorn, Frederick A. Wolf, Jamel C. Perkins, David L. Ulrich/2.20%, Gerard T. Mazurkiewicz *(18 Owners included in Index)*

Financial Data: *Fiscal Year End:*12/31 *Latest Annual Data:* 12/31/2006

Year	Sales	Net Income
2006	$527,048,000	$91,859,000
2005	$465,880,000	$92,859,000
2004	$276,444,000	$51,817,000

Curr. Assets:	$187,652,000	Curr. Liab.:	$6,010,019,000	P/E Ratio:	18.03
Plant, Equip.:	$97,180,000	Total Liab.:	$6,558,329,000	Indic. Yr. Divd.:	$0.560
Total Assets:	$7,945,526,000	Net Worth:	$1,387,197,000	Debt/ Equity:	0.2960

First Niles Financial Inc

55 N Main St., Niles, OH, 44446; *PH:* 1-330-652-2539

General		Stock	
Incorporation	DE	Price on:12/24/2007	NA
Employees	11	Stock Exchange	OTC
Auditor	Anness, Gerlach & Williams	Ticker Symbol	FNFI
Stk Agt	Computershare Investor Services LLC	Outstanding Shares	NA
Counsel	Silver, Freedman & Taff LLP	E.P.S	$0.57
DUNS No.	02-649-3226	Shareholders	NA

Business: The group's principal activity is to provide banking services. The group is a savings and loan holding company operating through its subsidiary, homes federal savings and loan association. The group provides services through its only office in nile, Ohio. The group attracts retail deposits from general public and applies those funds to the origination of loans for residential, consumer and nonresidential purposes.

Primary SIC and add'l.: 6035 6712

CIK No: 0001065823

Subsidiaries: Home Federal Savings and Loan Association of Niles

Officers: William Stephens/75/CEO, Pres., Daniel E. Csontos/45/Corp. Sec., Lawrence Safarek/58/VP

Directors: William Stephens/75/CEO, Pres., James P. Kramer/51/Dir., Robert I. Shaker/44/Dir.

Financial Data: *Fiscal Year End:*12/31 *Latest Annual Data:* 12/31/2005

Year	Sales	Net Income
2005	$5,482,000	$1,046,000
2004	$5,201,000	$1,032,000
2003	$5,442,000	$1,058,000

Curr. Assets:	$5,170,000	Curr. Liab.:	$82,120,000		
Plant, Equip.:	$330,000	Total Liab.:	$82,120,000	Indic. Yr. Divd.:	$0.640
Total Assets:	$98,516,000	Net Worth:	$16,396,000	Debt/ Equity:	NA

First Northern Community Bancorp

195 N First St., Dixon, CA, 95620; *PH:* 1-707-678-3041; *Fax:* 1-707-678-9734;
http:// www.thatsmybank.com

General - Incorporation	CA	Stock- Price on:12/24/2007	$17.75
Employees	242	Stock Exchange	OTC
Auditor	KPMG LLP	Ticker Symbol	FNRN
Stk Agt	First Northern Community Bancorp	Outstanding Shares	8,390,000
Counsel	NA	E.P.S.	$0.88
DUNS No.	NA	Shareholders	NA

Business: The group's principal activity is to provide commercial banking services. The services include accepting demand, interest bearing transaction, savings and time deposits, and making commercial, consumer, and real estate related loans. The group offers installment note collection, issues cashier's checks and money orders, sells travelers' checks, rents safe deposit boxes and provides other customary banking services. It also offers a broad range of alternative investment products and services. The group operates through its wholly owned subsidiary, first national bank of dixon. It has ten full service branches located in the solano county cities of dixon, fairfield, suisun city, vacaville, yolo county cities of winters, davis, west sacramento, woodland and downtown sacramento, sacramento county.

Primary SIC and add'l.: 6712 6022

CIK No: 0001114927

Subsidiaries: First Northern Bank

Officers: Owen J. Onsum/Dir., CEO, Pres./$904,027.00, Louise A. Walker/Sr. Exec. VP, CFO/$311,174.00, Robert M. Walker/Exec. VP - Commercial, Retail, Trust Divisions/$294,578.00, Patrick S. Day/Exec. VP, Chief Credit Officer/$152,503.00, Kimberly A. Debra/Sr. VP - Corporate Communications, Marketing, Bruce A. Orris/CIO, Sr. VP, Larry Miller/Sr. VP, Dir. - Human Resources

Directors: Owen J. Onsum/Dir., CEO, Pres., Lori J. Aldrete/Dir., Frank J. Andrews/Dir., John F. Hamel/Dir., Diane P. Hamlyn/Dir., Gregory Dupratt/Dir., Foy S. McNaughton/Dir., John M. Carbahal/Dir., David W. Schulze/Dir., Andrew Scott Wallace/Dir.

Owners: Foy S. McNaughton, David W. Schulze/2.30%, Andrew S. Wallace, Gregory DuPratt, Louise A. Walker/2.90%, Insiders/16.90%, Diane P. Hamlyn, John M. Carbahal, Lori J. Aldrete, Owen J. Onsum/6.40%, John F. Hamel/1.10%, Patrick S. Day, Robert M. Walker/1.60%, Frank J. Andrews

Financial Data: Fiscal Year End:12/31   Latest Annual Data: 12/31/2006

Year	Sales	Net Income
2006	$53,359,000	$8,810,000
2005	$46,622,000	$8,688,000
2004	$36,833,000	$6,707,000

Curr. Assets:	$101,833,000	Curr. Liab.:	$623,235,000	P/E Ratio:	19.51
Plant, Equip.:	$8,435,000	Total Liab.:	$623,235,000	Indic. Yr. Divd.:	NA
Total Assets:	$685,225,000	Net Worth:	$61,990,000	Debt/ Equity:	NA

First of Long Island Corp

10 Glen Head Rd., Glen Head, NY, 11545; *PH:* 1-516-671-4900; *Fax:* 1-516-676-7900;
http:// www.fnbli.com; *Email:* customerservice@fnbli.com

General - Incorporation	NY	Stock- Price on:12/24/2007	$20.2
Employees	214	Stock Exchange	NDQ
Auditor	Crowe Chizek & Co. LLC	Ticker Symbol	FLIC
Stk Agt	Registrar & Transfer Co	Outstanding Shares	7,610,000
Counsel	Schupbach, Williams & Pavone	E.P.S.	$1.44
DUNS No.	15-650-6776	Shareholders	NA

Business: The group's principal activity is to provide financial services which include deposit products like checking accounts, money market type accounts, savings accounts, escrow service and iola (interest on lawyer) accounts and time deposit accounts. The lending activities include construction loans, commercial and residential mortgage loans, home equity loans and lines, consumer loans and letters of credit. In addition, it offers investment services, insurance, ATM banking, telephone banking, collection services, counter checks and certified checks, night depository services, safe deposit boxes and other financial services. The group's customers are privately owned businesses, professionals, consumers, public bodies and other organizations, located in nassau and suffolk counties.

Primary SIC and add'l.: 6712 6022

CIK No: 0000740663

Subsidiaries: First National Bank of Long Island, First of Long Island Agency, Inc

Officers: Michael N. Vittorio/Dir., CEO, Pres./$538,569.00, Arthur J. Lupinacci/67/Exec. VP/$505,726.00, Richard Kick/50/Sr. VP/$323,933.00, Brian J. Keeney/59/Sr. VP, Mark D. Curtis/53/CFO , Exec. VP, Cashier/$311,379.00, Donald L. Manfredonia/56/Sr. VP/$372,899.00, Joseph G. Perri/56/Sr. VP, John Grasso/49/Exec. VP

Directors: Michael N. Vittorio/Dir., CEO, Pres., Walter C. Teagle/58/Chmn., Stephen V. Murphy/62/Dir., Allen E. Busching/76/Dir., Paul T. Canarick/51/Dir., Alexander L. Cover/64/Dir., Beverly Ann Gehlmeyer/76/Dir., William H.J. Hoefling/57/Dir., Howard Thomas Hogan/63/Dir., Douglas J. Maxwell/66/Dir.

Owners: Insiders/18.29%, Beverly Ann Gehlmeyer/0.78%, William H. J. Hoefling/0.10%, Zachary Levy/9.43%, Mark D. Curtis/0.31%, Donald L. Manfredonia/0.96%, Michael N. Vittorio/0.33%, Alexander L. Cover/0.03%, Walter C. Teagle, Paul T. Canarick/10.09%, Stephen V. Murphy/0.04%, Arthur J. Lupinacci, Howard Thomas Hogan/1.55%, Sidney Canarick/10.09%, Douglas J. Maxwell (17 Owners included in Index)

Financial Data: Fiscal Year End:12/31   Latest Annual Data: 12/31/2006

Year	Sales	Net Income
2006	$54,933,000	$11,227,000
2005	$49,262,000	$12,277,000
2004	$44,543,000	$12,081,000

Curr. Assets:	$23,790,000	Curr. Liab.:	$858,605,000	P/E Ratio:	14.13
Plant, Equip.:	$8,695,000	Total Liab.:	$858,605,000	Indic. Yr. Divd.:	$0.560
Total Assets:	$954,166,000	Net Worth:	$95,561,000	Debt/ Equity:	NA

First Ottawa Bancshares Inc

701-705 Lasalle St., Ottawa, IL, 61350; *PH:* 1-815-434-0044; *Fax:* 1-815-434-0307;
http:// www.firstottawa.com; *Email:* info@firstottawa.com

General - Incorporation	DE	Stock- Price on:12/24/2007	$71
Employees	82	Stock Exchange	OTC
Auditor	BKD LLP	Ticker Symbol	FOTB
Stk Agt	NA	Outstanding Shares	NA
Counsel	NA	E.P.S.	$3.81
DUNS No.	NA	Shareholders	NA

Business: The group's principal activity is to provide general banking services of the acceptance of deposits and lending of loans. It is a bank holding company for its wholly-owned subsidiary, first national bank of ottawa. The acceptance of deposits includes demand, savings and time accounts and the servicing of such accounts. The loan portfolio comprises of commercial, agricultural, consumer, real estate, installment loans and personal loans. The group also provides services tailored to the needs of customers such as trust operations, farm management, safe deposit operations, sale of traveler's checks, cashier's checks and foreign currency and other special services.

Primary SIC and add'l.: 6021 6712

CIK No: 0001099668

Subsidiaries: First Ottawa Financial Corp., The First National Bank of Ottawa

Officers: Joachim J. Brown/Vice Chmn. - First Ottawa Financial Corporation, CEO, Pres./$283,804.00, Vincent G. Easi/CFO/$98,088.00, Cheryl D. Gage/Dir., Corp. Sec., Donald J. Harris/Dir., Exec. VP, COO/$161,925.00, Patrick D. Fayhee/Exec. VP, Chief Lending Officer/$176,788.00, Mark D. Dunavan/Chief Trust Officer, Steven M. Gonzalo/CTO, Exec. VP/$133,517.00

Directors: Joachim J. Brown/Vice Chmn. - First Ottawa Financial Corporation, CEO, Pres., Thomas P. Rooney/Chmn. First Ottawa Bancshares - Inc, The First National Bank, Ottawa, First Ottawa Financial Corporation, Bradley J. Armstrong/Vice Chmn. - First Ottawa Bancshares, Inc, The First National Bank, Ottawa, Patty P. Godfrey/Dir., Thomas E. Haeberle/Dir., John L. Cantlin/Dir., Cheryl D. Gage/Dir., Corp. Sec., Donald J. Harris/Dir., Exec. VP, COO, William J. Walsh/Dir.

Owners: Thomas E. Haeberle/2.90%, Vincent G. Easi, Steven M. Gonzalo, William J. Walsh/3.10%, Thomas P. Rooney, Patty P. Godfrey/4.10%, Donald J. Harris, Erika L. Schmidt/7.70%, Joachim J. Brown/1.20%, John L. Cantlin, Bradley J. Armstrong, Patrick D. Fayhee, Insiders/15.20%

Financial Data: Fiscal Year End:12/31   Latest Annual Data: 03/31/2007

Year	Sales	Net Income
2007	NA	NA
2006	$17,717,000	$2,335,000
2005	$16,750,000	$2,545,000

Curr. Assets:	$27,740,000	Curr. Liab.:	$250,341,000		
Plant, Equip.:	$7,753,000	Total Liab.:	$254,544,000	Indic. Yr. Divd.:	NA
Total Assets:	$278,053,000	Net Worth:	$23,509,000	Debt/ Equity:	NA

First Pactrust Bancorp Inc

610 Bay Blvd., Chula Vista, CA, 91910; *PH:* 1-619-691-1519; *Fax:* 1-619-691-1350;
http:// www.pacifictrustbank.com; *Email:* fptb@pacifictrustbank.com

General - Incorporation	MD	Stock- Price on:12/24/2007	$24.16
Employees	105	Stock Exchange	NDQ
Auditor	Crowe Chizek & Co. LLC	Ticker Symbol	FPTB
Stk Agt	Registrar & Transfer Co	Outstanding Shares	4,400,000
Counsel	Keefe, Bruyette & Woods	E.P.S.	$1.02
DUNS No.	NA	Shareholders	NA

Business: The group's principal activity is to provide a variety of banking services in the United States. It provides a variety of deposit accounts having a wide range of interest rates and terms, which generally include savings accounts, money market deposit and term certificate accounts and checking accounts. Its lending portfolio includes one-to four-family residential mortgage loans, construction loans, consumer loans and adjustable-rate mortgage loans. The consumer loans portfolio includes a variety of secured consumer loans including home equity lines of credit, new and used auto loans, boat and recreational vehicle loans and other loans secured by savings deposits. The group is a bank holding company, which operates through pacific trust bank, and eight full service banking offices located in san diego and riverside counties in California.

Primary SIC and add'l.: 6035 6712

CIK No: 0001169770

Subsidiaries: Pacific Trust Bank

Officers: Hans R. Ganz/Dir., CEO, Pres./$732,600.00, Regan J. Lauer/Sr. VP, Controller/$236,451.00, Rachel M. Carrillo/Sr. VP - Branch Operations/$234,898.00, James P. Sheehy/Exec. VP, Sec., Treasurer/$329,447.00, Melanie M. Stewart/Exec. VP - Lending/$365,999.00, Lisa R. Goodwin/Sr. VP - Information Systems/$227,652.00

Directors: Hans R. Ganz/Dir., CEO, Pres., Alvin L. Majors/Chmn., Kenneth W. Scholz/Dir., Francis P. Burke/Dir., Donald M. Purdy/Dir., Donald A. Whitacre/Dir.

Owners: Lisa R. Goodwin/1.08%, James P. Sheehy/1.67%, Insiders/18.34%, Francis P. Burke/1.63%, Donald M. Purdy/1.63%, Donald A. Whitacre/1.47%, Kenneth W. Scholz/1.63%, Regan J. Lauer, Seymour Holtzman/6.89%, Rachel M. Carrillo, First Manhattan Co./6.75%, First PacTrust Bancorp/10.27%, Melanie M. Stewart/2.12%, Hans R. Ganz/4.69%, Investors of America Limited Partnership/11.85% (16 Owners included in Index)

Financial Data: Fiscal Year End:12/31   Latest Annual Data: 12/31/2006

Year	Sales	Net Income
2006	$47,731,000	$4,714,000
2005	$37,795,000	$4,807,000
2004	$33,283,000	$5,075,000

Curr. Assets:	$18,945,000	Curr. Liab.:	$726,602,000	P/E Ratio:	21.96
Plant, Equip.:	$4,910,000	Total Liab.:	$726,602,000	Indic. Yr. Divd.:	$0.740
Total Assets:	$808,343,000	Net Worth:	$81,741,000	Debt/ Equity:	NA

First Place Financial Corp

185 E Market St., Warren, OH, 44481; *PH:* 1-330-373-1221; *Fax:* 1-330-393-5578;
http:// www.firstplacebank.net

General - Incorporation	DE	**Stock**- Price on:12/24/2007	$21.48
Employees	753	Stock Exchange	NDQ
Auditor	Crowe Chizek & Co. LLC	Ticker Symbol	FPFC
Stk Agt	Registrar & Transfer Co	Outstanding Shares	17,430,000
Counsel	NA	E.P.S	$1.46
DUNS No.	01-274-8419	Shareholders	NA

Business: The group's principal activities are to accept deposits from the general public and investing those deposits. These deposits are invested in one-to four-family residential mortgage loans, automobile and home equity loans. The deposits are also invested in commercial real estate, commercial and construction loans. The operations of the group are conducted through 24 full-service banking facilities in trumbull, mahoning and portage counties in Ohio and 12 loan production offices located throughout Ohio. In fiscal 2003, the group acquired apb financial group, ltd., majority ownership in titleworks agency, llc. And remaining interest in coldwell banker first place real estate, ltd. On 03-May-2004 group acquired the weigel,lackey & ross insurance agency in Poland, Ohio and on 28-May-2004, franklin bancorp inc.

Primary SIC and add'l.: 6712 6035

CIK No: 0001068912

Subsidiaries: First Place Bank, First Place Capital Trust, First Place Capital Trust II, First Place Capital Trust III, First Place Holdings, Inc., The Northern Savings & Loan Company

Officers: Steven R. Lewis/Dir., CEO, Pres., Craig L. Johnson/Regional Pres., Corp. Dir. - Commercial RE, First Place Bank, Robert J. Kowalski/Corporate Exec. VP - Human Resources, First Place Bank, Kenton A. Thompson/Regional Pres., Corp. Dir. - BFS, First Place Bank, Debra Bish/Corporate Exec. VP - Marketing, First Place Bank, David W. Gifford/Interim CFO, Craig J. Carr/Corporate Exec. VP, General Counsel, Sec., Bruce R. Wenmoth/Corporate Exec. VP - Retail Lending, First Place Bank, Dominique K. Stoeber/Corporate Exec. VP - Retail Banking, First Place Bank, Timothy A. Beaumont/Corporate Exec. VP, Chief Credit Officer - First Place Bank, Brian E. Hoopes/CIO - First Place Bank, Corporate Exec. VP, Albert P. Blank/Pres., COO - First Place Bank/$349,541.00

Directors: Steven R. Lewis/Dir., CEO, Pres., Samuel A. Roth/Chmn., William A. Russell/Dir., Jeffrey B. Ohlemacher/Dir., Jeffrey E. Rossi/Dir., Gary A. Bitonte/Dir., Robert P. Grace/Dir., Donald Cagigas/Dir., Ronald P. Volpe/Dir., Earl T. Kissell/Dir., Thomas M. Humphries/Dir., Robert L. Wagmiller/Dir., Marie Izzo Cartwright/Dir.

Owners: Albert P. Blank, Paul S. Musgrove, Ronald P. Volpe, Barclays Global Investors UK Holdings Limited/5.60%, Steven R. Lewis/2.10%, Insiders/8.50%, Jeffrey E. Rossi, William A. Russell, Jeffrey B. Ohlemacher, First Place Bank Employee Stock Ownership Plan/5.00%, Dimensional Fund Advisors LP/8.60%, Gary A. Bitonte, Marie Izzo Cartwright, Earl T. Kissell, Kenton A. Thompson *(21 Owners included in Index)*

Financial Data: *Fiscal Year End:*06/30 *Latest Annual Data:* 06/30/2007

Year	Sales	Net Income
2007	$218,752,000	$25,624,000
2006	$178,981,000	$23,044,000
2005	$146,627,000	$18,938,000

Curr. Assets:	$77,511,000	**Curr. Liab.:**	$2,104,760,000	**P/E Ratio:**	14.42
Plant, Equip.:	$35,485,000	**Total Liab.:**	$2,801,636,000	**Indic. Yr. Divd.:**	$0.620
Total Assets:	$3,113,210,000	**Net Worth:**	$311,574,000	**Debt/ Equity:**	1.2071

First Potomac Realty Trust

7600 Wisconsin Ave., 11th Fl., Bethesda, MD, 20814; ***PH:*** 1-301-986-9200; ***Fax:*** 1-301-986-5554; ***http://*** www.first-potomac.com

General - Incorporation	MD	**Stock**- Price on:12/24/2007	$23.57
Employees	119	Stock Exchange	NYSE
Auditor	KPMG LLP	Ticker Symbol	FPO
Stk Agt	American Stock Transfer & Trust Co.	Outstanding Shares	24,210,000
Counsel	NA	E.P.S	$0.03
DUNS No.	NA	Shareholders	NA

Business: The groups principle activities include owning, developing and operating industrial and flex properties. In the year 2006, the group acquired 14 properties. The group operates from the United States. The group's quarterly revenue for September 2007 was 31.19 millions of USD.

Primary SIC and add'l.: 6798

CIK No: 0001254595

Subsidiaries: 1400 Cavalier, LLC, 1434 Crossways Boulevard I, LLC, 1434 Crossways Boulevard II, LLC, 1441 Crossways Boulevard II, LLC, 15395 John Marshall Highway, LLC, 403 & 405 Glenn Drive Manager, LLC, 403 & 405 Glenn Drive, LLC, 4212 Tech Court, LLC, Airpark Place Holdings, LLC, Airpark Place, LLC, AP Indian Creek, LLC, Aquia One, LLC, Aquia Two, LLC, Bren Mar Holdings, LLC, Bren Mar, LLC 99 Subsidiaries included in the Index

Officers: Douglas J. Donatelli/Chmn., CEO, Barry H. Bass/CFO, Exec. VP, James H. Dawson/COO, Exec. VP, Joel F. Bonder/Exec. VP, General Counsel, Sec., Nicholas R. Smith/Exec. VP, Chief Investment Officer, Michael H. Comer/Chief Accounting Officer, Sr. VP, Timothy M. Zulick/Sr. VP - Leasing, Anthony R. Beck/Regional VP, GM - Southern Virginia, Mary T. Wacker/Regional VP, GM - Northern Virginia, John E. Sadlik/VP - Construction, Tripp Sullivan/Contact - Corporate Communications, Kelly Crough/Leasing Contact - Maryland, Montgomery County, Michele Salvino/Leasing Contact - Maryland, All Other Areas, Ed Zaptin/Leasing Contact - Northern Virginia, Tony Beck/Leasing Contact - Southern Virginia

Directors: Douglas J. Donatelli/Chmn., CEO, Louis T. Donatelli/Trustee, Robert H. Arnold/Trustee, Richard B. Chess/Trustee, John Roderick Heller/Trustee, Michael R. McCullough/Trustee, Alan G. Merten/Trustee, Terry L. Stevens/Trustee, Roderick Heller/70/Dir.

Owners: Terry L. Stevens, Robert H. Arnold, Roderick J. Heller, Richard B. Chess, Insiders/5.47%, Joel F. Bonder, Michael R. McCullough, Nicholas R. Smith, Michael H. Comer, Douglas J. Donatelli/1.40%, Barry H. Bass, James H. Dawson, Timothy M. Zulick, Louis T. Donatelli/1.76%, Alan G. Merten

Financial Data: *Fiscal Year End:*12/31 *Latest Annual Data:* 12/31/2006

Year	Sales	Net Income
2006	$104,536,000	$10,031,000
2005	$77,633,000	$1,350,000
2004	$42,112,000	$2,630,000

Curr. Assets:	$50,552,000	**Curr. Liab.:**	$11,318,000	**P/E Ratio:**	62.03
Plant, Equip.:	$884,882,000	**Total Liab.:**	$630,981,000	**Indic. Yr. Divd.:**	$1.360
Total Assets:	$994,567,000	**Net Worth:**	$363,586,000	**Debt/ Equity:**	1.7384

First Pulaski National Corp

206 S 1st St., Pulaski, TN, 38478; ***PH:*** 1-931-363-2585; ***Fax:*** 1-931-363-7574; ***http://*** www.fnbforyou.com

General - Incorporation	TN	**Stock**- Price on:12/24/2007	NA
Employees	NA	Stock Exchange	NA
Auditor	Putman & Hancock	Ticker Symbol	NA
Stk Agt	NA	Outstanding Shares	NA
Counsel	NA	E.P.S	NA
DUNS No.	00-894-4167	Shareholders	NA

Business: The group's principal activities are to provide general commercial, retail banking and consumer finance businesses. The group operates through its subsidiaries, first national bank of pulaski and bank of belfast. The group operates principally in two market areas, giles county, Tennessee and lincoln county, Tennessee. The group offers a wide range of banking services, including checking, savings and money market deposit accounts, certificates of deposit and loans for consumer, commercial and real estate purposes. On 12-Apr-2002, the corporation merged the bank of belfast into first national bank of pulaski.

Primary SIC and add'l.: 6021 6712

CIK No: 0000354706

Subsidiaries: First National Bank of Pulaski, First Pulaski Reinsurance Company

Owners: Donald A. Haney/0.38%, Tracy Porterfield/0.23%, Gregory G. Dugger/0.50%, James K. Blackburn, Wade Boggs/0.75%, Insiders/8.81%, Bill Yancey/0.55%, James Rand Hayes/1.49%, Mark A. Hayes/1.10%, James H. Butler/0.58%, David E. Bagley/0.63%, Charles D. Haney/0.70%, Linda Lee Rogers/0.30%, Whitney R. Stevens, James T. Cox/1.15%

First Real Estate Investment Trust of New Jersey

505 Main St. , Hackensack, NJ, 07602; ***PH:*** 1-201-488-6400

General - Incorporation	NJ	**Stock**- Price on:12/24/2007	$26.5
Employees	23	Stock Exchange	OTC
Auditor	Eisner LLP	Ticker Symbol	FREVS
Stk Agt	Registrar & Transfer Co	Outstanding Shares	6,760,000
Counsel	NA	E.P.S	$1.29
DUNS No.	NA	Shareholders	NA

Business: The groups principle activities include acquiring, developing, constructing and holding real estate properties. The group operates through two segments namely commercial properties and residential properties. The group operates from the United States.

Primary SIC and add'l.: 6798

CIK No: 0000036840

Subsidiaries: Damascus Centre, LLC, Grande Rotunda, LLC, Pierre Towers, LLC, S And A Commercial Associates Limited Partnership, Wayne Preakness, LLC, Westwood Hills, LLC

Owners: Insiders/24.10%, Ronald J. Artinian/7.00%, Robert S. Hekemian/6.60%, Alan L. Aufzien, Herbert C. Klein/5.30%, Donald W. Barney/5.00%

Financial Data: *Fiscal Year End:*10/31 *Latest Annual Data:* 10/31/2006

Year	Sales	Net Income
2006	$38,305,000	$5,158,000
2005	$33,667,000	$4,456,000
2004	$30,356,000	$15,210,000

Curr. Assets:	$15,097,000	**Curr. Liab.:**	$12,295,000	**P/E Ratio:**	37.86
Plant, Equip.:	$207,308,000	**Total Liab.:**	$209,814,000	**Indic. Yr. Divd.:**	$0.400
Total Assets:	$234,786,000	**Net Worth:**	$24,972,000	**Debt/ Equity:**	8.3176

First Regional Bancorp

1801 Century Pk. E, Ste. 800, Los Angeles, CA, 90067; ***PH:*** 1-310-552-1776; ***Fax:*** 1-310-552-1772; ***http://*** www.firstregional.com

General - Incorporation	CA	**Stock**- Price on:12/24/2007	$26.23
Employees	264	Stock Exchange	NDQ
Auditor	Deloitte & Touche LLP	Ticker Symbol	FRGB
Stk Agt	Mellon Investor Services LLC	Outstanding Shares	12,310,000
Counsel	Horgan, Rosen, Beckham Et Al	E.P.S	$2.90
DUNS No.	03-762-8583	Shareholders	NA

Business: The group's principal activity is to provide a full range of banking services in southern California. The group accepts all types of demand, savings, and time certificates of deposit. The group originates loans such as commercial, real estate, construction loans, equipment financing and short-term loans. It provides standard banking services which include, telephone transfers, wire transfers, travelers' checks, credit card deposit and clearing services. In addition, the group also provides administrative services for self directed retirement plans, trust services for living trusts, investment agency accounts, ira rollovers and all forms of court-related matters.

Primary SIC and add'l.: 6712 6022

CIK No: 0000356708

Subsidiaries: First Regional Bank, First Regional Statutory Trust I, First Regional Statutory Trust II, First Regional Statutory Trust III, First Regional Statutory Trust IV, First Regional Statutory Trust V, Trust Administration Services Corp.

Owners: Richard E. Schreiber, Anthony H. Gartshore/2.85%, Fred M. Edwards, Jack A. Sweeney/28.26%, Insiders/37.41%, Wellington Management Company, LLP/5.25%, Steven J. Sweeney/3.45%, Lawrence J. Sherman/1.45%, Elizabeth Thompson, Thomas E. McCullough/2.04%, Gary M. Horgan

Financial Data: *Fiscal Year End:*12/31 *Latest Annual Data:* 12/31/2006

Year	Sales	Net Income
2006	$170,055,000	$38,336,000
2005	$112,610,000	$26,525,000
2004	$60,789,000	$11,084,000

Curr. Assets:	$216,174,000	**Curr. Liab.:**	$1,834,579,000	**P/E Ratio:**	9.04
Plant, Equip.:	$3,838,000	**Total Liab.:**	$1,927,626,000	**Indic. Yr. Divd.:**	NA
Total Assets:	$2,074,636,000	**Net Worth:**	$147,010,000	**Debt/ Equity:**	0.5919

First Reliance Bancshares Inc

2170 W Palmetto St., Florence, SC, 29501; ***PH:*** 1-843-662-8802; ***Fax:*** 1-843-662-8373; ***http://*** www.firstreliance.com; ***Email:*** info@firstreliance.com

General - Incorporation	SC	**Stock**- Price on:12/24/2007	$14.2
Employees	129	Stock Exchange	OTC
Auditor	Elliot Davis LLC	Ticker Symbol	FSRL
Stk Agt	Registrar & Transfer Co	Outstanding Shares	3,440,000
Counsel	NA	E.P.S	$0.97
DUNS No.	NA	Shareholders	NA

Business: The group's principal activity is to provide community-oriented commercial banking services. It is a holding company and operates all its activities through the subsidiary, first reliance bank. The bank provides a broad range of consumer and commercial banking services, concentrating on individuals and small and medium-sized businesses desiring a high level of personalized services. The deposit services include checking accounts, now accounts, savings accounts and other time deposits. The loan products offered by the bank include commercial and consumer loans, and real estate construction and acquisition loans. As on 31-Dec-2003, the group operated through its main office and one branch office located at florence, South Carolina.

Primary SIC and add'l.: 6712 6022

CIK No: 0001172102

Subsidiaries: First Reliance Bank, First Reliance Capital Trust I

Officers: F. R. Saunders/Dir., CEO, Pres., Leonard A. Hoogenboom/Organizer, Chmn., John M. Jebaily/Organizer, Dir., Jim Roberts/Sr. VP - Operations, Jeffrey Paolucci/Dir., Sr. VP, CFO, Sec., Nick Sherfesee/Marketing Pres. - Executive, Andrew G. Kampiziones/Organizer, Dir., Jess Nance/Sr. VP, Chief Credit Officer, Ken Cox/Sr. VP - Mortgage Banking, Pamela Anderson/Sr. VP - People Management, Thomas C. Ewart/Sr. VP, Chief Banking Officer, Lee D. Daugherty/VP, Community Banking Officer, Richard N. McIntyre/Marketing Pres. - Lexington, Karl H. Zerbst/Marketing Pres. - Charleston, Ricky Cox/VP - City Executive, Florence Region *(16 Officers included in Index)*

Directors: F. R. Saunders/Dir., CEO, Pres., Leonard A. Hoogenboom/Organizer, Chmn., Jeffrey Paolucci/Dir., Sr. VP, CFO, Sec., Andrew G. Kampiziones/Organizer, Dir., Dale A. Porter/Dir., John M. Jebaily/Organizer, Dir., Brian Newman/Member - Advisory Board, Barry Obrien/Member - Advisory Board, Ian Shaw/Member - Advisory Board, Ian Smith/Member - Advisory Board, Mindy Taylor/Member - Advisory Board, Berend Van Der Meer/Member - Advisory Board, Munford J. Scott/Dir., Paul C. Saunders/Dir., Daniel T. Turner/Dir. *(29 Directors included in Index)*

Owners: Joe A. Willis/1.45%, F. R. Saunders/5.84%, Daniel T. Turner/2.47%, Insiders/21.49%, Dale A. Porter/3.56%, Andrew G. Kampiziones, Dale C. Lusk, Service Capital Partners/5.84%, Thomas C. Ewart, Jeffrey A. Paolucci/1.05%, Munford J. Scott, John M. Jebaily, Paul C. Saunders/5.52%, Leonard A. Hoogenboom, Jess A. Nance

Financial Data: **Fiscal Year End:**12/31 **Latest Annual Data:** 12/31/2006

Year	Sales	Net Income
2006	$36,307,000	$3,246,000
2005	$26,003,000	$1,948,000
2004	$15,746,000	$1,339,000

Curr. Assets:	$33,928,000	**Curr. Liab.:**	$410,324,000	**P/E Ratio:**	14.95
Plant, Equip.:	$15,157,000	**Total Liab.:**	$422,117,000	**Indic. Yr. Divd.:**	NA
Total Assets:	$456,211,000	**Net Worth:**	$34,093,000	**Debt/ Equity:**	0.2937

First Robinson Financial Corp

501 E Main St., Robinson, IL, 62454; *PH:* 1-618-544-8621; *Fax:* 1-618-544-7506; *http://* www.frsb.net

General - Incorporation	DE	**Stock**- Price on:12/24/2007	$32
Employees	40	Stock Exchange	OTC
Auditor	BKD LLP	Ticker Symbol	FRFC
Stk Agt	Registrar & Transfer Co	Outstanding Shares	NA
Counsel	Silver, Freedman & Taff LLP	E.P.S	$1.98
DUNS No.	06-084-9114	Shareholders	NA

Business: The group's principal activity is to accept deposits from the general public and invests them in various loans. The deposits products include passbook savings, now accounts, super now accounts, certificate accounts, ira accounts, limited accounts and non-interest bearing accounts. The loan products include conventional, first mortgage loans secured by one- to four-family residences, consumer loans, commercial and agricultural real estate loans, commercial business and agricultural finance loans. The group operates through its wholly owned subsidiary, first robinson savings bank. The group conducts its business through its main office and three branch offices located in crawford county, Illinois. The customers of the group consist of individuals and small businesses.

Primary SIC and add'l.: 6712 6021

CIK No: 0001035991

Subsidiaries: First Robinson Savings Bank, National Association

Officers: Rick L. Catt/55/Dir., CEO, Pres./$145,750.00, Norma Carder/Executive Dir. - Crawford County Development Association, First Robinson Savings Bank NA, Jamie E. McReynolds/44/VP, CFO, Sec., Jo Drennen/Administrator - Community Contact - First Robinson Savings Bank NA

Directors: Rick L. Catt/55/Dir., CEO, Pres., Robin E. Guyer/60/Dir., Douglas J. Goodwine/46/Dir., Scott F. Pulliam/51/Dir., William K. Thomas/Dir., Donald K. Inboden/75/Dir., Steven E. Neeley/54/Dir.

Owners: Insiders/30.90%, Rick L. Catt/3.80%, Donald K. Inboden/3.20%, William K. Thomas/3.90%, Scott F. Pulliam/4.30%, Douglas J. Goodwine/1.90%, First Robinson Savings Bank/5.40%, First Robinson Financial Corporation Employee Stock Ownership Plan/13.50%, Steven E. Neeley/8.50%, Robin E. Guyer

Financial Data: **Fiscal Year End:**03/31 **Latest Annual Data:** 03/31/2007

Year	Sales	Net Income
2007	$8,094,000	$1,013,000
2006	$7,037,000	$984,000
2005	$6,553,000	$858,000

Curr. Assets:	$8,034,000	**Curr. Liab.:**	$86,526,000	**P/E Ratio:**	15.61
Plant, Equip.:	$2,651,000	**Total Liab.:**	$98,012,000	**Indic. Yr. Divd.:**	$0.650
Total Assets:	$109,428,000	**Net Worth:**	$11,416,000	**Debt/ Equity:**	NA

First Security Group Inc

531 Broad St., Chattanooga, TN, 37402; *PH:* 1-423-266-2000; *Fax:* 1-423-267-3383; *http://* www.fsgbank.com

General - Incorporation	TN	**Stock**- Price on:12/24/2007	$11.09
Employees	354	Stock Exchange	NDQ
Auditor	Joseph Decosimo & Co. PLLC	Ticker Symbol	FSGI
Stk Agt	Registrar & Transfer Co	Outstanding Shares	17,610,000
Counsel	NA	E.P.S	$0.66
DUNS No.	NA	Shareholders	NA

Business: The groups principle activity is to provide finance, banking and business management services. The group also provides construction equipment, tractor trucks and trailers for sale and lease. The group operates from United States.

Primary SIC and add'l.: 5110

CIK No: 0001138817

Subsidiaries: Dalton Whitfield Bank, First State Bank, Frontier Bank, FSGBank, National Association, Kenesaw Leasing, S Leasing

Officers: Rodger B. Holley/Chmn., CEO, Pres./$798,535.00, Lloyd L. Montgomery/Dir., COO, Pres./$358,494.00, William L. Lusk/CFO, Exec. VP, Sec./$283,711.00

Directors: Rodger B. Holley/Chmn., CEO, Pres., Lloyd L. Montgomery/Dir., COO, Pres., Ray D. Marler/Dir., Randall L. Gibson/Dir., Ralph L. Kendall/Dir., Harold J.C. Anders/Dir., Carol H. Jackson/Dir., William B. Kilbride/Dir.

Owners: Harold J.C. Anders, Carol H. Jackson, William L. Lusk, Insiders/5.74%, Rodger B. Holley/1.80%, Lloyd L. Montgomery, OZ Management, L.L.C./5.05%, ClearBridge Advisors, LLC/5.49%, Ralph L. Kendall, William B. Kilbride, Ray D. Marler, Randal L. Gibson

Financial Data: **Fiscal Year End:**12/31 **Latest Annual Data:** 12/31/2006

Year	Sales	Net Income
2006	$85,941,000	$11,112,000
2005	$65,268,000	$9,571,000
2004	$44,122,000	$4,267,000

Curr. Assets:	$35,610,000	**Curr. Liab.:**	$956,967,000	**P/E Ratio:**	17.06
Plant, Equip.:	$40,048,000	**Total Liab.:**	$985,015,000	**Indic. Yr. Divd.:**	$0.200
Total Assets:	$1,129,803,000	**Net Worth:**	$144,788,000	**Debt/ Equity:**	0.2180

First Solar Inc

4050 E Cotton Ctr. Blvd., Bldg. 6, Ste. 68, Phoenix, AZ, 85040; *PH:* 1-602-414-9300; *Fax:* 1-602-414-9400; *http://* www.firstsolar.com; *Email:* info@firstsolar.com

General - Incorporation	DE	**Stock**- Price on:12/24/2007	$80.07
Employees	723	Stock Exchange	NDQ
Auditor	PricewaterhouseCoopers LLP	Ticker Symbol	FSLR
Stk Agt	Computershare Trust Co	Outstanding Shares	72,360,000
Counsel	NA	E.P.S	$1.37
DUNS No.	NA	Shareholders	NA

Business: The groups principle activities include designing and manufacturing thin film semiconductor technology. The groups product is a solar module. Specific customers of the group include Blitzstrom GmbH, Conergy AG, Gehrlicher Umweltschonende Energiesysteme GmbH, Juwi Solar GmbH, Phnix Sonnenstrom AG and Reinecke + Pohl Sun Energy AG. The group operates from Germany and other. The group's quarterly revenue for September 2007 was 159.01 millions of USD.

Primary SIC and add'l.: 3629 3674

CIK No: 0001274494

Subsidiaries: First Solar Electric Company, LLC, First Solar Electric Contracting, Inc., First Solar FE Holdings Pte. Ltd., First Solar GmbH, First Solar Holdings GmbH, First Solar Malaysia SDM. BHD., First Solar Manufacturing GmbH, First Solar Property, LLC, First Solar US Manufacturing, LLC, Minera Teloro S.A. de C.V.

Officers: Michael J. Ahearn/Chmn., CEO, Bruce Sohn/Dir., Pres., Jens Meyerhoff/CFO, Kenneth M. Schultz/VP - Sales, Marketing, Paul Kacir/VP, General Counsel, Carol Campbell/VP - Human Resources

Directors: Michael J. Ahearn/Chmn., CEO, Bruce Sohn/Dir., Pres., James F. Nolan/Dir., Thomas J. Presby/Dir., Michael Sweeney/Dir., Paul H. Stebbins/Dir., Craig Kennedy/Dir., Jose H. Villarreal/Dir.

Owners: JCL Holdings, LLC/16.70%, Kenneth M. Schultz/1.00%, Thomas J. Presby, John T. Walton/37.00%, Paul I. Kacir, Michael Sweeney, Goldman, Sachs& Co./5.90%, Jens Meyerhoff, Paul H. Stebbins, Michael J. Ahearn/7.60%, Bruce Sohn, Insiders/10.30%, James F. Nolan, George A. Hambro/1.30%

Financial Data: **Fiscal Year End:**12/30 **Latest Annual Data:** 12/30/2006

Year	Sales	Net Income
2006	$134,974,000	$3,974,000
2005	$48,063,000	-$6,462,000
2004	$13,522,000	-$16,771,000

Curr. Assets:	$26,553,000	**Curr. Liab.:**	$33,913,000	**P/E Ratio:**	89.97
Plant, Equip.:	$73,778,000	**Total Liab.:**	$88,755,000	**Indic. Yr. Divd.:**	NA
Total Assets:	$101,884,000	**Net Worth:**	$13,129,000	**Debt/ Equity:**	0.1882

First Sound Bank WA

925 4th Ave. Ste. 2350, Seattle, WA, 98104; *PH:* 1-206-515-2004; *http://* www.firstsoundbank.com; *Email:* customerservice@firstsoundbank.com

General - Incorporation		**Stock**- Price on:12/24/2007	$15.2
Employees	NA	Stock Exchange	OTC
Auditor	NA	Ticker Symbol	FSWA
Stk Agt	NA	Outstanding Shares	NA
Counsel	NA	E.P.S	NA
DUNS No.	NA	Shareholders	NA

Business: The groups principal activity is to provide banking services. Services of the group include checking and saving services, loans, cash management, ATM and debit card, merchant services, courier services bankcard and online banking. Customers served by the group include small and medium-sized businesses, not-for-profit organizations, entrepreneurs, professionals, and service companies. The group operates from Washington in the United States.

Primary SIC and add'l.: 6029

CIK No:

Officers: Donald L. Hirtzel/Chmn., CEO, Steven M. Shaughnessy/Dir., Pres., Amanda D. Adams/Loan Operations Administrator, Michael Atmoko/Credit Analyst, Joshua Bolinger/Cash Management Associate, Rebecca Borek/Sr. VP, Relationship Mgr., Sam Byeon/Credit Analyst, Cyndi Child/Project Mgr., Kathy Emery/Sr. Customer Service Representative, Suzanne Goff/VP, Relationship Mgr., Erin Hayden/Assist. VP, Assistant Operations Mgr., Amber Klein/VP, Relationship Mgr., Shawne Lang/Loan Operations Specialist, Andy Leikin/VP, Relationship Mgr., John Maihofer/Cash Management Officer *(32 Officers included in Index)*

Directors: Donald L. Hirtzel/Chmn., CEO, Steven M. Shaughnessy/Dir., Pres., Kathleen Y. Titcomb/Dir., Steven J. Schwartz/Dir., Michael O. Evered/Dir., James H. Jackson/Dir., Pamela R. Myers/Dir.

Curr. Assets:	$214,000	**Curr. Liab.:**	$28,000		
Plant, Equip.:	$3,000	**Total Liab.:**	$28,000	**Indic. Yr. Divd.:**	NA
Total Assets:	$232,000	**Net Worth:**	$204,000	**Debt/ Equity:**	NA

First South Bancorp Inc

1450 John B. White Sr. Blvd., Spartanburg, SC, 29306; *PH:* 1-864-595-0455; *Fax:* 1-864-587-2781; *http://* www.firstsouthbancorp.com; *Email:* info@firstsouthbancorp.com

General - Incorporation ....SC
Employees ....NA
Auditor ....Cherry, Bekaert & Holland LLP
Stk Agt....Registrar & Transfer Co
Counsel....Rodman Holscher Francisco & Peck
DUNS No. ....NA

Stock- Price on:12/24/2007 ....$28
Stock Exchange....OTC
Ticker Symbol....FSBS
Outstanding Shares ....NA
E.P.S....$1.71
Shareholders....NA

Business: The group's principal activities are to provide banking services through two branch offices located in spartanburg county and South Carolina. The group's business primarily consists of accepting deposits and making loans. The group seeks deposit accounts from household and businesses in its primary market areas by offering a full range of savings accounts, retirement accounts, checking accounts, money market accounts and time certificate deposit. The group also makes commercial, real estate and installment loans on a secured basis, to borrowers in and around spartanburg and richland counties.

Primary SIC and add'l.: 6022 6712

CIK No: 0001097631

Subsidiaries: First South Bank

Officers: Barry L. Slider/55/Dir., CEO, Pres./$352,518.00, Lewis V. Shuler/CFO, Exec. VP, Sec./$182,135.00

Directors: Barry L. Slider/55/Dir., CEO, Pres., Roger A.F. Habisreutinger/66/Chmn., Chandrakant V. Shanbhag/58/Dir., Herman E. Ratchford/75/Dir., David G. White/52/Dir., Harold E. Fleming/67/Dir., Joel C. Griffin/54/Dir.

Owners: Insiders/38.52%, Joel C. Griffin/1.51%, Barry L. Slider/5.21%, Harold E. Fleming/1.43%, Herman E. Ratchford/10.62%, David G. White/3.15%, Chandrakant V. Shanbhag/6.90%, Lewis V. Shuler/2.12%, Roger A. F. Habisreutinger/7.58%

Financial Data: **Fiscal Year End:**12/31 **Latest Annual Data:** 12/31/2006

Year	Sales	Net Income
2006	$77,011,000	$17,192,000
2005	$61,383,000	$14,129,000
2004	$48,930,000	$11,712,000

Curr. Assets:	$32,808,000	**Curr. Liab.:**	$800,188,000		
Plant, Equip.:	$9,532,000	**Total Liab.:**	$831,751,000	**Indic. Yr. Divd.:**	$0.760
Total Assets:	$910,548,000	**Net Worth:**	$78,797,000	**Debt/ Equity:**	NA

First South Bancorp Inc/VA

1311 Carolina Ave., Washington, NC, 27889; *PH:* 1-252-946-4178; *http://* www.firstsouthbancorp.com; *Email:* onlinesupport@firstsouthnc.com

General - Incorporation ....VA
Employees 259
Auditor ....Dixon Hughes PLLC
Stk Agt....Registrar & Transfer Co
Counsel....Rodman Holscher Francisco & Peck
DUNS No. 07-558-2650

Stock- Price on:12/24/2007 ....$27.27
Stock Exchange....NDQ
Ticker Symbol....FSBK
Outstanding Shares 9,940,000
E.P.S....$1.71
Shareholders....NA

Business: The group's principal activities are to accept deposits from general public and invest these funds in loans secured by first mortgages on owner-occupied, single-family residences in the bank's market area, commercial real estate loans, commercial business loans and consumer loans. The group operates through its subsidiary first south bank. The group has offices throughout eastern North Carolina, located in beaufort, craven, cumberland, edgecombe, lenoir, nash, pasquotank, pitt and robeson counties. The group's major customers are pcs phosphate, weyerhaeuser company, dupont, abbott laboratories, east carolina university, pitt memorial hospital, kelly springfield tire company, fort bragg, pope air force base, converse, campbell soup and kaiser-roth hosiery among others.

Primary SIC and add'l.: 6022 6712 6022

CIK No: 0001027183

Subsidiaries: First South Bank, First South Investments, Inc, First South Leasing, LLC, First South Preferred Trust I

Officers: Thomas A. Vann/Dir., CEO, Pres./$813,804.00, William L. Wall/CFO, Exec. VP, Sec./$155,260.00, Lillian Moye/Administrative Assist. - Kinston, Evelyn Arrington/Branch Mgr. - Rocky Mount, Elizabeth Williford/Branch Mgr. - Washington, Wayne Champion/Branch Mgr. - Durham, Diane Dorman/Retail Sales Assoc., Fayetteville, Brenda Young/Retail Sales Assoc., Fayetteville, Everett Kelly/Branch Mgr. - Greenville, April Veir/Branch Mgr. - Kill Devil Hills, Charlie Ruffin/Construction Lender - Wilmington, Meg Howdy/Branch Mgr. - Washington, Dennis Nichols/City Exec., New Bern, Trish Dagnino/Branch Mgr. - New Bern, Grant Price/Mortgage Loan Officer - Fayetteville *(51 Officers included in Index)*

Directors: Thomas A. Vann/Dir., CEO, Pres., Marshall T. Singleton/68/Dir., Linley H. Gibbs/76/Dir., Frederick N. Holscher/59/Dir., Frederick H. Howdy/76/Dir., Charles E. Parker/71/Dir., H. D. Reaves/70/Dir.

Owners: Frederick H. Howdy/2.06%, Charles E. Parker/1.63%, Thomas A. Vann/5.90%, Frederick N. Holscher/1.15%, H.D. Reaves, Insiders/18.40%, Linley H. Gibbs/1.86%, Marshall T. Singleton/2.56%

Financial Data: **Fiscal Year End:**12/31 **Latest Annual Data:** 12/31/2006

Year	Sales	Net Income
2006	$77,011,000	$17,192,000
2005	$61,383,000	$14,129,000
2004	$48,930,000	$11,712,000

Curr. Assets:	$32,808,000	**Curr. Liab.:**	$800,188,000	**P/E Ratio:**	15.85
Plant, Equip.:	$9,532,000	**Total Liab.:**	$831,751,000	**Indic. Yr. Divd.:**	$0.760
Total Assets:	$910,548,000	**Net Worth:**	$78,797,000	**Debt/ Equity:**	0.1977

First Standard Bank CA

1000 Wilshire Blvd, Ste. 100, Los Angeles, CA, 90017; *PH:* 1-213-892-9999; *Fax:* 1-213-892-1199; *http://* www.firststandardbank.com

General - Incorporation ....
Employees ....NA
Auditor ....Kim & Lee Corporation
Stk Agt ....U.S. Stock Transfer Corp
Counsel....NA
DUNS No. ....NA

Stock- Price on:12/24/2007 ....$10
Stock Exchange....OTC
Ticker Symbol....FSTA
Outstanding Shares ....NA
E.P.S....NA
Shareholders....NA

Business: The groups principal activity is to provide commercial banking services. The services of the group include personal and business banking, savings, loans, credit and deposit and online banking services. Customers served by the group include small and medium-sized businesses, professionals and residents. The group operates from the United States.

Primary SIC and add'l.: 6022

CIK No:

Officers: Bon Tai Goo/Dir., CEO, Pres., Yong Ku Choe/CFO, Exec. VP, Jackie Shin/Mgr. - Accounting, Ki Hong/Sr. VP, SBA Loan Mgr., James C. Hong/Exec. VP, Chief Credit Officer, Justin Jung/FVP, Branch Mgr., Man Sup Chang/VP, Int'l Deputy Mgr., James Jeong/Contact - SBA Lending, Julie Y. Kim/FVP, Note Dept Mgr.

Directors: Bon Tai Goo/Dir., CEO, Pres., Soo Hun Jung/Chmn., Donald H. Kasle/Dir., Ernest E. Dow/Dir., Jason Hwang/Dir., Ock Hee Kim/Dir., Jong Hyun Lee/Dir., Richard S. Mack/Dir., Susan Park/Dir., Yong Sin Shin/Dir., Byung Ha Yu/Dir.

First State BanCorp

7900 Jefferson NE, Albuquerque, NM, 87109; *PH:* 1-505-241-7500; *Fax:* 1-505-241-7572; *http://* www.fsbnm.com

General - Incorporation ....NM
Employees 864
Auditor ....KPMG LLP
Stk Agt....Registrar & Transfer Co
Counsel....Marshall G. Martin
DUNS No. 36-255-7498

Stock- Price on:12/24/2007 ....$20.93
Stock Exchange....NDQ
Ticker Symbol....FSNM
Outstanding Shares 20,450,000
E.P.S....$1.34
Shareholders....NA

Business: The group's principal activity is to provide commercial banking services to businesses through its subsidiary bank, First State Bank of Taos. The financial services are provided mainly to commercial and individual customers. The services offered include checking accounts, short and medium term loans, revolving credit facilities, inventory and accounts receivable financing and equipment financing. In addition, the group also provides residential and small commercial construction lending, residential mortgage loans, various savings programs, installment and personal loans, safe deposit services and credit cards. The group operates thirty branch offices, including twenty-three in New Mexico, six offices in Colorado and one office in Utah.

Primary SIC and add'l.: 6712 6022

CIK No: 0000897861

Subsidiaries: Access Anytime Bancorp, Inc., Depository Institution, Federal Reserve Board, First Community Bank, First State Bancorporation, Nasdaq Stock Market (Nasdaq), New Mexico Financial Corporation (NMFC), Prompt Corrective Action

Officers: Michael R. Stanford/Dir., CEO, Pres./$760,199.00, Christopher C. Spencer/Sr. VP, CFO/$299,564.00, Heather Bandow/Branch Services Mgr. - Deer Valley, Jean Kuszmar/Branch Mgr. - SUN City, Janie Gilmont/Branch Mgr. - Lafayette 95th Street, Stephanie Sherrell/VP, Branch Mgr. - Midvale, Kelly Whallon/Branch Mgr., VP - Camelback, Barbara Nolan/Branch Mgr., VP - Phoenix Downtown, Rose Garcia/Branch Mgr. - Littleton, Jan Wright/Branch Services Mgr. - Longmont, Pat Walton/Branch Mgr. - Longmont Main, Micki Hass/Branch Mgr. - Louisville, Suzy Schmidt/Branch Mgr. - Boulder West, Karen Schwartz/Branch Mgr. - Colorado Springs Tejon, Judy Goodson/Branch Mgr. - Denver Lodo *(77 Officers included in Index)*

Directors: Michael R. Stanford/Dir., CEO, Pres., Leonard J. Delayo/Chmn., Douglas M. Smith/Dir., Bradford M. Johnson/Dir., Lowell A. Hare/Dir., A. J. Wells/68/Dir., James A. Wells/Dir., Nedra Matteucci/Dir., Daniel H. Lopez/Dir., Patrick H. Dee/Dir., Exec. VP, COO, Bank Pres., Herman N. Wisenteiner/Dir., Kathleen L. Avila/Dir., Linda Childears/Dir.

Owners: Lowell A. Hare, Nedra Matteucci, Herman N. Wisenteiner, St. Denis J. Villere & Company, LLC/7.90%, Douglas M. Smith, Christopher C. Spencer, Leonard J. DeLayo, Michael R. Stanford/1.85%, Kathleen L. Avila, Marshall G. Martin, Insiders/4.97%, Patrick H. Dee/1.20%, A. J. Wells

Financial Data: **Fiscal Year End:**12/31 **Latest Annual Data:** 12/31/2006

Year	Sales	Net Income
2006	$201,464,000	$22,775,000
2005	$138,587,000	$21,398,000
2004	$107,633,000	$15,225,000

Curr. Assets:	$98,259,000	**Curr. Liab.:**	$2,425,778,000	**P/E Ratio:**	15.62
Plant, Equip.:	$65,407,000	**Total Liab.:**	$2,496,680,000	**Indic. Yr. Divd.:**	$0.360
Total Assets:	$2,801,572,000	**Net Worth:**	$304,892,000	**Debt/ Equity:**	0.2857

First Sunamerica Life Insurance Co

733 Third Ave., New York, NY, 10017; *PH:* 1-212-551-5440

General - Incorporation ....NY
Employees ....NA
Auditor ....PricewaterhouseCoopers LLP
Stk Agt ....NA
Counsel....NA
DUNS No. 60-698-6909

Stock- Price on:12/24/2007 ....NA
Stock Exchange....NDQ
Ticker Symbol....FMFC
Outstanding Shares ....NA
E.P.S....NA
Shareholders....NA

Business: The group's principle activity is to sell and administer fixed and variable annuity for retirement savings. The group is a wholly owned subsidiary of American international group inc and an indirect wholly owned subsidiary of sunamerica inc. The variable annuity products of the group offer investors a broad spectrum of fund alternatives, with a choice of investment managers, as well as guaranteed fixed rate account options. The group issues portfolio of single premium fixed and flexible premium variable annuities that provide one, three, five, seven, or ten year fixed interest rate guarantees. The group also offers fixed rate account option on its variable annuity contracts with similar guarantees. The group operates from United States.

Primary SIC and add'l.: 6311

CIK No: 0000926897

First Trust Bank NC

1420 E Third St., Charlotte, NC, 28204; *PH:* 1-704-377-3936; *Fax:* 1-704-377-8869; *http://* www.firsttrustnc.com

General - Incorporation		Stock- Price on:12/24/2007	$19.05
Employees	42	Stock Exchange	OTC
Auditor	NA	Ticker Symbol	NCFT
Stk Agt	Registrar & Transfer Co	Outstanding Shares	NA
Counsel	NA	E.P.S.	NA
DUNS No.	NA	Shareholders	NA

Business: The group's principle activity is to provide banking services. The group's services inclue peersonel and business banking, and credit card services. The group operates from United States.

Primary SIC and add'l.: 6022

CIK No:

Officers: James T. Bolt/Dir., CEO, Pres., Greg Silliman/VP, Commercial Banking Officer - Concord, David Steen/VP, Commercial Banking Officer - Mooresville, Rosemary Harrington/VP, Branch Administrator - Third Street, Ellie McIntire/VP, Commercial Banking Officer - Southpark, Warren Miller/VP, Commercial Banking Officer - Southpark, Chris Sharpe/VP, Commercial Banking Officer - Monroe, Jean Galloway/Sr. VP, CFO, Catherine Humphrey/VP, Business Development Officer - Mooresville, Stacy MacLure/Assist. VP, Commercial Banking Officer - Third Street, Ellen Stahlsmith/Sr. VP, Commercial Banking Officer - Third Street, John Keane/Sr. VP, Chief Credit Officer, Buddy Barlow/VP, Commercial Banking Officer - Concord, Karl Cahoon/VP, Commercial Banking Officer - Monroe, Bill Elder/Sr. VP, Sr. Loan Officer - Third Street

Directors: James T. Bolt/Dir., CEO, Pres., William D. Shuford/Vice Chmn., William C. Godley/Chmn., William G. Seymour/Dir., Erman J. Evans/Dir., James E. Harris/Dir., Elaine M. Lyerly/Dir., Elizabeth Nisbet Miller/Dir., Gary C. Baucom/Dir., Bruce Berryhill/Dir., Francis Armistead Cash/Dir., Catherine M. Connor/Dir.

Financial Data: Fiscal Year End:NA **Latest Annual Data:** 12/31/2002

Year	Sales		Net Income
2002	$9,168,000		$1,510,000
2001	$8,638,000		$870,000
2000	$6,011,000		$115,000
Curr. Assets:	$9,439,000	Curr. Liab.:	$158,665,000	
Plant, Equip.:	$676,000	Total Liab.:	$160,136,000	Indic. Yr. Divd.: NA
Total Assets:	$173,310,000	Net Worth:	$13,174,000	Debt/ Equity: 0.3200

First United Corp

19 S 2nd St., Oakland, MD, 21550; *PH:* 1-301-334-9471; *Fax:* 1-301-334-5784; *http://* www.mybankfirstunited.com

General - Incorporation	MD	Stock- Price on:12/24/2007	$19.7
Employees	352	Stock Exchange	NDQ
Auditor	Beard Miller Company LLP	Ticker Symbol	FUNC
Stk Agt	Mellon Investor Services LLC	Outstanding Shares	6,150,000
Counsel	NA	E.P.S.	$2.00
DUNS No.	NA	Shareholders	NA

Business: The group operates through its subsidiaries whose principle activity is to provide banking services. The groups services include checking, savings, and money market deposit accounts, business loans, personal loans, mortgage loans and lines of credit. The products of the group include safe deposit and night depository facilities, and insurance. The group operates from Garrett, Allegany, Washington and Frederick. The assets of the group for the year 2006 were $1,349,317 (thousands).

Primary SIC and add'l.: 6712 6021

CIK No: 0000763907

Subsidiaries: First United Bank & Trust, First United Insurance Agency, Inc, First United Insurance Group, LLC, OakFirst Loan Center, Inc, OakFirst Loan Center, LLC

Officers: William B. Grant/54/Chmn., CEO/$985,413.00, Robert W. Kurtz/61/Dir., Pres. - CRO, Sec., Treasurer/$269,611.00, Jeannette N. Fitzwater/47/Sr. VP, Dir. - Human Resources, Eugene D. Helbig/Sr. VP, Sr. Trust Officer/$194,425.00, Steven M. Lantz/51/Chief Lending Officer, Sr. VP/$209,597.00, Robin M. Murray/49/Sr. VP, Dir. - Retail Banking, Carissa L. Rodeheaver/41/CFO/$188,239.00, Frederick A. Thayer/49/Sr. VP, Dir. - Marketing, Strategic Planning

Directors: William B. Grant/54/Chmn., CEO, John W. McCullough/58/Dir., Raymond F. Hinkle/71/Dir., Robert W. Kurtz/61/Dir., Pres. - CRO, Sec., Treasurer, Elaine L. McDonald/59/Dir., Donald E. Moran/77/Dir., Gary R. Ruddell/59/Dir., Kathryn M. Burkey/57/Dir., David J. Beachy/67/Dir., Karen F. Myers/56/Dir., Robert I. Rudy/55/Dir., Richard G. Stanton/68/Dir., Robert G. Stuck/61/Dir., Andrew H. Walls/Dir., Faye E. Cannon/58/Dir. *(16 Directors included in Index)*

Owners: Firstoak & Corporation/7.04%, Karen F. Myers/0.14%, Andrew N. Walls, Robert I. Rudy, Carissa L. Rodeheaver/0.02%, William B. Grant/0.15%, Richard G. Stanton/0.23%, Robert W. Kurtz/0.06%, Donald E. Moran/2.20%, Kathryn M. Burkey, John W. McCullough/0.08%, Paul Cox, Eugene D. Helbig, Steven M. Lantz/0.03%, Robert G. Stuck/0.05% *(21 Owners included in Index)*

Financial Data: Fiscal Year End:12/31 **Latest Annual Data:** 12/31/2006

Year	Sales		Net Income
2006	$94,310,000		$12,577,000
2005	$83,969,000		$12,151,000
2004	$73,653,000		$7,627,000
Curr. Assets:	$47,488,000	Curr. Liab.:	$1,086,131,000	P/E Ratio: 10.09
Plant, Equip.:	$29,852,000	Total Liab.:	$1,252,461,000	Indic. Yr. Divd.: $0.800
Total Assets:	$1,349,317,000	Net Worth:	$96,856,000	Debt/ Equity: 1.6676

First Valley Bancorp Inc CT

4 Riverside Ave., Bristol, CT, 06010; *PH:* 1-860-582-8868; *http://* www.valleybankct.com

General - Incorporation	CT	Stock- Price on:12/24/2007	$20.45
Employees	52	Stock Exchange	NA
Auditor	Whittlesey & Handley,P.C.	Ticker Symbol	NA
Stk Agt	Registrar & Transfer Co	Outstanding Shares	1,190,000
Counsel	NA	E.P.S.	$0.23
DUNS No.	NA	Shareholders	NA

Business: The groups principle activities include attracting deposits from the general public and investing deposits in small business, commercial real estate, and residential real estate and consumer loans. The group operates from the United States.

Primary SIC and add'l.: 6029

CIK No: 0001318849

Subsidiaries: FVB Capital Trust I, Valley Bank

Officers: Robert L. Messier/65/Dir., CEO, Pres., Mark J. Blum/54/Dir., CFO, Pres., Tony Mattioli/Contact - Valley Bank, Rebecca White/Mortgage Dept Mgr. - Valley Bank, Anthony M. Mattioli/Sr. Lending Officer, Exec. VP

Directors: Robert L. Messier/65/Dir., CEO, Pres., James J. Pryor/71/Chmn. - Valley Bank, David J. Preleski/Dir. - Valley Bank, Thomas P. O'Brien/62/Dir., Mark J. Blum/54/Dir., CFO, Pres., Thomas O. Barnes/Dir. - Valley Bank, James G. Biondi/70/Dir., Bonnie Crane/Dir. - Valley Bank, Edmund D. Donovan/Dir. - Valley Bank, David W. Florian/Dir. - Valley Bank, Mark A. Gibson/Dir. - Valley Bank, Edward T. McPhee/Dir. - Valley Bank

Owners: Robert L. Messier/2.40%, Mark J. Blum/0.70%, David J. Preleski/1.00%, Bonnie Crane/1.40%, Mark A. Gibson/0.40%, Thomas P. O'Brien/3.30%, Anthony M. Mattioli/0.60%, Edmund D. Donovan/1.50%, Insiders/3.20%, James J. Pryor/3.70%, David W. Florian/6.10%, James G. Biondi/4.50%, Thomas O. Barnes/3.60%, Leo G. Charette/5.20%, Edward T. McPhee/5.30%

Financial Data: Fiscal Year End:12/31 **Latest Annual Data:** 12/31/2006

Year	Sales		Net Income
2006	$11,268,000		$573,000
2005	$7,984,000		$749,000
Curr. Assets:	$26,160,000	Curr. Liab.:	$164,758,000	P/E Ratio: 88.91
Plant, Equip.:	$2,321,000	Total Liab.:	$182,616,000	Indic. Yr. Divd.: NA
Total Assets:	$193,147,000	Net Worth:	$10,531,000	Debt/ Equity: 1.4358

First Vietnamese American Bank

8990 Westminster Blvd., Westminster, CA, 92683; *PH:* 1-714-894-3105; *Fax:* 1-714-894-2802; *https://* www.fvab.com

General - Incorporation		Stock- Price on:12/24/2007	$9.4
Employees	NA	Stock Exchange	OTC
Auditor	NA	Ticker Symbol	FVAB
Stk Agt	NA	Outstanding Shares	NA
Counsel	NA	E.P.S.	NA
DUNS No.	NA	Shareholders	NA

Business: The groups principal activity is to provide banking services. The group operates from the United States.

Primary SIC and add'l.: 8742

CIK No:

Curr. Assets:	$51,171,000	Curr. Liab.:	$93,048,000	P/E Ratio: 1.97
Plant, Equip.:	$601,292,000	Total Liab.:	$822,092,000	Indic. Yr. Divd.: NA
Total Assets:	$703,060,000	Net Worth:	-$119,032,000	Debt/ Equity: NA

First West Virginia Bancorp Inc

1701 Warwood Ave., Wheeling, WV, 26003; *PH:* 1-304-277-1100; *Fax:* 1-304-277-4705; *http://* www.progbank.com

General - Incorporation	WV	Stock- Price on:12/24/2007	$19.5
Employees	110	Stock Exchange	AMEX
Auditor	S R Snodgrass, A.C	Ticker Symbol	FWV
Stk Agt	Registrar & Transfer Co	Outstanding Shares	1,530,000
Counsel	NA	E.P.S.	$1.246
DUNS No.	03-012-6999	Shareholders	NA

Business: The group's principal activity is to provide consumer and commercial banking services to individuals, businesses, professionals and governments. It is a holding company and operates its activities through the wholly owned subsidiary, progressive bank n.a. The loan portfolio of the bank consists primarily of loans secured by real estate to consumers and businesses. The group also engages in commercial loans and general consumer loans to individuals. The bank offers a wide range of both personal and commercial types of deposit accounts and services as a means of gathering funds. Deposit accounts and services available include, non-interest bearing demand checking, interest bearing checking, savings, money market, certificates of deposit, individual retirement accounts, and christmas club accounts. It provides banking services in Ohio, brooke, marshall, upshur, lewis and wetzel counties and a portion of the west bank of the Ohio river.

Primary SIC and add'l.: 6022 6712

CIK No: 0000037049

Subsidiaries: Progressive Bank, N.A. of Wheeling

Officers: Sylvan J. Dlesk/Chmn., CEO, Pres., Stephanie A. Laflam/Sec., Connie R. Tenney/VP, Nancy J. Ritter/VP, Francie P. Reppy/Exec. VP, Chief Administrative Officer, CFO, Nada E. Beneke/Dir., Assist. Sec.

Directors: Sylvan J. Dlesk/Chmn., CEO, Pres., Laura G. Inman/Vice Chmn., Nada E. Beneke/Dir., Assist. Sec., Gary W. Glessner/Dir., James C. Inman/Dir., Clark R. Morton/Dir., Thomas A. Noice/Dir., William G. Petroplus/Dir., Thomas L. Sable/Dir.

Owners: James C. Inman/7.85%, Francie P. Reppy, Cede& Co./59.81%, William G. Petroplus, Gary W. Glessner, Thomas L. Sable, Nada E. Beneke/2.82%, Thomas A. Noice, Insiders/25.74%, Laura G. Inman/7.85%, Sylvan J. Dlesk/10.56%, Clark R. Morton/3.07%

Financial Data: Fiscal Year End:12/31 **Latest Annual Data:** 12/31/2006

Year	Sales		Net Income
2006	$15,205,000		$2,144,000
2005	$14,506,000		$2,262,000
2004	$14,690,000		$2,637,000
Curr. Assets:	$12,635,000	Curr. Liab.:	$228,588,000	P/E Ratio: 15.21
Plant, Equip.:	$4,334,000	Total Liab.:	$229,160,000	Indic. Yr. Divd.: $0.760
Total Assets:	$254,438,000	Net Worth:	$25,277,000	Debt/ Equity: 0.0907

Firstbank Corp

311 Woodworth Ave., Alma, MI, 48801; *PH:* 1-989-463-3131; *Fax:* 1-989-466-2042; *http://* www.firstbank-corp.com

General - Incorporation	MI	Stock- Price on:12/24/2007	$19.46
Employees	405	Stock Exchange	NDQ
Auditor	Crowe Chizek & Co. LLC	Ticker Symbol	FBMI
Stk Agt	Registrar & Transfer Co	Outstanding Shares	6,520,000
Counsel	Varnum Riddering S & H LLP	E.P.S.	$1.42
DUNS No.	15-650-4664	Shareholders	NA

Business: The group's principal activity is to provide commercial banking services through 37 branches located in the state of Michigan. The services include accepting checking, savings and time deposits and making commercial, mortgage, home improvement, automobile and other consumer loans. The group also offers trust services through its subsidiary and securities brokerage services through arrangements with third party brokerage firms.

Primary SIC and add'l.: 6022 6712

CIK No: 0000778972

Subsidiaries: 1st Armored, Inc., 1st Title, Inc., C.A. Hanes Realty, Inc., Firstbank (Mt. Pleasant), Firstbank (Mt. Pleasant) Mortgage Company, Firstbank - Alma, Firstbank - Alma Mortgage Company, Firstbank - Lakeview, Firstbank - Lakeview Mortgage Company, Firstbank - St. Johns, Firstbank - St. Johns Mortgage Company, Firstbank - West Branch, Firstbank - West Branch Mortgage Company, Gladwin Land Company, KCB Title Insurance Agency, LLC 19 Subsidiaries included in the Index

Officers: Thomas R. Sullivan/Dir., CEO, Pres. - Firstbank Corporation/$361,320.00, William L. Benear/VP/$203,063.00, Dale A. Peters/VP/$204,608.00, David L. Miller/VP, James E. Wheeler/VP/$208,795.00, Douglas J. Ouellette/VP, David M. Brown/VP, Samuel G. Stone/CFO, Exec. VP/$264,092.00, Richard D. Rice/VP, Thomas O. Schlueter/VP

Directors: Thomas R. Sullivan/Dir., CEO, Pres. - Firstbank Corporation, William E. Goggin/Chmn., Kenneth A. Rader/Chmn. - Firstbank, Lakeview, Kenneth V. Miller/Chmn. - Keystone, Dana R. Hodges/Chmn. - Firstbank, Donald A. Rademacher/Chmn. - Firstbank, St. Johns, Joseph M. Clark/Chmn. - Firstbank, West Branch, Bryon A. Bernard/Dir. - Firstbank, West Branch, Robert T. Griffin/Dir. - Firstbank, West Branch, Charles A. Hanes/Dir. - Firstbank, West Branch, Christine R. Juarez/Dir. - Firstbank, West Branch, Norman J. Miller/Dir. - Firstbank, West Branch, Jeffrey C. Schubert/Dir. - Firstbank, West Branch, Camila J. Steckling/Dir. - Firstbank, West Branch, Sara Clark-Pierson/Dir. - Firstbank, St. Johns *(56 Directors included in Index)*

Owners: Edward B. Grant, James E. Wheeler, Dale A. Peters, David W. Fultz, William L. Benear, David D. Roslund, Samuel A. Smith, Samuel G. Stone, Jeff A. Gardner, Thomas R. Sullivan, Insiders/4.61%, William E. Goggin, Duane A. Carr

Financial Data: Fiscal Year End:12/31   Latest Annual Data: 12/31/2006

Year		Sales		Net Income
2006		$80,919,000		$10,208,000
2005		$62,862,000		$10,110,000
2004		$54,198,000		$10,358,000
Curr. Assets:	$73,825,000	Curr. Liab.:	$978,326,000	P/E Ratio:	13.70
Plant, Equip.:	$20,232,000	Total Liab.:	$999,019,000	Indic. Yr. Divd.:	$0.900
Total Assets:	$1,095,092,000	Net Worth:	$96,073,000	Debt/ Equity:	0.2106

Firstbank Financial Services Inc

120 Keys Ferry St., Mcdonough, GA, 30253; *PH:* 1-678-583-2265; *http://* www.firstbankofhenry.com; *Email:* investorinfo@firstbankfinancialservices.com

General - Incorporation	GA	**Stock**- Price on:12/24/2007	$12.75
Employees	48	Stock Exchange	OTC
Auditor	Mauldin & Jenkins, LLC	Ticker Symbol	FBFS
Stk Agt	NA	Outstanding Shares	2,830,000
Counsel	NA	E.P.S.	$0.57
DUNS No.	NA	Shareholders	NA

Business: The group operates through its subsidiary whose principle activity is to provide banking services. Services of the group include interest-bearing and noninterest-bearing checking accounts, statement savings accounts, money market deposits, certificates of deposit and individual retirement accounts. The Bank complements its lending and deposit products by offering ATM and debit cards, travelers checks, official checks, credit cards, direct deposit, automatic transfers, savings bonds, night depository, stop payments, collections, wire transfers and overdraft The group operates from Henry County in the United States.

Primary SIC and add'l.: 6035

CIK No: 0001316410

Subsidiaries: FirstBank Financial Services

Officers: Thaddeus M. Williams/Dir., CEO, Pres., Lisa J. Maxwell/CFO, Exec. VP, William M. Waller/Exec. VP, Sr. Lending Officer - Bank

Directors: Thaddeus M. Williams/Dir., CEO, Pres., Don H. Cagle/Chmn., Larry D. Adams/Vice Chmn., Wiley A. Brown/Dir., James T. Chafin/Dir., William L. Craddock/Dir., Luther M. Denney/Dir., Milton S. Goggins/Dir., Richard A. Grimes/Dir., Larry M. Phillips/Dir., Robert J. McDonald/Dir.

Owners: Larry D. Adams/3.60%, Insiders/23.90%, Thaddeus M. Williams/2.00%, Larry Max Phillips/2.70%, William Lee Craddock/3.00%, Wiley A. Brown/2.50%, Richard Allen Grimes/2.10%, Luther Martin Denney/1.60%, Don H. Cagle/2.00%, Lisa J. Maxwell/0.30%, James Troy Chafin/1.90%, William M. Waller/0.40%, Milton Stanley Goggins/1.90%, Estate of James Randall Dixon/7.09%

Financial Data: Fiscal Year End:12/31   Latest Annual Data: 12/31/2006

Year		Sales		Net Income
2006		$19,195,000		$2,562,000
2005		$13,881,000		$2,544,000
Curr. Assets:	$17,452,000	Curr. Liab.:	$216,411,000	P/E Ratio:	18.96
Plant, Equip.:	$6,013,000	Total Liab.:	$249,327,000	Indic. Yr. Divd.:	NA
Total Assets:	$277,080,000	Net Worth:	$27,753,000	Debt/ Equity:	NA

FirstBank NW Corp

1300 16th Ave., Clarkston, WA, 99403; *PH:* 1-509-295-5100; *http://* www.fbnw.com

General - Incorporation	WA	**Stock**- Price on:12/24/2007	$19.06
Employees	405	Stock Exchange	NA
Auditor	Moss Adams LLP	Ticker Symbol	NA
Stk Agt	Cranford N. J.	Outstanding Shares	6,520,000
Counsel	Breyer & Assocaite PC	E.P.S.	$1.42
DUNS No.	07-574-5109	Shareholders	NA

Business: The group's principal activity is to provide community-oriented banking services in the market area of Idaho and Washington. It is a holding company of firstbank northwest bank and tri star financial corporation. The group accepts deposits from the general public and originates various kinds of loans. The loans provided include residential mortgage loans, commercial and agricultural real estate loans. The group operates twenty full time banking offices through out United States. The group also has

six real estate loan production offices and six commercial and agricultural production centers in lewiston, moscow, coeur d'alene and boise, Idaho, spokane, Washington and baker city, Oregon. The loans are made to borrowers residing in the counties in which the group's offices are located and in the surrounding countries. On 31-Oct-2003, the group acquired Oregon trail financial corp.

Primary SIC and add'l.: 6035 6712

CIK No: 0001035513

Subsidiaries: FirstBank Northwest, Pioneer Development Corporation, Tri-Star Financial Corporation

Financial Data: Fiscal Year End:03/31   Latest Annual Data: 12/31/2006

Year		Sales		Net Income
2006		$80,919,000		$10,208,000
2005		$62,862,000		$10,110,000
2004		$54,198,000		$10,358,000
Curr. Assets:	$73,825,000	Curr. Liab.:	$978,326,000	P/E Ratio:	13.42
Plant, Equip.:	$20,232,000	Total Liab.:	$999,019,000	Indic. Yr. Divd.:	$0.900
Total Assets:	$1,095,092,000	Net Worth:	$96,073,000	Debt/ Equity:	0.2106

FirstCity Financial Corp

6400 Imperial Dr., Waco, TX, 76712; *PH:* 1-254-761-2800; *http://* www.fcfc.com; *Email:* info@fcfc.com

General - Incorporation	DE	**Stock**- Price on:12/24/2007	$9.98
Employees	214	Stock Exchange	NDQ
Auditor	KPMG LLP	Ticker Symbol	FCFC
Stk Agt	American Stock Transfer & Trust Co.	Outstanding Shares	11,320,000
Counsel	NA	E.P.S.	$0.447
DUNS No.	12-660-8462	Shareholders	NA

Business: The group's principal activities are acquisition, management, servicing and resolution of portfolio assets. The activities of the group are divided into two reportable segments: portfolio asset acquisition and resolution where in the subsidiary acquires and resolves portfolios of performing and non performing commercial and consumer loans and other assets that are generally acquired at a discount to face value. Consumer lending activities which include the origination, acquisition and servicing of sub-prime consumer loans principally secured by automobiles with the intention of selling the acquired loans in securitization transactions.

Primary SIC and add'l.: 6141 6162 6153

CIK No: 0000828678

Subsidiaries: Bosque Asset Corp., Bosque Asset Funding, L.P, Bosque Asset GP Corp, Bosque Leasing GP Corp, Bosque Leasing, L.P, Calibat Fund Limited Liability Company, Community Development Investments, LLC, DFC Asset Corp, Diversified Financial Systems, L.P., EuroTex Partners GP Corp., EuroTex Partners,Ltd., F& C Delaware Holdings Corporation, F& C Texas Holdings Corporation, FC Assets Corp, FC Assets Five Corp. 66 Subsidiaries included in the Index

Owners: James C. Holmes, Jeffery Leu, Heartland Advisors,Inc./10.67%, First ManhattanCo./8.43%, Robert E. Garrison/1.10%, Dane Fulmer, F&C Asset Managementplc./5.10%, Richard J. Vander Woude, Dimensional Fund AdvisorsLP/5.82%, Richard E. Bean/2.94%, Ivan C. Wilson, Terry R. DeWitt/1.80%, Michael D. Hunter, Insiders/15.47%, James T. Sartain/5.71% *(17 Owners included in Index)*

Financial Data: Fiscal Year End:12/31   Latest Annual Data: 12/31/2006

Year		Sales		Net Income
2006		$28,387,000		$9,802,000
2005		$24,093,000		$8,231,000
2004		$36,054,000		$63,634,000
Curr. Assets:	$19,400,000	Curr. Liab.:	NA	P/E Ratio:	15.35
Plant, Equip.:	NA	Total Liab.:	$192,200,000	Indic. Yr. Divd.:	NA
Total Assets:	$297,663,000	Net Worth:	$103,893,000	Debt/ Equity:	1.0424

FirstEnergy Corp

76 S Main St., Akron, OH, 44308; *PH:* 1-800-633-4766; *Fax:* 1-330-384-3866; *http://* www.firstenergycorp.com

General - Incorporation	OH	**Stock**- Price on:12/24/2007	$65.88
Employees	13,739	Stock Exchange	NYSE
Auditor	PricewaterhouseCoopers LLP	Ticker Symbol	FE
Stk Agt	FirstEnergy Securities Transfer Co	Outstanding Shares	304,830,000
Counsel	NA	E.P.S.	$4.18
DUNS No.	79-924-9461	Shareholders	NA

Business: The groups principle activities include exploring, producing, transmitting and marketing electricity and oil and natural gas. The group operates through three segments namely regulated, competitive and other. The group operates from United States.

Primary SIC and add'l.: 6719 4911

CIK No: 0001031296

Subsidiaries: Centerior Funding Corporation., Cleveland Electric Financing Trust, Shippingport Capital Trust

Officers: Anthony J. Alexander/Dir., CEO, Pres./$12,753,330.00, Thomas M. Welsh/Sr. VP, Assist. to CEO, Tony C. Banks/VP - Business Development, Performance, Management, David C. Luff/Sr. VP - Governmental Affairs, Donald R. Schneider/Sr. VP - Energy Delivery, Customer Service, Edward J. Udovich/Assist. Corp. Sec., Douglas S. Elliott/Pres. - Pennsylvania Operations, James M. Murray/Pres. - Ohio Operations, Lynn M. Cavalier/Sr. VP - Human Resources, David M. Blank/VP - Rates, Regulatory Affairs, William D. Byrd/VP - Corporate Risk, Chief Risk Officer, Mary Beth Carroll/VP - Corporate Affairs, Community Involvement, Thomas A. Clark/VP - Customer Service, Service Area Development, Kathryn W. Dindo/VP, Ralph J. Dinicola/VP - Communications *(54 Officers included in Index)*

Directors: Anthony J. Alexander/Dir., CEO, Pres., George M. Smart/Non - Exec. Chmn., Carol A. Cartwright/Dir., Wes M. Taylor/Dir., Ernest J. Novak/Dir., William T. Cottle/Dir., Paul T. Addison/Dir., Robert C. Savage/70/Dir., Russell W. Maier/71/Dir., Robert B. Heisler/Dir., Catherine A. Rein/Dir., Jesse T. Williams/Dir., Michael J. Anderson/Dir.

Owners: Richard H. Marsh, State Street Bank and Trust Company, Trustee, Ernest J. Novak, Catherine A. Rein, Jesse T. Williams, Wes M. Taylor, Paul T. Addison, Leila L. Vespoli, Insiders, Robert B. Heisler, William T. Cottle, Gary R. Leidich, Carol A. Cartwright, Robert C. Savage, Richard R. Grigg *(21 Owners included in Index)*

Financial Data: Fiscal Year End:12/31   Latest Annual Data: 12/31/2006

Year	Sales	Net Income
2006	$11,501,000,000	$1,254,000,000
2005	$11,989,000,000	$861,000,000
2004	$12,453,046,000	$878,175,000

Curr. Assets:	$2,083,000,000	Curr. Liab.:	$5,255,000,000	P/E Ratio:	15.54
Plant, Equip.:	$14,667,000,000	Total Liab.:	$22,161,000,000	Indic. Yr. Divd.:	$2.000
Total Assets:	$31,196,000,000	Net Worth:	$9,035,000,000	Debt/Equity:	1.0297

FirstFed Bancorp Inc

1630 4th Ave. N, Bessemer, AL, 35020; PH: 1-205-428-8472; http:// www.firstfedbessemer.com

General - Incorporation	DE	Stock - Price on:12/24/2007	$17.9101
Employees	102	Stock Exchange	NA
Auditor	KPMG LLP	Ticker Symbol	NA
Stk Agt	Registrar & Transfer Co	Outstanding Shares	5,880,000
Counsel	NA	E.P.S.	$0.83
DUNS No.	80-665-6393	Shareholders	NA

Business: The group's principal activities are to accept deposits from the general public and invest them in one-to-four family residential mortgage loans, commercial mortgage loans, commercial and consumer loans. The group serves as the holding group for first federal savings bank and first state bank of bibb county. It serves through its home office in bessemer and 7 other branches, one each in centreville, hoover, hueytown, pelham, vance, west blocton and woodstock.

Primary SIC and add'l.: 6035 6712

CIK No: 0000876947

Subsidiaries: First Financial Bank, First State Corp.

Financial Data: Fiscal Year End:12/31 Latest Annual Data: 12/31/2006

Year	Sales	Net Income
2006	$34,240,000	$5,341,000
2005	$23,020,000	$3,837,000
2004	$15,463,000	$2,072,000

Curr. Assets:	$44,532,000	Curr. Liab.:	$404,922,000	P/E Ratio:	21.58
Plant, Equip.:	$4,558,000	Total Liab.:	$404,922,000	Indic. Yr. Divd.:	$0.320
Total Assets:	$453,448,000	Net Worth:	$48,526,000	Debt/Equity:	NA

FirstFed Financial Corp

401 Wilshire Blvd., Santa Monica, CA, 90401; PH: 1-310-319-6000; Fax: 1-310-319-2100; http:// www.firstfedca.com

General - Incorporation	DE	Stock - Price on:12/24/2007	$60.15
Employees	603	Stock Exchange	NYSE
Auditor	Grant Thornton LLP	Ticker Symbol	FED
Stk Agt	Registrar & Transfer Co	Outstanding Shares	16,520,000
Counsel	NA	E.P.S.	$7.24
DUNS No.	18-468-6913	Shareholders	NA

Business: The group's principal activities are to accept savings and checking deposits from the general public and use them to originate real estate, business and consumer loans. It also provides various deposit accounts including passbook accounts, money market deposit accounts, interest bearing checking accounts and certificates of deposit. The group's lending activities include single family and multi-family residential loans, real estate loans, commercial business loans and consumer loans. The operations are conducted through twenty-nine retail savings branches located in southern California. In addition to its retail branches, it also operates a call center that conducts transactions with customers by telephone.

Primary SIC and add'l.: 6712 6035

CIK No: 0000810536

Subsidiaries: First Federal Bank of California, Oceanside Insurance Agency, Inc, Santa Monica Capital Group, Seaside Financial Corporation

Officers: Douglas J. Goddard/Investor Relation Officer/$495,365.00, Edward O. Lanchantin/44/Exec. VP - Commercial Banking Group, Brian Leonard/43/Exec. VP, Pres. - Residential Wholesale Lending, James P. Giraldin/COO, Pres./$1,676,399.00, Wayne McCoy/Contact, Ed Rockland/Contact, Kendon Studebaker/Contact, Linda Waring/Contact, Mike Posner/Contact

Directors: Brian E. Argrett/44/Dir.

Owners: Brian E. Argrett, James P. Giraldin, AXA Financial, Inc./5.10%, William P. Rutledge, Mellon Financial Group/5.93%, William G. Ouchi, Christopher M. Harding, Shannon Millard, Jesse Casso, John R. Woodhull, Advisory Research, Inc./7.84%, Douglas J. Goddard, Wellington Management Company, LLP/7.27%, Dimensional Fund Advisors, LP/6.53%, David Anderson (23 Owners included in Index)

Financial Data: Fiscal Year End:12/31 Latest Annual Data: 12/31/2006

Year	Sales	Net Income
2006	$728,872,000	$129,090,000
2005	$500,872,000	$91,698,000
2004	$284,018,000	$65,842,000

Curr. Assets:	$205,902,000	Curr. Liab.:	$8,490,872,000		
Plant, Equip.:	$17,663,000	Total Liab.:	$8,590,872,000	Indic. Yr. Divd.:	NA
Total Assets:	$9,295,587,000	Net Worth:	$704,715,000	Debt/Equity:	0.1368

Firstgold Corp

3108 Gabbert Dr. Ste. 210, Cameron Park, CA, 95682; PH: 1-530-677-5974; http:// www.firstgoldcorp.com; Email: info@firstgoldcorp.com

General - Incorporation	DE	Stock - Price on:12/24/2007	$0.605
Employees	2	Stock Exchange	OTC
Auditor	Singer Lewak Greenbaum & Goldstein	Ticker Symbol	FGOC
Stk Agt	Transfer Online, Inc.	Outstanding Shares	86,640,000
Counsel	NA	E.P.S.	-$0.08
DUNS No.	NA	Shareholders	NA

Business: The groups principal activities include acquiring, developing and exploring gold bearing properties. The group has posted a $243,204 reclamation bond with the Nevada Bureau of Mining regulations and reclamation. The group operates from the continental United States.

Primary SIC and add'l.: 1041

CIK No: 0000878808

Officers: Scott Dockter/CEO/$192,000.00, James W. Kluber/CFO/$166,000.00, Stephen Tibbals/Mine Mgr.

Directors: Scott Dockter/CEO, Stephen Akerfeldt/64/Chmn., Terry Lynch/Dir., Donald Heimler/Dir., Fraser Berrill/Dir.

Owners: Insiders/23.20%, Scott A. Dockter/16.70%, 1346049 Ontario LTD/12.40%, Stephen Akerfeldt, Fraser Berrill, Terrence Lynch, Cornell Capital Partners, LP/7.30%, Donald Heimler, James Kluber/2.70%

Financial Data: Fiscal Year End:01/31 Latest Annual Data: 01/31/2007

Year	Sales	Net Income
2007	NA	-$4,728,000
2006	NA	-$2,645,000
2005	NA	-$1,278,000

Curr. Assets:	$413,000	Curr. Liab.:	$1,927,000		
Plant, Equip.:	$928,000	Total Liab.:	$6,479,000	Indic. Yr. Divd.:	NA
Total Assets:	$2,233,000	Net Worth:	-$4,246,000	Debt/Equity:	NA

Firstline Environmental Solutions Inc

20189 56th Ave., Ste. 203, Langley, BC, V3A 3Y6; PH: 1-866-848-2940

General - Incorporation	FL	Stock - Price on:12/24/2007	NA
Employees	NA	Stock Exchange	NA
Auditor	Moore & Assoc., Chartered	Ticker Symbol	NA
Stk Agt	Fidelity Transfer Co.	Outstanding Shares	NA
Counsel	NA	E.P.S.	NA
DUNS No.	NA	Shareholders	NA

Business: The group's principal activities include developing both a mining property and remediating soils contaminated with heavy metals. The group utilizing existing mining technologies and techniques FLRS embarked on a two-year research and development program to refine the processes and equipment needed to bring their goals to fruition.

Primary SIC and add'l.: 1040

CIK No: 0001338118

Subsidiaries: Firstline Recovery Systems Inc

Officers: Thomas Hatton/65/Dir., CEO, Pres., Jordan Graham/Investor Relations Officer, Evan Brett/Dir., Sec., Dorlyn Evancic/44/Dir., CFO, Treasurer, Manning Elliot/Auditor, Eric Littman/Corporate State Attorney, Dennis Brovarone/Securities Attorney

Directors: Thomas Hatton/65/Dir., CEO, Pres., Evan Brett/Dir., Sec., Dorlyn Evancic/44/Dir., CFO, Treasurer

Owners: Evan Brett/3.90%, Insiders/15.90%, Fu Kwai Enterprises Ltd./8.30%, Thomas Hatton/3.80%, Dorlyn Evancic/8.20%, Great West Management Corp./14.90%

Financial Data: Fiscal Year End:05/31 Latest Annual Data: 05/31/2006

Year	Sales	Net Income
2006	NA	-$422,000

Curr. Assets:	$15,000	Curr. Liab.:	$939,000		
Plant, Equip.:	$60,000	Total Liab.:	$939,000	Indic. Yr. Divd.:	NA
Total Assets:	$174,000	Net Worth:	-$765,000	Debt/Equity:	NA

FirstMerit Corp

3 Cascade Plz., 7th Fl., Akron, OH, 44308; PH: 1-330-996-6300; Fax: 1-330-384-7133; http:// www.firstmerit.com

General - Incorporation	OH	Stock - Price on:12/24/2007	$21.5
Employees	2,755	Stock Exchange	NDQ
Auditor	PricewaterhouseCoopers LLP	Ticker Symbol	FMER
Stk Agt	American Stock Transfer & Trust Co.	Outstanding Shares	80,470,000
Counsel	NA	E.P.S.	$1.23
DUNS No.	02-734-5412	Shareholders	NA

Business: The group's principle activities are to provide banking, fiduciary, financial, insurance and investment services. The banking services include accepting a variety of demand, savings and time deposits and granting of commercial and consumer loans for financing real and personal property. In addition, it provides automated banking programs, credit and debit cards, rental of safe deposit boxes, letters of credit, leasing, discount brokerage and estate and trust services. The noon-banking services include insurance sales, credit life, credit accident and health insurance, securities brokerage services, equipment lease financing and other financial services. The group's offices span a total of 21 counties in Ohio including ashland, ashtabula, crawford, cuyahoga, Delaware, erie, franklin, geauga, huron, knox, lake, lorain, madison, medina, portage, richland, seneca, stark, summit, wayne and wood counties and lawrence county in Pennsylvania. The group's quarterly revenue for Sep'07 was 30.26 millions of USD.

Primary SIC and add'l.: 6211 6712 6022 6411

CIK No: 0000354869

Subsidiaries: Abell& Associates, Inc., Alpha Equipment Group, Inc., Citizens Savings Corporation of Stark County, FirstMerit Bank, National Association, FirstMerit Capital TrustI, FirstMerit Community Development Corporation, FirstMerit Credit Life Insurance Company, FirstMerit Insurance Agency, Inc., FirstMerit Leasing Company, FirstMerit Mortgage Corporation, FirstMerit Mortgage Reinsurance Company, Inc., FirstMerit Moss Creek Ventures, LLC, FirstMerit Securities, Inc., FirstMerit TitleAgency, Ltd., FirstMerit Wealth Management Services, Inc. 22 Subsidiaries included in the Index

Officers: Daniel K. McGill/CEO, Pres. - Central Ohio Region, Nicholas V. Browning/CEO, Pres. - Akron Region, Ronald H. Paydo/CEO, Pres. - Midwest, Old Phoenix Region, David J. Janus/CEO, Pres. - Cleveland Region, William G. Lamb/CEO, Pres. - Erie, Elyria Shores Region, Bruce M. Kephart/CEO, Pres. - Northeast Region, Gene P. Gottfried/CEO, Pres. - Mid Ohio Region, Donald H. Kincade/CEO, Pres. - Toledo Region, Paul G. Greig/Chmn., CEO, Pres./$2,205,723.00, Sue E. Zazon/CEO, Pres. - Columbus Region, Thomas P. O'Malley/Investor Relations Officer, William P. Richgels/Exec. VP, Chief Credit Officer, Julie Anne Robbins/Exec. VP - Retail, Jack R. Gravo/61/Exec. VP, Christopher J. Mauer/Exec. VP - Human Resources (21 Officers included in Index)

Directors: Paul G. Greig/Chmn., CEO, Pres., Cary R. Blair/Dir., Terry L. Haines/Dir., Steven H. Baer/58/Dir., Robert W. Briggs/Dir., Karen S. Belden/Dir., Richard J. Colella/Dir., Philip A. Lloyd/Dir., John C. Blickle/Dir., Richard N. Seaman/Dir., Michael J. Hochschwender/Dir., Gina D. France/49/Dir., Clifford J. Isroff/Dir.

Owners: Philip A. Lloyd/1.35%, Clifford J. Isroff, Gina D. France, Terry E. Patton, John C. Blickle, Terrence E. Bichsel, Michael J. Hochschwender, Karen S. Belden, Robert P. Brecht, John R. Cochran/1.54%, Paul G. Greig, Cary R. Blair, Terry L. Haines, Roger T. Read, George P. Paidas (20 Owners included in Index)

Financial Data: *Fiscal Year End:*12/31 *Latest Annual Data:* 12/31/2006

Year	Sales	Net Income
2006	$798,989,000	$94,946,000
2005	$731,912,000	$130,483,000
2004	$674,677,000	$103,214,000

Curr. Assets:	$696,817,000	*Curr. Liab.:*	$8,942,234,000	*P/E Ratio:*	17.92
Plant, Equip.:	$122,954,000	*Total Liab.:*	$9,406,461,000	*Indic. Yr. Divd.:*	$1.160
Total Assets:	$10,252,572,000	*Net Worth:*	$846,111,000	*Debt/ Equity:*	0.2417

FirstService Corp

FirstService Bldg., 1140 Bay St., Ste. 4000, Toronto, ON, M5S 2B4; *PH:* 1-416-960-9500; *http://* www.firstservice.com

General - Incorporation ....ON	**Stock**- Price on:12/24/2007 ....$36.64
Employees 16,000	Stock Exchange..NDQ
Auditor ....PricewaterhouseCoopers LLP	Ticker Symbol...FSRV
Stk Agt....................Equity Transfer Services Inc	Outstanding Shares 29,800,000
Counsel......................Shearman & Sterling LLP	E.P.S..$1.08
DUNS No...24-815-8024	Shareholders..NA

Business: The group's principle activity is to provide property and business services to residential, corporate and public sector customers in the United States and Canada. The property services division provides residential property management, integrated security services and consumer services. The business services division provides customer support and fulfillment and business process outsourcing services to corporations and government agencies. The group's quarterly revenue for September 2007 was 427.73 millions of USD.

Primary SIC and add'l.: 8748 7382 7389 6531 0782

CIK No: 0000913353

Subsidiaries: American Pool Enterprises,Inc, BDP Business Data Services,Ltd., BLW,Inc. (d/b/a Security Services and Technologies (SST), DDS Distribution Services,Ltd., Dickinson Management,Inc., FirstService (U.S.A.) Security HoldingsInc., FirstService (U.S.A.),Inc., FirstService ContinentalInc., FirstService Delaware,LLC, FirstService Delaware,LP, FirstService FinancialInc., FirstService GP,Inc., FirstService Nova Scotia Corp., FirstService WattsLtd., Greenspace ServicesLtd. 25 Subsidiaries included in the Index

Officers: Douglas P. Frye/CEO - Commercial Real Estate Services, Jay S. Hennick/Dir., CEO, Founder, Gene Gomberg/CEO - Residential Property Management, Frank Brewer/CEO - Integrated Security Service, Elias Mulamoottil/VP - Corporate Development, Greg Power/Deputy GM, Michael H. Appleton/Corp. Sec., Douglas G. Cooke/VP, Corporate Controller, Christian Mayer/Dir. - Financial Reporting, Scott D. Patterson/COO, Pres., John B. Friedrichsen/CFO, Sr. VP, Lynda A. Cralli/Assist. Corp. Sec., Richard M. Strunin/Pres. - Residential Property Management, Roman Kocur/MD - Corporate Development, Neil D. Chander/Dir. - Tax Planning, Compliance *(16 Officers included in Index)*

Directors: Jay S. Hennick/Dir., CEO, Founder, Peter F. Cohen/Chmn., Steven S. Rogers/Dir., Michael D. Harris/Dir., David R. Beatty/Dir., Bernard I. Ghert/Dir., Brendan Calder/Dir.

Financial Data: *Fiscal Year End:*03/31 *Latest Annual Data:* 3/31/2007

Year	Sales	Net Income
2007	$1,359,686,000	$34,863,000
2006	$1,068,134,000	$69,497,000
2005	$812,290,000	$23,207,000

Curr. Assets:	$362,357,000	*Curr. Liab.:*	$256,827,000		
Plant, Equip.:	$66,297,000	*Total Liab.:*	$503,817,000	*Indic. Yr. Divd.:*	NA
Total Assets:	$816,998,000	*Net Worth:*	$264,875,000	*Debt/ Equity:*	1.0340

Firstwave Technologies Inc

7000 Central Pkwy., NE, Ste. 330, Atlanta, GA, 30328; *PH:* 1-678-672-3100; *Fax:* 1-678-672-3131; *http://* www.firstwave.com; *Email:* info@firstwave.net

General - Incorporation ....GA	**Stock**- Price on:12/24/2007 ....$2.02
Employees 16	Stock Exchange..OTC
Auditor ....Cherry, Bekaert & Holland LLP	Ticker Symbol...FSTW
Stk Agt..............................Wachovia Bank N.A	Outstanding Shares 2,890,000
Counsel.......Powell, Goldstein, Frazer & Murphy	E.P.S...-$0.11
DUNS No..13-132-0707	Shareholders..NA

Business: The group's principle activity is to provide Internet-based customer relationship management (ecrm) solutions. The group's ecrm solution optimizes and strengthens the relationship between a company and its customers. The group sells and supports three products: firstwave ecrm, takecontrol(R) and firstwave for unix. Firstwave ecrm is a Web-based application that fulfills and manages e-business needs of a company in the area of sales, marketing and support. Takecontrol(R) is a microsoft(R) windows-based integrated client/server that automates the marketing, sales and customer service operations for companies. Firstwave for unix is character based crm solution. The group has licensed its products to users located in 13 countries. The group's quarterly revenue for Sep'07 was 0.59 millions of USD.

Primary SIC and add'l.: 7373 7372

CIK No: 0000897078

Owners: Roger A. Babb/1.50%, Gregory O. Sargent/30.50%, Bjurman, Barry & Associates/4.20%, Sigmund I. Mosley/1.20%, Insiders/34.60%, John N. Spencer/1.40%, Richard T. Brock/25.10%

Financial Data: *Fiscal Year End:*12/31 *Latest Annual Data:* 12/31/2006

Year	Sales	Net Income
2006	$2,694,000	$172,000
2005	$3,224,000	-$1,708,000
2004	$7,400,000	-$4,638,000

Curr. Assets:	$2,170,000	*Curr. Liab.:*	$976,000		
Plant, Equip.:	$55,000	*Total Liab.:*	$976,000	*Indic. Yr. Divd.:*	NA
Total Assets:	$3,824,000	*Net Worth:*	$2,848,000	*Debt/ Equity:*	NA

Fischer-Watt Gold Company

2582 Taft Ct, Lakewood, CO, 80215; *PH:* 1-303-232-0292; *http://* www.fischer-watt.com; *Email:* info@fischer-watt.com

General - Incorporation .... NV	**Stock**- Price on:12/24/2007 ....$0.0775
Employees ....NA	Stock Exchange..OTC
Auditor ....Stark Winter Schenkein & Co., LLP	Ticker Symbol...FWGO
Stk Agt ....Fidelity Transfer Co	Outstanding Shares 70,520,000
Counsel..NA	E.P.S..$0.016
DUNS No..NA	Shareholders..NA

Business: The groups principle activities include mining and exploring mineral. The group operates from Nevada in the United States.

Primary SIC and add'l.: 1041

CIK No: 0000844788

Subsidiaries: Minera Montoro, S. A. de C. V.

Officers: Peter Bojtos/Chmn., CEO, Pres., Gerald D. Helgeson/Sec. - Corporation

Directors: Peter Bojtos/Chmn., CEO, Pres., George J. Beattie/Dir., William Rapaglia/Dir., James M. Seed/Dir.

Owners: William Rapaglia, Peter Bojtos/5.30%, James M. Seed/27.40%, Gerald D. Helgeson, George Beattie/5.40%, Cede & Co./56.90%, Insiders/39.40%

Financial Data: *Fiscal Year End:*01/31 *Latest Annual Data:* 1/31/2007

Year	Sales	Net Income
2007	NA	$308,000
2006	$44,000	-$225,000
2005	NA	-$475,000

Curr. Assets:	$466,000	*Curr. Liab.:*	$2,016,000	*P/E Ratio:*	7.75
Plant, Equip.:	NA	*Total Liab.:*	$2,016,000	*Indic. Yr. Divd.:*	NA
Total Assets:	$466,000	*Net Worth:*	-$1,550,000	*Debt/ Equity:*	NA

Fiserv Inc

255 Fiserv Dr., Brookfield, WI, 53045; *PH:* 1-262-879-5000; *Fax:* 1-262-879-5013; *http://* www.fiserv.com

General - Incorporation ....WI	**Stock**- Price on:12/24/2007 ....$58.22
Employees 23,000	Stock Exchange..NDQ
Auditor ....Deloitte & Touche LLP	Ticker Symbol...FISV
Stk Agt ....Computershare Trust Co	Outstanding Shares 168,190,000
Counsel...........................Charles W. Sprague	E.P.S..$2.53
DUNS No......................................05-707-3744	Shareholders..NA

Business: The group's principle activity is to provide data processing and information management systems. The group provides services include financial institution outsourcing, systems and services, which provides account and transaction processing systems and services. The health plan management service provides services for the administration of health plans to customers nationwide. The securities processing and trust services provides securities processing products and services and retirement plan administration services to brokerage firms, investment advisers and financial institutions. The group also provides plastic card issuance, design, personalization and mailing services and document management products. The group operates from United States.

Primary SIC and add'l.: 7374 6371 6289 6091

CIK No: 0000798354

Subsidiaries: Administrative Services Group, Inc., Advanced Insurance Coverages, Inc., Agio Insurance Agency, Inc., Artius, Inc., Aspen Investment Alliance, Inc., Avidyn Health, LLLP, AVIDYN Holdings, Inc., Benefit Control Management, LLC, Benefit Planners Limited, LLP, Benesight, Inc., Benesight.com, Incorporated, BillMatrix Corporation, BMC Government Services, Inc., BMC Processing, Inc., BMC Resources, Inc. 103 Subsidiaries included in the Index

Officers: Jeffery W. Yabuki/48/Dir., CEO, Pres./$4,412,169.00, Norman J. Balthasar/61/COO, Sr. Exec. VP/$3,196,295.00, Thomas Hirsch/44/CFO, Exec. VP, Treasurer/$724,134.00, Tom W. Warsop/42/Group Pres. - Financial Institutions, Rahul Gupta/49/Group Pres. - Payments, Industry Products, Bridie A. Fanning/40/Exec. VP - Human Resources, David Banks/VP - Investor Relations, Dean C. Schmelzer/57/Group Pres. - Marketing, Sales, Charles W. Sprague/58/Exec. VP, General Counsel, Chief Administrative Officer, Douglas J. Craft/54/Group Pres. - Operations, Thomas A. Neill/59/Group Pres. - Depository Institution Processing/$1,579,590.00, James Cox/44/Exec. VP - Mergers, Acquisitions

Directors: Jeffery W. Yabuki/48/Dir., CEO, Pres., Donald F. Dillon/68/Chmn., Gerald J. Levy/76/Dir., Daniel P. Kearney/68/Dir., Thomas C. Wertheimer/67/Dir., Glenn M. Renwick/52/Dir., Leslie M. Muma/Dir., Doyle R. Simons/44/Dir., Kim M. Robak/52/Dir.

Owners: Gerald J. Levy, Kenneth R. Jensen, Michael D. Gantt, Norman J. Balthasar, Kim M. Robak, Thomas A. Neill, Barclays Global Investors/8.20%, Thomas C. Wertheimer, Jeffery W. Yabuki, Donald F. Dillon/2.10%, Thomas J. Hirsch, William L. Seidman, Glenn M. Renwick, Daniel P. Kearney, Insiders/4.20%

Financial Data: *Fiscal Year End:*12/31 *Latest Annual Data:* 12/31/2006

Year	Sales	Net Income
2006	$4,544,151,000	$449,914,000
2005	$4,059,478,000	$516,438,000
2004	$3,729,746,000	$377,642,000

Curr. Assets:	$786,554,000	*Curr. Liab.:*	$613,368,000	*P/E Ratio:*	23.01
Plant, Equip.:	$248,040,000	*Total Liab.:*	$3,782,301,000	*Indic. Yr. Divd.:*	NA
Total Assets:	$6,207,923,000	*Net Worth:*	$2,425,622,000	*Debt/ Equity:*	0.3382

Fisher Communications Inc

100 4th Ave. N, Ste. 510, Seattle, WA, 98109; *PH:* 1-206-404-7000; *Fax:* 1-206-404-6037; *http://* www.fsci.com; *Email:* info@fsci.com

General - Incorporation .... WA	**Stock**- Price on:12/24/2007 ....$12.97
Employees 812	Stock Exchange..NDQ
Auditor ....PricewaterhouseCoopers LLP	Ticker Symbol...FSCI
Stk Agt ....EquiServe Trust Co N.A	Outstanding Shares 8,720,000
Counsel..NA	E.P.S..$2.00
DUNS No......................................00-924-8816	Shareholders..NA

Business: The group's principal activities are the television and radio broadcasting, proprietary real estate development and management and other media operations including program production as well as satellite and fiber transmission. The group operates through three subsidiaries, namely, fisher broadcasting company, fisher media services company and fisher properties, inc. As of 31-Dec-2002, the group's broadcasting subsidiary owned and operated eleven network-affiliated television stations and 29 radio stations. The television and radio stations are located in Washington, Oregon, Idaho and Montana, with two fox-affiliated television stations located in augusta and columbus, Georgia.

Primary SIC and add'l.: 4841 4833 4832 6719 6531

CIK No: 0001034669

Subsidiaries: Fisher Broadcasting Idaho TV, LLC, Fisher Broadcasting Oregon TV, LLC, Fisher Broadcasting Portland TV, LLC, Fisher Broadcasting S.E. Idaho TV, LLC, Fisher Broadcasting Seattle Radio, LLC, Fisher Broadcasting Seattle TV, LLC, Fisher Broadcasting Washington TV, LLC, Fisher Broadcasting Company, Fisher Media Services Company, Fisher Mills Inc., Fisher Properties Inc., Fisher Radio Regional Group Inc.

Officers: Colleen B. Brown/Dir., CEO, Pres./$1,062,582.00, Connie Williamson/Station Mgr. - Roseburg, OR Marketing, Ken Messer/VP, GM - Yakima, WA Marketing, Tri Cities, WA Marketing, Lewiston, ID Marketing, Ken Croes/Station Mgr. - Coos Bay, OR Marketing, Lawrence P. Roberts/VP - Special Projects, Jim Clayton/VP, GM - Seattle, WA Marketing, Seattle Radio, Robert Thomas/VP, GM - Boise, ID Marketing, Greg Raschio/VP, GM - Eugene, OR Marketing, Coos Bay, OR Marketing, Roseburg, OR Marketing, Jodi A. Colligan/VP - Finance/$284,511.00, Kelly D. Alford/VP, Dir. - Engineering, Joseph L. Lovejoy/Sr. VP/$220,053.00, Robert I. Dunlop/40/Sr. VP - Developing Media/$415,995.00, John N. Tamerlano/VP - Sales, David Praga/Station Mgr. - Tri Cities, WA Marketing, Gina Berger/VP, GM - Idaho Falls, ID Marketing, Pocatello, ID Marketing *(23 Officers included in Index)*

Directors: Colleen B. Brown/Dir., CEO, Pres., Phelps K. Fisher/Chmn., Richard L. Hawley/Dir., William W. Warren/Dir., George F. Warren/Dir., James W. Cannon/80/Dir., Jerry A. St Dennis/Dir., Deborah L. Bevier/Dir., Donald G. Graham/Dir., Brian P. McAndrews/Dir., Michael D. Wortsman/Dir.

Owners: Carol H. Fratt, Phelps K. Fisher/3.00%, Donald G. Graham/5.20%, Joseph L. Lovejoy, James W. Cannon, Jodi A. Colligan, Colleen B. Brown, Judith A. Endejan, Donald G. Graham/9.30%, William W. Warren/3.80%, Insiders/0.28%, George F. Warren/6.60%, Robert I. Dunlop

Financial Data: Fiscal Year End:12/31 Latest Annual Data: 12/31/2006

Year	Sales	Net Income
2006	$154,699,000	$16,836,000
2005	$149,319,000	-$5,072,000
2004	$153,866,000	-$11,953,000

Curr. Assets:	$57,058,000	Curr. Liab.:	$26,044,000	P/E Ratio:	6.55
Plant, Equip.:	$150,819,000	Total Liab.:	$258,012,000	Indic. Yr. Divd.:	NA
Total Assets:	$497,577,000	Net Worth:	$239,565,000	Debt/ Equity:	0.6095

Fit For Business International Inc

3155 E Patrick Ln., Ste. 1, Las Vegas, NV, 89120; **PH:** 1-61-733673355; **http://** www.fitforbusiness.com.au; **Email:** enquiries@fitforbusiness.com.au

General - Incorporation	NV	Stock - Price on:12/24/2007	$0.015
Employees	NA	Stock Exchange	OTC
Auditor	Mendoza Berger & Co.	Ticker Symbol	FFBU
Stk Agt	Standard Registrar & Transfer Co Inc.	Outstanding Shares	NA
Counsel	NA	E.P.S.	NA
DUNS No.	NA	Shareholders	NA

Business: The groups principle activity is to provide health services in the business department. Services provided by the group in the health department include health risk assessment, behavior modification techniques, walking based fitness program, smoking cessation program, individual counseling of employees and preventative measures from diseases. The group operates from Nevada in the United States.

Primary SIC and add'l.: 5122

CIK No: 0001312623

Officers: Mark A. Poulsen/Chmn., CEO, Pres., Prins Ralston/COO, Sr. VP, Anthony F. Head/Dir., Sr. VP - Sales, Sandra L. Wendt/CFO, VP - Administration

Directors: Mark A. Poulsen/Chmn., CEO, Pres., Anthony F. Head/Dir., Sr. VP - Sales

Owners: Sandra L. Wendt/1.83%, Cede & Co./20.24%, Mark A. Poulsen/48.81%, Insiders/50.04%

Financial Data: Fiscal Year End:06/30 Latest Annual Data: 06/30/2007

Year	Sales	Net Income
2007	$12,000	$659,000
2006	$10,000	-$1,678,000

Curr. Assets:	$5,000	Curr. Liab.:	$1,654,000		
Plant, Equip.:	$30,000	Total Liab.:	$1,961,000	Indic. Yr. Divd.:	NA
Total Assets:	$1,209,000	Net Worth:	-$752,000	Debt/ Equity:	NA

FitMedia Inc

338 8th Ave. W , Ste. 304B, Vancouver, BC, V5Y 3X2; **PH:** 1-604-723-0954; **http://** www.fitmedia.net; **Email:** tim@fitmedia.net

General - Incorporation	DE	Stock - Price on:12/24/2007	$0.355
Employees	NA	Stock Exchange	OTC
Auditor	Manning Elliott LLP	Ticker Symbol	FTME
Stk Agt	Independent Stock Transfer Agency	Outstanding Shares	NA
Counsel	NA	E.P.S.	$0.18
DUNS No.	NA	Shareholders	NA

Business: The group's principal activities include producing, distributing and selling DVDs related to exercise, health lifestyles and physical and mental fitness. The group operates from the United States.

Primary SIC and add'l.: 7389

CIK No: 0001322729

Officers: Timothy J. Crottey/42/Chmn., CEO, CFO, Pres., Principal Accounting Officer, Treasurer, Sec.

Directors: Timothy J. Crottey/42/Chmn., CEO, CFO, Pres., Principal Accounting Officer, Treasurer, Sec., Roman Onufrijchuk/Dir.

Owners: Shouren Zhao/93.20%, Insiders/93.20%

Financial Data: Fiscal Year End:01/31 Latest Annual Data: 1/31/2007

Year	Sales	Net Income
2007	NA	-$45,000

Curr. Assets:	$5,000	Curr. Liab.:	$29,000	P/E Ratio:	1.97
Plant, Equip.:	$2,000	Total Liab.:	$29,000	Indic. Yr. Divd.:	NA
Total Assets:	$13,000	Net Worth:	-$16,000	Debt/ Equity:	NA

Fittipaldi Logistics Inc

903 Clint Moore Rd., Boca Raton, FL, 33487; **PH:** 1-561-998-7557; **Fax:** 1-561-998-7821; **http://** www.emmologic.com; **Email:** ir@emmologic.com

---

General - Incorporation	NV	Stock - Price on:12/24/2007	$0.028
Employees	17	Stock Exchange	OTC
Auditor	Sherb & Co., LLP	Ticker Symbol	FPLD
Stk Agt	Madison Stock Transfer, Inc.	Outstanding Shares	144,870,000
Counsel	NA	E.P.S.	-$0.053
DUNS No.	NA	Shareholders	NA

Business: The groups principle activity is to provide pertinent, real time information to the worldwide transportation and security industries. In March 2005, the group acquired Commodity Express Transportation. The group operates from the United States.

Primary SIC and add'l.: 4731

CIK No: 0001082733

Subsidiaries: Freight Rate, Inc

Officers: Frank P. Reilly/CEO, Orin S. Neiman/CEO - Fittipaldi Carriers, John M. Urbanowicz/Exec. VP - Information Technology

Directors: Richard Hersh/Chmn.

Owners: Robert F. Green/6.40%, Carmelo Luppino/9.50%, The Amber Capital Fund Ltd./6.80%, Richard Hersh/12.80%, Jeffrey L. Zimmerman/5.40%, Insiders/15.60%, Richard Hersh/12.80%, Arthur Notini/9.20%, Chris Bake/4.70%, The Black Diamond Fund, LLLP/7.20%, Insiders/15.60%, Frank P. Reilly/3.20%, Michael Garnick/11.20%

Financial Data: Fiscal Year End:06/30 Latest Annual Data: 06/30/2007

Year	Sales	Net Income
2007	$22,707,000	-$6,748,000
2006	$29,995,000	-$5,598,000
2005	$9,248,000	-$6,561,000

Curr. Assets:	$3,267,000	Curr. Liab.:	$8,117,000		
Plant, Equip.:	$383,000	Total Liab.:	$8,225,000	Indic. Yr. Divd.:	NA
Total Assets:	$5,252,000	Net Worth:	-$2,973,000	Debt/ Equity:	NA

Five Star Products Inc

750 Commerce Dr., East Hanover, NJ, 06825; **PH:** 1-203-336-7900; **Fax:** 1-203-336-7930; **http://** www.fivestargroup.com; **Email:** info@fivestarproducts.com

General - Incorporation	DE	Stock - Price on:12/24/2007	$0.58
Employees	219	Stock Exchange	OTC
Auditor	Eisner LLP	Ticker Symbol	FSPX
Stk Agt	Computershare Investor Services LLC	Outstanding Shares	16,360,000
Counsel	NA	E.P.S.	$0.08
DUNS No.	83-942-2243	Shareholders	NA

Business: The group's principal activity is the wholesale distribution of home decorating hardware and finishing products in the northeastern United States. The group is composed of two strategically located warehouse distribution centers and office locations in New Jersey and Connecticut. The group distributes paint sundry items, interior and exterior stains, brushes, rollers, caulking compounds and hardware products to retail dealers in the northeast region. The products are distributed to retail dealers, which include lumber yards, 'do-it yourself' centers, hardware stores and paint stores principally in the northeast region.

Primary SIC and add'l.: 5198 5023 3429

CIK No: 0000922408

Subsidiaries: Five Star Group, Inc.

Officers: John C. Belknap/62/Dir., CEO, Pres., Ira J. Sobotko/51/Sr. VP - Finance, Sec., Treasurer, Robert Przyborowski/Sales Engineer - Northeast, Brandon Belcher/Area Mgr. - Southwest, Michael Baxter/Regional Mgr. - West, Neal W. Collins/47/VP, Assist. Sec., Walt Cooper/Regional Mgr. - Central, Mike Paipal/Reg Engineering Specialist - Central, Richard D. Byerly/Regional Mgr. - Southwest, Bruce Sherman/56/Dir., Exec. VP, Terry Stysly/VP - Worldwide Sales, Thomas Gladden/International Sales Mgr., Chris Piekos/Research, Development Dir., Rick Dufresne/Regional Mgr. - Northeast

Directors: John C. Belknap/62/Dir., CEO, Pres., Leslie S. Flegel/71/Chmn., Bruce Sherman/56/Dir., Exec. VP, Carll Tucker/57/Dir., Harvey P. Eisen/65/Dir.

Owners: S. Leslie Flegel/17.77%, Insiders/17.77%, National Patent Development Corporation/69.92%

Financial Data: Fiscal Year End:12/31 Latest Annual Data: 12/31/2006

Year	Sales	Net Income
2006	$108,088,000	$285,000
2005	$106,451,000	-$287,000
2004	$101,982,000	$1,140,000

Curr. Assets:	$33,439,000	Curr. Liab.:	$29,777,000	P/E Ratio:	9.67
Plant, Equip.:	$530,000	Total Liab.:	$29,783,000	Indic. Yr. Divd.:	NA
Total Assets:	$34,497,000	Net Worth:	$4,714,000	Debt/ Equity:	NA

Five Star Quality Care Inc

400 Ctr. St., Newton, MA, 02458; **PH:** 1-617-796-8387; **Fax:** 1-617-796-8385; **http://** www.fivestarqualitycare.com; **Email:** info@5sqc.com

General - Incorporation	MD	Stock - Price on:12/24/2007	$7.71
Employees	11,960	Stock Exchange	AMEX
Auditor	Ernst & Young LLP	Ticker Symbol	
Stk Agt	Wells Fargo Shareowner Services	Outstanding Shares	31,680,000
Counsel	Sullivan & Worcester LLP	E.P.S.	-$0.44
DUNS No.	NA	Shareholders	

Business: The groups principle activity is to operates independent living and congregate care communities. The group operates from the United States. The groups quarterly revenue for September 2007 was 247.76 millions of USD.

Primary SIC and add'l.: 8059 8051 8361 8052

CIK No: 0001159281

Subsidiaries: Affiliates Insurers Limited, Alliance Pharmacy Services, LLC, CCC Boynton Beach, Inc., Five Star Advertising, Inc., Five Star Insurance, Inc., Five Star MD Homes LLC, Five Star Procurement Group Trust, Five Star Quality Care Trust, Five Star Quality Care-Ainsworth, LLC, Five Star Quality Care-Ashland, LLC, Five Star Quality Care-AZ, LLC, Five Star Quality Care-Blue Hill, LLC, Five Star Quality Care-CA II, INC., Five Star Quality Care-CA II, LLC, Five Star Quality Care-CA, Inc. 140 Subsidiaries included in the Index

Officers: Evrett W. Benton/CEO, Pres., Sec./$882,563.00, Timothy A. Bonang/Mgr. - Investor Relations, Bruce J. MacKey/Dir., CFO, Treasurer, Assist. Sec./$528,759.00, Rosemary Esposito/COO, Sr. VP/$566,405.00, Maryann Hughes/VP, Dir. - Human Resources/$323,949.00, William J. Sheehan/Dir. - Internal Audit, Compliance, Barry M. Portnoy/MD, Gerald M. Martin/MD, Katie Johnston/Investor Relations Analyst

Directors: Bruce M. Gans/61/Dir., Barbara D. Gilmore/Dir., Arthur G. Koumantzelis/Dir.

Owners: Evrett W. Benton, Barry M. Portnoy, Barbara D. Gilmore, Mazama Capital Management, Inc./6.70%, Insiders/2.00%, Bruce J. Mackey, JP Morgan Chase & Co./5.90%, Mellon Financial Corporation/5.50%, Lazard Asset Management LLC/7.20%, The Guardian Life Insurance Company of America/5.30%, Gerard M. Martin, Arthur G. Koumantzelis, Rosemary Esposito, Maryann Hughes, Bruce M. Gans

Financial Data: Fiscal Year End:12/31 Latest Annual Data: 12/31/2006

Year	Sales	Net Income
2006	$827,337,000	-$116,665,000
2005	$757,527,000	-$84,159,000
2004	$628,005,000	$3,291,000

Curr. Assets:	$205,760,000	Curr. Liab.:	$132,929,000		
Plant, Equip.:	$114,898,000	Total Liab.:	$298,981,000	Indic. Yr. Divd.:	NA
Total Assets:	$366,411,000	Net Worth:	$67,430,000	Debt/ Equity:	NA

Flagship Global Health Inc

Formerly: Finity Holdings Inc
432 Pk. Ave. S, 13th Fl., New York, NY, 10016; **PH:** 1-212-340-9111

General - Incorporation .... DE	Stock - Price on:12/24/2007 .... NA
Employees .... NA	Stock Exchange.................................... OTC
Auditor .............................J.H. Cohn, LLP	Ticker Symbol..................................... FGHH
Stk Agt.. NA	Outstanding Shares .... NA
Counsel...............Eric Grant & Richard Plestina	E.P.S.. NA
DUNS No. .... NA	Shareholders...................................... NA

Business: The group's principal activity was to provide credit and debit card services, document management, distribution services and processing services. The group's services were used for automatic teller machines transactions, debit terminal transactions and electronic benefits transfer systems transactions. The group's services served as a link between consumers, merchants and financial institutions by capturing initial transaction at the point of sale, giving the merchant credit for the transaction, posting the transaction in financial institution and customer's account. On Jun 5, 2001, the group sold both its subsidiaries finity corporation and fi-scrip. The group is a shell corporation, and is currently seeking for acquisitions.

Primary SIC and add'l.: 6211 4215 6719 7374 7331 7379

CIK No: 0001051985

Owners: Michael Holland/0.32%, Benjamin Safirstein/3.26%, Stephen J. OBrien/16.29%, Philip Barak/0.96%, Richard Torykian/0.21%, Richard Howard/0.82%, Insiders/11.11%, Brandon Fradd/7.71%, Laurus Master Fund, Ltd./9.39%, Fred Nazem/30.49%, John H. Flood/5.38%, Michael Huckabee/0.11%, Barbara McNeil, Brian Stafford/0.32%, FrontPoint Partners, LLC/9.80%

Curr. Assets:	$1,105,000	Curr. Liab.:	$6,178,000		
Plant, Equip.:	$434,000	Total Liab.:	$9,128,000	Indic. Yr. Divd.:	NA
Total Assets:	$2,584,000	Net Worth:	-$6,543,000	Debt/ Equity:	NA

Flagstar Bancorp Inc

5151 Corporate Dr., Troy, MI, 48098; **PH:** 1-248-312-2000; **http://** www.flagstar.com

General - Incorporation .... MI	Stock - Price on:12/24/2007 ....$12.8
Employees 2,954	Stock Exchange................................. NYSE
Auditor ....Virchow, Krause & Co. LLP	Ticker Symbol...................................... FBC
Stk Agt.......................Registrar & Transfer Co	Outstanding Shares 60,450,000
Counsel... NA	E.P.S... -$0.04
DUNS No. 17-736-0351	Shareholders...................................... NA

Business: The group's principal activity is that of a bank holding company. It operates in two segments namely, banking operations and home lending operations. The banking group offers a comprehensive line of consumer and commercial financial products and services to individuals and small and middle market businesses through 99 banking centers and 145 automated teller machines located in Michigan and Indiana. The home lending group's most significant activity is the origination and acquisition of residential mortgage loans carried out from 128 home loan centers in 25 states. In addition, the bank provides business financial products and services and a 24-hour telephone and Internet banking service.

Primary SIC and add'l.: 6035 6712

CIK No: 0001033012

Subsidiaries: Douglas Insurance Agency, Inc., Flagstar Bank, FSB, Flagstar Commercial Corporation, Flagstar Credit Corporation, Flagstar Investment Group, Inc., Flagstar Statutory Trust II, Flagstar Statutory Trust III, Flagstar Statutory Trust IV, Flagstar Statutory Trust V, Flagstar Statutory Trust VI, Flagstar Statutory Trust VII, Flagstar Statutory Trust VIII, Flagstar Title Insurance Agency, Inc.

Officers: Mark T. Hammond/CEO, Pres./$1,875,641.00, Valerie Wilton/Commercial Loan Servicing, Jackson, Jon W. Stuckey/Commercial Loan Officer - Covering Southern Michigan, Western Michigan, Indiana, Steven L. Sanders/Commercial Loan Officer - Covering Southern Michigan, Western Michigan, Indiana, Paul D. Borja/47/CFO, Exec. VP/$583,504.00, Peter W. Smith/Commercial Lending Mgr., Sr. VP - Flagstar Bank, Sandy Calamari/Administrative Assist. - Peter Smith, Flagstar Bank, Michael Tesler/Commercial Lender, Georgia, Flagstar Bank, John Groll/Commercial Lender, Texas, Flagstar Bank, Greg Vincent/Commercial Lender, Texas, Flagstar Bank, Heather Hensley/Contact - Customer Service, Flagstar Bank, Tim Link/Loan Document Processor, Flagstar Bank, Jeff Ciochetto/Commercial Banking Mgr., First VP - Flagstar Bank, Joe Lathrop/Commercial Lender, Michigan, Jackson, Flagstar Bank, Miriam Cox/Contact - Customer Service, Flagstar Bank *(45 Officers included in Index)*

Directors: Thomas J. Hammond/64/Chmn., Robert O. Rondeau/42/Dir., Kirstin A. Hammond/42/Dir., Chief Investment Officer, Jay J. Hansen/44/Dir., Michael Lucci/68/Dir., Richard S. Elsea/78/Dir., Robert W. Dewitt/68/Dir., Charles Bazzy/78/Dir.

Owners: Thomas J. Hammond/17.60%, Michael Lucci, Jay J. Hansen, Paul D. Borja, Frank DAngelo, Charles Bazzy, Carrie C. Langdon/5.30%, Janet G. Hammond/7.00%, Kirstin A. Hammond, Dimensional FundAdvisors LP/6.40%, Mark T. Hammond/10.50%, Insiders/29.20%, Robert O. Rondeau, Brian B. Tauber, Richard S. Elsea *(17 Owners included in Index)*

Financial Data: Fiscal Year End:12/31 Latest Annual Data: 12/31/2006

Year	Sales	Net Income
2006	$1,009,190,000	$75,202,000
2005	$868,111,000	$79,865,000
2004	$819,558,000	$143,754,000

Curr. Assets:	$329,994,000	Curr. Liab.:	$14,124,394,000	P/E Ratio:	16.00
Plant, Equip.:	$300,238,000	Total Liab.:	$14,684,971,000	Indic. Yr. Divd.:	$0.400
Total Assets:	$15,497,205,000	Net Worth:	$812,234,000	Debt/ Equity:	NA

Flamel Technologies

1825 K St., Ste. 1210, Washington, DC, 20006; **PH:** 1-202-862-8400; **Fax:** 1-202-862-3933; **http://** www.flamel-technologies.fr; **Email:** info@flamel.com

General - Incorporation ... Republic Of France	Stock - Price on:12/24/2007 ....$21.6
Employees 306	Stock Exchange................................... NDQ
Auditor .... Ernst & Young LLP	Ticker Symbol.................................... FLML
Stk Agt.. NA	Outstanding Shares 23,990,000
Counsel.. NA	E.P.S... -$1.57
DUNS No. 57-633-4411	Shareholders...................................... NA

Business: The group's principal activities are the development of innovative drugs for the pharmaceutical, agrochemical and ophthalmic sectors. To facilitate this development the group has entered into partnerships with corning inc.; merck & co., inc.; monsanto company and novo nordisk a/s.

Primary SIC and add'l.: 5995 5122 2834

CIK No: 0001012477

Subsidiaries: Flamel Technologies, Inc

Officers: Stephen H. Willard/Dir., CEO, Roger Kravtzoff/Preclinical, Early Clinical Development Dir., Rafael Jorda/COO, Exec. VP, Dir. - Manufacturing, Development, Sian Crouzet/Controller - Administrative, Financial Dir., Catherine Castan/Dir. - Research & Development Micropump, Head - Micropump Team, Katherine Hanras/Dir. - Analytical Department, Nigel McWilliam/Dir. - Business Development, USA, Kenneth Lundstrom/Dir. - Research, Christian Kalita/Chief Pharmacist, David Weber/Dir. - Purchasing Operations, Michel Finance/CFO, Exec. VP, Charles Marlio/Dir. - Strategic Planning, Investor Relations, Frederick Simonin/Marketing Analyst, Andrew Francis/VP - Business Development, Yves Bourboulou/Industrial Dir. *(21 Officers included in Index)*

Directors: Stephen H. Willard/Dir., CEO, Elie Vannier/Chmn., Cornelis Boonstra/Dir., Frederic Lemoine/Dir., John L. Vogelstein/Dir., Lodewijk J.R. De Vink/Dir.

Owners: Charles Mosseri-Marlio/0.24%, You Ping Chan/0.19%, Elie Vannier, Andrew Francis/0.53%, David Weber/0.19%, Knoll Capital Management, LP/8.80%, Remi Meyrueix/0.66%, Rafael Jorda/1.27%, Frdric Lemoine/0.20%, Katherine Hanras/0.16%, Greenlight Capital Management/6.44%, Lodewijk de Vink, Glenhill Advisors, LLC/4.97%, Yves Bourboulou/0.29%, Christian Kalita/0.22% *(26 Owners included in Index)*

Financial Data: Fiscal Year End:12/31 Latest Annual Data: 12/31/2006

Year	Sales	Net Income
2006	$23,020,000	-$35,201,000
2005	$23,598,000	-$27,377,000
2004	$55,410,000	$12,499,000

Curr. Assets:	$76,779,000	Curr. Liab.:	$21,314,000		
Plant, Equip.:	$25,705,000	Total Liab.:	$41,868,000	Indic. Yr. Divd.:	NA
Total Assets:	$114,894,000	Net Worth:	$73,026,000	Debt/ Equity:	NA

Flanders Corp

2399 26th Ave. N, St. Petersburg, FL, 33734; **PH:** 1-727-822-4411; **Fax:** 1-727-823-5510; **http://** www.flanderscorp.com; **Email:** customerservice@corp.precisionaire.com

General - Incorporation .... NC	Stock - Price on:12/24/2007 ....$7.34
Employees 3,067	Stock Exchange................................... NDQ
Auditor .... Pender Newkirk & Co	Ticker Symbol.................................... FLDR
Stk Agt ....OTC Stock Transfer, Inc.	Outstanding Shares 26,570,000
Counsel.. NA	E.P.S... -$0.91
DUNS No. 94-145-2237	Shareholders...................................... NA

Business: The group's principal activity is to design, manufacture and market air filters and related products. It provides complete environmental control systems for end uses ranging from controlling contaminants in residences and commercial office buildings through specialized manufacturing environments for semiconductors and pharmaceuticals. The group also produces glass-based air filter media. The products are utilized by industries, including those associated with commercial and residential heating, ventilation and air conditioning systems. It is also used in industries like semiconductor manufacturing, ultra-pure materials, biotechnology, pharmaceuticals, synthetics, nuclear power and nuclear materials processing. The major customers of the group are abbott laboratories, the home depot inc, motorola inc, merck & co inc, upjohn co, wal-Mart stores inc, westinghouse electric corp and several large computer chip manufacturers. The group operates only in United States.

Primary SIC and add'l.: 3569 3564 3599

CIK No: 0000799526

Subsidiaries: Global Containment Systems, Inc.

Officers: Steven K. Clark/54/CEO, Pres., John Hodson/44/CFO, James B. Mercer/60/VP - Operations

Directors: Robert R. Amerson/52/Chmn., David M. Mock/52/Dir., Peter Fredericks/45/Dir., Michael Steele/49/Dir., Harry L. Smith,/38/Dir., Kirk Dominick/41/Dir., Jeffrey G. Korn/51/Dir.

Owners: Insiders/37.48%, David Mock, Peter Fredericks, James L. Mercer, Atlas Master Fund, Ltd/5.09%, William D. Mitchum, Robert Kelly Barnhill, Heartland Advisors/11.16%, Robert R. Amerson/30.18%, Harry L. Smith/5.27%

Financial Data: Fiscal Year End:12/31 Latest Annual Data: 12/31/2006

Year	Sales	Net Income
2006	$238,378,000	$2,050,000
2005	$229,276,000	$12,506,000
2004	$199,933,000	$9,770,000

Curr. Assets:	$121,251,000	Curr. Liab.:	$53,284,000		
Plant, Equip.:	$77,349,000	Total Liab.:	$99,725,000	Indic. Yr. Divd.:	NA
Total Assets:	$207,104,000	Net Worth:	$107,379,000	Debt/ Equity:	0.3036

Flanigan's Enterprises Inc

5059 NE 18th Ave., Fort Lauderdale, FL, 33334; **PH:** 1-954-377-1961; **Fax:** 1-954-351-1245; **http://** www.flanigans.net; **Email:** rachel@flanigans.net

Fort Lauderdale, FL, 33334; *PH:* 1-954-377-1961; *Fax:* 1-954-351-1245; *http://* www.flanigans.net; *Email:* rachel@flanigans.net

General - Incorporation	FL	*Stock* - Price on:12/24/2007	$11.25
Employees	690	Stock Exchange	AMEX
Auditor	Rachlin Cohen & Holtz LLP	Ticker Symbol	BDL
Stk Agt	Registrar & Transfer Co	Outstanding Shares	1,890,000
Counsel	NA	E.P.S.	$0.50
DUNS No.	03-429-2268	Shareholders	NA

Business: The group's principal activities are to own and operate restaurants with lounges, package liquor stores and entertainment oriented units. It operates 16 units which include 7 restaurants, 4 combination package liquor store and restaurants and package stores, 4 package stores and 1 club and seven additional units which have been franchised. Restaurants provide efficient service of alcoholic beverages and full food service with abundant portions, reasonably priced, served in a relaxed, friendly and casual atmosphere. Package liquor stores emphasize high volume business by providing customers with a wide variety of brand name and private label merchandise at discount prices. The group's package liquor stores are operated under the servicemark big daddy's liquor and the restaurants are operated under the servicemark flanigan's seafood bar and grill.

Primary SIC and add'l.: 5813 6794 5921

CIK No: 0000012040

Subsidiaries: CIC Investors #13, Limited Partnership, CIC Investors #60, Limited Partnership, CIC Investors #65, Limited Partnership, CIC Investors #70, Limited Partnership, CIC Investors #75, Limited Partnership, CIC Investors #80, Limited Partnership, CIC Investors #95, Limited Partnership, Flanigans Enterprises, Inc. of Georgia, Flanigans Enterprises, Inc. of Pa., Flanigans Management Services, Inc., Seventh Street Corp.

Officers: James G. Flanigan/CEO, Compliance Officer, Pres., Jean Picard/VP - Package Operations, August Bucci/63/Dir., COO, Exec. VP, Jeffrey D. Kastner/General Counsel, Sec.

Directors: Germaine M. Bell/75/Dir., August Bucci/63/Dir., COO, Exec. VP, Patrick J. Flanigan/47/Dir., Barbara J. Kronk/42/Dir., Christopher O'Neil/42/Dir., Michael B. Flanigan/Dir., Michael Roberts/Dir.

Owners: James G. Flanigan, Robino Stortini Holdings LLC, Ann N. Flanigan, Insiders, Patrick J. Flanigan, Jeffrey D. Kastner, Michael B. Flanigan

Financial Data: Fiscal Year End:10/01   Latest Annual Data: 9/30/2006

Year	Sales		Net Income
2006	$55,014,000		$1,250,000
2005	$49,032,000		$1,107,000
2004	$45,933,000		$440,000
Curr. Assets:	$6,315,000	*Curr. Liab.:* $4,919,000	*P/E Ratio:* 22.50
Plant, Equip.:	$18,939,000	*Total Liab.:* $10,100,000	*Indic. Yr. Divd.:* NA
Total Assets:	$27,398,000	*Net Worth:* $10,792,000	*Debt/ Equity:* 0.5911

Flatbush Federal Bancorp Inc

2146 Nostrand Ave., Brooklyn, NY, 11210; *PH:* 1-718-859-6800; *Fax:* 1-718-421-3210; *http://* www.flatbush.com

General - Incorporation	Federal	*Stock* - Price on:12/24/2007	$7
Employees	40	Stock Exchange	OTC
Auditor	Beard Miller Co. LLP	Ticker Symbol	FLTB
Stk Agt	Registrar & Transfer Co	Outstanding Shares	2,760,000
Counsel	NA	E.P.S.	$0.18
DUNS No.	NA	Shareholders	NA

Business: The group's principal activity is to attract deposits from public and invest these deposits in loans and securities. The various types of loan are one- to four-family residential mortgage loans, commercial real estate loans, construction loans and loans guaranteed by the small business administration. The group's operates in brooklyn, queens and long island in New York.

Primary SIC and add'l.: 6035 6712

CIK No: 0001243496

Subsidiaries: Flatbush Federal Savings and Loan Association

Owners: Patricia A. McKinley, John D. Antoniello, John S. Lotardo, Flatbush Federal Bancorp, MHC/53.71%, Jesus R. Adia, Charles J. Vorbach, Alfred S. Pantaleone, Anthony J. Monteverdi/1.33%, Insiders/3.04%, John F. Antoniello

Financial Data: Fiscal Year End:12/31   Latest Annual Data: 12/31/2006

Year	Sales		Net Income
2006	$9,124,000		$195,000
2005	$7,919,000		$368,000
2004	$7,258,000		$278,000
Curr. Assets:	$4,744,000	*Curr. Liab.:* $136,128,000	*P/E Ratio:* 38.89
Plant, Equip.:	$2,902,000	*Total Liab.:* $139,336,000	*Indic. Yr. Divd.:* NA
Total Assets:	$154,382,000	*Net Worth:* $15,046,000	*Debt/ Equity:* NA

Fleetwood Enterprises Inc

3125 Myers St., Riverside, CA, 92503; *PH:* 1-951-351-3500; *Fax:* 1-951-351-3312; *http://* www.fleetwood.com

General - Incorporation	DA	*Stock* - Price on:12/24/2007	$9.53
Employees	11,500	Stock Exchange	NYSE
Auditor	Ernst & Young LLP	Ticker Symbol	FLE
Stk Agt	Computershare Investor Services LLC	Outstanding Shares	64,050,000
Counsel	Gibson, Dunn & Crutcher LLP	E.P.S.	-$1.13
DUNS No.	00-194-6979	Shareholders	NA

Business: The groups principle activity is to provide recreational vehicles and manufactured homes. The group operates from United States.

Primary SIC and add'l.: 9999 1531 6331 2451 2499 5271 3792

CIK No: 0000314132

Subsidiaries: C.V. Aluminum,Inc., Continental Lumber Products,Inc., Expression Homes Corporation, Fleetwood Canada Ltd., Fleetwood Capital Trust I, Fleetwood Folding Trailers,Inc., Fleetwood General Partner of Texas,Inc, Fleetwood Holdings,Inc., Fleetwood Holidays,Inc., Fleetwood Home Centers of Nevada,Inc., Fleetwood Home Centers of Texas,Inc., Fleetwood Homes Investment,Inc, Fleetwood Homes of Arizona,Inc., Fleetwood Homes of California,Inc., Fleetwood Homes of Florida,Inc. 78 Subsidiaries included in the Index

Officers: Elden L. Smith/Dir., CEO, Pres./$2,497,574.00, Kathy A. Munson/Dir. - Investor Relations, Boyd R. Plowman/CFO, Exec. VP/$1,149,530.00, Charles E. Lott/Pres. - Fleetwood Housing Group/$741,073.00, Andrew M. Griffiths/Chief Accounting Officer, Sr. VP, Larry L.

MacE/Pres. - Fleetwood Supply Group, Leonard J. McGill/Sr. VP, General Counsel, Sec./$545,352.00, Lyle N. Larkin/VP, Treasurer, Assist. Sec., Michael B. Shearin/Sr. VP - Human Resources, Administration, James F. Smith/VP, Controller - Operations, Paul C. Eskritt/Pres. - Fleetwood Recreational Vehicle Group/$569,010.00

Directors: Elden L. Smith/Dir., CEO, Pres., Thomas B. Pitcher/Chmn., James L. Doti/Dir., Daniel D. Villanueva/Dir., Loren K. Carroll/Dir., David S. Engelman/Dir., Paul D. Borghesani/Dir., Margaret S. Dano/Dir., Douglas M. Lawson/Dir., Michael J. Hagan/Dir., John T. Montford/Dir.

Owners: Paul C. Eskritt, James L. Doti, Leonard J. McGill, Columbia Wanger Asset Management, L.P./7.30%, David S. Engelman, John T. Montford, Paul D. Borghesani, Insiders/2.70%, Boyd R. Plowman, Michael J. Hagan, Wells Fargo& Company/16.10%, SLS Management, LLC/11.80%, First Pacific Advisors,Inc./13.10%, M.A.M Investments Ltd./6.90%, Elden L. Smith (22 Owners included in Index)

Financial Data) Fiscal Year End:04/30   Latest Annual Data: 04/29/2007

Year	Sales		Net Income
2007	$2,007,922,000		-$89,961,000
2006	$2,432,400,000		-$28,437,000
2005	$2,374,712,000		-$161,459,000
Curr. Assets:	$513,932,000	*Curr. Liab.:* $287,872,000	
Plant, Equip.:	$217,458,000	*Total Liab.:* $691,090,000	*Indic. Yr. Divd.:* NA
Total Assets:	$862,035,000	*Net Worth:* $170,945,000	*Debt/ Equity:* NA

Fleurs De Vie Inc

500 Domaine des Bois, Echenevex, 01170; *PH:* 33 4 50 42 62 32; *Fax:* 33 4 50 42 62 33; *http://* www.fleursdevie.com; *Email:* info@fleursdevie.com

General - Incorporation	NV	*Stock* - Price on:12/24/2007	$1.75
Employees	NA	Stock Exchange	OTC
Auditor	Malone & Bailey, PC	Ticker Symbol	FDVE
Stk Agt	Pacific Stock Transfer Company	Outstanding Shares	1,860,000
Counsel	NA	E.P.S.	-$0.02
DUNS No.	NA	Shareholders	NA

Business: The groups principle activity is to provide upscale custom floral design services and finished natural floral products to the general public. Services of the group include pre-event conferences and surveys with client, determining budget constraints and developing design schemes, pricing for custom designed and specified floral arrangements, developing coherent floral themes for events, preparing detailed pricing, production, delivery and placement of arrangements and accessories. The group operates from the United States.

Primary SIC and add'l.: 5992

CIK No: 0001341780

Officers: Harold A. Yount/54/Dir., CEO, CFO, Pres., Sec., Treasurer, Brenda P. Yount/52/VP

Directors: Harold A. Yount/54/Dir., CEO, CFO, Pres., Sec., Treasurer

Owners: Insiders, Brenda P. Yount, David M. Loev, Harold A. Yount

Financial Data: Fiscal Year End:12/31   Latest Annual Data: 12/31/2006

Year	Sales		Net Income
2006	$7,000		-$31,000
Curr. Assets:	$0	*Curr. Liab.:* $13,000	
Plant, Equip.:	NA	*Total Liab.:* $59,000	*Indic. Yr. Divd.:* NA
Total Assets:	$0	*Net Worth:* -$58,000	*Debt/ Equity:* NA

Flexible Solutions International Inc

615 Discovery St., Victoria, BC, V8T 5G4 ; *PH:* 1-250-477-9969; *http://* www.flexiblesolutions.com; *Email:* infowatersavr@flexiblesolutions.com

General - Incorporation	NV	*Stock* - Price on:12/24/2007	$3.04
Employees	26	Stock Exchange	AMEX
Auditor	Cinnamon, Jang, Willoughby & Co	Ticker Symbol	FSI
Stk Agt	Computershare Trust Co	Outstanding Shares	14,060,000
Counsel	Tatko Inc	E.P.S.	-$0.07
DUNS No.	NA	Shareholders	NA

Business: The group's principal activity is to develop, manufacture and market specialty chemicals and chemical dispensers, which slow down the evaporation of water. The group's products are heat$avr and water$avr. The heat$avr is used in swimming pools and spas that forms a thin, invisible layer on the surface of water which reduces the amount of water evaporation and heat loss from the pool. The heat$avr is marketed to residential market primarily in the form of tropical fish dispenser. Water$avr is used for water conservation in irrigation canals, aquaculture and reservoirs where its use slows down water loss due to evaporation. The products are marketed in Canada, the United States and Australia. On 09-Jun-2004, the group acquired assets of donlar corporation.

Primary SIC and add'l.: 2899

CIK No: 0001069394

Subsidiaries: Flexible Ltd

Officers: Daniel B. O'Brien/51/Dir., CEO - Principal Financial, Accounting Officer, Robert N. O'Brien/Dir., Chief Scientist, Grant Moonie/Contact - Pool Product Division, Jason Bloom/VP - Corporate Comm, Mike Stover/Contact - N America Sales, Marketing, Damera Fry/Contact - Accounting, David Verlee/Contact - Europe, Asia Sales, Marketing, Jill Sanden/Contact - Accounting

Directors: Daniel B. O'Brien/51/Dir., CEO - Principal Financial, Accounting Officer, Robert N. O'Brien/Dir., Chief Scientist, Dale Friend/51/Dir., Eric Hodges/59/Dir., John H. Bientjes/54/Dir.

Owners: Daniel B. OBrien/36.40%, John Bientjes/0.30%, Insiders/51.30%, Robert N. OBrien/14.60%

Financial Data: Fiscal Year End:12/31   Latest Annual Data: 12/31/2006

Year	Sales		Net Income
2006	$8,374,000		-$1,164,000
2005	$6,709,000		-$1,177,000
2004	$3,393,000		-$1,258,000
Curr. Assets:	$3,799,000	*Curr. Liab.:* $444,000	
Plant, Equip.:	$4,101,000	*Total Liab.:* $444,000	*Indic. Yr. Divd.:* NA
Total Assets:	$8,486,000	*Net Worth:* $8,042,000	*Debt/ Equity:* NA

Flexpoint Sensor Systems Inc

106 W 12200 S, Draper, UT, 84020; *PH:* 1-805-668-5111; *Fax:* 1-800-568-2405; *http://* www.flexpoint.com

General - Incorporation	DE	Stock- Price on:12/24/2007	$1.12
Employees	11	Stock Exchange	OTC
Auditor	Hansen, Barnett & Maxwell, P.C.	Ticker Symbol	FLXT
Stk Agt	Colonial Stock Transfer Co Inc	Outstanding Shares	23,290,000
Counsel	NA	E.P.S	-$0.09
DUNS No.	NA	Shareholders	NA

Business: The group is a development stage enterprise. The company designs, engineers and manufactures sensors and related equipment. The company currently markets proprietary patented sensor technology. The company became publicly held in Sept 1998. The group's quarterly revenue for Sep'07 was 0.01 millions of USD.

Primary SIC and add'l.: 8711

CIK No: 0000925660

Subsidiaries: Sensitron, Inc

Officers: Clark M. Mower/Dir., CEO, Pres.

Directors: Clark M. Mower/Dir., CEO, Pres., John A. Sindt/Chmn., Ruland J. Gill/Dir.

Owners: Clark M. Mower/3.80%, Fred B. Atkinson, Insiders/11.70%, Ruland J. Gill/1.00%, John A. Sindt/6.60%, First Equity Holdings Corp./24.70%

Financial Data: *Fiscal Year End:*12/31 *Latest Annual Data:* 12/31/2006

Year	Sales	Net Income
2006	$102,000	-$2,513,000
2005	$13,000	-$1,770,000
2004	$345,000	-$4,511,000

Curr. Assets:	$802,000	Curr. Liab.:	$48,000		
Plant, Equip.:	$1,076,000	Total Liab.:	$48,000	Indic. Yr. Divd.:	NA
Total Assets:	$8,792,000	Net Worth:	$8,744,000	Debt/ Equity:	NA

flexSCAN Inc

27201 Puerta Real Ste. 350, Mission Viejo, CA, 92691; *PH:* 1-949-609-1966;
http:// www.flexscan.com

General - Incorporation	NV	Stock- Price on:12/24/2007	NA
Employees	NA	Stock Exchange	OTC
Auditor	Rotenberg & Co., LLP	Ticker Symbol	FXSC
Stk Agt	OTC Stock Transfer, Inc.	Outstanding Shares	NA
Counsel	NA	E.P.S	-$0.28
DUNS No.	NA	Shareholders	NA

Business: The groups principle activity is to provide technical medical information management to the healthcare consumer. Customers of the group include marketers, advertisers, and researchers. The group operates from Nevada in the United States.

Primary SIC and add'l.: 8099

CIK No: 0000216593

Subsidiaries: FCA Acquisition Corp.

Officers: Thomas Banks/Chmn., CEO, Kenneth Westbrook/58/Dir., Pres.

Directors: Thomas Banks/Chmn., CEO, Kenneth Westbrook/58/Dir., Pres., Maurice J. Dewald/67/Dir., Jonathan C. Javitt/52/Dir.

Owners: Michael Cranford, Jeffrey C. Barbakow/36.30%, Kenneth Westbrook/2.70%, Heidi Patterson/18.30%, Insiders/55.80%, Francis X. Pisano/2.20%, Maurice J. DeWald, Thomas Banks/29.10%, Jonathan Javitt

Financial Data: *Fiscal Year End:*06/30 *Latest Annual Data:* 06/30/2006

Year	Sales	Net Income
2006	$135,000	-$9,878,000
2004	NA	-$8,000

Curr. Assets:	NA	Curr. Liab.:	$3,000		
Plant, Equip.:	NA	Total Liab.:	$3,000	Indic. Yr. Divd.:	NA
Total Assets:	NA	Net Worth:	-$3,000	Debt/ Equity:	NA

Flexsteel Industries Inc

PO Box 877, Dubuque, IA, 52004; *PH:* 1-563-556-7730; *Fax:* 1-563-556-8345;
http:// www.flexsteel.com

General - Incorporation	MN	Stock- Price on:12/24/2007	$14
Employees	2,400	Stock Exchange	NDQ
Auditor	Deloitte & Touche LLP	Ticker Symbol	FLXS
Stk Agt	Wells Fargo Shareowner Services	Outstanding Shares	6,570,000
Counsel	Irving C. Macdonal	E.P.S	$1.51
DUNS No.	00-514-6048	Shareholders	NA

Business: The group's principle activity is to design, manufacture and sell upholstered furniture and seating products for residential, commercial and recreational vehicle seating use. The group operates in two segments: seating products: manufactures a broad line of upholstered furniture for residential, recreational vehicle and commercial seating markets. The products are sold primarily throughout the United States by its internal sales force and various independent representatives. Retail stores: involves the operation of three retail furniture stores that offer the group's residential seating products for sale directly to consumers. The group's total revenue for the year 2007 was 425.40 millions of USD.

Primary SIC and add'l.: 2521 2512 2519 2599 2522 2531

CIK No: 0000037472

Subsidiaries: Desert Dreams, Inc, DMI Furniture, Inc

Officers: Ronald J. Klosterman/60/Dir., CEO, Pres., Donald D. Dreher/CEO, Pres. - DMI Furniture, Inc, Patrick M. Crahan/60/Dir., Sr. VP - Commercial Seating, James E. Gilbertson/58/VP - Vehicle Seating, Thomas D. Burkart/65/Sr. VP - Vehicle Seating, Timothy E. Hall/CFO, VP - Finance, Sec., Jeffrey T. Bertsch/53/Sr. VP, James R. Richardson/64/Dir., Sr. VP - Sales, Marketing, Charles P. Piekenbrock/Dir. - Retail Development

Directors: Ronald J. Klosterman/60/Dir., CEO, Pres., Bruce L. Boylen/76/Chmn., Patrick M. Crahan/60/Dir., Sr. VP - Commercial Seating, Mary C. Bottie/50/Dir., Thomas E. Holloran/79/Dir., Robert E. Deignan/69/Dir., James R. Richardson/64/Dir., Sr. VP - Sales, Marketing

Owners: Insiders/23.00%, Dimensional Fund Advisors, Inc./6.50%, Eric S. Rangen, Robert E. Deignan, Timothy E. Hall, Ronald J. Klosterman/1.90%, Thomas D. Burkart/1.70%, Bruce L. Boylen, Bruce K. Lauritsen/2.80%, Thomas E. Holloran, Patrick M. Crahan/2.60%, Donald D. Dreher, Towle & Co./5.00%, Lynn J. Davis, Jeffrey T. Bertsch/5.40% *(17 Owners included in Index)*

Financial Data: *Fiscal Year End:*06/30 *Latest Annual Data:* 06/30/2007

Year	Sales	Net Income
2007	$425,400,000	$9,334,000
2006	$426,408,000	$4,718,000
2005	$410,023,000	$6,044,000

Curr. Assets:	$145,387,000	Curr. Liab.:	$48,400,000	P/E Ratio:	18.42
Plant, Equip.:	$24,158,000	Total Liab.:	$75,823,000	Indic. Yr. Divd.:	$0.520
Total Assets:	$183,326,000	Net Worth:	$107,502,000	Debt/ Equity:	0.1972

Flextronics International Ltd

2090 Fortune Dr., San Jose, CA, 95131; *PH:* 1-408-576-7000; *Fax:* 1-408-576-7454;
http:// www.flextronics.com; *Email:* houstonsales@flextronics.com

General - Incorporation	Singapore	Stock- Price on:12/24/2007	$11.125
Employees	116,000	Stock Exchange	NDQ
Auditor	Deloitte & Touche LLP	Ticker Symbol	FLEX
Stk Agt	Computershare Investor Services LLC	Outstanding Shares	608,650,000
Counsel	Curtis Mallet-Prevost C & M LLP	E.P.S	$0.76
DUNS No.	59-524-0953	Shareholders	NA

Business: The group's principal's activity is the provision of electronics manufacturing services to original equipment manufacturers in the handheld electronics devices, information technologies infrastructure, communications infrastructure, computer and office automation, and consumer devices industries. It also provides a network of design, engineering and manufacturing operations in 28 countries across four continents. The company provides complete product design and technology services, logistics services, such as materials procurement, inventory management, vendor management. Packaging and distribution, and automation of key components of the supply chain through advanced information technologies. Operations are carried out in Singapore, the People's Republic of China, Malaysia, the United States of America, Mexico, Brazil, Sweden, Finland, France, Germany, Scotland, the United Kingdom, Austria, hungary and Ireland.

Primary SIC and add'l.: 3575 4812 3672 3577

CIK No: 0000866374

Subsidiaries: 2005878 Ontario Inc., Add Plus Precision Engineering Pte. Ltd., Astron Group Limited, Avnisoft Corporation, AvniSoft Systems Private Limited, Brady Industrial Hungary Kft., Charter Pacific Industries Ltd., Chatham International Holdings B.V., Chatham Technologies Do Brasil Ltda, Chatham Technologies Holding France S.A.S., Chemtech (UK)Ltd, DII Europe B.V., DII International Holdings B.V., Emuzed India PVT Ltd., Emuzed, Inc. 249 Subsidiaries included in the Index

Officers: Mike McNamara/Dir., CEO, Thomas J. Smach/CFO, Christopher Collier/Sr. VP - Finance, Principal Accounting Officer

Directors: Mike McNamara/Dir., CEO, Michael E. Marks/Chmn., Raymond H. Bingham/Dir., James A. Davidson/Dir., Ajay B. Shah/Dir., Richard L. Sharp/Dir., Ambassador Rockwell A. Schnabel/Dir., Lip-Bu Tan/Dir.

Owners: James A. Davidson, Entities associated with Capital Group International, Inc./6.86%, Raymond H. Bingham, Ajay B. Shah, Entities associated with Franklin Resources, Inc./6.02%, Werner Widmann, Nicholas E. Brathwaite, Peter Tan, Richard L. Sharp, Insiders/3.72%, Capital Research and Management Company/5.93%, Michael M. McNamara/1.13%, Wellington Management Company, LLP/5.98%, Michael E. Marks/1.59%, Entities associated with FMR Corp./11.46% *(19 Owners included in Index)*

Financial Data: *Fiscal Year End:*03/31 *Latest Annual Data:* 03/31/2007

Year	Sales	Net Income
2007	$18,853,688,000	$508,638,000
2006	$15,287,976,000	$141,162,000
2005	$15,908,223,000	$339,871,000

Curr. Assets:	$5,591,047,000	Curr. Liab.:	$4,488,068,000	P/E Ratio:	12.64
Plant, Equip.:	$1,998,706,000	Total Liab.:	$6,164,715,000	Indic. Yr. Divd.:	NA
Total Assets:	$12,341,374,000	Net Worth:	$6,176,659,000	Debt/ Equity:	0.2418

Flight Safety Technologies Inc

28 Cottrell St., Mystic, CT, 06355; *PH:* 1-860-245-0191; *Fax:* 1-860-437-4587;
http:// www.flysafetech.com

General - Incorporation	NV	Stock- Price on:12/24/2007	$1.7001
Employees	9	Stock Exchange	AMEX
Auditor	Wolf & Co. P.C	Ticker Symbol	FLT
Stk Agt	Pacific Stock Transfer Company	Outstanding Shares	8,220,000
Counsel	NA	E.P.S	-$0.359
DUNS No.	NA	Shareholders	NA

Business: The group's principle activity is to develop technologies to enhance aviation safety and reduce airport delays. The group is engaged in the development of two proprietary sensor technologies: socrates and unicorn. Socrates is designed to detect clear air turbulence, microbursts, and aircraft generated vortices, which result in hazardous conditions to safe air travel. Unicorn is a technology that is being designed based upon an arrangement of radar which gives both visual and audible warning indication of approaching aircraft to pilots. Since the group generated no additional revenues from providing staffing and production services, it discontinued these activities. The group's total revenue for the year 2007 was 1.55 millions of USD.

Primary SIC and add'l.: 7389

CIK No: 0001144879

Subsidiaries: Flight Safety Technologies Operating, Inc

Officers: Samuel A. Kovnat/Founder, Chmn., CEO, Pres./$199,750.00, William B. Cotton/Dir., Pres./$181,200.00, David D. Cryer/CFO, Treasurer, Sec., Robert C. Knight/VP - Administration, General Counsel, Neal E. Fine/Sr. VP - Technology, David C. Kring/Sr. Principal Engineer, Robert L. Cooperman/Sr. Principal Engineer, Robert Oneill/Program Mgr., Richard M. Williams/Consultant, Joseph L. Chovan/Consultant

Directors: Samuel A. Kovnat/Founder, Chmn., CEO, Pres., Jackson Kemper/Dir., Kenneth Wood/Dir., Frank L. Rees/Dir., Senator Larry Pressler/Dir., Joseph J. Luca/Dir., William B. Cotton/Dir., Pres., Wes Cummins/Dir., James A. Swartz/Dir.

Owners: Bryant R. Riley/11.72%, Robert C. Knight/1.78%, James A. Schwartz/2.55%, Larry L. Pressler/1.20%, Joseph J. Luca/1.32%, Frank L. Rees/6.97%, Kenneth S. Wood/1.32%, William B. Cotton/4.92%, David D. Cryer/1.81%, Wes Cummins/4.34%, Samuel A. Kovnat/7.17%, Insiders/35.37%, Jackson Kemper/1.99%

Financial Data: *Fiscal Year End:*05/31 *Latest Annual Data:* 5/31/2006

Year	Sales	Net Income
2006	$3,870,000	-$2,258,000
2005	$3,311,000	-$1,412,000
2004	$3,594,000	-$424,000

Curr. Assets:	$6,648,000	**Curr. Liab.:**	$832,000		
Plant, Equip.:	$182,000	**Total Liab.:**	$832,000	**Indic. Yr. Divd.:**	NA
Total Assets:	$7,157,000	**Net Worth:**	$6,325,000	**Debt/ Equity:**	NA

FLIR Systems Inc

27700A SW Pkwy. Ave., Wilsonville, OR, 97070; *PH:* 1-503-498-3547; *Fax:* 1-503-498-3904;
http:// www.flir.com

General - Incorporation ... OR
Employees ... 1,917
Auditor ... KPMG LLP
Stk Agt ... Mellon Investor Services LLC
Counsel ... Ater Wynne LLP
DUNS No. ... 09-129-6244

Stock- Price on:12/24/2007 ... $42.24
Stock Exchange ... NDQ
Ticker Symbol ... FLIR
Outstanding Shares ... 66,290,000
E.P.S ... $1.61
Shareholders ... NA

Business: The group's principal activities are to design, manufacture and market thermal imaging systems and infrared camera systems for a wide variety of applications in the commercial, industrial and government markets. The group operates in two segments: thermography and imaging. The thermography segment consists of a broad range of commercial and industrial applications utilizing infrared cameras to provide precise temperature measurement. The imaging segment offers a variety of products, which allow the user to see in total darkness and through obsurants such as smoke, haze and fog. The products of imaging segment include hand-held systems used for reconnaissance, surveillance and law enforcement and others.the major customers are dometic and foreign government agencies. The group operates in the United States, Canada and Europe. In 2003, the group acquired indigo systems corporation, a producer of infrared detectors and infrared camera subsystem and cameras.

Primary SIC and add'l.: 3829 3812

CIK No: 0000354908

Subsidiaries: FLIR Systems CV, FLIR Systems International Ltd., FLIR Systems Ltd, Indigo Systems Corporation., Scientific Materials Corporation

Officers: Earl R. Lewis/Chmn., CEO, Pres./$1,973,605.00

Directors: Earl R. Lewis/Chmn., CEO, Pres., William W. Crouch/Dir., Angus L. MacDonald/Dir., John D. Carter/Dir., John C. Hart/Dir., Michael T. Smith/Dir., Steven E. Wynne/Dir.

Owners: Angus L. Macdonald, William W. Crouch, EARNEST Partners, LLC/13.00%, Columbia Wanger Asset Management, L.P./5.80%, John C. Hart, Insiders/6.70%, Steven E. Wynne, FMR Corp./13.00%, John D. Carter, William A. Sundermeier, Andrew C. Teich, T. Rowe Price Associates, Inc./9.40%, Michael T. Smith, Stephen M. Bailey, Franklin Resources, Inc./9.90% *(17 Owners included in Index)*

Financial Data: *Fiscal Year End:*12/31 *Latest Annual Data:* 12/31/2006

Year	Sales	Net Income
2006	$575,000,000	$100,896,000
2005	$508,561,000	$90,765,000
2004	$482,651,000	$71,495,000

Curr. Assets:	$486,470,000	**Curr. Liab.:**	$170,373,000	**P/E Ratio:**	26.24
Plant, Equip.:	$92,156,000	**Total Liab.:**	$399,396,000	**Indic. Yr. Divd.:**	NA
Total Assets:	$798,148,000	**Net Worth:**	$398,752,000	**Debt/ Equity:**	0.4803

FLORIDA CMNTY BANKS

1400 N 15th St., Immokalee, FL, 34142; *PH:* 1-239-657-3171; *Fax:* 1-239-657-8482;
http:// www.floridacommunitybank.net

General - Incorporation ... FL
Employees ... 170
Auditor ... Schauer Taylor, PC
Stk Agt ... NA
Counsel ... NA
DUNS No. ... NA

Stock- Price on:12/24/2007 ... $33.5
Stock Exchange ... OTC
Ticker Symbol ... FLCM
Outstanding Shares ... 6,590,000
E.P.S ... $3.40
Shareholders ... NA

Business: The group's principle activity is to provide banking services. The group also provides personal, business and online banking services. The group's products include deposit accounts and loans. The group operates from United States.

Primary SIC and add'l.: 6022

CIK No: 0001170902

Officers: Stephen L. Price/Chmn., CEO, Pres./$671,800.00, Richard L. Bennett/62/Sr. VP, Larry T. Hall/67/Dir., Pres. - Labelle, Guy W. Harris/49/CFO, VP/$205,200.00, Raymond T. Holland/61/Sr. VP/$108,960.00, Robert K. Mays/50/Exec. VP, John G. Tamblyn/61/Dir., Pres. - Lee County/$165,385.00

Directors: Stephen L. Price/Chmn., CEO, Pres., Lewis J. Nobles/Dir., Beauford E. Davidson/Dir., James E. Williams/Dir., Daniel G. Rosbough/Dir., James W. O'Quinn/Dir., Patrick B. Langford/Dir., Jon R. Olliff/Dir., Kenneth J. Curtis/Dir. Emeritus, T. T. Knight/Dir. Emeritus, William G. Price/Dir. Emeritus, Robert A. Roberts/Dir. Emeritus, Larry T. Hall/67/Dir., Pres. - Labelle, John G. Tamblyn/61/Dir., Pres. - Lee County

Owners: Larry T. Hall, Raymond T. Holland, Stephen L. Price/3.39%, John G. Tamblyn, Insiders/23.35%, Guy W. Harris/2.71%

Financial Data: *Fiscal Year End:*12/31 *Latest Annual Data:* 12/31/2006

Year	Sales	Net Income
2006	$89,491,000	$23,146,000
2005	$61,702,000	$18,218,000
2004	$43,358,000	$12,242,000

Curr. Assets:	$27,252,000	**Curr. Liab.:**	$893,924,000	**P/E Ratio:**	9.85
Plant, Equip.:	$16,859,000	**Total Liab.:**	$926,111,000	**Indic. Yr. Divd.:**	$0.500
Total Assets:	$1,016,677,000	**Net Worth:**	$90,567,000	**Debt/ Equity:**	0.3247

Florida East Coast Industries Inc

One Malaga St., St Augustine, FL, 32084; *PH:* 1-904-396-6600; *Fax:* 1-651-738-4000;
http:// www.feci.com

General - Incorporation ... FL
Employees ... 1,053
Auditor ... KPMG LLP
Stk Agt ... Wachovia Bank N.A
Counsel ... Heidi J. Eddins
DUNS No. ... 61-194-0610

Stock- Price on:12/24/2007 ... $83.06
Stock Exchange ... NA
Ticker Symbol ... NA
Outstanding Shares ... 35,720,000
E.P.S ... $1.52
Shareholders ... NA

Business: The group's principal activity is to provide rail transportation services and real estate services. It operates through two segments: railway segment and realty segment. Through its subsidiary Florida east coast railway, llc provides freight transportation along the east coast of Florida between jacksonville and miami. The group also develops, manages, leases, operates and sells selected commercial and industrial properties, through it's subsidiary flagler development company.

Primary SIC and add'l.: 6517 6552 4011

CIK No: 0000740796

Subsidiaries: Beacon Station 22, 23 and 24 Limited Partnership, FDC Land Holdings, LLC, FEC Highway Services, Inc., Flagler Development Company, Flagler Development Realty, Inc., Flagler Transportation Services, Inc., Florida East Coast Deliveries, Inc., Florida East Coast Railway, LLC, Florida Express Logistics, Inc., GCC Beacon 22, 23 & 24, LLC, GCC Weston Office, Inc., Gran Central Deerwood North, LLC, Railroad Track Construction Corporation

Officers: Adolfo Henriques/Chmn., CEO, Pres., Armando Codina/Dir., Pres., CEO - Flagler Development Group, Mark A. Leininger/VP, Controller - Feci, Heidi J. Eddins/Exec. VP, Sec., General Counsel, Daniel H. Popky/CFO, Exec. VP, John D. McPherson/Exec. VP - Feci, Pres. - FEC Railway, Amy W. Bramlitt/VP, Controller, Bradley D. Lehan/VP, Treasurer - Feci, Jorge B. San Miguel/Exec. VP, Chief Investment Officer, Brian J. Nicholson/Dir. - Communications, Edward Manno Shumsky/Chief Human Resources Officer, Exec. VP

Directors: Adolfo Henriques/Chmn., CEO, Pres., Armando Codina/Dir., Pres., CEO - Flagler Development Group, Joseph Nemec/Dir., James E. Jordan/Dir., Gilbert H. Lamphere/Dir., Wellford L. Sanders/Dir., Jorge Perez/Dir., David M. Foster/Dir., Rosa Sugranes/Dir., George R. Zoffinger/Dir.

Financial Data: *Fiscal Year End:*12/31 *Latest Annual Data:* 12/31/2006

Year	Sales	Net Income
2006	$458,202,000	$63,119,000
2005	$362,346,000	$49,366,000
2004	$378,187,000	$80,598,000

Curr. Assets:	$79,040,000	**Curr. Liab.:**	$106,151,000	**P/E Ratio:**	54.64
Plant, Equip.:	$1,179,641,000	**Total Liab.:**	$676,019,000	**Indic. Yr. Divd.:**	$0.280
Total Assets:	$1,394,826,000	**Net Worth:**	$713,236,000	**Debt/ Equity:**	0.4844

Florida Gaming Corp

3500 NW 37th Ave., Miami, FL, 33142; *PH:* 1-305-633-6400; *Fax:* 1-305-638-1330;
http:// www.fla-gaming.com

General - Incorporation ... DE
Employees ... 63
Auditor ... King & Co. PSC
Stk Agt ... Continental Stock Transfer & Trust Co
Counsel ... NA
DUNS No. ... 08-453-1987

Stock- Price on:12/24/2007 ... $26.25
Stock Exchange ... OTC
Ticker Symbol ... FGMG
Outstanding Shares ... 3,340,000
E.P.S ... -$1.79
Shareholders ... NA

Business: The group's principal activity is to own and operate three jai-alai fronton and inter-track pari-mutuel wagering facilities located in south and central Florida. The term pari-mutuel wagering refers to the betting by the members of the public against each other. The group's operations include inter-track pari-mutuel wagering on jai-alai, horse racing, dog racing, sale of food and alcoholic beverages. Other operations of the group include owning and managing real estate.

Primary SIC and add'l.: 7948 5813

CIK No: 0000312065

Subsidiaries: Florida Gaming Centers, Inc., Tara Club Estates, Inc.

Officers: Bennett Collett/CEO, Bennett W. Collett/52/Chmn., CEO, W. B. Collett/Chmn., CEO, Stuart Neiman/Assist. GM, Corp Dir. - Marketing, Advirtising, David Dodd/Assist. GM, Mgr. - Mutuels, B. J. Moriatis/Office Mgr., Kimberly R. Tharp/50/CFO, Sec., Treasurer, Daniel Licciardi/Exec. VP, Michael Moriatis/Dir. - Security, Daniel Michelena/Dir. - Player Personnel, Luis Echaniz/Player's Mgr., Jackie Wilcher/Mgr. - Admissions, Boutique, Christian Cotabarren/Governor, Holly Benson/Sec. - Dept, Business, Prof Regulation, David J. Roberts/Dir. - Division, Pari, Mutuel Wagering *(17 Officers included in Index)*

Directors: Bennett W. Collett/52/Chmn., CEO, W. B. Collett/Chmn., CEO, William Haddon/76/Dir., Roland M. Howell/Dir., George Galloway/75/Dir.

Owners: Kimberly R. Tharp, Freedom Financial Corporation, Ramsey Asset, W. B. Collett, Roland M. Howell, Insiders, George W. Galloway, William C. Haddon, Daniel Licciardi, W. B. Collett

Financial Data: *Fiscal Year End:*12/31 *Latest Annual Data:* 12/31/2006

Year	Sales	Net Income
2006	$17,404,000	-$565,000
2005	$18,332,000	-$2,832,000
2004	$9,466,000	-$3,931,000

Curr. Assets:	$3,834,000	**Curr. Liab.:**	$3,476,000		
Plant, Equip.:	$9,697,000	**Total Liab.:**	$9,945,000	**Indic. Yr. Divd.:**	NA
Total Assets:	$14,227,000	**Net Worth:**	$4,282,000	**Debt/ Equity:**	1.7884

Florida Power & Light Co

700 Universe Blvd., Juno Beach, FL, 33408; *PH:* 1-561-694-4000; *Fax:* 1-561-694-4620;
http:// www.fpl.com

General - Incorporation ... FL
Employees ... 10,400
Auditor ... Deloitte & Touche LLP
Stk Agt ... Computershare Investor Services LLC
Counsel ... NA
DUNS No. ... 00-692-2371

Stock- Price on:12/24/2007 ... $59.3
Stock Exchange ... NA
Ticker Symbol ... NA
Outstanding Shares ... 406,420,000
E.P.S ... $3.38
Shareholders ... NA

Business: The group's principal activities are to generate, transmit, distribute and sell electric energy. The group is a wholly owned subsidiary of fpl group, inc. The group, through its 173 franchises, supplies electric service to various municipalities and counties in Florida. The group owns and operates four nuclear units, two at turkey point and two at st. Lucie.

Primary SIC and add'l.: 4911

CIK No: 0000037634

Subsidiaries: Bay Loan and Investment Bank, Florida Power & Light Company, FPL Energy, LLC, FPL Group Capital Inc, Palms Insurance Company, Limited

Officers: Armando J. Olivera/Pres., Michael L. Leighton/VP, Chief Development Officer, Paul W. Hamilton/VP - Governmental Affairs, State, James A. Keener/VP - Transmission, Substation, Dennis M. Klinger/VP - Information Management, Randall R. Labauve/VP - Environmental Services, Marlene M. Santos/VP - Customer Service, William G. Walker/VP - Regulatory Affairs, Al Alfonso/VP - Distribution

Financial Data: *Fiscal Year End:* 12/31 *Latest Annual Data:* 12/31/2006

Year	Sales		Net Income
2006	$15,710,000,000		$1,281,000,000
2005	$11,846,000,000		$885,000,000
2004	$10,522,000,000		$887,000,000
Curr. Assets:	$4,999,000,000	**Curr. Liab.:** $6,493,000,000	**P/E Ratio:** 20.03
Plant, Equip.:	$24,499,000,000	**Total Liab.:** $26,061,000,000	**Indic. Yr. Divd.:** $1.640
Total Assets:	$35,991,000,000	**Net Worth:** $9,930,000,000	**Debt/ Equity:** 0.9209

Florida Power Corp

299 First Ave. N, St. Petersburg, FL, 33701; *PH:* 1-727-820-5151; *Fax:* 1-727-384-7865; *http://* www.progress-energy.com

General - Incorporation	FL	**Stock** - Price on:12/24/2007	$75
Employees	NA	Stock Exchange	OTC
Auditor	Deloitte & Touche LLP	Ticker Symbol	FLPXM
Stk Agt..... Computershare Investor Services LLC		Outstanding Shares	NA
Counsel	NA	E.P.S	NA
DUNS No.	00-692-3700	Shareholders	NA

Business: The group's principle activities include generating, purchasing, transmiting, distributing and marketing electricity. The group provides services to approximately 1.5 million customers in west central Florida. The group is interconnected with 20 municipal and 9 rural electric cooperative systems. The group uses coal, gas, oil and nuclear fuel to generate electricity. Major customers of the group include seminole electric cooperative, inc, Florida municipal power agency, Florida power and light and tampa electric group. The group operates from United States.

Primary SIC and add'l.: 4911

CIK No: 0000037637

Subsidiaries: Carolina Power & Light Company d/b/a Progress Energy Carolinas, Inc., Florida Power Corporation d/b/a/ Progress Energy Florida, Inc., Florida Progress Corporation, Progress Capital Holdings, Inc., Progress Energy Service Company, LLC, Progress Fuels Corporation, Progress Telecom, LLC, Progress Telecommunications Corporation, Progress Ventures, Inc. d/b/a Progress Energy Ventures, Inc., PV Holdings, Inc., Strategic Resource Solutions Corp.

Officers: Jeffrey J. Lyash/Dir., Pres., CEO - Progress Energy Florida, Michael E. Williams/Sr. VP - Power Operations Progress Energy, Jeffrey M. Stone/46/Chief Accounting Officer, Joel Y. Kamya/VP - Progress Energy Florida, Robert H. Bazemore/VP - Progress Energy Florida, Peter M. Scott/58/CFO, Exec. VP, C. S. Hinnant/Sr. VP, Chief Nuclear Officer - Progress Energy Florida, Jeffrey A. Corbett/Dir., Sr. VP - Progress Energy Florida, Rodney E. Gaddy/VP - Progress Energy Florida, Laura M. Boisvert/VP - Progress Energy Florida, Robert F. Caldwell/VP - Regulated Commercial Operations - Progress Energy Florida, Mark Wimberly/VP - Progress Energy Florida, Dale J. Oliver/VP - Transmission Operations, Planning Progress Energy Florida, Joseph W. Donahue/VP - Progress Energy Florida, Mark A. Myers/VP - Corporate Planning - Progress Energy Florida Progress Energy *(20 Officers included in Index)*

Directors: Jeffrey J. Lyash/Dir., Pres., CEO - Progress Energy Florida, Robert B. McGehee/64/Chmn., Jeffrey A. Corbett/Dir., Sr. VP - Progress Energy Florida, William D. Johnson/54/Dir., Fred N. Day/64/Dir., John R. McArthur/52/Dir.

Florida Progress Corp

410 S Wilmington St., Raleigh, Raleigh, NC, 27601; *PH:* 1-919-546-6111; *http://* www.fpc.com

General - Incorporation	FL	**Stock** - Price on:12/24/2007	NA
Employees	NA	Stock Exchange	NYSE
Auditor	Deloitte & Touche LLP	Ticker Symbol	NA
Stk Agt..... Computershare Investor Services LLC		Outstanding Shares	NA
Counsel	NA	E.P.S	NA
DUNS No.	03-262-8596	Shareholders	NA

Business: The group's principle activities include generation, purchase, transmission, distribution and sale of electric energy. The electric fuels corpn operations include coal mining, procurement and transportation services to Florida power corpn and other external customers. Other diversified operations include activities in leveraged leasing, commercial finance, life insurance, real estate and technology development. The group operates from United States.

Primary SIC and add'l.: 6719 6311 6517 4911 4491

CIK No: 0000357261

Subsidiaries: Progress Fuels, Winchester Production Company, Ltd

Officers: Jeffrey J. Lyash/Pres., CEO - Progress Energy Florida, Michael A. Lewis/VP - Distribution Engineering - Operations Progress Energy Florida, Robert H. Bazemore/VP - Capital Planning, Jeffrey A. Corbett/Sr. VP - Energy Delivery Progress Energy Florida, Martha W. Barnwell/VP - North Coastal Region Progress Energy Florida, Tucker R. Mann/VP - Customer - Marketing Services Progress Energy Florida, David J. Maxon/VP - North Central Region Progress Energy Florida, Laura M. Boisvert/VP - South Central Region Progress Energy Florida, David Sorrick/VP - Power Generation, Mark Wimberly/VP - South Coastal Region, Joel Y. Kamya/VP - Plant Construction Progress Energy Florida, Dale E. Young/VP - Crystal River Nuclear Plant Progress Energy Florida, Paula Sims/Sr. VP - Power Operations, C. S. Hinnant/Sr. VP, Chief Nuclear Officer - Nuclear Generation, Mark A. Myers/VP - Corporate Planning Progress Energy Florida *(19 Officers included in Index)*

Directors: James E. Bostic/Dir.

Florida Public Utilities Co

401 S Dixie Hwy., West Palm Beach, FL, 33401; *PH:* 1-561-832-2461; *Fax:* 1-561-833-8562; *http://* www.fpuc.com; *Email:* centralflorida@fpuc.com

General - Incorporation	FL	**Stock** - Price on:12/24/2007	$12.03
Employees	351	Stock Exchange	AMEX
Auditor	BDO Seidman LLP	Ticker Symbol	FPU
Stk Agt ..... American Stock Transfer & Trust Co.		Outstanding Shares	6,030,000
Counsel	NA	E.P.S	$0.57
DUNS No.	00-692-4427	Shareholders	NA

Business: The group's principal activities are to purchase, transmit, distribute and sell electricity and natural gas. The group also distributes propane gas through a non-regulated subsidiary. The group operates in three segments namely electric, natural gas and a non-regulated segment, propane gas. It operates in five divisions namely, south Florida, central Florida, northwest Florida, northeast Florida and nature coast.

Primary SIC and add'l.: 4932 4941 4911

CIK No: 0000037643

Subsidiaries: Flo-Gas Corporation

Officers: John T. English/Chmn., CEO, Pres./$322,493.00, Charles L. Stein/58/COO, Sr. VP/$320,213.00, George M. Bachman/CFO, Treasurer, Sec./$240,810.00, Ellen Terry Benoit/Dir. - Investor

Directors: John T. English/Chmn., CEO, Pres., Paul L. Maddock/Dir., Troy W. Maschmeyer/Dir., Richard C. Hitchins/Dir., Ellen Terry Benoit/Dir. - Investor, Dennis S. Hudson/Dir.

Owners: Paul L. Maddock, Troy W. Maschmeyer, Dennis S. Hudson, Ellen Terry Benoit/3.55%, George M. Bachman, Richard C. Hitchins, Charles L. Stein, Insiders/5.28%, Gabelli Funds Inc. et al/9.94%, John T. English, Atlee M. Kohl/5.34%, Wachovia Corporation/5.05%

Financial Data: *Fiscal Year End:* 12/31 *Latest Annual Data:* 12/31/2006

Year	Sales		Net Income
2006	$134,393,000		$4,169,000
2005	$130,023,000		$4,248,000
2004	$110,039,000		$3,594,000
Curr. Assets:	$20,151,000	**Curr. Liab.:** $33,097,000	**P/E Ratio:** 19.40
Plant, Equip.:	$129,211,000	**Total Liab.:** $132,741,000	**Indic. Yr. Divd.:** $0.450
Total Assets:	$180,913,000	**Net Worth:** $48,172,000	**Debt/ Equity:** NA

Florida Rock Industries Inc

155 E 21st St., Jacksonville, FL, 32206; *PH:* 1-904-355-1781; *Fax:* 1-904-355-0817; *http://* www.flarock.com

General - Incorporation	FL	**Stock** - Price on:12/24/2007	$68.73
Employees	3,464	Stock Exchange	NA
Auditor	KPMG LLP	Ticker Symbol	NA
Stk Agt ..... American Stock Transfer & Trust Co.		Outstanding Shares	65,950,000
Counsel	Lewis S. Lee	E.P.S	$2.73
DUNS No.	00-985-7855	Shareholders	NA

Business: The group's principal activities are to provide basic construction materials. The group has three business segments: construction aggregates, concrete products and cement and calcium products. The construction aggregates segment is engaged in the mining, processing, distribution and sale of sand, gravel and crushed stone. The concrete products segment produces and sells ready mix concrete, concrete block, prestressed concrete and other building materials. The cement and calcium products segment is in the sale of portland and masonry cement, calcium products and importation of cement and slag. Substantially all operations are conducted in Florida, Virginia, Georgia, Maryland, Washington dc, Tennessee, North Carolina and Delaware. The group also has operations in new brunswick, Canada.

Primary SIC and add'l.: 3273 4731 1429 1442 3271

CIK No: 0000037651

Subsidiaries: Administration & Accounting Co., American Materials Technologies LLC, ARL Development Corp., ARL Services Inc., Arundel Risk Managers, Inc., Arundel Sand & Gravel Company, Atlantic Coast Materials, LLC, BWIP, Inc., Charlotte County Ports, LTD, Chesapeake Marine, Columbus Quarry LLC, Concrete Engineering Inc., D C Materials, Inc., Flacem, LLC., Florida Cement, Inc. 40 Subsidiaries included in the Index

Officers: John D. Milton/63/Dir., Exec. VP, Treasurer, CFO, Wallace A. Patzke/61/VP, Controller, Chief Accounting Officer, H. W. Walton/63/VP - Environmental, Safety, Health, Organizational Development, John W. Green/56/Assist. Sec., Scott L. McCaleb/56/VP - Corporate Development, Clarron E. Render/66/Pres. - Northern Concrete Group, John D. Baker/60/Dir., Pres., Chief, Executive Officer, Thompson S. Baker/50/Dir., Pres. - Aggregates Group, George J. Hossenlopp/65/VP, Michael P. Oates/48/VP - Human Resources, Barbara C. Johnston/55/Sec., General Counsel

Directors: Edward L. Baker/73/Chmn., John D. Milton/63/Dir., Exec. VP, Treasurer, CFO, John A. Delaney/52/Dir., Dix J. Druce/61/Dir., William P. Foley/63/Dir., William H. Walton/56/Dir., A. R. Carpenter/66/Dir., John D. Baker/60/Dir., Pres., Chief, Executive Officer, Thompson S. Baker/50/Dir., Pres. - Aggregates Group, Luke E. Fichthorn/67/Dir., Francis X. Knott/63/Dir.

Owners: Baker Holdings, L.P./16.70%, Luke E. Fichthorn, Thompson S. Baker, Dix J. Druce, Edward L. Baker/2.00%, John A. Delaney, John D. Milton, William P. Foley, Clarron E. Render, Francis X. Knott, Cynthia L. Baker Trust, John D. Baker/21.90%, A. R. Carpenter, Insiders/25.35%, William H. Walton

Financial Data: *Fiscal Year End:* 09/30 *Latest Annual Data:* 9/30/2006

Year	Sales		Net Income
2006	$1,367,789,000		$211,409,000
2005	$1,153,452,000		$157,653,000
2004	$948,519,000		$113,670,000
Curr. Assets:	$305,191,000	**Curr. Liab.:** $151,266,000	**P/E Ratio:** 25.18
Plant, Equip.:	$698,199,000	**Total Liab.:** $320,364,000	**Indic. Yr. Divd.:** $0.600
Total Assets:	$1,236,260,000	**Net Worth:** $915,896,000	**Debt/ Equity:** NA

Flotek Industries Inc

7030 Empire Central Dr., Houston, TX, 77040; *PH:* 1-713-849-9911; *Fax:* 1-713-896-4511; *http://* www.flotekind.com

General - Incorporation	DE	**Stock** - Price on:12/24/2007	$59.63
Employees	246	Stock Exchange	AMEX
Auditor	UHY LLP	Ticker Symbol	FTK
Stk Agt ..... Pacific Corporate Trust Co		Outstanding Shares	9,080,000
Counsel	NA	E.P.S	$0.91
DUNS No.	24-980-6381	Shareholders	NA

Business: The group operates through its subsidiaries whose principle activities include developing, manufacturing, packaging and selling chemicals used in oil and gas well cementing, stimulation and production, designs and manufactures specialized cementing equipment, and manufactures and markets downhole pump components, and provides patented and proprietary manufactured goods and services to organizations engaged in energy exploration, development, processing and transportation of related products. The group operates from United States.

Primary SIC and add'l.: 1389 2899 6719 3561

CIK No: 0000928054

Subsidiaries: CESI Chemical, Inc, Equipment Specialties, Inc., Esses, Inc., Flotek Paymaster, Inc., Harmon Machine Works, Inc, Material Translogistics, Inc., Padko International, Inc., Petrovalve Intl (Barbados), Inc, Petrovalve International, Inc, Petrovalve, Inc., Plainsman Technology, Inc., Spidle Sales & Services, Inc, Trinity Tool, Inc., Turbeco, Inc., USA Petrovalve, Inc.

Officers: Jerry D. Dumas/72/Chmn., CEO, Pres., Lisa B. Meier/35/CFO, VP, Rosalie Melia/Corp. Sec.

Directors: Jerry D. Dumas/72/Chmn., CEO, Pres., Glenn S. Penny/Dir., William R. Ziegler/Dir., Gary M. Pittman/Dir., John W. Chisholm/Dir., Richard O. Wilson/Dir., Barry S. Stewart/Dir.

Owners: William R. Ziegler/3.70%, John W. Chisholm/2.30%, Jerry D. Dumas/4.90%, Gary M. Pittman/1.10%, Barry E. Stewart, Millenco, L.L.C./5.90%, Insiders/13.30%, Richard R. Wilson, TOSI, LP/8.20%, Lisa G. Meier, Palo Alto Investors, LLC/13.10%

Financial Data: *Fiscal Year End:*12/31 *Latest Annual Data:* 12/31/2006

Year	Sales	Net Income
2006	$100,642,000	$11,350,000
2005	$52,869,000	$7,720,000
2004	$21,881,000	$2,154,000

Curr. Assets:	$38,064,000	**Curr. Liab.:**	$20,662,000	**P/E Ratio:**	70.99
Plant, Equip.:	$19,302,000	**Total Liab.:**	$29,381,000	**Indic. Yr. Divd.:**	NA
Total Assets:	$82,890,000	**Net Worth:**	$53,509,000	**Debt/ Equity:**	0.7220

Flow International Corp

23500 64th Ave. S, Kent, WA, 98032; ***PH:*** 1-253-850-3500; ***Fax:*** 1-253-813-9377; ***http://*** www.flowcorp.com; ***Email:*** info@flowcorp.com

General		**Stock**	
Incorporation	WA	Price on:12/24/2007	$12.76
Employees	688	Stock Exchange	NDQ
Auditor	Deloitte & Touche LLP	Ticker Symbol	FLOW
Stk Agt	Mellon Investor Services LLC	Outstanding Shares	37,270,000
Counsel	Preston Gates & Ellis	E.P.S	$0.04
DUNS No.	05-406-5057	Shareholders	NA

Business: The group's principal activities are to design, develop, manufacture, market, install and service ultrahigh-pressure (uhp) products, water-jet cutting, cleaning systems and specialized robotics systems. These products are used to cut both metallic and nonmetallic materials in many industry segments, which include aerospace, automotive, disposable products, food, glass, job shop, sign, metal cutting, marble, tile and other stone cutting and paper industries. The group also manufactures robotics articulation equipment used in the cutting and cleaning processes. It also provides isostatic and flexform presses to the automotive, aerospace and medical industries. It operates mainly in the United States, Europe and Asia. The primary manufacturing facilities are located in kent and Washington. The group discontinued the operations of decommissioning of oil wells in fiscal 2004.

Primary SIC and add'l.: 3569 7359

CIK No: 0000713002

Subsidiaries: Caitra Technologies Incorporated, CIS Acquisition Corporation, Flow Asia Corporation, Flow Asia International Corporation, Flow Automation Systems Corporation, Flow Europe, GmbH, Flow Holdings GmbH (SAGL) Limited Liability Company, Flow Iberica, S.R.L., Flow Italia, S.R.L., Flow Japan Corporation, Flow Korea Corporation, Flow Latino Americana Comercio Ltda., Flow Surface Prep/Europe, SAGL, Flow U.K., Ltd., Flow Ultra High Pressure Waterjet Technology (Shanghai) Co., Ltd. 18 Subsidiaries included in the Index

Officers: Charles M. Brown/49/CEO, Pres., Karen A. Carter/43/VP - Global Operations, Jeffrey L. Hohman/54/Exec. VP, GM, Scott G. Rollins/44/CIO, Theresa F. Treat/51/VP - Human Resources

Directors: Charles M. Brown/49/CEO, Pres., Jerry L. Calhoun/64/Dir.

Owners: Thomas C. Johnson, Lorenzo C. Lamadrid, Arlen I. Prentice, Richard A. LeBlanc, Richard P. Fox, Jan K. Ver Hagen, Michael J. Ribaudo, Insiders/5.30%, Jeffery Hohman, Jerry L. Calhoun, Rainier Investment Management, Inc/6.45%, Stephen R. Light/2.20%, Douglas P. Fletcher, Kathryn L. Munro, Third Point LLC/14.70%

Financial Data: *Fiscal Year End:*04/30 *Latest Annual Data:* 04/30/2007

Year	Sales	Net Income
2007	$217,279,000	$3,670,000
2006	$205,432,000	$7,410,000
2005	$172,966,000	-$21,197,000

Curr. Assets:	$100,042,000	**Curr. Liab.:**	$57,638,000	**P/E Ratio:**	31.90
Plant, Equip.:	$11,085,000	**Total Liab.:**	$62,128,000	**Indic. Yr. Divd.:**	NA
Total Assets:	$119,268,000	**Net Worth:**	$57,140,000	**Debt/ Equity:**	0.0427

Flowers Foods Inc

1919 Flowers Cir., Thomasville, GA, 31757; ***PH:*** 1-229-226-9110; ***Fax:*** 1-229-225-3806; ***http://*** www.flowersfoods.com

General		**Stock**	
Incorporation	GA	Price on:12/24/2007	$33.75
Employees	7,800	Stock Exchange	NYSE
Auditor	PricewaterhouseCoopers LLP	Ticker Symbol	FLO
Stk Agt	SunTrust Bank	Outstanding Shares	60,840,000
Counsel	NA	E.P.S	$0.97
DUNS No.	NA	Shareholders	NA

Business: The groups principle activities include producing and marketing bakery products. The groups products include breads, buns, rolls, snack cakes and pastries. The groups products are sold under the brand names Flowers, Nature's Own, Whitewheat, Cobblestone Mill, Captain John Derst and Dandee. The group operates from United States.

Primary SIC and add'l.: 2038 5461 2053 2052 2051

CIK No: 0001128928

Subsidiaries: Austin Baking Co., LLC, Bailey Street Bakery, LLC, Corpus Christi Baking Co., LLC, Derst Baking Company, LLC, El Paso Baking Company de Mexico, S.A. de C. V., Flowers Bakeries Brands, Inc., Flowers Bakery of Atlanta, LLC, Flowers Bakery of Cleveland, LLC, Flowers Bakery of Crossville, LLC, Flowers Bakery of Fort Smith, LLC, Flowers Bakery of London, LLC, Flowers Bakery of Montgomery, LLC, Flowers Bakery of Suwanee, LLC, Flowers Bakery of Texarkana, LLC, Flowers Bakery of Winston-Salem, LLC 66 Subsidiaries included in the Index

Officers: George E. Deese/62/Chmn., CEO, Pres./$3,271,350.00, Mary Krier/VP - Communications, Stephen R. Avera/52/Sr. VP, Sec., General Counsel/$887,315.00, Allen L. Shiver/52/COO, Pres./$1,005,988.00, Marta Jones Turner/54/Sr. VP - Corporate Relations, Gene D. Lord/60/COO, Pres./$1,105,607.00, Jimmy M. Woodward/47/CFO, Sr. VP/$1,085,754.00, Michael A. Beaty/57/Sr. VP - Supply Chain, Lisa R. Hay/Shareholder Relations Specialist, Steve R. Kinsey/47/CFO, Sr. VP

Directors: George E. Deese/62/Chmn., CEO, Pres., Melvin T. Stith/62/Dir., Benjamin H. Griswold/69/Dir., Jackie M. Ward/70/Dir., Franklin L. Burke/67/Dir., Joe E. Beverly/67/Dir., Joseph L. Lanier/76/Dir., Manuel A. Fernandez/62/Dir., Amos R. McMullian/71/Dir., J. V. Shields/70/Dir., Martin C. Wood/65/Dir.

Owners: J. V. Shields/7.51%, Amos R. McMullian/2.45%, Joseph L. Lanier, Melvin T. Stith, Jackie M. Ward, Gene D. Lord, Benjamin H. Griswold, Jimmy M. Woodward, Gabelli Asset Management, Inc./5.14%, Franklin L. Burke, Martin C. Wood/3.81%, Manuel A. Fernandez, George E. Deese/1.10%, Insiders/15.92%, Allen L. Shiver *(17 Owners included in Index)*

Financial Data: *Fiscal Year End:*12/31 *Latest Annual Data:* 12/30/2006

Year	Sales	Net Income
2006	$1,888,654,000	$81,043,000
2005	$1,715,869,000	$61,231,000

Curr. Assets:	$237,570,000	**Curr. Liab.:**	$174,275,000	**P/E Ratio:**	23.94
Plant, Equip.:	$468,303,000	**Total Liab.:**	$334,135,000	**Indic. Yr. Divd.:**	$0.500
Total Assets:	$851,069,000	**Net Worth:**	$512,371,000	**Debt/ Equity:**	0.0887

Flowserve Corp

5215 N O'Connor Blvd., Ste. 2300, Irving, TX, 75039; ***PH:*** 1-972-443-6500; ***Fax:*** 1-972-443-6800; ***http://*** www.flowserve.com

General		**Stock**	
Incorporation	NY	Price on:12/24/2007	$72.06
Employees	14,000	Stock Exchange	NYSE
Auditor	PricewaterhouseCoopers LLP	Ticker Symbol	FLS
Stk Agt	National City Bank	Outstanding Shares	57,050,000
Counsel	NA	E.P.S	$2.82
DUNS No.	NA	Shareholders	NA

Business: The groups principle activities include manufacturing and aftermarket servicing of flow control systems. The group operates through three segments namely, flowserve pump, flow control and flow solutions. In the year 2006, the group acquired Canada Alloy Castings. The group operates from the United States and Canada. The group's quarterly revenue for September 2007 was 919.25 millions of USD.

Primary SIC and add'l.: 3491 3594 3432 3492 3494 3499 3593

CIK No: 0000030625

Subsidiaries: Arabian Seals Company, Ltd., Argus GmbH & Co. K.G., Audco India Ltd., Audco Italiana Srl, Audco Limited, BW/IP New Mexico, Inc., Deutsche Ingersoll-Dresser Pumpen GmbH, Ebara-Byron Jackson, Ltd., Fabromatic B.V., Flowcom Insurance Company, Inc., Flowserve Al Mansoori Services Company, Ltd., Flowserve (Austria) GmbH, Flowserve (Mauritius) Corporation, Flowserve (Thailand) Limited, Flowserve Abahsain Co. Ltd. 112 Subsidiaries included in the Index

Officers: Lewis M. Kling/Dir., CEO, Pres./$6,850,839.00, Andrew J. Beall/Pres. - Flow Solutions Division, Sr. VP, Deborah K. Bethune/VP - Tax, Mark A. Blinn/44/CFO, Sr. VP/$2,376,174.00, Mark D. Dailey/Sr. VP - Human Resources, Chief Compliance Officer, Paul W. Fehlman/VP, Treasurer, Thomas E. Ferguson/Pres. - Flowserve Pump Division, Sr. VP/$2,217,185.00, Richard J. Guiltinan/VP, Chief Accounting Officer, Linda P. Jojo/CIO, Sr. VP, Thomas L. Pajonas/Pres. - Flow Control Division, Sr. VP/$2,104,908.00, Jerry L. Rockstroh/Sr. VP - Supply Chain, Continuous Improvement, Ronald F. Shuff/Sr. VP, Sec., General Counsel/$2,116,302.00

Directors: Lewis M. Kling/Dir., CEO, Pres., Kevin E. Sheehan/Chmn., Christopher A. Bartlett/Dir., John R. Friedery/Dir., Rick J. Mills/Dir., Charles M. Rampacek/Dir., Diane C. Harris/Dir., Michael F. Johnston/Dir., James O. Rollans/Dir., William C. Rusnack/Dir., Roger L. Fix/Dir., Joe E. Harlan/Dir.

Owners: Kevin E. Sheehan, Diane C. Harris, Mark A. Blinn, Charles M. Rampacek, Ronald F. Shuff, Hugh K. Coble, George T. Haymaker, Hotchkis and Wiley Capital Management, LLC/14.27%, Christopher A. Bartlett, Thomas E. Ferguson, William C. Rusnack, Lewis M. Kling, Roger L. Fix, Thomas L. Pajonas, GAMCO Investors, Inc./7.74% *(19 Owners included in Index)*

Financial Data: *Fiscal Year End:*12/31 *Latest Annual Data:* 12/31/2006

Year	Sales	Net Income
2006	$3,061,063,000	$115,032,000
2005	$2,695,277,000	$11,835,000
2004	$2,638,199,000	$24,200,000

Curr. Assets:	$1,302,881,000	**Curr. Liab.:**	$884,036,000	**P/E Ratio:**	31.47
Plant, Equip.:	$442,892,000	**Total Liab.:**	$1,848,649,000	**Indic. Yr. Divd.:**	$0.600
Total Assets:	$2,869,235,000	**Net Worth:**	$1,020,586,000	**Debt/ Equity:**	0.5478

Fluor Corp

6700 Las Colinas Blvd., Irving, TX, 75039; ***PH:*** 1-469-398-7000; ***Fax:*** 1-469-398-7255; ***http://*** www.fluor.com

General		**Stock**	
Incorporation	DE	Price on:12/24/2007	$106.21
Employees	37,560	Stock Exchange	NYSE
Auditor	Ernst & Young LLP	Ticker Symbol	FLR
Stk Agt	Mellon Investor Services LLC	Outstanding Shares	88,180,000
Counsel	NA	E.P.S	$3.92
DUNS No.	NA	Shareholders	NA

Business: The groups principle activity is to provide professional services on a global basis in the fields of engineering, procurement, construction and maintenance. The group operates through five segments namely oil and gas, industrial and infrastructure, government, global services and power. The group operates from United States and Canada.

Primary SIC and add'l.: 6719 8712 8748 8742 8741 4911 9199

CIK No: 0001124198

Subsidiaries: ADP Marshall Contractors, nc., ADP Marshall Lmted, ADP/FD of Neada, nc., alley Corrdor Constructors, alley nfrastructure Group, LLC, Alutq Federal Serces Lmted Lablty Company, Alutq-Fluor Constructors, LLC, Ambt Technology Lmted, AMECO Carbbean, nc., Ameco Chle S.A, AMECO Holdngs, nc., Ameco Mexco Admnstracon y Sercos, S. de R.L. de C., Ameco Mnng Serces S.R.L, Ameco Peru S.A.C, AMECO Project Serces, nc. 376 Subsidiaries included in the Index

Officers: Alan L. Boeckmann/Chmn., CEO/$10,746,300.00, Dwayne Wilson/Pres., Wendy Hallgren/VP - Corporate Compliance, Kent Smith/Sr. VP - Business Development, Robert J. Fluor/VP - Global Public Affairs, Jeff L. Faulk/Sr. Group Pres. - Overseeing/$1,552,622.00, Lawrence N. Fisher/Chief Legal Officer - Law/$2,823,429.00, Kenneth H. Lockwood/VP - Corporate Finance, Investor Relations, John L. Hopkins/Group Pres., Stephen B. Dobbs/Sr. Group Pres., Ken Oscar/Contact - Sales, David Durham/Contact - Sales Department, Energy, David Seaton/Group Pres. - Energy, Chemicals, Greg Meyer/Contact - Sales, Keith Stephens/Contact - Media *(25 Officers included in Index)*

Directors: Alan L. Boeckmann/Chmn., CEO, James T. Hackett/Dir., Peter J. Fluor/Dir., Joseph Wilson Prueher/Dir., Vilma S. Martinez/Dir., Dean R. OHare/Dir., Robin W. Renwick/Dir., Peter S. Watson/Dir., Suzanne H. Woolsey/Dir., Ilesanmi Adesida/Dir., Peter K. Barker/Dir., Kent Kresa/Dir.

Owners: Joseph W. Prueher, Peter S. Watson, Jeffery L. Faulk, Alan L. Boeckmann, Vilma S. Martinez, Capital Group International, Inc. and related entities/15.20%, Insiders/0.90%, Robin W. Renwick, AXA Financial,Inc. and related entities/6.20%, Dean R. OHare, Michael D. Steuert, Steven H. Gilbert, James T. Hackett, Suzanne H. Woolsey, Peter J. Fluor *(19 Owners included in Index)*

Financial Data: *Fiscal Year End:*12/31 *Latest Annual Data:* 12/31/2006

Year	Sales		Net Income
2006	$14,078,506,000		$263,452,000
2005	$13,161,051,000		$227,273,000
2004	$9,380,277,000		$186,695,000

Curr. Assets:	$3,323,586,000	**Curr. Liab.:**	$2,406,267,000	**P/E Ratio:**	36.62
Plant, Equip.:	$692,126,000	**Total Liab.:**	$3,144,398,000	**Indic. Yr. Divd.:**	$0.800
Total Assets:	$4,874,870,000	**Net Worth:**	$1,730,472,000	**Debt/ Equity:**	0.1206

Flushing Financial Corp

1979 Marcus Ave., Ste. E140, Lake Success, NY, 11042; ***PH:*** 1-718-961-5400; ***http://*** www.flushingsavings.com

General - Incorporation	DE	**Stock**- Price on:12/24/2007	$16.04
Employees	260	Stock Exchange	NDQ
Auditor	PricewaterhouseCoopers LLP	Ticker Symbol	FFIC
Stk Agt	Computershare Trust Co	Outstanding Shares	21,120,000
Counsel	Hughes Hubbard & Reed LLP	E.P.S	$1.06
DUNS No.	93-028-5895	Shareholders	NA

Business: The group's principal activity is to provide general banking services in the New York city. The group accepts retail deposits from the general public and invests the same in origination and purchases of residential mortgage loans, property loans, commercial real estate loans, government securities and other marketable securities. The group also originates co-operative apartment loans, small business administration loans and construction and consumer loans. Investments include the United States government and federal agency securities, corporate fixed income securities and other marketable securities. The group operates through 10 offices in the New York city.

Primary SIC and add'l.: 6035 6712

CIK No: 0000923139

Subsidiaries: Flushing Financial Capital Trust I, Flushing Preferred Funding Corporation, Flushing Savings Bank, Flushing Service Corporation., FSB Properties, Inc.

Officers: John R. Buran/Dir., CEO, Pres./$1,153,660.00, David W. Fry/CFO, Sr. VP, Treasurer/$386,184.00, Francis W. Korzekwinski/Exec. VP, Chief - Real Estate Lending/$410,439.00, Henry A. Braun/Sr. VP/$460,268.00, Maria A. Grasso/COO, Exec. VP, Theresa Kelly/Sr. VP, Ronald Hartmann/Sr. VP, Chris Hwang/Sr. VP, A. J. Jin/Sr. VP, Jeoung Jin/41/Sr. VP, Dir. - Asian Markets

Directors: John R. Buran/Dir., CEO, Pres., Gerard P. Tully/Chmn., Jeoung Jin/41/Sr. VP, Dir. - Asian Markets

Owners: Donna M. OBrien/0.08%, Henry A. Braun/0.46%, Louis C. Grassi/0.40%, Gerard P. Tully/1.47%, James D. Bennett/0.48%, Janus Capital Management LLC/6.30%, John E. Roe, Insiders/11.27%, Steven J. DIorio/0.08%, Michael J. Russo/1.19%, Robert L. Callicutt/0.13%, David W. Fry/0.19%, John R. Buran/1.31%, Francis W. Korzekwinski/0.44%, Thomson Horstmann& Bryant, Inc/5.80% *(21 Owners included in Index)*

Financial Data: *Fiscal Year End:*12/31 *Latest Annual Data:* 12/31/2006

Year	Sales		Net Income
2006	$168,179,000		$21,639,000
2005	$139,733,000		$23,542,000
2004	$124,767,000		$22,649,000

Curr. Assets:	$42,583,000	**Curr. Liab.:**	$1,968,295,000	**P/E Ratio:**	15.57
Plant, Equip.:	$23,042,000	**Total Liab.:**	$2,618,106,000	**Indic. Yr. Divd.:**	$0.480
Total Assets:	$2,836,521,000	**Net Worth:**	$218,415,000	**Debt/ Equity:**	2.7826

FMC Corp

1735 Market St., Philadelphia, PA, 19103; ***PH:*** 1-215-299-6000; ***Fax:*** 1-215-299-5998; ***http://*** www.fmc.com

General - Incorporation	DE	**Stock**- Price on:12/24/2007	$86.09
Employees	5,000	Stock Exchange	NYSE
Auditor	KPMG LLP	Ticker Symbol	FMC
Stk Agt	National City Bank	Outstanding Shares	38,290,000
Counsel	NA	E.P.S	$1.34
DUNS No.	00-914-6945	Shareholders	NA

Business: The groups principle activity is to produce chemicals for agriculture, industries and consumer markets. The group operates in three segments: agricultural products, specialty chemicals and industrial chemicals. The agricultural products segment manufactures and sells a portfolio of crop protection, structural pest control, turf and ornamental products around the world. The group operates from United States.

Primary SIC and add'l.: 2899 3339 2819 2879

CIK No: 0000037785

Subsidiaries: Electro Quimica Mexicana, S.A. de C.V., FMC (Shanghai) Chemical Technology Consulting Co. Ltd., FMC Agricultural Products International, AG, FMC Agroquimica de Mexico S.A. de C.V., FMC Asia Pacific Inc., FMC Australasia Pty. Ltd., FMC BioPolymer AS, FMC BioPolymer France SAS, FMC BioPolymer Germany G.m.b.H., FMC Chemical International, AG, FMC Chemical S.p.r.l., FMC Chemicals (Malaysia) Sdn. Bhd., FMC Chemicals (Thailand) Limited, FMC Chemicals Italy srl., FMC Chemicals KK 41 Subsidiaries included in the Index

Officers: William G. Walter/Chmn., CEO, Pres./$7,879,809.00, Theodore H. Butz/VP, GM - Specialty Chemicals/$1,528,178.00, Gerald R. Prout/VP - Government, Public Affairs, Kenneth R. Garrett/VP - Human Resources, Corporate Communications, Milton Steele/VP, GM - Agricultural Products/$2,149,017.00, Michael D. Wilson/VP, GM - Industrial Chemicals/$1,195,832.00, Kim W. Foster/CFO, Sr. VP/$2,432,171.00, Andrea E. Utecht/VP, General Counsel, Sec.

Directors: William G. Walter/Chmn., CEO, Pres., Paul J. Norris/Dir., Peter G. D'Aloia/63/Dir., William F. Reilly/Dir., Edward J. Mooney/Dir., Scott C. Greer/Dir., Enrique J. Sosa/Dir., Patricia A. Buffler/Dir., Vincent R. Volpe/Dir.

Owners: Edward J. Mooney, Theodore H. Butz, Paul J. Norris, Patricia A. Buffler, Milton Steele, Peter G. DAloia, James R. Thompson, Scott C. Greer, William F. Reilly, Michael D. Wilson, William G. Walter/1.60%, Kim W. Foster, Insiders/3.50%, Enrique Sosa

Financial Data: *Fiscal Year End:*12/31 *Latest Annual Data:* 12/31/2006

Year	Sales		Net Income
2006	$2,347,000,000		$132,000,000
2005	$2,150,200,000		$116,600,000
2004	$2,051,200,000		$160,200,000

Curr. Assets:	$1,067,800,000	**Curr. Liab.:**	$702,500,000	**P/E Ratio:**	24.18
Plant, Equip.:	$1,025,100,000	**Total Liab.:**	$1,656,500,000	**Indic. Yr. Divd.:**	$0.420
Total Assets:	$2,735,000,000	**Net Worth:**	$1,019,500,000	**Debt/ Equity:**	0.4864

FMC Technologies Inc

1803 Gears Rd., Houston, TX, 77067; ***PH:*** 1-281-591-4000; ***Fax:*** 1-281-591-4102; ***http://*** www.fmctechnologies.com; ***Email:*** corporate.info@fmcti.com

General - Incorporation	DE	**Stock**- Price on:12/24/2007	$75.55
Employees	11,000	Stock Exchange	NYSE
Auditor	KPMG LLP	Ticker Symbol	FTI
Stk Agt	National City Bank	Outstanding Shares	64,940,000
Counsel	Wachtell, Lipton, Rosen & Katz	E.P.S	$4.33
DUNS No.	NA	Shareholders	NA

Business: The group's principle activities include designing, manufacturing and supporting technologically sophisticated systems and products. The group operates in United States, Norway and other countries.

Primary SIC and add'l.: 2899 3556 5084 3728 3533

CIK No: 0001135152

Subsidiaries: CDS Engineering BV, FMC Airline Equipment Europe, S.L., FMC FoodTech Inc., FMC FoodTech S.L., FMC Kongsberg Holding AS, FMC Kongsberg Metering AS, FMC Kongsberg Services Limited, FMC Kongsberg Subsea AS, FMC Production Services AS, FMC Subsea Service, Inc., FMC Technologies A.G., FMC Technologies AS, FMC Technologies Australia Ltd., FMC Technologies B.V., FMC Technologies Canada Company 36 Subsidiaries included in the Index

Officers: Peter D. Kinnear/Dir., CEO, Pres./$4,307,147.00, Michael W. Murray/VP - Human Resources, Administration, David W. Grzebinski/Treasurer, Jeffrey W. Carr/VP, General Counsel, Sec., Robert L. Potter/Sr. VP - Energy Processing, Global Surface Wellhead, William H. Schumann/CFO, Sr. VP/$2,940,704.00, John T. Gremp/Exec. VP - Energy Systems/$2,212,188.00, Charles H. Cannon/Sr. VP - FMC Foodtech - Airport Systems/$2,187,309.00, Tore Halvorsen/Sr. VP - Global Subsea Production Systems, Randall S. Ellis/CIO, VP, Ronald D. Mambu/VP, Controller

Directors: Peter D. Kinnear/Dir., CEO, Pres., Joseph H. Netherland/Chmn., Asbjorn Larsen/Dir., Mike R. Bowlin/Dir., Maury C. Devine/Dir., Thomas M. Hamilton/Dir., Edward J. Mooney/Dir., Richard A. Pattarozzi/Dir., James M. Ringler/Dir., James R. Thompson/Dir., Philip J. Burguieres/Dir.

Owners: Charles H. Cannon, Thomas M. Hamilton, James M. Ringler, Philip J. Burguieres, Capital Research and Management Company/5.37%, Columbia Wanger Asset Management, L.P./6.95%, Joseph H. Netherland, James R. Thompson, Edward J. Mooney, Maury C. Devine, John T. Gremp, Mike R. Bowlin, Richard A. Pattarozzi, Peter D. Kinnear, T. Rowe Price Associates, Inc./11.04% *(18 Owners included in Index)*

Financial Data: *Fiscal Year End:*12/31 *Latest Annual Data:* 12/31/2006

Year	Sales		Net Income
2006	$3,790,700,000		$276,300,000
2005	$3,226,700,000		$106,100,000
2004	$2,767,700,000		$116,700,000

Curr. Assets:	$1,690,200,000	**Curr. Liab.:**	$1,208,200,000	**P/E Ratio:**	18.12
Plant, Equip.:	$445,700,000	**Total Liab.:**	$1,593,500,000	**Indic. Yr. Divd.:**	NA
Total Assets:	$2,487,800,000	**Net Worth:**	$886,000,000	**Debt/ Equity:**	0.2399

FMS Financial Corp

3 Sunset Rd. , Burlington, NJ, 08016; ***PH:*** 1-970-867-3319; ***http://*** www.flushingsavings.com; ***Email:*** fmsbank@fmsbank.com

General - Incorporation	NJ	**Stock**- Price on:12/24/2007	$30.41
Employees	344	Stock Exchange	NA
Auditor	PricewaterhouseCoopers LLP	Ticker Symbol	NA
Stk Agt	Computershare Trust Co	Outstanding Shares	6,540,000
Counsel	Malizia, Spidi & Fisch	E.P.S	$0.75
DUNS No.	36-441-8343	Shareholders	NA

Business: The group's principal activities are to originate loans and generate deposits from the public. The loans offered include consumer, commercial, and construction loans. The group invests these loans in the United States government securities and mortgage-related securities. The other services include accepting of money market deposits, checking accounts, savings and certificates of deposits. The operations are conducted through 40 branches located at burlington, camden and mercer counties in New Jersey.

Primary SIC and add'l.: 6035 6712

CIK No: 0000839845

Subsidiaries: Farmers and Mechanics Bank

Officers: John R. Buran/CEO, Pres., Craig W. Yates/65/Dir., CEO, Pres., Theresa Kelly/Sr. VP, Ronald Hartmann/Sr. VP, Chris Hwang/Sr. VP, A. J. Jin/Sr. VP, James E. Igo/51/Sr. VP, Sr. Lending Officer, Thomas M. Topley/47/Sr. VP - Operations, Corp. Sec., Channing L. Smith/64/CFO, VP, Maria A. Grasso/COO, Exec. VP, David W. Fry/Sr. VP, Treasurer, Henry A. Braun/Sr. VP, Francis W. Korzekwinski/Exec. VP

Directors: Craig W. Yates/65/Dir., CEO, Pres., Gerald P. Tully/Chmn., Joseph W. Clarke/70/Dir., George J. Barber/86/Dir., Edward J. Staats/63/Dir., Vincent R. Farias/61/Dir., Mary Wells/65/Dir.

Owners: Craig W. Yates/21.18%, Mary Wells, Frances E. Yates/9.11%, George J. Barber, Joseph W. Clarke, Vincent R. Farias, James E. Igo, Channing L. Smith, Insiders/29.95%, Dominic W. Flamini, Roy D. Yates/7.14%, Thomas M. Topley, Edward J. Staats

Financial Data: Fiscal Year End:12/31 Latest Annual Data: 12/31/2006

Year	Sales	Net Income
2006	$68,156,000	$5,319,000
2005	$63,336,000	$6,718,000
2004	$61,884,000	$8,768,000
Curr. Assets: $116,133,000	**Curr. Liab.:** $1,049,767,000	**P/E Ratio:** 40.55
Plant, Equip.: $33,739,000	**Total Liab.:** $1,109,753,000	**Indic. Yr. Divd.:** $0.120
Total Assets: $1,188,112,000	**Net Worth:** $78,361,000	**Debt/ Equity:** 0.3243

FNB Bancorp

975 El Camino Real, South San Francisco, CA, 94080; *PH:* 1-650-588-6800; *Fax:* 1-650-588-9695; *http://* www.fnbnorcal.com

General - Incorporation	CA	Stock - Price on:12/24/2007	$30.5
Employees	183	Stock Exchange	OTC
Auditor	Moss Adams LLP	Ticker Symbol	FNBG
Stk Agt	U.S. Stock Transfer Corp	Outstanding Shares	2,860,000
Counsel	NA	E.P.S.	$2.14
DUNS No.	NA	Shareholders	NA

Business: The group's principal activity is to provide commercial banking services to individuals and small to mid-sized businesses through twelve banking offices in sam mateo and san francisco counties. The depository products of the group include checking accounts, savings accounts, interest-bearing negotiable orders of withdrawal (now) accounts, money market accounts and certificates of deposit. The loan products of the group include real estate loans, construction loans, commercial loans and consumer loans. In addition, the group provides travelers checks and cashiers checks, automated teller machine (ATM) services, couriers, appointment banking businesses, Internet banking and other customary commercial banking services.

Primary SIC and add'l.: 6021 6712

CIK No: 0001163199

Subsidiaries: First National Bank

Officers: Thomas C. McGraw/Dir., CEO, Sec./$296,573.00, Anthony J. Clifford/Dir., COO, Exec. VP/$296,451.00, Jim D. Black/Dir., Pres./$334,408.00, Shirley Cabanero/Finance Officer, Dee Canepa/Branch Mgr. - Daly City, Jaye Fraser/Branch Mgr. - Colma, Sara Watson/Branch Mgr. - Half Moon Bay, Gary Moore/Branch Mgr. - Pacifica, Matthew Butler/Branch Mgr. - South San Francisco, Hem Patel/Branch Mgr. - Pacifica, Derek Chan/Branch Mgr. - San Francisco, Financial District, Charles R. Key/VP, Dir. - Information Technology, David A. Curtis/CFO, Sr. VP/$17,275.00, Mark Gueco/Branch Mgr. - South San Francisco, Nathalia Kelsey/Branch Mgr. - Redwood City *(17 Officers included in Index)*

Directors: Thomas C. McGraw/Dir., CEO, Sec., Michael R. Wyman/Chmn., Anthony J. Clifford/Dir., COO, Exec. VP, Jim D. Black/Dir., Pres., Mike Pacelli/Dir., Edward J. Watson/Dir., Neil J. Vanucci/Dir., Lisa Angelot/Dir., Merrie Turner Lightner/Dir.

Owners: Thomas G. Atwood/10.06%, Michael R. Wyman/1.13%, Jim D. Black, Cede & Co./43.57%, Neil J. Vannucci/2.16%, Thomas C. McGraw/5.07%, The Ricco Lagomarsino Trust/9.87%, Insiders/10.60%

Financial Data: Fiscal Year End:12/31 Latest Annual Data: 12/31/2006

Year	Sales	Net Income
2006	$43,466,000	$7,582,000
2005	$34,674,000	$5,728,000
2004	$27,864,000	$4,688,000
Curr. Assets: $45,717,000	**Curr. Liab.:** $519,207,000	**P/E Ratio:** 13.44
Plant, Equip.: $13,476,000	**Total Liab.:** $519,207,000	**Indic. Yr. Divd.:** $0.600
Total Assets: $581,270,000	**Net Worth:** $62,063,000	**Debt/ Equity:** NA

FNB Corp

105 Arbor Dr., Christiansburg, VA, 24073; *PH:* 1-540-382-4951; *Fax:* 1-540-381-6785; *http://* www.fnbonline.com

General - Incorporation		Stock - Price on:12/24/2007	$16.86
Employees	1,487	Stock Exchange	NYSE
Auditor	NA	Ticker Symbol	FNB
Stk Agt	Registrar & Transfer Co	Outstanding Shares	60,360,000
Counsel	n	E.P.S.	$1.16
DUNS No.	NA	Shareholders	NA

Business: The groups principal activity is to provide commercial banking services. The group also provides commercial and retail banking products and services. The groups services include checking, savings and time deposits, individual retirement accounts, merchant bankcard processing, residential and commercial mortgages, home equity loans, commercial loans, consumer installment loans and agricultural loans. The group operates from the United States.

Primary SIC and add'l.: 6712 6021 6712 6712 6021 6021

CIK No: 0001010961

Subsidiaries: First National Bank, FNB (VA) Statutory Trust II, FNB Financial Services, Inc., FNBO Co., Inc.

Officers: D. W. Shilling/61/CEO, Pres. - Bedford Federal Savings Bank, Exec. VP, William P. Heath/CEO, Pres., Scott D. Free/Treasurer, Bartley Parker/Investor Relations Officer, Kathryn Lima/Contact - Media, James G. Orie/Chief Legal Officer, David B. Mogle/Sec., Stephen J. Gurgovits/Pres., Brian F. Lilly/CFO, Gregory W. Feldmann/51/COO, Marketing Pres., Dir. - Wealth, Daniel A. Becker/65/CFO, Exec. VP

Directors: William P. Heath/CEO, Pres., Jon T. Wyatt/Chmn., Glen C. Combs/Dir., Douglas Covington/Dir., Beverley E. Dalton/Dir., Daniel D. Hamrick/Dir., Courtney F. Hoge/Dir., Steven D. Irvin/Dir., Harold K. Neal/Dir., Kendall O. Clay/Dir., Raymond D. Smoot/Dir., Charles W. Steger/Dir.

Owners: Keith J. Houghton, Daniel A. Becker, Harold K. Neal/1.05%, Beverley E. Dalton, Jon T. Wyatt, Glen C. Combs, Insiders/4.63%, Douglas Covington, William P. Heath, David W. DeHart, Courtney F. Hoge, Charles W. Steger, Kendall O. Clay, Steven D. Irvin, Daniel D. Hamrick *(17 Owners included in Index)*

Financial Data: Fiscal Year End:12/31 Latest Annual Data: 12/31/2006

Year	Sales	Net Income
2006	$421,697,000	$67,649,000
2005	$368,792,000	$55,258,000
2004	$332,589,000	$61,795,000
Curr. Assets: $123,834,000	**Curr. Liab.:** $4,736,752,000	**P/E Ratio:** 14.53
Plant, Equip.: $86,532,000	**Total Liab.:** $5,470,220,000	**Indic. Yr. Divd.:** $0.960
Total Assets: $6,007,592,000	**Net Worth:** $537,372,000	**Debt/ Equity:** 1.2106

FNB Corp/FL

F.n.b. Corporation, One F.n.b. Blvd., Hermitage, PA, 16148; *PH:* 1-724-981-6000; *http://* www.fnbcorporation.com

General - Incorporation	FL	Stock - Price on:12/24/2007	$33.64
Employees	464	Stock Exchange	NYSE
Auditor	Ernst & Young LLP	Ticker Symbol	NA
Stk Agt	Registrar & Transfer Co	Outstanding Shares	7,370,000
Counsel	Cohen & Girgsby	E.P.S.	$2.34
DUNS No.	08-063-4595	Shareholders	NA

Business: The group's principal activities are to provide an array of financial services to consumers and small-to medium-size businesses. It provides commercial banking services including demand and time deposit accounts, installment loans, personal and corporate fiduciary services. In addition to these, it provides various alternative investment products including mutual funds and annuities. The group owns and operates regional community banks, an insurance agency, a consumer finance company and first national trust company. During 2003, the group acquired charter banking corp and southern exchange bank. On 30-Jul-2004, the group acquired morrell, butz, and junker, inc.

Primary SIC and add'l.: 6021 6712 6141

CIK No: 0000037808

Subsidiaries: First National Bank of Pennsylvania, First National Insurance Agency, LLC, Regency Finance Company

Officers: James Morrell/Pres., CEO - First National Insurance Agency, LLC, Robert T. Rawl/Pres., CEO - Regency Finance Company, Stephen J. Gurgovits/CEO, Pres./$1,082,516.00, Gary J. Roberts/58/CEO, Pres./$842,873.00, Kim Craig/Pres., CEO - FNB Wealth Management, Jennifer Defazio/Contact - Shareholder Relation, Kathryn Lima/Contact - Media, Jeffrey W. Wagner/Sr. VP, Chief Investment Officer - Investment Strategy Group, FNB Wealth Management, Robert N. Swansboro/Assist. VP - Discipline, Research Mgr. - FNB Wealth Management, John C. Ayre/VP, Sr. Portfolio Mgr. - Portfolio Management Group, FNB Wealth Management, John Grazioli/Assist. VP, Portfolio Mgr. - FNB Wealth Management, Michael J. Basile/Assist. VP, Portfolio Mgr. - FNB Wealth Management, Mary Kay Schrock/Assist. VP, Portfolio Mgr. - FNB Wealth Management, Samuel A. Piccioni/Sr. VP, Sr. Relationship Mgr. - FNB Wealth Management, David B. Buckiso/Managing Executive, First National Trust Company *(47 Officers included in Index)*

Directors: Peter Mortensen/72/Chmn., Archie O. Wallace/73/Dir., Henry M. Ekker/69/Dir., William B. Campbell/69/Dir., Brian F. Lilly/Dir., CFO, Harry F. Radcliffe/57/Dir., William J. Strimbu/47/Dir., Earl K. Wahl/67/Dir., David J. Malone/53/Dir., Ron Kenny/Member - Advisory Board, FNB Capital Corporation, Jonathan King/Member - Advisory Board, James J. Cesare/Member - Advisory Board, Michael A. Monteleone/Member - Advisory Board, Kurt F. Buseck/Member - Advisory Board, Dawne S. Hickton/50/Dir. *(18 Directors included in Index)*

Owners: John W. Roseu, Robert B. Goldstein, Insiders/2.40%, Archie O. Wallace, Earl K. Wahl, Perkins, Wolf, McDonnell & Co./3.40%, Peter Mortensen, Dawne S. Hicktonu, William B. Campbellu, Henry M. Ekker, Harry F. Radcliffeu, David J. Malone, Janus Capital Management LLC/3.40%, Barclays Global Investors, NA/7.61%, James G. Orie *(21 Owners included in Index)*

Financial Data: Fiscal Year End:12/31 Latest Annual Data: 12/31/2006

Year	Sales	Net Income
2006	$109,991,000	$17,912,000
2005	$97,016,000	$17,533,000
2004	$84,810,000	$14,247,000
Curr. Assets: $47,477,000	**Curr. Liab.:** $1,325,616,000	**P/E Ratio:** 14.50
Plant, Equip.: $26,831,000	**Total Liab.:** $1,345,298,000	**Indic. Yr. Divd.:** $0.280
Total Assets: $1,518,715,000	**Net Worth:** $173,417,000	**Debt/ Equity:** 0.0712

FNB Corp/VA

105 Arbor Dr., Christiansburg, VA, 24068; *PH:* 1-540-382-4951; *Fax:* 1-540-381-6785; *http://* www.fnbonline.com; *Email:* mprater@fnbonline.com

General - Incorporation	VA	Stock - Price on:12/24/2007	$33.64
Employees	464	Stock Exchange	NDQ
Auditor	Brown, Edwards & Co LLP	Ticker Symbol	FNBP
Stk Agt	Registrar & Transfer Co	Outstanding Shares	7,370,000
Counsel	NA	E.P.S.	$2.15
DUNS No.	01-115-1912	Shareholders	NA

Business: The group's principal activity is to provide general and commercial banking services through its wholly owned subsidiary, first national bank. The group's deposit product include checking, savings and time deposits, individual retirement accounts, merchant bankcard processing. The lending products include residential and commercial mortgages, home equity loans, credit card and consumer installment loans, agricultural loans, investment loans, small business, fha and sba guaranteed loans, commercial loans, lines and letters of credit as well as trust services. The services are provided primarily in montgomery county, Virginia and surrounding counties, the cities of roanoke and salem, Virginia and roanoke and contiguous counties including bedford and franklin, Virginia through 55 banking facilities and 52 ATMs. On 01-Aug-2003, the group acquired bedford bancshares inc. On 30-Jun-2004, the group acquired morrell, butz, and junker, inc.

Primary SIC and add'l.: 6712 6021

CIK No: 0001010961

Subsidiaries: Bedford Federal Savings Bank, First National Bank, Fnb (va) Statutory Trust I, Fnb (va) Statutory Trust Ii, FNB Financial Services, Inc, FNB Salem Bank and Trust, N.A., FNBO Co., Inc., National Association

Officers: William P. Heath/CEO, Pres./$345,905.00, Gregory W. Feldmann/COO, Pres., CEO - First National Bank/$223,328.00, Kay O. McCoy/56/Exec. VP, Dir. - Retail Banking, Wooddell B. Nester/Exec. VP, Chief Systems Officer, Michael Whitmore/Contact, Rhonda Frazier/Contact, Chris Lewis/Contact - Investor Relations, David W. Dehart/Marketing Pres. - New River Valley, Dir. -

Commercial Banking/$189,106.00, Don W. Shilling/Pres. - Marketing, Central Virginia, Keith J. Houghton/Exec. VP, Chief Credit, Risk Officer/$172,798.00, Connie G. Kesler/Mgr. - Relationship, Lynchburg, Rebecca Sparks/Mgr. - Retail, Moneta, Daniel A. Becker/65/Exec. VP/$187,170.00, Rhonda Long/Mgr. - Retail, Bedford, Valerie McCraw/Mgr. - Retail, Forest *(40 Officers included in Index)*

Directors: Jon T. Wyatt/Chmn., Charles William Steger/Dir., Glen C. Combs/Dir., Raymond D. Smoot/Dir., Daniel D. Hamrick/Dir., Steven D. Irvin/Dir., Beverley English Dalton/Dir., Kendall O. Clay/Dir., Douglas H. Covington/Dir., Courtney F. Hoge/Dir., Harold K. Neal/Dir.

Owners: Kendall O. Clay, Steven D. Irvin, Daniel D. Hamrick, Raymond D. Smoot, Charles W. Steger, Daniel A. Becker, Harold K. Neal/1.05%, Beverley E. Dalton, Courtney F. Hoge, Insiders/4.63%, Keith J. Houghton, Glen C. Combs, Gregory W. Feldmann, Jon T. Wyatt, William P. Heath *(17 Owners included in Index)*

Financial Data: *Fiscal Year End:* 12/31 *Latest Annual Data:* 12/31/2006

Year	Sales	Net Income
2006	$109,991,000	$17,912,000
2005	$97,016,000	$17,533,000
2004	$84,810,000	$14,247,000

Curr. Assets:	$47,477,000	Curr. Liab.:	$1,325,616,000	P/E Ratio:	14.38
Plant, Equip.:	$26,831,000	Total Liab.:	$1,345,298,000	Indic. Yr. Divd.:	$0.840
Total Assets:	$1,518,715,000	Net Worth:	$173,417,000	Debt/ Equity:	0.0712

FNB United Corp

Formerly: FNB Corp/NC

150 S Fayetteville St., Asheboro, NC, 27203; *PH:* 1-336-626-8300; *Fax:* 1-336-625-2452; *http://* www.fnbonline.com; *Email:* customerservice@myyesbank.com

General		Stock	
Incorporation	NC	Price on:12/24/2007	$15.87
Employees	545	Stock Exchange	NDQ
Auditor	Dixon Hughes PLLC	Ticker Symbol	NA
Stk Agt	Registrar & Transfer Co	Outstanding Shares	11,360,000
Counsel	NA	E.P.S	$1.14
DUNS No.	84-923-9223	Shareholders	NA

Business: The group's principal activity is to provide loan, deposit, cash management, investment and trust services to individual and business customers in North Carolina. The banking services offered include regular checking accounts, interest checking accounts, money market accounts, savings accounts, certificates of deposit, individual retirement accounts, debit cards, credit cards and loans, both secured and unsecured, for business, agricultural and personal use. The financial services offered include Internet banking, cash management, investment and trust services. The group conducts all of its operations in chatham, montgomery, moore, randolph, richmond and Scotland counties in North Carolina. On 01-Apr-2003, the group acquired dover mortgage company.

Primary SIC and add'l.: 6021 6712

CIK No: 0000764811

Subsidiaries: Dover Mortgage Company, First National Bank and Trust Company, First National Investor Services, Inc, FNB United Statutory Trust I, Premier Investment Services, Inc

Officers: Michael C. Miller/57/Chmn., CEO, Pres./$527,020.00, Gregory W. Feldmann/COO, Robert O. Bratton/59/VP, Jerry A. Little/64/Treasurer, Sec./$295,105.00, David W. Dehart/Pres. - Marketing, New River Valley, Dir. - Commercial Banking, Keith J. Houghton/Exec. VP, Chief Credit, Risk Officer, Don W. Shilling/Pres. - Marketing, Central Virginia, Wooddell B. Nester/Exec. VP, Chief Systems Officer, Larry Campbell/63/VP/$277,060.00, Charles M. McGuire/Pres. - Marketing, Roanoke Valley, Dir. - Retail, Private Banking, Joseph W. Beury/Exec. VP, Dir. - Wealth Management, William B. Littreal/CFO, Exec. VP

Directors: Michael C. Miller/57/Chmn., CEO, Pres., Lynn S. Lloyd/57/Dir., J. M. Ramsay/60/Dir., James M. Campbell/69/Dir., Ray H. McKenney/53/Dir., Robert P. Huntley/70/Dir., Carl G. Yale/56/Dir., Darrell L. Frye/62/Dir., Thomas A. Jordan/68/Dir., Richard K. Pugh/73/Dir., Eugene B. McLaurin/51/Dir., Glen C. Combs/Dir., Beverley English Dalton/Dir., Steven D. Irvin/Dir., Raymond D. Smoot/Dir. *(25 Directors included in Index)*

Owners: Robert P. Huntley, Richard K. Pugh, Reynolds R. Neely/1.38%, Larry R. Campbell, James M. Campbell, Mark R. Hensley, Jerry A. Little, Jacob F. Alexander, J. M. Ramsay, Larry E. Brooks, Darrell L. Frye, Michael C. Miller, Ray H. McKenney, Thomas A. Jordan, Eugene B. McLaurin *(20 Owners included in Index)*

Financial Data: *Fiscal Year End:* 12/31 *Latest Annual Data:* 12/31/2006

Year	Sales	Net Income
2006	$123,143,000	$12,187,000
2005	$69,341,000	$9,937,000
2004	$54,109,000	$6,598,000

Curr. Assets:	$108,340,000	Curr. Liab.:	$1,509,999,000	P/E Ratio:	13.92
Plant, Equip.:	$45,691,000	Total Liab.:	$1,607,237,000	Indic. Yr. Divd.:	$0.600
Total Assets:	$1,814,905,000	Net Worth:	$207,668,000	Debt/ Equity:	0.3965

FNBH Bancorp Inc

101 E Grand River, Howell, MI, 48843; *PH:* 1-517-546-3150; *Fax:* 1-517-546-6275; *http://* www.fnbsite.com

General		Stock	
Incorporation	MI	Price on:12/24/2007	NA
Employees	NA	Stock Exchange	OTC
Auditor	BDO Seidman LLP, KPMG LLP	Ticker Symbol	FNHM
Stk Agt	American Stock Transfer & Trust Co.	Outstanding Shares	NA
Counsel	NA	E.P.S	$0.13
DUNS No.	78-747-5300	Shareholders	NA

Business: The group's principal activities are the provision of commercial and personal banking services. These services include checking accounts, savings accounts, certificates of deposit, commercial loans, real estate loans, installment loans, collections, travelers' checks, night depository, safe deposit box, U.S. Savings bonds and trust services. The group operates through eight offices within the four communities it serves, all of which are located in livingston county, Michigan.

Primary SIC and add'l.: 6021 6712

CIK No: 0000943119

Subsidiaries: First National Bank in Howell, H.B. Realty Co

Officers: James R. McAuliffe/Dir., CEO, Pres., Douglas A. Schyck/Sr. VP - Commercial Lender, Nancy Morgan/Sr. VP - Human Resources/$161,710.00, Carol Czekaj/VP - 1st National Wealth Management, Patricia Griffith/VP, Dir. - Operations, Janice Trouba/Sr. VP, CFO/$192,944.00, Violet Gintsis/Sr. VP - Sr. Lender/$209,516.00, Jane Sutterfield/VP - Commercial Lender, Charity Stulz/Branch Mgr., Kimberlee Foster/Controller, Jeff Billig/VP - Commercial Lender, Lauri L. Trapp/Branch Mgr., Scott Peters/VP - Commercial Lender, Dennis P. Gehringer/Sr. VP - Commercial Lender, Randy Greene/Branch Mgr. *(21 Officers included in Index)*

Directors: James R. McAuliffe/Dir., CEO, Pres., Randolph E. Rudisill/Vice Chmn., Rickard W. Scofield/Chmn., Michael R. Yost/Dir., John M. Pfeffer/Dir., Steven T. Walsh/44/Dir., Helen V.W. McGarry/Dir. Emeritus, Richard F. Hopper/Dir., Athena Bacalis/Dir., Barbara Draper/Dir., Gary R. Boss/Dir., Donald K. Burkel/Dir. Emeritus, Harry Griffith/Dir. Emeritus, Dona Scott Laskey/Dir.

Owners: Insiders/3.00%, Richard F. Hopper, Athena Bacalis, Randolph E. Rudisill, Dona Scott Laskey/2.00%, Gary R. Boss, Steven T. Walsh, John M. Pfeffer, Janice Trouba, Rickard W. Scofield, James R. McAuliffe, Barbara Draper, Michael R. Yost, Nancy Morgan

Financial Data: *Fiscal Year End:* 12/31 *Latest Annual Data:* 12/31/2006

Year	Sales	Net Income
2006	$35,850,000	$5,586,000
2005	$33,135,000	$6,507,000
2004	$29,102,000	$6,291,000

Curr. Assets:	$31,187,000	Curr. Liab.:	$410,422,000		
Plant, Equip.:	$11,512,000	Total Liab.:	$423,903,000	Indic. Yr. Divd.:	$0.840
Total Assets:	$473,896,000	Net Worth:	$49,992,000	Debt/ Equity:	0.1003

FNBH Bancorp Inc MI

101 E Grand River, Howell, MI, 48844; *PH:* 1-517-546-3150; *Fax:* 1-517-546-6275; *http://* www.fnbsite.com

General		Stock	
Incorporation	MI	Price on:12/24/2007	$23.95
Employees	120	Stock Exchange	OTC
Auditor	BDO Seidman, LLP	Ticker Symbol	NA
Stk Agt	American Stock Transfer & Trust Co.	Outstanding Shares	3,040,000
Counsel	NA	E.P.S	-$1.66
DUNS No.	NA	Shareholders	NA

Business: The group operates through its subsidiary whose principal activity is to provide banking services. Services of the group include checking accounts, savings accounts, certificates of deposit, commercial loans, real estate loans, installment loans, trust and investment services, collections, travelers checks, night depository, safe deposit box and United States savings bonds. The group operates from Livingston County, Michigan in the United States.

Primary SIC and add'l.: 6021

CIK No: 0000943119

Subsidiaries: First National Bank in Howell, H.B. Realty Co

Officers: James R. McAuliffe/Dir., CEO, Pres., Violet Gintsis/Sr. VP - Sr. Lender, Nancy Morgan/Sr. VP - Human Resources, Janice Trouba/Sr. VP, CFO, Dennis P. Gehringer/Sr. VP - Commercial Lender, Douglas A. Schyck/Sr. VP - Commercial Lender, Jeff Billig/VP - Commercial Lender, Carol Czekaj/VP - 1st National Wealth Management, Patricia Griffith/VP, Dir. - Operations, Robert Laura/VP, Head - 1st National Wealth Management, Jane Sutterfield/VP - Commercial Lender, Michael N. Wieclaw/VP, Chief Credit, Risk Officer, Scott Peters/VP - Commercial Lender, Edward Barrett/Commercial Lender, Gabi Bresett/BSA Officer and Deposit Operations *(22 Officers included in Index)*

Directors: James R. McAuliffe/Dir., CEO, Pres., Rickard W. Scofield/Chmn., Randolph E. Rudisill/Vice Chmn., Athena Bacalis/Dir., Gary R. Boss/Dir., Dona Scott Laskey/Dir. - Attorney, Barbara Draper/Dir., Richard F. Hopper/Dir., John M. Pfeffer/Dir., Michael R. Yost/Dir., Donald K. Burkel/Dir. Emeritus, Harry Griffith/Dir. Emeritus, Helen V.W. McGarry/Dir. Emeritus

Owners: Steven T. Walsh, John M. Pfeffer, Barbara Draper, Randolph E. Rudisill, Janice Trouba, Athena Bacalis, Insiders/3.00%, Michael R. Yost, James R. McAuliffe, Gary R. Boss, Rickard W. Scofield, Nancy Morgan, Dona Scott Laskey/2.00%, Richard F. Hopper

Financial Data: *Fiscal Year End:* 12/31 *Latest Annual Data:* 12/31/2006

Year	Sales	Net Income
2006	$35,850,000	$5,586,000
2005	$33,135,000	$6,507,000
2004	$29,102,000	$6,291,000

Curr. Assets:	$31,187,000	Curr. Liab.:	$410,422,000		
Plant, Equip.:	$11,512,000	Total Liab.:	$423,903,000	Indic. Yr. Divd.:	$0.840
Total Assets:	$473,896,000	Net Worth:	$49,992,000	Debt/ Equity:	NA

FNX Mining Co Inc

55 University Ave., Ste 700, Toronto, ON, M5J 2H7; *PH:* 1-416-628-5929; *http://* www.fnxmining.com; *Email:* info@fnxmining.com

General		Stock	
Incorporation	ON	Price on:12/24/2007	$30.23
Employees	NA	Stock Exchange	NA
Auditor	KPMG LLP	Ticker Symbol	NA
Stk Agt	Mellon Trust Co	Outstanding Shares	NA
Counsel	NA	E.P.S	NA
DUNS No.	NA	Shareholders	NA

Business: The groups principle activities include exploring, developing and mining mineral properties. The group produces and sells nickel, copper, platinum, palladium, gold and cobalt. The group operates from Canada.

Primary SIC and add'l.: 1041

CIK No: 0001191679

Subsidiaries: Aurora Holdings Limited

Officers: John W. Lill/Dir., CEO, Pres., Terry MacGibbon/Executive Chmn., David W. Constable/VP - Investor Relations, Corp. Sec., Anthony P. Makuch/COO, Sr. VP, John Marrington/VP - Operations, GM, Ronald P. Gagel/Sr. VP, CFO, Catharine Farrow/VP - Exploration, Gord Morrison/Sr. VP - Corporate Development

Directors: John W. Lill/Dir., CEO, Pres., Terry MacGibbon/Executive Chmn., Robert Cudney/Dir., Donald M. Ross/Dir., Daniel G. Innes/Dir., Robert B. Low/Dir., Duncan Gibson/Dir., John Lydall/Dir.

Foamex International Inc

1000 Columbia Ave., Linwood, PA, 19061; *PH:* 1-610-859-3000; *Fax:* 1-610-859-3035; *http://* www.foamex.com; *Email:* foamexinfo@foamex.com

General - Incorporation: DE
Employees: 5,000
Auditor: KPMG LLP, Deloitte & Touche LLP
Stk Agt: Mellon Investor Services LLC
Counsel: NA
DUNS No.: 61-997-1039

Stock - Price on:12/24/2007: NA
Stock Exchange: OTC
Ticker Symbol: FMXI
Outstanding Shares: NA
E.P.S.: NA
Shareholders: NA

Business: The group's principle activities are to manufacture and distribute flexible polyurethane and advanced polymer foam products. The group's operating segments are foam product, automotive, carpet cushion products and technical products. Foam product segment includes manufacturing and sales of cushioning foams for bedding, furniture, packaging, health care applications and foam-based consumer products. Automotive products segment distributes automotive foam products and laminates. Carpet cushion product segment manufactures and distributes rebond, prime, felt and rubber carpet padding. Technical product segment manufactures and markets reticulated and other specialty foams used for reservoiring, filtration, gasketing and sealing applications. Other include certain manufacturing operations in Mexico city. The major customer of the group include johnson controls. The group operates in the United States, Canada, Asia and Mexico. The group's quarterly revenue for Sep'07 was 290.82 millions of USD.

Primary SIC and add'l.: 2519 3086 3069

CIK No: 0000912908

Subsidiaries: Administration Foamex, S.A. de C.V., Corte y Costura Foamex, S.A. de C.V., FMXI, Inc., Foamex Asia, Inc., Foamex Aviation, Inc., Foamex Canada Inc., Foamex Capital Corporation, Foamex Carpet Cushion LLC, Foamex de Acuna, S.A. de C.V., Foamex de Cuautitlan, S.A. de C.V., Foamex de Juarez, S.A. de C.V., Foamex de Mexico, S.A. de C.V., Foamex Delaware, Inc., Foamex L.P., Foamex Latin America, Inc. 21 Subsidiaries included in the Index

Officers: John G. Johnson/Dir., CEO, Pres., Raymond E. Mabus/59/Chmn., CEO, Stephen E. Stockwell/62/Exec. VP - Carpet Cushion Products, Gregory J. Christian/42/Dir., Pres., Chief Restructuring Officer, Andrew Thompson/Exec. VP - Business Management, Marketing, Robert M. Larney/CFO, Exec. VP, James Gamache/Exec. VP - Sales, Supply Chain, Craig I. Barkhouse/Sr. VP - Asian Operations, Chiu Chan/Sr. VP - Research, Development, Ken Crawford/Sr. VP - Manufacturing, Fred P. Rullo/Sr. VP - Foam Products Sales, East, Donald W. Phillips/Exec. VP - Automotive Products, Robert S. Graham/Sr. VP - Finance, Accounting, Darrell Nance/Exec. VP - Foam Products West, Vincent A. Bonaddio/Sr. VP - Plant Consolidation Projects *(19 Officers included in Index)*

Directors: John G. Johnson/Dir., CEO, Pres., Raymond E. Mabus/59/Chmn., CEO, Gregory J. Christian/42/Dir., Pres., Chief Restructuring Officer, Seth Charnow/Dir., Gregory E. Poling/Dir., Thomas M. Hudgins/Dir., Eugene I. Davis/Dir., Robert B. Burke/Dir.

Owners: John G. ohnson, Robert M. Larney, Donald W. Phillips, Goldman, Sachs & Co/19.60%, Paul A. Haslanger, Andrew M. Thompson, Sigma Capital Management, Inc/9.30%, James B. Gamache, Gregory E. Poling, Greywolf Capital Management LP/5.40%, D. E. Shaw Laminar Portfolios, L.L.C/24.40%, Thomas M. Hudgins, Eugene I. Davis, Gregory J. Christian, Insiders

Focus Enhancements Inc

1370 Dell Ave., Campbell, CA, 95008; ***PH:*** 1-408-866-8300; ***Fax:*** 1-408-866-4859; ***http://*** www.focusinfo.com; ***Email:*** info@focusinfo.com

General - Incorporation: DE
Employees: 143
Auditor: Burr, Pilger & Mayer LLP
Stk Agt: American Stock Transfer & Trust Co.
Counsel: NA
DUNS No.: 78-580-1853

Stock - Price on:12/24/2007: $1.08
Stock Exchange: NDQ
Ticker Symbol: FCSE
Outstanding Shares: 78,290,000
E.P.S.: -$0.17
Shareholders: NA

Business: The group's principal activity is to design proprietary video scan conversion, application specific integrated circuits (asics), digital-video conversion and video production equipment. Semiconductor products include the fs400, fs450 and fs460 series asics for scaling, scan conversion, Internet TV and interactive TV applications. Commercial products for video presentation include desktop PC-to-TV scan converters, scalers, and line quadruplers. Video production equipments include application controllers, edit controllers, mixers, and character and effects generators. The products and technologies are sold through original equipment manufacturers (OEMs) and resellers to the broadcast, education, cable, business, industrial, presentation, Internet, gaming, home video production and home theater markets. In Sept 2003, the group acquired dvunlimited. On 02-Mar-2004, the group acquired como computer & motion gmbh.

Primary SIC and add'l.: 5045

CIK No: 0000884719

Subsidiaries: COMO Computer & Motion GmbH

Officers: Brett A. Moyer/Dir., CEO, Pres., Peter T. Mor/VP - Engineering, Operations, Michael Ngo/Contact Person - Career, Elizabeth Fisher/Contact Person - Career, Gary L. Williams/Sec., VP - Finance, CFO, Thomas M. Hamilton/Exec. VP, GM - Focus Semiconductor Group, Michael F. Conway/Sr. VP - Strategy, Business Development, Norman Schlomka/Sr. VP - European Operations

Directors: Brett A. Moyer/Dir., CEO, Pres., William N. Jasper/Chmn., William B. Coldrick/Vice Chmn., Carl E. Berg/Dir., Sam Runco/Dir., Tommy Eng/Dir., Michael L. D'Addio/Dir.

Owners: 033 Asset Management/9.40%, Insiders/10.10%, William N. Jasper, Tommy Eng, Brett A. Moyer, Thomas M. Hamilton, Michael F. Conway, Michael L. DAddio, Gary L. Williams, Peter T. Mor, Ingalls & Snyder LLC/6.80%, Sam Runco, William B. Coldrick, Norman Schlomka, Carl E. Berg/6.50% *(16 Owners included in Index)*

Financial Data: ***Fiscal Year End:***12/31 ***Latest Annual Data:*** 12/31/2006

Year	Sales	Net Income
2006	$37,478,000	-$15,923,000
2005	$24,551,000	-$15,368,000
2004	$20,015,000	-$10,985,000

Curr. Assets:	$15,436,000	**Curr. Liab.:**	$13,026,000		
Plant, Equip.:	$980,000	**Total Liab.:**	$23,972,000	**Indic. Yr. Divd.:**	NA
Total Assets:	$29,980,000	**Net Worth:**	$6,008,000	**Debt/ Equity:**	1.3584

Focus Media Holding Ltd

28-30/f, Zhao Feng World Trade Bldg., 369 Jiangsu Rd., Shanghai, 100032; ; ***http://*** www.focusmedia.cn

General - Incorporation: Cayman Islands
Employees: 3,548
Auditor: Deloitte Touche Tohmatsu CPA Ltd.
Stk Agt: Dexia Corporate Srvcs Hong Kong Ltd.
Counsel: Simpson Thacher & Bartlett LLP
DUNS No.: NA

Stock - Price on:12/24/2007: $46.43
Stock Exchange: NDQ
Ticker Symbol: FMCN
Outstanding Shares: 107,180,000
E.P.S.: $1.12
Shareholders: NA

Business: The groups principle activity is to provide out of home advertising services. In the year 2006, the group acquierd Framedia and E-Times, Focus Media Wireless, Target Media and Dotad Media Holdings. Specific customer of the group is Portland Outdoor Advertising Co., Ltd. The group operates from China. The group's quarterly revenue for September 2007 was 151.39 millions of USD.

Primary SIC and add'l.: 7312

CIK No: 0001330017

Subsidiaries: Beijing Focus Media Wireless Technology Co., Ltd., Capital Beyond Limited, Changsha Century Focus Media Advertising Company Ltd., Chongqing Geyang Focus Media Advertising Company Ltd., Dalian Focus Media Advertising Company Ltd., Defeng Information & Technology (Shanghai) Co., Ltd., Dongguan Focus Media Advertising & Communication Co., Ltd., Focus Media (China) Holding Limited, Focus Media Changsha Limited, Focus Media Dalian Limited, Focus Media Hebei Limited, Focus Media Qingdao Limited, Focus Media Technology (Shanghai) Company Ltd., Focus Media Tianjin Limited, Fuzhou Focus Culture Communication Company Ltd. 55 Subsidiaries included in the Index

Officers: Jason Nanchun Jiang/Chmn., CEO, Daniel Mingdong Wu/CFO, Diana Congrong Chen/COO, Cindy Yan Chan/Chief Strategy Officer, Acer Jiawei Zhang/VP - In, Store Network, Ergo Xueyuan Liu/VP - Commercial Location Network, July Lilin Wang/36/Chief Accounting Officer, Jie Chen/Mgr. - Investor Relations

Directors: Jason Nanchun Jiang/Chmn., CEO, David Feng Yu/Co - Chmn., Jimmy Wei Yu/Dir., Daqing Qi/Dir., Neil Nanpeng Shen/Dir., Fumin Zhuo/Dir., Charles Guo Wei Cao/Dir., Zhi Tan/Dir., Pres., David Zhang/Dir.

Owners: Total Team Investments Limited/5.80%, Jason Nanchun Jiang/9.95%, Zhi Tan/5.80%

Financial Data: ***Fiscal Year End:***12/31 ***Latest Annual Data:*** 12/31/2006

Year	Sales	Net Income
2006	$211,905,000	$83,198,000
2005	$68,229,000	$23,548,000
2004	$29,210,000	$373,000

Curr. Assets:	$243,323,000	**Curr. Liab.:**	$51,837,000	**P/E Ratio:**	53.58
Plant, Equip.:	$70,249,000	**Total Liab.:**	$55,498,000	**Indic. Yr. Divd.:**	NA
Total Assets:	$1,106,242,000	**Net Worth:**	$1,050,744,000	**Debt/ Equity:**	NA

Foldera Inc

17011 Beach Blvd., Ste. 1500, Huntington Beach, CA, 92647; ***PH:*** 1-480-659-8036; ***http://*** www.foldera.com

General - Incorporation: NV
Employees: 60
Auditor: Kabani & Co.,Inc.
Stk Agt: Holladay Stock Transfer, Inc.
Counsel: NA
DUNS No.: NA

Stock - Price on:12/24/2007: $0.38
Stock Exchange: OTC
Ticker Symbol: FDRA
Outstanding Shares: NA
E.P.S.: -$0.112
Shareholders: NA

Business: The groups principal activity is to distribute golf-related merchandise in the retail golf industry. Services of the group include training, fitness and swing mechanics programs for beginning golfers. The group operates from Nevada in the United States.

Primary SIC and add'l.: 5090

CIK No: 0000717945

Subsidiaries: Taskport, Inc

Officers: Daniel P. O'Shea/CTO, Sr. VP, Suyen Castellon/Dir., Sec., Ken Loyd/VP - Sales, Chief Marketing Officer, Susan Hunnel/Human Resources, Finance Administrator, Hien Ma/Software Architect, Reid Dabney/CFO, Blake Hunnel/CIO, Shane Belovsky/VP - Customer Relations, Hugh Dunkerley/COO, Pres., Brian Ismay/Lead Systems Engineer, Allen H. Lin/Dir. - Software Analysis, Ken Mason/Lead Software Architect, Lillian Wei/Lead Software Engineer, Huey La/Sr. Systems Engineer, David Simmons/Chief Software Architect *(24 Officers included in Index)*

Directors: Richard P. Lusk/Chmn., Simon J. Aspinall/Dir., Danilo Cacciamatta/Dir., Suyen Castellon/Dir., Sec., Michael J. Arrington/Dir., David Churbuck/Member - Advisory Board, Jnan Dash/Dir.

Owners: Richard Lusk/24.50%, Suyen Castellon/24.50%, Jnan Dash, Daniel OShea/1.80%, Vision Opportunity Master Fund Ltd./34.30%, Insiders/27.10%

Financial Data: ***Fiscal Year End:***12/31 ***Latest Annual Data:*** 12/31/2006

Year	Sales	Net Income
2006	NA	-$12,033,000
2005	NA	-$26,000

Curr. Assets:	$6,066,000	**Curr. Liab.:**	$1,750,000		
Plant, Equip.:	$1,692,000	**Total Liab.:**	$1,872,000	**Indic. Yr. Divd.:**	NA
Total Assets:	$7,859,000	**Net Worth:**	$5,987,000	**Debt/ Equity:**	0.0433

Fonar Corp

110 Marcus Dr., Melville, NY, 11747; ***PH:*** 1-631-694-2929; ***Fax:*** 1-631-753-5150; ***http://*** www.fonar.com; ***Email:*** info@fonar.com

General - Incorporation: DE
Employees: 409
Auditor: Marcum & Kliegman LLP
Stk Agt: Computershare Trust Co
Counsel: NA
DUNS No.: 03-704-8154

Stock - Price on:12/24/2007: $5.12
Stock Exchange: NDQ
Ticker Symbol: FONR
Outstanding Shares: 5,250,000
E.P.S.: -$4.04
Shareholders: NA

Business: The group's principal activity is to design, manufacture, sell and service magnetic resonance imaging scanners. The group also provides physician and diagnostic management services. These services include providing office equipment, staffing, administrative, billing and collections, cost saving programs and marketing services to physicians. The products include stand-up mri scanner, the open sky mri, fonar 360, the quad mri scanner and the echo mri scanner. The principal markets for the group's scanners are hospitals and private scanning centers. It currently manages eleven diagnostic imaging centers and six physical therapy and rehabilitation practices located principally in the New York state and Florida. In Apr 2003, the group discontinued a&a services.

Primary SIC and add'l.: 3845 8748 8741

CIK No: 0000355019

Subsidiaries: Central Health Care Management Company, Inc., Dynamic Services, Inc., Health Management Corporation of America, HMCM, Inc., MR Scanning Center Management Company

Officers: Raymond V. Damadian/Chmn., Principal Executive Officer, Acting Principal Financial Officer, David B. Terry/VP - Administration, Sec., Daniel Culver/Dir. - Communications

Directors: Raymond V. Damadian/Chmn., Principal Executive Officer, Acting Principal Financial Officer, Charles N. OData/72/Dir., Robert Djerejian/77/Dir., Claudette J.V. Chan/70/Dir., Robert J. Janoff/81/Dir.

Owners: Insiders/2.54%, Insiders/99.98%, Claudette Chan, Insiders/6.13%, Raymond V. Damadian/99.98%, Robert J. Janoff, Charles N. O'Data, Raymond V. Damadian/6.09%, Raymond V. Damadian/2.46%, Claudette Chan, Robert J. Janoff

Financial Data: Fiscal Year End:06/30 Latest Annual Data: 06/30/2007

Year	Sales	Net Income
2007	$33,212,000	-$25,539,000
2006	$33,076,000	-$29,963,000
2005	$104,899,000	$1,014,000

Curr. Assets:	$38,872,000	Curr. Liab.:	$24,634,000		
Plant, Equip.:	$6,667,000	Total Liab.:	$26,114,000	Indic. Yr. Divd.:	NA
Total Assets:	$57,230,000	Net Worth:	$30,419,000	Debt/ Equity:	0.0635

Fonix Corp

9350 S 150 E, Ste. 700, Sandy, UT, 84070; *PH:* 1-801-553-6600; *Fax:* 1-801-553-6707; *http://* www.fonix.com

General - Incorporation .... DE	Stock- Price on:12/24/2007 ....$0.001
Employees .... NA	Stock Exchange..OTC
Auditor ....Hansen, Barnett & Maxwell	Ticker Symbol... FNIX
Stk Agt..............Continental Stock Transfer & Trust Co	Outstanding Shares 1,710,000,000
Counsel.. NA	E.P.S. ....-$0.004
DUNS No. 87-830-7925	Shareholders...NA

Business: The group's principle activity is to develop speech synthesis equipment, compression and neural network technologies and other human-computer interface technologies and products. The group offers its speech-enabling technologies to markets for embedded automotive and wireless and mobile devices, computer telephony and server solutions and personal software for consumer applications. Revenues are generated through licensing of speech-enabling technologies, maintenance contracts and services. On 26-Feb-2004, the group acquired ltel holdings corp. The group's quarterly revenue for Sep'07 was 0.34 millions of USD.

Primary SIC and add'l.: 7373 7389 6794

CIK No: 0000855585

Subsidiaries: Fonix Sales, Group, Ltd., Fonix Speech Inc., Fonix Telecom, Inc., Fonix UK Ltd., Fonix/AcuVoice, Inc, Fonix/Papyrus Corporation., LTEL Acquisition Corp., TOE Acquisition Corporation.

Officers: Thomas A. Murdock/Chmn., CEO, Pres., William A. Maasberg/Dir., COO, Roger D. Dudley/Dir., Exec. VP, CFO, Michelle Aamodt/Dir. - Investor Relations

Directors: Thomas A. Murdock/Chmn., CEO, Pres., William A. Maasberg/Dir., COO, Roger D. Dudley/Dir., Exec. VP, CFO

Owners: Roger D. Dudley/31.51%, Insiders/41.00%, William A. Maasberg, Thomas A. Murdock/40.98%

Financial Data: Fiscal Year End:12/31 Latest Annual Data: 12/31/2006

Year	Sales	Net Income
2006	$1,329,000	-$21,943,000
2005	$16,191,000	-$22,631,000
2004	$14,902,000	-$15,148,000

Curr. Assets:	$9,000	Curr. Liab.:	$52,966,000		
Plant, Equip.:	$48,000	Total Liab.:	$55,954,000	Indic. Yr. Divd.:	NA
Total Assets:	$2,805,000	Net Worth:	-$53,149,000	Debt/ Equity:	NA

Food Technology Service Inc

502 Prairie Mine Rd., Mulberry, FL, 33860; *PH:* 1-863-425-0039; *Fax:* 1-863-425-5526; *http://* www.foodtechservice.com; *Email:* info@ftsi.us

General - Incorporation .... FL	Stock- Price on:12/24/2007 ....$2.51
Employees 12	Stock Exchange..NDQ
Auditor .... Faircloth & Assoc. P.A	Ticker Symbol..VIFL
Stk Agt..... American Stock Transfer & Trust Co.	Outstanding Shares 2,750,000
Counsel.. NA	E.P.S. $0.31
DUNS No. 15-645-7152	Shareholders...NA

Business: The group's principal activity is to own and operate an irradiation facility. This facility uses gamma radiation produced by cobalt 60 to treat and process various foods for insect disinfestation, shelf life extension and control certain disease causing microorganisms. The irradiation facility is used to irradiate fruits, vegetables, poultry, red meat and other food products. The group markets its irradiation process as a substitute and a complement to other food processing methods such as canning, freezing, heat pasteurization and fumigation. The group also provides contract sterilization service to the food packaging, medical device and food ingredient industries. The facility of the group is located in mulberry, Florida.

Primary SIC and add'l.: 7389

CIK No: 0000868267

Officers: Richard G. Hunter/55/CEO, CFO, Pres./$210,870.00, Jim Jones/VP - Sales, Marketing, Susan Lefrancois/Dir. - Regulatory Affairs, Quality Assurance

Directors: Ronald Thomas/55/Dir., David Nicholds/60/Dir., Samuel P. Bell/67/Dir., John Corley/62/Dir., John T. Sinnott/58/Dir.

Owners: Samuel Bell, MDS (Canada) Inc./35.40%, Insiders/37.10%, John Corley, David Nicholds, Ronald Thomas, John Sinnott, Richard G. Hunter

Financial Data: Fiscal Year End:12/31 Latest Annual Data: 12/31/2006

Year	Sales	Net Income
2006	$1,772,000	$739,000
2005	$1,704,000	$139,000
2004	$1,318,000	-$106,000

Curr. Assets:	$816,000	Curr. Liab.:	$886,000		
Plant, Equip.:	$3,474,000	Total Liab.:	$1,133,000	Indic. Yr. Divd.:	NA
Total Assets:	$4,956,000	Net Worth:	$3,824,000	Debt/ Equity:	0.0627

Foodarama Supermarkets Inc

922 Hwy. 33, Bldg 6, Freehold, NJ, 07728; *PH:* 1-732-462-4700; *http://* www.firstrepublic.com

General - Incorporation .... NJ	Stock- Price on:12/24/2007 ....NA
Employees .... NA	Stock Exchange..NA
Auditor ....Amper, Politziner & Mattia P.C	Ticker Symbol... NA
Stk Agt .... American Stock Transfer & Trust Co.	Outstanding Shares ....NA
Counsel.....................Giordano, Halleran & Ciesla	E.P.S. ....NA
DUNS No. 00-891-2230	Shareholders...NA

Business: The group's principal activities are the retail sale of food and non-food products. The group operates a chain of twenty-four supermarkets, two liquor stores and two garden centers. It also operates a central food processing facility to supply meat, various prepared salads, prepared foods and other items, and a central baking facility which supplies bakery products. The group features fresh fish-on-ice, prime meat service butcher departments, in-store bakeries, international foods, meals to go, salad bars, bulk foods and pharmacies. The group operates only in the United States.

Primary SIC and add'l.: 5461 5451 5411 5421 5999 5499 5912

CIK No: 0000037914

Subsidiaries: New Linden Price Rite, Inc., ShopRite of Malverne, Inc., ShopRite of Reading, Inc.

Foot Locker Inc

112 W 34th St., New York, NY, 10120; *PH:* 1-212-720-3700; *Fax:* 1-212-720-4397; *http://* www.footlocker-inc.com

General - Incorporation .... NY	Stock- Price on:12/24/2007 ....$21.12
Employees 16,806	Stock Exchange..NYSE
Auditor .... KPMG LLP	Ticker Symbol..FL
Stk Agt .... Bank of New York	Outstanding Shares 155,330,000
Counsel.. NA	E.P.S. $0.51
DUNS No. 60-245-8531	Shareholders...NA

Business: The group's principle activity is to retail athletic footwear and apparel. The groups products are sold under the brand name Foot Locker, Footaction, Lady Foot Locker, Kids Foot Locker and Champs Sports. The group operates from United States, Canada, Europe, Australia, and New Zealand.

Primary SIC and add'l.: 5661 3949 5699

CIK No: 0000850209

Subsidiaries: Eastbay, Inc., FL Canada Holdings, Inc., FL Corporate NY, LLC, FL Europe Holdings, Inc., FL Finance (Europe) Limited, FL Retail NY, LLC, FL Retail Operations LLC, FL Specialty NY, LLC, FL Specialty Operations LLC, FLE C.V., FLE CV Management, Inc., FLE Holdings, BV, Foot Locker Artigos desportivos e de tempos livres, Lda., Foot Locker Atlantic City, LLC, Foot Locker Australia, Inc. 42 Subsidiaries included in the Index

Officers: Richard T. Mina/CEO, Pres. - Foot Locker, Inc USA, Ron Halls/CEO, Pres. - Foot Locker - Inc, International/$1,437,551.00, Matthew D. Serra/Chmn., CEO, Pres./$5,672,903.00, Laurie J. Petrucci/Human Resources, Robert W. McHugh/CFO/$1,456,881.00, Gary M. Bahler/General Counsel, Sec./$1,464,785.00, Peter D. Brown/CIO - Investor Relations, Jeffrey L. Berk/Real Estate, Joseph N. Bongiorno/VP - Logistics, Peter M. Cupps/VP - Corporate Shared Services, Dennis E. Sheehan/VP, Deputy General Counsel, James T. Bulzis/VP - Global Sourcing, Team Edition, Patricia A. Peck/Human Resources, Bernard F. Steenman/Risk Management, Giovanna Cipriano/Chief Accounting Officer *(17 Officers included in Index)*

Directors: Matthew D. Serra/Chmn., CEO, Pres., Purdy Crawford/Dir., Nicholas Dipaolo/Dir., Christopher A. Sinclair/Dir., Dona D. Young/Dir., James E. Preston/Dir., Cheryl N. Turpin/Dir., Alan Feldman/Dir., Philip H. Geier/Dir., David Y. Schwartz/Dir., Jarobin Gilbert/Dir., Matthew M. McKenna/Dir.

Owners: Matthew D. Serra, David Y. Schwartz, Insiders, Alan D. Feldman, Ronald J. Halls, Purdy Crawford, Gary M. Bahler, Jarobin Gilbert, Cheryl Nido Turpin, Richard T. Mina, Nicholas DiPaolo, Lord, Abbett & Co. LLC/6.54%, Philip H. Geier, Dona D. Young, James E. Preston *(18 Owners included in Index)*

Financial Data: Fiscal Year End:01/29 Latest Annual Data: 2/3/2007

Year	Sales	Net Income
2007	$5,750,000,000	$251,000,000
2006	$5,653,000,000	$264,000,000
2005	$5,355,000,000	$293,000,000

Curr. Assets:	$2,034,000,000	Curr. Liab.:	$516,000,000	P/E Ratio:	15.84
Plant, Equip.:	$654,000,000	Total Liab.:	$954,000,000	Indic. Yr. Divd.:	$0.500
Total Assets:	$3,249,000,000	Net Worth:	$2,295,000,000	Debt/ Equity:	0.0962

Foothills Resources Inc

4540 California Ave., Ste. 550, Bakersfield, CA, 93309; *PH:* 1-661-716-1320; *http://* www.foothills-resources.com; *Email:* info@foothills-resources.com

General - Incorporation .... NV	Stock- Price on:12/24/2007 ....$0.9
Employees 11	Stock Exchange..OTC
Auditor .... Cawley, Gillespie & Assoc., Inc	Ticker Symbol..FTRS
Stk Agt .... Nevada Agency & Trust Company	Outstanding Shares 60,380,000
Counsel.. NA	E.P.S. ....-$0.13
DUNS No. .... NA	Shareholders...NA

Business: The group's principle activities include exploring, and developming oil and natural gas opportunities. The group operates from United States.

Primary SIC and add'l.: 1382

CIK No: 0001133494

Officers: Dennis B. Tower/Dir., CEO/$218,334.00, John L. Moran/Dir., Pres./$218,334.00, Kirk W. Bosche/CFO/$246,715.00, James H. Drennan/VP - Land, Legal, Michael L. Moustakis/VP - Engineering, Stuart A. Gordon/Chief Geologist

Directors: Dennis B. Tower/Dir., CEO, John L. Moran/Dir., Pres., John A. Brock/Dir., Frank P. Knuettel/Dir., David A. Melman/Dir., Christopher P. Moyes/Dir.

Owners: John L. Moran/8.00%, John A. Brock, Goldman, Sachs& Co./12.30%, David A. Melman, James H. Drennan, Dennis B. Tower/8.20%, Insiders/24.90%, Kirk W. Bosche/5.60%, Frank P. Knuettel, Michael L. Moustakis, Christopher P. Moyes/2.60%

Financial Data: Fiscal Year End:12/31 Latest Annual Data: 12/31/2006

Year	Sales	Net Income
2006	$4,853,000	-$3,764,000
2005	NA	-$332,000
2004	NA	-$31,000

Curr. Assets:	$11,170,000	Curr. Liab.:	$5,109,000	P/E Ratio:	1.97
Plant, Equip.:	$64,931,000	Total Liab.:	$35,345,000	Indic. Yr. Divd.:	NA
Total Assets:	$77,567,000	Net Worth:	$42,222,000	Debt/ Equity:	NA

Footstar Inc New

933 MacArthur Blvd., Mahwah, NJ, 07430; *PH:* 1-201-934-2000; *Fax:* 1-201-934-0398;
http:// www.footstar.com

General - Incorporation	DE	**Stock** - Price on:12/24/2007	$0.35
Employees	1,210	Stock Exchange	OTC
Auditor	Amper, Politziner & Mattia, P.C.	Ticker Symbol	FTAR
Stk Agt.	NA	Outstanding Shares	20,960,000
Counsel	NA	E.P.S.	$2.25
DUNS No.	NA	Shareholders	NA

Business: The group's principle activity is to sells family footwear through licensed footwear departments and wholesale arrangements. The group operates through two segments namely Athletic and Meldisco. The group operates from the United States.

Primary SIC and add'l.: 5661

CIK No: 0001011308

Subsidiaries: Footstar Corporation, Footstar HQ LLC

Officers: Jeffrey A. Shepard/Dir., CEO, Pres./$3,881,157.00, William Lenich/Exec. VP - Footstar - Inc./$1,581,529.00, Dennis Lee/Sr. VP - Human Resources Footstar, Inc., Mike Lynch/Sr. VP, CFO/$669,121.00, Randy Proffitt/Sr. VP - Store Operations/$1,081,984.00, Maureen Richards/Sr. VP, General Counsel - Corporate Secretary Footstar, Inc/$1,429,812.00, Gail Anderson/Contact - Communication, Compliance, Routing Manual

Directors: Jeffrey A. Shepard/Dir., CEO, Pres., Jonathan M. Couchman/Chmn., Eugene I. Davis/Dir., Adam W. Finerman/Dir., Alan Kelly/Dir., Gerald F. Kelly/Dir., Michael O'Hara/Dir., Alan I. Weinstein/Dir., Steven D. Scheiwe/Dir.

Owners: Alan Kelly, Maureen Richards, FMR Corp./9.68%, Michael A. O'Hara, Alan I. Weinstein, Adam W. Finerman, William Lenich, Randall Proffitt, Gerald F. Kelly, George A. Sywassink, Insiders/8.56%, Dimensional Fund Advisors Inc./5.28%, Jonathan M. Couchman/4.74%, Michael J. Lynch, Jeffrey A. Shepard *(17 Owners included in Index)*

Financial Data: *Fiscal Year End:*12/31   *Latest Annual Data:* 12/30/2006

Year	Sales	Net Income
2006	$666,700,000	$45,300,000
2005	$715,400,000	$24,400,000

Curr. Assets:	$315,700,000	**Curr. Liab.:**	$240,700,000		
Plant, Equip.:	$28,900,000	**Total Liab.:**	$281,200,000	**Indic. Yr. Divd.:**	NA
Total Assets:	$356,700,000	**Net Worth:**	$75,500,000	**Debt/ Equity:**	NA

Forbes Medi-Tech Inc

750 W Pender St., Ste. 200, Vancouver, BC, V6C 2T8; *PH:* 1-604-689-5899;
http:// www.forbesmedi.com; *Email:* info@forbesmedi.com

General - Incorporation	Canada	**Stock** - Price on:12/24/2007	$0.7525
Employees	35	Stock Exchange	NDQ
Auditor	KPMG LLP	Ticker Symbol	FMTI
Stk Agt.	Pacific Corporate Trust Co	Outstanding Shares	38,400,000
Counsel	Cawkell Broadie Glaister LLP	E.P.S.	-$0.406
DUNS No.	NA	Shareholders	NA

Business: The group's principle activities are developing and commercialising nutraceutical and pharmaceutical products derived from nature. It conducts research and development focused on the commercialization of healthcare and pharmaceutical products derived from forest industry by-products and other plant-based products. The group is currently focuses its product development efforts on plant sterols known for their cholesterol-lowering properties and which are also essential building blocks in the production of steroid-based pharmaceutical products. It is also currently focused on three market segments; nutraceuticals, pharmaceuticals steroids and prescription pharmaceuticals. The group's quarterly revenue for September 2007 was 2.40 millions of CAD.

Primary SIC and add'l.: 2833 2834 6794

CIK No: 0001087477

Subsidiaries: Forbes Medi-Tech (USA) Inc., Forbes Medi-Tech Capital Inc., Forbes Research & Manufacturing Inc., Phyto-Source LP, Phyto-Venture, LLC

Officers: Charles A. Butt/Dir., CEO, Pres., Laura Wessman/Sr. VP - Operations, Darren Seed/Dir. - Investor Relations, Michelle Martin/Mgr. - Human Resources, Susan Ben-Oliel/Sr. Dir. - Intellectual Property, John Nestor/Chief Scientific Officer, David Goold/CFO, Jeffrey J.E. Motley/VP - Marketing, Sales, David Stewart/VP - Regulatory Affairs, Nutraceutical, Scientific Services, Jerzy Zawistowski/VP - Functional Foods, Nutraceuticals, Member - Advisory Board, Daniel J. Rader/Member - Medical Scientific Advisory Board

Directors: Charles A. Butt/Dir., CEO, Pres., Donald Buxton/Chmn., Steven Nissen/Chmn. - Medical Scientific Advisory Board, Peter J. Jones/Chmn. - Functional Foods, Nutraceuticals Advisory Board, Jiri Frohlich/Member - Medical Scientific Advisory Board, Harvey G. Anderson/Member - Functional Foods, Nutraceuticals Advisory Board, Atif Awad/Member - Functional Foods, Nutraceuticals Advisory Board, Nitin Kaushal/Dir., Thomas A. Pearson/Member - Medical Scientific Advisory Board, Steven Haffner/Member - Medical Scientific Advisory Board, Percy Skuy/Dir., Joe Dunne/Dir., Lily C. Yang/Dir., G. Mazza/Member - Functional Foods, Nutraceuticals Advisory Board, Bruce E. McDonald/Member - Functional Foods, Nutraceuticals Advisory Board *(19 Directors included in Index)*

Financial Data: *Fiscal Year End:*12/31   *Latest Annual Data:* 12/31/2006

Year	Sales	Net Income
2006	$6,214,000	-$9,337,000
2005	$18,023,000	-$9,491,000
2004	$14,589,000	-$5,032,000

Curr. Assets:	$20,186,000	**Curr. Liab.:**	$3,504,000		
Plant, Equip.:	$474,000	**Total Liab.:**	$4,322,000	**Indic. Yr. Divd.:**	NA
Total Assets:	$21,785,000	**Net Worth:**	$17,462,000	**Debt/ Equity:**	NA

Force Protection Inc

9801 Hwy. 78, Ladson, SC, 29456; *PH:* 1-843-740-7015; *Fax:* 1-843-329-0380;
http:// www.forceprotectioninc.com; *Email:* info@forceprotection.net

General - Incorporation	NV	**Stock** - Price on:12/24/2007	NA
Employees	327	Stock Exchange	NDQ
Auditor	Jaspers & Hall, P.C	Ticker Symbol	FRPT
Stk Agt.	Integrity Stock Transfer, Inc.	Outstanding Shares	NA
Counsel	NA	E.P.S.	$0.60
DUNS No.	87-809-0687	Shareholders	NA

Business: The group's principal activity is to design, manufacture and distribute mine protected vehicles. The products combine innovative designs with power, safety, handling and stability to create vehicles designed to protect and save lives. These boats offer fire and de-watering pumps, watertight emergency equipment compartments and capacity for 5-7 passengers. The mine protected vehicles were designed to protect personnel during transport, removal of unexploded ordnance or land mine, route clearance, humanitarian de-mining and other missions that require protection from landmines and hostile fire.

Primary SIC and add'l.: 3732 3711

CIK No: 0001032863

Subsidiaries: Force Protection Industries, Inc, TSG International, Inc

Officers: Gordon McGilton/CEO/$1,192,028.00, Michael Durski/CFO, David Hubbard/CIO, Daniel Busher/Exec. VP, Kirk Daniel/VP - Quality Processes, John Wall/VP - Legal Affairs, Denise D. Speaks/General Counsel, Phillip Owens/VP - Integrated Logistics Support, Michael Aldrich/VP - Marketing, Government Relations/$566,963.00, Damon Walsh/VP - Program Management, Raymond Pollard/COO/$283,941.00, Richard Hamilton/VP - Finance, Wayne Phillips/VP - Business Development, Mike Gilbert/VP - Engineering/$160,000.00, Craig A. Whitt/VP - Manufacturing Engineering *(19 Officers included in Index)*

Directors: Roger Thompson/63/Dir.

Owners: Midsummer Investment Ltd./6.40%, Wellington Management Co., LLC/5.60%, Raymond Pollard, Scott R. Ervin, Frank Kavanaugh/3.30%, Michael Moody, Roger Thompson, Gordon McGilton, Jack Davis, Insiders/3.40%

Financial Data: *Fiscal Year End:*12/31   *Latest Annual Data:* 12/31/2006

Year	Sales	Net Income
2006	$196,017,000	$18,197,000
2005	$49,713,000	-$14,405,000
2004	$10,273,000	-$10,246,000

Curr. Assets:	$262,663,000	**Curr. Liab.:**	$56,369,000		
Plant, Equip.:	$8,964,000	**Total Liab.:**	$56,537,000	**Indic. Yr. Divd.:**	NA
Total Assets:	$274,391,000	**Net Worth:**	$217,855,000	**Debt/ Equity:**	NA

Ford Motor Co

1 American Rd., Dearborn, MI, 48126; *PH:* 1-313-322-3000; *Fax:* 1-313-845-6073;
http:// www.ford.com; *Email:* gpipas@ford.com

General - Incorporation	DE	**Stock** - Price on:12/24/2007	$8.91
Employees	283,000	Stock Exchange	NYSE
Auditor	PricewaterhouseCoopers LLP	Ticker Symbol	F
Stk Agt.	Computershare Trust Co	Outstanding Shares	1,880,000,000
Counsel	NA	E.P.S.	-$2.88
DUNS No.	00-134-4746	Shareholders	NA

Business: The group's principle activity is to produce vehicles including cars and trucks. The group operates from United States and Canada.

Primary SIC and add'l.: 3713 3714 7353 3711 7513 6141

CIK No: 0000037996

Subsidiaries: 3000 Schaefer Road Company, CAB East Holdings, LLC, Closed Joint Stock Company Ford Motor Company, Ford Automotive International Holding, S.L., Ford Capital B.V., Ford Credit Auto Receivables Two, LLC, Ford Credit Floorplan Corporation, Ford Credit Floorplan, LLC, Ford Credit International, Inc., Ford Espana S.A., Ford European Holdings LLC, Ford Global Technologies, LLC, Ford Holdings LLC, Ford International Capital Corporation, Ford Mexico Holdings, Inc. 32 Subsidiaries included in the Index

Officers: John Fleming/Group VP - Ford Motor Co, CEO, Pres. - Ford, Europe, Geoff P. Polites/VP - Ford Motor Co, CEO - Jaguar, Land Rover, Louise K. Goeser/VP - Ford Motor Co, CEO, Pres. - Ford, Mexico, Alan Mulally/Dir., CEO, Pres./$28,183,480.00, Fredrik Arp/VP - Ford Motor Co, CEO, Pres. - Volvo Cars, Michael E. Bannister/Exec. VP - Ford Motor Co, Chmn., CEO - Ford Motor Credit Company, Alex P. Ver/VP - Ford Motor Co-CEO, COO - Automotive Component Holdings, William Clay Ford/Exec. Chmn./$10,497,290.00, J. C. Mays/Group VP - Design, Chief Creative Officer, Francisco N. Codina/56/Group VP - North America Marketing, Sales, Service, Richard Parry-Jones/CTO, Group VP, Ziad S. Ojakli/Group VP - Government, Community Relationsgovernment, Community Relations, Joe W. Laymon/Group VP - Human Resources, Labor Affairs, Edsel B. Ford/59/Dir. - Consultant, Bennie W. Fowler/VP - Quality *(43 Officers included in Index)*

Directors: Alan Mulally/Dir., CEO, Pres., William Clay Ford/Exec. Chmn., John R.H. Bond/66/Dir., Richard A. Manoogian/71/Dir., Homer A. Neal/65/Dir., Gerald L. Shaheen/64/Dir., Stephen G. Butler/60/Dir., Jorma Ollila/Dir., Kimberly A. Casiano/50/Dir., Irvine O. Hockaday/71/Dir., Edsel B. Ford/59/Dir. - Consultant, Ellen R. Marram/60/Dir., John L. Thornton/Dir.

Owners: Richard A. Manoogian, Lewis W. K. Booth, Mark A. Schulz, Homer A. Neal, Stephen G. Butler, Donat R. Leclair, Donat R. Leclair, Ellen R. Marram, William Clay Ford, Edsel B. Ford, Insiders, Richard A. Manoogian, John L. Thornton, James J. Padilla, Jorma Ollila *(24 Owners included in Index)*

Financial Data: *Fiscal Year End:*12/31   *Latest Annual Data:* 12/31/2006

Year	Sales	Net Income
2006	$160,123,000,000	-$12,613,000,000
2005	$176,896,000,000	$1,440,000,000
2004	$171,652,000,000	$3,487,000,000

Curr. Assets:	$49,244,000,000	**Curr. Liab.:**	$52,544,000,000		
Plant, Equip.:	$38,505,000,000	**Total Liab.:**	$280,860,000,000	**Indic. Yr. Divd.:**	$0.200
Total Assets:	$278,554,000,000	**Net Worth:**	-$3,465,000,000	**Debt/ Equity:**	NA

Ford Motor Credit Co

One American Rd. , Dearborn, MI, 48126; *PH:* 1-800-244-4199; *Fax:* 1-313-323-6975;
http:// www.fordcredit.com

General - Incorporation	DE	**Stock** - Price on:12/24/2007	NA
Employees	300,000	Stock Exchange	NA
Auditor	PricewaterhouseCoopers LLP	Ticker Symbol	NA
Stk Agt.	NA	Outstanding Shares	NA
Counsel	NA	E.P.S.	NA
DUNS No.	00-134-4746	Shareholders	NA

Business: The group's principal activity is to provide a wide variety of automotive financial services to and through automotive dealers throughout the world. The categories of financing products include retail financing, wholesale financing and other financing. Retail financing includes purchase of retail installment sale contracts and retail lease contracts from dealers and to offer finance to commercial customers. Wholesale financing consist of offering loans to dealers to finance the purchase of vehicle

inventory also known as floorplan financing. Other financing includes offering loan to dealers for working capital, improvements to dealership facilities and to purchase and finance dealership real estate. The group provides vehicle and dealer financing in 36 countries to more than 10 million customers and 12,500 automotive dealers. The group conducts insurance operations through its wholly owned subsidiary, the American road insurance company.

Primary SIC and add'l.: 6321 6159 6141

CIK No: 0000038009

Subsidiaries: The American Road Insurance Company

Officers: Michael E. Bannister/Chmn., CEO, Kenneth R. Kent/Vice Chmn., CFO, Treasurer, John T. Noone/Dir., Exec. VP, Pres. - Global Marketing, Sales, Terry D. Chenault/Dir., Exec. VP

Directors: Michael E. Bannister/Chmn., CEO, Kenneth R. Kent/Vice Chmn., CFO, Treasurer, John T. Noone/Dir., Exec. VP, Pres. - Global Marketing, Sales, Terry D. Chenault/Dir., Exec. VP, Donat R. Leclair/Dir., Ann Marie Petach/Dir., Peter J. Daniel/Dir.

ForeFront Holdings Inc

Formerly: Datrek Miller International Inc
835 Bill Jones Indl. Dr., Springfield, TN, 37172; **PH:** 1-615-384-1286; **http://** www.datrek.com

General - Incorporation	FL	Stock - Price on:12/24/2007	NA
Employees	168	Stock Exchange	NA
Auditor	Marcum & Kliegman LLP	Ticker Symbol	NA
Stk Agt	Nevada Agency & Trust Company	Outstanding Shares	NA
Counsel	NA	E.P.S.	-$1.33
DUNS No.	NA	Shareholders	NA

Business: The group operates through its subsidiaries whose principle activity is to provide Internet-related services, including Web hosting, dial-up and wireless technologies, high speed connectivity and disaster recovery. The group operates from United States.

Primary SIC and add'l.: 7375 6719

CIK No: 0001103121

Subsidiaries: Datrek Professional Bags, Inc., Miller Golf Company

Officers: Richard M. Gozia/Chmn., Interim CEO, Stan J. Harris/49/CEO - Forefront Group, Inc, Richard A. Oleksyk/45/Pres., COO - Forefront Group, Inc, Randy Frapart/CFO, Exec. VP

Directors: Richard M. Gozia/Chmn., Interim CEO, Osmo A. Hautanen/54/Dir., Christopher J. Holiday/61/Dir.

Owners: Randall J. Frapart, Richard M. Gozia, Stanford International Bank Ltd./80.60%, Osmo A. Hautanen, Christopher J. Holiday, Michael S. Hedge, Insiders/81.50%

Financial Data: Fiscal Year End:12/31   Latest Annual Data: 12/31/2005

Year	Sales	Net Income
2005	$26,691,000	-$6,892,000
2004	$9,265,000	-$6,208,000
2003	NA	-$190,000

Curr. Assets:	$11,458,000	Curr. Liab.:	$8,902,000		
Plant, Equip.:	$875,000	Total Liab.:	$12,541,000	Indic. Yr. Divd.:	NA
Total Assets:	$14,785,000	Net Worth:	$2,244,000	Debt/ Equity:	NA

Foresight Financial Inc

340 50 Ave. SE, Calgary, AB, T2G 2B1; **PH:** 1-403-239-2821; **Fax:** 1-403-214-3302; **http://** www.foresightfg.com

General - Incorporation		Stock - Price on:12/24/2007	$22.2
Employees	NA	Stock Exchange	OTC
Auditor	NA	Ticker Symbol	FGFH
Stk Agt.	NA	Outstanding Shares	NA
Counsel	NA	E.P.S.	NA
DUNS No.	NA	Shareholders	NA

Business: The groups principal activity is to provide personalized insurance and retirement planning services. The services of the group include life insurance, disability insurance, critical illness, long-term care, wealth accumulation and group insurance. The group operates from Alberta in the United States.

Primary SIC and add'l.: 6411

CIK No:

Officers: Stephen G. Gaddis/Dir., Pres., CEO, Investor Relations Officer, Dean E. Cooke/Sr. VP - Finance, Consolidated Operations, Aaron Patterson/CIO, Douglas M. Cross/Dir., Exec. VP, Denise K. Osadjan/VP, Internal Audit Corp. Sec., Sandra J. Spinker/VP - Consolidated Operations

Directors: Stephen G. Gaddis/Dir., Pres., CEO, Investor Relations Officer, John L. Jeschke/Chmn., James A. Schneiderman/Dir., Douglas M. Cross/Dir., Exec. VP, Robert W. Stenstrom/Dir., Richard L. Weigle/Dir., Carolyn S. Sluiter/Dir., Douglas A. Wagner/Dir.

Financial Data: Fiscal Year End:NA   Latest Annual Data: 12/31/2002

Year	Sales	Net Income
2002	$32,065,000	$4,620,000
2001	$33,343,000	$2,946,000
2000	$25,627,000	$1,780,000

Curr. Assets:	$28,264,000	Curr. Liab.:	$411,045,000		
Plant, Equip.:	$6,637,000	Total Liab.:	$426,306,000	Indic. Yr. Divd.:	$0.280
Total Assets:	$464,443,000	Net Worth:	$38,137,000	Debt/ Equity:	NA

Forest City Enterprises Inc

1100 Terminal Tower, 50 Public Sq., Cleveland, OH, 44113; **PH:** 1-216-621-6060; **Fax:** 1-216-263-4808; **http://** www.forestcity.net; **Email:** humanresources@forestcity.net

General - Incorporation	OH	Stock - Price on:12/24/2007	$64.59
Employees	3,604	Stock Exchange	NYSE
Auditor	PricewaterhouseCoopers LLP	Ticker Symbol	FCE-A
Stk Agt	National City Bank	Outstanding Shares	102,590,000
Counsel	NA	E.P.S.	$1.04
DUNS No.	00-281-3582	Shareholders	NA

Business: The group's principal activities are organized into four groups: commercial group, residential group, land development group and lumber trading group. The commercial group owns, develops, acquires and operates regional malls, specialty/urban retail centers, office buildings, hotels and mixed-use projects. The residential group owns, develops, acquires, leases and manages residential rental properties. The land development group acquires and sells land and developed lots to residential,

commercial and industrial customers. In addition, it owns and develops land into master-planned communities and mixed-use projects. The lumber trading group sells lumber in all 50 states and Canadian provinces. The group's markets include Boston, denver, los angeles, New York, philadelphia, richmond, san francisco and Washington.

Primary SIC and add'l.: 6512 6531 5031

CIK No: 0000038067

Subsidiaries: FC Basketball, Inc., Forest City Central Station, Inc., Forest City Commercial Group, Inc., Forest City Commercial Holdings, Inc., Forest City East Coast, Inc., Forest City Equity Services, Inc., Forest City Land Group, Inc., Forest City N.Y. Group, Inc., Forest City Rental Properties Corporation, Forest City Residential Group, Inc., Forest City Stapleton, Inc., Playhouse Square Investment, Inc., Simi Valley Town and Country, Inc.

Officers: Charles A. Ratner/Dir., CEO, Pres./$1,748,029.00, Samuel H. Miller/Chmn., Treasurer/$803,654.00, James A. Ratner/Dir., Exec. VP/$1,254,508.00, Allan C. Krulak/VP, Dir. - Community Affairs, James J. Prohaska/COO, Exec. VP, Thomas T. Kmiecik/Assist. Treasurer, Ed Pelavin/Pres., Bruce C. Ratner/Dir., Exec. VP - East Coast Development, Joanne M. Minieri/Pres., David J. Larue/COO, Pres. - Forest City Commercial Group, Brian Jones/Pres. - Forest City West, Commercial Group, Andrew Passen/Exec. VP - Human Resources, Robert G. O'Brien/Exec. VP - Finance, Investment, Charles Rau/CTO, VP, Geralyn M. Presti/Sr. VP, General Counsel, Assist. Sec. *(141 Officers included in Index)*

Directors: Charles A. Ratner/Dir., CEO, Pres., Samuel H. Miller/Chmn., Treasurer, Albert B. Ratner/Chmn., Bruce C. Ratner/Dir., Exec. VP - East Coast Development, Stan Ross/Dir., Jerry V. Jarrett/Dir., Brian J. Ratner/Dir., Louis Stokes/Dir., James A. Ratner/Dir., Exec. VP, Deborah R. Salzberg/Dir., Scott S. Cowen/Dir., Michael P. Esposito/Dir., Joan K. Shafran/Dir., Ronald A. Ratner/Dir., Exec. VP

Owners: Third Avenue Management LLC, Miller Ratner, Third Avenue Management LLC/21.38%, Abraham Miller, Private Capital Management, L.P./11.44%, Miller Ratner/17.26%, Joseph Shafran, Columbia Wanger Asset Management, L.P., Columbia Wanger Asset Management, L.P., Abraham Miller, Private Capital Management, L.P., Joseph Shafran

Financial Data: Fiscal Year End:01/31   Latest Annual Data: 1/31/2007

Year	Sales	Net Income
2007	$1,168,835,000	$177,251,000
2006	$1,200,775,000	$83,519,000
2005	$1,041,851,000	$85,206,000

Curr. Assets:	$834,289,000	Curr. Liab.:	$772,964,000	P/E Ratio:	62.11
Plant, Equip.:	$7,143,295,000	Total Liab.:	$7,580,692,000	Indic. Yr. Divd.:	$0.280
Total Assets:	$8,981,604,000	Net Worth:	$1,025,811,000	Debt/ Equity:	6.6365

Forest Laboratories Inc

909 3rd Ave., New York, NY, 10022; **PH:** 1-212-421-7850; **Fax:** 1-212-750-9152; **http://** www.frx.com; **Email:** investorrelations@frx.com

General - Incorporation	DE	Stock - Price on:12/24/2007	$45.73
Employees	5,126	Stock Exchange	NYSE
Auditor	BDO Seidman LLP	Ticker Symbol	FRX
Stk Agt	Mellon Investor Services LLC	Outstanding Shares	320,020,000
Counsel	NA	E.P.S.	$1.41
DUNS No.	00-128-8281	Shareholders	NA

Business: The groups principle activities include identifying, developing and delivering pharmaceutical products for treatment of nervous, cardiovascular and respiratory health conditions. The groups products include include Lexapro, Namenda, Benicar and Campral. In the year 2007 the group acquired Cerexa, Inc. The group operates from United States.

Primary SIC and add'l.: 2834 8731

CIK No: 0000038074

Subsidiaries: Forest Finance B.V., Forest Healthcare B.V., Forest Laboratories Holdings Ltd., Forest Laboratories Ireland Ltd., Forest Laboratories UK Ltd., Forest Pharmaceuticals, Inc., Forest Tosara Ltd., FRXC Company, Inc., Inwood Laboratories, Inc.

Officers: Howard Solomon/Chmn., CEO/$5,402,282.00, Ivan Gergel/48/Sr. VP - Scientific Affairs/$2,062,235.00, Francis I. Perier/48/CFO, Sr. VP - Finance/$1,482,347.00, Elaine Hochberg/51/Sr. VP - Marketing/$2,656,807.00, Lawrence S. Olanoff/COO, Pres.

Directors: Howard Solomon/Chmn., CEO, Dan L. Goldwasser/68/Dir., George S. Cohan/84/Dir., Lester B. Salans/72/Dir., William J. Candee/81/Dir., Nesli Basgoz/50/Dir.

Owners: Capital Group International, Inc./16.46%, Francis I. Perier, Elaine Hochberg, William J. Candee, Capital Research and Management Company/8.81%, Howard Solomon/1.99%, Dan L. Goldwasser, Lawrence S. Olanoff, George S. Cohan, Insiders/2.53%, Wellington Management Company, LLP/10.74%, Ivan Gergel, Clearbridge Advisors, LLC/7.42%, Capital Guardian Trust Company/8.81%, Barclays Global Investors, NA./9.80% *(19 Owners included in Index)*

Financial Data: Fiscal Year End:03/31   Latest Annual Data: 3/31/2007

Year	Sales	Net Income
2007	$3,441,785,000	$454,103,000
2006	$2,962,390,000	$708,514,000
2005	$3,159,639,000	$838,805,000

Curr. Assets:	$2,422,717,000	Curr. Liab.:	$627,608,000	P/E Ratio:	32.43
Plant, Equip.:	$361,086,000	Total Liab.:	$628,559,000	Indic. Yr. Divd.:	NA
Total Assets:	$3,653,372,000	Net Worth:	$3,024,813,000	Debt/ Equity:	NA

Forest Oil Corp

707 - 17th St., Ste. 3600, Denver, CO, 80202; **PH:** 1-303-812-1400; **Fax:** 1-303-812-1602; **http://** www.forestoil.com

General - Incorporation	NY	Stock - Price on:12/24/2007	$43.7
Employees	585	Stock Exchange	NYSE
Auditor	Ernst & Young	Ticker Symbol	FST
Stk Agt	Mellon Investor Services LLC	Outstanding Shares	63,050,000
Counsel	Vinson & Elkins LLP	E.P.S.	$2.42
DUNS No.	00-790-9948	Shareholders	NA

Business: The group's principal activity is to acquire, explore, develop, produce and market natural gas and liquids. It conducts the oil and gas operations through five business units: gulf coast: comprises onshore and offshore region interests in the gulf of Mexico. Western United States: comprises of interests in Oklahoma, Utah, Wyoming and west Texas. Alaska: operations primarily located in the cook inlet area. Canada: include interests in the plains region in alberta, the foothills region of alberta and british columbia and the northwest territories. Marketing and processing conducts marketing and trading activities in Canada. In addition, it also has interests in other countries including South Africa, gabon, Italy, Germany, albania and romania.

FormFactor Inc

Primary SIC and add'l.: 1311 1321 1389

CIK No: 0000038079

Subsidiaries: Canadian Forest Oil Ltd., Forest Energy Resources, Inc., Forest Oil Panhandle Resources L.P., Forest Oil Permian Corporation

Officers: Craig H. Clark/Dir., CEO, Pres./$4,409,492.00, Cecil N. Colwell/Sr. VP - Worldwide Drilling, Leonard C. Gurule/Sr. VP - Alaska/$917,581.00, David H. Keyte/CFO, Exec. VP/$1,851,423.00, Matthew A. Wurtzbacher/Sr. VP - Corporate Planning, Development/$902,923.00, Paul J. Dusha/VP - Human Resources, James R. Good/Pres. - Canadian Forest Oil, Rick Hatcher/CTO, VP, Michael N. Kennedy/MD - Capital Markets, Treasurer, Cyrus D. Marter/VP, General Counsel, Sec., J. C. Ridens/Sr. VP - Southern Region/$903,796.00, Timothy F. Savoy/VP - Operations Support, Victor A. Wind/Corporate Controller - Principal Accounting, Robert B. Wofford/VP - oil, gas Marketing, Scott R. Woodall/Sr. VP - Western Region *(18 Officers included in Index)*

Directors: Craig H. Clark/Dir., CEO, Pres., Forrest E. Hoglund/Chmn., Dod A. Fraser/Dir., James D. Lightner/Dir., Cortlandt S. Dietler/Dir., William L. Britton/Dir., Patrick R. McDonald/Dir., James H. Lee/Dir.

Owners: William L. Britton, Artisan Partners Limited Partnership/5.34%, Leonard C. Gurule, Wachovia Corporation/5.38%, Patrick R. McDonald, Janus Capital Management LLC./8.33%, Loren K. Carroll, FMR Corporation/12.26%, Craig H. Clark/1.31%, J. C. Ridens, Matthew A. Wurtzbacher, T. Rowe Price Associates, Inc./5.95%, James D. Lightner, Insiders/3.26%, David H. Keyte *(20 Owners included in Index)*

Financial Data: Fiscal Year End:12/31 **Latest Annual Data:** 12/31/2006

Year	Sales	Net Income
2006	$819,992,000	$168,502,000
2005	$1,072,045,000	$151,568,000
2004	$912,898,000	$122,551,000

Curr. Assets:	$261,000,000	**Curr. Liab.:**	$263,941,000	**P/E Ratio:**	16.19
Plant, Equip.:	$2,789,926,000	**Total Liab.:**	$1,755,066,000	**Indic. Yr. Divd.:**	NA
Total Assets:	$3,189,072,000	**Net Worth:**	$1,434,006,000	**Debt/ Equity:**	0.8653

ForeverGreen Worldwide Corp

Formerly: Whole Living Inc
972 N 1430 W, Orem, UT, 84057; **PH:** 1-801-655-5500

General - Incorporation	NV	Stock - Price on:12/24/2007	NA
Employees	20	Stock Exchange	OTC
Auditor	Chisholm Bierwolf & Nilson LLC	Ticker Symbol	FVRG
Stk Agt	Standard Registrar & Transfer Co Inc.	Outstanding Shares	NA
Counsel	NA	E.P.S.	NA
DUNS No.	NA	Shareholders	NA

Business: The group's principal activities are to manufacture and distribute natural food products, oils and bath salts to improve mental and physical performance. The group operates through its wholly-owned subsidiary brian garden, inc. The group has divided nutrition into three categories: primary nutrition: includes fruits, vegetables, nuts, seeds, grains and legumes; secondary nutrition: includes all pills, essential oils, vitamins, shakes and powders and empty nutrition: includes processed, fast food, microwavable, junk food, chemically fortified and nutritionally emptied food. The group markets its products in the United States, Canada, Australia, New Zealand and Japan.

Primary SIC and add'l.: 6719 2099 2844

CIK No: 0001091983

Subsidiaries: Brain Garden, Inc.

Officers: Chris Patterson/41/Sec., COO, General Counsel

Directors: Kevin Howard/52/Dir.

Owners: George H. Brimhall/26.70%, First Equity Holdings Corp./10.90%, Kevin Howard/1.00%, Robert Reitz, Brenda Huang, Ronald Williams/15.30%, Insiders/18.00%

Financial Data: Fiscal Year End:12/31 **Latest Annual Data:** 12/31/2006

Year	Sales	Net Income
2006	$3,492,000	-$1,244,000
2005	$3,796,000	-$2,037,000
2004	$6,759,000	-$2,498,000

Curr. Assets:	$1,824,000	**Curr. Liab.:**	$5,573,000		
Plant, Equip.:	$497,000	**Total Liab.:**	$6,857,000	**Indic. Yr. Divd.:**	NA
Total Assets:	$16,084,000	**Net Worth:**	$9,227,000	**Debt/ Equity:**	NA

Forlink Software Corp Inc

Shenzhou Mansion 9f, Zhongguancun, S No.31, Beijing, 100081; **PH:** 86-10-68118866;
http:// www.forlink.com

General - Incorporation	NV	Stock - Price on:12/24/2007	$0.12
Employees	NA	Stock Exchange	OTC
Auditor	BDO McCabe Lo Ltd.	Ticker Symbol	FRLK
Stk Agt	Nevada Agency & Trust Company	Outstanding Shares	NA
Counsel	NA	E.P.S.	NA
DUNS No.	NA	Shareholders	NA

Business: The groups principle activities include developing and selling network software systems and providing enterprise application system integration services. In March 2005, the group acquired Qingdao Jiashi Technologies Limited and Xiamen Kuanshi Technologies Limited. The group operates from Nevada in the United States.

Primary SIC and add'l.: 7372

CIK No: 0000866458

Subsidiaries: Beijing Forlink Hua Xin Technology Co. Ltd, Beijing Forlink Kuanshi Technologies Limited, Forlink Technologies (Chengdu) Limited, Forlink Technologies (Guangxi) Limited, Forlink Technologies (Hong Kong) Limited, Forlink Technologies Co., Ltd, Qingdao Jiashi Technologies Limited, Xiamen Kuanshi Technologies Limited

Officers: Yi He/Chmn., CEO/$18,566.00, Hongkeung Lam/Dir., CFO, Grace Tan/Contact - Investor Relations

Directors: Yi He/Chmn., CEO, Hongkeung Lam/Dir., CFO, Guoliang Tian/Dir., Yu Fang/Dir., Zhenying Sun/Dir.

Owners: Insiders/54.80%, Lam Honkeung/11.70%, Statelink International Group, Ltd./14.50%, He Yi/28.70%, Zeng Jing/6.40%, Zhenying Sun/14.50%

Financial Data: Fiscal Year End:12/31 **Latest Annual Data:** 12/31/2006

Year	Sales	Net Income
2006	$6,918,000	$305,000
2005	$5,912,000	-$1,394,000
2004	$10,000,000	$468,000

Curr. Assets:	$2,591,000	**Curr. Liab.:**	$4,346,000		
Plant, Equip.:	$729,000	**Total Liab.:**	$4,346,000	**Indic. Yr. Divd.:**	NA
Total Assets:	$9,326,000	**Net Worth:**	$4,979,000	**Debt/ Equity:**	NA

Formation Capital Corp

999 W Hastings St., Ste. 1510, Vancouver, BC, V6C 2W2; **PH:** 1-604-682-6229;
http:// www.formcap.com; **Email:** inform@formcap.com

General - Incorporation	Canada	Stock - Price on:12/24/2007	NA
Employees	NA	Stock Exchange	OTC
Auditor	Deloitte & Touche LLP	Ticker Symbol	FCACF
Stk Agt	Computershare Investor Services LLC	Outstanding Shares	NA
Counsel	NA	E.P.S.	NA
DUNS No.	NA	Shareholders	NA

Business: The group's principle activity is to operate mineral exploration properties. The group's primary assets include the Idaho Cobalt Project (ICP) and the Big Creek Hydrometallurgical Complex that includes the Sunshine Precious Metals Refinery. The group's flagship property, the Idaho Cobalt Project, is a 100 % owned unique high-grade, primary cobalt deposit that is metallurgically favourable for the production of high purity cobalt products. The mine is forecast to produce approximately 3.3 million pounds of cobalt. Another of its wholly owned subsidiaries, the Big Creek Hydrometallurgical Complex was purchased in 2002. The Sunshine Silver Refinery section of the facility, operational since the summer of 2004, is currently producing high purity precious metal bullion for its clients and continues to attract new customers. The group operates from United States.

Primary SIC and add'l.: 1090

CIK No: 0000861987

Officers: Mari-Ann Green/Chmn., CEO, Scott J. Bending/Dir., Pres., W. G. Scales/Dir., Exec. VP, Paul J. Farquharson/CFO, Sr. VP, Jeffrey T.K. Fraser/Corp. Sec., E. R. Honsinger/VP - Corporate Communications, Alan D. Vichert/VP - Risk Management, John Allen/Metallurgical, Environmental Consultant, Mike Irish/Mgr. - Metallurgy, Patrick M. Fadyshen/VP - Marketing, Sales, Conrad Parrish/Environmental Mgr., Jim Orpet/Additional Environmental Consultants, Karen Kuzis/Additional Environmental Consultants

Directors: Mari-Ann Green/Chmn., CEO, Scott J. Bending/Dir., Pres., W. G. Scales/Dir., Exec. VP, David Stone/Dir., Robert Metka/Dir., James B. Engdahl/Dir., Robert J. Quinn/Dir.

Forme Capital Inc

730 W Randolph St., 6th Fl., Chicago, IL, 60661; **PH:** 1-312-454-0312

General - Incorporation	DE	Stock - Price on:12/24/2007	$0.55
Employees	NA	Stock Exchange	OTC
Auditor	Comiskey & Company	Ticker Symbol	FOCP
Stk Agt	Transfer Company Of America	Outstanding Shares	12,720,000
Counsel	NA	E.P.S.	$0.00
DUNS No.	NA	Shareholders	NA

Business: The groups principal activities include creating and spinning off to its stockholders of six blind pool companies. The group is now seeking an acquisition and/or merger transaction, and is effectively a blind pool company. The group operates from Delaware in the United States.

Primary SIC and add'l.: 6799

CIK No: 0000808047

Officers: Bartly J. Loethen/44/Chmn., Pres. VP, CFO, Treasurer

Directors: Bartly J. Loethen/44/Chmn., Pres. VP, CFO, Treasurer

Owners: Castle Bison, Inc./19.16%, Stallion Ventures, LLC/45.72%, Insiders/14.16%

Financial Data: Fiscal Year End:04/30 **Latest Annual Data:** 04/30/2007

Year	Sales	Net Income
2007	NA	-$13,000
2006	NA	-$2,000
2005	NA	-$1,000

Curr. Assets:	NA	**Curr. Liab.:**	$10,000		
Plant, Equip.:	NA	**Total Liab.:**	$10,000	**Indic. Yr. Divd.:**	NA
Total Assets:	NA	**Net Worth:**	-$10,000	**Debt/ Equity:**	NA

FormFactor Inc

7005 Sfront Rd., Livermore, CA, 94551; **PH:** 1-925-290-4000; **Fax:** 1-925-290-4010;
http:// www.formfactor.com; **Email:** info@formfactor.com

General - Incorporation	DE	Stock - Price on:12/24/2007	$40.92
Employees	936	Stock Exchange	NDQ
Auditor	PricewaterhouseCoopers LLP	Ticker Symbol	FORM
Stk Agt	EquiServe Trust Co N.A	Outstanding Shares	47,780,000
Counsel	NA	E.P.S.	$1.62
DUNS No.	NA	Shareholders	NA

Business: The group's principle activities include designing, developing, manufacturing, selling and supporting precision, high performance advanced semiconductor wafer probe cards. The group is based in livermore, California and manufacturing locations. The group has offices in California, Japan, hungary, Germany and South Korea.

Primary SIC and add'l.: 3674

CIK No: 0001039399

Subsidiaries: FormFactor Europe Ltd., FormFactor Germany GmbH, FormFactor Hungary Licensing LLC, FormFactor Korea, Inc., FormFactor, KK

Officers: Igor Y. Khadros/Dir., CEO/$2,488,137.00, Yoshikazu Hatsukano/Sr. VP - Strategic Intiatives, Chmn. - Formfactor KK, Peter B. Mathews/Sr. VP - New Buisness Development, Benjamin N. Eldridge/CTO - Sr.VP - Research, Development/$1,322,821.00, Ronald C. Foster/Sr. VP, CFO/$1,055,134.00, Richard M. Freeman/Sr. VP - Operations, Stuart L. Merkadeau/Sr. VP, General Counsel, Sec./$1,221,416.00, Henry I. Feir/VP - Human Resources, Stefen Zschiegner/VP - Marketing, Roger Hitchcock/VP - World Wide Sales, Thomas P. Ho/VP - Application, Service

Directors: Igor Y. Khadros/Dir., CEO, James A. Prestridge/Chmn., William H. Davidow/Dir., Carl G. Everett/Dir., Homa Bahrami/Dir., Thomas J. Campbell/Dir., Harvey A. Wagner/Dir., Lothar Mair/Dir.

Owners: James A. Prestridge, PRIMECAP Management Company/5.24%, Entities affiliated with Franklin Resources, Inc./5.95%, Carl G. Everett, Ronald C. Foster, Entities affiliated with FMR Corp./13.27%, Harvey A. Wagner, Goldman Sachs Asset Management, L.P./6.75%, Stuart L. Merkadeau, Thomas J. Campbell, Lothar Maier, Homa Bahrami, Insiders/7.32%, Benjamin N. Eldridge, Joseph R. Bronson (16 Owners included in Index)

Financial Data: **Fiscal Year End:** 12/31 **Latest Annual Data:** 12/30/2006

Year	Sales	Net Income
2006	$369,213,000	$57,217,000
2005	$237,495,000	$30,182,000
2004	$177,762,000	$25,178,000

Curr. Assets:	$292,544,000	**Curr. Liab.:**	$60,434,000	**P/E Ratio:**	29.44
Plant, Equip.:	$81,588,000	**Total Liab.:**	$63,572,000	**Indic. Yr. Divd.:**	NA
Total Assets:	$381,361,000	**Net Worth:**	$317,789,000	**Debt/ Equity:**	0.0147

Formula Systems (1985) Ltd

3 Abba Eban Blvd, Herzlia, 46120; **PH:** 972-99598800; **http://** www.formulasystems.com; **Email:** mktng@formula.co.il

General - Incorporation	Israel	**Stock** - Price on:12/24/2007	$13.9
Employees	5,950	Stock Exchange	NDQ
Auditor	Ziv Haft	Ticker Symbol	FORTY
Stk Agt.	Ziv Haft	Outstanding Shares	13,200,000
Counsel	NA	E.P.S.	$2.57
DUNS No.	60-003-7014	Shareholders	NA

Business: The group's principal activities are the provision of software consulting services and development of proprietary software products and computer based business solutions. The group operates in two principal business areas, software services and proprietary software solutions. The software services division designs, develops and implements innovative business-critical information technology solutions. The proprietary software solutions division designs, develops and markets proprietary software solutions for sale in selected niche markets worldwide.

Primary SIC and add'l.: 7373

CIK No: 0001045986

Subsidiaries: BluePhoenix Solutions Ltd., Formula Vision Technologies, Magic Software Enterprises Ltd., Matrix IT Ltd., nextSource Inc., Sapiens International Corporation N.V.

Officers: Nurit Keren/Mgr. - Community Relations

Directors: Guy Bernstein/40/Chmn., Tal Barnoach/45/Dir., Ronnie Vinkler/62/Dir., Ofer Lavie/63/Dir.

Owners: Menora Mivtachim Holdings Ltd./7.50%, Emblaze Ltd./50.10%, Clal Insurance Enterprises Holdings Ltd./5.40%

Financial Data: **Fiscal Year End:** 12/31 **Latest Annual Data:** 12/31/2006

Year	Sales	Net Income
2006	$492,735,000	$10,015,000
2005	$506,371,000	$183,000
2004	$456,610,000	$8,099,000

Curr. Assets:	$304,056,000	**Curr. Liab.:**	$178,191,000	**P/E Ratio:**	12.64
Plant, Equip.:	$18,457,000	**Total Liab.:**	$442,214,000	**Indic. Yr. Divd.:**	$1.130
Total Assets:	$595,504,000	**Net Worth:**	$153,290,000	**Debt/ Equity:**	NA

Forrester Research Inc

400 Technology Sq., Cambridge, MA, 02139; **PH:** 1-617-613-6000; **Fax:** 1-617-613-5200; **http://** www.forrester.com; **Email:** investor@forrester.com

General - Incorporation	DE	**Stock** - Price on:12/24/2007	$26.84
Employees	693	Stock Exchange	NDQ
Auditor	BDO Seidman LLP	Ticker Symbol	FORR
Stk Agt.	EquiServe Trust Co N.A	Outstanding Shares	22,930,000
Counsel	Ropes & Gray LLP	E.P.S.	$0.82
DUNS No.	10-676-5928	Shareholders	NA

Business: The group's principal activity is to conduct research and analyze the impact of emerging technologies on business, consumers and society. It provides the customers with a comprehensive and integrated perspective on technology and business, which is called the wholeview (TM). The group has developed a technology platform called forrester eresearch(r). The technology allows the group to conduct, design, sell, and deliver research over the Internet in a format, specifically developed to maximize its impact and effectiveness. The products and services include technographics(R), techstrategy(tm), techrankings(tm), strategy research and other data analysis and assessment tools. It markets its products and services to the senior management, business strategists and marketing and technology professionals at global 3,500 companies. During the year 2003, the group acquired giga information group, inc.

Primary SIC and add'l.: 7389 8731

CIK No: 0001023313

Subsidiaries: Forrester Beteiligungs GmbH, Forrester Research (Canada) Inc., Forrester Research APS, Forrester Research Australia Pty. Ltd., Forrester Research GmbH, Forrester Research GmbH & Co. KG, Forrester Research Israel Limited, Forrester Research KK, Forrester Research Limited, Forrester Research S.r.l., Forrester Research SAS, Forrester Research, B.V., Forrester Verwaltungs GmbH, Giga Information Group Limited, Whitcomb AB 16 Subsidiaries included in the Index

Officers: George F. Colony/Chmn., CEO, Dennis Van Lingen/MD - Marketing, Strategy Client Group, Chief Europe - Middle East, Africa Officer, Mark R. Nemec/MD - Technology Industry Client Group, Michael A. Doyle/CFO, Elizabeth Lemons/Chief People Officer, Brian E. Kardon/Chief Strategy, Marketing Officer, Gail S. Mann/Chief Legal Officer, Sec., Julie Meringer/MD - Information Technology Client Group, George M. Orlov/CIO, CTO, Charles Rutstein/COO

Directors: George F. Colony/Chmn., CEO, Michael H. Welles/Dir., Henk W. Broeders/Dir., Robert M. Galford/Dir., George R. Hornig/Dir., Gretchen G. Teichgraeber/Dir.

Owners: George F. Colony/34.30%, Brian Kardon, Michael Welles, Insiders/35.80%, U.S. TrustCorporation/6.05%, Morgan Stanley/5.60%, Daniel Mahoney, Charles Rutstein, Robert Galford

Financial Data: **Fiscal Year End:** 12/31 **Latest Annual Data:** 12/31/2006

Year	Sales	Net Income
2006	$181,473,000	$17,756,000
2005	$153,229,000	$11,348,000
2004	$138,479,000	$4,132,000

Curr. Assets:	$298,879,000	**Curr. Liab.:**	$132,605,000	**P/E Ratio:**	38.34
Plant, Equip.:	$5,611,000	**Total Liab.:**	$139,238,000	**Indic. Yr. Divd.:**	NA
Total Assets:	$384,143,000	**Net Worth:**	$244,905,000	**Debt/ Equity:**	NA

Forster Drilling Corp

2425 Fountain View Dr., Ste. 305, Houston, TX, 77057; **PH:** 1-713-266-8125; **Fax:** 1-713-266-8024; **http://** www.forsterdrilling.com

General - Incorporation	NV	**Stock** - Price on:12/24/2007	$1.35
Employees	4	Stock Exchange	OTC
Auditor	Mantyla McReynolds, LLC	Ticker Symbol	FODL
Stk Agt	Computershare Investor Services LLC	Outstanding Shares	45,480,000
Counsel	NA	E.P.S.	-$0.11
DUNS No.	NA	Shareholders	NA

Business: The groups principle activities include refurbishing drilling rigs and deploying them for use by oil and natural gas producers. In June 2006, the group acquired Forster Drilling Corporation. The group operates from New Mexico.

Primary SIC and add'l.: 7353

CIK No: 0000744667

Subsidiaries: Forster Drilling, Inc., Forster Exploration & Production, Inc., Forster Tool & Supply, Inc.

Officers: Fred Forster/Chmn., CEO, Pres., Roxanne M. Cort/47/General Counsel, Bud Najvar/CFO, Cullen Hudnall/GM - Fabrication, Refurbishing, Machining, Garrick Clayton/COO

Directors: Fred Forster/Chmn., CEO, Pres., Frederick C. Doutel/Dir., Fred Forster/Dir., Scott W. Thompson/Dir.

Owners: WLT Reification Trust, F. E. Forster, Bud Najvar, Insiders, Fred Forster, Roxanne M. Cort, William A. Silvey, Scott W. Thompson, Forster Family Trust

Financial Data: **Fiscal Year End:** 11/30 **Latest Annual Data:** 11/30/2006

Year	Sales	Net Income
2006	$2,545,000	-$5,055,000
2005	NA	-$39,000
2004	NA	-$11,000

Curr. Assets:	$553,000	**Curr. Liab.:**	$3,357,000		
Plant, Equip.:	$6,733,000	**Total Liab.:**	$4,047,000	**Indic. Yr. Divd.:**	NA
Total Assets:	$7,374,000	**Net Worth:**	$3,328,000	**Debt/ Equity:**	NA

Forsyth Bancshares Inc

501 Tri County Plaza, Highways 9 And 20, Cumming, GA, 30040; **PH:** 1-770-886-9500

General - Incorporation	GA	**Stock** - Price on:12/24/2007	NA
Employees	NA	Stock Exchange	NA
Auditor	Mauldin & Jenkins LLC	Ticker Symbol	NA
Stk Agt	NA	Outstanding Shares	NA
Counsel	NA	E.P.S.	NA
DUNS No.	15-099-6270	Shareholders	NA

Business: The group's principal activity is to provide banking services in cumming, Georgia and the surrounding area, including forsyth county. The group accepts deposits, originates various loans and provides other banking services to individuals, small to medium-sized businesses and professionals. The deposit products include checking, now, savings accounts and other time deposits, ranging from daily money market accounts to longer-term certificates of deposit. In addition, the group provides other services including certain retirement account services, safe deposit boxes, traveler's checks, direct deposits of payroll, social security checks and automatic drafts. The group originates various loans including commercial, consumer and real estate loans.

Primary SIC and add'l.: 6712 6022

CIK No: 0001021479

Subsidiaries: The Citizens Bank of Forsyth County

Fort Dearborn Income Securities Inc

1 North Wacker Dr., Chicago, IL, 60606; **PH:** 1-212-882-5575

General - Incorporation	DE	**Stock** - Price on:12/24/2007	$14.52
Employees	NA	Stock Exchange	NYSE
Auditor	Ernst & Young, LLP	Ticker Symbol	FDI
Stk Agt	EquiServe Trust Co N.A	Outstanding Shares	8,780,000
Counsel	NA	E.P.S.	$1.17
DUNS No.	NA	Shareholders	NA

Business: The groups principle activity is to invest in long-term and fixed-income debt securities. The group operates from the United States. The groups quarterly revenue for September 2007 was 4.11 millions of USD.

Primary SIC and add'l.: 6726

CIK No: 0000038188

Officers: Mark F. Kemper/50/Sec., VP, Joseph J. Allessie/43/VP, Assist. Sec., Thomas Disbrow/42/VP - Treasurer, Principal Accounting Officer, Michael J. Flook/43/VP, Assist. Treasurer, Joanne M. Kilkeary/40/VP, Assist. Treasurer, Tammie Lee/37/VP, Assist. Sec., Joseph McGill/46/VP, Chief Compliance Officer, Eric Sanders/43/VP, Assistance Sec., Andrew Shoup/52/VP, COO, Kai R. Sotorp/49/Pres., Keith Weller/47/VP, Assist. Sec., Nancy Osborn/42/VP, Assist. Treasurer

Directors: Frank K. Reilly/72/Chmn., Adela Cepeda/50/Dir., Mikesell J. Thomas/57/Dir., Edward M. Roob/74/Dir.

Owners: Doliver Capital Advisors, Inc/11.50%

Financial Data: **Fiscal Year End:** 09/30 **Latest Annual Data:** 9/30/2006

Year	Sales	Net Income
2006	$8,169,000	$4,625,000
2005	$9,476,000	$6,028,000
2004	$9,527,000	$7,138,000

Curr. Assets:	$1,622,000	**Curr. Liab.:**	$2,185,000	**P/E Ratio:**	31.47
Plant, Equip.:	NA	**Total Liab.:**	$2,185,000	**Indic. Yr. Divd.:**	$0.800
Total Assets:	$140,847,000	**Net Worth:**	$138,662,000	**Debt/ Equity:**	NA

Fortissimo Acquisition Corp

14 Hamelacha St., Pk. Afek, Rosh Ha'ayin, 48091; **PH:** 972-39157400; **Fax:** 972-39157411; **http://** www.ffcapital.com; **Email:** info@ffcapital.com

General - Incorporation	DE	Stock - Price on:12/24/2007	$5.69
Employees	NA	Stock Exchange	OTC
Auditor	Goldstein Golub Kessler LLP	Ticker Symbol	FSMO
Stk Agt	American Stock Transfer & Trust Co.	Outstanding Shares	NA
Counsel	NA	E.P.S.	NA
DUNS No.	NA	Shareholders	NA

Business: The group's principle activity is to invest primarily in public and private technology companies that require a capital infusion to expand their business. Customers served include the technology industry. The group operates from United States.

Primary SIC and add'l.: 6770

CIK No: 0001349318

Owners: Shmoulik Barashi/21.00%, Eli Blatt/21.00%, Yair Seroussi/0.90%, Insiders/21.00%, Michael Chill/0.90%, Sapling. LLC/8.90%, Marc Lesnick/21.00%, Weiss Asset Management LLC/10.10%, Hummingbird Management LLC/7.80%, Yuval Cohen/21.00%, Fortissimo Capital Fund GP, L.P./21.00%, Yochai Hacohen/21.00%

Financial Data: Fiscal Year End:12/31   Latest Annual Data: 12/31/2006

Year	Sales	Net Income
2006	NA	$89,000

Curr. Assets:	$27,291,000	Curr. Liab.:	$546,000		
Plant, Equip.:	NA	Total Liab.:	$5,794,000	Indic. Yr. Divd.:	NA
Total Assets:	$27,291,000	Net Worth:	$21,496,000	Debt/ Equity:	NA

Fortress International Group Inc

Formerly: Fortress America Acquisition Corp
9841 Broken Land Pk.way, Columbia, MD, 21046; **PH:** 1-410-312-9988;
http:// www.fortressamerica.net

General - Incorporation	DE	Stock - Price on:12/24/2007	$4.91
Employees	NA	Stock Exchange	NDQ
Auditor	Goldstein Golub Kessler LLP	Ticker Symbol	FIGI
Stk Agt	Continental Stock Transfer & Trust Co	Outstanding Shares	11,400,000
Counsel	FindLaw Corporate Counsel	E.P.S.	NA
DUNS No.	NA	Shareholders	NA

Business: The groups principal activity is to provide products and services that provide vital protection from security threats and natural disasters for people, physical assets, and critical infrastructure. Customers of the group include government and commercial users. In January 2007, the group acquired Vortech, L.L.C. The group operates from the United States.

Primary SIC and add'l.: 8742

CIK No: 0001320760

Officers: Tom Rosato/Dir., CEO, Gerard J. Gallagher/Dir., COO, Pres., John McNamara/Investor Relation Officer

Directors: Tom Rosato/Dir., CEO, Thomas C. McMillen/Vice Chmn., Harvey L. Weiss/Chmn., David J. Mitchell/Dir., Donald L. Nickles/Dir., William Jews/Dir., John Morton/Dir., Asa Hutchinson/Dir., Gerard J. Gallagher/Dir., COO, Pres.

Owners: David J. Mitchell, Hummingbird Management, LLC and Hummingbird Capital, LLC, Donald L. Nickles, Gerard J. Gallagher, Thomas P. Rosato, William L. Jews, Searock Capital Management, LLC and Seth Turkletaub, John Morton, Wellington Management Company, LLP, Andrew M. Weiss and Weiss Asset Management, LLC, Robert I. Green, Harvey L. Weiss, Asa Hutchinson, The Pinnacle Fund, L.P. and Barry M. Kitt, Thomas C. McMillen (17 Owners included in Index)

Financial Data: Fiscal Year End:12/31   Latest Annual Data: 12/31/2006

Year	Sales	Net Income
2006	$1,667,000	$645,000
2005	$525,000	$132,000

Curr. Assets:	$44,685,000	Curr. Liab.:	$2,061,000		
Plant, Equip.:	NA	Total Liab.:	$10,450,000	Indic. Yr. Divd.:	NA
Total Assets:	$46,046,000	Net Worth:	$35,596,000	Debt/ Equity:	NA

Fortuna Gaming Corp

3273 E Warm Springs Rd., Las Vegas, NV, 89120; **PH:** 1-888-304-1055;
http:// www.fortunagamingcorp.com; **Email:** info@fortunaroyale.com

General - Incorporation	NV	Stock - Price on:12/24/2007	$0.26
Employees	NA	Stock Exchange	OTC
Auditor	Moore & Associates	Ticker Symbol	FGAM
Stk Agt	Continental Stock Transfer & Trust Co	Outstanding Shares	NA
Counsel	Stepp Law Group	E.P.S.	NA
DUNS No.	NA	Shareholders	NA

Business: The groups principal activities include developing and licensing software and services for the online and mobile gaming industry. The group was reorganized to focus on the emerging European and Asian gambling marketplace. In mid-2006 the company changed its direction from acquiring an online gaming company to licensing its own suite of games. The group operates from the United States and the United Kingdom.

Primary SIC and add'l.: 7900

CIK No: 0001210536

Subsidiaries: Fortuna Gaming Corp. Limited, Fortuna Gaming UKLimited

Officers: Richard Von Raffay/Dir., CEO, CFO, Pres.

Directors: Richard Von Raffay/Dir., CEO, CFO, Pres.

Owners: Insiders/1.47%

Financial Data: Fiscal Year End:10/31   Latest Annual Data: 10/31/2006

Year	Sales	Net Income
2006	NA	-$1,976,000
2005	NA	-$3,022,000
2004	NA	-$29,000

Curr. Assets:	$9,000	Curr. Liab.:	$1,547,000		
Plant, Equip.:	$7,000	Total Liab.:	$1,547,000	Indic. Yr. Divd.:	NA
Total Assets:	$16,000	Net Worth:	-$1,532,000	Debt/ Equity:	NA

Fortune Brands Inc

520 Lake Cook Rd., Deerfield, IL, 60015; **PH:** 1-847-484-4400; **Fax:** 1-847-478-0073;
http:// www.fortunebrands.com; **Email:** mail@fortunebrands.com

General - Incorporation	DE	Stock - Price on:12/24/2007	$83.38
Employees	36,251	Stock Exchange	NYSE
Auditor	PricewaterhouseCoopers LLP	Ticker Symbol	FO
Stk Agt	Common & Preferred Stock	Outstanding Shares	152,760,000
Counsel	NA	E.P.S.	$4.89
DUNS No.	00-126-5768	Shareholders	NA

Business: The groups principle activity is to manufacture home products, spirits and wine, golf and office products. The groups products include omega kitchen and bath cabinets, locks and tool storage products. In the year 2007, the group acquired Simonton Holdings, Inc. The group operates from United States.

Primary SIC and add'l.: 2678 2085 3949 6719 3429

CIK No: 0000789073

Subsidiaries: 1700 Insurance Company Ltd., Acushnet Canada Inc., Acushnet Cayman Limited, Acushnet Company, Acushnet Europe Ltd., Acushnet Foot Joy (Thailand) Limited, Acushnet GmbH, Acushnet International Inc., Acushnet Japan, Inc., Acushnet Lionscore, Ltd., Acushnet Nederland B.V., Acushnet Sverige AB, Alberta Distillers Limited, ALC Holding Company, American Lock Company 68 Subsidiaries included in the Index

Officers: Norman H. Wesley/Chmn., CEO/$10,797,920.00, Mark A. Roche/Sr. VP, General Counsel, Sec./$3,053,095.00, Anthony J. Diaz/VP - Investor Relations, Clarkson C. Hine/VP - Corporate Communications, Lauren S. Tashma/VP, Assoc. General Counsel, Gary L. Tobison/VP, Chief Internal Auditor, Christopher J. Klein/Sr. VP - Strategy, Corporate Development/$2,853,105.00, Craig P. Omtvedt/CFO, Sr. VP/$4,828,706.00, Bruce A. Carbonari/Dir., COO, Pres., Elizabeth R. Lane/VP - Compensation, Benefits, Charlie Ryan/VP - Taxes, Allan J. Snape/VP - Business Development, Edward Wiertel/VP, Corporate Controller, Mark Hausberg/Sr. VP - Finance, Treasurer/$1,596,632.00

Directors: Norman H. Wesley/Chmn., CEO, Patricia O. Ewers/Dir., Bruce A. Carbonari/Dir., COO, Pres., Richard A. Goldstein/Dir., Pierre E. Leroy/Dir., David A.D. MacKay/Dir., Eugene A. Renna/Dir., Anne M. Tatlock/Dir., David M. Thomas/Dir., Peter M. Wilson/Dir.

Owners: Richard A. Goldstein, Eugene A. Renna, David D.A. Mackay, Peter M. Wilson, Mark A. Roche, Insiders/1.46%, Christopher J. Klein, Bruce A. Carbonari, Patricia O. Ewers, Gordon R. Lohman, Craig P. Omtvedt, Mark Hausberg, Norman H. Wesley, Pierre E. Leroy, Anne M. Tatlock (16 Owners included in Index)

Financial Data: Fiscal Year End:12/31   Latest Annual Data: 12/31/2006

Year	Sales	Net Income
2006	$8,769,000,000	$830,100,000
2005	$7,061,200,000	$621,100,000
2004	$6,145,200,000	$783,800,000

Curr. Assets:	$3,930,100,000	Curr. Liab.:	$2,515,400,000	P/E Ratio:	17.05
Plant, Equip.:	$1,948,500,000	Total Liab.:	$9,380,600,000	Indic. Yr. Divd.:	$1.680
Total Assets:	$14,668,300,000	Net Worth:	$4,728,000,000	Debt/ Equity:	1.0876

Fortune Industries Inc

Formerly: Fortune Diversified Industries Inc
Attn: Amy Gallo, 6402 Corporate Dr., Indianapolis, IN, 46268; **PH:** 1-317-532-1374;
http:// www.fdvi.net

General - Incorporation	IN	Stock - Price on:12/24/2007	$3.6
Employees	580	Stock Exchange	AMEX
Auditor	Somerset Cpas, P.C	Ticker Symbol	FFI
Stk Agt	American Stock Transfer & Trust Co.	Outstanding Shares	10,820,000
Counsel	NA	E.P.S.	-$0.72
DUNS No.	19-846-8654	Shareholders	NA

Business: The group's principal activity is to operate business under two segments namely: manufacturing and distribution segment and wireless infrastructure segment. Manufacturing and distribution segment is conducted through nor-cote and kingston subsidiaries. Nor-cote manufactures uv curable screen printing inks. Nor-cote inks are printed on plastic, metals and other substrates that are compatible with the uv curing process. Kingston is a manufacturer's representative and distributor for national companies in the electronic, sound, security and video markets. Kingston offers the latest technology in tvs, sound systems, electronic locking devices, wire, cable and fiber optics and intercom systems. Wireless infrastructure segment is conducted through pdh, cornerstone wireless, cornerstone construction, ttc and starquest. During the fiscal year 2003, the group established a professional business solutions segment with its acquisition of psm, psm ii and pro staff.

Primary SIC and add'l.: 5065 7812 7032 4899 5064

CIK No: 0000851249

Subsidiaries: Century II ASO, Inc., Century II Services, Inc., Century II Staffing TN, Inc., Century II Staffing USA, Inc., Century II Staffing, Inc., Commercial Solutions, Inc., Cornerstone Wireless Construction Services, Inc., Cornerstone Wireless Services Incorporated, CSM, Inc., Ink Source, Inc., Innovative Telecommunications Consultants, Inc., International, Inc.), James H. Drew Corporation, Kingston Sales Corp., Magtech Services, Inc. 30 Subsidiaries included in the Index

Officers: John F. Fisbeck/Dir., CEO, Pres., Amy E. Gallo/CFO

Directors: John F. Fisbeck/Dir., CEO, Pres., Carter M. Fortune/Chmn., David A. Berry/Dir., Nolan R. Lackey/Dir., Andy P. Rayl/Dir.

Owners: Fortune Industries, Inc, Insiders, Insiders, Carter M. Fortune, David A. Berry, John F. Fisbeck, Insiders, Nolan R. Lackey

Financial Data: Fiscal Year End:08/31   Latest Annual Data: 8/31/2006

Year	Sales	Net Income
2006	$157,113,000	$2,219,000
2005	$113,096,000	-$2,317,000
2004	$66,882,000	$2,402,000

Curr. Assets:	$48,824,000	Curr. Liab.:	$25,441,000		
Plant, Equip.:	$6,323,000	Total Liab.:	$53,335,000	Indic. Yr. Divd.:	NA
Total Assets:	$74,285,000	Net Worth:	$20,950,000	Debt/ Equity:	2.1425

Fortune Oil & Gas Inc

1656 Martin Dr., Ste. 305, White Rock, BC, V4A 6E7; **PH:** 1-604-530385;
http:// www.fortuneoilandgas.com; **Email:** info@fortuneoilandgas.com

General - Incorporation	NV	**Stock**- Price on:12/24/2007	$0.007
Employees	NA	Stock Exchange	OTC
Auditor	Dale Matheson Carr-Hilton Labonte	Ticker Symbol	FOGC
Stk Agt	Signature Stock Transfer, Inc.	Outstanding Shares	NA
Counsel	Richardson & Patel	E.P.S	NA
DUNS No.	NA	Shareholders	NA

Business: The group operates through its subsidiaries whose principle activities include exploring and producing oil and gas properties. The group also provides floating storage and off-loading tankers. The group operates from United States.

Primary SIC and add'l.: 1311

CIK No: 0001119949

Subsidiaries: A Barbados company, British West Indies, Fortune Pacific Management Ltd., Fortune Ship Management Ltd., Indo-Pacific Oil & Gas, Inc., Indo-Pacific Resources Java Ltd., Malta company

FortuNet Inc

2950 S Highland Dr., Ste. C, Las Vegas, NV, 89109; *PH:* 1-702-796-9090; *Fax:* 1-702-796-9069; *http://* www.fortunet.com; *Email:* sales@fortunet.com

General - Incorporation	NV	**Stock**- Price on:12/24/2007	NA
Employees	47	Stock Exchange	NDQ
Auditor	Schechter Dokken Kanter	Ticker Symbol	FNET
Stk Agt	Continental Stock Transfer & Trust Co	Outstanding Shares	11,350,000
Counsel	NA	E.P.S	$0.41
DUNS No.	NA	Shareholders	NA

Business: The groups principle activity is to manufacture gaming product. The groups product is wireless bingo. The group products sold under the trade names WIN-WIN, BingoStar(R) and AIMS(TM). Customers served by the group include commercial casino, tribal casino and charitable bingo. The group operates from International and domestic. The group's quarterly revenue for September 2007 was 4.27 millions of USD.

Primary SIC and add'l.: 7999 7379

CIK No: 0001337899

Subsidiaries: Millennium Games, Inc.

Officers: Yuri Itkis/66/Chmn., CEO, Boris Itkis/39/Co - Founder, Dir., CTO, Dir. - Engineering, William R. Jacques/59/CFO, Controller, Jack B. Coronel/42/Chief Marketing Officer, Dir. - Compliance, Strategic Development

Directors: Yuri Itkis/66/Chmn., CEO, Boris Itkis/39/Co - Founder, Dir., CTO, Dir. - Engineering, Merle Berman/61/Dir., Bradley P. Forst/Dir., Harlan W. Goodson/Dir., Darrel Johnson/58/Dir.

Owners: Jack B. Coronel, Boris Itkis, Bradley P. Forst, William R. Jacques, Harlan W. Goodson, Merle Berman, Insiders/74.30%, Arthur Schleifer, Yuri Itkis/72.80%

Financial Data: *Fiscal Year End:*12/31 *Latest Annual Data:* 3/31/2007

Year	Sales	Net Income
2007	NA	NA
2006	NA	NA
2005	$14,685,000	$2,225,000

Curr. Assets:	$30,021,000	*Curr. Liab.:*	$997,000	*P/E Ratio:*	10.09
Plant, Equip.:	$6,642,000	*Total Liab.:*	$997,000	*Indic. Yr. Divd.:*	NA
Total Assets:	$37,600,000	*Net Worth:*	$36,603,000	*Debt/ Equity:*	NA

Forum Energy Corp

46 Royal Ridge Rise Nw, Calgary, AB, T3G 4V2; *PH:* 1-403-290-1676; *http://* www.fecresources.com

General - Incorporation	Canada	**Stock**- Price on:12/24/2007	$0.035
Employees	NA	Stock Exchange	OTC
Auditor	Amisano Hanson	Ticker Symbol	FECOF
Stk Agt	Computershare Investor Services LLC	Outstanding Shares	234,140,000
Counsel	Eiseman Levine L & K	E.P.S	-$0.016
DUNS No.	NA	Shareholders	NA

Business: The group's principle activities include exploring and developing natural resource properties primarily oil and natural gas; and participates in the drilling of wells. The group operates from United States.

Primary SIC and add'l.: 1311 1381

CIK No: 0000849997

Subsidiaries: Pacific Geothermal Energy Inc, TEPCO Ltd., Tracer Petroleum International Ltd

Officers: Larry Youell/Dir., CEO, Pres., Riaz Sumar/Dir., CFO

Directors: Larry Youell/Dir., CEO, Pres., Barry Stansfield/Chmn., Riaz Sumar/Dir., CFO, Walter W. Brown/Dir., Mark Crandall/49/Dir., Michael Whiting/Dir.

Owners: Eastmark Limited/8.54%, CEDE & Co./14.44%, Barry Stansfield, CDS & Co./16.47%, Riaz Sumar, Langley Park Investments Plc./11.53%, Asian Coast International/8.67%, Insiders/3.87%, Mark Crandall/3.70%, Larry Youell, Indexa Corp./12.81%, Asian Coast International Limited/8.73%

Financial Data: *Fiscal Year End:*12/31 *Latest Annual Data:* 12/31/2006

Year	Sales	Net Income
2006	NA	-$4,733,000
2005	NA	$17,720,000
2004	NA	-$5,993,000

Curr. Assets:	$463,000	*Curr. Liab.:*	$3,342,000		
Plant, Equip.:	$4,000	*Total Liab.:*	$3,342,000	*Indic. Yr. Divd.:*	NA
Total Assets:	$16,589,000	*Net Worth:*	$13,247,000	*Debt/ Equity:*	NA

Forward Air Corp

430 Airport Rd., Greeneville, TN, 37745; *PH:* 1-423-636-7000; *Fax:* 1-423-636-7279; *http://* www.forwardair.com; *Email:* customs@forwardair.com

General - Incorporation	TN	**Stock**- Price on:12/24/2007	$35.24
Employees	1,225	Stock Exchange	NDQ
Auditor	Ernst & Young LLP	Ticker Symbol	FWRD
Stk Agt	Suntrust Bank	Outstanding Shares	30,170,000
Counsel	NA	E.P.S	$1.47
DUNS No.	04-890-7794	Shareholders	NA

Business: The group's principal activity is to provide air freight services to freight forwarders, integrated air cargo carriers and airlines. It provides scheduled ground transportation of cargo. It operates a network of 80 terminals located on or near airports in the United States and Canada, including a central sorting facility in columbus, Ohio and regional hubs serving key markets. Its operations involve receiving deferred freight shipments at its terminals and transporting them by truck to the terminal nearest their destination. Air freight forwarder customers include ait freight systems, associated global systems, danzas/aei, exel and pilot air freight. Airline customers include british airways, continental, northwest airlines, united airlines and virgin Atlantic. Integrated air cargo carrier customers include dhl worldwide express, emery worldwide, federal express and ups.

Primary SIC and add'l.: 4731 4213

CIK No: 0000912728

Subsidiaries: Forward Air, Inc

Officers: Bruce A. Campbell/Chmn., CEO, Pres./$778,496.00, Chris C. Ruble/Sr. VP - Operations/$466,404.00, Rodney L. Bell/CFO, Sr. VP, Treasurer/$487,744.00, Craig A. Drum/Sr. VP - Sales/$440,375.00, Matthew J. Jewell/Sr. VP, General Counsel, Sec./$494,079.00, Michael P. McLean/VP, Controller

Directors: Bruce A. Campbell/Chmn., CEO, Pres., Ray A. Mundy/Dir., Richard W. Hanselman/Dir., Michael G. Lynch/Dir., John C. Langley/Dir., Clyde B. Preslar/Dir., Robert C. Campbell/Dir., Tracy A. Leinbach/Dir., Gary L. Paxton/Dir.

Owners: Craig A. Drum, Rodney L. Bell, Ray A. Mundy, Federated Investors, Inc./6.60%, Kayne Anderson Rudnick Investment Management, LLC/6.10%, John C. Langley, Columbia Wanger Asset Management, L.P./7.20%, Wellington Management Company, LLP/13.50%, Bruce A. Campbell/1.50%, Clyde B. Preslar, Andrew C. Clarke, Chris C. Ruble, Matthew J. Jewell, Michael G. Lynch, Richard W. Hanselman *(16 Owners included in Index)*

Financial Data: *Fiscal Year End:*12/31 *Latest Annual Data:* 12/31/2006

Year	Sales	Net Income
2006	$352,758,000	$48,923,000
2005	$320,934,000	$44,909,000
2004	$282,197,000	$34,421,000

Curr. Assets:	$127,563,000	*Curr. Liab.:*	$19,133,000	*P/E Ratio:*	23.18
Plant, Equip.:	$53,315,000	*Total Liab.:*	$27,787,000	*Indic. Yr. Divd.:*	$0.280
Total Assets:	$213,014,000	*Net Worth:*	$185,227,000	*Debt/ Equity:*	0.0042

Forward Industries Inc

1801 Green Rd., Ste. E, Pompano Beach, FL, 33064; *PH:* 1-954-419-9544; *Fax:* 1-954-419-9735; *http://* www.forwardindustries.com; *Email:* info@forwardindustries.com

General - Incorporation	NY	**Stock**- Price on:12/24/2007	$3.37
Employees	49	Stock Exchange	NDQ
Auditor	Kaufman, Rossin & Co. P.A	Ticker Symbol	FORD
Stk Agt	American Stock Transfer & Trust Co.	Outstanding Shares	7,860,000
Counsel	NA	E.P.S	-$0.07
DUNS No.	00-128-3282	Shareholders	NA

Business: The group's principle activity is to design, manufacture and market customized soft-sided carrying cases made from leather, nylon, vinyl and other synthetic fabrics. The products are utilized for transporting portable electronic products such as cellular telephones, medical instruments and computers. The group operates through its wholly owned subsidiary, koszegi industries inc. It markets its products to original equipment manufacturers, principally in the communications, medical and testing and measurement equipment industries. Substantially all of the group's products are manufactured in China. Major customers of the group for fiscal 2003 were motorola and abbot labs. International sales accounted for 40% of fiscal 2003 revenues. In 2004, the group acquired abbot laboratories. The group's quarterly revenue for Sep'07 was 4.44 millions of USD.

Primary SIC and add'l.: 3172 3199

CIK No: 0000038264

Subsidiaries: Forward Innovations GmbH, Koszegi Asia Ltd, Koszegi Industries Inc

Officers: Jerome E. Ball/Chmn., CEO, Steven A. Malsin/Sec., Douglas W. Sabra/CFO, VP, Michael Schiffman/Dir., COO, Pres.

Directors: Jerome E. Ball/Chmn., CEO, Bruce Galloway/Dir., Norman Ricken/Dir., Michael Schiffman/Dir., COO, Pres., Edwin A. Levy/Dir., Louis Lipschitz/Dir.

Owners: Jerome E. Ball/4.90%, Edwin Levy, Bruce Galloway, Insiders/10.10%, Louis Lipschitz, Norman Ricken, Barclays Global Investor NA/6.30%, Michael Schiffman/4.20%

Financial Data: *Fiscal Year End:*09/30 *Latest Annual Data:* 9/30/2006

Year	Sales	Net Income
2006	$30,608,000	$1,541,000
2005	$51,869,000	$9,434,000
2004	$20,073,000	$1,939,000

Curr. Assets:	$27,540,000	*Curr. Liab.:*	$2,832,000	*P/E Ratio:*	25.92
Plant, Equip.:	$190,000	*Total Liab.:*	$2,832,000	*Indic. Yr. Divd.:*	NA
Total Assets:	$27,782,000	*Net Worth:*	$24,950,000	*Debt/ Equity:*	NA

Fossil Inc

2280 N Greenville Ave., Richardson, TX, 75082; *PH:* 1-972-234-2525; *Fax:* 1-972-234-4669; *http://* www.fossil.com; *Email:* ir@fossil.com

General - Incorporation	DE	**Stock**- Price on:12/24/2007	$30.25
Employees	7,160	Stock Exchange	NDQ
Auditor	Deloitte & Touche LLP	Ticker Symbol	FOSL
Stk Agt	Mellon Investor Services LLC	Outstanding Shares	67,460,000
Counsel	Jenkens & Gilchrist	E.P.S	$1.50
DUNS No.	11-864-3956	Shareholders	NA

Business: The group's principal activities are to design, develop, market and distribute watches, accessories and apparel. The market for watch products in the United States can be divided into four segments: fine watches, fine premium branded and designer watches, watches sold by mass marketers and moderately priced watches. Fine watches are made of precious metals or stainless steel and set with precious gems. The accessories include products such as small leather goods, handbags, belts, costume jewelery and sunglasses. The products are sold to departmental stores and specialty retail stores in over 90 countries worldwide, and through a network of independent distributors. The group has international operations in Europe, South and Central America, the Caribbean, Canada, the Far East, Australia and the Middle East. The group acquired Tempus International Corp in 2004.

Primary SIC and add'l.: 3911 3851 3171 3873 3172

CIK No: 0000883569

Subsidiaries: Arrow Merchandising, Inc., FDT, Ltd. (Design Time, Ltd.), Fossil (Asia) Holding Ltd., Fossil (Asia) Ltd, Fossil (Australia) Pty Ltd., Fossil (East) Limited, Fossil (Gibraltar) Ltd., Fossil (New Zealand) Ltd., Fossil (Newtime) Ltd., Fossil Austria GmbH, Fossil Canada, Inc., Fossil Europe B.V., Fossil Europe GmbH, Fossil European Services Co, GmbH, Fossil France SA 50 Subsidiaries included in the Index

Officers: Kosta N. Kartsotis/Dir., CEO, Jal S. Shroff/Dir., MD - Fossil East, Mike L. Kovar/Sr. VP, CFO, Treasurer, Harold Brooks/Pres. - Fashion Watch Division, Michael W. Barnes/Dir., COO, Pres., Jennifer Pritchard/Pres. - Retail Division, Livio Galanti/Exec. VP

Directors: Kosta N. Kartsotis/Dir., CEO, Tom Kartsotis/Chmn., Mark D. Quick/Vice Chmn., Jal S. Shroff/Dir., MD - Fossil East, Kenneth W. Anderson/Dir., Donald Stone/Dir., Michael Steinberg/Dir., Alan Gold/Dir., Michael W. Barnes/Dir., COO, Pres., Elaine B. Agather/Dir., James M. Zimmerman/Dir.

Owners: Donald J. Stone, Insiders/34.30%, Royce & Associates, LLC/8.37%, FMR Corp./10.68%, Kosta N. Kartsotis/13.80%, Michael W. Barnes, Alan J. Gold, Mark D. Quick, Mike Kovar, Harold S. Brooks, Jal S. Shroff/1.80%, Capital Research and Management Company/5.65%, Kenneth W. Anderson, Stephen Bock, Wellington Management Company, LLP/7.54% (17 Owners included in Index)

Financial Data: Fiscal Year End:12/31   Latest Annual Data: 01/06/2007

Year	Sales	Net Income
2007	$1,213,965,000	$77,582,000
2005	$1,040,468,000	$78,059,000
2004	$781,175,000	$68,335,000

Curr. Assets:	$505,869,000	Curr. Liab.:	$185,800,000	P/E Ratio:	21.76
Plant, Equip.:	$148,150,000	Total Liab.:	$216,070,000	Indic. Yr. Divd.:	NA
Total Assets:	$744,746,000	Net Worth:	$526,149,000	Debt/ Equity:	NA

Foster Wheeler Ltd

Perryville Corporate Pk., Clinton, NJ, 08809; *PH:* 1-908-730-4000; *Fax:* 1-908-730-5315; *http://* www.fwc.com; *Email:* fw@fwc.com

General - Incorporation	Bermuda	Stock - Price on:12/24/2007	$102.4
Employees	11,992	Stock Exchange	NDQ
Auditor	PricewaterhouseCoopers LLP	Ticker Symbol	FWLT
Stk Agt	Mellon Investor Services LLC	Outstanding Shares	70,420,000
Counsel	NA	E.P.S.	$4.55
DUNS No.	00-133-9456	Shareholders	NA

Business: The group's principle activities are to design, engineer and construct petroleum, chemical and alternative-fuels facilities. The group also manufactures steam generating and auxiliary equipment. The group's operations are conducted through two business segments: engineering and construction group and energy equipment group. The engineering and construction group designs, engineers and constructs petroleum, chemical and alternative-fuels facilities and related infrastructure, including power generation and distribution facilities. This segment also provides environmental remediation services. The energy equipment group designs, manufactures and erects steam generating and auxiliary equipment for power stations and industrial markets worldwide. This segment also provides research analysis and experimental work in fluid dynamics, heat transfer, combustion and fuel technology. The group's quarterly revenue for Sep'07 was 1,299.87 millions of USD.

Primary SIC and add'l.: 3511 8711

CIK No: 0001130385

Subsidiaries: 4900 Singleton L.P., 8925 Rehco Inc., A/C Power, Barsottis Inc., BSF China Company Limited, BSF Global Limited, Calabria Ambiente S.p.A., Camden County Energy Recovery Associates L.P., Camden County Energy Recovery Corp., CEG Nouvelle Caledonie, Centro Energia Ferrara S.p.A., Centro Energia Gas S.p.A., Centro Energia Teverola S.p.A., Chiyoda-Foster Wheeler and Company LLC, Conequip S.A. 188 Subsidiaries included in the Index

Officers: Umberto Della Sala/CEO - Global E, C Group/$4,258,267.00, Raymond J. Milchovich/Chmn., CEO, Pres./$10,591,030.00, David Wardlaw/52/VP - Project Risk Management Group, Steve Spicer/Contact - Foster Wheeler International Corporation, Steve Sock/Contact - Business Development, Brian K. Ferraiol/52/VP, Controller/$773,714.00, Rakesh K. Jindal/49/VP - Tax, Rhonda Campbell/Contact - Foster Wheeler Fired Heaters, Andre Robini/Pres. - Foster Wheeler France, Thierry Desmaris/49/VP - Corporate Development, John T. La Duc/65/CFO, Exec. VP/$1,777,863.00, Peter J. Ganz/46/Exec. VP, General Counsel, Sec./$1,675,061.00, Francis Ong/GM - Foster Wheeler, B Sdn Bhd, Renato Corno/Contact - Equipment Division, Giampiero Caronno/Contact - Equipment Division (33 Officers included in Index)

Directors: Raymond J. Milchovich/Chmn., CEO, Pres., Stephanie Hanbury-Brown/Dir., Eugene D. Atkinson/Dir., Diane C. Creel/Dir., James D. Woods/Dir., Ralph Alexander/Dir., Robert C. Flexon/Dir.

Owners: Raymond J. Milchovich, Brian K. Ferraioli, Peter J. Ganz, Diane C. Creel, Insiders, Franco Baseotto, Robert C. Flexon, Ziff Asset Management, L.P./5.00%, Eugene D. Atkinson, Umberto della Sala, Stephanie Hanbury-Brown, James D. Woods, John T. La Duc

Financial Data: Fiscal Year End:12/30   Latest Annual Data: 12/29/2006

Year	Sales	Net Income
2006	$3,495,048,000	$261,984,000
2005	$2,199,955,000	-$109,749,000
2004	$2,661,324,000	-$285,294,000

Curr. Assets:	$1,049,298,000	Curr. Liab.:	$1,261,421,000	P/E Ratio:	20.56
Plant, Equip.:	$280,305,000	Total Liab.:	$2,686,052,000	Indic. Yr. Divd.:	NA
Total Assets:	$2,187,539,000	Net Worth:	-$525,565,000	Debt/ Equity:	0.9379

Foundation Coal Holdings Inc

999 Corporate Blvd., Ste. 300, Linthicum Heights, MD, 21090; *PH:* 1-410-689-7500; *Fax:* 1-410-689-7511; *http://* www.foundationcoal.com; *Email:* ircommunications@foundationcoal.com

General - Incorporation	DE	Stock - Price on:12/24/2007	$40.14
Employees	3,150	Stock Exchange	NYSE
Auditor	Ernst & Young LLP	Ticker Symbol	FCL
Stk Agt	Bank of New York	Outstanding Shares	45,210,000
Counsel	NA	E.P.S.	$0.02
DUNS No.	NA	Shareholders	NA

Business: The groups principle activity is to produce coal. The group operates through three segments namely, powder river basin, northern Appalachia and central Appalachia. The group operates from the United States. The groups quarterly revenue for September 2007 was 359.06 millions of USD.

Primary SIC and add'l.: 1222 1221

CIK No: 0001301063

Subsidiaries: Alliance Power Marketing, Inc., Barbara Holdings Inc., Castle Gate Holding Company, Coal Gas Recovery, LP, Cumberland Coal Resources, LP, Delta Mine Holding Company, Emerald Coal Resources, LP, Energy Development Corporation, FC 2 Corp., Foundation American Coal Company, LLC, Foundation American Coal Holding, LLC, Foundation Coal Corporation, Foundation Coal Development Corporation, Foundation Coal Resources Corporation, Foundation Coal West, Inc. 53 Subsidiaries included in the Index

Officers: James F. Roberts/58/Chmn., CEO, Pres., Frank J. Wood/55/CFO, Sr. VP, Chris Hanko-Hayhurst/Sr. Human Resources Representative, Emerald, Kathy Richards/Sr. Human Resources Representative, Cumberland, Ryan Anderson/Mgr. - Human Resources, Wyoming, Kim Coleman/Supervisor, Human Resources, Eagle Butte, Greg A. Walker/Sr. VP, General Counsel, Sec., James A. Olsen/57/Sr. VP - Development, Information Technology, James J. Bryja/52/Sr. VP - Operations, Klaus-Dieter Beck/53/Sr. VP - Planning, Engineering, Kurt D. Kost/52/Exec. VP, Michael R. Peelish/47/Sr. VP - Safety, Human Resources, Scott A. Pack/49/Sr. VP - Sales, Marketing, Pres. - Foundation Energy Sales, Inc, William F. Davison/VP - Sales, Marketing, Eastern Sales, Larry M. Deal/VP - Sales, Marketing, Western Sales (20 Officers included in Index)

Directors: James F. Roberts/58/Chmn., CEO, Pres., William J. Crowley/Dir., David I. Foley/40/Dir., Michael P. Giftos/Dir., Alex T. Krueger/34/Dir., Joel Richards/61/Dir., Robert C. Scharp/Dir., Thomas V. Shockley/63/Dir.

Owners: Insiders, Scott A. Pack, Kurt D. Kost, James F. Roberts, Alex T. Krueger, FMR Corp/9.20%, Joel Richards, James J. Bryja, Frank J. Wood, Michael R. Peelish, Michael P. Giftos, James A. Olsen, T. Rowe Price Associates, Inc/10.20%, William J. Crowley, Thomas V. Shockley (20 Owners included in Index)

Financial Data: Fiscal Year End:12/31   Latest Annual Data: 12/31/2006

Year	Sales	Net Income
2006	$1,470,321,000	$31,419,000
2005	$1,316,929,000	$88,903,000
2004	$444,596,000	$14,477,000

Curr. Assets:	$240,647,000	Curr. Liab.:	$203,598,000		
Plant, Equip.:	$656,622,000	Total Liab.:	$1,651,767,000	Indic. Yr. Divd.:	$0.200
Total Assets:	$1,949,580,000	Net Worth:	$297,813,000	Debt/ Equity:	2.0152

Founders Community Bank

237 Higuera St., San Luis Obispo, CA, 93401; *PH:* 1-805-543-6500; *Fax:* 1-805-543-6599; *http://* www.founderscommunitybank.com; *Email:* mail@fcbslo.com

General - Incorporation		Stock - Price on:12/24/2007	$20.75
Employees	NA	Stock Exchange	NA
Auditor	NA	Ticker Symbol	NA
Stk Agt	Computershare Trust CO.	Outstanding Shares	NA
Counsel	NA	E.P.S.	NA
DUNS No.	NA	Shareholders	NA

Business: The groups principal activity is to provide community-banking services. The group operates from the United States.

Primary SIC and add'l.: 6022

CIK No:

Officers: Thomas J. Sherman/Dir., CEO, Pres., Mandy Leastman/CFO, Exec. VP

Directors: Thomas J. Sherman/Dir., CEO, Pres., Fred Russell/Dir., Michael D. Patrick/Dir., Richard H. Porter/Dir., Andrew G. Blodgett/Dir., William A. Hares/Dir., Todd J. Mirolla/Dir., Robert E. Olson/Dir., Greg Morris/Dir.

Foundry Networks Inc

4980 Great America Pkwy., Santa Clara, CA, 95054; *PH:* 1-408-207-1700; *Fax:* 1-408-207-1709; *http://* www.foundrynet.com; *Email:* info@foundrynet.com

General - Incorporation	DE	Stock - Price on:12/24/2007	$16.88
Employees	719	Stock Exchange	NDQ
Auditor	Ernst & Young LLP	Ticker Symbol	FDRY
Stk Agt	U.S. Stock Transfer Corp	Outstanding Shares	145,690,000
Counsel	Venture Law Group	E.P.S.	$0.44
DUNS No.	NA	Shareholders	NA

Business: The group's principle activities include designing, developing, manufacturing and marketing a comprehensive, end-to-end suite of data networking solutions. The products of the group's are ethernet layer 2 and layer 3 switches, metro routers, and Internet traffic management products. The customers include Internet and metro service providers, and enterprises such as e-commerce sites, entertainment, health and wellness, financial and manufacturing companies, universities, and government agencies. The group operates in the United States, barbados, Brazil, France, Canada, Germany, the Netherlands, the United Kingdom, Singapore, Japan and Italy.

Primary SIC and add'l.: 7372 8744 7373

CIK No: 0001090071

Subsidiaries: Foundry Networks Canada Co., Foundry Networks do Brasil Ltda., Foundry Networks France SARL, Foundry Networks GmbH, Foundry Networks Holding Co., Foundry Networks International Inc., Foundry Networks Italia Srl., Foundry Networks Japan KK, Foundry Networks Japan-US., LLC., Foundry Networks Ltd., Foundry Networks Nederland BV, Foundry Networks Singapore, PTE Ltd.

Officers: Bobby R. Johnson/51/CEO, Pres./$3,129,637.00, Richard Bridges/VP - Operations, Tim Heffner/VP - Corporate Development/$1,595,340.00, Robert W. Schiff/51/VP, GM - Small, Medium Systems/$1,381,111.00, Benjamin D. Taft/VP - Marketing Communications, John Burger/VP - Hardware Engineering, Antoine Gayon/Country Mgr. - France, Yamil Jimenez/Contact - Mexico Sales Office, Woody Akin/Sr. VP - Worldwide Sales, Ken Cheng/VP, GM - High Value Systems Business Unit/$2,094,038.00, Lisa McGill/VP - Human Resources, Facilities, Bob Schiff/VP, GM - Enterprise Business Unit, Paul Twombly/VP - Customer Service/$1,654,165.00, Pavel Radda/Contact - Media, Worldwide, Michael Iburg/Treasurer (20 Officers included in Index)

Directors: Alfred J. Amoroso/58/Chmn., Nicholas C. Keating/66/Dir., Steven J. Young/46/Dir., Alan L. Earhart/64/Dir.

Owners: Nicholas C. Keating, Bobby R. Johnson/8.15%, Timothy D. Heffner/1.00%, Insiders/11.35%, Steven J. Young, Paul L. Twombly, Laurence L. Akin, Robert Schiff, Alan L. Earhart, Royce& Associates, LLC/10.12%, Ken K. Cheng, Alfred J. Amoroso

Financial Data: Fiscal Year End:12/31   Latest Annual Data: 12/31/2006

Year	Sales	Net Income
2006	$473,280,000	$38,698,000
2005	$403,856,000	$56,013,000
2004	$409,104,000	$47,967,000

Curr. Assets:	$848,753,000	**Curr. Liab.:**	$113,437,000	**P/E Ratio:**	43.28
Plant, Equip.:	$11,103,000	**Total Liab.:**	$137,295,000	**Indic. Yr. Divd.:**	NA
Total Assets:	$1,095,390,000	**Net Worth:**	$958,095,000	**Debt/ Equity:**	NA

Fountain Powerboat Industries Inc

1653 Whichards Beach Rd., Washington, NC, 27889; ***PH:*** 1-252-975-2000; ***Fax:*** 1-252-975-6793; ***http://*** www.fountainpowerboats.com

General - Incorporation	NV	**Stock**- Price on:12/24/2007	$2.65
Employees	448	Stock Exchange	AMEX
Auditor	Dixon Hughes PLLC	Ticker Symbol	FPB
Stk Agt	First Citizens Bank & Trust Co	Outstanding Shares	4,830,000
Counsel	Ward & Smith	E.P.S	-$0.95
DUNS No.	05-675-0003	Shareholders	NA

Business: The group's principal activities are designing, manufacturing and selling offshore sport boats, sport cruisers, sport fishing boats and sport yachts. The group builds custom racing boats, outboard powered center consoles, and outboard or stern drive cabin model offshore sport fishing boats ranging from 27' to 47' of inboard/outboard design. Various military support craft are also produced by the group for domestic and international government agencies. The products of the group are sold through a network of 44 dealers throughout the United States and through 3 dealers internationally. The products are sold in the United States, Canada, Central and South America, Middle East, Europe and Asia.

Primary SIC and add'l.: 3732

CIK No: 0000764858

Subsidiaries: Fountain Powerboat Industries, Inc, Fountain Powerboats, Inc

Officers: Reginald M. Fountain/67/Chmn., CEO, Irving L. Smith/64/CFO, David R. Knight/50/Pres., Marty Tullio/Investor Relations Counsel, Roger F. Scott/Dir., Sec.

Directors: Reginald M. Fountain/67/Chmn., CEO, Guy L. Hecker/Dir., Mark L. Spencer/Dir., David C. Miller/Dir., Anthony J. Romersa/Dir., Anthony A. Sarandes/Dir., Craig F. Goess/Dir., Roger F. Scott/Dir., Sec.

Owners: Irving L. Smith, Insiders/51.53%, David C. Miller, Mark L. Spencer, Triglova Finanz, A. G./6.51%, Goodman & Company, Investment Counsel Ltd./5.71%, Reginald M. Fountain/51.15%, Anthony A. Sarandes

Financial Data: ***Fiscal Year End:***06/30 ***Latest Annual Data:*** 6/30/2006

Year	**Sales**	**Net Income**
2006	$79,226,000	$2,405,000
2005	$71,182,000	$756,000
2004	$59,297,000	$609,000

Curr. Assets:	$17,135,000	**Curr. Liab.:**	$13,233,000		
Plant, Equip.:	$17,108,000	**Total Liab.:**	$28,767,000	**Indic. Yr. Divd.:**	NA
Total Assets:	$37,860,000	**Net Worth:**	$9,094,000	**Debt/ Equity:**	4.7002

Four Oaks Fincorp Inc

6114 US 301 S, Four Oaks, NC, 27524; ***PH:*** 1-919-963-2177; ***Fax:*** 1-919-963-4169; ***http://*** portal.fxfn.com

General - Incorporation	NC	**Stock**- Price on:12/24/2007	$22.75
Employees	156	Stock Exchange	OTC
Auditor	Dixon Hughes PLLC	Ticker Symbol	FOFN
Stk Agt	Registrar & Transfer Co	Outstanding Shares	5,600,000
Counsel	NA	E.P.S	$0.94
DUNS No.	NA	Shareholders	NA

Business: The group's principle activity is to provide banking services in North Carolina. Deposit products of the group include checking accounts, savings accounts, now accounts, money market accounts, certificates of deposit, student checking and savings program. The loan portfolio includes agriculture, real estate, personal uses, home improvement and automobiles and equity lines of credit. It also provides services such as individual retirement accounts, safe deposit boxes, money orders, and electronic funds transfer services. Financial services also include a complete line of insurance and investment services, including financial strategies, mutual funds, annuities, insurance, stock brokerage, ira's, employee benefit plans and 401(k) s. The group's customers are individuals and small to medium-size businesses located in johnston county and surrounding areas. The operations of the group are carried through its head office in four oaks and nine branch offices.

Primary SIC and add'l.: 6022 6712

CIK No: 0001040799

Subsidiaries: Four Oaks Bank & Trust Company, Four Oaks Mortgage Company, L.P., Four Oaks Mortgage Services, LLC

Officers: Ayden R. Lee/Chmn., CEO, Pres./$350,866.00, Wendell Leon Hiatt/Exec. VP, Chief Administrative Officer, Lauren K. McLeod/Program Coordinator, Nancy S. Wise/CFO, Exec. VP/$163,757.00, Bruce Behrendt/VP - City Executive, Charlene Browning/Assist. VP, Branch Mgr. - Zebulon, Corey B. Culp/Financial Specialist, Miranda D. Matthews/Financial Representative, CSR, Jeff D. Pope/Exec. VP, Branch Administrator/$165,471.00, Wanda J. Blow/Investor Relation Officer, Christopher P. Vasques/Division Sr. VP - Investment, Clifton L. Painter/Sr. Exec. VP, COO/$181,442.00, Rene M. Karsko/Financial Specialist, John Wood/Sr. VP - City Executive, Benson, Tim Barbour/VP, Branch Mgr. - Benson *(27 Officers included in Index)*

Directors: Ayden R. Lee/Chmn., CEO, Pres., William J. Edwards/Dir., Percy Y. Lee/Dir., Michael A. Weeks/Dir., Warren L. Grimes/Dir., Paula Canaday Bowman/Dir., Max R. Raynor/Dir., William Ashley Turner/Dir.

Owners: Percy Y. Lee/1.00%, Debra C. Turner/5.30%, Ayden R. Lee/2.70%, Michael A. Weeks, William Ashley Turner/5.30%, Leon W. Hiatt, William J. Edwards, Paula Canaday Bowman/1.20%, Clifton L. Painter, Jeff D. Pope, Max R. Raynor, Warren L. Grimes, Insiders/13.00%, Nancy S. Wise

Financial Data: ***Fiscal Year End:***12/31 ***Latest Annual Data:*** 12/31/2006

Year	**Sales**	**Net Income**
2006	$45,214,000	$7,017,000
2005	$33,264,000	$5,003,000
2004	$25,597,000	$4,375,000

Curr. Assets:	$21,325,000	**Curr. Liab.:**	$470,126,000	**P/E Ratio:**	20.87
Plant, Equip.:	$11,630,000	**Total Liab.:**	$558,814,000	**Indic. Yr. Divd.:**	$0.320
Total Assets:	$608,137,000	**Net Worth:**	$49,323,000	**Debt/ Equity:**	1.6244

Fox & Hound Restaurant Group

1551 N Waterfront Pkwy., Ste. 310, Wichita, KS, 67206; ***PH:*** 1-316-634-0505; ***Fax:*** 1-316-634-6060; ***http://*** www.tentcorp.com; ***Email:*** investorrelations@fhrg.com

General - Incorporation	DE	**Stock**- Price on:12/24/2007	$22.29
Employees	NA	Stock Exchange	NA
Auditor	KPMG LLP	Ticker Symbol	NA
Stk Agt	Wachovia Bank N.A	Outstanding Shares	NA
Counsel	Foulston & Siefkin	E.P.S	NA
DUNS No.	16-001-5681	Shareholders	NA

Business: The group's principal activities are to own and operate a chain of 66 entertainment restaurant locations under the trade names, fox and hound English pub & grille (fox & hound), bailey's pub & grille (bailey's). Its restaurant concepts combines a comfortable and inviting social gathering place, full menu and full service bar, state-of-the art audio and video systems for sports entertainment, traditional games of skill such as pocket billiards and a late-night dining and entertainment alternative all in single location. At 22-Mar-2004, the group owned and operated fifty fox & hound units and sixteen bailey's units in Alabama, Arizona, Arkansas, Colorado, Georgia, Illinois, Indiana, Kansas, Louisiana, Michigan, Missouri, Nebraska, New Mexico, North Carolina, Ohio, Oklahoma, Pennsylvania, South Carolina, Tennessee, Texas and Virginia.

Primary SIC and add'l.: 5812 7999 5813 2099

CIK No: 0001035374

Subsidiaries: 505 Entertainment, Ltd., Alabama Fox & Hound, Inc., Baileys Sports Grill, Bryant Beverage Corporation, Campbell Beverage Corp., Downtown Beverage Corp., F & H of Iowa, Inc., F & H of Kennesaw, Inc., F & H Restaurant Corp., F & H Restaurant of Georgia, Inc., F & H Restaurants of Texas, Inc., Fox & Hound Club, Fox & Hound II, Inc., Fox & Hound of Arizona, Inc., Fox & Hound of Austin, Ltd. 58 Subsidiaries included in the Index

Officers: Steven M. Johnson/Dir., CEO, Gary M. Judd/Dir., Pres., Jeff Runion/GM - Fox, Hound Smokehouse, Tavern, Phoenix, Peoria, Arizona, Mike Murphy/GM - Fox, Hound Smokehouse, Tavern, Tucson, Arizona, Mariah Ruehl/Event Coordinator - Fox, Hound Smokehouse, Tavern, Tucson, Arizona, Kelly Thrush/GM - Fox, Hound Smokehouse, Tavern, Denver, Arapahoe Road, Colorado, Jon Davis/GM - Fox, Hound Smokehouse, Tavern, Denver, Bowles Avenue, Colorado, Janelle Beluscak/Event Coordinator - Fox, Hound Smokehouse, Tavern, Denver, Lone Tree, Colorado, Jordan Welker/GM - Bailey's Sports Grille, Columbia, Michelle Mamielle/Event Coordinator - Bailey's Sports Grille, Greenville, Jack Cardinal/Event Coordinator - Bailey's Pub, Grille, Atlanta, Kennesaw, Mike Zurn/GM - Fox, Hound English Pub, Grille, Montgomery, Louis Elliott/GM - Fox, Hound Pub, Grille, Birmingham, Danielle Hardaman/Event Coordinator - Fox, Hound Pub, Grille, Birmingham, Jennifer Kurth/Human Resources Mgr. *(146 Officers included in Index)*

Directors: Steven M. Johnson/Dir., CEO, Dennis L. Thompson/Chmn., Gary M. Judd/Dir., Pres., Wells C. Hall/Dir., John D. Harkey/Dir., Nestor R. Weigand/Dir., James T. Morton/Dir., James K. Zielke/Dir., CFO - Treasury, Sec., Gene E. Street/Dir.

Fox Chase Bancorp Inc

4390 Davisville Rd., Hatboro, PA, 19040; ***PH:*** 1-215-682-7400; ***Fax:*** 1-215-682-4147; ***http://*** www.foxchasebank.com

General - Incorporation	USA	**Stock**- Price on:12/24/2007	$13.6
Employees	131	Stock Exchange	NDQ
Auditor	KPMG LLP	Ticker Symbol	FXCB
Stk Agt	Registrar & Transfer Co	Outstanding Shares	14,680,000
Counsel	NA	E.P.S	$0.25
DUNS No.	NA	Shareholders	NA

Business: The group operates through its subsidiaries whose principle activity is to provide financial products and services. The groups services include mortgage, multi family and commercial real estate, construction, commercial and consumer loans. The group operates from Richboro, Willow Grove, Warminster, Lahaska, Hatboro, Media and Exton, Pennsylvania, and Ocean City, Marmora and Egg Harbor Township, New Jersey. The assets of the group for the year 2006 were $756,985 (thousands).

Primary SIC and add'l.: 6712 6035 6035 6712

CIK No: 0001359111

Subsidiaries: Fox Chase Bank, Fox Chase Financial, Inc

Officers: Thomas M. Petro/Dir., CEO, Pres., Mary Regnery/Head - Human Resources, James V. Schermerhorn/Exec. VP, Chief Lending Officer, Roger Deacon/Exec. VP, Chief Accounting Officer, Rich Fuchs/Exec. VP, Chief Deposit Officer, Jerry D. Holbrook/CFO, Exec. VP, Dave Kowalek/Exec. VP, Chief Credit Officer, Keiron G. Lynch/51/Exec. VP, Chief Administrative Officer, Kerry Lynch/Exec. VP, Chief Administrative Officer

Directors: Thomas M. Petro/Dir., CEO, Pres., Roger H. Ballou/Dir., Richard E. Bauer/Dir., Todd S. Benning/Dir., Richard M. Eisenstaedt/Dir., Laura M. Mercuri/Dir., Anthony A. Nichols/Dir., Peter A. Sears/Dir.

Owners: Peter A. Sears, Richard E. Bauer, Todd S. Benning, Roger H. Ballou, Thomas M. Petro, Fox Chase MHC/55.50%, Richard M. Eisenstaedt, James V. Schermerhorn, Anthony A. Nichols, David C. Kowalek, Insiders/1.23%, Laura M. Mercuri, Keiron G. Lynch, Jerry D. Holbrook

Financial Data: ***Fiscal Year End:***12/31 ***Latest Annual Data:*** 12/31/2006

Year	**Sales**	**Net Income**
2006	$39,326,000	$3,634,000

Curr. Assets:	$137,838,000	**Curr. Liab.:**	$629,078,000	**P/E Ratio:**	54.40
Plant, Equip.:	$14,287,000	**Total Liab.:**	$631,340,000	**Indic. Yr. Divd.:**	NA
Total Assets:	$756,985,000	**Net Worth:**	$125,645,000	**Debt/ Equity:**	NA

Foxby Corp

11 Hanover Sq, New York, NY, 10005; ***PH:*** 1-800-278-4353; ***Fax:*** 1-718-236-2641; ***http://*** www.foxbycorp.com; ***Email:*** info@FoxbyCorp.com

General - Incorporation		**Stock**- Price on:12/24/2007	$2.75
Employees	NA	Stock Exchange	AMEX
Auditor	Tait, Weller & Baker LLP	Ticker Symbol	FXX
Stk Agt	American Stock Transfer & Trust Co.	Outstanding Shares	2,600,000
Counsel	NA	E.P.S	$0.73
DUNS No.	NA	Shareholders	NA

Business: The groups principle activity is to provide investment management services of equity, gold mutual funds and closed end funds. The group also provides Internet and Internet related activities. The group operates from United States.

Primary SIC and add'l.: 6726

CIK No: 0001068897

Officers: Thomas B. Winmill/Chmn., Pres., Thomas O'Malley/CFO, John F. Ramirez/VP, Sec., Heidi Keating/VP

Directors: Thomas B. Winmill/Chmn., Pres., Bruce B. Huber/Dir., James E. Hunt/Dir., Peter K. Werner/Dir., Bassett S. Winmill/Dir.

Owners: Investor Service Center, Inc., Bassett S. Winmill, Winmill & Co. Incorporated, CSS, LLC, Thomas B. Winmill, Investment Partners Asset Management, Inc.

Financial Data: Fiscal Year End:12/31 Latest Annual Data: 12/31/2006

Year	Sales	Net Income
2006	$1,442,000	$1,048,000
2005	$380,000	-$186,000
2004	$1,214,000	-$452,000

Curr. Assets:	$3,000	Curr. Liab.:	$43,000		
Plant, Equip.:	NA	Total Liab.:	$1,001,000	Indic. Yr. Divd.:	$0.020
Total Assets:	$8,562,000	Net Worth:	$7,560,000	Debt/ Equity:	NA

FoxHollow Technologies Inc

740 Bay Rd., Redwood City, CA, 94063; *PH:* 1-650-421-8400; *Fax:* 1-650-421-8781; *http://* www.foxhollowtech.com; *Email:* info@foxhollowtech.com

General - Incorporation	DE	Stock- Price on:12/24/2007	$21.14
Employees	553	Stock Exchange	NA
Auditor	PricewaterhouseCoopers LLP	Ticker Symbol	NA
Stk Agt	Mellon Investor Services LLC	Outstanding Shares	29,610,000
Counsel	NA	E.P.S.	$0.06
DUNS No.		Shareholders	NA

Business: The groups principle activities include designing, developing, manufacturing and selling medical devices. The products of the group include SilverHawk and Rinspirator. for September 2006, the group acquired Kerberos Proximal Solutions, Inc. The group operates from the United States.

Primary SIC and add'l.: 3842 3841 3823 3845

CIK No: 0001217688

Subsidiaries: EOP-Industrial Portfolio, L.L.C, Kerberos Proximal Solutions, Inc.

Officers: John B. Simpson/Founder, CEO, Ronald T. Steckel/54/COO, Matthew B. Ferguson/CFO, Daniel J. Lerner/Sr. VP - Molecular Programs, Ronald W. Songer/Sr. VP - Research, Development, Douglas S. Rohlen/39/Pres. - Strategic Operations, Kevin D. Cordell/Sr. VP - Global Sales, Michael P. Ennen/VP - Global Marketing, William J. Olson/VP - Corporate Development

Directors: John B. Simpson/Founder, CEO, Jeffrey Child/47/Dir., Sanford Fitch/66/Dir., Tom Hinohara/56/Dir., Myrtle Potter/Dir., Michael S. Hunt/Dir., Richard N. Kender/Dir.

Owners: Insiders/23.20%, Michael S. Hunt, Jeffrey B. Child, Merck & Co., Inc./10.90%, Entities affiliated with Capital Research & Management Company/10.70%, Sanford Fitch, Persons and Entities affiliated with Palo Alto Investors, LLC/5.90%, John B. Simpson/20.30%, Richard N. Kender, Tomoaki Hinohara, Myrtle S. Potter, Douglas S. Rohlen/1.70%, Matthew B. Ferguson

Financial Data: Fiscal Year End:12/31 Latest Annual Data: 12/31/2006

Year	Sales	Net Income
2006	$193,085,000	-$12,229,000
2005	$128,156,000	-$11,611,000
2004	$38,552,000	-$29,875,000

Curr. Assets:	$206,363,000	Curr. Liab.:	$53,829,000	P/E Ratio:	352.33
Plant, Equip.:	$8,328,000	Total Liab.:	$60,963,000	Indic. Yr. Divd.:	NA
Total Assets:	$247,112,000	Net Worth:	$186,149,000	Debt/ Equity:	NA

FPB Bancorp Inc

1301 SE Port St. Lucie Blvd., Port St. Lucie, FL, 34952; *PH:* 1-772-398-1388; *Fax:* 1-772-398-1399; *http://* www.1stpeoplesbank.com

General - Incorporation	FL	Stock - Price on:12/24/2007	$16.06
Employees	64	Stock Exchange	NDQ
Auditor	Hacker, Johnson & Smith PA	Ticker Symbol	FPBI
Stk Agt	NA	Outstanding Shares	2,000,000
Counsel	NA	E.P.S.	$0.28
DUNS No.	NA	Shareholders	NA

Business: The groups principal activity is to provide retail and commercial banking services. The groups services include deposit accounts and loans. The financial products of the group include commercial, residential and consumer loan. The group operates from the United States. The assets of the group for the year 2006 were $153.4 (million).

Primary SIC and add'l.: 6712 6022

CIK No: 0001162245

Subsidiaries: First Peoples Bank

Officers: David W. Skiles/Dir., CEO, Pres./$212,094.00, Marge Riley/COO, Exec. VP/$146,202.00, Michelle Sias/VP - Commerical Lending, Ryan Coughlin/AVP - Commercial Lending, Nancy E. Aumack/Sr. VP, CFO/$128,366.00, Stephen J. Krumfolz/Sr. VP - Commercial, SBA Lending, Lee P. Brown/Sr. VP - Commercial Lending, Fort Pierce Area Executive, Melissa M. Favorite/Sr. VP - Deposit Operations, William V. West/Sr. VP - Commercial Lending, Stuart Area Executive, Randy J. Riley/Sr. VP - Commercial Lending, Vero Beach Area Executive, Thomas W. Eby/Sr. VP, Mortgage Lending Mgr., David P. Hoffman/VP - Sr. Consumer Lender, Sarah Baker/AVP, Stuart Branch Mgr., Christina Saltos/AVP, Port St. Lucie Branch Mgr., Brenda Parmelee/AVP, Ft. Pierce Branch Mgr. (20 Officers included in Index)

Directors: David W. Skiles/Dir., CEO, Pres., John R. Baker/Vice Chmn., Gary A. Berger/Chmn., Paul A. Zinter/Dir., Robert L. Seeley/Dir., Robert L. Schweiger/Dir., Donald J. Cuozzo/Dir., Paul J. Miret/Dir.

Owners: Paul A. Zinter/1.95%, Lee P. Brown/1.46%, Melissa M. Favorite, Donald J. Cuozzo/2.83%, Stephen J. Krumfolz, Thomas W. Eby, Nancy E. Aumack/1.14%, Ann L. Decker, Robert L. Seeley, Robert L. Schweiger/3.77%, Randy J. Riley/1.64%, William V. West/1.30%, John R. Baker/1.09%, David W. Skiles/3.41%, Paul J. Miret/2.48% (18 Owners included in Index)

Financial Data: Fiscal Year End:12/31 Latest Annual Data: 12/31/2006

Year	Sales	Net Income
2006	$11,450,000	$631,000
2005	$8,173,000	$765,000
2004	$5,104,000	$123,000

Curr. Assets:	$6,250,000	Curr. Liab.:	$131,560,000	P/E Ratio:	57.36
Plant, Equip.:	$4,278,000	Total Liab.:	$132,376,000	Indic. Yr. Divd.:	NA
Total Assets:	$153,439,000	Net Worth:	$21,063,000	Debt/ Equity:	NA

FPIC Insurance Group Inc

225 Water St., Ste. 1400, Jacksonville, FL, 32202; *PH:* 1-904-354-2482; *Fax:* 1-904-475-1159; *http://* www.fpic.com; *Email:* ir@fpic.com

General - Incorporation	FL	Stock - Price on:12/24/2007	$41.76
Employees	160	Stock Exchange	NDQ
Auditor	PricewaterhouseCoopers LLP	Ticker Symbol	FPIC
Stk Agt	Computershare Investor Services LLC	Outstanding Shares	9,730,000
Counsel	Leboeuf, Lamb, Greene & Macrae	E.P.S.	$4.50
DUNS No.	04-087-0446	Shareholders	NA

Business: The group's principal activities are to provide property, casualty, medical professional liability and legal professional liability insurance products. The group provides services for physicians, dentists, hospitals and other healthcare communities. The group offers insurance for medical professionals, managed care liability insurance, professional and comprehensive general liability, insurance coverages, stop loss insurance, third party administration and group accident and insurance coverage services.

Primary SIC and add'l.: 6321

CIK No: 0001010247

Subsidiaries: Administrators For The Professions, Inc. (AFP), Anesthesiologists Professional Assurance Company, First Professionals Insurance Company, Inc. (First Professionals), FPIC Insurance Agency, Inc., FPIC Intermediaries, Inc., FPIC Services, Inc., Group Data Corporation, Insurance Services, Inc., Interlex Insurance Company, Intermed Insurance Company (Intermed), Physicians Reciprocal Managers, Inc., Professional Medical Administrators, LLC., The Tenere Group, Inc. (Tenere), Trout Insurance Services, Inc.

Officers: John R. Byers/Dir., CEO, Pres./$1,921,335.00, Becky Thackery/VP, Dir. - Internal Audit, Charles Divita/CFO/$613,618.00, Pamela Deyo Harvey/VP, Controller, Robert E. White/Pres. - First Professionals Insurance Company, Inc, Malcolm T. Graham/General Counsel, Sec.

Directors: John R. Byers/Dir., CEO, Pres., Kenneth M. Kirschner/Chmn., John K. Anderson/58/Vice Chmn., Robert O. Baratta/Dir., Guy T. Selander/Dir., Richard J. Bagby/Dir., M. C. Harden/54/Dir., John G. Rich/Dir., David M. Shapiro/Dir., Joan D. Ruffier/Dir., Terence P. McCoy/62/Dir.

Owners: M. C. Harden, Robert O. Baratta, Robert E. White, Guy T. Selander, Joan D. Ruffier, Richard J. Bagby, Terence P. McCoy, Charles Divita, John K. Anderson, John R. Byers/0.04%, David M. Shapiro, Insiders/0.09%, Kenneth M. Kirschner, John G. Rich

Financial Data: Fiscal Year End:12/31 Latest Annual Data: 12/31/2006

Year	Sales	Net Income
2006	$259,772,000	$51,588,000
2005	$294,757,000	$35,022,000
2004	$236,807,000	$28,181,000

Curr. Assets:	$440,302,000	Curr. Liab.:	$24,136,000	P/E Ratio:	7.34
Plant, Equip.:	NA	Total Liab.:	$933,805,000	Indic. Yr. Divd.:	NA
Total Assets:	$1,219,059,000	Net Worth:	$285,254,000	Debt/ Equity:	0.1587

FPL Group Inc

700 Universe Blvd., Juno Beach, FL, 33408; *PH:* 1-561-694-4000; *Fax:* 1-561-694-4620; *http://* www.fplgroup.com

General - Incorporation	FL	Stock- Price on:12/24/2007	$58.96
Employees	10,400	Stock Exchange	NYSE
Auditor	Deloitte & Touche LLP	Ticker Symbol	FPL
Stk Agt	Computershare Investor Services LLC	Outstanding Shares	406,420,000
Counsel	NA	E.P.S.	$3.38
DUNS No.	12-272-3174	Shareholders	NA

Business: The group operates through its subsidiary whose principle activity is to provide electricity-related services. The group also provides fiber optical services. The group operates from United States.

Primary SIC and add'l.: 4931 6719 4911

CIK No: 0000753308

Subsidiaries: Bay Loan and Investment Bank, Florida Power & Light Company, FPL Energy, LLC, FPL Group Capital Inc, Palms Insurance Company, Limited

Officers: Lewis Hay/Chmn., CEO/$9,503,110.00, Edward F. Tancer/Sr. VP, General Counsel, Robert L. McGrath/Sr. VP - Engineering, Construction, Corporate Services, Mary Lou Kromer/VP - Marketing, Communications, Michael OSullivan/Sr. VP - Development, FPL Energy, LLC, Moray P. Dewhurst/CFO, Sr. VP - Finance, Michael K. Davis/Controller, Chief Accounting Officer, Alissa E. Ballot/VP, Corp. Sec., Mark Maisto/Pres. - Commodities Marketing, Retail Markets, FPL Energy, LLC, Mark R. Sorensen/CFO, VP - Finance - FPL Energy, LLC, Paul I. Cutler/Treasurer, Michael L. Leighton/VP, Chief Development Officer - Florida Power, Light Company, James L. Robo/COO, Pres./$3,132,651.00, Robert H. Escoto/Sr. VP - Human Resources, Antonio Rodriguez/Sr. VP - Power Generation Division (32 Officers included in Index)

Directors: Lewis Hay/Chmn., CEO, Michael H. Thaman/Dir., Robert M. Beall/Dir., Sherry S. Barrat/Dir., Paul R. Tregurtha/Dir., Hyatt J. Brown/Dir., James L. Camaren/Dir., Brian J. Ferguson/Dir., Rudy E. Schupp/Dir., Hansel E. Tookes/Dir., Toni Jennings/Dir., Oliver D. Kingsley/Dir.

Owners: Toni Jennings, James L. Robo, Lewis Hay, Rudy E. Schupp, James L. Camaren, Brian J. Ferguson, Armando J. Olivera, Michael H. Thaman, Fidelity Management Trust Company, Insiders, Hansel E. Tookes, Capital Research and Management Company, Paul R. Tregurtha, Hyatt J. Brown, Sherry S. Barrat (18 Owners included in Index)

Financial Data: Fiscal Year End:12/31 Latest Annual Data: 12/31/2006

Year	Sales	Net Income
2006	$15,710,000,000	$1,281,000,000
2005	$11,846,000,000	$885,000,000
2004	$10,522,000,000	$887,000,000

Curr. Assets:	$4,999,000,000	Curr. Liab.:	$6,493,000,000	P/E Ratio:	17.44
Plant, Equip.:	$24,499,000,000	Total Liab.:	$26,061,000,000	Indic. Yr. Divd.:	$1.640
Total Assets:	$35,991,000,000	Net Worth:	$9,930,000,000	Debt/ Equity:	0.9209

FrameWaves Inc

1981 E 4800 S Ste. 100, Saltlake, UT, 84117; *PH:* 1-801-272-9294

General - Incorporation	NV	Stock - Price on:12/24/2007	$0.12
Employees	NA	Stock Exchange	OTC
Auditor	Burnham & Schumm P.C.	Ticker Symbol	FWAV
Stk Agt	Interwest Transfer Company, Inc.	Outstanding Shares	NA
Counsel	NA	E.P.S	-$0.01
DUNS No.	NA	Shareholders	NA

Business: The groups principle activity is to provide recruiting services. The groups service area includes the research and development, engineering, marketing, sales, information technology and manufacturing industries. The group operates from United States.

Primary SIC and add'l.: 7600

CIK No: 0000788611

Officers: Thomas A. Thomsen/32/Dir., Pres., Dianne Hatton-Ward/51/Dir., VP, Susan Santage/46/Dir., Sec., Treasurer

Directors: Thomas A. Thomsen/32/Dir., Pres., Dianne Hatton-Ward/51/Dir., VP, Susan Santage/46/Dir., Sec., Treasurer

Owners: Thomas A. Thomsen, Susan Santage/0.27%, Dianne Hatton-Ward/0.27%, Insiders/0.60%

Financial Data: *Fiscal Year End:*12/31 *Latest Annual Data:* 12/31/2006

Year	Sales	Net Income
2006	NA	-$6,000
2005	NA	-$6,000
2004	NA	-$7,000

Curr. Assets:	$3,000	Curr. Liab.:	$15,000		
Plant, Equip.:	NA	Total Liab.:	$15,000	Indic. Yr. Divd.:	NA
Total Assets:	$3,000	Net Worth:	-$13,000	Debt/ Equity:	NA

France Telecom

225 Liberty St., Ste. 4301, New York, NY, 10281; *PH:* 1-212-332-2100; *http://* www.francetelecom.fr

General - Incorporation	France	Stock - Price on:12/24/2007	$28.14
Employees	203,008	Stock Exchange	NYSE
Auditor	Ernst & Young LLP	Ticker Symbol	FTE
Stk Agt	Bank of New York	Outstanding Shares	NA
Counsel	NA	E.P.S	$2.76
DUNS No.	26-652-9601	Shareholders	NA

Business: The group's principle activity is the provision of a wide range of telecommunications services to residential, professional and large business customers. Major lines of business include providing public fixed-line voiced telephone services, leased lines and data transmission services, mobile telecommunications services, telecommunications equipment sales and rentals, cable television and broadcasting services, information services, Internet and wireless applications. Brands include orange, wanadoo, equant, numeris, neostrada and minitel.

Primary SIC and add'l.: 4813 4812 1731 3669 4899 4822

CIK No: 0001038143

Subsidiaries: France Telecom Cble, France Telecom Capital Dveloppement

Officers: Sanjiv Ahuja/51/CEO, Sr. Exec. VP, Didier Lombard/66/Chmn., CEO, Gervais Pellissier/49/Sr. Exec., VP - Group Finance, Georges Penalver/52/Sr. Exec., VP - Group Strategic Marketing, Product Factory, Home, Olaf Swantee/Sr. Exec., VP - Personal Communication Services, UK, Europe, Middle East, Barbara Dalibard/50/Sr. Exec., VP - Enterprise Communication Services, Louis-Pierre Wenes/49/Sr. Exec., VP - Group Transformation, French Operations, Olivier Barberot/54/Sr. Exec. VP - Group Human Resources - Poland, Jean-Yves Larrouturou/47/Sr. Exec., VP, Group General Sec., Jean-Philippe Vanot/56/Sr. Exec., VP - Group Networks - Information Systems

Directors: Didier Lombard/66/Chmn., CEO, Stephane Tierce/Dir., Arnaud Lagardere/Dir., Henri Martre/Dir., Jean-Michel Gaveau/Dir., Claudie Haignere/Dir., Bruno Bezard/Dir., Marcel Roulet/Dir., Jacques De Larosiere/Dir., Jean-Paul Gristi/Dir., Rene Bernardi/Dir., Henri Serres/Dir., Helene Adam/Dir., Jean Simonin/Dir., Bernard Dufau/Dir.

Financial Data: *Fiscal Year End:*12/31 *Latest Annual Data:* 12/31/2006

Year	Sales	Net Income
2006	$68,262,151,000	$6,973,825,000
2005	$58,567,396,000	$6,747,527,000
2004	$64,341,011,000	$4,037,260,000

Curr. Assets:	$19,519,315,000	Curr. Liab.:	$36,291,086,000	P/E Ratio:	12.64
Plant, Equip.:	$36,651,528,000	Total Liab.:	$102,320,609,000	Indic. Yr. Divd.:	$1.360
Total Assets:	$123,656,657,000	Net Worth:	$21,336,048,000	Debt/ Equity:	NA

Franchise Capital Corp

7400 E McDonald, Ste 121, Scottsdale, AZ, 85050; *PH:* 1-480-355-8142; *http://* www.franchisecapitalcorp.com; *Email:* ir@franchisecapitalcorp.com

General - Incorporation	NV	Stock - Price on:12/24/2007	$0.015
Employees	1	Stock Exchange	OTC
Auditor	Epstein Weber & Conover, PLC	Ticker Symbol	FCCN
Stk Agt	Transfer Online, Inc.	Outstanding Shares	921,820,000
Counsel	NA	E.P.S	-$0.007
DUNS No.	NA	Shareholders	NA

Business: The group's principal activity is to acquire assets within restaurant industry. It is in the development stage. The group intends to develop and franchise casual dining restaurants.

Primary SIC and add'l.: 5812

CIK No: 0001160598

Subsidiaries: Comstock Jakes Franchise Company, Cousin Vinnies Franchise Company, Fathom Business Systems, Inc, Fit N Healthy Caf, Kirby Foos Asian Grill Franchise Company, Kokopelli Franchise Company

Officers: Steven Peacock/Interim CEO, Interim Pres., Interim Chief Compliance Officer, CFO

Directors: Robert McCoy/Chmn., James Bickel/Dir., Gary Nerison/Dir.

Owners: Robert McCoy, Insiders

Financial Data: *Fiscal Year End:*06/30 *Latest Annual Data:* 06/30/2006

Year	Sales	Net Income
2006	$2,000	-$934,000
2005	NA	-$773,000
2004	$109,000	-$5,405,000

Curr. Assets:	NA	Curr. Liab.:	$177,000		
Plant, Equip.:	NA	Total Liab.:	$398,000	Indic. Yr. Divd.:	NA
Total Assets:	$432,000	Net Worth:	$34,000	Debt/ Equity:	NA

Franklin Bank Corp

9800 Richmond Ave., Ste. 680, Houston, TX, 77042; *PH:* 1-713-339-8900; *Fax:* 1-713-343-8122; *http://* www.bankfranklin.com; *Email:* investorrelations@bankfranklin.com

General - Incorporation	DE	Stock - Price on:12/24/2007	$15.58
Employees	627	Stock Exchange	NDQ
Auditor	Deloitte & Touche LLP	Ticker Symbol	FBTX
Stk Agt	Bank of New York	Outstanding Shares	23,610,000
Counsel	NA	E.P.S	$0.60
DUNS No.	NA	Shareholders	NA

Business: The group's principal activity is to offer mortgage banking, commercial banking and community banking products through its subsidiary, franklin bank. Mortgage banking originate, acquire and sell residential mortgage loans through two channels, retails and wholesale. As of 30-Sep-2003, the group had 31 retail mortgage offices in 14 states throughout the United States. Community banking offers a wide variety of small business and consumer banking products. On 02-Mar-2004, the group acquired lost pines bancshares, inc.

Primary SIC and add'l.: 6035 6712

CIK No: 0001207070

Subsidiaries: FBC Holdings, LLC., Franklin Bank Capital Trust I., Franklin Bank, S.S.B., Franklin Capital Trust II., Franklin Capital Trust III., Franklin Capital Trust IV.

Officers: Anthony J. Nocella/Dir., CEO, Pres./$1,273,477.00, Daniel E. Cooper/Exec. VP, MD - Mortgage Banking, Franklin Bank, SSB, William L. Rayburn/Advisory Dir. - Franklin Bank, SSB, Herbert L. Wade/Advisory Dir. - Franklin Bank, SSB, Michael H. Gentry/Advisory Dir. - Franklin Bank, SSB, Samuel H. Harrison/Advisory Dir. - Franklin Bank, SSB, David W. Hickson/Advisory Dir. - Franklin Bank, SSB, Thomas B. McDade/Advisory Dir. - Franklin Bank, SSB, Charles A. Ellison/Advisory Dir. - Franklin Bank, SSB, Hank McQuaide/Advisory Dir. - Franklin Bank, SSB, Charles A. Sippial/Advisory Dir. - Franklin Bank, SSB, Jack M. Threadgill/Advisory Dir. - Franklin Bank, SSB, William D. Barkley/Advisory Dir. - Franklin Bank, SSB, Travis B. Bryan/Advisory Dir. - Franklin Bank, SSB, Homer R. Callaway/Advisory Dir. - Franklin Bank, SSB *(50 Officers included in Index)*

Directors: Anthony J. Nocella/Dir., CEO, Pres., Lewis S. Ranieri/Chmn., Lawrence Chimerine/Dir., David M. Golush/Dir., John B. Selman/Dir., James A. Howard/Dir., Robert A. Perro/Dir., William B. Rhodes/Dir., Alan E. Master/Dir., Andy Black/Dir., COO, Pres. - Franklin Bank, SSB

Owners: James A. Howard, Jan Scofield, Glenn E. Mealey, Max Epperson, Russell McCann, Barclays Global Investors, NA/5.30%, Russell Workman, NWQ Investment Management Company, LLC/5.80%, William B. Rhodes/3.00%, David M. Golush, Michael Davitt, Lewis S. Ranieri/4.10%, Dimensional FundAdvisors LP/8.20%, Lawrence Chimerine, Andy Black *(22 Owners included in Index)*

Financial Data: *Fiscal Year End:*12/31 *Latest Annual Data:* 12/31/2006

Year	Sales	Net Income
2006	$308,205,000	$19,380,000
2005	$215,958,000	$26,296,000
2004	$131,003,000	$23,149,000

Curr. Assets:	$86,783,000	Curr. Liab.:	$4,941,709,000	P/E Ratio:	24.73
Plant, Equip.:	$50,239,000	Total Liab.:	$5,104,641,000	Indic. Yr. Divd.:	NA
Total Assets:	$5,537,367,000	Net Worth:	$432,726,000	Debt/ Equity:	0.2455

Franklin Covey PFD A

2200 W Pkwy. Blvd., Salt Lake City, UT, 84119; *PH:* 1-801-817-1776; *http://* www.franklincovey.com

General - Incorporation	UT	Stock - Price on:12/24/2007	$23.99
Employees	NA	Stock Exchange	OTC
Auditor	KPMG LLP	Ticker Symbol	FCVYP
Stk Agt	NA	Outstanding Shares	NA
Counsel	NA	E.P.S	NA
DUNS No.	NA	Shareholders	NA

Business: The groups principle activity is to provide timeless and universal curriculum and effectiveness tools. Products of the group include planning pages, binders, electronic solutions, books, audio learning systems including multi-tape, CDs and workbook sets, CD-ROM software products and calendars. Customers of the group include Fortune 100 companies; Fortune 500 companies the United States and foreign governmental agencies, including the United States Department of Defense. The group operates through two segments namely Consumer Solutions Business Unit and Organizational Solutions Business Unit. The group operates from the United States, Australia, Brazil, Canada, Japan, Mexico and the United Kingdom.

Primary SIC and add'l.: 2780

CIK No: 0000886206

Subsidiaries: Franklin Covey Brasil Ltda., Franklin Covey Canada, Ltd., Franklin Covey Catalog Sales, Inc., Franklin Covey Client Sales, Inc., Franklin Covey de Mexico S. de R.L. de C.V., Franklin Covey Europe, Ltd., Franklin Covey Ireland Limited, Franklin Covey Japan Co. Ltd., Franklin Covey Marketing, Ltd., Franklin Covey Mexico, Inc., Franklin Covey Middle East W.L.L., Franklin Covey Printing, Inc., Franklin Covey Product Sales, Inc., Franklin Covey Proprietary Limited, Franklin Covey Services, L.L.C. 17 Subsidiaries included in the Index

Officers: Robert A. Whitman/Chmn., CEO, Robert W. Bennett/Pres. - Organizational Strategic Business Unit, Sarah E. Merz/Pres., GM - Consumer, Small Business Uni, Stephen D. Young/CFO, Corp. Sec.

Directors: Robert A. Whitman/Chmn., CEO, Stephen R. Covey/Vice Chmn., Joel C. Peterson/Dir., Kay E. Stepp/Dir., Robert H. Daines/Dir., Dennis G. Heiner/Dir., Clayton M. Christensen/Dir., E. J. Garn/Dir., Donald J. McNamara/Dir.

Owners: Robert A. Whitman/10.50%, Donald J. McNamara/27.20%, Joel C. Peterson/1.00%, Sarah Merz, E. J. Garn, Stephen D. Young, Knowledge Capital Investment/26.90%, Stephen R. Covey/5.30%, Robert W. Bennett, Robert H. Daines, Insiders/41.00%, Clayton M. Christensen, Kay E. Stepp, Dimensional Fund Advisors, Inc./7.70%, Dennis G. Heiner

Franklin Credit Mgmt Corp

101 Hudson St., 25th Fl., New Jersey, NJ, 07302; ***PH:*** 1-201-604-1800; ***Fax:*** 1-201-604-4400; ***http://*** www.franklincredit.com

General - Incorporation	DE	***Stock***- Price on:12/24/2007	$4.76
Employees	232	Stock Exchange	NDQ
Auditor	Deloitte & Touche LLP	Ticker Symbol	FCMC
Stk Agt	Computershare Investor Services LLC	Outstanding Shares	8,030,000
Counsel	NA	E.P.S	-$0.98
DUNS No.	79-721-0150	Shareholders	NA

Business: The group's principal activity is to provide specialty consumer finance and asset management services. It operates through two segments: portfolio asset acquisition and resolution and mortgage banking. The portfolio asset acquisition and resolution segment acquires performing, nonperforming, nonconforming and subperforming notes receivable and promissory notes from financial institutions and mortgage and finance companies. This segment services and collects such notes receivable through enforcement of terms of original note, modification of original note terms and if necessary, liquidation of the underlying collateral. The mortgage-banking segment originates or purchases, sub prime residential mortgage loans for individuals whose credit histories, income and other factors cause them to be classified as nonconforming borrowers.

Primary SIC and add'l.: 6162 6153

CIK No: 0000831246

Subsidiaries: 6 Harrison Corp, Accredit 75, Accu 95 Corp, Accu 99 Corp, Ark 38 Corp, Beach Funding Corp, Branford 55 Corp, Cal Second 49 Corp, Cape 77 Corp, Capt 47 Corp, Century 78 Corp, Coast 56 Corp, Coast 62 Corp, Coast 74 Corp, Coast 96 Corp 247 Subsidiaries included in the Index

Officers: Gordon Jardin/Dir., CEO, Stephen T. Hague/Exec. VP - Franklin Credit's Acquisitions Department, Paul D. Colasono/CFO/$522,554.00, William Sullivan/Dir., COO/$358,117.00, Michael Blair/COO - Loan Servicing, Richard W. Payne/Pres. - Tribeca Lending Corporation

Directors: Gordon Jardin/Dir., CEO, Thomas J. Axon/Chmn., William Sullivan/Dir., COO, Michael L. Bertash/Dir., Frank B. Evans/Dir., Allan R. Lyons/Dir., Steven W. Lefkowitz/Dir.

Owners: William F. Sullivan, Insiders/62.20%, Frank B. Evans/10.90%, Paul D. Colasono, Jeffrey R. Johnson, Robert M. Chiste, Steven W. Lefkowitz/3.80%, Michael Bertash, Joseph Caiazzo/2.40%, Alexander Gordon Jardin/1.50%, Thomas J. Axon/42.60%, Allan R. Lyons/1.10%

Financial Data: ***Fiscal Year End:***12/31 ***Latest Annual Data:*** 03/31/2007

Year	Sales	Net Income
2007	$42,542,000	-$1,954,000
2006	$163,753,000	-$1,761,000
2005	$121,399,000	$7,869,000

Curr. Assets:	$94,202,000	***Curr. Liab.:***	$40,970,000		
Plant, Equip.:	$26,694,000	***Total Liab.:***	$1,620,804,000	***Indic. Yr. Divd.:***	NA
Total Assets:	$1,668,358,000	***Net Worth:***	$47,553,000	***Debt/ Equity:***	37.0063

Franklin Electric Co Inc

400 E Spring St., Bluffton, IN, 46714; ***PH:*** 1-260-824-2900; ***Fax:*** 1-260-824-2909; ***http://*** www.franklinelect.com

General - Incorporation	IN	***Stock***- Price on:12/24/2007	$46.02
Employees	3,100	Stock Exchange	NDQ
Auditor	Deloitte & Touche LLP	Ticker Symbol	FELE
Stk Agt	Shareholder Services Group	Outstanding Shares	23,140,000
Counsel	NA	E.P.S	$1.59
DUNS No.	00-516-1674	Shareholders	NA

Business: The group's principal activities are to design, manufacture and distribute motors, electronic controls and related parts and equipment. The business consists of two operating segments that offer different products: the motor segment and the electronic controls segment. The motor segment designs, manufactures and sells motors and related parts and equipment for use in submersible water and fueling systems and in a wide variety of industrial motor products. The electronic controls segment designs and manufactures electronic controls for the principal purpose of being a supplier to the motor segment. The products include electric submersible water and fueling systems motors; fueling systems and industrial motor products and electronic drives and controls. These products are marketed to the original equipment manufacturers in the United States, Canada, Europe, Australia, South Africa, Mexico, Japan and China.

Primary SIC and add'l.: 3621

CIK No: 0000038725

Subsidiaries: Advanced Polymer Technology, Inc., Coverco S.r.l., EBW, Inc., Franklin Electric (Australia) Pty. Ltd., Franklin Electric (South Africa) Pty. Ltd., Franklin Electric (Suzhou) Co., Ltd., Franklin Electric B.V., Franklin Electric Europa GmbH, Franklin Electric International, Inc., Franklin Electric Manufacturing, Inc., Franklin Electric Sales, Inc., Franklin Electric spol s.r.o., Franklin Electric Subsidiaries, Inc. [inactive], Franklin Electric Trading (Shanghai) Co., Ltd., Franklin Fueling Systems, GmbH 23 Subsidiaries included in the Index

Officers: Scott R. Trumbull/Chmn., CEO/$2,686,693.00, Kirk M. Nevins/VP - Chmn.'s Office, Thomas A. Miller/VP, Peter C. Maske/Sr. VP/$896,982.00, Gregg C. Sengstack/Sr. VP/$686,802.00, Thomas J. Strupp/CFO, VP, Sec. - Water Transfer Systems/$645,600.00, Gary D. Ward/VP, Dir. - Human Resources, Robert J. Stone/Sr. VP/$587,494.00, Daniel J. Crose/VP, Dir. - Operations, Delancey W. Davis/VP - Engineering, Electronic Technology

Directors: Scott R. Trumbull/Chmn., CEO, David M. Wathen/Dir., Diana S. Ferguson/44/Dir., Thomas L. Young/Dir., Jerome D. Brady/Dir., David A. Roberts/Dir., Howard B. Witt/Dir.

Owners: Jerome D. Brady, Diana S. Ferguson, Patricia Schaefer/8.65%, Select Equity Group, Inc./14.42%, T. Rowe Price Associates, Inc./6.76%, Peter-Christian Maske, Wells Fargo Bank Minnesota, N.A./6.57%, Thomas L. Young, Gregg C. Sengstack, David M. Wathen, Howard B. Witt, Robert J. Stone, Scott R. Trumbull/1.23%, Thomas J. Strupp, Insiders/4.34% *(17 Owners included in Index)*

Financial Data: ***Fiscal Year End:***12/31 ***Latest Annual Data:*** 12/30/2006

Year	Sales	Net Income
2006	$557,948,000	$56,998,000
2005	$439,559,000	$46,009,000

Curr. Assets:	$203,020,000	***Curr. Liab.:***	$64,022,000	***P/E Ratio:***	20.64
Plant, Equip.:	$95,732,000	***Total Liab.:***	$112,200,000	***Indic. Yr. Divd.:***	$0.480
Total Assets:	$379,762,000	***Net Worth:***	$267,562,000	***Debt/ Equity:***	0.1475

Franklin Electronic Publishers Inc

1 Franklin Plz., Burlington, NJ, 08016; ***PH:*** 1-609-386-2500; ***Fax:*** 1-609-387-1787; ***http://*** www.franklin.com; ***Email:*** service@franklin.com

General - Incorporation	PA	***Stock***- Price on:12/24/2007	$2.36
Employees	185	Stock Exchange	AMEX
Auditor	Radin, Glass & Co. LLP	Ticker Symbol	FEP
Stk Agt	Registrar & Transfer Co	Outstanding Shares	8,220,000
Counsel	Rosenman & Colin	E.P.S	$0.19
DUNS No.	05-998-3189	Shareholders	NA

Business: The group's principal activity is to design, develop, publish and market electronic books and electronic organizers. The electronic books are battery-powered devices that incorporate the text of a reference work, general literature or database and permit the user to read selected portions on a display screen. The group currently markets electronic reference products in various categories including electronic format monolingual and bilingual dictionaries, version of the bible, encyclopedias, educational publications and medical publications. The group has international operations in the United Kingdom, France, Canada, Germany, Belgium, Mexico and Australia. Franklin(R), bookman(R), ebookman, spelling ace(R), wordmaster(R), seiko(R), next century(R) and language master and rolodex(R) are the certain trademark rights owned by the group.

Primary SIC and add'l.: 7372 7375 3579 2741

CIK No: 0000356841

Subsidiaries: Franklin Electronic Publishers (Deutschland) GmbH, Franklin Electronic Publishers (Europe) Ltd, Franklin Electronic Publishers (France) S.A.R.L, Franklin Electronic Publishers (HK) Ltd., Franklin Electronic Publishers Australia (Aust) Pty Ltd, Franklin Electronic Publishers Benelux N.V., Franklin Electronic Publishers de Mexico, S.A. de C.V, Franklin Electronic Publishers Euro-Holdings B.V, Franklin Electronic Publishers Southern Europe, Franklin Electronic Publishers, Ltd

Officers: Barry J. Lipsky/Dir., CEO, Pres./$402,900.00, Arnold D. Levitt/CFO, Sr. VP, Treasurer/$284,800.00, Michael A. Crincoli/VP - North American Operations/$202,425.00, Walter Schillings/MD - European Operations/$242,438.00, Matthew Baile/VP - Product Development/$216,000.00

Directors: Barry J. Lipsky/Dir., CEO, Pres., Edward H. Cohen/69/Dir., Leonard M. Lodish/64/Dir., James Meister/66/Dir., Howard L. Morgan/62/Dir., Jerry R. Schubel/72/Dir., James H. Simons/70/Dir., William H. Turner/68/Dir.

Owners: Marcy Lewis/8.10%, James Meister/1.30%, Michael A. Crincoli, Insiders/23.10%, Arnold D. Levitt/3.00%, Howard L. Morgan/2.00%, Shining Sea Limited/20.50%, Leonard M. Lodish/1.40%, William H. Turner/1.50%, Matthew T. Baile, Edward H. Cohen/1.40%, Barry J. Lipsky/6.90%, Jerry R. Schubel/1.50%, Dimensional Fund Advisors/5.50%, Walter Schillings *(16 Owners included in Index)*

Financial Data: ***Fiscal Year End:***03/31 ***Latest Annual Data:*** 03/31/2007

Year	Sales	Net Income
2007	$52,213,000	-$3,180,000
2006	$59,622,000	$2,012,000
2005	$62,146,000	$2,403,000

Curr. Assets:	$26,537,000	***Curr. Liab.:***	$8,415,000		
Plant, Equip.:	$1,607,000	***Total Liab.:***	$14,769,000	***Indic. Yr. Divd.:***	NA
Total Assets:	$43,021,000	***Net Worth:***	$28,252,000	***Debt/ Equity:***	NA

Franklin Financial Services Corp

20 S Main St., Chambersburg, PA, 17201; ***PH:*** 1-717-264-6116; ***Fax:*** 1-717-261-3545; ***http://*** www.fmtrustonline.com

General - Incorporation	PA	***Stock***- Price on:12/24/2007	$27.39
Employees	230	Stock Exchange	OTC
Auditor	Beard Miller Co. LLP	Ticker Symbol	FRAF
Stk Agt	Fulton Financial Advisors	Outstanding Shares	3,840,000
Counsel	NA	E.P.S	$2.16
DUNS No.	13-076-1596	Shareholders	NA

Business: The group's principal activities are to provide commercial, retail banking and trust services to businesses, individuals and government entities. The group operates through its subsidiary farmers and merchants trust company of chambersberg. The group's services include accepting and maintaining checking, savings and time deposit accounts; providing investment and trust services; making loans and providing safe deposit facilities. The group's lending activities include commercial, agricultural and industrial loans; installment and revolving loans to consumers; residential mortgage loans and construction loans. The group operates through 15 service offices located in franklin and cumberland counties.

Primary SIC and add'l.: 6022 6712

CIK No: 0000723646

Subsidiaries: Farmers and Merchants Trust Company of Chambersburg, Franklin Financial Properties Corp., Franklin Future Fund Inc.

Officers: William E. Snell/Dir., CEO, Pres./$285,733.00, Jerry Slothower/Investment Counselor - Ritner Highway Office, Carlisle, F&M Trust, Cathy Angle/Investor Relation Officer, Greg Frentzen/Investment Counselor - Waynesboro, Greencastle, F&M Trust, Diana Sponseller/Investment Counselor - Lincoln Way East Office, F&M Trust, Jack Turner/Investment Counselor - Shippensburg Office, F&M Trust, Avis Polk/Investment Counselor - Memorial Square Office, Chambersburg, F&M Trust

Directors: William E. Snell/Dir., CEO, Pres., Charles M. Sioberg/Chmn., Allan E. Jennings/Dir., Jeryl C. Miller/65/Dir., Stephen E. Patterson/61/Dir., Kurt E. Suter/Dir., Martha B. Walker/58/Dir., Warren G. Elliott/Dir., Donald A. Fry/56/Dir., Huber H. McCleary/Dir., Stanley J. Kerlin/53/Dir., Martin R. Brown/55/Dir.

Owners: Kurt E. Suter, Charles S. Bender/1.83%, Huber H. McCleary/1.40%, Allen C. Rebok, Warren G. Elliott, Insiders/6.37%, Donald A. Fry, Stephen E. Patterson, Ronald L. Cekovich, Stanley J. Kerlin, Jeryl C. Miller, Martin R. Brown, Michael E. Kugler, Martha B. Walker, Mark R. Hollar *(18 Owners included in Index)*

Financial Data: ***Fiscal Year End:***12/31 ***Latest Annual Data:*** 12/31/2006

Year	Sales	Net Income
2006	$49,180,000	$7,570,000
2005	$37,188,000	$6,112,000
2004	$32,084,000	$5,192,000

Curr. Assets:	$22,148,000	***Curr. Liab.:***	$680,405,000	***P/E Ratio:***	12.68
Plant, Equip.:	$13,101,000	***Total Liab.:***	$727,719,000	***Indic. Yr. Divd.:***	$1.040
Total Assets:	$799,333,000	***Net Worth:***	$71,614,000	***Debt/ Equity:***	0.4625

Franklin Lake Resources Inc

172 Starlite St., South San Francisco, CA, 94080; **PH:** 1-650-588-0425; **Fax:** 1-650-588-5869; **http://** www.fklr.com

General - Incorporation	NV	**Stock** - Price on:12/24/2007	$0.15
Employees	1	Stock Exchange	OTC
Auditor	Madsen & Assoc. CPAs, Inc	Ticker Symbol	FKLR
Stk Agt	Computershare Investor Services LLC	Outstanding Shares	18,030,000
Counsel	NA	E.P.S.	-$0.02
DUNS No.	24-828-3160	Shareholders	NA

Business: The group's principal activities are to explore and develop mineralized properties. The group develops the sites where the precious metals can be found and then develops processes for extracting then from the earth. The ores and bottom ash extracted were sold to a refiner for extraction of precious metals. The group is a development stage company.

Primary SIC and add'l.: 1481 1499 1081

CIK No: 0000879519

Officers: Gregory Ofiesh/Dir., CEO, Acting CFO, Pres.,, Peter Boyle/Dir., VP - Regulatory Affairs, Sec., Richard S. Kunter/Dir., VP - Research, Development, Roger Graham/Dir., VP - Operations, Michael Dwyer/Assist.

Directors: Gregory Ofiesh/Dir., CEO, Acting CFO, Pres.,, Peter Boyle/Dir., VP - Regulatory Affairs, Sec., Kamal Alawas/Dir., Paul A. Kaser/Dir., Richard S. Kunter/Dir., VP - Research, Development, Roger Graham/Dir., VP - Operations, Stanley R. Combs/Dir.

Owners: Insiders/72.00%, Prudent Bear Fund/3.90%, Peter Boyle/4.50%, Stanley Combs, Paul Kaser/1.80%, Roger Graham/4.50%, Gregory Ofiesh/61.10%, Forrest Godde/3.70%

Financial Data: Fiscal Year End:10/31   Latest Annual Data: 10/31/2006

Year	Sales	Net Income
2006	NA	-$338,000
2005	$5,000	-$325,000
2004	NA	-$345,000

Curr. Assets:	$36,000	Curr. Liab.:	$29,000		
Plant, Equip.:	NA	Total Liab.:	$29,000	Indic. Yr. Divd.:	NA
Total Assets:	$81,000	Net Worth:	$52,000	Debt/ Equity:	NA

Franklin Resources Inc

1 Franklin Pkwy., Bldg. 970, 1st Fl., San Mateo, CA, 94403; **PH:** 1-650-312-2000; **Fax:** 1-650-312-5606; **http://** www.franklintempleton.com

General - Incorporation	DE	**Stock** - Price on:12/24/2007	$134.83
Employees	8,000	Stock Exchange	NYSE
Auditor	PricewaterhouseCoopers LLP	Ticker Symbol	BEN
Stk Agt	Franklin Templeton Investor Services	Outstanding Shares	NA
Counsel	NA	E.P.S.	$7.03
DUNS No.	60-997-6543	Shareholders	NA

Business: The group's principle activities are carried out in two segments: investment management: provides investment advisory, fund administration, distribution and related services. Banking/finance: provides consumer lending and selected retail-banking services to individuals. The group also provides transfer agency, fund administration, shareholder processing, custodial, trustee and other fiduciary services. Major portion of revenues is derived from providing investment management, administration, distribution and related services to the sponsored investment products. It has operations in the United States, Canada, the bahamas, Europe, Asia, South America, Africa and Australia. On 01-Oct-2003, the group acquired darby overseas investments ltd and darby overseas partners lp. The group's total revenue for the year 2007 was 6,205.77 millions of USD.

Primary SIC and add'l.: 6719 6211 6282 6153 6099

CIK No: 0000038777

Subsidiaries: Asia Infrastructure Mezzanine Capital Management Co., Ltd., C&EE General Partner Ltd., C&EE Private Equity Partners L.P., Darby Asia Investors (HK), Ltd., Darby Asia Investors, Ltd., Darby CEE Founder Partner II, LLC, Darby Converging Europe founder Partner, L.P., Darby Emerging Markets Income Investments LLC, Darby Emerging Markets Income Investments, Ltd., Darby Emerging Markets Investments, LDC, Darby Europe Mezzanine Management, Darby Global SICAV Managers, LLC, Darby Holdings, Inc., Darby Latin American Mezzanine Investments, Darby Overseas Investments, Ltd. 101 Subsidiaries included in the Index

Officers: Gregory E. Johnson/Dir., CEO, Pres., Vijay C. Advani/Exec. VP - Global Advisor Services, Leslie M. Kratter/Sr. VP, Assist. Sec., Penelope S. Alexander/VP - Human Resources, US, Rick Frisbie/Sr. VP, Chief Administrative Officer, Craig S. Tyle/Exec. VP, General Counsel, William Y. Yun/Exec. VP - Institutional, Lisa Gallegos/Dir. - Media, Stacey Johnston/Mgr. - Media, Matt Walsh/Public Relations Consultant, Contact - Media, Holly Gibson Brady/VP - Media, Jennifer J. Bolt/Exec. VP - Operations, Technology, Donna S. Ikeda/VP - Human Resources, International, Murray L. Simpson/Exec. VP, Holly E. Gibson/VP - Corporate Communications (17 Officers included in Index)

Directors: Gregory E. Johnson/Dir., CEO, Pres., Charles B. Johnson/Chmn., Rupert H. Johnson/Vice Chmn., Samuel H. Armacost/Dir., Louis E. Woodworth/Dir., Charles Crocker/Dir., Robert D. Joffe/Dir., Joseph R. Hardiman/Dir., Peter M. Sacerdote/Dir., Anne M. Tatlock/Dir., Thomas H. Kean/Dir., Chutta Ratnathicam/Dir., Laura Stein/Dir.

Owners: AXA Financial, Inc./6.50%, Robert D. Joffe, Rupert H. Johnson/15.54%, Vijay C. Advani, Charles B. Johnson/17.86%, Peter M. Sacerdote, Louis E. Woodworth, Joseph R. Hardiman, Gregory E. Johnson, Laura Stein, Insiders/35.04%, Charles Crocker, Jennifer J. Bolt, Thomas H. Kean, William Y. Yun (19 Owners included in Index)

Financial Data: Fiscal Year End:09/30   Latest Annual Data: 9/30/2006

Year	Sales	Net Income
2006	$5,050,726,000	$1,267,568,000
2005	$4,310,098,000	$1,057,631,000
2004	$3,438,208,000	$706,664,000

Curr. Assets:	$5,272,191,000	Curr. Liab.:	$1,593,432,000		
Plant, Equip.:	$506,291,000	Total Liab.:	$2,719,335,000	Indic. Yr. Divd.:	$0.600
Total Assets:	$9,499,859,000	Net Worth:	$6,684,728,000	Debt/ Equity:	0.1200

Franklin Street Properties Corp

401 Edgewater Pl., Ste. 200, Wakefield, MA, 01880; **PH:** 1-781-557-1300; **Fax:** 1-781-246-2807; **http://** www.franklinstreetproperties.com; **Email:** investorrelations@franklinstreetproperties.com

General - Incorporation	MD	**Stock** - Price on:12/24/2007	$17.55
Employees	37	Stock Exchange	AMEX
Auditor	Ernst & Young LLP	Ticker Symbol	FSP
Stk Agt	Wells fargo Shareowner Services	Outstanding Shares	70,030,000
Counsel	NA	E.P.S.	NA
DUNS No.	NA	Shareholders	NA

Business: The groups principle activities include financing, acquiring and operating real estate properties. The group operates through two segments namely, real estate operations and banking services. In the year 2006, the group acquired five real estate investment trust. The group's quarterly revenue for September 2007 was 30.26 millions of USD.

Primary SIC and add'l.: 6798

CIK No: 0001031316

Subsidiaries: FSP 380 Interlocken Corp., FSP 390 Interlocken LLC, FSP Addison Circle Corp., FSP Austin N.W. Limited Partnership, FSP Blue Lagoon Drive Corp., FSP Bollman Place Limited Partnership, FSP Collins Crossing Corp., FSP Eldridge Green Corp., FSP Forest Park IV NC Limited Partnership, FSP Goldentop Technology Center Limited Partnership, FSP Greenwood Plaza Corp., FSP Hillview Center Limited Partnership, FSP Holdings LLC, FSP Innsbrook Corp., FSP Investments LLC 32 Subsidiaries included in the Index

Officers: George J. Carter/Chmn., CEO, Pres./$231,000.00, Barbara J. Fournier/Dir., VP, COO, Treasurer, Sec./$568,917.00, John G. Demeritt/CFO/$520,167.00, Janet P. Notopoulos/Dir., VP, William W. Gribbell/Exec. VP - Investment Sales/$1,113,286.00, Scott R. MacPhee/Exec. VP/$1,302,143.00, Scott H. Carter/Sr. VP - In, House Counsel, Jeffrey B. Carter/Sr. VP, Dir. - Acquisitions, Donna M. Brownell/VP - Operations, Andrew J. Klouse/VP - Finance, Stephen W. Garvey/Investment Executive, Investment Sales, Patrick M. Gorman/Investment Executive, Investment Sales, Adam R. Norris/Investment Executive, Investment Sales, Eric W. Nyland/Investment Executive, Investment Sales, Jeffrey E. Witherell/Investment Executive, Investment Sales (20 Officers included in Index)

Directors: George J. Carter/Chmn., CEO, Pres., Barbara J. Fournier/Dir., VP, COO, Treasurer, Sec., Janet P. Notopoulos/Dir., VP, Barry Silverstein/Non - Management Dir., Dennis J. McGillicuddy/Dir., John N. Burke/Dir., Georgia Murray/Dir.

Owners: Georgia Murray, John G. Demeritt, Scott R. MacPhee, Janet P. Notopoulos, George J. Carter/1.18%, John N. Burke, William W. Gribbell, Barry Silverstein/8.98%, Barbara J. Fournier, Insiders/15.86%, Dennis J. McGillicuddy/4.86%

Financial Data: Fiscal Year End:12/31   Latest Annual Data: 12/31/2006

Year	Sales	Net Income
2006	$114,368,000	$110,929,000
2005	$96,393,000	$75,116,000
2004	$100,052,000	$47,763,000

Curr. Assets:	$83,037,000	Curr. Liab.:	$29,662,000	P/E Ratio:	12.45
Plant, Equip.:	$852,862,000	Total Liab.:	$33,355,000	Indic. Yr. Divd.:	NA
Total Assets:	$955,317,000	Net Worth:	$921,962,000	Debt/ Equity:	NA

Franklin Towers Enterprises Inc

5 Ash Dr., Center Barnstead, NH, 03225; **PH:** 1-702-943-0714

General - Incorporation	NV	**Stock** - Price on:12/24/2007	$1.2
Employees	NA	Stock Exchange	OTC
Auditor	Wolinetz, Lafazan & Co., P.c.	Ticker Symbol	FRTW
Stk Agt	NA	Outstanding Shares	30,250,000
Counsel	NA	E.P.S.	-$0.01
DUNS No.	NA	Shareholders	NA

Business: The groups principal activities include manufacturing, processing, and distributing frozen Pan Asian foods. Products of the group include snacks, vegetables, fish, meat and fruit. The group operates from Nevada in the United States.

Primary SIC and add'l.: 2221

CIK No: 0001365669

Officers: Kelly Fan/38/Dir., CEO, Pres., Treasurer, Patricia E. Dowell/59/Sec.

Directors: Kelly Fan/38/Dir., CEO, Pres., Treasurer

Owners: Insiders/25.10%, Kelly Fan/1.10%, Dingliang Kuang/24.00%, Xinshengxiang Industrial Development Co., Ltd./18.80%

Financial Data: Fiscal Year End:09/30   Latest Annual Data: 12/31/2006

Year	Sales	Net Income
2006	NA	-$119,000

Curr. Assets:	$17,000	Curr. Liab.:	$22,000		
Plant, Equip.:	NA	Total Liab.:	$42,000	Indic. Yr. Divd.:	NA
Total Assets:	$17,000	Net Worth:	-$24,000	Debt/ Equity:	NA

FranklinCovey Co

2200 W Pkwy. Blvd., Salt Lake City, UT, 84119; **PH:** 1-801-817-1776; **Fax:** 1-801-817-8069; **http://** www.franklincovey.com; **Email:** comments@franklincovey.com

General - Incorporation	UT	**Stock** - Price on:12/24/2007	$7.97
Employees	1,237	Stock Exchange	NYSE
Auditor	KPMG LLP	Ticker Symbol	FC
Stk Agt	Zions First National Bank	Outstanding Shares	19,410,000
Counsel	Parr Waddups Brown Gee & Loveless	E.P.S.	$0.91
DUNS No.	11-340-2713	Shareholders	NA

Business: The group's principal activity is to offer integrated training and performance enhancement solutions to organizations and individuals. The group manufactures and distributes products designed to improve organization and individual effectiveness through proven leadership and productivity principles. It also provides products and services to a number of U.S. & foreign governmental agencies, including U.S. Department of defence & educational institutions. These products and services are available through professional consulting services, public workshops, catalogs, retail stores and the Internet. The group's best known products include the franklin planner and the 7 habits of highly effective people.

Primary SIC and add'l.: 8748 8211 2731

CIK No: 0000886206

Subsidiaries: Franklin Covey Brasil Ltda., Franklin Covey Canada, Ltd., Franklin Covey Catalog Sales, Inc., Franklin Covey Client Sales, Inc., Franklin Covey de Mexico S. de R.L. de C.V., Franklin Covey Europe, Ltd., Franklin Covey Ireland Limited, Franklin Covey Japan Co. Ltd., Franklin Covey Marketing, Ltd., Franklin Covey Mexico, Inc., Franklin Covey Middle East W.L.L., Franklin Covey Printing, Inc., Franklin Covey Product Sales, Inc., Franklin Covey Proprietary Limited, Franklin Covey Services, LLC 17 Subsidiaries included in the Index

Officers: Robert A. Whitman/Chmn., CEO, Robert William Bennett/Pres. - Organizational Strategic Business Unit, Stephen D. Young/CFO, Corp. Sec., Sarah E. Merz/Pres., GM - Consumer, Small Business Unit, Richard Putnam/Primary Investor Relations Officer

Directors: Robert A. Whitman/Chmn., CEO, Stephen R. Covey/Vice Chmn., Clayton M. Christensen/Dir., Robert H. Daines/Dir., E. J. Garn/Dir., Dennis G. Heiner/Dir., Donald J. McNamara/Dir., Joel C. Peterson/Dir., Kay E. Stepp/Dir.

Owners: Stephen R. Covey/5.30%, Robert H. Daines, Insiders/41.00%, Clayton M. Christensen, Robert W. Bennett, Stephen D. Young, Sarah Merz, Joel C. Peterson/1.00%, Donald J. McNamara/27.20%, Knowledge Capital Investment/26.90%, Robert A. Whitman/10.50%, Dimensional Fund Advisors, Inc./7.70%, Dennis G. Heiner, E. J. JakeGarn, Kay E. Stepp

Financial Data: *Fiscal Year End:*08/31 *Latest Annual Data:* 8/31/2006

Year		Sales		Net Income
2006		$278,623,000		$28,573,000
2005		$283,542,000		$10,186,000
2004		$275,434,000		-$10,150,000
Curr. Assets:	$87,120,000	**Curr. Liab.:**	$48,448,000	**P/E Ratio:** 8.48
Plant, Equip.:	$33,318,000	**Total Liab.:**	$83,210,000	**Indic. Yr. Divd.:** NA
Total Assets:	$216,559,000	**Net Worth:**	$133,349,000	**Debt/ Equity:** NA

Frawley Corp

5737 Kanan Rd., Pmb 188, Agoura Hills, CA, 91301; *PH:* 1-818-735-6640

General - Incorporation	DE	**Stock**- Price on:12/24/2007	NA
Employees	NA	Stock Exchange	OTC
Auditor	Larue, Corrigan & Mccormick LLP	Ticker Symbol	FRWL
Stk Agt	NA	Outstanding Shares	NA
Counsel	NA	E.P.S.	NA
DUNS No.	05-149-7527	Shareholders	NA

Business: The group's principal activity is development of real estate. The real estate investment consists of approximately 57 acres of largely undeveloped land in the santa monica mountains, northwest of los angeles. The group is continuing to pursue various options with respect to selling a significant portion of its real estate.

Primary SIC and add'l.: 6552 6531

CIK No: 0000038824

Officers: Sheila Callahan/25/Dir., Sec.

Directors: Sheila Callahan/25/Dir., Sec.

Owners: Joseph P. Frawley/13.20%, Mary Louise Frawley/11.50%, Joan Frawley Desmond/8.70%, Michael P. Frawley/10.90%, Insiders/10.90%, Eileen Frawley Callahan/8.20%

Fred's Inc

4300 New Getwell Rd., Memphis, TN, 38118; *PH:* 1-901-365-8880; *Fax:* 1-901-328-0354; *http://* www.fredsinc.com; *Email:* vote@fredsinc.com

General - Incorporation	TN	**Stock** - Price on:12/24/2007	$13.54
Employees	10,010	Stock Exchange	NDQ
Auditor	BDO Seidman LLP	Ticker Symbol	FRED
Stk Agt	American Stock Transfer & Trust Co.	Outstanding Shares	40,070,000
Counsel	Baker, Donelson, Bearman & Caldwell	E.P.S.	$0.67
DUNS No.	00-586-6116	Shareholders	NA

Business: The groups principle activity is to provide general merchandise through its retail discount stores and full-service pharmacies. The groups products include apparel, electronic products, fragrances for men and women and seasonal items. The group operates from United States.

Primary SIC and add'l.: 5632 5113 5993 5311 5912

CIK No: 0000724571

Subsidiaries: Freds Capital Finance, Inc., Freds Capital Management Company, Inc., Freds Stores of Tennessee, Inc., Insurance Value Protection Group, LTD, National Equipment Management and Leasing, Inc.

Officers: Michael J. Hayes/Chmn., CEO/$356,748.00, Charles S. Vail/Corp. Sec., VP - Legal Services, General Counsel, John D. Reier/Dir., Pres./$449,645.00, Gerald E. Thompson/COO, Exec. VP, James R. Fennema/Exec. VP, General Merchandise Mgr./$314,887.00, Dennis K. Curtis/Exec. VP - Store Operations/$268,381.00, Jerry A. Shore/CFO, Exec. VP/$315,683.00, John A. Casey/Exec. VP - Pharmacy Acquisitions, Rick A. Chambers/Exec. VP - Pharmacy Operations

Directors: Michael J. Hayes/Chmn., CEO, John D. Reier/Dir., Pres., Roger T. Knox/Dir., John R. Eisenman/Dir., Mary B. McNabb/Dir., Thomas J. Tashjian/Dir., Michael T. McMillan/Dir.

Owners: John R. Eisenman, Michael J. Hayes/6.40%, John D. Reier, Thomas H. Tashjian, Mary B. McNabb, Michael T. McMillan, Insiders/8.10%, James Fennema, Jerry A. Shore, Dimensional Fund Advisors LP/7.90%, Roger T. Knox, Dennis K. Curtis

Financial Data: *Fiscal Year End:*01/28 *Latest Annual Data:* 2/3/2007

Year		Sales		Net Income
2007		$1,767,239,000		$26,746,000
2006		$1,589,342,000		$26,094,000
2005		$1,441,781,000		$27,952,000
Curr. Assets:	$367,718,000	**Curr. Liab.:**	$127,829,000	**P/E Ratio:** 20.21
Plant, Equip.:	$138,421,000	**Total Liab.:**	$146,441,000	**Indic. Yr. Divd.:** $0.080
Total Assets:	$515,709,000	**Net Worth:**	$369,268,000	**Debt/ Equity:** 0.0063

Frederick County Bancorp Inc

30 W Patrick St., Frederick, MD, 21701; *PH:* 1-301-620-1400; *http://* www.fcbmd.com

General - Incorporation	MD	**Stock**- Price on:12/24/2007	$27.05
Employees	53	Stock Exchange	OTC
Auditor	McGladrey & Pullen LLP	Ticker Symbol	FCBI
Stk Agt	Registrar & Transfer Co	Outstanding Shares	1,460,000
Counsel	NA	E.P.S.	$1.16
DUNS No.	NA	Shareholders	NA

Business: The group's principal activities are to provide commercial banking services. The commercial banking services are provided to corporations, partnerships, small and medium-sized businesses and sole proprietorships as well as to non-profit organizations and associations and investors living or working in frederick county. The commercial loan portfolio consists of term loans, lines of credit and owner occupied commercial real estate loans provided to primarily locally based borrowers. Traditional installment loans and personal lines of credit are available on a selective basis. The service area of the group is frederick county, Maryland.

Primary SIC and add'l.: 6022 6712

CIK No: 0001258831

Subsidiaries: Frederick County Bank

Officers: Martin S. Lapera/CEO, Pres., Fern W. Mercer/Sr. VP, Jay M. House/Sr. VP - Operations, Craig P. Russell/Sr. VP - Commercial Loans, Terrence P. Lee/Sr. VP - Commercial Loans, William R. Talley/CFO, Exec. VP, Wanda S. Shade/Sr. VP - Commercial Services, Retail Banking, Denise Guyton-Boyer/Sr. VP - Commercial Loans

Directors: Raymond Raedy/Dir., John N. Burdette/Dir., William J. Kissner/Dir., William S. Fout/Dir., Helen G. Hahn/Dir., George E. Dredden/Dir., Kenneth G. McCombs/Dir., John Denham Crum/Dir., Emil D. Bennett/Dir., Farhad Memarsadeghi/Dir.

Owners: Insiders/33.75%, Denham J. Crum/2.51%, Martin S. Lapera/7.38%, Kenneth G. McCombs/3.87%, George E. Dredden, John N. Burdette/2.85%, Helen G. Hahn, William J. Kissner/4.40%, Farhad Memarsadeghi/3.86%, William R. Talley/2.57%, William S. Fout/2.22%, Raymond Raedy/3.37%, Emil D. Bennett/2.59%

Financial Data: *Fiscal Year End:*12/31 *Latest Annual Data:* 12/31/2006

Year		Sales		Net Income
2006		$14,073,000		$1,920,000
2005		$11,001,000		$1,832,000
2004		$7,851,000		$1,518,000
Curr. Assets:	$28,689,000	**Curr. Liab.:**	$210,872,000	**P/E Ratio:** 23.32
Plant, Equip.:	$4,362,000	**Total Liab.:**	$217,058,000	**Indic. Yr. Divd.:** NA
Total Assets:	$234,951,000	**Net Worth:**	$17,893,000	**Debt/ Equity:** 0.3378

Freedom Bank FL

4200 4th St. N Ste. D, Saint Petersburg, FL, 33703; *PH:* 1-727-527-2265; *http://* www.freedombankfl.net

General - Incorporation	NA	**Stock**- Price on:12/24/2007	$11.6
Employees	NA	Stock Exchange	OTC
Auditor	NA	Ticker Symbol	FBBF
Stk Agt	NA	Outstanding Shares	NA
Counsel	NA	E.P.S.	NA
DUNS No.	NA	Shareholders	NA

Business: The groups principal activity is to provide banking services. The services of the group include providing loans, deposit, overdraft protection, safe deposit boxes, credit cards, merchant services, cash management and online banking. The group operates from the United States.

Primary SIC and add'l.: 6021

CIK No:

Officers: Chris Draper/Residential Banker Mgr.

Freedom Bank of Virginia

10555 Main St. 1, Fairfax, VA, 22030; *PH:* 1-703-242-5300; *Fax:* 1-703-242-5303; *http://* www.freedombankva.com; *Email:* Info@freedombankva.com

General - Incorporation	NA	**Stock**- Price on:12/24/2007	$14.4
Employees	NA	Stock Exchange	OTC
Auditor	NA	Ticker Symbol	FDVA
Stk Agt	NA	Outstanding Shares	NA
Counsel	NA	E.P.S.	NA
DUNS No.	NA	Shareholders	NA

Business: The groups principal activity is to provide banking services. The services of the group include business and consumer loans, certificates of deposit, IRA investment, cash management, commercial lending, online banking, real state lending, overdraft protection, ATM and debit cards and safe deposit boxes. Customers served by the group include individuals, small and medium size businesses, and professionals. The group operates from Virginia in the United States.

Primary SIC and add'l.: 6512

CIK No:

Officers: John T. Rohrback/CEO, Pres., Karin M. Johns/CFO, Exec. VP, Deborah L. Nelson/Assist. Branch Mgr. - Vienna Branch, Fares Hakim/Branch Mgr., Michael J. Crawford/Business Development Officer, Frozan Pacha/Fairfax Branch, Teller, Veronika G. Cavero/Assist. Branch Mgr., Alicia G. Bez/Loan Clerk, Jennifer A. Hassenpflug/Administrative Assist., Thyda P. Price/VP, BSA Risk Management Officer, Leigh Carey/Mortgage Loan Processor, Closer, George J. Decker/VP - Mortgage Loan Origination Department, Gregory L. Montgomery/Sr. VP - Government Contracting Group, Henry L. Finch/Sr. VP, Relationship Management Officer, Jeremiah D. Behan/Sr. VP - Real Estate Lending Division *(30 Officers included in Index)*

Directors: Richard C. Litman/Chmn., Arlene L. Pripeton/Chmn. - Advisory Board, Darren Bernstein/Member - Advisory Board, William C. Bogart/Member - Advisory Board, Louis M. Cocks/Member - Advisory Board, Jimmy B. Contristan/Member - Advisory Board, Michael A. Falke/Member - Advisory Board, John R. Herbert/Member - Advisory Board, David C. Knapp/Member - Advisory Board, Michael A. Miranda/Dir., Terry L. Collins/Dir., Norman P. Horn/Dir., David C. Karlgaard/Dir., Alvin E. Nashman/Dir., Russell E. Sherman/Dir. *(40 Directors included in Index)*

Freedom Financial Group Inc

3058 E Elm St. , Springfield, MO, 65802; *PH:* 1-417-886-6600; *http://* www.ffgrp.net; *Email:* investor-relations@ffgrp.net

General - Incorporation	DE	**Stock**- Price on:12/24/2007	NA
Employees	NA	Stock Exchange	OTC
Auditor	BKD LLP	Ticker Symbol	FFGR
Stk Agt	Wells Fargo Bank, N.A.	Outstanding Shares	NA
Counsel	NA	E.P.S.	NA
DUNS No.	NA	Shareholders	NA

Business: The group is a specialized consumer finance company engaged in the purchasing, servicing and collection of motor vehicle retail installment contracts originated by independent automobile dealerships. The focus is on acquiring consumer installment contracts collateralized by motor vehicles

ranging in age from one to eight years old at the date of acquisition, entered into with purchasers who have sub-prime credit (i.e., purchasers who, due to poor credit ratings or other circumstances, have limited or no access to traditional sources of consumer credit) but meet certain underwriting requirements. The group is a Delaware corporation formed in 2001.

Primary SIC and add'l.: 6141

CIK No: 0001314386

Subsidiaries: The Credit Group Inc.

Officers: Jerry Fenstermaker/Dir., CEO, Trent Taylor/Assist. VP - Acquisitions, Buyer, Dan Graham/CFO, Staff Accountant, Sr. Mgr., James K. Browne/46/VP

Directors: Jerry Fenstermaker/Dir., CEO, Vernon S. Schweigert/69/Chmn., Steve Gore/Dir., Robert T. Chancellor/Dir., Troy A. Compton/Dir.

Owners: Daniel F. Graham/2.00%, James K. Browne, Jerald L. Fenstermaker/7.00%, Robert T. Chancellor, Insiders/9.80%, Troy A. Compton

Freegold Ventures Ltd

2303 W 41st Ave., Vancouver, BC, V6M 2A3; **PH:** 1-604-685-1870;
http:// www.freegoldventures.com

General - Incorporation .... BC	**Stock**- Price on:12/24/2007 ....$1.51
Employees .... NA	Stock Exchange...OTC
Auditor ....Pricewaterhousecoopers LLP	Ticker Symbol...FGOVF
Stk Agt.........................Staley Okada & Partners	Outstanding Shares ....NA
Counsel..NA	E.P.S...NA
DUNS No..NA	Shareholders...NA

Business: The group's principle activities include acquiring and developing platinum, palladium, rhodium and gold projects in North America. The group operates from United States.

Primary SIC and add'l.: 1041 1099

CIK No: 0001064052

Subsidiaries: Free Gold Recovery USA, Inc, Free Gold Recovery, USA

Officers: Steve Manz/CEO, Pres., Taryn Downing/VP - Administration, Corp. Sec., Gord Steblin/CFO, Michael Gross/VP - Exploration, Kristina Walcott/VP - Business Development, Edward D. Fields/Almaden Project Mgr., Curtis Freeman/Golden Summit Project Mgr., Jeffrey L. Woods/VP - Project Development, Spiros Cacos/Mgr. - Investor Relations

Directors: Harry Barr/Chmn., Bernard Barlin/Dir., Colin Bird/Dir., Hubert Marleau/Dir., Morris Medd/Dir.

Owners: Clifford Berger/5.74%, Gerard Pollino/5.25%, Cede & Co/8.00%, CDS & Company/60.37%

Financial Data: Fiscal Year End:12/31   Latest Annual Data: 12/31/2006

Year	Sales	Net Income
2006	NA	-$4,076,000
2005	NA	-$2,098,000
2004	NA	-$1,881,000

Curr. Assets:	$649,000	**Curr. Liab.:**	$1,340,000		
Plant, Equip.:	$54,000	**Total Liab.:**	$1,340,000	**Indic. Yr. Divd.:**	NA
Total Assets:	$820,000	**Net Worth:**	-$521,000	**Debt/ Equity:**	NA

Freeport McMoran Copper & Gold Inc

1615 Poydras St., New Orleans, LA, 70112; **PH:** 1-504-582-4000; **http://** www.fcx.com;
Email: ir@fmi.com

General - Incorporation .... DE	**Stock**- Price on:12/24/2007 ....$82.58
Employees 9,661	Stock Exchange.......................................NYSE
Auditor .... Ernst & Young LLP	Ticker Symbol..FCX
Stk Agt.................Mellon Investor Services LLC	Outstanding Shares 381,140,000
Counsel..NA	E.P.S..$8.46
DUNS No................................02-252-7808	Shareholders...NA

Business: The groups' principle activity is to operate copper and gold mining properties. The group operates through two segments include mining and exploration, and smelting and refining. The group operates from United The group operates from United States.

Primary SIC and add'l.: 1041 1021

CIK No: 0000831259

Subsidiaries: Atlantic Copper, S.A., FM Services Company, PT Freeport Indonesia, PT Irja Eastern Minerals, PT Puncakjaya Power Indonesia Same

Officers: Richard C. Adkerson/Dir., CEO/$32,110,650.00, Lynne M. Cooney/VP, Assist.To The Chmn., Kathleen L. Quirk/CFO, Exec. VP, Treasurer/$4,815,907.00, Javier Targhetta/Pres., Dir. - PT Irja Eastern Minerals, William L. Collier/VP - Communications, Armando Mahler/Dir., Pres., GM, Michael J. Arnold/Exec. VP, Chief Administrative Officer/$5,656,625.00, Dean T. Falgoust/VP, General Counsel, August Kafiar/Dir., Deputy Pres., Exec. VP, David R. Potter/Exec. VP - Exploration, James D. Miller/VP - Safety, Environmental Affairs, George D. MacDonald/VP - Exploration, Rusdian Lubis/Dir., Deputy Pres., Exec. VP, Frank D. Reuneker/Exec. VP - Security, Russell W. King/Sr. VP - International Relations, Federal Government Affairs (21 Officers included in Index)

Directors: Richard C. Adkerson/Dir., CEO, B. M. Rankin/Vice Chmn., James R. Moffett/Chmn., Robert J. Allison/Dir., Stephen H. Siegele/Dir., Stapleton J. Roy/Dir., Charles C. Krulak/Dir., Jon C. Madonna/Dir., Dustan E. McCoy/Dir., Gabrielle K. McDonald/Dir., Robert A. Day/Dir., H. A. Kissinger/Dir. Emeritus, Devon H. Graham/Dir., Taylor J. Wharton/Dir., Gerald J. Ford/Dir. (17 Directors included in Index)

Owners: James R. Moffett, Bennett J. Johnston, Adrianto Machribie, Devon H. Graham, Jon C. Madonna, Gabrielle K. McDonald, Robert J. Allison, Stapleton J. Roy, Michael J. Arnold, Bobby Lee Lackey, Stephen H. Siegele, Robert A. Day, B. M. Rankin, Insiders/1.20%, Mark J. Johnson (19 Owners included in Index)

Financial Data: Fiscal Year End:12/31   Latest Annual Data: 12/31/2006

Year	Sales	Net Income
2006	$5,790,500,000	$1,456,509,000
2005	$4,179,118,000	$995,127,000
2004	$2,371,866,000	$202,267,000

Curr. Assets:	$2,151,037,000	**Curr. Liab.:**	$972,449,000		
Plant, Equip.:	$3,098,502,000	**Total Liab.:**	$2,731,673,000	**Indic. Yr. Divd.:**	$1.250
Total Assets:	$5,389,802,000	**Net Worth:**	$2,445,101,000	**Debt/ Equity:**	0.7262

Freescale Semiconductor Inc

6501 William Cannon Dr. W, Austin, TX, 78735; **PH:** 1-512-895-2000; **Fax:** 1-512-895-2652;
http:// www.freescale.com

General - Incorporation .... DE	**Stock**- Price on:12/24/2007 ....$39.99
Employees .... NA	Stock Exchange.......................................NYSE
Auditor ....KPMG LLP	Ticker Symbol..FSL
Stk Agt ....Mellon Investor Services LLC	Outstanding Shares ....NA
Counsel.......................................John Torres	E.P.S...NA
DUNS No..NA	Shareholders...NA

Business: The group's principal activity is to design, manufacture and market embedded semiconductors for the automotive, consumer industrial, networking and wireless markets. The group operates in three business groups: transportation and standard products group: manufactures and markets components of embedded control systems like microcontrollers, embedded microprocessors and digital signal processors; networking and computing systems group: manufactures and markets embedded processors and related connectivity products for the wired and wireless networking and computing markets and wireless and mobile solutions group: designs, manufactures and markets semiconductors for wireless mobile devices, such as cellular phones, smart phones, personal data assistants, two-way messaging devices, global positioning systems, mobile gaming devices and wireless consumer electronics. The group has its operations in more than 30 countries.

Primary SIC and add'l.: 3674

CIK No: 0001272547

Subsidiaries: Freescale Halbleiter Deutschland GmbH, Freescale Semiconductor Hong Kong Limited, Freescale Semiconductor Japan Limited, Freescale Semiconductor Singapore Pte. Ltd.

Officers: Michel Mayer/Chmn., CEO, Joe Yiu/Sr. VP, Chmn. - Asia, Pacific, Paul E. Grimme/Sr. VP, GM Transportation - Standard Products Group, Sandeep Chennakeshu/Sr. VP, GM - Wireless, Mobile Systems Group, Janelle Monney/Sr. VP - Business Operations, Corporate Communications, Marketing Services, Dale Weisman/Contact - Media Relations, Jennifer Richard/Contact - Media Relations Wireless, Mobile Systems Group, Wmsg, Andy North/Contact - Media Relations Technology Solutions Organization, Kurt Twining/Sr. VP - Human Resources, Security, Sumit Sadana/Sr. VP - Strategy, Business Development, Alex Pepe/Sr. VP - Manufacturing, Denis Griot/Sr. VP, GM Europe - Middle East, Africa, EMEA Region, John D. Torres/Sr. VP, General Counsel, Sec., David Perkins/Opening General Session, Alan Campbell/Sr. VP, CFO (28 Officers included in Index)

Directors: Michel Mayer/Chmn., CEO, Joe Yiu/Sr. VP, Chmn. - Asia, Pacific

FreeSeas Inc

93 Akti Miaouli, Piraeus; **PH:** 30-302104528770; **http://** www.freeseas.gr; **Email:** info@feeseas.gr

General - Incorporation .... Marshall Islands	**Stock**- Price on:12/24/2007 ....$6.62
Employees 3	Stock Exchange...NDQ
Auditor ....PricewaterhouseCoopers LLP	Ticker Symbol...FREE
Stk Agt .....American Stock Transfer & Trust Co.	Outstanding Shares 6,290,000
Counsel..NA	E.P.S...-$0.78
DUNS No..NA	Shareholders...NA

Business: The groups principle activity is to provide shipping services. In the year 2005, the group merged with Trinity Partners Acquisition Company Inc. Specific customer of the group is Express Sea Transport Corporation. The group operates from Europe, South America, Asia and Africa. The group's quarterly revenue for September 2007 was 4.88 millions of USD.

Primary SIC and add'l.: 4412

CIK No: 0001325159

Subsidiaries: Adventure Four S.A, Adventure Three S.A., Adventure Two S.A.

Officers: Ion G. Varouxakis/37/Chmn., CEO, Pres., Interim CFO, Kostas Koutsoubelis/Dir., VP, Treasurer, Dimitris D. Papadopoulos/CFO, Alexis Varouxakis/Sec., Thomas J. Rozycki/Investor Relations

Directors: Ion G. Varouxakis/37/Chmn., CEO, Pres., Interim CFO, Kostas Koutsoubelis/Dir., VP, Treasurer, Focko H. Nauta/Dir., Matthew W. McCleery/Dir., Dimitrios N. Panagiotopoulos/Dir.

Owners: Ion G. Varouxakis/12.10%, Hummingbird Management, LLC/2.50%, Insiders/12.10%, FS Holdings Limited/14.80%

Financial Data: Fiscal Year End:12/31   Latest Annual Data: 12/31/2006

Year	Sales	Net Income
2006	$11,727,000	-$3,324,000
2005	$10,326,000	$152,000

Curr. Assets:	$1,417,000	**Curr. Liab.:**	$10,260,000	**P/E Ratio:**	57.36
Plant, Equip.:	$19,369,000	**Total Liab.:**	$16,079,000	**Indic. Yr. Divd.:**	NA
Total Assets:	$23,086,000	**Net Worth:**	$7,007,000	**Debt/ Equity:**	NA

FreeStar Technology Corp

Ave. Sarasota No.20, 8-th Fl., Torre Empresarial AIRD, La Julia, Santo Domingo; ;
http:// www.freestartech.com; **Email:** info@freestartech.com

General - Incorporation .... NV	**Stock**- Price on:12/24/2007 ....$0.18
Employees .... NA	Stock Exchange...OTC
Auditor ... Russell Bedford Stefanou Mirchandani	Ticker Symbol..FSRT
Stk Agt .....American Stock Transfer & Trust Co.	Outstanding Shares ....NA
Counsel..NA	E.P.S...NA
DUNS No..NA	Shareholders...NA

Business: The group's principal activity is to develop hardware and software solutions to secure e-commerce and payment transactions. The group operates in two business segments: paysafe system, which sells epaypad and related services and rahaxi payment processing, which generates fees from processing online point of sale terminal transactions in Finland. The group provides online connectivity to all finnish banks, including nordea sampo and oko and the domestic bank credit card company, luottokunta and provides processing services for over 1,300 merchants. The e-payments and e-commerce market is comprised of debit and credit card issuers, switch interchanges, transaction acquirers and generators, including automated teller machine networks, retail merchant locations and the Internet. On 26-Sep-2002 and 15-10-2003, the group acquired rahaxi processing oy and 87% of interest in transaxis inc. The group's operations are principally in Dominican Republic and helsinki Finland.

Primary SIC and add'l.: 7375 7373

CIK No: 0001102301

Subsidiaries: FreeStar Dominicana, FreeStar Technologies Ireland, Ltd, FSRC Processing Oy, Rahaxi Processing Oy

Officers: Paul Egan/Dir., CEO, Pres., Fionn Stakelum/38/Dir, Dir. - European Operations, Carl M. Hessel/45/Dir., VP - International Investor Relations, Alexander Randarevich/Information Technology Mgr., Ciaran Egan/Dir., CFO, Sec., Treasurer, Jose Enrique Perez/CTO, Paul Warren/European Sales Dir.

Directors: Paul Egan/Dir., CEO, Pres., Fionn Stakelum/38/Dir, Dir. - European Operations, Carl M. Hessel/45/Dir., VP - International Investor Relations, Ciaran Egan/Dir., CFO, Sec., Treasurer

Owners: Fionn Stakelum/25.00%, Carl M. Hessel/6.60%, Insiders/100.00%, Insiders/25.30%, Paul Egan/10.90%, Ciaran Egan/7.50%, Paul Egan/100.00%, Ciaran Egan/75.00%, Insiders/100.00%, Fionn Stakelum/0.90%

Financial Data: Fiscal Year End:06/30 Latest Annual Data: 06/30/2007

Year	Sales	Net Income
2007	$3,780,000	-$16,305,000
2006	$2,098,000	-$14,000,000
2005	$1,603,000	-$22,102,000

Curr. Assets:	$3,519,000	Curr. Liab.:	$1,071,000		
Plant, Equip.:	$126,000	Total Liab.:	$1,071,000	Indic. Yr. Divd.:	NA
Total Assets:	$8,388,000	Net Worth:	$7,317,000	Debt/ Equity:	NA

FreightCar America Inc

17 Johns St., Johnstown, PA, 15901; *PH:* 1-814-533-5000; *Fax:* 1-814-533-5010; *http://* www.freightcaramerica.com

General - Incorporation	DE	**Stock** - Price on:12/24/2007	$50.15
Employees	1,429	Stock Exchange	NDQ
Auditor	Deloitte & Touche LLP	Ticker Symbol	RAIL
Stk Agt	National City Bank	Outstanding Shares	12,260,000
Counsel	NA	E.P.S	$10.20
DUNS No.	NA	Shareholders	NA

Business: The groups principle activity is to manufacture aluminum bodied railcars. The products of the group include BethGon Series, AutoFlood Series, Aluminum Vehicle Carrier and Intermodal Double Stack Railcar. The group products sold under the trade name BethGon. In the year 2005, the group merged with FCA Acquisition Corp. Specific customers of the group include CIT Group Equipment Financing, Inc. and General Electric Capital Rail Services Corporation. The group operates from Danville, Illinois, Johnstown, Pennsylvania and Roanoke, Virginia.

Primary SIC and add'l.: 5088 3799 3799 3743 5088 3743

CIK No: 0001320854

Subsidiaries: Freight Car Services, Inc., FreightCar Roanoke, Inc., JAC Intermedco, Inc., JAC Operations, Inc., JAC Patent Company, JAIX Leasing Company, Johnstown America Corporation

Officers: Bill Hutzel/VP - Sales, Eastern Region, Mike Kelly/VP - Sales, Midwest Region, Ted Baun/VP - Sales, Western Region, Bill Wiles/VP - Automotive Products, Kevin Knarr/Mgr. - Customer Service, Sean Hankinson/Product Line Mgr., Mike Crisafulli/Product Line Mgr., Tim Mann/Product Line Mgr. - International Sales, Ron Marhefka/Product Line Mgr. - Steel Open Top Railcars, Kevin P. Bagby/56/VP - Finance, CFO, Treasurer, Sec., Glen T. Karan/57/VP - Planning, Administration, Edward J. Whalen/59/Sr. VP - Marketing, Sales, Peter Dworakowski/International Program Mgr.

Directors: Thomas M. Fitzpatrick/55/Chmn., Carl S. Soderstrom/54/Dir., James D. Cirar/61/Dir., Robert N. Tidball/69/Dir., Thomas A. Madden/54/Dir.

Owners: Camillo M. Santomero, Citadel Limited Partnership/7.80%, James D. Cirar, Thomas M. Fitzpatrick, Kenneth D. Bridges, Insiders, Robert N. Tidball, Thomas A. Madden, Putnam, LLC/5.10%, Wellington Management Company, LLP/8.10%, Barclays Global Investors, NA./13.40%, S. Carl Soderstrom

Financial Data: Fiscal Year End:12/31 Latest Annual Data: 12/31/2006

Year	Sales	Net Income
2006	$1,444,800,000	$128,733,000
2005	$927,187,000	$45,693,000
2004	$482,180,000	-$24,860,000

Curr. Assets:	$343,545,000	Curr. Liab.:	$156,988,000	P/E Ratio:	4.92
Plant, Equip.:	$25,905,000	Total Liab.:	$216,112,000	Indic. Yr. Divd.:	$0.240
Total Assets:	$419,981,000	Net Worth:	$203,869,000	Debt/ Equity:	NA

Fremont General Corp

2425 Olympic Blvd., 3rd Fl., Santa Monica, CA, 90404; *PH:* 1-310-315-5500; *Fax:* 1-310-315-5599; *http://* www.fremontgeneral.com

General - Incorporation	NV	**Stock** - Price on:12/24/2007	$12.27
Employees	3,200	Stock Exchange	NYSE
Auditor	Ernst & Young LLP	Ticker Symbol	FMT
Stk Agt	Mellon Investor Services LLC	Outstanding Shares	77,860,000
Counsel	Wilson Sonsini Goodrich & Rosati	E.P.S	$2.21
DUNS No.	07-795-8130	Shareholders	NA

Business: The group's principal activities are to provide financial services including origination of commercial and residential real estate loans and syndicated commercial loans on a nationwide basis. The lending is done on a senior and secured basis, minimizing credit exposure through conservative loan underwriting and appropriating loan to collateral valuations and cash flow coverages. Loans are originated through independent loan brokers. It provides deposit accounts including certificates of deposit and installment investment certificates through its 17 branches in California. The deposit accounts are insured by the federal deposit insurance corporation.

Primary SIC and add'l.: 6712 6021

CIK No: 0000038984

Subsidiaries: Fremont General Credit Corporation, Fremont Investment & Loan

Officers: Louis J. Rampino/Dir., CEO, Pres., Alan W. Faigin/Sr. VP, General Counsel, Chief Legal Officer, Wayne R. Bailey/Dir., Exec. VP, COO, Ronald J. Nicolas/Sr. VP, Treasurer, CFO, Chief Accounting Officer, Raymond G. Meyers/Sr. VP, Chief Administrative Officer

Directors: Louis J. Rampino/Dir., CEO, Pres., James A. McIntyre/Chmn., Dickinson C. Ross/Dir., Russell K. Mayerfeld/Dir., Robert F. Lewis/Dir., Thomas W. Hayes/Dir., Wayne R. Bailey/Dir., Exec. VP, COO

Owners: Harbinger Capital Partners Master FundI, Ltd./8.80%, Patrick E. Lamb, Insiders/13.40%, James A. McIntyre/10.70%, Thomas W. Hayes, Kyle R. Walker, Magnetar Investment Management, LLC/6.20%, Russell K. Mayerfeld, Robert F. Lewis, Louis J. Rampino/1.20%, Dickinson C. Ross, Howard Amster/8.90%, Wayne R. Bailey

Financial Data: Fiscal Year End:12/31 Latest Annual Data: 12/31/2005

Year	Sales	Net Income
2005	$1,274,843,000	$327,948,000
2004	$1,167,888,000	$353,756,000
2003	$903,665,000	$256,261,000

Curr. Assets:	$810,766,000	Curr. Liab.:	$9,550,993,000	P/E Ratio:	5.55
Plant, Equip.:	$99,075,000	Total Liab.:	$10,127,307,000	Indic. Yr. Divd.:	$0.480
Total Assets:	$11,484,113,000	Net Worth:	$1,356,806,000	Debt/ Equity:	0.2190

Fremont Michigan Insuracorp Inc

933 E Main St., Fremont, MI, 49412; *PH:* 1-231-924-0300; *Fax:* 1-888-968-3664; *http://* www.fmic.com; *Email:* info@fmic.com

General - Incorporation	MI	**Stock** - Price on:12/24/2007	$25.15
Employees	NA	Stock Exchange	OTC
Auditor	BDO Seidman, LLP	Ticker Symbol	FMMH
Stk Agt	Registrar & Transfer Co	Outstanding Shares	1,730,000
Counsel	NA	E.P.S	$3.61
DUNS No.	NA	Shareholders	NA

Business: The groups principle activity is to provide insurance services. The groups insurance products include homeowners, mobilowners, personal auto, dwelling, business owners, commercial package, commercial auto and workers compensation. The group operates through four segments namely personal, commercial, farm and marine. The group operates from Michigan in the United States.

Primary SIC and add'l.: 6331

CIK No: 0001271245

Subsidiaries: Fremont Insurance Company

Officers: Richard E. Dunning/Dir., CEO, Pres., William A. Hall/62/VP - Commercial Lines, Agency Relations, Marvin R. Deur/56/Sr. VP - Administration, Treasurer, Kurt M. Dettmer/40/VP, Marketing Mgr. - Fremont Insurance, Kevin G. Kaastra/37/VP - Finance, Harry L. Wiberg/Dir. - Fremont Insurance

Directors: Richard E. Dunning/Dir., CEO, Pres., Donald Vansingel/Chmn., William L. Johnson/Vice Chmn., Jack G. Hendon/Dir., Kenneth J. Schuiteman/Dir., Michael A. De Kuiper/Dir., Donald E. Bradford/Dir., Jack A. Siebers/Dir., Don Wilson/Dir., Monica C. Holmes/Dir.

Owners: Richard E. Dunning/3.30%, Jack G. Hendon, Donald VanSingel, Donald E. Bradford, Monica C. Holmes, William A. Hall/1.30%, Harold L. Wiberg, Michael A. DeKuiper, Jack A. Siebers, Kenneth J. Schuiteman, Kevin G. Kaastra, Marvin R. Deur/1.60%, Kurt M. Dettmer, William L. Johnson, Donald C. Wilson *(17 Owners included in Index)*

Financial Data: Fiscal Year End:12/31 Latest Annual Data: 12/31/2006

Year	Sales	Net Income
2006	$42,074,000	$7,215,000
2005	$41,214,000	$9,082,000
2004	$28,663,000	$1,513,000

Curr. Assets:	$20,415,000	Curr. Liab.:	$6,867,000	P/E Ratio:	6.97
Plant, Equip.:	$1,771,000	Total Liab.:	$51,447,000	Indic. Yr. Divd.:	NA
Total Assets:	$85,877,000	Net Worth:	$34,430,000	Debt/ Equity:	NA

Frequency Electronics Inc

55 Charles Lindbergh Blvd., Mitchel Field, NY, 11553; *PH:* 1-516-794-4500; *Fax:* 1-516-794-4340; *http://* www.freqelec.com; *Email:* ir@freqelec.com

General - Incorporation	DE	**Stock** - Price on:12/24/2007	$9.95
Employees	425	Stock Exchange	NDQ
Auditor	PricewaterhouseCooper	Ticker Symbol	FEIM
Stk Agt	American Stock Transfer & Trust Co.	Outstanding Shares	8,680,000
Counsel	Cadwalader, Wickersham & Taft LLP	E.P.S	$0.05
DUNS No.	00-132-1611	Shareholders	NA

Business: The group's principal activities are to design, develop and manufacture products for satellite, terrestrial voice, video and data telecommunications. The group operates in four segments: commercial communications segment consists of time and frequency control products used in satellites and terrestrial cellular telephone or other ground-based telecommunications. Us government segment consists of time and frequency control products used in terrestrial and space applications by the defense department and other us government agencies. Gillam-fei segment consists of wireline synchronization and network monitoring systems. Fei-zyfer segment provides global positioning system (gps) technologies into systems and subsystems for secure communications in government, commercial and other locator applications. Customers of the group include motorola corporation and space systems loral. On 09-May-2003, the group acquired zyfer,inc.

Primary SIC and add'l.: 3679 3829 3825 3625

CIK No: 0000039020

Subsidiaries: FEI Communications, Inc, FEI Government Systems, Inc, FEI-Asia, FEI-Zyfer, Inc, Gillam-FEI, Russian-based Morion, Inc

Officers: Martin B. Bloch/71/Dir., CEO, Pres./$682,520.00, Harry Newman/60/Sec., Leonard Martire/70/VP - Marketing/$299,801.00, Alan Miller/58/Treasurer, CFO/$227,775.00, Oleandro Mancini/58/VP - Business Development/$317,562.00, Markus Hechler/61/Exec. VP, Pres. - FEI Government Systems, Inc, Assist. Sec./$329,820.00, Charles S. Stone/76/VP - Low Noise Development, Thomas McClelland/52/VP - Commercial Products, Steven Strang/43/Pres. - FEI, Zyfer, Hugo Fruehauf/68/CTO, Adrian Lalicata/VP - RF

Directors: Martin B. Bloch/71/Dir., CEO, Pres., Joseph P. Franklin/73/Chmn., Joel Girsky/68/Dir., Robert S. Foley/79/Dir., Donald E. Shapiro/75/Dir., Richard Schwartz/71/Dir.

Owners: Robert S. Foley, Joel Girsky, Frequency Electronics, Inc.,/6.40%, Alan Miller, Dimensional Fund Advisors, Inc./7.30%, Oleandro Mancini, DePrince Race & Zollo, Inc./15.20%, Joseph P. Franklin/1.90%, Richard Schwartz, Martin B. Bloch/10.70%, Donald E. Shapiro, Markus Hechler/1.20%, Inverness Counsel, Inc./5.60%, Leonard Martire, Insiders/21.80%

Financial Data: Fiscal Year End:04/30 Latest Annual Data: 04/30/2007

Year	Sales	Net Income
2007	$56,206,000	-$257,000
2006	$52,810,000	$4,798,000
2005	$55,173,000	$5,037,000

Curr. Assets:	$66,763,000	Curr. Liab.:	$6,988,000	P/E Ratio:	62.19
Plant, Equip.:	$6,663,000	Total Liab.:	$16,108,000	Indic. Yr. Divd.:	$0.200
Total Assets:	$86,741,000	Net Worth:	$70,633,000	Debt/ Equity:	NA

Fresenius Medical Care Corp

Else-Kroner Strasse 1, Bad Homburg, 61352; *PH:* 49-61726092525; *http://* www.fmc-ag.com

General - Incorporation	Germany	**Stock**- Price on:12/24/2007	$45.92
Employees	47,521	Stock Exchange	NYSE
Auditor	KPMG LLP	Ticker Symbol	FMS
Stk Agt	Bank of New York	Outstanding Shares	NA
Counsel	NA	E.P.S.	NA
DUNS No.	31-497-8834	Shareholders	NA

Business: The group's principal activity is to design and develop customized computer servers and network appliances. The infrastructure server products include specialized custom servers, which are configured with single, dual or quad Intel Pentium III, IV or Xeon processors. The customers of the group includes to departments, agencies and offices of the federal government and selected businesses. The group conducts its business under the trademarks of SteelCloud, Dunn Computer Corporation, and IDP.

Primary SIC and add'l.: 3841 2836 2834 2835 8071

CIK No: 0001019600

Subsidiaries: Fresenius Medical Care AG, Fresenius Medical Care Holdings Inc., National Medical Care, Inc.

Officers: Roberto Fuste/56/Member - Management Board, Lawrence A. Rosen/50/CFO, Michael Brull/Mgr. - Human Resources, Andrea Bolting/Schweinfurt Plant, Human Resources, Svenja Grotzfeld/Dir. - Human Resources, Dieter Perinotto/Mgr. - Human Resources, Ursula Schmidt/Mgr. - Human Resources, Joachim Weith/Sr. VP - Corporate Communications, Public Affairs, Andrea Ukena/Sr. Mgr. - Human Resources, Carola Maurer/Mgr. - Human Resources, Silke Waldschmitt/Mgr. - Human Resources, Joachim Umbach/Mgr. - Human Resources, Ruth Koster/St Wendel Plant, Human Resources, Mats Wahlstrom/54/Pres., Emanuele Gatti/52/Member - Management Board *(23 Officers included in Index)*

Directors: Ben Lipps/68/Chmn., Gerd Krick/Chmn., Dieter Schenk/Vice Chmn., Ulf M. Schneider/Member - Supervisory Board, Germany, Bernd Fahrholz/Member - Supervisory Board, Attorney, Walter L. Weisman/Member - Supervisory Board, John Gerhard Kringel/Member - Supervisory Board, William P. Johnston/Member - Supervisory Board

Financial Data: *Fiscal Year End:*12/31 *Latest Annual Data:* 12/31/2006

Year	Sales		Net Income
2006	$8,499,038,000		$536,746,000

Curr. Assets:	$3,411,916,000	**Curr. Liab.:**	$2,375,705,000		
Plant, Equip.:	$1,722,392,000	**Total Liab.:**	$6,920,691,000	**Indic. Yr. Divd.:**	NA
Total Assets:	$13,044,681,000	**Net Worth:**	$4,870,162,000	**Debt/ Equity:**	NA

Fresh Del Monte Produce Inc

PO Box 149222, Coral Gables, FL, 33114; *PH:* 1-305-520-8400; *Fax:* 1-305-567-0320; *http://* www.freshdelmonte.com

General - Incorporation	Cayman Islands	**Stock**- Price on:12/24/2007	$23.39
Employees	37,500	Stock Exchange	NYSE
Auditor	Ernst & Young LLP	Ticker Symbol	FDP
Stk Agt	Mellon Investor Services LLC	Outstanding Shares	57,710,000
Counsel	NA	E.P.S.	$1.44
DUNS No.	01-795-7304	Shareholders	NA

Business: The group's principal activities are production, distribution and marketing of fresh and packaged fresh cut produce. The products of the group include bananas, pineapples, melons, grapes, citrus, apples, pears, peaches, plums, nectarines, apricots, kiwi, plantains, vidalia(R) sweet onions and various greens. The products are sold in Europe, North America, South America and the Asia-pacific region under the brand name del monte (r). The products are also sold under the registered trademarks utc (R), fielder (R), rosy(R) and purple mountain (r). These products are distributed through retail stores, wholesalers, independent distributors and food service operators in more than 50 countries around the world. On 21-Nov-2003, the group acquired expans sp. Z o.o. (expans) and standard fruit and vegetable co inc. On 11-Aug-2004, the group acquired can-AM express inc and rln leasing inc.

Primary SIC and add'l.: 0161 0175 2033

CIK No: 0001047340

Subsidiaries: Agencia Maritima de Costa Rica Amarco, S.A., Agricola UAC Limitada, Agricola Villa Alegre Acquisition Corp., Agricola Villa Alegre Limitada, Agrinanas Development Co., Inc., Alcantara Shipping Corporation, Alcazar Shipping Corporation, Algeciras Shipping Corporation, Alhambra Shipping Corporation, Alicante Shipping Corporation, Almeria Shipping Corporation, Altara Shipping Corporation, Amalgamated Fisheries Co. (Pty) Ltd., Andalucia Shipping Corporation, Bananeros S.A. (Conserba or C.I. Conserba) 164 Subsidiaries included in the Index

Officers: Mohammad Abu-Ghazaleh/Chmn., CEO, Antolin D. Saiz/VP - Internal Audit, Jose Luis Bendicho/VP - South America, John F. Inserra/CFO, Exec. VP, Paul Rice/Sr. VP - North America Operations, Bruce A. Jordan/Sr. VP, General Counsel, Sec., Jimenez Tenazas/Sr. VP - Asia Pacific, Christine Cannella/Assist. VP - Investor Relations, Marissa R. Tenazas/VP - Human Resources, Helmuth Lutty/VP - Shipping Operations, Hani El-Naffy/COO, Pres., Linda Conway/VP - Integration, Special Projects, Jean-Pierre Bartoli/Sr. VP - Europe, Africa, Middle East, Emanuel Lazopoulos/Sr. VP - North America Sales, Product Management, Jose Antonio Yock/Sr. VP - Central America *(16 Officers included in Index)*

Directors: Mohammad Abu-Ghazaleh/Chmn., CEO, Maher Abu-Ghazaleh/Dir., Salvatore H. Alfiero/Dir., Amir Abu-Ghazaleh/Dir., Edward L. Boykin/Dir., Michael J. Berthelot/Dir., John H. Dalton/Dir.

Owners: Wafa Abu-Ghazaleh, Mohammad Abu-Ghazaleh, Amir Abu-Ghazaleh, Maher Abu-Ghazaleh, Brandes Investment Partners, LP, Maha Abu-Ghazaleh, Nariman Abu-Ghazaleh, Oussama Abu-Ghazaleh, IAT Group Inc., FMR Corporation, Letko, Brosseau& Associates Inc., Hanan Abu-Ghazaleh, Sumaya Abu-Ghazaleh, Fatima Abu-Ghazaleh, Insiders

Financial Data: *Fiscal Year End:*12/30 *Latest Annual Data:* 12/29/2006

Year	Sales		Net Income
2006	$3,214,300,000		-$145,100,000
2005	$3,259,700,000		$106,600,000
2004	$2,906,000,000		$139,200,000

Curr. Assets:	$742,300,000	**Curr. Liab.:**	$442,400,000	**P/E Ratio:**	62.19
Plant, Equip.:	$914,700,000	**Total Liab.:**	$980,800,000	**Indic. Yr. Divd.:**	$0.200
Total Assets:	$2,058,000,000	**Net Worth:**	$1,069,200,000	**Debt/ Equity:**	NA

Fresno First Bank CA

7690 N Palm Ave. Ste. 101, Fresno, CA, 93711; *PH:* 1-559-439-0200; *http://* www.fresnofirstbank.com

General - Incorporation		**Stock**- Price on:12/24/2007	$13.6
Employees	NA	Stock Exchange	OTC
Auditor	NA	Ticker Symbol	FSNF
Stk Agt	NA	Outstanding Shares	NA
Counsel	NA	E.P.S.	NA
DUNS No.	NA	Shareholders	NA

Business: The groups principle activity is to provide recruiting services. The groups service area includes the research and development, engineering, marketing, sales, information technology and manufacturing industries. The group operates from United States.

Primary SIC and add'l.: 6022

CIK No:

Officers: Richard Whitsell/Dir., CEO, Pres., Teresa Palsgaard/VP, Commercial Relationship Mgr., Jay Roll/VP - Commercial Lender, Jeanette Gregory/VP - Personal Banker, Kenneth Herron/Sr. VP, Sr. Loan Officer, Evangelina Gonzalez/Sr. VP, Sr. Operating Officer, Debbie Cameron/VP, Executive Sec., Lanny Chan/VP - Personal Banker, Steve Canfield/CFO

Directors: Richard Whitsell/Dir., CEO, Pres., Brad L. Smith/Vice Chmn., David Price/Chmn., Robert Kubo/Dir., Morris Garcia/Dir., Jack Holt/Dir., Mark Saleh/Dir., Joel Slonski/Dir., Al Smith/Dir., Daniel Suchy/Dir., Lorrie Lorenz/Dir., Pablo Aleman/Dir.

Frezer Inc

1010 University Ave., Ste 40, San Diego, CA, 92103; *PH:* 1-619-702-1404; *http://* www.frezer.net

General - Incorporation	NV	**Stock**- Price on:12/24/2007	$0.15
Employees	3	Stock Exchange	OTC
Auditor	Chang G. Park, Cpa	Ticker Symbol	FRZR
Stk Agt	Colonial Stock Transfer Co Inc	Outstanding Shares	82,830,000
Counsel	NA	E.P.S.	-$0.04
DUNS No.	NA	Shareholders	NA

Business: The group's activity is to research and develop regenerative medicines. The group's R&D unit works on creating stem cell therapies.

Primary SIC and add'l.: 8731

CIK No: 0001328888

Subsidiaries: Bio-Matrix Scientific Group, Inc

Owners: Kevin R. Keating/2.00%, Insiders/2.00%, KI Equity Partners IV, LLC/84.50%

Financial Data: *Fiscal Year End:*12/31 *Latest Annual Data:* 12/31/2006

Year	Sales		Net Income
2006	NA		-$1,046,000

Curr. Assets:	$11,000	**Curr. Liab.:**	$107,000		
Plant, Equip.:	NA	**Total Liab.:**	$107,000	**Indic. Yr. Divd.:**	NA
Total Assets:	$15,000	**Net Worth:**	-$92,000	**Debt/ Equity:**	NA

Friedman Billings Ramsey Group Inc

1001 19th St. N, Arlington, VA, 22209; *PH:* 1-703-312-9500; *Fax:* 1-703-312-9501; *http://* www.fbr.com; *Email:* ir@fbr.com

General - Incorporation	VA	**Stock**- Price on:12/24/2007	$6.41
Employees	3,019	Stock Exchange	NYSE
Auditor	PricewaterhouseCoopers LLP	Ticker Symbol	FBR
Stk Agt	American Stock Transfer & Trust Co.	Outstanding Shares	174,430,000
Counsel	NA	E.P.S.	-$1.38
DUNS No.	NA	Shareholders	NA

Business: The group's principal activities are to provide investment banking, institutional brokerage, asset management and private client services through its operating subsidiaries. In addition, the group invests in mortgage-backed securities and merchant banking opportunities. The group focuses capital and financial expertise on six industry sectors: financial services, real estate, technology, healthcare, energy and diversified industrials. In mar 2003, the group merged with fbr asset investment corporation. As a result of the merger, the group will elect reit status for tax purposes. Fbr asset investment corporation is a real estate investment trust that invests in mortgage-backed securities and makes opportunistic investments in debt and equity securities of companies in real estate-related and other businesses.

Primary SIC and add'l.: 6211 6798 6719

CIK No: 0001209028

Subsidiaries: FBR Asset Management Holdings, Inc., FBR Bancorp, Inc., FBR Capital Markets Holdings, Inc., Fbr Ccp, Ltd., FBR Fund Advisers, Inc., FBR Investment Management, Inc., FBR Investment Services, Inc., FBR Investments, LLC, FBR NIM Investments, LLC, FBR Securitization, Inc., FBR TRS Holdings, Inc., FBR Trust Investments, LLC, FBRC, Ltd., First NLC Financial Services, Inc., First NLC Financial Services, LLC 28 Subsidiaries included in the Index

Officers: Dorian A. Prosdocimi/MD, CEO - International Business in London, Neal S. Henschel/Chmn., CEO - First NLC, Eric F. Billings/Chmn., CEO, Kurt R. Harrington/CFO, Exec. VP, Rock J. Tonkel/Dir., COO, Pres., William J. Ginivan/Exec. VP, General Counsel, Richard J. Hendrix/COO, Pres., Robert J. Kiernan/Sr. VP, Controller, Chief Accounting Officer, Philip J. Facchina/Sr. MD, Group Head - Technology, Media, Telecommunications, Patrick J. Keeley/Sr. MD, Group Head - Energy, Natural Resources, Ann M. Griffith/Dir. - Regulatory Affairs, Compliance, Ben Purser/Dir. - Operational Analysis, Shannon H. Small/Sr. VP, Dir. - Marketing, Communications, Timothy Wood/CIO, James Gargiulo/Sr. VP, Chief - Human Capital *(107 Officers included in Index)*

Directors: Neal S. Henschel/Chmn., CEO - First NLC, Eric F. Billings/Chmn., CEO, John T. Wall/Dir., Rock J. Tonkel/Dir., COO, Pres., Peter A. Gallagher/Dir., Russell C. Lindner/Dir., Daniel J. Altobello/Dir., Ralph S. Michael/Dir., Wallace L. Timmeny/Dir., Stephen D. Harlan/Dir.

Owners: Eric F. Billings, Daniel J. Altobello, Eric F. Billings/61.00%, William J. Ginivan, Russell W. Ramsey/7.20%, Kurt R. Harrington, Russell W. Ramsey, Insiders/70.60%, Peter A. Gallagher, John T. Wall, Insiders/2.10%, Ralph S. Michae, Richard J. Hendrix, Wallace L. Timmeny, Russell C. Lindner *(18 Owners included in Index)*

Financial Data: *Fiscal Year End:*12/31 *Latest Annual Data:* 12/31/2006

Year	Sales		Net Income
2006	$1,007,904,000		-$67,275,000
2005	$995,306,000		-$170,910,000
2004	$1,052,102,000		$349,559,000

Curr. Assets:	$454,516,000	**Curr. Liab.:**	$7,190,949,000		
Plant, Equip.:	$44,111,000	**Total Liab.:**	$12,046,030,000	**Indic. Yr. Divd.:**	$0.200
Total Assets:	$13,352,518,000	**Net Worth:**	$1,171,045,000	**Debt/ Equity:**	7.9771

Friedman Industries Inc

4001 Homestead Rd., Houston, TX, 77028; *PH:* 1-713-672-9433; *Fax:* 1-903-758-2265; *http://* www.friedmanindustries.com

General - Incorporation	TX	Stock- Price on:12/24/2007	$9.27
Employees	140	Stock Exchange	AMEX
Auditor	Ernst & Young LLP	Ticker Symbol	FRD
Stk Agt	American Stock Transfer & Trust Co.	Outstanding Shares	6,710,000
Counsel	Fulbright & Jaworski LLP	E.P.S.	$0.75
DUNS No.	00-842-9730	Shareholders	NA

Business: The group's principal activity is to manufacture, process and distribute pipe and steel. The group operates in two product and service groups: coil products and tubular products. The coil product segment purchases hot-rolled steel coils and processes steel coils into flat sheet and plate steel. The tubular product segment purchases, processes, manufactures and markets tubular products. The principal customers of the group are steel distributors and customers fabricating steel products such as storage tanks, steel buildings, farm machinery and equipment and similar other products. The coil processing plants of the group are located at lone star, Texas and hickman, Arkansas.

Primary SIC and add'l.: 3312
CIK No: 0000039092
Subsidiaries: Royal Fasteners Corporation
Officers: William E. Crow/61/Dir., CEO, Pres./$368,131.00, Bruce Boykin/Sales, Flat Roll Division, Tom Thompson/Sr. VP - Sales/$314,250.00, Jim Newsom/Sales, Flat Roll Division, Mark Settlage/Credit Mgr., Robert Sparkman/VP - Sales, Flat Roll Division, Bruce Crockett/Sales, Texas Tubular, Howard Henderson/VP, Plant Mgr. Texas Tubular Division, Connie Mack Hughes/Assist. Sales Mgr. - Texas Tubular, Jonathon Holcomb/Contact - Sales, XSCP, Ben Harper/Sr. VP - Finance/$314,250.00, Michael Thompson/Sales, Texas Tubular, Carol Sewell/Mgr. - Accounting Payable, Ron Welling/Mgr. - Sales, Texas Tubular Division, Ronald Burgerson/VP *(16 Officers included in Index)*
Directors: William E. Crow/61/Dir., CEO, Pres., Jack Friedman/Chmn., Harold Friedman/Co - Chmn., Alan M. Rauch/73/Dir., Joe L. Williams/62/Dir., Charles W. Hall/78/Dir., Durga D. Agrawal/63/Dir., Hershel M. Rich/83/Dir.
Owners: William E. Crow, Ben Harper, Joe L. Williams, Charles W. Hall, Alan M. Rauch, Dimensional Fund Advisors LP/7.60%, Hershel M. Rich, Insiders/8.20%, LSV Asset Management/5.60%, Jack Friedman/5.40%, Harold Friedman

Financial Data: *Fiscal Year End:* 03/31   *Latest Annual Data:* 03/31/2007

Year	Sales	Net Income
2007	$199,727,000	$7,018,000
2006	$181,900,000	$6,454,000
2005	$188,022,000	$6,246,000

Curr. Assets:	$47,551,000	Curr. Liab.:	$18,383,000	P/E Ratio:	9.76
Plant, Equip.:	$7,774,000	Total Liab.:	$18,834,000	Indic. Yr. Divd.:	$0.320
Total Assets:	$55,931,000	Net Worth:	$37,097,000	Debt/ Equity:	NA

Friendly Ice Cream Corp

1855 Boston Rd., Wilbraham, MA, 01095; *PH:* 1-413-543-2400; *http://* www.friendlys.com

General - Incorporation	MA	Stock- Price on:12/24/2007	$15.19
Employees	12,800	Stock Exchange	NA
Auditor	Ernst & Young LLP	Ticker Symbol	NA
Stk Agt	Bank of New York	Outstanding Shares	8,160,000
Counsel	NA	E.P.S.	$0.10
DUNS No.	00-111-6557	Shareholders	NA

Business: The group's principal activities are to manufacture and distribute ice cream and operate full service restaurants. As on 28-Dec-2003, the group owned and operated 380 full service restaurants and franchised 157 full-service restaurants and 6 non-traditional units. It operates in three segments: restaurant, foodservice and franchise. The restaurant segment offers wide variety of breakfast, lunch and dinner items. Foodservice segment manufactures and distributes packaged frozen dessert products to friendly's restaurants, supermarkets and other retail locations. The group has more than 100 food and dessert item in its menu.

Primary SIC and add'l.: 2024 6794 5812
CIK No: 0000039135
Subsidiaries: Friendlys Realty II, LLC, Restaurant Insurance Corporation
Officers: George M. Condos/52/Dir., CEO, Pres., Florence A. Tassinari/Controller, Kenneth D. Green/Sr. VP - Operations, Gregory A. Pastore/VP, General Counsel, Clerk, Paul V. Hoagland/Exec. VP - Administration, CFO, Garrett J. Ulrich/VP - Human Resources
Directors: George M. Condos/52/Dir., CEO, Pres., Donald N. Smith/Chmn., Perry D. Odak/Dir., Burton J. Manning/Dir., Steven L. Ezzes/Dir., Michael J. Daly/Dir.
Owners: Kevin Douglas/10.30%, The Lion Fund L.P./11.60%, Paul V. Hoagland, Burton J. Manning, Michael J. Daly, Kenneth D. Green, Gregory A. Pastore, Perry D. Odak, Insiders/16.00%, Donald N. Smith/12.40%, Bank of America Corporation/5.30%, Garrett J. Ulrich, Steven L. Ezzes, FMR Corp./5.70%, Prestley S. Blake/12.90%

Financial Data: *Fiscal Year End:* 01/01   *Latest Annual Data:* 12/31/2006

Year	Sales	Net Income
2006	$531,455,000	$4,946,000
2005	$574,497,000	-$3,417,000

Curr. Assets:	$58,111,000	Curr. Liab.:	$68,691,000	P/E Ratio:	151.90
Plant, Equip.:	$137,425,000	Total Liab.:	$347,063,000	Indic. Yr. Divd.:	NA
Total Assets:	$220,167,000	Net Worth:	-$126,896,000	Debt/ Equity:	NA

Frisch's Restaurants Inc

2800 Gilbert Ave., Cincinnati, OH, 45206; *PH:* 1-513-961-2660; *Fax:* 1-513-559-5160; *http://* www.frischs.com

General - Incorporation	OH	Stock- Price on:12/24/2007	$31.5
Employees	4,800	Stock Exchange	AMEX
Auditor	Grant Thornton LLP	Ticker Symbol	FRS
Stk Agt	Continental Stock Transfer & Trust Co	Outstanding Shares	5,110,000
Counsel	NA	E.P.S.	$1.80
DUNS No.	00-699-9437	Shareholders	NA

Business: The group's principal activity is to operate restaurants and license others to operate family restaurants. The family-style restaurants are operated under the name 'frisch's big boy' and grill buffet style restaurants under the name 'golden corral'. The restaurants also have 'drive-thru' service. Big boy

restaurants offer double-Deck hamburger sandwich, onion rings, hot fudge cake, sandwiches, pasta, roast beef, chicken and seafood dinners, desserts, non-alcoholic beverages and other items. Golden corral restaurant offers meat including fried and rotisserie chicken, meat loaf, pot roast, fish and a carving station that rotates hot roast beef, ham and turkey. As of 30-May-2004, the group operated 88 family-style restaurants and 26 grill-buffet style family restaurants. Additionally, the group licensed 31 'big boy' restaurants to other operators. All of these restaurants are currently located in various markets of Ohio, Kentucky and Indiana.

Primary SIC and add'l.: 5812
CIK No: 0000039047
Subsidiaries: Frisch Indiana, Inc., Frisch Kentucky LLC, Frisch Ohio, Inc., Frisch Pennsylvania, Inc., Frisch West Virginia, Inc.
Officers: Craig F. Maier/Dir., CEO, Pres./$681,158.00, Donald H. Walker/CFO/$274,094.00, Lindon C. Kelley/Regional Dir./$205,665.00, Michael R. Dunham/Regional Dir./$263,484.00, Kenneth C. Hull/VP - Development, Franchising/$200,304.00, Donald A. Bodner/Assist. Sec.
Directors: Craig F. Maier/Dir., CEO, Pres., Daniel W. Geeding/Chmn., Dale P. Brown/Dir., Jerome P. Montopoli/Dir., Lorrence T. Kellar/Dir., Karen F. Maier/Dir., Blanche F. Maier/Dir., William J. Reik/Dir., Robert J. Dourney/50/Dir.
Owners: Reik & Co., LLC/12.80%, Blanche F. Maier/33.30%, Karen F. Maier/16.40%, Royce & Associates, LLC/7.40%, Craig F. Maier/24.60%, River Road Asset Management, LLC/4.90%

Financial Data: *Fiscal Year End:* 05/30   *Latest Annual Data:* 05/29/2007

Year	Sales	Net Income
2007	$289,934,000	$9,268,000
2006	$292,218,000	$9,160,000
2005	$279,247,000	$14,741,000

Curr. Assets:	$12,063,000	Curr. Liab.:	$30,583,000	P/E Ratio:	16.94
Plant, Equip.:	$157,448,000	Total Liab.:	$74,601,000	Indic. Yr. Divd.:	$0.440
Total Assets:	$175,283,000	Net Worth:	$100,681,000	Debt/ Equity:	0.2634

Front Range Capital Corp

1020 Century Dr., Ste. 202, Louisville, CO, 80027; *PH:* 1-303-926-0300

General - Incorporation	CO	Stock- Price on:12/24/2007	$13
Employees	NA	Stock Exchange	OTC
Auditor	McGladrey & Pullen LLP	Ticker Symbol	FRGC
Stk Agt	NA	Outstanding Shares	NA
Counsel	Louisville Law Firm	E.P.S.	NA
DUNS No.	NA	Shareholders	NA

Business: The groups principle activity is to provide commercial banking services. The groups business banking services include checking, savings, loans, cards, cash management, merchant services and online banking. In March 2007, the group is acquired by First State Bancorporation. The group operates from United States.

Primary SIC and add'l.: NA
CIK No: 0001813964
Subsidiaries: Delaware business trust, Front Range Capital Trust I, Heritage Bank

Financial Data: *Fiscal Year End:* 12/31   *Latest Annual Data:* 12/31/2004

Year	Sales	Net Income
2004	$27,078,000	$1,059,000
2003	$26,882,000	$776,000
2002	$25,869,000	$1,440,000

Fronteer Development Group

1055 W Hastings St., Ste. 1650, Vancouver, BC, V6E 2E9; *PH:* 1-604-632-4677; *http://* www.fronteergroup.com; *Email:* info@fronteergroup.com

General - Incorporation	Canada	Stock- Price on:12/24/2007	$12.7501
Employees	14	Stock Exchange	AMEX
Auditor	PricewaterhouseCoopers LLP	Ticker Symbol	FRG
Stk Agt	Equity Transfer Services Inc	Outstanding Shares	67,860,000
Counsel	Goodman & Carr LLP	E.P.S.	$0.058
DUNS No.	NA	Shareholders	NA

Business: The group's principle activity is to explore mineral mineral properties located in the Northwest Territories, the province of Labrador, the province of Ontario, western Turkey and Mexico. The group operates from United States.

Primary SIC and add'l.: 1400
CIK No: 0001271129
Subsidiaries: Aurora Energy Resources Inc., Berkley Homes (Pickering) Inc., Fronteer de Mexico S.A. de C.V., Fronteer Eurasia Madencilik Limited Sirketi, Fronteer Holdings Inc., Fronteer Investment Inc.
Officers: Mark O'Dea/Dir., CEO, Pres., Sean Tetzlaff/CFO, Corp. Sec., Ian Cunningham-Dunlop/VP - Exploration, Jim Lincoln/VP - Operations, Chris Lee/Chief Geoscientist, Camon Mak/Mgr. - Investor Relations
Directors: Mark O'Dea/Dir., CEO, Pres., Oliver Lennox-King/Chmn., George Bell/Dir., Donald McInnes/Dir., Lyle Hepburn/Dir., Scott Hand/Dir., Jo Mark Zurel/Dir.

Financial Data: *Fiscal Year End:* 12/31   *Latest Annual Data:* 12/31/2006

Year	Sales	Net Income
2006	NA	-$20,201,000
2005	NA	-$10,951,000
2004	NA	-$5,482,000

Curr. Assets:	$38,369,000	Curr. Liab.:	$1,180,000		
Plant, Equip.:	$3,676,000	Total Liab.:	$2,529,000	Indic. Yr. Divd.:	NA
Total Assets:	$68,771,000	Net Worth:	$66,242,000	Debt/ Equity:	NA

Frontier Airlines Inc

7001 Tower Rd., Denver, CO, 80249; *PH:* 1-720-374-4200; *Fax:* 1-720-374-4375; *http://* www.flyfrontier.com; *Email:* earlyreturns@flyfrontier.com

General - Incorporation	DE	**Stock**- Price on:12/24/2007	$5.83
Employees	3,851	Stock Exchange	NDQ
Auditor	KPMG LLP	Ticker Symbol	FRNT
Stk Agt	Mellon Investor Services LLC	Outstanding Shares	36,640,000
Counsel	NA	E.P.S.	$0.07
DUNS No.	83-115-3622	Shareholders	NA

Business: The group's principal activity is to operate as a scheduled passenger airline based in denver, Colorado. The group, in conjunction with frontier jetexpress operated by mesa air group, operates routes linking its denver hub to forty-eight cities in twenty two states spanning the United States from coast to coast and to two cities in Mexico. It currently uses up to sixteen gates at the denver international airport ("Dia"), where it operates approximately 204 daily system flight departures and arrivals. It generally provides seats at discount fares on flights booked within 14 days of travel. It has twenty-eight leased jets and nine owned airbus aircraft. The fleets include three boeing 737-200s, sixteen larger boeing 737-300s ,twenty six airbus a319s and six airbus a318s.

Primary SIC and add'l.: 4512

CIK No: 0000921929

Officers: Sean E. Menke/Dir., CEO, Pres., Cathy Bradley/VP - Inflight Services, Ted Christie/VP - Finance, Gerry Coady/CIO, VP, Dennis Crabtree/VP - Safety, Security, Cameron Kenyon/VP - Flight Operations, Ann Block/Sr. VP - People, David Sislowski/Sr. VP, General Counsel, Elissa A. Potucek/VP - Controller, Treasurer, Ron McClellan/VP - Maintenance - Engineering, Cliff C. Van Leuven/VP - Customer Service, Airport guy, Chris Collins/COO, Exec. VP, John Happ/Sr. VP - Marketing, Planning, Paul Tate/Sr. VP, CFO, Joe Hodas/Dir. - Corporate Communications

Directors: Sean E. Menke/Dir., CEO, Pres., Paul S. Dempsey/Vice Chmn., Jeff S. Potter/Dir., Larae B. Orullian/Dir., Patricia A. Engels/Dir., James B. Upchurch/Dir., Robert D. Taylor/Dir., Dale D. Browning/Dir.

Financial Data: *Fiscal Year End:*03/31 **Latest Annual Data:** 3/31/2007

Year	Sales		Net Income
2007	$1,170,949,000		-$20,370,000
2006	$994,273,000		-$13,971,000

Curr. Assets:	$340,405,000	**Curr. Liab.:**	$359,326,000		
Plant, Equip.:	$605,131,000	**Total Liab.:**	$833,372,000	**Indic. Yr. Divd.:**	NA
Total Assets:	$1,042,868,000	**Net Worth:**	$209,496,000	**Debt/ Equity:**	2.1571

Frontier Energy Corp

PO Box 6282, China Village, ME, 04926; *PH:* 1-207-445-5274; *http://* www.frontierenergy.org; *Email:* infomail@frontierenergy.org

General - Incorporation	NV	**Stock**- Price on:12/24/2007	NA
Employees	NA	Stock Exchange	NA
Auditor	De Joya Griffith & Company LLC	Ticker Symbol	NA
Stk Agt	Standard Registrar & Transfer Co Inc.	Outstanding Shares	NA
Counsel	NA	E.P.S.	NA
DUNS No.	NA	Shareholders	NA

Business: The groups principal activities include exploring and developing oil and natural gas property. In January 2005, the group acquired copper, gold and platinum mineral properties. The group operates from Central Alberta in the United States.

Primary SIC and add'l.: 1381

CIK No: 0000793981

Subsidiaries: Technical Services & Logistics Inc

Officers: Robert Genesi/70/Dir., CEO, Principal Financial Officer, Pres., Chris Bitely/Contact, Joel Glatz/Contact, Brad Taylor/Contact

Directors: Robert Genesi/70/Dir., CEO, Principal Financial Officer, Pres., Don Huang/69/Dir.

Owners: Insiders/21.00%, Robert Genesi/21.00%

Frontier Financial Corp

332 SW Everett Mall Way, Everett, WA, 98204; *PH:* 1-425-514-0700; *Fax:* 1-425-514-0718; *http://* www.frontierbank.com; *Email:* ebanking@frontierbank.com

General - Incorporation	WA	**Stock**- Price on:12/24/2007	$23.95
Employees	721	Stock Exchange	NDQ
Auditor	Moss Adams LLP	Ticker Symbol	FTBK
Stk Agt	NA	Outstanding Shares	44,510,000
Counsel	NA	E.P.S.	$1.57
DUNS No.	10-370-4847	Shareholders	NA

Business: The group's principal activity is to provide general banking services including the acceptance of demand, time and savings deposits and origination of loans. It is a financial holding company and conducts its operations through its subsidiary, frontier bank. As of Dec 31, 2003, the bank has 38 offices located in clallam, jefferson, king, kitsap, pierce, skagit, snohomish and whatcom counties. It provides a wide range of consumer banking services including savings accounts, checking accounts, safe deposit facilities, time deposits, installments and commercial lending and other business related financial services. The group also provides discount brokerage services, trust services, home, construction and commercial long-term financing. In addition, the group markets annuities, life insurance products and mutual funds.

Primary SIC and add'l.: 6712 6022

CIK No: 0000716457

Subsidiaries: FFP, Incorporated, Inc., Frontier Bank

Officers: John J. Dickson/Dir., CEO/$795,429.00, James F. Felicetty/Sec., Treasurer, Lyle E. Ryan/COO, Pres./$471,744.00, Carol E. Wheeler/CFO/$293,501.00, Connie Pachek/Exec. VP - Operations - Human Resources/$361,931.00

Directors: John J. Dickson/Dir., CEO, Robert J. Dickson/Chmn., David Cuthill/Dir., William H. Lucas/Dir., William J. Robinson/Dir., Patrick Fahey/Dir., Jim Mulligan/Dir. Emeritus, Don Regan/Dir. Emeritus, Roger Rice/Dir. Emeritus, Darrell J. Storkson/Dir., Edward C. Rubatino/Dir., Michael J. Clementz/Dir., George Barber/Dir. Emeritus, Edward D. Hansen/Dir., Mark O. Zenger/Dir. *(16 Directors included in Index)*

Owners: David M. Cuthill, William J. Robinson/1.44%, Darrell J. Storkson/1.22%, Connie Pachek, John J. Dickson/1.89%, Robert J. Dickson/1.39%, Carol E. Wheeler, Edward C. Rubatino/1.25%, Lyle E. Ryan, Lucy DeYoung, Mark O. Zenger, Edward D. Hansen, William H. Lucas, George E. Barber, James W. Ries *(19 Owners included in Index)*

Financial Data: *Fiscal Year End:*12/31 **Latest Annual Data:** 12/31/2006

Year	Sales		Net Income
2006	$265,792,000		$68,910,000
2005	$192,172,000		$51,584,000
2004	$154,216,000		$43,045,000

Curr. Assets:	$122,895,000	**Curr. Liab.:**	$2,817,322,000	**P/E Ratio:**	15.45
Plant, Equip.:	$30,026,000	**Total Liab.:**	$2,843,181,000	**Indic. Yr. Divd.:**	$0.660
Total Assets:	$3,238,464,000	**Net Worth:**	$395,283,000	**Debt/ Equity:**	0.0131

Frontier Oil Corp

10000 Memorial Dr., Ste. 600, Houston, TX, 77024; *PH:* 1-713-688-9600; *Fax:* 1-713-688-0616; *http://* www.frontieroil.com; *Email:* ir@frontieroil.com

General - Incorporation	WY	**Stock**- Price on:12/24/2007	$43.94
Employees	747	Stock Exchange	NYSE
Auditor	Deloitte & Touche LLP	Ticker Symbol	FTO
Stk Agt	Wells Fargo Bank, N.A.	Outstanding Shares	110,190,000
Counsel	NA	E.P.S.	NA
DUNS No.	07-938-9086	Shareholders	NA

Business: The group's principle activities include refining, marketing crude oil and petroleum products. The groups petroleum products include gasoline, diesel fuel, jet fuel, asphalt, chemicals and petroleum coke. The group operates from United States.

Primary SIC and add'l.: 2911 5172 6719

CIK No: 0000110430

Subsidiaries: Frontier El Dorado Refining Company, Frontier Holdings Inc., Frontier Oil and Refining Company, Frontier Pipeline Inc., Frontier Refining & Marketing Inc, Frontier Refining Inc., Wainoco Oil & Gas Company, Wainoco Resources Inc

Officers: James R. Gibbs/Chmn., CEO, Pres./$8,792,928.00, Currie J. Bechtol/VP, General Counsel, Sec./$1,824,264.00, Doug Aron/VP - Corporate Finance, Gerald B. Faudel/VP - Corporate Relations, Jon D. Galvin/VP, Michael C. Jennings/CFO, Exec. VP/$1,778,992.00, Paul Eisman/Exec. VP - Refining, Marketing Operations/$1,449,692.00, Nancy J. Zupan/VP, Controller/$989,070.00

Directors: James R. Gibbs/Chmn., CEO, Pres., Douglas Y. Bech/Dir., Michael T. Dossey/Dir., Paul B. Loyd/Dir., James H. Lee/Dir., Clyde G. Buck/Dir., Michael E. Rose/Dir.

Owners: James H. Lee, Jon D. Galvin, Nancy J. Zupan, Paul W. Eisman, Michael C. Jennings, Douglas Y. Bech, FMR Corp/11.20%, Michael T. Dossey, James R. Gibbs/1.70%, Currie J. Bechtol, Insiders/3.00%, Clyde G. Buck, Michael E. Rose, Paul B. Loyd, BlackRock, Inc./5.40%

Financial Data: *Fiscal Year End:*12/31 **Latest Annual Data:** 12/31/2006

Year	Sales		Net Income
2006	$4,795,953,000		$379,277,000
2005	$4,001,162,000		$272,532,000
2004	$2,861,716,000		$69,764,000

Curr. Assets:	$939,216,000	**Curr. Liab.:**	$459,698,000		
Plant, Equip.:	$536,805,000	**Total Liab.:**	$748,071,000	**Indic. Yr. Divd.:**	$0.200
Total Assets:	$1,523,925,000	**Net Worth:**	$775,854,000	**Debt/ Equity:**	0.1819

Frontline Ltd

Par-La-Ville Pl, 14 Par-La-Ville Rd., Hamilton; ; *http://* www.frontline.bm

General - Incorporation	Bermuda	**Stock**- Price on:12/24/2007	$45.26
Employees	42	Stock Exchange	NYSE
Auditor	Grant Thornton, LLP	Ticker Symbol	FRO
Stk Agt	Mellon Investor Services LLC	Outstanding Shares	74,830,000
Counsel	NA	E.P.S.	$6.77
DUNS No.	NA	Shareholders	NA

Business: The group's principal activity is the operation of crude oil tankers and dry bulk carriers. The group is also involved in the charter, purchase and sale of vessels. The group operates two sizes of tankers namely, crude carriers or VLCCS and Suezmaxes. The group also operates a fleet of dry bulk carriers. The customers of the group include oil companies, petroleum products traders, and government agencies. In January 2005 the group acquired the VLCCs Front Century, Front Champion and Oscilla. The groups operates subsidiaries and partnerships located in Bermuda, Liberia, Norway, panama, Singapore and Sweden.

Primary SIC and add'l.: 4412

CIK No: 0000913290

Subsidiaries: formed Ship Finance, Frontline Shipping II, Golden Ocean Group Limited, Independent Tankers Corporation

Officers: John Fredriksen/Chmn., CEO, Pres., Bjorn Sjaastad/CEO - Frontline Management AS, Cathrine Fosse/Treasurer, Tor Olav Troim/Dir., VP, Inger M. Klemp/CFO - Frontline Management AS, Bengt Neteland/VP - Finance

Directors: John Fredriksen/Chmn., CEO, Pres., Kate Blankenship/Dir., Tor Olav Troim/Dir., VP, Frixos Savvides/Dir.

Owners: Hemen Holding Ltd. and associated companies/34.85%, Insiders/35.14%, Kate Blankenship, John Fredriksen/34.85%, Inger M. Klemp, Tor Olav Troim

Financial Data: *Fiscal Year End:*12/31 **Latest Annual Data:** 12/31/2006

Year	Sales		Net Income
2006	$1,583,863,000		$516,000,000
2005	$1,513,833,000		$606,839,000
2004	$1,855,666,000		$1,023,382,000

Curr. Assets:	$1,112,142,000	**Curr. Liab.:**	$443,916,000		
Plant, Equip.:	$3,239,503,000	**Total Liab.:**	$3,380,255,000	**Indic. Yr. Divd.:**	$6.000
Total Assets:	$4,589,937,000	**Net Worth:**	$668,560,000	**Debt/ Equity:**	NA

Frozen Food Express Industries Inc

1145 Empire Central Pl., Dallas, TX, 75247; *PH:* 1-214-630-8090; *Fax:* 1-214-819-5559; *http://* www.ffeinc.com

General - Incorporation	TX	**Stock**- Price on:12/24/2007	$10.74
Employees	2,633	Stock Exchange	NDQ
Auditor	KPMG LLP	Ticker Symbol	FFEX
Stk Agt	EquiServe Trust Co N.A	Outstanding Shares	17,310,000
Counsel	NA	E.P.S.	$0.01
DUNS No.	05-013-4964	Shareholders	NA

Business: The group's principle activities are to provide motor carrier transportation of perishable commodities, full-truckload and less-than-truckload services throughout North America. The group's services include full truckload, dedicated fleets, less-than-truckload and distribution services. Full-truckload has a single destination weighing between 20,000 and 40,000 pounds from a single shipper. Dedicated fleets enter into a contract with customers involving the assignment of specific trucks and drivers to handle transportation needs. Less-than-truckload use multi-compartment refrigerated trailers to carry goods requiring different temperatures on one trailer to customers. Distribution services deliver cargo to end users such as grocery stores, food brokers and drug stores within a single metropolitan area. The group's quarterly revenue for Sep'07 was 114.73 millions of USD.

Primary SIC and add'l.: 4231 4213

CIK No: 0000039273

Subsidiaries: Conwell Cartage, Inc., Conwell Corporation, Conwell, LLC, FFE Logistics, Inc., FFE Transportation Services, Inc., FFE, Inc., FX Holdings, Inc., Lisa Motor Lines, Inc.

Officers: Stoney M. Stubbs/71/Chmn., CEO, Pres./$656,662.00, Charles G. Robertson/COO, Exec. VP/$168,951.00, Leonard W. Bartholomew/Sec., Thomas G. Yetter/56/Dir., Sr. VP, CFO, Treasurer/$290,619.00, Stoney Russell Stubbs/44/Dir., COO, Sr. VP/$333,239.00

Directors: Stoney M. Stubbs/71/Chmn., CEO, Pres., Leroy Hallman/93/Dir., Michael T. O'Connor/53/Dir., Mike W. Baggett/61/Dir., Jerry T. Armstrong/69/Dir., Brian R. Blackmarr/66/Dir., Thomas G. Yetter/56/Dir., Sr. VP, CFO, Treasurer, Stoney Russell Stubbs/44/Dir., COO, Sr. VP, Barrett D. Clark/36/Dir.

Owners: Russell S. Stubbs/1.79%, Lucile B. Fielder/9.36%, Leroy Hallman, Mike W. Baggett, Thomas G. Yetter, Delaware Charter Guarantee & Trust Company/11.52%, Stoney M. Stubbs/9.57%, Sarah M. Daniel/9.96%, Michael T. O'Connor, Charles G. Robertson/4.69%, Dalton, Greiner, Hartman, Maher & Co./8.16%, Jerry T. Armstrong, William Blair & Company, L.L.C./5.96%, Insiders/12.44%, Dimensional Fund Advisors, Inc./8.69% *(16 Owners included in Index)*

Financial Data: *Fiscal Year End:*12/31 *Latest Annual Data:* 12/31/2006

Year	Sales	Net Income
2006	$483,721,000	$11,226,000
2005	$524,127,000	$20,437,000
2004	$474,430,000	$10,754,000

Curr. Assets:	$86,186,000	*Curr. Liab.:*	$44,773,000	*P/E Ratio:*	21.48
Plant, Equip.:	$97,808,000	*Total Liab.:*	$69,231,000	*Indic. Yr. Divd.:*	$0.120
Total Assets:	$191,762,000	*Net Worth:*	$122,531,000	*Debt/ Equity:*	NA

FSI International Inc

3455 Lyman Blvd., Chaska, MN, 55318; ***PH:*** 1-952-448-5440; ***Fax:*** 1-952-448-2825; ***http://*** www.fsi-intl.com; ***Email:*** fsi@fsi-intl.com

General - Incorporation	MN	**Stock**- Price on:12/24/2007	$3.36
Employees	560	Stock Exchange	NDQ
Auditor	KPMG LLP	Ticker Symbol	FSII
Stk Agt	Computershare Investor Services LLC	Outstanding Shares	30,420,000
Counsel	Luke R. Komarek	E.P.S	-$0.06
DUNS No.	06-654-2911	Shareholders	NA

Business: The group's principal activity is to design, develop, manufacture, market and support surface conditioning equipment. The equipment is used in the fabrication of microelectronics such as advanced semiconductor devices and thin film heads. The group operates in two divisions: surface conditioning division and polaris systems and supply services division. The surface conditioning division markets and services equipment that uses wet, vapor, cryogenic and other chemistry techniques to clean, strip or etch the surfaces of silicon wafers. The polaris systems and supply services division supplies photoresist processing equipment and services for the semiconductor and thin film head markets. The group markets its products in North America, Europe, Asia-Pacific and Japan, primarily through two affiliated distributors.

Primary SIC and add'l.: 5065 3674

CIK No: 0000841692

Subsidiaries: FSI International (France) SARL, FSI International (Germany) GmbH, FSI International (Holding) B.V., FSI International (Italy) S.r.l., FSI International (Korea) Co., Ltd., FSI International (Shanghai) Co., Ltd., FSI International (UK)Limited, FSI International Asia, Ltd., FSI Internafional Israel, Ltd., FSI International Netherlands B.V., FSI International Semiconductor Equipment Pte Ltd, FSI Malaysia SDN GHD, SCD Mountain View, Inc., Semiconductor Systems, Inc.

Officers: Donald Mitchell/Chmn., CEO, John Ely/VP - Global Sales, Service, Mike Baxter/VP - Engineering, Operations, John Walker/VP - Strategic Initiatives, Scott Becker/VP - Marketing, Stefano Avezzu/VP, GM - European Business, Patricia Hollister/CFO, Assist. Sec., Benno Sand/Exec. VP - Business Development, Investor Relations, Sec., Hosung Song/GM - Korea, Alan Tai/GM - Southeast Asia, Greater China Region

Directors: Donald Mitchell/Chmn., CEO, James Bernards/Dir., Willem Maris/Dir., Terrence Glarner/Dir., David Smith/Dir.

Owners: David V. Smith, Westcliff Capital Management, LLC/6.10%, Dimensional FundAdvisors LP/7.90%, Terrence W. Glarner, Insiders/6.00%, John C. Ely, Willem D. Maris, Benno G. Sand/1.10%, State of Wisconsin Investment Board/11.50%, Chapman Capital LLC/7.60%, James A. Bernards, Rutabaga Capital Management/5.30%, Donald S. Mitchell/2.80%, Patricia M. Hollister

Financial Data: *Fiscal Year End:*08/27 *Latest Annual Data:* 8/26/2006

Year	Sales	Net Income
2006	$113,241,000	-$7,287,000
2005	$86,370,000	-$3,302,000
2004	$114,404,000	$141,000

Curr. Assets:	$97,426,000	*Curr. Liab.:*	$28,675,000		
Plant, Equip.:	$30,918,000	*Total Liab.:*	$29,425,000	*Indic. Yr. Divd.:*	NA
Total Assets:	$139,797,000	*Net Worth:*	$110,372,000	*Debt/ Equity:*	0.0099

FTD Group Inc

3113 Woodcreek Dr., Downers Grove, IL, 60515; ***PH:*** 1-630-719-7800; ***Fax:*** 1-630-719-6170; ***http://*** www.ftd.com

General - Incorporation	DE	**Stock**- Price on:12/24/2007	$17.65
Employees	745	Stock Exchange	NYSE
Auditor	Ernst & Young LLP	Ticker Symbol	FTD
Stk Agt	Computershare Trust Co	Outstanding Shares	28,940,000
Counsel	NA	E.P.S	$1.02
DUNS No.	NA	Shareholders	NA

Business: The groups principle activity is to provide floral related products and services. The group operates through two segments namely, florist and consumer. In the year 2006, the group acquired Interflora Holdings Limited and Interflora, Inc. The group operates from the United States and Canada. The group's total revenue in the year 2007 was 613.01 millions of USD.

Primary SIC and add'l.: 5961 5947 5992 5999

CIK No: 0001283157

Subsidiaries: Florists Transworld Delivery Inc., Flowers USA Inc., FTD Canada Inc., FTD Holdings Incorporated, FTD International Corporation, FTD UK Holdings Limited, FTD, Inc, FTD.COM INC., Interflora, Interflora British Unit, Interflora Flowers Limited, Interflora Group Limited, Interflora Holdings Limited, Interflora Inc., Interflora Investments Limited 22 Subsidiaries included in the Index

Officers: Michael J. Soenen/38/Dir., CEO, Pres., Steve Richards/49/Exec. VP, CEO - Interflora Holdings, George T. Kanganis/52/Exec. VP - Sales, William J. Van Cleave/44/Exec. VP - Ftdcom, Anthony M. Dillon/51/CTO, Becky A. Sheehan/42/CFO, Jon R. Burney/66/VP, General Counsel, Sec., Lawrence W. Johnson/41/Exec. VP - Florist Segment

Directors: Michael J. Soenen/38/Dir., CEO, Pres., Peter J. Nolan/50/Chmn., Robert S. Apatoff/50/Dir., Adam M. Aron/54/Dir., John M. Baumer/41/Dir., Ted C. Nark/50/Dir., William J. Chardavoyne/56/Dir., Timothy J. Flynn/36/Dir., Thomas M. White/51/Dir., Carrie A. Wolfe/38/Dir.

Owners: William J. Chardavoyne, Green Equity Investors IV, L.P., Thomas M. White, Becky A. Sheehan, FMR Corp., Insiders, Stephen W. Richards, Michael J. Soenen, Peter J. Nolan, Robert S. Apatoff, Jon R. Burney, Adam M. Aron, Carrie A. Wolfe, John M. Baumer, Barclays Global Investors N.A. *(18 Owners included in Index)*

Financial Data: *Fiscal Year End:*06/30 *Latest Annual Data:* 6/30/2006

Year	Sales	Net Income
2006	$465,133,000	$25,543,000
2005	$437,795,000	-$22,600,000

Curr. Assets:	$46,525,000	*Curr. Liab.:*	$70,481,000	*P/E Ratio:*	17.30
Plant, Equip.:	$19,214,000	*Total Liab.:*	$353,001,000	*Indic. Yr. Divd.:*	$0.650
Total Assets:	$570,737,000	*Net Worth:*	$217,736,000	*Debt/ Equity:*	1.2459

FTI Consulting Inc

500 E Pratt St., Ste. 1400, Baltimore, MD, 21202; ***PH:*** 1-410-951-4800; ***Fax:*** 1-410-951-4895; ***http://*** www.fticonsulting.com; ***Email:*** info@fticonsulting.com

General - Incorporation	MD	**Stock**- Price on:12/24/2007	$37.21
Employees	2,079	Stock Exchange	NYSE
Auditor	Ernst & Young LLP	Ticker Symbol	FCN
Stk Agt	American Stock Transfer & Trust Co.	Outstanding Shares	42,730,000
Counsel	NA	E.P.S	$1.81
DUNS No.	06-903-1169	Shareholders	NA

Business: The group's principal activities are to provide turnaround, restructuring , bankruptcy and related consulting services. The group's skilled professionals assist distressed companies in improving their financial position, or their creditors or other stakeholders, in maximizing their claims. It helps the distressed companies implement their plans by providing interim management teams. It offers engineering and scientific consulting services, accident reconstruction, fire investigation and equipment procurement. The group also provides other consulting services such as corporate recovery, forensic accounting, fraud investigation and asset tracing, regulatory. The group advises clients in all phases of litigation, including pre-filing, discovery, jury selection, trial preparation, expert testimony and the actual trial. In 2002 the group acquired the business recovery services division and completed the acquisition of technology and financial consulting inc.

Primary SIC and add'l.: 8711 8399 7389 8111

CIK No: 0000887936

Subsidiaries: Competition Policy Associates, Inc., FTI Cambio LLC, FTI Capital Advisors, LLC, FTI Compass, LLC, FTI Consulting Limited, FTI Financial Services Limited, FTI Investigations, LLC, Fti Ip, LLC, FTI Repository Services, LLC, FTI Ringtail (AUST) PTY LTD, FTI, LLC, Lexecon, LLC, Reynolds Technologies International, LLC, Technology& Financial Consulting, Inc., Teklicon, Inc.

Officers: Jack B. Dunn/Dir., CEO, Pres./$3,290,935.00, Charles Boryenace/VP, Controller, Dominic Dinapoli/COO, Exec. VP/$3,263,865.00, Liz Behrmann/Dir. - Human Resources, Greg Wills/CIO, John A. MacColl/Exec. VP, Chief Risk Management Officer/$1,765,927.00, David G. Bannister/Exec. VP, Chief Development Officer, Richard Davis/VP - Strategic Planning, Adam Cohen/Sr. MD - Technology, New York, NY, Albert Conly/Sr. MD - Corporate Finance, Dallas, TX, Keith Cooper/Sr. MD - Corporate Finance, Atlanta, GA, Stephen Coulombe/Sr. MD - Corporate Finance, Boston, MA, Debra Cabral/MD - FD Dittus, Strategic Communications, Washington, DC, Jorge Celaya/CFO, Exec. VP, Joanne F. Catanese/Assoc. General Counsel, Sec. *(100 Officers included in Index)*

Directors: Jack B. Dunn/Dir., CEO, Pres., Dennis J. Shaughnessy/Chmn., Denis J. Callaghan/Dir., Matthew F. McHugh/Dir., Gary C. Wendt/Dir., Mark H. Berey/Dir., George P. Stamas/Dir., Gerard E. Holthaus/Dir., Brenda J. Bacon/Dir., James W. Crownover/Dir.

Owners: T. Rowe Price Associates, Inc./5.60%, George P. Stamas, Eric B. Miller, David G. Bannister, John A. MacColl, Jack B. Dunn/1.50%, Curt A. H. Jeschke, James W. Crownover, Brenda J. Bacon, Matthew F. McHugh, Dominic DiNapoli, Insiders/5.58%, Mark H. Berey, Gary C. Wendt, Dennis J. Shaughnessy/1.24% *(19 Owners included in Index)*

Financial Data: *Fiscal Year End:*12/31 *Latest Annual Data:* 12/31/2006

Year	Sales	Net Income
2006	$707,933,000	$42,024,000
2005	$539,545,000	$56,368,000
2004	$427,005,000	$42,878,000

Curr. Assets:	$294,949,000	*Curr. Liab.:*	$178,459,000	*P/E Ratio:*	28.19
Plant, Equip.:	$51,326,000	*Total Liab.:*	$826,056,000	*Indic. Yr. Divd.:*	NA
Total Assets:	$1,391,156,000	*Net Worth:*	$565,100,000	*Debt/ Equity:*	0.9381

FTS Group Inc

7610 W Hillsborough Ave., Tampa, FL, 33615; ***PH:*** 1-813-868-3600; ***Fax:*** 1-215-689-2748; ***http://*** www.ftsgroup.tv; ***Email:*** ftsgroup@aol.com

General - Incorporation	NV	**Stock**- Price on:12/24/2007	$0.025
Employees	49	Stock Exchange	OTC
Auditor	R. E. Bassie & Co	Ticker Symbol	FLIP
Stk Agt	Securities Transfer Corp	Outstanding Shares	153,320,000
Counsel	NA	E.P.S	$0.005
DUNS No.	NA	Shareholders	NA

Business: The group's principal activity is to sell accessories and components of wireless phones in the United States. The group's products include rechargeable batteries, personal and portable hands free kits, hands free installation kits, portable and vehicle antennas, in-car and travel chargers. It also sells fashionable accessory faceplates and colored housings for cellular phones, plain and colored phone carrying cases and two-way and pager accessories. The company sells its products through independent contractors. On 02-Mar-2004, the group acquired all clear wireless, inc.

Primary SIC and add'l.: 5731

CIK No: 0001062663

Subsidiaries: Dish Networks, Inc, FTS Wireless Inc

Owners: Whalehaven Capital Fund Limited/7.60%, Scott Gallagher/7.30%, David R. Rasmussen/1.10%, Bristol Investment Fund, LTD./5.10%, Insiders/8.40%

Financial Data: Fiscal Year End:12/31   Latest Annual Data: 12/31/2006

Year	Sales	Net Income
2006	$6,678,000	$1,231,000
2005	$1,311,000	-$3,627,000
2004	$712,000	-$2,328,000

Curr. Assets:	$867,000	**Curr. Liab.:**	$3,612,000	**P/E Ratio:**	0.71
Plant, Equip.:	$304,000	**Total Liab.:**	$5,065,000	**Indic. Yr. Divd.:**	NA
Total Assets:	$6,719,000	**Net Worth:**	$1,654,000	**Debt/ Equity:**	0.8784

Fuego Entertainment Inc

8010 NW 156th St., Miami Lakes, FL, 33016; **PH:** 1-305-823-9999; *http://* www.fuegoentertainment.net; **Email:** ir@fuegoentertainment.net

General - Incorporation	NV	Stock - Price on:12/24/2007	$0.2
Employees	NA	Stock Exchange	OTC
Auditor	Braverman International, P.C.	Ticker Symbol	FUGO
Stk Agt	First American Stock Transfer, Inc.	Outstanding Shares	35,610,000
Counsel	NA	E.P.S.	-$0.01
DUNS No.	NA	Shareholders	NA

Business: The groups principle activities include directing, producing, marketing, and distributing entertainment products. The groups entertainment products include feature and short films, documentaries, television shows, music, and tour productions. The group operates from Nevada in the United States.

Primary SIC and add'l.: 7929

CIK No: 0001336277

Officers: Hugo M. Cancio/42/Dir., CEO, Pres., Treasurer, Sec., Dan York/Investor Relations Contact

Directors: Hugo M. Cancio/42/Dir., CEO, Pres., Treasurer, Sec., Felix Danciu/Dir., Parnell F. Delcham/Dir., Marc Bodin/Dir.

Owners: Insiders/0.70%, Hugo M. Cancio/0.54%, Ciocan Entertainment Film & Music Group, LLC/0.16%

Financial Data: Fiscal Year End:05/31   Latest Annual Data: 05/31/2007

Year	Sales	Net Income
2007	$184,000	-$506,000

Curr. Assets:	$41,000	**Curr. Liab.:**	$152,000	**P/E Ratio:**	1.97
Plant, Equip.:	$39,000	**Total Liab.:**	$416,000	**Indic. Yr. Divd.:**	NA
Total Assets:	$193,000	**Net Worth:**	-$223,000	**Debt/ Equity:**	NA

Fuel Systems Solutions Inc

3030 S Susan St., Santa Ana, CA, 92704; **PH:** 1-714-656-1200; **Fax:** 1-714-656-1400; *http://* www.impco.ws

General - Incorporation	DE	Stock - Price on:12/24/2007	$15.94
Employees	694	Stock Exchange	NDQ
Auditor	BDO Seidman, LLP	Ticker Symbol	FSYS
Stk Agt	Mellon Investor Services LLC	Outstanding Shares	15,130,000
Counsel	NA	E.P.S.	-$0.01
DUNS No.	NA	Shareholders	NA

Business: The groups principal activities include designing, manufacturing, marketing and supplying natural gas and propane. The group operates from the United States.

Primary SIC and add'l.: 3714

CIK No: 0001340786

Officers: Mariano Costamagna/57/Dir., CEO, Pres., Thomas M. Costales/61/CFO, Sec.

Directors: Mariano Costamagna/57/Dir., CEO, Pres., John Jacobs/54/Dir., Norman L. Bryan/67/Dir., David J. Power/75/Dir., Aldo Zanvercelli/68/Dir.

Owners: AMVESCAP PLC/5.50%, Pier Antonio Costamagna/22.50%, Marco Di Toro, FMR Corp./7.00%, Aldo Zanvercelli, Mariano Costamagna/22.50%, Insiders/23.20%, John R. Jacobs, Roberto Olivo, Thomas M. Costales, Marco Seimandi, Norman L. Bryan, Douglas R. King, T. Rowe Price Associates, Inc./4.90%, David J. Power

Financial Data: Fiscal Year End:12/31   Latest Annual Data: 12/31/2006

Year	Sales	Net Income
2006	$220,816,000	$6,912,000

Curr. Assets:	$120,007,000	**Curr. Liab.:**	$63,756,000	**P/E Ratio:**	4.92
Plant, Equip.:	$21,287,000	**Total Liab.:**	$87,734,000	**Indic. Yr. Divd.:**	NA
Total Assets:	$198,512,000	**Net Worth:**	$110,778,000	**Debt/ Equity:**	NA

Fuel Tech

512 Kingsland Dr., Batavia, IL, 60510; **PH:** 1-630-845-4500; **Fax:** 1-630-845-4501; *http://* www.fuel-tech.com

General - Incorporation	Netherlands	Stock - Price on:12/24/2007	$33.8852
Employees	137	Stock Exchange	NDQ
Auditor	Ernst & Young LLP	Ticker Symbol	FTEK
Stk Agt	Mellon Investor Services LLC	Outstanding Shares	22,200,000
Counsel	NA	E.P.S.	$0.187
DUNS No.	85-546-5027	Shareholders	NA

Business: The group operates through its with subsidiaries whose principle activity is to develop and license air pollution control processes, including the reduction of oxides of nitrogen from flue gas from boilers, furnaces and other stationary combustion sources. The group operates from United States.

Primary SIC and add'l.: 2899 6719 6794

CIK No: 0000846913

Subsidiaries: Fuel-tech N.v

Officers: John F. Norris/Dir., CEO, Pres./$2,305,819.00, Ralph E. Bailey/Exec. Chmn., Vincent J. Arnone/CFO, Sr. VP, Treasurer/$931,068.00, Charles W. Grinnell/Dir., VP, General Counsel, Corp. Sec., Vincent M. Albanese/Sr. VP - Regulatory Affairs/$620,939.00, Stephen P. Brady/Sr. VP - Sales, Marketing/$896,822.00, Michael P. Maley/Sr. VP - International Business Development, Project Execution/$1,325,552.00, Nolan R. Schwartz/57/VP - Corporate Development, Tracy H. Krumme/VP - Investor Relations, Corporate Communications, Ellen T. Albrecht/35/VP, Controller, William E. Cummings/51/VP - Sales, Kevin R. Dougherty/46/VP - Business Development, Marketing, Timothy Eibes/51/VP - Project Execution, Linda M. Lin/VP - China, Pacific Rim, Christopher R. Smyrniotis/55/Dir. - Marketing, Technology

Directors: John F. Norris/Dir., CEO, Pres., Ralph E. Bailey/Exec. Chmn., Douglas G. Bailey/Dep. Chmn., Miguel Espinosa/Dir., Thomas L. Jones/Dir., John D. Morrow/Dir., Charles W. Grinnell/Dir., VP, General Counsel, Corp. Sec., Samer S. Khanachet/Dir., Thomas S. Shaw/Dir.

Owners: John F. Norris, Vincent J. Arnone, Ralph E. Bailey/19.83%, Fidelity Management& Research Company/10.73%, Samer S. Khanachet, Douglas G. Bailey/6.36%, Thomas S. Shaw, Insiders/28.80%, Miguel Espinosa, Stephen P. Brady, Charles W. Grinnell, John D. Morrow, Thomas L. Jones

Financial Data: Fiscal Year End:12/31   Latest Annual Data: 12/31/2006

Year	Sales	Net Income
2006	$75,115,000	$6,826,000
2005	$52,928,000	$7,588,000
2004	$30,832,000	$1,572,000

Curr. Assets:	$56,220,000	**Curr. Liab.:**	$17,505,000	**P/E Ratio:**	181.20
Plant, Equip.:	$4,051,000	**Total Liab.:**	$18,005,000	**Indic. Yr. Divd.:**	NA
Total Assets:	$65,660,000	**Net Worth:**	$47,655,000	**Debt/ Equity:**	NA

FuelCell Energy Inc

3 Great Pasture Rd., Danbury, CT, 06813; **PH:** 1-203-825-6000; **Fax:** 1-203-825-6100; *http://* www.fuelcellenergy.com

General - Incorporation	DE	Stock - Price on:12/24/2007	$7.62
Employees	384	Stock Exchange	NDQ
Auditor	KPMG LLP	Ticker Symbol	FCEL
Stk Agt	Continental Stock Transfer & Trust Co	Outstanding Shares	67,940,000
Counsel	NA	E.P.S.	-$1.52
DUNS No.	05-062-7884	Shareholders	NA

Business: The group's principal activity is to develop and manufacture fuel cell power plants for clean, efficient and reliable electric power generation. The group is developing the carbonate fuel cell products under the trademark of direct fuel cell (r). The systems generate electricity directly from hydrocarbon fuels like natural gas and methanol. The dfc300a, dfc1500 and dfc3000 range of products have a capacity upto 250 kw, 1 mw and 2 mw, respectively and can be scaled for distributed applications up to 50 mw. The products are designed to meet the requirements of commercial and industrial customers like wastewater treatment plants, data centers, manufacturing and industrial facilities, office buildings, hospitals, universities, hotels, as well as in grid support applications for utility customers. In Apr 2004, the group discontinued teg business segment.

Primary SIC and add'l.: 3629 8731

CIK No: 0000886128

Subsidiaries: 1065918 Alberta Ltd., Alliance Chico, LLC, Alliance Monterey, LLC, Alliance Star Energy, LLC, Alliance TST Energy, LLC, FuelCell Energy, Ltd.

Officers: Daniel R. Brdar/Chmn., CEO, Pres., Christopher R. Bentley/Exec. VP - Government Research & Development Operations, Strategic Manufacturing Development, Joseph G. Mahler/Sr. VP, CFO, Sec., Treasurer - Corporate Strategy, Bruce A. Ludemann/Sr. VP - Sales, Marketing

Directors: Daniel R. Brdar/Chmn., CEO, Pres., John A. Rolls/Dir., Michael Bode/Dir., George K. Petty/Dir., James D. Gerson/Dir., William A. Lawson/Dir., Thomas L. Kempner/Dir., Glenn H. Epstein/Dir., Richard A. Bromley/Dir.

Owners: George K. Petty, John A. Rolls, Thomas L. Kempner, Daniel R. Brdar, William A. Lawson, POSCO Power/6.69%, Insiders/6.89%, Blackrock Inc./6.57%, James D. Gerson/2.19%, The TCW Group, Inc./6.40%, Michael Bode/4.80%, Warren D. Bagatelle/1.84%, Christopher R. Bentley, Joseph G. Mahler, Bruce A. Ludemann (16 Owners included in Index)

Financial Data: Fiscal Year End:10/31   Latest Annual Data: 10/31/2006

Year	Sales	Net Income
2006	$33,288,000	-$76,105,000
2005	$30,370,000	-$68,186,000
2004	$31,386,000	-$86,443,000

Curr. Assets:	$133,709,000	**Curr. Liab.:**	$27,841,000		
Plant, Equip.:	$48,136,000	**Total Liab.:**	$35,242,000	**Indic. Yr. Divd.:**	NA
Total Assets:	$206,652,000	**Net Worth:**	$100,795,000	**Debt/ Equity:**	0.0067

FuelNation Inc

4121 SW 45th Ave., Ste 1301, Davie, FL, 33314; **PH:** 1-954-587-3775; **Fax:** 1-954-587-3776; *http://* www.fuelnation.com; **Email:** sales@fuelnation.com

General - Incorporation	FL	Stock - Price on:12/24/2007	$0.022
Employees	NA	Stock Exchange	OTC
Auditor	Moore Stephens Ellis Foster Ltd	Ticker Symbol	FLNA
Stk Agt	Continental Stock Transfer & Trust Co	Outstanding Shares	54,210,000
Counsel	NA	E.P.S.	-$0.031
DUNS No.	NA	Shareholders	NA

Business: The group's principal activity is to provide real-time e-commerce communications in petroleum marketing and energy services. These operations are conducted through strategic alliances, which principally are engaged in advanced technology and services solutions for the petroleum marketing industry, such as oil companies, marketers, transports, gas stations and convenience stores worldwide. The group is in its development stage.

Primary SIC and add'l.: 7375 7371

CIK No: 0000910111

Officers: Christopher R. Salmonson/CEO, Pres., Trevor Klein/Dir. - Finance

Directors: William C. Schlecht/Dir., Shaikh Isa Mohammed Isa Alkhalifa/Dir.

Financial Data: Fiscal Year End:12/31   Latest Annual Data: 12/31/2002

Year	Sales	Net Income
2002	NA	-$4,425,000
2001	NA	-$28,497,000
2000	NA	-$1,205,000

Curr. Assets:	$581,000	**Curr. Liab.:**	$2,215,000		
Plant, Equip.:	$127,000	**Total Liab.:**	$5,763,000	**Indic. Yr. Divd.:**	NA
Total Assets:	$1,461,000	**Net Worth:**	-$4,302,000	**Debt/ Equity:**	NA

FUJIFILM Holdings Corp

200 Summit Lake Dr., Valhalla, NY, 10595; *PH:* 1-914-789-8100; *Fax:* 1-914-789-8295; *http://* www.fujifilmholdings.com

General - Incorporation
Employees....NA
Auditor....NA
Stk Agt.... Morgan ADR Service Center, Citibank
Counsel....NA
DUNS No....NA

Stock- Price on:12/24/2007....$44.23
Stock Exchange....NDQ
Ticker Symbol....FUJI
Outstanding Shares....NA
E.P.S....NA
Shareholders....NA

Business: The groups principal activity is to manufacture and market imaging and information systems. The products of the group include color films, conventional cameras, digital cameras, lab equipment, color paper and chemicals, printers and facsimiles. The group operates from the United States, Japan, America, Europe and Asia.

Primary SIC and add'l.: 3861 3577 5047 3827 3572 5169 3695 3841 2899 3826 3579 5043

CIK No:

Officers: Shigetaka Komori/Dir., CEO, Pres., Toshio Takahashi/Dir., CFO, Shinpei Ikenoue/Dir., Sr. VP, Nobuoki Okamura/Dir., Corporate VP, Noboru Sasaki/Dir., Corporate VP, Yasutomo Maeda/Corporate VP, Kouichi Tamai/Corporate VP, Keiichi Inuzuka/Corporate Auditor, Kiichiro Furusawa/Corporate Auditor, Masahiro Miki/Corporate Auditor, Daisuke Ogawa/Corporate Auditor, Yoshikazu Aoki/Corporate VP, Toshimitsu Kawamura/Corporate VP

Directors: Shigetaka Komori/Dir., CEO, Pres., Toshio Takahashi/Dir., CFO, Shinpei Ikenoue/Dir., Sr. VP, Teisuke Kitayama/Dir., Tadashi Sasaki/Dir., Nobuoki Okamura/Dir., Corporate VP, Noboru Sasaki/Dir., Corporate VP, Tadahito Yamamoto/Dir.

Full House Resorts Inc

4670 S Ft. Apache Rd., Ste. 190, Las Vegas, NV, 89147; *PH:* 1-702-221-7800; *Fax:* 1-702-221-8101; *http://* www.fullhouseresorts.com

General - Incorporation....DE
Employees....9
Auditor....Piercy, Bowler, Taylor & Kern
Stk Agt....American Stock Transfer & Trust Co.
Counsel....NA
DUNS No....80-680-5636

Stock- Price on:12/24/2007....$3.71
Stock Exchange....AMEX
Ticker Symbol....FLL
Outstanding Shares....19,320,000
E.P.S....$0.03
Shareholders....NA

Business: The group's principal activities are to develop destination resorts and entertainment, gaming and commercial centers. The group's joint ventures are located at Delaware, Oregon and California. Mill casino-north bend at Oregon has 250 video lottery terminals, 9 blackjack tables and nine poker tables, a restaurant and buffet, a saloon, a bingo hall an snack bar. Midway slots and simulcast-harrington at Delaware features 1,400 gaming devices, 450-seat buffet, 50 seat dinner and gift shop. The group is also into the development of projects in battle creek, Michigan and southern California.

Primary SIC and add'l.: 5812 6719 7999

CIK No: 0000891482

Subsidiaries: Full House Subsidiary of Nevada, Inc., Full House Subsidiary, Inc., Gaming Entertainment (California), LLC, Gaming Entertainment (Delaware), LLC, Gaming Entertainment (Michigan), LLC, Gaming Entertainment (Montana) LLC, Gaming Entertainment (New Mexico) LLC, Gaming Entertainment (Oklahoma) LLC, Gaming Entertainment (Santa Fe) LLC, Manuelito LLC

Officers: Andre M. Hilliou/Dir., CEO/$649,076.00, Barth F. Aaron/Sec., General Counsel, Mark J. Miller/Sr. VP, CFO, Dir., Wesley T. Elam/VP - Operations, Project Management/$271,117.00, Key Personnel/VP - Indian Gaming Development, James Meier/VP - Finance, William Schmitt/Integrated Corporate Relations

Directors: Andre M. Hilliou/Dir., CEO, Michael J. Paulson/Chmn., Carl G. Braunlich/Dir., Lee A. Iacocca/Dir., Mark J. Miller/Sr. VP, CFO, Dir., Kathleen M. Caracciolo/Dir., Ken Adams/Dir.

Owners: Mark J. Miller, Kenneth R. Adams, Andre Hilliou/1.50%, Insiders/28.40%, James Meier, Carl G. Braunlich, William P. McComas/8.00%, Allen E. Paulson Living Trust/16.40%, Greg Violette/1.50%, Lee A. Iacocca/7.40%, Wesley T. Elam, Michael J. Paulson/17.00%, LKL Family Limited Partnership/5.40%, Barth Aaron

Financial Data: *Fiscal Year End:*12/31 *Latest Annual Data:* 12/31/2006

Year	Sales	Net Income
2006	$3,860,000	$640,000
2005	$3,701,000	$839,000
2004	$3,586,000	$320,000

Curr. Assets:	$22,309,000	**Curr. Liab.:**	$7,001,000	**P/E Ratio:**	185.50
Plant, Equip.:	$130,000	**Total Liab.:**	$7,001,000	**Indic. Yr. Divd.:**	NA
Total Assets:	$40,156,000	**Net Worth:**	$31,120,000	**Debt/ Equity:**	0.2272

FullCircle Registry Inc

161 Alpine Dr., Shelbyville, KY, 40065; *PH:* 1-502-410-4500; *Fax:* 1-502-964-8069; *http://* www.fullcircleregistry.com

General - Incorporation....NV
Employees....2
Auditor....Chisholm Bierwolf & Nilson LLC
Stk Agt....Interwest Transfer Company, Inc.
Counsel....Lehman Walstrand & Associates
DUNS No....NA

Stock- Price on:12/24/2007....$0.022
Stock Exchange....OTC
Ticker Symbol....FLCR
Outstanding Shares....85,730,000
E.P.S....$0.00
Shareholders....NA

Business: The group's principal activity is to electronically store and retrieve critical and important documents. The system is designed to allow medical personnel to quickly obtain critical information about the customers' special medical needs, wishes and emergency contact information through the use of coded customer ids and personal identification numbers (pins). The system also serves as a 'digital safe deposit box' with password protection for customer storage of other important documents or information such as deeds, passport, family photos, financial records, legal records and other documents. This documents are scanned into secured electronic database. On 15-Apr-2004, the group acquired security promotions marketing.

Primary SIC and add'l.: 7375

CIK No: 0001127993

Subsidiaries: AskPhysicians.com, Inc

Officers: Trent Oakley/CEO, Pres., Dennis McDonough/CIO

Directors: Alec G. Stone/Chmn., Isaac Boutwell/Dir., David Allen/Dir., Norman Frohreich/Dir.

Owners: Insiders/36.36%, Isaac Boutwell/24.25%, Alec Stone/10.68%, Trent Oakley/1.30%, David E. Allen

Financial Data: *Fiscal Year End:*12/31 *Latest Annual Data:* 12/31/2006

Year	Sales	Net Income
2006	$25,000	-$340,000
2005	$105,000	-$293,000
2004	$59,000	-$241,000

Curr. Assets:	$1,000	**Curr. Liab.:**	$481,000		
Plant, Equip.:	$11,000	**Total Liab.:**	$481,000	**Indic. Yr. Divd.:**	NA
Total Assets:	$330,000	**Net Worth:**	-$150,000	**Debt/ Equity:**	NA

FullNet Communications Inc

201 Robert S Kerr Ave., Ste. 210, Oklahoma City, OK, 73102; *PH:* 1-405-236-8200; *Fax:* 1-405-236-8201; *http://* web.fullnet.net; *Email:* sales@fullnet.net

General - Incorporation....OK
Employees....13
Auditor....Murrell, Hall, McIntosh & Co., PLLP
Stk Agt....Securities Transfer Corp
Counsel....NA
DUNS No....NA

Stock- Price on:12/24/2007....$0.04
Stock Exchange....OTC
Ticker Symbol....FULO
Outstanding Shares....6,740,000
E.P.S....-$0.07
Shareholders....NA

Business: The group's principal activity is to provide integrated communication and network solutions to individuals, businesses, organizations, educational institutions and government agencies. The group provides high quality, reliable and scalable Internet solutions to customers through its subsidiaries fullnet, inc., fulltel, inc. And fullweb, inc. The Internet connections provided by the group are dial-up connections and leased line connections. Dial-up connection method of service connects the user to the Internet through the use of a modem and standard telephone line. Leased line method of connection gives the user a full-time high-speed connection to the Internet through the point-of-presence.

Primary SIC and add'l.: 7375 7379

CIK No: 0001092570

Subsidiaries: Full Web, Inc., FullNet, Inc., FullSolutions, Inc., FullTel

Officers: Timothy J. Kilkenny/49/Chmn., CEO, Roger P. Baresel/52/Dir., CFO, Pres., Sec., Patricia R. Shurley/51/VP - Finance, Jason C. Ayers/Contact - Employment, Michael D. Tomas/35/VP - Technology

Directors: Timothy J. Kilkenny/49/Chmn., CEO, Roger P. Baresel/52/Dir., CFO, Pres., Sec.

Owners: Laura L. Kilkenny/6.90%, Roger P. Baresel/8.10%, Patricia R. Shurley/4.20%, Generation Capital Associates/9.90%, Michael D. Tomas/3.80%, Greg Lowney Snyder/5.90%, Jason C. Ayers/5.70%, Insiders/45.10%, Rupinder Sidu/5.20%, Karen Gustafson Kusnick/5.90%, Timothy J. Kilkenny/23.20%

Financial Data: *Fiscal Year End:*12/31 *Latest Annual Data:* 12/31/2006

Year	Sales	Net Income
2006	$1,769,000	-$479,000
2005	$2,379,000	$74,000
2004	$2,261,000	$226,000

Curr. Assets:	$136,000	**Curr. Liab.:**	$2,510,000		
Plant, Equip.:	$699,000	**Total Liab.:**	$2,578,000	**Indic. Yr. Divd.:**	NA
Total Assets:	$901,000	**Net Worth:**	-$1,677,000	**Debt/ Equity:**	NA

Fulton Bancshares Corp

100 Lincoln Way E, Mcconnellsburg, PA, 17233; *PH:* 1-717-485-3144; *http://* www.fcnbtc.com

General - Incorporation....PA
Employees....230
Auditor....Smith Elliott Kearns & Co. LLC
Stk Agt....Fulton Financial Advisors
Counsel....NA
DUNS No....00-893-6973

Stock- Price on:12/24/2007....$27.39
Stock Exchange....NA
Ticker Symbol....NA
Outstanding Shares....3,840,000
E.P.S....$2.16
Shareholders....NA

Business: The group's principal activities are to provide commercial and consumer banking services. The group accepts time, demand and savings deposits and originating secured and unsecured commercial, consumer, mortgage and construction loans. The group also offers trust services, bank by mail, direct deposit, drive-in banking, federal tax depository, automatic teller machine, night deposit services, notary public services, deposit boxes, travelers' checks, money bonds, individual retirement accounts and utility and municipal payments. The group operates seven branch offices located in mcconnellsburg, warfordsburg, hustontown, orbisonia and st. Thomas. The subsidiaries of the group are fulton county national bank and trust and fulton county community development corporation.

Primary SIC and add'l.: 6712 6021

CIK No: 0000850626

Subsidiaries: Fulton County Community Development Corporation, Fulton County National Bank and Trust, Pennsylvania

Financial Data: *Fiscal Year End:*12/31 *Latest Annual Data:* 12/31/2006

Year	Sales	Net Income
2006	$49,180,000	$7,570,000
2005	$37,188,000	$6,112,000
2004	$32,084,000	$5,192,000

Curr. Assets:	$22,148,000	**Curr. Liab.:**	$680,405,000	**P/E Ratio:**	12.68
Plant, Equip.:	$13,101,000	**Total Liab.:**	$727,719,000	**Indic. Yr. Divd.:**	$1.040
Total Assets:	$799,333,000	**Net Worth:**	$71,614,000	**Debt/ Equity:**	0.4625

Fulton Financial Corp

1 Penn Sq., Lancaster, PA, 17604; *PH:* 1-717-291-2411; *Fax:* 1-717-295-4792; *http://* www.fult.com

General - Incorporation ....PA
Employees 4,400
Auditor ....KPMG LLP
Stk Agt.... Fulton Financial Advisors
Counsel.... Barley, Snyder, Senft & Cohen
DUNS No. 07-954-6545

Stock- Price on:12/24/2007 ....$14.7
Stock Exchange....NDQ
Ticker Symbol....FULT
Outstanding Shares 173,170,000
E.P.S....$0.92
Shareholders....NA

Business: The group's principal activity is to provide banking and financial services to businesses and consumers through its wholly-owned banking subsidiaries. The group directly owns 100% of the common stock of eleven community banks, two financial services companies and eight non-bank entities. The personal banking services include various checking and savings products, certificates of deposit and individual retirement accounts. The commercial lending options include commercial, financial, and agricultural and real estate loans. In addition, construction lending, equipment leasing, credit cards, letters of credit, cash management services and traditional deposit products are offered to commercial customers. The group offers investment management, trust, brokerage, insurance and investment advisory services in the market areas serviced by the subsidiary banks. On 01-Apr-2004 the group acquired resource bankshares corporation.

Primary SIC and add'l.: 6712 6022

CIK No: 0000700564

Subsidiaries: Central Pennsylvania Financial Corp., Danville, Pennsylvania 17821, Delaware National Bank, FFC Management, Inc., FFC Penn Square, Inc., First Washington State Bank, FNB Bank, N.A., Fulton Bank, Fulton Financial Advisors, Fulton Financial Realty Company, Fulton Insurance Services Group, Inc., Fulton Reinsurance Company, LTD, Hagerstown Trust Company, Lafayette Ambassador Bank, Lancaster, Pennsylvania 17604 32 Subsidiaries included in the Index

Officers: Scott R. Smith/Chmn., CEO, Pres./$1,360,969.00, Charles J. Nugent/Sr. Exec. VP, CFO/$812,299.00, Laura J. Wakeley/VP - Corporate Communications, Craig H. Hill/Sr. Exec. VP - Human Resources, James E. Shreiner/Sr. Exec. VP - Administrative Services/$490,727.00, Philip E. Wenger/Sr. Exec. VP - Community Banking/$554,945.00, Beth Ann L. Chivinski/Exec. VP, Controller, Richard J. Ashby/Sr. Exec. VP - Community Banking/$695,034.00

Directors: Scott R. Smith/Chmn., CEO, Pres., Jeffrey G. Albertson/Dir., John M. Bond/Dir., Gary A. Stewart/Dir., George W. Hodges/Dir., Patrick J. Freer/Dir., Rufus Ayers Fulton/Dir., John Osborne Shirk/Dir., Craig A. Dally/Dir., Willem Kooyker/Dir., Donald W. Lesher/Dir., Carolyn R. Holleran/Dir., Donald M. Bowman/Dir., Abraham S. Opatut/Dir., Thomas W. Hunt/Dir.

Owners: Willem Kooyker, Craig A. Dally, Scott R. Smith, Rufus A. Fulton, Jeffrey G. Albertson, Donald M. Bowman, James E. Shreiner, Carolyn R. Holleran, Insiders/3.24%, Abraham S. Opatut, Charles J. Nugent, Donald W. Lesher, George W. Hodges, John O. Shirk, Gary A. Stewart *(20 Owners included in Index)*

Financial Data: *Fiscal Year End:*12/31 *Latest Annual Data:* 12/31/2006

Year	Sales	Net Income
2006	$1,014,382,000	$185,527,000
2005	$770,065,000	$166,074,000
2004	$632,507,000	$152,917,000

Curr. Assets:	$455,031,000	**Curr. Liab.:**	$11,974,701,000	**P/E Ratio:**	14.70
Plant, Equip.:	$191,401,000	**Total Liab.:**	$13,402,654,000	**Indic. Yr. Divd.:**	$0.600
Total Assets:	$14,918,964,000	**Net Worth:**	$1,516,310,000	**Debt/ Equity:**	1.0357

Fundtech Ltd

30 Montgomery St., Ste. 501, Jersey City, NJ, 07302; ***PH:*** 1-201-946-1100; ***Fax:*** 1-201-946-1313; ***http://*** www.fundtech.com

General - Incorporation ....Israel
Employees 606
Auditor ....Brightman Almagor & Co
Stk Agt.... American Stock Transfer & Trust Co.
Counsel.... Weil, Gotshal & Manges LLP
DUNS No. ....NA

Stock- Price on:12/24/2007 ....$14.71
Stock Exchange....NDQ
Ticker Symbol....FNDT
Outstanding Shares 15,070,000
E.P.S....$0.37
Shareholders....NA

Business: The group's principle activity is the provision of end-to-end financial transaction processing software solutions for financial institutions (fiscal). These solutions are divided into three groups: payment processing, foreign exchange settlement processing and delivery channels for fi cash management products.

Primary SIC and add'l.: 7372 5072

CIK No: 0001054836

Subsidiaries: Biveroni Batschelet Partners AG, Cashtech Solutions India Private Limited, Datasphere SA, Fundtech Australia Pty Limited, Fundtech Corporation, Fundtech International, LLC, Fundtech U.K. Limited, Radius Partners, Inc.

Officers: Reuven Ben Menachem/Co - Founder, CEO, Leslie Bertha/Exec. VP - Fundtech North America, Michael Sgroe/COO, Pres., Yoram Bibring/CFO, Moti Porath/Exec. VP - Business Development, Brian Jou/Exec. VP - Global Product Management, Gil Gadot/Exec. VP - Technology, Joseph P. Mazzetti/Exec. VP - Corporate Development

Directors: Reuven Ben Menachem/Co - Founder, CEO, Tsvi Gal/48/Dir.

Owners: Insiders/7.00%, Clal Industries and Investments Ltd/33.40%, Cannell Capital LLC/17.50%, Reuven BenMenachem/2.60%, Michael Sgroe/1.50%

Financial Data: *Fiscal Year End:*12/31 *Latest Annual Data:* 12/31/2006

Year	Sales	Net Income
2006	$85,509,000	$3,751,000
2005	$74,466,000	$4,336,000
2004	$58,537,000	$2,467,000

Curr. Assets:	$74,833,000	**Curr. Liab.:**	$20,039,000	**P/E Ratio:**	181.20
Plant, Equip.:	$11,944,000	**Total Liab.:**	$22,277,000	**Indic. Yr. Divd.:**	NA
Total Assets:	$112,063,000	**Net Worth:**	$89,786,000	**Debt/ Equity:**	NA

Furniture Brands International Inc

101 S Hanley Rd., St. Louis, MO, 63105; ***PH:*** 1-314-863-1100; ***Fax:*** 1-314-863-5306; ***http://*** www.furniturebrands.com

General - Incorporation ....DE
Employees 13,800
Auditor ....KPMG LLP
Stk Agt.... American Stock Transfer & Trust Co.
Counsel....NA
DUNS No. 00-626-6738

Stock- Price on:12/24/2007 ....$14.53
Stock Exchange....NYSE
Ticker Symbol....FBN
Outstanding Shares 48,350,000
E.P.S....-$0.06
Shareholders....NA

Business: The groups principle activity is to operate residential furniture stores. The group products are sold under the brand names Broyhill, Henredon, Laneventure and Pearson. The group operates from United States.

Primary SIC and add'l.: 2517 2511

CIK No: 0000050957

Subsidiaries: Action Transport, Inc., Broyhill Furniture Industries, Inc., Broyhill Home Furnishings, Inc., Broyhill Retail, Inc., Broyhill Transport, Inc., Classic Design Furnishings, Inc., D-H Retail Space, Inc., Decorative Hardware Solutions (L) Bhd., Drexel Heritage Furniture Industries, Inc., Fayette Enterprises, Inc., HDM Furniture Industries, Inc., Henredon Designer Showrooms, Inc., Henredon Furniture Industries, Inc., Henredon Transportation Company, Hickory Business Furniture, Inc. 27 Subsidiaries included in the Index

Officers: Wilbert G. Holliman/Chmn., CEO/$2,093,556.00, Denise L. Ramos/51/CFO, Sr. VP, Treasurer/$983,987.00, Steven W. Alstadt/Controller, Chief Accounting Officer, John Tom Foy/Dir., COO, Pres./$1,535,161.00, Lynn Chipperfield/Sr. VP, Sec./$976,429.00

Directors: Wilbert G. Holliman/Chmn., CEO, Aubrey B. Patterson/Dir., John R. Jordan/Dir., Albert E. Suter/Dir., Lee M. Liberman/Dir., John Tom Foy/Dir., COO, Pres., Richard B. Loynd/Dir., Bob L. Martin/Dir., Katherine Button Bell/Dir., Matthew E. Rubel/Dir.

Owners: Franklin Resources, Inc./6.00%, J. T. Foy, D. L. Ramos, L. M. Liberman, A. E. Suter, LSV Asset Management/5.70%, A. B. Patterson, L. Chipperfield, M. E. Rubel, Insiders/2.60%, W. G. Holliman/1.20%, J. R. Jordan, R. B. Loynd, FMR Corp./6.00%, Goldman Sachs Asset Management, L. P./8.60% *(22 Owners included in Index)*

Financial Data: *Fiscal Year End:*12/31 *Latest Annual Data:* 12/31/2006

Year	Sales	Net Income
2006	$2,418,175,000	$55,055,000
2005	$2,386,774,000	$61,436,000
2004	$2,447,430,000	$91,567,000

Curr. Assets:	$941,174,000	**Curr. Liab.:**	$188,556,000	**P/E Ratio:**	25.49
Plant, Equip.:	$221,398,000	**Total Liab.:**	$647,488,000	**Indic. Yr. Divd.:**	$0.640
Total Assets:	$1,558,203,000	**Net Worth:**	$910,715,000	**Debt/ Equity:**	0.0008

FUSA Capital Corp

1420 5th Ave. Fl 22, Seattle, WA, 98101; ***PH:*** 1-206-274-5107; ***http://*** www.fusacapital.com; ***Email:*** investors@searchformedia.com

General - Incorporation ....NV
Employees ....NA
Auditor ....Braverman International, P.C.
Stk Agt .... Pacific Stock Transfer Company
Counsel....NA
DUNS No. ....NA

Stock- Price on:12/24/2007 ....$0.95
Stock Exchange....OTC
Ticker Symbol....FSAC
Outstanding Shares 59,910,000
E.P.S....-$0.01
Shareholders....NA

Business: The groups principle activities include refinement and marketing audio and video search engine technologies. In March 2005, the group acquired FUSA Technology Investments Corp. The group operates from Nevada in the United States.

Primary SIC and add'l.: 4813

CIK No: 0001131903

Officers: Jenifer Osterwalder/42/Dir., CEO, Principal Accounting Officer, Pres., Treasurer, Sec., David Clarke/VP - Business Development, Tommy Jo St. John/CTO

Directors: Jenifer Osterwalder/42/Dir., CEO, Principal Accounting Officer, Pres., Treasurer, Sec., Alexander Khersonski/35/Dir.

Owners: Jenifer Osterwalder/9.80%, Insiders/22.70%, Tommy Jo St. John/12.50%, Alexander Khersonski/0.30%

Financial Data: *Fiscal Year End:*12/31 *Latest Annual Data:* 12/31/2006

Year	Sales	Net Income
2006	$14,000	-$435,000
2005	$0	-$4,091,000
2004	NA	-$76,000

Curr. Assets:	$98,000	**Curr. Liab.:**	$49,000		
Plant, Equip.:	$29,000	**Total Liab.:**	$49,000	**Indic. Yr. Divd.:**	NA
Total Assets:	$130,000	**Net Worth:**	$80,000	**Debt/ Equity:**	NA

Fushi International Inc

Formerly: Parallel Technologies Inc
1 Shuang Qiang Rd., Jinzhou, Dalian, 116100; ***PH:*** 86-411-877-03333; ***http://*** www.ptnet.com

General - Incorporation ....NV
Employees ....NA
Auditor ....Moore Stephens Wurth F & T LLP
Stk Agt .... Jersey Transfer & Trust Co
Counsel....NA
DUNS No. ....NA

Stock- Price on:12/24/2007 ....$13.15
Stock Exchange....NA
Ticker Symbol....NA
Outstanding Shares ....NA
E.P.S....$1.153
Shareholders....NA

Business: The groups principle activity is to provide network services and solutions. The group also provides voice, data and video solutions with cable infrastructure services. The groups solutions include cabling infrastructure, network infrastructure, IP converged solutions, application convergence and national project management. The group operates from United States.

Primary SIC and add'l.: 6770

CIK No: 0000710846

Subsidiaries: Bimetallic Cable, Co., Ltd., Dalian Diversified Product Inspections, Dalian Fushi Bimetallic Wire, Diversified Product Inspections, Inc., Manufacturing, Co., Ltd

Officers: Li Fu/42/Chmn., CEO/$240,000.00, Dale S. Klein/CEO, Pres., Chunyan Xu/52/Supervisory Dir., Jeanna Tuset/Dir. - Finance, Pat Siebenaler/Dir. - National Project Management, Yue Mathus Yang/40/Dir., VP, GM/$180,000.00, Wenbing Chris Wang/37/CFO, Treasurer, Sec./$120,000.00, Xishan Yang/70/Chief Engineer, Exec. VP - Research & Development, Chuck Warner/Project Dir., Randy Wood/Project Dir., Mark Lundberg/Project Dir., Ben Swenka/Technology Dir., Mark Torguson/Network Solutions Dir., Yang Roy Yu/26/Exec. VP - Finance, Accounting

Directors: Li Fu/42/Chmn., CEO, Yue Mathus Yang/40/Dir., VP, GM, John D. Kuhns/58/Dir., Pat Siebenaler/Dir. - National Project Management

Owners: Pope Asset Management LLC, Jiping Hua, Chunyan Xu, Insiders, Barry Raeburn, Feng Bai, Li Fu, John D. Kuhns, Yue Mathus Yang, Xishan Yang, Wenbing Chris Wang

Financial Data: *Fiscal Year End:*12/31 *Latest Annual Data:* 12/31/2006

Year	Sales	Net Income
2006	$67,596,000	$17,810,000
2005	$33,709,000	$7,799,000

Curr. Assets:	$38,827,000	***Curr. Liab.:***	$20,772,000		
Plant, Equip.:	$47,256,000	***Total Liab.:***	$31,028,000	***Indic. Yr. Divd.:***	NA
Total Assets:	$96,162,000	***Net Worth:***	$65,134,000	***Debt/ Equity:***	NA

Fusion Telecommunications International Inc

420 Lexington Ave., Ste. 1718, New York, NY, 10170; ***PH:*** 1-212-201-2400; ***Fax:*** 1-212-972-7884; ***http://*** www.fusiontel.com; ***Email:*** info@fusiontel.com

General - Incorporation DE; Employees 86; Auditor Rothstein, Kass & Company, P.C.; Stk Agt Continental Stock Transfer & Trust Co; Counsel Gersten, Wolf, & Marcus, LLP; DUNS No. NA

Stock- Price on:12/24/2007 $0.56; Stock Exchange AMEX; Ticker Symbol FSN; Outstanding Shares 26,970,000; E.P.S -$0.41; Shareholders NA

Business: The groups principle activity is to provide internet access, telecommunication service and private network. The group operates through two segments namely, voice to carriers, and consumers and others. The group operates from the United States.The group's quarterly revenue for September 2007 was 13.36 millions of USD.

Primary SIC and add'l.: 4813 4822 4899 7389

CIK No: 0001071411

Subsidiaries: African Communications Company S.A., Efonica, FL-LLC, Fusion Caribbean Limited., Fusion Jamaica Limited, Fusion Jordan Corp., Fusion Mya Communications, LLC., Fusion Romania Corp., Fusion Telco S.A., Fusion Turkey, LLC., Fusion VoIP Acquisition Corp., Intercontinental Communications Group, Inc., International Telecom Partners, LLC., Latin Overseas Communications Corp., Ldts Uzak Mesafe Telekomunikasyon VE Letism Hizmetleril SAN.TIC.A.S. (LDTS),, Seamless International Communications, LLC. 16 Subsidiaries included in the Index

Officers: Matthew D. Rosen/Dir., CEO, Pres./$579,250.00, Roger Karam/40/Vice Chmn., Pres. - Efonica/$332,959.00, Bruce Lawson/VP - International Business Development, Asia, Barbara Hughes/VP - Finance/$191,126.00, Charles Whiting/Sr. VP - Technical Operations/$182,668.00, Jan Sarro/VP - Sales, Marketing/$153,961.00, Philip D. Turits/Co - Founder, Dir., Treasurer, Gordon Hutchins/59/Exec. VP - Operations/$280,199.00, Joel H. Maloff/CTO, Exec. VP, Eric D. Ram/Exec. VP - International/$147,891.00, Don Hutchins/Exec. VP - Operations, Ibrahim Choueiry/VP - International Sales, Michael Adams/VP - International Carrier Sales, Jerry Bir/VP - Operations

Directors: Matthew D. Rosen/Dir., CEO, Pres., Marvin S. Rosen/Co - Founder, Chmn., John H. Sununu/Chmn. - Advisory Board, Paul C. O'Brien/Dir., Patrick A. Bello/Member - Advisory Board, Jack Rosen/Member - Advisory Board, Evelyn Langlieb Greer/Dir., Fred P. Hochberg/Dir., Raymond E. Mabus/Dir., Dennis Mehiel/Dir., Alan M. Braverman/Member - Advisory Board, Frederic V. Salerno/Member - Advisory Board, Philip D. Turits/Co - Founder, Dir., Treasurer, Alan E. Brumberger/Dir., Michael J. Del Giudice/Dir. *(18 Directors included in Index)*

Owners: Evelyn Langlieb Greer, Charles Whiting, Eric D. Ram, Gordon Hutchins, Raymond E. Mabus, Jan Sarro, Marvin S. Rosen/8.80%, Julius Erving, Joel Maloff, Alan E. Brumberger/1.10%, Insiders/33.70%, Philip D. Turits/7.50%, Barbara Hughes, Sandy Beach Investments/5.30%, Paul C. OBrien *(20 Owners included in Index)*

Financial Data: ***Fiscal Year End:***12/31 ***Latest Annual Data:*** 12/31/2006

Year	Sales	Net Income
2006	$47,087,000	-$13,351,000
2005	$49,365,000	-$9,395,000
2004	$49,558,000	-$5,030,000

Curr. Assets:	$10,603,000	***Curr. Liab.:***	$13,327,000		
Plant, Equip.:	$6,422,000	***Total Liab.:***	$14,127,000	***Indic. Yr. Divd.:***	NA
Total Assets:	$27,573,000	***Net Worth:***	$13,446,000	***Debt/ Equity:***	NA

Futura Banc Corp

529 N Cleveland Massillon Rd., Akron, OH , 44333; ***PH:*** 1-330-670-8080; ***http://*** www.champaignbank.com

General - Incorporation; Employees NA; Auditor NA; Stk Agt NA; Counsel NA; DUNS No. NA

Stock- Price on:12/24/2007 $20.75; Stock Exchange OTC; Ticker Symbol FUBK; Outstanding Shares NA; E.P.S NA; Shareholders NA

Business: The groups principal activity is to provide financial banking services. The services of the group include business and personal banking, investment management, mortgage loans, retail and trust services. The group operates from the United States.

Primary SIC and add'l.: 6021

CIK No:

Officers: Michael J. Lamping/Chmn., CEO, Pres. - Champaign Bank, George E. Geissbuhler/Contact - Investor Relations, Steven Jefferis/Contact - Investor Relations, Robert A. Lucas/Contact - Investor Relations

Directors: Michael J. Lamping/Chmn., CEO, Pres. - Champaign Bank, Thomas J. Crowley/Dir. Emeriti, Gregg N. Bedell/Dir., Barry W. Boerger/Dir., Robert J. Gantzer/Dir., Jerry L. Gecowets/Dir., Lilli A. Johnson/Dir., Allen R. Maurice/Dir., David A. Shiffer/Dir., Richard A. Weidrick/Dir.

Futuremedia Plc

Nile House, Nile St., Brighton, BN1 1HW; ***PH:*** 44-1273829700; ***http://*** www.futuremedia.co.uk; ***Email:*** fm@futuremedia.co.uk

General - Incorporation UK; Employees NA; Auditor BDO Stoy Hayward LLP; Stk Agt NA; Counsel Brown Rudnick Berlack Israels LLP; DUNS No. 22-525-8250

Stock- Price on:12/24/2007 NA; Stock Exchange NDQ; Ticker Symbol FMDAY; Outstanding Shares NA; E.P.S -$6.98; Shareholders NA

Business: The group's principal activity is the provision of e-learning solutions to the corporate market. The group's main elements of services are the development and distribution of its Web-based learning management systems, "Solstra"; the development and distribution of its e-learning solution; "Easycando"; project management and instructional design of e-learning content; aggregation, brokerage and distribution of e-learning content and applications technologies from third party vendors; and consulting and other professional services to support the development and the successful implementation of e-learning solutions.

Primary SIC and add'l.: 7374 5045

CIK No: 0000906476

Subsidiaries: Activna Objects Ltd, C2W Ltd., Easycando.com Ltd., Futuremedia (BVI) Ltd, Futuremedia America Inc., Futuremedia Group, Futuremedia Interactive Ltd., Futuremedia Sverige AB, Lasermedia International Ltd., Lasermedia UK Ltd, Open Training AB, Temp Ltd

Officers: G. Oleary/Dir., Interim CEO, George O'Leary/CEO, Robert Goad/VP

Directors: Jan Vandamme/Chmn., Michiel Steel/Non Exec. Dir., M. Lebenberg/Non Exec. Dir., B. McNutt/Non Exec. Dir., Jacob Matthew/Dir.

Owners: M. Pilsworth/0.07%, M. Steel/0.07%, J. Vandannne/0.34%, Le Shark Limited/6.08%, Peter Machin/0.10%, Insiders/8.33%, National Air Cargo/30.55%, T. Bingham/7.47%, L. Fertig/0.27%

Financial Data: ***Fiscal Year End:***04/30 ***Latest Annual Data:*** 06/30/2006

Year	Sales	Net Income
2006	$6,243,000	-$791,000
2005	$29,854,000	-$7,550,000

Curr. Assets:	$9,497,000	***Curr. Liab.:***	$20,038,000		
Plant, Equip.:	$1,092,000	***Total Liab.:***	$30,604,000	***Indic. Yr. Divd.:***	NA
Total Assets:	$33,872,000	***Net Worth:***	$3,268,000	***Debt/ Equity:***	NA

Futures Portfolio Fund LP

2099 Gaither Rd., Ste. 200, Rockville, MD, 20850; ***PH:*** 1-240-631-9808

General - Incorporation MD; Employees NA; Auditor Mcgladrey & Pullen, LLP; Stk Agt NA; Counsel NA; DUNS No. NA

Stock- Price on:12/24/2007 NA; Stock Exchange NA; Ticker Symbol NA; Outstanding Shares NA; E.P.S NA; Shareholders NA

Business: The group's principle activities include mining and producing minerals. The group operates from United States.

Primary SIC and add'l.: 6221

CIK No: 0000861441

Officers: Kenneth E. Steben/Dir., CEO, Pres., Mary E. Ganoe/Chief Compliance Officer, Sec., Barbara M. Rittenhouse/Dir., Controller, Michael D. Bulley/51/Dir., VP - Research, Risk Management, Corp. Sec.

Directors: Kenneth E. Steben/Dir., CEO, Pres., Barbara M. Rittenhouse/Dir., Controller, Michael D. Bulley/51/Dir., VP - Research, Risk Management, Corp. Sec.

Owners: Brain F. Hull, Kenneth E. Steben, Insiders

FX Energy Inc

3006 Highland Dr., Ste. 206, Salt Lake City, UT, 84106; ***PH:*** 1-801-486-5555; ***Fax:*** 1-801-486-5575; ***http://*** www.fxenergy.com

General - Incorporation NV; Employees 42; Auditor PricewaterhouseCoopers LLP; Stk Agt Fidelity Transfer Co; Counsel James R. Kruse; DUNS No. 82-574-7827

Stock- Price on:12/24/2007 $10.04; Stock Exchange NDQ; Ticker Symbol FXEN; Outstanding Shares 35,700,000; E.P.S -$0.3; Shareholders NA

Business: The group's principle activity is to explore, develop and produce oil and gas in the United States and Poland. The group operates in two business segments: exploration and production and oilfield services. Exploration and production activities consist of oil sales from the group's producing properties in the United States, oil and gas sale from the group's producing properties in Poland. Oilfield services segment is comprised of contract drilling and well servicing fees generated by the group's oilfield servicing equipment in Montana. The group's quarterly revenue for Sep'07 was 5.24 millions of USD.

Primary SIC and add'l.: 1382 1381

CIK No: 0000907649

Subsidiaries: Frontier Exploration Company, Fx Drilling Company, Inc., Fx Energy Netherlands B.v., Fx Energy Netherlands Partnership C.v., Fx Energy Poland Sp. Zo.o, Fx Producing Company, Inc., Karpaty Production Company Sp. Zo.o, Sudety Mining Company Sp. Zo.o, Warmia Petroleum Company Sp. Zo.o

Officers: David Pierce/Dir., CEO, Pres./$700,106.00, Tom Lovejoy/Chmn., Exec. VP, Aleksander Nowak/Dir. - Export, Marketing Division, Jerzy Maclolek/Inside Dir., VP - International Exploration/$574,944.00, Zbigniew Tatys/VP - Pogc, General Dir. - Upstream, Exploration, Production Division, Richard Hardman/Dir., Sr. Technical Advisor, Bhoopal R. Naini/Member - Technical Team, Andrew W. Pierce/60/VP - Operations/$561,091.00, Scott J. Duncan/59/VP - Investor Relations, Sec., Clay Newton/51/VP - Finance, Treasurer, Chief Accounting Officer/$438,025.00

Directors: David Pierce/Dir., CEO, Pres., Tom Lovejoy/Chmn., Exec. VP, David Worrell/Dir., Jerzy Maclolek/Inside Dir., VP - International Exploration, Richard Hardman/Dir., Sr. Technical Advisor, Dennis B. Goldstein/Dir., Arnold S. Grundvig/Dir., Allen H. Turner/Dir.

Owners: David N. Pierce/1.30%, Dennis B. Goldstein, James Shawn Chalmers/5.20%, Richard F. Hardman, Jerzy B. Maciolek, Potomac Capital Management/5.10%, Arnold S. Grundvig, David L. Worrell, Thomas B. Lovejoy/2.10%, Cascoh, Inc./5.70%, Insiders/7.40%

Financial Data: ***Fiscal Year End:***12/31 ***Latest Annual Data:*** 12/31/2006

Year	Sales	Net Income
2006	$8,229,000	-$13,767,000
2005	$5,937,000	-$11,423,000
2004	$3,806,000	-$12,620,000

Curr. Assets:	$18,208,000	***Curr. Liab.:***	$6,241,000		
Plant, Equip.:	$19,695,000	***Total Liab.:***	$7,202,000	***Indic. Yr. Divd.:***	NA
Total Assets:	$39,167,000	***Net Worth:***	$31,965,000	***Debt/ Equity:***	NA

G & K Services Inc

5995 Opus Pkwy., Ste. 500, Minnetonka, MN, 55343; **PH:** 1-952-912-5500; **Fax:** 1-952-912-5999; **http://** www.gkcares.com

General - Incorporation	MN	**Stock**- Price on:12/24/2007	$38.35
Employees	9,685	Stock Exchange	NDQ
Auditor	Ernst & Young LLP	Ticker Symbol	GKSR
Stk Agt	Wells Fargo Bank Minnesota N.A	Outstanding Shares	21,520,000
Counsel	Maslon Edelman Borman & Brand	E.P.S.	$2.17
DUNS No.	02-292-7230	Shareholders	NA

Business: The group's principal activity is to provide corporate identity apparel and facility services programs to a wide variety of industrial, service and high-technology companies. The business apparel and facility services programs provide rental-lease or purchase options to meet varied customer needs including heavy-industrial, light-manufacturing, service businesses, corporate casual and executive apparel. The facility services programs provide a wide range of dust control and maintenance products and services. This includes several floor mat offerings (traction control, logo, message, scraper and anti-fatigue), dust and wet mops, wiping towels, fender covers, selected linen items and several restroom products. The group operates in over 130 north American locations serving customers in 46 states and 2 Canadian provinces. On 13-Aug-2004, the group acquired keefer laundry ltd.

Primary SIC and add'l.: 7213 2326

CIK No: 0000039648

Subsidiaries: G&K Services Canada Inc., G&K Services, Co., Les Services G&K (Quebec) Inc.

Officers: Richard L. Marcantonio/Chmn., CEO, David M. Miller/Pres. - US Rental Operations, Douglas A. Milroy/Pres. - Direct Purchase, Business Devlopment, Jacqueline T. Punch/Sr. VP - Human Resources, Damian J. Luna/Sr. VP - Sales, Richard J. Stutz/Sr. VP - Operations, Sourcing, Robert G. Wood/Pres. - G, K Services Canada Inc, Jeffrey L. Wright/Sr. VP, CFO, John P. Wallace/Sr. VP - Marketing

Directors: Richard L. Marcantonio/Chmn., CEO, Michael G. Allen/Dir., John S. Bronson/Dir., Ernest J. Mrozek/Dir., Alice M. Richter/Dir., Paul Baszucki/Dir., Lenny M. Pippin/Dir., Patrick J. Doyle/Dir., Wayne M. Fortun/Dir.

Owners: John S. Bronson, David M. Miller, Robert G. Wood, Richard L. Marcantonio, Insiders/2.27%, Alice M. Richter, Paul Baszucki, Thomas J. Dietz, Lenny M. Pippin, Wayne M. Fortun, T. Rowe Price Associates, Inc./11.37%, Ernest J. Mrozek, Michael G. Allen, Barclays Global Investors NA/5.49%, Douglas A. Milroy (20 Owners included in Index)

Financial Data: Fiscal Year End:07/02 **Latest Annual Data:** 06/30/2007

Year	Sales	Net Income
2007	$929,542,000	$43,190,000
2006	$880,843,000	$41,851,000
2005	$788,775,000	$39,927,000

Curr. Assets:	$207,367,000	**Curr. Liab.:**	$128,394,000	**P/E Ratio:**	19.57
Plant, Equip.:	$240,609,000	**Total Liab.:**	$377,324,000	**Indic. Yr. Divd.:**	$0.160
Total Assets:	$802,747,000	**Net Worth:**	$425,423,000	**Debt/ Equity:**	0.2764

G-III Apparel Group Ltd

512 7th Ave., New York, NY, 10018; **PH:** 1-212-403-0500; **Fax:** 1-212-403-0551; **http://** www.g-iii.com

General - Incorporation	DE	**Stock**- Price on:12/24/2007	$16.6
Employees	510	Stock Exchange	NDQ
Auditor	Ernst & Young LLP	Ticker Symbol	GIII
Stk Agt	Wells Fargo Bank, N.A.	Outstanding Shares	16,370,000
Counsel	Fulbright & Jaworski LLP	E.P.S.	$1.05
DUNS No.	60-621-3023	Shareholders	NA

Business: The group's principle activities are to design, manufacture, import and market outerwear and sportswear. The products of the group include coats, jackets, pants, skirts and other sportswear items under licensed proprietary labels and private retail labels. The group operates through two product segments namely licensed apparel and non-licensed apparel. The licensed apparel segment includes sales of apparel brands licensed by the group from third parties. The non-licensed apparel segment includes sales of apparel under the group's own brands and private label brands owned by retailers. The trademarks of the group include g-iii, j.l. Colebrook, jlc, colebrook & co., sienna, 58 sports (& design), ladies first by g-iii/carl banks, American classics by colebrook, black rivet & design {lower diamond}, siena studio, and sports 58 (& design). The group operates and markets in United States of America, Canada and Europe. The group's total revenue for the year 2007 was 271.19 millions of USD.

Primary SIC and add'l.: 2331 2386 2337 2311

CIK No: 0000821002

Officers: Morris Goldfarb/Chmn., CEO/$2,110,811.00, Jeanette Nostra-Katz/Pres./$746,769.00, Wayne Miller/COO/$976,638.00, Neal Nackman/CFO/$436,120.00, Erich Bennet/Contact - Izod, Jordan Williams/Contact - Sean John, Deshane Granger/Contact - Sean John Junior Sportswear, Bob Metz/Contact - Eliza J, James R. Palczynski/Investor Relation Officer, Casey Vieira/Contact - Black Rivet Men's, Marc Rothstein/Contact - Calvin Klein, Tanya Spivey/Contact - Cole Haan Men's, Women's, Donna Bonetti/Contact - Ellen Tracy, Kyle Sanborn/Contact - Hot Markets, Brian Moorstein/Contact - Jones New York Outerwear (24 Officers included in Index)

Directors: Morris Goldfarb/Chmn., CEO, Sammy Aaron/Vice Chmn., Laura Pomerantz/60/Dir., Richard White/54/Dir.

Owners: Richard White, Pieter Deiters, Carl Katz, Laura Pomerantz, Prentice Capital Management, LP/6.90%, Buckingham Capital Management Incorporated/6.80%, Willem van Bokhorst, Neal S. Nackman, Jeanette Nostra, Thomas J. Brosig, Wayne S. Miller, Deborah Gaertner, Insiders/22.90%, Morris Goldfarb/20.10%, Alan Feller (16 Owners included in Index)

Financial Data: Fiscal Year End:01/31 **Latest Annual Data:** 1/31/2007

Year	Sales	Net Income
2007	$427,017,000	$13,189,000
2006	$324,072,000	$7,092,000
2005	$214,278,000	$703,000

Curr. Assets:	$126,129,000	**Curr. Liab.:**	$44,271,000	**P/E Ratio:**	15.66
Plant, Equip.:	$5,641,000	**Total Liab.:**	$57,888,000	**Indic. Yr. Divd.:**	NA
Total Assets:	$173,530,000	**Net Worth:**	$115,642,000	**Debt/ Equity:**	0.1136

G. Willi-Food International Ltd

3, Nahal Snir St., Northen Industrial Zone, Yavne, 81224; **PH:** 972-89322233; **http://** www.willi-food.co.il; **Email:** import@willi-food.co.il

General - Incorporation	Israel	**Stock**- Price on:12/24/2007	$8.199
Employees	114	Stock Exchange	NDQ
Auditor	Brightman Almagor & Co	Ticker Symbol	WILC
Stk Agt	NA	Outstanding Shares	10,270,000
Counsel	NA	E.P.S.	$0.24
DUNS No.	60-055-2079	Shareholders	NA

Business: The groups principle activity is to import, market and distribute food products including canned vegetables, pickled olives and other pickled vegetables, packaged fruit, canned fish edible oils, dried fruit and nuts, coffee creamers, jams, halva, pasta, tahini, butter cookies, dairy products and certain frozen and chilled products. The group operates from United States.

Primary SIC and add'l.: 5149

CIK No: 0001030997

Subsidiaries: Bank Leumi LeIsrael Ltd, United Mizrahi Bank Ltd, United Mizrahi Bank Ltd., Vitarroz Corp., Willi USA Holdings, Inc

Officers: Joseph Williger/Dir., CEO, Zwi Williger/Chmn., COO, Christopher Chu/Investor Relations Officer, Chen Shlein/CFO

Directors: Joseph Williger/Dir., CEO, Zwi Williger/Chmn., COO, Ariel Herzfeld/53/External Dir.

Owners: Willi Food, Joseph Williger, Zvi Williger

Financial Data: Fiscal Year End:12/31 **Latest Annual Data:** 12/31/2006

Year	Sales	Net Income
2006	$45,316,000	$6,773,000
2005	$36,125,000	$1,678,000
2004	$39,689,000	$2,596,000

Curr. Assets:	$41,919,000	**Curr. Liab.:**	$7,760,000	**P/E Ratio:**	181.20
Plant, Equip.:	$10,123,000	**Total Liab.:**	$11,416,000	**Indic. Yr. Divd.:**	NA
Total Assets:	$52,064,000	**Net Worth:**	$40,648,000	**Debt/ Equity:**	NA

G/O Business Solutions Inc

14360 Sylvanfield, Houston, TX, 77014; **PH:** 1-713-827-0588; **Fax:** 1-832-422-2612; **http://** www.gobusinesssolutions.com; **Email:** info@gobizs.com

General - Incorporation	CO	**Stock**- Price on:12/24/2007	$0.51
Employees	NA	Stock Exchange	OTC
Auditor	HJ & Associates, LLC	Ticker Symbol	GOBS
Stk Agt	American Stock Transfer & Trust Co.	Outstanding Shares	21,630,000
Counsel	NA	E.P.S.	-$0.02
DUNS No.	NA	Shareholders	NA

Business: The groups principal activities include purchasing, training and selling thoroughbred horses. The group operates from the United States and Europe.

Primary SIC and add'l.: 6770

CIK No: 0000928447

Subsidiaries: Waterbury Resources, Inc.

Owners: John Ellis, David M. Klausmeyer, Sand Hills Partners, LLC, David R. Strawn, George R. Jarkesy, Sand Hills General Partners, Insiders, SH Celera Capital Corporation

Financial Data: Fiscal Year End:12/31 **Latest Annual Data:** 12/31/2006

Year	Sales	Net Income
2006	$2,000	-$179,000
2005	NA	-$72,000
2004	NA	-$62,000

Curr. Assets:	$16,000	**Curr. Liab.:**	$136,000		
Plant, Equip.:	NA	**Total Liab.:**	$136,000	**Indic. Yr. Divd.:**	NA
Total Assets:	$16,000	**Net Worth:**	-$120,000	**Debt/ Equity:**	NA

Gabelli Asset Mgmt Inc

One Corporate Ctr., 401 Theodore Fremd Ave., Rye, NY, 10580; **PH:** 1-914-921-3700; **http://** www.gabelli.com

General - Incorporation	NY	**Stock**- Price on:12/24/2007	$55.85
Employees	200	Stock Exchange	NYSE
Auditor	Ernst & Young LLP	Ticker Symbol	NA
Stk Agt	State Street Bank & Trust Co.	Outstanding Shares	28,170,000
Counsel	NA	E.P.S.	$2.84
DUNS No.	NA	Shareholders	NA

Business: The group's principal activity is to provide investment advisory and brokerage services to mutual fund, institutional and high net worth investors, primarily in the United States. The group manages assets on a discretionary basis and invests in a variety of U.S. And international securities through various investment styles. The group conducts business through three subsidiaries: gamco investors, inc, gabelli securities, inc. It acts as an underwriter and distributor of open-end mutual funds and provides institutional research through gabelli & company, inc., the broker-dealer subsidiary.

Primary SIC and add'l.: 6719 6282 6211

CIK No: 0001060349

Subsidiaries: Gabelli & Company, Inc., Gabelli & Partners LLC, Gabelli Advisers, Inc., Gabelli Asset Management (UK) Limited, Gabelli Convertible Holdings, LLC, Gabelli Direct, Inc., Gabelli Fixed Income Distributors, Inc., Gabelli Fixed Income LLC, Gabelli Fixed Income, Inc., Gabelli Funds, LLC, Gabelli Securities, Inc., GAMCO Asset Management Inc.

Officers: Mario J. Gabelli/Chmn., CEO, Chief Investment Officer/$58,616,320.00, Charles L. Minter/Portfolio Mgr., Christopher J. McDonald/Portfolio Mgr., Barbara Marcin/Portfolio Mgr., Lawrence J. Haverty/Assoc. Portfolio Mgr., Joshua W. Fenton/Portfolio Mgr., Elizabeth M. Lilly/Portfolio Mgr., Caesar M.P. Bryan/Portfolio Mgr., Barry M. Abramson/Portfolio Mgr., Evan D. Miller/Portfolio Mgr., Vincent Hugonnard Roche/Portfolio Mgr., Laura S. Linehan/Portfolio Mgr. - Microcap Team, Walter K. Walsh/Portfolio Mgr., Nancy E. Stuebe/Portfolio Mgr., Martin Weiner/Portfolio Mgr. (22 Officers included in Index)

Directors: Mario J. Gabelli/Chmn., CEO, Chief Investment Officer, Eugene R. McGrath/Dir.

Owners: Richard L. Bready, Royce& Associates, LLC/8.10%, Robert S. Prather, Douglas R. Jamieson, James E. McKee, Cascade Investment, L.L.C./11.30%, Bruce N. Alpert, James E. McKee, Insiders/99.10%, Artisan Partners L.P./8.80%, Douglas R. Jamieson, Edwin L. Artzt, Insiders/1.40%, Frederick J. Mancheski/25.60%, Mario J. Gabelli/99.00% (19 Owners included in Index)

Financial Data: Fiscal Year End:12/31 **Latest Annual Data:** 12/31/2006

Year	Sales	Net Income
2006	$261,463,000	$69,518,000
2005	$252,363,000	$63,391,000
2004	$255,163,000	$62,559,000

Curr. Assets:	$232,791,000	**Curr. Liab.:**	$132,815,000	**P/E Ratio:**	19.67
Plant, Equip.:	$1,459,000	**Total Liab.:**	$367,571,000	**Indic. Yr. Divd.:**	$0.120
Total Assets:	$837,231,000	**Net Worth:**	$448,741,000	**Debt/ Equity:**	0.3276

Gabriel Technologies Corp

4538 S 140th St., Omaha, NE, 68137; *PH:* 1-402-614-0258; *Fax:* 1-402-614-0498; *http://* www.gabrieltechnologies.com; *Email:* info@gabrieltechnologies.com

General - Incorporation .... DE
Employees 29
Auditor .... Williams & Webster, P.S
Stk Agt .... Colonial Stock Transfer Co Inc
Counsel .... Heskett & Heskett
DUNS No. .... NA

Stock- Price on:12/24/2007 .... $0.25
Stock Exchange .... OTC
Ticker Symbol .... GWLK
Outstanding Shares 38,510,000
E.P.S .... -$0.38
Shareholders .... NA

Business: The group's principal activities are to develop and market a real-time video insertion system. It also places computer-generated electronic images into live and pre-recorded television broadcasts of sports and entertainment programs. The electronic image range from simple corporate names or logos to sophisticated multi-media 3-D animated productions. The live video insertion system l-vis(R) has been used to insert images, including advertising images and program enhancements, into both live and pre-recorded television broadcasts. The l-vis(R) system is an integrated hardware and software system. The group also provides video insertion services and live telecast events worldwide. The customers of the group include cbs, espn, televisa, TV azteca, philadelphia eagles, Dallas cowboys, philadelphia phillies, indy racing league, volkswagen, telcel, heineken, ford, kodak and fedex.

Primary SIC and add'l.: 7311 7373 7372 7310

CIK No: 0001009833

Subsidiaries: Gabriel Technologies, LLC, Trace Technologies, LLC

Officers: Keith R. Feilmeier/58/Chmn., CEO, Principal Financial Officer, Pres., Allan Angus/56/CTO, Robert Weinberg/54/VP - Operations, Ron Gillum/Media Contact, Thomas Joseph Obrien/Principal Executive Officer, Principal Financial Officer, Acting COO

Directors: Keith R. Feilmeier/58/Chmn., CEO, Principal Financial Officer, Pres., Steven Campisi/49/Dir., Dennis Blackman/55/Dir., Roy G. Breeling/62/Dir., Jerry Suess/60/Dir., Darius Anderson/42/Dir., Matthew Gohd/51/Dir.

Owners: Dennis Blackman, Matthew Gohd/5.44%, Elliot Broidy/9.60%, Nicholas Fegen/9.35%, Roy G. Breeling, Darius Anderson/1.06%, Insiders/24.37%, Keith R. Feilmeier/10.66%, Jerry Suess/5.66%, Maurice Shanley/2.69%

Financial Data: *Fiscal Year End:*06/30 *Latest Annual Data:* 06/30/2006

Year	Sales	Net Income
2006	$1,242,000	-$14,550,000
2005	$922,000	-$3,446,000
2004	NA	$13,771,000

Curr. Assets:	$1,972,000	**Curr. Liab.:**	$6,178,000		
Plant, Equip.:	$1,165,000	**Total Liab.:**	$6,636,000	**Indic. Yr. Divd.:**	NA
Total Assets:	$19,204,000	**Net Worth:**	$12,568,000	**Debt/ Equity:**	NA

Gaiam Inc

360 Interlocken Blvd, Ste. 300, Broomfield, CO, 80021; *PH:* 1-303-222-3600; *Fax:* 1-303-222-3700; *http://* www.gaiam.com; *Email:* investorrelations@gaiam.com

General - Incorporation .... CO
Employees 363
Auditor ... Ehrhardt Keefe Steiner & Hottman P.C
Stk Agt .... Computershare Trust Co
Counsel ...... Bartlit Beck Herman Palenchar Scott
DUNS No. .... NA

Stock- Price on:12/24/2007 .... $17.15
Stock Exchange .... NDQ
Ticker Symbol .... GAIA
Outstanding Shares 24,650,000
E.P.S $0.25
Shareholders .... NA

Business: The group's principle activity is to provide a broad selection of information, products and services to customers who value natural health, personal development and renewable energy. The products include solar panels and accessories, air filters, natural lighting, yoga information and accessories, natural cleaners and others. The group's products and lifestyle solutions are categorized into five main sectors of the lifestyles of health and sustainability market: sustainable economy, healthy living, alternative healthcare, personal development, ecological lifestyles. The group operates in two business segments: business to business: includes sales to retailers, corporate accounts and through the media. Direct to consumer: conducts business through catalogs, print advertising and e-commerce. During 2003, the group acquired majority interest in leisure systems international. The group's quarterly revenue for Sep'07 was 70.32 milllions of USD.

Primary SIC and add'l.: 7375

CIK No: 0001089872

Subsidiaries: Gaiam Americas,Inc., Gaiam Direct,Inc., Gaiam Energy Tech,Inc., Gaiam International B.V., Gaiam International C.V., Gaiam International II,Inc., Gaiam International III,Inc., Gaiam International,Inc., Gaiam Limited, Gaiam Media,Inc., Gaiam Shared Services,Inc., Gaiam Travel,Inc., Gaiam West,Inc., Gaiam.com,Inc., GT Direct,Inc. 17 Subsidiaries included in the Index

Officers: Jirka Rysavy/53/Chmn., CEO, Founder/$296,712.00, Lynn Powers/57/Dir., Pres./$1,516,371.00, Vilia Valentine/CFO/$266,967.00

Directors: Jirka Rysavy/53/Chmn., CEO, Founder, Paul H. Ray/64/Dir., Ted Nark/48/Dir., Barnet M. Feinblum/59/Dir., Lynn Powers/57/Dir., Pres., James Argyropoulos/62/Dir., Barbara Mowry/59/Dir.

Owners: Jirka Rysavy/26.44%, Jirka Rysavy/100.00%, Paul Ray, Barbara Mowry, Mazama Capital Management, Inc./6.36%, Barnet Feinblum, Prentice Capital Management, LP/22.24%, Columbia Wagner Asset Management, L.P./7.01%, Arbor Capital Management LLC/5.38%, Vilia Valentine, Goodwood Inc./5.42%, James Argyropoulos/1.67%, John Jackson, Insiders/29.40%, Insiders/100.00% *(17 Owners included in Index)*

Financial Data: *Fiscal Year End:*12/31 *Latest Annual Data:* 12/31/2006

Year	Sales	Net Income
2006	$219,480,000	$5,644,000
2005	$142,492,000	$1,336,000
2004	$96,657,000	-$4,638,000

Curr. Assets:	$166,847,000	**Curr. Liab.:**	$26,700,000	**P/E Ratio:**	61.25
Plant, Equip.:	$7,784,000	**Total Liab.:**	$26,700,000	**Indic. Yr. Divd.:**	NA
Total Assets:	$250,968,000	**Net Worth:**	$218,606,000	**Debt/ Equity:**	NA

Gainsco Inc

3333 Lee Pkwy., Ste. 1200, Dallas, TX, 75219; *PH:* 1-972-629-4301; *Fax:* 1-972-629-4302; *http://* www.gainsco.com; *Email:* ir@gainsco.com

General - Incorporation .... TX
Employees 391
Auditor .... KPMG LLP
Stk Agt .... Continental Stock Transfer & Trust Co
Counsel .... Jackson Walker
DUNS No. 03-790-2590

Stock- Price on:12/24/2007 .... $6.32
Stock Exchange .... AMEX
Ticker Symbol .... GAN
Outstanding Shares 24,910,000
E.P.S $0.20
Shareholders .... NA

Business: The group's principal activity is to provide property and casualty insurance to the nonstandard personal automobile market. Its insurance operations were conducted through two insurance companies: general agents insurance company of America Inc and MGA Insurance Company Inc. The group markets nonstandard personal auto line of insurance on an admitted basis through approximately 1,000 non-affiliated retail agencies. The group operates in the United States.

Primary SIC and add'l.: 6719 6331

CIK No: 0000786344

Subsidiaries: DLT Insurance Adjusters, Inc., GAINSCO Service Corp., General Agents Insurance Company of America, Inc., Lalande Financial Group, Inc., MGA Agency, Inc., MGA Insurance Company, Inc., National Specialty Lines, Inc., Risk Retention Administrators Inc.

Officers: Glenn W. Anderson/Dir., CEO, Pres./$876,484.00, Robert W. Stallings/Chmn., Chief Strategic Officer/$706,476.00, Terence J. Lynch/Sr. Management, Investments, James R. Reis/Exec. VP, Chief Risk Management Officer/$404,621.00, Richard M. Buxton/Corporate Affairs, Human Resources/$244,831.00, Daniel J. Coots/CFO/$244,583.00, John S. Daniels/General Counsel, Sec., Michael S. Johnston/Sr. Management, Southeast Region, Donna K. Dibiaso/Product Management, Paul Andy Jordan/Corporate Marketing, Brian L. Kirkham/Sr. Management, Southwest Region, Phillip J. West/Sr. Management, Information Technology, Wade E. Chance/Sr. Management, South Central Region

Directors: Glenn W. Anderson/Dir., CEO, Pres., Robert W. Stallings/Chmn., Chief Strategic Officer, Robert J. Boulware/Dir., John C. Goff/Dir., Joel C. Puckett/Dir., Harden H. Wiedemann/Dir., Sam Rosen/Dir., John H. Williams/Dir.

Owners: Richard M. Buxton, Harden H. Wiedemann, Insiders/70.40%, James R. Reis/11.30%, Daniel J. Coots, Robert W. Stallings/22.50%, Sam Rosen, Glenn W. Anderson/1.80%, John H. Williams, Joel C. Puckett, Robert J. Boulware, Goff Moore Strategic Partners/34.10%

Financial Data: *Fiscal Year End:*12/31 *Latest Annual Data:* 12/31/2006

Year	Sales	Net Income
2006	$206,477,000	$11,388,000
2005	$99,587,000	$8,872,000
2004	$48,877,000	$5,509,000

Curr. Assets:	$147,108,000	**Curr. Liab.:**	$26,940,000	**P/E Ratio:**	31.60
Plant, Equip.:	$2,379,000	**Total Liab.:**	$204,596,000	**Indic. Yr. Divd.:**	NA
Total Assets:	$289,332,000	**Net Worth:**	$84,736,000	**Debt/ Equity:**	0.5460

Galaxy Energy Corp

1331 17th St., Ste. 1050, Denver, CO, 80202; *PH:* 1-303-293-2300; *Fax:* 1-303-293-2417; *http://* www.galaxyenergy.com; *Email:* info@galaxyenergy.com

General - Incorporation .... CO
Employees 7
Auditor .... Hein & Assoc. LLP
Stk Agt .... Nevada Agency & Trust Company
Counsel .... NA
DUNS No. .... NA

Stock- Price on:12/24/2007 .... $0.1575
Stock Exchange .... AMEX
Ticker Symbol .... GAX
Outstanding Shares 83,680,000
E.P.S .... -$0.276
Shareholders .... NA

Business: The group's principal activities are oil and gas exploration and production. It is organized for the purpose of engaging in the acquisition, exploration and development of coal bed methane ("Cbm") and other unconventional and conventional natural gas properties primarily in Wyoming, Texas and other areas that offer exploitation opportunities for natural gas. The group conducts exploration activities to locate natural gas and crude petroleum and is in its development stage. On 13-Nov-2002, the group acquired dolphin energy corporation and on 2-Jun-2003, it acquired pannonian international ltd

Primary SIC and add'l.: 1311 1099

CIK No: 0001132784

Subsidiaries: Dolphin Energy Corporation, Pannonian International

Officers: Marc E. Bruner/Dir., CEO, Pres., Brad Long/Investor Relations Officer, Tina Cameron/Renmark Financial Communications, Montreal, Richard E. Kurtenbach/52/VP - Administration, Controller, Christopher S. Hardesty/CFO, Sr. VP, Sec., Treasurer, Cecil D. Gritz/Dir., COO, Thomas G. Fails/Pres. - Pannonian International

Directors: Marc E. Bruner/Dir., CEO, Pres., James M. Edwards/Dir., Cecil D. Gritz/Dir., COO, Robert Thomas Fetters/Dir., Nathan C. Collins/Dir., Ronald P. Trout/68/Dir.

Owners: Resource Venture Management/5.90%, Marc A. Bruner/14.00%, Cecil D. Gritz, Christopher S. Hardesty, Ronald P. Trout, Bruner Group, LLP/5.40%, James Edwards, Insiders/4.50%, Nathan C. Collins, Robert Thomas Fetters, Marc E. Bruner/2.50%

Financial Data: *Fiscal Year End:*11/30 *Latest Annual Data:* 11/30/2006

Year	Sales	Net Income
2006	$1,274,000	-$26,163,000
2005	$16,785,000	$1,883,000
2004	$14,162,000	$1,462,000

Curr. Assets:	$1,802,000	**Curr. Liab.:**	$21,671,000		
Plant, Equip.:	$44,915,000	**Total Liab.:**	$39,840,000	**Indic. Yr. Divd.:**	NA
Total Assets:	$47,760,000	**Net Worth:**	$7,920,000	**Debt/ Equity:**	5.0448

Galaxy Nutritional Foods Inc

5955 T. G. Lee Blvd, Ste. 201, Orlando, FL, 32822; *PH:* 1-407-855-5500; *Fax:* 1-407-855-1099; *http://* www.galaxyfoods.com; *Email:* galxquality@galaxyfoods.com

General - Incorporation .... DE
Employees 26
Auditor .... BDO Seidman LLP
Stk Agt .... Continental Stock Transfer & Trust Co
Counsel .... Proskauer Rose LLP
DUNS No. 08-396-5152

Stock- Price on:12/24/2007 .... $0.6
Stock Exchange .... OTC
Ticker Symbol .... GXYF
Outstanding Shares 17,110,000
E.P.S $0.09
Shareholders .... NA

Business: The group's principal activity is to develop, manufacture and market cheese, dairy related products and other cheese alternatives. The group also manufactures and markets organic soy-based, rice-based and non-dairy cheese products. The products are sold under the brand names veggie milk(tm), veggie slice(tm), soyco(R), soymage(R), wholesome valley(R), rice slice(tm), veggy singles(R), lite bakery(R) and veggie lite bakery(R) and the veggie natures alternatives to milk(R) and line of vegan dairy alternatives made with soy. The group also manufactures and markets non-branded and private label cheese products. The group has a licensing arrangement with tropicana(R) to manufacture, distribute and market its ultra smoothie(tm) product. The group distributes its products through supermarket chains, health food stores, restaurant chains, cafeterias, hospitals and schools. The customers are situated throughout the United States and in fourteen other countries.

Primary SIC and add'l.: 2044 2022

CIK No: 0000819527

Officers: Michael E. Broll/Dir., CEO, Thomas J. Perno/VP - Operations, Salvatore J. Furnari/CFO, John W. Jackson/VP - Global Sales, Kulbir Sabharwal/VP - Technical Services, Leann Hitchcock/Sec. Compliance Mgr., Internal Auditor, Dawn M. Robert/Investor Relation Officer, Hilary Taube/Marketing Dir.

Directors: Michael E. Broll/Dir., CEO, David H. Lipka/Chmn., Peter J. Jungsberger/Dir., Robert S. Mohel/Dir.

Owners: Frederick A. DeLuca/50.30%, BC Advisors LLC/6.40%, Fromageries Bel S.A./6.50%, John Hancock Advisers LLC/6.70%, Royce & Associates LLC/10.50%, Angelo S. Morini/13.40%

Financial Data: Fiscal Year End:03/31 **Latest Annual Data:** 3/31/2007

Year	Sales	Net Income
2007	$27,162,000	$146,000
2006	$37,776,000	-$24,149,000
2005	$44,510,000	-$3,860,000

Curr. Assets:	$4,171,000	Curr. Liab.:	$3,465,000	P/E Ratio:	60.00
Plant, Equip.:	$90,000	Total Liab.:	$6,336,000	Indic. Yr. Divd.:	NA
Total Assets:	$4,365,000	Net Worth:	-$1,972,000	Debt/ Equity:	NA

Gallaher Group Plc

Members Hill Brooklands Rd. , Weybridge, KT13 OQU; *PH:* 44-1932859777;
http:// www.gallaher-group.com; *Email:* info@gallaherltd.com

General - Incorporation	UK	Stock - Price on:12/24/2007	NA
Employees	11,100	Stock Exchange	OTC
Auditor	PricewaterhouseCoopers LLP	Ticker Symbol	GLHGF
Stk Agt	Bank of New York	Outstanding Shares	NA
Counsel	Simmons & Simmons	E.P.S.	NA
DUNS No.	37-848-6914	Shareholders	NA

Business: The group's principal activity is the manufacture, marketing and distribution of tobacco and tobacco related products. Brands include benson and hedges, silk cut, mayfair, sovereign, sobranie, dorchester, troika, ld, memphis, milde sorte, ronson, blend, hamlet, old holborn, amber leaf and condor. The group has manufacturing plants in the United Kingdom, Russia, the republic of Ireland, kazakhstan, Austria, Sweden and ukraine.

Primary SIC and add'l.: 2131 2121 2111

CIK No: 0001037333

Subsidiaries: Austria Tabak GmbH, Austria Tabak GmbH & Co KG, Benson & Hedges Limited, Cita Tabacos de Canarias SL, Gallaher (Dublin) Limited, Gallaher Asia Limited, Gallaher Austria Tabak Europe GmbH & Co. KG, Gallaher Belgium SA, Gallaher Canarias SA, Gallaher France EURL, Gallaher Hellas SA, Gallaher International Limited, Gallaher Italia SRL, Gallaher Kazakhstan LLC, Gallaher Limited 26 Subsidiaries included in the Index

Gallery of History Inc

3601 W Sahara Ave., Las Vegas, NV, 89102; *PH:* 1-702-364-1000; *Fax:* 1-702-364-1285;
http:// www.galleryofhistory.com

General - Incorporation	NV	Stock - Price on:12/24/2007	$1.93
Employees	8	Stock Exchange	NDQ
Auditor	Piercy, Bowler, Taylor & Kern	Ticker Symbol	HIST
Stk Agt	Continental Stock Transfer & Trust Co	Outstanding Shares	5,630,000
Counsel	NA	E.P.S.	-$0.09
DUNS No.	03-309-9326	Shareholders	NA

Business: The group's principle activities are to market historical documents such as letters, documents and signatures of presidents and other political and governmental figures, significant physicians, inventors, nobel prize winners, explorers, aviators, scientists, entertainers, actors, artists, musicians and famous personalities in sports. The group markets its products through direct sales approach via auctions and a catalog program. The group's customers are autograph dealers, auction houses and corporations. The group's inventory of documents currently consists of approximately 181,000 different documents. Retail sales of documents are made from a gallery located at its headquarters in las vegas, Nevada. The group's total revenue of the year 2007 was 0.63 millions of USD.

Primary SIC and add'l.: 5999

CIK No: 0000763730

Subsidiaries: 3601 West Sahara Corp., Gallery of History Auctions Inc., International Stolen Art & Documents Clearinghouse Corp

Officers: Todd M. Axelrod/Chmn., CEO, Pres./$7,644.00, Dana Merrill/Editor, Rod Lynam/Dir., CFO, Treasurer, Assist. Sec., William Benzenhafer/Archives Mgr., Gary Harris/Archivist, Robert Wais/Digital Archivist, Kathy Boyle/Editorial Assist., Betty J. Kartes/Editorial Assist., Ruth Canvasser/Editorial Assist., Don Prince/Sr. VP

Directors: Todd M. Axelrod/Chmn., CEO, Pres., Roger Schneier/64/Dir., Michael Rosenman/46/Dir., Rod Lynam/Dir., CFO, Treasurer, Assist. Sec., Peter Kuhr/60/Dir.

Owners: Insiders/82.50%, Todd M. Axelrod/82.00%, Roger Schneier/1.30%, Rod R. Lynam, Gerald Newman/8.80%

Financial Data: Fiscal Year End:09/30 **Latest Annual Data:** 9/30/2006

Year	Sales	Net Income
2006	$679,000	-$534,000
2005	$1,121,000	-$819,000
2004	$1,139,000	-$867,000

Curr. Assets:	$6,531,000	Curr. Liab.:	$1,683,000		
Plant, Equip.:	$1,100,000	Total Liab.:	$3,016,000	Indic. Yr. Divd.:	NA
Total Assets:	$9,000,000	Net Worth:	$5,985,000	Debt/ Equity:	NA

GamePlan Inc

6619 S Dixie Hwy., Ste. No. 333, Miami, FL, 33143; *PH:* 1-775-853-3980; *Fax:* 1-305-232-7372;
http:// www.gameplaninc.com; *Email:* masolutions@gameplaninc.com

General - Incorporation	NV	Stock - Price on:12/24/2007	$0.15
Employees	NA	Stock Exchange	OTC
Auditor	Mantyla McReynolds LLC	Ticker Symbol	GPLA
Stk Agt	Nevada Agency & Trust Company	Outstanding Shares	15,230,000
Counsel	NA	E.P.S.	$0.00
DUNS No.	NA	Shareholders	NA

Business: The group is exploring new ideas for its planned principal operations. The plan is based on concepts related to providing legal services. The plan envisions the creation of multiple new subsidiaries and divisions for the purpose of providing a variety of new integrated products and services. The products and services include financial services, insurance products, digital escrow services, advanced digital research, an Internet clicks to bricks site, and member legal service organizations of licensed attorneys.

Primary SIC and add'l.: 9999

CIK No: 0001095146

Subsidiaries: Gameplaninc.com

Officers: Robert G. Berry/72/Dir., CEO, CFO, Pres., Sec., Neal H. Bendesky/Pres., Robert J. Ruf/Exec. VP

Directors: Robert G. Berry/72/Dir., CEO, CFO, Pres., Sec., John Sien/59/Dir.

Owners: Jon T. Jenkins/39.60%, Insiders/39.60%, Robert G. Berry/39.60%

Financial Data: Fiscal Year End:12/31 **Latest Annual Data:** 12/31/2006

Year	Sales	Net Income
2006	NA	-$58,000
2005	$0	-$62,000
2004	NA	-$45,000

Curr. Assets:	$1,000	Curr. Liab.:	$1,000		
Plant, Equip.:	NA	Total Liab.:	$645,000	Indic. Yr. Divd.:	NA
Total Assets:	$1,000	Net Worth:	-$643,000	Debt/ Equity:	NA

Games On Demand International Inc

Arcade At Royal Palm 1 950 S Pine Island Rd. , Ste 150A-106, Plantation, FL, 33324;
PH: 1-954-727-8393; *http://* www.gamesondemand.com.au

General - Incorporation	DE	Stock - Price on:12/24/2007	NA
Employees	NA	Stock Exchange	NA
Auditor	NA	Ticker Symbol	NA
Stk Agt	NA	Outstanding Shares	NA
Counsel	NA	E.P.S.	NA
DUNS No.	NA	Shareholders	NA

Business: The group's principle activities include developing, manufacturing and marketing patented device to sterilize water for lubricating dentist drills. The group is also in the process of acquiring gaming technology to enable develop, upgrade and support Internet based games and software. The groups gaming facility is designed for online game players and is limited exclusively to online video game-play. The group also provides online games network. The group operates from United States.

Primary SIC and add'l.: 7389

CIK No: 0001324637

Gamestop Corp

625 Westport Pkwy., Grapevine, TX, 76051; *PH:* 1-817-424-2000; *Fax:* 1-817-424-2002;
http:// www.gamestop.com; *Email:* investorrelations@gamestop.com

General - Incorporation	DE	Stock - Price on:12/24/2007	$39.91
Employees	12,000	Stock Exchange	NYSE
Auditor	BDO Seidman, LLP	Ticker Symbol	GME
Stk Agt	Bank of New York	Outstanding Shares	158,460,000
Counsel	NA	E.P.S.	$1.08
DUNS No.	NA	Shareholders	NA

Business: The groups principal activity is to retail video game products and PC entertainment software. The group also sells new and used video game hardware, video game software and accessories. The group operates through four geographic segments namely, the United States, Australia, Canada and Europe. The group operates from the United States, Australia, Canada and Europe. Of the total sales in the year 2006, the United States segment accounted for $4,269.5, Canada $319.7, Australia $288.1 and Europe $441.6 (thousands).

Primary SIC and add'l.: 5731 5734 5945

CIK No: 0001326380

Subsidiaries: EB Catalog Company Inc, EB Games Finland Oy AB, EB Games Management Services A, EB Games Sweden AB, EB Games Trading GmbH, EB International Holdings Inc., EB Luxembourg Holdings Sarl, EB World. Com Pty. Ltd., Elbo Inc., Electronics Boutique Australia Pty. Ltd., Electronics Boutique Canada Inc., Electronics Boutique Denmark ApS., Electronics Boutique Holdings Corp., Electronics Boutique Norway AS., GameStop (LP) LLC 31 Subsidiaries included in the Index

Officers: Richard R. Fontaine/Chmn., CEO, Daniel A. Dematteo/Vice Chmn., COO, Steven R. Morgan/Pres., David W. Carlson/CFO, Exec. VP, Assist. Sec., Ronald Freeman/Exec. VP - Distribution, Michael N. Rosen/Dir., Sec., Matt Hodges/Dir. - Investor Relations, Robert A. Lloyd/46/Chief Accounting Officer, Sr. VP, Scott W. Shaver/Sec., Tony D. Bartel/44/Exec. VP - Merchandising, Marketing

Directors: Richard R. Fontaine/Chmn., CEO, Daniel A. Dematteo/Vice Chmn., COO, Leonard Riggio/Dir., Michael N. Rosen/Dir., Sec., Stephanie M. Shern/Dir., Edward A. Volkwein/Dir., Gerald R. Szczepanski/Dir., James J. Kim/72/Dir., Stanley Steinberg/Dir., Jerome L. Davis/Dir., Lawrence S. Zilavy/Dir., Steven R. Koonin/Dir.

Owners: Richard R. Fontaine/1.10%, Jerome L. Davis, FMR Corp./9.30%, Gerald R. Szczepanski, Insiders/12.70%, Edward A. Volkwein, Steven R. Morgan, Michael N. Rosen, Stephanie M. Shern, Ronald Freeman, Lawrence S. Zilavy, Stanley Steinberg, James J. Kim/1.40%, David W. Carlson, Leonard Riggio/8.60% (16 Owners included in Index)

Financial Data: Fiscal Year End:01/28 **Latest Annual Data:** 2/3/2007

Year	Sales	Net Income
2007	$5,318,900,000	$158,250,000
2006	$3,091,783,000	$100,784,000
2005	$1,842,806,000	$60,926,000

Curr. Assets:	$1,440,341,000	Curr. Liab.:	$1,087,057,000	P/E Ratio:	36.95
Plant, Equip.:	$456,463,000	Total Liab.:	$1,973,706,000	Indic. Yr. Divd.:	NA
Total Assets:	$3,349,584,000	Net Worth:	$1,375,878,000	Debt/ Equity:	0.4977

GameTech International Inc

900 Sandhill Rd., Reno, NV, 89521; **PH:** 1-775-850-6000; **Fax:** 1-775-850-6090;
http:// www.gametech-inc.com; **Email:** hr@gtiemail.com

General - Incorporation	DE	Stock - Price on:12/24/2007	$9.57
Employees	200	Stock Exchange	NDQ
Auditor	Grant Thornton LLP	Ticker Symbol	GMTC
Stk Agt	Mellon Investor Services LLC	Outstanding Shares	12,580,000
Counsel	NA	E.P.S.	$0.34
DUNS No.	83-600-1321	Shareholders	NA

Business: The group's principal activities are to design, develop and market interactive electronic bingo systems. The group rents these systems under operating type leases on month to month and long term contracts. The group currently markets a fixed-base system with light pen- or touch screen-activated monitors, and portable hand-held systems that can be played anywhere within a bingo hall. The group's bingo system allows players to play up to 600 electronic bingo card images during one bingo game. The group operates in 46 states excluding Arkansas, Hawaii, Tennessee, and Utah and the district of columbia.
Primary SIC and add'l.: 3944
CIK No: 0001045014
Subsidiaries: Bingo Card Minder Corporation, Bingo Technologies Corporation, GameTech Arizona Corporation, GameTech Canada Corporation, GameTech International, Inc.
Officers: Jay Meilstrup/Dir., CEO, Pres., Justin K. Goodman/VP - Research, Development, Ann D. McKenzie/Corporate Controller, Pat Crawford/VP - Business Affairs, Tracy C. Pearson/CFO, Treasurer, Sec.
Directors: Jay Meilstrup/Dir., CEO, Pres., Richard T. Fedor/Chmn., Richard Irvine/Dir., Don Whitaker/Dir., Scott Shackelton/Dir.
Owners: Insiders/23.40%, Delta Partners LLC/12.30%, Jay M. Meilstrup/2.10%, Richard H. Irvine, Donald K. Whitaker, Scott H. Shackelton
Financial Data: Fiscal Year End:10/31   Latest Annual Data: 10/31/2006

Year	Sales	Net Income
2006	$49,289,000	$4,383,000
2005	$49,651,000	$1,336,000
2004	$51,490,000	-$9,906,000

Curr. Assets:	$23,984,000	Curr. Liab.:	$8,572,000	P/E Ratio:	26.58
Plant, Equip.:	$22,868,000	Total Liab.:	$9,380,000	Indic. Yr. Divd.:	NA
Total Assets:	$59,214,000	Net Worth:	$49,834,000	Debt/ Equity:	0.7075

GameZnFlix Inc

1535 Blackjack Rd. , Franklin, KY, 42134; **PH:** 1-270-598-0385; **http://** www.gameznflix.com; **Email:** info@gameznflix.com

General - Incorporation	NV	Stock - Price on:12/24/2007	$0.0005
Employees	45	Stock Exchange	OTC
Auditor Child, Van Wagoner & Bradshaw, PLLC		Ticker Symbol	GMFX
Stk Agt	Interwest Transfer Company, Inc.	Outstanding Shares	6,490,000,000
Counsel	NA	E.P.S.	-$2.999
DUNS No.	NA	Shareholders	NA

Business: The group's principal activity is to rental on-line dvds and video games to it's subscribers. The group provides a large selection of video game rental choices to it's customers on a monthly subscription basis. The customers can sign-up via the Web page and get the games shipped to them through first class mail. The distribution centers are located in a home-based office space in franklin, Kentucky, with veegeez maintaining one location and a distribution center in a home-based office space in santa clarita, California. The group operates solely in the United States.
Primary SIC and add'l.: 7841
CIK No: 0001099234
Subsidiaries: GameZnFlix Racing and Merchandising, Inc.
Officers: John Fleming/CEO, Arthur De Joya/42/CFO
Owners: John Fleming/22.40%, Insiders/39.64%, Mark Crist/1.81%, Arthur De Joya/15.43%
Financial Data: Fiscal Year End:12/31   Latest Annual Data: 12/31/2006

Year	Sales	Net Income
2006	$1,885,000	-$10,840,000
2005	$676,000	-$4,240,000
2004	$287,000	-$9,717,000

Curr. Assets:	$2,026,000	Curr. Liab.:	$859,000		
Plant, Equip.:	$579,000	Total Liab.:	$862,000	Indic. Yr. Divd.:	NA
Total Assets:	$6,713,000	Net Worth:	$5,851,000	Debt/ Equity:	NA

Gaming & Entertainment Group Ltd

4501 Hayvenhurst Ave., Encino, CA, 91436; **PH:** 1-818-400-5930; **Fax:** 1-413-723-2141;
http:// www.gaming-group.com; **Email:** admin@gaming-group.com

General - Incorporation	UT	Stock - Price on:12/24/2007	$0.015
Employees	2	Stock Exchange	OTC
Auditor	J. H. Cohn LLP	Ticker Symbol	GMEI
Stk Agt	NA	Outstanding Shares	19,830,000
Counsel	NA	E.P.S.	-$0.048
DUNS No.	75-446-4709	Shareholders	NA

Business: The group's principal activity is the development of Internet casino gambling technology and related software applications.
Primary SIC and add'l.: 7993 7999
CIK No: 0001100356
Subsidiaries: G.E.T. (Holdings) Limited, Gaming & Entertainment Limited, Gaming & Entertainment Technology Pty Limited
Officers: Tibor N. Vertes/58/Chmn., CEO, Gregory L. Hrncir/41/Dir., Pres., Simon Daniel/34/CTO
Directors: Tibor N. Vertes/58/Chmn., CEO, Gregory L. Hrncir/41/Dir., Pres.
Owners: Jay Sanet/0.50%, Gregory L. Hrncir/12.00%, Insiders/46.10%, Tibor N. Vertes/33.60%, Cantor G&W (Nevada), L.P./40.10%

Financial Data: Fiscal Year End:12/31   Latest Annual Data: 12/31/2006

Year	Sales	Net Income
2006	$141,000	-$1,119,000
2005	$1,275,000	-$1,473,000
2004	$312,000	-$3,206,000

Curr. Assets:	$73,000	Curr. Liab.:	$1,057,000		
Plant, Equip.:	$31,000	Total Liab.:	$2,410,000	Indic. Yr. Divd.:	NA
Total Assets:	$104,000	Net Worth:	-$2,306,000	Debt/ Equity:	NA

Gaming Partners International Corp

1700 Industrial Rd., Las Vegas, NV, 89102; **PH:** 1-702-384-2425; **Fax:** 1-702-384-1965;
http:// www.gpigaming.com; **Email:** info@gpigaming.com

General - Incorporation	NV	Stock - Price on:12/24/2007	$13.7799
Employees	760	Stock Exchange	NDQ
Auditor	Moss Adams LLP	Ticker Symbol	GPIC
Stk Agt	American Stock Transfer & Trust Co.	Outstanding Shares	8,100,000
Counsel	NA	E.P.S.	-$0.068
DUNS No.	NA	Shareholders	NA

Business: The group's principle activities are to manufacture and supply casino table game equipment. The products of the group include casino chips, table game layouts, playing cards, dice, gaming furniture and miscellaneous table accessories such as chip trays, drop boxes and dealing shoes. The group designs and manufactures casino chips to meet a variety of customer preferences and specifications, including size, weight, ability to stack, ease of handling, texture, color, graphics, durability, security and anti-counterfeit features. It also has retail sales outlets, which provide casino-quality products. The group has its manufacturing facilities located at the United States and Mexico and operates through its sales offices. The group's quarterly revenue for Sep'07 was 15.20 millions of USD.
Primary SIC and add'l.: 3999 3944 2759 3949
CIK No: 0000918580
Subsidiaries: Gaming Partners International SAS, Gaming Partners International USA, Inc, GPI Mexicana, S.A. de C.V.
Officers: Gerard P. Charlier/Dir., CEO, Pres., Sec./$306,668.00, Laura McAllister Cox/Chief Legal, Gaming Compliance Officer/$219,674.00, David W. Grimes/CFO/$4,608.00
Directors: Gerard P. Charlier/Dir., CEO, Pres., Sec., Paul S. Dennis/Dir., Eric P. Endy/Dir., Alain Thieffry/Dir., Elisabeth Carrette/Dir., Robert J. Kelly/Dir., Charles R. Henry/Dir., Martin A. Berkowitz/59/Dir.
Owners: Robert J. Kelly, Elisabeth Carrette/49.30%, Charles R. Henry, Magnet Fund, L.P./7.96%, Insiders/60.44%, Eric P. Endy/3.36%, Paul S. Dennis, Gerard P. Charlier/8.17%, Alain Thieffry
Financial Data: Fiscal Year End:12/31   Latest Annual Data: 12/31/2006

Year	Sales	Net Income
2006	$73,954,000	$5,129,000
2005	$57,121,000	$4,328,000
2004	$44,585,000	$2,614,000

Curr. Assets:	$26,241,000	Curr. Liab.:	$11,454,000		
Plant, Equip.:	$14,567,000	Total Liab.:	$14,385,000	Indic. Yr. Divd.:	$0.130
Total Assets:	$46,969,000	Net Worth:	$32,584,000	Debt/ Equity:	0.0759

GammaCan International Inc

39 Jerusalem St., Kiryat Ono, 55423; **PH:** 972-37382616; **Fax:** 972-36356015;
http:// gammacan.com; **Email:** Info@GammaCan.com

General - Incorporation	DE	Stock - Price on:12/24/2007	$0.46
Employees	NA	Stock Exchange	OTC
Auditor	Kesselman & Kesselman	Ticker Symbol	GCAN
Stk Agt	NA	Outstanding Shares	NA
Counsel	NA	E.P.S.	NA
DUNS No.	NA	Shareholders	NA

Business: The groups principal activities include developing and commercializing therapies to treat cancer and other disease. The product of the group is intravenous immunoglobulin. The group operates from the Israel and the United States.
Primary SIC and add'l.: 2836
CIK No: 0001141222
Subsidiaries: ARP Biomed, Ltd., GammaCan, Ltd
Officers: Patrick Schnegelsberg/CEO/$593,641.00, Steven Katz/Chmn., Pres., Yonit Bomstein/VP - Research, Development, Jacob Nusbacher/Dir. - Medical, Scientific Affairs, Liat Ben David/Dir. - Clinical Affairs, Vered Caplan/VP - Corporate Development/$111,609.00, Yehuda Shoenfeld/Chief Scientist, Chaime Orlev/CFO/$270,930.00
Directors: Steven Katz/Chmn., Pres., Yair Aloni/Dir., Shmuel Levi/Dir., Josef Neuhaus/Dir., Albert Passner/Dir., David Sidransky/Member - Advisory Board, Richard Spritz/Member - Advisory Board, Yosef Yarden/Member - Advisory Board, Lynn M. Schuchter/Member - Advisory Board, Pearl E. Grimes/Member - Advisory Board
Owners: MM&B Holdings/11.20%, Josef Neuhaus, Andrew Lessman/15.70%, Insiders/12.10%, Yair Aloni, Jonathan Glaser/12.50%, Patrick Schnegelsberg, Zeev Bronfeld/8.70%, Chaime Orlev, Vered Caplan/8.70%, Yehuda Shoenfeld/1.60%, Shmuel Levi
Financial Data: Fiscal Year End:09/30   Latest Annual Data: 9/30/2006

Year	Sales	Net Income
2006	NA	-$2,065,000
2005	NA	-$1,199,000
2004	NA	-$498,000

Curr. Assets:	$551,000	Curr. Liab.:	$329,000		
Plant, Equip.:	$25,000	Total Liab.:	$361,000	Indic. Yr. Divd.:	NA
Total Assets:	$620,000	Net Worth:	$259,000	Debt/ Equity:	NA

Gammon Gold Inc

Formerly: Gammon Lake Resources Inc
PO Box 2067, 1601 Lower Water St., Ste.402, Summit Pl., Halifax, NS, B3J 2Z1; ;
http:// www.gammonlake.com

General - Incorporation	QC	**Stock**- Price on:12/24/2007	$13.13
Employees	NA	Stock Exchange	AMEX
Auditor	KPMG LLP	Ticker Symbol	GRS
Stk Agt	Computershare Investor Services LLC	Outstanding Shares	105,090,000
Counsel	NA	E.P.S	-$0.76
DUNS No.	NA	Shareholders	NA

Business: The groups principle activities include exploring and developing gold and silver properties. The group operates from the Mexico. The group's quarterly revenue for September 2007 was 0.08 millions of USD.

Primary SIC and add'l.: 1081

CIK No: 0001078217

Officers: Russell Barwick/Dir., CEO, Fred George/Chmn., Pres., Luis Chavez/Dir., Corp. Dir. - Mexican Operations, Glenn Hynes/CFO, Exec. VP, Dave Keough/COO, Exec. VP

Directors: Russell Barwick/Dir., CEO, Fred George/Chmn., Pres., Luis Chavez/Dir., Corp. Dir. - Mexican Operations, Dale Hendrick/Dir., Kent L. Noseworthy/Dir., Frank Conte/Dir., Canek Rangel/Dir.

Financial Data: *Fiscal Year End:*12/31 *Latest Annual Data:* 12/31/2006

Year	*Sales*	*Net Income*
2006	NA	NA
2005	$1,164,000	-$26,896,000

Curr. Assets:	$34,372,000	*Curr. Liab.:*	$2,951,000		
Plant, Equip.:	$68,312,000	*Total Liab.:*	$10,965,000	*Indic. Yr. Divd.:*	NA
Total Assets:	$118,677,000	*Net Worth:*	$107,712,000	*Debt/ Equity:*	NA

Gander Mountain Co

180 E 5th St., Ste. 1300, St. Paul, MN, 55101; ***PH:*** 1-651-325-4300; ***Fax:*** 1-651-325-2003; ***http://*** www.gandermountain.com; ***Email:*** investorrelations@gandermountain.com

General - Incorporation	MN	**Stock**- Price on:12/24/2007	$12.25
Employees	2,400	Stock Exchange	NDQ
Auditor	Ernst & Young LLP	Ticker Symbol	GMTN
Stk Agt	Wells Fargo Bank, N.A.	Outstanding Shares	20,280,000
Counsel	NA	E.P.S	-$0.79
DUNS No.	NA	Shareholders	NA

Business: The group's principal activity is the retail sale of hunting, fishing and family camping equipment and accessories. The group's retail stores sell national, regional and owned brand outdoor equipment, accessories, related technical apparel and footwear. Some of the national brands sold by the stores include browning, remington and winchester in hunting equipment; shimano, berkley, daiwa and mepps in fishing equipment and coleman, katadyn, eureka and kelty in outdoor camping accessories. At 31-Jan-2004, the group owned and operated 66 stores in Wisconsin, Minnesota, Michigan, Illinois, Indiana, Ohio, New York, Pennsylvania and Iowa.

Primary SIC and add'l.: 5941

CIK No: 0001277475

Officers: Mark R. Baker/Dir., CEO, Pres., Eric R. Jacobsen/Sr. VP, General Counsel, Sec., Richard J. Vazquez/Exec. VP - Merchandising, Marketing, Dennis M. Lindahl/Exec. VP, Treasurer, Andrew P. Carlin/Sr. VP - Store Operations, Robert J. Vold/CFO, Sr. VP, Treasurer, Joann B. Boldt/Sr. VP - Human Resources

Directors: Mark R. Baker/Dir., CEO, Pres., Ronald A. Erickson/Vice Chmn., David C. /Chmn., Gerald A. Erickson/Dir., Karen M. Bohn/Dir., Marshall L. Day/Dir., Richard C. Dell/Dir.

Owners: David C. Pratt, Robert J. Vold, Insiders, Charles E. Pihl, Richard C. Dell, Gratco, LLC, Richard J. Vazquez, Ronald A. Erickson, Karen M. Bohn, Brian A. Erickson, Neal D. Erickson, Richard D. Erickson, Sharon K. Link, Mark R. Baker, David C. Pratt *(20 Owners included in Index)*

Financial Data: *Fiscal Year End:*01/28 *Latest Annual Data:* 2/3/2007

Year	*Sales*	*Net Income*
2007	$911,438,000	-$13,242,000
2006	$804,474,000	-$13,307,000
2005	$642,140,000	$1,570,000

Curr. Assets:	$371,480,000	*Curr. Liab.:*	$281,062,000		
Plant, Equip.:	$144,439,000	*Total Liab.:*	$324,826,000	*Indic. Yr. Divd.:*	NA
Total Assets:	$521,617,000	*Net Worth:*	$196,791,000	*Debt/ Equity:*	0.0950

Gannett Co Inc

7950 Jones Branch Dr., McLean, VA, 22107; ***PH:*** 1-703-854-6000; ***Fax:*** 1-703-854-2046; ***http://*** www.gannett.com

General - Incorporation	DE	**Stock**- Price on:12/24/2007	$55.02
Employees	49,675	Stock Exchange	NYSE
Auditor	Ernst & Young LLP	Ticker Symbol	GCI
Stk Agt	Wells Fargo Bank, N.A.	Outstanding Shares	234,670,000
Counsel	NA	E.P.S	$4.97
DUNS No.	00-220-5698	Shareholders	NA

Business: The groups principle activity is to publish newspapers and operating broadcasting stations. The group operates through two segments namely newspaper publishing and broadcasting. The group operates from United States, United Kingdom, Europe and Asia.

Primary SIC and add'l.: 2711 2721 7319 4833

CIK No: 0000039899

Subsidiaries: 101, INC., Action Advertising, Inc., Alexandria Newspapers, Inc., Arkansas Television Company, Baxter County Newspapers, Inc., California Newspapers, Inc., Cape Publications, Inc., CARANTIN& CO., INC., Central Newspapers, Inc., CHILDRENS EDITION, INC., Citizen Publishing Company, Combined Communications Corporation Of Oklahoma, Inc., Des Moines Press Citizen LLC, Des Moines Register And Tribune Company, Detroit Free Press, Inc. 80 Subsidiaries included in the Index

Officers: Paul Davidson/Chmn., CEO - Newsquest plc, Craig A. Dubow/53/Chmn., CEO, Pres./$8,150,444.00, George R. Gavagan/VP, Controller, Jane Ann Wimbush/VP - Internal Audit, Dave Lougee/Pres. - Gannett Broadcasting, Todd A. Mayman/VP, Assoc. General Counsel, Sec., Chief Governance Officer, Roxanne V. Horning/Sr. VP - Gannett Human Resources, Barbara W. Wall/VP, Assoc. General Counsel, Craig A. Moon/Pres. - Publisher, USA Today/$2,063,469.00, Roger L. Ogden/62/Sr. VP - Design, Innovation, Strategy/$2,408,456.00, John A. Williams/Pres. - Gannett Digital, Kurt Wimmer/Sr. VP, General Counsel, Philip R. Currie/Sr. VP - News, Newspaper Division, Lynn Beall/Exec. VP - Gannett Broadcasting, Karen R. Moreno/Pres. - Gannett Supply *(23 Officers included in Index)*

Directors: Paul Davidson/Chmn., CEO - Newsquest plc, Craig A. Dubow/53/Chmn., CEO, Pres., Neal Shapiro/50/Dir., Marjorie Magner/58/Dir., Charles B. Fruit/61/Dir., John Jeffry Louis/45/Dir., Duncan M. McFarland/64/Dir., Donna E. Shalala/67/Dir., Karen Hastie Williams/63/Dir., Arthur H. Harper/52/Dir.

Owners: Roger L. Ogden, Arthur H. Harper, John Jeffry Louis, Louis D. Boccardi, Karen Hastie Williams, Marjorie Magner, Thomas L. Chapple, Duncan M. McFarland, Douglas H. McCorkindale/1.20%, Gracia C. Martore, Donna E. Shalala, Brandes Investment Partners, L.P./6.60%, Susan Clark-Johnson, Craig A. Dubow, Insiders/2.20% *(16 Owners included in Index)*

Financial Data: *Fiscal Year End:*12/25 *Latest Annual Data:* 12/31/2006

Year	*Sales*	*Net Income*
2006	$8,033,354,000	$1,160,782,000
2005	$7,598,939,000	$1,244,654,000
2004	$7,381,283,000	$1,317,186,000

Curr. Assets:	$1,532,019,000	*Curr. Liab.:*	$1,116,948,000	*P/E Ratio:*	11.41
Plant, Equip.:	$2,775,422,000	*Total Liab.:*	$7,817,230,000	*Indic. Yr. Divd.:*	$1.600
Total Assets:	$16,223,804,000	*Net Worth:*	$8,382,263,000	*Debt/ Equity:*	0.6215

Gap Inc

2 Folsom St., San Francisco, CA, 94105; ***PH:*** 1-650-952-4400; ***Fax:*** 1-415-427-2553; ***http://*** www.gap.com; ***Email:*** businessdirect@gapinc.com

General - Incorporation	DE	**Stock**- Price on:12/24/2007	$19.46
Employees	154,000	Stock Exchange	NYSE
Auditor	Deloitte & Touche LLP	Ticker Symbol	GPS
Stk Agt	Wells Fargo Shareowner Services	Outstanding Shares	815,930,000
Counsel	NA	E.P.S	$0.87
DUNS No.	04-862-6915	Shareholders	NA

Business: The groups principle activity is to provide retail food services. The groups products include bakery, delicatessen, pharmacy, floral, fresh fish and cheese. In the year 2007, the group acquired Pathmark Stores, Inc. The group operates from United States.

Primary SIC and add'l.: 5651 5641 5611 5621 5632

CIK No: 0000039911

Subsidiaries: Banana Republic (Apparel), LLC, Banana Republic (East) L.P., Banana Republic (Holdings), LLC, Banana Republic (ITM) Inc., Banana Republic (Japan) Y.K., Banana Republic, LLC, Direct Consumer Services, LLC, F&T Services LLC, Forth& Towne (Apparel) LLC, Forth& Towne (ITM) Inc., Forth& Towne LLC, Gap (Apparel), LLC, Gap (Canada) Inc., Gap (France) S.A.S., Gap (ITM) Inc. 61 Subsidiaries included in the Index

Officers: Glenn K. Murphy/46/Chmn., CEO, Jack Calhoun/Pres. - Banana Republic, Stephen Sunnucks/Pres. - Europe, Dawn Robertson/Pres. - Old Navy/$903,796.00, Sabrina Simmons/Exec. VP - Finance, Acting CFO, Toby Lenk/Pres. - Gap Inc Direct, Eva Sage-Gavin/Exec. VP - Human Resources, Corporate Communications/$1,057,841.00, Michael B. Tasooji/CIO, Exec. VP, Art Peck/Exec. VP - Strategy, Operations, Marka Hansen/Pres. - Gap Brand/$2,549,193.00, Lauri M. Shanahan/Chief Legal, Administrative Officer, Corp. Sec.

Directors: Glenn K. Murphy/46/Chmn., CEO, Bob L. Martin/59/Dir., Domenico De Sole/64/Dir., Jorge P. Montoya/61/Dir., Kneeland C. Youngblood/52/Dir., Penelope L. Hughes/48/Dir., Donald G. Fisher/79/Dir., Adrian D.P. Bellamy/66/Dir., Howard P. Behar/63/Dir., Mayo A. Shattuck/53/Dir., Robert J. Fisher/53/Dir., Doris F. Fisher/76/Dir., James M. Schneider/55/Dir.

Owners: Byron H. Pollitt, Doris F. Fisher/8.10%, Jenny J. Ming, Fisher Core Holdings L.P./12.40%, Eva M. Sage-Gavin, James M. Schneider, Adrian D. P. Bellamy, Paul S. Pressler, Jorge P. Montoya, Bob L. Martin, Mayo A. Shattuck, Marka V. Hansen, Penelope L. Hughes, William S. Fisher/17.60%, Robert J. Fisher/17.90% *(22 Owners included in Index)*

Financial Data: *Fiscal Year End:*01/28 *Latest Annual Data:* 2/3/2007

Year	*Sales*	*Net Income*
2007	$15,943,000,000	$778,000,000
2006	$16,023,000,000	$1,113,000,000
2005	$16,267,000,000	$1,150,000,000

Curr. Assets:	$5,029,000,000	*Curr. Liab.:*	$2,272,000,000	*P/E Ratio:*	22.37
Plant, Equip.:	$3,197,000,000	*Total Liab.:*	$3,370,000,000	*Indic. Yr. Divd.:*	$0.320
Total Assets:	$8,544,000,000	*Net Worth:*	$5,174,000,000	*Debt/ Equity:*	0.0352

Garb Oil & Power Corp

1588 S Main St., Ste 200, Second Fl., Salt Lake City, UT, 84115; ***PH:*** 1-800-832-9865; ***Fax:*** 1-800-832-9867; ***http://*** www.garb-oil.com; ***Email:*** sales@garb-oil.com

General - Incorporation	UT	**Stock**- Price on:12/24/2007	$0.03
Employees	NA	Stock Exchange	NA
Auditor	HJ & Assoc. LLC	Ticker Symbol	NA
Stk Agt	Atlas Stock Transfer Corp	Outstanding Shares	22,870,000
Counsel	NA	E.P.S	-$0.02
DUNS No.	00-648-5627	Shareholders	NA

Business: The group's principal activities are to purchase property and develop technology related to the production of electricity by burning used rubber and pyrolysis. The group develops processes to recover crumb rubber or other recyclable rubber, oil by-products, commercially marketable char and steel from scrap tires. The group also repairs truck tires of all sizes and markets processes which utilize scrap tires and municipal waste to generate steam for the production of electricity. The group is a development stage company.

Primary SIC and add'l.: 4911 7534

CIK No: 0000798371

Subsidiaries: Garbalizer Corporation of America, Rialto Power Corporation, Utah Truck Tire, Inc

Owners: Garbalizer Corporation/42.70%, Ralph C. Alexander/4.10%, LTD II Enterprises/4.40%, Insiders/46.30%, Commodities Trading Corporation/2.20%, Bill Anderson/1.30%, A/S Parkveien 55/4.60%

Financial Data: *Fiscal Year End:*06/30 *Latest Annual Data:* 6/30/2006

Year	*Sales*	*Net Income*
2006	$318,000	-$576,000
2005	$591,000	-$34,000
2004	$150,000	-$196,000

Curr. Assets:	$21,000	*Curr. Liab.:*	$2,095,000		
Plant, Equip.:	$1,000	*Total Liab.:*	$2,095,000	*Indic. Yr. Divd.:*	NA
Total Assets:	$22,000	*Net Worth:*	-$2,073,000	*Debt/ Equity:*	NA

Gardant Pharmaceuticals Inc

Formerly: Bioaccelerate Holdings Inc
712 Fifth Ave., 19th Fl., New York, NY, 10019; *PH:* 1-212-897-6849; *http://* www.bioaccelerate.com

General - Incorporation	NV	**Stock**- Price on:12/24/2007	$0.05
Employees	NA	Stock Exchange	NA
Auditor	Stark Winter Schenkein & Co. LLP	Ticker Symbol	NA
Stk Agt	Interwest Transfer Company, Inc.	Outstanding Shares	NA
Counsel	NA	E.P.S.	NA
DUNS No.	NA	Shareholders	NA

Business: The group's principle activity is to seek new business opportunities and investigate potential acquisitions. The group is a development stage company. The group designed and manufactured mobile kiosks for use as drive-through beverage units and intended to distribute or lease the kiosks to third parties that are engaged or plan to engage in the drive-through sale of coffee, espresso, juice, or other beverages. On 23-Sep-2004, the group acquired bioaccelerate inc. The group operates from United States.

Primary SIC and add'l.: 9999

CIK No: 0001119700

Subsidiaries: Cengent

Financial Data: *Fiscal Year End:*12/31 *Latest Annual Data:* 12/31/2004

Year	Sales	Net Income
2004	NA	-$157,147,000
2003	NA	-$7,000
2002	NA	-$26,000

Curr. Assets:	$1,423,000	**Curr. Liab.:**	$10,887,000		
Plant, Equip.:	$1,092,000	**Total Liab.:**	$17,168,000	**Indic. Yr. Divd.:**	NA
Total Assets:	$5,465,000	**Net Worth:**	-$11,703,000	**Debt/ Equity:**	NA

Gardner Denver Inc

1800 Gardner Expwy., Quincy, IL, 62305; *PH:* 1-217-222-5400; *Fax:* 1-217-228-8243; *http://* www.gardnerdenver.com

General - Incorporation	DE	**Stock**- Price on:12/24/2007	$43.75
Employees	6,000	Stock Exchange	NYSE
Auditor	KPMG LLP	Ticker Symbol	GDI
Stk Agt	National City Bank	Outstanding Shares	52,880,000
Counsel	NA	E.P.S.	$3.31
DUNS No.	82-644-8615	Shareholders	NA

Business: The groups principle activity is to provide compressed air and gas, vacuum and fluid transfer technology. The groups products include pumps and compressors, gasoline vapor and refrigeration recovery, printing, packaging and laboratory equipment. The group operates from United States.

Primary SIC and add'l.: 3564 3563 3561

CIK No: 0000916459

Subsidiaries: Air-Relief, Inc., Allen-Stuart Equipment Company, Inc. , Bellis& Morcom Limited, Belliss& Morcom Brasil Ltda., Bottarini S.p.A., Da More, Inc., Emco Wheaton Corp., Emco Wheaton GmbH, Emco Wheaton U.K. Ltd., Emco Wheaton USA, Inc., Gardner Denver (Deutschland) GmbH, Gardner Denver Australia Pty Ltd., Gardner Denver Belgium NV, Gardner Denver Drum Ltd., Gardner Denver Elmo France SARL 98 Subsidiaries included in the Index

Officers: Ross J. Centanni/Chmn., CEO, Pres./$5,129,122.00, Tracy D. Pagliara/VP - Administration, General Counsel, Sec./$1,138,814.00, Helen W. Cornell/CFO, VP - Finance/$1,223,473.00, Dennis J. Shull/VP, GM - Gardner Denver Compressor Division/$1,162,975.00, Richard C. Steber/VP, GM - Gardner Denver Engineered Products Division/$1,028,681.00, David J. Antoniuk/VP, Corporate Controller, Winfried Kaiser/VP, GM - Gardner Denver Blower Division, James J. Kregel/VP, GM - Gardner Denver Thomas Products Division, Duane T. Morgan/VP, GM - Gardner Denver Fluid Transfer Division

Directors: Ross J. Centanni/Chmn., CEO, Pres., David D. Petratis/Dir., Frank J. Hansen/Dir., Diane K. Schumacher/Dir., Donald G. Barger/Dir., Thomas M. McKenna/Dir., Raymond R. Hipp/Dir., Richard L. Thompson/Dir., Charles L. Szews/Dir.

Owners: Raymond R. Hipp, Ross J. Centanni/2.20%, David D. Petratis, Helen W. Cornell, Richard C. Steber, Frank J. Hansen, Tracy D. Pagliara, Donald G. Barger, Dennis J. Shull, Insiders/3.70%, Richard L. Thompson, Diane K. Schumacher

Financial Data: *Fiscal Year End:*12/31 *Latest Annual Data:* 12/31/2006

Year	Sales	Net Income
2006	$1,669,176,000	$132,908,000
2005	$1,214,552,000	$66,951,000
2004	$739,539,000	$37,123,000

Curr. Assets:	$579,718,000	**Curr. Liab.:**	$326,344,000	**P/E Ratio:**	14.98
Plant, Equip.:	$276,493,000	**Total Liab.:**	$897,701,000	**Indic. Yr. Divd.:**	NA
Total Assets:	$1,750,231,000	**Net Worth:**	$852,530,000	**Debt/ Equity:**	0.4009

Garmin Ltd

1200 E 151st St., Olathe, KS, 66062; *PH:* 1-913-397-8200; *Fax:* 1-913-397-8282; *http://* www.garmin.com; *Email:* investor.relations@garmin.com

General - Incorporation	Cayman Islands	**Stock**- Price on:12/24/2007	$69.989
Employees	4,751	Stock Exchange	NDQ
Auditor	Ernst & Young LLP	Ticker Symbol	GRMN
Stk Agt.	UMB Bank, N.A.	Outstanding Shares	216,300,000
Counsel	NA	E.P.S.	$3.00
DUNS No.	NA	Shareholders	NA

Business: The group's principal activity is to design, develop, manufacture and market navigation, communications and information devices. The group operates under two business segments: consumer products and aviation products. Consumer products include portable global positioning system (gps) receivers and accessories for marine, recreation, land and automotive use sold primarily to retail outlets. Aviation products include portable and panel mount avionics for visual flight rules and instrument flight rules navigation. Aviation products are sold primarily to retail outlets and certain aircraft manufacturers. The products of the group are sold under the brand name, garmin. The group has operations in North America, Asia and Europe. The group acquired ups aviation technologies on 22-Aug-2003.

Primary SIC and add'l.: 3812

CIK No: 0001121788

Subsidiaries: Everest Indemnity Insurance Company, Everest Insurance Company of Canada, Everest National Insurance Company, Everest Re Holdings, Ltd., Everest Reinsurance Company, Everest Reinsurance Holdings, Inc., Everest Security Insurance Company, Mt. McKinley Managers, LLC

Officers: Min Kao/Chmn., CEO/$371,711.00, Clifton A. Pemble/Dir., VP - Engineering/$581,181.00, Gary Kelley/VP - Marketing, Andrew Etkind/VP, General Counsel, Sec./$504,854.00, Kevin Rauckman/CFO, Treasurer/$478,583.00, Brian J. Pokorny/VP - Operations/$468,165.00, Ted Gartner/Sr. Media Relations Specialist - Garmin, Jessica Myers/Sr. Media Relations Specialist, Ed Link/VP - Information Technology, Laurie Minard/VP - Human Resources, Jon Cassat/VP - Communications, Dan Bartel/VP - Worldwide Sales, MD - Garmin Europe

Directors: Min Kao/Chmn., CEO, Gary Burrell/Chmn. Emeritus, Donald H. Eller/Dir., Thomas A. McDonnell/Dir., Gene M. Betts/Dir., Clifton A. Pemble/Dir., VP - Engineering, Charles W. Peffer/Dir.

Owners: Gary L. Burrell/13.80%, Insiders/46.70%, Min H. Kao/20.90%, Ruey-Jeng Kao/6.00%, Donald H. Eller, Thomas A. McDonnell, Clifton A. Pemble, Gene M. Betts, Kevin Rauckman, Andrew R. Etkind, Brian J. Pokorny, Charles W. Peffer

Financial Data: *Fiscal Year End:*12/25 *Latest Annual Data:* 12/30/2006

Year	Sales	Net Income
2006	$1,774,000,000	$514,123,000
2005	$1,027,773,000	$311,219,000
2004	$762,549,000	$205,700,000

Curr. Assets:	$801,167,000	**Curr. Liab.:**	$195,485,000	**P/E Ratio:**	27.05
Plant, Equip.:	$179,173,000	**Total Liab.:**	$204,971,000	**Indic. Yr. Divd.:**	$0.750
Total Assets:	$1,362,235,000	**Net Worth:**	$1,157,264,000	**Debt/ Equity:**	0.0001

Gartner Inc

56 Top Gallant Rd., Stamford, CT, 06902; *PH:* 1-203-964-0096; *Fax:* 1-866-618-0806; *http://* www.gartner.com

General - Incorporation	DE	**Stock**- Price on:12/24/2007	$24.57
Employees	3,784	Stock Exchange	NYSE
Auditor	KPMG LLP	Ticker Symbol	IT
Stk Agt	American Stock Transfer & Trust Co.	Outstanding Shares	104,040,000
Counsel	Wilson Sonsini Goodrich & Rosati	E.P.S.	$0.48
DUNS No.	09-722-0180	Shareholders	NA

Business: The group's principal activity is to provide research and analysis on information technology, computer hardware, software, communications and related technology industries. It operates through three business segments: research, consulting and events. The research segment reviews new products and technologies, provides quantitative market research and analyzes industry trends. The consulting segment includes consulting, measurement engagements and strategic advisory services, which provide comprehensive assessments of cost performance, efficiency and quality for all areas of information technology. The events consists of symposia, conferences and exhibitions focused on the information technology industry. The group provides comprehensive coverage of the it industry to approximately 10,000 client organizations.

Primary SIC and add'l.: 7389 8733 7379 8742

CIK No: 0000749251

Subsidiaries: 1422722 Ontario Inc., ATEM Netherlands ApS, Computer & Communications Information Group, Inc.(dba Datapro Information Services), Computer Consultancy Group (Management) Limited, Computer Financial Consultants (Management) Limited, Computer Financial Consultants, Inc., Computer Financial Consultants, Limited, Dataquest Australia Pty. Ltd., Dataquest, Inc., Decision Drivers, Inc., G.G. Canada, Inc., G.G. Credit, Inc., G.G. Properties, Ltd., G.G. West Corporation, Garter Group Taiwan 79 Subsidiaries included in the Index

Officers: Gene Hall/Dir., CEO, Marizete Ferreira/Regional Operations Specialist - Brazil, Darko Hrelic/CIO, Sr. VP, Carina Forsling/Public Relations Mgr. - EMEA, Laurence Goasduff/Public Relations Mgr. - EMEA, Hanne Main/VP - Public Relations, Susan Moore/Mgr. - Australia, New Zealand, Takako Imaizumi/Public Relations Specialist - Japan, Andrew Spender/VP - Corporate Communications, Chris Lafond/CFO, Exec. VP/$1,572,888.00, Robin Kranich/Sr. VP - End User Programs, Peter Sondergaard/Sr. VP - Research/$1,173,662.00, Joseph T. Waters/49/Sr. VP, Chief Marketing Officer, Lew Schwartz/Sr. VP, General Counsel, Corp. Sec./$1,143,433.00, Alister Christopher/Sr. VP - Worldwide Events (25 Officers included in Index)

Directors: Gene Hall/Dir., CEO, James C. Smith/Chmn., Jeffrey Ubben/Dir., Maynard G. Webb/Dir., Michael J. Bingle/Dir., John R. Joyce/Dir., Anne Sutherland Fuchs/Dir., Richard J. Bressler/49/Dir., Russell P. Fradin/52/Dir., Max D. Hopper/Dir., Stephen G. Pagliuca/Dir., William O. Grabe/Dir.

Owners: Anne Sutherland Fuchs, Jeffrey W. Ubben/19.80%, Max D. Hopper, Peter Sondergaard, Robert C. Patton, Lewis G. Schwartz, Richard J. Bresser, Silver Lake Partners, L.P. and affiliates/12.70%, Stephen G. Pagliuca, Michael J. Bingle/12.70%, William O. Grabe, James C. Smith, Eugene A. Hall/1.00%, Christopher Lafond, John R. Joyce/12.70% (18 Owners included in Index)

Financial Data: *Fiscal Year End:*12/31 *Latest Annual Data:* 12/31/2006

Year	Sales	Net Income
2006	$1,060,321,000	$58,192,000
2005	$989,004,000	-$2,437,000
2004	$893,821,000	$16,889,000

Curr. Assets:	$484,033,000	**Curr. Liab.:**	$803,883,000	**P/E Ratio:**	51.19
Plant, Equip.:	$59,715,000	**Total Liab.:**	$1,013,475,000	**Indic. Yr. Divd.:**	NA
Total Assets:	$1,039,793,000	**Net Worth:**	$26,318,000	**Debt/ Equity:**	4.8266

Garuda Capital Corp

1576 Rand Ave., Vancouver, BC, V6P 3G2; *PH:* 1-604-266-9539; *http://* www.garudacapital.com; *Email:* info@garudacapital.com

General - Incorporation	NV	**Stock**- Price on:12/24/2007	NA
Employees	NA	Stock Exchange	OTC
Auditor	Ernst & Young LLP	Ticker Symbol	GRUA
Stk Agt	Pacific Stock Transfer Company	Outstanding Shares	NA
Counsel	NA	E.P.S.	NA
DUNS No.	NA	Shareholders	NA

Business: The group's principal activities are to process and market specialty food products and herbal medication to wholesale and retail customers. The group operates through its subsidiaries, garuda ventures Canada inc., garuda gold corp., hagensborg foods ltd., hagensborg seafoods ltd., natural program inc. And natural program ltd. The group manufactures and markets gourmet chocolates and other gourmet products. The seafood products include smoked salmon, shrimp, rainbow trout with dill, crab and lobster. The group also develops and markets Chinese herbs and herbal remedies for common health problems.
Primary SIC and add'l.: 2834 2066 2091
CIK No: 0001116539
Subsidiaries: Garuda Exploration Inc., Garuda Gold Corporation, Garuda Minerals Inc, Hagensborg Foods Ltd, Hagensborg Seafoods Ltd, Natural Program Inc, Natural Program Ltd
Officers: Robin C. Relph/Dir., CEO, Pres.
Directors: Robin C. Relph/Dir., CEO, Pres., Juergen Wolf/Dir.
Owners: Insiders/24.10%, Robin C. Relph/21.40%, Jurgen Wolf/3.30%
Financial Data: *Fiscal Year End:*06/30 *Latest Annual Data:* 06/30/2006

Year	Sales	Net Income
2006	$769,000	-$2,052,000
2005	$702,000	-$1,968,000
2004	$1,236,000	-$845,000

Curr. Assets:	$420,000	**Curr. Liab.:**	$806,000		
Plant, Equip.:	$246,000	**Total Liab.:**	$821,000	**Indic. Yr. Divd.:**	NA
Total Assets:	$666,000	**Net Worth:**	-$155,000	**Debt/ Equity:**	NA

Gas Transporter of the South Inc

Don Bosco 3672, 5th Fl., Buenos Aires; *PH:* 54-1148659050; *http://* www.tgs.com.ar

General - Incorporation	AR	**Stock**- Price on:12/24/2007	NA
Employees	NA	Stock Exchange	NYSE
Auditor	Price Waterhouse & Co. S.R.L.	Ticker Symbol	NA
Stk Agt	CT Corporation	Outstanding Shares	NA
Counsel	NA	E.P.S	NA
DUNS No.	NA	Shareholders	NA

Business: The group's principal activities are the transportation of gas, production and distribution of lgn, and the provision of midstream services. Midstream services offers integral solutions on the natural gas materials from the mouth of the well to the transportation systems and consist of the preparation and compression of gas and services related to the construction, operation and maintenance of gas pipelines and treatment and compression plant for natural gas. In addition, the group also provides telecommunication services. The group operates in Argentina.
Primary SIC and add'l.: 4925 4924 4922
CIK No: 0000931427
Subsidiaries: Telcosur
Officers: Jorge Casagrande/CEO, Pablo Ferrero/CEO, Gonzalo Castro Olivera/Mgr. - Finance, IR, Mario Yaniskowski/Contact - Media Relation, Francisco Vila/Investor Relations Officer, Carlos Ariosa/Legal Affairs VP, Juan Martin Encina/VP - Human Resources, Jorge Garcia/Marketing VP, Eduardo Pawluszek/CFO, Daniel Perrone/Regulatory, Institutional Affairs VP, Alejandro Basso/Planning, Control VP, Oscar Sardi/Services VP, Jorge Bonetto/Operations VP
Directors: Joao Ferreira Bezerra De Souza/Chmn., Mariano Pablo Gonzalez/Vice Chmn., Rigoberto Mejia/Dir., Luis Blaquier/Dir., Gabriel Marchione/Alternate Dir., Diego Alberto Guerri/Dir., Hugo Guardia/Alternate Dir., Joaquin Acuna/Alternate Dir., Andrea Patricia Gribov/Alternate Dir., Carolina Sigwald/Dir., Carlos Alberto Seijo/Dir., Gustavo Sebastian Viramonte/Dir., Diego Petrecolla/Alternate Dir., Esteban Diez Pena/Alternate Dir., Oscar Marano/Dir.
(18 Directors included in Index)
Owners: D. E. Shaw/8.42%, CIESA/51.00%, CIESA/4.30%

Gasco Energy Inc

8 Inverness Dr. E, Ste. 100, Englewood, CO, 80112; *PH:* 1-303-483-0044; *Fax:* 1-303-483-0011; *http://* www.gascoenergy.com

General - Incorporation	NV	**Stock**- Price on:12/24/2007	$2.7
Employees	21	Stock Exchange	AMEX
Auditor	Hein & Assoc. LLP	Ticker Symbol	GSX
Stk Agt	Computershare Trust Co	Outstanding Shares	96,100,000
Counsel	NA	E.P.S	-$0.65
DUNS No.	NA	Shareholders	NA

Business: The group's principal activity is the exploration, development, acquisition and production of crude oil and natural gas in the western United States. The group is a natural gas and petroleum exploitation and development company engaged in locating and developing hydrocarbon prospects, primarily in the rocky mountain region. The group's principal business is the acquisition of leasehold interests in petroleum and natural gas rights, either directly or indirectly, and the exploitation and development of properties subject to these leases. The principal markets for these commodities are natural gas transmission pipeline companies, utilities, refining companies and private industry end-users.
Primary SIC and add'l.: 1311 1382
CIK No: 0001086319
Subsidiaries: Gasco Production Company, Myton Oilfield Rentals, LLC, Riverbend Gas Gathering, LLC, San Joaquin Oil & Gas, Ltd
Officers: Mark A. Erickson/Dir., CEO, Pres./$835,935.00, Robin Dean/Geological Mgr./$330,902.00, Shawn C. Elworthy/Field Superintendent, John D. Longwell/VP, Operations Mgr./$398,786.00, Suzie Wright/Mgr. - Corporate Administration, Michael K. Decker/COO, Exec. VP/$817,830.00, Peggy Herald/VP - Accounting, Administration, Chief Accounting Officer, King W. Grant/Exec. VP, CFO, Corp. Sec./$781,670.00, Charles H. Wilson/Drilling Mgr., David R. Smith/Land Mgr., Keith Doss/Controller
Directors: Mark A. Erickson/Dir., CEO, Pres., Charles B. Crowell/Vice Chmn., Marc A. Bruner/Chmn., Carmen J. Lotito/Dir., Richard J. Burgess/Dir., John A. Schmit/Dir., Richard S. Langdon/Dir., Carl Stadelhofer/Dir.
Owners: Gregory M. Pek/1.98%, Ian Robinson/1.25%, Richard N. Jeffs/17.26%, Gasco Energy, Inc./25.05%, Insiders/25.05%, Eugene Sweeney/2.47%, Shawne Malone/0.84%, Michael L. Nazmack/1.25%
Financial Data: *Fiscal Year End:*12/31 *Latest Annual Data:* 12/31/2006

Year	Sales	Net Income
2006	$25,675,000	-$55,818,000
2005	$16,863,000	-$38,000
2004	$3,592,000	-$4,206,000

Curr. Assets:	$33,431,000	**Curr. Liab.:**	$22,301,000		
Plant, Equip.:	$129,652,000	**Total Liab.:**	$88,283,000	**Indic. Yr. Divd.:**	NA
Total Assets:	$165,454,000	**Net Worth:**	$77,172,000	**Debt/ Equity:**	0.9877

Gastar Exploration Ltd

1331 Lamar St., Ste. 1080, Houston, TX, 77010; *PH:* 1-713-739-1800; *Fax:* 1-713-739-0458; *http://* www.gastar.com; *Email:* ir@gastar.com

General - Incorporation	AB	**Stock**- Price on:12/24/2007	$2.15
Employees	19	Stock Exchange	AMEX
Auditor	BDO Seidman, LLP	Ticker Symbol	GST
Stk Agt	Mellon Trust Co	Outstanding Shares	205,340,000
Counsel	NA	E.P.S	-$0.3
DUNS No.	NA	Shareholders	NA

Business: The groups principle activities include exploring, developing and producing natural gas and oil. The group operates from the United States, Canada and Australia. The groups quarterly revenue for September 2007 was 9.78 millions of USD.
Primary SIC and add'l.: 1311
CIK No: 0001170154
Subsidiaries: Gastar Exploration New South Wales, Inc., Gastar Exploration Texas LP, Gastar Exploration USA, Inc., Gastar Exploration Victoria, Inc.
Officers: Russell J. Porter/Chmn., CEO, Pres., Michael Gerlich/CFO, David R. Rhodes/VP - Completion, Production, Gene Beck/VP - Drilling, Henry J. Hansen/VP - Land, Sara-Lane Sirey/Corp. Sec., Jeffrey C. Pettit/VP, COO, Frederick E. Beck/48/VP - Drilling
Directors: Russell J. Porter/Chmn., CEO, Pres., Abby Badwi/Dir., Thomas Crow/Dir., Bob Penner/Dir., John M. Selser/Dir.
Owners: Michael A. Gerlich, Abby F. Badwi, Geostar Corporation/8.10%, Russell J. Porter/1.40%, Richard A. Kapuscinski, Palo Alto Investors, LLC/5.60%, Ospraie Management, LLC/6.30%, Chesapeake Energy Corporation/16.50%, Thomas L. Crow, Insiders/1.90%
Financial Data: *Fiscal Year End:*12/31 *Latest Annual Data:* 12/31/2006

Year	Sales	Net Income
2006	$26,765,000	-$84,839,000
2005	$27,442,000	-$25,692,000

Curr. Assets:	$54,482,000	**Curr. Liab.:**	$31,173,000		
Plant, Equip.:	$160,826,000	**Total Liab.:**	$129,800,000	**Indic. Yr. Divd.:**	NA
Total Assets:	$228,142,000	**Net Worth:**	$98,342,000	**Debt/ Equity:**	1.0602

Gatehouse Media Inc

350 Willowbrook Office Pk., Fairport, NY, 14450; *PH:* 1-585-598-0030; *Fax:* 1-585-248-2631; *http://* gatehousemedia.com

General - Incorporation	DE	**Stock**- Price on:12/24/2007	$18.93
Employees	4,000	Stock Exchange	NYSE
Auditor	KPMG LLP	Ticker Symbol	GHS
Stk Agt	Bank of New York	Outstanding Shares	39,140,000
Counsel	NA	E.P.S	-$0.22
DUNS No.	NA	Shareholders	NA

Business: The groups principle activity is to publish newspapers and online media. The groups products include 74 daily newspapers, 226 weekly newspapers, 113 shoppers and 230 locally focused websites. The group acquired two daily, three weekly newspapers and two shopper publications in the Northeast region in the year 2006 and one daily, 13 weekly, 10 shopper and one niche publication in the Atlantic region in the year 2007. The group operates from the United States. The group's quarterly revenue for September 2007 was 163.39 millions of USD.
Primary SIC and add'l.: 2711 8999
CIK No: 0001368900
Subsidiaries: ENHE Acquisition, LLC, Enterprise NewsMedia Holding, LLC, Enterprise NewsMedia, LLC, Enterprise Publishing Company, LLC, GateHouse Media Arizona Holdings, Inc., GateHouse Media Arkansas Holdings, Inc., GateHouse Media California Holdings, Inc., GateHouse Media Colorado Holdings, Inc., GateHouse Media Corning Holdings, Inc., GateHouse Media Directories Holdings, Inc., GateHouse Media Freeport Holdings, Inc., GateHouse Media Holdco Inc., GateHouse Media Illinois Holdings, Inc., GateHouse Media Iowa Holdings, Inc., GateHouse Media Kansas Holdings, Inc. 38 Subsidiaries included in the Index
Officers: Michael E. Reed/Dir., CEO, Mark R. Thompson/CFO, Paul Ameden/CIO, Bill Blevins/VP - Online Operations, Brad Dennison/VP - News Operations, Scott T. Champion/Co - Pres. - Co - COO Gatehouse Media Western Region, Randall W. Cope/Co - Pres. - Co - COO Gatehouse Southern Midwest Region, Kirk A. Davis/Pres. - Publisher, Gatehouse Media New England, Gene A. Hall/Exec. VP - Northern Midwest, Linda A. Hill/Corporate Controller, Amy V. Kahn/Dir. - Human Resources, Kelly M. Luvison/Exec. VP - Atlantic Region, Polly G. Sack/General Counsel, Caroll Stacklin/Dir. - Strategic Operations
Directors: Michael E. Reed/Dir., CEO, Wesley R. Edens/Chmn., Martin Bandier/Dir., Richard L. Friedman/Dir., Burl Osborne/Dir., Howard Rubin/Dir., Kevin M. Sheehan/Dir.
Owners: Insiders/42.80%, Fortress Investment Holdings LLC/40.30%, Howard Rubin, Randall W. Cope, Polly G. Sack, Scott T. Champion, Burl Osborne, Richard L. Friedman, GPS Partners LLC/4.20%, Martin Bandier, Wesley R. Edens/40.50%, Kevin M. Sheehan, Mark R. Thompson, Michael E. Reed
Financial Data: *Fiscal Year End:*12/31 *Latest Annual Data:* 12/31/2006

Year	Sales	Net Income
2006	$314,930,000	-$1,574,000

Curr. Assets:	$144,604,000	**Curr. Liab.:**	$50,615,000	**P/E Ratio:**	36.95
Plant, Equip.:	$100,694,000	**Total Liab.:**	$694,639,000	**Indic. Yr. Divd.:**	$1.600
Total Assets:	$1,167,723,000	**Net Worth:**	$473,084,000	**Debt/ Equity:**	1.1794

Gateway Energy Corp

500 Dallas St., Ste. 2615, Houston, TX, 77002; *PH:* 1-713-336-0844; *Fax:* 1-713-336-0855; *http://* www.gatewayenergy.com; *Email:* info@gatewayenergy.com

General - Incorporation	DE	**Stock**- Price on:12/24/2007	$0.94
Employees	14	Stock Exchange	OTC
Auditor	Pannell Kerr Forster Of Texas, P.C	Ticker Symbol	GNRG
Stk Agt	American Stock Transfer & Trust Co.	Outstanding Shares	17,140,000
Counsel	NA	E.P.S	$0.13
DUNS No.	80-868-5549	Shareholders	NA

Business: The group's principal activities are to own and operate natural gas gathering, transportation and distribution systems and related facilities in Texas and Oklahoma. In addition, it operates offshore in Texas and federal waters of the gulf of Mexico. The group's systems include approximately 769 miles of pipeline. The group gathers natural gas from producing properties owned by others and transports that gas to primary transmission pipelines. In some cases, it assumes the title and markets the natural gas directly to the end users such as agricultural, residential, industrial and commercial users, as well as to marketing companies. The group owns a license in the us for a patented process that removes nitrogen from streams of natural gas.

Primary SIC and add'l.: 4923

CIK No: 0000040194

Subsidiaries: Fort Cobb Fuel Authority, LLC, Gateway Energy Marketing Company, Gateway Pipeline Company, Gateway Processing Company, Gateway-ADAC Pipeline, LLC, GatewayOffshore Pipeline Company

Officers: Robert Panico/Dir., CEO, Pres./$171,537.00, Chris Rasmussen/CFO/$103,143.00, Craig Ramsey/Dir. - Business Development, Mark Brandon/Mgr. - Engineering, Operations

Directors: Robert Panico/Dir., CEO, Pres., Steven W. Cattron/Chmn., Darby J. Sere/Dir., Chauncey J. Gundelfinger/Dir., John A. Raasch/Dir., Steven C. Scheler/Dir., Gordon L. Wright/Dir.

Owners: Insiders/12.90%, Robert Panico/1.10%, Darby J. Sere, Gordon L. Wright, Steven C. Scheler/1.60%, John A. Raasch/7.00%, John A. Raasch/7.00%, Christopher M. Rasmussen, Chauncey J. Gundelfinger/2.80%, Steven W. Cattron

Financial Data: Fiscal Year End:12/31 Latest Annual Data: 12/31/2006

Year	Sales	Net Income
2006	$10,174,000	$305,000
2005	$10,510,000	$1,755,000
2004	$22,969,000	-$800,000

Curr. Assets:	$2,898,000	Curr. Liab.:	$1,525,000	P/E Ratio:	18.80
Plant, Equip.:	$5,946,000	Total Liab.:	$2,033,000	Indic. Yr. Divd.:	NA
Total Assets:	$8,976,000	Net Worth:	$6,104,000	Debt/ Equity:	0.0141

Gateway Financial Holdings Inc

1580 Laskin Rd., Virginia Beach, VA, 23451; **PH:** 1-757-422-4055; **Fax:** 1-757-422-4056; **http://** www.trustgateway.com

General - Incorporation	NC	**Stock** - Price on:12/24/2007	$14.74
Employees	327	Stock Exchange	NDQ
Auditor	Dixon Hughes PLLC	Ticker Symbol	GBTS
Stk Agt	Computershare Trust Co	Outstanding Shares	11,060,000
Counsel	NA	E.P.S.	$0.86
DUNS No.	NA	Shareholders	NA

Business: The group's principal activity is to provide commercial and retail banking and brokerage services. The services include checking and savings accounts, commercial, installment and personal loans, safe deposit boxes and other associated services. The group acts as an agent providing brokerage services for non-bank investment products and services. In addition, it offers a debit card program, automated teller machines, drive-through facilities at its branches and Internet banking to both business and individual customers. The group operates in the northeastern coastal region of North Carolina, principally pasquotank and Washington counties and in the tidewater area of southeastern Virginia.

Primary SIC and add'l.: 6712 6211 6022

CIK No: 0001156953

Subsidiaries: Gateway Bank & Trust Co, Gateway Capital Statutory Trust I, Gateway Capital Statutory Trust II

Officers: Ben D. Berry/Chmn., CEO, Pres., Brian Hellenga/Pres., CEO - Gateway Insurance Services, Mark A. Jeffries/Controller, Eric Hickman/Marketing Pres. - Wilmington, Louis McClam/Marketing Pres. - Raleigh Region, George Thomas/Marketing Pres. - Albemarle Region, David R. Twiddy/COO, Pres., Donna C. Kitchen/Sr. Exec. VP, Chief Administrative Officer, Ronald K. Bennett/Marketing Pres. - Dare, Currituck Region, Theodore L. Salter/Sr. Exec. VP, CFO, Stephen C. Skinner/Marketing Pres. - Albemarle Region, Frank J. Horne/Sr. Exec. VP, Chief Risk Officer, Daniel J. Fisher/Sr. Exec. VP, Chief Credit Officer, Steve McNulty/Marketing Pres. - Norfolk, Chesapeake, Suffolk, Emporia Region, Eddie Campbell/Marketing Pres., Triangle Pres. - Private Banking (17 Officers included in Index)

Directors: Ben D. Berry/Chmn., CEO, Pres., Richard W. Whiting/Dir. Emeritus, Jimmie Dixon/Dir., Russell E. Twiford/Dir. Emeritus, William Brumsey/Dir., Spencer H. Barrow/Dir., Robert W. Luther/Dir., Robert Y. Green/Dir., William A. Paulette/Dir., Taylor W. Johnson/Dir., Frank T. Williams/Dir., Charles R. Franklin/Dir., William Taylor Johnson/Dir., William C. Owens/Dir., James H. Ferebee/Dir. (19 Directors included in Index)

Owners: W.C. Owens/1.50%, Frances Morrisette Norrell, Ollin B. Sykes, Billy Roughton, Robert Y. Green, David R. Twiddy/1.10%, Wellington Management Co LLP/9.62%, William Taylor Johnson, Ben D. Berry/1.70%, Theodore L. Salter, Jimmie Dixon/1.10%, Charles R. Franklin, James H. Ferebee/1.90%, Jerry T. Womack/5.60%, Robert Willard Luther (19 Owners included in Index)

Financial Data: Fiscal Year End:12/31 Latest Annual Data: 12/31/2006

Year	Sales	Net Income
2006	$84,577,000	$5,269,000
2005	$47,746,000	$3,939,000
2004	$25,489,000	$2,010,000

Curr. Assets:	$35,536,000	Curr. Liab.:	$945,408,000	P/E Ratio:	21.68
Plant, Equip.:	$38,456,000	Total Liab.:	$1,097,837,000	Indic. Yr. Divd.:	$0.320
Total Assets:	$1,207,477,000	Net Worth:	$109,640,000	Debt/ Equity:	1.6362

Gateway Inc

7565 Irvine Ctr. Dr., Irvine, CA, 92618; **PH:** 1-949-471-7000; **http://** www.gateway.com

General - Incorporation	DE	**Stock** - Price on:12/24/2007	$1.6899
Employees	1,700	Stock Exchange	NA
Auditor	Deloitte & Touche LLP	Ticker Symbol	NA
Stk Agt	UMB Bank, N.A.	Outstanding Shares	371,460,000
Counsel	NA	E.P.S.	$0.06
DUNS No.	15-207-2849	Shareholders	NA

Business: The group's principle activities include developing, marketing, manufacturing and supporting personal computers, consumer electronic products, enterprise systems, communications tools and applications. The group also provides training and related services. The group marketing product models include plasma, LCD, rear projection TVS, digital camera, printers, mobile PC accessories, monitors, CD and DVD burners, surge protectors and various PC accessories. The group operates from United States.

Primary SIC and add'l.: 3571 5961 7378

CIK No: 0000895812

Subsidiaries: AD Technologies LLC, Advanced Logic Research, Inc., Cowabunga Enterprises, Inc. dba Gateway.com, eMachines Asia, Ltd, eMachines Europe B.V., eMachines Internet Group, Inc., eMachines Ltd., eMachines, Inc., Gateway Accessory Stores, Inc., Gateway Asia, Inc., Gateway Canada Corp., Gateway Companies, Inc., Gateway Computers Ireland Limited, Gateway France SAS, Gateway International Computers Ltd. 25 Subsidiaries included in the Index

Officers: Edward J. Coleman/56/Dir., CEO/$927,122.00, Bart Brown/42/Sr. VP - Marketing, James Burdick/48/Sr. VP - Professional, Consumer Direct, Robert V. Davidson/53/Sr. VP - Worldwide Retail/$617,665.00, Jack Baikie/51/VP - Supply Chain, Gary Elsasser/39/Sr. VP - Products, Chuck May/55/Sr. VP - Product Planning, Retail, Kyle Price/47/VP - Quality, Lazane Smith/53/Sr. VP - Human Resources, Customer Support Services, Neal West/48/VP, Corporate Controller, Bob Davidson/53/Sr. VP - Worldwide Retail, Michael R. Tyler/51/Sr. VP, Chief Legal, Administrative Officer, Sec., Bruce K. Riggs/45/Sr. VP - Retail/$605,814.00, John Goldsberry/53/CFO, Sr. VP/$1,226,055.00

Directors: Edward J. Coleman/56/Dir., CEO, Richard D. Snyder/Chmn., Douglas L. Lacey/Dir., Janet M. Clarke/Dir., George H. Krauss/Dir., Quincy L. Allen/Dir., Paul E. Weaver/Dir., Scott Galloway/Dir., Dave Russell/Dir., Joseph G. Parham/Dir.

Owners: Joseph G. Parham, Bruce K. Riggs, Firebrand/Harbinger Group/10.80%, Edward J. Coleman, Robert V. Davidson, Scott Galloway, Theodore W. Waitt/17.50%, Insiders/1.40%, Janet M. Clarke, John P. Goldsberry, Paul E. Weaver, Richard D. Snyder, Brandes Investment Partners, L.P./10.70%, Edward D. Fisher, Quincy L. Allen (17 Owners included in Index)

Financial Data: Fiscal Year End:12/31 Latest Annual Data: 12/31/2006

Year	Sales	Net Income
2006	$3,980,803,000	$9,643,000
2005	$3,854,061,000	$6,161,000
2004	$3,649,734,000	-$567,618,000

Curr. Assets:	$1,251,093,000	Curr. Liab.:	$1,018,934,000	P/E Ratio:	28.17
Plant, Equip.:	$110,931,000	Total Liab.:	$1,384,809,000	Indic. Yr. Divd.:	NA
Total Assets:	$1,656,235,000	Net Worth:	$269,008,000	Debt/ Equity:	1.1623

GATX Corp

500 W Monroe St., Chicago, IL, 60661; **PH:** 1-312-621-6200; **Fax:** 1-312-621-6648; **http://** www.gatx.com; **Email:** contactgatx@gatx.com

General - Incorporation	NY	**Stock** - Price on:12/24/2007	$49.57
Employees	2,340	Stock Exchange	NYSE
Auditor	Ernst & Young LLP	Ticker Symbol	GMT
Stk Agt	Mellon Investor Services LLC	Outstanding Shares	51,080,000
Counsel	NA	E.P.S.	$3.54
DUNS No.	00-516-1476	Shareholders	NA

Business: The group's principal activity is to provide leasing and financing services. It specializes in railcar, locomotive and aircraft operating leasing. The group operates through three segments: gatx rail, gatx air and gatx specialty finance. Gatx rail leases rail equipment including tank cars, freight cars and locomotives. The air unit leases aircraft used by commercial airlines. The aircraft are purchased in the secondary and from two manufacturers: airbus industries and the boeing company. The specialty finance unit invests in, arranges and manages various marine assets and industries.

Primary SIC and add'l.: 6159 6719 7372 7359 4741

CIK No: 0000040211

Subsidiaries: 3140172 Canada, Inc., American Steamship Company., GATX Beteiligungs GmbH., GATX Financial Corporation., GATX Rail Locomotive Group, LLC., GATX Spanish Holding Corporation, S.L. ., GATX Terminals Overseas Holding Corporation., GATX Third Aircraft Corporation., KVG Kesselwagen Vermietgesellschaft GmbH, KVG Kesselwagen Vermietgesellschaft mbH., O'Farrell Leasing (Holdings) Limited, O'Farrell Leasing Limited

Officers: Brian A. Kenney/Chmn., CEO, Pres./$2,282,172.00, Johannes Mansbart/CEO - Gatx Rail Europe, Daniel Penovich/MD, VP - Marketing, Shipper Sales, Rob Zmudka/VP - Regional Sales, Midwestern US, Al Smith/VP - Locomotive Marketing, Midwestern US, Tom Clark/Mgr. - Accounting, Midwestern US, Martin Passini/Mgr. - Accounting, Midwestern US, George Economy/Mgr. - Accounting, Midwestern US, John Sweeney/Mgr. - Accounting, Midwestern US, William M. Muckian/Sr. VP, Controller, Chief Accounting Officer, Robert C. Lyons/CFO, Sr. VP/$793,478.00, Deborah A. Golden/VP, General Counsel, Sec./$697,681.00, Rhonda S. Johnson/Dir. - Investor Relations, Irma Dominguez/Investor Relations Coordinator, Clifford J. Porzenheim/Sr. VP - Strategic Growth (58 Officers included in Index)

Directors: Brian A. Kenney/Chmn., CEO, Pres., Richard Fairbanks/Dir., Rod F. Dammeyer/Dir., Deborah M. Fretz/Dir., James M. Denny/Dir., Marla C. Gottschalk/Dir., Mark G. McGrath/Dir., Michael E. Murphy/Dir., Casey J. Sylla/Dir., Ernst A. Haberli/Dir., David S. Sutherland/Dir.

Owners: GAMCO Investors, Inc./6.68%, State Farm Mutual Automobile Insurance Company/11.52%, Lord, Abbett & Co. LLC/5.86%

Financial Data: Fiscal Year End:12/31 Latest Annual Data: 12/31/2006

Year	Sales	Net Income
2006	$1,229,100,000	$111,700,000
2005	$1,134,600,000	-$14,300,000
2004	$1,231,400,000	$169,600,000

Curr. Assets:	$775,700,000	Curr. Liab.:	$159,600,000	P/E Ratio:	27.39
Plant, Equip.:	$3,078,700,000	Total Liab.:	$3,481,000,000	Indic. Yr. Divd.:	$0.960
Total Assets:	$4,644,000,000	Net Worth:	$1,163,000,000	Debt/ Equity:	1.9042

GATX Financial Corp

500 W Monroe St. , Chicago, IL, 60661; **PH:** 1-415-955-3200; **http://** www.gatx.com

General - Incorporation	DE	**Stock** - Price on:12/24/2007	NA
Employees	NA	Stock Exchange	NA
Auditor	Ernst & Young LLP	Ticker Symbol	NA
Stk Agt	Mellon Investor Services LLC	Outstanding Shares	NA
Counsel	NA	E.P.S.	NA
DUNS No.	04-327-2426	Shareholders	NA

Business: The group's principal activities are to provide asset-based financing, structures transactions for investment by other lessors and manages lease portfolios. These activities are carried out through four operating segments: gatx rail, gatx air, gatx technology services and gatx specialty finance. Gatx rail is engaged in leasing rail equipment, including tank cars, freight cars and locomotives. Rail provides both full service leases and net leases. Gatx air is engaged in leasing newer, narrow-body aircraft

widely used by commercial airlines throughout the world. Gatx technology services is an independent lessor of information technology equipment in North America. In addition, technology has ownership interests in technology leasing companies in the United Kingdom and Germany. Gatx specialty finance is comprised of the former specialty finance and venture finance business units.

Primary SIC and add'l.: 6159 7359

CIK No: 0000357019

Subsidiaries: American Steamship Company, GATX Corporation

Officers: Brian A. Kenney/Chmn., CEO, Pres., Robert C. Lyons/Dir., CFO, William M. Muckian/VP, Controller, Chief Accounting Officer

Directors: Brian A. Kenney/Chmn., CEO, Pres., Robert C. Lyons/Dir., CFO

Gaylord Entertainment Co

1 Gaylord Dr., Nashville, TN, 37214; **PH:** 1-615-316-6000; **Fax:** 1-615-316-6555; **http://** www.gaylordentertainment.com; **Email:** investorrelations@gaylordentertainment.com

General - Incorporation	DE	Stock- Price on:12/24/2007	$55.04
Employees	8,983	Stock Exchange	NYSE
Auditor	Ernst & Young LLP	Ticker Symbol	GET
Stk Agt.	SunTrust Bank	Outstanding Shares	NA
Counsel	Bass, Berry & Sims PLC	E.P.S	$0.34
DUNS No.	00-790-6860	Shareholders	NA

Business: The group's principal activity is to offer hospitality and entertainment services. The operations of the group are carried through four business segments: hospitality, opry and attractions, resortquest and corporate and other. The hospitality segment comprises the operations of the Gaylord Hotel Properties and the Radisson Hotel at Opryland. The opry and attractions segment represents Nashville-area attractions, including the Grand Ole Opry, General Jackson Showboat, Ryman Auditorium, Springhouse Golf Club and the Wildhorse Saloon. The resortquest is a provider of vacation condominium and home rental property management services in premier destination resort locations in the United States and Canada, with a branded network of vacation rental properties. Corporate and other consists of ownership interests in certain entities including corporate expenses. On 20-Nov-2003, the group acquired Resortquest International Inc.

Primary SIC and add'l.: 7011 4841 4832

CIK No: 0001040829

Subsidiaries: Abbott & Andrews Realty, LLC, Abbott Resorts,LLC, Accommodations Center, Inc., Aspen Lodging Company, LLC, Base Mountain Properties, Inc., Brindley & Brindley Realty & Development, Inc., Catering Concepts, LLC, CCK Holdings,LLC, Coastal Resorts Management, Inc., Coastal Resorts Realty, LLC, Coates, Reid & Waldron, Inc., Collection of Fine Properties,Inc., Columbine Management Company, Corporate Magic, Inc., Country Music Television International, Inc. 79 Subsidiaries included in the Index

Officers: Colin V. Reed/Chmn., CEO, Pres./$3,960,303.00, Stephen G. Buchanan/Sr. VP - Media, Entertainment, Sheldon Suga/Sr. VP, GM - Gaylord National Resort, Convention Center, Kemp Gallineau/Sr. VP, GM - Gaylord Palms Resort, Convention Center, Rob Tanner/Dir. - Investor Relations, Rod Connor/Sr. VP, Chief Administrative Officer, Mark Fioravanti/Sr. VP, Treasurer - Gaylord Entertainment/$862,351.00, Carter R. Todd/Sr. VP, General Counsel, Sec./$741,421.00, Melissa J. Buffington/Sr. VP - Human Resources, Communications, John P. Caparella/COO, Exec. VP - Gaylord Hotels/$1,041,705.00, John A. Imaizumi/Sr. VP, GM - Gaylord Texan Resort, Convention Center, Bennett D. Westbrook/Sr. VP - Development, Design, Construction, David C. Kloeppel/CFO, Exec. VP/$2,028,091.00, Arthur Keith/Sr. VP, GM - Gaylord Opryland Resort, Convention Center, Rich Maradik/CIO, Sr. VP

Directors: Colin V. Reed/Chmn., CEO, Pres., Brad R. Martin/Dir., Michael J. Bender/Dir., Ralph D. Horn/Dir., Gordon E. Gee/Dir., Michael D. Rose/Dir., Michael I. Roth/Dir., Ellen R. Levine/Dir.

Owners: Ralph Horn, Robert P. Bowen, Gabelli Funds/10.40%, Gordon E. Gee, David C. Kloeppel, Colin V. Reed/2.30%, Insiders/6.00%, Michael I. Roth, Mark Fioravanti, Ellen Levine, Michael D. Rose, John P. Caparella, Carter R. Todd, Michael J. Bender, E. K. Gaylord/1.50%

Financial Data: Fiscal Year End:12/31 **Latest Annual Data:** 12/31/2006

Year	Sales	Net Income
2006	$947,922,000	-$79,435,000
2005	$868,789,000	-$33,950,000
2004	$749,453,000	-$53,638,000

Curr. Assets:	$737,671,000	Curr. Liab.:	$895,011,000	P/E Ratio:	100.07
Plant, Equip.:	$1,638,443,000	Total Liab.:	$1,834,493,000	Indic. Yr. Divd.:	NA
Total Assets:	$2,632,519,000	Net Worth:	$798,026,000	Debt/ Equity:	1.0833

GB&T Bancshares Inc

500 Jesse Jewell Pkwy. SE, Gainesville, GA, 30501; **PH:** 1-770-532-1212; **Fax:** 1-770-531-7368; **http://** www.gbt.com

General - Incorporation	GA	Stock- Price on:12/24/2007	$16.39
Employees	505	Stock Exchange	NDQ
Auditor	Mauldin & Jenkins LLC	Ticker Symbol	GBTB
Stk Agt.	Registrar & Transfer Co	Outstanding Shares	14,180,000
Counsel	NA	E.P.S	-$0.1
DUNS No.	NA	Shareholders	NA

Business: The group's principal activities are the provision of commercial banking services through four branches located in gainesville and oakwood, Georgia. The group conducts its business through two wholly-owned subsidiaries namely gainesville bank & trust and united bank & trust. The services offered include checking accounts, money market accounts, savings accounts, certificates of deposit, commercial, small business, real estate, consumer, home equity, automobile and credit card loans. The other banking services offered are drive-up and night depository facilities, 24-hour automated teller machines, Internet and telephone banking and limited trust services.

Primary SIC and add'l.: 6712 6022

CIK No: 0001061068

Subsidiaries: Community Trust Bank, First National Bank of Gwinnett, First National Bank of the South, Gainesville Bank & Trust, GB&T Bancshares, Inc., GB&T Bancshares, Inc. Statutory Trust II, HomeTown Bank of Villa Rica, Southern Heritage Bancorp, Inc. Statutory Trust I, United Bank & Trust

Officers: Richard A. Hunt/Dir., CEO, Pres./$634,861.00, Gregory L. Hamby/Exec. VP, Chief Finanical Officer/$311,727.00, Alan A. Wayne/Sec., Michael Banks/Investor Relations Contact, Sid Sims/Exec. VP, Chief Credit Officer

Directors: Richard A. Hunt/Dir., CEO, Pres., Philip A. Wilheit/Chmn., Samuel L. Oliver/Vice Chmn., James L. Lester/Dir., John E. Mansour/Dir., Lowell S. Cagle/Dir., Bennie E. Hewett/Dir., John W. Darden/Dir., James H. Moore/Dir., William A. Foster/Dir., Alan T. Maxwell/Dir., Anna B. Williams/Dir.

Owners: James H. Moore, Samuel L. Oliver, Bennie E. Hewett, Richard A. Hunt, Alan T. Maxwell, Insiders/8.14%, James L. Lester, William A. Foster, Alan A. Wayne, Anna B. Williams, Dimensional Fund Advisors LP/7.95%, Gregory L. Hamby, Lowell S. Cagle, Philip A. Wilheit/1.53%, John W. Darden (16 Owners included in Index)

Financial Data: Fiscal Year End:12/31 **Latest Annual Data:** 12/31/2006

Year	Sales	Net Income
2006	$137,104,000	$9,521,000
2005	$102,446,000	$11,991,000
2004	$70,052,000	$9,838,000

Curr. Assets:	$29,169,000	Curr. Liab.:	$1,527,870,000	P/E Ratio:	26.02
Plant, Equip.:	$41,776,000	Total Liab.:	$1,667,038,000	Indic. Yr. Divd.:	$0.380
Total Assets:	$1,900,376,000	Net Worth:	$233,338,000	Debt/ Equity:	0.5457

GBC Bancorp Inc

165 Nash St., Lawrenceville, GA, 30045; **PH:** 1-770-995-0000; **http://** www.generalbankusa.com

General - Incorporation	GA	Stock- Price on:12/24/2007	NA
Employees	NA	Stock Exchange	NA
Auditor	Mauldin & Jenkins LLC	Ticker Symbol	NA
Stk Agt.	NA	Outstanding Shares	NA
Counsel	NA	E.P.S	NA
DUNS No.	17-959-0419	Shareholders	NA

Business: The group's principal activity is to provide a wide range of commercial banking services to its customers in gwinnett county and to the parts of cobb, dekalb and fulton counties. The group accepts demand, time, savings and other deposits from the public and originates commercial, consumer, real estate and other loans. The principal sources of funds for the group's loans and investments are demand, time, savings, and other deposits (including negotiable orders of withdrawal or now accounts), amortization and prepayments of loans and borrowings. The sources of income for the group are interest and fees collected on loans, interest and dividends collected on other investments and service charges.

Primary SIC and add'l.: 6022 6712

CIK No: 0001026231

Subsidiaries: Gwinnett Banking Company

Gehl Co

143 Water St., West Bend, WI, 53095; **PH:** 1-262-334-9461; **Fax:** 1-262-338-7517; **http://** www.gehl.com

General - Incorporation	WI	Stock- Price on:12/24/2007	$30.41
Employees	855	Stock Exchange	NDQ
Auditor	PricewaterhouseCoopers LLP	Ticker Symbol	GEHL
Stk Agt.	NA	Outstanding Shares	12,220,000
Counsel	NA	E.P.S	$1.97
DUNS No.	00-607-0031	Shareholders	NA

Business: The group's principal activities are to design, manufacture, sell and finance equipment used in the light construction equipment and the agriculture equipment industries. Construction equipment is comprised of skid loaders, telescopic handlers, asphalt pavers, compact-excavators, and min-loaders and is sold to contractors, owner operators, rental stores and municipalities. Agriculture equipment is sold to customers in the dairy and livestock industries, and includes a broad range of products including haymaking, forage harvesting, materials handling, manure handling and feedmaking equipment. The group's patents and trademarks are the gehl(R) name, the mustang(R) name, the dynalift(R) name, the edgetm name and the scavenger(R) manure spreader.

Primary SIC and add'l.: 3531 3523

CIK No: 0000856386

Subsidiaries: Compact Equipment Attachments, Inc., Gehl Europe GmbH, Gehl Funding II, LLC, Gehl Funding LLC, Gehl Power Products, Inc., Gehl Receivables II, LLC, Gehl Receivables LLC, Mustang Manufacturing Company, Inc.

Officers: William D. Gehl/Chmn., CEO/$1,962,648.00

Directors: William D. Gehl/Chmn., CEO, Bruce D. Hertzke/56/Dir.

Owners: Daniel L. Miller, Richard J. Fotsch, Michael J. Mulcahy, William D. Gehl/3.50%, Kenneth H. Feucht, Hermann Viets, Manitou BF S.A, Marcel-Claude Braud, Malcolm F. Moore, Manitou BF S.A, Insiders/5.60%, Westfield Capital Management, Thomas M. Rettler, Westfield Capital Management, Dimensional Fund Advisors Inc. (21 Owners included in Index)

Financial Data: Fiscal Year End:12/31 **Latest Annual Data:** 12/31/2006

Year	Sales	Net Income
2006	$486,217,000	$19,507,000
2005	$478,214,000	$21,800,000
2004	$361,598,000	$13,387,000

Curr. Assets:	$291,033,000	Curr. Liab.:	$89,504,000		
Plant, Equip.:	$32,415,000	Total Liab.:	$134,329,000	Indic. Yr. Divd.:	NA
Total Assets:	$365,110,000	Net Worth:	$230,781,000	Debt/ Equity:	0.1660

GelStat Corp

7760 France Ave. S, 11th Fl., Minneapolis, MN, 55435; **PH:** 1-888-713-2092; **Fax:** 1-888-512-3766; **http://** www.gelstat.com; **Email:** info@gelstat.com

General - Incorporation	MN	Stock- Price on:12/24/2007	$0.22
Employees	11	Stock Exchange	OTC
Auditor	Virchow, Krause & Co. LLP	Ticker Symbol	GSAC
Stk Agt.	Wells Fargo Shareowner Services	Outstanding Shares	15,580,000
Counsel	NA	E.P.S	-$0.41
DUNS No.	NA	Shareholders	NA

Business: The group's principal activity is to research, develop and market over-the-counter and other non-prescription consumer healthcare products. The group's first product, gelstattm migraine is a patent pending solution, which is designed to provide acute relief from migraine headaches. The group's product gelstattm migraine is designed to designed to provide acute relief from migraine headaches. The operations are carried on in the United States.

Primary SIC and add'l.: 2834

CIK No: 0000890725

Subsidiaries: GS Pharma, Inc.

Financial Data: Fiscal Year End:12/31 **Latest Annual Data:** 12/31/2004

Year	Sales	Net Income
2004	$245,000	-$6,223,000
2003	NA	-$1,473,000
2002	NA	$1,463,000

Curr. Assets:	$2,342,000	Curr. Liab.:	$1,112,000		
Plant, Equip.:	$111,000	Total Liab.:	$1,112,000	Indic. Yr. Divd.:	NA
Total Assets:	$2,560,000	Net Worth:	$1,448,000	Debt/ Equity:	NA

Gem Solutions Inc

Formerly: Stellar Technologies Inc
7935 Airport Pulling Rd., Ste. 201, Naples, FL, 34109; ; http:// www.stellartechnologies.com

General - Incorporation	CO	Stock- Price on:12/24/2007	$0.007
Employees	23	Stock Exchange	NA
Auditor	Malone & Bailey, P.C	Ticker Symbol	NA
Stk Agt.... Computershare Investor Services LLC		Outstanding Shares	29,390,000
Counsel	NA	E.P.S.	-$0.276
DUNS No.	NA	Shareholders	NA

Business: The group's principle activity is to provide photography and related digital services to the travel industry. It created digital brochures for hotels, resorts, restaurants and airlines through digital archiving of high-resolution color images. In Apr 2002, the company terminated its digital service activities and implemented a new business plan. It is in the development stage company and intends to engage in the business of acquiring, exploring and developing natural gas and oil properties. The group operates from United States.
Primary SIC and add'l.: 7389
CIK No: 0001132590
Subsidiaries: CompuSven, Inc, GeM Solutions (Canada), Inc, GeM Solutions, Inc.
Owners: Strand Properties Corporation, John E. Baker, Donald R. Innis, Millennium International Pension Plan/12.40%, Paul Modie/6.50%, Moonlight Investments, Ltd./9.40%, Millennium International Pension Plan, SPH Profit Sharing Plan/6.20%, Trident Growth Fund, L.P., Strand Properties Corporation/6.50%, Alta Fin B.V./6.20%, S G Private Banking (Suisse) SA/7.80%, Mark G. Sampson, SPH Profit Sharing Plan, Dromen Securities Ltd. *(22 Owners included in Index)*
Financial Data: Fiscal Year End:06/30 Latest Annual Data: 6/30/2006

Year	Sales	Net Income
2006	$871,000	-$5,076,000
2005	$883,000	-$6,027,000
2004	$109,000	-$1,581,000

Curr. Assets:	$794,000	Curr. Liab.:	$2,772,000		
Plant, Equip.:	$136,000	Total Liab.:	$2,803,000	Indic. Yr. Divd.:	NA
Total Assets:	$2,185,000	Net Worth:	-$618,000	Debt/ Equity:	NA

Gemco Minerals Inc

No. 203 - 20189 56th Ave., Langley, BC, V3A 3Y6; PH: 1-866-848-2940;
http:// www.gemcominerals.net; Email: info@gemcominerals.net

General - Incorporation	FL	Stock - Price on:12/24/2007	$0.21
Employees	NA	Stock Exchange	OTC
Auditor Cinnamon Jang Willoughby & Company		Ticker Symbol	GMML
Stk Agt. Interwest Transfer Company, Inc.		Outstanding Shares	NA
Counsel	Dennis Brovarone	E.P.S.	NA
DUNS No.	NA	Shareholders	NA

Business: The groups principal activities include acquiring and exploring mineral properties. The group operates from British Columbia in Canada and in the United States.
Primary SIC and add'l.: 1040
CIK No: 0001338118
Subsidiaries: Firstline Recovery Systems Inc
Officers: Thomas Hatton/Dir., Pres., Dorlyn Evancic/43/Dir., CFO, Evan Brett/Dir., Sec., Jordan Graham/Investor Relations Officer, Manning Elliot/Auditor, Eric Littman/Corporate State Attorney, Dennis Brovarone/Securities Attorney
Directors: Thomas Hatton/Dir., Pres., Dorlyn Evancic/43/Dir., CFO, Evan Brett/Dir., Sec.
Owners: Evan Brett/3.90%, Dorlyn Evancic/8.20%, Fu Kwai Enterprises Ltd./8.30%, Thomas Hatton/3.80%, Great West Management Corp./14.90%, Insiders/15.90%
Financial Data: Fiscal Year End:05/31 Latest Annual Data: 05/31/2007

Year	Sales	Net Income
2007	NA	-$464,000
2006	NA	-$422,000

Curr. Assets:	$12,000	Curr. Liab.:	$848,000		
Plant, Equip.:	$73,000	Total Liab.:	$848,000	Indic. Yr. Divd.:	NA
Total Assets:	$198,000	Net Worth:	-$649,000	Debt/ Equity:	NA

Gemini Explorations Inc

2601 Centenary Blvd, Miami, FL, 33126; PH: 1-403-697-4877; http:// www.geminiexploration.com

General - Incorporation	NV	Stock- Price on:12/24/2007	NA
Employees	NA	Stock Exchange	OTC
Auditor	NA	Ticker Symbol	GXPI
Stk Agt.	NA	Outstanding Shares	NA
Counsel	NA	E.P.S.	NA
DUNS No.	NA	Shareholders	NA

Business: The groups principal activities include acquiring and exploring mineral properties. In March 2007, the group acquired interest in two mineral claims located in the Province of British Columbia, Canada. The group operates from Canada and the United States.
Primary SIC and add'l.: 1311
CIK No: 0001373693
Officers: Michael Hill/CEO, Pres., Sec., Treasurer, Dir., Carlos Alberto Vera/Sr. Geologist, Mgr. - Geological Staff, Minera Primecap Geological Services, Juan Fernando Restrepo/GM - Minera Primecap Geological Services
Directors: Michael Hill/CEO, Pres., Sec., Treasurer, Dir., Oscar Fernandez/Dir.
Owners: Oscar Fernandez/1.70%, Michael Hill/8.30%, Insiders/10.00%

Curr. Assets:	$288,601,000	Curr. Liab.:	$60,332,000		
Plant, Equip.:	$202,428,000	Total Liab.:	$88,065,000	Indic. Yr. Divd.:	NA
Total Assets:	$576,836,000	Net Worth:	$488,771,000	Debt/ Equity:	NA

Gemplus International

46a Ave. J.f. Kennedy, Grand Duchy, Grand Duchy, L-1855; ; http:// www.gemplus.com

General - Incorporation	Luxembourg	Stock- Price on:12/24/2007	NA
Employees	6,347	Stock Exchange	NA
Auditor	PricewaterhouseCoopers LLP	Ticker Symbol	NA
Stk Agt	NA	Outstanding Shares	NA
Counsel	NA	E.P.S.	NA
DUNS No.	40-078-6760	Shareholders	NA

Business: The group's principle activity is to provide smart card enabled technology, products and services for secured wireless communications and transactions specialising in the telecommunications, financial services (banking and retail), government ID and corporate security sector. The group operates through two divisions namely telecommunications and security services. The group operates from United States.
Primary SIC and add'l.: 8999 7389 3695 7372 4899
CIK No: 0001128749
Subsidiaries: Gemplus Corp., Gemplus Finance S.A., Gemplus GmbH, Gemplus Industrial S.A. de C.V., Gemplus Japan Co. Ltd, Gemplus Limited, Gemplus Microelectronics Asia Pte Limited, Gemplus S.A., Gemplus Technologies Asia Pte Ltd, Setec Oy

Gemstar-TV Guide International Inc

6922 Hollywood Blvd., Los Angeles, CA, 90028; PH: 1-323-817-4600; Fax: 1-323-817-4623;
http:// www.gemstartvguide.com; Email: investor@tvguide.com

General - Incorporation	DE	Stock- Price on:12/24/2007	$5.04
Employees	1,691	Stock Exchange	NDQ
Auditor	Ernst & Young LLP	Ticker Symbol	GMST
Stk Agt ..... American Stock Transfer & Trust Co.		Outstanding Shares	428,030,000
Counsel	NA	E.P.S.	$0.49
DUNS No.	93-794-1615	Shareholders	NA

Business: The group's principal activities are to develop, license, market and distribute technologies, products and services. It operates in four segments: publishing segment, cable and satellite segment, consumer electronic licensing segment and corporate segment. Publishing segment consists of print and electronic publishing units and websites including TV guide magazine, TV guide online and skymall. Cable and satellite segment includes operations of TV guide channel, TV guide interactive, tvg network tvg, uvtv, spacecom and other businesses. Consumer electronics licensing segment licenses video recording technology under vcr plus+ brand, showview and video plus+ brands and g-code and digital recording devices such as digital video recorders. Corporate segment provides corporate management, corporate legal, corporate finance and other functions.during Mar 2004 the group disposed its sng segment.
Primary SIC and add'l.: 4841 3651 7819 2721 7372
CIK No: 0000923282
Subsidiaries: Canada Services, Inc., Cim/tvg, LLC(50% Owned), Colorado City Cablevision, Inc., Continental Paper Company, DirectCom Networks, Inc., EuroMedia Group, Inc., G-TV Guide, LLC, Gemstar (B.V.I.) Limited, Gemstar Development Corporation, Gemstar Development Limited, Gemstar Marketing GmbH, Gemstar Multimedia Ltd., Gemstar Technology Development Limited, Gemstar-TV Guide Europe SARL, Gemstar-TV Guide Interactive, LLC 91 Subsidiaries included in the Index
Officers: Richard Battista/Dir., CEO/$1,679,940.00, Ryan O'Hara/Pres. - TV Guide Channel, TV Guide Spot, Michael Mckee/COO, Pres. - Interactive Program Guides/$1,403,770.00, Stephen H. Kay/Exec. VP, General Counsel/$1,083,248.00, Tonia O'Connor/Exec. VP - Distribution, Richard Cusick/Sr. VP, GM - Digital Media, Peter C. Halt/Chief Accounting Officer, Sr. VP, Ajay Singh Bedi/CFO, Exec. VP/$813,582.00, Scott J. Crystal/Pres. - TV Guide Magazine/$1,248,685.00, Alan Cohen/Exec. VP, Chief Marketing Officer, Steve Shannon/Exec. VP, GM - Product Development, Dustin Finer/Sr. VP - Human Resources, David Nathanson/Sr. VP, GM - TVG Network, Sanjay Reddy/Sr. VP - Business Development, Strategic Planning, Robert L. Carl/Analyst, Investor Relations Officer *(23 Officers included in Index)*
Directors: Richard Battista/Dir., CEO, Anthea Disney/63/Chmn., James P. OShaughnessy/Dir., Ruthann Quindlen/Dir., Nicholas Donatiello/Dir., David F. Devoe/Dir., Peter Chernin/Dir., Rupert K. Murdoch/Dir., James E. Meyer/Dir.
Owners: Insiders/41.50%, Ruthann Quindlen, Wellington Management Company, LLP/5.20%, James E. Meyer, Rupert K. Murdoch/41.00%, News Corporation/41.00%, James P. OShaughnessy, Bedi Singh, Nicholas Donatiello, Scott J. Crystal, Richard Battista, Stephen H. Kay, Michael McKee
Financial Data: Fiscal Year End:12/31 Latest Annual Data: 12/31/2006

Year	Sales	Net Income
2006	$571,254,000	$72,464,000
2005	$604,192,000	$54,815,000
2004	$732,300,000	-$94,461,000

Curr. Assets:	$700,583,000	Curr. Liab.:	$265,772,000	P/E Ratio:	21.00
Plant, Equip.:	$68,182,000	Total Liab.:	$770,612,000	Indic. Yr. Divd.:	NA
Total Assets:	$1,223,737,000	Net Worth:	$453,125,000	Debt/ Equity:	0.0219

Gen-Probe Inc

10210 Genetic Ctr. Dr., San Diego, CA, 92121; PH: 1-858-410-8000; Fax: 1-858-410-8625;
http:// www.gen-probe.com; Email: marketing@gen-probe.com

General - Incorporation	DE	Stock- Price on:12/24/2007	$55.53
Employees	925	Stock Exchange	NDQ
Auditor	Ernst & Young LLP	Ticker Symbol	GPRO
Stk Agt	Mellon Investor Services LLC	Outstanding Shares	52,450,000
Counsel	Latham & Watkins	E.P.S.	$1.53
DUNS No.	NA	Shareholders	NA

Business: The group's principle activity is to develop, manufacture and market nucleic acid probe-based products. These products are used for the clinical diagnosis of human diseases and for screening donated human blood. The group earns through product sales, research revenue and royalty and license revenue. Product sales include sale of clinical diagnostic products and sales or rental revenue related to delivery of the group's proprietary instrument platforms for performing its diagnostic tests. Research revenue is recognized over the agreements that are earned or reimbursable costs incurred related to that agreement. Royalty revenue includes manufacture, sale or use of the group's products or

technologies under license arrangements with third parties. The group has operations in the United States, France, Australia, Singapore, New Zealand, Italy, Japan and other countries. On 07-Aug-2003, it acquired additional 65.6% of molecular light technology limited. The group's quarterly revenue for Sep'07 was 101.73 millions of USD.

Primary SIC and add'l.: 8731 3821

CIK No: 0000820237

Subsidiaries: Bioanalysis Limited, Gen-Probe International, Inc., Gen-Probe Sales & Service, Inc., Gen-Probe UK Limited, Molecular Light Technology Limited, Molecular Light Technology Research Limited

Officers: Henry L. Nordhoff/Chmn., CEO, Pres./$3,802,646.00, Stephen J. Kondor/Sr. VP - Sales, Marketing, Gurney I. Lashley/VP - Supply Chain Management, Daniel L. Kacian/Exec. VP, Chief Scientist/$1,260,573.00, Christina Yang/Sr. VP - Clinical, Regulatory, Quality, Lynda A. Merrill/VP - Industrial Relationships, William R. Bowen/Sr. VP, General Counsel, Sec./$971,131.00, Herm Rosenman/Sr. VP - Finance, CFO/$892,704.00, Lyle J. Arnold/VP - Research, Martin B. Edelshain/Sr. VP - Corporate Strategy, Paul Gargan/VP - Business Development, Robert B. Blake/VP - Instrument Systems, Tammy J. Brach/VP - Program Management, Fritz L. Eibel/VP - Marketing, Brian B. Hansen/VP - North American Sales *(18 Officers included in Index)*

Directors: Henry L. Nordhoff/Chmn., CEO, Pres., John C. Martin/Dir., Mae C. Jemison/Dir., Abraham D. Sofaer/Dir., Armin M. Kessler/Dir., Phillip M. Schneider/Dir., John W. Brown/Dir., Raymond V. Dittamore/Dir.

Owners: Armin M. Kessler, Brian A. McNamee, Abraham D. Sofaer, Niall M. Conway, Larry T. Mimms, Orbimed Advisors LLC/7.32%, Insiders/3.49%, Phillip M. Schneider, Morgan Stanley/6.80%, Raymond V. Dittamore, John W. Brown, Henry L. Nordhoff/1.29%, William R. Bowen, Mae C. Jemison, Herm Rosenman *(17 Owners included in Index)*

Financial Data: **Fiscal Year End:**12/31 **Latest Annual Data:** 12/31/2006

Year		Sales			Net Income
2006		$354,764,000			$59,498,000
2005		$305,965,000			$60,089,000
2004		$269,707,000			$54,575,000
Curr. Assets:	$390,687,000	**Curr. Liab.:**	$48,625,000	**P/E Ratio:**	37.02
Plant, Equip.:	$134,614,000	**Total Liab.:**	$53,631,000	**Indic. Yr. Divd.:**	NA
Total Assets:	$623,839,000	**Net Worth:**	$570,208,000	**Debt/ Equity:**	0.0232

Genaera Corp

5110 Campus Dr., Plymouth Meeting, PA, 19462; ***PH:*** 1-610-941-4020; ***Fax:*** 1-610-941-5399; ***http://*** www.genaera.com; ***Email:*** info@genaera.com

General - Incorporation	DE	**Stock**- Price on:12/24/2007	$2.77
Employees	43	Stock Exchange	NDQ
Auditor	KPMG LLP	Ticker Symbol	GENR
Stk Agt	StockTrans, Inc.	Outstanding Shares	17,480,000
Counsel	Dechert LLP	E.P.S	-$0.82
DUNS No.	55-548-6851	Shareholders	NA

Business: The group's principal activity is to develop medicines for serious diseases from genomics and natural products. The research and development efforts of the group are focused on anti-angiogenesis, respiratory diseases, obesity, and infectious diseases. The products of the group include squalamine, which is the lead product candidate in anti-angiogenesis. Trodulamine, formerly known as produlestan, is the group's second natural aminosterol product. The group has maintained a respiratory product development program designed to discover and develop treatment alternatives for respiratory diseases.

Primary SIC and add'l.: 2834

CIK No: 0000880431

Officers: John L. Armstrong/Dir., CEO, Pres./$1,085,429.00, John A. Skolas/CFO, Exec. VP, General Counsel, Sec./$616,145.00, Michael Gast/Exec. VP - Clinical Research, Development/$368,516.00, Henry R. Wolfe/Sr. VP - Business Development and Research & Development, Leanne M. Kelly/CFO, Sr. VP, Sec., Susan Neath/Contact - Media Inquiries

Directors: John L. Armstrong/Dir., CEO, Pres., Zola P. Horovitz/Chmn., Peter J. Savino/Dir., James B. Wyngaarden/Dir., Mitchell D. Kaye/Dir., Robert F. Shapiro/Dir., Osagie O. Imasogie/Dir., Frank R. Ecock/Dir.

Owners: Frank R. Ecock, Insiders/1.75%, Michael J. Gast, Zola P. Horovitz, RA Capital Biotech Fund, L.P./6.05%, Robert F. Shapiro, John L. Armstrong, Xmark Opportunity Partners Fund, LLC/9.71%, Osagie O. Imasogie, James B. Wyngaarden, John A. Skolas, Peter J. Savino, Lloyd I. Miller/5.88%

Financial Data: **Fiscal Year End:**12/31 **Latest Annual Data:** 12/31/2006

Year		Sales			Net Income
2006		$892,000			-$21,234,000
2005		$446,000			-$26,361,000
2004		$873,000			-$17,873,000
Curr. Assets:	$34,435,000	**Curr. Liab.:**	$2,427,000		
Plant, Equip.:	$759,000	**Total Liab.:**	$4,197,000	**Indic. Yr. Divd.:**	NA
Total Assets:	$35,250,000	**Net Worth:**	$31,053,000	**Debt/ Equity:**	NA

Genco Shipping & Trading Ltd

299 Pk. Ave., 20th Fl., New York, NY, 10171; ***PH:*** 1-646-443-8550; ***Fax:*** 1-646-443-8551; ***http://*** gencoshipping.com

General - Incorporation	Marshall Islands	**Stock**- Price on:12/24/2007	NA
Employees	NA	Stock Exchange	NYSE
Auditor	Deloitte & Touche LLP	Ticker Symbol	GNK
Stk Agt	Mellon Investor Services LLC	Outstanding Shares	NA
Counsel	NA	E.P.S	$2.61
DUNS No.	NA	Shareholders	NA

Business: The groups principle activity is to provide shipping services. The group transport iron ore, coal, grain and steel products. Specific customers of the group include Lauritzen Bulkers, Cargill, BHP, NYK Europe and HMMC. The group operates from the United States. The group's quarterly revenue for September 2007 was 45.63 millions of USD.

Primary SIC and add'l.: 4412

CIK No: 0001326200

Subsidiaries: Genco Acheron Limited, Genco Beauty Limited, Genco Carrier Limited, Genco Commander Limited, Genco Explorer Limited, Genco Glory Limited, Genco Knight Limited, Genco Leader Limited, Genco Marine Limited, Genco Muse Limited, Genco Pioneer Limited, Genco Progress Limited, Genco Prosperity Limited, Genco Reliance Limited, Genco Ship Management LLC 21 Subsidiaries included in the Index

Officers: Robert Gerald Buchanan/Pres., Principal Executive Officer, John C. Wobensmith/CFO, Principal Accounting Officer, Sec., Treasurer

Directors: Peter C. Georgiopoulos/Chmn., Stephen A. Kaplan/Dir., Nathaniel C.A. Kramer/Dir., Mark F. Polzin/Dir., Robert C. North/Dir., Basil G. Mavroleon/Dir., Harry A. Perrin/Dir.

Owners: Stephen A. Kaplan/15.80%, John C. Wobensmith, Basil G. Mavroleon, Robert Gerald Buchanan, Fleet Acquisition LLC/15.80%, James B. Ford/15.80%, Insiders/14.60%, Nathaniel C.A. Kramer, Mark F. Polzin, Robert C. North, Harry A. Perrin, Peter C. Georgiopoulos/14.07%

Financial Data: **Fiscal Year End:**12/31 **Latest Annual Data:** 12/31/2006

Year		Sales			Net Income
2006		$133,232,000			$63,522,000
2005		$116,906,000			$54,482,000
Curr. Assets:	$88,118,000	**Curr. Liab.:**	$15,173,000	**P/E Ratio:**	13.95
Plant, Equip.:	$481,111,000	**Total Liab.:**	$224,729,000	**Indic. Yr. Divd.:**	$2.640
Total Assets:	$578,262,000	**Net Worth:**	$353,533,000	**Debt/ Equity:**	NA

Gencor Industries Inc

5201 N Orange Blossom Trl., Orlando, FL, 32810; ***PH:*** 1-407-290-6000; ***Fax:*** 1-407-578-0577; ***http://*** www.gencor.com

General - Incorporation	DE	**Stock**- Price on:12/24/2007	$10.25
Employees	346	Stock Exchange	OTC
Auditor	Moore Stephens Lovelace P.A	Ticker Symbol	GNCI
Stk Agt	Continental Stock Transfer & Trust Co	Outstanding Shares	9,610,000
Counsel	Randolph H. Fields	E.P.S	$1.20
DUNS No.	05-210-1409	Shareholders	NA

Business: The group's principal activity is to design and manufacture machinery and related equipment used primarily for the production of asphalt and highway construction materials. The group's products include asphalt plants, combustion systems and fluid heat transfer systems. The products are sold primarily to the highway construction industry and are manufactured in two facilities in the United States and two facilities located in the United Kingdom.

Primary SIC and add'l.: 3599

CIK No: 0000064472

Subsidiaries: Bituma Corporation, Bituma-Stor, Inc., CPM Brazil, Inc., Equipment Services Group, Inc., Gencor International Limited, General Combustion Corporation, General Combustion Limited

Officers: E. J. Elliott/Chmn., CEO, David F. Brashears/Sr. VP - Technology, Marc G. Elliott/Pres., Scott W. Runkel/CFO, Treasurer, John E. Elliott/Exec. VP, Jeanne M. Lyons/Sec.

Directors: E. J. Elliott/Chmn., CEO, Russell R. Lee/Dir., David A. Air/Dir., Randolph H. Fields/Dir.

Owners: E. J. Elliott/82.10%, Marc G. Elliott/6.20%, Lloyd I. Miller/5.30%, Insiders/31.20%, Insiders/88.20%, Scott W. Runkel, E. J. Elliott/14.70%, John E. Elliott/9.80%, Mark Shefts/6.30%, David F. Brashears/1.50%, Marc G. Elliott/4.60%, Harvey Houtkin/26.20%, Jeanne M. Lyons

Financial Data: **Fiscal Year End:**09/30 **Latest Annual Data:** 9/30/2006

Year		Sales			Net Income
2006		$67,107,000			$11,587,000
2005		$48,140,000			$31,307,000
Curr. Assets:	$67,634,000	**Curr. Liab.:**	$11,888,000	**P/E Ratio:**	8.54
Plant, Equip.:	$12,949,000	**Total Liab.:**	$17,931,000	**Indic. Yr. Divd.:**	NA
Total Assets:	$80,974,000	**Net Worth:**	$63,043,000	**Debt/ Equity:**	NA

GenCorp Inc

Hwy. 50 and Aerojet Rd., Rancho Cordova, CA, 95670; ***PH:*** 1-916-355-4000; ***Fax:*** 1-916-351-8668; ***http://*** www.gencorp.com; ***Email:*** ir@gencorp.com

General - Incorporation	OH	**Stock**- Price on:12/24/2007	$12.5
Employees	3,144	Stock Exchange	NYSE
Auditor	Ernst & Young LLP	Ticker Symbol	GY
Stk Agt	Bank of New York	Outstanding Shares	56,100,000
Counsel	NA	E.P.S	$0.90
DUNS No.	00-131-6330	Shareholders	NA

Business: The group's principal activity is to operate through four segments; gdx automotive, aerospace and defense, fine chemicals and real estate. The gdx automotive segment develops , manufactures and markets highly-engineered, extruded and molded rubber and plastic sealing systems for vehicle bodies and windows. The aerospace and defense segment develops and produces solid and liquid rocket propulsion systems and related defense products and services. The fine chemicals segment supplies special intermediates and active pharmaceutical ingredients primarily to pharmaceutical and biotechnology companies. The real estate segment consists of development, sale, acquisition and leasing of the group's real estate assets. On 17-Oct-2003, the group acquired the assets of Atlantic research corporation. During the second quarter of the year 2004, the group discontinued its gdx automotive segment.

Primary SIC and add'l.: 3812 3061 2833 3764 3769 6531

CIK No: 0000040888

Subsidiaries: Aerojet International, Inc., Aerojet Investments Ltd., Aerojet Ordnance Tennessee, Inc., Aerojet-General Corporation, AGC Office 1 LLC, BPOU LLC, Chemical Construction Corporation, Cordova Chemical Company, Cordova Chemical Company of Michigan, GDX Automotive (Pribor) s.r.o., GDX Automotive Corvol SAS, GDX Automotive SAS, GDX LLC, Gen II Services, Inc., Gen III Services, Inc. 31 Subsidiaries included in the Index

Officers: Terry L. Hall/54/Dir., CEO, Pres., Robert G. Hall/Assist. Sec., Michael F. Martin/VP, Scott J. Neish/VP, Pres. - Aerojet, General Corporation, Leon R. Blackburn/VP, Controller, William M. Lau/VP, Treasurer, Yasmin R. Seyal/Sr. VP, CFO, Chris W. Conley/VP - Environmental Health, Safety, Bryan P. Ramsey/VP - Human Resources, Linda B. Cutler/VP - Corporate Communications, Mark A. Whitney/Sr. VP, General Counsel, Sec.

Directors: Terry L. Hall/54/Dir., CEO, Pres., James M. Osterhoff/72/Dir., David A. Lorber/30/Dir., Todd R. Snyder/45/Dir., Sheila E. Widnall/70/Dir., Charles F. Bolden/61/Dir., James J. Didion/68/Dir., Timothy A. Wicks/43/Dir., Robert C. Woods/56/Dir.

Owners: James J. Didion, Terry L. Hall, Todd R. Snyder, Insiders/2.10%, Michael F. Martin, Timothy A. Wicks, David A. Lorber, Robert J. Anderson, Robert C. Woods, Sheila E. Widnall, Scott J. Neish, Yasmin R. Seyal, Charles F. Bolden, James M. Osterhoff, Mark A. Whitney

Financial Data: **Fiscal Year End:**11/30 **Latest Annual Data:** 11/30/2006

Year	Sales	Net Income
2006	$621,100,000	-$38,500,000
2005	$624,000,000	-$230,000,000
2004	$499,000,000	-$398,000,000

Curr. Assets:	$283,200,000	**Curr. Liab.:**	$279,200,000	**P/E Ratio:**	113.64
Plant, Equip.:	$175,000,000	**Total Liab.:**	$1,117,400,000	**Indic. Yr. Divd.:**	NA
Total Assets:	$1,021,400,000	**Net Worth:**	-$96,000,000	**Debt/ Equity:**	NA

Gene Logic Inc

50 W Watkins Mill Rd., Gaithersburg, MD, 20878; *PH:* 1-301-987-1700; *Fax:* 1-301-987-1701; *http://* www.genelogic.com; *Email:* info@genelogic.com

General - Incorporation .... DE
Employees 151
Auditor .... Ernst & Young LLP
Stk Agt .... Mellon Investor Services LLC
Counsel ...... Venable, Baetjer, Howard & Civiletti
DUNS No. 93-266-1275

Stock- Price on:12/24/2007 .... $1.39
Stock Exchange .... NDQ
Ticker Symbol .... GLGC
Outstanding Shares 32,010,000
E.P.S .... -$1.56
Shareholders .... NA

Business: The group's principal activity is to provide services to organizations involved in the drug discovery and development business. These services are organized into two segments: information services and contract study services. The information services segment is based on the group's gene expression reference database, the geneexpress system, for research related to drug discovery and optimization. The contract study services business consists of services related to drug development, including primarily preclinical toxicity and pharmacology studies and related laboratory services and, to a lesser extent, phase i clinical trial services. Geneexpress(R), toxexpress(R) bioexpresstm, ascentatm, genesistm enterprise system and genechip(R) are the registered trademarks of the group. The customers of the group include pharmaceutical and biotechnology companies and U.S. Government agencies. The group acquired therimmune research corporation on 01-arp-2003.

Primary SIC and add'l.: 8731

CIK No: 0001043914

Subsidiaries: Gene Logic K.K., Gene Logic Laboratories Inc, Gene Logic Ltd.

Officers: Charles L. Dimmler/Dir., CEO, Pres., Joanne M. Smith-Farrell/VP - Corporate Development, Strategy/$277,399.00, V. W. Brinkerhoff/Sr. VP - Administration, GM - Gene Logic Laboratories/$358,507.00, Louis A. Tartaglia/44/Chief Scientific Officer/$878,499.00, Philip L. Rohrer/CFO/$343,883.00, Dudley F. Staples/Sr. VP, Sec., General Counsel/$289,833.00, Christopher Culotta/Dir. - Strategic Communications, Investor Relations, Albert J. Risdorfer/VP - Human Resources, Thomas Barnes/Sr. VP - Drug Repositioning Discovery, Larry Tiffany/Sr. VP, GM - Genomics

Directors: Charles L. Dimmler/Dir., CEO, Pres., Stark J. Thompson/Chmn., Anthony G. Gorry/Dir., Mark J. Gabrielson/Dir., Lloyd I. Miller/Dir., Michael J. Brennan/Dir., Mark D. Gessler/Dir., Frank L. Douglas/Dir., David L. Urdal/Dir.

Owners: V. W. Brinkerhoff, Dimensional Fund Advisors Inc./8.10%, Insiders/22.00%, Mark D. Gessler/2.80%, Anthony G. Gorry, Charles L. Dimmler/1.00%, Michael J. Brennan/1.80%, Lloyd I. Miller/14.10%, Louis A. Tartaglia, Renaissance Technologies, Corp./5.40%, Stark J. Thompson, Dudley F. Staples, Philip L. Rohrer/1.40%, Frank L. Douglas

Financial Data: *Fiscal Year End:*12/31 *Latest Annual Data:* 12/31/2006

Year	Sales	Net Income
2006	$24,346,000	-$54,710,000
2005	$79,370,000	-$48,304,000
2004	$75,937,000	-$28,520,000

Curr. Assets:	$61,017,000	**Curr. Liab.:**	$17,803,000		
Plant, Equip.:	$12,829,000	**Total Liab.:**	$19,183,000	**Indic. Yr. Divd.:**	NA
Total Assets:	$90,273,000	**Net Worth:**	$71,090,000	**Debt/ Equity:**	0.0010

Genelabs Technologies Inc

505 Penobscot Dr., Redwood City, CA, 94063; *PH:* 1-650-369-9500; *Fax:* 1-650-368-0709; *http://* www.genelabs.com; *Email:* info@genelabs.com

General - Incorporation .... CA
Employees 67
Auditor .... Ernst & Young LLP
Stk Agt .... Mellon Investor Services LLC
Counsel .... Skadden, Meagher & Flom LLP
DUNS No. 18-069-5348

Stock- Price on:12/24/2007 .... $2.33
Stock Exchange .... NDQ
Ticker Symbol .... GNLB
Outstanding Shares 29,980,000
E.P.S .... -$0.25
Shareholders .... NA

Business: The group's principal activity is to discover and develop pharmaceutical products. The group is currently pursuing regulatory approval of prestara (TM), its investigational drug for women with systemic lupus erythematosus. It is also pursuing the discovery of antiviral compounds for the treatment of hepatitis c virus ('hcv') infections and is advancing its hcv research program into preclinical development. In addition, the group has established a portfolio of patents and patent applications based on inventions arising from its research and development activities. Trademarks include prestara (TM), anastar (TM) and aslera (TM).

Primary SIC and add'l.: 2834 2835 8731

CIK No: 0000874443

Subsidiaries: Accelerated Clinical Research Organization, Inc., Genelabs Diagnostic, Inc., Genelabs Europe B.V

Officers: James A.D. Smith/Dir., CEO, Pres./$601,881.00, Roy J. Wu/VP - Business Development/$401,178.00, Ronald C. Griffith/Chief Scientific Officer/$497,097.00, Heather Criss Keller/VP - Business Strategy, Sec., Kenneth E. Schwartz/VP - Medical Affairs/$398,907.00, Frederick W. Driscoll/CFO

Directors: James A.D. Smith/Dir., CEO, Pres., Irene A. Chow/Chmn. - Genelabs Technologies, Inc, Alan Y. Kwan/Dir., Richard J. Whitley/Member - Scientific Advisory Board, Charles Cantor/Member - Scientific Advisory Board, H. H. Haight/Dir., David A. Stevens/Member - Scientific Advisory Board, Arthur Gray/Dir., John Fried/Member - Scientific Advisory Board, Leslie J. Browne/Dir., Matthew J. Pfeffer/Dir., Stanley M. Lemon/Member - Scientific Advisory Board

Owners: Insiders/3.20%, Arthur Gray, Lehman Brothers Holdings Inc./6.40%, Ronald C. Griffith, Roy J. Wu, Irene A. Chow, Kenneth E. Schwartz, Alan Y. Kwan, James A. D. Smith, Biotechnology Value Fund, LP/5.40%, Arnhold and S. Bleichroeder Advisers, LLP/6.00%, H. H. Haight

Financial Data: *Fiscal Year End:*12/31 *Latest Annual Data:* 12/31/2006

Year	Sales	Net Income
2006	$11,209,000	-$8,685,000
2005	$6,849,000	-$10,842,000
2004	$5,556,000	-$13,511,000

Curr. Assets:	$19,839,000	**Curr. Liab.:**	$10,008,000		
Plant, Equip.:	$1,011,000	**Total Liab.:**	$19,066,000	**Indic. Yr. Divd.:**	NA
Total Assets:	$22,072,000	**Net Worth:**	$3,006,000	**Debt/ Equity:**	NA

GeneLink Inc

123 Town Sq. Pl., No. 313, Ste. 313, Jersey City, NJ, 07310; *PH:* 1-800-558-4363; *http://* www.bankdna.com; *Email:* info@genelink.info

General - Incorporation .... PA
Employees 14
Auditor .... Buckno, Lisicky & Co
Stk Agt .... StockTrans, Inc.
Counsel .... NA
DUNS No. .... NA

Stock- Price on:12/24/2007 .... $0.1
Stock Exchange .... OTC
Ticker Symbol .... GNLK
Outstanding Shares 44,100,000
E.P.S .... -$0.03
Shareholders .... NA

Business: The group's principle activity is to provide public safe collection and preservation of a family's dna material for later use by the family to identify and potentially prevent inherited diseases. The group has developed a dna collection kit for the collection of dna specimens of its clients. The dna will be stored for 75-year intervals. The group has also developed three proprietary genetic indicator tests and has filed three patent applications. These tests are designed to measure genes that can contribute to disease and aging, predict an individual's risk for skin aging, and predict an individual's susceptibility to obesity. The group operates from United States.

Primary SIC and add'l.: 2835

CIK No: 0000941020

Subsidiaries: Dermagenetics, Inc.

Officers: Monte Taylor/Dir., CEO, Acting CFO/$112,486.00, Bernard L. Kasten/Exec. Chmn., John H. Souza/Dir., Dir. - Business Development, Robert P. Ricciardi/Dir., Chief Scientific Officer/$116,924.00

Directors: Monte Taylor/Dir., CEO, Acting CFO, Bernard L. Kasten/Exec. Chmn., John H. Souza/Dir., Dir. - Business Development, James W. Simpkins/Member - Scientific Advisory Board, Donald J. Cannon/Member - Scientific Advisory Board, Robert P. Ricciardi/Dir., Chief Scientific Officer, Harold H. Harrison/Member - Scientific Advisory Board, Robert P.K. Keller/Member - Scientific Advisory Board, Robert Hoekstra/Dir.

Owners: Robert Hoekstra/6.10%, Monte E. Taylor, Bernard L. Kasten/7.50%, Robert P. Ricciardi/6.10%, Insiders/2.14%, John R. and Maria D. DePhillipo/10.70%, John H. Souza/3.30%, Kenneth R. Levine/6.70%

Financial Data: *Fiscal Year End:*12/31 *Latest Annual Data:* 12/31/2006

Year	Sales	Net Income
2006	$176,000	-$578,000
2005	$397,000	-$1,053,000
2004	$305,000	-$2,115,000

Curr. Assets:	$202,000	**Curr. Liab.:**	$1,109,000		
Plant, Equip.:	$132,000	**Total Liab.:**	$1,732,000	**Indic. Yr. Divd.:**	NA
Total Assets:	$714,000	**Net Worth:**	-$1,018,000	**Debt/ Equity:**	NA

Genentech Inc

1 DNA Way, South San Francisco, CA, 94080; *PH:* 1-650-225-1000; *Fax:* 1-650-225-6000; *http://* www.gene.com

General - Incorporation .... DE
Employees 10,533
Auditor .... Ernst & Young LLP
Stk Agt .... Computershare Trust Co
Counsel .... NA
DUNS No. 08-012-9000

Stock- Price on:12/24/2007 .... $76.83
Stock Exchange .... NYSE
Ticker Symbol .... DNA
Outstanding Shares 1,050,000,000
E.P.S $2.44
Shareholders .... NA

Business: The group's principal activities are to discover, develop, manufacture and commercialize biotherapeutics for unmet medical needs. The group manufactures and markets 13 biotechnology products and licenses several additional products to other companies. Activase, avastintm, cathflo activase, herceptin, lucentistm, nutropin depot, nutropin aq, nutropin, protropin, pulmozyme, raptivatm,tnkasetm, rituxan, etc. Are some of the registered trademarks owned by the group. The group also provides certain customer service programs relating to products. The group has foreign operations in Asia-Pacific, Canada, Switzerland, Germany, France, Italy, great britan and other countries. The major customers of the group are amerisource/bergen, corp., cardinal health, inc. And mckesson, inc.

Primary SIC and add'l.: 2834 8731 2836

CIK No: 0000318771

Officers: Arthur D. Levinson/Chmn., CEO/$17,124,020.00, Susan D. Desmond-Hellmann/Pres. - Product Development/$7,820,142.00, Roy C. Hardiman/VP - Corporate Law, Assist. Sec., Stephen G. Juelsgaard/Exec. VP, Sec., Chief Compliance Officer/$4,896,340.00, Robert L. Garnick/Sr. VP - Regulatory - Quality, Compliance, Sean A. Johnston/Sr. VP, General Counsel, Vishva Dixit/VP - Early Discovery Research, Staff Scientists, Corsee D. Sanders/VP - Design, Analysis, Technology, Administration, Data Development Organization, Richard H. Scheller/Exec. VP - Research/$4,992,779.00, William N. Anderson/VP - Sales, Marketing, Immunology, Robert Andreatta/Controller, Chief Accounting Officer, Scott Carmer/VP - Sales, Marketing, Rituxan Immunology, Jennifer E. Cook/VP - Product Portfolio Management, Ashraf Hanna/VP - Alliance Management, Pipeline, Portfolio Planning, Gary Harbour/VP - Commercial Quality, South San Francisco *(79 Officers included in Index)*

Directors: Arthur D. Levinson/Chmn., CEO, Debra L. Reed/51/Dir., Charles A. Sanders/75/Dir., Herbert W. Boyer/Co - Founder, Member - Scientific Resource Board, William M. Burns/60/Dir., Erich Hunziker/54/Dir., Jonathan K.C. Knowles/60/Dir.

Owners: Debra L. Reed, Susan D. Desmond-Hellmann, FMR Corp./5.39%, Charles A. Sanders, Insiders, Richard H. Scheller, Arthur D. Levinson, David A. Ebersman, Roche Holdings, Inc./55.80%, Herbert W. Boyer, Stephen G. Juelsgaard

Financial Data: *Fiscal Year End:*12/31 *Latest Annual Data:* 12/31/2006

Year	Sales	Net Income
2006	$9,284,000,000	$2,113,000,000
2005	$6,633,372,000	$1,278,991,000
2004	$4,621,157,000	$784,816,000

Curr. Assets:	$5,704,000,000	**Curr. Liab.:**	$2,157,000,000	**P/E Ratio:**	31.49
Plant, Equip.:	$4,173,000,000	**Total Liab.:**	$5,364,000,000	**Indic. Yr. Divd.:**	NA
Total Assets:	$14,842,000,000	**Net Worth:**	$9,478,000,000	**Debt/ Equity:**	0.2233

Gener8xion Entertainment Inc

3400 Cahuenga Blvd., Hollywood, CA, 90068; *PH:* 1-323-874-9888; *Fax:* 1-323-876-5217; *http://* www.8x.com; *Email:* info@8x.com

General - Incorporation	DE	**Stock** - Price on:12/24/2007	$0.35
Employees	NA	Stock Exchange	OTC
Auditor	Stonefield Josephson, Inc	Ticker Symbol	GNXE
Stk Agt	OTC Corporate Transfer Service Co	Outstanding Shares	18,040,000
Counsel	NA	E.P.S	-$0.1
DUNS No.	15-480-6756	Shareholders	NA

Business: The group's recently began leasing specialized equipment to the entertainment industry and intends to be a provider of sound stages and production facilities to the entertainment industry worldwide. In addition, the group intends to develop and produce full-length motion pictures through autonomous entities. On 13-Sep-2002, the group acquired gamogen inc. In may 2003 the group acquired luso American securities Portugal. The company is development stage company.

Primary SIC and add'l.: 7359 7812

CIK No: 0000803034

Subsidiaries: CDMI Productions, Inc.

Officers: Matthew Crouch/Chmn., CEO, Richard J. Cook/Exec. VP, Marilyn Harris Beaubien/CFO, Marcos M. De Mattos/VP, Carlos D. De Mattos/Dir., Pres.

Directors: Matthew Crouch/Chmn., CEO, Ric Wake/Dir., John R. Dempsey/Dir., Tom Newman/Dir., Carlos D. De Mattos/Dir., Pres., William Barnett/Dir.

Owners: Carlos D. De Mattos/16.00%, Marcos M. De Mattos/3.00%, Richard Cook/4.00%, Insiders/78.00%, William B. Barnett, Tom Newman, Marilyn Beaubien/2.00%, John R. Demsey, Matthew Crouch/47.00%, Ric Wake, Yale Farar/6.00%

Financial Data: *Fiscal Year End:*10/31 *Latest Annual Data:* 10/31/2006

Year	Sales	Net Income
2006	$5,708,000	-$5,768,000
2005	$451,000	-$1,213,000
2004	$52,000	-$77,000

Curr. Assets:	$6,302,000	**Curr. Liab.:**	$7,365,000		
Plant, Equip.:	$326,000	**Total Liab.:**	$7,365,000	**Indic. Yr. Divd.:**	NA
Total Assets:	$7,068,000	**Net Worth:**	-$297,000	**Debt/ Equity:**	NA

General American Investors Inc

450 Lexington Ave. Rm 3300, New York, NY, 10017; *PH:* 1-212-916-8400; *http://* www.generalamericaninvestors.com; *Email:* InvestorRelations@gainv.com

General - Incorporation	DE	**Stock** - Price on:12/24/2007	$41.36
Employees	NA	Stock Exchange	NYSE
Auditor	Ernst & Young, LLP	Ticker Symbol	GAM
Stk Agt	Mellon Investor Services	Outstanding Shares	29,540,000
Counsel	NA	E.P.S	$3.21
DUNS No.	NA	Shareholders	NA

Business: The groups principal activity is to invest in various industries, including oil and natural gas, finance and insurance, retail trade, healthcare, communications and information services, consumer products and services, building and real estate, technology, computer software and systems, machinery and equipment, electronics, mining and semiconductors. The group operates from the United States.

Primary SIC and add'l.: 6282

CIK No: 0000040417

Officers: Spencer Davidson/Dir., CEO, Pres., Portfolio Mgr., Andrew V. Vindigni/Sr. VP - Analyst Coverage, Banking, Insurance, Financial Services Industries, Jesse Stuart/VP - Analyst With General Industry Responsibilities, Sally A. Lynch/VP - Analyst Coverage, Biotechnology, Pharmaceutical Industries, Michael W. Robinson/Sr. Securities Analyst, Analyst With General Industry Responsibilities, Harold J. Kingsberg/Consultant - Analyst Coverage, Retail Trade Industry, Peter P. Donnelly/VP - Securities Trader, Eugene S. Stark/VP - Administration, Principal Financial Officer, Chief Compliance Officer, Diane G. Radosti/Treasurer, Principal Accounting Officer - Accounting Operations, Craig Grassi/Assist. VP, Dir. - Information Technology, Carole Anne Clementi/Corp. Sec. - Office Management, Shareholder Relations, Maureen E. Lobello/Assist. Sec. - Benefits Administration

Directors: Spencer Davidson/Dir., CEO, Pres., Portfolio Mgr., Lawrence B. Buttenwieser/Chmn., Arthur G. Altschul/Dir., Lewis B. Cullman/Dir., Gerald M. Edelman/Dir., John D. Gordan/Dir., Sidney R. Knafel/Dir., Ellen D. Shuman/Dir., Joseph T. Stewart/Dir., Raymond S. Troubh/Dir., Rodney B. Berens/Dir., Daniel M. Neidich/Dir.

Owners: Insiders/8.19%, Carole Anne Clementi, Arthur G. Altschul/2.10%, Ellen D. Shuman, Insiders/1.30%, Eugene S. Stark, John D. Gordan, John D. Gordan/1.19%, Gerald M. Edelman/0.01%, Lawrence B. Buttenwieser/2.13%, Peter P. Donnelly, Raymond S. Troubh/0.16%, Maureen E. LoBello/0.01%, Richard R. Pivirotto/0.01%, Sidney R. Knafel/0.13% *(23 Owners included in Index)*

Financial Data: *Fiscal Year End:*12/31 *Latest Annual Data:* 12/31/2006

Year	Sales	Net Income
2006	$159,740,000	$147,380,000
2005	$185,384,000	$172,071,000
2004	$119,685,000	$108,389,000

Curr. Assets:	$4,340,000	**Curr. Liab.:**	$22,120,000	**P/E Ratio:**	36.95
Plant, Equip.:	NA	**Total Liab.:**	$25,441,000	**Indic. Yr. Divd.:**	$3.000
Total Assets:	$1,424,894,000	**Net Worth:**	$1,399,453,000	**Debt/ Equity:**	NA

General Cable Corp

4 Tesseneer Dr., Highland Heights, KY, 41076; *PH:* 1-859-572-8000; *Fax:* 1-859-572-8458; *http://* www.generalcable.com; *Email:* info@generalcable.com

General - Incorporation	DE	**Stock** - Price on:12/24/2007	$75.19
Employees	7,700	Stock Exchange	NYSE
Auditor	Deloitte & Touche LLP	Ticker Symbol	BGC
Stk Agt	Chase Mellon Shareholder Services LLC	Outstanding Shares	52,280,000
Counsel	NA	E.P.S	$3.26
DUNS No.	84-791-4173	Shareholders	NA

Business: The groups principle activities include developing, designing, manufacturing, marketing and distributing copper, aluminum and fiber optic wire and cable products. The groups products include automotive and cordset products, and electric utility, fiber optic, military and mining cables. Customers served by the group include the energy, industrial, specialty and communications markets. The group operates from United States.

Primary SIC and add'l.: 3357

CIK No: 0000886035

Subsidiaries: Dominion Wire and Cables Ltd., General Cable Automotriz, S.A. de C.V., General Cable Canada, Ltd., General Cable Celcat Energia e Telecommunicaciones SA, General Cable Company, General Cable Corporation, General Cable de Latinoamerica, S.A. de C.V., General Cable de Mexico del Norte, S.A. de C.V., General Cable Holdings (Spain) SRL, General Cable Holdings de Mexico, S.A. de C.V., General Cable Holdings New Zealand, General Cable Industries Inc, General Cable Industries, LLC, General Cable Investments, SGPS SA., General Cable New Zealand Limited 22 Subsidiaries included in the Index

Officers: Gregory B. Kenny/Dir., CEO, Pres./$3,151,681.00, Domingo Goenaga/CEO, Sr. VP, Pres. - General Cable Europe, Campbell Whyte/CEO, Pres. - General Cable Oceania, Elizabeth W. Taliaferro/CIO, Sr. VP, Mark A. Thackeray/Sr. VP - North American Operations, Roderick MacDonald/Sr. VP - Sales, Business Development, Peter J. Olmsted/Sr. VP - Human Resources, Brian J. Robinson/CFO, Sr. VP, Treasurer, Roger A. Roundhouse/Sr. VP, GM - Specialty Wire Harnesses, Gregory J. Lampert/Sr. VP, GM - Data Communications Cables, Carol Brand Products, Michael P. Dickerson/VP - Finance, Investor Relations, James Freestone/VP - Technology, North America, James W. Barney/Sr. VP, GM - Telecommunications Business, Corporate Development, Robert J. Siverd/Exec. VP, General Counsel, Sec./$1,060,790.00, Michael J. Andrews/Sr. VP, GM - Utility, Industrial Cables

Directors: Gregory B. Kenny/Dir., CEO, Pres., John E. Welsh/57/Non - Exec. Chmn., Robert L. Smialek/Dir., Gregory E. Lawton/Dir., Craig P. Omtvedt/Dir.

Owners: Gregory B. Kenny/1.35%, Robert J. Siverd, Christopher F. Virgulak, Insiders/2.54%, JPMorgan Chase & Co./5.23%, Fidelity Management & Research Corp./5.91%, Gregory E. Lawton, John E. Welsh, Craig P. Omtvedt, Robert L. Smialek

Financial Data: *Fiscal Year End:*12/31 *Latest Annual Data:* 12/31/2006

Year	Sales	Net Income
2006	$3,665,100,000	$135,300,000
2005	$2,380,800,000	$39,200,000
2004	$1,970,700,000	$37,900,000

Curr. Assets:	$1,734,300,000	**Curr. Liab.:**	$995,200,000	**P/E Ratio:**	23.06
Plant, Equip.:	$416,700,000	**Total Liab.:**	$1,784,300,000	**Indic. Yr. Divd.:**	NA
Total Assets:	$2,218,700,000	**Net Worth:**	$434,400,000	**Debt/ Equity:**	1.5625

General Communication Inc

PO Box 99016, Anchorage, AK, 99509; *PH:* 1-907-868-5600; *Fax:* 1-907-868-5676; *http://* www.gci.com

General - Incorporation	AK	**Stock** - Price on:12/24/2007	$12.82
Employees	1,264	Stock Exchange	NDQ
Auditor	KPMG LLP	Ticker Symbol	GNCMA
Stk Agt	Mellon Investor Services LLC	Outstanding Shares	53,630,000
Counsel	NA	E.P.S	NA
DUNS No.	01-119-9767	Shareholders	NA

Business: The group's principle activity is to operate under four segments: long-distance services: provides services to commercial, government, other telecommunications companies and residential customers, through the networks of fiber optic cables, digital microwave, fixed and transportable satellite earth stations and others. Cable television services: provides services throughout Alaska. Local access services: provides facilities based local exchange services in anchorage and fairbanks. Internet services: provides wholesale and retail Internet services. The group also provides other services such as managed services, private line and private network services, broadband services, lease and sales of capacity on two undersea fiber optic cables. The group's quarterly revenue for Sep'07 was 133.86 millions of USD.

Primary SIC and add'l.: 4813 4841 7375

CIK No: 0000808461

Subsidiaries: Alaska United Fiber System Partnership, GCI American Cablesystems, Inc., GCI Cable, Inc., GCI Cablesystems of Alaska, Inc., GCI Communication Corp., GCI Fiber Communication, Co., Inc., GCI Holdings, Inc., GCI, Inc., Potter View Development Co., Inc., WOK 1, Inc., WOK 2, Inc.

Officers: Ronald A. Duncan/Co - Founder, Dir., CEO, Pres., Gregory W. Pearce/45/VP, GM - Commercial Services, Dana L. Tindall/Sr. VP - Legal, Regulatory, Governmental Affairs/$514,595.00, John Lowber/Sr. VP, CFO/$715,516.00, Bruce Broquet/VP - Finance, Gregory F. Chapados/50/Sr. VP - Federal Affairs, Business Development, Wilson G. Hughes/Exec. VP, GM/$812,178.00, Terry J. Nidiffer/57/VP - Product Management, Data, Entertainment, Paul E. Landes/50/VP, GM - Consumer Services, Martin E. Cary/43/VP, GM - Managed Broadband Services, Gina R. Borland/45/VP - Product Management, Voice, Messaging, Richard D. Westlund/64/Sr. VP, GM - Network Access Services/$893,476.00, William C. Behnke/Sr. VP - Strategic Initiatives, Richard P. Dowling/Sr. VP - Corporate Development

Directors: Ronald A. Duncan/Co - Founder, Dir., CEO, Pres., Stephen M. Brett/67/Chmn., Stephen R. Mooney/48/Dir., William P. Glasgow/49/Dir., Jerry A. Edgerton/66/Dir., Scott M. Fisher/42/Dir., James M. Schneider/55/Dir.

Owners: Ronald A. Duncan/14.10%, Robert M. Walp/6.20%, Dana L. Tindall, Gary Magness/13.30%, Richard D. Westlund, Wellington Management/9.40%, James M. Schneider, Wilson G. Hughes/1.70%, Insiders/8.40%, Stephen M. Brett, Wilson G. Hughes, GCI Qualified Employee Stock Purchase Plan/2.50%, GCI Qualified Employee Stock Purchase Plan/7.70%, Gary Magness, Westport Asset Management, Inc./5.60% *(28 Owners included in Index)*

Financial Data: *Fiscal Year End:*12/31 *Latest Annual Data:* 12/31/2006

Year	Sales	Net Income
2006	$477,482,000	$18,520,000
2005	$443,026,000	$20,831,000
2004	$424,826,000	$21,252,000

Curr. Assets:	$173,308,000	**Curr. Liab.:**	$78,936,000		
Plant, Equip.:	$484,873,000	**Total Liab.:**	$669,186,000	**Indic. Yr. Divd.:**	NA
Total Assets:	$914,659,000	**Net Worth:**	$245,473,000	**Debt/ Equity:**	1.9330

General Components Inc

6767 W Tropicana Ave., Ste. 207, Las Vegas, NV, 89103; *PH:* 1-702-248-1047; *http://* www.gciworld.com

General - Incorporation: NV; Employees: NA; Auditor: Weinberg & Co., P.A; Stk Agt: Pacific Stock Transfer Company; Counsel: Loeb & Loeb; DUNS No.: NA

Stock- Price on:12/24/2007: NA; Stock Exchange: OTC; Ticker Symbol: GCPN; Outstanding Shares: NA; E.P.S: NA; Shareholders: NA

Business: The groups principle activites include developing, manufacturing and marketing broadband networking products and systems. Products of the group include cables, patch cords, panels, adapters, converters, switches and wireless devices. The group markets its products under the brandnames General Components and Reachhome. The group operates from the United States and Hong Kong.

Primary SIC and add'l.: 3661

CIK No: 0001160764

Subsidiaries: GCI Cayman

Officers: Zhang Zhengyu/50/Chmn., CEO/$10,076.00, Ma Qing/46/Dir., CFO, Treasurer/$17,633.00, Li Ming/43/Dir., Sec., Pres.

Directors: Zhang Zhengyu/50/Chmn., CEO, Simon Mu/51/Dir., Ma Qing/46/Dir., CFO, Treasurer, Li Ming/43/Dir., Sec., Pres.

Owners: Full Wisdom International Limited/6.40%, Simon Mu/3.70%, Ma Qing/9.30%, Full Talent Limited/29.60%, Marvel Sight Limited/9.30%, Smooth Wealth Group Limited/16.10%, Insiders/65.00%, Zhang Zhengyu/35.90%, Ming Li/16.10%

General Dynamics Corp

2941 Fairview Pk. Dr., Ste. 100, Falls Church, VA, 22042; *PH:* 1-703-876-3000; *Fax:* 1-703-876-3125; *http://* www.gendyn.com; *Email:* wm4gd@gendyn.com

General - Incorporation: DE; Employees: 81,000; Auditor: KPMG LLP; Stk Agt: EquiServe Trust Co N.A; Counsel: Robert H Duesenberg; DUNS No.: 00-138-1284

Stock- Price on:12/24/2007: $79.56; Stock Exchange: NYSE; Ticker Symbol: GD; Outstanding Shares: 404,830,000; E.P.S: $1.44; Shareholders: NA

Business: The groups principle activity is to provide aerospace, combat and marine systems, and Information systems and technologies. The group operates from United States.

Primary SIC and add'l.: 1241 3795 3812 1221 7379 3731

CIK No: 0000040533

Subsidiaries: American Overseas Marine Corporation, Anghel Labratories, Inc., Bath Iron Works Australia Corporation, Bath Iron Works Corporation, Braintree I Maritime Corp., Braintree II Maritime Corp., Braintree III Maritime Corp., Braintree IV Maritime Corp., Braintree V Maritime Corp., Concord I Maritime Corporation, Concord II Maritime Corporation, Concord III Maritime Corporation, Concord IV Maritime Corporation, Concord V Maritime Corporation, Convair Aircraft Corporation 59 Subsidiaries included in the Index

Officers: Nicholas D. Chabraja/Chmn., CEO/$14,504,740.00, Gerard J. Demuro/Exec. VP - Group Exec., Information Systems, Technology/$2,486,128.00, Bryan T. Moss/68/Exec. VP - Group Exec., Aerospace/$2,172,110.00, Hugh L. Redd/CFO, Sr. VP/$1,770,043.00, Joseph T. Lombardo/Exec. VP - Aerospace, Pres., Tommy R. Augustsson/VP - Information Technology, David D. Baier/VP - Taxes, Michael E. Chandler/VP, Pres. - Information Technology, Randy M. Collins/VP - Financial Planning, Analysis, Henry C. Eickelberg/VP - Human Capital Processes, Larry R. Flynn/Pres., VP, David H. Fogg/VP, Treasurer, Frederick J. Harris/VP, Pres. - Nassco, Preston A. Henne/VP, Sr. VP - Programs, Engineering, Test, Gulfstream Aerospace, Jeffrey Kudlac/VP - Real Estate *(37 Officers included in Index)*

Directors: Nicholas D. Chabraja/Chmn., CEO, Deborah J. Lucas/Dir., George A. Joulwan/Dir., Carl E. Mundy/Dir., John M. Keane/Dir., James S. Crown/Dir., Charles H. Goodman/Dir., Lester L. Lyles/Dir., William P. Fricks/Dir., Jay L. Johnson/Dir., Paul G. Kaminski/Dir., Robert Walmsley/Dir.

Owners: Nicholas D. Chabraja, Longview Asset Management, LLC/8.20%, Marsico Capital Management, LLC/6.10%, Michael J. Mancuso, Bryan T. Moss, Robert Walmsley, Jay L. Johnson, Lester L. Lyles, Insiders/7.60%, The Northern Trust Company/8.30%, Hugh L. Redd, James S. Crown/4.00%, George A. Joulwan, Capital Research and Management Company/7.80%, William P. Fricks *(22 Owners included in Index)*

Financial Data: Fiscal Year End:12/31 Latest Annual Data: 12/31/2006

Year	Sales	Net Income
2006	$24,063,000,000	$1,856,000,000
2005	$21,244,000,000	$1,461,000,000
2004	$19,178,000,000	$1,227,000,000

Curr. Assets:	$9,880,000,000	**Curr. Liab.:**	$7,824,000,000	**P/E Ratio:**	16.93
Plant, Equip.:	$2,168,000,000	**Total Liab.:**	$12,549,000,000	**Indic. Yr. Divd.:**	$1.160
Total Assets:	$22,376,000,000	**Net Worth:**	$9,827,000,000	**Debt/ Equity:**	0.2761

General Electric Capital Corp

3135 Easton Tpke., Fairfield, CT, 06828; *PH:* 1-203-373-2211; *Fax:* 1-203-373-2884; *http://* www.gecapital.com

General - Incorporation: DE; Employees: NA; Auditor: KPMG LLP; Stk Agt: Bank of New York; Counsel: NA; DUNS No.: 00-698-4256

Stock- Price on:12/24/2007: $25.19; Stock Exchange: NYSE; Ticker Symbol: GEA; Outstanding Shares: NA; E.P.S: NA; Shareholders: NA

Business: The group's principle activities are to provide financial services for the distribution and sale of consumer and other products of its parent company. The group is a wholly owned subsidiary of general electric capital services, inc., which in turn is owned by general electric company. The group operates in four segments: ge commercial finance, ge consumer finance, ge equipment management, and ge insurance. These segments provide a wide variety of financing, asset management, and insurance products and services. Products and services include credit card loans, personal loans, revolving credit, auto leasing, loans and financing leases for capital assets, inventory financing, mortgages servicing and insurance services. The group operates primarily in the United States, Canada, Europe and the pacific basin. During 2003, the group acquired first national bank, allbank and the retail sales finance business of conseco

Primary SIC and add'l.: 6159 7359 6153 7515 6351

CIK No: 0000040554

Subsidiaries: Genworth Financial Inc.

Officers: Jeffrey R. Immelt/Dir., CEO, Philip D. Ameen/Sr. VP, Controller, Keith S. Sherin/Dir., CFO

Directors: Jeffrey R. Immelt/Dir., CEO, Keith S. Sherin/Dir., CFO, Ronald R. Pressman/Dir., Brackett B. Denniston/Dir., Pamela Daley/Dir., Jeffrey S. Bornstein/Dir., Kathryn A. Cassidy/Dir., David R. Nissen/Dir., Robert C. Wright/Dir., James A. Colica/Dir., Michael A. Neal/Dir., John M. Samuels/Dir., Charles E. Alexander/Dir., Deborah M. Reif/Dir., John G. Rice/Dir. *(16 Directors included in Index)*

Financial Data: Fiscal Year End:12/31 Latest Annual Data: 12/31/2006

Year	Sales	Net Income
2006	$59,733,000,000	$10,386,000,000
2005	$56,010,000,000	$9,926,000,000
2004	$59,347,000,000	$8,034,000,000

Curr. Assets:	$47,622,000,000	**Curr. Liab.:**	$184,452,000,000		
Plant, Equip.:	$58,216,000,000	**Total Liab.:**	$485,072,000,000	**Indic. Yr. Divd.:**	NA
Total Assets:	$543,665,000,000	**Net Worth:**	$56,585,000,000	**Debt/ Equity:**	4.8361

General Electric Capital Services Inc

260 Long Ridge Rd. , Stamford, CT, 06927; *PH:* 1-203-357-4000; *http://* www.ge.com

General - Incorporation: DE; Employees: NA; Auditor: KPMG LLP; Stk Agt: Bank of New York; Counsel: NA; DUNS No.: 00-698-4256

Stock- Price on:12/24/2007: NA; Stock Exchange: NYSE; Ticker Symbol: fcj; Outstanding Shares: NA; E.P.S: NA; Shareholders: NA

Business: The group's principal activities are providing credit card loans, personal loans, mortgage servicing, auto leasing, consumer savings and insurance services. The services are provided through its wholly owned subsidiaries, general electric capital corporation and global insurance holding corporation. The group operates in four segments: ge commercial finance, ge consumer finance, ge equipment management and ge insurance. These segments provide a wide variety of financing, asset management, and insurance products and services. Products and services include creditcard loans, personal loans, revolving credit, auto leasing, loans and financing leases for capital assets, inventory financing, mortgages servicing and insurance services. The group operates primarily in the United States, Canada, Europe and the pacific basin. In Jun 2004 the group acquired wmc finance co & ikon office solutions

Primary SIC and add'l.: 6153 7359 6321 6331 6159 6311 6351

CIK No: 0000797463

Subsidiaries: General Electric Capital Corporation

Officers: Jeffrey R. Immelt/51/Dir., CEO, Keith S. Sherin/Dir., CFO, Philip D. Ameen/Sr. VP, Controller

Directors: Jeffrey R. Immelt/51/Dir., CEO, Deborah M. Reif/Dir., John G. Rice/Dir., Lloyd G. Trotter/Dir., David R. Nissen/Dir., Michael A. Neal/Dir., Brackett B. Denniston/Dir., Robert C. Wright/Dir., Keith S. Sherin/Dir., CFO, Jeffrey S. Bornstein/Dir., Kathryn A. Cassidy/Dir., Pamela Daley/Dir., John M. Samuels/Dir., Charles E. Alexander/Dir., Ronald R. Pressman/Dir. *(16 Directors included in Index)*

General Electric Co

3135 Easton Tpke., Fairfield, CT, 06828; *PH:* 1-203-373-2211; *Fax:* 1-203-373-3131; *http://* www.ge.com; *Email:* russell.wilkerson@ge.com

General - Incorporation: NY; Employees: 319,000; Auditor: KPMG LLP; Stk Agt: Bank of New York; Counsel: NA; DUNS No.: 00-136-7960

Stock- Price on:12/24/2007: $38.8; Stock Exchange: NYSE; Ticker Symbol: GE; Outstanding Shares: 10,290,000,000; E.P.S: $2.15; Shareholders: NA

Business: The group's principle is to provide imaginative idea in to leading products and services that helps to solve some of the world toughest problem. The group's products include GE cafe(TM),GE monogram(C) and GE profile(TM). The group's services include healthcare, media and entertainment, and security services. The group operates from United States.

Primary SIC and add'l.: 3080 6159 3724 3511 4911 3639 3845

CIK No: 0000040545

Subsidiaries: American Silicones, Inc., Amersham Biosciences Holding AB, Amersham plc, Bently Nevada, LLC, Cardinal Cogen, Inc., Caribe GE International of Puerto Rico, Inc., Datex-Ohmeda, Inc., Everest VIT, Inc., GE Aviation Service Operation Pte Ltd, GE Caledonian Limited, GE Canada Company, GE Drives & Controls, Inc., GE Druck Holdings Limited, GE Energy Europe B.V., GE Energy Parts, Inc. 71 Subsidiaries included in the Index

Officers: James P. Campbell/CEO, Pres. - GE Consumer, Industrial, Mark W. Begor/CEO, Pres. - GE Money Americas, Jeff R. Garwood/CEO, Pres. - GE Water, Process Technologies, Jay Ireland/CEO, Pres. - GE Asset Management, Omar S. Ishrak/CEO, Pres. - Clinical Systems, GE Healthcare, Richard Laxer/CEO, Pres. - GE Capital Solutions, Dean Seavers/CEO, Pres. - GE Security, Mark L. Vachon/CEO, Pres. - Global Diagnostic Imaging - GE Healthcare, Jeffrey A. Zucker/42/CEO, Pres., John G. Rice/51/Vice Chmn. - GE, CEO, Pres. - GE Infrastructure/$12,817,730.00, Charlene T. Begley/CEO, Pres. - GE Enterprise Solutions, William H. Cary/CEO, Pres. - GE Money Europe, Middle East, Africa, EMEA, John Dineen/CEO, Pres. - GE Transportation, John Krenicki/45/CEO, Pres. - GE Energy, Ronald R. Pressman/CEO, Pres. - GE Real Estate *(45 Officers included in Index)*

Directors: Jeffrey R. Immelt/52/Chmn., CEO, Michael A. Neal/Vice Chmn., CEO, Pres. - GE Commercial Finance, John G. Rice/51/Vice Chmn. - GE, CEO, Pres. - GE Infrastructure, Lloyd G. Trotter/Vice Chmn., Keith S. Sherin/Vice Chmn., CFO, William M. Castell/Dir., Douglas A. Warner/Dir., Claudio X. Gonzalez/Dir., Robert W. Lane/Dir., Rochelle B. Lazarus/Dir., Robert J. Swieringa/Dir., James I. Cash/Dir., Andrea Jung/Dir., Sam Nunn/Dir., Ann M. Fudge/Dir. *(21 Directors included in Index)*

Owners: Rochelle B. Lazarus3, Michael A. Neal, Alan G. Lafley, Sam Nunn, Robert C. Wright, Andrea Jung, Keith S. Sherin3, Robert W. Lane, Ann M. Fudge, Roger S. Penske, Douglas A. Warner, Robert J. Swieringa, Ralph S. Larsen, Claudio X. Gonzalez, William M. Castell *(18 Owners included in Index)*

Financial Data: Fiscal Year End:12/31 Latest Annual Data: 12/31/2006

Year	Sales	Net Income
2006	$163,391,000,000	$20,829,000,000
2005	$150,242,000,000	$16,711,000,000
2004	$152,866,000,000	$16,819,000,000

Curr. Assets:	$87,456,000,000	**Curr. Liab.:**	$220,514,000,000	**P/E Ratio:**	19.21
Plant, Equip.:	$74,966,000,000	**Total Liab.:**	$577,347,000,000	**Indic. Yr. Divd.:**	$1.120
Total Assets:	$697,239,000,000	**Net Worth:**	$112,314,000,000	**Debt/ Equity:**	2.4093

General Employment Enterprises Inc

1 Tower Ln., Ste. 2100, Oakbrook Terrace, IL, 60181; *PH:* 1-630-954-0400; *Fax:* 1-630-954-0447;
http:// www.generalemployment.com; *Email:* investorrelations@genp.com

General - Incorporation	IL	*Stock* - Price on:12/24/2007	$1.99
Employees	150	Stock Exchange	AMEX
Auditor	BDO Seidman LLP	Ticker Symbol	JOB
Stk Agt	Continental Stock Transfer & Trust Co	Outstanding Shares	5,150,000
Counsel	Herbert F. Imhoff, Jr.	E.P.S.	$0.20
DUNS No.	00-553-9010	Shareholders	NA

Business: The group's principle activities are to provide professional staffing services through a network of branch offices located in the United States. The group specializes in providing information technology, engineering, accounting and other professionals to clients on either a regular placement basis or a temporary contract basis. The services are marketed to prospective clients through telephone marketing by employment consultants and through mailing of employment bulletins listing candidates available for placement and contract employees available for assignment. The group markets its services using the trade names: general employment, omni one, business management personnel and triad personnel services. The group operated in 21 branch offices located in 11 states in 2003. The group's total revenue for the year 2007 was 19.69 millions of USD.

Primary SIC and add'l.: 7363 7361
CIK No: 0000040570
Subsidiaries: Triad Personnel Services, Inc.
Officers: Herbert F. Imhoff/Chmn., CEO, Marilyn L. White/VP, Kimberly Cullen/Branch Mgr. - Massachusetts, Doris A. Bernar/Mgr. - Communications, Assist. Corp. Sec., Michael Coleman/Branch Mgr. - Massachusetts, Rick Mowery/Branch Mgr. - North Carolina, Tim Schwenk/Branch Mgr. - Ohio, Michele Leblanc/Branch Mgr. - Texas, Nancy C. Frohnmaier/VP, Corp. Sec., Kent M. Yauch/Dir., VP, CFO, Treasurer, Brenda Randazzo/Branch Mgr. - Arizona, Dave Bond/Branch Mgr. - California, North, Lara Bojarsky/Branch Mgr. - California, South, Dave Wysock/Branch Mgr. - Lllinois, Frank Anichini/Branch Mgr. - Lllinois *(16 Officers included in Index)*
Directors: Herbert F. Imhoff/Chmn., CEO, Kent M. Yauch/Dir., VP, CFO, Treasurer, Dennis W. Baker/Dir., Sheldon Brottman/Dir., Delain G. Danehey/Dir., Joseph F. Lizzadro/Dir., Andrew Dailey/Dir.
Owners: Spectrum Galaxy Fund Ltd./5.90%, Kent M. Yauch, Sheldon Brottman/1.20%, Delain G. Danehey, Marilyn L. White/1.17%, Herbert F. Imhoff/11.35%, Dennis W. Baker, Joseph F. Lizzadro, Daniel Zeff/9.98%, Insiders/15.74%

*Financial Data: Fiscal Year End:*09/30 *Latest Annual Data:* 9/30/2006

Year	Sales	Net Income
2006	$20,068,000	$1,002,000
2005	$20,348,000	$671,000
2004	$17,981,000	-$1,397,000

Curr. Assets:	$8,474,000	*Curr. Liab.:*	$2,423,000	*P/E Ratio:*	9.95
Plant, Equip.:	$801,000	*Total Liab.:*	$2,423,000	*Indic. Yr. Divd.:*	NA
Total Assets:	$9,275,000	*Net Worth:*	$6,852,000	*Debt/ Equity:*	NA

General Finance Corp

39 Dundonald St., Port Of Spain; *PH:* 34-868625368; *http://* www.gfc.co.tt; *Email:* gfc@gfc.co.tt

General - Incorporation	CA	*Stock* - Price on:12/24/2007	$7.88
Employees	NA	Stock Exchange	AMEX
Auditor	Grobstein, Horwath & Company LLP	Ticker Symbol	GFN
Stk Agt	NA	Outstanding Shares	NA
Counsel	NA	E.P.S.	-$0.01
DUNS No.	NA	Shareholders	NA

Business: The group's principal activities include merging, capital stock exchanging, and asset acquiring. The group operates from the United States.

Primary SIC and add'l.: 6141
CIK No: 0001342287
Subsidiaries: GFN Australasia Finance Pty. Limited, GFN Australasia Pty. Holdings Pty. Limited
Officers: John O. Johnson/47/COO
Owners: Olawalu Holdings, LLC, Insiders, Robert Allan, Lawrence Glascott, Ronald L. Havner, Charles E. Barrantes, David M. Connell, Manuel Marrero, Ronald F. Valenta, Neil Gagnon, Jonathan Gallen, James B. Roszak, Gilder, Gagnon, Howe & Co. LLC, Jack Silver, John O. Johnson

*Financial Data: Fiscal Year End:*12/31 *Latest Annual Data:* 12/31/2006

Year	Sales	Net Income
2006	NA	$457,000

Curr. Assets:	$68,112,000	*Curr. Liab.:*	$3,797,000		
Plant, Equip.:	$3,000	*Total Liab.:*	$16,965,000	*Indic. Yr. Divd.:*	NA
Total Assets:	$69,128,000	*Net Worth:*	$52,163,000	*Debt/ Equity:*	NA

General Growth Properties Inc

110 N Wacker Dr., Chicago, IL, 60606; *PH:* 1-312-960-5000; *Fax:* 1-312-960-5475;
http:// www.generalgrowth.com

General - Incorporation	DE	*Stock* - Price on:12/24/2007	$56.47
Employees	4,700	Stock Exchange	NYSE
Auditor	Deloitte & Touche LLP	Ticker Symbol	GGP
Stk Agt	Mellon Investor Services LLC	Outstanding Shares	245,090,000
Counsel	NA	E.P.S.	$1.10
DUNS No.	NA	Shareholders	NA

Business: The groups principle activities include operating, developing and managing retail and other rental property like shopping centers. The group operates through two segments namely, retail and other, and master planned communities. The group operates from the United States. The groups quarterly revenue for September 2007 was 864.26 millions of USD.

Primary SIC and add'l.: 6798
CIK No: 0000895648
Subsidiaries: 10 CCC Business Trust, 10000 West Charleston Boulevard, LLC, 10450 West Charleston Boulevard, LLC, 1450 CENTER CROSSING DRIVE, LLC, 1451 CENTER CROSSING DRIVE, LLC, 1551 HILLSHIRE DRIVE, LLC, 1645 VILLAGE CENTER CIRCLE, LLC, 170

RETAIL ASSOCIATES, LTD., 20 CCC BUSINESS TRUST, 30 CCC BUSINESS TRUST, 500 WEST ASSOCIATES, LLC, 500 WEST CAPITAL, L.C., A/T ROUSE LIMITED PARTNERSHIP, THE, ABBEY ACQUISITION LLC, ACAPURANA PARTICIPACOES LTDA 853 Subsidiaries included in the Index
Officers: John Bucksbaum/Chmn., CEO/$237,200.00, Robert A. Michaels/64/Dir., COO, Pres./$4,752,833.00, Joel Bayer/44/Chief Investment Officer, Sr. VP, Thomas D'Alesandro/53/Sr. VP - Development/$1,244,542.00, Libby Scott/Contact - Leasing Information, Lincolnshire Commons, Amy MacLaren/Contact - Leasing Information, Palladio at Broadstone, Babette Israwi/Contact - Leasing Information, Marya Haluska/Contact - Leasing Information, Fran Martin/Specialty Leasing Representative, Austin Bluffs Plaza, Janet Henderson/GM - Austin Bluffs Plaza, Dewey Richardson/GM - Cache Valley Marketplace, Kathy Bennett Santelli/Leasing Representative - Cache Valley Marketplace, Deron Hansen/Specialty Leasing Representative, Country Hills Plaza, Stacey Dinkel/GM - Canyon Pointe, Sandy Ray/Leasing Representative - Center Pointe Plaza *(84 Officers included in Index)*
Directors: John Bucksbaum/Chmn., CEO, Matthew Bucksbaum/82/Chmn. Emeritus, Robert A. Michaels/64/Dir., COO, Pres., Bernard Freibaum/55/Dir., CFO, Exec. VP, Alan Cohen/47/Dir., Anthony Downs/77/Dir., Adam Metz/46/Dir., Thomas Nolan/50/Dir., John Riordan/70/Dir., Beth Stewart/51/Dir.
Owners: John Riordan, Anthony Downs, FMR Corp./11.40%, Thomas DAlesandro, Matthew Bucksbaum/1.60%, Adam Metz, Davis Selected Advisers, L.P./6.60%, Alan Cohen, Robert Michaels, Thomas Nolan, John Bucksbaum, Beth Stewart, General Trust Company, as trustee/20.60%, Insiders/6.50%, Bernard Freibaum/2.70% *(16 Owners included in Index)*

*Financial Data: Fiscal Year End:*12/31 *Latest Annual Data:* 12/31/2006

Year	Sales	Net Income
2006	$3,256,283,000	$59,273,000
2005	$3,073,416,000	$75,553,000
2004	$1,802,845,000	$267,852,000

Curr. Assets:	$505,800,000	*Curr. Liab.:*	$1,050,192,000	*P/E Ratio:*	51.34
Plant, Equip.:	$21,894,730,000	*Total Liab.:*	$23,577,366,000	*Indic. Yr. Divd.:*	NA
Total Assets:	$25,241,445,000	*Net Worth:*	$1,664,079,000	*Debt/ Equity:*	12.4359

General Maritime Corp

299 Pk. Ave., New York, NY, 10171; *PH:* 1-212-763-5600; *Fax:* 1-212-763-5602;
http:// www.generalmaritimecorp.com; *Email:* info@generalmaritimecorp.com

General - Incorporation	MH	*Stock* - Price on:12/24/2007	$27.93
Employees	530	Stock Exchange	NYSE
Auditor	Deloitte & Touche LLP	Ticker Symbol	GMR
Stk Agt	Mellon Investor Services LLC	Outstanding Shares	32,900,000
Counsel	Kramer, Levin, Naftalis & Frankel	E.P.S.	$1.97
DUNS No.	NA	Shareholders	NA

Business: The group's principal activity is to provide international transportation services of crude oil within the Atlantic basin. The group's fleet is comprised of both aframax and suezmax tankers. The group's vessels are currently operating in the Atlantic basin which consists primarily of ports in the Caribbean, south and Central America, the United States, western Africa and the north sea. The vessels are primarily available for charter on a voyage or time basis. Voyage and time charters are available for varying periods, ranging from a single trip to a long-term arrangement. Commercial firms such as oil companies and governmental agencies both foreign and domestic on a worldwide basis charter the vessels. At 31-Dec-2003, the group operated 42 vessels.

Primary SIC and add'l.: 4412
CIK No: 0001127269
Subsidiaries: General Maritime Management (Hellas) Ltd., General Maritime Management (Portugal) Ltd., General Maritime Management (UK) LLC, General Maritime Management LLC, Genmar Kentucky Ltd., Genmar Trader Ltd., Genmar West Virginia Ltd., GMR Administration Corp., GMR Agamemnon LLC, GMR Ajax LLC, GMR Alexandra LLC, GMR Alta LLC, GMR Argus LLC, GMR Ariston LLC, GMR Baltic LLC 66 Subsidiaries included in the Index
Officers: Peter C. Georgiopoulos/Chmn., CEO, Founder/$4,771,436.00, Jeffrey D. Pribor/CFO/$1,560,774.00, John C. Georgiopoulos/VP, Chief Administrative Officer, Treasurer/$1,232,962.00
Directors: Peter C. Georgiopoulos/Chmn., CEO, Founder, John P. Tavlarios/Dir., William J. Crabtree/Dir., John O. Hatab/Dir., Rex W. Harrington/Dir., Peter S. Shaerf/Dir., Stephen A. Kaplan/Dir.
Owners: Peter S. Bell, William J. Crabtree, FMR Corp./15.40%, Stephen A. Kaplan, Bergesen Worldwide Ltd./11.70%, Peter C. Georgiopoulos/11.40%, John P. Tavlarios, John O. Hatab, Jeffrey D. Pribor, John C. Georgiopoulos, Rex W. Harrington, Insiders/13.00%, Peter S. Shaerf

*Financial Data: Fiscal Year End:*12/31 *Latest Annual Data:* 12/31/2006

Year	Sales	Net Income
2006	$325,984,000	$156,831,000
2005	$567,901,000	$212,357,000
2004	$701,291,000	$315,109,000

Curr. Assets:	$137,865,000	*Curr. Liab.:*	$27,147,000	*P/E Ratio:*	9.94
Plant, Equip.:	$678,359,000	*Total Liab.:*	$79,777,000	*Indic. Yr. Divd.:*	$2.000
Total Assets:	$843,690,000	*Net Worth:*	$763,913,000	*Debt/ Equity:*	1.9860

General Metals Corp

Formerly: Interactive Multimedia Network Inc
1 E Liberty St., Ste. 6000, Reno, NV, 89501; *PH:* 1-480-603-5100; *http://* www.imnetinc.com

General - Incorporation	DE	*Stock* - Price on:12/24/2007	$0.334
Employees	NA	Stock Exchange	OTC
Auditor	Moore & Assoc. Chartered	Ticker Symbol	GNMT
Stk Agt	Jersey Transfer & Trust Co	Outstanding Shares	NA
Counsel	NA	E.P.S.	NA
DUNS No.	NA	Shareholders	NA

Business: The group's principle activities are marketing and branding through multiple media channels for the purpose of facilitating sales of a variety of consumer products and services. It has two operating subsidiaries best health, inc and New Jersey corporation which focuses on the development and marketing of consumer products in the the health and wellness markets. The channels used for distribution include Internet, online computer services, broadcast, cable and satellite television and retail exposure. It derives revenue from marketing fees charged to clients, commissions earned on the sale of clients' products and services and wholesale and retail sales of its own products.

Primary SIC and add'l.: 7311 7379
CIK No: 0001060910

Subsidiaries: General Gold Corporation

Officers: Stephen B. Parent/63/Dir., CEO, Pres./$134,000.00, David J. Salari/51/Dir., COO, Daniel Forbush/55/Dir., CFO/$24,000.00

Directors: Stephen B. Parent/63/Dir., CEO, Pres., Daniel Forbush/55/Dir., CFO, David J. Salari/51/Dir., COO, Leslie James Porter/43/Dir., John R. Rose/65/Dir.

Owners: Fastmarine Group Ltd./6.46%, Aegan Capital Management/5.68%, David Salari/1.18%, Daniel Forbush/0.65%, Insiders/13.13%, Grassy Mole Enterprises Ltd./12.91%, Leslie James Porter/0.90%, Stephen Parent/10.41%

Financial Data: Fiscal Year End:04/30   Latest Annual Data: 4/30/2006

Year	Sales	Net Income
2006	NA	-$419,000
2005	$1,000	-$142,000
2004	$54,000	-$57,000

Curr. Assets:	$205,000	Curr. Liab.:	$68,000		
Plant, Equip.:	$84,000	Total Liab.:	$68,000	Indic. Yr. Divd.:	NA
Total Assets:	$289,000	Net Worth:	$221,000	Debt/ Equity:	NA

General Mills Inc

PO Box 9452, Minneapolis, MN, 55440; *PH:* 1-800-248-7310; *Fax:* 1-763-764-8330; *http://* www.generalmills.com

General - Incorporation	DE	**Stock**- Price on:12/24/2007	$59.1
Employees	28,100	Stock Exchange	NYSE
Auditor	KPMG LLP	Ticker Symbol	GIS
Stk Agt	Wells Fargo Bank Minnesota N.A	Outstanding Shares	346,360,000
Counsel	NA	E.P.S.	$3.31
DUNS No.	00-625-0740	Shareholders	NA

Business: The groups principle activities include producing and marketing packaged consumer food products. The groups products include cereals, desserts, flour and baking mixes, dinner and side dish, organic products, and snacks. The group operates through three segments namely us retail, bakeries and foodservice and international. The group operates from United States.

Primary SIC and add'l.: 2024 2099 2026 2051 2052 2043

CIK No: 0000040704

Subsidiaries: AESR, LLC, Cereales Partners Latin America LLC, Colombo, Inc., Croissant King Pty Limited, D.h. Austral (uruguay) Sociedad Anonima, Elysees Consult S.a., FYL CORP., GARDETTOS BAKERY, INC., Gcf Servicios De Mexico S. De R.l. De C.v., General Mills (suisse) Sve Sarl, General Mills Argentina L.s., LLC, General Mills Argentina S.a., General Mills Asia Pacific Limited, General Mills Asia Pte. Ltd., General Mills Australia Pty Ltd 162 Subsidiaries included in the Index

Officers: Kendall J. Powell/CEO/$4,647,516.00, Christi L. Strauss/CEO, Sr. VP - Cereal Partners Worldwide, James A. Lawrence/55/Vice Chmn., CFO/$5,233,990.00, Siri S. Marshall/Sr. VP, General Counsel, Sec., Robert F. Waldron/Sr. VP, Pres. - Yoplait USA, Maria Morgan/VP, Pres. - Small Planet Foods, Donal Leo Mulligan/VP, Treasurer, James H. Murphy/VP, Pres. - Meals, Ann W.H. Simonds/Pres. - Baking Products, Michael A. Peel/Sr. VP - Human Resources, Corporate Services, Marc Y. Belton/Exec. VP - Worldwide Health, Brand, New Business Development, Jeffrey J. Rotsch/Exec. VP - Worldwide Sales, Channel Development/$4,592,329.00, Ian R. Friendly/COO, Exec. VP - US Retail, Christina L. Shea/Sr. VP - External Relations, Pres. - General Mills Community Action, Foundation, Kimberly A. Nelson/VP, Pres. - Snacks Unlimited *(26 Officers included in Index)*

Directors: Stephen W. Sanger/Chmn., James A. Lawrence/55/Vice Chmn., CFO, Michael A. Spence/Dir., Robert L. Ryan/Dir., Dorothy A. Terrell/63/Dir., Heidi G. Miller/Dir., Hilda Ochoa-Brillembourg/Dir., Raymond V. Gilmartin/Dir., William T. Esrey/Dir., Steve Odland/Dir., Judith Richards Hope/Dir., Michael D. Rose/Dir., Paul Danos/Dir.

Owners: R. L. Ryan, Insiders/3.50%, D. A. Terrell, A. M. Spence, Capital Research and Management Company/6.50%, S. W. Sanger/1.30%, M. D. Rose, S. Odland, H. G. Miller, P. Danos, J. R. Hope, J. A. Lawrence, R. G. Darcy, K. J. Powell, J. J. Rotsch *(18 Owners included in Index)*

Financial Data: Fiscal Year End:05/28   Latest Annual Data: 05/27/2007

Year	Sales	Net Income
2007	$12,442,000,000	$1,144,000,000
2006	$11,640,000,000	$1,090,000,000
2005	$11,244,000,000	$1,240,000,000

Curr. Assets:	$3,215,000,000	Curr. Liab.:	$2,757,000,000	P/E Ratio:	18.70
Plant, Equip.:	$3,111,000,000	Total Liab.:	$12,901,000,000	Indic. Yr. Divd.:	$1.480
Total Assets:	$18,448,000,000	Net Worth:	$5,248,000,000	Debt/ Equity:	0.5309

General Motors Acceptance Corp

Mail Code: 482-b08-d76, 200 Renaissance Ctr., Detroit, MI, 48265; *PH:* 1-313-656-6278; *http://* www.gmacfs.com

General - Incorporation	DE	**Stock**- Price on:12/24/2007	$7.2
Employees	33	Stock Exchange	NA
Auditor	Deloitte & Touche LLP	Ticker Symbol	NA
Stk Agt	Computershare Investor Services LLC	Outstanding Shares	4,090,000
Counsel	NA	E.P.S.	-$0.18
DUNS No.	12-053-0084	Shareholders	NA

Business: The group's principal activities are to provide automotive financial services to and through franchised general motors dealers throughout the world. The group is a wholly owned subsidiary of general motors corporation. The operations are conducted through three segments: financing, mortgage and insurance. Financing segment offers a wide variety of automotive financial services to and through general motors and other automobile dealerships. The group also provides commercial financing and factoring services to businesses in other industries. Mortgage operations originate, purchase, service and securitize residential and commercial mortgage loans and mortgage related products. Insurance operations insures and reinsures automobile service contracts, personal automobile insurance coverages and selected commercial insurance coverages.

Primary SIC and add'l.: 6162 9999 6141 6411

CIK No: 0000040729

Subsidiaries: General Motors Corporation, Semperian

Officers: Jim Jones/CEO - Rescap, Eric A. Feldstein/CEO, Sanjiv Khattri/CFO, Exec. VP, Richard Colgan/Contact - Gmac, Canada, Kenneth Fischbach/Contact - Rescap, Mark F. Bole/Exec. VP - International Operations, Barbara J. Stokel/Exec. VP - North American Automotive Operations, William F. Muir/Pres., William B. Solomon/Group VP, General Counsel, Cherri M. Musser/Group VP, CIO, David C. Walker/Group VP - Global Borrowings, Cathy Quenneville/Corp. Sec., Bruce J. Paradis/59/Exec. VP - Rescap, Linda K. Zukauckas/VP, Corporate Controller

Directors: Ezra J. Merkin/54/Chmn., Mark A. Neporent/50/Dir., Douglas A. Hirsch/45/Dir., Robert W. Scully/57/Dir., Lenard B. Tessler/55/Dir., Frank W. Bruno/42/Dir., Seth P. Plattus/46/Dir., Michael S. Klein/44/Dir., Richard G. Wagoner/54/Dir., Walter G. Borst/46/Dir., Frederick A. Henderson/49/Dir., Mark R. Laneve/48/Dir., T. K. Duggan/56/Dir.

Financial Data: Fiscal Year End:12/31   Latest Annual Data: 12/31/2006

Year	Sales	Net Income
2006	$21,659,000	$1,859,000
2005	$17,683,000	-$3,543,000
2004	$11,208,000	$8,072,000

Curr. Assets:	$4,232,000	Curr. Liab.:	$10,932,000		
Plant, Equip.:	$76,547,000	Total Liab.:	$23,377,000	Indic. Yr. Divd.:	NA
Total Assets:	$84,703,000	Net Worth:	$61,326,000	Debt/ Equity:	0.3032

General Motors Corp

PO Box 33170, Detroit, MI, 48232; *PH:* 1-313-556-5000; *Fax:* 1-313-556-5108; *http://* www.gm.com

General - Incorporation	DE	**Stock**- Price on:12/24/2007	$35.96
Employees	280,000	Stock Exchange	NYSE
Auditor	Deloitte & Touche LLP	Ticker Symbol	GM
Stk Agt	Computershare Trust Co	Outstanding Shares	565,740,000
Counsel	NA	E.P.S.	-$65.48
DUNS No.	00-535-6613	Shareholders	NA

Business: The group's principle activity is to manufacture automobiles including cars and trucks. The group products are sold under the brand names Buick, Cadillac, Chevrolet, GMC, GM Daewoo, Holden, HUMMER, Opel, Pontiac, Saab, Saturn and Vauxhall. The group operates from United States.

Primary SIC and add'l.: 7379 3714 3711 6141

CIK No: 0000040730

Subsidiaries: 1908 Holdings Ltd., 3096169 Nova Scotia Company, 4309642 Canada, Inc., ABA Seguros, S.A. de C.V., Adam Opel GmbH, Aisin GM Allison Co., Ltd., Alexium Financial Services, Inc., Annunciata Corporation, Argonaut Holdings, Inc., Autofinanciamiento GMAC, S.A. de C.V., Banco General Motors S.A., Basic Credit Holding Company, LLC, BOCO (Proprietary) Limited, Cadillac Polanco, S.A. de C.V., Canadian Lease Auto Receivable Corporation 291 Subsidiaries included in the Index

Officers: Richard G. Wagoner/Chmn., CEO, Nancy C. Everett/CEO, GM Asset Management, Michael A. Grimaldi/CEO, GM, Pres., VP, GM - Daewoo Auto - Technology, GMDT, Frederick A. Henderson/Vice Chmn., CFO/$5,192,838.00, Chris Gubbey/Chmn., MD, GM Holden Ltd, Robert A. Lutz/Vice Chmn. - Global Product Development/$8,444,043.00, Gary A. White/GM - North America, VP - Vehicle Line Exec., Full Size Truck Team, David W. Meline/GM, North America VP, Michael P. Millikin/Assoc. General Counsel, Nicholas S. Cyprus/Controller, Chief Accounting Officer, Raymond P. Wexler/Chief Tax Officer, Jaime Ardila/MD, Pres., GM do Brasil, Ralph J. Szygenda/Group VP, CIO, Bo I. Andersson/Group VP - Global Purchasing, Supply Chain, Edward T. Welburn/GM, VP - Global Design *(54 Officers included in Index)*

Directors: Richard G. Wagoner/Chmn., CEO, Frederick A. Henderson/Vice Chmn., CFO, Chris Gubbey/Chmn., MD, GM Holden Ltd, Eckhard Pfeiffer/Dir., Kathryn V. Marinello/Dir., Erroll B. Davis/Dir., Percy N. Barnevik/Dir., Erskine B. Bowles/Dir., John H. Bryan/Dir., Armando M. Codina/Dir., George M.C. Fisher/Dir., Karen Katen/Dir., Kent Kresa/Dir., Ellen J. Kullman/Dir., Philip A. Laskawy/Dir.

Owners: A. M. Codina, J. M. Devine, R. A. Lutz, G. R. Wagoner, P. A. Laskawy, E. Pfeiffer, T. A. Gottschalk, State Street Bank and Trust Company/14.80%, E. J. Kullman, Insiders, J. H. Bryan, K. Katen, G. M.C. Fisher, G. L. Cowger, K. Kresa *(22 Owners included in Index)*

Financial Data: Fiscal Year End:12/31   Latest Annual Data: 12/31/2006

Year	Sales	Net Income
2006	$207,349,000,000	-$1,978,000,000
2005	$192,604,000,000	-$10,567,000,000
2004	$193,517,000,000	$2,804,000,000

Curr. Assets:	$64,480,000,000	Curr. Liab.:	$69,036,000,000		
Plant, Equip.:	$53,728,000,000	Total Liab.:	$190,443,000,000	Indic. Yr. Divd.:	$1.000
Total Assets:	$186,192,000,000	Net Worth:	-$5,441,000,000	Debt/ Equity:	NA

General Steel Holdings Inc

Haitong Plz., 10th Fl., Bldg. A, No.3 Nanlishi Ave., Xicheng District, Beijing, 100037; *PH:* 86-5942713; *http://* www.gshi-steel.com; *Email:* info@gshi-steel.com

General - Incorporation	NV	**Stock**- Price on:12/24/2007	$3.89
Employees	NA	Stock Exchange	AMEX
Auditor	MSW Frazer & Torbet	Ticker Symbol	GSI
Stk Agt	Pacific Stock Transfer Company	Outstanding Shares	NA
Counsel	NA	E.P.S.	NA
DUNS No.	09-266-6262	Shareholders	NA

Business: The groups principle activity is to manufacture hot rolled carbon and silicon steel sheets. The groups products include carbon steel, silicon steel, special steel pipe, and rebar and round bar. The group's products sold under the brand name Qiu Steel. The group operates from United States.

Primary SIC and add'l.: NA

CIK No: 0001239188

Subsidiaries: General Steel Investment Co., Ltd., Tianjin Daqiuzhuang Metal Sheet Co., Ltd

Officers: Sheng Zuo Yu/Dir., CEO, Pres., Henry Yu/CEO - China, Vicky Cheng/Contact - China, Yale Yu/Contact - Investor Relations, China, Yong Zu Zhang/Mgr. - Merchandizing, John Chen/Dir., CFO, Xiao Gang Su/42/Mgr. - Human Resources Department, Tong Sheng Fan/Mgr. - Sales, Guo Sheng Zhao/Dir., Chief Engineer, Chun Wen Han/Dir., Controller, Dong Guo Wang/Dir., CTO, Guang Zhi Wang/GM, Qi Hou/Mgr. - Production, Yan Zuo Yu/Mgr. - Equipment, Wen Yu Liu/Mgr. - Human Resources

Directors: Sheng Zuo Yu/Dir., CEO, Pres., John Chen/Dir., CFO, Guo Sheng Zhao/Dir., Chief Engineer, Chun Wen Han/Dir., Controller, Ross Warner/43/Dir., John Wong/40/Dir., Lian Hui Tian/66/Dir.

Owners: Ross Warner, John Chen, Sheng Guo Zhao, Insiders/82.20%, Yu Wen Liu, Wen Chun Han, Matlin Patterson Global/6.81%, Zuo Sheng Yu/73.00%, Xiao Gang Su, John Wong

Financial Data: Fiscal Year End:12/31   Latest Annual Data: 12/31/2006

Year	Sales	Net Income
2006	$139,495,000	$1,033,000
2005	$89,740,000	$2,740,000
2004	$87,832,000	$915,000

Curr. Assets:	$44,690,000	**Curr. Liab.:**	$51,396,000		
Plant, Equip.:	$26,607,000	**Total Liab.:**	$51,396,000	**Indic. Yr. Divd.:**	NA
Total Assets:	$73,822,000	**Net Worth:**	$14,060,000	**Debt/ Equity:**	NA

Generex Biotechnology Corp

33 Harbour Sq., Ste. 202, Toronto, ON, M5J 2G2; ***PH:*** 1-416-364-2551; ***Fax:*** 1-416-364-9363; ***http://*** www.generex.com; ***Email:*** info@generex.com

General		**Stock**	
Incorporation	DE	Price on:12/24/2007	$1.67
Employees	23	Stock Exchange	NDQ
Auditor	Danziger Hochman Partners LLP	Ticker Symbol	GNBT
Stk Agt	StockTrans, Inc.	Outstanding Shares	108,980,000
Counsel	Eckert Seamens Cherin & Mellott	E.P.S	-$0.25
DUNS No.	NA	Shareholders	NA

Business: The group's principal activity is the research and development of drug delivery systems and technology. Its current focus is the development of its proprietary technology for the administration of formulations of large molecule drugs to the oral (Buccal) cavity using a hand-held aerosol applicator. In Sep-2003, the group commenced a 90 day study in 80 type 2 diabetic patients with poorly controlled blood glucose. The group continues to conduct limited clinical trials in the United States and other countries. The group is in development stage. On 08-Aug-2003, the group acquired Antigen Express Inc.

Primary SIC and add'l.: 8731

CIK No: 0001059784

Subsidiaries: Antigen Express, Inc., Generex (Bermuda), Inc., Generex Pharmaceuticals (USA) LLC., Generex Pharmaceuticals, Inc.

Officers: Anna E. Gluskin/Chmn., CEO, Pres., Slava Jarnitskii/Financial Controller, Rose C. Perri/Dir., CFO, COO, Treasurer, Sec., Gerald Bernstein/Dir., VP - Medical Affairs, Mark Fletcher/Exec. VP, General Counsel, Eric Von Hofe/VP - Generex, Pres. - Antigen Express, Roberto Cid/VP - Marketing, Sales Latin, South America, Minzhen Xu/VP - Biology, Antigen, Craig Kulman/Contact - Investor Relations, George Markus/Mgr. - Regulatory Affairs

Directors: Anna E. Gluskin/Chmn., CEO, Pres., Peter Amanatides/Dir., Rose C. Perri/Dir., CFO, COO, Treasurer, Sec., Gerald Bernstein/Dir., VP - Medical Affairs, John Barratt/Dir., Brian T. McGee/Dir., Nola E. Masterson/Dir., Jaime Davidson/Dir.

Owners: Mark Fletcher/1.00%, Nola Masterson, Mindy J. Allport-Settle, John P. Barratt, EBI, Inc. In Trust/1.30%, Anna E. Gluskin/2.60%, GHI, Inc. In Trust/1.70%, David E. Wires, Rose C. Perri/4.90%, Gerald Bernstein, Brian T. McGee, Peter G. Amanatides, Insiders/10.00%

Financial Data: ***Fiscal Year End:***07/31 ***Latest Annual Data:*** 07/31/2007

Year	Sales	Net Income
2007	$180,000	-$23,505,000
2006	$175,000	-$67,967,000
2005	$392,000	-$24,002,000

Curr. Assets:	$52,819,000	**Curr. Liab.:**	$6,033,000		
Plant, Equip.:	$2,586,000	**Total Liab.:**	$8,641,000	**Indic. Yr. Divd.:**	NA
Total Assets:	$64,105,000	**Net Worth:**	$55,464,000	**Debt/ Equity:**	0.0706

Genesco Inc

Genesco Pk., 1415 Murfreesboro Rd., Nashville, TN, 37202; ***PH:*** 1-615-367-7000; ***Fax:*** 1-615-367-8278; ***http://*** www.genesco.com; ***Email:*** investorrelations@genesco.com

General		**Stock**	
Incorporation	TN	Price on:12/24/2007	$53
Employees	5,600	Stock Exchange	NYSE
Auditor	Ernst & Young LLP	Ticker Symbol	GCO
Stk Agt	EquiServe Trust Co N.A	Outstanding Shares	22,750,000
Counsel	NA	E.P.S	$1.65
DUNS No.	00-136-7549	Shareholders	NA

Business: The group's principal activity is the retail and wholesale distribution of branded footwear. In addition, it also designs, sources, markets and distributes footwear under the johnston & murphy brand and the licensed dockers brand, to more than 1,000 retail stores in the United States. The group operates under five segments: journeys: operates 665 retail footwear chains under the name journeys and journeys kidz. Jarman: operates 233 retail footwear chains under the name jarman and underground station. Johnston & murphy: operates 148 retail stores and factory stores under the name johnston & murphy, as well as conducts direct marketing and wholesale distribution of footwear. Dockers footwear: comprises of dockers footwear. Hat world/lids: comprises of hat world, lids, hat zone and cap factory retail headwear operations. All the segments sell footwear products at either retail or wholesale. On 01-Apr-2004, the group acquired hat world corporation.

Primary SIC and add'l.: 5139 3144 5661 3143

CIK No: 0000018498

Subsidiaries: Beagen Street Corporation, Flagg Bros. of Puerto Rico, Inc., GCO Canada Inc., GCO Properties, Inc., Genesco Brands, Inc., Genesco Global, Inc., Genesco Merger Company Inc., Genesco Netherlands BV, Genesco Virgin Islands, Genesco World Apparel, Ltd., Hat World Corporation, Hat World, Inc., Hatworld.com, Inc.

Officers: Hal N. Pennington/Chmn., CEO/$3,409,389.00, John W. Clinard/Sr. VP - Administration, Human Resources, Claire S. McCall/Dir. - Corporate Relations, Kenneth J. Kocher/Sr. VP, Pres. - Hat World, James S. Gulmi/CFO, Sr. VP - Finance/$1,139,637.00, Robert J. Dennis/COO, Pres./$2,098,197.00, James C. Estepa/56/Sr. VP/$1,685,426.00, Jonathan D. Caplan/54/Sr. VP/$1,225,814.00, Mimi E. Vaughn/Sr. VP - Strategy, Business Development, Paul D. Williams/VP, Chief Accounting Officer, Roger G. Sisson/Sr. VP, Corp. Sec., General Counsel, Matthew N. Johnson/VP - Finance, Treasurer

Directors: Hal N. Pennington/Chmn., CEO, Ben T. Harris/Dir., William A. Williamson/Dir., Marty G. Dickens/Dir., Leonard L. Berry/Dir., Robert V. Dale/Dir., Matthew C. Diamond/Dir., William F. Blaufuss/Dir., James S. Beard/Dir., James W. Bradford/Dir., Kathleen Mason/Dir.

Owners: Marty G. Dickens, William F. Blaufuss, William A. Williamson, Citadel Limited Partnership, Hazel Grossman, Michael A. Roth, A group consisting of Barclays Global Investors, NA, A group consisting of Octavian Master Fund, L.P., FMR Corp., Ben T. Harris, James S. Bradford, Kathleen Mason, Insiders, James S. Beard, Leonard L. Berry *(24 Owners included in Index)*

Financial Data: ***Fiscal Year End:***01/28 ***Latest Annual Data:*** 2/3/2007

Year	Sales	Net Income
2007	$1,460,478,000	$67,646,000
2006	$1,283,876,000	$62,686,000
2005	$1,112,681,000	$48,249,000

Curr. Assets:	$335,066,000	**Curr. Liab.:**	$134,736,000	**P/E Ratio:**	23.14
Plant, Equip.:	$222,334,000	**Total Liab.:**	$324,147,000	**Indic. Yr. Divd.:**	NA
Total Assets:	$729,373,000	**Net Worth:**	$405,226,000	**Debt/ Equity:**	NA

Genesee & Wyoming Inc

66 Field Point Rd., Greenwich, CT, 06830; ***PH:*** 1-203-629-3722; ***Fax:*** 1-203-661-4106; ***http://*** www.gwrr.com; ***Email:*** ccomm@gwrr.com

General		**Stock**	
Incorporation	DE	Price on:12/24/2007	$30.7
Employees	2,677	Stock Exchange	NYSE
Auditor	PricewaterhouseCoopers LLP	Ticker Symbol	GWR
Stk Agt	Computershare Investor Services LLC	Outstanding Shares	40,090,000
Counsel	Simpson Thacher & Bartlett LLP	E.P.S	$1.37
DUNS No.	09-360-9113	Shareholders	NA

Business: The group's principal activities are the operation of short line and regional freight railroads, the provision of freight car switching and rail-related services. The operations are conducted in the United States, Australia, Canada, Mexico and Bolivia. The group transports coke, ores, paper, petroleum, grains, alumina, forest products and other commodities. The group operates railroads under a fifty percent joint venture with the australian railroad group pty ltd in Australia. In 2003, the group operated approximately 8,100 miles of owned, jointly owned or leased tracks as well as over 3,000 additional miles under track access arrangements. During 2003, the group acquired chattahoochee industrial railroad, Arkansas Louisiana and Mississippi railroad company and fordyce & princeton railroad company.

Primary SIC and add'l.: 4011 4013

CIK No: 0001012620

Subsidiaries: Allegheny & Eastern Railroad, LLC, AN Railway LLC, Arkansas Louisiana & Mississippi Railroad Company, Atlantic and Western Railway LP, Bay Line Railroad LLC, Breaux Bridge Railroad, Inc., Buffalo & Pittsburgh Railroad, Inc., Chattahoochee Industrial Railroad, Commonwealth Railway, Inc., Compaa de Ferrocarriles Chiapas-Mayab, S.A. de C.V., Corpus Christi Terminal Railroad, Inc., East Tennessee Railway LP, Emons Finance Corp., Emons Industries, Inc., Emons Railroad Group, Inc. 77 Subsidiaries included in the Index

Officers: John C. Hellmann/Dir., CEO, Pres./$2,353,253.00, Mortimer B. Fuller/Exec. Chmn./$4,075,322.00, David L. Powell/VP - Motive Power, Richard T. O'Donnell/VP - Tax, Gerald A. Sattora/VP - Accounting, Controller, Mark W. Hastings/Exec. VP - Corporate Development, David J. Collins/Sr. VP - New York, Pennsylvania Region, Kym Fullgrabe/Project Coordinator, Ian Hall/GM - Transportation, Bill Fleer/Assist. Chief Engineer, Renu Duchesne/VP - Administration, Controller - Vice - President Administration et Controleur, Jean-Marc Montigny/VP - Transportation - Labour Relation, VP - Transport et Relations de Travail - GWC, GM - Directeur General, QGR, Bruce A. Carswell/Sr. VP - Oregon Region, James N. Davis/Sr. VP - Rocky Mountain Region, Gerald T. Gates/Sr. VP - Southern Region *(92 Officers included in Index)*

Directors: John C. Hellmann/Dir., CEO, Pres., Mortimer B. Fuller/Exec. Chmn., Robert M. Melzer/Dir., Oivind Lorentzen/Dir., Mark A. Scudder/Dir., Philip J. Ringo/Dir., John M. Randolph/Dir., David C. Hurley/Dir., Douglas M. Young/Dir., Louis S. Fuller/Dir., Peter O. Scannell/Dir.

Owners: Philip J. Ringo, Insiders/76.20%, David C. Hurley, Mark A. Scudder, Mortimer B. Fuller/1.60%, Wellington Management Company,/13.80%, John C. Hellmann, Louis S. Fuller/1.00%, Allison M. Fergus, Marsico Capital Management,LLC/7.60%, Peter O. Scannell, James W. Benz, Louis S. Fuller/17.00%, John C. Hellmann/1.10%, Robert M. Melzer *(23 Owners included in Index)*

Financial Data: ***Fiscal Year End:***12/31 ***Latest Annual Data:*** 12/31/2006

Year	Sales	Net Income
2006	$478,846,000	$134,003,000
2005	$385,389,000	$50,135,000
2004	$303,784,000	$37,619,000

Curr. Assets:	$390,919,000	**Curr. Liab.:**	$233,138,000	**P/E Ratio:**	9.65
Plant, Equip.:	$573,292,000	**Total Liab.:**	$620,877,000	**Indic. Yr. Divd.:**	NA
Total Assets:	$1,141,064,000	**Net Worth:**	$520,187,000	**Debt/ Equity:**	0.4575

Genesee Corp B

600 Powers Bldg., 16 W St., Rochester, NY, 14614; ***PH:*** 1-716-454-1250

General		**Stock**	
Incorporation	NY	Price on:12/24/2007	$2.1
Employees	NA	Stock Exchange	NA
Auditor	PricewaterhouseCoopers LLP	Ticker Symbol	NA
Stk Agt	NA	Outstanding Shares	1,670,000
Counsel	NA	E.P.S	NA
DUNS No.	NA	Shareholders	NA

Business: The group operates through its subsidiaries whose principal activities include conducting dry food processing and packaging, equipment leasing and real estate investment. The group operates from New York in the United States.

Primary SIC and add'l.: 2082

CIK No: 0000040934

Subsidiaries: GBC Liquidating Corp., Genesee Ventures, Inc.

Officers: Steven M. Morse/44/Pres., Treasurer, Sec.

Directors: Stephen B. Ashley/68/Dir.

Owners: Charles S. Wehle/35.20%, Henry S. Wehle/20.00%, Elizabeth R. Wehle Trust/5.80%

Genesis Bioventures Inc

10940 Wilshire Blvd., Ste 600, Los Angeles, CA, 90024; ***PH:*** 1-310-443-4102; ***Fax:*** 1-310-443-4103; ***http://*** www.gnsbio.com; ***Email:*** info@runonideas.com

General		**Stock**	
Incorporation	NY	Price on:12/24/2007	$0.09
Employees	5	Stock Exchange	NA
Auditor	Jaspers & Hall, P.C.	Ticker Symbol	NA
Stk Agt	Olde Monmouth Stk Trnsfer Co. Inc.	Outstanding Shares	76,090,000
Counsel	NA	E.P.S	-$0.1
DUNS No.	NA	Shareholders	NA

Business: The group's principal activity is to develop and market breast cancer risk assessment tool. The group is a development stage company. It is involved with portfolio companies, which are involved in cancer therapy and neurodegenerative diagnostics. It also serves as a strategic advisor in key aspects of science, product commercialization, business issues and financial development by providing management expertise aimed at transforming promising medical technology into successful commercial products. The group has selected the areas of oncology and neurology as its primary sectors of interest, based on the perceived market potential for new treatments and diagnostics.

Primary SIC and add'l.: 2834 8731

CIK No: 0001084966

Subsidiaries: Biomedical Diagnostics, LLC

Officers: Douglas C. Lane/Chmn., CEO, Pres., Kaspar Baenziger/Business Advisor, Lou Lome/Scientific Advisor, Jeffrey A. Conrad/Dir., Sec., Ivan Labat/Scientific Advisor, William A. Collins/Business Advisor, Michael R. Petriella/Business Advisor

Directors: Douglas C. Lane/Chmn., CEO, Pres., John D. Todd/Chmn. - Scientific Advisory Board, Jonathan F. Atzen/Dir., Antony S. Dyakowski/59/Dir., Ian B. Woods/64/Dir., Jeffrey A. Conrad/Dir., Sec., Barrett S. Evans/Dir., Robert F. Lutz/Dir., Victor A. Voebel/Dir.

Owners: The Lutz Family Trust/5.90%, Insiders/33.70%, eFund Capital Management, LLC/13.60%, Victor Voebel/7.40%, Douglas Lane/6.60%

Financial Data: ***Fiscal Year End:***12/31 ***Latest Annual Data:*** 12/31/2006

Year	Sales	Net Income
2006	NA	-$6,425,000
2005	NA	-$6,002,000
2004	NA	-$5,018,000

Curr. Assets:	$309,000	**Curr. Liab.:**	$4,319,000		
Plant, Equip.:	$1,000	**Total Liab.:**	$4,319,000	**Indic. Yr. Divd.:**	NA
Total Assets:	$3,816,000	**Net Worth:**	-$504,000	**Debt/ Equity:**	NA

Genesis Energy LP

500 Dallas St., Ste. 2500, Houston, TX, 77002; ***PH:*** 1-713-860-2500; ***Fax:*** 1-713-860-2640; ***http://*** www.genesiscrudeoil.com

General - Incorporation	DE	***Stock*** - Price on:12/24/2007	$33
Employees	NA	Stock Exchange	AMEX
Auditor	Deloitte & Touche LLP	Ticker Symbol	GEL
Stk Agt	American Stock Transfer & Trust Co.	Outstanding Shares	13,780,000
Counsel	NA	E.P.S.	$0.18
DUNS No.	NA	Shareholders	NA

Business: The groups principle activities include operating, developing and acquiring oil and gas properties. The group operates through three segments namely, pipeline transportation, crude oil gathering and marketing, and industrial gases. In the year 2006, the group acquired 50% partnership interest in Sandhill Group, LLC. The group operates from the Gulf Coast region of the United States.

Primary SIC and add'l.: 5171 4612 4612

CIK No: 0001022321

Subsidiaries: Genesis CO2 Pipeline, L.P., Genesis Crude Oil, L.P., Genesis Energy Finance Corporation, Genesis Natural Gas Pipeline, L.P., Genesis Pipeline Texas, L.P., Genesis Pipeline USA, L.P., Genesis Syngas Investments, L.P.

Officers: Grant E. Sims/Dir., CEO, Joe Mueller/Contact, Joseph A. Blount/COO, Pres., Brad Graves/Exec. VP - Business Development, Ross A. Benavides/CFO, General Counsel, Sec., Kerry W. Mazoch/VP - Crude Oil, Karen N. Pape/VP, Controller, Kirk Kitchens/Contact - Dallas, North Texas, Bill Rigney/Contact - West Texas, New Mexico, Mark Harrell/Contact - West Texas, New Mexico, Eddie Stutts/Contact - East Texas, North Louisiana, South Arkansas, Gary Taub/Contact - Mississippi, South Louisiana, Alabama, Florida, Jim Buford/Contact - Mississippi, South Louisiana, Alabama, Florida, Kathy Warren/Mgr. - Division Orders, Jodi Hasley/Contact - Tariffs, Statements

Directors: Grant E. Sims/Dir., CEO, Gareth Roberts/Chmn., Phil Rykhoek/Dir., Conley J. Stone/Dir., Mark C. Allen/Dir., Ronald T. Evans/Dir., Herbert I. Goodman/Dir., Susan O. Rheney/Dir.

Owners: Grant E. Sims, Genesis Energy, Inc./7.40%, Ross A. Benavides, James E. Davison/14.30%, Ronald T. Evans, Davison Petroleum Products, L.L.C./32.70%, Conley J. Stone, Herbert I. Goodman, Susan O. Rheney, Swank Capital, L.L.C.,/6.00%, Phil Rykhoek, Karen N. Pape, James E. Davison/5.10%, Gareth Roberts, Davison Transport, Inc./8.40% *(16 Owners included in Index)*

Financial Data: ***Fiscal Year End:***12/31 ***Latest Annual Data:*** 12/31/2006

Year	Sales	Net Income
2006	$918,369,000	$8,381,000
2005	$1,078,739,000	$3,415,000
2004	$927,143,000	-$1,412,000

Curr. Assets:	$99,992,000	**Curr. Liab.:**	$95,912,000	**P/E Ratio:**	183.33
Plant, Equip.:	$31,316,000	**Total Liab.:**	$105,425,000	**Indic. Yr. Divd.:**	$0.920
Total Assets:	$191,087,000	**Net Worth:**	$85,662,000	**Debt/ Equity:**	0.1210

Genesis HealthCare Corp

101 E State St., Kennett Square, PA, 19348; ***PH:*** 1-610-444-6350; ***http://*** www.genesishcc.com

General - Incorporation	PA	***Stock*** - Price on:12/24/2007	$68.6
Employees	35,500	Stock Exchange	NA
Auditor	KPMG LLP	Ticker Symbol	NA
Stk Agt	Mellon Investor Services LLC	Outstanding Shares	19,720,000
Counsel	NA	E.P.S.	$1.64
DUNS No.	NA	Shareholders	NA

Business: The groups principle activity is to operate assisted living and skilled nursing facilities. The groups services include alzheimers care, orthopedic rehabilitation, ventilator care and dialysis care. The group operates from United States.

Primary SIC and add'l.: 8059 8051 8082

CIK No: 0001236736

Subsidiaries: Academy Nursing Home, Inc., ADS Apple Valley Limited Partnership, ADS Apple Valley, Inc., ADS Consulting, Inc., ADS Danvers ALF, Inc., ADS Dartmouth ALF, Inc., ADS Group, Inc.(The), ADS Hingham ALF, Inc., ADS Hingham Limited Partnership, ADS Hingham Nursing Facility, Inc., ADS Home Health, Inc., ADS Management, Inc., ADS Palm Chelmsford, Inc., ADS Recuperative Center Limited Partnership, ADS Recuperative Center, Inc. 304 Subsidiaries included in the Index

Officers: George V. Hager/Chmn., CEO, James W. Tabak/Sr. VP - Human Resources, James V. McKeon/CFO, Exec. VP, Eileen M. Coggins/Sr. VP, General Counsel, Corp. Sec., David C. Almquist/Exec. VP, Pres. - Southern Area, Barbara J. Hauswald/Sr. VP - Planning, Development, Richard Pell/Sr. VP - Administration, Richard P. Blinn/Exec. VP, Pres. - Northeast Area, Irene Fleshner/Sr. VP - Clinical Practice, Outcomes Management, Robert A. Reitz/COO, Exec. VP, Deborah Soutar/Sr. VP, Chief Learning Officer, Richard L. Castor/CIO, Sr. VP, Paul D. Bach/Exec. VP, Pres. - Central Area, A. T. Locilento/Sr. VP - Human Development, Dan Hirschfeld/Pres. - Genesis Rehab Services *(17 Officers included in Index)*

Directors: George V. Hager/Chmn., CEO, Terry Allison Rappuhn/Dir., Charlene Connolly Quinn/Dir., John F. Depodesta/Dir., Robert H. Fish/Dir., Charles W. McQueary/Dir., Kevin M. Kelley/Dir., Michael J. Gallagher/Dir.

Owners: Mellon Financial Corporation/6.10%, A. T. Locilento, Charles W. McQueary, Donald Smith & Co., Inc./6.47%, Kevin M. Kelley, George V. Hager/1.12%, Northbrook GH, LLC/5.10%, Robert H. Fish, Charlene Connolly Quinn, Copper Arch Capital, LLC/5.53%, Richard P. Blinn, Robert A. Reitz, Michael J. Gallagher, Dimensional Fund Advisors, Inc./5.25%, John F. DePodesta *(22 Owners included in Index)*

Financial Data: ***Fiscal Year End:***09/30 ***Latest Annual Data:*** 9/30/2006

Year	Sales	Net Income
2006	$1,770,298,000	$35,877,000
2005	$1,711,433,000	$46,068,000
2004	$1,529,892,000	$29,073,000

Curr. Assets:	$430,457,000	**Curr. Liab.:**	$208,262,000	**P/E Ratio:**	41.83
Plant, Equip.:	$877,075,000	**Total Liab.:**	$772,056,000	**Indic. Yr. Divd.:**	NA
Total Assets:	$1,472,530,000	**Net Worth:**	$700,474,000	**Debt/ Equity:**	0.6364

Genesis Microchip Inc

2525 Augustine Dr., Santa Clara, CA, 95054; ***PH:*** 1-408-919-8400; ***Fax:*** 1-408-986-9644; ***http://*** www.gnss.com; ***Email:*** sales-americas@gnss.com

General - Incorporation	DE	***Stock*** - Price on:12/24/2007	$8.82
Employees	595	Stock Exchange	NDQ
Auditor	KPMG LLP	Ticker Symbol	GNSS
Stk Agt	Mellon Investor Services LLC	Outstanding Shares	37,180,000
Counsel	NA	E.P.S.	-$4.68
DUNS No.	24-708-5087	Shareholders	NA

Business: The group's principal activities are to design, develop and market integrated circuits that receive and process digital video and graphic images. These solutions translate video, graphics and image sources for viewing on various display systems such as flat panel computer monitors, digital crt monitors and digital television. The group supplies these solutions to the digital image processing markets for use in medical imaging, aerospace, video editing and television broadcasting. The group sells and markets its products through various subsidiaries located not only in the United States but also in Japan, China, Taiwan, South Korea and rest of the world.

Primary SIC and add'l.: 3679 6719 3577

CIK No: 0001161396

Subsidiaries: Faroudja Laboratories, Inc., Faroudja, Inc., Genesis Microchip (Canada) Co., Genesis Microchip (Delaware) Inc., Genesis Microchip (India) Pvt. Ltd., Genesis Microchip GmbH, Genesis Microchip KK, Genesis Microchip Limited Partnership, Genesis Microchip LLC, Sage, Inc., Smart Yantra Technologies Pvt. Ltd.

Officers: Elias Antoun/Dir., CEO/$1,887,855.00, Hildy Shandell/Sr. VP - Corporate Development/$513,184.00, Behrooz Yadegar/Sr. VP - Product Development/$530,939.00, Pamela Goncalves/Contact - Investor Relations, Media Inquiries, Graham Loveridge/VP - TV Marketing, Paula Ewanich/VP - Human Resources, Linda Millage/Interim Principal Accounting Officer, Sr. Dir. - Finance, Mary Ann Baker/VP - Operations, Jeffrey Lin/General Counsel, Sec., Robert Haefling/GM, Sr. VP - Displayport, Monitor Business, Ernest Lin/Sr. VP - Worldwide Sales

Directors: Elias Antoun/Dir., CEO, Jeffrey Diamond/Chmn., Tim Christoffersen/Dir., Chandrashekar M. Reddy/Dir., Robert H. Kidd/Dir., Jon Castor/Dir., Chieh Chang/Dir.

Owners: Robert H. Kidd, Chandrashekar M. Reddy, Elias Antoun/1.10%, Jon Castor, Tzoyao Chan, Raphael Mehrbians, Hildy Shandell, Behrooz Yadegar, Anders Frisk, Tim Christoffersen, Chieh Chang, Jeffrey Diamond, DeutscheBank AG/8.50%, Sonar Capital Management LLC/6.10%, Michael Healy *(16 Owners included in Index)*

Financial Data: ***Fiscal Year End:***03/31 ***Latest Annual Data:*** 03/31/2007

Year	Sales	Net Income
2007	$214,617,000	-$144,341,000
2006	$269,506,000	$18,390,000
2005	$204,115,000	-$9,447,000

Curr. Assets:	$244,772,000	**Curr. Liab.:**	$40,254,000		
Plant, Equip.:	$16,459,000	**Total Liab.:**	$40,254,000	**Indic. Yr. Divd.:**	NA
Total Assets:	$479,677,000	**Net Worth:**	$439,423,000	**Debt/ Equity:**	NA

Genesis Pharmaceuticals Enterprises Inc

Formerly: Genesis Technology Group Inc
7900 Glades Rd., Ste. 420, Boca Raton, FL, 33434; ***PH:*** 1-561-988-9880; ***http://*** www.genesis-technology.net

General - Incorporation	FL	***Stock*** - Price on:12/24/2007	$0.1399
Employees	2	Stock Exchange	NA
Auditor	Sherb & Co. LLP	Ticker Symbol	NA
Stk Agt	Computershare Investor Services LLC	Outstanding Shares	84,640,000
Counsel	NA	E.P.S.	-$0.009
DUNS No.	NA	Shareholders	NA

Business: The group's principal activity is to assist western companies in entering the Chinese market for business development. The group acts as a resource for companies that desire expertise in marketing, distribution, manufacturing, forming joint ventures or establishing a base in China. As a part of that strategy, the group is a member of the shanghai technology stock (property rights) exchange, an organization that promotes the influx of technology into China. The group's key area of focus is the life and health science arena in China. Life and health science is compromised of different but related industries such as environmental science, biotechnology, pharmaceuticals and healthcare development. In addition to its consulting services, it has also acquired companies in the United States and China for the purposes of further developing these companies, with operational, managerial and financial support.

Primary SIC and add'l.: 7389

CIK No: 0001091164

Subsidiaries: Extrema LLC, Genesis (Hong Kong) OEM Direct, Ltd., Genesis China, Inc, Genesis Equity Partners LLC, Genesis Latin America LLC, Genesis Systems, Inc., Shanghai Chorry Technology Development Co., Limited

Officers: Gary L. Wolfson/59/Dir., CEO, Adam Wasserman/43/CFO, Kenneth Clinton/37/Dir., Pres.

Directors: Gary L. Wolfson/59/Dir., CEO, Kenneth Clinton/37/Dir., Pres., Shaohua Tan/45/Dir., Rodrigo Arboleda/66/Dir.

Owners: Gary Wolfson/14.30%, Kenneth Clinton/13.50%, Rodrigo Arboleda, Insiders/31.00%, Shaohua Tan/3.30%, Adam Wasserman/1.47%

Financial Data: ***Fiscal Year End:***09/30 ***Latest Annual Data:*** 9/30/2006

Year	Sales	Net Income
2006	$6,750,000	$2,910,000
2005	$155,000	-$3,727,000
2004	$23,387,000	-$1,591,000

Curr. Assets:	$1,301,000	Curr. Liab.:	$433,000	P/E Ratio:	11.66
Plant, Equip.:	$16,000	Total Liab.:	$433,000	Indic. Yr. Divd.:	NA
Total Assets:	$7,232,000	Net Worth:	$5,221,000	Debt/ Equity:	NA

Genesys

Immeuble LAcropole 954-980, Ave. Jean Mermoz, Montpellier, 34000; *PH:* 33-0499132767; *http://* www.genesys.com

General - Incorporation......................France	Stock- Price on:12/24/2007 ....NA
Employees 1,018	Stock Exchange.....................................OTC
Auditor ...:.............................. Ernst & Young LLP	Ticker Symbol.................................GNSYY
Stk Agt....................................Bank of New York	Outstanding Shares ....NA
Counsel..NA	E.P.S...NA
DUNS No. ....NA	Shareholders..NA

Business: The group's principle activity is the provision of teleconferencing services. The company specialises in three types of teleconference services: telephone conferencing, which consists of connecting more than three people together by telephone; graphic audio conferencing, which allows the participants to present and exchange text, tables, charts etc and work through computers as well as communicate through the telephone; video conferencing, which allows the voices of the participants to be exchanged along with moving images of them. The company also offers a range of Web conferencing services including live audio streaming, live data streaming, recorded audio and data streaming as well as multi conference manager ip.

Primary SIC and add'l.: 7389

CIK No: 0001125276

Subsidiaries: Genesys Conferencing Europe SAS, Genesys Conferencing, Inc.

Officers: Francois Legros/Chmn., CEO, Stephen Sperling/Exec. VP - Production, Infrastructure, Denise Persson/Exec. VP - Marketing, Olivier Fourcade/Exec. VP - Asia Pacific, Andrew Lazarus/CFO, Exec. VP, Jim Lysinger/Exec. VP - Sales, Marketing, Shelly Robertson/COO, Exec. VP, Jim Huzell/Pres.

Directors: Francois Legros/Chmn., CEO, David Detert/Dir., Patrick Jones/Dir., Frederic Spagnou/Dir., Bo Dimert/Dir., Tim Samples/Dir.

*Financial Data: Fiscal Year End:*12/31   *Latest Annual Data:* 12/31/2005

Year	Sales	Net Income
2005	$168,101,000	$4,573,000
2004	$189,703,000	-$97,807,000
2003	$200,284,000	-$14,256,000

Curr. Assets:	$47,430,000	Curr. Liab.:	$39,960,000		
Plant, Equip.:	$26,007,000	Total Liab.:	$129,593,000	Indic. Yr. Divd.:	NA
Total Assets:	$119,623,000	Net Worth:	-$9,970,000	Debt/ Equity:	NA

GeneThera Inc

3930 Youngfield St., Wheat Ridge, CO, 80033; *PH:* 1-303-463-6371; *Fax:* 1-303-463-6377; *http://* www.genethera.net

General - Incorporation...............................FL	Stock- Price on:12/24/2007 ....$0.033
Employees 4	Stock Exchange.....................................OTC
Auditor .... Jaspers & Hall, P.C.	Ticker Symbol.....................................GTHA
Stk Agt................... Florida Atlantic Stock Transfer, Inc.	Outstanding Shares 37,810,000
Counsel..NA	E.P.S. ....-$0.035
DUNS No. ....NA	Shareholders..NA

Business: The group's principal activity is to develop therapeutic vaccines for the detection and prevention of food contaminating pathogens, veterinary diseases, and diseases affecting human health. The group publishes a news catalog to market its products, which includes family health news containing articles on health, nutrition, lifestyle and innovative health products and therapies. The products cater to agriculture, veterinary and health care industries. On 23-Mar-2003, the group acquired genethera, inc.

Primary SIC and add'l.: 8731 2834 2721

CIK No: 0001017110

Subsidiaries: Family Health News, VDx, Inc., Wisconsin Corporation

Officers: Tony Milici/Chmn., CEO, Pres., Tannya Irizarry/Chief Administrative Officer, Jose R. Sandoval/Consulting Controller, James Huang/Consulting Scientist

Directors: Tony Milici/Chmn., CEO, Pres., Thomas J. Slaga/Dir., Steven M. Grubner/Dir.

Owners: Antonio Milici/49.50%, Tannya L. Irizarry/3.00%, 0711005 BC Ltd. Marketing Group/6.20%, Insiders/58.70%

*Financial Data: Fiscal Year End:*12/31   *Latest Annual Data:* 12/31/2006

Year	Sales	Net Income
2006	$150,000	-$1,483,000
2005	$191,000	-$3,625,000
2004	$25,000	-$5,756,000

Curr. Assets:	$26,000	Curr. Liab.:	$1,418,000		
Plant, Equip.:	$363,000	Total Liab.:	$1,418,000	Indic. Yr. Divd.:	NA
Total Assets:	$395,000	Net Worth:	-$1,024,000	Debt/ Equity:	NA

Genetic Technologies Ltd

60-66 Hanover St., Fitzroy, Victoria, 3065; ; *http://* www.gtg.com.au

General - Incorporation...................Australia	Stock- Price on:12/24/2007 ....$3.65
Employees 49	Stock Exchange.....................................NDQ
Auditor .... Ernst & Young LLP	Ticker Symbol.....................................GENE
Stk Agt....................................Bank of New York	Outstanding Shares 11,800,000
Counsel..NA	E.P.S. ....-$0.3
DUNS No. ....NA	Shareholders..NA

Business: The groups principle activities include research, developing and manufacturing biopharmaceutical products. The group operates through four segments include licensing, testing, research, and corporate. The group operates from United States.

Primary SIC and add'l.: 2836

CIK No: 0001166272

Subsidiaries: AgGenomics Pty. Limited, GeneType Pty. Limited, Gtech International Resources Limited

Officers: Michael Ohanessian/44/CEO, Luisa M. Ashdown/GM - Licensing, Andrea Tobisch/Contact - Media, Gene Technologies Media Releases, Jonathan S. Whitty/GM - Medical Diagnostics, Thomas G. Howitt/44/Company Sec., CFO, Gary Cobon/Chief Scientific Officer, Everard Hunder/Media, Mgr. - Communications, Australia, Ian W. Smith/GM - DNA Profiling, Catherine M. Barclay/GM - Human Resources

Directors: Henry Bosch/76/Chmn., Mervyn Jacobson/66/Non Exec. Dir., Fred Bart/54/Non Exec. Dir., John S. Dawkins/61/Non Exec. Dir., Thomas G. Howitt/44/Company Sec., CFO, David Carruthers/60/Non Exec. Dir.

Owners: Mervyn Jacobson/41.65%, David Carruthers/0.04%, Fred Bart/7.15%, Henry Bosch/0.07%

*Financial Data: Fiscal Year End:*06/30   *Latest Annual Data:* 6/30/2006

Year	Sales	Net Income
2006	$7,345,000	-$4,020,000
2005	$7,220,000	-$5,743,000
2004	$2,645,000	-$4,817,000

Curr. Assets:	$9,715,000	Curr. Liab.:	$2,187,000		
Plant, Equip.:	$1,682,000	Total Liab.:	$3,229,000	Indic. Yr. Divd.:	NA
Total Assets:	$16,653,000	Net Worth:	$13,424,000	Debt/ Equity:	NA

Geneva Resources Inc

Formerly: Geneva Gold Corp
1005 Terminal Way, Ste. 110, Reno, NV, 89502; *PH:* 1-775-348-9330; *http://* www.genevagoldcorp.com

General - Incorporation ....NV	Stock- Price on:12/24/2007 ....NA
Employees ....NA	Stock Exchange.....................................OTC
Auditor ....Dale Matheson Carr-Hilton LaBonte LLP	Ticker Symbol.....................................GVRS
Stk Agt.................... Pacific Stock Transfer Co.	Outstanding Shares ....NA
Counsel..NA	E.P.S...NA
DUNS No. ....NA	Shareholders..NA

Business: The groups principal activities include identifying parcels of land and reclaiming and stabilizing these lands in preparation for construction. The group operates from Canada and the United States.

Primary SIC and add'l.: 1000

CIK No: 0001318196

Officers: Marcus M. Johnson/Dir., CEO, Pres., Bruce D. Horton/62/Dir., Chief Financia Officer, Sec., Treasurer, Duncan Bain/Dir., Consulting Geologist

Directors: Marcus M. Johnson/Dir., CEO, Pres., Bruce D. Horton/62/Dir., Chief Financia Officer, Sec., Treasurer, Stephen Jewett/69/Dir., Mark Campbell/Dir., Duncan Bain/Dir., Consulting Geologist, Stacey Kivel/41/Dir.

Owners: Steve Jewett, Bruce D. Horton, Marcus Johnson/15.98%, Insiders/17.96%, Mark Campbell, Stacey Kivel/0.01%, Petaquilla Minerals, Ltd./9.71%, Duncan Bain

Curr. Assets:	$6,000	Curr. Liab.:	$1,490,000		
Plant, Equip.:	NA	Total Liab.:	$1,490,000	Indic. Yr. Divd.:	NA
Total Assets:	$6,000	Net Worth:	-$1,485,000	Debt/ Equity:	NA

Genex Pharmaceutical Inc

1801 Guangyin Bldg., Youyibeilu, Hexi District, Tianjin City, 300074; *PH:* 86-22-2337-0440; *http://* www.genexpharm.com

General - Incorporation .... DE	Stock- Price on:12/24/2007 ....$0.25
Employees ....NA	Stock Exchange.....................................OTC
Auditor ....Schwartz Levitsky Feldman LLP	Ticker Symbol.....................................GENX
Stk Agt............Interwest Transfer Company, Inc.	Outstanding Shares 3,950,000
Counsel..NA	E.P.S. $1.59
DUNS No. ....NA	Shareholders..NA

Business: The groups principle activities include developing and marketing medical therapies to the dermatology market. The groups products include Oracea(R), Alcortin(TM) and Novacort(TM). The group operates from United States.

Primary SIC and add'l.: NA

CIK No: 0001197380

Subsidiaries: Tianjin Zhongjin Biology Development Co., Ltd.

Owners: Fuzhi Song/0.74%, Deshun Song/0.08%, Insiders/0.74%

*Financial Data: Fiscal Year End:*12/31   *Latest Annual Data:* 12/31/2005

Year	Sales	Net Income
2005	$2,491,000	$625,000
2004	$2,350,000	$1,013,000

Curr. Assets:	$5,614,000	Curr. Liab.:	$1,634,000	P/E Ratio:	0.16
Plant, Equip.:	$131,000	Total Liab.:	$1,678,000	Indic. Yr. Divd.:	NA
Total Assets:	$5,745,000	Net Worth:	$4,067,000	Debt/ Equity:	NA

Genio Group Inc

400 Garden City Plz., Garden City, NY, 11530; *PH:* 1-516-873-2000

General - Incorporation .... DE	Stock- Price on:12/24/2007 ....$0.004
Employees ....NA	Stock Exchange.....................................OTC
Auditor ....Sherb & Co., LLP	Ticker Symbol.....................................GNOI
Stk Agt...........................Interwest Transfer Co.	Outstanding Shares 55,680,000
Counsel..NA	E.P.S. ....-$0.006
DUNS No. ....NA	Shareholders..NA

Business: The groups principal activity is to acquire the operating business of other companies. The group operates from the United States.

Primary SIC and add'l.: 3944 3944

CIK No: 0001100779

Subsidiaries: Genio Inc.

Officers: Steven A. Horowitz/48/Chmn., CEO, CFO

Directors: Steven A. Horowitz/48/Chmn., CEO, CFO

Owners: Steven A. Horowitz/4.99%, Insiders/4.99%

Financial Data: *Fiscal Year End:*09/30 *Latest Annual Data:* 9/30/2006

Year	Sales	Net Income
2006	NA	-$539,000
2005	$320,000	-$3,136,000
2004	$4,000,000	-$9,997,000

Curr. Assets:	NA	**Curr. Liab.:**	$3,905,000		
Plant, Equip.:	NA	**Total Liab.:**	$3,905,000	**Indic. Yr. Divd.:**	NA
Total Assets:	NA	**Net Worth:**	-$3,905,000	**Debt/ Equity:**	NA

Genitope Corp

6900 Dumbarton Cir., Fremont, CA, 94555; *PH:* 1-510-284-3000; *Fax:* 1-512-284-3100; *http://* www.genitope.com; *Email:* info@genitope.com

General - Incorporation .... DE
Employees 170
Auditor .... Deloitte & Touche, LLP
Stk Agt .... Mellon Investor Services LLC
Counsel .... Intellectual Property Counsel
DUNS No. .... NA

Stock- Price on:12/24/2007 .... $3.89
Stock Exchange .... NDQ
Ticker Symbol .... GTOP
Outstanding Shares 41,570,000
E.P.S. .... -$1.65
Shareholders .... NA

Business: The group's principle activities include research and developing immunotherapies for the treatment of cancer. Immunotherapies are treatments that utilize the immune system to combat diseases. The group's product, myvax personalized immunotherapy, is a patient-specific active immunotherapy that is based on the genetic makeup of a patient's tumor and is designed to activate a patient's immune system to identify and attack cancer cells. Myvax is currently in a pivotal phase 3 clinical trial and additional phase 2 clinical trials for the treatment of b-cell non-hodgkin's lymphoma. The group operates in the domestic market. The group operates from United States.

Primary SIC and add'l.: 2836

CIK No: 0001028358

Subsidiaries: Corixa Corporation, Genitrix, LLC, Genius Products, Inc., Genlyte Thomas Group LLC

Officers: Dan W. Denney/Chmn., CEO, Founder/$1,998,762.00, Laura Randall Woodhead/VP - Legal Affairs, David H. Miller/VP - Information Technology, Thomas Theriault/VP - Research, Development, Michael J. Buckley/VP - Manufacturing/$526,184.00, John Vuko/CFO, VP - Finance/$797,723.00, Gregory Ennis/Dir., MD - Peninsula Equity Partners LLC, Mary Ellen Rybak/Chief Medical Officer, VP - Medical Affairs, Thomas Dezao/VP - Strategic Marketing, Sales, Claude Miller/VP - Regulatory Affairs, Quality, Kent R. McGaughy/Dir. - Principal, Cpmg

Directors: Dan W. Denney/Chmn., CEO, Founder, Gregory Ennis/Dir., MD - Peninsula Equity Partners LLC, Stanford C. Finney/Dir., Gordon D. Denney/Dir., William A. Hasler/Dir., Kent R. McGaughy/Dir. - Principal, Cpmg

Owners: Thomas DeZao, Gregory Ennis/2.10%, Insiders/30.00%, Michael Buckley, CPMG, Inc./17.00%, Dan W. Denney/4.50%, Gordon D. Denney, William A. Hasler, Ronald L. Goode, John M. Vuko, Claude Miller, Kent R. McGaughy/17.00%, Stanford C. Finney/5.20%, Bonnie Charpentier

Financial Data: *Fiscal Year End:*12/31 *Latest Annual Data:* 12/31/2006

Year	Sales	Net Income
2006	NA	-$48,912,000
2005	NA	-$30,424,000
2004	NA	-$27,026,000

Curr. Assets:	$54,994,000	**Curr. Liab.:**	$12,027,000		
Plant, Equip.:	$93,479,000	**Total Liab.:**	$57,577,000	**Indic. Yr. Divd.:**	NA
Total Assets:	$160,423,000	**Net Worth:**	$102,846,000	**Debt/ Equity:**	0.5417

Genius Products Inc

2230 Broadway, Santa Monica, CA, 90404; *PH:* 1-310-453-1222; *Fax:* 1-310-453-0074; *http://* www.geniusproducts.com; *Email:* info1@geniusproducts.com

General - Incorporation .... DE
Employees 149
Auditor .... Ernst & Young, LLP
Stk Agt .... Interwest Transfer Company, Inc.
Counsel .... NA
DUNS No. .... NA

Stock- Price on:12/24/2007 .... $2.77
Stock Exchange .... OTC
Ticker Symbol .... GNPI
Outstanding Shares 65,870,000
E.P.S. $0.47
Shareholders .... NA

Business: The group's principal activities are to produce, publish and distribute classical, instrumental and vocal compact discs, cassettes, videos and digital video discs for children under a variety of proprietary and third party brands. It markets the products at retail outlets nationwide and through commercial retail websites on the Internet and distributes in over 8000 retail locations in the United States. The group also sells, on a wholesale basis, fine and costume jewelry and its major jewelry customer is a United States television shopping network. It designs its jewelry products and uses independent foreign manufacturing facilities to produce them. The group owns the right to publish dvds, video and audio cds under the following major brands: baby genius, kid genius, bozo the clown, guess how much i love you, raggedy ann and rainbow fish.

Primary SIC and add'l.: 3652 9651 7812 7822

CIK No: 0001098016

Subsidiaries: American Vantage Media Corporation

Officers: Trevor Drinkwater/Dir., CEO, Michel Urich/General Counsel, Philip Crimaldi/Contact - Dan Klores Communications, Rodney Satterwhite/COO, Amanda Thorn/Contact - Dan Klores Communications, Ed Byrnes/63/Exec. VP - Finance, Gary Davis/Contact - WWE Public Relations, Sandra Carreon-John/Contact - Espn Public Relations, John Mueller/CFO, Christine Martinez/GM, Exec. VP, Michael Radiloff/Exec. VP - Marketing, Mitch Budin/Exec. VP - Sales, John Mills/Investor Relation Officer, Anne Rakunas/Investor Relation Officer, Steve Wegner/Contact - Public Relations Inquiries *(16 Officers included in Index)*

Directors: Trevor Drinkwater/Dir., CEO, Stephen K. Bannon/Chmn., Brad Ball/Dir., James G. Ellis/Dir., Herbert Hardt/Dir., Larry Madden/Dir., Irwin Reiter/Dir.

Owners: Rodney Satterwhite, Herbert Hardt, Wellington Management Company LLP/12.58%, Michel Urich, Christine Martinez, Mitch Budin, John Mueller, Insiders/8.01%, W-G Holding Corp., Stephens Investment Management, LLC/5.40%, The Weinstein Company Holdings LLC/98.57%, Stephen K. Bannon, Trevor Drinkwater/3.11%, Michael Radiloff, James G. Ellis *(17 Owners included in Index)*

Financial Data: *Fiscal Year End:*12/31 *Latest Annual Data:* 12/31/2006

Year	Sales	Net Income
2006	$119,011,000	$8,840,000
2005	$22,328,000	-$17,161,000
2004	$16,630,000	-$6,046,000

Curr. Assets:	$4,632,000	**Curr. Liab.:**	$924,000	**P/E Ratio:**	19.79
Plant, Equip.:	NA	**Total Liab.:**	$13,945,000	**Indic. Yr. Divd.:**	NA
Total Assets:	$89,428,000	**Net Worth:**	$75,483,000	**Debt/ Equity:**	NA

Genlyte Group Inc

10350 Ormsby Pk. Pl., Ste. 601, Louisville, KY, 40223; *PH:* 1-502-420-9500; *Fax:* 1-502-420-9540; *http://* www.genlyte.com; *Email:* genlyteboard@genlytegroup.com

General - Incorporation .... DE
Employees 6,386
Auditor .... PricewaterhouseCoopers LLP
Stk Agt .... Shareholder Services Group
Counsel .... NA
DUNS No. 13-048-3597

Stock- Price on:12/24/2007 .... $83.23
Stock Exchange .... NDQ
Ticker Symbol .... GLYT
Outstanding Shares 28,440,000
E.P.S. $4.98
Shareholders .... NA

Business: The group's principal activities are to design, manufacture and sell lighting fixtures and controls for a wide variety of applications in the commercial, industrial and residential markets. The group operates in three industry segments: commercial lighting, residential lighting and other lighting. The group operates through its divisions namely: Capri/Omega, Chloride Systems, Controls, Crescent, Day-Brite, Gardco, Hadco, Lightolier, Stonco, Thomas Residential, and Wide-Lite in the United States and Canlyte, Ledalite, Lumec, and Thomas Lighting Canada in Canada. The group operates in the United States, Mexico and Canada. On 12-May-2004, the group acquired USS Manufacturing Inc.

Primary SIC and add'l.: 3645 3648 3646

CIK No: 0000833076

Subsidiaries: Canlyte Inc., Genlyte Canadian Holdings LLC, Genlyte Holdings Inc., Genlyte Intangible Inc., Genlyte International Acquisitions, Genlyte Lighting Corp., Genlyte Nova Scotia CGP, Genlyte Nova Scotia CLP, Genlyte Receivables Corporation, Genlyte Thomas Group LLC, Genlyte Thomas Group Nova Scotia ULC, GTG Intangible Holdings LLP, GTG International Acquisitions LP, Ledalite Architectural Products, Lightolier De Mexico S.A. De C.V. 25 Subsidiaries included in the Index

Officers: Larry K. Powers/Chmn., CEO, Pres./$3,109,858.00, Zia Eftekhar/Dir., VP/$1,434,979.00, Daniel R. Fuller/VP, General Counsel, Assist. Corp. Sec., Raymond L. Zaccagnini/VP - Administration, Corp. Sec./$815,166.00, Ronald D. Schneider/VP - Operations/$769,819.00, William G. Ferko/CFO, VP/$1,244,995.00

Directors: Larry K. Powers/Chmn., CEO, Pres., Zia Eftekhar/Dir., VP, David M. Engelman/Dir., Robert D. Nixon/Dir., William A. Trotman/Dir., John T. Baldwin/Dir.

Owners: Insiders/3.00%, FMR Corp./9.90%, Ronald D. Schneider, William G. Ferko, Glenn W. Bailey Irrevocable Trust/7.50%, Raymond L. Zaccagnini, Robert D. Nixon, Larry K. Powers/1.30%, Columbia Wanger Asset Management/11.10%, Zia Eftekhar, John T. Baldwin

Financial Data: *Fiscal Year End:*12/31 *Latest Annual Data:* 12/31/2006

Year	Sales	Net Income
2006	$1,484,833,000	$154,481,000
2005	$1,252,194,000	$84,844,000
2004	$1,179,069,000	$58,253,000

Curr. Assets:	$513,046,000	**Curr. Liab.:**	$341,297,000	**P/E Ratio:**	16.92
Plant, Equip.:	$179,516,000	**Total Liab.:**	$480,417,000	**Indic. Yr. Divd.:**	NA
Total Assets:	$1,186,185,000	**Net Worth:**	$705,768,000	**Debt/ Equity:**	0.0840

Genoil Inc

101- 6 Ave. SW, Ste 650, Calgary, AB, T2P 3P4; *PH:* 1-403-750-3450; *http://* www.genoil.net; *Email:* ir@genoil.net

General - Incorporation .... Canada
Employees .... NA
Auditor .... BDO Dunwoody LLP
Stk Agt .... Computershare Trust Co of Canada
Counsel .... NA
DUNS No. .... NA

Stock- Price on:12/24/2007 .... $0.56
Stock Exchange .... OTC
Ticker Symbol .... GNOLF
Outstanding Shares .... NA
E.P.S. .... NA
Shareholders .... NA

Business: The group's principle activities include acquiring, developing and exploring oil upgrading properties. The group also provides technologies in hydrogen addition upgrading and oil water separation. The group converts heavy hydrocarbon feeds into lighter synthetic crude. The synthetic product is used to reduced levels of contaminants include sulphur, nitrogen and metals. The group suite of oil water separation technologies includes the Maxis 3-phase separator and Crystal 2-phase water-polishing unit. The groups markets include steel mills, power plants, aboard ships and any other process applications where hydrocarbons must be separated from water. Several units are in operation, with clients including the US Navy. The group operates from United States.

Primary SIC and add'l.: 1389

CIK No: 0001261002

Subsidiaries: Crystal Clear Solutions Ltd. Genoil, Genoil (USA) Inc., Velox Corporation, Hydrogen Solutions Inc

Officers: David Lifschultz/Chmn., CEO, James Runyan/COO, Exec. VP, Peter Chung/VP - Engineering, Paul Costinel/Mgr. - Oil Water Separation, David Kippen/39/CFO, John Noble/VP - Global Sales, Marketing

Directors: David Lifschultz/Chmn., CEO, Lawrence Lifschultz/59/Dir., Brian Korney/Dir., Adam G. Hedayat/58/Dir., Joseph C. Fatony/Dir., Henry Bloomfield/Dir.

Owners: David Lifschultz/24.50%

Financial Data: *Fiscal Year End:*12/31 *Latest Annual Data:* 12/31/2005

Year	Sales	Net Income
2005	NA	-$9,353,000
2004	$116,000	-$7,585,000

Curr. Assets:	$1,315,000	**Curr. Liab.:**	$1,394,000		
Plant, Equip.:	$1,882,000	**Total Liab.:**	$3,817,000	**Indic. Yr. Divd.:**	NA
Total Assets:	$5,562,000	**Net Worth:**	$1,744,000	**Debt/ Equity:**	NA

Genomic Health Inc

301 Penobscot Dr., Redwood City, CA, 94063; *PH:* 1-650-556-9300; *Fax:* 1-650-556-1132; *http://* www.genomichealth.com; *Email:* investors@genomichealth.com

General - Incorporation	DE	**Stock**- Price on:12/24/2007	NA
Employees	191	Stock Exchange	NDQ
Auditor	Ernst & Young LLP	Ticker Symbol	GHDX
Stk Agt	Computershare Investor Services LLC	Outstanding Shares	24,630,000
Counsel	NA	E.P.S	-$1.17
DUNS No.	NA	Shareholders	NA

Business: The groups principle activities include developing and commercializing genomic clinical diagnostic tests. The groups services include Medicare and Medicaid. The groups product is Oncotype DX. The group operates from the United States. The group's quarterly revenue for September 2007 was 15.90 millions of USD.

Primary SIC and add'l.: 2835 8731 8734

CIK No: 0001131324

Subsidiaries: Oncotype Laboratories, Inc

Officers: Randy Scott/Chmn., CEO/$433,700.00, Kim Popovits/COO, Pres./$509,700.00, Joffre Baker/Chief Scientific Officer/$475,400.00, Steve Shak/Chief Medical Officer/$475,400.00, Brad Cole/CFO, Exec. VP/$514,900.00

Directors: Randy Scott/Chmn., CEO, Julian Baker/Dir., Brook Byers/Dir., Fred Cohen/Dir., Samuel Colella/Dir., Michael Goldberg/Dir., Randall Livingston/Dir., Woodrow Myers/Dir.

Owners: Steven Shak/2.00%, Kimberly J. Popovits/1.90%, Samuel D. Colella/9.70%, Insiders/51.60%, Entities Affiliated with TPG Ventures/7.80%, Entities Affiliated with Baker Brothers Advisors/12.00%, Entities Affiliated with Kleiner Perkins Caufield & Byers/6.80%, Joffre B. Baker/1.90%, Bradley G. Cole, Randall S. Livingston, Julian C. Baker/12.00%, Randal W. Scott/9.20%, Brook H. Byers/6.80%, Fred E. Cohen/8.00%, Michael D. Goldberg *(18 Owners included in Index)*

Financial Data: ***Fiscal Year End:***12/31 ***Latest Annual Data:*** 12/31/2006

Year	Sales	Net Income
2006	$29,174,000	-$28,920,000
2005	$5,202,000	-$31,361,000
2004	$327,000	-$24,995,000

Curr. Assets:	$47,686,000	***Curr. Liab.:***	$10,151,000		
Plant, Equip.:	$9,421,000	***Total Liab.:***	$16,195,000	***Indic. Yr. Divd.:***	NA
Total Assets:	$58,024,000	***Net Worth:***	$41,829,000	***Debt/ Equity:***	0.1327

Gensym Corp

52 Second Ave, Burlington, MA, 01803; ***PH:*** 1-617-547-2500; ***http://*** www.gensym.com

General - Incorporation	DE	**Stock**- Price on:12/24/2007	$1.6
Employees	65	Stock Exchange	NA
Auditor	Vitale, Caturano & Co., Ltd.	Ticker Symbol	NA
Stk Agt	NA	Outstanding Shares	7,880,000
Counsel	Hale & Dorr LLP	E.P.S	$0.00
DUNS No.	16-133-2556	Shareholders	NA

Business: The group's principal activity is to provide operations management and expert systems software products and services. Its products emulate the reasoning of human experts, using process knowledge and often real-time data and make recommendations or take direct operational actions based on such reasoning. Products include g2 (R), neuron-line(R), optegrity (TM), intelligent objects (TM), integrity (TM), rethink(R) and e-scor. In addition, the group provides customer support, education and consulting and implementation services. The group's products are sold to end users, value-added resellers, systems integrators and original equipment manufacturers. Customers include abb, dow chemical, dupont, eli lilly, exxonmobil, siemens, shell and toyota, the us department of defense, nasa, computer sciences corporation, ericsson, motorola and pivetal. The group operates in the United States, the United Kingdom and other parts of Europe.

Primary SIC and add'l.: 7372

CIK No: 0001005387

Subsidiaries: Gensym B.V., Gensym International Corporation, Gensym Japan Corporation, Gensym Ltd., Gensym MENA, Gensym S.A., Gensym Securities Corporation, Gensym Srl.

Officers: Robert Ashton/CEO, Pres., Stephen Allison/VP - Finance, CFO, Philippe Printz/VP - Engineering

Directors: David Smith/Chmn., John A. Shane/Dir., Thomas E. Swithenbank/Dir.

Owners: Phillipe C. Printz, David A. Smith, Stephen D. Allison, John A. Shane/1.80%, Robert B. Ashton/16.67%, Johann Magnusson Gedda/12.24%, Insiders/21.16%, Lowell B. Hawkinson/8.17%, Thomas E. Swithenbank/1.49%

Financial Data: ***Fiscal Year End:***12/31 ***Latest Annual Data:*** 12/31/2006

Year	Sales	Net Income
2006	$16,935,000	-$794,000
2005	$17,665,000	-$663,000
2004	$17,621,000	$894,000

Curr. Assets:	$6,643,000	***Curr. Liab.:***	$6,791,000		
Plant, Equip.:	$561,000	***Total Liab.:***	$7,798,000	***Indic. Yr. Divd.:***	NA
Total Assets:	$7,336,000	***Net Worth:***	-$462,000	***Debt/ Equity:***	NA

Genta Inc

200 Connell Dr., Berkeley Heights, NJ, 07922; ***PH:*** 1-908-286-9800; ***Fax:*** 1-908-464-1701; ***http://*** www.genta.com

General - Incorporation	DE	**Stock**- Price on:12/24/2007	$0.2932
Employees	55	Stock Exchange	NDQ
Auditor	Deloitte & Touche LLP	Ticker Symbol	GNTA
Stk Agt	Mellon Investor Services LLC	Outstanding Shares	183,720,000
Counsel	NA	E.P.S	-$1.75
DUNS No.	60-283-4483	Shareholders	NA

Business: The group's principle activity is to identify, develop and commercialize novel drugs for cancer and related diseases. The research program of the group is focused mainly on dna/rna medicines and small molecules. Dna/rna medicines are based on chemical modifications of either deoxyribonucleic acid or dna or ribonucleic acid or rna. Ganitetm, which forms part of small molecules program, is the first commercial product of the group. Ganitetm has been approved by the U.S. Food and drug administration for treatment of cancer-related hypercalcemia that is resistant to hydration. The group derives its revenues from three segments: product sales, license fees and royalties and development funding. The group's quarterly revenue for Sep'07 was 0.12 millions of USD.

Primary SIC and add'l.: 8731 2836 2834

CIK No: 0000880643

Officers: Raymond P. Warrell/Chmn., CEO/$3,294,286.00, Loretta M. Itri/Pres. - Pharmaceutical Development, Chief Medical Officer/$1,444,900.00, Richard J. Moran/Sr. VP, CFO/$451,400.00, Bharat M. Mehta/VP - Manufacturing Operations, Bob D. Brown/VP - Research, Technology, Thomas N. Julian/VP - Technology Development, Lloyd Sanders/Sr. VP - Commercial Operations/$392,829.00

Directors: Raymond P. Warrell/Chmn., CEO, Daniel D. Von Hoff/Dir., Douglas G. Watson/Dir., Christopher Parios/Dir., Martin Driscoll/Dir.

Owners: Raymond P. Warrell/4.10%, Loretta M. Itri, Christopher P. Parios, Richard J. Moran, Lloyd W. Sanders, Daniel D. Von Hoff, Martin J. Driscoll, Douglas G. Watson, Betsy McCaughey, Insiders/5.10%

Financial Data: ***Fiscal Year End:***12/31 ***Latest Annual Data:*** 12/31/2006

Year	Sales	Net Income
2006	$708,000	-$56,781,000
2005	$26,585,000	-$2,203,000
2004	$15,127,000	-$32,685,000

Curr. Assets:	$49,818,000	***Curr. Liab.:***	$37,136,000		
Plant, Equip.:	$271,000	***Total Liab.:***	$37,136,000	***Indic. Yr. Divd.:***	NA
Total Assets:	$51,778,000	***Net Worth:***	$14,642,000	***Debt/ Equity:***	NA

GenTek Inc

90 E Halsey Rd., Parsippany, NJ, 07054; ***PH:*** 1-973-515-3221; ***Fax:*** 1-973-515-3229; ***http://*** www.gentek-global.com; ***Email:*** info@gentek-global.com

General - Incorporation	DE	**Stock**- Price on:12/24/2007	$35.73
Employees	1,525	Stock Exchange	NDQ
Auditor	Deloitte & Touche LLP	Ticker Symbol	GETI
Stk Agt	Wells Fargo Shareowner Services	Outstanding Shares	10,390,000
Counsel	NA	E.P.S	-$0.15
DUNS No.	NA	Shareholders	NA

Business: The group's principal activity is to manufacture telecommunications equipment, industrial components and performance chemicals. It operates through three business segments: communications: provides global products, systems and services, including copper and fiber-optic cabling & connection products, for local & wide area data & communication networks. Manufacturing segment provides a broad range of engineered components and services to the automotive, appliance and electronic and industrial markets. Performance products segment manufactures a broad range of products and services to four principal markets: environmental services, pharmaceutical and personal care, chemical processing and technology. The group operates in the United States, Canada, Australia, Austria, China, Germany, great Britain, India, Indonesia, Ireland & Mexico. The group emerged from bankruptcy in nov 2003. The group discontinued its operations of krone communications in mar 2004.

Primary SIC and add'l.: 3714 3661 2298 2819 3264

CIK No: 0001077552

Subsidiaries: 1279597 Ontario Inc., Alembic Manufacturing Ltd., Balcrank Products Inc., Big T-2 Company LLC, Binderline Draftline, Inc., Defiance Kinematics Inc., Defiance Precision Products Inc., Defiance Precision Products Management LLC, Defiance Precision Products Manufacturing LLC, Defiance Testing & Engineering Services, Inc., Defiance, Inc., DTA Development, LLC, Fini Enterprises, Inc., General Chemical Canada Holdings Inc., General Chemical LLC 44 Subsidiaries included in the Index

Officers: William E. Redmond/Dir., CEO, Pres./$1,939,174.00, Greg Gilbert/VP, General Mgr. - GT Technologies, Thomas B. Testa/CFO, VP/$809,379.00, Robert Novo/VP - Human Resources, Environmental, Health, Safety/$684,184.00, Vincent J. Opalewski/VP, General Mgr. - General Chemical Performance Chemicals/$574,808.00

Directors: William E. Redmond/Dir., CEO, Pres., John G. Johnson/Chmn., John F. McGovern/Dir., Kathleen R. Flaherty/Dir., Henry L. Druker/Dir., Richard A. Rubin/Dir.

Owners: Henry L. Druker, James Imbriaco, Insiders, Pamet Capital Management, LLC, John F. McGovern, Robert D. Novo, William E. Redmond, Kathleen R. Flaherty, Hawkeye Capital, Shapiro Capital Management Company, Inc., Abrams Capital, LLC, Tontine Capital Partners, L.P., John G. Johnson, Mark McGrath, Chesapeake Partners Management Co., Inc. *(25 Owners included in Index)*

Financial Data: ***Fiscal Year End:***12/31 ***Latest Annual Data:*** 12/31/2006

Year	Sales	Net Income
2006	$611,368,000	-$2,103,000
2005	$919,962,000	-$822,000
2004	$843,919,000	$195,318,000

Curr. Assets:	$282,946,000	***Curr. Liab.:***	$135,175,000		
Plant, Equip.:	$232,180,000	***Total Liab.:***	$634,273,000	***Indic. Yr. Divd.:***	NA
Total Assets:	$730,206,000	***Net Worth:***	$95,933,000	***Debt/ Equity:***	2.8126

Gentex Corp

600 N Centennial St., Zeeland, MI, 49464; ***PH:*** 1-616-772-1800; ***Fax:*** 1-616-772-7348; ***http://*** www.gentex.com

General - Incorporation	MI	**Stock**- Price on:12/24/2007	$19.49
Employees	2,393	Stock Exchange	NDQ
Auditor	Ernst & Young LLP	Ticker Symbol	GNTX
Stk Agt	American Stock Transfer & Trust Co.	Outstanding Shares	142,710,000
Counsel	Varnum Riddering S & H LLP	E.P.S	$0.77
DUNS No.	06-585-5363	Shareholders	NA

Business: The group's principal activities are to design, develop, manufacture and market proprietary electro-optical products. The products include automatic-dimming rearview mirrors for the automotive industry and fire protection products for the commercial building industry. The automatic-dimming rearview mirrors comprise of interior nvs(R) mirrors, exterior nvs(R) mirror sub-assemblies, nvs(R) headlamp control mirror, the nvs(R) lighted mirror with led map lamps and others. The principal customers for the rear-view mirrors include general-motors corporation, mercedes-benz, chrysler corporation and ford motor company. The fire protection products include smoke detectors, remote signaling electronic horns, strobe warning lights and evacuation speakers. The fire protection products are directly marketed to fire protection and security product distributors and electrical wholesale houses. The group operates in the United States, Japan, Germany, United Kingdom.

Primary SIC and add'l.: 5090 3714 3669

CIK No: 0000355811

Subsidiaries: E.C. Aviation Services Inc., Gentex (Shanghai) Electronic Technology Co Inc., Gentex France SAS, Gentex GmbH, Gentex Holdings Inc., Gentex International Corporation, Gentex Japan, Inc, Gentex Mirrors Ltd, Gentex Technologies Korea Co Ltd

Officers: Fred Bauer/Chmn., CEO/$806,612.00, Craig Piersma/Dir. - Corporate Communications, Bruce Los/VP - Human Resources, John Carter/VP - Engineering, Mechanical/$451,288.00, Mark Newton/VP - Purchasing, Photonics, Tom Ludema/VP - Quality Assurance, Scott Edwards/VP - Fire Protection Products, Enoch Jen/56/Sr. VP/$468,866.00, John Arnold/VP - Operations, Jim Hollars/Sr. VP - International, Steve Dykman/VP - Finance, CFO, Robert Vance/VP - Business Development, Japanese Automakers, Tom Guarr/VP - Chemical Research, Bill Tonar/VP - Advanced Materials, Process Development, Dennis Alexejun/VP - North American Automotive Marketing/$386,413.00 *(17 Officers included in Index)*

Directors: Fred Bauer/Chmn., CEO, James Wallace/66/Dir.

Owners: John Carter, Fidelity Management and Research/8.20%, Kenneth La Grand, Arlyn Lanting, Enoch Jen, Wallace Tsuha, Fred Bauer/4.20%, Frederick Sotok, Insiders/5.80%, Garth Deur, Rande Somma, Dennis Alexejun, Capital Research and Management Company/10.80%, John Mulder, Gary Goode

Financial Data: ***Fiscal Year End:***12/31 ***Latest Annual Data:*** 12/31/2006

Year	Sales	Net Income
2006	$572,267,000	$108,761,000
2005	$536,484,000	$109,528,000
2004	$505,666,000	$112,657,000

Curr. Assets:	$446,878,000	***Curr. Liab.:***	$57,363,000	***P/E Ratio:***	25.31
Plant, Equip.:	$184,134,000	***Total Liab.:***	$82,334,000	***Indic. Yr. Divd.:***	$0.380
Total Assets:	$785,028,000	***Net Worth:***	$702,694,000	***Debt/ Equity:***	NA

Gentium SpA

Piazza XX Settembre 2, Villa Guardia, Como, 22079; ***PH:*** 39-031385217; ***Fax:*** 39-031385241; ***http://*** www.gentium.it

General - Incorporation	Italy	***Stock***- Price on:12/24/2007	$16.96
Employees	65	Stock Exchange	NDQ
Auditor	Reconta Ernst & Young SPA	Ticker Symbol	GENT
Stk Agt	Bank of New York	Outstanding Shares	14,190,000
Counsel	NA	E.P.S.	-$3.71
DUNS No.	NA	Shareholders	NA

Business: The groups principle activities include researching, discovering and developing drugs. The products of the group include Defibrotide, Urokinase, Calcium heparin and Sulglicotide. Specific customer of the group is Crinos Industria Farmacobiologica. The group operates from the United States and Korea. The group's quarterly revenue for September 2007 was 1.20 millions of USD.

Primary SIC and add'l.: 2834 2833

CIK No: 0001314755

Officers: Laura Ferro/Dir., CEO, Pres., Giorgio Iacobone/Chmn., Statutory Auditor, Carlo Ciardiello/Member - Statutory Auditors, Salvatore Calabrese/VP - Finance, Sec., Armando Cedro/53/Chief - Manufacturing, Gary G. Gemignani/CFO, Exec. VP, Romano Chiapponi/Alternate Member - Statutory Auditors, Massimo Iacobelli/Sr. VP, Scientific Dir., Augusto Belloni/Member - Statutory Auditors, Domenico Ferrari/Alternate Member - Statutory Auditors

Directors: Laura Ferro/Dir., CEO, Pres., Giorgio Iacobone/Chmn., Statutory Auditor, Richard E. Champlin/Member - Scientific Advisory Board, Ralph B. D'Agostino/Member - Scientific Advisory Board, Stephen Fredd/Member - Scientific Advisory Board, Luca Breveglieri/Dir., Alessandro M. Gianni/Member - Scientific Advisory Board, Cy Stein/Member - Scientific Advisory Board, Peter Levitch/Member - Scientific Advisory Board, Malcolm Sweeney/59/Dir., Gigliola Bertoglio/Dir., Lee M. Nadler/Dir., Andrea Zambon/Dir., Kenneth Anderson/Dir., Marco Codella/Dir. *(16 Directors included in Index)*

Owners: Insiders, Claudio Cavazza, Millenco, L.L.C., Biomedical Offshore Value Fund, Ltd., FinSirton S.p.A., Paolo Cavazza, Clipper Bay & Co., Biomedical Value Fund, L.P., Capital Research and Management Company, Sigma Tau Finanziaria S.p.A., Great Point Partners, LLC, Millennium Management, L.L.C., Israel A. Englander, Jeffrey R. Jay, SMALLCAP World Fund, Inc.

Financial Data: ***Fiscal Year End:***12/31 ***Latest Annual Data:*** 12/31/2006

Year	Sales	Net Income
2006	$5,709,000	-$18,970,000
2005	$4,312,000	-$14,591,000
2004	$4,767,000	-$9,066,000

Curr. Assets:	$27,510,000	***Curr. Liab.:***	$9,629,000	***P/E Ratio:***	53.58
Plant, Equip.:	$12,403,000	***Total Liab.:***	$18,096,000	***Indic. Yr. Divd.:***	NA
Total Assets:	$46,729,000	***Net Worth:***	$28,633,000	***Debt/ Equity:***	NA

Gentiva Health Services Inc

3 Huntington Quadrangle, Ste. 200S, Melville, NY, 11747; ***PH:*** 1-631-501-7000; ***Fax:*** 1-631-501-7148; ***http://*** www.gentiva.com

General - Incorporation	DE	***Stock***- Price on:12/24/2007	$19.56
Employees	7,600	Stock Exchange	NDQ
Auditor	PricewaterhouseCoopers LLP	Ticker Symbol	GTIV
Stk Agt	Computershare Investor Services LLC	Outstanding Shares	27,610,000
Counsel	NA	E.P.S.	$0.83
DUNS No.	NA	Shareholders	NA

Business: The group's principal activity is to provide health services in the United States. It operates licensed and medicare-certified nursing agencies located in 35 states. The agencies provide various combinations of skilled nursing and therapy services, paraprofessional nursing services and homemaker services to pediatric, adult and elder patients. The group's carecentrix operation provides an array of outsourcing services and coordinates the delivery of home nursing services, acute and chronic infusion therapies, durable medical equipment, and respiratory products and services for managed care organizations and health plans. The services of the group are conducted through more than 250 locations and deliver a wide range of services principally through its gentiva health services and carecentrix(R) brands. On 28-Mar-2003, the group acquired first home care-houston inc.

Primary SIC and add'l.: 8082 8099

CIK No: 0001096142

Subsidiaries: Access Home Health of Florida, Inc., Capital CareResources of South Carolina Inc., Capital CareResources, Inc., Capital Health Management Group, Inc., Chattahoochee Valley Home Care Services, Inc., Chattahoochee Valley Home Health, Inc., CHMG Acquisition Corp., CHMG of Atlanta, Inc., CHMG of Columbus, Inc., CHMG of Griffin, Inc., Commonwealth Home Care, Inc., Eastern Carolina Home Health Agency, Inc., ECT, Inc., Gentiva CareCentrix (Area One) Corp., Gentiva CareCentrix (Area Three) Corp. 71 Subsidiaries included in the Index

Officers: Ron Malone/Chmn., CEO/$1,893,236.00, Brian Jones/CIO, VP, Mary Morrisey-Gabriel/Sr. VP, Chief Marketing Officer, Susan Sender/VP, Chief Nursing Executive, Murray Mease/VP - Carecentrix, John Potapchuk/Exec. VP, CFO, Investor Contact/$893,606.00, Steve Paige/Sr. VP, General Counsel, Sec./$712,175.00, Tony Strange/Exec. VP, Pres. - Gentiva Home Health, Bob Creamer/Sr. VP - Nursing Operations, Brian Silva/Sr. VP - Human Resources, John Camperlengo/VP, Deputy General Counsel, Chief Compliance Officer, Robert Creamer/Sr. VP - Carecentrix/$590,324.00, Anthony H. Strange/Exec. VP, Pres. - Gentiva Home Health/$806,007.00, Thomas Boelsen/VP - Carecentrix, David Gieringer/VP, Controller

Directors: Ron Malone/Chmn., CEO, Stuart Olsten/Dir., Stuart R. Levine/Dir., John A. Quelch/Dir., Victor F. Ganzi/Dir., Josh S. Weston/79/Dir., Gail R. Wilensky/Dir., Raymond S. Troubh/81/Dir., Rodney D. Windley/Dir., Mary O'Neil Mundinger/Dir.

Owners: John R. Potapchuk, Ronald A. Malone/2.00%, Dimensional Fund Advisors LP/6.80%, Barclays Global Investors, NA/5.00%, Westfield Capital Management Co. LLC/5.70%, John A. Quelch, Stuart R. Levine, WS Capital, L.L.C./8.00%, Josh S. Weston, Robert Creamer, Stuart Olsten, Victor F. Ganzi, Rodney D. Windley/5.80%, Anthony H. Strange/1.10%, Insiders/12.00% *(21 Owners included in Index)*

Financial Data: ***Fiscal Year End:***01/01 ***Latest Annual Data:*** 12/31/2006

Year	Sales	Net Income
2006	$1,106,588,000	$20,776,000
2005	$845,764,000	$26,488,000

Curr. Assets:	$281,160,000	***Curr. Liab.:***	$165,411,000	***P/E Ratio:***	23.57
Plant, Equip.:	$49,684,000	***Total Liab.:***	$569,557,000	***Indic. Yr. Divd.:***	NA
Total Assets:	$843,882,000	***Net Worth:***	$274,325,000	***Debt/ Equity:***	NA

Gentry Resources Ltd

101 6th Ave. SW, Ste. 2500, Calgary, AB, T2P 3G9; ***PH:*** 1-403-264-6161; ***http://*** www.gentryresources.com; ***Email:*** hugh@gentryresources.com

General - Incorporation	Canada	***Stock***- Price on:12/24/2007	$3.3721
Employees	NA	Stock Exchange	OTC
Auditor	Collins Barrow Calgary LLP	Ticker Symbol	GYRLF
Stk Agt	Registrar & Transfer Agent	Outstanding Shares	NA
Counsel	Blake, Cassels & Graydon LLP	E.P.S.	NA
DUNS No.	NA	Shareholders	NA

Business: The group's principle activities include exploring and developing petroleum and natural gas properties in Canada. In 2001 the company drilled 7 wells which resulted in 4 gas wells, 1 oil well and 2 standing cased wells. The company holds interests in some of western Canada's highest-quality producing units and in west Africa's offshore. As on 01-Mar-2001 the company amalgamated with sloane petroleums inc. During 2001 the company's oil production came from saskatchewan and gas production was generated in alberta. The group operates from United States.

Primary SIC and add'l.: 4924 1382 2911

CIK No: 0001067483

Subsidiaries: Gentry Resources (Saskatchewan) Ltd.

Officers: Hugh G. Ross/Dir., CEO, Pres., Gordon R. Mckay/VP - Exploration, COO, Robert J. Poole/VP - Operations, Corporation, Ketan Panchmatia/VP - Finance, CFO, Sec., Treasurer, Roger Fullerton/Mgr. - Investor Relations, Connie Nischuk/Corporate Administrator, Harley Kempthorne/VP - Engineering, Greg Groten/VP - Exploration, Larry Buzan/VP - Land, Negotiations

Directors: Hugh G. Ross/Dir., CEO, Pres., Bruce A. MacDonald/Dir., Michael Halvorson/Dir., Walter O'Donoghue/Dir., Dean G. Prodan/Dir., Robert R. Rooney/Dir.

Owners: Ketan Panchmatia, Michael Halvorson, Hugh G. Ross, Dean G. Prodan, Harley Kempthorne, A. Bruce Macdonald, Lawrence B. Buzan, Gordon R. McKay, Robert J. Poole, Walter O'Donoghue

Financial Data: ***Fiscal Year End:***12/31 ***Latest Annual Data:*** 12/31/2006

Year	Sales	Net Income
2006	$45,221,000	$2,480,000
2005	$55,483,000	$8,482,000
2004	$25,452,000	$3,541,000

Curr. Assets:	$10,804,000	***Curr. Liab.:***	$51,403,000		
Plant, Equip.:	$108,338,000	***Total Liab.:***	$67,754,000	***Indic. Yr. Divd.:***	NA
Total Assets:	$131,066,000	***Net Worth:***	$63,312,000	***Debt/ Equity:***	NA

Genuine Parts Co

2999 Cir. 75 Pkwy., Atlanta, GA, 30339; ***PH:*** 1-770-953-1700; ***Fax:*** 1-770-956-2211; ***http://*** www.genpt.com

General - Incorporation	GA	***Stock***- Price on:12/24/2007	$50.17
Employees	32,000	Stock Exchange	NYSE
Auditor	Ernst & Young LLP	Ticker Symbol	GPC
Stk Agt	Computershare Investor Services LLC	Outstanding Shares	170,380,000
Counsel	Alston & Bird LLP	E.P.S.	$2.92
DUNS No.	00-692-4948	Shareholders	NA

Business: The groups principle activity is to provide automotive replacement parts, industrial replacement parts, office products and electrical and electronic materials. The group operates from United States, Canada and Mexico.

Primary SIC and add'l.: 5085 5013 5044 5065 5063

CIK No: 0000040987

Subsidiaries: 1st Choice Auto Parts, Inc., Altrom America Corp., Automoteur Terrebonne Ltee, BALKAMP, Centre Di Culasses Du Quebec Inc., EIS de MEXICO, Eis Dominican Republic, LLC, Eis Holdings (canada), Inc., EIS, INC., Garanat Inc., Genuine Parts Finance Company, Genuine Parts Holdings, Ulc, Genuine Parts Investment Company, Gpc Mexico, S.a. De C.v., Gpc Procurement Company 33 Subsidiaries included in the Index

Officers: Thomas C. Gallagher/Chmn., CEO, Pres./$3,837,348.00, Jerry W. Nix/Vice Chmn., CFO, Exec. VP - Finance/$1,684,965.00, Carol B. Yancey/Sr. VP - Finance, Corp. Sec., Larry R. Samuelson/Pres. - US Automotive Parts Group/$1,445,374.00, Robert J. Susor/Exec. VP/$1,403,311.00, Bruce R. Clayton/Sr. VP - Human Resources/$734,667.00, Sid Jones/Investor Relations Officer

Directors: Thomas C. Gallagher/Chmn., CEO, Pres., Jerry W. Nix/Vice Chmn., CFO, Exec. VP - Finance, Gary W. Rollins/Dir., Michael M.E. Johns/Dir., Hicks J. Lanier/Dir., George C. Guynn/65/Dir., Larry L. Prince/Dir., Lawrence G. Steiner/Dir., Wendy B. Needham/Dir., John D. Johns/Dir., Jean Douville/Dir., Mary B. Bullock/Dir., Richard W. Courts/Dir.

Owners: Mary B. Bullock, Bruce R. Clayton/1.80%, Larry L. Prince, John D. Johns, Gary W. Rollins, Hicks J. Lanier, Insiders/3.10%, Richard W. Courts, Larry R. Samuelson, Lawrence G. Steiner, Thomas C. Gallagher, Jerry W. Nix/1.90%, George C. Guynn, Dodge& Cox/11.10%, Robert J. Susor *(18 Owners included in Index)*

Financial Data: ***Fiscal Year End:***12/31 ***Latest Annual Data:*** 12/31/2006

Year	Sales	Net Income
2006	$10,457,942,000	$475,405,000
2005	$9,783,050,000	$437,434,000
2004	$9,097,267,000	$395,552,000

Curr. Assets:	$3,835,127,000	Curr. Liab.:	$1,198,768,000	P/E Ratio:	17.85
Plant, Equip.:	$429,260,000	Total Liab.:	$1,886,277,000	Indic. Yr. Divd.:	$1.460
Total Assets:	$4,496,984,000	Net Worth:	$2,549,991,000	Debt/ Equity:	0.1916

GenVec Inc

65 W Watkins Mill Rd., Gaithersburg, MD, 20878; *PH:* 1-240-632-0740; *Fax:* 1-240-632-0735; *http://* www.genvec.com

General - Incorporation	DE	**Stock**- Price on:12/24/2007	NA
Employees	109	Stock Exchange	NDQ
Auditor	KPMG LLP	Ticker Symbol	GNVC
Stk Agt	American Stock Transfer & Trust Co.	Outstanding Shares	73,610,000
Counsel	Arnold & Porter LLP	E.P.S	-$0.28
DUNS No.	80-672-9547	Shareholders	NA

Business: The group's principal activities are to develop innovative therapeutics to treat serious and life-threatening diseases such as cancer, heart disease and diseases of the eye. The group is also developing cell transplantation technology for the treatment of human diseases which are characterized by cell dysfunction or cell death. The products of the group are tnferade, biobypass and adpedf. On 21-Aug-2003, the group acquired diacrin inc.

Primary SIC and add'l.: 8731 2834

CIK No: 0000934473

Officers: Paul H. Fischer/Dir., CEO, Pres./$626,800.00, Bryan T. Butman/Sr. VP - Vector Operations/$320,993.00, Nita U. Patel/VP - Regulatory Affairs, Robert J. Walden/Executive Dir. - Finance, Richter C. King/Sr. VP - Research/$333,812.00, Douglas J. Swirsky/CFO, Treasurer, Corp. Sec./$172,012.00, Milan Kovacevic/VP - Clinical Operations, Mark O. Thornton/Sr. VP - Product Development/$146,499.00

Directors: Paul H. Fischer/Dir., CEO, Pres., Zola P. Horovitz/Chmn., Harold R. Werner/Dir., Stelios Papadopoulos/Dir., William N. Kelley/Dir., Wayne T. Hockmeyer/Dir., Joshua Ruch/Dir., Barbara H. Franklin/Dir., Marc R. Schneebaum/Dir.

Owners: Joshua Ruch/4.90%, Paul H. Fischer/1.20%, Mark O. Thornton, Douglas J. Swirsky, Bryan T. Butman, Insiders/12.20%, Harold R. Werner/4.90%, Landesbank Berlin AG/6.30%, Richter C. King, William N. Kelley, Wayne T. Hockmeyer, Zola P. Horovitz

Financial Data: Fiscal Year End:12/31 **Latest Annual Data:** 12/31/2006

Year	Sales	Net Income
2006	$18,923,000	-$19,272,000
2005	$26,554,000	-$13,992,000
2004	$11,853,000	-$18,894,000

Curr. Assets:	$37,211,000	Curr. Liab.:	$7,146,000		
Plant, Equip.:	$2,921,000	Total Liab.:	$9,377,000	Indic. Yr. Divd.:	NA
Total Assets:	$40,168,000	Net Worth:	$30,791,000	Debt/ Equity:	0.0611

Genworth Financial Inc

6620 W Broad St., Richmond, VA, 23230; *PH:* 1-804-281-6000; *Fax:* 1-804-662-2414; *http://* www.genworth.com; *Email:* contactus@genworth.com

General - Incorporation	DE	**Stock**- Price on:12/24/2007	$35.81
Employees	7,200	Stock Exchange	NYSE
Auditor	KPMG LLP	Ticker Symbol	GNW
Stk Agt	Bank of New York	Outstanding Shares	434,870,000
Counsel	NA	E.P.S	$3.01
DUNS No.	NA	Shareholders	NA

Business: The groups principle activity is to provide trust solutions. The groups services include term care and medicare supplement insurance, and related financial and wellness advisory services.

Primary SIC and add'l.: 6321 6311

CIK No: 0001276520

Subsidiaries: American Agriculturist Services, Inc., American Mayflower Life Insurance Company of New York, Assigned Settlement, Inc., Assocred SA, Brookfield Life Assurance Company Limited, California Benefits Dental Plan, Capital Brokerage Corporation (also doing business as Genworth Financial Brokerage Corporation (Indiana) (Minnesota) (New Mexico) (Texas), Centurion Capital Group Inc., Centurion Financial Advisers Inc., Centurion-Hesse Investment Management Corp., Centurion-Hinds Investment Management Corp., CFI Administrators Limited, CFI Pensions Trustees Limited, Consolidated Insurance Group Limited, Dental Holdings, Inc. 98 Subsidiaries included in the Index

Officers: Michael D. Fraizer/Chmn., CEO, Pres., Robert J. Brannock/Pres. - European, Canadian Operations, Marcia Cantor Grable/Chief Risk Dir. - European, Canadian Operations, William C. Goings/Pres. - Life Insurance, Retirement, Protection Segment, Jean S. Peters/Sr. VP - Strategic Analysis, Thomas H. Mann/Exec. VP - Genworth, International, US Mortgage Insurance, Michael S. Laming/Sr. VP - Human Resources, Mark W. Griffin/Chief Investment Officer, Sr. VP, Brian L. Hurley/Pres. - International Development, Australian Operations, Samuel D. Marsico/Sr. VP, Chief Risk Officer, Kevin D. Schneider/Pres. - US Mortgage Insurance, Pamela S. Schutz/Exec. VP - Genworth, Retirement, Protection Segment, Ronald D. Cordes/Pres. - Managed Money, Retirement, Protection Segment, Christopher Grady/Pres. - Retirement Income, Retirement, Protection Segment, Shailesh Shah/Pres. - Institutional, Retirement, Protection Segment *(35 Officers included in Index)*

Directors: Michael D. Fraizer/Chmn., CEO, Pres., Frank J. Borelli/Dir., Thomas B. Wheeler/Dir., Nancy J. Karch/Dir., Robert J. Kerrey/Dir., Saiyid T. Naqvi/Dir., James S. Riepe/Dir., Barrett A. Toan/Dir., James A. Parke/Dir.

Owners: George R. Zippel, Insiders, Hotchkis and Wiley Capital Management, LLC/6.20%, Victor C. Moses, Pamela S. Schutz, Thomas H. Mann, Nancy J. Karch, Richard P. McKenney, James S. Riepe, Michael D. Fraizer, Massachusetts Financial Services Company/7.20%, AXA Financial, Inc. and affiliates/7.10%, James A. Parke, NWQ Investment Management Company, LLC/5.30%

Financial Data: Fiscal Year End:12/31 **Latest Annual Data:** 12/31/2006

Year	Sales	Net Income
2006	$11,029,000,000	$1,328,000,000
2005	$10,504,000,000	$1,221,000,000
2004	$11,057,000,000	$1,157,000,000

Curr. Assets:	$20,023,000,000	Curr. Liab.:	$199,000,000	P/E Ratio:	12.56
Plant, Equip.:	NA	Total Liab.:	$95,891,000,000	Indic. Yr. Divd.:	$0.360
Total Assets:	$110,871,000,000	Net Worth:	$13,330,000,000	Debt/ Equity:	0.5032

Genzyme Corp

500 Kendall St., Cambridge, MA, 02142; *PH:* 1-617-252-7500; *Fax:* 1-617-252-7600; *http://* www.genzyme.com

General - Incorporation	MA	**Stock**- Price on:12/24/2007	$64.41
Employees	9,000	Stock Exchange	NDQ
Auditor	PricewaterhouseCoopers LLP	Ticker Symbol	GENZ
Stk Agt	American Stock Transfer & Trust Co.	Outstanding Shares	264,050,000
Counsel	Palmer & Dodge LLP	E.P.S	-$0.04
DUNS No.	02-532-2157	Shareholders	NA

Business: The group's principle activities are carried out through three main business divisions: genzyme general, genzyme molecular oncology and genzyme biosurgery. Genzyme general develops and markets therapeutic proteins, surgical and diagnostic products, genetic diagnostic services, and pharmaceuticals. Genzyme biosurgery is organized into three business units: orthopaedics, cardiothoracic and biosurgical specialties. Biosurgery develops and markets instruments, devices, biomaterials and biotherapeutic products to improve or replace surgery, with an emphasis on the orthopaedics and cardiothoracic markets. Genzyme molecular oncology develops gene-based approaches to cancer therapy through genomics. The group's quarterly revenue for Sep'07 was 960.16 millions of USD.

Primary SIC and add'l.: 2836 2835 2834 8731 8071

CIK No: 0000732485

Subsidiaries: BioMarin/Genzyme LLC, Genzyme Europe B.V., Genzyme Flanders N.V., Genzyme GmbH, Genzyme International Holdings Limited, Genzyme Ireland Limited, Genzyme Limited, Genzyme Pharmaceuticals AG, Genzyme Polyclonals S.A.S., Genzyme Securities Corporation, Imtix SangStat (Switzerland) GmbH, SangStat Atlantique S.A.S., SangStat Luxembourg S.r.l.

Officers: Henri A. Termeer/Chmn., CEO, Pres./$22,448,920.00, Alison Lawton/Sr. VP - Regulatory Affairs, Corporate Quality Systems, Mara G. Aspinall/Pres. - Genetics, Sanford D. Smith/Pres. - International Group, Richard A. Moscicki/Sr. VP - Medical, Clinical, Regulatory Affairs, Chief Medical Officer, John M. McPherson/Sr. VP - Cell and Protein Research & Development, Thomas J. Desrosier/Sr. VP, General Counsel, Chief Patent Counsel, Earl M. Collier/Exec. VP/$3,027,653.00, Mary McGrane/VP - Government Relations, John Butler/Pres. - Genzyme Renal, Roger W. Louis/VP - Healthcare, Regulatory Counsel, Chief Compliance Officer, Peter T. Traynor/VP, Corporate Controller, Peter Wirth/Exec. VP - Legal, Corporate Development, Chief Legal Officer, Sec./$3,192,418.00, Donald E. Pogorzelski/Pres. - Genzyme Diagnostics, James A. Geraghty/Sr. VP *(26 Officers included in Index)*

Directors: Henri A. Termeer/Chmn., CEO, Pres., Connie Mack/67/Dir., Charles L. Cooney/Dir., Robert J. Carpenter/Dir., Victor J. Dzau/Dir., Richard F. Syron/Dir., Senator Connie Mack/Dir., Gail K. Boudreaux/Dir., Douglas A. Berthiaume/Dir.

Owners: Insiders/2.90%, Henry E. Blair, Gail K. Boudreaux, Michael S. Wyzga, Henri A. Termeer/1.50%, Victor J. Dzau, Connie Mack, UBS AG/6.28%, Douglas A. Berthiaume, Sands Capital Management, LLC/5.41%, Peter Wirth, Charles L. Cooney, Richard F. Syron, Robert J. Carpenter, Marsico Capital Management, LLC/6.91% *(18 Owners included in Index)*

Financial Data: Fiscal Year End:12/31 **Latest Annual Data:** 12/31/2006

Year	Sales	Net Income
2006	$3,187,013,000	-$16,797,000
2005	$2,734,842,000	$441,489,000
2004	$2,201,145,000	$86,527,000

Curr. Assets:	$1,989,501,000	Curr. Liab.:	$651,439,000	P/E Ratio:	429.40
Plant, Equip.:	$1,610,593,000	Total Liab.:	$1,530,477,000	Indic. Yr. Divd.:	NA
Total Assets:	$7,191,188,000	Net Worth:	$5,660,711,000	Debt/ Equity:	0.1358

GEO Group Inc (The)

One Pk. Pl., 621 Northwest 53rd St., Ste. 700, Boca Raton, FL, 33487; *PH:* 1-568-931-0101; *Fax:* 1-569-299-7635; *http://* www.thegeogroupinc.com

General - Incorporation	FL	**Stock**- Price on:12/24/2007	$28.35
Employees	10,253	Stock Exchange	NYSE
Auditor	Ernst & Young LLP	Ticker Symbol	GEO
Stk Agt	Mellon Investor Services LLC	Outstanding Shares	50,420,000
Counsel	NA	E.P.S	$0.88
DUNS No.	NA	Shareholders	NA

Business: The group's principal activity is to offer correctional and related institutional services to federal, state, local and overseas government agencies. Correctional services include the management of a broad spectrum of facilities, including male and female adult facilities, juvenile facilities, community corrections, work programs, prison industries, substance abuse treatment facilities and mental health, geriatric and other special needs institutions. Other management contracts include psychiatric health care, electronic home monitoring, prisoner transportation, correctional health services and facility maintenance. The group has an in-house capability for the design of new facilities and offers a full privatization package to government agencies, including financing of new projects. The group has 41 correctional, detention and healthcare facilities. The group operates in the United States, Europe, Australia, Canada, New Zealand and South Africa.

Primary SIC and add'l.: 1542 8744 8331 8322

CIK No: 0000923796

Subsidiaries: Australasian Correction Services Pty Limited, Australasian Correctional Investments Limited, Canadian Correctional Management, Inc., Correctional Services Corporation, CSC Management De Puerto Rico, Inc., CSC of Tacoma, LLC, FF&E, Inc., GEO Australasia Pty Limited, GEO Care, Inc., GEO Design Services, Inc., GEO International Holdings, Inc., GEO NZ Limited, GEO RE Holdings, LLC, Miramichi Youth Centre Management, Inc., Pacific Rim Employment Pty Limited 29 Subsidiaries included in the Index

Officers: George C. Zoley/Chmn., CEO, Founder/$3,299,032.00, Wayne H. Calabrese/Vice Chmn., COO, Pres./$1,989,005.00, John J. Bulfin/Sr. VP, General Counsel, Corp. Sec./$644,977.00, John M. Hurley/Sr. VP, Pres. - US Corrections/$691,888.00, Jorge A. Dominicis/Sr. VP - Residential Treatment Services, Donald H. Keens/Sr. VP, Pres. - International Services, John G. O'Rourke/CFO/$832,512.00, Thomas M. Wierdsma/Sr. VP - Project Development, Ron Maddux/Contact

Directors: George C. Zoley/Chmn., CEO, Founder, Wayne H. Calabrese/Vice Chmn., COO, Pres., Anne Newman Foreman/Dir., Norman A. Carlson/Dir., John M. Perzel/Dir., Richard H. Glanton/Dir., John M. Palms/Dir.

Owners: John J. Bulfin, John M. Hurley, Artisan Partners Limited Partnership/5.62%, Anne N. Foreman, John M. Perzel, Norman A. Carlson, Wayne H. Calabrese/1.92%, Wells Fargo& Company/11.39%, George C. Zoley/2.69%, Richard H. Glanton, Insiders/6.78%, John M. Palms, Delaware Management Holdings/6.21%, John G. ORourke

Financial Data: Fiscal Year End:01/01 **Latest Annual Data:** 12/31/2006

Year	Sales	Net Income
2006	$860,882,000	$30,031,000
2005	$614,548,000	$16,815,000

Curr. Assets:	$322,754,000	Curr. Liab.:	$173,703,000	P/E Ratio:	33.35
Plant, Equip.:	$288,984,000	Total Liab.:	$493,546,000	Indic. Yr. Divd.:	NA
Total Assets:	$743,453,000	Net Worth:	$248,610,000	Debt/ Equity:	0.9446

Geocom Resources Inc

114 W Magnolia St. Ste. 143, Bellingham, WA, 98225; *PH*: 1-360-392-2898; *Fax*: 1-360-733-3941; *http://* www.geocom-resources.com; *Email*: info@geocom-resources.com

General - Incorporation	NV	**Stock** - Price on:12/24/2007	$0.255
Employees	NA	Stock Exchange	OTC
Auditor	Staley, Okada & Partners	Ticker Symbol	GOCM
Stk Agt	Nevada Agency & Trust Company	Outstanding Shares	27,200,000
Counsel	NA	E.P.S.	-$0.052
DUNS No.	NA	Shareholders	NA

Business: The groups principal activities include exploring and developing mineral resource. The group operates from the United States.

Primary SIC and add'l.: 1481

CIK No: 0001141787

Subsidiaries: Minera Geocom Resources-Chile Limitada

Officers: John E. Hiner/59/Dir., CEO, Pres., Paul Chung/Dir., CFO, Treasurer, Sec., James Chapman/South American Exploration Mgr., Jeffrey A. Jaacks/Chief Geochemist, John Bengelsdorf/Project Geologist, Andrew Stewart/Dir. - Counsel, Bernard Pinsky/Outside Counsel

Directors: John E. Hiner/59/Dir., CEO, Pres., Paul Chung/Dir., CFO, Treasurer, Sec., Andrew Stewart/Dir. - Counsel, Talal Yassin/Dir., Clyde Harrison/Dir.

Owners: John Hiner/7.00%, Talal Yassin/8.40%, Paul Chung/5.90%, Insiders/29.80%, Andrew Stewart/8.40%

Financial Data: Fiscal Year End:06/30 Latest Annual Data: 03/31/2007

Year	Sales	Net Income
2007	NA	NA
2006	NA	NA

GeoEye Inc

Formerly: Orbimage Inc
21700 Atlantic Blvd., Dulles, VA, 20166; *PH*: 1-703-480-7500; *http://* www.orbimage.com

General - Incorporation	DE	**Stock** - Price on:12/24/2007	$22.25
Employees	318	Stock Exchange	NDQ
Auditor	BDO Seidman LLP	Ticker Symbol	GEOY
Stk Agt	Bank of New York	Outstanding Shares	17,510,000
Counsel	NA	E.P.S.	$2.67
DUNS No.	NA	Shareholders	NA

Business: The group's principal activity is providing geospatial imagery products and services. The imagery products are available in both high and low resolutions and can be downlinked in real time to customer ground stations worldwide. The group also offers fish finding maps via. the 'SeaStar Pro Fisheries Information Service' to fishing customers worldwide. Services include image processing services. The group serves the U.S. government and commercial customers.

Primary SIC and add'l.: 4899

CIK No: 0001040570

Subsidiaries: Orbimage Merger Sub Inc, Orbimage Si Holdco Inc., SI Opco

Officers: Angela Galyean/45/VP - Human Resources, Thornton W. Wilt/62/VP - North American Sales

Owners: Henry Dubois, James M. Simon, Redwood Master Fund, Insiders, Mark Brender, Lawrence A. Hough, Concordia Advisors LLC, Deephaven Capital Management LLC, Credit Suisse, Harbinger Capital Partners Master Fund, Ltd., Ahab Partners, Matthew M. OConnell, Joseph M. Ahearn, William L. Warren, William W. Sprague (18 Owners included in Index)

Financial Data: Fiscal Year End:12/31 Latest Annual Data: 06/30/2007

Year	Sales	Net Income
2007	NA	NA
2006	$151,168,000	$23,406,000
2005	$40,702,000	-$24,255,000

Curr. Assets:	$228,177,000	Curr. Liab.:	$95,780,000		
Plant, Equip.:	$67,389,000	Total Liab.:	$528,699,000	Indic. Yr. Divd.:	NA
Total Assets:	$691,817,000	Net Worth:	$163,118,000	Debt/ Equity:	1.5085

GeoGlobal Resources Inc

605- 1 St. SW, Ste. #310, Calgary, AB, T2P 3S9; *PH*: 1-403-777-9250; *http://* www.geoglobal.com; *Email*: nfo@geoglobal.com

General - Incorporation	DE	**Stock** - Price on:12/24/2007	$5.4
Employees	7	Stock Exchange	AMEX
Auditor	Ernst & Young LLP	Ticker Symbol	GGR
Stk Agt	Computershare Trust Co	Outstanding Shares	66,230,000
Counsel	William S. Clarke P.A	E.P.S.	-$0.05
DUNS No.	NA	Shareholders	NA

Business: The group's principle activity is to provide engaged in the exploration for and development of oil and natural gas reserves. The group has been granted exploration rights in three exploration blocks, of which two are located onshore in the state of gujarat in western India and the third is offshore eastern India. The group's quarterly revenue for September 2007 is 43.02 millions of USD.

Primary SIC and add'l.: 7375 7372 7378

CIK No: 0000896726

Subsidiaries: GeoGlobal Resources (Barbados) Inc., GeoGlobal Resources (Canada) Inc., GeoGlobal Resources (India) Inc.

Officers: Jean Paul Roy/Dir., CEO, Pres./$964,780.00, Vincent J. Roy/Consultant - Management Information Systems, Allan J. Kent/Dir., Exec. VP, CFO/$755,500.00, Grahame M. Notman/Advisor to The Board, Wilsonville, Canada, Miles Leggett/Geoscience Specialist, B. Mohapatra/Country Mgr.

- Indiaveritas, Keisha N. Hyde/Legal Counsel, Maureen T. Gallagher/Technical Consultant, Allan G. Lye/Technical Consultants, Carla D. Boland/Contact - Investor Relations, Corporate Affairs, Ajay Kalsi/Advisor to The Board, Delhi, India, Mccarthy Tetrault/Legal Counsel, Gregory R. Harris/Legal Counsel, Patti J. Price/Corp. Sec., William S. Clarke/Legal Counsel

Directors: Jean Paul Roy/Dir., CEO, Pres., Peter R. Smith/Chmn., Michael J. Hudson/Dir., Brent J. Peters/Dir., Allan J. Kent/Dir., Exec. VP, CFO, Avinash Chandra/Dir.

Owners: Jean Paul Roy/49.20%, Insiders/51.30%, Peter R. Smith, Brent J. Peters, Michael J. Hudson, Allan J. Kent/1.40%, Avinash Chandra

Financial Data: Fiscal Year End:12/31 Latest Annual Data: 12/31/2006

Year	Sales	Net Income
2006	NA	-$1,151,000
2005	NA	-$481,000
2004	NA	-$867,000

Curr. Assets:	$32,597,000	Curr. Liab.:	$1,955,000		
Plant, Equip.:	$9,906,000	Total Liab.:	$1,955,000	Indic. Yr. Divd.:	NA
Total Assets:	$46,094,000	Net Worth:	$44,139,000	Debt/ Equity:	NA

Geokinetics Inc

One Riverway, Ste 2100, Houston, TX, 77056; *PH*: 1-713-850-7600; *Fax*: 1-713-850-7330; *http://* www.geokineticsinc.com

General - Incorporation	DE	**Stock** - Price on:12/24/2007	$33.45
Employees	663	Stock Exchange	OTC
Auditor	UHY LLP	Ticker Symbol	GKNT
Stk Agt	Mellon Investor Services LLC	Outstanding Shares	NA
Counsel	NA	E.P.S.	-$2.49
DUNS No.	07-464-3768	Shareholders	NA

Business: The group's principal activities are to provide seismic acquisition and high-end seismic data processing services to the oil and gas industry. The group operates through seismic acquisition and data processing segments. Seismic acquisition is engaged in land-based and transition zone seismic acquisition services, on a contract basis. The group's equipment enables to collect both 2-d and 3-D seismic acquisition data. The majority of the seismic acquisition activities have been in the gulf coast and rocky mountain region of the United States. Seismic data processing center operates a high-capacity clustered processing environment built around sun microsystems and intel computers. This enables to replace high-end sun microsystems servers with low-cost computer clusters. The group processes land and marine seismic data and provides a suite of seismic interpretation products and services.

Primary SIC and add'l.: 6719 1382

CIK No: 0000314606

Subsidiaries: Geophysical Development Corporation, Quantum Geophysical Services, Inc., Quantum Geophysical, Inc., Trace Energy Services Ltd., Trace Energy Services, Inc.

Officers: Richard F. Miles/59/Dir., CEO, Pres./$480,827.00, Chin H. Yu/35/VP - Finance, Assist. Sec./$146,942.00, Michael A. Dunn/53/VP - Business Development, Scott A. McCurdy/CFO, VP/$378,682.00, Lee M. Bell/60/Pres. - Processing, Interpretation/$203,200.00, Lynn A. Turner/58/Exec. VP - US Operations, Michael A. Schott/VP - Financial Reporting, Compliance, Chief Accounting Officer, Jim White/Exec. VP - North America Operations/$1,282,367.00, Pete Northmore/VP - Geophysical Services

Directors: Richard F. Miles/59/Dir., CEO, Pres., William R. Ziegler/65/Chmn., Christopher M. Harte/60/Dir., Steven A. Webster/56/Dir., Gary M. Pittman/44/Dir., Robert L. Cabes/38/Dir., Christopher D. Strong/49/Dir.

Owners: Robert L. Cabes, Lee M. Bell, Maple Leaf Partners, L.P./8.58%, Gary M. Pittman, Christopher M. Harte, David A. Johnson/1.41%, Chin H. Yu, Maple Leaf Offshore, Ltd./5.68%, Michael A. Dunn, Richard F. Miles, Lynn A. Turner, William R. Ziegler/8.89%, James C. White, Dane Andreeff/14.71%, Steven A. Webster/13.44% (19 Owners included in Index)

Financial Data: Fiscal Year End:12/31 Latest Annual Data: 12/31/2006

Year	Sales	Net Income
2006	$225,183,000	-$4,176,000
2005	$62,175,000	-$1,922,000
2004	$43,145,000	-$441,000

Curr. Assets:	$97,911,000	Curr. Liab.:	$83,445,000	P/E Ratio:	33.35
Plant, Equip.:	$116,602,000	Total Liab.:	$271,038,000	Indic. Yr. Divd.:	NA
Total Assets:	$299,633,000	Net Worth:	$28,595,000	Debt/ Equity:	NA

GeoMet Inc

909 Fannin, Ste. 1850, Houston, TX, 77010; *PH*: 1-713-659-3855; *Fax*: 1-713-659-3856; *http://* www.geometinc.com

General - Incorporation	DE	**Stock** - Price on:12/24/2007	$8
Employees	77	Stock Exchange	NDQ
Auditor	Deloitte & Touche, LLP	Ticker Symbol	GMET
Stk Agt	American Stock Transfer & Trust Co.	Outstanding Shares	38,720,000
Counsel	NA	E.P.S.	$0.18
DUNS No.	NA	Shareholders	NA

Business: The groups principal activities include exploring, developing, and producing natural gas. The groups operates through two segments namely natural gas exploration, development and production, and gas marketing. Specific customer of the group is Shamrock Energy LLC. The group operates from the United States and Canada. Of the total assets in the year 2006, natural gas exploration, development and production accounted for $331,807,648 and gas marketing $9,266,426.

Primary SIC and add'l.: 1311

CIK No: 0001352302

Subsidiaries: GeoMet Gathering Company, LLC, GeoMet Operating Company, Inc, Hudsons Hope Gas, Ltd., Shamrock Energy LLC

Officers: Darby J. Sere/Chmn., CEO, Pres./$539,337.00, William C. Rankin/CFO, Exec. VP/$403,062.00, Brett S. Camp/Sr. VP - Operations/$285,200.00, Philip G. Malone/Dir., Sr. VP - Exploration/$285,200.00, Steve Smith/Treasurer, Frank C. Turner/Controller

Directors: Darby J. Sere/Chmn., CEO, Pres., Philip G. Malone/Dir., Sr. VP - Exploration, Hord J. Armstrong/Dir., James C. Crain/Dir., Stanley L. Graves/Dir., Charles D. Haynes/Dir., Howard W. Keenan/Dir.

Owners: William C. Rankin/3.00%, Charles D. Haynes, Philip G. Malone/2.30%, Darby J. Ser/3.60%, Yorktown Energy Partners IV, L.P./41.70%, Howard W. Keenan/41.70%, Insiders/51.70%, Brett S. Camp/2.30%, Hord J. Armstrong, James C. Crain, Stanley L. Graves

Financial Data: Fiscal Year End:12/31 Latest Annual Data: 12/31/2006

Year	Sales	Net Income
2006	$58,137,000	$17,296,000
2005	$41,980,000	-$1,573,000
2004	$21,466,000	$3,836,000

Curr. Assets:	$17,316,000	Curr. Liab.:	$18,940,000		
Plant, Equip.:	$315,873,000	Total Liab.:	$125,187,000	Indic. Yr. Divd.:	NA
Total Assets:	$335,195,000	Net Worth:	$210,008,000	Debt/ Equity:	0.3579

GeoPharma Inc

6950 Bryan Dairy Rd., Largo, FL, 33777; *PH:* 1-727-544-8866; *Fax:* 1-727-544-4386; *http://* www.onlineihp.com

General - Incorporation	FL	**Stock** - Price on:12/24/2007	$4.05
Employees	150	Stock Exchange	NDQ
Auditor	Brimmer, Burek & Keelan LLP	Ticker Symbol	GORX
Stk Agt	Registrar & Transfer Co	Outstanding Shares	9,860,000
Counsel	NA	E.P.S.	-$0.16
DUNS No.	NA	Shareholders	NA

Business: The group's principal activities are to manufacture, pack and distribute private label dietary supplements, over-the-counter drugs and health and beauty care products. The group develops and manufactures branded dietary supplements and health and beauty care products for distribution through various outlets. The group's products are sold under the trademarks lean proteintm, nutrisuretm, physician pharmaceuticaltm 12-and arth-aidtm. It has network of brokers and distributors located across the United States and Canada. The group products marketed to wholesale, retail and institutional customers.

Primary SIC and add'l.: 2833 5122

CIK No: 0001098315

Subsidiaries: Belcher Capital Corporation, Belcher Pharmaceuticals, Inc, Breakthrough Engineered Nutrition, Inc, Breakthrough Marketing, Inc, Go2pbm Services, Inc, Ihp Marketing, Inc

Officers: Mihir K. Taneja/CEO, Sec., Dir., Carol Dore-Falcone/Dir., VP, CFO, Kotha S. Sekharam/Dir., Pres., Leonardo G. Zangani/Investor Relation Officer

Directors: Mihir K. Taneja/CEO, Sec., Dir., Jugal K. Taneja/Chmn., Shan Shikarpuri/Dir., Kotha S. Sekharam/Dir., Pres., George L. Stuart/Dir., Barry H. Dash/Dir., Carol Dore-Falcone/Dir., VP, CFO

Owners: Barry H. Dash, Carnegie Capital/6.80%, Kotha S. Sekharam/5.50%, Shan Shikarpuri, Jugal K. Taneja/22.60%, William L. LaGamba/2.50%, Insiders/49.10%, Theodore A. Stautburg, Mandeep K. Taneja/2.50%, Mihir K. Taneja/9.70%, Carol Dore-Falcone/2.80%, Rafick Henein, George Stuart

Financial Data: Fiscal Year End:03/31   Latest Annual Data: 03/31/2007

Year	Sales	Net Income
2007	$59,792,000	$2,507,000
2006	$49,744,000	$1,789,000
2005	$28,230,000	-$882,000

Curr. Assets:	$19,803,000	Curr. Liab.:	$11,224,000	P/E Ratio:	45.00
Plant, Equip.:	$9,659,000	Total Liab.:	$14,309,000	Indic. Yr. Divd.:	NA
Total Assets:	$38,169,000	Net Worth:	$24,772,000	Debt/ Equity:	0.0969

GeoResources Inc

1407 W Dakota Pkwy., Ste. 1-B, Williston, ND, 58801; *PH:* 1-701-572-2020; *Fax:* 1-701-572-0277; *http://* www.georesources.net; *Email:* geoi@geoi.net

General - Incorporation	CO	**Stock** - Price on:12/24/2007	$7.4
Employees	13	Stock Exchange	NDQ
Auditor	Richey, May & Co. LLP	Ticker Symbol	GEOI
Stk Agt	Wells Fargo Shareowner Services	Outstanding Shares	NA
Counsel	Jones & Keller	E.P.S.	NA
DUNS No.	04-264-8139	Shareholders	NA

Business: The group's principal activities are explore, develop and produce oil and gas and mines leonardite (oxidized lignite coal). It operates through three primary segments: oil and gas exploration and production; oil and gas drilling and leonardite mining and processing. The group manufactures leonardite-based products, which are sold as oil and gas drilling mud additivés. The group operates a leonardite mine and processing plant in Williston, North Dakota. The group owns a non-producing silver property in Arizona and minor amount of geothermal and other mineral rights in Oregon.

Primary SIC and add'l.: 1381 1311 1221

CIK No: 0000041023

Subsidiaries: Belmont Natural Resource Company, Western Star Drilling Company

Officers: Frank A. Lodzinski/59/Dir., CEO, Pres., Jeffrey P. Vickers/Principal Executive Officer, Collis P. Chandler/39/Dir., COO, Exec. VP - Northern Region

Directors: Frank A. Lodzinski/59/Dir., CEO, Pres., Nick L. Voller/56/Dir., Collis P. Chandler/39/Dir., COO, Exec. VP - Northern Region, Christopher W. Hunt/40/Dir., Jay F. Joliat/52/Dir., Scott R. Stevens/35/Dir., Michael A. Vlasic/48/Dir.

Owners: Wachovia Capital Partners 2005, LLC, Michael A. Vlasic, Jay F. Joliat, Howard E. Ehler, Collis P. Chandler, Insiders, Frank A. Lodzinski, Chandler Energy, LLC, Vlasic FAL, L.P., Francis M. Mury, Robert J. Anderson, Christopher W. Hunt

Financial Data: Fiscal Year End:12/31   Latest Annual Data: 12/31/2006

Year	Sales	Net Income
2006	$8,878,000	$1,742,000
2005	$7,995,000	$2,179,000
2004	$6,820,000	$1,106,000

Curr. Assets:	$2,516,000	Curr. Liab.:	$2,045,000		
Plant, Equip.:	$14,226,000	Total Liab.:	$5,603,000	Indic. Yr. Divd.:	NA
Total Assets:	$16,741,000	Net Worth:	$11,139,000	Debt/ Equity:	NA

George Foreman Enterprises Inc

100 N Wilkes-barre Blvd., 4th Fl., Wilkes-barre, PA, 18702; *PH:* 1-570-822-6277

General - Incorporation	DE	**Stock** - Price on:12/24/2007	NA
Employees	6	Stock Exchange	OTC
Auditor	Parente Randolph, LLC	Ticker Symbol	GFME
Stk Agt	Computershare Investor Services LLC	Outstanding Shares	NA
Counsel	NA	E.P.S.	-$0.57
DUNS No.	NA	Shareholders	NA

Business: The group's principle activity is to provide customize music CD compilations and music downloads. These products were sold through Internet, marketing partners, strategic alliances and direct mail order promotions. On 3-Jan-2001, the company ceased the operations. The company is seeking acquisitions of companies with a view of refocusing its strategic direction. The group operates from United States.

Primary SIC and add'l.: 5735

CIK No: 0001079786

Subsidiaries: George Foreman Management, Inc

Officers: Seymour Holtzman/Co - Chmn., CEO, Jeremy Anderson/CFO, Efrem Gerszberg/34/Dir., Pres., George Foreman/33/Dir., Sr. VP, Georg Foreman/Exec. VP, Richard Huffsmith/VP, General Counsel

Directors: Seymour Holtzman/Co - Chmn., CEO, George Foreman/Co - Chmn., Efrem Gerszberg/34/Dir., Pres., Jesse Choper/73/Dir., George Foreman/33/Dir., Sr. VP

Owners: Jesse Choper/1.00%, Jeremy Anderson, Efrem Gerszberg/6.00%, Insiders/71.00%, George Foreman/37.00%, Seymour Holtzman/52.00%, George Foreman/2.00%

Financial Data: Fiscal Year End:12/31   Latest Annual Data: 12/31/2006

Year	Sales	Net Income
2006	NA	-$1,787,000
2005	NA	-$10,113,000
2004	NA	-$760,000

Curr. Assets:	$1,879,000	Curr. Liab.:	$286,000		
Plant, Equip.:	NA	Total Liab.:	$471,000	Indic. Yr. Divd.:	NA
Total Assets:	$3,653,000	Net Worth:	$1,263,000	Debt/ Equity:	NA

Georgetown Bancorp Inc MA

2 E Main St., Georgetown, MA, 01833; *PH:* 1-978-352-8600; *http://* www.georgetownsb.com; *Email:* customerinfo@georgetownsb.com

General - Incorporation		**Stock** - Price on:12/24/2007	$7.9
Employees	37	Stock Exchange	OTC
Auditor	NA	Ticker Symbol	GTWN
Stk Agt	Registrar & Transfer Co	Outstanding Shares	2,700,000
Counsel	NA	E.P.S.	-$0.2
DUNS No.	NA	Shareholders	NA

Business: The group operates through its subsidiary whose principle activity is to attract retail deposits from the general public. Services of the group include providing commercial and industrial loans, commercial real estate loans, and consumer loans. The group operates from Georgetown in the United States.

Primary SIC and add'l.: 6036

CIK No: 0001302709

Subsidiaries: Georgetown Savings Bank, Georgetown Securities Corporation

Officers: Robert E. Balletto/CEO, Pres./$215,596.00, Joseph Kennedy/Sr. VP, CFO/$140,812.00

Directors: Anthony S. Conte/42/Dir., Mary L. Williams/56/Dir., Calvin H. Pingree/Dir., Richard F. Spencer/63/Dir., David H. Condon/63/Dir., Stephen L. Flynn/52/Dir., Thomas L. Hamelin/52/Dir.

Owners: Insiders/60.00%, Georgetown Bancorp, M.H.C./57.20%

Financial Data: Fiscal Year End:06/30   Latest Annual Data: 06/30/2007

Year	Sales	Net Income
2007	$9,649,000	-$464,000
2006	$8,637,000	-$380,000
2005	$7,532,000	$228,000

Curr. Assets:	$6,285,000	Curr. Liab.:	$109,282,000		
Plant, Equip.:	$4,816,000	Total Liab.:	$147,472,000	Indic. Yr. Divd.:	NA
Total Assets:	$165,082,000	Net Worth:	$17,610,000	Debt/ Equity:	NA

Georgia Bancshares Inc

100 W Pk. Dr., Peachtree City, GA, 30269; *PH:* 1-770-631-9488; *Fax:* 1-770-487-4098; *http://* www.bankofgeorgia.com

General - Incorporation	GA	**Stock** - Price on:12/24/2007	$17.5
Employees	NA	Stock Exchange	OTC
Auditor	Porter Keadle Moore LLP	Ticker Symbol	GABA
Stk Agt	First Citizens Bank & Trust Co	Outstanding Shares	2,810,000
Counsel	NA	E.P.S.	$1.06
DUNS No.	NA	Shareholders	NA

Business: The group's principal activity is to provide commercial and retail banking services. The services are offered to individuals and small-to medium-sized businesses in peachtree city, the rest of fayette county and portions of coweta county in Georgia. The group offers a full range of deposit services including checking accounts, now accounts, savings accounts and other time deposits of various types, ranging from daily money market accounts to longer-term certificates of deposit. The lending activities of the group include real estate, commercial and consumer loans. The group also offers traditional products such as safe deposit boxes, ATM cards, debit cards, travelers checks, direct deposit of payroll and social security checks and automatic drafts for various accounts.

Primary SIC and add'l.: 6712 6022

CIK No: 0001163308

Subsidiaries: The Bank of Georgia

Officers: Ira P. Shepherd/Dir., CEO, Pres., Lynn C. Gable/Investor Relation Officer, Pat Shepherd/Investor Relations Officer

Directors: Ira P. Shepherd/Dir., CEO, Pres., Enrico A. Stanziale/Chmn., Joseph Stephen Black/Vice Chmn., Malcolm R. Godwin/Dir., Rick A. Duncan/Dir., James H. Webb/Dir., Arlie C. Aukerman/Dir., Dale K. Geeslin/Dir., William Robert Hancock/Dir., Donnie H. Russell/Dir., Vincent M. Rossetti/Dir., Thomas G. Sellmer/Dir.

Financial Data: Fiscal Year End:12/31   Latest Annual Data: 12/31/2004

Year	Sales	Net Income
2004	$14,254,000	$1,846,000
2003	$11,584,000	$1,323,000
2002	$9,985,000	$592,000

Curr. Assets:	$11,359,000	Curr. Liab.:	$221,741,000	P/E Ratio:	16.67
Plant, Equip.:	$6,213,000	Total Liab.:	$228,443,000	Indic. Yr. Divd.:	$0.400
Total Assets:	$249,550,000	Net Worth:	$21,106,000	Debt/ Equity:	NA

Georgia Gulf Corp

115 Perimeter Ctr. Pl., Ste. 460, Atlanta, GA, 30346; *PH:* 1-770-395-4500; *Fax:* 1-770-395-4529;
http:// www.ggc.com

General - Incorporation ... DE
Employees ... 6,654
Auditor ... Deloitte & Touche LLP
Stk Agt ... Computershare Ltd.
Counsel ... Joel I. Beerman
DUNS No. ... 12-095-7840

Stock- Price on:12/24/2007 ... $18.7099
Stock Exchange ... NYSE
Ticker Symbol ... GGC
Outstanding Shares ... 34,400,000
E.P.S. ... -$2.51
Shareholders ... NA

Business: The groups principle activities include manufacturing and marketing chlorovinyls and aromatics. The groups products include chlorine, caustic soda, vinyl resins and vinyl compounds, cumene, phenol and acetone. The group operates from United States.

Primary SIC and add'l.: 2812 2819 2869 2865

CIK No: 0000805264

Subsidiaries: Georgia Gulf Chemicals& Vinyls, LLC, Georgia Gulf Europe, ApS, Georgia Gulf Lake Charles, LLC, GGRC Corp., Great River Oil& Gas Corporation

Officers: Edward A. Schmitt/Chmn., CEO, Pres./$6,024,408.00, William H. Doherty/53/VP - Custom Products, Mark J. Seal/VP - Outdoor Building Products/$1,553,607.00, Douglas C. Shannon/56/VP - Procurement, Joel I. Beerman/VP, General Counsel, Sec./$1,523,280.00, Paul D. Carrico/57/VP - Chemicals, Vinyls/$1,764,060.00, James T. Matthews/CFO, VP - Finance, Treasurer/$1,460,693.00, James L. Worrell/VP - Human Resources, Mark Badger/VP - Marketing, Corporate Communications, Angie Tickle/Mgr. - Investor Relations, Will Hinson/Mgr. - Legislative, Community, Public Affairs

Directors: Edward A. Schmitt/Chmn., CEO, Pres., Yoshi Kawashima/Dir., Patrick J. Fleming/Dir., Dennis M. Chorba/Dir., John E. Akitt/Dir., Charles L. Henry/Dir., Jerry R. Satrum/Dir.

Owners: Barclays Global Investors, NA./5.85%, James T. Matthews, Yoshi Kawashima, Joel I. Beerman, Edward A. Schmitt/2.67%, Dennis M. Chorba/1.68%, Paul D. Carrico, FMR Corporation/13.43%, Jerry R. Satrum/2.18%, Capital Group International,Inc./7.71%, Insiders/9.48%, John E. Akitt, Patrick J. Fleming, Mark J. Seal, Charles L. Henry

Financial Data: *Fiscal Year End:*12/31 *Latest Annual Data:* 12/31/2006

Year	Sales	Net Income
2006	$2,427,843,000	$48,539,000
2005	$2,273,719,000	$95,503,000
2004	$2,206,239,000	$105,892,000

Curr. Assets:	$695,006,000	**Curr. Liab.:**	$492,051,000		
Plant, Equip.:	$1,092,923,000	**Total Liab.:**	$2,064,704,000	**Indic. Yr. Divd.:**	$0.320
Total Assets:	$2,458,227,000	**Net Worth:**	$393,523,000	**Debt/ Equity:**	3.8553

Georgia Power Co

241 Ralph McGill, Blvd. NE, Atlanta, GA, 30308; *PH:* 1-404-506-5000; *Fax:* 1-404-506-6526;
http:// www.georgiapower.com

General - Incorporation ... GA
Employees ... 26,091
Auditor ... Deloitte & Touche LLP
Stk Agt ... Southern Company Services
Counsel ... Troutman Saunders LLP
DUNS No. ... 00-692-4989

Stock- Price on:12/24/2007 ... $34.74
Stock Exchange ... NYSE
Ticker Symbol ... GAH
Outstanding Shares ... 751,810,000
E.P.S. ... $2.25
Shareholders ... NA

Business: The group's principle activities include generating, purchasing and distributing electricity within the state of Georgia. The group is a wholly owned subsidiary of southern group, which provides utility services. The services are provided at retail in over 600 communities, as well as in rural areas and at wholesale currently to opc, meag, dalton and the city of hampton. The group operates from United States.

Primary SIC and add'l.: 4911

CIK No: 0000041091

Subsidiaries: Alabama Power Capital Trust IV, Alabama Power Capital Trust V, Alabama Power Capital Trust VI, Alabama Power Capital Trust VII, Alabama Power Capital Trust VIII, Alabama Power Company, Alabama Property Company, Georgia Power Capital Trust IV, Georgia Power Capital Trust IX, Georgia Power Capital Trust V, Georgia Power Capital Trust VI, Georgia Power Capital Trust VII, Georgia Power Capital Trust VIII, Georgia Power Capital Trust X, Georgia Power Capital Trust XI 37 Subsidiaries included in the Index

Officers: Michael D. Garrett/Dir., CEO, Pres./$2,891,052.00, Cliff S. Thrasher/CFO, Exec. VP, Treasurer/$794,192.00, Christopher C. Womack/Exec. VP - External Affairs/$850,863.00, Judy M. Anderson/Sr. VP - Charitable Giving, Richard L. Holmes/Sr. VP - Metro Region, Doug Jones/Sr. VP - Fossil, Hydro Power, James H. Miller/Sr. VP, General Counsel/$905,767.00, Leslie R. Sibert/VP - Transmission, Lamont E. Houston/Sr. VP - Customer Service, Sales, Anthony Wilson/VP - Distribution, Mickey A. Brown/Exec. VP - Customer Services/$1,038,138.00

Directors: Michael D. Garrett/Dir., CEO, Pres., Robert L. Brown/Dir., Anna R. Cablik/Dir., David M. Ratcliffe/Dir., Gary D. Thompson/Dir., Richard W. Ussery/Dir., William Jerry Vereen/Dir., Jenner E. Wood/Dir., Ronald D. Brown/54/Dir., Jimmy Tallent/Dir., Gus H. Bell/70/Dir.

Owners: Mickey A. Brown, Insiders, Christopher C. Womack, Robert L. Brown, Cliff S. Thrasher, Ronald D. Brown, Douglas E. Jones, Gary D. Thompson, James H. Miller, David M. Ratcliffe, Judy M. Anderson, Michael D. Garrett, Gus H. Bell, William J. Vereen, Anna R. Cablik *(17 Owners included in Index)*

Financial Data: *Fiscal Year End:*12/31 *Latest Annual Data:* 12/31/2006

Year	Sales	Net Income
2006	$14,356,000,000	$1,573,000,000
2005	$13,554,000,000	$1,591,000,000
2004	$11,902,000,000	$1,532,000,000

Curr. Assets:	$4,019,000,000	**Curr. Liab.:**	$6,353,000,000	**P/E Ratio:**	15.79
Plant, Equip.:	$32,231,000,000	**Total Liab.:**	$30,743,000,000	**Indic. Yr. Divd.:**	$1.610
Total Assets:	$42,858,000,000	**Net Worth:**	$12,115,000,000	**Debt/ Equity:**	1.1634

Georgia-Carolina Bancshares Inc

3527 Wheeler Rd., Augusta, GA, 30909; *PH:* 1-706-731-6600; *Fax:* 1-706-731-6601;
http:// www.firstbankofga.com

General - Incorporation ... GA
Employees ... 156
Auditor ... Cherry, Bekaert & Holland LLP
Stk Agt ... NA
Counsel ... Smith, Gambrell & Russell
DUNS No. ... NA

Stock- Price on:12/24/2007 ... $13.2
Stock Exchange ... OTC
Ticker Symbol ... GECR
Outstanding Shares ... 3,390,000
E.P.S. ... $1.00
Shareholders ... NA

Business: The group's principal activities are to provide banking services. The deposit products of the group include commercial and consumer interest bearing and non-interest bearing deposit accounts. These accounts consist of checking accounts, money market accounts, negotiable order of withdrawal (now) accounts, individual retirement accounts, certificates of deposit and regular savings accounts. The lending products of the group include commercial and business credit services, as well as various consumer credit services, including home mortgage loans, automobile loans, lines of credit, home equity loans, home improvement loans and credit card accounts.

Primary SIC and add'l.: 6022 6712

CIK No: 0001044082

Subsidiaries: First Bank of Georgia

Officers: Remer Y. Brinson/Dir., CEO, Pres./$277,619.00, Patti Plummer/Mortgage Officer - Augusta, GA, First Bank, Georgia, Lisa D. Hayes/Assist. VP, Controller - First Bank, Georgia, Amy M. Sykes/Assist. VP, Human Resources Mgr., Sandra S. Davis-Attaway/Sr. VP, Office Mgr. Daniel Village Office Augusta - GA, First Bank, Georgia, Bradley J. Gregory/Sr. VP, CFO/$99,208.00, Cedric J. Johnson/Sr. VP, Community Development Officer Medical Center Office Augusta - GA, First Bank, Georgia, William W. McCartney/Sr. VP - Investment Consultant FB Financial Services, First Bank, Georgia, Cameron W. Nixon/Sr. VP, Sr. Lending Officer, Donald H. Skinner/Sr. VP - City Executive Columbia County Martinez, GA, Marie B. Sutton/COO, Sr. VP - First Bank, Georgia, James W. Brantley/VP, Office Mgr. Main Office Augusta - GA, First Bank, Georgia, Yvonne Davis/VP - Business Banker Main Office Augusta, GA, First Bank, Georgia, Joyce Frankenfield/VP - Internal Audit Coordinator, First Bank, Georgia, George Lokey/VP - City Executive Hill Street Office Thomson, GA, First Bank, Georgia *(45 Officers included in Index)*

Directors: Remer Y. Brinson/Dir., CEO, Pres., Montague A. Miller/Chmn., Adarsh K. Gulati/Advisory Dir., George H. Inman/76/Dir., Gary J. Waters/Advisory Dir., First Bank - Georgia, Charles Webster/Advisory Dir., First Bank - Georgia, Jim Whitehead/Advisory Dir., First Bank - Georgia, Connie H. Cheatham/Advisory Dir., First Bank - Georgia, Clayton P. Boardman/Dir., R. W. Culpepper/Dir. - First Bank, Georgia, Larry Demeyers/Dir., Phillip G. Farr/Dir., Karen M. Foushee/Dir., Samuel A. Fowler/Dir., Arthur J. Gay/Dir. *(42 Directors included in Index)*

Owners: Larry DeMeyers, Hugh L. Hamilton/1.52%, Bradley J. Gregory, Arthur J. Gay, Robert N. Wilson/1.43%, William G. Hatcher/1.45%, Phillip G. Farr, John W. Lee/4.51%, George H. Inman/1.48%, Julian W. Osbon/2.63%, Joseph D. Greene/1.58%, David W. Joesbury/1.46%, James L. Lemley/1.85%, Montague A. Miller/1.17%, Randal J. Hall *(20 Owners included in Index)*

Financial Data: *Fiscal Year End:*12/31 *Latest Annual Data:* 12/31/2006

Year	Sales	Net Income
2006	$35,135,000	$2,897,000
2005	$31,207,000	$3,455,000
2004	$26,659,000	$3,502,000

Curr. Assets:	$14,029,000	**Curr. Liab.:**	$379,903,000	**P/E Ratio:**	15.53
Plant, Equip.:	$11,254,000	**Total Liab.:**	$385,345,000	**Indic. Yr. Divd.:**	NA
Total Assets:	$417,471,000	**Net Worth:**	$32,126,000	**Debt/ Equity:**	NA

GeoVax Labs Inc

1256 Briarcliff Rd., Atlanta, GA, 30306; *PH:* 1-404-727-0971; *Fax:* 1-404-712-9357;
http:// www.geovax.com

General - Incorporation ... IL
Employees ... 8
Auditor ... Tripp, Chafin & Causey, LLC
Stk Agt ... American Stock Transfer & Trust Co.
Counsel ... NA
DUNS No. ... NA

Stock- Price on:12/24/2007 ... $0.29
Stock Exchange ... OTC
Ticker Symbol ... GOVX
Outstanding Shares ... 712,830,000
E.P.S. ... -$0.01
Shareholders ... NA

Business: The groups principle activities include developing, licensing and commercializing the manufacture and sale of human vaccines for diseases caused by Human Immunodeficiency Virus and other infectious agents. for September 2006, the group merged with Dauphin Technology, Inc. The group operates from the United States.

Primary SIC and add'l.: 3571

CIK No: 0000832489

Subsidiaries: GeoVax, Inc

Officers: Donald G. Hildebrand/Founder, Chmn., CEO, Pres./$108,074.00, Andrew J. Kandalepas/Vice Chmn., Sr. VP/$2,573,467.00, Mark W. Reynolds/CFO, Sec./$15,192.00

Directors: Donald G. Hildebrand/Founder, Chmn., CEO, Pres., Andrew J. Kandalepas/Vice Chmn., Sr. VP, Harriet L. Robinson/Geovax Member - Scientific Advisory Board Chmn., John N. Spencer/Dir., Dean G. Kollintzas/Dir., Robert T. McNally/Dir.

Owners: Insiders/13.80%, Donald G. Hildebrand/10.50%, Andrew J. Kandalepas/3.10%, Harriet L. Robinson/9.60%, John N. Spencer, Dean G. Kollintzas, Emory University/32.80%, Mark W. Reynolds, Robert T. McNally

Financial Data: *Fiscal Year End:*12/31 *Latest Annual Data:* 03/31/2007

Year	Sales	Net Income
2007	NA	NA
2006	$853,000	-$584,000
2005	NA	-$1,409,000

Curr. Assets:	$2,126,000	**Curr. Liab.:**	$193,000		
Plant, Equip.:	$105,000	**Total Liab.:**	$193,000	**Indic. Yr. Divd.:**	NA
Total Assets:	$2,396,000	**Net Worth:**	$2,203,000	**Debt/ Equity:**	NA

Gerber Scientific Inc

83 Gerber Rd. W, South Windsor, CT, 06074; *PH:* 1-860-644-1551; *Fax:* 1-860-643-7039;
http:// www.gerberscientific.com

General - Incorporation ... CT
Employees ... 2,250
Auditor ... PricewaterhouseCoopers LLP
Stk Agt ... Mellon Investor Services LLC
Counsel ... Richard F. Treacy
DUNS No. ... 00-115-8195

Stock- Price on:12/24/2007 ... $11.65
Stock Exchange ... NYSE
Ticker Symbol ... GRB
Outstanding Shares ... 23,120,000
E.P.S. ... $0.56
Shareholders ... NA

Business: The group's principal activity is to supply manufacturing systems with innovative computer-based systems, equipment and software. It operates through three principal segments: sign making and specialty graphics, apparel and flexible materials and ophthalmic lens processing. Sign making and specialty graphics develops, manufactures and supplies computerized sign-making and specialty graphics systems. Apparel and flexible materials provide computer-aided design and computer-aided manufacturing systems for producing industrial, commercial and retail goods for a variety of industries. Ophthalmic lens processing develops, manufactures and distributes a range of fully integrated, computer-based laboratory production solutions to ophthalmic professionals around the world.

Primary SIC and add'l.: 3841 7373

CIK No: 0000041133

Subsidiaries: Gerber Coburn Optical (Australia) Pty., Ltd., Gerber Coburn Optical (U.K.), Ltd., Gerber Coburn Optical International, Inc., Gerber Scientific (Shanghai) Co. Ltd., Gerber Scientific International A/S, Gerber Scientific International Italy S.R.L., Gerber Scientific International Limited, Gerber Scientific International Ltd., Gerber Scientific International Pte., Ltd., Gerber Scientific International, Inc., Gerber Scientific UK, Ltd., Gerber Technology Aktiebalag, Gerber Technology GmbH, Gerber Technology LDA, Gerber Technology NV/SA 35 Subsidiaries included in the Index

Officers: Marc T. Giles/CEO, Pres./$1,867,463.00, Jay Zager/CFO, Exec. VP/$819,890.00, Bernard J. Demko/Sr. VP - Gerber Scientific Operations/$578,705.00, William V. Grickis/Sr. VP, General Counsel, Sec., Gregory A. Wolf/Sr. VP, Stephen Lovass/Sr. VP/$494,460.00, John R. Hancock/Sr. VP, James S. Arthurs/Sr. VP/$622,735.00, Rodney Larson/Sr. VP

Directors: Donald P. Aiken/Chmn., Joseph H. Gerber/Founder, Edward G. Jepsen/Dir., Randall D. Ledford/Dir., John R. Lord/Dir., Carole F. St. Mark/Dir., Jerry W. Vereen/Dir.

Owners: Marc T. Giles/1.20%, Insiders/4.50%, Donald P. Aiken, Robert A. Towbin, John R. Lord, Jerry W. Vereen, Edward G. Jepsen, Randall D. Ledford, Jay Zager, James S. Arthurs, Barclays Global Investors, NA./5.30%, Bernard J. Demko, Royce& Associates, LLC/6.70%, Bear Stearns Asset Management Inc./6.20%, Wells Fargo& Company/7.20% *(19 Owners included in Index)*

Financial Data: ***Fiscal Year End:***04/30 ***Latest Annual Data:*** 04/30/2007

Year	Sales	Net Income
2007	$574,798,000	$13,508,000
2006	$530,418,000	$2,644,000
2005	$517,322,000	-$5,561,000

Curr. Assets:	$194,878,000	**Curr. Liab.:**	$113,753,000	**P/E Ratio:**	22.84
Plant, Equip.:	$36,982,000	**Total Liab.:**	$191,481,000	**Indic. Yr. Divd.:**	NA
Total Assets:	$335,962,000	**Net Worth:**	$144,481,000	**Debt/ Equity:**	NA

Gerdau Ameristeel Corp

4221 W Boy Scout Blvd., Ste. 600, Tampa, FL, 33607; ***PH:*** 1-813-286-8383; ***Fax:*** 1-813-207-2328; ***http://*** www.gerdauameristeel.com

General - Incorporation	ON	**Stock**- Price on:12/24/2007	$15.63
Employees	9,000	Stock Exchange	NYSE
Auditor	PricewaterhouseCoopers LLP	Ticker Symbol	GNA
Stk Agt	Mellon Trust Co	Outstanding Shares	305,520,000
Counsel	NA	E.P.S.	$1.38
DUNS No.	NA	Shareholders	NA

Business: The group's principal activity is steel production. The group produces reinforcing steel in the United States and is also a major supplier of merchant bars, wire rod, nails, welded wire mesh, railroad spikes, and light structural shapes. The company has the capacity to manufacture over 8.4 million tons of mill finished steel products annually. Through an integrated network of minimills, steel scrap recycling facilities, and downstream operations, the company serves customers in the eastern two-thirds of North America. The company serves steel service centers, and original equipment manufacturers (OEMs) and its customer base includes commercial, industrial, highway and residential building contractors, reinforcing steel fabricators, steel service centers, metal manufacturers, railroads, building material dealers, steel joist producers, and coal mine roof bolt manufacturers. The company's products are used in a variety of industries including construction, automotive, mining, and cellular and electrical transmission. The company operates 15 electric steel mills in North America (including one 50% owned minimill), 15 scrap recycling facilities and 36 downstream operations, including a collated nail and welded wire mesh manufacturing facility in New Orleans, Louisiana, railroad track spike operations in Lancaster, South Carolina, and Paragould, Arkansas, a concrete products facility in North Jackson, Ohio, and a grinding ball plant in Duluth, Minnesota. The company is headquartered in Toronto, with executive offices in Tampa, Fla. Brazilian-based Gerdau S.A. (a leading producer of long steel products in Brazil, Chile, Uruguay, Argentina) is Ameristeel's majority shareholder.

Primary SIC and add'l.: 3312

CIK No: 0001203748

Subsidiaries: 1062316 Ontario limited, 1300554 Ontario Limited, 1551533 Ontario Limited, 3038482 Nova Scotia Company, 3100361 Nova Scotia Company, Acierco S.A., AmeriSteel Bright Bar, Inc., Bradley Steel Processors Inc., Canadian Guide Rail Corporation, Co-Steel Benefit Plans Inc., Co-Steel Benefit Plans USA Inc., Co-Steel C.S.M. Corp., Co-Steel Dofasco LLC, Co-Steel Liquidity Management Hungary Limited Liability Company, Co-Steel UKLimited 36 Subsidiaries included in the Index

Officers: Mario Longhi/Dir., CEO, Pres., Tom J. Landa/VP - Finance, CFO, Assist. Sec., Greg W. Bott/VP - Beaumont Mill, Van S. Taylor/Assist. VP - Atlantic Reinforcing Steel Region, Donald R. Shumake/VP - Jacksonville Mill, Michael P. Christy/VP - Procurement, Logistics, Barbara R. Smith/Assist. VP, Corporate Treasurer, Dir. Finance and Planning, Robert L. Thompson/VP - Recycling, Glen A. Beeby/VP - Northern Mill Region, Yuan C. Wang/VP - Manitoba Mill, Wilburn G. Manuel/VP - Southern Mill Region, James S. Rogers/VP - Human Resources, Edward C. Woodrow/VP - Cartersville Mill, Matthew C. Yeatman/VP - Scrap Procurement, Operations, Roger D. Paiva/VP - Whitby Mill *(34 Officers included in Index)*

Directors: Mario Longhi/Dir., CEO, Pres., Phillip E. Casey/Chmn., Joseph J. Heffernan/Dir., Andre Gerdau Johannpeter/Dir., Jorge Gerdau Johannpeter/Dir., Frederico Gerdau Johannpeter/Dir., Spencer J. Lanthier/Dir., Arthur R.A. Scace/Dir., Richard H. McCoy/Dir., Claudio Gerdau Johannpeter/Dir.

Owners: Robert E. Lewis, Mario Longhi, Claudio Gerdau Johannpeter, Joseph J. Heffernan, Phillip E. Casey, Andr Gerdau Johannpeter, Frederico C. Gerdau Johannpeter, Insiders, Neal J. McCullohs, Jorge Gerdau Johannpeter, Arthur Scace, Spencer J. Lanthier, Gerdau S.A.

Financial Data: ***Fiscal Year End:***12/31 ***Latest Annual Data:*** 12/31/2006

Year	Sales	Net Income
2006	$4,464,203,000	$378,646,000
2005	$3,897,143,000	$301,995,000
2004	$3,009,854,000	$337,669,000

Curr. Assets:	$1,597,043,000	**Curr. Liab.:**	$525,691,000		
Plant, Equip.:	$1,119,458,000	**Total Liab.:**	$1,324,254,000	**Indic. Yr. Divd.:**	$0.080
Total Assets:	$3,176,388,000	**Net Worth:**	$1,852,134,000	**Debt/ Equity:**	NA

Gerdau SA

Formerly: Gerdau

Av. Farrapos 1811, Porto Alegre, Rio Grande do Sul, 90220-005; ; ***http://*** www.gerdau.com.br

General - Incorporation	Brazil	**Stock**- Price on:12/24/2007	$25.09
Employees	25,254	Stock Exchange	NYSE
Auditor	PricewaterhouseCoopers LLP	Ticker Symbol	GGB
Stk Agt	Mellon Trust Co	Outstanding Shares	662,520,000
Counsel	NA	E.P.S.	$2.23
DUNS No.	NA	Shareholders	NA

Business: The group's principal activities are the production of concrete reinforced bars, wire rods, bars and shapes, ingots, billets and other related activities. The important markets are automobile industry, home appliances, civil construction, etc. The group has production units in Brazil, uruguay, Chile, Canada, Argentina and the United States.

Primary SIC and add'l.: 3312 3321

CIK No: 0001073404

Subsidiaries: Aceros Cox S.A., Ameristeel Bright Bar Inc., Diaco S.A., Gerdau Aominas S.A., Gerdau Aos Especiais S.A., Gerdau Aos Longos S.A., Gerdau Ameristeel Corp. and subsidiaries, Gerdau Ameristeel MRM Special Sections Inc., Gerdau Ameristeel Perth Amboy Inc., Gerdau Ameristeel Sayreville Inc., Gerdau Ameristeel US Inc., Gerdau Aza S.A., Gerdau Comercial de Aos S.A., Gerdau Laisa S.A., Maranho Gusa S.A. Margusa 18 Subsidiaries included in the Index

Officers: Andre Bier Johannpeter/45/CEO, VP, Jorge Gerdau Johannpeter/Chmn., Pres., Claudio Johannpeter/Dir., COO, VP, Filipe Affonso Ferreira/42/Controller, Exec. VP, Frederico Carlos Gerdau Johannpeter/Dir., VP, Mario Longhi Filho/Dir., VP, Paulo Fernando Bins De Vasconcellos/Dir., VP, Ricardo Gehrke/50/Exec. VP, Marcio Pinto/Dir., Exec. VP, Egon Handel/Board Of Auditor - Effectives, Carlos Roberto Schroder/Board Of Auditor - Effectives, Eduardo Grande Bittencourt/Board Of Auditor - Substitutes, Domingos Matias Urroz Lopes/Board Of Auditor - Substitutes, Germano Gerdau Johannpeter/Dir., VP, Klaus Gerdau Johannpeter/Dir., VP *(30 Officers included in Index)*

Directors: Jorge Gerdau Johannpeter/Chmn., Pres., Claudio Johannpeter/Dir., COO, VP, Frederico Carlos Gerdau Johannpeter/Dir., VP, Mario Longhi Filho/Dir., VP, Paulo Fernando Bins De Vasconcellos/Dir., VP, Marcio Pinto/Dir., Exec. VP, Nestor Mundstock/Dir., Osvaldo B. Schirmer/Dir., CFO, Exec. VP, Geraldo Toffanello/Dir., Germano Gerdau Johannpeter/Dir., VP, Klaus Gerdau Johannpeter/Dir., VP, Affonso Celso Pastore/Dir., Andre Pinheiro De Lara Resende/Dir., Oscar De Paula Bernardes Neto/Dir., Expedito Luz/Dir., General Sec. *(16 Directors included in Index)*

Owners: Germano H. Gerdau Johannpeter/1.14%, Expedito Luz, Sirleu Jos Protti, Claudio Johannpeter, Andr Pinheiro de Lara Resende, Carlos Joo Petry, Sta. Felicidade Com. Imp. Exp. de Prod. Sid. Ltda/3.28%, Frederico C. Gerdau Johannpeter/1.09%, Jorge Gerdau Johannpeter, Carlos Joo Petry, Claudio Johannpeter, Insiders/3.43%, Insiders, Jorge Gerdau Johannpeter, BNDES Participaes S.A. BNDESPAR/7.39% *(30 Owners included in Index)*

Financial Data: ***Fiscal Year End:***12/31 ***Latest Annual Data:*** 12/31/2006

Year	Sales	Net Income
2006	$11,844,230,000	$1,513,808,000
2005	$8,894,432,000	$1,117,521,000
2004	$6,952,149,000	$1,158,358,000

Curr. Assets:	$7,084,430,000	**Curr. Liab.:**	$2,924,303,000		
Plant, Equip.:	$5,990,629,000	**Total Liab.:**	$9,558,224,000	**Indic. Yr. Divd.:**	$0.580
Total Assets:	$14,488,865,000	**Net Worth:**	$4,930,641,000	**Debt/ Equity:**	NA

German American Bancorp

711 Main St., Jasper, IN, 47546; ***PH:*** 1-812-482-1314; ***Fax:*** 1-812-482-0721; ***http://*** www.germanamericanbancorp.com

General - Incorporation	IN	**Stock**- Price on:12/24/2007	$13.74
Employees	395	Stock Exchange	NDQ
Auditor	Crowe Chizek & Co. LLC	Ticker Symbol	GABC
Stk Agt	UMB Bank, N.A.	Outstanding Shares	11,030,000
Counsel	NA	E.P.S.	$0.84
DUNS No.	00-693-8849	Shareholders	NA

Business: The group's principal activities are to provide retail, commercial banking and mortgage banking services. In addition, it also provides trust and brokerage services, title insurance, personal, corporate and casualty insurance products. The group operates through five affiliated community banks with twenty-seven banking offices, five independent insurance agencies located in eight contiguous southwestern Indiana counties and a business lending center in evansville, Indiana. The eight Indiana counties are daviess, dubois, gibson, knox, martin, perry, pike and spencer. On 02-Sep-2003, the group acquired hoosierland agency and stafford williams agency.

Primary SIC and add'l.: 6021 6712 6331

CIK No: 0000714395

Subsidiaries: Allied Premium Finance Company, Citizens State Bank, CSB Investment Center, Inc., CSB Investment Company, Inc., CSB Investments, LLC, FAB Investment Center, Inc., FAB Investment Company, Inc., FAB Investments of Nevada, LLC, Financial Services of Southern Indiana, Inc., First American Bank, First State Bank, Southwest Indiana, First Title Insurance Company, GAB Investment Center, Inc., GAB Investment Company, Inc., GAB Investments, LLC 28 Subsidiaries included in the Index

Officers: Mark A. Schroeder/54/Dir., CEO, Pres./$493,968.00, Therese Volz/Mortgage, Equity Loan Specialist - Main Office, Mortgage Originator, Tracey Gutgsell/Financial Consultant, Jeff Tooley/Sr. Financial Consultant, Brian Simpson/Financial Consultant, Andy Ellermann/Financial Consultant, Ryan Oberhausen/Financial Consultant, Josh Morrison/Mortgage, Equity Loan Specialist, Clay W. Ewing/52/Pres. - Retail Financial Services/$268,284.00, Stan J. Ruhe/56/Exec. VP - Credit Administration/$183,445.00, Kenneth L. Sendelweck/53/Sec., Pres. - Commercial Financial Services/$289,262.00, Bradley M. Rust/41/CFO, Sr. VP - Accounting, Finance/$194,851.00, Alex Knepp/Financial Consultant, Erich Raasch/Financial Consultant, Gene Mattingly/Sr. Financial Consultant *(19 Officers included in Index)*

Directors: Mark A. Schroeder/54/Dir., CEO, Pres., Richard E. Forbes/60/Dir., U. Butch Klem/57/Dir., Michael J. Voyles/59/Dir., David J. Lett/55/Dir., Gene C. Mehne/63/Dir., Larry J. Seger/57/Dir., Christina M. Ernst/58/Dir., Douglas A. Bawel/52/Dir., Butch U. Klem/57/Dir.

Owners: Stan J. Ruhe, Mark A. Schroeder, Kenneth L. Sendelweck, Insiders, William R. Hoffman, Christina M. Ernst, Bradley M. Rust, Chet L. Thompson, Clay W. Ewing, Richard E. Forbes, David J. Lett/1.10%, Gene C. Mehne/2.20%, Michael J. Voyles, Butch U. Klem/1.20%, Larry J. Seger

Financial Data: ***Fiscal Year End:***12/31 ***Latest Annual Data:*** 12/31/2006

Year	Sales	Net Income
2006	$78,984,000	$10,221,000
2005	$64,391,000	$9,721,000
2004	$61,008,000	$7,239,000

Curr. Assets:	$46,336,000	Curr. Liab.:	$1,001,033,000	P/E Ratio:	16.55
Plant, Equip.:	$24,090,000	Total Liab.:	$1,001,033,000	Indic. Yr. Divd:	$0.560
Total Assets:	$1,093,424,000	Net Worth:	$92,391,000	Debt/ Equity:	NA

Geron Corp

230 Constitution Dr., Menlo Park, CA, 94025; *PH:* 1-650-473-7700; *Fax:* 1-650-473-7750; *http://* www.geron.com; *Email:* info@geron.com

General - Incorporation .... DE
Employees... 103
Auditor .... Ernst & Young LLP
Stk Agt........................ U.S. Stock Transfer Corp
Counsel .... Latham & Watkins
DUNS No. 85-885-4490

Stock - Price on:12/24/2007 ....$7.3
Stock Exchange...NDQ
Ticker Symbol...GERN
Outstanding Shares 72,870,000
E.P.S..-$0.54
Shareholders..NA

Business: The group's principal activity is to discover, develop and commercialize therapeutic and diagnostic products for applications in oncology and regenerative medicine and research tools for drug discovery. Product development programs are based upon three patented technologies: telomerase, human embryonic stem cells and nuclear transfer. Telomerase are the ends of chromosomes that protect chromosomes from degradation and act as a molecular clock for cellular aging. Human embryonic stem cells are potential source for the manufacture of replacement cells and tissues for organ repair applications in regenerative medicine. Nuclear transfer technology is developed to produce genetically matched cells that would not be rejected by the patient's immune system. This technology is used for repairing organs damaged by chronic degenerative disease. The group operates solely in the domestic market.

Primary SIC and add'l.: 8731 2836 2835

CIK No: 0000886744

Subsidiaries: TA Therapeutics, Ltd

Officers: Thomas B. Okarma/Dir., CEO, Pres./$1,296,977.00, David J. Earp/Chief Patent Counsel, Sr. VP - Business Development, Calvin B. Harley/Chief Scientific Officer/$585,205.00, David L. Greenwood/Exec. VP, CFO, Treasurer, Sec./$914,401.00, Jane S. Lebkowski/Sr. VP - Regenerative Medicine, Melissa A. Kelly Behrs/Sr. VP - Therapeutic Development, Oncology, David Schull/Media Inquiries, Media, Investor Relations, Tracey Milani/Contact - Investor, Media Inquiries, Alan B. Colowick/Pres. - Oncology

Directors: Thomas B. Okarma/Dir., CEO, Pres., Alexander E. Barkas/Chmn., Patrick J. Zenner/Dir., Charles J. Homcy/Dir., John P. Walker/Dir., Thomas D. Kiley/Dir., Edward V. Fritzky/Dir.

Owners: Insiders/7.00%, Edward V. Fritzky, Alexander E. Barkas, Patrick J. Zenner, Jane S. Lebkowski, David J. Earp, David L. Greenwood/1.22%, Thomas B. Okarma/1.97%, John P. Walker, Thomas D. Kiley, Calvin B. Harley, Charles J. Homcy

Financial Data: *Fiscal Year End:*12/31   *Latest Annual Data:* 12/31/2006

Year	Sales	Net Income
2006	$3,277,000	-$31,365,000
2005	$6,158,000	-$33,528,000
2004	$1,053,000	-$80,405,000

Curr. Assets:	$217,153,000	Curr. Liab.:	$46,776,000		
Plant, Equip.:	$2,482,000	Total Liab.:	$46,881,000	Indic. Yr. Divd.:	NA
Total Assets:	$220,800,000	Net Worth:	$173,919,000	Debt/ Equity:	NA

Getting Ready Corp

8990 Wembley Ct., Sarasota, FL, 34238; *PH:* 1-941-966-6955; *http://* www.gettingreadycorp.com; *Email:* info@gettingreadycorp.com

General - Incorporation .... DE
Employees..3
Auditor ....Pender Newkirk & Co
Stk Agt................................ Island Stock Transfer
Counsel ....NA
DUNS No. ....NA

Stock - Price on:12/24/2007 ....$1.95
Stock Exchange...OTC
Ticker Symbol...GTRY
Outstanding Shares 18,330,000
E.P.S..-$0.07
Shareholders..NA

Business: The group intends to open Mother Supercare Centers in target areas across the United States. The Mother Supercare Centers will provide women who are planning to start a family, are pregnant or have recently had a baby, with a one-stop destination offering pregnancy, childbirth and parenting educational classes, nutritional counseling health and fitness classes and training and spa services, retail catalog and internet shopping for women's and infant's products related to pregnancy through the infant's first year of life.

Primary SIC and add'l.: 7200

CIK No: 0001302554

Officers: Glenn L. Halpryn/49/Chmn., CEO, Pres., Alan Jay Weisberg/61/Dir., CFO, Noah M. Silver/49/Dir., VP, Sec., Treasurer

Directors: Glenn L. Halpryn/49/Chmn., CEO, Pres., Alan Jay Weisberg/61/Dir., CFO, Noah M. Silver/49/Dir., VP, Sec., Treasurer, Curtis Lockshin/47/Dir.

Owners: Steven Jerry Glauser/9.40%, Noah M. Silver/1.20%, Frost Gamma Investments Trust/32.10%, Jane Hsiao/8.10%, Curtis Lockshin, Stephen H. Bittel/6.30%, Insiders/7.00%, Ernest M. Halpryn/7.20%, Alan Jay Weisberg, Glenn L. Halpryn/5.50%

Financial Data: *Fiscal Year End:*09/30   *Latest Annual Data:* 9/30/2006

Year	Sales	Net Income
2006	NA	-$465,000

Curr. Assets:	NA	Curr. Liab.:	$625,000		
Plant, Equip.:	NA	Total Liab.:	$625,000	Indic. Yr. Divd.:	NA
Total Assets:	NA	Net Worth:	-$625,000	Debt/ Equity:	NA

Getty Images Inc

601 N 34th St., Seattle, WA, 98103; *PH:* 1-206-925-5000; *Fax:* 1-206-925-5001; *http://* www.gettyimages.com

General - Incorporation .... DE
Employees...1,750
Auditor .... PricewaterhouseCoopers LLP
Stk Agt ....Bank of New York
Counsel ....NA
DUNS No. 02-846-4894

Stock - Price on:12/24/2007 ....$49.73
Stock Exchange...NYSE
Ticker Symbol...GYI
Outstanding Shares 59,220,000
E.P.S...$2.14
Shareholders..NA

Business: The group's principal activity is to provide e-commerce visual content and related products and services to businesses worldwide. The group provides a variety of visual content products including creative imagery, news and sports photography, archival imagery, illustrations and related products and services. It provides imagery products through its creative photography collections, getty images film, getty images editorial and hulton or archive. The products and services are provided through its Website, CD-roms, catalogs and the group operate company-owned offices serving customers in approximately 35 countries. The customers include advertising and design agencies, publishing and media companies and corporate communications departments. The group operates in the unites states, United Kingdom, Germany, France, Canada Australia and in other foreign contries. In 2003, the group acquired imagedirect, inc, mission studios limit and the image bank .

Primary SIC and add'l.: 7389 6794

CIK No: 0001047202

Subsidiaries: 3032097 Nova Scotia Limited, All-Sport (UK) Limited, Allsport Australia Pty Limited, Allsport Photographic Limited, Allsport Photographic Share Scheme Trustees Limited, Amana Europe Limited, Amana France S.A.S., Amana Germany GmbH, Amana Images Limited, Amana Italy S.r.l., Bavaria Bildagentur Verwaltungsgesellschaft GmbH, Bongarts Sportfotografie GmbH, Colorific Photo Library Limited, Digital Vision (US) Limited, Digital Vision GmbH 95 Subsidiaries included in the Index

Officers: Tom Oberdorf/CFO, Sr. VP/$589,307.00, Alan Pickerill/Dir. - Investor Relations, Nicholas E. Evans-Lombe/41/Exec. VP - Imagery, Products, Services, John McKay/Sr. VP, General Counsel, Bruce Livingstone/Sr. VP, Jeff Beyle/Sr. VP - Business Development, Linda J. Ranz/39/Sr. VP - Technology, Jim Gurke/Sr. VP - Human Resources, Chief - Staff, Bo Olofsson/Sr. VP - Global Sales/$982,943.00, Jack Sansolo/64/Sr. VP - Marketing, Chief Marketing Officer/$907,716.00, Nick Evans-Lombe/Sr. VP - Imagery, Services/$731,022.00, Michael Teaster/VP - Business Development, Image Partners

Directors: Mark H. Getty/Chmn., Christopher H. Sporborg/Dir., Andrew S. Garb/Dir., James N. Bailey/Dir., Jonathan D. Klein/Dir., Alan G. Spoon/Dir., Michael A. Stein/Dir.

Owners: Michael A. Stein, Mark H. Getty/1.87%, Jonathan D. Klein/1.94%, Alan G. Spoon, Nicholas E. Evans-Lombe, Getty Investments, L.L.C./13.97%, Capital Group International Inc./13.91%, Bo T. Olofsson, Blum Capital Partners LP/5.76%, Capital Research & Management Company/8.53%, Christopher H. Sporborg, James N. Bailey, FMR Corp/8.27%, Elizabeth J. Huebner, Insiders/4.68% *(17 Owners included in Index)*

Financial Data: *Fiscal Year End:*12/31   *Latest Annual Data:* 12/31/2006

Year	Sales	Net Income
2006	$806,589,000	$130,428,000
2005	$733,729,000	$149,703,000
2004	$622,427,000	$106,650,000

Curr. Assets:	$487,025,000	Curr. Liab.:	$133,201,000	P/E Ratio:	21.34
Plant, Equip.:	$147,133,000	Total Liab.:	$466,147,000	Indic. Yr. Divd.:	NA
Total Assets:	$1,714,384,000	Net Worth:	$1,248,237,000	Debt/ Equity:	0.2051

Getty Realty Corp

125 Jericho Tpke., Ste. 103, Jericho, NY, 11753; *PH:* 1-516-478-5400; *Fax:* 1-516-478-5476; *http://* www.gettyrealty.com; *Email:* investorrelations@gettyrealty.com

General - Incorporation .... MD
Employees... 16
Auditor .... PricewaterhouseCoopers LLP
Stk Agt ....Registrar & Transfer Co
Counsel ....NA
DUNS No. ....NA

Stock - Price on:12/24/2007 ....$28.07
Stock Exchange...NYSE
Ticker Symbol...GTY
Outstanding Shares 24,760,000
E.P.S...$1.74
Shareholders..NA

Business: The groups principal activities include owning and leasing retail motor fuel store properties. The group operates from the United States.

Primary SIC and add'l.: 6798

CIK No: 0001052752

Subsidiaries: AOC Transport, Inc., Getty CT Leasing, Inc., Getty Kingston Corporation, Getty NY Leasing, Inc., Getty Properties Corp., Getty Saugerties Corporation, Getty TM Corp., Getty VA Leasing, Inc., GettyMart, Inc., Leemilts Flatbush Avenue, Inc., Leemilts Petroleum, Inc., Power Test Realty Company Limited Partnership, Slattery Group, Inc.

Officers: Leo Liebowitz/Chmn., CEO/$443,841.00, Andrew M. Smith/Pres., Sec./$260,045.00, Kevin C. Shea/Exec. VP/$283,024.00, Thomas J. Stirnweis/VP, Treasurer, CFO/$277,601.00

Directors: Leo Liebowitz/Chmn., CEO, Howard Safenowitz/Dir., Milton Cooper/Dir., Philip E. Coviello/Dir., David B. Driscoll/Dir.

Owners: Howard Safenowitz/12.10%, Leo Liebowitz/12.20%, Andrew M. Smith, Philip E. Coviello, Milton Cooper/5.40%, Thomas Stirnweis, Kevin C. Shea, Insiders/30.00%

Financial Data: *Fiscal Year End:*12/31   *Latest Annual Data:* 12/31/2006

Year	Sales	Net Income
2006	$72,405,000	$42,725,000
2005	$71,377,000	$45,448,000
2004	$66,331,000	$39,352,000

Curr. Assets:	$1,195,000	Curr. Liab.:	$21,313,000		
Plant, Equip.:	$267,469,000	Total Liab.:	$83,708,000	Indic. Yr. Divd.:	$1.860
Total Assets:	$309,283,000	Net Worth:	$225,575,000	Debt/ Equity:	0.2003

Gevity HR Inc

9000 Town Ctr. Pkwy., Bradenton, FL, 34202; *PH:* 1-941-741-4300; *Fax:* 1-941-744-8030; *http://* www.gevityhr.com

General - Incorporation .... FL
Employees...1,000
Auditor ....Deloitte & Touche LLP
Stk Agt ..... American Stock Transfer & Trust Co.
Counsel ....NA
DUNS No. 92-756-3882

Stock - Price on:12/24/2007 ....$21.885
Stock Exchange...NDQ
Ticker Symbol...GVHR
Outstanding Shares 24,450,000
E.P.S...$0.82
Shareholders..NA

Business: The group's principal activities are to provide professional employer services to small and medium sized businesses. The services include payroll administration, risk management, benefits administration, unemployment services and human resources consulting services. The payroll

administration services include record keeping, making payroll tax deposits, reporting payroll taxes and related matters. Risk management services includes conducting of on-site safety inspections and review the clients' loss history and recommend control options. In the human resource consulting services the group provides consultation to its clients in the recruitment, selection and development of human capital. On 17-Nov-2003, the group acquired the hr outsourcing portfolio of teamstaff inc. As of 31-Dec-2003, the group served more than 7,500 clients by providing professional employer services. On 29-Mar-2004, acquired hr outsourcing portfolio of privately held epix holdings corporation.

Primary SIC and add'l.: 7363 8742

CIK No: 0001035185

Subsidiaries: Concorda Insurance Company Limited, Gevity HR IV, L.P., Gevity HR IX, L.P., Gevity HR VI, L.P., Gevity HR VII, L.P., Gevity HR VIII, L.P., Gevity HR X, L.P., Gevity HR XI, LLC, Gevity HR XII Corp., Gevity HR, L.P., Gevity HRII, L.P., Gevity HRIII, L.P., Gevity HRV, L.P., Gevity Insurance Agency, Inc., Gevity XIV, LLC 16 Subsidiaries included in the Index

Officers: Erik Vonk/55/Chmn., CEO/$1,882,092.00, Michael Lavington/Chmn., CEO - Designate, Paul Benz/CIO/$284,192.00, Patrick C. Lee/Dir. - Investor, Media Relations, Eddie Hightower/Corp. Sec., John Hale/VP - Information Technology, Application Architecture, Development, Nick Iacono/VP - Enterprise Transformation, Julie Johnson/VP - Finance, Sales, Service, Marketing, Anne-Marie Megela/VP - Financial Management, Clifford M. Sladnick/Chief Administrative Officer/$825,200.00, Jim Hardee/Chief Sales, Marketing Officer, Garry Welsh/CFO, John Bilello/VP - Finance, Alejandro Figueroa/VP - Information Technology, Edwin Hightower/Sec., VP, General Counsel *(28 Officers included in Index)*

Directors: Erik Vonk/55/Chmn., CEO, Michael Lavington/Chmn., CEO - Designate, Paul Daoust/Dir., Jeffrey A. Sonnenfeld/Dir., Jonathan H. Kagan/Dir., Darcy E. Bradbury/51/Dir., David S. Katz/Dir., George B. Beitzel/Dir., Edwin Hightower/Sec., VP, General Counsel, Todd F. Bourell/Dir., Daniel J. Sullivan/Dir.

Owners: Artisan Partners Limited Partnership/12.41%, Insiders/6.76%, Jeffrey A. Sonnenfeld, ValueAct Capital Management, L.P./13.46%, Jonathan H. Kagan, Peter C. Grabowski, Clifford M. Sladnick, Michael J. Lavington, Paul R. Daoust, Paul E. Benz, Erik Vonk/5.23%, James E. Cowie, Tracer Capital Management, L.P./7.77%, George B. Beitzel, Barclays Global Investors, NA/5.80% *(18 Owners included in Index)*

Financial Data: Fiscal Year End:12/31　Latest Annual Data: 12/31/2006

Year	Sales	Net Income
2006	$647,967,000	$35,263,000
2005	$608,797,000	$37,378,000
2004	$585,481,000	$34,618,000

Curr. Assets:	$218,986,000	Curr. Liab.:	$229,639,000		
Plant, Equip.:	$23,847,000	Total Liab.:	$232,508,000	Indic. Yr. Divd.:	$0.360
Total Assets:	$374,560,000	Net Worth:	$142,052,000	Debt/ Equity:	0.0164

GFI Group Inc

100 Wall St., New York, NY, 10005; **PH:** 1-212-968-4100; **Fax:** 1-212-968-4124; http:// www.gfigroup.com

General - Incorporation	DE	**Stock**- Price on:12/24/2007	$73.41
Employees	1,438	Stock Exchange	NDQ
Auditor	Deloitte & Touche LLP	Ticker Symbol	GFIG
Stk Agt	EquiServe Trust Co N.A	Outstanding Shares	28,930,000
Counsel	NA	E.P.S.	$2.35
DUNS No.	NA	Shareholders	NA

Business: The groups principle activity is to provide derivatives products and related securities. The groups service is brokerage. The products of the group include credit derivatives and bond instruments. The products of the group include GFI CreditMatch(R) and GFI ForexMatch(TM). Specific customers of the group include Barclays Bank, Citigroup, Credit Suisse, Deutsche Bank, Goldman Sachs, JPMorgan Chase, Lehman Brothers, Merrill Lynch, Morgan Stanley and UBS. The group operates from North America and Europe. The group's quarterly revenue for September 2007 was 254.74 millions of USD.

Primary SIC and add'l.: 6211 6289

CIK No: 0001292426

Subsidiaries: Amerex Brokers LLC, Christopher Street Capital Limited, Dvega Limited, Fenics Limited, Fenics Software Inc., Fenics Software Limited, GFI (HK) Brokers Limited, GFI (HK) Securities LLC, GFI Advisory (China) Co. Limited, GFI Brokers (SA) (PTY) Limited, GFI Brokers Limited, GFI Brokers LLC, GFI Group LLC, GFI Group Pte. Limited, GFI Holdings Limited 22 Subsidiaries included in the Index

Officers: Michael Gooch/Chmn., CEO, Colin Heffron/Dir., Pres., Ron Levi/COO, Donald P. Fewer/Sr. MD, Head - Credit Product Brokerage, Jurgen Breuer/Sr. MD, James A. Peers/CFO, Christopher J. Giancarlo/Exec. VP - Corporate Development, Scott Pintoff/General Counsel, Corp. Sec., Ian Clague/MD - North America, Nick Brown/MD - North America, Julian Swain/MD, Scott Fitzpatrick/Global Head - Sales, Sheena Griffiths/Global Dir. - Human Resources, Mark Souffir/MD, Scott Tatham/MD

Directors: Michael Gooch/Chmn., CEO, Colin Heffron/Dir., Pres., Geoffrey Kalish/Dir., John W. Ward/Dir., Marisa Cassoni/Dir., John R. MacDonald/Dir.

Owners: Geoffrey Kalish, Ronald Levi, Colin Heffron, Entities Affiliated with Jersey Partners Inc./43.00%, John W. Ward, John R. MacDonald, Marisa Cassoni, Insiders/43.40%, Michael Gooch/43.10%

Financial Data: Fiscal Year End:12/31　Latest Annual Data: 12/31/2006

Year	Sales	Net Income
2006	$747,183,000	$61,078,000
2005	$533,592,000	$48,103,000
2004	$385,020,000	$23,123,000

Curr. Assets:	$490,072,000	Curr. Liab.:	$244,378,000		
Plant, Equip.:	$47,166,000	Total Liab.:	$369,140,000	Indic. Yr. Divd.:	NA
Total Assets:	$699,609,000	Net Worth:	$330,469,000	Debt/ Equity:	NA

GFR Pharmaceuticals Inc

11450-201A St., Maple Ridge, BC, V2X 0Y4; **PH:** 1-604-460-8440; **Fax:** 1-604-648-8221; http:// www.gfrpharma.com; **Email:** sales@gfrpharma.com

General - Incorporation	NV	**Stock**- Price on:12/24/2007	$0.31
Employees	NA	Stock Exchange	OTC
Auditor	Robison, Hill & Co.	Ticker Symbol	GFRP
Stk Agt	Pacific Stock Transfer Company	Outstanding Shares	NA
Counsel	NA	E.P.S.	NA
DUNS No.	NA	Shareholders	NA

Business: The groups principle activity is to manufacturer nutritional supplement products. The group operates from Canada and the United States. The specific customer of the group is Prairie Naturals, Inc.

Primary SIC and add'l.: 2834

CIK No: 0001096294

Subsidiaries: GFR Health, Inc., GFR Pharma, Ltd., Nutritionals(USA) Direct.com

Officers: Jie Su/45/Dir., CEO, Pres., Zhi Dong Wang/41/Dir., CFO, VP, John Speers/Research, Development Mgr., Sam Elliott/Graphic Designer, Mark Likness/GM, Marc Casavant/CFO, Maribel Aloria/Dir. - Quality Control, Rosemarie Pierce/Holistic Pharmacist

Directors: Jie Su/45/Dir., CEO, Pres., Zhi Dong Wang/41/Dir., CFO, VP

Owners: Li An Guo/38.00%, Insiders/38.00%

Financial Data: Fiscal Year End:12/31　Latest Annual Data: 12/31/2006

Year	Sales	Net Income
2006	$1,543,000	$620,000
2005	$6,536,000	$109,000
2004	$5,860,000	$103,000

Curr. Assets:	$725,000	Curr. Liab.:	$1,443,000	P/E Ratio:	2.50
Plant, Equip.:	$5,272,000	Total Liab.:	$1,834,000	Indic. Yr. Divd.:	NA
Total Assets:	$5,997,000	Net Worth:	$4,163,000	Debt/ Equity:	NA

GFSI Inc

9700 Commerce Pkwy, Lenexa, KS, 66219; **PH:** 1-913-888-0445; http:// www.gearforsports.com; **Email:** corpcontact@gearforsports.com

General - Incorporation	DE	**Stock**- Price on:12/24/2007	NA
Employees	NA	Stock Exchange	NDQ
Auditor	KPMG LLP	Ticker Symbol	NA
Stk Agt	NA	Outstanding Shares	NA
Counsel	NA	E.P.S.	NA
DUNS No.	06-796-3967	Shareholders	NA

Business: The group's principal activity is to design, manufacture and market custom designed sportswear and activewear with logos and insignia of resorts, corporations, national associations, colleges and professional sports leagues and teams. It is a wholly owned subsidiary of gfsi holdings, inc. The products of the group include fleecewear, outerwear, polo shirts, woven shirts, sweaters, t-shirts and bottoms, women's and other apparel items and accessories. The group markets its products to destination resorts, family entertainment companies, hotel chains, golf clubs, cruise lines, casinos, United States military bases and a diverse group of corporations. The group markets its products under the trade names: gear for sports(R) brand name, champion(R), pro gear(R), big cotton(R), winning ways(R), and yikes(r).

Primary SIC and add'l.: 2326 2339 2329

CIK No: 0001036327

Subsidiaries: CC Products, Inc, Event 1, Inc, GFSI Canada Company, GFSI Holdings, Inc

Officers: Larry Graveel/COO, Pres.

GFY Foods Inc

601 Deerfield Pkwy, Buffalo Grove, IL, 60089; **PH:** 1-847-353-7554; http:// www.gfyfoodsinc.com

General - Incorporation	NV	**Stock**- Price on:12/24/2007	$0.3
Employees	NA	Stock Exchange	OTC
Auditor	Smith & Co	Ticker Symbol	GFYX
Stk Agt	Standard Registrar & Transfer Co Inc.	Outstanding Shares	NA
Counsel	Grateful Internet Associates	E.P.S.	NA
DUNS No.	NA	Shareholders	NA

Business: The group owns and operates a beverage and food restaurant in Illinois. Prior to 2004, the group was operating in oil and natural gas exploration and oil and natural gas producing properties. The group also continues to to explore investment opportunities in the oil and natural gas exploration arena.

Primary SIC and add'l.: 5812

CIK No: 0001145421

Subsidiaries: GFY, Inc.

Financial Data: Fiscal Year End:12/31　Latest Annual Data: 3/31/2004

Year	Sales	Net Income
2004	$27,000	-$1,911,000
2003	$1,000	-$1,730,000

Curr. Assets:	$2,588,000	Curr. Liab.:	$1,332,000		
Plant, Equip.:	$30,000	Total Liab.:	$1,346,000	Indic. Yr. Divd.:	NA
Total Assets:	$5,398,000	Net Worth:	$4,052,000	Debt/ Equity:	NA

Giant Industries Inc

23733 N Scottsdale Rd. , Scottsdale, AZ, 85255; **PH:** 1-480-585-8888; http:// www.giant.com

General - Incorporation	DE	**Stock**- Price on:12/24/2007	NA
Employees	2,632	Stock Exchange	NA
Auditor	Deloitte & Touche LLP	Ticker Symbol	NA
Stk Agt	Computershare Trust Co	Outstanding Shares	NA
Counsel	NA	E.P.S.	NA
DUNS No.	03-590-3194	Shareholders	NA

Business: The group operates through its subsidiaries whose principle activities include refining and marketing petroleum products. The groups refining products include gasoline, diesel fuel and food oil products. The group operates from United States, New Mexico, Colorado, and Arizona.

Primary SIC and add'l.: 5541 2911

CIK No: 0000856465

Subsidiaries: Ciniza Production Company, Dial Oil Co., Giant Four Corners, Inc., Giant Industries Arizona, Inc., Giant Mid-Continent, Inc., Giant Pipeline Company, Giant Stop-N-Go of New Mexico, Inc., Giant Yorktown Holding Company, Giant Yorktown, Inc., Navajo Convenient Stores Co., LLC, Phoenix Fuel Co., Inc., San Juan Refining Company

Officers: Fred L. Holliger/60/Chmn., CEO, Kim H. Bullerdick/54/Sr. VP, General Counsel, Sec., Natalie Dopp/36/VP - Human Resources, Jeff D. Perry/52/CIO, Leland S. Gould/51/Exec. VP - Governmental Affairs, Real Estate, Robert C. Sprouse/Exec. VP - Retail Group, Mark B. Cox/49/CFO, Exec. VP, Treasurer, Assist. Sec., Morgan Gust/60/Pres., Renee Dahl/Contact - Unbranded Marketing, Korbi Hart/Contact - Unbranded Marketing, Joe Dinapoli/Contact - Unbranded Marketing, James Marker/Marketing Mgr. - Branded Marketing

Directors: Fred L. Holliger/60/Chmn., CEO, Donald M. Wilkinson/70/Dir., George M. Rapport/64/Dir., Brooks J. Klimley/50/Dir., Larry L. Deroin/66/Dir.

Owners: Morgan Gust, Kim H. Bullerdick, Gabelli entities/8.60%, Fred L. Holliger, Mark B. Cox, Jack W. Keller, Larry DeRoin, George Rapport, Donald M. Wilkinson, Insiders/1.24%, Barclays entities/7.60%

Giant Motorsports Inc

13134 State Rte. 62, Salem, OH, 44460; *PH:* 1-440-439-9480; *Fax:* 1-440-439-9253; *http://* www.giantcorporate.com; *Email:* info@giantcorporate.com

General - Incorporation	NV	**Stock** - Price on:12/24/2007	$0.28
Employees	136	Stock Exchange	OTC
Auditor	Bagell, Josephs, Levine & Co. LLC	Ticker Symbol	GMOS
Stk Agt	Pacific Stock Transfer Company	Outstanding Shares	12,210,000
Counsel	NA	E.P.S.	$0.00
DUNS No.	NA	Shareholders	NA

Business: The group's principle activity is to market Honda products. The group sells new and used motorcycles, ATV's, personal watercraft, snowmobiles, parts, and accessories. The group also provides mechanical and financial services. The group's selling motorcycle brand names include Harley-Davidson, Honda, Yamaha, Suzuki, and Kawasaki. The group operates from United States.

Primary SIC and add'l.: NA

CIK No: 0001204947

Subsidiaries: Chicago Cycle, Inc, Giant Motorsports Acceptance Group, Inc, W.W. Cycles, Inc.

Owners: Gregory A. Haehn/25.40%, Insiders/65.80%, Russell A. Haehn/43.80%

Financial Data: *Fiscal Year End:*12/31 *Latest Annual Data:* 12/31/2006

Year	Sales	Net Income
2006	$100,752,000	-$181,000
2005	$105,605,000	-$9,000
2004	$79,951,000	$958,000

Curr. Assets:	$25,351,000	**Curr. Liab.:**	$25,429,000
Plant, Equip.:	$2,004,000	**Total Liab.:**	$25,450,000	**Indic. Yr. Divd.:**	NA
Total Assets:	$29,086,000	**Net Worth:**	$3,636,000	**Debt/ Equity:**	NA

Gibraltar Industries Inc

3556 Lake Shore Rd., Buffalo, NY, 14219; *PH:* 1-716-826-6500; *Fax:* 1-716-826-1589; *http://* www.gibraltar1.com

General - Incorporation	DE	**Stock** - Price on:12/24/2007	$21.64
Employees	3,460	Stock Exchange	NDQ
Auditor	Ernst & Young LLP	Ticker Symbol	ROCK
Stk Agt	American Stock Transfer & Trust Co.	Outstanding Shares	29,840,000
Counsel	NA	E.P.S.	$0.54
DUNS No.	05-996-1847	Shareholders	NA

Business: The group's principal activities are to process, manufacture and distribute a broad range of steel and other metal products. It operates in three segments: processed steel products, building products and heat-treating. The processed steel products segment produces a variety of cold-rolled strip steel products, coated sheet steel products and strapping products. Building products segment includes the processing of sheet steel to produce a variety of building and construction products. Heat-treating segment provides a wide range of processes, which refine the metallurgical properties of customer-owned metal products. The group's products and services are marketed in the United States, Canada and Mexico. During the year 2003, the group acquired construction metals inc and air vent inc and in 06-Jan-2004, it acquired renown specialties company ltd and in 13-Aug-2004, it acquried portals plus incorporated.

Primary SIC and add'l.: 3316

CIK No: 0000912562

Subsidiaries: Air Vent Inc., Alabama Metal Industries Corporation, AMICO Canada, Inc., Appleton Supply Co., Inc., B & W Heat Treating Corp., B&W Leasing LLC, B&W of Michigan, Inc., Brazing Concepts Company, Carolina Commercial Heat Treating, Inc., Cleveland Pickling, Inc., Construction Metals, LLC, Diamond Perforated Metals, Inc., Gator Grate, Inc., Gibraltar Construction Products, Inc., Gibraltar International, Inc. 38 Subsidiaries included in the Index

Officers: Brian J. Lipke/Chmn., CEO/$2,650,778.00, Paul M. Murray/Sr. VP - Human Resources, Organizational Development/$301,046.00, Henning N. Kornbrekke/COO, Pres./$2,015,383.00, Kenneth P. Houseknecht/VP - Communications, Investor Relations, Cliff A. Tucker/Group Pres. - Building Products, David W. Kay/Exec. VP, CFO, Treasurer/$804,803.00, Robert C. Brunson/Group Pres. - Building Products, Joseph D. Smith/Pres. - Alabama Metal Industries Corporation, Timothy J. Heasley/Sr. VP, Corporate Controller/$323,762.00, Dave A. McCartney/VP - Information Systems, John E. Wagner/VP - Supply Chain Management, Thomas A. Blanchard/Pres. - Processed Metals Group, Kevin Cullen/VP - Operations

Directors: Brian J. Lipke/Chmn., CEO, David N. Campbell/Dir., Arthur A. Russ/Dir., Gerald S. Lippes/Dir., Robert E. Sadler/Dir., William P. Montague/Dir., William J. Colombo/Dir.

Owners: Brian J. Lipke/3.83%, Dimensional Fund Advisors Inc./7.81%, Gerald S. Lippes, Insiders/4.21%, Meredith A. Lipke/2.58%, William P. Montague, Robert E. Sadler, Timothy Heasley, Curtis W. Lipke/1.83%, William J. Colombo, David W. Kay, Arthur A. Russ, Columbia Wanger Asset Management LP/10.82%, NWQ Investment Management Company LLC/7.55%, Eric R. Lipke/6.34% *(20 Owners included in Index)*

Financial Data: *Fiscal Year End:*12/31 *Latest Annual Data:* 12/31/2006

Year	Sales	Net Income
2006	$1,303,355,000	$57,269,000
2005	$1,178,236,000	$43,472,000
2004	$1,014,664,000	$50,782,000

Curr. Assets:	$455,780,000	**Curr. Liab.:**	$124,415,000	**P/E Ratio:**	17.31
Plant, Equip.:	$243,138,000	**Total Liab.:**	$602,640,000	**Indic. Yr. Divd.:**	$0.200
Total Assets:	$1,152,868,000	**Net Worth:**	$550,228,000	**Debt/ Equity:**	0.7546

Giga-tronics Inc

4650 Norris Canyon Rd., San Ramon, CA, 94583; *PH:* 1-925-328-4650; *Fax:* 1-925-328-4700; *http://* www.gigatronics.com; *Email:* info@gigatronics.com

General - Incorporation	CA	**Stock** - Price on:12/24/2007	$1.75
Employees	120	Stock Exchange	NDQ
Auditor	Perry-Smith LLP	Ticker Symbol	GIGA
Stk Agt	American Stock Transfer & Trust Co.	Outstanding Shares	4,810,000
Counsel	Bingham McCutchen	E.P.S.	-$0.033
DUNS No.	02-178-2669	Shareholders	NA

Business: The group's principal activity is to design, manufacture and market various test and measurement equipment. The products of the group are used in the development, test and maintenance of wireless communications products and systems, flight navigational equipment, electronic defense systems, automatic testing systems, commercial telecommunications, radar and electronic warfare. Presently the group holds 22 patents. The group distributes its products in the United States, Asia and Europe. Dymatix segment was discontinued during Jun 2003.

Primary SIC and add'l.: 3829 3826 3825

CIK No: 0000719274

Subsidiaries: ASCOR, Inc., Microsource, Inc.

Officers: John R. Regazzi/Dir., CEO, Pres. - Instrument Division/$162,462.00, Jeffrey T. Lum/Pres. - Ascor Inc/$144,324.00, Patrick J. Lawlor/VP - Finance, CFO, Sec.

Directors: John R. Regazzi/Dir., CEO, Pres. - Instrument Division, George H. Bruns/Chmn., Ken A. Harvey/Dir., James A. Cole/Dir., Garrett A. Garrettson/Dir., Robert C. Wilson/Dir.

Owners: Insiders/14.27%, John R. Regazzi/1.15%, Robert C. Wilson, Garrett A. Garrettson, George H. Bruns/10.85%, Jeffrey T. Lum, Kenneth A. Harvey, James A. Cole

Financial Data: *Fiscal Year End:*03/25 *Latest Annual Data:* 06/30/2007

Year	Sales	Net Income
2007	$4,628,000	$92,000
2006	$20,620,000	-$961,000
2005	$21,477,000	$612,000

Curr. Assets:	$12,155,000	**Curr. Liab.:**	$4,158,000
Plant, Equip.:	$1,251,000	**Total Liab.:**	$4,537,000	**Indic. Yr. Divd.:**	NA
Total Assets:	$13,733,000	**Net Worth:**	$9,196,000	**Debt/ Equity:**	NA

Gigabeam Corp

4021 Stirrup Creek Dr., Ste. 400, Druham, NC, 27703; *PH:* 1-919-206-4420; *Fax:* 1-919-544-8470; *http://* www.gigabeam.com; *Email:* sales@gigabeam.com

General - Incorporation	DE	**Stock** - Price on:12/24/2007	$2.66
Employees	20	Stock Exchange	NDQ
Auditor	BDO Seidman, LLP	Ticker Symbol	GGBM
Stk Agt	Continental Stock Transfer & Trust Co	Outstanding Shares	6,550,000
Counsel	NA	E.P.S.	-$3.36
DUNS No.	NA	Shareholders	NA

Business: The groups principal activities include designing, developing, selling, leasing, installing and servicing communications links. The products of the group include GigaBeam GigE unit, GigaBeam OC-48 unit and GigaBeam OC-192 unit. Customers served by the group include carriers and network integrators, value added resellers, government and enterprise entities. The group products sold under the trade name WiFiber(TM). The group operates from the United States. The net sale of the group for the year 2006 was $1,196,512.

Primary SIC and add'l.: 3661 3663 4822 4812 3669 7389 4899

CIK No: 0001279831

Subsidiaries: GigaBeam Service Corporation

Officers: Louis Slaughter/Chmn., CEO, Douglas Lockie/Co - Founder, Dir., CTO, Pres., Leighton J. Stephenson/59/CFO, VP - Finance, Administration, Duane D. Butler/VP - Link Operations, Caroline Baldwin Kahl/50/VP, Corporate Counsel, Sec., Don E. Peck/VP - Engineering, Manufacturing, Jay S. Lawrence/COO, Pres., VP - Sales, John Krzywicki/VP - Marketing, Strategy, Business Development, James Kennett/VP - Business Development, Robert Sutherland/53/Dir. - Engineering, Scott Wetenkamp/57/Engineering Consultant, Craig Hinkley/Outside Advisor, Edwin F. Johnson/Outside Advisor, David Rutledge/Outside Advisor, Bill Carey/Contact - Sales *(16 Officers included in Index)*

Directors: Louis Slaughter/Chmn., CEO, Douglas Lockie/Co - Founder, Dir., CTO, Pres., David A. Buckel/45/Dir., Richard Fiorentino/Dir., Merrill A. McPeak/Dir., Roger M. Widmann/Dir.

Owners: Don E. Peck/1.40%, Merrill A. McPeak, Ameristock Corp./9.34%, Insiders/39.15%, Edward S. Gutman/5.40%, Richard I. Fiorentino, Louis S. Slaughter/17.73%, Harvey Silverman/8.17%, John E. Krzywicki, Douglas G. Lockie/17.09%, Duane D. Butler

Financial Data: *Fiscal Year End:*12/31 *Latest Annual Data:* 12/31/2006

Year	Sales	Net Income
2006	$4,824,000	-$20,235,000
2005	$1,197,000	-$15,306,000
2004	NA	-$7,505,000

Curr. Assets:	$9,652,000	**Curr. Liab.:**	$3,337,000
Plant, Equip.:	$1,987,000	**Total Liab.:**	$4,429,000	**Indic. Yr. Divd.:**	NA
Total Assets:	$12,266,000	**Net Worth:**	$7,837,000	**Debt/ Equity:**	0.0053

GigaMedia Ltd

14th Floor, 122 Tunhwa N Rd., Taipei, 10595; *PH:* 886-6287707966; *http://* www.gigamedia.com.tw.

General - Incorporation	Singapore	**Stock** - Price on:12/24/2007	$14.2
Employees	323	Stock Exchange	NDQ
Auditor	GHP Horwath, P.C	Ticker Symbol	GIGM
Stk Agt	Bank of New York	Outstanding Shares	51,990,000
Counsel	NA	E.P.S.	$0.59
DUNS No.	NA	Shareholders	NA

Business: The group's principle activity is the provision of broadband Internet access services through the cable television infrastructure in Taiwan. It also provides Internet content services through the Web site, www.gigigaga.com, which is a Chinese-language broadband Web destination.

Primary SIC and add'l.: 7375 5065 7373 7372

CIK No: 0001105101

Subsidiaries: Bridgepoint International Limited, Cambridge Entertainment Software Limited, Cambridge Interactive Development Corporation, Cambridge Interactive Development Corporation (Quebec) Inc., FunTown Hong Kong Limited, FunTown World Limited, GigaMedia Asia Limited, GigaMedia China Limited, GigaMedia Finance International Limited, GigaMedia International Holdings Limited, Hoshin GigaMedia Center, Inc., Implus International Limited, Internet Media Licensing Ltd., Koos Broadband Telecom Co., Ltd.

Officers: Arthur Wang/Dir., CEO, Joseph Shea/Exec. VP, Robert J. Cahill/42/Head - Entertainment Software Business, Kenny Ching-Kun Huang/43/Sr. VP, Jennifer Tseng/Sr. VP, General Counsel, Falco Mai/Chief Administrative Officer, Exec. VP, Michel Chu/CTO, Exec. VP, Thomas Hui/Dir., CFO, COO, Pres., Chen-Wen Tarn/48/Head - Internet Access Services Business, Brad Miller/Dir. - Investor Relations, Samuel Chou/Head - Online Games Business

Directors: Arthur Wang/Dir., CEO, Daniel Chuen-Tai Wu/Chmn., Howe Yong Lee/Dir., Nancy Jing-Ying Hu Zee/Dir., Michael Y.J. Ding/Dir., Nelson Chang/Dir., Yichin Lee/Dir., Thomas Hui/Dir., CFO, COO, Pres., Gilbert Bao/Dir., Emmet Yu-Jui Hsu/Dir.

Financial Data: *Fiscal Year End:* 12/31 *Latest Annual Data:* 12/31/2006

Year	Sales	Net Income
2006	$94,292,000	$30,784,000
2005	$44,187,000	$6,336,000
2004	$99,819,000	$1,682,000

Curr. Assets:	$64,176,000	**Curr. Liab.:**	$45,207,000		
Plant, Equip.:	$10,098,000	**Total Liab.:**	$48,532,000	**Indic. Yr. Divd.:**	NA
Total Assets:	$182,619,000	**Net Worth:**	$134,087,000	**Debt/ Equity:**	NA

Gilat Satellite Networks Ltd

1750 Old Meadow Rd., McLean, VA, 22102; *PH:* 1-703-848-1000; *Fax:* 1-703-848-1010; *http://* www.gilat.com; *Email:* info@gilat.com

General - Incorporation	Israel	**Stock**- Price on:12/24/2007	$9.4
Employees	950	Stock Exchange	NDQ
Auditor	Kost Forer Gabbay & Kasierer	Ticker Symbol	GILT
Stk Agt	American Stock Transfer & Trust Co.	Outstanding Shares	38,820,000
Counsel	Arnold & Porter LLP	E.P.S	$0.52
DUNS No.	60-008-2523	Shareholders	NA

Business: The group's principle activity is the provision of products and services for satellite-based communication networks. The company designs, develops, manufactures, markets and services products that enable complete end-to-end telecommunications and data networking solutions. These products also enable broadband Internet solutions, based on very small aperture terminal (vsat) satellite earth stations, related central station equipment and software. The company provides service offerings which include access to satellite transponder capacity, installation of network equipment, on-line network monitoring and network maintenance and repair services. The company sells its products and services to postal, telephone and telegraph organizations and other major carriers, resellers and other companies in the usa, Europe, south and Latin America, Asia, South Africa and other countries. The group's quarterly revenue for Sep '07 was 71.55 millions of USD.

Primary SIC and add'l.: 7373 3669 4899

CIK No: 0000897322

Subsidiaries: Gilat Colombia S.A. E.S.P, Gilat to Home Peru S.A, Spacenet Inc

Officers: Amiram Levinberg/Chmn., CEO, Erez Antebi/CEO - Gilat Network Systems, GNS, Andreas Georghiou/CEO - Spacenet Inc, Yoav Leibovitch/Exec. VP - Corporate Development, Joshua Levinberg/Exec. VP - Corporate Business Development, Strategy, Rachel Prishkolnik/Dir., Corp. Sec., Tal Payne/CFO, Rocio D. Campo/Pres., Ayelet Shaked/Dir. - Investor Relations, Rachel Levine/Investor Relations Officer - USA, Noam Tepper/Contact - Financial Access

Directors: Amiram Levinberg/Chmn., CEO, Haim Benjamini/69/Dir., Jeremy Blank/Dir., Leora Meridor/Dir., Karen Sarid/Dir., Izhak Tamir/Dir., Rachel Prishkolnik/Dir., Corp. Sec., Ehud Ganani/Dir.

Owners: Mivtach Shamir Finance Ltd./5.71%, York Capital Management/20.77%, Insiders/5.85%

Financial Data: *Fiscal Year End:* 12/31 *Latest Annual Data:* 12/31/2006

Year	Sales	Net Income
2006	$248,710,000	$10,487,000
2005	$209,395,000	-$3,716,000
2004	$241,498,000	-$11,535,000

Curr. Assets:	$258,203,000	**Curr. Liab.:**	$137,569,000		
Plant, Equip.:	$121,366,000	**Total Liab.:**	$228,155,000	**Indic. Yr. Divd.:**	NA
Total Assets:	$440,214,000	**Net Worth:**	$212,059,000	**Debt/ Equity:**	NA

Gildan Activewear Inc

725 Monte de Liesse, Montreal, PQ, H4T 1P5; *PH:* 1-514-735-2023; *Fax:* 1-514-735-6810; *http://* www.gildan.com; *Email:* investors@gildan.com

General - Incorporation	QC	**Stock**- Price on:12/24/2007	$35.61
Employees	15,000	Stock Exchange	NYSE
Auditor	KPMG LLP	Ticker Symbol	GIL
Stk Agt	Computershare Investor Services LLC	Outstanding Shares	120,350,000
Counsel	NA	E.P.S	$0.79
DUNS No.	24-529-0549	Shareholders	NA

Business: The group's principal activity is to manufacture and sell active wear apparel in the Canadian, United States, European and international apparel markets. The group's products are sold under gildan active wear brand. The group's product lines include t-shirts, placket collar golf shirts and sweatshirts in both 100% cotton and 50% polyester blends. The group sells its products as blanks, which are ultimately decorated with designs and logos for sale to consumers. Its operations include knitting, dyeing, finishing, cutting and sewing.

Primary SIC and add'l.: 2389 2399 5651 2331

CIK No: 0001061894

Subsidiaries: Gildan Activewear (Eden) Inc., Gildan Activewear (UK)Limited, Gildan Activewear (US Holdings) Inc., Gildan Activewear Castaos, Gildan Activewear Clercine, Gildan Activewear Dominican Republic Textile Company Inc., Gildan Activewear Honduras Textiles Company, Gildan Activewear Malone, Gildan Activewear Mexico, Gildan Activewear Properties (BVI)Inc., Gildan Activewear Properties Dominican Republic, Gildan Activewear Rivas, Gildan Activewear San Antonio, Gildan Activewear San Jos, Gildan Activewear San Marcos 20 Subsidiaries included in the Index

Officers: Glenn J. Chamandy/Dir., CEO, Pres., Claude Guay/CIO, Exec. VP, Cam Gentile/Exec. VP - Organizational Development, Change Management, Eric Lehman/Exec. VP - Supply Chain, Michael R. Hoffman/Pres. - Gildan Activewear SRL, Laurence G. Sellyn/Exec. VP, Chief Financial, Administrative Officer, Georges Sam Yu Sum/Exec. VP - Operations, Benito Masi/Exec. VP - Manufacturing, William H. Nichol/Pres. - Gildan Retail

Directors: Robert M. Baylis/Chmn., Pierre Robitaille/Dir., William D. Anderson/Dir., Richard P. Strubel/Dir., Gonzalo F. Valdes-Fauli/Dir., Sheila Obrien/Dir.

Financial Data: *Fiscal Year End:* 10/02 *Latest Annual Data:* 10/1/2006

Year	Sales	Net Income
2006	$773,190,000	$106,227,000
2005	$653,851,000	$85,629,000
2004	$533,368,000	$59,456,000

Curr. Assets:	$274,184,000	**Curr. Liab.:**	$95,373,000		
Plant, Equip.:	$211,693,000	**Total Liab.:**	$161,410,000	**Indic. Yr. Divd.:**	NA
Total Assets:	$489,907,000	**Net Worth:**	$328,498,000	**Debt/ Equity:**	NA

Gilead Sciences Inc

333 Lakeside Dr., Foster City, CA, 94404; *PH:* 1-650-574-3000; *Fax:* 1-650-578-9264; *http://* www.gilead.com

General - Incorporation	DE	**Stock**- Price on:12/24/2007	$78.98
Employees	2,515	Stock Exchange	NDQ
Auditor	Ernst & Young LLP	Ticker Symbol	GILD
Stk Agt	Mellon Investor Services LLC	Outstanding Shares	416,920,000
Counsel	Cooley Godward LLP	E.P.S	NA
DUNS No.	18-504-9848	Shareholders	NA

Business: The groups principle activities include developing and commercializing therapeutics in areas of unmet medical need including life threatening diseases. The groups products include Truvada, Viread, Atripla and Emtriva. The group operates from United States.

Primary SIC and add'l.: 6794 8731 2834

CIK No: 0000882095

Subsidiaries: Bristol-Myers Squibb& Gilead Sciences, LLC, Gilead Biopharmaceutics Ireland Corporation, Gilead Holdings, LLC, Gilead Sciences (NZ), Gilead Sciences Canada, Inc., Gilead Sciences Europe Ltd., Gilead Sciences GmbH, Gilead Sciences Hellas EPE, Gilead Sciences Holding LLC, Gilead Sciences International Ltd., Gilead Sciences Limited, Gilead Sciences Ltd., Gilead Sciences Luxembourg S.a.r.l., Gilead Sciences Pty Limited, Gilead Sciences SARL 21 Subsidiaries included in the Index

Officers: John C. Martin/Dir., CEO, Pres./$9,608,496.00, William A. Lee/Sr. VP - Research, Norbert W. Bischofberger/Exec. VP - Research, Development, Chief Scientific Officer/$4,242,611.00, Bruce A. Montgomery/Sr. VP, Head - Respiratory Therapeutics, Kristen M. Metza/Sr. VP - Human Resources, Susan Hubbard/Investor Relations Officer, Andre Torres/Investor Relations Officer, Ruey-Li Hwang/Investor Relations Officer, Paul Carter/Sr. VP - International Commercial Operations, James R. Meyers/Sr. VP - Commercial Operations, North America, Patrick O'Brien/Investor Relations Officer, Kevin Young/Exec. VP - Commercial Operations/$3,355,196.00, John F. Milligan/CFO, Exec. VP/$4,214,450.00, John J. Toole/54/Sr. VP - Clinical Research/$2,413,728.00, Gregg H. Alton/Sr. VP, General Counsel, Sec. *(17 Officers included in Index)*

Directors: John C. Martin/Dir., CEO, Pres., Bernard M. Wagner/Chmn. - Scientific Advisory Board, James M. Denny/Chmn., Richard M. Whitley/Member - Scientific Advisory Board, Carla A. Hills/Dir., Paul Berg/81/Dir., Etienne F. Davignon/Dir., Nicholas G. Moore/Dir., John F. Cogan/Dir., John W. Madigan/Dir., Gordon E. Moore/Dir., George P. Shultz/Dir., Gayle Edlund Wilson/Dir., Jacqueline K. Barton/Member - Scientific Advisory Board, Francis V. Chisari/Member - Scientific Advisory Board *(21 Directors included in Index)*

Owners: John J. Toole, John W. Madigan, Insiders/2.60%, James M. Denny, Axa Financial, Inc./7.50%, Gordon E. Moore, Paul Berg, John F. Cogan, Norbert W. Bischofberger, Gayle E. Wilson, US Bank FBO Essentia Health Services, Nicholas G. Moore, Radcliffe SPC, Ltd. for and on behalf of the ClassA Convertible Crossover Segregated Portfolio, Carla A. Hills, UBS Securities LLC *(21 Owners included in Index)*

Financial Data: *Fiscal Year End:* 12/31 *Latest Annual Data:* 12/31/2006

Year	Sales	Net Income
2006	$3,026,139,000	-$1,189,957,000
2005	$2,028,400,000	$813,914,000
2004	$1,324,621,000	$449,371,000

Curr. Assets:	$2,429,206,000	**Curr. Liab.:**	$764,276,000		
Plant, Equip.:	$361,299,000	**Total Liab.:**	$2,217,172,000	**Indic. Yr. Divd.:**	NA
Total Assets:	$4,085,981,000	**Net Worth:**	$1,815,718,000	**Debt/ Equity:**	0.5456

Gilman & Ciocia Inc

11 Raymond Ave., Poughkeepsie, NY, 12603; *PH:* 1-845-486-0900; *Fax:* 1-845-483-9332; *http://* www.gtax.com

General - Incorporation	DE	**Stock**- Price on:12/24/2007	$0.1
Employees	205	Stock Exchange	OTC
Auditor	Radin, Glass & Co. LLP	Ticker Symbol	GTAX
Stk Agt	Corporate Stock Transfer, Inc.	Outstanding Shares	9,690,000
Counsel	NA	E.P.S	$0.25
DUNS No.	10-826-6966	Shareholders	NA

Business: The group's principal activities are providing income tax preparations and financial planning services to individuals and businesses. The group attracts business through direct mail advertising, promotions and seminars. A large majority of the company's clients are first introduced to the group's products by direct mail advertising. The group provides federal, state and local tax preparation services to individuals predominantly in the middle and upper income group through 43 offices operating in 5 states across the United States. The group in addition, provides financial planning services like securities brokerage services and insurance agency services.

Primary SIC and add'l.: 7291 7331 6211 6411

CIK No: 0000914142

Subsidiaries: Asset & Financial Planning, Ltd., GC Capital Corp, Prime Capital Services, Inc, Prime Financial Services, Inc

Officers: Michael Ryan/Dir., CEO, Pres., Carole Enisman/Exec. VP - Operation, Ted Finkelstein/VP, General Counsel, Kathryn Travis/Sec., Karen Fisher/42/Chief Accounting Officer

Directors: Michael Ryan/Dir., CEO, Pres., James Ciocia/Chmn., Edward H. Cohen/Dir., Allan Page/Dir., Frederick Wasserman/Dir., Nelson Obus/Dir., John F. Levy/Dir.

Owners: Wynnefield Small Cap Value Offshore Fund, Ltd, Wynnefield Partners Small Cap Value LP, Ralph Porpora, James Ciocia, Ted Finkelstein, Edward Cohen, Wynnefield Partners Small Cap Value LP, Insiders, WebFinancial Corporation, Carole Enisman, Kathryn Travis, Prime Partners II, LLC, Karen Fisher, Nelson Obus, Allan Page *(17 Owners included in Index)*

Financial Data: *Fiscal Year End:*06/30   *Latest Annual Data:* 06/30/2007

Year	Sales	Net Income
2007	$53,052,000	$793,000
2006	$53,621,000	-$2,555,000
2005	$56,083,000	-$1,826,000

Curr. Assets:	$6,405,000	**Curr. Liab.:**	$21,001,000		
Plant, Equip.:	$1,273,000	**Total Liab.:**	$21,816,000	**Indic. Yr. Divd.:**	NA
Total Assets:	$16,636,000	**Net Worth:**	-$5,180,000	**Debt/ Equity:**	NA

Girasolar Inc

Formerly: Legend Investment Corp
173 Pk. Land Plz., Ste. B, Ann Arbor, MI, 48103; *PH:* 1-734-418-3004;
http:// www.legendinvestment.com

General - Incorporation .... DE	**Stock**- Price on:12/24/2007 ....$0.35
Employees ....NA	Stock Exchange..NA
Auditor .... Gruber & Co., LLC	Ticker Symbol..NA
Stk Agt....... Olde Monmouth Stk Trnsfer Co. Inc.	Outstanding Shares ....NA
Counsel .... Lehman & Eilen	E.P.S..NA
DUNS No. ....NA	Shareholders..NA

Business: The group's principal activity is to develop, produce, and market sports entertainment products, primarily in sports such as extreme fighting, professional boxing, and mixed martial arts. Extreme fighting is a no-holds-barred combination of martial arts and wrestling. The group intends to plan, promote, manage, and coordinate professional combat sports events for live audiences and for television broadcasts.

Primary SIC and add'l.: 6799

CIK No: 0001307901

Subsidiaries: Legend Credit, Inc., Online Enterprises, Inc.

Officers: James Miller/Pres.

Owners: Barton PK, LLC/50.00%, Insiders/11.00%, Barton PK, LLC/11.00%, Peter Klamka/11.00%, ISA BV/50.00%, GiraSolar BV/35.00%

Financial Data: *Fiscal Year End:*12/31   *Latest Annual Data:* 12/31/2005

Year	Sales	Net Income
2005	NA	-$435,000
2004	NA	-$375,000

Curr. Assets:	$6,733,000	**Curr. Liab.:**	$8,981,000		
Plant, Equip.:	$24,000	**Total Liab.:**	$9,001,000	**Indic. Yr. Divd.:**	NA
Total Assets:	$12,941,000	**Net Worth:**	$3,940,000	**Debt/ Equity:**	NA

GiveMePower Corp

5925 12th St. SE, Ste. 230, Calgary, AB, T2H 2M3; *PH:* 1-403-287-6001; *Fax:* 1-403-287-6002;
http:// www.givemepower.com; *Email:* info@givemepower.com

General - Incorporation .... NV	**Stock**- Price on:12/24/2007 ....NA
Employees ....NA	Stock Exchange...OTC
Auditor .... Malone & Bailey, P.C	Ticker Symbol...GMPW
Stk Agt................................ Fidelity Transfer Co	Outstanding Shares ....NA
Counsel... Sichenzia Ross Friedman Ference LLP	E.P.S..NA
DUNS No. ....NA	Shareholders..NA

Business: The group's principal activity is to market software geared to end users and developers involved in the design, manufacture and construction of engineered products. The group operates in two segments: the retail products segment include the sale of pre-packaged software and related solutions and services for businesses and individuals involved in the design, construction and management of man-made structures and manufactured products. The embedded products segment includes licensing technologies and providing related services to OEM hardware manufacturers and third-party software developers. The group's principal products include powercad ce viewer(tm), powercad ce classic(tm), powercad ce pro(tm), powercad lt+(TM), powercad classic(tm), powercad pro(tm) and powercad architect(tm) . The group's products and services are sold primarily in North America through it's wholly owned subsidiary givemepower inc.

Primary SIC and add'l.: 7374 7373 7372

CIK No: 0001064722

Subsidiaries: GiveMePower, Inc

Officers: William V. Walton/Dir., CEO, Pres., Principal Financial Officer, Principal Accounting Officer, Dave Wilkinson/VP - Information, Technology, D. C. Walton/VP - Client Relations, Tim Nye/Advisory Counsel, Janeen Norman-Lando/Media, Public Relations Mgr.

Directors: William V. Walton/Dir., CEO, Pres., Principal Financial Officer, Principal Accounting Officer, Richard Cheyne/Dir., Jeffrey Fajgenbaum/Dir., Doug Reid/Dir.

Owners: Wilfried Grabert/7.50%, Douglas Reid, W.V. Walton Family Trust/6.97%, Insiders/7.50%, Robert Grabert/5.90%, Jeffrey Fajgenbaum, Scott Sabins Profit Sharing Plan/9.20%, Richard Cheyne

Financial Data: *Fiscal Year End:*06/30   *Latest Annual Data:* 06/30/2006

Year	Sales	Net Income
2006	$185,000	-$1,561,000
2005	$190,000	-$787,000
2004	$117,000	-$1,454,000

Curr. Assets:	$18,000	**Curr. Liab.:**	$1,026,000		
Plant, Equip.:	$3,000	**Total Liab.:**	$1,276,000	**Indic. Yr. Divd.:**	NA
Total Assets:	$21,000	**Net Worth:**	-$1,254,000	**Debt/ Equity:**	NA

Given Imaging Ltd

5555 Oakbrook Pkwy., No. 355, Norcross, GA, 30093; *PH:* 1-770-662-0870; *Fax:* 1-770-662-0510;
http:// www.givenimaging.com

General - Incorporation ....Israel	**Stock**- Price on:12/24/2007 ....$26.16
Employees 400	Stock Exchange..NDQ
Auditor .... Somekh Chaikin	Ticker Symbol...GIVN
Stk Agt ..... American Stock Transfer & Trust Co.	Outstanding Shares 28,690,000
Counsel.......................Zellermayer, Pelossof & Co	E.P.S...$0.13
DUNS No. ....NA	Shareholders..NA

Business: The groups principle activity is to develop a proprietary wireless imaging system that represents a new approach to visual examination of gastrointestinal tract. The group operates from United States.

Primary SIC and add'l.: 3845

CIK No: 0001126140

Subsidiaries: Given Imaging B.V., Given Imaging GmbH, Given Imaging KK, Given Imaging Pty. Ltd., Given Imaging s.a.s., Given Imaging, Inc.

Officers: Nachum Shamir/Dir., CEO, Pres., Chris Rowland/Pres., Manfred Gehrtz/Pres. - International, Mark Gilreath/Chief Marketing Officer, Ori Braun/Sr. VP - Business Development, Kazem Samandari/Sr. VP - Asia Pacific, Japan Region, Yuval Yanai/CFO, Kevin Rubey/COO

Directors: Nachum Shamir/Dir., CEO, Pres., Israel Makov/Chmn., Arie Mientkavitch/Dir., Doron Birger/Dir., Dennert Ware/Dir., Michael Grobstein/Dir., A. Leowenstein/Dir., James M. Cornelius/Dir.

Owners: James M. Cornelius, Michael Grobstein, Doron Birger/25.40%, OrbiMed Advisors LLC, OrbiMed Capital LLC and Samuel D. Isaly/6.40%, Nachum Shamir, Manfred Gehrtz, Christopher Rowland, Eyal Lifschitz, IDB Holding Corporation Ltd./39.40%, Insiders/43.90%, Anat Loewenstein, AXA Assurances I.A.R.D. Mutuelle, AXA Assurances Vie Mutuelle,/13.10%, Kevin Rubey, Yuval Yanai, Chen Barir *(16 Owners included in Index)*

Financial Data: *Fiscal Year End:*12/31   *Latest Annual Data:* 12/31/2006

Year	Sales	Net Income
2006	$95,029,000	-$1,508,000
2005	$86,776,000	$6,343,000
2004	$65,020,000	$2,888,000

Curr. Assets:	$103,069,000	**Curr. Liab.:**	$24,054,000		
Plant, Equip.:	$14,811,000	**Total Liab.:**	$50,391,000	**Indic. Yr. Divd.:**	NA
Total Assets:	$158,177,000	**Net Worth:**	$107,786,000	**Debt/ Equity:**	NA

Glacier Bancorp Inc

49 Commons Loop, Kalispell, MT, 59901; *PH:* 1-406-751-4200; *Fax:* 1-406-751-4729;
http:// www.glacierbancorp.com; *Email:* investor@glacierbancorp.com

General - Incorporation ....MT	**Stock**- Price on:12/24/2007 ....$21.44
Employees 1,236	Stock Exchange..NDQ
Auditor .... BKD LLP	Ticker Symbol..GBCI
Stk Agt .... American Stock Transfer & Trust Co.	Outstanding Shares 52,690,000
Counsel.. Hash & O'brien	E.P.S...$1.26
DUNS No. ....NA	Shareholders..NA

Business: The group's principal activity is to provide banking services to individual and corporate customers in Montana. The group's subsidiaries are glacier bank, first security bank of missoula, western security bank, mountain west bank in Idaho, big sky western bank, valley bank of helena, glacier bank of whitefish and glacier capital trust i. The banking products and services offered include transaction and savings deposits, commercial, consumer and real estate loans and mortgage origination services. The group also provides brokerage services through raymond james financial services, a non-affiliated company. The group acquired pend oreille bancorp and its subsidiary pend oreille bank on 15-Jul-2003. As on 31-Dec-2003, the group has 54 banking offices throughout Montana, Idaho and Utah and as on 04-Jun-2004, the group acquired ione branch in ione, Washington.

Primary SIC and add'l.: 6712 6022

CIK No: 0000868671

Subsidiaries: Big Sky Western Bank, Citizens (ID) Statutory Trust I, Citizens Community Bank, First National Bank - West, First Security Bank of Missoula, Glacier Bank, Glacier Bank of Whitefish, Glacier Capital Trust I, Glacier Capital Trust II, Mountain West Bank in Idaho, Valley Bank of Helena, Western Security Bank

Officers: Michael J. Blodnick/Dir., CEO, Pres./$666,683.00, James H. Strosahl/66/Exec. VP, Sec./$508,193.00, Ron Copher/CFO, Treasurer, Don Chery/Exec. VP, Chief Administrative Officer

Directors: Michael J. Blodnick/Dir., CEO, Pres., Everit A. Sliter/Chmn., Craig A. Langel/Dir., James M. English/Dir., John W. Murdoch/Dir., Jon W. Hippler/Dir., Peter L. Larson/Dir., Allen J. Fetscher/Dir., Douglas J. McBride/Dir.

Owners: T. Rowe Price Associates, Inc./7.70%, Columbia Wanger Asset Management, L.P./8.30%, James H. Strosahl/0.21%, Insiders/4.53%

Financial Data: *Fiscal Year End:*12/31   *Latest Annual Data:* 09/30/2007

Year	Sales	Net Income
2007	$94,908,000	$17,639,000
2006	$87,575,000	$17,030,000
2005	$234,749,000	$52,373,000

Curr. Assets:	$198,746,000	**Curr. Liab.:**	$3,696,312,000	**P/E Ratio:**	17.43
Plant, Equip.:	$112,243,000	**Total Liab.:**	$4,011,596,000	**Indic. Yr. Divd.:**	$0.520
Total Assets:	$4,467,739,000	**Net Worth:**	$456,143,000	**Debt/ Equity:**	0.2635

Glacier Water Services Inc

1385 Pk. Ctr. Dr., Vista, CA, 92081; *PH:* 1-760-560-1111; *Fax:* 1-760-560-3333;
http:// www.glacierwater.com

General - Incorporation .... DE	**Stock**- Price on:12/24/2007 ....$37
Employees ....NA	Stock Exchange...OTC
Auditor ....KPMG LLP	Ticker Symbol...GWSV
Stk Agt .... Mellon Investor Services LLC	Outstanding Shares 2,600,000
Counsel..........Milbank, Tweed Hadley & McCoy	E.P.S..-$1.88
DUNS No. 10-627-0861	Shareholders..NA

Business: The group's principal activity is to provide drinking water to consumers through self-service vending machines. The water vending machines reduce impurities in the water through a combination of micron filtration, reverse osmosis, carbon absorption and ultraviolet sterilization. The group's machines are placed at supermarkets and other retail outlets under commission arrangements with the retailers. The group's machines are primarily located throughout the sunbelt and midwest regions of the United States. The group operated approximately 15,500 machines in 39 states. On Oct 7, 2003, the company acquired 100% outstanding common stock of the water island, inc.

Primary SIC and add'l.: 5962

CIK No: 0000883505

Subsidiaries: Glacier Water Trust I

Officers: Brian H. McInerney/CEO, Steven L. Murphy/COO, David W. Walters/CFO, Dave Walters/Investor Relation

Directors: Charles A. Norris/Chmn.

Financial Data: Fiscal Year End:01/02 Latest Annual Data: 1/2/2005

Year	Sales	Net Income
2005	$76,261,000	-$2,357,000
2003	$72,316,000	-$1,400,000
2002	$71,029,000	-$2,573,000

Curr. Assets:	$13,074,000	Curr. Liab.:	$6,865,000		
Plant, Equip.:	$43,520,000	Total Liab.:	$72,990,000	Indic. Yr. Divd.:	NA
Total Assets:	$66,724,000	Net Worth:	-$6,266,000	Debt/ Equity:	NA

Gladstone Commercial Corp

1521 Westbranch Dr., Ste. 200, McLean, VA, 22102; *PH:* 1-703-287-5800; *Fax:* 1-703-287-5801; *http://* www.gladstonecommercial.com; *Email:* info@gladstonecapital.com

General		Stock	
Incorporation	MD	Price on:12/24/2007	$19.85
Employees	NA	Stock Exchange	NDQ
Auditor	PricewaterhouseCoopers LLP	Ticker Symbol	GOOD
Stk Agt	Bank of New York	Outstanding Shares	8,570,000
Counsel	NA	E.P.S	$0.27
DUNS No.	NA	Shareholders	NA

Business: The groups principle activity is to provide real estate investment services. The investments products of the group include working capital reserves, mortgage loans and mortgage backed securities. The groups operates through two segments namely real estate leasing and real estate lending. The group operates from the United States. The group's quarterly revenue for September 2007 was 8.36 millions of USD.

Primary SIC and add'l.: 6798

CIK No: 0001234006

Subsidiaries: 2525 N Woodlawn Vstrm Wichita KS, LLC, 260 Springside Drive, Akron OH LLC, 3094174 Nova Scotia Company, 3094175 Nova Scotia Company, ACI06 Champaign IL LLC, AFL05 Duncan SC LLC, AFL05 Duncan SC Member LLC, CI05 Clintonville WI LLC, CMI04 Canton NC LLC, CMS06-3 LLC, COCO04 Austin TX GP LLC, COCO04 Austin TX, L.P., Corning Big Flats LLC, Dorval Property Trust, EE, 208 South Rogers Lane, Raleigh NC LLC 52 Subsidiaries included in the Index

Officers: David J. Gladstone/Founder, Chmn., CEO, Terry Lee Brubaker/Vice Chmn., COO, Sec., Bill Cooke/MD, Brian Eick/MD, David Meier/MD, John Sateri/MD, John Weller/MD, Erika Highland/Principal, Debbie Peterson/Assoc., Christopher Seneta/Assoc., Kristina A. Wilmer/Assoc., Joy Beck/Analyst, Arnett James/Analyst, Katie Swanson/Analyst, Jack Dellafiora/Chief Compliance Officer - Gladstone Companies *(57 Officers included in Index)*

Directors: David J. Gladstone/Founder, Chmn., CEO, Terry Lee Brubaker/Vice Chmn., COO, Sec., Anthony W. Parker/61/Dir., Paul W. Adelgren/Dir., John H. Outland/Dir., George Stelljes/Dir., Pres., Chief Investment Officer, David A.R. Dullum/59/Dir., Maurice W. Coulon/64/Dir., Gerard Mead/63/Dir., Michela A. English/57/Dir.

Owners: Anthony W. Parker, Gary Gerson, George Stelljes/1.50%, Harry Brill, Gerard Mead, Avenir Corporation/10.27%, Persons associated with CF Advisors, LLC/5.67%, Prudential Financial, Inc/5.64%, David Gladstone/4.10%, Insiders/6.89%, John H. Outland, Terry Lee Brubaker, Michela A. English, Paul Adelgren, Maurice W. Coulon (16 Owners included in Index)

Financial Data: Fiscal Year End:12/31 Latest Annual Data: 12/31/2006

Year	Sales	Net Income
2006	$25,946,000	$4,373,000
2005	$13,465,000	$3,602,000
2004	$4,312,000	$1,624,000

Curr. Assets:	$37,454,000	Curr. Liab.:	$2,698,000		
Plant, Equip.:	$235,118,000	Total Liab.:	$163,542,000	Indic. Yr. Divd.:	$1.440
Total Assets:	$315,766,000	Net Worth:	$152,224,000	Debt/ Equity:	NA

Glamis Gold Ltd

5190 Neil Rd., Ste. 310, Reno, NV, 89502; *PH:* 1-775-827-4600; *http://* www.glamis.com

General		Stock	
Incorporation	Canada	Price on:12/24/2007	$23.98
Employees	3,509	Stock Exchange	NYSE
Auditor	KPMG LLP	Ticker Symbol	NA
Stk Agt	Computershare Trust Co of Canada	Outstanding Shares	703,830,000
Counsel	Lang Michener Lawrence & Shaw	E.P.S	$0.41
DUNS No.	24-368-9346	Shareholders	NA

Business: The group's principal activities are the exploration, mine development and extraction of gold and other precious metals. On 16-Jul-2002, the group acquired francisco gold corp.

Primary SIC and add'l.: 1041

CIK No: 0000782819

Financial Data: Fiscal Year End:12/31 Latest Annual Data: 12/31/2006

Year	Sales	Net Income
2006	$1,056,300,000	-$161,500,000
2005	$597,183,000	-$134,909,000
2004	$191,016,000	$49,879,000

Curr. Assets:	$555,200,000	Curr. Liab.:	$352,900,000		
Plant, Equip.:	$75,700,000	Total Liab.:	$5,291,700,000	Indic. Yr. Divd.:	$0.180
Total Assets:	$17,677,800,000	Net Worth:	$12,137,400,000	Debt/ Equity:	NA

Glassmaster Co

PO Box 788, Lexington, SC, 29071; *PH:* 1-803-359-2594; *Fax:* 1-269-345-5613; *http://* www.glassmaster.com; *Email:* request@gcontrols.com

General		Stock	
Incorporation	SC	Price on:12/24/2007	NA
Employees	175	Stock Exchange	OTC
Auditor	Elliott Davis LLC	Ticker Symbol	GLMA
Stk Agt	BB&T Corporate Trust Services	Outstanding Shares	NA
Counsel	NA	E.P.S	-$0.34
DUNS No.	00-334-2243	Shareholders	NA

Business: The group's principle activities are to manufacture thermoplastic and thermoset plastic materials, industrial controls and electronics and to market a broad range of product lines to customers across multiple industries. The group operates under two segments: industrial products and controls and electronics. Industrial products consist of extruded synthetic monofilaments and pultruded fiberglass and composites. Controls and electronics segment consists of mechanical and electronic controls, electronic controls, electronic test equipment and circuit boards. The products of the group are marketed by in house sales efforts and commissioned sales representatives to original equipment manufacturers and distributors. The group markets its products throughout North America, Europe, South America and the Pacific Rim.

Primary SIC and add'l.: 3083 3679

CIK No: 0000109870

Subsidiaries: Glassmaster Controls Company, IncMichigan, Glassmaster Marine, LLC

Officers: Angelika Guldt/Corporate Communications, Nathan G. Leaphart/CFO

Owners: Raymond M. Trewhella/6.80%, Stephen W. Trewhella/20.60%, John W. Begg/2.20%, Harold S. Trewhella, M. L. Chavis/12.00%, Neil A. McLeod, James S. Burroughs/4.50%, George L. Husong, Paul B. Trewhella/2.20%, Insiders/57.30%, Nathan G. Leaphart, Stephen W. Trewhella/6.60%, James F. Kane/1.30%

Financial Data: Fiscal Year End:08/31 Latest Annual Data: 08/31/2006

Year	Sales	Net Income
2006	$20,413,000	-$725,000
2005	$18,248,000	$101,000
2004	$15,750,000	-$9,000

Curr. Assets:	$6,731,000	Curr. Liab.:	$10,651,000		
Plant, Equip.:	$2,960,000	Total Liab.:	$11,551,000	Indic. Yr. Divd.:	NA
Total Assets:	$11,602,000	Net Worth:	$51,000	Debt/ Equity:	NA

GlaxoSmithKline Plc

1 Franklin Plz., Philadelphia, PA, 19101; *PH:* 1-215-751-4000; *Fax:* 1-215-751-3233; *http://* www.gsk.com

General		Stock	
Incorporation	UK	Price on:12/24/2007	$51.98
Employees	102,695	Stock Exchange	NYSE
Auditor	PricewaterhouseCoopers LLP	Ticker Symbol	GSK
Stk Agt	Bank of New York	Outstanding Shares	NA
Counsel	NA	E.P.S	$3.74
DUNS No.	NA	Shareholders	NA

Business: The group's principal activities are the creation and discovery, development, manufacture and marketing of pharmaceutical products, including vaccines, over-the-counter medicines and health-related consumer products. The group's principal pharmaceutical products include medicines in the following therapeutic areas: central nervous system, respiratory, anti-virals, anti-bacterials, vaccines, oncology and emesis, metabolic, cardiovascular and urogenital. The group has operational headquarters in philadelphia, and research triangle park, usa, and operations in some 117 countries, with products sold in over 130 countries. The principal research and development facilities are in the UK, the usa, Japan, Italy and Belgium. During the year 2003, the group acquired europharm holdings sa.

Primary SIC and add'l.: 2834 5122

CIK No: 0001131399

Subsidiaries: SmithKline Beecham plc

Officers: Jean-Pierre D. Garnier/Dir., CEO, Bob Ingram/Vice Chmn. - Pharmaceuticals, John Clarke/Pres. - Consumer Healthcare, Julian Heslop/Dir., CFO, Marc Dunoyer/Pres. - Pharmaceuticals Japan, Duncan Learmouth/Sr. VP - Corporate Communications, Community Partnerships, Bill Louv/Sr. VP - Information Technology, CIO, Smith Barney/Contact - Corporate Share Dealing Facility, Claire Dixon/Contact - Consumer Healthcare, Dan Phelan/Sr. VP - Human Resources, Russell Greig/Pres. - Pharmaceuticals International, Rupert Bondy/Sr. VP, General Counsel, David Stout/Pres. - Pharmaceutical Operations, Chris Viehbacher/Pres. - US Pharmaceuticals, Andrew Witty/Pres. - Pharmaceuticals Europe *(18 Officers included in Index)*

Directors: Jean-Pierre D. Garnier/Dir., CEO, Christopher Gent/Chmn., Moncef Slaoui/Dir., Ian Prosser/Dir., Lawrence Culp/Non - Exec. Dir., Deryck Maughan/Non - Exec. Dir., Ronaldo D. Schmitz/Non - Exec. Dir., Julian Heslop/Dir., CFO, Crispin Davis/Non - Exec. Dir., Daniel Podolsky/Non - Exec. Dir., Tom De Swaan/Non - Exec. Dir., Robert Wilson/Non - Exec. Dir., Roy Anderson/Non - Exec. Dir., Stephanie Burns/Non - Exec. Dir.

Financial Data: Fiscal Year End:12/31 Latest Annual Data: 12/31/2006

Year	Sales	Net Income
2006	$45,500,098,000	$8,747,382,000
2005	$37,272,528,000	$5,740,589,000
2004	$39,223,649,000	$5,263,471,000

Curr. Assets:	$21,534,427,000	Curr. Liab.:	$14,232,862,000		
Plant, Equip.:	$13,402,203,000	Total Liab.:	$37,918,381,000	Indic. Yr. Divd.:	$2.130
Total Assets:	$105,807,073,000	Net Worth:	$67,888,692,000	Debt/ Equity:	NA

Glen Burnie Bancorp

106 Padfield Blvd., Glen Burnie, MD, 21061; *PH:* 1-410-766-3300; *Fax:* 1-410-787-8581; *http://* www.thebankofglenburnie.com

General		Stock	
Incorporation	MD	Price on:12/24/2007	$17.33
Employees	119	Stock Exchange	NDQ
Auditor	Trice Geary & Myers LLC	Ticker Symbol	GLBZ
Stk Agt	Registrar & Transfer Co	Outstanding Shares	2,490,000
Counsel	NA	E.P.S	$1.08
DUNS No.	NA	Shareholders	NA

Business: The group's principal activities are to provide commercial and retail banking services including acceptance of demand and time deposits and origination of loans. The group's lending activities include residential and commercial real estate loans, construction loans, land acquisition and development loans, commercial loans and consumer installment lending, including indirect automobile lending. The group accepts regular savings accounts, money market deposit accounts, demand deposit accounts, now checking accounts, ira and sep accounts, christmas club accounts and certificates of deposit. The group's services are provided in anne arundel county and surrounding areas of central Maryland through its head office and six branches.

Primary SIC and add'l.: 6712 6022

CIK No: 0000890066

Subsidiaries: Glen Burnie Statutory Trust I

Officers: William F. Kuethe/Dir., CEO, Pres./$132,637.00, John E. Porter/CFO, Sr. VP/$133,015.00, Michael G. Livingston/Dir., Exec. VP/$208,564.00, Frederick W. Kuethe/Dir., VP, Barbara J. Elswick/Sec.

Directors: William F. Kuethe/Dir., CEO, Pres., John E. Demyan/Chmn., Charles Lynch/Dir., Shirley E. Boyer/Dir., Mary Lipin Wilcox/Dir., Michael G. Livingston/Dir., Exec. VP, Thomas Clocker/Dir., Norman Harrison/Dir., Karen B. Thorwarth/Dir., Edward Maddox/Dir., William N. Scherer/Dir., Frederick W. Kuethe/Dir., VP

Owners: John E. Demyan/9.44%, Charles Lynch Lynch, Insiders/20.03%, Edward L. Maddox/0.26%, Thomas Clocker/0.40%, Shirley E. Boyer/0.78%, Eugene P. Nepa/7.66%, Marrian K. McCormick/5.52%, Karen B. Thorwarth/0.80%, William N. Scherer, William F. Kuethe/2.13%, Michael G. Livingston/0.13%, Norman E. Harrison/0.30%, Frederick W. Kuethe/5.29%, Mary Lou Wilcox/0.80%

Financial Data: Fiscal Year End:12/31 Latest Annual Data: 12/31/2006

Year	Sales	Net Income
2006	$19,900,000	$2,720,000
2005	$18,211,000	$2,775,000
2004	$18,033,000	$3,056,000

Curr. Assets:	$14,947,000	Curr. Liab.:	$276,062,000	P/E Ratio:	15.90
Plant, Equip.:	$3,456,000	Total Liab.:	$289,544,000	Indic. Yr. Divd.:	$0.480
Total Assets:	$317,746,000	Net Worth:	$28,201,000	Debt/ Equity:	0.4281

Glenayre Technologies Inc

825 8th Ave., 23rd Fl., New York, NY, 10019; *PH:* 1-212-333-8400; *http://* www.glenayre.com

General - Incorporation .... DE
Employees 2,193
Auditor .... Ernst & Young LLP
Stk Agt...... American Stock Transfer & Trust Co.
Counsel .... NA
DUNS No. 61-971-4850

Stock- Price on:12/24/2007 .... NA
Stock Exchange .... NDQ
Ticker Symbol .... EDCI
Outstanding Shares .... NA
E.P.S. .... -$0.03
Shareholders .... NA

Business: The group's principal activity is to provide communication solutions for communications service providers, including wireless, traditional and broadband carriers. The communications messaging systems consist of enhanced services and unified communications solutions and products. The enhanced services and unified communications platforms include integrated messaging and personal communications applications, such as call answering, voice messaging, fax messaging and unified communications. The services include installation, project management of turnkey systems, training and customization. Major customers include nextel communications, voice stream, verizon wireless, alltel, us cellular, cricket communications, kpn telecom, cosmote, smart and starhub.

Primary SIC and add'l.: 7376 3663 4812 4813

CIK No: 0000808918

Subsidiaries: Entertainment Distribution Company (USA), LLCDelaware, U.S.A., Entertainment Distribution Company GMBH Germany, Entertainment Distribution Company Netherlands, Entertainment Distribution Company, LLCDelaware, U.S.A., Entertainment Distribution Holdings GMBH Germany, Glenayre (India) Private Limited India, Glenayre Administracion, S.A. de C.V. Mexico, Glenayre de Mexico S.A. de C.V. Mexico, Glenayre Digital Systems, Inc. North Carolina, U.S.A., Glenayre Electronics (Beijing) Co., Ltd. China, Glenayre Electronics (Hong Kong) Limited Hong Kong, Glenayre Electronics (Korea) Limited Korea, Glenayre Electronics (Proprietary) Limited South Africa, Glenayre Electronics (UK) Limited United Kingdom, Glenayre Electronics Europe B.V. Netherlands 27 Subsidiaries included in the Index

Officers: Oscar Rodriguez/CEO - IP Unity Glenayre, James Caparro/56/Dir., CEO, Pres./$1,068,169.00, Stan Chilton/Sr. VP - Service, Operations, Quality, Dick Kramlich/Co - Founder, Dir., General Partner, Matthew K. Behrent/37/Sr. VP, Chief Acquisitions Officer/$698,553.00, Jordan M. Copland/46/CFO, Exec. VP, Treasurer, Sec./$872,450.00, Keith Bhatia/Sr. VP - Americas, GM Japan, Stan Little/Sr. VP - Marketing, Business Development, Sonny Bettis/CTO, Steve Whipps/Sr. VP - EMEA

Directors: James Caparro/56/Dir., CEO, Pres., Ramon D. Ardizzone/70/Vice Chmn., Clarke H. Bailey/53/Chmn., Donald S. Bates/79/Dir., Howard W. Speaks/60/Dir., Cliff O. Bickell/65/Dir., John J. Hurley/73/Dir., Peter W. Gilson/68/Dir., Greg Tarr/Member - Board of Advisor, Steve Craddock/Member - Board of Advisor, Horace H. Sibley/68/Dir., Matt Murphy/Dir., Gerd Goette/Dir., Dick Kramlich/Co - Founder, Dir., General Partner, Augie Cruciotti/Dir. *(18 Directors included in Index)*

Owners: Matthew Behrent, Robert L. Chapman/9.66%, Debra L. Ziola, John J. Hurley, Howard W. Speaks, Cliff O. Bickell, Peter W. Gilson, Ramon D. Ardizzone, Dimensional Fund Advisors, Inc./5.12%, Horace H. Sibley, Donald S. Bates, Clarke H. Bailey/1.47%, State of Wisconsin Investment Board/9.66%, Insiders/3.42%

Financial Data: Fiscal Year End:12/31 Latest Annual Data: 12/31/2006

Year	Sales	Net Income
2006	$348,528,000	$4,025,000
2005	$267,818,000	$7,975,000
2004	$50,575,000	$4,519,000

Curr. Assets:	$169,150,000	Curr. Liab.:	$109,276,000		
Plant, Equip.:	$59,219,000	Total Liab.:	$206,039,000	Indic. Yr. Divd.:	NA
Total Assets:	$324,236,000	Net Worth:	$112,785,000	Debt/ Equity:	NA

Glencairn Gold Corp

6 Adelaide St. E, Ste. 500, Toronto, ON, M5C 1H6; *PH:* 1-416-860-0919; *Fax:* 1-416-367-0182; *http://* www.glencairngold.com

General - Incorporation .... ON
Employees 948
Auditor .... PricewaterhouseCoopers LLP
Stk Agt............ Equity Transfer Services Inc
Counsel............ Cassels Brock & Blackwell LLP
DUNS No. .... NA

Stock- Price on:12/24/2007 .... $0.56
Stock Exchange .... NA
Ticker Symbol .... NA
Outstanding Shares 241,250,000
E.P.S. .... -$0.047
Shareholders .... NA

Business: The Group's principal activity is to explore, extract, process and develop gold mines in Limon Mine in Nicaragua and constructing the Bellavista Mine in Costa Rica. The Group owns exploration properties in Nicaragua and Canada and is engaged in exploring for gold on certain Nicaraguan properties. Bellavista poured its first gold in the second quarter of 2005

Primary SIC and add'l.: 1040

CIK No: 0001311967

Subsidiaries: Black Hawk Mining Inc., Triton Mining (USA) LLC, Triton Mining Corporation

Officers: Peter Tagliamonte/Dir., CEO, Pres., Lorna D. MacGillivray/Corp. Sec., General Counsel, Bill Pearson/Exec. VP - Exploration, Graham Speirs/COO, Tina Cameron/Contact, Denis Arsenault/CFO

Directors: Peter Tagliamonte/Dir., CEO, Pres., Stan Bharti/Chmn., George Faught/Dir., Bruce Humphrey/Dir., Joe Milbourne/Dir., Patrick J. Mars/Dir., Ronald P. Gagel/Dir.

Financial Data: Fiscal Year End:12/31 Latest Annual Data: 12/31/2006

Year	Sales	Net Income
2006	$52,150,000	-$10,640,000
2005	$23,996,000	-$8,652,000
2004	$19,669,000	-$8,626,000

Curr. Assets:	$30,519,000	Curr. Liab.:	$15,328,000		
Plant, Equip.:	$65,272,000	Total Liab.:	$18,301,000	Indic. Yr. Divd.:	NA
Total Assets:	$96,564,000	Net Worth:	$78,263,000	Debt/ Equity:	NA

Glimcher Realty Trust

150 E Gay St., Columbus, OH, 43215; *PH:* 1-614-621-9000; *Fax:* 1-614-621-9321; *http://* www.glimcher.com; *Email:* grtinfo@glimcher.com

General - Incorporation .... MD
Employees 603
Auditor .... BDO Seidman, LLP
Stk Agt .... Computershare Investor Services LLC
Counsel .... NA
DUNS No. .... NA

Stock- Price on:12/24/2007 .... $27.13
Stock Exchange .... NYSE
Ticker Symbol .... GRT
Outstanding Shares 37,110,000
E.P.S. .... NA
Shareholders .... NA

Business: The groups principle activities include owning, acquiring, developing and operating retail properties. In the year 2006, the group acquired Tulsa mall in Oklahoma. The group operates from the United States. The group's quarterly revenue for September 2007 was 75.27 millions of USD.

Primary SIC and add'l.: 6798 6798

CIK No: 0000912898

Subsidiaries: California Retail Security, Inc, Catalina Partners, L, Charlotte Eastland Mall, LLC,, Colonial Park Mall LP,, Colonial Park Trust,, Dayton Mall Venture LLC,, EM Columbus II, LLC,, EM Columbus, LLC,, Fairfield Village, LLC,, GB Northtown, LLC,, GDC Retail, Inc, GDC Retail, LLC,, Glimcher Ashland Venture, LLC,, Glimcher Auburn, Inc, Glimcher Colonial Park Mall, Inc 84 Subsidiaries included in the Index

Officers: Michael P. Glimcher/Dir., CEO, Pres./$1,045,937.00, Marshall A. Loeb/COO, Pres./$530,247.00, Jed Reichard/VP - Regional Property Management, Grace E.E. Schmitt/VP - Human Resources, George A. Schmidt/Exec. VP, Chief Investment Officer/$479,625.00, Mark E. Yale/CFO, Exec. VP, Treasurer/$401,495.00, Thomas J. Drought/Sr. VP, Dir. - Leasing/$346,723.00, Ken Cannon/Sr. VP - Development, Antonio R. Marshall/VP - Design, Construction, Carrie Dworek/VP - Leasing, Melissa Indest/VP - Finance, Accounting, Christopher Lavender/VP - Development, Armand Mastropietro/VP - Property Management, Kim A. Rieck/Sr. VP, General Counsel, Sec., David Stec/VP, Regional Leasing Dir. *(18 Officers included in Index)*

Directors: Michael P. Glimcher/Dir., CEO, Pres., Herbert Glimcher/Chmn., Howard Gross/Trustee, Philip G. Barach/Trustee, Wayne S. Doran/Trustee, Niles C. Overly/Trustee, Alan R. Weiler/Trustee, William S. Williams/Trustee, David M. Aronowitz/Trustee

Owners: Alan R. Weiler, Niles C. Overly, Cohen & Steers, Inc./15.70%, George A. Schmidt, David M. Aronowitz, Deutsche Bank AG/8.99%, Alan R. Weiler, Thomas J. Drought, William S. Williams, The Vanguard Group, Inc./6.41%, Howard Gross, Herbert Glimcher/6.28%, Insiders/9.58%, Heitman Real Estate/5.51%, Michael P. Glimcher/2.02% *(19 Owners included in Index)*

Financial Data: Fiscal Year End:12/31 Latest Annual Data: 12/31/2006

Year	Sales	Net Income
2006	$309,264,000	-$77,165,000
2005	$334,859,000	$20,850,000
2004	$345,089,000	$51,755,000

Curr. Assets:	$64,116,000	Curr. Liab.:	$81,001,000		
Plant, Equip.:	$1,686,073,000	Total Liab.:	$1,661,813,000	Indic. Yr. Divd.:	NA
Total Assets:	$1,888,820,000	Net Worth:	$225,235,000	Debt/ Equity:	7.4410

Global Agri Med Technologies Inc

400 Grove St. , Glen Rock, NJ, 07452; *PH:* 1-201-445-7399

General - Incorporation .... NJ
Employees .... NA
Auditor .... Drakeford & Drakeford, LLC
Stk Agt .... Interstate Transfer Company
Counsel .... NA
DUNS No. .... NA

Stock- Price on:12/24/2007 .... NA
Stock Exchange .... NA
Ticker Symbol .... NA
Outstanding Shares .... NA
E.P.S. .... NA
Shareholders .... NA

Business: The group's principle activities include developing and marketing medical devices through product awareness, promotional campaigns and development of key manufacturing and distributor relationships. The group intends to develop and maintain favorable relationships with suppliers and members of its distribution channels. The group operates from United States, Chile, United Kingdom and Singapore.

Primary SIC and add'l.: 2835

CIK No: 0001257514

Subsidiaries: D-Lanz Development Group, Inc

Owners: Roger Fidler/71.70%, Insiders/71.70%, Scantek Medical, Inc./20.00%

Global Aircraft Solutions Inc

6901 S Pk. Ave., Tucson, AZ, 85706; *PH:* 1-520-294-3481; *Fax:* 1-520-741-1430; *http://* www.globalaircraftsolutions.com

General - Incorporation .... NV
Employees 170
Auditor .... Epstein, Weber & Conover, PLC
Stk Agt .... NA
Counsel .... NA
DUNS No. .... NA

Stock- Price on:12/24/2007 .... $0.7
Stock Exchange .... OTC
Ticker Symbol .... GACF
Outstanding Shares 39,650,000
E.P.S. $0.001
Shareholders .... NA

Business: The group operates through its subsidiaries whose principle activities include establishing, maintaining and administering the equity and debt funding of acquired subsidiaries and to maintain the capitalization of these subsidiaries. The group operates through three segments namely aircraft maintenance, aircraft trading and part sales. Specific customers of the group include Jets MD Lease, MD Leasego, Ltd., Aircraft LLC and Jetran. The group operates from the United States.

Primary SIC and add'l.: 4581

CIK No: 0000854171

Subsidiaries: Hamilton Aerospace Technologies, Inc., World Jet Corporation,

Officers: Ian Herman/Chmn., CEO, John B. Sawyer/Dir., Pres., Alan R. Abate/VP - Hamilton Aerospace Technologies, Patricia Graham/VP - Finance, Hamilton Aerospace Technologies, David T. Querio/VP - Operations, Hamilton Aerospace Technologies, Gordon Dito Hamilton/Dir. - Hamilton Aerospace Technologies, Govindarajan Sankar/48/CFO

Directors: Ian Herman/Chmn., CEO, John B. Sawyer/Dir., Pres.

Owners: Ian M. Herman/6.09%, Lawrence Mulcahy, Silverpoint/5.00%, Delta Offshore/7.49%, Ewing & Partners/14.16%, Seymour Siegel, Barron Partners/15.23%, John B. Sawyer/5.80%, Contrarian Capital Management, LLC/9.98%, Insiders/12.16%, Doucet Capital, LLC/5.00%

Financial Data: Fiscal Year End:12/31   **Latest Annual Data:** 12/31/2006

Year	Sales	Net Income
2006	$34,542,000	$826,000
2005	$41,229,000	$3,123,000
2004	$30,851,000	$2,291,000

Curr. Assets:	$20,786,000	Curr. Liab.:	$12,151,000	P/E Ratio:	700.00
Plant, Equip.:	$1,521,000	Total Liab.:	$12,720,000	Indic. Yr. Divd.:	NA
Total Assets:	$28,474,000	Net Worth:	$15,754,000	Debt/ Equity:	0.0133

Global Axcess Corp

224 Ponte VeDr.a Pk. Dr., Ponte Vedra Beach, FL, 32082; **PH:** 1-904-280-3950; **Fax:** 1-904-280-8588; http:// www.glxs.biz

General - Incorporation	NV	**Stock**- Price on:12/24/2007	$0.295
Employees	51	Stock Exchange	OTC
Auditor	Kirland, Russ, Murphy & Tapp, P.A.	Ticker Symbol	GAXC
Stk Agt	Oxford Transfer & Registrar	Outstanding Shares	20,970,000
Counsel	NA	E.P.S.	$0.02
DUNS No.	NA	Shareholders	NA

Business: The groups principle activity is to provide ATM branding and processing services. The group operates from the United States.

Primary SIC and add'l.: 7379 3578 6199 7379 6099 7374 6099 3578 7374

CIK No: 0000852570

Subsidiaries: Axcess Technology Corporation, Axcess Technology Corporation, Pty Ltd, Cash Axcess Corporation, Pty Ltd, EFT Integration Corporation, Nationwide Money Services Inc

Officers: George A. McQuain/Dir., CEO, Pres., Michael J. Loiacono/CFO, Chief Accounting Officer/$93,801.00, Sharon Jackson/Corp. Sec., John C. Rawlins/Exec. VP - Sales, Heather Webb/VP - Operations

Directors: George A. McQuain/Dir., CEO, Pres., Joseph M. Loughry/Chmn., Lock Ireland/Vice Chmn., Robert Landis/Dir., Alan W. Rossiter/Dir., Walter Howell/Dir.

Owners: Robert Landis/0.40%, Joe Loughry/0.25%, George A. McQuain/0.63%, Insiders/3.07%, Lock Ireland/1.43%, Rennaissance U.S. Growth Investment Trust PLC/15.60%, Michael Loiacono/0.02%, BFS U.S. Special Opportunities Trust PLC/15.89%, Rennaissance Capital Growth & Income Fund III, Inc./11.61%, Sharon Jackson/0.23%, Al Rossiter/0.11%

Financial Data: Fiscal Year End:12/31   **Latest Annual Data:** 12/31/2006

Year	Sales	Net Income
2006	$21,437,000	-$4,864,000
2005	$19,595,000	-$723,000
2004	$13,908,000	$1,140,000

Curr. Assets:	$2,797,000	Curr. Liab.:	$6,343,000		
Plant, Equip.:	$6,207,000	Total Liab.:	$14,462,000	Indic. Yr. Divd.:	NA
Total Assets:	$26,091,000	Net Worth:	$11,629,000	Debt/ Equity:	NA

Global Beverage Solutions Inc

12607 Hiddencreek Way, Ste S, Cerritos, CA, 90703; **PH:** 1-918-459-9689; **Fax:** 1-562-623-4050; http:// www.globalbeveragesolutions.com; **Email:** investors@bluetorchinc.net

General - Incorporation	NV	**Stock**- Price on:12/24/2007	$0.07
Employees	NA	Stock Exchange	OTC
Auditor	Turner, Stone & Co. LLP	Ticker Symbol	GBVS
Stk Agt.	Routh Stock Transfer	Outstanding Shares	147,270,000
Counsel	NA	E.P.S.	-$0.14
DUNS No.	NA	Shareholders	NA

Business: The group's principal activity is to sell sporting goods and apparels. The group offers a full range of t-shirt, hooded and unhooded sweatshirts (printables), along with denim and cut and sew items. The group has signed an agreement with federation group of Australia to acquire all international trademarks to hot tuna, xisle, piranha, piranha boy and piranha girl apparels. The hot tuna consists of printables, denim, cut and sew which targets 16 to 25 year old male/female core surf participants, the xisle with its mid-tier sporting goods targets 13 to 18 year old male/female casual action sports participant and piranha boy and piranha girl consists of children's labels. The group is in development stage.

Primary SIC and add'l.: 3949 2339 2329

CIK No: 0001084133

Subsidiaries: Total Sports Distribution, Inc, Unboxed Distribution, Inc.

Officers: Jerry Pearring/CEO, Pres.

Directors: Ross Silvey/Chmn., Terry Turner/Dir.

Owners: Ruettiger Family Trust/6.03%, XStream Beverage Network, Inc/45.62%

Financial Data: Fiscal Year End:12/31   **Latest Annual Data:** 12/31/2006

Year	Sales	Net Income
2006	$125,000	-$7,306,000
2005	$14,000	-$1,706,000
2004	NA	-$2,583,000

Curr. Assets:	NA	Curr. Liab.:	$152,000		
Plant, Equip.:	NA	Total Liab.:	$1,487,000	Indic. Yr. Divd.:	NA
Total Assets:	$1,576,000	Net Worth:	$89,000	Debt/ Equity:	0.3463

Global Business Services Inc

261 S Robertson Blvd, Ste. 200, Beverly Hills, CA, 90211; **PH:** 1-310-288-4585; **Fax:** 1-310-623-1853; http:// www.energetics.biz

General - Incorporation	DE	**Stock**- Price on:12/24/2007	$0.011
Employees	NA	Stock Exchange	NA
Auditor	Berkovits, Lago & Co LLP	Ticker Symbol	NA
Stk Agt.	Pacific Stock Transfer Company	Outstanding Shares	NA
Counsel	NA	E.P.S.	NA
DUNS No.	NA	Shareholders	NA

Business: The group's principal activities are to own, operate and franchise retail stores that provide postal, shipping and other business services and supplies. The group owns and operates seven retail stores in California and Arizona under the name postal connections. The group's postal connections stores offer a broad range of products and services for postal, business and communications support. The services and products offered at postal connections stores include private mail and parcel receiving, shipping, business support products and services, communications services and convenience items and services. During fiscal 2003, the group discontinued the art and direct ownership of corporate retail stores.

Primary SIC and add'l.: 7389

CIK No: 0001082431

Owners: Insiders/13.16%, Harvey Judkowitz/1.00%, Stephen M. Thompson/11.20%, George Marlowe/1.00%, World Call Funding, Inc./6.80%

Financial Data: Fiscal Year End:06/30   **Latest Annual Data:** 6/30/2005

Year	Sales	Net Income
2005	$914,000	-$2,754,000
2004	$2,695,000	-$467,000
2003	$746,000	-$3,291,000

Curr. Assets:	$438,000	Curr. Liab.:	$2,356,000		
Plant, Equip.:	$11,000	Total Liab.:	$3,398,000	Indic. Yr. Divd.:	NA
Total Assets:	$682,000	Net Worth:	-$2,716,000	Debt/ Equity:	NA

Global Cash Access Holdings Inc

3525 E Post Rd., Ste. 120, Las Vegas, NV, 89120; **PH:** 1-702-855-3000; **Fax:** 1-866-672-4371; http:// www.globalcashaccess.com; **Email:** corpinfo@gcamail.com

General - Incorporation	DE	**Stock**- Price on:12/24/2007	$16.22
Employees	354	Stock Exchange	NYSE
Auditor	Deloitte & Touche LLP	Ticker Symbol	GCA
Stk Agt	American Stock Transfer & Trust Co.	Outstanding Shares	83,040,000
Counsel	n	E.P.S.	$0.35
DUNS No.	NA	Shareholders	NA

Business: The groups principle activity is to provide cash access products and related services. The group also provides check verification and warranty services to gaming establishments that cash patron checks. The group operates through four segments namely, cash advance, ATM, check services and credit reporting services. The group operates from the United States. The group's quarterly revenue for September 2007 was 156.57 millions of USD.

Primary SIC and add'l.: 7375 7389 7379 4822 7999 3578 7374 5046 6141 6099

CIK No: 0001318568

Subsidiaries: Arriva Card, Inc., CashCall Systems Inc., Central Credit, LLC, GCA (Macau) S.A., Global Cash Access (Belgium) S.A., Global Cash Access (BVI)Inc., Global Cash Access (HK)Ltd., Global Cash Access (UK)Limited, Global Cash Access Switzerland A.G., Global Cash Access, Inc., Innovative Funds Transfer, LLC*

Officers: Kirk Sanford/41/Dir., CEO, CFO, Pres., Harry C. Hagerty/47/CFO, Exec. VP, Kathryn S. Lever/39/Exec. VP, General Counsel, Diran Kludjian/Exec. VP - Sales GCA, Kurt Sullivan/Exec. VP - Check Services, Central Credit SAG, Thomas Sears/48/Exec. VP - Card Services, Cashless Gaming, Udai Puramsetti/Primary Investor Relations Officer

Directors: Kirk Sanford/41/Dir., CEO, CFO, Pres., Karim Maskatiya/Co - Founder, Co - Chmn., Walter G. Kortschak/Co - Chmn., Robert Cucinotta/Co - Founder, Dir., Charles J. Fitzgerald/Dir., Miles E. Kilburn/Dir., William H. Harris/52/Dir., Geoff Judge/Dir., Fred C. Enlow/Dir.

Owners: Summit Partners, Robert Cucinotta, Kathryn S. Lever, Thomas Sears, Harry C. Hagerty, Geoff Judge, FMR Corp., Walter G. Kortschak, Charles J. Fitzgerald, M&C International, William H. Harris, Fred C. Enlow, Kirk Sanford, Karim Maskatiya, Miles E. Kilburn (17 Owners included in Index)

Financial Data: Fiscal Year End:12/31   **Latest Annual Data:** 03/31/2007

Year	Sales	Net Income
2007	NA	$3,000
2006	$548,148,000	$26,609,000
2005	$454,080,000	$22,591,000

Curr. Assets:	$192,208,000	Curr. Liab.:	$43,665,000	P/E Ratio:	47.71
Plant, Equip.:	$20,454,000	Total Liab.:	$456,490,000	Indic. Yr. Divd.:	NA
Total Assets:	$588,647,000	Net Worth:	$132,157,000	Debt/ Equity:	2.0769

Global Casinos Inc

5455 Spine Rd., Ste. C, Boulder, CO, 80301; **PH:** 1-303-527-2903; http:// www.globalcasinos.com

General - Incorporation	UT	**Stock**- Price on:12/24/2007	$0.85
Employees	32	Stock Exchange	OTC
Auditor	Schumacher & Assoc., Inc	Ticker Symbol	GBCS
Stk Agt	American Stock Transfer & Trust Co.	Outstanding Shares	5,200,000
Counsel	NA	E.P.S.	$0.00
DUNS No.	83-606-5789	Shareholders	NA

Business: The group's principal activity is to acquire and operate casinos, gaming properties and other related interests. The games provided include casino, bingo, lotto, table games, sports betting and pari-mutuel wagering. The group also leases space to bingo hall operators. The subsidiaries include casinos u.s.a. Global Alaska corporation, global central corporation, global casinos international inc. And woodbine corporation. The group operates 22 casinos in the black hawk market and 5 casinos located approximately one mile west in central city. The group has 9,582 slot machines in the black hawk market and 1,599 in the central city market.

Primary SIC and add'l.: 7999 7993 7011 6519

CIK No: 0000727346

Subsidiaries: Casinos Usa, Inc

Officers: Clifford L. Neuman/60/Dir., Interim Pres., Pete Bloomquist/51/Dir., Sec., Todd Huss/56/CFO

Directors: Clifford L. Neuman/60/Dir., Interim Pres., Pete Bloomquist/51/Dir., Sec.

Owners: Insiders/12.40%, Clifford L. Neuman/9.80%, Pete Bloomquist/1.90%, Todd Huss/0.70%

Financial Data: Fiscal Year End:06/30   **Latest Annual Data:** 6/30/2006

Year	Sales	Net Income
2006	$3,957,000	$117,000
2005	$3,925,000	$942,000
1998	$11,335,000	-$2,289,000

Curr. Assets:	$1,314,000	***Curr. Liab.:***	$620,000	***P/E Ratio:***	21.25
Plant, Equip.:	$3,899,000	***Total Liab.:***	$2,556,000	***Indic. Yr. Divd.:***	NA
Total Assets:	$5,314,000	***Net Worth:***	$2,758,000	***Debt/ Equity:***	0.6482

Global Concepts Ltd

14 Garrison Inn Ln., Garrison, VA, 10524; *PH:* 1-845-424-4100; *http://* www.globalc.com; *Email:* info@tliusa.com

General - Incorporation .... CO	***Stock***- Price on:12/24/2007 .... $0.0007
Employees .... NA	Stock Exchange .... OTC
Auditor .... Bagell, Josephs, Levine & Co. LLC	Ticker Symbol .... GCCP
Stk Agt .... American Registrar & Transfer Co	Outstanding Shares .... NA
Counsel .... NA	E.P.S .... NA
DUNS No. .... NA	Shareholders .... NA

Business: The group's principal activity is to manufacture and distribute the "Advanced Medical Diagnostics Hiv (1 & 2) Rapid Test." effective as of Jun 30, 2003, the group terminated the operations of xcalibur xpress, the only operation which had been continuing prior to that date. At present the group has only one business operation: its newly acquired subsidiary, advanced medical diagnostics llc. On Jun 1, 2004 the group acquired the entire membership interest in advanced medical diagnostics llc ("Amd").

Primary SIC and add'l.: 4731

CIK No: 0001055313

Subsidiaries: Advanced Medical Diagnostics, LLC

Financial Data: ***Fiscal Year End:***12/31 ***Latest Annual Data:*** 12/31/2004

Year	Sales	Net Income
2004	$5,286,000	-$3,955,000
2003	$66,000	-$2,329,000
2002	$3,621,000	-$760,000

Curr. Assets:	$2,451,000	***Curr. Liab.:***	$4,683,000		
Plant, Equip.:	$146,000	***Total Liab.:***	$7,182,000	***Indic. Yr. Divd.:***	NA
Total Assets:	$4,270,000	***Net Worth:***	-$2,912,000	***Debt/ Equity:***	NA

Global Crossing Ltd

200 Pk. Ave., Ste. 300, Florham Park, NJ, 07932; *PH:* 1-973-937-0100; *Fax:* 1-973-360-0148; *http://* www.globalcrossing.com

General - Incorporation .... Bermuda	***Stock***- Price on:12/24/2007 .... $20.05
Employees 3,626	Stock Exchange .... NDQ
Auditor .... Ernst & Young LLP	Ticker Symbol .... GLBC
Stk Agt .... Computershare Investor Services LLC	Outstanding Shares 36,920,000
Counsel .... NA	E.P.S .... -$10.57
DUNS No. 87-565-4055	Shareholders .... NA

Business: The group's principle activity is to provide broadband services to global enterprises. The company provides services in two segments. Telecommunications services segment offersa variety of integrated telecommunications services through global fiber optic network. Installation and maintenance services segment, consisting of the company's global marine business, installs andmaintains undersea fiber optic cable systems for carrier customers worldwide. The company also has international operations in the Netherlands, Germany, England and other foreign countries. The company acquired ixnet, inc. And its parent company, ipc communications in 2000. The group's quarterly revenue for Sep '07 was 594.00 millions of USD.

Primary SIC and add'l.: 4813 7375

CIK No: 0001061322

Subsidiaries: ALC Communications Corporation, Ameritel Management, Inc., Atlantic Crossing Holdings U.K. Limited, Atlantic Crossing Ltd., Budget Call Long Distance, Inc., Business Telemanagement, Inc., Equal Access Networks, LLC, G C Peru S.R.L., G.C. St. Croix Company, Inc., GC Dev. Co., Inc., GC Hungary Holdings Vagyonkezel Korltolt Felelssg Trsasg, GC Landing Co. GmbH, GC Mart LLC, GC Pacific Landing Corp., GC Pan European Crossing Belgie b.v.b.a. 114 Subsidiaries included in the Index

Officers: John Legere/Dir., CEO/$4,783,283.00, Jose Antonio Rios/62/International Pres., Chmn. - Global Crossing UK/$1,601,858.00, Daniel J. Enright/Exec. VP - Global Operations, Mitchell C. Sussis/Sec., VP, Deputy General Counsel, Robert A. Klug/40/Chief Accounting Officer, Neil Barua/Chief Administrative Officer, David Carey/Exec. VP - Strategy, Corporate Development, Edward T. Higase/Exec. VP - Worldwide Carrier Services, Anthony D. Christie/Exec. VP - MD - United Kingdom, Europe/$924,864.00, Hector R. Alonso/MD - Latin America, Gary Breauninger/Chief Marketing Officer, Exec. VP, Suzanne Lipton/VP - Investor Relations, Antonio Suarez/Sr. Mgr. - Investor Relations, Gino Mathew/Sr. Mgr. - Investor Relations, Daniel J. Wagner/43/CIO, Exec. VP - Enterprise Services *(19 Officers included in Index)*

Directors: John Legere/Dir., CEO, Lodewijk Christiaan Van Wachem/Chmn., Peter S. Lim Huat/Vice Chmn., Robert Sachs/Dir., Lee Theng Kiat/Dir., Pete Aldridge/Dir., Archie Clemins/Dir., Donald L. Cromer/Dir., Richard R. Erkeneff/Dir., Charles MacAluso/Dir., Michael Rescoe/Dir.

Owners: Insiders/3.40%, Jose A. Rios, E. C. Aldridge, Michael Rescoe, John J. Legere, Robert J. Sachs, Lee Theng Kiat, Archie Clemins, Jean F. Mandeville, Charles Macaluso, Richard R. Erkeneff, Steven T. Clontz, John B. McShane, Peter Seah Lim Huat, Donald L. Cromer *(18 Owners included in Index)*

Financial Data: ***Fiscal Year End:***12/31 ***Latest Annual Data:*** 12/31/2006

Year	Sales	Net Income
2006	$1,871,000,000	-$324,000,000
2005	$1,968,000,000	-$354,000,000
2004	$2,487,000,000	-$336,000,000

Curr. Assets:	$797,000,000	***Curr. Liab.:***	$896,000,000		
Plant, Equip.:	$1,132,000,000	***Total Liab.:***	$2,239,000,000	***Indic. Yr. Divd.:***	NA
Total Assets:	$2,044,000,000	***Net Worth:***	-$195,000,000	***Debt/ Equity:***	NA

Global Digital Solutions Inc

PO Box 670, Coeur dAlene, ID, 83816; *PH:* 1-208-665-9998; *http://* www.globaldigitalsolutions.com

General - Incorporation .... NJ	***Stock***- Price on:12/24/2007 .... $0.02
Employees .... NA	Stock Exchange .... NA
Auditor .... Rubin, Brown, Gornstein & Co. LLP	Ticker Symbol .... NA
Stk Agt .... Continental Stock Transfer & Trust Co	Outstanding Shares .... NA
Counsel .... NA	E.P.S .... NA
DUNS No. .... NA	Shareholders .... NA

Business: The group's principal activity is to distribute cosmetic and beauty products at retail and wholesale levels. The products are purchased from a number of unaffiliated suppliers and manufacturers and thereafter sold on its premises to retail 'walk-in' customers or directly to beauty salons. The beauty and cosmetic products consist of shampoos, conditioners, mousse, setting/styling and spray gels, lotions, lipstick and nail products and hair sprays as well as beauty and cosmetic related appliances such as blow dryers, curling irons, mirrors, air diffusers and hair trimmers. The group distributes its products to approximately 200 nail and beauty salons. The group operates in the northern and central state of New Jersey, essex, hudson, bergen, passaic, morris and union.

Primary SIC and add'l.: 5087

CIK No: 0001011662

Subsidiaries: Pacific Comtel Monterey, Inc.

Financial Data: ***Fiscal Year End:***12/31 ***Latest Annual Data:*** 6/30/2004

Year	Sales	Net Income
2004	$8,745,000	-$7,279,000
2003	$193,000	-$85,000
2002	$216,000	-$319,000

Curr. Assets:	$496,000	***Curr. Liab.:***	$4,470,000		
Plant, Equip.:	$209,000	***Total Liab.:***	$4,480,000	***Indic. Yr. Divd.:***	NA
Total Assets:	$1,216,000	***Net Worth:***	-$3,264,000	***Debt/ Equity:***	NA

Global Diversified Industries Inc

1200 Airport Dr., Chowchilla, CA, 93610; *PH:* 1-559-665-5800; *Fax:* 1-559-665-5700; *http://* www.gdvi.net; *Email:* ir@gdvi.net

General - Incorporation .... NV	***Stock***- Price on:12/24/2007 .... $0.019
Employees 145	Stock Exchange .... OTC
Auditor .... RBS Mirchandani LLP	Ticker Symbol .... GDVI
Stk Agt .... Fidelity Transfer Co	Outstanding Shares 163,460,000
Counsel .... NA	E.P.S .... -$0.002
DUNS No. .... NA	Shareholders .... NA

Business: The group's principal activities are to design, manufacture and market pre-fabricated, modular type structures such as classrooms and office buildings. The product lines consist of a variety of re-locatable and portable classroom designs, including both single-story and two-story floor plans. The group operates three wholly owned subsidiaries: lutrex enterprises inc, mbs construction inc and global modular inc. Lutrex enterprises inc holds equipment and inventory for the group. Mbs construction inc a modular contractor specializing in modular construction site work and renovation. Global modular inc manufactures and markets modular type structures. On 28-Feb-2003, the group acquired mbs construction inc.

Primary SIC and add'l.: 6719 1542

CIK No: 0001090461

Subsidiaries: Global Modular, Inc.

Officers: Phil Hamilton/61/Chmn., CEO, Pres., Adam Debard/41/Dir., Sec., Treasurer

Directors: Phil Hamilton/61/Chmn., CEO, Pres., Adam Debard/41/Dir., Sec., Treasurer

Owners: Insiders/28.09%, Hamilton Trust/2.99%, Adam Debard/3.07%, Rebecca Manadic/19.00%

Financial Data: ***Fiscal Year End:***04/30 ***Latest Annual Data:*** 4/30/2006

Year	Sales	Net Income
2006	$14,921,000	$597,000
2005	$9,206,000	$502,000
2004	$3,828,000	-$428,000

Curr. Assets:	$6,870,000	***Curr. Liab.:***	$3,621,000		
Plant, Equip.:	$1,779,000	***Total Liab.:***	$4,456,000	***Indic. Yr. Divd.:***	NA
Total Assets:	$9,716,000	***Net Worth:***	$5,259,000	***Debt/ Equity:***	0.1614

Global Employment Holdings Inc

10375 Pk. Meadows Dr., Ste. 375, Littleton, CO, 80124; *PH:* 1-303-216-9500; *Fax:* 1-303-216-9533; *https://* www.gesnetwork.com

General - Incorporation .... DE	***Stock***- Price on:12/24/2007 .... $3.75
Employees 19,710	Stock Exchange .... OTC
Auditor .... Mayer Hoffman Mccann, P.C	Ticker Symbol .... GEYH
Stk Agt .... NA	Outstanding Shares 6,020,000
Counsel .... NA	E.P.S $1.69
DUNS No. .... NA	Shareholders .... NA

Business: The groups principle activity is to provide recruiting services. The groups service area includes the research and development, engineering, marketing, sales, information technology and manufacturing industries. The group operates from United States.

Primary SIC and add'l.: 7363

CIK No: 0001348155

Subsidiaries: Global Employment Solutions inc

Officers: Howard Brill/37/Dir., CEO, Pres., Dan Hollenbach/52/CFO, Stephen Pennington/65/Pres. - Staffing Services, Steven List/38/Dir., COO, Terry Koch/54/Pres. - PEO Services

Directors: Jay Wells/45/Chmn., Charles Gwirtsman/54/Dir., Luci Staller Altman/41/Dir., Richard Goldman/51/Dir.

Owners: Richard Goldman, Dan Hollenbach/1.60%, Luci Staller Altman, Steven List/3.20%, Charles Gwirtsman/18.90%, Stephen Pennington/5.90%, Howard Brill/16.30%, Jay Wells, Terry Koch/2.40%, Insiders/45.40%, Robert Larkin/2.70%

Financial Data: ***Fiscal Year End:***12/30 ***Latest Annual Data:*** 12/31/2006

Year	Sales	Net Income
2006	$128,790,000	$1,309,000

Curr. Assets:	$28,234,000	***Curr. Liab.:***	$34,284,000	***P/E Ratio:***	2.50
Plant, Equip.:	$1,168,000	***Total Liab.:***	$74,830,000	***Indic. Yr. Divd.:***	NA
Total Assets:	$57,202,000	***Net Worth:***	-$19,641,000	***Debt/ Equity:***	NA

Global Energy Inc

520 1122 Mainland St., Vancouver, BC, V6B 5L1; *PH:* 1-778-688-9194;
http:// www.globalenergyinc.com

General - Incorporation	NV	Stock- Price on:12/24/2007	$2.05
Employees	NA	Stock Exchange	OTC
Auditor	Vellmer & Chang	Ticker Symbol	GEYI
Stk Agt	Holladay Stock Transfer, Inc.	Outstanding Shares	NA
Counsel	NA	E.P.S.	NA
DUNS No.	NA	Shareholders	NA

Business: The group's principle activity is to provide consumer credit tracking and loyalty programs for specialized market niches focused toward the resort and cruise markets through the use of smart cards designed to eliminate growing transaction charges by creating an internal credit system for each client while adding photo identification for security verification. The group operates from United States.

Primary SIC and add'l.: 7372

CIK No: 0001090967

Officers: Christopher Kape/34/Dir., CEO, Pres., Treasurer, Sec.

Directors: Christopher Kape/34/Dir., CEO, Pres., Treasurer, Sec.

Owners: Carrigain Investment Ltd./66.50%

Financial Data: Fiscal Year End:12/31 Latest Annual Data: 12/31/2006

Year	Sales	Net Income
2006	NA	-$69,000
2005	NA	$6,000
2004	$58,000	-$47,000

Curr. Assets:	$11,000	Curr. Liab.:	$56,000		
Plant, Equip.:	NA	Total Liab.:	$56,000	Indic. Yr. Divd.:	NA
Total Assets:	$11,000	Net Worth:	-$45,000	Debt/ Equity:	NA

Global Entertainment Corp

4909 E McDowell Rd., Ste. 104, Phoenix, AZ, 85008; *PH:* 1-480-994-0772; *Fax:* 1-480-994-0759;
http:// www.globalentertainment2000.com

General - Incorporation	NV	Stock- Price on:12/24/2007	$4.9
Employees	88	Stock Exchange	AMEX
Auditor	Semple, Marchal & Cooper, LLP	Ticker Symbol	GEE
Stk Agt	Stalt, Inc.	Outstanding Shares	6,510,000
Counsel	NA	E.P.S.	-$0.72
DUNS No.	NA	Shareholders	NA

Business: The group's principal activity is that of a holding company. The group activities include sports management, arena development and management, licensing, ticketing and marketing. The sports management includes designing, managing the construction of multipurpose sports and entertainment arenas. The group solely operates in the United States of America.

Primary SIC and add'l.: 7999 6719

CIK No: 0000885780

Subsidiaries: Cragar Industries, Encore Facility Management, Global Entertainment Marketing Systems, Global Entertainment Ticketing, International Coliseums Company, Western Professional Hockey League

Officers: Richard Kozuback/Dir., CEO, Pres./$214,017.00, Craig J. Johnson/CFO, Exec. VP - Global Entertainment/$172,327.00, James Yeager/58/Sr. VP - Treasurer, James Domaz/52/VP, General Counsel, Sec., Steve Bielewicz/Pres. - Global Development

Directors: Richard Kozuback/Dir., CEO, Pres., James Treliving/Chmn., Donald R. Head/Dir., Terry S. Jacobs/Dir., Michael L. Hartzmark/Dir., Mark Schwartz/Dir., Michael L. Bowlin/Dir., Stephen A. McConnell/Dir., George Melville/Dir.

Owners: Mark Schwartz/2.23%, Ron Thom/5.70%, Terry S. Jacobs/1.42%, Donald R. Head/2.90%, Stephen A. McConnell/0.30%, Richard Kozuback/8.36%, Rudy R. Miller/7.84%, Insiders/28.02%, Dolores Hartzmark/5.02%, Michael L. Hartzmark/1.08%, WPHL Holdings, Inc./42.25%, James Treliving/5.19%, Michael L. Bowlin/0.15%, George Melville/6.40%

Financial Data: Fiscal Year End:05/31 Latest Annual Data: 5/31/2006

Year	Sales	Net Income
2006	$14,266,000	$245,000
2005	$13,473,000	$436,000
2004	$5,253,000	$848,000

Curr. Assets:	$11,941,000	Curr. Liab.:	$5,288,000		
Plant, Equip.:	$222,000	Total Liab.:	$5,746,000	Indic. Yr. Divd.:	NA
Total Assets:	$16,761,000	Net Worth:	$11,015,000	Debt/ Equity:	NA

Global Entertainment Holdings/Equities Inc

23760 Oakfield Rd., Hidden Hills, CA, 91302; *PH:* 1-818-884-2777; *Fax:* 1-818-884-3443;
http:// www.globalentertainmentco.com; *Email:* sales@globalentertainmentinc.com

General - Incorporation	CO	Stock- Price on:12/24/2007	NA
Employees	26	Stock Exchange	NA
Auditor	Spector & Wong, LLP	Ticker Symbol	NA
Stk Agt	Corporate Stock Transfer, Inc.	Outstanding Shares	NA
Counsel	NA	E.P.S.	-$0.02
DUNS No.	NA	Shareholders	NA

Business: The group's principal activity is to provide business development support and administrative assistance. The assistance is mainly provided for technology-driven subsidiaries that license, develop and host Internet software applications and operate Web publishing sites in the on-line gaming sector. The group's two segment services: management and marketing services and software development service are managed in two geographical segments, the United States of America and Netherlands antilles. The group operate through its subsidiaries: interactive gaming and wagering n v ("Igw") and prevail on-line inc ("Prevail"). Igw develops, licenses and hosts Internet and telephony based gaming software. Prevail, provides information about the on-line gaming industry through four Web site locations.

Primary SIC and add'l.: 6719 7375 7372 7319

CIK No: 0001096050

Subsidiaries: IGW Software, N.V.

Officers: Jacob Dadon/26/Dir., CEO, CFO, Pres., Lydia Dadon/50/Dir., Sec.

Directors: David Dadon/56/Chmn.

Owners: Insiders/36.79%, Lydia Dadon/12.26%, Darryl Dadon/9.60%, Giants Entertainment, Inc./17.90%, Barry Dadon/9.60%, Jacob Dadon/12.26%, David Dadon/12.26%, Mazelle Dadon/9.60%, Jacqueline Dadon/9.60%

Financial Data: Fiscal Year End:12/31 Latest Annual Data: 12/31/2006

Year	Sales	Net Income
2006	NA	-$1,105,000
2005	$4,236,000	$713,000
2004	$4,196,000	-$748,000

Curr. Assets:	$61,256,000	Curr. Liab.:	$1,933,000		
Plant, Equip.:	$122,000	Total Liab.:	$1,966,000	Indic. Yr. Divd.:	NA
Total Assets:	$61,391,000	Net Worth:	$59,425,000	Debt/ Equity:	0.0005

Global Environmental Energy Corp

2005 Beechgrove Pl, Utica, NY, 13501; *PH:* 1-315-724-8370; *http://* www.greatchinaholdings.com

General - Incorporation	Bahamas	Stock- Price on:12/24/2007	$0.12
Employees	NA	Stock Exchange	OTC
Auditor	Kempisty & Company CPAs, P.C.	Ticker Symbol	GEECF
Stk Agt	North American Transfer Co	Outstanding Shares	NA
Counsel	NA	E.P.S.	NA
DUNS No.	NA	Shareholders	NA

Business: The groups principal activities include producing and exploring oil, gas and alternative energy sources. The group operates through two segments namely biosphere process system and oil and gas development. The group operates from the United States.

Primary SIC and add'l.: 5047

CIK No: 0000840823

Subsidiaries: Biosphere Development Corp, Sahara Petroleum Exploration Corp

Officers: Christopher A. McCormack/Chmn., CEO, Salim Ghafari/Dir., VP - Middle Eastern Operations, CFO

Directors: Christopher A. McCormack/Chmn., CEO, Salim Ghafari/Dir., VP - Middle Eastern Operations, CFO

Owners: International Environmental Energy Corp/16.59%, Salter Overseas SA Genve Switzerland/9.78%, Christopher McCormack/4.76%

Financial Data: Fiscal Year End:05/31 Latest Annual Data: 5/31/2006

Year	Sales	Net Income
2006	NA	-$54,931,000
2005	NA	-$26,500,000
2004	NA	-$9,511,000

Curr. Assets:	NA	Curr. Liab.:	$0		
Plant, Equip.:	NA	Total Liab.:	$55,612,000	Indic. Yr. Divd.:	NA
Total Assets:	$3,000	Net Worth:	-$55,610,000	Debt/ Equity:	NA

Global ePoint Inc

339 S Cheryl Ln., City Of Industry, CA, 91789; *PH:* 1-909-869-1688; *Fax:* 1-909-598-5808;
http:// www.globalepoint.com; *Email:* info@globalepoint.com

General - Incorporation	NV	Stock- Price on:12/24/2007	$0.45
Employees	91	Stock Exchange	OTC
Auditor	Vasquez & Co. LLP	Ticker Symbol	GEPT
Stk Agt	American Stock Transfer & Trust Co.	Outstanding Shares	19,510,000
Counsel	NA	E.P.S.	-$1.2
DUNS No.	61-675-4446	Shareholders	NA

Business: The group's principal activities are to provide computers, computing solutions, and digital video products. The group operates in two segments: contract manufacturing division and digital technology division. Contract manufacturing division manufactures customized computing systems for the industrial, business and consumer markets, with the capability of specialized, custom-manufacture of other electronic products and systems. The industrial and business application provided includes mainly X-ray scanning equipment used in airports. Digital technology segment designs and markets digital video, audio and data transmission and recording products, primarily for surveillance systems. On 08-Aug-2003, the group acquired mcdigit inc.

Primary SIC and add'l.: 3571 3577 3669 7382

CIK No: 0000896195

Subsidiaries: Best Logic, LLC, Global AirWorks, Inc., Global Telephony, Inc., McDigit, Inc.

Officers: Toresa Lou/Dir., CEO - Global Epoint, John Pan/Chmn., CFO, Pres., Sec. - Global Epoint, John Price/VP - Finance, Daryl F. Gates/Dir. - Consultant, Ricky Frick/Pres. - Aviation Division

Directors: Toresa Lou/Dir., CEO - Global Epoint, John Pan/Chmn., CFO, Pres., Sec. - Global Epoint, John K. Yuan/Dir., Daryl F. Gates/Dir. - Consultant, James D. Smith/Dir., Arik Arad/Dir., Joseph R. Hermosillo/Dir.

Owners: Insiders/33.80%, Toresa Lou/7.80%, James D. Smith, Iroquois Capital LP/30.29%, Joseph R. Hermosillo, John Yuan, Arik Arad, John Pan/25.05%, Daryl F. Gates

Financial Data: Fiscal Year End:12/31 Latest Annual Data: 12/31/2006

Year	Sales	Net Income
2006	$32,904,000	-$11,214,000
2005	$32,748,000	-$7,254,000
2004	$21,076,000	-$5,013,000

Curr. Assets:	$8,969,000	Curr. Liab.:	$14,399,000		
Plant, Equip.:	$1,674,000	Total Liab.:	$16,396,000	Indic. Yr. Divd.:	NA
Total Assets:	$22,533,000	Net Worth:	$6,137,000	Debt/ Equity:	NA

Global Gold Corp

104 Field Point Rd. , Greenwich, CT, 06830; *PH:* 1-203-422-2300; *Fax:* 1-203-422-2330;
http:// www.globalgoldcorp.com; *Email:* ggc@globalgoldcorp.com

General - Incorporation	DE	Stock- Price on:12/24/2007	$0.81
Employees	81	Stock Exchange	OTC
Auditor	Allen G. Roth P.A	Ticker Symbol	NA
Stk Agt	American Registrar & Transfer Co	Outstanding Shares	33,450,000
Counsel	NA	E.P.S.	-$0.21
DUNS No.	03-822-1495	Shareholders	NA

Business: The group's principal activity is to develop copper/gold property in the chanaral district iii in Chile. The group has pursued various mining and other business opportunities. The group is currently in the development stage.

Primary SIC and add'l.: 3695 1041 6719

CIK No: 0000319671

Subsidiaries: Global Gold Armenia LLC, Global Gold Mining LLC

Officers: Z. Van Krikorian/Chmn., CEO/$603,989.00, Drury J. Gallagher/Treasurer, Sec./$359,233.00, Ted Urquhart/VP, Lester S. Caesar/Controller, Michael T. Mason/63/COO, Pres./$275,208.00, Hrayr Agnerian/Sr. VP, Jan Dulman/CFO/$123,334.00, W. E.S. Urquhart/57/VP - South American Operations

Directors: Z. Van Krikorian/Chmn., CEO, Ian Hague/Dir., Nicholas J. Aynilian/Dir., Harry J. Gilmore/Dir.

Owners: Harry Gilmore, Firebird Global Master Fund, LTD/12.62%, Farallon Capital Management, LLC/17.38%, W. E.S. Urquhart, Michael T. Mason/1.64%, Hrayr Agnerian, Firebird Avrora Fund, LTD/7.17%, Drury J. Gallagher/9.25%, Lester Caesar, Firebird Republic Fund, LTD/7.18%, Nicholas J. Aynilian/4.93%, Van Z. Krikorian/7.00%, Jan Dulman, Chasm Lake Management Services, LLC/7.38%, Insiders/22.82% (16 Owners included in Index)

Financial Data: Fiscal Year End:12/30 **Latest Annual Data:** 12/31/2006

Year	Sales	Net Income
2006	$6,000	-$5,296,000
2005	NA	-$2,309,000
2004	NA	-$688,000

Curr. Assets:	$7,758,000	Curr. Liab.:	$1,651,000		
Plant, Equip.:	$1,737,000	Total Liab.:	$1,651,000	Indic. Yr. Divd.:	NA
Total Assets:	$15,468,000	Net Worth:	$13,817,000	Debt/ Equity:	NA

Global Green Solutions Inc

Ste. 1010, 789 W Pender St., Vancouver, V6C1H2; **PH:** 1-604-408-0153;
http:// www.globalgreensolutionsinc.com/s/Home.asp; **Email:** enquiries@globalgreencompany.com

General - Incorporation	NV	Stock- Price on:12/24/2007	$1
Employees	NA	Stock Exchange	OTC
Auditor	Morgan & Company	Ticker Symbol	GGRN
Stk Agt	Pacific Stock Transfer Company	Outstanding Shares	NA
Counsel	NA	E.P.S.	NA
DUNS No.	NA	Shareholders	NA

Business: The groups principal activity is to provide eco-technology solutions. Services of the group include reduction of greenhouse gas emissions, renewable energy utilization and carbon credit generation. The group operates from Americas, Europe, Middle East, Africa, Australia and Asia.

Primary SIC and add'l.: 2860

CIK No: 0001277576

Subsidiaries: Global Green Solutions Ltd., Global Green Solutions Pty Ltd

Officers: Doug Frater/57/Pres., CEO, Robert M. Baker/54/Corporate Sec., Arnold Hughes/54/CFO, Corporate Treas., Craig Harting/57/COO, Michael Gilbert/VP-Strategy & Development

Directors: Elden Schorn/68/Chmn.

Owners: Robert M. Baker/11.86%, Elden Schorn/12.06%, Craig Harting/12.06%, Timothy Brock/12.11%, Doug Frater/1.42%

Financial Data: Fiscal Year End:11/30 **Latest Annual Data:** 11/30/2006

Year	Sales	Net Income
2006	NA	-$5,568,000
2005	NA	-$54,000

Curr. Assets:	$907,000	Curr. Liab.:	$584,000		
Plant, Equip.:	$10,000	Total Liab.:	$584,000	Indic. Yr. Divd.:	NA
Total Assets:	$1,310,000	Net Worth:	$726,000	Debt/ Equity:	NA

Global Imaging Systems Inc

PO Box 273478, Tampa, FL, 33688; **PH:** 1-813-960-5508; **Fax:** 1-813-264-7877;
http:// www.global-imaging.com

General - Incorporation	DE	Stock- Price on:12/24/2007	NA
Employees	4,230	Stock Exchange	NA
Auditor	Ernst & Young LLP	Ticker Symbol	NA
Stk Agt	Wachovia Bank N.A	Outstanding Shares	NA
Counsel	Hogan & Hartson LLP	E.P.S.	NA
DUNS No.	84-985-2389	Shareholders	NA

Business: The group's principal activity is to provide office technology solutions to middle-Market businesses in the United States. It also provides contract services for automated office equipment, including copiers, facsimile machines, printers, network integration solutions and electronic presentation systems. It offers solutions incorporating products from konica minolta, canon, ricoh, sharp, hewlett-packard, IBM, microsoft, infocus, sony and other companies from a network of 173 locations in 28 states and in the district of columbia. On 15-Mar-2004, the group acquired advanced document solutions, on 10-May-2004, imagine technology group, inc and on 27-Sep-2004, image manufacturing inc.

Primary SIC and add'l.: 7359 5045 5044 7377

CIK No: 0001050167

Subsidiaries: American Photocopy Equipment Company of Pittsburgh, LLC, Arizona Office Technologies, Inc., AV Presentations, Inc., Berney Office Solutions, LLC, Boise Office Equipment, Inc., Business Equipment Unlimited, Cameron Office Products, LLC, Capitol Office Solutions, LLC, Carolina Office Systems, Inc., Carr Business Systems, Inc., Centre Business Products, Inc., Commercial Equipment Company, Connecticut Business Systems, LLC, Conway Office Products, LLC, Copier Sales Consultants, Inc. 39 Subsidiaries included in the Index

Officers: Dan Cooper/Sr. VP - Sales, CEO - Electronic Systems Group, Jim Arnold/CEO - Lewan Group, Brian Landgren/Pres. - Northwest Group, Ed Bass/VP - Finance, Joseph Payne/Pres. - MWB Business Systems, Dan Brady/Pres. - Michigan Group, Todd Johnson/Sr. VP - Acquisitions, Steve Rolla/Pres. - Capitol Group, Wilson Vega/Pres. - Connecticut Group, Phil Lampugnano/Pres. - Chicago Office Technologies Group, Paul Mosely/Pres. - Conway Group, Mike Mueller/Pres. - Dahill Group, Dan Boylan/Pres. - Southern Business Communications Group, Dick Peterson/Pres. - Amcom Group, Mitch Cohen/Pres. - Carr Group (30 Officers included in Index)

Directors: Tom Johnson/Chmn., Edward J. Smith/Dir., Lazane Smith/Dir., Edward N. Patrone/Dir., Eric McCarthey/Dir., Mark Harris/Dir., Michael E. Shea/Dir., Daniel T. Hendrix/Dir.

Global Immune Technologies Inc

Formerly: Secureview Systems Inc
1111-207 W Hastings St., Vancouver, BC, A1 V6G 3J4; **PH:** 1-604-351-9443

General - Incorporation	Canada	Stock- Price on:12/24/2007	$0.07
Employees	5	Stock Exchange	NA
Auditor	SF Partnership LLP	Ticker Symbol	NA
Stk Agt	Pacific Corporate Trust Co	Outstanding Shares	NA
Counsel	NA	E.P.S.	NA
DUNS No.	NA	Shareholders	NA

Business: The group's principle activity is to seek potential business opportunities. The group operates from United States.

Primary SIC and add'l.: 6799

CIK No: 0001105284

Officers: Donald L. Perks/56/Dir., CEO, CFO, Pres.

Directors: Donald L. Perks/56/Dir., CEO, CFO, Pres., Piers Vanziffle/60/Dir.

Owners: J&J Rentals, Inc./6.20%, Capital Associates/15.40%, Azimuth Corporation/6.20%

Financial Data: Fiscal Year End:03/31 **Latest Annual Data:** 03/31/2007

Year	Sales	Net Income
2007	NA	NA
2006	NA	-$96,000
2005	NA	$49,000

Curr. Assets:	$0	Curr. Liab.:	$446,000		
Plant, Equip.:	NA	Total Liab.:	$446,000	Indic. Yr. Divd.:	NA
Total Assets:	$0	Net Worth:	-$446,000	Debt/ Equity:	NA

Global Industries Ltd

8000 Global Dr., Carlyss, LA, 70665; **PH:** 1-337-583-5000; **Fax:** 1-337-583-5100;
http:// www.globalind.com

General - Incorporation	LA	Stock- Price on:12/24/2007	$25.38
Employees	2,982	Stock Exchange	NDQ
Auditor	Deloitte & Touche LLP	Ticker Symbol	GLBL
Stk Agt	American Stock Transfer & Trust Co.	Outstanding Shares	117,120,000
Counsel	NA	E.P.S.	$1.54
DUNS No.	80-680-8309	Shareholders	NA

Business: The group's principal activity is to provide a comprehensive and integrated range of marine construction and support services in the gulf of Mexico, west Africa, Asia-Pacific, Latin America and the Middle East. These services include pipeline construction, platform installation and removal and diving services. The group also operates other offshore support vessels internationally to support its offshore construction services. Offshore construction services performed by the group include pipelay, derrick and related services. At 31-Dec-2003, the group's fleet consisted of sixty-eight vessels. The customers of the group primarily include oil and gas producers and pipeline companies.

Primary SIC and add'l.: 1623 8711 1389 1629

CIK No: 0000895663

Subsidiaries: de R.L. de C.V., GIL Holdings, LLC, GIL Mauritius Holdings, Ltd., GLBL Holdings, LLC, Global Asia Pacific Industries, Sdn. Bhd., Global Construction Mauritius Services, Ltd., Global Divers and Contractors, LLC, Global Industries (B)Sdn. Bhd., Global Industries Asia Pacific Pte, Ltd., Global Industries Australia Holdings Pty Ltd., Global Industries International, L.P., Global Industries International, LLC, Global Industries Mexico Holdings, S., Global Industries Offshore Hong Kong Limited, Global Industries Offshore Labuan Ltd. 46 Subsidiaries included in the Index

Officers: B. K. Chin/Dir., CEO/$1,485,980.00, James J. Dore/Sr. VP - Asia Pacific, India, Mediterranean, The Middle East/$1,122,276.00, Peter S. Atkinson/CFO, VP/$1,572,425.00, Timothy W. Miciotto/Sr. VP, Financial Advisor to The Pres., Eduardo Borja/VP - Latin America Business Unit, James F. Gallagher/VP - Investor Relations, Marketing Services, Russell J. Robicheaux/Chief Administrative Officer, General Counsel/$734,307.00, Byron W. Baker/Sr. VP - Gulf, Mexico/$851,463.00, Peter R. Buchler/VP - Commercial, Subcontracts, Kenneth A. Caldwell/VP - West Africa Business Unit, Worldwide Quality Management, Aaron Cooley/VP - Worldwide Estimating, Project Policies, William A. Cummings/VP - Human Resources, Ashit Jain/VP - Asia Pacific, India, Middle East, Anne G. Schreiber/Mgr. - Investor Relations, Steve Spease/VP - Worldwide Project Managment (18 Officers included in Index)

Directors: B. K. Chin/Dir., CEO, William J. Dore/Chmn., Founder, Luis Tellez/Dir., Edgar G. Hotard/Dir., James L. Payne/Dir., R. A. Pattarozzi/Dir., John A. Clerico/Dir., Larry E. Farmer/Dir., Larry R. Dickerson/Dir., Cindy B. Taylor/Dir., Michael J. Pollock/Dir., Edward P. Djerejian/Dir., James C. Day/Dir.

Owners: Wells Fargo & Company/15.20%, FMR Corporation/8.00%, B. K. Chin, Insiders/23.50%, Edward P. Djerejian, James J. Dor, Lawrence R. Dickerson, Michael J. Pollock, John A. Clerico, Russell J. Robicheaux, Edgar G. Hotard, Byron W. Baker, James L. Payne, Richard A. Pattarozzi, Larry E. Farmer (18 Owners included in Index)

Financial Data: Fiscal Year End:12/31 **Latest Annual Data:** 12/31/2006

Year	Sales	Net Income
2006	$1,234,849,000	$199,745,000
2005	$688,615,000	$34,758,000
2004	$463,331,000	$22,432,000

Curr. Assets:	$683,138,000	Curr. Liab.:	$223,012,000	P/E Ratio:	14.02
Plant, Equip.:	$316,876,000	Total Liab.:	$345,432,000	Indic. Yr. Divd.:	NA
Total Assets:	$1,070,997,000	Net Worth:	$725,565,000	Debt/ Equity:	0.0852

Global Innovation Corp

901 Hensley Ln., Wylie, TX, 75098; **PH:** 1-214-291-1427; **Fax:** 1-800-303-9266;
http:// www.integratedperformsys.com

General - Incorporation	NY	Stock- Price on:12/24/2007	$0.35
Employees	225	Stock Exchange	OTC
Auditor	KBA Group LLP	Ticker Symbol	GINV
Stk Agt	NA	Outstanding Shares	10,180,000
Counsel	NA	E.P.S.	-$0.02
DUNS No.	NA	Shareholders	NA

Business: The groups principle activities include designing manufacturing printed circuit boards. Products of the group include antenna and metal back radio frequency circuit boards. Customers of the group include commercial companies, the military and military suppliers. The specific customers served by the group include L-3 Communications, Raytheon, Lockheed Martin, Tyco Power Systems, Invensys, General Electric and Adtran.

Primary SIC and add'l.: 3672

CIK No: 0001069562

Subsidiaries: Best Circuit Boards, Inc. d/b/a Lone Star Circuits, LSC Asset Acquisition Corp., Performance Interconnect Corp., Varga Investments, Inc.

Officers: Brad Jacoby/51/Chmn., CEO, Brent Nolan/COO, Pres., Brad Peters/41/CFO, VP, Bryan Nolan/Dir. - Operations, Greg Mitchell/Dir. - Engineering, Product Development, Oscar Cammuse/Dir. - Quality, Tom Holder/Dir. - Value Add Services, Kathy Atterbury/Mgr. - Accounting, Jeannie Nolan/Mgr. - Accounting, Greg Thomas/Mgr. - Accounting

Directors: Brad Jacoby/51/Chmn., CEO

Owners: Brent Nolan/13.30%, Ronald D. Allen/9.30%, Insiders/68.50%, Brad Jacoby/51.40%

Financial Data: Fiscal Year End:07/31 Latest Annual Data: 7/31/2006

Year	Sales	Net Income
2006	$34,604,000	$315,000
2005	$31,143,000	-$11,596,000
2003	$5,466,000	-$4,757,000

Curr. Assets:	$9,097,000	Curr. Liab.:	$4,966,000		
Plant, Equip.:	$2,011,000	Total Liab.:	$12,201,000	Indic. Yr. Divd.:	NA
Total Assets:	$22,816,000	Net Worth:	$10,615,000	Debt/ Equity:	1.0806

Global Matrechs Inc

90 Grove St., Ridgefield, CT, 06877; **PH:** 1-203-431-6665; **Fax:** 1-203-431-8304; **http://** www.globalmatrechs.com; **Email:** info@globalmatrechs.com

General - Incorporation	DE	Stock- Price on:12/24/2007	NA
Employees	2	Stock Exchange	OTC
Auditor	Sherb & Co. LLP	Ticker Symbol	GBMR
Stk Agt	American Stock Transfer & Trust Co.	Outstanding Shares	NA
Counsel	NA	E.P.S	-$0.228
DUNS No.	NA	Shareholders	NA

Business: The group's principal activity is to manufacture and market products related to licensed technologies from eurotech, ltd. The licensed technologies include ekor, hybrid non-isocyanate polyurethane, emr/ac, rad-x, firesil, lem and rbhm. The products developed through ekor technology include sealer plus, foam, grout, matrix, stonestore. Rad-x is a technology used as an interior fire-resistant fixative for equipment or facilities with contaminated surfaces. The group has operation in the United States. In 2003, the group has discontinued the operations of hosting and Web site maintenance business.

Primary SIC and add'l.: 7372 7379

CIK No: 0001021226

Subsidiaries: True To Form, Ltd

Officers: Michael Sheppard/Chmn., CEO, Pres., Ivan K.F. Gothner/Dir., Sec.

Directors: Michael Sheppard/Chmn., CEO, Pres., Ivan K.F. Gothner/Dir., Sec., Thomas L. Folsom/Dir.

Financial Data: Fiscal Year End:12/31 Latest Annual Data: 12/31/2005

Year	Sales	Net Income
2005	$0	-$6,110,000
2004	$1,000	-$2,998,000
2003	$8,000	-$1,581,000

Curr. Assets:	$275,000	Curr. Liab.:	$7,309,000		
Plant, Equip.	NA	Total Liab.:	$11,520,000	Indic. Yr. Divd.:	NA
Total Assets:	$577,000	Net Worth:	-$10,943,000	Debt/ Equity:	NA

Global Med Technologies Inc

4925 Robert J, Mathews Pkwy., Ste. 100, El Dorado Hills, CA, 95762; ; **http://** www.globalmedtech.com; **Email:** info@wyndgate.com

General - Incorporation	CO	Stock- Price on:12/24/2007	$0.8
Employees	83	Stock Exchange	OTC
Auditor	Ehrhardt Keefe Steiner & Hottman P.C	Ticker Symbol	GLOB
Stk Agt	Computershare Investor Services LLC	Outstanding Shares	23,210,000
Counsel	NA	E.P.S	$0.03
DUNS No.	60-693-9924	Shareholders	NA

Business: The group's principal activities are to design, develop, market and support information management software products. The group's products include Internet-based software applications safetrace(R) and safetrace tx tm, a transfusion management information system designed to be used by hospitals and centralized transfusion centers to help insure the quality of blood transfused into patient-recipients. These systems help to integrate hospitals with blood centers and provide a vein-to-vein(TM) tracking of the blood supply. Safetrace tx.com(TM) provides hospitals and blood centers with a coordinated system that fully integrates blood inventory, testing and management-improving blood safety, reducing waste and improving patient care. The products of the group are sold to blood banks, hospitals, centralized transfusion centers and other healthcare related facilities.

Primary SIC and add'l.: 7372 7379

CIK No: 0001009463

Subsidiaries: PeopleMed.com, Inc.

Officers: Michael I. Ruxin/Chmn., CEO, Thomas F. Marcinek/COO, Pres., Gerald F. Willman/Sr. VP - International Business Development, Timothy J. Pellegrini/VP - Operations, Miklos Csore/VP - Research, Development, Scott Dustin/VP - Domestic Sales, Marketing, Darren Craig/Mgr. - Finance

Directors: Michael I. Ruxin/Chmn., CEO, Robert R. Gilmore/56/Dir., Sarah L. Eames/49/Dir., T. Kendall Hunt/64/Dir.

Owners: Thomas F. Marcinek, Crestview Capital Master,LLC/8.00%, Kendall T. Hunt, Magnetar Capital Master,Fund Ltd./7.60%, Insiders/3.80%, Shepherd Investments International, Ltd./6.60%, Futuristic Image Builder/13.10%, Michael I. Ruxin/3.60%

Financial Data: Fiscal Year End:12/31 Latest Annual Data: 12/31/2006

Year	Sales	Net Income
2006	$12,362,000	$1,381,000
2005	$11,204,000	-$10,819,000
2004	$6,884,000	-$766,000

Curr. Assets:	$7,123,000	Curr. Liab.:	$6,951,000	P/E Ratio:	40.00
Plant, Equip.:	$269,000	Total Liab.:	$7,013,000	Indic. Yr. Divd.:	NA
Total Assets:	$7,392,000	Net Worth:	$379,000	Debt/ Equity:	0.0781

Global Music International Inc

30 Grassy Plain St., Ste. 7, Bethel, CT, 06801; ; **http://** www.imntv.com; **Email:** info@imntv.com

General - Incorporation	FL	Stock- Price on:12/24/2007	$1.7
Employees	2	Stock Exchange	OTC
Auditor	Carlin, Charron & Rosen, LLP	Ticker Symbol	GMUS
Stk Agt	Florida Atlantic Stock Transfer, Inc.	Outstanding Shares	22,180,000
Counsel	NA	E.P.S	-$0.13
DUNS No.	NA	Shareholders	NA

Business: The groups principle activities include operating music website and airing music videos submitted by artists and bands. The group operates from the United States and China.

Primary SIC and add'l.: 4841

CIK No: 0001308841

Officers: James Fallacaro/61/Chmn., CEO, Pres., Christopher Mauritz/41/Dir., CTO, Exec. VP, Ji Shen/40/Dir., VP - China Operations, Corinne Fallacaro/50/Sec., Treasurer, David R. Allen/53/CFO

Directors: James Fallacaro/61/Chmn., CEO, Pres., Christopher Mauritz/41/Dir., CTO, Exec. VP, Ji Shen/40/Dir., VP - China Operations

Owners: James Fallacaro, Insiders, Corinne Fallacaro, Ji Shen, Christopher Mauritz

Financial Data: Fiscal Year End:06/30 Latest Annual Data: 06/30/2007

Year	Sales	Net Income
2007	$73,000	-$2,566,000
2006	$55,000	-$694,000
2005	NA	-$233,000

Curr. Assets:	$134,000	Curr. Liab.:	$2,290,000		
Plant, Equip.:	$26,000	Total Liab.:	$2,290,000	Indic. Yr. Divd.:	NA
Total Assets:	$160,000	Net Worth:	-$2,130,000	Debt/ Equity:	NA

Global Pari-mutuel Services Inc

Formerly: Orbis Development Inc
2533 N Carson St., Carson City, NV, 89706; **PH:** 1-480-883-2272

General - Incorporation	NV	Stock- Price on:12/24/2007	NA
Employees	NA	Stock Exchange	NA
Auditor	Hansen, Barnett & Maxwell	Ticker Symbol	NA
Stk Agt	OTC Corporate Transfer Service Co	Outstanding Shares	NA
Counsel	NA	E.P.S	-$0.12
DUNS No.	NA	Shareholders	NA

Business: The group's principle activity is to provide merchant portfolio services. The company will act as the intermediary in the exchange of information between merchants and credit card issuers before credit card transactions are processed and settled. The company will offer orbis payment solution, which will allow the customers of the company to initiate, authorize, process and manage credit card transactions in a real-time, online environment. The company will provide pari-mutuel wagering support services, in which the holders of winning tickets divide the total amount of money bet on a race, after subtracting taxes, racetrack fees and other expenses. In Feb 2003, it discontinued its operations of ATM debit card services business. The group operates from United States.

Primary SIC and add'l.: 7372

CIK No: 0001137417

Subsidiaries: Racing Services de Mexico

Officers: James A. Egide/74/Chmn., Founder, Principal Executive Officer, Michael D. Bard/61/Dir., Principal Accounting Officer

Directors: Joseph P. Neglia/78/Vice Chmn., James A. Egide/74/Chmn., Founder, Principal Executive Officer, Michael D. Bard/61/Dir., Principal Accounting Officer, Keith Cannon/66/Dir.

Owners: Andrew Broughton/6.20%, Michael D. Bard/2.89%, C. R. Fedrick/5.18%, Keith Cannon/1.95%, Heritage Limited/17.47%, AMEJ Foundation/8.98%, James A. Egide/18.85%, Joseph P. Neglia/9.80%

Financial Data: Fiscal Year End:12/31 Latest Annual Data: 12/31/2006

Year	Sales	Net Income
2006	$1,000	-$854,000
2005	$1,000	-$183,000
2004	NA	-$223,000

Curr. Assets:	$54,000	Curr. Liab.:	$322,000		
Plant, Equip.:	NA	Total Liab.:	$498,000	Indic. Yr. Divd.:	NA
Total Assets:	$54,000	Net Worth:	-$844,000	Debt/ Equity:	NA

Global Partners LP

800 S St., Waltham, MA, 02453; **PH:** 1-781-894-8800; **Fax:** 1-781-398-4160; **http://** www.globalp.com

General - Incorporation	DE	Stock- Price on:12/24/2007	$36.61
Employees	180	Stock Exchange	NYSE
Auditor	Ernst& Young LLP	Ticker Symbol	GLP
Stk Agt	American Stock Transfer & Trust Co.	Outstanding Shares	11,280,000
Counsel	Vinson & Elkins LLP,	E.P.S	$1.27
DUNS No.	NA	Shareholders	NA

Business: The groups principal activity is to distribute gasoline, distillates and residual oil to wholesalers, retailers and commercial customers. The groups products include distillates, gasoline and residual oil. The group operates through two segments namely, wholesale and commercial. The group operates from the United States and England. Of the total sales in the year 2006, wholesale segment accounted for $4,071,608 and commercial $400,810 (thousands).

Primary SIC and add'l.: 5172

CIK No: 0001323468

Subsidiaries: Chelsea Sandwich LLC, Glen Hes Corp., Global Companies LLC, Global Montello Corp., Global Operating LLC, GLP Finance Corp.

Officers: Eric Slifka/Dir., CEO, Pres., Thomas J. Hollister/CFO, COO, Edward J. Faneuil/Exec. VP, General Counsel, Sec., Charles A. Rudinsky/Exec. VP, Treasurer, Chief Accounting Officer

Directors: Eric Slifka/Dir., CEO, Pres., Alfred A. Slifka/Chmn., Richard Slifka/Vice Chmn., David K. McKown/Dir., Robert J. McCool/Dir., Kenneth I. Watchmaker/Dir.

Owners: Andrew Slifka, Sandwich Terminal, L.L.C., Richard Slifka, Larea Holdings LLC, Thomas J. Hollister, Global Petroleum Corp., Karen Dattilo, Edward J. Fancuil, Chelsea Terminal Limited Partnership, Insiders/1.10%, Thomas A. McManmon, Kayne Anderson Capital Advisors L.P./15.30%, Montello Oil Corporation, Eric Slifka, Larea Holdings II LLC *(20 Owners included in Index)*

Financial Data: Fiscal Year End:12/31 Latest Annual Data: 12/31/2006

Year	Sales	Net Income
2006	$4,472,418,000	$33,461,000
2005	$4,045,858,000	$18,101,000

Curr. Assets:	$596,073,000	**Curr. Liab.:**	$447,790,000	**P/E Ratio:**	47.71
Plant, Equip.:	$31,657,000	**Total Liab.:**	$535,648,000	**Indic. Yr. Divd.:**	$1.920
Total Assets:	$638,887,000	**Net Worth:**	$103,239,000	**Debt/ Equity:**	0.8062

Global Payment Technologies Inc

170 Wilbur Pl., Bohemia, NY, 11716; *PH:* 1-631-563-2500; *Fax:* 1-631-563-2630; *http://* www.gptx.com; *Email:* customerservice@gptx.com

General - Incorporation .... DE
Employees 102
Auditor .... Eisner LLP
Stk Agt...... American Stock Transfer & Trust Co.
Counsel............ Jenkens & Gilchrist Parker
DUNS No. 60-324-7016

Stock- Price on:12/24/2007 .... $0.65
Stock Exchange .... OTC
Ticker Symbol .... GPTX
Outstanding Shares 6,220,000
E.P.S .... -$0.85
Shareholders .... NA

Business: The group's principal activities are to design, manufacture and market currency validation systems including paper currency validators and stackers. The validators are used for receiving and authenticating paper currencies in a variety of automated machines. Gaming and related equipment, beverage and vending machines and retail equipment that dispense products, services, coinage and other currencies also use these validators for authentication. The note stackers of the company are designed to store validated paper currency and are also used to record and store information on contents usually in secure removable cassettes. The group's principal products include three basic validator models gii, argus(tm) and aurora and a range of comprehensive currency databases and note stacker configurations. The operations of the company are based in the United States, Australia, Russia, Latin America, South Africa, Europe and southeast Asia.

Primary SIC and add'l.: 3578

CIK No: 0000933020

Subsidiaries: Abacus Financial Management Systems Ltd., USA, Ecash Holdings Pty. Ltd., Evolve Corporation PLC, Global Payment Technologies (Europe) Limited, Global Payment Technologies Australia Pty. Ltd., Global Payment Technologies, Inc.

Officers: Stephen Nevitt/Dir., CEO, Pres., Thomas Oliveri/Dir., Exec. VP, COO, William McMahon/VP, CFO, Sec.

Directors: Stephen Nevitt/Dir., CEO, Pres., Richard Gerzof/Chmn., Thomas Oliveri/Dir., Exec. VP, COO, William Wood/Dir., Matthew Dollinger/Dir., Elliot Goldberg/Dir. - Chariman

Owners: William McMahon/3.90%, William Wood/4.70%, Matthew Dollinger, Elliot Goldberg, Richard Gerzof/7.90%, Stephen Nevitt/7.70%, Doucet Capital LLC/5.20%, Insiders/22.30%

Financial Data: Fiscal Year End:09/30 Latest Annual Data: 9/30/2006

Year	Sales	Net Income
2006	$14,303,000	-$4,143,000
2005	$25,886,000	-$573,000
2004	$24,381,000	-$1,690,000

Curr. Assets:	$9,873,000	**Curr. Liab.:**	$2,806,000		
Plant, Equip.:	$1,249,000	**Total Liab.:**	$2,846,000	**Indic. Yr. Divd.:**	NA
Total Assets:	$11,683,000	**Net Worth:**	$8,837,000	**Debt/ Equity:**	0.0012

Global Payments Inc

10 Glenlake Pkwy. NE, North Tower, Atlanta, GA, 30328; *PH:* 1-770-829-8000; *Fax:* 1-770-829-8224; *http://* www.globalpaymentsinc.com

General - Incorporation .... GA
Employees 4,277
Auditor .... Deloitte & Touche LLP
Stk Agt............ Suntrust Bank Atlanta Georgia
Counsel............ Suellyn P. Tornay
DUNS No. .... NA

Stock- Price on:12/24/2007 .... $41
Stock Exchange .... NYSE
Ticker Symbol .... GPN
Outstanding Shares 80,710,000
E.P.S $1.77
Shareholders .... NA

Business: The group's principal activity is to provide electronic transaction processing services. The group provides services through its merchant services and funds transfer offerings. Merchant service offerings include credit and debit card transaction processing, business-to-business purchase card transaction processing and checking verification and terminal management services. The electronic funds transfer offerings include services such as cash management, account balance reporting, management information and deposit reporting to domestic and international financial institutions, corporations and government agencies. The group markets its products and services throughout the United States, Canada and Europe. On 12-Nov-2003, the group acquired Latin America money services llc and on 20-Feb-2004, 52.6% interest in muzo.

Primary SIC and add'l.: 7374

CIK No: 0001123360

Subsidiaries: DolEx Belgium, S.P.R.L, Dolex CE, LP, DolEx Dollar Express, Inc., Dolex Envios, S.A. de C.V., DolEx Europe, S.L., Global Payment Holding Company, Global Payment Systems LLC, Global Payment Systems of Canada, Ltd., Global Payments Acquisition Corp 1 B.V., Global Payments Acquisition Corp 2 B.V., Global Payments Acquisition Corp 3 B.V., Global Payments Acquisition PS 1 C.V., Global Payments Acquisition PS 2 C.V., Global Payments Asia Pacific Processing Company Limited, Global Payments Asia-Pacific (Hong Kong Holding) Limited 44 Subsidiaries included in the Index

Officers: Paul R. Garcia/Chmn., CEO, Pres./$3,470,153.00, Suellyn P. Tornay/Exec. VP - Human Resources, Corporate Communications/$845,179.00, Carl J. Williams/Pres. - World, Wide Payment Processing/$1,592,823.00, Joseph C. Hyde/CFO, Exec. VP/$1,089,291.00, James G. Kelly/COO, Sr. Exec. VP/$1,708,331.00, Morgan Schuessler/Exec. VP - Human Resources, Corporate Communications

Directors: Paul R. Garcia/Chmn., CEO, Pres., Gerald J. Wilkins/Dir., Alan M. Silberstein/Dir., Michael W. Trapp/Dir., Edwin H. Burba/Dir., William I. Jacobs/Dir., Alex W. Hart/Dir., Raymond L. Killian/Dir., Ruth Ann Marshall/Dir.

Owners: Joseph C. Hyde, Suellyn P. Tornay, Paul R. Garcia/1.30%, Edwin H. Burba, Gerald J. Wilkins, William I. Jacobs, Ruth Ann Marshall, EARNEST Partners, LLC/8.90%, Raymond L. Killian, Alan M. Silberstein, Insiders/3.15%, Michael W. Trapp, Carl J. Williams, Alex W. Hart, T. Rowe Price Associates, Inc./10.10% *(16 Owners included in Index)*

Financial Data: Fiscal Year End:05/31 Latest Annual Data: 05/31/2007

Year	Sales	Net Income
2007	$1,061,523,000	$142,985,000
2006	$908,056,000	$125,524,000
2005	$784,331,000	$92,896,000

Curr. Assets:	$348,406,000	**Curr. Liab.:**	$149,655,000	**P/E Ratio:**	23.43
Plant, Equip.:	$107,977,000	**Total Liab.:**	$235,459,000	**Indic. Yr. Divd.:**	$0.080
Total Assets:	$1,018,678,000	**Net Worth:**	$770,223,000	**Debt/ Equity:**	NA

Global Power Equipment Group Inc

6120 S Yale, Ste. 1480, Tulsa, OK, 74136; *PH:* 1-918-488-0828; *Fax:* 1-918-488-8389; *http://* www.globalpower.com

General - Incorporation .... DE
Employees 1,805
Auditor .... PricewaterhouseCoopers LLP
Stk Agt .... Computershare Investor Services LLC
Counsel............ John Matheson
DUNS No. .... NA

Stock- Price on:12/24/2007 .... $2.2
Stock Exchange .... OTC
Ticker Symbol .... GEGQQ
Outstanding Shares 47,130,000
E.P.S .... -$0.03
Shareholders .... NA

Business: The group's principal activities are to design, engineer and fabricate equipment for gas turbine power plants. It operates through two segments: heat recovery equipment: includes heat recovery steam generators, specialty boilers and related products. These products are marketed under the deltak brand name. Auxiliary power equipment: includes filter houses, inlet systems, gas and steam turbine enclosures, exhaust systems and diverter dampers. The brand names of these products are braden and consolidated fabricators. The group also provides value-added services such as engineering, retrofit, upgrade, maintenance and repair. The major customers are general electric and the southern company. On Jul 30, 2004, the company purchased a 90 percent interest in nanjing boiler works (nbw).

Primary SIC and add'l.: 3511 3699

CIK No: 0001136294

Subsidiaries: Braden Construction Services, Inc., Braden Manufacturing, LLC, Braden Manufacturing, S.A. de C.V., Braden-Europe B.V., CFI Mexicana, S.A. de C.V., Deltak B.V., Deltak Construction Services, Inc., Deltak Israel Ltd., Deltak Power Equipment, Deltak, LLC, Global Power Asia Limited, Global Power Equipment, Global Power Equipment Group Brazil, Global Power Equipment Group International, Nanjing Deltak Power Equipment Co. Ltd. 16 Subsidiaries included in the Index

Officers: Gene Schockemoehl/Sr. VP, Pres. Braden Manufacturing - LLC, John Matheson/Dir., Pres., Chief Executive Officier, Dan Daniels/Sr. VP, Pres. Williams Industrial Services Group - LLC, Candice Cheeseman/VP, General Counsel, Sec., Mike Hanson/VP - Finance, CFO, Marty Musselman/Deltak, Jan Ferlin/Braden Manufacturing, Moe Edwards/Contact - CFI, Jeff Davis/Pres. - Deltak Specialty Boiler Systems Division, Deltak, LLC

Directors: Ira Kleinman/Dir., Bengt Sohlen/Dir., Stephen Eisenstein/Dir., John Matheson/Dir., Pres., Chief Executive Officier, Adrian Doherty/Dir., Michael Greenwood/Dir., Jerry Ryan/Dir.

Financial Data: Fiscal Year End:12/31 Latest Annual Data: 12/31/2004

Year	Sales	Net Income
2004	$233,692,000	-$705,000
2003	$263,778,000	$19,784,000
2002	$586,805,000	$51,877,000

Curr. Assets:	$177,520,000	**Curr. Liab.:**	$119,721,000		
Plant, Equip.:	$22,983,000	**Total Liab.:**	$202,845,000	**Indic. Yr. Divd.:**	NA
Total Assets:	$366,894,000	**Net Worth:**	$162,420,000	**Debt/ Equity:**	NA

Global Precision Medical Inc

1489 Marine Dr., Ste. 536, W. Vancouver, BC, V7T 1B8; *PH:* 1-604-926-2939

General - Incorporation .... WY
Employees .... NA
Auditor .... BDO Dunwoody LLP
Stk Agt .... Pacific Corporate Trust Co
Counsel............ NA
DUNS No. .... NA

Stock- Price on:12/24/2007 .... $0.06
Stock Exchange .... NA
Ticker Symbol .... NA
Outstanding Shares .... NA
E.P.S .... NA
Shareholders .... NA

Business: The group's principal activity is to develop and commercialize medical device technology. The group has the license for developing a medical device known as uro-stent which is used for the prevention of lumen restriction associated with bph. The group was an exploration stage company prior to 23-Sep- 2002, after which it changed its activities from mining exploration and into the medical device industry.

Primary SIC and add'l.: 3841

CIK No: 0001095556

Subsidiaries: Global Precision Medical (USA) Inc.

Officers: Lindsay Semple/62/Dir., CEO, James Elliott/48/Dir., CTO

Directors: Lindsay Semple/62/Dir., CEO, James Elliott/48/Dir., CTO, Boris Weiss/42/Dir.

Owners: GLENFIELD PARTNERS LIMITED/27.32%, James R. ELLIOTT/6.13%, Ilona M. GOGNIAT/21.71%, LEDDING Gregory/4.77%, Lindsay SEMPLE/5.95%, Boris Weiss/1.08%, Insiders/12.60%

Financial Data: Fiscal Year End:12/31 Latest Annual Data: 12/31/2006

Year	Sales	Net Income
2006	NA	-$30,000
2005	NA	-$49,000
2004	NA	-$2,668,000

Curr. Assets:	$10,000	**Curr. Liab.:**	$162,000		
Plant, Equip.:	NA	**Total Liab.:**	$162,000	**Indic. Yr. Divd.:**	NA
Total Assets:	$10,000	**Net Worth:**	-$152,000	**Debt/ Equity:**	NA

Global Preferred Holdings Inc

PO Box 1561, Suwanee, GA, 30024; *PH:* 1-770-248-3311; *http://* www.gphre.com

General - Incorporation .... DE
Employees .... NA
Auditor .... Marcum & Kliegman LLP
Stk Agt .... NA
Counsel............ NA
DUNS No. 84-060-8012

Stock- Price on:12/24/2007 .... NA
Stock Exchange .... NA
Ticker Symbol .... NA
Outstanding Shares .... NA
E.P.S .... NA
Shareholders .... NA

Business: The group's principal activity is to provide reinsurance for variable universal life insurance and variable annuity products. The group is a holding company, owning all of the outstanding capital stock of global preferred re limited. The group writes three types of reinsurance on a quota share basis namely renewable term, coinsurance and modified coinsurance. The group's reinsurance business is based on the relationship with independent agents of world financial group, inc.

Primary SIC and add'l.: 6311

CIK No: 0000947716

Subsidiaries: Global Preferred Re Limited, Global Preferred Resources, Inc, Global Preferred Solutions, Inc, Preferred Advantage Insurance Services, Inc.

Officers: Edward F. McKernan/Dir., CEO, Pres., Thomas W. Montgomery/59/Dir., Exec. VP - World Leadership Group, Caryl P. Shepherd/VP, Treasurer, Bradley E. Barks/CFO, Sr. VP - Finance, David W. McLeroy/VP - Financial Projects, Andre J. Dill/Sec., Mgr. - Codan Services, Ltd, Lisa J. Marshall/Contact

Directors: Edward F. McKernan/Dir., CEO, Pres., Simon C. Scupham/Dir., Thomas W. Montgomery/59/Dir., Exec. VP - World Leadership Group, Milan M. Radonich/Dir.

Global Realty Development Corp

11555 Heron Bay Blvd., Ste. 200, Coral Springs, FL, 33076; *PH:* 1-954-509-9830;
Fax: 1-954-603-0523; *http://* www.grdcorporation.com; *Email:* info@grdcorporation.com

General - Incorporation	DE	Stock- Price on:12/24/2007	$0.55
Employees	4	Stock Exchange	OTC
Auditor	Meyler & Company, LLC	Ticker Symbol	GRLY
Stk Agt..... Computershare Investor Services LLC		Outstanding Shares	99,530,000
Counsel	NA	E.P.S.	-$0.08
DUNS No.	NA	Shareholders	NA

Business: The group operates through its subsidiary whose principle activity is to provide the real estate development services. The group operates from the United States and Australia.

Primary SIC and add'l.: 6500

CIK No: 0001118629

Subsidiaries: Australian Agriculture and Property Management Limited, No. 2 Holdings Pty. Ltd., Victorian Land Holdings Pty. Ltd.

Officers: Robert Kohn/Dir., CEO, Roger Charles Davis/Dir., CFO, Jon Sparks/Pres. - TFM Music Production Division, Roy Sciacca/Managing Partner, TFM Group, Mario Rivera/Exec. VP - TFM Group, Peter Voss/International Corporate Development

Directors: Robert Kohn/Dir., CEO, Roger Charles Davis/Dir., CFO

Owners: Nick Corcoris/8.48%, Kathryn Voss/24.89%, Jennifer Corcoris/8.48%, Michael J. Corcoris/21.21%, Peter Voss/24.89%, Roger Davis, Insiders

Financial Data: Fiscal Year End:12/31 Latest Annual Data: 12/31/2006

Year	Sales	Net Income
2006	$4,699,000	-$6,894,000
2005	$132,000	-$10,643,000
2004	$5,021,000	-$2,872,000

Curr. Assets:	$2,942,000	Curr. Liab.:	$6,587,000	P/E Ratio:	21.50
Plant, Equip.:	$31,381,000	Total Liab.:	$29,496,000	Indic. Yr. Divd.:	NA
Total Assets:	$42,826,000	Net Worth:	$13,330,000	Debt/ Equity:	NA

Global Resource Corp

408 Bloomfield Dr, Unit 3, West Berlin, NJ, 08091; *PH:* 1-856-767-5661;
http:// www.globalresourcecorp.com

General - Incorporation	NV	Stock- Price on:12/24/2007	NA
Employees	NA	Stock Exchange	OTC
Auditor	Bagell, Josephs, Levine & Co., L.I.c.	Ticker Symbol	GBRC
Stk Agt.......... Olde Monmouth Stock Transfer Co		Outstanding Shares	NA
Counsel	NA	E.P.S.	-$0.18
DUNS No.	NA	Shareholders	NA

Business: The group's principle activities include petroleum research, engineering, development and manufacturing services. The group also provides innovation and new technologies to the petrochemical industries. The group operates from United States.

Primary SIC and add'l.: 3559

CIK No: 0001128949

Subsidiaries: Advanced Hyperbaric Industries, Inc, NutraTek , LLC

Officers: Frank Pringle/Chmn., CEO, Pres., Jeffrey J. Andrews/Dir., Sec., Treasurer, CFO, Jerry Meddick/Business Development, Diane Rudderow/Accounting, Paul Gilgallon/Contact - NON US Investor Relation, Jimmy Villabolos/Pres., Hawk Hogan/Chief Engineer, Jay Gill/Sales

Directors: Frank Pringle/Chmn., CEO, Pres., Jeffrey J. Andrews/Dir., Sec., Treasurer, CFO, Frederick A. Clark/45/Dir.

Owners: Olde Monmouth Stock Transfer Co., Inc., Trustee Mobilestream Oil, Inc./5.00%, Insiders/73.10%, Olde Monmouth Stock Transfer Co., Inc., Trustee Carbon Recovery Corporation/5.00%, Frank G. Pringle/73.10%, Lois Augustine Pringle/8.80%

Financial Data: Fiscal Year End:03/31 Latest Annual Data: 3/31/2006

Year	Sales	Net Income
2006	NA	-$165,000
2005	NA	-$629,000

Curr. Assets:	$1,770,000	Curr. Liab.:	$352,000		
Plant, Equip.:	$489,000	Total Liab.:	$445,000	Indic. Yr. Divd.:	NA
Total Assets:	$2,404,000	Net Worth:	$1,959,000	Debt/ Equity:	NA

Global Sources Ltd

c/o Media Data Systems Pte Ltd, Raffles City, 911707; *PH:* 65-65472800;
http:// www.globalsources.com; *Email:* service@globalsources.com

General - Incorporation	Bermuda	Stock- Price on:12/24/2007	$21.02
Employees	NA	Stock Exchange	NDQ
Auditor	Ernst & Young LLP	Ticker Symbol	GSOL
Stk Agt..... Computershare Investor Services LLC		Outstanding Shares	42,340,000
Counsel	NA	E.P.S.	$0.67
DUNS No.	NA	Shareholders	NA

Business: The groups principle activity is to provide information and integrated marketing services. The groups services include media, online and print. The groups operates through two segments namely online and other media services, and exhibitions. The group operates from Asia, the United States and Europe. The group's quarterly revenue for September 2007 was 33.78 millions of USD.

Primary SIC and add'l.: 7379 4899 2741 2721 7375

CIK No: 0001110650

Subsidiaries: A.S. Mediaconsult Limited, ASM Business Services Limited, China Media Advertising, Inc., E-Commerce International Ltd., Earldom Computer Software (Shenzhen) Co., Ltd., Earldom Limited, eMedia Asia Ltd., Equitable Accounting Services Limited, Event Marketing Services Limited, Export Media Ltd., Fertile Valley Pte Ltd, Floro Company Limited, Fortune Valley Ltd., Global Alliance Investment Holdings Limited, Global Alliance Investment Management Limited 43 Subsidiaries included in the Index

Officers: Merle Hinrichs/Chmn., CEO, Sarah Benecke/Executive Dir., Craig Pepples/COO, Eddie Heng/Dir., CFO, Spenser Au/Pres. - Asian Sales, Peter Zapf/VP - E, Commerce Services, Mark Saunderson/Pres. - Electronics Business Unit, James Strachan/Exec. VP - Corporate Development, Bill Georgiou/CIO

Directors: Merle Hinrichs/Chmn., CEO, Sarah Benecke/Executive Dir., Eddie Heng/Dir., CFO, Roderick Chalmers/Dir., David Jones/Dir., James Watkins/Dir., Jeffrey Steiner/Dir., Robert Lees/Dir.

Owners: Jeffrey J. Steiner/1.20%, Hung Lay Si Co. Ltd/8.20%, Appleby Trust/5.10%, Merle A. Hinrichs/61.30%, Insiders/63.20%

Financial Data: Fiscal Year End:12/31 Latest Annual Data: 12/31/2006

Year	Sales	Net Income
2006	$156,481,000	$27,880,000
2005	$112,194,000	$13,378,000
2004	$105,846,000	$15,769,000

Curr. Assets:	$190,564,000	Curr. Liab.:	$82,018,000		
Plant, Equip.:	$28,374,000	Total Liab.:	$87,238,000	Indic. Yr. Divd.:	NA
Total Assets:	$220,889,000	Net Worth:	$133,651,000	Debt/ Equity:	NA

Global Svcs PTR

3130 Fairview Pk. Dr., Ste.500, Falls Church, VA, 22042;

General - Incorporation	DE	Stock- Price on:12/24/2007	$1.7
Employees	NA	Stock Exchange	OTC
Auditor	BDO Seidman, LLP	Ticker Symbol	GSPA
Stk Agt..... American Stock Transfer & Trust Co.		Outstanding Shares	NA
Counsel	NA	E.P.S.	$0.05
DUNS No.	NA	Shareholders	NA

Business: The group's principle activity is to serve vehicle to effect a merger, capital stock exchange, asset acquisition, or other similar business combination with an entity that has operating business. The company was founded in 2005 and is based in Falls Church, Virginia. The group operates from United States.

Primary SIC and add'l.: 6770

CIK No: 0001336262

Owners: Millennium Management L.L.C./5.10%, Fir Tree Recovery Master Fund, L.P./2.40%, Satellite Fund Management LLC/8.03%, Israel A. Englander/5.10%, The Baupost Group, L.L.C./9.72%, Millenco, L.L.C./5.10%, Fir Tree, Inc./9.80%, Abhishek Jain, Pentagram Partners, L.P./14.13%, Satellite Asset Management, L.P./8.03%, Andrew M. Weiss/11.60%, Richard Jacinto/14.13%, Sapling LLC/7.40%, Insiders

Financial Data: Fiscal Year End:12/31 Latest Annual Data: 07/31/2007

Year	Sales	Net Income
2007	NA	$501,000
2006	NA	$153,000

Curr. Assets:	$995,000	Curr. Liab.:	$78,000		
Plant, Equip.:	NA	Total Liab.:	$6,361,000	Indic. Yr. Divd.:	NA
Total Assets:	$32,484,000	Net Worth:	$26,123,000	Debt/ Equity:	NA

Global Svcs PTR CL B

3130 Fairview Pk. Dr., Ste.500, Falls Church, VA, 22042; *PH:* 1-703-373-3143

General - Incorporation	DE	Stock- Price on:12/24/2007	$5.1
Employees	NA	Stock Exchange	OTC
Auditor	BDO Seidman, LLP	Ticker Symbol	GSPAB
Stk Agt..... American Stock Transfer & Trust Co.		Outstanding Shares	NA
Counsel	NA	E.P.S.	NA
DUNS No.	NA	Shareholders	NA

Business: The groups principle activity is to provide recruiting services. The groups service area includes the research and development, engineering, marketing, sales, information technology and manufacturing industries. The group operates from United States.

Primary SIC and add'l.: 6770

CIK No: 0001336262

Owners: The Baupost Group, L.L.C./9.72%, Millennium Management L.L.C./5.10%, Pentagram Partners, L.P./14.13%, Andrew M. Weiss/11.60%, Satellite Asset Management, L.P./8.03%, Richard Jacinto/14.13%, Satellite Fund Management LLC/8.03%, Insiders, Millenco, L.L.C./5.10%, Israel A. Englander/5.10%, Fir Tree Recovery Master Fund, L.P./2.40%, Fir Tree, Inc./9.80%, Sapling LLC/7.40%, Abhishek Jain

Global Tech Appliances Inc

12/f., Kin Teck Industrial Bldg., 26 Wong Chuk Hang Rd., Aberdeen;

General - Incorporation British Virgin Islands		Stock- Price on:12/24/2007	$3.0401
Employees	2,383	Stock Exchange	NYSE
Auditor	Ernst & Young LLP	Ticker Symbol	GAI
Stk Agt..... American Stock Transfer & Trust Co.		Outstanding Shares	NA
Counsel	Calfee, Halter & Griswold	E.P.S.	-$0.65
DUNS No.	66-318-2533	Shareholders	NA

Business: The groups principle activities include designing and manufacturing of a wide range of small household appliances, including kitchen appliances such as breadmakers and coffeemakers, personal, beauty and healthcare products such as hair dryers and curling irons, travel products and accessories such as irons and hair setters, and garment care products such as steam and dry irons. The group operates from United States.

Primary SIC and add'l.: 3634
CIK No: 0001057708
Subsidiaries: Consotium Investment (BVI) Limited, Dongguan Lite Array Company Limited, Dongguan Litewell (OLED) Technology Co., Ltd., Dongguan Wing Shing Electrical Products Factory Company Limited, Global Appliances Holdings Limited, Global Auto Limited, Global Digital Imaging Limited, Global Display Holdings Limited, Global Lite Array (BVI) Limited, Global Optics Limited, Global Rich Innovation Limited, Global-Tech USA, Inc., GT Investment (BVI) Limited, Kwong Lee Shun Trading Company Limited, Lite Array Holdings Limited 24 Subsidiaries included in the Index
Owners: Kwong Ho Sham, Patrick Po-On Hui, Wing Shing Holdings Company Limited, Barry J. Buttifant, Kin Shek Leung, Brian Yuen, Ken Ying-Keung Wong, John C.K. Sham, Insiders
Financial Data: Fiscal Year End:03/31   Latest Annual Data: 03/31/2007

Year	Sales	Net Income
2007	$60,291,000	-$1,167,000
2006	$73,812,000	-$11,223,000
2005	$41,851,000	-$18,623,000

Curr. Assets:	$71,764,000	**Curr. Liab.:**	$18,692,000		
Plant, Equip.:	$24,165,000	**Total Liab.:**	$18,731,000	**Indic. Yr. Divd.:**	NA
Total Assets:	$98,080,000	**Net Worth:**	$79,349,000	**Debt/ Equity:**	NA

Global Telecom & Technology Inc

8484 WestPk. Dr., Ste. 720, Mclean, VA, 22102; **PH:** 1-703-442-5500; **Fax:** 1-703-442-5501; http:// www.gt-t.net; **Email:** info@gt-t.net

General - Incorporation	DE	**Stock** - Price on:12/24/2007	$2.5
Employees	92	Stock Exchange	OTC
Auditor	J.H. Cohn, LLP	Ticker Symbol	GTLT
Stk Agt	American Stock Transfer & Trust CO.	Outstanding Shares	11,730,000
Counsel	NA	E.P.S.	-$0.95
DUNS No.	NA	Shareholders	NA

Business: The groups principal activity is to acquire the operating business of other companies. The group operates from the United States.
Primary SIC and add'l.: 7378 7373 7371 7379
CIK No: 0001315255
Officers: Richard D. Calder/Dir., CEO, Pres., Brian H. Thompson/Executive Chmn., Todd Vecchio/Sr. VP - Corporate Development, Kevin Welch/CFO, John G. Hendler/Sr. VP - Global Sales, J. D. Darby/VP - Marketing, Media Contact, Trish Drennan/Investor Contact
Directors: Richard D. Calder/Dir., CEO, Pres., Brian H. Thompson/Executive Chmn., Michael D. Keenan/Dir., Didier Delepine/Dir., Rhodric C. Hackman/Dir., Morgan Obrien/Dir., Howard Janzen/Dir., Sudhakar Shenoy/Dir., Joseph S. Bruno/59/Dir.
Owners: J. Carlo Cannell, Lior Samuelson, Howard Janzen, Sudhakar Shenoy, Rhodric C. Hackman, Michael D. Keenan, Morgan E. OBrien, David Ballarini, Todd Vecchio, Alex Mandl, Goldman Sachs Asset Management, L.P, Kevin J. Welch, H. Brian Thompson, Millenco, L.L.C., S. Joseph Bruno (17 Owners included in Index)
Financial Data: Fiscal Year End:12/31   Latest Annual Data: 12/31/2006

Year	Sales	Net Income
2006	$10,471,000	-$1,847,000
2005	NA	$1,369,000

Curr. Assets:	$23,733,000	**Curr. Liab.:**	$46,059,000		
Plant, Equip.:	$890,000	**Total Liab.:**	$54,482,000	**Indic. Yr. Divd.:**	NA
Total Assets:	$98,275,000	**Net Worth:**	$43,793,000	**Debt/ Equity:**	0.1949

Global Traffic Network Inc

800 2nd Ave., 5th Fl., New York, NY, 10017; **PH:** 1-212-896-1255; http:// www.globaltrafficnetwork.com; **Email:** ctninfo@globaltrafficnetwork.com

General - Incorporation	DE	**Stock** - Price on:12/24/2007	$6.98
Employees	84	Stock Exchange	NDQ
Auditor	Bdo Kendalls (nsw)	Ticker Symbol	GNET
Stk Agt	Wells Fargo Bank, N.A.	Outstanding Shares	12,870,000
Counsel	NA	E.P.S.	-$0.09
DUNS No.	NA	Shareholders	NA

Business: The groups principle activity is to provide customized traffic and news reports. The groups services include radio traffic reports, radio news reports and TV reports. Customers served by the group include radio stations, television stations. The group operates from Australia and Canada. The group's quarterly revenue for September year 2007 was 10.98 millions of USD.
Primary SIC and add'l.: 4832 7812 4899
CIK No: 0001344907
Subsidiaries: Canadian Traffic Network ULC, Global Traffic Canada, Inc, The Australia Traffic Network Pty Limited
Officers: William L. Yde/Chmn., CEO, Pres., Dale C. Arfman/Dir., Treasurer, Sec., Scott E. Cody/CFO, COO, Ivan N. Shulman/Exec. VP, Dir. - International Sales, William Pezzimenti/Pres., Sales Dir. Australia Traffic Network
Directors: William L. Yde/Chmn., CEO, Pres., Dale C. Arfman/Dir., Treasurer, Sec., Shane E. Coppola/Dir., Robert L. Johander/Dir., Stuart R. Romenesko/Dir., Gary S. Worobow/Dir., Gary O. Benson/Dir.
Owners: William Pezzimenti, Stuart R. Romenesko, William L. Yde/21.64%, Gary O. Benson, Ivan N. Shulman, Robert L. Johander Revocable Trust/4.87%, Scott E. Cody, Shane E. Coppola, Insiders/36.37%, Gary L. Worobow, Metro Networks Communications, Inc./8.54%, Kern Capital Management LLC/5.97%, Dale C. Arfman/13.92%
Financial Data: Fiscal Year End:06/30   Latest Annual Data: 06/30/2007

Year	Sales	Net Income
2007	$31,699,000	-$2,017,000
2006	$19,502,000	-$2,996,000

Curr. Assets:	$19,874,000	**Curr. Liab.:**	$7,172,000		
Plant, Equip.:	$4,188,000	**Total Liab.:**	$8,680,000	**Indic. Yr. Divd.:**	NA
Total Assets:	$24,288,000	**Net Worth:**	$15,608,000	**Debt/ Equity:**	0.0667

Global Wataire Inc

Formerly: International Development Corp
534 Delaware Ave., Ste. 412, Buffalo, NY, 14202; **PH:** 1-716-332-7150; http:// www.ozolutions.com

General - Incorporation	NV	**Stock** - Price on:12/24/2007	$0.12
Employees	3	Stock Exchange	OTC
Auditor	Rotenberg & Co. LLP	Ticker Symbol	GWTE
Stk Agt	Transfer Online, Inc.	Outstanding Shares	9,720,000
Counsel	NA	E.P.S.	-$0.16
DUNS No.	NA	Shareholders	NA

Business: The groups principal activities are the distribution and marketing of water purification systems using ozone, ultra violet and activated water treatment systems. Ozone water treatment systems use ozonation treatment of water with ozone gas. This system includes an ozone generator that applies electrical discharge to oxygen or ambient air to produce ozone and a transfer system for injecting the ozone into a water stream to oxidize or purify the water. Ultra violet water treatment systems do not use chemicals and are capable of disinfecting water faster than chlorine. Activated water treatment systems use water flow over ceramic granules to generate, from the resulting friction, electric charges in the water. The group has distributor agreement with hankin, through which it markets and sells the hankin water treatment products. The products of the group are marketed in Canada, Mexico and the Caribbean zone including panama, Costa Rica, El Salvador and Peru.
Primary SIC and add'l.: 5074 3589
CIK No: 0001121901
Subsidiaries: BUFFALO, FreshWater Technologies Inc
Officers: Sydney A. Harland/57/Dir., CEO, Pres., Edmund Gorman/62/Dir., CFO, Sec., Mark Hollingworth/49/VP
Directors: Sydney A. Harland/57/Dir., CEO, Pres., Edmund Gorman/62/Dir., CFO, Sec., Robert Glassen/61/Dir.
Owners: Betty-Ann Harland/66.00%, Betty-Ann Harland/100.00%, Betty-Ann Harland/25.00%
Financial Data: Fiscal Year End:08/31   Latest Annual Data: 08/31/2007

Year	Sales	Net Income
2007	$62,000	-$1,407,000
2006	NA	-$198,000
2005	$16,000	-$1,131,000

Curr. Assets:	NA	**Curr. Liab.:**	$666,000		
Plant, Equip.:	NA	**Total Liab.:**	$666,000	**Indic. Yr. Divd.:**	NA
Total Assets:	$66,000	**Net Worth:**	-$600,000	**Debt/ Equity:**	NA

Global Wireless Satellite Ntwrks USA Inc

11555 Heron Bay Blvd., Ste. 200, Coral Springs, FL, 33076; **PH:** 1-954-603-0522; http:// www.grdcorporation.com

General - Incorporation	DE	**Stock** - Price on:12/24/2007	NA
Employees	3	Stock Exchange	NA
Auditor	Meyler & Co. LLC	Ticker Symbol	NA
Stk Agt	Computershare Trust Co	Outstanding Shares	NA
Counsel	NA	E.P.S.	-$0.07
DUNS No.	NA	Shareholders	NA

Business: The group's intends to acquire properties and businesses. Prior to this the group had intended to develop, manufacture and market advanced uninterruptible power supplies for the telecommunication industry. The group no longer continues in this business.
Primary SIC and add'l.: 3612 6719
CIK No: 0001118629
Subsidiaries: Australian Agriculture and Property Management Limited, Holdings Pty. Ltd, Victorian Land Holdings Pty. Ltd
Officers: Robert Kohn/Dir., CEO, Roy Sciacca/CEO - MJD Films, Managing Partner, TFM Group, Mario Rivera/Exec. VP - TFM Group, Peter Voss/International Corporate Development, Roger Charles Davis/Dir., CFO, Jon Sparks/Pres. - TFM Music Production Division
Directors: Robert Kohn/Dir., CEO, Roger Charles Davis/Dir., CFO
Owners: Kathryn Voss/24.89%, Roger Davis, Jennifer Corcoris/8.48%, Michael J. Corcoris/21.21%, Insiders, Nick Corcoris/8.48%, Peter Voss/24.89%
Financial Data: Fiscal Year End:12/31   Latest Annual Data: 12/31/2006

Year	Sales	Net Income
2006	$4,699,000	-$6,894,000
2005	$132,000	-$10,643,000
2004	$5,021,000	-$2,872,000

Curr. Assets:	$2,942,000	**Curr. Liab.:**	$6,587,000		
Plant, Equip.:	$31,381,000	**Total Liab.:**	$29,497,000	**Indic. Yr. Divd.:**	NA
Total Assets:	$42,826,000	**Net Worth:**	$13,330,000	**Debt/ Equity:**	1.3777

Global-E Investments Inc

2090 E University Ste. 112, Tempe, Scottsdale, AZ, 85281; **PH:** 1-480-990-0007

General - Incorporation	NV	**Stock** - Price on:12/24/2007	$0.075
Employees	NA	Stock Exchange	OTC
Auditor	Moore & Assoc., Chartered	Ticker Symbol	NAUG
Stk Agt	Holladay Stock Transfer, Inc.	Outstanding Shares	9,840,000
Counsel	NA	E.P.S.	-$0.17
DUNS No.	NA	Shareholders	NA

Business: The group's principle activity is to provide customized management solutions to new and existing golf course property owners. The services provided by the group include financial planning, oversight of daily course operations, designing and implementing marketing initiatives and advertising programs, turf maintenance, course presentation, food and beverage sales, accounting procedures, staff recruitment and employer relations. The group is in development stage. The group operates in the United States. The group serves the golf club companies.
Primary SIC and add'l.: 8741
CIK No: 0001285828
Subsidiaries: Navicom Corporation, Navicom GPS, Inc.
Officers: Scott Miller/CEO, Faith Forbis/CFO
Financial Data: Fiscal Year End:12/31   Latest Annual Data: 6/30/2006

Year	Sales	Net Income
2006	$11,684,000	-$447,000
2004	$10,000	-$13,000

Curr. Assets:	$2,330,000	**Curr. Liab.:**	$3,481,000		
Plant, Equip.:	$41,000	**Total Liab.:**	$3,481,000	**Indic. Yr. Divd.:**	NA
Total Assets:	$5,986,000	**Net Worth:**	$2,505,000	**Debt/ Equity:**	2.7734

GlobalOptions Group Inc

75 Rockefeller Plz., 27th Fl., New York, NY, 10019; *PH:* 1-212-445-6262; *Fax:* 1-212-445-0053; *http://* www.globaloptionsgroup.com; *Email:* info@globaloptionsgroup.com

General - Incorporation: NV
Employees: NA
Auditor: Marcum & Kliegman LLP
Stk Agt: Continental Stock Transfer & Trust Co
Counsel: NA
DUNS No.: NA

Stock - Price on:12/24/2007: NA
Stock Exchange: NDQ
Ticker Symbol: GLOI
Outstanding Shares: NA
E.P.S: NA
Shareholders: NA

Business: The groups principle activity is to provide risk mitigation services. Services of the group include risk management and security, investigations and litigation support, and crisis management and corporate governance. Customers served by the group include Fortune 500 corporations, governmental organizations and individuals. The group operates through three segments namely Confidential Business Resources, James Lee Witt Associates and SafirRosetti. The group operates from the United States.

Primary SIC and add'l.: 8742

CIK No: 0001294649

Subsidiaries: GlobalOptions Management, Inc., GlobalOptions, Inc, The Bode Technology Group, Inc

Officers: Harvey W. Schiller/Chmn., CEO, James Lee Witt/CEO - Globaloptions, James Lee Witt Division, Globaloptions, Inc, Howard Safir/Chmn., CEO - Safirrosetti, Wesley Clark/Vice Chmn. - Sr. Advisor, James Lee Witt Associates, Mark C. Merritt/Sr. VP - James Lee Witt Associates, Richard Rosetti/Regional MD - Safirrosetti, Washington, DC, Adam Safir/General Counsel - Safirrosetti, Barry W. Scanlon/Sr. VP - James Lee Witt Associates, Allen Lux/VP - Business Development, Fraud, SIU Services, Rusty Aaronson/VP - Eastern Region, Fraud, SIU Services, David W. Nicastro/Founder - CPP, CFE, Pres. - Secure Source, Chris Witty/Primary Investor Relations Officer, Michael A. Gomez/VP - Western Region, Pate Felts/COO - James Lee Witt Associates, LLC, Anneilia J. Holton-Williams/Dir. - Southeast Region, James Lee Witt Associates, LLC *(21 Officers included in Index)*

Directors: Harvey W. Schiller/Chmn., CEO, Per-Olof Loof/Vice Chmn., Rodney E. Slater/Member - Sr. Advisory Board, Vice Chmn. - James Lee Witt Associates, Wesley Clark/Vice Chmn. - Sr. Advisor, James Lee Witt Associates, Frances D. Cook/Member - Sr. Advisory Board, William S. Sessions/Member - Sr. Advisory Board, William H. Webster/Member - Sr. Advisory Board, Arnold Burns/Member - Business Advisory Board, Andrew Kaslow/Member - Business Advisory Board, Sanford R. Climan/Member - Business Advisory Board, John Oswald/Member - Sr. Advisory Board, Neil C. Livingstone/Member - Sr. Advisory Board, Daniel L. Burstein/Dir., Ronald M. Starr/Dir., John P. Bujouves/Dir.

Owners: Howard Safir/2.70%, Harvey W. Schiller/3.20%, James Lee Witt, Daniel L. Burstein/3.10%, Per-Olof Loof, Jeffrey O. Nyweide/1.40%, Rising Wolf II, LLC/2.90%, Ronald M. Starr, Insiders/14.00%, John P. Bujouves/1.80%, Thomas P. Ondeck

Curr. Assets:	$41,906,000	**Curr. Liab.:**	$14,387,000		
Plant, Equip.:	$798,000	**Total Liab.:**	$15,327,000	**Indic. Yr. Divd.:**	NA
Total Assets:	$69,226,000	**Net Worth:**	$53,899,000	**Debt/ Equity:**	0.0116

GlobalSantaFe Corp

15375 Memorial Dr., Houston, TX, 77079; *PH:* 1-281-925-6000; *Fax:* 1-281-925-6010; *http://* www.globalsantafe.com

General - Incorporation: Cayman Islands
Employees: 5,962
Auditor: PricewaterhouseCoopers LLP
Stk Agt: Computershare Investor Services LLC
Counsel: NA
DUNS No.: 14-711-0530

Stock - Price on:12/24/2007: $72.98
Stock Exchange: NA
Ticker Symbol: NA
Outstanding Shares: 227,970,000
E.P.S: $4.98
Shareholders: NA

Business: The group's principal activity is to provide offshore contract drilling and offshore drilling management services. The offshore contract drilling services are provided on a day rate basis and offshore drilling management services on a day rate or completed-project, fixed-price (turnkey) basis.the group's operations include oil and gas exploration, development and production activities through its wholly owned subsidiary, challenger minerals inc. The group's owned fleet currently includes 13 floating rigs, 45 cantilevered jackup rigs, 31 land rigs and one platform rig. Its mobile offshore drilling rigs include six cantilevered heavy-duty harsh environment jackups, 39 cantilevered jackups, nine semisubmersibles, three ultra-deepwater, dynamically positioned drillships and one moored drillship. The operations are conducted mainly in the United States, the United Kingdom, nigeria, egypt, trinidad and tabago and other foreign countries.

Primary SIC and add'l.: 1321 1311 1382

CIK No: 0001038914

Subsidiaries: Applied Drilling Technology Inc., Campeche Drilling Services Inc., Challenger Minerals (Nigeria) Limited, Challenger Minerals (North Sea) Limited, Challenger Minerals Inc., Covent GardenServicos de Marketing LDA, Eaton Industries of Houston, Inc., Entities Holdings, Inc., Global Marine do Brasil Perfuracoes Ltda., Global Marine Inc., Global Offshore Drilling Limited, GlobalSantaFe (Africa) Inc., GlobalSantaFe (Labuan) Inc., GlobalSantaFe (Norge) AS, GlobalSantaFe AG 94 Subsidiaries included in the Index

Officers: Jon A. Marshall/Dir., CEO, Pres./$12,060,990.00, Roger B. Hunt/Sr. VP - Marketing/$4,271,379.00, James L. McCulloch/Sr. VP, General Counsel/$2,507,749.00, Marion M. Woolie/Sr. VP - Operations/$3,440,142.00, Matt W. Ralls/COO, Exec. VP/$5,896,688.00, Michael R. Dawson/Sr. VP, CFO/$1,869,160.00, Robert L. Herrin/VP, Controller, Richard J. Hoffman/VP - Investor Relations, Alexander A. Krezel/VP, Corp. Sec., Assoc. General Counsel, Myrtle Penelton/VP - Tax, Anil B. Shah/VP, Treasurer, John L. Truschinger/CIO, VP, Sherry Richard/Sr. VP - Human Resources, Blake R. Simmons/Sr. VP - Operations

Directors: Jon A. Marshall/Dir., CEO, Pres., Robert E. Rose/Chmn., Richard W. Anderson/Dir., Thomas W. Cason/Dir., Richard L. George/Dir., Edward R. Muller/Dir., Stephen J. Solarz/Dir., Carroll W. Suggs/Dir., John L. Whitmire/Dir.

Owners: Robert E. Rose, Edward R. Muller, Jon A. Marshall, James L. McCulloch, Richard L. George, Richard W. Anderson, Matt W. Ralls, John L. Whitmire, Stephen J. Solarz, Roger B. Hunt, Insiders, Thomas W. Cason, Wellington Management Company, LLP/6.70%, Michael R. Dawson, Carroll W. Suggs *(16 Owners included in Index)*

Financial Data: **Fiscal Year End:**12/31 **Latest Annual Data:** 12/31/2006

Year	Sales	Net Income
2006	$3,312,600,000	$1,006,400,000
2005	$2,263,500,000	$423,100,000
2004	$1,723,700,000	$143,700,000

Curr. Assets:	$1,233,700,000	**Curr. Liab.:**	$563,100,000		
Plant, Equip.:	$4,514,600,000	**Total Liab.:**	$1,373,100,000	**Indic. Yr. Divd.:**	NA
Total Assets:	$6,220,200,000	**Net Worth:**	$4,847,100,000	**Debt/ Equity:**	0.1426

GlobalSCAPE Inc

6000 NW Pkwy., Ste. 100, San Antonio, TX, 78249; *PH:* 1-210-308-8267; *Fax:* 1-210-308-8297; *http://* www.globalscape.com

General - Incorporation: DE
Employees: 56
Auditor: PMB Helin Donovan, LLP
Stk Agt: Mellon Investor Services LLC
Counsel: NA
DUNS No.: NA

Stock - Price on:12/24/2007: $3.9
Stock Exchange: AMEX
Ticker Symbol: GSB
Outstanding Shares: 17,230,000
E.P.S: $0.20
Shareholders: NA

Business: The group's principle activity is to develop and distribute Internet related software, including file management, content management and Web development tools. The products include windows(R) -based, browser-based and server software applications. The customers include Web development and information technology professionals. The consumers who are actively involved in moving and managing Web site content, corporate and personal data are also the customers of the group. Globalscape(R), cuteftp pro(R), cuteftp(R), cutezip(R), cutehtml(R), cutemap(R) and cutesite builder(R) are registered trademarks of the group. The group has operations in the United States of America and also generates revenue from customers in western Europe, Canada and Australia. The group's quarterly revenue for Sep'07 was 3.90 millions of USD.

Primary SIC and add'l.: 7319 7372 7375

CIK No: 0001112920

Subsidiaries: GlobalSCAPE Limited, LLC, GlobalSCAPE Texas, LP, GS General, LLC

Officers: Charles R. Poole/65/Dir., CEO, Pres./$254,274.00, Kelly E. Simmons/CFO, Ellen Ohlenbusch/VP - Marketing, Strategic Alliances, Doug Conyers/VP - Professional Services, Gregory Hoffer/CTO, VP, Jeffrey Gehring/VP - Sales/$235,985.00, Timothy J. Barton/VP - Operations/$170,827.00, Earl K. Posey/VP - Investor Relations, Business Operations/$167,251.00

Directors: Charles R. Poole/65/Dir., CEO, Pres., Thomas W. Brown/Chmn., David L. Mann/Dir., Phillip M. Renfro/Dir., Frank M. Morgan/Dir.

Owners: Bernard N. Schneider, Sandra Poole-Christal, Jeffrey Gehring, Thomas W. Brown, SF Capital Partners, Ltd., Frank M. Morgan, Chuck T. Shavit, Philip M. Renfro, Edward Antoian, Michael A. Roth, Brian J. Stark, Charles R. Poole, David L. Mann, Insiders, Earl K. Posey *(17 Owners included in Index)*

Financial Data: **Fiscal Year End:**12/31 **Latest Annual Data:** 12/31/2006

Year	Sales	Net Income
2006	$10,974,000	$1,963,000
2005	$6,679,000	$1,447,000
2004	$4,931,000	$200,000

Curr. Assets:	$6,415,000	**Curr. Liab.:**	$3,666,000	**P/E Ratio:**	35.45
Plant, Equip.:	$232,000	**Total Liab.:**	$6,795,000	**Indic. Yr. Divd.:**	NA
Total Assets:	$16,368,000	**Net Worth:**	$9,573,000	**Debt/ Equity:**	NA

Globalstar Inc

461 S Milpitas Blvd., Milpitas, CA, 95035; *PH:* 1-408-933-4000; *Fax:* 1-408-933-4100; *http://* www.globalstar.com; *Email:* sales@globalstar.com

General - Incorporation: DE
Employees: 343
Auditor: Crowe Chizek & Co. LLP
Stk Agt: NA
Counsel: NA
DUNS No.: NA

Stock - Price on:12/24/2007: $10.52
Stock Exchange: NDQ
Ticker Symbol: GSAT
Outstanding Shares: 76,590,000
E.P.S: -$0.17
Shareholders: NA

Business: The groups principle activity is to provide mobile voice and data communications services via satellite. The groups services include mobile voice and data satellite communications, fixed voice and data satellite, satellite data modem and asset tracking and remote monitoring. The products of the group include voice and data equipment, data-only equipment and multi channel modem. Customers served by the group include oil and gas, government, mining, forestry, commercial fishing, utilities, military, transportation and heavy construction. The group operates from the United States, Canada, Europe and Central and South America. The group's quarterly revenue for September 2007 was 25.96 millions of USD.

Primary SIC and add'l.: 3669 4789 4899 7389 4812

CIK No: 0001366868

Subsidiaries: Astral Technologies Investment Ltd., ATSS Canada,Inc., GCL Licensee LLC, Globalstar Americas Acquisitions, Ltd., Globalstar Americas Holding Ltd., Globalstar Americas Telecommunications Ltd., Globalstar C, LLC, Globalstar Canada Satellite Co., Globalstar Caribbean Ltd., Globalstar Colombia, Ltda., Globalstar de El Salvador, SA de CV, Globalstar de Venezuela, C.A., Globalstar Europe Satellite Services, Ltd., Globalstar Europe, S.A.R.L., Globalstar Gateway Company S.A. 27 Subsidiaries included in the Index

Officers: James Monroe/Chmn., CEO, Anthony J. Navarra/Pres. - Global Operations, Fuad Ahmad/CFO, VP, Megan L. Fitzgerald/Sr. VP - Strategic Initiatives, Space Operations, Dennis C. Allen/Sr. VP - Sales, Marketing, Steven Bell/Sr. VP - International Sales, Marketing, Customer Care, Robert D. Miller/Sr. VP - Engineering, Ground Operations, William F. Adler/VP - Legal, Regulatory Affairs, Paul A. Monte/VP - Engineering, Product Development

Directors: James Monroe/Chmn., CEO, Peter J. Dalton/Dir., James F. Lynch/Dir., Richard S. Roberts/Dir., Kenneth E. Jones/Dir., Patrick J. McIntyre/Dir.

Owners: Anthony J. Navarra, Columbia Ventures Corporation, Peter J. Dalton, Globalstar Holdings, LLC, Thermo Funding Company LLC, QUALCOMM Incorporated, Globalstar Satellite, LP, Steven Bell, James Monroe, Insiders

Financial Data: **Fiscal Year End:**12/31 **Latest Annual Data:** 12/31/2006

Year	Sales	Net Income
2006	$136,671,000	$23,623,000
2005	$127,147,000	$18,719,000
2004	$84,368,000	$370,000

Curr. Assets: $116,552,000 **Curr. Liab.:** $59,716,000 **P/E Ratio:** 526.00
Plant, Equip.: $136,722,000 **Total Liab.:** $66,055,000 **Indic. Yr. Divd.:** NA
Total Assets: $331,701,000 **Net Worth:** $260,697,000 **Debt/ Equity:** 0.0010

Globalwise Investments Inc

2157 S Lincoln St., Salt Lake City, UT, 84106; ***PH:*** 1-801-323-2395

General - Incorporation .... NV
Employees .... NA
Auditor .... Chisholm, Bierwolf & Nilson, LLC
Stk Agt .... Colonial Stock Transfer Co Inc
Counsel .... NA
DUNS No. .... NA

Stock- Price on:12/24/2007 .... NA
Stock Exchange .... OTC
Ticker Symbol .... GWIV
Outstanding Shares .... NA
E.P.S. .... NA
Shareholders .... NA

Business: The groups principal activities include seeking, investigating, and acquiring interest in a business opportunity. The group operates from the United States. The group is a development stage company.

Primary SIC and add'l.: 6799

CIK No: 0001081745

Officers: Donald R. Mayer/68/Dir., Pres., Linda L. Perry/63/Dir., Sec., Treasurer

Directors: Donald R. Mayer/68/Dir., Pres., Linda L. Perry/63/Dir., Sec., Treasurer

Owners: Donald R. Mayer, Brent Nelson/18.70%, Insiders

Globe Bancorp Inc

4051 Veterans Blvd., Ste. 100, Metairie, LA, 70002; ***PH:*** 1-504-887-0057

General - Incorporation .... LA
Employees .... NA
Auditor .... NA
Stk Agt .... Registrar and Transfer Co.
Counsel .... NA
DUNS No. .... NA

Stock- Price on:12/24/2007 .... $21.05
Stock Exchange .... OTC
Ticker Symbol .... GLBP
Outstanding Shares .... NA
E.P.S. .... NA
Shareholders .... NA

Business: The groups principal activities include attracting deposits from the general public and using those funds to originate loans secured by one- to four-family residential loans. Services of the group include commercial real estate loans, construction loans and consumer loans. The group operates from the United States.

Primary SIC and add'l.: 6712 6162 6021 6163

CIK No: 0001136645

Financial Data: ***Fiscal Year End:***12/31 ***Latest Annual Data:*** 12/31/2003

Year	Sales	Net Income
2003	$1,746,000	$158,000
2002	$2,012,000	$200,000
2001	$1,797,000	$68,000

Curr. Assets: $1,776,000 **Curr. Liab.:** $26,234,000
Plant, Equip.: $120,000 **Total Liab.:** $26,391,000 **Indic. Yr. Divd.:** NA
Total Assets: $31,941,000 **Net Worth:** $5,550,000 **Debt/ Equity:** NA

Globecomm Systems Inc

45 Oser Ave., Hauppauge, NY, 11788; ***PH:*** 1-631-231-9800; ***Fax:*** 1-631-231-1557; ***http://*** www.globecommsystems.com

General - Incorporation .... DE
Employees 192
Auditor .... Ernst & Young LLP
Stk Agt .... American Stock Transfer & Trust Co.
Counsel .... Brobeck, Phleger & Harrison
DUNS No. 87-891-5701

Stock- Price on:12/24/2007 .... $14.09
Stock Exchange .... NDQ
Ticker Symbol .... GCOM
Outstanding Shares 16,330,000
E.P.S. $0.60
Shareholders .... NA

Business: The group's principal activity is to design, engineer, integrate and install satellite-based ground segment systems and network solutions for communications requirements. The services offered include wide area network connectivity, broadband connectivity to end users, Internet connectivity, content delivery network services, media distribution and other network services. The customers of the group are communications service providers, commercial enterprises, multinational corporations, Internet service providers, broadcasters and other content providers and government entities.

Primary SIC and add'l.: 3669 4899

CIK No: 0001031028

Subsidiaries: Globecomm NetworkServices Corporation, Globecomm Systems Europe Limited, GSI Properties Corp

Officers: David E. Hershberg/70/Chmn., CEO, Founder, Paul J. Johnson/51/Sr. VP - Customer Relations, Contracts, Paul Eterno/51/VP - Human Resources, Andrew C. Melfi/53/CFO, VP, Treasurer, Kenneth A. Miller/62/Dir., Pres., Stephen C. Yablonski/60/Sr. VP - Sales - Marketing, Product Development, Donald G. Woodring/59/VP - Network - Systems Analysis

Directors: David E. Hershberg/70/Chmn., CEO, Founder, Kenneth A. Miller/62/Dir., Pres., Richard E. Caruso/61/Dir., Robert A. Towbin/72/Dir., Jack A. Shaw/68/Dir., C. J. Waylan/65/Dir., Brian T. Maloney/53/Dir., Harry L. Hutcherson/64/Dir.

Owners: David E. Hershberg/4.15%, Richard E. Caruso, Stephen C. Yablonski, Jack A. Shaw, Kenneth A. Miller, Harry L. Hutcherson, Robert A. Towbin, Insiders/7.44%, Brown Advisory Securities LLC/7.69%, Andrew C. Melfi, C. J. Waylan, Brian T. Maloney, Paul J. Johnson

Financial Data: ***Fiscal Year End:***06/30 ***Latest Annual Data:*** 6/30/2006

Year	Sales	Net Income
2006	$126,036,000	$4,492,000
2005	$109,584,000	$4,814,000
2004	$87,236,000	-$1,341,000

Curr. Assets: $69,560,000 **Curr. Liab.:** $25,865,000 **P/E Ratio:** 35.23
Plant, Equip.: $15,510,000 **Total Liab.:** $26,218,000 **Indic. Yr. Divd.:** NA
Total Assets: $93,234,000 **Net Worth:** $67,016,000 **Debt/ Equity:** NA

Globetech Ventures Corp

Ste. 804 - 750 W Pender St., Vancouver, BC, V6C 2T8; ***PH:*** 1-604-488-1011; ***http://*** globetechventures.com

General - Incorporation .... BC
Employees .... NA
Auditor .... MacKay LLP
Stk Agt .... Pacific Corporate Trust Co
Counsel .... Gergory S. Yanke
DUNS No. .... NA

Stock- Price on:12/24/2007 .... $0.21
Stock Exchange .... OTC
Ticker Symbol .... GTVCF
Outstanding Shares .... NA
E.P.S. .... NA
Shareholders .... NA

Business: The group's principal activity is to identify, acquire, develop and market Internet-related products. Through translationwave.com, the group provides translation services to and from English, Spanish, portuguese, Italian, Japanese, german, korean, Chinese, russian and French. Products and services include multilingual text translation, document translation, bulk files translation, multilingual email translation, multilingual live chat and forum translation, as well as wireless multilingual translation for text, instant messaging and email. The group's real-time wireless translation services are provided to over 2 million users through the telus mobility(R) wireless Web network. The group acquired a 20% interest in translationwave inc on 19-Apr-2001.

Primary SIC and add'l.: 1099

CIK No: 0000947994

Officers: Casey Forward/Dir., CEO, Ping Shen/CFO, John Kowalchuk/Exploration Mgr., David M. Stone/Consultant

Directors: Casey Forward/Dir., CEO, K. Sachdeva/Dir., Arnold Abramson/Dir., Ian Bartholomew/Dir.

Owners: Insiders, YOUNG.JT/TEN, JOAO LUIS PULGATTI & JOHN/12.80%

Financial Data: ***Fiscal Year End:***09/30 ***Latest Annual Data:*** 9/30/2006

Year	Sales	Net Income
2006	NA	-$480,000
2004	NA	-$5,751,000
2003	NA	-$35,000

Curr. Assets: $4,000 **Curr. Liab.:** $584,000
Plant, Equip.: $1,000 **Total Liab.:** $584,000 **Indic. Yr. Divd.:** NA
Total Assets: $5,000 **Net Worth:** -$579,000 **Debt/ Equity:** NA

GlobeTel Communications Corp

101 NE 3rd Ave., Ste. 1500, Fort Lauderdale, FL, 33301; ***PH:*** 1-954-332-3752; ***Fax:*** 1-954-332-3738; ***http://*** www.globetel.net; ***Email:*** info@globetel.net

General - Incorporation .... DE
Employees .... NA
Auditor .... Dohan & Co
Stk Agt .... American Stock Transfer & Trust Co.
Counsel .... NA
DUNS No. 92-725-6586

Stock- Price on:12/24/2007 .... $0.242
Stock Exchange .... OTC
Ticker Symbol .... GTEL
Outstanding Shares .... NA
E.P.S. .... NA
Shareholders .... NA

Business: The group's principal activity is to provide telecommunication services, involving Internet telephony using voice over Internet protocol technology and equipment. The group offers to its customers a full portfolio of telecommunications services including: international voice, data service, international prepaid calling services, enhanced service platform, international subscription programs for international calling. It has virtual networks serving callers in venezuela, Australia, China, Brazil, Philippines and Malaysia.

Primary SIC and add'l.: 4899

CIK No: 0000919742

Subsidiaries: Centerline Communications, LLC, EQ8, LLC, G Link Solutions, LLC, Lonestar Communications LLC, Sanswire Networks, LLC, Volta Communications, LLC

Officers: Jonathan D. Leinwand/Dir., CEO, Robert Bleckman/Dir. - Investor Relations

Directors: Jonathan D. Leinwand/Dir., CEO, Przemyslaw L. Kostro/Chmn.

Owners: Jonathan Leinwand/1.10%, Przemyslaw L. Kostro/7.25%, Insiders/9.35%

GlobeTrac Inc

29 Abingson Rd., Kensington, London, W8 6AH; ***PH:*** 800-648-4287; ***http://*** www.globetrac.com

General - Incorporation .... DE
Employees .... NA
Auditor .... Mendoza Berger & Co., LLP
Stk Agt .... NA
Counsel .... Stepp Law Group Plc
DUNS No. .... NA

Stock- Price on:12/24/2007 .... $0.01
Stock Exchange .... OTC
Ticker Symbol .... GBTR
Outstanding Shares .... NA
E.P.S. .... NA
Shareholders .... NA

Business: The group's principal activities are to sell, market, distribute and install global wireless tracking and telematics equipment. Commercial markets include fleets, couriers, security firms, transportation industry and utilities. The group offers to its clients an end-to-end platform of wireless and mobile services using a Global System for Mobile communications/ General Packet Radio Service ("GSM/GPRS") network that provides commercial fleets with affordable vehicle tracking, communications and telematics services delivered over the Internet. The software can instantly track and locate the clients' vehicles.

Primary SIC and add'l.: 3812 4822 7375

CIK No: 0001143238

Subsidiaries: Global Axxess, GlobeTrac Limited

Officers: John Dacosta/CEO, CFO, Pres., Treasurer, Corp. Sec.

Directors: David Patriquin/65/Dir.

Owners: Insiders/20.40%, Gregory M. Pek/18.10%, Jim Pratt/15.80%, David Patriquin/4.60%

Financial Data: ***Fiscal Year End:***12/31 ***Latest Annual Data:*** 12/31/2006

Year	Sales	Net Income
2006	$135,000	-$186,000
2005	$124,000	-$161,000
2004	$25,000	-$1,364,000

Curr. Assets: $90,000 **Curr. Liab.:** $3,191,000
Plant, Equip.: NA **Total Liab.:** $3,191,000 **Indic. Yr. Divd.:** NA
Total Assets: $90,000 **Net Worth:** -$3,102,000 **Debt/ Equity:** NA

Globix Corp

2200 W Pk. Dr., Westborough, MA, 01581; ***PH:*** 1-508-616-7800; ***http://*** www.globix.com

General - Incorporation	DE	**Stock**- Price on:12/24/2007	$42.4
Employees	330	Stock Exchange	OTC
Auditor	Amper, Politziner & Mattia P.C	Ticker Symbol	GBIXQ
Stk Agt	Mellon Investor Services LLC	Outstanding Shares	NA
Counsel	NA	E.P.S	NA
DUNS No.	88-440-1845	Shareholders	NA

Business: The group's principal activity is to provide Internet solutions to businesses. The solutions include secure and fault-tolerant Internet data centers, premium network services, complex Internet based managed and applications services. Premium network services include providing of high performance network connectivity to the Internet. The Internet based services include dedicated hosting, streaming media, content delivery services and messaging services. The group provides its solutions to various industries such as media and publishing, financial services, retail, healthcare and technology. The group operates in Europe and the United States. On 31-Oct-2003 the group acquired aptegrity inc.

Primary SIC and add'l.: 7374 7373 7372 7375

CIK No: 0001003111

Subsidiaries: 415 Greenwich GC Tenant LLC, 415 Greenwich GC, LLC, 415 Greenwich MM LLC, ATC Merger Corp., BLP Acquisition LLC, Globix (Netherlands) BV, Globix AB, Globix Denmark ApS, Globix GmbH, Globix Holdings (UK) Limited, Globix Internet Services GmbH, Globix Limited, GLX Leasing Limited, NEON Communications, Inc., NEON Connect, Inc. 20 Subsidiaries included in the Index

Officers: Kurt J. Van Wagenen/CEO, Pres., Eric J. Sandman/42/Sr. VP, CFO, Gene M. Bauer/Sr. VP, General Counsel, Sec., Patrick J. Coughlin/VP - Sales, Marketing, Russell E. Schomber/VP - Engineering, James J. Capuano/VP - Operations, John P. Stack/VP - Finance, Corporate Controller

Directors: Ted S. Lodge/Chmn., Jose A. Cecin/44/Dir., John H. Forsgren/61/Dir., Peter L. Herzig/45/Dir., Steven G. Lampe/48/Dir., Steven G. Singer/46/Dir., Raymond L. Steele/72/Dir.

Owners: John H. Forsgren, Ted S. Lodge, Singer Children Management Trust, John P. Stack, LC Capital Master Fund Ltd., Loeb Partners Corporation, Gene M. Bauer, Steven G. Lampe, Insiders, MacKay Shields LLC, Greywolf Capital Management L.P., Jos A. Cecin, JGD Management Corp., RCN Corporation, Steven G. Singer *(17 Owners included in Index)*

Globus International Resources Corp

80 Wall St., Ste. 518, New York, NY, 10005; ***PH:*** 1-212-558-6100; ***Fax:*** 1-212-558-6060; ***http://*** www.globuscorp.com; ***Email:*** globus@globuscorp.com

General - Incorporation	NV	**Stock**- Price on:12/24/2007	$0.005
Employees	NA	Stock Exchange	OTC
Auditor	Arthur Yorkes & Co	Ticker Symbol	GBIR
Stk Agt	Continental Stock Transfer & Trust Co	Outstanding Shares	NA
Counsel	NA	E.P.S	NA
DUNS No.	NA	Shareholders	NA

Business: The group's principle activities include distributing and exporting dairy and meat products, seafood, instant soups, deli products and non-food products such as auto parts and clothing. The group operates from United States.

Primary SIC and add'l.: 5141

CIK No: 0001033114

Subsidiaries: Globus Cold Storage Corp, Shuttle International

Officers: Yuri Greene/66/Co - CEO, Herman Roth/Co - CEO

Directors: Yuri Greene/66/Co - CEO, Herman Roth/Co - CEO, Serge Pisman/42/Dir.

Owners: Yury Greene/15.10%, Serge Pisman/13.30%, Insiders/43.50%, Herman Roth/15.10%, Atlantic Investment Aps./22.90%

Financial Data: ***Fiscal Year End:***09/30 ***Latest Annual Data:*** 9/30/2003

Year	Sales	Net Income
2003	$6,803,000	-$1,939,000
2002	$11,790,000	$131,000
2001	$9,010,000	$7,000

Curr. Assets:	$1,405,000	**Curr. Liab.:**	$2,973,000		
Plant, Equip.:	$319,000	**Total Liab.:**	$3,983,000	**Indic. Yr. Divd.:**	NA
Total Assets:	$1,906,000	**Net Worth:**	-$2,077,000	**Debt/ Equity:**	NA

GlowPoint Inc

225 Long Ave., Hillside, NJ, 07205; ***PH:*** 1-973-282-2000; ***Fax:*** 1-973-391-1901; ***http://*** www.glowpoint.com; ***Email:*** info@glowpoint.com

General - Incorporation	DE	**Stock**- Price on:12/24/2007	$0.65
Employees	59	Stock Exchange	OTC
Auditor	Eisner LLP	Ticker Symbol	GLOW
Stk Agt	American Stock Transfer & Trust Co.	Outstanding Shares	47,210,000
Counsel	David W. Robinson	E.P.S	-$0.16
DUNS No.	NA	Shareholders	NA

Business: The group's principal activities are to provide single source of video communication solutions that encompass the entire video communications value chain. The group is into the business of selling, installing and servicing video, audio systems, data products and voice communication systems to commercial and institutional customers located principally within the United States. The group integrates major video communications equipment manufacturers, including the picturetel corporation and polycom inc. The group also operates glowpoint network service, which provides customers with two-way video communications and services. The customer base of the group includes over 3,000 companies with approximately 22,000 videoconferencing endpoints. On Sept 23, 2003, the group sold substantially all of the assets of our video solutions business.

Primary SIC and add'l.: 5065 4899 3661 3669

CIK No: 0000746210

Subsidiaries: AllComm Products Corporation, Glowpoint, Inc., Virtual DSL Communications Corp., VTC Resources, Inc

Officers: Michael Brandofino/Dir., CEO, Pres./$332,248.00, Joseph Laezza/COO/$325,671.00, Edwin Heinen/CFO, Exec. VP - Finance/$280,925.00, David W. Robinson/Exec. VP, General Counsel/$227,871.00

Directors: Michael Brandofino/Dir., CEO, Pres., Peter Rust/Dir., Dean Hiltzik/Dir., Richard Reiss/Dir., Aziz Ahmad/Dir., Bami Bastani/Dir., James S. Lusk/Dir.

Owners: James Lusk, Richard Reiss/7.70%, Joseph Laezza/1.10%, North Sound Capital LLC/4.90%, Dean Hiltzik, Coghill Capital Management LLC/9.90%, Smithfield Fiduciary LLC/4.90%, Michael Brandofino/2.40%, Insiders/16.70%, Peter Rust, David W. Robinson/1.40%, Bami Bastani, Aziz Ahmad, Edwin F. Heinen/1.70%, David Trachtenberg *(16 Owners included in Index)*

Financial Data: ***Fiscal Year End:***12/31 ***Latest Annual Data:*** 12/31/2006

Year	Sales	Net Income
2006	$19,511,000	-$10,790,000
2004	$15,995,000	-$17,413,000
2003	$10,311,000	-$22,439,000

Curr. Assets:	$5,228,000	**Curr. Liab.:**	$17,096,000		
Plant, Equip.:	$2,762,000	**Total Liab.:**	$17,096,000	**Indic. Yr. Divd.:**	NA
Total Assets:	$8,393,000	**Net Worth:**	-$11,591,000	**Debt/ Equity:**	NA

GlycoGenesys Inc

8th Floor, 31 St. James Ave., Boston, MA, 02116; ***PH:*** 1-617-422-0674; ***Fax:*** 1-617-422-0675; ***http://*** www.glycogenesys.com

General - Incorporation	NV	**Stock**- Price on:12/24/2007	$0.16
Employees	NA	Stock Exchange	NDQ
Auditor	Deloitte & Touche LLP	Ticker Symbol	GLGS
Stk Agt	Computershare Investor Services LLC	Outstanding Shares	NA
Counsel	McDermott Will & Emery	E.P.S	NA
DUNS No.	83-807-1256	Shareholders	NA

Business: The group's principal activities are to develop pharmaceutical products based on carbohydrate compounds and related technologies. The group has developed a drug called gcs-100 aimed at treating multiple forms of cancer. It also develops two agricultural products and continues to seek strategic alternatives, including the sale, of its agricultural product business area. It conducts its business through its three wholly owned subsidiaries, international gene group, inc, safescience products, inc and safescience newco ltd. International gene group, inc. ("Igg") develops human therapeutics. Igg is focused on developing gcs-100, a complex carbohydrate intended to fight cancerous tumors and metastasis. Safescience products develops agriculture products and markets chemically safe consumer and commercial products. The group terminated joint venture with elan international services ltd.

Primary SIC and add'l.: 2836 2834

CIK No: 0000946661

Subsidiaries: International Gene Group, Inc., SafeScience Products, Inc.

Officers: Gary Neumayer/Treasurer, Chief Compliance Officer

GMAC LLC

200 Renaissance Ctr., Detroit, MI, 48265; ***PH:*** 1-313-556-5000; ***Fax:*** 1-815-282-6156; ***http://*** www.gmacfs.com

General - Incorporation	DE	**Stock**- Price on:12/24/2007	$23.23
Employees	31,400	Stock Exchange	NYSE
Auditor	Deloitte & Touche LLP	Ticker Symbol	GJM
Stk Agt	Computershare Investor Services	Outstanding Shares	NA
Counsel	NA	E.P.S	NA
DUNS No.	NA	Shareholders	NA

Business: The groups principal activity is to provide automotive finance services. The group operates through two segments namely, North American automotive finance operations and international automotive finance operations. The group operates from the United States, Canada, Europe, Latin America and Asia Pacific. Of the total assets in the year 2006, the North American automotive finance operations accounted for $127,822 and international automotive finance operations $25,588 (millions).

Primary SIC and add'l.: 6331 6162 6163 6141

CIK No: 0000040729

Subsidiaries: American Suzuki Financial Services Company LLC, Autofinanciamiento GMAC, S.A. de C.V., Banco GMAC S.A., Basic Credit Holding Company, L.L.C., Capital Auto Receivables LLC, Central Originating Lease, LLC, G.M.A.C. Financiera de Colombia S.A. Compania de Financiamiento Comercial, G.M.A.C. Comercio e Aluguer de Veiculos, Lda., Gamma Auto Receivables LLC, General Motors Acceptance Corporation (N.Z.) Limited, General Motors Acceptance Corporation (U.K.) plc, General Motors Acceptance Corporation de Portugal, Instituicao Financiera de Credito, SA, General Motors Acceptance Corporation del Peru S.A., General Motors Acceptance Corporation Hungary Commercial Limited Liability Company, General Motors Acceptance Corporation Italia S.p.A. 96 Subsidiaries included in the Index

Officers: Eric Feldstein/CEO, T. K. Duggan/56/Co - Founder - Managing Principal, Durham Asset Management, Lenard B. Tessler/55/MD - Cerberus, William F. Muir/53/Pres., Sanjiv Khattri/43/CFO, Exec. VP, Bruce J. Paradis/59/Exec. VP - Rescap, Barbara J. Stokel/55/Exec. VP - North American Operations, Mark F. Bole/44/Exec. VP - International Operations, William B. Solomon/54/Group VP, General Counsel, Cherri M. Musser/56/Group VP, CIO, David C. Walker/47/Group VP - Global Borrowings, Linda K. Zukauckas/46/VP, Corporate Controller, Cathy L. Quenneville/48/Corp. Sec.

Directors: Ezra J. Merkin/54/Chmn., Robert W. Scully/57/Dir., T. K. Duggan/56/Co - Founder - Managing Principal, Durham Asset Management, Douglas A. Hirsch/45/Founder, Managing Partner - Seneca Capital, Mark A. Neporent/50/Dir., Frank W. Bruno/42/Dir., Seth P. Plattus/46/Dir., Michael S. Klein/44/Dir., Richard G. Wagoner/54/Dir., Frederick A. Henderson/49/Dir., Mark R. Laneve/48/Dir., Walter G. Borst/46/Dir.

Financial Data: ***Fiscal Year End:***12/31 ***Latest Annual Data:*** 12/31/2006

Year	Sales	Net Income
2006	$35,723,000,000	$2,125,000,000
2005	$33,222,000,000	$2,394,000,000
2004	$30,312,000,000	$2,913,000,000

Curr. Assets:	$19,405,000,000	**Curr. Liab.:**	$16,958,000,000	**P/E Ratio:**	47.71
Plant, Equip.:	$5,284,000,000	**Total Liab.:**	$273,070,000,000	**Indic. Yr. Divd.:**	NA
Total Assets:	$287,439,000,000	**Net Worth:**	$14,369,000,000	**Debt/ Equity:**	NA

Gmarket Inc

LIG Tower 6-8 Fl., 649-11, Yeoksam-Dong, Gangnam-Gu, Seoul, 135912; ***PH:*** 82-2208183676; ***Fax:*** 82-230165452; ***http://*** global.gmarket.co.kr; ***Email:*** global@gmarket.co.kr

General - Incorporation	Republic of Korea	**Stock**- Price on:12/24/2007	$20.93
Employees	374	Stock Exchange	NDQ
Auditor	NA	Ticker Symbol	GMKT
Stk Agt	Citibank N.A	Outstanding Shares	49,510,000
Counsel	NA	E.P.S	$0.57
DUNS No.	NA	Shareholders	NA

Business: The groups principal activity is to provide online auction services. The groups service is retail e-commerce. The group operates from the United States.

Primary SIC and add'l.: 2353 2331 2341 2337 2251 5136 2335 2329 2361 2252 2369 2321 5992 2342 5621 5699 2389 5632 2339 5947 2322 2519 2325 5712 3131 5945 2311 2392 5137 5331 3143 5641 5139 5092 5021 5941 2387 3144 5611 5399 5963 5734 5722 7319 3949 5651 5193 3965 5912 5949 3915 5944 5719 3942 3944 3961 5023 5999 5064 2844 5661 3149 3142 5731 5961 3171 5131 5091 7631

CIK No: 0001365241

Officers: Young Bae Ku/Dir., CEO, Duckjun Lee/CFO, Dae Sik Yang/CTO, Kwang Jin Ryoo/VP - e- Marketing Operations, Paul J. Lee/General Counsel, Chang Sun Jo/Sr. VP - Marketing, Business Development

Directors: Young Bae Ku/Dir., CEO, Ki Hyung Lee/Chmn., Sang Kyu Lee/Dir., John E. Milburn/Dir., Massoud Entekhabi/Dir., Hakkyun Kim/Dir., Joon-Ho Hahm/Dir., Greg Mrva/Dir., Seok-Heon Kim/45/Dir., Dean Geehun Kim/Dir.

Owners: Young Bae Ku/5.50%, Yahoo! Korea Corporation/9.10%, Ki Hyung Lee/7.30%, Insiders/15.20%, Kwang Jin Ryoo, Dae Sik Yang/1.20%, Sang Kyu Lee, Yahoo! Inc/1.00%, Techno Pacific Assets Limited, Interpark Corporation/29.50%

Financial Data: ***Fiscal Year End:*** 12/31 ***Latest Annual Data:*** 12/31/2006

Year	Sales	Net Income
2006	$166,558,000	$17,589,000

Curr. Assets:	$236,302,000	**Curr. Liab.:**	$151,108,000	**P/E Ratio:**	46.72
Plant, Equip.:	$21,161,000	**Total Liab.:**	$152,617,000	**Indic. Yr. Divd.:**	NA
Total Assets:	$268,102,000	**Net Worth:**	$115,485,000	**Debt/ Equity:**	NA

GMH Communities Trust

10 Campus Blvd., Newtown Square, PA, 19073; ***PH:*** 1-610-355-8000; ***Fax:*** 1-610-355-8001; ***http://*** www.gmhcommunities.com

General - Incorporation	MD	***Stock*** - Price on:12/24/2007	$10.13
Employees	1,103	Stock Exchange	NYSE
Auditor	Ernst & Young LLP	Ticker Symbol	GCT
Stk Agt	Computershare Trust Co	Outstanding Shares	41,570,000
Counsel	NA	E.P.S.	$0.66
DUNS No.	NA	Shareholders	NA

Business: The groups principle activities include owning, developing, constructing and operating student-housing properties. The group also provides consulting services. The group operates through three segments namely, student housing owned properties, student housing management and military housing. In the year 2006, the group acquired 21 properties. The group operates from the United States. The group's quarterly revenue for September 2007 was 78.97 millions of USD.

Primary SIC and add'l.: 6798

CIK No: 0001293200

Subsidiaries: 12thStreet Associates Intermediate, LLC, 12thStreet Associates, LLC, 3175 JFK Associates, LP, 353 Associates, 353 Associates GP, LLC, Abbott Road Associates Intermediate, LLC, Abbott Road Associates, LLC, AETC Housing LP, Alexander Road Associates Intermediate, LLC, Alexander Road Associates, LLC, Belle Chase Associates Intermediate II, LLC, Belle Chase Associates Intermediate, LLC, Belle Chase Associates, LLC, Bethel Avenue Associates Intermediate, LLC, Bethel Avenue Associates, LLC 217 Subsidiaries included in the Index

Officers: Gary M. Holloway/Chmn., CEO, Pres., Bruce F. Robinson/Trustee, Pres. - GMH Military Housing, John Deriggi/Pres. - College Park Communities, Chief Investment Officer, Joseph M. MacChione/Exec. VP, General Counsel, Sec., Patrick J. O' Grady/CFO, Exec. VP, Marina Dikos/VP, Chief Accounting Officer, Joe Calabrese/Financial Relations Board, Investor Relations Contact

Directors: Gary M. Holloway/Chmn., CEO, Pres., Bruce F. Robinson/Trustee, Pres. - GMH Military Housing, Frederick F. Buchholz/Trustee, James W. Eastwood/Trustee, Michael D. Fascitelli/Trustee, Steven J. Kessler/Trustee, Denis Nayden/Trustee, Dennis J. O'Leary/Trustee, Richard A. Silfen/Trustee

Owners: James W. Eastwood, Bruce F. Robinson/2.40%, Denis J. Nayden, FMR Corp./15.00%, Heitman Real Estate Securities LLC/11.50%, Gary M. Holloway/20.00%, The Vanguard Group,Inc./6.10%, Joseph M. Macchione, John DeRiggi, JP Morgan Chase& Co./6.10%, Franklin Resources,Inc./7.10%, Cohen& Steers/11.20%, Michael D. Fascitelli, Insiders/31.10%, Vornado Realty Trust/20.20% *(20 Owners included in Index)*

Financial Data: ***Fiscal Year End:*** 12/31 ***Latest Annual Data:*** 12/31/2006

Year	Sales	Net Income
2006	$293,131,000	-$4,986,000
2005	$224,152,000	$6,059,000
2004	$83,878,000	-$37,002,000

Curr. Assets:	$59,387,000	**Curr. Liab.:**	$42,547,000	**P/E Ratio:**	47.71
Plant, Equip.:	$1,600,992,000	**Total Liab.:**	$1,456,690,000	**Indic. Yr. Divd.:**	$0.660
Total Assets:	$1,713,990,000	**Net Worth:**	$257,300,000	**Debt/ Equity:**	NA

GMX Resources Inc

9400 N Broadway, Ste. 600, Oklahoma City, OK, 73114; ***PH:*** 1-405-600-0711; ***Fax:*** 1-405-600-0600; ***http://*** www.gmxresources.com

General - Incorporation	OK	***Stock*** - Price on:12/24/2007	$37.58
Employees	99	Stock Exchange	NDQ
Auditor	Smith, Carney & Co., P.c.	Ticker Symbol	GMXR
Stk Agt	UMB Bank, N.A.	Outstanding Shares	13,270,000
Counsel	NA	E.P.S.	$0.79
DUNS No.	NA	Shareholders	NA

Business: The group's principal activities are to acquire, explore and develop properties for the production of crude oil and natural gas. The operations are conducted in oklahama, Kansas, Louisiana, New Mexico and Texas. Natural gas customers include marketing affiliates of the major pipeline companies, natural gas marketing companies, and a variety of commercial and public authorities, industrial, and institutional end-users that ultimately consume the gas.

Primary SIC and add'l.: 1381

CIK No: 0001127342

Subsidiaries: Diamond Blue Drilling Co., Endeavor Pipeline, Inc.

Officers: Ken L. Kenworthy/Dir., CEO, Pres., Ken L. Kenworthy/Dir., CFO, Exec. VP, James Merrill/Controller - Accounting Department, Amber Croisant/Office Mgr., Administrator - Revenue Distribution, Payroll, Accounting Department, Charles Pope/Engineer - Drilling, Completions Mgr. - Production, Engineering Department, Wayne Smith/Petroleum Engineer - Production, Engineering Department, Tracie Billings/Operations Assist. - Production, Engineering Department, Brett Stephens/Operations Analyst - Production, Engineering Department, Dianne Newman/Operations Assist. - Production, Engineering Department, Stephanie Estel/Production Analyst, Production, Engineering Department, Marilyn Leonard/Geology Technician, Technical Department, Bill Welch/Data Base Analyst, Technical Department, Keith Leffel/VP - Gas Marketing, April Mitchell/General Office Clerk, Stephanie Mullin/Accounts Payable, Accounting Department *(27 Officers included in Index)*

Directors: Ken L. Kenworthy/Dir., CEO, Pres., Jon W. McHugh/Dir., T. J. Boismier/Dir., Steven Craig/Dir., Ken L. Kenworthy/Dir., CFO, Exec. VP

Owners: Ken L. Kenworthy/6.20%, T. J. Boismier, Karen Kenworthy/5.20%, Investment Management, Inc/5.96%, Insiders/13.10%, Steven Craig, Centennial Energy Partners, L.L.C.,/17.18%, Jon W. McHugh, Newton Family Group/6.78%, Ken L. Kenworthy/6.50%, Gary D. Jackson

Financial Data: ***Fiscal Year End:*** 12/31 ***Latest Annual Data:*** 12/31/2006

Year	Sales	Net Income
2006	$32,033,000	$8,975,000
2005	$19,193,000	$7,156,000
2004	$7,834,000	$1,442,000

Curr. Assets:	$13,624,000	**Curr. Liab.:**	$28,974,000	**P/E Ratio:**	56.94
Plant, Equip.:	$196,656,000	**Total Liab.:**	$78,842,000	**Indic. Yr. Divd.:**	NA
Total Assets:	$210,323,000	**Net Worth:**	$131,481,000	**Debt/ Equity:**	0.0709

GoAmerica Inc

433 Hackensack Ave., 3rd Fl., Hackensack, NJ, 07601; ***PH:*** 1-201-996-1717; ***Fax:*** 1-201-996-1772; ***http://*** www.goamerica.com; ***Email:*** investors@goamerica.com

General - Incorporation	DE	***Stock*** - Price on:12/24/2007	$5.46
Employees	34	Stock Exchange	NDQ
Auditor	WithumSmith & Brown, P.C	Ticker Symbol	GOAM
Stk Agt	American Stock Transfer & Trust Co.	Outstanding Shares	2,460,000
Counsel	Hale & Dorr LLP	E.P.S.	-$1.104
DUNS No.	NA	Shareholders	NA

Business: The group's principal activity is to develop and distribute wireless data technology, applications and software. The solutions address the productivity and communications needs of enterprise customers and consumers. The group's proprietary technology called go.Web(tm) allows customers to open, edit, fax and forward email attachments; remotely access and manage documents, send instant messages and queue requests when a device is outside of a wireless service area. Its wireless data solutions are designed for people who are deaf, hard of hearing or speech impaired. The group also distributes wireless communication devices to the customers of its wireless services and procures subscribers on behalf of various wireless network providers and earthlink inc.

Primary SIC and add'l.: 4822 4899

CIK No: 0001101268

Subsidiaries: GoAmerica Communications Corp., GoAmerica Marketing, Inc., HOSLS Acquisition Corporation, Hotpaper.com, Inc., HOVRS Acquisition Corporation, OutBack Resource Group, Inc., Wynd Communications Corporation

Officers: Dan Luis/CEO, Rick Personette/VP - Sales, Mark Stern/VP - Product Management, Accessible Communication Services, Jesse Odom/CTO, Joe Karp/VP - Marketing, Donald Barnhart/CFO

Directors: Sue Decker/Dir., Janice Dehesh/Dir.

Owners: Insiders/18.00%, Aaron Dobrinsky/2.40%, Wayne D. Smith/2.40%, Sue D. Decker, Joseph Korb/1.30%, David Lyons, King Lee/1.00%, Daniel R. Luis/4.00%, Janice Dehesh, Jesse Odom/2.70%, Donald Barnhart/2.60%

Financial Data: ***Fiscal Year End:*** 12/31 ***Latest Annual Data:*** 12/31/2006

Year	Sales	Net Income
2006	$12,776,000	-$1,960,000
2005	$8,078,000	-$4,372,000
2004	$6,222,000	-$4,444,000

Curr. Assets:	$6,323,000	**Curr. Liab.:**	$2,706,000		
Plant, Equip.:	$755,000	**Total Liab.:**	$2,818,000	**Indic. Yr. Divd.:**	NA
Total Assets:	$13,879,000	**Net Worth:**	$11,061,000	**Debt/ Equity:**	NA

GoFish Corp

500 3rd St., Ste. 260, San Francisco, CA, 94107; ***PH:*** 1-415-738-8705; ***Fax:*** 1-415-738-8834; ***http://*** www.gofish.com

General - Incorporation		***Stock*** - Price on:12/24/2007	$1.04
Employees	22	Stock Exchange	OTC
Auditor	Rowbotham & Co. LLP	Ticker Symbol	GOFH
Stk Agt	NA	Outstanding Shares	24,130,000
Counsel	NA	E.P.S.	-$0.8
DUNS No.	NA	Shareholders	NA

Business: The groups principal activities include programming and operating a platform, which provides original short-form and programmed user-generated video content. The services of the group include video community, custom channels and branded programming. The group operates from Canada.

Primary SIC and add'l.: 2741

CIK No: 0001349274

Officers: Michael Downing/Co - Founder, Chmn., CEO, Tabreez Verjee/Pres., Nate Wright/Investor Relation - Marketing Street Partners, Joann Horne/Invester Relation, Marketing Street Partner, C. J. Bowden/VP - Branded Entertainment - Program Development, Sales , Lori Maclas/VP - Program Development, Marketing, David Fisch/VP - Branded Entertainment - Program Development, Product Management, Lennox Vernon/Chief Accounting Officer & Dir. - Operations

Directors: Michael Downing/Co - Founder, Chmn., CEO, Peter Guber/Dir., Riaz Valani/Dir.

Owners: Michael Downing/6.80%, Peter Guber, Riaz Valani/18.40%, Tabreez Verjee/18.00%, Insiders/25.50%

Financial Data: ***Fiscal Year End:*** 12/31 ***Latest Annual Data:*** 12/31/2006

Year	Sales	Net Income
2006	$26,000	-$5,312,000

Curr. Assets:	$5,332,000	**Curr. Liab.:**	$954,000		
Plant, Equip.:	$157,000	**Total Liab.:**	$954,000	**Indic. Yr. Divd.:**	NA
Total Assets:	$5,499,000	**Net Worth:**	$4,545,000	**Debt/ Equity:**	NA

Gol Intelligent Airlines Inc

Rua Tamoios 246, Jardim Aeroporto, Sao Paulo, 4630000; *PH:* 55-1150334226;
http:// www.voegol.com.br

General - Incorporation	Brazil	Stock- Price on:12/24/2007	NA
Employees	NA	Stock Exchange	NA
Auditor	Ernst & Young LLP	Ticker Symbol	NA
Stk Agt.	NA	Outstanding Shares	NA
Counsel.	NA	E.P.S	NA
DUNS No.	NA	Shareholders	NA

Business: The groups principle activity is to provide low fare airline services. The group provides airline services in South American countries. The group operates from Brazil, Argentina, Chile, Peru, Paraguay and Uruguay.

Primary SIC and add'l.: NA

CIK No: 0001291733

Subsidiaries: Gol, GOL Finance LLP, GOL Transportes Areos S.A

Officers: Constantino De Oliveira/Chmn., CEO, Pres., Constantino De Oliveira/CEO, Pres., David Barioni Neto/49/Exec. VP - Technical, Fernando Rockert De Magalhaes/VP - Technical, Richard F. Lark/CFO, VP - Finance, Investor Relations Officer, Tarcisio Geraldo Gargioni/61/VP - Marketing, Services, Wilson Maciel Ramos/VP - Planning, Administration

Directors: Constantino De Oliveira/Chmn., CEO, Pres., Henrique Constantino/Dir., Alvaro De Souza/Dir., Antonio Kandir/Dir., Ricardo Constantino/Dir., Joaquim Constantino Neto/Dir., Luiz Kaufmann/Dir.

Owners: Insiders/3.04%, Fundo de Investimento em Participaes Asas/35.79%, Fundo de Investimento em Participaes Asas/100.00%, Insiders

Gol Linhas Aereas Inteligentes S.A.

Rua Gomes de Carvalho, 1629 Vila Olmpia, So Paulo, Rio de Janeiro; ; *http://* www.voegol.com.br;
Email: contactus@golnaweb.com.br

General - Incorporation		Stock- Price on:12/24/2007	$34.07
Employees	8,840	Stock Exchange	NYSE
Auditor	NA	Ticker Symbol	GOL
Stk Agt.	Bank of New York	Outstanding Shares	196,210,000
Counsel.	NA	E.P.S	$1.40
DUNS No.	NA	Shareholders	NA

Business: The groups principle activity is to provide airline services. The group operates from Brazil, Argentina, Bolivia, Chile, Paraguay and Uruguay. The groups quarterly revenue for September 2007 was 1,303.54 millions of USD.

Primary SIC and add'l.: 4512 4513

CIK No:

Officers: Constantino De Oliveira/38/Dir., CEO, Pres., Richard F. Lark/VP - Finance, CFO, Investor Relations Officer, Tarcisio Geraldo Gargioni/VP - Marketing, Services, Wilson Maciel Ramos/VP - Planning, Administration, Fernando Rockert De Magalhaes/VP - Technical

Directors: Constantino De Oliveira/38/Dir., CEO, Pres., Constantino De Oliveira/Chmn., Henrique Constantino/Dir., Joaquim Constantino Neto/Dir., Ricardo Constantino/Dir., Alvaro De Souza/Dir., Antonio Kandir/Dir., Luiz Kaufmann/Dir.

Financial Data: Fiscal Year End:NA *Latest Annual Data:* 12/31/2006

Year		Sales		Net Income
2006		$1,778,305,000		$266,200,000
2005		$1,140,296,000		$219,263,000
2004		$738,730,000		$144,933,000
Curr. Assets:	$1,314,932,000	Curr. Liab.:	$467,888,000	P/E Ratio: 24.69
Plant, Equip.	$504,781,000	Total Liab.:	$960,382,000	Indic. Yr. Divd.: $0.490
Total Assets:	$1,991,793,000	Net Worth:	$1,031,411,000	Debt/ Equity: 0.0132

Golar LNG Ltd

Par La Ville Pl., Fourth Fl., 14 Par La Ville Rd., Hamilton; ; *http://* www.golargas.com;
Email: golarlng@golar.com

General - Incorporation	Bermuda	Stock- Price on:12/24/2007	$17.01
Employees	585	Stock Exchange	NDQ
Auditor	PricewaterhouseCoopers LLP	Ticker Symbol	GLNG
Stk Agt.	NA	Outstanding Shares	65,560,000
Counsel.	NA	E.P.S	$1.49
DUNS No.	NA	Shareholders	NA

Business: The group's principle activity is transportation of gas and other bulk cargo. The company owns and operates a fleet of six lng carriers. The company plans to expand and diversify its lng shipping operations. The company has integrated into other lng activities such as liquefaction and regasification, also has entered into construction contracts for four lng carries to be delivered in 2003 and 2004. The year 2001 marked the first full year of operation for the two newcomers in the Atlantic basin lng trade, nigeria lng and Atlantic lng in trinidad. The year under review also marked the the first time lng from the Middle East was sold on a long term contract to Europe or the usa.

Primary SIC and add'l.: 4412

CIK No: 0001207179

Subsidiaries: Aurora Management Inc., Faraway Maritime Shipping Inc., Golar 2215 (UK) Limited, Golar 2226 (UK) Limited, Golar Freeze (UK) Limited, Golar FSRU 1 Corporation, Golar Gas Holding Company Inc., Golar Gimi (UK) Limited, Golar Hilli (UK) Limited, Golar International Ltd., Golar Khannur (UK) Limited, Golar LNG 1444 Corporation, Golar LNG 1460 Corporation, Golar LNG 2215 Corporation, Golar LNG 2220 Corporation 27 Subsidiaries included in the Index

Officers: Gary Smith/CEO - Golar Managment, UK Ltd, John Fredriksen/Chmn., Pres., Graeme McDonald/Group Techanical Dir. - Golar Managment, UK Ltd, Tor Olav Troim/Vice Presidant, Dir., Georgina Sousa/Dir., Company Sec., Charlie Peile/Exec. Vice Presidant, Head - Commercial, Golar Managment, UK Ltd, Ian Walker/Commercial Mgr. - Golar Managment, UK Ltd, Graham Robjohns/CFO - Golar Managment, UK Ltd, Brian Tienzo/Finance Mgr. - Golar Managment, UK Ltd, Hugo Skar/Preoject Mgr. - Golar Managment, UK Ltd, Jan Flatseth/GM, Tom Christiansen/Fleet Mgr.

Directors: John Fredriksen/Chmn., Pres., Tor Olav Troim/Vice Presidant, Dir., Kate Blankenship/Dir., Frixos Savvides/Dir., Georgina Sousa/Dir., Company Sec.

Owners: Insiders/48.18%, World Shipholding Ltd./47.65%

Financial Data: Fiscal Year End:12/31 *Latest Annual Data:* 12/31/2005

Year		Sales		Net Income
2005		$171,042,000		$34,529,000
2004		$163,410,000		$55,833,000
2003		$132,765,000		$39,570,000
Curr. Assets:	$132,332,000	Curr. Liab.:	$128,357,000	
Plant, Equip.:	$1,515,538,000	Total Liab.:	$2,059,145,000	Indic. Yr. Divd.: $2.000
Total Assets:	$2,566,189,000	Net Worth:	$507,044,000	Debt/ Equity: NA

Gold Banc Corp Inc

11301 Nall Ave, Leawood, KS, 66211; *PH:* 1-913-451-8050; *http://* www.goldbanc.com

General - Incorporation	KS	Stock- Price on:12/24/2007	NA
Employees	NA	Stock Exchange	NA
Auditor	KPMG LLP	Ticker Symbol	NA
Stk Agt	American Stock Transfer & Trust Co.	Outstanding Shares	NA
Counsel.	Stinson, Mag & Fizzell	E.P.S	NA
DUNS No.	92-819-6740	Shareholders	NA

Business: The group's principal activity is to provide community banking and related financial services. It is a financial holding company and conducts activities through its subsidiaries, gold bank-Kansas, gold bank-Oklahoma and gold bank-Florida. As of 31, dec 2003, the group operates with 40 offices in 21 communities in Kansas, Missouri, Oklahoma and Florida. The non-bank financial services provided by the group are securities brokerage, investment management, trust, insurance agency, investment advisory, title insurance services, and merchant banking services.

Primary SIC and add'l.: 6021 6712

CIK No: 0001015610

Subsidiaries: Central Oklahoma Leasing Authority, Inc., GBC Kansas, Inc., GBS Holding Company, LLC, Gold Banc Acquisition Corporation VIII, Inc., Gold Banc Acquisition Corporation X, Inc., Gold Banc Mortgage, Inc., Gold Banc Trust III, Gold Bank, Gold Bank Capital Trust V, Gold Bank Trust IV, Gold Capital Management, Inc, Gold Financial Services, Inc., Gold IHC-I, LLC, Gold Insurance Agency, Inc., Gold Investment Advisors, Inc. 23 Subsidiaries included in the Index

Gold Fields Ltd

24 St. Andrews Rd., Parktown, Johannesburg, 02193; *PH:* 1-27-11-644-2525;
http:// www.goldfields.co.za/company_executive_committee.asp?navDisplay=Company;
Email: cain.farrel@goldfields.co.za

General - Incorporation	South Africa	Stock- Price on:12/24/2007	$16.48
Employees	46,663	Stock Exchange	NYSE
Auditor	PricewaterhouseCoopers LLP	Ticker Symbol	GFI
Stk Agt.	Bank of New York	Outstanding Shares	650,410,000
Counsel.	Paul C Pretorius	E.P.S	$0.58
DUNS No.	NA	Shareholders	NA

Business: The group's principal activity is the production of precious metals with mining operations conducted in Australia, ghana and South Africa. In addition, exploration for gold and other precious metals is conducted worldwide. On 30-Oct-2002, the group disposed st helena mine.

Primary SIC and add'l.: 1041

CIK No: 0001172724

Subsidiaries: Abosso Goldfields Limited, Driefontein Consolidated (Proprietary) Limited, GFI Mining South Africa (Proprietary) Ltd, Gold Fields Ghana Limited, St. Ives Gold Mining Company Pty Ltd., The Ghana Chamber of Mines

Officers: Ian D. Cockerill/54/Dir., CEO, Terence P. Goodlace/49/Exec. VP, Head - South African Operations, Wiillie Jan Jacobsz/47/Sr. VP - North American Investor Relations, Sustainable Development, Jimmy Wd Dowsley/50/Sr. VP - Corporate Development, John A. Munro/40/Exec. VP, Head - Corporate Development, Nerina Bodasing/33/Sr. VP, Head - Investor Relations, Corporate Affairs, Italia Boninelli/52/Sr. VP, Head - Human Resources, Michael D. Fleischer/47/General Counsel, James J. Komadina/51/Sr. VP - Development Projects, Francie Whitley/Investor Relations Officer, Themba J. Nkosi/57/Sr. VP - Human Resources, Transformation, Rosemary Noge/Mgr. - Sustainable Development, Jolene Pienaar/Bursaries Officer, Glenn R. Baldwin/36/Exec. VP, Head - International Operations, Cain Farrel/58/Corp. Sec. (16 Officers included in Index)

Directors: Ian D. Cockerill/54/Dir., CEO, Alan J. Wright/67/Chmn., Chris I. Von Christierson/60/Dir., Donald M J Ncube/61/Dir., Gill Marcus/59/Dir., Tokyo Mg Sexwale/55/Dir., Nicholas J. Holland/49/Dir., CFO, Michael J. McMahon/61/Dir., Wiillie Jan Jacobsz/47/Sr. VP - North American Investor Relations, Sustainable Development, Rupert L. Pennant-Rea/60/Dir., Patrick J. Ryan/71/Dir., Kofi D. Ansah/Dir., Artem Grigorian/51/Dir., John G. Hopwood/60/Dir.

Owners: U.S. Retail ADR& Brokerage/6.72%, Capital Research& Management Company/7.41%, BlackRock Investment Management/8.40%, Public Investment Commissioner/5.04%

Financial Data: Fiscal Year End:06/30 *Latest Annual Data:* 6/30/2006

Year		Sales		Net Income
2006		$2,282,000,000		$138,500,000
2005		$1,893,100,000		-$206,200,000
2004		$1,727,300,000		$48,900,000
Curr. Assets:	$555,800,000	Curr. Liab.:	$376,800,000	
Plant, Equip.:	$3,018,500,000	Total Liab.:	$1,990,300,000	Indic. Yr. Divd.: $0.250
Total Assets:	$3,971,200,000	Net Worth:	$1,855,800,000	Debt/ Equity: NA

Gold Hill Corp

2233 W Lindsey, Ste. 117, Norman, OK, 73069; *PH:* 1-405-329-0930

General - Incorporation	CO	Stock- Price on:12/24/2007	NA
Employees	NA	Stock Exchange	OTC
Auditor	Ron Kirkpatrick	Ticker Symbol	GOHL
Stk Agt.	Corporate Stock Transfer, Inc.	Outstanding Shares	NA
Counsel.	NA	E.P.S	NA
DUNS No.	NA	Shareholders	NA

Business: The group's principle activity is to operate oil and gas exploration properties. During the year, the group has abandoned all of its mining claims and leases due to failure to discover economic amounts of gold to the depths drilled. The group is a development stage group and the management plans to obtain operating capital through joint ventures, geological consulting services and private placements of restricted stock. The group operates from United States.

Primary SIC and add'l.: 1381

CIK No: 0000774491

Officers: Susan Nash/Sec., Treasurer, T. J. Simek/Dir., VP, Earl W. Smith/Dir., Pres.

Directors: Paul W. Smith/Dir., T. J. Simek/Dir., VP, Earl W. Smith/Dir., Pres.

Gold Kist Inc

244 Perimeter Ctr Pkwy Ne, Atlanta, GA, 30346; *PH:* 1-404-393-5000; *http://* www.goldkist.com

General - Incorporation	GA	**Stock**- Price on:12/24/2007	NA
Employees	16,800	Stock Exchange	NA
Auditor	KPMG Peat Marwick	Ticker Symbol	NA
Stk Agt	SunTrust Bank	Outstanding Shares	NA
Counsel	NA	E.P.S	NA
DUNS No.	NA	Shareholders	NA

Business: The group's principle activity is to provide chicken food services. The group operates from United States.

Primary SIC and add'l.: 2015

CIK No: 0000215994

Gold Reserve Inc

926 W Sprague Ave., Ste. 200, Spokane, WA, 99201; *PH:* 1-509-623-1500; *Fax:* 1-509-623-1634; *http://* www.goldreserveinc.com; *Email:* info@goldreserveinc.com

General - Incorporation	Canada	**Stock**- Price on:12/24/2007	$5.59
Employees	65	Stock Exchange	AMEX
Auditor	PricewaterhouseCoopers LLP	Ticker Symbol	GRZ
Stk Agt	Computershare Trust Co	Outstanding Shares	41,870,000
Counsel	Fasken Martineau Baker & McKenzie	E.P.S	-$0.31
DUNS No.	NA	Shareholders	NA

Business: The group's principle activities include acquiring, exploring gold and copper mining properties. The group operates from United States.

Primary SIC and add'l.: 1041 6719 1021

CIK No: 0001072725

Subsidiaries: Gold Reserve Corporation, Great Basin Energies, MGC Ventures Inc.

Officers: Rockne J. Timm/Dir., CEO, Robert A. McGuinness/VP - Finance, CFO, Douglas A. Belanger/Dir., Pres., Mary E. Smith/VP - Administration, Sec., Arturo Rivero/Pres. - Gold Reserve de Venezuela, James P. Geyer/Dir., Sr. VP, Douglas E. Stewart/VP - Project Development

Directors: Rockne J. Timm/Dir., CEO, James H. Coleman/Chmn., Patrick D. McChesney/Dir., James P. Geyer/Dir., Sr. VP, Chris D. Mikkelsen/Dir., Jean Charles Potvin/Dir., Douglas A. Belanger/Dir., Pres.

Financial Data: **Fiscal Year End:**12/31 **Latest Annual Data:** 12/31/2006

Year	Sales	Net Income
2006	$8,252,000	-$6,977,000
2005	$1,403,000	-$5,878,000
2004	$900,000	-$10,360,000

Curr. Assets:	$31,534,000	**Curr. Liab.:**	$2,223,000		
Plant, Equip.:	$32,610,000	**Total Liab.:**	$2,223,000	**Indic. Yr. Divd.:**	NA
Total Assets:	$65,916,000	**Net Worth:**	$61,963,000	**Debt/ Equity:**	NA

Gold Resource Corp

222 Milwaukee St., Ste. 301, Denver, CO, 80206; *PH:* 1-303-320-7708; *Fax:* 1-303-320-7835; *http://* www.goldresourcecorp.com

General - Incorporation	CO	**Stock**- Price on:12/24/2007	$3.59
Employees	3	Stock Exchange	OTC
Auditor	Stark Winter Schenkein & Co., LLP	Ticker Symbol	GORO
Stk Agt	Corporate Stock Transfer, Inc.	Outstanding Shares	28,170,000
Counsel	NA	E.P.S	-$0.24
DUNS No.	NA	Shareholders	NA

Business: The groups principal activities include exploring and developing mineral resource. The group operates from the United States.

Primary SIC and add'l.: 1241

CIK No: 0001160791

Subsidiaries: Don David Gold, S.A. de C.V., Golden Trump S.A. de C.V

Officers: William W. Reid/Chmn., CEO, Pres., David Reid/58/Dir., VP - Exploration, Sec., Treasurer, Jose Perez Reynoso/Mgr. - Mexican Operations, Monty Jennings/CFO, Frank L. Jennings/57/CFO

Directors: William W. Reid/Chmn., CEO, Pres., David Reid/58/Dir., VP - Exploration, Sec., Treasurer, Bill M. Conrad/Dir.

Owners: William W. Reid/15.70%, Beth Reid/15.70%, Bill M. Conrad/2.00%, David C. Reid/14.60%, Insiders/31.00%

Financial Data: **Fiscal Year End:**12/31 **Latest Annual Data:** 12/31/2006

Year	Sales	Net Income
2006	NA	-$2,687,000

Curr. Assets:	$7,866,000	**Curr. Liab.:**	$451,000		
Plant, Equip.:	$96,000	**Total Liab.:**	$451,000	**Indic. Yr. Divd.:**	NA
Total Assets:	$7,964,000	**Net Worth:**	$7,513,000	**Debt/ Equity:**	NA

Goldcorp Inc

Pk. Pl., Ste. 3400-666 Burrard St., Vancouver, BC, V6C 2X8; *PH:* 1-604-696-3000; *http://* www.goldcorp.com; *Email:* info@goldcorp.com

General - Incorporation	Canada	**Stock**- Price on:12/24/2007	$24.4
Employees	3,509	Stock Exchange	NYSE
Auditor	Deloitte & Touche, LLP	Ticker Symbol	GG
Stk Agt	Mellon Trust Co	Outstanding Shares	703,830,000
Counsel	NA	E.P.S	$0.39
DUNS No.	NA	Shareholders	NA

Business: The group's principle activity of the company is to produce gold. The company explores and develops mines for precious metals and gold. The company operates in two segments: gold bullion and industrial minerals. The company's gold mines include red lake mine located in northern ontario and the wharf mine located in South Dakota.

Primary SIC and add'l.: 1474 1041

CIK No: 0000919239

Subsidiaries: Cayman Pampas Ltd., Compania Minera Pefia de Bernat, S.A. de C.V., Desarrollos Mineros San Luis, S.A. de C.v., Luismin S.A. de C.V., minera Alumbrera Ltd., Musto Explorations (Bermuda) Ltd, Peak Gold Mines Pty Ltd, Wharf Resources (U.S.A.) Inc., Wharf Resources Ltd., Wheaton Minerals Asia pacific Pty Limited, Wheaton River (Cayman Islands) Ltd., Wheaton River Cayman pampas Ltd.

Officers: Ian Telfer/Chmn., CEO, Pres., Eduardo Luna/Exec. VP, Charles Jeannes/Exec. VP - Corporate Development, Tim Miller/VP - Central, South America, Wendy Louie/VP, Controller, Mark Ruus/VP - Tax, Lindsay Hall/CFO, Exec. VP, Julio Carvalho/Exec. VP - Central, South America, Steve Reid/COO, Exec. VP, Rohan Hazelton/VP - Finance, Paula Rogers/VP, Treasurer, Paul M. Stein/Corp. Sec., Anna M. Tudela/Dir. - Legal, Assist. Corp. Sec., Salvador Garcia/VP - Mexico

Directors: Ian Telfer/Chmn., CEO, Pres., Doug Holtby/Vice Chmn., Peter Dey/Dir., John Bell/Dir., Larry Bell/Dir., Beverley Anne Briscoe/Dir., Anna M. Tudela/Dir. - Legal, Assist. Corp. Sec., Kevin McArthur/Dir., Randy Reifel/Dir., Dan Rovig/Dir., Kenneth Williamson/Dir.

Financial Data: **Fiscal Year End:**12/31 **Latest Annual Data:** 12/31/2006

Year	Sales	Net Income
2006	$1,056,300,000	-$161,500,000
2005	$597,183,000	-$134,909,000
2004	$191,016,000	$49,879,000

Curr. Assets:	$555,200,000	**Curr. Liab.:**	$352,900,000		
Plant, Equip.:	$75,700,000	**Total Liab.:**	$5,540,400,000	**Indic. Yr. Divd.:**	$0.180
Total Assets:	$17,677,800,000	**Net Worth:**	$12,137,400,000	**Debt/ Equity:**	NA

Golden Aria Corp

700 W Pender St., No. 604, Vancouver, BC, V6C 1G8; *PH:* 1-604-602-1633

General - Incorporation	NV	**Stock**- Price on:12/24/2007	$0.55
Employees	NA	Stock Exchange	OTC
Auditor	Vellmer & Chang	Ticker Symbol	GARA
Stk Agt	Nevada Agency and Trust Co.	Outstanding Shares	NA
Counsel	NA	E.P.S	NA
DUNS No.	NA	Shareholders	NA

Business: The groups principal activity is to explore minerals. In April 2005, the group acquired mineral claims in Eureka County, Nevada. The group operates from the United States and Canada.

Primary SIC and add'l.: 1081

CIK No: 0001346022

Officers: Gerald Carlson/Dir., Pres., Diane Rees/CFO - Secretaries, Dir., Chris Bunka/48/Dir., CFO

Directors: Gerald Carlson/Dir., Pres., Diane Rees/CFO - Secretaries, Dir., Chris Bunka/48/Dir., CFO

Owners: Gerald Carlson/4.95%, Chris Bunka/10.12%, Insiders/15.07%, Piranah Investment Corporation/9.09%

Financial Data: **Fiscal Year End:**08/31 **Latest Annual Data:** 08/31/2006

Year	Sales	Net Income
2006	NA	-$200,000

Curr. Assets:	$166,000	**Curr. Liab.:**	$53,000		
Plant, Equip.:	$0	**Total Liab.:**	$53,000	**Indic. Yr. Divd.:**	NA
Total Assets:	$166,000	**Net Worth:**	$113,000	**Debt/ Equity:**	NA

Golden Cycle Gold Corp

1515 S Tejon St., Ste. 201, Colorado Springs, CO, 80906; *PH:* 1-719-471-9013; *Fax:* 1-719-520-1442; *http://* www.goldencycle.com; *Email:* info@goldencycle.com

General - Incorporation	CO	**Stock**- Price on:12/24/2007	$6.1
Employees	2	Stock Exchange	NYSE
Auditor	Ehrhardt Keefe Steiner & Hottman P.C	Ticker Symbol	GCGC
Stk Agt	American Stock Transfer & Trust Co.	Outstanding Shares	NA
Counsel	Robert H. Haines	E.P.S	NA
DUNS No.	06-275-1615	Shareholders	NA

Business: The group's principal activity is to acquire and develop mining properties. The group is in participation with cripple creek & victor gold mining company and joint venture with anglogold, Colorado. The joint venture engages in gold mining activity in the cripple creek area of Colorado. The group also participates in mining in certain areas of the Philippines, through a subsidiary, golden cycle Philippines inc by an agreement with benguet corporation, a philippine mining company.

Primary SIC and add'l.: 1041 1044

CIK No: 0000719754

Subsidiaries: Golden Cycle Gold Exploration Inc., Golden Cycle Philippines Inc.

Officers: Herbert R. Hampton/58/Dir., CEO, Pres./$253,625.00, Barbara E. Woodside/Corp. Sec., Kenneth G. Sam/Corporate Counsel, Jason G. Brenkert/Corporate Counsel

Directors: Herbert R. Hampton/58/Dir., CEO, Pres., James C. Ruder/75/Chmn., Taki N. Anagnoston/73/Dir., Donald L. Gustafson/66/Dir., Robert T. Thul/60/Dir.

Owners: Taki N. Anagnoston/5.50%, Insiders/10.50%, Donald L. Gustafson, David W. Tice & Associates, LLC/13.50%, Herbert R. Hampton/2.90%, James C. Ruder, Robert T. Thul, MIDAS Fund, Inc./20.20%

Golden Eagle International Inc

9661 S 700 E, Salt Lake City, UT, 84070; *PH:* 1-801-619-9320; *Fax:* 1-801-619-1747; *http://* www.geii.com; *Email:* info@geii.com

General - Incorporation	CO	**Stock**- Price on:12/24/2007	$0.024
Employees	35	Stock Exchange	OTC
Auditor	Chisholm Bierwolf & Nilson LLC	Ticker Symbol	MYNG
Stk Agt	Computershare Investor Services LLC	Outstanding Shares	790,000,000
Counsel	Hamilton Lehrer & Dargan P.A	E.P.S	-$0.007
DUNS No.	92-633-9334	Shareholders	NA

Business: The group's principal activities are to acquire, develop and operate gold, silver and other mineral properties. The group is a publicly-traded mining company. The group acquired 100% of the buen futuro mining claim in the precambrian shield geological formation. The group completed the acquistion of the cobra claim, an additional 22,500 acres of prime ground in the ascension gold-copper trend. In the fourth quarter of 2003, the group was no longer an exploration or a developiment stage company.

Primary SIC and add'l.: 1041 1044

CIK No: 0000869531

Subsidiaries: Eagle Mining of Bolivia, Ltd., Golden Eagle Bolivia Mining, S.A, Golden eagle International, Inc.

Officers: Terry C. Turner/Chmn., CEO, Pres., Michael H. Biste/Chief Geologist - Geii Bolivia, Marco Antonio Venegas/CFO - Geii Bolivia, Tracy A. Madsen/CFO, Corp. Sec., Hugo Aparicio/Mine Superintendent, Geii Bolivia

Directors: Terry C. Turner/Chmn., CEO, Pres., H. E. Dunham/Dir., Mac Delozier/Dir., Alvaro Riveros/Dir., Kevin K. Pfeffer/Dir.

Owners: Kevin Pfeffer/7.24%, Lone Star Equity Group/10.14%, Insiders, Atlas Precious Metals, Inc./2.97%, Terry C. Turner, Golden Eagle Mineral Holding, Inc./32.49%, Tracy A. Madsen

Financial Data: Fiscal Year End:12/31   Latest Annual Data: 12/31/2006

Year	Sales	Net Income
2006	NA	-$4,276,000
2005	NA	-$2,039,000
2004	$1,322,000	-$5,878,000

Curr. Assets:	$22,000	Curr. Liab.:	$804,000		
Plant, Equip.:	$5,480,000	Total Liab.:	$4,781,000	Indic. Yr. Divd.:	NA
Total Assets:	$5,501,000	Net Worth:	$720,000	Debt/ Equity:	NA

Golden Enterprises Inc

1 Golden Flake Dr., Birmingham, AL, 35205; **PH:** 1-205-323-6161; **Fax:** 1-205-458-7327; **http://** www.goldenflake.com

General - Incorporation	DE	**Stock**- Price on:12/24/2007	$3.12
Employees	991	Stock Exchange	NDQ
Auditor	Dudley, Hopton-Jones	Ticker Symbol	GLDC
Stk Agt	Bank of New York	Outstanding Shares	11,840,000
Counsel	Spain & Gillon	E.P.S.	$0.16
DUNS No.	00-400-8975	Shareholders	NA

Business: The group's principle activities are to manufacture and distribute snack food products through its wholly owned subsidiary golden flake snack foods inc. The snack food products include potato chips, tortilla chips, corn chips, fried pork skins, baked and fried cheese curls, onion rings and buttered popcorn. These products are packaged in flexible bags or other suitable wrapping material. Products such as cakes and cookie items, canned dips, pretzels, peanut butter crackers, cheese crackers and dried meat products, products manufactured by others are also sold by the group under the golden flake label. The products are sold through the group's own sales organization and independent distributors to commercial establishments which sell food products in Alabama, Tennessee, Kentucky, Georgia, Florida, Mississippi, Louisiana, North Carolina, South Carolina, Arkansas and Missouri in the United States. The group's total revenue for the year 2007 was 110.83 millions of USD.

Primary SIC and add'l.: 2052 6719 2096

CIK No: 0000042228

Subsidiaries: Golden Flake Snack Foods, Inc.

Officers: Mark W. McCutcheon/Dir., CEO, Pres./$312,749.00, Randy Bates/53/Exec. VP - Sales Marketing, Transportation/$174,919.00, Patty Townsend/49/CFO, VP, Sec./$121,276.00, David Jones/Exec. VP - Operations, Human Resources, Quality Control, Golden Flakesnack Foods, Inc/$172,919.00

Directors: Mark W. McCutcheon/Dir., CEO, Pres., John S. Stein/71/Chmn., Wallace J. Nall/68/Dir., John P. McKleroy/64/Dir., Joann F. Bashinsky/76/Dir., Edward R. Pascoe/71/Dir., Wayne F. Pate/73/Dir., James I. Rotenstreich/70/Dir., John S.P. Samford/58/Dir.

Owners: James I. Rotenstreich, Randy Bates, Insiders/6.30%, John P. McKleroy, John S. Stein/2.40%, SYB, Inc./44.60%, John S. P. Samford, David Jones, F. Wayne Pate/1.20%, Edward R. Pascoe, Joann F. Bashinsky, Mark W. McCutcheon, The Estate of Sloan Y. Bashinsky,/8.50%

Financial Data: Fiscal Year End:06/03   Latest Annual Data: 06/01/2007

Year	Sales	Net Income
2007	$110,827,000	$1,213,000
2006	$106,547,000	$289,000
2005	$103,144,000	-$15,000

Curr. Assets:	$15,109,000	Curr. Liab.:	$9,781,000	P/E Ratio:	52.00
Plant, Equip.:	$14,247,000	Total Liab.:	$13,495,000	Indic. Yr. Divd.:	$0.130
Total Assets:	$34,402,000	Net Worth:	$20,907,000	Debt/ Equity:	NA

Golden Goliath Resources Ltd

675 W Hastings St., Ste. 711, Vancouver, BC, V6B 1N2; **PH:** 1-604-682-2950; **http://** www.goldengoliath.com

General - Incorporation	Canada	**Stock**- Price on:12/24/2007	NA
Employees	NA	Stock Exchange	NA
Auditor	Morgan & Co	Ticker Symbol	NA
Stk Agt	Computershare Trust Co	Outstanding Shares	NA
Counsel	Stephen Pearce	E.P.S.	NA
DUNS No.	NA	Shareholders	NA

Business: The group has financed its operations through funds raised in loans, public/private placements of common shares, shares issued for property, shares issued in debt settlements, and shares issued upon exercise of stock options and share purchase warrants. The group operates from United States.

Primary SIC and add'l.: 1400

CIK No: 0001127307

Subsidiaries: Minera Delta S.A. de C.V.

Officers: Paul J. Sorbara/CEO, Pres., Stephen Pearce/CFO

Owners: Paul J. Sorbara/5.00%, Marc Legault/1.00%, Rob Hutchison/1.00%, Insiders/13.00%, Edward K. Sorbara/1.00%, Richard Hughes/1.00%, Stephen Pearce/1.00%, Daniel Nofrietta Fernandez/3.00%, Andrew Robertson/1.00%

Golden Hand Resources Inc

110 E 59th St., New York, NY, 10022; **PH:** 1-212-557-9000; **http://** www.brainstorm-cell.com

General - Incorporation	WA	**Stock**- Price on:12/24/2007	$0.33
Employees	12	Stock Exchange	NA
Auditor	Kost Forer Gabbay & Kasierer	Ticker Symbol	NA
Stk Agt	First American Stock Transfer, Inc.	Outstanding Shares	24,770,000
Counsel	Brl Law Group LLC	E.P.S.	-$0.24
DUNS No.	NA	Shareholders	NA

Business: The group's principle activity is to market licensed product line. The group's licensed product lines include high-tech instruments that are used to record information transferred from distant sources like aircraft and satellites. The group operates from United States.

Primary SIC and add'l.: 5065

CIK No: 0001137883

Subsidiaries: BrainStorm Cell Therapeutics Ltd

Officers: Rami Efrati/CEO, Holly G. Atkinson/Dir. - Business Development, Chaim Lebovitz/Pres., Yoram Drucker/COO, Principal Executive Officer, David Stolick/CFO, Avinoam Kadouri/Chief Technology Advisor, Eldad Melamed/Chief Medical Advisor, Co - Dir., Scientific Team Member, Daniel Offen/Chief Scientist, Warren C. Olanow/Scientific Advisor, Andres Lozano/Scientific Advisor, Jeffrey Kordower/Scientific Advisor

Directors: Irit Arbel/Founder, Michael D. Greenfield/48/Dir., Robert Shorr/Dir., Moshe Lion/Dir., Jonathan C. Javitt/Dir.

Owners: Daniel Offen/9.90%, Ramot at Tel Aviv University Ltd./20.70%, Yoram Drucker/4.30%, Malcom S. Taub/5.50%, Eldad Melamed/9.90%, Insiders/16.80%, Robert Shorr, Basad Holdings Ltd./6.60%, David Stolick/1.60%, Zegal & Ross Capital/10.70%, Michael Greenfield, Irit Arbel/9.90%

Financial Data: Fiscal Year End:03/31   Latest Annual Data: 3/31/2006

Year	Sales	Net Income
2006	NA	-$3,317,000
2005	NA	-$18,840,000

Curr. Assets:	$365,000	Curr. Liab.:	$1,067,000		
Plant, Equip.:	$411,000	Total Liab.:	$8,770,000	Indic. Yr. Divd.:	NA
Total Assets:	$860,000	Net Worth:	-$7,911,000	Debt/ Equity:	NA

Golden Hope Resources Corp

2549 W Main St., Ste. 202, Littleton, Colorado, CO, 80120; **PH:** 1-303-798-5235; **http://** www.eternalenergy.com

General - Incorporation	NV	**Stock**- Price on:12/24/2007	NA
Employees	1	Stock Exchange	NA
Auditor	Kelly & Co	Ticker Symbol	NA
Stk Agt	Holladay Stock Transfer, Inc.	Outstanding Shares	NA
Counsel	NA	E.P.S.	-$0.11
DUNS No.	NA	Shareholders	NA

Business: The group's principal activity is to engage in the acquisition, exploration and development of natural resource properties.

Primary SIC and add'l.: 1000

CIK No: 0001282613

Officers: Bradley M. Colby/51/Dir., CEO, CFO, Pres., Treasurer, Sec., Craig Phelps/VP - Engineering, Jamie Kelley/Contact

Directors: Bradley M. Colby/51/Dir., CEO, CFO, Pres., Treasurer, Sec., John Anderson/Dir., Paul Rumler/Dir.

Owners: RAB Special Situations (Master) Fund Ltd./7.10%, John Anderson/0.50%, Bradley M. Colby/9.20%, Insiders/9.60%, Dennis Eldjarnson/6.60%

Financial Data: Fiscal Year End:12/31   Latest Annual Data: 12/31/2006

Year	Sales	Net Income
2006	NA	$3,135,000
2005	NA	-$230,000
2004	NA	-$34,000

Curr. Assets:	$2,380,000	Curr. Liab.:	$2,293,000		
Plant, Equip.:	$1,262,000	Total Liab.:	$2,293,000	Indic. Yr. Divd.:	NA
Total Assets:	$6,646,000	Net Worth:	$4,353,000	Debt/ Equity:	NA

Golden Patriot Corp

1979 Marcus Ave., Ste. 210, Lake Success, NY, 11042; **PH:** 1-212-760-0500; **http://** www.goldenpatriotcorp.com; **Email:** info@goldenpatriotcorp.com

General - Incorporation	NV	**Stock**- Price on:12/24/2007	$0.038
Employees	NA	Stock Exchange	OTC
Auditor	Amisano Hanson	Ticker Symbol	GPTC
Stk Agt	Computershare Trust Co	Outstanding Shares	81,660,000
Counsel	NA	E.P.S.	-$0.015
DUNS No.	NA	Shareholders	NA

Business: The groups principal activities include exploring and developing oil and gas properties. The group operates from California in the United States.

Primary SIC and add'l.: 1382

CIK No: 0001080036

Officers: Bradley Rudman/Dir., CFO, Pres., Negar Towfigh/35/Corp. Sec.

Directors: Bradley Rudman/Dir., CFO, Pres., Steven Goldberg/Dir.

Owners: Bradley Rudman/1.30%, Negar Towfigh/0.80%, Nathan Nock/25.50%, Insiders/2.80%, Steven Goldberg/0.80%

Financial Data: Fiscal Year End:04/30   Latest Annual Data: 4/30/2006

Year	Sales	Net Income
2006	NA	-$2,136,000
2005	NA	-$365,000
2004	NA	-$3,520,000

Curr. Assets:	$263,000	Curr. Liab.:	$317,000		
Plant, Equip.:	$1,000	Total Liab.:	$2,193,000	Indic. Yr. Divd.:	NA
Total Assets:	$335,000	Net Worth:	-$1,858,000	Debt/ Equity:	NA

Golden Phoenix Minerals Inc

1675 E Prater Way, Ste. 102, Sparks, NV, 89434; *PH:* 1-775-853-4919; *Fax:* 1-775-853-5010; *http://* www.golden-phoenix.com; *Email:* investor@golden-phoenix.com

General - Incorporation .... MN	Stock - Price on:12/24/2007 .... $0.41
Employees 34	Stock Exchange .... OTC
Auditor .... HJ & Assoc. LLC	Ticker Symbol .... GPXM
Stk Agt .... Nevada Agency & Trust Company	Outstanding Shares 190,920,000
Counsel .... Charles Clayton	E.P.S. .... -$0.023
DUNS No. 83-319-5209	Shareholders .... NA

Business: The group's principal activities are to explore, operate and develop mineral properties in Nevada and other parts of the western United States. The group controls its mineral property interests through ownership, leases, and mining claims. The group is planning exploration and development of selected properties with the intent of conducting precious and base mining and production operations. It will also provide joint venture opportunities to other large mining companies to work with the company in these activities. In 2003, the group began formal operation of its mineral ridge property. On Jul 18, 2003, the group signed a joint venture agreement for its borealis gold project with gryphon gold corporation, a Nevada incorporated company.

Primary SIC and add'l.: 1481 1041

CIK No: 0001042784

Subsidiaries: Gryphon Gold Corporation

Officers: David A. Caldwell/Dir., CEO/$486,664.00, Robert P. Martin/Pres./$339,317.00, Wayne Colwell/Dir. - Laboratory Services, Donald R. Prahl/COO/$126,021.00, Larry A. Kitchen/Controller, Lari Marlow/Financial Controller, Sr. Accountant, Paul Knopick/Public Relation, E, E Communication, Dennis P. Gauger/CFO/$17,353.00, Craig Patrick/VP - Corporate Development

Directors: David A. Caldwell/Dir., CEO, David W. Payne/Member - Advisory Board, Daniel Breckenridge/Member - Advisory Board, Jeffrey Tissier/Dir., Ronald L. Parratt/Dir., William R. Thomson/Member - Advisory Board, Corby G. Anderson/Dir., Kent D. Aveson/33/Dir.

Owners: Ronald L. Parratt, Kenneth S. Ripley/1.60%, Dennis P. Gauger, Kent D. Aveson, Insiders/5.39%, Corby G. Anderson, Jeffrey Tissier, David Caldwell/1.18%, Donald R. Prahl, RBC Dexia Investor Services Trust/7.96%, Crestview Capital Marter, LLC/5.13%, Robert P. Martin/1.87%

Financial Data: Fiscal Year End:12/31   Latest Annual Data: 12/31/2006

Year	Sales	Net Income
2006	$177,000	-$4,081,000
2005	$746,000	-$5,942,000
2004	$1,560,000	-$6,470,000

Curr. Assets:	$1,179,000	Curr. Liab.:	$6,618,000		
Plant, Equip.:	$1,295,000	Total Liab.:	$10,046,000	Indic. Yr. Divd.:	NA
Total Assets:	$5,033,000	Net Worth:	-$4,971,000	Debt/ Equity:	NA

Golden Queen Mining Co Ltd

6411 Imperial Ave., Vancouver, BC, V7W 2J5; *PH:* 1-604-921-7570; *Fax:* 1-604-921-9446; *http://* www.goldenqueen.com; *Email:* info@goldenqueen.com

General - Incorporation .... BC	Stock - Price on:12/24/2007 .... NA
Employees .... NA	Stock Exchange .... OTC
Auditor .... BDO Dunwoody LLP	Ticker Symbol .... GQMNF
Stk Agt .... Computershare Trust Co of Canada	Outstanding Shares .... NA
Counsel .... Morton & Co	E.P.S. .... NA
DUNS No. 93-283-3346	Shareholders .... NA

Business: The group's principle activity is to acquire and maintain gold mining properties for exploration, future development and production. The group's activities involve bringing to operation a precious metals mine located in kern county, California. The group is in the development stage. The group operates from United States.

Primary SIC and add'l.: 1041

CIK No: 0001025362

Subsidiaries: Golden Queen Mining Company, Inc.

Officers: Lutz H. Klingmann/Dir., CEO, Pres., Principal Financial Officer/$111,116.00, Keith Gainey/Accountant

Directors: Lutz H. Klingmann/Dir., CEO, Pres., Principal Financial Officer, Edward G. Thompson/Chmn., Chester Shynkaryk/Dir., Gordon Gutrath/Dir., Landon Clay/Dir.

Owners: GORDON C. GUTRATH, Landon T. Clay/22.91%, Insiders/26.51%, David T. Lu/5.43%, CHESTER SHYNKARYK, Sprott Asset Management Inc./9.19%, EDWARD G. THOMPSON, LUTZ H. KLINGMANN/1.03%

Financial Data: Fiscal Year End:12/31   Latest Annual Data: 12/31/2006

Year	Sales	Net Income
2006	NA	-$4,910,000
2005	NA	-$1,476,000
2004	NA	-$1,772,000

Curr. Assets:	$5,566,000	Curr. Liab.:	$1,139,000		
Plant, Equip.:	$224,000	Total Liab.:	$1,272,000	Indic. Yr. Divd.:	NA
Total Assets:	$6,036,000	Net Worth:	$4,764,000	Debt/ Equity:	NA

Golden River Resources Corp

Level 8, 580 St Kilda Rd., Melbourne, Victoria, 3004; ; *http://* www.bayresourcesltd.com; *Email:* investors@goldenriverresources.com

General - Incorporation .... DE	Stock - Price on:12/24/2007 .... $0.12
Employees .... NA	Stock Exchange .... OTC
Auditor .... Peter J Lee	Ticker Symbol .... GORV
Stk Agt .... Bank of New York	Outstanding Shares .... NA
Counsel .... NA	E.P.S. .... NA
DUNS No. .... NA	Shareholders .... NA

Business: The group's principal activity is to currently look out for opportunities in the mining and exploration industry in North America, Canada and Latin America. The group is currently into exploration of gold in the highly prospective committee bay greenstone belt in Canada. It's major asset has been its 24% holding in the stock of scnv acquisition corporation which is involved in the research and development of high efficiency, low pollution or pollution-free products and technologies in the energy conversion and conservation fields.

Primary SIC and add'l.: 1041

CIK No: 0000814904

Subsidiaries: Bay Resources (Asia) Pty Ltd, Baynex.com Pty Ltd, Golden Bull Resources Corporation

Officers: Joseph Gutnick/Chmn., CEO, Pres., Craig Alford/VP - Exploration, Peter Lee/Dir., Sec., CFO

Directors: Joseph Gutnick/Chmn., CEO, Pres., David Tyrwhitt/Dir., Peter Lee/Dir., Sec., CFO, Mordechai Gutnick/Dir.

Owners: Peter James Lee, RAB Special Situations (Master) Fund Limited, Insiders, Stera Gutnick, David Stuart Tyrwhitt, Mordechai Zev Gutnick

Financial Data: Fiscal Year End:06/30   Latest Annual Data: 6/30/2006

Year	Sales	Net Income
2006	NA	-$970,000
2005	NA	-$1,982,000
2004	NA	-$1,190,000

Curr. Assets:	$1,535,000	Curr. Liab.:	$396,000		
Plant, Equip.:	$7,000	Total Liab.:	$396,000	Indic. Yr. Divd.:	NA
Total Assets:	$1,543,000	Net Worth:	$1,147,000	Debt/ Equity:	NA

Golden Spirit Mining Ltd

Formerly: Golden Spirit Minerals Ltd
1288 Alberni St., Ste. 806, Vancouver, BC, V6E 4N5; *PH:* 1-888-488-6882

General - Incorporation .... DE	Stock - Price on:12/24/2007 .... $0.31
Employees .... NA	Stock Exchange .... OTC
Auditor .... Dale Matheson Carr-Hilton Labonte	Ticker Symbol .... GSPT
Stk Agt .... Alexis Stock Transfer	Outstanding Shares .... NA
Counsel .... NA	E.P.S. .... -$0.108
DUNS No. .... NA	Shareholders .... NA

Business: The group's principal activity is to operate Internet-related businesses. It is developing its own websites aimed at the Far East markets. The group's current project is an online casting agency designed to connect talent with casting agents and producers. The talent directory will give both the experienced and the aspiring model or actor or entertainer unique opportunities to have his or her photo appear before the professionals who are continually in search of talent and fresh new faces. For a yearly subscription fee, an industry professional will be able to post his or her name, specifications, experience, training and special skills and scanned high resolution photos to be stored in the talent database on Website. The group is in the development stage.

Primary SIC and add'l.: 7375

CIK No: 0001076262

Subsidiaries: British Virgin Islands, PDTech.com

Officers: Carlton Parfitt/Dir., Sec., Robert Klein/Dir., Pres.

Directors: Carlton Parfitt/Dir., Sec., Robert Klein/Dir., Pres.

Owners: CEDE & Co./41.60%

Financial Data: Fiscal Year End:12/31   Latest Annual Data: 12/31/2006

Year	Sales	Net Income
2006	$19,000	-$2,954,000
2005	NA	-$1,842,000
2004	NA	-$1,883,000

Curr. Assets:	$32,000	Curr. Liab.:	$382,000		
Plant, Equip.:	$0	Total Liab.:	$382,000	Indic. Yr. Divd.:	NA
Total Assets:	$53,000	Net Worth:	-$329,000	Debt/ Equity:	NA

Golden Star Resources Ltd

10901 W Toller Dr., Ste. 300, Littleton, CO, 80127; *PH:* 1-303-830-9000; *Fax:* 1-303-830-9094; *http://* www.gsr.com; *Email:* info@gsr.com

General - Incorporation .... Canada	Stock - Price on:12/24/2007 .... $3.74
Employees 1,800	Stock Exchange .... AMEX
Auditor .... PricewaterhouseCoopers LLP	Ticker Symbol .... GSS
Stk Agt .... Mellon Trust Co	Outstanding Shares 233,190,000
Counsel .... NA	E.P.S. $0.06
DUNS No. 88-307-3538	Shareholders .... NA

Business: The group's principal activity is to produce gold. The acquisition, exploration, development and production of gold are carried out in several areas in Africa, South America and ghana. The group own 90% equity interest in bogoso gold limited, which owns gold mines in ghana.

Primary SIC and add'l.: 1499 1041

CIK No: 0000903571

Subsidiaries: Bogoso Gold Limited, Bogoso Holdings, Caystar Holdings, Euro Resources S.a., St. Jude Resources Ltd., Wasford Holdings, Wexford Goldfields Limited

Officers: Peter Bradford/Dir., CEO, Pres./$534,910.00, Richard Gray/VP - Wassa, Bruce Higson-Smith/VP - Corporate Development, Investor Relations, Colin Belshaw/VP, GM - Bogoso, Prestear/$225,391.00, Roger Palmer/VP - Finance, Controller/$231,435.00, Anne Hite/Mgr. - Investor Relations, Peter Bourke/VP - Technical Services, Tom Mair/Sr. VP, CFO, Ted Strickler/VP - Human Resources, Administration, Mark Thorpe/VP - Sustainability, Mitchel S. Wasel/VP - Exploration

Directors: Peter Bradford/Dir., CEO, Pres., David Fagin/Dir., Ian MacGregor/Dir., Jim Askew/Dir., Michael Martineau/Dir., Lars-Eric Johansson/Dir., Michael Terrell/Dir.

Owners: Bruce Higson-Smith, Michael P. Martineau, Ian MacGregor, Thomas G. Mair, Peter J. Bradford, Colin Belshaw, Douglas A. Jones, Insiders/2.75%, David K. Fagin, Lars-Eric Johansson, James E. Askew, Michael A. Terrell

Financial Data: Fiscal Year End:12/31   Latest Annual Data: 12/31/2006

Year	Sales	Net Income
2006	$128,690,000	$57,875,000
2005	$95,465,000	-$13,531,000
2004	$65,029,000	$2,642,000

Curr. Assets:	$90,534,000	Curr. Liab.:	$69,151,000	P/E Ratio:	31.17
Plant, Equip.:	$501,032,000	Total Liab.:	$198,775,000	Indic. Yr. Divd.:	NA
Total Assets:	$606,095,000	Net Worth:	$404,418,000	Debt/ Equity:	0.1278

Golden State BUS BK

PO Box 430, Upland, CA , 91785; *PH:* 1-909-981-8000; *Fax:* 1-909-579-6373; *http://* goldenstatebusinessbank.com

CA , 91785; *PH:* 1-909-981-8000; *Fax:* 1-909-579-6373; *http://* goldenstatebusinessbank.com

General - Incorporation		*Stock*- Price on:12/24/2007	$14.25
Employees	NA	Stock Exchange	OTC
Auditor	NA	Ticker Symbol	GSBB
Stk Agt	NA	Outstanding Shares	NA
Counsel	NA	E.P.S.	NA
DUNS No.	NA	Shareholders	NA

Business: The groups principle activity is to provide recruiting services. The groups service area includes the research and development, engineering, marketing, sales, information technology and manufacturing industries. The group operates from United States.

Primary SIC and add'l.: 6022

CIK No:

Officers: Ralph Wiita/Dir., CEO, Pres., Jami Schaffer/VP, Sr. Loan Officer - Dealer Center, Cathy Allan/VP, Relationship Mgr. - Upland Branch, Maricela Miranda/Assist. VP, Compliance Officer - Upland Branch, Blanca Nieves/Credit Analyst, Trainee, Loan Department, Normita Forbes/Utility, Loan Department, Annmarie Paolino/Exec. VP, Sr. Loan Officer - Construction Loan Departmen, Desirae M. Lopez/Teller, Upland Branch, Debi Hill/VP, Branch Mgr. - Brea Office, Nina Moores/VP, Branch Mgr. - Brea Office, Ruth Hernandez/New Accounting Representative, Brea Office, Grace Ramos/Utility, Teller, Brea Office, Anne Kellenberger/VP, Credit Service Mgr. - Loan Department, Jenny Stachurski/Branch Specialist - Upland Branch, Darriana Davis/Teller, Upland Branch *(22 Officers included in Index)*

Directors: Ralph Wiita/Dir., CEO, Pres., Michael E. MacKe/Chmn., Philip Arciero/Dir., Frank Caliri/Dir., Raymond L. Crebs/Dir., Mark Leggio/Dir., Bernard A. Kloenne/Dir., Christopher M. Leggio/Dir., Robert C. Osborn/Dir., Rudolph F. Silva/Dir., Sec.

Golden Telecom Inc

2831 29th St., NW, Washington, DC, 20008; *PH:* 1-202-332-5997; *Fax:* 1-202-332-4877; *http://* www.goldentelecom.ru; *Email:* ir@gti.ru

General - Incorporation	DE	*Stock*- Price on:12/24/2007	$50.85
Employees	4,218	Stock Exchange	NDQ
Auditor	Ernst & Young LLC	Ticker Symbol	GLDN
Stk Agt	Mellon Investor Services LLC	Outstanding Shares	36,720,000
Counsel	Cahill Gordon & Reindel LLP	E.P.S.	$3.77
DUNS No.	NA	Shareholders	NA

Business: The group's principal activities are to provide integrated telecommunications and Internet services to businesses and other high-usage customers and telecommunications operators. The group operates in four segments: business and corporate services, carrier and operator services, consumer Internet services and mobile services. Business and corporate services provides business and corporate services including voice and data services to corporate clients. Carrier and operator services provides a range of carrier and operator services including voice and data services to foreign and russian telecommunications and mobile operators. Consumer Internet services provides dial-up Internet accesses to the consumer market. Mobile services include voicemail, roaming and messaging services on a subscription and prepaid basis. The group acquired sibchallenge telecom, oao comincom, oao combellga and samara-telecom in 2003 and st-holdings and sp buzton in 2004.

Primary SIC and add'l.: 4899 4813 7375 7389

CIK No: 0001089874

Subsidiaries: Agama Ltd., Agency of Business Communication (ADS) LLC, Antel Rascom Ltd., Buzton, Andizhan Branch, Buzton, Bukhara Branch, Buzton, Fergana Branch, Buzton, Gulistan Branch, Buzton, Jizzakh Branch, Buzton, Karshi Branch, Buzton, Namangan Branch, Buzton, Naroi Branch, Buzton, Nukus Branch, Buzton, Samarkand Branch, Buzton, Termez Branch, Buzton, Ugrench Branch 85 Subsidiaries included in the Index

Officers: Jean-Pierre Vandromme/54/Dir., CEO/$6,796,964.00, Boris Svetlichny/Sr. VP, CFO, Treasurer/$1,202,644.00, Ilya Smirnov/VP, Acting General Counsel, Corp. Sec., Kevin Cuffe/48/VP, Head - BCS, Customer Care Business Units/$1,327,565.00, Michael Wilson/39/VP, Corporate Controller, Principal Accounting Officer/$651,805.00, Fred Ledbetter/Sr. VP, Chief Marketing Officer, Andrey Patoka/VP, MD - International, Regional Business Unit, Alexander Vinogradov/Pres./$669,942.00, Dmitry Bragin/VP, Head - Consumer Marketing Solutions Business Unit, Mikhail Afonin/VP - Mergers, Acquisitions, Aleksey Goryachkin/CTO, VP, Olga Novikova/VP, Head - Human Resources, Administrative Divisions, Alexander Shinkarev/VP, Head - Business Development, Strategic Planning Division, Svetlana Kostyukova/VP - Customer Care Business Unit, Vladislav Terekhin/VP - Corporate Security - Business Support

Directors: Jean-Pierre Vandromme/54/Dir., CEO, Alexy Reznikovich/Chmn., Petr Aven/53/Chmn., Patrick Gallagher/53/Dir., David Herman/62/Dir., Kjell Johnsen/40/Dir., Oleg Malis/33/Dir., David Smyth/48/Dir., Vladimir Bulgak/66/Dir., Thor A. Halvorsen/54/Dir.

Owners: Alexey Khudyakov, Michael Wilson, Oleg Malis, Vladimir Bulgak, Sunbird Limited/29.20%, Ronny Naevdal, Alexander Vinogradov, OAO Rostelecom/11.00%, Derek Bloom, Boris Svetlichny, David Smyth, David Herman, Kjell Johnsen, Insiders, Patrick Gallagher *(19 Owners included in Index)*

Financial Data: Fiscal Year End:12/31 Latest Annual Data: 12/31/2006

Year	Sales	Net Income
2006	$854,617,000	$85,500,000
2005	$667,379,000	$76,073,000
2004	$583,978,000	$64,783,000

Curr. Assets:	$231,405,000	*Curr. Liab.:*	$188,591,000	*P/E Ratio:*	23.01
Plant, Equip.:	$552,341,000	*Total Liab.:*	$290,014,000	*Indic. Yr. Divd.:*	$1.920
Total Assets:	$1,107,190,000	*Net Worth:*	$817,176,000	*Debt/ Equity:*	NA

Golden Valley Bank CA

190 Cohasset Rd. , Ste. 170, Chico, CA, 95926; *PH:* 1-530-892-2440; *http://* www.goldenvalleybank.com; *Email:* contact@goldenvalleybank.com

General - Incorporation		*Stock*- Price on:12/24/2007	$11
Employees	NA	Stock Exchange	OTC
Auditor	NA	Ticker Symbol	GVYB
Stk Agt	NA	Outstanding Shares	NA
Counsel	NA	E.P.S.	NA
DUNS No.	NA	Shareholders	NA

Business: The group's principle activity is to provide banking services. The group also provides personal and business banking services. The group operates from United States.

Primary SIC and add'l.: 6022

CIK No:

Officers: Mark Francis/Dir., CEO, Pres., Hilary Schwartz/Client Services, Shannon Moore/Client Services, Jessica Hays/Client Services, James Doss/Chief Credit Officer, Matt Moseley/Commercial Banking Officer, Sheryl Rollins/Relationship Banking Officer, Denise Fawns/Sr. Loan Document Specialist, Marci Ryther/Sr. Credit Analyst, Relationship Specialist, Jacqueline Smith/Accounting Services Specialist, Amber Coley/New Accounting, Jaclyn Foreman/Client Services, Dawna Hoofard/CFO, Tracie Cvitkovich/Executive Administrative Assist., Jeremy Stone/Sr. Commercial Relationship Mgr. *(28 Officers included in Index)*

Directors: Mark Francis/Dir., CEO, Pres., Robert D. Harp/Vice Chmn., Howard W. Isom/Chmn., Kenneth R. Grossman/Dir., Douglas Guillon/Dir., Donald J. Hubbard/Dir., Gary Katz/Dir., Syl Lucena/Dir., Audrey Z. Tennis/Dir., Donald R. Wallrich/Dir., Dan Cargile/Dir., Scott R. Chalmers/Dir., Marilyn Everett/Dir.

Golden West Brewing Company Inc

945 W 2nd St., Chico, CA, 95928; *PH:* 1-530-894-7906

General - Incorporation	DE	*Stock*- Price on:12/24/2007	$0.4
Employees	7	Stock Exchange	OTC
Auditor	Schumacher & Associates, Inc.	Ticker Symbol	NA
Stk Agt	Corporate Stock Transfer, Inc.	Outstanding Shares	2,820,000
Counsel	Clifford Neuman	E.P.S.	-$0.43
DUNS No.	NA	Shareholders	NA

Business: The group operates through its subsidiary whose principle activities include manufacturing and distributing craft beer. Products of the group include Organic Ale, Organic Pilsner, Organic Porter and Organic India Pale Ale. In August 2005, the group acquired Butte Creek Brewing Company, LLC. The group operates from the United States.

Primary SIC and add'l.: 2082

CIK No: 0001304409

Subsidiaries: Golden West Brewing Company

Officers: John C. Power/45/Dir., CEO, CFO, Pres., Principal Accounting Officer

Directors: John C. Power/45/Dir., CEO, CFO, Pres., Principal Accounting Officer, Brian Power/41/Dir.

Owners: John Gibbs/22.90%, Insiders/33.40%, John C. Power/22.00%, Butte Creek Brewing Company, LLC/7.10%, Allan W. Williams/5.70%

Financial Data: Fiscal Year End:12/31 Latest Annual Data: 12/31/2006

Year	Sales	Net Income
2006	$984,000	-$1,030,000

Curr. Assets:	$318,000	*Curr. Liab.:*	$551,000		
Plant, Equip.:	$276,000	*Total Liab.:*	$1,248,000	*Indic. Yr. Divd.:*	NA
Total Assets:	$623,000	*Net Worth:*	-$625,000	*Debt/ Equity:*	NA

Golden West Financial Corp

1901 Harrison St., 1901 Harrison St., Oakland, CA, 94612; *PH:* 1-510-466-3402; *http://* www.gdw.com

General - Incorporation	DE	*Stock*- Price on:12/24/2007	$53.12
Employees	108,238	Stock Exchange	NA
Auditor	Deloitte & Touche LLP	Ticker Symbol	NA
Stk Agt	American Stock Transfer & Trust Co.	Outstanding Shares	1,910,000,000
Counsel	NA	E.P.S.	$4.79
DUNS No.	06-415-9833	Shareholders	NA

Business: The group's principal activities are to attract funds from the investing public and capital markets and investing those funds in loans. The group offers loans secured by residential real estate and mortgage backed securities. The group also accepts deposits. Various categories of deposits accepted by the group include passbook, checking, certificates of deposit and money market deposit accounts. The group operates through 479 branch offices in 38 states in the United States.

Primary SIC and add'l.: 6712 6035

CIK No: 0000042293

Subsidiaries: Atlas Advisers, Inc., Atlas Securities, Inc., World Savings Bank, FSB, World Savings Bank, FSB (TEXAS), World Savings Insurance Agency, Inc.

Financial Data: Fiscal Year End:12/31 Latest Annual Data: 06/30/2007

Year	Sales	Net Income
2007	NA	$3,131,000,000
2006	$46,810,000,000	$7,791,000,000
2005	$35,908,000,000	$6,643,000,000

Curr. Assets:	$94,763,000,000	*Curr. Liab.:*	$465,683,000,000	*P/E Ratio:*	11.21
Plant, Equip.:	$6,141,000,000	*Total Liab.:*	$634,304,000,000	*Indic. Yr. Divd.:*	$2.240
Total Assets:	$707,121,000,000	*Net Worth:*	$69,716,000,000	*Debt/ Equity:*	2.0395

Goldeneye Capital Group Inc

PO Box 110310, Naples, FL, 34108; *PH:* 1-239-598-2300

General - Incorporation	NV	*Stock*- Price on:12/24/2007	NA
Employees	NA	Stock Exchange	NA
Auditor	Child, Sullivan & Co	Ticker Symbol	NA
Stk Agt	Manhattan Transfer Registrar Co	Outstanding Shares	NA
Counsel	NA	E.P.S.	NA
DUNS No.	NA	Shareholders	NA

Business: The group has not yet identified any business opportunity or plans. The group operates from United States.

Primary SIC and add'l.: 9995

CIK No: 0001097885

Goldfield Corp (The)

100 Rialto Pl., Ste. 500, Melbourne, FL, 32901; *PH:* 1-327-224-1700; *Fax:* 1-323-308-1163; *http://* www.goldfieldcorp.com; *Email:* investorrelations@goldfieldcorp.com

General - Incorporation .... DE	**Stock**- Price on:12/24/2007 ....$0.93
Employees...120	Stock Exchange..AMEX
Auditor .... KPMG LLP	Ticker Symbol..GV
Stk Agt...... American Stock Transfer & Trust Co.	Outstanding Shares 25,450,000
Counsel LeBoeuf, Lamb, Greene & MacRae LLP	E.P.S...$0.06
DUNS No..................................05-210-1185	Shareholders...NA

Business: The group's principal activities are electrical construction and real estate development. The group's subsidiary, southeast power corporation, constructs transmission lines, distributes systems and substations and maintains electrical facilities for utilities and industrial consumers. The group also installs fiber optic cable for fiber optic cable manufacturers, telecommunication companies and electric utilities. Under its real estate development activities the group is involved in the development of small, high-end, waterfront condominium projects.

Primary SIC and add'l.: 1731 3357 6531

CIK No: 0000042316

Subsidiaries: Bayswater Development Corporation, Cape Club of Brevard, Inc., Country Club Point of Brevard, Inc., Florida Coastal Homes, Inc., Florida Transport Corporation, Oak Park of Brevard, Inc., Pineapple House of Brevard, Inc., Riomar of Brevard, Inc., Southeast Power Corporation

Officers: John H. Sottile/Chmn., CEO, Pres./$672,466.00, Stephen R. Wherry/Sr. VP, CFO/$261,289.00, Mary Manger/Sec.

Directors: John H. Sottile/Chmn., CEO, Pres., Dwight W. Severs/Dir., Al M. Marino/Dir., John P. Fazzini/Dir., Harvey C. Eads/Dir., Thomas E. Dewey/Dir., Danforth E. Leitner/Dir.

Owners: Danforth E. Leitner, Stephen R. Wherry, Harvey C. Eads, Thomas E. Dewey, John P. Fazzini, Al Marino/2.83%, Dwight W. Severs, Robert L. Jones/1.18%, John H. Sottile/5.02%, Insiders/9.77%

Financial Data: Fiscal Year End:12/31   Latest Annual Data: 12/31/2006

Year		Sales		Net Income
2006		$47,496,000		$2,996,000
2005		$39,344,000		$2,322,000
2004		$32,688,000		-$388,000
Curr. Assets:	$30,889,000	**Curr. Liab.:**	$14,573,000	**P/E Ratio:** 15.50
Plant, Equip.:	$10,176,000	**Total Liab.:**	$17,558,000	**Indic. Yr. Divd.:** NA
Total Assets:	$41,904,000	**Net Worth:**	$24,346,000	**Debt/ Equity:** 0.1512

Goldleaf Financial Solutions Inc

Formerly: Private Business Inc
9020 Overlook Blvd., 3rd Fl., Brentwood, TN, 37027; **PH:** 1-615-221-8400;
http:// www.privatebusiness.com

General - Incorporation .... TN	**Stock** - Price on:12/24/2007 ....$5.23
Employees...343	Stock Exchange...NDQ
Auditor ....Grant Thornton LLP	Ticker Symbol...GFSI
Stk Agt.......................................Suntrust Bank	Outstanding Shares 17,270,000
Counsel...................Brobeck, Phleger & Harrison	E.P.S...-$1.22
DUNS No...NA	Shareholders...NA

Business: The group's principal activity is to provide solutions that enable community banks market and manage accounts receivable financing. The group's products include business manager, insurance manager, linemanager, collection manager and identification manager. The business manager software enables the network of client banks to purchase accounts receivable from their small business customers. The banks then process, bill and track those receivables on an ongoing basis. Insurance manager enables smaller community banks to provide an array of insurance products. Linemanager is an information tool, enabling asset-based lenders to monitor the activity and quality of the assets that are the collateral to the loans.

Primary SIC and add'l.: 7379 7389

CIK No: 0001069469

Subsidiaries: Captiva Financial Solutions, LLC, a Tennessee corporation, Forseon Corporation, a Delaware corporation, Goldleaf Technologies, Inc., a Delaware corporation, KVI Capital, LLC, a Tennessee corporation, Private Business Insurance, LLC, a Tennessee corporation, Towne Services, Inc., a Georgia corporation

Officers: Lynn G. Boggs/Dir., CEO/$1,441,730.00, Henry M. Baroco/COO, Pres./$580,010.00, Scott R. Meyerhoff/Exec. VP/$594,890.00, Todd W. Shiver/Exec. VP - Sales, Marketing, Matthew W. Pribus/Exec. VP, John R. Polchin/CFO

Directors: Lynn G. Boggs/Dir., CEO, Robert A. McCabe/Chmn., John D. Schneider/Dir., Bill Mathis/Dir., Beck A. Taylor/Dir., Lawrence A. Hough/Dir., David W. Glenn/Dir., David B. Ingram/Dir.

Owners: Paul McCulloch/1.19%, Lynn G. Boggs/1.74%, Robert A. McCabe, Lawrence A. Hough, Lightyear Fund, L.P./13.78%, Scott R. Meyerhoff, John D. Schneider, Peninsula Capital Management, LP/11.42%, Scott J. Craighead, David B. Ingram, Wellington Management Co LLP/12.07%, Alydar Partners LLC/8.22%, Henry M. Baroco/1.23%, Wellington Trust Company NA/5.46%, Castine Capital Management/5.47% (16 Owners included in Index)

Financial Data: Fiscal Year End:12/31   Latest Annual Data: 12/31/2006

Year		Sales		Net Income
2006		$55,651,000		-$2,972,000
2005		$38,351,000		$2,335,000
2004		$39,649,000		$2,570,000
Curr. Assets:	$22,392,000	**Curr. Liab.:**	$16,685,000	
Plant, Equip.:	$3,266,000	**Total Liab.:**	$26,050,000	**Indic. Yr. Divd.:** NA
Total Assets:	$75,304,000	**Net Worth:**	$49,254,000	**Debt/ Equity:** 0.1830

Goldman Sachs Group Inc (The)

85 Brd St., 17th Fl., New York, NY, 10004; **PH:** 1-212-902-1000; http:// www.gs.com;
Email: gs-investor-relations@gs.com

General - Incorporation .... DE	**Stock**- Price on:12/24/2007 ....$229.51
Employees..30,335	Stock Exchange...NYSE
Auditor ....PricewaterhouseCoopers LLP	Ticker Symbol...GS
Stk Agt.....................Mellon Investor Services LLC	Outstanding Shares 434,900,000
Counsel...NA	E.P.S...$21.43
DUNS No...NA	Shareholders...NA

Business: The group's principle activity is to provide a wide range of services to substantial and diversified clients including corporations, financial institutions, governments and high-net-worth individuals. The group's client services include institutional portal, investment and merchant banking, private wealth management, and security and trading services. The group is divided into three segments including investment banking, trading and principle investments, and asset management and security services. The group operates from United States.

Primary SIC and add'l.: 6099 6211 6221 6282

CIK No: 0000886982

Subsidiaries: Chiltern Trust, ELQ Investors, LTD, Goldman Sachs (Asia) Finance, Goldman Sachs (Asia) Finance Holdings LLC, Goldman Sachs (Asia) LLC, Goldman Sachs (Asia) Securities Limited, Goldman Sachs (Cayman) Holding Company, Goldman Sachs (Japan) Ltd., Goldman Sachs (UK)L.L.C., Goldman Sachs Asset Management Co., Ltd., Goldman Sachs Asset Management International, Goldman Sachs Asset Management, L.P., Goldman Sachs Capital Markets, L.P., Goldman Sachs Credit Partners L.P., Goldman Sachs Execution & Clearing, L.P. 58 Subsidiaries included in the Index

Officers: Lloyd C. Blankfein/Chmn., CEO, John F.W . Rogers/MD, Sec. to The Board, David A. Viniar/CFO, Exec. VP, Gary D. Cohn/Dir., Co - COO, Pres., Jon Winkelried/Dir., Co - COO, Pres., Edward C. Forst/Exec. VP, Chief Administrative Officer, Gregory K. Palm/Exec. VP, General Counsel, Sec. - Corporation, Esta E. Stecher/Exec. VP, General Counsel, Sec. - Corporation, Kevin W. Kennedy/Exec. VP - Human Capital Management, MD, Alan M. Cohen/Exec. VP, Global Head - Compliance, MD, Beverly L. OToole/Assist. Sec.

Directors: Lloyd C. Blankfein/Chmn., CEO, John S. Weinberg/Vice Chmn., Rajat K. Gupta/Dir., Ruth J. Simmons/Dir., Stephen Friedman/Dir., Lois D. Juliber/Dir., John H. Bryan/Dir., Edward M. Liddy/Dir., Lord Browne/59/Dir., Claes Dahlback/Dir., James A. Johnson/Dir., Gary D. Cohn/Dir., Co - COO, Pres., Jon Winkelried/Dir., Co - COO, Pres.

Owners: Stephen Friedman, William W. George, Rajat K. Gupta, Edward M. Liddy, Insiders, Ruth J. Simmons, Barclays Global Investors, N.A. and other related entities/5.80%, Jon Winkelried, Gary D. Cohn, Claes Dahlbck, David A. Viniar, John H. Bryan, Parties to Shareholders Agreement/9.20%, James A. Johnson, (18 Owners included in Index)

Financial Data: Fiscal Year End:11/25   Latest Annual Data: 11/24/2006

Year		Sales		Net Income
2006		$69,353,000,000		$9,537,000,000
2005		$43,391,000,000		$5,626,000,000
2004		$29,839,000,000		$4,553,000,000
Curr. Assets:	$149,346,000,000	**Curr. Liab.:**	$398,830,000,000	**P/E Ratio:** 10.71
Plant, Equip.:	$4,083,000,000	**Total Liab.:**	$504,491,000,000	**Indic. Yr. Divd.:** $1.400
Total Assets:	$531,379,000,000	**Net Worth:**	$25,079,000,000	**Debt/ Equity:** 10.8294

Goldman Sachs Hedge Fund Partners II LLC

701 Mount Lucas Rd., Princeton, NJ, 08540; **PH:** 1-609-497-5500

General - Incorporation .... DE	**Stock**- Price on:12/24/2007 ....NA
Employees...NA	Stock Exchange...NA
Auditor .... Ernst & Young LLP	Ticker Symbol..NA
Stk Agt ....Registrar & Transfer Co	Outstanding Shares ....NA
Counsel...NA	E.P.S..NA
DUNS No...NA	Shareholders...NA

Business: The groups principle activity is to provide global investment banking, securities and investment management services. The company is limited liability group operating out of Delaware as an investment fund. As on 31/12/2004, the group had approximately $960.3 million net assets under management. Goldman Sachs Hedge Fund Strategies, LLC serves as the group's managing member. The group operates from United States.

Primary SIC and add'l.: 6211

CIK No: 0001260502

Goldman Sachs Hedge Fund Partners LLC

701 Mount Lucas Rd., Princeton, NJ, 08540; **PH:** 1-609-497-5500

General - Incorporation .... DE	**Stock**- Price on:12/24/2007 ....NA
Employees...NA	Stock Exchange...NA
Auditor .... Ernst & Young LLP	Ticker Symbol..NA
Stk Agt ....Registrar & Transfer Co	Outstanding Shares ....NA
Counsel...NA	E.P.S..NA
DUNS No...NA	Shareholders...NA

Business: The group's principle activity is to provide global investment banking, securities and investment management services. The group is limited liability group operating out of Delaware as an investment fund. The group had approximately $960.3 million net assets under management. Goldman Sachs Hedge Fund Strategies, LLC serves as the group's managing member. The group operates from United States.

Primary SIC and add'l.: 6211

CIK No: 0001173394

Subsidiaries: The Goldman Sachs Group, Inc.

Officers: Thomas Dobler/42/VP, Head - GTT, Peter Ort/37/MD, Head - Gels, Kent A. Clark/43/Dir., MD, Chief Investment Officer, Hugh J. Lawson/39/Dir., MD, Global Head - Product Management, Jennifer Barbetta/35/Dir., MD, CFO, Omar Asali/37/MD, Head - GED, Melanie Owen/30/VP, Head - GRV

Directors: Tobin V. Levy/64/Dir., Kent A. Clark/43/Dir., MD, Chief Investment Officer, Hugh J. Lawson/39/Dir., MD, Global Head - Product Management, Jennifer Barbetta/35/Dir., MD, CFO

Goldmountain Exploration Corp

Formerly: Konigsberg Corp
30-70 E Beaver Creek Rd., Richmond Hill, On, L4B 3B2; **PH:** 1-905-882-7044;
http:// www.konigsbergcorp.com

General - Incorporation	NV	Stock - Price on:12/24/2007	NA
Employees	NA	Stock Exchange	OTC
Auditor	Telford Sadovnick, PLLC	Ticker Symbol	GMEX
Stk Agt	Transfer Online, Inc	Outstanding Shares	NA
Counsel	NA	E.P.S.	NA
DUNS No.	NA	Shareholders	NA

Business: The groups principal activities include acquiring and exploring mineral properties. The group operates from the United States and Canada.

Primary SIC and add'l.: 1000

CIK No: 0001326780

Subsidiaries: KONIGSBERG EXPLORATIONS INC.

Officers: Darin W. Wagner/Dir., Pres., CEO - WTM, TSX, Adam R. Cegielski/Dir., Pres.

Directors: Darin W. Wagner/Dir., Pres., CEO - WTM, TSX, Adam R. Cegielski/Dir., Pres., Peter Megaw/Member - Advisory Board

Owners: Insiders/49.40%, Adam R. Cegielski/49.40%

Financial Data: Fiscal Year End:03/31 Latest Annual Data: 3/31/2007

Year	Sales	Net Income
2007	NA	-$685,000
2006	NA	-$72,000

Curr. Assets:	$20,000	Curr. Liab.:	$30,000		
Plant, Equip.:	$1,060,000	Total Liab.:	$30,000	Indic. Yr. Divd.:	NA
Total Assets:	$1,080,000	Net Worth:	$1,050,000	Debt/ Equity:	NA

GoldSpring Inc

8585 E Hartford Dr., Ste. 400, Scottsdale, AZ, 85255; *PH:* 1-480-505-4040; *Fax:* 1-775-847-4762; http:// www.goldspring.us

General - Incorporation	FL	Stock - Price on:12/24/2007	$0.0013
Employees	18	Stock Exchange	OTC
Auditor	Jewett, Schwartz, & Assoc.	Ticker Symbol	GSPG
Stk Agt	Corporate Stock Transfer, Inc.	Outstanding Shares	1,260,000,000
Counsel	NA	E.P.S.	-$0.004
DUNS No.	NA	Shareholders	NA

Business: The group's principal activity is to produce precious metals through state-of-the-art and conventional recovery methods. The group operates through the spring valley and gold canyon gold placer properties of harlesk Nevada inc. The properties consist of 21 unpatented placer claims covering approximately 850 acres located about 30 miles southeast of reno, Nevada. It also owns a copper ore recovery project known as the big mike project located in winnemucca, Nevada. On 01-Nov-2003, the group acquired plum mining company and assets of ecovery inc.

Primary SIC and add'l.: 1099 1041

CIK No: 0001120970

Officers: Robert T. Faber/Chmn., Principal Executive Officer, Principal Financial Officer, Pres., Robert S. Kant/Securities Counsel, Lawrence H. Wolfe/Independent Accountant, Jim Golden/49/COO

Directors: Robert T. Faber/Chmn., Principal Executive Officer, Principal Financial Officer, Pres., Todd S. Brown/Dir., Christopher L. Aguilar/Dir., Stanley A. Hirschman/Dir., William J. Nance/Dir., Rex L. Outzen/Dir.

Owners: John W. Winfield, Capital Ventures International, Christopher L. Aguilar, Robert T. Faber, Longview Equity Fund and Longview International Equity Fund, Longview Fund, L.P., Insiders

Financial Data: Fiscal Year End:12/31 Latest Annual Data: 12/31/2006

Year	Sales	Net Income
2006	$1,255,000	-$4,417,000
2005	$2,632,000	-$11,353,000
2004	$955,000	-$9,570,000

Curr. Assets:	$799,000	Curr. Liab.:	$18,631,000		
Plant, Equip.:	$2,378,000	Total Liab.:	$19,253,000	Indic. Yr. Divd.:	NA
Total Assets:	$3,554,000	Net Worth:	-$15,699,000	Debt/ Equity:	NA

Golf Rounds.com Inc

111 Village Pk.way Bldg., Ste. 2, Marietta, GA, 30067; *PH:* 1-770-951-0984

General - Incorporation	DE	Stock - Price on:12/24/2007	$0.8303
Employees	NA	Stock Exchange	OTC
Auditor	Weinberg & Company, P.A.	Ticker Symbol	TEEE
Stk Agt	American Stock Transfer & Trust Co.	Outstanding Shares	3,450,000
Counsel	NA	E.P.S.	-$0.01
DUNS No.	NA	Shareholders	NA

Business: The groups principal activity is in the wholesale distribution of aluminum alloys, steel and other specialty metals and serves as a vehicle for the acquisition of a target business. The group operates from the United States.

Primary SIC and add'l.: 6794

CIK No: 0000319016

Subsidiaries: DPE Acquisition Corp.

Officers: Robert H. Donehew/56/Dir., Pres., Treasurer, Sec.

Directors: Robert H. Donehew/56/Dir., Pres., Treasurer, Sec., Anthony Charos/44/Dir.

Owners: David S. Nagelberg/12.50%, Asset Value Holdings, Inc./5.80%, Robert H. Donehew/11.80%, John W. Galuchie/6.20%, Shamrock Associates/11.90%, Paul O. Koether/14.10%, Galt Asset Management/5.80%, Ronald I. Heller/10.70%, Insiders/15.10%, Anthony Charos/3.90%

Financial Data: Fiscal Year End:08/31 Latest Annual Data: 08/31/2006

Year	Sales	Net Income
2006	NA	-$88,000
2005	NA	-$104,000
2004	NA	-$366,000

Curr. Assets:	$2,255,000	Curr. Liab.:	$3,000		
Plant, Equip.:	NA	Total Liab.:	$3,000	Indic. Yr. Divd.:	NA
Total Assets:	$2,255,000	Net Worth:	$2,252,000	Debt/ Equity:	NA

Golf Trust of America Inc

72 Persimmon Ridge Dr., Louisville, KY, 40245; *PH:* 1-502-241-0456; *http://* www.golftrust.com

General - Incorporation	MD	Stock - Price on:12/24/2007	$2.6
Employees	508	Stock Exchange	AMEX
Auditor	BDO Seidman, LLP	Ticker Symbol	GTA
Stk Agt	Mellon Investor Services LLC	Outstanding Shares	7,320,000
Counsel	NA	E.P.S.	-$0.47
DUNS No.	NA	Shareholders	NA

Business: The groups principle activities include operating and acquiring upscale golf courses. The group operates from the United States. The group's quarterly revenue for September 2007 was 5.14 millions of USD.

Primary SIC and add'l.: 7997

CIK No: 0001024126

Subsidiaries: Golf Host Securities,Inc., Golf Trust of America, L.P., GTA Black Bear, LLC, GTA GP,Inc., GTA IB Condominium, LLC, GTA IB Golf Resort, LLC, GTA IB Management, LLC, GTA IB Operations, LLC, GTA IB, LLC, GTA LP,Inc., GTA Stonehenge, LLC, GTA Tierra Del Sol, LLC

Owners: Tracy S. Clifford, Edward L. Wax, Jay A. Gottlieb/8.28%, Merrill Lynch, Pierce, Fenner & Smith, Inc./5.06%, Jonathan M. Couchman/4.46%, William Vlahos/14.62%, Jan H. Loeb/11.54%, Bradley W. Blair/3.67%, Insiders/41.66%, Odyssey Value Advisors, LLC/9.57%

Financial Data: Fiscal Year End:12/31 Latest Annual Data: 12/31/2006

Year	Sales	Net Income
2006	NA	$83,000
2005	$712,000	-$6,073,000
2004	NA	-$12,238,000

Curr. Assets:	$5,116,000	Curr. Liab.:	$13,408,000	P/E Ratio:	183.33
Plant, Equip.:	$55,592,000	Total Liab.:	$32,213,000	Indic. Yr. Divd.:	NA
Total Assets:	$66,078,000	Net Worth:	$13,865,000	Debt/ Equity:	NA

GolfGear International Inc

12771 Pala Dr, Garden Grove, CA, 92841; *PH:* 1-714-899-4274

General - Incorporation	NV	Stock - Price on:12/24/2007	$0.004
Employees	NA	Stock Exchange	OTC
Auditor	Corbin & Co LLP	Ticker Symbol	GEAR
Stk Agt	Pacific Stock Transfer Company	Outstanding Shares	NA
Counsel	NA	E.P.S.	NA
DUNS No.	NA	Shareholders	NA

Business: The group's principal activities are to design, develop and market golf clubs and golf related products intended to improve the quality and performance of a golfer's game. The group utilizes its proprietary patented forged face insert technology to provide a full line of golf equipment. It markets a full range of patented metal woods and irons marketed under various names, including tsunami titanium drivers. The group offers these drivers in several sizes ranging from 300 cc's to 340 cc's. The principal product line of the group consists of the tsunami woods and irons. The group also markets a line of leading edge putters called the claw as well as a full line of junior clubs under the brand name players golf. The group operates in the United States, Far East and Europe.

Primary SIC and add'l.: 3949

CIK No: 0001053210

Subsidiaries: Bel Air Players Group, Inc, GearFit Golf Company, Leading Edge Acquisition, Inc., Pacific Golf Holdings, Inc

Financial Data: Fiscal Year End:12/31 Latest Annual Data: 12/31/2003

Year	Sales	Net Income
2003	$1,973,000	-$4,158,000
2002	$1,546,000	-$4,273,000
2001	$2,143,000	-$1,017,000

Curr. Assets:	$536,000	Curr. Liab.:	$2,780,000		
Plant, Equip.:	$34,000	Total Liab.:	$2,780,000	Indic. Yr. Divd.:	NA
Total Assets:	$650,000	Net Worth:	-$2,130,000	Debt/ Equity:	NA

Golfsmith International Holdings Inc

11000 N IH-35, Austin, TX, 78753; *PH:* 1-512-837-8810; *Fax:* 1-512-837-1245; http:// www.golfsmith.com

General - Incorporation	DE	Stock - Price on:12/24/2007	$6.78
Employees	880	Stock Exchange	NDQ
Auditor	Ernst& Young LLP	Ticker Symbol	GOLF
Stk Agt	National City Bank	Outstanding Shares	15,770,000
Counsel	Scott Wood	E.P.S.	-$0.76
DUNS No.	NA	Shareholders	NA

Business: The groups principle activity is to retailing golf and tennis equipment, apparel and accessories. The products of the group include apparel and footwear, golf balls, racquets and club components. The group products sold under the trade name Golfsmith (R), Black Cat (R), Crystal Cat (R), Killer Bee (R), Lynx (R), Parallax (R), Predator (R) and Snake Eyes (R). Customers served by the group include direct to consumer, store and international distributors and other. The group operates from the United States. The group's quarterly revenue for September 2007 was 106.53 millions of USD.

Primary SIC and add'l.: 3949 5091 5941

CIK No: 0001202273

Subsidiaries: Golfsmith International, Inc

Officers: James D. Thompson/Dir., CEO, Pres., Virginia Bunte/Sr. VP, CFO, Treasurer, Fred Quandt/Sr. VP - Merchandising, David Pritchett/Sr. VP - Retail Operations, Andrew Spratt/VP - Information Services, Kathryn Ingerly/VP - Finance, Michael Polishook/VP - Sales, New Business Development, Adrian Gonzalez/VP - Store Administration, Guest Experience, Jeff Sheets/VP - Research, Development, Matthew Corey/VP - Marketing, Brand, David Lowe/VP - Brands, Golf Instruction, Gillian Felix/Sr. VP - Human Resources, Guest Experience, Joseph J. Kester/VP - Field Operations, Scott R. Wood/General Counsel, Sec.

Directors: James D. Thompson/Dir., CEO, Pres., Martin E. Hanaka/Chmn., Thomas Hardy/Dir., Glenda Chamberlain/Dir., Roberto Buaron/Dir., Noel Wilens/Dir., James Long/Dir., Marvin E. Lesser/Dir., Thomas Berglund/Dir.

Owners: Roberto Buaron, Franklin Paul, Martin Hanaka, Kenneth Brugh, Marvin E. Lesser, James D. Thompson, Thomas G. Hardy, BlackRock, Inc., Atlantic Equity Partners III, L.P., Wellington Management Company, LLP, Glenda Chamberlain, David Pritchett, Frederick Quandt, Lawrence Mondry, Virgina Bunte (*18 Owners included in Index*)

Financial Data: Fiscal Year End:12/31 Latest Annual Data: 12/30/2006

Year	**Sales**	**Net Income**
2006	$357,890,000	-$7,018,000
2005	$323,794,000	$2,958,000

Curr. Assets:	$83,964,000	**Curr. Liab.:**	$61,164,000		
Plant, Equip.:	$46,570,000	**Total Liab.:**	$147,709,000	**Indic. Yr. Divd.:**	NA
Total Assets:	$204,836,000	**Net Worth:**	$57,127,000	**Debt/ Equity:**	NA

Good Buddys Coffee Express Inc

7 Richmond Ln., Blythewood, SC, 29016; *PH:* 1-803-920-4620

General - Incorporation	FL	**Stock**- Price on:12/24/2007	NA
Employees	NA	Stock Exchange	NA
Auditor	NA	Ticker Symbol	NA
Stk Agt	NA	Outstanding Shares	NA
Counsel	NA	E.P.S	NA
DUNS No.	NA	Shareholders	NA

Business: The group's principle activity is to operate restaurant. The group operates from United States.

Primary SIC and add'l.: 5810

CIK No: 0001221749

Officers: Scott Massey/36/Chmn., Pres., Principal Executive Officer

Directors: Scott Massey/36/Chmn., Pres., Principal Executive Officer, Phillips N. Dee/40/Dir.

Owners: Insiders/64.22%, Scott Massey/63.24%, Phillips N. Dee

Good Harbor PTR CL A

4100 N Fairfax Dr., Arlington, VA, 22203; *PH:* 1-703-812-9199; *http://* www.goodharborpartners.com

General - Incorporation	DE	**Stock**- Price on:12/24/2007	$1.01
Employees	NA	Stock Exchange	OTC
Auditor	NA	Ticker Symbol	GHBAA
Stk Agt	American Stock Transfer & Trust Co.	Outstanding Shares	NA
Counsel	NA	E.P.S	$0.09
DUNS No.	NA	Shareholders	NA

Business: The groups principal activities include identifying, researching and negotiating the purchase of business meeting the requirements and standards of business plan. The group operates from the United States.

Primary SIC and add'l.: 6770

CIK No: 0001337009

Officers: Ralph S. Sheridan/Dir., CEO, Sec., Thomas J. Colatosti/Dir., Pres., Treasurer

Directors: Ralph S. Sheridan/Dir., CEO, Sec., Richard A. Clarke/Chmn., Roger W. Cressey/Vice Chmn., Thomas J. Colatosti/Dir., Pres., Treasurer, John C. Mallon/Dir., Brian L. Stafford/Dir., John S. Tritak/Dir.

Owners: Jack Silver/1.70%, Pequot Capital Management, Inc./5.20%, Fir Tree Recovery Master Fund, LP/2.30%, Ralph S. Sheridan, Jack Silver/12.20%, Pequot Capital Management, Inc./6.50%, Sapling, LLC/7.30%, Weiss Asset Management, LLC/12.90%, The Baupost Group, LLC/6.50%, Pentagram Partners, LP/8.50%, Satellite Asset Management, LP/8.30%, Context Capital Management, LLC/8.10%

Financial Data: **Fiscal Year End:**12/31 **Latest Annual Data:** 12/31/2006

Year	**Sales**	**Net Income**
2006	NA	$906,000

Curr. Assets:	$56,214,000	**Curr. Liab.:**	$139,000		
Plant, Equip.:	NA	**Total Liab.:**	$11,084,000	**Indic. Yr. Divd.:**	NA
Total Assets:	$56,214,000	**Net Worth:**	$45,130,000	**Debt/ Equity:**	NA

Good Harbor PTR CL B

79 Byron Rd., Weston, MA, 02493; *PH:* 1-617-237-1014

General - Incorporation	DE	**Stock**- Price on:12/24/2007	$5.1
Employees	NA	Stock Exchange	OTC
Auditor	NA	Ticker Symbol	GHBBB
Stk Agt	NA	Outstanding Shares	NA
Counsel	NA	E.P.S	NA
DUNS No.	NA	Shareholders	NA

Business: The group is a development-stage blank check company formed for the purpose of effecting a merger, capital stock exchange, asset acquisition or other similar business combination with an entity that has an operating business in the security industry. The Company does not have any specific merger, capital stock exchange, asset acquisition or other business combination under consideration and it has not (nor has anyone on its behalf), directly or indirectly, contacted, or been contacted by, any potential target business or had any discussions, formal or otherwise, with respect to such a transaction. The group operates from United States.

Primary SIC and add'l.: 6770

CIK No: 0001337009

Officers: Ralph S. Sheridan/Dir., CEO, Sec., Thomas J. Colatosti/Dir., Pres., Treasurer

Directors: Ralph S. Sheridan/Dir., CEO, Sec., Richard A. Clarke/Chmn., Roger W. Cressey/Vice Chmn., Thomas J. Colatosti/Dir., Pres., Treasurer, John C. Mallon/Dir., Brian L. Stafford/Dir., John S. Tritak/Dir.

Owners: Ralph S. Sheridan, Sapling, LLC/7.30%, Satellite Asset Management, LP/8.30%, Context Capital Management, LLC/8.10%, Pequot Capital Management, Inc./5.20%, Pequot Capital Management, Inc./6.50%, Weiss Asset Management, LLC/12.90%, Pentagram Partners, LP/8.50%, Jack Silver/1.70%, Fir Tree Recovery Master Fund, LP/2.30%, Jack Silver/12.20%, The Baupost Group, LLC/6.50%

Good Times Restaurants Inc

601 Corporate Cir., Golden, CO, 80401; *PH:* 1-303-384-1400; *Fax:* 1-303-273-0177; *http://* www.goodtimesburgers.com

General - Incorporation	NV	**Stock**- Price on:12/24/2007	$5.39
Employees	89	Stock Exchange	NDQ
Auditor	Hein & Assoc. LLP	Ticker Symbol	GTIM
Stk Agt	Computershare Trust Co	Outstanding Shares	3,840,000
Counsel	NA	E.P.S	$0.03
DUNS No.	61-409-7145	Shareholders	NA

Business: The group's principal activities are to develop, own, operate and franchise hamburger-oriented drive-through restaurants. The group's major trademarks include good times! drive thru burgers, mighty deluxe, wild fries and spoonbender. The business operations are primarily in Colorado and operates eleven company-owned restaurants, nine joint-venture restaurants and sixteen franchised restaurants.

Primary SIC and add'l.: 5812 7011 6719

CIK No: 0000825324

Subsidiaries: Good Times Drive Thru Inc

Officers: Boyd E. Hoback/Dir., CEO, Pres., Eric W. Reinhard/Chmn., Officer, Scott G. Lefever/VP - Operations, Robert D. Turrill/VP - Marketing, Susan M. Knutson/Controller

Directors: Boyd E. Hoback/Dir., CEO, Pres., Eric W. Reinhard/Chmn., Officer, Richard J. Stark/Dir., Geoffrey R. Bailey/Dir., Ron Goodson/Dir., Alan A. Teran/Dir., David Grissen/Dir.

Owners: Geoffrey R. Bailey, Alan A. Teran, Richard J. Stark, The Erie County Investment Co., Boyd E. Hoback, Insiders, David Grissen, Paul T. Bailey, Commonwealth Equity Services, LLP, The Bailey Company, LLLP, Ron Goodson, Eric W. Reinhard, Scott G. LeFever

Financial Data: **Fiscal Year End:**09/30 **Latest Annual Data:** 9/30/2006

Year	**Sales**	**Net Income**
2006	$20,935,000	$17,000
2005	$16,961,000	-$418,000
2004	$15,781,000	-$665,000

Curr. Assets:	$3,047,000	**Curr. Liab.:**	$1,500,000		
Plant, Equip.:	$7,202,000	**Total Liab.:**	$3,816,000	**Indic. Yr. Divd.:**	NA
Total Assets:	$10,693,000	**Net Worth:**	$6,082,000	**Debt/ Equity:**	0.0421

Goodman Global Inc

2550 N Loop W, Ste. 400, Houston, TX, 77092; *PH:* 1-713-861-2500; *Fax:* 1-713-861-3207; *http://* www.goodmanmfg.com

General - Incorporation	DE	**Stock**- Price on:12/24/2007	$21.5
Employees	4,878	Stock Exchange	NYSE
Auditor	NA	Ticker Symbol	GGL
Stk Agt	Computershare Investor Services	Outstanding Shares	68,910,000
Counsel	NA	E.P.S	$1.42
DUNS No.	NA	Shareholders	NA

Business: The groups principal activities include manufacturing and marketing heating, ventilation and air conditioning products. The groups products include pumps, gas furnaces, packages units, air handlers, package terminal air conditioners, evaporator coils and accessories. The groups products marketed under the brand names Goodman(R), Amana(R) and Quietflex(R). The group operates from the United States. The groups total sales in the year 2006 were $1,794,753 (thousands).

Primary SIC and add'l.: 5075 3585 3564

CIK No: 0001314655

Subsidiaries: AsureCare Corp., Goodman Appliance Holding Company, Goodman Canada, L.L.C., Goodman Company Canada, Goodman Company, L.P., Goodman Distribution, Inc., Goodman Global Holdings, Inc., Goodman Holding Company, Goodman Holding Company, L.L.C., Goodman II Holdings Company, L.L.C., Goodman Manufacturing Company, L.P., Goodman Manufacturing I LLC, Goodman Manufacturing II LLC, Goodman Sales Company, Nitek Acquisition Company, L.P. 18 Subsidiaries included in the Index

Officers: Charles A. Carroll/58/Dir., CEO, Pres., Lawrence M. Blackburn/53/CFO, Exec. VP, Principal Financial Officer, Ben D. Campbell/51/Exec. VP, Sec., General Counsel, Donald R. King/51/Exec. VP - Human Resources, Peter H. Alexander/69/Sr. VP - Independent Distribution, Samuel G. Bikman/39/Sr. VP - Logistics, Business Development, Gary L. Clark/45/Sr. VP - Marketing, James L. Mishler/53/Pres. - Company Owned Distribution, Sr. VP, Terrance M. Smith/58/CIO, Sr. VP, William L. Topper/51/Sr. VP - Operations, Michael J. Bride/44/VP - Sales, Amana, Mark M. Dolan/48/VP, Corporate Controller, Treasurer, Ardee Toppe/44/Pres., VP, GM - Quietflex, Neelkanth S. Gupte/44/VP - Engineering

Directors: Charles A. Carroll/58/Dir., CEO, Pres., Laurence M. Berg/41/Dir., Anthony M. Civale/33/Dir., John B. Goodman/44/Dir., Steven Martinez/39/Dir., David Bechhofer/51/Dir., Jeffrey Benjamin/46/Dir., John J. Hannan/55/Dir., David W. Oskin/65/Dir., James H. Schultz/59/Dir., Michael D. Weiner/55/Dir.

Owners: Sam Houston Viterbo Abell 1991 Trust/1.26%, Meg Goodman Daniel 1984 Grantor Trust, John Bailey Goodman Jr. 1991 Trust/1.89%, Jeffrey Benjamin, Harold G. Goodman 1984 Grantor Trust, Donald R. King, Michael D. Weiner, William L. Topper, John Bailey Goodman 1984 Grantor Trust, Lawrence M. Blackburn/1.46%, Hutton Gregory Goodman 1994 Trust, Harriett Elizabeth Goodman 1991 Trust/1.89%, John J. Hannan, Frio Holdings LLC/41.05%, Harold Viterbo Goodman II 1994 Trust *(30 Owners included in Index)*

Financial Data: **Fiscal Year End:**NA **Latest Annual Data:** 12/31/2006

Year	**Sales**	**Net Income**
2006	$1,794,753,000	$64,167,000
2005	$1,565,406,000	$24,880,000

Curr. Assets:	$604,489,000	**Curr. Liab.:**	$247,309,000	**P/E Ratio:**	16.93
Plant, Equip.:	$172,246,000	**Total Liab.:**	$1,102,886,000	**Indic. Yr. Divd.:**	NA
Total Assets:	$1,623,971,000	**Net Worth:**	$521,085,000	**Debt/ Equity:**	1.5835

Goodrich Corp

Four Coliseum Ctr., 2730 W Tyvola Rd., Charlotte, NC, 28217; *PH:* 1-704-423-7000; *Fax:* 1-704-423-5540; *http://* www.goodrich.com; *Email:* corporate.communications@goodrich.com

General - Incorporation	NY	**Stock**- Price on:12/24/2007	$58.61
Employees	23,400	Stock Exchange	NYSE
Auditor	Ernst & Young LLP	Ticker Symbol	GR
Stk Agt	Bank of New York	Outstanding Shares	NA
Counsel	NA	E.P.S	$3.33
DUNS No.	00-446-7452	Shareholders	NA

Business: The group's principle activity is to provide systems and services to the aerospace, defense and homeland security markets. The group operates from North America, Europe and Asia.

Primary SIC and add'l.: 3728 7699

CIK No: 0000042542

Subsidiaries: A-Chem (U.K.) Limited, Advanced Egress Systems, Inc., ALA Corporation, AMI Industries FSC, Inc., AMI Industries, Inc., AS Engineering, Inc., BFGoodrich Capital, Brecksville Road Realty (I), LLC, CII Holdings Inc, CMK Corporation, Delavan European Marketing Company Limited, Delavan Inc, Delavan Limited, Delavan Spray, LLC, Delfzijl Resin C.V. 112 Subsidiaries included in the Index

Officers: Marshall O. Larsen/Chmn., CEO, Pres./$15,833,650.00, Cynthia M. Egnotovich/50/VP, Segment Pres. - Nacelles, Interior Systems, Jennifer Pollino/43/Sr. VP - Human Resources, Joseph F. Andolino/VP - Business Development, Tax, Janet Slakman/Assist. Sec., William G. Stiehl/VP - Internal Audit, Kelly Chopus/Sec. - Foundation, Lisa Bottle/VP - Corporate Communications, Terrence G. Linnert/Exec. VP - Administration, General Counsel/$5,022,310.00, John J. Grisik/Exec. VP - Operational Excellence, Technology/$5,168,844.00, John J. Carmola/Segment Pres. - Actuation, Landing Systems/$3,080,638.00, Jerry Witowski/Segment Pres. - Electronic Systems, Sally L. Geib/VP, Assoc. General Counsel, Sec., Scott Cottrill/VP, Controller, Houghton Lewis/VP, Treasurer *(17 Officers included in Index)*

Directors: Marshall O. Larsen/Chmn., CEO, Pres., Thomas A. Young/Dir., Lloyd W. Newton/Dir., William R. Holland/Dir., James W. Griffith/Dir., James R. Wilson/Dir., Douglas E. Olesen/Dir., Alfred M. Rankin/Dir., Harris E. Deloach/Dir., Diane C. Creel/Dir., George A. Davidson/Dir., John P. Jumper/Dir.

Owners: Thomas A. Young, William R. Holland, Alfred M. Rankin, Douglas E. Olesen, Diane C. Creel, Insiders/1.30%, Scott E. Kuechle, John J. Carmola, Terrence G. Linnert, Harris E. DeLoach, John J. Grisik, George A. Davidson, Marshall O. Larsen, Vanguard Windsor Funds/6.50%, James W. Griffith *(16 Owners included in Index)*

Financial Data: ***Fiscal Year End:***12/31 ***Latest Annual Data:*** 12/31/2006

Year	Sales	Net Income
2006	$5,878,300,000	$482,100,000
2005	$5,396,500,000	$263,600,000
2004	$4,724,500,000	$172,200,000

Curr. Assets:	$3,007,500,000	**Curr. Liab.:**	$1,632,600,000		
Plant, Equip.:	$1,327,700,000	**Total Liab.:**	$4,924,500,000	**Indic. Yr. Divd.:**	$0.800
Total Assets:	$6,901,200,000	**Net Worth:**	$1,976,700,000	**Debt/ Equity:**	0.8988

Goodrich Petroleum Corp

808 Travis St., Ste. 1320, Houston, TX, 77002; ***PH:*** 1-713-780-9494; ***Fax:*** 1-713-780-9254; ***http://*** www.goodrichpetroleum.com

General - Incorporation	DE	**Stock**- Price on:12/24/2007	$36.51
Employees	84	Stock Exchange	NYSE
Auditor	KPMG LLP	Ticker Symbol	GDP
Stk Agt	Computershare Investor Services LLC	Outstanding Shares	28,300,000
Counsel	NA	E.P.S	-$2.1
DUNS No.	03-685-3778	Shareholders	NA

Business: The group's principal activities are exploration, exploitation, development and production of oil and natural gas properties. A majority of proved oil and natural gas reserves are in the transition zone of south Louisiana and in north Louisiana, the gulf coast of Texas and east Texas. The group owns working and overriding royalty interests in 85 active oil and gas wells located in 22 fields in four states.

Primary SIC and add'l.: 1311

CIK No: 0000943861

Subsidiaries: Drilling & Workover Company, Inc, Goodrich Petroleum Company, Goodrich Petroleum Company LLC, LECE, Inc

Officers: Walter G. Goodrich/Vice Chmn., CEO/$1,392,850.00, James B. Davis/Sr. VP - Engineering, Operations/$619,201.00, Andrew W. Bagot/VP - Geology, James G. Marston/VP - Land, Mark E. Ferchau/Exec. VP/$972,617.00, Robert C. Turnham/COO, Pres./$1,258,500.00, David R. Looney/CFO, Exec. VP/$773,892.00, Jan L. Schott/VP, Controller, Lloyd Armstrong/VP - Operational Accounting, Tom S. Nemec/VP - Project Management, James Marston/VP, Kristie Oviedo/Investor Relations Officer, Robert Turnham/Pres.

Directors: Walter G. Goodrich/Vice Chmn., CEO, Patrick E. Malloy/Chmn., John Callaghan/Dir., Arthur A. Seeligson/Dir., Gene Washington/Dir., Geraldine A. Ferraro/Dir., Josiah T. Austin/Dir., Michael J. Perdue/Dir., Henry Goodrich/Dir.

Owners: Henry Goodrich/1.20%, Walter G. Goodrich/4.40%, Steven A. Webster, John T. Callaghan, Robert C. Turnham/1.10%, Insiders/46.10%, Patrick E. Malloy/18.80%, Michael J. Perdue, Gene Washington, FMR Corp/13.20%, Arthur A. Seeligson, Mark E. Ferchau, Josiah T. Austin/19.90%, Geraldine Ferraro, James B. Davis *(16 Owners included in Index)*

Financial Data: ***Fiscal Year End:***12/31 ***Latest Annual Data:*** 03/31/2007

Year	Sales	Net Income
2007	$23,542,000	$1,036,000
2006	$116,154,000	$1,639,000
2005	$68,333,000	-$17,450,000

Curr. Assets:	$41,170,000	**Curr. Liab.:**	$63,337,000		
Plant, Equip.:	$420,620,000	**Total Liab.:**	$274,131,000	**Indic. Yr. Divd.:**	NA
Total Assets:	$479,264,000	**Net Worth:**	$205,133,000	**Debt/ Equity:**	0.8457

Goodyear Tire & Rubber Com (The)

1144 E Market St., Akron, OH, 44316; ***PH:*** 1-330-796-2121; ***Fax:*** 1-330-796-2222; ***http://*** www.goodyear.com

General - Incorporation	OH	**Stock**- Price on:12/24/2007	$34.65
Employees	77,000	Stock Exchange	NYSE
Auditor	PricewaterhouseCoopers LLP	Ticker Symbol	GT
Stk Agt	Computershare Investor Services LLC	Outstanding Shares	182,050,000
Counsel	NA	E.P.S	-$2.87
DUNS No.	00-446-7924	Shareholders	NA

Business: The groups principle activity is to manufacture tires and rubber products. The group's products include Eagle F1all season,. The group operates from United States. The group operates from United States.

Primary SIC and add'l.: 3052 2869 3011 5013

CIK No: 0000042582

Subsidiaries: 4 Fleet Group GmbH, Abacom (Pty.) Ltd., Air Treads New Zealand Limited, AOT Canada Ltd., Artic (Zambia) Limited, Artic Retreading Products (Pty) Ltd., Beaurepaires for Tyre Limited, Belt Concepts of America, Inc., Cegyco S.A., Celeron Corporation, Compania Anonima Goodyear de Venezuela, Compania Goodyear del Peru, S.A., Compania Goodyear S. de R.L. de C.V., Corporacion Industrial Mercurio S.A. de C.V., Cosmoflex, Inc. 200 Subsidiaries included in the Index

Officers: Robert J. Keegan/Chmn., CEO, Pres., Lawrence D. Mason/48/Pres. - Consumer Tires, North American Tire, Darren Wells/43/Sr. VP - Finance, Strategy, Arthur De Bok/46/Pres. - European Union, Isabel H. Jasinowski/59/VP - Government Relations, Jarro F. Kaplan/Pres. - Eastern Europe, Africa, Middle East, Richard J. Kramer/45/Pres. - North American Tire, Christopher W. Clark/57/Sr. VP - Global Sourcing, Damon J. Audia/37/VP, Treasurer, Charles L. Sinclair/57/Sr. VP - Global Communications, Joseph M. Gingo/64/Exec. VP - Quality Systems, CTO, Eduardo A. Fortunato/55/Pres. - Latin America Region, Pierre E. Cohade/47/Pres. - Asia Pacific Region, Kathleen T. Geier/52/Sr. VP - Human Resources, Thomas C. Harvie/65/Sr. VP, General Counsel, Sec. *(26 Officers included in Index)*

Directors: Robert J. Keegan/Chmn., CEO, Pres., Denise M. Morrison/54/Dir., James C. Boland/68/Dir., John G. Breen/73/Dir., Gary D. Forsee/Dir., William J. Hudson/73/Dir., Steven A. Minter/69/Dir., Rodney ONeal/54/Dir., Shirley D. Peterson/66/Dir., Thomas H. Weidemeyer/60/Dir., Michael R. Wessel/48/Dir., Craig G. Sullivan/67/Dir.

Owners: Thomas H. Weidemeyer, Richard J. Kramer, LSV Asset Management/5.20%, Steven A. Minter, Brandes Investment Partners, L.P./12.90%, Thomas C. Harvie, James C. Boland, John G. Breen, Craig G. Sullivan, Insiders/1.50%, Robert J. Keegan, Jonathan D. Rich, Joseph M. Gingo, Gary D. Forsee, William J. Hudson *(17 Owners included in Index)*

Financial Data: ***Fiscal Year End:***12/31 ***Latest Annual Data:*** 12/31/2006

Year	Sales	Net Income
2006	$20,258,000,000	-$330,000,000
2005	$19,723,000,000	$228,000,000
2004	$18,370,400,000	$114,800,000

Curr. Assets:	$10,179,000,000	**Curr. Liab.:**	$4,666,000,000		
Plant, Equip.:	$5,377,000,000	**Total Liab.:**	$16,910,000,000	**Indic. Yr. Divd.:**	NA
Total Assets:	$17,029,000,000	**Net Worth:**	-$758,000,000	**Debt/ Equity:**	NA

Google Inc

1600 Amphitheatre Pkwy., Mountain View, CA, 94043; ***PH:*** 1-650-253-0000; ***Fax:*** 1-650-253-0001; ***http://*** www.google.com

General - Incorporation	DE	**Stock**- Price on:12/24/2007	$509.97
Employees	10,674	Stock Exchange	NDQ
Auditor	Ernst & Young LLP	Ticker Symbol	GOOG
Stk Agt	Computershare Trust Co	Outstanding Shares	311,550,000
Counsel	NA	E.P.S	$12.31
DUNS No.	NA	Shareholders	NA

Business: The groups principle activity is to provide advertising and global Internet search solutions through its Internet site. In the year 2007, the group acquires Adscape Media Inc. The group operates from United States.

Primary SIC and add'l.: 7375

CIK No: 0001288776

Subsidiaries: Applied Semantics, Inc., dMarc Broadcasting, Inc., Google (Hong Kong) Limited, Google Akwan Internet Ltda., Google Australia Pty Limited, Google Brasil Internet Ltda, Google Canada Corporation, Google Denmark ApS, Google France SarL, Google Germany GmbH, Google International GmbH, Google International LLC, Google Ireland Holdings Limited, Google Ireland Limited, Google Italy s.r.l. 37 Subsidiaries included in the Index

Officers: Eric Schmidt/Chmn., CEO, David C. Drummond/Sr. VP - Corporate Development, Chief Legal Officer, Sergey Brin/34/Dir., Co - Founder, Pres. - Technology, Shona Brown/Sr. VP - Business Operations, David Eun/VP - Content Partnerships, Udi Manber/VP - Engineering, Marissa Mayer/VP - Search Products, User Experience, Douglas Merrill/VP - Engineering, David Fischer/VP - Online Sales, Operations, David Radcliffe/VP - Real Estate, Sheryl Sandberg/VP - Global Online Sales, Operations, Susan Wojcicki/VP - Product Management, Larry Brilliant/Exec. Dir. - Googleorg, Omid Kordestani/Sr. VP - Global Sales, Business Development, Stuart Feldman/VP - Engineering *(47 Officers included in Index)*

Directors: Eric Schmidt/Chmn., CEO, Larry Page/Dir., Arthur D. Levinson/Dir., Paul S. Otellini/Dir., John L. Hennessy/Dir., Sergey Brin/34/Dir., Co - Founder, Pres. - Technology, John L. Doerr/Dir., Ann Mather/Dir., Ram K. Shriram/Dir., Shirley M. Tilghman/Dir.

Owners: Jonathan Rosenberg, K. Ram Shriram/2.10%, Insiders, Paul S. Otellini, John L. Hennessy, George Reyes, David Drummond, Eric Schmidt, Eric Schmidt/13.30%, Ann Mather, Capital Research & Management Company/5.70%, Shona Brown, Entities affiliated with Fidelity/11.10%, Jonathan Rosenberg, Arthur D. Levinson *(27 Owners included in Index)*

Financial Data: ***Fiscal Year End:***12/31 ***Latest Annual Data:*** 12/31/2006

Year	Sales	Net Income
2006	$10,604,917,000	$3,077,446,000
2005	$6,138,560,000	$1,465,397,000
2004	$3,189,223,000	$399,119,000

Curr. Assets:	$13,039,847,000	**Curr. Liab.:**	$1,304,587,000	**P/E Ratio:**	44.23
Plant, Equip.:	$2,395,239,000	**Total Liab.:**	$1,433,511,000	**Indic. Yr. Divd.:**	NA
Total Assets:	$18,473,351,000	**Net Worth:**	$17,039,840,000	**Debt/ Equity:**	NA

Gorman-Rupp Co (The)

PO Box 1217, Mansfield, OH, 44901; ***PH:*** 1-419-755-1011; ***Fax:*** 1-419-755-1233; ***http://*** www.gormanrupp.com; ***Email:*** gradmin@gormanrupp.com

General - Incorporation	OH	**Stock**- Price on:12/24/2007	$32.95
Employees	1,049	Stock Exchange	AMEX
Auditor	Ernst & Young LLP	Ticker Symbol	GRC
Stk Agt	National City Bank	Outstanding Shares	13,360,000
Counsel	NA	E.P.S	$1.55
DUNS No.	00-415-4038	Shareholders	NA

Business: The group's principle activities are to design, manufacture and market pumps and related fluid control equipment for use in water, wastewater, construction, industrial, petroleum, original equipment, agricultural, fire protection, military and other liquid-handling applications. The principal products are pumps and fluid control products. The group produces variety of pumps such as self priming centrifugal, standard centrifugal, magnetic drive centrifugal, axial and mixed flow, rotary gear, diaphragm, bellows and oscillating. The pumps are used in X-ray processing, gas air conditioning, floor cleaning equipment, office copy machines, instrumentation and ice cube making machinery, etc. The products are sold in the United States and Canada through a network of 1,000 distributors, manufacturers' representative, direct sales and through wholly owned subsidiaries. The operations of the group are carried out in the United States. The group's quarterly revenue for Sep'07 was 74.63 millions of USD.

Primary SIC and add'l.: 3561

CIK No: 0000042682

Subsidiaries: American Machine and Tool Co., Inc, Gorman-Rupp of Canada Limited, Patterson Pump Company, The Gorman-Rupp International Company

Officers: Jeffrey S. Gorman/CEO, Pres./$411,877.00, David P. Emmens/Corporate Counsel, Sec., Judith L. Sovine/Treasurer/$212,323.00, Lee Wilkins/VP - Human Resources/$148,470.00, Robert E. Kirkendall/Sr. VP, CFO/$287,929.00, William D. Danuloff/CIO, VP/$200,817.00

Owners: Insiders/14.09%, James C. Gorman/7.95%, Jeffrey S. Gorman/5.24%, Unicredito Italiano/6.20%

Financial Data: Fiscal Year End:12/31 Latest Annual Data: 12/31/2006

Year	Sales	Net Income
2006	$270,910,000	$19,072,000
2005	$231,249,000	$10,903,000
2004	$203,554,000	$9,277,000

Curr. Assets:	$120,118,000	Curr. Liab.:	$27,646,000	P/E Ratio:	22.41
Plant, Equip.:	$52,351,000	Total Liab.:	$59,398,000	Indic. Yr. Divd.:	$0.480
Total Assets:	$187,540,000	Net Worth:	$128,142,000	Debt/ Equity:	NA

Gottaplay Interactive Inc

Formerly: Donobi Inc

3256 Chico Way Nw, Bremerton, WA, 98312; **PH:** 1-360-782-4477; http:// www.gottaplay.com

General - Incorporation	NV	**Stock**- Price on:12/24/2007	$1.6
Employees	12	Stock Exchange	OTC
Auditor	Lake & Associates CPA'S LLC	Ticker Symbol	GTAP
Stk Agt	Colonial Stock Transfer Co Inc	Outstanding Shares	31,100,000
Counsel	NA	E.P.S.	NA
DUNS No.	NA	Shareholders	NA

Business: The groups principle activity is to provide online video game rental services. The group operates through two segments namely on-line video game and Internet service provider. The group operates from the United States.

Primary SIC and add'l.: 7372

CIK No: 0000831232

Officers: John P. Gorst/Chmn., CEO, Carroll M. Benton/CFO, Chief Administrative Officer, Sec., Treasurer, Dir. - Gottaplay, William M. Wright/Dir., COO, Asra Rasheed/Pres.

Directors: John P. Gorst/Chmn., CEO, Carroll M. Benton/CFO, Chief Administrative Officer, Sec., Treasurer, Dir. - Gottaplay, William M. Wright/Dir., COO

Owners: John P. Gorst/11.29%, Mark H. Levin/10.29%, Asra Rasheed/6.13%, Carroll M. Benton/11.28%, THI Inc, LLC/8.31%, Insiders/41.60%, William M. Wright/1.43%, Norm Johnson, Whispering Pines Development, Ltd./5.12%

Curr. Assets:	$331,000	Curr. Liab.:	$2,970,000		
Plant, Equip.:	$282,000	Total Liab.:	$3,055,000	Indic. Yr. Divd.:	NA
Total Assets:	$1,679,000	Net Worth:	-$1,376,000	Debt/ Equity:	NA

Gottschalks Inc

7 River Pk. Pl. E, Fresno, CA, 93720; **PH:** 1-559-434-4800; **Fax:** 1-559-434-4666; http:// www.gottschalks.com

General - Incorporation	DE	**Stock**- Price on:12/24/2007	$12.86
Employees	4,100	Stock Exchange	NYSE
Auditor	Deloitte & Touche LLP	Ticker Symbol	GOT
Stk Agt	Mellon Investor Services LLC	Outstanding Shares	13,670,000
Counsel	O'melveny & Myers	E.P.S.	-$0.25
DUNS No.	14-757-5138	Shareholders	NA

Business: The group's principle activity is to operate department and specialty store chain business. The Department Stores Offer A Wide Range Of Better To Moderate Brand-Name And Private-Label Merchandise, Including Men's, Women's, Juniors And Children's Apparel, Cosmetics, Shoes, Fine Jewelry And Accessories And Home Furnishings Including China, Housewares, Domestics, Small Electric Appliances And Furniture And Mattresses. The Group Currently Operates 63 Full-Line Gottschalks Department Stores Located In 6 Western States, With 39 Stores Located In California, 12 In Washington, 6 In Alaska And 2 In Each Of Oregon, Nevada And Idaho. It Also Operates 11 Village East And Gottschalks Specialty Stores. The group operates from United States.

Primary SIC and add'l.: 5399 5311

CIK No: 0000790414

Subsidiaries: El Corte Ingles (ECI), Gottschalks Credit Receivables Corporation(GCRC)

Officers: James Famalette/Chmn., CEO, Pres./$652,709.00, Gregory J. Ambro/COO, Exec. VP/$415,662.00, Michael Schmidt/Sr. VP, Dir. - Stores/$343,071.00

Directors: James Famalette/Chmn., CEO, Pres., Joe Levy/Chmn. Emeritus, Philip S. Schlein/73/Dir., Sharon Levy/Dir., James Czech/Dir., Tom H. McPeters/Dir., Jorge Pont Sanchez/Dir., Joseph J. Penbera/Dir., Frederick R. Ruiz/65/Dir., Dale D. Achabal/Dir., O. J. Woodward/Dir.

Owners: Michael J. Schmidt, Dimensional Fund/7.90%, James O. Woodward, The Harris Company/15.30%, Cramer Rosenthal/5.70%, Scott G. Manson, Pequot Capital Management, Inc./4.20%, Joe Levy/9.10%, Gregory J. Ambro, Insiders/13.90%, James R. Famalette/2.80%, Jana Partners LLC/5.30%, Robert C. Wiser, Frederick R. Ruiz, Gary L. Gladding (18 Owners included in Index)

Financial Data: Fiscal Year End:01/28 Latest Annual Data: 2/3/2007

Year	Sales	Net Income
2007	$687,481,000	$2,649,000
2006	$676,826,000	$5,200,000
2005	$668,613,000	$5,281,000

Curr. Assets:	$202,372,000	Curr. Liab.:	$85,071,000	P/E Ratio:	91.86
Plant, Equip.:	$134,696,000	Total Liab.:	$225,474,000	Indic. Yr. Divd.:	NA
Total Assets:	$350,066,000	Net Worth:	$124,592,000	Debt/ Equity:	1.0119

Gourmet Herb Growers Inc

2302 Parleys Way, Salt Lake City, UT, 84109; **PH:** 1-801-466-4614

General - Incorporation	NV	**Stock**- Price on:12/24/2007	$1.02
Employees	NA	Stock Exchange	OTC
Auditor	Pritchett, Siler & Hardy, P.C.	Ticker Symbol	GMHB
Stk Agt	Interwest Transfer Company, Inc.	Outstanding Shares	NA
Counsel	homas G. Kimble & Associates, P.C.	E.P.S.	-$0.01
DUNS No.	NA	Shareholders	NA

Business: The groups principal activity is to investigate potential acquisitions with other companies. The group operates from the United States.

Primary SIC and add'l.: 6770

CIK No: 0001059885

Officers: Thomas G. Kimble/62/Dir., Pres., Sec. - Treas

Directors: Thomas G. Kimble/62/Dir., Pres., Sec. - Treas

Owners: Insiders/63.00%, Lynn Dixon/9.00%, Brenda White/9.00%, Melissa Epperson/9.00%, Thomas G. Kimble/63.00%

Financial Data: Fiscal Year End:12/31 Latest Annual Data: 12/31/2006

Year	Sales	Net Income
2006	NA	-$10,000
2005	NA	-$7,000
2004	NA	-$7,000

Curr. Assets:	NA	Curr. Liab.:	$1,000		
Plant, Equip.:	NA	Total Liab.:	$1,000	Indic. Yr. Divd.:	$0.250
Total Assets:	NA	Net Worth:	-$1,000	Debt/ Equity:	NA

Gouverneur Bancorp Inc

42 Church St., Gouverneur, NY, 13642; **PH:** 1-315-287-2600; **Fax:** 1-315-287-3340; http:// www.gouverneurbank.com; **Email:** gsla@bankmail.com

General - Incorporation	DE	**Stock**- Price on:12/24/2007	$10.75
Employees	33	Stock Exchange	AMEX
Auditor	NA	Ticker Symbol	GOV
Stk Agt	NA	Outstanding Shares	2,300,000
Counsel	NA	E.P.S.	$0.41
DUNS No.	NA	Shareholders	NA

Business: The groups principle activity is to provide banking services. The group operates from the United States.

Primary SIC and add'l.: 6035 6712

CIK No: 0001063942

Subsidiaries: Gouverneur Savings and Loan Association.

Officers: Richard F. Bennett/Dir., Pres., CEO - Gouverneur Savings, Loan Association, Frank Langevin/Dir., Chmn. - Gouverneur Savings, Loan Association, Robert Leader/Dir. - Gouverneur Savings, Loan Association, Timothy Monroe/Dir. - Gouverneur Savings, Loan Association, Toby F. Morrow/Dir. - Gouverneur Savings, Loan Association, Joseph Pistolesi/Dir. - Gouverneur Savings, Loan Association, Larry Straw/Dir. - Gouverneur Savings, Loan Association, Robert Twyman/CFO - Gouverneur Savings, Loan Association, Kathleen McIntosh/Treasurer - Gouverneur Savings, Loan Association, John Bartlett/VP - Gouverneur Savings, Loan Association, Charles Vanvleet/VP - Gouverneur Savings, Loan Association, Thomas Penn/VP - Gouverneur Savings, Loan Association, Cheryl Hay/Assist. Sec. - Gouverneur Savings, Loan Association, Richard Jones/Dir. - Gouverneur Savings, Loan Association

Owners: Timothy J. Monroe, Richard E. Jones, Robert J. Leader/1.57%, Cambray Mutual Holding Company/57.07%, Insiders/9.28%, Frank Langevin/1.59%, Toby F. Morrow, Third Avenue Management/6.19%, Richard F. Bennett/2.99%, Joseph C. Pistolesi

Financial Data: Fiscal Year End:09/30 Latest Annual Data: 09/30/2006

Year	Sales	Net Income
2006	$8,448,000	$1,300,000
2005	$7,030,000	$1,032,000
2004	$5,866,000	$860,000

Curr. Assets:	$4,707,000	Curr. Liab.:	$74,970,000	P/E Ratio:	24.43
Plant, Equip.:	$2,225,000	Total Liab.:	$110,220,000	Indic. Yr. Divd.:	$0.320
Total Assets:	$130,075,000	Net Worth:	$19,855,000	Debt/ Equity:	NA

Government Properties Trust Inc

13625 California St., Ste. 310, Omaha, NE, 68154; **PH:** 1-402-391-0010; http:// www.gptrust.com

General - Incorporation	MD	**Stock**- Price on:12/24/2007	NA
Employees	NA	Stock Exchange	NA
Auditor	Ernst & Young LLP	Ticker Symbol	NA
Stk Agt	LaBranche & Co Inc.	Outstanding Shares	NA
Counsel	NA	E.P.S.	NA
DUNS No.	NA	Shareholders	NA

Business: The groups principle activities include buying, owning and managing recently built office properties. In the year 2006, the group acquired Denver EPA property, Riverside property and Harlingen USCIS property. The group operates from the United States.

Primary SIC and add'l.: 6798

CIK No: 0001266112

Subsidiaries: Acquest Government Leases, LLC, Buffalo NY SSA, LLC, Charleston Federal Courthouse, LLC, Charleston SS, LLC, Clarksburg GSA, LLC, Dallas SSA, LP, DEA Bakersfield, LLC, Denver EPA LLC, GPT Portland, OR 1201 Lloyd, LLC, GPT Riverside CA, Inc., GPT Vicksburg, MS, Inc., Harlingen USCIS LP, Kingsport SSA, LLC, Lenexa FDA, LLC, Loudoun Building, LLC 22 Subsidiaries included in the Index

Officers: Thomas D. Peschio/CEO, Pres., James E. Okell/Dir. - Acquisition Processing, Edward C. Fuxa/Dir. - Accounting, Finance, John V. Hrupek/Mgr. - Asset Acquisition, Willard H. Rosegay/Acquisition Coordinator, Nancy D. Olson/CFO, Treasurer, Gary L. Marron/Dir. - Asset Management, Oscar P. Peterson/Dir. - Asset Acquisition, Beth Schulze/Mgr. - Accounting, Scott M. Hedrick/Asset Mgr., James P. Dugdale/Acquisition Coordinator, Virginia M. Larsen/Contract Administrator, Melinda Gruhn/Administrative Assist.

Directors: Jerry D. Bringard/Chmn., Philip S. Cottone/Dir., Robert M. Ames/Dir., Robert A. Peck/Dir., Richard H. Schwachter/Dir.

Owners: Royce& Associates, LLC/5.74%, Hotchkis and Wiley Capital Management, LLC/7.25%, Jerry D. Bringard, Philip S. Cottone, Robert M. Ames, Insiders/1.20%, Thomas D. Peschio, Robert A. Peck, Richard H. Schwachter, Wells Fargo& Company/7.44%, Nancy D. Olson, Cadmus Capital Management, LLC/5.21%

GP Strategies Corp

6095 Marshalee Dr., Ste. 300, Elkridge, MD, 21075; *PH:* 1-410-379-3600; *Fax:* 1-410-540-5302; *http://* www.gpstrategies.com; *Email:* info@gpworldwide.com

General - Incorporation............................ DE	Stock - Price on:12/24/2007 ....$10.8
Employees...1,599	Stock Exchange..NYSE
Auditor ....KPMG LLP	Ticker Symbol..GPX
Stk Agt..... Computershare Investor Services LLC	Outstanding Shares 16,490,000
Counsel...NA	E.P.S..$0.53
DUNS No. 00-167-2633	Shareholders...NA

Business: The group's principal activity is to operate through three business segments: manufacturing and process: provides technology based training, engineering and consulting services to automotive, steel, food and beverage industries. Information technology: provides information technology training programs and solutions including enterprise solutions and comprehensive career training programs. Simulation: provides real-time simulation, homeland security and engineering services for the energy, process and military industries. Optical plastics: manufactures and distributes coated and molded plastic products such as shields and facemasks and non-optical plastic products. Home improvement distribution: distributes paint sundry items, interior and exterior stains, brushes, rollers, caulking compounds and hardware products on a regional basis. In 2003, the group acquired additional 36% interest in gse systems inc.

Primary SIC and add'l.: 7389 5198 3089 8742 8299

CIK No: 0000070415

Subsidiaries: General Physics Corporation

Officers: Scott N. Greenberg/51/Dir., CEO, Douglas E. Sharp/Pres., Sharon Esposito-Mayer/CFO, Exec. VP, Karl Baer/Exec. VP, Larry T. Davis/Exec. VP, Kenneth L. Crawford/Sr. VP, General Counsel, Sec.

Directors: Scott N. Greenberg/51/Dir., CEO, Harvey P. Eisen/Chmn., Ogden R. Reid/Dir., Richard C. Pfenniger/52/Dir., Jerome I. Feldman/80/Dir., Marshall S. Geller/69/Dir.

Owners: Sharon Esposito-Mayer, Richard C. Pfenniger, Jerome I. Feldman/1.60%, Dimensional Fund Advisors LP/7.80%, Pequot Capital Management, Inc./7.20%, Ogden R. Reid, Caxton Associates LLC/8.20%, Royce & Associates, LLC/5.10%, Douglas E. Sharp, Karl Baer, Scott N. Greenberg, Harvey P. Eisen/2.10%, Insiders/6.90%, Marshall S. Geller/1.30%

Financial Data: *Fiscal Year End:*12/31   *Latest Annual Data:* 12/31/2006

Year		Sales		Net Income
2006		$178,783,000		$6,642,000
2005		$175,555,000		$7,213,000
2004		$193,973,000		$22,520,000
Curr. Assets:	$52,956,000	Curr. Liab.:	$29,814,000	P/E Ratio: 24.55
Plant, Equip.:	$1,859,000	Total Liab.:	$41,669,000	Indic. Yr. Divd.: NA
Total Assets:	$121,400,000	Net Worth:	$79,731,000	Debt/ Equity: 0.1059

GPC-Biotech

610 Lincoln St., Waltham, MA, 02451; *PH:* 1-781-466-4400; *http://* www.gpc-biotech.com

General - Incorporation....................Germany	Stock - Price on:12/24/2007 ....$26.63
Employees..245	Stock Exchange...NDQ
Auditor .... Ernst & Young AG	Ticker Symbol...GPCB
Stk Agt..............................Bank of New York	Outstanding Shares 35,950,000
Counsel...NA	E.P.S..-$3.33
DUNS No. ....NA	Shareholders...NA

Business: The groups principle activities include discovering, developing and commercializing new anticancer drugs. The group operates from United States.

Primary SIC and add'l.: NA

CIK No: 0001117629

Subsidiaries: GPC Biotech Inc.

Officers: Margaret Ference/49/VP - US Sales, Leon Kentner/50/VP, Quality AssuranceVP - Quality Assurance, Ramona Lloyd/44/VP - World Wide Regulatory Affairs - Quality Compliance, Gerhard Muller/VP - Drug Discovery, Benno Rattel/49/VP - Nonclinical Development, Anne Marie Robertson/45/VP - World Wide Marketing - Product Planning, Hemanshu Shah/VP - Commercial Operations, Brent Hatzis-Schoch/VP, General Counsel, Gregory H. Hamm/VP - Corporate Integration, VP - Bioinformatics, Information Technology, Marcel Rozencweig/Sr. VP - Clinical Science, Drug Evaluation, John P. Richard/Sr. Business Advisor

Directors: Jurgen Drews/Chmn. - Supervisory Board, Michael Lytton/Vice Chmn. - Supervisory Board, Metin Colpan/Member - Supervisory Board, Donald Soltysiak/Member - Supervisory Board, James Frates/Member - Supervisory Board, Peter Preuss/Member - Supervisory Board

Financial Data: *Fiscal Year End:*12/31   *Latest Annual Data:* 12/31/2006

Year		Sales		Net Income
2006		$29,936,000		-$84,516,000
2005		$11,063,000		-$73,678,000
2004		$17,258,000		-$54,476,000
Curr. Assets:	$132,290,000	Curr. Liab.:	$32,670,000	
Plant, Equip.:	$5,623,000	Total Liab.:	$53,266,000	Indic. Yr. Divd.: NA
Total Assets:	$141,957,000	Net Worth:	$88,691,000	Debt/ Equity: NA

GPS Industries Inc

5500 152nd St., Ste. 214, Surrey, BC, V3S 5J9; *PH:* 1-604-576-7442; *Fax:* 1-604-576-7460; *http://* www.gpsindustries.com; *Email:* info@gpsindustries.com

General - Incorporation.............................NV	Stock - Price on:12/24/2007 ....$0.116
Employees..NA	Stock Exchange...OTC
Auditor .... Sherb & Co. LLP	Ticker Symbol...GPSN
Stk Agt.................Signature Stock Transfer, Inc.	Outstanding Shares ....NA
Counsel...NA	E.P.S...$2.63
DUNS No. ....NA	Shareholders...NA

Business: The group's principal activity is the development of golf course management technology. It designs, develops and manufactures its inforemer line of products and other recreational devices that utilize a patented combination of global positioning systems (gps), two way messaging systems and Internet technology. The group provides precision guidance around courses and delivers pinpoint accuracy locations. The group is in the process of developing a hand-held global positioning satellite (gps) technology and has not yet determined the ultimate economic viability of the technology. At 31-Dec-2003, the group had substantially all of its assets and operations in Canada.

Primary SIC and add'l.: 7389

CIK No: 0000029233

Subsidiaries: Inforetech Golf Technology 2000 Inc., Optimal Golf Solutions, Inc

Officers: Robert C. Silzer/Founder, Chmn., CEO, Pres., Peter Nesveda/Contact - International Investor Relations, Peter Lesyk/VP - Wireless Solutions, Rob Silzer/Dir. - Fire At The Flag, Steven Barrett/Chief Marketing Officer, Marc Potter/Exec. VP, Glenn Pierce/Exec. VP, Ryan Gray/Contact - Investor Relations, Keith Andrews/Dir. - Business Development, Don Adamson/Dir. - Golf Development, Michael Martin/58/Principal Accounting Officer, Controller, Alex Doaga/CTO, Exec. VP, Julius Farkas/Dir. - Manufacturing

Directors: Robert C. Silzer/Founder, Chmn., CEO, Pres., Rick Horrow/Chmn. - Gpsi Advisory Board, Geoff Hunter/Dir., Bob Linn/Dir., Brian Burke/Member - Advisory Board, Bart Collins/Dir., Stephen Johnston/Member - Advisory Board, Douglas J. Wood/Dir., Greg Norman/Member - Advisory Board, Howdy Giles/Member - Board Of Advisor, Jeffrey Lurie/Member - Advisory Board, Nathaniel Crosby/Member - Advisory Board

Owners: Bart Collins, Alex Doaga, Robert C. Silzer, Gregory John Norman, Great White Shark Enterprises, Inc., Doug Wood, Istithmar PJSC, Insiders

Financial Data: *Fiscal Year End:*12/31   *Latest Annual Data:* 12/31/2006

Year		Sales		Net Income
2006		$6,576,000		-$5,442,000
2005		$5,818,000		-$17,191,000
2004		$2,184,000		-$8,960,000
Curr. Assets:	$10,171,000	Curr. Liab.:	$15,200,000	
Plant, Equip.:	$109,000	Total Liab.:	$17,509,000	Indic. Yr. Divd.: NA
Total Assets:	$11,936,000	Net Worth:	-$5,573,000	Debt/ Equity: NA

Graco Inc

88 11th Ave. NE, Minneapolis, MN, 55413; *PH:* 1-612-623-6000; *Fax:* 1-612-378-3505; *http://* www.graco.com

General - Incorporation .... MN	Stock - Price on:12/24/2007 ....$40.55
Employees...2,300	Stock Exchange..NYSE
Auditor ....Deloitte & Touche LLP	Ticker Symbol...GGG
Stk Agt.........................Wells Fargo Bank, N.A.	Outstanding Shares 66,520,000
Counsel...NA	E.P.S...$2.27
DUNS No. 00-625-3223	Shareholders...NA

Business: The group's principal activity is to manufacture, market and supplies equipment systems for the management of fluids in industrial and commercial settings. The group operates through three segments: contractor equipment: designs and markets sprayers for the application of paint and other architectural coatings and for the high-pressure cleaning of equipment and structures. Industrial/automotive equipment: designs and markets sealants and adhesives, liquid finishing and protective coatings. Lubrication equipment: designs and markets products for the lubrication and maintenance of vehicles and other equipment. The group's customers include the manufacturing, process, construction and maintenance industries.

Primary SIC and add'l.: 3563 3823 3491 3594 3569 5084

CIK No: 0000042888

Subsidiaries: Decker Industries, Inc., Graco Australia Pty Ltd., Graco Canada Inc., Graco do Brasil Limitada, Graco Fluid Equipment (Shanghai) Co., Ltd., Graco Fluid Equipment (Suzhou) Co., Ltd., Graco GmbH, Graco Hong Kong Ltd, Graco K.K., Graco Korea Inc., Graco Ltd., Graco Minnesota Inc., Graco N.V., Graco S.A.S., Gusmer Canada Ltd. 21 Subsidiaries included in the Index

Officers: Patrick J. McHale/CEO, Pres., Karen Park Gallivan/VP, General Counsel, Sec., Fred A. Sutter/VP, GM - Applied Fluid Technologies Division/$725,870.00, Charles L. Rescorla/VP - Manufacturing, Distribution Operations/$1,016,269.00, James A. Graner/CFO, Treasurer/$1,163,252.00, Dale D. Johnson/VP, GM - Contractor Equipment Division, Christian D. Koch/VP, GM - Asia Pacific, David M. Lowe/VP, GM - Industrial Products Division, Simon Paulis/VP, GM - Europe, Mark W. Sheahan/Chief Administrative Officer, Primary Investor Relations Officer, Brian J. Zumbolo/VP, GM - Lubrication Equipment Division

Directors: Lee R. Mitau/Chmn., Marti Morfitt/Dir., Jack W. Eugster/Dir., Kevin J. Gilligan/Dir., William J. Carroll/Dir., David A. Roberts/60/Dir., William G. Van Dyke/Dir., Robert G. Bohn/Dir., Mark H. Rauenhorst/Dir., William R. Van Sant/Dir., James H. Moar/Dir.

Owners: Jack W. Eugster, Mark H. Rauenhorst, James A. Graner, Kevin J. Gilligan, Marti Morfitt, Dale D. Johnson, Lee R. Mitau, William G. Van Dyke, Insiders/3.00%, James H. Moar, Charles L. Rescorla, William R. VanSant, William J. Carroll, David A. Roberts, Fred A. Sutter (17 Owners included in Index)

Financial Data: *Fiscal Year End:*12/30   *Latest Annual Data:* 12/29/2006

Year		Sales		Net Income
2006		$816,468,000		$149,766,000
2005		$731,702,000		$125,854,000
2004		$605,032,000		$108,681,000
Curr. Assets:	$227,226,000	Curr. Liab.:	$96,773,000	P/E Ratio: 18.77
Plant, Equip.:	$94,510,000	Total Liab.:	$140,877,000	Indic. Yr. Divd.: $0.660
Total Assets:	$371,714,000	Net Worth:	$230,837,000	Debt/ Equity: NA

GrafTech International Ltd

12900 Snow Rd., Parma, OH, 44130; *PH:* 1-216-676-2000; *Fax:* 1-216-676-2526; *http://* www.graftech.com

General - Incorporation .... DE	Stock - Price on:12/24/2007 ....$16.35
Employees...2,757	Stock Exchange..NYSE
Auditor ....PricewaterhouseCoopers LLP	Ticker Symbol..GTI
Stk Agt..... Computershare Investor Services LLC	Outstanding Shares 99,310,000
Counsel...NA	E.P.S...$1.60
DUNS No. 87-717-6578	Shareholders...NA

Business: The group's principal activities are to manufacture and provide graphite and carbon electrodes and cathodes. These are used in electric arc furnace steel production and aluminum smelting. The group also manufactures other natural and synthetic graphite and carbon products and provide services to, the fuel cell power generation, electronics, semiconductor, transportation, chemical, petrochemical markets and other metal industries. The group operates in two divisions: synthetic graphite division and graphite and carbon division. Synthetic graphite division manufactures and delivers graphite electrodes, cathodes and advanced synthetic graphite products and materials. Graphite electrodes are used in the production of steel in electric arc furnaces and refining steel in ladle furnaces. Cathodes are used in aluminum smelting. The trademarks of the group include grafcell(R), egraf(R), grafoil(R), grafguard(R) and grafshield(r).

Primary SIC and add'l.: 3624

CIK No: 0000931148

Subsidiaries: Advanced Energy Technology Inc., Carbone Savoie Brasil Holdings Brasil S.A., Carbone Savoie Brasil S.A., Carbone Savoie S.A.S., GrafTech Finance Inc., GrafTech Global Enterprises Inc., GrafTech S.p.A, Graphite Electrode Network LLC, UCAR Carbon (Malaysia) Sdn. Bhd., UCAR Carbon Company Inc., UCAR Carbon Mexicana, S.A. de C.V, UCAR Carbon S.A, UCAR Carbon Technology LLC, UCAR Electrodos Iberica, S.L, UCAR Grafit OAO 25 Subsidiaries included in the Index

Officers: Craig S. Shular/54/Chmn., CEO, Pres./$2,489,645.00, Pieter J. Barnard/VP, Mark Widmar/CFO/$856,300.00, Gary Whitaker/VP, General Counsel, Sec./$561,165.00, Hermanus L. Pretorius/Pres. - Advanced Graphite, Carbon/$823,758.00

Directors: Craig S. Shular/54/Chmn., CEO, Pres., Mary B. Cranston/59/Dir., Michael C. Nahl/64/Dir., Harold E. Layman/60/Dir., Ferrell P. McClean/60/Dir., John R. Hall/74/Dir., Frank A. Riddick/50/Dir., Eugene R. Cartledge/77/Dir.

Owners: Frank A. Riddick, Mary B. Cranston, NWQ Investment Management Company, LLC/9.70%, Petrus J. Barnard, Ferrell P. McClean, Gary R. Whitaker, Mark R. Widmar, Hermanus L. Pretorius, Harold E. Layman, Barclays Global Fund Advisors/7.53%, Wells Fargo & Company/8.07%, Craig S. Shular/1.30%, John R. Hall, Insiders/2.67%, Royal Capital Management LLC/7.59% *(19 Owners included in Index)*

Financial Data: *Fiscal Year End:*12/31 *Latest Annual Data:* 12/31/2006

Year	Sales	Net Income
2006	$855,433,000	$91,334,000
2005	$886,699,000	-$125,180,000
2004	$848,000,000	$17,000,000

Curr. Assets:	$569,245,000	**Curr. Liab.:**	$220,591,000	**P/E Ratio:**	11.20
Plant, Equip.:	$291,555,000	**Total Liab.:**	$1,016,399,000	**Indic. Yr. Divd.:**	NA
Total Assets:	$906,201,000	**Net Worth:**	-$113,920,000	**Debt/ Equity:**	NA

Graham Corp

20 Florence Ave., Batavia, NY, 14020; *PH:* 1-585-343-2216; *Fax:* 1-585-343-1177; *http://* www.graham-mfg.com; *Email:* applicationengineering@graham-mfg.com

General - Incorporation	DE	**Stock**- Price on:12/24/2007	$25.9
Employees	265	Stock Exchange	AMEX
Auditor	Deloitte & Touche LLP	Ticker Symbol	GHM
Stk Agt	Mellon Investor Services LLC	Outstanding Shares	3,890,000
Counsel	NA	E.P.S	$2.81
DUNS No.	00-212-3941	Shareholders	NA

Business: The group's principal activities are to design and manufacture vacuum and heat transfer equipment. It supplies steam jet ejector vacuum systems, surface condensers for steam turbines, liquid ring vacuum pumps and compressors, dry pumps, rotary piston pumps, oil sealed rotary vane pumps, atmospheric air operated ejectors. It also supplies various types of heat exchangers such as heliflow and plate and frame exchangers. It combines various products into packaged systems for sale in a variety of industrial markets, including oil refining, chemical, petrochemical, power, pulp and paper, other process applications and shipbuilding. The group's operations are located in the United States and the United Kingdom.

Primary SIC and add'l.: 3443 3563

CIK No: 0000716314

Subsidiaries: Graham Vacuum and Heat Transfer Limited (GVHT

Officers: Ronald J. Hansen/CFO, VP - Finance, Administration, James R. Lines/47/COO, Pres.

Directors: Jerald D. Bidlack/72/Chmn., Frederick D. Berkeley/Founder, Russel H. Lemcke/68/Dir., Helen H. Berkeley/79/Dir., Harold M. Graham/Founder, Frederick D. Berkeley/Founder, Cornelius S. Van Rees/79/Dir., William C. Denninger/57/Dir., Frederick D. Berkeley/Founder

Owners: William C. Denninger, Insiders/10.30%, Cornelius S. Van Rees/1.00%, Ronald J. Hansen, Stephen P. Northrup, James R. Lines, Royce & Associates, LLC/10.70%, Jerald D. Bidlack/1.30%, James J. Malvaso, Russel H. Lemcke/1.70%, Helen H. Berkeley/4.60%

Financial Data: *Fiscal Year End:*03/31 *Latest Annual Data:* 03/31/2007

Year	Sales	Net Income
2007	$65,822,000	$5,761,000
2006	$55,208,000	$3,586,000
2005	$41,333,000	-$2,906,000

Curr. Assets:	$27,395,000	**Curr. Liab.:**	$10,616,000	**P/E Ratio:**	14.08
Plant, Equip.:	$7,954,000	**Total Liab.:**	$13,449,000	**Indic. Yr. Divd.:**	$0.100
Total Assets:	$40,556,000	**Net Worth:**	$27,107,000	**Debt/ Equity:**	0.0003

Gramercy Capital Corp

420 Lexington Ave., New York, NY, 10170; *PH:* 1-212-297-1000; *Fax:* 1-212-297-1090; *http://* www.gramercycapitalcorp.com

General - Incorporation	MD	**Stock**- Price on:12/24/2007	$30.23
Employees	NA	Stock Exchange	NYSE
Auditor	Ernst & Young LLP	Ticker Symbol	GKK
Stk Agt	Wells Fargo Bank, N.A.	Outstanding Shares	26,050,000
Counsel	NA	E.P.S	$2.54
DUNS No.	NA	Shareholders	NA

Business: The groups principle activity is to provide loan services. In the year 2005, the group acquired 200 Franklin Square Drive. The group operates from the United States. The groups quarterly revenue for September 2007 was 90.21 millions of USD.

Primary SIC and add'l.: 6798

CIK No: 0001287701

Subsidiaries: GIT Trading Corp., GKK Capital LP, GKK Trading Corp., Gramercy Investment Trust, Gramercy Warehouse Funding I LLC, Gramercy Warehouse Funding II LLC

Officers: Marc Holliday/Dir., CEO, Pres., Andrew S. Levine/Sec., Hugh F. Hall/40/Dir., COO, Robert R. Foley/CFO, Andrew Mathias/Chief Investment Officer, Gregory F. Hughes/Chief Credit Officer, Heidi Gillette/Investor Relations Officer

Directors: Marc Holliday/Dir., CEO, Pres., Stephen L. Green/70/Chmn., Allan J. Baum/50/Dir., Hugh F. Hall/40/Dir., COO, Paul J. Konigsberg/70/Dir., Charles S. Laven/55/Dir., Jeffrey E. Kelter/52/Dir.

Owners: Robert R. Foley, Hugh F. Hall, Allan J. Baum, Marc Holliday, Paul J. Konigsberg, Gregory F. Hughes, SL Green Realty Corp./24.70%, Insiders/3.60%, Jeffrey E. Kelter, Cohen & Steers, Inc./8.50%, Neuberger Berman, LLC/7.60%, Stephen L. Green, Andrew Mathias, Charles S. Laven

Financial Data: *Fiscal Year End:*12/31 *Latest Annual Data:* 03/31/2007

Year	Sales	Net Income
2007	$68,134,000	$17,049,000
2006	$198,215,000	$55,902,000
2005	$88,085,000	$31,371,000

Curr. Assets:	$385,689,000	**Curr. Liab.:**	$319,869,000	**P/E Ratio:**	11.90
Plant, Equip.:	$99,821,000	**Total Liab.:**	$2,305,453,000	**Indic. Yr. Divd.:**	$2.520
Total Assets:	$2,766,113,000	**Net Worth:**	$460,660,000	**Debt/ Equity:**	4.4105

Gran Tierra Energy Inc

300, 611-10th Ave. S.W., Calgary, AB, T2R 0B2; *PH:* 1-403-265-3221; *Fax:* 1-403-265-3242; *http://* www.grantierra.com; *Email:* info@grantierra.com

General - Incorporation	NV	**Stock**- Price on:12/24/2007	$1.37
Employees	NA	Stock Exchange	OTC
Auditor	Deloitte & Touche LLP	Ticker Symbol	GTRE
Stk Agt	Island Stock Transfer	Outstanding Shares	NA
Counsel	NA	E.P.S	NA
DUNS No.	NA	Shareholders	NA

Business: The groups principle activities include exploring and producing oil and natural gas. The group acquired, Argosy Energy International and Argosy Energy Corp in June 2006, and Dong Won Corporation for September 2005. Specific customer of the group is Ecopetrol (government agency). The group operates from Colombia and Argentina.

Primary SIC and add'l.: 1311

CIK No: 0001273441

Subsidiaries: 1203647 Alberta, Inc., Gran Tierra Argentina SA, Gran Tierra Energy Inc., Gran Tierra Goldstrike Inc., PCESA

Officers: Dana Coffield/50/Dir., CEO, Pres./$270,108.00, Martin Eden/CFO, Max Wei/VP - Operations/$214,868.00, Rafael Orunesu/Pres. - Gran Tierra Energy Argentina/$213,807.00, Edgar Dyes/Pres. - Gran Tierra Energy Colombia/$163,750.00

Directors: Dana Coffield/50/Dir., CEO, Pres., Jeffrey Scott/Chmn., Walter Dawson/Dir., Verne Johnson/Dir., Nadine C. Smith/Dir., James Hart/54/Dir.

Owners: Verne Johnson/1.96%, Jeffrey Scott/2.78%, Walter Dawson/3.22%, Greywolf Capital Management LP/10.69%, Nadine C. Smith/2.26%, Martin Eden, Max Wei/1.97%, Edgar Dyes, US Global Investors, Inc./6.99%, Rafael Orunesu/2.05%, Dana Coffield/2.11%, Millennium Global Investments Limited/5.26%, Insiders/16.48%

Financial Data: *Fiscal Year End:*12/31 *Latest Annual Data:* 12/31/2006

Year	Sales	Net Income
2006	$12,073,000	-$5,824,000
2005	$1,059,000	-$2,220,000

Curr. Assets:	$33,374,000	**Curr. Liab.:**	$19,100,000	**P/E Ratio:**	53.55
Plant, Equip.:	$56,093,000	**Total Liab.:**	$29,716,000	**Indic. Yr. Divd.:**	NA
Total Assets:	$105,911,000	**Net Worth:**	$76,195,000	**Debt/ Equity:**	NA

Grand Peak Capital Corp

Formerly: Black Mountain Capital Corp
555 Burrard St., Ste. 900, Vancouver, BC, V7X 1M8;

General - Incorporation	Canada	**Stock**- Price on:12/24/2007	$0.125
Employees	NA	Stock Exchange	NA
Auditor	Davidson & Co LLP	Ticker Symbol	NA
Stk Agt	Computershare Trust Co	Outstanding Shares	NA
Counsel	NA	E.P.S	NA
DUNS No.	83-612-3422	Shareholders	NA

Business: The group's principle activity is to performs private equity and merchant banking services, including asset-based commercial lending, and formerly developed, published, and distributed interactive multimedia software titles. The group operates from United States.

Primary SIC and add'l.: 7372 6159 6799

CIK No: 0000781885

Subsidiaries: Alliance Imaging Group Inc., Cross Creek Finance Group Ltd., Digital Labs Inc., Midland Holland Ltd., Pearson Finance Group Ltd.

Officers: Navchand Jagpal/CEO, CFO, Pres., Sec., Dir.

Directors: Navchand Jagpal/CEO, CFO, Pres., Sec., Dir., Mahmoud S. Aziz/Dir., Greg MacRae/Dir., Lewis J. Dillman/Dir.

Financial Data: *Fiscal Year End:*12/31 *Latest Annual Data:* 12/31/2006

Year	Sales	Net Income
2006	NA	-$77,000
2005	$52,000	-$389,000
2004	$61,000	-$1,524,000

Curr. Assets:	$448,000	**Curr. Liab.:**	$411,000		
Plant, Equip.:	NA	**Total Liab.:**	$411,000	**Indic. Yr. Divd.:**	NA
Total Assets:	$448,000	**Net Worth:**	$38,000	**Debt/ Equity:**	NA

Grand Toys International Inc

1710 Trans Canada Hwy., Dorval, QC, H9P 1H7; *PH:* 1-514-685-2180; *Fax:* 1-514-685-2825; *http://* www.grand.com

General - Incorporation		**Stock**- Price on:12/24/2007	NA
Employees	NA	Stock Exchange	NDQ
Auditor	NA	Ticker Symbol	GRIN
Stk Agt	NA	Outstanding Shares	NA
Counsel	NA	E.P.S	NA
DUNS No.	NA	Shareholders	NA

Business: The groups principle activities include developing, manufacturing and distributing toy products. The groups services include printing and packaging, party goods, and mould. The products of the group include Novelty books, Board books, paperboard, puzzles, board games and photo albums. The group products sold under the trade name KORD. Specific customers of the group include Toys R Us, Mamas & Papas Ltd. And, Eveil and Jeux. The group operates from the United States, Asia, Europe, Canada, Africa and other.

Primary SIC and add'l.: 5090

CIK No: 0000814463

GrandSouth Bancorp

381 Halton Rd., Greenville, SC, 29607; *PH:* 1-864-770-1000; *Fax:* 1-864-770-1081;
http:// www.grandsouth.com

General - Incorporation	SC	**Stock**- Price on:12/24/2007	$13.5
Employees	66	Stock Exchange	OTC
Auditor	Elliot Davis LLC	Ticker Symbol	GRRB
Stk Agt	NA	Outstanding Shares	3,370,000
Counsel	NA	E.P.S	$0.74
DUNS No.	NA	Shareholders	NA

Business: The group's principal activity is to provide commercial banking services. These services include business and personal checking accounts, now accounts, savings accounts, money market accounts, various term certificates of deposit, ira accounts and other deposit services. The group offers secured and unsecured, short-to-intermediate term loans, with floating and fixed interest rates for commercial, consumer and residential purposes. The other services offered by the group include residential mortgage loan origination services, safe deposit boxes, night depository service, visa(R) and mastercard(R) charge cards, tax deposits and traveler's checks. The group operates through 147 branch locations, located in greenville county of greenville.

Primary SIC and add'l.: 6022 6712

CIK No: 0001126961

Subsidiaries: GrandSouth Bank

Owners: Blanton S. Phillips, Mason Y. Garrett/18.00%, Harold E. Garrett/4.20%, Hunter S. Howard, Baety O. Gross/1.10%, Calhoun J. Pruitt, Insiders/36.10%, J. B. Garrett/3.00%, Michael L. Gault/1.90%, Ronald K. Earnest/6.00%

Financial Data: *Fiscal Year End:*12/31 *Latest Annual Data:* 12/31/2006

Year	Sales	Net Income
2006	$24,370,000	$3,260,000
2005	$16,703,000	$2,361,000
2004	$10,910,000	$1,319,000

Curr. Assets:	$19,804,000	**Curr. Liab.:**	$268,923,000	**P/E Ratio:**	16.27
Plant, Equip.:	$5,269,000	**Total Liab.:**	$280,840,000	**Indic. Yr. Divd.:**	$0.080
Total Assets:	$300,310,000	**Net Worth:**	$19,470,000	**Debt/ Equity:**	0.4087

Grandview Gold Inc

360 Bay St., Ste. 500, Toronto, ON, M5H 2V6; *PH:* 1-416-486-3444;
http:// www.grandviewgold.com; *Email:* info@grandviewgold.com

General - Incorporation	ON	**Stock**- Price on:12/24/2007	$0.4319
Employees	NA	Stock Exchange	OTC
Auditor	McCarney Greenwood LLP	Ticker Symbol	GVGDF
Stk Agt	Equity Transfer Services Inc	Outstanding Shares	NA
Counsel	WeirFoulds LLP	E.P.S	NA
DUNS No.	NA	Shareholders	NA

Business: The group's principle activity is to explore and develop high-grade gold properties in the major gold camps of North America. The group currently has three significant projects underway, covering approximately 5,800 hectares (21+square miles). The three properties are located in three of the highest gold producing areas of North America; the Carlin Trend in Nevada, U.S.A., the Bissett Gold Camp in Manitoba and Red Lake in Ontario, Canada. The group is currently an exploration stage company and are not engaged in any mining operations. The exploration interest of the group are an option to acquire a 60% interest in the Pony Creek and the Elliot Dome Property which are both located in Elko County on the Carlin Trend in Nevada. The group owns 100% interest in 8 mining claims of approximately 60 hectares in the Red Lake Area in Northwestern Ontario.

Primary SIC and add'l.: 1000

CIK No: 0001313974

Officers: Michael Hitch/Chmn., CEO, Paul Sarjeant/Dir., CEO, Pres., Sophie Tsementzis/Executive Assist. - Investor Relations, Ernest Cleave/CFO, Alex Korboukh/Mgr. - Exploration Canada, Martin Tuchscherer/Chief Geologist, Peter MacDonald/Exploration Geologist, Thomas Kulh/Sr. Geologist, Brian Goss/Exploration Geologist, Monte M. Swan/Consulting Geologist, Stanley B. Keith/Consulting Geologist

Directors: Michael Hitch/Chmn., CEO, Paul Sarjeant/Dir., CEO, Pres., Ian Grant/Dir., Richard D. Brown/Dir., Peter Born/Dir.

Financial Data: *Fiscal Year End:*05/31 *Latest Annual Data:* 5/31/2006

Year	Sales	Net Income
2006	NA	-$3,334,000

Curr. Assets:	$3,844,000	**Curr. Liab.:**	$383,000		
Plant, Equip.:	NA	**Total Liab.:**	$383,000	**Indic. Yr. Divd.:**	NA
Total Assets:	$4,950,000	**Net Worth:**	$4,568,000	**Debt/ Equity:**	NA

Granite City Food & Brewery Ltd

5402 Parkdale Dr., Ste. 101, Minneapolis, MN, 55416; *PH:* 1-952-215-0660; *Fax:* 1-952-525-2021;
http:// www.gcfb.net

General - Incorporation	MN	**Stock**- Price on:12/24/2007	$5.6
Employees	1,300	Stock Exchange	NDQ
Auditor	Schechter Dokken Kanter	Ticker Symbol	GCFB
Stk Agt	Wells Fargo Bank Minnesota N.A	Outstanding Shares	15,990,000
Counsel	Briggs & Morgan	E.P.S	-$0.44
DUNS No.	NA	Shareholders	NA

Business: The group's principal activities are to develop and operate casual dining restaurants featuring on-premise breweries. The group is developing these restaurant-microbreweries, known as the granite city food & brewery in selected markets throughout the United States. The restaurants offer a wide variety of menu items which includes high quality food and prepared fresh daily, combined with freshly brewed hand crafted beers made on-premise. The group's popular items include granite city ale, cheddar soup, chicken caesar chalupa, grilled chicken and bruschetta salad, Chinese pasta salad, grilled london broil with bourbon onion sauce, southern fried chicken breast sandwich, honey rosemary filet mignon and the granite city walleye. The group operates at st. Cloud, Minnesota, sioux falls, North Dakota, South Dakota, fargo, west des moines, cedar rapids and davenport.

Primary SIC and add'l.: 7011

CIK No: 0001048620

Subsidiaries: Granite City Olathe, Inc., Granite City West Wichita, Inc., Granite City Wichita, Inc., Granite City of Kansas Ltd.

Officers: Steven J. Wagenheim/Dir., CEO, Pres./$754,536.00, Monica Underwood/Corporate Controller/$147,797.00, Michael Dewitte/Mgr. - Davenport, Iowa, Janelle Adams/Mgr. - Eagan, Minnesota, Matt Vobroucek/Mgr. - East Peoria, Illinois, Zach Saueressing/Mgr. - Fargo, North Dakota, Grant Lowe/Mgr. - Kansas City Speedway, Kansas, Kenny O'Rourke/Mgr. - Kansas City, Missouri, Brad McKinnon/Mgr. - Cedar Rapids, Iowa, Brian Higgins/Mgr. - Clive, Iowa, Brooke Barnes/Mgr. - Lincoln, Nebraska, Russ Carroll/Mgr. - Madison, Wisconsin, Tony Donatelle/Mgr. - Maple Grove, Minnesota, Michael Pettys/Mgr. - Rockford, Illinois, Adam Seymour/Mgr. - Rogers, Arkansas *(24 Officers included in Index)*

Directors: Steven J. Wagenheim/Dir., CEO, Pres., James G. Gilbertson/47/Dir., Eugene E. McGowan/72/Dir., Arthur E. Pew/75/Dir., Dermot F. Rowland/71/Dir., Bruce H. Senske/53/Dir.

Owners: Monica A. Underwood, Steven J. Wagenheim/10.30%, Gary M. Winston/6.00%, Perkins Capital Management, Inc./5.40%, William Blair & Company, LLC/8.50%, Arthur E. Pew/9.00%, Dermot F. Rowland, Solstice Capital Management, LLC/6.00%, James G. Gilbertson, Bruce H. Senske, Timothy R. Cary/1.80%, Peter P. Hausback, Eugene E. McGowan/2.50%, Andrew J. Redleaf/5.70%, Insiders/17.90% *(17 Owners included in Index)*

Financial Data: *Fiscal Year End:*12/27 *Latest Annual Data:* 12/26/2006

Year	Sales	Net Income
2006	$58,328,000	-$5,531,000
2005	$36,205,000	-$3,667,000
2004	$30,756,000	-$725,000

Curr. Assets:	$9,824,000	**Curr. Liab.:**	$3,607,000		
Plant, Equip.:	$21,950,000	**Total Liab.:**	$18,287,000	**Indic. Yr. Divd.:**	NA
Total Assets:	$32,169,000	**Net Worth:**	$13,882,000	**Debt/ Equity:**	1.3842

Granite Community Bank

4100 Douglas Blvd, Granite Bay, CA, 95746; *PH:* 1-916-788-8200; *http://* www.granitecb.com;
Email: customerservice@granitecb.com

General - Incorporation		**Stock**- Price on:12/24/2007	$16
Employees	NA	Stock Exchange	OTC
Auditor	NA	Ticker Symbol	GCBK
Stk Agt	David Caulkins	Outstanding Shares	NA
Counsel	NA	E.P.S	NA
DUNS No.	NA	Shareholders	NA

Business: The groups principal activity is to provide banking services. The services of the group include personal and business loans, direct deposit payroll, courier services, debit and ATM cards, cashiers and travelers check, cash management, safe deposit boxes and online banking. The group operates from the United States.

Primary SIC and add'l.: 6036

CIK No:

Officers: David Kaiser/CEO, Pres., David Caulkins/Sr. VP, CFO, Carol Garcia/VP, Marketing Dir., Dave Potter/Pres., Commercial Loan Officer, William Reynolds/VP, Commercial Loan Officer, Linda Le Sage/VP, Mortgage Loan Mgr.

Directors: Kirk Doyle/Chmn., Mark Davis/Dir., Ronald L. Feist/Dir., Alan Frumkin/Dir., Marcus J. Lo Duca/Dir., Irma McClure/Dir., Geotgene Waterman/Dir., Damon G. Eberhart/Dir.

Granite Construction Inc

585 W Beach St., Watsonville, CA, 95076; *PH:* 1-831-724-1011; *Fax:* 1-831-722-9657;
http:// www.graniteconstruction.com; *Email:* info@gcinc.com

General - Incorporation	DE	**Stock**- Price on:12/24/2007	$66.7
Employees	5,200	Stock Exchange	NYSE
Auditor	PricewaterhouseCoopers LLP	Ticker Symbol	GVA
Stk Agt	Registrar & Transfer Co	Outstanding Shares	41,940,000
Counsel	NA	E.P.S	$2.35
DUNS No.	00-691-4642	Shareholders	NA

Business: The groups principle activity is to build roads, tunnels, bridges, airports and other infrastructure-related projects. The group also produces sand, gravel, ready-mix and asphalt concrete, and other construction materials. The groups services include site preparation and infrastructure services for residential development, commercial and industrial buildings, plants and other facilities. The group operates through two business segments namely branch and heavy construction division. The group operates from United States.

Primary SIC and add'l.: 1611 1629 6719

CIK No: 0000861459

Subsidiaries: GILC Incorporated, Granite Construction Company, Granite Construction Northeast, Inc., Wilder Construction Company

Officers: William G. Dorey/Dir., CEO, Pres./$2,266,765.00, Bob Leonetti/Mgr. - Business Development, Granite Construction Northeast, Mark E. Boitano/COO, Exec. VP/$1,052,770.00, John A. Franich/VP, Granite West Mgr. - Construction, Mary McCann-Jenni/VP, Controller, Brian Dowd/VP, Dir. - Human Resources, Jigisha Desai/VP, Treasurer, J. C. Miseroy/Projects Exec., Michael Futch/VP, General Counsel, Randy Kremer/VP, Mgr. Construction Materials, William E. Barton/CFO, Sr. VP/$1,211,278.00, James H. Roberts/Sr. VP, Granite West Mgr./$841,473.00, Michael F. Donnino/Sr. VP, Granite East Mgr./$391,692.00

Directors: William G. Dorey/Dir., CEO, Pres., David H. Watts/Chmn., Rebecca A. McDonald/Dir., Fernando J. Niebla/Dir., James W. Bradford/Dir., William H. Powell/Dir., Gary M. Cusumano/Dir., David H. Kelsey/Dir., Claes G. Bjork/Dir.

Owners: William H. Powell, Insiders/2.09%, Rebecca A. McDonald, James H. Roberts, David H. Watts, Michael F. Donnino, Mark E. Boitano, William E. Barton, William G. Dorey, Barclays Global Investors, NA/16.86%, Gary M. Cusumano, Emben & Co./14.08%, Claes G. Bjork, David H. Kelsey, James W. Bradford *(16 Owners included in Index)*

Financial Data: *Fiscal Year End:*12/31 *Latest Annual Data:* 06/30/2007

Year	Sales	Net Income
2007	$770,876,000	$43,846,000
2006	$2,969,604,000	$80,509,000
2005	$2,641,352,000	$83,150,000

Curr. Assets:	$1,083,205,000	**Curr. Liab.:**	$763,443,000	**P/E Ratio:**	30.74
Plant, Equip.:	$429,966,000	**Total Liab.:**	$922,762,000	**Indic. Yr. Divd.:**	$0.400
Total Assets:	$1,632,838,000	**Net Worth:**	$694,544,000	**Debt/ Equity:**	0.1023

Grant Life Sciences Inc

3550 Wilshire Blvd. 17th, Los Angeles, CA, 90010; *PH:* 1-213-637-5692; *Fax:* 1-213-637-5691; *http://* www.grantlifesciences.com

General - Incorporation	NV	Stock - Price on:12/24/2007	NA
Employees	NA	Stock Exchange	OTC
Auditor ...Singer Lewak Greenbaum & Goldstein		Ticker Symbol	GLIF
Stk Agt	Interstate Transfer Company	Outstanding Shares	NA
Counsel	NA	E.P.S.	$0.006
DUNS No.	NA	Shareholders	NA

Business: The groups principal activity is to develop antibody-based screening tests to screen woman for cervical cancer and pre-cancerous conditions. The group operates from the United States Canada, Western Europe and Japan.

Primary SIC and add'l.: 8748

CIK No: 0001210336

Subsidiaries: Impact Diagnostics, Inc.

Officers: Hun Chi-Lin/Dir., Pres., Chief Scientific Officer, Michael L. Ahlin/Dir., VP, Indira Pottathil/Dir. - International Marketing, Seth Yakatan/Consultant - Business Development, Doyle R. Judd/CFO, Dawne Anderson/Corporate Assist. - Accounting Payable

Directors: Stan Yakatan/Chmn., Yao Xiong Hu/Member - Scientific Advisory Board, Hun Chi-Lin/Dir., Pres., Chief Scientific Officer, Michael L. Ahlin/Dir., VP, Raveendran Pottathil/Member - Scientific Advisory Board, Jack Levine/57/Dir., Kim Liao/Dir. - Asian Business Developoment

Owners: Michael Ahlin/2.70%, Stan Yakatan/1.50%, Insiders/7.00%, Hun-Chi Lin/1.00%, Don Rutherford/1.00%, Jack Levine/1.10%

Financial Data: Fiscal Year End:12/31   Latest Annual Data: 12/31/2006

Year	Sales	Net Income
2006	NA	-$3,385,000
2005	$73,000	-$4,634,000
2004	NA	-$1,910,000

Curr. Assets:	$296,000	Curr. Liab.:	$846,000		
Plant, Equip.:	$11,000	Total Liab.:	$7,037,000	Indic. Yr. Divd.:	NA
Total Assets:	$377,000	Net Worth:	-$6,660,000	Debt/ Equity:	NA

Grant Prideco Inc

400 N Sam Houston Pkwy. E, Ste. 900, Houston, TX, 77060; *PH:* 1-281-878-8000; *http://* www.grantprideco.com

General - Incorporation	DE	Stock - Price on:12/24/2007	$58.23
Employees	4,857	Stock Exchange	NYSE
Auditor	Deloitte & Touche LLP	Ticker Symbol	GRP
Stk Agt	American Stock Transfer & Trust Co.	Outstanding Shares	127,450,000
Counsel	NA	E.P.S.	$4.08
DUNS No.	NA	Shareholders	NA

Business: The groups principle activity is to provide drilling products and technology. The groups products include drill pipe, drill collars, heavy weight drill pipe, landing strings and accessories. Customers served by the group include oil and gas drilling contractors. The group operates from United States.

Primary SIC and add'l.: 3533

CIK No: 0001097313

Subsidiaries: C.M.A. Canavera S.R.L., Enerpro de Mexico, S.A. de C.V., GP Expatriate Services, Inc., GP USA Holding, LLC, Gpex, L.p., Grant Prideco (Singapore) Ptd. Ltd., Grant Prideco Asia (Singapore) Pte Ltd, Grant Prideco Canada Ltd., Grant Prideco de Venezuela, S.A., Grant Prideco Equipamentos para Petroleo Ltda., Grant Prideco European Holding, LLC, Grant Prideco Finance, LLC, Grant Prideco Holding, LLC, Grant Prideco Jersey Limited, Grant Prideco Limited 62 Subsidiaries included in the Index

Officers: Michael McShane/Chmn., CEO, Pres./$6,447,584.00, Toni Plympton/Import, Export Support, Bryan Bennett/Contact - Expeditor, Buyer, Jim Breihan/Pres. - Tubular Technology, Services, Ralph Best/Dir. - Supply Chain Management, Mike Johnston/Mgr. - Supply Chain Management, Mike Jordan/Import, Export Administrator, Iain Kinloch/Mgr. - Supply Chain Management, Ronda Roush/Coordinator, Logistics, Traffic, Loretta Wilson/Contact - Licensee Support Services, Marty Coffman/Contact - Licensee Support Services, Jason Travis/Contact - Licensee Support Services, Randall Edwards/Sr. VP - Sales, Marketing, Mike Reeves/VP, GM - Intelliserv Network, Nelson Allen/Regional Mgr. - North, South America (60 Officers included in Index)

Directors: Michael McShane/Chmn., CEO, Pres., Eliot M. Fried/Dir., Joseph E. Reid/Dir., Dennis R. Hendrix/Dir., Robert K. Moses/Dir., David J. Butters/Dir., Sheldon B. Lubar/Dir., Gary W. Childress/Dir., VP, Harold E. Layman/Dir., David A. Trice/Dir.

Owners: ClearBridge Advisors, LLC/11.30%, T. Rowe Price Associates, Inc./5.20%, Philip A. Choyce, Sheldon B. Lubar, David L. Butters, Eliot M. Fried, Insiders/3.00%, Harold E. Layman, Dennis R. Hendrix, David R. Black, Robert K. Moses, John D. Deane, David A. Trice, Matthew D. Fitzgerald, Michael McShane (16 Owners included in Index)

Financial Data: Fiscal Year End:12/31   Latest Annual Data: 12/31/2006

Year	Sales	Net Income
2006	$1,835,693,000	$464,584,000
2005	$1,349,997,000	$189,004,000
2004	$945,643,000	$55,266,000

Curr. Assets:	$947,446,000	Curr. Liab.:	$307,339,000	P/E Ratio:	15.20
Plant, Equip.:	$305,524,000	Total Liab.:	$641,662,000	Indic. Yr. Divd.:	NA
Total Assets:	$2,022,067,000	Net Worth:	$1,362,883,000	Debt/ Equity:	0.1806

Graphic Packaging Corp

814 Livingston Ct., Marietta, GA, 30067; *PH:* 1-770-644-3000; *Fax:* 1-770-644-2962; *http://* www.graphicpkg.com

General - Incorporation	DE	Stock - Price on:12/24/2007	$4.91
Employees	7,700	Stock Exchange	NYSE
Auditor	PricewaterhouseCoopers LLP	Ticker Symbol	GPK
Stk Agt	Wells Fargo Shareowner Services	Outstanding Shares	200,930,000
Counsel	NA	E.P.S.	-$0.5
DUNS No.	NA	Shareholders	NA

Business: The groups principle activity is to provide packaging solutions. The group operates through two business segments namely paperboard packaging and containerboard/other. The group operates from United States.

Primary SIC and add'l.: 2657 2653 2671

CIK No: 0000886239

Subsidiaries: Electro Rent (Tianjin) Rental Co., Ltd, Electro Rent Asia, Inc, Electro Rent Europe NV, ER International, Inc, Genstar Rental Electronics, Inc.

Officers: David W. Scheible/Dir., CEO, Pres./$1,502,679.00, Robert M. Simko/Sr. VP - Paperboard, Wayne E. Juby/Sr. VP - Human Resources Since, Steven D. Saucier/Sr. VP - Paperboard Operations, Donald W. Sturdivant/Sr. VP - Consumer Products Division, GPC, Michael R. Schmal/Sr. VP - Beverage/$1,121,882.00, Stephen Hellrung/Sr. VP, General Counsel, Sec., Daniel J. Blount/CFO, Sr. VP/$1,085,987.00, Deborah R. Frank/VP, Controller, Michael P. Doss/41/Sr. VP - Consumer Products Packaging

Directors: David W. Scheible/Dir., CEO, Pres., Stephen M. Humphrey/63/Vice Chmn., John R. Miller/Non - Exec. Chmn., Harold R. Logan/Dir., William R. Fields/Dir., Kevin J. Conway/Dir., Jeffrey H. Coors/Dir., Robert W. Tieken/Dir., Andrea G. Botta/Dir., John D. Beckett/Dir.

Owners: Stephen M. Humphrey/1.81%, David W. Scheible, EXOR Group S.A./9.98%, Harold R. Logan, William R. Fields, TPG BCH Entities/38.55%, Clayton, Dubilier & Rice Fund V Limited Partnership/9.98%, Robert W. Tieken, Daniel J. Blount, HWH Investment PTE Ltd./3.08%, John D. Beckett, Grover C. Coors Trust/14.94%, Jeffrey H. Coors/18.42%, John R. Miller, Michael R. Schmal (16 Owners included in Index)

Financial Data: Fiscal Year End:12/31   Latest Annual Data: 12/31/2006

Year	Sales	Net Income
2006	$2,413,000,000	-$100,500,000
2005	$2,384,000,000	-$91,100,000
2004	$2,386,500,000	-$60,900,000

Curr. Assets:	$564,300,000	Curr. Liab.:	$420,300,000		
Plant, Equip.:	$1,489,900,000	Total Liab.:	$3,051,900,000	Indic. Yr. Divd.:	NA
Total Assets:	$3,233,600,000	Net Worth:	$181,700,000	Debt/ Equity:	13.0625

GraphOn Corp

5400 Soquel Ave., Ste. A2, Santa Cruz, CA, 95062; *PH:* 1-603-225-3525; *Fax:* 1-831-475-3017; *http://* www.graphon.com; *Email:* info@graphon.com

General - Incorporation	DE	Stock - Price on:12/24/2007	$0.155
Employees	34	Stock Exchange	OTC
Auditor	Macias Gini & Co LLP	Ticker Symbol	GOJO
Stk Agt	American Stock Transfer & Trust Co.	Outstanding Shares	46,850,000
Counsel	Sonnenschein Nath & Rosenthal LLP	E.P.S.	-$0.09
DUNS No.	NA	Shareholders	NA

Business: The group's principal activities are to develop, market, sell and support business infrastructure software. The software empowers a diverse range of desktop computing devices (desktops) to access server-based windows, unix and linux applications from any location, over network or Internet connections. The software architecture provides application developers with the ability to relocate traditional desktop applications to be run entirely on a server or host computer, over any connection from any location. The technology allows the user to interface with an application as if it were running on the user's desktop computer.

Primary SIC and add'l.: 7372

CIK No: 0001021435

Subsidiaries: GraphOn NES Sub LLC

Officers: Robert Dilworth/Chmn., CEO, William Swain/CFO, Sec., Tom Castanzo/Asia, Pacific, Sales, Mark Miller/Eastern United States, Sales

Directors: Robert Dilworth/Chmn., CEO, Gordon Watson/Dir., August P. Klein/Dir., Michael Volker/Dir.

Owners: Michael Volker, Globis Capital Partners/7.80%, August P. Klein/1.20%, Ralph Wesinger/8.60%, Orin Hirschman/18.00%, Insiders/11.20%, Robert Dilworth/1.90%, Gordon Watson, William Swain/1.60%, Insiders/6.30%

Financial Data: Fiscal Year End:12/31   Latest Annual Data: 12/31/2006

Year	Sales	Net Income
2006	$5,171,000	-$3,035,000
2005	$5,180,000	-$1,147,000
2004	$3,530,000	-$1,428,000

Curr. Assets:	$3,683,000	Curr. Liab.:	$1,946,000		
Plant, Equip.:	$129,000	Total Liab.:	$3,601,000	Indic. Yr. Divd.:	NA
Total Assets:	$7,453,000	Net Worth:	$3,852,000	Debt/ Equity:	NA

Gravity Company Ltd

14F Meritz Tower, 825-2 Yeoksam-dong, Gangnam-gu, Seoul; ; *http://* www.gravity.co.kr; *Email:* erick@gravity.co.kr

General - Incorporation	Republic of Korea	Stock - Price on:12/24/2007	$6.4
Employees	NA	Stock Exchange	NDQ
Auditor	Samil PricewaterhouseCoopers	Ticker Symbol	GRVY
Stk Agt	Bank of New York	Outstanding Shares	27,800,000
Counsel	NA	E.P.S.	-$0.33
DUNS No.	NA	Shareholders	NA

Business: The groups principle activities include developing and distributing online games. The products of the group include Ragnarok Online, Requiem, Time N Tales and Emil Chronicle Online. In the year 2005, the group acquires TriggerSoft Corporation and NEOCYON, Inc. The group operates from Korea, Japan, Taiwan and Thailand, the United States and China. The group's quarterly revenue for September 2007 was 9,341.00 millions of KRW.

Primary SIC and add'l.: 7372

CIK No: 0001313310

Subsidiaries: Cybermedia International, Inc, Gravity Entertainment Corporation, Gravity Interactive, Inc, Mados, Inc, NEOCYON, Inc, TriggerSoft Corporation

Officers: Ryu Young/Chmn., CEO, Pres., Representative Dir., Seung Taik Baik/Executive Dir., Chief Marketing Officer, Kyu Hyeong Lee/Sr. Exec. VP - Human Resources, Chief Compliance Officer, Jonathan J. Lee/CFO, Investor Relations Officer

Directors: Ryu Young/Chmn., CEO, Pres., Representative Dir., Jungil Lee/Dir., William Woojae Hahn/Dir., Kwangsuk Lee/Dir.

Owners: LaGrange Capital Administration, L.L.C./5.00%, Ramius Capital Group, L.L.C./9.20%, Government of Singapore Investment Corporation Pte Ltd/6.00%, Moon Capital Master Fund Ltd./8.50%, EZER, Inc./52.40%

Financial Data: Fiscal Year End:12/31   Latest Annual Data: 12/31/2006

Year	Sales	Net Income
2006	$44,046,000	-$23,942,000
2005	$52,856,000	-$3,000,000
2004	$66,323,000,000	$28,883,000,000

Curr. Assets:	$94,842,000	Curr. Liab.:	$17,411,000		
Plant, Equip.:	$12,034,000	Total Liab.:	$26,288,000	Indic. Yr. Divd.:	NA
Total Assets:	$131,786,000	Net Worth:	$105,498,000	Debt/ Equity:	NA

Gray Peaks Inc

1320 Tower Rd., Schaumburg, IL, 60173; *PH:* 1-847-598-3700; *Fax:* 1-847-598-3704; *http://* www.graypeaks.com; *Email:* info@graypeaks.com

General - Incorporation	DE	**Stock**- Price on:12/24/2007	NA
Employees	NA	Stock Exchange	OTC
Auditor	McGladrey & Pullen LLP	Ticker Symbol	GRPK
Stk Agt	NA	Outstanding Shares	NA
Counsel	NA	E.P.S	NA
DUNS No.	NA	Shareholders	NA

Business: The groups principal activity is to provide wireless business solutions to the transportation industry. Services of the group include mobile tracking solutions, ruggedized, low-power asset management solution targeting trailers, cargo containers, and other mobile assets and ruggedized, vehicle performance and data communications solution targeting the transportation and mobile worker marketplaces consisting of LTL, service, and utility vehicles. The group operates from the United States.

Primary SIC and add'l.: 7389

CIK No: 0001295702

Officers: Bary Bertiger/Co - CEO, Executive Dir., Tim R. Sensenig/Chmn., CEO, Bernard Asher/Pres., Co - Founder, Treasurer, Michael L. Shelton/Member - Advisory Board, COO, Sherry May/41/VP - Sales

Directors: Tim R. Sensenig/Chmn., CEO, Bary Bertiger/Co - CEO, Executive Dir., Bernard Asher/Pres., Co - Founder, Treasurer, Michael L. Shelton/Member - Advisory Board, COO, Michael Proffitt/Dir., David Cairns/Dir., Jack Schang/Member - Advisory Board, Llew Keltner/Member - Advisory Board, Robert E. Cawthorn/Member - Advisory Board

Owners: Insiders/55.90%, Bary Bertiger/6.00%, David C. Cairns/3.50%, Tim R. Sensenig/38.70%, Investors Insurance Group, Inc/14.30%, Tall Trees Capital, LLC/6.00%, Sensenig Family Irrevocable/21.10%, Michael L. Shelton

Financial Data: Fiscal Year End:12/31 **Latest Annual Data:** 12/31/2006

Year	Sales	Net Income
2006	NA	-$1,982,000

Curr. Assets:	$2,000	Curr. Liab.:	$1,122,000		
Plant, Equip.:	$2,000	Total Liab.:	$1,122,000	Indic. Yr. Divd.:	NA
Total Assets:	$4,000	Net Worth:	-$1,119,000	Debt/ Equity:	NA

Gray Television Inc

4370 Peachtree Rd. NE, Atlanta, GA, 30319; *PH:* 1-404-504-9828; *Fax:* 1-404-261-9607; *http://* www.graycommunications.com

General - Incorporation	GA	**Stock**- Price on:12/24/2007	$9.52
Employees	2,117	Stock Exchange	NYSE
Auditor	PricewaterhouseCoopers LLP	Ticker Symbol	GTN
Stk Agt	Mellon Investor Services LLC	Outstanding Shares	47,900,000
Counsel	NA	E.P.S	NA
DUNS No.	04-297-3875	Shareholders	NA

Business: The group's principle activities are to provide television broadcasting, publishing and paging operations. The broadcasting segment operates thirteen television stations located in the southern, southwestern and midwestern United States. The publishing segment operates four daily newspapers in four different markets located in Georgia and Indiana, and an area weekly advertising only publication in Georgia. The paging operations are located in Florida, Georgia, and Alabama. Television station revenues are primarily derived from local, regional and national advertising, network compensation and studio and tower space rental and commercial production activities. The group has 29 television stations serving 25 television markets. The group's quarterly revenue for Sep'07 was 73.58 millions of USD.

Primary SIC and add'l.: 4812 2711 4813

CIK No: 0000043196

Subsidiaries: Gray Television Group, Inc., Gray Television Licensee, Inc., Gray Texas LLC, Gray Texas LP, Wvlt-tv, Inc.

Officers: Mack J. Robinson/84/Chmn., CEO/$814,096.00, Robert S. Prather/Dir., COO, Pres./$2,423,108.00, Robert A. Beizer/VP - Law, Development, Sec./$367,627.00, Tracey Jones/Regional VP, GM - WHSV, Frank J. Jonas/Regional VP - Midwest, GM Wowt, Wayne M. Martin/Regional VP - Television, GM Wkyt, James C. Ryan/CFO, Sr. VP/$567,843.00, Pat Dalbey/Regional VP, GM - WTVY, Nick Waller/Regional VP, GM - WCTV, Don Ray/Regional VP, GM - WSAZ, Bob Smith/Regional VP, GM - WMTV, Jackson S. Cowart/Chief Accounting Officer, Charlie Peterson/Regional VP - Texas, GM Kktv

Directors: Mack J. Robinson/84/Chmn., CEO, Hilton H. Howell/Vice Chmn., Richard L. Boger/Dir., Ray Deaver/Dir., Hugh Norton/Dir., William E. Mayher/Dir., Robert S. Prather/Dir., COO, Pres., T. L. Elder/Dir., Zell Miller/Dir., Howell W. Newton/Dir., Harriett J. Robinson/Dir.

Owners: Wellington Management Company, L.L.P./9.00%, Howell W. Newton, Ray M. Deaver, William E. Mayher, Insiders/5.30%, Robert S. Prather/1.50%, Highland Capital Management L.P./10.60%, Richard L. Boger, Hilton H. Howell, Richard L. Boger, Hugh E. Norton, Hilton H. Howell, Zell B. Miller, T. L. Elder, Robert S. Prather *(30 Owners included in Index)*

Financial Data: Fiscal Year End:12/31 **Latest Annual Data:** 12/31/2006

Year	Sales	Net Income
2006	$332,137,000	$11,711,000
2005	$261,553,000	$3,362,000
2004	$346,567,000	$44,285,000

Curr. Assets:	$80,158,000	Curr. Liab.:	$63,801,000		
Plant, Equip.:	$187,120,000	Total Liab.:	$1,211,082,000	Indic. Yr. Divd.:	$0.120
Total Assets:	$1,628,287,000	Net Worth:	$379,754,000	Debt/ Equity:	2.4031

Graybar Electric Co Inc

34 N Meramec Ave., St Louis, MO, 63105; *PH:* 1-314-512-9200; *http://* www.graybar.com

General - Incorporation	NY	**Stock**- Price on:12/24/2007	NA
Employees	NA	Stock Exchange	NDQ
Auditor	Ernst & Young LLP	Ticker Symbol	NA
Stk Agt	NA	Outstanding Shares	NA
Counsel	NA	E.P.S	NA
DUNS No.	00-190-3202	Shareholders	NA

Business: The group's principle activity is to distribute electrical and communication products. The group provides integrated supply services to contractors, industrial plants, telephone companies, power plants and commercial users. The products of the group include wire, cable, conduit, wiring devices, tools, motor controls, transformers, lamps, lighting fixtures and hardware, power transmission equipment, telephone station apparatus, data products. The group operates from United States, Puerto Rico, Mexico and Canada.

Primary SIC and add'l.: 5063 5065

CIK No: 0000205402

Subsidiaries: Commonwealth Controls Corporation, Distribution Associates, Inc., Graybar Business Services, Inc., Graybar Canada Limited, Graybar Commerce Corporation, Graybar Electric Canada Limited, Graybar Electric de Mexico, S. de R.L. de C.V., Graybar Electric Limited, Graybar Financial Services, Inc., Graybar International, Inc., Graybar Newfoundland Limited, Graybar Services, Inc.

Officers: Robert A. Reynolds/Chmn., CEO, Pres./$1,567,482.00, L. R. Giglio/53/Dir., Sr. VP - Operations, R. D. Offenbacher/57/Dir., Sr. VP - Sales, Marketing/$638,699.00, R. A. Cole/58/Dir., District VP, D. B. D'Alessandro/47/Dir., CFO, Sr. VP/$565,854.00, T. F. Dowd/64/Dir., Sr. VP, Sec., General Counsel/$551,993.00, K. M. Mazzarella/48/Dir., Sr. VP - Human Resources, Strategic Planning, D. E. Desousa/49/Dir., Sr. VP - Sales, Distribution/$706,625.00, R. C. Lyons/51/Dir., District VP, R. L. Nowak/61/Dir., District VP

Directors: Robert A. Reynolds/Chmn., CEO, Pres., L. R. Giglio/53/Dir., Sr. VP - Operations, R. D. Offenbacher/57/Dir., Sr. VP - Sales, Marketing, R. A. Cole/58/Dir., District VP, D. B. D'Alessandro/47/Dir., CFO, Sr. VP, T. F. Dowd/64/Dir., Sr. VP, Sec., General Counsel, K. M. Mazzarella/48/Dir., Sr. VP - Human Resources, Strategic Planning, T. S. Gurganous/58/Dir., D. E. Desousa/49/Dir., Sr. VP - Sales, Distribution, F. H. Hughes/61/Dir., K. B. Sparks/62/Dir., R. C. Lyons/51/Dir., District VP, R. L. Nowak/61/Dir., District VP

Owners: T. F. Dowd, T. S. Gurganous, K. B. Sparks, D. E. DeSousa, R. D. Offenbacher, K. M. Mazzarella, D. B. D'Alessandro, R. A. Reynolds, R. A. Cole, R. C. Lyons, L. R. Giglio, Insiders, R. L. Nowak

Graymark Productions Inc

101 N Robinson Ave., Ste. 920, Oklahoma City, OK, 73102; *PH:* 1-405-601-5300; *Fax:* 1-405-601-4550; *http://* www.graymarkproductions.com; *Email:* Megan@Graymark.net

General - Incorporation	OK	**Stock**- Price on:12/24/2007	$0.45
Employees	3	Stock Exchange	OTC
Auditor	Murrell, Hall, McIntosh & Co., PLLP	Ticker Symbol	GRMK
Stk Agt	UMB Bank, N.A.	Outstanding Shares	8,740,000
Counsel	NA	E.P.S	-$0.22
DUNS No.	NA	Shareholders	NA

Business: The groups principle activities include developing, financing and creating feature-length movies and promoting and marketing movies in media markets. The group operates from the United States and Canada.

Primary SIC and add'l.: 7812

CIK No: 0001272597

Subsidiaries: Graymark Productions, L.L.C, Out of the Blue Productions, LLC

Officers: John Simonelli/Chmn., CEO, Gray Frederickson/COO, Pres., Mark R. Kidd/CFO, Sec., Albert S. Ruddy/Consulting Producer, Jonny Talley/Reception, Office Assist., Amy Briede/Contact Person, Harry G. Frederickson/70/COO, Pres.

Directors: John Simonelli/Chmn., CEO, Fred Roos/Dir., George Kiersch/Dir., Lewis B. Moon/Dir., Stanton Nelson/Dir.

Owners: Oliver Company Holdings, LLC, SXJE, LLC and Sam Eyde, W. Ransome Oliver, John Simonelli, Insiders, RTO Management, L.L.C., Mark R. Kidd, Stanton Nelson, Lewis P. Zeidner, Peter E. Hoffman, Lewann, Ltd., Greg Luster, Roy T. Oliver, RTO Capital Holdings, Ltd., Vahid Salalati

Financial Data: Fiscal Year End:12/31 **Latest Annual Data:** 12/31/2006

Year	Sales	Net Income
2006	$404,000	-$2,215,000
2005	$450,000	-$551,000
2004	NA	-$396,000

Curr. Assets:	$856,000	Curr. Liab.:	$1,492,000		
Plant, Equip.:	$12,000	Total Liab.:	$2,939,000	Indic. Yr. Divd.:	NA
Total Assets:	$3,308,000	Net Worth:	$369,000	Debt/ Equity:	NA

Great American Bancorp Inc

1311 S Neil St., Champaign, IL, 61820; *PH:* 1-217-356-2265; *Fax:* 1-217-356-2502; *http://* www.greatamericanbancorp.com; *Email:* jadams@356bank.com

General - Incorporation	DE	**Stock**- Price on:12/24/2007	$33.2
Employees	NA	Stock Exchange	OTC
Auditor	NA	Ticker Symbol	GTPS
Stk Agt	NA	Outstanding Shares	NA
Counsel	NA	E.P.S	$0.62
DUNS No.	NA	Shareholders	NA

Business: The group operates through its subsidiary whose principal activity is to provide banking and financial services. The other services of the group include brokerage activities and sale of tax-deferred annuities. The group operates from the United States.

Primary SIC and add'l.: 6035 6712

CIK No: 0000943064

Officers: George R. Rouse/Dir., CEO, Pres., Jane F. Adams/CFO, Sec., Treasurer

Directors: George R. Rouse/Dir., CEO, Pres., Ronald E. Guenther/Chmn., Clinton C. Atkins/Dir., Ronald Kiddoo/Dir., Jack B. Troxell/Dir.

Financial Data: Fiscal Year End:12/31 **Latest Annual Data:** 12/31/2003

Year	Sales	Net Income
2003	$11,768,000	$1,470,000
2002	$13,595,000	$1,904,000
2001	$13,829,000	$1,201,000

Curr. Assets:	$44,062,000	**Curr. Liab.:**	$139,664,000	**P/E Ratio:**	53.55
Plant, Equip.:	$6,299,000	**Total Liab.:**	$141,814,000	**Indic. Yr. Divd.:**	NA
Total Assets:	$159,450,000	**Net Worth:**	$17,636,000	**Debt/ Equity:**	NA

Great American Family Parks Inc

208 S Academy Ave., Ste 130, Eagle, ID, 83616; ***PH:*** 1-208-342-8888; ***http://*** www.weloveparks.com

General - Incorporation .... NV
Employees 17
Auditor .... Madsen & Assoc. CPAs, Inc
Stk Agt .... OTC Stock Transfer, Inc.
Counsel .... NA
DUNS No. .... NA

Stock- Price on:12/24/2007 .... $0.12
Stock Exchange .... OTC
Ticker Symbol .... GFAM
Outstanding Shares 51,890,000
E.P.S $0.01
Shareholders .... NA

Business: The group's principle activity is buying and managing profitable regional theme parks and themed amusement attractions in the United States. By building a family of parks each with up to 1 million annual attendees, the company is in the process of developing a series of compatible, yet distinct entertainment and amusement products, including themed amusement parks, associated products, food and beverage, and multimedia offerings. One of the area's most popular attractions, the 500-acre Pine Mountain Wild Animal Safari located in Pine Mountain, Georgia, offers a unique, hands-on safari experience. Visitors can see, touch and feed hundreds of exotic animals from every continent - a true worldwide safari. Crossroads Convenience Center (CCC) is a retail and food service center. Their primary revenue stream at CCC is the sale of fuel with additional revenues derived from high-margin food and beverage, and lotto ticket sales. CCC services facilities in the Boise Idaho and surrounding area. Locations serviced include The Idaho Center (an athletic and entertainment facility), the new Boise State University campus, and surrounding entertainment and commercial facilities. Noble Romans Pizza and Tuscano's Italian Style Subs, part of the national Noble Romans food service company. The dual branded restaurants have been integrated into the food service operations of Wild Animal Safari Park

Primary SIC and add'l.: 7990

CIK No: 0001297937

Subsidiaries: Crossroads Convenience Center LLC, GFAM Management Corporation, Wild Animal Safari, Inc

Officers: Larry L. Eastland/Chmn., CEO, Pres., Dale W. Van Voorhis/Pres. - Gfam Management, Richard W. Jackson/Dir., CFO, Treasurer, Tristan R. Pico/Dir., Sec., Ashley Jennette Hull/Administrative Dir., Jason Hull/Information Technology Mgr.

Directors: Larry L. Eastland/Chmn., CEO, Pres., Jim Meikle/Dir., Richard W. Jackson/Dir., CFO, Treasurer, Tristan R. Pico/Dir., Sec., Jeffrey Lococo/Dir., Christopher Eastland/Dir., Jane Klosterman/Dir.

Owners: Jane Klosterman/6.10%, Richard Jackson, Jeffrey Lococo, Jay Pitlake/6.70%, Tristan Pico, EDLA FLP/19.30%, Christopher L. Eastland, Insiders/29.00%, James Meikle/3.00%, Larry L. Eastland/19.30%

Financial Data: ***Fiscal Year End:***12/31 ***Latest Annual Data:*** 12/31/2006

Year	Sales	Net Income
2006	$9,329,000	$423,000
2005	$6,978,000	-$828,000

Curr. Assets:	$1,483,000	**Curr. Liab.:**	$379,000		
Plant, Equip.:	$4,693,000	**Total Liab.:**	$2,563,000	**Indic. Yr. Divd.:**	NA
Total Assets:	$6,559,000	**Net Worth:**	$3,997,000	**Debt/ Equity:**	0.5409

Great American Financial Resources Inc

250 E 5th St., Cincinnati, OH, 45202; ***PH:*** 1-513-333-5300; ***http://*** www.gafri.com;
Email: mmuething@gafri.com

General - Incorporation .... DE
Employees 1,000
Auditor .... Ernst & Young LLP
Stk Agt.. New York Drops-Mellon Investor Srvcs
Counsel .... NA
DUNS No. 18-005-2144

Stock- Price on:12/24/2007 .... $24.07
Stock Exchange .... NA
Ticker Symbol .... NA
Outstanding Shares 47,730,000
E.P.S $1.69
Shareholders .... NA

Business: The group's principle activities are to market retirement products, primarily fixed and variable annuities and various forms of life and supplemental health insurance. The operations are carried on through three divisions, life and annuity, supplemental insurance and ga life of Puerto Rico. Life and annuity provides fixed and variable annuity products and traditional life insurance products. Annuity products are sold through agents to employees of primary and secondary educational institutions, hospitals and in the non-qualified markets. Supplemental insurance provides a variety of supplemental health and life products through independent agents. Ga life of Puerto Rico markets in-home life and supplemental health products through a network of group-employed agents.

Primary SIC and add'l.: 6371 6311

CIK No: 0000894651

Subsidiaries: AAG Holding Company, Inc., American Annuity Group Capital Trust II, Annuity Investors Life Insurance Company, Great American Life Assurance Company of Puerto Rico, Inc., Great American Life Insurance Company, Loyal American Holding Corporation, Loyal American Life Insurance Company, Manhattan National Life Insurance Company, United Teacher Associates Insurance Company

Officers: Craig S. Lindner/Dir., CEO, Pres., Byron Buescher/Sr. VP, Jeffrey G. Hester/Controller, Christopher P. Miliano/CFO, Exec. VP, Treasurer, Mark F. Muething/Exec. VP, General Counsel, Sec., Malott W. Nyhart/Exec. VP, Michael J. Prager/Exec. VP, Chief Actuary, Charles R. Scheper/COO, Richard L. Magoteaux/CFO, Exec. VP, John B. Berding/Exec. VP - Investments, Mathew T. Dutkiewicz/Exec. VP, Adrienne S. Kessling/Sr. VP, Billy B. Hill/Pres. - UTA1, James E. Moffett/Exec. VP - Operations, Brad Wolfram/Exec. VP *(20 Officers included in Index)*

Directors: Craig S. Lindner/Dir., CEO, Pres., Carl H. Lindner/Dir., Kenneth C. Ambrecht/Dir., Ronald G. Joseph/Dir., Robert A. Adams/Dir., John T. Lawrence/Dir., William R. Martin/Dir.

Owners: Mark F. Muething, Kenneth C. Ambrecht, Carl H. Lindner/1.10%, Insiders/4.70%, James E. Moffett, American Financial Group, Inc./81.10%, Richard L. Magoteaux, John T. Lawrence, Charles R. Scheper, Thomas E. Mischell, Christopher P. Miliano, William R. Martin, Michael J. Prager, Robert A. Adams, Theodore H. Emmerich *(19 Owners included in Index)*

Financial Data: ***Fiscal Year End:***12/31 ***Latest Annual Data:*** 12/31/2006

Year	Sales	Net Income
2006	$1,044,000,000	$98,900,000
2005	$988,100,000	$69,900,000
2004	$1,045,400,000	$101,800,000

Curr. Assets:	$1,241,600,000	**Curr. Liab.:**	$298,300,000	**P/E Ratio:**	14.24
Plant, Equip.:	NA	**Total Liab.:**	$12,261,400,000	**Indic. Yr. Divd.:**	$0.100
Total Assets:	$13,335,400,000	**Net Worth:**	$1,074,000,000	**Debt/ Equity:**	0.2534

Great Atlantic & Pacific Tea Co Inc

2 Paragon Dr., Montvale, NJ, 07645; ***PH:*** 1-973-323-6691; ***Fax:*** 1-973-323-3442;
http:// www.aptea.com; ***Email:*** apcustomerrel@aptea.com

General - Incorporation .... MD
Employees 12,920
Auditor .... Ernst & Young, LLP
Stk Agt ..... American Stock Transfer & Trust Co.
Counsel .... NA
DUNS No. 00-136-7366

Stock- Price on:12/24/2007 .... $34.2
Stock Exchange .... NYSE
Ticker Symbol .... GAP
Outstanding Shares 41,800,000
E.P.S $0.64
Shareholders .... NA

Business: The group's principal activity is to operate conventional supermarkets, combination food and drug stores and discount food stores. It sells groceries, meats, fresh produce and other items commonly offered in supermarkets. In addition, many stores have bakery, delicatessen, pharmacy, floral, fresh fish and cheese departments and on-site banking. The group's operations are carried out in 10 U.S. States, the district of columbia, and ontario, Canada. Trade marks of the group include a&p(R), super fresh(R), sav-a-center(R), farmer jack(R), waldbaum's(tm), super foodmart, ultra food & drug, dominion(R), food basics(R), the barn markets(R) and the food emporium(r). As on 28-Feb-2004, the group operated 633 retail stores and served as wholesaler to 63 franchise stores in Canada.

Primary SIC and add'l.: 5411 2051 2024 2095 5141

CIK No: 0000043300

Subsidiaries: 1046 Yonkers Ave. Corp., 111 North Ave. Realty Corp., 1282891 Ontario Inc., 2008 Broadway, Inc., 3328155 Canada Inc., 3399486 Canada Inc., 3467210 Canada Inc., 3499031 Canada Inc., 3557588 Canada Inc., 3714683 Canada Inc., 3864715 Canada Inc., A & P Wine & Spirits, Inc., A&p Drug Mart Limited, A&p Properties Limited, Amboy Road Development Corp. 97 Subsidiaries included in the Index

Officers: Eric Claus/CEO, Pres./$1,948,974.00, Christian W.E. Haub/Executive Chmn./$1,941,084.00, Brenda Galgano/Sr. VP, CFO/$793,491.00, Allan Richards/Sr. VP - Human Resources, Labor Relations, Legal Services/$774,275.00, Paul Wiseman/Sr. VP - Store Operations/$915,045.00, Jennifer MacLeod/Sr. VP - Marketing, Communications, Rebecca Philbert/Sr. VP - Merchandising, Supply, Logistics, Harry L. Rubinstein/Sr. Dir. Properties - Administration, Timothy S. Huttleston/Sr. Dir. - Real Estate Development, John Majczan/Dir. - Real Estate, David E. Brecher/Real Estate Mgr., Janet Sides/Real Estate Mgr.

Directors: Christian W.E. Haub/Executive Chmn., Andreas Guldin/46/Dir.

Owners: John D. Barline, Eric Claus, Goodwood, Inc., Brenda Galgano, Andreas Guldin, Jens-Jrgen Bckel, Tengelmann Warenhandelsgesellschaft KG, John E. Metzger, Christian W. E. Haub, Karl-Erivan Warder Haub, Insiders, Edward Lewis, Dan Kourkoumelis, Maureen B. Tart-Bezer, Prentice Capital Management LP *(19 Owners included in Index)*

Financial Data: ***Fiscal Year End:***02/25 ***Latest Annual Data:*** 2/24/2007

Year	Sales	Net Income
2007	$6,850,268,000	$26,893,000
2006	$8,740,347,000	$392,630,000
2005	$10,854,911,000	-$188,098,000

Curr. Assets:	$1,164,681,000	**Curr. Liab.:**	$1,078,202,000	**P/E Ratio:**	53.44
Plant, Equip.:	$1,515,700,000	**Total Liab.:**	$2,564,112,000	**Indic. Yr. Divd.:**	NA
Total Assets:	$2,801,968,000	**Net Worth:**	$233,802,000	**Debt/ Equity:**	0.7294

Great Basin Financial Corp

PO Box 2808, Elko, NV, 89801; ***PH:*** 1-775-753-3800; ***Fax:*** 1-775-753-8836;
http:// www.greatbasinbank.com

General - Incorporation ....
Employees .... NA
Auditor .... NA
Stk Agt .... Great Basin Financial Corp
Counsel .... NA
DUNS No. .... NA

Stock- Price on:12/24/2007 .... $9.75
Stock Exchange .... OTC
Ticker Symbol .... GBFL
Outstanding Shares 2,580,000
E.P.S .... NA
Shareholders .... NA

Business: The groups principle activity is to provide recruiting services. The groups service area includes the research and development, engineering, marketing, sales, information technology and manufacturing industries. The group operates from United States.

Primary SIC and add'l.: 6022

CIK No:

Great Basin Gold Ltd

101 Carson Rd., Unit 5, Battle Mountain, NV, 89820; ***PH:*** 1-775-635-3323; ***Fax:*** 1-775-635-3399;
http:// www.greatbasingold.com; ***Email:*** info@hdgold.com

General - Incorporation .... BC
Employees .... NA
Auditor .... KPMG LLP
Stk Agt .... Computershare Trust Co of Canada
Counsel .... NA
DUNS No. 24-750-5209

Stock- Price on:12/24/2007 .... $2.54
Stock Exchange .... AMEX
Ticker Symbol .... GBN
Outstanding Shares .... NA
E.P.S .... -$0.28
Shareholders .... NA

Business: The group's principal activities are to acquire and explore mineral property interests in United States and Canada. Detail engineering and economic analysis are conducted by the group of high-grade, high-quality gold mineral deposits. The group has acquired ivanhoe property and casino property. The ivanhoe project hosts a number of gold-silver vein systems with high indicated grades that are potentially amenable to underground mining. The casino project hosts mineralizations that is potentially exploitable by open pit mining. The operations of the group are through its wholly owned subsidiary great basin gold inc.

Primary SIC and add'l.: 1041 1044

CIK No: 0000865492

Subsidiaries: Antler Peak Gold Inc., Great Basin Gold Inc., Great Basin Gold RSA (Proprietary) Limited, N5C Resources Inc., N6C Resources Inc., Pacific Sentinel Resources Inc., Rodeo Creek Gold Inc., Southgold Exploration (Proprietary) Limited, Touchstone Resources Company

Officers: Ferdinand Dippenaar/Dir., CEO, Pres., Dawie Mostert/VP - Human Capital, Boniface Ngarachu/Organizational Effectiveness, Change Specialist, Gernot Wober/Exploration Mgr., Josh Mashigo/GM, Dawn Black/Sr. Exploration Geologist, Zelda Smit/CFO, Louis Scheepers/Sr. Mgr. - Project Development, Peter Ott/Burnstone Mine Mgr., Mike Baynes/Ore Reserve Mgr., Gerhard Combrink/Business Services, Financial Mgr., Kenneth Mbewe/Human Capital Mgr., Duduzile Ratshefola/Corporate Social Responsibility Mgr., John Haan/GM, Paul Huet/Mine Mgr. *(22 Officers included in Index)*

Directors: Ferdinand Dippenaar/Dir., CEO, Pres., Ronald W. Thiessen/Chmn., Barry T. Coughlan/Dir., David J. Copeland/Dir., David Elliott/Dir., Wayne H. Kirk/Dir., Sipho A. Nkosi/Dir., Walter T. Segsworth/Dir.

Financial Data: *Fiscal Year End:*12/31 *Latest Annual Data:* 12/31/2006

Year	Sales	Net Income
2006	NA	-$9,905,000
2005	NA	-$1,303,000
2004	NA	-$5,490,000

Curr. Assets:	$30,169,000	*Curr. Liab.:*	$1,142,000		
Plant, Equip.:	$1,264,000	*Total Liab.:*	$18,528,000	*Indic. Yr. Divd.:*	NA
Total Assets:	$128,701,000	*Net Worth:*	$110,173,000	*Debt/ Equity:*	NA

Great China International Holdings Inc

C Site 25-26F President Building, No. 69 Heping N St., Shenyang, Heping District, 110003; *PH:* 86-2422813888; *http://* www.greatchinaholdings.com

General - Incorporation	NV	*Stock*- Price on:12/24/2007	$3.75
Employees	NA	Stock Exchange	OTC
Auditor	Murrell, Hall, McIntosh & Co., PLLP	Ticker Symbol	GCIH
Stk Agt	Signature Stock Transfer	Outstanding Shares	NA
Counsel	NA	E.P.S.	NA
DUNS No.	NA	Shareholders	NA

Business: The groups principle activities include developing, selling and managing commercial and residential real estate investment. In July 2005, the group acquired Silverstrand International Holdings Limited. The group operates from China and the United States. The group's quarterly revenue for September 2007 was 1.91 millions of USD.

Primary SIC and add'l.: 6500
CIK No: 0000828878
Subsidiaries: Shenyang Jitian Property Co. Ltd., Shenyang Maryland International Industry Company Limited, Silverstrand International Holdings Limited

Officers: Frank Jiang/53/Chmn., CEO, Pres., Danny Sui Keung Chau/51/CFO
Directors: Frank Jiang/53/Chmn., CEO, Pres., Chen Jin Rong/49/Dir., Duan Jing Shi/56/Dir., Wang Li Rong/Dir., Wang Jian Guo/Dir., Duan Jingshi/Dir.
Owners: Chen Jin Rong/0.10%, Wang Li Rong/0.80%, Frank Jiang/69.40%, Wang Jian Guo/0.10%, Duan Jing Shi/0.80%, Insiders/71.00%

Financial Data: *Fiscal Year End:*12/31 *Latest Annual Data:* 12/31/2006

Year	Sales	Net Income
2006	$12,738,000	-$3,747,000
2005	$26,524,000	$80,000
2004	NA	-$34,000

Curr. Assets:	$16,663,000	*Curr. Liab.:*	$67,842,000		
Plant, Equip.:	$53,267,000	*Total Liab.:*	$69,841,000	*Indic. Yr. Divd.:*	NA
Total Assets:	$69,929,000	*Net Worth:*	$88,000	*Debt/ Equity:*	NA

Great China Mining Inc

Formerly: China NetTV Holdings Inc
World Trade Ctr., Ste. 536, 999 Canada Pl., Vancouver, BC, V6C 3E2; *PH:* 1-604-641-1366; *http://* greatchinamining.com

General - Incorporation	NV	*Stock*- Price on:12/24/2007	NA
Employees	NA	Stock Exchange	NA
Auditor	Clancy & Co. PLLC	Ticker Symbol	NA
Stk Agt	Nevada Agency & Trust Company	Outstanding Shares	NA
Counsel	Michael A. Littman	E.P.S.	NA
DUNS No.	NA	Shareholders	NA

Business: The group's principal activity is to develop gold and other mineral deposits in tibet and other areas of China. On 07-Jul-2003, the group acquired honglu investment holdings inc.
Primary SIC and add'l.: 3663 1081 3679
CIK No: 0001080759
Subsidiaries: Great China Mining (Canada), Inc.

Great Lakes Aviation Ltd

1022 Airport Pkwy., Cheyenne, WY, 82001; *PH:* 1-307-432-7000; *Fax:* 1-307-432-7001; *http://* www.greatlakesav.com; *Email:* custrel@greatlakesav.com

General - Incorporation	IA	*Stock*- Price on:12/24/2007	$2.7
Employees	557	Stock Exchange	OTC
Auditor	KPMG LLP	Ticker Symbol	GLUX
Stk Agt	Wells Fargo Bank, N.A.	Outstanding Shares	14,070,000
Counsel	Briggs & Morgan	E.P.S.	$1.15
DUNS No.	86-870-7662	Shareholders	NA

Business: The group's principle activity is to provide aviation services. The group is a regional air carrier, providing scheduled passenger and airfreight services. The group now operates under its own name and as a code-sharing partner with united and frontier. As of 29-Feb-2004, the group provided passenger service to 40 airports in 11 states with 1,293 scheduled departures each week. The group has 33 beechcraft model 1900d aircraft, 19-passenger aircraft and 7 embraer brasilia model 120 30-passenger aircraft on its fleet. The group provides direct and connecting service to and from three major cities. The group operated 91 departures daily from denver, 2 departures daily from minneapolis and 3 departures daily from phoenix. The group operates from United States.

Primary SIC and add'l.: 4512 4731
CIK No: 0000914397
Owners: Charles R. Howell, Michael E. Tennenbaum, Ivan L. Simpson, Vernon A. Mickelson, Tennenbaum & Co., LLC, Insiders, Raytheon Aircraft Credit Corporation, Iowa Great Lakes Flyers, Inc., Michael L. Tuinstra, Douglas G. Voss, Gayle R. Brandt

Financial Data: *Fiscal Year End:*12/31 *Latest Annual Data:* 12/31/2006

Year	Sales	Net Income
2006	$87,614,000	$15,679,000
2005	$76,393,000	$1,181,000
2004	$76,348,000	$5,629,000

Curr. Assets:	$12,270,000	*Curr. Liab.:*	$17,081,000	*P/E Ratio:*	2.27
Plant, Equip.:	$69,056,000	*Total Liab.:*	$85,184,000	*Indic. Yr. Divd.:*	NA
Total Assets:	$82,312,000	*Net Worth:*	-$2,872,000	*Debt/ Equity:*	NA

Great Lakes Bancorp Inc

2421 Main St., Buffalo, NY, 14214; *PH:* 1-716-961-1900; *Fax:* 1-716-961-0976; *http://* greatlakesbancorp.com

General - Incorporation	DE	*Stock*- Price on:12/24/2007	$13.78
Employees	101	Stock Exchange	NYSE
Auditor	Freed Maxick & Battaglia, Cpas, P.C	Ticker Symbol	GLK
Stk Agt	Registrar & Transfer Co	Outstanding Shares	10,920,000
Counsel	NA	E.P.S.	-$0.149
DUNS No.	NA	Shareholders	NA

Business: The groups principle activity is to provide banking services. The groups services include business checking and savings accounts, commercial loans and merchant banking services. The group provides lending services include consumer loans, mortgage loans, commercial loans and wholesale loans. The group operates from United States.

Primary SIC and add'l.: NA
CIK No: 0001217730
Subsidiaries: Great Lakes Bancorp Statutory Trust I, Greater Buffalo Savings Bank
Officers: Andrew W. Dorn/Dir., Pres., CEO - Greater Buffalo Saving Bank, Douglas Carlson/Mgr. - Lockport, Greater Buffalo Saving Bank, Timothy Mayer/Branch Mgr. - North Tonawanda, Greater Buffalo Saving Bank, Penny Morgante/Mgr. - Main, Jewett, Greater Buffalo Saving Bank, Michele Walczak/Branch Mgr. - Orchard Park, Greater Buffalo Saving Bank, Mark Priester/Mgr. - Snyder, Greater Buffalo Saving Bank, Dal Giuliani/Mgr. - Town, Tonawanda, Greater Buffalo Saving Bank, Jodie Alexander/Mgr. - West Amherst, Greater Buffalo Saving Bank, Mary Jo Suffoletta/Mgr. - West Seneca, Greater Buffalo Saving Bank, Jamel Perkins/CIO, Exec. VP - Greater Buffalo Saving Bank, Michael Rogers/Exec. VP, CFO - Greater Buffalo Saving Bank, Peter Babiarz/Exec. VP, Chief Credit Officer - Greater Buffalo Saving Bank, Robert McKnight/Exec. VP, Chief Lending Officer - Greater Buffalo Saving Bank, Lawrence A. Schiavi/Exec. VP - Mortgage Banking Division - Greater Buffalo Saving Bank, Ramon Morales/Mgr. - Connecticut Street, Greater Buffalo Saving Bank *(21 Officers included in Index)*
Directors: Andrew W. Dorn/Dir., Pres., CEO - Greater Buffalo Saving Bank, Barry M. Snyder/Chmn., William A. Evans/Vice Chmn., John W. Rose/Dir. - Greater Buffalo Saving Bank, James A. Smith/Dir. - Greater Buffalo Saving Bank, Charles G. Cooper/Dir. - Greater Buffalo Saving Bank, Frederick A. Wolf/Dir. - Greater Buffalo Saving Bank, Louis Sidoni/Founder, Dir. Emeritus - Greater Buffalo Saving Bank, Carrie B. Frank/Dir. - Greater Buffalo Saving Bank, Robert B. Goldstein/Dir. - Greater Buffalo Saving Bank, Gerard T. Mazurkiewicz/Dir. - Greater Buffalo Saving Bank, Acea M. Mosey-Pawlowski/Dir. - Greater Buffalo Saving Bank

Financial Data: *Fiscal Year End:*12/31 *Latest Annual Data:* 12/31/2006

Year	Sales	Net Income
2006	$44,915,000	-$896,000
2005	$49,546,000	-$34,450,000
2004	$42,921,000	-$3,912,000

Curr. Assets:	$21,643,000	*Curr. Liab.:*	$736,530,000		
Plant, Equip.:	$24,765,000	*Total Liab.:*	$748,902,000	*Indic. Yr. Divd.:*	NA
Total Assets:	$884,412,000	*Net Worth:*	$135,510,000	*Debt/ Equity:*	0.7105

Great Northern Iron Ore Properties

W 1290 First National Bank Bldg, 332 Minnesota St., Saint Paul, MN, 55101; *PH:* 1-651-224-2385

General - Incorporation	MN	*Stock*- Price on:12/24/2007	$115
Employees	10	Stock Exchange	NYSE
Auditor	Ernst & Young LLP	Ticker Symbol	GNI
Stk Agt	Wells Fargo Shareowner Services	Outstanding Shares	1,500,000
Counsel	NA	E.P.S.	$10.98
DUNS No.	NA	Shareholders	NA

Business: The groups principal activity is to invest in mineral properties. The group operates from the United States.
Primary SIC and add'l.: 1011
CIK No: 0000043410
Officers: Joseph S. Micallef/74/Trustee, CEO, Pres., Robert A. Stein/69/Exec. Dir., Trustee, COO, Thomas A. Janochoski/49/CFO, VP, Sec.
Directors: Joseph S. Micallef/74/Trustee, CEO, Pres., Roger W. Staehle/74/Trustee, Robert A. Stein/69/Exec. Dir., Trustee, COO, John H. Roe/68/Trustee, Thomas A. Janochoski/49/CFO, VP, Sec.

Financial Data: *Fiscal Year End:*12/31 *Latest Annual Data:* 12/31/2006

Year	Sales	Net Income
2006	$17,555,000	$14,773,000
2005	$18,361,000	$15,721,000
2004	$14,447,000	$12,242,000

Curr. Assets:	$10,667,000	*Curr. Liab.:*	$5,034,000	*P/E Ratio:*	11.94
Plant, Equip.:	$4,122,000	*Total Liab.:*	$6,349,000	*Indic. Yr. Divd.:*	$11.200
Total Assets:	$18,510,000	*Net Worth:*	$12,161,000	*Debt/ Equity:*	NA

Great Panther Resources Ltd

1177 W Hastings St., Ste. 2100, Vancouver, BC, V6E 2K9x; *PH:* 1-604-608-1766; *http://* www.greatpanther.com; *Email:* info@greatpanther.com

General - Incorporation	BC	*Stock*- Price on:12/24/2007	NA
Employees	NA	Stock Exchange	AMEX
Auditor	KPMG LLP	Ticker Symbol	NA
Stk Agt	Computershare Trust Co	Outstanding Shares	NA
Counsel	M. Michael Sikula Law Corp	E.P.S.	NA
DUNS No.	NA	Shareholders	NA

Business: The group's principle activities include acquiring, exploring and developing mineral resource properties that have a potential for success. The group has combined experienced management and access to capital with the acquisition and development of high quality silver and gold projects, to offer shareholders strong leverage to rising silver and gold prices. The four main projects that the company is handling are Topia mine, Guanajuato project, Virimoa gold project, and San Antonio project. The group operates from United States.

Primary SIC and add'l.: 1000

CIK No: 0001300050

Subsidiaries: Metalicos de Durango, S.A. de C.V., Minera de Villa Seca, S.A. de C.V., Minera Mexicana el Rosario, S.A. de C.V, New Age Investments Inc.

Officers: Robert A. Archer/Dir., CEO, Pres., Francisco Ramos Sanchez/VP - Operations, Interim GM - Guanajuato Mine Complex, Robert Brown/VP - Exploration, Wendy Ratcliffe/Company Sec., Brad Aelicks/Investor Relation Officer, Don Mosher/Investor Relation Officer, Raakel Iskanius/CFO, Javier Ramirez Vargas/GM - Topia Mine, Bill Vanderwall/Exploration Mgr. - Mexico, Reg Advocaat/Mgr. - Corporate Development, Ramos F. Sanchez/VP - Operations

Directors: Robert A. Archer/Dir., CEO, Pres., Kaare G. Foy/Chmn., Malcolm A. Burne/Dir., John T. Kopcheff/Dir., Michael A. Turko/Dir.

Great Pee Dee Bancorp Inc

901 Chesterfield Hwy., Cheraw, SC, 29520; *PH:* 1-843-537-7656; *Fax:* 1-843-537-4436; *http://* www.sentrybankandtrust.com

General - Incorporation	DE	**Stock** - Price on:12/24/2007	$15.25
Employees	NA	Stock Exchange	NDQ
Auditor	Dixon Odom	Ticker Symbol	PEDE
Stk Agt	Registrar & Transfer Co	Outstanding Shares	1,790,000
Counsel	Luse Gorman Pomerenk & Schick PC	E.P.S	$0.68
DUNS No.	13-146-2657	Shareholders	NA

Business: The group principal activities are to provide financial services through 2 full banking offices located in cheraw and florence, South Carolina. The group's operations are conducted through its subsidiary sentry bank & trust. Its lending activities include one to four family residential loans, commercial real estate loans, construction loans and home improvement loans. The group offers a variety of deposits consisting of passbook accounts, checking accounts, money market accounts, fixed term certificates of deposit, individual retirement accounts and savings accounts. The group through its subsidiary conducts its primary business in chesterfield, marlboro and florence counties, South Carolina.

Primary SIC and add'l.: 6712 6035

CIK No: 0001046587

Subsidiaries: Sentry Bank & Trust

Officers: John S. Long/Dir., Pres., CEO - Sentry Bank, Trust, John M. Digby/Dir., CFO, Treasurer, Michael Blakeley/City Executive, Florence SC, Sentry Bank, Trust, Charlotte King/Personal Banker Loan Officer - Marketing Street Office, Sentry Bank, Trust, Kellie Joyner/Personal Banker Loan Officer - Cheraw Main Office, Sentry Bank, Trust, Teresa Ward/Customer Service - Representative, Marketing Street Office, Sentry Bank, Trust, Wayne Howle/Branch Mgr. - Raymond James Sentry Investment Svc, Sentry Bank, Trust, Amanda Fenters/Customer Service Representative, Cheraw Main Office, Sentry Bank, Trust, Marion Brooks-Byrd/Personal Banker Loan Officer - Florence Office, Sentry Bank, Trust, Richard White/City Executive, Cheraw SC, Barbara Shirley/Registered Sales Assist. - Raymond James, Raymond James

Directors: John S. Long/Dir., Pres., CEO - Sentry Bank, Trust, James C. Crawford/Chmn., Herbert W. Watts/Dir., William R. Butler/Dir., Malloy H. Evans/Dir., Robert M. Bennett/Dir., Henry P. Duvall/Dir., John M. Digby/Dir., CFO, Treasurer

Owners: Herbert W. Watts/6.90%, First Citizens Bancorporation of South Carolina, Inc./6.60%, The Great Pee Dee Bancorp, Inc./8.30%

Financial Data: *Fiscal Year End:*06/30 *Latest Annual Data:* 06/30/2007

Year	Sales	Net Income
2007	$15,665,000	$1,543,000
2006	$13,838,000	$1,599,000
2005	$10,687,000	$1,164,000

Curr. Assets:	$5,728,000	**Curr. Liab.:**	$162,446,000	**P/E Ratio:**	17.13
Plant, Equip.:	$5,127,000	**Total Liab.:**	$186,167,000	**Indic. Yr. Divd.:**	$0.640
Total Assets:	$212,706,000	**Net Worth:**	$26,540,000	**Debt/ Equity:**	0.8924

Great Plains Energy Inc

PO Box 418679, Kansas City, MO, 64141; *PH:* 1-816-556-2200; *http://* www.greatplainsenergy.com; *Email:* custserv@kcpl.com

General - Incorporation	MO	**Stock** - Price on:12/24/2007	$29.48
Employees	2,470	Stock Exchange	NYSE
Auditor	Deloitte & Touche LLP	Ticker Symbol	GXP
Stk Agt	UMB Bank, N.A.	Outstanding Shares	86,000,000
Counsel	NA	E.P.S	$1.72
DUNS No.	NA	Shareholders	NA

Business: The groups principle activity is to provide electricity. The group also provides energy management services. The group operates from United States.

Primary SIC and add'l.: 4924 4911 6719

CIK No: 0001143068

Subsidiaries: Custom Energy Holdings, LLC, Innovative Energy Consultants Inc., Kansas City Power & Light Company, KLT Energy Services Inc., KLT Inc, Strategic Energy, LLC

Officers: Shahid Malik/CEO, Pres. - Strategic Energy/$1,740,959.00, Michael J. Chesser/Chmn., CEO/$3,068,017.00, Stephen T. Easley/Sr. VP - Supply, Kansas City Power, Light, Lori Wright/Controller, Todd A. Kobayashi/VP - Energy Resource Management, Kansas City Power, Light, Eula Jones/Investor Relations Officer, William H. Downey/Dir., COO, Pres./$1,754,233.00, Mark English/General Counsel, Kevin Bryant/VP - Energy Solutions, Kansas City Power, Light, John Marshall/Sr. VP - Delivery, Kansas City Power, Light/$1,024,417.00, David Price/VP - Construction, Kansas City Power, Light, Barbara Curry/Sr. VP - Corporate Services, Corp. Sec., Chris B. Giles/VP - Regulatory Affairs, Kansas City Power, Light, Dana Crawford/VP - Plant Operations, Kansas City Power, Light, William P. Herdegen/VP - Customer Operations, Kansas City Power, Light *(22 Officers included in Index)*

Directors: Michael J. Chesser/Chmn., CEO, Mark A. Ernst/Dir., William K. Hall/Dir., Luis A. Jimenez/Dir., Linda H. Talbott/Dir., Randall C. Ferguson/Dir., William H. Downey/Dir., COO, Pres., William C. Nelson/Dir., Robert H. West/Dir., David L. Bodde/Dir., James A. Mitchell/Dir.

Owners: Luis A. Jimenez, David L. Bodde, John R. Marshall, Shahid Malik, James A. Mitchell, Linda H. Talbott, Terry Bassham, Randall C. Ferguson, Mark A. Ernst, Insiders, Michael J. Chesser, Robert H. West, William H. Downey, William K. Hall, William C. Nelson

Financial Data: *Fiscal Year End:*12/31 *Latest Annual Data:* 12/31/2006

Year	Sales	Net Income
2006	$2,675,349,000	$127,630,000
2005	$2,604,882,000	$162,310,000
2004	$2,464,018,000	$180,811,000

Curr. Assets:	$570,782,000	**Curr. Liab.:**	$1,202,993,000	**P/E Ratio:**	17.65
Plant, Equip.:	$3,066,201,000	**Total Liab.:**	$2,954,744,000	**Indic. Yr. Divd.:**	$1.660
Total Assets:	$4,335,660,000	**Net Worth:**	$1,380,916,000	**Debt/ Equity:**	0.9098

Great Southern Bancorp Inc

1451 E Battlefield, Springfield, MO, 65804; *PH:* 1-417-887-4400; *Fax:* 1-417-888-4315; *http://* www.greatsouthernbank.com

General - Incorporation	MD	**Stock** - Price on:12/24/2007	$27.73
Employees	581	Stock Exchange	NDQ
Auditor	BKD LLP	Ticker Symbol	GSBC
Stk Agt	Registrar & Transfer Co	Outstanding Shares	13,640,000
Counsel	Carnahan, Evans, Cantwell & Brown	E.P.S	$2.25
DUNS No.	04-795-4243	Shareholders	NA

Business: The group's principal activity is to provide banking services. The group originates residential and commercial real estate loans, automobile loans, home equity loans, loans secured by savings deposits, home improvement loans, guaranteed student loans and unsecured consumer loans. The deposit products include time, demand and saving. The group also offers insurance, travel, discount brokerage and related services. The operations of the group are carried out through 29 branches offices located in the southwestern and central Missouri.

Primary SIC and add'l.: 6712 6022

CIK No: 0000854560

Subsidiaries: GSB Two LLC

Officers: Joseph W. Turner/43/Dir., CEO, Pres./$665,333.00, Connie Hopper/Summit Club Contact, Steven G. Mitchem/Chief Lending Officer, Sr. VP/$257,255.00, Rex A. Copeland/Sr. VP, CFO/$228,033.00, Douglas W. Marrs/VP - Operations, Mike Stuck/Commercial Lender, Osage Beach, Curt Morgret/Marketing Mgr., Chris Jones/Commercial Lender LPO, Jill Bolding/Commercial Lender LPO, Ron Pender/Marketing Mgr., Henry Heimsoth/Marketing Mgr., Daren Bruschi/Commercial Lender LPO, Kevin Baker/Marketing Mgr., Carol Hanson/Commercial Lenderlpo, Kevin Saettele/Commercial Lender *(33 Officers included in Index)*

Directors: Joseph W. Turner/43/Dir., CEO, Pres., William V. Turner/75/Chmn., Julie Turner Brown/46/Dir., Earl A. Steinert/71/Dir., Thomas J. Carlson/55/Dir., William E. Barclay/78/Dir., Larry D. Frazier/70/Dir.

Owners: Robert M. Mahoney/7.24%, Gary D. Lewis, Earl A. Steinert/6.26%, Thomas J. Carlson, Steven G. Mitchem, Rex A. Copeland, William E. Barclay, Joseph W. Turner/12.85%, William V. Turner/4.04%, Julie Turner Brown/11.84%, Insiders/24.68%, Larry D. Frazier

Financial Data: *Fiscal Year End:*12/31 *Latest Annual Data:* 12/31/2006

Year	Sales	Net Income
2006	$179,714,000	$30,743,000
2005	$143,388,000	$22,671,000
2004	$110,724,000	$26,880,000

Curr. Assets:	$149,043,000	**Curr. Liab.:**	$2,038,956,000	**P/E Ratio:**	12.11
Plant, Equip.:	$31,185,000	**Total Liab.:**	$2,064,730,000	**Indic. Yr. Divd.:**	$0.680
Total Assets:	$2,240,308,000	**Net Worth:**	$175,578,000	**Debt/ Equity:**	0.1422

Great Western Bancorp Inc

9290 W Dodge Rd., Ste. 203, Omaha, NE, 68114; *PH:* 1-402-952-6000; *Fax:* 1-402-333-8339; *http://* www.greatwesternbank.com

General - Incorporation	IA	**Stock** - Price on:12/24/2007	NA
Employees	NA	Stock Exchange	NA
Auditor	BKD LLP	Ticker Symbol	NA
Stk Agt	NA	Outstanding Shares	NA
Counsel	Baird, Holm, Hamann & Strashei LLP	E.P.S	NA
DUNS No.	NA	Shareholders	NA

Business: The group's principal activity is to offer financial services. The group is a multi bank holding group for f and m bank, rushmore bank and trust, citizens bank, citizens bank of princeton and citizens bank of carlisle. The services include real estate mortgage loans, commercial loans, agricultural loans and individual loans. The deposit services include demand deposits, now, money market and savings deposits and certificate of deposits. It operates through 16 banking locations in Nebraska, 21 banking locations in South Dakota, 24 banking locations in southern Iowa and 1 banking locations in northern Missouri and 1 banking location in northeastern Kansas.

Primary SIC and add'l.: 6022 6712

CIK No: 0001088381

Subsidiaries: Great Western Bank, Clive, Great Western Bank, Omahal, Great Western Bank, Watertown, Great Western Service Corporation, Great Western Statutory Trust IV, GWB Capital Trust II, GWB Capital Trust III, GWB Capital Trust V

Great Wolf Resorts Inc

1400 Great Wolf Dr., Wisconsin Dells, WI, 53965; *PH:* 1-608-253-2222; *Fax:* 1-608-661-4701; *http://* greatwolfresorts.com; *Email:* info@greatwolfresorts.com

General - Incorporation	DE	**Stock** - Price on:12/24/2007	$14.62
Employees	2,300	Stock Exchange	NDQ
Auditor	Deloitte& Touche LLP	Ticker Symbol	WOLF
Stk Agt	Computershare Investor Services LLC	Outstanding Shares	30,680,000
Counsel	NA	E.P.S	-$1.67
DUNS No.	NA	Shareholders	NA

Business: The groups principle activity is to provide resort services. The groups services include themed restaurants, ice cream shop and confectionery, snack bar, cub club, game arcade and gift shop. The group products sold under the trade names Great Wolf Lodge(R) and Blue Harbor Resort. Customer served by the group is family with children. The group operates from Niagara Falls, Ontario and Canada. The group's quarterly revenue for September 2007 was 50.90 millions of USD.

Primary SIC and add'l.: 7996 7011

CIK No: 0001294538

Subsidiaries: BHMH, LLC, Blue Harbor Resort Condominium, LLC, Blue Harbor Resort Sheboygan, LLC, GLGB Manager III, LLC, Grapevine Beverage, Inc., Great Bear Lodge of Wisconsin Dells, LLC, Great Lakes Services, LLC, Great Wolf Capital Trust I, Great Wolf Lodge Kansas SPE, LLC, Great Wolf Lodge of Chehalis, LLC, Great Wolf Lodge of Grapevine, LLC, Great Wolf Lodge of Kansas City, LLC, Great Wolf Lodge of PKI, LLC, Great Wolf Lodge of the Poconos, LLC, Great Wolf Lodge of Traverse City, LLC 29 Subsidiaries included in the Index

Officers: John Emery/Dir., CEO, Alexander P. Lombardo/Investor Relation Officer, Michael J. Schroeder/General Counsel, Corp. Sec., Alissa N. Nolan/MD - International, Andrew Wilson/Media Contact, Katie McCall/Media Contact, Jennifer Beranek/Media Contact

Directors: John Emery/Dir., CEO, Joseph V. Vittoria/Chmn., Elan Blutinger/Dir., Randy Churchey/Dir., Michael M. Knetter/Dir., Edward H. Rensi/Dir., Howard Silver/Dir.

Owners: Hayground Cove Asset Management LLC/7.80%, State of Wisconsin Investment Board/6.70%, Randy Churchey, James A. Calder, Hernan R. Martinez, Insiders/7.40%, Kimberly K. Schaefer/2.90%, John Emery/2.50%, Elan Blutinger, Michael J. Schroeder, Alissa N. Nolan, Baron Capital Group, Inc./9.70%, Howard Silver, Bill Croke, Alexander P. Lombardo (16 Owners included in Index)

Financial Data: Fiscal Year End:12/31 Latest Annual Data: 12/31/2006

Year	Sales	Net Income
2006	$148,648,000	-$49,250,000
2005	$139,415,000	-$24,413,000
2004	$69,887,000	-$16,784,000

Curr. Assets:	$109,144,000	Curr. Liab.:	$53,779,000		
Plant, Equip.:	$489,968,000	Total Liab.:	$365,930,000	Indic. Yr. Divd.:	NA
Total Assets:	$683,439,000	Net Worth:	$317,509,000	Debt/ Equity:	0.9069

Great-West Life & Annuity Insurance Co

8515 E Orchard Rd. , Greenwood Village, CO, 80111; **PH:** 1-303-689-3831;
http:// www.greatwest.com

General - Incorporation	CO	**Stock**- Price on:12/24/2007	NA
Employees	NA	Stock Exchange	NA
Auditor	Deloitte & Touche LLP	Ticker Symbol	NA
Stk Agt.	NA	Outstanding Shares	NA
Counsel	NA	E.P.S	NA
DUNS No.	NA	Shareholders	NA

Business: The group's principle activity is to sell life insurance, accident and health insurance and annuities. The group operates from United States.

Primary SIC and add'l.: 6321 6311

CIK No: 0000744455

Officers: Raymond L. McFeetors/CEO, Pres., Lisa Gigax/Dir. - Corporate Affairs, Kent G. Boyer/51/Sr. VP - Specialty Risk, Miles R. Edwards/48/Sr. VP - Fascore Operations, Christopher M. Knackstedt/39/Sr. VP - Healthcare Management, Scot A. Miller/49/Sr. VP - Financial Services Systems, Neil J. Waldron/55/Sr. VP - Group Health, George C. Bogdewiecz/56/Sr. VP - Human Resources, Loren Finkelstein/Mgr. - Public Relations

Directors: John L. Bernbach/Dir., Alain Louvel/62/Dir., Jeffrey R. Orr/49/Dir.

Owners: Insiders, K. P. Kavanagh, W. Mackness, O. T. Dackow, J. E.A. Nickerson, D. A. Nield, D. A. Nield, R. J. Orr, R. L. McFeetors, R. Gratton, C. P. Nelson, M. T.G. Graye, R. F. Rivers, A. Desmarais, K. P. Kavanagh (24 Owners included in Index)

Greater Atlantic Financial Corp

10700 Pk.ridge Blvd., Ste. P50, Reston, VA, 20191; **PH:** 1-703-391-1300; **Fax:** 1-703-391-1506;
http:// www.gab.com

General - Incorporation	DE	**Stock**- Price on:12/24/2007	NA
Employees	115	Stock Exchange	OTC
Auditor	BDO Seidman LLP	Ticker Symbol	GAFC
Stk Agt.	American Stock Transfer & Trust Co.	Outstanding Shares	NA
Counsel	Muldoon Murphy & Faucette	E.P.S	$0.31
DUNS No.	NA	Shareholders	NA

Business: The group's principal activity is to provide banking services to customers through nine branch offices. The lending services provided by the group include origination and sale of single-family mortgage loans, multi-family residential and second mortgage loans. The group operates through two segments: banking and mortgage banking. The banking segment provides retail consumer and small businesses with deposit products such as demand, transaction, savings accounts and certificates of deposit and lending products, such as residential and commercial real estate, construction and development, consumer and commercial business loans. The banking segment also invests in residential real estate loans purchased from gamc and others. The mortgage-banking segment originates and sells residential real estate loans. The group offers banking services to customers through the nine bank branches located throughout the greater Washington, DC/Baltimore metropolitan area.

Primary SIC and add'l.: 6035 6712

CIK No: 0001082735

Subsidiaries: federally-chartered savings bank, Greater Atlantic Capital Trust I., Greater Atlantic Mortgage Corporation, The bank

Officers: Carroll E. Amos/60/CEO, Pres., Edward C. Allen/60/Sr. VP, James B. Vito/82/Managing General Partner, David E. Ritter/58/CFO, Sr. VP

Directors: Carroll E. Amos/60/CEO, Pres., Charles W. Calomiris/50/Chmn., Paul J. Cinquegrana/66/Dir., Jeffrey W. Ochsman/55/Dir.

Owners: Robert I. Schattner/14.30%, Jenifer Calomiris/6.12%, George W. Calomiris/6.40%, Charles W. Calomiris/5.85%, Katherine Calomiris Tompros/6.12%, The Ochsman Children Trust/7.89%

Financial Data: Fiscal Year End:09/30 Latest Annual Data: 09/30/2006

Year	Sales	Net Income
2006	$19,499,000	-$5,571,000
2005	$25,753,000	-$1,558,000
2004	$29,176,000	-$3,192,000

Curr. Assets:	$21,877,000	Curr. Liab.:	$286,711,000		
Plant, Equip.:	$2,764,000	Total Liab.:	$296,369,000	Indic. Yr. Divd.:	NA
Total Assets:	$305,219,000	Net Worth:	$8,850,000	Debt/ Equity:	NA

Greater Bay Bancorp

1900 University Ave., 6th Fl., East Palo Alto, CA, 94303; **PH:** 1-415-375-1555;
http:// www.gbbk.com

General - Incorporation	CA	**Stock**- Price on:12/24/2007	$27.7
Employees	1,895	Stock Exchange	NA
Auditor	PricewaterhouseCoopers LLP	Ticker Symbol	NA
Stk Agt.	Wells Fargo Shareowner Services	Outstanding Shares	51,120,000
Counsel	Manatt, Phelps & Phillips LLP	E.P.S	$1.32
DUNS No.	18-276-3201	Shareholders	NA

Business: The group's principle activity is to operate in four segments: community banking: originates loans, provides deposit products, cash management and international trade finance services, traveler's checks, safe deposit and other services. The group operates 45 offices located in California. Specialty finance: provides specialty finance products that include loans to smaller businesses, asset-based lending, accounts receivable factoring, loans and lease products for the dental and veterinary health professions and capital lease equipment financing. Trust services: provides trust services including custodial, investment management, estate planning resources and employee benefit plan services. Insurance brokerage services: provides commercial insurance brokerage and employee benefits consulting services throughout the United States. The group acquired sullivan & curtis insurance brokers in 2003.

Primary SIC and add'l.: 6712 6022 6331 6411

CIK No: 0000775473

Subsidiaries: ABD Financial Services, Inc., ABD Insurance& Financial Services, CNB Investment Trust I, CNB Investment Trust II, Epic Funding Corporation, GBB Capital II, GBB Capital III, GBB Capital IV, GBB Capital V, GBB Capital VI, GBB Capital VII, Greater Bay Bank, National Association, Lucini/Parish Insurance Inc., Mid- Peninsula Capital LLC, Pacific Business Funding Corporation 16 Subsidiaries included in the Index

Officers: Byron A. Scordelis/Dir., CEO, Pres./$2,249,926.00, Robert B. Kaplan/Dir. - Sr. Executive, Consultant, Colleen Anderson/Exec. VP, Peggy Hiraoka/Exec. VP - Human Resources, Kamran Husain/Sr. VP, Controller, Chief Accounting Officer, Linda M. Iannone/Sr. VP, General Counsel, Corp. Sec., Kenneth A. Shannon/Exec. VP, Chief Risk Officer, James S. Westfall/CFO, Exec. VP

Directors: Byron A. Scordelis/Dir., CEO, Pres., John M. Gatto/Vice Chmn., Duncan L. Matteson/Chmn., Linda R. Meier/Dir., James C. Thompson/Dir., Frederick J. De Grosz/Dir., Glen McLaughlin/Dir., Robert B. Kaplan/Dir. - Sr. Executive, Consultant, Thomas E. Randlett/Dir., George M. Marcus/Dir., Arthur K. Lund/Dir., Daniel G. Libarle/Dir.

Owners: Glen McLaughlin/0.19%, Byron A. Scordelis/0.37%, Insiders/4.41%, John M. Gatto/0.33%, Ariel Capital Management, LLC/8.20%, Robert B. Kaplan/0.02%, Thomas E. Randlett/0.03%, James C. Thompson/0.28%, James S. Westfall/0.09%, Barclays Global Investors, NA/5.39%, Linda R. Meier/0.09%, Kenneth A. Shannon/0.12%, Frederick J. de Grosz/0.97%, Arthur K. Lund/0.29%, Peggy Hiraoka/0.08% (19 Owners included in Index)

Financial Data: Fiscal Year End:12/31 Latest Annual Data: 12/31/2006

Year	Sales	Net Income
2006	$665,135,000	$89,612,000
2005	$602,715,000	$97,227,000
2004	$563,084,000	$92,919,000

Curr. Assets:	$199,516,000	Curr. Liab.:	$5,257,183,000	P/E Ratio:	20.98
Plant, Equip.:	$86,263,000	Total Liab.:	$6,518,761,000	Indic. Yr. Divd.:	$0.640
Total Assets:	$7,371,134,000	Net Worth:	$839,512,000	Debt/ Equity:	1.1431

Greater China Media & Entertainment Corp

10th Fl. Bldg. A Tongyongguoji Ctr., No. 3 Jianguomenwai Rd., Chaoyang District, Beijing, 100101;
PH: 86-1059212222; **Fax:** 86-1059212228; http:// www.greaterchinamedia.com

General - Incorporation	NV	**Stock**- Price on:12/24/2007	$0.14
Employees	NA	Stock Exchange	OTC
Auditor	Michael T. Studer CPA P.C.	Ticker Symbol	GCME
Stk Agt.	NA	Outstanding Shares	NA
Counsel	NA	E.P.S	NA
DUNS No.	NA	Shareholders	NA

Business: The groups principal activity is to provide media and entertainment broadcast. Services of the group include program production, management, promotion and distribution. The group operates from China and the United States.

Primary SIC and add'l.: 7812

CIK No: 0001321366

Subsidiaries: Beijing New-Element Co., Ltd., Beijing Star King Talent Agency Ltd., Co., Triumph Research Limited

Officers: Jake Wei/Chmn., Principal Accounting Officer, Principal Financial Officer, John Hui/Dir., Pres., Principal Executive Officer, Xiao Lin Liu/Dir., GM, Zhao Liu/GM, Yi Wu Feng/GM

Directors: Jake Wei/Chmn., Principal Accounting Officer, Principal Financial Officer, John Hui/Dir., Pres., Principal Executive Officer, Yi Wang/46/Dir., Xiao Lin Liu/Dir., GM

Owners: Zhang JianPing/44.80%

Financial Data: Fiscal Year End:09/30 Latest Annual Data: 03/31/2007

Year	Sales	Net Income
2007	NA	NA
2006	NA	NA

Curr. Assets:	$56,000	Curr. Liab.:	$181,000		
Plant, Equip.:	NA	Total Liab.:	$181,000	Indic. Yr. Divd.:	NA
Total Assets:	$56,000	Net Worth:	-$126,000	Debt/ Equity:	NA

Greater Community Bancorp

55 Union Blvd., Totowa, NJ, 07511; **PH:** 1-973-942-1111; **Fax:** 1-973-942-9816;
http:// www.greatercommunity.com; **Email:** info@greatercommunity.com

General - Incorporation	NJ	**Stock**- Price on:12/24/2007	$15.31
Employees	177	Stock Exchange	NDQ
Auditor	McGladrey & Pullen LLP	Ticker Symbol	GFLS
Stk Agt.	Registrar & Transfer Co	Outstanding Shares	8,450,000
Counsel	Williams, Caliri, Miller Et Al	E.P.S	$0.68
DUNS No.	14-742-0186	Shareholders	NA

Business: The group's principal activities are to provide a range of lending, depository and related financial services to individual consumers, business and governmental units through 15 full service offices located in bergen and passaic counties, New Jersey. The group operates through three operating subsidiaries, greater community bank, bergen commercial bank and rock community bank. The group's lending services include commercial and residential real estate loans, short and medium term loans,

revolving credit arrangements, lines of credit and consumer installment loans. The deposit accounts include consumer and commercial checking accounts and now accounts. In addition, the group provides bookkeeping, data processing and management information systems and various other banking related services.

Primary SIC and add'l.: 6022 6712

CIK No: 0000773845

Subsidiaries: BCB Investment Company, Inc. , Bergen Commercial Bank, GCB Realty, LLC, GCB CapitalTrust II , GCB Capital Trust II, GCB Realty,LLC, Great Falls InvestmentCompany, Inc. , GreaterCommunity Bank , Greater Community Tax Services LLC , Greater Community Title LLC, Greater CommunityServices, Inc. , Greater Community 1031 Exchange Services LLC, Greater Community, Greater Community 1031 Exchange Services LLC, Greater Community Bank 28 Subsidiaries included in the Index

Officers: Anthony M. Bruno/Chmn., CEO, Pres., Naqi A. Naqvi/Sr. VP, Chief Auditor/$153,540.00, Stephen J. Mauger/Sr. VP, CFO, Treasurer, Jeannette Chardavoyne/VP, Sec., Roger Tully/58/Exec. VP - Greater Community Bancorp

Directors: Anthony M. Bruno/Chmn., CEO, Pres., Robert C. Soldoveri/Dir., Alfred R. Urbano/Dir., William T. Ferguson/Dir., David Waldman/Dir., Charles J. Volpe/Dir., Marino A. Bramante/Dir., Angelo J. Genova/Dir.

Owners: Charles J. Volpe/1.28%, William T. Ferguson/0.89%, Alfred R. Urbano/3.50%, Stephen J. Mauger/0.08%, Angelo J. Genova/0.01%, Mary E. Smith/0.08%, Robert C. Soldoveri/0.06%, Anthony M. Bruno/2.60%, Insiders/12.98%, Naqi A. Naqvi/0.34%, David Waldman/0.32%, M. A. Bramante/1.68%, Mark C. Campbell/1.96%

Financial Data: Fiscal Year End:12/31   **Latest Annual Data:** 12/31/2006

Year	Sales	Net Income
2006	$61,178,000	$5,553,000
2005	$54,883,000	$8,854,000
2004	$46,739,000	$7,786,000

Curr. Assets:	$84,319,000	Curr. Liab.:	$844,749,000	P/E Ratio:	26.40
Plant, Equip.:	$10,948,000	Total Liab.:	$883,394,000	Indic. Yr. Divd.:	NA
Total Assets:	$950,969,000	Net Worth:	$67,575,000	Debt/ Equity:	0.3616

Greater Sacramento Bancorp

1750 Howe Ave., Ste. 100, Sacramento, CA, 95825; **PH:** 1-916-648-2100; **Fax:** 1-916-648-2622; *http://* www.bankofsacramento.com; **Email:** bank@bankofsacramento.com

General - Incorporation		Stock - Price on:12/24/2007	$21
Employees	NA	Stock Exchange	OTC
Auditor	NA	Ticker Symbol	GSCB
Stk Agt	U.S. Stock Transfer Corp	Outstanding Shares	2,040,000
Counsel	NA	E.P.S.	NA
DUNS No.	NA	Shareholders	NA

Business: The groups principal activity is to provide commercial banking services. The services of the group include deposit accounts, loans, courier service, equipment leasing, cash management, business online banking, ACH services, lockbox services, zero balance accounts, and merchant card services, business credit cards, federal tax deposits, night depository, safe deposit boxes, telephone transfers/requests, travelers checks, and wire transfers, investment broker services, sweep accounts services, ATM cards, and online banking services. Customers served by the group include small-to medium size businesses, professionals, and individuals.

Primary SIC and add'l.: 6712 6022

CIK No: 0001317628

Officers: William J. Martin/Dir., CEO, Pres., Andrew S. Popovich/Sr. VP, CFO, Kathleen M. Thomas/Dir. - Executive, VP, COO

Directors: William J. Martin/Dir., CEO, Pres., Kip S. Skidmore/Chmn., Alison Buhler/Dir., Kathleen M. Thomas/Dir. - Executive, VP, COO, Gary S. Ravel/Dir., Mark L. Ures/Dir., Cecil L. Wetsel/Dir., George R. Wong/Dir., Gregory A. Meredith/Dir., Frank L. Vellutini/Dir., Richard D. Wilbur/Dir.

Green Dolphin Systems Inc

26 Voyager Ct. S, Toronto, ON, M9W 5M7 ; **PH:** 1-870-120-2324; **Fax:** 1-865-922-6946; *http://* www.greendolphin.net; **Email:** sales@greendolphin.net

General - Incorporation	DE	Stock - Price on:12/24/2007	NA
Employees	4	Stock Exchange	NA
Auditor	Rotenberg & Co. LLP	Ticker Symbol	NA
Stk Agt	NA	Outstanding Shares	NA
Counsel	NA	E.P.S.	$0.06
DUNS No.	NA	Shareholders	NA

Business: The group's principal activities are developing, testing, producing and marketing a line of specialty chemical products. The products are used for ceiling and wall cleaning, fabric protection, fire retardation applications, graffiti removal, smoke and odor elimination, non-slip protection, mold and mildew control, sanitization, laundry and dry cleaning solutions. The group also manufactures and markets a line of waterproofing products for wood, concrete and stonework. The products of the group are renew 4000, green dolphin non-slip, protection plus 2000, fire sate 108 wood, fire safe 701 fabric, penta seal 6f, shield kote, g.d. Orange cleaner/degreaser, turbo kleen, g.d. Graffiti remover, enviro-zyme, liquid enzyme, enviro-kleen super, pure-n-fresh, air-o-kleen, ultra oxi renew and fabric fresh 101. Major trademarks are green dolphin, fire safe 108 wood, fire poly np-30 paint, safe-n-dry, rain guard, shield kote, secure-step and protection plus 2000.

Primary SIC and add'l.: 2842

CIK No: 0001110304

Financial Data: Fiscal Year End:12/31   **Latest Annual Data:** 12/31/2005

Year	Sales	Net Income
2005	$608,000	-$433,000
2004	$656,000	-$92,000
2003	$768,000	-$373,000

Curr. Assets:	$93,000	Curr. Liab.:	$588,000		
Plant, Equip.:	$0	Total Liab.:	$588,000	Indic. Yr. Divd.:	NA
Total Assets:	$262,000	Net Worth:	-$326,000	Debt/ Equity:	NA

Green Energy Group Inc

Formerly: Pro Card Corp
1016 Clemons St., Ste. 302, Jupiter, FL, 33477; **PH:** 1-561-745-6789

General - Incorporation	FL	Stock - Price on:12/24/2007	NA
Employees	NA	Stock Exchange	NA
Auditor	Wieseneck, Andres & Co P.A	Ticker Symbol	NA
Stk Agt	Florida Atlantic Stock Transfer	Outstanding Shares	NA
Counsel	NA	E.P.S.	-$0.004
DUNS No.	NA	Shareholders	NA

Business: The group's principle activities include producing and selling renewable enwergy-biodiesal.The group operates from United States.

Primary SIC and add'l.: 9995

CIK No: 0001321500

Subsidiaries: eCom eCom.com, Inc

Officers: Barney A. Richmond/56/Chmn., Sec., Richard C. Turner/48/Dir., Treasurer, Mark S. Hiltwein/CFO, Exec. VP, Timothy D. Davis/Sr. VP, General Counsel, Sec., Sean S. Sullivan/Pres. - Commercial, Packaging

Directors: Barney A. Richmond/56/Chmn., Sec., Richard C. Turner/48/Dir., Treasurer, Patrice M. Daniels/Dir., Leonard C. Green/Dir., Mark J. Griffin/Dir., Robert T. Kittel/Dir., Robert Obernier/Dir.

Owners: Barney A. Richmond/21.40%, United States Financial Group, Inc./6.50%, Richard C. Turner/1.70%, American Capital Holdings, Inc./16.20%, Insiders/23.10%

Financial Data: Fiscal Year End:05/31   **Latest Annual Data:** 05/31/2006

Year	Sales	Net Income
2006	NA	-$291,000
2005	$1,000	-$131,000
2004	$62,000	-$408,000

Curr. Assets:	$67,000	Curr. Liab.:	$155,000		
Plant, Equip.:	$0	Total Liab.:	$876,000	Indic. Yr. Divd.:	NA
Total Assets:	$67,000	Net Worth:	-$809,000	Debt/ Equity:	NA

Green Mountain Coffee Roasters Inc

33 Coffee Ln., Waterbury, VT, 05676; **PH:** 1-802-244-5621; **Fax:** 1-802-244-5436; *http://* www.GreenMountainCoffee.com; **Email:** investor.services@gmcr.com

General - Incorporation	DE	Stock - Price on:12/24/2007	$79.52
Employees	782	Stock Exchange	NDQ
Auditor	PricewaterhouseCoopers LLP	Ticker Symbol	GMCR
Stk Agt	Continental Stock Transfer & Trust Co	Outstanding Shares	7,770,000
Counsel	NA	E.P.S.	NA
DUNS No.	03-770-4855	Shareholders	NA

Business: The group's principal activity is to distribute roasted coffee primarily in the northeastern United States. The arabica coffee is roasted and sold in over 90 coffee selections through a multi-channel distribution network in wholesale and consumer direct operations. The coffee selections include single-origins, estates, certified organics, fair trade, proprietary blends and flavored coffees that are sold under the green mountain coffee roaster(R) and frontier(R) organic coffee brands. The group serves supermarkets, specialty food stores, convenience stores, food service, hotel, restaurant, university, and travel and office coffee service customers. The coffee is sold to more than 7,000 wholesale customers. The wholesale customers are educated about the origin and preparation of coffee through on-site training, tours, manuals and hands-on learning experiences known as coffee college. The group also has a direct mail operation-serving customers nationwide.

Primary SIC and add'l.: 5149 5963

CIK No: 0000909954

Officers: Robert P. Stiller/Chmn., CEO, Pres., Stephen J. Sabol/VP - Development, Scott R. McCreary/COO, Frances G. Rathke/CFO, Sec., Treasurer, Kathryn S. Brooks/VP - Human Resources, Organizational Development, Maureen Martin/Investor Services Coordinator

Directors: Robert P. Stiller/Chmn., CEO, Pres., William D. Davis/Dir., Jules A. Del Vecchio/Dir., Hinda Miller/Dir., David E. Moran/Dir., Barbara D. Carlini/Dir.

Owners: William D. Davis, Kathryn S. Brooks, Robert P. Stiller/30.60%, Barbara D. Carlini, Brown Capital Management/9.90%, Natcan Investment Management Inc./5.20%, Frances G. Rathke, Scott R. McCreary, Hinda Miller, David E. Moran, Jules A. delVecchio, James E. Travis, Essex Investment Management LLC./5.10%, Insiders/34.90%

Financial Data: Fiscal Year End:09/24   **Latest Annual Data:** 9/30/2006

Year	Sales	Net Income
2006	$225,323,000	$8,443,000
2005	$161,536,000	$8,956,000
2004	$137,444,000	$7,825,000

Curr. Assets:	$67,959,000	Curr. Liab.:	$38,809,000		
Plant, Equip.:	$48,811,000	Total Liab.:	$159,066,000	Indic. Yr. Divd.:	NA
Total Assets:	$234,006,000	Net Worth:	$74,940,000	Debt/ Equity:	1.2384

Green Plains Renewable Energy Inc

105 N 31st Ave., Ste.103, Omaha, NE, 68131; **PH:** 1-402-884-8700; **Fax:** 1-402-884-8776; *http://* www.gpreethanol.com; **Email:** info@gpreethanol.com

General - Incorporation	IO	Stock - Price on:12/24/2007	$18.29
Employees	8	Stock Exchange	NDQ
Auditor	L.L. Bradford & Company, LLC	Ticker Symbol	GPRE
Stk Agt	Pacific Stock Transfer Company	Outstanding Shares	6,000,000
Counsel	NA	E.P.S.	-$0.74
DUNS No.	NA	Shareholders	NA

Business: The groups principal activity is to produce ethanol and animal feed products. The product of the group is dry mill ethanol. In February 22, 2006 the group acquired Superior Ethanol, LLC. The group operates from the United States.

Primary SIC and add'l.: 2869 2865 5169

CIK No: 0001309402

Subsidiaries: Superior Ethanol, LLC

Officers: Wayne B. Hoovestol/Dir., CEO, COO, Barry A. Ellsworth/53/CEO, Pres., Dan E. Christensen/Dir., Exec. VP - Construction, Treasurer, Sec., Brian D. Peterson/Dir., Exec. VP, Jerry Peters/CFO

Directors: Wayne B. Hoovestol/Dir., CEO, COO, Barry A. Ellsworth/53/CEO, Pres., Robert D. Vavra/Chmn., Dan E. Christensen/Dir., Exec. VP - Construction, Treasurer, Sec., David A. Hart/Dir., Stephen R. Nicholson/Dir., Herschel C. Patton/Dir., Brian D. Peterson/Dir., Exec. VP, Michael A. Warren/Dir.

Owners: Insiders/29.60%, Herschel C. Patton/1.20%, Michael A. Warren, Gary Parker/7.20%, Jerry L. Peters, Dan E. Christensen/1.40%, David A. Hart, Robert D. Vavra, Brian D. Peterson/3.60%, Stephen R. Nicholson/1.60%, Wayne B. Hoovestol/14.10%

Financial Data: Fiscal Year End:11/30 Latest Annual Data: 11/30/2006

Year	Sales	Net Income
2006	NA	$918,000
2005	NA	-$398,000

Curr. Assets:	$44,196,000	Curr. Liab.:	$9,781,000		
Plant, Equip.:	$47,082,000	Total Liab.:	$10,111,000	Indic. Yr. Divd.:	NA
Total Assets:	$96,007,000	Net Worth:	$85,896,000	Debt/ Equity:	0.0966

Greenbrier Cos Inc

1 Ctr. pointe Dr., Ste. 200, Lake Oswego, OR, 97035; *PH:* 1-503-684-7000; *Fax:* 1-503-684-7553; *http://* www.gbrx.com

General		Stock	
Incorporation	DE	Price on:12/24/2007	$31.86
Employees	3,661	Stock Exchange	NYSE
Auditor	Deloitte & Touche LLP	Ticker Symbol	GBX
Stk Agt	First Chicago Trust Co Of New York	Outstanding Shares	15,990,000
Counsel	Tonkon Torp LLP	E.P.S	$1.18
DUNS No.	02-500-4318	Shareholders	NA

Business: The group's principal activities are to manufacture and supply transportation equipment and to provide services to the railroad and related industries. The group operates in two segments: manufacturing segment and leasing and services segment. Manufacturing segment produces double-stack intermodal railcars, conventional railcars, marine vessels and industrial forgings. Leasing and other related services segment performs repair and refurbishment activities for both intermodal and conventional railcars. The customers of the group includes class i railroads, regional and short-line railroads, other leasing companies, shippers, carriers and other transportation companies. Ttx and bnsf are the major customers of the group.

Primary SIC and add'l.: 6159 3743

CIK No: 0000923120

Subsidiaries: Autostack Company LLC, Greenbrier Europe B.V., Greenbrier Germany GmbH, Greenbrier Leasing Company LLC, Greenbrier Leasing Limited, Greenbrier Leasing Limited Partner, LLC, Greenbrier Leasing, L.P., Greenbrier Management Services, LLC, Greenbrier Railcar LLC., Greenbrier U.K. Limited, Greenbrier-Concarril LLC, Gunderson LLC, Gunderson Marine LLC, Gunderson-Concarril, S.A. de C.V., Nova Scotia Limited

Officers: William A. Furman/Dir., CEO, Pres., Maren C. Malik/VP - Administration, Linda M. Olinger/VP, Corporate Controller, James T. Sharp/Pres. - Greenbrier Leasing Corporation, Sandy Stephenson/Mgr. - Communications, Dick Tierney/Contact - Autostack, Julie Ward/Public Relations, Alejandro Centurion/52/Sr. VP - Manufacturing Operations, Mark J. Rittenbaum/Sr. VP, Treasurer, Larry G. Brady/69/CFO, Sr. VP, Kenneth D. Stephens/Corp. Sec., Mark J. Eitzen/VP, GM, Charles A. Garman/VP - Marine Sales, Marketing, Thomas Mueller/Dir. - Sales, Greenbrier Europe, Cornelia Schaffner/Assist. *(19 Officers included in Index)*

Directors: William A. Furman/Dir., CEO, Pres., Benjamin R. Whiteley/Chmn., Charles J. Swindells/Dir., Graeme A. Jack/Dir., Victor Atiyeh/Dir., Duane C. McDougall/56/Dir., Daniel A. Oneal/Dir., Bruce C. Ward/Dir., Donald A. Washburn/Dir.

Owners: Larry G. Brady, Tontine Capital Partners, L.P./11.50%, Daniel A. ONeal, Graeme A. Jack, Robin D. Bisson, Duane C. McDougall, Keeley Asset Management Corp/10.10%, Mark J. Rittenbaum, James A. Sharp, Bruce C. Ward, Victor G. Atiyeh, FMR Corporation/10.60%, OppenheimerFunds, Inc./10.30%, Donald A. Washburn, Benjamin R. Whiteley *(18 Owners included in Index)*

Financial Data: Fiscal Year End:08/31 Latest Annual Data: 8/31/2006

Year	Sales	Net Income
2006	$953,823,000	$39,598,000
2004	$729,451,000	$20,778,000
2003	$434,991,000	$4,317,000

Curr. Assets:	$423,666,000	Curr. Liab.:	$204,793,000	P/E Ratio:	24.14
Plant, Equip.:	$416,259,000	Total Liab.:	$658,033,000	Indic. Yr. Divd.:	$0.320
Total Assets:	$877,314,000	Net Worth:	$219,281,000	Debt/ Equity:	2.8123

Greene County Bancorp Inc

302 Main St., Catskill, NY, 12414; *PH:* 1-518-943-2600; *Fax:* 1-518-943-4431; *http://* www.thebankofgreenecounty.com

General		Stock	
Incorporation	US	Price on:12/24/2007	$13.6
Employees	89	Stock Exchange	NDQ
Auditor	PricewaterhouseCoopers LLP	Ticker Symbol	GCBC
Stk Agt	Computershare Investor Services LLC	Outstanding Shares	4,310,000
Counsel	Luse Gorman Pomerenk & Schick	E.P.S	$0.50
DUNS No.	NA	Shareholders	NA

Business: The group's principal activity is to accept deposits from the general public and using such funds to originate one-to four-family residential mortgage loan, commercial real estate loans, home equity loans, consumer loans and commercial business loans and investment securities. The group is a one-bank holding company for greene county savings bank, a community oriented state-chartered mutual savings bank. The group offers a variety of deposits consisting of savings, now accounts, money market accounts, certificates of deposit and non-interest bearing checking accounts. The group also offers iras. The group operates through six full service banking services in greene county and southern albany county, New York.

Primary SIC and add'l.: 6035 6712

CIK No: 0001070524

Subsidiaries: Greene County Commercial Bank, The Bank of Greene County

Officers: Donald Gibson/CEO, Dir., Pres./$113,030.00, Michelle M. Plummer/Exec. VP, CFO, COO/$149,190.00, Kelly MacFarlane/Branch Mgr. - Greenport Office, Bank, Greene County, Robin Siter/Branch Mgr. - Chatham Office, Bank, Greene County, Ellen De Lucia/Sr. VP - Facilities Construction, Maintenance, Bank, Greene County, Gary R. Pollard/Sr. VP - Comm Lending, Bank, Greene County, Kathleen P. Proper/Assist. Treasurer, Branch Mgr. - Cairo Office, Bank, Greene County, Colleen Selkirk/Branch Mgr. - W Coxsackie Office, Bank, Greene County, Amanda Anderson/Branch Mgr. - Catskill Office, Bank, Greene County, Kathy Bagley/Branch Mgr. - Catskill Commons Office, Bank, Greene County, Brian G. Whiteman/Branch Mgr. - Greenville Office, Bank, Greene County, Linda Kuever/Branch Mgr. - Tannersville Office, Bank, Greene County, Darla Knoll/Branch Mgr. - Westerlo Office, Bank, Greene County, Kathleen Passaro/Branch Mgr. - Hudson Office, Bank, Greene County, Bruce P. Egger/Sr. VP, Sec./$138,010.00 *(30 Officers included in Index)*

Directors: Martin C. Smith/Chmn., David H. Jenkins/Dir., Arthur Place/Dir., Paul Slutzky/Dir., Walter H. Ingalls/Dir. - Bank, Greene County, Dennis R. O'Grady/Dir., Charles H. Schaefer/Dir., Bruce J. Whittaker/Dir.

Owners: Insiders, Stephen E. Nelson, J. Bruce Whittaker, Dennis R. OGrady, Bruce P. Egger, Greene County Bancorp, MHC, Charles H. Schaefer, David H. Jenkins, Paul Slutzky, Greene County Bancorp, MHC, Martin C. Smith, Michelle M. Plummer, Donald Gibson

Financial Data: Fiscal Year End:06/30 Latest Annual Data: 06/30/2007

Year	Sales	Net Income
2007	$20,926,000	$2,259,000
2006	$17,937,000	$2,243,000
2005	$16,779,000	$2,949,000

Curr. Assets:	$17,588,000	Curr. Liab.:	$268,984,000		
Plant, Equip.:	$10,805,000	Total Liab.:	$273,984,000	Indic. Yr. Divd.:	$0.500
Total Assets:	$307,565,000	Net Worth:	$33,581,000	Debt/ Equity:	NA

Greene County Bancshares Inc

100 N Main St., Greeneville, TN, 37743; *PH:* 1-423-639-5111; *http://* www.mybankconnection.com

General		Stock	
Incorporation	TN	Price on:12/24/2007	NA
Employees	561	Stock Exchange	NDQ
Auditor	Dixon Hughes PLLC	Ticker Symbol	GRNB
Stk Agt	Illinois Stock Transfer Co.	Outstanding Shares	NA
Counsel	NA	E.P.S	$2.41
DUNS No.	00-338-6497	Shareholders	NA

Business: The group's principal activity is to attract deposits from the general public and provide commercial, real estate and consumer loans. It also provides collection and other banking services including finance, acceptance and title subsidiary corporations. The banking operations are conducted through its wholly owned subsidiary, greene county bank. It provides trust and money management services to its customers. At 31-Dec-2003, it operated through 36 full service offices. On 21-Nov-2003, the group acquired independent bankshares corporation.

Primary SIC and add'l.: 6712 6022

CIK No: 0000764402

Subsidiaries: Fairway Title Company, GCB Acceptance Corporation, Greene County Bank, Greene County Capital Trust I, Greene County Capital Trust II, Superior Financial Services,Inc.

Officers: Stan R. Pucket/Chmn., CEO, James E. Adams/CFO, Exec. VP, Ronald E. Mayberry/Dir., Regional Pres. - Sumner, Lawrence Counties, Kenneth R. Vaught/Dir., COO, Pres.

Directors: Stan R. Pucket/Chmn., CEO, Martha M. Bachman/Dir., Bill Terry Leonard/Dir., Philip M. Bachman/Dir., W. T. Daniels/Dir., Robert K. Leonard/Dir., Ronald E. Mayberry/Dir., Regional Pres. - Sumner, Lawrence Counties, Bruce Campbell/Dir., Jerald K. Jaynes/Dir., Charles H. Whitfield/Dir., John Tolsma/Dir., Robin R. Haynes/Dir., Kenneth R. Vaught/Dir., COO, Pres., Charles S. Brooks/Dir.

Owners: Bruce Campbell, Martha Bachman/8.96%, Ronald E. Mayberry, Bill Adams, Insiders/13.03%, Charles S. Brooks, Bobby Leonard, Steve L. Droke, W.T. Daniels, Jerald K. Jaynes, James E. Adams, Stan R. Puckett/1.43%, Wellington Management Company, LLP/5.23%, Phil M. Bachman/8.99%, Kenneth R. Vaught *(21 Owners included in Index)*

Financial Data: Fiscal Year End:12/31 Latest Annual Data: 12/31/2006

Year	Sales	Net Income
2006	$138,135,000	$21,262,000
2005	$101,947,000	$14,163,000
2004	$78,104,000	$12,008,000

Curr. Assets:	$70,640,000	Curr. Liab.:	$1,574,780,000		
Plant, Equip.:	$57,258,000	Total Liab.:	$1,588,183,000	Indic. Yr. Divd.:	$0.520
Total Assets:	$1,772,654,000	Net Worth:	$184,471,000	Debt/ Equity:	NA

Greenfield Online Inc

21 River Rd., Wilton, CT, 06897; *PH:* 1-203-834-8585; *Fax:* 1-203-834-8686; *http://* www.greenfield.com

General		Stock	
Incorporation	DE	Price on:12/24/2007	$15.66
Employees	675	Stock Exchange	NDQ
Auditor	PricewaterhouseCoopers LLP	Ticker Symbol	SRVY
Stk Agt	Registrar & Transfer Co	Outstanding Shares	25,600,000
Counsel	Preston Gates & Ellis	E.P.S	$0.45
DUNS No.	NA	Shareholders	NA

Business: The group's principal activity is to provide Internet survey solutions to the global marketing research industry. The group's customers include taylor nelson sofres intersearch, gfk-custom research, inc., hall and partners, synovate, inc. And arbor, inc

Primary SIC and add'l.: 8713 7372 7371 7379

CIK No: 0001108906

Subsidiaries: Ciao France SAS, Ciao Holding GmbH, Ciao International, Inc., Ciao Romania S.R.L., Ciao Spain, S.L., Ciao, GmbH, Greenfield Online Canada, ltd., Greenfield Online Europe, Ltd., Greenfield Online Private Ltd., Rapidata.net, Inc., SRVY Acquisition GmbH, Zing Wireless, Inc.

Officers: Albert Angrisani/Dir., CEO, Pres./$2,608,173.00, Jonathan A. Flatow/VP - Corporate Development, General Counsel/$499,659.00, Keith Price/Exec. VP/$607,315.00, Hugh Davis/Co - Founder, Exec. VP, David St. Pierre/CTO, Andrew C. Ellis/MD - Asia/$462,225.00, Robert E. Bies/CFO, Exec. VP/$548,386.00, Nicolas Metzke/Sr. VP, MD - Europe

Directors: Albert Angrisani/Dir., CEO, Pres., Peter Sobiloff/Chmn., Joel R. Mesznik/Dir., Burton J. Manning/Dir., Joseph A. Ripp/Dir., Hugh Davis/Co - Founder, Exec. VP, Lise J. Buyer/Dir., Charles W. Stryker/Dir.

Owners: Burda Digital Ventures GmbH/5.03%, Burton J. Manning, Entities Affiliated with Insight Venture Associates III, L.L.C./15.21%, Andrew C. Ellis, Joel R. Mesznik/1.39%, Keith Price, Albert Angrisani/2.45%, Jonathan A. Flatow, Insiders/9.46%, Robert E. Bies, Lise J. Buyer, Joseph A. Ripp, Entities Affiliated with Cannell Capital, LLC/6.31%, Burgundy Asset Management Ltd./7.70%, Charles W. Stryker *(17 Owners included in Index)*

Financial Data: Fiscal Year End:12/31 Latest Annual Data: 12/31/2006

Year	Sales	Net Income
2006	$100,342,000	$8,454,000
2005	$89,179,000	-$65,959,000
2004	$44,428,000	$5,718,000

Curr. Assets:	$66,980,000	Curr. Liab.:	$26,654,000	P/E Ratio:	42.32
Plant, Equip.:	$6,447,000	Total Liab.:	$30,223,000	Indic. Yr. Divd.:	NA
Total Assets:	$179,844,000	Net Worth:	$149,621,000	Debt/ Equity:	NA

Greenhill & Co Inc

300 Pk. Ave., 23rd Fl., New York, NY, 10022; *PH:* 1-212-389-1500; *Fax:* 1-212-389-1700; *http://* www.greenhill-co.com; *Email:* investorrelations@greenhill-co.com

General - Incorporation	DE	Stock - Price on:12/24/2007	$65.08
Employees	201	Stock Exchange	NYSE
Auditor	Ernst & Young LLP	Ticker Symbol	GHL
Stk Agt	American Stock Transfer & Trust Co.	Outstanding Shares	28,470,000
Counsel	NA	E.P.S.	$1.90
DUNS No.	94-748-6460	Shareholders	NA

Business: The groups principal activities are to provide financial advisory and merchant banking services. Financial advisory services include underwriting services, retainer services and investment advisory services. Merchant banking services consists of management fees on the merchant banking activities, gain or loss on investments in the merchant banking funds and other merchant banking services. The group provides strategic and financial advice to us and non-us clients in mergers, acquisitions, restructuring, and other corporate financial matters.

Primary SIC and add'l.: 8748 8741

CIK No: 0001282977

Subsidiaries: GCP Managing Partner II, L.P., GCP Managing Partner, L.P., Greenhill & Co. Cayman Limited, Greenhill & Co. Europe Limited, Greenhill & Co. International LLP, Greenhill & Co., LLC, Greenhill Aviation Co., LLC, Greenhill Capital Partners, LLC

Officers: Scott L. Bok/Dir., Co - CEO, MD - New York Office/$12,804,340.00, Simon A. Borrows/Dir., Co - CEO, MD - London/$7,577,342.00, Kenneth S. Crews/MD - Dallas, Gregory R. Miller/MD - New York, Timothy M. George/MD - New York, Richard Steinman/MD - New York, Richard Morse/MD - London, Brian Phillips/MD - London, Brad J. Crompton/MD - Toronto, Julie Betts/Assoc. - London, Pieter-Jan Bouten/Assoc. - London, Ben Loomes/VP - London, James R.C. Lupton/MD - London, Cyrus Hormazdi/Assoc. - New York, James B. Lockhart/Assoc. - New York *(108 Officers included in Index)*

Directors: Scott L. Bok/Dir., Co - CEO, MD - New York Office, Simon A. Borrows/Dir., Co - CEO, MD - London, Robert F. Greenhill/Chmn., John C. Danforth/Dir., Stephen L. Key/Dir., Isabel V. Sawhill/Dir., Steven F. Goldstone/Dir.

Owners: Isabel V. Sawhill, Steven F. Goldstone, Timothy M. George/5.40%, Stephen L. Key, James R. C. Lupton/5.40%, Robert H. Niehaus/4.10%, Robert F. Greenhill/17.30%, Morgan Stanley/8.00%, John C. Danforth, Simon A. Borrows/5.40%, Insiders/33.10%, John D. Liu, Scott L. Bok/5.40%, FMR Corp./7.80%

*Financial Data: Fiscal Year End:*12/31 *Latest Annual Data:* 12/31/2006

Year	Sales	Net Income
2006	$290,646,000	$75,666,000
2005	$221,152,000	$55,532,000
2004	$151,853,000	$38,316,000

Curr. Assets:	$86,570,000	Curr. Liab.:	$120,439,000	P/E Ratio:	34.25
Plant, Equip.:	$14,260,000	Total Liab.:	$139,939,000	Indic. Yr. Divd.:	$1.000
Total Assets:	$297,731,000	Net Worth:	$155,561,000	Debt/ Equity:	0.1999

Greenland Corp

100 E San Marcos Blvd., Ste. 400, San Marcos, CA, 92069; *PH:* 1-760-510-5900; *http://* www.greenlandcorp.com

General - Incorporation	NV	Stock - Price on:12/24/2007	$0.0009
Employees	NA	Stock Exchange	OTC
Auditor	Kabani & Co, Inc	Ticker Symbol	GRLC
Stk Agt	Computershare Investor Services LLC	Outstanding Shares	NA
Counsel	NA	E.P.S.	NA
DUNS No.	87-825-3798	Shareholders	NA

Business: The group's principle activity is to produce, distribute and market advanced automatic check cashing machines similar to bank ATMs through the wholly owned subsidiary check central, inc. The group allocates resources and assesses the performance of its sales activities in two segments: processing and sales segments. Processing segment provides customer service and earns fee through check cashing transaction and sales segment sells and distributes automatic check cashing machines. The group develops, manufactures and delivers limited number of freestanding kiosks, under the brand name maxcash abm. The group markets and sells its products throughout the United States and grants unsecured credit to its customers.

Primary SIC and add'l.: 7372 3578

CIK No: 0000852127

Subsidiaries: ExpertHR Inc, Kabani & Company, Inc.

Owners: Lawrence S. Hershfield, Whitebox Advisors LLC

*Financial Data: Fiscal Year End:*12/31 *Latest Annual Data:* 12/31/2004

Year	Sales	Net Income
2004	$2,319,000	-$3,219,000
2003	$5,953,000	-$3,536,000
2002	NA	-$5,714,000

Curr. Assets:	$315,000	Curr. Liab.:	$9,042,000		
Plant, Equip.:	$29,000	Total Liab.:	$9,042,000	Indic. Yr. Divd.:	NA
Total Assets:	$353,000	Net Worth:	-$8,689,000	Debt/ Equity:	NA

Greenman Technologies Inc

12498 Wyoming Ave. S, Savage, MI, 55378; *PH:* 1-800-526-0860; *http://* www.greenman.biz; *Email:* info@tirerecyclersgmt.com

General - Incorporation	DE	Stock - Price on:12/24/2007	$0.31
Employees	79	Stock Exchange	OTC
Auditor	Schechter Dokken Kanter	Ticker Symbol	GMTI
Stk Agt	American Stock Transfer & Trust Co.	Outstanding Shares	21,580,000
Counsel	Morse, Barnes-Brown & Pendleton	E.P.S.	-$0.02
DUNS No.	83-762-0772	Shareholders	NA

Business: The group's principal activity is to collect, process and market scrap tires in whole, shredded or granule form. The scrap tires are collected from local, regional and national tire stores, tire manufacturing plants and illegal tire piles. These tires are collected, processed and sold as alternative fuel by pulp and paper producers, a substitute for crushed stone in civil engineering, as feedstock and heavy-duty roofing shingles. The group operates in California, Georgia, Iowa, Minnesota, Tennessee and Wisconsin and supplies whole tires to cement kilns located in Florida, Georgia, Illinois, Missouri, Tennessee and Texas. On 21-Jul-2004, the group acquired American tire disposal inc.

Primary SIC and add'l.: 7534

CIK No: 0000932699

Subsidiaries: GreenMan Technologies of California, Inc., GreenMan Technologies of Georgia, Inc., GreenMan Technologies of Iowa, Inc., GreenMan Technologies of Minnesota, Inc., GreenMan Technologies of Oklahoma, Inc., GreenMan Technologies of South Carolina, Inc., GreenMan Technologies of Tennessee, Inc., GreenMan Technologies of Wisconsin, Inc., Technical Tire Recycling, Inc.

Officers: Lyle Jensen/56/Dir., CEO, Pres., Charles E. Coppa/CFO, Treasurer, Sec., Mark T. Maust/VP

Directors: Lyle Jensen/56/Dir., CEO, Pres., Maurice E. Needham/66/Chmn., Lew F. Boyd/61/Dir., Nicholas Debenedictis/47/Dir., Allen Kahn/85/Dir.

Owners: Lew F. Boyd/1.85%, Nicholas DeBenedictis/3.30%, Laurus Master Fund, Ltd./4.99%, Charles E. Coppa/3.44%, Robert H. Davis/3.27%, Maurice E. Needham/10.63%, Lyle Jensen/2.63%, Allen Kahn/20.77%, Insiders/40.09%

*Financial Data: Fiscal Year End:*09/30 *Latest Annual Data:* 9/30/2006

Year	Sales	Net Income
2006	$17,608,000	-$3,706,000
2005	$22,075,000	-$15,173,000
2004	$30,777,000	-$2,645,000

Curr. Assets:	$3,470,000	Curr. Liab.:	$7,460,000		
Plant, Equip.:	$5,807,000	Total Liab.:	$20,923,000	Indic. Yr. Divd.:	NA
Total Assets:	$9,510,000	Net Worth:	-$11,413,000	Debt/ Equity:	NA

Greens Worldwide Inc

346 Woodland Church Rd., Hertford, NC, 27944; *PH:* 1-252-264-2064; *Fax:* 1-252-264-2068; *http://* www.usprogolftour.com

General - Incorporation	AZ	Stock - Price on:12/24/2007	NA
Employees	NA	Stock Exchange	OTC
Auditor	Most & Co LLP	Ticker Symbol	GRWW
Stk Agt	Computershare Trust Co	Outstanding Shares	NA
Counsel	NA	E.P.S.	$1.37
DUNS No.	NA	Shareholders	NA

Business: The group is in development stage. It plans to develop 23 acres of property located near las vegas strip. On 31-Oct-2003 the group discontinued its sports themed restaurant and bar, pro shop, and five 18-hole natural grass putting courses. The group operates from United States.

Primary SIC and add'l.: 9999

CIK No: 0001072971

Subsidiaries: BreakThru Media, ILX Resorts Incorporated, US Pro Golf Tour

Officers: Thomas R. Kidd/CEO, Pres.

Owners: Insiders/9.85%, Golden Gate Investors, Inc./1.26%, SportsQuest, Inc./100.00%, Thomas R. Kidd/9.85%

*Financial Data: Fiscal Year End:*12/31 *Latest Annual Data:* 12/31/2005

Year	Sales	Net Income
2005	$99,000	-$1,718,000
2004	NA	-$58,000
2003	$106,000	-$4,094,000

Curr. Assets:	$95,000	Curr. Liab.:	$754,000		
Plant, Equip.:	$39,000	Total Liab.:	$912,000	Indic. Yr. Divd.:	NA
Total Assets:	$464,000	Net Worth:	-$447,000	Debt/ Equity:	NA

Greenville Federal Financial Corp

690 Wagner Ave., Greenville, OH, 45331; *PH:* 1-937-548-4158; *http://* www.greenvillefederal.com

General - Incorporation	OH	Stock - Price on:12/24/2007	$9.55
Employees	36	Stock Exchange	OTC
Auditor	BKD, LLP	Ticker Symbol	GVFF
Stk Agt	Illinois Stock Transfer Co	Outstanding Shares	2,290,000
Counsel	NA	E.P.S.	$0.30
DUNS No.	NA	Shareholders	NA

Business: The groups principle activities include attracting deposits and using these deposits to originate loans to individuals and businesses. The group provides loans including residential real estate loans nonresidential real estate, commercial and consumer loans. The group operates from the United States.

Primary SIC and add'l.: 6035

CIK No: 0001330365

Subsidiaries: Greenville Federal

Officers: David M. Kepler/Dir., CEO, Pres./$171,654.00, Susan J. Allread/CFO, Sec.

Directors: David M. Kepler/Dir., CEO, Pres., James W. Ward/63/Chmn., David R. Wolverton/71/Dir., George S. Luce/46/Dir., David Feltman/73/Dir., Richard J. Obrien/62/Dir., Eunice F. Steinbrecher/67/Dir.

Owners: Insiders/5.32%, Eunice F. Steinbrecher/0.74%, David T. Feltman/0.66%, George S. Luce, David R. Wolverton/0.96%, James W. Ward/0.52%, David M. Kepler/1.38%, Richard J. OBrien/0.30%

*Financial Data: Fiscal Year End:*06/30 *Latest Annual Data:* 06/30/2007

Year	Sales	Net Income
2007	$8,296,000	$641,000
2006	NA	NA

Curr. Assets:	$4,077,000	Curr. Liab.:	$106,091,000		
Plant, Equip.:	$2,269,000	Total Liab.:	$106,964,000	Indic. Yr. Divd.:	$0.280
Total Assets:	$129,708,000	Net Worth:	$22,744,000	Debt/ Equity:	NA

Greer Bancshares Inc SC

1111 W Poinsett St., Greer, SC, 29650; *PH:* 1-864-877-2000; *http://* www.greerstatebank.com

General - Incorporation....SC
Employees....83
Auditor....Dixon Hughes PLLC
Stk Agt....NA
Counsel....NA
DUNS No.....NA

Stock- Price on:12/24/2007....$23
Stock Exchange....OTC
Ticker Symbol....GRBS
Outstanding Shares....2,480,000
E.P.S....$1.09
Shareholders....NA

Business: The groups principal activity is to provide the commercial banking services. Services of the group include checking, savings, brokered deposits and time deposits, loans for business, real estate, personal use, home improvements and automobiles, ravelers checks, safe deposit boxes, direct deposit of payroll and social security checks and Automated Teller Machine services. The group operates from the United States.

Primary SIC and add'l.: 6021

CIK No: 0001145547

Subsidiaries: Greer Capital Trust I, Greer Capital Trust II, Greer Financial Services Corporation, Greer State Bank

Owners: Steven M. Bateman, Dennis R. Hennett, Paul D. Lister/4.90%, David M. Rogers, Raj K. S. Dhillon, Kenneth M. Harper, Theron C. Smith, Harold K. James/2.10%, Gary M. Griffin/1.90%, Mark S. Ashmore, Pierce E. Williams, Walter M. Burch/2.30%, Insiders/21.40%, Victor K. Grout, Don C. Wall/5.50% *(17 Owners included in Index)*

Financial Data: **Fiscal Year End:**12/31 **Latest Annual Data:** 12/31/2006

Year	Sales	Net Income
2006	$24,556,000	$3,153,000
2005	$17,721,000	$2,795,000
2004	$13,405,000	$2,560,000

Curr. Assets:	$14,396,000	**Curr. Liab.:**	$254,460,000	**P/E Ratio:**	21.50
Plant, Equip.:	$6,632,000	**Total Liab.:**	$337,120,000	**Indic. Yr. Divd.:**	$0.680
Total Assets:	$359,662,000	**Net Worth:**	$22,542,000	**Debt/ Equity:**	3.2120

Greif Inc

425 Winter Rd., Delaware, OH, 43015; *PH:* 1-740-549-6000; *Fax:* 1-740-549-6100;
http:// www.greif.com

General - Incorporation....DE
Employees....9,025
Auditor....Ernst & Young LLP
Stk Agt....National City Bank
Counsel....NA
DUNS No.....00-428-2661

Stock- Price on:12/24/2007....$60
Stock Exchange....NYSE
Ticker Symbol....GEF
Outstanding Shares....46,600,000
E.P.S....$2.23
Shareholders....NA

Business: The groups principle activity is to produce industrial packaging products. The groups products include steel, fiber and plastic drums, intermediate bulk containers, closure systems for industrial packaging products and polycarbonate water bottles, which are complemented with a variety of value-added services, including blending, packaging, logistics and warehousing. The group operates through three business segments including industrial packaging and services, paper, packaging and services, and timber. The group operates from United States.

Primary SIC and add'l.: 2674 2653 5099 2631 3412 2431 2655

CIK No: 0000043920

Subsidiaries: American Flange& Manufacturing Co. Inc., Austro Fass Vertriebs GmbH (51%), Balmer Lawrie Van Leer Ltd (40.06%), CorrChoice LLC, Ecocontainer (UK) Ltd., Emballagefabrieken Verma BV, GCC Drum, Inc, GCC Fibre Drum, Inc., Greif (Ningbo) Packaging Co., Ltd., Greif (Shanghai) Packaging Co. LTD, Greif (Taicang) Packaging Co Ltd, Greif AquaPack Sp. Z.o.o., Greif Argentina S.A., Greif Asia Pacific Investments PTY Limited, Greif Australia Administration Pty Limited 117 Subsidiaries included in the Index

Officers: Michael J. Gasser/Chmn., CEO, Pres., David B. Fischer/COO, Pres., C. F. Chong/Contact - Malaysia, Rob Zimmerman/Contact - South Africa, Ronald L. Brown/Sr. VP - Global Sourcing, Supply Chain, Michael C. Patton/Sr. VP, Divisional Pres. - Paper, Packaging, Services, Industrial Packaging, Services, North America, Gary R. Martz/Sr. VP, General Counsel, Pres. - Soterra, Donald S. Huml/CFO, Exec. VP, Necip Bulut/Contact - Turkey, Igor Pastukh/Contact - Ukraine, Tammy Drumheller/Contact - United States, East, Al Clark/Contact - United States, Midwest, Dee Dee Reichstadt/Contact - US, West, Southwest, Jimmy Lack/Contact - Intermediate Bulk Containers, Rick Volker/Contact - Water Bottles *(59 Officers included in Index)*

Directors: Michael J. Gasser/Chmn., CEO, Pres., Patrick J. Norton/Dir., William B. Sparks/Dir., Robert C. MacAuley/Dir. - Distinguished, Judith Hook/Dir., Daniel J. Gunsett/Dir., Bruce A. Edwards/Dir., Michael H. Dempsey/Dir., Charles R. Chandler/Dir., Vicki L. Avril/Dir.

Owners: Charles R. Chandler, Judith D. Hook, William B. Sparks, Ronald L. Brown, David B. Fischer, Vicki L. Avril, Daniel J. Gunsett, Michael H. Dempsey, Mary T. McAlpin/5.49%, Virginia D. Ragan/5.54%, David B. Fischer, Patrick J. Norton, Michael J. Gasser, Judith D. Hook/3.38%, Robert C. Macauley/9.40% *(24 Owners included in Index)*

Financial Data: **Fiscal Year End:**10/31 **Latest Annual Data:** 10/31/2006

Year	Sales	Net Income
2006	$2,628,475,000	$142,119,000
2005	$2,424,297,000	$104,656,000
2004	$2,209,282,000	$47,769,000

Curr. Assets:	$793,037,000	**Curr. Liab.:**	$491,299,000	**P/E Ratio:**	26.91
Plant, Equip.:	$940,949,000	**Total Liab.:**	$1,339,115,000	**Indic. Yr. Divd.:**	$1.120
Total Assets:	$2,188,001,000	**Net Worth:**	$844,011,000	**Debt/ Equity:**	0.8133

Grey Wolf Inc

10370 Richmond Ave., Ste. 600, Houston, TX, 77042; *PH:* 1-713-435-6100; *Fax:* 1-713-435-6170;
http:// www.gwdrilling.com

General - Incorporation....TX
Employees....3,400
Auditor....KPMG LLP
Stk Agt......American Stock Transfer & Trust Co.
Counsel....Porter & Hedges LLP
DUNS No.....06-356-9313

Stock- Price on:12/24/2007....$8.4
Stock Exchange....AMEX
Ticker Symbol....GW
Outstanding Shares....184,870,000
E.P.S....$0.95
Shareholders....NA

Business: The group's principal activity is to provide contract land drilling services to the oil and gas industry in the United States. As on 30-Jun-2003, the group had a fleet of 117 rigs, 80 of which are marketed and 37 are held in inventory. The group operates through six drilling markets in the United States: ark-la-tex; gulf coast; Mississippi/Alabama; south Texas; rocky mountain and west Texas. Majority of the rigs are located in the ark-la-tex; gulf coast; Mississippi/Alabama; south Texas markets. The group's customers include independent producers and major oil and gas companies. On 06-Apr-2004, the group acquired new patriot drilling corp.

Primary SIC and add'l.: 1381

CIK No: 0000320186

Subsidiaries: DI Energy, Inc., DI/Perfensa, Inc., Drillers Inc., DI de Venezuela, Grey Wolf Drilling Company L.P., Grey Wolf Drilling de Mexico, S. de R.L. de C.V., Grey Wolf Drilling de Venezuela, Grey Wolf Drilling International, Ltd., Grey Wolf Holdings Company, Grey Wolf International de Mexico, S. de R.L. de C.V., Grey Wolf International, Inc., Grey Wolf LLC, Grey Wolf Mexico Holdings LLC, Murco Drilling Corp., Perforaciones Andinas, S.A., Servicios Grey Wolf, S. de R.L. de C.V.

Officers: Thomas P. Richards/Chmn., CEO, Pres./$2,361,888.00, Edward S. Jacob/Sr. VP - Operations/$745,261.00, Robert J. Proffit/Sr. VP - Human Resources/$450,701.00, Kent D. Cauley/VP, Controller/$368,905.00, Donald J. Guedry/VP, Treasurer, Forrest M. Conley/VP - Ark, La, Tex Division, Dale Love/VP - Gulf Coast Division, Ray Smith/VP - Rocky Mountain Division, David W. Wehlmann/CFO, Exec. VP, Sec., David J. Crowley/COO, Exec. VP, Jay Minmier/VP - South Texas Division, Burley Lett/Operations Mgr. - Mid Continent Division

Directors: Thomas P. Richards/Chmn., CEO, Pres., William R. Ziegler/Vice Chmn., Robert E. Rose/Dir., Steven A. Webster/Dir., Frank M. Brown/Dir., William T. Donovan/Dir., Trevor M. Turbidy/Dir.

Owners: Frank M. Brown, Putnam, LLC d/b/a/ Putman Investments/5.70%, Kent D. Cauley, Edward S. Jacob, Steven A. Webster/1.40%, Donald J. Guedry, David W. Wehlmann, William R. Ziegler/0.80%, Thomas P. Richards/0.50%, Trevor Turbidy, William T. Donovan/0.50%, Insiders/9.00%, FMR Corp/8.70%, Robert E. Rose, Robert J. Proffit

Financial Data: **Fiscal Year End:**12/31 **Latest Annual Data:** 12/31/2006

Year	Sales	Net Income
2006	$945,527,000	$219,951,000
2005	$696,979,000	$120,637,000
2004	$424,634,000	$8,078,000

Curr. Assets:	$451,846,000	**Curr. Liab.:**	$147,082,000	**P/E Ratio:**	8.84
Plant, Equip.:	$608,136,000	**Total Liab.:**	$553,190,000	**Indic. Yr. Divd.:**	NA
Total Assets:	$1,086,984,000	**Net Worth:**	$533,794,000	**Debt/ Equity:**	0.4710

Greystone Logistics Inc

1613 E 15th St., Tulsa, OK, 74120; *PH:* 1-918-583-7441; *Fax:* 1-918-583-7442;
http:// www.greystonelogistics-glgi.com

General - Incorporation....OK
Employees....75
Auditor..... Murrell, Hall, McIntosh & Co., PLLP
Stk Agt....Continental Stock Transfer & Trust Co
Counsel....NA
DUNS No.....NA

Stock- Price on:12/24/2007....$0.26
Stock Exchange....OTC
Ticker Symbol....GLGI
Outstanding Shares....26,060,000
E.P.S....-$0.1
Shareholders....NA

Business: The group's principal activities are to manufacture and distribute plastic pallets and plastic injection molding machines and systems. The group's operations are carried out through its wholly owned subsidiary, plastic pallet production, inc. It holds a patent for the original design of materials handling plastic pallet and on plastic injection molding machine used to produce such pallets. The group's product line include hawker(tm) fr, tank(tm), tank(tm) 3-runner, granada(tm), granada(tm) 3 runner, ap, ap 3-runner, stackable and nestable.

Primary SIC and add'l.: 3599 3089

CIK No: 0001088413

Subsidiaries: Greystone Manufacturing, LLC, Plastic Pallet Production, Inc

Officers: Warren F. Kruger/Dir., CEO, Pres., Robert H. Nelson/62/CFO

Directors: Warren F. Kruger/Dir., CEO, Pres., Robert B. Rosene/53/Dir.

Owners: Marshall S. Cogan, Paul A. Kruger, Robert H. Nelson, Commerce Plastics, Hildalgo Trading Company, LC, GLOG Investment, L.L.C., Insiders, Warren F. Kruger, Robert B. Rosene

Financial Data: **Fiscal Year End:**05/31 **Latest Annual Data:** 5/31/2006

Year	Sales	Net Income
2006	$15,956,000	-$2,335,000
2005	$9,306,000	-$10,422,000
2004	$6,965,000	-$2,975,000

Curr. Assets:	$1,483,000	**Curr. Liab.:**	$5,848,000		
Plant, Equip.:	$8,028,000	**Total Liab.:**	$16,734,000	**Indic. Yr. Divd.:**	NA
Total Assets:	$9,663,000	**Net Worth:**	-$7,071,000	**Debt/ Equity:**	NA

Griffin Land & Nurseries Inc

1 Rockefeller Plz., New York, NY, 10020; *PH:* 1-212-218-7910; *Fax:* 1-212-218-7917;
http:// www.imperialnurseries.com

General - Incorporation....DE
Employees....206
Auditor....PricewaterhouseCoopers LLP
Stk Agt....Mellon Investor Services LLC
Counsel....Latham & Watkins
DUNS No.....05-550-7677

Stock- Price on:12/24/2007....$34.73
Stock Exchange....NDQ
Ticker Symbol....GRIF
Outstanding Shares....5,140,000
E.P.S....$1.12
Shareholders....NA

Business: The group's principal activities are the real estate business and to provide landscape nursery operations. The group operates in two business segments: landscape nursery segment and real estate segment. The landscape nursery segment includes growing containerized landscape products for garden center operators and landscape nursery mass merchandisers. The largest portion of container-grown product consists of broadleaf evergreens, including azaleas and rhododendron, juniper and deciduous shrubs. The real estate business is comprised of the ownership, construction and management of commercial and industrial properties and the development of residential subdivisions.

Primary SIC and add'l.: 6552 6519 0181

CIK No: 0001037390

Subsidiaries: General Cigar Co., Inc, Imperial Nurseries, Inc., Linguaphone Group Ltd.

Officers: Frederick M. Danziger/68/Dir., CEO, Pres., Anthony J. Galici/50/CFO, VP, Sec.

Directors: Frederick M. Danziger/68/Dir., CEO, Pres., David M. Danziger/42/Dir., Winston J. Churchill/67/Dir., Edgar M. Cullman/90/Dir., Thomas C. Israel/64/Dir., Alan Plotkin/62/Dir., David F. Stein/67/Dir.

Owners: Susan R. Cullman, David M. Danziger, Winston J. Churchill, Gabelli Funds,Inc. et al, David F. Stein, Frederick M. Danziger, Thomas C. Israel, B. Bros. Realty LLC, Edgar M. Cullman, Alan Plotkin, Lucy C. Danziger, Insiders, Louise B. Cullman, Anthony J. Galici, John L. Ernst *(16 Owners included in Index)*

Financial Data: **Fiscal Year End:**12/03 **Latest Annual Data:** 12/2/2006

Year	Sales	Net Income
2006	$53,231,000	-$432,000
2005	$41,889,000	-$1,368,000
2004	$41,270,000	$30,988,000

Curr. Assets:	$83,070,000	Curr. Liab.:	$8,149,000		
Plant, Equip.:	$89,087,000	Total Liab.:	$55,793,000	Indic. Yr. Divd.:	NA
Total Assets:	$188,650,000	Net Worth:	$132,857,000	Debt/ Equity:	0.3644

Griffon Corp

100 Jericho Quadrangle, Jericho, NY, 11753; *PH:* 1-516-938-5544; *Fax:* 1-516-938-5644; *http://* www.griffoncorp.com

General - Incorporation	DE	*Stock*- Price on:12/24/2007	$22.29
Employees	5,700	Stock Exchange	NYSE
Auditor	PricewaterhouseCoopers LLP	Ticker Symbol	GFF
Stk Agt	American Stock Transfer & Trust Co.	Outstanding Shares	29,820,000
Counsel	NA	E.P.S.	$0.71
DUNS No.	05-059-0710	Shareholders	NA

Business: The groups principle activity is to manufacture garage doors, fireplaces, floor coverings and cabinets. The group operates through four business segments namely garage doors, installation services, specialty plastic films, and electronic information and communication systems segments. The group operates from United States.

Primary SIC and add'l.: 3442 3081 3812 1796

CIK No: 0000050725

Subsidiaries: Clopay Corporation, Clopay Plastics Products Company, Telephonics Corporation

Officers: Patrick Alesia/VP, Treasurer, Sec., Ethics Officer, Eric P. Edelstein/58/Exec. VP, CFO, David E. Troller/VP, Chief Legal Officer, Sec., Clopay Ethics Liaison Officer, Gerald Raymon/General Counsel, Telephonics Ethics Liaison Officer, Franklin H. Smith/57/Exec. VP

Directors: Harvey R. Blau/73/Chmn., Robert G. Harrison/71/Dir., Henry A. Alpert/60/Dir., Bertrand M. Bell/78/Dir., Martin S. Sussman/70/Dir., Joseph J. Whalen/76/Dir., Ronald J. Kramer/49/Dir., Donald J. Kutyna/74/Dir., James W. Stansberry/80/Dir., Blaine V. Fogg/67/Dir., Clarence A. Hill/87/Dir., William H. Waldorf/69/Dir., Gordon E. Fornell/Dir., James A. Mitarotonda/Dir.

Owners: Ronald J. Kramer, Barington Capital Group, L.P./5.50%, Insiders/14.70%, Griffon Corporation Employee Stock Ownership Plan/8.10%, James A. Mitarotonda/5.50%, NWQ Investment Management Company, LLC/15.30%, Patrick L. Alesia, Donald J. Kutyna, Martin S. Sussman, Clarence A. Hill, Joseph J. Whalen, Harvey R. Blau/7.90%, Bertrand M. Bell, Blaine V. Fogg, Robert G. Harrison *(19 Owners included in Index)*

Financial Data: Fiscal Year End:09/30   Latest Annual Data: 9/30/2006

Year	Sales	Net Income
2006	$1,636,580,000	$51,786,000
2005	$1,401,993,000	$48,813,000
2004	$1,393,809,000	$53,859,000

Curr. Assets:	$545,004,000	Curr. Liab.:	$236,299,000	P/E Ratio:	14.96
Plant, Equip.:	$231,975,000	Total Liab.:	$515,769,000	Indic. Yr. Divd.:	NA
Total Assets:	$928,214,000	Net Worth:	$412,445,000	Debt/ Equity:	0.5813

Grill Concepts Inc

11661 San Vicente Blvd., Ste. 404, Los Angeles, CA, 90049; *PH:* 1-310-820-5559; *Fax:* 1-310-820-6530; *http://* www.dailygrill.com; *Email:* info@thegrill.com

General - Incorporation	DE	*Stock*- Price on:12/24/2007	$7.17
Employees	1,242	Stock Exchange	NDQ
Auditor	Moss Adams LLP	Ticker Symbol	GRIL
Stk Agt	Securities Transfer Corp	Outstanding Shares	6,520,000
Counsel	Herzog, Fisher, Grayson & Wolfe	E.P.S.	$0.39
DUNS No.	60-967-1516	Shareholders	NA

Business: The group's principal activity is to develop and operate casual dining restaurants under the name daily grill and fine dining restaurants under the name the grill on the alley. In addition, the group owns and operates or has management or licensing agreements with respect to, other restaurant properties. At 28-Dec-2003, the group had 14 restaurants and managed or licensed 8 additional restaurants.

Primary SIC and add'l.: 5812

CIK No: 0000895041

Subsidiaries: 612 Flower Daily Grill, LLC, Alcoli 66, Inc., C.T.S. Investments, Chicago - The Grill on the Alley, LLC, EMNDEE, Inc., Formerly Grill Concepts Acquisition Corp., Inc., Formerly Magellan Restaurants, Formerly Uno Concepts, Inc., GC Dallas Ventures LP, GCI-CC, Inc., GCI-MP, Inc, Grill Concepts - D.C., Inc., Grill Concepts CD, Inc., Grill Concepts Chicken Daily, LLC, Grill Concepts Management, Inc. 26 Subsidiaries included in the Index

Officers: Philip Gay/50/Dir., CEO, Pres./$366,823.00, Mike Weinstock/Chmn., Exec. VP, Wayne Lipschitz/CFO, VP, Ryan Handel/GM - Brentwood, Linda Gwinnett/GM - Burbank, Coni Zingarelli/Dir. - Special Events, Terri Henry/VP - Marketing, Jim Snodgrass/Area Dir., Chris Gehrke/Dir. - Human Resources, Rob Robertson/GM - Irvine, Susan Carnes/GM - Los Angeles, Burke Schechtel/Dir. - Restaurant Development, Toni Shizuru/Dir. - Performance, Development, Steve Grant/Area Dir., John Sola/Sr. VP - Culinary/$241,774.00 *(38 Officers included in Index)*

Directors: Philip Gay/50/Dir., CEO, Pres., Mike Weinstock/Chmn., Exec. VP, Bob Spivak/Founder, Bruce Schwartz/68/Dir., Robert Spivak/64/Dir., Robert Fell/65/Dir., Glenn Golenberg/67/Dir., Stephen Ross/59/Dir.

Owners: Stephen Ross/2.90%, Richard Dantas, Mackenzie Financial Corp/5.40%, Louie Feinstein, Bruce Schwartz, Glenn Golenberg, Michael Weinstock/8.00%, Robert Spivak/8.40%, Keith Wolff/5.60%, Aaron Ferrer/6.40%, Eaturna LLC/14.40%, Philip Gay, John Sola, Insiders/21.30%, Lewis Wolff/5.10%

Financial Data: Fiscal Year End:12/25   Latest Annual Data: 12/31/2006

Year	Sales	Net Income
2006	$80,662,000	$3,029,000
2005	$70,688,000	$939,000
2004	$63,659,000	$38,000

Curr. Assets:	$8,104,000	Curr. Liab.:	$11,676,000		
Plant, Equip.:	$15,139,000	Total Liab.:	$22,088,000	Indic. Yr. Divd.:	NA
Total Assets:	$30,598,000	Net Worth:	$6,962,000	Debt/ Equity:	0.1813

Groen Brothers Aviation Inc

2640 W California Ave., Salt Lake City, UT, 84104; *PH:* 1-801-973-0177; *Fax:* 1-801-973-4027; *http://* www.gbagyros.com; *Email:* sales@groenbros.com

General - Incorporation	UT	*Stock*- Price on:12/24/2007	$0.15
Employees	66	Stock Exchange	OTC
Auditor	HJ & Assoc., LLC	Ticker Symbol	GNBA
Stk Agt	Atlas Stock Transfer Corp	Outstanding Shares	152,980,000
Counsel	NA	E.P.S.	-$0.16
DUNS No.	80-088-6392	Shareholders	NA

Business: The group's principal activity is to develop and manufacture hawk gyroplane and other gyroplane models. The gyroplane aircraft gets its lift from rotor blades and thrust from an engine-driven propeller. A gyroplane's rotor blades turn freely in flight and are tilted back to catch the air. The rushing air spins the rotor as its propeller thrusts the aircraft forward. The gyroplanes are easier to operate and less expensive to maintain than helicopters. The aircrafts are marketed to the law enforcement agencies, public service organizations and military.

Primary SIC and add'l.: 3721

CIK No: 0000870743

Subsidiaries: American Autogyro Inc., Groen Brothers Aviation USA, Inc

Officers: David Groen/Chmn., CEO, Pres., Al W. Waddill/VP - Sales, Dan Banks/Customer Support Mgr., Thomas E. Winn/VP - Corporate Planning, Quality Assurance, Dennis P. Gauger/VP - Finance, CFO, Corp. Sec., Treasurer, Nathan W. Drage/Corporate Counsel, J. Jaap Van Der Westhuizen/VP - Engineering, CTO, Robin H.H. Wilson/Exec. VP, Head - Business Development, Bruce M. Tinnesand/VP - Manufacturing, David L. Whetten/VP - Marketing, Jason Chen/VP - Business Development Asia, Terry Brandt/VP - Flight Operations, Raymond W. Prouty/Aeronautical Engineer - Consultants, Barnes W. McCormick/Aeronautical Engineer - Consultant, Dan M. Somers/Aeronautical Engineer - Consultant *(19 Officers included in Index)*

Directors: David Groen/Chmn., CEO, Pres.

Owners: David Groen/73.20%, David Groen/10.60%, Margaret Groen/6.00%, Robin Wilson/3.70%, Margaret Groen/8.90%, Insiders/91.10%, Robin Wilson/8.90%, Insiders/16.40%, Dennis Gauger/8.90%, Dennis Gauger/2.10%

Financial Data: Fiscal Year End:06/30   Latest Annual Data: 6/30/2006

Year	Sales	Net Income
2006	$3,115,000	-$20,081,000
2005	$864,000	-$13,354,000
2004	$509,000	-$12,522,000

Curr. Assets:	$1,755,000	Curr. Liab.:	$62,242,000		
Plant, Equip.:	$513,000	Total Liab.:	$69,469,000	Indic. Yr. Divd.:	NA
Total Assets:	$2,268,000	Net Worth:	-$67,201,000	Debt/ Equity:	NA

Grosvenor Explorations Inc

1533 Eagle Mountain Dr., Coquitlam, BC, V3E 2ZS3; *PH:* 1-632-887-2131

General - Incorporation	NV	*Stock*- Price on:12/24/2007	NA
Employees	NA	Stock Exchange	OTC
Auditor	Madsen & Associates, CPA's Inc.	Ticker Symbol	GVXP
Stk Agt	Empire Stock Transfer Inc.	Outstanding Shares	NA
Counsel	NA	E.P.S.	NA
DUNS No.	NA	Shareholders	NA

Business: The groups principal activity is to explore minerals. The group operates from the United States and Canada.

Primary SIC and add'l.: 1000

CIK No: 0001351765

Subsidiaries: Grosvenor Explorations Ltd.

Officers: Alexander Ibsen/67/Dir., CEO, Pres., Patrick Grant/59/Dir., CFO, Chief Accounting Officer, Sec., Treasurer

Directors: Alexander Ibsen/67/Dir., CEO, Pres., Patrick Grant/59/Dir., CFO, Chief Accounting Officer, Sec., Treasurer

Owners: Alexander Ibsen/44.75%, Patrick Grant/26.73%, Insiders/71.48%

Group 1 Automotive Inc

950 Echo Ln., Ste. 100, Houston, TX, 77024; *PH:* 1-713-647-5700; *Fax:* 1-713-647-5858; *http://* www.group1auto.com; *Email:* investorrelations@group1auto.com

General - Incorporation	DE	*Stock*- Price on:12/24/2007	$41.66
Employees	8,800	Stock Exchange	NYSE
Auditor	Ernst & Young LLP	Ticker Symbol	GPI
Stk Agt	Mellon Investor Services LLC	Outstanding Shares	24,280,000
Counsel	NA	E.P.S.	$3.23
DUNS No.	62-791-2553	Shareholders	NA

Business: The group's principle activity is to provide new, used cars and light trucks. The group also provides maintenance and repair services. In the year 2007, the group acquired Chandlers Garage Holdings Ltd. The group operates from United States.

Primary SIC and add'l.: 5511 5012 6141 5521

CIK No: 0001031203

Subsidiaries: Amarillo Motors-C, Ltd, Amarillo Motors-F, Ltd, Amarillo Motors-J, Ltd, Amarillo Motors-SM, Ltd, Bob Howard Automotive-East, Inc, Bob Howard Chevrolet, Inc, Bob Howard Dodge, Inc, Bob Howard Motors, Inc, Bob Howard Nissan, Inc, Bohn Holdings-DC, Inc, Bohn Holdings-F, Inc, Bohn Holdings-GM, Inc, Bohn Holdings-S, Inc, Bohn-DC, LLC, Bohn-FII, LLC 148 Subsidiaries included in the Index

Officers: Earl J. Hesterberg/Dir., CEO, Pres./$2,392,311.00, Brooks J. O'Hara/VP - Human Resources, Randy L. Callison/Sr. VP - Operations, Corporate Development/$755,851.00, Peter C. Delongchamps/VP - Manufacturer Relations, Public Affairs, John C. Rickel/CFO, Sr. VP/$941,378.00, Wade D. Hubbard/VP - Fixed Operations, Darryl M. Burman/VP, General Counsel, Corp. Sec./$122,817.00, Philip W. Bres/VP - Variable Operations, James R. Druzbik/VP - Information Systems, Gigi L. Myung/VP - Purchasing, Lance A. Parker/VP, Corporate Controller, Kim Craig/Dir., Treasurer, Steve J. Waller/VP - Corporate Development

Directors: Earl J. Hesterberg/Dir., CEO, Pres., John L. Adams/Chmn., Louis E. Lataif/Dir., Stephen D. Quinn/Dir., Max P. Watson/Dir., Kim Craig/Dir., Treasurer, Robert E. Howard/Dir., Beryl Raff/Dir., Terry J. Strange/Dir.

Owners: Louis E. Lataif, John C. Rickel, Insiders/1.40%, Randy L. Callison, Stephen D. Quinn, Terry J. Strange, Darryl M. Burman, Barclays Global Investors, N.A/10.90%, Dimensional Fund Advisors Inc./6.70%, Goldman Sachs Asset Management, LP/11.80%, American Century Companies,Inc./7.60%, Earl J. Hesterberg, Max P. Watson, Robert E. Howard, John L. Adams

Financial Data: *Fiscal Year End:*12/31 *Latest Annual Data:* 12/31/2006

Year	Sales	Net Income
2006	$6,083,484,000	$88,390,000
2005	$5,969,590,000	$54,231,000
2004	$5,435,033,000	$27,781,000

Curr. Assets:	$1,178,012,000	Curr. Liab.:	$940,958,000	P/E Ratio:	12.11
Plant, Equip.:	$230,385,000	Total Liab.:	$1,421,115,000	Indic. Yr. Divd.:	$0.560
Total Assets:	$2,113,955,000	Net Worth:	$692,840,000	Debt/ Equity:	0.6942

Groupe Danone

100 Hillside Ave., Greenburgh, NY, 10603; *PH:* 1-914-872-8400; *http://* www.danonegroup.com

General - Incorporation	France	Stock- Price on:12/24/2007	$15.29
Employees	88,124	Stock Exchange	OTC
Auditor	PricewaterhouseCoopers LLP	Ticker Symbol	GDNNY
Stk Agt	Citibank N.A	Outstanding Shares	2,610,000,000
Counsel	NA	E.P.S	$0.74
DUNS No.	27-524-2634	Shareholders	NA

Business: The group's principal activity is food producing, originating in the merger between two glass producers, boussois and souchon neuvesel. Fresh dairy products: yoghurts, infant foods (bledina), low-fat products, bio products; beverages: bottled water (evian, volvic and wahaha) and beer (mahou); biscuits: sweet, savoury and low-calorie biscuits (lu, jacob's, grany and vitalinea); other food business: sauces produced by hp foods, lea & perrins and amoy.

Primary SIC and add'l.: 2023 2082 2086 2051 2099 3221 5149

CIK No: 0001048515

Officers: Franck Riboud/53/Chmn., CEO, Simon Israel/Chmn. - Asia, Pacific, Jacques Vincent/62/Vice Chmn., COO, Antoine Giscard Destaing/Exec. VP - Finance - Strategy, Information Systems, Georges Casala/Exec. VP - Biscuits, Cereal Products, Franck Mougin/Exec. VP - Human Resources, Bernard Hours/52/Dir., Exec. VP - Fresh Dairy Products, Thomas Kunz/Exec. VP - Beverages, Philippe-Loic Jacob/Company Sec., Sven Thormahlen/VP - Research - Development

Directors: Franck Riboud/53/Chmn., CEO, Simon Israel/Chmn. - Asia, Pacific, Jacques Vincent/62/Vice Chmn., COO, Bruno Bonnell/50/Dir., Hakan Mogren/64/Dir., Michel David-Weill/76/Dir., Emmanuel Faber/44/Dir., Richard Goblet Dalviella/60/Dir., Hirokatsu Hikanu/71/Dir., Jacques-Alexandre Nahmias/61/Dir., Christian Laubie/70/Dir., Bernard Hours/52/Dir., Exec. VP - Fresh Dairy Products, Benoit Potier/51/Dir., Jean Laurent/64/Dir.

Owners: Caisse des Dpts et Consignations/3.60%, FCPE GROUPE DANONE/1.50%, Public/78.00%, Eurazeo/5.40%, Sofina and Glaces de Moustier/2.00%, Predica/1.70%, The Company and its subsidiaries/7.80%

Financial Data: *Fiscal Year End:*12/31 *Latest Annual Data:* 12/31/2006

Year	Sales	Net Income
2006	$18,580,582,000	$1,750,718,000
2005	$15,425,626,000	$1,581,174,000
2004	$18,692,280,000	$544,396,000

Curr. Assets:	$8,125,126,000	Curr. Liab.:	$5,608,634,000		
Plant, Equip.:	$3,987,306,000	Total Liab.:	$14,566,870,000	Indic. Yr. Divd.:	$0.230
Total Assets:	$22,453,022,000	Net Worth:	$7,886,152,000	Debt/ Equity:	NA

Grubb & Ellis Co

2215 Sanders Rd. , Ste. 400, Northbrook, IL, 60062; *PH:* 1-847-753-7500; *http://* www.grubb-ellis.com; *Email:* corporatecommunications@grubb-ellis.com

General - Incorporation	DE	Stock- Price on:12/24/2007	$12.74
Employees	5,000	Stock Exchange	NYSE
Auditor	Ernst & Young LLP	Ticker Symbol	GBE
Stk Agt	Computershare Investor Services LLC	Outstanding Shares	25,910,000
Counsel	Robert J. Walner	E.P.S	$0.46
DUNS No.	00-922-8198	Shareholders	NA

Business: The group's principal activity is to provide services to real estate owners or investors and tenants. The services provided by the group include transaction services involving leasing, acquisitions, dispositions and property and facilities management services. The group also provides consulting and strategic services with respect to commercial real estate. The group through its offices, affiliates and alliance provides a full range of real estate services, including transaction, management and consulting services, to users and investors worldwide. The group through professionals arranges and advises the sale, acquisition or lease of business properties as industrial, retail and office buildings, as well as the acquisition and disposition of multi-family properties and commercial land. The group operates under the trade name grubb & ellis. During Feb, the group disposed wadley-donovan group.

Primary SIC and add'l.: 8741

CIK No: 0000216039

Subsidiaries: Aequus Property Management Company, Crane Realty & Management Co., Crane Realty Services, Inc., GEMS Korea, LLC, GEMS Mexicana, S. DE R.L. DE C.V., GEMS of Sweden, AB, Grubb & Ellis Advisers of California, Inc., Grubb & Ellis Affiliates, Inc., Grubb & Ellis Asset Services Company, Grubb & Ellis Consulting Services Company, Grubb & Ellis Europe, Inc., Grubb & Ellis Institutional Properties, Inc., Grubb & Ellis Management Services of Brazil LTDA, Grubb & Ellis Management Services of Canada, Inc., Grubb & Ellis Management Services of Michigan, Inc. (GEMS of Michigan) 30 Subsidiaries included in the Index

Officers: Mark E. Rose/Dir., CEO, Duke Suwyn/Pres., CEO - Industrial, Mike Wafer/Sr. VP - Industrial, Bob Sticht/Sr. VP - Industrial, Rob Stillwell/VP - Industrial, Ron Washle/Sr. VP - Industrial, Xavier Wasiak/Sr. VP - Industrial Group, Industrial, David Williams/Sr. VP, MD - Industrial, Charles Dilks/VP - Office, Keith Lavey/Assoc. VP - Office, Beau Barrett/Managing Partner, Investment, Tucker J. Brooks/Assoc. Retail, Jason Brumm/Sr. Associate, Multi Housing, Megan Byrne/Assoc. Retail, Don Cape/Principal - Sales Associate, Industrial *(523 Officers included in Index)*

Directors: Mark E. Rose/Dir., CEO, Michael C. Kojaian/Chmn., Anthony G. Antone/Dir., Robert J. McLaughlin/Dir., Joseph F. Moravec/Dir., Rodger D. Young/Dir., Steve Smith/MD - Corporate Services Group

Owners: Donald D. Olinger, Frances Lewis, Robert H. Osbrink, Rodger D. Young, Robert Z. Slaughter, Persons affiliated with Kojaian Ventures, L.L.C/29.00%, Mark E. Rose/1.70%, Persons affiliated with Kojaian Holdings LLC/9.40%, Michael C. Kojaian/38.40%, Robert J. McLaughlin, Insiders/41.00%, Joseph F. Moravec, Anthony G. Antone, Maureen A. Ehrenberg

Financial Data: *Fiscal Year End:*06/30 *Latest Annual Data:* 6/30/2006

Year	Sales	Net Income
2006	$490,127,000	$4,911,000
2005	$463,535,000	$13,267,000
2004	$440,554,000	$14,194,000

Curr. Assets:	$42,864,000	Curr. Liab.:	$32,871,000		
Plant, Equip.:	$9,908,000	Total Liab.:	$82,697,000	Indic. Yr. Divd.:	NA
Total Assets:	$94,223,000	Net Worth:	$11,526,000	Debt/ Equity:	NA

Gruma

Calzada Del Valle 407 Ote, Colonia Del Valle, San Pedro Garza Garcia Nl, 66220; *PH:* 52-8183993312; *http://* www.gruma.com

General - Incorporation	Mexico	Stock- Price on:12/24/2007	$13.52
Employees	16,582	Stock Exchange	NYSE
Auditor	PricewaterhouseCoopers LLP	Ticker Symbol	GMK
Stk Agt	Citibank N.A	Outstanding Shares	120,640,000
Counsel	NA	E.P.S	$1.32
DUNS No.	81-046-0329	Shareholders	NA

Business: The group's principal activities are the manufacturing and sale of corn flour, packaged tortilla, wheat flour and other related products. It operates in Mexico, venezuela, Central America, Europe and in the United States of America. Brands include maseca, mission, guerrero, reposada, selecta, poderosa, mision, tortirica, masarica, tortimasa, tosty, juana and robin hood.

Primary SIC and add'l.: 2041 0111 2051 2099 3556

CIK No: 0001053947

Subsidiaries: Azteca Milling LP, Derivados de Maz Seleccionado, DEMASECA, C.A. (DEMASECA), Gruma Centroamrica, LLC, Gruma Corporation, Grupo Industrial Maseca, S.A. de C.V. (GIMSA), Investigacin de Tecnologa Avanzada, S.A. de C.V., Molinera de Mxico, S.A. de C.V. (Molinera de Mxico), Molinos Nacionales, C.A. (MONACA) (MONACA), Productos y Distribuidora Azteca, S.A. de C.V. (PRODISA)

Officers: Jairo Senise/CEO, Juan A. Gonzalez Moreno/Dir., CEO, Jose De La Pena Y Angelini/CEO - Gruma Latin America, Juan A. Quiroga Garcia/Dir., Chief Corporate Officer, Leonel Garza Ramirez/Chief Procurement Officer, Norma Morales/Investor Relations Officer, Homero Huerta Moreno/Chief Administrative Officer, Joaquin Rubio Lamas/Sr. VP - Manufacturing, Procurement, Rafael Abreu/Sr. VP - Commercial Operations, Gruma Mexico, Felipe Rubio Lamas/CTO - Corn Flour, Tortilla Production, Juan Fernando Roche/MD - Mission Foods, Eduardo Sastre/Pres. - Corporate Communications, Salvador Vargas Guajardo/General Counsel, Rogelio Sanchez/Investor Relations Officer, Lilia Gomez/Investor Relations Officer *(29 Officers included in Index)*

Directors: Juan A. Gonzalez Moreno/Dir., CEO, Roberto Gonzalez Barrera/Chmn., Javier Velez Bautista/51/Dir., Roberto Hernandez Ramirez/Dir., Adrian Sada Gonzalez/Dir., Roberto Gonzalez Moreno/Dir., Carlos Hank Rhon/Dir., Juan Manuel Ley Lopez/Dir., Juan A. Quiroga Garcia/Dir., Chief Corporate Officer, Federico Gorbea Quintero/Dir., Ismael Roig/Dir., Juan Diez-canedo Ruiz/Dir., Bernardo Quintana Isaac/Dir., Hector Rangel Domene/Dir., Alfonso Romo Garza/Dir.

Owners: Roberto Gonzalez Barrera/45.76%, Insiders/0.04%, Archer-Daniels-Midland/27.13%

Financial Data: *Fiscal Year End:*12/31 *Latest Annual Data:* 12/31/2006

Year	Sales	Net Income
2006	$2,844,708,000	$134,413,000
2005	$2,480,852,000	$110,732,000
2004	$2,241,826,000	$69,718,000

Curr. Assets:	$912,940,000	Curr. Liab.:	$487,730,000		
Plant, Equip.:	$1,446,523,000	Total Liab.:	$1,519,060,000	Indic. Yr. Divd.:	$0.310
Total Assets:	$2,764,910,000	Net Worth:	$1,245,850,000	Debt/ Equity:	NA

Grupo Aeroportuario del Centro Norte S.A.B. de C.V.

Aeropuerto Internacional de Monterrey, Zona de Carga, Carretera Miguel Aleman Km. 24., Apodaca, 66600; *PH:* 52-8186254300; *http://* ir.oma.aero

General - Incorporation		Stock- Price on:12/24/2007	$27.26
Employees	930	Stock Exchange	NDQ
Auditor	NA	Ticker Symbol	OMAB
Stk Agt	NA	Outstanding Shares	400,000,000
Counsel	NA	E.P.S	$0.11
DUNS No.	NA	Shareholders	NA

Business: The groups principle activity is to provide recruiting services. The groups service area includes the research and development, engineering, marketing, sales, information technology and manufacturing industries. The group operates from United States.

Primary SIC and add'l.: 4581 4581

CIK No:

Officers: Ruben Gerardo Lopezbarrera/CEO, Victor Humberto Bravo Martin/CFO, Nicolas Etienne Marcel Claude/COO, Manuel De La Torre Melendez/General Counsel, Jose Ignacio De La Pena/Infrastructure, Maintenance Dir., Porfirio Gonzalez Alvarez/Airports Dir., Maria Victoria Zapata Guerrero/Dir. - Human Resources, Jean Philippe Frederic Percheron/Commercial, Marketing Dir.

Directors: Bernardo Quintana Isaac/Chmn., Fernando Flores Perez/Dir., Jose Luis Guerrero alvarez/Dir., Sergio F. Montano Leon/Dir., Alonso Quintana Kawage/Dir., Luis Fernando Zarate Rocha/Dir., Luis Guillermo Zazueta Dominguez/Dir., Alberto Mulas Alonso/Dir., Salvador Gomez Alva/Dir., Manuel Francisco Arce Rincon/Dir., Alberto Felipe Mulas Alonso/Dir., Jean Marie Chevallier Jacque Follain/Dir., Fernando Perez Flores/Dir.

Financial Data: *Fiscal Year End:*12/31 *Latest Annual Data:* 12/31/2006

Year	Sales	Net Income
2006	$150,910,000	$49,083,000
2005	$122,238,000	$31,479,000

Curr. Assets:	$191,690,000	Curr. Liab.:	$16,478,000	P/E Ratio:	115.26
Plant, Equip.:	$163,684,000	Total Liab.:	$80,705,000	Indic. Yr. Divd.:	$0.710
Total Assets:	$548,505,000	Net Worth:	$467,800,000	Debt/ Equity:	NA

Grupo Aeroportuario Del Pacifico S.A. de C.V.

Avenida Mariano Otero No. 1249-B, Torre Pacifico, Piso 6, Rinconada del Bosque, Guadalajara, Jalisco, 45140; *PH:* 52-3338801100; *Fax:* 52-3336714582; *http://* www.aeropuertosgap.com.mx; *Email:* info@aeropuertosgap.com.mx

General - Incorporation		Stock - Price on:12/24/2007	$49.66
Employees	1,072	Stock Exchange	NYSE
Auditor	NA	Ticker Symbol	PAC
Stk Agt	Bank of New York	Outstanding Shares	56,090,000
Counsel	NA	E.P.S.	$1.86
DUNS No.	NA	Shareholders	NA

Business: The groups principle activities include operating, maintenance and developing airport systems. The group operates from the Mexico. The groups quarterly revenue for September 2007 was 878.33 millions of MXN.

Primary SIC and add'l.: 3721

CIK No:

Officers: Jorge Sales Martinez/CEO, Javier Antonio Gamez Vega/Airport Mgr. - Los Mochis, Cesar Sanchez Resendiz/Airport Mgr. - Mexicali, Guillermo Villalba Morales/Airport Mgr. - La Paz, Manuel Sanson Suarez/Technical Operating Dir., Roman Araiza/Airport Mgr. - Aguascalientes, Dante Homero Rios Concha/Airport Mgr. - Hermosillo, Rodrigo Guzman Perera/CFO, Carlos Criado Alonso/Dir. - Commercial Activity, Sergio Enrique Flores Ochoa/General Counsel, Miguel Aliaga Gargollo/Investor Relations Officer, Martin Pablo Zazueta Chavez/Airport Mgr. - Guadalajara, Enrique Valle Alvarez/Airport Mgr. - Tijuana, Javier Martinez De Escobar/Airport Mgr. - Los Cabos, Jose Gomez Diaz/Airport Mgr. - Puerto (17 Officers included in Index)

Directors: Eduardo Sanchez Navarro Redo/Chmn., Javier Marin San Andres/Dir., Ernesto Vega Velasco/Dir., Henry R. Davis Signoret/Dir., Laura Diez Barroso Azcarraga/Alternate Dir., Rodrigo Marabini Ruiz/Alternate Dir., Vicente Alonso Diego/Alternate Dir., Manuel Garcia Buey/Dir., Jorge Luis Valdespino Rivera/Dir. - Human Resources, Alfonso Pasquel Barcenas/Dir., Carlos Laviada Ocejo/Alternate Dir., Demetrio Ullastres Llorente/Dir., Francisco Glennie Y Graue/Dir., Javier F. Fernandez Carbajal/Dir., Rincon J.M. Gallardo Puron/Dir. (16 Directors included in Index)

Financial Data: Fiscal Year End: NA   *Latest Annual Data:* 12/31/2006

Year	Sales		Net Income
2006	$271,826,000		$102,074,000
2005	$238,281,000		$82,639,000
2004	$196,476,000		-$10,394,000
Curr. Assets:	$145,293,000	Curr. Liab.:	$24,750,000	P/E Ratio: 11.94
Plant, Equip.:	$219,154,000	Total Liab.:	$33,314,000	Indic. Yr. Divd.: $1.880
Total Assets:	$1,178,322,000	Net Worth:	$1,145,008,000	Debt/ Equity: NA

Grupo Aeroportuario del Sureste S.A. de C.V.

Bosque de Alisos 47A - Piso 4, Bosques De Las Lomas, C.P, 5120; *PH:* 52-5552840400; *http://* www.asur.com

General - Incorporation		Stock - Price on:12/24/2007	$53.45
Employees	NA	Stock Exchange	NYSE
Auditor	NA	Ticker Symbol	ASR
Stk Agt	Bank of New York	Outstanding Shares	30,000,000
Counsel	NA	E.P.S	$2.53
DUNS No.	NA	Shareholders	NA

Business: The groups principle activity is to operate airports. The group operates from the Mexico. The groups quarterly revenue for September 2007 was 688.01 millions of MXN.

Primary SIC and add'l.: 4581

CIK No:

Financial Data: Fiscal Year End: NA   *Latest Annual Data:* 12/31/2006

Year	Sales		Net Income
2006	$207,776,000		$38,601,000
2005	$191,934,000		$42,031,000
2004	$177,245,000		$22,287,000
Curr. Assets:	$154,470,000	Curr. Liab.:	$23,127,000	P/E Ratio: 11.94
Plant, Equip.:	$292,260,000	Total Liab.:	$23,824,000	Indic. Yr. Divd.: $0.700
Total Assets:	$740,009,000	Net Worth:	$716,186,000	Debt/ Equity: NA

Grupo Casa Saba

Paseo De La Reforma 215, Colonia Lomas De Chapultepec, Mexico City, 11000; *PH:* 52-5552846600; *http://* www.casasaba.com

General - Incorporation	Mexico	Stock - Price on:12/24/2007	$32.64
Employees	5,319	Stock Exchange	NYSE
Auditor	Salles, Sainz-Grant Thornton	Ticker Symbol	SAB
Stk Agt	NA	Outstanding Shares	NA
Counsel	Mijares Angoitia Corts Y Fuentes	E.P.S.	$3.111
DUNS No.	NA	Shareholders	NA

Business: The group's principal activity is the distribution of pharmaceutical products, health-and-beauty aids, entertainment products including magazines and books, non-perishable food products, and electronic and office items. The group distributes these products through its 22 distribution networks/centers to supermarket chains, both private and governmental pharmacies, and to its retail customers throughout Mexico.

Primary SIC and add'l.: 5122 5149 5999

CIK No: 0000906779

Subsidiaries: Alta del Centro, S.A. de C.V., Bloques y Ladrillos, S.A. de C.V., Capa S.A. de C.V., Casa Saba, S.A. de C.V., Centennial S.A. de C.V., Distribuidora Casa Saba, S.A. de C.V., Distribuidora Drogueros, S.A. de C.V., Distribuidora Eclipse, S.A. de C.V., Drogueros S.A. de C.V., Estrella del Este, S.A. de C.V., Estrella del Pacfico, S.A. de C.V., Grupo Mexatar, S.A. de C.V., Inmobiliaria Iliria, S.A. de C.V., Inmobiliaria Osa Mayor, S.A. de C.V., Inmobiliaria Perceval, S.A. de C.V. 24 Subsidiaries included in the Index

Officers: Manuael Saba Ades/Vice Chmn., CEO, Gabriel Saba. D'Jamus/Deputy Chief, Exec. VP, Oscar Gutierrez/Purchasing Dir., Hector Manzano/Dir. - Operations, Sales, Northern Zone, Alejandro Sadurni/CFO, Norberto Mouret/Dir. - Human Resources, Jesus Guerra/Legal Affairs Dir., Jorge Garcia/Information Technology Dir., Juan Restrepo/Dir. - Operations, Southern Zone

Directors: Manuael Saba Ades/Vice Chmn., CEO, Alberto Saba Ades/Vice Chmn., Moises Saba Ades/Vice Chmn., Isaac Saba Raffoul/Chmn., Jose Ellstein Japchik/Dir., Gabriel Alarcon Velazquez/71/Dir., Patricio Alejandro Trad Cepeda/36/Dir.

Owners: Insiders/85.00%, Isaac Saba Raffoul/85.00%

Financial Data: Fiscal Year End: 12/31   *Latest Annual Data:* 12/31/2006

Year	Sales		Net Income
2006	$2,182,784,000		$84,823,000
2005	$2,042,196,000		$64,963,000
2004	$1,833,609,000		$57,836,000
Curr. Assets:	$821,995,000	Curr. Liab.:	$389,978,000	
Plant, Equip.:	$106,814,000	Total Liab.:	$466,656,000	Indic. Yr. Divd.: $0.590
Total Assets:	$963,260,000	Net Worth:	$496,604,000	Debt/ Equity: NA

Grupo Financiero Galicia

Tte. Gral. Juan D Peron 456, Buenos Aires, 1038; *PH:* 54-1143437528; *http://* www.gfgsa.com

General - Incorporation	AR	Stock - Price on:12/24/2007	$10.02
Employees	6,849	Stock Exchange	NDQ
Auditor	Price Waterhouse & Co. S.R.L.	Ticker Symbol	GGAL
Stk Agt	Bank of New York	Outstanding Shares	124,140,000
Counsel	NA	E.P.S.	-$0.23
DUNS No.	NA	Shareholders	NA

Business: The group's principal activity is the provision of financial and banking services in Argentina and uruguay. It has also expanded its business to include insurance and credit cards. It has joined a unit of Portugal telecom to provide online b2b services in Latin America as well as life insurance selling through its alliance with hartford life.

Primary SIC and add'l.: 6211 6021

CIK No: 0001114700

Subsidiaries: Galicia (Cayman) Ltd, Galicia Pension Fund Ltd., Galicia Uruguay, Galval Agente de Valores S.A, Net Investment BV, Tradecom International N.V

Officers: Antonio R. Garces/Chmn., CEO, Jose Luis Gentile/Chief Accounting Officer, Pablo E. Firvida/VP - Investor Relations, Enrique M. Garda Olaciregui/CFO

Directors: Antonio R. Garces/Chmn., CEO, Federico Braun/Vice Chmn., Abel Ayerza/Dir., Luis O. Oddone/Dir., Luis S. Monsegur/Alternate Dir., Silvestre V. Moret/Dir., Eduardo J. Zimmermann/Dir., Maria Ofelia H. De Escasany/Alternate Dir., Pablo Gutierrez/Alternate Dir., Enrique C. Martin/Dir., Eduardo J. Escasany/Dir., Pedro A. Richards/Dir., Sergio Grinenco/Alternate Dir., Alejandro Rojas Lagarde/Alternate Dir.

Owners: Members of the families that are shareholders of EBA Holding S.A./10.70%, The Bank of New York/44.20%, Met AFJP S.A./5.20%, BBVA Consolidar AFJP S.A./5.80%, Banco Santander Central Hispano/8.60%, EBA Holding S.A./100.00%

Financial Data: Fiscal Year End: 12/31   *Latest Annual Data:* 12/31/2006

Year	Sales		Net Income
2006	$1,012,796,000		$1,150,532,000
2005	$1,003,119,000		$240,874,000
2004	$646,486,000		-$366,000
Curr. Assets:	$2,745,788,000	Curr. Liab.:	$3,632,181,000	
Plant, Equip.:	$197,245,000	Total Liab.:	$7,229,180,000	Indic. Yr. Divd.: NA
Total Assets:	$7,276,772,000	Net Worth:	$47,592,000	Debt/ Equity: NA

Grupo Industrial Maseca

Av La Clinica 2520, Edilicia Delta 1er. Pisa, Col Serloma, Monterey, 64710; *PH:* 52-8183993300; *http://* www.gimsa.com; *Email:* contactogimsa@gruma.com

General - IncorporationUnited Mexican States		Stock - Price on:12/24/2007	NA
Employees	NA	Stock Exchange	NYSE
Auditor	PricewaterhouseCoopers S.C	Ticker Symbol	NA
Stk Agt	NA	Outstanding Shares	NA
Counsel	NA	E.P.S.	NA
DUNS No.	81-140-3997	Shareholders	NA

Business: The group's principal activity is the production, distribution and sale of corn flour in Mexico which is then used in the preparation of tortillas and other related products. Its sole brand is maseca.

Primary SIC and add'l.: 2041 5149

CIK No: 0000914596

Subsidiaries: Arrendadora de Maquinaria de Chihuahua, S.A. de C.V., Compaa Nacional Almacenadora, S.A. de C.V., Harinera de Maz de Jalisco, S.A. de C.V., Harinera de Maz de Mexicali, S.A. de C.V., Harinera de Veracruz, S.A. de C.V., Harinera de Yucatn, S.A. de C.V., Molinos Azteca de Chalco, S.A. de C.V., Molinos Azteca de Chiapas, S.A. de.C.V., Molinos Azteca de Jalisco, S.A. de C.V., Molinos Azteca de Veracruz, S.A. de C.V., Molinos Azteca, S.A. de C.V.

Officers: Jairo Senise/CEO, Guillermo N. Cubas Cordero/VP - Marketing, Rafael A. Garate Munoz/COO - Agroinsa, Luis Lauro Garza Villezca/VP - Human Resources, Roberto Gonzalez Alcala/MD - Gruma Mexico, Christian Martinez Gonzalez/VP - Strategic Planning, Business Solutions, Ramiro Martinez Guerra/VP - Administration, Salvador Moreno Hernandez/VP - Institutional Relations, Raul A. Pelaez Cano/CFO, Juan A. Quiroga Garcia/Sr. Corporate Controller, Joaquin Rubio Lamas'/Sr. VP - Manufacturing, Procurement, Salvador V. Guajardo/General Counsel, Gillermo Arteaga MacKinney/VP - New Product Development, Juan A. Quiroga Garcia/Dir., Sr. Corporate Controller, Norma Morales/Investor Relations Officer (19 Officers included in Index)

Directors: Roberto Gonzalez Moreno/Chmn., Juan B. Guichard Michel/Dir., Jose De La Pena Y Angelini/Dir., Juan Diez-canedo Ruiz'/Dir., Juan A. Quiroga Garcia/Dir., Sr. Corporate Controller, Ernesto Enriquez Uso/Dir., Raul A. Pelaez Cano/Dir., Rodolfo F. Barrera Villarreal/Dir., Hector Rangel Domene/Dir.

Grupo Radio Centro

Constituyentes 1154, 7th Fl., Col Lomas Altas; *PH:* 52-5557284800; *http://* www.radiocentro.com

General		**Stock**	
Incorporation	Mexico	Price on:12/24/2007	$12.8965
Employees	422	Stock Exchange	NYSE
Auditor	Bernardo Soto Penafiel	Ticker Symbol	RC
Stk Agt	NA	Outstanding Shares	54,170,000
Counsel	Cleary Gottlieb Steen & Hamilton	E.P.S	$0.39
DUNS No.	81-196-9922	Shareholders	NA

Business: The group's principle activities are the production and broadcasting of musical programs, news, interviews and special event programs. Its revenue is derived primarily from the sale of commercial air time to advertising agencies and businesses. At 31-Dec-2003, the group owned 8 AM and 5 FM radio stations and manages and operates an additional FM station. Of the 14 radio stations it owns or operates, the group operates 5 AM and 6 FM stations in Mexico city, the remaining 3 stations, including 1 in Mexico city, are currently managed and operated by third parties pursuant to operating agreements. The group also acts as the national sales representative for, and provides programming to, a network of affiliates in Mexico under the trade name organizacion impulsora de radio. The group's quarterly revenue for Sep '07 was 177.28 millions of MXN.

Primary SIC and add'l.: 4832

CIK No: 0000906526

Subsidiaries: Desarrollos Empresariales, S.A. de C.V., Emisora 1150, S.A. de C.V., Enlaces Troncales, S.A. de C.V., Estacion Alfa, S.A. de C.V., GRC Medios, S.A. de C.V., GRC Publicidad, S.A. de C.V., GRC Radiodifusion, S.A., Inmobiliaria Radio Centro, S.A. de C.V., Promo Red, S.A. de C.V., Promotora Tecnica de Servicios Profesionales, S.A. de C.V., Publicidad y Promociones Internacionales, S.A. de C.V., Radio Centro Publicidad, S.A. de C.V., Radio Red, S.A. de C.V., Radio Red-FM, S.A. de C.V., Radio Sistema Mexicano, S.A. 24 Subsidiaries included in the Index

Officers: Sergio L. Gonzalez/Operations Dir., Luis A. Cepero/Audio Engineering Dir., Rodolfo C. Nava/Treasurer, Financial Information Mgr., Luis M. Carrasco N/Commercial Dir., Alvaro F. De La Mora/General Counsel, Ana Maria Aguirre/Dir., Advisor, Rafael G. Aguirre/Dir., Advisor, Jose Manuel Aguirre/Dir., Advisor

Directors: Maria Esther Aguirre/Vice Chmn., Francisco Aguirre/Chmn., Jose Manuel Aguirre/Dir., Advisor, Rafael G. Aguirre/Dir., Advisor, Thomas Harold R. Moffet/66/Dir., Luis De La F. Baca/62/Dir., Pedro N. Beltran/64/Dir., Ana Maria Aguirre/Dir., Advisor, Jose Manuel G. Aguirre/45/Dir., Luis Alfonso Cervantes Muniz/52/Dir.

Owners: Old Controlling Trust/7.20%, New Controlling Trust/44.40%

Financial Data: ***Fiscal Year End:***12/31 ***Latest Annual Data:*** 12/31/2006

Year	Sales	Net Income
2006	$73,677,000	$38,792,000
2005	$55,619,000	$6,107,000
2004	$49,454,000	$1,808,000

Curr. Assets:	$36,070,000	**Curr. Liab.:**	$24,152,000		
Plant, Equip.:	$42,163,000	**Total Liab.:**	$29,932,000	**Indic. Yr. Divd.:**	NA
Total Assets:	$152,909,000	**Net Worth:**	$122,977,000	**Debt/ Equity:**	NA

Grupo Simec S.A. de C.V.

Av. Lazaro Cardenas 601, Colonia La Nogalera, Guadalajara, Jalisco, 44440; ;
http:// www.gsimec.com.mx

General		**Stock**	
Incorporation		Price on:12/24/2007	$13.01
Employees	NA	Stock Exchange	AMEX
Auditor	NA	Ticker Symbol	SIM
Stk Agt	Bank of New York	Outstanding Shares	158,210,000
Counsel	NA	E.P.S	$0.93
DUNS No.	NA	Shareholders	NA

Business: The groups principle activities include manufacturing and producing small and medium-sized structural steel products. The groups products include I-beams, channels and angles, steel bars and rebar. The group operates from the United States, South America, Canada and Europe.

Primary SIC and add'l.: 3316 3315

CIK No:

Owners: SEYCO Estructuras S.A. de C.V./1.00%, Industrial de Herramientas CH, S.A. de C.V./1.00%, Aceros y Laminados Sigosa, S.A. de C.V/1.00%, Compaia Mexicana de Tubos, S.A. de C.V/1.00%, Public Investors./16.00%, Operadora de Manufacturera de Tubos, S.A. de C.V./5.00%, Industrias CH/55.00%, Tuberas Procarsa, S.A. de C.V./20.00%

Financial Data: ***Fiscal Year End:***NA ***Latest Annual Data:*** 12/31/2006

Year	Sales	Net Income
2006	$2,105,577,000	$199,137,000
2005	$1,198,109,000	$118,154,000
2004	$509,761,000	$123,683,000

Curr. Assets:	$883,860,000	**Curr. Liab.:**	$260,340,000	**P/E Ratio:**	24.43
Plant, Equip.:	$737,492,000	**Total Liab.:**	$697,469,000	**Indic. Yr. Divd.:**	NA
Total Assets:	$1,664,577,000	**Net Worth:**	$967,108,000	**Debt/ Equity:**	NA

Grupo Televisa, S.A.B.

Formerly: Grupo Televisa S.A.
Avenida Vasco De Quiroga No. 2000, Colonia Santa Fe, Mexico, DF 01210; ;
http:// www.televisa.com

General		**Stock**	
Incorporation	United Mexican States	Price on:12/24/2007	$28.52
Employees	NA	Stock Exchange	NYSE
Auditor	Ernst & Young LLP	Ticker Symbol	TV
Stk Agt	Bank of New York	Outstanding Shares	574,270,000
Counsel	NA	E.P.S	$1.20
DUNS No.	NA	Shareholders	NA

Business: The groups principle activity is to produce Spanish language television programs. The group operates through ten segments. In the year 2005, the group acquired Editora Cinco. The group operates from the United States, Mexico and Canada.

Primary SIC and add'l.: 4833

CIK No: 0000912892

Subsidiaries: Altavista Sur Inmobiliaria, S.A. de C.V., Apuestas Internacionales, S.A. de C.V., Argos Comunicacion, S.A. de C.V., Atmore Investment, A.V.V., Audiomaster 3000, S.A. de C.V., Bay City Television, Inc. ., BouncyNet, Inc. and subsidiary, Cablestar, S.A. de C.V. ., Cablevision, S.A. de C.V., Cadena de las Americas, S.A. de C.V., Cadena Radiodifusora Mexicana, S.A. de C.V., Cadena Televisora del Norte, S.A. de C.V., Campus America, S.A. de C.V., Canal 23 de Ensenada, S.A. de C.V. ., Canal XXI, S.A. de C.V. 193 Subsidiaries included in the Index

Officers: Emilio Azcarraga Jean/40/Chmn., CEO, Pres., Jean Paul Broc Haro/46/CEO - Cablevision, Eduardo Michelsen Delgado/37/CEO - Editorial Televisa, Javier Merida Guzman/CEO - Radiopolis, Alexandre Penna/CEO - Innova, Jorge Eduardo Murguia Orozco/58/VP - Production, Grupo Televisa, Rafael Carabias Principe/64/Dir., CFO - La Sexta, Julio Barba Hurtado/75/Dir., Legal Advisor to The Pres. - Grupo Televisa, Jose Antonio Baston Patino/40/Dir., Corporate VP - Television, Grupo Televisa, Alfonso De Angoitia Noriega/46/Dir., Exec. VP, Manuel Cutillas Covani/Dir. - Grupo Bacardi Limited, Bernardo Gomez Martinez/41/Dir., Exec. VP, Alejandro Quintero Iniguez/58/Dir., Corporate VP - Sales, Marketing, Grupo Televisa, Lucrecia Aramburuzabala Larregui De Fernandez/41/Private Investor, Felix Araujo Ramirez/57/Dir., VP - Telesistema Mexicano *(17 Officers included in Index)*

Directors: Emilio Azcarraga Jean/40/Chmn., CEO, Pres., Alfonso De Angoitia Noriega/46/Dir., Exec. VP, Julio Barba Hurtado/75/Dir., Legal Advisor to The Pres. - Grupo Televisa, Jose Antonio Baston Patino/40/Dir., Corporate VP - Television, Grupo Televisa, Alberto Bailleres Gonzalez/77/Dir., Manuel Jorge Cutillas/76/Dir., Carlos Fernandez Gonzalez/42/Dir., Bernardo Gomez Martinez/41/Dir., Exec. VP, Claudio X. Gonzalez Laporte/Dir., Roberto Hernandez Ramirez/66/Dir., Enrique Krauze Kleinbort/61/Dir., German Larrea Mota Velasco/55/Dir., Gilberto Perezalonso Cifuentes/65/Dir., Alejandro Quintero Iniguez/58/Dir., Corporate VP - Sales, Marketing, Grupo Televisa, Fernando Senderos Mestre/58/Dir. *(35 Directors included in Index)*

Owners: Capital Research and Management Co/5.00%, Azcrraga Trust/0.10%, Cascade Investment, L.L.C/5.10%, Azcrraga Trust/0.10%, Cascade Investment, L.L.C/4.90%, Inbursa Trust/2.50%, Inbursa Trust/2.70%, Azcrraga Trust/0.10%, Inbursa Trust/2.70%, Azcrraga Trust/43.70%, Cascade Investment, L.L.C/2.60%, Capital Research and Management Co/2.70%, Morgan Stanley Investment Management Inc/5.90%, Cascade Investment, L.L.C/5.10%, Morgan Stanley Investment Management Inc/3.00% *(20 Owners included in Index)*

Financial Data: ***Fiscal Year End:***12/31 ***Latest Annual Data:*** 12/31/2006

Year	Sales	Net Income
2006	$3,520,075,000	$743,058,000
2005	$3,020,737,000	$634,696,000
2004	$2,629,488,000	$311,490,000

Curr. Assets:	$4,408,051,000	**Curr. Liab.:**	$2,314,832,000	**P/E Ratio:**	11.94
Plant, Equip.:	$1,899,535,000	**Total Liab.:**	$4,455,255,000	**Indic. Yr. Divd.:**	$0.160
Total Assets:	$7,658,045,000	**Net Worth:**	$3,202,791,000	**Debt/ Equity:**	NA

Grupo TMM

Avenida De La Cuspideno. 4755, Col. Parque del Pedregal, C.P. 14010, Mexico City, 14010;
PH: 52-5556298866; ***http://*** www.grupotmm.com; ***Email:*** grupotmm@tmm.com.mx

General		**Stock**	
Incorporation	Mexico	Price on:12/24/2007	$3.48
Employees	5,054	Stock Exchange	NYSE
Auditor	Pricewaterhousecoopers S.c.	Ticker Symbol	TMM
Stk Agt	Citibank N.A	Outstanding Shares	56,960,000
Counsel	NA	E.P.S	-$0.79
DUNS No.	NA	Shareholders	NA

Business: The group's principle activities are the provision of specialized maritime transportation services which includes transport of vehicles and trucks, refined petroleum and chemical products, chartering of supply ships and ship lorry services; land operations which include autotransport and logistics services; and port, terminal and railway operations services. The group's quarterly revenue for Sep '07 was 76.92 millions of USD.

Primary SIC and add'l.: 4010 4499 4231 4789

CIK No: 0001163560

Subsidiaries: Administracion Porturaria Integral de Acapulco S.A. de C.V., Autotransportacion y Distribucion Logistica, S.A. de C.V. (Trucking), Lacto Comercial Organizada, S.A. de C.V. (Trucking), Maritima Mexicana, S.A. de C.V., Marmex Offshore, S.A. de C.V., New Marmex, S.A. de C.V., Seglo, S.A. de C.V. (Logistics), Servicios Mexicanos en Remolcadores, S.A. de C.V. (Tugboats), Terminal Maritima de Tuxpan, S.A. de C.V. (Ports), TMM Logistics, S.A. de C.V. (Logistics), Transportacin Martima Mexicana, S.A. de C.V.

Officers: Brad L. Skinner/60/CEO, Sr. VP, TMM Logistics, Investor Relations, Jose F. Serrano/68/Chmn., CEO, Javier Segovia/47/Pres., Elvira Ruiz Carreno/54/Dir. - Corporate Audit, Juan Fernandez/39/CFO, Horacio Reyes/Dir. - Administrative, Planning Corporate, Silverio Di Costanzo/52/Dir. - Maritime Transportation, Ignacio Rodriguez/52/Dir., Sec., Juan Vergara/50/Corp. Dir. - Human Resources, Marcoflavio Rigada/36/Chief Legal Officer, Miguel Casanueva/58/Dir. - Ports, Terminals

Directors: Jose F. Serrano/68/Chmn., CEO, Ramon Serrano/Vice Chmn., Maria Serrano/Vice Chmn., Sergio Chedraui/32/Dir., Antonio Cue Sanchez-Navarro/41/Alternate Dir., Jaime Zabludovsky/52/Alternate Dir., Paloma Serrano De Chedarui/27/Alternate Dir., Jose Serrano Cuevas/28/Alternate Dir., Elvira Ruiz Carreno/54/Dir. - Corporate Audit, Jose Luis Salas/54/Dir., Lorenzo Cue Sanchez-Navarro/Dir., Luis Martinez/67/Dir., Ignacio Rodriguez/52/Dir., Sec.

Owners: Ramn Serrano Segovia/7.00%, Steinberg Asset Management/5.70%, Jos F. Serrano Segovia/11.40%, Beck Mack & Oliver./6.90%

Financial Data: ***Fiscal Year End:***12/31 ***Latest Annual Data:*** 12/31/2006

Year	Sales	Net Income
2006	$248,148,000	$75,550,000
2005	$306,599,000	$111,618,000
2004	$251,001,000	-$115,793,000

Curr. Assets:	$168,686,000	**Curr. Liab.:**	$102,544,000		
Plant, Equip.:	$282,811,000	**Total Liab.:**	$452,788,000	**Indic. Yr. Divd.:**	NA
Total Assets:	$635,615,000	**Net Worth:**	$182,827,000	**Debt/ Equity:**	NA

Gryphon Gold Gorporation

1130 W Pender St., Ste. 810, Vancouver, BC, V6E A4A; ***PH:*** 1-888-261-2229;
Fax: 1-604-608-3262; ***http://*** www.gryphongold.com

General		**Stock**	
Incorporation	NV	Price on:12/24/2007	$0.75
Employees	NA	Stock Exchange	OTC
Auditor	Ernst & Young LLP	Ticker Symbol	GYPH
Stk Agt.	Computershare Investor Services LLC	Outstanding Shares	NA
Counsel	NA	E.P.S	NA
DUNS No.	NA	Shareholders	NA

Business: The groups principal activities include acquiring, exploring, and developing gold properties. The group operates from the United States.

Primary SIC and add'l.: 1040

CIK No: 0001262751

Subsidiaries: Borealis Mining Company

Officers: Mike Longinotti/CFO/$398,237.00, Raj Kang/Corporate Controller, Treasurer, Sec., Steve Craig/VP - Exploration, Geological Team/$213,359.00, Dave Harvey/District Exploration Mgr. - Geological Team, Roger Steininger/Chief Consulting Geologist, Anthony D.J. Ker/Dir., Exec. VP, Sec., Treasurer, Jerry Baughman/VP - Corporate Development, Lisanna Lewis/Office Mgr., Matt Bender/VP - Borealis Project Development, Glen Kile/Consultant, Malcolm Gander/Consultant, Susan Judy/Consultant

Directors: Albert J. Matter/Chmn., Donald Gentry/Dir., Donald Ranta/64/Dir., Richard Hughes/Dir., Rohan Hazelton/Dir., Anthony D.J. Ker/Dir., Exec. VP, Sec., Treasurer

Owners: Anthony Ker/2.77%, Geologic Resource Fund/10.77%, Albert Matter/4.32%, Gerry W. Baughman and Fabiola Baughman/9.99%, Standard Bank plc/5.57%, Insiders/11.02%, Michael Longinotti/0.78%

Financial Data: *Fiscal Year End:*03/31   *Latest Annual Data:* 03/31/2007

Year	Sales	Net Income
2007	NA	-$8,737,000
2006	NA	-$5,602,000

Curr. Assets:	$9,582,000	**Curr. Liab.:**	$1,208,000		
Plant, Equip.:	$2,051,000	**Total Liab.:**	$1,227,000	**Indic. Yr. Divd.:**	NA
Total Assets:	$11,693,000	**Net Worth:**	$10,466,000	**Debt/ Equity:**	0.0032

GS AgriFuels Corp

1 Penn Plz Ste. 1612, New York, NY, 10119; *PH:* 1-212-994-5374; *Fax:* 1-646-572-6336; *http://* www.gs-agrifuels.com; *Email:* info@gs-agrifuels.com

General - Incorporation	DE	**Stock**- Price on:12/24/2007	$1.15
Employees	NA	Stock Exchange	OTC
Auditor	Rosenberg,Baker & Berman and Co.	Ticker Symbol	GSGF
Stk Agt	David Gonzalez	Outstanding Shares	29,010,000
Counsel	NA	E.P.S.	-$0.26
DUNS No.	NA	Shareholders	NA

Business: The groups principal activities include producing and selling clean fuels from agriproducts. The services of the group include fuel production and oilseeds crushing. Products of the group include biodiesel, ethanol and synthetic fuel. The group operates from the United States.

Primary SIC and add'l.: 2899

CIK No: 0001120802

Officers: Thomas Scozzafava/CEO, Pres., Paul T. Miller/VP - Oilseed Processing, Pres. - Sustainable Systems, Robert N. Turnbull/GM, Edward R. Carroll/CFO

Directors: Kevin Kreisler/Chmn.

Owners: Kevin Kreisler/100.00%, Thomas W. Scozzafava

Financial Data: *Fiscal Year End:*12/31   *Latest Annual Data:* 12/31/2006

Year	Sales	Net Income
2006	$52,000	-$2,549,000
2005	NA	-$425,000
2004	NA	-$56,000

Curr. Assets:	$3,225,000	**Curr. Liab.:**	$13,795,000		
Plant, Equip.:	NA	**Total Liab.:**	$33,203,000	**Indic. Yr. Divd.:**	NA
Total Assets:	$29,631,000	**Net Worth:**	-$3,572,000	**Debt/ Equity:**	NA

GS Cleantech Corp

Formerly: Veridium Corp
One Penn Plz., Ste. 1612, New York, NY, 10119; *PH:* 1-212-994-5374; *http://* www.veridium.com

General - Incorporation	DE	**Stock**- Price on:12/24/2007	$0.006
Employees	58	Stock Exchange	NA
Auditor	Rosenberg Rich Baker Berman & Co.	Ticker Symbol	NA
Stk Agt	American Stock Transfer & Trust Co.	Outstanding Shares	410,660,000
Counsel	NA	E.P.S.	-$0.024
DUNS No.	11-286-1422	Shareholders	NA

Business: The group's principal activity is to provide environmental services. It uses patented and proprietary green technologies to minimize and eliminate the need for disposal and reduce the burden on natural resources by recycling and mining industrial hazardous wastes. The group's business model is to develop the domestic hazardous waste management market organically and acquisitively, leveraging the operational efficiencies made possible by its unique green technologies to recycle, reuse and mine all reusable resources from hazardous wastes in safe, compliant and profitable manner. On 22-Jan-2003, the group acquired vulcan waste systems inc.

Primary SIC and add'l.: 4959 3341

CIK No: 0001269127

Subsidiaries: American Metals Recovery, Corp, Veridium Environmental Corporation, Veridium Recovery Systems

Officers: David Winsness/39/CEO, Pres., Kevin Kreisler/35/Chmn., CFO

Directors: Kevin Kreisler/35/Chmn., CFO

Owners: Insiders, Insiders/100.00%, Kevin Kreisler/100.00%

Financial Data: *Fiscal Year End:*12/31   *Latest Annual Data:* 12/31/2006

Year	Sales	Net Income
2006	$14,435,000	-$9,869,000
2005	$13,962,000	-$5,698,000
2004	$13,195,000	-$6,971,000

Curr. Assets:	$5,006,000	**Curr. Liab.:**	$20,135,000		
Plant, Equip.:	$2,848,000	**Total Liab.:**	$23,170,000	**Indic. Yr. Divd.:**	NA
Total Assets:	$14,380,000	**Net Worth:**	-$8,790,000	**Debt/ Equity:**	NA

GS Energy Corp

1 Penn Plz Ste. 1612, New York, NY, 10119; *PH:* 1-212-994-5374; *Fax:* 1-646-572-6336; *http://* www.gs-energy.com

General - Incorporation	DE	**Stock** - Price on:12/24/2007	$0.0007
Employees	NA	Stock Exchange	OTC
Auditor	Rich Baker Berman & Company, P.A.	Ticker Symbol	GSEG
Stk Agt	Olde Monmouth Stk Trnsfer Co. Inc.	Outstanding Shares	2,500,000,000
Counsel	NA	E.P.S.	$0.00
DUNS No.	NA	Shareholders	NA

Business: The groups principle activity is to manufacture specialty metal. The services of the group include bulb eater product line, EasyPak Recycling Program, pre-paid ground transportation services. The group operates from North America.

Primary SIC and add'l.: 3441

CIK No: 0001127242

Owners: Insiders/7.70%, Insiders/100.00%, Kevin Kreisler/100.00%, James Grainer/7.70%, Insiders/100.00%, Kevin Kreisler/100.00%

Financial Data: *Fiscal Year End:*12/31   *Latest Annual Data:* 12/31/2006

Year	Sales	Net Income
2006	$5,845,000	-$1,023,000
2005	$2,427,000	-$1,876,000
2004	$1,000	-$277,000

Curr. Assets:	$2,236,000	**Curr. Liab.:**	$1,981,000		
Plant, Equip.:	$945,000	**Total Liab.:**	$2,343,000	**Indic. Yr. Divd.:**	NA
Total Assets:	$4,087,000	**Net Worth:**	$1,744,000	**Debt/ Equity:**	0.2159

GS Financial Corp

3798 Veterans Blvd., Metairie, LA, 70002; *PH:* 1-504-457-6220; *Fax:* 1-504-457-6227; *http://* www.gsfinancialcorp.com

General - Incorporation	LA	**Stock**- Price on:12/24/2007	$20.43
Employees	43	Stock Exchange	NDQ
Auditor	Laporte, Sehrt, Romig & Hand	Ticker Symbol	GSLA
Stk Agt	Registrar & Transfer Co	Outstanding Shares	1,230,000
Counsel	Bruce A. Scott	E.P.S.	$1.61
DUNS No.	84-064-1963	Shareholders	NA

Business: The group's principal activity is financial services to individuals, corporate entities and other organizations. The group operates through its subsidiary, guaranty savings and homestead association. The services are provided to commercial, small business and retail customers, offering a variety of transaction and savings deposit products and secured loan products.

Primary SIC and add'l.: 6035 6712

CIK No: 0001029630

Subsidiaries: Guaranty Savings and Homestead Association.

Officers: Lettie R. Moll/Corp. Sec./$148,358.00

Owners: Bruce A. Scott/13.20%, Stephen L. Cory/1.90%, Lettie R. Moll/1.40%, Andrew J. Bower, Insiders/31.20%, Ralph Weber/1.90%, Albert J. Zahn/3.00%, Edward J. Bourgeois, Guaranty Savings Bank 401(k) Plan/14.20%, Philip J. Timyan/9.90%, Jeffrey A. Miller/5.20%, Bradford A. Glazer/2.80%, Donald C. Scott/10.30%, Hayden W. Wren, Stephen E. Wessel

Financial Data: *Fiscal Year End:*12/31   *Latest Annual Data:* 03/31/2007

Year	Sales	Net Income
2007	NA	NA
2006	NA	NA
2005	$10,467,000	-$3,676,000

Curr. Assets:	$13,121,000	**Curr. Liab.:**	$139,796,000	**P/E Ratio:**	12.69
Plant, Equip.:	$4,042,000	**Total Liab.:**	$141,216,000	**Indic. Yr. Divd.:**	$0.400
Total Assets:	$168,380,000	**Net Worth:**	$27,164,000	**Debt/ Equity:**	NA

GSE Systems Inc

7133 Rutherford Rd., Ste. 200, Baltimore, MD, 21244; *PH:* 1-410-277-3740; *Fax:* 1-410-277-5287; *http://* www.gses.com; *Email:* investor@gses.com

General - Incorporation	DE	**Stock**- Price on:12/24/2007	$6.55
Employees	135	Stock Exchange	AMEX
Auditor	KPMG LLP	Ticker Symbol	GVP
Stk Agt	Continental Stock Transfer & Trust Co	Outstanding Shares	13,120,000
Counsel	NA	E.P.S.	$0.073
DUNS No.	82-643-3658	Shareholders	NA

Business: The group's principal activity is to provides simulation solutions and services to the nuclear and fossil electric utility industry, chemical and petrochemical industries. The group also provides plant monitoring, security access and control, and signal analysis monitoring and optimization software primarily to the power industry. The products include java applications and development environment, simexec, extreme i/s, pegasus surveillance and diagnosis system, simon and vista pin. The customers include ameren, Arizona public service, carolina power and light company, commonwealth edison company, eskom South Africa, karnaraft sakerhet & utbildning ab, korean electric power company, nationalina elecktrischecka kompania, orgrez sc, battelle's pacific northwest national laboratory, Taiwan power company, and west bengal development corp.

Primary SIC and add'l.: 7372 7373

CIK No: 0000944480

Subsidiaries: GSE Engineering Systems (Beijing) Company, Ltd, GSE Erudite Software, Inc., GSE Government & Military Simulation Systems, Inc., GSE Power Systems AB, GSE Power Systems, Inc., GSE Process Solutions, BV, GSE Process Solutions, Inc., GSE Services Company LLC, MSHI, Inc.

Officers: John V. Moran/Dir., CEO/$371,765.00, Gill R. Grady/Sr. VP/$211,350.00, Harold D. Paris/Sr. VP, Jeffery G. Hough/CFO - CPA/$205,810.00, Chin-Our Jerry Jen/Pres./$201,088.00, Jean-Marc Holt/MD - GSE Power Systems AB, Michael Feldman/Dir., Exec. VP

Directors: John V. Moran/Dir., CEO, Jerome I. Feldman/Chmn., Sheldon L. Glashow/Dir., Michael Feldman/Dir., Exec. VP, Scott Greenberg/Dir., Roger Hagengruber/Dir., Joseph Lewis/Dir., George Pedersen/Dir., Lee Tawes/Dir.

Owners: Chin-Our Jerry Jen, Wells Fargo & Company/12.30%, Insiders/9.10%, Jack Silver/5.10%, Michael D. Feldman/2.50%, Jeffery G. Hough, Sheldon L. Glashow, Westcliff Capital Management, LLC/10.60%, Scott N. Greenberg, Hal D. Paris, Kaizen Management, LP/7.60%, Lee O. Tawes/3.10%, Gill R. Grady, Peninsula Capital Management, LP/5.40%, Jerome I. Feldman/2.50% *(20 Owners included in Index)*

Financial Data: *Fiscal Year End:*12/31   *Latest Annual Data:* 12/31/2006

Year	Sales	Net Income
2006	$27,502,000	-$346,000
2005	$21,950,000	-$4,795,000
2004	$29,514,000	$118,000

Curr. Assets:	$12,299,000	**Curr. Liab.:**	$10,836,000	**P/E Ratio:**	78.92
Plant, Equip.:	$354,000	**Total Liab.:**	$11,087,000	**Indic. Yr. Divd.:**	NA
Total Assets:	$18,448,000	**Net Worth:**	$7,361,000	**Debt/ Equity:**	0.0456

GSI Commerce Inc

935 1st Ave., King of Prussia, PA, 19406; *PH:* 1-610-491-7000; *http://* www.gsicommerce.com

General - Incorporation	DE	Stock- Price on:12/24/2007	$22.78
Employees	2,521	Stock Exchange	NDQ
Auditor	Deloitte & Touche LLP	Ticker Symbol	GSIC
Stk Agt	American Stock Transfer & Trust Co.	Outstanding Shares	46,360,000
Counsel	NA	E.P.S.	$1.09
DUNS No.	17-818-5393	Shareholders	NA

Business: The group's principal activity is to provide an e-commerce platform that enables retailers, branded manufacturers, entertainment companies and professional sports organizations to operate e-commerce businesses. The e-commerce platform includes Web site design, e-commerce technology, managed hosting, order fulfillment, customer service, merchandising and order management, online merchandising, customer relationship management, content development and online marketing. The e-commerce also includes the sale of products through online retail stores over the Internet and direct response television campaigns. The group operates e-commerce businesses for 40 partners in the United States. The group generally operates each of these e-commerce businesses based on one of three models, or a combination of those models — gsi-owned inventory model, partner-owned inventory model or business-to-business model.

Primary SIC and add'l.: 7372 5091 3149 7375 5139

CIK No: 0000828750

Subsidiaries: 1075 First Global Associates, LLC, 7601 Trade Port Drive, LLC, 935 HQ Associates, LLC, 935 KOP Associates, LLC, ASFD Corporate Gifts, Inc., ASFD, Inc., Blue Route, Inc., Global-QVC Solutions, Inc, GSI Call Center, Inc., GSI Commerce Sales, Inc, GSI Commerce Services, Inc, GSI Commerce Solutions, Inc, GSI Consignment Services, Inc, GSI Equipment, Inc., GSI Legacy Holdings, Inc. 18 Subsidiaries included in the Index

Officers: Michael G. Rubin/Chmn., CEO, Pres./$923,575.00, Robert W. Liewald/Exec. VP - Merchandising, Steven Davis/Exec. VP - International, Pres. - GSI Commerce Europe, Stephen J. Gold/CIO, Exec. VP/$884,018.00, Jim Flanagan/Exec. VP - Human Resources, Damon Mintzer/Exec. VP - Sales/$859,136.00, Arthur H. Miller/Exec. VP, General Counsel, Michael R. Conn/Sr. VP - Finance, CFO/$676,740.00, Robert Wuesthoff/Exec. VP - Global Operations/$746,614.00, Greg Ryan/Dir. - Corporate Communications

Directors: Michael G. Rubin/Chmn., CEO, Pres., Jeffrey F. Rayport/Dir., Michael S. Perlis/Dir., Ronald D. Fisher/Dir., Mark S. Menell/Dir., Jeffrey M. Branman/Dir., Michael J. Donahue/Dir., John A. Hunter/Dir., Andrea M. Weiss/Dir.

Owners: Insiders/19.00%, Damon Mintzer, Mark S. Menell, John A. Hunter, FMR Corp./9.96%, Ronald D. Fisher, Robert Wuesthoff, Robert J. Blyskal, Stephen J. Gold, Michael J. Donahue, Michael S. Perlis, Liberty Media Corporation/19.97%, Andrea M. Weiss, Comcast Corporation/5.57%, Prudential Financial, Inc./6.22% (*21 Owners included in Index*)

Financial Data: Fiscal Year End:12/31   Latest Annual Data: 12/30/2006

Year	Sales	Net Income
2006	$609,553,000	$53,701,000
2005	$440,392,000	$2,699,000

Curr. Assets:	$218,683,000	Curr. Liab.:	$108,879,000	P/E Ratio:	20.71
Plant, Equip.:	$87,851,000	Total Liab.:	$179,473,000	Indic. Yr. Divd.:	NA
Total Assets:	$332,646,000	Net Worth:	$153,173,000	Debt/ Equity:	0.3379

GSI Group Inc

39 Manning Rd., Billerica, MA, 01821; *PH:* 1-978-439-5511; *Fax:* 1-978-663-0044; *http://* www.gsig.com

General - Incorporation	NB	Stock- Price on:12/24/2007	$10.22
Employees	1,347	Stock Exchange	NDQ
Auditor	Ernst & Young LLP	Ticker Symbol	GSIG
Stk Agt	Computershare Trust Co	Outstanding Shares	42,370,000
Counsel	NA	E.P.S.	$0.45
DUNS No.	NA	Shareholders	NA

Business: The group's principle activities are the designing, developing and marketing laser based advanced manufacturing systems. The group operates in two segments: laser systems and waveprecision. The laser systems designs, develops, manufactures and markets laser-based advanced manufacturing systems and components. This segment also includes computer-chip memory repair processing, wafer and die marking, component placement on ace-mount printed circuits, hybrid circuit trim and circuit trim on silicon. These products are sold to semiconductor and electronic industries. The waveprecision provides precision optics for dense wave division multiplexing networks. The trademarks and trade names of the group include wafermark (R), super softmark (R), drillstar(R) and waveprecision. The group's products are sold in the United States, Europe, Japan, latin and South America, Asia-pacific and other countries. The group's quarterly revenue for Sep'07 was 83.95 millions of USD.

Primary SIC and add'l.: 3674 3699 3679 7379 4899

CIK No: 0001076930

Subsidiaries: 124988 Ontario Inc., General Scanning Limited, General Scanning Securities Corp., General Scanning VI Export Corp. -FSC, GSI Life Science Trust, GSI Lumonics Asia Pacific Ltd., GSI Lumonics Corporation, GSI Lumonics GmbH, GSI Lumonics Hungary Trade Company Limited by Shares, GSI Lumonics Japan KK, GSI Lumonics Life Science Trust, GSI Lumonics Limited, GSI Lumonics Trust Inc., GSI Lumonics, SARL, GSLI Investments, Inc. 25 Subsidiaries included in the Index

Officers: Sergio Edelstein/Dir., CEO, Pres./$817,977.00, Thomas R. Swain/62/Pres. - Finance/$407,918.00, Kurt A. Pelsue/55/CTO, VP - Technology, Felix I. Stukalin/VP - Business Development, Robert L. Bowen/CFO, VP/$533,165.00, Daniel J. Lyne/VP, General Counsel/$449,167.00, Nino Federico/57/VP, GM/$492,964.00, Anthony J. Bellantuoni/VP - Human Resources, Stephen Kew/54/MD - GSI Group Laser Division, Ray Sansouci/57/VP - General Manger, Precision Motion Division

Directors: Sergio Edelstein/Dir., CEO, Pres., Richard B. Black/73/Dir., Phillip A. Griffiths/69/Dir., Byron O. Pond/71/Dir., Benjamin J. Virgilio/68/Dir., Garrett A. Garrettson/64/Dir., Marina Hatsopoulos/42/Dir.

Owners: Richard B. Black, Felix Stukalin, Thomas R. Swain, Insiders/5.00%, Stephen Webb, Franklin Resources Inc./9.30%, T. Rowe Price Associates Inc./5.30%, Ray Sansouci, Charles D. Winston, FMR Corp/6.30%, Byron O. Pond, Phillip A. Griffiths, Sumitomo Heavy Industries Ltd./9.80%, Garrett A. Garrettson, Stephen Kew (*24 Owners included in Index*)

Financial Data: Fiscal Year End:12/31   Latest Annual Data: 09/28/2007

Year	Sales	Net Income
2007	$83,952,000	$7,772,000
2006	$79,458,000	$4,725,000
2005	$260,784,000	$9,657,000

Curr. Assets:	$290,803,000	Curr. Liab.:	$43,303,000	P/E Ratio:	25.55
Plant, Equip.:	$33,511,000	Total Liab.:	$68,332,000	Indic. Yr. Divd.:	NA
Total Assets:	$411,405,000	Net Worth:	$343,073,000	Debt/ Equity:	0.0040

GSV Inc

191 Post Rd. W, Westport, CT, 06880; *PH:* 1-203-221-2690; *Fax:* 1-203-221-2691; *http://* www.gsv.com; *Email:* contact@gsv.com

General - Incorporation	DE	Stock- Price on:12/24/2007	$0.22
Employees	1	Stock Exchange	OTC
Auditor	UHY LLP	Ticker Symbol	GSVI
Stk Agt	American Stock Transfer & Trust Co.	Outstanding Shares	7,500,000
Counsel	NA	E.P.S.	$0.01
DUNS No.	87-822-1191	Shareholders	NA

Business: The group's principal activity is to manage and develop oil and gas properties. The group is also seeking out new business operations through an acquisition and merger. The group operates solely in the United States.

Primary SIC and add'l.: 1389 6552

CIK No: 0001051591

Subsidiaries: Cybershop Holding Corp., Cybershop, LLC

Officers: Gilad Gat/CEO, Michael J. Moldowan/Consultant, Walter Epstein/Consultant, James Morgan Cole/Geologist, Consultant, Ron De Jong/Investor Information

Directors: Sagi Matza/Chmn.

Owners: Sagi Matza/76.40%, Gilad Gat, Yoav Bitter, Doron Ofer/16.00%, Insiders/77.00%

Financial Data: Fiscal Year End:12/31   Latest Annual Data: 12/31/2006

Year	Sales	Net Income
2006	$264,000	-$166,000
2005	$714,000	-$157,000
2004	$431,000	-$535,000

Curr. Assets:	$142,000	Curr. Liab.:	$744,000		
Plant, Equip.:	$197,000	Total Liab.:	$944,000	Indic. Yr. Divd.:	NA
Total Assets:	$2,706,000	Net Worth:	$1,762,000	Debt/ Equity:	0.1119

GTC Biotherapeutics Inc

175 Crossing Blvd., Framingham, MA, 01702; *PH:* 1-508-620-9700; *Fax:* 1-508-370-3797; *http://* www.gtc-bio.com

General - Incorporation	MA	Stock- Price on:12/24/2007	$1.19
Employees	143	Stock Exchange	NDQ
Auditor	PricewaterhouseCoopers LLP	Ticker Symbol	GTCB
Stk Agt	American Stock Transfer & Trust Co.	Outstanding Shares	77,910,000
Counsel	NA	E.P.S.	-$0.44
DUNS No.	80-793-4260	Shareholders	NA

Business: The group's principal activity is the application of transgenic technology to the development and production of recombinant proteins for therapeutic and other biomedical uses. It has several partnerships with pharmaceutical and other biotechnology companies to develop monoclonal antibodies and immunoglobulin (ig) fusion proteins transgenically. The group's operations in goat husbandry, breeding, milking and clarification to intermediate bulk material occur at the company's biopharmaceutical farm production facilities in central Massachusetts. It also develops transgenic production processes for other proteins, including a malaria merozoite surface protein (msp-1) for use in a malaria vaccine. Its corporate partners include abbott, alexion, bristol-myers squibb, centocor, elan, immunogen, and progenics.

Primary SIC and add'l.: 8071 2836 8731

CIK No: 0000904973

Subsidiaries: ATIII LLC, GTC Biotherapeutics U.K. Ltd., GTC Holding Ltd., GTC Japan Limited, GTC NZ Limited, GTC Securities Corporation, Taurus hSA LLC, TSI Corporation

Officers: Geoffrey F. Cox/Chmn., CEO, Pres./$667,518.00, John B. Green/Sr. VP - Finance, CFO/$402,829.00, Thomas E. Newberry/VP - Corporate Communications, Daniel S. Woloshen/Sr. VP, General Counsel/$337,461.00, Carol A. Ziomek/VP - Development, Suzanne Groet/VP - Therapeutic Protein Development, Gregory Liposky/Sr. VP - Operations/$389,357.00, Richard A. Scotland/Sr. VP - Regulatory Affairs, Harry M. Meade/Sr. VP - Research, Development/$394,800.00, Francesca Devellis/Contact - Media, Investor Relations, Ashley Lawton/VP - Business Development, Frederick J. Finnegan/VP - Commercial Development

Directors: Geoffrey F. Cox/Chmn., CEO, Pres., Robert W. Baldridge/Dir., James A. Geraghty/Dir., Michael J. Landine/Dir., Alan W. Tuck/Dir., Kenneth A. Bauer/Dir., Marvin L. Miller/Dir., Francis J. Bullock/Dir., Pamela W. McNamara/Dir., Christian Bechon/Dir.

Owners: LFB Biotechnologies, S.A.S.U/19.80%, William Harris Investors, Inc./8.90%, Michael J. Landine, James A. Geraghty, Genzyme Corporation/5.50%, Christian Bchon/100.00%, Christian Bchon/19.80%, John B. Green, Daniel S. Woloshen, Francis J. Bullock, Robert W. Baldridge, Gregory F. Liposky, Alan W. Tuck, Pamela W. McNamara, Marvin L. Miller (*20 Owners included in Index*)

Financial Data: Fiscal Year End:01/01   Latest Annual Data: 12/31/2006

Year	Sales	Net Income
2006	$6,128,000	-$35,345,000
2005	$6,626,000	-$29,493,000

Curr. Assets:	$48,218,000	Curr. Liab.:	$18,836,000		
Plant, Equip.:	$15,336,000	Total Liab.:	$35,279,000	Indic. Yr. Divd.:	NA
Total Assets:	$73,235,000	Net Worth:	$37,956,000	Debt/ Equity:	0.2885

GTC Telecom Corp

PO Box 1680, Costa Mesa, CA, 92628; *PH:* 1-714-549-7700; *Fax:* 1-714-549-7707; *http://* www.gtctelecom.com; *Email:* comments@teamgtc.com

General - Incorporation	NV	Stock- Price on:12/24/2007	NA
Employees	NA	Stock Exchange	OTC
Auditor	Squar, Milner, Raehl & Williamson	Ticker Symbol	GTCC
Stk Agt	Alpha Tech Stock Transfer Ltd	Outstanding Shares	NA
Counsel	NA	E.P.S.	NA
DUNS No.	NA	Shareholders	NA

Business: The group's principal activities are to provide telecommunication services and Internet related services. The group's telecommunication related services includes providing long distance telephone and calling card services under a variety of plans such as outbound service, inbound toll-free 800 service and dedicated private line service for data. The group's Internet related services provide international PC-to-phone telecommunication services, Web page hosting and a variety of Internet related services. The group provides services to small and medium sized businesses and residential customers throughout the United States.

Primary SIC and add'l.: 4813 7375

CIK No: 0001081919

Subsidiaries: CallingPlanet.com, Inc., Curbside Communications, Inc., ecallingcards.com, Inc., Perfexa Solutions, Inc.

Officers: Clayton Miller/Investor Relations

Owners: Rapaport Family Trust/11.88%, Gerald A. DeCiccio/1.72%, Insiders/18.32%, Reet Trust/6.61%, Eric Clemons/3.41%, Paul Sandhu/13.19%

Curr. Assets:	$564,000	Curr. Liab.:	$5,490,000		
Plant, Equip.:	$340,000	Total Liab.:	$5,734,000	Indic. Yr. Divd.:	NA
Total Assets:	$978,000	Net Worth:	-$5,005,000	Debt/ Equity:	NA

GTECH Holdings Corp

55 Tecnology Way, West Greenwich, RI, 02817; **PH:** 1-401-392-1000; **http://** www.gtech.com

General - Incorporation	DE	Stock- Price on:12/24/2007	NA
Employees	NA	Stock Exchange	NA
Auditor	Ernst & Young LLP	Ticker Symbol	NA
Stk Agt	Bank of New York	Outstanding Shares	NA
Counsel	Cowards & Angell	E.P.S.	NA
DUNS No.	60-820-8286	Shareholders	NA

Business: The group's principal activity is to provide online lottery transaction processing systems. It provides a full range of lottery technology services, including the design, assembly, installation, operation, maintenance and marketing of online lottery systems and instant ticket support systems. Its lottery system consists of numerous lottery terminals located in retail outlets, central computer systems, systems software and game software and communications equipment which connects the terminals and the central computer systems. The group provides its products and services to governmental lottery authorities and governmental licensees. It operates online lottery systems for or supplies equipment and services to the online lottery authorities in the United States. The group acquired Spielo Manufacturing Incorporated on 30-Apr-2004, on 05-May-2004 Leeward Islands Lottery Holding Company Inc and on 09-Sep-2004, acquired Billbird S.A.

Primary SIC and add'l.: 7379 7999 3575

CIK No: 0000857323

Subsidiaries: Anguilla Lottery and Gaming Company, Ltd., Antigua Lottery Company, Ltd., Beijing GTECH Computer Technology Company Ltd., BillBird S.A., BTN Telecomunicacoes Ltda., Cam Galaxy Group Ltd., Caribbean Cricket Lottery, Inc., Caribbean Lottery Services, Inc., Curacao Lottery Company, N.V., Data Transfer Systems, Inc., DataTrans Sp. z.o.o., Dreamport do Brasil Ltda., Dreamport International, Inc., Dreamport Suffolk Corporation, Dreamport, Inc. 90 Subsidiaries included in the Index

Officers: Bruce W. Turner/Dir., CEO, Atul Bali/Sr. VP - Corporate Development, Strategic Planning, Jeff Hecht/Sr. Mgr. - Field Services, Daniel Smith/Regional Dir. - Field Services, Donald R. Sweitzer/Sr. VP - Global Business Development, Public Affairs, Jaymin B. Patel/COO, Pres., Larry Wetsch/Sales Mgr., Al Nigro/Sr. Accounting Executive, Ross Dalton/Sr. VP - Printed Products, Licensed Content Markets, Alan Eland/Sr. VP - Gtech Americas, Dan Donohue/Sr. Accounting Executive, Great Lakes Region, Ashley E. Kisla/Dir. - Operations, Marketing, Matthew Cedor/Dir. - Business Development, Seth Levine/Service Supervisor, Declan Harkin/Sr. VP - Gtech International *(31 Officers included in Index)*

Directors: Bruce W. Turner/Dir., CEO, Robert M. Dewey/Vice Chmn., Lorenzo Pellicioli/Chmn., Rosario Bifulco/Dir., Pietro Boroli/Dir., Paolo Ceretti/Dir., Anthony Ruys/Dir., James F. McCann/Dir., Marco Drago/Dir., Marco Sala/Dir., Severino Salvemini/Dir., Gianmario Tondato Da Ruos/Dir.

GTREX Capital Inc

43180 Business Pk. Dr., Ste. 202, Temecula, CA, 92590; **PH:** 1-949-330-7140; **Fax:** 1-951-587-8866; **http://** www.gtrexcapital.com; **Email:** investors@gtrexcapital.com

General - Incorporation	DE	Stock- Price on:12/24/2007	$0.0046
Employees	1	Stock Exchange	OTC
Auditor	Chisholm, Beirwolf & Nilson, LLC	Ticker Symbol	GRXI
Stk Agt	Transfer Online, Inc.	Outstanding Shares	1,960,000,000
Counsel	NA	E.P.S.	$0.00
DUNS No.	NA	Shareholders	NA

Business: The groups principle activity is to provide investment services. The group operates from the United States.

Primary SIC and add'l.: 7389

CIK No: 0000944020

Subsidiaries: Global Travel Exchange, Inc.

Officers: Steven R. Peacock/Consultant CEO, Ron Lindsay/Pres., Ronald Lindsay/47/Interim Pres.

Directors: Gary Nerison/Chmn., James Bickel/Dir., Robert McCoy/Dir.

Owners: Insiders/3.00%, Ronald Lindsay/1.00%, Robert McCoy, Gary Nerison/1.00%, James Bickel/1.00%

Financial Data: *Fiscal Year End:*12/31 **Latest Annual Data:** 12/31/2006

Year	Sales	Net Income
2006	$57,000	-$1,812,000
2005	$12,000	-$1,795,000
2004	NA	-$777,000

Curr. Assets:	$24,000	Curr. Liab.:	$412,000		
Plant, Equip.:	$27,000	Total Liab.:	$412,000	Indic. Yr. Divd.:	NA
Total Assets:	$314,000	Net Worth:	-$98,000	Debt/ Equity:	NA

GTSI Corp

3901 Stonecroft Blvd., Chantilly, VA, 20151; **PH:** 1-703-502-2000; **Fax:** 1-703-222-5204; **http://** www.gtsi.com

General - Incorporation	DE	Stock- Price on:12/24/2007	$13.25
Employees	719	Stock Exchange	NDQ
Auditor	Ernst & Young LLP	Ticker Symbol	GTSI
Stk Agt	American Stock Transfer & Trust Co.	Outstanding Shares	9,620,000
Counsel	NA	E.P.S.	$0.46
DUNS No.	10-793-9357	Shareholders	NA

Business: The group's principal activities are distribution of unix workstation hardware, software and networking products to the federal government market. The group also performs network integration services like configuring, installing and maintaining microcomputers in local area networks. The group offers its customers a convenient and cost-effective centralized source for microcomputer and workstation products through its competitive pricing, broad product selection and procurement expertise. The major trademark of the group is "Gtsi". The products of the group consist of microcomputer and workstation hardware, software and peripherals. The group's customers are primarily federal, state and local government agencies and prime contractors to the government, including systems integrators. The group has operations in United States.

Primary SIC and add'l.: 7374 5045 3577

CIK No: 0000850483

Subsidiaries: GTSI Financial Services, Technology Logistics, Inc

Officers: Jim Leto/Dir., CEO, Pres., Leslie Barry/VP - Government Affairs, Business Development, Robert E. Mitchell/Sr. VP - Operations, CIO/$555,201.00, Bill Weber/Sr. VP - Professional Services, P. Jayachandran/VP - Marketing, Mark Smith/VP - Supply Chain, William Weber/Sr. VP/$540,496.00, Peter Whitfield/VP - Internal Audit, Business Process Improvement, Cathy Finotti/VP - Financial Operations, Scott W. Friedlander/Exec. VP/$840,733.00, Paul Liberty/VP - Corporate Affairs, Investor Relations, Bridget Atkinson/VP - Human Resources, Organizational Development, Joseph D. Ragan/CFO, Sr. VP - Finance/$429,884.00, Charles Deleon/Sr. VP, General Counsel, Todd Leto/Sr. VP - Sales

Directors: Jim Leto/Dir., CEO, Pres., Daniel R. Young/Dir., Steven Kelman/Dir., Barry L. Reisig/Dir., John M. Toups/Dir., Lee Johnson/Dir., Tom Hewitt/Dir., Keith Kellogg/Dir.

Owners: James J. Leto/1.10%, William Weber, Rowe T. Price/6.30%, Scot T. Edwards, Lee Johnson/2.00%, Thomas A. Mutryn, Linwood A. (Chip) Lacy, Jr./14.50%, Peninsula Capital Management, Inc./12.60%, Dimensional Fund Advisors, Inc./8.10%, Steven Kelman/1.10%, Robert E. Mitchell, Joseph Keith Kellogg, Scott W. Friedlander, Joseph Ragan, Thomas L. Hewitt *(20 Owners included in Index)*

Financial Data: *Fiscal Year End:*12/31 **Latest Annual Data:** 12/31/2006

Year	Sales	Net Income
2006	$850,189,000	-$3,014,000
2005	$882,012,000	-$13,673,000
2004	$1,076,148,000	$10,264,000

Curr. Assets:	$290,307,000	Curr. Liab.:	$220,110,000		
Plant, Equip.:	$13,627,000	Total Liab.:	$253,998,000	Indic. Yr. Divd.:	NA
Total Assets:	$330,681,000	Net Worth:	$76,683,000	Debt/ Equity:	0.3452

GTx Inc

3 N Dunlap St., Van Vleet Bldg., Memphis, TN, 38163; **PH:** 1-901-523-9700; **Fax:** 1-901-523-9772; **http://** www.gtxinc.com; **Email:** investor.relations@gtxinc.com

General - Incorporation	DE	Stock- Price on:12/24/2007	$17.22
Employees	91	Stock Exchange	NDQ
Auditor	Ernst & Young LLP	Ticker Symbol	GTXI
Stk Agt	Computershare Ltd.	Outstanding Shares	34,880,000
Counsel	NA	E.P.S.	-$1.05
DUNS No.	NA	Shareholders	NA

Business: The group's principal activity is the discovery, development and commercialization of therapeutics related to the treatment of serious men's health conditions. The group has two product candidates that are in human clinical trials, acapodene and andarine. The group is a development stage company. As on 6-Feb-2004, the group completed an initial public offering.

Primary SIC and add'l.: 2834

CIK No: 0001260990

Subsidiaries: Johnson & Johnson

Officers: Mitchell S. Steiner/47/Vice Chmn., CEO/$472,333.00, Mark E. Mosteller/CFO, VP, Treasurer/$378,935.00, James T. Dalton/VP - Preclinical Research, Development/$343,733.00, Henry P. Doggrell/VP, General Counsel, Sec./$371,832.00, Marc S. Hanover/45/Dir., COO, Pres./$325,046.00, Greg Deener/VP - Sales, Marketing, Gary K. Barnette/VP - Clinical Research, Development Strategy, Ronald A. Morton/Chief Medical Officer, VP, Jeff Hesselberg/VP - Regulatory Affairs

Directors: Mitchell S. Steiner/47/Vice Chmn., CEO, J. R. Hyde/65/Chmn., Michael G. Carter/69/Dir., Marc S. Hanover/45/Dir., COO, Pres., Rosemary Mazanet/52/Dir., Andrew M. Clarkson/70/Dir., John H. Pontius/52/Dir., Timothy R.G. Sear/70/Dir., Kenneth J. Glass/61/Dir., Robert W. Karr/59/Dir.

Owners: Rosemary Mazanet, Visium Asset Management, LLC/6.80%, Timothy R. G. Sear, Gary K. Barnette, Insiders/51.30%, James T. Dalton, Marc S. Hanover/5.20%, J. R. Hyde/31.40%, Robert W. Karr, FMR Corp./10.40%, Oracle Investment Management, Inc./5.10%, Larry N. Feinberg/6.90%, Mark E. Mosteller, Gregory A. Deener, John H. Pontius/11.00% *(19 Owners included in Index)*

Financial Data: *Fiscal Year End:*12/31 **Latest Annual Data:** 12/31/2006

Year	Sales	Net Income
2006	$7,505,000	-$35,510,000
2005	$3,782,000	-$36,839,000
2004	$1,867,000	-$22,348,000

Curr. Assets:	$121,700,000	Curr. Liab.:	$10,337,000		
Plant, Equip.:	$1,448,000	Total Liab.:	$32,206,000	Indic. Yr. Divd.:	NA
Total Assets:	$129,255,000	Net Worth:	$97,049,000	Debt/ Equity:	0.0001

Guangshen Railway Co Ltd

No. 1052 Heping Rd. , Shenzhen, 518010; **PH:** 86-75525587920; **http://** www.gsrc.com

General - Incorporation	China	Stock- Price on:12/24/2007	$41.19
Employees	9,411	Stock Exchange	NYSE
Auditor	PricewaterhouseCoopers LLP	Ticker Symbol	GSH
Stk Agt	Morgan ADR Service Center	Outstanding Shares	NA
Counsel	NA	E.P.S.	$1.41
DUNS No.	65-451-8398	Shareholders	NA

Business: The group's principle activities are railway passenger and freight transportation services between guangzhou and shenzhen. Other activities include provision of railway facilities and technical services, sales of food, beverages and merchandise in railway stations and on trains. Operations of the group are carried out in the People's Republic of China.

Primary SIC and add'l.: 4731 4789 7699 5812 8322 4226 4011

CIK No: 0001012139

Subsidiaries: Dongguan Changsheng Enterprise Company, Guangzhou East Station Dongqun Trade and Commerce Service Company, Shenzhen Fu Yuan Enterprise Development Company, Shenzhen Guangshen Railway Civil Engineering Company, Shenzhen Guangshen Railway Economic and Trade Enterprise Company, Shenzhen Guangshen Railway Travel Service Ltd., Shenzhen Jian Kai Trade Company, Shenzhen Jing Ming Industrial & Commercial Company Limited, Shenzhen Longgang Pinghu Qun Yi Railway Store Loading and Unloading Company, Shenzhen Nantie Construction Supervision Company, Shenzhen Railway Property Management Company Limited, Shenzhen Railway Station Passenger Services Company Limited, Shenzhen Railway Station Travel Service Company, Shenzhen Road Multi-modal Transportation Company Limited, Shenzhen Yuezheng Enterprise Company Limited

Officers: Wu Weimin/50/Deputy GM, Chen Ruixing/45/Supervisor, Li Jin/47/Supervisor, Li Zhiming/46/Supervisor, Guo Xiangdong/42/Dir., Company Sec., Sec. Of The Board, Chen Yunzhong/55/Supervisor, Yao Xiaocong/54/Chief Accountant, Wang Jianping/44/Supervisor, Hang Dong/46/Deputy GM, Luo Jiancheng/35/GM, Assist., Yang Yiping/58/Dir., GM

Directors: He Yuhua/55/Dir., Chmn., Wu Houhui/59/Dir., Chang Loong Cheong/62/Dir., Wen Weiming/45/Dir., Yang Jinzhong/56/Dir., Deborah Kong/48/Dir., Yang Yiping/58/Dir., GM, Cao Jianguo/49/Dir., Wilton Chau Chi Wai/46/Dir.

Owners: Sumitomo Life Insurance Company/6.07%, Baring Asset Management Limited/5.31%, Guangzhou Railway (Group) Company/20.20%, Sumitomo Mitsui Asset Management Company, Limited/6.07%, Guangzhou Railway (Group) Company/41.00%, Guangzhou Railway (Group) Company/51.38%

Financial Data: ***Fiscal Year End:***12/31 ***Latest Annual Data:*** 12/31/2006

Year	Sales	Net Income
2006	$460,830,000	$98,527,000
2005	$404,559,000	$77,945,000
2004	$366,043,000	$72,320,000

Curr. Assets:	$835,292,000	***Curr. Liab.:***	$286,727,000		
Plant, Equip.:	$1,548,812,000	***Total Liab.:***	$535,951,000	***Indic. Yr. Divd.:***	$0.520
Total Assets:	$3,120,913,000	***Net Worth:***	$2,584,962,000	***Debt/ Equity:***	NA

GuangZhou Global Telecom Inc

Formerly: Avalon Development Enterprises Inc

Rm. 1802, N Tower, Suntec Plaza, No. 197 Guangzhou Ave. N, Guangzhou, Guangdong; ***PH:*** 44-120-724-56131

General - Incorporation	FL	**Stock**- Price on:12/24/2007	NA
Employees	NA	Stock Exchange	OTC
Auditor	Jewett, Schwartz, Wolfe & Assoc.	Ticker Symbol	GZGT
Stk Agt	Holladay Stock Transfer, Inc.	Outstanding Shares	NA
Counsel	NA	E.P.S	-$0.31
DUNS No.	NA	Shareholders	NA

Business: The groups principle activity is to provide recruiting services. The groups service area includes the research and development, engineering, marketing, sales, information technology and manufacturing industries. The group operates from United States.

Primary SIC and add'l.: 4899

CIK No: 0001346287

Officers: Yankuan Li/51/Chmn., CEO, Yiwen Wu/44/Dir., COO, Zhihan Hu/44/Dir., CFO

Directors: Yiwen Wu/44/Dir., COO, Zhihan Hu/44/Dir., CFO

Owners: Zhihan Hu/0.02%, Insiders/23.83%, Yankuan Li/23.30%, Yiwen Wu/0.50%

Financial Data: ***Fiscal Year End:***12/31 ***Latest Annual Data:*** 12/31/2006

Year	Sales	Net Income
2006	$19,000	-$10,000

Curr. Assets:	$0	***Curr. Liab.:***	NA		
Plant, Equip.:	NA	***Total Liab.:***	NA	***Indic. Yr. Divd.:***	NA
Total Assets:	$0	***Net Worth:***	$0	***Debt/ Equity:***	NA

Guaranty Federal Bancshares Inc

1341 W Battlefield, Springfield, MO, 65807; ***PH:*** 1-417-520-4333; ***Fax:*** 1-417-520-3607; ***http://*** www.gfed.com

General - Incorporation	DE	**Stock**- Price on:12/24/2007	$30.2
Employees	114	Stock Exchange	NDQ
Auditor	BKD LLP	Ticker Symbol	GFED
Stk Agt	Registrar & Transfer Co	Outstanding Shares	2,890,000
Counsel	Manatt, Phelps & Phillips LLP	E.P.S	$2.29
DUNS No.	94-729-1894	Shareholders	NA

Business: The group's principal activities are to accept retail deposits from the general public and invest them in one-to four-family residential mortgage loans, multi-family residential mortgage loans, commercial real estate loans, consumer and other loans. The deposits of the group include fixed-term certificates, passbook savings, money market, individual retirement accounts and now accounts. The other services provided by the group include mutual funds, fixed and variable annuities, unit investment trusts, individual stocks and bonds and life insurance. The operations are conducted through its main office in springfield, greene county, Missouri and three full-service branch offices in springfield, four in-store branches located in the dillons supermarkets in springfield and one in-store in walmart supercenter in nixa, Missouri.

Primary SIC and add'l.: 6712 6035

CIK No: 0001046203

Subsidiaries: Guaranty Financial Services of Springfield, Inc, Gurantee Federal Bank, Gurantee Federal Bank Trust I, Gurantee Federal Bank Trust II

Officers: Shaun A. Burke/Dir., CEO, Pres./$384,588.00, Rachel Godden/Consumer Lender, Carter Peters/CFO, COO, Exec. VP/$151,205.00, Bruce Winston/Sr. VP/$108,485.00, Crystal Colton/Mortgage Lender, Becky Scorse/Sr. VP - Commercial Lending, Guaranty Bank, Dana Elwell/Sr. VP - Mortgage Lending, Guaranty Bank, Susan Johanson/Consumer Lender, Michael Mattson/Exec. VP, Chief Lending Officer - Guaranty Bank, Teresa E. Blair/Sr. VP, Sr. Operations Officer - Guaranty Bank, Ken Johnston/CIO, VP - Guaranty Bank, Linda Lindsay/VP - Information Systems, Guaranty Bank, Kenton Devries/Sr. VP - Commercial Lending, Guaranty Bank, Doug Thornsberry/Sr. VP - Commercial Lending, Guaranty Bank, Scott Noskowiak/VP - Mortgage Lending, Guaranty Bank *(31 Officers included in Index)*

Directors: Shaun A. Burke/Dir., CEO, Pres., Jack L. Barham/74/Vice Chmn., Don M. Gibson/Chmn., James R. Batten/45/Dir., Kurt D. Hellweg/50/Dir., Tim Rosenbury/51/Dir., Wayne V. Barnes/76/Dir., Gregory V. Ostergren/52/Dir., James L. Sivils/43/Dir.

Owners: James L. Sivils, Insiders/10.20%, Tim Rosenbury, Michael H. Mattson, Don M. Gibson/1.60%, Wayne V. Barnes/2.40%, Carter Peters, Shaun A. Burke/1.00%, Kurt D. Hellweg/1.10%, Guaranty Bank/9.80%, Gregory V. Ostergren/1.50%

Financial Data: ***Fiscal Year End:***12/31 ***Latest Annual Data:*** 12/31/2006

Year	Sales	Net Income
2006	$38,911,000	$6,509,000
2005	$30,882,000	$5,899,000
2004	$24,159,000	$4,285,000

Curr. Assets:	$18,566,000	***Curr. Liab.:***	$464,258,000	***P/E Ratio:***	13.19
Plant, Equip.:	$8,040,000	***Total Liab.:***	$479,946,000	***Indic. Yr. Divd.:***	$0.680
Total Assets:	$524,845,000	***Net Worth:***	$44,899,000	***Debt/ Equity:***	0.3444

Guardian Technologies International Inc

516 Herndon Pkwy., Ste. A, Herndon, VA, 20170; ***PH:*** 1-703-464-5495; ***Fax:*** 1-703-464-8530; ***http://*** www.guardiantechintl.com; ***Email:*** info@guardiantechintl.com

General - Incorporation	DE	**Stock**- Price on:12/24/2007	$0.83
Employees	33	Stock Exchange	OTC
Auditor	Goodman & Co. LLP	Ticker Symbol	GDTI
Stk Agt	Signature Stock Transfer, Inc.	Outstanding Shares	35,160,000
Counsel	NA	E.P.S	-$0.34
DUNS No.	62-113-3321	Shareholders	NA

Business: The group's principal activity is to design, develop and deliver advanced software and advanced intelligent reasoning solutions to commercial clients and U.S. Governmental agencies. The groups software and reasoning solutions will help its clients to radically improve the quality and velocity of decision-making, organizational productivity and efficiency of cognitive labor intensive processes. On 27-Jun-2003, the group acquired rjl marketing services inc. Prior to this the group activity was to fabricate and erect structural steel for governmental, military, commercial and industrial construction projects. On 27-Jul-2004, the group acquired wise systems ltd.

Primary SIC and add'l.: 3482 6799 3499 1791

CIK No: 0000873198

Subsidiaries: Guardian Healthcare UK, Ltd., RJL Marketing Services, Inc, Wise Systems, Ltd.

Officers: Michael W. Trudnak/Chmn., CEO, Bill Donovan/COO, Pres., Steven Lancaster/VP - Corporate Development, Richard Borrelli/VP - Business Development Healthcare Systems, Greg Hare/CFO, John Paganini/Sr. Dir. - Product Management Healthcare Systems, Andrew Underhill/Dir. - Technical Services Healthcare Systems

Directors: Michael W. Trudnak/Chmn., CEO

Owners: Gregory E. Hare, Steve V. Lancaster/2.10%, Michael W. Trudnak/15.20%, Darrell E. Hill/2.10%, Charles T. Nash, Tobin Family Trust/6.00%, Robert A. Dishaw/13.40%, Sean W. Kennedy, Gina Marie Lindsey, Insiders/21.60%, William J. Donovan/2.90%

Financial Data: ***Fiscal Year End:***12/31 ***Latest Annual Data:*** 12/31/2006

Year	Sales	Net Income
2006	$488,000	-$10,094,000
2005	$432,000	-$13,147,000
2004	$101,000	-$29,220,000

Curr. Assets:	$948,000	***Curr. Liab.:***	$3,419,000		
Plant, Equip.:	$612,000	***Total Liab.:***	$6,710,000	***Indic. Yr. Divd.:***	NA
Total Assets:	$3,710,000	***Net Worth:***	-$2,999,000	***Debt/ Equity:***	NA

Guess ? Inc

1444 S Alameda St., Los Angeles, CA, 90021; ***PH:*** 1-213-765-3100; ***Fax:*** 1-213-744-7838; ***http://*** www.guess.com

General - Incorporation	DE	**Stock**- Price on:12/24/2007	$48.2
Employees	8,800	Stock Exchange	NYSE
Auditor	KPMG LLP	Ticker Symbol	GES
Stk Agt	Computershare Trust Co	Outstanding Shares	NA
Counsel	NA	E.P.S	$1.82
DUNS No.	02-745-1731	Shareholders	NA

Business: The group's principal activities are to design, market, distribute and license lifestyle collections of casual apparel and accessories for men, women and children that reflect the American lifestyle and European fashion sensibilities. The apparel line includes a full collection of denim and cotton clothing including jeans, pants, overalls, skirts, dresses, shorts, blouses, shirts, jackets and knitwear. The group also grants licenses to manufacture and distribute products, which complement its apparel lines. The trademarks of the group include guess, guess?, guess u.s.a., guess jeans, triangle design, question mark and triangle design, brand g, a stylized g, guess kids, baby guess and guess collection. The products of the group are sold in the United States, Canada, Europe, Asia, South America, Mexico, Middle East and Africa.

Primary SIC and add'l.: 5136 2339 6794 2325 2337 5137 2321

CIK No: 0000912463

Subsidiaries: Guess France SAS, Guess Italia, S.r.l., Guess Operations Ireland Limited, Guess Swiss SAGL, Guess UK Limited, Guess.com, Inc., Guess? Apparel Retail, B.V., Guess? Asia Limited, Guess? Canada Corporation, Guess? Europe, B.V., Guess? IP GP LLC, Guess? IP Holder L.P., Guess? IP LP LLC, Guess? Licensing, Inc., Guess? Retail, Inc. 18 Subsidiaries included in the Index

Officers: Paul Marciano/Vice Chmn., CEO/$17,114,070.00

Directors: Paul Marciano/Vice Chmn., CEO, Maurice Marciano/Chmn., Carlos Alberini/Dir., Anthony Chidoni/Dir., Alice T. Kane/Dir., Alex Yemenidjian/Dir., Kay Isaacson-Leibowitz/Dir., Judith Blumenthal/Dir.

Owners: Maurice Marciano/24.06%, Insiders/42.41%, Nancy Shachtman, Karen Neuburger, Carlos Alberini, Paul Marciano/17.93%, Kay Isaacson-Leibowitz, Alex Yemenidjian, Dennis Secor, Stephen Pearson, Alice Kane, Anthony Chidoni, Michael Relich

Financial Data: ***Fiscal Year End:***12/31 ***Latest Annual Data:*** 12/31/2006

Year	Sales	Net Income
2006	$1,185,184,000	$123,168,000
2005	$936,092,000	$58,813,000
2004	$729,262,000	$29,566,000

Curr. Assets:	$558,892,000	Curr. Liab.:	$283,896,000	P/E Ratio:	31.92
Plant, Equip.:	$164,262,000	Total Liab.:	$401,113,000	Indic. Yr. Divd.:	$0.320
Total Assets:	$836,925,000	Net Worth:	$431,060,000	Debt/ Equity:	0.0365

Guidant Corp

111 Monument Cir., 29th Fl., Indianapolis, IN, 46204; *PH:* 1-317-971-2000; *http://* www.guidant.com

General - Incorporation ....IN	**Stock**- Price on:12/24/2007 ....$16.01
Employees...28,600	Stock Exchange...NA
Auditor .... Ernst & Young LLP	Ticker Symbol...NA
Stk Agt.................Mellon Investor Services LLC	Outstanding Shares 1,480,000,000
Counsel..NA	E.P.S..$0.40
DUNS No.......................................87-726-0471	Shareholders..NA

Business: The group's principal activity is to provide therapeutic medical solutions for customers, patients and health care systems. The group develops, manufactures and markets products and services that focus on the treatment of coronary arrhythmias, heart failure, coronary artery disease and biliary and artery diseases. The group's products include coronary stent systems, dilatation catheters, intravascular radiotherapy systems and related accessories, implantable defibrillator systems, implantable pacemaker systems, angioplasty systems, cardiac surgery systems, implantable cardiac resynchronization therapy. The group has principal operations in the United States, Europe, Asia and Japan. In 2003, the group acquired Medivas, LLC, Biosensors International, Bioabscorbable Vascular Soulutions and X Technologies Inc. In Jun 2003, the group discontinued Ancure Endograft System product line and operations in Brazil. On 09-Feb-2004, the group acquired AFX Inc.

Primary SIC and add'l.: 3845 3841

CIK No: 0000929987

Subsidiaries: 4105 Lexington, LLC, Advanced Cardiovascular Systems, Inc., AFx, Inc., Arter Re Insurance Co. Ltd., Bioerodible Vascular Solutions, Cardiac Pacemakers, Inc., Cardio Thoracic Systems, Inc., EndoVascular Technologies, Inc., Guidant Aparelhos Medicos LOA, Guidant Australia Pty Ltd., Guidant Belgium S.A., Guidant Canada Corporation, Guidant CR Sro, Guidant do Brasil Ltda., Guidant Endovascular Solutions, Inc. 47 Subsidiaries included in the Index

Financial Data: *Fiscal Year End:*12/31 *Latest Annual Data:* 12/31/2006

Year	Sales	Net Income
2006	$7,821,000,000	-$3,577,000,000
2005	$6,283,000,000	$628,000,000
2004	$5,624,000,000	$1,062,000,000

Curr. Assets:	$4,901,000,000	Curr. Liab.:	$2,630,000,000	P/E Ratio:	40.03
Plant, Equip.:	$1,726,000,000	Total Liab.:	$15,798,000,000	Indic. Yr. Divd.:	NA
Total Assets:	$31,096,000,000	Net Worth:	$15,298,000,000	Debt/ Equity:	0.5722

Guideline Inc

Formerly: Find/svp Inc
625 Ave. Of The Americas, New York, NY, 10011; *PH:* 1-212-645-4500; *http://* www.guideline.com

General - Incorporation ....NY	**Stock**- Price on:12/24/2007 ....$1.2
Employees...239	Stock Exchange...NA
Auditor ....Deloitte & Touche LLP	Ticker Symbol...NA
Stk Agt..........................Computershare Trust Co	Outstanding Shares 20,950,000
Counsel............................. Kane Kessler P.C	E.P.S...$0.011
DUNS No.......................................07-328-5629	Shareholders..NA

Business: The group's principal activities are to provide consulting, quantitative market research and outsourced information services. The group operates in four business segments: quick consulting service ('qcs') provides clients with access to the expertise of the group's staff and information resources on day-to-day business related topics. The strategic consulting and research group ('scrg') provides in-depth custom research and intelligence information. The quantitative market research provides full service quantitative custom market research services such as large-scale consumer surveys both domestically and internationally. Teltech provides outsourced information and consulting services to customers in research and development and related technical sectors on subscription basis. At 31-Dec-2003, it had 1,331 subscription customers and 8,938 holders of the membership card. On 01-Apr-2003 and 01-Jul-2003, it acquired guideline research corp and teltech respectively.

Primary SIC and add'l.: 8742 8732

CIK No: 0000801338

Subsidiaries: Atlantic Research & Consulting, Inc., Find/SVP Internet Services, Inc., Find/SVP Published Products, Inc., Guideline Research Corp., Signia Partners, Inc., Ttech Acquisition Corp., Washington Researchers, Ltd.

Officers: David M. Walke/Chmn., CEO, Walter Dempsey/Sr. MD - On, Demand Business Research, Peter Stone/CFO, David Magnani/Sr. MD, Richard Forzani/VP - Sales, Ty Albert/MD - Guideline Chicago, Brian Methvin/MD - Competitive Intelligence Business Unit, Costas Pavlides/MD - Guideline Boston, Robert Reitter/MD - Guideline Legal, Morris S. Whitcup/MD - Guideline Pharmaceutical, Healthcare, Frank Dudley/VP - Marketing, Jack Foreman/VP - Product, Channel Development, Tom McGillis/VP - Human Resources, Stacey Fisher/Contact - Investor Relations

Directors: David M. Walke/Chmn., CEO, Andrew P. Garvin/Founder, Warren Struhl/Dir., Denise Shapiro/Dir., Brian Ruder/Dir., Regina Paolillo/Dir.

Owners: Zesiger Capital Group LLC/8.50%, Performance Capital/6.70%, Andrew P. Garvin/3.20%, David Walke/10.90%, Austin W. Marxe/19.40%, Marc Litvinoff/1.00%, Peter Stone, Wynnefield Partners/11.40%, Scott A. Gerard, Petra Mezzanine Fund, L.P./3.40%, Denise Shapiro, Petra Mezzanine Fund, L.P./100.00%, Brian Ruder, Martin Franklin/6.50%, Regina Paolillo *(17 Owners included in Index)*

Financial Data: *Fiscal Year End:*12/31 *Latest Annual Data:* 12/31/2006

Year	Sales	Net Income
2006	$46,285,000	$1,034,000
2005	$43,034,000	$452,000
2004	$38,437,000	-$1,945,000

Curr. Assets:	$13,390,000	Curr. Liab.:	$13,601,000	P/E Ratio:	109.09
Plant, Equip.:	$2,228,000	Total Liab.:	$16,283,000	Indic. Yr. Divd.:	NA
Total Assets:	$40,166,000	Net Worth:	$23,209,000	Debt/ Equity:	0.0901

Guilin Paper Inc

Formerly: LogSearch Inc
3632-13 St. Sw, Calgary, AB, T2T 3R1; *PH:* 1-403-689-3901

General - Incorporation ....NV	**Stock**- Price on:12/24/2007 ....$0.9
Employees...NA	Stock Exchange..OTC
Auditor ....Bateman & Co., Inc., P.C.	Ticker Symbol..GUPR
Stk Agt ....Interwest Transfer Company, Inc.	Outstanding Shares ....NA
Counsel..NA	E.P.S..NA
DUNS No..NA	Shareholders..NA

Business: The group's principal activity is to markets software database management and analysis system known as Leadscan. The products of the group include LeadScan system and well log search software. The group operates from the United States.

Primary SIC and add'l.: 7371

CIK No: 0001288837

Officers: Fangde Zhang/CEO, Mingzhu Zhang/CFO

Directors: Biao Tan/Chmn.

Owners: Shaoqiu Li/3.90%, Insiders/24.51%, Fangde Zhang/12.44%, Jianqiang Peng/3.90%, Biao Tan/37.44%, Jiajie Chen/4.26%

Financial Data: *Fiscal Year End:*10/31 *Latest Annual Data:* 10/31/2006

Year	Sales	Net Income
2006	NA	-$35,000

Curr. Assets:	$14,000	Curr. Liab.:	$6,000		
Plant, Equip.:	NA	Total Liab.:	$6,000	Indic. Yr. Divd.:	NA
Total Assets:	$14,000	Net Worth:	$8,000	Debt/ Equity:	NA

Gulf & Orient Steamship Company Ltd

601 S State St., Salt Lake City, UT, 84101; *PH:* 1-801-550-5800

General - Incorporation ....CO	**Stock**- Price on:12/24/2007 ....$0.3
Employees...NA	Stock Exchange..OTC
Auditor ....NA	Ticker Symbol..GLFO
Stk Agt ....OTC Stock Transfer, Inc.	Outstanding Shares ....NA
Counsel..NA	E.P.S..-$0.01
DUNS No..NA	Shareholders..NA

Business: The groups principle activity is to provide recruiting services. The groups service area includes the research and development, engineering, marketing, sales, information technology and manufacturing industries. The group operates from United States.

Primary SIC and add'l.: 6770

CIK No: 0001365388

Officers: Michael Vardakis/43/Dir., Pres., Melissa Ladakis/Dir., Sec., Treasurer

Directors: Michael Vardakis/43/Dir., Pres., Melissa Ladakis/Dir., Sec., Treasurer

Owners: Vincent Lombardi/44.62%, Michael Vardakis/44.35%

Financial Data: *Fiscal Year End:*12/31 *Latest Annual Data:* 12/31/2006

Year	Sales	Net Income
2006	NA	-$31,000

Curr. Assets:	$0	Curr. Liab.:	$87,000		
Plant, Equip.:	NA	Total Liab.:	$87,000	Indic. Yr. Divd.:	NA
Total Assets:	$0	Net Worth:	-$87,000	Debt/ Equity:	NA

Gulf Coast Oil & Gas Inc

5847 San Felipe, Ste. 1700, Houston, TX, 77057; ; *http://* www.gcoil.com; *Email:* info@gcoil.com

General - Incorporation ....NV	**Stock**- Price on:12/24/2007 ....$0.0033
Employees...1	Stock Exchange..OTC
Auditor ....Pollard-Kelley Auditing Services, Inc	Ticker Symbol...GCOG
Stk Agt ....Pacific Stock Transfer Company	Outstanding Shares 182,050,000
Counsel..NA	E.P.S..-$0.004
DUNS No..NA	Shareholders..NA

Business: The groups principal activity is to develop oil and gas properties. The group operates from the Gulf of Texas and Louisiana in the United States.

Primary SIC and add'l.: 1000

CIK No: 0001108943

Officers: Rahim Rayani/Chmn., CEO, Pres., Channon C. Bourgeois/Technical Advisor

Directors: Rahim Rayani/Chmn., CEO, Pres.

Owners: Insiders/9.98%, Rahim Rayani/9.98%

Financial Data: *Fiscal Year End:*12/31 *Latest Annual Data:* 12/31/2006

Year	Sales	Net Income
2006	$29,000	-$755,000
2005	NA	-$187,000
2003	NA	-$94,000

Curr. Assets:	$750,000	Curr. Liab.:	$326,000		
Plant, Equip.:	$3,000	Total Liab.:	$2,300,000	Indic. Yr. Divd.:	NA
Total Assets:	$1,866,000	Net Worth:	-$435,000	Debt/ Equity:	NA

Gulf Island Fabrication Inc

583 Thompson Rd., Houma, LA, 70363; *PH:* 1-985-872-2100; *Fax:* 1-985-872-2129; *http://* www.gulfisland.com; *Email:* info@gulfisland.com

General - Incorporation .... LA	**Stock**- Price on:12/24/2007 ....$34.82
Employees...1,800	Stock Exchange...NDQ
Auditor .... Ernst & Young LLP	Ticker Symbol...GIFI
Stk Agt ..... American Stock Transfer & Trust Co.	Outstanding Shares 14,150,000
Counsel..........Jones, Walker, Waechter, Poitevent	E.P.S...$1.83
DUNS No.......................................13-924-0618	Shareholders..NA

Business: The group's principle activities are to provide fabrication of offshore drilling and production platforms and other specialized structures used in the development and production of offshore oil and gas reserves. The structures and equipment fabricated by the group include jackets and deck sections of fixed production platforms, hull and deck sections of floating production platforms, piles,

wellhead protectors, subsea templates and various production, compressor and utility modules and offshore living quarters. The group provides services including offshore interconnect pipe hook-up, inshore marine construction, manufacture and repair of pressure vessels and steel warehousing and sales. It also produces and repairs pressure vessels used in the oil and gas industry, refurbish existing platforms and fabricate various other types of steel structures. The major customers are el paso corporation, j. Ray mcdermott sa and kerr mcgee corporation. The group's quarterly revenue for Sep'07 was 124.90 millions of USD.

Primary SIC and add'l.: 3441

CIK No: 0001031623

Subsidiaries: Dolphin Services, LLC, G. M. Fabricators, L.P, Gulf Island, LLC, Southport, LLC

Officers: William G. Blanchard/CEO, Pres. - Gulf Island, LLC/$213,802.00, Johannes Ikdal/CEO, Pres. - Gulf Marine Fabricators, Robert C. Anderson/51/CEO, Pres. - Gulf Marine Fabricators, Fabrication Subsidiary, William Fromenthal/CEO, Pres. - Dolphin Services, LLC, Kerry J. Chauvin/Chmn., CEO/$892,675.00, Murphy Bourke/Exec. VP - Marketing/$396,691.00, Deborah Kern-Knoblock/Corp. Sec. - Investor Relations, Randy Munson/Contact - Sales, Marketing Offices, Roy Francis/Contact - Sales, Marketing, Ray Avet/Contact - Sales, Marketing, David Daigneault/Contact - Sales, Marketing, Robin Seibert/CFO, VP - Finance, Treasurer, Roy Brearwood/Controller, Eric Maier/Contact - Sales, Marketing, Kirk Meche/Exec. VP - Operations/$437,695.00 *(16 Officers included in Index)*

Directors: Kerry J. Chauvin/Chmn., CEO, John A. Wishart/49/Dir., Alden J. Laborde/92/Dir., Huey J. Wilson/80/Dir., David W. Sverre/52/Dir., Ken C. Tamblyn/64/Dir., Gregory J. Cotter/59/Dir., John P. Laborde/58/Dir.

Owners: Kirk J. Meche, Huey J. Wilson/3.20%, Alden J. Laborde/7.50%, Insiders/12.80%, Gregory J. Cotter, St. Denis J. Villere & Company, L.L.C./9.10%, Aransas Partners/11.30%, John P. Laborde, Murphy A. Bourke, Hugh J. Kelly, Joseph P. Gallagher, Kerry J. Chauvin/1.10%, Ken C. Tamblyn

Financial Data: ***Fiscal Year End:***12/31 ***Latest Annual Data:*** 12/31/2006

Year	Sales	Net Income
2006	$312,181,000	$21,325,000
2005	$188,545,000	$12,987,000
2004	$173,878,000	$12,042,000

Curr. Assets:	$94,765,000	**Curr. Liab.:**	$40,214,000	**P/E Ratio:**	18.92
Plant, Equip.:	$155,440,000	**Total Liab.:**	$50,692,000	**Indic. Yr. Divd.:**	$0.400
Total Assets:	$251,448,000	**Net Worth:**	$200,756,000	**Debt/ Equity:**	NA

Gulf Power Co

One Energy Pl., Pensacola, FL, 32520; ***PH:*** 1-850-444-6111; ***http://*** www.gulfpower.com

General - Incorporation	FL	**Stock** - Price on:12/24/2007	$23.21
Employees	NA	Stock Exchange	NYSE
Auditor	Deloitte & Touche LLP	Ticker Symbol	GUI
Stk Agt	NA	Outstanding Shares	NA
Counsel	Beggs & Lane	E.P.S	NA
DUNS No.	00-692-3429	Shareholders	NA

Business: The group's principal activities are generating, purchasing, distributing and selling of electricity in the northwest portion of Florida. The group is a wholly owned subsidiary of the southern company. The group distributes electricity in retail to 71 communities including pensacola, panama city and fort walton beach as well as in rural areas. Electricity in also distributed at wholesale to a non-affiliated utility companies and municipality.

Primary SIC and add'l.: 4911

CIK No: 0000044545

Subsidiaries: Alabama Power Capital Trust IV, Alabama Power Capital Trust V, Alabama Power Capital Trust VI, Alabama Power Capital Trust VII, Alabama Power Capital Trust VIII, Alabama Power Company, Alabama Property Company, Georgia Power Capital Trust IV, Georgia Power Capital Trust IX, Georgia Power Capital Trust V, Georgia Power Capital Trust VI, Georgia Power Capital Trust VII, Georgia Power Capital Trust VIII, Georgia Power Capital Trust X, Georgia Power Capital Trust XI 38 Subsidiaries included in the Index

Officers: Susan N. Story/Dir., CEO, Pres., Bernard Jacob/VP - Customer Operations, Ronnie Labrato/CFO, VP, Controller, Michael D. Garrett/58/Exec. VP, James H. Miller/58/Sr. VP, General Counsel, Christopher C. Womack/49/Exec. VP, Mickey A. Brown/60/Exec. VP, Bentina Terry/VP - External Affairs, Corporate Services, Ted McCullough/VP - Generation, John Hutchinson/Mgr. - Public Affairs, Lynn Erickson/Corporate Communications Supervisor

Directors: Susan N. Story/Dir., CEO, Pres., Ledon C. Anchors/Dir., William C. Cramer/Dir., Fred C. Donovan/Dir., William A. Pullum/Dir., Winston E. Scott/Dir.

Owners: Bernard P. Jacob, Fred C. Donovan, The Southern Company, Francis M. Fisher, William A. Pullum, Winston E. Scott, LeDon C. Anchors, William C. Cramer, Penny M. Manuel, Insiders, Susan N. Story, Ronnie R. Labrato

Financial Data: ***Fiscal Year End:***12/31 ***Latest Annual Data:*** 12/31/2006

Year	Sales	Net Income
2006	$1,203,914,000	$79,289,000
2005	$1,083,622,000	$75,970,000
2004	$960,131,000	$68,440,000

Curr. Assets:	$374,924,000	**Curr. Liab.:**	$345,548,000		
Plant, Equip.:	$1,750,614,000	**Total Liab.:**	$1,652,579,000	**Indic. Yr. Divd.:**	NA
Total Assets:	$2,340,489,000	**Net Worth:**	$687,910,000	**Debt/ Equity:**	0.9038

Gulf United Energy Inc

3555 Timmons., Ste. 1510, Houston, TX, 77027; ***PH:*** 1-713-942-6575; ***http://*** www.gulfunitedenergy.com

General - Incorporation	NV	**Stock** - Price on:12/24/2007	$1.01
Employees	NA	Stock Exchange	OTC
Auditor	Morgan & Company	Ticker Symbol	GLFE
Stk Agt	NA	Outstanding Shares	NA
Counsel	Brewer and Pritchard	E.P.S	-$0.01
DUNS No.	NA	Shareholders	NA

Business: The groups principal activities include designing, constructing, operating and maintaining natural gas pipeline between Valladoloid, Cancun and Punta Venado, and liquified natural gas storage and re-gasification facility. The group operates from the United States.

Primary SIC and add'l.: 1000

CIK No: 0001312165

Officers: Don W. Wilson/Dir., Pres., David Pomerantz/CFO, Bill St. John/Sr. Advisor, International Exploration, John B. Connally/Sr. Advisor, Houston, Texas, John L. Dragonetti/Sr. Advisor, Middle East Affairs, Dubai, United Arab Emirates

Directors: Don W. Wilson/Dir., Pres.

Owners: Don W. Wilson/7.59%, Insiders/7.59%

Financial Data: ***Fiscal Year End:***08/31 ***Latest Annual Data:*** 8/31/2006

Year	Sales	Net Income
2006	NA	-$32,000
2005	NA	-$17,000

Curr. Assets:	$3,000	**Curr. Liab.:**	$41,000		
Plant, Equip.:	NA	**Total Liab.:**	$41,000	**Indic. Yr. Divd.:**	NA
Total Assets:	$3,000	**Net Worth:**	-$38,000	**Debt/ Equity:**	NA

Gulf Western Petroleum Corp

Formerly: Georgia Exploration Inc

4801 Woodway Dr., Ste. 306, Houston, TX, 77056; ***PH:*** 1-713-355-7001

General - Incorporation	NV	**Stock** - Price on:12/24/2007	NA
Employees	NA	Stock Exchange	NA
Auditor	Gbh Cpas, P.C	Ticker Symbol	NA
Stk Agt	Corporate Stock Transfer, Inc.	Outstanding Shares	NA
Counsel	NA	E.P.S	NA
DUNS No.	NA	Shareholders	NA

Business: The groups principal activities include exploring and developing natural gas and oil reserves. The group operates from the United States.

Primary SIC and add'l.: 1311

CIK No: 0001359699

Officers: Milton W. Cox/Chmn., CEO, Bassam Nastat/Dir., Pres., Don L. Sytsma/Dir., CFO, Michael M. Tindle/Dir. - Field Operations, Paul Moase/Financing Advisor

Directors: Milton W. Cox/Chmn., CEO, Bassam Nastat/Dir., Pres., Don L. Sytsma/Dir., CFO, Jay Timothy Altum/Dir., Arden T. McCracken/Dir., Tim J. Altum/53/Dir.

Owners: Metage Funds Limited/23.30%, Arden T. McCracken, Milton Cox/30.50%, Bassam Nastat/17.70%, Donald L. Sytsma/13.70%, Insiders/60.60%, Tim J. Altum

Curr. Assets:	$212,000	**Curr. Liab.:**	$2,333,000		
Plant, Equip.:	$7,929,000	**Total Liab.:**	$4,866,000	**Indic. Yr. Divd.:**	NA
Total Assets:	$8,197,000	**Net Worth:**	$3,330,000	**Debt/ Equity:**	NA

Gulfmark Offshore Inc

10111 Richmond Ave., Ste. 340, Houston, TX, 77042; ***PH:*** 1-713-963-9522; ***Fax:*** 1-713-963-9796; ***http://*** www.gulfmark.com

General - Incorporation	DE	**Stock** - Price on:12/24/2007	$53.32
Employees	1,243	Stock Exchange	NYSE
Auditor	UHY LLP	Ticker Symbol	GLF
Stk Agt	American Stock Transfer & Trust Co.	Outstanding Shares	22,870,000
Counsel	NA	E.P.S	$5.15
DUNS No.	61-505-6884	Shareholders	NA

Business: The group's principal activity is to operate offshore support vessels, principally in the north sea, southeast Asia and Brazil. The group transports materials, supplies and personnel to and from offshore platforms, drilling rig and performs anchor handling and towing services. The customers of the group include integrated oil companies, large independent oil and natural as exploration, production companies working in international markets, and foreign government organizations. The majority of operations are conducted in the north sea, with the balance in offshore southeast Asia, Brazil and west Africa.

Primary SIC and add'l.: 4412

CIK No: 0001030749

Subsidiaries: Chalvoyage (M)Sdn. Bhd., GM Offshore, Inc., Gulf Channel Offshore Servicos LDA, Gulf Marine Far East PTE, Ltd., Gulf Marine Servicos Maritimos do Brasil Limitada, Gulf Offshore Guernsey, Ltd., Gulf Offshore Marine International B.V., Gulf Offshore Marine International, S. de R.L., Gulf Offshore N.S. Limited, Gulf Offshore Norge AS, GulfMark Capital, LLC, GulfMark de Mexico, S. de R.L. de C.V., GulfMark Norge AS, GulfMark North Sea Limited, GulfMark Oceans, L.P. 22 Subsidiaries included in the Index

Officers: Bruce A. Streeter/Dir., CEO, Pres./$1,991,417.00, David Rosenwasser/Mgr. - Operations, Gulf Marine Servicos Maritimos DO Brasil Limitada, Arne Lier/GM - Gulf Offshore Norge, Steve Wilson/Mgr. - Chartering , Gulf Offshore North SEA, LTD, Mario Madalena/Mgr. - Administrative, Gulf Marine DO Brasil Ltda, Martin Watts/Area Dir. - Gulf Marine FAR East PTE LTD, Steven Yong/Mgr. - Operations, Gulf Marine FAR East PTE LTD, Thor Skandsen/Mgr. - Accounting, Gulf Offshore Norge, John Scott/Mgr. - Operations, Gulf Offshore North SEA, LTD, Edward A. Guthrie/CFO, Exec. VP - Finance/$1,335,087.00, Carla A. Mashinski/VP - Accounting, Chief Accounting Officer, Trond Forland/Mgr. - Chartering, Gulf Offshore Norge, Carla S. Mashinski/45/Controller, Assist. Sec./$640,555.00, Erik Utne Eikhaugen/Mgr. - Operations, Gulf Offshore Norge, David Kenwright/MD - Gulf Offshore North SEA, LTD *(18 Officers included in Index)*

Directors: Bruce A. Streeter/Dir., CEO, Pres., David J. Butters/Chmn., Robert T. Oconnell/Dir., Rex C. Ross/64/Dir., Peter I. Bijur/Dir., Marshall A. Crowe/Dir., Louis S. Gimbel/Dir., Sheldon S. Gordon/Dir., Robert B. Millard/Dir.

Owners: Marshall A. Crowe, Sheldon S. Gordon, Steinberg Asset Management, LLC/8.91%, Rex C. Ross, Louis S. Gimbel/1.78%, Estabrook Capital Management LLC/5.14%, Lehman Brothers Holdings Inc./9.55%, Insiders/14.54%, Robert B. Millard/3.45%, Dimensional Fund Advisors LP/5.54%, Bruce A. Streeter/2.86%, Robert T. OConnell, John E. Leech/1.46%, Peter I. Bijur, David J. Butters/3.16% *(17 Owners included in Index)*

Financial Data: ***Fiscal Year End:***12/31 ***Latest Annual Data:*** 12/31/2006

Year	Sales	Net Income
2006	$250,921,000	$89,729,000
2005	$204,042,000	$38,390,000
2004	$139,312,000	-$4,631,000

Curr. Assets:	$143,112,000	**Curr. Liab.:**	$38,164,000	**P/E Ratio:**	10.64
Plant, Equip.:	$571,989,000	**Total Liab.:**	$209,401,000	**Indic. Yr. Divd.:**	NA
Total Assets:	$750,829,000	**Net Worth:**	$541,428,000	**Debt/ Equity:**	0.2810

Gulfport Energy Corp

14313 N May Ave., Ste. 100, Oklahoma City, OK, 73134; **PH:** 1-405-848-8807; **Fax:** 1-405-848-8816; **http://** www.gulfportenergy.com

General - Incorporation	DE	**Stock**- Price on:12/24/2007	$18.87
Employees	151	Stock Exchange	NDQ
Auditor	Grant Thornton LLP	Ticker Symbol	GPOR
Stk Agt	American Stock Transfer & Trust Co.	Outstanding Shares	35,100,000
Counsel	NA	E.P.S	$0.99
DUNS No.	15-474-5392	Shareholders	NA

Business: The group's principal activities are exploration, development and production of crude oil and gas. As on 01-Jan-2004, the group had 22 mmboe proved reserves. The operations are concentrated in two fields: west cote blanche bay and the hackberry fields. It owns interests in a number of producing oil and gas properties along the Louisiana fields.

Primary SIC and add'l.: 1311

CIK No: 0000874499

Officers: James D. Palm/Dir., CEO/$585,178.00, Michael G. Moore/Sr. VP, CFO/$404,925.00, Stuart Maier/Contact - Geology, Geophysics, Randy Wilson/Contact - Geology, Geophysics, Jay Thomas/Land Management, Business Ventures, Sandy Holmes/Contact - Royalty Owner Relations, Kit Coffin/Human Resources, John Kilgallon/Contact - Investor Relations, Corporate Affairs

Directors: James D. Palm/Dir., CEO, Mike Liddell/Chmn., David L. Houston/Dir., Scott E. Streller/Dir.

Owners: David L. Houston, Scott E. Streller, Charles E. Davidson/41.30%, Mike Liddell/4.10%, Michael G. Moore, Southpoint Capital Advisor, LP/8.10%, Luxor Capital Group/8.40%, Insiders/4.60%, James D. Palm, Robert E. Brooks

Financial Data: *Fiscal Year End:*12/31 *Latest Annual Data:* 12/31/2006

Year	Sales	Net Income
2006	$60,390,000	$27,808,000
2005	$27,559,000	$10,895,000
2004	$23,190,000	$4,304,000

Curr. Assets:	$19,927,000	**Curr. Liab.:**	$26,108,000	**P/E Ratio:**	19.06
Plant, Equip.:	$157,674,000	**Total Liab.:**	$71,342,000	**Indic. Yr. Divd.:**	NA
Total Assets:	$195,151,000	**Net Worth:**	$123,809,000	**Debt/ Equity:**	0.2371

GVI Security Solutions Inc

2801 Trade Ctr Dr., Ste. 120, Carrollton, TX, 75007; **PH:** 1-972-245-7353; **Fax:** 1-972-245-7333; **http://** www.gviss.com; **Email:** npaciotti@gviss.com

General - Incorporation	DE	**Stock**- Price on:12/24/2007	$0.8
Employees	42	Stock Exchange	OTC
Auditor	Mercadien, P.C	Ticker Symbol	GVSS
Stk Agt	Continental Stock Transfer & Trust Co	Outstanding Shares	28,130,000
Counsel	NA	E.P.S	-$0.23
DUNS No.	NA	Shareholders	NA

Business: The group's principle activity is to provide video surveillance and security solutions to the professional, homeland security, retail and business-to-business security markets. The group also offers other security products such as digital recording, software systems and networking products. Customers of the group include retail outlets such as warehouse clubs, mass-Market retailers and specialty electronics stores, distributors and system integrators that specialize in video surveillance and security products and services. Products are distributed in north, central and South America. It operates sales and distribution centers in Dallas, Texas, Mexico, sao paulo, Brazil and bogota, Colombia. The group acquired gvi security inc in 2004. The group's quarterly revenue for Sep'07 was 10.76 millions of USD.

Primary SIC and add'l.: 7372 7382 3663 3651

CIK No: 0001021444

Subsidiaries: GVI Security Solutions, Inc., GVI Security, Inc., Rapor, Inc.

Officers: Steven E. Walin/Dir., CEO, Aldo Cindo/Contact - Customer Service, Canada, Joseph F. Restivo/Dir., CFO, Fernando Tomasiello/Sr. VP - Sales, International, Michael Capulli/Sr. VP - Sales, North America, Joel Schaffer/Dir. - Product Management, Ramon Duran/Product Development Mgr. - Cctv, Melissa A. Viviano/Regional Sales Mgr. - Northeast, E. N. Simon/Regional Sales Mgr. - Central, Chistopher Thomas/Regional Sales Mgr. - Western, Manuel Pecino/Dir. - Technical Services, Susan Wells/Customer Service Mgr., Victor Pena/Contact - Customer Service, Shirlie Kirk/Contact - Customer Service, Abby Davis/Contact - Customer Service *(22 Officers included in Index)*

Directors: Steven E. Walin/Dir., CEO, David Weiner/Chmn., Gary Freeman/Dir., Craig Ellins/Dir., Moshe Zarmi/Dir., Joseph F. Restivo/Dir., CFO

Owners: Moshe Zarmi, Gary Freeman, HG Investments, LLC/9.80%, Steven Walin/4.20%, Joseph Restivo/4.20%, Richard Kall/9.20%, David Weiner/10.10%, Craig Ellins, Insiders/19.50%, Europa International, Inc./12.40%, Fred Knoll/12.40%, Steven Kolow/19.70%

Financial Data: *Fiscal Year End:*12/31 *Latest Annual Data:* 12/31/2006

Year	Sales	Net Income
2006	$43,973,000	-$16,491,000
2005	$41,166,000	-$13,020,000
2004	$66,206,000	-$7,178,000

Curr. Assets:	$15,846,000	**Curr. Liab.:**	$17,850,000		
Plant, Equip.:	$384,000	**Total Liab.:**	$17,912,000	**Indic. Yr. Divd.:**	NA
Total Assets:	$16,472,000	**Net Worth:**	-$1,440,000	**Debt/ Equity:**	NA

Gymboree Corp

500 Howard St., San Francisco, CA, 94105; **PH:** 1-415-278-7000; **Fax:** 1-415-278-7100; **http://** www.gymboree.com

General - Incorporation	DE	**Stock**- Price on:12/24/2007	$41.27
Employees	4,300	Stock Exchange	NDQ
Auditor	Deloitte & Touche LLP	Ticker Symbol	GYMB
Stk Agt	Computershare Ltd.	Outstanding Shares	30,780,000
Counsel	Perkins Coie LLP	E.P.S	$2.51
DUNS No.	03-885-5029	Shareholders	NA

Business: The group's principal activity is to sell high quality apparel, accessories, and play programs for children and parent-child developmental play programs designed to enhance early childhood development through fun-filled sensory and motor activities that engage children ages newborn to four years old through sight, touch, sound and movement. The major brands of the group are gymboree (R), janie and jack and play and music(R) brands. The group operates its stores in the United States, Canada, Ireland and the United Kingdom, primarily in regional shopping malls and in selected suburban and urban locations. On 31-Jul-2004, the group operated 646 retail stores, including 596 stores in the United States, 28 stores in Canada and 22 stores in Europe, as well as an online store at www.gymboree.com and www.janieandjack.com.

Primary SIC and add'l.: 2300 3944

CIK No: 0000786110

Subsidiaries: Gym-Mark, Inc., Gymboree Industries Ltd, Gymboree Logistics Partnership, Gymboree Manufacturing, Inc, Gymboree of Ireland, Ltd., Gymboree Operations, Inc., Gymboree Play Program, Inc, Gymboree Retail Stores, Inc, Gymboree U.K. Leasing Ltd., Gymboree U.K. Ltd., Gymboree, Inc., a, The Gymboree Stores, Inc

Officers: Matthew K. McCauley/35/Chmn., CEO/$3,434,661.00, Blair W. Lambert/Dir., CFO, COO/$1,629,887.00, Marina Armstrong/Sr. VP - Stores, Human Resources, Play, Music, Sec./$1,656,698.00, Kip M. Garcia/Pres./$1,683,182.00, Lynda G. Gustafson/VP, Corporate Controller/$489,427.00

Directors: Matthew K. McCauley/35/Chmn., CEO, Gary M. Heil/Dir., Blair W. Lambert/Dir., CFO, COO, John C. Pound/Dir., William U. Westerfield/Dir., Daniel R. Lyle/Dir.

Owners: Insiders/5.20%, Barclays Global Investors, N.A./6.70%, Blair W. Lambert, Daniel R. Lyle, FMR Corporation/11.30%, Barbara L. Rambo, Gary M. Heil, Matthew K. McCauley/1.80%, Marina Armstrong/1.30%, Lynda G. Gustafson, Kip M. Garcia, John C. Pound, William U. Westerfield, Goldman Sachs Asset Management, L.P./10.00%

Financial Data: *Fiscal Year End:*01/28 *Latest Annual Data:* 2/3/2007

Year	Sales	Net Income
2007	$791,638,000	$60,250,000
2006	$678,453,000	$33,684,000
2005	$594,478,000	$8,644,000

Curr. Assets:	$293,846,000	**Curr. Liab.:**	$132,136,000	**P/E Ratio:**	21.27
Plant, Equip.:	$150,251,000	**Total Liab.:**	$178,481,000	**Indic. Yr. Divd.:**	NA
Total Assets:	$454,208,000	**Net Worth:**	$275,727,000	**Debt/ Equity:**	NA

Gyrodyne Co of America Inc

102 Flowerfield St., St James, NY, 11780; **PH:** 1-631-584-5400; **Fax:** 1-631-584-7075; **http://** www.gyrodyne.com; **Email:** lierardi@gyrodyne.com

General - Incorporation	NY	**Stock**- Price on:12/24/2007	$58.01
Employees	8	Stock Exchange	NDQ
Auditor	Holtz Rubenstein Reminick LLP	Ticker Symbol	GYRO
Stk Agt	Registrar & Transfer Co	Outstanding Shares	1,290,000
Counsel	NA	E.P.S	$3.06
DUNS No.	00-204-0061	Shareholders	NA

Business: The group's principal activity is to lease industrial and commercial real estate to diversified entities located in long island, New York. It owns 314 acre site, primarily zoned for light industry and has 184,000 square feet of rental space and 59 tenants. It also invests as a passive investor in citrus grove partnerships.

Primary SIC and add'l.: 6552 6519

CIK No: 0000044689

Subsidiaries: Flowerfield Properties, Inc

Officers: Stephen V. Maroney/Dir., CEO, CFO, Pres., Treasurer, Frank D. Alessandro/Controller, Peter Pitsiokos/COO, Corp. Sec., Chief Compliance Officer, Marigene Gallicchio/Executive Assist., Lynn Ierardi/Accounting, Clint Borkstrom/Property Mgr.

Directors: Stephen V. Maroney/Dir., CEO, CFO, Pres., Treasurer, Paul L. Lamb/Chmn., Philip F. Palmedo/Dir., Robert H. Beyer/Dir., Elliot H. Levine/Dir., Richard B. Smith/Dir., Nader G.M. Salour/Dir., Ronald J. MacKlin/Dir.

Owners: Paul L. Lamb/1.89%, River Road Asset Management/6.16%, AmTrust Capital Management/5.89%, Stephen V. Maroney/6.29%, Peter Pitsiokos/1.25%, Insiders/11.61%, Richard B. Smith, Bulldog Investors/17.43%, Ronald J. Macklin, Gerard Scollan/7.06%, Nader G.M. Salour, Philip F. Palmedo, Robert H. Beyer/1.07%

Financial Data: *Fiscal Year End:*04/30 *Latest Annual Data:* 4/30/2006

Year	Sales	Net Income
2006	$1,627,000	$13,115,000
2005	$2,039,000	-$138,000

Curr. Assets:	$28,028,000	**Curr. Liab.:**	$1,085,000	**P/E Ratio:**	19.80
Plant, Equip.:	$1,111,000	**Total Liab.:**	$10,443,000	**Indic. Yr. Divd.:**	NA
Total Assets:	$30,580,000	**Net Worth:**	$20,137,000	**Debt/ Equity:**	NA

H & R Block Inc

1 H&R Block Way, Kansas City, MO, 64105; **PH:** 1-816-854-3000; **Fax:** 1-816-854-8500; **http://** www.handrblock.com; **Email:** mediadesk@hrblock.com

General - Incorporation	MO	**Stock**- Price on:12/24/2007	$23.24
Employees	16,000	Stock Exchange	NYSE
Auditor	KPMG LLP	Ticker Symbol	HRB
Stk Agt	Mellon Investor Services LLC	Outstanding Shares	322,930,000
Counsel	James H. Ingraham	E.P.S	-$2.94
DUNS No.	04-395-1235	Shareholders	NA

Business: The group's principle activities are to provide tax services, financial advice, investment and mortgage products and consulting services. The group operates in five segments. The U.S. Tax operations and international tax operations segment provides income tax return preparation services, electronic filing services and other services related to income tax return preparation in the United States, Canada, Australia and the United Kingdom. The mortgage operations segment originate, service and sell conforming and nonconforming mortgage loans in the United States. The investment services segment provides investment advice, brokerage services and investment planning. The business services segment provides accounting, tax, consulting, payroll, employee benefits and capital market services to individuals in the United States. The international tax operations segment provides tax return preparation, electronic filing and related services. The group's total revenue for the year 2007 was 4,021.27 millions of USD.

Primary SIC and add'l.: 6162 7291 7379 6211 7389

CIK No: 0000012659

Subsidiaries: 2430472 Nova Scotia Co., 4230 West Green Oaks, Inc., AcuLink Mortgage Solutions, LLC, AcuLink of Alabama, LLC, BFC Transactions, Inc., Birchtree Financial Services, Inc., Birchtree Insurance Agency, Inc., Black Orchard Financial, Inc., Block Financial Corporation, Companion Insurance, Ltd., Companion Mortgage Corporation, Credit Union Jobs, LLC, Equico Europe Limited, Equico, Inc., Financial Marketing Services, Inc. 75 Subsidiaries included in the Index

Officers: Mark A. Ernst/Chmn., CEO, Pres., Joan Cohen/Pres. - H, R Block Financial Advisors, Thomas M. Bloch/Dir. - Educator, Tom Allanson/Group Pres. - Digital Tax Solutions, William L. Trubeck/CFO, Exec. VP, Marc West/Group Pres. - Commercial Markets, Bret G. Wilson/Sec., Steve Tait/Pres. - RSM Mcgladrey Business Services Inc, Tim Gokey/Group Pres. - Retail Tax Services, Brad C. Iversen/Sr. VP, Chief Marketing Officer, Tammy S. Serati/Sr. VP - Human Resources, Jeffrey E. Nachbor/43/Sr. VP, Corporate Controller, Kathy Barney/Pres. - H, R Block Bank, Scott Dudley/Assist. VP - Investor Relations, Rich Agar/CIO, Sr. VP *(16 Officers included in Index)*

Directors: Mark A. Ernst/Chmn., CEO, Pres., Henry W. Bloch/Co - Founder, Jerry D. Choate/Dir., Donna R. Ecton/Dir., Henry F. Frigon/Dir., Roger W. Hale/Dir., Len J. Lauer/Dir., David Baker Lewis/Dir., Tom D. Seip/Dir., Louis W. Smith/Dir., Rayford Wilkins/Dir., Richard C. Breeden/Dir., Robert A. Gerard/Dir., Edward L. Shaw/Dir., Kenneth G. Baum/Dir.

Owners: Tom D. Seip, Ariel Capital Management, Inc./0.05%, Timothy C. Gokey, Richard C. Breeden/1.84%, Steven Tait, Jerry D. Choate, William L. Trubeck, Roger W. Hale, David B. Lewis, Insiders/3.64%, Harris Associates L.P./0.07%, Mark A. Ernst, Henry F. Frigon, Nicholas J. Spaeth, T. Rowe Price Associates, Inc./0.10% *(20 Owners included in Index)*

Financial Data: *Fiscal Year End:*04/30 *Latest Annual Data:* 04/30/2007

Year	Sales	Net Income
2007	$4,021,274,000	-$433,653,000
2006	$4,872,801,000	$490,408,000
2005	$4,420,019,000	$623,910,000

Curr. Assets:	$3,454,292,000	**Curr. Liab.:**	$5,176,352,000	**P/E Ratio:**	31.84
Plant, Equip.:	$379,066,000	**Total Liab.:**	$6,084,994,000	**Indic. Yr. Divd.:**	$0.570
Total Assets:	$7,499,493,000	**Net Worth:**	$1,414,499,000	**Debt/ Equity:**	NA

H&E Equipment Services Inc

11100 Mead Rd., Ste. 200, Baton Rouge, LA, 70816; ***PH:*** 1-225-298-5200; ***Fax:*** 1-225-298-5377; ***http://*** www.he-equipment.com

General		**Stock**	
Incorporation	DE	Price on:12/24/2007	$26.74
Employees	1,677	Stock Exchange	NDQ
Auditor	BDO Seidman, LLP	Ticker Symbol	HEES
Stk Agt	Continental Stock Transfer & Trust Co	Outstanding Shares	38,180,000
Counsel	NA	E.P.S.	$1.79
DUNS No.	NA	Shareholders	NA

Business: The groups principle activity is to provide heavy construction and industrial equipment. The products of the group include aerial platform equipment, cranes, earthmoving equipment and industrial lift trucks. The groups operates through five segments namely equipment rentals, new equipment sales, used equipment sales, parts sales, and repair and maintenance services. Customers served by the group include industrial and commercial companies, construction contractors, manufacturers, public utilities, municipalities and maintenance contractors. The group operates from West Coast, Intermountain, Southwest, Gulf Coast and Southeast in United States. In February 28, 2006, the group acquired Eagle High Reach Equipment, Inc. The group's quarterly revenue for September 2007 was 270.59 millions of USD.

Primary SIC and add'l.: 5063 7353 5082 7359 5085 5084

CIK No: 0001339605

Subsidiaries: GNE Investments, Inc., Great Northern Equipment, Inc., H&E California Holding, LLC, H&E Equipment Services (California), LLC, H&E Finance Corp.

Officers: John M. Engquist/Dir., CEO, Pres., Joe Mancaruso/Contact - Boise, ID, C. J. Nichols/Contact - Alexandria, Larry Levet/Contact - Baton Rouge, Tom Diano/Contact - Belle Chasse, Curt Lear/Contact - Jacksonville, Art Hutchins/Contact - Orlando, Darin Odey/Contact - Pompano Beach, Joe Villarosa/Contact - Tampa, Scott Patch/Contact - Atlanta, Calvin Canter/Contact - Arden, Alfred Anaya/Contact - Albuquerque, Ed Allan/Contact - Corpus Christi, Bob Martin/Contact - Dallas, Steve Flood/Contact - Houston *(68 Officers included in Index)*

Directors: John M. Engquist/Dir., CEO, Pres., Gary W. Bagley/Chmn., Keith E. Alessi/Dir., Lawrence C. Karlson/Dir., John T. Sawyer/Dir., Paul Arnold/Dir., Bruce C. Bruckmann/Dir.

Owners: John T. Sawyer, Leslie S. Magee, John M. Engquist/11.80%, Bruckmann, Rosser, Sherrill& Co. L.P./13.35%, Bruckmann, Rosser, Sherrill& Co.II L.P./24.36%, Keith E. Alessi, William W. Fox, Gary W. Bagley, John D. Jones, Bruckman, Rosser, Sherrill& Co., Inc., Bradley W. Barber, Lawrence C. Karlson, Insiders/53.31%, Bruce C. Bruckmann/39.04%, Dale W. Roesener/1.12% *(16 Owners included in Index)*

Financial Data: *Fiscal Year End:*12/31 *Latest Annual Data:* 12/31/2006

Year	Sales	Net Income
2006	$804,369,000	$32,714,000
2005	$600,210,000	$28,160,000
2004	$478,172,000	-$13,737,000

Curr. Assets:	$249,922,000	**Curr. Liab.:**	$251,798,000		
Plant, Equip.:	$470,117,000	**Total Liab.:**	$524,358,000	**Indic. Yr. Divd.:**	NA
Total Assets:	$759,942,000	**Net Worth:**	$235,584,000	**Debt/ Equity:**	1.6148

H&Q Healthcare Investors

30 Rowes Wharf, Ste. 430, Boston, MA, 02110; ***PH:*** 1-617-574-0537; ***Fax:*** 1-617-772-8577; ***http://*** www.hqcm.com; ***Email:*** info@hqcm.com

General		**Stock**	
Incorporation	MA	Price on:12/24/2007	$17.4
Employees	NA	Stock Exchange	NYSE
Auditor	Deloitte & Touche, LLP	Ticker Symbol	HQH
Stk Agt	State Street Bank and Trust Co	Outstanding Shares	22,730,000
Counsel	NA	E.P.S.	$3.243
DUNS No.	NA	Shareholders	NA

Business: The groups principal activity is to invest in sectors including, biopharmaceuticals, drug delivery, drug discovery technologies, generic pharmaceuticals, healthcare services, and medical devices and diagnostics. The group operates from the United States.

Primary SIC and add'l.: 6199

CIK No: 0000805267

Officers: Daniel R. Omstead/CEO, Pres., Christopher F. Brinzey/Sr. VP - Research, Eric Oddleifson/73/Sr. Adviser, Oleg M. Pohotsky/60/Self, Employed Financial Consultant, Frank T. Gentile/Sr. VP - Research, Jason C. Akus/VP - Research, Peter Savitscus/Head - Trading, Carolyn Haley/Chief Compliance Officer, VP - Fund Administration, Betty Chang/Mgr. - Fund Administration, Regulatory Affairs, Amy Scott Boudnitskii/Assist. to Pres.

Directors: Lawrence S. Lewin/70/Chmn., Robert P. Mack/72/Trustee, Uwe E. Reinhardt/70/Dir., Lucinda H. Stebbins/62/Trustee

Financial Data: *Fiscal Year End:*09/30 *Latest Annual Data:* 9/30/2006

Year	Sales	Net Income
2006	$24,375,000	-$15,013,000
2005	$68,526,000	$62,621,000
2004	$33,989,000	$13,364,000

Curr. Assets:	$2,599,000	**Curr. Liab.:**	$1,830,000	**P/E Ratio:**	11.94
Plant, Equip.:	NA	**Total Liab.:**	$1,830,000	**Indic. Yr. Divd.:**	$1.520
Total Assets:	$386,931,000	**Net Worth:**	$385,101,000	**Debt/ Equity:**	NA

H&Q Life Sciences Investors

30 Rowes Wharf Fl 4, Boston, MA, 02110; ***PH:*** 1-617-310-0500; ***http://*** www.hqcm.com; ***Email:*** info@hqcm.com

General		**Stock**	
Incorporation	MA	Price on:12/24/2007	$13.77
Employees	NA	Stock Exchange	NYSE
Auditor	Deloitte & Touche, LLP	Ticker Symbol	HQL
Stk Agt	Computershare Investor Services	Outstanding Shares	19,640,000
Counsel	NA	E.P.S.	$2.515
DUNS No.	NA	Shareholders	NA

Business: The groups principal activity is to invest in life sciences companies. The group operates from the United States.

Primary SIC and add'l.: 6036

CIK No: 0000884121

Officers: Daniel R. Omstead/CEO, Pres.

Directors: Lawrence S. Lewin/70/Chmn., Robert P. Mack/72/Trustee, Eric Oddleifson/73/Trustee, Oleg M. Pohotsky/60/Trustee, Uwe E. Reinhardt/70/Trustee, Lucinda H. Stebbins/62/Trustee

Financial Data: *Fiscal Year End:*NA *Latest Annual Data:* 09/30/2007

Year	Sales	Net Income
2007	$55,100,000	$50,512,000
2006	$16,036,000	-$21,446,000
2005	$48,237,000	$44,763,000

Curr. Assets:	$1,375,000	**Curr. Liab.:**	$2,695,000	**P/E Ratio:**	11.94
Plant, Equip.:	NA	**Total Liab.:**	$2,695,000	**Indic. Yr. Divd.:**	$1.240
Total Assets:	$270,814,000	**Net Worth:**	$268,119,000	**Debt/ Equity:**	NA

H.B. Fuller Co

1200 Willow Lake Blvd., PO Box 64683, St. Paul, MN, 55110; ***PH:*** 1-651-236-5900; ***http://*** www.hbfuller.com

General		**Stock**	
Incorporation	MN	Price on:12/24/2007	$28.05
Employees	3,721	Stock Exchange	NYSE
Auditor	KPMG LLP	Ticker Symbol	FUL
Stk Agt	Wells Fargo Shareholder Services	Outstanding Shares	60,660,000
Counsel	Rick Baker	E.P.S.	$2.48
DUNS No.	00-615-9776	Shareholders	NA

Business: The group's principle activity is to manufacture and market adhesives and specialty chemical products. It operates under two business segments: global adhesives and full-valu/specialty. The global adhesive segment comprises of industrial and performance adhesives products. The products are used in various markets including assembly, packaging, converting, nonwoven, automotive, graphic arts and footwear. The full-valu/specialty segment produces and supplies specialty chemical products that are used in various applications. These applications include ceramic tile application, hvac insulation, powder coatings applied to metal surfaces for office furniture, appliances and lawn and garden equipment, specialty hot melt products for packaging applications and others. The group has sales operations in 33 countries throughout North America, Europe, Latin America and the Asia/pacific region. The group's quarterly revenue for Sep'07 was 367.89 millions of USD.

Primary SIC and add'l.: 2891 2851

CIK No: 0000039368

Subsidiaries: Adalis Corporation, Adhesivos H.B. Fuller (Sul) Ltda.1, Autotek Sealants, Inc., B. Fuller International Inc., Centro de Pinturas Glidden-Protecto, S.A., Changchun EFTEC Chemical Products Ltd., Chemical Supply Corporation, Chemical Supply Peruana, S.A.2, D Plast - EFTEC a.s., D Plast - EFTEC NN, D Plast - EFTEC RT, D Plast - EFTEC SK, s.r.o., Datac Ltd.1, Deco Tintas Comerciales, S.A.1, Deco Tintas de El Salvador, S.A.1 118 Subsidiaries included in the Index

Officers: Michele Volpi/Dir., CEO, Pres., Ramon Tico/VP - Latin America, Jan Muller/VP - Europe, Jay Scripter/VP - North America, Timothy Keenan/VP, General Counsel, Corp. Sec., James C. McCreary/VP, Interim CFO, Controller, Cheryl Reinitz/VP, Treasurer, Ann Parriott/VP - Human Resources, Fabrizio Corradini/VP, Chief Strategy Officer, Kevin Gilligan/VP - Asia Pacific, Monica Moretti/VP, Chief Marketing Officer

Directors: Michele Volpi/Dir., CEO, Pres., Lee R. Mitau/Chmn., Knut Kleedehn/Dir., Michael J. Losh/Dir., Juliana Chugg/Dir., John C. Van Roden/Dir., Alfredo L. Rovira/Dir., Richard L. Marcantonio/Dir., William R. Van Sant/Dir.

Owners: Albert P.L. Stroucken/1.83%, Alfredo L. Rovira, Knut Kleedehn, John A. Feenan, Edwin J. Snyder, Lee R. Mitau, Michael J. Losh, Barclays Global Investors, NA and Fund Advisors/5.32%, William R. Van Sant, Richard L. Marcantonio, Stephen J. Large, Mairs and Power, Inc./7.37%, Insiders/2.58%, Michele Volpi, John C. van Roden

Financial Data: *Fiscal Year End:*12/03 *Latest Annual Data:* 12/2/2006

Year	Sales	Net Income
2006	$1,472,391,000	$134,213,000
2005	$1,512,193,000	$61,576,000
2004	$1,409,606,000	$35,603,000

Curr. Assets:	$582,434,000	**Curr. Liab.:**	$261,858,000	**P/E Ratio:**	12.14
Plant, Equip.:	$298,852,000	**Total Liab.:**	$506,753,000	**Indic. Yr. Divd.:**	$0.260
Total Assets:	$1,107,557,000	**Net Worth:**	$584,443,000	**Debt/ Equity:**	0.2018

H2Diesel Holdings Inc

11111 Katy Fwy., Ste. 910, Houston, TX, 33498; ***PH:*** 1-713-973-5720

General		**Stock**	
Incorporation	FL	Price on:12/24/2007	$6.7
Employees	3	Stock Exchange	OTC
Auditor	Imowitz Koenig & Co., LLP	Ticker Symbol	HTWO
Stk Agt	Olde Monmouth Stk Trnsfer Co. Inc.	Outstanding Shares	17,090,000
Counsel	NA	E.P.S.	-$0.55
DUNS No.	NA	Shareholders	NA

Business: The groups principal activity is to produce bio-diesel fuel. The group operates from the United States.

Primary SIC and add'l.: 2860

CIK No: 0001268236

Subsidiaries: H2Diesel, Inc.

Owners: David H. Goebel, Ferdinando Petrucci/5.18%, Xethanol Corporation/33.88%, Michael Burstein, Phil E. Pearce, The River Trust/5.73%, Connie Lausten, Andrea Festuccia, Lee S. Rosen/19.21%, James Robert Sheppard, Insiders/25.65%, Lee Rosen 2006 Irrevocable Trust I/12.10%, Steven F. Gilliland, David A. Gillespie, John Mack

Financial Data: Fiscal Year End:12/31 **Latest Annual Data:** 12/31/2006

Year	Sales	Net Income
2006	NA	-$5,392,000
2005	$63,000	-$71,000
2004	$161,000	-$115,000

Curr. Assets:	$1,102,000	**Curr. Liab.:**	$1,690,000		
Plant, Equip.:	NA	**Total Liab.:**	$6,495,000	**Indic. Yr. Divd.:**	NA
Total Assets:	$9,163,000	**Net Worth:**	$2,669,000	**Debt/ Equity:**	NA

Habasit Holding USA Inc

Formerly: Summa Industries
21250 Hawthorne Blvd., Ste. 500, Torrance, CA, 90503; **PH:** 1-310-792-7024;
http:// www.summaindustries.com

General - Incorporation	DE	**Stock**- Price on:12/24/2007	NA
Employees	NA	Stock Exchange	NA
Auditor	PricewaterhouseCoopers LLP	Ticker Symbol	NA
Stk Agt	U.S. Stock Transfer Corp	Outstanding Shares	NA
Counsel	NA	E.P.S.	NA
DUNS No.	04-876-3320	Shareholders	NA

Business: The group's principle activities include developing and manufacturing proprietary plastic products for diverse industrial and commercial markets, primarily located in the United States. It designs and manufactures injection-molded and formed plastic optical components, molded plastic modular conveyor belt and chain, plastic fittings, valves, filters and tubing, molded plastic coil forms and , motors, relays and switches and other molded and extruded plastic components for diverse industries. The group also performs additional production operations including laser cutting, machining and welding of plastic parts, vacuum deposition, coating, assembly and testing. The group operates from United States.

Primary SIC and add'l.: 3089 3559 3569 6719 3728

CIK No: 0000062262

Subsidiaries: Aquarius Brands, Inc, Central Valley Manufacturing, Inc, Fullerton Holdings, Inc, Genesta, Inc., an Ontario, KVP Falcon Plastic Belting, Inc, KVP Holdings, Inc, LexaLite International Corporation, Plastic Specialties, Inc, Plastron Industries, Inc

Officers: James R. Swartwout/CEO, Paul A. Walbrun/VP, Controller

Habersham Bancorp

282 Historic Hwy. 441 N, Cornelia, GA, 30531; **PH:** 1-706-778-1000; **Fax:** 1-706-778-6886;
http:// www.habcorp.com

General - Incorporation	GA	**Stock**- Price on:12/24/2007	$20.0123
Employees	180	Stock Exchange	NDQ
Auditor	Porter Keadle Moore LLP	Ticker Symbol	HABC
Stk Agt	Suntrust Bank	Outstanding Shares	2,970,000
Counsel	NA	E.P.S.	$1.58
DUNS No.	03-633-6782	Shareholders	NA

Business: The group's principal activity is to operate a full service commercial banking business that provides customary banking services. These services include checking and savings accounts, various types of time deposits, safe deposit facilities and individual retirement accounts. The group also makes secured and unsecured loans and provides other financial services to its customers. The group offers trust services including trust administration, asset management services and other services in the area of personal trusts.

Primary SIC and add'l.: 6712 6022

CIK No: 0000754597

Subsidiaries: Advantage Insurers, Inc., Habersham Bank

Officers: David D. Stovall/Dir., CEO, Pres./$364,371.00, Annette Banks/61/CFO, VP/$96,554.00, Edward D. Ariail/Dir., VP, Corp. Sec./$213,662.00, Bonnie C. Bowling/49/COO/$205,166.00

Directors: David D. Stovall/Dir., CEO, Pres., Thomas A. Arrendale/Chmn., Calvin B. Wilbanks/Vice Chmn., Edward D. Ariail/Dir., VP, Corp. Sec., Michael C. Martin/Dir., Michael L. Owen/Dir., Ben F. Cheek/Dir., James A. Stapleton/Dir.

Owners: Edward D. Ariail, Michael L. Owen, Ben F. Cheek, Michael C. Martin, Calvin R. Wilbanks, John Robert Arrendale, Matthew Byrnes, David D. Stovall, Insiders, James A. Stapleton, Bonnie C. Bowling, Cyndae Arrendale Bussey, Thomas A. Arrendale, Annette Banks

Financial Data: Fiscal Year End:12/31 **Latest Annual Data:** 12/31/2006

Year	Sales	Net Income
2006	$38,129,000	$5,293,000
2005	$29,593,000	$3,813,000
2004	$25,174,000	$2,343,000

Curr. Assets:	$93,456,000	**Curr. Liab.:**	$498,261,000	**P/E Ratio:**	12.67
Plant, Equip.:	$13,462,000	**Total Liab.:**	$500,174,000	**Indic. Yr. Divd.:**	NA
Total Assets:	$555,738,000	**Net Worth:**	$55,564,000	**Debt/ Equity:**	NA

Haemonetics Corp

400 Wood Rd., Braintree, MA, 02184; **PH:** 1-781-848-7100; **Fax:** 1-781-356-3558;
http:// www.haemonetics.com

General - Incorporation	MA	**Stock**- Price on:12/24/2007	$52.31
Employees	1,826	Stock Exchange	NYSE
Auditor	Ernst & Young LLP	Ticker Symbol	HAE
Stk Agt	Registrar & Transfer Co	Outstanding Shares	26,540,000
Counsel	NA	E.P.S.	$1.84
DUNS No.	05-782-7420	Shareholders	NA

Business: The group's principal activities are to design, manufacture and market automated systems and single use consumables for collecting, processing and surgical salvation of blood for blood donors and patients. It also develops and markets associated data management systems through its subsidiary fifth dimension information systems. Its direct customers are blood and plasma collectors, hospitals and hospital service providers. The group's product line includes donor products and patient products. The group operates in the United States, Europe and Japan.

Primary SIC and add'l.: 3841

CIK No: 0000313143

Officers: Brad Nutter/Dir., CEO, Pres./$4,422,391.00, Ulrich Eckert/VP - Sales, Marketing, Donor, Plasma Divisons Europe, Brian Concannon/COO/$926,843.00, Pam Spear/VP - Quality Systems, James O'Shaughnessy/General Counsel, Remi Corlin/Pres. - Asia Pacific, Joseph Forish/VP - Human Resources, Tom Lawlor/Pres. - Patient Division, Nereyda Garcia/Chief Ethics Officer, Stephen Swenson/VP, GM - Global Plasma Business, Tony Pare/VP, GM - Services Business, Christopher Lindop/VP - Finance, CFO/$1,406,284.00, Dottie Barr/ERP Program Mgr., Mark Beucler/VP, GM - Global Distribution Channel Management, Susan Hanlon/VP - Planning, Control *(24 Officers included in Index)*

Directors: Brad Nutter/Dir., CEO, Pres., Ronald A. Matricaria/Chmn., Mark Kroll/Dir., Richard Meelia/Dir., Lawrence Best/Dir., Ronald Gelbman/Dir., Ronald Merriman/Dir., Susan Bartlett Foote/Dir., Pedro Granadillo/Dir.

Owners: Ronald J. Ryan/0.02%, Brad Nutter/1.77%, Capital Research & Management Co./7.43%, Lawrence C. Best/0.52%, Ronald L. Merriman/0.10%, Peter Allen/0.37%, Susan Bartlett Foote/0.12%, Pedro P. Granadillo/0.14%, Brian Concannon/0.39%, Robert Ebbeling/0.43%, Ronald G. Gelbman/0.21%, Insiders/4.32%, Ronald A. Matricaria/0.18%, Neuberger Berman, LLC./8.70%, Mark W. Kroll/0.10% *(16 Owners included in Index)*

Financial Data: Fiscal Year End:04/01 **Latest Annual Data:** 3/31/2007

Year	Sales	Net Income
2007	$449,607,000	$49,109,000
2006	$419,733,000	$69,076,000
2005	$383,598,000	$39,639,000

Curr. Assets:	$343,611,000	**Curr. Liab.:**	$87,922,000	**P/E Ratio:**	28.43
Plant, Equip.:	$69,337,000	**Total Liab.:**	$112,622,000	**Indic. Yr. Divd.:**	NA
Total Assets:	$467,757,000	**Net Worth:**	$355,135,000	**Debt/ Equity:**	NA

Haggar Corp

Two Colinas Crossing, 11511 Luna Rd., Dallas, TX, 75234; **PH:** 1-214-352-8481;
http:// www.haggarcorp.com

General - Incorporation	NV	**Stock**- Price on:12/24/2007	NA
Employees	NA	Stock Exchange	NA
Auditor	PricewaterhouseCoopers LLP	Ticker Symbol	NA
Stk Agt	Mellon Investor Services LLC	Outstanding Shares	NA
Counsel	NA	E.P.S.	NA
DUNS No.	NA	Shareholders	NA

Business: The group's principal activity is to design, manufacture, import and sell casual and dress men's and women's apparel products. The products of the group include pants, shorts, suits, sportcoats, sweaters, shirts, dresses, skirts and vests in wide varieties of colors, sizes, fabrics and styles. The group's operations are carried out through the following segments: the wholesale segment designs, manufactures, imports and markets casual and dress men's and women's apparel to retailers throughout North America and the United Kingdom. The retail segment markets haggar(R) branded products through 70 company operated stores located in the group's Dallas headquarters and in outlet malls throughout the United States. The licensing segment generates royalty income by licensing the group's trademarks for use by other manufacturers of specified products in specified geographic areas.

Primary SIC and add'l.: 2325 2311 2321 2339

CIK No: 0000892533

Hain Celestial Group Inc

58 S Service Rd. , Melville, NY, 11747; **PH:** 1-631-730-2200; **Fax:** 1-631-730-2550;
http:// www.hain-celestial.com

General - Incorporation	DE	**Stock**- Price on:12/24/2007	$28.55
Employees	2,074	Stock Exchange	NDQ
Auditor	Ernst & Young LLP	Ticker Symbol	HAIN
Stk Agt	Continental Stock Transfer & Trust Co	Outstanding Shares	39,680,000
Counsel	Cahill Gordon & Reindel LLP	E.P.S.	$1.11
DUNS No.	82-470-0850	Shareholders	NA

Business: The group's principal activities are to manufacture, market, distribute and sell natural, specialty, organic and snack food products. Natural and organic food products include non-dairy drinks (soy and rice milk), popcorn cakes, cookies, crackers, flour, hot and cold cereals, pasta, baby food, condiments, canned and instant soups, chilis, packaged grain, nut butters, nutritional oils and other food products. Snack food products include potato and vegetable chips, organic tortilla chips, pretzels, popcorn and potato chips. Meat alternative products include soy protein meat alternative products. Medically-directed and weight management products include sugar-free, fructose sweetened and low sodium products. The brand names include celestial seasonings(R) teas, hain pure foods(R), westbrae(R), westsoy(R), arrowhead mills(R), health valley(R) and others. In 2003, the group acquired imagine foods inc., grains noirs nv, acirca inc. And on 25-Feb-2004 acquired natumi ag

Primary SIC and add'l.: 5142 5149 5145

CIK No: 0000910406

Subsidiaries: Acirca, Inc., AMI Operating, Inc., Arrowhead Mills, Inc., Botalia Pharmaceutical, Inc., Celestial Beverages, Inc., Celestial Seasonings, Inc., Dana Alexander, Inc., DeBoles Nutritional Foods, Inc., Fruit Specialties B.V., Grains Noirs SA, Hain Celestial Belgium BVBA, Hain Celestial Europe B.V., Hain Celestial UK Limited, Hain Europe NV, Hain Frozen Foods UK Limited 39 Subsidiaries included in the Index

Officers: Philippe Woitrin/CEO - Hain Celestial Europe, Irwin D. Simon/Chmn., CEO, Pres., Ellen B. Deutsch/Sr. VP, Chief Growth Officer, Maureen M. Putman/Chief Marketing Officer - Grocery, Snacks, Cecilia G. Atkinson/GM - Celestial Seasonings, Joseph A. Depippo/Pres. - Hain Pure Protein, Beena G. Goldenberg/GM - Hain Celestial Canada, David Arrow/MD - Hain Celestial UK, Adam S. Levit/Chief Sales Officer - Grocery, Snacks, Mary Celeste Anthes/VP - Investor Relations, John Carroll/Exec. VP, Pres. - Grocery, Snacks, Andrew H. Jacobson/Pres. - Personal Care, Ira J. Lamel/CFO, Exec. VP, Treasurer, Sec., Benjamin Brecher/Sr. VP - Special Projects

Directors: Irwin D. Simon/Chmn., CEO, Pres., Barry A. Alperin/Dir., Daniel R. Glickman/Dir., Andrew R. Heyer/Dir., Roger Meltzer/Dir., Beth L. Bronner/Dir., Larry S. Zilavy/Dir., Richard C. Berke/Dir., Jack Futterman/Dir., Marina Hahn/Dir., Mitchell A. Ring/Dir., Lewis D. Schiliro/Dir.

Owners: Irwin D. Simon/7.00%, Ira J. Lamel, Barry J. Alperin, Marina Hahn, Lewis D. Schiliro, BlackRock, Inc. and affiliates/8.40%, Insiders/9.90%, Cooke & Bieler LP/8.20%, Andrew R. Heyer, Mitchell A. Ring, Dimensional Fund Advisors Inc./7.30%, Beth L. Bronner, Daniel R. Glickman, Roger Meltzer, Larry S. Zilavy (17 Owners included in Index)

Financial Data: Fiscal Year End:06/30　Latest Annual Data: 6/30/2006

Year	Sales	Net Income
2006	$738,557,000	$37,067,000
2005	$619,967,000	$21,870,000
2004	$544,058,000	$27,008,000

Curr. Assets:	$260,476,000	Curr. Liab.:	$86,042,000	P/E Ratio:	25.72
Plant, Equip.:	$119,830,000	Total Liab.:	$256,357,000	Indic. Yr. Divd.:	NA
Total Assets:	$877,684,000	Net Worth:	$616,401,000	Debt/ Equity:	0.2322

Hair Therapists Inc

10940 Wilshire Blvd., Ste. 1600, Los Angeles, NV, 90024; **PH:** 1-310-443-4151

General - Incorporation	NV	Stock- Price on:12/24/2007	NA
Employees	NA	Stock Exchange	NA
Auditor Morgenstern, Svoboda & Baer CPA's PC		Ticker Symbol	NA
Stk Agt	NA	Outstanding Shares	NA
Counsel	NA	E.P.S.	$0.17
DUNS No.	NA	Shareholders	NA

Business: The group's principle activity is to provide hair services in Las Vegas, NV. Prior to execution of its original business plan, management discovered that the group was under-capitalized and unable to pursue its original business plan. The group has subsequently become a blank check group. Its current purpose is to seek a merger or business acquisition transaction. The group operates from United States.

Primary SIC and add'l.: 6770

CIK No: 0001336644

Officers: Xin Zhang/39/Dir., CFO, Jing Xie/Dir., Sec.

Directors: Xin Zhang/39/Dir., CFO, Jing Xie/Dir., Sec.

Owners: Insiders/34.50%, Xiao Jun/23.40%, Jiangping Jiang/34.50%

Financial Data: Fiscal Year End:12/31　Latest Annual Data: 12/31/2006

Year	Sales	Net Income
2006	$10,014,000	$2,558,000

Curr. Assets:	$7,462,000	Curr. Liab.:	$3,655,000		
Plant, Equip.:	$52,000	Total Liab.:	$3,655,000	Indic. Yr. Divd.:	NA
Total Assets:	$7,564,000	Net Worth:	$3,909,000	Debt/ Equity:	NA

Halifax Corp

5250 Cherokee Ave., Alexandria, VA, 22312; **PH:** 1-703-750-2202; **Fax:** 1-703-658-2444; **http://** www.hxcorp.com; **Email:** info@hxcorp.com

General - Incorporation	VA	Stock- Price on:12/24/2007	$3
Employees	436	Stock Exchange	AMEX
Auditor	Grant Thornton LLP	Ticker Symbol	HX
Stk Agt	American Stock Transfer & Trust Co	Outstanding Shares	3,180,000
Counsel	NA	E.P.S.	-$0.81
DUNS No.	04-135-3715	Shareholders	NA

Business: The group's principal activities are to provide information technology services and solutions to commercial and government organizations. The services provided by the group include seat management enterprises maintenance solutions, network security solutions, ebusiness/egovernment development, communication services. The group also provides consultation, integration, networking, maintenance and installation and training for computer systems, communications systems and simulation systems and the management, operations and maintenance support of military bases, prisons, waterways, major office complexes and communication sites. The group provides services to major manufactures including IBM, compaq, dell, gateway, hewlett packard and lexmark. On 29-Aug-2003, the group acquired microserv inc.

Primary SIC and add'l.: 7375 7378 8711

CIK No: 0000720671

Subsidiaries: Halifax Engineering, Inc., Halifax Realty, Inc

Officers: Charles L. McNew/Dir., CEO, Pres., Charles A. Harper/VP - Strategic Development, Hugh Foley/VP - Operations, Arthur Whalen/VP - Planning, Pricing, Jamie P. Cox/Corporate Controller, Joseph Sciacca/VP - Finance, CFO, Doug Reece/VP - Sales, Marketing

Directors: Charles L. McNew/Dir., CEO, Pres., John H. Grover/Chmn., John Toups/Dir., Daniel R. Young/Dir., Gerald F. Ryles/Dir., Thomas L. Hewitt/Dir., Arch C. Scurlock/Dir.

Owners: Douglas H. Reece, Hugh M. Foley/1.60%, Gary M. Lukowski/5.00%, Nancy M. Scurlock/12.60%, John M. Toups/1.70%, Insiders/19.00%, Joseph Sciacca/3.10%, Jai N. Gupta/6.10%, Gerald F. Ryles/3.40%, Arch C. Scurlock, Charles L. McNew/5.30%, John H. Grover/2.00%, Thomas L. Hewitt/1.40%, The Arch C. Scurlock Childrens Trust/12.60%, Daniel R. Young/1.30%

Financial Data: Fiscal Year End:03/31　Latest Annual Data: 3/31/2006

Year	Sales	Net Income
2006	$54,911,000	$1,536,000
2005	$62,006,000	-$1,411,000
2004	$49,537,000	$4,228,000

Curr. Assets:	$20,857,000	Curr. Liab.:	$11,183,000		
Plant, Equip.:	$1,381,000	Total Liab.:	$19,446,000	Indic. Yr. Divd.:	NA
Total Assets:	$27,409,000	Net Worth:	$7,963,000	Debt/ Equity:	NA

Hallador Petroleum Co

1660 Lincoln St., Ste. 2700, Denver, CO, 80264; **PH:** 1-303-839-5504; **http://** www.sino-land.com

General - Incorporation	CO	Stock- Price on:12/24/2007	$3.25
Employees	4	Stock Exchange	OTC
Auditor	Ehrhardt Keefe Steiner & Hottman P.C	Ticker Symbol	HPCO
Stk Agt	Computershare Trust Co	Outstanding Shares	12,170,000
Counsel	NA	E.P.S.	-$0.15
DUNS No.	08-265-3858	Shareholders	NA

Business: The group's principal activities are to explore, develop and produce oil and natural gas in the United States. The group also trades and acquires non-producing oil and gas mineral leases and fee-simple minerals. The oil and gas is used for heating, manufacturing, power and transportation.

Primary SIC and add'l.: 1311

CIK No: 0000788965

Officers: Victor P. Stabio/60/Dir., CEO, CFO, Pres., Brent K. Bilsland/34/Dir., Pres.

Directors: Victor P. Stabio/60/Dir., CEO, CFO, Pres., David Hardie/59/Chmn., Cortlandt S. Dietler/86/Dir., Steven Hardie/54/Dir., Bryan H. Lawrence/64/Dir., Brent K. Bilsland/34/Dir., Pres.

Owners: Cortlandt S. Dietler/1.00%, Victor P. Stabio/3.00%, Bryan H. Lawrence/54.00%, Insiders/85.00%, David Hardie/29.00%, Lubar & Associates/6.00%

Financial Data: Fiscal Year End:12/31　Latest Annual Data: 12/31/2006

Year	Sales	Net Income
2006	$2,468,000	-$824,000
2005	$1,646,000	$162,000
2004	$1,072,000	$9,870,000

Curr. Assets:	$8,782,000	Curr. Liab.:	$5,613,000		
Plant, Equip.:	$46,513,000	Total Liab.:	$33,644,000	Indic. Yr. Divd.:	NA
Total Assets:	$61,823,000	Net Worth:	$28,179,000	Debt/ Equity:	0.9276

Halliburton Co

5 Houston Ctr., 1401 McKinney, Ste. 2400, Houston, TX, 77010; **PH:** 1-713-759-2600; **http://** www.halliburton.com; **Email:** investors@halliburton.com

General - Incorporation	DE	Stock- Price on:12/24/2007	$35.9
Employees	104,000	Stock Exchange	NYSE
Auditor	KPMG LLP	Ticker Symbol	HAL
Stk Agt	Mellon Investor Services LLC	Outstanding Shares	914,050,000
Counsel	NA	E.P.S.	$3.32
DUNS No.	04-329-6920	Shareholders	NA

Business: The groups principle activity is to provide energy services. The group operates though two segments namely drilling and evaluation, and completion and production. The group's services include real time, sand controle, and pipe line and process services. The group operates from United States.

Primary SIC and add'l.: 1389 1629

CIK No: 0000045012

Subsidiaries: Baroid International Trading, LLC, Bitc (us) LLC, BITC Holdings (US) LLC, Breswater Marine Contracting B.V., Brown & Root Toll Road Investment Partners, Inc., Devonport Management Limited, Devonport Royal Dockyard Limited, DII Industries, LLC, Halliburton Affiliates, LLC, Halliburton AS, Halliburton Canada Holdings, Inc., Halliburton Energy Cayman Islands Limited, Halliburton Energy Services, Inc., Halliburton Group Canada, Halliburton Group Canada Inc. 29 Subsidiaries included in the Index

Officers: David J. Lesar/Chmn., CEO, Pres./$15,295,790.00, Evelyn M. Angelle/VP - Investor Relations, Katy Eichelberger/Representative, Public Relations, Sherry D. Williams/VP, Sec., Mark A. McCollum/Chief Accounting Officer, Sr. VP/$1,597,469.00, Andrew Lane/COO, Exec. VP/$3,315,798.00, Albert O. Cornelison/Exec. VP, General Counsel, Donald A. Deline/VP - Government Affairs, Christopher C. Gaut/CFO, Exec. VP/$3,494,559.00, Craig Nunez/Sr. VP, Treasurer, Lawrence Pope/VP - Human Resources, Administration, David R. Smith/61/VP - Tax, Cathy G. Mann/Dir. - Communications, Melissa Norcross/Mgr. - Public Relations, Zelma Branch/Sr. Representative, Public Relations

Directors: David J. Lesar/Chmn., CEO, Pres., W. R. Howell/Dir., Robert L. Crandall/Dir., Alan M. Bennett/Dir., Jay A. Precourt/Dir., Debra L. Reed/Dir., Malcolm S. Gillis/Dir., Kenneth T. Derr/Dir., James R. Boyd/Dir., Landis J. Martin/Dir.

Owners: Ray L. Hunt, Debra L. Reed, Capital Research and Management Company/6.30%, Wellington Management Company, LLP/6.00%, Alliance Bernstein L.P./8.30%, David J. Lesar

Financial Data: Fiscal Year End:12/31　Latest Annual Data: 12/31/2006

Year	Sales	Net Income
2006	$22,576,000,000	$2,348,000,000
2005	$20,994,000,000	$2,358,000,000
2004	$20,466,000,000	-$979,000,000

Curr. Assets:	$11,183,000,000	Curr. Liab.:	$4,727,000,000	P/E Ratio:	15.54
Plant, Equip.:	$3,048,000,000	Total Liab.:	$8,997,000,000	Indic. Yr. Divd.:	$0.360
Total Assets:	$16,820,000,000	Net Worth:	$7,376,000,000	Debt/ Equity:	0.3528

Hallmark Financial Services Inc

777 Main St., Ste. 1000, Fort Worth, TX, 76102; **PH:** 1-817-348-1600; **Fax:** 1-817-348-1815; **http://** www.hallmarkgrp.com

General - Incorporation	NV	Stock- Price on:12/24/2007	$12.37
Employees	347	Stock Exchange	NDQ
Auditor	KPMG LLP	Ticker Symbol	HALL
Stk Agt	Securities Transfer Corp	Outstanding Shares	20,770,000
Counsel	NA	E.P.S.	$1.21
DUNS No.	60-102-4003	Shareholders	NA

Business: The group's principal activities are to market, underwrite and finance non-standard automobile insurance, claims adjusting and other insurance related services. It provides services through its subsidiaries American hallmark general agency inc, hallmark claims services inc and hallmark finance corporation. The group provides insurance through a reinsurance arrangement with an unaffiliated company, state and county mutual fire insurance company. Through state & county, the group provides insurance for drivers who do not qualify for standard-rate insurance. The group also writes non-standard automobile liability and physical damage coverages. The non-standard personal automobile insurance is marketed in Texas, New Mexico and Arizona and commercial insurance in Texas, New Mexico, Idaho, Oregon and Washington.

Primary SIC and add'l.: 6331 6411 6719

CIK No: 0000819913

Subsidiaries: ACO Holdings, Inc, Aerospace Claims Management Group, Inc., Aerospace Flight, Inc., Aerospace Holdings, LLC, Aerospace Insurance Managers, Inc, Aerospace Special Risk, Inc., Allrisk Insurance Agency, Inc, American Hallmark Agencies, Inc, American Hallmark General Agency, Inc., Effective Claims Management, Inc, Gulf States Insurance Company, Hallmark Claims Service, Inc., Hallmark Finance Corporation, Hallmark General Agency, Inc, Hallmark Underwriters, Inc 21 Subsidiaries included in the Index

Officers: Mark J. Morrison/CEO, Pres./$530,396.00, Mark E. Schwarz/Executive Chmn./$182,838.00, Gregory P. Birdsall/CIO, Richard N. Gibson/Chief Actuary, Jeffrey R. Passmore/Chief Accounting Officer, Sr. VP/$223,470.00, Kevin T. Kasitz/Exec. VP - Commercial Lines, COO, Pres. - HGA Operating Unit/$342,125.00, Brookland F. Davis/Exec. VP - Personal Lines, Pres. - Phoenix Operating Unit/$348,546.00, Cecil R. Wise/Sec., Donald E. Meyer/Pres. - TGA Operating Unit/$318,549.00, Curtis R. Donnell/Pres. - Aerospace Operating Unit/$256,600.00

Directors: Mark E. Schwarz/Executive Chmn., James H. Graves/Dir., George R. Manser/Dir., Scott T. Berlin/Dir.

Owners: Mark E. Schwarz, Newcastle Special Opportunity Fund I, L.P., Jeffrey R. Passmore, George R. Manser, Insiders, Brookland F. Davis, James H. Graves, Donald E. Meyer, Mark J. Morrison, Newcastle Partners, L.P., Kevin T. Kasitz, Curtis R. Donnell, Thomas G. Berlin, Newcastle Special Opportunity Fund II, L.P., Scott T. Berlin

Financial Data: Fiscal Year End: 12/31   **Latest Annual Data:** 12/31/2006

Year	Sales	Net Income
2006	$202,741,000	$9,191,000
2005	$87,035,000	$9,186,000
2004	$63,121,000	$5,849,000

Curr. Assets:	$172,824,000	Curr. Liab.:	$24,532,000	P/E Ratio:	10.57
Plant, Equip.:	$1,644,000	Total Liab.:	$265,222,000	Indic. Yr. Divd.:	NA
Total Assets:	$415,953,000	Net Worth:	$150,731,000	Debt/ Equity:	0.2307

Hallwood Group Inc

1306 Countryside Pl Se, Smyrna, GA, 30080; **PH:** 1-770-436-5027; **http://** www.hallwood.com

General - Incorporation	DE	**Stock**- Price on:12/24/2007	$92
Employees	447	Stock Exchange	AMEX
Auditor	Deloitte & Touche LLP	Ticker Symbol	HWG
Stk Agt	Computershare Investor Services LLC	Outstanding Shares	1,520,000
Counsel	NA	E.P.S.	-$9.29
DUNS No.	NA	Shareholders	NA

Business: The group operates through its subsidiaries whose principle activities include manufacturing and marketing textile products. The group operates through two segments namely, textile products and energy. The group operates from the United States. The groups quarterly revenue for September 2007 was 32.58 millions of USD.

Primary SIC and add'l.: 8742

CIK No: 0000355766

Subsidiaries: Brookwood Companies Incorporated

Officers: Amber M. Brookman/66/CEO, Pres. - Brookwood Companies Incorporated/$586,600.00, Anthony J. Gumbiner/Chmn., CEO/$1,287,200.00, Charles A. Crocco/Dir. - Attorney, Joseph T. Koenig/Treasurer, Assist. Sec., Peter A. Landolfo/Dir. - Consultant, William L. Guzzetti/COO, Pres./$323,826.00, Melvin J. Melle/CFO, VP, Sec./$223,289.00

Directors: Anthony J. Gumbiner/Chmn., CEO, Charles A. Crocco/Dir. - Attorney, Peter A. Landolfo/Dir. - Consultant, Thomas J. Talbot/Dir., Garrett W. Smith/Dir., Garrett M. Smith/46/Dir.

Owners: Charles A. Crocco/1.00%, Insiders/67.80%, Advisory Research, Inc./8.10%, Melvin J. Melle/0.80%, Anthony J. Gumbiner/66.00%, Thomas J. Talbot

Financial Data: Fiscal Year End: 12/31   **Latest Annual Data:** 12/31/2006

Year	Sales	Net Income
2006	$112,154,000	-$6,725,000
2005	$134,607,000	$26,342,000
2004	$137,280,000	$94,485,000

Curr. Assets:	$52,812,000	Curr. Liab.:	$14,014,000	P/E Ratio:	24.43
Plant, Equip.:	$13,853,000	Total Liab.:	$24,631,000	Indic. Yr. Divd.:	NA
Total Assets:	$107,597,000	Net Worth:	$81,966,000	Debt/ Equity:	NA

Halo Resources Ltd

Commerce Ct. N, 25 King St. W, Ste. 2900A, Toronto, ON, M5L 1G3; **PH:** 1-416-368-7045; **http://** www.halores.com; **Email:** info@halores.com

General - Incorporation	Canada	**Stock**- Price on:12/24/2007	$0.4841
Employees	NA	Stock Exchange	OTC
Auditor	D&H Group LLP	Ticker Symbol	HLOSF
Stk Agt	Computershare Trust Co	Outstanding Shares	NA
Counsel	NA	E.P.S.	NA
DUNS No.	NA	Shareholders	NA

Business: The group's principle activities include exploring and developing crude oil and natural gas properties in the United States. The group operates from United States.

Primary SIC and add'l.: 1311

CIK No: 0001050807

Subsidiaries: Trimark Inc, Trimark Resources Inc.

Officers: Lynda Bloom/Dir., CEO, Pres., Nick Demare/Dir., CFO, Harvey Lim/Corp. Sec., Tom H. Healy/Dir., COO, Sr. VP

Directors: Lynda Bloom/Dir., CEO, Pres., Marc Cernovitch/Chmn., Ewan Downie/Dir., Andrew Carter/Dir., William Lee/Dir., Tom H. Healy/Dir., COO, Sr. VP, Nick Demare/Dir., CFO

Owners: Nick DeMare/2.23%, Harvey Lim/0.49%, Wolfden Resources Inc/6.04%, William Lee/0.47%, Ewan Downie/3.27%, Tom Healy/1.21%, Andrew Carter/0.52%, Marc Cernovitch/1.61%, Lynda Bloom/0.71%

Financial Data: Fiscal Year End: 08/31   **Latest Annual Data:** 8/31/2006

Year	Sales	Net Income
2006	$15,000	-$2,921,000
2005	$26,000	-$21,404,000
2004	$62,000	-$338,000

Curr. Assets:	$368,000	Curr. Liab.:	$12,728,000		
Plant, Equip.:	$270,000	Total Liab.:	$12,728,000	Indic. Yr. Divd.:	NA
Total Assets:	$11,716,000	Net Worth:	-$1,012,000	Debt/ Equity:	NA

Halo Technology Holdings Inc

Formerly: WARP Technology Holdings Inc
151 Railrd. Ave., 3rd Fl., Greenwich, CT, 06830; **PH:** 1-203-422-2950; **http://** www.haloholdings.com

General - Incorporation	NV	**Stock**- Price on:12/24/2007	NA
Employees	234	Stock Exchange	NA
Auditor	Mahoney Cohen & Co. CPA, P.C	Ticker Symbol	NA
Stk Agt	Pacific Stock Transfer Company	Outstanding Shares	NA
Counsel	NA	E.P.S.	NA
DUNS No.	NA	Shareholders	NA

Business: The group's principal activity is to develop warp 2063 application pre-processor, a computer network appliance. The pre-processor improves the speed and reliability of Internet, intranet and extranet-based applications, transactions and information requests. The group operates through its subsidiary warp solutions, inc. On 13-Jan-2003, the group acquired spidersoftware inc.

Primary SIC and add'l.: 7379

CIK No: 0001125052

Subsidiaries: 6043577 Canada, Inc., David Corporation, Empagio, Inc, Gupta Technologies GmbH, Gupta Technologies, LLC, Gupta Technologies, LLC, Gupta Technologies, S.A. de C.V., Kenosia Corporation, Process Software, LLC, Profitkey International, LLC, Revcast, LLC, Spider Software, Inc., Tenebril, Inc, Warp Solutions, Inc., Warp Solutions, Ltd.

Officers: Ron Bienvenu/Chmn., CEO, Ernest Mysogland/Chief Legal Officer, Jude Sullivan/Dir. - M, A, Business Development, David E. Oliver/Dir., Private Investor

Directors: Ron Bienvenu/Chmn., CEO, David Howitt/Dir., Gordon O. Rapkin/Dir., David E. Oliver/Dir., Private Investor, David Skriloff/Dir.

Curr. Assets:	$5,946,000	Curr. Liab.:	$29,151,000
Plant, Equip.:	$433,000	Total Liab.:	$60,295,000	Indic. Yr. Divd.:	NA
Total Assets:	$59,704,000	Net Worth:	-$8,342,000	Debt/ Equity:	NA

Halozyme Therapeutics Inc

11588 Sorrento Valley Rd., Ste. 17, San Diego, CA, 92121; **PH:** 1-858-794-8889; **Fax:** 1-858-259-2539; **http://** www.halozyme.com; **Email:** ir@halozyme.com

General - Incorporation	NV	**Stock**- Price on:12/24/2007	NA
Employees	34	Stock Exchange	NDQ
Auditor	Cacciamatta Accountancy Corp	Ticker Symbol	HALO
Stk Agt	Corporate Stock Transfer, Inc.	Outstanding Shares	NA
Counsel	NA	E.P.S.	-$0.27
DUNS No.	NA	Shareholders	NA

Business: The group's principal activity is to develop and commercialize recombinant human enzymes for the infertility, ophthalmology and oncology markets. The group's business is in the development stage. Its portfolio of products in development stage is based on intellectual property covering the family of human enzymes known as hyaluronidases. The group's first hyaluronidase enzyme, recombinant human pH20 or rhuph20, is the platform for three different products, including a medical device, a drug enhancement agent and a therapeutic biologic.

Primary SIC and add'l.: 7389

CIK No: 0001159036

Subsidiaries: Baxter Healthcare Corporation

Officers: Jonathan E. Lim/Dir., CEO, Pres./$428,148.00, Mark A. Wilson/VP - Business Development, Richard C. Yocum/VP - Clinical Development, Medical Affairs/$333,200.00, Don A. Kennard/VP - Regulatory Affairs, Quality Assurance/$272,334.00, David A. Ramsay/CFO, VP/$266,754.00, Gregory I. Frost/Dir., VP, Chief Scientific Officer/$335,543.00, Robert L. Little/VP, Chief Commercial Officer, William Fallon/VP - Manufacturing, Operations, Eleanor Tang/Investor Relations Contact

Directors: Jonathan E. Lim/Dir., CEO, Pres., Kenneth J. Kelley/Chmn., Gregory I. Frost/Dir., VP, Chief Scientific Officer, Connie L. Matsui/Dir., Kathryn E. Falberg/Dir., Steven T. Thornton/Dir., Robert L. Engler/Dir., John S. Patton/Dir., Randal J. Kirk/Dir.

Owners: Kenneth J. Kelley, Insiders/24.40%, Randal J. Kirk/14.40%, David A. Ramsay/1.00%, Robert L. Engler, Gregory I. Frost/5.10%, Richard C. Yocum, Don A. Kennard, QVT Financial LP/7.70%, Jonathan E. Lim/3.60%, John S. Patton, Connie L. Matsui, Kathryn E. Falberg, Steven T. Thornton

Financial Data: Fiscal Year End: 12/31   **Latest Annual Data:** 12/31/2006

Year	Sales	Net Income
2006	$982,000	-$14,752,000
2005	$127,000	-$13,275,000
2004	NA	-$9,091,000

Curr. Assets:	$45,594,000	Curr. Liab.:	$4,251,000		
Plant, Equip.:	$498,000	Total Liab.:	$23,011,000	Indic. Yr. Divd.:	NA
Total Assets:	$46,091,000	Net Worth:	$23,081,000	Debt/ Equity:	NA

Hamilton Biophile Co

4127 N.w. 27th Ln., Gainesville, FL, 32606; **PH:** 1-352-373-2565

General - Incorporation	NV	**Stock**- Price on:12/24/2007	NA
Employees	NA	Stock Exchange	NA
Auditor	NA	Ticker Symbol	NA
Stk Agt	NA	Outstanding Shares	NA
Counsel	NA	E.P.S.	NA
DUNS No.	NA	Shareholders	NA

Business: The group's principle activity is to provide transfer technolgies. The group operates from United States.

Primary SIC and add'l.: 3990

CIK No: 0000726608

Hammonds Industries Inc

Formerly: Unlimited Coatings Corp
601 Cien St., Ste. 235, Kemah, TX, 77565; **PH:** 1-281-334-9479

General - Incorporation	NV	**Stock**- Price on:12/24/2007	NA
Employees	NA	Stock Exchange	NA
Auditor	Glo Cpas, LLP	Ticker Symbol	NA
Stk Agt	Colonial Stock Transfer Co Inc	Outstanding Shares	NA
Counsel	NA	E.P.S.	NA
DUNS No.	NA	Shareholders	NA

Business: The group's principal activity is to distribute polyurethane chemicals, coatings, and spray-on bedliners for trucks. The primary target for the group subsidiary Marald, Inc.'s truck bed liners was the auto dealers market, which dealers sell liners to, as part of the accessory package at the point of sale of the truck, and can be included as part of the financing package. Other targets for the subsidiary included leasing companies that serviced large fleet customers and local accessory installers. The former potential fleet customers of the subsidiary included businesses with delivery services such as soft drink distributors, construction companies, and lawn care services. The group sold 100% of its investment in Marald, Inc. to American International Industries Inc.

Primary SIC and add'l.: 6770

CIK No: 0001300524

Subsidiaries: American International Industries, Inc.

Owners: Insiders/45.41%, Carl Hammond/44.30%, American International Industries, Inc./45.10%, Gary D. Woerz/0.30%

Financial Data: Fiscal Year End:12/31 Latest Annual Data: 12/31/2006

Year	Sales	Net Income
2006	$6,467,000	-$2,447,000
2005	$3,395,000	-$1,195,000
2004	NA	-$7,000

Curr. Assets:	$3,382,000	Curr. Liab.:	$1,628,000		
Plant, Equip.:	$782,000	Total Liab.:	$6,526,000	Indic. Yr. Divd.:	NA
Total Assets:	$10,384,000	Net Worth:	$3,858,000	Debt/ Equity:	1.2850

Hampshire First Bank

221 Main St., Nashua, NH, 03060; **PH:** 1-603-578-2652; **http://** www.hampshirefirst.com; **Email:** CustomerService@HampshireFirst.com

General - Incorporation		Stock - Price on:12/24/2007	$10
Employees	NA	Stock Exchange	OTC
Auditor	NA	Ticker Symbol	HFBN
Stk Agt	Registrar & Transfer Co	Outstanding Shares	NA
Counsel	NA	E.P.S.	NA
DUNS No.	NA	Shareholders	NA

Business: The groups principal activity is to provide banking services. The services of the group include personal banking, business banking, lending services and online banking. The group operates from Manchester in the United States.

Primary SIC and add'l.: 6022

CIK No:

Officers: James Dunphy/CEO, Pres., Thomas Wiggins/CFO, Katherine Meyer/VP - Operations, Donna Upson/VP - Commercial Lending, Aaron Holt/Commercial Loan Officer, Michelle Johnson/Loan Administration, Michele Popham/Customer Service Representative, Laura Mckay/Head - Teller, Alyson Hatfield/Teller, Jay Dinkel/Dir. - Communty Banking, Lisa Wrisley/Electronic Banking Officer, Alan Manoian/Lending, Economic Development Officer, Bonnie White/VP - Retail Banking

Hampshire Funding Inc

One Granite Pl, Concord, NH, 03301; **PH:** 1-800-258-3648

General - Incorporation	NH	Stock - Price on:12/24/2007	NA
Employees	NA	Stock Exchange	NYSE
Auditor	Ernst & Young LLP	Ticker Symbol	cik
Stk Agt.	NA	Outstanding Shares	NA
Counsel	NA	E.P.S.	NA
DUNS No.	08-340-2438	Shareholders	NA

Business: The group's principal activity is to conduct programs for the initial and periodic cash purchases of mutual fund shares. Under the program, the activities include purchase of mutual fund shares by the participants by making initial and periodic cash purchase with automatic reinvestment of all distributions. Participants obtain insurance coverage through a series of insurance premium loans offered by the group. The loans offered are secured by participants' initial and periodic purchases of mutual fund shares. The group is a wholly-owned subsidiary of jefferson-pilot corporation.

Primary SIC and add'l.: 6153

CIK No: 0000205422

Hampshire Group Ltd

215 Commerce Blvd, Anderson, SC, 29625; **PH:** 1-864-231-1200; **Fax:** 1-864-231-1201; **http://** www.hamp.com; **Email:** hr@hamp.com

General - Incorporation	DE	Stock - Price on:12/24/2007	NA
Employees	370	Stock Exchange	OTC
Auditor	Deloitte & Touche LLP	Ticker Symbol	HAMP
Stk Agt	Bank of New York	Outstanding Shares	NA
Counsel	Willkie Farr & Gallagher LLP	E.P.S.	-$0.12
DUNS No.	08-847-0802	Shareholders	NA

Business: The group's principal activities are the design and sale of apparel and real estate investments. The group operates through two subsidiaries namely, hampshire designers inc and hampshire investments limited. Hampshire designers inc sells women's and men's branded and private-label sweaters and women's related sportswear. The products include designers originals studio(R) and moving bleu(R) sweaters, business-casual line for women and requirements(R) and nouveaux(R) labeled blazers, pants, shirts and sweaters. The products are distributed through mass merchandisers, specialty retail stores and catalog companies. Hampshire investments limited purchases real properties located primarily in the United States, Russia and eastern Europe for the purpose of holding as long-term investments. It has subsidiaries located in the cayman islands and the czech republic.

Primary SIC and add'l.: 2339 2253 6799

CIK No: 0000887150

Subsidiaries: Hampshire Designers, Inc., Item Eyes, Inc., Keynote Services, Limited, SB Corporation

Officers: Michael S. Culang/58/Interim CEO, Pres., Jeffrey B. Meier/60/VP - Global Sourcing, David Brooks/Contact - Sales Office, Showrooms, Shane Hunter/Contact - Sales Office, Showrooms, Jonathan W. Norwood/39/CFO, VP, Treasurer, Heath L. Golden/33/General Counsel, VP - Administration, Sec.

Directors: Michael C. Jackson/Interim Chmn., Harvey L. Sperry/Dir., Irwin W. Winter/Dir., Joel Goldberg/Dir., Ludwig Kuttner/Dir.

Owners: Peter Woodworth/5.30%, AMVESCAP PLC/10.30%, Heartland Advisors, Inc./5.90%, Joel H. Goldberg, Irwin W. Winter, Ludwig Kuttner/31.10%, Charles Clayton/2.00%, River Road Asset Management/5.90%, FMR Corp./12.00%, Insiders/33.20%, Harvey L. Sperry, Michael C. Jackson

Financial Data: Fiscal Year End:12/31 Latest Annual Data: 12/31/2006

Year	Sales	Net Income
2006	$347,919,000	$4,302,000
2005	$324,281,000	$11,414,000
2004	$301,999,000	$13,725,000

Curr. Assets:	$141,050,000	Curr. Liab.:	$47,791,000		
Plant, Equip.:	$1,964,000	Total Liab.:	$48,328,000	Indic. Yr. Divd.:	NA
Total Assets:	$155,905,000	Net Worth:	$107,577,000	Debt/ Equity:	NA

Hampton Roads Bankshares Inc

999 Waterside Dr., Ste. 200, Norfolk, VA, 23510; **PH:** 1-757-217-1000; **Fax:** 1-757-217-3656; **http://** www.bankofhamptonroads.com

General - Incorporation	VA	Stock - Price on:12/24/2007	$14.52
Employees	159	Stock Exchange	NDQ
Auditor	KPMG LLP	Ticker Symbol	HMPR
Stk Agt	Registrar & Transfer Co	Outstanding Shares	10,270,000
Counsel	NA	E.P.S.	$0.64
DUNS No.	NA	Shareholders	NA

Business: The group's principal activity is to provide general community and commercial banking services. The group serves as a holding company for bank of hampton roads and operates through 15 branches located in chesapeake, suffolk, norfolk and Virginia beach, Virginia. The group attract deposits and lends or invest those deposits on profitable terms to individuals and small to medium sized businesses. The deposits are in varied form of both demand and time accounts including checking accounts, interest checking, money market accounts, savings accounts, certificates of deposit and ira accounts. Loans consist of secured or unsecured loans including loans to individuals and businesses for personal, household, family purposes, working capital, plant expansion and equipment purchases.

Primary SIC and add'l.: 6712 6022

CIK No: 0001143155

Subsidiaries: Bank of Hampton Roads Inc, Bank of Hampton Roads Service Corporation, Hampton Roads Investments Inc

Officers: Jack W. Gibson/Dir., CEO, Pres./$1,078,269.00, Douglas J. Glenn/Dir., Exec. VP, General Counsel, Member - Advisory Board, Pembroke Bank, Hampton Roads, Tiffany K. Glenn/Sr. VP, Marketing Officer, Corp. Sec., Investor Relations Officer, Donald W. Fulton/CFO, Sr. VP/$248,944.00, Gregory P. Marshall/Sr. VP, Commercial Loan Officer, Julie R. Anderson/Sr. VP, Chief Credit Officer/$354,822.00, Renee R. McKinney/Sr. VP, Branch Administrator/$221,643.00

Directors: Jack W. Gibson/Dir., CEO, Pres., Emil A. Viola/Chmn., Bobby L. Ralph/Dir., W. L. Witt/Dir., Cynthia W. Snyman/Member - Advisory Board, Corporate Landing, Bank, Hampton Roads, Patricia M. Windsor/Dir., David E. Kellam/Member - Advisory Board, Corporate Landing, Bank, Hampton Roads, Warren L. Aleck/Member - Advisory Board, Indian River, Bank, Hampton Roads, Neal S. Windley/Member - Advisory Board, Princess Anne, Bank, Hampton Roads, Durwood S. Curling/Member - Advisory Board, Princess Anne, Bank, Hampton Roads, James S. Creekmore/Member - Advisory Board, Princess Anne, Bank, Hampton Roads, Charles G. Hackworth/Member - Advisory Board, South Norfolk, Bank, Hampton Roads, James W. McNeil/Member - Advisory Board, South Norfolk, Bank, Hampton Roads, Richard G. Pretlow/Member - Advisory Board, South Norfolk, Bank, Hampton Roads, John F. Elizabeth/Member - Advisory Board, South Norfolk, Bank, Hampton Roads (101 Directors included in Index)

Owners: Julie R. Anderson, Roland Carroll Smith/1.01%, Patricia M. Windsor, Insiders/17.44%, Emil A. Viola/4.58%, Herman A. Hall/1.65%, Robert R. Kinser, Jordan E. Slone, John Sheldon Clark/5.26%, Gregory P. Marshall, Bobby L. Ralph, Douglas J. Glenn, Renee R. McKinney, Jack W. Gibson/4.78%, Donald W. Fulton (16 Owners included in Index)

Financial Data: Fiscal Year End:12/31 Latest Annual Data: 12/31/2006

Year	Sales	Net Income
2006	$33,419,000	$6,036,000
2005	$27,773,000	$5,507,000
2004	$21,859,000	$4,134,000

Curr. Assets:	$29,080,000	Curr. Liab.:	$402,734,000	P/E Ratio:	22.69
Plant, Equip.:	$12,184,000	Total Liab.:	$406,137,000	Indic. Yr. Divd.:	$0.440
Total Assets:	$476,299,000	Net Worth:	$70,163,000	Debt/ Equity:	NA

Hamptons Luxury Homes Inc

PO Box 871, Bridgehampton, NY, 11932; **PH:** 1-631-537-1600; **Fax:** 1-631-537-3951; **http://** www.hlxhomes.com; **Email:** info@hlxhomes.com

General - Incorporation	DE	Stock - Price on:12/24/2007	$0.05
Employees	11	Stock Exchange	OTC
Auditor	Most & Company, LLP	Ticker Symbol	HLXH
Stk Agt	Manhattan Transfer Registrar Co	Outstanding Shares	57,970,000
Counsel	NA	E.P.S.	$0.003
DUNS No.	NA	Shareholders	NA

Business: The groups principle activities include building and maintaining custom homes, luxury vacation homes and ultra-luxury estate homes. In April 2006, the group acquired Telemark, Inc. The group operates from Bridgehampton, New York in the United States. The group's quarterly revenue for September 2007 was 3.74 millions of USD.

Primary SIC and add'l.: 1521

CIK No: 0001034674

Subsidiaries: DWD Construction Services, Inc, Telemark Inc.

Officers: Roy Dalene/50/Chmn., CEO, Pres., Frank Dalene/CFO, VP, Beverly Jedynak/Contact - Financial Public Relations, Martin E. Janis/Financial Public Relations

Directors: Roy Dalene/50/Chmn., CEO, Pres.

Owners: Roy Dalene/38.79%, Robert A. Wilson/18.11%, Frank Dalene/38.64%, Insiders/77.43%

Financial Data: Fiscal Year End:12/31 Latest Annual Data: 12/31/2006

Year	Sales	Net Income
2006	$4,558,000	-$177,000

Curr. Assets:	$654,000	Curr. Liab.:	$277,000		
Plant, Equip.:	$308,000	Total Liab.:	$799,000	Indic. Yr. Divd.:	NA
Total Assets:	$1,020,000	Net Worth:	$221,000	Debt/ Equity:	NA

Hana Biosciences Inc

7000 Shoreline Ct., Ste. 370, South San Francisco, CA, 94080; *PH:* 1-650-588-6404;
Fax: 1-650-588-2787; *http://* www.hanabiosciences.com; *Email:* info@hanabiosciences.com

General - Incorporation	DE	**Stock** - Price on:12/24/2007	$1.71
Employees	36	Stock Exchange	NDQ
Auditor	J.H. Cohn LLP	Ticker Symbol	HNAB
Stk Agt	Corporate Stock Transfer, Inc.	Outstanding Shares	29,310,000
Counsel	NA	E.P.S.	-$1.755
DUNS No.	NA	Shareholders	NA

Business: The groups principal activities include acquiring, developing, and commercializing innovative products. The groups services include Chemotherapy and Supportive care. The group products sold under the trade names Alocrest(TM), Talvesta(TM) and Zensana(TM). The group operates from the United States.

Primary SIC and add'l.: 2834 2835 2833 3841 3845 3843 2836

CIK No: 0001140028

Officers: Mark J. Ahn/45/Dir., CEO, Pres./$3,772,794.00, Steven R. Deitcher/Dir., CEO, Pres., Acting Exec. VP, Chief Medical Officer, Fred L. Vitale/VP, Chief Business Officer/$906,898.00, Michael S. Imperiale/VP - Clinical Research Operations, Remy Bernarda/Dir. - Investor Relations, Gregory I. Berk/49/Sr. VP, Chief Medical Officer/$1,610,272.00, John Iparraguirre/CFO, VP, Sec./$389,220.00, Alex Tkachenko/VP - Corporate Development, Strategic Planning

Directors: Mark J. Ahn/45/Dir., CEO, Pres., Steven R. Deitcher/Dir., CEO, Pres., Acting Exec. VP, Chief Medical Officer, Leon Rosenberg/Chmn., Isaac Kier/Dir., Arie Belldegrun/Dir., Michael Weiser/Dir., Lyn Wiesinger/Dir., Ken Anderson/Member - Scientific Advisory Board, James O. Armitage/Member - Scientific Advisory Board, Robert A. Figlin/Member - Scientific Advisory Board, Hagop M. Kantarjian/Member - Scientific Advisory Board, Thomas Lynch/Member - Scientific Advisory Board, Nicholas Vogelzang/Member - Scientific Advisory Board

Owners: D. E. Shaw & Co., L.P./8.88%, Larry Gellman/8.23%, Mark J. Ahn/4.97%, Leon E. Rosenberg, Sectoral Asset Management Inc./6.12%, Michael Weiser/2.20%, Arie S. Belldegrun, Fred L. Vitale/1.36%, Insiders/11.28%, Isaac Kier/1.66%, John P. Iparraguirre, Gregory I. Berk, James E. Flynn/5.61%

Financial Data: *Fiscal Year End:*12/31 *Latest Annual Data:* 12/31/2006

Year	Sales	Net Income
2006	NA	-$44,788,000
2005	NA	-$10,043,000
2004	NA	-$7,330,000

Curr. Assets:	$35,755,000	**Curr. Liab.:**	$5,935,000		
Plant, Equip.:	$424,000	**Total Liab.:**	$5,935,000	**Indic. Yr. Divd.:**	NA
Total Assets:	$36,305,000	**Net Worth:**	$30,370,000	**Debt/ Equity:**	NA

Hanaro Telecom Inc

43, Taepyeongno 2-Ga, Jung-Gu, Seoul, 100733; *PH:* 850-262664319; *http://* www.hanaro.com;
Email: ir@hanaro.com

General - Incorporation	Korea	**Stock** - Price on:12/24/2007	$9.5
Employees	1,461	Stock Exchange	OTC
Auditor	Deloitte Anjin LLC	Ticker Symbol	HANAY
Stk Agt	Korean Securities Depository	Outstanding Shares	NA
Counsel	NA	E.P.S.	NA
DUNS No.	NA	Shareholders	NA

Business: The group's principal activities are the provision of voice, data service, broadband Internet access bundled with voice telephony, multimedia content and other corporate data services as well as building its own network.

Primary SIC and add'l.: 4813 4899

CIK No: 0001108838

Subsidiaries: Hanaro Dream Corp, Hanaro Realty Development & Management Co., Ltd, Hanaro Telephone & Internet Information, Inc, Hanaromedia

Officers: Soon-Yub Kwon/CEO, Sang Jin Jeun/Sr. VP, Head - Communications Unit, Soon Man Hong/Head - Marketing HQ, Eric Choi/Sr. Exec. VP, Head - Sales Channel Management Headquarters, Young Bo Chang/Head - Financial Management Unit, Matt Lee/Head - Sales Operations Headquarters, Byung-Moo Park/Representative Dir., Jin Ha Kim/Sr. Exec. VP, Head - Technology Headquarters, Chong H. Park/43/Head - GR External Collaboration, Strategy HQ, Sang Hwan Oh/Sr. VP, Head - Honam Branch, Sang Soo Lee/Sr. VP, Head - Gangnam Branch, Myung Hun Choi/Sr. VP, Head - Chungcheng Branch, Dominic A. Gomez/COO, Kyu Shik Shin/Head - Corporate, Sales Headquarters, Park Byung-Moo/Representative Dir. *(18 Officers included in Index)*

Directors: David Yeung/Dir., Paul Chen/Dir., Sun W. Kim/Dir., Varun Bery/Dir., Park Sung-Kyu/Dir., Kim Sun-Woo/Dir., Steven J. Schneider/Dir., Afshin Mohebbi/Dir., Peter Whang/Dir., Wilfried Kaffenberger/Dir.

Financial Data: *Fiscal Year End:*12/31 *Latest Annual Data:* 12/31/2005

Year	Sales	Net Income
2005	$1,573,609,000	-$201,200,000
2004	$1,400,414,000	$14,346,000
2003	$1,160,643,000	-$139,252,000

Curr. Assets:	$436,916,000	**Curr. Liab.:**	$634,500,000		
Plant, Equip.:	$2,314,737,000	**Total Liab.:**	$1,446,546,000	**Indic. Yr. Divd.:**	NA
Total Assets:	$3,027,616,000	**Net Worth:**	$1,581,070,000	**Debt/ Equity:**	NA

Hancock Fabrics Inc

1 Fashion Way, Baldwyn, MS, 38824; *PH:* 1-662-365-6000; *http://* www.hancockfabrics.com

General - Incorporation	DE	**Stock** - Price on:12/24/2007	NA
Employees	6,200	Stock Exchange	OTC
Auditor	PricewaterhouseCoopers LLP	Ticker Symbol	HKFIQ
Stk Agt	Continental Stock Transfer & Trust Co	Outstanding Shares	NA
Counsel	NA	E.P.S.	-$2.22
DUNS No.	03-345-2954	Shareholders	NA

Business: The group's principal activity is the retail and wholesale distribution of fabrics and related accessories to the sewing and home decorating markets. The group offers a wide selection of apparel fabrics, home decorating products, notions, sewing machines, patterns, quilting materials and supplies and related items. The group operates an Internet store under its two domain names, hancockfabrics.com and homedecoratingaccents.com. At 02-Feb-2004, the group operates 433 stores in 42 states.

Primary SIC and add'l.: 5949 5131

CIK No: 0000812906

Subsidiaries: Hancock Fabrics of MI, Inc., Hancock Fabrics, LLC, hancockfabrics.com, Inc., HF Enterprises, Inc., HF Merchandising, HF Resources, Inc., Sewing Centers, LLC

Officers: Jane F. Aggers/57/Dir., CEO, Pres., Wellford L. Sanders/60/Chmn., MD - Wachovia Securities, Larry D. Fair/Primary IR Contact, Clayton E. Stallings/49/Sr. VP - Store Operations, Dean W. Abraham/Sr. VP - Store Operations, William A. Sheffield/Sr. VP - Distribution, William D. Smothers/Sr. VP - Real Estate

Directors: Jane F. Aggers/57/Dir., CEO, Pres., Wellford L. Sanders/60/Chmn., MD - Wachovia Securities, Bernard J. Wein/Dir., Don L. Fruge/Dir., Roger T. Knox/Dir., Donna L. Weaver/Dir.

Owners: Donna L. Weaver/0.67%, Bernard J. Wein/0.17%, T. Rowe Price Associates, Inc./12.14%, Dean W. Abraham/0.25%, Don L. Frug/0.35%, Bruce D. Smith/0.88%, Rutabaga Capital Management/8.28%, Insiders/4.16%, Clayton E. Stallings/0.21%, Babson Capital Management LLC/8.09%, Wells Fargo & Company/11.31%, Dimensional Fund Advisors Inc./6.38%, Roger T. Knox/0.28%, Wellford L. Sanders, Jane F. Aggers/1.24%

Financial Data: *Fiscal Year End:*01/30 *Latest Annual Data:* 01/28/2006

Year	Sales	Net Income
2006	$403,237,000	-$30,251,000
2005	$426,691,000	$1,758,000
2004	$443,605,000	$17,428,000

Curr. Assets:	$162,334,000	**Curr. Liab.:**	$75,690,000		
Plant, Equip.:	$57,142,000	**Total Liab.:**	$117,843,000	**Indic. Yr. Divd.:**	NA
Total Assets:	$249,423,000	**Net Worth:**	$131,580,000	**Debt/ Equity:**	NA

Hancock Holding Co

One Hancock Plz., 2510 14th St., Gulfport, MS, 39502; *PH:* 1-228-214-5242;
http:// www.hancockbank.com

General - Incorporation	MS	**Stock** - Price on:12/24/2007	$38.24
Employees	1,848	Stock Exchange	NDQ
Auditor	KPMG LLP	Ticker Symbol	HBHC
Stk Agt	NA	Outstanding Shares	32,390,000
Counsel	NA	E.P.S.	$2.93
DUNS No.	12-269-4490	Shareholders	NA

Business: The group's principal activity is to provide commercial banking services through 101 banking offices and 140 automated teller machines in the states of Mississippi and Louisiana. It provides commercial, consumer and mortgage loans and depository accounts services. Its other activities include providing trust services, consumer financing services; mortgage lending; owning, managing and maintaining certain real property; providing general insurance agency services; holding investment securities; marketing credit life insurance; and providing discount investment brokerage services. The customers include individuals and small to middle market businesses. On 31-Dec-2003, the group acquired Magna Insurance Company, on 22-Feb-2003 two Dryades Savings Bank branches located in Metairie, LA and Kenner, LA and on 12-Mar-2004, acquired Guaranty National Bank.

Primary SIC and add'l.: 6712 6021

CIK No: 0000750577

Subsidiaries: Hancock Bank, Hancock Bank of Florida, Hancock Bank of Louisiana, Hancock Bank Securities Corp, LLC., Hancock Insurance Agency, Hancock Insurance Agency of AL, Inc., Hancock Investment Services of MS, Inc, Hancock Investment Services,Inc., Harrison Finance Company, Harrison Life Insurance Company, HBLA Properties, LLC, Magna Insurance Company, The Gulfport Building, Inc., Town Properties, Inc.

Officers: Carl J. Chaney/Dir., CEO, CFO/$674,767.00, John M. Hairston/Dir., CEO, COO/$663,057.00, Alfreda A. Horne/Sr. VP, Auditor, Clifton J. Saik/Exec. VP - Executive, Wealth Management/$564,307.00, Richard T. Hill/Exec. VP - Executive, Retail Banking/$441,534.00, Alfred G. Rath/Exec. VP, CCO/$504,554.00, Michael M. Achary/CFO, Sr. VP, Shane D. Loper/COO, Sr. VP, Edward G. Francis/Sr. VP - Executive, Commercial Banking, Robert E. Easterly/Exec. VP - Hancock Bank, Louisiana, Joy L. Phillips/Sr. VP, General Counsel, Leo W. Seal/Dir., Pres.

Directors: Carl J. Chaney/Dir., CEO, CFO, John M. Hairston/Dir., CEO, COO, George A. Schloegel/Chmn., Robert W. Roseberry/Dir., Charles H. Johnson/Dir., James B. Estabrook/Dir., James H. Horne/Dir., Joseph F. Boardman/Dir., Frank E. Bertucci/Dir., Alton G. Bankston/Dir., Leo W. Seal/Dir., Pres., Don P. Descant/Dir., John H. Pace/Dir., Christine L. Pickering/Dir., Anthony J. Topazi/Dir.

Owners: James H. Horne/0.09%, Robert W. Roseberry/0.45%, Insiders/17.35%, George A. Schloegel/1.93%, Alfred G. Rath/0.15%, Shane D. Loper, John M. Hairston/0.49%, Joseph F. Boardman, Hancock Bank Trust Department/11.75%, Leo W. Seal/12.46%, Anthony J. Topazi/0.00%, John H. Pace/0.01%, Michael M. Achary/0.08%, James B. Estabrook, Richard T. Hill/0.26% *(25 Owners included in Index)*

Financial Data: *Fiscal Year End:*12/31 *Latest Annual Data:* 12/31/2006

Year	Sales	Net Income
2006	$453,332,000	$101,802,000
2005	$361,953,000	$54,032,000
2004	$317,055,000	$61,704,000

Curr. Assets:	$488,424,000	**Curr. Liab.:**	$5,301,773,000	**P/E Ratio:**	13.05
Plant, Equip.:	$141,122,000	**Total Liab.:**	$5,406,155,000	**Indic. Yr. Divd.:**	$0.960
Total Assets:	$5,964,565,000	**Net Worth:**	$558,410,000	**Debt/ Equity:**	NA

Handheld Entertainment Inc

539 Bryant St., Ste. 403, San Francisco, CA, 94107; *PH:* 1-415-495-6470; *Fax:* 1-415-882-5400;
http:// www.zvue.com; *Email:* info@hheld.com

General - Incorporation	DE	**Stock** - Price on:12/24/2007	$1.51
Employees	25	Stock Exchange	NDQ
Auditor	Salberg & Co., P.A	Ticker Symbol	ZVUE
Stk Agt	American Stock Transfer & Trust Co.	Outstanding Shares	17,000,000
Counsel	NA	E.P.S.	-$0.82
DUNS No.	NA	Shareholders	NA

Business: The groups principal activity is to provide video entertainment content. The products of the group include digital media content and portable media players. The group products sold under the trade names ZVUE and Ztunes. In the year 2007, the group acquired Gareth Coote and Putfile Limited. Specific customers of the group include Wal-Mart, Best Buy, Target, and Toys(R). The group operates from the United States. The sale of the group for the year 2006 was $3,779,692.

Primary SIC and add'l.: 3651

CIK No: 0001309710

Subsidiaries: Dorks LLC, Putfile, Ltd.

Subsidiaries: Dorks LLC, Putfile, Ltd.

Officers: Jeff Oscodar/CEO, Pres., Tim Keating/COO, Garrett Cecchini/60/Founder, Exec. VP, Sec., Carl Page/CTO, Bill Bush/CFO, Greg Sutyak/Exec. VP - Finance, Operations, Larry Gitlin/VP - Business Development, Ted Richards/Exec. Dir. - Creative, Peter A. Evers/Contact - Press Relations, William J. Bush/43/CFO, Assist. Sec.

Directors: Bill Keating/Chmn., William Keating/51/Chmn., Geoff Mulligan/Dir., Garrett Cecchini/60/Founder, Exec. VP, Sec., Carl Goldfischer/Dir., David Hadley/Dir., Robert Austrian/Dir.

Owners: William J. Bush/1.20%, Insiders/29.20%, Carl Goldfischer, Carl Page/16.00%, David Hadley/1.10%, William Keating/1.30%, Jeffrey Oscodar/4.00%, Tim Keating/1.20%, Gordon Robert Page/10.50%, Geoff Mulligan/1.60%, Robert Austrian

Financial Data: Fiscal Year End: 12/31 **Latest Annual Data:** 12/31/2006

Year	Sales	Net Income
2006	$3,780,000	-$12,180,000
2005	$7,000	-$37,000

Curr. Assets:	$5,346,000	**Curr. Liab.:**	$4,984,000		
Plant, Equip.:	$117,000	**Total Liab.:**	$7,384,000	**Indic. Yr. Divd.:**	NA
Total Assets:	$9,127,000	**Net Worth:**	$1,743,000	**Debt/ Equity:**	0.0732

Handleman Co

500 Kirts Blvd., Troy, MI, 48084; **PH:** 1-248-362-4400; **http://** www.handleman.com; **Email:** investors@handleman.com

General - Incorporation	MI	Stock - Price on:12/24/2007	$7.01
Employees	2,600	Stock Exchange	NYSE
Auditor	PricewaterhouseCoopers LLP	Ticker Symbol	HDL
Stk Agt	Mellon Investor Services LLC	Outstanding Shares	20,300,000
Counsel	Honigman Miller Schwartz & Cohn	E.P.S.	-$3.31
DUNS No.	00-695-8243	Shareholders	NA

Business: The group's principle activities are to provide category management services and distribute pre-recorded music. It operates through two segments: handleman entertainment resources ('h.e.r') and north coast entertainment ('nce'). The handleman entertainment resources segment distributes pre-recorded music and provides category management services to mass merchants in the United States, United Kingdom, Canada and only category management services in Mexico, Brazil and Argentina. As a category manager, the group manages an assortment of titles to optimize sales in retail stores and provides direct-to-store shipments, marketing of the selections, in-store merchandising and product exchange. The north coast entertainment segment provides music and video products. On 11-Dec-2003, the group completed the sale of anchor bay entertainment business unit, within the nce segment, and now operates only through the h.e.r segment. Customers include wal-Mart and kmart corporation. The group's total revenue for the year 2007 was 1,324.48 millions of USD.

Primary SIC and add'l.: 5099 7822 6794

CIK No: 0000314727

Subsidiaries: Artist to Market Distribution LLC, Crave Entertainment ., Crave Entertainment Group ., Entertainment Fulfillment Services LLC, Handleman Canada ., Handleman Category Management Company, Handleman Company of Canada Limited, Handleman de Mexico S.A. de C.V., Handleman dergentina S.R.L., Handleman do Brasil Commercial Ltda., Handleman Entertainment Resources LLC, Handleman Ontario Ltd., Handleman Real Estate LLC, Handleman UK Limited, Hanleydvertising Company 20 Subsidiaries included in the Index

Officers: Stephen Strome/Chmn., CEO/$1,970,550.00, Thomas C. Braum/53/Sr. VP, CFO/$704,705.00, Mark J. Albrecht/50/Sr. VP - Human Resources, Organizational Development, Ronnie W. Lund/45/Sr. VP - Product Management, Logistics, Business Processes, Donald M. Genotti/50/VP, Corporate Controller, Khaled Haram/44/CIO, Sr. VP/$907,630.00, Robert E. Kirby/51/Dir., COO, Pres./$1,164,054.00

Directors: Stephen Strome/Chmn., CEO, Elizabeth A. Chappell/Dir., Ralph J. Szygenda/Dir., James B. Nicholson/Dir., Thomas S. Wilson/Dir., Eugene A. Miller/Dir., Irvin D. Reid/Dir., Daniel P. Miller/Dir., Lloyd E. Reuss/Dir., Robert E. Kirby/51/Dir., COO, Pres., Adam D. Sexton/Dir.

Owners: Stephen Strome/2.20%, Century Management/9.20%, Franklin Advisory Services, LLC/8.90%, Dimensional Fund Advisors, Inc./8.40%, Ralph J. Szygenda, Donald Smith & Co., Inc./6.70%, Robert E. Kirby, Aegis Financial/7.00%, Daniel P. Miller, Mark J. Albrecht, Elizabeth A. Chappell, Lloyd E. Reuss, James B. Nicholson, Insiders/3.80%, Eugene A. Miller *(21 Owners included in Index)*

Financial Data: Fiscal Year End: 04/29 **Latest Annual Data:** 04/28/2007

Year	Sales	Net Income
2007	$1,324,483,000	-$53,428,000
2006	$1,312,404,000	$13,568,000
2005	$1,260,585,000	$34,196,000

Curr. Assets:	$409,154,000	**Curr. Liab.:**	$176,277,000		
Plant, Equip.:	$62,124,000	**Total Liab.:**	$185,726,000	**Indic. Yr. Divd.:**	$0.320
Total Assets:	$494,592,000	**Net Worth:**	$308,866,000	**Debt/ Equity:**	NA

Handy Hardware Wholesale Inc

8300 Tewantin Dr., Houston, TX, 77061; **PH:** 1-713-644-1495; **Fax:** 1-713-644-3167; **http://** www.handyhardware.com

General - Incorporation	TX	Stock - Price on:12/24/2007	NA
Employees	NA	Stock Exchange	NA
Auditor	BKD LLP	Ticker Symbol	NA
Stk Agt	NA	Outstanding Shares	NA
Counsel	NA	E.P.S.	NA
DUNS No.	02-660-0569	Shareholders	NA

Business: The group's principle activity is to provide warehouse facilities and centralized purchasing services to hardware dealers. The group sells products used in retail hardware, building material and home center stores, plant nurseries, marine, industrial and automotive stores. The group offers advertising and other services, merchandise to its member-dealers at its cost plus a markup charge resulting in lower price. The group operates with the trade name, handy hardware stores that buys merchandise from vendors in large quantity lots, warehouses them and resells it in smaller lots to its member-dealers. The member-dealers are located in Texas, Louisiana, Oklahoma, Arkansas, Alabama, Mississippi, Florida, Colorado, New Mexico, Mexico and Central America.

Primary SIC and add'l.: 5070 5072 5030

CIK No: 0000354053

Hanesbrands Inc

1000 E Hanes Mill Rd., Winston-Salem, NC, 27105; **PH:** 1-336-519-4400; **http://** www.hanesbrands.com; **Email:** ir@hanesbrands.com

General - Incorporation	MD	Stock - Price on:12/24/2007	$27.23
Employees	49,000	Stock Exchange	NYSE
Auditor	PricewaterhouseCoopers LLP	Ticker Symbol	HBI
Stk Agt	Computershare Investor Services LLC	Outstanding Shares	96,420,000
Counsel	NA	E.P.S.	$0.89
DUNS No.	NA	Shareholders	NA

Business: The groups principle activities include designing, manufacturing, sourcing and selling apparel. The groups products include t-shirts, bras, panties, mens underwear, kids underwear, socks, hosiery, casual wear and active wear. The groups products marketed under the brand names include Hanes, Champion, Playtex, Bali, Just My Size, barely there and Wonderbra. The group operates through four segments namely, innerwear, outerwear, hosiery and international. The group operates from the United States, Brazil, Canada, Argentina, Germany, Mexico and 13 other countries. The group's quarterly revenue for September 2007 was 1,153.61 millions of USD.

Primary SIC and add'l.: 2322 5137 2321 2252 2339 2384 5136 2369 2251 2342 2325 2341 2329 2331 2389

CIK No: 0001359841

Subsidiaries: Allende Internacional S. de R.L. de C.V., BA International, L.L.C., Bal-Mex S. de R.L. de C.V., Bali Dominicana Textiles, S.A., Bali Dominicana, Inc., Canadelle Holdings Corporation Limited, Canadelle LP, Caribesock, Inc., Caribetex, Inc., Cartex Manufacturera S. A., CASA International, LLC, Caysock, Inc., Caytex, Inc., Caywear, Inc., Ceiba Industrial, S. de R.L. 99 Subsidiaries included in the Index

Officers: Richard A. Noll/Dir., CEO, Lee A. Chaden/Executive Chmn., Joia M. Johnson/Exec. VP, General Counsel, Corp. Sec., Gerald W. Evans/Exec. VP, Chief Global Supply Chain Officer, Kevin D. Hall/Exec. VP, Chief Marketing Officer, Joan P. McReynolds/Exec. VP, Chief Customer Officer, Kevin W. Oliver/Exec. VP - Human Resources, Lee E. Wyatt/CFO, Exec. VP

Directors: Richard A. Noll/Dir., CEO, Lee A. Chaden/Executive Chmn., Harry Allyn Cockrell/57/Dir., Charles W. Coker/74/Dir., Bobby J. Griffin/58/Dir., James C. Johnson/55/Dir., Jessica T. Mathews/61/Dir., Patrick J. Mulcahy/63/Dir., Alice M. Peterson/54/Dir., Andrew J. Schindler/62/Dir.

Owners: Insiders, Lee E. Wyatt, Kevin W. Oliver, Lee A. Chaden, Gerald W. Evans, Capital Research and Management Company/14.80%, Richard A. Noll, Joan P. McReynolds, Charles W. Coker, Michael Flatow

Financial Data: Fiscal Year End: 07/01 **Latest Annual Data:** 12/30/2006

Year	Sales	Net Income
2006	$2,250,473,000	$74,139,000

Curr. Assets:	$2,071,180,000	**Curr. Liab.:**	$611,181,000	**P/E Ratio:**	11.94
Plant, Equip.:	$556,866,000	**Total Liab.:**	$3,366,349,000	**Indic. Yr. Divd.:**	NA
Total Assets:	$3,435,620,000	**Net Worth:**	$69,271,000	**Debt/ Equity:**	NA

Hanger Orthopedic Group Inc

2 Bethesda Metro Ctr., Ste. 1200, Bethesda, MD, 20814; **PH:** 1-301-986-0701; **Fax:** 1-301-986-0702; **http://** www.hanger.com; **Email:** info@hanger.com

General - Incorporation	DE	Stock - Price on:12/24/2007	$10.99
Employees	3,303	Stock Exchange	NYSE
Auditor	PricewaterhouseCoopers LLP	Ticker Symbol	HGR
Stk Agt	Mellon Investor Services LLC	Outstanding Shares	22,350,000
Counsel	Foley & Lardner LLP	E.P.S.	$0.49
DUNS No.	15-466-6218	Shareholders	NA

Business: The group's principal activity is to own and operate orthotic and prosthetic patient-care centers in the United States. The group operates under two segments: patient-care centers and distribution. The patient-care centers segment consists of the o&p patient-care centers, fabrication centers of o&p components and opnet. The patient-care centers provide services to design and fit o&p devices to patients. It designs, fabricates and maintains braces and other devices that provide external support to patients. It also designs, fabricates and maintains artificial limbs for patients who are without limbs. The distribution segment distributes purchased o&p products and components to both the o&p industry and the group's own patient-care practices. During 2003, the group acquired advanced bio-mechanics inc, advanced prosthetic svcs inc, adl prosthetic & orthotic svcs inc and during 2004, the group acquired the brace shop prosthetic orthotic centers inc

Primary SIC and add'l.: 8069 3842 8093

CIK No: 0000722723

Subsidiaries: ABI Orthotic/Prosthetic Laboratories, Ltd., Advanced Bio-Mechanics, Inc., Certified Orthotic & Prosthetic Associates, Inc., Conner Brace Co., Inc., DOBI-Symplex, Inc., Dosteon Solutions, LLC, Elite Care, Inc., Eugene Teufel & Son Orthotics & Prosthetics, Inc., Fortitude Medical Specialists, Inc., Greater Chesapeake Orthotics & Prosthetics, Inc., Hanger Europe, N.V., Hanger Prosthetics & Orthotics East, Inc., Hanger Prosthetics & Orthotics West, Inc., Hanger Prosthetics & Orthotics, Inc., Hanger Services Corporation 28 Subsidiaries included in the Index

Officers: Ivan R. Sabel/Chmn., CEO, Thomas F. Kirk/Dir., COO, Pres./$1,271,294.00, Ronald N. May/Pres. - Southern Prosthetic Supply, Inc, George E. McHenry/CFO, Richmond L. Taylor/Pres. - Hanger Prosthetics, Orthotics Inc, Hai Tran/Treasurer

Directors: Ivan R. Sabel/Chmn., CEO, Eric Green/Dir., Thomas F. Kirk/Dir., COO, Pres., Thomas P. Cooper/Dir., Edmond E. Charrette/Dir., Cynthia Feldmann/Dir., Isaac Kaufman/Dir., H. E. Thranhardt/Dir., Bennett Rosenthal/Dir.

Owners: George E. McHenry/0.80%, Richmond L. Taylor/1.40%, Greywolf Capital Management, L.P./7.00%, Insiders/10.60%, H. E. Thranhardt/1.70%, Putnam Investment Management, L.L.C./6.60%, Prides Capital, L.L.C./6.20%, Isaac Kaufman, Dimensional Fund Advisors, Inc./8.50%, Ron May/0.10%, Eric Green/0.10%, Ares Management, L.L.C./23.50%, Lazard Asset Management, L.L.C./6.50%, Edmond Charrette, Thomas P. Cooper *(18 Owners included in Index)*

Financial Data: Fiscal Year End: 12/31 **Latest Annual Data:** 12/31/2006

Year	Sales	Net Income
2006	$598,766,000	$3,434,000
2005	$578,241,000	$17,753,000
2004	$568,721,000	-$23,394,000

Curr. Assets:	$215,112,000	**Curr. Liab.:**	$57,904,000		
Plant, Equip.:	$42,294,000	**Total Liab.:**	$551,445,000	**Indic. Yr. Divd.:**	NA
Total Assets:	$719,122,000	**Net Worth:**	$167,677,000	**Debt/ Equity:**	2.3758

Hangman Productions Inc

1223 Wilshire Blvd, Ste 912, Santa Monica, CA, 90403; *PH:* 1-310-795-0252;
http:// www.hangmanproductions.com

General - Incorporation	UT	Stock - Price on:12/24/2007	$1.01
Employees	3	Stock Exchange	OTC
Auditor	Mantyla McReynolds	Ticker Symbol	HGMP
Stk Agt	NA	Outstanding Shares	1,490,000
Counsel	NA	E.P.S	-$0.01
DUNS No.	NA	Shareholders	NA

Business: The group's principal activity is to seek undiscovered screenwriters, and develop a pipeline between talented screenwriters and the filmmaking industry, as well as develop and produce independent film projects. The company is an emerging film production company. The company help screenwriters showcase their talent along with forging relationships within the film industry, helping to bridge the gap between screenwriters and Hollywood decision makers In November 2001, the company changed its name to "Hangman Productions".

Primary SIC and add'l.: 7812
CIK No: 0001299864
Officers: James P. Doolin/31/Dir., CEO, CFO, Pres., Shane E. Thueson/31/Dir., VP
Directors: James P. Doolin/31/Dir., CEO, CFO, Pres., Shane E. Thueson/31/Dir., VP, John K. Winchester/32/Dir.
Owners: Leonard W. Burningham, James P. Doolin, Shane E. Thueson, Quad D LTD Partnership, John K. Winchester, Michael J. Doolin, Insiders

*Financial Data: Fiscal Year End:*12/31 *Latest Annual Data:* 12/31/2006

Year	Sales	Net Income
2006	$4,000	-$20,000
2005	NA	-$29,000

Curr. Assets:	$0	Curr. Liab.:	$21,000		
Plant, Equip.:	NA	Total Liab.:	$21,000	Indic. Yr. Divd.:	NA
Total Assets:	$0	Net Worth:	-$21,000	Debt/ Equity:	NA

Hankersen International Corp

3rd Fl., A Tower Of Chuang Xin, Information Bldg., 72 Second Keji Rd., Hi Tech Zone, XIAN, 710075; *PH:* 86-13301996766

General - Incorporation	DE	Stock - Price on:12/24/2007	NA
Employees	NA	Stock Exchange	OTC
Auditor	MS Group CPA LLC	Ticker Symbol	HKRS
Stk Agt	NA	Outstanding Shares	NA
Counsel	NA	E.P.S	NA
DUNS No.	NA	Shareholders	NA

Business: The groups principle activity is to produce cork-building material. The group markets its product under the brand name Hanxin. The group acquired Hanxin International Holding Co., Ltd., in August 2005, and Export Co. Ltd., in the year 2005. The group operates from China, India, the United States, Germany and Japan.

Primary SIC and add'l.: 2400
CIK No: 0001104040
Subsidiaries: Hanxin Science and Technology Co., Ltd., Kushi Sub, Inc, Xi An Cork Investments Consultative Management Co
Officers: Pengcheng Chen/Dir., CEO, Yi Tong/CFO, Pingjun Zhang/CTO, Yinquan Su/Sr. Technical Consultant, Shibin Hu/Sr. Technical Consultant
Directors: Pengcheng Chen/Dir., CEO, Fangshe Zhang/Chmn.
Owners: Insiders/60.01%, Pengcheng Chen/32.08%, Fangshe Zhang/27.93%

*Financial Data: Fiscal Year End:*12/31 *Latest Annual Data:* 12/31/2006

Year	Sales	Net Income
2006	$12,042,000	$633,000

Curr. Assets:	$6,695,000	Curr. Liab.:	$1,920,000		
Plant, Equip.:	$3,591,000	Total Liab.:	$3,284,000	Indic. Yr. Divd.:	NA
Total Assets:	$14,029,000	Net Worth:	$10,745,000	Debt/ Equity:	NA

Hanmi Financial Corp

3660 Wilshire Blvd., Penthouse Ste. A, Los Angeles, CA, 90010; *PH:* 1-213-382-2200;
Fax: 1-213-384-0990; *http://* www.hanmifinancial.com

General - Incorporation	DE	Stock - Price on:12/24/2007	$17.04
Employees	589	Stock Exchange	NDQ
Auditor	KPMG LLP	Ticker Symbol	HAFC
Stk Agt	U.S. Stock Transfer Corp	Outstanding Shares	48,830,000
Counsel	NA	E.P.S	$1.16
DUNS No.	NA	Shareholders	NA

Business: The group's principal activity is to provide banking services to individuals and small to medium-sized businesses. The group has fifteen full service branch offices. The products and services of the group include commercial, installment and real estate loans, issuance and collection of letters of credit, international collection, import/export financing and small business administration guaranteed loans. On 22-Apr-2004, the group acquired pacific union bank.

Primary SIC and add'l.: 6022 6712
CIK No: 0001109242
Subsidiaries: Hanmi Bank
Officers: Sung W. Sohn/Dir., Pres., CEO - Hanmi Bank/$1,646,439.00, Inkyoung An/FVP, Operations Mgr. - Wilshire Branch, Anna Y. Cheong/AVP, Loan Officer - Western Branch, Suk Jin Yoon/Sr. VP, Branch Mgr. - Wilshire Branch, Stephanie Yoon/Primary Investor Relations Officer, Haekyong Kim/Sr. VP, Deputy Chief Credit Officer - Hanmi Bank, Woo Young Choung/Sr. VP, Branch Mgr. - Cerritos Branch, Prakash Ajwani/FVP, Marketing Officer - Cerritos Branch, Samuel Song/VP, Loan Mgr. - Vermont Branch, Seung Hee Cho/FVP - Operations Mgr. - Vermont Branch, Michelle Kwon/FVP, Branch Mgr. - West Garden Grove Branch, Hyung Suk Hahm/AVP, Loan Officer - West Garden Grove Branch, Eunice Lee/FVP, Operations Mgr. - West Garden Grove Branch, Jae Ho Lee/FVP, Branch Mgr. - West Torrance Branch, Sun Hyung Kim/VP, Operation Officer - West Torrance Branch (*62 Officers included in Index*)

Directors: Sung W. Sohn/Dir., Pres., CEO - Hanmi Bank, Richard B.C. Lee/Chmn. - Hanmi Bank, Joon I. Ahn/Dir. - Hanmi Bank, Joon Hyung Lee/Dir., Chang Kyu Park/Dir. - Hanmi Bank, Joseph K. Rho/Dir. - Hanmi Bank, Won R. Yoon/Dir. - Hanmi Bank, Ki Tae Hong/Dir. - Hanmi Bank, Mark K. Mason/Dir. - Hanmi Bank
Owners: Kurt M. Wegleitner/0.01%, Joon I. Ahn/2.41%, Richard B. C. Lee/2.48%, Insiders/16.65%, FMR Corporation/8.43%, Christian M. Mitchell, Won R. Yoon/3.45%, Michael J. Winiarski/0.03%, Chang Kyu Park/2.13%, Kraig A. Kupiec/0.06%, Joseph K. Rho/3.27%, William J. Ruh/0.14%, Joon Hyung Lee/2.41%, Barclays Global Investors/5.26%, Sung Won Sohn/0.34%

*Financial Data: Fiscal Year End:*12/31 *Latest Annual Data:* 12/31/2006

Year	Sales	Net Income
2006	$295,793,000	$65,649,000
2005	$231,323,000	$58,229,000
2004	$161,765,000	$36,700,000

Curr. Assets:	$168,823,000	Curr. Liab.:	$3,144,737,000	P/E Ratio:	13.21
Plant, Equip.:	$20,075,000	Total Liab.:	$3,238,126,000	Indic. Yr. Divd.:	$0.240
Total Assets:	$3,725,243,000	Net Worth:	$487,117,000	Debt/ Equity:	NA

Hanover Capital Mortgage Holdings Inc

200 Metroplex Dr., Ste. 100, Edison, NJ, 08817; *PH:* 1-732-548-0101; *Fax:* 1-732-548-0286;
http:// www.hanovercapitalholdings.com; *Email:* info@hanovercapitalholdings.com

General - Incorporation	MD	Stock - Price on:12/24/2007	$4.48
Employees	53	Stock Exchange	AMEX
Auditor	Grant Thornton LLP	Ticker Symbol	HCM
Stk Agt	Computershare Trust Co	Outstanding Shares	8,070,000
Counsel	NA	E.P.S	-$5.56
DUNS No.	NA	Shareholders	NA

Business: The groups principle activity is to provide finance to the real estate properties. The group operates from the United States. The groups quarterely revenue for September 2007 was 6.19 millions of USD.

Primary SIC and add'l.: 6798
CIK No: 0001040719
Subsidiaries: Hanover Capital Partners 2, Ltd., Hanover Capital Securities, Inc., Hanover SPC-A, Inc., Hanover Statutory Trust I, Hanover Statutory Trust II, HDMF-I LLC, HDMF-II LLC, HDMF-II Realty Corp., Pedestal Capital Markets, Inc.
Officers: John A. Burchett/Chmn., CEO, Pres./$397,411.00, Irma N. Tavares/COO/$315,885.00, Harold F. McElraft/CFO, Treasurer/$256,364.00, James C. Strickler/MD/$259,000.00, Suzette N. Berrios/VP, General Counsel
Directors: John A. Burchett/Chmn., CEO, Pres., John A. Clymer/Dir., John N. Rees/Dir., James F. Stone/Dir.
Owners: Douglas L. Jacobs, Irma N. Tavares/3.13%, Joseph J. Freeman, Joyce S. Mizerak/3.29%, Insiders/19.00%, James C. Strickler, George J. Ostendorf/3.06%, John A. Burchett/8.97%, John A. Clymer, James F. Stone, Harold F. McElraft, John N. Rees

*Financial Data: Fiscal Year End:*12/31 *Latest Annual Data:* 03/31/2007

Year	Sales	Net Income
2007	NA	NA
2006	$25,801,000	-$2,926,000
2005	$42,000,000	$1,366,000

Curr. Assets:	$15,634,000	Curr. Liab.:	$197,240,000	P/E Ratio:	24.43
Plant, Equip.:	$788,000	Total Liab.:	$246,686,000	Indic. Yr. Divd.:	$0.600
Total Assets:	$304,269,000	Net Worth:	$57,583,000	Debt/ Equity:	NA

Hanover Gold Company Inc

424 S Sullivan Rd. , Ste. 306, Veradale, WA, 99037; *PH:* 1-509-891-8817

General - Incorporation	DE	Stock - Price on:12/24/2007	$0.1
Employees	NA	Stock Exchange	OTC
Auditor	DeCoria, Maichel & Teague P.S.	Ticker Symbol	HVGO
Stk Agt	Jersey Transfer & Trust Co	Outstanding Shares	NA
Counsel	NA	E.P.S	$0.00
DUNS No.	NA	Shareholders	NA

Business: The groups principal activities include acquiring and exploring mining claims. Services of the group include diamond drilling, mapping and sampling, lithologic logging of drill holes, metallurgical testing, assaying, and aerial surveying. The group operates from southwestern Montana in the United States.

Primary SIC and add'l.: 1781 9999 6726
CIK No: 0000778165
Officers: Terrence J. Dunne/59/Chmn., Pres.
Directors: Terrence J. Dunne/59/Chmn., Pres., Daniel Mckinney/57/Dir., Hobart Teneff/87/Dir., Paul E. Fredericks/52/Dir.
Owners: Terrence Dunne/6.42%, Estate of Neal A. Degerstrom/11.53%, Margaret A. Nierengarten/6.78%

*Financial Data: Fiscal Year End:*12/31 *Latest Annual Data:* 12/31/2006

Year	Sales	Net Income
2006	NA	-$66,000
2005	NA	-$27,000
2004	NA	-$219,000

Curr. Assets:	$324,000	Curr. Liab.:	$4,000		
Plant, Equip.:	$400,000	Total Liab.:	$4,000	Indic. Yr. Divd.:	NA
Total Assets:	$724,000	Net Worth:	$720,000	Debt/ Equity:	NA

Hanover Insurance Group Inc

Formerly: Allmerica Financial Corp
440 Lincoln St., Worcester, MA, 01653; *PH:* 1-508-855-1000; *http://* www.allmerica.com

General - Incorporation	DE	Stock - Price on:12/24/2007	$48.14
Employees	4,000	Stock Exchange	NYSE
Auditor	PricewaterhouseCoopers LLP	Ticker Symbol	NA
Stk Agt	NA	Outstanding Shares	51,480,000
Counsel	Ropes & Gray LLP	E.P.S	$4.26
DUNS No.	00-695-6858	Shareholders	NA

Business: The groups principle activity is to provide insurance services. The group operates through three business segments namely personal lines, commercial lines, and other property and casualty. The group operates from United States.

Primary SIC and add'l.: 6331 6719 6321 6311

CIK No: 0000944695

Subsidiaries: AFC Capital Trust I, Allmerica Financial Alliance Insurance Company, Allmerica Financial Benefit Insurance Company, Allmerica Financial Insurance Brokers, Inc., Allmerica Financial Services Insurance Agency, Inc., Allmerica Funding Corp., Allmerica Investment Insurance Agency, Inc. of Georgia, Allmerica Investment Insurance Agency, Inc. of Kentucky, Allmerica Investments Insurance Agency of Florida, Inc., Allmerica Investments Insurance Agency, Inc. of Alabama, Allmerica Investments Insurance Agency, Inc. of Mississippi, Allmerica Plus Insurance Agency, Inc., AMGRO Receivables Corporation, AMGRO, INC., Citizens Insurance Company of America 32 Subsidiaries included in the Index

Officers: Frederick H. Eppinger/49/Dir., CEO, Pres./$6,485,786.00, Edward J. Parry/48/CFO, Exec. VP/$2,757,434.00, Mark J. Welzenbach/VP - Claims, Marita Zuraitis/Pres. - Property, Casualty Companies/$2,841,422.00, Bryan D. Allen/VP, Chief Human Resources Officer, Charles F. Cronin/VP, Sec., Gregory D. Tranter/CIO, VP/$1,294,731.00, Kendall J. Huber/Sr. VP, General Counsel/$1,554,579.00, Kristen M. Albright/VP, Chief Actuary, Warren E. Barnes/VP, Corporate Controller, Mark R. Desrochers/VP - State Management, David J. Firstenberg/Pres. - Commercial Lines, James S. Hyatt/Regional Pres. - Southeast, Richard W. Lavey/Regional Pres. - Northeast, Douglas H. McDonough/Regional Pres. - Southeast (23 Officers included in Index)

Directors: Frederick H. Eppinger/49/Dir., CEO, Pres., Kevin Condron/63/Dir., Wendell J. Knox/60/Dir., Gail L. Harrison/61/Dir., Joseph R. Ramrath/51/Dir., Michael P. Angelini/65/Dir., Neal F. Finnegan/70/Dir., David J. Gallitano/60/Dir., Robert J. Murray/67/Dir.

Owners: Kendall J. Huber, Edward J. Parry, Robert J. Murray, Wendell J. Knox, Neal F. Finnegan, Gail L. Harrison, Michael P. Angelini, Gregory Tranter, Insiders/2.30%, David J. Gallitano, Frederick H. Eppinger/1.10%, Joseph R. Ramrath, Kevin P. Condron, Herbert M. Varnum, Marita Zuraitis

Financial Data: Fiscal Year End:12/31 **Latest Annual Data:** 12/31/2006

Year	Sales	Net Income
2006	$2,644,100,000	$170,300,000
2005	$2,624,300,000	-$325,200,000
2004	$3,111,000,000	$125,300,000

Curr. Assets:	$2,307,900,000	**Curr. Liab.:**	$980,700,000		
Plant, Equip.:	NA	**Total Liab.:**	$7,857,400,000	**Indic. Yr. Divd.:**	$0.400
Total Assets:	$9,856,600,000	**Net Worth:**	$1,999,200,000	**Debt/ Equity:**	0.2609

Hansen Medical Inc

308 N Bernardo Ave., Mountain View, CA, 94043; **PH:** 1-650-404-5800; **Fax:** 1-650-404-5901; http:// www.hansenmedical.com

General - Incorporation	DE	**Stock** - Price on:12/24/2007	$19.64
Employees	96	Stock Exchange	NDQ
Auditor	Pricewaterhousecoopers LLP	Ticker Symbol	HNSN
Stk Agt	Mellon Investor Services LLC	Outstanding Shares	21,660,000
Counsel	NA	E.P.S	-$1.83
DUNS No.	NA	Shareholders	NA

Business: The groups principal activities include developing and manufacturing medical robotics design. The products of the group include Sensei(TM) Robotic Catheter System and Sensei system. The group products sold under the trade names Hansen Medical, Sensei, Artisan, intellisense, Elite, Hansen Artisan and Hansen Elite. In March 2005, the groups acquired endoVia Medical, Inc. Customer served by the group is academic institution. The group operates from the United States.

Primary SIC and add'l.: 3842

CIK No: 0001276591

Officers: Frederic H. Moll/Dir., CEO, Gary C. Restani/Dir., COO, Pres., Robert G. Younge/CTO, Sean M. Murphy/Sr. VP - Engineering, David C. Lundmark/VP - Intellectual Property, Legal Affairs, Jed A. Palmacci/VP - Sales, Service, Daniel T. Wallace/VP - Advanced Applications, Steven M. Van Dick/CFO, VP - Finance, Administration, Thomas A. Kramer/VP - Clinical Affairs, Judy Bartlett-Roberto/VP - Marketing

Directors: Frederic H. Moll/Dir., CEO, Russell C. Hirsch/Chmn., John G. Freund/Dir., Gary C. Restani/Dir., COO, Pres., Christopher P. Lowe/Dir., Joseph M. Mandato/Dir., Thomas C. McConnell/Dir., James M. Shapiro/Dir.

Owners: Robert G. Younge, Russell C. Hirsch, Christopher P. Lowe, Insiders, James M. Shapiro, Entities affiliated with Prospect Venture PartnersII, L.P., De Novo VenturesII, L.P., Steven M. VanDick, Entities affiliated with Vanguard Ventures, Joseph M. Mandato, Gary C. Restani, Thomas C. McConnell, John G. Freund, Thomas Weisel Healthcare Venture Partners, L.P., Entities affiliated with Skyline Ventures (17 Owners included in Index)

Financial Data: Fiscal Year End:12/31 **Latest Annual Data:** 12/31/2006

Year	Sales	Net Income
2006	NA	-$26,004,000
2005	NA	-$21,403,000
2004	NA	-$7,089,000

Curr. Assets:	$90,944,000	**Curr. Liab.:**	$4,551,000		
Plant, Equip.:	$1,706,000	**Total Liab.:**	$8,018,000	**Indic. Yr. Divd.:**	NA
Total Assets:	$92,790,000	**Net Worth:**	$84,772,000	**Debt/ Equity:**	0.0357

Hansen Natural Corp

1010 Railroad St., Corona, CA, 92882; **PH:** 1-951-739-6200; **Fax:** 1-951-739-6220; http:// www.hansens.com

General - Incorporation	DE	**Stock** - Price on:12/24/2007	$44.92
Employees	377	Stock Exchange	NDQ
Auditor	Deloitte & Touche LLP	Ticker Symbol	HANS
Stk Agt	American Stock Transfer & Trust Co.	Outstanding Shares	90,060,000
Counsel	Whitman Bred Abbott & Morgan	E.P.S	$1.09
DUNS No.	62-543-7488	Shareholders	NA

Business: The group's principal activity is to market, sell and distribute beverage category drinks. These include natural sodas, fruit juices, energy drinks, sparkling lemonades and orangeades, non-carbonated ready-to-drink iced teas, lemonades, juice cocktails and energy sports drinks, children's multi-vitamin juice drinks and nutrition bars and cereals. The group also markets and distributes energy drinks under the monster(tm) brand name. In addition, it markets nutrition bars and cereals under the

hansen's(R) brand name. Its fruit juices for toddlers and malt-based drinks are marketed under the junior juice(R) and the hard e(tm) brand names. The group's operations are conducted through wholly owned subsidiaries hansen beverage company ('hbc') and hard energy beverage company ('heb'). The customers of the group include, costco, trader joe's, sam's club, vons, ralph's, wal-Mart, safeway and albertson's.

Primary SIC and add'l.: 6719 5149

CIK No: 0000865752

Subsidiaries: Hansen Foods, Inc., Hansen Natural Corporation

Officers: Rodney C. Sacks/Chmn., CEO/$2,583,549.00, Hilton H. Schlosberg/55/Vice Chmn., CFO, COO, Sec./$2,573,164.00, Thomas J. Kelly/54/VP - Finance, Sec. - HBC/$256,583.00, Michael B. Schott/60/Sr. VP - National Sales, Monster Beverage Division, HBC/$627,287.00, Mark J. Hall/52/Pres. - Monster Beverage Division, HBC/$1,541,789.00, Roger Pondel/Contact - Investor Relations, Judy Lin Sfetcu/Contact - Investor Relations, Kirk Blower/57/Sr. VP - Non - Carbonated Products - HBC

Directors: Rodney C. Sacks/Chmn., CEO, Hilton H. Schlosberg/55/Vice Chmn., CFO, COO, Sec., Sydney Selati/Dir., Harold C. Taber/55/Dir., Norman C. Epstein/Dir., Benjamin M. Polk/Dir., Mark S. Vidergauz/Dir.

Owners: Barclay's Global Investors, NA/4.40%, Mark Vidergauz, Hilrod Holdings II, L.P./0.50%, Harold Taber, Mark Hall, Benjamin Polk, Hilton H. Schlosberg/17.80%, Rodney C. Sacks/18.20%, HRS Holdings, L.P./0.80%, Brandon Limited Partnership No. 2/8.30%, Fidelity Low Priced Stock Fund/7.30%, Brandon Limited Partnership No. 1/1.30%, Norman Epstein, Hilrod Holdings, L.P./4.40%, Kirk Blower (17 Owners included in Index)

Financial Data: Fiscal Year End:12/31 **Latest Annual Data:** 12/31/2006

Year	Sales	Net Income
2006	$605,774,000	$97,949,000
2005	$348,886,000	$62,776,000
2004	$180,341,000	$20,387,000

Curr. Assets:	$275,157,000	**Curr. Liab.:**	$62,843,000	**P/E Ratio:**	41.21
Plant, Equip.:	$5,565,000	**Total Liab.:**	$83,288,000	**Indic. Yr. Divd.:**	NA
Total Assets:	$308,372,000	**Net Worth:**	$225,084,000	**Debt/ Equity:**	NA

Hanson Plc

1 Grosvenor Pl., Londonengland, SW1X7JH; ; http:// www.hansonplc.com

General - Incorporation	UK	**Stock** - Price on:12/24/2007	$106.85
Employees	25,900	Stock Exchange	NA
Auditor	Ernst & Young LLP	Ticker Symbol	NA
Stk Agt	Citibank Shareholder Services	Outstanding Shares	142,460,000
Counsel	NA	E.P.S	$5.45
DUNS No.	NA	Shareholders	NA

Business: The group's principal activity is the manufacture and supply of building materials to the construction industry worldwide. The group's product includes asphalt, cement, crushed rock, ready-mixed concrete, sand and gravel, bricks, concrete pipe and products, roofing tiles, building stone, recycled materials and pre-cast concrete. Its key markets are North America and the United Kingdom where the operating groups are hanson aggregates and hanson building products. The group's other operations are hanson Australia, hanson continental Europe and marine and hanson Asia-Pacific. The group operates in North America, the United Kingdom, Australia, continental Europe and Asia-Pacific.

Primary SIC and add'l.: NA

CIK No: 0001265725

Subsidiaries: Hanson Australia Funding Limited

Officers: Alan Murray/CEO, Jim Kitzmiller/Pres., CEO - Hanson Aggregates North America, Richard Manning/Pres., CEO - Hanson Building Products North America, Justin Read/MD - Hanson Continental Europe, David Szymanski/MD - Hanson Building Products UK, Leslie Cadzow/Chief Executive - Hanson Australia, Asia Pacific, Patrick O'Shea/MD - Hanson Aggregates UK, Graham Dransfield/57/Legal Dir., Pavi Binning/Dir. - Finance, Gemma Parsons/Assist., Company Sec., Paul Tunnacliffe/Company Sec., Brigitte Fickel/Corporate Responsibility Contact, David Weeks/Group Enquirie, Jeremy Smith/Group Enquirie, Australia, Asia Pacific, Terry Demler/Group Enquirie, Building Products North America

Directors: Mike Welton/61/Chmn., Jim Leng/62/Sr. Non Exec. Dir., Frank Blount/69/Non Exec. Dir., John Brady/56/Non Exec. Dir., Sam Laidlaw/52/Non Exec. Dir., Baroness Noakes/59/Non Exec. Dir.

Financial Data: Fiscal Year End:12/31 **Latest Annual Data:** 12/31/2006

Year	Sales	Net Income
2006	$8,096,373,000	$711,937,000
2005	$6,393,977,000	$797,935,000
2004	$6,674,320,000	$372,990,000

Curr. Assets:	$3,991,862,000	**Curr. Liab.:**	$3,053,257,000		
Plant, Equip.:	$5,697,063,000	**Total Liab.:**	$7,683,589,000	**Indic. Yr. Divd.:**	$2.130
Total Assets:	$13,146,345,000	**Net Worth:**	$5,449,237,000	**Debt/ Equity:**	NA

Harbor Florida Bancshares Inc

100 S Second St. , Fort Pierce, FL, 34950; **PH:** 1-772-461-2414; http:// www.harborfederal.com

General - Incorporation	DE	**Stock** - Price on:12/24/2007	$33.78
Employees	31,270	Stock Exchange	NDQ
Auditor	KPMG LLP	Ticker Symbol	NCEM
Stk Agt	Mellon Investor Services	Outstanding Shares	575,760,000
Counsel	Fee, Koblegard & Deross	E.P.S	$3.32
DUNS No.	96-963-1589	Shareholders	NA

Business: The group's principal activity is to provide a wide range of banking services that include acceptance of deposits and using the funds to originate various loans. It provides a number of different deposit accounts, including regular savings, interest-bearing checking or now accounts, non-interest checking, money market accounts, term certificate accounts and individual retirement accounts. The group's loan portfolio consists of commercial real estate, residential real estate and commercial business and consumer loans. In addition, it also provides investment and insurance services. The group operates through thirty-three full-service banking offices, one loan production office, three insurance agency locations and one in-store branch location. On 27-Mar-2003, the group acquired david g. Willbur insurance agency.

Primary SIC and add'l.: 6712 6035

CIK No: 0001029407

Subsidiaries: Appraisal Analysts, Inc., H. F. Development Company, Inc., Harbor Florida Financial Services, Inc., Harbor Insurance Agency, Inc.

Financial Data: Fiscal Year End:09/30 **Latest Annual Data:** 12/31/2006

Year	Sales	Net Income
2006	NA	NA
2005	NA	NA
2004	NA	NA

Curr. Assets:	$5,072,503,000	**Curr. Liab.:**	$96,887,366,000	**P/E Ratio:**	10.17
Plant, Equip.:	$2,204,172,000	**Total Liab.:**	$125,609,839,000	**Indic. Yr. Divd.:**	$1.640
Total Assets:	$140,190,842,000	**Net Worth:**	$14,581,003,000	**Debt/ Equity:**	2.0345

Hardinge Inc

1 Hardinge Dr., Elmira, NY, 14902; *PH:* 1-607-734-2281; *Fax:* 1-607-732-4925;
http:// www.hardinge.com

General - Incorporation	NY	**Stock**- Price on:12/24/2007	$35.45
Employees	1,457	Stock Exchange	NDQ
Auditor	Ernst & Young LLP	Ticker Symbol	HDNG
Stk Agt	Computershare Investor Services LLC	Outstanding Shares	8,890,000
Counsel	NA	E.P.S	$2.21
DUNS No.	00-220-4063	Shareholders	NA

Business: The group's principle activities are to design, manufacture and distribute metal cutting lathes, grinding machines, machining centers and tooling and accessories related to metal cutting machines. Turning machines, or lathes, are power-driven machines used to remove material from a rough-formed part by moving multiple cutting tools arranged on a turret assembly against the surface of a part rotating at very high speeds in a spindle mechanism. The group produces computer numerically controlled ('cnc') machines, which uses commands from an on-board computer to control the movement of cutting tools and rotation speeds of the part being produced. The group markets its products in the United States, western Europe, Canada, China, Mexico, Japan, Australia and other foreign countries through its direct sales force and through distributors and manufacturers' representatives. The group's quarterly revenue for Sep'07 was 83.68 millions of USD.

Primary SIC and add'l.: 3541 3545

CIK No: 0000313716

Subsidiaries: Canadian Hardinge Machine Tools, Ltd., Hardinge China Limited, Hardinge Machine (Shanghai) Co., Ltd., Hardinge Machine Tools, Ltd., Hardinge Taiwan Precision Machinery Limited, Hardinge, GmbH, HTT Hauser Tripet Tschudin, AG, L. Kellenberger& Co., AG

Officers: Patrick J. Ervin/51/Chmn., CEO, Pres./$925,985.00, Charles Trego/57/Sr. VP, CFO/$367,335.00, Joseph T. Colvin/VP, GM - Workholding Operations, Jurg Kellenberger/VP - Grinding Operations, Douglas C. Tifft/53/Sr. VP - Administration/$247,650.00, Beth Tranter/Dir. - Corporate Accounting, Thomas Doud/Media Contact - Turning, Milling, Grinding

Directors: Patrick J. Ervin/51/Chmn., CEO, Pres., Douglas A. Greenlee/60/Dir., John J. Perrotti/47/Dir., Mitchell I. Quain/56/Dir., Kyle H. Seymour/47/Dir., Daniel J. Burke/67/Dir., Philip J. Hunter/65/Dir.

Owners: Douglas A. Greenlee, John J. Perrotti, Daniel J. Burke, Franklin Resources, Inc./10.20%, Dimensional Fund Advisors LP/8.22%, Philip J. Hunter, FMR Corp./10.01%, Mitchell I. Quain, Douglas C. Tifft, Jeffrey L. Gendell/8.18%, Kyle H. Seymour, Patrick J. Ervin/1.40%, Insiders/3.40%

Financial Data: **Fiscal Year End:**12/31 **Latest Annual Data:** 12/31/2006

Year	Sales	Net Income
2006	$326,621,000	$13,950,000
2005	$289,925,000	$7,006,000
2004	$232,054,000	$4,392,000

Curr. Assets:	$227,638,000	**Curr. Liab.:**	$70,644,000	**P/E Ratio:**	16.04
Plant, Equip.:	$64,052,000	**Total Liab.:**	$173,551,000	**Indic. Yr. Divd.:**	$0.200
Total Assets:	$330,660,000	**Net Worth:**	$157,109,000	**Debt/ Equity:**	0.4384

Hardwood Doors & Milling Specialities Inc

1667 K St., Nw, Ste. 1230, Washington, DC, 20006; *PH:* 1-202-223-4401

General - Incorporation	NV	**Stock**- Price on:12/24/2007	$0.08
Employees	10	Stock Exchange	OTC
Auditor	Malone & Bailey, P.C	Ticker Symbol	CBRE
Stk Agt	Pacific Stock Transfer Company	Outstanding Shares	NA
Counsel	Vinson & Elkins LLP	E.P.S	-$0.182
DUNS No.	NA	Shareholders	NA

Business: The group's principle activity is to seek, investigate, and if warranted, acquire an interest in a business opportunity. We are not restricting our search to any particular industry or geographical area. We may therefore engage in essentially any business in any industry. The group's management has unrestricted discretion in seeking and participating in a business opportunity, subject to the availability of such opportunities, economic conditions and other factors. The group operates from United States.

Primary SIC and add'l.: 7389

CIK No: 0001124074

Subsidiaries: Calibre Energy

Financial Data: **Fiscal Year End:**12/31 **Latest Annual Data:** 12/31/2006

Year	Sales	Net Income
2006	$554,000	-$10,259,000
2005	$21,000	-$1,902,000

Curr. Assets:	$2,003,000	**Curr. Liab.:**	$4,732,000		
Plant, Equip.:	$14,600,000	**Total Liab.:**	$4,786,000	**Indic. Yr. Divd.:**	NA
Total Assets:	$17,140,000	**Net Worth:**	$12,354,000	**Debt/ Equity:**	NA

Harford Bank MD

8 W Bel Air Ave., Aberdeen, MD, 21001; *PH:* 1-410-272-5000; *Fax:* 1-410-272-0533;
http:// www.harfordbank.com

General - Incorporation		**Stock**- Price on:12/24/2007	$44.75
Employees	NA	Stock Exchange	OTC
Auditor	NA	Ticker Symbol	HFBK
Stk Agt	NA	Outstanding Shares	NA
Counsel	NA	E.P.S	NA
DUNS No.	NA	Shareholders	NA

Business: The group's principle activity is to provide banking services. The group also provides loans. The group operates from United States.

Primary SIC and add'l.: 6029

CIK No: 0001218371

Financial Data: **Fiscal Year End:**NA **Latest Annual Data:** 12/31/2002

Year	Sales	Net Income
2002	$9,986,000	$1,809,000
2001	$10,545,000	$1,754,000
2000	$10,322,000	$1,551,000

Curr. Assets:	$14,672,000	**Curr. Liab.:**	$140,110,000		
Plant, Equip.:	$4,025,000	**Total Liab.:**	$142,258,000	**Indic. Yr. Divd.:**	$1.120
Total Assets:	$160,423,000	**Net Worth:**	$18,165,000	**Debt/ Equity:**	NA

Harley-Davidson Inc

8969 N Port Washington Rd., Milwaukee, WI, 53201; *PH:* 1-414-342-4680; *Fax:* 1-888-224-2453;
http:// www.harley-davidson.com

General - Incorporation	WI	**Stock**- Price on:12/24/2007	$59.87
Employees	9,704	Stock Exchange	NYSE
Auditor	Ernst & Young LLP	Ticker Symbol	HOG
Stk Agt	Computershare Investor Services LLC	Outstanding Shares	257,530,000
Counsel	NA	E.P.S	$4.06
DUNS No.	10-222-4623	Shareholders	NA

Business: The group's principle activity is to provide motorcycles and branded products. The group also provide rental and rider education services. The group operates through two segments namely motorcycles and related products and financial services segment. The group operates from United States, Canada and Europe.

Primary SIC and add'l.: 6282 3751 6159 6399 5561

CIK No: 0000793952

Subsidiaries: Buell Distribution Company, LLC, Buell Motorcycle Company, LLC, Eaglemark Customer Funding Corporation-IV, Eaglemark Savings Bank, H-D Capitol Drive, LLC, H-d F&r, LLC, H-D Franklin, LLC, H-D Group LLC, H-D Michigan, Inc., H-D Milwaukee, LLC, H-D Pilgrim Road, LLC, H-D Tomahawk Industrial Park, LLC, H-D Tomahawk Kaphaem Road, LLC, H-D Tomahawk Somo, LLC, Harley-Davidson Asia, Inc. 55 Subsidiaries included in the Index

Officers: James L. Ziemer/Dir., CEO, Pres./$4,337,718.00, Gail A. Lione/VP, General Counsel, Sec./$1,628,009.00, Thomas E. Bergmann/41/CFO, VP/$1,170,759.00, Joanne M. Bischmann/46/VP - Marketing, Harley, Davidson Motor Company, James M. Brostowitz/55/VP, Treasurer, Chief Accounting Officer/$1,035,854.00, Karl M. Eberle/59/VP, GM - Kansas City Operations, Harley, Davidson Motor Company, Jon R. Flickinger/50/VP - Harley, Davidson Motor Company, John A. Hevey/50/VP - Strategic Planning, New Business Development, Harley, Davidson Motor Company, Ronald M. Hutchinson/60/VP - New Business, Harley, Davidson Motor Company, James A. McCaslin/59/COO, Pres. - Harley, Davidson Motor Company/$1,860,068.00, Harold A. Scott/59/VP - Human Resources, Harley, Davidson Motor Company, Kenneth W. Sutton/59/VP - Engineering, Harley, Davidson Motor Company

Directors: James L. Ziemer/Dir., CEO, Pres., Jeffrey L. Bleustein/Chmn., Richard I. Beattie/Dir., George H. Conrades/Dir., Sara L. Levinson/Dir., Donald A. James/Dir., James A. Norling/Dir., Judson C. Green/Dir., Barry K. Allen/Dir., George L. Miles/Dir., Jochen Zeitz/Dir.

Owners: James M. Brostowitz, Ronald M. Hutchinson, George L. Miles, Donald A. James, Insiders/1.10%, James A. Norling, Capital Research and Management Company/5.10%, Davis Selected Advisers, L.P./9.20%, Gail A. Lione, Sara L. Levinson, James L. Ziemer, Judson C. Green, James A. McCaslin, Richard I. Beattie, Barry K. Allen *(18 Owners included in Index)*

Financial Data: **Fiscal Year End:**12/31 **Latest Annual Data:** 12/31/2006

Year	Sales	Net Income
2006	$6,185,577,000	$1,043,153,000
2005	$5,673,832,000	$959,604,000
2004	$5,320,452,000	$889,766,000

Curr. Assets:	$3,550,633,000	**Curr. Liab.:**	$1,595,677,000		
Plant, Equip.:	$1,024,469,000	**Total Liab.:**	$2,775,413,000	**Indic. Yr. Divd.:**	NA
Total Assets:	$5,532,150,000	**Net Worth:**	$2,756,737,000	**Debt/ Equity:**	0.3155

Harleysville Group Inc

355 Maple Ave., Harleysville, PA, 19438; *PH:* 1-215-256-5000; *Fax:* 1-215-256-5799;
http:// www.harleysvillegroup.com; *Email:* information@harleysvillegroup.com

General - Incorporation	DE	**Stock**- Price on:12/24/2007	$32.61
Employees	1,898	Stock Exchange	NDQ
Auditor	KPMG LLP	Ticker Symbol	HGIC
Stk Agt	Mellon Investor Services LLC	Outstanding Shares	31,930,000
Counsel	NA	E.P.S	$2.94
DUNS No.	06-180-5396	Shareholders	NA

Business: The group's principal activity is to provide property and casualty insurance products. It provides personal and commercial property and casualty coverages including automobile, homeowners, commercial multi-peril and workers compensation. The group operates a network of regional insurers in the eastern and midwestern United States through approximately 1,700 insurance agencies. Its regional offices are maintained in Georgia, Indiana, Maryland, Massachusetts, Michigan, Minnesota, New Jersey, New York, North Carolina, Pennsylvania, Tennessee and Virginia.

Primary SIC and add'l.: 6331 6719

CIK No: 0000792013

Subsidiaries: Harleysville Insurance Company, Harleysville Insurance Company of New Jersey, Harleysville Insurance Company of New York, Harleysville Insurance Company of Ohio, Harleysville Lake States Insurance Company, Harleysville Preferred Insurance Company, Harleysville Worcester Insurance Company, Harleysville-Atlantic Insurance Company, Mid-America Insurance Company

Officers: Michael L. Browne/CEO, Pres./$2,559,217.00, Thomas E. Clark/Sr. VP - Field Operations, Allan R. Becker/Sr. VP, Chief Actuary, Robert A. Kauffman/Sr. VP, Sec., General Counsel, Chief Governance Officer, Mark R. Cummins/Exec. VP, Chief Investment Officer, Treasurer/$778,609.00, Dennis J. Otmaskin/Pres. - Northeast Operation, Donna M. Jallick/VP - Flood Operations, Kevin J. McArdle/VP - Communications, Robert R. Southard/Regional Operations Resident VP - Atlanta Office, Kevin M. Toth/Sr. VP - Claims, Theodore A. Majewski/Sr. VP - Personal Lines, Donna M. Dever/Sr. VP - Business Process Improvement, William J. Shelow/Pres., COO - Harleysville Life Insurance Company, William D. Granato/Regional Pres. - Midwest Operation, Jeffrey D. Brown/Regional Operations Resident VP - Michigan Office *(40 Officers included in Index)*

Owners: Michael L. Browne, Dimensional Fund, Akhil Tripathi, Catherine B. Strauss, William W. Scranton, Thacher W. Brown, William E. Storts, Frank E. Reed, Lowell R. Beck, Mark R. Cummins, Jerry S. Rosenbloom, Mirian M. Graddick-Weir, Harleysville Mutual, Arthur E. Chandler, Insiders

Financial Data: *Fiscal Year End:*12/31 *Latest Annual Data:* 12/31/2006

Year	Sales	Net Income
2006	$999,171,000	$111,069,000
2005	$948,340,000	$61,431,000
2004	$953,392,000	$46,878,000

Curr. Assets:	$430,066,000	**Curr. Liab.:**	$98,184,000	**P/E Ratio:**	11.09
Plant, Equip.:	$16,690,000	**Total Liab.:**	$2,278,822,000	**Indic. Yr. Divd.:**	$0.760
Total Assets:	$2,990,984,000	**Net Worth:**	$712,162,000	**Debt/ Equity:**	0.3415

Harleysville National Corp

483 Main St., Harleysville, PA, 19438; *PH:* 1-215-256-8851; *Fax:* 1-215-256-3065;
http:// www.harleysvillebank.com

General - Incorporation	PA	**Stock**- Price on:12/24/2007	$16.28
Employees	740	Stock Exchange	NDQ
Auditor	Grant Thornton LLP	Ticker Symbol	HNBC
Stk Agt	American Stock Transfer & Trust Co.	Outstanding Shares	28,970,000
Counsel	NA	E.P.S	$1.15
DUNS No.	00-893-6098	Shareholders	NA

Business: The group's principal activities are to provide commercial banking and trust services to customers located in eastern Pennsylvania. These services include acceptance of time and demand deposits, originating secured and unsecured commercial loans, construction and mortgage loans, financing of commercial transactions and performing corporate pension and personal trust services. The deposits are insured by the federal deposit insurance corporation. As on 31-Dec-2003, the group operates 40 branch offices located in montgomery, bucks, chestier, berks, carbon, wayne, monroe, lehigh, northampton and schuylkill counties, Pennsylvania. On 30-Apr-2004, the group acquired millennium bank & cumberland advisors, inc.

Primary SIC and add'l.: 6712 6022

CIK No: 0000702902

Subsidiaries: Harleysville Management Services, LLC, Harleysville National Bank and Trust Company., Harleysville Statutory Trust I, HNB Auto Sales, LLC, HNC Financial Company, HNC Insurance Agency, Inc, HNC Reinsurance Company, HNC Statutory Trust II, HNC Statutory Trust III

Officers: Demetra M. Takes/Exec. VP, CEO, Pres. - Harleysville National Bank/$542,803.00, Paul D. Geraghty/Dir., CEO, Pres., Liz Chemnitz/Investment Relations Officer, Michael B. High/COO, Exec. VP/$519,616.00, Jo Ann M. Bynon/Sr. VP, Sec., John W. Eisele/67/Exec. VP/$369,138.00, George S. Rapp/CFO, Exec. VP, Treasurer/$245,661.00, James F. McGowan/Exec. VP/$220,748.00, Lewis C. Cyr/Exec. VP, Chief Lending Officer

Directors: Demetra M. Takes/Exec. VP, CEO, Pres. - Harleysville National Bank, Paul D. Geraghty/Dir., CEO, Pres., Walter E. Daller/Chmn., James A. Wimmer/Dir., Leeann B. Bergey/Dir., Stephanie S. Mitchell/Dir., Harold A. Herr/Dir., Thomas C. Leamer/Dir., Walter R. Bateman/Dir., Ross A. Myers/Dir.

Owners: Ross A. Myers, James F. McGowan, John W. Eisele, Gregg J. Wagner, LeeAnn B. Bergey, Stephanie S. Mitchell, Harold A. Herr, Insiders/7.00%, Michael B. High, George S. Rapp, Walter R. Bateman, Demetra M. Takes, Walter E. Daller/2.75%, Thomas C. Leamer, Mikkalya W. Murray *(16 Owners included in Index)*

Financial Data: *Fiscal Year End:*12/31 *Latest Annual Data:* 06/30/2007

Year	Sales	Net Income
2007	$57,966,000	$7,079,000
2006	$65,541,000	$13,272,000
2005	$181,729,000	$38,828,000

Curr. Assets:	$139,820,000	**Curr. Liab.:**	$2,646,410,000	**P/E Ratio:**	13.02
Plant, Equip.:	$33,785,000	**Total Liab.:**	$2,955,077,000	**Indic. Yr. Divd.:**	$0.800
Total Assets:	$3,249,828,000	**Net Worth:**	$294,751,000	**Debt/ Equity:**	1.2027

Harleysville Savings Financial Corp

271 Main St., Harleysville, PA, 19438; *PH:* 1-215-256-8828; *Fax:* 1-215-513-9393;
http:// www.harleysvillesavings.com; *Email:* info@harleysvillesavings.com

General - Incorporation	PA	**Stock**- Price on:12/24/2007	$16.5042
Employees	67	Stock Exchange	NDQ
Auditor	Deloitte & Touche LLP	Ticker Symbol	HARL
Stk Agt	Registrar & Transfer Co	Outstanding Shares	3,870,000
Counsel	Elias, Matz, Tierman & Herrick	E.P.S	$0.83
DUNS No.	NA	Shareholders	NA

Business: The group's principal activity is to provide banking services to individuals and corporates in Pennsylvania. It is a holding company for harleysville savings bank. The group attracts attract deposits from the general public through a variety of deposit programs and investing such deposits principally in first mortgage loans secured by residential properties. It also originates a variety of consumer loans, predominately home equity loans and lines of credit also secured by residential properties. It serves its customers through its full-service branch network as well as through remote ATM locations, the Internet and telephone banking.

Primary SIC and add'l.: 6035 6712

CIK No: 0001107160

Subsidiaries: Harleysville Savings Bank

Officers: Ronald B. Geib/CEO, Pres., Brendan J. McGill/Sr. VP - Treasurer, CFO

Directors: Edward J. Molnar/Chmn., Sanford L. Alderfer/Dir., David J. Friesen/64/Dir., George W. Meschter/Dir., Philip A. Clemens/Dir., Mark R. Cummins/Dir., Charlotte A. Hunsberger/Dir., James L. Rittenhouse/Dir.

Owners: David J. Friesen/1.20%, Charlotte A. Hunsberger, Edward J. Molnar/2.80%, Mark R. Cummins/3.50%, Philip A. Clemens/1.20%, First Manhattan Company/7.10%, Harleysville Savings Financial/5.50%, Stephen J. Kopenhaver, George W. Meschter/1.40%, Insiders/14.80%, Ronald B. Geib/2.90%, Adrian D. Gordon, Sanford L. Alderfer, Sheri Strouse, Brendan J. McGill *(16 Owners included in Index)*

Financial Data: *Fiscal Year End:*09/30 *Latest Annual Data:* 9/30/2006

Year	Sales	Net Income
2006	$40,391,000	$4,202,000
2005	$37,368,000	$5,004,000
2004	$34,244,000	$4,850,000

Curr. Assets:	$14,020,000	**Curr. Liab.:**	$725,982,000	**P/E Ratio:**	17.67
Plant, Equip.:	$8,014,000	**Total Liab.:**	$727,166,000	**Indic. Yr. Divd.:**	$0.680
Total Assets:	$775,638,000	**Net Worth:**	$48,471,000	**Debt/ Equity:**	NA

Harman International Industries Inc

1101 Pennsylvania Ave. N W, Ste. 1010, Washington, DC, 20004; *PH:* 1-516-255-4545;
http:// www.harman.com

General - Incorporation	DE	**Stock**- Price on:12/24/2007	$117.46
Employees	11,246	Stock Exchange	NYSE
Auditor	KPMG LLP	Ticker Symbol	HAR
Stk Agt	Mellon Investor Services LLC	Outstanding Shares	65,150,000
Counsel	NA	E.P.S	$4.10
DUNS No.	04-765-3555	Shareholders	NA

Business: The groups principle activities include developing, manufacturing and marketing of high-fidelity audio products and electronic systems. The group operates through three business segments namely automotive, consumer and professional. The group operates from United States.

Primary SIC and add'l.: 3651

CIK No: 0000800459

Subsidiaries: AKG Acoustics GmbH, AKG Acoustics Limited, Amek Systems and Controls Ltd., Amek Technology Group Limited, Becker Automotive (Pty) Ltd., Becker Service und Verwaltungs GmbH, BSS Audio, CAudio, Crown Audio, Inc., Digital Audio Research Limited, Fosgate, Inc., Harman Kardon, Incorporated, Harman Audio de Mexico S.A. de CV, Harman Becker Automotive Electronic Systems Suzhou Co. Ltd., Harman Becker Automotive Systems (Michigan), Inc. 78 Subsidiaries included in the Index

Officers: Dinesh C. Paliwal/50/Vice Chmn., CEO, Pres., Helmut Schinagel/55/CEO - Automotive, Sidney Harman/90/Exec. Chmn., Kevin L. Brown/48/CFO, Exec. VP, Assist. Sec., Sandra B. Robinson/49/VP - Financial Operations, Chief Accounting Officer, Edwin C. Summers/61/VP, General Counsel, Sec., Gina Harman/59/Pres. - Consumer, Erich A. Geiger/61/Exec. VP, Chief Strategy Officer, CTO, Blake Augsburger/45/Pres. - Professional

Directors: Dinesh C. Paliwal/50/Vice Chmn., CEO, Pres., Sidney Harman/90/Exec. Chmn., Edward H. Meyer/81/Dir., Shirley Mount Hufstedler/83/Dir., Ann McLaughlin Korologos/66/Dir., Harald Einsmann/74/Dir., Brian F. Carroll/37/Dir.

Owners: Insiders/7.00%, Edward H. Meyer, Dinesh Paliwal, FMR Corp./10.60%, Ann M. Korologos, Gina Harman, T. Rowe Price Associates, Inc./13.90%, Shirley M. Hufstedler, Capital Research and Management Company/12.70%, Sidney Harman/5.40%, Kevin Brown, The Growth Fund of America/5.60%, Erich A. Geiger

Financial Data: *Fiscal Year End:*06/30 *Latest Annual Data:* 6/30/2006

Year	Sales	Net Income
2006	$3,247,897,000	$255,295,000
2005	$3,030,889,000	$232,848,000
2004	$2,711,374,000	$157,883,000

Curr. Assets:	$1,249,357,000	**Curr. Liab.:**	$869,001,000	**P/E Ratio:**	24.89
Plant, Equip.:	$521,935,000	**Total Liab.:**	$1,123,781,000	**Indic. Yr. Divd.:**	$0.050
Total Assets:	$2,354,661,000	**Net Worth:**	$1,228,164,000	**Debt/ Equity:**	0.1022

Harmonic Inc

549 Baltic Way, Sunnyvale, CA, 94089; *PH:* 1-408-542-2500; *Fax:* 1-408-542-2511;
http:// www.harmonicinc.com

General - Incorporation	DE	**Stock**- Price on:12/24/2007	$8.67
Employees	639	Stock Exchange	NDQ
Auditor	PricewaterhouseCoopers LLP	Ticker Symbol	HLIT
Stk Agt	Mellon Investor Services LLC	Outstanding Shares	79,360,000
Counsel	Wilson Sonsini Goodrich & Rosati	E.P.S	$0.27
DUNS No.	60-278-8580	Shareholders	NA

Business: The group's principal activity is to design, manufacture and market a variety of broadband solutions. The products are classified as broadband access networks: include optical transmission products, node platforms and return path products and element management hardware and software. These systems provide enhanced network reliability and allow broadband service providers to deliver advanced services, including two-way interactive services. Convergent systems: include encoders, multiplexers and modulators. These digital video solutions enable satellite, cable, telco, broadcast and wireless operators around the world to offer digital video services and advanced data services. In addition, the group provides professional services and systems support to its customers worldwide.

Primary SIC and add'l.: 3663 3661

CIK No: 0000851310

Subsidiaries: Harmonic (Asia Pacific) Ltd., Harmonic (UK)Ltd., Harmonic Europe S.A.S., Harmonic Germany GmbH, Harmonic International Inc., Harmonic International Limited, Harmonic Lightwaves (Israel) Ltd., Harmonic Video Systems Ltd.

Officers: Patrick Harshman/Dir., CEO, Pres./$842,515.00, Mark E. Renfroe/VP - Americas Sales, Robin N. Dickson/CFO/$626,146.00, Michael Newman/Investor Relations Officer - Harmonic Streetconnect, Neven Haltmayer/VP - Research, Development/$322,758.00, Charles Bonasera/VP - Operations/$66,524.00, Matthew Aden/VP - Worldwide Sales, Service, Nimrod Ben-Natan/VP - Product Marketing, Solutions, Strategy, Anne Lynch/VP - Human Resources, David Price/VP - Business Development, Marketing Communications, Glen Sakata/VP - EMEA Sales, David Trescot/VP - Rhozet Business Unit, Raymond Tse/VP - Apac Sales, Excluding China, Tony Xu/VP - China Sales, Sarah Lum/Sr. Mgr. - Public Relations

Directors: Patrick Harshman/Dir., CEO, Pres., Anthony J. Ley/Chmn., David R. Van Valkenburg/Dir., William F. Reddersen/Dir., Lewis Solomon/Dir., Floyd E. Kvamme/Dir., Harold Covert/Dir., Patrick Gallagher/Dir.

Owners: Barclays Global Investors, NA/5.40%, Neven Haltmayer, Lewis Solomon, Insiders/3.40%, Anthony J. Ley/1.40%, Michel L. Vaillaud, Patrick J. Harshman, Robin N. Dickson, Floyd E. Kvamme, David R. Van Valkenburg, William F. Reddersen

Financial Data: *Fiscal Year End:*12/31 *Latest Annual Data:* 12/31/2006

Year	Sales	Net Income
2006	$247,684,000	$1,007,000
2005	$257,378,000	-$5,731,000
2004	$248,306,000	$1,574,000

Curr. Assets:	$211,968,000	**Curr. Liab.:**	$114,570,000	**P/E Ratio:**	41.29
Plant, Equip.:	$14,816,000	**Total Liab.:**	$136,828,000	**Indic. Yr. Divd.:**	NA
Total Assets:	$281,962,000	**Net Worth:**	$145,134,000	**Debt/ Equity:**	0.0577

Harmony Gold Mining Co Ltd

Ste No. 1, Private Bag X1, Melrose Arch, 2076; *PH:* 27-114112000; *Fax:* 27-116923879;
http:// www.harmony.co.za/about/management.asp

General - Incorporation	South Africa	**Stock**- Price on:12/24/2007	$14.64
Employees	44,000	Stock Exchange	NYSE
Auditor	PricewaterhouseCoopers LLP	Ticker Symbol	HMY
Stk Agt	Bank of New York	Outstanding Shares	398,740,000
Counsel	NA	E.P.S	NA
DUNS No.	36-678-1243	Shareholders	NA

Business: The group's principal activity is the operation of an underground and open pit gold mining, exploration and related activities in South Africa, australasia, russian federation and Peru. The group's main operations are located in the free state, evander, randfontein and west rand regions of the witwatersrand basin, as well as in the kraaipan greenstone belt of the north west province, where the kalgold open pit mine is situated. The group's offshore operations include operations in Australia, and investments in abelle ltd and highland gold ltd. During 2003, the group acquired 16% of high river gold, 87% of abelle ltd and its 50% joint acquisition of a 34.5% in anglovaal mining ltd. On 15-Jul-2003, the group acquired 11.5% in avgold ltd from anglo South Africa capital ltd.

Primary SIC and add'l.: 1044 1041

CIK No: 0001023514

Subsidiaries: ARMgold Limited, ARMgold/Harmony Freegold Joint Venture Company (Pty) Ltd, Avgold Limited, Evander Gold Mines Limited, Harmony Gold (Australia) (Pty) Limited, Kalahari Goldridge Mining Company Limited, Randfontein Estates Limited, save for Harmony Gold (Australia) (Pty) Limited

Officers: Z. B. Swanepoel/Dir. - Executive, T. S.A. Grobicki/Dir. - Executive, N. Qangule/Financial Dir., Amelia Soares/GM - Investor Relations, Lizelle Du Toit/Investor Relations Officer, Marian Van Der Walt/Company Sec., Abre Van Vuuren/47/Human Resources Mgr., Bob Atkinson/COO, Graham Briggs/52/Dir., Acting Chief Executive Officer

Directors: Patrice Motsepe/45/Non Exec. Chmn., Modise Motloba/41/Dir., Andre Wilkens/58/Dir., Graham Briggs/52/Dir., Acting Chief Executive Officer, Cedric Savage/68/Dir., Fikile De Buck/47/Non Exec. Dir., Cathie Markus/51/Non Exec. Dir., Z. B. Swanepoel/Dir. - Executive, Joaquim Chissano/67/Dir., Simo Lushaba/40/Non Exec. Dir., T. S.A. Grobicki/Dir. - Executive

Financial Data: *Fiscal Year End:*06/30 *Latest Annual Data:* 06/30/2007

Year	Sales	Net Income
2007	$1,346,596,000	-$295,435,000
2006	$1,263,333,000	-$155,725,000
2005	$1,265,200,000	-$616,467,000

Curr. Assets:	$428,345,000	**Curr. Liab.:**	$343,802,000		
Plant, Equip.:	$3,306,555,000	**Total Liab.:**	$1,536,835,000	**Indic. Yr. Divd.:**	NA
Total Assets:	$4,462,199,000	**Net Worth:**	$2,925,364,000	**Debt/ Equity:**	NA

Harold's Stores Inc

5919 Maple Ave., Dallas, TX, 75235; ***PH:*** 1-214-366-0600; ***Fax:*** 1-214-366-1061;
http:// www.harolds.com

General - Incorporation	OK	**Stock**- Price on:12/24/2007	$0.25
Employees	362	Stock Exchange	OTC
Auditor Ernst & Young LLP, BDO Seidman LLP		Ticker Symbol	HLDI
Stk Agt	UMB Bank, N.A.	Outstanding Shares	6,130,000
Counsel	NA	E.P.S	-$1.74
DUNS No.	17-701-0956	Shareholders	NA

Business: The group's principal activities are to operate a chain of traditional, classic styled ladies and men's specialty apparel stores. The group offers quality apparel to quality-conscious consumers primarily in the thirty to fifty year old age groups. The group operates through 39 full-price retail stores and 3 outlet stores to clear markdowns and slow-moving merchandise. In addition to the stores, the group has a direct response mail order catalog business and also sells merchandise online through its Website. The women's apparel includes coordinated sportswear, dresses, outerwear, shoes and accessories. The men's apparel product line includes tailored clothing, furnishings, sportswear and shoes. The trademarks of the group are harold's, harold powell, old school clothing company and oscc bespoke.

Primary SIC and add'l.: 5632 5621 5699 5611

CIK No: 0000818682

Officers: Ronald S. Staffieri/58/Dir., CEO, Cherryl Sergeant/57/VP - Merchandising, Jodi L. Taylor/46/CFO, Sec., Kenneth C. Row/43/Exec. VP - Marketing, Curtis E. Elliott/44/VP - Planning, Allocation, Mary E. Davich/49/VP - Ladies Merchandising

Directors: Ronald S. Staffieri/58/Dir., CEO, William E. Haslam/49/Chmn., James D. Abrams/63/Dir., Leonard M. Snyder/60/Dir., Robert L. Anderson/66/Dir., Clark J. Hinkley/66/Dir., Margaret A. Gilliam/69/Dir.

Owners: Rebecca Powell Casey, Arvest Bank Group, Inc., Margaret A. Gilliam, Ronald de Waal, Curtis E. Elliott, Kenneth C. Row, Ronald S. Staffieri, Robert L. Anderson, Elizabeth M. Powell Trust B, Jodi L. Taylor, James D. Abrams, Arvest Trust Company, N.A., Michael T. Casey, William E. Haslam, Mary E. Davich *(19 Owners included in Index)*

Financial Data: *Fiscal Year End:*01/28 *Latest Annual Data:* 2/3/2007

Year	Sales	Net Income
2007	$86,328,000	-$11,230,000
2006	$88,247,000	-$5,980,000
2005	$89,357,000	$95,000

Curr. Assets:	$28,579,000	**Curr. Liab.:**	$34,491,000		
Plant, Equip.:	$9,921,000	**Total Liab.:**	$67,067,000	**Indic. Yr. Divd.:**	NA
Total Assets:	$38,500,000	**Net Worth:**	-$28,567,000	**Debt/ Equity:**	NA

Harrah's Entertainment Inc

1 Caesars Palace Dr., Las Vegas, NV, 89109; ***PH:*** 1-702-407-6000; ***Fax:*** 1-702-407-6037;
http:// www.harrahs.com

General - Incorporation	DE	**Stock**- Price on:12/24/2007	$85.35
Employees	85,000	Stock Exchange	NYSE
Auditor	Deloitte & Touche LLP	Ticker Symbol	HET
Stk Agt	Bank of New York	Outstanding Shares	186,680,000
Counsel	NA	E.P.S	$3.42
DUNS No.	05-680-2986	Shareholders	NA

Business: The groups principle activity is to provide casino-entertainments. The group operates from United States.

Primary SIC and add'l.: 7999 7011 5813 5812 7993

CIK No: 0000858339

Subsidiaries: Aegean Management Corporation, AJP Holdings, LLC, AJP Parent, LLC, Asian Financial Syndicate,Inc., Aster Insurance Ltd., Atlantic City Country Club,Inc., Atlantic City Showboat,Inc., Atlantic HMO,Inc., B I Gaming Corporation, Bally Data Systems,Inc., Ballys Casino Management,Inc., Ballys Land Ventures,Inc., Ballys Louisiana,Inc., Ballys Manager,Inc., Ballys Maryland,Inc. 234 Subsidiaries included in the Index

Officers: Gary W. Loveman/Chmn., CEO, Pres./$14,239,850.00, Stephen Brammell/Sr. VP, General Counsel/$1,669,664.00, Tom Jenkin/Pres. - Western Division, Jonathan S. Halkyard/CFO, Treasurer/$1,167,519.00, Anthony D. McDuffie/Sr. VP, Controller, Chief Accounting Officer, Mary Thomas/Sr. VP - Human Resources, Michael D. Cohen/Corp. Sec., Virginia E. Shanks/47/Sr. VP - Acquisition Marketing/$1,459,860.00, John Payne/Pres. - Central Division, Jan L. Jones/Sr. VP - Communications, Government Relations, Carlos J. Tolosa/Pres. - Eastern Division, David Norton/Sr. VP - Relationship Marketing, Ginny Shanks/Sr. VP - Brand Management, Tim Stanley/Sr. VP - Innovation, Gaming, CIO

Directors: Gary W. Loveman/Chmn., CEO, Pres., Charles L. Atwood/58/Vice Chmn., Boake A. Sells/69/Dir., Frank J. Biondi/62/Dir., Robert G. Miller/62/Dir., Barbara T. Alexander/58/Dir., Christopher J. Williams/49/Dir., Stephen F. Bollenbach/64/Dir., Ralph Horn/66/Dir., Gary G. Michael/66/Dir., Brad R. Martin/55/Dir.

Owners: Charles L. Atwood, Gary W. Loveman, Robert G. Miller, Virginia E. Shanks, Ralph Horn, Private Capital Management, L.P./5.80%, Capital Research and Management Company/5.00%, Timothy J. Wilmott, Boake A. Sells, Stephen F. Bollenbach, Insiders/1.90%, Brad R. Martin, Stephen H. Brammell, Christopher J. Williams, Frank J. Biondi *(19 Owners included in Index)*

Financial Data: *Fiscal Year End:*12/31 *Latest Annual Data:* 12/31/2006

Year	Sales	Net Income
2006	$9,673,900,000	$535,800,000
2005	$7,111,000,000	$236,400,000
2004	$4,548,326,000	$367,709,000

Curr. Assets:	$1,630,800,000	**Curr. Liab.:**	$2,241,000,000	**P/E Ratio:**	24.96
Plant, Equip.:	$14,408,300,000	**Total Liab.:**	$16,161,400,000	**Indic. Yr. Divd.:**	$1.600
Total Assets:	$22,284,900,000	**Net Worth:**	$6,071,100,000	**Debt/ Equity:**	1.9509

Harrington West Financial Group Inc

610 Alamo Pintado Rd., Solvang, CA, 93463; ***PH:*** 1-805-688-6644; ***Fax:*** 1-805-688-4959;
http:// www.lospadresbank.com; ***Email:*** info@lospadresbank.com

General - Incorporation	DE	**Stock**- Price on:12/24/2007	$15.9
Employees	189	Stock Exchange	NDQ
Auditor	Crowe Chizek & Co. LLP	Ticker Symbol	HWFG
Stk Agt	LPMC	Outstanding Shares	5,550,000
Counsel	Kelley, Drye & Warren	E.P.S	$0.98
DUNS No.	NA	Shareholders	NA

Business: The group's principal activity is that of a holding group. It is a holding group for los padres bank, a federally chartered savings bank. The group operates twelve branch offices located on the central coast of California and in the Kansas city metropolitan area. It accepts deposits and originates single-family and multi-family residential, commercial real estate, commercial business and consumer loans. In addition, the group provides trust and investment management services to individuals and small institutional customers using a customized investment allocation approach and low fee, indexed mutual funds through harrington wealth management subsidiary.

Primary SIC and add'l.: 6035 6712

CIK No: 0001063997

Subsidiaries: InterNetwork Experts, Inc, Stratasoft, Inc, Valerent, Inc

Officers: Craig J. Cerny/Chmn., CEO/$592,744.00, Susan C. Weber/61/Sr. VP/$224,163.00, Lori Greener/Branch Mgr. - Overland Park, Kansas Branch, Kim D. Chambers/40/Sr. VP, Mortgage Lending Mgr., Kerry Steele/52/Sr. VP, CFO/$154,582.00, Trudy Perry/Branch Mgr. - Atascadero Branch, LOS Padres Bank, Kerry Semonsen/Loan Officer - Atascadero Branch, Los Padres Bank, Gussie Hampson/Branch Mgr. - Pismo Beach, Five Cities Branch, Los Padres Bank, Herb Jones/Loan Officer - Pismo Beach, Five Cities Branch, Los Padres Bank, Dianne Pearson/Branch Mgr. - Santa Maria Branch, Los Padres Bank, Mike Pitts/Commercial Loan Officer - Santa Maria Branch, Los Padres Bank, Jan Brink/Branch Mgr. - Solvang Branch, Corporate Office, Los Padres Bank, Alan Hitt/Loan Officer - Solvang Branch, Corporate Office, Los Padres Bank, Rakesh Prajapati/Branch Mgr. - Goleta Branch, Los Padres Bank, Martha Dowden/Branch Mgr. - Ojai Branch, Los Padres Bank *(24 Officers included in Index)*

Directors: Craig J. Cerny/Chmn., CEO, John J. McConnell/Dir., Tim Hatlestad/Dir., William W. Phillips/Dir., COO, Pres., William D. Ross/79/Dir., Paul O. Halme/Dir.

Owners: Mark R. Larrabee/0.70%, Douglas T. Breeden/8.10%, The Banc Funds Co. LLC/7.50%, Northaven Management Inc./5.50%, Paul O. Halme/0.70%, Susan C. Weber/1.70%, William D. Ross/2.10%, Kerril Steele/0.10%, Timothy Hatlestad/0.40%, Insiders/24.10%, Craig J. Cerny/12.30%, John J. McConnell/1.90%, William W. Phillips/2.90%

Financial Data: *Fiscal Year End:*12/31 *Latest Annual Data:* 12/31/2006

Year	Sales	Net Income
2006	$79,165,000	$8,228,000
2005	$66,940,000	$8,336,000
2004	$56,675,000	$8,209,000

Curr. Assets:	$27,584,000	**Curr. Liab.:**	$1,059,903,000	**P/E Ratio:**	12.52
Plant, Equip.:	$15,581,000	**Total Liab.:**	$1,086,775,000	**Indic. Yr. Divd.:**	$0.500
Total Assets:	$1,154,473,000	**Net Worth:**	$67,698,000	**Debt/ Equity:**	0.3724

Harris & Harris Group Inc

111 W 57th St., Ste. 1100, New York, NY, 10019; ***PH:*** 1-212-582-0900; ***Fax:*** 1-212-582-9563;
http:// www.tinytechvc.com; ***Email:*** admin@tinytechvc.com

General - Incorporation	NY	**Stock**- Price on:12/24/2007	$11.46
Employees	10	Stock Exchange	NDQ
Auditor	PricewaterhouseCoopers LLP	Ticker Symbol	TINY
Stk Agt	Bank of New York	Outstanding Shares	21,340,000
Counsel	NA	E.P.S	-$0.74
DUNS No.	17-511-5658	Shareholders	NA

Business: The group's principle activity is to operate as a venture capital investment company, which invests in private development or start-up companies. The group has made initial investments exclusively in tiny technology, defined by it as nanotechnology, microsystems and microelectromechanical systems. The group performs follow-on investments in the rest of its venture

capital portfolio and the group now has 13 investments in tiny technologies. The group operates as an internally managed investment company whereby the officers and employees, under the general supervision of the board of directors, conduct its operations. The group's quarterly revenue for Sep'07 was 0.74 millions of USD.

Primary SIC and add'l.: 6799

CIK No: 0000893739

Subsidiaries: Harris & Harris Enterprises, Inc.

Officers: Charles E. Harris/Chmn., MD, CEO/$2,937,854.00, Douglas W. Jamison/Pres., MD, CFO, COO/$949,634.00, Daniel B. Wolfe/Principal Since, Sr. Associate, VP, Alexei A. Andreev/Exec. VP, MD/$945,677.00, Sandra Matrick Forman/General Counsel, Chief Compliance Officer, Dir. - Human Resources/$613,175.00, Misti Ushio/VP - Associate, Michael A. Janse/Exec. VP, MD, Susan T. Harris/63/Sec.

Directors: Charles E. Harris/Chmn., MD, CEO, James E. Roberts/Dir., Morgan G. Browne/Dir., Mark A. Parsells/Dir., Wayne C. Bardin/Dir., Douglas W. Jamison/Pres., MD, CFO, COO, Dugald A. Fletcher/Dir., Lori D. Pressman/Dir., Kelly S. Kirkpatrick/Dir., Phillip A. Bauman/Dir., Charles E. Ramsey/Dir., W. Dillaway Ayres/57/Dir., Richard P. Shanley/61/Dir.

Owners: Douglas W. Jamison, Kelly S. Kirkpatrick, Mark A. Parsells, Charles E. Ramsey, Insiders/6.00%, Phillip A. Bauman, Sandra M. Forman, Charles E. Harris/5.00%, Daniel V. Leff, Morgan G. Browne, Alexei A. Andreev, Daniel B. Wolfe, Lori D. Pressman, Wayne C. Bardin, James E. Roberts *(16 Owners included in Index)*

Financial Data: ***Fiscal Year End:***12/31 ***Latest Annual Data:*** 12/31/2006

Year	Sales	Net Income
2006	$3,029,000	-$11,773,000
2005	$15,750,000	$6,716,000
2004	$638,000	-$2,066,000

Curr. Assets:	$3,517,000	***Curr. Liab.:***	$4,377,000		
Plant, Equip.:	$275,000	***Total Liab.:***	$4,398,000	***Indic. Yr. Divd.:***	NA
Total Assets:	$118,329,000	***Net Worth:***	$113,930,000	***Debt/ Equity:***	NA

Harris Corp

1025 W Nasa Blvd, Melbourne, FL, 32919; ***PH:*** 1-321-727-9100; ***http://*** www.harris.com

General - Incorporation	DE	***Stock***- Price on:12/24/2007	$53.14
Employees	13,900	Stock Exchange	NYSE
Auditor	Ernst & Young LLP	Ticker Symbol	HRS
Stk Agt	Harris Trust & Savings Bank	Outstanding Shares	134,280,000
Counsel	NA	E.P.S	$3.57
DUNS No.	00-420-3337	Shareholders	NA

Business: The groups principle activity is to provide communications and information technology (IT) solutions for government and commercial markets. The group operates through four business segments namely Government Communications Systems, RF Communications, Broadcast Communications and Harris Stratex Networks, Inc. (Harris Stratex Networks). On June 15, 2007, Harris acquired Multimax Incorporated (Multimax). The group operates from United States.

Primary SIC and add'l.: 3812 3663 3661

CIK No: 0000202058

Subsidiaries: American Coastal Insurance Ltd., BG-COM Information and Communication Limited Partnership, BWA Technology, Inc., Digital Automation (Canada) Ltd., Drake Automation, Inc., Eagle Technology, Inc., Encoda Systems de Mexico SA de CV, Eyeon Software, Inc., HAL Technologies, Inc., Harris Asia Pacific Sdn. Bhd, Harris Australia Pty. Ltd., Harris Canada Holdings Inc., Harris Canada, Inc., Harris Cayman, Ltd., Harris Communication (Netherlands) BV 62 Subsidiaries included in the Index

Officers: Howard L. Lance/52/Chmn., CEO, Pres., Michael C. Tuttle/Sr. Exec. Mgr. - Accounting, US Navy, George Cronin/Sr. Exec. Mgr. - Accounting, National Security, Fred Dubay/Sr. Exec. Mgr. - Accounting, National Reconnaissance Office, NRO, National Geospatial, Intelligence Agency, NGA, Roger W. Anderson/Sr. Exec. Mgr. - Accounting, Other Intelligence Community, Duane Selby/Sr. Exec. Mgr. - Accounting, Russell Gaspard/Sr. Exec. Mgr. - Accounting, Space Primes, Terrence L. Casto/Sr. Exec. Mgr. - Accounting, Ground Primes, Wesley W. Winn/Sr. Exec. Mgr. - Accounting, Department, State, Government Communications Systems, Robert T. Coulson/Sr. Exec. Mgr. - Accounting, Department, Transportation, Jeff Perry/VP - Business Development, Dana A. Mehnert/Pres. - RF Communications, Mike Thomas/VP, Controller - Business Operations, Stephen Marschilok/VP, GM - International Defense Products, System RF Communications, Gerald Woolever/National Exec. Mgr. - Department, Homeland Security *(47 Officers included in Index)*

Directors: Howard L. Lance/52/Chmn., CEO, Pres., Lewis Hay/52/Dir., Stephen P. Kaufman/66/Dir., Gregory T. Swienton/58/Dir., Thomas A. Dattilo/57/Dir., Leslie F. Kenne/60/Dir., David B. Rickard/61/Dir., James C. Stoffel/62/Dir., Karen Katen/59/Dir., Hansel E. Tookes/60/Dir., Terry D. Growcock/62/Dir.

Owners: Gregory T. Swienton, Thomas A. Dattilo, Hansel E. Tookes, Terry D. Growcock, David B. Rickard, Robert K. Henry, Jeffrey S. Shuman, Lewis Hay, FMR Corp./11.20%, Insiders, Leslie F. Kenne, James C. Stoffel, Howard L. Lance, Timothy E. Thorsteinson, Stephen P. Kaufman *(18 Owners included in Index)*

Financial Data: ***Fiscal Year End:***07/01 ***Latest Annual Data:*** 6/30/2006

Year	Sales	Net Income
2006	$3,474,800,000	$237,900,000
2005	$3,000,600,000	$202,200,000
2004	$2,518,600,000	$132,800,000

Curr. Assets:	$1,553,800,000	***Curr. Liab.:***	$542,800,000	***P/E Ratio:***	15.58
Plant, Equip.:	$283,300,000	***Total Liab.:***	$947,000,000	***Indic. Yr. Divd.:***	$0.600
Total Assets:	$2,225,800,000	***Net Worth:***	$1,278,800,000	***Debt/ Equity:***	NA

Harris Interactive Inc

60 Corporate Woods, Rochester, NY, 14623; ***PH:*** 1-585-272-8400; ***Fax:*** 1-585-272-8680; ***http://*** www.harrisinteractive.com; ***Email:*** info@harrisinteractive.com

General - Incorporation	DE	***Stock***- Price on:12/24/2007	$5.38
Employees	958	Stock Exchange	NDQ
Auditor	PricewaterhouseCoopers LLP	Ticker Symbol	HPOL
Stk Agt	American Stock Transfer & Trust Co.	Outstanding Shares	52,730,000
Counsel	Harris Beach & Wilcox	E.P.S	$0.17
DUNS No.	NA	Shareholders	NA

Business: The group's principal activity is to provide market research, polling and consulting services. It uses Internet-based and traditional methodologies to provide customers with critical market knowledge in many industries. The group services its clients through six distinct operating groups: strategic marketing solutions/business and consumer research; health care, youth & public policy research; customer loyalty management; hi Europe; harris interactive Japan; and harris interactive service bureau. The group conducts: custom research - Internet-based and traditional studies conducted on specific issues for specific customers; multi-client research - Internet-based studies conducted on issues of general interest and sold to numerous clients; and service bureau research - Internet-based research conducted for other research firms. In 2004, the group acquired novatris s.a. And wirthlinworldwide.

Primary SIC and add'l.: 8742

CIK No: 0001094238

Subsidiaries: GSBC Ohio Corporation, Harris Interactive Asia, LLC, Harris Interactive International Inc, Harris Interactive UK Limited, HI UK Holdings Limited, Louis Harris & Associates, Inc, Novatris, S.A, Romtec UK Limited, Teligen UK Limited, The Wirthlin Group International, LLC, Wirthlin Europe Limited, Wirthlin UK Limited, Wirthlin Worldwide, LLC

Officers: Gregory T. Novak/Dir., CEO, Pres./$1,344,656.00, David B. Vaden/Pres. - North America, Global Operations/$825,988.00, Dee T. Allsop/Pres. - US Solutions Research Groups, Dennis K. Bhame/Exec. VP - Human Resources, Leonard E. Bayer/Dir., Exec. VP, Chief Scientist, Member - Research, Development, CTO, Anthony P. Venus/Pres. - North Asia, Tracey McNerney/Public Relations, Media Relations, George H. Terhanian/Pres. - Europe, Global Internet Research/$404,330.00, Katherine A. Binns/Pres. - US Industry Research Groups, James E. Fredrickson/Exec. VP - Research Operations, Kyle R. Karnes/Exec. VP - Corporate Development, Eric W. Narowski/Principal Accounting Officer, VP, Corporate Controller, Michelle F. O'Neill/Pres. - US Industry Research Groups, Ronald E. Salluzzo/CFO, Exec. VP, Treasurer, Sec./$750,793.00, Ali M. Mirza/Pres. - South Asia

Directors: Gregory T. Novak/Dir., CEO, Pres., George Bell/Chmn., Howard L. Shecter/Dir., Subrata K. Sen/Dir., Stephen D. Harlan/Dir., Antoine Treuille/Dir., Leonard E. Bayer/Dir., Exec. VP, Chief Scientist, Member - Research, Development, CTO, David Brodsky/Dir., James R. Riedman/Dir.

Owners: Dimensional Fund Advisors LP/9.60%, Stephen D. Harlan, David B. Vaden, Antoine G. Treuille, Financiere de Sainte-Marine/8.20%, David Brodsky, Ronald E. Salluzzo, Howard L. Shecter, Subrata K. Sen, Gregory T. Novak/1.70%, Leonard R. Bayer/3.40%, George H. Terhanian, James R. Riedman, George Bell, Insiders/9.40% *(16 Owners included in Index)*

Financial Data: ***Fiscal Year End:***06/30 ***Latest Annual Data:*** 6/30/2006

Year	Sales	Net Income
2006	$216,011,000	$9,460,000
2005	$196,965,000	$1,583,000
2004	$146,032,000	$29,918,000

Curr. Assets:	$111,297,000	***Curr. Liab.:***	$49,788,000	***P/E Ratio:***	35.87
Plant, Equip.:	$9,759,000	***Total Liab.:***	$53,279,000	***Indic. Yr. Divd.:***	NA
Total Assets:	$254,557,000	***Net Worth:***	$201,278,000	***Debt/ Equity:***	NA

Harry Winston Diamond Corp

Formerly: Aber Diamond Corp

PO Box 4569, Sta. A, Toronto, ON, M5W 4T9; ***PH:*** 1-416-362-2237; ***http://*** www.aber.ca

General - Incorporation	Canada	***Stock***- Price on:12/24/2007	$39.301
Employees	NA	Stock Exchange	NDQ
Auditor	KPMG LLP	Ticker Symbol	ABER
Stk Agt	Mellon Trust Co	Outstanding Shares	NA
Counsel	Stikeman Elliott	E.P.S	NA
DUNS No.	24-673-3638	Shareholders	NA

Business: The group's principal activities are to explore, develop and market Canadian diamonds. The group holds 40% interest in diavik diamonds project.

Primary SIC and add'l.: 1499

CIK No: 0000841071

Subsidiaries: Aber Diamond Mines Ltd

Officers: Robert A. Gannicott/Chmn., CEO, Harsh B. Dalal/VP - Sales, Greg R. Rieveley -/VP - Internal Audit, Business Development, Beth Bandler/VP, General Counsel, Michael A. Ballantyne/VP - Northwest Territories, Aber Diamond Corporation, Lyle R. Hepburn/Corp. Sec., James R.W. Pounds/Sr. VP - Diamond Management, Charles Stanley/Dir. - Marketing Research, Wendy Kei/Corporate Controller, Kevin P. Marchant/VP - Production, Alice Murphy/CFO, VP, Raymond N. Simpson/VP - Corporate Development

Directors: Robert A. Gannicott/Chmn., CEO, Roger Jb Phillimore/Corp. Dir., Lars-Eric Johansson/Dir., John M. Willson/Corp. Dir., Laurent E. Mommeja/Dir., Lyndon Lea/Dir., Thomas J. O'Neill/Dir.

Financial Data: ***Fiscal Year End:***01/31 ***Latest Annual Data:*** 1/31/2007

Year	Sales	Net Income
2007	$558,793,000	$98,497,000
2006	$505,234,000	$81,253,000
2005	$385,402,000	$58,331,000

Curr. Assets:	$413,930,000	***Curr. Liab.:***	$249,957,000		
Plant, Equip.:	$384,532,000	***Total Liab.:***	$786,101,000	***Indic. Yr. Divd.:***	NA
Total Assets:	$1,259,875,000	***Net Worth:***	$473,689,000	***Debt/ Equity:***	NA

Harsco Corp

350 Poplar Church Rd., Camp Hill, PA, 17011; ***PH:*** 1-717-763-7064; ***Fax:*** 1-717-763-6424; ***http://*** www.harsco.com

General - Incorporation	DE	***Stock***- Price on:12/24/2007	$51.76
Employees	21,500	Stock Exchange	NYSE
Auditor	PricewaterhouseCoopers LLP	Ticker Symbol	HSC
Stk Agt	Mellon Investor Services LLC	Outstanding Shares	84,160,000
Counsel	NA	E.P.S	$3.08
DUNS No.	00-300-2268	Shareholders	NA

Business: The groups principle activity is to provide industrial services and engineered products. The group operates through three segments namely Mill Services, Access Services and Gas Technologies. Customers served by the group include the steel, construction, railways, and energy industries. In 2007, the group acquired Excell Materials, Inc. (Excell), Alexander Mill Services International, and ZETA-TECH Associates, Inc. The group operates from United States.

Primary SIC and add'l.: 3492 4932 1629 3441

CIK No: 0000045876

Subsidiaries: AluServ Middle East W.L.L., Andamios Patentados, S.A. de C.V., Ashland Recovery Inc., BC Nord S.A.S., BC S.A.S., Becema S.A.S., Braddock Recovery Inc., Carbofer International GmbH, Companhia de Tratamento de Sucatas, Limitada, Czech Slag - Nova Hut s.r.o., ECR Inc., Electroforjados Nacionales, S.A. de C.V., Evulca S.A.S., Faber Prest (Overseas) Limited, Faber Prest (Pacific) Limited 187 Subsidiaries included in the Index

Subsidiaries: AluServ Middle East W.L.L., Andamios Patentados, S.A. de C.V., Ashland Recovery Inc., BC Nord S.A.S., BC S.A.S., Becema S.A.S., Braddock Recovery Inc., Carbofer International GmbH, Companhia de Tratamento de Sucatas, Limitada, Czech Slag - Nova Hut s.r.o., ECR Inc., Electroforjados Nacionales, S.A. de C.V., Evulca S.A.S., Faber Prest (Overseas) Limited, Faber Prest (Pacific) Limited 187 Subsidiaries included in the Index

Officers: Derek C. Hathaway/Chmn., CEO/$3,409,495.00, Salvatore D. Fazzolari/Dir., CFO, Pres., Treasurer/$1,195,395.00, Eugene M. Truett/VP - Investor Relations, Credit, Mark E. Kimmel/General Counsel, Corp. Sec./$502,981.00, Michael H. Kolinsky/VP - Taxes, Stephen J. Schnoor/VP, Controller, Scott H. Gerson/CIO, VP, Geoffrey D.H. Butler/Dir., Sr. VP - Operations/$2,085,659.00, Kenneth Julian/Dir. - Communications, Public, Media Inquiries, Richard C. Neuffer/Group Pres./$732,036.00, Gary J. Findling/VP, Treasurer, Michael A. Higgins/VP - Internal Audit

Directors: Derek C. Hathaway/Chmn., CEO, Robert C. Wilburn/Dir., Jerry J. Jasinowski/Dir., James I. Scheiner/Dir., Joseph P. Viviano/Dir., Carolyn F. Scanlan/Dir., Salvatore D. Fazzolari/Dir., CFO, Pres., Treasurer, Andrew J. Sordoni/Dir., Geoffrey D.H. Butler/Dir., Sr. VP - Operations, Kathy G. Eddy/Dir., Howard D. Pierce/Dir., D. H. Pierce/66/Dir.

Owners: C. F. Scanlan, J. J. Jasinowski, R. C. Neuffer, S. D. Fazzolari, A. J. Sordoni, D. H. Pierce, Insiders, J. P. Viviano, D. C. Hathaway, R. C. Wilburn, M. E. Kimmel, Earnest Partners LLC/8.10%, G. D. H. Butler, J. I. Scheiner, K. G. Eddy

Financial Data: Fiscal Year End:12/31   Latest Annual Data: 06/30/2007

Year	Sales	Net Income
2007	$946,149,000	$83,070,000
2006	$3,423,293,000	$196,398,000
2005	$2,766,210,000	$156,657,000

Curr. Assets:	$1,231,622,000	Curr. Liab.:	$910,775,000	P/E Ratio:	20.87
Plant, Equip.:	$1,322,467,000	Total Liab.:	$2,180,059,000	Indic. Yr. Divd.:	$0.780
Total Assets:	$3,326,423,000	Net Worth:	$1,146,364,000	Debt/ Equity:	0.7365

Hartcourt Co Inc

Rm. 304-306, Yong Teng Plz., No. 1065, Wu Zhong Rd., Shanghai, 210013; PH: 86-21 6272 3088; Fax: 86-21 6249 9758; http:// www.hartcourt.com; Email: info@hartcourt.com

General - Incorporation	UT	Stock - Price on:12/24/2007	$0.069
Employees	NA	Stock Exchange	OTC
Auditor	Kabani & Co, Inc	Ticker Symbol	HRCT
Stk Agt	Signature Stock Transfer, Inc.	Outstanding Shares	NA
Counsel	Zhonglun Law Firm	E.P.S.	NA
DUNS No.	15-971-5960	Shareholders	NA

Business: The group's principle activity is to sell a broad range of white box desktops, branded monitors and notebooks, PC components and peripherals. It has 33 retail stores in China primarily engaged in the sales of above mentioned computer hardware peripherals. The principal market for its products is China.it has entered into a conditional sales and purchase agreement to obtained 51% interest of shanghai computer servicenet co, ltd. ltd was stroke off, hartcourt capital ltd was stroked off in Aug 2003 & sold all its 58.53% equity interest in financial telecom limited.

Primary SIC and add'l.: 4899 7375

CIK No: 0000949427

Subsidiaries: Ai-Asia Information (Shanghai) Inc., Ai-Asia, Inc., Control Tech Electronics (Shanghai) Co., Ltd., Hartcourt Capital Inc., Hartcourt China Inc., Hartcourt Hi-tech Investment (Shanghai) Inc., Shanghai Huaqing Enterprise Development Co., Ltd., Shanghai Jiumeng Information Technology Co., Ltd.

Officers: Victor Zhou/Dir., CEO, Yungeng Hu/Dir., CFO, Pres., Tingting Ni/Investor Relations Officer

Directors: Victor Zhou/Dir., CEO, Billy Wang/Chmn., Wilson Li/Dir., Geoffrey Wei/Dir., Yungeng Hu/Dir., CFO, Pres.

Owners: Billy Y. Wang/4.70%, Wilson Li, Yungeng Hu/2.10%, Insiders/9.90%, Victor Zhou/2.00%, Geoffrey Wei

Financial Data: Fiscal Year End:05/31   Latest Annual Data: 05/31/2007

Year	Sales	Net Income
2007	NA	-$3,786,000
2006	$42,090,000	-$2,835,000
2005	$19,678,000	$123,000

Curr. Assets:	$7,444,000	Curr. Liab.:	$5,929,000		
Plant, Equip.:	$115,000	Total Liab.:	$5,929,000	Indic. Yr. Divd.:	NA
Total Assets:	$9,533,000	Net Worth:	$2,866,000	Debt/ Equity:	NA

Harte-Hanks Inc

200 Concord Plz. Dr., San Antonio, TX, 78216; PH: 1-210-829-9000; Fax: 1-210-829-9403; http:// www.harte-hanks.com; Email: marie_hull@harte-hanks.com

General - Incorporation	DE	Stock - Price on:12/24/2007	$25.82
Employees	6,338	Stock Exchange	NYSE
Auditor	KPMG LLP	Ticker Symbol	HHS
Stk Agt	Computershare Trust Co	Outstanding Shares	73,310,000
Counsel	Hughes & Luce LLP	E.P.S.	$1.26
DUNS No.	04-701-1085	Shareholders	NA

Business: The group's principal activity are to provide direct and interactive marketing services. The group operates through two segments: direct marketing and shoppers. The direct marketing segment offers a complete range of specialized, coordinated and integrated direct marketing services. The customers of this segment include retailers, banks, mutual fund, pharmaceutical and insurance companies, healthcare organizations and telecommunications firms. The shoppers segment produces weekly advertising publications delivered by third-class mail to all households in a particular geographic area. The group operates in the United States, Europe, Australia and South America. On 27-Feb-2004, the group acquired avellino technologies ltd.

Primary SIC and add'l.: 7331 7389 2741

CIK No: 0000045919

Subsidiaries: Avellino Technologies, Inc., Harte-Hanks CRM Services Belgium NV, Harte-Hanks Data Services LLC, Harte-Hanks Data Technologies, Inc., Harte-Hanks Direct Marketing/Baltimore, Inc., Harte-Hanks Direct Marketing/Cincinnati, Inc., Harte-Hanks Direct Marketing/Dallas, L.P., Harte-Hanks Direct Marketing/Fullerton, Inc., Harte-Hanks Direct Marketing/Jacksonville, LLC, Harte-Hanks Direct Marketing/Kansas City, LLC, Harte-Hanks Direct, Inc., Harte-Hanks do Brazil Consultoria e Servicos Ltda., Harte-Hanks Market Intelligence Espaa LLC, Harte-Hanks Market Intelligence Europe B.V., Harte-Hanks Market Intelligence GmbH 36 Subsidiaries included in the Index

Officers: Richard Hochhauser/Dir., CEO/$2,792,005.00, Dave Lagreca/VP - Direct Marketing, Bryan Pechersky/Sr. VP, General Counsel, Sec., Tann Tueller/VP - Direct Marketing, Mike Paulsin/VP - Shoppers, Federico Ortiz/VP - Tax, Jessica Huff/VP - Finance, Chief Accounting Officer, Spencer Joyner/VP - Direct Marketing, Dean Blythe/CFO, Pres./$815,739.00, Peter Gorman/Exec. VP, Pres. - Shoppers/$999,581.00, James Davis/Sr. VP - Direct Marketing, Bill Goldberg/Sr. VP - Direct Marketing, Gary Skidmore/Exec. VP, Pres. - Direct Marketing/$754,034.00, Robert J. Colucci/VP - Direct Marketing, Loren Dalton/VP - Shoppers (17 Officers included in Index)

Directors: Richard Hochhauser/Dir., CEO, Houston Harte/Vice Chmn., Larry Franklin/Chmn., David Copeland/Dir., Judy C. Odom/Dir., William Gayden/Dir., Christopher Harte/Dir., William Farley/Dir.

Owners: Peter E. Gorman, Christopher M. Harte/2.40%, Houston H. Harte/13.40%, Larry Franklin/14.70%, Richard M. Hochhauser/1.50%, William K. Gayden, William F. Farley, Dean H. Blythe, Judy C. Odom, Gary J. Skidmore, Kathy S. Calta, Shelton Family Foundation/6.30%, Ariel Capital Management, Inc./11.20%, Insiders/34.00%, David L. Copeland/12.20%

Financial Data: Fiscal Year End:12/31   Latest Annual Data: 12/31/2006

Year	Sales	Net Income
2006	$1,184,688,000	$111,792,000
2005	$1,134,993,000	$114,458,000
2004	$1,030,461,000	$97,568,000

Curr. Assets:	$279,975,000	Curr. Liab.:	$171,236,000	P/E Ratio:	18.85
Plant, Equip.:	$116,591,000	Total Liab.:	$475,809,000	Indic. Yr. Divd.:	$0.280
Total Assets:	$969,285,000	Net Worth:	$493,476,000	Debt/ Equity:	0.4259

Hartford Financial Services Group Inc

Hartford Plz., 690 Asylum Avenue, Hartford, CT, 06115; PH: 1-860-547-5000; http:// www.thehartford.com; Email: media.relations@thehartford.com

General - Incorporation	DE	Stock - Price on:12/24/2007	$98.95
Employees	31,000	Stock Exchange	NYSE
Auditor	Deloitte & Touche LLP	Ticker Symbol	HIG
Stk Agt	Bank of New York	Outstanding Shares	316,660,000
Counsel	NA	E.P.S.	$9.49
DUNS No.	00-593-0458	Shareholders	NA

Business: The group's principle activity is to provide investment products including annuities, mutual funds, college savings plans, and life insurance, group and employee benefits, and automobile, homeowners' and business insurance. In December 13, 2007 the group acquired Boston-Based Sun Life Retirement Services (U.S.), Inc. The group operates from United States.

Primary SIC and add'l.: 6331 6311

CIK No: 0000874766

Subsidiaries: 1810 Corporation, 1stAgChoice, Inc., Access CoverageCorp Technologies, Inc., Access CoverageCorp, Inc., American Maturity Life Insurance Company, BMG Capital Advisors Group, LLC, Brazilcap Capitalizacao S.A., Business Management Group, Inc., Canada Life Fundo De Pensao, CCS Commercial, LLC, Charles Stedman & Co., Inc., CIAXA Capitalizacao S.A., Claimplace, Inc., Downlands Liability Management Ltd., Ersatz Corporation 55 Subsidiaries included in the Index

Officers: Ramani Ayer/Chmn., CEO, Pres./$17,487,730.00, Thomas M. Marra/Dir., COO, Pres., Exec. VP/$8,592,238.00, David K. Zwiener/Dir., COO, Exec. VP, Pres. - Property, Casualty Operations/$8,556,727.00, Neal S. Wolin/Exec. VP, General Counsel/$4,085,297.00, David M. Johnson/CFO, Exec. VP/$4,690,891.00, Ann M. De Raismes/Exec. VP - Human Resources, David M. Znamierowski/Chief Investment Officer, Pres. - Hartford Investment Management Company, Richard G. Costello/VP, Corp. Sec., John C. Walters/Co - COO - Hartford Life, Pres. - US Wealth Management, Lizabeth H. Zlatkus/Co - COO - Hartford Life, Pres. - International Wealth Management, Group Benefits, Alan J. Kreczko/Exec. VP, General Counsel, Eileen Whelley/Exec. VP - Human Resources, Robert J. Price/57/Sr. VP, Controller

Directors: Ramani Ayer/Chmn., CEO, Pres., Charles B. Strauss/Dir., Ramon De Oliveira/52/Dir., Robert W. Selander/Dir., Edward J. Kelly/Dir., Gail J. McGovern/Dir., Paul G. Kirk/Dir., Michael G. Morris/60/Dir., Thomas M. Marra/Dir., COO, Pres., Exec. VP, Patrick H. Swygert/Dir., David K. Zwiener/Dir., COO, Exec. VP, Pres. - Property, Casualty Operations, Trevor Fetter/Dir.

Owners: Ramon de Oliveira, Michael G. Morris, Neal S. Wolin, Insiders/1.10%, Edward J. Kelly, Robert W. Selander, Gail J. McGovern, Ramani Ayer, David K. Zwiener, State Street Bank and Trust Company/5.70%, Thomas M. Marra, David M. Johnson, Patrick H. Swygert, Trevor Fetter, FMR Corp/7.27% (17 Owners included in Index)

Financial Data: Fiscal Year End:12/31   Latest Annual Data: 12/31/2006

Year	Sales	Net Income
2006	$26,500,000,000	$2,745,000,000
2005	$27,083,000,000	$2,274,000,000
2004	$22,693,000,000	$2,115,000,000

Curr. Assets:	$10,670,000,000	Curr. Liab.:	$6,219,000,000	P/E Ratio:	10.43
Plant, Equip.:	$791,000,000	Total Liab.:	$307,834,000,000	Indic. Yr. Divd.:	$2.000
Total Assets:	$326,710,000,000	Net Worth:	$18,876,000,000	Debt/ Equity:	0.2354

Hartford Life Inc

200 Hopmeadow St., Simsbury, CT, 06089; PH: 1-860-547-5000; http:// www.thehartford.com

General - Incorporation	DE	Stock - Price on:12/24/2007	NA
Employees	NA	Stock Exchange	NA
Auditor	Deloitte & Touche LLP	Ticker Symbol	NA
Stk Agt	Bank of New York	Outstanding Shares	NA
Counsel	NA	E.P.S.	NA
DUNS No.	61-446-8049	Shareholders	NA

Business: The group operates through its subsidiaries whose principle activity is to provide investment products, such as individual variable and fixed rate annuities, deferred compensation plan services and mutual funds for savings and retirement needs; underwrite and sell variety of individual life insurance products; and sells group life and disability insurance, and corporate-owned life insurance. The group operates from United States.

Primary SIC and add'l.: 6719 6211 6311

CIK No: 0001032204

Subsidiaries: Hartford Financial Services Group, Inc., Hartford Holdings, Inc, Hartford Life and Accident Insurance Company, HIMCO, HL Investment Advisors, LLC, PLANCO Financial Services, LLC, Planco, LLC

Officers: Ramani Ayer/Chmn., CEO, Lizabeth H. Zlatkus/Co - COO - Hartford Life, Pres. - International Wealth Management, Group Benefits, David K. Zwiener/Dir., Exec. VP, Ann De Raismes/Exec. VP - Human Resources, David M. Znamierowski/Chief Investment Officer, Pres. -

Hartford Investment Management Company, Thomas M. Marra/Dir., Exec. VP, David M. Johnson/CFO, Exec. VP, Neal S. Wolin/Pres., COO - Property, Casualty Operations, John C. Walters/Co - COO - Hartford Life, Pres. - US Wealth Management, Alan J. Kreczko/Exec. VP, General Counsel, Eileen Whelley/Exec. VP - Human Resources

Directors: Ramani Ayer/Chmn., CEO, Ramon De Oliveira/Dir., Thomas M. Marra/Dir., Exec. VP, David K. Zwiener/Dir., Exec. VP, Edward J. Kelly/Dir., Paul G. Kirk/Dir., Gail J. McGovern/Dir., Michael G. Morris/Dir., Robert W. Selander/Dir., Charles B. Strauss/Dir., Patrick H. Swygert/Dir., Trevor Fetter/Dir.

Hartford Life Insurance Co

200 Hopmeadow St., Simsbury, CT, 06070; *PH:* 1-860-547-5000; *http://* www.thehartford.com

General - Incorporation	CT	**Stock** - Price on:12/24/2007	NA
Employees	NA	Stock Exchange	NA
Auditor	Deloitte & Touche LLP	Ticker Symbol	NA
Stk Agt	NA	Outstanding Shares	NA
Counsel	NA	E.P.S.	NA
DUNS No.	04-303-1459	Shareholders	NA

Business: The group's principal activities are to provide financial services and insurance products such as variable annuities and individual and corporate owned life insurance. The group is organized into three reportable operating segments: investment products, individual life and corporate owned life insurance ('coli'). The investment products segment focuses, through the sale of individual variable and fixed annuities, retirement plan services and other investment products. Through the individual life segment the group earns fees, based on policyholders' account values, for managing variable annuity assets and maintaining policyholder accounts. The group includes in 'other' corporate items not directly allocable to any of its reportable operating segments. The group is a wholly owned subsidiary of hartford life and accident insurance company.

Primary SIC and add'l.: 6311 6321

CIK No: 0000045947

Subsidiaries: Hartford International Life Reassurance Corporation, Hartford Life and Annuity Insurance Company, Servus Life Insurance Company

Officers: Ramani Ayer/Chmn., CEO - Hartford, David M. Znamierowski/Chief Investment Officer, Pres. - Hartford Investment Management Company, Edward J. Kelly/Dir. - Hartford Financial Services Group, Inc, Michael G. Morris/Dir. - Hartford Financial Services Group, Inc, John C. Walters/Co - COO - Hartford Life, Pres. - US Wealth Management, Thomas M. Marra/Dir., Exec. VP, COO, Ernest M. McNeill/Chief Accounting Officer, Sr. VP, Lizabeth H. Zlatkus/Co - COO - Hartford Life, Pres. - International Wealth Management, Group Benefits, Charles B. Strauss/Dir. - Hartford Financial Services Group, Inc, David K. Zwiener/Dir., COO, Pres. Property - Casualty Operations, The Hartford Financial Services Group, Inc, Ramon De Oliveira/Dir. - Hartford Financial Services Group Inc, Robert W. Selander/Dir. - Hartford Financial Services Group Inc, Patrick H. Swygert/Dir. - Hartford Financial Services Group Inc, Neal S. Wolin/Pres., COO - Property, Casualty Operations, David M. Johnson/CFO, Exec. VP (*19 Officers included in Index*)

Directors: Paul G. Kirk/Dir. - Hartford Financial Services Group Inc, Gail J. McGovern/Dir. - Hartford Financial Services Group Inc

Hartmarx Corp

101 N Wacker Dr., Chicago, IL, 60606; *PH:* 1-312-372-6300; *Fax:* 1-312-444-2710; *http://* www.hartmarx.com; *Email:* getinfo@hartmarx.com

General - Incorporation	DE	**Stock** - Price on:12/24/2007	$6.33
Employees	4,000	Stock Exchange	NYSE
Auditor	PricewaterhouseCoopers LLP	Ticker Symbol	HMX
Stk Agt	EquiServe Trust Co N.A	Outstanding Shares	36,440,000
Counsel	NA	E.P.S.	$0.08
DUNS No.	00-512-0100	Shareholders	NA

Business: The group's principal activities are to manufacture and market men's and women's apparel. The operations are comprised of the men's apparel group and women's apparel group. The men's apparel group designs, manufactures and markets men's tailored clothing, slacks, sportswear and dress furnishings. The women's apparel group markets women's career apparel, sportswear and accessories. The brand names include hart schaffner & marx(R), hickey-freeman(R), sansabelt(R), racquet club(R), palm beach(R), brannoch(R), barrie pace(R), hawksley & wight(R), desert classic(R), pusser's of the west indies(R), cambridge(R), coppley(R), keithmoor(R) and royal shirt (TM). The products are sold to department stores, specialty retail stores, off-price marketers, catalogs and through electronic commerce channels.

Primary SIC and add'l.: 5621 2311 2329 2321 5611 6719

CIK No: 0000723371

Subsidiaries: Anniston Sportswear Corporation, Consolidated Apparel Group, Inc., Coppley Apparel Group Limited ., Direct Route Marketing Corporation, Exclusively Misook Apparel, Inc., Hart Schaffner& Marx, Hickey-Freeman Co., Inc., HMX Luxury, Inc., HMX Sportswear, Inc., International Womens Apparel, Inc., Jaymar-Ruby, Inc. (d/b/a Trans-Apparel Group), M. Wile& Company, Inc. (d/b/a HMX Tailored, Inc.), National Clothing Company, Inc., Simply Blue Apparel, Inc., Universal Design Group, Ltd.

Officers: Homi B. Patel/58/Chmn., CEO, Pres., Taras R. Proczko/Sr. VP, General Counsel, Sec., Glenn R. Morgan/CFO, Exec. VP, Raymond C. Giuriceo/VP, MD - International Marketing, Andrew A. Zahr/VP, Controller

Directors: Homi B. Patel/58/Chmn., CEO, Pres., Michael B. Rohlfs/56/Dir., Elbert O. Hand/68/Dir., Dipak C. Jain/50/Dir., Michael F. Anthony/52/Dir., Jeffrey A. Cole/66/Dir., James P. Dollive/56/Dir., Raymond F. Farley/83/Dir., Stuart L. Scott/69/Dir.

Owners: Homi B. Patel/2.39%, Jeffrey A. Cole, Elbert O. Hand, Andrew A. Zahr, Dipak C. Jain, Dimensional Fund Advisors, Inc./8.70%, Michael F. Anthony, Stuart L. Scott, Raymond C. Giuriceo, Vanguard Fiduciary Trust Company,/5.96%, James P. Dollive, Raymond F. Farley, Abdullah Taha Bakhsh/15.83%, Glenn R. Morgan, Insiders/4.90% (*18 Owners included in Index*)

Financial Data: Fiscal Year End:11/30 Latest Annual Data: 11/30/2006

Year	Sales	Net Income
2006	$600,463,000	$7,286,000
2005	$600,285,000	$23,555,000
2004	$588,858,000	$15,865,000

Curr. Assets:	$293,130,000	**Curr. Liab.:**	$95,145,000	**P/E Ratio:**	158.25
Plant, Equip.:	$33,964,000	**Total Liab.:**	$212,428,000	**Indic. Yr. Divd.:**	NA
Total Assets:	$473,084,000	**Net Worth:**	$260,656,000	**Debt/ Equity:**	0.4245

Hartville Group Inc

3840 Greentree Ave. SW, Canton, OH, 44706; *PH:* 1-330-484-8080; *http://* www.hartvillegroup.com

General - Incorporation	NV	**Stock** - Price on:12/24/2007	$0.123
Employees	78	Stock Exchange	OTC
Auditor	BDO Seidman LLP	Ticker Symbol	HVLL
Stk Agt	OTC Corporate Transfer Service Co	Outstanding Shares	56,270,000
Counsel	NA	E.P.S.	-$0.24
DUNS No.	NA	Shareholders	NA

Business: The group's principal activity is to sell sickness and accident insurance policies for domestic household pets. The group operates though its subsidiaries: petsmarketing insurance.com agency inc, hartville equestrian inc and hartville insurance company ltd. The activities of the group are carried out through three segments: holding company, insurance agency and reinsurance company. The insurance agency sells proprietary health insurance plans for domestic pets. The reinsurance company reinsures pet health insurance originated by the agency.

Primary SIC and add'l.: 6719 6321

CIK No: 0001126960

Subsidiaries: Hartville Re, Petsmarketing Insurance.com Agency, Inc., Wag N Pet, Inc.

Officers: Dennis Rushovich/Dir., CEO/$338,700.00, Christopher Edgar/Chief Marketing Officer/$681,700.00, Hirsch C. Ribakow/Exec. VP - Insurance - Compliance/$172,347.00, Christopher R. Sachs/Dir., Sec., CFO/$266,815.00, Amy Glynn/Investor Relation Officer

Directors: Dennis Rushovich/Dir., CEO, Nicholas Leighton/Chmn., Christopher R. Sachs/Dir., Sec., CFO, Alan Kaufman/Dir., Michel Amsalem/Dir.

Owners: Christopher Edgar/18.40%, Nicholas J. Leighton, Alan J. Kaufman/1.30%, Christopher R. Sachs/4.80%, Crescent International, Ltd./8.60%, Hirsch C. Ribakow/2.10%, Insiders/75.10%, Michel Amsalem/69.10%, Dennis C. Rushovich/5.20%

Financial Data: Fiscal Year End:12/31 Latest Annual Data: 12/31/2006

Year	Sales	Net Income
2006	$6,719,000	-$11,163,000
2005	$4,439,000	-$8,017,000
2004	$4,224,000	-$8,144,000

Curr. Assets:	$3,935,000	**Curr. Liab.:**	$1,611,000		
Plant, Equip.:	$863,000	**Total Liab.:**	$3,224,000	**Indic. Yr. Divd.:**	NA
Total Assets:	$6,204,000	**Net Worth:**	$2,981,000	**Debt/ Equity:**	0.2527

Harvard Bioscience Inc

84 October Hill Rd., Ste. 7, Holliston, MA, 01746; *PH:* 1-508-893-8999; *Fax:* 1-508-429-5732; *http://* www.harvardbioscience.com; *Email:* info@harvardbioscience.com

General - Incorporation	DE	**Stock** - Price on:12/24/2007	$5.15
Employees	270	Stock Exchange	NDQ
Auditor	KPMG LLP	Ticker Symbol	HBIO
Stk Agt	Registrar & Transfer Co	Outstanding Shares	30,580,000
Counsel	Goodwin Procter LLP	E.P.S.	-$0.08
DUNS No.	NA	Shareholders	NA

Business: The group's principal activities are to develop, manufacture and market innovative, research enabling tools used in drug discovery at pharmaceutical and biotechnology companies, universities and government laboratories. These tools are designed to accelerate the speed and to reduce the cost at which the group's customers can discover and commercialize new drugs. In Mar 1996, the group focussed on developing tools to alleviate two critical bottlenecks in the drug discovery process: proteomics during the target validation stage and admet screening during the secondary screening stage of the drug discovery process. The group sells these instruments, devices and consumables through its catalog, distributors and Web site. The group distributes most of its products directly through its operations in the United States, the United Kingdom, Germany, France and Canada on 03-Mar-2004, the group acquired kd scientific inc.

Primary SIC and add'l.: 3826

CIK No: 0001123494

Subsidiaries: Asys Hitech GmbH, Biochrom Ltd., Cartesian Technology, Inc., Ealing Scientific Ltd., Genomic Solutions (CDN), Inc., Genomic Solutions Canada Inc., Genomic Solutions, Inc., Genomic Solutions, Ltd., Harvard Apparatus FSC, Inc., Harvard Apparatus, Ltd., Harvard Apparatus, SARL, HBIO Securities Corp., Hoefer, Inc., Hugo Sachs Elektronik Harvard Apparatus GmbH, KDS, Inc. 20 Subsidiaries included in the Index

Officers: Chane Graziano/Dir., CEO/$1,247,038.00, Bryce Chicoyne/CFO/$414,615.00, David Strack/Pres. - Genomic Solutions, Inc, Union Biometrica INC, David Parr/MD - Biochrom Business Unit, David Green/Dir., Pres./$1,010,404.00, Mark Norige/Pres. - Harvard Apparatus Business Unit/$406,237.00, Susan Luscinski/COO/$503,243.00

Directors: Chane Graziano/Dir., CEO, Robert Dishman/Dir., George Uveges/Dir., David Green/Dir., Pres., Neal J. Harte/Dir., John Kennedy/Dir., Earl R. Lewis/Dir.

Owners: Mark Norige/1.10%, Earl R. Lewis, Neal J. Harte, HSO Limited Partnership/10.80%, David Green/6.50%, Robert Dishman, FMR Corp./8.90%, John F. Kennedy, Chane Graziano/14.20%, Bryce Chicoyne, LeRoy C. Kopp/5.00%, Susan M. Luscinski/1.70%, George Uveges, Insiders/23.80%, Dimensional Fund Advisors LP/5.80% (*16 Owners included in Index*)

Financial Data: Fiscal Year End:12/31 Latest Annual Data: 12/31/2006

Year	Sales	Net Income
2006	$76,181,000	-$2,341,000
2005	$67,431,000	-$31,877,000
2004	$92,597,000	$2,329,000

Curr. Assets:	$53,285,000	**Curr. Liab.:**	$14,684,000		
Plant, Equip.:	$4,610,000	**Total Liab.:**	$21,345,000	**Indic. Yr. Divd.:**	NA
Total Assets:	$93,228,000	**Net Worth:**	$71,883,000	**Debt/ Equity:**	0.0205

Harvest Community Bank

285 N Broadway, Pennsville, NJ, 08070; *PH:* 1-856-678-4555; *http://* www.harvestcommunitybank.com

General - Incorporation		**Stock** - Price on:12/24/2007	$11.6
Employees	NA	Stock Exchange	OTC
Auditor	NA	Ticker Symbol	HCBP
Stk Agt	NA	Outstanding Shares	NA
Counsel	NA	E.P.S.	NA
DUNS No.	NA	Shareholders	NA

Business: The group's principle activity is to provide banking and financial services. The group's services include online banking services. The group operates from United States.

Primary SIC and add'l.: 6029

CIK No:

Officers: Dennis H. Engle/Dir., CEO, Pres.

Directors: Dennis H. Engle/Dir., CEO, Pres., Michael A. Williams/Chmn., David L. Sickler/Dir., Lee C. Williams/Dir., Ernest A. Bickford/Dir., Anthony W. Carapella/Dir., Michael E. Cinkala/Dir., John H. Coombs/Dir., Ronald W. Gregory/Dir., Grant Harris/Dir., Gordon J. Ostrum/Dir., David J. Puma/Dir.

Harvest Energy Trust

330 5 Ave. SW , Ste. 2100, Calgary, AB, T2P 0L4; **PH:** 1-403-265-1178; **Fax:** 1-403-265-3490; **http://** www.harvestenergy.ca; **Email:** information@harvestenergy.ca

General - Incorporation	AO	Stock - Price on:12/24/2007	$31.59
Employees	924	Stock Exchange	NYSE
Auditor	KPMG LLP	Ticker Symbol	HTE
Stk Agt	Valient Trust Co	Outstanding Shares	130,070,000
Counsel	NA	E.P.S.	$0.69
DUNS No.	NA	Shareholders	NA

Business: The groups principle activities include exploiting, developing and holding petroleum and natural gas properties through its investments. The group operates through two segments namely, petroleum and natural gas, and refining and marketing. The group operates from the United States. The group's quarterly revenue for September 2007 was 1,007.79 millions of CAD.

Primary SIC and add'l.: 1311

CIK No: 0001309799

Subsidiaries: Trust Indenture between Harvest Operations

Officers: John Zahary/CEO, Pres., Rob Morgan/COO - Upstream, Jacob Roorda/VP - Corporate, Stephen F. Saunders/Assist., Corp. Sec., David J. Rain/Corp. Sec., Robert Fotheringham/CFO - Calgary, Alberta, Gary Boukall/VP - Geosciences, Calgary, Alberta, James Sheasby/VP - Engineering, Calgary, Alberta, Neil Sinclair/VP - Operations, Calgary, Alberta, Phillip L. Reist/VP, Controller - Calgary, Alberta, Dean Beacon/Treasurer

Directors: Bruce Chernoff/Chmn., Kevin Bennett/Dir., Dale Blue/Dir., David J. Boone/Dir., John A. Brussa/Dir., William Friley/Dir., Verne Johnson/Dir., Hector McFadyen/Dir.

Financial Data: Fiscal Year End:12/31 Latest Annual Data: 12/31/2006

Year	Sales	Net Income
2006	$1,191,211,000	-$402,312,000
2005	$374,476,000	$96,365,000

Curr. Assets:	$279,136,000	Curr. Liab.:	$315,560,000	P/E Ratio:	11.94
Plant, Equip.:	$3,770,347,000	Total Liab.:	$2,638,360,000	Indic. Yr. Divd.:	$3.660
Total Assets:	$4,930,263,000	Net Worth:	$2,291,904,000	Debt/ Equity:	NA

Harvest Natural Resources Inc

1177 EnclAve. Pkwy., Ste. 300, Houston, TX, 77077; **PH:** 1-281-899-5700; **Fax:** 1-281-899-5702; **http://** www.harvestnr.com; **Email:** questions@harvestnr.com

General - Incorporation	DE	Stock - Price on:12/24/2007	$12.3
Employees	274	Stock Exchange	NYSE
Auditor	PricewaterhouseCoopers LLP	Ticker Symbol	HNR
Stk Agt	Wells Fargo Bank Minnesota N.A	Outstanding Shares	37,550,000
Counsel	NA	E.P.S.	-$0.45
DUNS No.	36-067-2851	Shareholders	NA

Business: The group's principle activities are acquisition, development, production and disposition of oil and gas properties. The group operates through geographical segments namely, Venezuela, Russia, and United States and Other.

Primary SIC and add'l.: 1311

CIK No: 0000845289

Subsidiaries: Energy International Financial Institution, Ltd., Harvest Vinccler, C.A.

Officers: James A. Edmiston/Dir., CEO, Pres., Kurt A. Nelson/VP, Controller, Chief Accounting Officer/$417,304.00, Keith L. Head/VP, General Counsel, Corp. Sec., Karl L. Nesselrode/VP - Engineering, Business Development/$545,138.00, Steven W. Tholen/CFO, Sr. VP, Treasurer/$617,225.00, Kerry R. Brittain/61/Sr. VP, General Counsel, Corp. Sec/$860,709.00, Byron A. Dunn/Sr. VP - Corporate Development/$606,960.00

Directors: James A. Edmiston/Dir., CEO, Pres., Stephen D. Chesebro/Chmn., Patrick M. Murray/Dir., H. H. Hardee/Dir., John U. Clarke/Dir., Michael J. Stinson/Dir.

Owners: James A. Edmiston, Michael J. Stinson, H. H. Hardee, Patrick M. Murray, Steven W. Tholen/1.70%, Kurt A. Nelson, Insiders/5.60%, Karl L. Nesselrode, John U. Clarke, Kerry R. Brittain, Stephen D. Chesebro, Byron A. Dunn

Financial Data: Fiscal Year End:12/31 Latest Annual Data: 12/31/2006

Year	Sales	Net Income
2006	$59,506,000	-$58,562,000
2005	$236,941,000	$50,839,000
2004	$186,066,000	$34,360,000

Curr. Assets:	$199,778,000	Curr. Liab.:	$82,214,000		
Plant, Equip.:	$3,320,000	Total Liab.:	$149,191,000	Indic. Yr. Divd.:	NA
Total Assets:	$422,711,000	Net Worth:	$244,886,000	Debt/ Equity:	0.2385

Harvey Electronics Inc

205 Chubb Ave., Lyndhurst, NJ, 07071; **PH:** 1-201-842-0078; **Fax:** 1-201-842-0660; **http://** www.harveyonline.com

General - Incorporation	NY	Stock - Price on:12/24/2007	$1.66
Employees	128	Stock Exchange	OTC
Auditor	Ernst & Young LLP	Ticker Symbol	HRVE
Stk Agt	Registrar & Transfer Co	Outstanding Shares	NA
Counsel	NA	E.P.S.	-$5.31
DUNS No.	01-340-6475	Shareholders	NA

Business: The group's principle activities include retail sale, service and custom installation of audio, video, home theater equipment and other consumer electronics products. The products of the group include high fidelity components and systems, digital versatile disc players (DVD), high definition

television (hdtv), direct view projection, plasma flat-screen and LCD flat panel television sets, audio/video furniture, digital satellite systems, conventional telephones, service contracts and related accessories. The group currently operates nine locations: seven harvey specialty retail stores and two bang & olufsen branded stores. The group operates from United States.

Primary SIC and add'l.: 5731

CIK No: 0000046043

Officers: Martin W. McClanan/Interim CEO, Victor Buszko/Store Mgr., Paul Adams/Custom Installation Project Mgr. - Eatontown, Bridgewater, Janina Majchrzak/Dir. - Human Resources, David Claflin/Store Mgr., Andrew Siok/Store Mgr., Dylan Craig/VP - Custom Installation, Tom Destio/Dir. - Custom Sales, Jaron Argiz/Assist. Dir. - New Construction, Bill Ace/Project Mgr., Bill Woessner/Custom Installation Project Mgr. - Manhattan, Al Urbieta/Custom Installation Project Mgr. - Greenwich, Darrin Zirpoli/Custom Installation Project Mgr. - Greenvale, Robert Kohlhase/Custom Installation Project Mgr. - Paramus, Jeffrey Taylor/Contact - Web Site (22 Officers included in Index)

Directors: Andrew D. Stackpole/44/Chmn., Scott Galloway/42/Dir., Ron L. Jones/64/Dir., Charles M. Berger/71/Dir., Michael E. Recca/Dir., Robert E. Albus/61/Dir., Ira J. Lamel/60/Dir., Patrick E. Hobbs/47/Dir., Jonathan Stearns/48/Dir., William F. Kenny/76/Dir., Fredric J. Gruder/61/Dir., Nicholas A. Marshall/75/Dir.

Owners: SBA Receiver for Inter-Equity Capital Partners, L.P./12.20%, Insiders/62.00%, Dylan M. Craig, Richard McGlenn/12.50%, Joseph J. Calabrese/4.80%, Charles M. Berger/10.00%, Ronald I. Heller/4.90%, Scott Galloway/3.40%, Andrew D. Stackpole/56.90%, Roland W. Hiemer/2.60%, Michael A. Beck/4.70%, Michael E. Recca/1.10%

Financial Data: Fiscal Year End:10/29 Latest Annual Data: 10/28/2006

Year	Sales	Net Income
2006	$36,065,000	-$3,238,000
2005	$40,444,000	-$830,000
2004	$43,198,000	$1,274,000

Curr. Assets:	$8,692,000	Curr. Liab.:	$5,520,000		
Plant, Equip.:	$2,318,000	Total Liab.:	$7,629,000	Indic. Yr. Divd.:	NA
Total Assets:	$12,799,000	Net Worth:	$5,170,000	Debt/ Equity:	1.1372

Harvey Westbury Corp

18b E 5th St., Paterson, NJ, 07524; **PH:** 1-973-684-0800; **http://** www.harveywestbury.com

General - Incorporation	NV	Stock - Price on:12/24/2007	$0.021
Employees	NA	Stock Exchange	OTC
Auditor	NA	Ticker Symbol	HVYW
Stk Agt	Interstate Transfer Company	Outstanding Shares	NA
Counsel	NA	E.P.S.	NA
DUNS No.	NA	Shareholders	NA

Business: The group's principal activity is distribution and packaging services. The group offers services to automotive and marine retailers and distributors. While not engaged in any formal contracts with identified volumes, it has arrangements to provide private labels of Warren Distribution for Polar products and CarQuest Inc. for CarQuest products. Other products are packaged under different brand names.

Primary SIC and add'l.: 5013

CIK No: 0001327037

Subsidiaries: Harvey NY

Hasbro Inc

1027 Newport Ave., Pawtucket, RI, 02862; **PH:** 1-401-431-8697; **Fax:** 1-401-431-8535; **http://** www.hasbro.com; **Email:** customersupport@hasbro.com

General - Incorporation	RI	Stock - Price on:12/24/2007	$30.99
Employees	5,800	Stock Exchange	NYSE
Auditor	KPMG LLP	Ticker Symbol	HAS
Stk Agt	Computershare Investor Services LLC	Outstanding Shares	159,370,000
Counsel	NA	E.P.S.	$1.78
DUNS No.	00-120-0443	Shareholders	NA

Business: The groups principle activity is to manufacture childrens and family leisure time and entertainment products and services. The groups products include trading card, roleplaying, plug and play and digital versatile disc (DVD) games, including electronic learning aids and puzzles. The group operates from United States.

Primary SIC and add'l.: 3944 3942 5092

CIK No: 0000046080

Subsidiaries: Company S.A., Group Grosvenor Plc., Hasbro (Schweiz) AG, Hasbro Asia-Pacific Marketing Ltd., Hasbro Australia Limited, Hasbro Australia Pty Ltd, Hasbro B.V., Hasbro Canada, Hasbro Canada Corporation / Corporation, Hasbro Chile LTDA, Hasbro de Mexico S.R.L. de C.V., Hasbro Deutschland GmbH, Hasbro Far East LTD, Hasbro France S.A.S., Hasbro Hellas Industrial & Commercial 32 Subsidiaries included in the Index

Officers: Alfred J. Verrecchia/65/Dir., CEO, Pres./$8,406,288.00, Barry Nagler/51/Sr. VP, General Counsel, Sec./$1,834,082.00, Brian Goldner/44/COO/$4,273,990.00, David D.R. Hargreaves/55/CFO, Exec. VP - Finance, Global Operations/$2,209,986.00, Simon Gardner/47/Pres. - Hasbro Europe/$1,755,150.00, Deborah Thomas Slater/44/Sr. VP, Controller, Martin R. Trueb/55/Sr. VP, Treasurer, Frank P. Bifulco/58/Pres. - North American Sales

Directors: Alfred J. Verrecchia/65/Dir., CEO, Pres., Alan G. Hassenfeld/59/Chmn., Frank J. Biondi/63/Dir., Gordon E. Gee/64/Dir., John M. Connors/65/Dir., Paula Stern/63/Dir., Jack M. Greenberg/65/Dir., Michael W.O. Garrett/65/Dir., Basil L. Anderson/63/Dir., Alan R. Batkin/63/Dir., Claudine B. Malone/71/Dir., Edward M. Philip/42/Dir.

Owners: Claudine B. Malone, Basil L. Anderson, Michael W.O. Garrett, Insiders/12.60%, Gordon E. Gee, Jack M. Connors, Alan R. Batkin, Barry Nagler, Jack M. Greenberg, Barclays Global Investors, NA/6.10%, Brian Goldner, Alan G. Hassenfeld/10.30%, George W. Lucas/8.90%, State Street Bank and Trust Company/6.30%, Alfred J. Verrecchia/1.20% (20 Owners included in Index)

Financial Data: Fiscal Year End:12/25 Latest Annual Data: 12/31/2006

Year	Sales	Net Income
2006	$3,151,481,000	$230,055,000
2005	$3,087,627,000	$212,075,000
2004	$2,997,510,000	$195,977,000

Curr. Assets:	$1,718,315,000	Curr. Liab.:	$905,893,000	P/E Ratio:	20.52
Plant, Equip.:	$181,726,000	Total Liab.:	$1,559,015,000	Indic. Yr. Divd.:	$0.640
Total Assets:	$3,096,905,000	Net Worth:	$1,537,890,000	Debt/ Equity:	0.3229

Hastings Entertainment Inc

3601 Plains Blvd., Amarillo, TX, 79102; *PH:* 1-806-351-2300; *Fax:* 1-806-467-8330;
http:// www.gohastings.com; *Email:* irelations@hastings-ent.com

General - Incorporation	TX	**Stock**- Price on:12/24/2007	$7.24
Employees	2,011	Stock Exchange	NDQ
Auditor	Ernst & Young LLP	Ticker Symbol	HAST
Stk Agt	Mellon Investor Services LLC	Outstanding Shares	10,940,000
Counsel	NA	E.P.S.	$0.84
DUNS No.	NA	Shareholders	NA

Business: The groups principle activity is to retailing multimedia entertainment product. The products of the group include music, books, video, rental, video games, boutique, consumables and other. The group's quarterly revenue for September 2007 was 122.28 millions of USD. The group operates from Alabama, Arkansas, Georgia, Kentucky, New Mexico, Tennessee and Indiana.

Primary SIC and add'l.: 3652 5192 5192 5961 5735 5045 7841 5734 5735 7372 5961 7372 3652 5734 7841 5045

CIK No: 0001054579

Subsidiaries: College Stores, Inc., Hastings Internet, Inc., Hastings Properties, Inc.

Officers: John H. Marmaduke/Chmn., CEO, Pres./$868,441.00, Alan Van Ongevalle/Sr. VP - Merchandising/$304,269.00, Dan Crow/VP - Finance, CFO/$395,095.00, John Hintz/VP - Information Technology, Kevin Ball/VP - Marketing, Phil McConnell/VP - Product, Natalya A. Ballew/Corp. Sec.

Directors: John H. Marmaduke/Chmn., CEO, Pres., Jeffrey G. Shrader/Dir., Daryl L. Lansdale/Dir., Ann S. Lieff/Dir., Frank O. Marrs/Dir., Danny W. Gurr/Dir.

Owners: Alan Van Ongevalle/1.20%, Stephen S. Marmaduke/14.82%, Jeff Ostler, Daryl L. Lansdale, John Hintz, Danny W. Gurr, Phil McConnell, Kevin J. Ball, Frank O. Marrs, Insiders/32.27%, Jeffrey G. Shrader/2.55%, John H. Marmaduke/28.02%, Dan Crow/1.80%, Michael Rigby, Ann S. Lieff *(16 Owners included in Index)*

Financial Data: Fiscal Year End:01/31 Latest Annual Data: 1/31/2007

Year	Sales	Net Income
2007	$548,332,000	$5,019,000
2006	$537,931,000	$5,695,000
2005	$542,016,000	$5,809,000

Curr. Assets:	$185,638,000	**Curr. Liab.:**	$113,697,000	**P/E Ratio:**	14.78
Plant, Equip.:	$69,353,000	**Total Liab.:**	$159,945,000	**Indic. Yr. Divd.:**	NA
Total Assets:	$257,498,000	**Net Worth:**	$97,553,000	**Debt/ Equity:**	0.4737

Hauppauge Digital Inc

91 Cabot Ct., Hauppauge, NY, 11788; *PH:* 1-631-434-1600; *Fax:* 1-631-434-3198;
http:// www.hauppauge.com; *Email:* techsupport@hauppauge.com

General - Incorporation	DE	**Stock**- Price on:12/24/2007	$5.25
Employees	141	Stock Exchange	NDQ
Auditor	BDO Seidman LLP	Ticker Symbol	HAUP
Stk Agt	North American Transfer Co	Outstanding Shares	9,960,000
Counsel	Certilman Balin Adler & Hyman LLP	E.P.S.	$0.38
DUNS No.	87-826-3664	Shareholders	NA

Business: The group's principle activity is to design, manufacture and market video computer boards and video conferencing boards. The products are manufactured and sold for the personal computer market and the apple(R) macintosh(R) market. The operations are divided into three product lines that are sold under the wintv(r): analog tvreceivers, digital TV receivers and personal video recorders. The analog TV receiver product line allows PC users to watch cable TV on their PC screen in a resizable window. The wintv digital TV receivers can receive digital TV transmissions and display the digital TV show in a window on the user's PC screen. The PC-based personal video recording (pvr) products allow PC users to watch and record TV shows with instant replay and program pause functions. The products are sold domestically and internationally through sales offices in New York, California, Germany, the United Kingdom, France, Singapore, Netherlands and the People's Republic of China. The group's total revenue for the year 2007 was 110.90 millions of USD.

Primary SIC and add'l.: 3679 5065 3577

CIK No: 0000930803

Subsidiaries: Hauppauge Computer Works Gmbh, Hauppauge Computer Works Inc., Hauppauge Computer Works Limited, Hauppauge Computer Works Sarl., Hauppauge Computer Works, Ltd., Hauppauge Digital Asia Pte Ltd., Hauppauge Digital Europe Sarl., Hauppauge Digital Taiwan, HCW Distributing Corp.

Officers: Kenneth H. Plotkin/Chmn., CEO, Pres., Jerry Tucciarone/Hauppauge Investor Relations, Gerald Tucciarone/CFO, Treasurer, John Casey/VP - Technology

Directors: Kenneth H. Plotkin/Chmn., CEO, Pres., Christopher G. Payan/Dir., Bernard Herman/Dir., Neal Page/Dir., Seymour G. Siegel/Dir., Robert S. Nadel/Dir., Steven J. Kuperschmid/Dir.

Owners: Christopher G. Payan, Robert S. Nadel, Dorothy Plotkin/5.60%, Bruce Willins, Bernard Herman, Insiders/13.30%, Laura Aupperle/9.70%, Seymour G. Siegel, Kenneth Plotkin/8.20%, Neal Page, Gerald Tucciarone, John Casey/1.60%

Financial Data: Fiscal Year End:09/30 Latest Annual Data: 9/30/2006

Year	Sales	Net Income
2006	$97,662,000	$2,410,000
2005	$78,458,000	$1,387,000
2004	$65,340,000	$1,825,000

Curr. Assets:	$35,955,000	**Curr. Liab.:**	$18,871,000	**P/E Ratio:**	14.58
Plant, Equip.:	$612,000	**Total Liab.:**	$18,871,000	**Indic. Yr. Divd.:**	NA
Total Assets:	$36,650,000	**Net Worth:**	$17,780,000	**Debt/ Equity:**	NA

Havas

350 Hudson St., New York, NY, 10014; *PH:* 1-212-886-2000; *Fax:* 1-212-886-2016;
http:// www.havas.com

General - Incorporation	France	**Stock**- Price on:12/24/2007	$5.6
Employees	NA	Stock Exchange	OTC
Auditor	Ernst & Young LLP	Ticker Symbol	HAVSF
Stk Agt	NA	Outstanding Shares	NA
Counsel	NA	E.P.S.	-$0.39
DUNS No.	NA	Shareholders	NA

Business: The groups principle activity is to provide advertising and media on a worldwide scale. The group is divided into following divisions namely euro rscg worldwide: marketing services, corporate communication, interactive media, healthcare, targeted consumer access; arnold worldwide partners: global marketing; media planning group: media consulting and buying; diversified agencies group: public relations, marketing services, interactive media, design, human resources, advertising. The group operates from United States.

Primary SIC and add'l.: 7319 8743 8732 7311 7331

CIK No: 0001107470

Subsidiaries: Arnold Worldwide LLC, Betc Euro Rscg, Brann LLC., Ehs Brann Ltd, Euro Rscg 4d, Euro Rscg C&o., Euro Rscg Direct Response LLC., Euro Rscg Healthview, Inc., Euro Rscg London, Euro Rscg New York, Inc., Euro Rscg Riley., Euro Rscg Worldwide, Inc, EWDB Ltd, Havas Holdings Ltd, Havas Holdings, Inc. 22 Subsidiaries included in the Index

Officers: David Jones/Global CEO - Euro Rscg Worldwide, Fernando Rodes Vila/Dir., CEO, Mercedes Erra/Executive Co - Chmn. - Euro Rscg Worldwide, Stephane Fouks/Executive Co - Chmn. - Euro Rscg Worldwide, Jacques Seguela/Dir. - Executive Vice - President, Chief Creative Officer, Remi Babinet/Chief Creative Officer - Euro Rscg Worldwide, Herve Philippe/CFO

Directors: Fernando Rodes Vila/Dir., CEO, Ed Eskandarian/Vice Chmn., Vincent Bollore/Chmn., Richard F. Colker/Dir., Pierre Lescure/Dir., Jacques Seguela/Dir. - Executive Vice - President, Chief Creative Officer, Patrick Soulard/Dir., Thierry Marraud/Dir., Leopoldo Rodes Castane/Dir.

Financial Data: Fiscal Year End:12/31 Latest Annual Data: 12/31/2005

Year	Sales	Net Income
2005	$1,730,408,000	$65,142,000
2004	$1,977,016,000	$45,025,000
2003	$1,921,171,000	-$532,884,000

Curr. Assets:	$2,725,304,000	**Curr. Liab.:**	$2,833,085,000		
Plant, Equip.:	$121,993,000	**Total Liab.:**	$3,655,058,000	**Indic. Yr. Divd.:**	NA
Total Assets:	$5,161,615,000	**Net Worth:**	$1,506,557,000	**Debt/ Equity:**	NA

Haverty Furniture Companies Inc

780 Johnson Ferry Rd. NE, Ste. 800, Atlanta, GA, 30342; *PH:* 1-404-443-2900;
Fax: 1-404-443-4180; *http://* www.havertys.com

General - Incorporation	MD	**Stock**- Price on:12/24/2007	$12.16
Employees	4,500	Stock Exchange	NYSE
Auditor	Ernst & Young LLP	Ticker Symbol	HVT
Stk Agt	Suntrust Bank	Outstanding Shares	22,700,000
Counsel	NA	E.P.S.	$0.43
DUNS No.	00-692-5036	Shareholders	NA

Business: The group's principal activity is the retail distribution of home furnishings. It provides a wide selection of furniture and accessories. The group carries multiple lines of furniture, enabling the consumer, to select from broad product choices. The merchandise includes living room furniture, bedroom furniture, dining room furniture and bedding. The group markets many brand names such as broyhill, thomasville, lane, bernhardt, la-z-boy, sealy and serty. As a service to its customers, the group offers a revolving charge credit plan with credit limits determined through its on-line credit approval system. As on 31-Dec-2003, the group operated 113 stores serving 74 cities in 15 states.

Primary SIC and add'l.: 5712 7389

CIK No: 0000216085

Subsidiaries: Havertys Capital, Inc., Havertys Credit Services, Inc., Havertys Enterprises, Inc.

Officers: Clarence H. Smith/57/Dir., CEO, Pres./$668,177.00, Thomas P. Curran/Sr. VP - Marketing, Justin P. Seamonds/VP, Controller, Allan J. Deniro/Chief People Officer, Janet E. Taylor/46/VP, General Counsel, Rawson Haverty/52/Dir., Sr. VP - Real Estate, Development/$380,866.00, Dennis L. Fink/CFO, Exec. VP/$509,909.00, Steven G. Burdette/46/Sr. VP - Operations, Jenny Hill Parker/VP, Sec., Treasurer, Edward J. Clary/CIO, Tony M. Wilkerson/Exec. VP - Merchandising/$454,407.00

Directors: Clarence H. Smith/57/Dir., CEO, Pres., Clarence H. Ridley/66/Chmn., John T. Glover/62/Dir., Phillip L. Humann/62/Dir., Al Trujillo/48/Dir., Frank S. McGaughey/59/Dir., Fred L. Schuermann/62/Dir., Mylle H. Mangum/61/Dir., Rawson Haverty/52/Dir., Sr. VP - Real Estate, Development, Vicki R. Palmer/55/Dir., Terence F. McGuirk/57/Dir.

Owners: Donald Smith & Co., Inc./7.37%, Dimensional Fund Advisors LP/8.20%, Tony M. Wilkerson/1.08%, Mylle H. Mangum, Ben M. Haverty/5.44%, Vicki R. Palmer, Clarence H. Smith/1.06%, Fred L. Schuermann, Third Avenue Management LLC/13.45%, AXA/5.46%, Clarence H. Ridley, Rawson Haverty, Al Trujillo, Clarence H. Smith/13.85%, T. Rowe Price Associates, Inc./11.96% *(30 Owners included in Index)*

Financial Data: Fiscal Year End:12/31 Latest Annual Data: 12/31/2006

Year	Sales	Net Income
2006	$859,101,000	$16,000,000
2005	$831,164,000	$15,054,000
2004	$788,664,000	$22,636,000

Curr. Assets:	$219,309,000	**Curr. Liab.:**	$124,619,000	**P/E Ratio:**	28.28
Plant, Equip.:	$221,245,000	**Total Liab.:**	$177,831,000	**Indic. Yr. Divd.:**	$0.270
Total Assets:	$469,754,000	**Net Worth:**	$291,923,000	**Debt/ Equity:**	0.0942

Hawallan Electric Co Inc

900 Richards St., Honolulu, HI, 96813; *PH:* 1-808-543-5662; *http://* www.heco.com

General - Incorporation	HI	**Stock**- Price on:12/24/2007	$23.29
Employees	3,447	Stock Exchange	NA
Auditor	KPMG LLP	Ticker Symbol	NA
Stk Agt	Continental Stock Transfer & Trust Co	Outstanding Shares	81,960,000
Counsel	NA	E.P.S.	$0.89
DUNS No.	00-692-6927	Shareholders	NA

Business: The group's principal activity is to generate, purchase, transmit, distribute and sell electric power in the islands of hawaii, oahu, maui, lanai and molokai in Hawaii. Its service areas include suburban communities, resorts, U.S. Armed forces installations and agricultural operations. The group operates through its operating subsidiaries: maui electric company limited (meco) and Hawaii electric light company, inc. (helco). The group is a wholly owned subsidiary of hawaiian electric industries, inc.

Primary SIC and add'l.: 4911

CIK No: 0000046207

Subsidiaries: AdCommunications, Inc, American Savings Bank, F.S.B., American Savings Investment Services Corp., Bishop Insurance Agency of Hawaii, Inc, Hawaii Electric Light Company, Inc., Hawaiian Electric Company, Inc., Hawaiian Electric Industries Capital Trust II, Hawaiian Electric Industries Capital Trust III, HECO Capital Trust III, HEI Diversified, Inc, HEI Properties, Inc, Hycap Management, Inc, Maui Electric Company, Limited, Pacific Energy Conservation Services, Inc, Renewable Hawaii, Inc 16 Subsidiaries included in the Index

Officers: Michael T. May/Dir., CEO, Pres., Bill Carreira/Mgr. - Accounting, William A. Bonnet/64/VP - Government, Community Affairs, Lynne T. Unemori/48/VP - Corporate Relations, Marsha Tam/Mgr. - Accounting, Corinne Chang/Mgr. - Accounting, Bill Lane/Mgr. - Accounting, Steve Luckett/Mgr. - Accounting, Patti Young/Mgr. - Accounting, Candace Oyasato/Mgr. - Accounting, Dan Sakamoto/Mgr. - Accounting, Ruby Shimabukuro/Mgr. - Accounting, Darlene Bajadali/Mgr. - Accounting, Edward L. Reinhardt/Pres., Member - Advisory Board, Maui Electric Company, Limited, Warren H.W. Lee/Pres., Member - Advisory Board, Hawaii Electric Light Company, Inc *(27 Officers included in Index)*

Directors: Michael T. May/Dir., CEO, Pres., Constance H. Lau/Chmn., Anne M. Takabuki/Dir., David C. Cole/Dir., David M. Nakada/Dir., Barry K. Taniguchi/Dir., Crystal K. Rose/Dir., James K. Scott/Dir., Timothy E. Johns/Dir., Thomas B. Fargo/Dir., Bert A. Kobayashi/Dir., Martin B. Luna/Member - Advisory Board, Maui Electric Company, Limited, Boyd P. Mossman/Member - Advisory Board, Maui Electric Company, Limited, Carol R. Ignacio/Member - Advisory Board, Hawaii Electric Light Company, Inc, Jeffrey N. Watanabe/Member - Advisory Board, Maui Electric Company, Limited *(16 Directors included in Index)*

Owners: David M. Nakada, Timothy E. Johns, Anne M. Takabuki, Thomas L. Joaquin, David C. Cole, Karl E. Stahlkopf, Michael T. May, Robert A. Alm, Tayne S. Y. Sekimura, Bert A. Kobayashi, Insiders

Financial Data: ***Fiscal Year End:***12/31 ***Latest Annual Data:*** 12/31/2006

Year		Sales		Net Income	
2006		$2,460,904,000		$108,001,000	
2005		$2,215,564,000		$126,689,000	
2004		$1,924,057,000		$109,652,000	
Curr. Assets:	$505,940,000	**Curr. Liab.:**	$4,917,325,000	**P/E Ratio:**	23.06
Plant, Equip.:	$2,647,490,000	**Total Liab.:**	$8,761,676,000	**Indic. Yr. Divd.:**	$1.240
Total Assets:	$9,891,209,000	**Net Worth:**	$1,095,240,000	**Debt/ Equity:**	2.5677

Hawallan Electric Industries Inc

900 Richards St., Honolulu, HI, 96813; ***PH:*** 1-808-543-5662; ***Fax:*** 1-808-543-7602; ***http://*** www.hei.com; ***Email:*** invest@hei.com

General - Incorporation	HI	Stock - Price on:12/24/2007	$23.28
Employees	3,447	Stock Exchange	NYSE
Auditor	KPMG LLP	Ticker Symbol	HE
Stk Agt	Continental Stock Transfer & Trust Co	Outstanding Shares	81,960,000
Counsel	Watanabe Ing & Komeiji LLP	E.P.S	$0.89
DUNS No.	10-390-1773	Shareholders	NA

Business: The groups principle activity is to supply power. The group also provides financial services to individuals and businesses. The group operates from United States.

Primary SIC and add'l.: 6035 6552 4911 4424 6719

CIK No: 0000354707

Subsidiaries: AdCommunications, Inc., American Savings Bank, F.S.B., American Savings Investment Services Corp., Bishop Insurance Agency of Hawaii, Inc., Hawaii Electric Light Company, Inc., Hawaiian Electric Company, Inc., Hawaiian Electric Industries Capital Trust II, Hawaiian Electric Industries Capital Trust III, HECO Capital Trust III, HEI Diversified, Inc., HEI Properties, Inc., Hycap Management, Inc., Maui Electric Company, Limited, Pacific Energy Conservation Services, Inc., Renewable Hawaii, Inc. 16 Subsidiaries included in the Index

Officers: Michael T. May/Dir., CEO, Pres. - Hawaiian Electric Company, Inc/$1,163,047.00, Constance H. Lau/Dir., CEO, Pres./$3,701,320.00, Curtis Y. Harada/Controller/$331,095.00, Karl E. Stahlkopf/67/Sr. VP - Energy Solutions, CTO - Heco, Thomas L. Joaquin/64/Sr. VP - Operations, Heco, Warren H.W. Lee/Member - Advisory Board, Hawaii Electric Light Company, Inc, Suzy P. Hollinger/Mgr. - Treasury, Investor Relations, William A. Bonnet/64/VP - Government, Community Affairs, Heco, Amy E. Ejercito/49/VP - Corporate Excellence, Heco, Boyd P. Mossman/Member - Advisory Board, Maui Electric Company, Limited, Edward L. Reinhardt/Pres., Member - Advisory Board, Maui Electric Company, Limited, Carol R. Ignacio/Member - Advisory Board, Hawaii Electric Light Company, Inc, Molly M. Egged/57/Sec. - Heco, Martin B. Luna/Member - Advisory Board, Maui Electric Company, Limited, Patricia U. Wong/VP - Administration, Corp. Sec./$473,784.00 *(24 Officers included in Index)*

Directors: Constance H. Lau/Dir., CEO, Pres., Jeffrey N. Watanabe/Chmn., Diane J. Plotts/Dir. - Business Advisor, Maurice A. Myers/Dir., Victor Hao Li/Dir., Barry K. Taniguchi/Dir., Thomas B. Fargo/Dir., James K. Scott/Dir., Kelvin H. Taketa/Dir., Bill D. Mills/Dir., Shirley J. Daniel/Dir., Don E. Carroll/Dir., David C. Cole/Dir. - Hawaiian Electric Company, Inc, Timothy E. Johns/Dir. - Hawaiian Electric Company, Inc, Bert A. Kobayashi/Dir. - Hawaiian Electric Company, Inc *(21 Directors included in Index)*

Owners: Barry K. Taniguchi, Diane J. Plotts, Michael T. May, Victor Hao Li, Curtis Y. Harada, Insiders, Bill D. Mills, Shirley J. Daniel, Kelvin H. Taketa, Maurice A. Myers, Don E. Carroll, Robert F. Clarke, Constance H. Lau, Patricia U. Wong, Thomas B. Fargo *(18 Owners included in Index)*

Financial Data: ***Fiscal Year End:***12/31 ***Latest Annual Data:*** 12/31/2006

Year		Sales		Net Income	
2006		$2,460,904,000		$108,001,000	
2005		$2,215,564,000		$126,689,000	
2004		$1,924,057,000		$109,652,000	
Curr. Assets:	$505,940,000	**Curr. Liab.:**	$4,917,325,000	**P/E Ratio:**	23.05
Plant, Equip.:	$2,647,490,000	**Total Liab.:**	$8,761,676,000	**Indic. Yr. Divd.:**	$1.240
Total Assets:	$9,891,209,000	**Net Worth:**	$1,095,240,000	**Debt/ Equity:**	2.5677

Hawallan Holdings Inc

3375 Koapaka St., G-350, Honolulu, HI, 96819; ***PH:*** 1-808-835-3700; ***Fax:*** 1-808-835-3690; ***http://*** www.hawaiianair.com

General - Incorporation	DE	Stock - Price on:12/24/2007	$3.78
Employees	3,454	Stock Exchange	AMEX
Auditor	Ernst & Young LLP	Ticker Symbol	HA
Stk Agt	Mellon Investor Services LLC	Outstanding Shares	46,580,000
Counsel	Dow, Lohnes & Albertson	E.P.S	-$0.38
DUNS No.	NA	Shareholders	NA

Business: The group's principal activity is to provide scheduled transportation of passengers, cargo and mail. Scheduled passenger airline service consists of, on an average, 150 flights per day with daily service between Hawaii and las vegas, Nevada and the five key United States west coast gateway cities of los angeles, san diego and san francisco, California, seattle, Washington and portland, Oregon. The group also provides charter service from honolulu to las vegas and to anchorage, Alaska and from los angeles to papeete, tahiti. The group operates a fleet of boeing 717-200 and 767-300 aircrafts. The group's inter-island operations provide service to six major hawaiian islands of oahu, Hawaii, maui, kauai, molokai and lanai.

Primary SIC and add'l.: 6719 4512 4522 4513

CIK No: 0001172222

Subsidiaries: Hawaiian Airlines, Inc

Officers: Mark B. Dunkerley/44/Dir., CEO, Pres., Charles R. Nardello/Sr. VP - Operations, Karen A. Berry/VP - Finance, Louis D. Saint-Cyr/VP - Inflight Services, Glenn G. Taniguchi/Sr. VP - Marketing, Sales, Blaine J. Miyasato/VP - Customer Services, David J. Osborne/CIO, Exec. VP, Peter R. Ingram/Exec. VP, CFO, Treasurer, Barbara D. Falvey/Sr. VP - Human Resources, Rick Peterson/VP - Marketing, Sales, Hoyt H. Zia/Sr. VP, General Counsel, Corp. Sec., Kenneth E. Rewick/VP - Flight Operations, Donald A.E. Sealey/VP - Corporate Audit, Keoni Wagner/VP - Public Affairs, Andrew Greenebaum/Investor Relations Officer *(16 Officers included in Index)*

Directors: Mark B. Dunkerley/44/Dir., CEO, Pres., Lawrence S. Hershfield/Chmn., Gregory S. Anderson/51/Dir., Thomas B. Fargo/Dir., Randall L. Jenson/Dir., Bert T. Kobayashi/Dir., Eric Nicolai/Dir., William S. Swelbar/Dir., Sean Kim/Dir., Crystal Rose/Dir., Todd L. Budge/Dir.

Owners: Randall L. Jenson, Thomas B. Fargo, Barbara D. Falvey, QVT Hawaiian LLC/8.80%, Schultze Asset Management, LLC/5.00%, Association of Flight Attendants/100.00%, William S. Swelbar, Canyon Capital Advisors LLC/8.60%, Mark B. Dunkerley/1.90%, Gregory S. Anderson, Peter R. Ingram, Insiders/13.10%, RC Aviation Management, LLC/10.60%, RC Aviation LLC/6.60%, Norman H. Davies *(23 Owners included in Index)*

Financial Data: ***Fiscal Year End:***12/31 ***Latest Annual Data:*** 12/31/2006

Year		Sales		Net Income	
2006		$888,047,000		-$40,547,000	
2005		$504,323,000		-$12,366,000	
2004		NA		-$7,262,000	
Curr. Assets:	$259,696,000	**Curr. Liab.:**	$293,851,000		
Plant, Equip.:	$272,614,000	**Total Liab.:**	$736,316,000	**Indic. Yr. Divd.:**	NA
Total Assets:	$819,953,000	**Net Worth:**	$83,637,000	**Debt/ Equity:**	4.9253

Hawk Corp

200 Public Sq., Ste. 1500, Cleveland, OH, 44114; ***PH:*** 1-216-861-3553; ***Fax:*** 1-216-861-4546; ***http://*** www.hawkcorp.com

General - Incorporation	DE	Stock - Price on:12/24/2007	$12.75
Employees	1,115	Stock Exchange	AMEX
Auditor	Ernst & Young LLP	Ticker Symbol	HWK
Stk Agt	National City Bank	Outstanding Shares	9,020,000
Counsel	Kohrman Jackson & Krantz	E.P.S	$1.665
DUNS No.	60-692-4793	Shareholders	NA

Business: The group's principal activities are to design, manufacture and market specialized components used in aerospace, industrial and commercial applications. The group operates in three business segments: friction products, precision components and performance automotive. The friction products segment engineers, manufactures and markets specialized components used in aerospace, industrial and commercial applications. The precision components segment manufactures components used in industrial applications. The performance automotive segment manufactures and markets high friction material for use in racing car brakes and clutch and drive train components. The group's registered trademarks are hawk(R), wellman friction products(R) and fibertuff(r). During 2003, the group discontinued motor segment, manufacturer of die-cast aluminium rotors for fractional and sub-fractional horsepower electric motors. The group operates in the United States, Canada, Italy and China.

Primary SIC and add'l.: 3499 3463 3714 3621 6719

CIK No: 0000849240

Subsidiaries: Allegheny Clearfield, Inc., Friction Products Co., Hawk Composites (Suzhou) Company Limited, Hawk International Trading (Shanghai) Company, Ltd., Hawk Mauritius, LTD., Hawk MIM, Inc., Hawk Motors de Mexico, S. de R.L. de C.V., Hawk Motors Monterrey, S.A. de C.V., Hawk Motors, Inc., Hawk Precision Components Group, Inc., Helsel, Inc., Logan Metal Stampings, Inc., Net Shape Technologies LLC, Quarter Master Industries, Inc., S. K. Wellman Corp. 23 Subsidiaries included in the Index

Officers: Ronald E. Weinberg/Chmn., CEO, Pres./$1,191,580.00, Sheila Wulff/Mgr. - Corporate Treasury, Benefit Services, Thomas A. Gilbride/VP - Finance/$333,908.00, Joseph J. Levanduski/CFO, VP, Controller/$405,675.00, Byron S. Krantz/Sec., Chris Disantis/Pres. - Wellman Products Group, Hawk Racing/$552,906.00

Directors: Ronald E. Weinberg/Chmn., CEO, Pres., Norman C. Harbert/74/Founder, Dir., Andrew T. Berlin/47/Dir., Paul R. Bishop/64/Dir., Jack F. Kemp/72/Dir., Dan T. Moore/68/Dir.

Owners: Ronald E. Weinberg/15.30%, Jack F. Kemp, FMR Corp./7.60%, Dan T. Moore, Insiders/100.00%, Norman C. Harbert/13.90%, Paul R. Bishop, Insiders/35.60%, Wellington Trust Company, NA/5.10%, Andrew T. Berlin, Discovery Group I/8.40%, Joseph J. Levanduski, Byron S. Krantz/10.00%, Ronald E. Weinberg/45.00%, Wellington Management Company LLP/11.80% *(20 Owners included in Index)*

Financial Data: ***Fiscal Year End:***12/31 ***Latest Annual Data:*** 12/31/2006

Year		Sales		Net Income	
2006		$212,050,000		$2,969,000	
2005		$265,434,000		-$1,344,000	
2004		$241,188,000		$1,141,000	
Curr. Assets:	$173,961,000	**Curr. Liab.:**	$57,194,000	**P/E Ratio:**	7.63
Plant, Equip.:	$39,409,000	**Total Liab.:**	$182,525,000	**Indic. Yr. Divd.:**	NA
Total Assets:	$229,254,000	**Net Worth:**	$46,729,000	**Debt/ Equity:**	1.8341

Hawkins Inc

3100 E Hennepin Ave., Minneapolis, MN, 55413; ***PH:*** 1-612-331-6910; ***Fax:*** 1-612-331-5304; ***http://*** www.hawkinschemical.com

General - Incorporation	MN	Stock - Price on:12/24/2007	$15.34
Employees	235	Stock Exchange	NDQ
Auditor	Deloitte & Touche LLP	Ticker Symbol	HWKN
Stk Agt	Wells Fargo Shareowner Services	Outstanding Shares	10,260,000
Counsel	NA	E.P.S	$0.78
DUNS No.	04-119-9639	Shareholders	NA

Business: The group's principal activity is the formulation, blending and distribution of bulk and specialty chemicals. The group operates through two segments: water treatment and the industrial. The water treatment segment provides water and wastewater treatment equipment and chemicals. This segment also provides services relating to the testing of water samples and distribution of the group's products. The industrial segment provides industrial chemicals and services to the energy, electronics, chemical processing, pulp and paper, medical device and plating industries. This segment also provides products and services to food manufacturers and processing plants.

Primary SIC and add'l.: 2899 5169

CIK No: 0000046250

Officers: Daniel E. Soderlund/VP - Pharmaceutical Group/$258,845.00, Steve Berge/Dir. - Technical Services, Joshua Van Vooren/Sales, Marketing Mgr., Julie Miriovsky/Marketing Specialist, Chris Meyer/Sr. Sales Representative, Bill Fraser/Sales Representative, Kelly Greenleaf/Sales Representative, Sarah Ashbach/Sales Representative, Bryon Smith/Customer Service Representative, Ron Larson/Customer Service Representative, Greg Christianson/Customer Service Representative, Faith Pranno/HRT Consultant, Fritz J. Wagner/Business Mgr. - Manufactured Products, Specialty Chemicals, Nick Corriere/Sales, GM - Metro, Wisconsin, Sue Niemela/Sales, Laboratory, Technical Service *(19 Officers included in Index)*

Directors: Howard M. Hawkins/64/Dir., Duane M. Jergenson/61/Dir., Daryl I. Skaar/66/Dir., James A. Faulconbridge/40/Dir.

Owners: Royce & Associates, LLC/12.40%, Duane M. Jergenson, Marvin E. Dee, Insiders/3.50%, Hawkins, Inc. Employee Stock Ownership Plan and Trust/15.10%, Eapen Chacko, Daryl I. Skaar, Keenan A. Paulson, Daniel E. Soderlund, James A. Faulconbridge, John R. Sevenich, Howard M. Hawkins/2.00%, John R. Hawkins, John S. McKeon, Robert G. Gey

Financial Data: Fiscal Year End:04/02   Latest Annual Data: 04/01/2007

Year	Sales	Net Income
2007	$160,405,000	$8,069,000
2006	$143,331,000	$8,886,000
2005	$115,280,000	$8,092,000

Curr. Assets:	$35,723,000	**Curr. Liab.:**	$14,258,000	**P/E Ratio:**	19.42
Plant, Equip.:	$30,974,000	**Total Liab.:**	$15,458,000	**Indic. Yr. Divd.:**	$0.440
Total Assets:	$87,658,000	**Net Worth:**	$72,200,000	**Debt/ Equity:**	NA

Hawthorn Bancshares Inc

Formerly: Exchange Bancshares Inc
PO Box 177, Luckey, OH, 43443; *PH:* 1-419-833-3401; *http://* www.theexchangebank.com

General - Incorporation	OH	**Stock**- Price on:12/24/2007	$45.5
Employees	NA	Stock Exchange	NDQ
Auditor	Clifton Gunderson LLP	Ticker Symbol	HWBK
Stk Agt	Illinois Stock Transfer Co	Outstanding Shares	NA
Counsel	Dinsmore & Shohl	E.P.S.	NA
DUNS No.	83-599-3676	Shareholders	NA

Business: The group's principal activity is to provide a wide range of commercial and retail banking services to individuals, firms and corporations in wood and lucas counties. The group is a one-bank holding company operating through its wholly owned subsidiary, the exchange bank. The services provided by the group include accepting of time, savings, money market and demand deposits accounts and providing commercial, industrial, agricultural, real estate and consumer installment loans. Besides, the group also provides credit card lending, safe deposit box rental, automated teller machines and other services.

Primary SIC and add'l.: 6022 6712

CIK No: 0000720912

Subsidiaries: The Exchange Bank

Financial Data: Fiscal Year End:12/31   Latest Annual Data: 12/31/2004

Year	Sales	Net Income
2004	$5,442,000	-$564,000
2002	$7,803,000	-$1,090,000
2001	$8,967,000	$602,000

Curr. Assets:	$3,289,000	**Curr. Liab.:**	$82,421,000		
Plant, Equip.:	$3,318,000	**Total Liab.:**	$82,421,000	**Indic. Yr. Divd.:**	NA
Total Assets:	$90,719,000	**Net Worth:**	$8,298,000	**Debt/ Equity:**	NA

Hayes Lemmerz International Inc

15300 Centennial Dr., Northville, MI, 48168; *PH:* 1-734-737-5000; *Fax:* 1-734-737-2003; *http://* www.hayes-lemmerz.com

General - Incorporation	DE	**Stock**- Price on:12/24/2007	$5.43
Employees	8,500	Stock Exchange	NDQ
Auditor	KPMG LLP	Ticker Symbol	HAYZ
Stk Agt	Mellon Investor Services LLC	Outstanding Shares	99,070,000
Counsel	NA	E.P.S.	-$4.27
DUNS No.	NA	Shareholders	NA

Business: The group's principle activities are to design, engineer and manufacture steel and aluminum wheels and components. The group operates in three segments: automotive wheels segment: includes a wide range of wheels, for passenger cars and light trucks. Components segment: includes wheel-end attachments, such as axle assemblies and automotive brake components, consisting primarily of composite metal drums, full cast drums and cast iron hubs for drum-type brakes and cast iron rotors for disc brakes. Other segment: includes commercial highway vehicle wheels, rims and brake products sold by the group to truck manufacturers and aftermarket distributors. The customers of the group are general motors, ford, daimler chrysler, bmw, volkswagen, nissan and honda. The group's total revenue for the year 2007 was 2,056.20 millions of USD.

Primary SIC and add'l.: NA

CIK No: 0001237941

Subsidiaries: Automotive Overseas Investments, Borlem Aluminio S.A., Borlem S.A. Emprendimentos Industriais, CMI Europe Netherlands Holdings B.V., CMI Monterrey S.A. de C.V., Emac R&d Corporation, European Commercial Wheels, B.V.B.A., Hayes Lemmerz Inci Jant Sanayi, A.S, Hayes Lemmerz Jantas Jant Sanayi ve Ticaret A.S., Hayes Lemmerz Alukola, s.r.o., Hayes Lemmerz Aluminio S. de R. L. de C.V., Hayes Lemmerz Alutechnologie, s.r.o., Hayes Lemmerz Autokola, a.s, Hayes Lemmerz Barcelona, S.A., Hayes Lemmerz Belgie, B.V.B.A. 77 Subsidiaries included in the Index

Officers: Curtis J. Clawson/Chmn., CEO, Pres., James A. Yost/CFO, Exec. VP, Mark A. Brebberman/Corporate Controller, Eric Moraw/Corporate Treasurer, John A. Salvette/VP - Business Development, Fred Bentley/COO, Daniel M. Sandberg/VP - Global Materials, Logistics, Patrick C. Cauley/VP, General Counsel, Sec., Marika Diamond/Dir. - Worldwide Public Relations, Communication, Advertising

Directors: Curtis J. Clawson/Chmn., CEO, Pres., Mohsen Sohi/Dir., James L. Bayless/Dir., Cynthia Feldmann/Dir., Richard F. Wallman/Dir., William H. Cunningham/Dir., Henry D.G. Wallace/Dir., George T. Haymaker/Dir.

Owners: Rutabaga Capital Management/11.00%, Credit Suisse/5.80%, Amalgamated Gadget, L.P./8.60%, Insiders/3.60%, Mohsen Sohi, Curtis J. Clawson/2.10%, George T. Haymaker, Richard F. Wallman, James A. Yost, Henry D. G. Wallace, Patrick C. Cauley, William H. Cunningham, Daniel M. Sandberg, Fred Bentley

Financial Data: Fiscal Year End:01/31   Latest Annual Data: 1/31/2007

Year	Sales	Net Income
2007	$2,056,200,000	-$166,900,000
2006	$2,277,200,000	-$457,500,000
2005	$2,244,500,000	-$62,300,000

Curr. Assets:	$580,600,000	**Curr. Liab.:**	$438,900,000		
Plant, Equip.:	$680,700,000	**Total Liab.:**	$1,532,100,000	**Indic. Yr. Divd.:**	NA
Total Assets:	$1,691,200,000	**Net Worth:**	$101,800,000	**Debt/ Equity:**	5.0866

HAZ Holdings Inc

Formerly: Nannaco Inc
34211 Pacific Hwy. S, Ste. 2, Federal, WA, 98003; *PH:* 1-253-874-4100

General - Incorporation	TX	**Stock**- Price on:12/24/2007	NA
Employees	NA	Stock Exchange	OTC
Auditor	Salberg & Co P.A	Ticker Symbol	HAZH
Stk Agt	Computershare Trust Co	Outstanding Shares	NA
Counsel	NA	E.P.S.	NA
DUNS No.	NA	Shareholders	NA

Business: The group's principal activity is to provide surface cleaning, surface protection, surface restoration and other services to commercial businesses, as well to the owners of historical buildings. The group operated under the trade name surface pro in order to relate to the principal business activity. As of Sept 2003, the group ceased all operating activities and has disposed of most of its assets. The group has entered a new development phase, while formulating a plan to improve it financial position.

Primary SIC and add'l.: 7349 7699

CIK No: 0001112748

Financial Data: Fiscal Year End:09/30   Latest Annual Data: 09/30/2004

Year	Sales	Net Income
2004	$16,000	-$6,400,000
2003	$68,000	-$977,000
2002	$138,000	-$268,000

Curr. Assets:	NA	**Curr. Liab.:**	$841,000		
Plant, Equip.:	NA	**Total Liab.:**	$841,000	**Indic. Yr. Divd.:**	NA
Total Assets:	NA	**Net Worth:**	-$841,000	**Debt/ Equity:**	NA

HCA Inc

One Pk. Plz., Nashville, TN, 37203; *PH:* 1-615-344-9551; *http://* www.hcahealthcare.com

General - Incorporation	DE	**Stock**- Price on:12/24/2007	NA
Employees	NA	Stock Exchange	NA
Auditor	Ernst & Young LLP	Ticker Symbol	NA
Stk Agt	National City Bank	Outstanding Shares	NA
Counsel	NA	E.P.S.	NA
DUNS No.	05-066-8656	Shareholders	NA

Business: The group's principle activity is to provide health care services by operating hospitals and related health care entities. The group operates from United States.

Primary SIC and add'l.: 6719 8082 8063 6321 8062 8011

CIK No: 0000860730

Subsidiaries: AAL Holdings, Inc., AC Med, LLC, Acadiana Care Center, Inc., Acadiana Practice Management, Inc., Acadiana Regional Pharmacy, Inc., ACH, Inc., Acworth Imaging Center, LLC, AHN Holdings, Inc., Alabama-Tennessee Health Network, Inc., Alaska Regional Hospital, Albany Family Practice, LLC, Albany Neurosurgery Center, LLC, Aligned Business Consortium Group, L.P., All About Learning, LLC, All About Staffing of Texas, Inc. 1776 Subsidiaries included in the Index

Officers: Jack O. Bovender/Chmn., CEO, Robert A. Waterman/Sr. VP, General Counsel, Richard M. Bracken/Dir., COO, Pres., Rosalyn S. Elton/Sr. VP - Operations Finance, Chuck J. Hall/55/Pres. - Eastern Group, Sam R. Hankins/CFO - Outpatient Services Group, Beverly B. Wallace/Pres. - Financial Services Group, Bruce A. Moore/Pres. - Outpatient Services Group, Samuel N. Hazen/Pres. - Western Group, Richard J. Shallcross/CFO - Western Group, Alan R. Yuspeh/Sr. VP, Chief Ethics, Compliance Officer, Carl V. George/Sr. VP - Development, John M. Steele/Sr. VP - Human Resources, David G. Anderson/Sr. VP - Finance, Treasurer, Noel Brown Williams/CIO, Sr. VP *(24 Officers included in Index)*

Directors: Jack O. Bovender/Chmn., CEO, Richard M. Bracken/Dir., COO, Pres., Thomas F. Frist/Co - Founder, Dir., Christopher J. Birosak/Dir., George A. Bitar/Dir., John Connaughton/Dir., Thomas F. Frist/Dir., Chris Gordon/Dir., Michael W. Michelson/Dir., James C. Momtazee/Dir., Steve Pagliuca/Dir., Peter Stavros/Dir., Nathan C. Thorne/Dir.

Owners: Richard M. Bracken, Hercules Holding II, LLC/97.50%, Samuel N. Hazen, Insiders/2.00%, Jack O. Bovender, R. Milton Johnson, Paul W. Rutledge

HCB Financial Corp

150 W Court St., Hastings, MI , 49058; *PH:* 1-269-945-2401; *Fax:* 1-269-945-9777; *https://* www.hastingscitybank.com

General - Incorporation		**Stock**- Price on:12/24/2007	$27.6
Employees	NA	Stock Exchange	OTC
Auditor	NA	Ticker Symbol	HCBN
Stk Agt	NA	Outstanding Shares	NA
Counsel	NA	E.P.S.	NA
DUNS No.	NA	Shareholders	NA

Business: The groups principle activity is to provide recruiting services. The groups service area includes the research and development, engineering, marketing, sales, information technology and manufacturing industries. The group operates from United States.

Primary SIC and add'l.: 6021

CIK No:

HCC Insurance Holdings Inc

13403 NW Fwy., Houston, TX, 77040; ***PH:*** 1-713-690-7300; ***Fax:*** 1-713-462-2401; ***http://*** www.hcch.com; ***Email:*** investorrelations@hcch.com

General - Incorporation	DE	***Stock*** - Price on:12/24/2007	$33.85
Employees	1,660	Stock Exchange	NYSE
Auditor	PricewaterhouseCoopers LLP	Ticker Symbol	HCC
Stk Agt	American Stock Transfer & Trust Co.	Outstanding Shares	112,100,000
Counsel	Haynes & Boone	E.P.S	$3.18
DUNS No.	78-112-0100	Shareholders	NA

Business: The groups principle activity is to provide insurance services. The groups services include specialized property and casualty, surety and group life, accident and health insurance coverages and related agency and reinsurance brokerage services to commercial customers and individuals. The group also underwrites insurance both on a direct and reinsurance basis. The group operates from United States, the United Kingdom, Spain, Bermuda and Ireland.

Primary SIC and add'l.: 6331 6311

CIK No: 0000888919

Subsidiaries: American Contractors Indemnity Company, Avemco Corporation, Avemco Insurance Agency, Inc., Avemco Insurance Company, Avemco Services, Inc., cineFinance Insurance Services, LLC, Continental Underwriters Ltd., Covenant Claims Service, LLC, Covenant Underwriters Ltd., Credance Limited, Credit Shield Limited, De Montfort Group Limited, De Montfort Holdings Limited, De Montfort Investments Limited, Dickson Manchester & Company, Limited 103 Subsidiaries included in the Index

Officers: Matthew R. Fairfield/CEO, Head - International Operations, HCC Global Financial Products, Frank J. Bramanti/Dir., CEO/$733,786.00, William F. Hubbard/CEO, Pres. - HCC Specialty Underwriters, Carl C. Petty/CEO, Pres. - Perico Life Insurance Company, Elder H. Brown/CEO, Pres. - Continental Underwriters, Property, Casualty Operations, Cory L. Moulton/CEO - Professional Indemnity Agency, Russell J. Benzies/CEO - Illium Managing Agency, Ltd, Charles L.C. Manchester/CEO - HCC International Insurance Company, Dean E. Carberry/MD - Rattner Mackenzie, Bermuda, Nicholas I. Hutton-Penman/COO - HCC Insurance Holdings, International, Michael J. Donovan/Sr. VP - Aviation Divisions, Insurance Company Subsidiaries, Andrew G. Stone/Pres., Head - US Operations, HCC Global Financial Products, Steven A.F. Ahern/MD - Rattner Mackenzie, UK, Larry Stewart/Sr. VP, Chief Underwriting Officer - HCC Life Insurance Company, Mark R. Sanderford/CFO, COO - HCC Life Insurance Company *(44 Officers included in Index)*

Directors: Frank J. Bramanti/Dir., CEO, Robert J. Dickerson/Dir., James E. Oesterreicher/Dir., Christopher J.B. Williams/Dir., Walter M. Duer/Dir., Allan W. Fulkerson/Dir., Patrick B. Collins/Dir., Michael A.F. Roberts/Dir., John N. Molbeck/Dir., COO, Pres., James R. Crane/54/Dir., Edward H. Ellis/Dir., CFO, Exec. VP, James C. Flagg/Dir.

Owners: Edward H. Ellis, Robert J. Dickerson, Michael J. Schell, Michael A. F. Roberts, Wachovia Corporation/4.96%, James R. Crane, John N. Molbeck, Allan W. Fulkerson, Barry J. Cook, James C. Flagg, Patrick B. Collins, Insiders/1.37%, Frank J. Bramanti, Ariel Capital Management, LLC/10.87%, Walter M. Duer

Financial Data: ***Fiscal Year End:***12/31 ***Latest Annual Data:*** 12/31/2006

Year	***Sales***	***Net Income***
2006	$2,075,295,000	$342,285,000
2005	$1,642,688,000	$191,192,000
2004	$1,283,154,000	$163,025,000

Curr. Assets:	$3,200,163,000	***Curr. Liab.:***	$4,222,220,000	***P/E Ratio:***	10.64
Plant, Equip.:	NA	***Total Liab.:***	$5,587,329,000	***Indic. Yr. Divd.:***	$0.400
Total Assets:	$7,630,132,000	***Net Worth:***	$2,042,803,000	***Debt/ Equity:***	0.1398

HCSB Financial Corp

5201 Broad St., Loris, SC, 29569; ***PH:*** 1-843-716-4272 ; ***Fax:*** 1-843-716-6136; ***http://*** www.horrycountystatebank.com; ***Email:*** customerservice@horrycountystatebank.com

General - Incorporation	SC	***Stock*** - Price on:12/24/2007	$22
Employees	132	Stock Exchange	OTC
Auditor	Elliott Davis LLC	Ticker Symbol	HCFB
Stk Agt	First Citizens Bank of NC	Outstanding Shares	3,570,000
Counsel	NA	E.P.S	$0.72
DUNS No.	NA	Shareholders	NA

Business: The group's principal activity is to provide commercial banking business. These services are offered for individuals and businesses in horry and marion counties in South Carolina and columbus and brunswick counties in North Carolina. Deposit products include checking accounts, savings accounts, certificate of deposits and money market accounts. The group provides commercial loans, consumer loans, agricultural and construction loans. The group offers a broad array of non-deposit services including trading of mutual funds, stocks and bonds, estate and retirement planning, life insurance plans and discount brokerage services.

Primary SIC and add'l.: 6712 6022

CIK No: 0001091491

Subsidiaries: HCSB Financial Trust I, Horry County State Bank

Officers: James R. Clarkson/57/CEO, Pres., Principal Accounting Officer, Principal Financial Officer/$242,503.00, Annette Stroud/Assist. VP, Branch Operations Officer - Downtown Conway, Jimmy Nealey/VP, Loris City Exec. Officer - Broad Street, Marie Jeffers/VP, Branch Mgr. - Carolina Forest Office, Debbie Guyette/VP, Branch Mgr. - Myrtle Beach, Annette Suggs/Mgr. - Branch Operations, Ruth Bell/VP, Branch Mgr. - Homewood, Bernice Hammond/VP, Branch Mgr. - Mt. Olive, Amy Cannon/Assist. VP, Branch Mgr. - Little River, Clay Harrelson/Assist. VP, Branch Mgr. - Meeting Street, Ann Marion/Assist. VP, Branch Mgr. - Socastee, Charles Sprinkle/VP, Branch Mgr. - Windy Hill, Walter Williamson/VP, Mgr. - Tabor City, Denise Floyd/Investor Relations Officer, Richard Carroll/Assist. VP, Branch Mgr. - Conway Office

Directors: Johnny C. Allen/61/Dir., Clay D. Brittain/53/Dir., Russell R. Burgess/65/Dir., Singleton D. Bailey/57/Dir., Franklin C. Blanton/63/Dir., William H. Caines/71/Dir., Lavelle J. Coleman/68/Dir., Larry G. Floyd/67/Dir., Boyd R. Ford/68/Dir., Tommie W. Grainger/69/Dir., Randy B. Hardee/50/Dir., Gwyn G. McCutchen/64/Dir., Freddie T. Moore/67/Dir., Carroll D. Padgett/60/Dir., Michael S. Addy/56/Dir. *(16 Directors included in Index)*

Owners: Insiders/14.05%, Boyd R. Ford/3.06%, Johnny C. Allen, Freddie T. Moore, Franklin C. Blanton/2.40%, William H. Caines, Tommie W. Grainger/1.39%, Russell R. Burgess, Rachel B. Broadhurst, Gwyn G. McCutchen, Clay D. Brittain, Lavelle J. Coleman, Randy B. Hardee, Larry G. Floyd, Singleton D. Bailey/1.21% *(19 Owners included in Index)*

Financial Data: ***Fiscal Year End:***12/31 ***Latest Annual Data:*** 12/31/2006

Year	***Sales***	***Net Income***
2006	$26,284,000	$2,805,000
2005	$21,147,000	$2,408,000
2004	$17,328,000	$2,055,000

Curr. Assets:	$31,581,000	***Curr. Liab.:***	$319,313,000	***P/E Ratio:***	30.56
Plant, Equip.:	$16,234,000	***Total Liab.:***	$331,187,000	***Indic. Yr. Divd.:***	NA
Total Assets:	$359,537,000	***Net Worth:***	$28,350,000	***Debt/ Equity:***	0.2136

HDFC Bank Ltd

HDFC Bank House, Senapati Bapat Marg, Lower Parel, Mumbai, Maharashtra, 400 013; ; ***http://*** www.hdfcbank.com

General - Incorporation	India	***Stock*** - Price on:12/24/2007	$84.68
Employees	21,477	Stock Exchange	Nyse
Auditor	Deloitte Haskins & Sells	Ticker Symbol	HDB
Stk Agt	NA	Outstanding Shares	105,070,000
Counsel	NA	E.P.S	$3.12
DUNS No.	NA	Shareholders	NA

Business: The group's principal activities are to provide banking and other financial services. The group's wholesale banking operations includes a wide array of commercial, transactional and electronic banking products through innovative product development and a well integrated approach to relationship management to corporate and institutional clients. The treasury services of the group consist of foreign exchange & derivatives, money markets & debt securities and equities investments & advisory. The retail banking services includes ATMs, phone banking and net banking; and capital markets infrastructure which provides transactional banking and payment services for capital market related payments such as dividends, interests, etc. And strategic investments. The group operates through 312 outlets in 163 cities in India.

Primary SIC and add'l.: 6021

CIK No: 0001144967

Officers: Sudhir Joshi/61/Head - Treasury, C. N. Ram/51/Head - Information Technology, Bharat Shah/61/Head - Merchant Services, G. Subramanian/61/Head - Audit, Compliance, Vigilance, A. Rajan/56/Head - Operations, Abhay Aima/45/Head - Equities, Private Banking, Third Party Products, Kaizad Bharucha/42/Head - Credit, Marketing Risk, Pralay Mondal/42/Head - Retail Assets, Credit Cards, Mandeep Maitra/42/Head - Human Resources, Ashish Parthasarthy/40/Head - Trading, Rahul N. Bhagat/44/Head - Retail Liabilities, Marketing, P. V. Ananthakrishnan/48/Head - Capital Markets, Commodity Business, Bhavesh Zaveri/42/Head - Wholesale Banking Operations, Aseem Dhru/37/Head - Business Banking, Commercial Transportation Group, Shyamal Saxena/40/Head - Branch Banking *(19 Officers included in Index)*

Directors: Jagdish Capoor/Chmn., Arvind Pande/Dir., Gautam Divan/Dir., Pandit Palande/Dir., Ashim Samanta/Dir., Renu Karnad/Dir., Paresh Sukthankar/Dir., C. M. Vasudev/Dir., Aditya Puri/Dir., Vineet Jain/Dir., Keki M. Mistry/Dir., Harish Engineer/Dir.

Owners: HDFC group/21.56%, Insiders/0.82%, Bennett Coleman group/5.07%

Financial Data: ***Fiscal Year End:***03/31 ***Latest Annual Data:*** 03/31/2007

Year	***Sales***	***Net Income***
2007	$1,987,100,000	$256,100,000
2006	$1,261,700,000	$206,500,000
2005	$858,800,000	$151,500,000

Curr. Assets:	$2,630,900,000	***Curr. Liab.:***	$21,200,700,000		
Plant, Equip.:	$241,200,000	***Total Liab.:***	$21,987,800,000	***Indic. Yr. Divd.:***	$0.520
Total Assets:	$23,507,700,000	***Net Worth:***	$1,519,900,000	***Debt/ Equity:***	NA

Head

1 Selleck St., Norwalk, CT, 06855; ***PH:*** 1-203-855-8666; ***http://*** www.head.com

General - Incorporation	Netherlands	***Stock*** - Price on:12/24/2007	$4.19
Employees	1,966	Stock Exchange	NYSE
Auditor	PricewaterhouseCoopers LLP	Ticker Symbol	HED
Stk Agt	Cede & Co	Outstanding Shares	36,260,000
Counsel	NA	E.P.S	-$0.35
DUNS No.	NA	Shareholders	NA

Business: The groups principle activity is to design and manufacture sports goods in the field of skiing, tennis, squash & diving. The grouop produces the following brand names: head (alpine skis & boots, snow board equipment, athletic footwear as well as tennis & squash racquets); tyrolia (ski bindings); penn (tennis & squash balls); mares & dacor (diving equipment). The group operates from United States.

Primary SIC and add'l.: 3149 3949 3021

CIK No: 0001123455

Subsidiaries: Head Austria GmbH, Head Germany GmbH, Head Holding Unternehmensbeteiligung GmbH, Head International GmbH, Head Sport AG, Head Sport sro, Head Switzerland AG, Head Technology GmbH, Head Tyrolia Sports SA, Head UK Ltd, Head USA Inc, Head/Tyrolia Sports Canada Inc, HTM Head Tyrolia Mares Iberica SL, HTM Sport sro, HTM Sport- und Freizeitgerate AG 20 Subsidiaries included in the Index

Officers: Johan Eliasch/Chmn., CEO, Head NV, Gerald Skrobanek/Exec. VP - Diving Division, Robert Marte/Exec. VP - Racquets Sports Division, Klaus Hotter/Exec. VP - Ski Division, Georg Kroell/Exec. VP - Licensing Division, Edgar Pollmann/Exec. VP - Operations, George F. Nicolai/Member - Management Board, Ralph Bernhart/CFO, Gunter Hagspiel/VP - Finance - Controlling, Vicki Booth/Investor Relations

Directors: Johan Eliasch/Chmn., CEO, Head NV, William S. Cohen/Member - Supervisory Board, Viktor Klima/Member - Supervisory Board, Jurgen Hintz/Member - Supervisory Board

Financial Data: ***Fiscal Year End:***12/31 ***Latest Annual Data:*** 12/31/2006

Year	***Sales***	***Net Income***
2006	$484,236,000	$760,000
2005	$446,882,000	$7,994,000
2004	$467,014,000	-$36,935,000

Curr. Assets:	$367,873,000	***Curr. Liab.:***	$134,669,000		
Plant, Equip.:	$81,622,000	***Total Liab.:***	$352,090,000	***Indic. Yr. Divd.:***	$0.570
Total Assets:	$557,579,000	***Net Worth:***	$205,489,000	***Debt/ Equity:***	NA

Headwaters Inc

10653 S River Front Pkwy., Ste. 300, S Jordan, UT, 84095; *PH:* 1-801-984-9400;
Fax: 1-801-984-9460; *http://* www.covol.com; *Email:* smadden@headwaters.com

General - Incorporation	DE	**Stock** - Price on:12/24/2007	$17.51
Employees	4,300	Stock Exchange	NYSE
Auditor	Ernst & Young LLP	Ticker Symbol	HW
Stk Agt..... American Stock Transfer & Trust Co.		Outstanding Shares	42,180,000
Counsel	NA	E.P.S.	$0.47
DUNS No.	78-619-5701	Shareholders	NA

Business: The group's principal activities are to develop and commercialize its chemical technologies, which are used to produce alternative fuel from coal derivatives and to develop and deploy alternative energy technologies. Alternative energy segment includes traditional coal-based solid alternative fuel business. It also develops and commercializes catalysts and catalytic processes for producing chemicals and converting low-value fossil fuels into high-value alternative fuels. Ccp segment includes supply of post-combustion services and technologies to the coal-fired electric utility industry. The construction materials segment produces and sells standard masonry, stucco construction materials and supplies packaged products and blocks as well as value added technology products. On 12-Apr-2004, the group acquired vfl technology corp.
Primary SIC and add'l.: 4953 2999
CIK No: 0001003344
Subsidiaries: Atlantic Shutter Systems, Inc., Best Masonry & Tool Supply, LLC, Blue Flint Ethanol LLC, Chihuahua Stone LLC, Covol Coal Company, LLC, Covol Engineered Fuels, LC, Covol Services Corporation, Degussa Headwaters Korea Co., Ltd., Degussa Headwaters LLP, Don's Building Supply, LLC, Eldorado G-Acquisition Co., Eldorado SC-Acquisition Co., Eldorado Stone Acquisition Co., LLC, Eldorado Stone Funding Co., LLC, Eldorado Stone LLC 45 Subsidiaries included in the Index
Officers: Kirk A. Benson/Chmn., CEO, Harlan M. Hatfield/VP, Sec., General Counsel, Steven G. Stewart/Treasurer, Scott K. Sorensen/46/CFO, Sharon A. Madden/Dir. - Investor Relations
Directors: Kirk A. Benson/Chmn., CEO, William S. Dickinson/Dir., James A. Herickhoff/Dir., Malyn K. Malquist/Dir., E. J. Garn/Dir., Sam R. Christensen/Dir., Raymond J. Weller/Dir., Blake O. Fisher/Dir.
Owners: William S. Dickinson, Raymond J. Weller, John N. Lawless, Sam R. Christensen, Michael S. Lewis, EARNEST Partners, LLC/10.10%, Kenneth R. Frailey, Blake O. Fisher, Franklin Resources, Inc./7.00%, Insiders/8.10%, Waddell and Reed, Inc./7.00%, James A. Herickhoff, Kirk A. Benson/3.90%, Scott K. Sorensen, Malyn K. Malquist *(16 Owners included in Index)*
Financial Data: *Fiscal Year End:*09/30 *Latest Annual Data:* 9/30/2006

Year	Sales	Net Income
2006	$1,121,387,000	$102,058,000
2005	$1,064,639,000	$121,278,000
2004	$553,955,000	$64,317,000

Curr. Assets:	$310,037,000	Curr. Liab.:	$164,741,000	P/E Ratio:	6.87
Plant, Equip.:	$213,406,000	Total Liab.:	$860,771,000	Indic. Yr. Divd.:	NA
Total Assets:	$1,661,729,000	Net Worth:	$800,958,000	Debt/ Equity:	0.6967

Health Anti Aging Lifestyle Opts Inc

580 Hornby St., Ste. 210, Vancouver, BC, V6C 3B6; *PH:* 1-604-687-6991;
http:// www.haloonair.com

General - Incorporation	UT	**Stock** - Price on:12/24/2007	$0.05
Employees	NA	Stock Exchange	OTC
Auditor	Vellmer & Chang	Ticker Symbol	HLOI
Stk Agt	Signature Stock Transfer, Inc.	Outstanding Shares	NA
Counsel	NA	E.P.S.	NA
DUNS No.	NA	Shareholders	NA

Business: The group's principal activities are to develop multimedia products and services related to the health, wellness and anti-aging industry. The group's multimedia products develops, produces, commercializes and distributes content based research, education and information related to health, wellness and anti-aging, including issues related to the body/mind/spirit connection. The group also has radio broadcasting in the United States called halo-radio. Halo-radio is broadcast via the talk radio network into approximately 59 u s cities.
Primary SIC and add'l.: 8099 4832
CIK No: 0000805902
Officers: Peter Hogendoorn/53/Dir., CEO, Pres., Bruce Schmidt/56/Dir., CFO, Sec., Treasurer, Principal Accounting Officer
Directors: Peter Hogendoorn/53/Dir., CEO, Pres., Bruce Schmidt/56/Dir., CFO, Sec., Treasurer, Principal Accounting Officer
Financial Data: *Fiscal Year End:*12/31 *Latest Annual Data:* 12/31/2006

Year	Sales	Net Income
2006	$0	-$22,000
2005	$0	-$22,000
2004	$0	-$34,000

Curr. Assets:	$39,000	Curr. Liab.:	$21,000		
Plant, Equip.:	NA	Total Liab.:	$21,000	Indic. Yr. Divd.:	NA
Total Assets:	$39,000	Net Worth:	$18,000	Debt/ Equity:	NA

Health Benefits Direct Corp

100 Matsonford Rd., 5 Radnor Corporate Ctr., Ste. 555, Radnor, PA, 19087; *Fax:* 1-954-944-4010;
http:// www.healthbenefitsdirect.com; *Email:* info@hbdc.com

General - Incorporation	DE	**Stock** - Price on:12/24/2007	$2.45
Employees	191	Stock Exchange	OTC
Auditor	Sherb & Co., LLP	Ticker Symbol	HBDT
Stk Agt.	NA	Outstanding Shares	34,070,000
Counsel	NA	E.P.S.	NA
DUNS No.	NA	Shareholders	NA

Business: The groups principle activity is to provide services in the direct marketing of health and life insurance and related products to individuals, families and groups. In April 2006, the group merged with ISG Merger Acquisition Corp. The group operates from the United States.
Primary SIC and add'l.: 6411
CIK No: 0001309442

Subsidiaries: HBDC II, Inc., Health Benefits Direct II, LLC, Health Benefits Direct III, LLC, Insurance Specialist Group, Insurint Corporation, Platinum Partners, LLC
Officers: Alvin H. Clemens/Chmn., CEO, Charles A. Eissa/Dir., COO, Pres., Anthony R. Verdi/CFO, Ivan M. Spinner/Sr. VP
Directors: Alvin H. Clemens/Chmn., CEO, Warren V. Musser/Vice Chmn., Charles A. Eissa/Dir., COO, Pres., Paul Soltoff/Dir., John Harrison/Dir., James C. Jensen/Dir., Sanford Rich/Dir., L. J. Rowell/Dir., Frederick C. Tecce/73/Dir.
Owners: Frederick C. Tecce, Alvin H. Clemens/12.00%, John Harrison/1.20%, Sanford Rich, Charles A. Eissa/5.40%, Ivan M. Spinner, Anthony R. Verdi/1.20%, Insiders/28.70%, Paul Soltoff, James C. Jensen, L. J. Rowell/1.00%, Warren V. Musser/3.00%
Financial Data: *Fiscal Year End:*12/31 *Latest Annual Data:* 12/31/2006

Year	Sales	Net Income
2006	$12,240,000	-$13,968,000
2005	$2,660,000	-$3,171,000

Curr. Assets:	$5,313,000	Curr. Liab.:	$7,807,000		
Plant, Equip.:	$1,483,000	Total Liab.:	$7,807,000	Indic. Yr. Divd.:	NA
Total Assets:	$12,237,000	Net Worth:	$4,431,000	Debt/ Equity:	NA

Health Care Property Investors Inc

3760 Kilroy Airport Way, Suite, CA, 90806; ; *http://* www.hcpi.com

General - Incorporation	MD	**Stock** - Price on:12/24/2007	$29.4
Employees	165	Stock Exchange	NA
Auditor	Ernst & Young LLP	Ticker Symbol	NA
Stk Agt	Bank of New York	Outstanding Shares	206,020,000
Counsel	NA	E.P.S.	$3.77
DUNS No.	NA	Shareholders	NA

Business: The groups principle activity is to operate health care properties. The group operates through two segments namely, medical office buildings and triple-net leased. In the year 2006, the group acquired 13 medical office buildings. The group operates from the United States. The group's quarterly revenue for September 2007 was 284.25 millions of USD.
Primary SIC and add'l.: 6512
CIK No: 0000765880
Subsidiaries: AHP of Nevada, Inc., AHP of Washington, Inc., Annapolis Assisted Living, LLC, ARC Holland Real Estate Holdings, LLC, ARC LaBarc Real Estate Holdings, LLC, ARC Richmond Place Real Estate Holdings, LLC, ARC Sun City Real Estate Holdings, LLC, Aurora HCP, LLC, Aurora MOB Owner, LLC, Baytown MOB Partners, Ltd., Birmingham HCP, LLC, Brentwood MOB Owners, LLC, Charles Pavilion Holdings, LLC 100%, CNL Retirement Aur1 California A Pack, LP, Davis North I, LLC 558 Subsidiaries included in the Index
Officers: James F. Flaherty/Chmn., CEO/$4,324,449.00, Charles Elcan/Exec. VP - Medical Office Properties/$1,382,092.00, Paul Gallagher/Exec. VP, Chief Investment Officer/$1,405,476.00, Stephen R. Maulbetsch/51/Exec. VP - Strategic Development/$1,275,201.00, Edward J. Henning/Exec. VP, General Counsel, Corp. Sec., Thomas D. Kirby/Sr. VP - Acquisitions, Dispositions, Mark Wallace/Exec. VP, CFO, Treasurer/$1,160,073.00, Marshall D. Lees/Exec. VP, Donald McNutt/Exec. VP - Operations, George P. Doyle/Chief Accounting Officer, Sr. VP
Directors: James F. Flaherty/Chmn., CEO, Mary A. Cirillo-Goldberg/Dir., Robert R. Fanning/Dir., David B. Henry/Dir., Michael D. Mckee/Dir., Harold M. Messmer/Dir., Peter L. Rhein/Dir., Kenneth B. Roath/Dir., Richard M. Rosenberg/Dir., Joseph P. Sullivan/Dir.
Owners: David B. Henry, Paul F. Gallagher, Insiders/2.35%, Mark A. Wallace, James F. Flaherty, Mary A. Cirillo-Goldberg, Stephen R. Maulbetsch, Peter L. Rhein, Joseph P. Sullivan, Robert R. Fanning, Charles A. Elcan, Kenneth B. Roath, Michael D. McKee, Richard M. Rosenberg, The Vanguard Group,Inc./5.50% *(16 Owners included in Index)*
Financial Data: *Fiscal Year End:*12/31 *Latest Annual Data:* 12/31/2006

Year	Sales	Net Income
2006	$619,087,000	$417,547,000
2005	$477,276,000	$173,057,000
2004	$428,684,000	$169,040,000

Curr. Assets:	$91,713,000	Curr. Liab.:	$182,810,000		
Plant, Equip.:	$8,026,703,000	Total Liab.:	$6,718,713,000	Indic. Yr. Divd.:	$1.780
Total Assets:	$10,012,749,000	Net Worth:	$3,294,036,000	Debt/ Equity:	1.4011

Health Care REIT Inc

1 SeaGate, Ste. 1500, Toledo, OH, 43603; *PH:* 1-419-247-2800; *Fax:* 1-419-247-2826;
http:// www.hcreit.com; *Email:* info@hcreit.com

General - Incorporation	DE	**Stock** - Price on:12/24/2007	$41.32
Employees	113	Stock Exchange	NYSE
Auditor	Ernst & Young LLP	Ticker Symbol	HCN
Stk Agt	Mellon Investor Services LLC	Outstanding Shares	80,520,000
Counsel	NA	E.P.S.	$1.25
DUNS No.	NA	Shareholders	NA

Business: The groups principle activity is to operate medical properties. The groups services include assisted living facilities, skilled nursing facilities, hospitals, long-term acute care hospitals and medical office buildings. The group operates through two segments including investment properties and operating properties. The group operates from the United States. The group's quarterly revenue for September 2007 was 125.08 millions of USD.
Primary SIC and add'l.: 6798
CIK No: 0000766704
Subsidiaries: 111 Lazelle Road East, LLC, 130 Buena Vista Street, LLC, 1425 Yorkland Road, LLC, 1785 Freshley Avenue, LLC, 1850 Crown Park Court, LLC, 1920 Cleveland Road West, LLC, 209 Merriman Road, L.L.C., 222 East Beech Street Jefferson, L.L.C., 5166 Spanson Drive SE, LLC, 5700 Karl Road, LLC, 721 Hickory Street, LLC, Brierbrook Partners, LLC, CAL-GAT Limited Partnership, CAL-LAK Limited Partnership, Cooper Holding, L.L.C. 235 Subsidiaries included in the Index
Officers: George L. Chapman/Chmn., CEO/$3,748,916.00, Raymond W. Braun/Dir., Pres./$1,321,227.00, Frederick L. Farrar/Exec. VP/$3,778,335.00, Michael A. Crabtree/VP, Treasurer, Scott A. Estes/Sr. VP, CFO/$570,132.00, Charles J. Herman/Exec. VP, Chief Investment Officer, Erin C. Ibele/Sr. VP - Administration, Corp. Sec., Daniel R. Loftus/Sr. VP, Jeffrey H. Miller/Exec. VP, General Counsel
Directors: George L. Chapman/Chmn., CEO, Fred S. Klipsch/Vice Chmn., Raymond W. Braun/Dir., Pres., William C. Ballard/Dir., Pier C. Borra/Dir., Thomas J. Derosa/Dir., Jeffrey H. Donahue/Dir., Peter J. Grua/Dir., Sharon M. Oster/Dir., Scott R. Trumbull/Dir.

Owners: Raymond W. Braun, Morgan Stanley/5.97%, Insiders, William C. Ballard, Frederick L. Farrar, Cohen& Steers Capital Management, Inc./7.85%, Sharon M. Oster, Peter J. Grua, Pier C. Borra, George L. Chapman, Thomas J. DeRosa, ING Clarion Real Estate Securities, L.P./5.31%, The Vanguard Group, Inc./5.36%, Scott A. Estes, Scott R. Trumbull *(17 Owners included in Index)*

Financial Data: Fiscal Year End:12/31 **Latest Annual Data:** 12/31/2006

Year	Sales	Net Income
2006	$322,824,000	$102,750,000
2005	$281,847,000	$84,286,000
2004	$251,395,000	$85,371,000

Curr. Assets:	$132,360,000	**Curr. Liab.:**	$101,588,000	**P/E Ratio:**	33.06
Plant, Equip.:	$3,935,851,000	**Total Liab.:**	$2,299,589,000	**Indic. Yr. Divd.:**	$2.640
Total Assets:	$4,280,610,000	**Net Worth:**	$1,978,793,000	**Debt/ Equity:**	1.1452

Health Discovery Corp

1116 S Old Temple Rd. , Lorena, TX, 76655; *PH:* 1-512-583-4500;
http:// www.healthdiscoverycorp.com; *Email:* info@healthdiscoverycorp.com

General - Incorporation	TX	Stock - Price on:12/24/2007	$0.1
Employees	5	Stock Exchange	OTC
Auditor	Porter Keadle Moore LLP	Ticker Symbol	HDVY
Stk Agt	Corporate Stock Transfer, Inc.	Outstanding Shares	116,490,000
Counsel	Mr. Williams	E.P.S.	-$0.02
DUNS No.	NA	Shareholders	NA

Business: The group's principle activity is to develop technology for a wireless telephone system. The group was formed in 1997 for the purpose of developing and exploiting a wireless telephone technology intended to eliminate the need for expensive control towers and related equipment currently in use in the cellular communications industry. The group does not have any revenue producing operation presently. The group's quarterly revenue for Sep'07 was 0.02 millions of USD.

Primary SIC and add'l.: 4899
CIK No: 0001141788
Officers: Stephen D. Barnhill/Chmn., CEO, Ramananda K. Madyastha/Sr. VP - Research, Development, Hong Zhang/Sr. VP - Computational Medicine, Robert S. Braswell/52/Dir., Sr. VP, Daniel R. Furth/Principal Financial Officer, Exec. VP, Sec., Treasurer
Directors: Stephen D. Barnhill/Chmn., CEO, Herbert A. Fritsche/Chmn. - Scientific Advisory Board, Kary Mullis/Member - Scientific Advisory Board, Robert S. Braswell/52/Dir., Sr. VP, Thomas A. Stamey/Member - Scientific Advisory Board, Vladimir Vapnik/Member - Scientific Advisory Board, Isabelle Guyon/Member - Scientific Advisory Board, Bernhard Scholkopf/Member - Scientific Advisory Board, Ken Welsh/Member - Scientific Advisory Board, Tin-Chuen Yeung/Member - Scientific Advisory Board, William M. Goldstein/Dir., William F. Quirk/Dir., Richard Caruso/Dir., Jimmy Woodward/Dir.
Owners: William Goldstein/9.90%, Stephen D. Barnhill/20.38%, William Quirk/16.21%, Insiders/40.58%, Daniel R. Furth/5.60%

Financial Data: Fiscal Year End:12/31 **Latest Annual Data:** 12/31/2006

Year	Sales	Net Income
2006	$204,000	-$2,596,000
2005	$227,000	-$3,159,000
2004	$0	-$2,205,000

Curr. Assets:	$750,000	**Curr. Liab.:**	$490,000		
Plant, Equip.:	$15,000	**Total Liab.:**	$2,157,000	**Indic. Yr. Divd.:**	NA
Total Assets:	$4,070,000	**Net Worth:**	$1,914,000	**Debt/ Equity:**	1.0917

Health Enhancement Products Inc

7740 E Evans Rd., Ste. A101, Scottsdale, AZ, 85260; *PH:* 1-480-385-3800; *Fax:* 1-480-385-3801;
http:// www.heponline.com; *Email:* investors@heponline.com

General - Incorporation	NV	Stock - Price on:12/24/2007	$0.61
Employees	7	Stock Exchange	OTC
Auditor	Wolinetz, Lafazan & Company, P.C.	Ticker Symbol	HEPI
Stk Agt	Interwest Transfer Company, Inc.	Outstanding Shares	42,340,000
Counsel	NA	E.P.S.	-$0.06
DUNS No.	NA	Shareholders	NA

Business: The groups principle activities include selecting and marketing the natural and herbal products. The product of the group is ProAlgaZyme. The group markets its products under the brandname ProAlgaZyme(TM). The group operates from the United States.

Primary SIC and add'l.: 2000
CIK No: 0001101026
Subsidiaries: Health Enhancement Corporation
Officers: Tiffany Thomas/Biologist, John Gorman/Sales Mgr., Janet Crance/CFO
Directors: Michael Tempesta/Member - Scientific Advisory Board, Hamilton Jordan/Member - Scientific Advisory Board, Matt Vincent/Member - Scientific Advisory Board, Mark Anderson/Member - Scientific Advisory Board
Owners: Kae Park/8.40%, Howard R. Baer/24.30%, John Gorman, Insiders/1.10%, John Gantt/10.70%, William J. Rogers/9.70%, Janet L. Crance, Tom Ingolia

Financial Data: Fiscal Year End:12/31 **Latest Annual Data:** 12/31/2006

Year	Sales	Net Income
2006	$297,000	-$3,541,000
2005	$96,000	-$5,957,000
2004	$49,000	-$3,859,000

Curr. Assets:	$56,000	**Curr. Liab.:**	$1,092,000		
Plant, Equip.:	$132,000	**Total Liab.:**	$1,154,000	**Indic. Yr. Divd.:**	NA
Total Assets:	$322,000	**Net Worth:**	-$833,000	**Debt/ Equity:**	NA

Health Fitness Corp

3600 American Blvd. W, Ste. 560, Bloomington, MN, 55431; *PH:* 1-952-831-6830;
Fax: 1-952-897-5173; *http://* www.hfit.com; *Email:* info@hfit.com

General - Incorporation	MN	Stock - Price on:12/24/2007	$2.9
Employees	833	Stock Exchange	OTC
Auditor	Grant Thornton LLP	Ticker Symbol	HFIT
Stk Agt	Computershare Trust Co	Outstanding Shares	19,690,000
Counsel	Fredrikson & Byron	E.P.S.	$0.12
DUNS No.	18-319-6138	Shareholders	NA

Business: The group principal activity is to provide fitness and wellness management services and programs to corporations, hospitals, communities and universities. Fitness center based services include the development, marketing and management of corporate, hospital and community-based fitness centers, health related programming and on-site physical therapy and occupational health services. The group also provides injury prevention programs and on-site physical therapy services. The group is under contract to manage 187 corporate and 8 hospital, community or university based fitness centers. The group conducts its operations primarily in the United States and Canada. On 08-Dec-2003, the group acquired business assets of the health & fitness services division of johnson & johnson health care systems inc.

Primary SIC and add'l.: 7991
CIK No: 0000886432
Subsidiaries: Fitness Centers of America, Inc., Health Fitness Corporation of Canada, Inc., Health Fitness Rehab, Inc.
Officers: Gregg O. Lehman/CEO, Pres., Peter Egan/Chief Science Officer, John Ellis/CIO, Mike Seethale/National VP - New Business Development, Katherine Meacham Hamlin/VP - Health Management Accounting Services/$183,466.00, David Hurt/VP - Fitness Management Accounting Services, Wesley W. Winnekins/CFO, Treasurer/$235,970.00, Brian Gagne/National VP - Operations/$202,837.00, Scott Kinzer/National VP - Business Development, Jeanne Crawford/VP - Human Resources, Debra Marshall/VP - Marketing
Owners: Gruber & McBaine Capital Management/7.25%, Jerry V. Noyce/2.90%, Pequot Capital Management, Inc./12.03%, Jeanne C. Crawford, James A. Bernards, Insiders/11.81%, Perkins Capital Management, Inc./13.41%, Rodney A. Young, Magnetar Capital Master Fund, Ltd./9.73%, John C. Penn, Linda Hall Whitman, James K. Ehlen, Brian Gagne, Wesley W. Winnekins, Mark W. Sheffert *(18 Owners included in Index)*

Financial Data: Fiscal Year End:12/31 **Latest Annual Data:** 12/31/2006

Year	Sales	Net Income
2006	$63,579,000	$3,025,000
2005	$54,942,000	$1,345,000
2004	$52,455,000	$1,674,000

Curr. Assets:	$14,312,000	**Curr. Liab.:**	$8,521,000	**P/E Ratio:**	24.17
Plant, Equip.:	$768,000	**Total Liab.:**	$8,521,000	**Indic. Yr. Divd.:**	NA
Total Assets:	$32,318,000	**Net Worth:**	$23,798,000	**Debt/ Equity:**	NA

Health Management Associates Inc

5811 Pelican Bay Blvd., Ste. 500, Naples, FL, 34108; *PH:* 1-239-598-3131; *Fax:* 1-239-598-2705;
http:// www.hma-corp.com; *Email:* info@hma.org

General - Incorporation	DE	Stock - Price on:12/24/2007	$11.41
Employees	34,500	Stock Exchange	NYSE
Auditor	Ernst & Young LLP	Ticker Symbol	HMA
Stk Agt	American Stock Transfer & Trust Co.	Outstanding Shares	242,310,000
Counsel	NA	E.P.S.	$0.39
DUNS No.	08-619-0493	Shareholders	NA

Business: The groups principle activity is to provide general acute care health services. The group provides medical and surgical services include inpatient care, intensive and cardiac care, diagnostic services and emergency services. The group provides outpatient services include one-day surgery, laboratory, X-ray, respiratory therapy, cardiology and physical therapy. The groups specialty services include oncology, radiation therapy, CT scanning, MRI imaging, lithotripsy and full service obstetrics. The group operates from United States.

Primary SIC and add'l.: 8063 8062
CIK No: 0000792985
Subsidiaries: Alabama HMA Physician Management, Inc., Amory HMA Physician Management Group, Inc., Amory HMA, Inc., Anniston HMA, Inc., Augusta HMA, Inc., Bartow HMA, Inc., Biloxi H.M.A., Inc., Biloxi HMA Physician Management, Inc., Brandon HMA, Inc., Brooksville HMA Physician Management, Inc., Canton HMA, Inc., Carlisle HMA Physician Management, Inc., Carlisle HMA, Inc., Chester HMA Physician Management, Inc., Chester HMA, Inc. 115 Subsidiaries included in the Index
Officers: Burke W. Whitman/52/Dir., CEO, Pres./$3,015,882.00, Kelly E. Curry/COO, Exec. VP, Joseph C. Meek/VP, Corporate Treasurer, John C. Merriwether/VP - Financial Relations, Peter E. Farnham/CFO, Sr. VP/$1,071,366.00, Jon P. Vollmer/Exec. VP - Operations/$984,336.00, Timothy R. Parry/Sr. VP, General Counsel, Peter M. Lawson/Exec. VP - Operations/$978,818.00
Directors: Burke W. Whitman/52/Dir., CEO, Pres., William J. Schoen/73/Chmn., Joseph V. Vumbacco/63/Vice Chmn., Donald E. Kiernan/67/Dir., Robert A. Knox/56/Dir., William E. Mayberry/78/Dir., Randolph W. Westerfield/66/Dir., Kent P. Dauten/52/Dir., William C. Steere/71/Dir., Vicki A. O'Meara/Dir.
Owners: Jon P. Vollmer, Burke W. Whitman, T. Rowe Price Associates, Inc./5.40%, Private Capital Management/7.80%, William C. Steere, William E. Mayberry, FMR Corp./11.00%, Randolph W. Westerfield, Donald E. Kiernan, Vicki A. OMeara, Insiders/6.00%, Wellington Management Company/6.10%, William J. Schoen/4.20%, Kent P. Dauten, Robert E. Farnham *(19 Owners included in Index)*

Financial Data: Fiscal Year End:09/30 **Latest Annual Data:** 12/31/2006

Year	Sales	Net Income
2006	$4,056,599,000	$182,749,000
2005	$3,588,822,000	$353,077,000
2004	$3,205,885,000	$325,099,000

Curr. Assets:	$988,155,000	**Curr. Liab.:**	$1,068,857,000	**P/E Ratio:**	29.26
Plant, Equip.:	$2,032,752,000	**Total Liab.:**	$1,652,884,000	**Indic. Yr. Divd.:**	$0.240
Total Assets:	$3,988,171,000	**Net Worth:**	$2,289,459,000	**Debt/ Equity:**	52.7594

Health Net Inc

21650 Oxnard St., Woodland Hills, CA, 91367; *PH:* 1-818-676-6000; *Fax:* 1-818-676-8591;
http:// www.healthnet.com; *Email:* investor.relations@healthnet.com

General - Incorporation	DE	**Stock**- Price on:12/24/2007	$53.82
Employees	9,725	Stock Exchange	NYSE
Auditor	Deloitte & Touche LLP	Ticker Symbol	HNT
Stk Agt	Wells Fargo Bank, N.A.	Outstanding Shares	112,250,000
Counsel	NA	E.P.S	$1.40
DUNS No.	79-833-0908	Shareholders	NA

Business: The group's principle activity is to provide managed health care services. The group operates through two segments namely health plan services and government contracts. The group operates from United States.

Primary SIC and add'l.: 8099

CIK No: 0000916085

Subsidiaries: Catalina Behavioral Health Services, Inc. (AZ), East Los Angeles Doctors Hospital, Inc. (CA), Employ Better Care, Inc. (PA), FH Assurance Company (Cayman Islands), FH Surgery Centers, Inc. (CA), FH Surgery Limited, Inc. (CA), FOHP, Inc. (NJ), Foundation Health Facilities, Inc. (CA), Greater Atlantic Health Service, Inc. (DE), Greater Atlantic Preferred Plus, Inc. (PA), Greater Sacramento Surgery Center Limited Partnership (CA), Health Management Center, Inc. (MA), Health Net Community Solutions, Inc., Health Net Federal Services of Hawaii, Inc. (HI), Health Net Federal Services, LLC(DE) 53 Subsidiaries included in the Index

Officers: Steven Sell/CEO, Pres. - MHN, Jay M. Gellert/Dir., CEO, Pres./$5,232,780.00, Stephen D. Lynch/Pres. - Regional Health Plans/$1,693,829.00, John P. Sivori/Pres. - Health Net Pharmaceutical Services, Sr. VP, Linda V. Tiano/Sr. VP, General Counsel, Sec., David W. Olson/Sr. VP - Corporate Communications, James E. Woys/Pres. - Government, Specialty Services/$2,181,624.00, Karin D. Mayhew/Sr. VP - Organization Effectiveness, Joseph C. Capezza/CFO, Mark S. El-Tawil/Chief Sr. Products Officer, Steven H. Nelson/Pres. - Health Net, Northeast, Inc

Directors: Jay M. Gellert/Dir., CEO, Pres., Roger F. Greaves/Chmn., Patrick Foley/Dir., Gale S. Fitzgerald/Dir., Theodore F. Craver/Dir., Frederick C. Yeager/Dir., Thomas T. Farley/Dir., Vicki B. Escarra/Dir., Bruce G. Willison/Dir.

Owners: Wellington Management Company, LLP/6.12%, Thomas T. Farley, Roger F. Greaves, Gale S. Fitzgerald, Stephen D. Lynch, Bruce G. Willison, Frederick C. Yeager, Legg Mason Capital Management, Inc./17.64%, Insiders/3.32%, Curtis B. Westen, Steve H. Nelson, Theodore F. Craver, AMVESCAP PLC and related entities/5.16%, Jay M. Gellert/2.14%, Patrick Foley *(17 Owners included in Index)*

Financial Data: ***Fiscal Year End:***12/31 ***Latest Annual Data:*** 12/31/2006

Year	Sales	Net Income
2006	$12,908,350,000	$329,313,000
2005	$11,940,533,000	$229,785,000
2004	$11,646,393,000	$42,604,000

Curr. Assets:	$3,217,846,000	***Curr. Liab.:***	$2,109,503,000	***P/E Ratio:***	17.59
Plant, Equip.:	$151,184,000	***Total Liab.:***	$2,518,057,000	***Indic. Yr. Divd.:***	NA
Total Assets:	$4,297,022,000	***Net Worth:***	$1,778,965,000	***Debt/ Equity:***	0.2147

Health Sciences Group Inc

Howard Hughes Ctr, 6080 Ctr. Dr., 6th Fl., Los Angeles, CA, 90045; ***PH:*** 1-310-242-6700; ***Fax:*** 1-310-362-8607; ***http://*** www.healthsciencesgroup.com

General - Incorporation	DE	**Stock**- Price on:12/24/2007	NA
Employees	2	Stock Exchange	OTC
Auditor	Corbin & Co LLP	Ticker Symbol	HESG
Stk Agt	Transfer Online, Inc.	Outstanding Shares	NA
Counsel	NA	E.P.S	-$0.126
DUNS No.	NA	Shareholders	NA

Business: The group's principal activity is to acquire and integrate into a collaborative network, companies operating in the field of pharmaceuticals, nutraceuticals and biotechnology. The group will leverage the benefits of its public status, the knowledge of its executive management team and access to capital resources of its strategic investors to assist in developing the business strategies, operations and management teams of companies it acquires. The group acquired quality botanical ingredients, inc on 25-Feb-2003.

Primary SIC and add'l.: 2834

CIK No: 0001127696

Subsidiaries: UTEK Corporation

Officers: Stuart Avery Gold/CEO, Fred E. Tannous/CFO, Co - Chmn.

Directors: Fred E. Tannous/CFO, Co - Chmn., Bill Glaser/Chmn., William T. Walker/75/Dir., Merrill A. McPeak/71/Dir.

Owners: Insiders/23.80%, Fred E. Tannous/8.00%, UTEK Corporation/6.85%, Stuart Avery Gold/0.68%, Sid L. Anderson/0.65%, Merrill A. McPeak/0.68%, William T. Walker, Bill Glaser/8.26%

Financial Data: ***Fiscal Year End:***12/31 ***Latest Annual Data:*** 12/31/2005

Year	Sales	Net Income
2005	$60,000	-$5,750,000
2004	$3,257,000	-$10,442,000
2003	$17,771,000	-$7,419,000

Curr. Assets:	$131,000	***Curr. Liab.:***	$5,029,000		
Plant, Equip.:	NA	***Total Liab.:***	$6,240,000	***Indic. Yr. Divd.:***	NA
Total Assets:	$4,156,000	***Net Worth:***	-$4,911,000	***Debt/ Equity:***	NA

Health Systems Solutions Inc

405 N Reo St., Ste. 300, Tampa, FL, 33609; ***PH:*** 1-813-282-3303; ***Fax:*** 1-813-282-8907; ***http://*** www.hqsonline.com

General - Incorporation	NV	**Stock**- Price on:12/24/2007	$0.7
Employees	84	Stock Exchange	OTC
Auditor	Sherb & Co. LLP	Ticker Symbol	HSSO
Stk Agt	Florida Atlantic Stock Transfer, Inc.	Outstanding Shares	6,410,000
Counsel	NA	E.P.S	-$0.66
DUNS No.	NA	Shareholders	NA

Business: The group is in development stage. The group operates from United States.

Primary SIC and add'l.: 6799

CIK No: 0001093913

Subsidiaries: Healthcare Quality Solutions, Inc

Officers: B. M. Milvain/71/Dir., CEO, Pres./$180,996.00, Stanley Vashovsky/Chmn., CEO, Michael G. Levine/CFO, Exec. VP, Susan Baxter Gibson/50/CFO, VP, Tom Lillis/Sr. VP, Winston Charlton/Dir. - Customer Support, Information Management Services, Virginia Tomic/VP - Product Management, Marketing, Fred Tanzer/Dir. - Implementation Services, Ted E. Weaver/CTO

Directors: B. M. Milvain/71/Dir., CEO, Pres., Stanley Vashovsky/Chmn., CEO, Batsheva Schreiber/61/Dir., Steven Katz/60/Dir., Randall J. Frapart/49/Dir., Wayne Leroux/65/Dir.

Owners: Susan Baxter Gibson, Steven Katz, Stanford International Bank Ltd./82.50%, Batsheva Schreiber, Insiders/2.30%, B. M. Milvain/1.90%

Financial Data: ***Fiscal Year End:***12/31 ***Latest Annual Data:*** 12/31/2006

Year	Sales	Net Income
2006	$6,577,000	-$2,456,000
2005	$4,213,000	-$490,000
2004	$3,638,000	-$1,125,000

Curr. Assets:	$1,589,000	***Curr. Liab.:***	$2,491,000		
Plant, Equip.:	$275,000	***Total Liab.:***	$2,491,000	***Indic. Yr. Divd.:***	NA
Total Assets:	$5,839,000	***Net Worth:***	$3,348,000	***Debt/ Equity:***	NA

HealthAxis Inc

7301 N State Hwy. 161, Ste. 300, Irving, TX, 75039; ***PH:*** 1-972-443-5000; ***Fax:*** 1-972-556-0572; ***http://*** www.healthaxis.com

General - Incorporation	PA	**Stock**- Price on:12/24/2007	$1.73
Employees	72	Stock Exchange	NDQ
Auditor	McGladrey & Pullen LLP	Ticker Symbol	HAXS
Stk Agt	Mellon Investor Services LLC	Outstanding Shares	8,620,000
Counsel	NA	E.P.S	-$0.04
DUNS No.	15-729-4612	Shareholders	NA

Business: The group's principal activity is to provide software and application integration services that assists the clients in using the Internet for health insurance distribution and administration. The group operates through three segments: benefit administration and claims processing system, Web connectivity products and business processing outsourcing services. The benefit administration and processing system provides Web-enabled systems for administration and processing of health insurance claims. The Web connectivity products provide Web-enabled platforms and solutions for self-service individuals, enrollment, sale/distribution and post-sale administration of group and individual insurance policies. The business process outsourcing services provides electronic data capture, imaging, storage and retrieval of health insurance claims, attachments and other correspondence.

Primary SIC and add'l.: 7379

CIK No: 0000768892

Subsidiaries: Healthaxis Imaging Services, LLC., Healthaxis Limited Partner, LLC, Healthaxis Managing Partner, LLC., Healthaxis, Ltd., Healthaxis.com, Inc., Satellite Image Systems (Jamaica) Limited

Officers: Paula Ringlbauer/55/VP - Product Management

Owners: LB I Group Inc./7.90%, Lewis Asset Management/27.80%, Sharad K. Tak/47.30%, Kevin F. Hickey, James W. McLane/4.20%, James J. Byrne, Barry L. Reisig, Roxanne Seale, Ronald K. Herbert, Insiders/11.80%, Brent J. Webb/1.50%, John W. Coyle, Lawrence F. Thompson, Adam J. Gutstein, Thomas L. Cunningham *(16 Owners included in Index)*

Financial Data: ***Fiscal Year End:***12/31 ***Latest Annual Data:*** 12/31/2006

Year	Sales	Net Income
2006	$16,674,000	-$526,000
2005	$15,705,000	-$2,251,000
2004	$16,162,000	-$5,958,000

Curr. Assets:	$6,849,000	***Curr. Liab.:***	$5,294,000		
Plant, Equip.:	$1,550,000	***Total Liab.:***	$6,996,000	***Indic. Yr. Divd.:***	NA
Total Assets:	$21,318,000	***Net Worth:***	$14,322,000	***Debt/ Equity:***	0.0637

Healthcare Acquisition Corp

One Pk. Pl., Ste. 450, Annapolis, MD, 21401; ***PH:*** 1-410-269-2600

General - Incorporation	DE	**Stock**- Price on:12/24/2007	$7.52
Employees	NA	Stock Exchange	NA
Auditor	Mccarter & English, LLP	Ticker Symbol	NA
Stk Agt	Continental Stock Transfer & Trust Co	Outstanding Shares	11,650,000
Counsel	NA	E.P.S	-$1.3
DUNS No.	NA	Shareholders	NA

Business: The groups principle activities include acquiring and operating healthcare centers. The group operates from the United States.

Primary SIC and add'l.: 2834

CIK No: 0001326190

Subsidiaries: PAI Acquisition Corp

Officers: Derace L. Schaffer/59/Vice Chmn., CEO, John Pappajohn/79/Chmn., Sec., Matthew P. Kinley/40/Dir., Pres., Treasurer

Directors: Derace L. Schaffer/59/Vice Chmn., CEO, John Pappajohn/79/Chmn., Sec., Matthew P. Kinley/40/Dir., Pres., Treasurer, Edward B. Berger/78/Dir., Wayne A. Schellhammer/55/Dir.

Owners: Edward B. Berger, Insiders/24.35%, Derace L. Schaffer/9.53%, Sapling, LLC/6.00%, John Pappajohn/9.53%, Wayne A. Schellhammer, QVT Financial LP/5.50%, Andrew M. Weiss/5.30%, Matthew P. Kinley/4.79%, Fir Tree Recovery Master Fund, LP/2.88%

Financial Data: ***Fiscal Year End:***12/31 ***Latest Annual Data:*** 12/31/2006

Year	Sales	Net Income
2006	$1,085,000	-$187,000
2005	$586,000	$277,000

Curr. Assets:	$71,739,000	***Curr. Liab.:***	$1,046,000	***P/E Ratio:***	88.47
Plant, Equip.:	NA	***Total Liab.:***	$1,046,000	***Indic. Yr. Divd.:***	NA
Total Assets:	$71,739,000	***Net Worth:***	$57,114,000	***Debt/ Equity:***	NA

Healthcare Business Services Groups Inc

1126 W Foothill Blvd, Ste. 105, Upland, CA, 91786; ***PH:*** 1-909-608-2035; ***Fax:*** 1-909-608-1081; ***http://*** www.thenewhbsgi.com; ***Email:*** info@hbsgi.com

General - Incorporation	NV	**Stock**- Price on:12/24/2007	$0.007
Employees	13	Stock Exchange	OTC
Auditor	Kabani & Company, Inc.	Ticker Symbol	HBSV
Stk Agt	Pacific Stock Transfer Company	Outstanding Shares	50,390,000
Counsel	NA	E.P.S	-$0.077
DUNS No.	NA	Shareholders	NA

Business: The groups principle activity is to provide medical billing services. The group operates from the United States.

Primary SIC and add'l.: 8721

CIK No: 0001192069

Subsidiaries: AutoMed Software Corp., HEALTHCARE BUSINESS SERVICES GROUPS, INC, Silver Shadow Properties, LLC.

Officers: Chandana Basu/51/Dir., CEO, Treasurer, COO

Directors: Chandana Basu/51/Dir., CEO, Treasurer, COO, Narinder Grewal/54/Dir., Bharati Shah/60/Dir.

Owners: Chandana Basu/57.11%, Abhijit Bhattacharya/6.35%, Insiders/65.45%, Shahandana Z.U. Garcia/5.95%, Arjinderpal Singh Sekhon/1.98%

Financial Data: ***Fiscal Year End:***12/31 ***Latest Annual Data:*** 12/31/2006

Year	Sales	Net Income
2006	$1,012,000	-$2,998,000
2005	$1,565,000	-$1,236,000
2004	$1,667,000	-$1,879,000

Curr. Assets:	NA	***Curr. Liab.:***	$5,144,000		
Plant, Equip.:	$41,000	***Total Liab.:***	$5,144,000	***Indic. Yr. Divd.:***	NA
Total Assets:	$84,000	***Net Worth:***	-$5,061,000	***Debt/ Equity:***	NA

Healthcare Realty Trust Inc

3310 W End Ave., Ste. 700, Nashville, TN, 37203; ***PH:*** 1-615-269-8175; ***Fax:*** 1-615-269-8461; ***http://*** www.healthcarerealty.com; ***Email:*** communications@healthcarerealty.com

General - Incorporation	MD	**Stock**- Price on:12/24/2007	$29.31
Employees	201	Stock Exchange	NYSE
Auditor	BDO Seidman, LLP	Ticker Symbol	HR
Stk Agt	Computershare Investor Services LLC	Outstanding Shares	47,820,000
Counsel	NA	E.P.S	$1.33
DUNS No.	NA	Shareholders	NA

Business: The groups principal activities include owning, acquiring, managing and developing real estate properties associated with healthcare services. The group also provides mortgage financing on healthcare facilities. In the year 2006, the group acquired three properties. The group operates from the United States.

Primary SIC and add'l.: 6798

CIK No: 0000899749

Subsidiaries: 593HR, Inc., Bellaire Medical Plaza SPE, LLC, Chippenham Medical Offices SPE, LLC, Durham Medical Office Building, Inc., Healthcare Acquisition of Texas, Inc., Healthcare Realty Services Incorporated, HR Farmington, LLC, HR Novi, LLC, HR Acquisition I Corporation, HR Acquisition of Alabama, Inc., HR Acquisition of Pennsylvania, Inc., HR Acquisition of San Antonio, Ltd., HR Acquisition of Virginia Limited Partnership, HR Assets, Inc. (inactive), HR Assets, LLC 46 Subsidiaries included in the Index

Officers: David R. Emery/Chmn., CEO/$1,331,147.00, Charles Raymond Fernandez/64/CEO, Chief Medical Officer - Piedmont Clinic, Atlanta, Georgia, Glenn D. Herndon/Assoc. VP, Controller - not Pictured, Amy A. Byrd/VP, National Asset Mgr., J.D. Carter Steele/58/Sr. VP/$434,742.00, Gilbert T. Irvin/VP - Operations, Anne C. Barbour/VP, National Asset Mgr., Chad D. McIntyre/Assoc. VP, Dir. - Operations, Julie A. Wilson/VP, National Asset Mgr., Steve L. Standifer/VP - Design, Construction, Revell M. Lester/Assoc. VP - Project Development Services, Stephen D. Denney/Assoc. VP - Real Estate Investments, James C. Douglas/VP - Asset Administration, Todd J. Meredith/VP - Real Estate Investments, Matthew J. Lederer/Assoc. VP - Real Estate Investments *(33 Officers included in Index)*

Directors: David R. Emery/Chmn., CEO, Marliese E. Mooney/Dir., Knox J. Singleton/Dir., Dan S. Wilford/Dir., Batey M. Gresham/Dir., Bruce D. Sullivan/Dir., Edwin B. Morris/Dir., Raymond C. Fernandez/Dir., Errol L. Biggs/Dir.

Owners: Dan S. Wilford, Bruce D. Sullivan, Edwin B. Morris, All executive officers and directors as a group/2.30%, David R. Emery/2.01%, The Vanguard Group, Inc./5.82%, Marliese E. Mooney, Insiders/6.24%, Batey M. Gresham, Scott W. Holmes, Douglas B. Whitman, Errol L. Biggs, Carter J.D. Steele, Charles Raymond Fernandez, John Knox Singleton *(16 Owners included in Index)*

Financial Data: ***Fiscal Year End:***12/31 ***Latest Annual Data:*** 12/31/2006

Year	Sales	Net Income
2006	$264,882,000	$39,719,000
2005	$254,536,000	$52,668,000
2004	$234,069,000	$55,533,000

Curr. Assets:	$1,950,000	***Curr. Liab.:***	$32,448,000	***P/E Ratio:***	33.06
Plant, Equip.:	$1,558,620,000	***Total Liab.:***	$908,967,000	***Indic. Yr. Divd.:***	$1.540
Total Assets:	$1,734,639,000	***Net Worth:***	$825,672,000	***Debt/ Equity:***	NA

Healthcare Services Group Inc

3220 Tillman Dr., Ste. 300, Bensalem, PA, 19020; ***PH:*** 1-215-639-8191; ***Fax:*** 1-215-639-2152; ***http://*** www.hcsgcorp.com; ***Email:*** info@hcsgcorp.com

General - Incorporation	PA	**Stock**- Price on:12/24/2007	$28.08
Employees	23,600	Stock Exchange	NDQ
Auditor	Grant Thornton LLP	Ticker Symbol	HCSG
Stk Agt	American Stock Transfer & Trust Co.	Outstanding Shares	27,730,000
Counsel	Olshan Grundman Frome Et Al	E.P.S	$0.65
DUNS No.	08-419-2111	Shareholders	NA

Business: The group's principal activity is to provide management and administrative services to the housekeeping, laundry, linen, facility maintenance and food service departments of the health care industry. Housekeeping services include cleaning, disinfecting and sanitizing resident areas in the facilities. Laundry and linen services involve laundering and processing of the residents' personal clothing. Food services consist of the development of a menu that meets the residents' dietary needs, purchasing and preparing the food to assure the residents receive an appetizing meal, and participation in monitoring the residents' on-going nutrition status. Maintenance services consist of repair and maintenance of laundry equipment, plumbing and electrical systems, as well as carpentry and painting.

Primary SIC and add'l.: 7349 5812 7219 7213

CIK No: 0000731012

Subsidiaries: HCSG Supply, Inc, Huntingdon Holdings, Inc

Officers: Daniel P. McCartney/Chmn., CEO/$1,055,120.00, Thomas Cook/COO, Pres./$1,074,468.00

Directors: Daniel P. McCartney/Chmn., CEO, Dino D. Ottaviano/60/Dir.

Owners: Insiders/12.50%, Robert L. Frome, Daniel P. McCartney/8.50%, Barton D. Weisman, Wells Capital Management Incorporated/7.10%, Thomas A. Cook/2.00%, Richard W. Hudson, John M. Briggs, Robert J. Moss, Joseph F. McCartney, Pequot Capital Management, Inc./6.00%, James L. DiStefano, Advisory Research Inc./8.80%

Financial Data: ***Fiscal Year End:***12/31 ***Latest Annual Data:*** 12/31/2006

Year	Sales	Net Income
2006	$511,631,000	$25,452,000
2005	$466,291,000	$19,096,000
2004	$442,568,000	$14,699,000

Curr. Assets:	$168,237,000	***Curr. Liab.:***	$27,610,000	***P/E Ratio:***	29.87
Plant, Equip.:	$4,875,000	***Total Liab.:***	$50,079,000	***Indic. Yr. Divd.:***	$0.430
Total Assets:	$215,556,000	***Net Worth:***	$165,477,000	***Debt/ Equity:***	NA

Healthcare Technologies Ltd

32 Hashacham St., Petach Tikva, 49170; ***PH:*** 972-39277227; ***Fax:*** 972-39277228; ***http://*** www.hctech.com; ***Email:*** contact@hctech.com

General - Incorporation	Israel	**Stock**- Price on:12/24/2007	$1.2157
Employees	115	Stock Exchange	NDQ
Auditor	Kost Forer Gabbay & Kasierer	Ticker Symbol	HCTL
Stk Agt	Continental Stock Transfer & Trust Co	Outstanding Shares	7,700,000
Counsel	NA	E.P.S	$0.03
DUNS No.	60-011-4474	Shareholders	NA

Business: The groups principle activities include development, manufacturing and marketing of medical diagnostic kits for diagnosing infectious diseases, in particular sexually transmitted diseases and diseases of the urinary and respiratory tracts as well as detection of drugs of abuse and the diagnosis of thyroid conditions, fertility hormones and other steroid-related disorders, and monitoring of certain therapeutic drugs and tumor markers; and imports, markets, distributes and sells products for the biotechnology industry, including instruments and reagents, filtration systems and membranes, analytical and laboratory systems, and consumables. The group operates from United States.

Primary SIC and add'l.: 5049 2835

CIK No: 0000835688

Subsidiaries: Diatech Diagnostica Inc, Gamida Gen Marketing Ltd., Gamida MedEquip Ltd., Procognia (Israel) Ltd, Pronto Technologies Ltd. (Pronto), The Gamidor Group

Officers: Moshe Rehuveni/Dir., CEO, Eran Rotem/Dir., CFO

Directors: Moshe Rehuveni/Dir., CEO, Daniel Kropf/Chmn., Israel Amir/Dir., Rolando Eisen/Dir., Luly Gurevich/Dir., Elan Penn/External Dir., Eran Rotem/Dir., CFO, Yacob Ofer/Dir., Varda Rotter/External Dir., Ethan Rubinstein/Dir., Samuel Pinchas/Dir., Martin J. Lee/Dir.

Owners: Gamida for Life B.V./62.00%

Financial Data: ***Fiscal Year End:***12/31 ***Latest Annual Data:*** 12/31/2006

Year	Sales	Net Income
2006	$13,656,000	$210,000
2005	$12,053,000	$276,000
2004	$12,130,000	-$359,000

Curr. Assets:	$7,672,000	***Curr. Liab.:***	$5,055,000		
Plant, Equip.:	$2,197,000	***Total Liab.:***	$6,779,000	***Indic. Yr. Divd.:***	NA
Total Assets:	$14,094,000	***Net Worth:***	$7,315,000	***Debt/ Equity:***	NA

HealthExtras Inc

800 King Farm Blvd., Rockville, MD, 20850; ***PH:*** 1-301-548-2900; ***Fax:*** 1-301-548-2991; ***http://*** www.healthextras.com; ***Email:*** management@catalystrx.com

General - Incorporation	DE	**Stock**- Price on:12/24/2007	$29.58
Employees	410	Stock Exchange	NDQ
Auditor	PricewaterhouseCoopers LLP	Ticker Symbol	HLEX
Stk Agt	American Stock Transfer & Trust Co.	Outstanding Shares	41,950,000
Counsel	Dewey Ballantine	E.P.S	$0.84
DUNS No.	NA	Shareholders	NA

Business: The group's principal activities are to provide pharmacy benefit management ('pbm') services and supplemental benefit programs. The group operates in two segments namely, pharmacy benefit management and supplemental benefits. The pharmacy benefit management segment includes network pharmacy claims processing, mail order services, benefit design consultation, drug utilization review and formulary management services. The supplemental benefits segment operates under the brand name 'healthextras.' supplemental benefits programs developed by healthextras are offered to individuals and small businesses. Additionally, it operates a nationwide network of over 53,000 retail pharmacies. The group has operations in the United States. The group's clients include managed-care organizations, self-insured employers and third-party administrators. On 22-Jun-2004 group acquired managed healthcare systems inc.

Primary SIC and add'l.: 7375 6324

CIK No: 0001090403

Subsidiaries: Catalyst Consultants, Catalyst Rx, Catalyst Rx Government Services, Inc., EBRx, Inc., HealthExtras Benefits Administrator, Inc., Managed Care of America, Inc., Managed Healthcare Systems, Inc., U.S. Scripts, Inc.

Officers: David T. Blair/Dir., CEO, Thomas M. Farah/General Counsel, Corp. Sec., Nick J. Grujich/COO, Exec. VP, Michael P. Donovan/CFO, Exec. VP

Directors: David T. Blair/Dir., CEO, Edward S. Civera/Chmn., Steven B. Epstein/Dir., William E. Brock/Dir., Dale B. Wolf/Dir., Michael R. McDonnell/Dir., Thomas L. Blair/Dir., Daniel J. Houston/Dir., Kenneth A. Samet/Dir.

Owners: Michael R. McDonnell, David T. Blair/2.80%, Michael P. Donovan/1.90%, William E. Brock, Insiders/13.80%, T. Rowe Price Associates, Inc./7.60%, Artisan Partners Limited Partnership/5.20%, Kenneth A. Samet, Steven B. Epstein, Richard W. Hunt, Principal Financial Group, Inc./12.60%, Dale B. Wolf, Thomas L. Blair/8.10%, Nick J. Grujich, Edward S. Civera *(16 Owners included in Index)*

Financial Data: ***Fiscal Year End:***12/31 ***Latest Annual Data:*** 12/31/2006

Year	Sales	Net Income
2006	$1,271,006,000	$31,574,000
2005	$694,519,000	$22,980,000
2004	$521,325,000	$16,383,000

Curr. Assets:	$267,574,000	Curr. Liab.:	$181,797,000	P/E Ratio:	33.24
Plant, Equip.:	$12,859,000	Total Liab.:	$194,729,000	Indic. Yr. Divd.:	NA
Total Assets:	$436,024,000	Net Worth:	$240,047,000	Debt/ Equity:	NA

HealthGrades Inc

500 Golden Ridge Rd., Ste. 100, Golden, CO, 80401; *PH:* 1-303-716-0041; *Fax:* 1-303-716-1298; *http://* www.healthgrades.com; *Email:* media@healthgrades.com

General - Incorporation	DE	Stock- Price on:12/24/2007	$6.39
Employees	123	Stock Exchange	NDQ
Auditor	Grant Thornton LLP	Ticker Symbol	HGRD
Stk Agt...... American Stock Transfer & Trust Co.		Outstanding Shares	29,790,000
Counsel	Morgan, Lewis & Bockius LLP	E.P.S.	$0.19
DUNS No.	94-918-8064	Shareholders	NA

Business: The group's principle activity is to provide healthcare ratings, advisory services and other healthcare information. Ratings and advisory provides marketing arrangements for hospitals and licensing of its content. Physician practice services provides management services to physician practices. The customers of the group include healthcare providers, employees, health plans, insurance companies and consumers. The group provides basic and expanded profile information for a variety of providers and facilities. The group's quarterly revenue for Sep'07 was 8.11 millions of USD.

Primary SIC and add'l.: 8099 8093

CIK No: 0001027915

Officers: Kerry R. Hicks/Chmn., CEO/$499,079.00, Allen Dodge/CFO, Exec. VP/$228,328.00, Sarah P. Loughran/Exec. VP/$249,535.00, David G. Hicks/Exec. VP/$254,352.00, Tod Baker/Sr. VP - Internet Patient Acquisition, Kirk Schreck/Sr. VP - Provider Sales, Samantha Collier/Sr. VP - Medical Affairs, Chief Medical Officer

Directors: Kerry R. Hicks/Chmn., CEO, Leslie S. Matthews/Dir., John Quattrone/Dir., J. D. Kleinke/Dir., Mary Boland/Dir., Michael J. Beaudoin/Dir.

Owners: Steve Wood, Janus Capital Management LLC/5.70%, Healthinvest Partners AB/5.40%, Leslie S. Matthews, Sarah Loughran/5.20%, Insiders/26.00%, J. D. Kleinke, Kerry R. Hicks/14.10%, Allen Dodge/2.60%, Magnetar Capital Partners LP/8.60%, David G. Hicks/5.60%, John Quattrone, FMR Corp./14.40%, Mary Boland

Financial Data: Fiscal Year End:12/31 Latest Annual Data: 12/31/2006

Year	Sales	Net Income
2006	$27,770,000	$3,182,000
2005	$20,808,000	$4,140,000
2004	$14,538,000	$1,782,000

Curr. Assets:	$25,632,000	Curr. Liab.:	$18,604,000	P/E Ratio:	33.63
Plant, Equip.:	$1,766,000	Total Liab.:	$18,876,000	Indic. Yr. Divd.:	NA
Total Assets:	$31,020,000	Net Worth:	$12,143,000	Debt/ Equity:	0.0003

HealthMarkets Inc

Formerly: UICI
9151 Blvd. 26, North Richland Hills, TX, 76180; *PH:* 1-817-255-5200; *http://* www.healthmarkets.com

General - Incorporation	DE	Stock- Price on:12/24/2007	NA
Employees	NA	Stock Exchange	NA
Auditor	KPMG LLP	Ticker Symbol	NA
Stk Agt	Mellon Investor Services LLC	Outstanding Shares	NA
Counsel	NA	E.P.S.	NA
DUNS No.	13-955-2087	Shareholders	NA

Business: The group's principal activity is to provide health and life insurance to self-employed individuals and individuals who work for small businesses. The group operates through insurance segment includes the self-employed agency division, the group insurance division, the life insurance division and other insurance division.

Primary SIC and add'l.: 6141 6321 6719 6311

CIK No: 0000773660

Subsidiaries: AMLI Realty Company, Benefit Administration for the Self-Employed, LLC, CFLD-I, Inc., Fidelity First Insurance Company, Financial Services Reinsurance, Ltd., MCIS, LLC, Mid-West National Life Insurance Company of Tennessee, New United Agency, Inc., Performance Driven Awards, Inc., Resolution Reinsurance Intermediaries, LLC, Success Driven Awards, Inc., The Chesapeake Life Insurance Company, The MEGA Life and Health Insurance Company, The National Student Association, LLC, U.S. Managers Life Insurance, Ltd. 20 Subsidiaries included in the Index

Officers: William J. Gedwed/Dir., CEO, Pres./$4,284,302.00, Brian W. Harrigan/Pres., CEO - ZON Re, USA, LLC, Troy A. McQuagge/Pres. - Healthmarkets Agency Marketing Group, Chmn. - UGA, Association Field Services, Cornerstone America/$5,111,483.00, Phillip J. Myhra/54/Exec. VP - Insurance Group/$5,864,139.00, Michael A. Colliflower/Exec. VP, General Counsel, Peggy G. Simpson/Corp. Sec., Asher M. Schoor/Sr. VP, James N. Plato/Pres. - Healthmarkets Life Insurance Operations/$1,918,279.00, Anthony M. Garcia/Exec. VP - Sales, Cornerstone America, Michael Boxer/CFO, Exec. VP/$382,725.00, Nancy G. Cocozza/Exec. VP, Katherine D. Phillips/VP, Chief Compliance Officer, Assoc. General Counsel, Jack V. Heller/Exec. VP - Sales, UGA, Susan Stead/Regulatory Advisory Panel Member, Jose Montemayor/Regulatory Advisory Panel Member (23 Officers included in Index)

Directors: William J. Gedwed/Dir., CEO, Pres., Allen F. Wise/Chmn., Chinh F. Chu/Dir., Adrian M. Jones/Dir., Matthew Kabaker/Dir., Andrew S. Kahr/Dir., Kamil M. Salame/Dir., Steven J. Shulman/Dir., Nathaniel M. Zilkha/32/Dir., Harvey C. Demovick/Dir., Sumit Rajpal/Dir., Mural R. Josephson/Dir.

Owners: Goldman Sachs Investor Group/22.20%, Steven J. Shulman, Insiders/1.10%, William J. Gedwed, Blackstone Investor Group/54.10%, Mark D. Hauptman, William J. Truxal, Allen F. Wise, Trustees under the HealthMarkets Agents Total Ownership Fund Trust/7.70%, Trustees under the Dynamic Equity Fund Program Trust/3.50%, Phillip J. Myhra, DLJ Investor Group/11.10%, James N. Plato, Michael E. Boxer, Troy A. McQuagge

HealthSouth Corp

1 HealthS Pkwy., Birmingham, AL, 35243; *PH:* 1-205-967-7116; *Fax:* 1-205-969-3543; *http://* www.healthS.com

General - Incorporation	DE	Stock- Price on:12/24/2007	$19.51
Employees	21,000	Stock Exchange	NYSE
Auditor	Pricewaterhousecoopers LLP	Ticker Symbol	HLS
Stk Agt	Mellon Investor Services LLC	Outstanding Shares	78,740,000
Counsel	NA	E.P.S.	NA
DUNS No.	NA	Shareholders	NA

Business: The group's principle activity is to provide rehabilitative health care and ambulatory surgery services. The group operates through five segments namely, inpatient, surgery centers, outpatient, diagnostic, and corporate and other. The group operates from the United States. The group's quarterly revenue for September 2007 was 431.60 millions of USD.

Primary SIC and add'l.: 8069 8051 8052

CIK No: 0000785161

Subsidiaries: 2121 Surgery Center, Limited Partnership, Advantage Health Corporation, Advantage Health Harmarville Rehabilitation Corporation, Advantage Rehabilitation Clinics, Inc., Alaska Surgery Center, Inc., All Care Surgery Center, Inc., Antelope Valley Surgery Center, L.P., Arcadia Outpatient Surgery Center, L.P., Arthroscopic & Laser Surgery Center of San Diego, L.P., Auburn Surgical Center, L.P., Aurora Surgery Center Limited Partnership, Austin Center For Outpatient Surgery, L.P., Bakersfield Physicians Plaza Surgical Center, L.P., Baton Rouge Rehab, Inc., Beaumont Rehab Associates LP 311 Subsidiaries included in the Index

Officers: Jay Grinney/Dir., CEO, Pres./$2,632,862.00, Michael D. Snow/53/COO, Exec. VP/$1,365,329.00, John L. Workman/CFO, Exec. VP/$1,119,982.00, John P. Whittington/Exec. VP, General Counsel, Sec., John Markus/Chief Compliance Officer, Exec. VP/$702,592.00, Joseph T. Clark/52/Pres. - Surgery Centers Division, Gregory R. Brophy/48/Pres. - Diagnostic Division, Diane L. Munson/57/Pres. - Outpatient Division, Mark J. Tarr/Exec. VP - Operations/$635,568.00, James C. Foxworthy/Chief Administrative Officer, Exec. VP/$698,254.00

Directors: Jay Grinney/Dir., CEO, Pres., Jon F. Hanson/Chmn., Edward A. Blechschmidt/Dir., Donald L. Correll/Dir., Yvonne M. Curl/Dir., Charles M. Elson/Dir., Leo I. Higdon/Dir., John E. Maupin/Dir., Edward L. Shaw/Dir., John W. Chidsey/Dir.

Owners: James C. Foxworthy, John Markus, Donald L. Correll, Edward L. Shaw, Charles M. Elson, Leo I. Higdon, Jay Grinney, Iridian Asset Management LLC/8.93%, Highfields Capital Management LP/8.38%, Insiders, TIAA-CREF Investment Management, LLC/9.11%, Edward A. Blechschmidt, John L. Workman, Michael D. Snow, Mark J. Tarr (18 Owners included in Index)

Financial Data: Fiscal Year End:12/31 Latest Annual Data: 12/31/2006

Year	Sales	Net Income
2006	$3,000,100,000	-$625,000,000
2005	$3,207,728,000	-$445,994,000
2004	$3,753,781,000	-$174,470,000

Curr. Assets:	$880,300,000	Curr. Liab.:	$1,261,600,000		
Plant, Equip.:	$1,096,000,000	Total Liab.:	$5,156,800,000	Indic. Yr. Divd.:	NA
Total Assets:	$3,359,600,000	Net Worth:	-$2,184,600,000	Debt/ Equity:	NA

Healthsport Inc

Formerly: Team Sports Entertainment Inc
7633 E 63rd Pl., Ste. 220, Tulsa, OK, 74133; *PH:* 1-877-570-4776; *http://* www.ideaseg.com

General - Incorporation	DE	Stock- Price on:12/24/2007	$2.2
Employees	NA	Stock Exchange	NA
Auditor	Creason & Assoc. PLLC	Ticker Symbol	NA
Stk Agt	Guest & Co. PC	Outstanding Shares	NA
Counsel	NA	E.P.S.	NA
DUNS No.	83-545-9710	Shareholders	NA

Business: The group's principle activity is to locate and negotiate with a business entity for the merger of that target business into the company thereafter. On 13-Sep-2004, the group acquired idea management group inc. The group operates from United States.

Primary SIC and add'l.: 7948

CIK No: 0000777516

Subsidiaries: Idea Management Group, Inc, Maxx Motorsports, Inc, Strategic Gaming Consultants, LLC, World Championship Poker, Inc

Officers: Daniel J. Kelly/46/CEO, Pres., Ross E. Silvey/79/Dir., Acting CFO, Principal Financial Officer

Directors: Ross E. Silvey/79/Dir., Acting CFO, Principal Financial Officer, Jason Freeman/33/Dir., Hank Durschlag/44/Dir.

Owners: Ross E. Silvey, Clay Cooley, Trustee/6.46%, Hank Durschlag/2.84%, Jason Freeman, Daniel J. Kelly/2.97%, Charles W. Clark/4.38%, Insiders/6.19%

Financial Data: Fiscal Year End:12/31 Latest Annual Data: 12/31/2006

Year	Sales	Net Income
2006	$1,000	-$1,438,000
2005	NA	-$1,906,000
2004	NA	-$1,016,000

Curr. Assets:	$968,000	Curr. Liab.:	$58,000		
Plant, Equip.:	NA	Total Liab.:	$58,000	Indic. Yr. Divd.:	NA
Total Assets:	$4,652,000	Net Worth:	$4,594,000	Debt/ Equity:	NA

Healthspring Inc

44 Vantage Way, Ste. 300, Nashville, TN, 37228; *PH:* 1-615-291-7000; *Fax:* 1-615-401-4566; *http://* www.myhealthspring.com

General - Incorporation	DE	Stock- Price on:12/24/2007	$18.36
Employees	1,200	Stock Exchange	NYSE
Auditor	KPMG LLP	Ticker Symbol	HS
Stk Agt ..... American Stock Transfer & Trust Co.		Outstanding Shares	57,340,000
Counsel	NA	E.P.S.	$1.42
DUNS No.	NA	Shareholders	NA

Business: The groups principle activity is to manage care organization. The group also provides health insurance program for citizens aged 65 and older, disabled persons, and persons suffering from end stage renal disease. The group operates from the United States. The group's quarterly revenue for September 2007 was 366.34 millions of USD.

Primary SIC and add'l.: 6324

CIK No: 0001339553

Subsidiaries: GulfQuest, L.P., HealthSpring Employer Services, Inc., HealthSpring Life & Health Insurance Company, Inc., HealthSpring Management of America, LLC, HealthSpring Management, Inc., HealthSpring of Alabama, Inc., HealthSpring of Illinois I, Inc., HealthSpring of Tennessee, Inc., HealthSpring USA, LLC, HouQuest, L.L.C., NewQuest Management of Alabama, LLC, NewQuest Management of Florida, LLC, NewQuest Management of Illinois, LLC, NewQuest, Inc., NewQuest, LLC 19 Subsidiaries included in the Index

Officers: Herbert A. Fritch/Chmn., CEO, Pres., Kevin M. McNamara/Exec. VP, CFO, Treasurer, Gentry J. Barden/Sr. VP, Corporate General Counsel, Sec., David L. Terry/Sr. VP, Chief Actuary, Gerald V. Coil/COO, Exec. VP, Craig S. Schub/Sr. VP, Chief Marketing Officer, Mark A. Tulloch/Sr. VP - Managed Care Operations

Directors: Herbert A. Fritch/Chmn., CEO, Pres., Robert Z. Hensley/Dir., Russell K. Mayerfeld/Dir., Joseph P. Nolan/Dir., Martin S. Rash/Dir., Bruce M. Fried/Dir., Benjamin Leon/63/Dir., Sharad Mansukani/Dir.

Owners: Russell K. Mayerfeld, FMR Corp./7.50%, Martin S. Rash, Perry Corp./9.20%, Bruce M. Fried, Gentry J. Barden, Kevin M. McNamara, Joseph P. Nolan/4.70%, Robert Z. Hensley, Insiders/17.00%, Daniel L. Timm, Jeffrey L. Rothenberger, Craig S. Schub, Herbert A. Fritch/10.10%

Financial Data: Fiscal Year End:12/31 Latest Annual Data: 12/31/2006

Year	Sales	Net Income
2006	$1,308,956,000	$80,836,000
2005	$856,763,000	$29,256,000

Curr. Assets:	$382,162,000	Curr. Liab.:	$238,538,000	P/E Ratio:	12.16
Plant, Equip.:	$8,831,000	Total Liab.:	$267,363,000	Indic. Yr. Divd.:	NA
Total Assets:	$842,645,000	Net Worth:	$575,282,000	Debt/ Equity:	NA

HealthStream Inc

209 10th Ave. S, Ste. 450, Nashville, TN, 37203; *PH:* 1-615-301-3100; *Fax:* 1-615-301-3200; *http://* www.healthstream.com; *Email:* contact@healthstream.com

General - Incorporation	TN	Stock - Price on:12/24/2007	$3.4
Employees	160	Stock Exchange	NDQ
Auditor	Ernst & Young LLP	Ticker Symbol	HSTM
Stk Agt	Suntrust Bank	Outstanding Shares	22,220,000
Counsel	Bass, Berry & Sims PLC	E.P.S.	$0.10
DUNS No.	NA	Shareholders	NA

Business: The group's principal activity is to provide Web-based solutions and services to meet the training and education needs of the healthcare industry. The group has two operating segments: healthcare organisations and professionals and pharmaceutical and medical device companies. The group provides event development and registration services, custom development services and translation of content into an interactive experience and assists in the development of other educational activities, provided through the Internet. Within healthcare organizations, the group focuses on expanding the Internet-based application service provider or asp e-learning solutions to hospitals and long-term care and outpatient facilities.

Primary SIC and add'l.: 7375 8299

CIK No: 0001095565

Subsidiaries: Data Management & Research, Inc, Education Design, Inc.

Officers: Robert A. Frist/Chmn., CEO, Pres./$254,113.00, Susan A. Brownie/43/CFO/$226,891.00, Arthur E. Newman/Exec. VP/$275,127.00, Edward J. Pearson/Sr. VP/$154,976.00, Kevin P. O'Hara/Sr. VP, General Counsel, Mollie Condra/Dir. - Investor Relations, Communications

Directors: Robert A. Frist/Chmn., CEO, Pres., James F. Daniell/Dir., Thompson S. Dent/Dir., Linda Rebrovick/Dir., William W. Stead/Dir., Frank E. Gordon/Dir., Ron Hinds/Dir., Jeffrey L. McLaren/Dir., Michael Shmerling/Dir., Gerard M. Hayden/Dir., Dale W. Polley/Dir.

Owners: Jeffrey L. McLaren/1.60%, Insiders/32.70%, Thompson S. Dent, T. Rowe Price Associates, Inc./11.20%, Robert A. Frist/25.70%, William W. Stead, Gerard M. Hayden, Morgan Stanley Dean Witter & Co./5.40%, Dale Polley, Ronald Hinds, Susan A. Brownie, James F. Daniell, Linda Rebrovick, Arthur E. Newman/1.70%, Frank Gordon/1.10% *(17 Owners included in Index)*

Financial Data: Fiscal Year End:12/31 Latest Annual Data: 12/31/2006

Year	Sales	Net Income
2006	$31,783,000	$2,500,000
2005	$27,359,000	$1,913,000
2004	$20,057,000	-$1,048,000

Curr. Assets:	$22,211,000	Curr. Liab.:	$11,063,000	P/E Ratio:	42.50
Plant, Equip.:	$2,184,000	Total Liab.:	$11,374,000	Indic. Yr. Divd.:	NA
Total Assets:	$41,008,000	Net Worth:	$29,634,000	Debt/ Equity:	NA

HealthTronics Inc

1301 Capital of Texas Hwy., Ste. 200B, Austin, TX, 78746; *PH:* 1-512-328-2892; *Fax:* 1-512-439-8303; *http://* www.healthtronics.com

General - Incorporation	GA	Stock - Price on:12/24/2007	$4.6
Employees	293	Stock Exchange	NDQ
Auditor	KPMG LLP	Ticker Symbol	HTRN
Stk Agt	American Stock Transfer & Trust Co.	Outstanding Shares	35,420,000
Counsel	Miller & Martin	E.P.S.	$0.21
DUNS No.	NA	Shareholders	NA

Business: The group's principal activity is to provide state-of-the-art noninvasive treatment solutions for certain urologic and orthopaedic conditions. The products are manufactured by high medical technologies of Switzerland and philips medical systems of Germany and are marketed throughout Europe. The medical devices include the ossatron orthopaedic shock wave system, the lithotron kidney lithotripter and the lithotron ultra endourology workstation. The group operates approximately 80 lithotripsy devices and 58 ossatron machines throughout 40 states in North America. The lithotripsy and orthotripsy services are provided to doctors, medical facilities and directly to patients. On 05-Mar-2004, the group acquired hmt holding, ag.

Primary SIC and add'l.: 3842 7352

CIK No: 0001018871

Subsidiaries: Advanced Urology Services, LLC, AK Specialty Vehicles B.V., AK Specialty Vehicles, Ltd., Alabama Renal Stone Institute, Inc.,, Alaska Extracorporeal Shockwave Therapy, LLC, Allied Urological Services, LLC, Aluminum Body Corporation,, AmCare Health Services, Inc.,, AMCARE, Inc.,, ARKLATX Mobile Lithotripter Limited, Bay Area Partners, Ltd., Big Sky Urological Services, L.P., Buckeye Urological Services, LP, California Lithotripters Limited Partnership II, L.P., California Lithotripters Limited Partnership IV, L.P. 151 Subsidiaries included in the Index

Officers: Sam B. Humphries/Dir., CEO, Pres.

Directors: Sam B. Humphries/Dir., CEO, Pres., Steven R. Hicks/Chmn., Mark G. Yudof/Dir., Kenneth S. Shifrin/Dir., Perry W. Waughtal/Dir., Argil J. Wheelock/Dir., Timothy J. Lindgren/Dir., Donny R. Jackson/Dir., Kevin A. Richardson/Dir.

Owners: Chris B. Schneider, Richard A. Rusk, Steven R. Hicks, Insiders/21.80%, James S.B. Whittenburg, Donny R. Jackson, Kevin A. Richardson/14.70%, Perry M. Waughtal, Mark G. Yudof, William A. Searles, Argil J. Wheelock/4.00%, Sam B. Humphries, Kenneth S. Shifrin/1.00%, Dimensional Fund Advisors LP/6.10%, Kennedy Capital Management, Inc./5.90% *(19 Owners included in Index)*

Financial Data: Fiscal Year End:12/31 Latest Annual Data: 12/31/2006

Year	Sales	Net Income
2006	$142,891,000	$8,683,000
2005	$267,694,000	$9,188,000
2004	$193,076,000	$878,000

Curr. Assets:	$71,825,000	Curr. Liab.:	$30,123,000		
Plant, Equip.:	$35,528,000	Total Liab.:	$61,112,000	Indic. Yr. Divd.:	NA
Total Assets:	$346,733,000	Net Worth:	$255,517,000	Debt/ Equity:	0.0207

Healthways Inc

Formerly: American Healthways Inc
3841 Green Hills Village Dr., Nashville, TN, 37215; *PH:* 1-615-665-1122; *http://* www.americanhealthways.com

General - Incorporation	DE	Stock - Price on:12/24/2007	$48.4
Employees	2,855	Stock Exchange	NDQ
Auditor	Ernst & Young LLP	Ticker Symbol	AMHC
Stk Agt	National City Bank	Outstanding Shares	35,060,000
Counsel	NA	E.P.S.	$1.19
DUNS No.	05-995-1988	Shareholders	NA

Business: The group's principal activity is to provide care enhancement and disease management services to health plans and hospitals. The group's reportable segments are the types of customers, hospital or health plan, who contract for its services. The group's integrated care enhancement product line includes programs for people with diabetes, coronary artery disease (cad), heart failure (hf), asthma, chronic obstructive pulmonary disease (copd), end-stage renal disease (esrd), acid-related stomach disorders, atrial fibrillation, decubitus ulcer, fibromyalgia, hepatitis c, inflammatory bowel disease, irritable bowel syndrome, low-back pain, osteoarthritis, osteoporosis and urinary incontinence. On 05-Sep-2003, the group acquired statusone health systems inc.

Primary SIC and add'l.: 8069 8744

CIK No: 0000704415

Subsidiaries: American Healthways Government Services, Inc., American Healthways Services, Inc., Axonal Information Solutions, Inc., CareSteps.com, Inc., Healthways International GmbH, Healthways International Limited, Healthways International, Inc., Healthways International, S.a.r.l., Population Health Support, LLC, StatusOne Health Systems, LLC

Officers: Ben R. Leedle/Dir., CEO, Pres., Dexter W. Shurney/Chief Medical Officer, VP, Matthew E. Kelliher/Exec. VP - International Business, Robert E. Stone/Chief Strategy Officer, Exec. VP, Mary A. Chaput/CFO, Exec. VP, James Pope/COO, Exec. VP, Mary D. Hunter/Exec. VP, Robert L. Chaput/CIO, Exec. VP, Donald B. Taylor/Exec. VP - Sales, Marketing, John E. Anderson/Member - Medical Advisory Counsel, Charles H. Booras/Member - Medical Advisory Counsel, Richard S. Chung/Member - Medical Advisory Counsel, Kenan E. Haver/Member - Medical Advisory Counsel, Leonard Mastbaum/Member - Medical Advisory Counsel, Maura J. McGuire/Member - Medical Advisory Counsel *(24 Officers included in Index)*

Directors: Ben R. Leedle/Dir., CEO, Pres., Thomas G. Cigarran/Chmn., Henry D. Herr/Dir., Warren C. Neel/Dir., William C. O'Neil/Dir., Jack Wickens/Dir., Alison Taunton-Rigby/Dir., Ben L. Lytle/Dir., Mary Jane England/Dir., John W. Ballantine/Dir., Cris J. Bisgard/Dir.

Owners: Ben L. Lytle, Alison Taunton Rigby, Henry D. Herr, T. Rowe Price Associates, Inc./5.93%, FMR Corp./9.78%, Mary Jane England, Robert E. Stone, Wasatch Advisors, Inc./9.55%, Warren C. Neel, Thomas G. Cigarran/1.73%, William Blair & Company LLC/12.55%, Jay C. Bisgard, Insiders/8.16%, Mary A. Chaput, William C. O'Neil *(23 Owners included in Index)*

Financial Data: Fiscal Year End:08/31 Latest Annual Data: 8/31/2007

Year	Sales	Net Income
2007	$615,586,000	$45,121,000
2006	$412,308,000	$37,151,000
2005	$312,504,000	$33,084,000

Curr. Assets:	$151,431,000	Curr. Liab.:	$140,639,000	P/E Ratio:	38.41
Plant, Equip.:	$58,722,000	Total Liab.:	$466,095,000	Indic. Yr. Divd.:	NA
Total Assets:	$828,845,000	Net Worth:	$362,750,000	Debt/ Equity:	NA

Hearst Argyle Television Inc

300 W 57th St., New York, NY, 10019; *PH:* 1-212-887-6800; *Fax:* 1-212-887-6855; *http://* www.hearstargyle.com

General - Incorporation	DE	Stock - Price on:12/24/2007	$24.73
Employees	2,938	Stock Exchange	NYSE
Auditor	Deloitte & Touche LLP	Ticker Symbol	HTV
Stk Agt	Computershare Investor Services LLC	Outstanding Shares	93,620,000
Counsel	Clifford Chance Rogers & Wells LLP	E.P.S.	$0.80
DUNS No.	87-774-9861	Shareholders	NA

Business: The group's principal activity is to operate network-affiliated television stations and radio stations. It operates in the commercial television broadcasting segment. As of 31-Dec-2003, the group owned and operated 24 television stations and managed two network-affiliated and one independent television stations and two radio stations in the United States. The group owns 10 NBC affiliates and 12 ABC affiliated stations. The group also develops and manages local news, information and entertainment Web sites through local partnerships with Internet Broadcasting Systems, Inc. In addition, the group provides human resources support to corporations.

Primary SIC and add'l.: 4832 4833

CIK No: 0000949536

Subsidiaries: Arkansas Hearst-argyle Television, Inc., California, DELAWARE, Des Moines Hearst-argyle Television, Inc., Hatv Investments, Inc., Hearst-argyle Capital Trust, Hearst-argyle Properties, Inc., Hearst-argyle Sports, Inc., Hearst-argyle Stations, Inc., Jackson Hearst-argyle Television, Inc., Ketv Hearst-argyle Television, Inc., Khbs Hearst-argyle Television, Inc., Kmbc Hearst-argyle Television, Inc., Koat Hearst-argyle Television, Inc., NEVADA 27 Subsidiaries included in the Index

Officers: David J. Barrett/Dir., CEO, Pres./$2,435,942.00, Philip M. Stolz/Sr. VP/$1,054,789.00, Harry T. Hawks/CFO, Exec. VP/$955,852.00, Steven A. Hobbs/Exec. VP, Chief Legal, Development Officer/$819,676.00, Martin Faubell/VP - Engineering, Ellen McClain/VP - Finance, Candy Altman/VP - News, Terry MacKin/Exec. VP/$1,110,107.00, Brian A. Bracco/VP - News, Frederick I. Young/Sr. VP - News, Emerson Coleman/VP - Programming, Frank Biancuzzo/Sr. VP, Kathleen Keefe/VP - Sales, Marv Danielski/VP - Marketing, Creative Services, Alvin R. Lustgarten/VP - Administration, Information Technology *(16 Officers included in Index)*

Directors: David J. Barrett/Dir., CEO, Pres., Victor F. Ganzi/Chmn., Caroline L. Williams/Dir., Bob Marbut/Dir., Gilbert C. Maurer/Dir., John G. Conomikes/Dir., David Pulver/Dir., Frank A. Bennack/Presiding Dir., William Randolph Hearst/Dir., George R. Hearst/Dir., Ken J. Elkins/Dir.

Owners: Caroline L. Williams, Bob Marbut, Hearst Broadcasting, Inc./52.70%, Gilbert C. Maurer, David Pulver, Private Capital Management/16.20%, Steven A. Hobbs, Harry T. Hawks, Insiders/5.30%, Frank A. Bennack, David J. Barrett/1.80%, George R. Hearst, Terry Mackin, William Randolph Hearst, Hearst Broadcasting, Inc./100.00% *(20 Owners included in Index)*

Financial Data: Fiscal Year End:12/31 **Latest Annual Data:** 12/31/2006

Year	Sales	Net Income
2006	$785,402,000	$98,723,000
2005	$706,883,000	$100,217,000
2004	$779,879,000	$123,942,000

Curr. Assets:	$258,685,000	**Curr. Liab.:**	$250,254,000	**P/E Ratio:**	28.43
Plant, Equip.:	$295,094,000	**Total Liab.:**	$2,075,281,000	**Indic. Yr. Divd.:**	$0.280
Total Assets:	$3,958,088,000	**Net Worth:**	$1,882,807,000	**Debt/ Equity:**	0.4955

Heartland Bancshares Inc

420 N Morton St., Franklin, IN, 46131; *PH:* 1-317-738-3915

General - Incorporation	IN	**Stock** - Price on:12/24/2007	$15
Employees	NA	Stock Exchange	OTC
Auditor	Crowe Chizek & Co. LLC	Ticker Symbol	HRTB
Stk Agt	NA	Outstanding Shares	NA
Counsel	NA	E.P.S.	NA
DUNS No.	83-390-5730	Shareholders	NA

Business: The group's principal activities are to provide commercial and retail banking services through its subsidiary, heartland community bank. The group accepts deposits from the general public and uses them to originate commercial, residential real estate and consumer loans and purchasing certain investments. The group's deposit activities include demand deposits, savings deposit, money market deposits and certificates of deposits. The group's lending activities include real estate loans, consumer loans, residential mortgages and commercial loans. The group also sells mutual funds and other non-deposit investment products through a full-service brokerage department. The group operates through offices located in franklin, greenwood, and bargersville, Indiana.

Primary SIC and add'l.: 6712 6022

CIK No: 0001042905

Subsidiaries: Heartland Community Bank, Heartland Statutory Trust (IN)

Financial Data: Fiscal Year End:12/31 **Latest Annual Data:** 12/31/2004

Year	Sales	Net Income
2004	$11,196,000	$1,224,000
2003	$11,452,000	$414,000
2002	$12,907,000	-$1,213,000

Curr. Assets:	$15,377,000	**Curr. Liab.:**	$167,176,000		
Plant, Equip.:	$2,354,000	**Total Liab.:**	$172,331,000	**Indic. Yr. Divd.:**	$0.200
Total Assets:	$185,837,000	**Net Worth:**	$13,506,000	**Debt/ Equity:**	1.0041

Heartland Express Inc

901 N Kansas Ave., North Liberty, IA, 52317; *PH:* 1-319-626-3600; *Fax:* 1-319-626-3355; *http://* www.heartlandexpress.com; *Email:* sales@heartlandexpress.com

General - Incorporation	NV	**Stock** - Price on:12/24/2007	$16.11
Employees	3,317	Stock Exchange	NDQ
Auditor	KPMG LLP	Ticker Symbol	HTLD
Stk Agt	NA	Outstanding Shares	98,250,000
Counsel	NA	E.P.S.	$0.87
DUNS No.	00-986-5684	Shareholders	NA

Business: The group's principal activity is to provide nationwide transportation of general commodities to major shippers. The group uses late-model equipment and a combined fleet of group-owned and owner-operator tractors. Its primary traffic lanes are between customer locations towards the east of the rocky mountains, with selected service to the west. It operates 7 specialized regional distribution operations near atlanta, Georgia; carlisle, Pennsylvania; columbus, Ohio; jacksonville, Florida kingsport, Tennessee; chester, Virginia and olive branch, Mississippi. The short-haul operations concentrate on freight movements generally within a 400-mile radius of the regional terminal and are designed to meet the needs of significant customers in those regions. The group's primary customers include retailers and manufacturers.

Primary SIC and add'l.: 4210 4212 4213

CIK No: 0000799233

Subsidiaries: A & M Express, Inc., Heartland Equipment, Inc., Heartland Express, Inc. of Iowa

Officers: Russell A. Gerdin/Chmn., CEO/$300,000.00, John P. Cosaert/60/CFO, Exec. VP - Finance, Treasurer/$310,999.00, Richard L. Meehan/62/Exec. VP - Marketing, Operations/$310,999.00, Michael J. Gerdin/38/Dir., Pres./$166,112.00, Thomas E. Hill/54/VP, Controller, Sec./$163,910.00

Directors: Russell A. Gerdin/Chmn., CEO, Michael J. Gerdin/38/Dir., Pres., Richard O. Jacobson/71/Dir., Allen J. Benjamin/61/Dir., Lawrence D. Crouse/67/Dir., James G. Pratt/59/Dir.

Owners: Benjamin J. Allen, James G. Pratt, John P. Cosaert, Richard L. Meehan, Lord, Abbett & Co. LLC/5.40%, Lawrence D. Crouse/6.10%, Russell A. Gerdin/24.20%, Insiders/41.00%, Richard O. Jacobson, Michael J. Gerdin/12.20%, Thomas E. Hill

Financial Data: Fiscal Year End:12/31 **Latest Annual Data:** 12/31/2006

Year	Sales	Net Income
2006	$571,919,000	$87,171,000
2005	$523,793,000	$71,906,000
2004	$457,086,000	$62,447,000

Curr. Assets:	$410,675,000	**Curr. Liab.:**	$116,423,000	**P/E Ratio:**	18.52
Plant, Equip.:	$248,031,000	**Total Liab.:**	$174,046,000	**Indic. Yr. Divd.:**	$0.080
Total Assets:	$669,070,000	**Net Worth:**	$495,024,000	**Debt/ Equity:**	NA

Heartland Financial USA Inc

1398 Central Ave., Dubuque, IA, 52001; *PH:* 1-563-589-2100; *Fax:* 1-563-589-2011; *http://* www.htlf.com

General - Incorporation	DE	**Stock** - Price on:12/24/2007	$24.75
Employees	959	Stock Exchange	NDQ
Auditor	KPMG LLP	Ticker Symbol	HTLF
Stk Agt	Heartland Financial USA Inc	Outstanding Shares	16,450,000
Counsel	Barack Ferrazzano Kirschbaum Et Al	E.P.S.	$0.06
DUNS No.	80-784-4170	Shareholders	NA

Business: The group's principal activity is to provide full service retail banking services. The services provided by the group include checking accounts, now accounts, savings accounts, certificate of deposit, individual retirement accounts, visa debit cards, trust services, home equity, commercial and industrial loans, consumer loans, real estate loans and agricultural loans. These services are provided to individuals, corporations and partnerships. The group is a multi bank holding company that operates through 7 bank subsidiaries and 8 non-bank subsidiaries. The bank subsidiaries operate 37 banking locations in Iowa, Illinois, Wisconsin and New Mexico. On 02-Jun-2004, the group acquired rocky mountain bancorporation inc.

Primary SIC and add'l.: 6211 6022 6712

CIK No: 0000920112

Subsidiaries: Arizona Bank & Trust, an Arizona state bank with its main office located in Chandler, Arizona, Autorent Wisconsin, Inc., Citizens Finance Co., DB&T Community Development Corp., DB&T Insurance, Inc., DBT Investment Corporation, Dubuque Bank and Trust Company, an Iowa state bank with its main office located in Dubuque, Iowa, Econo Lease, Inc, First Community Bank, an Iowa state bank with its main office located in Keokuk, Iowa, Galena State Bank and Trust Company, an Illinois state bank with its main office located in Galena, Illinois, Heartland Community Development, Inc., Heartland Financial Capital Trust II, Heartland Financial Statutory Trust II, Heartland Financial Statutory Trust III, Heartland Financial Statutory Trust IV 24 Subsidiaries included in the Index

Officers: Lynn B. Fuller/Chmn., CEO, Pres./$732,382.00, John K. Schmidt/Dir., Exec. VP, CFO, COO - Investor Relations Contact/$445,344.00, Kenneth J. Erickson/Exec. VP, Chief Credit Officer/$336,442.00, Lisan Adams/VP - Retirement Services, Eric R. Foy/Financial Advisor - Retirement Services, Neal Hoppe/Retirement Services Supervisor, Joan Goddard/Retirement Services Officer, Jill Gansemer/Education Consultant, Lois K. Pearce/VP, Corp. Sec. - Transfer Agent, Edward H. Everts/Sr. VP - Operations/$262,125.00, Janet M. Quick/VP - Finance, Paul J. Peckosh/Sr. VP - Trust, Douglas J. Horstmann/Sr. VP - Lending/$283,127.00, David J. Kapler/VP, General Counsel, Assist Corp. Sec., Jacquie M. Manternach/VP - Finance *(20 Officers included in Index)*

Directors: Lynn B. Fuller/Chmn., CEO, Pres., Mark C. Falb/Vice Chmn., Thomas L. Flynn/Vice Chmn., John W. Cox/Dir., Ronald A. Larson/Dir., John K. Schmidt/Dir., Exec. VP, CFO, COO - Investor Relations Contact, James F. Conlan/Dir.

Owners: John W. Cox, Mark C. Falb, Thomas L. Flynn, Douglas J. Horstmann/1.10%, John K. Schmidt/1.30%, Kenneth J. Erickson/1.30%, Heartland Partnership, L.P./5.10%, Ronald A. Larson, Insiders/11.80%, James F. Conlan, Edward H. Everts/1.00%, Lynn B. Fuller/4.40%, Lynn S. Fuller/8.40%, Dubuque Bank and Trust Company/12.70%

Financial Data: Fiscal Year End:12/31 **Latest Annual Data:** 12/31/2006

Year	Sales	Net Income
2006	$221,702,000	$25,102,000
2005	$195,598,000	$22,726,000
2004	$159,235,000	$20,252,000

Curr. Assets:	$50,711,000	**Curr. Liab.:**	$2,624,008,000	**P/E Ratio:**	15.66
Plant, Equip.:	$110,142,000	**Total Liab.:**	$2,848,531,000	**Indic. Yr. Divd.:**	$0.400
Total Assets:	$3,058,242,000	**Net Worth:**	$209,711,000	**Debt/ Equity:**	1.0706

Heartland Inc

3300 Fernbrook Ln. N, Ste. 180, Plymouth, MN, 55447; *PH:* 1-763-557-2900; *http://* www.heartlandinc.com

General - Incorporation	MD	**Stock** - Price on:12/24/2007	$0.25
Employees	68	Stock Exchange	OTC
Auditor	Meyler & Co. LLC	Ticker Symbol	HTLJ
Stk Agt	Securities Transfer Corp	Outstanding Shares	36,450,000
Counsel	NA	E.P.S.	-$0.06
DUNS No.	NA	Shareholders	NA

Business: The group's principal activity is to operate diversified businesses. It develops intelligence visual software solutions for wireless and mobile devices. The software decodes barcodes and other visual symbols in mobile handsets and pda's that have integrated digital cameras. In 2003, the group acquired pmi wireless, inc. And mound technologies, inc. Pmi plans to deliver customer premise equipment for broadband wireless access systems in the ism, wll, mmds and unii frequency bands. It also expects to deliver wireless services. Mound is involved in the fabricated metals industry as well as industrial property management. Freedom products of Ohio, a wholly owned subsidiary of mound, manufactures products for the heavy machinery industry and has the ability to do complete assembly and testing. The group's present mission is to become a leading diversified group with business interests in well established service organizations and capital goods manufacturing companies.

Primary SIC and add'l.: 3429 6531 3441 7372

CIK No: 0001084415

Subsidiaries: Evans Columbus, LLC of Columbus, Freedom Products, Karkela Construction, Inc. of St. Louis Park, Monarch Homes, Inc. of Ramsey, Mound Technologies, Inc. of Springboro

Officers: Thomas C. Miller/52/Dir., COO

Directors: Thomas C. Miller/52/Dir., COO

Owners: Trent Sommerville/9.08%, John E. Gracik/4.86%, First Union Venture Group, LLC/5.23%, Insiders/17.38%, John Zavoral/3.10%, Kenneth B. Farris/1.55%, Jerry Gruenbaum/3.44%, Thomas Miller/3.30%

Financial Data: Fiscal Year End:12/31 **Latest Annual Data:** 12/31/2006

Year	Sales	Net Income
2006	$20,224,000	$4,103,000
2005	$40,675,000	-$13,535,000
2004	$7,389,000	-$765,000

Curr. Assets:	$5,754,000	**Curr. Liab.:**	$6,260,000		
Plant, Equip.:	$944,000	**Total Liab.:**	$7,164,000	**Indic. Yr. Divd.:**	NA
Total Assets:	$8,069,000	**Net Worth:**	$906,000	**Debt/ Equity:**	0.8018

Heartland Oil and Gas Corp

14255 US HWY 1, Ste. 209, Juno Beach, FL, 33408; *PH:* 1-561-630-2977; *Fax:* 1-561-630-2241; *http://* www.heartlandoilandgas.com; *Email:* info@heartlandoilandgas.com

General		**Stock**	
Incorporation	NV	Price on:12/24/2007	$0.107
Employees	5	Stock Exchange	OTC
Auditor	Staley, Okada & Partners	Ticker Symbol	HTOG
Stk Agt	Registrar & Transfer Co	Outstanding Shares	97,700,000
Counsel	NA	E.P.S	-$1.66
DUNS No.	NA	Shareholders	NA

Business: The group's principle activities are to acquire, explore and develop oil and gas properties to determine whether they contain economically recoverable resources. Oil and gas properties are located primarily in Kansas. The group is considered to be in the development stage, since revenues have not been attained and planned operations have not commenced.

Primary SIC and add'l.: 1382

CIK No: 0001075636

Subsidiaries: Far East International Petroleum Company (FEIPCO), Heartland Oil and Gas, Inc

Officers: Philip Winner/Dir., CEO, Pres., Eileen Himes/Controller, Robert Poley/Dir., CFO, Said Abdallah/53/COO, Steven A. Fall/58/CFO, Interim Pres., Jack Baker/Contact - Investor Information

Directors: Philip Winner/Dir., CEO, Pres., Robert Poley/Dir., CFO, John Martin/Dir., Todd MacKintosh/Dir., Christopher J. McCauley/Dir., Kamal Abdallah/Dir.

Owners: UPDA Corp./52.00%, Philip Winner/1.20%, Insiders/1.20%

Financial Data: *Fiscal Year End:*12/31 *Latest Annual Data:* 12/31/2006

Year	Sales	Net Income
2006	$399,000	-$1,456,000
2005	NA	-$41,575,000
2004	NA	-$1,683,000

Curr. Assets:	$259,000	**Curr. Liab.:**	$283,000		
Plant, Equip.:	$5,097,000	**Total Liab.:**	$510,000	**Indic. Yr. Divd.:**	NA
Total Assets:	$5,356,000	**Net Worth:**	$4,847,000	**Debt/ Equity:**	NA

Heartland Payment Systems Inc

90 Nassau St., Princeton, NJ, 08542; *PH:* 1-609-683-3831; *Fax:* 1-609-683-3815; *http://* www.heartlandpaymentsystems.com; *Email:* heartland_ir@gregoryfca.com

General		**Stock**	
Incorporation	DE	Price on:12/24/2007	$26.33
Employees	2,026	Stock Exchange	NYSE
Auditor	Deloitte & Touche LLP	Ticker Symbol	HPY
Stk Agt	Registrar & Transfer Co	Outstanding Shares	37,790,000
Counsel	NA	E.P.S	NA
DUNS No.	NA	Shareholders	NA

Business: The group's principle activity is to provide credit and debit card, payroll and related processing services. The group also provides the following time and money-saving benefits; fraud monitoring services to minimize potential losses, assistance in resolving disputed transactions, fully disclosed fees and agreement terms, simple, clear monthly statements, specialized applications for restaurants and hotels/resorts, and automatic or manual batch closing. Today, the company has become one of the largest payment processors, with $35 billion of annual processing volume from current merchants. The company operates throughout the United States and has its corporate headquarters in Princeton, New Jersey. It has its satellite offices in Berea, Ohio; Frisco, Texas; and Scottsdale, Arizona. Its service centre in Jeffersonville, Ind. The group operates from United States.

Primary SIC and add'l.: 7389

CIK No: 0001144354

Subsidiaries: Heartland Payroll Company

Officers: Robert O. Carr/Chmn., CEO, Pres./$350,000.00, Thomas M. Sheridan/62/Exec. Dir., Chief Portfolio Officer/$222,150.00, Sanford C. Brown/Chief Sales Officer/$525,586.00, Robert H.B. Baldwin/53/CFO, Sec./$260,001.00, Brooks L. Terrell/44/CTO/$223,600.00, Charles H.N. Kallenbach/General Counsel, Chief Legal Officer, Sec.

Directors: Robert O. Carr/Chmn., CEO, Pres., Thomas M. Sheridan/62/Exec. Dir., Chief Portfolio Officer, Mitchell L. Hollin/Dir., Marc J. Ostro/Dir., George F. Raymond/Dir., Scott L. Bok/Dir., Robert H. Niehaus/Dir., Jonathan J. Palmer/Dir., Richard W. Vague/Dir.

Owners: Jonathan J. Palmer, Robert H.B. Baldwin, Thomas M. Sheridan, Brooks L. Terrell, LLR Equity Partners, L.P. and affiliated investment fund, Carr Holdings, L.L.C., Mitchell L. Hollin, Robert O. Carr, Robert H. Niehaus, Marc J. Ostro, Greenhill Capital Partners, L.P. and affiliated investment funds, George F. Raymond, Insiders, Sanford C. Brown, Scott L. Bok

Financial Data: *Fiscal Year End:*12/31 *Latest Annual Data:* 12/31/2006

Year	Sales	Net Income
2006	$1,097,041,000	$28,544,000
2005	$834,577,000	$19,093,000
2004	$602,749,000	$8,855,000

Curr. Assets:	$165,516,000	**Curr. Liab.:**	$90,701,000		
Plant, Equip.:	$23,135,000	**Total Liab.:**	$112,475,000	**Indic. Yr. Divd.:**	$0.300
Total Assets:	$251,768,000	**Net Worth:**	$139,293,000	**Debt/ Equity:**	NA

HearUSA Inc

1250 Northpoint Pkwy., West Palm Beach, FL, 33407; *PH:* 1-561-478-8770; *Fax:* 1-800-323-3277; *http://* www.hearx.com; *Email:* info@hearusa.com

General		**Stock**	
Incorporation	DE	Price on:12/24/2007	$1.74
Employees	576	Stock Exchange	AMEX
Auditor	BDO Seidman LLP	Ticker Symbol	EAR
Stk Agt	American Stock Transfer & Trust Co.	Outstanding Shares	37,120,000
Counsel	Bryan Cave LLP	E.P.S	-$0.14
DUNS No.	19-451-1085	Shareholders	NA

Business: The group's principal activities are operating a chain of hearing care centers throughout the United States. The group provides full range of audiological products and services for the hearing impaired. The group serves three geographic markets: Florida, the northeast and California, through its joint venture hearx west llc. As of Dec 27, 2003, the group operated 31 centers in Florida, 15 in New Jersey, 15 in New York, 9 in Massachusetts, 8 in Ohio, 8 in Michigan, 2 in Wisconsin, 6 in Minnesota, 8 in Missouri, 14 in Washington and 22 hearx west centers in California.

Primary SIC and add'l.: 9999 8049 7389

CIK No: 0000821536

Subsidiaries: 3371727 Canada, Inc., Auxiliary Health Benefits Corporation D/B/A National Ear Care Plan, HEARx Acquisition, ULC., HEARx Canada, Inc., HEARx West, Inc., HEARx West, LLC., Helix Hearing Care of America (USA) Corp., Helix Hearing Care of America Corp.

Owners: Paul A. Brown/6.87%, Joseph L. Gitterman, Michel Labadie/6.32%, Gino Chouinard/1.24%, Thomas W. Archibald, Insiders/18.09%, Kenneth Schofield/1.14%, Stephen J. Hansbrough/1.44%, Jack Silver/7.94%, David J. McLachlan

Financial Data: *Fiscal Year End:*12/31 *Latest Annual Data:* 12/30/2006

Year	Sales	Net Income
2006	$88,786,000	-$3,174,000
2005	$76,672,000	-$583,000
2004	$72,301,000	-$2,759,000

Curr. Assets:	$17,086,000	**Curr. Liab.:**	$20,205,000		
Plant, Equip.:	$3,474,000	**Total Liab.:**	$47,745,000	**Indic. Yr. Divd.:**	NA
Total Assets:	$68,982,000	**Net Worth:**	$21,237,000	**Debt/ Equity:**	1.9671

Hecla Mining Co

6500 N Mineral Dr., Ste. 200, Coeur dAlene, ID, 83815; *PH:* 1-208-769-4100; *Fax:* 1-208-769-7612; *http://* www.hecla-mining.com; *Email:* hmc-info@hecla-mining.com

General		**Stock**	
Incorporation	DE	Price on:12/24/2007	NA
Employees	1,163	Stock Exchange	Nyse
Auditor	PricewaterhouseCoopers LLP	Ticker Symbol	HL
Stk Agt	American Stock Transfer & Trust Co.	Outstanding Shares	120,260,000
Counsel	NA	E.P.S	$0.44
DUNS No.	00-692-7610	Shareholders	NA

Business: The group's principle activity is to explore, develop and mine precious and nonferrous metals, including gold, silver, lead, zinc and certain industrial minerals. The group's revenue and profitability are strongly influenced by global prices of silver, gold, lead and zinc. The principal producing properties of the group in 2003 included the san sebastian silver unit, located in the state of durango, Mexico, la camorra gold unit, located in the state of bolivar, venezuela, greens creek silver unit, located on the admiralty island, near juneau, Alaska, lucky friday unit, located in northern Idaho. The group's quarterly revenue for Sep'07 was 49.23 millions of USD.

Primary SIC and add'l.: 1044 1041

CIK No: 0000719413

Subsidiaries: 2056672 Ontario Limited, Burke Trading Inc., Drake-Bering Holdings B.V., El Callao Gold Mining Company, El Callao Gold Mining Company de Venezuela, Hecla Alaska LLC, Hecla Ventures Corp., Industrias Hecla S.A. de C.V., Minera Hecla S.A. de C.V., Minera Hecla Venezolana

Officers: Phillips S. Baker/Dir., CEO/$1,522,867.00, Ronald W. Clayton/Sr. VP - Operations/$582,485.00, Vicki Veltkamp/VP - Investor, Public Relations, Michael H. Callahan/VP/$601,482.00, Lewis E. Walde/CFO, VP/$498,642.00, Dean W. McDonald/VP - Exploration, Philip C. Wolf/Sr. VP, General Counsel/$670,252.00, Don Poirier/VP - Corporate Development, Jay S. Layman/49/VP - Corporate Development

Directors: Phillips S. Baker/Dir., CEO, Ted Crumley/Chmn., John H. Bowles/Dir., Terry V. Rogers/Dir., Charles B. Stanley/Dir., David J. Christensen/Dir., George R. Nethercutt/Dir., Anthony P. Taylor/Dir.

Owners: Michael H. Callahan, Jay S. Layman, Dean W.A. McDonald, Lewis E. Walde, Wentworth, Hauser & Violich, Inc/5.00%, David J. Christensen, Anthony P. Taylor, Royce & Associates, LLC/8.70%, Insiders, Anthony P. Taylor, George R. Nethercutt, Insiders/1.40%, Jorge E. Ordonez, Charles L. McAlpine, John H. Bowles *(20 Owners included in Index)*

Financial Data: *Fiscal Year End:*12/31 *Latest Annual Data:* 12/31/2006

Year	Sales	Net Income
2006	$217,417,000	$69,122,000
2005	$110,161,000	-$25,360,000
2004	$130,826,000	-$6,134,000

Curr. Assets:	$165,561,000	**Curr. Liab.:**	$52,317,000		
Plant, Equip.:	$125,986,000	**Total Liab.:**	$121,541,000	**Indic. Yr. Divd.:**	NA
Total Assets:	$346,269,000	**Net Worth:**	$224,728,000	**Debt/ Equity:**	NA

Hector Communications Corp

211 S Main St., Hector, MN, 55342; *PH:* 1-612-848-6611; *http://* www.hectorcom.com

General		**Stock**	
Incorporation	MN	Price on:12/24/2007	$13
Employees	71	Stock Exchange	NA
Auditor	PricewaterhouseCoopers	Ticker Symbol	NA
Stk Agt	Wells Fargo Bank Minnesota N.A	Outstanding Shares	5,120,000
Counsel	Lindquist & Vennum PLLP	E.P.S	$6.96
DUNS No.	61-496-2629	Shareholders	NA

Business: The group's principal activity is to provide local telephone, cable television and Internet access services. The group operates through two segments hector communications corporation and its subsidiaries, and alliance telecommunications corporation and its subsidiaries. Principal services provided by the group are local network, network access, video services, nonregulated services and Internet services. The local network provides basic telephone services for residential and business customers. The network access provides intrastate and interstate exchange services to long distance carriers. The video services provide cable television services. The nonregulated services provide fiber optic transport facilities, sell and lease customer premise telephone equipment, provide inside wiring services, sell and lease other facilities for private line and other communications services. The Internet services provide digital subscriber lines to the customers.

Primary SIC and add'l.: 4841 4813 4899 6719

CIK No: 0000863437

Subsidiaries: Alliance Telecommunications Corporation, Arrowhead Communications Corporation, Cannon Communications Corp., Eagle Valley Telephone Company, Felton Telephone Company, Granada Telephone Company, Hager TeleCom, Inc., Hastad Engineering Co., Indianhead Communications Corporation, Indianhead Telephone Company, Loretel Financial Systems, Inc., Loretel Systems, Inc., Mustang Communications Corporation, North American Communications Corporation, OU Connection, Inc. 17 Subsidiaries included in the Index

Officers: Curtis A. Sampson/Chmn., CEO, Steven H. Sjogren/Dir., COO, Pres., Richard A. Primuth/Legal Counsel, Charles A. Braun/CFO, Paul N. Hanson/VP, Treasurer, Sec., Dir.

Directors: Curtis A. Sampson/Chmn., CEO, Steven H. Sjogren/Dir., COO, Pres., Luella Gross Goldberg/Dir., James O. Ericson/Dir., Paul A. Hoff/Dir., Wayne E. Sampson/Dir., Ronald J. Bach/Dir., Gerald D. Pint/Dir., Paul N. Hanson/VP, Treasurer, Sec., Dir.

Financial Data: *Fiscal Year End:*12/31 *Latest Annual Data:* 12/31/2006

Year	Sales	Net Income
2006	$16,882,000	$35,111,000
2005	$17,345,000	$5,460,000
2004	$15,101,000	$3,292,000

Curr. Assets: $2,059,528,724,000 **Curr. Liab.:** NA **P/E Ratio:** 1.87
Plant, Equip.: NA **Total Liab.:** NA **Indic. Yr. Divd.:** $0.400
Total Assets: $2,059,528,724,000 **Net Worth:** NA **Debt/ Equity:** 0.0014

Heelys Inc

3200 Belmeade Dr., Ste. 100, Carrollton, TX, 75006; *PH:* 1-214-390-1831; *Fax:* 1-214-390-1661; *http://* www.heelys.com

General - Incorporation DE
Employees 41
Auditor Deloitte & Touche LLP
Stk Agt American Stock Transfer & Trust Co.
Counsel NA
DUNS No. NA

Stock- Price on:12/24/2007 $26.71
Stock Exchange NDQ
Ticker Symbol HLYS
Outstanding Shares 27,060,000
E.P.S. $1.66
Shareholders NA

Business: The groups principal activities include designing, marketing and distributing sports products. The product of the group is wheeled footwear. The group products sold under the trade name HEELYS. Specific customer of the group is A.G. Corporation, Big 5 Sporting Goods and The Sports Authority. The group operates from the United States, the United Kingdom, Canada and Ireland. The net sale of the group for the year 2006 was 71,101 (thousands).

Primary SIC and add'l.: 5139 5091

CIK No: 0001373980

Subsidiaries: Heeling Holding Corporation, Heeling Management Corp, Heeling Sports Limited

Officers: Michael G. Staffaroni/Dir., CEO, Pres., Michael W. Hessong/VP - Finance, CFO, Treasurer, Sec., James S. Peliotes/VP - Marketing, Robert W. Byrne/VP - Design, Development, Patrick F. Hamner/Sr. VP, Charles D. Beery/Sr. VP - Global Sales, John W. O'Neil/VP - International, William D. Albers/VP - Sourcing

Directors: Michael G. Staffaroni/Dir., CEO, Pres., Gary L. Martin/Chmn., James T. Kindley/Dir., Jeffrey G. Peterson/Dir., Roger R. Adams/Dir., Samuel B. Ligon/Dir., Richard E. Middlekauff/Dir.

Owners: Insiders, James T. Kindley, Roger R. Adams, Richard E. Middlekauff, Patrick F. Hamner, Michael W. Hessong, William R. Thomas, Samuel B. Ligon, Jeffrey G. Peterson, Capital Southwest Venture Corporation, Michael G. Staffaroni, Charles D. Beery

Financial Data: **Fiscal Year End:**12/31 **Latest Annual Data:** 12/31/2006

Year	Sales	Net Income
2006	$188,208,000	$29,174,000
2005	$43,950,000	$4,347,000
2004	$21,310,000	$803,000

Curr. Assets: $105,096,000 **Curr. Liab.:** $12,568,000 **P/E Ratio:** 16.09
Plant, Equip.: $393,000 **Total Liab.:** $12,568,000 **Indic. Yr. Divd.:** NA
Total Assets: $106,338,000 **Net Worth:** $93,770,000 **Debt/ Equity:** NA

HEI Inc

1495 Steiger Lake Ln., Victoria, MN, 55386; *PH:* 1-952-443-2500; *Fax:* 1-952-443-2668; *http://* www.heii.com; *Email:* headqtrs@heii.com

General - Incorporation MN
Employees 466
Auditor KPMG LLP, Virchow, Krause & Co LLP
Stk Agt Wells Fargo Shareowner Services
Counsel Brown & Wood LLP
DUNS No. 04-539-7270

Stock- Price on:12/24/2007 $1.17
Stock Exchange OTC
Ticker Symbol HEII
Outstanding Shares 9,510,000
E.P.S. -$0.59
Shareholders NA

Business: The group's principal activities are to design and manufacture ultraminiature microelectronic devices and high technology products. These devices consist of placing or assembling one or more integrated circuits or 'chips' and other passive electrical components onto a ceramic or organic substrate. This assembly of microelectronic embodies the end products of the customers including hearing aids, defibrillators and communication components. The products also include quality flex circuits and performance laminate based substrates. The group also manufactures wireless smart cards and other ultra-miniature radio frequency applications. The group operates in the United States of America. On 28-Jan-2003, the group acquired certain assets & liabilities of Colorado medtech, inc.'s Colorado operations.

Primary SIC and add'l.: 5047 3841 3669 9999

CIK No: 0000351298

Subsidiaries: Cross Technology, Inc.

Officers: Mark B. Thomas/CEO, CFO, Treasure, Sec. Principal Executive Officer, Principal Financial Officer

Directors: Thomas F. Leahy/Chmn., Robert Heller/Dir., Timothy F. Floeder/Dir., Michael J. Evers/Dir.

Owners: Robert W. Heller, Michael J. Evers, Scott M. Stole, Minneapolis Portfolio Management Group, LLC/9.30%, Timothy F. Floeder, Insiders/12.40%, George M. Heenan, Thomas F. Leahy/11.80%, Mack V. Traynor

Financial Data: **Fiscal Year End:**08/31 **Latest Annual Data:** 9/2/2006

Year	Sales	Net Income
2006	$52,631,000	-$6,057,000
2005	$56,631,000	$355,000
2004	$43,320,000	-$7,009,000

Curr. Assets: $18,025,000 **Curr. Liab.:** $13,493,000
Plant, Equip.: $7,717,000 **Total Liab.:** $18,108,000 **Indic. Yr. Divd.:** NA
Total Assets: $26,872,000 **Net Worth:** $8,764,000 **Debt/ Equity:** 0.4153

HEICO Corp

3000 Taft St., Hollywood, FL, 33021; *PH:* 1-954-987-4000; *Fax:* 1-954-987-8228; *http://* www.heico.com

General - Incorporation FL
Employees 1,843
Auditor Deloitte & Touche LLP
Stk Agt Susquehanna Investment Group
Counsel NA
DUNS No. 80-957-0781

Stock- Price on:12/24/2007 $42.7
Stock Exchange NYSE
Ticker Symbol HEI
Outstanding Shares 25,780,000
E.P.S. $1.45
Shareholders NA

Business: The group's principal activities are to design, manufacture and market aerospace, defense and electronics related products and services throughout the United States and internationally. It operates under two segments: the flight support group: designs, engineers, manufactures, repairs and overhauls engine parts and components such as combustion chambers, gas flow transition ducts, airfoils and various other engine and airframe parts. The electronic technologies group: manufactures various types of electrically engineered products such as power supplies, shielding for communications, computer and aerospace applications, infrared simulation and test equipment. The group's customers consist of domestic and foreign commercial and cargo airlines, other after market suppliers of aircraft engine and airframe materials. The group acquired sierra microwave technology, inc. in dec 2003.

Primary SIC and add'l.: 3728 3724

CIK No: 0000046619

Subsidiaries: Aero Design, Inc, Aircraft Technology, Inc., Analog Modules, Inc, Aviation Facilities, Inc, Connectronics Corporation, Connectronics, Corp, Future Aviation, Inc, HEICO Aerospace Corporation, HEICO Aerospace Parts Corp, HEICO Electronic Technologies Corp, HVT Group, Inc, Inertial Airline Services, Inc., Jet Avion Corporation, Jetseal, Inc, Leader Tech, Inc 24 Subsidiaries included in the Index

Officers: Laurans A. Mendelson/Chmn., CEO, Pres., Victor H. Mendelson/Dir., Pres. - Electronic Technologies Group, General Counsel, Eric A. Mendelson/Dir., Pres. - Flight Support Group

Directors: Laurans A. Mendelson/Chmn., CEO, Pres., Samuel L. Higginbottom/Dir., Victor H. Mendelson/Dir., Pres. - Electronic Technologies Group, General Counsel, Eric A. Mendelson/Dir., Pres. - Flight Support Group, Albert Morrison/Dir., Joseph W. Pallot/Dir., Alan Schriesheim/Dir., Wolfgang Mayrhuber/Dir., Frank J. Schwitter/Dir.

Owners: Wolfgang Mayrhuber, Barclays Global Reporting Grou/5.30%, Samuel L. Higginbottom, Joseph W. Pallot, JPMorgan Chase & Co./6.72%, Victor H. Mendelson/6.64%, Thomas S. Irwin/4.74%, Victor H. Mendelson/1.31%, Mendelson Reporting Group/2.54%, Rene Plessner Reporting Group/5.19%, Thomas S. Irwin, Samuel L. Higginbottom, Albert Morrison, Eric A. Mendelson/1.13%, Susquehanna Investment Group/7.90% *(32 Owners included in Index)*

Financial Data: **Fiscal Year End:**10/31 **Latest Annual Data:** 10/31/2006

Year	Sales	Net Income
2006	$392,190,000	$31,888,000
2005	$269,647,000	$22,812,000
2004	$215,744,000	$20,630,000

Curr. Assets: $180,021,000 **Curr. Liab.:** $65,503,000 **P/E Ratio:** 32.85
Plant, Equip.: $49,489,000 **Total Liab.:** $154,256,000 **Indic. Yr. Divd.:** $0.080
Total Assets: $534,815,000 **Net Worth:** $317,258,000 **Debt/ Equity:** 0.1433

Heidrick & Struggles International Inc

233 S Wacker Dr., Ste. 4200, Chicago, IL, 60606; *PH:* 1-312-496-1200; *Fax:* 1-312-496-1290; *http://* www.heidrick.com

General - Incorporation DE
Employees 1,550
Auditor KPMG LLP
Stk Agt Mellon Investor Services LLC
Counsel NA
DUNS No. 00-552-5159

Stock- Price on:12/24/2007 $49.7
Stock Exchange NDQ
Ticker Symbol HSII
Outstanding Shares 17,990,000
E.P.S. $2.84
Shareholders NA

Business: The group's principal activity is to provide executive search and leadership consulting services. The group helps its clients build leadership teams by facilitating the recruitment, development and retention of personnel for their executive management positions. In addition to executive search, the group provides other leadership services, including executive assessment, placement of interim executive management and through an alliance, executive coaching. The clients of the group include: Fortune 500 companies, major non-U.S. Companies, middle market and emerging growth companies, governmental and not-for-profit organizations and other leading private and public entities. The group operates principally in North America, Latin America, Europe and Asia-Pacific.

Primary SIC and add'l.: 7361

CIK No: 0001066605

Subsidiaries: Beijing Heidrick& Struggles International Management Consulting Company Limited, H&s Software Development And Knowledge Management Centre Private Limited, HEIDRICK& STRUGGLES (INDIA) PRIVATE LIMITED, HEIDRICK& STRUGGLES (KOREA), INC., a, HEIDRICK& STRUGGLES AB, HEIDRICK& STRUGGLES AG, HEIDRICK& STRUGGLES ARGENTINA, S.A., HEIDRICK& STRUGGLES ASIA-PACIFIC, LTD., HEIDRICK& STRUGGLES AUSTRALIA, LTD., HEIDRICK& STRUGGLES BV, HEIDRICK& STRUGGLES CANADA, INC., HEIDRICK& STRUGGLES CONSULTORES de GESTAO Lda, HEIDRICK& STRUGGLES DE CHILE LIMITADA, HEIDRICK& STRUGGLES DO BRASIL LTDA, HEIDRICK& STRUGGLES DUTCH PARTNERSHIP 37 Subsidiaries included in the Index

Officers: Kevin L. Kelly/CEO/$2,222,272.00, Thomas J. Friel/60/Partner - Washington DC/$2,984,091.00, David G. Pumphrey/Partner - Sydney, Charles Moore/Managing Partner - Singapore, Eileen A. Kamerick/CFO, Chief Administrative Officer/$1,721,260.00, Kelvin Thompson/Managing Partner - San Francisco/$1,749,635.00, Gerry Davis/Regional Managing Partner, Asia Pacific, David Peters/Regional Managing Partner, EMEA, Patricia R. Willard/Principal, Bernard Zen-Ruffinen/Managing Partner - Zurich, Pat Friel/Partner - Washington DC, Joe Haberman/Practice Leader - Washington DC, Daan De Roos/Managing Partner - Amsterdam, Per Insinger/Partner - Amsterdam, Filip Lerno/Managing Partner - Brussels *(24 Officers included in Index)*

Directors: Gerard R. Roche/Sr. Chmn., Richard L. Beattie/Chmn., Michael Franzino/59/Chmn. - Global Markets, John A. Fazio/Dir., Robert E. Knowling/Dir., Jill Kanin-Lovers/Dir., Antonio Borges/Dir., Douglas C. Yearley/72/Dir., Gary E. Knell/Dir., Paul Unruh/Dir.

Owners: Thomas J. Friel/3.40%, Gerard R. Roche/1.30%, Vincent C. Perro, Skyline Asset Management, L.P./4.60%, Douglas C. Yearley, Barclays Global Investors. NA/4.20%, Robert E. Knowling, Kelvin J.R. Bolli-Thompson, Eileen A. Kamerick, Paul V. Unruh, Richard I. Beattie, John A. Fazio, Wachovia Corporation/4.40%, Jill Kanin-Lovers, Antonio Borges *(21 Owners included in Index)*

Financial Data: **Fiscal Year End:**12/31 **Latest Annual Data:** 12/31/2006

Year	Sales	Net Income
2006	$501,994,000	$34,243,000
2005	$432,850,000	$39,218,000
2004	$398,176,000	$82,308,000

Curr. Assets:	$333,678,000	**Curr. Liab.:**	$202,592,000	**P/E Ratio:**	19.04
Plant, Equip.:	$18,648,000	**Total Liab.:**	$256,065,000	**Indic. Yr. Divd.:**	$0.520
Total Assets:	$519,770,000	**Net Worth:**	$263,705,000	**Debt/ Equity:**	NA

Heinz Co

600 Grant St., Pittsburgh, PA, 15219; ***PH:*** 1-412-456-5700; ***Fax:*** 1-412-456-6128; ***http://*** www.heinz.com; ***Email:*** ted.smyth@us.hjheinz.com

General - Incorporation .... PA
Employees 36,000
Auditor .... PricewaterhouseCoopers LLP
Stk Agt .... Mellon Bank N.A
Counsel .... Latham & Watkins
DUNS No. 00-431-8846

Stock- Price on:12/24/2007 .... $46.61
Stock Exchange .... NYSE
Ticker Symbol .... HNZ
Outstanding Shares 323,760,000
E.P.S $2.55
Shareholders .... NA

Business: The groups principle activities include manufacturing and marketing processed food products. The groups products include ketchup, condiments, sauces, soups, beans, pasta meals, seafood, and infant foods. The group operates from North America, Europe, Asia-Pacific and Africa.

Primary SIC and add'l.: 2038 2099 2034 2033 2092 2023 2035

CIK No: 0000046640

Subsidiaries: H. J. Heinz B.V, H. J. Heinz Company Australia Limited, H. J. Heinz Company Limited, H. J. Heinz Company of Canada Ltd., H. J. Heinz Company, L.P., H. J. Heinz Finance Company, Heinz Investments Ltd., Heinz Italia S.r.l, Heinz Management LLC, Heinz Watties Limited, HP Foods Limited, ProMark Brands, Inc., PT Heinz ABC Indonesia, Shanghai Guofu LongFong Co., Ltd.

Officers: William R. Johnson/Chmn., CEO, Pres./$14,990,520.00, David C. Moran/CEO, Exec. VP - Heinz North America/$2,298,273.00, Scott C. O'Hara/CEO, Exec. VP, Pres. - Heinz Europe, Jeffrey P. Berger/Exec. VP, Chmn. - Global Foodservice/$2,786,355.00, Rene D. Biedzinski/Corp. Sec., Dave J. Gaertner/VP - North American Business Development, Corporate Real Estate, Arthur B. Winkleblack/CFO, Exec. VP/$2,366,828.00, Michael D. Milone/Sr. VP - Australia, New Zealand, Rest, World, Edward A. Aiello/VP - Global Insurance, Leonard A. Cullo/VP, Treasurer, Mitchell A. Ring/Sr. VP - Global Initiatives, Patrycja Hatalska/Contact - Heinz Poland, Ros Kohler/Human Resources, Corporate Affairs Mgr. - Heinz Australia, Theodore N. Bobby/Sr. VP, General Counsel, John C. Crowe/VP - Taxes *(34 Officers included in Index)*

Directors: William R. Johnson/Chmn., CEO, Pres., Charles E. Bunch/Dir., Leonard S. Coleman/Dir., John G. Drosdick/Dir., Edith E. Holiday/Dir., Candace Kendle/Dir., Dean R. OHare/Dir., Dennis H. Reilley/Dir., Lynn C. Swann/Dir., Thomas J. Usher/Dir., Nelson Peltz/Dir., Michael F. Weinstein/Dir.

Owners: Charles E. Bunch, D. E.I. Smyth, William R. Johnson/1.30%, Trian Fund Management, L.P./5.90%, Insiders/8.20%, John G. Drosdick, Lynn C. Swann, Leonard S. Coleman, Dean R. OHare, Nelson Peltz/5.90%, Michael F. Weinstein, Jeffrey P. Berger, Candace Kendle, Edith E. Holiday, David C. Moran *(19 Owners included in Index)*

Financial Data: ***Fiscal Year End:***05/03 ***Latest Annual Data:*** 05/02/2007

Year	Sales	Net Income
2007	$9,001,630,000	$785,746,000
2006	$8,643,438,000	$645,603,000
2005	$8,912,297,000	$752,699,000

Curr. Assets:	$2,703,935,000	**Curr. Liab.:**	$2,018,231,000	**P/E Ratio:**	19.75
Plant, Equip.:	$1,900,557,000	**Total Liab.:**	$7,568,792,000	**Indic. Yr. Divd.:**	$1.520
Total Assets:	$9,737,767,000	**Net Worth:**	$2,048,823,000	**Debt/ Equity:**	2.1758

Helen of Troy Ltd

1 Helen of Troy Plz., El Paso, TX, 79912; ***PH:*** 1-915-225-8000; ***Fax:*** 1-915-225-8004; ***http://*** www.helenoftroyusa.com

General - Incorporation .... Bermuda
Employees 901
Auditor .... KPMG LLP
Stk Agt ..... Computershare Investor Services LLC
Counsel .... NA
DUNS No. 04-612-0994

Stock- Price on:12/24/2007 .... $28.26
Stock Exchange .... NDQ
Ticker Symbol .... HELE
Outstanding Shares .... NA
E.P.S $1.68
Shareholders .... NA

Business: The group's principal activities are to design, develop and markets hair care appliances including hair dryers, curling irons, brush irons, lighted mirrors, hair brushes, combs and skin care liquids and powders and other personal care products. The group operates in two segments: north American segment and international segment. North American segment markets the products in the United States and Canada. The international segment markets the products outside the United States and Canada. The group markets its products under the trademarks vidal sassoon, revlon, helen of troy, sable, salon edition, hot tools and gallery series. The group markets its products to retailers, distributors and the professional hair care market in the United States, Canada, Europe, Mexico, Hong Kong and other countries. On 29-Apr-2004, the group sold its interest in tactica international inc.

Primary SIC and add'l.: 2844 3999 3634

CIK No: 0000916789

Subsidiaries: Asia Pacific Liaison Services Limited, DCNL, Inc., Fontelux Trading, S.A., H.O.T. (Luxembourg) SARL, H.O.T. Cayman Holding, Helen of Troy (Cayman) Limited, Helen of Troy (Far East) Limited, Helen of Troy Canada, Inc., Helen of Troy Chile, S.A., Helen of Troy Comercial Offshore de Macau Limitada, Helen of Troy Consulting (Shenzhen) Company Limited, Helen of Troy Costa Rica, S.A., Helen of Troy de Mexico S.de R.L. de C.V., Helen of Troy do Brasil Ltda., Helen of Troy GmbH 36 Subsidiaries included in the Index

Officers: Gerald J. Rubin/Chmn., CEO, Pres./$4,771,555.00, Arthur A. August/Pres. - Professional Division, James Cooper/VP - Product Procurement, Forecasting, Jack Jancin/Sr. VP - Idelle Labs, John Boomer/VP - Corporate Business Development, Scott Thrasher/VP - Sales, Appliances, Rick Oppenheim/Corporate Financial Controller, Michael Cafaro/Sr. VP - New Product Development, Engineering, Deanna Nasser/Corporate Treasurer, John Hunnicutt/VP - Marketing, Idelle Labs, Carlos Jovel/VP - International, Latin, Central America, Mary Esther Minjares/VP - Customer Services, Alan Ames/Sr. VP - Sales, Accessories, Omar A. Tovar/VP, Chief Logistics Officer, Alex Lee/Pres. - OXO International *(27 Officers included in Index)*

Directors: Gerald J. Rubin/Chmn., CEO, Pres., Darren Woody/Dir., Byron H. Rubin/Dir., Adolpho R. Telles/Dir., Timothy F. Meeker/Dir., John Butterworth/Dir., Stanlee N. Rubin/Dir., Gary B. Abromovitz/Dir.

Owners: Insiders/21.27%, Columbia Wanger Asset Management, LP/5.23%, Thomas J. Benson, Daren G. Woody, Byron H. Rubin, Darren G. Woody, Timothy F. Meeker, Timothy F. Meeker, Gerald J. Rubin/20.16%, Gary B. Abromovitz, Thomas J. Benson, Vincent D. Carson, Gerald J. Rubin, Vincent D. Carson, Stanlee N. Rubin *(21 Owners included in Index)*

Financial Data: ***Fiscal Year End:***02/28 ***Latest Annual Data:*** 2/28/2007

Year	Sales	Net Income
2007	$634,932,000	$50,087,000
2006	$589,747,000	$49,310,000
2005	$581,549,000	$76,450,000

Curr. Assets:	$373,218,000	**Curr. Liab.:**	$135,087,000	**P/E Ratio:**	16.82
Plant, Equip.:	$96,669,000	**Total Liab.:**	$378,855,000	**Indic. Yr. Divd.:**	NA
Total Assets:	$906,272,000	**Net Worth:**	$527,417,000	**Debt/ Equity:**	0.4550

Helios & Matheson North America Inc

Formerly: A Consulting Team Inc (The)
200 Pk. Ave. S, Ste. 901, New York, NY, 10003; ***PH:*** 1-212-979-8228; ***http://*** www.tact.com

General - Incorporation .... NY
Employees 90
Auditor .... Grant Thornton, LLP
Stk Agt .... Mellon Investor Services LLC
Counsel .... Orrick, Herrington & Sutcliffe LLP
DUNS No. 15-479-9944

Stock- Price on:12/24/2007 .... NA
Stock Exchange .... NA
Ticker Symbol .... NA
Outstanding Shares .... NA
E.P.S .... -$0.13
Shareholders .... NA

Business: The group's principal activities are to provide technology-based consulting services and enterprise-wide information technology consulting, software and solutions. The information technology consulting services include technology infrastructure advisory services and systems architecture design for clients. The group markets and distributes a number of software products developed by independent software developers. The clients consist of Fortune 1000 companies and other large organizations that operate in a wide range of industries. The group delivers e-services solutions from Web strategy and design through Web development and integration, to Web application hosting.

Primary SIC and add'l.: 7371 7379

CIK No: 0001040792

Subsidiaries: International Object Technology, Inc., TACT Global Services Private Limited

Officers: Shmuel Bentov/Chmn., CEO, Pres./$381,004.00, Michael Prude/COO/$225,000.00, Salvatore M. Quadrino/CFO/$169,822.00

Directors: Shmuel Bentov/Chmn., CEO, Pres., Rabin Dhoble/Dir., Shankar Ram/Dir., Dan Thomas/Dir., S. Jambunathan/Dir., Divya Ramachandran/Dir., Kishan Gramma Ananthram/Dir.

Owners: Helios & Matheson Information Technology Ltd./52.00%, Steven Mukamal, Shmuel BenTov, Rabin Dhoble, William Miller, Michael Prude, Insiders

Financial Data: ***Fiscal Year End:***12/31 ***Latest Annual Data:*** 12/31/2006

Year	Sales	Net Income
2006	$24,940,000	$852,000
2005	$26,432,000	-$484,000
2004	$25,035,000	$1,237,000

Curr. Assets:	$8,001,000	**Curr. Liab.:**	$2,580,000		
Plant, Equip.:	$457,000	**Total Liab.:**	$2,580,000	**Indic. Yr. Divd.:**	NA
Total Assets:	$9,789,000	**Net Worth:**	$7,209,000	**Debt/ Equity:**	NA

Helix BioMedix Inc

22122 20th Ave. SE, Ste. 204, Bothell, WA, 98021; ***PH:*** 1-425-402-8400; ***Fax:*** 1-425-806-2999; ***http://*** www.helixbiomedix.com

General - Incorporation .... DE
Employees 8
Auditor .... KPMG LLP
Stk Agt .... U.S. Stock Transfer Corp
Counsel .... NA
DUNS No. 78-135-1747

Stock- Price on:12/24/2007 .... $0.85
Stock Exchange .... OTC
Ticker Symbol .... HXBM
Outstanding Shares 25,650,000
E.P.S .... -$0.14
Shareholders .... NA

Business: The group's principal activity is to engage in the research, development and commercialization of bioactive peptides (small proteins). The research is conducted both internally and in conjunction with a research and development arrangement with Louisiana state university, in the field of biotechnology. The group's technology consists of a proprietary library of bioactive peptides which are harnessed to develop products for various non-pharmaceutical applications including skin care products, biocides and commercial disinfectants and pharmaceutical products to aid in wound healing and treating infectious diseases.

Primary SIC and add'l.: 8731 2836

CIK No: 0000831749

Subsidiaries: Helix International, Inc

Officers: Stephen R. Beatty/Dir., CEO, Pres./$499,520.00, David S. Drajeske/VP - Business Development/$315,921.00, Timothy Falla/VP, Chief Scientific Officer/$328,778.00, David H. Kirske/CFO, VP/$299,174.00

Directors: Stephen R. Beatty/Dir., CEO, Pres., Richard M. Cohen/55/Dir., Randall L.W. Caudill/Dir., Weston Anson/65/Dir., John Fiddes/Dir., Barry L. Seidman/Dir., Daniel O. Wilds/Dir., Jeffrey A. Miller/Dir., David Oconnor/71/Dir., John F. Clifford/Dir., William Baker/Member - Scientific Advisory Board, Robert E.W. Hancock/Member - Scientific Advisory Board, Robin Cooper/Member - Scientific Advisory Board

Owners: Barry L. Seidman/8.40%, David S. Drajeske, John C. Fiddes, Daniel O. Wilds, Stephen R. Beatty/3.60%, Frank T. Nickell/29.30%, David H. Kirske, David M. OConnor, Insiders/16.90%, Richard M. Cohen, Jeffrey A. Miller/1.50%, Randall L.W. Caudill/1.60%, Timothy J. Falla/1.90%, Weston Anson

Financial Data: ***Fiscal Year End:***12/31 ***Latest Annual Data:*** 12/31/2006

Year	Sales	Net Income
2006	$71,000	-$3,828,000
2005	$108,000	-$3,277,000
2004	$94,000	-$3,109,000

Curr. Assets:	$2,344,000	**Curr. Liab.:**	$256,000		
Plant, Equip.:	$195,000	**Total Liab.:**	$256,000	**Indic. Yr. Divd.:**	NA
Total Assets:	$3,054,000	**Net Worth:**	$2,798,000	**Debt/ Equity:**	NA

Helix Energy Solutions Group Inc

400 N Sam Houston Pkwy. E, Ste. 400, Houston, TX, 77060; ***PH:*** 1-281-618-0400; ***Fax:*** 1-281-618-0501; ***http://*** www.helixesg.com

General - Incorporation	MN	Stock- Price on:12/24/2007	$40.24
Employees	2,300	Stock Exchange	NYSE
Auditor	Ernst& Young LLP	Ticker Symbol	HLX
Stk Agt	Wells Fargo Bank, N.A.	Outstanding Shares	91,310,000
Counsel	NA	E.P.S.	$3.76
DUNS No.	NA	Shareholders	NA

Business: The groups principle activities include constructing and maintaining pipelines, production platforms, risers and subsea production systems. The groups services include air and saturation diving, salvage work and shallow water pipelay. Customers served by the group include oil and gas producers and suppliers, pipeline transmission companies and offshore engineering and construction firms. The groups operates through three segments namely contracting services, shelf contracting and production facilities. Specific customers of the group include Louis Dreyfus Energy Services and Shell Offshore, Inc. The group operates from the United States. The group's quarterly revenue for September 2007 was 460.57 millions of USD.

Primary SIC and add'l.: 1389 1382 1311

CIK No: 0000866829

Subsidiaries: Box Brothers Realty Investments Company, Box Resources, Inc., Cal Dive I-Title XI, Inc., Cal Dive International, Inc., Cal Dive Offshore Ltd., Canyon Offshore International Corp, Canyon Offshore Limited, Canyon Offshore, Inc., CB Farms, Inc., CKB & Associates, Inc., CKB Petroleum, Inc., Energy Resource Technology (U.K.) Limited, Energy Resource Technology GOM, Inc., Helix Energy Limited, Helix Energy Services Pte. Limited. 31 Subsidiaries included in the Index

Officers: Quinn J. Hebert/Pres., CEO - Cal Dive International, Inc, Owen Kratz/Executive Chmn., Bart H. Heijermans/COO, Exec. VP, Wade A. Pursell/Sr. VP, CFO, Corporate Treasurer, Alisa B. Johnson/Sr. VP, General Counsel, Corp. Sec., Phil Moore/MD - Helix Energy Limited, Cory Weinbel/GM - Production Facilities, Martin R. Ferron/Dir., COO, Pres., Michael McEvilly/VP - Capital Projects, Brent Shinall/VP - Supply Chain Management, William E. Morrice/VP - Global Well Operations, GM - Well Ops UK, Stephen Rogers/VP - International Business Development, Michael C. Overman/Deputy General Counsel, Assist. Sec., Erik Heyman/Deputy General Counsel, Assist. Sec., Cliff Chamblee/Pres. - Canyon Offshore, Inc. *(23 Officers included in Index)*

Directors: Owen Kratz/Executive Chmn., Martin R. Ferron/Dir., COO, Pres., Gordon F. Ahalt/Dir., Bernard J. Duroc-Danner/Dir., John V. Lovoi/Dir., William T. Porter/Dir., William L. Transier/Dir., Tony Tripodo/Dir., James A. Watt/Dir.

Owners: James A. Watt, Bart H. Heijermans, Neuberger Berman, LLC/8.90%, Martin R. Ferron, Insiders/7.20%, William L. Transier, William T. Porter, Anthony Tripodo, Gordon F. Ahalt, John V. Lovoi, Owen Kratz/5.90%, Greenlight Capital, L.L.C./7.30%, Wade A. Pursell, Lloyd A. Hajdik, Bernard Duroc-Danner

Financial Data: Fiscal Year End:12/31   **Latest Annual Data:** 12/31/2006

Year	Sales	Net Income
2006	$1,366,924,000	$347,394,000
2005	$799,472,000	$152,568,000
2004	$543,392,000	$82,659,000

Curr. Assets:	$923,900,000	Curr. Liab.:	$613,376,000	P/E Ratio:	10.70
Plant, Equip.:	$2,212,458,000	Total Liab.:	$2,764,239,000	Indic. Yr. Divd.:	NA
Total Assets:	$4,290,187,000	Net Worth:	$1,525,948,000	Debt/ Equity:	NA

Hellenic Telecommun Organization

99 Kifissias Ave., Maroussi, Athens; *PH:* 30-210 6111574; *http://* www.ote.gr

General - Incorporation	Greece	Stock- Price on:12/24/2007	$15.43
Employees	14,739	Stock Exchange	NYSE
Auditor	KPMG Kyriacou Certified Auditors AE	Ticker Symbol	OTE
Stk Agt	Puglisi & Associates	Outstanding Shares	980,300,000
Counsel	George Gerapetritis	E.P.S.	$0.85
DUNS No.	42-300-4498	Shareholders	NA

Business: The groups principle activities include provision and maintenance of a national and international communication network. Customers served by the group include telecommunication, television and marine industries. The group operates from United States.

Primary SIC and add'l.: 4822 4812 3663 1731

CIK No: 0001071170

Subsidiaries: Albanian Mobile Communications, Armenian Telephone Company, CosmoBulgaria Mobile, Cosmofon, CosmoONE Hellas Market Site S.A., Cosmote Romania, EDEKTOTE S.A., EOS High Technology Applications SA, HATWAVE Hellenic-American Telecommunications Wave Ltd., Hellas Sat Consortium Limited, Hellas Sat S.A., Hellascom International S.A., Infote S.a., Lofos Pallini S.A., Multicom S.A. 33 Subsidiaries included in the Index

Officers: Panagis Vourloumis/Chmn., CEO, Konstantinos Kappos/53/CIO, Andreas Karageorgos/56/Chief Regional Officer, Nikolaos Tsatsanis/59/Chief Human Recourses Officer, Christos Katsaounis/45/Chief Officer - National Wholesale Services, Paraskevas Passias/42/General Counsel, Christini Spanoudaki/48/CFO, Maria Efthimerou/53/CTO, Kosmas Liaros/46/Chief Internal Audit Officer, Konstantinos M. Ploumpis/39/General Dir. - Regulatory Affairs, Dimitris Tzelepis/Head - Investor Relations, Nektarios Papagiannakopoulos/Sr. Financial Analyst, Daria Kozanoglou/Investor Relations Officer, Communications Officer, Marilli Diamanti/Investor Relations Officer, Coordinator, Evangelos Martigopoulos/49/MD - Cosmote *(17 Officers included in Index)*

Directors: Panagis Vourloumis/Chmn., CEO, Iakovos Georganas/Vice Chmn., Georgios Bitros/Dir., Charalambos Dimitriou/Dir., Ilias Gounaris/Dir., George Gerapetritis/Dir., Xeni Skorini-Paparrigopoulou/Dir., Nikolaos Stefanou/Dir., Panagiotis Tambourlos/Dir., Georgios Tzovlas/Dir., Theodoros E. Veniamis/Dir.

Owners: Andreas Karageorgos, Konstantinos Kappos, Christos Katsaounis, Nikos Stefanou

Financial Data: Fiscal Year End:12/31   **Latest Annual Data:** 12/31/2006

Year	Sales	Net Income
2006	$7,773,134,000	$672,033,000
2005	$6,479,852,000	-$345,726,000
2004	$7,073,050,000	$233,722,000

Curr. Assets:	$5,094,510,000	Curr. Liab.:	$3,814,479,000	P/E Ratio:	16.82
Plant, Equip.:	$8,364,893,000	Total Liab.:	$12,338,204,000	Indic. Yr. Divd.:	$0.370
Total Assets:	$16,994,638,000	Net Worth:	$4,656,434,000	Debt/ Equity:	NA

Helmerich & Payne Inc

1437 S Boulder Ave., Tulsa, OK, 74119; *PH:* 1-918-742-5531; *Fax:* 1-918-742-0237; *http://* www.hpinc.com; *Email:* investor.relations@hpinc.com

General - Incorporation	DE	Stock- Price on:12/24/2007	$36.04
Employees	5,697	Stock Exchange	Nyse
Auditor	Ernst & Young LLP	Ticker Symbol	HP
Stk Agt	UMB Bank, N.A.	Outstanding Shares	103,310,000
Counsel	NA	E.P.S.	$3.75
DUNS No.	00-330-5224	Shareholders	NA

Business: The group's principal activity is the contract drilling of oil and gas wells for others. In addition, the group owns, develops and operates commercial real estate. The group is organized into two separate autonomous operating entities. The contract drilling operations consist of contracting company-owned drilling equipment primarily to major oil and gas exploration companies. The group's domestic contract drilling is conducted primarily in Oklahoma, Texas, Wyoming and Louisiana and offshore from platforms in the gulf of Mexico and offshore California. The primary international areas of operation of the group include venezuela, Colombia, Ecuador, Argentina and Bolivia. The group's real estate investments are located in tulsa, Oklahoma. The primary areas of operation include a major shopping center and several multi-tenant warehouses.

Primary SIC and add'l.: 4924 1311 6531 2819 1382

CIK No: 0000046765

Subsidiaries: Fishercorp, Inc., H&P Finco, H&P Invest Ltd., Helmerich & Payne (Africa) Drilling Co., Helmerich & Payne (Argentina) Drilling Co, Helmerich & Payne (Australia) Drilling Co, Helmerich & Payne (Boulder) Drilling Co, Helmerich & Payne (Colombia) Drilling Co., Helmerich & Payne (Gabon) Drilling Co, Helmerich & Payne (Peru) Drilling Co., Sucursal del Peru, Helmerich & Payne (Peru) Drilling Co., Sucursal del Peru,Lima, Helmerich & Payne de Venezuela, C.A, Helmerich & Payne del Ecuador, Inc, Helmerich & Payne International Drilling Co., Helmerich & Payne Properties, Inc. 20 Subsidiaries included in the Index

Officers: Hans W. Helmerich/CEO, Pres., Douglas E. Fears/CFO, VP, John W. Lindsay/Exec. VP, Steven R. MacKey/VP, Sec., General Counsel, Alan M. Orr/Exec. VP

Directors: W. H. Helmerich/Chmn., William L. Armstrong/Dir., Glenn A. Cox/Dir., Edward B. Rust/Dir., Paula Marshall/Dir., John D. Zeglis/Dir., Randy A. Foutch/Dir.

Owners: Paula Marshall, Hans Helmerich, Alan M. Orr, John D. Zeglis, Goldman Sachs Asset Management, L.P., State Farm Mutual Automobile, John W. Lindsay, George S. Dotson, Douglas E. Fears, Steven R. Mackey, Insiders, Glenn A. Cox, William L. Armstrong, W. H. Helmerich, Edward B. Rust

Financial Data: Fiscal Year End:09/30   **Latest Annual Data:** 9/30/2006

Year	Sales	Net Income
2006	$1,224,813,000	$293,858,000
2005	$800,726,000	$127,606,000
2004	$620,928,000	$4,359,000

Curr. Assets:	$428,691,000	Curr. Liab.:	$264,548,000	P/E Ratio:	9.61
Plant, Equip.:	$1,483,134,000	Total Liab.:	$670,948,000	Indic. Yr. Divd.:	$0.180
Total Assets:	$2,134,712,000	Net Worth:	$1,381,892,000	Debt/ Equity:	0.2103

HemaCare Corp

15350 Sherman Way, Ste. 350, Van Nuys, CA, 91406; *PH:* 1-818-226-1968; *Fax:* 1-818-251-5300; *http://* www.hemacare.com; *Email:* mailroom@hemacare.com

General - Incorporation	CA	Stock- Price on:12/24/2007	$1.82
Employees	188	Stock Exchange	OTC
Auditor	Stonefield Josephson, Inc	Ticker Symbol	HEMA
Stk Agt	U.S. Stock Transfer Corp	Outstanding Shares	8,740,000
Counsel	Shepherd, Mullin, Rechter Et Al	E.P.S.	$0.16
DUNS No.	09-443-8447	Shareholders	NA

Business: The group is providing blood products and blood services to hospitals and medical centers primarily in California. The group operates through two segments namely: blood products and blood services. Blood product segment collects, processes and distributes blood products and donor testing. Blood services segment performs therapeutic apheresis, stem cell collection procedures and other therapeutic services provided to patients. The group has developed a customized blood service program designed to meet the requirements of each individual customer.

Primary SIC and add'l.: 2836 8099

CIK No: 0000801748

Subsidiaries: Comprehensive Blood Services, Inc., Coral Blood Services, Inc., HemaBiologics, Inc.

Officers: Judi Irving/50/Dir., CEO, Pres./$512,000.00, Julian Steffenhagen/Chmn., Interim CEO, Robert S. Chilton/CFO, Exec. VP/$308,000.00, Joshua Levy/National Dir. - Medical/$265,000.00, David Ciavarella/Dir. - Medical, Jacquelyn Hedlund/Dir. - Medical, Coral Blood Services, Melanie Osby/Assist. Dir. - Medical

Directors: Judi Irving/50/Dir., CEO, Pres., Julian Steffenhagen/Chmn., Interim CEO, Terry Van Der Tuuk/Dir., Steven Gerber/Dir., Teresa S. Sligh/Dir.

Owners: Praetorian Capital Management, LLC/14.90%, Steven B. Gerber/3.90%, Insiders/20.60%, Joshua Levy/5.70%, Robert S. Chilton/1.50%, Judi Irving/4.20%, Terry Van Der Tuuk/1.80%, Julian L. Steffenhagen/3.30%, Wellington Management Company, LLP/7.20%, John W. Egan/9.10%, D Carnegie& Co AB/9.10%, Teresa S Sligh

Financial Data: Fiscal Year End:12/31   **Latest Annual Data:** 12/31/2006

Year	Sales	Net Income
2006	$36,484,000	$1,851,000
2005	$31,227,000	$1,655,000
2004	$26,836,000	$1,545,000

Curr. Assets:	$10,528,000	Curr. Liab.:	$8,280,000		
Plant, Equip.:	$4,778,000	Total Liab.:	$9,194,000	Indic. Yr. Divd.:	NA
Total Assets:	$19,047,000	Net Worth:	$9,853,000	Debt/ Equity:	0.0545

Hemagen Diagnostics Inc

9033 Red Branch Rd., Columbia, MD, 21045; *PH:* 1-443-367-5500; *Fax:* 1-410-997-7812; *http://* www.hemagen.com; *Email:* info@hemagen.com

General - Incorporation	DE	Stock- Price on:12/24/2007	$0.22
Employees	46	Stock Exchange	OTC
Auditor	Grant Thornton LLP	Ticker Symbol	HMGN
Stk Agt	Continental Stock Transfer & Trust Co	Outstanding Shares	15,230,000
Counsel	Keating, Muething & Klekamp	E.P.S.	-$0.027
DUNS No.	14-782-7216	Shareholders	NA

Business: The group's principal activities are to develop, manufacture and market medical diagnostic test kits and materials for manufacturers of diagnostic test kits. The test kits are used as an aid in diagnosis of autoimmune and infectious diseases and for research purposes. The research works are undertaken on

diseases such as polymyositis, tissue disease, cytomegalovirus infections, chagas disease, wegeners disease, bilary cirrhosis, chicken pox, german measles, etc. The major products are elisa assays, immunofluorescence products, hemagglutination assays, clinical chemistry reagents products and analyst system products. The group also manufacturers and markets fda-cleared clinical chemistry analyzer. The products are marketed directly to clinical laboratories, blood banks and through multinational distributors of medical diagnostics. The operations are based in the United States and Brazil.

Primary SIC and add'l.: 3845 2835

CIK No: 0000892822

Subsidiaries: Hemagen Diagnosticos Comercio

Officers: William P. Hales/45/Chmn., CEO, Pres., Laura A. Bell/40/Controller

Directors: William P. Hales/45/Chmn., CEO, Pres., Edward T. Lutz/61/Dir., Alan S. Cohen/81/Dir., Richard W. Edwards/48/Dir.

Owners: Insiders/24.20%, Alan S. Cohen/1.70%, Edward T. Lutz, William P. Hales/21.30%, Jonathan E. Rothschild/7.40%, Richard W. Edwards

Financial Data: Fiscal Year End:09/30 Latest Annual Data: 9/30/2006

Year	Sales	Net Income
2006	$7,250,000	$313,000
2005	$7,586,000	-$1,337,000
2004	$7,471,000	-$3,599,000

Curr. Assets:	$4,183,000	Curr. Liab.:	$1,256,000		
Plant, Equip.:	$171,000	Total Liab.:	$5,097,000	Indic. Yr. Divd.:	NA
Total Assets:	$4,389,000	Net Worth:	-$708,000	Debt/ Equity:	NA

Hemcure Inc

5353 Manhattan Cir., Ste 101, Boulder, CO, 80303; *PH:* 1-303-499-6000; *http://* www.hemcure.com

General - Incorporation	MN	Stock - Price on:12/24/2007	$2
Employees	NA	Stock Exchange	OTC
Auditor	Kabani & Co.,Inc.	Ticker Symbol	HMCU
Stk Agt	Computershare Trust Co	Outstanding Shares	NA
Counsel	NA	E.P.S.	NA
DUNS No.	NA	Shareholders	NA

Business: The groups principle activity is to treat hemorrhoid problem without surgery. The group utilizes FDA approved treatment methods performed by physicians in a professional medical office. The group operates from United States.

Primary SIC and add'l.: 6770

CIK No: 0000810208

Officers: Arthur Liu/68/Chmn., CEO, CFO, Joseph Major/Medical Dir., Celia Cheng/64/Dir., Sec., Donald North/34/VP - Engineering

Directors: Arthur Liu/68/Chmn., CEO, CFO, Amy Liu,/32/Dir., Celia Cheng/64/Dir., Sec.

Owners: Arthur Liu, Funds to which RENN Capital Group serves as an investment advisor, Vision Opportunity Master Fund Ltd., Insiders, Renaissance US Growth Investment Trust PLC,

Financial Data: Fiscal Year End:06/30 Latest Annual Data: 6/30/2006

Year	Sales	Net Income
2006	NA	-$33,000

Curr. Assets:	$1,000	Curr. Liab.:	$1,000		
Plant, Equip.:	NA	Total Liab.:	$1,000	Indic. Yr. Divd.:	NA
Total Assets:	$1,000	Net Worth:	-$1,000	Debt/ Equity:	NA

Hemispherx Biopharma Inc

1 Penn Ctr., 1617 JFK Blvd., 6th Fl., Philadelphia, PA, 19103; *PH:* 1-215-988-0080; *Fax:* 1-215-988-1739; *http://* www.hemispherx.net; *Email:* info@hemispherx.net

General - Incorporation	DE	Stock - Price on:12/24/2007	$1.35
Employees	52	Stock Exchange	AMEX
Auditor	BDO Seidman LLP	Ticker Symbol	HEB
Stk Agt	Continental Stock Transfer & Trust Co	Outstanding Shares	71,990,000
Counsel	Schnader, Harrison, Segal & Lewis	E.P.S.	-$0.28
DUNS No.	05-860-8076	Shareholders	NA

Business: The group's principal activity is to develop therapeutic products for the treatment of viral diseases and certain cancers. The group's proprietary drug technology utilizes specifically configured ribonucleic acid (MA) and is protected by more than 300 patents worldwide. The products of the group include Ampligen, Oragent Drugs. Ampligen is being developed clinically for three anti-viral indications: myalgic encephalomyelitis, human immunodeficiency virus associated disorders and chronic hepatitis B virus infection.

Primary SIC and add'l.: 8731 2836 2834

CIK No: 0000946644

Subsidiaries: Hemispherx Biopharma Europe, S.A.

Officers: William A. Carter/Chmn., CEO, Pres./$2,186,764.00, Carol A. Smith/VP - Manufacturing Quality Assurance, Process Development/$169,963.00, Robert Hansen/VP - Manufacturing/$166,917.00, David R. Strayer/Dir. - Medical, Regulatory Affairs/$244,344.00, Robert E. Peterson/CFO/$696,998.00, Mei-June Liao/56/VP - Regulatory Affairs, Quality Control, Research, Development/$186,406.00, Dianne Will/Contact - Corporate Communications, Investor Relations, Rolf Reininghaus/Contact - Biovail, Syed Zaki Sallahudin/Contact - California Institute, Molecular Medicine, Cimm, Howard Urnovitz/Contact - Chronix Biomedical, James Tuite/Contact, Anthony Bonelli/COO, Pres./$210,601.00

Directors: William A. Carter/Chmn., CEO, Pres., William M. Mitchell/Dir., Ransom W. Ethridge/Dir., Richard C. Piani/Dir., Steven D. Spence/Dir., Iraj E. Kiani/Dir., Jack M. Gwaltney/Member - Scientific Advisory Board, Luc Montagnier/Dir., Member - Scientific Advisory Board, James J. Rahal/Member - Scientific Advisory Board

Owners: Robert E. Peterson, Insiders/11.50%, Steven Spence, Robert Hansen, Carol A. Smith, Richard C. Piani, David R. Strayer, William M. Mitchell, William A. Carter/8.00%, Ransom W. Etheridge/1.00%, Iraj-Eqhbal Kiani, Anthony Bonelli, Mei-June Liao

Financial Data: Fiscal Year End:12/31 Latest Annual Data: 12/31/2006

Year	Sales	Net Income
2006	$933,000	-$19,399,000
2005	$1,083,000	-$12,446,000
2004	$1,229,000	-$24,140,000

Curr. Assets:	$23,239,000	Curr. Liab.:	$6,680,000		
Plant, Equip.:	$5,344,000	Total Liab.:	$6,680,000	Indic. Yr. Divd.:	NA
Total Assets:	$31,431,000	Net Worth:	$24,751,000	Debt/ Equity:	NA

HemoBioTech Inc

5001 Spring Valley Rd., Ste. 1040- W, Dallas, TX, 75244; *PH:* 1-972-455-8950; *Fax:* 1-972-455-8951; *http://* hemobiotech.com; *Email:* info@hemobiotech.com

General - Incorporation	DE	Stock - Price on:12/24/2007	$2.02
Employees	5	Stock Exchange	OTC
Auditor	Eisner LLP	Ticker Symbol	HMBT
Stk Agt	Continental Stock Transfer & Trust Co	Outstanding Shares	18,440,000
Counsel	NA	E.P.S.	-$0.18
DUNS No.	NA	Shareholders	NA

Business: The groups principal activity is to provide biopharmaceutical product. The product of the group is HemoTech. The group markets its product under the brand name HemoTech(TM). The group operates from the United States.

Primary SIC and add'l.: 7379

CIK No: 0001301348

Officers: Arthur P. Bollon/Chmn., CEO, Pres., Mark J. Rosenblum/54/CFO, Sec., Mario Feola/Chief Medical Officer, Jan Simoni/Acting VP - Research, Development, Advisor, Tom G. Shires/Scientific Advisor

Directors: Arthur P. Bollon/Chmn., CEO, Pres., Ghassan Nino/Co - Founder, Vice Chmn., Robert Baron/Dir., Robert Comer/Dir., Walter Haeussler/Dir., Bernhard Mittemeyer/Dir., Frederick Frank/Member - Advisory Board, Ronald Blanck/Member - Scientific Advisory Board, Lawrence Helson/Dir., Member - Scientific Advisory Board

Owners: Nino Partners, LLC, Renaissance US Growth Investment Trust PLC, Renn Capital Group, Inc., Renaissance Capital Growth & Income Fund III, Inc., Robert Comer, Insiders, Ghassan Nino, Texas Tech University System, Robert Baron, Walter Haeussler, Jan Simoni, Arthur P. Bollon, Mark J. Rosenblum, Meyers Associates, L.P., Russell Cleveland *(19 Owners included in Index)*

Financial Data: Fiscal Year End:12/31 Latest Annual Data: 12/31/2006

Year	Sales	Net Income
2006	NA	-$2,571,000
2005	NA	-$3,454,000

Curr. Assets:	$4,247,000	Curr. Liab.:	$171,000		
Plant, Equip.:	$12,000	Total Liab.:	$171,000	Indic. Yr. Divd.:	NA
Total Assets:	$4,259,000	Net Worth:	$4,088,000	Debt/ Equity:	NA

HemoSense Inc

651 River Oaks Pkwy., San Jose, CA, 95134; *PH:* 1-408-719-1393; *Fax:* 1-408-719-1184; *http://* www.hemosense.com

General - Incorporation	DE	Stock - Price on:12/24/2007	$8.15
Employees	79	Stock Exchange	AMEX
Auditor	PricewaterhouseCoopers LLP	Ticker Symbol	HEM
Stk Agt	Computershare Trust Co	Outstanding Shares	13,200,000
Counsel	NA	E.P.S.	-$0.52
DUNS No.	NA	Shareholders	NA

Business: The groups principle activities include developing, manufacturing and selling easy-to-use, handheld blood coagulation monitoring systems. The groups products marketed under the INRatio System(R). The group operates from the United States, Germany and Spain.

Primary SIC and add'l.: 3829 3841 3829

CIK No: 0001127393

Officers: James D. Merselis/Dir., CEO, Pres., Harvey Schloss/Dir., Independent Consultant, Timothy I. Still/Exec. VP, Chief Commercial Officer, Gordon Sangster/CFO, VP - Finance, William Dippel/Exec. VP - Operations, Research, Development, Gregory M. Ayers/45/Medical Device Consultant

Directors: James D. Merselis/Dir., CEO, Pres., Edward F. Brennan/Dir., Richard P. Powers/Dir., Harvey Schloss/Dir., Independent Consultant, Robert D. Ulrich/Dir., Kurt C. Wheeler/Dir.

Owners: JPMorgan Asset Management, Inc./10.70%, Vanguard V, L.P./5.30%, Insiders/3.60%, Entities affiliated with Balyasny Asset Management/5.60%, New Enterprise Associates 12, Limited Partnership/13.60%, W Capital Partners Ironworks, L.P./6.30%, Gregory M. Ayers, Entities affiliated with MPM Capital/33.20%

Financial Data: Fiscal Year End:09/30 Latest Annual Data: 9/30/2006

Year	Sales	Net Income
2006	$16,257,000	-$10,885,000
2005	$8,768,000	-$11,746,000
2004	$3,250,000	-$10,261,000

Curr. Assets:	$15,978,000	Curr. Liab.:	$5,283,000		
Plant, Equip.:	$501,000	Total Liab.:	$8,173,000	Indic. Yr. Divd.:	NA
Total Assets:	$16,850,000	Net Worth:	$8,677,000	Debt/ Equity:	0.3921

Hendrx Corp

3051 Boones Ln, Ellicott City, MD, 21042; *PH:* 1-410-418-5118; *http://* www.hendrx.com

General - Incorporation	NV	Stock - Price on:12/24/2007	$0.32
Employees	NA	Stock Exchange	OTC
Auditor	Chisholm, Bierwolf & Nilson, LLC	Ticker Symbol	HDRX
Stk Agt	Holladay Stock Transfer, Inc.	Outstanding Shares	NA
Counsel	NA	E.P.S.	NA
DUNS No.	NA	Shareholders	NA

Business: The groups principle activities include researching, developing, manufacturing and marketing the distribution of water generation, filtration, ionization, desalinization, and purification devices. The groups products line includes Atmospheric Water Generation units, Alkaline Calcium Ionic Water Dispensers, and Reverse Osmosis systems. Specific customer of the group is Librex Group S.A.L. The group operates from the, United States, United Arab, Australia, Lebanon, Malaysia, Saudi Arabia, Thailand, Israel, India, Indonesia, Italy and Canada. The group's quarterly revenue for September 2007 was 0.40 milions of USD.

Primary SIC and add'l.: 8732

CIK No: 0001082696

Officers: George Solymar/Dir., CEO, Cherry Cai/CFO, Principal Accounting Officer, David Tjahjadi/VP - Business Development

Directors: George Solymar/Dir., CEO, Hendrik Tjandra/Chmn., Nadir Walji/Dir.

Owners: Insiders/37.50%, Pictet Funds/5.40%, Robert De Costa, Hendrik Tjandra/37.50%

Financial Data: Fiscal Year End:12/31 Latest Annual Data: 12/31/2006

Year	Sales	Net Income
2006	$2,248,000	-$2,974,000
2005	$4,471,000	-$2,951,000
2004	$255,000	$106,000

Curr. Assets:	$2,331,000	Curr. Liab.:	$3,810,000	
Plant, Equip.:	$5,826,000	Total Liab.:	$4,810,000	Indic. Yr. Divd.: NA
Total Assets:	$42,805,000	Net Worth:	$37,995,000	Debt/ Equity: NA

Hennessy Advisors Inc

7250 Redwood Blvd., Ste. 200, Novato, CA, 94945; *PH:* 1-415-899-1555; *Fax:* 1-415-899-1559; *http://* www.hennessyadvisors.com; *Email:* steady@hennessyadvisors.com

General - Incorporation	CA	*Stock*- Price on:12/24/2007	$13.12
Employees	12	Stock Exchange	OTC
Auditor	Pisenti & Brinker LLP	Ticker Symbol	HNNA
Stk Agt	Firstar Bank, N.A.	Outstanding Shares	5,700,000
Counsel	NA	E.P.S.	$0.70
DUNS No.	NA	Shareholders	NA

Business: The group's principal activity is provide investment advisory services to five no-loan mutual funds and networth investors. The investment advisory services of the group include investment research, supervision of investments, conducting clients' investment programs that include evaluation, sale and reinvestment of assets, the placement of orders for purchase and sale of securities. The group solicits brokers to execute transactions and also prepares and distributes reports and statistical information. The shareholder services primarily involve the handling of shareholder inquiries and providing written materials regarding the mutual fund operations and performance. The group operates in the United States.

Primary SIC and add'l.: 6282

CIK No: 0001145255

Officers: Neil J. Hennessy/Dir., CEO, Pres., Teresa M. Nilsen/Dir., CFO, Exec. VP, Sec., Daniel B. Steadman/Dir., Exec. VP, Keith Grady/Marketing Maker

Directors: Neil J. Hennessy/Dir., CEO, Pres., Teresa M. Nilsen/Dir., CFO, Exec. VP, Sec., Thomas L. Seavey/Dir., Charles W. Bennett/Dir., Henry Hansel/Dir., Rodger Offenbach/Dir., Brian A. Hennessy/Dir., Daniel B. Steadman/Dir., Exec. VP, Daniel G. Libarle/Dir.

Owners: Brian A. Hennessy/4.70%, Insiders/47.50%, Daniel B. Steadman/0.80%, Charles W. Bennett/0.30%, Thomas L. Seavey/1.30%, Teresa M. Nilsen/2.10%, Neil J. Hennessy/35.60%, Daniel G. Libarle/1.80%, Henry Hansel/2.90%, Rodger Offenbach/2.30%

Financial Data: Fiscal Year End:09/30 *Latest Annual Data:* 9/30/2006

Year	Sales	Net Income
2006	$16,934,000	$4,403,000
2005	$11,997,000	$3,139,000
2004	$9,545,000	$2,765,000

Curr. Assets:	$12,280,000	Curr. Liab.:	$4,339,000	P/E Ratio: 17.49
Plant, Equip.:	$383,000	Total Liab.:	$14,157,000	Indic. Yr. Divd.: $0.050
Total Assets:	$33,107,000	Net Worth:	$18,950,000	Debt/ Equity: 0.3587

Henry Bros. Electronics Inc

Formerly: Diversified Security Solutions Inc
280 Midland Ave, Saddle Brook, NJ, 07663; *PH:* 1-201-794-6500; *http://* www.hbe-inc.com

General - Incorporation	DE	*Stock*- Price on:12/24/2007	$3.67
Employees	172	Stock Exchange	NA
Auditor	Demetrius & Co LLC	Ticker Symbol	NA
Stk Agt	Continental Stock Transfer & Trust Co	Outstanding Shares	5,900,000
Counsel	NA	E.P.S.	-$0.31
DUNS No.	NA	Shareholders	NA

Business: The group's principle activities are to design, integrate, manufacture, install and maintain security and control systems. The group manufactures, develops and assembles various security related products, used in installations and for sales to other integrators. As a security integrator, the group designs, customizes, installs, connects and maintains closed circuit television and access control systems for customers in the private and public sectors under the trade names, hbe and henry bros. Electronics. The group provides technology-based security solutions for medium and large commercial and governmental facilities in the United States. The group also provides a full range of security integration services, which include consulting and planning, engineering and design, systems installation and management, systems training and maintenance and technical support.

Primary SIC and add'l.: 3577 7382 1731

CIK No: 0001099918

Subsidiaries: Airorlite Communications, Inc., Diversified Security Solutions, Inc., Henry Bros. Electronics, Inc., Henry Bros. Electronics, LLC, National Safe of California, Inc., Securus, Inc., Viscom Products, Inc.

Officers: James E. Henry/Chmn., CEO, Founder, Mike Tiffin/VP - HBE Arizona, Alex Pavlis/VP - HBE California, Brian Reach/Dir., COO, Emil Marone/CTO, John A. Batsch/Dir. - Operations, Viscom, Jim Williams/VP, GM - CIS Subsidiary, Lee Masoian/Pres. - Airorlit, Theodore Gjini/VP - HBE New York Metro, Bruce Debon/Dir. - Business Development, Dssi, Jeffrey H. Marcus/VP - General Managersecurus, Chris Peckham/Chief Information, Security Officer, John Hopkins/CFO, Brian Smith/Corporate Controller, David Fitzgerald/VP - Business Development (*16 Officers included in Index*)

Directors: James E. Henry/Chmn., CEO, Founder, Joseph P. Ritorto/Dir., Brian Reach/Dir., COO, Robert L. De Lia/Dir., James W. Power/Dir., David Sands/Dir.

Owners: John P. Hopkins, Joseph P. Ritorto, James E. Henry/23.60%, Insiders/29.10%, James W. Power, Brian Reach/3.30%, Robert De Lia, David Sands

Financial Data: Fiscal Year End:12/31 *Latest Annual Data:* 12/31/2006

Year	Sales	Net Income
2006	$42,133,000	-$2,260,000
2005	$42,156,000	$1,108,000
2004	$29,726,000	$44,000

Curr. Assets:	$23,471,000	Curr. Liab.:	$13,469,000	
Plant, Equip.:	$2,402,000	Total Liab.:	$17,360,000	Indic. Yr. Divd.: NA
Total Assets:	$31,372,000	Net Worth:	$14,011,000	Debt/ Equity: 0.0334

Henry County Bancshares Inc

4806 N Henry Blvd., Stockbridge, GA, 30281; *PH:* 1-770-474-7293; *Fax:* 1-770-474-8053; *http://* www.firststateonline.com

General - Incorporation	GA	*Stock*- Price on:12/24/2007	NA
Employees	NA	Stock Exchange	NA
Auditor	Mauldin & Jenkins LLC	Ticker Symbol	NA
Stk Agt	NA	Outstanding Shares	NA
Counsel	NA	E.P.S.	NA
DUNS No.	NA	Shareholders	NA

Business: The group's principle activity is to provide full service commercial banking, consumer banking and variety of deposit services. The group operates through its wholly owned subsidiaries first metro mortgage co and the first state bank. The group's lending activity include commercial, consumer installment, real estate, home equity and second mortgage loans, with particular emphasis on short and medium term obligations. It also offers on-line banking services to its customers.

Primary SIC and add'l.: 6712 6021

CIK No: 0000706465

Subsidiaries: The First State Bank

Officers: David H. Gill/Dir., CEO, Pres., Thomas L. Redding/Sr. VP, CFO, Lisa C. Carter/VP, Br Mgr., Judy C. Coker/VP, Br Mgr., Paul E. Cross/VP, Sally L. Fitzgerald/VP, Randall A. Holcomb/VP, Teena H. Lee/VP, Bonnie J. Lecroy/Mgr. - Locust Grove, James W. Love/VP, Donald L. Mason/VP, Elizabeth A. McCullough/VP, John H. Moore/VP, Judith A. Morrow/VP, Br Mgr., Dianne Pulliam/Mgr. - First Metro Mortgage (*31 Officers included in Index*)

Directors: David H. Gill/Dir., CEO, Pres., Robert O. Linch/Chmn., Mary Lynn E. Lambert/Dir., Phillip H. Cook/Dir., William C. Strom/Dir., Exec. VP - CCO, Paul J. Cates/Dir., H. K. Elliott/Dir., G. R. Foster/Dir., Edwin C. Kelley/Dir., Ronald M. Turpin/Dir., James C. Waggoner/Dir.

Owners: James C. Waggoner, Thomas L. Redding, David H. Gill, Ronald M. Turpin, Mary Lynn E. Lambert, Insiders/11.25%, William C. Strom, H. K. Elliott/1.39%, Paul J. Cates, G. R. Foster, Phillip H. Cook, Robert O. Linch/6.29%, Edwin C. Kelley

Henry Schein Inc

135 Duryea Rd., Melville, NY, 11747; *PH:* 1-631-843-5500; *Fax:* 1-631-843-5658; *http://* www.henryschein.com

General - Incorporation	DE	*Stock*- Price on:12/24/2007	$52.86
Employees	11,000	Stock Exchange	NDQ
Auditor	BDO Seidman LLP	Ticker Symbol	HSIC
Stk Agt	Continental Stock Transfer & Trust Co	Outstanding Shares	88,840,000
Counsel	Proskauer Rose	E.P.S.	$1.99
DUNS No.	01-243-0880	Shareholders	NA

Business: The group's principle activity is to distribute healthcare products and services. The group operates through four segments include Dental, Medical, International, and Technology. The groups customers include dental practices and laboratories, physician practices and veterinary clinics, as well as government and other institutions. The group operates from United States.

Primary SIC and add'l.: 7389 5047 7372

CIK No: 0001000228

Subsidiaries: Dentrix Dental Systems, Inc, Henry Schein Europe, Inc., Henry Schein Financial Services, Inc., Henry Schein Holding GmbH, HSI Service Corp.

Officers: Stanley M. Bergman/Chmn., CEO/$2,818,157.00, Leonard A. David/Corporate Sr. VP, Chief Compliance Officer, James P. Breslawski/Dir., COO, Pres./$1,539,337.00, Michael Racioppi/Pres. - Medical Group, Stanley Komaroff/Sr. Advisor, Mark E. Mlotek/Dir., Exec. VP - Corporate Business Development/$1,235,770.00, Gerald A. Benjamin/Dir., Exec. VP, Chief Administrative Officer/$1,236,351.00, Michael Zack/Corporate Sr. VP, Pres. - International Group, Steven Paladino/Dir., CFO, Exec. VP/$1,250,672.00, Susan Vassallo/VP - Corporate Communications, Neal Goldner/VP - Investor Relations

Directors: Stanley M. Bergman/Chmn., CEO, Barry J. Alperin/Dir., Norman S. Matthews/Dir., Philip A. Laskawy/Dir., James P. Breslawski/Dir., COO, Pres., Donald J. Kabat/Dir., Margaret A. Hamburg/Dir., Mark E. Mlotek/Dir., Exec. VP - Corporate Business Development, Gerald A. Benjamin/Dir., Exec. VP, Chief Administrative Officer, Paul Brons/Dir., Steven Paladino/Dir., CFO, Exec. VP, Marvin H. Schein/Dir., Louis W. Sullivan/Dir.

Owners: Gerald A. Benjamin, Paul Brons, James P. Breslawski, Insiders/3.50%, Margaret A. Hamburg, Steven Paladino, Barry J. Alperin, Norman S. Matthews, Neuberger Berman, Inc./5.60%, Mark E. Mlotek, Stanley M. Bergman/1.40%, T. Rowe Price Associates, Inc./7.40%, Louis W. Sullivan, Marvin H. Schein, Philip A. Laskawy (*16 Owners included in Index*)

Financial Data: Fiscal Year End:12/31 *Latest Annual Data:* 12/30/2006

Year	Sales	Net Income
2006	$5,153,097,000	$163,759,000
2005	$4,635,929,000	$151,326,000
2004	$4,060,266,000	$128,183,000

Curr. Assets:	$1,584,409,000	Curr. Liab.:	$724,114,000	
Plant, Equip.:	$190,746,000	Total Liab.:	$1,341,223,000	Indic. Yr. Divd.: NA
Total Assets:	$2,583,120,000	Net Worth:	$1,229,544,000	Debt/ Equity: 0.3098

Hepalife Technologies Inc

60 State St., Ste. 700, Boston, MA, 02109; *PH:* 1-800-518-4879; *http://* www.hepalife.com; *Email:* info@hepalife.com

General - Incorporation	FL	*Stock*- Price on:12/24/2007	$0.81
Employees	NA	Stock Exchange	OTC
Auditor	Peterson Sullivan, PLLC	Ticker Symbol	HPLF
Stk Agt	Holladay Stock Transfer	Outstanding Shares	NA
Counsel	NA	E.P.S.	-$0.06
DUNS No.	NA	Shareholders	NA

Business: The groups principal activities include identifying and developing cell-based technologies and products. The product of the group is PICM-19 Cell Line. The group operates from the United Sates.

Primary SIC and add'l.: 3841

CIK No: 0001054274

Subsidiaries: Phoenix BioSystems, Inc

Officers: Frank Menzler/Dir., CEO, Pres./$56,250.00, Harmel S. Rayat/Chmn., Sec., Treasurer, CFO

Directors: Frank Menzler/Dir., CEO, Pres., Harmel S. Rayat/Chmn., Sec., Treasurer, CFO, Javier Jimenez/Non - Exec. Dir., Paul Coussens/Member - Scientific Advisory Board, Michael Ott/Member - Scientific Advisory Board, Joerg C. Gerlach/Member - Scientific Advisory Board, Stephen R. Ash/Member - Scientific Advisory Board, Aly El-Banayosy/Member - Scientific Advisory Board

Owners: Frank Menzler/3.00%, Insiders/64.00%, Harmel S. Rayat/61.00%

Financial Data: *Fiscal Year End:*12/31 *Latest Annual Data:* 12/31/2006

Year	Sales	Net Income
2006	NA	-$4,654,000
2005	NA	-$2,814,000
2004	NA	-$1,436,000

Curr. Assets:	$257,000	**Curr. Liab.:**	$1,339,000		
Plant, Equip.:	$23,000	**Total Liab.:**	$1,339,000	**Indic. Yr. Divd.:**	NA
Total Assets:	$280,000	**Net Worth:**	-$1,059,000	**Debt/ Equity:**	NA

Herbalife Ltd

1800 Century Pk. E, Los Angeles, CA, 90067; *PH:* 1-310-410-9600; *Fax:* 1-310-258-7019; *http://* www.herbalife.com

General - Incorporation	Cayman Islands	***Stock***- Price on:12/24/2007	$40.15
Employees	3,644	Stock Exchange	NYSE
Auditor	KPMG LLP	Ticker Symbol	HLF
Stk Agt	Mellon Investor Services LLC	Outstanding Shares	71,840,000
Counsel	NA	E.P.S.	$2.42
DUNS No.	NA	Shareholders	NA

Business: The groups principle activity is to sell weight management, nutritional supplement and personal care products. In the year 2005, the group acquired Stauber Performance ingredients. The group operates from the United States, Mexico and other countries. The group's quarterly revenue for September 2007 was 529.54 millions of USD.

Primary SIC and add'l.: 5963 2833

CIK No: 0001180262

Subsidiaries: H & L (Suzhou) Health Products Ltd, Herbalife (N.Z.) Limited,, Herbalife (U.K.) Limited,, Herbalife Australasia Pty Ltd, Herbalife Denmark ApS,, Herbalife Europe Limited,, Herbalife Hungary Trading, Ltd, Herbalife Indonesia,, Herbalife Internacional de Mexico, S.A. de C.V, Herbalife International (Thailand) Ltd,, Herbalife International Argentina, S.A, Herbalife International Belgium, S.A./N.V, Herbalife International Communications, Inc, Herbalife International de Espana, S.A, Herbalife International Deutschland GmbH, 55 Subsidiaries included in the Index

Officers: Michael O. Johnson/Dir., CEO/$4,555,721.00, Gregory Probert/51/COO, Pres./$3,142,698.00, Brett Chapman/52/General Counsel, Corp. Sec./$1,447,343.00, Richard Goudis/CFO/$1,535,712.00, Paul Noack/46/Chief Strategic Officer/$1,542,954.00, Steve Henig/65/Chief Scientific Officer

Directors: Michael O. Johnson/Dir., CEO, Peter M. Castleman/51/Chmn., Leroy T. Barnes/Dir., Richard P. Bermingham/Dir., David D. Halbert/52/Dir., Peter Maslen/Dir., Colombe M. Nicholas/Dir., Valeria Rico/Dir., John Tartol/Dir., Leon Waisbein/Dir.

Owners: FMR Corp./9.10%, Daniel J. OBrien/26.00%, Michael R. Stone/0.40%, John Tartol, Peter Maslen, Valeria Rico, Michael O. Johnson/2.90%, David D. Halbert, Peter M. Castleman/25.90%, Paul Noack, Whitney Private Debt Fund, L.P./0.10%, Gregory Probert, WhitneyV, L.P./24.50%, Brett R. Chapman, Whitney Strategic PartnersV, L.P./0.20% *(22 Owners included in Index)*

Financial Data: *Fiscal Year End:*12/31 *Latest Annual Data:* 12/31/2006

Year	Sales	Net Income
2006	$1,885,534,000	$143,139,000
2005	$1,566,750,000	$93,140,000
2004	$1,309,663,000	-$14,311,000

Curr. Assets:	$455,707,000	**Curr. Liab.:**	$323,492,000	**P/E Ratio:**	19.03
Plant, Equip.:	$105,266,000	**Total Liab.:**	$663,043,000	**Indic. Yr. Divd.:**	$0.800
Total Assets:	$1,016,933,000	**Net Worth:**	$353,890,000	**Debt/ Equity:**	NA

Herborium

Formerly: Pacific Magtron International Corp
3 Oak St., Teaneck, NJ, 07666; *PH:* 1-201-836-2424; *http://* www.pacmag.com

General - Incorporation	NV	***Stock***- Price on:12/24/2007	$0.019
Employees	1	Stock Exchange	NA
Auditor	Berenson LLP	Ticker Symbol	NA
Stk Agt	NA	Outstanding Shares	114,070,000
Counsel	NA	E.P.S.	-$0.005
DUNS No.	NA	Shareholders	NA

Business: The group's principal activity is wholesale distribution of electronic products, computer components and peripheral equipment and information technology solutions. The group operates in three segments. Pmi, pmiga and lw. Pmi segment includes distribution of computer related multimedia hardware components and software. Pmiga segment includes distribution of pmi's products in the eastern United States. Lw segment provides consumers a convenient way to purchase computer products via the Internet. The group disposed of frontline network consulting inc. (fnc) and lea publishing inc in 2003. In 2003 the group dissolved pmi capital corporation (pmicc) a wholly-owned subsidiary of pmic, formed for the purpose of acquiring companies or assets deemed suitable for pmic's organization.

Primary SIC and add'l.: 5045 7375

CIK No: 0001077050

Subsidiaries: LiveWarehouse, Inc., Pacific Magtron (GA), Inc., Pacific Magtron, Inc.

Officers: Agnes P. Olszewski/51/Dir., CEO, CFO, Pres., James P. Gilligan/56/Dir., Consultant

Directors: Agnes P. Olszewski/51/Dir., CEO, CFO, Pres., James P. Gilligan/56/Dir., Consultant, Max G. Ansbacher/71/Dir., Wayne I. Danson/54/Dir.

Owners: Agnes P. Olszewski/39.30%, Wayne I. Danson, James P. Gilligan/37.70%, Insiders/77.70%, Max G. Ansbacher

Financial Data: *Fiscal Year End:*12/31 *Latest Annual Data:* 11/30/2006

Year	Sales	Net Income
2006	$828,000	-$340,000
2005	$9,984,000	-$1,679,000
2004	$71,474,000	-$1,134,000

Curr. Assets:	$74,000	**Curr. Liab.:**	$222,000		
Plant, Equip.:	NA	**Total Liab.:**	$313,000	**Indic. Yr. Divd.:**	NA
Total Assets:	$74,000	**Net Worth:**	-$239,000	**Debt/ Equity:**	NA

Hercules Inc

1313 N Market St., Wilmington, DE, 19894; *PH:* 1-302-594-7151; *Fax:* 1-302-594-5400; *http://* www.herc.com

General - Incorporation	DE	***Stock***- Price on:12/24/2007	$19.18
Employees	4,430	Stock Exchange	NYSE
Auditor	BDO Seidman LLP	Ticker Symbol	HPC
Stk Agt	Mellon Investor Services LLC	Outstanding Shares	116,590,000
Counsel	NA	E.P.S.	$3.42
DUNS No.	00-131-5647	Shareholders	NA

Business: The groups principle activities include manufacturing and marketing chemical specialties used in making a variety of products for home, office and industrial markets. Customers served by the group include the pulp and paper, paints and adhesives, construction materials, food, pharmaceutical and personal care industries. The group operates from United States.

Primary SIC and add'l.: 2819 2869 2842 2821 2861 3081 2899

CIK No: 0000046989

Subsidiaries: Abieta Chemie GmbH, Aqualon Company, Aqualon France B.V., Athens Holdings Inc., Covington Holdings Inc., Curtis Bay Insurance Co. Ltd., East Bay Realty Services, Inc., ES FiberVisions ApS, ES FiberVisions Holding ApS, ES FiberVisions Hong Kong Ltd., Ever Success Overseas Limited, FiberVisions (China) A/S, FiberVisions (China) Textile Products Ltd., FiberVisions GmbH, FiberVisions Incorporated 74 Subsidiaries included in the Index

Officers: Craig A. Rogerson/CEO, Pres./$5,400,717.00, Edward V. Carrington/VP - Human Resources/$815,760.00, Richard G. Dahlen/Chief Legal Officer, John E. Panichella/VP/$1,385,898.00, Israel J. Floyd/Corp. Sec., General Counsel, Vincenzo M. Romano/54/VP - Taxes, Stuart C. Shears/57/VP, Treasurer, Paul C. Raymond/VP - Hercules Incorporated/$946,094.00, Allen A. Spizzo/CFO, VP/$1,402,169.00, Stuart L. Fornoff/Dir. - Investor Relations, Corporate Analysis, Fred G. Aanonsen/60/VP, Controller

Directors: John K. Wulff/59/Non - Exec. Chmn., Jeffrey M. Lipton/65/Dir., Anna C. Catalano/48/Dir., Burton M. Joyce/66/Dir., Thomas P. Gerrity/66/Dir., Joe B. Wyatt/72/Dir., John C. Hunter/61/Dir., Robert D. Kennedy/74/Dir.

Owners: J. M. Lipton, J. K. Wulff, J. E. Panichella, B. M. Joyce, State Street Bank and Trust Company/8.40%, J. C. Hunter, T. P. Gerrity, A. C. Catalano, A. A. Spizzo, Sasco Capital, Inc./5.60%, AXA Assurances I.A.R.D. Mutuelle/5.70%, J. B. Wyatt, R. D. Kennedy, Insiders/2.10%, GAMCO Investors, Inc./5.40% *(18 Owners included in Index)*

Financial Data: *Fiscal Year End:*12/31 *Latest Annual Data:* 12/31/2006

Year	Sales	Net Income
2006	$2,035,300,000	$238,700,000
2005	$2,068,800,000	-$41,100,000
2004	$1,997,000,000	$27,000,000

Curr. Assets:	$984,500,000	**Curr. Liab.:**	$629,600,000	**P/E Ratio:**	7.24
Plant, Equip.:	$600,400,000	**Total Liab.:**	$2,552,900,000	**Indic. Yr. Divd.:**	$0.200
Total Assets:	$2,808,500,000	**Net Worth:**	$242,900,000	**Debt/ Equity:**	2.7626

Hercules Offshore Inc

9 Greenway Plz., Ste. 2220, Houston, TX, 77046; *PH:* 1-713-350-5100; *Fax:* 1-713-979-5105; *http://* www.herculesoffshore.com

General - Incorporation	DE	***Stock***- Price on:12/24/2007	$34.89
Employees	920	Stock Exchange	NDQ
Auditor	Grant Thornton LLP	Ticker Symbol	HERO
Stk Agt	American Stock Transfer & Trust Co.	Outstanding Shares	32,260,000
Counsel	NA	E.P.S.	$3.73
DUNS No.	NA	Shareholders	NA

Business: The groups principle activity is to provide shallow water drilling and lift boat services. The groups services include contract drilling and marine. The groups operates through four segments namely domestic contract drilling services, international contract drilling services, domestic marine services and international marine services. Specific customers of the group include Chevron Corporation and Bois dArc Energy, Inc. The group operates from the United States, Gulf, Mexico, Qatar and India. The group's quarterly revenue for September 2007 was 294.37 millions of USD.

Primary SIC and add'l.: 1381 7359 6719 7353

CIK No: 0001330849

Subsidiaries: Hercules Drilling Company, LLC, Hercules International Asset Company, Ltd., Hercules International Drilling, Ltd., Hercules International Finance Company, Ltd., Hercules International Holdings, Ltd., Hercules International Management Company, Ltd., Hercules International Offshore, Ltd., Hercules Liftboat Company, LLC, Hercules Marketing International, Ltd., Hercules Offshore (Nigeria) Limited, Hercules Offshore International, LLC, Hercules Offshore Services, LLC, Hercules Oilfield Services, Ltd.

Officers: Randall D. Stilley/Dir., CEO, Pres., Troy L. Carson/VP, Corporate Controller, Laura D. Guthrie/VP - Human Resources, Terry L. Carr/VP - Worldwide Operations, Hercules Drilling Company, LLC, Todd Pellegrin/MD - West Africa, Hercules Liftboat Company, LLC, Don P. Rodney/Pres., Dir. - Hercules International Holdings, Ltd, James W. Noe/Sr. VP, General Counsel, Chief Compliance Officer, Sec., James C. Bryan/VP - Human Resources, Stephen M. Butz/VP - Finance, Treasurer, Richard E. McClaine/VP - Health, Safety, Environmental, Randal R. Reed/Pres. - Hercules Liftboat Company, LLC, John T. Rynd/COO, Exec. VP, Lisa W. Rodriguez/CFO, Sr. VP

Directors: Randall D. Stilley/Dir., CEO, Pres., John T. Reynolds/Chmn., Thomas R. Bates/Dir., Gardner G. Parker/Dir., Steven A. Webster/Dir., Thomas J. Madonna/Dir., Thierry Pilenko/Dir., Thomas N. Amonett/Dir., Suzanne V. Baer/Dir., Thomas M. Hamilton/Dir.

Owners: F. Gardner Parker, James W. Noe, Thomas R. Bates/4.90%, AMVESCAP PLC/5.20%, Steven A. Manz, Thomas J. Madonna, John T. Rynd, John T. Reynolds/4.90%, Randal R. Reed, Steven A. Webster/2.30%, Insiders/17.70%, Randall D. Stilley/3.00%, Thierry Pilenko, Don P. Rodney, Thomas E. Hord

Financial Data: *Fiscal Year End:*12/31 *Latest Annual Data:* 12/31/2006

Year	Sales	Net Income
2006	$344,312,000	$119,050,000
2005	$161,334,000	$27,456,000

Curr. Assets:	$180,223,000	**Curr. Liab.:**	$69,326,000	**P/E Ratio:**	9.35
Plant, Equip.:	$415,864,000	**Total Liab.:**	$210,730,000	**Indic. Yr. Divd.:**	NA
Total Assets:	$605,581,000	**Net Worth:**	$394,851,000	**Debt/ Equity:**	0.2123

hereUare Inc

Formerly: Peoplenet International Corp
5201 Great America Pk.way, Ste. 446, Santa Clara, CA, 95054; *PH:* 1-408-988-1888;
http:// www.peoplenet.com

General - Incorporation	DE	**Stock**- Price on:12/24/2007	NA
Employees	10	Stock Exchange	NA
Auditor	Kabani & Co, Inc	Ticker Symbol	NA
Stk Agt	NA	Outstanding Shares	NA
Counsel	NA	E.P.S.	-$0.171
DUNS No.	NA	Shareholders	NA

Business: The group focuses on development and sales of communication software solutions and management of media-related programs. The software solutions include a controlled and safe Internet browser for children and a multiple-module Web-based email and office automation bundle. The company is currently seeking merger opportunities with other software companies.

Primary SIC and add'l.: 7375 7372 7812

CIK No: 0001145906

Subsidiaries: Completo Communications Corporation, Pacific Systems Control Technology

Officers: Benedict Van/Chmn., CEO, Anthony K. Chan/Dir., CFO

Directors: Benedict Van/Chmn., CEO, Anthony K. Chan/Dir., CFO, James McCargo/Dir., David A. Brewer/Dir., Gregory B. Pelling/Dir.

Owners: Benedict Van/7.90%, Gregory B. Pelling/0.51%, Adel M. Ali/9.63%, James McCargo/0.98%, David A. Brewer/0.88%, PeopleWeb Communications, Inc./9.41%, Anthony K. Chan/2.47%, ECapital Group, Inc./40.68%, Insiders/12.02%

Financial Data: *Fiscal Year End:*12/31 *Latest Annual Data:* 12/31/2006

Year	Sales	Net Income
2006	$38,000	-$13,485,000
2005	$9,000	-$1,035,000
2004	$10,000	-$507,000

Curr. Assets:	$435,000	**Curr. Liab.:**	$459,000		
Plant, Equip.:	$258,000	**Total Liab.:**	$459,000	**Indic. Yr. Divd.:**	NA
Total Assets:	$1,903,000	**Net Worth:**	$1,443,000	**Debt/ Equity:**	NA

Heritage Commerce Corp

150 Almaden Blvd., San Jose, CA, 95113; *PH:* 1-408-947-6900; *Fax:* 1-408-947-6910;
http:// www.heritagecommercecorp.com

General - Incorporation	CA	**Stock**- Price on:12/24/2007	$24.49
Employees	196	Stock Exchange	NDQ
Auditor	Deloitte & Touche, LLP	Ticker Symbol	HTBK
Stk Agt	U.S. Stock Transfer Corp	Outstanding Shares	11,640,000
Counsel	NA	E.P.S.	$1.28
DUNS No.	04-234-2076	Shareholders	NA

Business: The group's principal activity is to provide commercial loans, real estate, construction, small business administration, inventory, accounts receivable and equipment loans. The group also accepts checking, savings and time deposits, now and money market deposit accounts, traveler's checks and safe deposit. In addition, the group provides other non-banking services. The group issues visa and master card credit cards through a correspondent bank. The group is a multi-bank holding company for heritage bank of commerce, heritage bank east bay and heritage bank south valley.

Primary SIC and add'l.: 6022 6712

CIK No: 0001053352

Subsidiaries: Heritage Bank of Commerce - State of Incorporation, Heritage Capital Trust I, Heritage Commerce Corp Statutory Trust I, Heritage Commerce Corp Statutory Trust III, Heritage Statutory Trust II

Officers: Walter T. Kaczmarek/Dir., CEO, Pres./$907,471.00, William J. Del Biaggio/Founder Chmn., VP/$306,431.00, Rebecca A. Levey/Sr. VP - Marketing, Shareholder Relations, Corp. Sec., Richard E. Hagarty/Exec. VP, Chief Credit Officer/$289,002.00, Raymond Parker/Exec. VP - Banking Division/$582,002.00, James A. Mayer/Pres. - Diablo Valley Banking Region, Lawrence D. McGovern/CFO, Exec. VP/$439,544.00

Directors: Walter T. Kaczmarek/Dir., CEO, Pres., Jack W. Conner/Chmn., William J. Del Biaggio/Founder Chmn., VP, Frank G. Bisceglia/Dir., Louis O. Normandin/Dir., Humphrey P. Polanen/Dir., Robert T. Moles/Dir., James R. Blair/Dir., Mark E. Lefanowicz/Dir., John J. Hounslow/Dir., Charles J. Toeniskoetter/Dir., Jack L. Peckham/Dir., Ranson W. Webster/Dir.

Owners: Dennis M. Casagrande/4.66%, Kenneth V. Stevens/4.40%, Alfred D. McKelvy/1.11%, Alfred D. McKelvy/1.16%, Robert C. Philcox/2.29%, William Keller/0.77%, Kenneth R. Mercer/1.00%, John J. Hounslow/6.73%, Insiders/29.23%, James A. Mayer/5.99%, Uri Eliahu/1.39%, Randy B. Williams/1.45%, Mark E. Lefanowicz/2.46%, William Keller/0.77%, James A. Mayer/6.04% *(26 Owners included in Index)*

Financial Data: *Fiscal Year End:*12/31 *Latest Annual Data:* 12/31/2006

Year	Sales	Net Income
2006	$82,797,000	$17,270,000
2005	$73,179,000	$14,446,000
2004	$62,651,000	$8,478,000

Curr. Assets:	$86,305,000	**Curr. Liab.:**	$890,616,000	**P/E Ratio:**	17.37
Plant, Equip.:	$2,539,000	**Total Liab.:**	$914,318,000	**Indic. Yr. Divd.:**	$0.320
Total Assets:	$1,037,138,000	**Net Worth:**	$122,820,000	**Debt/ Equity:**	0.1880

Heritage Financial Corp

201 5th Ave. SW, Olympia, WA, 98501; *PH:* 1-360-943-1500; *Fax:* 1-360-943-8046;
http:// www.heritagebankwa.com

General - Incorporation	WA	**Stock**- Price on:12/24/2007	$23.22
Employees	233	Stock Exchange	NDQ
Auditor	KPMG LLP	Ticker Symbol	HFWA
Stk Agt	U.S. Stock Transfer Corp	Outstanding Shares	6,590,000
Counsel	Gerrish, Smith & McCreary	E.P.S.	$1.57
DUNS No.	82-482-8966	Shareholders	NA

Business: The group's principal activity is to provide commercial and savings bank services. As a holding company, the group operates through its wholly owned subsidiaries, heritage bank and central valley bank. The activities include lending loans and accepting deposits from the small businesses and the general public. Loans consist of residential construction loans, income property loans and consumer loans. Heritage bank operates from its main office in olympia, Washington and its eleven branch offices located in thurston, pierce and mason counties. Central valley bank operates from its main office in toppenish, Washington and its five branch offices located in yakima and kittitas counties.

Primary SIC and add'l.: 6022 6712

CIK No: 0001046025

Subsidiaries: Central Valley Bank, N.A., Heritage Bank

Officers: Brian L. Vance/Dir., CEO, Pres./$320,638.00, Lisa L. Welander/CIO, VP, Donald J. Hinson/Sr. VP, CFO

Directors: Brian L. Vance/Dir., CEO, Pres., Donald V. Rhodes/Chmn., John A. Clees/Dir., Gary B. Christensen/Dir., Philip S. Weigand/Dir., James P. Senna/Dir., Jeffrey S. Lyon/Dir., Daryl D. Jensen/Dir., Brian S. Charneski/Dir., Peter N. Fluetsch/Dir., Kimberly T. Ellwanger/Dir.

Owners: Gary B. Christensen, Peter N. Fluetsch, Daryl D. Jensen/2.63%, Gregory D. Patjens, Philip S. Weigand/2.05%, John A. Clees/1.31%, Michael D. Broadhead/1.20%, Donald V. Rhodes/6.20%, Edward D. Cameron, Insiders/20.79%, James P. Senna/1.28%, Jeffrey S. Lyon, Brian S. Charneski, Kimberly T. Ellwanger, Brian L. Vance/3.04%

Financial Data: *Fiscal Year End:*12/31 *Latest Annual Data:* 12/31/2006

Year	Sales	Net Income
2006	$63,191,000	$10,547,000
2005	$52,058,000	$10,476,000
2004	$45,442,000	$9,585,000

Curr. Assets:	$30,729,000	**Curr. Liab.:**	$770,883,000	**P/E Ratio:**	14.88
Plant, Equip.:	$15,906,000	**Total Liab.:**	$774,254,000	**Indic. Yr. Divd.:**	$0.840
Total Assets:	$852,893,000	**Net Worth:**	$78,639,000	**Debt/ Equity:**	0.0392

Heritage Financial Group

721 N Westover Blvd., Albany, GA, 31721; *PH:* 1-229-878-2047; *Fax:* 1-229-878-2054;
http:// www.eheritagebank.com

General - Incorporation	USA	**Stock**- Price on:12/24/2007	$15.36
Employees	128	Stock Exchange	NDQ
Auditor	Mauldin & Jenkins,Crtfd Pub. Acct.	Ticker Symbol	HBOS
Stk Agt	Registrar & Transfer Co	Outstanding Shares	10,890,000
Counsel	NA	E.P.S.	$0.24
DUNS No.	NA	Shareholders	NA

Business: The groups principal activity is to provide banking services. The groups services include commercial banking and small business lending, indirect auto lending, retail banking, brokerage investment and mortgage lending. The financial products of the group include commercial real estate, commercial and industrial, consumer, construction and land and mortgage loans. The group operates from Southwest Georgia and Central Florida in the United States. The assets of the group for the year 2006 were $413,330 (thousands).

Primary SIC and add'l.: 6712 6035 6712 6062 6062

CIK No: 0001320002

Subsidiaries: A&B Real Estate Ventures, LLC, Heritage Real Estate Holdings, HeritageBank of the South

Officers: Leonard O. Dorminey/55/CEO, Pres., Joseph C. Burger/71/Vice Chmn., Sec., Tammy W. Burdette/48/CFO, Joshua Buck/Financial Advisor, Jim Burton/Registered Representative, Clark Ulrich/Financial Advisor, Jerry Jensen/Assoc., Rodney Tieken/Assoc., Quinn Campbell/Financial Advisor, Kirk Chugg/Financial Advisor, Laura Guthrie/Registered Representative, Calvin Welling/Pres., Terry Bexell/Sr. Associate, Stephen Stringham/Registered Representative, Jared Van Orden/Investment Advisor Representative *(27 Officers included in Index)*

Directors: Leonard O. Dorminey/55/CEO, Pres., Antone D. Lehr/67/Chmn., Douglas J. McGinley/59/Dir., Carol W. Slappey/52/Dir., Keith J. Land/56/Dir., Lee J. Stanley/60/Dir.

Owners: Edward J. Cassity, Mitchell O. Smith/0.20%, Carol W. Slappey/0.55%, James L. Stanley/0.22%, Antone D. Lehr/0.34%, Insiders/3.71%, Tammy W. Burdette/0.38%, Keith J. Land, Leonard O. Dorminey/1.04%, James H. Moore, Fred F. Sharpe/0.04%, Joseph C. Burger, Heath T. Fountain, Douglas J. McGinley/0.24%, Heritage, MHC/72.26% *(16 Owners included in Index)*

Financial Data: *Fiscal Year End:*12/31 *Latest Annual Data:* 12/31/2006

Year	Sales	Net Income
2006	$28,277,000	$2,354,000
2005	$24,582,000	$2,950,000
2004	$23,235,000	$3,533,000

Curr. Assets:	$26,901,000	**Curr. Liab.:**	$306,685,000	**P/E Ratio:**	64.00
Plant, Equip.:	$13,138,000	**Total Liab.:**	$350,521,000	**Indic. Yr. Divd.:**	NA
Total Assets:	$413,330,000	**Net Worth:**	$62,809,000	**Debt/ Equity:**	0.6271

Heritage Oaks Bancorp

545 Twelfth St., Paso Robles, CA, 93446; *PH:* 1-805-239-5200; *Fax:* 1-805-238-6257;
http:// www.heritageoaksbancorp.com; *Email:* info@heritageoaksbank.com

General - Incorporation	CA	**Stock**- Price on:12/24/2007	$17.9
Employees	212	Stock Exchange	NDQ
Auditor	Vavrinek, Trine, Day & Co. LLP	Ticker Symbol	HEOP
Stk Agt	American Stock Transfer & Trust Co.	Outstanding Shares	6,410,000
Counsel	NA	E.P.S.	$0.99
DUNS No.	10-306-5686	Shareholders	NA

Business: The group's principal activity is to provide commercial banking services in California. The group's business is conducted through its subsidiary, heritage oaks bank. The group accepts demand, savings and time deposits and originates commercial, real estate, sba, agricultural, credit card and consumer loans. It also provides installment note collection, issues cashiers checks and money orders, sells travelers checks and provides bank-by-mail, night depository, safe deposit boxes and other customary banking services. The group's branches are located in the cities of arroyo grande, morro bay, paso robles and san luis obispo.

Primary SIC and add'l.: 6712 6022

CIK No: 0000921547

Subsidiaries: CCMS Systems, Inc, Heritage Oaks Bank, Heritage Oaks Capital Trust I

Officers: Lawrence P. Ward/Dir., CEO, Pres./$645,076.00, Paul Tognazzini/Exec. VP, Chief Lending Officer/$267,836.00, Margaret A. Torres/CFO, Exec. VP/$308,841.00, Gwen R. Pelfrey/Exec. VP, Chief Administrative Officer/$253,765.00, Mark W. Stasinis/Exec. VP, Southern Regional Mgr./$267,542.00, Joni Watson/Exec. VP, Human Resources Officer, Craig Heyl/Exec. VP, Client Services Officer

Directors: Lawrence P. Ward/Dir., CEO, Pres., Donald H. Campbell/Vice Chmn., Bobbie Ray Bryant/75/Chmn., Ole K. Viborg/76/Dir., Daniel J. O'Hare/Dir., Alexander F. Simas/Dir., Mark C. Fugate/Dir., Kenneth L. Dewar/Dir., Dolores T. Lacey/Dir., Merle F. Miller/Dir., Michael J. Morris/Dir., Michael J. Behrman/Dir., Michael Pfau/Dir.

Owners: Ole K. Viborg/6.31%, Donald H. Campbell, Paul Tognazzini/1.13%, Daniel J. O'Hare, Michael J. Morris, Merle F. Miller/5.92%, Lawrence P. Ward/5.21%, Insiders/31.78%, B. R. Bryant/6.30%, Margaret A. Torres, Kenneth L. Dewar, Gwen R. Pelfrey/1.14%, Mark W. Stasinis, Dee T. Lacey, Mark C. Fugate/1.39% *(16 Owners included in Index)*

Financial Data: *Fiscal Year End:*12/31 *Latest Annual Data:* 12/31/2006

Year	Sales	Net Income
2006	$41,362,000	$6,662,000
2005	$35,184,000	$6,637,000
2004	$28,312,000	$4,584,000

Curr. Assets:	$23,352,000	*Curr. Liab.:*	$471,885,000	*P/E Ratio:*	17.72
Plant, Equip.:	$14,581,000	*Total Liab.:*	$492,302,000	*Indic. Yr. Divd.:*	$0.320
Total Assets:	$541,774,000	*Net Worth:*	$49,472,000	*Debt/ Equity:*	0.3224

Heritage Worldwide Inc

337 Ave. De Bruxelles, La Seyne-sur-mer, 83507; ***PH:*** 011-33-494-109810

General - Incorporation	DE	***Stock***- Price on:12/24/2007	$0.4
Employees	NA	Stock Exchange	OTC
Auditor	Sherb & Co. LLP	Ticker Symbol	HWWI
Stk Agt	Interwest Transfer Company, Inc.	Outstanding Shares	NA
Counsel	NA	E.P.S	NA
DUNS No.	NA	Shareholders	NA

Business: The groups principle activities include seek potential business opportunities. The group operates from United States.

Primary SIC and add'l.: 6799

CIK No: 0001034682

Subsidiaries: OS MXM, Inc., Poly Implant Protheses, SA, Poly Implantes Protesis Espana SL

Owners: Claude Couty, Jean-Claude Mas, Milo Finance, S.A, MediCor Ltd, Insiders

Financial Data: *Fiscal Year End:*06/30 *Latest Annual Data:* 6/30/2006

Year	Sales	Net Income
2006	$15,269,000	$607,000
2005	$13,572,000	$881,000
2004	$11,730,000	-$5,630,000

Curr. Assets:	$12,297,000	*Curr. Liab.:*	$7,401,000		
Plant, Equip.:	$2,104,000	*Total Liab.:*	$11,184,000	*Indic. Yr. Divd.:*	NA
Total Assets:	$16,193,000	*Net Worth:*	$4,066,000	*Debt/ Equity:*	1.0055

Herley Industries Inc

101 N Pointe Blvd., Lancaster, PA, 17601; ***PH:*** 1-717-735-8117; ***Fax:*** 1-717-397-9503; ***http://*** www.herley.com; ***Email:*** ir@herley.com

General - Incorporation	DE	***Stock***- Price on:12/24/2007	$17.94
Employees	1,014	Stock Exchange	NDQ
Auditor	Marcum & Kliegman, LLP	Ticker Symbol	HRLY
Stk Agt	American Stock Transfer & Trust Co.	Outstanding Shares	13,980,000
Counsel	NA	E.P.S	$0.45
DUNS No.	00-241-7004	Shareholders	NA

Business: The group's principal activities are to provide microwave products and systems to defense and aerospace entities. The group operates in the defense electronics and commercial technologies markets. In the defense electronics market, the group designs and manufactures microwave components and subassemblies, which are embedded in a variety of radars, flight instrumentation, weapons sensors, electronic warfare systems and guidance systems. Commercial technologies are comprised of scientific products and medical products. The group's customers include the U.S. Government, foreign governments and aerospace companies. On 29-Sep-2004, the group acquired reliable system services.

Primary SIC and add'l.: 3812 3663

CIK No: 0000047035

Subsidiaries: Communication Techniques, Inc., EW Simulation Technology Limited (EWST)

Officers: Myron Levy/Chmn., CEO, Anello C. Garefino/VP - Finance, John M. Kelley/Pres., John A. Thonet/Dir., Sec., Richard Poirier/VP, John Carroll/VP - Human Resources, Rozalie Schachter/VP - Strategic Initiatives, GM Herley Farmingdale, Kevin J. Purcell/CFO, VP, Peg Guzzetti/Investor Contact

Directors: Myron Levy/Chmn., CEO, Edward A. Bogucz/Dir., Edward K. Walker/Dir., John A. Thonet/Dir., Sec., Carlos Campbell/67/Dir., Rodert M. Moore/Dir.

Owners: Third Avenue Management, Inc./19.60%, John M. Kelley, Myron Levy/10.20%, Edward K. Walker, Robert M. Moore, Insiders/12.70%, Kevin J. Purcell, GAMCO Investors/10.60%, John A. Thonet, Lee N. Blatt/10.10%, Jeffrey L. Markel, Edward A. Bogucz, Dimensional Fund Advisors, Inc./8.40%, Carlos C. Campbell

Financial Data: *Fiscal Year End:*07/31 *Latest Annual Data:* 07/29/2007

Year	Sales	Net Income
2007	$163,140,000	$3,118,000
2006	$176,268,000	$10,354,000
2005	$151,415,000	$10,781,000

Curr. Assets:	$154,119,000	*Curr. Liab.:*	$23,846,000	*P/E Ratio:*	897.00
Plant, Equip.:	$25,968,000	*Total Liab.:*	$35,471,000	*Indic. Yr. Divd.:*	NA
Total Assets:	$220,971,000	*Net Worth:*	$185,500,000	*Debt/ Equity:*	0.0307

Herman Miller Inc

855 E Main Ave., Zeeland, MI, 49464; ***PH:*** 1-616-654-3000; ***Fax:*** 1-616-654-5234; ***http://*** www.hermanmiller.com

General - Incorporation	MI	***Stock***- Price on:12/24/2007	$34.77
Employees	6,054	Stock Exchange	NDQ
Auditor	Ernst & Young LLP	Ticker Symbol	NA
Stk Agt	EquiServe Trust Co N.A	Outstanding Shares	63,500,000
Counsel	NA	E.P.S	$2.19
DUNS No.	00-601-2801	Shareholders	NA

Business: The groups principle activity is to provide office furniture and services for the healthcare, educational and residential industries. The group operates from United States.

Primary SIC and add'l.: 2522 2541 2521 2542

CIK No: 0000066382

Subsidiaries: Coro Acquisition Corporation-California, Geiger International, Inc., Herman Miller (Australia) Pty., Ltd., Herman Miller Canada, Herman Miller Global Customer Solutions, Inc., Herman Miller Italia S.p.A., Herman Miller Japan, Ltd., Herman Miller Mexico S.A. de C.V., Herman Miller, Ltd., Integrated Metal Technologies, Inc., Meridian, Inc., Milsure Insurance, Ltd., Office Pavilion South Florida, Inc., OP Corporate Furnishings, Inc., OP Spectrum LLP 17 Subsidiaries included in the Index

Officers: Brian C. Walker/Dir., CEO, Pres./$2,582,429.00, Charles J. Vranian/58/Exec. VP - North American Emerging Markets, Joseph M. Nowicki/Treasurer, VP - Investor Relations, Andrew J. Lock/Exec. VP, Chief Administrative Officer/$817,708.00, John P. Portlock/Exec. VP - Herman Miller International/$943,661.00, Gary S. Miller/Exec. VP, Chief Development Officer/$827,177.00, Curt Pullen/CFO, James E. Christenson/61/Sr. VP - Legal Services, Sec., Donald D. Goeman/Exec. VP - Operations, Kenneth L. Goodson/56/Exec. VP - Operations, Kristen L. Manos/49/Exec. VP - North American Office Learning Environments

Directors: Brian C. Walker/Dir., CEO, Pres., Michael A. Volkema/Chmn., Paget L. Alves/Dir., John R. Hoke/Dir., James R. Kackley/Dir., Douglas D. French/Dir., David O. Ulrich/Dir., Mary Vermeer Andringa/Dir., Lord Brian Griffiths/Dir., Barry J. Griswell/Dir., William C. Pollard/Dir., Dorothy A. Terrell/Dir.

Owners: Ariel Capital Management, Inc./11.36%, John Portlock/0.15%, Gary S. Miller/0.46%, Brian C. Walker/0.50%, Elizabeth A. Nickels/0.38%, Rainier Investment Management, Inc./5.68%, Barclays Global Fund Advisors/9.95%, Insiders/3.42%, Andrew J. Lock/0.07%, Columbia Wanger Asset Management, L.P./6.75%

Financial Data: *Fiscal Year End:*06/03 *Latest Annual Data:* 06/02/2007

Year	Sales	Net Income
2007	$1,918,900,000	$129,100,000
2006	$1,737,200,000	$99,200,000
2005	$1,515,600,000	$68,000,000

Curr. Assets:	$390,200,000	*Curr. Liab.:*	$299,400,000	*P/E Ratio:*	18.69
Plant, Equip.:	$203,300,000	*Total Liab.:*	$529,400,000	*Indic. Yr. Divd.:*	$0.350
Total Assets:	$668,000,000	*Net Worth:*	$138,400,000	*Debt/ Equity:*	1.0137

Hersha Hospitality Trust

44 Hersha Dr., Harrisburg, PA, 17102; ***PH:*** 1-717-236-4400; ***Fax:*** 1-717-774-7383; ***http://*** www.hersha.com

General - Incorporation	MD	***Stock***- Price on:12/24/2007	$12.06
Employees	21	Stock Exchange	AMEX
Auditor	KPMG LLP	Ticker Symbol	HT
Stk Agt	American Stock Transfer & Trust Co.	Outstanding Shares	40,770,000
Counsel	Hunton & Williams	E.P.S	$0.18
DUNS No.	NA	Shareholders	NA

Business: The groups principle activity is to invest in real estate properties. The group operates from the United States. The group's quarterly revenue for September 2007 was 68.83 millions of USD.

Primary SIC and add'l.: 7011 6798

CIK No: 0001063344

Subsidiaries: 1244 Associates, 2144 Associates - Hershey, 2144 Associates - New Columbia, 2144 Associates - Selinsgrove, 2444 Associates, 2844 Associates, 3044 Associates, 3144 Associates, 315 Trumbull Street Associates, LLC, 3544 Associates, 44 Aarti Associates, LP, 44 Alexandria Hotel Management, LLC, 44 Alexandria Hotel, LLC, 44 Bridgewater, LLC, 44 Brookhaven, LLC 155 Subsidiaries included in the Index

Officers: Jay H. Shah/Trustee, CEO/$489,924.00, Kiran P. Patel/Trustee, Corp. Sec., Michael R. Gillespie/Chief Accounting Officer/$169,679.00, Neil H. Shah/COO, Pres. - Hersha Hospitality Trust/$447,013.00, William J. Walsh/VP - Asset Management, Ashish R. Parikh/CFO/$307,556.00, Robert C. Hazard/VP - Acquisitions, Development, David L. Desfor/Treasurer, Corp. Sec.

Directors: Jay H. Shah/Trustee, CEO, Hasu P. Shah/Chmn., Thomas S. Capello/Trustee, Michael A. Leven/Trustee, John M. Sabin/Trustee, Donald J. Landry/Trustee, Kiran P. Patel/Trustee, Corp. Sec., Kiran D. Patel/64/Trustee

Owners: K. D. Patel/1.11%, Hasu P. Shah/1.04%, Morgan Stanley/9.41%, Jay H. Shah/2.71%, Michael A. Leven, Ashish R. Parikh, Wellington Management Company LLP/6.08%, Kiran P. Patel, Kensington Investment Group, Inc./5.69%, Barclays Global Investors, NA/5.67%, Michael R. Gillespie, Insiders/7.97%, Deutsche BANK AG/8.98%, Shreenathji Enterprises, Ltd., Donald J. Landry *(19 Owners included in Index)*

Financial Data: *Fiscal Year End:*12/31 *Latest Annual Data:* 12/31/2006

Year	Sales	Net Income
2006	$147,888,000	$5,098,000
2005	$80,899,000	$3,297,000
2004	$50,562,000	$2,049,000

Curr. Assets:	$23,634,000	*Curr. Liab.:*	$27,022,000		
Plant, Equip.:	$807,784,000	*Total Liab.:*	$636,589,000	*Indic. Yr. Divd.:*	$0.720
Total Assets:	$968,208,000	*Net Worth:*	$331,619,000	*Debt/ Equity:*	1.7506

Hershey Co (The)

100 Crystal A Dr., Hershey, PA, 17033; ***PH:*** 1-717-534-4200; ***Fax:*** 1-800-539-0261; ***http://*** www.hersheys.com

General - Incorporation	DE	***Stock***- Price on:12/24/2007	$50.54
Employees	12,800	Stock Exchange	NYSE
Auditor	KPMG LLP	Ticker Symbol	HSY
Stk Agt	Mellon Investor Services LLC	Outstanding Shares	228,570,000
Counsel	NA	E.P.S	$1.35
DUNS No.	00-300-2052	Shareholders	NA

Business: The group's principle activities include manufacturing, distributing and marketing confectionery and grocery products. The group sells its confectionery products in the form of bar goods, bagged and boxed items and grocery products in the form of baking ingredients, chocolate drink mixes, peanut butter, dessert toppings and beverages. The groups products are sold under the brand names Hershey's, Reese's and Hershey's Kisses. The group operates in United States, Canada and Mexico.

Primary SIC and add'l.: 2052 2064 2099 2032 2066

CIK No: 0000047111

Subsidiaries: Hershey Canada, Inc., Hershey Chocolate & Confectionery Corporation, Hershey Chocolate of Virginia, Inc

Officers: Richard H. Lenny/56/Chmn., CEO, Pres./$11,349,910.00, Andrew W. Jacobs/VP - Wal*mart Global, Thaddeus J. Jastrzebski/VP - Finance, Planning, International Commercial Group, Bryon L. Klemens/VP - Finance, Planning, North American Commercial Group, David G. Onorato/VP - Global Convenience Stores, Specialty Retail, Donald A. Mastrorocco/VP - Quality, Regulatory Compliance, Bruce A. Brown/VP - Business Process Optimization, Michelle J. Gloeckler/VP - Strategic Customers, Thomas K. Hernquist/Sr. VP, Global Chief Growth Officer/$1,436,391.00, Burton H. Snyder/Sr. VP, General Counsel, Sec., Gregg A. Tanner/51/Sr. VP - Global Operations, David J. West/45/Dir., Pres./$1,507,644.00, Humberto P. Alfonso/CFO, Sr. VP, Vincent R. Clempson/Assist. Sec., Joseph A. Cottonaro/Assist. Sec., Assist. Treasurer *(47 Officers included in Index)*

Directors: Richard H. Lenny/56/Chmn., CEO, Pres., Marie J. Toulantis/54/Dir., David J. West/45/Dir., Pres., Alfred F. Kelly/50/Dir., Jon A. Boscia/56/Dir., Robert H. Campbell/71/Dir., Robert F. Cavanaugh/49/Dir., Gary P. Coughlan/64/Dir., Harriet Edelman/52/Dir., Bonnie G. Hill/66/Dir., Mackey J. McDonald/61/Dir.

Owners: David J. West, Insiders/1.40%, Jon A. Boscia, Thomas K. Hernquist, Marie J. Toulantis, MiltonHersheySchoolTrust/99.70%, DavisSelectedAdvisers,L.P./6.30%, Hershey Trust Company, Gary P. Coughlan, John P. Bilbrey, Marcella K. Arline, Alfred F. Kelly, Harriet Edelman, Robert F. Cavanaugh, Richard H. Lenny *(19 Owners included in Index)*

Financial Data: Fiscal Year End:12/31 **Latest Annual Data:** 12/31/2006

Year	Sales		Net Income
2006	$4,944,230,000		$559,061,000
2005	$4,835,974,000		$493,244,000
2004	$4,429,248,000		$590,879,000
Curr. Assets: $1,417,812,000	**Curr. Liab.:**	$1,453,538,000	**P/E Ratio:** 22.56
Plant, Equip.: $1,651,300,000	**Total Liab.:**	$3,474,142,000	**Indic. Yr. Divd.:** $1.190
Total Assets: $4,157,565,000	**Net Worth:**	$683,423,000	**Debt/ Equity:** 2.0108

Hertz Corp

225 Brae Blvd, Park Ridge, NJ, 07656; *PH:* 1-800-654-3131; *http://* www.hertz.com

General - Incorporation	DE	Stock- Price on:12/24/2007	NA
Employees	NA	Stock Exchange	NA
Auditor ....PricewaterhouseCoopers LLP		Ticker Symbol	NA
Stk Agt.......First Chicago Trust Co of New York		Outstanding Shares	NA
Counsel	NA	E.P.S.	NA
DUNS No.	00-556-9314	Shareholders	NA

Business: The group's principle activities are to provide car rental services, renting and leasing of industrial, construction and materials handling equipment. The group maintains a network of company-owned car rental locations both in the United States and in Europe. The group rents a broad range of earthmoving equipment, material handling equipment, aerial and electrical equipment, air compressors, small tools, compaction equipment and construction-related trucks.

Primary SIC and add'l.: 6411 7515 7353 7514

CIK No: 0000047129

Subsidiaries: Hertz Equipment Rental Corporation, Hertz International, Ltd., Hertz System, Inc.

Officers: Mark P. Frissora/Chmn., CEO, Michel Taride/Exec. VP, Pres. - Hertz Europe Limited, Charles L. Shafer/Sr. VP - Quality Assurance, Administration, Richard J. Foti/Staff VP, Controller, Elyse Douglas/CFO, Exec. VP, Joseph R. Nothwang/Exec. VP, Pres. - Vehicle Rental, Leasing, The Americas, Pacific, John A. Thomas/Exec. VP - Supply Chain Management, Leighanne Baker/Sr. VP, Chief Human Resources Officer, Joseph F. Eckroth/CIO, Sr. VP, Robert W. Davis/Interim Staff VP, Controller, Anthony Fiore/Interim Treasurer, Staff VP - Global Tax, Gerald A. Plescia/Exec. VP, Harold E. Rolfe/Sr. VP, General Counsel, Sec.

Directors: Mark P. Frissora/Chmn., CEO, Henry C. Wolf/Dir., George W. Tamke/Dir., Nathan K. Sleeper/34/Dir., Brian A. Bernasek/Dir., Barry H. Beracha/Dir., Carl T. Berquist/Dir., Michael J. Durham/Dir., David H. Wasserman/41/Dir., Gregory S. Ledford/50/Dir., George A. Bitar/Dir., Robert F. End/52/Dir.

Owners: Craig R. Koch, Joseph R. Nothwang, ML Global Private Equity Fund, L.P./23.55%, Barry H. Beracha, Mark P. Frissora, Paul J. Siracusa, Michael J. Durham, CMC-Hertz Partners, L.P./7.80%, Carl T. Berquist, Clayton, Dubilier & Rice Fund VII, L.P./24.17%, Gerald A. Plescia, Carlyle Partners IV, L.P./23.86%, Michel Taride, Henry C. Wolf, Insiders

Hertz Global Holdings Inc

225 Brae Blvd., Park Ridge, NJ, 07656; *PH:* 1-201-307-2000; *Fax:* 1-201-307-2644; *http://* www.hertz.com; *Email:* investorrelations@hertz.com

General - Incorporation	DE	Stock- Price on:12/24/2007	$25.62
Employees	31,500	Stock Exchange	NYSE
Auditor ....PricewaterhouseCoopers LLP		Ticker Symbol	HTZ
Stk Agt ....Computershare Trust Co		Outstanding Shares	321,350,000
Counsel	NA	E.P.S.	$0.58
DUNS No.	NA	Shareholders	NA

Business: The groups principle activity is to provide cars and their equipment on the rent. The group operates through two segments namely, car rental and equipment rental. In the year 2005, the group acquired Ford Holdings LLC. The group operates from the United States, the United Kingdom, France, Spain, Netherlands, Switzerland, Norway, Belgium, Denmark and Greece.

Primary SIC and add'l.: 7514 7353 7510 7359 7353 7359 7514

CIK No: 0001364479

Subsidiaries: 3198872 Nova Scotia Company, Apex Processing Limited, Brae Holding Corp., Car Rental Systems Do Brasil Locacao De Veiculos Ltda., CCMG HERC Sub, Inc., CMGC Canada Acquisition ULC, Daimler Hire Limited, Dan Ryan Car Rentals Ltd., Equipole Finance Services SAS, Equipole S.A., EVZ LLC, Executive Ventures, Ltd., HC Partnership, HCM Marketing Corporation, Hertz (Cayman Islands) Limited 105 Subsidiaries included in the Index

Officers: Mark P. Frissora/Chmn., CEO, Paul J. Siracusa/63/CFO, Exec. VP, John A. Thomas/Exec. VP, Leighanne Baker/Chief Human Resources Officer, Sr. VP, Joseph F. Eckroth/CIO, Sr. VP, Robert W. Davis/Interim Staff VP, Controller, Anthony Fiore/Interim Treasurer, Staff VP - Global Tax, Joseph R. Nothwang/Exec. VP, Brian J. Kennedy/66/Exec. VP - Marketing, Sales, Gerald A. Plescia/Pres. - Herc, Exec. VP, Michel Taride/Pres. - Hertz Europe Limited, Exec. VP, Harold E. Rolfe/Sr. VP, General Counsel, Sec., Charles L. Shafer/Sr. VP - Quality Assurance, Administration, Richard J. Foti/61/Controller, Elyse Douglas/CFO, Exec. VP

Directors: Mark P. Frissora/Chmn., CEO, George W. Tamke/Dir., Nathan K. Sleeper/Dir., David H. Wasserman/Dir., Brian A. Bernasek/Dir., Gregory S. Ledford/Dir., George A. Bitar/Dir., Robert F. End/Dir., Barry H. Beracha/Dir., Carl T. Berquist/Dir., Michael J. Durham/Dir., Henry C. Wolf/Dir.

Owners: Henry C. Wolf, CMC-Hertz Partners, L.P./6.25%, Merrill Lynch, Pierce, Fenner & Smith Incorporated/0.01%, Gregory S. Ledford, ML Global Private Equity Fund, L.P./10.38%, CEP II U.S. Investments, L.P./2.41%, Investment Funds Associated/18.90%, Michel Taride, Carlyle Partners IV, L.P./15.99%, Barry H. Beracha, FMR Corp. and related entities/5.79%, Mark P. Frissora, Craig R. Koch, Carl T. Berquist, ML Hertz Co-Investor, L.P./1.00% *(25 Owners included in Index)*

Financial Data: Fiscal Year End:NA **Latest Annual Data:** 12/31/2006

Year	Sales		Net Income
2006	$8,058,405,000		$115,943,000
Curr. Assets: $3,365,648,000	**Curr. Liab.:**	$1,723,745,000	**P/E Ratio:** 44.17
Plant, Equip.: $11,173,565,000	**Total Liab.:**	$16,142,839,000	**Indic. Yr. Divd.:** NA
Total Assets: $18,677,401,000	**Net Worth:**	$2,534,562,000	**Debt/ Equity:** 4.7353

Heska Corp

3760 Rocky Mountain Ave., Loveland, CO, 80538; *PH:* 1-970-493-7272; *Fax:* 1-970-619-3003; *http://* www.heska.com; *Email:* investorrelations@heska.com

General - Incorporation	DE	Stock- Price on:12/24/2007	$2.382
Employees	299	Stock Exchange	NDQ
Auditor ...Ehrhardt Keefe Steiner & Hottman P.C		Ticker Symbol	HSKA
Stk Agt ....Computershare Trust Co		Outstanding Shares	50,950,000
Counsel.........Wilson Sonsini Goodrich & Rosati		E.P.S.	$0.10
DUNS No.	60-363-1326	Shareholders	NA

Business: The group's principal activities are to discover, develop, manufacture and market companion animal health products and delivery of diagnostic services to veterinarians. The group operates in two segments namely companion animal health and animal health segment. The companion animal health segment sells pharmaceuticals, vaccine and diagnostic products, veterinary diagnostic and patient monitoring instruments, offers diagnostic services and performs a variety of research and development activities. The animal health segment manufactures food animal vaccine and pharmaceutical products that are marketed and distributed by third parties. The group manufactures and markets its products in two major geographic areas, North America and Europe.

Primary SIC and add'l.: 2834 8731

CIK No: 0001038133

Subsidiaries: Diamond Animal Health, Inc., Heska Holding AG

Officers: Robert B. Grieve/Chmn., CEO/$689,460.00, Jason A. Napolitano/CFO, Exec. VP, Sec./$431,850.00, Joseph H. Ritter/Exec. VP - Global Business Operations/$339,212.00, Michael A. Bent/VP, Controller, Principal Accounting Officer/$270,481.00, Malcolm A. Hammerton/VP - Information Technology, Michael J. McGinley/GM - Heska Des Moines, VP - Operations, Technical Affairs, Mark D. Cicotello/VP - Human Resources, Donald L. Wassom/MD - Heska AG, Dir. - Global Allergy, Todd M. Gilson/VP - Marketing, Lynn G. Snodgrass/Sr. Dir. - Sales, Nancy Wisnewski/VP - Research, Development, Heller Ehrman/General Counsel, John R. Flanders/VP, General Counsel, Corp. Sec.

Directors: Robert B. Grieve/Chmn., CEO

Owners: Elisabeth DeMarse, John F. Sasen, State of Wisconsin Investment Board/18.40%, Zesiger Capital Group LLC/14.10%, Jason A. Napolitano/3.50%, Insiders/25.80%, Barr A. Dolan/12.40%, Irwin G. Gordon, Entities associated with Charter Ventures/11.80%, Peter Eio, William A. Aylesworth, Robert B. Grieve/5.00%, Carol T. Verser/1.20%, Joseph H. Ritter, Michael A. Bent

Financial Data: Fiscal Year End:12/31 **Latest Annual Data:** 12/31/2006

Year	Sales		Net Income
2006	$75,060,000		$1,828,000
2005	$69,437,000		$282,000
2004	$67,691,000		-$4,815,000
Curr. Assets: $30,652,000	**Curr. Liab.:**	$21,980,000	**P/E Ratio:** 23.82
Plant, Equip.: $6,948,000	**Total Liab.:**	$31,747,000	**Indic. Yr. Divd.:** NA
Total Assets: $38,495,000	**Net Worth:**	$6,748,000	**Debt/ Equity:** 0.2855

Hesperia Holding Inc

9780 "E" Ave., Hesperia, CA, 92345; *PH:* 1-760-244-8787; *Fax:* 1-760-244-2215; *http://* www.hesperiatrussinc.com

General - Incorporation	NV	Stock- Price on:12/24/2007	$0.03
Employees	NA	Stock Exchange	OTC
Auditor ... Russell Bedford Stefanou Mirchandani		Ticker Symbol	HSPR
Stk Agt .... Pacific Stock Transfer Company		Outstanding Shares	NA
Counsel	NA	E.P.S.	NA
DUNS No.	NA	Shareholders	NA

Business: The group's principal activity is to design, manufacture and provide custom designed wood trusses to the residential construction market. The product lines include roof and floor trusses. The floor trusses are used for multi-story structures and are also used as substitutes for floor joints. The floor trusses are open Web, providing space for plumbing, electrical and ductwork. Roof trusses are used for both single-story and multi-story structures. The primary customers of the group include general contractors, framing contractors, owner builders and resale distributors.

Primary SIC and add'l.: 5039

CIK No: 0001109329

Subsidiaries: Hesperia Truss, Inc., Pahrump Valley Truss, Inc.

Financial Data: Fiscal Year End:12/31 **Latest Annual Data:** 12/31/2004

Year	Sales		Net Income
2004	$11,267,000		-$2,348,000
2003	$8,142,000		-$677,000
Curr. Assets: $1,085,000	**Curr. Liab.:**	$1,186,000	
Plant, Equip.: $302,000	**Total Liab.:**	$2,277,000	**Indic. Yr. Divd.:** NA
Total Assets: $1,387,000	**Net Worth:**	-$891,000	**Debt/ Equity:** NA

Hess Corp

Formerly: Amerada Hess Corp

1185 Ave. Of The Americas, Newyork, NY, 10036; *PH:* 1-212-997-8500; *http://* www.hess.com

General - Incorporation	DE	**Stock**- Price on:12/24/2007	$60.85
Employees	13,700	Stock Exchange	NYSE
Auditor	Ernst & Young LLP	Ticker Symbol	HES
Stk Agt	Bank of NY Shareholder Relations	Outstanding Shares	317,280,000
Counsel	NA	E.P.S	$5.27
DUNS No.	00-697-9785	Shareholders	NA

Business: The group's principle activities include exploration and production of crude oil and natural gas. The group also refines and markets refined petroleum products, natural gas and electricity. The group operates from United States.

Primary SIC and add'l.: 2992 1311 2911

CIK No: 0000004447

Subsidiaries: Amerada Hess (Azerbaijan) Limited, Amerada Hess (Denmark) ApS, Amerada Hess (GEA)Limited, Amerada Hess (Thailand) Limited, Amerada Hess Energy Limited, Amerada Hess Limited, Amerada Hess Norge A/ S, Amerada Hess Oil and Gas Holdings Inc., Amerada Hess Production Gabon, Hess Energy Trading Company, LLC, Hess Oil Virgin Islands Corp., Hovensa LLC, Samara Nafta, Tioga Gas Plant, Inc.

Officers: John B. Hess/Chmn., CEO/$15,010,130.00, G. Shearer/CEO, Sr. VP - Hess LNG, W. Drennen/Sr. VP - Global Exploration, New Ventures, R. J. Lawlor/VP - Sales, Retail Marketing, D. K. Kirshner/VP - Supply, Trading, J. Simon/Sr. VP - Global Production, J. R. Wilson/VP - Investor Relations, K. B. Wilcox/VP, Controller, P. R. Walton/CIO, VP, R. Vogel/VP, Treasurer, J. C. Stein/VP, Chief Risk Officer, E. S. Smith/VP - Marketing, Refining Strategy, H. I. Small/VP - Global Business Improvement, J. J. Lynett/VP - Corporate Tax, J. J. Scelfo/Sr. VP - Finance, Corporate Development *(45 Officers included in Index)*

Directors: John B. Hess/Chmn., CEO, Nicholas F. Brady/Dir., Barclay J. Collins/Dir., Exec. VP, General Counsel, Craig G. Matthews/Dir., Frank A. Olson/Dir., Thomas H. Kean/Dir., Risa Lavizzo-Mourey/Dir., Edith E. Holiday/Dir., John J. O'Connor/Dir., Exec. VP, Pres. - Worldwide Exploration, Production, Ernst H. Von Metzsch/Dir., Borden F. Walker/Dir., Exec. VP, Pres. - Marketing, Refining, Robert N. Wilson/Dir., John H. Mullin/Dir.

Owners: Insiders, Capital Research and Management Company, John J. OConnor, J. Barclay Collins, F. Borden Walker, Frank A. Olson, Craig G. Matthews, Robert N. Wilson, Massachusetts Financial Services Company, John H. Mullin, Nicholas F. Brady, Edith E. Holiday, Risa Lavizzo-Mourey, John P. Rielly, John B. Hess *(18 Owners included in Index)*

Financial Data: ***Fiscal Year End:***12/31 ***Latest Annual Data:*** 12/31/2006

Year	Sales	Net Income
2006	$28,720,000,000	$1,916,000,000
2005	$23,255,000,000	$1,242,000,000
2004	$17,126,000,000	$977,000,000

Curr. Assets:	$5,848,000,000	**Curr. Liab.:**	$6,739,000,000	**P/E Ratio:**	12.13
Plant, Equip.:	$12,308,000,000	**Total Liab.:**	$14,293,000,000	**Indic. Yr. Divd.:**	$0.400
Total Assets:	$22,404,000,000	**Net Worth:**	$8,111,000,000	**Debt/ Equity:**	0.4773

Hewitt Assoc Inc

100 Half Day Rd., Lincolnshire, IL, 60069; ***PH:*** 1-847-295-5000; ***Fax:*** 1-847-295-7634; ***http://*** www.hewitt.com

General - Incorporation	DE	**Stock**- Price on:12/24/2007	$31.93
Employees	24,000	Stock Exchange	NYSE
Auditor	Ernst & Young LLP	Ticker Symbol	HEW
Stk Agt	Computershare Investor Services LLC	Outstanding Shares	110,240,000
Counsel	NA	E.P.S	-$1.62
DUNS No.	NA	Shareholders	NA

Business: The groups principle activity is to provide human resource benefits, outsourcing and consulting services. In the year 2007 the group acquired RealLife HR. The group operates from United States.

Primary SIC and add'l.: 8742 8721 7379

CIK No: 0001168478

Subsidiaries: Becketts Limited, Cyborg Systems (Africa) Pty Limited, Empresas Hewitt S. de R.L. de C.V., HA Insurance Services, Inc., Hewitt (Hong Kong) Limited, Hewitt Associates, Hewitt Associates (Chile) Limitada, Hewitt Associates (Europe) Ltd., Hewitt Associates (India) Pvt. Ltd., Hewitt Associates (Thailand) Limited, Hewitt Associates B.V, Hewitt Associates BPO Limited, Hewitt Associates Caribe, Inc, Hewitt Associates Consulting (Malaysia) Sdn. Bhd., Hewitt Associates Consulting (Shanghai) Co. Ltd. 57 Subsidiaries included in the Index

Officers: Russ Fradin/Chmn., CEO, Monica Burmeister/Global Chief - Consulting Operations, Perry Brandorff/Pres. - Human Resources Consulting, Julie Gordon/Dir., Pres. - Client, Marketing Leadership, Steven Kyono/Sr. VP, General Counsel, Corp. Sec., Tracy Keogh/Sr. VP - Human Resources, Rajeev Grover/Human Resources Outsourcing, Asia, Pacific Leader, Steve Fein/Benefits Outsourcing Sales, Marketing, Product Strategy Leader, Brad Anderson/CIO, Eric Fiedler/Human Resources Consulting, Asia, Pacific Leader, Rohail Khan/Benefits Outsourcing Operations Leader, Jim Konieczny/Multi Process Human Resources Outsourcing Leader, John Park/CFO, Roger Parkin/Human Resources Consulting, Europe Leader, Carlos A. Raposo/Human Resources Outsourcing, Latin America Leader *(20 Officers included in Index)*

Directors: Russ Fradin/Chmn., CEO, Cary D. McMillan/Dir., Steven A. Denning/Dir., Steven P. Stanbrook/Dir., Michele M. Hunt/Dir., Michael E. Greenlees/Dir., Thomas J. Neff/Dir., Julie Gordon/Dir., Pres. - Client, Marketing Leadership, Cheryl Francis/Dir., Alex Mandl/Dir.

Owners: Steven A. Denning, Michele M. Hunt, Thomas J. Neff, Cary D. McMillan, Michael E. Greenlees, Julie S. Gordon, Ariel Capital Management, LLC,, Insiders, John J. Park, Alex J. Mandl, John M. Ryan, Cheryl A. Francis, General Atlantic Partners, LLC, Russell P. Fradin, Perry O. Brandorff *(16 Owners included in Index)*

Financial Data: ***Fiscal Year End:***09/30 ***Latest Annual Data:*** 06/30/2007

Year	Sales	Net Income
2007	NA	NA
2006	$2,857,161,000	-$115,938,000
2005	$2,898,450,000	$134,732,000

Curr. Assets:	$1,244,833,000	**Curr. Liab.:**	$815,712,000		
Plant, Equip.:	$411,205,000	**Total Liab.:**	$1,511,309,000	**Indic. Yr. Divd.:**	NA
Total Assets:	$2,767,678,000	**Net Worth:**	$1,256,369,000	**Debt/ Equity:**	0.1854

Hewlett-Packard Company

3000 Hanover St., Palo Alto, CA, 94304; ***PH:*** 1-650-857-1501; ***Fax:*** 1-650-857-5518; ***http://*** www.hp.com

General - Incorporation	DE	**Stock**- Price on:12/24/2007	$45.64
Employees	156,000	Stock Exchange	NYSE
Auditor	Ernst & Young LLP	Ticker Symbol	HPQ
Stk Agt	Computershare Investor Services LLC	Outstanding Shares	2,620,000,000
Counsel	NA	E.P.S	$2.30
DUNS No.	00-912-2532	Shareholders	NA

Business: The groups principle activity is to provide products, technologies, software, solutions and services. The groups services include personal computing, access devices, imaging, printing related products, network management software, server technology and enterprise system. The group operates through seven segments namely, enterprise storage and servers (ESS), HP services (HPS), software, the personal systems group (PSG), the imaging and printing group (IPG), HP financial services (HPFS), and corporate investments. In the year 2005, the group acquired Peregrine Systems, Inc., SAC, LLC, AppIQ, Inc. and Snapfish. The group operates from the United States. The group's total revenue in the year 2007 was 104,286.00 millions of USD.

Primary SIC and add'l.: 7389 7379 3578 3571 3669 3572 3577 7372 3575 3695 3579 7373 3661 7371

CIK No: 0000047217

Subsidiaries: China HewlettPackard Company Limited, Compaq Latin America Corporation, Compaq Trademark B.V., Computer Insurance Company, HewlettPackard (Canada) Co., HewlettPackard (M)Sdn. Bhd., HewlettPackard (Manufacturing)Ltd., HewlettPackard (Nigeria) Limited, HewlettPackard (Romania) SRL, HewlettPackard (Schweiz) GmbH, HewlettPackard (Thailand) Limited, HewlettPackard ApS, HewlettPackard Argentina S.R.L., HewlettPackard Asia Pacific Pte.Ltd., HewlettPackard Australia Pty. Limited 97 Subsidiaries included in the Index

Officers: Mark V. Hurd/Chmn., CEO, Pres., Todd Bradley/Exec. VP - Personal Systems Group, Beth Howe/Investor Relations Officer, Dave Hill/Investor Relations Officer, Prith Banerjee/Dir. - HP Labs, Sr. VP - Research, Michael Mendenhall/Chief Marketing Officer, Sr. VP, Jon Flaxman/Chief Administrative Officer, Exec. VP, Michael J. Holston/Exec. VP, General Counsel, Sec., Vyomesh Joshi/Exec. VP - Imaging, Printing Group, Cathie Lesjak/CFO, Exec. VP, Ann M. Livermore/Exec. VP - Technology Solutions Group, Randall D. Mott/CIO, Exec. VP, Marcela Perez De Alonso/Exec. VP - Human Resources, Shane Robison/Chief Strategy, Technology Officer, Exec. VP, Jim Burns/VP - Investor Relations *(17 Officers included in Index)*

Directors: Mark V. Hurd/Chmn., CEO, Pres., Joel Z. Hyatt/Dir., John R. Joyce/Dir., Lawrence T. Babbio/Dir., Sari M. Baldauf/Dir., Richard A. Hackborn/Dir., John H. Hammergren/Dir., Robert L. Ryan/Dir., Lucille S. Salhany/Dir., Kennedy G. Thompson/Dir.

Owners: Lawrence T. Babbio, Kennedy G. Thompson, Robert L. Ryan, Vyomesh I. Joshi, Mark V. Hurd, Richard A. Hackborn, Ann M. Livermore, John H. Hammergren, Robert P. Wayman, Insiders, Shane V. Robison, Lucille S. Salhany

Financial Data: ***Fiscal Year End:***10/31 ***Latest Annual Data:*** 10/31/2006

Year	Sales	Net Income
2006	$91,658,000,000	$6,198,000,000
2005	$86,696,000,000	$2,398,000,000
2004	$79,905,000,000	$3,497,000,000

Curr. Assets:	$48,264,000,000	**Curr. Liab.:**	$35,850,000,000	**P/E Ratio:**	18.48
Plant, Equip.:	$6,863,000,000	**Total Liab.:**	$43,837,000,000	**Indic. Yr. Divd.:**	$0.320
Total Assets:	$81,981,000,000	**Net Worth:**	$38,144,000,000	**Debt/ Equity:**	0.0640

Hexcel Corp

281 Tresser Blvd., 2 Stamford Pl., 16th Fl., Stamford, CT, 06901; ***PH:*** 1-203-969-0666; ***Fax:*** 1-203-358-3972; ***http://*** www.hexcel.com

General - Incorporation	DE	**Stock**- Price on:12/24/2007	$21.82
Employees	4,459	Stock Exchange	NYSE
Auditor	PricewaterhouseCoopers LLP	Ticker Symbol	HXL
Stk Agt	American Stock Transfer & Trust Co.	Outstanding Shares	94,310,000
Counsel	NA	E.P.S	$0.69
DUNS No.	00-911-8563	Shareholders	NA

Business: The group's principle activity is to manufacture advanced structural materials. The group operates in three segments namely, reinforcements, composites and structures. The reinforcements segment manufactures and sells industrial fabrics and other specialty reinforcement products made from a variety of fibers. This segment also weaves electronic fiberglass fabrics that are a substrate for printed circuit boards. The composites segment manufactures and sells carbon fibers, prepregs, honeycomb, structural adhesives and specially machined honeycomb parts. The structures segment manufactures and markets composite structures primarily for use in the aerospace industry. The group's products are used in commercial aerospace, space and defense, electronics, general industrial and recreation markets. The group operates in the United States and Europe and has sales offices located in the peoples republic of China and Australia. The group's quarterly revenue for Sep'07 was 281.10 millions of USD.

Primary SIC and add'l.: 2221 3229 3624

CIK No: 0000717605

Subsidiaries: ACM Holdings Corporation, Clark-Schwebel Holding Corp., CS Tech-Fab Holding, Inc., Hexcel Beta Corp., Hexcel Chemical Products Limited, Hexcel Composites GmbH, Hexcel Composites GmbH & Co. KG, Hexcel Composites Limited, Hexcel Composites S.A., Hexcel Composites S.L., Hexcel Composites S.P.R.L., Hexcel Composites S.r.l., Hexcel do Brasil Servicos S/C Ltda, Hexcel Europe Limited, Hexcel Far East 37 Subsidiaries included in the Index

Officers: David E. Berges/Chmn., CEO/$4,924,692.00, Mark I. Clair/48/VP, Corporate Controller, Chief Accounting Officer, Wayne C. Pensky/CFO, Sr. VP, William J. Fazio/53/Chief Accounting Officer, Corporate Controller, Stephen C. Forsyth/52/Exec. VP/$1,008,385.00, Ira J. Krakower/Sr. VP, General Counsel, Sec./$1,015,958.00, William Hunt/Pres./$1,535,240.00, Michael J. MacIntyre/Treasurer, Joseph H. Shaulson/42/Pres. - Reinforcements Business/$860,531.00, Robert G. Hennemuth/Sr. VP - Human Resources

Directors: David E. Berges/Chmn., CEO, Kim W. Foster/Dir., Jeffrey A. Graves/Dir., Joel S. Beckman/Dir., Arthur H. Bellows/Dir., Jeffrey C. Campbell/Dir., Sandra L. Derickson/Dir., David C. Hurley/Dir., Lynn Brubaker/Dir., David Pugh/Dir.

Owners: FMR Corp./13.70%, Joseph H. Shaulson, Sandra L. Derickson, Ira J. Krakower, Lord, Abbett & Co. LLC/11.70%, Joel S. Beckman, Earnest Partners LLC/10.20%, Jeffrey L. Gendell/8.90%, Ingalls & Snyder LLC/5.70%, William Hunt, Stephen C. Forsyth, Westfield Capital Management Company, LLC/6.10%, David E. Berges/1.60%, Arthur H. Bellows, David C. Hurley *(19 Owners included in Index)*

Financial Data: ***Fiscal Year End:***12/31 ***Latest Annual Data:*** 12/31/2006

Year	Sales	Net Income
2006	$1,193,100,000	$65,900,000
2005	$1,161,400,000	$141,300,000
2004	$1,074,500,000	$28,800,000

Curr. Assets:	$425,800,000	Curr. Liab.:	$219,300,000	P/E Ratio:	27.97
Plant, Equip.:	$376,300,000	Total Liab.:	$711,300,000	Indic. Yr. Divd.:	NA
Total Assets:	$1,012,900,000	Net Worth:	$301,600,000	Debt/ Equity:	1.2594

HF Financial Corp

225 S Main Ave., Sioux Falls, SD, 57104; **PH:** 1-605-333-7556; **Fax:** 1-605-333-7621; **http://** www.homefederal.com

General - Incorporation	DE	Stock- Price on:12/24/2007	$17.6
Employees	312	Stock Exchange	NDQ
Auditor	Eide Bailly LLP	Ticker Symbol	HFFC
Stk Agt	Mellon Investor Services LLC	Outstanding Shares	4,000,000
Counsel	Gray, Plant, Mooty, Mooty & Bennett	E.P.S.	$1.39
DUNS No.	80-541-5205	Shareholders	NA

Business: The group's principal activity is to provide consumer and commercial banking services through its subsidiary, home federal bank. The group accepts deposits from the general public and uses such deposits to originate one-to four-family residential, consumer, multi-family, commercial real estate, construction, agricultural and commercial business loans. The consumer loan portfolio of the group includes automobile loans, home equity loans, credit card loans, loans secured by deposit accounts, student loans and mobile home loans. The services are provided through 34 bank centers.

Primary SIC and add'l.: 6712 6035

CIK No: 0000881790

Subsidiaries: HF Financial Corp., Home Federal Bank

Officers: Curtis L. Hage/Chmn., CEO, Pres., Pamela F. Russo/Corp. Sec., Darrel L. Posegate/Exec. VP, CFO, Treasurer, Mark S. Sivertson/Contact - Investment, Trust, Estate Services, Nicole Hurt/Contact - Investment, Trust, Estate Services, Rosanne Krier/Contact - Investment, Trust, Estate Services, Kent Wigg/Contact - Investment, Trust, Estate Services, Karen Beranek/Contact - Investment, Trust, Estate Services, Mary Johnson/Contact - Investment, Trust, Estate Services, Dianne Harris/Contact - Investment, Trust, Estate Services, Jamie Heetland/Contact - Investment, Trust, Estate Services, Diane Hovda/Contact - Investment, Trust, Estate Services

Directors: Curtis L. Hage/Chmn., CEO, Pres., Charles T. Day/60/Dir., Steven R. Sershen/Dir., Curtis J. Bernard/Dir., G. Pederson/Dir., Thomas L. Van Wyhe/Dir., Robert L. Hanson/Dir., Christine E. Hamilton/Dir.

Owners: Curtis L. Hage/5.60%, Steven R. Sershen, David A. Brown, William G. Pederson, Jeffrey L. Gendell/8.56%, Thomas L. Van Wyhe, Dimensional Fund Advisors,Inc/6.81%, Robert L. Hanson, Natalie A. Solberg, Christine E. Hamilton, Mark S. Sivertson/1.30%, HF Financial Corp./5.54%, Curtis J. Bernard, Insiders/12.39%, Darrel L. Posegate *(16 Owners included in Index)*

Financial Data: Fiscal Year End:06/30 Latest Annual Data: 06/30/2007

Year	Sales	Net Income
2007	$75,070,000	$5,383,000
2006	$66,262,000	$4,508,000
2005	$53,960,000	$5,165,000

Curr. Assets:	$33,917,000	Curr. Liab.:	$870,430,000	P/E Ratio:	13.23
Plant, Equip.:	$16,348,000	Total Liab.:	$905,236,000	Indic. Yr. Divd.:	$0.420
Total Assets:	$961,294,000	Net Worth:	$56,058,000	Debt/ Equity:	0.4507

Hi-Shear Technology Corp

24225 Garnier St., Torrance, CA, 90505; **PH:** 1-310-784-2100; **Fax:** 1-310-325-5354; **http://** www.hstc.com; **Email:** fo@hstc.com

General - Incorporation	DE	Stock- Price on:12/24/2007	$10.33
Employees	100	Stock Exchange	AMEX
Auditor	Raimondo Pettit Group	Ticker Symbol	HSR
Stk Agt	American Stock Transfer & Trust Co.	Outstanding Shares	6,780,000
Counsel	Jeffers, Shaff & Falk	E.P.S.	$0.579
DUNS No.	13-127-8558	Shareholders	NA

Business: The group's principal activity is to design and manufacture electronic, mechanical and pyrotechnic-Separation products for the aerospace industry. The products of the group are power cartridges/initiators, mechanical devices, electronic products, laser initiation systems, emergency cutters and automotive air bag inflators. The group's aerospace products are used primarily in commercial space satellites and launch vehicles, exploration missions, strategic missiles, advanced fighter aircraft and military systems. The customers of the group are lockheed martin, the boeing company, U.S. Army, U.S. Navy, U.S. Air force and nasa.

Primary SIC and add'l.: 3769 3679 3764 3489 3559 3728

CIK No: 0000918027

Officers: George W. Trahan/CEO, Pres./$667,225.00, Linda A. Nespole/Investor Relations Contact, Vaughn D. Williams/77/Mgr. - Marketing, Sales

Owners: George W. Trahan/38.30%, Insiders/69.20%, Thomas R. Mooney/30.60%, Jack Bunis, David W. Einsel

Financial Data: Fiscal Year End:05/31 Latest Annual Data: 05/31/2007

Year	Sales	Net Income
2007	$20,550,000	$3,418,000
2006	$21,052,000	$2,295,000
2005	$16,076,000	$215,000

Curr. Assets:	$15,036,000	Curr. Liab.:	$3,048,000	P/E Ratio:	20.66
Plant, Equip.:	$2,718,000	Total Liab.:	$3,498,000	Indic. Yr. Divd.:	$0.470
Total Assets:	$17,754,000	Net Worth:	$14,256,000	Debt/ Equity:	0.0050

Hi-Tech Pharmacal Co Inc

369 Bayview Ave., Amityville, NY, 11701; **PH:** 1-631-789-8228; **Fax:** 1-631-789-8429; **http://** www.hitechpharm.com

General - Incorporation	DE	Stock- Price on:12/24/2007	$12.08
Employees	224	Stock Exchange	NDQ
Auditor	Eisner LLP	Ticker Symbol	HITK
Stk Agt	Continental Stock Transfer & Trust Co	Outstanding Shares	11,440,000
Counsel	Tashlik, Goldwyn & Crandell P.C.	E.P.S.	-$0.34
DUNS No.	10-119-6749	Shareholders	NA

Business: The group's principal activities are to manufacture and sell prescription, over-the-counter generic drugs and nutritional products. These drugs are in liquid and semi-solid dosage forms including higher margin prescription products. The company sells its products in two primary markets: generic pharmaceuticals and branded products. The company markets its generic pharmaceuticals primarily under the hi-tech name. The company also markets a line of branded products primarily for people with diabetes, including diabetic tussin (R), diabetiderm (R), diabetisweet (R), diabetitrim(R) and multi-betic (r). The group markets more than 100 products to over 100 customers. The customers comprise of chain drug stores, drug wholesalers, managed care purchasing organizations, certain federal government agencies, generic distributors, mass merchandisers, and mail-order pharmacies. The brand names include h-t and rx choice.

Primary SIC and add'l.: 8731 2834

CIK No: 0000887497

Officers: David S. Seltzer/Dir., CEO, Pres., Tanya Akimova/54/Dir. - New Business Development, William Peters/CFO, VP, Elan Bar-Giora/Exec. VP - Operations, Gary M. April/51/Pres. - Health Care Products Division, Divisional VP - Sales, Edwin A. Berrios/56/VP - Sales, Marketing, Joanne Curri/68/Dir. - Regulatory Affairs, Polireddy Dondeti/43/Sr. Dir. - Research, Development, Jesse Kirsh/50/VP - Quality, Christopher Losardo/42/VP - Corporate Development, Pudpong Poolsuk/64/Sr. Dir. - Science, Margaret Santorufo/42/VP, Controller, James P. Tracy/64/VP - Information Systems, Arthur S. Goldberg/VP - Finance, Eyal Mares/45/VP - Operations

Directors: David S. Seltzer/Dir., CEO, Pres., Bernard Seltzer/Chmn., Anthony J. Puglisi/Dir., Reuben Seltzer/Dir., Bruce W. Simpson/Dir., Martin M. Goldwyn/Dir., Yashar Hirshaut/Dir., Robert Holster/Dir.

Owners: Columbia Management Advisors, Inc./7.90%, Martin M. Goldwyn, Galleon Group/5.70%, Insiders/34.40%, Royce & Associates LLC/7.40%, Estate of Bernard Seltzer/5.20%, Anthony J. Puglisi, Yashar Hirshaut, Bruce W. Simpson, Accipter Capital Management LLC/12.60%, Robert M. Holster, Visium Asset Management LLC/5.60%, David S. Seltzer/19.40%, Wellington Management Co., LLP/9.70%, William Peters *(16 Owners included in Index)*

Financial Data: Fiscal Year End:04/30 Latest Annual Data: 04/30/2007

Year	Sales	Net Income
2007	$58,898,000	-$2,036,000
2006	$78,020,000	$11,453,000
2005	$67,683,000	$8,288,000

Curr. Assets:	$75,205,000	Curr. Liab.:	$9,971,000		
Plant, Equip.:	$15,738,000	Total Liab.:	$11,937,000	Indic. Yr. Divd.:	NA
Total Assets:	$100,379,000	Net Worth:	$88,442,000	Debt/ Equity:	NA

HIA Inc

1105 W 122nd Ave, Westminster, CO, 80234; **PH:** 1-303-394-6040; **http://** www.hia-inc.com

General - Incorporation	NY	Stock- Price on:12/24/2007	NA
Employees	NA	Stock Exchange	NA
Auditor	Hein & Assoc. LLP	Ticker Symbol	NA
Stk Agt	Computershare Trust Co	Outstanding Shares	NA
Counsel	NA	E.P.S.	NA
DUNS No.	01-745-0180	Shareholders	NA

Business: The group's principal activity is to distribute turf irrigation equipment and commercial, industrial and residential well pumps and equipment on a wholesale basis. The business of the group is conducted through its wholly owned subsidiary, cps distributors, inc. The group carries a variety of brand name products, including pumps and water systems, water-conditioning equipment, pump and well accessories, pipe valves and fittings and sprinkler system equipment. The group serves customers in the rocky mountain region in five states consisting of Colorado, Wyoming, New Mexico, Kansas and Nebraska.

Primary SIC and add'l.: 5084 5083 6719

CIK No: 0000318189

Subsidiaries: CPS Distributors , Inc.

Officers: Gerry Bartley/Co - Founder, Pres., Mary Ann Bartley/Co - Founder, Exec. VP, Larry Diamond/VP - Business Development, Randy Carson/VP - Organizational Design, Transformation, Paula Kyburz/Specialties, Implementation, Clinical Applications, Benefits, Kevin J.M. Monn/Specialties, Implementation, Financial, Admin Applications, Benefits, Steve Robinson/Specialties, Implementation, Benefits, Pharmacy Applicationsspecialties, Implementation, Benefits, Pharmacy Applications, Lois Sakerka/Sr. Consultant, Clinical Applications, Pam Schutt/Specialties, Clinical Applications, Monte Prentice/Specialties, Interface Mgmt, Gary R. Smith/Specialties, Pharmacy, Amber Whipple/Specialties, HIM, Medical Records, Carla Daily-Goodright/Specialties, Clinical Applications, Implementations, Jim Kewley/Specialties, Pharmacy, Steve Coffey/Specialties, Accounting, Business Mgr. *(21 Officers included in Index)*

Directors: Gerry Bartley/Co - Founder, Pres., Mary Ann Bartley/Co - Founder, Exec. VP

Hibbett Sports Inc

Formerly: Hibbett Sporting Goods Inc
451 Indl. Ln., Birmingham, AL, 35211; **PH:** 1-205-942-4292; **http://** www.hibbett.com

General - Incorporation	DE	Stock- Price on:12/24/2007	$25.62
Employees	1,700	Stock Exchange	NDQ
Auditor	KPMG LLP	Ticker Symbol	HIBB
Stk Agt	SunTrust Bank	Outstanding Shares	31,240,000
Counsel	Latham & Watkins	E.P.S.	NA
DUNS No.	79-741-1964	Shareholders	NA

Business: The group's principal activity is the retail distribution of sporting goods. The group operates sporting goods stores that offers footwear, apparel and athletic equipment. The group solely operates in the United States of America. At 31-Jan-2004, the group operated 408 hibbett sports stores, sixteen smaller-format sports additions athletic shoe stores and four larger-format superstores in 21 states.

Primary SIC and add'l.: 5941 5699 5661

CIK No: 0001017480

Subsidiaries: Hibbett

Owners: Brian N. Priddy, Gary A. Smith, Michael J. Newsome, Wasatch Advisors, Inc./5.10%, Neuberger Berman, Inc./6.74%, Thomas A. Saunders, T. Rowe Price Associates, Inc./10.20%, Clyde B. Anderson, Insiders/1.90%

Financial Data: Fiscal Year End:01/28 Latest Annual Data: 2/3/2007

Year	Sales	Net Income
2007	$512,094,000	$38,073,000
2006	$440,269,000	$33,624,000
2005	$377,534,000	$25,147,000

Curr. Assets:	$166,889,000	Curr. Liab.:	$60,461,000	P/E Ratio:	22.47
Plant, Equip.:	$42,573,000	Total Liab.:	$76,212,000	Indic. Yr. Divd.:	NA
Total Assets:	$212,853,000	Net Worth:	$136,641,000	Debt/ Equity:	NA

Hickok Inc

10514 Dupont Ave., Cleveland, OH, 44108; *PH:* 1-216-761-9879; *http://* www.hickok-inc.com

General - Incorporation	OH	*Stock* - Price on:12/24/2007	$11.5
Employees	145	Stock Exchange	OTC
Auditor	Meaden & Moore Ltd	Ticker Symbol	HICKA
Stk Agt..... Computershare Investor Services LLC		Outstanding Shares	1,210,000
Counsel	Calfee, Halter & Griswold	E.P.S.	-$0.27
DUNS No.	00-420-4772	Shareholders	NA

Business: The group's principle activities are carried through two business segments: indicators and gauges develops and manufactures precision indicating instruments used in aircraft, locomotives and other applications, automotive diagnostic tools and equipment designs and markets instruments used to diagnose automotive electronic systems. The group's products and services are provided to automotive, aircraft and locomotive with sales to both original equipment manufacturers(OEMs) and to the automotive aftermarket in North America. The group's quarterly revenue for Sep'07 was 5.97 millions of USD.

Primary SIC and add'l.: 3743 3714 3724 3829

CIK No: 0000047307

Subsidiaries: Supreme Electronics Corp., Waekon Corp.

Officers: Robert L. Bauman/67/Dir., CEO, Pres., Gregory M. Zoloty/CFO, Sr. VP - Finance, Thomas F. Bauman/Sr. VP - Sales, Marketing, William A. Bruner/Sr. VP - Manufacturing Operations

Directors: Robert L. Bauman/67/Dir., CEO, Pres., Janet H. Slade/64/Chmn., Harold T. Hudson/68/Dir., James T. Martin/76/Dir., Michael L. Miller/66/Dir., Jim N. Moreland/76/Dir., Hugh S. Seaholm/56/Dir.

Owners: Insiders/20.20%, Gretchen L. Hickok/25.30%, Robert L. Bauman/9.50%, Koonce Securities Inc./18.67%, Glaubman Rosenberg & Robotti Fund, L.P./6.24%, Patricia H. Aplin, Robert E. Robotti/5.40%, Robert L. Bauman/26.30%, Janet H. Slade/22.50%, Patricia H. Aplin/25.90%, Gretchen L. Hickok, Insiders/48.80%, Janet H. Slade/1.40%, Thomas F. Bauman/2.20%

Financial Data: Fiscal Year End:09/30   Latest Annual Data: 9/30/2006

Year	Sales		Net Income
2006	$15,878,000		$804,000
2005	$9,671,000		-$1,574,000
2004	$15,721,000		$660,000
Curr. Assets:	$9,642,000	Curr. Liab.:	$2,852,000	
Plant, Equip.:	$890,000	Total Liab.:	$2,852,000	Indic. Yr. Divd.: $0.100
Total Assets:	$12,107,000	Net Worth:	$9,256,000	Debt/ Equity: NA

Hickory Tech Corp

221 E Hickory St., Mankato, MN, 56002; *PH:* 1-507-387-1151; *Fax:* 1-507-625-9191; *http://* www.hickorytech.com

General - Incorporation	MN	*Stock* - Price on:12/24/2007	$8.8
Employees	399	Stock Exchange	NDQ
Auditor	PricewaterhouseCoopers LLP	Ticker Symbol	HTCO
Stk Agt	Wells Fargo Bank Stock Transfer	Outstanding Shares	13,240,000
Counsel	NA	E.P.S.	$0.34
DUNS No.	14-758-7554	Shareholders	NA

Business: The group's principle activity is to operate incumbent local exchange carriers. The group operates in three segments: telecom sector, information solutions and enterprise solutions. The group's core business is the telecom sector, which consists of incumbent local exchange carriers (ilecs), competitive local exchange carrier (elec) and wireless telecommunications. Local exchange carriers connect customers to long distance service providers. Competitive local exchange carrier leverages its telecommunications services to customers and expands service into areas served by other ilecs. The group also provides data processing services to the telecommunications industry and data equipment sales and service as well as the sale, installation and ongoing service of voice over Internet protocol equipment. The group's quarterly revenue for Sep'07 was 35.86 millions of USD.

Primary SIC and add'l.: 3661 7374 4813

CIK No: 0000766561

Subsidiaries: Cable Network, Inc., Collins Communications Systems Co., Crystal Communications, Inc., Enventis Telecom, Inc., Heartland Telecommunications Company of Iowa, Inc., Mankato Citizens Telephone Company, Mid-Communications, Inc., National Independent Billing, Inc.

Officers: John W. Finke/Dir., CEO, Pres., David A. Christensen/Sr. VP, CFO/$216,867.00, Mary T. Jacobs/VP/$180,858.00, Lane C. Nordquist/VP/$216,369.00, Walt Prahl/Corporate VP, Pres. - Transport Solutions/$344,318.00, Damon D. Dutz/VP, John P. Morton/VP, Jennifer M. Spaude/Dir. - Public, Investor Relations

Directors: John W. Finke/Dir., CEO, Pres., James H. Holdrege/Vice Chmn., Wynn R. Kearney/Chmn., Dale Parker/Dir., Starr J. Kirklin/Dir., Lyle G. Jacobson/Dir., James W. Bracke/Dir., Robert D. Alton/Dir., Myrita P. Craig/Dir., Lyle T. Bosacker/Dir.

Owners: Lyle T. Bosacker/3.20%, Lane C. Nordquist, Dale E. Parker, Wynn R. Kearney/1.10%, Walter A. Prahl, David A. Christensen, Myrita P. Craig, QVT Financial LP/5.88%, Starr J. Kirklin, Lyle G. Jacobson, James W. Bracke, Insiders/8.70%, James H. Holdrege, Mary T. Jacobs, John W. Finke

Financial Data: Fiscal Year End:12/31   Latest Annual Data: 12/31/2006

Year	Sales		Net Income
2006	$132,901,000		$2,268,000
2005	$92,512,000		$8,529,000
2004	$90,515,000		$7,590,000
Curr. Assets:	$36,538,000	Curr. Liab.:	$28,807,000	P/E Ratio: 25.88
Plant, Equip.:	$152,835,000	Total Liab.:	$196,814,000	Indic. Yr. Divd.: $0.480
Total Assets:	$226,900,000	Net Worth:	$30,086,000	Debt/ Equity: 4.4900

HiEnergy Technologies Inc

1601 Alton Pkwy., Unit B, Irvine, CA, 92606; *PH:* 1-949-757-0855; *Fax:* 1-949-757-1477; *http://* www.hienergyinc.com; *Email:* hienergy@hienergyinc.com

General - Incorporation	DE	*Stock* - Price on:12/24/2007	NA
Employees	17	Stock Exchange	OTC
Auditor .. Singer Lewak Greenbaum & Goldstein		Ticker Symbol	HIET
Stk Agt...... American Stock Transfer & Trust Co.		Outstanding Shares	NA
Counsel	U.s. Federal, U.s. Attorney	E.P.S.	-$0.127
DUNS No.	NA	Shareholders	NA

Business: The group's principal activity is to develop technology capable of remote and non-intrusive, quantitative on-line deciphering of the chemical composition of substances, including explosives, biological weapons and illegal drugs. The group develops the atometer commercially known as the supersenzor which is used for airport security screening, border patrol/ customs control drug and contraband detection, bomb, biological and chemical weapons detection, including landmine clearance, carbomb detection, detecting of impurities in crude oil, coal and natural gas and fingerprinting of diamonds and other gemstones.

Primary SIC and add'l.: 7382

CIK No: 0001112424

Subsidiaries: HiEnergy Defense, Inc, HiEnergy Europe, Ltd, HiEnergy International, Inc, HiEnergy Leasing, Inc, HiEnergy Mfg Company

Owners: David R. Baker/1.81%, Bogdan C. Maglich/14.73%, William A. Nitze/1.13%, Insiders/19.53%, Peter J. Le Beau/0.66%, William J. Lacey, Roger W.A. Spillmann/0.73%

Financial Data: Fiscal Year End:04/30   Latest Annual Data: 4/30/2006

Year	Sales		Net Income
2006	NA		-$8,632,000
2005	NA		-$9,985,000
2004	NA		-$7,600,000
Curr. Assets:	$987,000	Curr. Liab.:	$4,506,000	
Plant, Equip.:	$789,000	Total Liab.:	$4,514,000	Indic. Yr. Divd.: NA
Total Assets:	$1,776,000	Net Worth:	-$2,739,000	Debt/ Equity: NA

Hifn Inc

750 University Ave., Los Gatos, CA, 95032; *PH:* 1-408-399-3500; *Fax:* 1-408-399-3501; *http://* www.hifn.com; *Email:* quality@hifn.com

General - Incorporation	DE	*Stock* - Price on:12/24/2007	$5.94
Employees	176	Stock Exchange	NDQ
Auditor	PricewaterhouseCoopers LLP	Ticker Symbol	HIFN
Stk Agt..... American Stock Transfer & Trust Co.		Outstanding Shares	14,080,000
Counsel........ Wilson Sonsini Goodrich & Rosati		E.P.S.	-$0.18
DUNS No.	01-817-4487	Shareholders	NA

Business: The group's principal activity is to design, develop and market high-performance, multi-protocol packet processors. Packet processors include semiconductor devices and software designed to enable secure, high-bandwidth network connectivity and efficient storage of business information. The packet processor products perform the computation and intensive tasks of compression, encryption and authentication, providing customers with high-performance, interoperable implementations of a wide variety of industry standard networking and storage protocols. The group's products are used in networking and storage equipment such as routers, remote access concentrators, switches, broadband access equipment, network interface cards, firewalls and back-up storage devices. The group acquired certain assets and intellectual property related to international business machines corporation's network processor product line in fiscal 2004.

Primary SIC and add'l.: 3577 3674 7372

CIK No: 0001065246

Subsidiaries: Hifn International, Hifn Limited, Hifn Netherlands B.V., Saian Microsystems, Inc.

Officers: Albert E. Sisto/Chmn., CEO, Barbara Newlon/Investor Relations, Mike Goldgof/VP - Product Marketing, Jiebing Wang/VP - Worldwide Engineering, GM - Hifn's China Product Operations, Douglas L. Whiting/Dir., Chief Scientist, Tom Moore/VP - Sales, Marketing, Russell Dietz/CTO, VP, William R. Walker/CFO, VP, John Matze/VP - Business Development

Directors: Albert E. Sisto/Chmn., CEO, Thomas Lawrence/Dir., Taher Elgamal/Dir., Douglas L. Whiting/Dir., Chief Scientist, Robert W. Johnson/Dir., Dennis Decoste/Dir.

Owners: Thomas A. Moore/1.60%, Russell S. Dietz, Austin Marxe & David Greenhouse/16.90%, Robert W. Johnson/3.60%, William R. Walker/1.30%, Columbia Management Advisors Inc./5.70%, Albert E. Sisto/1.30%, Dennis DeCoste, Dimensional Fund Advisors Inc./8.10%, Kamran Malik/1.10%, Taher Elgamal, CCM Master Qualified Fund, Ltd./10.10%, Laurence Lytton/7.30%, Douglas L. Whiting/2.70%, Christopher G. Kenber/3.40% (17 Owners included in Index)

Financial Data: Fiscal Year End:09/30   Latest Annual Data: 09/30/2007

Year	Sales		Net Income
2007	$42,967,000		-$2,541,000
2006	$43,764,000		-$8,724,000
2005	$46,394,000		-$5,216,000
Curr. Assets:	$46,990,000	Curr. Liab.:	$6,791,000	
Plant, Equip.:	$2,356,000	Total Liab.:	$6,791,000	Indic. Yr. Divd.: NA
Total Assets:	$57,476,000	Net Worth:	$50,685,000	Debt/ Equity: NA

High End Ventures Inc

1066 W Hastings St., Ste. 2610, Vancouver, BC, V6E 3X2; *PH:* 1-604-602-1717

General - Incorporation	CO	*Stock* - Price on:12/24/2007	$1.5
Employees	NA	Stock Exchange	OTC
Auditor .... Madsen & Associates, CPA's Inc.		Ticker Symbol	HEVE
Stk Agt	Stock Transfer Agent	Outstanding Shares	NA
Counsel	NA	E.P.S.	NA
DUNS No.	NA	Shareholders	NA

Business: The groups principal activity is to explore minerals. The group operates from the United States.

Primary SIC and add'l.: 1081

CIK No: 0001357694

Owners: Insiders/15.78%, Joseph H. Montgomery/18.93%, Thomas Forzani/15.78%

Financial Data: Fiscal Year End:09/30   Latest Annual Data: 9/30/2006

Year	Sales		Net Income
2006	NA		-$44,000
Curr. Assets:	$14,000	Curr. Liab.:	NA	
Plant, Equip.:	NA	Total Liab.:	NA	Indic. Yr. Divd.: NA
Total Assets:	$14,000	Net Worth:	$14,000	Debt/ Equity: NA

Highbury Financial Inc

535 Madison Ave., New York, NY, 10022; *PH:* 1-212-688-2341; *http://* www.highburyfinancial.com

General - Incorporation	DE	Stock - Price on:12/24/2007	$6.6
Employees	NA	Stock Exchange	OTC
Auditor	Goldstein Golub Kessler LLP	Ticker Symbol	HBRF
Stk Agt	Continental Stock Transfer & Trust Co	Outstanding Shares	9,530,000
Counsel	NA	E.P.S.	NA
DUNS No.	NA	Shareholders	NA

Business: The group operates through its subsidiary whose principle activity is to provide permanent capital solutions to investment management firms. The group operates from the United States.

Primary SIC and add'l.: 6282

CIK No: 0001335249

Subsidiaries: Aston Asset Management LLC

Officers: Richard S. Foote/Dir., CEO, Pres., Bradley R. Forth/CFO, Exec. VP, Sec., Devlin Lander/Investor Relations Officer - Integrated Corporate Relations, Inc

Directors: Richard S. Foote/Dir., CEO, Pres., Bruce R. Cameron/Chmn., Russell L. Appel/Dir., Aidan J. Riordan/36/Dir.

Owners: Wellington Management Company, LLP, Royce & Associates, LLC, Nisswa Master Fund Ltd., Woodbourne Partners, L.P., Jack Silver, Aidan J. Riordan, Insiders, Potomac Capital Management LLC, Second Curve Capital, LLC, Russell L. Appel, Bradley R. Forth, Richard S. Foote, Context Capital Management, LLC, Broad Hollow LLC, Talon Opportunity Partners, L.P. *(16 Owners included in Index)*

Financial Data: Fiscal Year End: 12/31 **Latest Annual Data:** 12/31/2006

Year	Sales	Net Income
2006	$3,828,000	-$12,463,000
2005	NA	-$2,000

Curr. Assets:	$10,130,000	Curr. Liab.:	$2,512,000		
Plant, Equip.:	$574,000	Total Liab.:	$3,138,000	Indic. Yr. Divd.:	NA
Total Assets:	$47,367,000	Net Worth:	$44,229,000	Debt/ Equity:	NA

Highland Hospitality Corp

8405 Greensboro Dr., Ste. 500, Mclean, VA, 22102; ; *http://* www.highlandhospitality.com

General - Incorporation	MD	Stock - Price on:12/24/2007	$19.21
Employees	16	Stock Exchange	NA
Auditor	KPMG LLP	Ticker Symbol	NA
Stk Agt	American Stock Transfer & Trust Co.	Outstanding Shares	61,450,000
Counsel	NA	E.P.S.	$0.49
DUNS No.	NA	Shareholders	NA

Business: The groups principle activity is to provide upscale full services, premium limited service and extended stay properties to the resort and airport markets. In the year 2006, the group acquired six properties. The group operates from the United States and Columbia.

Primary SIC and add'l.: 7011

CIK No: 0001262415

Subsidiaries: HH Annapolis Holding LLC, HH Annapolis LLC, HH Atlanta LLC, HH Baltimore Holdings LLC, HH Baltimore LLC, HH Boston Back Bay LLC, HH Churchill Hotel Associates, L.P., HH Denver LLC, HH DFW Hotel Associates, L.P., HH FP Portfolio Holding LLC, HH FP Portfolio LLC, HH Gaithersburg LLC, HH LC Portfolio LLC, HH Melrose Hotel Associates, L.P., HH Mexico Holding LLC 48 Subsidiaries included in the Index

Officers: James L. Francis/Dir., CEO, Pres., Douglas W. Vicari/Exec. VP, CFO, Treasurer, Patrick W. Campbell/Exec. VP, Chief Investment Officer, Tracy M.J Colden/Exec. VP, General Counsel, Corp. Sec.

Directors: James L. Francis/Dir., CEO, Pres., Bruce D. Wardinski/Chmn., John M. Elwood/Dir., Reeder W. Glass/Dir., John W. Hill/Dir., William L. Wilson/Dir., Thomas A. Natelli/Dir., Margaret A. Sheehan/Dir.

Owners: Insiders/3.50%, Margaret A. Sheehan, Tracy M.J. Colden, John M. Elwood, William L. Wilson, Columbia Wanger Asset Management, L.P./10.90%, Thomas A. Natelli, The Vanguard Group, Inc./5.70%, Douglas W. Vicari, John W. Hill, James L. Francis/1.20%, Patrick W. Campbell, Bruce D. Wardinski, Barclays Global Investors, NA/7.60%, Reeder W. Glass

Financial Data: Fiscal Year End: 12/31 **Latest Annual Data:** 12/31/2006

Year	Sales	Net Income
2006	$422,588,000	$32,875,000
2005	$251,215,000	$9,673,000
2004	$133,011,000	$4,266,000

Curr. Assets:	$76,774,000	Curr. Liab.:	$53,730,000	P/E Ratio:	39.20
Plant, Equip.:	$1,207,812,000	Total Liab.:	$703,063,000	Indic. Yr. Divd.:	$0.920
Total Assets:	$1,313,197,000	Net Worth:	$605,637,000	Debt/ Equity:	1.1464

Highlands Union Bank

113 Hardin Ln, Sevierville, TN, 37862; *PH:* 1-865-908-0455; *http://* www.hubank.com; *Email:* info@hubank.com

General - Incorporation	WV	Stock - Price on:12/24/2007	NA
Employees	NA	Stock Exchange	OTC
Auditor	S. B. Hoover & Co. LLP	Ticker Symbol	NA
Stk Agt		Outstanding Shares	NA
Counsel	Krauskopf & Baker	E.P.S.	NA
DUNS No.	15-653-1295	Shareholders	NA

Business: The group's principal activities are to provide full range of commercial banking services, life and accident insurance coverage and trust services. The group's accepts commercial deposit, individual deposits and demand deposits. The group lends real estate mortgage loans, real estate construction loans, commercial loans, consumer installment loans, agricultural loans and residential loans. The group also provides drive-in banking services and automated teller machine banking, through its insurance subsidiary. Also sells credit life accident and health insurance coverage. The group primarily operates in grant county, randolph county, hardy county, mineral county and the northwest pendleton county.

Primary SIC and add'l.: 6022 6712

CIK No: 0000756862

Subsidiaries: Capon Valley Bank, HBI Life Insurance Company, Inc., The Grant County Bank

Officers: Sam Neese/Dir., CEO

Directors: Sam Neese/Dir., CEO, William J. Singleton/Dir., Clydes B. Kiser/Dir., Samuel L. Neese/Dir., William E. Chaffin/Dir., Carter J. Lambert/Dir., Craig E. Kendrick/Dir., J. D. Morefield/Dir., James D. Moore/Dir., Charles P. Olinger/Dir., James T. Riffe/Dir., Ramsey H. White/Dir.

Owners: Alan R. Miller, John G. Van Meter/4.20%, Jack H. Walters, Kathy G. Kimble, Steven C. Judy, Insiders/8.20%, Clarence E. Porter, Courtney R. Tusing, Thomas B. McNeill/1.10%, Keith L. Wolfe, Leslie A. Barr, Alan L. Brill

Highveld Steel and Vanadium Corp Ltd

Old Pretoria Rd., Witbank, Mpumalanga, 1035; *PH:* 27-0136909911; *Fax:* 27-0136909033; *http://* www.highveldsteel.co.za, *Email:* general@hiveld.co.za

General - Incorporation		Stock - Price on:12/24/2007	$12.92
Employees	NA	Stock Exchange	NDQ
Auditor	NA	Ticker Symbol	HSVLY
Stk Agt	Bank of New York	Outstanding Shares	NA
Counsel	NA	E.P.S.	NA
DUNS No.	NA	Shareholders	NA

Business: The groups principal activity is to provide Vanadium, Steel and Ferro-alloys product. The products of the group include vanadium pentoxide, ferrovanadium and vanadium chemicals, vanadium slag, billets, slabs, ferrosilicon, electrode paste and char. The group operates from the United States.

Primary SIC and add'l.: 3312

CIK No: 0000800630

Officers: W. G. Ballandino/Dir., CEO, A. Diener/Dir., Company Sec., Sh Van Niekerk/GM - General Services, R. Wolar/Mgr. - Human Capital, Organisational Development, Security, S. N. Mafoane/GM - Human Resources, J. B. Price/GM - Ironmaking, Engineering Services, J. W. Swanepoel/GM - Steelmaking, Mills, J. Theiss/GM - Sheq, D. C. Pretorius/GM, CFO, M. Van In/GM - Information Technology, A. M. Visser/GM - Procurement, Stores, A. J. Vorster/GM - Sales, Marketing

Directors: W. G. Ballandino/Dir., CEO, L. Boyd/Chmn., C. B. Brayshaw/Dir., P. S. Tatyanin/Non Exec. Dir., A. Diener/Dir., Company Sec., G. C. Baizini/Dir., G. A. Mannina/Dir. - Swiss, Bjt Shongwe/Dir., J. W. Campbell/Dir., A. V. Frolov/Dir.

Financial Data: Fiscal Year End: 12/31 **Latest Annual Data:** 12/31/2006

Year	Sales	Net Income
2006	$991,674,000	$159,938,000
2005	$1,131,206,000	$302,920,000
2004	$893,890,000	$132,238,000

Curr. Assets:	$337,408,000	Curr. Liab.:	$305,794,000	P/E Ratio:	46.72
Plant, Equip.:	$303,926,000	Total Liab.:	$387,703,000	Indic. Yr. Divd.:	NA
Total Assets:	$656,565,000	Net Worth:	$268,863,000	Debt/ Equity:	NA

Highway Holdings Ltd

Ste. 810, Level 8, Landmark N, 39 Lung Sum Ave., Sheung Shui New Territories; *PH:* 852-24940923; *Fax:* 852-23434976; *http://* www.highwayholdings.com

General - Incorporation British Virgin Islands		Stock - Price on:12/24/2007	$4.41
Employees	1,250	Stock Exchange	NDQ
Auditor	Deloitte Touche Tohmatsu	Ticker Symbol	HIHO
Stk Agt	U.S. Stock Transfer Corp	Outstanding Shares	3,620,000
Counsel	NA	E.P.S.	$0.04
DUNS No.	66-306-4285	Shareholders	NA

Business: The group operates through its subsidiaries whose principle activity is to manufacture high quality metal parts, cameras and clocks for original equipment manufacturers, contract manufacturers and others. The group operates from United States.

Primary SIC and add'l.: 3861 3873 3469 6719

CIK No: 0001026785

Subsidiaries: Antemat Limited, Cavour Industrial Limited, Hi-Lite Camera Company, Hi-Lite Camera Company Limited, Kayser (Wuxi) Metal Precision Manufacturing Limited, Kayser Technik (Overseas) Inc, Kayser Technik Limited, Kienzle Bulgaria Limited, Kienzle Time (H.K.) Limited, Kienzle USA Ltd, Metal Precision Manufacturing Limited, Nissin Mechatronic Limited, Nissin Precision Metal, Saiwan Industries Limited

Owners: Shu Mui May Tsang, Kuang Yu Kevin Yang, Ping Yim Irene Wong, Roland W. Kohl, Cartwright Investments Limited, Brian Geary, Fong Po Shan, Shlomo Tamir, Dirk Hermann, Quan Vinh Can, Satoru Saito, Uri Bernhard Oppenheimer, George Leung Wing Chan, Tiko Aharonov

Financial Data: Fiscal Year End: 03/31 **Latest Annual Data:** 03/31/2007

Year	Sales	Net Income
2007	$31,469,000	$594,000
2006	$25,843,000	$42,000
2005	$27,678,000	-$152,000

Curr. Assets:	$16,102,000	Curr. Liab.:	$6,142,000		
Plant, Equip.:	$2,787,000	Total Liab.:	$6,617,000	Indic. Yr. Divd.:	$0.320
Total Assets:	$18,891,000	Net Worth:	$12,274,000	Debt/ Equity:	NA

Highwoods Properties Inc

3100 Smoketree Ct., Ste. 600, Raleigh, NC, 27604; *PH:* 1-919-872-4924; *Fax:* 1-919-873-0088; *http://* www.highwoods.com; *Email:* hiw-ir@highwoods.com

General - Incorporation	MD	Stock - Price on:12/24/2007	$40.65
Employees	476	Stock Exchange	NYSE
Auditor	Deloitte & Touche LLP	Ticker Symbol	HIW
Stk Agt	American Stock Transfer & Trust Co.	Outstanding Shares	56,880,000
Counsel	NA	E.P.S.	$1.41
DUNS No.	NA	Shareholders	NA

Business: The groups principle activities include owning, developing and operating suburban office, industrial and retail properties. The group customers include Federal Government, AT&T, T-Mobile USA, Volvo, Northern Telecom, Fluor Enterprises, Inc. and The Martin Agency. The group operates from the Southeastern and Midwestern United States. The groups quarterly revenue for September 2007 was 110.17 millions of USD.

Primary SIC and add'l.: 6798

CIK No: 0000921082

Subsidiaries: AP Southeast Portfolio Partners, L.P., Highwoods Finance LLC, Highwoods Realty Limited Partnership, Highwoods Services, Inc., Highwoods/Florida Holdings, L.P., Highwoods/Tennessee Holdings, L.P.

Officers: Edward J. Fritsch/Dir., CEO, Pres./$2,201,582.00, Michael E. Harris/COO, Exec. VP/$1,342,677.00, Julie M. Kelly/VP - Internal Audit, Compliance, Carman J. Liuzzo/VP - Investments, Dan Woodward/VP, Gene H. Anderson/Sr. VP - Atlanta, Dir./$738,480.00, Barrett Brady/Sr. VP, Daniel L. Clemmens/VP, Chief Accounting Officer, David J. Matthes/Corporate VP - Leasing, Art H. McCann/CIO, Jeffrey D. Miller/VP, General Counsel, Sec., Hugh Esleeck/Treasurer, Steven L. Guinn/VP - Memphis, Thomas Hill/VP, Paul W. Kreckman/VP *(21 Officers included in Index)*

Directors: Edward J. Fritsch/Dir., CEO, Pres., Temple O. Sloan/Chmn., Sherry A. Kellett/Dir., Thomas W. Adler/Dir., Gene H. Anderson/Sr. VP - Atlanta, Dir., Lawrence S. Kaplan/Dir., Glenn L. Orr/Dir., William F. Vandiver/66/Dir., Kay Nichols Callison/Dir.

Owners: The Vanguard Group, Inc./5.00%, Insiders/7.30%, Edward J. Fritsch/1.60%, Barclays Global Investors, NA/6.40%, AEW Capital Management, L.P./6.80%, Mack D. Pridgen, Cohen & Steers, Inc./6.30%, Lawrence S. Kaplan, William F. Vandiver, ING Groep N.V./10.70%, Michael E. Harris, Terry L. Stevens, Sherry A. Kellett, Gene H. Anderson/1.90%, Kay N. Callison/1.00% *(18 Owners included in Index)*

Financial Data: *Fiscal Year End:*12/31 *Latest Annual Data:* 12/31/2006

Year	Sales	Net Income
2006	$416,798,000	$53,744,000
2005	$410,701,000	$62,458,000
2004	$464,724,000	$41,577,000

Curr. Assets:	$110,428,000	*Curr. Liab.:*	$156,737,000	*P/E Ratio:*	28.83
Plant, Equip.:	$2,582,488,000	*Total Liab.:*	$1,737,122,000	*Indic. Yr. Divd.:*	NA
Total Assets:	$2,844,853,000	*Net Worth:*	$1,107,731,000	*Debt/ Equity:*	1.3629

Hiland Holdings GP LP

205 W Maple, Ste. 1100, Enid, OK, 73701; *PH:* 1-580-242-6040; *Fax:* 1-580-548-5188; *http://* www.hilandpartners.com

General - Incorporation	DE	Stock- Price on:12/24/2007	$31.82
Employees	NA	Stock Exchange	NDQ
Auditor	Grant Thornton, LLP	Ticker Symbol	HPGP
Stk Agt	American Stock Transfer & Trust Co.	Outstanding Shares	21,600,000
Counsel	NA	E.P.S.	$0.11
DUNS No.	NA	Shareholders	NA

Business: The groups principle activities include gathering, compressing, dehydrating, treating, processing and marketing natural gas. The groups services include fractionating natural gas liquids and providing air compression and water injection. The group operates from the United States. The group's quarterly revenue for September 2007 was 67.64 millions of USD.

Primary SIC and add'l.: 1389

CIK No: 0001363381

Subsidiaries: Continental Gas Operating, LP, Hiland Energy Partners, LLC, Hiland GP, LLC, Hiland LP, LLC, Hiland Operating, LLC, Hiland Partners GP, LLC, Hiland Partners GP,Inc., Hiland Partners, LLC, Hiland Partners, LP

Officers: Randy Moeder/47/Dir., CEO, Pres., Joseph Griffin/Dir., CEO, Pres., Mika Dick/Mgr. - Gas Supply, Vanessa Gainer/Dir. - Human Resources, Jason Vann/Dir. - Information Technology, Ken Maples/Dir., CFO, VP - Finance, Sec., Robert Shain/VP - Operations, Engineering, Ron Hill/VP - Business Development

Directors: Randy Moeder/47/Dir., CEO, Pres., Joseph Griffin/Dir., CEO, Pres., Harold Hamm/Chmn., Ken Maples/Dir., CFO, VP - Finance, Sec., Edward D. Doherty/Dir., Cheryl L. Evans/Dir., Michael L. Greenwood/Dir., Bobby B. Lyle/Dir., Shelby E. Odell/Dir., Rayford T. Reid/Dir., David L. Boren/Dir. - Hiland Partners GP, LLC, John T. McNabb/Dir. - Hiland Partners GP, LLC

Owners: Bobby B. Lyle, Harold Hamm/35.40%, Edward D. Doherty, Michael L. Greenwood, Harold Hamm HJ Trust/9.90%, Ken Maples, Randy Moeder/1.80%, Rayford T. Reid, Harold Hamm DST Trust/14.80%, Insiders/38.30%, Shelby E. Odell, Cheryl L. Evans

Financial Data: *Fiscal Year End:*12/31 *Latest Annual Data:* 12/31/2006

Year	Sales	Net Income
2006	$219,686,000	$2,363,000

Curr. Assets:	$41,207,000	*Curr. Liab.:*	$26,934,000	*P/E Ratio:*	64.00
Plant, Equip.:	$257,003,000	*Total Liab.:*	$314,041,000	*Indic. Yr. Divd.:*	$0.830
Total Assets:	$355,198,000	*Net Worth:*	$41,157,000	*Debt/ Equity:*	NA

Hiland Partners LP

205 W Maple, Ste. 1100, Enid, OK, 73701; *PH:* 1-580-242-6040; *Fax:* 1-580-548-5188; *http://* www.hilandpartners.com; *Email:* info@hilandpartners.com

General - Incorporation	DE	Stock- Price on:12/24/2007	$55.0199
Employees	95	Stock Exchange	NDQ
Auditor	Grant Thornton LLP	Ticker Symbol	HLND
Stk Agt	American Stock Transfer & Trust Co.	Outstanding Shares	9,290,000
Counsel	NA	E.P.S.	$1.137
DUNS No.	NA	Shareholders	NA

Business: The groups principle activities include gathering, compressing, dehydrating, treating, processing and marketing natural gas. The group operates from two segments namely midstream and compression. The groups services include dehydrating natural gas and remove impurities. The group operates from the United States. The group's quarterly revenue for September 2007 was 67.64 millions of USD.

Primary SIC and add'l.: 1389

CIK No: 0001306527

Subsidiaries: Continental Gas Operating, LP, Hiland Energy Partners, LLC, Hiland GP, LLC, Hiland LP, LLC, Hiland Operating, LLC

Officers: Joseph Griffin/Dir., CEO, Pres., Ron Hill/VP - Business Development, Ken Maples/Dir., CFO, VP - Finance, Sec., Robert Shain/VP - Operations, Engineering

Directors: Joseph Griffin/Dir., CEO, Pres., Harold Hamm/Chmn., Ken Maples/Dir., CFO, VP - Finance, Sec., David L. Boren/Dir., Edward D. Doherty/Dir., Michael L. Greenwood/Dir., John T. McNabb/Dir., Shelby E. Odell/Dir., Rayford T. Reid/Dir.

Owners: Harold Hamm/24.90%, Rayford T. Reid, John T. McNabb, Randy Moeder, Fiduciary Asset Management, LLC./7.40%, David L. Boren, Ken Maples, Insiders/26.10%, Kayne Anderson Capital Advisors, L.P./7.20%, Michael L. Greenwood, Robert Shain, Shelby E. Odell, Edward D. Doherty

Financial Data: *Fiscal Year End:*12/31 *Latest Annual Data:* 12/31/2006

Year	Sales	Net Income
2006	$219,686,000	$14,682,000
2005	$166,601,000	$10,337,000

Curr. Assets:	$40,804,000	*Curr. Liab.:*	$26,519,000	*P/E Ratio:*	48.39
Plant, Equip.:	$252,801,000	*Total Liab.:*	$176,070,000	*Indic. Yr. Divd.:*	NA
Total Assets:	$343,816,000	*Net Worth:*	$167,746,000	*Debt/ Equity:*	0.9859

Hilb Rogal & Hobbs Co

4951 Lake Brook Dr., Ste. 500, Glen Allen, VA, 23060; *PH:* 1-804-747-6500; *Fax:* 1-804-747-6046; *http://* www.hrh.com

General - Incorporation	VA	Stock- Price on:12/24/2007	$44.22
Employees	3,700	Stock Exchange	NYSE
Auditor	Ernst & Young LLP	Ticker Symbol	HRH
Stk Agt	Mellon Investor Services LLC	Outstanding Shares	36,770,000
Counsel	NA	E.P.S.	$2.40
DUNS No.	04-961-2914	Shareholders	NA

Business: The group's principle activity is to operate a network of wholly owned subsidiary insurance agencies. The group places various types of insurance, including property, casualty, marine, aviation and employee benefits, with insurance underwriters. The agencies operate approximately 100 offices in 25 states. The group also advises customers on risk management and employee benefits and provides claims administration and loss control consulting services. The group's client base ranges from personal to large national accounts and is primarily comprised of middle-Market and top-tier commercial and industrial accounts. The group's quarterly revenue for Sep'07 was 195.51 millions of USD.

Primary SIC and add'l.: 6411

CIK No: 0000814898

Subsidiaries: Bay Technology Group, LLC, Bliss& Glennon, Inc., Dominion Specialty Group, Inc., Ed Murray& Sons, Inc., Essenale, Ltd., Frank F. Haack& Associates, Inc., Freberg Environmental, Inc., Freberg& Company of Wyoming, Inc., Hilb Rogal& Hobbs Insurance Services of Aliso Viejo, LLC, Hilb Rogal& Hobbs Insurance Services of California, Inc., Hilb Rogal& Hobbs Insurance Services of Long Beach, LLC, Hilb Rogal& Hobbs of Alabama, Inc., Hilb Rogal& Hobbs of Appleton, Inc., Hilb Rogal& Hobbs of Arizona, Inc., Hilb Rogal& Hobbs of Atlanta, Inc. 72 Subsidiaries included in the Index

Officers: Martin L. Vaughan/60/Chmn., CEO/$1,840,687.00, Michael F. Crowley/Pres./$1,189,191.00, Michael Dinkins/CFO, Exec. VP/$628,323.00, Joseph Birriel/Sr. VP - Human Resources, Corporate Branding, Walter L. Smith/Sr. VP - Business Practices, Quality Assurance, Frank H. Beard/VP, National Dir. - Property, Casualty, Karl E. Manke/VP, National Dir. - Select Commercial, Personal Lines, Robert S. O'Brien/VP, National Dir. - Production, Sales Development, Thomas J. Stiles/VP, Regional Dir. - Southeast Region, Alice Edwards/HRH Complex Property Claims Practice Leader, Thomas Pegg/HRH Risk Control Practice Leader, Mark Mirek/HRH Property Risk Control Practice Leader, Viren R. Kapadia/CIO, Assist. VP, John P. McGrath/VP, Regional Dir. - Midwest Region, Timothy J. Korman/Exec. VP - Finance, Administration/$906,788.00 *(40 Officers included in Index)*

Directors: Martin L. Vaughan/60/Chmn., CEO, Thomas H. Obrien/71/Dir., Scott R. Royster/Dir., Robert H. Hilb/81/Dir., Theodore L. Chandler/55/Dir., Robert W. Fiondella/65/Dir., Warren M. Thompson/47/Dir., Norwood H. Davis/68/Dir., Julious P. Smith/65/Dir., Anthony F. Markel/66/Dir., Robert S. Ukrop/61/Dir.

Owners: Michael Dinkins, FMR Corp/5.29%, Insiders, Robert S. Ukrop, Robert H. Hilb, Timothy J. Korman, Westport Asset Management, Inc./7.65%, Steven C. Deal, Theodore L. Chandler, Michael F. Crowley, Warren M. Thompson, Robert W. Fiondella, Southeastern Asset Management, Inc./9.86%, Lord, Abbett& Co. LLC/5.10%, Artisan Partners Limited Partnership/6.31% *(21 Owners included in Index)*

Financial Data: *Fiscal Year End:*12/31 *Latest Annual Data:* 12/31/2006

Year	Sales	Net Income
2006	$710,845,000	$87,031,000
2005	$673,885,000	$56,200,000
2004	$619,603,000	$81,414,000

Curr. Assets:	$596,372,000	*Curr. Liab.:*	$526,651,000	*P/E Ratio:*	18.43
Plant, Equip.:	$22,178,000	*Total Liab.:*	$834,778,000	*Indic. Yr. Divd.:*	$0.520
Total Assets:	$1,438,147,000	*Net Worth:*	$603,369,000	*Debt/ Equity:*	0.3844

Hill International Inc

303 Lippincott Ctr., Marlton, NJ, 08053; *PH:* 1-856-810-6200; *Fax:* 1-856-810-1309; *http://* www.hillintl.com

General - Incorporation	DE	Stock- Price on:12/24/2007	$7.37
Employees	NA	Stock Exchange	NDQ
Auditor	Amper, Politziner & Mattia P.c	Ticker Symbol	HINT
Stk Agt	Continental Stock Transfer & Trust Co	Outstanding Shares	24,600,000
Counsel	NA	E.P.S.	NA
DUNS No.	NA	Shareholders	NA

Business: The groups principle activity is to provide project management and construction claims services. The groups operates through two segments namely project management group and the construction claims group. Customers served by the group include United States federal government, foreign governments and private sector. The group operates from the United States, Europe, the Middle East and Asia Pacific. The group's quarterly revenue for September 2007 was 72.18 millions of USD.

Primary SIC and add'l.: 8711 8741 8713 8748 8712 8742

CIK No: 0001287808

Subsidiaries: Hill Construction Management Ltd., Hill International (Anatolia), Hill International (Bucharest) S.R.L., Hill International (Hellas) S.A., Hill International (Middle East) Ltd. (b), Hill International (Puerto Rico), Inc., Hill International (UK) Ltd., Hill International Rijeka d.o.o., Hill International S.A., Hill International Services Ltd., James R. Knowles (Australian Holdings) Pty. Ltd. (c), James R. Knowles (Holdings) Ltd., James R. Knowles (Worldwide) Ltd. (c), James R. Knowles Global Ltd. (c), Knowles Consultancy Services, Inc. 20 Subsidiaries included in the Index

Officers: Irvin E. Richter/Chmn., CEO, David L. Richter/Dir., COO, Pres., William H. Dengler/Sr. VP, General Counsel, Catherine H. Emma/Sr. VP, Chief Administrative Officer, Gregg D. Metzinger/VP - Global Recruiting, Staff Augmentation, John P. Paolin/VP - Marketing, Corporate Communications, Hans A. Van Winkle/Pres. - Project Management Group, Americas, Raouf S. Ghali/Pres. - Project Management Group, International, Stuart S. Richter/Sr. VP, Michael V. Griffin/Sr. VP, John W. Herzog/Sr. VP, Abdo E. Kardous/Sr. VP, MD - Middle East Operations, Clarke D. Pile/Sr. VP, Martin S. Brown/Sr. VP - Business Development, Frederic Z. Samelian/Pres. - Construction Claims Group *(33 Officers included in Index)*

Directors: Irvin E. Richter/Chmn., CEO, David L. Richter/Dir., COO, Pres., William J. Doyle/Dir., Eric S. Rosenfeld/Dir., Brian W. Clymer/Dir., Alan S. Fellheimer/Dir., Arnaud Ajdler/Dir.

Owners: Jack Silver/6.50%, John Fanelli, Eric S. Rosenfeld/7.80%, Raouf S. Ghali, Brahman Capital Corp./6.80%, Brady H. Richter/9.10%, Insiders/70.70%, Wells Fargo & Company/7.70%, Israel Englander/6.30%, Stuart S. Richter/2.50%, William J. Doyle, Alan S. Fellheimer, Brian W. Clymer, David L. Richter/15.70%, Arnaud Ajdler *(18 Owners included in Index)*

Financial Data: **Fiscal Year End:**12/31 **Latest Annual Data:** 12/30/2006

Year	Sales	Net Income
2006	$129,987,000	$8,580,000
2005	NA	$284,000
2004	NA	$70,000

Curr. Assets:	$37,127,000	**Curr. Liab.:**	$190,000		
Plant, Equip.:	NA	**Total Liab.:**	$7,520,000	**Indic. Yr. Divd.:**	NA
Total Assets:	$37,342,000	**Net Worth:**	$29,822,000	**Debt/ Equity:**	0.1966

Hillenbrand Industries Inc

1069 State Rte. , 46 E, Batesville, IN, 47006; ***PH:*** 1-812-934-7000; ***Fax:*** 1-812-931-3533; ***http://*** www.hillenbrand.com

General - Incorporation	IN	**Stock**- Price on:12/24/2007	$65.69
Employees	9,300	Stock Exchange	NYSE
Auditor	PricewaterhouseCoopers LLP	Ticker Symbol	HB
Stk Agt	Computershare Investor Services LLC	Outstanding Shares	61,680,000
Counsel	Bracewell & Patterson	E.P.S	$3.07
DUNS No.	05-065-6982	Shareholders	NA

Business: The groups principle activity is to provide health care services. The group also provides products for the death care industry. The groups products include patient support systems, non-invasive therapeutic products, burial and cremation caskets including containers and urns. The group operates from United States.

Primary SIC and add'l.: 3995 7352 3842 6311 2599 7359

CIK No: 0000047518

Subsidiaries: Advanced Respiratory, Inc., Allen Medical Systems, Inc., Batesville Casket Co. South Africa Pty, Ltd., Batesville Casket Company, Inc., Batesville Casket de Mexico, S.A. de C.V, Batesville Casket de Mexico, S.A. de C.V., Batesville Casket UK, Ltd., Batesville International Corporation, Batesville Logistics, Inc., Batesville Manufacturing, Inc., Batesville Services, Inc, Batesville Services, Inc., Cutler Property, Inc, Forethought Federal Savings Bank, Green Tree Manufacturing, Inc. 59 Subsidiaries included in the Index

Officers: Peter H. Soderberg/61/Dir., CEO, Pres., Kimbery K. Dennis/40/Sr. VP - Post Acute, Gary L. Larson/46/VP - Internal Audit, John Dickey/53/VP - Human Resources, Gregory N. Miller/44/CFO, Sr. VP, Patrick D. De Maynadier/47/VP, General Counsel, Sec., Mark R. Lanning/52/VP, Treasurer, Kenneth A. Camp/62/Sr. VP, Blair A. Rieth/VP - Investor Relations

Directors: Peter H. Soderberg/61/Dir., CEO, Pres., Rolf A. Classon/62/Chmn., Joanne C. Smith/Vice Chmn., Charles E. Golden/Dir., John A. Hillenbrand/Dir., August W. Hillenbrand/Dir., Ray J. Hillenbrand/Dir., Mark D. Ketchum/Dir., Eduardo R. Menasce/Dir., Ronald A. Malone/Dir., Jose A. Mejia/Dir., Patrick T. Ryan/Dir.

Owners: Ray J. Hillenbrand, Joanne C. Smith, Gregory N. Miller, Franklin Resources, Inc./5.10%, Franklin Mutual Advisers, LLC/5.30%, Eduardo R. Menasce, John A. Hillenbrand/1.70%, Charles E. Golden, Patrick D. de Maynadier, Barclays Global Investors, NA/5.00%, Peter H. Soderberg, Kenneth A. Camp, August W. Hillenbrand/5.20%, Rolf A. Classon, Kimberly K. Dennis *(16 Owners included in Index)*

Financial Data: **Fiscal Year End:**09/30 **Latest Annual Data:** 9/30/2006

Year	Sales	Net Income
2006	$1,962,900,000	$221,200,000
2005	$1,938,100,000	-$94,100,000
2004	$1,829,000,000	$143,000,000

Curr. Assets:	$763,900,000	**Curr. Liab.:**	$325,200,000	**P/E Ratio:**	18.00
Plant, Equip.:	$369,100,000	**Total Liab.:**	$820,500,000	**Indic. Yr. Divd.:**	$1.140
Total Assets:	$1,952,200,000	**Net Worth:**	$1,131,700,000	**Debt/ Equity:**	0.2855

Hillman Cos Inc

10590 Hamilton Ave., Cincinnati, OH, 45231; ***PH:*** 1-513-851-4900; ***Fax:*** 1-513-854-9977; ***http://*** www.hillmangroup.com; ***Email:*** info@hillmangroup.com

General - Incorporation	DE	**Stock**- Price on:12/24/2007	$29.35
Employees	NA	Stock Exchange	AMEX
Auditor	Grant Thornton, LLP	Ticker Symbol	HLM-P
Stk Agt	NA	Outstanding Shares	NA
Counsel	Morgan, Lewis & Bockius LLP	E.P.S	NA
DUNS No.	16-094-6992	Shareholders	NA

Business: The group operates through its subsidiaries whose principle activity is to provide merchandise services and products, such as fasteners and related hardware items, key duplication equipment, keys and related accessories and identification equipment and items to retail oulets, primarily hardware stores, home centers and mass merchants, and offers personalized inventory management systems of maintenance, repair and operations products to industrial manufacturing customers and maintenance and repair facilities, as well as provides systems, parts and engineering services for hydraulic, pneumatic, electronic and related systems to major industrial concerns throughout the u.s and Canada; and formerly installed and repair glass. The group operates from United States.

Primary SIC and add'l.: 5072 6719 5065

CIK No: 0001029831

Subsidiaries: Hillman Group Capital Trust, Hillman Investment Company, SunSource Integrated Services de Mexico S.A. de C.V., SunSource Technology Services, LLC, SunSub C, Inc., SunSub Holdings LLC, The Hillman Group Canada, Ltd., The Hillman Group, Inc.

Officers: Max W. Hillman/61/Dir., CEO, Pres., Richard P. Hillman/59/Pres. - Hillman Group, Inc, George L. Heredia/49/Sr. VP - Engraving, The Hillman Group, Inc, James P. Waters/46/CFO, Sec., Terry R. Rowe/53/Sr. VP - National Accounting Sales, The Hillman Group, Inc

Directors: Max W. Hillman/61/Dir., CEO, Pres., Peter M. Gotsch/43/Chmn., Maurice P. Andrien/66/Dir., Mark A. Dolfato/35/Dir., Larry Wilton/60/Dir., Andrew W. Code/49/Dir., Shael J. Dolman/36/Dir.

Owners: James P. Waters, Terry R. Rowe/7.07%, Insiders/100.00%, James P. Waters/0.38%, Terry R. Rowe/0.95%, Code Hennessy & Simmons IV LP/49.03%, George L. Heredia/0.97%, Richard P. Hillman/14.46%, George L. Heredia/1.05%, Richard P. Hillman/1.99%, Ontario Teachers Pension Plan/100.00%, Code Hennessy & Simmons IV LP/78.89%, Richard P. Hillman/0.88%, Max W. Hillman/5.10%, Insiders/14.16% *(33 Owners included in Index)*

Financial Data: **Fiscal Year End:**12/31 **Latest Annual Data:** 12/31/2006

Year	Sales	Net Income
2006	$423,901,000	-$7,648,000
2005	$382,512,000	-$3,654,000
2004	$273,374,000	$779,000

Curr. Assets:	$152,975,000	**Curr. Liab.:**	$47,092,000		
Plant, Equip.:	$59,061,000	**Total Liab.:**	$528,272,000	**Indic. Yr. Divd.:**	NA
Total Assets:	$653,584,000	**Net Worth:**	$47,233,000	**Debt/ Equity:**	10.6762

Hills Bancorp

131 Main St., Hills, IA, 52235; ***PH:*** 1-319-679-2291; ***Fax:*** 1-319-679-2180; ***http://*** www.hillsbank.com

General - Incorporation	IA	**Stock**- Price on:12/24/2007	$59.5
Employees	327	Stock Exchange	OTC
Auditor	KPMG LLP	Ticker Symbol	HBIA
Stk Agt	UMB Bank, N.A.	Outstanding Shares	4,500,000
Counsel	NA	E.P.S	$3.49
DUNS No.	10-737-1494	Shareholders	NA

Business: The group's principal activity is the provision of commercial banking services to individual, business, governmental units and institutional customers. The commercial banking services include acceptance of demand, savings and time deposits, making commercial, real estate, agricultural and consumer loans. The group administers estates, personal trusts, custodial services, pension plans and provides farm management and investment advisory services. The group operates in the communities of Iowa city, coralville, hills and north liberty.

Primary SIC and add'l.: 6022 6712

CIK No: 0000732417

Subsidiaries: Hills Bank and Trust Company

Officers: Dwight O. Seegmiller/55/Dir., CEO, Pres./$368,369.00, James G. Pratt/Chief Accounting Officer, Sec., Treasurer/$276,037.00, Richard W. Oberman/72/Dir., VP

Directors: Dwight O. Seegmiller/55/Dir., CEO, Pres., Donald H. Gringer/Dir., Willis M. Bywater/69/Dir., Thomas J. Gill/61/Dir., Michael E. Hodge/54/Dir., Richard W. Oberman/72/Dir., VP, Sheldon E. Yoder/55/Dir., James A. Nowak/60/Dir., Theodore H. Pacha/59/Dir., Ann Marie Rhodes/54/Dir., Ronald E. Stutsman/68/Dir.

Owners: James A. Nowak/0.07%, Ronald E. Stutsman/1.10%, Theodore H. Pacha/0.21%, Willis M. Bywater/1.59%, Hills Bank and Trust/9.00%, Michael E. Hodge/0.16%, James G. Pratt/1.56%, Ann Marie Rhodes/0.02%, Insiders/9.03%, Thomas J. Gill/0.18%, Donald H. Gringer/0.13%, Sheldon E. Yoder, Richard W. Oberman/1.05%, Michael S. Donovan/0.04%, Dwight O. Seegmiller/2.73%

Financial Data: **Fiscal Year End:**12/31 **Latest Annual Data:** 12/31/2006

Year	Sales	Net Income
2006	$102,229,000	$15,559,000
2005	$87,445,000	$15,202,000
2004	$77,866,000	$14,195,000

Curr. Assets:	$40,800,000	**Curr. Liab.:**	$1,169,972,000		
Plant, Equip.:	$22,061,000	**Total Liab.:**	$1,432,594,000	**Indic. Yr. Divd.:**	NA
Total Assets:	$1,551,233,000	**Net Worth:**	$118,639,000	**Debt/ Equity:**	NA

Hilltop Community Bancorp Inc NJ

385 Springfield Ave., Summit, NJ, 07901; ***PH:*** 1-908-522-0090; ***http://*** www.hilltopcommunitybank.com; ***Email:*** comments@hilltopcommunitybank.com

General - Incorporation		**Stock**- Price on:12/24/2007	$9
Employees	NA	Stock Exchange	OTC
Auditor	NA	Ticker Symbol	HTBC
Stk Agt	Registrar & Transfer Co	Outstanding Shares	1,890,000
Counsel	NA	E.P.S	NA
DUNS No.	NA	Shareholders	NA

Business: The groups principal activity is to provide banking services. The services of the group include consumer services, business services and online banking services. The group operates from the United States.

Primary SIC and add'l.: 6712

CIK No:

Officers: Mortimer J. O'Shea/Dir., CEO, Pres.

Directors: Mortimer J. O'Shea/Dir., CEO, Pres., Richard D. Wellbrock/Chmn., Donald W. Barney/Dir., Chandler F. Coddington/Dir., Daniel D. Cronheim/Dir., Peter J. Daley/Dir., Gregory O. Drummond/Dir., Terence Golden/Dir., Nancy J. King/Dir., Kenneth J. Mathews/Dir., Judith T. Page/Dir., Robert F. Tokash/Dir., Thomas D. Ucko/Dir.

Hilltop Holdings Inc

Formerly: Affordable Residential Communities Inc

E Belleview Ave., Ste. 200, Englewood, CO, 80111; ***PH:*** 1-303-291-0222; ***http://*** www.aboutarc.com

General - Incorporation	MD	**Stock**- Price on:12/24/2007	$12.04
Employees	901	Stock Exchange	NYSE
Auditor	PricewaterhouseCoopers LLP	Ticker Symbol	ARC
Stk Agt	American Stock Transfer & Trust Co.	Outstanding Shares	56,400,000
Counsel	NA	E.P.S	NA
DUNS No.	NA	Shareholders	NA

Business: The groups principle activities include acquiring, renovating, repositioning and operting manufactured home communities. In January 31, 2007, the group acquired NLASCO, Inc. The group operates from the United States.

Primary SIC and add'l.: 1522

CIK No: 0001265131

Subsidiaries: Affordable III, L.L.C., Affordable Residential Communities Inc., Affordable Residential Communities LP, American Summit Insurance Company, ARC AF Utilities LLC, ARC Arlington Lakeside LP, ARC Autumn Woods LLC, ARC BHA Utilities LLC, ARC BHC Utilities LLC, ARC Birchwood LLC, ARC Brookside Village LP, ARC Capital Trust I, ARC Cedar Knoll LLC, ARC Cedar Terrace LLC, ARC Communities 10 LLC 71 Subsidiaries included in the Index

Officers: Larry D. Willard/Dir., CEO, Pres., James F. Kimsey/Dir., COO, Pres., Scott L. Gesell/49/Exec. VP, General Counsel, Corp. Sec., Lawrence E. Kreider/60/Exec. VP, CFO, CIO

Directors: Larry D. Willard/Dir., CEO, Pres., Gerald J. Ford/Chmn., Charles R. Cummings/Dir., Markham J. Green/Dir., James R. Staff/Dir., James F. Kimsey/Dir., COO, Pres., Rhodes Bobbitt/Dir., Joris W. Brinkerhoff/Dir., Carl B. Webb/Dir., Clifton C. Robinson/70/Dir.

Owners: Charles R. Cummings, Clifton C. Robinson/2.10%, Carl B. Webb, Markham J. Green, Insiders/19.30%, Scott L. Gesell, James F. Kimsey, Gerald J. Ford/16.00%, Rhodes R. Bobbitt, Lawrence E. Kreider, Morgan Stanley/7.00%, James R. Staff, Joris W. Brinkerhoff, Larry D. Willard, Farallon Funds/9.60% *(16 Owners included in Index)*

Financial Data: Fiscal Year End:12/31 **Latest Annual Data:** 12/31/2006

Year	Sales	Net Income
2006	$244,111,000	-$17,418,000
2005	$254,513,000	-$184,473,000
2004	$222,657,000	-$85,693,000

Curr. Assets:	$70,620,000	**Curr. Liab.:**	$30,849,000		
Plant, Equip.:	$1,405,890,000	**Total Liab.:**	$1,095,323,000	**Indic. Yr. Divd.:**	NA
Total Assets:	$1,542,701,000	**Net Worth:**	$419,236,000	**Debt/ Equity:**	2.0513

Himax Technologies Inc

10F No. 605, Chungshan Rd., Tainan County, Hsinhua, 712; **PH:** 886-65050880; **Fax:** 886-65106620; *http://* www.himax.com.tw

General - Incorporation	Cayman Islands	**Stock** - Price on:12/24/2007	$5.75
Employees	NA	Stock Exchange	NDQ
Auditor	NA	Ticker Symbol	HIMX
Stk Agt	RBC Dexia Corp Srvcs Hong Kong Ltd	Outstanding Shares	195,760,000
Counsel	NA	E.P.S	$0.49
DUNS No.	NA	Shareholders	NA

Business: The groups principal activities include designing, developing and marketing flat panel displays product. The products of the group include display drivers. The group operates from China, Yokohama, Japan and Anyangsi Kyungkido and South Korea.

Primary SIC and add'l.: 3674

CIK No: 0001342338

Subsidiaries: Amazion Electronics, Inc., Himax Display, Inc., Himax Technologies Co., Ltd., Himax Technologies Inc., Himax Technologies Anyang Limited, Himax Technologies Limited, JC Investment Co., Ltd.

Officers: Jordan Wu/46/Dir., CEO, Pres., Chih Chung Tsai/51/CTO, Max Chan/40/CFO, Baker Bai/49/VP - Engineering Center, John Chou/48/QRA Center VP, Jackson Ko/Investor Relations Officer, Jessie Wang/Investor Relations Officer, Norman Hung/50/VP - Sales, Marketing

Directors: Jordan Wu/46/Dir., CEO, Pres., Biing-Seng Wu/49/Chmn., Jung-Chun Lin/58/Dir., Chun-Yen Chang/69/Dir., Yuan-Chuan Horng/55/Dir.

Owners: Baker Bai/1.15%, CMO/12.56%, Jordan Wu/5.52%, Norman Hung, Yuan-Chuan Horng, Max Chan, Chih-Chung Tsai/1.48%, John Chou, Insiders/24.82%, Biing-Seng Wu/15.98%, Chun-Yen Chang

Financial Data: Fiscal Year End:12/31 **Latest Annual Data:** 12/31/2006

Year	Sales	Net Income
2006	$744,518,000	$75,190,000
2005	$540,204,000	$61,558,000
2004	$300,273,000	$36,000,000

Curr. Assets:	$466,715,000	**Curr. Liab.:**	$153,279,000	**P/E Ratio:**	46.72
Plant, Equip.:	$38,895,000	**Total Liab.:**	$154,867,000	**Indic. Yr. Divd.:**	$0.200
Total Assets:	$518,794,000	**Net Worth:**	$363,927,000	**Debt/ Equity:**	NA

Hines Horticulture Inc

12621 Jeffrey Rd., Irvine, CA, 92620; **PH:** 1-949-559-4444; **Fax:** 1-949-786-0968; *http://* www.HinesHorticulture.com

General - Incorporation	DE	**Stock** - Price on:12/24/2007	$0.86
Employees	2,940	Stock Exchange	OTC
Auditor	KPMG LLP	Ticker Symbol	HORT
Stk Agt	American Stock Transfer & Trust Co.	Outstanding Shares	22,070,000
Counsel	Kirkland & Ellis LLP	E.P.S	-$1
DUNS No.	95-995-4397	Shareholders	NA

Business: The group's principal activity is to produce and distribute horticultural products. The group operates through nursery and color divisions. The nursery division produces approximately 4,300 varieties of ornamental shrubs and color plants through its 13 nursery facilities located in Arizona, California, Florida, Georgia, New York, Oregon, Pennsylvania, South Carolina and Texas. These products are sold to more than 2,000 retail and commercial customers, representing more than 8,000 outlets throughout the United States and Canada.

Primary SIC and add'l.: 0181

CIK No: 0001003515

Subsidiaries: Enviro-Safe Laboratories, Inc., Hines Horticulture, Inc., Hines Nurseries, Inc., Hines SGUS, Inc.

Officers: James R. Tennant/Chmn., CEO, Pres., Claudia M. Pieropan/CFO, Treasurer, Sec., Jeffery A. Dunbar/Sr. VP - Operations, Jim O'Donnell/VP - National Sales

Directors: James R. Tennant/Chmn., CEO, Pres., Stanley R. Fallis/Dir., Paul R. Wood/Dir., Ray E. Mabus/Dir., Hugh E. Sawyer/Dir.

Owners: Stan R. Fallis, Ray E. Mabus, Jeffrey Dunbar, Abbott Capital 1330 Investors I, LP, Boston Partners Asset Management, L.L.C., Lincoln B. Moehle, Madison Dearborn Capital Partners, L.P., Claudia M. Pieropan, Thomas R. Reusch, California State Teachers Retirement System, Robert A. Ferguson, James R. Tennant, Insiders, James J. O'Donnell

Financial Data: Fiscal Year End:12/31 **Latest Annual Data:** 12/31/2006

Year	Sales	Net Income
2006	$232,570,000	-$46,472,000
2005	$327,913,000	-$2,558,000
2004	$335,168,000	$8,236,000

Curr. Assets:	$193,333,000	**Curr. Liab.:**	$124,074,000		
Plant, Equip.:	$85,470,000	**Total Liab.:**	$331,126,000	**Indic. Yr. Divd.:**	NA
Total Assets:	$340,368,000	**Net Worth:**	$9,242,000	**Debt/ Equity:**	3.2888

Hingham Institution for Savings

55 Main St., Hingham, MA, 02043; **PH:** 1-781-749-2200; **Fax:** 1-781-749-7835; *http://* www.hinghamsavings.com

General - Incorporation		**Stock** - Price on:12/24/2007	$31.18
Employees	NA	Stock Exchange	NDQ
Auditor	NA	Ticker Symbol	HIFS
Stk Agt	Mellon Investor Services LLC	Outstanding Shares	2,120,000
Counsel	NA	E.P.S	NA
DUNS No.	NA	Shareholders	NA

Business: The groups principal activity is to provide banking services. The products of the group include personal and commercial real estate loan, a non profit concern, or a child's savings account. The group operates from Hull, South Hingham, Cohasset, North Scituate, and South Weymouth. The assets of the group for the year 2006 were $691,652,000.

Primary SIC and add'l.: 6035

CIK No:

Officers: Robert H. Gaughen/CEO, Pres., Deborah J. Jackson/Sr. VP, Treasurer, William M. Donovan/VP - Administration, Peter R. Smollett/VP - Commercial Lending, Shawn T. Sullivan/VP - Commercial Lending, Michael J. Sinclair/VP - Retail Lending, Thomas I. Chew/VP - Branch Operations, Edward P. Zec/VP, William G. Bowers/VP - Commercial Lending, Teresa Tseng/Mgr. - Hingham, Holly Hendrix/Mgr. - South Hingham, Virginia Walsh/Mgr. - Hull, Joanne Reynolds/Mgr. - Cohasset, Marjorie Young/Mgr. - North Scituate, Margaret Santacroce/Mgr. - South Weymouth *(16 Officers included in Index)*

Hirsch International Corp

50 Engineers Rd., Hauppauge, NY, 11788; **PH:** 1-631-436-7100; **Fax:** 1-631-436-7054; *http://* www.tajima-hirsch.com

General - Incorporation	DE	**Stock** - Price on:12/24/2007	$4.8199
Employees	99	Stock Exchange	NDQ
Auditor	BDO Seidman LLP	Ticker Symbol	HRSH
Stk Agt	American Stock Transfer & Trust Co.	Outstanding Shares	8,880,000
Counsel	Hale & Dorr LLP	E.P.S	$0.17
DUNS No.	07-853-5184	Shareholders	NA

Business: The group's principal activity is to provide electronic computer-controlled embroidery machinery and related value-added products and services. The group offers a complete line of technologically advanced single and multi-head embroidery machines, proprietary application software, a diverse line of embroidery parts, supplies, accessories and proprietary embroidery products. The group also provides a comprehensive service program and user training and support. During 2004, the group sold tajima usa inc. And discontinued hapl leasing subsidiary.

Primary SIC and add'l.: 3571 3552

CIK No: 0000915909

Subsidiaries: HAPL Leasing Co., Inc., Hirsch Business Concepts, LLC, Hometown Threads, LLC, Sedeco, Inc., SSE Acquisition Corp.

Officers: Paul Gallagher/CEO, Pres./$893,736.00, Beverly Eichel/CFO, Exec. VP/$469,771.00

Directors: Paul Gallagher/CEO, Pres.

Owners: Marvin Broitman, Beverly Eichel/4.20%, Paul Gallagher/12.10%, Insiders/100.00%, Insiders/26.80%, Paul Levine/11.40%, Henry Arnberg/10.10%, Henry Arnberg/100.00%, Mary Ann Domuracki, Christopher Davino

Financial Data: Fiscal Year End:01/28 **Latest Annual Data:** 12/31/2006

Year	Sales	Net Income
2006	$49,912,000	$1,332,000
2005	$43,641,000	-$1,772,000

Curr. Assets:	$26,331,000	**Curr. Liab.:**	$10,655,000	**P/E Ratio:**	21.91
Plant, Equip.:	$319,000	**Total Liab.:**	$10,775,000	**Indic. Yr. Divd.:**	NA
Total Assets:	$27,188,000	**Net Worth:**	$16,413,000	**Debt/ Equity:**	NA

Hitachi Ltd

50 Prospect Ave., Tarrytown, NY, 10591; **PH:** 1-914-332-5800; **Fax:** 1-914-332-5555; *http://* www.hitachi.com; **Email:** investor.info@hal.hitachi.com

General - Incorporation	Japan	**Stock** - Price on:12/24/2007	$74.06
Employees	384,444	Stock Exchange	NYSE
Auditor	Ernst & Young Shinnihon	Ticker Symbol	HIT
Stk Agt	The Industrial Bank Of Japan	Outstanding Shares	333,380,000
Counsel	NA	E.P.S	$0.88
DUNS No.	69-054-1503	Shareholders	NA

Business: The group's principal activity is to manufacture electronic and electrical equipment. The group's operations are divided into the following segments: information systems and electronics: manufacturing of computers, audio/visual equipment and development of software; electronic devices: manufacturing of semi-conductor equipment and test and measurement equipment: power and industrial systems: manufacturing of nuclear, thermal and hydroelectric power plants and control equipment; consumer products: manufacturing of air conditioners, household appliances and audio/visual products; materials: manufacturing of synthetic resin materials and products; services and others: general trading and financial services, transportation and property management.

Primary SIC and add'l.: 3629 4213 3571 3357 3639 3651 3829

CIK No: 0000047710

Subsidiaries: Automotive Systems, Babcock-Hitachi Kabushiki Kaisha, Chuo Shoji, Ltd., Densen Works, Hitachi Cable, Ltd., Fujitsu Hitachi Plasma Display Limited, Guangzhou Hitachi Elevator Co., Ltd., Head Office, Head Office, Hitachi Building Systems Co., Ltd., Head Office, Hitachi Software Engineering Co., Ltd., Hitachi (China), Ltd., Hitachi Air Conditioning Systems Co., Ltd., Hitachi America, Ltd., Hitachi Asia Ltd., Hitachi Automotive Products (USA), Inc., Hitachi Building Systems Co., Ltd. 73 Subsidiaries included in the Index

Officers: Etsuhiko Shoyama/Chmn., CEO, Masahiro Hayashi/Representative Exec. Officer, Exec. VP, Exec. Officer, Koichiro Nishikawa/Sr. VP, Exec. Officer, Junzo Kawakami/Representative Exec. Officer, Exec. VP, Exec. Officer, Masao Hisada/VP, Exec. Officer, Gaku Suzuki/VP, Exec. Officer, Kazuhiro Mori/Representative Exec. Officer, Exec. VP, Exec. Officer, Kazuo Furukawa/Dir., Representative Exec. Officer, Pres., Shozo Saito/Sr. VP, Exec. Officer, Mitsuo Yamaguchi/VP, Exec. Officer, Yasuhiko Honda/VP, Exec. Officer, Eiji Takeda/VP, Exec. Officer, Takao Koyama/VP, Exec. Officer, Kiyoshi Kozuka/VP, Exec. Officer, Kenji Ohno/VP, Exec. Officer *(31 Officers included in Index)*

Directors: Etsuhiko Shoyama/Chmn., CEO, Isao Uchigasaki/Dir., Tadamichi Sakiyama/Dir., Tohru Motobayashi/Dir., Toyoaki Nakamura/Dir., Representative Exec. Officer, Sr. VP, Exec. Officer, Yoshie Ota/Dir., Mitsuo Ohashi/Dir., Akihiko Nomiyama/Dir., Kenji Miyahara/Dir., Takeo Ueno/Dir., Michihiro Honda/Dir., Kazuo Furukawa/Dir., Representative Exec. Officer, Pres., Yoshiki Yagi/Dir.

Owners: The Master Trust Bank of Japan, Ltd./6.30%, State Street Bank and Trust Company/7.30%, NATS CUMCO/11.30%

Financial Data: *Fiscal Year End:*03/31 *Latest Annual Data:* 03/31/2007

Year	Sales	Net Income
2007	$87,107,176,000	-$278,792,000
2006	$80,450,809,000	$317,220,000
2005	$83,951,500,000	$478,913,000

Curr. Assets:	$46,190,148,000	**Curr. Liab.:**	$39,674,124,000		
Plant, Equip.:	$22,856,305,000	**Total Liab.:**	$69,712,427,000	**Indic. Yr. Divd.:**	$0.690
Total Assets:	$90,476,202,000	**Net Worth:**	$20,763,775,000	**Debt/ Equity:**	NA

Hittite Microwave Corp

20 Alpha Rd., Chelmsford, MA, 01824; *PH:* 1-978-250-3343; *Fax:* 1-978-250-3373; *http://* www.hittite.com; *Email:* ir@hittite.com

General		Stock	
Incorporation	DE	Price on:12/24/2007	NA
Employees	267	Stock Exchange	NDQ
Auditor	PricewaterhouseCoopers LLP	Ticker Symbol	HITT
Stk Agt	American Stock Transfer & Trust Co.	Outstanding Shares	NA
Counsel	NA	E.P.S.	NA
DUNS No.	NA	Shareholders	NA

Business: The groups principle activities include designing and developing circuits. The products of the group include amplifiers, attenuators, data converters, modulators, oscillators and power detectors. In August 2005, the group acquired Q-Dot, Inc. The group operates from Colorado Springs, Istanbul, Turkey, and Ottawa, Ontario, Canada, and has sales offices in China, Germany, Korea, Sweden and the United Kingdom. The group's quarterly revenue for September 2007 was 39.93 millions of USD.

Primary SIC and add'l.: 3674 3679 8711

CIK No: 0001130866

Subsidiaries: Hittite Microdalga Sanayi Ve Ticaret Ltd. Sirketi, Hittite Microwave Asia Co., Limited, Hittite Microwave Canada Inc., Hittite Microwave Co. Limited, Hittite Microwave Deutschland GmbH, Hittite Microwave Europe Limited, Hittite Microwave Nordic AB, Hittite Microwave Security Corporation

Officers: Stephen G. Daly/Chmn., CEO, Pres./$771,863.00, William W. Boecke/CFO, VP, Treasurer/$416,619.00, Michael J. Koechlin/Exec. VP - Engineering/$482,570.00, Norman G. Hildreth/VP - Sales, Marketing/$499,807.00, Brian Jablonski/VP - Operations/$304,660.00, Robert W. Sweet/Sec., Peter Denardo/Demer Investor Relations Officer - Counsel

Directors: Stephen G. Daly/Chmn., CEO, Pres., Yalcin Ayasli/Founder, Chmn. Emeritus, Bruce R. Evans/Dir., Rick D. Hess/Dir., Cosmo S. Trapani/Dir., Franklin Weigold/Dir.

Owners: Insiders/47.50%, Michael J. Koechlin, Franklin Weigold, William W. Boecke, Brian J. Jablonski, Ayasli Children LLC/14.40%, Rick D. Hess, Norman G. Hildreth, Stephen G. Daly, Cosmo S. Trapani, FMR Corp/10.90%, Bruce R. Evans

Financial Data: *Fiscal Year End:*12/31 *Latest Annual Data:* 12/31/2006

Year	Sales	Net Income
2006	$130,290,000	$42,690,000
2005	$80,677,000	$21,078,000
2004	$61,671,000	$13,414,000

Curr. Assets:	$140,827,000	**Curr. Liab.:**	$14,152,000		
Plant, Equip.:	$13,757,000	**Total Liab.:**	$15,328,000	**Indic. Yr. Divd.:**	NA
Total Assets:	$155,019,000	**Net Worth:**	$139,691,000	**Debt/ Equity:**	NA

HKN Inc

Formerly: Harken Energy Corp

580 Westlake Pk. Blvd. Ste. 600, Houston, TX, 77079; *PH:* 1-281-504-4000; *http://* www.harkenenergy.com

General		Stock	
Incorporation	DE	Price on:12/24/2007	NA
Employees	46	Stock Exchange	AMEX
Auditor	Hein & Assoc. LLP	Ticker Symbol	HEC
Stk Agt	American Stock Transfer & Trust Co.	Outstanding Shares	NA
Counsel	NA	E.P.S.	$0.32
DUNS No.	07-315-7521	Shareholders	NA

Business: The group's principal activities are to explore, develop and produce oil and gas both domestically and internationally through its various subsidiaries. Operations of the group are divided into two segments, north American operating segment and middle American operating segment. North American operating segment consists of exploration, development, production and acquisition efforts in the United States. Middle American operating segment currently consists of exploration, development, production and acquisition efforts in Colombia, Costa Rica, Peru and panama as well as potential future operations elsewhere in Central America and South America. The group also has oil and gas properties located in the western and panhandle regions of Texas.

Primary SIC and add'l.: 1382 1311

CIK No: 0000313478

Subsidiaries: GEMCBM Company (f/k/a Harken Gulf Exploration Company), Global Energy Development Ltd., Global Energy Development PLC (34% Owned), Global Energy Management Resources Inc., Gulf Energy Management Company, Harken de Colombia, Ltd., Harken de Panama Holdings Ltd., Harken de Panama Limited, Harken de Peru Holdings, Ltd., Harken del Peru Limitada, Harken Energy West Texas, Inc., Harken Exploration Company, Harken Operating Company, Inc., International Business Associates Holding Co., Ltd., International Business Associates, Ltd. 20 Subsidiaries included in the Index

Officers: Mikel D. Faulkner/Dir., CEO, Pres./$409,013.00, James W. Denny/59/CEO, Pres. - Gulf Energy Management Company/$352,893.00, Anna M. Williams/VP - Finance, CFO - Harken/$241,885.00, Elmer A. Johnston/VP, General Counsel, Sec. - Harken/$291,882.00, Kyle Willis/59/CFO, VP, Rodger L. Ehrlish/Treasurer

Directors: Mikel D. Faulkner/Dir., CEO, Pres., Alan G. Quasha/Chmn., H. A. Smith/Dir., Michael M. Ameen/Dir., William J. Petty/Dir.

Owners: William J. Petty, Mikel D. Faulkner, Lyford Investment Enterprises Ltd./29.71%, Michael M. Ameen, Insiders, The Tail Wind Fund Ltd./6.90%, James W. Denny, H. A. Smith, Rodger L. Ehrlish

Financial Data: *Fiscal Year End:*12/31 *Latest Annual Data:* 12/31/2006

Year	Sales	Net Income
2006	$28,967,000	-$855,000
2005	$40,134,000	$42,980,000
2004	$29,742,000	-$17,894,000

Curr. Assets:	$41,589,000	**Curr. Liab.:**	$12,627,000		
Plant, Equip.:	$51,503,000	**Total Liab.:**	$20,034,000	**Indic. Yr. Divd.:**	NA
Total Assets:	$125,149,000	**Net Worth:**	$105,115,000	**Debt/ Equity:**	0.0775

HLTH Corp

Formerly: Emdeon Corp

River Dr. Ctr. 2, 669 River Dr, Elmwood Park, NJ, 07407; *PH:* 1-201-703-3400; *http://* www.emdeon.com

General		Stock	
Incorporation	DE	Price on:12/24/2007	$14.06
Employees	2,260	Stock Exchange	NDQ
Auditor	Ernst & Young LLP	Ticker Symbol	HLTH
Stk Agt	American Stock Transfer & Trust Co.	Outstanding Shares	172,160,000
Counsel	NA	E.P.S.	$2.57
DUNS No.	93-371-2945	Shareholders	NA

Business: The group's principal activities are to provide a range of transaction and information services and technology solutions. It operates through four segments: the transaction services transmits electronic transactions between healthcare payers and physicians, pharmacies, dentists, hospitals and other healthcare providers. The physician services develops and markets information technology systems for healthcare providers, primarily under the medical manager network services brands. The portal services offers a variety of online resources and services for consumers and healthcare professionals. The plastic technologies develops, manufactures and distributes proprietary porous and solid plastic products used in healthcare, industrial and consumer applications. It sold the porex bio products, inc and porex medical products inc in 2003. It acquired the little blue book, advanced business fulfillment inc and medifax-edi inc. In 2003 and dakota imaging and vips in 2004.

Primary SIC and add'l.: 7374 6794 7375 3089 8099 7372

CIK No: 0001009575

Subsidiaries: 225 Summit Associates LLC, Adaptive Health Systems of Arizona, Inc., Advanced Business Fulfillment, LLC, BabyData.com, Inc., Benchmark Systems, Inc. of Louisiana, Boca Subsidiary Corp., CareInsite LLC, Claims Processing Service, Inc., CLD Corporation, Conceptis, Inc., Crescendo Medical Education LLC, Dakota Imaging, Inc., Dakota Imaging, S.A., Demand Management, Inc., Emdeon Corporation 86 Subsidiaries included in the Index

Officers: William G. Midgette/52/CEO - Porex Segment, Kevin M. Cameron/42/Dir., CEO/$6,843,998.00, Wayne T. Gattinella/56/CEO, Pres. - Webmd Segment/$2,585,752.00, Arthur Lehrer/58/CEO, Pres. - Vips Segment, Jennifer Newman/Contact - Media, Mark D. Funston/48/CFO, Exec. VP/$129,268.00, Risa Fisher/Contact - Investors, Charles A. Mele/52/Exec. VP, General Counsel, Sec./$2,442,339.00

Directors: Kevin M. Cameron/42/Dir., CEO, Martin J. Wygod/68/Chmn., Mark J. Adler/51/Dir., Paul A. Brooke/62/Dir., Neil F. Dimick/59/Dir., James V. Manning/61/Dir., Herman Sarkowsky/82/Dir., Joseph E. Smith/69/Dir.

Owners: Neil F. Dimick, FMR Corp./11.40%, Mark J. Adler, Paul A. Brooke, Wayne T. Gattinella, Kevin M. Cameron/1.50%, Insiders/10.40%, James V. Manning, Charles A. Mele/1.20%, Joseph E. Smith, Mark Funston, Martin J. Wygod/6.20%, CalPERS/PCG Corporate Partners LLC/5.90%, Herman Sarkowsky

Financial Data: *Fiscal Year End:*12/31 *Latest Annual Data:* 12/31/2006

Year	Sales	Net Income
2006	$1,098,608,000	$771,917,000
2005	$1,276,879,000	$72,974,000
2004	$1,160,351,000	$39,334,000

Curr. Assets:	$842,948,000	**Curr. Liab.:**	$204,609,000		
Plant, Equip.:	$72,040,000	**Total Liab.:**	$980,648,000	**Indic. Yr. Divd.:**	NA
Total Assets:	$1,451,943,000	**Net Worth:**	$372,527,000	**Debt/ Equity:**	1.4842

HMG/Courtland Properties Inc

1870 S Bayshore Dr., Coconut Grove, FL, 33133; *PH:* 1-305-854-6803

General		Stock	
Incorporation	DE	Price on:12/24/2007	$13
Employees	1	Stock Exchange	AMEX
Auditor	Berenfeld Spritzer Shechter & Sheer	Ticker Symbol	HMG
Stk Agt	NA	Outstanding Shares	1,020,000
Counsel	NA	E.P.S.	-$0.36
DUNS No.	NA	Shareholders	NA

Business: The groups principle activities include owning, developing and managing income-producing commercial properties. The group operates through three segments namely, real estate rentals, food and beverage sales, and other investments and related income. The group operates from the United States. The group's quarterly revenue for September 2007 was 2.55 millions of USD.

Primary SIC and add'l.: 6798

CIK No: 0000311817

Subsidiaries: 260 River Corp., Bayshore Landing, LLC, Bayshore Rawbar, LLC, Bayshore Restaurant, LLC, CII Spa, LLC, Courtland Bayshore Rawbar, LLC, Courtland Bayshore Restaurant LLC, Courtland Investments, Inc., Courtland Key West, Inc., Grove Isle Associates, Ltd., Grove Isle Club, Inc., Grove Isle Investments, Inc., Grove Isle Marina, Inc., Grove Isle Yacht Club Associates, Grove Spa, LLC 17 Subsidiaries included in the Index

Officers: Maurice Wiener/66/Chmn., CEO, Lawrence I. Rothstein/55/Dir., Pres., Treasurer, Sec., Carlos Camarotti/47/VP - Finance, Assist. Sec.

Directors: Maurice Wiener/66/Chmn., CEO, Lawrence I. Rothstein/55/Dir., Pres., Treasurer, Sec., Walter Arader/89/Dir., Harvey Comita/78/Dir., Clinton Stuntebeck/68/Dir.

Owners: Clinton Stuntebeck, Walter G. Arader, Maurice Wiener, Harvey Comita, Lawrence Rothstein, Insiders

Financial Data: *Fiscal Year End:*12/31 *Latest Annual Data:* 12/31/2006

Year	Sales	Net Income
2006	$11,341,000	-$661,000
2005	$9,581,000	-$403,000
2004	$5,472,000	$1,519,000

Curr. Assets:	$2,413,000	**Curr. Liab.:**	$1,749,000		
Plant, Equip.:	$16,213,000	**Total Liab.:**	$25,807,000	**Indic. Yr. Divd.:**	NA
Total Assets:	$42,730,000	**Net Worth:**	$16,923,000	**Debt/ Equity:**	1.2118

HMI Industries Inc

6000 Lombardo Ctr., Ste. 500, Seven Hills, OH, 44131; *PH:* 1-216-432-1990;
http:// www.filterqueen.com

General - Incorporation	DE	**Stock**- Price on:12/24/2007	NA
Employees	NA	Stock Exchange	NA
Auditor	PricewaterhouseCoopers LLP	Ticker Symbol	NA
Stk Agt	Mellon Investor Services LLC	Outstanding Shares	NA
Counsel	NA	E.P.S	NA
DUNS No.	NA	Shareholders	NA

Business: The group's principal activity is to manufacture and market filtration portable surface cleaners, central vacuum cleaning systems and portable room air cleaners. The high filtration portable surface cleaner and portable room air cleaner are sold under various brand names such as filter queen (R), princess (R), majestic (R), empress(R) and defender(R) (portable room air cleaner only). The central vacuum cleaning system is sold under the trade names vacu-queen(R) and majestic ii (r). The products are mainly sold in the United States, Canada, Europe and Asia.

Primary SIC and add'l.: 3635

CIK No: 0000046445

Subsidiaries: AdvantEdge Credit Management Services Inc., Health-Mor Acceptance Corporation, Health-Mor International Inc., HMI Acceptance Corporation, HMI Incorporated

HMN Financial Inc

1016 Civic Ctr. Dr. NW, Rochester, MN, 55901; *PH:* 1-507-535-1200; *Fax:* 1-507-535-1300;
http:// www.hmnf.com

General - Incorporation	DE	**Stock**- Price on:12/24/2007	$35.12
Employees	223	Stock Exchange	NDQ
Auditor	KPMG LLP	Ticker Symbol	HMNF
Stk Agt	Wells Fargo Shareowner Services	Outstanding Shares	4,310,000
Counsel	Faegre & Benson LLP	E.P.S	$2.83
DUNS No.	87-298-7409	Shareholders	NA

Business: The group's principal activities are accepting deposits from the general public and businesses and using such deposits to originate or purchase loans. The loan products of the group include one-to-four family residential, commercial real estate and multi-family mortgage loans, consumer loans, construction and commercial business loans. The group also invests in mortgage-backed and related securities, investment securities (consisting primarily of U.S. Government and government agency obligations) and other investments. The group serves the Minnesota counties of fillmore, freeborn, houston, mower, dodge, goodhue, wabasha, olmsted and winona and portions of steele through its main office and 9 branch offices. The group also serves the Iowa counties of marshall and tama through is branch offices located in marshalltown and toledo.

Primary SIC and add'l.: 6035 6712

CIK No: 0000921183

Subsidiaries: Home Federal Savings Bank, Osterud Insurance Agency, Inc., Security Finance Corporation

Officers: Cindy K. Hamlin/Sec.

Directors: Michael J. Fogarty/69/Dir., Malcolm W. McDonald/71/Dir., Allan R. Deboer/65/Dir.

Owners: Duane D. Benson, Susan K. Kolling/1.49%, Bradley C. Krehbiel, HMN Financial, Inc. Employee Stock Ownership Plan/18.93%, Malcolm W. McDonald, Michael J. Fogarty, Allan R. DeBoer, Dwain C. Jorgensen/1.42%, Karen L. Himle, Mahlon C. Schneider, Jeffrey L. Gendell/9.12%, Jon J. Eberle, Timothy R. Geisler, Dimensional FundAdvisors, Inc./6.92%, Michael McNeil/2.15% *(16 Owners included in Index)*

Financial Data: **Fiscal Year End:**12/31 **Latest Annual Data:** 12/31/2006

Year	Sales	Net Income
2006	$73,968,000	$8,428,000
2005	$66,839,000	$11,068,000
2004	$58,145,000	$9,290,000

Curr. Assets:	$48,837,000	**Curr. Liab.:**	$883,926,000	**P/E Ratio:**	16.49
Plant, Equip.:	$13,444,000	**Total Liab.:**	$884,647,000	**Indic. Yr. Divd.:**	$1.000
Total Assets:	$977,789,000	**Net Worth:**	$93,142,000	**Debt/ Equity:**	0.0130

HMS Holdings Corp

401 Pk. Ave. S, New York, NY, 10016; *PH:* 1-212-725-7965; *Fax:* 1-212-857-5973;
http:// www.hmsholdings.com; *Email:* ir@hmsy.com

General - Incorporation	NY	**Stock**- Price on:12/24/2007	$19.19
Employees	578	Stock Exchange	NDQ
Auditor	KPMG LLP	Ticker Symbol	HMSY
Stk Agt	Mellon Investor Services LLC	Outstanding Shares	23,570,000
Counsel	NA	E.P.S	$0.28
DUNS No.	NA	Shareholders	NA

Business: The group's principle activities are to provide revenue recovery, business process and business office outsourcing services to healthcare payors and providers. It the group helps its clients increase revenue, accelerate collections, and reduce operating and administrative costs. The group operates in two businesses through its wholly owned subsidiaries, health management systems, inc. And accordis inc. The group's clients consist of state health and human services agencies, county and municipal governments, public care hospitals and clinics, physician practices, nursing facilities, and emergency medical transport agencies. The group operates only in United States. The group's quarterly revenue for Sep'07 was 37.68 millions of USD.

Primary SIC and add'l.: 7375 8742

CIK No: 0001196501

Subsidiaries: Health Management Systems, Inc., HMS Business Services Inc., Reimbursement Services Group Inc.

Officers: Robert M. Holster/Chmn., CEO, Richard M. Lang/Chief Compliance Officer, William C. Lucia/COO, Pres., David Schmid/VP - Human Resources, Walter D. Hosp/CFO

Directors: Robert M. Holster/Chmn., CEO, William F. Miller/Dir., William W. Neal/Dir., Galen D. Powers/Dir., Richard H. Stowe/Dir., Ellen A. Rudnick/Dir., James T. Kelly/Dir., Michael A. Stocker/Dir., William S. Mosakowski/Dir.

Owners: Richard H. Stowe, AMVESCAP PLC/5.20%, William C. Lucia/1.80%, William W. Neal, Ellen A. Rudnick, William F. Miller/4.40%, Galen D. Powers, Insiders/21.20%, James T. Kelly/1.40%, Thomas G. Archbold, William S. Mosakowski/8.00%, Wells Fargo & Company/6.40%, FMR Corp./10.10%, Robert M. Holster/4.90%

Financial Data: **Fiscal Year End:**12/31 **Latest Annual Data:** 12/31/2006

Year	Sales	Net Income
2006	$87,940,000	$5,325,000
2005	$60,024,000	$8,027,000
2004	$85,193,000	$7,711,000

Curr. Assets:	$48,809,000	**Curr. Liab.:**	$23,545,000	**P/E Ratio:**	68.54
Plant, Equip.:	$9,924,000	**Total Liab.:**	$50,336,000	**Indic. Yr. Divd.:**	NA
Total Assets:	$157,243,000	**Net Worth:**	$106,907,000	**Debt/ Equity:**	0.1985

HNI Corp

408 E 2nd St., Muscatine, IA, 52761; *PH:* 1-563-272-7400; *Fax:* 1-563-272-7655;
http:// www.hnicorp.com

General - Incorporation	IA	**Stock**- Price on:12/24/2007	$41.54
Employees	13,400	Stock Exchange	NYSE
Auditor	PricewaterhouseCoopers LLP	Ticker Symbol	HNI
Stk Agt	Computershare Investor Services LLC	Outstanding Shares	47,930,000
Counsel	NA	E.P.S	$2.38
DUNS No.	00-526-9709	Shareholders	NA

Business: The groups principle activity is to provide office furniture and hearth products. The groups products include an array of gas, electric and wood burning fireplaces, inserts, stoves, facings and accessories. The group operates from United States.

Primary SIC and add'l.: 2521 3443 2542 2522 2541

CIK No: 0000048287

Subsidiaries: A&M Business Interior Services, LLC, Allsteel Inc., Business Environments LLC, Contract Resource Group LLC, Corporate Installations Minneapolis LLC, Emerald City Moving& Storage LLC, Fullmer Contract LLC, Hearth& Home Technologies Inc., HFM Partners, Hht LLC, HNI Asia LLC, HNI Asia Technology Services (Shenzhen) Limited, HNI International Inc., HNI Services LLC, HNI Technologies Inc. 32 Subsidiaries included in the Index

Officers: Stan A. Askren/Chmn., CEO, Pres./$2,354,759.00, Tamara S. Feldman/VP - Financial Reporting, Robert D. Hayes/VP - Business Analysis, General Auditor, Douglas L. Jones/CIO, VP, David C. Burdakin/Exec. VP, Brad D. Determan/Exec. VP - HNI Corporation, Jerald K. Dittmer/CFO, VP/$791,151.00, Jeffrey D. Lorenger/VP, General Counsel, Sec., Eric K. Jungbluth/Exec. VP - HON Company/$816,253.00, Marco V. Molinari/Pres. - HNI International Inc/$1,024,387.00, Gary L. Carlson/VP, Member - Community Relations, David W. Gardner/Pres. - Paoli, Thomas E. Hammer/VP - Continuous Improvement, Eugene Sung/Pres. - Allsteel Inc, Donald C. Wharton/Pres. - Gunlocke Company LLC *(20 Officers included in Index)*

Directors: Stan A. Askren/Chmn., CEO, Pres., Gary M. Christensen/Dir., Mary H. Bell/Dir., Abbie J. Smith/Dir., Miguel M. Calado/Dir., Cheryl A. Francis/Dir., John A. Halbrook/Dir., James R. Jenkins/Dir., Dennis J. Martin/Dir., Larry B. Porcellato/Dir., Joseph Scalzo/Dir., Brian E. Stern/Dir., Ronald V. Waters/Dir., Richard H. Stanley/Dir. Emeritus

Owners: Gary M. Christensen, Stan A. Askren, Brian E. Stern, David C. Burdakin, Jerald K. Dittmer, Richard H. Stanley, Terrence L. and Loretta B. Mealy/7.10%, Marco V. Molinari, Mary H. Bell, Ronald V. Waters, Dennis J. Martin, Cheryl A. Francis, Miguel M. Calado, Columbia Wanger Asset Management, L.P./6.30%, Joseph Scalzo *(22 Owners included in Index)*

Financial Data: **Fiscal Year End:**12/31 **Latest Annual Data:** 06/30/2007

Year	Sales	Net Income
2007	$618,160,000	$26,877,000
2006	$2,679,803,000	$123,375,000
2005	$2,450,572,000	$137,420,000

Curr. Assets:	$486,598,000	**Curr. Liab.:**	$358,174,000	**P/E Ratio:**	17.75
Plant, Equip.:	$294,660,000	**Total Liab.:**	$546,187,000	**Indic. Yr. Divd.:**	$0.780
Total Assets:	$1,140,271,000	**Net Worth:**	$593,944,000	**Debt/ Equity:**	0.5669

Hoku Scientific Inc

1075 Opakapaka St., Kapolei, HI, 96707; *PH:* 1-808-682-7800; *Fax:* 1-808-682-7807;
http:// www.hokuscientific.com

General - Incorporation	DE	**Stock**- Price on:12/24/2007	$6.95
Employees	NA	Stock Exchange	NDQ
Auditor	KPMG LLP	Ticker Symbol	HOKU
Stk Agt	Continental Stock Transfer & Trust Co	Outstanding Shares	16,500,000
Counsel	NA	E.P.S	NA
DUNS No.	NA	Shareholders	NA

Business: The groups principle activity is to provide clean energy technologies. The groups product is Hoku MEA. The groups operates through three segments namely Fuel Cells, Solar and Materials. Specific customers of the group include Sanyo Electric Co., Ltd. and Nissan Motor Co. Ltd. The group operates from the United States. The group's quarterly revenue for September 2007 was 0.24 millions of USD.

Primary SIC and add'l.: 3692 3674 3629

CIK No: 0001178336

Officers: Dustin M. Shindo/Chmn., CEO, Pres./$745,462.00, Karl M. Taft/CTO, Dir./$250,485.00, Darryl S. Nakamoto/CFO, Treasurer, Sec./$309,373.00, Scott B. Paul/VP - Business Development, General Counsel/$303,948.00, James E. McGrath/Technical Advisor

Directors: Dustin M. Shindo/Chmn., CEO, Pres., Karl M. Taft/CTO, Dir., Karl E. Stahlkopf/Dir., Kenton T. Eldridge/Dir., Dean K. Hirata/Dir.

Owners: Dean K. Hirata, Insiders/26.70%, Darryl S. Nakamoto, Karl E. Stahlkopf, Karl M. Taft/6.40%, Scott B. Paul, Dustin M. Shindo/18.10%, Kenton T. Eldridge

Curr. Assets:	$24,027,000	**Curr. Liab.:**	$3,131,000		
Plant, Equip.:	$5,795,000	**Total Liab.:**	$5,131,000	**Indic. Yr. Divd.:**	NA
Total Assets:	$30,625,000	**Net Worth:**	$25,494,000	**Debt/ Equity:**	NA

Hollis-Eden Pharmaceuticals Inc

4435 Egate Mall, Ste. 400, San Diego, CA, 92121; *PH:* 1-858-587-9333; *Fax:* 1-858-558-6470;
http:// www.holliseden.com; *Email:* Info@holliseden.com

General - Incorporation	DE	**Stock**- Price on:12/24/2007	$2.09
Employees	66	Stock Exchange	NDQ
Auditor	BDO Seidman LLP	Ticker Symbol	HEPH
Stk Agt	American Stock Transfer & Trust Co.	Outstanding Shares	28,950,000
Counsel	BDO Seidman LLP	E.P.S	-$0.91
DUNS No.	95-637-0282	Shareholders	NA

Business: The group's principle activity is to develop a series of proprietary immune regulating hormones (irhs) for the treatment of immune system and metabolic disorders. The purpose of irh therapy is to direct, through controlling gene expression, the production of key cytokines and enzymes that re-regulate immune and metabolic functions toward homeostasis, a profile that could be useful in a wide variety of diseases. The company has a number of investigational irhs under development, including neumune (he2100), which the company is co-developing with the U.S. Military for use in protecting the body's bone marrow from acute radiation injury and immunitin (he2000), which is infectious disease compound, is currently being studied in a number of infectious diseases. Additionally, the company is also developing irhs for protection from chemotherapy and other conditions of immune dysregulation. On 25-Feb-2004, the company acquired congressional pharmaceutical corporation. The group operates from United States.

Primary SIC and add'l.: 2834

CIK No: 0000899394

Officers: Richard B. Hollis/Founder, Chmn., CEO/$1,747,892.00, James M. Frincke/Chief Scientific Officer/$696,320.00, Dwight R. Stickney/VP - Medical Affairs, Robert L. Marsella/Sr. VP, Robert W. Weber/VP, Controller, Chief Accounting Officer, Christopher L. Reading/Exec. VP - Scientific Development/$468,745.00, Scott M. Freeman/Chief Medical Officer

Directors: Richard B. Hollis/Founder, Chmn., CEO, Jerome M. Hauer/55/Dir., Brendan R. McDonnell/44/Dir., Thomas C. Merigan/73/Dir., Marc R. Sarni/48/Dir., Salvatore J. Zizza/61/Dir.

Owners: Marc R. Sarni, Jerome M. Hauer, Christopher L. Reading, Gruber & McBaine Capital Management, L.L.C./6.30%, Daniel D. Burgess/1.40%, Insiders/19.30%, Thomas Charles Merigan/1.00%, James M. Frincke/2.10%, Eric J. Loumeau, Richard B. Hollis/12.10%, Salvatore J. Zizza, Brendan R. McDonnell

Financial Data: *Fiscal Year End:*12/31 *Latest Annual Data:* 12/31/2006

Year	Sales	Net Income
2006	$444,000	-$30,231,000
2005	$56,000	-$29,441,000
2004	$63,000	-$24,757,000

Curr. Assets:	$67,366,000	**Curr. Liab.:**	$6,734,000		
Plant, Equip.:	$1,051,000	**Total Liab.:**	$6,734,000	**Indic. Yr. Divd.:**	NA
Total Assets:	$68,512,000	**Net Worth:**	$61,778,000	**Debt/ Equity:**	NA

Holly Corp

100 Crescent Ct., Ste. 1600, Dallas, TX, 75201; *PH:* 1-214-871-3555; *Fax:* 1-214-871-3560; *http://* www.hollycorp.com; *Email:* investors@hollycorp.com

General - Incorporation	DE	**Stock**- Price on:12/24/2007	$75.62
Employees	859	Stock Exchange	NYSE
Auditor	Ernst & Young LLP	Ticker Symbol	HOC
Stk Agt	American Stock Transfer & Trust Co.	Outstanding Shares	55,050,000
Counsel	NA	E.P.S	$5.90
DUNS No.	00-896-5808	Shareholders	NA

Business: The group's principle activity is to provide petroleum refining and pipeline transportation services. The group's refined products include gasoline, diesel fuel and jet fuel. The group operates from United States.

Primary SIC and add'l.: 2911 5171 1311 4922

CIK No: 0000048039

Subsidiaries: Black Eagle, Inc., HEP Logistics Holdings, L.P., Holly Logistics Services, LLC, Holly Payroll Services, Inc., Holly Petroleum, Inc., Holly Pipeline, LLC, Holly Refining & Marketing Company, Holly Refining & Marketing Company Woods Cross, Holly Refining Communications, Inc., Holly Utah Holdings, Inc., Holly Western Asphalt Company, Lea Refining Company, Lorefco, Inc., Montana Refining Company, a Partnership (1), Montana Retail Corporation 27 Subsidiaries included in the Index

Officers: Matthew P. Clifton/Chmn., CEO/$6,133,120.00, James G. Townsend/VP - Special Projects, Stephen J. McDonnell/CFO, VP/$686,437.00, Mark A. Plake/VP, Controller, John W. Glancy/Sr. VP, General Counsel, Sec./$926,067.00, David L. Lamp/Exec. VP - Refining, Marketing/$1,251,507.00, Dean P. Ridenour/VP, Chief Accounting Officer/$657,837.00, Bruce R. Shaw/VP - Special Projects, David G. Blair/Sr. VP, Thomas G. Creery/VP - Crude Supply, Refinery Economics, Nancy F. Hartmann/VP - Human Resources, Neale M. Hickerson/VP - Investor Relations, Randall R. Howes/VP, Project Mgr., Lynn P. Keddington/VP - Woods Cross Refinery, Scott W. Louderback/VP - Merchant Crude Oil *(23 Officers included in Index)*

Directors: Matthew P. Clifton/Chmn., CEO, Paul T. Stoffel/Dir., Robert G. McKenzie/Dir., Jack P. Reid/Dir., Buford P. Berry/Dir., William J. Gray/Dir., Marcus R. Hickerson/Dir., Thomas K. Matthews/Dir.

Owners: Goldman Sachs Asset Management, L.P./12.70%, Dean P. Ridenour, Stephen J. McDonnell, John W. Glancy, Aronson& Johnson& Ortiz, LP/5.70%, Insiders/6.00%, Lamar Norsworthy/2.30%, Jack P. Reid/1.10%, David L. Lamp, Robert G. McKenzie, Paul T. Stoffel/1.10%, Thomas K. Matthews, Marcus R. Hickerson, Brown Brothers Harriman Trust Company of Texas/17.90%, Matthew P. Clifton *(17 Owners included in Index)*

Financial Data: *Fiscal Year End:*12/31 *Latest Annual Data:* 12/31/2006

Year	Sales	Net Income
2006	$4,023,217,000	$266,566,000
2005	$3,212,745,000	$167,658,000
2004	$2,246,373,000	$83,879,000

Curr. Assets:	$806,852,000	**Curr. Liab.:**	$559,393,000	**P/E Ratio:**	15.06
Plant, Equip.:	$405,470,000	**Total Liab.:**	$607,370,000	**Indic. Yr. Divd.:**	$0.480
Total Assets:	$1,237,869,000	**Net Worth:**	$466,094,000	**Debt/ Equity:**	NA

Holly Energy Partners LP

100 Crescent Ct., Ste. 1600, Dallas, TX, 75201; *PH:* 1-214-871-3555; *Fax:* 1-214-871-3560; *http://* www.hollyenergy.com; *Email:* investors@hollyenergy.com

General - Incorporation	DE	**Stock**- Price on:12/24/2007	$49.5
Employees	89	Stock Exchange	NYSE
Auditor	Ernst& Young LLP	Ticker Symbol	HEP
Stk Agt	NA	Outstanding Shares	16,110,000
Counsel	NA	E.P.S	$2.24
DUNS No.	NA	Shareholders	NA

Business: The groups principle activity is to operate a system of refined product pipelines and distribution terminals. In the year 2005, the group acquired Hollys Intermediate Pipelines. The group operates from the west Texas, New Mexico, Utah and Arizona. The groups quarterly revenue for September 2007 was 27.21 millions of USD.

Primary SIC and add'l.: 4613

CIK No: 0001283140

Subsidiaries: HEP Fin-Tex/Trust-River, L.P., HEP Logistics G.P., L.L.C, HEP Mountain Home, L.L.C., HEP Navajo Southern, L.P., HEP Pipeline Assets, L.P., HEP Pipeline G.P., L.L.C., HEP Pipeline, L.L.C., HEP Refining Assets, L.P., HEP Refining G.P., L.L.C., HEP Refining, L.L.C., HEP Woods Cross, L.L.C., Holly Energy Finance Corp., Holly Energy Partners Operating, L.P., Rio Grande Pipeline Company

Officers: Matthew P. Clifton/Chmn., CEO, David G. Blair/Sr. VP, Stephen J. McDonnell/CFO, VP, Dean P. Ridenour/Dir., VP, Chief Accounting Officer - Partnership, John W. Glancy/VP, General Counsel, James G. Townsend/53/VP - Pipeline Operations, Neale M. Hickerson/VP - Investor Relations, Nancy F. Hartmann/VP - Human Resources, Stephen D. Wise/Treasurer, Mark Cunningham/VP - Operations, Scott C. Surplus/VP - Risk Management

Directors: Matthew P. Clifton/Chmn., CEO, Dean P. Ridenour/Dir., VP, Chief Accounting Officer - Partnership, Bruce R. Shaw/Dir., Lamar Norsworthy/61/Dir., Charles M. Darling/Dir., Jerry W. Pinkerton/Dir., William P. Stengel/Dir.

Owners: Fiduciary Asset Management, LLC/11.60%, Jerry W. Pinkerton, Tortoise Capital Advisors LLC/7.00%, Holly Corporation, Stephen J. McDonnell, Dean P. Ridenour, Kayne Anderson Capital Advisors, L.P./9.60%, John W. Glancy, James G. Townsend, Charles M. Darling, Insiders/1.20%, HEP Logistics Holdings, L.P., Matthew P. Clifton, William P. Stengel, David G. Blair

Financial Data: *Fiscal Year End:*12/31 *Latest Annual Data:* 12/31/2006

Year	Sales	Net Income
2006	$89,194,000	$27,543,000
2005	$80,120,000	$26,816,000
2004	$67,766,000	$32,494,000

Curr. Assets:	$23,624,000	**Curr. Liab.:**	$14,174,000	**P/E Ratio:**	23.82
Plant, Equip.:	$160,484,000	**Total Liab.:**	$207,347,000	**Indic. Yr. Divd.:**	$2.860
Total Assets:	$243,573,000	**Net Worth:**	$36,226,000	**Debt/ Equity:**	5.7446

Hollywood Media Corp

2255 Glades Rd., Ste.219A, Boca Raton, FL, 33431; *PH:* 1-561-998-8000; *Fax:* 1-561-998-2974; *http://* www.hollywood.com; *Email:* ir@hollywood.com

General - Incorporation	FL	**Stock**- Price on:12/24/2007	$4.21
Employees	206	Stock Exchange	NDQ
Auditor	Kaufman, Rossin & Co. P.A	Ticker Symbol	HOLL
Stk Agt	American Stock Transfer & Trust Co.	Outstanding Shares	33,630,000
Counsel	NA	E.P.S	$0.06
DUNS No.	80-997-1377	Shareholders	NA

Business: The group's principle activities are to provide entertainment-related information, content and ticketing services. The operating segment of the group are broadway ticketing, data business, Internet ad sales and other and intellectual properties. Broadway ticketing, markets tickets to live theater events, online and offline, covering shows on broadway. Also markets tickets to the domestic and international travel professionals, travel agencies, operators and educational institutions. Data business, licenses entertainment content and data. Internet ad sales and other markets advertisements and provides show previews, showtimes, show synopses and box office results. Intellectual properties, owns or controls the exclusive rights to certain intellectual properties created by best-selling authors and media celebrities. The group's quarterly revenue for Spe'07 was 28.21 millions of USD.

Primary SIC and add'l.: 7313 5990 7819 7922

CIK No: 0000912544

Subsidiaries: Baseline Acquisitions Corp., Baseline, Inc., Big Online, Inc., Broadway.com, Inc., Cinemasonline Limited, Cinemasource UK Limited, Fedora, Inc., Hollywood Fan Sites, Inc., Hollywood Services, Inc., Hollywood Wrestling Venture LLC, Hollywood.com International, Inc., Hollywood.com, Inc., Hollywood.fr SARL, Independent Hollywood, Inc., NetCo Partners 25 Subsidiaries included in the Index

Officers: Mitchell Rubenstein/Chmn., CEO, Laurie S. Silvers/Pres., Scott Gomez/Chief Accounting Officer, Harry Hoffman/Cinematographer - Cinematography, Harry Wiland/Dir. - Production Credits, Producer, Joe Constantino/Cinematographer - Cinematography, Bob Fiori/Cinematographer - Cinematography, Gerald Cotts/Cinematographer - Cinematography

Directors: Mitchell Rubenstein/Chmn., CEO, David Hoffman/Dir., Harry Wiland/Dir. - Production Credits, Producer, Robert D. Epstein/64/Dir.

Owners: Gruber and McBaine Capital Management, LLC/9.57%, Deborah J. Simon, Harry T. Hoffman, Insiders/5.11%, 033 Asset Management, LLC/6.53%, CCM Master Qualified Fund, Ltd./9.65%, Scott Gomez, Robert E. McAllan, Mitchell Rubenstein and Laurie S. Silvers/4.05%, Ira A. Rosenberg, S.A.C. Capital Advisors, LLC/7.58%

Financial Data: *Fiscal Year End:*12/31 *Latest Annual Data:* 12/31/2006

Year	Sales	Net Income
2006	$115,895,000	$9,523,000
2005	$95,614,000	-$8,913,000
2004	$72,979,000	-$11,598,000

Curr. Assets:	$58,436,000	**Curr. Liab.:**	$42,055,000	**P/E Ratio:**	16.19
Plant, Equip.:	$2,053,000	**Total Liab.:**	$44,248,000	**Indic. Yr. Divd.:**	NA
Total Assets:	$100,010,000	**Net Worth:**	$55,699,000	**Debt/ Equity:**	0.0013

Holobeam Inc

540 Ravine Ct, Wyckoff, NJ, 07481; *PH:* 1-201-445-2420

General - Incorporation	DE	**Stock**- Price on:12/24/2007	NA
Employees	3	Stock Exchange	OTC
Auditor	R.A. Fredericks & Co. LLP	Ticker Symbol	HOOB
Stk Agt	Continental Stock Transfer & Trust Co	Outstanding Shares	NA
Counsel	NA	E.P.S	$1.39
DUNS No.	03-237-9109	Shareholders	NA

Business: The group's principal activities are rental and development of real estate and surgical staples and the technology used to apply the staples. The group has rented the two buildings it owns, both located at a&s drive, paramus, New Jersey. One building is rented to the sports authority, inc and the other to comp usa, both for retail purposes. The group is also involved in research and development of surgical staples. The group discontinued its efforts in engineering and development of electro-optical equipment. The group has several patents issued in connection with medical staples for use in internal surgery.

Primary SIC and add'l.: 6519 8731 3559

CIK No: 0000048105

Subsidiaries: Grupo Sanborns, S.A. de C.V., TPC Acquisition Corp.

Officers: Melvin S. Cook/76/Chmn., Pres., Ralph A. Fredericks/59/Dir., Treasurer, Beverly Cook/71/Sec.

Directors: Melvin S. Cook/76/Chmn., Pres., Ralph A. Fredericks/59/Dir., Treasurer, Cynthia R. Cook/42/Dir.

Owners: Melvin S. Cook/35.40%, Beverly Cook/24.00%, Insiders/81.70%, The Cook 2003 Insurance Trust/22.30%

Financial Data: *Fiscal Year End:*09/30   *Latest Annual Data:* 9/30/2006

Year	Sales	Net Income
2006	$2,145,000	$368,000
2005	$2,079,000	$481,000
2004	$2,058,000	$185,000

Curr. Assets:	$1,079,000	*Curr. Liab.:*	$793,000			
Plant, Equip.:	$4,322,000	*Total Liab.:*	$3,519,000	*Indic. Yr. Divd.:*	NA	
Total Assets:	$6,295,000	*Net Worth:*	$2,776,000	*Debt/ Equity:*	NA	

Hologic Inc

35 Crosby Dr., Bedford, MA, 01730; *PH:* 1-781-999-7300; *http://* www.hologic.com

General - Incorporation	DE	**Stock** - Price on:12/24/2007	$56.37
Employees	1,617	Stock Exchange	NDQ
Auditor	Ernst & Young LLP	Ticker Symbol	HOLX
Stk Agt	American Stock Transfer & Trust Co.	Outstanding Shares	53,890,000
Counsel	Brown Rudnick Berlack Israels LLP	E.P.S.	$1.73
DUNS No.	15-362-3137	Shareholders	NA

Business: The group's principal activities are to develop, manufacture and market diagnostic and medical imaging systems primarily serving the healthcare needs of women. The core women's healthcare business units are focused on bone densitometry, mammography, breast biopsy and on developing a direct-to-digital X-ray mammography system. In addition, the group develops, manufactures and supplies other X-ray based imaging systems, such as general-purpose direct-to-digital X-ray equipment and mini c-arm imaging products. The group has its operations in Netherlands, Belgium and France. The customers of the group include hospitals, imaging clinics, private practitioners, healthcare organizations and pharmaceutical companies.

Primary SIC and add'l.: 3844

CIK No: 0000859737

Subsidiaries: Direct Radiography Corp.

Officers: John W. Cumming/Dir., CEO, Robert Cascella/COO, Pres., Jay A. Stein/CTO, Glenn P. Muir/Dir., Exec. VP, CFO, John Pekarsky/Sr. VP - Sales, Strategic Accounting, Robert H. Lavallee/Sr. VP, Chief Accounting Officer, Principal Accounting Officer

Directors: John W. Cumming/Dir., CEO, Patrick J. Sullivan/Chmn., Sally W. Crawford/Dir., Daniel J. Levangie/Dir., William McDaniel/Dir., Elaine S. Ullian/Dir., Wayne Wilson/Dir., Glenn P. Muir/Dir., Exec. VP, CFO, Arthur G. Lerner/67/Dir., Irwin Jacobs/Dir., David R. Lavance/Dir., Nancy Leaming/Dir., Laurie L. Fajardo/Dir., Lawrence Levy/69/Dir.

Owners: Lawrence M. Levy, David R. LaVance, Arthur G. Lerner, Nancy L. Leaming, Laurie Fajardo, Glenn P. Muir/1.30%, John Pekarsky, Irwin Jacobs, John W. Cumming/1.50%, Jay A. Stein, Robert A. Cascella, Insiders/4.10%

Financial Data: *Fiscal Year End:*09/24   *Latest Annual Data:* 9/30/2006

Year	Sales	Net Income
2006	$462,680,000	$27,423,000
2005	$287,684,000	$28,256,000
2004	$228,705,000	$12,164,000

Curr. Assets:	$290,022,000	*Curr. Liab.:*	$174,279,000	*P/E Ratio:*	50.33
Plant, Equip.:	$61,723,000	*Total Liab.:*	$250,455,000	*Indic. Yr. Divd.:*	NA
Total Assets:	$856,205,000	*Net Worth:*	$605,750,000	*Debt/ Equity:*	0.0106

Home BancShares Inc

PO Box 966, Conway, AR, 72032; *PH:* 1-501-328-4715; *Fax:* 1-501-328-4679; *http://* www.homebancshares.com

General - Incorporation		**Stock** - Price on:12/24/2007	$22
Employees	562	Stock Exchange	NDQ
Auditor	BKD, LLP	Ticker Symbol	HOMB
Stk Agt	Computershare Investor Services LLC	Outstanding Shares	17,240,000
Counsel	NA	E.P.S.	NA
DUNS No.	NA	Shareholders	NA

Business: The group operates through its subsidiaries whose principle activity is to provide commercial and retail banking and financial services. The groups services include cash management, overdraft protection, direct deposit, travelers checks, safe deposit boxes, United States savings bonds and automatic account transfers. The products of the group include Insurance, single and multi-family real estate, Consumer, residential construction and commercial buildings loan. In the year 2005, the group acquired Marine Bancorp, Inc, Mountain View Bancshares, Inc. and White River Bancshares, Inc. The group operates from the United States. The assets of the group for the year 2006 were $2,190,648 (thousands).

Primary SIC and add'l.: 6022 6022 6712 6712

CIK No: 0001331520

Subsidiaries: CB Bancorp

Officers: John W. Allison/Chmn., CEO/$143,851.00, Robert Hunter Padgett/49/CEO, Pres., Dir. - Marine Bank, Robert F. Birch/58/CEO, Pres., Dir. - Twin City Bank, Tracy M. French/46/CEO, Pres., Dir. - Community Bank/$355,634.00, Michael L. Waddington/64/Dir., CEO - Bank, Mountain View, Ron W. Strother/Dir., COO, Pres./$378,456.00, Randy E. Mayor/CFO, Treasurer/$308,756.00, Brian S. Davis/Dir. - Financial Reporting, Investor Relations Officer, Randall C. Sims/Dir., Sec.

Directors: John W. Allison/Chmn., CEO, Michael L. Waddington/64/Dir., CEO - Bank, Mountain View, Robert H. Adcock/Vice Chmn., Richard H. Ashley/Vice Chmn., Dale A. Bruns/Dir., Ron W. Strother/Dir., COO, Pres., Richard A. Buckheim/Dir., Jack E. Engelkes/Dir., Frank D. Hickingbotham/71/Dir., Herren C. Hickingbotham/49/Dir., Randall C. Sims/Dir., Sec., William G. Thompson/Dir., James G. Hinkle/Dir., Alex R. Lieblong/Dir.

Owners: Insiders/35.30%, Frank D. Hickingbotham/3.60%, Dale A. Bruns, Randall C. Sims, Richard A. Buckheim, Randy E. Mayor, Alex R. Lieblong/3.20%, Herren C. Hickingbotham/1.30%, John W. Allison/15.20%, Tracy M. French, James G. Hinkle/1.00%, Ron W. Strother, Richard H. Ashley/6.20%, Robert H. Adcock/5.00%, Jack E. Engelkes *(16 Owners included in Index)*

Financial Data: *Fiscal Year End:*NA   *Latest Annual Data:* 12/31/2006

Year	Sales	Net Income
2006	$143,269,000	$15,918,000
2005	$102,276,000	$11,446,000
2004	$55,021,000	$9,159,000

Curr. Assets:	$82,439,000	*Curr. Liab.:*	$1,914,566,000	*P/E Ratio:*	21.36
Plant, Equip.:	$57,774,000	*Total Liab.:*	$1,959,229,000	*Indic. Yr. Divd.:*	NA
Total Assets:	$2,190,648,000	*Net Worth:*	$231,419,000	*Debt/ Equity:*	0.1884

Home City Financial Corp

2454 N Limestone St., Springfield, OH, 45503; *PH:* 1-937-390-0470; *Fax:* 1-937-390-0876; *http://* www.homecityfederal.com

General - Incorporation	OH	**Stock** - Price on:12/24/2007	$16
Employees	31	Stock Exchange	OTC
Auditor	BKD LLP	Ticker Symbol	HCFL
Stk Agt	Illinois Stock Transfer Co	Outstanding Shares	NA
Counsel	Gorman, Veskauf, Henson & Wineberg	E.P.S.	$0.94
DUNS No.	05-285-9980	Shareholders	NA

Business: The group's principal activities are to provide a variety of financial services to individuals and corporate customers through its offices located in springfield, Ohio. It operates through the wholly owned subsidiary, home city federal savings bank of springfield. The group's deposit products are now accounts, money market accounts, statement savings accounts, passbook savings accounts and term certificate accounts. The lending products include first and second mortgage loans secured by one-to-four-family residential real estate and nonresidential real estate, loans for the construction of residential real estate, loans secured by multifamily real estate, commercial loans and consumer loans. The group invests in U.S. Government and federal agency obligations, interest-bearing deposits in other financial institutions, mortgage-backed securities and municipal securities. The group also provides a variety of insurance products to individuals and corporate customers.

Primary SIC and add'l.: 6712 6035

CIK No: 0001022103

Subsidiaries: Homciti Service Corp, Home City Federal Savings Bank of Springfield

Officers: William J. Stapleton/55/CEO, COO, Pres. - City Federal Savings Bank, Don E. Lynam/54/Exec. VP - City Federal Savings Bank, Tom Jordan/VP - Loan Administration, City Federal Savings Bank, Wendy Hoewischer/Branch Administrator - City Federal Savings Bank, Donna M. Williams/VP - Operations, Margaret A. Detty/VP - City Federal Savings Bank, Charles A. Mihal/69/Sec., Treasurer, Peter E. Duffey/Assist. VP - Mortgage Loan Consultant, Cindy J. Gorby/Security Officer, Mgr. - City Federal Savings Bank, Debbie S. Moore/Bank Secrecy Act Officer, Gary D. Smart/Information Technology Coordinator, City Federal Savings Bank, Patti S. Ark/Compliance Officer, Auditor - City Federal Savings Bank, Bill A. Atkinson/Facilities, Purchasing, City Federal Savings Bank

Financial Data: *Fiscal Year End:*12/31   *Latest Annual Data:* 12/31/2005

Year	Sales	Net Income
2005	$9,746,000	$837,000
2004	$9,011,000	$682,000
2003	$9,425,000	$649,000

Curr. Assets:	$7,405,000	*Curr. Liab.:*	$103,533,000	*P/E Ratio:*	17.02
Plant, Equip.:	$3,398,000	*Total Liab.:*	$136,147,000	*Indic. Yr. Divd.:*	$0.480
Total Assets:	$149,553,000	*Net Worth:*	$13,406,000	*Debt/ Equity:*	NA

Home Depot Inc

2455 Paces Ferry Rd. NW, Atlanta, GA, 30339; *PH:* 1-770-433-8211; *Fax:* 1-770-384-2356; *http://* www.homedepot.com; *Email:* customercare@homedepot.com

General - Incorporation	DE	**Stock** - Price on:12/24/2007	$37.84
Employees	247,520	Stock Exchange	NYSE
Auditor	KPMG LLP	Ticker Symbol	HD
Stk Agt	EquiServe Trust Co N.A	Outstanding Shares	1,970,000,000
Counsel	NA	E.P.S.	$2.40
DUNS No.	07-227-1711	Shareholders	NA

Business: The group's principle activity is to operate stores for home improvement. The group's products include building materials and lawn and garden products. The group's services include everyday, home, credit center, home improvement loans, delivery, tool and truck rental, kids workshop and designing services. During the fiscal year ended January 28, 2007, the group acquired The Home Way. The group operates from United States.

Primary SIC and add'l.: 5198 5251 5211 5074

CIK No: 0000354950

Subsidiaries: HD Development of Maryland, Inc, Home Depot U.S.A., Inc.

Officers: Francis S. Blake/Chmn., CEO/$6,336,612.00, Robert P. Derodes/CIO, Exec. VP/$5,179,182.00, Joseph J. Deangelo/46/COO, Exec. VP, Carol B. Tome/CFO, Exec. VP - Corporate Services/$4,809,671.00, Diane Dayhoff/Sr. VP - Investor Relations, Annette Verschuren/Pres. - Home Depot Canada, Asia, Roger W. Adams/51/Sr. VP, Chief Marketing Officer, James C. Snyder/44/VP, Sec., Acting General Counsel, Craig Menear/Exec. VP - Merchandising, Jack A. Vanwoerkom/Exec. VP, General Counsel, Corp. Sec., Paul Raines/Exec. VP - US Stores, Tim Crow/Exec. VP - Human Resources, Marvin Ellison/Pres. - Northern Division, Joe Izganics/Pres. - Southern Division, Ricardo Saldivar/Pres. - Mexico Division *(17 Officers included in Index)*

Directors: Francis S. Blake/Chmn., CEO, Bonnie G. Hill/Dir., Kenneth G. Langone/Dir., Gregory D. Brenneman/Dir., Claudio X. Gonzalez/Dir., Milledge A. Hart/Dir., Angelo R. Mozilo/Dir., David H. Batchelder/Dir., Armando Codina/Dir., Lawrence R. Johnston/Dir., Helen Johnson-Leipold/Dir., John L. Clendenin/Dir., Laban P. Jackson/Dir.

Owners: Kenneth G. Langone, Frank L. Fernandez, Milledge A. Hart, Angelo R. Mozilo, Robert L. Nardelli, Insiders/3.26%, Lawrence R. Johnston, Robert P. DeRodes, Carol B. Tome, Helen Johnson-Leipold, Laban P. Jackson, Francis S. Blake, Thomas J. Ridge, Claudio X. Gonzalez, Bonnie G. Hill *(19 Owners included in Index)*

Financial Data: *Fiscal Year End:*01/29   *Latest Annual Data:* 1/28/2007

Year	Sales	Net Income
2007	$90,837,000,000	$5,761,000,000
2006	$81,511,000,000	$5,838,000,000
2005	$73,094,000,000	$5,001,000,000

Curr. Assets:	$14,190,000,000	*Curr. Liab.:*	$10,529,000,000	*P/E Ratio:*	13.56
Plant, Equip.:	$22,726,000,000	*Total Liab.:*	$14,749,000,000	*Indic. Yr. Divd.:*	$0.900
Total Assets:	$38,907,000,000	*Net Worth:*	$24,158,000,000	*Debt/ Equity:*	0.4651

Home Diagnostics Inc

2400 NW 55th Ct., Fort Lauderdale, FL, 33309; *PH:* 1-954-677-9201; *Fax:* 1-954-739-8506; *http://* www.homediagnostics.com; *Email:* professionals@hdidiabetes.com

General - Incorporation	DE	*Stock* - Price on:12/24/2007	$11.56
Employees	500	Stock Exchange	NDQ
Auditor	Pricewaterhousecoopers LLP	Ticker Symbol	HDIX
Stk Agt	American Stock Transfer & Trust Co.	Outstanding Shares	17,970,000
Counsel	NA	E.P.S	$0.52
DUNS No.	NA	Shareholders	NA

Business: The groups principal activities include developing, manufacturing and marketing blood glucose monitoring systems. The products of the group include biosensor and photometric. The group products sold under the trade names Prestige IQ(R), Gentle Draw(R), TRUEread(TM), TRUEresult(TM) and TRUEelement(TM). In May 10, 2005, the group acquired Home Diagnostics Limited. Specific customers of the group include AmerisourceBergen, Cardinal Health, McKesson, Morris & Dickson Co., LLC and Kinray, Inc. The group operates from Florida and Taiwan in the United States. The net sale of the group for the year 2006 was $112,628 (thousands).

Primary SIC and add'l.: 3845

CIK No: 0000884909

Subsidiaries: Applied Sciences Corporation, Home Diagnostics (Australia) Pty Ltd, Home Diagnostics (UK)Limited

Officers: Richard J. Damron/Dir., CEO, Pres./$1,011,467.00, Nick Laudico/Investor Relations Contact, Ronald L. Rubin/CFO, Sec./$676,937.00, Christopher J. Avery/MD - Diagnosys Medical Limited, Gregg A. Johnson/VP - Consumer Healthcare/$286,026.00, Robert Tsao/MD - Applied Sciences Corporation/$298,472.00, Gary T. Neel/VP - Research, Development, Daniel S. Falter/VP - Marketing, George S. Godfrey/VP - Operations, Scott I. Verner/Sr. VP - Sales, Marketing

Directors: Richard J. Damron/Dir., CEO, Pres., George H. Holley/Chmn., Donald P. Parson/Vice Chmn., Douglas G. Lindgren/Dir., Richard A. Upton/Dir., Tom Watlington/Dir.

Owners: Douglas G. Lindgren, George H. Holley/16.87%, Waddell & Reed Investment Management Company/5.59%, Ronald L. Rubin, Judy Salem/14.40%, Richard J. Damron/2.82%, Gregg A. Johnson, Donald P. Parson/5.01%, Fidelity Management and Research/5.34%, Richard A. Upton, Insiders/27.05%, Robert Tsao, Jon M. Schneider/1.84%

Financial Data: Fiscal Year End: 12/31   *Latest Annual Data:* 12/31/2006

Year	Sales	Net Income
2006	$112,628,000	$10,309,000
2005	$100,165,000	$5,932,000
2004	$85,082,000	$1,966,000

Curr. Assets:	$62,964,000	*Curr. Liab.:*	$20,563,000	*P/E Ratio:*	18.65
Plant, Equip.:	$17,933,000	*Total Liab.:*	$20,563,000	*Indic. Yr. Divd.:*	NA
Total Assets:	$117,676,000	*Net Worth:*	$97,113,000	*Debt/ Equity:*	NA

Home Federal Bancorp

501 Washington St., Columbus, IN, 47201; *PH:* 1-812-522-1592; *Fax:* 1-812-522-1611; *http://* www.homf.com

General - Incorporation	IN	*Stock* - Price on:12/24/2007	$28.51
Employees	270	Stock Exchange	NDQ
Auditor	Deloitte & Touche LLP	Ticker Symbol	HOMF
Stk Agt	Registrar and Transfer CO.	Outstanding Shares	3,510,000
Counsel	NA	E.P.S	NA
DUNS No.	NA	Shareholders	NA

Business: The group operates through its subsidiaries whose principle activity is to provide banking and financial services. The groups services include online banking and telephone banking. The products of the group include mortgage, residential, commercial and consumer loan. The group operates from the United States.

Primary SIC and add'l.: 6022 6712

CIK No: 0000867493

Subsidiaries: Home Federal Savings Bank, HomeFed Financial

Officers: John K. Keach/55/Chmn., CEO, Pres., Melissa A. McGill/Sr. VP, Controller, Principal Accounting Officer, Sean P. Watt/Sr. VP - Retail Branch Administration, Home Federal Bank, Charles R. Farber/58/Exec. VP, Elaine S. Pollert/47/Exec. VP, Steven D. Emerson/Exec. VP - Commercial Division, Len E. Williams/Dir., Pres., Robert A. Schoelkoph/CFO, Sr. VP, Roger D. Eisenbarth/Sr. VP, Chief Lending Officer - Home Federal Bank, Lynn A. Sander/Exec. VP - Retail Division, Denis J. Trom/Sr. VP - Human Resources, Home Federal Bank, Mark T. Gorski/43/CFO, VP, Treasurer, Sec., Principal Financial Officer, Cindy L. Bateman/Sr. VP - Commercial Banking Team Lead, Home Federal Bank

Directors: John K. Keach/55/Chmn., CEO, Pres., Len E. Williams/Dir., Pres., Robert A. Tinstman/Dir. - Home Federal Bank, Richard J. Navarro/Dir. - Home Federal Bank, Fred H. Helpenstell/Dir. - Home Federal Bank, Thomas W. Malson/Dir. - Home Federal Bank, Charles N. Hedemark/Dir. - Home Federal Bank, James R. Stamey/Dir. - Home Federal Bank, Harvard W. Nolting/68/Dir., John T. Beatty/57/Dir., David W. Laitinen/55/Dir., Harold Force/56/Dir., John M. Miller/57/Dir., William J. Blaser/58/Dir.

Owners: David W. Laitinen/1.00%, Mark T. Gorski, Charles R. Farber/1.00%, Financial Edge Fund, L.P./6.50%, Insiders/11.90%, John M. Miller, John T. Beatty, Harvard W. Nolting/1.80%, Harold Force, Thomson Horstmann & Bryant, Inc./7.00%, John K. Keach/5.70%, William J. Blaser

Financial Data: Fiscal Year End: 12/31   *Latest Annual Data:* 12/31/2006

Year	Sales	Net Income
2006	$64,614,000	$6,441,000
2005	$55,272,000	$6,102,000
2004	$52,429,000	$5,163,000

Curr. Assets:	$110,742,000	*Curr. Liab.:*	$800,288,000		
Plant, Equip.:	$17,232,000	*Total Liab.:*	$833,186,000	*Indic. Yr. Divd.:*	NA
Total Assets:	$904,467,000	*Net Worth:*	$71,281,000	*Debt/ Equity:*	0.2261

Home Federal Bancorp Inc

500 12th Ave. S, Nampa, ID, 83651; *PH:* 1-208-468-5189; *Fax:* 1-208-468-5001; *http://* www.myhomefed.com

General - Incorporation	IN	*Stock* - Price on:12/24/2007	$16.27
Employees	227	Stock Exchange	NDQ
Auditor	Moss Adams LLP	Ticker Symbol	HOME
Stk Agt	Registrar & Transfer Co	Outstanding Shares	15,190,000
Counsel	NA	E.P.S	$0.39
DUNS No.	NA	Shareholders	NA

Business: The groups principal activity is to provide banking and financial services. The financial products of the group include mortgages, residential real estate, residential development and construction, and commercial real estate loan .The group operates from the United States. The assets of the group for the year 2006 were $61,292 (thousands).

Primary SIC and add'l.: 6712 6035 6712 6035

CIK No: 0001283858

Subsidiaries: Home Federal Bank, Idaho Home Service Corporation

Officers: Daniel L. Stevens/Chmn., CEO, Pres., Robert A. Schoelkoph/Sr. VP, CFO, Roger D. Eisenbarth/Chief Lending Officer, Sr. VP, Lynn A. Sander/Exec. VP - Retail Division, Denis J. Trom/Sr. VP - Human Resources, Steven D. Emerson/Exec. VP - Commercial Division, Cindy L. Bateman/Sr. VP - Commercial Banking Team Lead, Sean P. Watt/Sr. VP - Retail Branch Administration

Directors: Daniel L. Stevens/Chmn., CEO, Pres., Len E. Williams/Dir., Robert A. Tinstman/Dir., Richard J. Navarro/Dir., Fred H. Helpenstell/Dir., Thomas W. Malson/Dir., Charles N. Hedemark/Dir., James R. Stamey/Dir.

Owners: Robert A. Tinstman, John L. Keeley/5.48%, Robert A. Schoelkoph, Len E. Williams, Fred H. Helpenstell, Lynn A. Sander, James R. Stamey, Daniel L. Stevens/1.08%, Richard J. Navarro, Home Federal MHC/58.84%, Charles N. Hedemark, Thomas W. Malson, Insiders/4.29%

Financial Data: Fiscal Year End: 12/31   *Latest Annual Data:* 9/30/2006

Year	Sales	Net Income
2006	$51,264,000	$6,212,000
2005	$44,518,000	$5,283,000
2004	$37,213,000	$4,684,000

Curr. Assets:	$21,410,000	*Curr. Liab.:*	$642,011,000	*P/E Ratio:*	41.72
Plant, Equip.:	$12,849,000	*Total Liab.:*	$653,423,000	*Indic. Yr. Divd.:*	$0.220
Total Assets:	$761,292,000	*Net Worth:*	$107,869,000	*Debt/ Equity:*	NA

Home Federal Bancorp Inc of Louisiana

624 Market St., Shreveport, LA, 71101; *PH:* 1-318-222-1145; *http://* www.myhomefed.com

General - Incorporation		*Stock* - Price on:12/24/2007	$10.5
Employees	17	Stock Exchange	OTC
Auditor	Laporte Sehrt, Romig Hand	Ticker Symbol	HFBL
Stk Agt	Registrar & Transfer Co	Outstanding Shares	3,450,000
Counsel	NA	E.P.S	$0.18
DUNS No.	NA	Shareholders	NA

Business: The groups principle activity is to hold common stock of Home Federal Savings and Loan. The group operates from the United States.

Primary SIC and add'l.: 6035

CIK No: 0001302901

Officers: Daniel R. Herndon/Chmn., CEO, Pres., Sean P. Watt/Sr. VP - Retail Branch Administration, Len E. Williams/Dir., Pres., Roger D. Eisenbarth/Chief Lending Officer, Sr. VP, Lynn A. Sander/Exec. VP - Retail Division, Denis J. Trom/Sr. VP - Human Resources, Clyde D. Patterson/Dir., Exec. VP, Denell W. Mitchell/51/Corp. Sec., Steven D. Emerson/Exec. VP - Commercial Division, Cindy L. Bateman/Sr. VP - Commercial Banking Team Lead

Directors: Daniel R. Herndon/Chmn., CEO, Pres., Walter T. Colquitt/Dir., Sidney D. York/Dir., Amos L. Wedgeworth/Dir., Clyde D. Patterson/Dir., Exec. VP, Scott D. Lawrence/Dir., David A. Herndon/Dir., Woodus K. Humphrey/Dir., Fred H. Helpenstell/Dir., Thomas W. Malson/Dir., Charles N. Hedemark/Dir., James R. Stamey/Dir., Robert A. Tinstman/Dir., Richard J. Navarro/Dir., Len E. Williams/Dir., Pres. (16 Directors included in Index)

Owners: Daniel R. Herndon/1.70%, Henry M. Hearne, Clyde D. Patterson, Walter T. Colquitt, Insiders/5.10%, Sidney D. York, Home Federal Mutual Holding/63.10%, Amos L. Wedgeworth, David A. Herndon, Scott D. Lawrence, Woodus K. Humphrey

Financial Data: Fiscal Year End: 06/30   *Latest Annual Data:* 06/30/2007

Year	Sales	Net Income
2007	$6,830,000	$637,000
2006	$5,808,000	$634,000
2005	$5,451,000	$850,000

Curr. Assets:	$4,471,000	*Curr. Liab.:*	$90,777,000		
Plant, Equip.:	$923,000	*Total Liab.:*	$90,973,000	*Indic. Yr. Divd.:*	$0.240
Total Assets:	$118,785,000	*Net Worth:*	$27,812,000	*Debt/ Equity:*	NA

Home Financial Bancorp

279 E Morgan St., Spencer, IN, 47460; *PH:* 1-812-829-2095; *Fax:* 1-812-829-3069; *http://* www.hfbancorp.com; *Email:* owencom@owencom.com

General - Incorporation	IN	*Stock* - Price on:12/24/2007	$4.9
Employees	NA	Stock Exchange	OTC
Auditor	NA	Ticker Symbol	HWEN
Stk Agt	Registrar & Transfer Co	Outstanding Shares	1,350,000
Counsel	NA	E.P.S	$0.13
DUNS No.	NA	Shareholders	NA

Business: The groups principal activities include attracting deposits from consumers and businesses, and purchasing and developing tracts of real estate. The services of the group include originating consumer, residential, multi-family, commercial real estate loans, and non-residential loans. The total assets of the group in the year 2006, was $69.65 (million).

Primary SIC and add'l.: 6036 6712

CIK No: 0001009242

Financial Data: Fiscal Year End: 06/30   *Latest Annual Data:* 6/30/2004

Year	Sales	Net Income
2004	$4,873,000	$361,000
2003	$5,486,000	$345,000
2002	$5,999,000	$500,000

Curr. Assets:	$3,982,000	*Curr. Liab.:*	$38,896,000	*P/E Ratio:*	37.69
Plant, Equip.:	$2,559,000	*Total Liab.:*	$56,300,000	*Indic. Yr. Divd.:*	$0.120
Total Assets:	$63,426,000	*Net Worth:*	$7,126,000	*Debt/ Equity:*	NA

Home Inns & Hotels Management Inc

No. 400 Tian Yao Qiao Rd., Shanghai, 200030; ; http:// english.homeinns.com

General - Incorporation.		**Stock**- Price on:12/24/2007 ....$31.6
Employees.....................................6,291		Stock Exchange...NDQ
Auditor ....PricewaterhouseCoopers		Ticker Symbol..HMIN
Stk Agt.............................Bank of New York		Outstanding Shares 32,960,000
Counsel...NA		E.P.S..$0.25
DUNS No. ....NA		Shareholders..NA

Business: The groups principal activity is to provide home and hotels services. The groups service is providing hotel rooms. The group operates from the United States and China.

Primary SIC and add'l.: 7011

CIK No: 0001376972

Subsidiaries: Hemei Hotel Management Company, Home Inns Hotel Management Co., Ltd., Home Inns& Hotels Management Limited

Officers: David Sun/Dir., CEO, May Wu/CFO, Rixin Liang/COO, Angela Li/Mgr. - Investor Relations

Directors: David Sun/Dir., CEO, Yunxin Mei/Co - Chmn., Neil Shen/Co - Chmn., Min Bao/Dir., James Jianzhang Liang/Dir., Kenneth Gaw/Dir., Terry Hu/Dir.

Owners: IDG Technology Venture Investments, L.P./4.71%, Rixin Liang/1.14%, Chung Lau/5.81%, James Jianzhang Liang/5.84%, Insiders/16.52%, AsiaStar IT Fund L.P./8.72%, Qi Ji/6.36%, Neil Nanpeng Shen/7.83%, David Jian Sun/1.02%, May Wu, Poly Victory Investments Limited/19.26%, Min Bao, Yunxin Mei

Financial Data: Fiscal Year End:12/31 Latest Annual Data: 12/31/2006

Year		Sales		Net Income
2006		$71,055,000		$6,009,000
2005		$33,653,000		$2,618,000
Curr. Assets:	$101,925,000	**Curr. Liab.:**	$41,418,000	**P/E Ratio:** 166.32
Plant, Equip.:	$58,695,000	**Total Liab.:**	$55,135,000	**Indic. Yr. Divd.:** NA
Total Assets:	$169,144,000	**Net Worth:**	$114,009,000	**Debt/ Equity:** NA

Home Loan Financial Corp New

401 Main St. , Coshocton, OH, 43812; *PH:* 1-740-622-0444

General - Incorporation..........................OH		**Stock**- Price on:12/24/2007 ....$14.8
Employees...NA		Stock Exchange...OTC
Auditor ....NA		Ticker Symbol..HLFN
Stk Agt.............Registrar and Transfer Co. serves		Outstanding Shares ....NA
Counsel...NA		E.P.S...NA
DUNS No. ....NA		Shareholders...NA

Business: The groups principle activity is to provide commercial and financial banking services. The services of the group include providing mortgage loans, commercial loans, consumer credits, mortgage-backed securities and trust and investments. The group operates from Ohio in the United States.

Primary SIC and add'l.: 6036 6712

CIK No: 0001050894

Subsidiaries: Coshocton County Title Agency, LLC, Home Loan Financial Services, Inc., The Home Loan Savings Bank

Financial Data: Fiscal Year End:06/30 Latest Annual Data: 06/30/2004

Year		Sales		Net Income
2004		$10,521,000		$1,785,000
2003		$10,560,000		$1,874,000
2002		$9,929,000		$1,475,000
Curr. Assets:	$3,994,000	**Curr. Liab.:**	$97,323,000	
Plant, Equip.:	$1,381,000	**Total Liab.:**	$137,721,000	**Indic. Yr. Divd.:** NA
Total Assets:	$160,030,000	**Net Worth:**	$22,309,000	**Debt/ Equity:** NA

Home Properties Inc

850 Clinton Sq., Rochester, NY, 14604; *PH:* 1-585-546-4900; *Fax:* 1-585-546-5433; http:// www.homeproperties.com; *Email:* yvonnew@homeproperties.com

General - Incorporation..........................MD		**Stock**- Price on:12/24/2007 ....$53.27
Employees...1,200		Stock Exchange...NYSE
Auditor ....PricewaterhouseCoopers LLP		Ticker Symbol..HME
Stk Agt.................Mellon Investor Services LLC		Outstanding Shares 33,240,000
Counsel............................Nixon Peabody LLP		E.P.S..$3.59
DUNS No. ....NA		Shareholders...NA

Business: The groups principle activities include owning, operating, acquiring, developing and rehabilitation apartment communities. In the year 2006, the group acquired eight communities. The group operates from the United States.

Primary SIC and add'l.: 6798 6798

CIK No: 0000923118

Subsidiaries: Arsenal Street Fee Holding, LLC, Arsenal Street Leasehold Holding, LLC, Barrington Gardens, LLC, Carriage Hill Venture, L.L.C., Carriage Park Associates, L.L.C., Century Investors, LLC, Cherry Hill Club, LLC, Cherry Hill Village Venture, L.L.C., Curren Terrace, L.L.C., Deerfield Woods Home Properties LLC, Dunedin I, LLC, Dunedin II, LLC, Dunedin, LLC, Hackensack Gardens Apartments, LLC, Hampton Lakes Associates, LLC 197 Subsidiaries included in the Index

Officers: Edward J. Pettinella/Dir., CEO, Pres./$1,917,053.00, Leonard F. Helbig/Dir. - Integra Realty Advisors, David P. Gardner/CFO, Exec. VP/$866,046.00, Ann M. McCormick/Exec. VP, General Counsel, Sec./$753,311.00, Scott A. Doyle/Sr. VP - Property Management/$576,296.00, Jodi A. Falk/Sr. VP, Chief Administrative, Information Officer, Robert J. Luken/Sr. VP, Chief Accounting Officer, Treasurer, Janine M. Schue/Sr. VP - Human Resources, John E. Smith/Sr. VP, Chief Investment Officer/$525,104.00, Lisa M. Critchley/Sr. VP - Human Resources

Directors: Edward J. Pettinella/Dir., CEO, Pres., Nelson B. Leenhouts/Co - Chmn., Norman Leenhouts/Co - Chmn., Josh E. Fidler/Dir., Alan L. Gosule/Dir., Roger W. Kober/Dir., Clifford W. Smith/Dir., Paul L. Smith/Dir., Thomas S. Summer/Dir., Amy L. Tait/Dir.

Owners: Josh E. Fidler, Leonard F. Helbig, Ann M. McCormick, Edward J. Pettinella/1.39%, William Balderston, Amy L. Tait, Thomas S. Summer, Norman P. Leenhouts, Alan L. Gosule, Scott A. Doyle, David P. Gardner, John H. Smith, Roger W. Kober, Nelson B. Leenhouts, Paul L. Smith

(17 Owners included in Index)

Financial Data: *Fiscal Year End:*12/31   *Latest Annual Data:* 12/31/2006

Year		Sales		Net Income
2006		$453,992,000		$110,485,000
2005		$443,801,000		$81,512,000
2004		$458,330,000		$47,022,000
Curr. Assets:	$127,499,000	**Curr. Liab.:**	$77,946,000	**P/E Ratio:** 17.41
Plant, Equip.:	$3,001,633,000	**Total Liab.:**	$2,484,801,000	**Indic. Yr. Divd.:** $2.640
Total Assets:	$3,240,418,000	**Net Worth:**	$755,617,000	**Debt/ Equity:** 3.1386

Home Solutions of America Inc

1500 Dr.agon St., Ste. B, Dallas, TX, 75207; *PH:* 1-214-623-8446; *Fax:* 1-214-333-9435; http:// www.hsoacorp.com; *Email:* contact@homcorp.com

General - Incorporation .... DE		**Stock**- Price on:12/24/2007 ....$5.96
Employees...458		Stock Exchange...NDQ
Auditor ....KMJ Corbin & Company LLP		Ticker Symbol..HSOA
Stk Agt...NA		Outstanding Shares 47,330,000
Counsel...NA		E.P.S..$0.51
DUNS No. 80-885-8146		Shareholders...NA

Business: The group's principal activity is to provide abatement services of indoor air contaminate for residential and commercial properties to customers located throughout California. It also provides services such as cleaning and fabric protection that protects furniture, carpet and draperies from stains and daily wear and tear, fire and water damage restoration that provides highly trained technicians to respond to fire, water and weather-related emergencies. The group's corporate operations are based in houston and Texas. The group acquired central taxes residential services, fiber seal systems lp and southern exposure unlimited of Florida inc in 2003.

Primary SIC and add'l.: 7389 4953 3679

CIK No: 0000855424

Subsidiaries: Fiber Seal Systems, L.P., Home Solutions Restoration of Louisiana, Inc., PW Stephens, Inc.

Owners: Frank J. Fradella/4.06%, Insiders/16.69%, Jeffrey M. Mattich, Charles P. McCusker, Willard W. Kimbrell, Patrick A. McGeeney, Dale W. Mars/3.04%, Michael S. Chadwick, Brian Marshall/8.59%, Stephen Scott Sewell/1.00%

Financial Data: *Fiscal Year End:*12/31 *Latest Annual Data:* 12/31/2006

Year		Sales		Net Income
2006		$127,220,000		$17,898,000
2005		$68,135,000		$7,185,000
2004		$31,121,000		$2,563,000
Curr. Assets:	$83,805,000	**Curr. Liab.:**	$43,366,000	**P/E Ratio:** 11.69
Plant, Equip.:	$6,129,000	**Total Liab.:**	$78,599,000	**Indic. Yr. Divd.:** NA
Total Assets:	$222,725,000	**Net Worth:**	$143,889,000	**Debt/ Equity:** 0.1685

Home System Group

1330 Ave. of the Americas, 21st Fl., New York, NY, 10019; *PH:* 1-646-200-6304; *Fax:* 1-213-223-2276; http:// www.homesystemgroup.com; *Email:* info@homesystemgroup.com

General - Incorporation		**Stock**- Price on:12/24/2007 ....$4.75
Employees...NA		Stock Exchange...OTC
Auditor ....NA		Ticker Symbol..HSYT
Stk Agt...NA		Outstanding Shares ....NA
Counsel...NA		E.P.S...NA
DUNS No. ....NA		Shareholders...NA

Business: The groups principle activity is to distribute home appliances and environmental products. Products of the group include gas grills, family-use water pumps, fruit processors, and other electrical appliances. In June 2006 the group acquired Oceanic International Limited and in August 2006, the group merged with Supreme Realty Investments, Inc., Specific customers of the group include Nexgrill Industries, Inc., Whalen Storage, and BTB Products, Inc. The group operates from Europe, America, and Australia.

Primary SIC and add'l.: 3441

CIK No:

Subsidiaries: Oceanic International (HK) Limited, Oceanic Well Profit Inc

Officers: Weiqiu Li/47/Chmn., CEO, Kin Wai Cheung/47/Dir., CFO, Jing Liu/37/Sec., Li Min Hong/GM, Dai Chun Ping/35/Engineer - Research & Development, Chen Ding Sun/Sr. Engineer, Zhou Jin Tong/Engineer, Mgr., Michelle Zheng/Contact, Liu Dong Bing/Finance Mgr., Li Wei Ming/Analyst, Liao Shi Fu/GM, Engineer, Wen Jie Su/Sr. VP, Liu Jing/Sec.

Directors: Weiqiu Li/47/Chmn., CEO, Kin Wai Cheung/47/Dir., CFO

Owners: Wei Qiu Li/3.30%, Insiders/5.90%, Yu Kaming/68.20%, Kin Wai Cheung/2.60%

Financial Data: *Fiscal Year End:*NA *Latest Annual Data:* 12/31/2006

Year		Sales		Net Income
2006		$26,391,000		$1,354,000
2005		$1,000		-$400,000
2004		$63,000		-$202,000
Curr. Assets:	$7,208,000	**Curr. Liab.:**	$3,445,000	
Plant, Equip.:	$1,000	**Total Liab.:**	$3,445,000	**Indic. Yr. Divd.:** NA
Total Assets:	$7,209,000	**Net Worth:**	$3,764,000	**Debt/ Equity:** NA

Home Valley Bancorp Inc OR

Towne Ctr., 4th & G St.s, Grants Pass, OR, 97528; *PH:* 1-541-476-4663; http:// www.homevalleybankonline.com

General - Incorporation		**Stock**- Price on:12/24/2007 ....$12.1
Employees .... NA		Stock Exchange...OTC
Auditor .... NA		Ticker Symbol..HVYB
Stk Agt.. NA		Outstanding Shares 1,910,000
Counsel.. NA		E.P.S..$0.11
DUNS No. .... NA		Shareholders...NA

Business: The groups principal activity is to provide community-banking services. The services of the group include checking account, certificates of deposit, overdraft protection, automatic payments, consumer, auto and business loans, merchant services, ATM/VISA check card and telephone and online banking. The group operates from the United States.

Primary SIC and add'l.: 6022

CIK No: 0001179011

Financial Data: Fiscal Year End:NA **Latest Annual Data:** 12/31/2002

Year	Sales	Net Income
2002	$5,889,000	$679,000

Curr. Assets:	$18,932,000	**Curr. Liab.:**	$80,721,000	**P/E Ratio:**	14.94
Plant, Equip.:	$2,573,000	**Total Liab.:**	$80,844,000	**Indic. Yr. Divd.:**	NA
Total Assets:	$86,338,000	**Net Worth:**	$5,494,000	**Debt/ Equity:**	NA

Homebanc Corp

2002 Summit Blvd., Ste. 100, Atlanta, GA, 30319; *PH:* 1-404-459-7400; *Fax:* 1-404-303-4069; *http://* www.homebanc.com

General - Incorporation	GA	**Stock**- Price on:12/24/2007	$1.49
Employees	1,199	Stock Exchange	OTC
Auditor	Ernst & Young LLP	Ticker Symbol	HMBN
Stk Agt	Computershare Trust Co	Outstanding Shares	51,450,000
Counsel	Alston & Bird LLP	E.P.S	-$0.63
DUNS No.	NA	Shareholders	NA

Business: The groups principle activity is to provide banking services. The group operates through two segments namely, mortgage investment operations and mortgage banking operations. The group operates from the United States.

Primary SIC and add'l.: 6162 6163 6798 6162 6163 6798

CIK No: 0001283683

Subsidiaries: BH Mortgage Partners, LLC*, HMB Acceptance Corp., HMB Mortgage Partners, LLC, HomeBanc Funding Corp., HomeBanc Funding Corp. II, HomeBanc Mortgage Corporation, HomeBanc Title Partners, LLC**

Officers: Kevin D. Race/Dir., CEO, CFO, COO, Pres./$999,849.00, Michael J. Barber/Exec. VP, Chief Accounting Officer, Nicolas V. Chater/Exec. VP, CFO - Homebanc Mortgage Corporation, John Kubiak/Exec. VP, Chief Investment Officer/$386,066.00, Charles W. McGuire/Exec. VP, General Counsel, Sec. - Homebanc Mortgage Corporation, D. Reighard/Exec. VP, Chief People Officer - Homebanc Mortgage Corporation/$365,452.00, Norbert Theisen/Exec. VP - Operations, Homebanc Mortgage Corporation, Debra F. Watkins/Exec. VP - Capital Markets, Homebanc Mortgage Corporation, Jacqueline E. Yeaney/39/Exec. VP, Chief Marketing Officer, Carol Knies/VP - Investor Relations

Directors: Kevin D. Race/Dir., CEO, CFO, COO, Pres., James B. Witherow/Chmn., Glenn T. Austin/Dir., Lawrence W. Hamilton/Dir., Warren Y. Jobe/Dir., Joel K. Manby/Dir., Robert C. Patton/Dir., Bonnie L. Phipps/Dir., John W. Spiegel/Dir.

Owners: Patrick S. Flood, Warren Y. Jobe, Kevin D. Race, Robert C. Patton, Wasatch Advisers, Inc/6.62%, UBS Global Asset Management (Americas), Inc/6.29%, Insiders, FMR Corp/16.57%, Bonnie L. Phipps, Paul Lopez, D.Ike Reighard, T. Rowe Price Associates, Inc/6.45%, John Kubiak, NWQ Investment Management Company, LLC/10.84%, James B. Witherow *(20 Owners included in Index)*

Financial Data: Fiscal Year End:12/31 **Latest Annual Data:** 12/31/2006

Year	Sales	Net Income
2006	$437,008,000	-$6,480,000
2005	$298,038,000	-$11,635,000
2004	$109,099,000	-$48,333,000

Curr. Assets:	$253,843,000	**Curr. Liab.:**	$1,536,614,000		
Plant, Equip.:	$45,406,000	**Total Liab.:**	$6,552,394,000	**Indic. Yr. Divd.:**	NA
Total Assets:	$6,822,664,000	**Net Worth:**	$270,270,000	**Debt/ Equity:**	21.7934

HomeFed Corp

1903 Wright Pl., Ste. 220, Carlsbad, CA, 92008; *PH:* 1-760-918-8200

General - Incorporation	DE	**Stock**- Price on:12/24/2007	$63
Employees	23	Stock Exchange	OTC
Auditor	PricewaterhouseCoopers LLP	Ticker Symbol	HOFD
Stk Agt	American Stock Transfer & Trust Co.	Outstanding Shares	8,270,000
Counsel	NA	E.P.S	$1.47
DUNS No.	19-975-4961	Shareholders	NA

Business: The group's principle activity is to provide banking services. The group attracting deposits from the public. Primarily loans secured by residential real estate. Dealings suspended in Apr 1992. The group operates from United States.

Primary SIC and add'l.: 6035

CIK No: 0000833795

Subsidiaries: Bird Ranch Development Company, LLC, CDS Devco, CDS Holding Corporation, Flat Rock Land Company, LLC, HomeFed Communities LLC, HomeFed Communities, Inc., HomeFed Realty, Inc., HomeFed Resources, Inc., Northfork Communities, Otay Land Company, LLC, Otay Valley Development Company, LLC, Paradise Glen Development Company, LLC, Paradise Valley Communities No.1, Paradise Valley LLC, Rampage Vineyard, LLC 21 Subsidiaries included in the Index

Officers: Paul J. Borden/Dir., Pres., Principal Executive Officer, Curt R. Noland/VP, Erin N. Ruhe/VP, Treasurer, Controller, Corinne A. Maki/Sec.

Directors: Joseph S. Steinberg/64/Chmn., Michael A. Lobatz/59/Dir., Ian M. Cumming/67/Dir., Timothy M. Considine/67/Dir., Patrick D. Bienvenue/53/Dir., Paul J. Borden/Dir., Pres., Principal Executive Officer

Owners: Timothy M. Considine, Joseph S. Steinberg/9.00%, Cumming Foundation/2.10%, Michael A. Lobatz, Patrick D. Bienvenue, The Steinberg Children Trust/0.30%, Paul J. Borden, Leucadia National Corporation/29.90%, Erin N. Ruhe, Ian M. Cumming/7.40%, Insiders/16.60%, Diane H. Steinberg/0.50%, Curt R. Noland, Beck, Mack & Oliver LLC/6.40%

Financial Data: Fiscal Year End:12/31 **Latest Annual Data:** 12/31/2006

Year	Sales	Net Income
2006	$69,442,000	$17,176,000
2005	$107,932,000	$31,792,000
2004	$81,671,000	$36,792,000

Curr. Assets:	$48,975,000	**Curr. Liab.:**	$10,699,000	**P/E Ratio:**	43.45
Plant, Equip.:	$79,341,000	**Total Liab.:**	$69,452,000	**Indic. Yr. Divd.:**	NA
Total Assets:	$237,299,000	**Net Worth:**	$154,780,000	**Debt/ Equity:**	0.0633

Homeland Precious Metals Corp

1489 Marine Dr., Ste. 136, West Vancouver, BC, V7T 1B8; *PH:* 1-604-922-6663; *Fax:* 1-604-922-2886; *http://* www.homelandpreciousmetals.com; *Email:* info@hpmef.com

General - Incorporation	BC	**Stock**- Price on:12/24/2007	$0.3
Employees	NA	Stock Exchange	OTC
Auditor	Robison, Hill & Co.	Ticker Symbol	HPMEF
Stk Agt	Holladay Stock Transfer, Inc.	Outstanding Shares	NA
Counsel	Conrad C. Lysiak	E.P.S	NA
DUNS No.	NA	Shareholders	NA

Business: The groups principal activities include finding and developing economical metal asset. The group operates from the United States, Canada and Mexico.

Primary SIC and add'l.: 1000

CIK No: 0001289634

Subsidiaries: Homeland Exploration, Inc

Officers: Bruce Johnstone/Dir., CEO, Pres., Conrad C. Lysiak/Legal Counsel

Directors: Bruce Johnstone/Dir., CEO, Pres., George Eliopulos/Dir., David Mallo/Dir., Douglas Turnbull/Member - Advisory Board, Ian E. Marshall/Member - Advisory Board, Gerry Humphries/Member - Advisory Board

Owners: George Eliopulos, Insiders/27.97%, Bruce E. Johnstone/26.64%, David Mallo

Financial Data: Fiscal Year End:03/31 **Latest Annual Data:** 03/31/2007

Year	Sales	Net Income
2007	NA	-$770,000
2006	NA	-$1,345,000
2005	NA	-$20,000

Curr. Assets:	$578,000	**Curr. Liab.:**	$22,000		
Plant, Equip.:	NA	**Total Liab.:**	$27,000	**Indic. Yr. Divd.:**	NA
Total Assets:	$584,000	**Net Worth:**	$556,000	**Debt/ Equity:**	NA

HomeLife Inc

1503 S Coast Dr., Ste. 204, Costa Mesa, CA, 92626; *PH:* 1-714-241-3030; *http://* www.homelifeus.com; *Email:* homelife@homelifeinc.com

General - Incorporation	NV	**Stock**- Price on:12/24/2007	$0.07
Employees	4	Stock Exchange	OTC
Auditor	Rotenberg & Co. LLP	Ticker Symbol	HMLF
Stk Agt	OTC Corporate Transfer Service Co	Outstanding Shares	12,370,000
Counsel	NA	E.P.S	-$0.04
DUNS No.	NA	Shareholders	NA

Business: The group's principal activity is to provide a broad range of services to its franchisees, licensees and consumers in the real estate marketplace. The group offers consumer-oriented real estate brokerage and finance services through subsidiaries and franchises. It utilizes both its proprietary 'supersystem' marketing system and business combinations and acquisitions to grow as a real estate services company. The group provides franchise services, mortgage financing, retail real estate and home warranty services. The franchise services include name recognition, advertising, training and recruiting for franchise offices. The trademarks include 'red carpet' and 'national real estate services'.

Primary SIC and add'l.: 7389 6794

CIK No: 0001024048

Subsidiaries: FamilyLife Realty Services inc., HomeLife Builders Realty, HomeLife California Properties Inc, HomeLife Realty Services, Inc., MaxAmerica Financial Services Inc., MaxAmerica Home Warranty Company ., MIT Holding Inc., National Sellers Network, Inc., Red Carpet Real Estate Services Inc., The Keim Group Ltd.

Officers: Andrew Cimerman/60/Dir., CEO, Pres., Charles Goodson/53/Dir., VP, Marie May/41/Dir., CFO, Sec.

Directors: Andrew Cimerman/60/Dir., CEO, Pres., Terry A. Lyles/49/Dir., Bryson F. Farrill/80/Dir., Charles Goodson/53/Dir., VP, Marie May/41/Dir., CFO, Sec.

Owners: Marie M. May/0.50%, Andrew Cimerman/72.80%, Insiders/73.50%, Terry Lyles/0.10%, Bryson F. Farrill

Financial Data: Fiscal Year End:05/31 **Latest Annual Data:** 05/31/2007

Year	Sales	Net Income
2007	$453,000	-$437,000
2006	$585,000	-$178,000
2005	$628,000	-$139,000

Curr. Assets:	$95,000	**Curr. Liab.:**	$335,000		
Plant, Equip.:	$2,000	**Total Liab.:**	$506,000	**Indic. Yr. Divd.:**	NA
Total Assets:	$366,000	**Net Worth:**	-$160,000	**Debt/ Equity:**	NA

Hometown Auto Retailers Inc

774 Straits Tpke., Watertown, CT, 06795; *PH:* 1-203-756-1300; *Fax:* 1-860-274-4137; *http://* www.hometownautoretailers.com; *Email:* investor@htauto.com

General - Incorporation	DE	**Stock**- Price on:12/24/2007	NA
Employees	297	Stock Exchange	NA
Auditor	BDO Seidman LLP	Ticker Symbol	NA
Stk Agt	Mellon Investor Services LLC	Outstanding Shares	NA
Counsel	NA	E.P.S	NA
DUNS No.	02-577-3693	Shareholders	NA

Business: The group's principle activity is to sell new and used cars, light trucks and replacement parts. The group also provides maintenance and repair services, related financing, insurance and service contracts. The group provides these services through 9 franchised dealerships. The group operates in New Jersey, New York, Connecticut, Massachusetts and Vermont. The group dealerships offer 10 American and Asian automotive brands. These brands include chevrolet, chrysler, dodge, ford, jeep, lincoln, mercury, oldsmobile, mazda and toyota. The group also arranges financing for their customers' vehicle purchases, sells vehicle service contracts and arranges selected types of credit insurance in connection with the financing of vehicle sales.

Primary SIC and add'l.: 5531 5511 7538 6141

CIK No: 0001061117

Subsidiaries: Bay State Realty Holdings, Inc., Brattleboro Realty Holdings, Inc., ERR Enterprises, Inc., Family Ford, Inc., Hometown Auto Framingham, Inc., Hometown Brattleboro, Inc., Hometown Emerson New Jersey, Inc., Hometown New Windsor, Inc., Hometown Newburgh, Inc., Morristown Auto Sales, Inc., Muller Automotive Group, Inc., Muller Chevrolet, Isuzu, Inc., Newburgh Realty Holding Co., Inc., Shakers Inc., Shakers Lincoln/Mercury Auto Care, Inc.

Homex Development Corp

Gd, Kamloops, BC, V2C 6B8; ***PH:*** 1-250-374-5769; ***http://*** www.homex.com.mx

General - Incorporation	Mexico	**Stock**- Price on:12/24/2007	$61.52
Employees	7,337	Stock Exchange	NYSE
Auditor	Galaz, Yamazaki, Ruiz Urquiza, S.C	Ticker Symbol	HXM
Stk Agt	Bank of New York	Outstanding Shares	55,980,000
Counsel	NA	E.P.S	$2.56
DUNS No.	NA	Shareholders	NA

Business: The groups principle activities include developing, constructing and sale of entry level, middle-income and upper-income housing in Mexico. The group operates from United States.

Primary SIC and add'l.: NA

CIK No: 0001293153

Subsidiaries: Administradora Picsa, S.A. de C.V., AeroHomex, S.A. de C.V., Altos Mandos de Negocios, S.A. de C.V., Casas Beta del Centro, S.A. de C.V., Casas Beta del Noroeste, S.A. de C.V, Casas Beta del Norte, S.A. de C.V., Desarrolladora de Casas del Noroeste, S.A. de C.V., Homex Atizapan, S.A. de C.V., Proyectos Inmobiliarios de Culiacan, S.A. de C.V.

Officers: Gerardo De Nicolas Gutierrez/40/Dir., CEO, Lorena Andrade/Contact - Media, Deborah Placencia/Contact - Land Reserve, Dalila Magana/Contact - Land Reserve, Ramon Lafarga Batiz/48/Administrative, Accounting Officer, Ruben Izabal Gonzalez/40/VP - Construction, Alberto Menchaca Valenzuela/VP - Affordable Entry Division, Carlos J. Moctezuma/Dir. - Investor Relations, Vania Fueyo/Investor Relation Officer, Alan Castellanos Carmona/CFO, Julian De Nicolas Gutierrez/VP - Middle Income Division, Daniel Leal Diaz-Conti/VP - Sales, Marketing, Marena Rubio/Investor Relations Officer

Directors: Gerardo De Nicolas Gutierrez/40/Dir., CEO, Eustaquio Tomas De Nicolas Gutierrez/47/Chmn., Gary R. Garrabrant/51/Vice Chmn., Jamie Z. Behar/Dir., Wilfrido Castillo Sanchez-Mejorada/Dir., Luis Alberto Harvey McKissack/48/Dir., Edward Lowenthal/Dir., Matthew M. Zell/Dir., Jose Ignacio De Nicolas Gutierrez/44/Dir., Rafael Matute Labrador/48/Dir.

Owners: Equity International Properties, Ltd./13.10%, De Nicols family/32.90%

Financial Data: ***Fiscal Year End:***12/31 ***Latest Annual Data:*** 12/31/2005

Year	Sales	Net Income
2005	$793,863,000	$113,088,000
2004	$476,555,000	$37,865,000
2003	$250,829,000	$21,283,000

Curr. Assets:	$1,124,436,000	**Curr. Liab.:**	$559,867,000	**P/E Ratio:**	24.03
Plant, Equip.:	$523,183,000	**Total Liab.:**	$1,085,732,000	**Indic. Yr. Divd.:**	NA
Total Assets:	$1,719,220,000	**Net Worth:**	$633,489,000	**Debt/ Equity:**	NA

Honat Bancorp Inc

PO Box 350, Honesdale, PA, 18431; ; ***http://*** www.hnbbank.com; ***Email:*** hnb@hnbbank.com

General - Incorporation		**Stock**- Price on:12/24/2007	$355
Employees	NA	Stock Exchange	OTC
Auditor	NA	Ticker Symbol	HONT
Stk Agt	NA	Outstanding Shares	NA
Counsel	NA	E.P.S	NA
DUNS No.	NA	Shareholders	NA

Business: The groups principal activity is to provide community banking services. The services of the group include originating loans, trust and investment, brokerage, consumer banking and online banking. The group operates from the United States.

Primary SIC and add'l.: 6712

CIK No:

Officers: William Schweighofer/CEO, Pres., Thomas Sheridan/COO, Exec. VP, Judy Cudo/Kingston Office Teller, Rachael Gallup/Kingston Office Teller, Joseph Killeen/VP - Kingston Office, Rose Antoine/Contact - HNB Mortgage Specialist, Alison Swanson/Contact - HNB Mortgage Specialist, Jeanette Johnston/Contact - HNB Mortgage Specialist, Betty Ditzel/Contact - HNB Mortgage Specialist, Marcy Swingle/VP - Kingston Office, Kathy Enslin/VP - HNB Uvest Division, Mark Graziadio/VP - HNB Uvest Division, Paul Vitiello/VP - HNB Uvest Division, James Jennings/VP - HNB, Brian Burd/Kingston Office Mgr. *(21 Officers included in Index)*

Directors: Roger Dirlam/Vice Chmn., John Burlein/Chmn., Harry Mattern/Dir., Kingston Solicitor/Dir., Paul Meagher/Dir.

Honda Motor Co Ltd

540 Madison Ave., 32nd Fl., New York, NY, 10022; ***PH:*** 1-212-355-9191; ***Fax:*** 1-212-813-0260; ***http://*** www.world.honda.com

General - Incorporation	Japan	**Stock**- Price on:12/24/2007	$35.85
Employees	144,785	Stock Exchange	NYSE
Auditor	KPMG Azsa & Co	Ticker Symbol	HMC
Stk Agt	Morgan ADR Service Center	Outstanding Shares	3,640,000,000
Counsel	NA	E.P.S	$1.75
DUNS No.	69-056-6815	Shareholders	NA

Business: The group's principal activities are to manufacture automobiles, motorcycles and power products. The group develops and manufactures a wide variety of products, ranging from small general-purpose engines to specialty sports cars that incorporate their internal combustion engine technology. The group also provides financing for the sale of its motorcycles, automobiles and power products. The group has got 439 subsidiaries and affiliates. It operates through 110 overseas production facilities in 31 overseas countries. The group operates in the following four segments: motorcycle business, automobile business, financial services and other. The group's major trademarks includes honda, acura, accord, civic, fit, odyssey, cr-v, pilot, mobilio, element, step wgn, mdx, stream, life, acty, vamos, that's, cub, wave and gold wing. The group has subsidiaries throughout the world including North America, pakistan, the Philippines, India, South America and Europe.

Primary SIC and add'l.: 3751 6141 3524 3711

CIK No: 0000715153

Subsidiaries: American Honda Finance Corporation, American Honda Motor Co., Inc., Asama Giken Co., Ltd., Asian Honda Motor Co., Ltd., Cardington Yutaka Technologies Inc., Celina Aluminum Precision Technology Inc., Honda Atlas Cars (Pakistan) Limited, Honda Australia Pty. Ltd., Honda Automobile (China) Co., Ltd., Honda Automobile (Thailand) Co., Ltd., Honda Automoveis do Brasil Ltda., Honda Bank Gmbh, Honda Canada Finance Inc., Honda Canada Inc., Honda Cars Philippines, Inc. 61 Subsidiaries included in the Index

Officers: Takeo Fukui/Dir., CEO, Pres., Representative Dir., Takanobu Ito/Dir. , Sr. Managing, Representative Dir., Minoru Harada/Dir. , Sr. Managing, Representative Dir., Atsuyoshi Hyogo/Dir., Sr. Managing, Representative Dir., Toru Onda/Dir., MD, Mikio Yoshimi/Dir. , Sr. Managing, Representative Dir., Hidenobu Iwata/Operating Officer, Fumihiko Saito/Corporate Auditor, Masaaki Kato/Dir., Sr. Managing, Representative Dir., Gen Tsujii/Operating Officer, Takashi Yamamoto/Managing Officer, Masaya Yamashita/Operating Officer, Koichi Fukuo/Operating Officer, Koukei Higuchi/Corporate Auditor, Hiroshi Okubo/Corporate Auditor *(46 Officers included in Index)*

Directors: Takeo Fukui/Dir., CEO, Pres., Representative Dir., Satoshi Aoki/Chmn., Akira Takano/Dir., MD, Toru Onda/Dir., MD, Mikio Yoshimi/Dir. , Sr. Managing, Representative Dir., Takanobu Ito/Dir. , Sr. Managing, Representative Dir., Minoru Harada/Dir. , Sr. Managing, Representative Dir., Satoru Kishi/Dir., Atsuyoshi Hyogo/Dir., Sr. Managing, Representative Dir., Masaaki Kato/Dir., Sr. Managing, Representative Dir., Satoshi Toshida/Dir., COO - Power Product Operations, Sho Minekawa/Dir., Tatsuhiro Oyama/Dir., MD, Kensaku Hogen/Dir., Shigeru Takagi/Dir., MD *(20 Directors included in Index)*

Financial Data: ***Fiscal Year End:***03/31 ***Latest Annual Data:*** 03/31/2007

Year	Sales	Net Income
2007	$94,240,690,000	$5,034,737,000
2006	$84,217,966,000	$5,074,781,000
2005	$80,445,977,000	$4,521,632,000

Curr. Assets:	$44,645,324,000	**Curr. Liab.:**	$36,443,980,000	**P/E Ratio:**	24.03
Plant, Equip.:	$20,526,965,000	**Total Liab.:**	$64,208,057,000	**Indic. Yr. Divd.:**	$0.310
Total Assets:	$102,310,250,000	**Net Worth:**	$38,102,194,000	**Debt/ Equity:**	NA

Honeywell International Inc

101 Columbia Rd., Morristown, NJ, 07962; ***PH:*** 1-973-455-2000; ***Fax:*** 1-973-455-4807; ***http://*** www.honeywell.com

General - Incorporation	DE	**Stock**- Price on:12/24/2007	NA
Employees	NA	Stock Exchange	NYSE
Auditor	PricewaterhouseCoopers LLP	Ticker Symbol	HON
Stk Agt	American Stock Transfer & Trust Co.	Outstanding Shares	779,720,000
Counsel	NA	E.P.S	$2.96
DUNS No.	NA	Shareholders	NA

Business: The groups principal activity is to manufacture aerospace products and services, control, sensing and security technologies. The group operates through four segments namely, aerospace, automation and control solutions, specialty materials, and transportation systems. In the year 2006, the group acquired Gardiner Groupe and UOP LLC. The group operates from the United States.

Primary SIC and add'l.: 3625 3824 3812 3825 3823 3724 3822 3728 3714

CIK No: 0000773840

Subsidiaries: AlliedSignal Aerospace Service Corporation, Grimes Aerospace Company, Honeywell ACSA Inc., Honeywell Aerospace UK, Honeywell Asia Pacific Inc., Honeywell Electronic Materials Inc., Honeywell GmbH, Honeywell HomeMed L.L.C., Honeywell Intellectual Properties Inc., Honeywell Limited, Honeywell Resins & Chemicals L.L.C., Honeywell Specialty Materials, L.L.C., Honeywell Technologies S.r.l., Honeywell Technology Solutions Inc., Honeywell UK Limited 18 Subsidiaries included in the Index

Officers: David M. Cote/54/Chmn., CEO/$27,695,650.00, Nance K. Dicciani/CEO, Pres. - Honeywell Specialty Materials, Roger Fradin/CEO, Pres. - Automation, Control Solutions/$6,102,578.00, Rob Gillette/CEO, Pres. - Aerospace/$5,851,916.00, Adriane M. Brown/CEO, Pres. - Transportation Systems, Mark James/Sr. VP - Human Resources, Communications, Thomas W. Weidenkopf/Sr. VP - Human Resources, Communications, Thomas F. Larkins/VP, Corp. Sec., David J. Anderson/CFO, Sr. VP/$7,623,081.00, Rhonda Germany/VP - Strategy, Business Development, Larry E. Kittelberger/Sr. VP - Technology, Operations/$6,401,052.00, Peter M. Kreindler/63/Sr. VP, General Counsel

Directors: David M. Cote/54/Chmn., CEO, Gordon M. Bethune/Dir., Jaime Chico Pardo/58/Dir., Scott D. Davis/56/Dir., Linnet F. Deily/62/Dir., Clive R. Hollick/62/Dir., James J. Howard/72/Dir., Ivan G. Seidenberg/61/Dir., Bradley T. Sheares/51/Dir., Eric K. Shinseki/65/Dir., John R. Stafford/Dir., Michael W. Wright/69/Dir.

Owners: FMR Corp./8.30%, Jaime Chico Pardo, Clive R. Hollick, Eric K. Shinseki, Roger Fradin, State Street Bank and Trust Company/10.60%, Gordon M. Bethune, Linnet F. Deily, Insiders, Russell E. Palmer, Ivan G. Seidenberg, James J. Howard, Robert J. Gillette, Larry E. Kittelberger, Michael W. Wright *(20 Owners included in Index)*

Financial Data: ***Fiscal Year End:***12/31 ***Latest Annual Data:*** 12/31/2006

Year	Sales	Net Income
2006	$31,367,000,000	$2,083,000,000
2005	$27,653,000,000	$1,655,000,000
2004	$25,601,000,000	$1,281,000,000

Curr. Assets:	$12,304,000,000	**Curr. Liab.:**	$10,135,000,000		
Plant, Equip.:	$4,797,000,000	**Total Liab.:**	$21,221,000,000	**Indic. Yr. Divd.:**	$1.000
Total Assets:	$30,941,000,000	**Net Worth:**	$9,720,000,000	**Debt/ Equity:**	NA

Hooker Furniture Corp

440 E Commonwealth Blvd., Martinsville, VA, 24112; ***PH:*** 1-276-632-0459; ***Fax:*** 1-276-632-0026; ***http://*** www.hookerfurniture.com

General - Incorporation	VA	**Stock**- Price on:12/24/2007	$22.34
Employees	1,050	Stock Exchange	NDQ
Auditor	KPMG LLP	Ticker Symbol	HOFT
Stk Agt	Wachovia Equity Services Group	Outstanding Shares	12,650,000
Counsel	McGuire-Woods	E.P.S	$1.18
DUNS No.	NA	Shareholders	NA

Business: The group's principal activity is to manufacture, import and sell household and office furniture to wholesale and retail merchandisers through out North America. The group's product line includes home office, occasional, dining, bedroom and residential furniture, wall systems and entertainment centers. The group provides furniture products in wood, veneers and finishes in European traditional, transitional, American traditional and country casual designs. The group's distribution network

includes independent furniture stores, department stores, specialty retailers, catalog merchandisers and national and regional furniture chains. These product lines cover major design categories including European traditional, transitional, American traditional and country and casual designs. On 02-Jan-2003, the group acquired bradington young, llc.

Primary SIC and add'l.: 2511 2521

CIK No: 0001077688

Subsidiaries: Bradington-Young LLC

Officers: Paul B. Toms/53/Chmn., CEO, Larry E. Ryder/CFO, Exec. VP - Finance, Administration, Douglas C. Williams/60/COO, Pres., Raymond T. Harm/58/Sr. VP - Sales, Michael P. Spece/55/Exec. VP - Merchandising, Design, Robert W. Sherwood/Sec.

Directors: Paul B. Toms/53/Chmn., CEO, Clyde J. Hooker/Chmn. Emeritus, Christopher W. Beeler/56/Dir., John L. Gregory/60/Dir., Mark F. Schreiber/65/Dir., David G. Sweet/61/Dir., Henry G. Williamson/60/Dir.

Owners: Franklin Resources, Inc./13.30%, Henry G. Williamson, Christopher W. Beeler, Douglas C. Williams, Insiders/4.80%, Michael P. Spece, Mark F. Schreiber, Scott C. Young, Larry E. Ryder, Barclays Global Investors, NA/5.70%, David G. Sweet, NWQ Investment Management Company, LLC/13.50%, Raymond T. Harm, Paul B. Toms/4.10%, Clyde J. Hooker/5.20% (18 Owners included in Index)

Financial Data: Fiscal Year End: 11/30 **Latest Annual Data:** 11/30/2006

Year		Sales		Net Income
2006		$350,026,000		$14,138,000
2005		$341,775,000		$12,485,000
2004		$345,944,000		$18,204,000
Curr. Assets:	$149,804,000	**Curr. Liab.:**	$25,776,000	
Plant, Equip.:	$29,215,000	**Total Liab.:**	$38,763,000	**Indic. Yr. Divd.:** $0.400
Total Assets:	$201,299,000	**Net Worth:**	$162,536,000	**Debt/ Equity:** 0.0487

Hooper Holmes Inc

170 Mount Airy Rd., Basking Ridge, NJ, 07920; **PH:** 1-908-766-5000; **Fax:** 1-908-953-6304; **http://** www.hooperholmes.com; **Email:** hholmes@hooperholmes.com

General - Incorporation	NY	**Stock** - Price on:12/24/2007	$3.25
Employees	3,270	Stock Exchange	AMEX
Auditor	KPMG LLP	Ticker Symbol	HH
Stk Agt	Registrar & Transfer Co	Outstanding Shares	68,540,000
Counsel	Robert W. Jewett	E.P.S.	-$1.28
DUNS No.	06-072-2915	Shareholders	NA

Business: The group's principal activity is to provide outsourced risk assessment services to the life and health insurance industry. The group operates through two segments, the health information business unit provides a full range of paramedical services to life insurance industries in the United States and u.k. The unit's core health information operations are portamedic, infolink, heritage labs and medical directs. The diversified business unit provides independent medical examinations, case management services primarily for property and casualty insurers and claim reviewers. The group operates through approximately 217 branch offices and 62 contract affiliate offices located in 50 states, the United Kingdom, guam and Puerto Rico. On 06-Jan-2004, the group acquired allegiance health services inc and in may 2004, assets and liabilities of mid-american agency services inc and Michigan evaluation group

Primary SIC and add'l.: 8099 7375

CIK No: 0000741815

Subsidiaries: Hooper Evaluations, Inc., Hooper Information Services, Inc., Mid-America Agency Services, Incorporated, TEG Enterprises, Inc.

Officers: James D. Calver/CEO, Pres./$856,268.00, Joseph A. Marone/VP/$181,956.00, William F. Kracklauer/Sr. VP, General Counsel, Corp. Sec., Robert William Jewett/55/Sr. VP, General Counsel, Sec./$226,574.00, Michael Shea/CFO, Sr. VP/$339,855.00, Bill Kracklauer/Sr. VP, General Counsel, Corp. Sec., Ron Levesque/Corp. Officer, Sr. VP, Chris Behling/Sr. VP, Business Development Officer, Chuck Groseth/Sr. VP, Mgr. - National Sales, Richard DAlesandro/Sr. VP - Administrative Services, Mark Patterson/Pres.- Heritage Labs, Steve Sherrill/Pres., Anthony Minichini/GM

Directors: Benjamin A. Currier/Chmn., Roy Bubbs/Dir., Elaine Rigolosi/Dir., Roy E. Lowrance/Dir., Kenneth Rossano/Dir., Quentin J. Kennedy/Dir., Paul W. Kolacki/66/Dir., John W. Remshard/Dir.

Owners: Wells Fargo & Company/10.30%, Ronald J. Levesque, Benjamin A. Currier, James D. Calver, Elaine L. Rigolosi, Heartland Advisors, Inc/5.10%, Dimensional Fund Advisors LP/8.10%, Royce & Associates, LLC/10.40%, John L. Spenser, Paul W. Kolacki, Putnam, LLC d/b/a Putnam Investments/7.70%, Kenneth R. Rossano/2.60%, Quentin J. Kennedy, Carlo J. Cannell/5.00%, Robert W. Jewett (19 Owners included in Index)

Financial Data: Fiscal Year End: 12/31 **Latest Annual Data:** 12/31/2006

Year		Sales		Net Income
2006		$293,862,000		-$85,181,000
2005		$320,346,000		-$96,623,000
2004		$327,748,000		$10,710,000
Curr. Assets:	$53,755,000	**Curr. Liab.:**	$33,757,000	
Plant, Equip.:	$15,839,000	**Total Liab.:**	$36,089,000	**Indic. Yr. Divd.:** NA
Total Assets:	$84,897,000	**Net Worth:**	$48,808,000	**Debt/ Equity:** NA

HopFed Bancorp Inc

2700 Ft. Campbell Blvd., Hopkinsville, KY, 42240; **PH:** 1-270-885-1171; **Fax:** 1-270-889-0313; **http://** www.bankwithheritage.com; **Email:** info@heritagebankky.com

General - Incorporation	DE	**Stock** - Price on:12/24/2007	$15.66
Employees	202	Stock Exchange	NDQ
Auditor	Rayburn, Bates & Fitzgerald, P.C	Ticker Symbol	HFBC
Stk Agt	Registrar & Transfer Co	Outstanding Shares	3,610,000
Counsel	Deatherage, Myers, Self & Lackey	E.P.S.	$1.10
DUNS No.	00-431-7934	Shareholders	NA

Business: The group's principal activity is to accept deposits from the general public and invest such deposits in loans secured by single family residential real estate and investment securities, including U.S. Government and agency securities and mortgage-backed securities. The group also originates single-family residential/construction loans and multi-family and commercial real estate loans, as well as loans secured by deposits, other consumer loans and commercial loans. It accepts deposits through offering money market accounts, passbook savings accounts, individual retirement accounts, and certificates of deposit that range in maturity from three months to five years. The group operates through its branch offices located in hopkinsville, murray, cadiz, elkton and benton

Primary SIC and add'l.: 6035 6712

CIK No: 0001041550

Subsidiaries: Fall & Fall Insurance, Inc., Heritage Bank, HopFed Capital Trust I

Officers: John E. Peck/Dir., CEO, Pres./$259,322.00, Michael L. Woolfolk/COO, Exec. VP/$193,832.00, Billy C. Duvall/CFO, VP, Treasurer/$138,391.00, Michael F. Stalls/VP, Chief Credit Officer/$155,245.00, Boyd M. Clark/Dir., Sr. VP, Sec./$125,285.00, Robert K. Burrow/Marketing Pres. - Fulton County Offices/$137,929.00, Connie Smith/Office Mgr. - Fulton, KY Carr Plaza Office, Paul Thurman/Marketing Pres. - Marshall County Offices, Brent Evans/Office Mgr. - Calvert City, KY Office, Dan Dickerson/Marketing Mgr. - Trigg County, KY Office, Tim Little/Marketing Mgr. - Todd County, KY Office, Cindy Fleming/Office Mgr. - Hopkinsville, KY Lafayette Road Office, Doug Lawson/Marketing Pres. - Calloway County, KY Office, Keith Bennett/Marketing Pres. - Montgomery, Houston Counties, TN/$313,758.00, Thomas Douthitt/Office Mgr. - Hopkinsville, KY Downtown Office (22 Officers included in Index)

Directors: John E. Peck/Dir., CEO, Pres., W. D. Kelley/Chmn., Gilbert E. Lee/Vice Chmn., Joseph H. Dempsey/Dir., Thomas I. Miller/Dir., Kerry B. Harvey/Dir., Boyd M. Clark/Dir., Sr. VP, Sec., Walton G. Ezell/Dir.

Owners: Kerry B. Harvey, WD Kelley/1.50%, Walton G. Ezell/1.60%, Thomas I. Miller, Insiders/11.90%, Billy C. Duvall, Boyd M. Clark/2.60%, Robert Burrow, Harry J. Dempsey/1.10%, Michael F. Stalls, John E. Peck/1.70%, Keith Bennett, Michael L. Woolfolk, Jeffrey L. Gendell/6.80%, Gilbert E. Lee/1.30%

Financial Data: Fiscal Year End: 12/31 **Latest Annual Data:** 12/31/2006

Year		Sales		Net Income
2006		$46,433,000		$3,908,000
2005		$34,198,000		$4,130,000
2004		$29,419,000		$3,991,000
Curr. Assets:	$26,692,000	**Curr. Liab.:**	$708,021,000	**P/E Ratio:** 14.24
Plant, Equip.:	$25,542,000	**Total Liab.:**	$718,618,000	**Indic. Yr. Divd.:** $0.480
Total Assets:	$770,888,000	**Net Worth:**	$52,270,000	**Debt/ Equity:** 0.1940

Horace Mann Educators Corp

1 Horace Mann Plz., Springfield, IL, 62715; **PH:** 1-217-789-2500; **Fax:** 1-217-788-5161; **http://** www.horacemann.com

General - Incorporation	DE	**Stock** - Price on:12/24/2007	$21.48
Employees	2,400	Stock Exchange	NYSE
Auditor	KPMG LLP	Ticker Symbol	HMN
Stk Agt	American Stock Transfer & Trust Co.	Outstanding Shares	43,190,000
Counsel	NA	E.P.S.	$2.09
DUNS No.	03-056-5147	Shareholders	NA

Business: The group's principle activity is to market and underwrite personal lines of property and casualty and life insurance and retirement annuities in the United States of America. The group markets its products primarily to educators and other employees of public schools and their families. The group's principal operating subsidiaries are horace mann life insurance company, horace mann insurance company, teachers insurance company, horace mann property and casualty insurance company and horace mann lloyds. The group's quarterly revenue for Sep'07 was 218.92 millions of USD.

Primary SIC and add'l.: 6331 6719 6411 6311

CIK No: 0000850141

Subsidiaries: Allegiance Life Insurance Company, Educators Life Insurance Company of America, Horace Mann General Agency, Inc., Horace Mann Insurance Company, Horace Mann Investors, Inc., Horace Mann Life Insurance Company, Horace Mann Lloyds, Horace Mann MGA and Brokerage of Florida, Inc., Horace Mann Property& Casualty Insurance Company, Horace Mann Service Corporation, Teachers Insurance Company

Officers: Louis G. Lower/Dir., CEO, Pres./$1,527,176.00, Douglas W. Reynolds/Exec. VP - Property, Casualty/$836,240.00, Peter H. Heckman/CFO, Exec. VP/$873,504.00, Dwayne D. Hallman/Sr. VP - Finance, Karen Ruffatto/Investor Relation Officer

Directors: Louis G. Lower/Dir., CEO, Pres., Joseph J. Melone/Dir., Jeffrey L. Morby/Dir., Charles A. Parker/Dir., Mary H. Futrell/Dir., Stephen J. Hasenmiller/Dir., Roger J. Steinbecker/Dir., Charles R. Wright/Dir., Gabriel L. Shaheen/Dir.

Owners: Roger J. Steinbecker, Jeffrey L. Morby, Mary H. Futrell, Peter H. Heckman, LSV Asset Management/5.00%, Joseph J. Melone, Barclays Global Investors, NA/5.50%, Shaun F. OMalley, William W. Abbott, Ariel Capital Management, LLC/18.20%, Stephen J. Hasenmiller, Paul D. Andrews, Insiders/5.70%, Frank DAmbra, Charles A. Parker (18 Owners included in Index)

Financial Data: Fiscal Year End: 12/31 **Latest Annual Data:** 12/31/2006

Year		Sales		Net Income
2006		$873,807,000		$98,708,000
2005		$869,412,000		$77,273,000
2004		$878,349,000		$56,313,000
Curr. Assets:	$495,472,000	**Curr. Liab.:**	NA	**P/E Ratio:** 10.18
Plant, Equip.:	NA	**Total Liab.:**	$5,672,606,000	**Indic. Yr. Divd.:** $0.420
Total Assets:	$6,329,687,000	**Net Worth:**	$657,081,000	**Debt/ Equity:** 0.8602

Horizon Bancorp

515 Franklin Sq., Michigan City, IN, 46360; **PH:** 1-219-874-9318; **Fax:** 1-219-874-9305; **http://** www.accesshorizon.com; **Email:** investorrelations@accesshorizon.com

General - Incorporation	IN	**Stock** - Price on:12/24/2007	$27.5
Employees	277	Stock Exchange	NDQ
Auditor	BKD LLP	Ticker Symbol	HBNC
Stk Agt	Registrar & Transfer Co	Outstanding Shares	3,200,000
Counsel	NA	E.P.S.	$2.49
DUNS No.	11-974-7624	Shareholders	NA

Business: The group's principle activities are to offer commercial and retail banking business, investment management services, commercial, personal property and casualty insurance services, retail lending and insurance credit life sales. The group's subsidiaries are horizon bank na and hbc insurance group. Horizon bank is a full service commercial bank offering a broad range of commercial and retail banking services, corporate and individual trust and agency services, commercial and personal property, casualty insurance services and other services incident to banking. Hbc insurance group offers credit life and accident and health insurance. The group maintains four facilities located within la porte county and three facilities located in porter county, Indiana. The group's quarterly income for Sep'07 was 2.27 millions of USD.

Primary SIC and add'l.: 6712 6022

CIK No: 0000706129

Subsidiaries: Alliance Financial Statutory Trust I, Horizon Bancorp Capital Trust II, Horizon Bank, National Association, Horizon Insurance Services, Inc., Horizon Investments, Inc, Horizon Statutory Trust I, Horizon Trust & Investment Management, National Association

Officers: Craig M. Dwight/Dir., CEO, Pres./$360,045.00, James H. Foglesong/CFO/$195,625.00, Thomas H. Edwards/Exec. VP/$227,840.00, Lawrence Mazur/Sec./$214,142.00, James D. Neff/Corp. Sec./$340,683.00

Directors: Craig M. Dwight/Dir., CEO, Pres., Robert C. Dabagia/Chmn., James B. Dworkin/Dir., Susan D. Aaron/Dir., Bruce E. Rampage/Dir., Peter L. Pairitz/Dir., Larry N. Middleton/Dir., Daniel F. Hopp/Dir., Spero W. Valavanis/Dir., Robert E. Swinehart/Dir., Robert E. McBride/Dir., Charley E. Gillispie/Dir.

Owners: Daniel F. Hopp, Susan D. Aaron, Robert C. Dabagia/1.10%, Peter L. Pairitz, James B. Dworkin, Spero W. Valavanis, Bruce E. Rampage, Lawrence J. Mazur/1.80%, Craig M. Dwight/2.80%, Robert E. McBride, James D. Neff/1.10%, Insiders/10.40%, Larry N. Middleton, Thomas H. Edwards/1.20%, James H. Foglesong *(17 Owners included in Index)*

Financial Data: Fiscal Year End:12/31   Latest Annual Data: 12/31/2006

Year	Sales	Net Income
2006	$79,581,000	$7,484,000
2005	$66,654,000	$7,091,000
2004	$53,657,000	$6,935,000

Curr. Assets:	$65,804,000	Curr. Liab.:	$999,586,000	P/E Ratio:	11.04
Plant, Equip.:	$23,394,000	Total Liab.:	$1,160,553,000	Indic. Yr. Divd.:	$0.600
Total Assets:	$1,222,430,000	Net Worth:	$61,877,000	Debt/ Equity:	2.9270

Horizon BanCorp Inc

515 Franklin Sq., Michigan City, IN, 46360; *PH:* 1-219-879-0211; *Fax:* 1-219-874-9305; *http://* www.accesshorizon.com; *Email:* InvestorRelations@accesshorizon.com

General - Incorporation	FL	*Stock-* Price on:12/24/2007	$13.55
Employees	35	Stock Exchange	OTC
Auditor	Francis & Co, CPAs	Ticker Symbol	HZNB
Stk Agt	Registrar & Transfer Co	Outstanding Shares	1,810,000
Counsel	NA	E.P.S	$0.86
DUNS No.	NA	Shareholders	NA

Business: The Group's principal activity is to provide commercial banking services. The services include personal and business checking accounts, savings and other time certificates of deposit. The services are provided to individuals, professional and business customers. The Group operates through two full service branches in Bradenton, Florida and has an ATM location in the Red Barn Market.Deposits by directors and their related interests, as of December 31, 2005 and 2004 approximated $4,720,955 and $2,981,439, respectively.

Primary SIC and add'l.: 6021

CIK No: 0001074458

Subsidiaries: Horizon Bank

Officers: Craig M. Dwight/Chmn., CEO - Horizon Bank, Charles S. Conoley/49/Dir., CEO, Pres./$219,595.00, James H. Foglesong/CFO, Thomas H. Edwards/Exec. VP, Mary McColl/Investor Relations Officer, Bradley N. Severson/45/Exec. VP/$144,825.00, Jeffrey S. Chapin/37/Sr. VP/$108,662.00, James D. Neff/Corp. Sec., Kathleen M. Jepson/59/Sr. VP

Directors: Craig M. Dwight/Chmn., CEO - Horizon Bank, Charles S. Conoley/49/Dir., CEO, Pres., Robert C. Dabagia/Chmn., Bruce E. Shackelford/52/Dir., Donald C. Miller/69/Dir., Clarence R. Urban/62/Dir., Maryann P. Turner/47/Dir., David K. Scherer/46/Dir., Elizabeth Thomason/64/Dir., Charley E. Gillispie/Dir., Robert E. McBride/Dir., Peter L. Pairitz/Dir., Robert E. Swinehart/Dir., Susan D. Aaron/Dir., James B. Dworkin/Dir. *(22 Directors included in Index)*

Owners: David K. Scherer/6.97%, Elizabeth Thomason/1.68%, John Falkner/8.30%, C. Donald Miller, Insiders/44.84%, Clarence R. Urban/7.93%, Jeffrey S. Chapin/1.09%, Michael Shannon Glasgow/7.24%, Barclay Kirkland/2.04%, Bruce E. Shackelford/2.20%, Kathleen M. Jepson/0.10%, Banc Fund VII, L.P./6.50%, Banc Fund IV, L.P./6.50%, Bradley N. Severson/1.84%, Mary Ann P. Turner/4.75% *(17 Owners included in Index)*

Financial Data: Fiscal Year End:12/31   Latest Annual Data: 12/31/2006

Year	Sales	Net Income
2006	$12,589,000	$1,846,000
2005	$9,267,000	$1,427,000
2004	$6,705,000	$851,000

Curr. Assets:	$4,673,000	Curr. Liab.:	$155,212,000	P/E Ratio:	15.40
Plant, Equip.:	$2,116,000	Total Liab.:	$155,704,000	Indic. Yr. Divd.:	$0.110
Total Assets:	$168,273,000	Net Worth:	$12,570,000	Debt/ Equity:	NA

Horizon Financial Corp

1500 Cornwall Ave., Bellingham, WA, 98225; *PH:* 1-360-733-3050; *Fax:* 1-360-733-7019; *http://* www.horizonbank.com; *Email:* investorrelations@horizonbank.com

General - Incorporation	WA	*Stock-* Price on:12/24/2007	NA
Employees	253	Stock Exchange	NDQ
Auditor	Moss Adams LLP	Ticker Symbol	HRZB
Stk Agt	American Stock Transfer & Trust Co.	Outstanding Shares	12,200,000
Counsel	Ludwigson, Thompson, Hayes & Bell	E.P.S	$1.60
DUNS No.	92-864-8831	Shareholders	NA

Business: The group's principal activities are to provide a range of commercial and mortgage lending to borrowers and customer services to depositors. The deposit products of the group include regular passbook and statement savings accounts, personal and business checking accounts, money market with and without check access and certificates of deposit accounts. Its loan products include loans on residential and non residential real estate properties, construction loans, home equity loans, home equity lines of credit, loans secured by personal property and certificate of deposit and unsecured loans. The group's operations are conducted through sixteen full service office facilities, three commercial loan centers, and three real estate loan centers located in whatcom, skagit, and snohomish counties in northwest Washington.

Primary SIC and add'l.: 6035 6712

CIK No: 0001002682

Subsidiaries: Bank Holding Company Act, Federal Reserve Act, and transactions, Horizon Bank, Real Estate Development, Westward Financial Services

Officers: Lawrence V. Evans/Chmn., CEO, Pres./$417,897.00, Kelli J. Holz/VP/$110,786.00, Richard P. Jacobson/VP, Corp. Sec./$239,626.00, Dennis C. Joines/Dir., Exec. VP/$342,691.00, Terry Aiello/Loan Specialist - Ferndale, Blaine Offices, Tiffany Bergsma-Evans/Loan Specialist - Cornwall Office, Loren Adkins/Loan Specialist - Barkley Office, Jeremey Beck/Loan Specialist - Cornwall Office, Marjorie Lavalley/Loan Specialist - Meridian Office, Kelly Gustafson/Loan Specialist -

Lynden Office, Eileen Hebert/Loan Specialist - Anacortes Office, Holly Peterson/Loan Specialist - Burlington Office, Eve Brown/Loan Specialist - Mount Vernon Office, Terri Hemmann/Loan Specialist - Everett Office, Krista Geiger/Loan Specialist - Lynnwood Office, Edmonds Office, Marysville Office *(17 Officers included in Index)*

Directors: Lawrence V. Evans/Chmn., CEO, Pres., Dennis C. Joines/Dir., Exec. VP, Robert C. Diehl/Dir., Richard R. Haggen/Dir., Fred R. Miller/Dir., James A. Strengholt/Dir., Gary E. Goodman/Dir., Robert C. Tauscher/Dir.

Owners: Dennis C. Joines, Robert C. Diehl, Robert C. Tauscher, James A. Strengholt, Lawrence V. Evans/2.39%, Steven L. Hoekstra, Gary E. Goodman, Fred R. Miller/1.12%, Richard P. Jacobson, Richard R. Haggen, Kelli J. Holz, Insiders/5.76%

Financial Data: Fiscal Year End:03/31   Latest Annual Data: 03/31/2007

Year	Sales	Net Income
2007	$98,448,000	$19,028,000
2006	$76,287,000	$15,655,000
2005	$58,699,000	$13,063,000

Curr. Assets:	$52,838,000	Curr. Liab.:	$985,040,000		
Plant, Equip.:	$28,356,000	Total Liab.:	$1,146,472,000	Indic. Yr. Divd.:	NA
Total Assets:	$1,270,327,000	Net Worth:	$123,855,000	Debt/ Equity:	1.2834

Horizon Health Corp

2941 S Lake Vista Dr., Lewisville Tx, TX, 75067; *PH:* 1-972-420-8200; *http://* www.horz.com

General - Incorporation	DE	*Stock-* Price on:12/24/2007	NA
Employees	2,914	Stock Exchange	NA
Auditor	PricewaterhouseCoopers LLP	Ticker Symbol	NA
Stk Agt	JP Morgan Chase Bank, N.A.	Outstanding Shares	NA
Counsel	Strasburger & Price	E.P.S	NA
DUNS No.	60-859-0105	Shareholders	NA

Business: The group's principle activity is to provide diversified health care services. The group operates in four segments: mental health contract management services: provides services to general acute care hospitals. Physical rehabilitation contract management: provides acute physical therapy, rehabilitation services, skilled nursing services and outpatient rehabilitation programs. Specialized temporary nurse: provides its specialized temporary nurse staffing services on an on-call, twenty-four hour per day, seven days a week, basis. Employee assistance programs: assist in the early identification and resolution of productivity problems associated with behavioral conditions or other personal concerns of employees and their dependants. On 01-Apr-2004, the group acquired the assets of northern Indiana hospital. On 01-Jun-2004, the group acquired the assets of psh acquisition corporation.

Primary SIC and add'l.: 6324

CIK No: 0000935007

Subsidiaries: AHG Partnership, Delaware Investment Associates, LLC, Employee Assistance Services, Inc., Friends Behavioral Health System, LP, Friends GP, LLC, Health and Human Resource Center, Inc., HHC Augusta, Inc., HHC Berkeley, Inc., HHC Conway Investment, Inc., HHC Cooper City, Inc., HHC Delaware, Inc., HHC Focus Florida, Inc., HHC Indiana, Inc., HHC Kingwood Investment, LLC, HHC Oconee, Inc. 37 Subsidiaries included in the Index

Officers: Ken Newman/Chmn., CEO, Pres., Frank J. Baumann/Pres. - Hospital Services, Michael Saul/Pres. - Behavioral Health Contract Management Services, Cindy Sheriff/Pres. - EAP Services, John E. Pitts/CFO, Exec. VP - Finance, David K. Meyercord/Exec. VP - Administration, General Counsel, David K. White/COO, Pres., Donald W. Thayer/Exec. VP - Acquisitions, Development, Paula Taylor/Contact - Investor Relations

Directors: Ken Newman/Chmn., CEO, Pres., George E. Bello/Dir., Michael R. Bowlin/Dir., James E. Buncher/Dir., Robert A. Lefton/Dir., William H. Longfield/Dir., Thomas C. Smith/Dir.

Owners: George E. Bello/3.70%, William H. Longfield, Insiders/12.20%, Ken Newman/6.20%, Michael R. Bowlin, Thomas C. Smith, Eagle Asset Management,Inc./6.90%, David K. White, Frank J. Baumann, Fidelity Management& Research Company/5.80%, David K. Meyercord, John E. Pitts, Donald W. Thayer, The Burton Partnership, Limited Partnership/7.60%, James E. Buncher *(18 Owners included in Index)*

Horizon Lines Inc

4064 Colony Rd., Ste. 200, Charlotte, NC, 28211; *PH:* 1-704-973-7000; *Fax:* 1-704-973-7075; *http://* www.horizonlines.com; *Email:* investor.relations@horizonlines.com

General - Incorporation	DE	*Stock-* Price on:12/24/2007	$33.11
Employees	1,878	Stock Exchange	NYSE
Auditor	Ernst & Young LLP	Ticker Symbol	HRZ
Stk Agt	Bank of New York	Outstanding Shares	33,640,000
Counsel	NA	E.P.S.	$2.272
DUNS No.	NA	Shareholders	NA

Business: The groups principle activity is to acquire vehicles. The group operates from the United States. The groups quarterly revenue for September 2007 was 321.14 millions of USD.

Primary SIC and add'l.: 4731 4424 7372

CIK No: 0001302707

Subsidiaries: H-Lines Finance Holding Corp., HLH, LLC, Horizon Lines Holding Corp., Horizon Lines of Alaska, LLC, Horizon Lines of Guam, LLC, Horizon Lines of Puerto Rico, Inc., Horizon Lines Ventures, LLC, Horizon Lines Vessels, LLC, Horizon Lines, LLC, Horizon Services Group, LLC, S-L Distribution Service, LLC, Sea-Logix, LLC, SL Payroll Services, LLC

Officers: Charles G. Raymond/Chmn., CEO, Pres., John W. Handy/Exec. VP, Kenneth L. Privratsky/Sr. VP, GM - Alaska Division, Horizon Lines, LLC, Mark M. Urbania/Sr. VP - Finance, Administration, CFO, Brian W. Taylor/Pres. - Horizon Logistics, LLC, John V. Keenan/Pres. - Horizon Lines, LLC, Mar F. Labrador/VP, GM - Hawaii, Micronesia Division, Horizon Lines, LLC, Gabriel M. Serra/Sr. VP, GM - Puerto Rico Division, Horizon Lines, LLC, Robert S. Zuckerman/VP, General Counsel, Sec., Michael T. Avara/VP - Investor Relations, Treasurer

Directors: Charles G. Raymond/Chmn., CEO, Pres., Norman Y. Mineta/Dir., Dan A. Colussy/Dir., Francis Jungers/Dir., James G. Cameron/Dir., Ernie L. Danner/Dir., William J. Flynn/Dir., James W. Down/Dir., Admiral Clark/Dir., Alex J. Mandl/Dir., Thomas P. Storrs/Dir.

Owners: Insiders/9.20%, James Down, James G. Cameron, Trafelet & Company, LLC/7.80%, Mark M. Urbania/1.30%, Charles G. Raymond/3.00%, Norman Y. Mineta, Steinberg Asset Management, LLC/6.20%, John V. Keenan/1.60%, Brian W. Taylor, Francis Jungers, John K. Castle, Ernie L. Danner, William J. Flynn, Dan A. Colussy *(16 Owners included in Index)*

Financial Data: Fiscal Year End:12/24   Latest Annual Data: 12/24/2006

Year	Sales	Net Income
2006	$1,156,892,000	$72,357,000
2005	$1,096,156,000	-$18,321,000

Curr. Assets:	$210,462,000	**Curr. Liab.:**	$143,351,000		
Plant, Equip.:	$200,597,000	**Total Liab.:**	$775,559,000	**Indic. Yr. Divd.:**	$0.440
Total Assets:	$927,319,000	**Net Worth:**	$151,760,000	**Debt/ Equity:**	2.4206

Horizon Offshore Inc

2500 City W Blvd., Ste. 2200, Houston, TX, 77042; ***PH:*** 1-713-361-2600; ***Fax:*** 1-713-361-2690;
http:// www.horizonoffshore.com; ***Email:*** investorrelations@horizonoffshore.com

General - Incorporation	DE	**Stock** - Price on:12/24/2007	$19.48
Employees	770	Stock Exchange	NDQ
Auditor	Grant Thornton LLP	Ticker Symbol	HOFF
Stk Agt	Mellon Investor Services LLC	Outstanding Shares	32,680,000
Counsel	Jones Walker Waechter Et Al	E.P.S.	$0.89
DUNS No.	11-010-1557	Shareholders	NA

Business: The group's principal activity is to provide marine construction services to the offshore oil and gas industry in the U.S. Gulf of Mexico, Latin America, southeast Asia and west Africa. The group's fleet consists of thirteen vessels, twelve of which are currently operational. The primary services of the group include: installing pipelines; providing pipebury, hook-up and commissioning services; installing production platforms and other structures; disassembling and salvaging production platforms and other structures and performing pipe spooling services. The customers of the group in the U.S. Have primarily been the oil and gas companies operating on the U.S. Outer continental shelf.

Primary SIC and add'l.: 1629

CIK No: 0001051431

Subsidiaries: Affiliated Marine Contractors, Inc., Bayou Marine Contractors, Inc., ECH Offshore, S.de R.L. de C.V., Fleet Pipeline Services, Inc., Gulf Offshore Construction, Inc., HOC Offshore, S.de R.L. de C.V, HoriZen, LLC, Horizon Group L.D.C., Horizon Marine Construction, Horizon Marine Construction Ltd., Horizon Marine Contractors, Horizon Offshore Contractors, Horizon Offshore Contractors, Inc., Horizon Offshore Contractors, Ltd., Horizon Offshore International Ltd. 28 Subsidiaries included in the Index

Owners: JPMorgan Chase & Co./7.50%, Ken R. LeSuer, Insiders/1.80%, David W. Sharp, William B. Gibbens, Raymond L. Steele, Ronald D. Mogel, George G. Reuter, Charles O. Buckner, John T. Mills, Cumberland Associates LLC/6.90%

Financial Data: ***Fiscal Year End:***12/31 ***Latest Annual Data:*** 06/30/2007

Year	Sales	Net Income
2007	$117,351,000	-$6,235,000
2006	$547,289,000	$67,010,000
2005	$325,044,000	-$71,056,000

Curr. Assets:	$307,235,000	**Curr. Liab.:**	$102,712,000	**P/E Ratio:**	11.51
Plant, Equip.:	$197,409,000	**Total Liab.:**	$225,684,000	**Indic. Yr. Divd.:**	NA
Total Assets:	$523,019,000	**Net Worth:**	$297,335,000	**Debt/ Equity:**	0.3167

Hormel Foods Corp

1 Hormel Pl., Austin, MN, 55912; ***PH:*** 1-507-437-5007; ***Fax:*** 1-507-437-5129;
http:// www.hormel.com

General - Incorporation	DE	**Stock** - Price on:12/24/2007	$37.4
Employees	18,100	Stock Exchange	NYSE
Auditor	Ernst & Young LLP	Ticker Symbol	HRL
Stk Agt	Wells Fargo Bank, N.A.	Outstanding Shares	137,670,000
Counsel	James W. Cavanaugh	E.P.S.	$2.10
DUNS No.	00-614-7383	Shareholders	NA

Business: The group's principle activities include manufacturing and marketing meat and food products. The group operates through segments include Grocery Products, Refrigerated Foods, Jennie-O Turkey Store, Specialty Foods, and All Other. The group operates from United States. In the year 2006, the group acquired Valley Fresh, Inc. and Provena Foods Inc.

Primary SIC and add'l.: 2011 2032

CIK No: 0000048465

Subsidiaries: Alma Foods, LLC, Beijing Hormel Business Management Co. Ltd., Beijing Hormel Foods Co. Ltd., Campoco,Inc., Century Foods International, LLC, Champ, LLC, Clougherty Packing, LLC, Creative Contract Packaging, LLC, Dans Prize,Inc., Diamond Crystal Brands,Inc., Diamond Crystal Bremen, LLC, Diamond Crystal Sales, LLC, Dold Foods, LLC, Dubuque Foods, LLC, FJ Foodservice, LLC 50 Subsidiaries included in the Index

Officers: Jeffrey M. Ettinger/Chmn., CEO, Pres., William F. Snyder/Sr. VP - Supply Chain, Joe C. Swedberg/VP - Legislative Affairs, Marketing Services, Gary J. Ray/Dir., Pres. - Protein Business Units, Kurt F. Mueller/VP, Sr. VP - Business Planning, Consumer Product Sales, James N. Sheehan/VP, Controller, Daniel A. Hartzog/VP, Sr. VP - Sales, Consumer Product Sales, Larry J. Pfeil/VP - Engineering, Richard A. Bross/Group VP, VP - Hormel Foods International, James M. Splinter/VP - Marketing, Consumer Products, Refrigerated Foods, Jack Yeo/Contact - Media, Joan Hanson/Contact - Media, Fred D. Halvin/Dir. - Investor Relations, James W. Cavanaugh/Sr. VP, General Counsel, Ronald W. Fielding/Exec. VP - Grocery Products, Mergers, Acquisitions *(35 Officers included in Index)*

Directors: Jeffrey M. Ettinger/Chmn., CEO, Pres., Hugh C. Smith/Dir., Robert C. Nakasone/Dir., Ronald D. Pearson/Dir., Gary J. Ray/Dir., Pres. - Protein Business Units, Michael J. McCoy/60/Dir., Jody H. Feragen/Dir., CFO, Sr. VP, John R. Block/Dir., Peter E. Gillette/Dir., Luella G. Goldberg/Dir., Susan I. Marvin/Dir., Dakota A. Pippins/Dir., John G. Turner/Dir., Terrell K. Crews/Dir., John L. Morrison/Dir. *(16 Directors included in Index)*

Owners: Jeffrey M. Ettinger, Robert C. Nakasone, The Hormel Foundation/47.06%, Luella G. Goldberg, Dakota A. Pippins, Terrell K. Crews, Elsa A. Murano, Barclays Global Investors, N.A./5.38%, Hugh C. Smith, John G. Turner, Gary J. Ray, John L. Morrison, Richard A. Bross, Michael J. McCoy, Ronald W. Fielding *(19 Owners included in Index)*

Financial Data: ***Fiscal Year End:***10/30 ***Latest Annual Data:*** 10/29/2006

Year	Sales	Net Income
2006	$5,745,481,000	$286,139,000
2005	$5,413,997,000	$253,459,000
2004	$4,779,875,000	$231,663,000

Curr. Assets:	$1,041,084,000	**Curr. Liab.:**	$583,172,000	**P/E Ratio:**	17.81
Plant, Equip.:	$877,676,000	**Total Liab.:**	$1,247,830,000	**Indic. Yr. Divd.:**	$0.600
Total Assets:	$2,822,406,000	**Net Worth:**	$1,574,576,000	**Debt/ Equity:**	0.1825

Hornbeck Offshore Services Inc

103 NPk. Blvd., Ste. 300, Covington, LA, 70433; ***PH:*** 1-985-727-2000; ***Fax:*** 1-985-727-2006;
http:// www.hornbeckoffshore.com; ***Email:*** ir@hornbeckoffshore.com

General - Incorporation	DE	**Stock** - Price on:12/24/2007	$40.12
Employees	742	Stock Exchange	NYSE
Auditor	Ernst & Young LLP	Ticker Symbol	HOS
Stk Agt	Mellon Investor Services LLC	Outstanding Shares	25,820,000
Counsel	NA	E.P.S.	$3.23
DUNS No.	NA	Shareholders	NA

Business: The group's principal activity is to provide technologically advanced, new generation osvs serving the offshore oil and gas industry. The group primarily operates in United States gulf of Mexico and in selected international markets. The focus of our osv business is on complex exploration and production activities, which include deepwater, deep well and other logistically demanding projects. The group is also engaged in transportation of petroleum products through our tug and tank barge segment serving the energy industry, primarily in the northeastern United States and Puerto Rico.

Primary SIC and add'l.: 4412

CIK No: 0001131227

Subsidiaries: operates offshore supply vessels

Officers: Todd M. Hornbeck/Chmn., CEO, Pres./$2,056,987.00, James O. Harp/CFO, Exec. VP/$989,231.00, Carl G. Annessa/COO, Exec. VP/$1,042,152.00, John Burns/Contact, Ben Todd/Dir. - Fleet Operations, Steve Welch/Dir. - Business Development

Directors: Todd M. Hornbeck/Chmn., CEO, Pres., Bruce W. Hunt/Dir., Patricia B. Melcher/Dir., Bernie W. Stewart/Dir., Steven W. Krablin/Dir., Larry D. Hornbeck/Dir., David A. Trice/Dir.

Owners: Bernie W. Stewart, James O. Harp, David A. Trice, Todd M. Hornbeck/2.70%, FMR Corp/10.70%, William Herbert Hunt Trust Estate/8.00%, Larry D. Hornbeck, Steven W. Krablin, Carl G. Annessa, Insiders/5.20%, John S. Cook, Samuel A. Giberga, Patricia B. Melcher, Bruce W. Hunt

Financial Data: ***Fiscal Year End:***12/31 ***Latest Annual Data:*** 12/31/2006

Year	Sales	Net Income
2006	$274,551,000	$75,715,000
2005	$182,586,000	$37,443,000
2004	$132,261,000	-$2,483,000

Curr. Assets:	$526,987,000	**Curr. Liab.:**	$37,726,000	**P/E Ratio:**	13.88
Plant, Equip.:	$531,951,000	**Total Liab.:**	$643,507,000	**Indic. Yr. Divd.:**	NA
Total Assets:	$1,098,380,000	**Net Worth:**	$454,873,000	**Debt/ Equity:**	1.1579

Hospira Inc

275 N Field Dr., Lake Forest, IL, 60045; ***PH:*** 1-224-212-2000; ***Fax:*** 1-224-212-3350;
http:// www.hospira.com

General - Incorporation	DE	**Stock** - Price on:12/24/2007	$38.85
Employees	13,000	Stock Exchange	NYSE
Auditor	Deloitte & Touche LLP	Ticker Symbol	HSP
Stk Agt	Computershare Investor Services LLC	Outstanding Shares	156,620,000
Counsel	NA	E.P.S.	$0.81
DUNS No.	NA	Shareholders	NA

Business: The groups principle activities include developing, manufacturing and marketing of specialty injectable pharmaceuticals and medication delivery systems that deliver drugs and intravenous fluids. In the year 2007 the group acquired Mayne Pharma Limited. The group operates from United States.

Primary SIC and add'l.: 2834 3845 3841

CIK No: 0001274057

Subsidiaries: Hospira, Hospira Bahamas (Donegal) Corp., Hospira Bahamas (Ireland) Corp., Hospira Bahamas (Irish Manufacturing) Ltd., Hospira Bahamas International Holdings Ltd., Hospira Chile Limitada, Hospira Enterprises B.V., Hospira Fleet Services, LLC, Hospira GmbH, Hospira Healthcare B.V., Hospira Healthcare B.V., Representative Office, Hospira Healthcare Corporation, Hospira Healthcare EPE, Hospira Healthcare SPRL, Hospira Holding Ltd. 42 Subsidiaries included in the Index

Officers: Christopher B. Begley/Chmn., CEO - Hospira, Inc/$5,285,090.00, Terrence C. Kearney/COO/$2,316,768.00, Edward A. Ogunro/Sr. VP - Research & Development, R&D, Medical Affairs, Chief Scientific Officer/$1,727,975.00, Brian J. Smith/Sr. VP, General Counsel, Sec./$1,619,274.00, Thomas E. Werner/CFO, Sr. VP - Finance/$365,317.00

Directors: Christopher B. Begley/Chmn., CEO - Hospira, Inc, John C. Staley/65/Dir., Irving W. Bailey/65/Dir., Jacque J. Sokolov/52/Dir., Ronald A. Matricaria/64/Dir., Roger W. Hale/64/Dir.

Owners: Edward A. Ogunro, David A. Jones, Christopher B. Begley, Brian J. Smith, Jacque J. Sokolov, Ronald A. Matricaria, Insiders, Roger W. Hale, Thomas E. Werner, Irving W. Bailey, Terrence C. Kearney

Financial Data: ***Fiscal Year End:***12/31 ***Latest Annual Data:*** 12/31/2006

Year	Sales	Net Income
2006	$2,688,505,000	$237,679,000
2005	$2,626,696,000	$235,638,000
2004	$2,645,036,000	$301,552,000

Curr. Assets:	$1,522,890,000	**Curr. Liab.:**	$606,226,000	**P/E Ratio:**	47.96
Plant, Equip.:	$1,039,431,000	**Total Liab.:**	$1,486,498,000	**Indic. Yr. Divd.:**	NA
Total Assets:	$2,847,587,000	**Net Worth:**	$1,361,089,000	**Debt/ Equity:**	1.8449

Hospitality Properites Trust

400 Ctr. St., Newton, MA, 02458; ***PH:*** 1-617-964-8389; ***Fax:*** 1-617-969-5730;
http:// www.hptreit.com; ***Email:*** info@hptreit.com

General - Incorporation	MD	**Stock** - Price on:12/24/2007	$42.61
Employees	NA	Stock Exchange	NYSE
Auditor	Ernst & Young LLP	Ticker Symbol	HPT
Stk Agt	Wells Fargo Shareowner Services	Outstanding Shares	93,870,000
Counsel	Sullivan & Worcester LLP	E.P.S.	$2.14
DUNS No.	NA	Shareholders	NA

Business: The groups principle activity is to operate hotels. The group operates from the United States, Canada and Puerto Rico. The groups quarterly revenue for September 2007 was 334.31 millions of USD.

Primary SIC and add'l.: 6798

CIK No: 0000945394

Subsidiaries: Candlewood Jersey City Urban Renewal, L.L.C., Harbor Court Associates, LLC, HH HPT Suite Properties LLC, HH HPTCW II Properties LLC, HH HPTCY Properties LLC, HH HPTMI III Properties LLC, HH HPTRI Properties LLC, HH HPTWN Properties LLC, HH CW MA Realty Trust, HPT CW Overland Park LLC, HPT CW Properties Trust, HPT HSD Properties Trust, HPT IHG Canada Corporation, HPT IHG Canada Properties Trust, HPT IHG GA Properties LLC 39 Subsidiaries included in the Index

Officers: John G. Murray/COO, Pres./$104,752.00, Mark L. Kleifges/Treasurer, CFO/$94,060.00, Ethan S. Bornstein/VP, Tim Bonang/Mgr. - Investor Relations, Carlynn Finn/Investor Relations Analyst

Directors: William J. Sheehan/Dir., Barry M. Portnoy/Managing Trustee, Adam D. Portnoy/Managing Trustee, Frank J. Bailey/Trustee, John L. Harrington/Trustee, William A. Lamkin/Trustee

Owners: John L. Harrington, Barry M. Portnoy, Adam D. Portnoy, Barclays Global Investors, N.A./6.80%, The Vanguard Group, Inc./5.30%, William A. Lamkin, Frank J. Bailey, Capital Research and Management Company/6.20%, Ethan S. Bornstein, John G. Murray, Insiders, Mark L. Kleifges

Financial Data: *Fiscal Year End:* 12/31 *Latest Annual Data:* 12/31/2006

Year	Sales	Net Income
2006	$1,039,415,000	$169,039,000
2005	$834,412,000	$129,903,000
2004	$645,368,000	$127,091,000

Curr. Assets:	$580,619,000	**Curr. Liab.:**	$310,093,000		
Plant, Equip.:	$3,334,179,000	**Total Liab.:**	$1,509,923,000	**Indic. Yr. Divd.:**	$3.040
Total Assets:	$3,957,463,000	**Net Worth:**	$2,447,540,000	**Debt/ Equity:**	NA

Host Hotels & Resorts Inc

6903 Rockledge Dr., Ste. 1500, Bethesda, MD, 20817; *PH:* 1-240-744-1000; *Fax:* 1-240-744-5125; *http://* hosthotels.com; *Email:* ir@hosthotels.com

General - Incorporation	MD	**Stock**- Price on:12/24/2007	$23.75
Employees	229	Stock Exchange	NYSE
Auditor	KPMG LLP	Ticker Symbol	HST
Stk Agt	Computershare Trust Co	Outstanding Shares	522,050,000
Counsel	NA	E.P.S.	$1.15
DUNS No.	NA	Shareholders	NA

Business: The groups principle activity is to provide lodging services. In the year 2006, the group acquired five hotels. The group operates from the United States. The group's quarterly revenue for September 2007 was 1,206.00 millions of USD.

Primary SIC and add'l.: 6798 7011

CIK No: 0001070750

Subsidiaries: Airport Hotels LLC, Ameliatel, a Florida GP, Atlanta II Limited Partnership, Beachfront Properties, Inc., Benjamin Franklin Hotel, Inc., Braintree TPP LLC, BRE/Swiss L.L.C., Brookfield TPP LLC, Calgary Charlotte Holdings Company, Calgary Charlotte Partnership, CB Realty Sales, Inc., CCC CMBS Corporation, CCES Chicago LLC, CCFH Maui LLC, CCFS Atlanta LLC 396 Subsidiaries included in the Index

Officers: Christopher J. Nassetta/45/Dir., CEO, Pres./$13,119,630.00, Edward W. Walter/Dir., CEO, Pres./$7,046,792.00, James F. Risoleo/Exec. VP, Chief Investment Officer/$5,308,816.00, Minaz Abji/Exec. VP - Asset Management/$3,091,443.00, Elizabeth A. Abdoo/Exec. VP, General Counsel, Sec./$2,632,125.00, Gregory J. Larson/Exec. VP - Corporate Strategy, Fund Management, Larry K. Harvey/CFO, Exec. VP, Treasurer, Pamela K. Wagoner/Sr. VP - Human Resources, Brian G. MacNamara/Sr. VP, Corporate Controller, Matthew L. Richardson/Chief Development Officer, Sr. VP

Directors: Christopher J. Nassetta/45/Dir., CEO, Pres., Edward W. Walter/Dir., CEO, Pres., Richard E. Marriott/Chmn., Ann McLaughlin Korologos/Dir., Robert M. Baylis/Dir., Terence C. Golden/Dir., Judith A. McHale/Dir., John B. Morse/Dir.

Owners: Insiders/3.70%, Morgan Stanley/5.10%, The Vanguard Group, Inc./5.60%, John B. Morse, Ann McLaughlin Korologos, Edward W. Walter, Barclays Global Investors, NA/9.40%, Elizabeth A. Abdoo, Christopher J. Nassetta/0.40%, Richard E. Marriott/3.00%, Judith A. McHale, James F. Risoleo/0.10%, Wellington Management Company, LLP/6.70%, Terence C. Golden, Robert M. Baylis (16 Owners included in Index)

Financial Data: *Fiscal Year End:* 12/31 *Latest Annual Data:* 12/31/2006

Year	Sales	Net Income
2006	$4,888,000,000	$738,000,000
2005	$3,881,000,000	$166,000,000
2004	$3,640,000,000	NA

Curr. Assets:	$609,000,000	**Curr. Liab.:**	$243,000,000		
Plant, Equip.:	$10,780,000,000	**Total Liab.:**	$6,586,000,000	**Indic. Yr. Divd.:**	$0.800
Total Assets:	$11,808,000,000	**Net Worth:**	$5,222,000,000	**Debt/ Equity:**	1.2181

Hosting Site Networks Inc

32 Poplar Pl., Fanwood, NJ, 10017; *PH:* 1-973-652-6333

General - Incorporation	DE	**Stock**- Price on:12/24/2007	NA
Employees	NA	Stock Exchange	OTC
Auditor	Most & Company, LLP	Ticker Symbol	HSNI
Stk Agt	Stock Transfer & Trust Co.	Outstanding Shares	NA
Counsel	NA	E.P.S.	NA
DUNS No.	NA	Shareholders	NA

Business: The groups principal activity is to provide Internet services. Services of the group include web hosting, web consulting and electronic mail. The group operates from the United States.

Primary SIC and add'l.: 7389

CIK No: 0001157817

Subsidiaries: HSN (NJ), INC

Owners: Scott Vicari/41.20%, Insiders/41.50%, Matthew Sebal, Ralph Brown

Hot Topic Inc

18305 E San Jose Ave., City of Industry, CA, 91748; *PH:* 1-626-839-4681; *Fax:* 1-626-839-4686; *http://* www.hottopic.com

General - Incorporation	CA	**Stock**- Price on:12/24/2007	$10.85
Employees	2,762	Stock Exchange	NDQ
Auditor	Ernst & Young LLP	Ticker Symbol	HOTT
Stk Agt	Wells Fargo Shareowner Services	Outstanding Shares	44,250,000
Counsel	Cooley Godward LLP	E.P.S.	$0.32
DUNS No.	60-322-6986	Shareholders	NA

Business: The group's principal activity is to offer a selection of music-licensed and music-influenced apparel, accessories and gift items for young men and women principally between the ages of 12 and 22. The group is a mall-based specialty retailer operating the hot topic and torrid store concepts. Torrid offers a selection of apparel, lingerie, shoes and accessories centered around various lifestyles for plus-size females between the ages of 15 and 29. At 31-Mar-2004, the group operated 513 hot topic stores in 49 states throughout the United States and Puerto Rico and 52 torrid stores in 22 states.

Primary SIC and add'l.: 5611 5699 5661 5947

CIK No: 0001017712

Subsidiaries: Hot Topic Administration, Inc., Hot Topic Merchandising, Inc., Hot Topic Tennessee, Inc., hottopic.com, Inc.

Officers: Elizabeth McLaughlin/47/Dir., CEO/$1,759,634.00, Jerry Cook/Pres., John Neppl/VP - Real Estate, Construction, Chris Kearns/Sr. VP, General Counsel, Sec., Darrell Kinsley/VP - Store Design, Visual Merchandising, James McGinty/CFO/$549,330.00, Tom Beauchamp/CIO, Sr. VP, Maria Comfort/Sr. VP, Chief Merchandising Officer/$586,421.00, Robin Elledge/Sr. VP - Human Resources, Chris Daniel/VP, Torrid General Merchandise Mgr./$917,295.00, Ed Gusman/VP - Hot Topic Store Operations, Lori Smith/VP - Torrid Store Operations, Mike Yoshida/VP - Finance, Megan Hall/Mgr. - Investor Relations, Gerald Cook/55/Pres./$843,501.00 (21 Officers included in Index)

Directors: Elizabeth McLaughlin/47/Dir., CEO, Bruce Quinnell/Chmn., Andy Schuon/Dir., Betsy McLaughlin/Dir., Kathleen Mason/Dir., Scott Hedrick/Dir., Cynthia Cohen/Dir., Corrado Federico/Dir.

Owners: Kathleen Mason, Christopher Daniel, Andrew Schuon, Corrado Federico, Cynthia Cohen, James McGinty, Maria Comfort, Scott W. Hedrick, Bruce Quinnell, Gerald Cook, Insiders/7.50%

Financial Data: *Fiscal Year End:* 01/28 *Latest Annual Data:* 2/3/2007

Year	Sales	Net Income
2007	$751,558,000	$13,626,000
2006	$725,142,000	$22,419,000
2005	$656,468,000	$39,673,000

Curr. Assets:	$147,051,000	**Curr. Liab.:**	$55,784,000	**P/E Ratio:**	33.91
Plant, Equip.:	$166,726,000	**Total Liab.:**	$96,814,000	**Indic. Yr. Divd.:**	NA
Total Assets:	$318,271,000	**Net Worth:**	$221,457,000	**Debt/ Equity:**	NA

Hotel Outsource Mgmt Intl Inc

80 Wall St., Ste 815, New York, NY, 10005; *PH:* 1-212-344-1600

General - Incorporation	DE	**Stock**- Price on:12/24/2007	$0.33
Employees	15	Stock Exchange	OTC
Auditor	Kingery & Crouse P.A	Ticker Symbol	HOUM
Stk Agt	Atlas Stock Transfer Corp	Outstanding Shares	40,000,000
Counsel	Staley, Okada & Partners	E.P.S.	$0.01
DUNS No.	NA	Shareholders	NA

Business: The group's principle activity is to provide hotel outsourcing and management services. The group also provides consulting services. The group's specific customers include Hyatt Regency Boston, Sheraton Diana Majestic Milano, Radisson Golden Sands, ArabellaSheraton Cape Town and Carlton Hotel Tel Aviv. The group operates from United States, Europe, South Africa, Australia and Israel.

Primary SIC and add'l.: NA

CIK No: 0001174814

Subsidiaries: HOMI - Malta, HOMI Europe SARL, HOMI Israel Ltd., HOMI South Africa (Proprietary) Limited South Africa, Hotel Outsource Services, Inc.

Owners: Ariel Almog/5.90%, Jacob Ronnel/6.00%, Avraham Bahry/8.90%, Rodia Mihali/6.00%, Yoav Ronnen/0.06%, Blackborn Financial Consulting (1999) LTD./9.00%, Insiders/20.90%

Financial Data: *Fiscal Year End:* 12/31 *Latest Annual Data:* 12/31/2006

Year	Sales	Net Income
2006	$3,261,000	-$303,000
2005	$2,814,000	-$128,000
2004	$1,647,000	-$732,000

Curr. Assets:	$1,572,000	**Curr. Liab.:**	$1,053,000	**P/E Ratio:**	33.00
Plant, Equip.:	$4,327,000	**Total Liab.:**	$2,328,000	**Indic. Yr. Divd.:**	NA
Total Assets:	$7,738,000	**Net Worth:**	$4,951,000	**Debt/ Equity:**	0.2217

House of Brussels Chocolates Inc

One Riverway, Ste 1700, Houston, TX, 77056; *PH:* 1-713-599-0800; *Fax:* 1-713-622-1937; *http://* www.brusselschocolates.com

General - Incorporation	NV	**Stock**- Price on:12/24/2007	$0.004
Employees	NA	Stock Exchange	OTC
Auditor	Ham, Langston & Brezina LLP	Ticker Symbol	HBSL
Stk Agt	American Stock Transfer & Trust Co.	Outstanding Shares	NA
Counsel	NA	E.P.S.	NA
DUNS No.	NA	Shareholders	NA

Business: The group's principal activity is to manufacture and distribute gourmet high quality belgian chocolate products. It operates through its licensed retail outlets and through a wholesale network in Canada, the United States and overseas. It manufactures all chocolate products at its high-quality manufacturing facility in vancouver, british columbia. Its main product is hedgehog, which has more than 100 products based on this. Other products include an assortment of tourist oriented truffles including some made with genuine maple syrup and some with Canadian ice wine, fine quality chocolate bars made in several distinct flavors, and low-carbohydrate chocolate bars and truffles. On 30-Jul-2004, the group acquired debas chocolate inc.

Primary SIC and add'l.: 2066

CIK No: 0001072367

Subsidiaries: Candy Jar, Inc., Chocomed Inc, DeBas Chocolates, Inc.

Financial Data: *Fiscal Year End:* 04/30 *Latest Annual Data:* 4/30/2005

Year	Sales	Net Income
2005	$7,492,000	-$4,855,000
2004	$2,481,000	-$3,768,000
2003	$3,047,000	-$489,000

Curr. Assets:	$4,086,000	Curr. Liab.:	$3,448,000		
Plant, Equip.:	$3,391,000	Total Liab.:	$3,854,000	Indic. Yr. Divd.:	NA
Total Assets:	$8,881,000	Net Worth:	$5,027,000	Debt/ Equity:	0.2171

House of Taylor Jewelry Inc

9200 Sunset Blvd., Ste. 425, West Hollywood, CA, 90069; *PH:* 1-310-860-2660;
Fax: 1-310-860-2661; *http://* www.hotj.com; *Email:* investor@pondel.com

General - Incorporation .... NV
Employees 15
Auditor .... Stonefield Josephson, Inc.
Stk Agt......................... U.S. Stock Transfer Corp
Counsel... NA
DUNS No.. NA

Stock- Price on:12/24/2007 .... $1.48
Stock Exchange.................................. NDQ
Ticker Symbol.................................... HOTJ
Outstanding Shares 40,340,000
E.P.S.. -$0.21
Shareholders..................................... NA

Business: The groups principle activities include designing and marketing jewelry products.The products of the group include earrings, rings, bracelets, necklaces, brooches, bangles and charms. The group products sold under the trade names Elizabeth(R), ET(R), House of Taylor Jewelry(R), Kathy Ireland Jewelry(R) and Mirabelle(R). The group operates from the United States. The group's quarterly revenue for September 2007 was 4.88 millions of USD.

Primary SIC and add'l.: 5094 3911

CIK No: 0001069249

Subsidiaries: Global Jewelry Concepts, Inc, Tech Line Jewelry, Inc

Officers: Jack Abramov/Chmn., CEO, Pres./$274,482.00, Monty Abramov/Dir., Exec. VP, Design Dir., Sec./$272,294.00, Bob Rankin/CFO

Directors: Jack Abramov/Chmn., CEO, Pres., Monty Abramov/Dir., Exec. VP, Design Dir., Sec., Larry Chimerine/Non Exec. Dir., Frank M. Devine/Non Exec. Dir., Peter Mainstain/Non Exec. Dir., John Moretz/Non Exec. Dir.

Owners: Special Situations Private Equity Fund LP/7.50%, Jack Abramov/8.30%, Insiders/17.20%, Sandbox Jewelry, LLC/15.40%, Rachel Abramov, Trustee/4.80%, Frank M. Devine, Interplanet Productions, Limited/35.10%, Larry Chimerine, Monty Abramov/8.30%

Financial Data: *Fiscal Year End:*12/31 *Latest Annual Data:* 12/31/2006

Year	Sales	Net Income
2006	$31,793,000	-$8,353,000
2005	NA	-$85,000

Curr. Assets:	$44,000	Curr. Liab.:	$91,000		
Plant, Equip.:	NA	Total Liab.:	$91,000	Indic. Yr. Divd.:	NA
Total Assets:	$44,000	Net Worth:	-$47,000	Debt/ Equity:	1.1052

HouseRaising Inc

11 Acland Cres, Toronto, ON, M1C 1N5; *PH:* 1-416-287-9554; *Fax:* 1-416-287-9554;
http:// www.houseraising.com; *Email:* info@houseraising.com

General - Incorporation .... NC
Employees .... NA
Auditor .... Traci J. Anderson, CPA
Stk Agt............... Florida Atlantic Stock Transfer, Inc.
Counsel... NA
DUNS No.. NA

Stock- Price on:12/24/2007 .... $0.17
Stock Exchange.................................. OTC
Ticker Symbol.................................... HRAI
Outstanding Shares 52,070,000
E.P.S.. -$0.09
Shareholders..................................... NA

Business: The group's principal activity is to provide installation services of structured wiring capacities to new home builders. It installs structured wiring capacities into newly constructed homes and retrofitting existing homes with the same integrated technology components and systems. The integrated technology and systems include security systems, Internet technology, satellite television delivery systems, indoor/outdoor lighting, solar energy systems and entertainment/communication technology.

Primary SIC and add'l.: 1731

CIK No: 0001168940

Subsidiaries: HouseRaising of Asheville, LLC, HouseRaising of Charleston, LLC, HouseRaising of Columbia, LLC, HouseRaising of Greater Charlotte, LLC, HouseRaising of Greenville, LLC, HouseRaising of Myrtle Beach, LLC, HouseRaising of the Gulf Coast, LLC, HouseRaising of Wilmington, LLC, HouseRaisingAcademy, LLC, HouseRaisingManagement, LLC, HouseRaisingMembership, LLC, HouseRaisingUSA, LLC

Officers: Gregory J. Wessling/Chmn., CEO, Kristy M. Carriker/Co - Founder, Dir., Sr. VP, Grant S. Neerings/Dir., CTO, Pres. - Houseraisingacademy, Richard A. Von Gnechten/CFO

Directors: Gregory J. Wessling/Chmn., CEO, Kristy M. Carriker/Co - Founder, Dir., Sr. VP, Robert M. Burroughs/Dir., Daniel S. Fogel/Dir., Grant S. Neerings/Dir., CTO, Pres. - Houseraisingacademy, James Oconnor/Dir., Elizabeth Ann McLemore/Dir.

Owners: Gregory J. Wessling, Linda W. McLemore, Linda W. McLemore, Robert V. McLemore Revoc. Trust, Estate of Robert V. McLemore, Estate of Robert V. McLemore, Gregory J. Wessling, Gregory J. Wessling, Robert V. McLemore Revoc. Trust, Estate of Robert V. McLemore

Financial Data: *Fiscal Year End:*12/31 *Latest Annual Data:* 12/31/2006

Year	Sales	Net Income
2006	$1,249,000	-$2,999,000
2005	$534,000	-$4,121,000
2004	$191,000	-$927,000

Curr. Assets:	$888,000	Curr. Liab.:	$4,795,000		
Plant, Equip.:	$254,000	Total Liab.:	$4,795,000	Indic. Yr. Divd.:	NA
Total Assets:	$14,919,000	Net Worth:	$10,125,000	Debt/ Equity:	NA

HouseValues Inc

11332 NE 122nd Way, Kirkland, WA, 98034; *PH:* 1-425-952-5500; *Fax:* 1-425-952-5809;
http:// www.housevalues.com; *Email:* info@housevalues.com

General - Incorporation .... WA
Employees 542
Auditor .... KPMG LLP
Stk Agt .... Mellon Investor Services LLC
Counsel .... Perkins Coie LLP
DUNS No.. NA

Stock- Price on:12/24/2007 .... $4.65
Stock Exchange.................................. NDQ
Ticker Symbol.................................... SOLD
Outstanding Shares 24,580,000
E.P.S.. -$0.31
Shareholders..................................... NA

Business: The groups principle activity is to provide comprehensive set of marketing and business management tools design. The products of the group include The Loan Page, JustListed Connect, HouseValue and Showcase. The group products sold under the trade name HouseValues(R) JustListed(R) and HomePages(TM). Customers served by the group include local real estate agents. The groups operates through two segments namely real estate and mortgage. In the year 2005, the group acquired The Loan Page, Inc. The group operates from the United States. The group's quarterly revenue for September 2007 was 13.80 millions of USD.

Primary SIC and add'l.: 7375 7379 7389

CIK No: 0001298978

Subsidiaries: FastStart Real Estate Services (California), Inc., FastStart Real Estate Services (Canada) Corporation, FastStart Real Estate Services, LLC, HouseValues Paymaster, LLC, HouseValues, LLC, Soar Solutions, Inc., The Loan Page, Inc.

Officers: Ian Morris/Dir., CEO, Pres., Barry Allen/CFO, Exec. VP - Operations, Mary Reeder/CTO, Jacqueline L. Davidson/VP - Finance, Ken Hansen/VP - Sales, Jill Maguire-Ward/VP - Human Resources, Richard Goebel/Chief Marketing Officer

Directors: Pete M. Higgins/Chmn., And Capital/Dir., Jon W. Gacek/Dir., Nicolas J. Hanauer/Dir.

Owners: Insiders/20.40%, Frank M. Higgins/5.60%, Nicolas J. Hanauer/6.30%, Jon W. Gacek, Thomas W. Smith/10.50%, Jacqueline L. Davidson, Ian Morris/4.00%, Gregg I. Eskenazi, Mark S. Powell/4.20%, Clayton W. Lewis, LMM, LLC/16.30%, Richard A. Mendenhall, Morgan Stanley/17.10%

Financial Data: *Fiscal Year End:*12/31 *Latest Annual Data:* 12/31/2006

Year	Sales	Net Income
2006	$98,243,000	-$3,138,000
2005	$86,710,000	$14,983,000
2004	$47,691,000	$7,458,000

Curr. Assets:	$83,836,000	Curr. Liab.:	$12,873,000		
Plant, Equip.:	$11,469,000	Total Liab.:	$15,709,000	Indic. Yr. Divd.:	NA
Total Assets:	$101,362,000	Net Worth:	$85,653,000	Debt/ Equity:	NA

Houston American Energy Corp

801 Travis St., Ste. 2020, Houston, TX, 77002; *PH:* 1-713-222-6966; *Fax:* 1-713-222-6440;
http:// www.houstonamericanenergy.com

General - Incorporation .... DE
Employees 2
Auditor .... Thomas Leger & Co. LLP
Stk Agt .... Atlas Stock Transfer Corp
Counsel... NA
DUNS No.. NA

Stock- Price on:12/24/2007 .... $5.08
Stock Exchange.................................. NDQ
Ticker Symbol.................................... HUSA
Outstanding Shares 27,820,000
E.P.S.. -$0.017
Shareholders..................................... NA

Business: The groups principle activities include exploring and producing oil and natural gas. The group operates from the Gulf region of the United States. The groups quarterly revenue for September 2007 was 1.17 millions of USD.

Primary SIC and add'l.: 1381 1382 1311 1321

CIK No: 0001156041

Officers: John F. Terwilliger/Chmn., CEO, Pres./$267,500.00, Norman T. Reynolds/Legal Counsel, Michelle Stojanik/Administrative Mgr., James J. Jacobs/CFO/$276,846.00

Directors: John F. Terwilliger/Chmn., CEO, Pres., Lee Tawes/Dir., Edwin C. Broun/55/Dir., Stephen P. Hartzell/Dir., John Boylan/Dir., Orrie Lee Tawes/60/Dir.

Owners: GLG Partners LP/5.10%, Northeast Securities, Inc./9.00%, Jay Jacobs, John Terwilliger/30.70%, Insiders/46.90%, Edwin Broun/3.70%, Lee O. Tawes/12.10%, Stephen Hartzell, John Boylan

Financial Data: *Fiscal Year End:*12/31 *Latest Annual Data:* 12/31/2006

Year	Sales	Net Income
2006	$3,203,000	-$512,000
2005	$2,875,000	-$502,000
2004	$1,182,000	$115,000

Curr. Assets:	$14,734,000	Curr. Liab.:	$532,000		
Plant, Equip.:	$5,248,000	Total Liab.:	$571,000	Indic. Yr. Divd.:	NA
Total Assets:	$19,986,000	Net Worth:	$19,415,000	Debt/ Equity:	NA

Houston Wire & Cable Company

10201 N Loop E, Houston, TX, 77029; *PH:* 1-713-609-2100; *Fax:* 1-713-609-2101;
http:// www.houwire.com

General - Incorporation .... DE
Employees 293
Auditor .... Ernst & Young LLP
Stk Agt ..... American Stock Transfer & Trust Co.
Counsel.............................. Schiff-Hardin
DUNS No.. NA

Stock- Price on:12/24/2007 .... $28.67
Stock Exchange.................................. NDQ
Ticker Symbol.................................... HWCC
Outstanding Shares 20,930,000
E.P.S.. $1.54
Shareholders..................................... NA

Business: The groups principal activity is to distribute wire and cable services. The groups services include custom color striping, full extranet capabilities and cable selection system. The products of the group include continuous armor, instrumentation and thermocouple, medium voltage, interlocked armor, and flexible and portable cord. The group products sold under the trade names LifeGuard(TM), DataGuard(R) and Houwire(R). Specific customers of the group include Border States Electric Supply, HD Supply, Inc, Consolidated Electrical Distributors, Inc. and Mayer Electric Supply Company, Inc. The group operates from the United States. The sale of the group for the year 2006 was $323,467 (thousands).

Primary SIC and add'l.: 4236 5063

CIK No: 0001356949

Subsidiaries: Advantage Wire & Cable and Cable Management Services Inc, HWC Wire & Cable Company

Officers: Charles A. Sorrentino/Dir., CEO, Pres., Richard Elwell/Regional Mgr. - Tampa, Florida, Nicol G. Graham/CFO, Treasurer, Sec., Eric W. Davis/VP, Controller, Ken Oakes/Regional Mgr. - Coatesville, Pennsylvania, Brian Domblesky/Distribution Center Mgr. - Coatesville, Pennsylvania, Phil Mitchell/Regional Mgr. - Kent, Washington, Mike Aders/Distribution Center Mgr. - Kent, Washington, Eric Blankenship/Region VP - Houston, Texas, Larry Scott/Region Distribution Center

Mgr. - Houston, Texas, Dave Cathcart/Regional Mgr. - Norwalk, California, Bill Bouldin/Region Distribution Center Mgr. - Norwalk, California, Marcus Jones/Region VP - Charlotte, North Carolina, Bill Ferguson/Regional Mgr. - Charlotte, North Carolina, Dave Campbell/Warehouse Mgr. - Charlotte, North Carolina *(22 Officers included in Index)*

Directors: Charles A. Sorrentino/Dir., CEO, Pres., Peter M. Gotsch/Chmn., Ian Stewart Farwell/Dir., Stewart I. Farwell/66/Dir., Robert G. Hogan/Dir., Scott L. Thompson/Dir., William H. Sheffield/Dir., Wilson B. Sexton/Dir.

Owners: Peter M. Gotsch/37.90%, Wilson B. Sexton, Robert G. Hogan, Stewart I. Farwell, Nicol G. Graham, Code, Hennessy& SimmonsII,L.P./37.90%, Wells Fargo and Company/9.00%, Gilder, Gagnon, Howe&Co.,LLC/5.10%, Insiders/46.20%, Charles A. Sorrentino/7.20%

Financial Data: Fiscal Year End:12/31 Latest Annual Data: 12/31/2006

Year	Sales	Net Income
2006	$323,467,000	$30,674,000
2005	$213,957,000	$12,514,000
2004	$172,723,000	$4,809,000

Curr. Assets:	$110,072,000	Curr. Liab.:	$23,131,000		
Plant, Equip.:	$2,973,000	Total Liab.:	$35,190,000	Indic. Yr. Divd.:	$0.300
Total Assets:	$116,864,000	Net Worth:	$81,674,000	Debt/ Equity:	0.0421

Hovnanian Enterprises Inc

110 W Front St., Red Bank, NJ, 07701; *PH:* 1-732-225-4001; *Fax:* 1-732-747-6835; *http://* www.khov.com

General - Incorporation	DE	**Stock**- Price on:12/24/2007	$19.08
Employees	6,239	Stock Exchange	NYSE
Auditor	Ernst & Young LLP	Ticker Symbol	HOV
Stk Agt	National City Bank	Outstanding Shares	62,200,000
Counsel	Simpson Thacher & Bartlett LLP	E.P.S	-$2.09
DUNS No	04-665-0388	Shareholders	NA

Business: The groups principle activities include designing, constructing, marketing single-family detached homes. The group also provide financing fiancing and home design galleries. The group operates from United States.

Primary SIC and add'l.: 6552 6361 1531 6163

CIK No: 0000357294

Subsidiaries: 12th Street Residential, Ltd., 77 Hudson Street Joint Development, LLC, Alford, LLC, Arrow Properties, Inc., Brightbeach Development, Ltd., Brightchase, Ltd., Brighton Homes at Walden Management, LLC, Brighton Homes at Walden, Ltd., Cambridge Mortgage Company, LLC, Cobblestone Square Developments, LLC, Dulles Coppermine, LLC, Eastern Title Agency, Inc., Edison Contract Services, LLC, Founders Title Agency of Maryland, LLC, Founders Title Agency, Inc. 536 Subsidiaries included in the Index

Officers: Ara K. Hovnanian/Dir., CEO, Pres., Paul W. Buchanan/Sr. VP, Corporate Controller, Larry J. Sorsby/Dir., CFO, Exec. VP, Robyn T. Mingle/Sr. VP - Human Resources, Peter S. Reinhart/Sr. VP, General Counsel, Geaton A. Decesaris/Pres. - Hovnanian Land Investment Group, Kevin C. Hake/Sr. VP - Finance, Treasurer, Mark S. Hodges/Sr. VP - Corporate Operations, John F. Ulen/CIO, VP, Michael P. Kehoe/Pres. - Eastern Title Agency, Affiliated Title Agencies, Dan A. Klinger/Pres. - K Hovnanian American Mortgage, LLC, Nicholas Pappas/Region Pres. - Southern California Coastal Region, Larry Young/Region Pres. - Northern California Region, Jim Rex/Region Pres. - Southern California Inland Region, Thomas J. Pellerito/Group Pres. *(18 Officers included in Index)*

Directors: Ara K. Hovnanian/Dir., CEO, Pres., Kevork S. Hovnanian/Chmn., John J. Robbins/Dir., Larry J. Sorsby/Dir., CFO, Exec. VP, Edward A. Kangas/Dir., Stephen D. Weinroth/Dir., Robert B. Coutts/Dir., Joseph A. Marengi/Dir.

Owners: Paul W. Buchanan/0.20%, Stephen D. Weinroth, Larry J. Sorsby, Robert B. Coutts, Insiders/90.70%, Kevin C. Hake/0.10%, EARNEST Partners, L.L.C./18.40%, FMR Corp./13.50%, Edward A. Kangas/0.10%, Kevork S. Hovnanian/73.60%, Joseph A. Marengi, Tontine Management, L.L.C./8.40%, John J. Robbins/0.10%, Ara K. Hovnanian/7.90%, Kevork S. Hovnanian/18.20% *(18 Owners included in Index)*

Financial Data: Fiscal Year End:10/31 Latest Annual Data: 10/31/2006

Year	Sales	Net Income
2006	$6,148,235,000	$149,533,000
2005	$5,348,417,000	$471,847,000
2004	$4,160,403,000	$348,681,000

Curr. Assets:	$4,481,313,000	Curr. Liab.:	$830,599,000		
Plant, Equip.:	$110,704,000	Total Liab.:	$3,405,387,000	Indic. Yr. Divd.:	NA
Total Assets:	$5,480,035,000	Net Worth:	$1,942,163,000	Debt/ Equity:	1.4344

Howard Bancorp MD

6011 University Blvd, Ellicott City, MD, 21043; *PH:* 1-410-750-0020; *Fax:* 1-410-750-8588; *http://* www.howardbank.com

General - Incorporation	MD	**Stock**- Price on:12/24/2007	$15
Employees	NA	Stock Exchange	OTC
Auditor	NA	Ticker Symbol	HBMD
Stk Agt	Registrar & Transfer Co	Outstanding Shares	NA
Counsel	NA	E.P.S	NA
DUNS No	NA	Shareholders	NA

Business: The group's principle activity is to provide banking services, The group also provides online banking services. The group operates from United States.

Primary SIC and add'l.: 6712

CIK No: 0001390162

Officers: Mary Ann Scully/Chmn., CEO, Pres., Paul G. Brown/Exec. VP, Charles E. Schwabe/Exec. VP, Sec., George C. Coffman/Exec. VP, Treasurer - Investor Relations Contact, Michele Healy/Mgr. - Ellicott City, Snowden River Branch, Howard Bank, Ana Liesch/Assist. Mgr. - Ellicott City, Snowden River Branch, Howard Bank, Marc Lee/Mgr. - Laurel, Maple Lawn Branch, Howard Bank, Frances Blyther/Assist. Mgr. - Laurel, Maple Lawn Branch, Howard Bank

Directors: Mary Ann Scully/Chmn., CEO, Pres., Steven W. Sachs/Dir., Robert N. Meyers/Dir., Richard H. Pettingill/Dir., Richard B. Talkin/Dir., Richard G. Arnold/Dir., Andrew E. Clark/Dir., Martha A. Clark/Dir., Bernaldo J. Dancel/Dir., Robert J. Hartson/Dir., John M. Kingsmore/Dir., Paul I. Latta/Dir., Kenneth C. Lundeen/Dir.

HPL Technologies Inc

2033 Gateway Pl., Ste. 400, San Jose, CA, 95110; *PH:* 1-408-437-1466; *http://* www.synopsys.com

General - Incorporation	DE	**Stock**- Price on:12/24/2007	$26.66
Employees	5,130	Stock Exchange	NA
Auditor	PricewaterhouseCoopers LLP	Ticker Symbol	NA
Stk Agt	NA	Outstanding Shares	143,360,000
Counsel. Heller Ehrman White & McAuliffe LLP		E.P.S	$0.56
DUNS No	NA	Shareholders	NA

Business: The group's principal activity is to provide yield optimization and productivity improvement solutions that enable semiconductor and flat panel display producers to enhance the efficiency. The software solutions integrate data sets from the process technology development, design, fabrication and test stages of the product development process. Its yield optimization solution consists of a software platform called yield director (TM) and numerous software modules, which are sold individually or in pre-configured groups. The modules include equipment commonality analysis, wafer zonal analysis and data mining.

Primary SIC and add'l.: 7372 7378

CIK No: 0001121980

Subsidiaries: Defect & Yield Management, Inc., FabCentric, Inc., Heuristic Physics Laboratories, Inc., HPL International Ltd., HPL Japan KK, HPL Technologies Private Limited, HPL Texas, Inc., HPL, Taiwan Inc., HPLA Limited Liability Company, TestChip Technologies, Inc.

Financial Data: Fiscal Year End:03/31 Latest Annual Data: 10/31/2006

Year	Sales	Net Income
2006	$1,095,560,000	$24,742,000
2005	$991,931,000	-$15,478,000
2004	$1,092,104,000	$74,337,000

Curr. Assets:	$894,490,000	Curr. Liab.:	$871,096,000		
Plant, Equip.:	$140,660,000	Total Liab.:	$994,655,000	Indic. Yr. Divd.:	NA
Total Assets:	$2,157,822,000	Net Worth:	$1,163,167,000	Debt/ Equity:	NA

HQ Sustainable Maritime Industries Inc

Ste. 788, Melbourne Towers 1511 3rd Ave., Seattle, WA, 98101; *PH:* 1-206-621-9888; *Fax:* 1-206-621-0318; *http://* www.hqfish.com; *Email:* sporns@hqfish.com

General - Incorporation	DE	**Stock**- Price on:12/24/2007	NA
Employees	400	Stock Exchange	AMEX
Auditor	Rotenberg & Co. LLP	Ticker Symbol	HQS
Stk Agt	American Stock Transfer & Trust Co.	Outstanding Shares	NA
Counsel	NA	E.P.S	$0.441
DUNS No	NA	Shareholders	NA

Business: The group's principle activity is to provide high quality aquatic products through an integrated business of aquaculture.this is done through cooperative supply agreements, ocean product harvesting and processing and sales of farm bred and ocean harvested aquatic products. It covers value added key areas along the production chain from a bio-secure and stable supply of tilapia and shrimp under stringently monitored conditions, processed in accordance with internationally recognised standards of hygiene. On 31-Aug-2004, the group acquired hainan jiahua marine bio-products company limited. The group's quarterly revenue for Sep'07 was 15.78 millions of USD.

Primary SIC and add'l.: 0919 0273

CIK No: 0000857073

Subsidiaries: Hainan Quebec Ocean Fishing Co. Ltd, HQ Sustainable Maritime Marketing Inc, Jade Profit Investment Limited, Jiahua Marine Bio-Products Company Limited, Sealink Wealth Limited

Officers: Norbert Sporns/53/Dir., CEO, Pres./$268,340.00, Lillian Wang Li/50/Chmn., Sec./$328,840.00, Qun Jie Tang/38/Chief Accountant, Wang Fu Hai/63/Dir., Chief Accounting, Finance Officer, Jie Liu/44/Plant Mgr., William Su/39/Compliance Mgr. - International Sales Liaison, Harry Wang Hua/44/Dir., COO/$242,000.00, He Jian Bo/40/Mgr. - Finance Department, Jean-Pierre Dallaire/58/CFO, Financial Controller/$179,565.00, Trond Ringstad/40/Exec. VP - Sales, Marketing/$62,500.00

Directors: Norbert Sporns/53/Dir., CEO, Pres., Lillian Wang Li/50/Chmn., Sec., Wang Fusheng/70/Honorary Chmn., Harry Wang Hua/44/Dir., COO, Wang Fu Hai/63/Dir., Chief Accounting, Finance Officer, Jacques Vallee/55/Dir., Fred Bild/70/Dir., Daniel Too/57/Dir., Joseph I. Emas/53/Dir., Andrew Intrater/45/Dir.

Owners: Insiders, Daniel Too, The Tail Wind Fund Ltd, Jean-Pierre Dallaire, Fred Bild, Sino-Sult Canada (S.S.C.) Limited, Red Coral Group Limited, Lillian Wang Li, Harry Wang Hua, Norbert Sporns

Financial Data: Fiscal Year End:12/31 Latest Annual Data: 12/31/2006

Year	Sales	Net Income
2006	$39,095,000	$874,000
2005	$27,553,000	$3,254,000
2004	$20,782,000	$2,130,000

Curr. Assets:	$30,440,000	Curr. Liab.:	$8,377,000		
Plant, Equip.:	$8,816,000	Total Liab.:	$12,246,000	Indic. Yr. Divd.:	NA
Total Assets:	$41,852,000	Net Worth:	$29,606,000	Debt/ Equity:	NA

HRPT Properties Trust

400 Ctr. St., Newton, MA, 02458; *PH:* 1-617-332-3990; *Fax:* 1-617-332-2261; *http://* www.hrpreit.com; *Email:* info@hrpreit.com

General - Incorporation	MD	**Stock**- Price on:12/24/2007	$10.7
Employees	NA	Stock Exchange	NYSE
Auditor	Ernst & Young LLP	Ticker Symbol	HRP
Stk Agt	Wells Fargo Shareowner Services	Outstanding Shares	211,930,000
Counsel	Sullivan & Worcester LLP	E.P.S	$0.41
DUNS No	NA	Shareholders	NA

Business: The groups principle activities include owning and operating real estate properties. The groups properties include office and industrial buildings, and leased industrial land. In the year 2006, the group acquired 64 properties. The group operates from the United States. The groups quarterly revenue for September 2007 was 211.22 millions of USD.

Primary SIC and add'l.: 6798

CIK No: 0000803649

Subsidiaries: 1600 Market Street Property Trust, 1735 Market Street Properties Trust, 4 Maguire Road Realty Trust, 47 Harvard Street Real Estate Trust, ALPHA BT LLC, Blue Dog Properties Trust, Bridgepoint Property Trust, Candler Associates, L.L.C., Candler Property Trust, Causeway Holdings, Inc., Cedars LA LLC, First Associates LLC, Fourth and Roma Property Trust, Franklin Plaza Property Trust, Hawaii 2x5 0 Properties Trust 83 Subsidiaries included in the Index

Officers: John A. Mannix/COO, Pres./$52,238.00, John C. Popeo/Treasurer, CFO/$52,238.00, Jennifer B. Clark/Sr. VP, David M. Lepore/Sr. VP, William J. Sheehan/Dir. - Internal Audit, Compliance, Timothy A. Bonang/Mgr. - Investor Relations, Katie Johnston/Investor Relations Analyst

Directors: Barry M. Portnoy/Managing Trustee, Adam D. Portnoy/Managing Trustee, Patrick F. Donelan/Trustee, William A. Lamkin/Trustee, Frederick N. Zeytoonjian/Trustee

Owners: David M. Lepore, John A. Mannix, John C. Popeo, Barclays Global Investors/5.00%, Jennifer B. Clark, Patrick F. Donelan, Barry M. Portnoy, Frederick N. Zeytoonjian, Insiders, The Vanguard Group,Inc/5.90%, William A. Lamkin, Adam D. Portnoy

Financial Data: *Fiscal Year End:* 12/31 *Latest Annual Data:* 12/31/2006

Year	Sales	Net Income
2006	$795,821,000	$250,580,000
2005	$710,758,000	$164,984,000
2004	$603,229,000	$162,829,000

Curr. Assets:	$211,984,000	**Curr. Liab.:**	$166,525,000	**P/E Ratio:**	26.10
Plant, Equip.:	$5,261,692,000	**Total Liab.:**	$2,625,181,000	**Indic. Yr. Divd.:**	$0.840
Total Assets:	$5,575,949,000	**Net Worth:**	$2,950,768,000	**Debt/ Equity:**	0.8526

HS3 Technologies Inc

1800 Boulder St., Ste. 600, Denver, CO, 80211; *PH:* 1-303-455-2550; *Fax:* 1-303-433-7242; *http://* www.hs3tech.com; *Email:* info@hs3tech.com

General - Incorporation	NV	Stock- Price on:12/24/2007	$0.17
Employees	6	Stock Exchange	OTC
Auditor	Gordon, Hughes & Banks, LLP	Ticker Symbol	HSTH
Stk Agt	Empire Stock Transfer Inc.	Outstanding Shares	33,970,000
Counsel	NA	E.P.S.	-$0.15
DUNS No.	NA	Shareholders	NA

Business: The groups principle activity is to provide Internet services and wireless technology. In November 2005, the group acquired ip-Colo, Inc., The group operates from the United States.

Primary SIC and add'l.: 7382

CIK No: 0001297203

Subsidiaries: Ip-Colo, Inc.

Officers: Mark Lana/55/Dir., CEO, Sec., Pres., Treasurer/$85,000.00, Scott Annis/CTO, Ryder Gaston/National Sales Mgr., Stan Smith/National Sales Mgr., Robert A. Morrison/Dir., Pres.

Directors: Mark Lana/55/Dir., CEO, Sec., Pres., Treasurer, Robert A. Morrison/Dir., Pres., Charles F. Ferris/61/Dir., Michael Yinger/51/Dir.

Owners: Insiders/20.64%, Robert A. Morrison/12.65%, Lougene Baird/6.80%, Mark Lana/7.99%

Financial Data: *Fiscal Year End:* 06/30 *Latest Annual Data:* 6/30/2006

Year	Sales	Net Income
2006	$42,000	-$445,000
2005	NA	-$33,000

Curr. Assets:	$145,000	**Curr. Liab.:**	$676,000		
Plant, Equip.:	$80,000	**Total Liab.:**	$676,000	**Indic. Yr. Divd.:**	NA
Total Assets:	$225,000	**Net Worth:**	-$451,000	**Debt/ Equity:**	NA

HSBC Finance Corp

2700 Sanders Rd., Prospect Heights, IL, 60070; *PH:* 1-847-564-6478; *Fax:* 1-847-205-7538; *http://* www.hsbcusa.com; *Email:* investor.relations@us.hsbc.com

General - Incorporation	DE	Stock- Price on:12/24/2007	NA
Employees	NA	Stock Exchange	NA
Auditor	KPMG LLP	Ticker Symbol	NA
Stk Agt	NA	Outstanding Shares	NA
Counsel	NA	E.P.S.	NA
DUNS No.	00-162-5888	Shareholders	NA

Business: The group's principal activity is to provide consumer lending products. The group operates in four segments: consumer, credit card services, international and all other. The consumer segment consists of lending, mortgage services, retail services and auto finance businesses. The credit card services segment consists of domestic mastercard and visa credit card business. The international segment consists of foreign operations in the United Kingdom, Canada and Europe. This segment offers secured and unsecured lines of credit and secured and unsecured closed-end loans primarily in the United Kingdom and Canada. The group's all other segment services include insurance and tax services, direct lending and commercial operations, corporate and treasury activities. On Mar 28, 2003, the group merged with hsbc holdings plc and became a wholly-owned subsidiary.

Primary SIC and add'l.: 6411 6141 6153 6719

CIK No: 0000354964

Subsidiaries: AHLIC Investment Holdings Corporation, Amstelveen FSC, Ltd., B.I.G. Insurance Agency, Inc., Beaver Valley, Inc., Bencharge Credit Service Holding Company, Beneficial (Hungary) Financial Services Limited, Beneficial Alabama Inc., Beneficial Arizona Inc., Beneficial Building Company Limited, Beneficial California Inc., Beneficial Colorado Inc., Beneficial Commercial Corporation, Beneficial Commercial Holding Corporation, Beneficial Company LLC(f/k/a Beneficial Corporation), Beneficial Connecticut Inc. 350 Subsidiaries included in the Index

Officers: Brendan P. McDonagh/Dir., CEO, Anthony J. Murphy/Sr. Exec. VP - Portfolio Management, Stuart G. Tait/MD - Taxpayer Financial Services, Christopher D. Spooner/57/Sr. Exec. VP, Niall S.K. Booker/Dir., COO, Iain J. MacKay/Exec. VP, Mark A. Melas/Exec. VP - Corporate Real Estate, David M. Neenan/MD - Canada, James E.C. Binyon/VP, Chief Accounting Officer, Patrick J. Burke/MD - Card Services, Patrick A. Cozza/Group Executive, Thomas M. Detelich/Group Executive, Gary R. Esposito/MD - Mortgage Services, John J. Haines/MD - Auto Finance, Joseph W. Hoff/MD - Retail Services *(23 Officers included in Index)*

Directors: Brendan P. McDonagh/Dir., CEO, Douglas J. Flint/Non Exec. Chmn., Niall S.K. Booker/Dir., COO, Louis Hernandez/Dir., William R.P. Dalton/64/Dir., Dudley J. Fishburn/Dir., Cyrus F. Freidheim/Dir., Larree M. Renda/Dir., Robert K. Herdman/Dir., George A. Lorch/Dir.

Owners: J. Dudley Fishburn, Insiders, Kenneth H. Robin, Walter G. Menezes, Gary G. Dillon, Larree M. Renda, Michael R. P. Smith, Douglas J. Flint, Thomas M. Detelich, William R. P. Dalton, George A. Lorch, Siddharth N. Mehta

HSBC Holdings Plc

HSBC Holdings plc, 8 Canada Sq., London, NY, E14 5HQ; *PH:* 1-212-525-5000; *http://* www.hsbc.com

General - Incorporation	UK	Stock- Price on:12/24/2007	$92.92
Employees	NA	Stock Exchange	NYSE
Auditor	KPMG Audit Plc	Ticker Symbol	HBC
Stk Agt	Computershare Investor Services LLC	Outstanding Shares	NA
Counsel	NA	E.P.S.	NA
DUNS No.	NA	Shareholders	NA

Business: The group's principal activities are banking and related financial services. It operates in Europe, Hong Kong, the rest Asia-pacific, including the Middle East and Africa, North America and South America through the following business groups: personal financial services which provides services to individual customers, including those who are self-employed; commercial banking which serves from sole proprietors, partnership, clubs, and associations to incorporated businesses and publicly quoted companies; corporate, investment banking and markets which provides financial solutions to government, corporate and institutional clients; private banking services include deposits and funds transfer, tax and trustee structures, asset and trust management, mutual funds, currency and securities transactions and lending.

Primary SIC and add'l.: 6311 6211 6021

CIK No: 0001089113

Officers: M. F. Geoghegan/54/Exec. Dir., Group CEO, M. R.P. Smith/51/Group GM, R. J. Arena/59/Group GM, M. J.W. King/51/Group GM, R. C.F. Or/58/Group GM, R. G. Barber/57/Sec., R. C. Picot/50/Group GM, D. J. Flint/53/Dir., Group Dir. - Finance, K. M. Harvey/47/Group GM, N. S.K. Booker/49/Group GM, P. A. Thurston/54/Group GM, S. T. Gulliver/48/Group MD, Z. J. Cama/60/Group GM, V. H.C. Cheng/59/Group MD, P. Y. Antika/47/Group MD *(30 Officers included in Index)*

Directors: M. F. Geoghegan/54/Exec. Dir., Group CEO, S. K. Green/59/Group Chmn., Baroness Dunn/68/Dep. Chmn., Brian Moffat/69/Dep. Chmn., Brian Williamson/63/Non - Exec. Dir., S. M. Robertson/67/Dir., G. Morgan/62/Dir., S. W. Newton/66/Non - Exec. Dir., J. D. Coombe/63/Dir., D. J. Flint/53/Dir., Group Dir. - Finance, J. W.J. Hughes-Hallett/58/Dir., H. Sohmen/68/Dir., Mark Moody-Stuart/67/Non - Exec. Dir., R. A. Fairhead/46/Dir., W. K.L. Fung/59/Dir.

Owners: S. K. Green, W. K L Fung, S. W. Newton, D. J. Flint, R. K F Chien, S. M. Robertson, S. Hintze, M. F. Geoghegan, Baroness Dunn, J. D. Coombe

Financial Data: *Fiscal Year End:* 12/31 *Latest Annual Data:* 12/31/2006

Year	Sales	Net Income
2006	$115,361,000,000	$16,358,000,000
2005	$93,494,000,000	$15,495,000,000
2004	$66,681,000,000	$12,506,000,000

Curr. Assets:	$337,874,000,000	**Curr. Liab.:**	$99,089,000,000	**P/E Ratio:**	24.03
Plant, Equip.:	$13,580,000,000	**Total Liab.:**	$1,604,087,000,000	**Indic. Yr. Divd.:**	NA
Total Assets:	$1,712,627,000,000	**Net Worth:**	$108,540,000,000	**Debt/ Equity:**	NA

HSBC USA Inc

452 5th Ave., New York, NY, 10018; *PH:* 1-716-841-7212; *http://* www.us.hsbc.com

General - Incorporation	MD	Stock- Price on:12/24/2007	$25.3
Employees	NA	Stock Exchange	OTC
Auditor	KPMG LLP	Ticker Symbol	HBAGP
Stk Agt	American Stock Transfer & Trust Co.	Outstanding Shares	NA
Counsel	NA	E.P.S.	NA
DUNS No.	07-279-6535	Shareholders	NA

Business: The group's principle activities are to provide banking and financial services. The group offers full range of banking products and services and also provides access to global markets through its affiliation with hsbc. The products offered by the group include installment and revolving term loans, deposits, insurance, estate planning, branch services, mutual funds, and other investment management services.

Primary SIC and add'l.: 6021 6712

CIK No: 0000083246

Subsidiaries: Alexandria Holdings, Inc., Beachhouse Properties, Inc., Cabot Park Holdings, Inc., Capco/Cove, Inc., Card-Flo #1, Inc., Card-Flo #3, Inc., CBS/Holdings, Inc., CC&H Holdings LLC, Cross Zou Holding Corp., Cross-LA Realty, Inc., Crossturkey, Inc., Delaware Credit Corp. (USA), Delaware Securities Processing Corp., Eagle Rock Holdings, Inc., Ellenville Holdings, Inc. 101 Subsidiaries included in the Index

Officers: Marlon Young/MD, CEO - Private Bank Americas, Paul J. Lawrence/46/Dir., CEO, Pres., Jeanne Ebersole/Exec. VP - Human Resources, Robert M. Butcher/64/Sr. Exec. VP, Chief Risk Officer, Carolyn M. Wind/Exec. VP, MD - Specialized Compliance, Mark Martinelli/Exec. VP - Audit, Gerard Mattia/Sr. Exec. VP, CFO, Kevin Newman/Sr. Exec. VP - Personal Financial Services, David C. Kotheimer/50/Sr. Exec. VP - Business Performance, Clive R. Bucknall/44/Exec. VP, Controller, Christopher Davies/Sr. Exec. VP - Commercial Banking, Mark A. Hershey/Sr. Exec. VP, Chief Credit Officer, Janet L. Burak/Sr. Exec. VP, General Counsel, David Dew/COO, Sr. Exec. VP, John J. McKenna/Sr. Exec. VP, CFO - Husi *(17 Officers included in Index)*

Directors: Paul J. Lawrence/46/Dir., CEO, Pres., Frances D. Fergusson/Dir., Sal H. Alfiero/Dir., Stuart T. Gulliver/Dir., James H. Cleave/Dir., James L. Morice/Dir., Donald K. Boswell/Dir., Peter Kimmelman/Dir., Richard A. Jalkut/Dir., Charles G. Meyer/Dir., Salvatore H. Alfiero/70/Dir., Michael F. Geoghegan/Dir.

Owners: Joseph A. Belfatto, Richard A. Jalkut, Insiders, Donald K. Boswell, Marlon Young, Frances D. Fergusson, John J. McKenna, Salvatore H. Alfiero, James L. Morice, Martin J.G. Glynn, Brendan McDonagh, Joseph M. Petri, Stuart T. Gulliver, Sandra L. Derickson, Janet L. Burak *(18 Owners included in Index)*

Huaneng Power International Inc

West Wing, Bldg. C , Tianyin Mansion, 2c, Fuxingmennan St., Beijing, 100031; *PH:* 86-1066491999; *Fax:* 86-1066491888; *http://* www.hpi.com.cn; *Email:* ir@hpi.com.cn

General - Incorporation	China	Stock- Price on:12/24/2007	NA
Employees	23,531	Stock Exchange	NYSE
Auditor	PricewaterhouseCoopers LLP	Ticker Symbol	HNP
Stk Agt	Bank of New York	Outstanding Shares	NA
Counsel	NA	E.P.S.	$3.16
DUNS No.	65-428-5220	Shareholders	NA

Business: The group's principal activity is the generation and sale of electric power to regional and provincial grid companies in China. Its power plants located in liaoning, hebei, jiangsu, fujian, guangdong, shanghai, zhejiang, shanxi and shandong provinces.

Primary SIC and add'l.: 4931 4911

CIK No: 0000929058

Officers: Guo Junming/43/Chmn. - Board of Supervisors, Sr. Accountant, Yu Ying/53/Vice Chairwoman, Board Of Supervisors - Sr. Economist, Qian Zhongwei/70/Dir., Sr. Engineer, Ding Shida/60/Dir., Sr. Engineer, Shan Qunying/55/Dir., Sr. Engineer, Huang Jian/46/Dir., VP, Sec., Sr. Accountant, Shen Zongmin/54/Member - Board Of Supervisors, Sr. Political Specialist, Na Xizhi/55/Dir., Pres., Sr. Engineer, Gu Jianguo/42/Member - Board Of Supervisors - Economist, Zou Cui/55/Member - Board Of Supervisors, Sr. Engineer, Wang Zhaobin/53/Dir., GM - Administration Department, Political Specialist, Member - Board Of Supervisors, Qu Xiaojun/VP, Lu Dan/VP, Fan Xiaxia/VP, Zhou Hui/Chief Accountant *(41 Officers included in Index)*

Directors: Huang Long/55/Vice Chmn., Huang Yongda/51/Vice Chmn., Li Xiaopeng/49/Chmn., Guo Junming/43/Chmn. - Board of Supervisors, Sr. Accountant, Yu Ying/53/Vice Chairwoman, Board Of Supervisors - Sr. Economist, Ding Shida/60/Dir., Sr. Engineer, Shen Zongmin/54/Member - Board Of Supervisors, Sr. Political Specialist, Na Xizhi/55/Dir., Pres., Sr. Engineer, Qian Zhongwei/70/Dir., Sr. Engineer, Huang Jian/46/Dir., VP, Sec., Sr. Accountant, Xia Donglin/47/Dir., Liu Jipeng/52/Dir., Xu Zujian/54/Dir. - Sr. Economist, Liu Shuyuan/58/Dir. - Sr. Economist, Wu Dawei/55/Dir., Sr. Engineer *(20 Directors included in Index)*

Financial Data: Fiscal Year End:12/31 **Latest Annual Data:** 12/31/2006

Year	Sales	Net Income
2006	$5,679,440,000	$819,799,000
2005	$4,969,490,000	$673,311,000

Curr. Assets:	$57,332,000	**Curr. Liab.:**	$2,928,558,000		
Plant, Equip.:	$164,088,000	**Total Liab.:**	$2,300,339,000	**Indic. Yr. Divd.:**	$2.700
Total Assets:	$729,066,000	**Net Worth:**	$312,714,000	**Debt/ Equity:**	0.8720

Hub Group Inc

3050 Highland Pkwy., Ste.100, Downers Grove, IL, 60515; **PH:** 1-630-271-3600;
Fax: 1-630-964-6475; **http://** www.hubgroup.com

General - Incorporation	DE	**Stock**- Price on:12/24/2007	$36.26
Employees	1,089	Stock Exchange	NDQ
Auditor	Ernst & Young LLP	Ticker Symbol	HUBG
Stk Agt	Computershare Investor Services LLC	Outstanding Shares	40,110,000
Counsel	NA	E.P.S	$1.40
DUNS No.	15-514-3480	Shareholders	NA

Business: The group's principle activity is to provide asset-light freight transportation management services. The group provides intermodal, truck brokerage and logistics services. The group operates from United States.

Primary SIC and add'l.: 4213 4731

CIK No: 0000940942

Subsidiaries: Hub Chicago Holdings, Inc., Hub City Terminals, Inc., Hub City Texas, L.P., Hub Freight Services, Inc., Hub Group Associates, Inc., Hub Group Atlanta, LLC, Hub Group Canada L.P., Hub Group Distribution Services, LLC, Hub Group Transport, LLC, Quality Services LLC

Officers: David P. Yeager/Vice Chmn., CEO/$1,605,818.00, Thomas M. White/50/CFO, Sr. VP, Treasurer/$894,296.00, Donald G. Maltby/Exec. VP - Logistics Services/$667,216.00, David C. Zeilstra/VP, Sec., General Counsel, Dennis R. Polsen/Exec. VP - Information Services, James B. Gaw/Exec. VP - Sales, Stephen P. Cosgrove/Exec. VP - Intermodal Operations, Administration, David L. Marsh/Exec. VP - Highway/$742,436.00, Mark A. Yeager/Dir., COO, Pres. - Field Operations/$1,148,562.00, Christopher R. Kravas/Exec. VP - Strategy, Yield Management, Terri A. Pizzuto/CFO, Exec. VP, Treasurer

Directors: David P. Yeager/Vice Chmn., CEO, Phillip C. Yeager/Chmn., Charles R. Reaves/Dir., Mark A. Yeager/Dir., COO, Pres. - Field Operations, Gary D. Eppen/Dir., Martin P. Slark/Dir.

Owners: Gary D. Eppen, FMR Corp./5.60%, Barclays/7.30%, Insiders/6.30%, David L. Marsh, David P. Yeager/2.40%, Charles R. Reaves, Thomas M. White, Phillip C. Yeager/2.50%, Martin P. Slark, Mark A. Yeager/2.90%, Donald G. Maltby, Friess Associates LLC/5.20%, Debra A. Jensen/1.70%

Financial Data: Fiscal Year End:12/31 **Latest Annual Data:** 12/31/2006

Year	Sales	Net Income
2006	$1,609,529,000	$48,686,000
2005	$1,531,499,000	$32,946,000
2004	$1,426,806,000	$17,279,000

Curr. Assets:	$221,229,000	**Curr. Liab.:**	$174,426,000	**P/E Ratio:**	27.68
Plant, Equip.:	$26,974,000	**Total Liab.:**	$225,704,000	**Indic. Yr. Divd.:**	NA
Total Assets:	$484,548,000	**Net Worth:**	$258,844,000	**Debt/ Equity:**	NA

Hubbell Inc

584 Derby Milford Rd., Orange, CT, 06477; **PH:** 1-203-799-4100; **Fax:** 1-203-799-4205;
http:// www.hubbell.com; **Email:** info@hubbell.com

General - Incorporation	CT	**Stock**- Price on:12/24/2007	$55.5
Employees	12,000	Stock Exchange	NYSE
Auditor	PricewaterhouseCoopers LLP	Ticker Symbol	HUB-B
Stk Agt	Mellon Investor Services LLC	Outstanding Shares	59,640,000
Counsel	NA	E.P.S	NA
DUNS No.	00-118-1858	Shareholders	NA

Business: The groups principle activities includes designing, manufacturing and selling of electrical and electronic products. The groups products include wiring and power systems, and telecom and data products. The group operates from United States.

Primary SIC and add'l.: 3643 3646 3648 3625 3644 3585 1731

CIK No: 0000048898

Subsidiaries: Artesanias Baja, S.A. de C.V., Bel Manufacturera, S.A. de C.V., Dual-Lite Manufacturing Inc., Fabrica de Pecas Electricas Delmar LTDA., GAI-Tronics Corporation, Gleason Reel Corp., Haefely Test AG, Harvey Hubbell Caribe, Inc., Hipotronics, Inc., Hubbell Building Automation, Inc., Hubbell Canada LP, Hubbell de Mexico, S.A. de C.V., Hubbell Distribution, Inc., Hubbell Incorporated (Delaware), Hubbell Industrial Controls, Inc. 20 Subsidiaries included in the Index

Officers: Timothy H. Powers/Chmn., CEO, Pres./$5,523,319.00, James K. Braun/VP - Planning, Development, Thomas R. Conlin/VP - Public Affairs, Gregory F. Covino/VP, Controller, Gary N. Amato/Group VP, James H. Biggart/VP, Treasurer, Stephen M. Mais/VP - Human Resources, Scott

H. Muse/Group VP/$1,247,441.00, Thomas P. Smith/Group VP, David G. Nord/CFO, Sr. VP/$1,428,304.00, Richard W. Davies/VP, General Counsel, Sec./$1,291,945.00, Charles M. Tencza/VP - Information Technology, Robert W. Murphy/Exec. VP - Marketing, Sales, William T. Tolley/Group VP

Directors: Timothy H. Powers/Chmn., CEO, Pres., Daniel J. Meyer/Dir., Richard J. Swift/Dir., George W. Edwards/Dir., Joel S. Hoffman/Dir., Richard E. Brooks/Dir., Andrew McNally/Dir., Jackson G. Ratcliffe/Dir., Daniel S. Van Riper/Dir., Anthony J. Guzzi/Dir.

Owners: Richard W. Davies, Adage Capital Partners, L.P., Andrew McNally/0.03%, George W. Edwards, Andrew McNally, Jackson G. Ratcliffe/1.04%, Cooke & Bieler, L.P./5.14%, George W. Edwards, Robert W. Murphy/0.20%, David G. Nord/0.07%, Timothy H. Powers/1.63%, Richard E. Brooks, G.Jackson Ratcliffe, Scott H. Muse/0.26%, Daniel J. Meyer *(33 Owners included in Index)*

Hudson City Bancorp Inc

W 80 Century Rd., Paramus, NJ, 07652; **PH:** 1-201-967-1900; **Fax:** 1-201-967-0332;
http:// www.hcsbonline.com

General - Incorporation	DE	**Stock**- Price on:12/24/2007	$12.44
Employees	1,168	Stock Exchange	NDQ
Auditor	KPMG LLP	Ticker Symbol	HCBK
Stk Agt	Mellon Investor Services LLC	Outstanding Shares	544,420,000
Counsel	Diefennbach, Witt & Birchby	E.P.S	$0.55
DUNS No.	NA	Shareholders	NA

Business: The groups principle activity is to provide banking services. The groups products include deposit products, residential real estate mortgage and consumer loans. The group operates from United States.

Primary SIC and add'l.: 6712 6036

CIK No: 0000921847

Subsidiaries: HC Value Broker Services, Inc, HudCiti Service Corporation, Hudson City Preferred Funding Corp., Hudson City Savings Bank

Officers: Ronald E. Hermance/Chmn., CEO, Pres./$5,329,535.00, Denis J. Salamone/55/Dir., COO, Sr. Exec. VP/$2,737,313.00, Ronald J. Butkovich/58/Sr. VP/$1,499,642.00, James A. Klarer/55/Sr. VP, Barry V. Corridon/59/Sr. VP - Mortgage Servicing, Thomas E. Laird/55/Sr. VP, Michael B. Lee/58/Sr. VP, Veronica A. Olszewski/48/Sr. VP, Corp. Sec., John M. Tassillo/73/Exec. VP, Treasurer/$1,396,570.00, James C. Kranz/59/CFO, Sr. VP/$960,116.00, Susan K. Munhall/Investment Relations Officer

Directors: Ronald E. Hermance/Chmn., CEO, Pres., Denis J. Salamone/55/Dir., COO, Sr. Exec. VP, Michael W. Azzara/61/Dir., Victoria H. Bruni/66/Dir., William G. Bardel/68/Dir., Scott A. Belair/60/Dir., William J. Cosgrove/75/Dir., Donald O. Quest/68/Dir., Joseph G. Sponholz/64/Dir.

Owners: John M. Tassillo, Human Resources Committee of Hudson/8.48%, Employee Stock Ownership Plan Trust/7.68%, Michael W. Azzara, Victoria H. Bruni, Denis J. Salamone, Donald O. Quest, William G. Bardel, Insiders/9.39%, Joseph G. Sponholz, William J. Cosgrove, Scott A. Belair, Ronald J. Butkovich, James C. Kranz, Ronald E. Hermance/1.11%

Financial Data: Fiscal Year End:12/31 **Latest Annual Data:** 12/31/2006

Year	Sales	Net Income
2006	$1,621,134,000	$288,579,000
2005	$1,186,915,000	$276,055,000
2004	$931,615,000	$239,266,000

Curr. Assets:	$376,475,000	**Curr. Liab.:**	$30,576,325,000		
Plant, Equip.:	$77,090,000	**Total Liab.:**	$30,576,325,000	**Indic. Yr. Divd.:**	$0.340
Total Assets:	$35,506,581,000	**Net Worth:**	$4,930,256,000	**Debt/ Equity:**	NA

Hudson Highland Group Inc

560 Lexington Ave., 4th & 5th Fl., New York, NY, 10022; **PH:** 1-212-351-7400;
Fax: 1-917-256-8592; **http://** www.hhgroup.com

General - Incorporation	DE	**Stock**- Price on:12/24/2007	$20.79
Employees	3,600	Stock Exchange	NDQ
Auditor	BDO Seidman LLP	Ticker Symbol	HHGP
Stk Agt	Bank of New York	Outstanding Shares	25,230,000
Counsel	NA	E.P.S	$1.21
DUNS No.	NA	Shareholders	NA

Business: The group principal activity is to provide professional staffing, retained executive search and human capital solutions. The group operates through two segments: hudson global resources and highland partners. Hudson global resources provides mid-level professional temporary personnel and permanent recruitment services & also provides a variety of other services in the area of human capital solutions like customized interactive recruiting and hr solutions, career transition, executive assessment and coaching. Highland partners offers a comprehensive range of executive search services on a retained basis aimed at recruiting senior level executives or professionals & also practice in assisting clients desiring to augment their boards of directors. The group operates in Australia, United Kingdom & continental Europe. On 31-Mar-2003, the group spun off from monster worldwide.

Primary SIC and add'l.: 8742 7375

CIK No: 0001210708

Subsidiaries: Balance Ervaring op Projectbasis B.V., Cornell Technical Services, Inc., De Witte& Morel Global Resources N.V., De Witte& Morel Global Resources S.A., Delta Search Group, Inc., HH Global Resources A.B., Highland Partners (Australia) Pty Ltd, Highland Partners Co (Canada), Highland Partners Limited, Hudson Global Resources (NZ) Ltd, Hudson Global Resources (Singapore) Pte Limited, Hudson Global Resources America, Inc., Hudson Global Resources AS, Hudson Global Resources Holding, Inc., Hudson Global Resources Hong Kong Limited 35 Subsidiaries included in the Index

Officers: Jon F. Chait/Chmn., CEO/$1,108,018.00, Stefanie Cross-Wilson/CEO - Asia, Helen Nugent/Exec. Chmn. - Hudson Australia, New Zealand, Donald E. Bielinski/Sr. VP, Chmn. - Hudson Asia Pac, Chmn. - Hudson Talent Management/$769,602.00, Mary Jane Raymond/CFO, Exec. VP/$1,674,786.00, Latham Williams/VP - Legal Affairs, Administration, David S. Reynolds/VP, Corporate Controller, Margaretta Noonan/Exec. VP, Chief Administrative Officer/$442,995.00, David F. Kirby/Investor Relations Officer, Sarah Kafenstok/Contact - Media, Richard S. Gray/51/Sr. VP - Marketing, Communications, Christine Raynaud/Pres. - Hudson Europe, Ralph L. O'Hara/63/VP, Global Controller, Gary Lazzarotto/MD - Australia, New Zealand, Rick Gray/Sr. VP - Marketing, Communications/$389,826.00 *(17 Officers included in Index)*

Directors: Jon F. Chait/Chmn., CEO, Jennifer Laing/Dir., John J. Haley/Dir., David G. Offensend/Dir., Robert B. Dubner/Dir., Richard J. Stolz/Dir.

Owners: Robert B. Dubner, John J. Haley, Kensico Capital/6.90%, Heartland Advisors, Inc./8.00%, Richard J. Stolz, David G. Offensend, Margaretta R. Noonan, Donald E. Bielinski, Perry Corp./9.10%, Jennifer Laing, Richard S. Gray, Mary Jane Raymond, Capital Management Corporation/10.10%, Artisan Partners Limited Partnership/7.80%, Insiders/3.90% *(16 Owners included in Index)*

Financial Data: *Fiscal Year End:*12/31 *Latest Annual Data:* 12/31/2006

Year	Sales	Net Income
2006	$1,373,473,000	$22,115,000
2005	$1,428,276,000	$5,313,000
2004	$1,256,354,000	-$26,775,000

Curr. Assets:	$280,107,000	**Curr. Liab.:**	$164,270,000	**P/E Ratio:**	17.47
Plant, Equip.:	$28,105,000	**Total Liab.:**	$177,839,000	**Indic. Yr. Divd.:**	NA
Total Assets:	$350,869,000	**Net Worth:**	$173,030,000	**Debt/ Equity:**	0.0013

Hudson Holding Corp

8311 Windbreak Trl. N, Minneapolis, MN, 55414; ***PH:*** 1-612-245-4773; ***http://*** www.hudsonvalleybank.com; ***Email:*** scracraft-fehler@qbs.com

General		Stock	
Incorporation	DE	Price on:12/24/2007	$0.5
Employees	78	Stock Exchange	OTC
Auditor	Eisner LLP	Ticker Symbol	HDHL
Stk Agt	Hudson Securities Inc	Outstanding Shares	36,730,000
Counsel	NA	E.P.S	-$0.05
DUNS No.	14-851-5059	Shareholders	NA

Business: The group's principle activities include developing and marketing clinical support and financial software services designed to aid physicians and other health care professionals. The group operates from United States.

Primary SIC and add'l.: 8099 7372

CIK No: 0000804157

Subsidiaries: Hudson Capital Markets, Inc, Hudson Securities, Inc, Hudson Technologies Inc

Officers: Martin C. Cunningham/Chmn., CEO/$208,792.00, Keith R. Knox/Dir., Pres., Sec., Principal Financial, Accounting Officer/$208,005.00, Mark Leventhal/52/Dir., Exec. VP/$212,538.00

Directors: Martin C. Cunningham/Chmn., CEO, Keith R. Knox/Dir., Pres., Sec., Principal Financial, Accounting Officer, Mark Leventhal/52/Dir., Exec. VP, Peter J. Zugschwert/Dir., Joanne V. Landau/Dir., Carmine V. Chiusano/Dir.

Owners: Keith R. Knox/11.40%, Steven L. Winkler/11.80%, Joanne V. Landau, Insiders/35.30%, Martin C. Cunningham/11.40%, Carmine V. Chiusano, Kenneth D. Pasternak/24.20%, Peter J. Zugschwert, Mark Leventhal/11.80%, South Ferry #2 LP/8.90%

Financial Data: *Fiscal Year End:*03/31 *Latest Annual Data:* 03/31/2007

Year	Sales	Net Income
2007	$20,852,000	-$383,000
2006	$20,228,000	$784,000
2005	NA	-$20,000

Curr. Assets:	$5,344,000	**Curr. Liab.:**	$2,774,000		
Plant, Equip.:	$176,000	**Total Liab.:**	$2,774,000	**Indic. Yr. Divd.:**	NA
Total Assets:	$10,866,000	**Net Worth:**	$8,093,000	**Debt/ Equity:**	NA

Hudson Technologies Inc

275 N Middletown Rd., Pearl River, NY, 10965; ***PH:*** 1-845-735-6000; ***Fax:*** 1-845-512-6070; ***http://*** www.hudsontech.com; ***Email:*** info@hudsontech.com

General		Stock	
Incorporation	NY	Price on:12/24/2007	$1.13
Employees	65	Stock Exchange	NDQ
Auditor	BDO Seidman LLP	Ticker Symbol	HDSN
Stk Agt	Continental Stock Transfer & Trust Co	Outstanding Shares	25,920,000
Counsel	NA	E.P.S	-$0.04
DUNS No.	78-261-9647	Shareholders	NA

Business: The group's principal activity is to provide innovative solutions to recurring problems within the refrigeration industry. The group also provides recovery and reclamation of refrigerants used in commercial air conditioning, industry processing and refrigeration systems. The group provides services that are performed at a customer's site through the use of portable, high volume, high-speed proprietary equipment, including the patented zugibeast(R) system. The group markets reclaimed and virgin refrigerants to a variety of customers in various segments of the air conditioning and refrigeration industry. The group provides a complete offering of refrigerant management services, which primarily include reclamation of refrigerants, testing and banking services tailored to individual customer requirements. The group operates through its wholly owned subsidiaries hudson technologies company and hudson holdings, inc.

Primary SIC and add'l.: 7623 7629

CIK No: 0000925528

Subsidiaries: Hudson Holdings, Inc., Hudson Technologies of Tennessee d/b/a Hudson Technologies Company

Officers: Kevin J. Zugibe/Chmn., CEO, Stephen P. Mandracchia/VP - Legal, Regulatory, James R. Buscemi/CFO, Joseph Longo/Dir. - Engineering, Riyaz Paper/Dir. - Energy Assets, Optimazition, Brian F. Coleman/COO, Pres., Charles F. Harkins/VP - Sales, Marketing

Directors: Kevin J. Zugibe/Chmn., CEO, Dominic J. Monetta/Dir., Vincent P. Abbatecola/Dir., Otto C. Morch/Dir., Robert L. Burr/Dir.

Owners: Stephen P. Mandracchia/12.67%, Robert L. Burr, Insiders/54.82%, Dominic J. Monetta, Vincent P. Abbatecola, Kevin J. Zugibe/37.35%, Charles F. Harkins/1.06%, Otto C. Morch, Brian F. Coleman/3.52%

Financial Data: *Fiscal Year End:*12/31 *Latest Annual Data:* 12/31/2006

Year	Sales	Net Income
2006	$23,451,000	$2,108,000
2005	$19,223,000	$2,270,000
2004	$14,613,000	$264,000

Curr. Assets:	$14,377,000	**Curr. Liab.:**	$8,418,000		
Plant, Equip.:	$2,984,000	**Total Liab.:**	$9,715,000	**Indic. Yr. Divd.:**	NA
Total Assets:	$17,723,000	**Net Worth:**	$8,008,000	**Debt/ Equity:**	0.1500

Hudson United Bancorp

1000 Macarthur Blvd., Mahwah, NJ, 07430; ***PH:*** 1-201-236-2600; ***http://*** www.tdbanknorth.com

General		Stock	
Incorporation	NJ	Price on:12/24/2007	NA
Employees	7,500	Stock Exchange	NA
Auditor	Ernst & Young LLP	Ticker Symbol	NA
Stk Agt	Mellon Investor Services LLC	Outstanding Shares	NA
Counsel	NA	E.P.S	NA
DUNS No.	10-759-5209	Shareholders	NA

Business: The group's principle activity is to provide commercial banking services to individual and corporate customers through its banking subsidiary, hudson united bank. The group is a holding company and operates over 205 branches located throughout the state of New Jersey; in the hudson valley area of New York state; in New York city; in southern Connecticut in the areas between greenwich and hartford; and in philadelphia and surrounding areas in Pennsylvania. Services offered by the group include imaged checking, savings and time deposit accounts; 24-hour telephone banking; Internet banking; trust services; cash management services; merchant services; safe deposit boxes; insurance, stock, bond and mutual fund sales. The services also include secured and unsecured personal and commercial loans; residential and commercial real estate loans; and international services including import and export financing, foreign currency purchases and letters of credit.

Primary SIC and add'l.: 6712 6022

CIK No: 0000703559

Subsidiaries: AMBA Realty Corporation, Flatiron Credit Company, Inc, Hendrick Hudson Corp. of New Jersey, HUB Mortgage Investments, Inc, HUBCO Capital Trust I, HUBCO Capital Trust II, Hudson Insurance Services Inc, Hudson Trader Brokerage Services, Hudson United Bank, Hudson United Capital Trust I, Hudson United Capital Trust II, Hudson United Statutory Trust I, JBI Capital Trust I, Jefferson Delaware, Inc., Lafayette Development Corp 21 Subsidiaries included in the Index

Hudson Valley Holding Corp

21 Scarsdale Rd., Yonkers, NY, 10707; ***PH:*** 1-914-961-6100; ***Fax:*** 1-914-961-7378; ***http://*** www.hudsonvalleybank.com; ***Email:*** info@hvbank.com

General		Stock	
Incorporation	NY	Price on:12/24/2007	$57
Employees	395	Stock Exchange	OTC
Auditor	Deloitte & Touche, LLP	Ticker Symbol	HUVL
Stk Agt	Hudson Valley Bank	Outstanding Shares	8,920,000
Counsel	NA	E.P.S	$3.39
DUNS No.	NA	Shareholders	NA

Business: The group operates through its subsidiary whose principal activity is to provide commercial services. Services of the group include lending, deposits, automated teller machines and other portfolio services. Customers served by the group include businesses, professionals, municipalities, organizations and individuals. In January 2006, the group acquired New York National Bank. The group operates from New York in the United States. The total assets of the group in the year 2006, was $2,220,594.

Primary SIC and add'l.: 6022 6712

CIK No: 0000722256

Subsidiaries: 369 East 149th Street Corp., A.R. Schmeidler& Co., Inc., Grassy Sprain Real Estate Holdings, Inc., Hudson Valley Bank, Hudson Valley Investment Corp., HVB Employment Corp., HVB Leasing Corp., HVB Realty Corp., NYNB Bank, Sprain Brook Realty Corp.

Officers: James J. Landy/Dir., CEO, Pres./$708,110.00, Joan T. Dupay/Sec. - Hudson Valley National Foundation, Andrew Reinhart/Treasurer - Hudson Valley National Foundation, Stephen R. Brown/Dir., CFO, Sr. Exec. VP, Treasurer/$612,499.00, James M. Coogan/Dir., Sec., Michael P. Maloney/Dir., Chief Banking Officer, Exec. VP - Hudson Valley Bank/$440,703.00, Michael Gilfeather/Exec. VP - Branch Administration, Hudson Valley Bank, Michael Goldrick/Exec. VP - Business, Professional Banking, Hudson Valley Bank, Daniel J. Harris/Chief Credit Officer, Mary Minieri/Administration, Vincent T. Palaia/Chief Lending Officer/$603,152.00, Frank J. Skuthan/Marketing Dir., Christopher Taylor/COO/$376,104.00, Wendy Croker/VP - Shareholder Relations, Esther Vincenty/CLE Administrator - Hudson Valley Bank *(31 Officers included in Index)*

Directors: James J. Landy/Dir., CEO, Pres., William E. Griffin/Chmn., William F. Banks/Member - Business Development Board, Hudson Valley Bank, William R. Bastardi/Member - Business Development Board, Hudson Valley Bank, Ellen M. Boyle/Member - Business Development Board, Hudson Valley Bank, Gerald M. Boyle/Member - Business Development Board, Hudson Valley Bank, Steven Brown/Member - Business Development Board, Hudson Valley Bank, Mae R. Carpenter/Member - Business Development Board, Hudson Valley Bank, Ernest R. Catenacci/Member - Business Development Board, Hudson Valley Bank, Paul F. Cocozza/Member - Business Development Board, Hudson Valley Bank, Cathy Alexis Comas/Member - Business Development Board, Hudson Valley Bank, Clifford Cook/Member - Business Development Board, Hudson Valley Bank, Jerry L. Crispino/Member - Business Development Board, Hudson Valley Bank, Joan P. Cunningham/Member - Business Development Board, Hudson Valley Bank, Joseph R. Curto/Member - Business Development Board, Hudson Valley Bank *(127 Directors included in Index)*

Owners: William E. Griffin/3.70%, Christopher J. Taylor, John A. Pratt/1.80%, Insiders/31.20%, Michael P. Maloney, Craig S. Thompson/2.30%, William J. Mulrow, Vincent T. Palaia/1.20%, Cecile D. Singer/1.00%, James J. Landy/1.80%, Gregory F. Holcombe/18.80%, Angelo R. Martinelli/2.40%, Bruno J. Gioffre, Marie A. Holcombe/18.80%, James M. Coogan/2.90% *(19 Owners included in Index)*

Financial Data: *Fiscal Year End:*12/31 *Latest Annual Data:* 12/31/2006

Year	Sales	Net Income
2006	$154,435,000	$34,059,000
2005	$119,825,000	$30,945,000
2004	$94,957,000	$27,540,000

Curr. Assets:	$90,584,000	**Curr. Liab.:**	$1,856,797,000		
Plant, Equip.:	$21,669,000	**Total Liab.:**	$2,106,168,000	**Indic. Yr. Divd.:**	$1.820
Total Assets:	$2,291,734,000	**Net Worth:**	$185,566,000	**Debt/ Equity:**	1.3095

Hudson's Grill International Inc

16970 Dallas Pkwy., Ste. 402, Dallas, TX, 75248; ***PH:*** 1-972-931-9237; ***Fax:*** 1-972-931-1326; ***http://*** www.hudsonsgrill.com; ***Email:*** getinfo@hudsonsgrill.com

General		Stock	
Incorporation	TX	Price on:12/24/2007	$0.07
Employees	1	Stock Exchange	OTC
Auditor	Whitley Penn LLP	Ticker Symbol	HGIIA
Stk Agt	Registrar & Transfer Co	Outstanding Shares	7,640,000
Counsel	NA	E.P.S	$0.03
DUNS No.	NA	Shareholders	NA

Business: The group's principle activity is to franchise full service restaurants. The group has eleven franchised restaurants which serve lunch and dinner and a wide range of alcoholic beverages. The group also provides management and support services to the franchised restaurants. The restaurants are currently operating in California, Michigan, Wisconsin and Texas. The group owns the trademark registrations for two hudson's grill logos and for the hudson's name. The group operates from United States.

Primary SIC and add'l.: 5812

CIK No: 0001104254

Officers: David L. Osborn/60/Dir., CEO, Pres., Barbara Amstutz/Sec.

Directors: David L. Osborn/60/Dir., CEO, Pres., Robert W. Fischer/57/Chmn., Anthony B. Duncan/52/Dir.

Owners: ANTHONY B. DUNCAN/9.01%, ROY J. MILLENDER/11.47%, Charles L. Boppell/6.59%, DAVID L. OSBORN/28.29%, Insiders, Barbara Amstutz, ROBERT W. FISCHER/4.47%, CLIFFORD J. OSBORN/13.79%

Financial Data: Fiscal Year End: 12/31 **Latest Annual Data:** 12/31/2006

Year	Sales	Net Income
2006	$468,000	-$58,000
2005	$455,000	$249,000
2004	$279,000	$43,000

Curr. Assets:	$44,000	Curr. Liab.:	$101,000		
Plant, Equip.:	$1,232,000	Total Liab.:	$1,193,000	Indic. Yr. Divd.:	NA
Total Assets:	$1,483,000	Net Worth:	$291,000	Debt/ Equity:	3.7337

Hughes Communications Inc

11717 Exploration Ln., Germantown, MD, 20876; **PH:** 1-301-428-5500; **Fax:** 1-301-428-1868; **http://** www.hughes.com

General - Incorporation	DE	Stock - Price on:12/24/2007	$52.91
Employees	1,828	Stock Exchange	NDQ
Auditor	Deloitte & Touche LLP	Ticker Symbol	HUGH
Stk Agt	American Stock Transfer & Trust Co.	Outstanding Shares	19,140,000
Counsel	NA	E.P.S.	$1.73
DUNS No.	NA	Shareholders	NA

Business: The groups principle activity is to provide satellite communications services and equipment. The groups operates through three segments namely VSAT, telecom systems, and parent and other. Customers served by the group include telecom carriers and government agencies. Specific customers of the group include Wal-Mart Stores, Inc., ExxonMobil Corporation, Blockbuster Entertainment Corp. and GTECH Corporation. The group operates from United States, India, North America, Europe, South America, Africa, Asia and the Middle East. The group's quarterly revenue for September 2007 was 233.70 millions of USD.

Primary SIC and add'l.: 3669 4899 7389 4822

CIK No: 0001345840

Subsidiaries: Electronic Systems Products, Inc, HNS Amricas Comunicaes Ltda., HNS de Mxico S.A. de C.V., HNS Finance Corp., HNS License Sub Limited, HNS License Sub, LLC, HNS Mauritius Ltd., HNS Participaes e Emprendimentos Ltda., HNS Real Estate, LLC, HNS-India VSAT, Inc., HNS-Shanghai, Inc., Hughes Communications India Limited (1), Hughes Network Systems (Beijing) Co., Ltd., Hughes Network Systems Europe Limited, Hughes Network Systems GmbH 23 Subsidiaries included in the Index

Officers: Pradman P. Kaul/Dir., CEO, Pres., Grant A. Barber/CFO, Exec. VP, Bahram Pourmand/Exec. VP, GM - International Division, Paul T. Gaske/Exec. VP, GM - North America Division, Adrian Morris/Exec. VP - Hughes Communications, Inc, Execvp, Engineering, Hughes Network Systems, LLC, Dean Manson/VP, General Counsel, Sec., Thomas J. McElroy/Chief Accounting Officer, Deepak V. Dutt/VP, Treasurer, Investor Relations Officer, Cleo V. Belmonte/Assist. Sec.

Directors: Pradman P. Kaul/Dir., CEO, Pres., Andrew D. Africk/Dir., Stephen H. Clark/Dir., Gene O. Gabbard/Dir., Jeffrey A. Leddy/Dir., Lawrence J. Ruisi/Dir., Aaron J. Stone/Dir., Michael D. Weiner/Dir.

Owners: Insiders/1.78%, Michael D. Weiner, Pradman P. Kaul, Adrian Morris, Harbinger Capital Partners/8.76%, Paul T. Gaske, Aaron J. Stone, Grant A. Barber, Lawrence J. Ruisi, Gene O. Gabbard, Apollo Investment Fund IV, L.P./64.84%, Bahram Pourmand, Jeffrey A. Leddy, Stephen H. Clark, Andrew D. Africk (16 Owners included in Index)

Financial Data: Fiscal Year End: 12/31 **Latest Annual Data:** 12/31/2006

Year	Sales	Net Income
2006	$858,699,000	-$39,113,000
2005	$615,000	$68,854,000

Curr. Assets:	$496,435,000	Curr. Liab.:	$224,306,000	P/E Ratio:	51.87
Plant, Equip.:	$312,497,000	Total Liab.:	$716,255,000	Indic. Yr. Divd.:	NA
Total Assets:	$931,644,000	Net Worth:	$215,389,000	Debt/ Equity:	2.6557

Hugoton Royalty Trust

901 Main St., 17th Fl., Dallas, TX, 75283; **PH:** 1-877-228-5083; **Fax:** 1-214-209-2431; **http://** www.hugotontrust.com

General - Incorporation	TX	Stock - Price on:12/24/2007	$26.05
Employees	NA	Stock Exchange	NYSE
Auditor	KPMG LLP	Ticker Symbol	HGT
Stk Agt	Chase Mellon Shareholder Services LLC	Outstanding Shares	40,000,000
Counsel	NA	E.P.S.	$1.70
DUNS No.	NA	Shareholders	NA

Business: The groups principal activity is to invest in real estate properties. The group operates from the United States.

Primary SIC and add'l.: 6792

CIK No: 0000862022

Subsidiaries: XTO Energy

Officers: Nancy G. Willis/VP, Louis G. Baldwin/CFO, Exec. VP - XTO Energy INC

Financial Data: Fiscal Year End: 12/31 **Latest Annual Data:** 12/31/2006

Year	Sales	Net Income
2006	$91,440,000	$90,911,000
2005	$105,242,000	$104,832,000
2004	$81,955,000	$81,597,000

Curr. Assets:	$1,813,000	Curr. Liab.:	$1,813,000	P/E Ratio:	15.32
Plant, Equip.:	NA	Total Liab.:	$1,813,000	Indic. Yr. Divd.:	$2.680
Total Assets:	$165,610,000	Net Worth:	$163,797,000	Debt/ Equity:	NA

Huifeng Bio-Pharmaceutical Technology Inc

16B/F Ruixin Rd. Bldg. No. 25, Gaoxin Rd. XI An, Shaanxi Province, 710075; **PH:** 86-2988246358; **http://** www.hfgb.cn

General - Incorporation	NV	Stock - Price on:12/24/2007	$0.51
Employees	NA	Stock Exchange	OTC
Auditor	Jimmy C.H. Cheung & Co	Ticker Symbol	HFGB
Stk Agt	Interwest Transfer Company, Inc.	Outstanding Shares	NA
Counsel	NA	E.P.S.	NA
DUNS No.	NA	Shareholders	NA

Business: The group's principle activity is to provide case management software for specialty courts. The products are focused on health professionals and those involved in fitness related businesses. The company was into marketing of vitamineralherb.com products to customers in Oklahoma and New Mexico. Vitamineralherb.com hosts an Internet Web site where health related products can be purchased for resale. In Mar 2002, the company terminated marketing of vitamins and related products and acquired icyberdata court manager suite, an Internet-based, multi-agency asp, which includes nine case management systems as on 31-Jan-2002. The company is in the development stage. The group operates from United States.

Primary SIC and add'l.: 7372

CIK No: 0001119951

Subsidiaries: Huifeng Biochemistry, Huifeng Engineering, Northwest BioTechnic Inc, Xian Huifeng Biochemistry Engineering Company Limited, Xian Huifeng Biochemistry Group Joint-Stock Company Limited

Officers: Jingan Wang/48/Chmn., CEO, Sanding Tao/40/CFO, Xinwen Hou/40/Dir., Sec.

Directors: Jingan Wang/48/Chmn., CEO, Xinwen Hou/40/Dir., Sec.

Owners: Sanding Tao/1.76%, Xinwen Hou/1.76%, Xian Runfeng Investment Ltd. Co./4.45%, Jingan Wang/39.56%, Insiders/47.53%

Financial Data: Fiscal Year End: 12/31 **Latest Annual Data:** 12/31/2006

Year	Sales	Net Income
2006	$3,077,000	$132,000
2005	$2,443,000	-$833,000
2004	$2,479,000	-$220,000

Curr. Assets:	$3,609,000	Curr. Liab.:	$710,000		
Plant, Equip.:	$3,338,000	Total Liab.:	$710,000	Indic. Yr. Divd.:	NA
Total Assets:	$7,083,000	Net Worth:	$5,921,000	Debt/ Equity:	NA

Huiheng Medical Inc

Formerly: Mill Basin Technologies Ltd
850 Third Ave., Ste. 1801, New York, NY, 10022; **PH:** 1-646-218-1400

General - Incorporation	NV	Stock - Price on:12/24/2007	$9
Employees	NA	Stock Exchange	NA
Auditor	Li & Company, PC	Ticker Symbol	NA
Stk Agt	NA	Outstanding Shares	NA
Counsel	NA	E.P.S.	NA
DUNS No.	NA	Shareholders	NA

Business: The groups principle activity is to provide recruiting services. The groups service area includes the research and development, engineering, marketing, sales, information technology and manufacturing industries. The group operates from United States.

Primary SIC and add'l.: 5211

CIK No: 0001353972

Officers: Hui Xiaobing/55/Chmn., CEO, Richard Rosenblum/48/Dir., CFO, Pres., David Stefansky/36/Dir., Sec.

Directors: Hui Xiaobing/55/Chmn., CEO, Richard Rosenblum/48/Dir., CFO, Pres., David Stefansky/36/Dir., Sec.

Owners: Insiders/78.18%, Hui Xiaobing/78.18%

Financial Data: Fiscal Year End: 11/30 **Latest Annual Data:** 11/30/2006

Year	Sales	Net Income
2006	NA	-$56,000

Curr. Assets:	NA	Curr. Liab.:	$25,000		
Plant, Equip.:	NA	Total Liab.:	$25,000	Indic. Yr. Divd.:	NA
Total Assets:	NA	Net Worth:	-$25,000	Debt/ Equity:	NA

Human BioSystems

1127 Harker Ave., Palo Alto, CA, 94301; **PH:** 1-650-323-0943; **http://** www.humanbiosystems.com; **Email:** hmasuda@humanbiosystems.com

General - Incorporation	CA	Stock - Price on:12/24/2007	$0.065
Employees	16	Stock Exchange	OTC
Auditor	LL Bradford & Co	Ticker Symbol	HBSC
Stk Agt	First American Stock Transfer, Inc.	Outstanding Shares	108,350,000
Counsel	NA	E.P.S.	-$0.036
DUNS No.	NA	Shareholders	NA

Business: The group's principle activity is to develop and provide economical, non-toxic methods of extending the shelf life and improving the quality of blood platelets and other biological material. The customers include blood banks, hospitals, clinics and similar organizations. The primary competitors of the group include dupont, baxter, lifecell, cerus and cryo life. The group is currently in the developmental stage. The group operates from United States.

Primary SIC and add'l.: 8731

CIK No: 0001070181

Officers: Harry Masuda/Dir., Co - Founder, CEO/$244,687.00, Paul Okimoto/Chmn., VP, Co - Founder/$94,640.00, David Winter/Pres., Luis Toledo/Chief Medical Officer

Directors: Harry Masuda/Dir., Co - Founder, CEO, Paul Okimoto/Chmn., VP, Co - Founder, Michael D. Strong/Member - Advisory Board, George Rubisson/Member - Advisory Board, Ed Snyder/Member - Advisory Board, Jose A. Venzor/Member - Advisory Board, Vincent A. Yalon/Member - Advisory Board, Bryan Flaherty/Member - Advisory Board, Richard Wells/Member - Advisory Board

Owners: Meiswinkel Investment Group/6.90%, Harry Masuda/3.01%, Larry McCleary/7.38%, David Winter/1.10%, Langley Park Investments/7.10%, Paul Okimoto/1.82%, Claude Luster, Insiders/14.51%

Financial Data: Fiscal Year End:12/31 Latest Annual Data: 12/31/2006

Year	Sales	Net Income
2006	NA	-$2,753,000
2005	NA	-$5,807,000
2004	NA	-$2,603,000

Curr. Assets:	$824,000	Curr. Liab.:	$1,363,000		
Plant, Equip.:	$41,000	Total Liab.:	$1,383,000	Indic. Yr. Divd.:	NA
Total Assets:	$920,000	Net Worth:	-$463,000	Debt/ Equity:	NA

Human Genome Sciences Inc

14200 Shady Grove Rd., Rockville, MD, 20850; *PH:* 1-301-309-8504; *Fax:* 1-301-309-8512; *http://* www.hgsi.com

General -		Stock-	
Incorporation	DE	Price on:12/24/2007	$9.86
Employees	770	Stock Exchange	NDQ
Auditor	Ernst & Young LLP	Ticker Symbol	HGSI
Stk Agt	American Stock Transfer & Trust Co.	Outstanding Shares	134,270,000
Counsel	NA	E.P.S.	-$1.77
DUNS No.	79-705-7437	Shareholders	NA

Business: The group's principal activity is to discover, develop, manufacture and market gene-based drugs to treat and cure disease. The group has ten products in clinical development, including drugs to treat such diseases as cancer, rheumatoid arthritis, lupus, hepatitis c, chronic venous ulcers, growth hormone deficiency and immunodeficiencies. The group focuses its internal product development efforts on novel human protein and antibody drugs discovered through genomics-based research and on new improved long-acting versions of existing protein drugs created using proprietary albumin fusion technology. The group uses collaborations for the development of gene therapy products, small molecule drugs and diagnostic products discovered using its genomics-based technology.

Primary SIC and add'l.: 2834 2835 8731

CIK No: 0000901219

Subsidiaries: Human Genome Sciences Europe GmbH, Human Genome Sciences Pacific Pty Ltd., Traville LLC

Officers: Thomas H. Watkins/Dir., CEO, Pres./$3,029,893.00, Curran M. Simpson/Sr. VP - Operations, Barry A. Labinger/Exec. VP, Chief Commercial Officer/$1,855,712.00, Timothy C. Barabe/CFO, Sr. VP/$626,441.00, Margery B. Fischbein/VP - Business Development, Strategic Planning, Randy Maddux/VP - Manufacturing Operations, Anthony /Mgr. - Manufacturing, Tricia /Payroll Supervisor, David C. Stump/Exec. VP - Research, Development/$1,828,443.00, Susan Bateson McKay/Sr. VP - Human Resources, Sally D. Bolmer/Sr. VP - Regulatory Affairs, Gilles Gallant/VP - Clinical Oncology, HGS Europe, Jerry Parrott/VP - Corporate Communications, Public Policy, Daniel Gold/Sr. VP - Manufacturing Alliances, Daniel Odenheimer/VP - Clinical Research, General Medicine *(22 Officers included in Index)*

Directors: Thomas H. Watkins/Dir., CEO, Pres., Argeris N. Karabelas/Chmn., Tuan Ha-Ngoc/Dir., Robert C. Young/Dir., Max Link/Dir., Augustine Lawlor/Dir., Richard J. Danzig/Dir., Jurgen Drews/Dir., Kevin P. Starr/45/Dir., William D. Young/Dir.

Owners: Robert C. Young, Curran M. Simpson, Max Link, Thomas H. Watkins, A. N. Karabelas, Taube Hodson Stonex Partners, Ltd./5.20%, Jrgen Drews, Susan Bateson McKay, Tuan Ha-Ngoc, FMR Corp./14.80%, Kevin P. Starr, Sid R. Bass Management Trust/7.80%, Barry A. Labinger, Wellington Management Company, LLP/8.30%, Richard J. Danzig *(19 Owners included in Index)*

Financial Data: Fiscal Year End:12/31 Latest Annual Data: 12/31/2006

Year	Sales	Net Income
2006	$25,755,000	-$251,173,000
2005	$19,113,000	-$239,439,000
2004	$3,831,000	-$242,898,000

Curr. Assets:	$392,049,000	Curr. Liab.:	$91,951,000		
Plant, Equip.:	$285,177,000	Total Liab.:	$935,745,000	Indic. Yr. Divd.:	NA
Total Assets:	$1,149,668,000	Net Worth:	$213,923,000	Debt/ Equity:	3.5130

Human Pheromone Sciences Inc

84 W Santa Clara St., Ste. 720, San Jose, CA, 95113; *PH:* 1-408-938-3030; *Fax:* 1-408-938-3025; *http://* www.naturalattraction.com; *Email:* nasupport@erox.com

General -		Stock-	
Incorporation	CA	Price on:12/24/2007	$0.82
Employees	2	Stock Exchange	OTC
Auditor	Singer Lewak Greenbaum & Goldstein	Ticker Symbol	EROX
Stk Agt	American Stock Transfer & Trust Co.	Outstanding Shares	4,150,000
Counsel	Heller Ehrman White & McAuliffe LLP	E.P.S.	$0.00
DUNS No.	78-270-9307	Shareholders	NA

Business: The group's principal activity is to develop and market consumer products containing human pheromones as a component. The group markets three fragrances, realm(R) women, realm(R) men and inner realm(r). The group sells these products through independent distributors in selected markets in south east Asia. The group also licenses the rights to sell these products to niche marketing, inc. The products include a full line of fragrance and bath and body products including eau de toilette, cologne, eau de parfume, lotion, bath and shower gel, after-shave balm, deodorant, talc, soap and body cream.

Primary SIC and add'l.: 2844 8731 6794

CIK No: 0000878616

Officers: Bernard I. Grosser/Scientist, Louis Monti/Scientist, Chloe Jennings-White/Scientist

Owners: Greg Fredrick/0.20%, Robert Marx/4.00%, Insiders/16.60%, Larry H. Schatz, L.P./7.20%, Bernard I. Grosser/5.20%, William P. Horgan/4.90%, Renovatio Global Funds, L.P./15.80%, Helen C. Leong/3.60%

Financial Data: Fiscal Year End:12/31 Latest Annual Data: 12/31/2006

Year	Sales	Net Income
2006	$1,227,000	-$111,000
2005	$414,000	-$934,000
2004	$1,140,000	-$542,000

Curr. Assets:	$2,073,000	Curr. Liab.:	$990,000		
Plant, Equip.:	$2,000	Total Liab.:	$1,711,000	Indic. Yr. Divd.:	NA
Total Assets:	$2,075,000	Net Worth:	$364,000	Debt/ Equity:	NA

Humana Inc

500 W Main St., Louisville, KY, 40202; *PH:* 1-502-580-1000; *Fax:* 1-502-580-3677; *http://* www.humana.com

General -		Stock-	
Incorporation	DE	Price on:12/24/2007	$61.47
Employees	22,300	Stock Exchange	NYSE
Auditor	PricewaterhouseCoopers LLP	Ticker Symbol	HUM
Stk Agt	National City Bank	Outstanding Shares	168,040,000
Counsel	NA	E.P.S.	$4.40
DUNS No.	04-994-4143	Shareholders	NA

Business: The group's principle activity is to guide consumers to make informed health and benefits decisions, and giving back to the communities we serve. The group operates from United States.

Primary SIC and add'l.: 6324

CIK No: 0000049071

Subsidiaries: American Tax Credit Corporate Georgia Fund III, LLC , Availity, LLC , CAC-Florida Medical Centers, LLC, Carenetwork, CareNetwork, Inc. Doing Business As:, CarePlus Health Plans, Inc. Doing Business As:, CarePlus Real Estate Holdings, LLC, CarePlus Transportation, LLC, ChoiceCare Network, ChoiceCare/Humana (IL, IN, KY, OH), Coastal Pediatric-Ormond, Coastal Pediatrics-Daytona, Coastal Pediatrics-Port Orange, Corphealth Healthcare, Inc., Corphealth, Inc. 100 Subsidiaries included in the Index

Officers: Michael B. McCallister/Dir., CEO, Pres./$5,798,613.00, Bruce J. Goodman/Sr. VP, Chief Service, Information Officer/$2,197,128.00, Bonnie Hathcock/Sr. VP, Chief Human Resources Officer, Arthur P. Hipwell/Sr. VP, Heidi S. Margulis/Sr. VP - Government Relations, James E. Murray/COO, Sr. VP/$2,778,690.00, Steven E. McCulley/VP, Controller, Principal Accounting Officer, James H. Bloem/CFO, Sr. VP/$2,103,072.00, Steve Moya/Sr. VP, Chief Marketing Officer, John M. Bertko/58/VP, Chief Actuary, Jonathan T. Lord/Sr. VP, Chief Innovation Officer/$2,086,710.00, Thomas J. Liston/VP - Strategy, Corporate Development, Kathleen Pellegrino/VP, Acting General Counsel, Tom Noland/Sr. VP - Corporate Communications, Bruce Perkins/Sr. VP - National Contracting, Puerto Rico Operations *(16 Officers included in Index)*

Directors: Michael B. McCallister/Dir., CEO, Pres., David A. Jones/Chmn., Frank A. Damelio/Dir., Roy W. Dunbar/Dir., Kurt J. Hilzinger/Dir., James J. O'Brien/Dir., Ann W. Reynolds/Dir., James O. Robbins/65/Dir., William J. McDonald/Dir.

Owners: James E. Murray, Frank A. DAmelio, Barclays Global Investors NA/10.80%, James H. Bloem, Vanguard Specialized Funds/5.10%, Ann W. Reynolds, Roy W. Dunbar, Kurt J. Hilzinger, Insiders/2.58%, Bruce J. Goodman, Michael B. McCallister, Wellington Management Company, LLP/5.40%, FMR Corp./5.50%, David A. Jones, Goldman Sachs Asset Management, L.P./6.20% *(16 Owners included in Index)*

Financial Data: Fiscal Year End:12/31 Latest Annual Data: 06/30/2007

Year	Sales	Net Income
2007	$6,426,797,000	$216,846,000
2006	$5,655,219,000	$155,021,000
2005	$14,418,127,000	$308,483,000

Curr. Assets:	$7,332,973,000	Curr. Liab.:	$5,191,812,000	P/E Ratio:	21.80
Plant, Equip.:	$545,004,000	Total Liab.:	$7,073,610,000	Indic. Yr. Divd.:	NA
Total Assets:	$10,127,496,000	Net Worth:	$3,053,886,000	Debt/ Equity:	0.4207

Hummingbird Ltd

1 Sparks Ave., Toronto, ON, M2H 2W1; *PH:* 1-416-496-2200; *http://* www.hummingbird.com

General -		Stock-	
Incorporation	Canada	Price on:12/24/2007	NA
Employees	NA	Stock Exchange	NA
Auditor	Deloitte & Touche LLP	Ticker Symbol	NA
Stk Agt	Mellon Trust Co	Outstanding Shares	NA
Counsel	DuMoulin Black	E.P.S.	NA
DUNS No.	24-803-1155	Shareholders	NA

Business: The group's principle activity is to design, manufacture and market enterprise software solutions. The products include enterprise information portal solutions and host access and network connectivity. The group offers a portfolio of modular and interoperable technologies comprised of portal, document, knowledge and records management, collaboration, search, retrieval, business intelligence and data transformation and connectivity. The group also provides a turnkey solution for rapid and cost-effective deployment of data marts. The operations of the group are carried out in Canada, the United States of America, Europe and Asia-Pacific.

Primary SIC and add'l.: 7372 4899 7379

CIK No: 0000919548

Hungarian Telephone & Cable Corp

1201 Third Ave., Ste. 3400, Seattle, WA, 98101; *PH:* 1-206-654-0204; *Fax:* 1-206-652-2911; *http://* www.htcc.hu; *Email:* budapest@htcc.hu

General -		Stock-	
Incorporation	DE	Price on:12/24/2007	$21.32
Employees	700	Stock Exchange	AMEX
Auditor	KPMG Hungaria Kft	Ticker Symbol	HTC
Stk Agt	Continental Stock Transfer & Trust Co	Outstanding Shares	16,430,000
Counsel	Shearman & Sterling LLP	E.P.S.	-$2.52
DUNS No.	79-691-1956	Shareholders	NA

Business: The group's principle activity is to provide basic telephone services. The operations of the group are located in three defined regions of the republic of hungary. The group owns and operates virtually all existing public telephone exchanges and local loop telecommunications network facilities in its operating areas. The group also provides non-cellular local voice telephone services, network services and pbx hardware and sales services. The group's quarterly revenue for Sep'07 was 116.14 millions of USD.

Primary SIC and add'l.: 4813

CIK No: 0000889949

Subsidiaries: Austrian Entity, Bulgarian Entity, Company for Telecommunication and Communication PanTel d.o.o. Novi Sad, HTCC Menedzsment es Tanacsado Kft., Hungarian Entities, Hungarotel Tavkozlesi Zrt., PanTel Romania SRL, PanTel Slovakia s.r.o., Pantel Tavkozlesi Kft., PanTel TechnoCom Kft., PanTel Telecommunications and Communications Services GmbH, PanTel Telekommunikacije in Kommunikacije d.o.o., PTB EAD, Romanian Entity, Serbia & Montenegro Entity 17 Subsidiaries included in the Index

Officers: Martin Lea/CEO, Pres., Peter T. Noone/General Counsel, Sec./$422,000.00, Robert Bowker/CFO

Directors: Jesper Theill Eriksen/Chmn., Carsten Dyrup Revsbech/Vice Chmn., Jens Due Olsen/Dir., Henrik Scheinemann/Dir., Peter Feiner/Dir., Ole Steen Andersen/Dir., Robert Dogonowski/Dir.

Owners: Ole Steen Andersen, Insiders/7.80%, Ole Bertram/2.80%, John B. Ryan, William T. McGann, Peter T. Noone

Financial Data: *Fiscal Year End:*12/31 *Latest Annual Data:* 12/31/2006

Year	Sales	Net Income
2006	$193,732,000	$21,124,000
2005	$110,240,000	$2,892,000
2004	$60,340,000	$16,242,000

Curr. Assets:	$79,829,000	**Curr. Liab.:**	$121,073,000		
Plant, Equip.:	$180,329,000	**Total Liab.:**	$245,780,000	**Indic. Yr. Divd.:**	NA
Total Assets:	$332,754,000	**Net Worth:**	$86,974,000	**Debt/ Equity:**	1.1572

Hunt J B Transport Services Inc

615 J.B. Hunt Corporate Dr., Lowell, AR, 72745; *PH:* 1-479-820-0000; *Fax:* 1-479-820-3418; *http://* www.jbhunt.com

General - Incorporation	AR	**Stock**- Price on:12/24/2007	$28.88
Employees	17,150	Stock Exchange	NYSE
Auditor	Ernst & Young LLP	Ticker Symbol	JBHT
Stk Agt	EquiServe Trust Co N.A	Outstanding Shares	141,180,000
Counsel	Wright, Lindsey & Jennings	E.P.S	$1.53
DUNS No.	00-633-8552	Shareholders	NA

Business: The group's principle activity is to provide transportation logistics in North America. The group operates in three segments: the truck (jbt) segment; the intermodal (jbi) segment and the dedicated contract services. The truck (jbt) segment includes full truck-load, dry-van freight that is primarily transported utilizing company-owned or controlled revenue equipment. Freight is typically transported over roads and highways. The intermodal (jbi) segment includes freight that is transported by rail over at least a portion of the movement. This may also include certain repositioning truck loads that are moved by jbi equipment or third-party carriers, in circumstances where the movement directs jbi equipment back towards intermodal operations. The dedicated contract services (dcs) segment usually includes company-owned revenue equipment and employee drivers who are assigned to a specific customer, traffic lane or service. The group's quarterly revenue for September 2007 was 891.64 millions of USD.

Primary SIC and add'l.: 4213

CIK No: 0000728535

Subsidiaries: FIS, Inc, Hunt Mexicana, S.A. de C.V, J.B. Hunt Corp., J.B. Hunt Logistics, Inc, J.B. Hunt Transport, Inc, L.A., Inc

Officers: Kirk Thompson/Dir., CEO, Pres./$1,313,695.00, Craig Harper/COO, Exec. VP - Operations/$674,660.00, Bob D. Ralston/Exec. VP - Equipment, Properties, Johnelle D. Hunt/Dir., Corp. Sec., Jerry W. Walton/CFO, Exec. VP - Finance, Administration/$748,194.00, John N. Roberts/Pres. - Dedicated Contract Services, Exec. VP - Enterprise Solutions, Paul R. Bergant/Chief Marketing Officer, Exec. VP - Marketing/$693,109.00, Kay Palmer/CIO, Exec. VP, Donald G. Cope/57/Sr. VP - Finance, Controller, Chief Accounting Officer, David N. Chelette/44/VP, Treasurer, Terrence D. Matthews/49/Sr. VP - Marketing, David G. Mee/47/Sr. VP - Tax, Risk Management

Directors: Kirk Thompson/Dir., CEO, Pres., Wayne Garrison/Chmn., Leland E. Tollett/Dir., Johnelle D. Hunt/Dir., Corp. Sec., James L. Robo/Dir., Coleman H. Peterson/Dir., John A. White/Dir., Bryan J. Hunt/Dir., Gary Charles George/57/Dir.

Owners: Coleman H. Peterson, Bryan Hunt, Johnelle Hunt/24.70%, Paul Bergant, Kirk Thompson, Wayne Garrison/5.90%, John A. White, Gary Charles George, Insiders/30.98%, Leland Tollett, James L. Robo, Craig Harper, Jerry W. Walton

Financial Data: *Fiscal Year End:*12/31 *Latest Annual Data:* 12/31/2006

Year	Sales	Net Income
2006	$3,327,987,000	$219,952,000
2005	$3,127,899,000	$207,311,000
2004	$2,786,154,000	$146,256,000

Curr. Assets:	$471,243,000	**Curr. Liab.:**	$478,730,000	**P/E Ratio:**	20.06
Plant, Equip.:	$1,283,551,000	**Total Liab.:**	$1,010,320,000	**Indic. Yr. Divd.:**	$0.360
Total Assets:	$1,770,057,000	**Net Worth:**	$759,737,000	**Debt/ Equity:**	NA

Huntington Bancshares Inc

208 S Us Hwy. 69, Huntington, TX, 75949; *PH:* 1-936-422-3000; *http://* www.huntington.com

General - Incorporation	MD	**Stock**- Price on:12/24/2007	$22.04
Employees	8,081	Stock Exchange	NDQ
Auditor	Deloitte & Touche, LLP	Ticker Symbol	HBAN
Stk Agt	Computershare Investor Services LLC	Outstanding Shares	235,910,000
Counsel	Deloitte & Touche LLP	E.P.S	$1.76
DUNS No.	04-643-1227	Shareholders	NA

Business: The groups principle activity is to provide banking services. The groups services include mortgage banking, automobile financing, equipment leasing and investment management services. In the year 2007 the group acquired Archer-Meek-Weiler Agency, Inc. The group operates from United States.

Primary SIC and add'l.: 6712 6021

CIK No: 0000049196

Subsidiaries: 41 South High Ltd, 7575 Corporation, Allen Edwin Home Mortgage, LLC, Arbors Apartments LLC, Arbors of Dublin LLC, Bosgraaf Capital Company, LLC, CB&T Capital Investment Company, Cheyenne Mountain Apartments LLC, Cheyenne Mountain/DEC LLC, Distinctive Mortgage Company, LLC, East Sound Realty, Inc., First Sunset Development, Inc., Forty-One Corporation, Fourteen Corporation, Haberer Registered Investment Advisor, Inc. 91 Subsidiaries included in the Index

Officers: Thomas E. Hoaglin/Chmn., CEO, Sharon Speyer/Regional Pres. - Northwest Ohio, Jayson Zatta/Regional Pres. - Ohio Valley Region, Vincent W. Locher/Regional Pres. - Pittsburgh, Stephen R. Sant/Regional Pres. - Western Pennsylvania, Clayton Rice/Regional Pres. - West Virginia, Daniel B. Benhase/Sr. Exec. VP - Private Financial Group, Jerry Kelsheimer/Regional Pres. - Greater Cleveland, Wilton Dolloff/Exec. VP - Operations, Technology, Jim Dunlap/Regional Banking Group Pres., Mary W. Navarro/Sr. Exec. VP, Regional Banking Group Pres., Richard A. Cheap/Exec. VP, General Counsel, Sec. - Cashier, James E. Kunk/Regional Pres. - Central Ohio, James W. Nelson/Exec. VP, Chief Risk Officer, Donald R. Kimble/CFO, Exec. VP *(25 Officers included in Index)*

Directors: Thomas E. Hoaglin/Chmn., CEO, Gerard P. Mastroianni/Dir., James D. Hilliker/Dir., Jonathan A. Levy/Dir., Kathleen H. Ransier/Dir., John B. Gerlach/Dir., Marty E. Adams/Dir., COO, Pres., Marylouise Fennell/Dir., Raymond J. Biggs/Dir., Don M. Casto/Dir., Michael J. Endres/Dir., Karen A. Holbrook/Dir., David P. Lauer/Dir., Wm. J. Lhota/Dir., Gene E. Little/Dir. *(16 Directors included in Index)*

Owners: Michael J. Endres, Insiders/3.02%, Thomas E. Hoaglin, Raymond J. Biggs, Don M. Casto, Daniel B. Benhase, Donald R. Kimble, Gene E. Little, Wm. J. Lhota, Kathleen H. Ransier, David L. Porteous, David P. Lauer, James W. Nelson, Karen A. Holbrook, Ronald C. Baldwin *(16 Owners included in Index)*

Financial Data: *Fiscal Year End:*12/31 *Latest Annual Data:* 12/31/2006

Year	Sales	Net Income
2006	$2,704,779,000	$461,221,000
2005	$2,282,102,000	$412,091,000
2004	$2,165,913,000	$398,925,000

Curr. Assets:	$1,630,971,000	**Curr. Liab.:**	$28,314,814,000	**P/E Ratio:**	11.72
Plant, Equip.:	$401,103,000	**Total Liab.:**	$32,314,693,000	**Indic. Yr. Divd.:**	$1.060
Total Assets:	$35,329,019,000	**Net Worth:**	$3,014,326,000	**Debt/ Equity:**	1.5245

HuntMountain Resources

1611 N Molter Rd. Ste. 201, Liberty Lake, WA, 99019; *PH:* 1-509-892-5287; *Fax:* 1-509-892-5318; *http://* www.huntmountain.com; *Email:* info@huntmountain.com

General - Incorporation	NV	**Stock**- Price on:12/24/2007	NA
Employees	4	Stock Exchange	OTC
Auditor	NA	Ticker Symbol	HNTM
Stk Agt	Computershare Trust Co	Outstanding Shares	32,270,000
Counsel	Dorsey & Whitney LLP	E.P.S	-$0.09
DUNS No.	NA	Shareholders	NA

Business: The groups principle activities include acquiring, exploring and developing mineral properties. The group operates from the United States and Argentina.

Primary SIC and add'l.: 1499

CIK No: 0000065224

Subsidiaries: Cerro Cazador S.A., HuntMountain Investments, LLC, HuntMountain Resources Ltd.

Officers: Tim Hunt/55/Chmn., CEO, Pres., Matthew Hughes/47/COO, Exec. VP, Ronald E. Schutz/58/CFO, Marc Lipsker/54/VP - Investor Relations, Kimberley R. Anderson/Legal Counsel, Bryn Harman/CFO

Directors: Tim Hunt/55/Chmn., CEO, Pres., Greg Lipsker/58/Vice Chmn., Randal L. Hardy/46/Dir., William R. Green/68/Dir., Eberhard A. Schmidt/70/Dir., Alastair H. Summers/71/Dir.

Owners: Randal L. Hardy/0.69%, Tim Hunt/75.68%, Ronald E. Schutz/0.34%, Gregory B. Lipsker/2.25%, Danilo Silva/0.31%, Alastair H. Summers/0.46%, William R. Green/3.22%, Insiders/80.96%, Matthew Hughes/0.36%, Eberhard A. Schmidt/0.48%

Financial Data: *Fiscal Year End:*12/31 *Latest Annual Data:* 12/31/2006

Year	Sales	Net Income
2006	$54,000	-$2,014,000
2005	$18,000	-$242,000
2004	$4,000	-$17,000

Curr. Assets:	$316,000	**Curr. Liab.:**	$61,000		
Plant, Equip.:	$8,000	**Total Liab.:**	$61,000	**Indic. Yr. Divd.:**	NA
Total Assets:	$401,000	**Net Worth:**	$340,000	**Debt/ Equity:**	NA

Huntsman Corp

500 Huntsman Way, Salt Lake City, UT, 84108; *PH:* 1-801-584-5700; *Fax:* 1-801-584-5781; *http://* www.huntsman.com

General - Incorporation	DE	**Stock**- Price on:12/24/2007	NA
Employees	15,000	Stock Exchange	NYSE
Auditor	Deloitte& Touche LLP	Ticker Symbol	HUN
Stk Agt	Bank of New York	Outstanding Shares	221,900,000
Counsel	NA	E.P.S	$0.89
DUNS No.	NA	Shareholders	NA

Business: The groups principle activity is to manufacture inorganic and commodity chemical products. The group operates through six segments namely, polyurethanes, materials and effects, performance products, pigments, polymers and base chemicals. The group operates from the United States. Of the total revenue in the year 2006, the polyurethanes 33%, materials and effects 16%, performance products 19%, pigments 10%, polymers 17% and base chemicals 5%. The group's quarterly revenue for September 2007 was 2,480.00 millions of USD.

Primary SIC and add'l.: 2821 2865 2843 2816 2869

CIK No: 0001307954

Subsidiaries: Airstar Corporation, Alta One Inc., Arabian Polyol Company Limited, Astorit AG, Avanti Switzerland (Monthey) SA, BASF Huntsman Shanghai Isocyanate Investment BV, Chemical Australia Property Trust, Chemical Blending Holland BV, Chemplex (NZ) Holdings Limited, CP Manufacturing Pty Limited, Eurofuels LLC, Eurogen C.V., Eurostar Industries LLC, Felgray Pty Limited, Gulf Advanced Chemical Industries Company Limited 208 Subsidiaries included in the Index

Officers: Peter R. Huntsman/Dir., CEO, Pres./$7,947,962.00, Kimo J. Esplin/CFO, Exec. VP/$3,014,031.00, Samuel D. Scruggs/Exec. VP, General Counsel, Sec./$2,932,114.00, Anthony P. Hankins/Division Pres. - Polyurethanes/$3,465,833.00, John R. Heskett/VP - Corporate Development, Investor Relations, James R. Moore/VP, Deputy General Counsel, Wade R. Rogers/VP - Global Human Resources, Maria Csiba-Womersley/CIO, VP, Paul G. Hulme/Division Pres. - Materials, Effects/$3,363,964.00, Thomas J. Keenan/Division Pres. - Pigments, Kevin J. Ninow/Division Pres. - Base Chemicals, Polymers, Donald J. Stanutz/Division Pres. - Performance Products, Michael J. Kern/Sr. VP - Environmental, Health, Safety, Russell R. Stolle/Sr. VP - Global Public Affairs, Communications, Brian V. Ridd/Sr. VP - Purchasing *(19 Officers included in Index)*

Directors: Peter R. Huntsman/Dir., CEO, Pres., Jon M. Huntsman/Chmn., Nolan D. Archibald/Dir., Marsha J. Evans/Dir., William H. Lichtenberger/Dir., David J. Matlin/46/Dir., Richard Michaelson/Dir., Christopher R. Pechock/43/Dir., Wayne A. Reaud/Dir., Alvin V. Shoemaker/Dir.

Owners: Alvin V. Shoemaker, MatlinPatterson Global Opportunities Partners L.P., Paul G. Hulme, Samuel D. Scruggs, Wayne E. Reaud, Insiders, Nolan D. Archibald, Kimo J. Esplin, Peter R. Huntsman, Jon M. Huntsman, Richard A. Michaelson, The Jon and Karen Huntsman Foundation, Marsha J. Evans, HMP Equity Trust, Huntsman Family Holdings Company LLC *(20 Owners included in Index)*

Financial Data: *Fiscal Year End:*12/31 *Latest Annual Data:* 12/31/2006

Year	Sales	Net Income
2006	NA	$29,400,000
2005	NA	$20,400,000
2004	NA	$36,800,000

Hurco Cos Inc

1 Technology Way, Indianapolis, IN, 46268; *PH:* 1-317-293-5309; *Fax:* 1-800-634-2416; *http://* www.hurco.com

General - Incorporation	IN	Stock - Price on:12/24/2007	$46.92
Employees	320	Stock Exchange	NDQ
Auditor	Crowe Chizek & Co. LLC	Ticker Symbol	HURC
Stk Agt	EquiServe Trust Co N.A	Outstanding Shares	6,390,000
Counsel	Baker & Daniels	E.P.S	$3.10
DUNS No.	04-458-1734	Shareholders	NA

Business: The group's principal activities are to design, develop, produce and market interactive, personal computer based, computer control systems and software and computerized machine systems. The group's products include computerized machine systems, such as milling machines, machining centers and metal forming systems and computer controlled systems and related software. The products are marketed through 346 independent agents and distributors in 35 countries throughout North America, Europe and Asia. It serves various industries, which include aerospace, defense, medical equipment, energy, transportation and computer industries. The group is operating in the United States, England, Germany, France, Italy, Singapore and China.

Primary SIC and add'l.: 7372 3546 3541

CIK No: 0000315374

Subsidiaries: Hurco (S.E. Asia) Pte Ltd., Hurco B.V., Hurco Europe Limited, Hurco GmbH, Hurco Manufacturing Ltd., Hurco S.a.r.l., Hurco S.r.l.

Officers: Michael Doar/Chmn., CEO - Hurco Companies, Inc, Sonja K. McClelland/Corporate Controller, Assist. Sec., James D. Fabris/COO, Pres., Stephen H. Cooper/Dir., Independent Business Consultant, John Oblazney/VP, Sec., Treasurer, CFO, Curtis O. Noel/Dir., Independent Business Consultant

Directors: Michael Doar/Chmn., CEO - Hurco Companies, Inc, Charlie Rentschler/Dir., Robert W. Cruickshank/Dir., Richard T. Niner/Dir., Stephen H. Cooper/Dir., Independent Business Consultant, Curtis O. Noel/Dir., Independent Business Consultant, Michael P. Mazza/43/Dir.

Owners: David E. Platts, Michael Doar/1.10%, Sonja K. McClelland, Royce & Associates, Inc./11.10%, Richard T. Niner/11.40%, Gerald V. Roch, Robert W. Cruickshank, Stephen H. Cooper, James D. Fabris, Michael P. Mazza, Charlie Rentschler, Insiders/13.60%, Systematic Financial Management LP/6.90%

Financial Data: *Fiscal Year End:*10/31 *Latest Annual Data:* 10/31/2006

Year		Sales		Net Income	
2006		$148,517,000		$15,479,000	
2005		$125,509,000		$16,443,000	
2004		$99,572,000		$6,269,000	
Curr. Assets:	$100,882,000	Curr. Liab.:	$44,340,000	P/E Ratio:	15.14
Plant, Equip.:	$9,150,000	Total Liab.:	$48,739,000	Indic. Yr. Divd.:	NA
Total Assets:	$124,114,000	Net Worth:	$75,375,000	Debt/ Equity:	NA

Huron Consulting Group Inc

550 W Van Buren St., Chicago, IL, 60607; *PH:* 1-312-583-8700; *Fax:* 1-312-583-8701; *http://* www.huronconsultinggroup.com

General - Incorporation	DE	Stock - Price on:12/24/2007	$69.98
Employees	1,035	Stock Exchange	NDQ
Auditor	PricewaterhouseCoopers LLP	Ticker Symbol	HURN
Stk Agt	Computershare Investor Services LLC	Outstanding Shares	18,650,000
Counsel	NA	E.P.S	$2.15
DUNS No.	NA	Shareholders	NA

Business: The groups principle activity is to provide financial and operational consulting services. The groups services include disputes and investigations, economic consulting and corporate advisory, valuation and interim management. The groups operates through two segments namely financial consulting and operational consulting. Customers served by the group include education, professional services, transportation services, healthcare, telecommunications, consumer products and industrial manufacturing. The group acquired Wellspring Partners LTD, Glass & Associates, Inc in the year 2007, MSGalt & Company, LLC, Document Review Consulting Services LLC in the year 2006 and Speltz & Weis LLC in the year 2005. The group operates from the United States. The group's quarterly revenue for September 2007 was 145.34 millions of USD.

Primary SIC and add'l.: 8748 7389 8742

CIK No: 0001289848

Subsidiaries: Aaxis Technologies, Inc, FAB Advisory Services, LLC, Huron (UK) Limited, Huron Consulting Group Holdings LLC, Huron Consulting Services LLC, Wellspring Management Services LLC

Officers: Gary E. Holdren/Chmn., CEO, Pres./$3,051,933.00, Gary L. Burge/CFO, VP, Treasurer/$843,916.00, Jeffrey H. Ellis/MD, Peter J. Eschenbach/MD, Kenneth Evola/MD, Wanda L. Forrest/MD, Robert Fraga/MD, Mukesh Gangwal/MD, Christopher Getner/MD, Dawn M. Gideon/MD, Scott M. Gillis/MD, Todd J. Glomb/MD, Jeffrey S. Gray/MD, Mark Grover/MD, David Hanfland/MD *(306 Officers included in Index)*

Directors: Gary E. Holdren/Chmn., CEO, Pres., George E. Massaro/Vice Chmn., Dubose Ausley/Dir., James D. Edwards/Dir., Eugene H. Lockhart/Dir., John McCartney/Dir., John S. Moody/Dir.

Owners: James D. Edwards, Mary M. Sawall, Daniel P. Broadhurst, Stanley N. Logan, George E. Massaro, John McCartney, Gary L. Burge, FMR Corporation/13.80%, DuBose Ausley, Gary E. Holdren/6.40%, Insiders/9.30%, John S. Moody, H. Eugene Lockhart, Wells Fargo& Company/7.00%

Financial Data: *Fiscal Year End:*12/31 *Latest Annual Data:* 12/31/2006

Year		Sales		Net Income	
2006		$321,918,000		$26,689,000	
2005		$225,962,000		$17,769,000	
2004		$173,911,000		$10,864,000	
Curr. Assets:	$106,409,000	Curr. Liab.:	$70,362,000	P/E Ratio:	39.54
Plant, Equip.:	$27,742,000	Total Liab.:	$82,864,000	Indic. Yr. Divd.:	NA
Total Assets:	$199,444,000	Net Worth:	$116,580,000	Debt/ Equity:	0.8624

Huron Valley ST MI

390 Spaulding Ave. Se, Grand Rapids, MI, 49546; *PH:* 1-616-942-3400

General - Incorporation		Stock - Price on:12/24/2007	NA
Employees	NA	Stock Exchange	OTC
Auditor	NA	Ticker Symbol	HVLME
Stk Agt	NA	Outstanding Shares	NA
Counsel	NA	E.P.S	NA
DUNS No.	NA	Shareholders	NA

Business: The groups principle activity is to provide recruiting services. The groups service area includes the research and development, engineering, marketing, sales, information technology and manufacturing industries. The group operates from United States.

Primary SIC and add'l.: 6022

CIK No: 0001212485

Hurray! Holding Company Ltd

15/F,Tower B,Gateway Plz., No.18 Xia Guang Li,N Rd., E Third Ring Chaoyang, Beijing, Hebei, 100027; *PH:* 86-1084555566; *Fax:* 86-1084555555; *http://* www.hurray.com.cn

General - Incorporation	Cayman Islands	Stock - Price on:12/24/2007	$4.74
Employees	NA	Stock Exchange	NDQ
Auditor	Deloitte Touche Tohmatsu CPA Ltd.	Ticker Symbol	HRAY
Stk Agt	Dexia Corporate Srvcs Hong Kong Ltd.	Outstanding Shares	21,680,000
Counsel	Morrison & Foerster LLP	E.P.S	NA
DUNS No.	NA	Shareholders	NA

Business: The groups principle activity is to provide music and music related products. The groups services include 2G, 2.5G and Software and system integration services. The products of the group include ringtones, ringbacktones, and truetones. The groups operates through two segments namely wireless value added services and software and system integration services. In the year 2005, the group acquired Beijing Hutong Wuxian Technology Co., Ltd., Guangzhou Piosan Information Technology Co., Ltd. and Beijing Hengji Weiye Electronic Commerce Co., Ltd. The group operates from China. The group's quarterly revenue for September 2007 was 13.62 millions of USD.

Primary SIC and add'l.: 7372 4899 7374

CIK No: 0001294435

Subsidiaries: Beijing Cool Young Information Technology Co., Ltd., Beijing Enterprise Network Technology Co., Ltd., Beijing Hengji Weiye Electronic Commerce Co., Ltd., Beijing Hurray! Freeland Digital Music Technology Co., Ltd., Beijing Hutong Wuxian Technology Co., Ltd., Beijing Palmsky Technology Co., Ltd., Beijing WVAS Solutions Ltd., Huayi Brothers Music, Hurray! Digital Music Technology Co., Ltd., Hurray! Solutions Ltd., Hurray! Times Communications (Beijing) Ltd., Shanghai Magma Digital Technology Co., Ltd.

Officers: Qindai Wang/Chmn., CEO, Pres., Sean Wang/Pres., Acting CFO, COO, Harry Yang/Sr. VP - Digital Music Content, Jiang Wang/Sr. VP, Shijie Wu/VP, Chief Engineer, Feng Wu/VP, Peifu Xie/VP, Hong Jiang/VP, Haoyu Yang/36/Sr. VP, Yuqi Shi/VP, May Pang/Sec.

Directors: Qindai Wang/Chmn., CEO, Pres., Jesse Liu/Dir., Robert Mao/Dir., Alan Powrie/Dir., Suberna Shringla/Dir., Songzuo Xiang/Dir., Shudan Zhang/Dir.

Owners: Jiang Wang, Alan Powrie, Shudan Zhang/4.29%, Harrison Youth Ltd./3.58%, Wellington Management Company, LLP/7.11%, Shaojian Sean Wang, Pleasant Season Ltd./8.68%, Jesse Liu/3.70%, Insiders/25.60%, Robert Mao, Xero Holdings Ltd./5.04%

Financial Data: *Fiscal Year End:*12/31 *Latest Annual Data:* 12/31/2006

Year		Sales		Net Income	
2006		$69,893,000		$5,804,000	
2005		$62,375,000		$18,619,000	
2004		$53,440,000		$17,240,000	
Curr. Assets:	$91,388,000	Curr. Liab.:	$12,960,000	P/E Ratio:	46.72
Plant, Equip.:	$1,954,000	Total Liab.:	$17,170,000	Indic. Yr. Divd.:	NA
Total Assets:	$139,990,000	Net Worth:	$122,820,000	Debt/ Equity:	NA

Husky Energy Inc

707 8th Ave. SW, Calgary, AB, T2P 3G7; *PH:* 1-403-298-6111; *http://* www.huskyenergy.ca

General - Incorporation	Canada	Stock - Price on:12/24/2007	NA
Employees	NA	Stock Exchange	NA
Auditor	KPMG LLP	Ticker Symbol	NA
Stk Agt	Computershare Trust Co	Outstanding Shares	NA
Counsel	NA	E.P.S	NA
DUNS No.	20-076-3860	Shareholders	NA

Business: The group's principle activities are to explore, develop, market, transport, process and sell crude oil, natural gas, synthetic crude oil and a range of derivative products in North America and internationally. The company operates in three business segments: upstream operations, midstream operations and refined products. Upstream segment explores and produces light, medium and heavy crude oil, natural gas and natural gas liquids from the company's 1,129 wells. Midstream segment focuses on upgrading of heavy crude oil feedstock into synthetic crude oil, marketing, development of pipelines and infrastructure facilities to support the upstream operations. Refined products segment refines crude oil and markets the refined petroleum products. The group's quarterly revenue for September 2007 was 4,351.00 millions of CAD.

Primary SIC and add'l.: 1389 1382 2911 1321 1381 1311

CIK No: 0000049279

Subsidiaries: Canterra Resources Canada Ltd. (formerly 147212 Canada Ltd.), HOI Resources Co., Husky (U.S.A.) Inc., Husky Energy International Corporation, Husky Energy International Sulphur Corporation, Husky Energy Marketing Inc., Husky Gas Marketing Inc., Husky Oil (Madura) Ltd., Husky Oil China Ltd., Husky Oil Limited, Husky Oil Limited (Husky Oil), Husky Oil Overseas Ltd., mean Husky Energy Inc., Renaissance Energy Ltd

Officers: John C.S. Lau/Dir., CEO, Pres., James D. Girgulis/VP - Legal, Corp. Sec., Bill Watson/VP - Engineering, Project Management, Husky Oil Operations Limited, Tanis Thacker/Mgr. - Investor Relations, P. A. Welch/MD, Pres., Geoffrey L. Barlow/CFO, VP, Michael J. Daguiar/VP - Finance, Husky Oil Operations Limited, Donald R. Ingram/Sr. VP - Midstream, Refined Products, Robert S. Coward/VP - Western Canadian Conventional Production, Husky Oil Operations Limited, Robert J. Peabody/COO - Operations, Refining, Ron Butler/VP - Corporate Administration, Husky Oil Operations Limited, Edward T. Connolly/VP - Heavy Oil, Husky Oil Operations Limited, Catherine J. Hughes/VP - Exploration, Production Services, Husky Oil Operations Limited, Garry P. Mihaichuk/VP - Oil Sands, Husky Oil Operations Limited, Ruud B. Zoon/VP - East Coast Operations, Husky Oil Operations Limited

Directors: John C.S. Lau/Dir., CEO, Pres., William Shurniak/Dep. Chmn., Victor T.K. Li/Co - Chmn., Canning K.N. Fok/Co - Chmn., Martin J.G. Glynn/Dir., Brent D. Kinney/Dir., Holger Kluge/Dir., Stanley T.L. Kwok/Dir., Frank J. Sixt/Dir., Eva L. Kwok/Dir., Donald R. Fullerton/Dir., Poh Chan Koh/Dir., Wayne E. Shaw/Dir.

Hutchinson Technology Inc

40 W Highland Pk., Hutchinson, MN, 55350; *PH:* 1-320-587-1605; *Fax:* 1-320-587-1404;
http:// www.htch.com; *Email:* connie.pautz@hti.htch.com

General - Incorporation	MN	*Stock* - Price on:12/24/2007	$18.34
Employees	5,433	Stock Exchange	NDQ
Auditor	Deloitte & Touche LLP	Ticker Symbol	HTCH
Stk Agt	Wells Fargo Shareowner Services	Outstanding Shares	26,030,000
Counsel	Faegre & Benson LLP	E.P.S.	$0.35
DUNS No.	00-645-6768	Shareholders	NA

Business: The group's principal activities are to manufacture and supply suspension assemblies for hard disk drives. Suspension assemblies are critical components of hard disk drives that hold the recording heads in position above the spinning magnetic disks. The group operates in two segments: the disk drive division and the biomeasurement division. The group supplies nearly all domestic and many foreign-based users of suspension assemblies, including alps, fujitsu, IBM and its affiliates, innovex, kaifa, maxtor, read-rite, sae magnetics/tdk, samsung, seagate technology, toshiba and western digital. The group operates in the United States, Thailand, China, Hong Kong, Japan, China, Indonesia, Mexico and other foreign countries.

Primary SIC and add'l.: 3572

CIK No: 0000772897

Subsidiaries: Hutchinson Technology Asia, Inc., Hutchinson Technology Service (Wuxi) Co., Ltd.

Officers: Wayne M. Fortun/Dir., CEO, Pres., Scott R. Schaefer/CTO, VP, Richard G. Fiedler/VP - Engineering, Disk Drive Components Division, Peter J. Ollmann/VP - Operations, Disk Drive Components Division, Peter Carlson/VP - Sales, Marketing, Disk Drive Components Division, David P. Radloff/VP - Corporate Finance, Chuck Ives/Mgr. - Investor Relations, Connie Pautz/Dir. - Corporate Communications, Kathleen S. Skarvan/VP, Pres. - Disk Drive Components Division, Ruth N. Bauer/Treasurer, John A. Ingleman/Sr. VP, CFO, Beatrice A. Graczyk/VP - Business Development, Peggy Steif Abram/Sec., Richard J. Penn/Sr. VP, Pres. - Biomeasurement Division, Rebecca A. Albrecht/VP - Human Resources (*16 Officers included in Index*)

Directors: Wayne M. Fortun/Dir., CEO, Pres., Jeffrey W. Green/Chmn., Russell Huffer/Dir., William T. Monahan/Dir., Richard B. Solum/Dir., Archibald Cox/Dir., Thomas W. Brunberg/Dir., Thomas R. Verhage/Dir.

Owners: William T. Monahan, Dimensional FundAdvisors LP/7.50%, Richard J. Penn, Raj Rajaratnam/6.40%, Thomas R. VerHage, Richard B. Solum, Archibald Cox, Insiders/6.80%, Wayne M. Fortun/2.40%, Barclays Global Investors, NA./5.10%, Kathleen S. Skarvan, OppenheimerFunds, Inc./8.70%, John A. Ingleman, Jeffrey W. Green, Scott R. Schaefer (*21 Owners included in Index*)

Financial Data: Fiscal Year End:09/25 Latest Annual Data: 9/24/2006

Year	Sales	Net Income
2006	$721,507,000	$20,476,000
2005	$631,581,000	$54,881,000
2004	$469,696,000	$73,113,000

Curr. Assets:	$384,796,000	*Curr. Liab.:*	$61,885,000		
Plant, Equip.:	$213,761,000	*Total Liab.:*	$214,840,000	*Indic. Yr. Divd.:*	NA
Total Assets:	$688,392,000	*Net Worth:*	$473,552,000	*Debt/ Equity:*	NA

Hutchison Telecommunications International Ltd

20/F, Hutchison Telecom Tower, 99 Cheung Fai Rd., Tsing Yi; *PH:* 852-21283222;
Fax: 852-28271371; *http://* www.htil.com

General - Incorporation	Cayman Islands	*Stock* - Price on:12/24/2007	$32.51
Employees	20,000	Stock Exchange	NYSE
Auditor	PricewaterhouseCoopers LLP	Ticker Symbol	HTX
Stk Agt	Citibank N.A	Outstanding Shares	317,730,000
Counsel	NA	E.P.S.	$28.21
DUNS No.	NA	Shareholders	NA

Business: The groups principal activity is to provide telecommunications. The group operates from Hong Kong, India, Israel, Thailand and other countries.

Primary SIC and add'l.: 4812 4813 7389 4822 4899

CIK No: 0001293257

Subsidiaries: Aircel Digilink India Limited, BFKT (Thailand) Limited, Fascel Limited, HCL Network Partnership, HTI (BVI) Finance Limited, Hutchison CAT Wireless MultiMedia Limited, Hutchison Essar Limited (formerly known as Hutchison Max Telecom Private Limited), Hutchison Essar Mobile Services Limited (formerly known as Hutchison Essar Telecom Limited), Hutchison Essar South Limited, Hutchison Global Communications Limited, Hutchison GlobalCentre Limited, Hutchison MultiMedia Services (Thailand) Limited, Hutchison MultiMedia Services Limited, Hutchison Telecom East Limited, Hutchison Telecommunication Services Limited 31 Subsidiaries included in the Index

Officers: Dennis Lui/57/Executive Dir., CEO, Chan Ting/58/Alternate Dir., Tim Pennington/48/Executive Dir., CFO, Edith Shih/Company Sec.

Directors: Dennis Lui/57/Executive Dir., CEO, Canning Fok/57/Chmn., Michael O'Connor/41/Non Exec. Dir., Frank Sixt/56/Non Exec. Dir., Kc Kwan/59/Dir., Susan Chow/55/Alternate Dir., Martin Michlmayr/37/Alternative Dir., Ragy Soliman/34/Alternate Dir., Chan Ting/58/Alternate Dir., John Stanton/53/Dir., Tim Pennington/48/Executive Dir., CFO, Aldo Mareuse/44/Non Exec. Dir., Kevin Westley/59/Dir., Cliff Woo/54/Alternate Dir., Kwan Kai Cheong/58/Non Exec. Dir. (*17 Directors included in Index*)

Owners: Dennis Pok Man Lui, Frank John SIX, John W. STANTON, FOK Kin-Ning Canning, CHAN Ting Yu, CHOW WOO Mo Fong, Susan, Insiders

Financial Data: Fiscal Year End:12/31 Latest Annual Data: 12/31/2006

Year	Sales	Net Income
2006	$4,292,411,000	-$63,400,000
2005	$3,141,924,000	-$118,035,000
2004	$14,960,000,000	-$247,000,000

Curr. Assets:	$1,619,974,000	*Curr. Liab.:*	$3,840,639,000		
Plant, Equip.:	$4,110,313,000	*Total Liab.:*	$8,250,847,000	*Indic. Yr. Divd.:*	NA
Total Assets:	$9,967,529,000	*Net Worth:*	$1,716,681,000	*Debt/ Equity:*	NA

Huttig Building Products Inc

555 Maryville University Dr., Ste. 240, St. Louis, MO, 63141; *PH:* 1-314-216-2600;
Fax: 1-314-216-2601; *http://* www.huttig.com

General - Incorporation	DE	*Stock* - Price on:12/24/2007	$7.55
Employees	1,900	Stock Exchange	NYSE
Auditor	KPMG LLP	Ticker Symbol	HBP
Stk Agt	National City Bank	Outstanding Shares	20,600,000
Counsel	NA	E.P.S.	-$0.66
DUNS No.	NA	Shareholders	NA

Business: The group's principal activity is to distribute building materials and wood products used in new residential construction, home improvement, remodeling and repair work. The group provides differentiated building products and excellent services for residential construction. The group provides doors, windows, specialty building materials, mouldings, lumber and other commodity building products.

Primary SIC and add'l.: 2421 2431 2541 2426 5031

CIK No: 0001093082

Subsidiaries: Huttig Building Materials, Inc., Huttig FSC, Inc., Huttig Texas Holdings, Inc., Huttig Texas Limited Partnership, Huttig, Inc.

Officers: Jon P. Vrabely/Dir., CEO, Pres./$490,899.00, David L. Fleisher/CFO, VP, Sec./$458,133.00, Richard A. Baltz/VP - Internal Audit, Darlene K. Schroeder/50/VP - Human Resources/$228,645.00, Rick P. Richardson/VP - West Region, Nikki Wildman/Mgr. - Marketing Services, Gary Fishman/Investor Relations Officer, Steven Anreder/Investor Relations Officer, Brian D. Robinson/CIO, VP/$253,210.00, Robert J. Pearce/VP - East Region, Greg W. Gurley/VP - Product Management, Marketing

Directors: Jon P. Vrabely/Dir., CEO, Pres., R. S. Evans/Chmn., Thayer E. Bigelow/Dir., Dorsey R. Gardner/Dir., Richard S. Forte/Dir., Donald L. Glass/Dir., Michael A. Lupo/Dir., Keith J. Matheney/Dir., Philippe J.C. Gastone/Dir., Delbert H. Tanner/Dir., Steven A. Wise/Dir.

Owners: Jon P. Vrabely, Insiders/7.10%, Richard S. Fort, Michael A. Lupo/2.60%, Brian D. Robinson, Donald L. Glass, David L. Fleisher, Philippe J. Gastone, Darlene K. Schroeder, Steven A. Wise, Hank J. Krey, R. S. Evans/2.70%, Delbert H. Tanner, Dorsey R. Gardner, Thayer E. Bigelow (*16 Owners included in Index*)

Financial Data: Fiscal Year End:12/31 Latest Annual Data: 12/31/2006

Year	Sales	Net Income
2006	$1,102,700,000	-$7,700,000
2005	$1,097,200,000	$18,400,000
2004	$938,400,000	$18,900,000

Curr. Assets:	$184,000,000	*Curr. Liab.:*	$84,700,000		
Plant, Equip.:	$30,000,000	*Total Liab.:*	$131,500,000	*Indic. Yr. Divd.:*	NA
Total Assets:	$241,200,000	*Net Worth:*	$109,700,000	*Debt/ Equity:*	0.5942

Hutton Holdings Corp

3945 S Wasatch Blvd., Ste. 282, Saltlake, UT, 84124; *PH:* 1-801-244-2423

General - Incorporation	NV	*Stock* - Price on:12/24/2007	$6
Employees	NA	Stock Exchange	OTC
Auditor	Robison, Hill & Co.	Ticker Symbol	HTTH
Stk Agt	Transfer Agency and Insurance	Outstanding Shares	NA
Counsel	NA	E.P.S.	NA
DUNS No.	NA	Shareholders	NA

Business: The groups principle activity is to provide mortgage brokerage services. The group operates from San Antonio, Texas in the United States.

Primary SIC and add'l.: 6163

CIK No: 0001156833

Officers: Lau Hing Bun/58/Dir., CEO, CFO

Directors: Lau Hing Bun/58/Dir., CEO, CFO, Douglas M. Goff/58/Dir.

Owners: Douglas Goff, IPacific Asset Management/8.96%, Lau Hing Bun/78.17%, Canary Global Investment, Inc./9.28%, Insiders/78.37%

Financial Data: Fiscal Year End:06/30 Latest Annual Data: 06/30/2007

Year	Sales	Net Income
2007	$152,000	-$15,000
2006	$338,000	$11,000
2005	$394,000	$17,000

Curr. Assets:	$19,000	*Curr. Liab.:*	$6,000		
Plant, Equip.:	$6,000	*Total Liab.:*	$6,000	*Indic. Yr. Divd.:*	NA
Total Assets:	$25,000	*Net Worth:*	$19,000	*Debt/ Equity:*	NA

Hybrid Technologies

Formerly: Whistler Investments Inc

5841 E Charleston, Ste. 230-145, Las Vegas, NV, 89142; *PH:* 1-818-780-2403;
http:// www.hybridtechnologies.com

General - Incorporation	NV	*Stock* - Price on:12/24/2007	NA
Employees	NA	Stock Exchange	NA
Auditor	Haynie & Co.	Ticker Symbol	NA
Stk Agt	Pacific Stock Transfer Company	Outstanding Shares	NA
Counsel	NA	E.P.S.	NA
DUNS No.	NA	Shareholders	NA

Business: The group's principle activities are the development and marketing of electric powered vehicles and products through three wholly owned subsidiaries. The global electric corp holds the licensing rights for all product development other than four-wheeled vehicles. R-electric car co holds the licensing rights for product development for product development for all four-wheeled vehicles. Solium power corp holds the rights for the advanced lithium/solar power system technology.

Primary SIC and add'l.: 3699

CIK No: 0001141263

Subsidiaries: Global Hybrid Corp, R.-Electric Car, Solium Power Corp, Zingo Telecom Inc, Zingo, Inc

Officers: Holly A. Roseberry/57/Dir., CEO, Pres., Mehboob Charania/52/Dir., Sec.

Directors: Holly A. Roseberry/57/Dir., CEO, Pres., Mehboob Charania/52/Dir., Sec., Brian Newman/57/Dir., Greg Navone/61/Dir.

Owners: Eurolink Corporation/37.20%, Holly Roseberry, Insiders, Esmeralda Development Ltd/5.50%, Rocamar Investments Ltd/5.90%

Hybrid Technologies Inc

5841 E Charleston, Ste. 230-145, Las Vegas, NV, 89142; ***PH:*** 1-928-778-1316;
Fax: 1-702-926-9508; ***http://*** www.hybridtechnologies.com; ***Email:*** info@hybridtechnologies.com

General - Incorporation	NV	**Stock** - Price on:12/24/2007	$3.25
Employees	NA	Stock Exchange	OTC
Auditor	Mason Russell West, LLC	Ticker Symbol	HYBT
Stk Agt	Pacific Stock Transfer Company	Outstanding Shares	NA
Counsel	NA	E.P.S	NA
DUNS No.	NA	Shareholders	NA

Business: The groups principle activities include developing and marketing electric powered vehicles and products and, providing telecommunications services through VoIP system that utilizes the Internet. The product of the group is neighborhood electric vehicle. The group operates from the United States.

Primary SIC and add'l.: 7389

CIK No: 0001141263

Subsidiaries: Global Hybrid Corp., R-Electric Car Co., Solium Power Corp., Zingo, Inc.

Officers: Holly A. Roseberry/56/Dir., CEO - Precident, Mehboob Charania/52/Dir., Sec., Richard Griffiths/Contact - Canadian Public Relations

Directors: Holly A. Roseberry/56/Dir., CEO - Precident, Mehboob Charania/52/Dir., Sec., Brian Newman/57/Dir., Gregory Navone/61/Dir.

Owners: Holly Roseberry, Rocamar Investments Ltd./5.90%, Esmeralda Development Ltd./5.50%, Insiders

Financial Data: *Fiscal Year End:*07/31 *Latest Annual Data:* 07/31/2006

Year	*Sales*	*Net Income*
2006	$390,000	-$13,127,000
2005	NA	-$2,919,000

Curr. Assets:	$887,000	*Curr. Liab.:*	$653,000		
Plant, Equip.:	$3,205,000	*Total Liab.:*	$1,681,000	*Indic. Yr. Divd.:*	NA
Total Assets:	$4,513,000	*Net Worth:*	$2,832,000	*Debt/ Equity:*	NA

Hydril Co

3300 N Sam Houston Pkwy E, Houston, TX, 77032; ***PH:*** 1-281-449-2000; ***http://*** www.hydril.com

General - Incorporation	DE	**Stock** - Price on:12/24/2007	NA
Employees	1,700	Stock Exchange	NA
Auditor	Deloitte & Touche LLP	Ticker Symbol	NA
Stk Agt	Mellon Investor Services LLC	Outstanding Shares	NA
Counsel	Baker & Botts LLP	E.P.S	NA
DUNS No.	NA	Shareholders	NA

Business: The group's principle activities include manufacturing and marketing premium connection and pressure control products used for oil and gas drilling and production. Premium connections are used in drilling environments where extreme pressure, corrosion and sensitive drilling. These harsh drilling conditions are typical for deep-formation, deepwater and horizontal wells. Pressure control products are safety devices that control and contain fluid and gas pressure during drilling, completion and maintenance of oil and gas wells. The group also provides after market replacement parts, repair and field services for group's installed base of pressure control equipment. The group's customer base consists of steel pipe distributors, major oil companies, independent oil and gas producers and drilling contractors. The group operates from United States.

Primary SIC and add'l.: 3533

CIK No: 0001116030

Subsidiaries: 3078778 Nova Scotia Company, 3083489 Nova Scotia Company, 3084408 Nova Scotia Company, Bettis de Mexico S.A. de C.V., Flowguard, Ltd., Hydril Acquisition Sub, Inc. LP, Hydril Canadian Company Limited Partnership, Hydril Company LP, Hydril General LLC, Hydril India JV, LLC, Hydril India Private Ltd., Hydril Jindal International Private Ltd., Hydril Limited LLC, Hydril Pressure Control S. de R.L. de C.V., Hydril Private Ltd. 22 Subsidiaries included in the Index

Officers: Christopher T. Seaver/59/Chmn., CEO, Pres., Charles E. Jones/48/COO, Exec. VP, Chris D. North/52/CFO, VP - Finance, Sec., Charles E. Chauviere/43/VP - Pressure Control, Neil G. Russell/62/Sr. VP - Premium Connections, Sr. VP - Business Development, Michael Danford/45/VP - Human Resources

Directors: Christopher T. Seaver/59/Chmn., CEO, Pres., Richard C. Seaver/85/Chmn. Emeritus, Jerry S. Cox/Dir., Patrick T. Seaver/Dir., Roger Goodan/Dir., Kenneth S. McCormick/Dir., Lew O. Ward/Dir., Gordon T. Hall/Dir., Don T. Stacy/Dir.

Owners: Neil G. Russell, Chris D. North, Charles E. Chauviere, Lew O. Ward, Don T. Stacy, Charles E. Jones, Insiders, Oppenheimer Funds, Inc., Mario J. Gabelli, Myron E. Harpole, The Seaver Institute, Roger Goodan, Blanche Ebert Seaver Endowment, Neuberger Berman Inc., Declaration of Trust *(20 Owners included in Index)*

HydroFlo Inc

2501 Reliance Ave., Apex, NC, 27539; ***PH:*** 1-919-772-9925; ***Fax:*** 1-919-355-1200;
http:// www.hydroflo.us; ***Email:*** postmaster@hydroflo-inc.com

General - Incorporation	NC	**Stock** - Price on:12/24/2007	$0.01
Employees	15	Stock Exchange	OTC
Auditor	Thomas Leger & Co., LLP	Ticker Symbol	HYRF
Stk Agt	Corporate Stock Transfer, Inc.	Outstanding Shares	NA
Counsel	NA	E.P.S	-$1.39
DUNS No.	NA	Shareholders	NA

Business: The group's principle activity is to provide wastewater treatment solutions for industrial and governmental entity customers. It designs, builds and installs aeration equipment used for pre-treatment of wastewater. The group's principal products are hydroflo plus system, an aeration system for sewage treatment in pipes prior to reaching treatment facilities and hydroflo ats system, a standardized system of applying oxygen to wastewater for purification purposes. It operates in the United States of America. On 4-Mar-2004, the group became a diversified internally managed closed-end investment group. On 04-Aug-2004, the group acquired arsenic removal technologies inc. The group operates from United States.

Primary SIC and add'l.: 3589

CIK No: 0001107809

Subsidiaries: HydroFlo Water Treatment, Inc, Metals & Arsenic Removal Technology, Inc, Safety Scan Technology, Inc, Ultra Choice Water, Inc

Officers: George A. Moore/Chmn., CEO

Directors: George A. Moore/Chmn., CEO, James Kelly/Dir., William Dobo/Dir.

Owners: Free Harbour Foundation/31.50%, Capital Access, Inc/19.00%

Financial Data: *Fiscal Year End:*06/30 *Latest Annual Data:* 6/30/2005

Year	*Sales*	*Net Income*
2005	NA	$18,888,000
2004	NA	-$590,000
2003	$244,000	-$1,154,000

Curr. Assets:	$3,000	*Curr. Liab.:*	$2,155,000		
Plant, Equip.:	$11,000	*Total Liab.:*	$2,155,000	*Indic. Yr. Divd.:*	NA
Total Assets:	$25,223,000	*Net Worth:*	$23,068,000	*Debt/ Equity:*	NA

Hydrogen Corp

936a Beachland Blvd, Ste 13, Vero Beach, FL, 32963; ***PH:*** 1-480-759-9400;
http:// www.hydrogenllc.net; ***Email:*** info@hydrogenllc.com

General - Incorporation	NV	**Stock** - Price on:12/24/2007	NA
Employees	29	Stock Exchange	NDQ
Auditor	Goldstein Golub Kessler LLP	Ticker Symbol	HYDG
Stk Agt	Computershare Trust Co	Outstanding Shares	NA
Counsel	NA	E.P.S	NA
DUNS No.	NA	Shareholders	NA

Business: The group's principle activity is to acquire management and opportunities for growth. On 02-Apr-2004, the company changed its name to chiste corporation. On 30-Jun-2003, the company sold its dyna-cam operating assets. The group operates from United States.

Primary SIC and add'l.: 3519

CIK No: 0001124394

Subsidiaries: HydroGen LLC

Officers: Leo Blomen/Chmn., CEO/$125,015.00, Joshua Tosteson/Dir., Pres./$426,909.00, Scott Schecter/CFO/$380,644.00, Scott Wilshire/COO/$363,195.00, Gregory Morris/Sr. VP, Christopher Garofalo/General Counsel

Directors: Leo Blomen/Chmn., CEO, Joshua Tosteson/Dir., Pres., Howard Yana Shapiro/Non Exec. Dir., John J. Freeh/Non Exec. Dir., Brian D. Bailys/Non Exec. Dir., Philip J. Kranenburg/Non Exec. Dir., Brian T. McGee/Non Exec. Dir., Michael E. Basham/Non Exec. Dir.

Owners: Insiders/10.60%, Pequot Capital Management, Inc./6.80%, Philip J. Kranenburg, John J. Freeh, Magnetar Capital Master Fund, Ltd./11.50%, Alysheba Funds/6.80%, Joshua Tosteson/4.40%, Howard-Yana Shapiro, Leo Blomen/3.40%, Scott Wilshire/0.50%, Federated Investors, Inc./9.60%, Michael E. Basham, Scott Schecter/1.40%, FuelCell Holdings, LLC/5.90%, Brian T. McGee *(17 Owners included in Index)*

Curr. Assets:	$25,613,000	*Curr. Liab.:*	$1,732,000		
Plant, Equip.:	$3,470,000	*Total Liab.:*	$1,852,000	*Indic. Yr. Divd.:*	NA
Total Assets:	$29,139,000	*Net Worth:*	$27,288,000	*Debt/ Equity:*	0.0062

Hydrogen Engine Center Inc

56 W 400 S, Ste. 220, Salt Lake City, UT, 84101; ***PH:*** 1-515-295-3178;
http:// www.hydrogenenginecenter.com; ***Email:*** info@hydrogenenginecenter.com

General - Incorporation	NV	**Stock** - Price on:12/24/2007	$1.7
Employees	25	Stock Exchange	OTC
Auditor	LWBJ, LLP	Ticker Symbol	HYEG
Stk Agt	Interstate Transfer Company	Outstanding Shares	26,080,000
Counsel	NA	E.P.S	-$0.26
DUNS No.	NA	Shareholders	NA

Business: The group's principal activities are limited to operating history and no representation is made, nor is any intended, that the company will be able to carry on future business activities successfully.

Primary SIC and add'l.: 1000

CIK No: 0001272703

Subsidiaries: Green Mt. Acquisitions, Inc., HEC Iowa

Officers: Theodore G. Hollinger/66/Dir., CEO, Pres., Michael A. Schiltz/VP - Engine Development, Tapan K. Bose/Pres. - HEC Canada, Sandra M. Batt/CFO, Don Vanderbrook/COO, Joe E. Lewis/VP - Engine Sales

Directors: Theodore G. Hollinger/66/Dir., CEO, Pres., Thomas Trimble/Dir., Edward T. Berg/58/Dir., Philip G. Ruggieri/54/Dir.

Owners: Philip G. Ruggieri, Edward T. Berg, Insiders/58.61%, Thomas O. Trimble, Tapan K. Bose, Gabriel Elias/7.18%, Sandra M. Batt, Michael A. Schiltz, Theodore G. Hollinger/57.65%

Financial Data: *Fiscal Year End:*12/31 *Latest Annual Data:* 12/31/2006

Year	*Sales*	*Net Income*
2006	$278,000	-$5,752,000
2005	$24,000	-$1,123,000
2004	NA	-$21,000

Curr. Assets:	$3,776,000	*Curr. Liab.:*	$2,193,000		
Plant, Equip.:	$3,274,000	*Total Liab.:*	$3,005,000	*Indic. Yr. Divd.:*	NA
Total Assets:	$7,050,000	*Net Worth:*	$4,045,000	*Debt/ Equity:*	0.3337

Hydrogen Hybrid Technologies Inc

Formerly: Eaton Laboratories Inc
1845 Sandstone Manor, Unit 11, Pickering, ON, L1W3X9; ***PH:*** 1-905-697-4880

General - Incorporation	NV	**Stock** - Price on:12/24/2007	$1.05
Employees	NA	Stock Exchange	NA
Auditor	Moore & Associates Chartered	Ticker Symbol	NA
Stk Agt	Empire Stock Transfer Inc.	Outstanding Shares	60,370,000
Counsel	NA	E.P.S	NA
DUNS No.	NA	Shareholders	NA

Business: The groups principal activity is to produce generic pharmaceutical products, through contract laboratories and contract manufacturing facilities, for pharmaceutical products that have lost their innovator patent. In January 2007, the group acquired Pinoak, Inc. The group operates from Nevada in the United States.

Primary SIC and add'l.: 3510

CIK No: 0001163002

Subsidiaries: IVPSA Corporation

Officers: T. J. Jesky/60/Dir., CFO, Pres., Sec.

Directors: T. J. Jesky/60/Dir., CFO, Pres., Sec.

Owners: HYHY ESOP/7.00%, Frank Carino/63.50%, Ira Lyons/3.10%, Insiders/3.10%, CHEC/3.10%

Financial Data: Fiscal Year End:12/31 Latest Annual Data: 12/31/2006

Year	Sales	Net Income
2006	NA	$0

Curr. Assets:	$0	Curr. Liab.:	$5,000	
Plant, Equip.:	NA	Total Liab.:	$5,000	Indic. Yr. Divd.: NA
Total Assets:	$0	Net Worth:	-$5,000	Debt/ Equity: NA

Hydrogen Power Inc

Formerly: Equitex Inc

1942 Westlake Ave., Ste. 1010, Seattle, WA, 98101; **PH:** 1-206-448-5073; *http://* www.equitex.net

General - Incorporation	DE	**Stock**- Price on:12/24/2007	$0.44
Employees	NA	Stock Exchange	NA
Auditor	Peterson Sullivan, PLLC	Ticker Symbol	NA
Stk Agt	Computershare Trust Co	Outstanding Shares	NA
Counsel	NA	E.P.S	-$2.04
DUNS No.	NA	Shareholders	NA

Business: The group's principal activity is to provide comprehensive cash access and consumer financial services to casinos and other gaming establishments. The group's approach is to provide its products and services principally on a fee basis taking minimal credit risk. It operates through its wholly-owned subsidiary chex services, inc. (chex) and majority-owned subsidiary denaris corporation (denaris). Chex provides comprehensive cash access services to casinos and other gaming facilities throughout the United States. Denaris was recently formed to develop stored value card programs. Stored value cards, which can be purchased by anyone without a credit check or intrusive personal information.

Primary SIC and add'l.: 6153 6159 6719

CIK No: 0000716101

Subsidiaries: Chex Services, Inc., Denaris Corporation, FastFunds Financial Corporation, Hydrogen Power, Inc., Key Financial Systems, Inc., Nova Financial Systems, Inc.

Officers: David J. Cade/CEO, James G. Matkin/65/Corp. Sec. - Special Counsel, Henry Fong/Dir., Financial, Accounting Officer, Thomas B. Olson/Corp. Sec., Ricky Gujral/Management Consultant to HPI, Exec. Officer, Dir. - Major Subsidiary, Michael Hines/51/CFO

Directors: Russell L. Casement/Dir., Henry Fong/Dir., Financial, Accounting Officer, Aaron A. Grunfeld/Dir., John J. Martin/59/Dir., James H. Diffendorfer/68/Dir., Virendra Chaudhary/Dir., Gurinder Dilawari/51/Dir.

Owners: James G. Matkin, Insiders/2.70%, Global Hydro Fuel Technologies, Inc./61.60%, John J. Martin/1.30%, James H. Diffendorfer

Financial Data: Fiscal Year End:12/31 Latest Annual Data: 12/31/2006

Year	Sales	Net Income
2006	$126,000	-$27,239,000
2005	$197,000	-$8,842,000
2004	$15,494,000	-$7,458,000

Curr. Assets:	$4,518,000	Curr. Liab.:	$6,556,000	
Plant, Equip.:	$78,000	Total Liab.:	$7,198,000	Indic. Yr. Divd.: NA
Total Assets:	$4,931,000	Net Worth:	-$2,434,000	Debt/ Equity: NA

Hydrogenics Corp

5985 McLaughlin Rd., Mississauga, ON, L5R 1B8; **PH:** 1-905-361-3660; **Fax:** 1-905-361-3626; *http://* www.hydrogenics.com; **Email:** info@hydrogenics.com

General - Incorporation	Canada	**Stock**- Price on:12/24/2007	$1.27
Employees	265	Stock Exchange	NDQ
Auditor	PricewaterhouseCoopers LLP	Ticker Symbol	NA
Stk Agt	Mellon Trust Co	Outstanding Shares	NA
Counsel	Osler, Hoskin & Harcourt	E.P.S	-$0.44
DUNS No.	NA	Shareholders	NA

Business: The group's principal activities are the designing, developing, manufacturing and selling of proton-exchange membrane, or pem, fuel cell automated test stations and fuel cell systems. The group focuses on the commercialization of proton exchange membrane (pem) fuel cells for clean power generation. The group develops and manufactures fully integrated pem fuel cell test and control systems, including related peripheral products and associated diagnostic and control equipment. The group's principal customers include automotive companies, fuel cell developers and component suppliers principally located in Canada, the United States and the United Kingdom. On 08-Jan-2003, the group acquired greenlight power technologies inc.

Primary SIC and add'l.: 3629

CIK No: 0001119985

Subsidiaries: Hydrogenics Europe NV, Hydrogenics GmbH, Hydrogenics Japan Inc, Hydrogenics Test Systems Inc, Hydrogenics USA, Inc., Stuart Energy, Stuart Energy Systems Corporation

Officers: Daryl Wilson/Dir., CEO, Pres., Pierre Rivard/Executive Chmn., Pres., Salil Munjal/VP - Corporate Development, General Counsel, Corp. Sec., Lawrence E. Davis/CFO, Joseph Cargnelli/Dir., CTO, John Werderman/VP - Business Development, Power Systems

Directors: Daryl Wilson/Dir., CEO, Pres., Pierre Rivard/Executive Chmn., Pres., Hugo Vandenborre/Vice Chmn., Douglas Alexander/Dir., James Sardo/Dir., William Szkodinski/Dir., Norman M. Seagram/Dir., Frank Colvin/Dir., Joseph Cargnelli/Dir., CTO

Financial Data: Fiscal Year End:12/31 Latest Annual Data: 12/31/2006

Year	Sales	Net Income
2006	$30,059,000	-$114,988,000
2005	$37,191,000	-$53,145,000
2004	$16,656,000	-$33,562,000

Curr. Assets:	$86,185,000	Curr. Liab.:	$30,189,000	
Plant, Equip.:	$5,435,000	Total Liab.:	$30,416,000	Indic. Yr. Divd.: NA
Total Assets:	$97,173,000	Net Worth:	$66,757,000	Debt/ Equity: NA

Hydromer Inc

35 Industrial Pkwy., Branchburg, NJ, 08876; **PH:** 1-908-722-5000; **Fax:** 1-908-526-3633; *http://* www.hydromer.com

General - Incorporation	NJ	**Stock**- Price on:12/24/2007	$1.85
Employees	85	Stock Exchange	OTC
Auditor	Rosenberg Rich Baker Berman & Co	Ticker Symbol	HYDI
Stk Agt	Registrar & Transfer Co	Outstanding Shares	4,670,000
Counsel	NA	E.P.S	-$0.02
DUNS No.	10-124-8508	Shareholders	NA

Business: The group's principal activity is to research and develop polymeric complexes. The polymeric complexes are used for commercial, medical and industrial fields. The group operates through two business segments; polymer research and medical products.the group owns process and application patents for hydromer & various trademarks including sea-slide(R), dermaseal(R), aquamere(tm), & t-hexx(r). It markets anti-fog, sea-slide(R) and cosmetic formulations. The products of the group include food packaging coating, drag reducing coating for boats and ships and water based formulations used as a component in beauty aids. The group owns patents for permanent anti-fog materials, hydrophilic polyurethane foams, hydrophilic polyurethane blends, hydrophilic polyvinylbutyral alloys, several biocompatible hydrogels and an anti-bacterial medical material. The major customers of the group are johnson & johnson's cordis division and wilson cook medical, inc.

Primary SIC and add'l.: 3841 3479 2821 3845

CIK No: 0000704432

Subsidiaries: Biosearch Medical Products, Inc., BMPI

Officers: Manfred F. Dyck/Chmn., CEO, Pres., Robert J. Moravsik/Sr. VP, General Counsel, Sec., Martin C. Dyck/Exec. VP - Operation, Robert Y. Lee/VP - Finance, CFO, Rainer Gruening/VP - Research & Development, John Konar/59/VP - Quality Assurance, Dir. - Human Resources

Directors: Manfred F. Dyck/Chmn., CEO, Pres., Dieter Heinemann/Dir., Ursula M. Dyck/Dir., Frederick Perl/Dir., Michal F. Ryan/Dir., Klaus Meckler/Dir., Robert H. Bea/Dir., Maxwell Borow/Dir.

Owners: Manfred F. Dyck, Ben Posdal, Insiders, Maxwell Borow, URSULA M. DYCK, Dieter Heinemann

Financial Data: Fiscal Year End:06/30 Latest Annual Data: 06/30/2007

Year	Sales	Net Income
2007	$8,099,000	-$107,000
2006	$7,870,000	-$779,000
2005	$8,486,000	$269,000

Curr. Assets:	$2,968,000	Curr. Liab.:	$1,998,000	
Plant, Equip.:	$3,377,000	Total Liab.:	$4,455,000	Indic. Yr. Divd.: NA
Total Assets:	$7,816,000	Net Worth:	$3,361,000	Debt/ Equity: 0.6070

Hydron Technologies Inc

4400 34th St. N, Ste. F, St. Petersburg, FL, 33714; **PH:** 1-727-342-5050; **Fax:** 1-727-344-3920; *http://* www.hydron.com

General - Incorporation	NY	**Stock**- Price on:12/24/2007	$0.25
Employees	18	Stock Exchange	OTC
Auditor	Sherb & Co., LLP	Ticker Symbol	HTEC
Stk Agt	Banyan Securities	Outstanding Shares	16,220,000
Counsel	Daszkalbolton LLP	E.P.S	-$0.04
DUNS No.	01-217-4397	Shareholders	NA

Business: The group's principle activity is to develop personal care and cosmetic products using hydron polymers, primarily for skin care and oral health care. The group's products are sold through direct response television, catalog sales and electronic sales via qvc. The group has 21 skin care products, 6 hair care products, 7 bath and body products and 2 sun care products. The group also markets polymer-based products for dental professionals. The group is expanding into markets in Australia, New Zealand and also in Europe. The group's total revenue for year 2007 was 0.89 millions of USD.

Primary SIC and add'l.: 2899 2844

CIK No: 0000028146

Owners: Insiders/53.63%, Douglas Reitz/9.65%, Karen Gray/1.00%, Ronald J. Saul/13.66%, David Pollock/11.08%, Richard Banakus/26.13%

Financial Data: Fiscal Year End:12/31 Latest Annual Data: 12/31/2006

Year	Sales	Net Income
2006	$1,474,000	-$552,000
2005	$1,463,000	-$772,000
2004	$1,185,000	-$856,000

Curr. Assets:	$344,000	Curr. Liab.:	$1,013,000	
Plant, Equip.:	$121,000	Total Liab.:	$1,037,000	Indic. Yr. Divd.: NA
Total Assets:	$898,000	Net Worth:	-$361,000	Debt/ Equity: NA

Hynes & Howes Insurance Counselors Inc

2920 Harrison St. , Davenport, IA, 52803; **PH:** 1-319-326-6401

General - Incorporation	IA	**Stock**- Price on:12/24/2007	NA
Employees	NA	Stock Exchange	NA
Auditor	Shapley, Shapley & Moorhead, P.C	Ticker Symbol	NA
Stk Agt	NA	Outstanding Shares	NA
Counsel	NA	E.P.S	NA
DUNS No.	10-852-4877	Shareholders	NA

Business: The group's principal activity is to invest in single family residences and to sell it on contract. The group was an independent insurance agency providing all types of casualty, fire and surety insurance. The group operates in the quad city metropolitan area of eastern Iowa and western Illinois.

Primary SIC and add'l.: 6153 6159

CIK No: 0000205462

Officers: Joseph Coon/47/Pres., Monica Wilcher/38/Sec.

Hypercom Corp

2851 W Kathleen Rd., Phoenix, AZ, 85053; *PH:* 1-602-504-5000; *Fax:* 1-602-504-4655; *http://* www.hypercom.com; *Email:* Info-US@hypercom.com

General - Incorporation	DE	Stock- Price on:12/24/2007	$5.85
Employees	1,358	Stock Exchange	NYSE
Auditor	Ernst & Young LLP	Ticker Symbol	HYC
Stk Agt	Computershare Trust Co	Outstanding Shares	53,250,000
Counsel	Snell & Wilmer	E.P.S.	-$0.2
DUNS No.	18-179-2714	Shareholders	NA

Business: The group's principal activity is to provide electronic payment solutions that add value at the point-of-sale (pos) for consumers, merchants and acquirers, such as banks and processing companies. Products include secure card payment terminals and peripheral devices, specialized networking equipment, software applications for e-commerce, mobile commerce, smart cards and traditional credit, charge and debit card transactions and related support and services. The group is also involved in micro-ticket leasing of payment terminals and other equipment. Pos systems develop, manufacture, market and support products that automate electronic payment transactions at the pos in merchant establishments. Network systems develop, manufacture, market and support enterprise-networking systems. The group operates in the United States, Latin America, Asia-pacific & Europe. During 2003, the group disposed of golden eagle leasing.

Primary SIC and add'l.: 3661 3577 7373 7377

CIK No: 0001045769

Subsidiaries: Empresa Brasileira Industrial, Comercial e Servicos Limitada, HBNet Canada Ltd., HBNet, Inc., Hypercom (Thailand) Co., Ltd., Hypercom Asia (Singapore) Pte. Ltd., Hypercom Asia Ltd., Hypercom Australia Pty., Ltd., Hypercom China Co. Ltd., Hypercom de Chile, S.A., Hypercom de Mexico, S.A. de C.V., Hypercom de Venezuela C.A., Hypercom Electronic Manufacturing (Shenzhen) Co. Ltd., Hypercom EMEA Ltd., Hypercom EMEA, Inc., Hypercom Far East Ltd. 27 Subsidiaries included in the Index

Officers: Douglas J. Reich/Sr. VP, General Counsel, Chief Compliance Officer, Corp. Sec., Scott M. Tsujita/Sr. VP - Finance, Treasury, Investor Relations, William Dowlin/Sr. VP - Manufacturing, Materials, Philippe Tartavull/COO, Pres., Thomas Liguori/CFO/$1,107,520.00

Directors: Daniel D. Diethelm/Chmn., Phillip J. Riese/Dir., Norman Stout/Dir., Ian Marsh/Dir.

Owners: Dreman Value Management, LLC/5.30%, Perry Corp./6.10%, Norman Stout, Insiders/2.10%, Dimensional Fund Advisors LP/5.40%, Wells Fargo & Company/5.60%, FMR Corp./15.00%, RLR Capital Partners, LP/5.10%, Jonatan Schmidt, O. B. Rawls, William Keiper, Thomas Liguori, Daniel D. Diethelm, Phillip J. Riese, Neil Hudd

Financial Data: Fiscal Year End:12/31 **Latest Annual Data:** 12/31/2006

Year	Sales	Net Income
2006	$248,565,000	$6,970,000
2005	$245,223,000	-$33,366,000
2004	$255,155,000	-$8,662,000

Curr. Assets:	$195,720,000	Curr. Liab.:	$53,797,000		
Plant, Equip.:	$27,261,000	Total Liab.:	$57,785,000	Indic. Yr. Divd.:	NA
Total Assets:	$236,716,000	Net Worth:	$178,931,000	Debt/ Equity:	NA

HyperDynamics Corp

1 Sugar Creek Ctr. Blvd., Ste. 125, Sugar Land, TX, 77478; *PH:* 1-713-353-9400; *Fax:* 1-713-353-9421; *http://* www.hypd.com; *Email:* info@hyperdynamics.com

General - Incorporation	DE	Stock- Price on:12/24/2007	$2.99
Employees	22	Stock Exchange	AMEX
Auditor	Malone & Bailey, PC	Ticker Symbol	HDY
Stk Agt	Fidelity Transfer Co	Outstanding Shares	48,930,000
Counsel	NA	E.P.S.	-$0.477
DUNS No.	NA	Shareholders	NA

Business: The groups principle activities include developing and providing integrated information technology services. The group operates from the United States. The groups quarterly revenue for September 2007 was 0.31 millions of USD.

Primary SIC and add'l.: 1311 1382

CIK No: 0000937136

Subsidiaries: GHRC, HYD Resources Corporation, SCS Corporation, SCS Guinea SARL, Trendsetter Production Company

Officers: Kent P. Watts/Chmn., CEO, CFO, Pres., Harry James Briers/Dir., Exec. VP, COO, Steven Plumb/CFO, Famourou Kourouma/VP - Guinea Affairs, Sarah Berel-Harrop/Corp. Sec., James R. Spear/VP, Chief Geophysicist - SCS Corporation, Phillip Bergman/Roher Public Relations

Directors: Kent P. Watts/Chmn., CEO, CFO, Pres., Harry James Briers/Dir., Exec. VP, COO, Harold A. Poling/Dir., Gene L. Stohler/Dir., Albert F. Young/Dir.

Owners: Harry Briers/2.00%, Insiders/19.00%, Steven Plumb, Harold Poling/1.00%, Gene L. Stohler, Michael Watts/8.00%, Albert F. Young, Kent Watts/15.00%

Financial Data: Fiscal Year End:06/30 **Latest Annual Data:** 06/30/2007

Year	Sales	Net Income
2007	$1,006,000	-$23,199,000
2006	$656,000	-$7,144,000
2005	$173,000	-$5,216,000

Curr. Assets:	$6,625,000	Curr. Liab.:	$2,621,000		
Plant, Equip.:	$4,849,000	Total Liab.:	$2,754,000	Indic. Yr. Divd.:	NA
Total Assets:	$11,480,000	Net Worth:	$8,726,000	Debt/ Equity:	NA

Hyperion Solutions Corp

5450 Great America Pkwy., Santa Clara, CA, 95054; *PH:* 1-408-744-9500; *http://* www.hyperion.com

General - Incorporation	DE	Stock- Price on:12/24/2007	NA
Employees	2,720	Stock Exchange	NDQ
Auditor	PricewaterhouseCoopers LLP	Ticker Symbol	HYSL
Stk Agt	Computershare Trust Co	Outstanding Shares	NA
Counsel. Heller Ehrman White & McAuliffe LLP		E.P.S.	NA
DUNS No.	78-313-6906	Shareholders	NA

Business: The group's principle activity is to provide business performance management software. This enables companies to translate strategies into plans, monitor execution and provide insight to manage and improve financial and operational performance. The group provides managers with reporting and analysis tools and packaged and custom applications that support a process for proactively managing their business to optimal performance against goals and for anticipating and forecasting results. The group

markets and sells the products in North America, Latin America, Europe and Asia-Pacific through its direct sales force and through original equipment manufacturers, value added resellers and independent distributors. In addition, the group offers support and services from offices in 20 countries and works with over 330 partners to provide solutions to more than 6,000 customer organizations worldwide.

Primary SIC and add'l.: 7379 7372

CIK No: 0001001113

Subsidiaries: HSC Acquisition Co., Hyperion Corporation of Canada Ltd., Hyperion Foreign Sales Corporation, Hyperion International Corporation, Hyperion KK, Hyperion Latin America Ltda., Hyperion Software Solutions Austria GmbH, Hyperion Solutions (Hong Kong) Ltd., Hyperion Solutions (UK)Limited, Hyperion Solutions AS, Hyperion Solutions Asia Pte. Ltd., Hyperion Solutions Australia Pty. Ltd., Hyperion Solutions China Ltd., Hyperion Solutions Denmark Aps, Hyperion Solutions Deutschland GmbH 24 Subsidiaries included in the Index

Officers: Godfrey Sullivan/54/Dir., CEO, Pres., Jeffrey R. Rodek/54/Exec. Chmn., Mark Cochran/VP, General Counsel, Corp. Sec., Howard Dresner/Chief Strategy Officer, Bill Gaylord/VP - Corporate Development, Robert Gersten/Chief Development Officer, John L. Kopcke/CTO, Steve McMahon/VP - Human Resources, Heidi Melin/Chief Marketing Officer, Robin Washington/CFO

Directors: Godfrey Sullivan/54/Dir., CEO, Pres., Jeffrey R. Rodek/54/Exec. Chmn., Gary G. Greenfield/52/Dir., Terry Carlitz/56/Dir., Yorgen Edholm/52/Dir., Henry Autry/59/Dir., Nanci Caldwell/50/Dir., John Riccitiello/48/Dir., Maynard Webb/52/Dir.

Hypertension Diagnostics Inc

2915 Waters Rd., Ste. 108, Eagan, MN, 55121; *PH:* 1-651-687-9999; *Fax:* 1-651-687-0485; *http://* www.hdi-pulsewave.com; *Email:* infoteam@hdii.com

General - Incorporation	MN	Stock- Price on:12/24/2007	$0.115
Employees	10	Stock Exchange	OTC
Auditor	Virchow, Krause & Co. LLP	Ticker Symbol	HDII
Stk Agt	Firstar Trust Co	Outstanding Shares	39,610,000
Counsel... Liner, Yankelevitz & Regenstreif LLP		E.P.S.	-$0.02
DUNS No.	61-256-5622	Shareholders	NA

Business: The group's principal activities are to design, develop, manufacture and market proprietary medical devices. These medical devices detect changes in the elasticity of both small and large arteries. The group currently markets three product versions, the hdi/pulsewave(TM) cr-2000 research cardiovascular profiling system, the cvprofilor(R) do-2020 cardiovascular profiling system and the cvprofilor(R) md-3000 cardiovascular profiling system. The model cr-2000 research system is being marketed worldwide and has a medical device ce mark allowing to be marketed as a medical device in the European market. In the United States the product is marketed for research purpose only and not for screening, diagnosing or monitoring the treatment of patients.

Primary SIC and add'l.: 3829 3845

CIK No: 0001058828

Officers: Mark Schwartz/Chmn., CEO, Greg H. Guettler/Pres., Mark Oneill/Mgr. - Finance, Accounting, Principal Financial Officer

Directors: Mark Schwartz/Chmn., CEO, Larry Leitner/55/Dir., Alan Stern/53/Dir., Kenneth W. Brimmer/53/Dir., Jay N. Cohn/78/Dir.

Owners: Kenneth W. Brimmer, Marten S. Hoekstra, Alan Stern, James K. Cummings, Marten S. Hoekstra, Mark N. Schwartz, Beljam Holdings, Ltd., Jonathan Gross, Larry Leitner, Beljam Holdings, Ltd., A Group Granting Proxies to Mark N. Schwartz, Jonathan Gross, James K. Cummings, Jonathan Gross, Weinstein Family Trust (45 Owners included in Index)

Financial Data: Fiscal Year End:06/30 **Latest Annual Data:** 06/30/2007

Year	Sales	Net Income
2007	$1,879,000	-$504,000
2006	$1,790,000	-$1,273,000
2005	$1,182,000	-$1,455,000

Curr. Assets:	$2,257,000	Curr. Liab.:	$489,000		
Plant, Equip.:	$82,000	Total Liab.:	$505,000	Indic. Yr. Divd.:	NA
Total Assets:	$2,346,000	Net Worth:	$1,840,000	Debt/ Equity:	NA

Hythiam Inc

11150 Santa Monica Blvd., Ste. 1500, Los Angeles, CA, 90025; *PH:* 1-310-444-4300; *Fax:* 1-310-444-5300; *http://* www.hythiam.com; *Email:* info@hythiam.com

General - Incorporation	DE	Stock- Price on:12/24/2007	$8.3
Employees	120	Stock Exchange	NDQ
Auditor	BDO Seidman LLP	Ticker Symbol	HYTM
Stk Agt ..... American Stock Transfer & Trust Co.		Outstanding Shares	44,480,000
Counsel	Cletha A. Walstrand	E.P.S.	-$1.04
DUNS No.	NA	Shareholders	NA

Business: The group's principle activity is to provide transportation and freight brokerage services in Alaska. The group transports goods overland by using trucks. The modes of transportation include rail, highway, water, air and pipeline transportation. The current operations of the transportation segment include local hauling of gravel products, asphalt, concrete material and ballast rock. The freight brokerage services of the group involve securing the loads that need to be hauled and contracting with other transportation service or independent providers to perform the job. The group operates a fleet of eight tractors and fourteen trailers. The group operates solely in the domestic market. The group operates from United States.

Primary SIC and add'l.: 4213

CIK No: 0001136174

Subsidiaries: Hythiam International (Cayman) Ltd., Hythiam International Sarl, Hythiam Switzerland Sarl, Quit System Italy Srl, Quit System Sarl, Quit Systems Spain Trading Sl

Officers: Terren S. Peizer/Chmn., CEO/$1,161,777.00, Arlandis Rush/VP - Government Affairs, Chris Hassan/Dir., Sr. Exec. VP, Sanjay Sabnani/Exec. VP - Strategic Development/$577,505.00, Chuck Timpe/61/CFO/$375,672.00, Donald R. Wesson/Sr. VP - Scientific Affairs, Richard A. Anderson/Dir., Sr. Exec. VP/$830,723.00, Anthony M. Lamacchia/Sr. Exec. VP/$466,532.00, Lawrence M. Weinstein/Sr. VP - Medical Affairs

Directors: Terren S. Peizer/Chmn., CEO, Ivan M. Lieberburg/Dir., Marc G. Cummins/Dir., Richard A. Anderson/Dir., Sr. Exec. VP, Leslie F. Bell/Dir., Andrea Grubb Barthwell/Dir.

Owners: Anthony M. LaMacchia, Monica Alfaro Welling, Terren S. Peizer/32.20%, Ivan M. Lieberburg, Fred Knoll/5.40%, Andrea Grubb Barthwell, Richard A. Anderson, Marc G. Cummins, Leslie F. Bell, Sanjay Sabnani, Insiders/35.70%, Herve de Kergrohen, Chuck Timpe

Financial Data: Fiscal Year End:12/31 **Latest Annual Data:** 12/31/2006

Year	Sales	Net Income
2006	$3,906,000	-$38,298,000
2005	$1,164,000	-$24,038,000
2004	$192,000	-$11,775,000

Curr. Assets:	$44,549,000	Curr. Liab.:	$9,451,000		
Plant, Equip.:	$3,711,000	Total Liab.:	$10,176,000	Indic. Yr. Divd.:	NA
Total Assets:	$52,205,000	Net Worth:	$42,029,000	Debt/ Equity:	0.3097

I C Isaacs & Co Inc

3840 Bank St., Baltimore, MD, 21224; **PH:** 1-410-649-4500; **Fax:** 1-410-276-4087;
http:// www.icisaacs.com; **Email:** ir@icisaacs.com

General - Incorporation.............................DE
Employees 110
Auditor ....BDO Seidman LLP
Stk Agt...... American Stock Transfer & Trust Co.
Counsel..NA
DUNS No. 10-147-7834

Stock- Price on:12/24/2007 ....$1.1
Stock Exchange..OTC
Ticker Symbol..ISAC
Outstanding Shares 12,280,000
E.P.S. ....-$1.23
Shareholders..NA

Business: The group's principal activities are to design and market branded jeanswear and sportswear products. Sportswear products include jeans, tee shirts, sweatshirts, shorts, knit and woven shirts and outerwear. The jeanswear and sportswear collections for men and women are marketed under the marithe and francois girbaud brandnames in the United States, Puerto Rico and Canada. These branded jeanswear and sportswear collections for young men and women include a variety of tops, bottoms and outerwear. The group's products are sold in over 3,600 specialty stores, specialty store chains and department stores. The group also operates a 70,000 square foot group-owned and operated distribution center in milford, Delaware to serve its customers in the United States.

Primary SIC and add'l.: 5611 2253 5621

CIK No: 0001041179

Subsidiaries: I.C. Isaacs & Company L.P., Isaacs Design, Inc.

Officers: Robert Stephen Stec/Dir., Interim CEO, Peter Rizzo/Dir., CEO/$695,849.00, Gregg Holst/CFO, Exec. VP/$537,119.00, Jesse De La Rama/53/COO/$420,000.00

Directors: Robert Stephen Stec/Dir., Interim CEO, Peter Rizzo/Dir., CEO, Neal J. Fox/Chmn., Oliver Bachellerie/Dir., Rene Faltz/Dir., Francois Girbaud/Dir., Jon Hechler/Dir., John McCoy/Dir.

Owners: Jon Hechler/1.60%, Robert Stephen Stec, Neal J. Fox, Buckingham Capital Management Inc./4.50%, Franois Girbaud/33.90%, Peter J. Rizzo/3.80%, Jeffrey L. Feinberg/12.10%, Ren Faltz, Jesse de la Rama, Insiders/42.20%, Olivier Bachellerie, John McCoy, Wurzburg Holding S.A./33.60%, Gregg A. Holst, Microcapital Fund LP/7.30%

Financial Data: Fiscal Year End:12/31 **Latest Annual Data:** 12/31/2006

Year	Sales	Net Income
2006	$82,236,000	$2,607,000
2005	$83,289,000	$6,411,000
2004	$80,649,000	$6,165,000

Curr. Assets:	$25,289,000	Curr. Liab.:	$10,138,000		
Plant, Equip.:	$3,233,000	Total Liab.:	$11,741,000	Indic. Yr. Divd.:	NA
Total Assets:	$28,809,000	Net Worth:	$17,068,000	Debt/ Equity:	NA

i-CABLE Communications Ltd

Cable Tv Tower, 9 Hoi Shing Rd., Tsuen Wan; **PH:** 852-21128899; **Fax:** 852-2112 7878;
http:// www.i-cable.com; **Email:** sales@i-cable.com

General - Incorporation.................Hong Kong
Employees 3,275
Auditor ....KPMG LLP
Stk Agt...Tengis Ltd
Counsel..NA
DUNS No. ....NA

Stock- Price on:12/24/2007 ....$25.55
Stock Exchange..NDQ
Ticker Symbol..ICAB
Outstanding Shares ....NA
E.P.S. ....NA
Shareholders..NA

Business: The group's principal activities are the provision of pay television and Internet and multimedia services. Other activities include advertising airtime, programme licensing, online shopping and investment holding. As of Dec 2003, the group serves 605,000 pay television subscribers and 225,000 broadband subscribers. Operations are carried out primarily in Hong Kong.

Primary SIC and add'l.: 7379 6719 4841 7375

CIK No: 0001097020

Subsidiaries: Apex Victory Limited, Cable Network Communications Limited, Guangzhou Dong Liang Cai Movie& Television Technology Consultation Company Limited, Guangzhou Kuan Xun Customer Services Company Limited, Hong Kong Cable Enterprises Limited, Hong Kong Cable News Express Limited, Hong Kong Cable News Express Limited (formerly New Television and Film International Limited; changed to current name on February8, 2005), Hong Kong Cable Television Limited, i-CABLE China Limited, i-CABLE Enterprises Limited, i-CABLE Entertainment Limited, i-CABLE Entertainment Limited (commenced business operation on August12, 2005), i-CABLE Media Limited, i-CABLE Media Limited (commenced business operation on August12, 2005), i-CABLE Network Limited 32 Subsidiaries included in the Index

Officers: Stephen T.H. Ng/54/Chmn., CEO, Felix W.K. Yip/49/VP - Human Resources, Administration, Audit, Simon K.K. Yu/54/VP - Network Operations, HKC, Siuming Y.M. Tsui/54/Executive Dir. - I Cable Entertainment Ltd, COO - I Cable Satellite Television Ltd, Pres. - Sundream Motion Pictures Ltd, Samuel C.C. Tsang/51/GM - Hong Kong Cable Enterprises Limited, Hong Kong Cable News Express Limited, Garmen K.Y. Chan/54/VP - External Affairs, Ronald Y.C. Chiu/55/Executive Dir. - i, Cable News Limited, i, Cable Sports Limited, Vincent T.Y. Lam/57/Executive Dir., David C.T. Wong/53/VP - i, Cable Enterprises Limited, Benjamin W. Tong/58/Executive Dir. - HKC, i, Cable Webserve Limited, William J.H. Kwan/44/Dir., CFO

Directors: Stephen T.H. Ng/54/Chmn., CEO, Siuming Y.M. Tsui/54/Executive Dir. - I Cable Entertainment Ltd, COO - I Cable Satellite Television Ltd, Pres. - Sundream Motion Pictures Ltd, Anthony K.K. Yeung/61/Dir., Gordon Y.S Wu/71/Dir., Dennis T.L. Sun/55/Dir., Ronald Y.C. Chiu/55/Executive Dir. - i, Cable News Limited, i, Cable Sports Limited, Vincent T.Y. Lam/57/Executive Dir., Benjamin W. Tong/58/Executive Dir. - HKC, i, Cable Webserve Limited, Peter S.O. Mak/59/Dir., William J.H. Kwan/44/Dir., CFO, Patrick Y.W. Wu/55/Dir.

Owners: Wheelock and Company Limited, Marathon Asset Management Limited, WF Investment Partners Limited, Wharf Communications Limited, Matthews International Capital Management, LLC, The Wharf (Holdings) Limited, HSBC Trustee (Guernsey) Limited

I-Flow Corp

20202 Windrow Dr., Lake Forest, CA, 92630; **PH:** 1-949-206-2700; **Fax:** 1-949-206-2600;
http:// www.iflo.com; **Email:** information@iflo.com

General - Incorporation ....DE
Employees 990
Auditor ....Deloitte & Touche LLP
Stk Agt...... American Stock Transfer & Trust Co.
Counsel...........Gibson, Dunn & Crutcher LLP
DUNS No. 17-510-1625

Stock- Price on:12/24/2007 ....$15.61
Stock Exchange..NDQ
Ticker Symbol..IFLO
Outstanding Shares 24,220,000
E.P.S. $0.55
Shareholders..NA

Business: The group's principal activities are to design, develop, manufacture and market technically advanced and low-cost ambulatory infusion systems. The customers of the group include hospitals and alternate site settings. The group manufactures compact, portable infusion pumps, catheters and pain kits that administer local anesthetic, chemotherapy, nutritional supplement and other medications. The group, through its wholly owned subsidiary infusystem inc provides rental of medical infusion pumps on a month-to-month basis. It markets its products through its distributors in Canada, Brazil, the Benelux Countries, Germany, England, Ireland, Italy, Mexico, Spain, Korea, Australia, New Zealand and Israel. The product line includes the on-q(R) post-operative pain relief system, painbuster(R) pain management system and c-bloc (TM) continuous nerve block system. The group sold spinal specialties on Nov 1, 2003.

Primary SIC and add'l.: 7352 3841

CIK No: 0000857728

Subsidiaries: Block Medical de Mexico, S.A. de C.V., InfuSystem, Inc.

Officers: Donald M. Earhart/Chmn., CEO, Pres./$2,371,684.00, James J. Dal Porto/Exec. VP, COO, Corp. Sec., James R. Talevich/CFO/$818,009.00, John Hicks/Investor Relations Officer

Directors: Donald M. Earhart/Chmn., CEO, Pres.

Owners: Joel S. Kanter, Capital Research and Management Company/6.00%, Donald M. Earhart/8.20%, Henry T. Tai/1.20%, Jack H. Halperin, Erik H. Loudon, James J. Dal Porto/2.10%, Wisconsin State Board of Investment/8.80%, James R. Talevich, Insiders/14.30%, John H. Abeles/1.50%

Financial Data: Fiscal Year End:12/31 **Latest Annual Data:** 12/31/2006

Year	Sales	Net Income
2006	$93,582,000	$13,674,000
2005	$100,644,000	-$8,405,000
2004	$71,145,000	-$17,110,000

Curr. Assets:	$76,690,000	Curr. Liab.:	$20,142,000	P/E Ratio:	28.38
Plant, Equip.:	$18,159,000	Total Liab.:	$20,142,000	Indic. Yr. Divd.:	NA
Total Assets:	$112,146,000	Net Worth:	$92,004,000	Debt/ Equity:	NA

I-many Inc

399 Thornall St., 12th Fl., Edison, NJ, 08837; **PH:** 1-800-832-0228; *http://* www.imany.com;
Email: info@imany.com

General - Incorporation ....DE
Employees 185
Auditor ....BDO Seidman, LLP
Stk Agt...... American Stock Transfer & Trust Co.
Counsel..........Testa, Hurwitz & Thibeault
DUNS No. ....NA

Stock- Price on:12/24/2007 ....$2.39
Stock Exchange..NDQ
Ticker Symbol..IMNY
Outstanding Shares 51,950,000
E.P.S. ....-$0.35
Shareholders..NA

Business: The group's principal activities are to provide software and Internet-based solutions and related professional services. The services of the group enable the clients to manage business-to-business relationships especially the complex contract purchasing relationships in the healthcare industry. The group serves manufacturers, purchasers, group purchasing organizations and parties involved in the purchase, sale and distribution of healthcare supplies and pharmaceutical products. The professional services group provides implementation and deployment services, training and customer support and consulting services. On 02-Apr-2004, the group acquired pricing analytics, inc.

Primary SIC and add'l.: 7379 7371

CIK No: 0001104017

Subsidiaries: ChiCor, Inc., I-many International Limited, I-many Software Private Limited, Intersoft International, Inc

Officers: John A. Rade/Chmn., CEO, Pres./$598,466.00, Todd A. Shytle/Sr. VP - Sales/$339,015.00, Kevin M. Harris/CFO/$308,040.00, Robert G. Schwartz/VP, General Counsel/$237,508.00, David Blumberg/Exec. VP - Fulfillment Services/$269,174.00, Michael T. Zuckerman/Sr. VP - Marketing, Lawrence Lindsey/Exec. VP - Product Operations

Directors: John A. Rade/Chmn., CEO, Pres., Reynolds C. Bish/Dir., Steven L. Fingerhood/Dir., Murray B. Low/49/Dir., Mark R. Mitchell/Dir., Karl E. Newkirk/Dir.

Owners: Diker Management, L.L.C/11.80%, Reynolds C. Bish, Murray B. Low, Mark R. Mitchell, Karl E. Newkirk, David L. Blumberg, Insiders/13.00%, Kevin M. Harris, Ramius Capital Group, L.L.C./12.90%, Todd A. Shytle, Robert G. Schwartz, John A. Rade, Neil Gagnon/5.60%, Steven L. Fingerhood/9.90%, ZF Partners, LP/9.90%

Financial Data: Fiscal Year End:12/31 **Latest Annual Data:** 12/31/2006

Year	Sales	Net Income
2006	$29,575,000	-$15,815,000
2005	$32,576,000	-$9,305,000
2004	$38,413,000	-$7,290,000

Curr. Assets:	$26,198,000	Curr. Liab.:	$23,151,000		
Plant, Equip.:	$1,341,000	Total Liab.:	$25,531,000	Indic. Yr. Divd.:	NA
Total Assets:	$36,985,000	Net Worth:	$11,454,000	Debt/ Equity:	0.0351

I-trax Inc

4 Hillman Dr., Ste. 130, Chadds Ford, PA, 19317; **PH:** 1-610-459-2405; **Fax:** 1-610-459-4705;
http:// www.i-trax.com

General - Incorporation ....DE
Employees 1,079
Auditor ....Goldstein Golub Kessler LLP
Stk Agt.................................StockTrans, Inc.
Counsel..........Akin, Gump, Strauss, Hauer & Feld LLP
DUNS No. ....NA

Stock- Price on:12/24/2007 ....$4.02
Stock Exchange..AMEX
Ticker Symbol..DMX
Outstanding Shares 40,200,000
E.P.S. $0.01
Shareholders..NA

Business: The group's principle activity is to provide corporate health management services to self-insured employers and business consortia. The health management services are designed to allow employers to contract directly for a wide range of employee healthcare needs. The group provides each

client with flexibility to meet its specific pharmacy, primary care, occupational health, corporate health, wellness, lifestyle management or disease management needs. The group operates through 160 locations in 32 states. On 22-Mar-2004, the group acquired meridian occupational healthcare associates inc. The group's quarterly revenue for Sep'07 was 35.15 millions of USD.

Primary SIC and add'l.: 7372

CIK No: 0001110189

Subsidiaries: American Occupational Health Management, Inc., CHD Meridian Healthcare LLC, CHDM, Inc., CHDM, LLC, Corporate Health Dimensions, Inc., Green Hills Insurance Company, I-trax Health Management Solutions, Inc, I-trax Health Management Solutions, LLC, Medicenter, Inc., Meridian COMP of New York, Inc

Officers: Dixon R. Thayer/Dir., CEO/$631,843.00, Thomas G. Lundquist/Chmn. - Medical Advisory Board, Exec. VP, Chief Medical Officer, Raymond J. Fabius/Pres., Chief Medical Officer/$577,465.00, David R. Bock/CFO, Exec. VP/$507,617.00, Robert W. Land/CIO

Directors: Dixon R. Thayer/Dir., CEO, Haywood D. Cochrane/Vice Chmn., Thomas G. Lundquist/Chmn. - Medical Advisory Board, Exec. VP, Chief Medical Officer, Frank A. Martin/Chmn., Arthur N. Leibowitz/Member - Medical Advisory Board, David Nash/Dir., Member - Medical Advisory Board, Stuart Ditcheck/Member - Medical Advisory Board, Craig A. Jones/Member - Medical Advisory Board, Michael O'Connell/Member - Medical Advisory Board, Philip D. Green/Dir., Jack A. Smith/Dir., Michael M.E. Johns/Member - Medical Advisory Board, Gail F. Lieberman/Dir., Gerald D. Mintz/Dir., Arthur Michael Feldman/Member - Medical Advisory Board

Owners: David Nash, Frank A. Martin/3.30%, Ashford Capital Management Inc./5.50%, Insiders/8.60%, Gail F. Lieberman, Perkins Capital Management, Inc./5.70%, Jack A. Smith, Dixon R. Thayer/1.00%, Philip D. Green, Yuri Rozenfeld, Haywood D. Cochrane/1.20%, Pequot Capital Management, Inc./6.40%, Gerald D. Mintz, David R. Bock/1.30%, Raymond J. Fabius/1.00%

Financial Data: ***Fiscal Year End:***12/31 ***Latest Annual Data:*** 12/31/2006

Year	Sales	Net Income
2006	$124,589,000	$1,766,000
2005	$115,887,000	-$14,072,000
2004	$76,402,000	-$3,937,000

Curr. Assets:	$29,788,000	***Curr. Liab.:***	$26,565,000	***P/E Ratio:***	201.00
Plant, Equip.:	$3,377,000	***Total Liab.:***	$37,696,000	***Indic. Yr. Divd.:***	NA
Total Assets:	$103,387,000	***Net Worth:***	$65,691,000	***Debt/ Equity:***	NA

I/OMagic Corp

4 Marconi, Irvine, CA, 92618; ***PH:*** 1-949-707-4800; ***Fax:*** 1-949-855-3550; ***http://*** www.iomagic.com; ***Email:*** sales@iomagic.com

General		***Stock***	
Incorporation	NV	Price on:12/24/2007	NA
Employees	NA	Stock Exchange	OTC
Auditor	Singer Lewak Greenbaum & Goldstein	Ticker Symbol	IOMG
Stk Agt	Transfer Online, Inc.	Outstanding Shares	NA
Counsel	NA	E.P.S	-$0.45
DUNS No.	NA	Shareholders	NA

Business: The groups principle activities include operating data storage industry and selling digital entertainment products. The products of the group include recordable compact disc drives, recordable digital video drives, universal serial bus and hard disk drives. The group markets its products under the brand names I/Omagic(R), Hi-Val(R) and Digital Research Technologies(R). Specific customers of the group include Best Buy, Best Buy Canada, Circuit City, CompUSA, Costco, Fred Meyer Stores, Micro Center, Office Depot and RadioShack. The group operates from North America. Of the total net sales in the year 2005, the United States accounted for 98% and Canada 2%. The group's quarterly revenue for Sep '07 was 5.77 millions of USD.

Primary SIC and add'l.: 3695 3572 3669 3663 3651 3343 3577

CIK No: 0001083663

Subsidiaries: IOM Holdings, Inc.

Officers: Thomas L. Gruber/63/CFO, COO

Owners: Tony Shahbaz/53.00%, Insiders/72.98%, Thomas L. Gruber, Sung Ki Kim/8.27%, Daniel Yao/8.04%, Steel Su/13.06%

Financial Data: ***Fiscal Year End:***12/31 ***Latest Annual Data:*** 12/31/2006

Year	Sales	Net Income
2006	$45,889,000	-$309,000
2005	$37,773,000	-$1,818,000
2004	$44,397,000	-$8,057,000

Curr. Assets:	$25,004,000	***Curr. Liab.:***	$19,118,000		
Plant, Equip.:	$194,000	***Total Liab.:***	$19,118,000	***Indic. Yr. Divd.:***	NA
Total Assets:	$25,602,000	***Net Worth:***	$6,484,000	***Debt/ Equity:***	NA

I2 Technologies Inc

1 i2 Pl., 11701 Luna Rd., Dallas, TX, 75234; ***PH:*** 1-469-357-1000; ***Fax:*** 1-469-357-1798; ***http://*** www.i2.com; ***Email:*** info@i2.com

General		***Stock***	
Incorporation	DE	Price on:12/24/2007	$18.06
Employees	1,340	Stock Exchange	NDQ
Auditor	Deloitte & Touche LLP	Ticker Symbol	ITWO
Stk Agt	Mellon Investor Services LLC	Outstanding Shares	21,200,000
Counsel	NA	E.P.S	$0.90
DUNS No.	62-232-6684	Shareholders	NA

Business: The group's principal activity is to provide enterprise supply chain management solutions including various supply chain software and service offerings. The supply chain management is the set of processes, technology and expertise involved in managing supply, demand and fulfillment throughout divisions within a company and with its customers, suppliers and partners. The group also provides content and services such as business optimization, technical consulting, training, solution maintenance, content management, software upgrades and development. The products of the group are marketed under the trademarks i2, rhythm, planet, tradematrix, global supply chain management and powering the bottom line. The group markets its software and services to customers located in the United States, Europe, Asia, Canada and Latin America.

Primary SIC and add'l.: 7372 7379

CIK No: 0001009304

Subsidiaries: Aspect Development Germany GmbH, Aspect Development International, Inc., Aspect Development K.K., Beijing i2 Technologies Company Ltd., ec-Content, Inc., FreightMatrix.com Europe B.V., FreightMatrix.com, Inc., i2 de Mexico S. de R.L.C.V., i2 Federal, Inc., i2 Technologies (Canada), Inc., i2 Technologies (Malaysia) Sdn Bhd, i2 Technologies (Netherlands) B.V., i2 Technologies (Schweiz) GmbH, i2 Technologies A/S, i2 Technologies China Ltd. 34 Subsidiaries included in the Index

Officers: Michael E. McGrath/Dir., CEO, Pres./$6,803,726.00, Hiten D. Varia/Exec. VP, Chief Customer Officer - Greater Asia, Pacific/$1,614,301.00, Pallab Chatterjee/Exec. VP, Solutions Officer, Chief Delivery Officer/$1,308,021.00, Michael Berry/CFO, Exec. VP/$1,224,953.00, Jana Wammack/Contact, R. M. Robin/57/VP - Human Resources, John Harvey/43/VP, General Counsel, John Cummings/Sr. VP, Chief Marketing Officer, Melis Jones/Aidmatrix Contact, Guy-Frederic Courtin/Industry Analyst Relation, Beth Elkin/Investor Relations Contact, Mette Krogh/Contact - EMEA Marketing, Kellie Nugent/Shelton Investor Relations, Dawn Kahle/Contact, Surku Sinnadurai/CIO, MD *(17 Officers included in Index)*

Directors: Michael E. McGrath/Dir., CEO, Pres., Sanjiv Sidhu/Founder, Chmn., Jackson L. Wilson/Dir., Harvey B. Cash/Dir., Richard L. Clemmer/Dir., Stephen Bradley/Dir., Lloyd G. Waterhouse/Dir.

Owners: Stephen P. Bradley, Lloyd G. Waterhouse, Jackson L. Wilson, Insiders/30.90%, Wells Fargo & Company/7.00%, Amalgamated Gadget, L.P/100.00%, Pallab K. Chatterjee, Luther King Capital Management Corporation/5.30%, Richard L. Clemmer, Sanjiv S. Sidhu/26.10%, Hiten D. Varia, Michael E. McGrath/4.40%, Barbara Stinnett, Amalgamated Gadget, L.P./17.70%, Michael Berry *(16 Owners included in Index)*

Financial Data: ***Fiscal Year End:***12/31 ***Latest Annual Data:*** 12/31/2006

Year	Sales	Net Income
2006	$279,677,000	$24,216,000
2005	$336,867,000	$87,329,000
2004	$389,334,000	-$1,352,000

Curr. Assets:	$148,953,000	***Curr. Liab.:***	$131,585,000	***P/E Ratio:***	20.52
Plant, Equip.:	$10,691,000	***Total Liab.:***	$215,407,000	***Indic. Yr. Divd.:***	NA
Total Assets:	$190,069,000	***Net Worth:***	-$25,338,000	***Debt/ Equity:***	NA

i2Telecom International Inc

5070 Old Ellis Point, Ste. 110, Roswell, GA, 30076; ***PH:*** 1-404-567-4750; ***Fax:*** 1-314-725-4073; ***http://*** www.i2telecom.com

General		***Stock***	
Incorporation	WA	Price on:12/24/2007	$0.118
Employees	10	Stock Exchange	OTC
Auditor	Freedman & Goldberg	Ticker Symbol	ITUI
Stk Agt	Continental Stock Transfer & Trust Co	Outstanding Shares	100,930,000
Counsel	NA	E.P.S	-$0.089
DUNS No.	NA	Shareholders	NA

Business: The group's principal activity is to provide low-cost telecommunications services employing next-generation voip technology. The group provides micro gateway adapters (internettalker(tm)), voip long distance and other enhanced communication services to subscribers. The group operations are based in boca raton, Florida; atlanta, Georgia; redwood city, California; and China.

Primary SIC and add'l.: 3669 7312

CIK No: 0000949371

Subsidiaries: i2 Telecom International Limited, i2 Telecom International, Inc., SuperCaller Community, Inc.

Officers: Paul R. Arena/Chmn., CEO/$111,708.00, James Rose/CTO/$124,574.00, David C. Burns/CFO, Douglas F. Bender/58/GM, Sr. VP - Operations/$99,499.00, Andrew Hellman/Investor Contact, Jerry Lumpkin/Sr. VP - Americas Sales, Fenn King/Sr. VP, GM - Asia Pacific

Directors: Paul R. Arena/Chmn., CEO, Christer D. Bylander/54/Dir.

Owners: Douglas Bender/2.40%, Christer D. Bylander/1.10%, Insiders/13.60%, Renaissance Capital/12.50%, Vestal Venture Capital/32.30%, Paul R. Arena/8.10%, Audrey L. Braswel/7.00%, James R. Rose/2.10%

Financial Data: ***Fiscal Year End:***12/31 ***Latest Annual Data:*** 12/31/2006

Year	Sales	Net Income
2006	$755,000	-$5,800,000
2005	$485,000	-$8,028,000
2004	$548,000	-$6,693,000

Curr. Assets:	$1,305,000	***Curr. Liab.:***	$9,044,000		
Plant, Equip.:	$764,000	***Total Liab.:***	$9,044,000	***Indic. Yr. Divd.:***	NA
Total Assets:	$5,447,000	***Net Worth:***	-$3,597,000	***Debt/ Equity:***	NA

IA Global Inc

101 California St., Ste. 2450, San Francisco, CA, 94111; ***PH:*** 1-415-946-8828; ***Fax:*** 1-415-946-8801; ***http://*** www.iaglobalinc.com; ***Email:*** support@iaglobalinc.com

General		***Stock***	
Incorporation	DE	Price on:12/24/2007	$0.42
Employees	198	Stock Exchange	AMEX
Auditor	Sherb & Co. LLP	Ticker Symbol	IAO
Stk Agt	American Stock Transfer & Trust Co.	Outstanding Shares	151,050,000
Counsel	NA	E.P.S	-$0.05
DUNS No.	NA	Shareholders	NA

Business: The group's principal activity is to provide streaming audio and video content over four Internet television networks. The group has a number of related Internet Web sites, commonly called a network, utilizing geographic location. Each site will offer original programming, in English, of local events, politics, entertainment, business and culture. The group's corner stone network is foreigntv.com, which features five channels. On 18-Mar-2004, the group acquired rex Tokyo company ltd.

Primary SIC and add'l.: 4841

CIK No: 0001077634

Subsidiaries: Collobration Co Ltd, Double R, Inc, Global Hotline, Inc, IA Partners Co Ltd, Inforidge Co Ltd, Rex Tokyo Co Ltd

Officers: Derek Schneideman/Chmn., CEO, Mark Scott/Dir., Chief Operating, Financial Officer/$377,521.00, Hideki Anan/Management Dir./$288,817.00

Directors: Derek Schneideman/Chmn., CEO, Clifford James Bernstein/Dir., Meiko Towada/Dir., Eric La Cara/Dir., Mark Scott/Dir., Chief Operating, Financial Officer, Raymond Christinson/Dir., Masazumi Ishii/Dir.

Owners: Hiroki Isobe/2.90%, Mark Scott, Kyo Nagae/1.00%, Baddas Investments Pty Ltd/7.10%, Derek Schneideman, Terra Firma Fund , Ltd./8.60%, Inter Asset Japan Co. Ltd./2.00%, PBAA Fund, Ltd./15.80%, Raymond Christinson, Inter Asset Japan LBO No. 1 Fund/19.40%, IA Turkey Equity Portfolio Ltd/1.60%, Clifford Bernstein, Derek Schneideman, McFraui Pty Ltd, ATF The McFraui Trust/19.60%, Eric La Cara *(17 Owners included in Index)*

Financial Data: *Fiscal Year End:*12/31   *Latest Annual Data:* 12/31/2006

Year	Sales	Net Income
2006	$19,139,000	-$3,770,000
2005	$45,079,000	-$2,071,000
2004	$31,550,000	-$1,443,000

Curr. Assets:	$10,576,000	**Curr. Liab.:**	$7,619,000		
Plant, Equip.:	$409,000	**Total Liab.:**	$12,381,000	**Indic. Yr. Divd.:**	NA
Total Assets:	$21,640,000	**Net Worth:**	$9,259,000	**Debt/ Equity:**	0.5143

IAMGOLD Corp

401 Bay St., Ste. 3200, Toronto, ON, M5H 2Y4; *PH:* 1-416-360-4710; *Fax:* 1-416-360-4750; *http://* www.iamgold.com; *Email:* info@iamgold.com

General - Incorporation..................Canada	Stock- Price on:12/24/2007 ....$7.72
Employees...3,300	Stock Exchange.....................................NYSE
Auditor ....KPMG LLP	Ticker Symbol...IAG
Stk Agt.... Computershare Trust Co (Can & Aus)	Outstanding Shares 292,980,000
Counsel .... Fraser, Milner, Casgrain LLP	E.P.S $0.29
DUNS No. ....NA	Shareholders..NA

Business: The group's principal activities are the development and exploration of precious metals in Africa and South America. The group also is a co-owner of two gold mines in west Africa. The group holds a 38 percent stake in sadiola gold mine and a 40 percent stake in the yatela gold mine which are located in mali, west Africa. On 07-Jan-2003, it acquired repadre capital corporation.

Primary SIC and add'l.: 1041 1044

CIK No: 0001203464

Officers: Joseph F. Conway/Dir., CEO, Pres., Grant A. Edey/Sr. VP - Finance, Paul B. Olmsted/Sr. VP - Corporate Development, John McCombe/Sr. VP - Africa, Luc Lessard/VP - Engineering, Construction, Lucie Desjardins/Sr. Legal Counsel, Assist. Corp. Sec., Glynnis Frelih/Corporate Controller, Larry E. Phillips/Sr. VP - Corporate Affairs, Carol T. Banducci/CFO, Michael Donnelly/Sr. VP - Exploration, Denis Miville-Deschenes/Sr. VP - Project Development, Janet Wilkinson/Sr. VP - Human Resources, Guy G. Dufresne/Engineer, Corp. Dir., Jacques Perron/Sr. VP - Americas, Claude Barjot/VP - African Affairs *(17 Officers included in Index)*

Directors: Joseph F. Conway/Dir., CEO, Pres., William D. Pugliese/Chmn., John E. Caldwell/Dir., Derek Bullock/Dir., Mahendra Naik/Dir., Donald K. Charter/Dir., Jean-Andre elie/Dir., Robert W. Dengler/Dir., Stephen Freedhoff/Dir., Peter C. Jones/Dir., John Shaw/Dir.

Financial Data: *Fiscal Year End:*12/31   *Latest Annual Data:* 12/31/2006

Year	Sales	Net Income
2006	$332,219,000	$65,175,000
2005	$145,241,000	$13,317,000
2004	$135,021,000	$12,011,000

Curr. Assets:	$318,567,000	**Curr. Liab.:**	$216,511,000		
Plant, Equip.:	$1,273,800,000	**Total Liab.:**	$505,325,000	**Indic. Yr. Divd.:**	$0.060
Total Assets:	$2,236,231,000	**Net Worth:**	$1,730,906,000	**Debt/ Equity:**	NA

IAS Communications Inc

Formerly: IAS Communications Inc
240 11780 Hammersmith Way, Richmond, BC, V7A 5E9; *PH:* 1-604-278-5996

General - Incorporation...........................OR	Stock- Price on:12/24/2007 ....$0.2
Employees...NA	Stock Exchange.....................................OTC
Auditor .... Smythe Ratcliffe LLP	Ticker Symbol.......................................IASCA
Stk Agt...........Nevada Agency & Trust Company	Outstanding Shares ....NA
Counsel ....James L. Vandeberg	E.P.S ....NA
DUNS No. ....NA	Shareholders..NA

Business: The group's principle activity is to commercialize advanced antennas for wireless communications markets, including cellular, meter reading and global positioning services. The group operates from United States.

Primary SIC and add'l.: 3679

CIK No: 0000945641

Officers: John G. Robertson/67/Chmn., CEO, Pres., Jennifer Lorette/36/Dir., Sec., Treasurer, James Vandeberg/64/Dir., CFO, COO

Directors: John G. Robertson/67/Chmn., CEO, Pres., Jennifer Lorette/36/Dir., Sec., Treasurer, James Vandeberg/64/Dir., CFO, COO

Owners: Insiders, Jennifer Lorette, SMR Investments, Robertson Family Trust, Access Information Services, Inc., John G. Robertson, JGR Petroleum Inc, James L. Vandeberg

Financial Data: *Fiscal Year End:*04/30   *Latest Annual Data:* 04/30/2007

Year	Sales	Net Income
2007	$24,000	-$25,000
2006	NA	-$59,000
2005	NA	-$43,000

Curr. Assets:	$230,000	**Curr. Liab.:**	$347,000		
Plant, Equip.:	NA	**Total Liab.:**	$347,000	**Indic. Yr. Divd.:**	NA
Total Assets:	$230,000	**Net Worth:**	-$117,000	**Debt/ Equity:**	NA

iBasis Inc

20 2nd Ave., Burlington, MA, 01803; *PH:* 1-781-505-7500; *Fax:* 1-781-505-7300; *http://* www.ibasis.net; *Email:* info@ibasis.net

General - Incorporation...........................DE	Stock- Price on:12/24/2007 ....$10.16
Employees...230	Stock Exchange.....................................NDQ
Auditor ....Deloitte & Touche LLP	Ticker Symbol..IBAS
Stk Agt........ EquiServe, Shareholder Services	Outstanding Shares 33,470,000
Counsel .... Hale & Dorr LLP	E.P.S ....-$0.07
DUNS No. ....NA	Shareholders..NA

Business: The group's principal activity is to provide advanced Internet-based communication services. The services of the group enable the telecommunications carriers and other communications service providers to offer international voice, fax and other value-added applications over the Internet. The group has deployed vocore hosted unified communication solution that permits the customers to offer a communications solution that unifies the storage of and access to email and voicemail messages. It also provides enhanced services, such as interactive voice response and customer service applications. The customers of the group include mci worldcom, cable & wireless and certain government-affiliated dominant carriers. The group operates through various service agreements with local service providers in the United States, Europe, Asia, the Middle East, Latin America, Africa and Australia.

Primary SIC and add'l.: 4813 7375

CIK No: 0001091756

Officers: Ofer Gneezy/Chmn., CEO, Pres., Dan Powdermaker/44/Sr. VP - Worldwide Sales, Chris Ward/Sr. Dir. - Marketing Communications, Hong Guo/Contact - Beijing, Tianmu Gao/Contact - Beijing, Jorge Hernandez/Contact - Amsterdam, Kinuyo Sakamoto/Contact - Japan, Natalia Kouksenko/Contact - Russia, CIS, Jayesh Patel/VP - Business Development, Strategy, Mark Flynn/Chief Legal Officer, Corp. Sec., Edwin Van Ierland/Sr. VP - Sales, Juan Ramos/VP - Latin America, Tamah Solomon Rosker/VP - Human Resources, Ajay T. Joseph/VP - Network Architecture, Engineering, John Tolton/VP - Asia Pacific Region *(22 Officers included in Index)*

Directors: Ofer Gneezy/Chmn., CEO, Pres., Frank W. King/Dir., Eelco Blok/Dir., Robert H. Brumley/Dir., Joost Farwerck/Dir., Charles Skibo/69/Dir., David S. Lee/70/Dir., Charles Corfield/Dir., Gordon J. Vanderbrug/Co - Founder, Dir., Exec. VP, Assist. Sec.

Owners: Paul H. Floyd, LC Capital Master Fund, Ltd./9.78%, Gordon J. VanderBrug/1.91%, Dan Powdermaker, KPN B.V./23.78%, Greywolf Capital Partners II LP/5.04%, Robert H. Brumley, Millennium Partners, L.P./5.07%, Richard G. Tennant, Charles Skibo, David Lee, Insiders/9.57%, Singer Children's Management Trust/6.29%, Frank W. King, Charles N. Corfield/1.52% *(16 Owners included in Index)*

Financial Data: *Fiscal Year End:*12/31   *Latest Annual Data:* 12/31/2006

Year	Sales	Net Income
2006	$511,083,000	-$2,194,000
2005	$385,485,000	-$1,676,000
2004	$263,678,000	-$17,536,000

Curr. Assets:	$123,396,000	**Curr. Liab.:**	$98,111,000		
Plant, Equip.:	$13,858,000	**Total Liab.:**	$100,283,000	**Indic. Yr. Divd.:**	NA
Total Assets:	$137,664,000	**Net Worth:**	$37,381,000	**Debt/ Equity:**	0.0201

IBERIABANK Corp

200 W Congress St., 12th Fl., Lafayette, LA, 70501; *PH:* 1-337-521-4012; *Fax:* 1-337-364-1171; *http://* www.iberiabank.com

General - Incorporation ....LA	Stock- Price on:12/24/2007 ....$49.98
Employees...692	Stock Exchange.....................................NDQ
Auditor .... Castaing, Hussey & Lolan, LLC	Ticker Symbol..IBKC
Stk Agt........................Registrar & Transfer Co	Outstanding Shares 12,890,000
Counsel ....Elias, Matz, Tierman & Herrick	E.P.S $3.35
DUNS No. 92-725-8202	Shareholders..NA

Business: The group's principal activity is to attract retail deposits from the general public and business community and utilizing these funds to originate loans. The deposit accounts are checking, savings and certificate of deposits. The group lends commercial, consumer and mortgage loans. Consumer loans consist of home equity loans, home equity lines of credit, automobile loans, indirect automobile loans, loans secured by deposit accounts and other consumer loans. The group also offers discount brokerage services and insurance services. The group operates 39 offices in south central Louisiana, north Louisiana and the greater new orleans area. On 28-Feb-2003, the group acquired acadiana bancshares, inc and on 29-Feb-2004, it acquired alliance bank.

Primary SIC and add'l.: 6022 6712

CIK No: 0000933141

Subsidiaries: Acadiana Holdings, LLC, Finesco, LLC, Iberia Financial Services, LLC, Iberiabank, Iberiabank Insurance Services, LLC, Jefferson Insurance Corporation

Officers: Daryl G. Byrd/Dir., CEO, Pres./$1,180,233.00, William E. Pratt/Vice Chmn. - Advisory Board,Northeast Louisiana, Iberiabank, John R. Davis/Sr. Exec. VP, Dir. - Financial Strategy, Mortgage, Title Insurance Companies/$584,993.00, Marilyn W. Burch/Exec. VP, Dir. - Corporate Operations, Anthony J. Restel/CFO, Chief Credit Officer, Sr. Exec. VP/$279,188.00, Michael J. Brown/Sr. Exec. VP, Regional Pres. - Marketing/$847,824.00, Michael A. Naquin/Sr. Exec. VP, Dir. - Retail Segment, Facilities, Treasury Management/$533,191.00, George J. Becker/Exec. VP, Corp. Sec., Dir. - Organizational Development, Taylor F. Barras/Pres. - Marketing, Member - Advisory Board, New Iberia, Iberiabank, Karl E. Hoefer/Pres. - Marketing, Member - Advisory Board, New Orleans, Iberiabank, E. Van Pardue/Pres. - Marketing, Member - Advisory Board, Northeast Louisiana, Iberiabank, Keith J. Short/Pres. - Marketing, Member - Advisory Board, Baton Rouge, Iberiabank, Pete M. Yuan/Pres. - Marketing, Member - Advisory Board, Lafayette, Iberiabank, Mark Evans/Pres. - Marketing, Beth Ardoin/Exec. VP, Dir. - Communications *(16 Officers included in Index)*

Directors: Daryl G. Byrd/Dir., CEO, Pres., William H. Fenstermaker/Chmn., Stewart E. Shea/Vice Chmn., Cecil C. Broussard/Co - Chmn., Member - Advisory Board, New Iberia, Iberiabank, Elton W. Kennedy/Chmn. - Advisory Board, Northeast Louisiana, Iberiabank, Steven W. Usdin/Member - Advisory Board, New Orleans, Iberiabank, Stephen F. Stumpf/Member - Advisory Board, New Orleans, Iberiabank, Jose S. Suquet/Member - Advisory Board, New Orleans, Iberiabank, Patrick J. Quinlin/Member - Advisory Board, New Orleans, Iberiabank, J. C. Rathborne/Member - Advisory Board, New Orleans, Iberiabank, James J. Reiss/Member - Advisory Board, New Orleans, Iberiabank, Benton J. Smallpage/Member - Advisory Board, New Orleans, Iberiabank, Dixon W. Abell/Member - Advisory Board, Northeast Louisiana, Iberiabank, Scott J. Cummins/Member - Advisory Board, Northeast Louisiana, Iberiabank, Randy L. Ewing/Member - Advisory Board, Northeast Louisiana, Iberiabank *(87 Directors included in Index)*

Owners: John R. Davis/1.42%, Michael A. Naquin, Miles O. Pollard, Stewart E. Shea, Anthony J. Restel, Michael J. Brown/1.38%, Elaine D. Abell, Harry V. Barton, Ernest P. Breaux, Larrey G. Mouton, Jefferson G. Parker, David H. Welch, Daryl G. Byrd/2.91%, James C. East/5.52%, Insiders/16.37% *(17 Owners included in Index)*

Financial Data: *Fiscal Year End:*12/31   *Latest Annual Data:* 12/31/2006

Year	Sales	Net Income
2006	$192,825,000	$35,695,000
2005	$161,509,000	$22,000,000
2004	$131,827,000	$27,339,000

Curr. Assets:	$84,905,000	**Curr. Liab.:**	$2,625,187,000	**P/E Ratio:**	14.88
Plant, Equip.:	$71,007,000	**Total Liab.:**	$2,883,495,000	**Indic. Yr. Divd.:**	$1.360
Total Assets:	$3,203,046,000	**Net Worth:**	$319,551,000	**Debt/ Equity:**	0.7102

Ibis Technology Corp

32 Cherry Hill Dr., Danvers, MA, 01923; *PH:* 1-978-777-4247; *Fax:* 1-978-777-6570;
http:// www.ibis.com; *Email:* info@ibis.com

General - Incorporation .... MA	Stock- Price on:12/24/2007 .... $1.53
Employees 45	Stock Exchange.. NDQ
Auditor .... KPMG LLP	Ticker Symbol... IBIS
Stk Agt.............. Continental Stock Transfer & Trust Co	Outstanding Shares 12,320,000
Counsel........... Mintz Levin Cohn Ferris Et Al	E.P.S.. -$0.417
DUNS No. 17-815-8564	Shareholders... NA

Business: The group's principal activities are to develop, manufacture and market silicon-on-insulator (soi) wafers formed by simox (separation by implantation of oxygen) technology. Simox-soi wafers are manufactured by the group using a specialized oxygen ion implanter, which is developed and manufactured by the group and is integrated with other specialized processes and characterization equipment.

Primary SIC and add'l.: 8733 3674

CIK No: 0000855182

Officers: Martin J. Reid/Chmn., CEO, Pres./$341,171.00, Angelo V. Alioto/Dir. - Sales, William J. Schmidt/CFO, Treasurer/$235,844.00, Robert P. Dolan/VP - Wafer Technology/$193,166.00, Charles M. McKenna/COO, Exec. VP/$251,548.00, Marianne Dunn/Assist. - Investor Relations

Directors: Martin J. Reid/Chmn., CEO, Pres., Robert L. Gable/Dir., Dimitri A. Antoniadis/Dir., Donald McGuinness/Dir., Leslie B. Lewis/Dir., Lamberto Raffaelli/Dir., Cosmo Trapani/Dir.

Owners: Charles M. McKenna, Special Situations Fund III QP, L.P. and its affiliated funds/19.90%, Robert L. Gable, Leslie B. Lewis, Dimitri Antoniadis, Cosmo S. Trapani, Martin J. Reid/2.70%, William J. Schmidt, Donald F. McGuinness, Lamberto Raffaelli, Robert P. Dolan, Insiders/5.40%

Financial Data: Fiscal Year End:12/31 Latest Annual Data: 12/31/2006

Year	Sales	Net Income
2006	$13,987,000	$405,000
2005	$602,000	-$9,245,000
2004	$7,926,000	-$10,919,000

Curr. Assets:	$9,028,000	Curr. Liab.:	$1,534,000	
Plant, Equip.:	$3,984,000	Total Liab.:	$1,534,000	Indic. Yr. Divd.: NA
Total Assets:	$13,789,000	Net Worth:	$12,255,000	Debt/ Equity: NA

iBIZ Technology Corp

2238 W Lone Cactus Dr., No. 200, Phoenix, AZ, 85027; *PH:* 1-623-492-9200;
http:// www.ibizcorp.com; *Email:* support@ibizcorp.com

General - Incorporation .... FL	Stock- Price on:12/24/2007 .... $0.0006
Employees .... NA	Stock Exchange.. OTC
Auditor .... Farber & Hass LLP	Ticker Symbol.. IBZTE
Stk Agt... NA	Outstanding Shares .... NA
Counsel... NA	E.P.S... NA
DUNS No. .... NA	Shareholders... NA

Business: The group's principle activity is to design, manufacture and distribute personal digital assistant accessories and other handheld computing devices. The group also markets LCD monitors, OEM notebook computers, third party software, and general-purpose financial application keyboards. The products of the group include aluminum hardcase, folding cradles, chargers, keysync keyboard, cables and travel kits. The group primarily operates through its subsidiary invnsys technology corporation. The products of the group are marketed and distributed directly to end users through direct sales force, regional resellers, value-added providers in the banking and point-of-sale market and Internet commerce sites. On 03-Feb-2004, the group acquired synosphere, llc.

Primary SIC and add'l.: 6719 7373 3575 3577 7375 3571

CIK No: 0001079893

Subsidiaries: iBIZ, Inc, Invnsys Technology Corporation, Qhost, Inc, Synosphere, LLC

Officers: Kenneth W. Schilling/CEO, Pres.

IBM Corp

1 New Orchard Rd., Armonk, NY, 10504; *PH:* 1-877-426-6006; *Fax:* 1-877-426-9226;
http:// www.ibm.com; *Email:* ews@us.ibm.com

General - Incorporation .... NY	Stock- Price on:12/24/2007 .... $106.6
Employees 366,486	Stock Exchange... NYSE
Auditor .... PricewaterhouseCoopers LLP	Ticker Symbol.. IBM
Stk Agt..... Computershare Investor Services LLC	Outstanding Shares 1,480,000,000
Counsel... NA	E.P.S.. $6.76
DUNS No. 00-136-8083	Shareholders... NA

Business: The group's principle activity is to provide business, technology and consulting services. The group's products include software, systems and server, semiconductors, small and medium business products, and workstations. The group's services include business consulting, outsourcing, application, and IT services. In September 2007, IBM completed the acquisition of DataMirror Corporation. The group operates from United States.

Primary SIC and add'l.: 3577 3571 7373 7371 3572 6159

CIK No: 0000051143

Subsidiaries: Compagnie IBM France, S.A.S., Companhia IBM Portuguesa, S.A., Grupo IBM Mexico, S.A. de C.V., IBM (International Business Machines)Turk Limited Sirketi, IBM (Schweiz)-IBM (Suisse)-IBM (Svizzera)-IBM (Switzerland), Ibm A/nz Holdings Pty. Limited, IBM Americas Holding Limited, IBM Argentina Sociedad Anonima, IBM Australia Limited, IBM Bahamas Limited, IBM Brasil Industria, Maquinas e Servicos Limitada, IBM Bulgaria Ltd., IBM Business Transformation Center, S.r.l., IBM Canada Credit Services Company, IBM Canada Holding Company, Limited Partnership 92 Subsidiaries included in the Index

Officers: Samuel J. Palmisano/56/Chmn., CEO, Pres./$24,463,790.00, Martin Schroeter/Treasurer, Rodney C. Adkins/Sr. VP - Development, Manufacturing, Linda S. Sanford/Sr. VP - Enterprise On Demand Transformation, Information Technology, Steven A. Mills/Sr. VP - Group Exec. IBM Software Group/$6,010,229.00, Robert W. Moffat/Sr. VP - Integrated Operations, Daniel E. O'Donnell/VP, Assist. General Counsel, Sec., Virginia M. Rometty/Sr. VP - IBM Global Business Services, Timothy S. Shaughnessy/VP, Controller, Robert C. Weber/Sr. VP - Legal, Regulatory Affairs, General Counsel, William M. Zeitler/Sr. VP - Group Exec., IBM Systems, Technology Group, Nicholas M. Donofrio/Exec. VP - Innovation, Technology/$6,292,426.00, Doug T. Elix/Sr. VP - Group Exec. Sales, Distribution/$6,060,149.00, Mark Loughridge/CFO, Sr. VP/$5,954,301.00, Randall J. MacDonald/Sr. VP - Human Resources (*20 Officers included in Index*)

Directors: Samuel J. Palmisano/56/Chmn., CEO, Pres., Kenneth I. Chenault/56/Dir., Sidney Taurel/59/Dir., Lorenzo H. Zambrano/63/Dir., Michael L. Eskew/58/Dir., Lucio A. Noto/69/Dir., Shirley Ann Jackson/61/Dir., James W. Owens/62/Dir., William R. Brody/Dir., Cathleen Black/63/Dir., Juergen Dormann/68/Dir., Joan E. Spero/63/Dir., Minoru Makihara/78/Dir.

Owners: M. Makihara, Insiders, N. M. Donofrio, S. J. Palmisano, J. Dormann, S. Taurel, C. Black, L. H. Zambrano, K. I. Chenault, D. T. Elix, S. A. Mills, J. E. Spero, M. Loughridge, C. M. Vest, L. A. Noto (*16 Owners included in Index*)

Financial Data: Fiscal Year End:12/31 Latest Annual Data: 06/30/2007

Year	Sales	Net Income
2007	$23,772,000,000	$2,261,000,000
2006	$91,424,000,000	$9,492,000,000
2005	$91,134,000,000	$7,934,000,000

Curr. Assets:	$44,660,000,000	Curr. Liab.:	$40,090,000,000	P/E Ratio: 17.03
Plant, Equip.:	$14,439,000,000	Total Liab.:	$74,727,000,000	Indic. Yr. Divd.: $1.600
Total Assets:	$103,233,000,000	Net Worth:	$28,506,000,000	Debt/ Equity: 0.5136

IBSG International Inc

1132 Celebration Blvd, Kissimmee, FL, 34747; *PH:* 1-321-939-6321; *http://* www.ibsgi.com

General - Incorporation .... FL	Stock- Price on:12/24/2007 .... $1.63
Employees 38	Stock Exchange.. OTC
Auditor ....HJ & Associates, LLC	Ticker Symbol.. IBIN
Stk Agt .... Florida Atlantic Stock Transfer, Inc.	Outstanding Shares 8,540,000
Counsel... NA	E.P.S.. $0.37
DUNS No. .... NA	Shareholders... NA

Business: The group operates through its subsidiaries whose principle activity is to provide software solutions. Markets served by the group include Small Business Development Centers, Fortune 1000 Corporations, Business Associations, Banking Institutions and International Economic Development Projects. The group operates from the United States and United Kingdom. The group's quarterly revenur for September 2007 was 3.99 millions of USD.

Primary SIC and add'l.: 7371

CIK No: 0001031905

Subsidiaries: Intelligent Business Systems Group, Inc, Secure Blue, Inc.

Officers: Michael Rivers/Chmn., CEO, Geoffrey Birch/Dir., Acting CFO, Michael Porter/Investor Relation Officer

Directors: Michael Rivers/Chmn., CEO, Jeffery Willmott/Dir., Geoffrey Birch/Dir., Acting CFO

Owners: Jeffrey Willmott, Geoffrey Birch, M&K Trust/12.90%, Insiders/12.90%

Financial Data: Fiscal Year End:12/31 Latest Annual Data: 12/31/2006

Year	Sales	Net Income
2006	$10,302,000	$1,828,000
2005	$7,226,000	$2,133,000
2004	$3,295,000	-$2,559,000

Curr. Assets:	$16,758,000	Curr. Liab.:	$6,290,000	P/E Ratio: 4.41
Plant, Equip.:	$641,000	Total Liab.:	$6,290,000	Indic. Yr. Divd.: NA
Total Assets:	$23,725,000	Net Worth:	$17,435,000	Debt/ Equity: NA

IBT Bancorp Inc

309 Main St., Irwin, PA, 15642; *PH:* 1-724-863-3100; *Fax:* 1-724-863-3069;
http:// www.myirwinbank.com

General - Incorporation .... PA	Stock- Price on:12/24/2007 .... $18.5
Employees 181	Stock Exchange... AMEX
Auditor ....Edwards Sauer & Owens, P.C	Ticker Symbol... IRW
Stk Agt ....Registrar & Transfer Co	Outstanding Shares 5,880,000
Counsel.............................. Malizia, Spidi & Fisch	E.P.S.. $1.33
DUNS No. .... NA	Shareholders... NA

Business: The group's principal activity is that of a commercial bank. The group provides mortgage, commercial and consumer banking business and trust and depository services to its customers. The group is a state chartered commercial banking institution that operates through its wholly owned banking subsidiary, irwin bank and trust company. The group provides residential mortgage loans, commercial mortgage loans and instalment loans. It offers a broad selection of deposit instruments including checking, regular savings, money market deposits, term certificate accounts and individual retirement accounts. The group's offices are located in the Pennsylvania counties of westmoreland and allegheny.

Primary SIC and add'l.: 6712 6022

CIK No: 0000801122

Subsidiaries: Irwin Bank & Trust Company, T.A. of Irwin, LP

Officers: Charles G. Urtin/Dir., CEO, Pres./$266,411.00, Raymond G. Suchta/Sr. VP, CFO/$115,075.00, Robert A. Bowell/Exec. VP, Chief Lending Officer/$156,902.00, David A. Finui/COO, Sr. VP/$126,013.00

Directors: Charles G. Urtin/Dir., CEO, Pres., Robert Rebich/Chmn., Thomas E. Deger/Dir., Charles W. Hengenroeder/Dir., Robert C. Whisner/Dir., Richard L. Ryan/Dir., John N. Brenzia/Dir., Grant J. Shevchik/Dir., Richard J. Hoffman/Dir.

Owners: Richard J. Hoffman, Insiders/10.12%, Robert A. Bowell, Robert C. Whisner/2.83%, Raymond G. Suchta, S&T Bancorp, Inc./8.10%, Thomas E. Deger, Charles G. Urtin/1.22%, John N. Brenzia, Charles W. Hergenroeder, Grant J. Shevchik, Robert Rebich/3.53%, Richard L. Ryan, David A. Finui

Financial Data: Fiscal Year End:12/31 Latest Annual Data: 12/31/2006

Year	Sales	Net Income
2006	$47,862,000	$8,456,000
2005	$42,406,000	$8,579,000
2004	$39,205,000	$6,085,000

Curr. Assets:	$20,055,000	Curr. Liab.:	$678,380,000	P/E Ratio: 13.91
Plant, Equip.:	$5,281,000	Total Liab.:	$678,380,000	Indic. Yr. Divd.: $1.000
Total Assets:	$740,962,000	Net Worth:	$62,581,000	Debt/ Equity: NA

IBT Bancorp Inc/MI

200 E Broadway St., Mount Pleasant, MI, 48858; *PH:* 1-989-772-9471;
http:// www.myirwinbank.com

General - Incorporation: MI
Employees: 303
Auditor: Rehmann Robson P.C
Stk Agt: Registrar & Transfer Co
Counsel: NA
DUNS No.: 60-324-3189

Stock- Price on:12/24/2007: $43.5
Stock Exchange: OTC
Ticker Symbol: IBTM
Outstanding Shares: 6,340,000
E.P.S: $1.17
Shareholders: NA

Business: The group's principle activity is to provide financial products and services to businesses, institutions and individuals in Michigan. The group operates its activities through seven wholly owned subsidiaries. The isabella bank and trust and farmers state bank of breckenridge offer banking services through 19 locations. The lending services include commercial real estate loans, lines of credit, residential real estate loans, consumer loans, student loans and credit cards. The deposits include interest and non-interest bearing checking accounts, savings accounts, money market accounts and certificates of deposit. In addition, the banks also offer other financial related products including trust services, title insurance, stocks, investment securities, bonds, mutual fund sales, 24 hour banking service through automatic teller machines and safe deposit box rentals. The group's quarterly income for Sep'07 was 2.02 millions of USD.

Primary SIC and add'l.: 6022 6712

CIK No: 0000842517

Subsidiaries: Farmers State Bank of Breckenridge, Financial Group Information Services, IB & T Employee Leasing, LLC, IBT Personnel, LLC, IBT Title and Insurance Agency, Inc., Isabella Bank and Trust

Officers: Dennis P. Angner/52/Dir., CEO, Pres./$360,344.00, Raymond G. Suchta/CFO, Sr. VP, Investor Relations Officer, David A. Finui/COO, Sr. VP, Debra Campbell/Sec., Robert A. Bowell/Exec. VP, Chief Lending Officer

Directors: Dennis P. Angner/52/Dir., CEO, Pres., Robert Rebich/Chmn., Thomas E. Deger/Dir., William J. Strickler/67/Dir., John N. Brenzia/Dir., Charles W. Hergenroeder/Dir., Richard J. Hoffman/Dir., Richard L. Ryan/Dir., Richard J. Barz/59/Dir., David W. Hole/70/Dir., Dale Weburg/64/Dir., Sandra L. Caul/64/Dir., Michael W. McGuire/58/Dir., James C. Fabiano/64/Dir., Joseph W. Manifold/56/Dir. *(19 Directors included in Index)*

Owners: Joseph W. Manifold, Insiders/6.96%, Kirk Faber/2.00%, Sandra L. Caul/0.14%, Leland T. Wallin/5.38%, Todd N. Taylor/5.76%, Timothy M. Miller/0.05%, Dale D. Weburg/0.79%, Jae A. Evans/0.65%, Todd Taylor/5.76%, William J. Strickler/1.18%, Peggy L. Wheeler/0.08%, Michael W. McGuire, Douglas D. McFarlane/0.01%, James Beckman/0.65% *(26 Owners included in Index)*

Financial Data: ***Fiscal Year End:*** 12/31 ***Latest Annual Data:*** 12/31/2006

Year	Sales	Net Income
2006	$53,807,000	$7,001,000

Curr. Assets:	$37,124,000	**Curr. Liab.:**	$733,659,000	**P/E Ratio:**	36.25
Plant, Equip.:	$20,754,000	**Total Liab.:**	$794,378,000	**Indic. Yr. Divd.:**	NA
Total Assets:	$910,127,000	**Net Worth:**	$115,749,000	**Debt/ Equity:**	0.5377

ICA Corp

12130 Brockton Ln., Minneapolis, MN, 55369; ***PH:*** 1-763-428-2800; ***Fax:*** 1-763-428-4230; ***http://*** www.icacorp.com; ***Email:*** info@icacorp.com

General - Incorporation: Mexico
Employees: 6,600
Auditor: Arturo Vargas Arellano
Stk Agt: American Stock Transfer & Trust Co.
Counsel: NA
DUNS No.: NA

Stock- Price on:12/24/2007: NA
Stock Exchange: NYSE
Ticker Symbol: NA
Outstanding Shares: NA
E.P.S: NA
Shareholders: NA

Business: The group's principal activities are carried out through four divisions: construction: provides projects which include heavy construction such as highways, bridges, tunnels and dams; industrial construction such as energy generating and petrochemical plants; and hydraulic project construction such as building, transportation and environmental infrastructure and gas pipelines. Real estate housing and development: develops, trades, owns, sells, assists, operates and administers real estate. Infrastructure operations: operates and maintains concessioned highways, bridges and tunnels, water supply systems, waste treatment and automobile parking facilities. Corporate and other: operates and distributes grain storage and provides corporate services. It operates in Mexico, Spain, the United States and Latin America.

Primary SIC and add'l.: 8741 1522 9532 1541 1611

CIK No: 0000885012

Subsidiaries: Constructora Internacional de Infraestructura., Constructoras ICA, Controladora de Empresas de Vivienda, Controladora de Operaciones de Infraestructura, Grupo Aeropotuario del Centro Norte, ICA - Fluor Daniel, ICA Panama, ICATECH Corporation, Ingenieros Civiles Asociados, Promotora e Inversora ADISA, Rodio/KronsaCimentaciones Especiales

Officers: Jose Luis Guerrero Alvarez/64/Dir., CEO, Sergio F. Montano Leon/60/Dir., Exec. VP - Administration, Jeff Hoaglund/Contact - Purchasing, Bob Elstad/Contact - Estimating, Expediting, Alonso Quintana Kawage/CFO, Jorge Aguirre Quintana/60/Dir., VP - Civil Construction, Luis Carlos Romandia Garcia/General Counsel, Sec., Steve Hoaglund/Pres., Terry Hoaglund/VP, Chris George/VP, Steve Brown/Sales Representative, Mike Ditscheit/Sales Representative, Jim Schoeplein/Sales Representative, Sheila Schoeplein/Sales Representative, Megan Mergenhagen/Sales Representative *(22 Officers included in Index)*

Directors: Jose Luis Guerrero Alvarez/64/Dir., CEO, Bernardo Quintana/66/Chmn., Angeles Espinosa Yglesias/65/Dir., Alberto Mulas Alonso/47/Dir., Jorge Borja Navarrete/65/Dir., Jorge Aguirre Quintana/60/Dir., VP - Civil Construction, Esteban Malpica Fomperosa/58/Dir., Elmer Franco Macias/67/Dir., Alberto Escofet Artigas/74/Dir., Emilio Carrillo Gamboa/70/Dir., Luis Fernando Zarate Rocha/64/Dir., Juan Claudio Salles Manuel/71/Dir., Fernando Ruiz Sahagun/Dir., Luis Rubio Friedberg/Dir., Guillermo Javier Haro/Dir. *(17 Directors included in Index)*

Owners: Management Trust/3.10%, Fundacion Trust/2.10%, Employee Trust, Foreign Employee Trust, Bernardo I. Quintana/7.90%

iCAD Inc

98 Spit Brook Rd., Ste. 100, Nashua, NH, 03062; ***PH:*** 1-603-882-5200; ***Fax:*** 1-603-880-3843 ; ***http://*** www.icadmed.com; ***Email:*** sales@icadmed.com

General - Incorporation: DE
Employees: 82
Auditor: BDO Seidman LLP
Stk Agt: Continental Stock Transfer & Trust Co
Counsel: McLaughlin & Stern
DUNS No.: 10-887-0254

Stock- Price on:12/24/2007: $3.38
Stock Exchange: NDQ
Ticker Symbol: ICAD
Outstanding Shares: 38,030,000
E.P.S: -$0.11
Shareholders: NA

Business: The group's principle activities include designing, engineering, developing, manufacturing and marketing digital image scanners, film digitizers and software. The products of the group are used in graphic arts, desktop publishing, medical imaging and life sciences markets. The group focuses on promoting its scanning technology for use in photo finishing and medical applications. The group is introducing new line of products linking photo labs and processors to the Internet and worldwide Web. The group sells its products through distributors, resellers, systems integrators and OEM's. On 31-Dec-2003, the group acquired cadx systems inc & qualia computing inc. The group operates from United States.

Primary SIC and add'l.: 3577

CIK No: 0000749660

Subsidiaries: CADx Systems, Inc., Qualia Acquisition Corporation

Officers: Ken Ferry/CEO, Pres./$775,484.00, Darlene Deptula-Hicks/CFO, Exec. VP - Finance/$207,323.00, Stacey M. Stevens/Sr. VP - Marketing, Strategy/$269,087.00, Jeffrey H. Barnes/Sr. VP - Sales/$332,913.00, Jonathan Go/Sr. VP - Research, Development/$132,308.00, Anne Marie Fields/Investor Relations Officer

Owners: Robert Howard/14.10%, Annette Heroux, Jeffrey Barnes, Lawrence Howard/3.30%, Stacey Stevens, Insiders/25.70%, Maha Sallam/4.50%, Donald Chapman/100.00%, Steven Rappaport, Donald Chapman/5.00%, Scott W. Parr/1.00%, Jonathan Go, Rachel Brem, Kenneth Ferry/2.30%, James Harlan/1.00% *(17 Owners included in Index)*

Financial Data: ***Fiscal Year End:*** 12/31 ***Latest Annual Data:*** 12/31/2006

Year	Sales	Net Income
2006	$19,721,000	-$6,638,000
2005	$19,770,000	-$4,758,000
2004	$23,308,000	-$828,000

Curr. Assets:	$10,558,000	**Curr. Liab.:**	$6,489,000		
Plant, Equip.:	$2,104,000	**Total Liab.:**	$12,318,000	**Indic. Yr. Divd.:**	NA
Total Assets:	$60,290,000	**Net Worth:**	$47,972,000	**Debt/ Equity:**	0.1180

Icagen Inc

4222 Emperor Blvd., Ste. 350, Durham, NC, 27703; ***PH:*** 1-919-941-5206; ***Fax:*** 1-919-941-0813; ***http://*** www.icagen.com; ***Email:*** investorsandpress@icagen.com

General - Incorporation: DE
Employees: 64
Auditor: Ernst & Young LLP
Stk Agt: Wachovia Bank N.A
Counsel: NA
DUNS No.: NA

Stock- Price on:12/24/2007: $2
Stock Exchange: NDQ
Ticker Symbol: ICGN
Outstanding Shares: 37,920,000
E.P.S: -$0.41
Shareholders: NA

Business: The groups principle activities include discovering, developing and commercializing novel drugs. The group operates from the United States and Japan. The group's quarterly revenue for September 2007 was 12.87 millions of USD.

Primary SIC and add'l.: 2834

CIK No: 0000902622

Officers: Kay P. Wagoner/Dir., CEO, Pres./$712,383.00, Richard D. Katz/Sr. VP - Finance, Corporate Development, CFO, Treasurer/$533,566.00, Edward P. Gray/Sr. VP - Intellectual Property, Chief Patent Counsel, Sec./$332,624.00, Seth V. Hetherington/Sr. VP - Clinical, Regulatory Affairs/$531,225.00, Douglas S. Krafte/VP - Biology, Gregory C. Rigdon/VP - New Product Development, Mark J. Suto/VP - Chemistry, Gregory S. Shotzberger/VP - Business Development, Robert J. Jakobs/Sr. Dir. - Finance, Assist. Sec.

Directors: Kay P. Wagoner/Dir., CEO, Pres., Charles A. Sanders/Chmn., David R. Williams/Member - Scientific Advisory Board, Anthony B. Evnin/Dir., Dennis B. Gillings/Dir., Gerry S. Oxford/Member - Scientific Advisory Board, Roy Swaringen/Member - Scientific Advisory Board, Dhirren Thakker/Member - Scientific Advisory Board, Andre L. Lamotte/Dir., Richard G. Morrison/Dir., Martin A. Simonetti/Dir., Adeoye Y. Olukotun/Dir., John Adelman/Member - Scientific Advisory Board, John Bettis/Member - Scientific Advisory Board, Carlo Brugnara/Member - Scientific Advisory Board *(17 Directors included in Index)*

Owners: Entities/individuals affiliated with Venrock Associates/8.20%, Insiders/17.40%, Heyward J. Hull, Martin A. Simonetti, Goldman, Sachs& Co./9.99%, Anthony B. Evnin/8.20%, QVT Fund LP/5.60%, Seth V. Hetherington, Entities/individuals affiliated with Greenway Capital/17.30%, Dennis B. Gillings/5.10%, Entities/individuals affiliated with PharmaBio Development Inc./5.10%, Kay P. Wagoner/2.20%, Adeoye Y. Olukotun, Charles A. Sanders, Entities/individuals affiliated with Alta Partners/8.20% *(19 Owners included in Index)*

Financial Data: ***Fiscal Year End:*** 12/31 ***Latest Annual Data:*** 12/31/2006

Year	Sales	Net Income
2006	$8,420,000	-$24,808,000
2005	$8,794,000	-$20,249,000
2004	$6,494,000	-$16,723,000

Curr. Assets:	$26,052,000	**Curr. Liab.:**	$6,481,000		
Plant, Equip.:	$1,566,000	**Total Liab.:**	$18,768,000	**Indic. Yr. Divd.:**	NA
Total Assets:	$30,815,000	**Net Worth:**	$12,047,000	**Debt/ Equity:**	0.0230

Icahn Enterprises LP

Formerly: American Real Estate Partners LP
767 5th Ave., Ste. 4700, New York, NY, 10153; ***PH:*** 1-212-702-4300; ***Fax:*** 1-914-242-9282; ***http://*** www.icahnenterprises.com; ***Email:*** ir@arep.com

General - Incorporation: DE
Employees: 13,370
Auditor: Grant Thornton LLP
Stk Agt: Registrar & Transfer Co
Counsel: NA
DUNS No.: NA

Stock- Price on:12/24/2007: $96.15
Stock Exchange: NDQ
Ticker Symbol: ACP
Outstanding Shares: 61,860,000
E.P.S: $11.77
Shareholders: NA

Business: The group operates through its subsidiaries whose operating businesses include gaming, real estate, and home fashion. The group operates through six segments namely, oil and gas, gaming, rental real estate, property development, associated resort activities and home fashion. The group acquired WestPoint International, Inc., and Aquarius Hotel and Casino in Nevada. The group operates from the United States.

Primary SIC and add'l.: 7999 7011 1522 1521 1541 6519 6552

CIK No: 0000813762

Subsidiaries: American Casino& Entertainment LLC, American Casino& Entertainment Properties LLC, American Entertainment Properties Corp., American Real Estate Holdings Limited Partnership, AREP Asset Management LLC, AREP Car Acquisition Corp., AREP Car Holdings Corp., AREP Home Fashion Holdings LLC, AREP New Jersey Land Holdings LLC, AREP Oil & Gas Corp., AREP Oil & Gas Holdings LLC, AREP Real Estate Holdings LLC, AREP Sands Holding, LLC, Aretex LLC, Arizona Charlies, LLC 32 Subsidiaries included in the Index

Officers: Keith A. Meister/34/Vice Chmn., Principal Executive Officer, Peter K. Shea/56/Pres., Hillel Moerman/35/CFO, Chief Accounting Officer

Directors: Carl C. Icahn/72/Chmn., Keith A. Meister/34/Vice Chmn., Principal Executive Officer, William A. Leidsdorf/62/Dir., James L. Nelson/58/Dir., Jack G. Wasserman/71/Dir., Vincent J. Intrieri/51/Dir.

Owners: Carl C. Icahn/90.00%, Carl C. Icahn/86.50%, Insiders/90.00%, Insiders/86.50%

Financial Data: Fiscal Year End:12/31 Latest Annual Data: 12/31/2006

Year	Sales	Net Income
2006	$1,477,930,000	$798,833,000
2005	$1,262,493,000	-$27,044,000
2004	$453,581,000	$160,973,000

Curr. Assets:	$3,055,838,000	Curr. Liab.:	$317,013,000	P/E Ratio:	7.16
Plant, Equip.:	$907,071,000	Total Liab.:	$1,641,871,000	Indic. Yr. Divd.:	NA
Total Assets:	$4,244,747,000	Net Worth:	$2,310,655,000	Debt/ Equity:	0.7137

iCarbon Corp

106 Lakeside Ave., Delano, PA, 18220; *PH:* 1-570-467-2222;
http:// www.graphitetechnologygroup.com

General - Incorporation	NV	Stock- Price on:12/24/2007	$0.38
Employees	NA	Stock Exchange	OTC
Auditor	L J Soldinger Associates, LLC	Ticker Symbol	ICRB
Stk Agt.	Stock Transfer & Trust Co	Outstanding Shares	NA
Counsel	NA	E.P.S.	NA
DUNS No.	NA	Shareholders	NA

Business: The groups principle activities include acquiring, exploring and developing natural gas and oil properties. The group operates from the United States.

Primary SIC and add'l.: 3624 1311 3624

CIK No: 0001093818

Subsidiaries: BPK Acquisition Corp., CSR-Waha Partners, L.P.

Owners: David Laudeman, Derek Hirsch/4.20%, Insiders/10.87%, Bertil Akesson, Thomas G. Dugan/1.10%, Budea Johns, James E. Olive/4.30%, Edward L. Ryan, Alvin B. Marshall

Financial Data: Fiscal Year End:12/31 Latest Annual Data: 12/31/2005

Year	Sales	Net Income
2005	$12,000	-$436,000
2004	$142,000	-$2,513,000
2003	$258,000	-$7,715,000

Curr. Assets:	$1,169,000	Curr. Liab.:	$2,009,000		
Plant, Equip.:	NA	Total Liab.:	$2,009,000	Indic. Yr. Divd.:	NA
Total Assets:	$1,169,000	Net Worth:	-$840,000	Debt/ Equity:	1.3787

ICB Financial CA

3999 E Inland Empire Blvd, Ontario, CA, 91764; *PH:* 1-909-481-8706; *Fax:* 1-909-481-9928;
http:// www.icbbank.com; *Email:* mailbox@inlandcommunitybank.com

General - Incorporation		Stock- Price on:12/24/2007	NA
Employees	NA	Stock Exchange	OTC
Auditor	NA	Ticker Symbol	ICBN
Stk Agt.	NA	Outstanding Shares	NA
Counsel	NA	E.P.S.	NA
DUNS No.	NA	Shareholders	NA

Business: The group's principle activity is to provide banking services. The group's deposit products include checking and saving accounts. The group also provides internet banking services. The group operates from United States.

Primary SIC and add'l.: 6712

CIK No: 0001359297

Officers: James S. Cooper/CEO, Pres., Tillie Ross/VP - BAY Area, Joelle Pavone-Higgins/Business Development Specialist, Robert S. Demallie/VP, Mgr., William Sorotsky/VP - LOS Angeles Area, David Weiss/VP, Mgr., James Walling/VP, Mgr. - Loma Linda, Russell Scranton/Sr. VP, Branch Administrator - Ontario, Robert C. Littlejohn/Exec. VP, Chief Credit Officer, Chief Administrative Officer, Richard Balogh/Exec. VP, Branch Administrator, Barbara Oliver/VP - Human Resources, Henry Wesolowski/VP, Controller, Cynthia Filbin/Sr. VP, Dir. - Operations, Roger Kaye/VP - Loan Administration, Robert McCullough/VP - Loan Administration *(23 Officers included in Index)*

IceWeb Inc

205 Van Buren St., Ste. 150, Herndon, VA, 20170; *PH:* 1-703-964-8000; *Fax:* 1-703-964-0160;
http:// www.iceweb.com; *Email:* info@iceweb.com

General - Incorporation	DE	Stock- Price on:12/24/2007	$0.64
Employees	25	Stock Exchange	OTC
Auditor	Sherb & Co. LLP	Ticker Symbol	IWEB
Stk Agt.	Olde Monmouth Stk Trnsfer Co. Inc.	Outstanding Shares	10,270,000
Counsel	NA	E.P.S.	-$0.38
DUNS No.	04-836-0093	Shareholders	NA

Business: The group's principal activity is to create, produce and deliver e-learning and marketing presentations. The service provided by the group includes iceshowtm for on-demand multimedia presentations and iceslidetm for powerpoint to flash conversion. The group has also added a new Website called learningstream.com to host pay-per-view online training courses for business professionals. It operates only in the United States.

Primary SIC and add'l.: 7375 7389 7372

CIK No: 0001097718

Subsidiaries: Propster, Inc.

Officers: John R. Signorello/41/Chmn., CEO, Mark B. Lucky/CFO

Directors: John R. Signorello/41/Chmn., CEO, Joseph L. Druzak/Dir., Harold F. Compton/58/Dir., Raymond Pirtle/65/Dir., Jack Bush/71/Dir.

Owners: Insiders/28.10%, Joseph L. Druzak/3.40%, Jack Bush/2.10%, Raymond H. Pirtle/1.40%, John R. Signorello/15.70%, Hal Compton/4.40%, Mark B. Lucky/1.10%

Financial Data: Fiscal Year End:09/30 Latest Annual Data: 9/30/2006

Year	Sales	Net Income
2006	$4,769,000	-$3,870,000
2005	$6,810,000	-$904,000
2004	$6,663,000	-$2,035,000

Curr. Assets:	$1,707,000	Curr. Liab.:	$3,334,000		
Plant, Equip.:	$425,000	Total Liab.:	$3,667,000	Indic. Yr. Divd.:	NA
Total Assets:	$2,596,000	Net Worth:	-$1,071,000	Debt/ Equity:	NA

ICF Corp

Formerly: Comc Inc
2840 Howe Rd., Ste. D, Martinez, CA, 94553; *PH:* 1-818-556-3333; *http://* www.comcinc.com

General - Incorporation	DE	Stock- Price on:12/24/2007	$0.04
Employees	150	Stock Exchange	NA
Auditor	Pisenti & Brinker LLP	Ticker Symbol	NA
Stk Agt	American Stock Transfer & Trust Co.	Outstanding Shares	9,030,000
Counsel	NA	E.P.S.	-$1.14
DUNS No.	19-517-8488	Shareholders	NA

Business: The group's principle activities are to design, implement, support and manage LAN/wan computer network systems, voice communication network systems and premise wiring for both data and voice. It also distributes and maintains equipment on behalf of major telecommunication equipment manufacturers. The group operates through two divisions: data and voice services and recruitment services. Its data and voice services division provides voice communications and data network design, equipment sales, installation, systems integration consulting and maintenance to Fortune 1000 companies and municipalities. Its recruitment services include technical employee recruitment, leasing and permanent placement services. The products are marketed to banking, insurance and financial services, education institutions, healthcare and medical institutions and retail and service industries.

Primary SIC and add'l.: 7371 1731 4813 7373 7389 7378

CIK No: 0000754568

Subsidiaries: ICF Communication Solutions, Inc

Financial Data: Fiscal Year End:12/31 Latest Annual Data: 12/31/2004

Year	Sales	Net Income
2004	$11,831,000	-$6,952,000
2003	$11,888,000	-$1,518,000
2002	$12,133,000	-$2,044,000

Curr. Assets:	$3,473,000	Curr. Liab.:	$12,778,000		
Plant, Equip.:	$724,000	Total Liab.:	$13,752,000	Indic. Yr. Divd.:	NA
Total Assets:	$8,106,000	Net Worth:	-$6,641,000	Debt/ Equity:	NA

ICF International Inc

9300 Lee Hwy., Fairfax, VA, 22031; *PH:* 1-703-934-3603; *Fax:* 1-703-934-3740;
http:// www.icfi.com; *Email:* info@icfi.com

General - Incorporation	DE	Stock- Price on:12/24/2007	$19.4
Employees	2,111	Stock Exchange	NDQ
Auditor	Grant Thornton LLP	Ticker Symbol	ICFI
Stk Agt	American Stock Transfer & Trust Co.	Outstanding Shares	14,140,000
Counsel	NA	E.P.S.	$2.37
DUNS No.	NA	Shareholders	NA

Business: The groups principle activity is to provide management, technology and policy consulting and implementation services. The groups services include advisory, implementation evaluation and improvement. The group acquired Synergy, Inc. and Caliber Associates, Inc. Specific customers of the group include Department of Defense, the Environmental Protection Agency, the Department of Homeland Security, the Department of Transportation, and the Department of Health and Human Services. The group operates from the United States, Europe and Canada. The group's quarterly revenue for September 2007 was 198.81 millions of USD.

Primary SIC and add'l.: 8742 8999 8999 7389 7373 7379 8748 7379 7371 7373 8748 8742 7389 7371

CIK No: 0001362004

Subsidiaries: Advanced Performance Consulting Group, Inc., Caliber Associates, Inc., Collins Management Consulting, Inc., CommentWorks.Com Company, L.L.C., Energy and Environmental Analysis, Incorporated, Fried& Sher, Inc., ICF Associates, L.L.C., ICF Biomedical Consulting, LLC, ICF Consulting Canada, Inc., ICF Consulting Group, Inc., ICF Consulting India Private Ltd., ICF Consulting Limited, ICF Consulting Pty, Ltd., ICF Consulting Services, L.L.C., ICF Consultoria do Brasil, Ltda. 26 Subsidiaries included in the Index

Officers: Edward H. Bersoff/Chmn., CEO, John Wasson/COO, Exec. VP, Alan Stewart/CFO, Judith Kassel/Exec. VP, General Counsel, Miriam Wardak/Sr. VP, Douglas Beck/Sr. VP, Donald Zimmerman/Exec. VP, Michael Byrne/Sr. VP - Homeland, National Security, Gerald Croan/Exec. VP - ICF Caliber, Ellen Glover/Exec. VP - Technology, Management Solutions, Sergio Ostria/Sr. VP - Environment, Transportation, Regulation, Isabel Reiff/Sr. VP, Philip Mihlmester/Sr. VP - Energy, Resources, Lynn Morgen/Contact - ICF Investor Relation, Betsy Brod/Contact - ICF Investor Relation

Directors: Edward H. Bersoff/Chmn., CEO, Srikant M. Datar/Dir., Joel R. Jacks/Dir., Sudhakar Kesavan/Dir., David C. Lucien/Dir., Peter M. Schulte/Dir.

Owners: Edward H. Bersoff, Sudhakar Kesavan, Alan Stewart, Joel R. Jacks, CM Equity Partners, L.P., CM Equity Partners, L.P., David C. Lucien, William Moody, CM Equity Partners II Co-Investors, L.P., CM Equity Partners II, L.P., Ellen Glover, Peter M. Schulte, CMEP Co-Investment ICF, L.P., John Wasson, Gerald Croan *(18 Owners included in Index)*

Financial Data: Fiscal Year End:12/31 Latest Annual Data: 12/31/2006

Year	Sales	Net Income
2006	$331,279,000	$11,867,000
2005	$177,218,000	$2,022,000
2004	$139,488,000	$3,017,000

Curr. Assets:	$118,698,000	Curr. Liab.:	$96,347,000	P/E Ratio:	11.90
Plant, Equip.:	$5,388,000	Total Liab.:	$101,880,000	Indic. Yr. Divd.:	NA
Total Assets:	$215,827,000	Net Worth:	$113,947,000	Debt/ Equity:	0.1518

ICICI Bank Ltd

ICICI Bank Towers, Bandra-Kurla Complex, Mumbai, Maharashtra, 400 051; ;
http:// www.icicibank.com

General - Incorporation	India	Stock- Price on:12/24/2007	$49.85
Employees	25,384	Stock Exchange	NYSE
Auditor	KPMG	Ticker Symbol	IBN
Stk Agt	3i Infotech	Outstanding Shares	451,430,000
Counsel	NA	E.P.S.	$1.65
DUNS No.	NA	Shareholders	NA

Business: The group's principal activities are to provide retail-banking, corporate banking, cash management and treasury management services. As on 31-Mar-2004, the group operates through 413 branches and 56 extension counters in India. The retail-banking services include mobilizing of funds from retail depositors and lending services namely credit cards, loans against deposits and securities. Corporate banking services include medium and short-term credit, fee and commission based services like documentary credits, letters of credit and forward contracts, accepts deposits from corporate customers. The cash and treasury management includes treasury operations of the bank through market operations and investing in various money market instruments, debt instruments, shares and debentures. On 07-May-2003, the group acquired transamerica apple distribution finance private limited.

Primary SIC and add'l.: 6035 6021 6211 6159

CIK No: 0001103838

Subsidiaries: Company Limited, ICICI Bank Canada, ICICI Bank Eurasia LLC, ICICI Bank UK Limited, ICICI Brokerage Services Limited, ICICI Home Finance Company Limited, ICICI International Limited, ICICI Investment Management Company Limited, ICICI Lombard General Insurance Company Limited, ICICI Property Trust, ICICI Prudential Life Insurance Company Limited, ICICI Securities Holdings Inc, ICICI Securities Inc, ICICI Securities Limited, ICICI Trusteeship Services Limited 20 Subsidiaries included in the Index

Officers: K. V. Kamath/Dir., MD, CEO, Vishakha Mulye/39/Group CFO, Sonjoy Chatterjee/Executive Dir., V. Vaidyanathan/Executive Dir., Pravir Vohra/54/Group CTO, Chanda Kochhar/Joint MD, Kalpana Morparia/Joint MD, Rakesh Jha/Contact - Operational, Financial Performance, Padmanabhan Iyer/Contact - Investor Services, Madhabi Puri-Buch/Executive Dir., K. Ramkumar/46/Group Chief Human Resources Officer, Rupesh Kumar/Contact - Operational, Financial Performance

Directors: K. V. Kamath/Dir., MD, CEO, Narayanan Vaghul/71/Chmn., Sonjoy Chatterjee/Executive Dir., Narendra Murkumbi/Dir., Madhabi Puri-Buch/Executive Dir., T. S. Vijayan/Dir., Sridar Iyengar/Dir., Prem V. Watsa/Dir., Marti G. Subrahmanyam/Dir., Ram Kishore Joshi/61/Dir., Mahendra Kumar Sharma/61/Dir., Kundapur Vaman Kamath/60/Dir., Anupam Puri/Dir., Vinod Rai/Dir., Nachiket Mor/44/Dir. *(19 Directors included in Index)*

Owners: Lakshmi Niwas Mittal, Mahendra Kumar Sharma, V. Vaidyanathan, Marti Gurunath Subrahmanyam, Pravir Vohra, Madhabi Puri-Buch, Narayanan Vaghul, Insiders, Chanda Kochhar, Life Insurance Corporation of India/7.60%, K. Ramkumar, Allamanda Investments Pte. Limited/7.30%, Nachiket Mor, Vishakha Mulye, Kundapur Vaman Kamath

*Financial Data: Fiscal Year End:*03/31 *Latest Annual Data:* 03/31/2007

Year	Sales			Net Income
2007	$9,784,544,000			$719,229,000
2006	$5,796,246,000			$524,071,000
2005	$2,911,000,000			$196,000,000
Curr. Assets:	$9,863,865,000	Curr. Liab.:	$58,644,965,000	P/E Ratio: 33.01
Plant, Equip.:	$1,053,675,000	Total Liab.:	$90,409,636,000	Indic. Yr. Divd.: $0.710
Total Assets:	$90,696,985,000	Net Worth:	$287,349,000	Debt/ Equity: NA

ICO Global Communications Holdings Ltd DE

11700 Plz. America Dr., Ste. 1010, Reston, VA, 20190; *PH:* 1-703-964-1400; *Fax:* 1-703-964-1401;
http:// www.ico.com

General - Incorporation		Stock- Price on:12/24/2007	$3.97
Employees	NA	Stock Exchange	NDQ
Auditor	NA	Ticker Symbol	ICOG
Stk Agt	NA	Outstanding Shares	NA
Counsel	NA	E.P.S.	NA
DUNS No.	NA	Shareholders	NA

Business: The groups principal activity is to provide satellite communications system.The groups services include voice, data and Internet. The products of the group include devices, handsets and cellular phones. The group operates from the United States.

Primary SIC and add'l.: 4899 4812

CIK No:

Subsidiaries: Closed Joint Stock Company ICO-R, Double Helix Investment Corp., Gatecom Brazil SA, Gatecom Leasing GmbH, Gatecom Mexico SA de CV, Gatecom Netherlands BV, ICO Communications Partners Ltd., ICO Global Communications (Holdings) PTE Ltd., ICO Global Communications (Operations) Limited, ICO Global Communications Canada Inc., ICO Global Communications Holdings (Netherlands Antilles) NV, ICO Global Communications Holdings BV, ICO Global Communications Israel Ltd., ICO Global Communications Services Inc., ICO Global Limited 30 Subsidiaries included in the Index

Officers: Timothy J. Bryan/Dir., CEO, Craig Jorgens/Pres., Donna P. Alderman/Dir., Exec. VP - Corporate Development, Strategy, John L. Flynn/Exec. VP, General Counsel, Corp. Sec., David Bagley/Sr. VP - Corporate Development, Suzanne Hutchings Malloy/Sr. VP - Regulatory Affairs, Dennis Schmitt/Sr. VP - Finance, David Zufall/Sr. VP - Network Systems, Robert S. Day/Sr. VP

Directors: Timothy J. Bryan/Dir., CEO, Craig O. McCaw/Chmn., Samuel L. Ginn/Dir., Donna P. Alderman/Dir., Exec. VP - Corporate Development, Strategy, Barry Rowan/Dir., Gerard R. Salemme/Dir., David Wasserman/Dir., Benjamin G. Wolff/Dir.

*Financial Data: Fiscal Year End:*NA *Latest Annual Data:* 12/31/2006

Year	Sales			Net Income
2006	NA			-$64,172,000
Curr. Assets:	$290,105,000	Curr. Liab.:	$64,506,000	
Plant, Equip.:	$318,936,000	Total Liab.:	$719,101,000	Indic. Yr. Divd.: NA
Total Assets:	$643,517,000	Net Worth:	-$75,584,000	Debt/ Equity: NA

ICO Inc

1811 Bering Dr., Ste. 200, Houston, TX, 77057; *PH:* 1-713-351-4100; *Fax:* 1-713-335-2201;
http:// www.icopolymers.com; *Email:* investorrelations@icopolymers.com

General - Incorporation	TX	Stock- Price on:12/24/2007	$9.99
Employees	831	Stock Exchange	NDQ
Auditor	PricewaterhouseCoopers LLP	Ticker Symbol	ICOC
Stk Agt	Computershare Investor Services LLC	Outstanding Shares	26,000,000
Counsel	NA	E.P.S.	$0.60
DUNS No.	07-079-6743	Shareholders	NA

Business: The group's principal activities are to manufacture engineered resins and provide specialized polymers processing services. The engineered resins manufactured are typically produced into a powder form. The customers mix these concentrates with polymer resins to give finished products the desired characteristics, such as color or protection from ultraviolet light. The group also provides toll processing services including ambient grinding, jet milling, compounding, and ancillary services for polymer resins produced in pellet form. The engineered resins are provided to the rotational molding industry worldwide. On 06-Sep-2002, the group completed the sale of substantially all of its oilfield services business to varco international, inc. The group operates in the polymers industry in the United States, Europe, Australia, New Zealand, Malaysia and Brazil. On 23-Jun-2004, the group acquired idockusa.

Primary SIC and add'l.: 2821

CIK No: 0000353567

Subsidiaries: Bayshore Industrial, L.P., Courtenay Polymers Pty Ltd., Ico (uk) Limited, ICO Europe B.V., ICO Global Services, Inc., ICO Holdings Australia Pty Limited, ICO Holdings New Zealand Limited, ICO Holland B.V., Ico P&o, Inc., ICO Polymers do Brasil Ltda., ICO Polymers France S.A.S., ICO Polymers Italy S.r.l., ICO Polymers North America, Inc., ICO Technology, Inc., J.R. Courtenay (N.Z.) Limited 18 Subsidiaries included in the Index

Officers: John A. Knapp/Dir., CEO, Pres., Bradley T. Leuschner/Chief Accounting Officer, Charlotte Fischer Ewart/General Counsel, Sec., Jon C. Biro/Dir., CFO, Treasurer, Stephen Barkmann/Pres. - Bayshore Industrial, Darek Bristow/Pres. - ICO Europe, Eric Persons/Pres. - ICO Polymers North America, Dario Masutti/Pres. - ICO Courtenay

Directors: John A. Knapp/Dir., CEO, Pres., Gregory T. Barmore/Chmn., Charles T. McCord/Dir., Jon C. Biro/Dir., CFO, Treasurer, Daniel R. Gaubert/Dir., David E.K. Frischkorn/Dir., John F. Gibson/Dir., Eric O. English/Dir., Warren W. Wilder/Dir.

Owners: Eric O. English, Dario E. Masutti, Gregory T. Barmore, David E.K. Frischkorn, Eric D. Parsons, John A. Knapp, Derek R. Bristow, Bradley T. Leuschner, John F. Gibson, Daniel R. Gaubert, Warren W. Wilder, Charlotte Fischer Ewart, Stephen E. Barkmann, Charles T. McCord, Jon C. Biro *(16 Owners included in Index)*

*Financial Data: Fiscal Year End:*09/30 *Latest Annual Data:* 9/30/2006

Year	Sales			Net Income
2006	$324,331,000			$12,004,000
2005	$296,606,000			$4,505,000
2004	$257,525,000			$257,000
Curr. Assets:	$136,100,000	Curr. Liab.:	$78,599,000	P/E Ratio: 18.85
Plant, Equip.:	$50,884,000	Total Liab.:	$106,244,000	Indic. Yr. Divd.: NA
Total Assets:	$197,961,000	Net Worth:	$91,717,000	Debt/ Equity: 0.3673

ICOA Inc

111 Airport Rd., Warwick, RI, 02889; *PH:* 1-401-352-2300; *Fax:* 1-401-352-2323;
http:// www.icoacorp.com; *Email:* investor@icoacorp.com

General - Incorporation	NV	Stock- Price on:12/24/2007	NA
Employees	NA	Stock Exchange	OTC
Auditor	Sherb & Co., LLP	Ticker Symbol	ICOA
Stk Agt	Signature Stock Transfer, Inc.	Outstanding Shares	NA
Counsel	NA	E.P.S.	-$0.011
DUNS No.	NA	Shareholders	NA

Business: The groups principle activities include selling, installing, supporting and providing wired and wireless Ethernet and Internet access services. The group acquired WiseTechnologies, Inc. in May 2005, and LinkSpot Technologies, Inc. and Cafe.com in July 2005. The group operates from the United States.

Primary SIC and add'l.: 4812 4899 4899 4812 4813

CIK No: 0000745084

Subsidiaries: Airport Network Solutions, Inc., AuthDirect, Inc, WebCenter Technologies, Inc

Officers: George Strouthopoulos/Chmn., CEO, Erwin Vahlsing/Dir., CFO, William D. Ankerstjerne/Dir. - Field Operations, Christopher Browne/Dir. - Operations

Directors: George Strouthopoulos/Chmn., CEO, Erwin Vahlsing/Dir., CFO

*Financial Data: Fiscal Year End:*12/31 *Latest Annual Data:* 12/31/2005

Year	Sales			Net Income
2005	$2,476,000			-$9,237,000
2004	$1,171,000			-$3,922,000
2003	$325,000			-$775,000
Curr. Assets:	$475,000	Curr. Liab.:	$8,668,000	
Plant, Equip.:	$1,693,000	Total Liab.:	$10,320,000	Indic. Yr. Divd.: NA
Total Assets:	$6,078,000	Net Worth:	-$4,242,000	Debt/ Equity: NA

ICON Health & Fitness Inc

1500 S 1000 W, Logan, UT, 84321; *PH:* 1-435-750-5000; *Fax:* 1-435-750-3917;
http:// www.iconfitness.com; *Email:* media@iconfitness.com

General - Incorporation	DE	Stock- Price on:12/24/2007	NA
Employees	NA	Stock Exchange	NA
Auditor	PricewaterhouseCoopers LLP	Ticker Symbol	NA
Stk Agt	NA	Outstanding Shares	NA
Counsel	NA	E.P.S.	NA
DUNS No.	08-392-2229	Shareholders	NA

Business: The group's principle activities include developing, manufacturing and distributing aerobic and anaerobic fitness equipment. The group also manufactures innovative line of products for the institutional fitness equipment under cardiovascular, strength training equipment and other equipment category. The brand names of the group include proform, nordictrack, healthrider, weslo, image, jumpking, free motion fitness and, under license, reebok, weider and gold's gym. The group operates from United States.

Primary SIC and add'l.: 3949
CIK No: 0000934798
Subsidiaries: HF Holdings, Inc, JumpKing, Inc
Officers: Colleen Logan/VP - Marketing

ICON Plc

South County Business Pk., Leopardstown, Dublin, 18; ; *http://* www.iconclinical.com

General - Incorporation .... Ireland	Stock- Price on:12/24/2007 ....$44.06
Employees..4,300	Stock Exchange..NDQ
Auditor ....KPMG LLP	Ticker Symbol..ICLR
Stk Agt................................. Bank of New York	Outstanding Shares 28,520,000
Counsel..................................A & l Goodbody	E.P.S..$1.60
DUNS No. 37-974-7041	Shareholders..NA

Business: The group's principal activity is the provision of clinical research and development services on a global basis to the pharmaceutical and biotechnology industries. The group specializes in the management, execution and analysis of complex, multinational clinical trials in most major therapeutic areas. Its operations are located in Ireland, the United Kingdom, United States, Germany, Australia, Argentina, France, Japan, Israel, Singapore, Canada, Sweden, the Netherlands, Latvia, South Africa and India. During fiscal 2003, the group acquired Barton & Polansky Associates Inc, Managed Clinical Solutions Inc, Medeval Group Ltd and Globomax Llc.
Primary SIC and add'l.: 8731
CIK No: 0001060955
Subsidiaries: ICON Clinical Research GmbH, ICON Clinical Research Limited, ICON Clinical Research, Inc.
Officers: Peter Gray/Dir., CEO, Ted Gastineau/CEO - Icon Medical Imaging, John Climax/Exec. Chmn., Josephine Coyle/VP - Corporate QA, Ciaran Murray/CFO, Robert Scott-Edwards/Pres. - Icon Central Laboratories, Peter Sowood/Chief Scientific Officer - Icon Clinical Research, Dan Weng/Pres. - Icon Clinical Research, ROW, Thomas Frey/Pres. - Icon Development Solutions, Malcolm Burgess/COO - Icon US, Sean Leech/Exec. VP - Commercial, Organisational Development, Bill Taaffe/Pres. - Corporate Development, Simon Holmes/Group Dir. - Marketing, Erica Verost/Mgr. - Marketing, Icon Clinical Research, David Vindel/Contact - Band, Brown Communications *(19 Officers included in Index)*
Directors: Peter Gray/Dir., CEO, John Climax/Exec. Chmn., William Taaffe/59/Dir., Ronan Lambe/68/Dir., Thomas Lynch/51/Dir., Edward Roberts/73/Dir., Shuji Higuchi/67/Dir., Bruce Given/53/Dir.
Owners: Insiders/13.60%, John Climax/6.90%, Wasatch Group Companies/5.70%, Fidelity Group Companies/12.30%

Financial Data: *Fiscal Year End:*12/31 *Latest Annual Data:* 12/31/2006

Year		Sales		Net Income
2006		$649,826,000		$38,304,000
2005		$469,583,000		$13,545,000
Curr. Assets:	$234,639,000	Curr. Liab.:	$109,351,000	P/E Ratio: 33.01
Plant, Equip.:	$45,286,000	Total Liab.:	$113,603,000	Indic. Yr. Divd.: NA
Total Assets:	$347,553,000	Net Worth:	$233,066,000	Debt/ Equity: NA

Iconix Brand Group Inc

215 W 40th St., 4th Fl., New York, NY, 10018; *PH:* 1-212-730-0030; *Fax:* 1-212-391-2057; *http://* iconixbrand.com; *Email:* info@iconixbrand.com

General - Incorporation .... DE	Stock- Price on:12/24/2007 ....$22.39
Employees..46	Stock Exchange..NDQ
Auditor ....BDO Seidman LLP	Ticker Symbol..ICON
Stk Agt..............Continental Stock Transfer & Trust Co	Outstanding Shares 56,650,000
Counsel..NA	E.P.S..$0.81
DUNS No. 09-482-5262	Shareholders..NA

Business: The group's principal activity is to design, market and distribute women's footwear, apparel and fashion products. The group is also a designer, distributor and marketer of jeans wears under the bongo brand. It also markets and distributes children's footwear trademarks and a variety of men's workboots, hiking boots, winter boots and outdoor casual shoes. The group also licenses the candie's and bongo brands for a variety of other product categories. The group has operations in the United States, Hong Kong and british virgin islands. During the year, the group exited the operating footwear business.
Primary SIC and add'l.: 2339 3144 2329
CIK No: 0000857737
Subsidiaries: Badgley Mischka Licensing LLC, Bright Star Footwear LLC, IP Holdings and Management Corporation, IP Holdings, LLC, IP Management, LLC, Licensing Acquisition Corp., Showroom Holding Co., Inc., Unzipped Apparel LLC
Officers: Neil Cole/Chmn., CEO, Pres./$615,745.00, Deborah Sorell Stehr/Sr. VP, General Counsel, Sec./$249,277.00, David Conn/Exec. VP/$333,486.00, Warren Clamen/CFO/$302,917.00, Dari Marder/Dir. - Advertising, Andrew Tarshis/Sr. VP - Business Affairs, Associate Counsel/$282,818.00
Directors: Neil Cole/Chmn., CEO, Pres., Drew Cohen/Dir., Barry Emanuel/Dir., Steven Mendelow/Dir., Peter F. Cuneo/Dir., Mark Friedman/Dir.
Owners: Mark Friedman, Barry Emanuel, Neil Cole/5.80%, Peter F. Cuneo, Drew Cohen, Insiders/8.10%, Warren Clamen, Deborah Sorell Stehr, William Sweedler, Steven Mendelow, Luxor Capital Group, LP/5.40%, Andrew Tarshis, David Conn, Fred M. Alger/5.60%

Financial Data: *Fiscal Year End:*01/31 *Latest Annual Data:* 12/31/2006

Year		Sales		Net Income
2006		$80,694,000		$32,501,000
2005		$30,156,000		$15,943,000
2004		$68,980,000		$241,000
Curr. Assets:	$99,829,000	Curr. Liab.:	$35,705,000	P/E Ratio: 27.64
Plant, Equip.:	$1,384,000	Total Liab.:	$235,595,000	Indic. Yr. Divd.: NA
Total Assets:	$701,052,000	Net Worth:	$465,457,000	Debt/ Equity: 0.7145

ICOP Digital Inc

16801 W 116th St., Lenexa, KS, 66219; *PH:* 1-913-338-5550; *http://* icopdigital.com; *Email:* info@icop.com

General - Incorporation .... CO	Stock- Price on:12/24/2007 ....$8.63
Employees..41	Stock Exchange..NDQ
Auditor ....Cordovano and Honeck, LLP	Ticker Symbol..ICOP
Stk Agt ....Computershare Trust Co	Outstanding Shares 7,230,000
Counsel..NA	E.P.S..-$0.57
DUNS No. ....NA	Shareholders..NA

Business: The groups principle activity is to protect people, assets and profits with security, surveillance and communication solutions. The group products sold under the trade names ICOP Model 20/20(R), Veil of Protection(TM) and ICOP Model 20/20-W(TM). The group operates from the United States. The group's quarterly revenue for September 2007 was 3.75 millions of USD.
Primary SIC and add'l.: 3699
CIK No: 0001094572
Officers: David C. Owen/Chmn., CEO/$1,488,802.00, Laura E. Owen/COO, Pres./$1,363,599.00, John Stransky/Dir. - Sales, David H. Nicholl/Dir. - Technology, Derick D. Shupe/CPA, CFO, Chief Lou Anemone/Board Advisor, Colonel John Garrett/Board Advisor, Tully Plessor/Board Advisor
Directors: David C. Owen/Chmn., CEO, Derrick L. Ashcroft/Dir., Noel Koch/Dir., Roger L. Mason/54/Dir.
Owners: Roger L. Mason/1.10%, Chester L.F. Paulson and Jacqueline M. Paulson/17.80%, Derrick L. Ashcroft, John C. Garrison, Paulson Family LLC/15.10%, Paulson Investment Company, Inc./14.80%, Noel Koch, Paulson Capital Corp./14.80%, Insiders/16.40%, Laura E. Owen/14.70%, Walrus Partners, LLC/5.50%, David C. Owen/14.70%

Financial Data: *Fiscal Year End:*12/31 *Latest Annual Data:* 12/31/2006

Year		Sales		Net Income
2006		$6,621,000		-$3,518,000
2005		$1,760,000		-$2,898,000
2004		$51,000		-$2,393,000
Curr. Assets:	$13,114,000	Curr. Liab.:	$739,000	
Plant, Equip.:	$840,000	Total Liab.:	$739,000	Indic. Yr. Divd.: NA
Total Assets:	$14,046,000	Net Worth:	$13,308,000	Debt/ Equity: NA

ICOS Vision Systems Corp

Research Pk. Haasrode, Esperantolaan 8, Heverlee, 3001; *PH:* 32-16398220; *Fax:* 32-16400067; *http://* www.icos.be; *Email:* info@icos.be

General - Incorporation .... Belgium	Stock- Price on:12/24/2007 ....NA
Employees..NA	Stock Exchange..OTC
Auditor ....Klynveld Peat Marwick Goerdeler	Ticker Symbol..IVISF
Stk Agt ....Mellon Investor Services LLC	Outstanding Shares ....NA
Counsel..........Brown, Rudnick, Freed & Gesmer	E.P.S..NA
DUNS No. 37-290-1926	Shareholders..NA

Business: The group's principle activities are the manufacture and distribution of vision systems and inspection systems for the semi-conductor and electronic assembly industries. The company operates under two product lines: the in-line vision or inspection systems and the stand alone machines. The in-line vision or inspection systems are small, fast and accurate modules, specially designed for easy integration in product lines and other chip manufacturing equipment. The stand-alone machines are used for inspection of finished ics, bumped wafers or tcps. The group has operations in Europe, Asia and the United States.

Primary SIC and add'l.: 3829
CIK No: 0001049253
Subsidiaries: ICOS Vision Systems (Shenzhen) Co. Ltd, ICOS Vision Systems GmbH, ICOS Vision Systems Inc., ICOS Vision Systems Korea Co. Ltd., ICOS Vision Systems Limited, ICOS Vision Systems Ltd., ICOS Vision Systems NV, ICOS Vision Systems Pte. Ltd.

Financial Data: *Fiscal Year End:*12/31 *Latest Annual Data:* 12/31/2005

Year		Sales		Net Income
2005		$95,443,000		$15,993,000
2004		$121,876,000		$27,924,000
2003		$56,201,000		$6,689,000
Curr. Assets:	$125,627,000	Curr. Liab.:	$33,171,000	
Plant, Equip.:	$11,999,000	Total Liab.:	$39,613,000	Indic. Yr. Divd.: NA
Total Assets:	$145,121,000	Net Worth:	$105,508,000	Debt/ Equity: NA

ICP Solar Technologies Inc

7075 Pl. Robert-Joncas, Unit 131, Montreal, QC, H4M 2Z2; *PH:* 1-514-270-5770; *Fax:* 1-514-270-3677; *http://* www.icpsolar.com; *Email:* info-customers@icpsolar.com

General - Incorporation .... NV	Stock- Price on:12/24/2007 ....$3.2
Employees..NA	Stock Exchange..OTC
Auditor ....Rsm Richter LLP	Ticker Symbol..ICPR
Stk Agt ....Equity Transfer Services	Outstanding Shares ....NA
Counsel..NA	E.P.S..NA
DUNS No. ....NA	Shareholders..NA

Business: The group's principle activity is to provide research, development, manufacturing, marketing and sales of solar energy products. The group's brands include ICP Solars brands include Sunsei(TM) Solar, Sunsei(TM) Construct, and Sunsei(TM). The group operates from United States.
Primary SIC and add'l.: 3674
CIK No: 0001281872
Officers: Sass Peress/Chmn., CEO, Leon Assayag/CFO, Arlene Ades/Exec. VP, Head North American Sales, Manuel Gomez/MD - EMEA, PAC, Europe, Africa, Asia, Pacific, Joel Cohen/36/Dir., Sec., Treasurer, Laurent Lafite/VP - Marketing, Global Strategy, Tom Clark/VP - North American Consumer Sales, Gary Jones/VP - Sales North America OEM Applications, Pascal Petit/Dir. - Sales EMEA, PAC
Directors: Sass Peress/Chmn., CEO, Paul Maycock/Dir., Dave McDowell/Dir., David Dangoor/Dir., Joel Cohen/36/Dir., Sec., Treasurer
Owners: Insiders, Joel Cohen, Equity Transfer & Trust Company, Bank Sal. Oppenheim jr cie, Sass Peress, Rahn & Bohmer Banquiers

Financial Data: *Fiscal Year End:*11/30 *Latest Annual Data:* 01/31/2007

Year		Sales		Net Income
2007		$7,603,000		-$2,627,000
2005		NA		-$72,000
Curr. Assets:	$50,000	Curr. Liab.:	$9,000	
Plant, Equip.:	$6,000	Total Liab.:	$9,000	Indic. Yr. Divd.: NA
Total Assets:	$56,000	Net Worth:	$47,000	Debt/ Equity: NA

ICT Group Inc

100 Brandywine Blvd., Newtown, PA, 18940; *PH:* 1-267-685-5000; *Fax:* 1-267-685-5705; *http://* www.ictgroup.com

General - Incorporation	PA	**Stock**- Price on:12/24/2007	$18.86
Employees	911	Stock Exchange	NDQ
Auditor	KPMG LLP	Ticker Symbol	ICTG
Stk Agt	American Stock Transfer & Trust Co.	Outstanding Shares	15,770,000
Counsel	NA	E.P.S.	$0.53
DUNS No.	10-884-5371	Shareholders	NA

Business: The group's principle activity is to provide global customer relationship management (crm) services. The group provides integrated telesolutions, e-solutions and market solutions to clients to identify, acquire, retain, service, measure and maximize the value of their customer relationships. The company provides services to the customers in the United States, Europe, Australia and Canada. The group through its customer contact center supports outbound and inbound telesales, customer management services, Web-enable center services and e-mail management processing for domestic and multinational corporations and institutions. The services are primarily provided to the insurance, financial, pharmaceutical, telecommunications/utilities, healthcare and information technology industries. The group's quarterly revenue for Sep'07 was 113.90 millions of USD.

Primary SIC and add'l.: 7389

CIK No: 0001013149

Subsidiaries: Eurotel Marketing Limited, Harvest Resources, Inc., ICT Australia Pty. Ltd., ICT Barbados, Inc., ICT Canada Marketing, Inc., ICT International, ICT Marketing Services of Asia Pacific Pte Ltd, ICT Marketing Services, Inc., ICTMarketingServicesofMexico,S.deR.L.deC.V., Yardley Enterprises, Inc.

Officers: John J. Brennan/Chmn., CEO, Pres./$2,416,856.00, Janice A. Jones/Sr. VP - Corporate Support Services, Gail Lebel/Sr. VP - Human Resources, John D. Campbell/Exec. VP - Global Sales/$447,996.00, Karen Batungbacal/Pres. - ICT Asia, Pacific, Jeffrey C. Moore/Sr. VP, General Counsel, Sec., Vincent A. Paccapaniccia/CFO, Exec. VP - Finance/$542,311.00, Pamela Goyke/Sr. VP - Systems, Technology, CIO, John Stoops/Independent Consultant, Martin Puttock/MD - ICT Europe, Steven Pink/VP, GM - ICT Europe, Orla Fitzpatrick/Dir. - Support Services, ICT Europe, Jo Teefy/Dir. - Human Resources, ICT Europe, Jack L. Magee/Exec. VP - Global Operations/$534,362.00, Timothy F. Kowalski/Exec. VP - Marketing, Technology Solutions

Directors: John J. Brennan/Chmn., CEO, Pres., Donald P. Brennan/Vice Chmn., Bernard Somers/Dir., Seth J. Lehr/Dir., Gordon Coburn/Dir.

Owners: John J. Brennan/37.40%, Bernard Somers, John A. Stoops, Insiders/42.60%, John L. Magee, Lloyd M. Wirshba, Gordon Coburn, Seth J. Lehr, Vincent A. Paccapaniccia, Eileen Brennan Oakley/7.50%, Donald P. Brennan/29.80%, Bear Stearns Asset Management Inc./8.80%, John D. Campbell

Financial Data: *Fiscal Year End:*12/31 *Latest Annual Data:* 12/31/2006

Year	Sales	Net Income
2006	$447,912,000	$16,811,000
2005	$401,334,000	$12,175,000
2004	$325,529,000	-$2,693,000

Curr. Assets:	$129,864,000	**Curr. Liab.:**	$50,341,000	**P/E Ratio:**	35.58
Plant, Equip.:	$61,667,000	**Total Liab.:**	$54,521,000	**Indic. Yr. Divd.:**	NA
Total Assets:	$215,666,000	**Net Worth:**	$161,145,000	**Debt/ Equity:**	NA

ICTS International

Biesbosch 225, Amstelveen; *PH:* 31-203471077; *Fax:* 31-206432412; *http://* www.icts-int.com; *Email:* mail@ictsinternational.com

General - Incorporation	Netherlands	**Stock**- Price on:12/24/2007	$2.7
Employees	NA	Stock Exchange	OTC
Auditor	Goldstein Golub Kessler LLP	Ticker Symbol	ICTSF
Stk Agt	NA	Outstanding Shares	NA
Counsel	McLaughlin & Stern	E.P.S.	NA
DUNS No.	41-939-3178	Shareholders	NA

Business: The group's principal activity is the provision of advanced aviation services. The group provides security services, passenger data analysis, passenger screening, air terminal checkpoints, electronic pre-screening, baggage reconciliation, lost luggage retrieval, document verification, consulting, training, quality auditing and aircraft handling. The group operates in the USA and Europe.

Primary SIC and add'l.: 4581

CIK No: 0001010134

Subsidiaries: Explore Atlantic City, LLC, Explore Baltimore, LLC, Explore Niagara, LLC, Explore USA, Inc, HLS, B.V., Huntleigh USA Corporation, ICTS Leasing B.V., ICTS Technologies B.V., ICTS Technologies USA, Inc., Icts Usa, Inc, International Security B.V., Procheck International B.V.

Officers: Ran Langer/Joint MD, Avraham Dan/Joint MD, CFO, Oded Shoham/MD - I-Sec. Technologies BV, Doron Zicher/GM - I-Sec. International Security BV, Alon Raich/32/Controller

Directors: Menachem J. Atzmon/Chmn., David Sass/Dir., Gordon Housmann/63/Member - Supervisory Board, Elie Housman/Dir., Lynda Davey/Dir., Albert Nissim/Dir., Phil Getter/Dir., Eytan Barak/64/Member - Supervisory Board

Owners: Elchauan Moaz & Affiliates/8.70%, Insiders/52.98%, Atzmon Family Trust/52.98%, Galladio Capital Management B.V./7.61%

ICU Medical Inc

951 Calle Amanecer, San Clemente, CA, 92673; *PH:* 1-949-366-2183; *Fax:* 1-949-366-8368; *http://* www.icumed.com; *Email:* customerservice@icumed.com

General - Incorporation	DE	**Stock**- Price on:12/24/2007	$42.71
Employees	1,819	Stock Exchange	NDQ
Auditor	McGladrey & Pullen LLP	Ticker Symbol	ICUI
Stk Agt	Mellon Investor Services LLC	Outstanding Shares	14,450,000
Counsel	NA	E.P.S.	$1.62
DUNS No.	11-838-0146	Shareholders	NA

Business: The group's principle activities include developing, manufacturing and selling proprietary, disposable medical connection systems for use in intravenous therapy applications. The group devices are designed to protect healthcare workers and their patients from exposure to infectious diseases such as hepatitis b and c and human immunodeficiency virus through accidental needlesticks. The products are clave, custom and generic iv systems, clc2000, click lock, mcgaw protected needle, mcgaw safeline products, lopez valve, rf100-rf150 and other products. The group has supply and distribution agreements with b.braun medical inc and abbott laboratories, both major iv product suppliers and commands a large share of the market. The customers include acute care hospitals, surgical centers and nursing homes. The group operates from United States.

Primary SIC and add'l.: 3829 3841

CIK No: 0000883984

Subsidiaries: Budget Medical Products, Inc., ICU Finance, Inc., ICU MedEurope (NZ) Limited, ICU MedEurope Limited, ICU Medical (Utah), Inc., ICU Medical de Mexico, S.A. de C.V., ICU Medical Europe S.r.l., ICU Medical Sales, Inc., MedScanSonics, Inc.

Officers: George A. Lopez/57/Chmn., CEO, Pres./$1,467,261.00, Alison Burcar/32/VP - Marketing, Steven C. Riggs/46/VP - Operations/$412,478.00, Francis J. O'Brien/62/CFO, Sec., Treasurer/$404,086.00, James Reitz/Dir. - Human Resources, Scott Lamb/Controller/$309,542.00, Richard A. Costello/41/VP - Sales/$312,836.00

Directors: George A. Lopez/57/Chmn., CEO, Pres., Jack W. Brown/65/Dir., John J. Connors/63/Dir., Michael T. Kovalchik/59/Dir., Joseph R. Saucedo/61/Dir., Richard H. Sherman/58/Dir., Robert S. Swinney/59/Dir.

Owners: Jack W. Brown, Insiders/26.00%, George A. Lopez, M.D. Second Family Limited Partnership/8.10%, Michael T. Kovalchik, Scott E. Lamb, Joseph R. Saucedo, Richard A. Costello, Robert S. Swinney, Francis J. O'Brien, Richard H. Sherman, Neuberger Berman, Inc/13.40%, John J. Connors, George A. Lopez/23.40%, Steven C. Riggs, Barclay's Global Investors NA/6.40% *(16 Owners included in Index)*

Financial Data: *Fiscal Year End:*12/31 *Latest Annual Data:* 12/31/2006

Year	Sales	Net Income
2006	$201,613,000	$25,660,000
2005	$157,532,000	$20,274,000
2004	$75,550,000	$5,000,000

Curr. Assets:	$171,438,000	**Curr. Liab.:**	$15,919,000	**P/E Ratio:**	26.36
Plant, Equip.:	$59,037,000	**Total Liab.:**	$19,003,000	**Indic. Yr. Divd.:**	NA
Total Assets:	$244,248,000	**Net Worth:**	$224,887,000	**Debt/ Equity:**	0.0111

Icy Splash Food & Beverage Inc

535 Wortman Ave., Brooklyn, NY, 11208; *PH:* 1-877-978-3624; *Fax:* 1-718-272-2764; *http://* www.icysplash.com; *Email:* info@icysplash.com

General - Incorporation	NY	**Stock**- Price on:12/24/2007	$0.02
Employees	NA	Stock Exchange	OTC
Auditor	Lazar Levine & Felix LLP	Ticker Symbol	IFBV
Stk Agt	Florida Atlantic Stock Transfer, Inc.	Outstanding Shares	NA
Counsel	NA	E.P.S.	NA
DUNS No.	NA	Shareholders	NA

Business: The group's principle activities include producing and distributing soft drinks and refreshing line of carbonated beverages. The company has two lines of soft drinks: icy splash (TM) clear and icy splash - second generation. The icy splash (TM) clear is a naturally fruit-flavored, clear, carbonated soda. This product is produced in four flavors: blackberry; wild cherry; lime kiwi and raspberry & boysenberry. The icy splash - second generation is a colored, fruit-flavored and carbonated soda. This product is produced in fourteen flavors: natural lemon tea; blue raspberry; orange; pineapple; fruit punch; root beer; black cherry; lemon lime; grape; kola champagne; strawberry; peach; ginger ale and cola. The products are offered to supermarket chains, grocery stores and convenience stores primarily in the New York, New Jersey and Connecticut area. In 2004, the company expanded its product line to include health & beauty aids (hba). The group operates from United States.

Primary SIC and add'l.: 2086

CIK No: 0001070906

Financial Data: *Fiscal Year End:*12/31 *Latest Annual Data:* 12/31/2004

Year	Sales	Net Income
2004	$1,679,000	-$130,000
2003	$683,000	-$41,000
2002	$401,000	-$522,000

Curr. Assets:	$600,000	**Curr. Liab.:**	$363,000		
Plant, Equip.:	$4,000	**Total Liab.:**	$363,000	**Indic. Yr. Divd.:**	NA
Total Assets:	$610,000	**Net Worth:**	$247,000	**Debt/ Equity:**	NA

ID Systems Inc

1 University Plz., 6th Fl., Hackensack, NJ, 07601; *PH:* 1-201-996-9000; *Fax:* 1-201-996-9144; *http://* www.id-systems.com; *Email:* info@id-systems.com

General - Incorporation	DE	**Stock**- Price on:12/24/2007	$14.1
Employees	89	Stock Exchange	NDQ
Auditor	Eisner LLP	Ticker Symbol	IDSY
Stk Agt	American Stock Transfer & Trust Co.	Outstanding Shares	11,380,000
Counsel	Orrick, Herrington & Sutcliffe LLP	E.P.S.	NA
DUNS No.	NA	Shareholders	NA

Business: The group's principle activities include design, developing and producing wireless monitoring and tracking products for securing enterprise assets. The group utilizes radio-frequency-based system and Internet-based data management systems in its solutions. The products are designed to enable users to reduce operating costs, increase security, improve safety, enhance service and increase profits. The main components of the wireless monitoring and tracking system are miniature computers called asset communicators that are attached to the objects that are being tracked or monitored. The products are focused to monitor, control and manage mobile assets such as industrial vehicles, rental vehicle fleets, railcars, packages and letters. The major customers are british airways, daimler chrysler, deere & co., ford, general motors, hallmark cards, the U.S. Postal service and the U.S. Navy. The group operates from United States.

Primary SIC and add'l.: 3669

CIK No: 0000049615

Officers: Jeffrey M. Jagid/Chmn., CEO/$695,448.00, Michael L. Ehrman/Exec. VP - Engineering/$579,411.00, Kenneth S. Ehrman/Dir., COO, Pres./$518,595.00, Ned Mavrommatis/CFO, Treasurer/$580,171.00, Peter Fausel/Exec. VP - Sales, Marketing, Customer Support, Curt Lloyd/Exec. VP - Operations

Directors: Jeffrey M. Jagid/Chmn., CEO, Lawrence Burstein/Dir., Michael Monaco/Dir., Beatrice Yormark/Dir., Kenneth S. Ehrman/Dir., COO, Pres.

Owners: Ned Mavrommatis/1.14%, Peter Fausel, Michael L. Ehrman/4.16%, Empire Capital Partners, L.P./7.81%, Kenneth S. Ehrman/5.87%, Jeffrey M. Jagid/5.21%, Artis Capital Management, LLC/18.45%, Michael Monaco, Beatrice Yormark, MFC Global Investment Management, LLC/6.28%, Oberweis Asset Management, Inc./5.36%, Lawrence Burstein, Insiders/17.14%, Luther King Capital Management Corporation/5.78%

Financial Data: Fiscal Year End:12/31 **Latest Annual Data:** 12/31/2006

Year	Sales	Net Income
2006	$24,740,000	-$1,616,000
2005	$19,004,000	$851,000
2004	$13,741,000	$398,000

Curr. Assets:	$83,391,000	**Curr. Liab.:**	$3,392,000		
Plant, Equip.:	$1,394,000	**Total Liab.:**	$3,621,000	**Indic. Yr. Divd.:**	NA
Total Assets:	$84,905,000	**Net Worth:**	$81,284,000	**Debt/ Equity:**	0.0026

Idacorp Inc

1221 W Idaho St., Boise, ID, 83702; **PH:** 1-208-388-2200; **Fax:** 1-208-388-6955;
http:// www.idacorpinc.com

General - Incorporation	ID	**Stock**- Price on:12/24/2007	$32.3
Employees	1,976	Stock Exchange	NYSE
Auditor	Deloitte & Touche LLP	Ticker Symbol	IDA
Stk Agt	Wells Fargo Bank, N.A.	Outstanding Shares	NA
Counsel	NA	E.P.S.	$2.05
DUNS No.	NA	Shareholders	NA

Business: The group's principal activity is to generate, transmit, distribute, sell and purchase electric energy. The group operates in three segments, utility operations, energy marketing and ifs. Utility operations are involved in the generation, purchase, transmission, distribution and sale of electric energy. Energy marketing segment markets electricity and natural gas. Ifs invest primarily in affordable housing developments, historic rehabilitation projects such as the el cortez hotel in san diego, California and the empire building in boise, Idaho.

Primary SIC and add'l.: 6719 4911 6531

CIK No: 0001057877

Subsidiaries: Equigy Development, L.P, Ida-West Energy Company, Idacomm, Inc., IDACORP Energy L.P., IDACORP Energy Services Company, IDACORP Financial Services, IDACORP Services Co, IDACORP Technologies, Inc, Idaho Energy Resources Company, Idaho Power Company, Idaho Solar Power, LLC, IdaTech, LLC, Pathnet/Idaho Power Equipment, LLC, RMC Holding, Inc, Velocitus, Inc

Officers: Lamont J. Keen/Dir., CEO, Pres./$1,420,655.00, Tom R. Saldin/Sr. VP, General Counsel, Sec./$735,687.00, Luci K. McDonald/VP - Human Resources, Dan B. Minor/Sr. VP - Delivery, Idaho Power/$642,320.00, Darrel T. Anderson/CFO, Sr. VP - Administrative Services/$787,345.00, John R. Gale/VP - Regulatory Affairs, Idaho Power, Greg W. Panter/VP - Public Affairs, Lori D. Smith/VP - Finance, Chief Risk Officer, Dennis G. Gribble/CIO, VP, Steve R. Keen/VP, Treasurer, Patrick A. Harrington/Corp. Sec. - Idaho Power, Idacorp, Inc, Lisa A. Grow/VP - Delivery Engineering, Operations, Idaho Power, Naomi C. Shankel/VP - Audit, Compliance, Idacorp, Inc, Idaho Power, Warren Kline/VP - Customer Service, Regional Operations, Lawrence F. Spencer/Dir. - Investor Relations *(17 Officers included in Index)*

Directors: Lamont J. Keen/Dir., CEO, Pres., Jon H. Miller/Chmn., Gary G. Michael/Dir., Peter S. O'Neill/Dir., Richard G. Reiten/Dir., Jan B. Packwood/Dir., Judith A. Johansen/Dir., Christine King/Dir., Joan H. Smith/Dir., Robert A. Tinstman/Dir., Thomas J. Wilford/Dir.

Owners: Joan H. Smith, Rotchford L. Barker, Insiders/1.80%, Jan B. Packwood, Jon H. Miller, Robert A. Tinstman, Thomas R. Saldin, Darrel T. Anderson, James C. Miller, Daniel B. Minor, Thomas J. Wilford, Christine King, Peter S. ONeill, Gary G. Michael, Richard G. Reiten *(16 Owners included in Index)*

Financial Data: Fiscal Year End:12/31 **Latest Annual Data:** 12/31/2006

Year	Sales	Net Income
2006	$926,291,000	$107,403,000
2005	$859,488,000	$63,661,000
2004	$844,491,000	$72,983,000

Curr. Assets:	$266,531,000	**Curr. Liab.:**	$410,334,000	**P/E Ratio:**	13.35
Plant, Equip.:	$2,440,156,000	**Total Liab.:**	$2,320,947,000	**Indic. Yr. Divd.:**	$1.200
Total Assets:	$3,445,130,000	**Net Worth:**	$1,124,183,000	**Debt/ Equity:**	0.8260

Idaho Bancorp ID

7661 W Riverside Dr., Ste. 201, Boise, ID, 83714; **PH:** 1-208-287-6505; **Fax:** 1-208-287-6502;
http:// www.idahobankingco.com

General - Incorporation		**Stock**- Price on:12/24/2007	$15.7
Employees	NA	Stock Exchange	OTC
Auditor	NA	Ticker Symbol	IDBC
Stk Agt	Registrar & Transfer Co	Outstanding Shares	1,820,000
Counsel	NA	E.P.S.	NA
DUNS No.	NA	Shareholders	NA

Business: The groups principal activity is to provide banking services. The services of the group include personal banking, business banking, mortgage and lending activities, and online banking. The group operates from the United States.

Primary SIC and add'l.: 6022

CIK No:

Officers: Alison Gillespie/VP, Mgr. - Morgage, Idaho Banking Company, Horace Hunt/Sr. Loan Officer - Mortgage, Idaho Banking Company, Jan Griffith/Loan Officer - Mortgage, Idaho Banking Company, Randy Bauer/Loan Officer - Mortgage, Idaho Banking Company, Kate Asbury/Loan Officer - Mortgage, Idaho Banking Company, Jackie Stearns/Loan Officer - Mortgage, Idaho Banking Company, Laurie Funston/Sr. Processor, Mortgage, Idaho Banking Company, Becky Rawlings/Processor, Mortgage, Idaho Banking Company, Pat Johnson/VP, Mgr. - Construction Department, Idaho Banking Company, Nick Barber/VP, Assist. Mgr. - Construction Department, Idaho Banking Company, Michael Shepard/AVP, Loan Officer - Construction Department, Idaho Banking Company, Ken Kean/AVP, Loan Officer - Construction Department, Idaho Banking Company, Roger Schumacher/Construction Loan Officer - Idaho Banking Company, Lynn Reynolds/Sr. Construction Loan Processor, Idaho Banking Company, Terry Disbennett/Construction Loan Processor, Idaho Banking Company *(17 Officers included in Index)*

Idaho General Mines Inc

1726 Cole Blvd., Ste. 115, Lakewood, CO, 80401; **PH:** 1-303-928-8599;
http:// www.idahogeneralmines.com

General - Incorporation	ID	**Stock**- Price on:12/24/2007	$6.45
Employees	8	Stock Exchange	AMEX
Auditor	Pricewaterhousecoopers LLP	Ticker Symbol	GMO
Stk Agt	Pacific Corporate Trust Co.	Outstanding Shares	NA
Counsel	NA	E.P.S.	NA
DUNS No.	NA	Shareholders	NA

Business: The group's principal activities are mineral exploration specializing in advanced-stage projects. The group's advance-stage projects includes molybdenum-porphyry deposits in central Nevada, and high-potential molybdenum, copper, and gold projects in the western United States. The group holds the Mount Hope Project in central Nevada, which contains large molybdenum-porphyry deposits. The company, based upon a feasibility study, plans to mine 920 million metric tonnes of mineralized material by open pit methods which will produce about 1.3 billion pounds of recoverable molybdenum during its 53-year lifetime. On 12, November, 2004, the company entered into an Option to Lease agreement all property and assets of the Mount Hope Molybdenum Property from Mt. Hope Mines, Inc. Exercise of the Option allows the company to proceed for the next 30 years with permitting, developing and mining the deposit and for so long thereafter as the company maintains an active operation.

Primary SIC and add'l.: 1000

CIK No: 0001275229

Subsidiaries: American Molybdenum, Inc, Kellogg Minerals, Inc

Officers: Bruce D. Hansen/50/Dir., CEO

Directors: Bruce D. Hansen/50/Dir., CEO

Owners: Citadel Limited Partnership/6.00%, Bruce D. Hansen/1.50%, Robert L. Russell/4.50%, John B. Benjamin, Insiders/10.70%, Richard Nanna, Gene W. Pierson, Mark A. Lettes, Sprott Asset Management Inc/8.30%, David A. Chaput, David R. Russell/2.20%, Norman A. Radford, Clint D. Coghill/25.80%, Ricardo Campoy

Financial Data: Fiscal Year End:12/31 **Latest Annual Data:** 12/31/2006

Year	Sales	Net Income
2006	NA	-$12,745,000
2005	NA	-$4,518,000
2004	NA	-$2,337,000

Curr. Assets:	$18,075,000	**Curr. Liab.:**	$970,000		
Plant, Equip.:	$8,315,000	**Total Liab.:**	$1,028,000	**Indic. Yr. Divd.:**	NA
Total Assets:	$26,391,000	**Net Worth:**	$25,363,000	**Debt/ Equity:**	0.0022

Idaho Independent Bank

7661 W Riverside Dr., Ste. 201, Boise, ID, 83714; **PH:** 1-208-287-6505; **Fax:** 1-208-287-6502;
https:// www.theidahobank.com

General - Incorporation		**Stock**- Price on:12/24/2007	$29.25
Employees	194	Stock Exchange	OTC
Auditor	NA	Ticker Symbol	IIBK
Stk Agt	Computershare Investor Services LLC	Outstanding Shares	5,610,000
Counsel	NA	E.P.S.	NA
DUNS No.	NA	Shareholders	NA

Business: The groups principal activity is to provide banking services. The services of the group include business and personal banking, originating loans, deposit and lending activities. The group operates from the United States.

Primary SIC and add'l.: 6712 6022 6162 6163

CIK No: 0001145724

Financial Data: Fiscal Year End:NA **Latest Annual Data:** 03/31/2003

Year	Sales	Net Income
2003	$6,028,000	$1,096,000
2002	$23,776,000	$4,004,000
2001	$23,496,000	$3,675,000

Curr. Assets:	$89,445,000	**Curr. Liab.:**	$295,114,000	**P/E Ratio:**	15.56
Plant, Equip.:	$9,997,000	**Total Liab.:**	$295,114,000	**Indic. Yr. Divd.:**	NA
Total Assets:	$325,597,000	**Net Worth:**	$30,483,000	**Debt/ Equity:**	NA

IdeaEdge Inc

Formerly: 1st Net Technologies Inc
6440 Lusk Blvd., Ste. 200, San Diego, CA, 92121; **PH:** 1-858-677-0080

General - Incorporation	CO	**Stock**- Price on:12/24/2007	$0.05
Employees	NA	Stock Exchange	NA
Auditor	Cordovano & Honeck LLP	Ticker Symbol	NA
Stk Agt	Computershare, Inc.	Outstanding Shares	42,360,000
Counsel	Donald A. Nunn	E.P.S.	-$0.01
DUNS No.	NA	Shareholders	NA

Business: The group's principle activity is to provide services in Internet commerce and services business. The company currently does not maintain any business operations. The group operates from United States.

Primary SIC and add'l.: 7375

CIK No: 0001062273

Subsidiaries: 1st Net Technologies, Inc, VOS Systems, Inc

Officers: James Collas/47/Dir., CEO, Chris Nicolaidis/47/Dir., VP - Business Development, Corp. Sec., Jonathan Shultz/48/CFO, Treasurer

Directors: James Collas/47/Dir., CEO, Chris Nicolaidis/47/Dir., VP - Business Development, Corp. Sec.

Owners: James Collas/23.20%, Jonathan Shultz, Jeffrey Hall/7.20%, Chris Nicolaidis/15.30%, Insiders/38.90%, Robert Wheat/8.40%

Financial Data: Fiscal Year End:09/30 **Latest Annual Data:** 9/30/2006

Year	Sales	Net Income
2006	$214,000	-$492,000
2005	$285,000	-$741,000
2004	NA	$38,000

Curr. Assets:	$104,000	**Curr. Liab.:**	$516,000		
Plant, Equip.:	$39,000	**Total Liab.:**	$1,192,000	**Indic. Yr. Divd.:**	NA
Total Assets:	$222,000	**Net Worth:**	-$970,000	**Debt/ Equity:**	NA

Ideal Accents Inc

50 Tiffield Rd., Unit 1, Scarborough, ON, M1V 5B7; **PH:** 1-416-904-1677;
http:// www.idealaccents.com

General - Incorporation	FL	**Stock**- Price on:12/24/2007	NA
Employees	NA	Stock Exchange	OTC
Auditor	Rotenberg & Co. LLP	Ticker Symbol	IACE
Stk Agt	Olde Monmouth Stk Trnsfer Co. Inc.	Outstanding Shares	NA
Counsel	NA	E.P.S.	NA
DUNS No.	NA	Shareholders	NA

Business: The groups principle activity is to provide automotive accessorizing related consulting services. The group operates from Canada.

Primary SIC and add'l.: NA

CIK No: 0001170161

Subsidiaries: Ideal Accents, Ideal Accents Inc.

Owners: James Erickson/1.77%, Joseph OConnor/30.52%, George Walch, Thomas Sullivan

Financial Data: Fiscal Year End:12/31   **Latest Annual Data:** 12/31/2006

Year	Sales	Net Income
2006	NA	-$104,000
2005	$139,000	$151,000
2004	$4,914,000	-$1,820,000

Curr. Assets:	NA	**Curr. Liab.:**	$557,000		
Plant, Equip.:	NA	**Total Liab.:**	$3,800,000	**Indic. Yr. Divd.:**	NA
Total Assets:	NA	**Net Worth:**	-$3,800,000	**Debt/ Equity:**	NA

Idearc Inc

2200 W Airfield Dr., D/FW Airport, TX, 75261; **PH:** 1-972-453-7000; **Fax:** 1-972-453-6869;
http:// www.idearc.com; **Email:** dmcanotices@idearc.com

General - Incorporation	DE	**Stock**- Price on:12/24/2007	$35.88
Employees	7,400	Stock Exchange	NYSE
Auditor	Ernst & Young LLP	Ticker Symbol	IAR
Stk Agt	Computershare Trust Co	Outstanding Shares	NA
Counsel	NA	E.P.S.	$2.88
DUNS No.	NA	Shareholders	NA

Business: The groups principle activity is to publish yellow pages directories. The group operates from the United States and Columbia. The groups quarterly revenue for September 2007 was 791.00 millions of USD.

Primary SIC and add'l.: 2721 2741

CIK No: 0001367396

Subsidiaries: Idearc Information Services Inc.*, Idearc Media Corp., Idearc Media Sales East Co., Idearc Media Sales West Inc., Idearc Media Sales East LLC, Idearc Media Services East Inc., Idearc Media Services West Inc., License Application Corporation**, Second License Application Corporation**, VIS Inceptor, LTD**

Officers: Katherine J. Harless/Dir., CEO, Pres./$1,780,845.00, Eric D. Chandler/Pres. - Internet, Andrew Coticchio/CFO, Exec. VP/$832,673.00, Frank P. Gatto/Pres. - Northeast/$776,824.00, Scott W. Hanle/Pres. - West, Independent/$712,687.00, Sandra Lee Henjum/Pres. - Southeast, Central, Samuel D. Jones/Sr. VP - Investor Relations Idearc Inc., Scott B. Laver/Pres. - Mid, Atlantic/$781,218.00, William G. Mundy/Exec. VP, General Counsel, Sec., Michael D. Pawlowski/Sr. VP, Chief Marketing Officer, Georgia R. Scaife/Sr. VP - Human Resources, Stephen Smith/42/CIO, Sr. VP, Janet P. Stevens/Sr. VP - Public Relations, Debbie Johnson/Contact - Community Programs Mgr., Jannie Luong/Media Contact (17 Officers included in Index)

Directors: Katherine J. Harless/Dir., CEO, Pres., John J. Mueller/Chmn., Jerry V. Elliot/Dir., Donald B. Reed/Dir., Stephen L. Robertson/Dir., Thomas S. Rogers/Dir., Paul E. Weaver/Dir.

Owners: Katherine J. Harless, Paul E. Weaver, Donald B. Reed, Jerry V. Elliott, John J. Mueller, Frank P. Gatto, Stephen L. Robertson, Andrew Coticchio, Insiders, Scott B. Laver, Scott W. Hanle, Thomas S. Rogers

Financial Data: Fiscal Year End:12/31   **Latest Annual Data:** 12/31/2006

Year	Sales	Net Income
2006	$3,221,000,000	$772,000,000

Curr. Assets:	$707,000,000	**Curr. Liab.:**	$692,000,000		
Plant, Equip.:	$143,000,000	**Total Liab.:**	$10,164,000,000	**Indic. Yr. Divd.:**	$1.370
Total Assets:	$1,318,000,000	**Net Worth:**	-$8,846,000,000	**Debt/ Equity:**	NA

Idenix Pharmaceuticals Inc

60 Hampshire St., Cambridge, MA, 02139; **PH:** 1-617-995-9800; **Fax:** 1-617-995-9801;
http:// www.idenix.com; **Email:** idenix@idenix.com

General - Incorporation	DE	**Stock**- Price on:12/24/2007	$6.31
Employees	277	Stock Exchange	NDQ
Auditor	PricewaterhouseCoopers LLP	Ticker Symbol	IDIX
Stk Agt	Computershare Trust Co	Outstanding Shares	56,170,000
Counsel	Wilmer Cutler Pickering H & D LLP	E.P.S.	-$1.58
DUNS No.	NA	Shareholders	NA

Business: The group's principal activity is to discover and develop drugs for the treatment of human viral and other infectious diseases. The group's current focus is on the treatment of infections caused by hepatitis b virus (hbv), hepatitis c virus (hcv) and human immunodeficiency virus (HIV). On Jul 27, 2004, the group completed its initial public offering.

Primary SIC and add'l.: 2834

CIK No: 0001093649

Subsidiaries: Idenix (Cayman) Limited, Idenix SARL, Novartis Pharma AG (Novartis), Ribapharm, Inc.

Officers: Jean-Pierre Sommadossi/Founder, CEO, Chmn. - Idenix/$1,873,921.00, Paul Fanning/VP - Human Resources, John F. Weidenbruch/Exec. VP, General Counsel/$450,977.00, Susan Koppy/Sr. VP - Business - Corporate Development, Guy MacDonald/Exec. VP - Operations/$779,149.00, David Standring/Sr. VP - Biology, Amy Sullivan/VP - Corporate Communications, Teri Dahlman/Sr. Mgr. - Corporate Communications, Ronald C. Renaud/CFO, Treasurer, Douglas L. Mayers/Chief Medical Officer, Exec. VP

Directors: Jean-Pierre Sommadossi/Founder, CEO, Chmn. - Idenix, Charles W. Cramb/Dir., Thomas Ebeling/Dir., Pamela Thomas-Graham/Dir., Wayne T. Hockmeyer/Dir., Thomas R. Hodgson/Dir., Robert Pelzer/Dir., Denise Pollard-Knight/Dir., Norman C. Payson/Dir., Norman C. Payson,/Dir.

Owners: Jean-Pierre Sommadossi/4.60%, Wayne T. Hockmeyer, Novartis AG/55.70%, David A. Arkowitz, Andrea J. Corcoran, Thomas R. Hodgson, MPM Capital L.P./5.80%, Charles W. Cramb, Insiders/6.00%, Guy Macdonald

Financial Data: Fiscal Year End:12/31   **Latest Annual Data:** 12/31/2006

Year	Sales	Net Income
2006	$67,377,000	-$75,087,000
2005	$64,718,000	-$50,777,000
2004	$95,389,000	-$6,244,000

Curr. Assets:	$147,605,000	**Curr. Liab.:**	$37,446,000		
Plant, Equip.:	$17,448,000	**Total Liab.:**	$86,440,000	**Indic. Yr. Divd.:**	NA
Total Assets:	$228,465,000	**Net Worth:**	$142,025,000	**Debt/ Equity:**	0.0097

Identix Inc

5600 Rowland Rd., Minnetonka, MN, 55343; **PH:** 1-952-932-0888; **http://** www.identix.com

General - Incorporation	DE	**Stock**- Price on:12/24/2007	$20
Employees	1,047	Stock Exchange	NA
Auditor	PricewaterhouseCoopers LLP	Ticker Symbol	NA
Stk Agt	Wells Fargo Shareowner Services	Outstanding Shares	72,840,000
Counsel	Heller Ehrman White & McAuliffe LLP	E.P.S.	NA
DUNS No.	10-210-6952	Shareholders	NA

Business: The group's principal activities are to provide fingerprint, facial and skin biometric technologies, as well as systems, and critical system components that empower the identification of individuals in large-scale ID and ID management programs. It provides live scan systems and services for biometric data capture, mobile systems for on-the-spot ID, and backend standards-based modules and software components for biometric matching and data mining. The group's offerings includes: live scan; ibis (identification based information system); abis (automated biometric identification system); enabling biometric technologies and biometric and other professional sevices. Its products serve industries and market segments such as government and law enforcement, transportation, healthcare and corporate enterprises. On 23-Feb-2004, the group acquired sylvan identix fingerprint centers, llc.

Primary SIC and add'l.: 7379 7372 3999 7382

CIK No: 0000735780

Subsidiaries: Biometric Applications & Technology, Inc., Identicator Technology, Inc., Identix Australia Pty Ltd., Identix Identification Services, Identix International, Inc., iTrust, Inc., Legislative Demographic Services, Inc., Visionics Corporation

Financial Data: Fiscal Year End:06/30   **Latest Annual Data:** 12/31/2006

Year	Sales	Net Income
2006	$164,386,000	-$31,037,000
2005	$66,224,000	-$7,353,000
2004	$67,466,000	-$6,997,000

Curr. Assets:	$82,002,000	**Curr. Liab.:**	$70,344,000		
Plant, Equip.:	$19,928,000	**Total Liab.:**	$160,140,000	**Indic. Yr. Divd.:**	NA
Total Assets:	$1,227,225,000	**Net Worth:**	$1,067,085,000	**Debt/ Equity:**	0.0922

Idera Pharmaceuticals Inc

Formerly: Hybridon Inc
167 Sidney St., Cambridge, MA, 02139; **PH:** 1-617-679-5500

General - Incorporation	DE	**Stock**- Price on:12/24/2007	$7.06
Employees	33	Stock Exchange	AMEX
Auditor	Ernst & Young LLP	Ticker Symbol	HBY
Stk Agt	Mellon Investor Services LLC	Outstanding Shares	21,250,000
Counsel	Hale & Dorr LLP	E.P.S.	-$0.84
DUNS No.	61-865-5609	Shareholders	NA

Business: The group's principal activity is to discover and develop therapeutics and diagnostics using synthetic dna. The group's activities are based on two technology platforms: immunomodulatory oligonucleotide (imo) technology that uses synthetic dna to modulate responses of the immune system. The imo compounds designed and developed by the group provide therapeutic benefits in the areas of cancer, allergic asthma and other allergies, infectious diseases and in combinations with vaccines and antibody therapies. The antisense technology uses synthetic dna to inhibit the production of disease-associated proteins at the cellular level. Antisense drug development technology involves the design and synthesis of synthetic dna to bind and inhibit the activity of messenger rna which codes for the production of disease-associated proteins. The trademarks of the group are hybridon (R), gem (R), amplivaxtm, cprtm, cyclicontm, imotm, imoxinetm, ypgtm, and yprtm.

Primary SIC and add'l.: 8731 8733

CIK No: 0000861838

Officers: Sudhir Agrawal/54/Dir., CEO, Chief Scientific Officer/$1,213,405.00, Robert G. Andersen/CFO, VP - Operations, Treasurer, Sec./$458,366.00, Robert W. Karr/59/Dir., Pres./$807,060.00, Timothy M. Sullivan/VP - Development Programs/$389,904.00

Directors: Sudhir Agrawal/54/Dir., CEO, Chief Scientific Officer, Youssef El Zein/59/Vice Chmn., James B. Wyngaarden/83/Chmn., Alison Taunton-Rigby/63/Dir., Robert W. Karr/59/Dir., Pres., William S. Reardon/61/Dir., Keith C. Hartley/65/Dir.

Owners: William S. Reardon, Felix J. Baker/27.90%, James B. Wyngaarden, Robert G. Andersen, Timothy M. Sullivan, Keith C. Hartley, Alison Taunton-Rigby, Youssef El Zein/8.70%, Sudhir Agrawal/4.60%, Optima Life Sciences Limited/6.70%, Insiders/14.70%, Merck& Co, Inc./8.90%, Robert W. Karr

Financial Data: Fiscal Year End:12/31   **Latest Annual Data:** 12/31/2006

Year	Sales	Net Income
2006	$2,421,000	-$16,525,000
2005	$2,467,000	-$13,706,000
2004	$943,000	-$12,735,000

Curr. Assets:	$39,002,000	**Curr. Liab.:**	$8,018,000		
Plant, Equip.:	$622,000	**Total Liab.:**	$28,304,000	**Indic. Yr. Divd.:**	NA
Total Assets:	$40,541,000	**Net Worth:**	$12,237,000	**Debt/ Equity:**	0.4115

IDEX Corp

630 Dundee Rd., Ste. 400, Northbrook, IL, 60062; *PH:* 1-847-498-7070; *Fax:* 1-847-498-3940; *http://* www.idexcorp.com; *Email:* careers@idexcorp.com

General - Incorporation	DE	**Stock**- Price on:12/24/2007	$37.57
Employees	4,863	Stock Exchange	NYSE
Auditor	Deloitte & Touche LLP	Ticker Symbol	IEX
Stk Agt	National City Bank	Outstanding Shares	81,120,000
Counsel	NA	E.P.S	$1.86
DUNS No.	18-358-0844	Shareholders	NA

Business: The group's principal activity is to manufacture pump products and engineered equipment. The group operates under three segments: pump products group, dispensing equipment group and other engineered products group. The pump product segment designs, produces and distributes a wide variety of industrial pumps, compressors, meters and related controls for the movement of liquids, air and gases. The dispensing equipment segment produces highly engineered equipment for dispensing, metering and mixing colorants, paints, inks, dyes and others. Other engineered products segment manufactures engineered banding and clamping devices, fire fighting pumps and rescue tools. In 2003, the group acquired Sponsler Co Inc and Classic Engineering Inc and in 2004, it acquired Manfred Vetter GMBH, Systec Inc, Scivex Inc and Tianjin Dinglee Machine and Motor Co Ltd.

Primary SIC and add'l.: 3569 3586 3541 3594 3429 3561

CIK No: 0000832101

Subsidiaries: Band-it Clamps (asia) Pte., Ltd., Band-it Company Ltd., Band-it-idex, Inc., Blagdon Holdings, Ltd., Blagdon Pump Ltd., Class 1, Inc., Classic Engineering Inc., Corken, Inc., Dominator Pump Ab, Fast & Fluid Management Iberica S.a., Fast & Fluid Management S.r.l., Fast & Fluid Management U.k. Limited, FAST and FLUID MANAGEMENT FRANCE SARL, Fluid Management Australia Pty., Ltd., Fluid Management Canada, Inc. 86 Subsidiaries included in the Index

Officers: Larry D. Kingsley/Chmn., CEO, Pres., Susan H. Fisher/48/Dir. - Corporate Communications, Divakar Kamath/58/CIO, Frank J. Notaro/44/VP, General Counsel, Sec./$769,911.00, Kimberly K. Bors/47/VP - Global Human Resources, Corporate Communications/$731,367.00, Dominic A. Romeo/48/CFO, VP/$1,325,488.00, Gerald F. Carter/44/VP - Tax, International Finance, Heath A. Mitts/37/VP - Corporate Finance, Daniel J. Salliotte/42/VP - Strategy, Business Development, Michael J. Yates/44/VP, Controller, Robert K. Brinley/53/Pres. - Health, Science Technologies, Robert W. Kreps/61/Pres. - Fire, Safety, Diversified Products, John L. McMurray/57/VP - Group Exec., Fluid, Metering Technologies/$1,096,227.00, Kelly D. Sloan/48/VP - Global Supply Chain, Operational Excellence, Bradley A. Spiegel/45/Pres. - Dispensing, VP - Commercial Excellence *(17 Officers included in Index)*

Directors: Larry D. Kingsley/Chmn., CEO, Pres., Bradley J. Bell/52/Dir., Exec. VP, Neil A. Springer/67/Dir., Michael T. Tokarz/55/Dir., Ruby R. Chandy/45/Dir., VP - Marketing, Commercial Excellence, Thermo Fisher Scientific, Frank S. Hermance/56/Dir., Gregory B. Kenny/52/Dir.

Owners: Dominic A. Romeo, Insiders/2.20%, Fidelity Management & Research/5.60%, Ruby R. Chandy, Bradley J. Bell, Gregory B. Kenny, Lawrence D. Kingsley, Ariel Capital Management, Inc./13.30%, Select Equity Group, Inc./7.70%, Kimberly K. Bors, Michael T. Tokarz, John L. McMurray, Frank S. Hermance, Frank J. Notaro, Neil A. Springer

Financial Data: **Fiscal Year End:**12/31 **Latest Annual Data:** 12/31/2006

Year	Sales	Net Income
2006	$1,154,940,000	$146,671,000
2005	$1,043,275,000	$109,803,000
2004	$928,297,000	$86,406,000

Curr. Assets:	$417,908,000	**Curr. Liab.:**	$187,252,000	**P/E Ratio:**	19.17
Plant, Equip.:	$165,949,000	**Total Liab.:**	$691,549,000	**Indic. Yr. Divd.:**	$0.480
Total Assets:	$1,670,821,000	**Net Worth:**	$979,272,000	**Debt/ Equity:**	0.2118

IDEXX Laboratories Inc

1 IDEXX Dr., Westbrook, ME, 04092; *PH:* 1-207-856-0300; *Fax:* 1-207-856-0346; *http://* www.idexx.com; *Email:* investorrelations@idexx.com

General - Incorporation	DE	**Stock**- Price on:12/24/2007	$90.93
Employees	3,900	Stock Exchange	NDQ
Auditor	PricewaterhouseCoopers LLP	Ticker Symbol	IDXX
Stk Agt	American Stock Transfer & Trust Co.	Outstanding Shares	30,980,000
Counsel	NA	E.P.S	$1.44
DUNS No.	10-818-3757	Shareholders	NA

Business: The group's principle activities are to develop, manufacture and distribute products and provide services for veterinary, food and water testing markets. The group operates under three divisions: companion animal group, water quality products and food diagnostics group. The group's products and services include point-of-care veterinary diagnostic products; laboratory and consulting services used by veterinarians; veterinary pharmaceutical products; information products and services, including software, used in veterinary practice management; diagnostic and health-monitoring products and services for production animals; products that test water for certain microbiological contaminants; and products that test milk for antibiotic residues. The products are marketed, sold and serviced in more than 50 countries through their marketing, sales and technical service groups, as well as through independent distributors and other resellers. The group's quarterly revenue for Sep'07 was 229.38 millions of USD.

Primary SIC and add'l.: 2834 3841 8734 3826

CIK No: 0000874716

Subsidiaries: Cardiopet Incorporated, Diavet Labor AG, Dr. Bommeli AG, Genera Technologies Limited, IDEXX Computer Systems, Inc., IDEXX Distribution, Inc., IDEXX Europe B.V, IDEXX GmbH, IDEXX Holding GmbH, IDEXX Laboratories (NZ) Limited, IDEXX Laboratories B.V, IDEXX Laboratories Canada Corporation, IDEXX Laboratories Inc., IDEXX Laboratories Italia S.r.l, IDEXX Laboratories Limited 34 Subsidiaries included in the Index

Officers: Jonathan W. Ayers/Chmn., CEO, Pres./$2,455,120.00, William C. Wallen/Chief Scientific Officer, Sr. VP/$1,130,357.00, Merilee Raines/CFO, Corporate VP, Treasurer/$702,126.00, Conan R. Deady/Corporate VP, General Counsel, Sec./$619,048.00, Sam S. Fratoni/Corporate VP, Ali Naqui/Corporate VP - Dairy, Water, Asia, Pacific, Latin America Operations, Elisabeth L. Richards/Contact - Corporate Business Communications, Thomas J. Dupree/Corporate VP - Companion Animal Group, William B. Goodspeed/Corporate VP - Production Animal Segment, Irene C. Kerr/Corporate VP - Worldwide Operations, James Polewaczyk/Corporate VP - Rapid Assay, Digital Radiography, Michael Williams/Corporate VP - Instrument Diagnostics

Directors: Jonathan W. Ayers/Chmn., CEO, Pres., Rebecca M. Henderson/48/Dir., Robert J. Murray/67/Dir., William T. End/61/Dir., Brian P. McKeon/46/Dir., Thomas Craig/53/Dir., Errol B. De Souza/55/Dir., Barry C. Johnson/64/Dir.

Owners: Insiders/3.88%, Thomas Craig, Conan R. Deady, William T. End, Robert S. Hulsy, Capital Research and Management Company/5.05%, Neuberger Berman, Inc./8.14%, William C. Wallen, Brian P. McKeon, Merilee Raines, Robert J. Murray, Errol B. DeSouza, Jonathan W. Ayers/1.86%, Rebecca M. Henderson, Ruane Cunniff& Goldfarb Inc./15.09%

Financial Data: **Fiscal Year End:**12/31 **Latest Annual Data:** 12/31/2006

Year	Sales	Net Income
2006	$739,117,000	$93,678,000
2005	$638,095,000	$78,254,000
2004	$549,181,000	$78,332,000

Curr. Assets:	$302,263,000	**Curr. Liab.:**	$124,743,000	**P/E Ratio:**	30.82
Plant, Equip.:	$99,628,000	**Total Liab.:**	$149,699,000	**Indic. Yr. Divd.:**	NA
Total Assets:	$559,560,000	**Net Worth:**	$409,861,000	**Debt/ Equity:**	0.0152

IDI Global Inc

462 E 800 N, Orem, UT, 84097; *PH:* 1-801-224-4444; *Fax:* 1-801-224-4457; *http://* www.idiglobal.com; *Email:* email@idiglobal.com

General - Incorporation	NV	**Stock**- Price on:12/24/2007	$0.008
Employees	NA	Stock Exchange	OTC
Auditor	HJ & Assoc., LLC	Ticker Symbol	IDIB
Stk Agt	Standard Registrar & Transfer Co Inc.	Outstanding Shares	19,110,000
Counsel	NA	E.P.S	-$0.055
DUNS No.	NA	Shareholders	NA

Business: The group operates through its subsidiaries whose principle activities include designing, developing and marketing web-based software applications and development tools. Services of the group include merchant account, web development, web hosting, and consulting. Products of the group include QuickSite Builder, Odyssey Billing System and ARRAY. The group acquired Mentoring of America, LLC and HG Marketing, Inc. in January 2005, and Circle Tree Media, Inc. in December 2005. The group operates from the United States.

Primary SIC and add'l.: 7379 7389 7376 7379 7375 7378 7374 7389 7374 7378 7376 7372 7375

CIK No: 0001110418

Subsidiaries: Chief Financial, Inc., IDI Small Business, IDI technology, Internet Development, Inc., Professional Consulting Services, Sports Media International, Inc., Worldwide Recruiting Solutions Inc.

Officers: Kevin Griffith/52/Chmn., CEO, Pres., Randy Lane/CEO - Idisb, Owned Subsidiary, IDI Global, Subsidiary, Idisb, Professional Consulting Services, Inc, Eugene Bergmann/49/Dir., Sec., Treasurer, Karl Ackerman/Pres. - Subsidiary, IDI Global, Sports Media International, Chris Matthews/Pres. - Idisb, Owned Subsidiary, IDI Global, Subsidiary, Idisb, Professional Consulting Services, Inc, Steve Weatherly/CFO, Mark Hildebrandt/VP - Operations, Dave Reed/VP - Technology

Directors: Kevin Griffith/52/Chmn., CEO, Pres., Eugene Bergmann/49/Dir., Sec., Treasurer

Owners: Insiders/36.19%, Kevin R. Griffith/36.19%

Financial Data: **Fiscal Year End:**12/31 **Latest Annual Data:** 12/31/2006

Year	Sales	Net Income
2006	$8,000,000	-$1,500,000
2005	$21,090,000	-$5,869,000
2004	$27,718,000	-$776,000

Curr. Assets:	$175,000	**Curr. Liab.:**	$4,004,000		
Plant, Equip.:	NA	**Total Liab.:**	$4,004,000	**Indic. Yr. Divd.:**	NA
Total Assets:	$986,000	**Net Worth:**	-$3,018,000	**Debt/ Equity:**	NA

IDM Pharma Inc

9 Pk.er, Ste. 100, Irvine, CA, 92618; *PH:* 1-949-470-4751; *Fax:* 1-949-470-6470; *http://* www.idm-biotech.com

General - Incorporation	DE	**Stock**- Price on:12/24/2007	$3.6
Employees	81	Stock Exchange	NDQ
Auditor	Ernst & Young LLP	Ticker Symbol	IDMI
Stk Agt	American Stock Transfer & Trust Co.	Outstanding Shares	17,960,000
Counsel	Cooley Godward LLP	E.P.S	-$1.41
DUNS No.	18-398-3576	Shareholders	NA

Business: The group's principal activities are to design and develop new class of drugs for the treatment of acute and chronic inflammatory diseases, infectious diseases and cancer. The group has a broad proprietary position covering epitope identification system, numerous epitopes for cancer and infectious disease vaccine targets and other vaccine technology. Epimmune(tm) , eis(tm), epigene(tm) and padre(tm) are the trademarks and immunosense is a service mark of the company. The group is in the research and preclinical development with therapeutic vaccines for breast, colon, lung and prostate cancers, hepatitis c, HIV and malaria.

Primary SIC and add'l.: 8731 2834

CIK No: 0000822206

Subsidiaries: IDM-Biotech, Ltd., Immuno-Designed Molecules S.A., Immuno-Designed Molecules, Inc.

Officers: Jean-Loup Romet-Lemonne/Dir., CEO/$636,592.00, Timothy P. Walbert/Dir., CEO, Pres., Robert J. De Vaere/Sr. VP - Finance, Administration, CFO, Jeffrey W. Sherman/Sr. VP - Research, Development, Chief Medical Officer, Timothy C. Melkus/VP - Business Development, Operations, Sylvie Gregoire/Executive Chairperson/$635,965.00, Bonnie Mills/VP - Clinical Operations/$329,713.00, Herve De Lamotte Duchesne/Acting Principal Financial, Accounting Officer - Principal Financial, Accounting Officer/$337,383.00

Directors: Jean-Loup Romet-Lemonne/Dir., CEO, Timothy P. Walbert/Dir., CEO, Pres., Donald Drakeman/Dir., Sylvie Gregoire/Executive Chairperson, John P. McKearn/Dir., Michael G. Grey/Dir., Robert Beck/Dir., Jean Deleage/Dir., Edward E. Penhoet/Dir.

Financial Data: **Fiscal Year End:**12/31 **Latest Annual Data:** 12/31/2006

Year	Sales	Net Income
2006	$11,286,000	-$23,455,000
2005	$8,539,000	-$39,209,000
2004	$9,647,000	-$3,882,000

Curr. Assets:	$15,154,000	**Curr. Liab.:**	$10,636,000		
Plant, Equip.:	$1,711,000	**Total Liab.:**	$14,186,000	**Indic. Yr. Divd.:**	NA
Total Assets:	$24,382,000	**Net Worth:**	$10,196,000	**Debt/ Equity:**	0.0317

iDNA Inc

Formerly: National Auto Credit Inc

415 Madison Ave., 7th Fl., New York, NY, 10017; **PH:** 1-212-644-1400

General - Incorporation	DE	Stock - Price on:12/24/2007	$0.46
Employees	80	Stock Exchange	NA
Auditor	Grant Thornton LLP	Ticker Symbol	NA
Stk Agt	American Stock Transfer & Trust Co.	Outstanding Shares	9,950,000
Counsel	NA	E.P.S	-$0.83
DUNS No.	05-837-6724	Shareholders	NA

Business: The group's principle activity is to provide funding, receivables management and collection services in the sub-prime used auto loan market to its member dealerships who in turn provide financing for their customers who have limited access to financing through more traditional consumer lending sources. The group operates from United States.

Primary SIC and add'l.: 5521 6141

CIK No: 0001004981

Subsidiaries: ARAC, Inc., Audience Response Systems, Inc., Campus Group Companies, Inc., Illumine Entertainment, Inc, NAC, Inc., National Cinemas, Inc., OMI Business Communications, Inc., Option Technologies Interactive, LLC, ZoomLot Corporation

Owners: Robert V. Cuddihy/3.50%, Henry Y. L. Toh/2.60%, Donald Shek/0.50%, John A. Gleason/2.60%, James M. Augur/0.50%, Campus Family 2000 Trust/16.30%, James McNamara/32.40%, Insiders/39.70%

Financial Data: Fiscal Year End:01/31   **Latest Annual Data:** 1/31/2007

Year	Sales	Net Income
2007	$15,444,000	-$7,580,000
2006	$14,090,000	-$501,000
2005	$11,343,000	-$3,164,000

Curr. Assets:	$3,735,000	Curr. Liab.:	$6,334,000		
Plant, Equip.:	$2,919,000	Total Liab.:	$19,275,000	Indic. Yr. Divd.:	NA
Total Assets:	$28,847,000	Net Worth:	$9,572,000	Debt/ Equity:	5.0622

IDO Security Inc

Formerly: Medical Exchange Inc

17 State St., New York, NY, 10004; **PH:** 1-212-269-4051

General - Incorporation	NV	Stock - Price on:12/24/2007	$6.9
Employees	NA	Stock Exchange	NA
Auditor	Amisano Hanson	Ticker Symbol	NA
Stk Agt	Nevada Agency & Trust Company	Outstanding Shares	NA
Counsel	NA	E.P.S	NA
DUNS No.	NA	Shareholders	NA

Business: The groups principle activity is to provide recruiting services. The groups service area includes the research and development, engineering, marketing, sales, information technology and manufacturing industries. The group operates from United States.

Primary SIC and add'l.: 8071

CIK No: 0001301367

Officers: Jorge Wolf/CEO, Henry Shabat/COO, Michael L. Goldberg/Dir., Pres., Gil Stiss/CTO, Dir.

Directors: Irit Reiner/48/Dir., Michael L. Goldberg/Dir., Pres., John Mitola/Dir., Amos Eiran/Dir., Gil Stiss/CTO, Dir.

Owners: Yoav Hirsch/7.21%, Gil Stiss/16.35%, Zeev Bronfeld/8.81%, Melton Management Limited/6.59%, EDA Capital Corporation/8.81%, Pentium Management Ltd./5.63%, ACC Holdings Ltd./8.81%, Adi Levy/8.65%, Zegal & Ross Capital LLC/8.81%, Rolfe Investment Ltd./8.81%

Financial Data: Fiscal Year End:06/30   **Latest Annual Data:** 6/30/2006

Year	Sales	Net Income
2006	NA	-$59,000
2005	NA	-$57,000

Curr. Assets:	$9,000	Curr. Liab.:	$24,000		
Plant, Equip.:	NA	Total Liab.:	$24,000	Indic. Yr. Divd.:	NA
Total Assets:	$18,000	Net Worth:	-$5,000	Debt/ Equity:	NA

IDS Life Insurance Co

50605 Ameriprise Financial Ctr., H27/5299, Minneapolis, MN, 55474; **PH:** 1-612-678-0175

General - Incorporation	MN	Stock - Price on:12/24/2007	NA
Employees	NA	Stock Exchange	NA
Auditor	Ernst & Young LLP	Ticker Symbol	NA
Stk Agt	NA	Outstanding Shares	NA
Counsel	NA	E.P.S	NA
DUNS No.	04-952-9035	Shareholders	NA

Business: The group's principal activity is to offer deferred annuities and universal life insurance products, primarily to individuals. The group offers single premium and flexible premium deferred annuities on both the fixed and variable dollar basis. The group's insurance products include fixed and variable universal life, whole life, single premium life and term products including waiver of premium and accidental death benefits. In addition, the group also markets disability income and long-term care insurance. The group is a wholly owned subsidiary of American express financial corporation.

Primary SIC and add'l.: 6321 6311

CIK No: 0000727892

Subsidiaries: American Centurion Life Assurance Company, American Enterprise Life Insurance Company, American Partners Life Insurance Company, IDS Life Insurance Compan

IDT Corp

520 Broad St., Newark, NJ, 07102; **PH:** 1-973-438-1000; **Fax:** 1-973-482-3971; http:// www.idt.net

General - Incorporation	DE	Stock - Price on:12/24/2007	$11.36
Employees	3,000	Stock Exchange	NYSE
Auditor	Ernst & Young LLP	Ticker Symbol	IDT
Stk Agt	American Stock Transfer & Trust Co.	Outstanding Shares	82,310,000
Counsel	Morrison & Foerster LLP	E.P.S	$0.71
DUNS No.	80-903-9910	Shareholders	NA

Business: The groups principle activity is to provide communication products and services for the telecommunications industry. The group operates through four business segments namely prepaid products, consumer phone services, wholesale telecommunications services and IDT energy. The group operates from United States.

Primary SIC and add'l.: 7375 7389 4813 6719

CIK No: 0001005731

Subsidiaries: 225 Old NB Road Inc., 226 Old NB Road, Corp., 60 Park Place Associates, LLC, 60 Park Place Holding Company Inc., ADSI Acquisition Corp., Advanced Data Services, Inc., Anchor Bay Entertainment Canada, Limited, Anchor Bay Entertainment UK Limited, Beltway Acquisition Corporation, Confie Seguros, Inc., CTM Brochure Display of Puerto Rico, Inc., CTM Brochure Display, Inc., D.p.s.i. Digital Production Solutions Israel Ltd., Dan Krech Productions Inc., Dipchip Corp. 111 Subsidiaries included in the Index

Officers: James A. Courter/Vice Chmn., CEO, Marc E. Knoller/Dir., Sr. VP, Ira A. Greenstein/Dir., Pres., Joyce J. Mason/Dir., General Counsel, Exec. VP, Corp. Sec., Douglas W. Mauro/Chief Tax Officer, Mitch Silberman/Chief Accounting Officer, Controller, Yona Katz/38/Exec. VP - Business Development, Kathleen B. Timko/Exec. VP - Technology, Marc J. Oppenheimer/51/Dir., CFO, Exec. VP, Treasurer, Stephen R. Brown/52/COO, Michael Leibov/Exec. VP - Business Development, Michael Rapaport/Investor Relations Officer, Moshe Kaganoff/Exec. VP - Strategic Planning, Morris Lichtenstein/49/COO, Ely D. Tendler/Exec. VP - Telecom Legal

Directors: James A. Courter/Vice Chmn., CEO, Howard S. Jonas/52/Chmn., Ira A. Greenstein/Dir., Pres., Joyce J. Mason/Dir., General Counsel, Exec. VP, Corp. Sec., Marc J. Oppenheimer/51/Dir., CFO, Exec. VP, Treasurer, James R. Mellor/78/Dir., Judah Schorr/56/Dir., Eric Cosentino/52/Dir., Marc E. Knoller/Dir., Sr. VP

Owners: Third Avenue Management, LLC, Southeastern Asset Management, Inc., Morris Lichtenstein/1.10%, Yona Katz, Stephen R. Brown, Howard S. Jonas, Judah Schorr, Eric F. Cosentino, Insiders, Insiders, Stephen R. Brown, James A. Courter, James A. Courter/5.00%, Fairholme Capital Management, L.L.C., Howard S. Jonas (34 Owners included in Index)

Financial Data: Fiscal Year End:07/31   **Latest Annual Data:** 07/31/2007

Year	Sales	Net Income
2007	$2,012,739,000	$58,624,000
2006	$2,226,422,000	-$178,654,000
2005	$2,468,522,000	-$43,814,000

Curr. Assets:	$1,243,171,000	Curr. Liab.:	$679,812,000	P/E Ratio:	11.47
Plant, Equip.:	$292,152,000	Total Liab.:	$916,260,000	Indic. Yr. Divd.:	$0.500
Total Assets:	$1,762,839,000	Net Worth:	$803,352,000	Debt/ Equity:	0.1469

IDX Systems Corp

40 Idx Dr., Burlington, VT, 05403; **PH:** 1-802-862-1022; **Fax:** 1-802-862-6848; http:// www.idx.com; **Email:** margo_happer@idx.com

General - Incorporation	VT	Stock - Price on:12/24/2007	$39.59
Employees	319,000	Stock Exchange	NDQ
Auditor	Ernst & Young LLP	Ticker Symbol	IDXC
Stk Agt	EquiServe Trust Co N.A	Outstanding Shares	10,290,000,000
Counsel	Hale & Dorr LLP	E.P.S	$2.07
DUNS No.	02-066-6681	Shareholders	NA

Business: The group's principle activity is to provide healthcare information systems and services to healthcare delivery enterprises. The group's core business segment, providing information systems, services and connectivity for group physician practices, hospitals and integrated delivery networks, operates under the idx(R) brand name and consists of software licensing, services and hardware sales. The principal markets for this segment include physician groups, management service organizations, hospitals and integrated delivery networks primarily located in the United States. The medical transcription services segment consists of edix, a provider of medical transcription outsourcing services. The principal markets for this segment include hospitals and large physician group practices primarily located in the United States, United Kingdom and Canada.

Primary SIC and add'l.: 6324 7379 7372 7373

CIK No: 0001001185

Subsidiaries: IDX Canada Inc, IDX Information Systems Corporation, IDX Investment Corporation, IDX Systems UK Limited, IDX Transportation Corporation, PointDX Software Development (Shanghai) Limited

Financial Data: Fiscal Year End:12/31   **Latest Annual Data:** 12/31/2006

Year	Sales	Net Income
2006	$163,391,000,000	$20,829,000,000
2005	$150,242,000,000	$16,711,000,000
2004	$152,866,000,000	$16,819,000,000

Curr. Assets:	$87,456,000,000	Curr. Liab.:	$220,514,000,000	P/E Ratio:	19.13
Plant, Equip.:	$74,966,000,000	Total Liab.:	$577,347,000,000	Indic. Yr. Divd.:	$1.120
Total Assets:	$697,239,000,000	Net Worth:	$112,314,000,000	Debt/ Equity:	2.4093

IEC Electronics Corp

105 Norton St., Newark, NY, 14513; **PH:** 1-315-331-7742; **Fax:** 1-315-331-3547; http:// www.iec-electronics.com

General - Incorporation	DE	Stock - Price on:12/24/2007	$1.8
Employees	240	Stock Exchange	OTC
Auditor	Rotenberg & Co. LLP	Ticker Symbol	IECE
Stk Agt	Mellon Investor Services LLC	Outstanding Shares	8,550,000
Counsel	Boylan Brown Code Vigdor Wilson LLP	E.P.S	$0.10
DUNS No.	00-246-3305	Shareholders	NA

Business: The group's principal activity is the manufacture and marketing of printed circuit board assemblies, systems and electronic products. The group provides a range of manufacturing and management services on either a turnkey or consignment basis. The services include material procurement and control, manufacturing and test engineering support, statistical quality assurance and complete resource management. The services are primarily for computers, computer peripheral equipment, medical instrumentation, measuring devices, office equipment, telecommunication equipment, industrial photography and imaging equipment. The group provides its services to multiple divisions and product lines of many of its customers and typically manufacturers for a number of each customers successive product generations.

Primary SIC and add'l.: 3672

CIK No: 0000049728

Subsidiaries: IEC Electronicos de Mexico, S. De R.L. De C.V

Officers: Barry W. Gilbert/Chmn., CEO, Jeffrey T. Schlarbaum/VP - Sales, Marketing, Don Doody/VP - Operations, Ron Pratt/CTO, Tim Fox/Dir. - Business Development, Brian Davis/CFO, VP, Controller, Kevin Taylor/Sales Representative - New England Area, Bob Gathercole/Sales Representative - New York, Jim Piampiano/Sales Representative - New York, Matt Raio/Sales Representative - Long Island NY, New Jersey, Andrew Tobolewski/Sales Representative - Western Pennsylvania, Tom Buroojy/Sales Representative - Southern New Jersey, Eastern Pennsylvania, Delaware, Ed Mihok/Sales Representative - Virginia, Rob Craig/Sales Representative - North Carolina, Eric Zepp/Sales Representative - Louisiana (19 Officers included in Index)

Directors: Barry W. Gilbert/Chmn., CEO

Owners: Insiders/22.05%, Barry W. Gilbert/4.48%, James C. Rowe/4.79%, Carl E. Sassano, Brian H. Davis/1.26%, Justin L. Vigdor/3.06%, Eben S. Moulton/4.46%, Jerold L. Zimmerman, Jeffrey T. Schlarbaum/2.51%, Donald S. Doody/1.46%

Financial Data: Fiscal Year End:09/30   Latest Annual Data: 9/30/2006

Year	Sales	Net Income
2006	$22,620,000	$215,000
2005	$19,066,000	$285,000
2004	$27,701,000	-$828,000

Curr. Assets:	$10,429,000	Curr. Liab.:	$8,227,000	P/E Ratio:	36.00
Plant, Equip.:	$1,260,000	Total Liab.:	$8,626,000	Indic. Yr. Divd.:	NA
Total Assets:	$11,718,000	Net Worth:	$3,092,000	Debt/ Equity:	0.1817

IEH Corp

140 58th St. Ste. 8e, Brooklyn, NY, 11220; PH: 1-718-492-4448; http:// www.iehcorp.com; Email: ieh@iehcorp.com

General - Incorporation	NY	Stock- Price on:12/24/2007	$2.35
Employees	83	Stock Exchange	OTC
Auditor	Jerome Rosenberg	Ticker Symbol	IEHC
Stk Agt	Registrar & Transfer Co	Outstanding Shares	2,300,000
Counsel	Goldstein & Digioia	E.P.S.	$0.14
DUNS No.	00-136-7630	Shareholders	NA

Business: The group's principle activities include designing, developing, manufacturing and distributing electronic printed circuit connectors and interconnection devices. The products are used in providing electrical connections between electronic component assemblies. Electronic connectors enable circuit boards and electronic components to communicate with each other, via direct electrical connection. The connectors also are fundamental to modular construction of electronic assemblies enabling the disconnection and removal of circuit boards and other electronic components for testing, repair, and replacement. The group solely operates in domestic market. The group serves the commercial and military marketplace, manufacturing connectors for avionics, electronics, satellite, radar systems, test equipment, medical electronic and related industries. The group operates from United States.

Primary SIC and add'l.: 3678

CIK No: 0000050292

Officers: Michael Offerman/Chmn., CEO, Pres., Rolando Velez/Mgr. - Accounting Receivable, Paul Tzetzos/Quality Mgr., Tim Wolfe/Sales Representative - Southern California, Southern Nevada, Baja California, Mexico, Joseph Roback/Sale Representative, New York, Alice Lee/Sales Representative - Taiwan, Michael Jumper/Sales Representative - Northern California, Northern Nevada, Bruce Metcalf/Sales Representative - Maine, Vermont, New Hamphire, Massachusetts, Rhode Island, Craig Holmgren/Sales Representative - Minnesota, Western Wisconsin, North Dakota, South Dakota, Todd Schwerm/Sales Representative - Eastern Wisconsin, Robert Knoth/CFO, Controller, Treasurer, Sec., Mark Iskin/Materials Dir., David Offerman/National Sales Mgr., Bill Jette/Sales Representative - Florida, Bobbie Gentile/Sales Representative - Illinois, Indiana, Kentucky, Ohio, Michigan, Western Pennsylvania (29 Officers included in Index)

Directors: Michael Offerman/Chmn., CEO, Pres., Allen Gottlieb/67/Dir., Murray Sennet/87/Dir.

Owners: Murray Sennet/1.10%, Robert Knoth, Hummingbird Management, LLC/5.50%, Nancy Lopez/8.20%, Insiders/41.19%, Michael Offerman/40.00%

Financial Data: Fiscal Year End:03/31   Latest Annual Data: 03/30/2007

Year	Sales	Net Income
2007	$6,256,000	$201,000
2006	$7,588,000	$1,138,000
2005	$5,321,000	$166,000

Curr. Assets:	$2,476,000	Curr. Liab.:	$1,392,000	P/E Ratio:	7.34
Plant, Equip.:	$1,200,000	Total Liab.:	$1,415,000	Indic. Yr. Divd.:	NA
Total Assets:	$3,699,000	Net Worth:	$2,283,000	Debt/ Equity:	0.0004

IElement Corp

17194 Preston Rd. Ste. 102, PMB 341, Dallas, TX, 75248; PH: 1-214-254-3425; Fax: 1-888-832-9422; http:// www.ielement.com; Email: investor@ielement.com

General - Incorporation	NV	Stock- Price on:12/24/2007	$0.011
Employees	NA	Stock Exchange	OTC
Auditor	Bagell, Levine & Company, LLC	Ticker Symbol	IELM
Stk Agt	Madison Stock Transfer, Inc.	Outstanding Shares	228,260,000
Counsel	NA	E.P.S.	-$0.013
DUNS No.	NA	Shareholders	NA

Business: The groups principle activity is to provide telecommunications services. The group operates from the United States.

Primary SIC and add'l.: 7389

CIK No: 0001043105

Subsidiaries: IElement Telephone of Arizona, Inc., IElement Telephone of California, Inc., IElement Telephone of Nevada, Inc., IElement, Inc.

Officers: Ivan Zweig/35/Chmn., CEO, Interim CFO, Lance Stovall/39/Dir., COO, Alex Ponnath/40/CTO

Directors: Ivan Zweig/35/Chmn., CEO, Interim CFO, Lance Stovall/39/Dir., COO, Ken Willey/Dir.

Owners: Alex Ponnath/1.63%, Gerd Weger/6.01%, Ivan Zweig/11.54%, Insiders/13.75%, Ken Willey, Lance Stovall

Financial Data: Fiscal Year End:03/31   Latest Annual Data: 03/31/2007

Year	Sales	Net Income
2007	$3,777,000	-$2,256,000
2006	$4,550,000	-$1,426,000
2005	$1,228,000	-$417,000

Curr. Assets:	$548,000	Curr. Liab.:	$2,479,000		
Plant, Equip.:	$514,000	Total Liab.:	$2,735,000	Indic. Yr. Divd.:	NA
Total Assets:	$1,124,000	Net Worth:	-$1,611,000	Debt/ Equity:	NA

IFF Inc

521 W 57th St., New York, NY, 10019; PH: 1-212-765-5500; Fax: 1-212-708-7132; http:// www.iff.com; Email: corporate.communications@iff.com

General - Incorporation	NY	Stock- Price on:12/24/2007	$51.43
Employees	5,087	Stock Exchange	NYSE
Auditor	PricewaterhouseCoopers LLP	Ticker Symbol	IFF
Stk Agt	American Stock Transfer & Trust Co.	Outstanding Shares	89,250,000
Counsel	Fulton, Rowe, Hart & Coon	E.P.S.	$2.76
DUNS No.	00-153-4833	Shareholders	NA

Business: The groups principle activity is to create and manufacture flavors and fragrances products. The groups products include toiletries, soaps, detergents, beverages and food products. The group operates from United States.

Primary SIC and add'l.: 2087 2844 2869

CIK No: 0000051253

Subsidiaries: A. Boake, Roberts And Company (Holding), Limited, Alva Insurance Ltd., Aromatics Holdings Limited, Asian Investments, Inc., Bush Boake Allen (Chile) S.A., Bush Boake Allen (Executive Pension Trustees) Limited, Bush Boake Allen (Jamaica) Limited, Bush Boake Allen (New Zealand) Limited, Bush Boake Allen (Nominees) Limited, Bush Boake Allen (Pension Trustees) Limited, Bush Boake Allen (SA) (Proprietary) Limited, Bush Boake Allen (Thailand) Limited, Bush Boake Allen (Works Pension Trustees) Limited, Bush Boake Allen Australia Pty Ltd., Bush Boake Allen Barbados Inc. 97 Subsidiaries included in the Index

Officers: Robert M. Amen/Chmn., CEO/$2,013,452.00, Joe A. Faranda/VP, Chief Marketing Officer, Douglas J. Wetmore/CFO, Sr. VP/$1,530,920.00, Steven J. Heaslip/Sr. VP - Human Resources, Liz Gomez/Investor Relations Officer, Carol Brys/Contact - Media, Melissa Sachs/Contact - Corporate, Fragrance Communications, James P. Huether/51/Controller, Dennis M. Meany/Sr. VP, General Counsel, Sec./$1,247,318.00, Nicolas Mirzayantz/Group Pres. - Fragrances/$1,274,090.00, Hernan Vaisman/Group Pres. - Flavors, Jim Dunsdon/Sr. VP, Transition Leader/$2,513,811.00

Directors: Robert M. Amen/Chmn., CEO, Gunter Blobel/Dir., Michael J. Cook/Dir., Marcello Bottoli/Dir., Linda Buck/Dir., Burton M. Tansky/Dir., Peter A. Georgescu/Dir., Arthur C. Martinez/Dir., Henry Howell/Dir., Alexandra A. Herzan/Dir., Margaret Hayes Adame/Dir.

Owners: William D. Van Dyke/5.59%, Alexandra A. Herzan, Pauline H. Van Dyke/5.73%, Peter A. Georgescu, Henry W. Howell, Douglas J. Wetmore, Richard A. Goldstein, Arthur C. Martinez, T. Rowe Price Associates, Inc./6.96%, Margaret Hayes Adame, Nicolas Mirzayantz, Insiders/2.03%, Gnter Blobel, Dennis M. Meany, Michael J. Cook (18 Owners included in Index)

Financial Data: Fiscal Year End:12/31   Latest Annual Data: 12/31/2006

Year	Sales	Net Income
2006	$2,095,390,000	$226,500,000
2005	$1,993,393,000	$193,066,000
2004	$2,033,653,000	$196,071,000

Curr. Assets:	$1,079,803,000	Curr. Liab.:	$446,771,000	P/E Ratio:	19.86
Plant, Equip.:	$495,124,000	Total Liab.:	$1,573,736,000	Indic. Yr. Divd.:	$0.920
Total Assets:	$2,478,904,000	Net Worth:	$905,168,000	Debt/ Equity:	0.8511

IFSA Strongman Inc

Formerly: Synerteck Inc
28-32 Wellington Rd., London, NW8 9SP; PH: 44-20-7060-4372; http:// www.synerteck.com

General - Incorporation	DE	Stock- Price on:12/24/2007	NA
Employees	NA	Stock Exchange	NA
Auditor	Bouwhuis, Morrill & Co LLC	Ticker Symbol	NA
Stk Agt	Colonial Stock Transfer Co Inc	Outstanding Shares	NA
Counsel	NA	E.P.S.	NA
DUNS No.	NA	Shareholders	NA

Business: The groups principle activity is to provide IT solutions and business services. The groups services include marketing technology, flash management, GUI design, web design, network design and hosting. The group operates from United States.

Primary SIC and add'l.: 7373

CIK No: 0001289630

Subsidiaries: IFSA Strongman, Inc

Financial Data: Fiscal Year End:12/31   Latest Annual Data: 12/31/2005

Year	Sales	Net Income
2005	$138,000	-$404,000
2004	$207,000	-$64,000

Curr. Assets:	$448,000	Curr. Liab.:	$377,000		
Plant, Equip.:	$90,000	Total Liab.:	$377,000	Indic. Yr. Divd.:	NA
Total Assets:	$1,864,000	Net Worth:	$1,486,000	Debt/ Equity:	NA

iGATE Corp

1000 Commerce Dr., Ste. 500, Pittsburgh, PA, 15275; PH: 1-412-787-2100; Fax: 1-412-494-9272; http:// www.igatecorp.com; Email: investor@igate.com

General - Incorporation	PA	Stock- Price on:12/24/2007	$8.19
Employees	6,900	Stock Exchange	NDQ
Auditor	PricewaterhouseCoopers LLP	Ticker Symbol	IGTE
Stk Agt	Mellon Investor Services LLC	Outstanding Shares	53,140,000
Counsel	NA	E.P.S.	$0.32
DUNS No.	18-175-9119	Shareholders	NA

Business: The group's principal activities are to provide information technology and offshore outsourcing services to large and medium-sized organizations. The group operates in three segments: igate solutions, igate professional services and igate corporate. Igate solutions segment provides offshore outsourcing of it services, it systems maintenance, applications implementation and related custom development of applications such as oracle, sap and peoplesoft. Igate professional services segment provides client-managed and supervised it staffing service offerings including enterprise resource package implementation and integration, application support services and client directed software design and customization. Igate corporate segment provides recruiting, placement services and conduct clinical trials. During the year the group acquired quintant inc, diagnosearch, ideaspace solutions ltd & certain businesses of it&t technology services ltd.

Primary SIC and add'l.: 7361 7372 7371

CIK No: 0001024732

Subsidiaries: Air2Web, Aqua Regia Tech. Ltd., Bluewater Information Convergence Inc. L.P., Brainbench, Inc., Chen& McGinley LLC, Diagno Search Ltd., Direct Resources Scotland, Ltd., eJiva, Inc., Escend Technologies, Inc., Global Financial Services of Nevada, Highgate Venture Management, LLC, Highgate Venture Partners I, L.P., Highgate Ventures I, L.P., iGATE Capital Management, Inc., iGATE Clinical Research International Inc. 48 Subsidiaries included in the Index

Officers: Sunil Wadhwani/Co - Founder, Co - Chmn., CEO, Phaneesh Murthy/CEO - Igate Global Solutions, Gordon J. Garrett/69/CEO - Interloci Management Inc, Ashok Trivedi/Co - Chmn., Pres., Michel Berty/Pres. - PAC US, Michael Zugay/CFO, Sr. VP, Edward Yourdon/Independent Software Engineering Consultant

Directors: Sunil Wadhwani/Co - Founder, Co - Chmn., CEO, Ashok Trivedi/Co - Chmn., Pres., Goran Lindahl/Dir.

Owners: Ed Yourdon, Goran Lindahl, Michel Berty, Michael Zugay, Phaneesh Murthy, Columbia Wanger Asset Management, L.P./11.30%, Ashok Trivedi/28.80%, Sunil Wadhwani/28.80%, Gordon J. Garrett, Insiders/59.90%, Steven Shangold

Financial Data: Fiscal Year End:12/31   Latest Annual Data: 12/31/2006

Year	Sales	Net Income
2006	$283,588,000	$8,704,000
2005	$275,992,000	$6,969,000
2004	$264,585,000	-$18,211,000

Curr. Assets:	$146,549,000	Curr. Liab.:	$33,162,000		
Plant, Equip.:	$29,867,000	Total Liab.:	$43,051,000	Indic. Yr. Divd.:	NA
Total Assets:	$190,774,000	Net Worth:	$133,351,000	Debt/ Equity:	NA

Igene Biotechnology Inc

9110 Red Branch Rd., Columbia, MD, 21045; **PH:** 1-410-997-2599; **Fax:** 1-410-730-0540; http:// www.igene.com

General - Incorporation	MD	Stock - Price on:12/24/2007	$0.04
Employees	12	Stock Exchange	OTC
Auditor	Berenson LLP	Ticker Symbol	IGNE
Stk Agt	American Stock Transfer & Trust Co.	Outstanding Shares	109,340,000
Counsel	NA	E.P.S.	-$0.007
DUNS No.	01-163-4268	Shareholders	NA

Business: The group's principal activity is to develop, manufacture and market industrial microbiology and related biotechnology products. Astaxin(R) is the main product of the group. Astaxin is a natural source of astaxanthin, a pigment which imparts the characteristic red color to the flesh of salmon, trout, prawns and certain other kind of fish and shellfish. The group's products are value added specialty biochemical products derived from abundant, inexpensive and renewable agricultural residues and wastes through fermentation, physical and chemical separation and related chemical and biochemical engineering technologies.

Primary SIC and add'l.: 2836 2048

CIK No: 0000793160

Subsidiaries: Igene Chile Comercial, Ltda, Igene Norway

Officers: Edward J. Weisberger/CFO, Patrick F. Monahan/Dir., VP, Dir. - Manufacturing, Sec., Claudio Gesche Montandon/Regional Mgr., Jorge Torres/Technical Support, Malin Nilsson/Operating, Logistics Mgr., Stephen F. Hiu/Dir., Pres., CTO, Dir. - Research, Development, Christine L. Fitch/Office Mgr., Robert Hodson/VP - Global Sales, Marketing

Directors: Michael G. Kimelman/Chmn., Thomas L. Kempner/Vice Chmn., Stephen F. Hiu/Dir., Pres., CTO, Dir. - Research, Development, Patrick F. Monahan/Dir., VP, Dir. - Manufacturing, Sec., Sidney R. Knafel/Dir.

Owners: Patrick F. Monahan, Fermic, Joseph C. Abeles, Sidney R. Knafel, Stephen F. Hiu, Insiders, Thomas L. Kempner, Edward J. Weisberger, Fraydun Manocherian, Michael G. Kimelman

Financial Data: Fiscal Year End:12/31   Latest Annual Data: 12/31/2006

Year	Sales	Net Income
2006	NA	-$1,156,000
2005	NA	-$1,415,000
2004	NA	-$1,310,000

Curr. Assets:	$36,000	Curr. Liab.:	$962,000		
Plant, Equip.:	$34,000	Total Liab.:	$16,274,000	Indic. Yr. Divd.:	NA
Total Assets:	$75,000	Net Worth:	-$16,419,000	Debt/ Equity:	NA

IGI Inc

105 Lincoln Ave., Buena, NJ, 08310; **PH:** 1-856-697-1441; **Fax:** 1-856-697-2259; http:// www.askigi.com

General - Incorporation	DE	Stock - Price on:12/24/2007	$0.7093
Employees	19	Stock Exchange	AMEX
Auditor	Amper, Politziner & Mattia P.C	Ticker Symbol	IG
Stk Agt	State Street Bank and Trust Co	Outstanding Shares	14,610,000
Counsel	NA	E.P.S.	-$0.106
DUNS No.	01-103-6910	Shareholders	NA

Business: The group's principal activities are to manufacture and market cosmetics and skin care products. The group's manufacturing operations include bulk manufacturing and testing of cosmetics, dermatologics, emulsions and shampoos. It's consumer products development efforts are directed towards novasome(R) encapsulation to improve performance and efficacy of pesticides, specialty and other chemicals, biocides, cosmetics, consumer products, flavors and dermatologic products. The group markets its skin care products through collaborative arrangements with major cosmetic and consumer products companies.

Primary SIC and add'l.: 2844

CIK No: 0000352998

Subsidiaries: IGI, Inc., Novavax, Inc

Officers: Rajiv Mathur/Dir., CEO, Pres., Carlene Lloyd/VP - Finance/$104,618.70, Nadya Lawrence/VP - Operations/$163,864.60

Directors: Rajiv Mathur/Dir., CEO, Pres., Frank Gerardi/Chmn., Stephen J. Morris/Dir., Terrence Odonnell/Dir., Jane E. Hager/Dir.

Owners: Sunil K. Pai/0.10%, Carlene Lloyd/0.50%, Terence O'Donnell/2.30%, Nadya Lawrence/1.80%, Pharmachem Laboratories, Inc./10.30%, Jane E. Hager/14.90%, Insiders/36.90%, Rajiv Mathur/0.10%

Financial Data: Fiscal Year End:12/31   Latest Annual Data: 12/31/2006

Year	Sales	Net Income
2006	$2,620,000	-$1,667,000
2005	$2,867,000	-$1,298,000
2004	$3,558,000	-$892,000

Curr. Assets:	$1,837,000	Curr. Liab.:	$2,891,000		
Plant, Equip.:	$2,396,000	Total Liab.:	$2,950,000	Indic. Yr. Divd.:	NA
Total Assets:	$5,143,000	Net Worth:	$2,193,000	Debt/ Equity:	NA

IGIA Inc

16 E 40th St., 12th Fl., New York, NY, 10016; **PH:** 1-212-575-0500; **Fax:** 1-212-354-5323; http:// www.igia.com

General - Incorporation	DE	Stock - Price on:12/24/2007	NA
Employees	30	Stock Exchange	OTC
Auditor	Russell Bedford Stefanou Mirchandani	Ticker Symbol	IGAI
Stk Agt	Transfer & Trust Co	Outstanding Shares	NA
Counsel	NA	E.P.S.	$0.00
DUNS No.	NA	Shareholders	NA

Business: The group's principal activity is to own, operate and manage talent management companies through its subsidiaries. Its talent management business is to represent talent including professional fashion models, commercial actors and theatrical actors. The talent management business of the group is based upon obtaining talent and matching talent to clientele. The group also provides hair, makeup and styling services for models, actors, actresses and celebrities. These services not only add value to the group's existing clients but also provide the group with entry into the celebrity/entertainment field. The clients of the group mainly include magazine publishing houses, designers, national retailers and catalogs including elle magazine, talbot's, nordstroms, banana republic and macy's. The group operates solely in the domestic market. On 21-Jun-2004, the group acquired tactica international inc.

Primary SIC and add'l.: 7389 6719 7363

CIK No: 0000919603

Subsidiaries: Kleenfast Inc., Shopflash, Inc., Tactica International Inc.

Owners: Avi Sivan/50.00%, Yehiel Ben-Harush, Prem Ramchandani/3.13%, Insiders/5.66%, Avi Sivan/2.50%, Prem Ramchandani/50.00%

Financial Data: Fiscal Year End:02/28   Latest Annual Data: 02/28/2007

Year	Sales	Net Income
2007	$6,020,000	$669,000
2006	$25,532,000	-$17,159,000
2005	$11,324,000	-$16,197,000

Curr. Assets:	$187,000	Curr. Liab.:	$29,960,000		
Plant, Equip.:	$115,000	Total Liab.:	$30,180,000	Indic. Yr. Divd.:	NA
Total Assets:	$410,000	Net Worth:	-$29,769,000	Debt/ Equity:	NA

Ignis Petroleum Group Inc

7160 Dallas Pkwy Ste. 380, Plano, TX, 75201; **PH:** 1-972-526-5250; **Fax:** 1-972-526-5251; http:// www.ignispetroleum.com

General - Incorporation	NV	Stock - Price on:12/24/2007	$0.095
Employees	3	Stock Exchange	OTC
Auditor	Hein & Assoc., LLP	Ticker Symbol	IGPG
Stk Agt	Empire Stock Transfer Inc.	Outstanding Shares	52,090,000
Counsel	NA	E.P.S.	-$0.03
DUNS No.	NA	Shareholders	NA

Business: The groups principle activities include exploring, developing, and producing crude oil and natural gas. In May 2005, the group acquired Sheer Ventures, Inc. The group operates from the United States.

Primary SIC and add'l.: 1311

CIK No: 0001296524

Subsidiaries: Ignis Petroleum Corporation

Officers: Michael P. Piazza/CEO, Pres., Shawn L. Clift/CFO, Joseph Gittelman/Exploration Advisor, Alexander Kulpecz/Executive Advisor, Frederick C. Stein/Operations Advisor, Eric Hanlon/Adviser, Mergers, Acquisitions, Partnerships

Directors: Geoffrey Lowndes Evett/Chmn., Roger A. Leopard/Dir.

Owners: Roger A. Leopard, Newton Properties, Inc/6.20%, Geoffrey Evett, Shawn Clift, Petrofinanz GMBH/11.70%, Philipp Buschmann/3.50%, Insiders/5.30%

Financial Data: Fiscal Year End:06/30   Latest Annual Data: 06/30/2007

Year	Sales	Net Income
2007	$1,410,000	$344,000
2006	$553,000	-$10,643,000
2005	NA	-$276,000

Curr. Assets:	$607,000	Curr. Liab.:	$2,813,000		
Plant, Equip.:	$316,000	Total Liab.:	$3,861,000	Indic. Yr. Divd.:	NA
Total Assets:	$1,576,000	Net Worth:	-$2,285,000	Debt/ Equity:	NA

IHOP Corp

450 N Brand Blvd., Glendale, CA, 91203; **PH:** 1-818-240-6055; **Fax:** 1-818-637-4730; http:// www.ihop.com

General - Incorporation	DE	Stock - Price on:12/24/2007	$54.59
Employees	267	Stock Exchange	NYSE
Auditor	Ernst & Young LLP	Ticker Symbol	IHP
Stk Agt	Mellon Investor Services LLC	Outstanding Shares	17,430,000
Counsel	NA	E.P.S.	$2.63
DUNS No.	03-086-5711	Shareholders	NA

Business: The group's principal activity is the development, operation and franchise of international house of pancakes restaurants primarily in the United States. At 31-Dec-2003, the group had 1,165 restaurants. Franchisees operated 991 of these restaurants, area licensees operated 130 restaurants and the group operated 44 restaurants. The restaurants feature table service and moderately priced, quality food and beverage items in an attractive and comfortable atmosphere. Although the restaurants are known for their pancakes, omelets and other breakfast specialties, they also offer lunch, dinner and snack items. They are open throughout the day and evening hours. Some operate 24 hours a day. The restaurants are located in 48 states and Canada. Trademarks and service marks include international house of pancakes, ihop and variations of each, as well as the home of the never empty coffee pot, rooty tooty fresh 'n fruity and harvest grain 'n nut.

Primary SIC and add'l.: 5812

CIK No: 0000049754

Subsidiaries: IHOP, restaurants, International House of Pancakes

Officers: Julia A. Stewart/36/Chmn., CEO/$6,013,073.00, Mark D. Weisberger/VP - Legal, Sec., General Counsel/$978,000.00, Patrick J. Piccininno/VP - Information Technology, Thomas G. Conforti/CFO/$868,614.00, Richard C. Celio/VP - Franchise, Development/$726,095.00, Carolyn P. Okeefe/Chief Marketing Officer, Dennis R. Farrow/COO/$813,692.00, Dustin Dixon/VP - Product, Quality Assurance, Procurement, Jim Peros/VP - Operations Services

Directors: Julia A. Stewart/36/Chmn., CEO, Larry Alan Kay/Dir., Patrick W. Rose/Dir., Michael S. Gordon/Dir., Gilbert T. Ray/Dir., Frank Edelstein/Dir., Caroline W. Nahas/Dir., Richard J. Dahl/Dir., Frederick H. Christie/Dir.

Owners: Mark D. Weisberger, Third Point LLC/7.20%, Richard J. Dahl, Dennis R. Farrow, MSD Capital, L.P./12.00%, Caroline W. Nahas, Neuberger Berman,Inc./8.80%, Richard C. Celio, Insiders/3.40%, Frederick H. Christie, Gilbert T. Ray, Michael S. Gordon, Julia A. Stewart/1.00%, Patrick W. Rose, Frank Edelstein *(19 Owners included in Index)*

Financial Data: *Fiscal Year End:*12/31 *Latest Annual Data:* 12/31/2006

Year	Sales	Net Income
2006	$349,560,000	$44,553,000
2005	$348,023,000	$43,937,000
2004	$359,002,000	$33,421,000

Curr. Assets:	$78,393,000	**Curr. Liab.:**	$64,105,000	**P/E Ratio:**	22.94
Plant, Equip.:	$309,737,000	**Total Liab.:**	$479,657,000	**Indic. Yr. Divd.:**	$1.000
Total Assets:	$768,870,000	**Net Worth:**	$289,213,000	**Debt/ Equity:**	1.2948

IHS Inc

15 Inverness Way E, Englewood, CO, 80112; ***PH:*** 1-303-790-0600; ***Fax:*** 1-303-754-3940; ***http://*** www.ihs.com; ***Email:*** investor_relations@ihs.com

General		**Stock**	
Incorporation	DE	Price on:12/24/2007	$45.9
Employees	2,500	Stock Exchange	NYSE
Auditor	Ernst & Young LLP	Ticker Symbol	IHS
Stk Agt	Computershare Trust Co	Outstanding Shares	58,580,000
Counsel	NA	E.P.S	$1.06
DUNS No.	NA	Shareholders	NA

Business: The groups principle activity is to provide critical technical information, decision-support tools and related services. The group operates through two segments namely, critical information and decision-support tools. In the year 2006, the group acquired Canadian Hydrodynamics Ltd., GeoPLUS and Construction Research Communications Limited. The group operates from the United States.

Primary SIC and add'l.: 7379 7375 4899 7375 7379 4899 7370 7389 7389

CIK No: 0001316360

Subsidiaries: DOREV,Inc., Dwights Acquisition Corp., IHS Energy Canada Ltd., IHS Energy Group Inc., IHS Group Holdings Limited., Information Handling Services Group Inc., Information Handling Services Inc., Petroconsultants SA, Petroleum Information/Dwights LLC., PID Acquisition Corp., Technical Indexes Limited.

Officers: Jerre L. Stead/Chmn., CEO, Daniel Yergin/Cera Chmn., Exec. VP - IHS, Karen Stolz/Global VP, Mark Kelly/Sr. VP - Finance, Mark Rose/Sr. VP, Chris Jones/Sr. VP - IHS Canadian Operations, Patricia F. Wonderley/VP, Philip H. Stark/VP, Charles Lucas-Clements/VP, MD Energy Consulting, Michael Sullivan/CFO, Exec. VP, Thomas Littman/Sr. VP - Technical Publishing, Andrew Sadler-Smith/Sr. VP - Europe, Middle East, Africa, EMEA, Paul Evenson/Sr. VP - Parts, Solutions, Wain Beard/Sr. VP - Americas, Asia Pacific, Engineering Segment, Todd Hyatt/Sr. VP - Finance, Engineering Segment *(27 Officers included in Index)*

Directors: Jerre L. Stead/Chmn., CEO, Daniel Yergin/Cera Chmn., Exec. VP - IHS, Christoph V. Grolman/Dir., Steven A. Denning/Dir., Ruann Ernst/Dir., Michael Klein/Dir., Richard W. Roedel/Dir., Michael V. Staudt/Dir., Michael C. Armstrong/Dir., Roger Holtback/Dir., Balakrishnan Iyer/Dir.

Owners: Michael J. Sullivan, Daniel Yergin, TBG Holdings N.V./20.60%, Richard W. Roedel, Urvanos Investments Limited/2.10%, Urvanos Investments Limited/100.00%, Entities affiliated with General Atlantic LLC/10.50%, Rowe T. Price/5.80%, Chares Picasso, Rohinton Mobed, Roger Holtback, Wellington Management/5.30%, Balakrishnan S. Iyer, Ruann F. Ernst, Michael v. Staudt *(22 Owners included in Index)*

Financial Data: *Fiscal Year End:*11/30 *Latest Annual Data:* 11/30/2006

Year	Sales	Net Income
2006	$550,770,000	$56,345,000
2005	$476,117,000	$41,797,000
2004	$393,969,000	$61,314,000

Curr. Assets:	$380,922,000	**Curr. Liab.:**	$338,471,000		
Plant, Equip.:	$53,096,000	**Total Liab.:**	$379,110,000	**Indic. Yr. Divd.:**	NA
Total Assets:	$944,301,000	**Net Worth:**	$565,191,000	**Debt/ Equity:**	NA

II-VI Inc

375 Saxonburg Blvd., Saxonburg, PA, 16056; ***PH:*** 1-724-352-4455; ***Fax:*** 1-724-352-5284; ***http://*** www.ii-vi.com; ***Email:*** info@ii-vi.com

General		**Stock**	
Incorporation	PA	Price on:12/24/2007	$27.19
Employees	1,690	Stock Exchange	NDQ
Auditor	Deloitte & Touche LLP	Ticker Symbol	IIVI
Stk Agt	American Stock Transfer & Trust Co.	Outstanding Shares	29,550,000
Counsel	NA	E.P.S	$1.32
DUNS No.	NA	Shareholders	NA

Business: The groups principle activities include developing, manufacturing and marketing technology materials and derivative precision components and products. The products of the group include military infrared optics, solid-state radiation sensors, silicon carbide substrates and thermoelectric coolers. Customers served by the group include high power industrial, medical and military laser systems. The group operates through four segments namely infrared optics, near-infrared optics, military infrared optics and compound semiconductor group. Specific customers of the group include Rofin-Sinar Technologies, Inc., Trumpf, Inc and John Deere and Caterpillar, Inc. The group operates from the United States, China, Germany, Japan and the United Kingdom. The group's quarterly revenue for September 2007 was 72.67 millions of USD.

Primary SIC and add'l.: 3679 3559 3674 3661 2851

CIK No: 0000820318

Subsidiaries: Exotic Electro-Optics, Inc., II-VI Belgium N.V., II-VI Delaware, Incorporated, II-VI Deutschland GmbH, II-VI Deutschland Holdings GmbH, II-VI Holdings B.V., II-VI International Pte., Ltd., II-VI Japan Incorporated, II-VI LOT Suisse S.a.r.l. (75%), II-VI Optics (Suzhou) Co. Ltd., II-VI Singapore Pte., Ltd., II-VI Technologies (Beijing), Co., Ltd., II-VI Trading (Suzhou) Co. Ltd., II-VI U.K. Limited, II-VI Vietnam Co. Ltd. 20 Subsidiaries included in the Index

Officers: Francis J. Kramer/59/Dir., COO, CEO, Pres./$1,353,575.00, Craig A. Creaturo/CFO, Treasurer/$538,401.00, Herman E. Reedy/Exec. VP - Infrared Optics/$518,916.00, Vincent D. Mattera/VP - Compound Semiconductor Group/$635,802.00, Robert D. German/Sec.

Directors: Francis J. Kramer/59/Dir., COO, CEO, Pres., Carl J. Johnson/66/Chmn., Joseph J. Corasanti/44/Dir., Thomas E. Mistler/66/Dir., Duncan A.J. Morrison/71/Dir., Peter W. Sognefest/67/Dir., Marc Y.E. Pelaez/62/Dir., Wendy F. Dicicco/41/Dir.

Owners: Insiders/19.20%, CARL J. JOHNSON/13.80%, COLUMBIA WANGER ASSET MANAGEMENT, L.P/8.60%, MARC Y.E. PELAEZ, HERMAN E. REEDY, PETER W. SOGNEFEST, CRAIG A. CREATURO, VINCENT D. MATTERA, JOSEPH J. CORASANTI, FRANCIS J. KRAMER/1.30%, DUNCAN A.J. MORRISON, JAMES MARTINELLI, THOMAS E. MISTLER/3.10%, WENDY F. DICICCO

Financial Data: *Fiscal Year End:*06/30 *Latest Annual Data:* 06/30/2007

Year	Sales	Net Income
2007	$263,195,000	$37,966,000
2006	$232,525,000	$10,794,000
2005	$194,040,000	$24,843,000

Curr. Assets:	$127,633,000	**Curr. Liab.:**	$45,035,000	**P/E Ratio:**	45.32
Plant, Equip.:	$77,713,000	**Total Liab.:**	$79,705,000	**Indic. Yr. Divd.:**	NA
Total Assets:	$250,296,000	**Net Worth:**	$170,591,000	**Debt/ Equity:**	0.0572

Ikanos Communications Inc

47669 Fremont Blvd., Fremont, CA, 94538; ***PH:*** 1-510-438-5349; ***Fax:*** 1-510-438-6245; ***http://*** www.ikanos.com; ***Email:*** sales@ikanos.com

General		**Stock**	
Incorporation	CA	Price on:12/24/2007	$7.19
Employees	279	Stock Exchange	NDQ
Auditor	PricewaterhouseCoopers LLP	Ticker Symbol	IKAN
Stk Agt	American Stock Transfer & Trust Co.	Outstanding Shares	28,360,000
Counsel	NA	E.P.S	-$1.59
DUNS No.	NA	Shareholders	NA

Business: The groups principle activity is to provide silicon and software. The groups services include high definition television, broadcast television, interactive television and streaming video and audio. The products of the group include VDSLx Physical Layer and ADSL2+ PHY. The group products sold under the trade names SmartLeap(TM) and CleverConnect(TM) Eagle(R) and Fusiv(R). Customers served by the group include original design manufacturers and contract manufacturers In August 2006, the group acquired Doradus Technologies, Inc. Specific customers of the group include Sumitomo Electric Industries, Ltd., Innomedia, Inc., Sagem and Woojyun Systec Co., Ltd. The group operates from Japan, France, Korea and Other.

Primary SIC and add'l.: 3674 3674 3661 3661

CIK No: 0001219210

Subsidiaries: Ikanos Communications (India) Private, Ltd, Ikanos Communications (Singapore) Private Limited, Ikanos Communications Europe SARL, Ikanos Communications GmbH, Ikanos Communications International, Inc., Ikanos Communications Japan KK

Officers: Daniel K. Atler/48/CEO, Pres., Michael Ricci/Dir., CEO, Pres., Yehoshua Rom/56/VP - Operations, Shekhar Khandekar/VP - Operations, Noah Mesel/VP, General Counsel, Sergio Henrique Abramoff/Sales Representative - Brazil, Paul Dietz/Sales Representative - Canada, Cory J. Sindelar/CFO, Rusty Counts/Sales Representative, John Groff/Sales Representative, Don Dabney/Sales Representative, Ken Storck/Sales Representative - Hoffman Estates, IL, Tammy Millsap/Sales Representative - Cedar Rapids, IA, John Eckart/Sales Representative - Overland Park, KS, Mike Hoekstra/Sales Representative - Durham, NC *(22 Officers included in Index)*

Directors: Michael Ricci/Dir., CEO, Pres., G. Venkatesh/Chmn., Paul Hansen/Dir., Danial Faizullabhoy/Dir., Michael Goguen/Dir., Michael Gulett/Dir.

Owners: David J. Greene and Company, LLC/5.10%, Rouben Toumani, Entities affiliated with Sequoia Capital/10.80%, Yehoshua Rom, Insiders/12.90%, Dean Westman, Derek Obata, Rajesh Vashist/1.40%, Gopal Venkatesh, Daniel K. Atler, Paul Hansen, Nick Shamlou, Michael Gulett, Michael L. Goguen/10.20%, Danial Faizullabhoy *(17 Owners included in Index)*

Financial Data: *Fiscal Year End:*12/31 *Latest Annual Data:* 12/31/2006

Year	Sales	Net Income
2006	$134,685,000	-$22,799,000
2005	$85,071,000	$2,742,000
2004	$66,676,000	-$8,464,000

Curr. Assets:	$140,665,000	**Curr. Liab.:**	$31,980,000		
Plant, Equip.:	$18,073,000	**Total Liab.:**	$32,967,000	**Indic. Yr. Divd.:**	NA
Total Assets:	$175,857,000	**Net Worth:**	$142,890,000	**Debt/ Equity:**	0.0056

IKON Office Solutions Inc

70 Valley Stream Pkwy., Malvern, PA, 19355; ***PH:*** 1-610-296-8000; ***Fax:*** 1-610-408-7025; ***http://*** www.ikon.com

General		**Stock**	
Incorporation	OH	Price on:12/24/2007	$14.89
Employees	25,000	Stock Exchange	NYSE
Auditor	PricewaterhouseCoopers LLP	Ticker Symbol	IKN
Stk Agt	National City Bank	Outstanding Shares	125,180,000
Counsel	NA	E.P.S	$0.91
DUNS No.	NA	Shareholders	NA

Business: The groups principle activity is to provide integrated document management systems and solutions. The group operates through two segments namely, IKON North America and IKON Europe. The group operates from the North America, the United Kingdom, Germany and Canada. The group's quarterly revenue for September 2007 was 1,064.71 millions of USD.

Primary SIC and add'l.: 5963 5112 5734 5044

CIK No: 0000003370

Subsidiaries: IKON Baja, S.A. de C.V., IKON Capital PLC, IKON Document Services Limited (Ireland), IKON Leasing GmbH, IKON Office Solutions (Holdings) France S.A.S. (IOSHF), IKON Office Solutions A/S (Denmark) (IOSD), IKON Office Solutions AB, IKON Office Solutions Dublin Limited, IKON Office Solutions Europe PLC (IOSE), IKON Office Solutions France S.A.S., IKON Office Solutions GmbH Hamburg, IKON Office Solutions GmbH Leipzig, IKON Office Solutions Group PLC (IOSG), IKON Office Solutions Holding GmbH (IOSH), IKON Office Solutions Italia S.r.l. 24 Subsidiaries included in the Index

Officers: Matthew J. Espe/Chmn., CEO, Pres., Brian D. Edwards/Sr. VP - US Sales, Services, Mark A. Hershey/Sr. VP, General Counsel, Sec., Jeffrey W. Hickling/Sr. VP - Operations, David Mills/VP - Ikon Europe, Dan Murphy/VP - Global Strategy, Communications, Richard Obetz/VP, Treasurer, Tracey Rothenberger/CIO, Sr. VP, Beth B. Sexton/Sr. VP - Human Resources, Theodore E. Strand/VP, Controller, Robert F. Woods/CFO, Sr. VP, Henry Miller/Investor Relations Officer, Wendy Pinckney/Contact - Media Relations

Directors: Matthew J. Espe/Chmn., CEO, Pres., Philip E. Cushing/Dir., Thomas R. Gibson/Dir., Richard A. Jalkut/Dir., Arthur E. Johnson/Dir., Kurt M. Landgraf/Dir., Gerald Luterman/Dir., William E. McCracken/Dir., William L. Meddaugh/Dir., Anthony P. Terracciano/Dir., Hellene S. Runtagh/59/Dir.

Financial Data: Fiscal Year End:09/30　Latest Annual Data: 9/30/2006

Year	Sales	Net Income
2006	$4,228,249,000	$106,202,000
2005	$4,377,305,000	$60,666,000
2004	$4,613,551,000	$83,694,000

Curr. Assets:	$1,379,574,000	Curr. Liab.:	$757,700,000		
Plant, Equip.:	$227,701,000	Total Liab.:	$1,545,566,000	Indic. Yr. Divd.:	$0.160
Total Assets:	$3,231,699,000	Net Worth:	$1,686,133,000	Debt/ Equity:	0.3772

Ikona Gear International Inc

101 Convention Ctr. Dr., Las Vegas, NV, 89109; **PH:** 1-604-523-5500; **http://** www.ikona.ca; **Email:** info@ikona.ca

General - Incorporation	NV	Stock- Price on:12/24/2007	$0.4
Employees	NA	Stock Exchange	OTC
Auditor	Dohan and Company CPAs, P.A.	Ticker Symbol	IKGI
Stk Agt	Signature Stock Transfer, Inc.	Outstanding Shares	NA
Counsel	NA	E.P.S	NA
DUNS No.	NA	Shareholders	NA

Business: The groups principle activity is to commercialize proprietary patented gearing technology. The group operates from the United States and Canada. The group's quartely revenue for Aug '07 was 0.59 millions of USD.

Primary SIC and add'l.: 3541

CIK No: 0001130809

Subsidiaries: Ikona Gear USA, Inc., Ikona Industries Corporation

Officers: Laith Nosh/Dir., CEO, Pres., Interim CFO, Joe Vosburgh/Dir., Exec. VP, George Stefan/COO, Sasha Tesic/Chief Engineer, Scott Rose/Ikona In, House Investor Relations, Marty Tullio/Ikona Institutional Investor Relations, Silvia Minka/Accounting Controller

Directors: Laith Nosh/Dir., CEO, Pres., Interim CFO, Joe Vosburgh/Dir., Exec. VP, Brendan J. Burns/45/Dir.

Owners: Brendan Burns/0.78%, Joe Vosburgh/1.22%, George Stefan/3.25%, Nasser M. Al-Jarallah/20.44%, Laith Nosh/15.59%, Insiders/24.09%, Sasha Tesic/3.25%

Financial Data: Fiscal Year End:08/31　Latest Annual Data: 08/31/2007

Year	Sales	Net Income
2007	$1,042,000	-$4,128,000
2006	$464,000	-$1,824,000
2005	$16,000	-$1,691,000

Curr. Assets:	$575,000	Curr. Liab.:	$1,240,000		
Plant, Equip.:	$124,000	Total Liab.:	$1,251,000	Indic. Yr. Divd.:	NA
Total Assets:	$972,000	Net Worth:	-$279,000	Debt/ Equity:	NA

Ikonics Corp

4832 Grand Ave., Duluth, MN, 55807; **PH:** 1-218-628-2217; **Fax:** 1-218-628-3245; **http://** www.ikonics.com; **Email:** info@ikonics.com

General - Incorporation	MN	Stock- Price on:12/24/2007	$9.6
Employees	70	Stock Exchange	NDQ
Auditor	McGladrey & Pullen LLP	Ticker Symbol	IKNX
Stk Agt	Wells Fargo Shareowner Services	Outstanding Shares	2,020,000
Counsel	Hanft Fride	E.P.S	$0.57
DUNS No.	NA	Shareholders	NA

Business: The group's principal activity is to develop, manufacture and market light sensitive liquid coatings and light sensitive films for commercial and industrial applications. It also markets ancillary chemicals and equipment to provide a full line of products and services to its customers. The products serve the screen printing and decorative sand blasting markets. The screen printing products are used by screen printers to create stencil images. The sand blasting products are used by consumers to create architectural glass, art pieces and awards. The group's products are used in textiles, billboards, electronics, glassware, fine China and many other industrial and commercial applications. The products of the group are films and emulsions. The products are marketed in the United States, western Europe, Latin America, Asia and other parts of the world.

Primary SIC and add'l.: 2869 3861

CIK No: 0001083301

Officers: William C. Ulland/Chmn., CEO, Pres./$212,489.00, Claude Piguet/Exec. VP/$134,309.00, Toshifumi Komatsu/VP - Technology/$113,880.00, Robert D. Banks/VP - International/$113,880.00, Parnell Thill/VP - Marketing, Jon Gerlach/CFO, VP - Finance/$114,930.00

Directors: William C. Ulland/Chmn., CEO, Pres., Charles H. Andresen/Dir., David O. Harris/Dir., Rondi Erickson/Dir., Leigh H. Severance/Dir., Gerald W. Simonson/Dir.

Owners: Charles H. Andresen/1.30%, Jon Gerlach, Rondi Erickson, William C. Ulland/11.57%, Toshifumi Komatsu, Gerald W. Simonson/5.59%, Insiders/33.66%, Claude P. Piguet/1.07%, Leigh Severance/8.66%, Joseph R. Nerges/10.27%, David O. Harris/4.43%, Robert D. Banks

Financial Data: Fiscal Year End:12/31　Latest Annual Data: 12/31/2006

Year	Sales	Net Income
2006	$14,889,000	$1,124,000
2005	$13,971,000	$908,000
2004	$13,682,000	$758,000

Curr. Assets:	$8,229,000	Curr. Liab.:	$879,000	P/E Ratio:	17.14
Plant, Equip.:	$992,000	Total Liab.:	$879,000	Indic. Yr. Divd.:	NA
Total Assets:	$10,743,000	Net Worth:	$9,864,000	Debt/ Equity:	NA

iLinc Communications Inc

2999 N 44th St., Ste. 650, Phoenix, AZ, 85018; **PH:** 1-602-952-1200; **Fax:** 1-602-952-0544; **http://** www.ilinc.com

General - Incorporation	DE	Stock- Price on:12/24/2007	$0.72
Employees	71	Stock Exchange	AMEX
Auditor	Epstein Weber & Conover, PLC	Ticker Symbol	ILC
Stk Agt	Continental Stock Transfer & Trust Co	Outstanding Shares	33,410,000
Counsel	Bogatin Law Firm	E.P.S	-$0.016
DUNS No.	NA	Shareholders	NA

Business: The group's principle activity is to develop and sell software that provides online training and real-time collaboration. The ilinc Web collaboration suite consists of four products: learnlinc(tm), meetinglinc(tm), conferenceline(tm) and supportlinc(tm). These products may be sold as a customer-hosted installation allowing the customer to purchase the entire suite for organization-wide use on an unlimited connection basis. The uses of the four-product suite of Web collaboration software include online business meetings, sales presentations, employee training sessions, product demonstrations and technical support assistance. The group discontinued its dental practice management business in fiscal 2004. The group acquired glyphics communications on 01-Jun-2004. The group's total revenue for year 2007 was 14.20 millions of USD.

Primary SIC and add'l.: 7375 7372

CIK No: 0001042291

Subsidiaries: Edge Acquisition Subsidiary, Inc., Liberty Acquisition Corporation, Pentegra Investments, Inc., Special Omega Acquisition Corporation, TW Acquisition Subsidiary, Inc.

Officers: James M. Powers/Chmn., CEO, Pres./$320,705.00, Mark Yeager/VP - Marketing/$145,236.00, James L. Dunn/Sr. VP, CFO, General Counsel/$186,945.00, Gary L. Moulton/Sr. VP - Audio Conferencing/$161,076.00, Jason Walker/VP - Sales, Frank X. Gartland/VP - Product Development, Technology, Kathy Sacks/Sacks Public Relations

Directors: James M. Powers/Chmn., CEO, Pres., James H. Collins/Dir., Kent Petzhold/Dir., Daniel T. Robinson/Dir., Michael T. Flynn/Dir.

Owners: Daniel T. Robinson, James M. Powers/6.00%, Gary Moulton/3.30%, Renaissance Capital Growth and Income Fund III, Inc./1.50%, Michael T. Flynn, James L. Dunn, Benjamin James Taylor/3.20%, Kent Petzold/1.70%, Craig W. Stull, Nathan Cocozza, Renaissance U.S. Growth and Income Trust PLC/2.90%, James H. Collins, Insiders/13.00%, Herald Investment Trust PLC/7.60%, US Special Opportunities Trust PLC/4.00% (16 Owners included in Index)

Financial Data: Fiscal Year End:03/31　Latest Annual Data: 03/31/2007

Year	Sales	Net Income
2007	$14,195,000	$56,000
2006	$12,532,000	-$1,171,000
2005	$10,369,000	-$5,327,000

Curr. Assets:	$2,715,000	Curr. Liab.:	$4,656,000		
Plant, Equip.:	$336,000	Total Liab.:	$11,630,000	Indic. Yr. Divd.:	NA
Total Assets:	$16,000,000	Net Worth:	$4,370,000	Debt/ Equity:	1.0266

Illinois Power Co

500 S 27th St., Decatur, IL, 62521; **PH:** 1-217-424-6600; **http://** www.illinoispower.com

General - Incorporation	IL	Stock- Price on:12/24/2007	$49
Employees	NA	Stock Exchange	OTC
Auditor	PricewaterhouseCoopers LLP	Ticker Symbol	ILLNP
Stk Agt	NA	Outstanding Shares	NA
Counsel	NA	E.P.S	NA
DUNS No.	00-693-3519	Shareholders	NA

Business: The group's principle activities include generating, transmiting, distributing and selling electric energy in Illinois; and distributes, transports and sells natural gas in Illinois. The group operates from United States.

Primary SIC and add'l.: 4931 4923

CIK No: 0000049816

Subsidiaries: AFS Development Company, LLC, Agricultural Research& Development Corp., Ameren Corporation, Ameren Development Company, Ameren Energy Communications, Inc., Ameren Energy Development Company, Ameren Energy Fuels and Services Company, Ameren Energy Generating Company, Ameren Energy Marketing Company, Ameren Energy Resources Company, Ameren Energy, Inc., Ameren ERC, Inc., Ameren Services Company, AmerenEnergy Medina Valley Cogen (No. 2) LLC, AmerenEnergy Medina Valley Cogen, (No. 4) LLC 73 Subsidiaries included in the Index

Financial Data: Fiscal Year End:12/31　Latest Annual Data: 12/31/2001

Year	Sales	Net Income
2001	$1,614,400,000	$166,200,000
2000	$1,585,600,000	$134,900,000
1999	$1,903,200,000	$113,100,000

Curr. Assets:	$280,000,000	Curr. Liab.:	$705,600,000		
Plant, Equip.:	$1,905,400,000	Total Liab.:	$3,639,200,000	Indic. Yr. Divd.:	NA
Total Assets:	$4,861,100,000	Net Worth:	$1,221,900,000	Debt/ Equity:	1.3140

Illinois Tool Works Inc

3600 W Lake Ave., Glenview, IL, 60026; **PH:** 1-847-724-7500; **Fax:** 1-847-657-4572; **http://** www.itw.com

General - Incorporation	DE	Stock- Price on:12/24/2007	$55.85
Employees	55,000	Stock Exchange	NYSE
Auditor	Deloitte & Touche LLP	Ticker Symbol	ITW
Stk Agt	Computershare Investor Services LLC	Outstanding Shares	556,720,000
Counsel	NA	E.P.S	$3.17
DUNS No.	80-151-3623	Shareholders	NA

Business: The groups principle activity is to manufacture engineered products and specialty systems. In the year 2007, the group acquired Quasar International, Inc. The group operates from United States.

Primary SIC and add'l.: 3565 6159 3625 3569 2891 2992

CIK No: 0000049826

Subsidiaries: 1245267 Ontario Limited, A 3 Sud S.r.l., A.J. Gerrard LLC, Accu-Lube Manufacturing GmbH, ACI Kardam Manufacturing Limited, Addix, S.A., Appleton Investments LLC, Asbury Place Venture, Auto Wax Company, Inc., AXA Power ApS, Azon Pty. Limited, B.C. Immo S.C.I., B.c.h. S.a.s., Bates Cargo-Pak ApS, Bay Area Labels 574 Subsidiaries included in the Index

Officers: David B. Speer/56/Chmn., CEO/$5,391,157.00, Philip M. Gresh/59/Exec. VP, Craig A. Hindman/53/Exec. VP, Allan C. Sutherland/44/Sr. VP - Leasing, Investments, Robert E. Brunner/Exec. VP, David C. Parry/Exec. VP, Sharon Brady/Sr. VP - Human Resources, Scott E. Santi/46/Exec. VP, Hugh J. Zentmyer/61/Exec. VP/$2,085,977.00, John L. Brooklier/VP - Investor Relations, Ronald D. Kropp/CFO/$633,349.00, James H. Wooten/Sr. VP, General Counsel, Sec., Russell M. Flaum/Exec. VP/$2,047,366.00, Roland M. Martel/Exec. VP, Lee A. Sheridan/VP - Research, Development *(16 Officers included in Index)*

Directors: David B. Speer/56/Chmn., CEO, Thomas J. Hansen/Vice Chmn., Robert C. McCormack/67/Dir., William F. Aldinger/59/Dir., Don H. Davis/67/Dir., Harold B. Smith/73/Dir., Susan Crown/48/Dir., James Skinner/62/Dir., Marvin D. Brailsford/68/Dir., Michael J. Birck/69/Dir., Robert S. Morrison/64/Dir.

Owners: Susan Crown, Robert C. McCormack/3.70%, David B. Speer, Insiders/11.40%, Harold B. Smith/10.80%, Robert S. Morrison, James W. Farrell, William F. Aldinger, Thomas J. Hansen, Michael J. Birck, Ronald D. Kropp, Don H. Davis, James A. Skinner, Hugh J. Zentmyer, Marvin D. Brailsford *(16 Owners included in Index)*

Financial Data: *Fiscal Year End:* 12/31 *Latest Annual Data:* 12/31/2006

Year	Sales	Net Income
2006	$14,055,049,000	$1,717,746,000
2005	$12,921,792,000	$1,494,869,000
2004	$11,731,425,000	$1,338,694,000

Curr. Assets:	$5,206,405,000	**Curr. Liab.:**	$2,636,584,000	**P/E Ratio:**	18.13
Plant, Equip.:	$2,053,457,000	**Total Liab.:**	$4,862,931,000	**Indic. Yr. Divd.:**	$1.120
Total Assets:	$13,880,439,000	**Net Worth:**	$9,017,508,000	**Debt/ Equity:**	0.1044

Illumina Inc

9885 Towne Ctr. Dr., San Diego, CA, 92121; *PH:* 1-858-202-4500; *Fax:* 1-858-202-4545; *http://* www.illumina.com; *Email:* info@illumina.com

General - Incorporation	DE	**Stock**- Price on:12/24/2007	$40.54
Employees	596	Stock Exchange	NDQ
Auditor	Ernst & Young LLP	Ticker Symbol	ILMN
Stk Agt	EquiServe Trust Co N.A	Outstanding Shares	53,610,000
Counsel	Brobeck, Phleger & Harrison	E.P.S.	-$5.43
DUNS No.	NA	Shareholders	NA

Business: The group's principal activity is to design and develop next-generation tools for the large-scale analysis of genetic variation and function. The group's patented bead array technology uses fiber optics to achieve a level of array miniaturization that allows for a new scale of experimentation. The tools provide information that could be used by life sciences and pharmaceutical companies to improve drugs and therapies, customize diagnoses and treatment and cure diseases. The group's complementary oligator technology permits parallel synthesis of the millions of different pieces of dna necessary to perform large-scale genetic analysis on arrays. Illumina(R) , arrays of arraystm, beadarraytm, goldengatetm and oligatortm are the group's trademarks. The group's technology has applicability across a wide variety of industries, including agriculture, petrochemicals and food and beverages.

Primary SIC and add'l.: 2834 3826 8731 2835

CIK No: 0001110803

Subsidiaries: CyVera Corporation, Illumina Canada, Illumina GmbH, Illumina K.K., Illumina Singapore Pte. Ltd., Illumina UK, Limited

Officers: Jay T. Flatley/Dir., CEO, Pres./$1,800,603.00, Christian Henry/CFO, VP/$658,923.00, Tristan Orpin/Sr. VP - Commercial Operations/$689,140.00, John R. Stuelpnagel/Dir., Co - Founder, COO, Sr. VP/$1,020,933.00, Christian G. Cabou/Sr. VP, General Counsel/$494,002.00, Arthur L. Holden/Sr. VP - Corporate, Marketing Development/$529,158.00, John West/Sr. VP, GM - DNA Sequencing

Directors: Jay T. Flatley/Dir., CEO, Pres., William H. Rastetter/Chmn., Daniel M. Bradbury/Dir., David R. Walt/Dir., John R. Stuelpnagel/Dir., Co - Founder, COO, Sr. VP, Karin Eastham/Dir., Paul C. Grint/Dir., Jack Goldstein/Dir., Blaine Bowman/Dir., Roy Whitfield/Dir.

Owners: William H. Rastetter, Tristan B. Orpin, John R. Stuelpnagel/1.12%, Christian G. Cabou, John West, Blaine A. Bowman, Federated Investors, Inc./5.78%, Karin Eastham, Daniel M. Bradbury, Paul Grint, Arthur L. Holden, Goldman Sachs Asset Management, L.P./6.66%, Christian O. Henry, FMR Corp./11.07%, Jay T. Flatley/1.79% *(18 Owners included in Index)*

Financial Data: *Fiscal Year End:* 01/01 *Latest Annual Data:* 12/31/2006

Year	Sales	Net Income
2006	$184,586,000	$39,968,000
2005	$50,583,000	-$6,225,000

Curr. Assets:	$193,726,000	**Curr. Liab.:**	$33,776,000		
Plant, Equip.:	$25,634,000	**Total Liab.:**	$53,242,000	**Indic. Yr. Divd.:**	NA
Total Assets:	$300,584,000	**Net Worth:**	$247,342,000	**Debt/ Equity:**	1.5040

ILOG

1195 W Freemont Ave., Sunnyvale, CA, 94087; *PH:* 1-400-991-7000; *Fax:* 1-400-991-7001; *http://* www.ilog.com; *Email:* info@ilog.com

General - Incorporation	France	**Stock**- Price on:12/24/2007	$12.57
Employees	720	Stock Exchange	NDQ
Auditor	Ernst & Young LLP	Ticker Symbol	ILOG
Stk Agt	Morgan Guaranty Trust Co	Outstanding Shares	18,970,000
Counsel	NA	E.P.S.	$0.09
DUNS No.	39-197-7824	Shareholders	NA

Business: The groups principle activity is to develop and market optimisation and visualisation software as reusable components. The groups products include ilog optimisation; ilog visualisation products and java components. Customers served by the group include telecommunications, manufacturing, transportation and defence. The group operates from United States.

Primary SIC and add'l.: 7379 7372

CIK No: 0001031140

Subsidiaries: ILOG (s) Pte Ltd., ILOG Australia PTY LTD, Sydney, ILOG GmbH, Bad Homburg, ILOG Ltd., London, ILOG Ltd., Tokyo, Ilog Sa, Madrid, ILOG Software Technology (Shanghai) CO. Ltd, Shanghai, ILOG, Inc., Mountain View

Officers: Bounthara Ing/Exec. VP, Deputy CEO - Ilog, Heads The Company's Asian Operations, Pierre Haren/Chmn., CEO, Janet Lowe/VP - Strategic Projects, Jean-Francois Abramatic/Chief Product Officer, Kim Funk/VP, General Counsel, Olivier Maurel/CIO, Edith Simchi-Levi/VP - Operations, Logictools Division, Robert Bixby/Chief Science Officer, Christian Deutsch/Chief Quality Officer, Eric Brisson/Exec. VP - Sales, Services, Jerome Arnaud/CFO

Directors: Pierre Haren/Chmn., CEO, Todd Lowe/Dir., Michel Alard/Dir., Pascal Brandys/Dir., Marc Fourrier/Dir., Richard Liebhaber/Dir., Stephane Lizeray/Dir., Pierre-Michel Peugnet/Dir., Marie-Claude Bernal/Dir.

Owners: Marc Fourrier/1.40%, Insiders/8.60%, Todd Lowe/1.60%, Pierre Haren/2.50%

Financial Data: *Fiscal Year End:* 06/30 *Latest Annual Data:* 06/30/2007

Year	Sales	Net Income
2007	$161,459,000	$4,864,000
2006	$133,559,000	$6,617,000
2005	$125,303,000	$6,727,000

Curr. Assets:	$108,259,000	**Curr. Liab.:**	$48,798,000	**P/E Ratio:**	33.01
Plant, Equip.:	$4,582,000	**Total Liab.:**	$49,950,000	**Indic. Yr. Divd.:**	NA
Total Assets:	$118,762,000	**Net Worth:**	$68,812,000	**Debt/ Equity:**	NA

ILX Resorts Inc

2111 E Highland Ave., Ste. 200, Phoenix, AZ, 85016; *PH:* 1-602-957-2777; *http://* www.ilxinc.com; *Email:* centralres@ilxresorts.com

General - Incorporation	AZ	**Stock**- Price on:12/24/2007	$9.4
Employees	490	Stock Exchange	AMEX
Auditor	Hansen, Barnett & Maxwell	Ticker Symbol	ILX
Stk Agt	Computershare Investor Services LLC	Outstanding Shares	3,490,000
Counsel	Squire, Sanders & Dempsey LLP	E.P.S.	-$0.19
DUNS No.	17-324-0458	Shareholders	NA

Business: The group's principal activity is to acquire, develop, and operate timeshare resorts in the western United States. These resorts are marketed by the group as vacation ownership resorts and marketing and selling vacation ownership interests in the timeshare resorts. It also provides unused and unsold inventory of units for rent and provides food, beverages and other services at the resorts. The group's current portfolio of resorts consists of six resorts in Arizona, one in Indiana, one in Colorado, one in san carlos, Mexico, and a land adjacent to an existing resort for which the it holds development rights.

Primary SIC and add'l.: 7011

CIK No: 0000819551

Subsidiaries: All-Star Resorts, Inc, Genesis Investment Group, Inc, Golden Eagle Realty, Inc, Golden Eagle Resort, Inc, Harbor Southwest Development, Inc, ILE Florida, Inc, ILE Sedona Incorporated, ILX Bell Rock Incorporated, ILX Tourist Station Incorporated, ILX-Bruno LLC, Kohls Ranch Water Company, Laveen Properties, Inc, Los Abrigados Partners Limited Partnership, Premiere Development Incorporated, Premiere Media Incorporated 24 Subsidiaries included in the Index

Officers: Joseph P. Martori/Chmn., CEO/$354,000.00, Nancy J. Stone/Vice Chmn., COO, Pres./$394,886.00, Margaret M. Eardley/CFO, Exec. VP/$235,092.00, Edward S. Zielinski/Dir., Exec. VP/$242,215.00, Thomas F. Dunlap/Exec. VP/$216,295.00, Ty D. Krehbiel/Exec. VP - Sales/$201,204.00, Patrick Crosser/Mgr. - Corporate Customer Service, Philip E. Baxter/Exec. VP - Development

Directors: Joseph P. Martori/Chmn., CEO, Nancy J. Stone/Vice Chmn., COO, Pres., Joseph P. Martori/Vice Chmn., Steven A. White/Dir., James W. Myers/Dir., Wayne M. Greenholtz/67/Dir., Steven R. Chanen/Dir., Edward S. Zielinski/Dir., Exec. VP, Patrick J. McGroder/Dir.

Owners: Joseph P. Martori/2.70%, Dimensional Fund Advisors Inc./6.90%, Ty D. Krehbiel, Steven R. Chanen, Margaret M. Eardley, Edward S. Zielinski/2.20%, ILX Resorts Incorporated Employee Stock Ownership Plan & Trust/18.30%, Nancy J. Stone/5.20%, Martori Enterprises Incorporated/19.90%, Joseph P. Martori/25.30%, Patrick J. McGroder/1.40%, Steven A. White, Wayne M. Greenholtz, Insiders/39.60%, Thomas F. Dunlap *(16 Owners included in Index)*

Financial Data: *Fiscal Year End:* 12/31 *Latest Annual Data:* 12/31/2006

Year	Sales	Net Income
2006	$54,493,000	$2,166,000
2005	$56,887,000	$6,244,000
2004	$60,064,000	$2,681,000

Curr. Assets:	$7,322,000	**Curr. Liab.:**	$5,576,000	**P/E Ratio:**	28.48
Plant, Equip.:	$39,708,000	**Total Liab.:**	$47,366,000	**Indic. Yr. Divd.:**	$0.500
Total Assets:	$87,234,000	**Net Worth:**	$37,801,000	**Debt/ Equity:**	1.0022

IMA Exploration Inc

837 W Hastings St., Ste. 709, Vancouver, BC, V6C 3N6; *PH:* 1-604-687-1828; *Fax:* 1-604-687-1858; *http://* www.imaexploration.com; *Email:* info@imaexploration.com

General - Incorporation	BC	**Stock**- Price on:12/24/2007	$0.42
Employees	NA	Stock Exchange	AMEX
Auditor	PricewaterhouseCoopers LLP	Ticker Symbol	IMR
Stk Agt	Computershare Trust Co	Outstanding Shares	NA
Counsel	NA	E.P.S.	-$0.05
DUNS No.	NA	Shareholders	NA

Business: The groups principal activity is to explore mineral resources properties. The group operates from the United States.

Primary SIC and add'l.: 1031 1044

CIK No: 0001102706

Subsidiaries: IMA Navidad (BVI) Inc, IMA Holdings Corp, IMA Latin America Inc, IMPSA Resources Corporation, Inversiones Mineras Argentinas S.A., Inversiones Mineras Argentinas Inc, Inversiones Mineras Australes S.A, Inversiones Mineras Argentinas Holdings (BVI) Inc, Minera IMP-Peru S.A.C, Punto Dorado SA

Officers: Joseph Grosso/Dir., CEO, Pres., Arthur Lang/Dir., CFO, David Terry/Dir., VP - Exploration, Nikolaos Cacos/VP - Corporate Development, Sean D. Hurd/VP - Corporate Communications

Directors: Joseph Grosso/Dir., CEO, Pres., Gerald Carlson/Chmn., Robert Stuart Angus/Dir., Leonard Harris/Dir., David J. Horton/Dir., Chet Idziszek/Dir., Arthur Lang/Dir., CFO, David Terry/Dir., VP - Exploration

Owners: Insiders/6.90%, Robert Stuart Angus/0.50%, Nikolaos Cacos/0.40%, Leonard Harris/0.20%, Chet Idziszek/0.50%, Gerald Carlson/0.60%, David Horton/0.30%, Arthur Lang/0.40%, Sean Hurd/0.60%, David Terry/0.40%, Joseph Grosso/3.20%

Financial Data: *Fiscal Year End:* 12/31 *Latest Annual Data:* 12/31/2006

Year	Sales	Net Income
2006	NA	-$6,927,000
2005	NA	-$11,472,000
2004	NA	-$7,584,000

Curr. Assets:	$7,977,000	**Curr. Liab.:**	$203,000		
Plant, Equip.:	NA	**Total Liab.:**	$203,000	**Indic. Yr. Divd.:**	NA
Total Assets:	$8,207,000	**Net Worth:**	$8,004,000	**Debt/ Equity:**	NA

Image Entertainment Inc

20525 Nordhoff St., Ste. 200, Chatsworth, CA, 91311; *PH:* 1-818-407-9100; *Fax:* 1-818-407-9151; *http://* www.image-entertainment.com; *Email:* intl@image-entertainment.com

General - Incorporation	DE	**Stock**- Price on:12/24/2007	$4.26
Employees	187	Stock Exchange	NDQ
Auditor	BDO Seidman LLP	Ticker Symbol	DISK
Stk Agt	Computershare Investor Services LLC	Outstanding Shares	21,580,000
Counsel	NA	E.P.S	-$0.59
DUNS No.	10-389-4044	Shareholders	NA

Business: The group's principle activities include acquiring and distributing entertainment programs for release on DVD. It acquires and exploits exclusive distribution rights to a diverse array of general and specialty programming, including music concerts, urban, youth culture/lifestyle, stand-up comedy, television and theatrical, foreign and silent films in DVD, CD and other home entertainment formats. It acquires related broadcast rights, including video-on-demand, broadband streaming, digital download, pay-per-view, in-flight, radio, satellite, cable and broadcast television. On 23-Sep-2003, the group sold its subsidiary DVD planet, inc and hence discontinued retail distribution business. The group operates in two segments: domestic and international. Domestic segment primarily consists of acquisition, production and distribution of exclusive DVD programming. International segment includes international sublicensing and worldwide broadcast rights exploitation. The group operates from United States.

Primary SIC and add'l.: 7822 7812

CIK No: 0000216324

Subsidiaries: Egami Media, Inc., Home Vision Entertainment, Inc., Image Entertainment (UK), Inc

Officers: Martin W. Greenwald/Chmn., CEO, Pres., Jeff M. Framer/CFO, David Borshell/COO

Directors: Martin W. Greenwald/Chmn., CEO, Pres., Gary Haber/Dir., Robert J. McCloskey/Dir., David Coriat/Dir., Ira S. Epstein/Dir., Trevenen M. Huxley/Dir.

Owners: Martin W. Greenwald/5.94%, Standard Broadcasting Corp. Ltd./7.09%, BTP Acquisition Company, LLC/38.34%, Ira S. Epstein, MMCAP International Inc. SPC and MM Asset Management Inc./5.02%, Jeff M. Framer/1.33%, Image Investors Co/27.79%, Robert J. McCloskey, David Borshell/1.62%, Insiders/9.32%, David Coriat, Gary Haber, Trevenen M. Huxley

Financial Data: *Fiscal Year End:*03/31 *Latest Annual Data:* 03/31/2007

Year	Sales	Net Income
2007	$99,751,000	-$12,611,000
2006	$111,902,000	-$207,000
2005	$118,383,000	$5,127,000

Curr. Assets:	$50,053,000	**Curr. Liab.:**	$46,032,000		
Plant, Equip.:	$7,804,000	**Total Liab.:**	$46,032,000	**Indic. Yr. Divd.:**	NA
Total Assets:	$87,675,000	**Net Worth:**	$41,643,000	**Debt/ Equity:**	NA

Image Sensing Systems Inc

500 Spruce Tree Ctr., 1600 University Ave. W, St. Paul, MN, 55104; *PH:* 1-651-603-7700; *Fax:* 1-651-603-7795; *http://* www.imagesensing.com; *Email:* imagesensing@imagesensing.com

General - Incorporation	MN	**Stock**- Price on:12/24/2007	$15.89
Employees	50	Stock Exchange	NDQ
Auditor	Grant Thornton LLP	Ticker Symbol	ISNS
Stk Agt	Continental Stock Transfer & Trust Co	Outstanding Shares	3,780,000
Counsel	Dorsey & Whitney LLP	E.P.S	$0.81
DUNS No.	62-160-7514	Shareholders	NA

Business: The group's principal activity is to develop and market video image processing technology and processing products for implementation in advanced traffic management systems, freeway incident detection and traffic data collection. The group also provides technical expertise in image processing, hardware and software design and traffic management and control. The products include autoscope(R) that converts video images of a traffic scene into digitized traffic data and transmits the same to local or remote locations for real-time traffic management or stored for later analysis. The customers include federal, state, city and county departments of transportation, road commissions, port, turnpike, tunnel and other transportation authorities. The group operates in the United States and Hong Kong.

Primary SIC and add'l.: 8748 3829

CIK No: 0000943034

Subsidiaries: Flow Traffic Ltd., Image Sensing Systems Europe Limited

Officers: Ken Aubrey/CEO, Pres., Greg Smith/CFO, Mats Johan Billow/MD - Flow Traffic Ltd, Durga Panda/Sr. VP - Sales, Marketing, Graham P. Heywood/MD - ISS Europe Ltd, Ken Partyka/Dir. - Hardware Engineering, Oran Ener/Dir. - Technical Services, Craig A. Anderson/VP - Marketing

Directors: James Murdakes/Chmn., Richard C. Magnuson/Dir., Panos G. Michalopoulos/Dir., Michael G. Eleftheriou/Dir., Sven Wehrwein/Dir.

Owners: Insiders/11.30%, James Murdakes/1.50%, Michael G. Eleftheriou, Walrus Partners, L.L.C./5.20%, Austin W. Marxe/22.40%, Nicusa Capital Partners L.P./5.40%, Panos G. Michalopoulos/9.30%, Heartland Advisors, Inc./5.60%, Brown Brothers Harriman & Co./5.10%

Financial Data: *Fiscal Year End:*12/31 *Latest Annual Data:* 12/31/2006

Year	Sales	Net Income
2006	$13,116,000	$3,105,000
2005	$11,002,000	$2,841,000
2004	$10,830,000	$2,694,000

Curr. Assets:	$19,652,000	**Curr. Liab.:**	$1,883,000		
Plant, Equip.:	$522,000	**Total Liab.:**	$1,891,000	**Indic. Yr. Divd.:**	NA
Total Assets:	$21,224,000	**Net Worth:**	$19,333,000	**Debt/ Equity:**	NA

Image Technology Laboratories Inc

602 Enterprise Dr., Kingston, NY, 12401; *PH:* 1-845-338-3366; *Fax:* 1-845-338-8880; *http://* www.imagetechlabs.com; *Email:* investorrelations@imagetechlabs.com

General - Incorporation	DE	**Stock**- Price on:12/24/2007	$0.17
Employees	8	Stock Exchange	OTC
Auditor	Berenson LLP	Ticker Symbol	IMTL
Stk Agt	NA	Outstanding Shares	15,240,000
Counsel	NA	E.P.S	-$0.02
DUNS No.	NA	Shareholders	NA

Business: The group's principle activity is to develop picture archive and communications software known as pacs for the use in the management of medical diagnostic images by hospitals. Pacs input and store diagnostic images in digital format from original imaging sources such as computerized tomography, magnetic resonance imaging, ultrasound, nuclear imaging and digital fluoroscopy. The product of the group is itlpacs, along with its pacs software system has automation of the total work flow, integration of patient data with digital images, radiologist designed user interface, quality review programs. In addition the group designed a proprietary display workstation that permits the simultaneous viewing of multiple diagnostic images together with relevant patient data. The group operates from United States.

Primary SIC and add'l.: 7372

CIK No: 0001110648

Officers: Barry Muradian/CEO, Pres., Lewis M. Edwards/Chmn., Principal Accounting Officer

Directors: Lewis M. Edwards/Chmn., Principal Accounting Officer, Robert G. Carpenter/70/Dir., Richard V. Norell/62/Dir., John J. Naccarato/75/Dir.

Owners: Insiders/32.71%, Richard V. Norell/2.23%, Valerie McDowell/33.33%, John J. Naccarato, Valerie McDowell/26.00%, Allen M. McDowell/7.44%, Valerie McDowell/100.00%, Lewis M. Edwards/27.43%, Lewis M. Edwards/33.33%, Insiders/33.33%, Robert G. Carpenter/2.59%

Financial Data: *Fiscal Year End:*12/31 *Latest Annual Data:* 12/31/2006

Year	Sales	Net Income
2006	$673,000	-$144,000
2005	$700,000	-$415,000
2004	$894,000	-$565,000

Curr. Assets:	$209,000	**Curr. Liab.:**	$456,000		
Plant, Equip.:	$118,000	**Total Liab.:**	$456,000	**Indic. Yr. Divd.:**	NA
Total Assets:	$328,000	**Net Worth:**	-$128,000	**Debt/ Equity:**	NA

Imagenetix Inc

10845 Rancho Bernardo Rd., Ste. 105, San Diego, CA, 92127; *PH:* 1-858-674-8455; *http://* www.imagenetix.net; *Email:* admin@imagenetix.net

General - Incorporation	NV	**Stock**- Price on:12/24/2007	$1.2
Employees	8	Stock Exchange	OTC
Auditor	HJ Assoc. & Consultants LLP	Ticker Symbol	IAGX
Stk Agt	Interwest Transfer Company, Inc.	Outstanding Shares	10,720,000
Counsel	NA	E.P.S	-$0.12
DUNS No.	60-684-3431	Shareholders	NA

Business: The group's principal activities are to develop, formulate and market natural-based nutritional supplements and skin care products. The products are proprietary in nature and are often supported by scientific studies. These products are offered primarily to network marketing companies such as nikken, avon and unicity network and to mass market distributors that sell to the large retail chains. The group's main product is called celadrin(tm). Celadrin(tm) is a nutritional supplement compound comprised of a complex of fatty acid esters, which plays a role in human and animal joint health. The group also develops patentable compounds for the purpose of entering into licensing agreements with pharmaceutical partners.

Primary SIC and add'l.: 2834 8731

CIK No: 0000839441

Subsidiaries: Imagenetix CA.

Officers: William P. Spencer/55/Dir., CEO, Pres., Debra L. Spencer/56/Dir., Sec., Treasurer, Derek Boosey/Contact - Sales, Lowell W. Giffhorn/61/CFO, Donald Radcliffe/Primary Investor Relations Officer

Directors: William P. Spencer/55/Dir., CEO, Pres., Robert L. Hesslink/Member - Advisory Board, Jeffrey G. McGonegal/57/Dir., Debra L. Spencer/56/Dir., Sec., Treasurer, Jonathan Adachi/Member - Advisory Board, Robert L. Beeten/Member - Advisory Board, Daniel D. Gallaher/Member - Advisory Board, William J. Kraemer/Member - Advisory Board, Lorna R. Vanderhaeghe/Member - Advisory Board, Robert Burg/51/Dir., Barry S. King/62/Dir., Robert Zurier/Member - Advisory Board

Owners: Derek C. Boosey/1.80%, Robert Burg, William P. Spencer/26.90%, Insiders/30.10%, Gary J. McAdam/22.50%, Barry S. King, James Scibelli/9.20%, Jeffrey G. McGonegal, Lowell W. Giffhorn/1.10%

Financial Data: *Fiscal Year End:*03/31 *Latest Annual Data:* 03/31/2007

Year	Sales	Net Income
2007	$5,597,000	-$668,000
2006	$7,650,000	-$593,000
2005	$7,574,000	$754,000

Curr. Assets:	$5,293,000	**Curr. Liab.:**	$870,000		
Plant, Equip.:	$98,000	**Total Liab.:**	$939,000	**Indic. Yr. Divd.:**	NA
Total Assets:	$5,894,000	**Net Worth:**	$4,955,000	**Debt/ Equity:**	0.0105

ImageWare Systems Inc

10883 Thornmint Rd., San Diego, CA, 92127; *PH:* 1-858-673-8600; *Fax:* 1-858-673-1770; *http://* www.iwsinc.com

General - Incorporation	DE	**Stock**- Price on:12/24/2007	$2.3
Employees	74	Stock Exchange	AMEX
Auditor	Stonefield Josephson, Inc	Ticker Symbol	IW
Stk Agt	Computershare Trust Co	Outstanding Shares	14,680,000
Counsel	Greenberg Traurig LLP	E.P.S	-$0.43
DUNS No.	NA	Shareholders	NA

Business: The group's principle activities include developing, selling and supporting modular software products used by law enforcement and public safety agencies to manage criminal history records and to investigate crime and designs systems which utilize digital imaging in the production of photo identification cards, documents and identification badging systems. The group operates from United States.

Primary SIC and add'l.: 7372 3572

CIK No: 0000941685

Subsidiaries: Digital Imaging International GmbH, E-Focus West LLC, I.W. Systems Canada Company, ImageWare Digital Photography Systems, LLC, ImageWare Systems ID Group, Inc., XImage Corporation

Officers: Jim Miller/Chmn., CEO, Bill Willis/Exec. VP, Wayne Wetherell/Sr. VP - Administration, CFO, Chuck Aubuchon/VP - Business Development, David Harding/CTO

Directors: Jim Miller/Chmn., CEO, John Callan/Dir., John Holleran/Dir., David Loesch/Dir., Patrick Downs/Dir., Steve Hamm/Dir., David W. Carey/Dir.

Owners: David Loesch, Wesley Hampton/6.68%, John Holleran, Wesley Hampton, James S. Miller/3.80%, David Harding, Gruber & McBaine Capital Management LLC/23.88%, Darrelyn Carpenter/11.90%, Wayne Wetherell/1.71%, William Willis, Howard Harrison/8.35%, John Callan, David Carey, Darrelyn Carpenter, Steve G. Hamm *(19 Owners included in Index)*

Financial Data: ***Fiscal Year End:***12/31 ***Latest Annual Data:*** 03/31/2007

Year	Sales	Net Income
2007	NA	NA
2006	$10,190,000	-$5,926,000
2005	$9,519,000	-$8,356,000

Curr. Assets:	$2,856,000	***Curr. Liab.:***	$5,213,000		
Plant, Equip.:	$352,000	***Total Liab.:***	$6,229,000	***Indic. Yr. Divd.:***	NA
Total Assets:	$7,549,000	***Net Worth:***	$1,320,000	***Debt/ Equity:***	NA

Imagin Molecular Corp

104 Chestnut St. 315, Hinsdale, IL, 60521; ***PH:*** 1-630-371-5583;
http:// www.imaginmolecularcorp.com; ***Email:*** contact@imaginmolecularcorp.com

General - Incorporation	DE	***Stock***- Price on:12/24/2007	$0.043
Employees	3	Stock Exchange	OTC
Auditor	Frank L. Sassetti & Co.	Ticker Symbol	NA
Stk Agt	Corporate Stock Transfer, Inc.	Outstanding Shares	68,660,000
Counsel	NA	E.P.S	NA
DUNS No.	NA	Shareholders	NA

Business: The groups principle activities include technical and educational services to diagnose and treat patients with coronary artery disease and patients having the risk of developing coronary heart disease. Services of the group include cardiovascular PET perfusion imaging and coronary disease reversal program. Customers served by the group include general and family persons, and internal medicine physicians. In April 2005, the group acquired Positron Acquisition Corp. The group operates from the United States. The group's quarterly revenue for Sep '07 was 0.07 millions of USD.

Primary SIC and add'l.: 8071

CIK No: 0001047540

Subsidiaries: Cipher Multimedia, Inc.,, Imagin Nuclear Partners Corporation

Owners: Insiders/1.73%, Patrick G. Rooney/22.90%, Neil Sy/0.54%, Imagin Diagnostic Centers, Inc/11.03%, Corey Conn/1.19%

Financial Data: ***Fiscal Year End:***12/31 ***Latest Annual Data:*** 12/31/2006

Year	Sales	Net Income
2006	$183,000	-$973,000
2005	$3,000	-$75,000
2004	$3,000	-$330,000

Curr. Assets:	$167,000	***Curr. Liab.:***	$848,000		
Plant, Equip.:	$235,000	***Total Liab.:***	$1,054,000	***Indic. Yr. Divd.:***	NA
Total Assets:	$1,989,000	***Net Worth:***	$935,000	***Debt/ Equity:***	NA

Imaging Diagnostic Systems Inc

6531 NW 18th Ct., Plantation, FL, 33313; ***PH:*** 1-954-581-9800; ***Fax:*** 1-954-581-0555;
http:// www.imds.com

General - Incorporation	FL	***Stock***- Price on:12/24/2007	$0.042
Employees	40	Stock Exchange	OTC
Auditor	Margolies, Fink & Wichrowski	Ticker Symbol	IMDS
Stk Agt	Jersey Transfer & Trust Co	Outstanding Shares	289,820,000
Counsel	NA	E.P.S	-$0.024
DUNS No.	86-754-1831	Shareholders	NA

Business: The group's principal activity is to develop medical imaging devices. These medical devices include the computed tomography laser mammography (ctlm(r)) that utilizes a proprietary laser and proprietary scanning geometry and reconstruction algorithms for the detection and analysis of tissue in the breast to indicate malignancy or benignancy. The group is in development stage and is currently conducting clinical trials for ctlm(r). In connection with the clinical trials, it is also developing a clinical atlas of the optical properties of benign and malignant tissues with respect to absorption and scattering parameters as laser light passes through the tissue. The ctlm(R) is designed to provide the physician with objective data for interpretation and further clinical work-up. The group has entered into distribution agreements with distributors in North America, the United Kingdom, bosnia, Brazil, Ecuador, egypt, Israel, jordan, Middle East, slovenia, syria and turkey.

Primary SIC and add'l.: 8731 3845

CIK No: 0000790652

Officers: Tim Hansen/Dir., CEO, Patrick J. Gorman/Co - Chmn., Certified Public Accountant, Allan L. Schwartz/Co - Founder, Dir., CFO, Exec. VP, Deborah Obrien/Sr. VP

Directors: Tim Hansen/Dir., CEO, Patrick J. Gorman/Co - Chmn., Certified Public Accountant, Sherman Lazrus/Co - Chmn., Jay S. Bendis/Co - Chmn., Allan L. Schwartz/Co - Founder, Dir., CFO, Exec. VP, Edward Rolquin/Dir.

Owners: Allan L. Schwartz/2.20%, Patrick J. Gorman/0.50%, Deborah OBrien/0.40%, Timothy B. Hansen/1.10%, Sherman Lazrus/0.30%, Linda B. Grable/6.20%, Jay S. Bendis/0.30%, Insiders/5.10%, Edward Rolquin/0.30%

Financial Data: ***Fiscal Year End:***06/30 ***Latest Annual Data:*** 6/30/2006

Year	Sales	Net Income
2006	$676,000	-$7,163,000
2005	$375,000	-$7,313,000
2004	$733,000	-$8,403,000

Curr. Assets:	$2,061,000	***Curr. Liab.:***	$924,000		
Plant, Equip.:	$2,031,000	***Total Liab.:***	$924,000	***Indic. Yr. Divd.:***	NA
Total Assets:	$4,365,000	***Net Worth:***	$3,441,000	***Debt/ Equity:***	NA

Imaging3 Inc

3200 W Valhalla Dr., Burbank, CA, 91505; ; ***http://*** www.imaging3.com; ***Email:*** info@imaging3.com

General - Incorporation	CA	***Stock***- Price on:12/24/2007	$0.105
Employees	9	Stock Exchange	OTC
Auditor	Kabani & Company, Inc.	Ticker Symbol	IMGG
Stk Agt	Mountain Share Transfer	Outstanding Shares	205,140,000
Counsel	NA	E.P.S	-$0.011
DUNS No.	NA	Shareholders	NA

Business: The groups principle activity is to develop proprietary medical technology designed to produce 3D medical diagnostic images. The group operates from the United States.

Primary SIC and add'l.: 3844

CIK No: 0001205181

Officers: Dean Janes/Chmn., CEO, Christopher Sohn/COO, Pres., Xavier Aguilera/Sr. VP, CFO, Michele Janes/VP - Administration

Directors: Dean Janes/Chmn., CEO

Owners: Xavier Aguilera, Christopher Sohn/11.00%, Dean Janes/34.00%

Financial Data: ***Fiscal Year End:***12/31 ***Latest Annual Data:*** 12/31/2006

Year	Sales	Net Income
2006	$1,386,000	-$2,122,000
2005	$2,096,000	-$1,220,000

Curr. Assets:	$627,000	***Curr. Liab.:***	$3,647,000		
Plant, Equip.:	$34,000	***Total Liab.:***	$3,647,000	***Indic. Yr. Divd.:***	NA
Total Assets:	$692,000	***Net Worth:***	-$2,955,000	***Debt/ Equity:***	NA

ImaRx Therapeutics Inc

1635 E 18th St., Tucson, AZ, 85719; ***PH:*** 1-520-770-1259; ***Fax:*** 1-520-791-2437;
http:// www.imarx.com; ***Email:*** imarx@imarx.com

General - Incorporation		***Stock***- Price on:12/24/2007	NA
Employees	NA	Stock Exchange	NDQ
Auditor	NA	Ticker Symbol	IMRX
Stk Agt	Registrar & Transfer Co	Outstanding Shares	NA
Counsel	NA	E.P.S	NA
DUNS No.	NA	Shareholders	NA

Business: The groups principal activities include developing and commercializing therapies for vascular disorders associated with blood clots. The group products sold under the trade name Abbokinase(R) Open-Cath-R(R) PROLYSE(TM) and SonoLysis (TM). The group operates from the United States.

Primary SIC and add'l.: 2834 2836

CIK No: 0001123695

Subsidiaries: ImaRx Europe Limited, ImaRx Newco, Ltd.

Officers: Bradford Zakes/Dir., CEO, Pres., Terry Matsunaga/VP - Research, Greg Cobb/37/CFO, Rajan Ramaswami/VP - Product Development, Lynne E. Weissberger/VP - Reg Affairs - Quality Assurance, Reg Comp, Reena Zutshi/VP - Operations, Garen Manvelian/Chief Medical Officer, Jennifer Marshall/VP - Corporate Development, Kevin Ontiveros/VP - Legal Affairs, General Counsel

Directors: Bradford Zakes/Dir., CEO, Pres., Richard L. Love/Chmn., James M. Strickland/Dir., Richard E. Otto/Dir., Philip C. Ranker/Dir., Thomas W. Pew/Dir., Andrei V. Alexandrov/Member - Scientific Advisory Board, George W. Keilman/Member - Scientific Advisory Board, Marie-Pierre Krafft/Member - Scientific Advisory Board, Katsuro Tachibana/Member - Scientific Advisory Board, Daniel Von Hoff/Member - Scientific Advisory Board

Owners: Bradford A. Zakes/1.50%, Thomas W. Pew, Evan and Susan Unger Family Trust/4.10%, Richard Otto, Lynne E. Weissberger, Walter Singleton, John A. Moore/3.60%, Richard Love, James M. Strickland/1.00%, Insiders/7.20%, Greg Cobb/1.40%, Rajan Ramaswami, Philip Ranker, Evan C. Unger/4.70%, ITX International Equity Corp./7.10% *(17 Owners included in Index)*

Imation Corp

1 Imation Pl., Oakdale, MN, 55128; ***PH:*** 1-888-466-3456; ***Fax:*** 1-888-704-4200;
http:// www.imation.com

General - Incorporation	DE	***Stock***- Price on:12/24/2007	$37.61
Employees	2,070	Stock Exchange	NYSE
Auditor	PricewaterhouseCoopers LLP	Ticker Symbol	IMN
Stk Agt	Shareholder Services Group	Outstanding Shares	35,190,000
Counsel	NA	E.P.S	$1.32
DUNS No.	93-358-8691	Shareholders	NA

Business: The groups principle activity is to provide removable data storage products. The groups products include 4mm and 8mm data cartridges, CD-RW Media, and DataGuard Vault(TM). The group also provides select flash and removable hardware and accessories for data storage media. The group operates from United States.

Primary SIC and add'l.: 3695 7374

CIK No: 0001014111

Subsidiaries: Global Data Media FZ-LLC, Glyphics Media Inc., Imation (Guangzhou) International Co. Ltd., Imation (Malaysia) SDN.BHD, Imation (Shanghai) Co. Ltd., Imation (Thailand) Ltd., Imation (Tianjin) International Co. Ltd., Imation ANZ Pty Ltd., Imation Argentina S.A.C.I.F.I.A, Imation Asia Pacific Pte Ltd., Imation Canada Inc., Imation Chile S.A., Imation Colombia S.A., Imation Corporation Japan, Imation Deutschland GmbH 40 Subsidiaries included in the Index

Officers: Frank P. Russomanno/60/Dir., CEO, Pres./$1,900,684.00, Jacqueline A. Chase/VP - Human Resources/$761,804.00, Paul R. Zeller/CFO, VP/$1,086,470.00, John L. Sullivan/Sr. VP, General Counsel, Corp. Sec./$926,876.00, Bradley D. Allen/VP - Investor Relations, Corporate Communications/$523,502.00, Peter A. Koehn/VP - Global Operations, James C. Ellis/VP - Strategy, M, A, Subodh K. Kulkarni/VP - Global Commercial Business, Research & Development and Manufacturing, Stephen F. Moss/VP, Chief Marketing Officer

Directors: Frank P. Russomanno/60/Dir., CEO, Pres., Linda W. Hart/Chmn., Glen A. Taylor/Dir., Charles Reich/Dir., Charles A. Haggerty/Dir., Ronald T. Lemay/Dir., Bruce A. Henderson/58/Dir., Daryl J. White/Dir., Michael S. Fields/Dir., White L. Matthews/Dir., Mark E. Lucas/Dir., Raymond Leung/Dir.

Owners: Dimensional FundAdvisors LP/5.90%, Insiders/2.60%, Ronald T. LeMay, Frank P. Russomanno, Private Capital Management, L.P./7.40%, FMR Corp./8.27%, Daryl J. White, Charles A. Haggerty, John L. Sullivan, Michael S. Fields, Barclays Global Investors, NA/5.17%, Linda W. Hart, Paul R. Zeller, Glen A. Taylor, Charles Reich *(19 Owners included in Index)*

Financial Data: ***Fiscal Year End:***12/31 ***Latest Annual Data:*** 12/31/2006

Year	Sales	Net Income
2006	$1,584,700,000	$76,400,000
2005	$1,258,100,000	$87,900,000
2004	$1,219,300,000	$29,900,000

Curr. Assets:	$876,900,000	***Curr. Liab.:***	$391,600,000	***P/E Ratio:***	18.17
Plant, Equip.:	$178,000,000	***Total Liab.:***	$436,600,000	***Indic. Yr. Divd.:***	$0.640
Total Assets:	$1,382,900,000	***Net Worth:***	$946,300,000	***Debt/ Equity:***	NA

IMAX Corp

2525 Speakman Dr., Mississauga, ON, L5K 1B1; *PH:* 1-905-403-6500; *http://* www.imax.com; *Email:* info@imax.com

General - Incorporation	Canada	**Stock** - Price on:12/24/2007	$4.31
Employees	376	Stock Exchange	NDQ
Auditor	PricewaterhouseCoopers LLP	Ticker Symbol	IMAX
Stk Agt	Computershare Trust Co	Outstanding Shares	40,280,000
Counsel	NA	E.P.S	-$0.645
DUNS No.	20-403-1801	Shareholders	NA

Business: The group's principle activities are to design, manufacture, market and lease proprietary projection and sound systems for imax theaters. The group develops digital re-mastering, post-production and distribution of films in the imax theater network. The group also provides other services to the imax theater network including maintenance services. The group operates through three segments: imax systems, films and other. The group's major brands include imax(R), the imax experience(R), an imax experience(R), imax(R) dmr(tm), imax(R) 3D and imax(R) dome. The group also owns the service mark imax theatre(tm). The group operates in Canada, the United States, Japan, Europe and other countries. The group's quarterly revenue for September 2007 was 29.80 millions of USD.

Primary SIC and add'l.: 7829 3861 7922 7822 7812

CIK No: 0000921582

Subsidiaries: 3D Sea II Ltd., Big Engine Films Inc., David Keighley Productions 70MM Inc., IMAX (Netherlands) B.V., IMAX Chicago Theatre LLC, Imax Ii U.s.a. Inc., IMAX Indianapolis LLC, IMAX Japan Inc., IMAX Minnesota Holding Co., IMAX Rhode Island Limited Partnership, IMAX Scribe Inc., IMAX Space Ltd., IMAX Theatre Holding Co., IMAX Theatre Holdings (OEI) Inc., IMAX Theatre Management Company 28 Subsidiaries included in the Index

Officers: Richard L. Gelfond/Co - Chmn., Co - CEO/$684,640.00, Bradley J. Wechsler/Co - Chmn., Co - CEO/$689,429.00, Greg Foster/Chmn., Pres. - Filmed Entertainment/$1,234,906.00, Mary G. Ruby/Sr. VP - Legal Affairs, Deputy General Counsel, Corp. Sec., Larry OReilly/Sr. VP - Theatre Development, Film Distribution, Mark Welton/Exec. VP - Theatre Operations, GM - Digital, Brian Bonnick/Sr. VP - Technology, Robert D. Lister/Exec. VP - Business, Legal Affairs, General Counsel/$605,367.00, David B. Keighley/Exec. VP, Pres. - Productions 70mm Inc/$575,893.00, Mary C. Sullivan/Sr. VP - Human Resources, Administration, Joseph Sparacio/CFO, Jeffrey Vance/37/Co - Controller, Vigna Vivekanand/38/Co - Controller

Directors: Richard L. Gelfond/Co - Chmn., Co - CEO, Bradley J. Wechsler/Co - Chmn., Co - CEO, Greg Foster/Chmn., Pres. - Filmed Entertainment, Neil S. Braun/55/Dir., Kenneth G. Copland/70/Dir., Garth M. Girvan/59/Dir., David Leebron/53/Dir., Marc A. Utay/48/Dir.

Owners: Edward MacNeil, Marc A. Utay/3.30%, Francis T. Joyce, Kenneth G. Copland, Garth M. Girvan, Insiders/17.80%, Richard L. Gelfond/6.60%, David B. Keighley, David W. Leebron, Greg Foster, Bradley J. Wechsler/6.50%, Neil S. Braun, Robert D. Lister

Financial Data: *Fiscal Year End:*12/31 *Latest Annual Data:* 12/31/2006

Year	Sales	Net Income
2006	$129,452,000	-$16,849,000
2005	$144,930,000	$14,382,000
2004	$135,980,000	$10,244,000

Curr. Assets:	$83,600,000	**Curr. Liab.:**	$69,720,000		
Plant, Equip.:	$24,639,000	**Total Liab.:**	$285,523,000	**Indic. Yr. Divd.:**	NA
Total Assets:	$227,291,000	**Net Worth:**	-$58,232,000	**Debt/ Equity:**	NA

Imclone Systems Inc

180 Varick St., 6th Fl., New York, NY, 10014; *PH:* 1-212-645-1405; *Fax:* 1-212-645-2054; *http://* www.imclone.com

General - Incorporation	DE	**Stock** - Price on:12/24/2007	$36.88
Employees	993	Stock Exchange	NDQ
Auditor	KPMG LLP	Ticker Symbol	IMCL
Stk Agt	KPMG LLP	Outstanding Shares	85,630,000
Counsel	Howard, Darby & Levin	E.P.S	$1.87
DUNS No.	13-134-5761	Shareholders	NA

Business: The group's principal activity is to conduct research and develop therapeutic products for the treatment of cancer and cancer related disorders. The group's product erbitux(tm) is a therapeutic monoclonal antibody that inhibits stimulation of epidermal growth factor (egf) receptor upon which certain solid tumors depend in order to grow. The group also develops the inhibitors of angiogenesis, which can be used to treat various kinds of cancer and other diseases. The group performs ongoing research which includes ongoing clinical programs of growth factor blockers, other tumor cell growth inhibitors and angiogenesis inhibitors.the group operates in the United States and Germany.

Primary SIC and add'l.: 6794 8731

CIK No: 0000765258

Subsidiaries: EndoClone Incorporated

Officers: John H. Johnson/Dir., CEO, Eric K. Rowinsky/Sr. VP, Chief Medical Officer/$769,454.00, Peter R. Borzilleri/Interim VP - Finance, Richard P. Crowley/Sr. VP - Biopharmaceutical Operations, Margaret Dalesandro/VP - Project Management, Daniel J. O'Connor/Sr. VP, General Counsel, Sec., David Schloss/VP - Human Resources, Larry Witte/Sr. VP - Research, Ana I. Stancic/51/Sr. VP - Finance/$496,587.00, Michael P. Bailey/Sr. VP - Commercial Operations

Directors: John H. Johnson/Dir., CEO, Carl C. Icahn/Chmn., Alexander J. Denner/Dir., Peter S. Liebert/Dir., David Sidransky/Dir., Jules Haimovitz/Dir., Andrew G. Bodnar/Dir., Thomas F. Deuel/Dir., Richard C. Mulligan/Dir., Charles Woler/Dir.

Owners: Richard C. Mulligan, ClearBridge Advisors, LLC/10.96%, Insiders/14.80%, Peter S. Liebert, Eric Rowinsky, Charles Woler, Alexander J. Denner, Richard Crowley, Carl C. Icahn/13.47%, David Sidransky, Vincent T. DeVita, Joseph L. Fischer, Ana I. Stancic, William R. Miller, Capital Group International, Inc/13.50% *(17 Owners included in Index)*

Financial Data: *Fiscal Year End:*12/31 *Latest Annual Data:* 12/31/2006

Year	Sales	Net Income
2006	$677,847,000	$370,674,000
2005	$383,673,000	$86,496,000
2004	$388,690,000	$113,653,000

Curr. Assets:	$1,270,232,000	**Curr. Liab.:**	$238,932,000	**P/E Ratio:**	19.72
Plant, Equip.:	$423,000,000	**Total Liab.:**	$1,080,187,000	**Indic. Yr. Divd.:**	NA
Total Assets:	$1,839,836,000	**Net Worth:**	$759,649,000	**Debt/ Equity:**	0.7464

IMCOR Pharmaceutical Co

4660 La Jolla Dr., Ste. 500, San Diego, CA, 92122; *PH:* 1-858-546-2955; *Fax:* 1-858-410-5602; *http://* www.imcorpharma.com

General - Incorporation	NV	**Stock** - Price on:12/24/2007	$0.01
Employees	NA	Stock Exchange	OTC
Auditor	Quar, Milner, Peterson LLP	Ticker Symbol	ICRP
Stk Agt	Computershare Investor Services LLC	Outstanding Shares	6,960,000
Counsel	NA	E.P.S	-$0.05
DUNS No.	NA	Shareholders	NA

Business: The group's principal activity is focused on developing and marketing medical imaging pharmaceutical products. The products include imagent (R), approved by the food and drug administration and two additional contrast agents in development called pH-50 and n1177. Imagent (R), an ultrasound imaging contrast agent improves the visualization of blood vessels for better diagnosis of diseases and assessment of organ function. Ph-50 is a blood pool contrast agent for use in computed tomography (ct) and X-ray imaging to diagnose diseased tissue in the cardiovascular system and other organs. The n1177 enables physicians to precisely locate tumorous nodes by first injecting the material in the vicinity of the tumor and then taking an image using a ct device.

Primary SIC and add'l.: 2834 3845 2835

CIK No: 0000761237

Subsidiaries: Sentigen, Ltd.

Officers: Brian M. Gallagher/60/Chmn., Acting Principal Financial Officer, Larry D. Grant/56/Financial Consultant, Jack Defranco/62/Acting Principal Executive Officer, COO

Directors: Brian M. Gallagher/60/Chmn., Acting Principal Financial Officer, Taffy J. Williams/58/Dir., Alan D. Watson/55/Dir., Darlene M. Deptula-Hicks/50/Dir., Richard T. Dean/60/Dir., Jonathan J. Fleming/50/Dir., Robert A. Ashley/50/Dir.

Owners: Richard T. Dean, Brian M. Gallagher/1.10%, Alan D. Watson, Insiders/67.90%, Darlene M. Deptula-Hicks, Jonathan Fleming/Oxford Bioscience/67.50%

Financial Data: *Fiscal Year End:*12/31 *Latest Annual Data:* 12/31/2006

Year	Sales	Net Income
2006	$1,200,000	-$350,000
2005	$726,000	-$17,698,000
2004	$355,000	-$21,673,000

Curr. Assets:	$1,340,000	**Curr. Liab.:**	$4,603,000		
Plant, Equip.:	NA	**Total Liab.:**	$4,603,000	**Indic. Yr. Divd.:**	NA
Total Assets:	$1,340,000	**Net Worth:**	-$3,263,000	**Debt/ Equity:**	NA

iMedia International Inc

1721 21st St., Santa Monica, CA, 90404; *PH:* 1-310-453-4499; *Fax:* 1-310-453-6120; *http://* www.imedia-intl.com; *Email:* info@imedia-intl.com

General - Incorporation	DE	**Stock** - Price on:12/24/2007	NA
Employees	43	Stock Exchange	OTC
Auditor	Weinberg & Co. P.A	Ticker Symbol	IMNL
Stk Agt	Interwest Transfer Company, Inc.	Outstanding Shares	NA
Counsel	NA	E.P.S	-$0.08
DUNS No.	NA	Shareholders	NA

Business: The group's principal activity is to produce interactive CD-ROM discs that promote a variety of content, messages and sponsor advertisements. The group operates through four operating units: imedia us, llc, hpi, las vegas previews, llc; and ipolitix, llc. Imedia us designs custom digital discs that allow the corporate sponsor or national brand to display their products and services. Hpi has the exclusive rights to produce and distribute the hollywood previews(tm) entertainment magazine in the United States. Las vegas previews, llc has completed a prototype destination disc magazine, entitled las vegas previews(tm) magazine. Ipolitix, llc creates interactive discs that promote political candidates, ballot initiatives and viewpoints. On Aug 29, 2003, the company acquired all of the capital stock of hollywood previews.

Primary SIC and add'l.: 7311

CIK No: 0001208498

Subsidiaries: Hollywood Previews, Inc.

Officers: Henry Williamson/Chmn., CEO, Shaun McClure/Producer, Tristan Davis/Producer, Tyler Mares/Contact - Design, Programming, Video Editing, Anthony J. Fidaleo/Dir., CFO, Exec. VP, COO, John Vivona/Universal Press Syndicate, Mindy Williford/Universal Press Syndicate, Jason Gandhi/VP - Technical Operations, Julie Rytand/Operations Dir., Scott Kapp/Dir., Co - Founder, Pres., Alex Ranarivelo/Contact - Design, Programming, Video Editing, Andrew Walkinshaw/Executive Producer, Brain Hunkins/Contact - Design, Programming, Video Editing

Directors: Henry Williamson/Chmn., CEO, David MacEachern/Co - Founder, Dir., Anthony J. Fidaleo/Dir., CFO, Exec. VP, COO, Scott Kapp/Dir., Co - Founder, Pres., Frank Unruh/Dir.

Owners: Franklin H. Unruh/15.20%, Midsummer Investment Ltd./6.40%, Insiders/53.20%, Waletta Far East Ltd./7.00%, Henry Williamson/4.20%, David G. MacEachern/14.80%, Anthony J. Fidaleo/2.70%, Crestview Capital Master LLC/6.40%, Scott Kapp/16.30%

Financial Data: *Fiscal Year End:*12/31 *Latest Annual Data:* 12/31/2005

Year	Sales	Net Income
2005	$5,932,000	-$12,271,000
2004	$2,291,000	-$4,915,000

Curr. Assets:	$3,260,000	**Curr. Liab.:**	$2,480,000		
Plant, Equip.:	$140,000	**Total Liab.:**	$7,595,000	**Indic. Yr. Divd.:**	NA
Total Assets:	$3,400,000	**Net Worth:**	-$5,048,000	**Debt/ Equity:**	NA

iMergent Inc

754 E Technology Ave., Orem, UT, 84097; *PH:* 1-801-227-0004; *Fax:* 1-801-226-8848; *http://* www.imergentinc.com; *Email:* investor_relations@imergentinc.com

General - Incorporation	DE	**Stock** - Price on:12/24/2007	$25.66
Employees	242	Stock Exchange	AMEX
Auditor	Tanner LC	Ticker Symbol	IIG
Stk Agt	Colonial Stock Transfer Co Inc	Outstanding Shares	12,320,000
Counsel	NA	E.P.S	$1.65
DUNS No.	NA	Shareholders	NA

Business: The group's principal activity is to provide Web-based technology solutions to small emerging companies and entrepreneurs seeking to establish an e-commerce presence on the Internet. The group's suite of services includes a 90-minute informational preview training session, followed by an eight hour Internet training workshop. At the end of the workshop, the attending small business owner

or entrepreneur can purchase a license to use its storesonline software and Website development platform, as well as an integrated package of services. These services include creation of ecommerce enabled websites, access to Internet marketing information, helpdesk technical support, tracking software to monitor site traffic, Internet classified advertisements and others. The group also offers programming to create distinctive Web page graphics and banners, websites with streaming audio and video content and pages powered by macromedia(R) flash.

Primary SIC and add'l.: 7379 7375 7372

CIK No: 0001075736

Subsidiaries: Galaxy Enterprises, Inc, Galaxy Mall, Inc, Internet Training Group, Inc, StoresOnline Inc, StoresOnline International, Inc., StoresOnline.com, Ltd

Officers: Donald L. Danks/Dir., CEO, Brandon Lewis/Dir., COO, Pres., Robert Lewis/CFO, David L. Rosenvall/CTO, Jeffrey G. Korn/Sec. - Counsel

Directors: Todd A. Goergen/Chmn., Robert Kamm/Dir., Brandon Lewis/Dir., COO, Pres., Craig W. Rauchle/Dir.

Owners: Donald Danks/4.80%, Brandon Lewis/3.00%, Todd Goergen/2.30%, Robert Lewis, Insiders/12.30%, David Rosenvall/1.10%, Robert Kamm, Wellington Management Co. LLP/12.60%, Steven Mihaylo/9.10%, Gruber & McBaine Capital Management LLC/5.10%, Craig Rauchle, Goldman Capital Management, Inc./5.70%

Financial Data: Fiscal Year End:06/30   Latest Annual Data: 06/30/2007

Year	Sales	Net Income
2007	$151,617,000	$24,001,000
2006	$185,089,000	$110,622,000
2005	$39,075,000	-$29,517,000

Curr. Assets:	$46,832,000	Curr. Liab.:	$27,340,000	P/E Ratio:	15.74
Plant, Equip.	$696,000	Total Liab.:	$36,033,000	Indic. Yr. Divd.:	$0.400
Total Assets:	$66,012,000	Net Worth:	$29,979,000	Debt/ Equity:	NA

IMI International Medical Innovations Inc

4211 Yonge St., Ste. 615, Toronto, ON, M2P 2A9; ; *http://* www.imimedical.com

General - Incorporation	Canada	Stock- Price on:12/24/2007	$1.06
Employees	NA	Stock Exchange	NA
Auditor	Ernst & Young LLP	Ticker Symbol	NA
Stk Agt	Equity Transfer Services Inc	Outstanding Shares	NA
Counsel	NA	E.P.S.	-$0.21
DUNS No.	NA	Shareholders	NA

Business: The groups principle activity is to provide non-invasive tests that detect early-stage cardiovascular disease and cancer. The groups products include PREVU* Skin Sterol Test, ColorectAlert(TM) and LungAlert(TM). The group operates from Canada.

Primary SIC and add'l.: 9999

CIK No: 0001179083

Officers: Brent Norton/Dir., CEO, Pres., Michael Evelegh/Exec. VP - Clinical, Regulatory Affairs, Laila Gurney/Dir. - Clinical, Quality, Regulatory Affairs, Tim Currie/VP - Corporate Development, Peter Horsewood/Dir. - Scientific Affairs, Ron Hosking/VP - Finance, CFO

Directors: Brent Norton/Dir., CEO, Pres., Stephen A. Wilgar/Chmn., Anthony F. Griffiths/Dir., Norman Marcon/Member - Scientific Advisory Board, Dennis L. Sprecher/Member - Scientific Advisory Board, John Bienenstock/Member - Scientific Advisory Board, David Rosenkrantz/Dir., Herbert A. Fritsche/Member - Scientific Advisory Board, Ronald D. Henriksen/Dir.

Owners: Anthony F. Griffiths/2.00%, Ronald Henriksen/0.20%, H.B. Brent Norton/9.40%, David A. Rosenkrantz/1.10%, Midsummer Investment Ltd/7.80%, Ronald G. Hosking/1.20%, Stephen A. Wilgar/1.20%, Tim Currie/0.10%, Michael Evelegh/1.50%

Financial Data: Fiscal Year End:12/31   Latest Annual Data: 12/31/2006

Year	Sales	Net Income
2006	$2,862,000	-$5,052,000
2005	$1,355,000	-$4,103,000
2004	$403,000	-$4,549,000

Curr. Assets:	$3,636,000	Curr. Liab.:	$1,627,000		
Plant, Equip.:	$268,000	Total Liab.:	$7,077,000	Indic. Yr. Divd.:	NA
Total Assets:	$4,530,000	Net Worth:	-$2,546,000	Debt/ Equity:	NA

Immediatek Inc

320 S Walton St., Dallas, TX, 75226; **PH:** 1-214-744-8801; *http://* www.immediatek.com; **Email:** info@immediatek.com

General - Incorporation	NV	Stock- Price on:12/24/2007	$3.5
Employees	2	Stock Exchange	OTC
Auditor	KBA Group, LLP	Ticker Symbol	IMKI
Stk Agt	Pacific Stock Transfer Company	Outstanding Shares	NA
Counsel	Zach Bair	E.P.S.	-$8.86
DUNS No.	NA	Shareholders	NA

Business: The group's principle activity is to provide cutting-edge software and technology solutions. The group offers it outsourcing solutions with available 24x7 teknet oncall technicians. On 27-Feb-2003, the group acquired key assets of LCD interactive, inc. It is a development stage group. The group operates from United States.

Primary SIC and add'l.: 7373 7372

CIK No: 0001084182

Subsidiaries: DiscLive, Inc.

Officers: Travis Hill/35/CEO/$45,000.00, Paul Marin/Dir., Pres., Sec., Principal Financial, Accounting Officer/$84,350.00

Directors: Paul Marin/Dir., Pres., Sec., Principal Financial, Accounting Officer, Darin Divinia/36/Dir., Corey Prestidge/34/Dir.

Owners: Paul Marin, Darin Divinia, Jess Morgan & Co Inc., Corey Prestidge, Radical Holdings LP, Radical Holdings LP, Insiders

Financial Data: Fiscal Year End:12/31   Latest Annual Data: 12/31/2006

Year	Sales	Net Income
2006	$50,000	-$627,000
2005	$141,000	-$1,943,000
2004	$1,099,000	-$2,149,000

Curr. Assets:	$1,062,000	Curr. Liab.:	$216,000		
Plant, Equip.:	$122,000	Total Liab.:	$216,000	Indic. Yr. Divd.:	NA
Total Assets:	$2,982,000	Net Worth:	-$234,000	Debt/ Equity:	NA

Immersion Corp

801 Fox Ln., San Jose, CA, 95131; **PH:** 1-408-467-1900; **Fax:** 1-408-467-1901; *http://* www.immersion.com

General - Incorporation	DE	Stock- Price on:12/24/2007	$13.148
Employees	140	Stock Exchange	NDQ
Auditor	Deloitte & Touche LLP	Ticker Symbol	IMMR
Stk Agt	EquiServe Trust Co N.A	Outstanding Shares	26,000,000
Counsel	DLA Piper Rudnick Gray Cary	E.P.S.	$4.09
DUNS No.	NA	Shareholders	NA

Business: The group's principle activity is to develop, manufacture, license and support a wide range of hardware and software technologies. These technologies enable users to interact with a multitude of computing and other devices using their sense of touch. The group operates under two segments: immersion computing, entertainment and industrial segment and medical segment. Immersion computing, entertainment and industrial segment develops and markets touchsense and force-feedback technology that enables software and hardware developers to bring realism into their computing and entertainment experience and industrial applications. Medical segment develops, manufactures and markets medical simulators that recreate realistic healthcare environments. The group operates in North America, Europe and the Far East.

Primary SIC and add'l.: 3577 7373 7372

CIK No: 0001058811

Subsidiaries: Immersion Canada, Inc.

Officers: Victor Viegas/Chmn., CEO, Pres./$489,871.00, Christophe Ramstein/Sr. VP - Research, Engineering, Michael Zuckerman/Sr. VP, GM - 3D Business Group/$667,403.00, Richard Vogel/Sr. VP, GM - Immersion Medical, Inc/$594,154.00, Stephen Ambler/CFO, VP - Finance/$385,592.00, Gayle Schaeffer/VP - Corporate Marketing, Laura A. Peter/VP, General Counsel, Mark Belinsky/VP, GM - Mobility, Gaming, Michael D. Levin/VP, GM - Touch Interface Products, Janice Passarello/VP - Human Resources

Directors: Victor Viegas/Chmn., CEO, Pres., John Hodgman/Dir., Robert Van Naarden/Dir., Jack Saltich/Dir., Emily Liggett/Dir., Anne Degheest/Dir.

Owners: Emily Liggett, John Hodgman, Victor Viegas/4.30%, Stephen Ambler, Austin W. Marxe/8.10%, Robert Van Naarden, Mazama Capital Management Inc./23.30%, Richard Vogel, Jonathan Rubinstein, Insiders/6.50%, Jack Saltich

Financial Data: Fiscal Year End:12/31   Latest Annual Data: 12/31/2006

Year	Sales	Net Income
2006	$27,853,000	-$10,424,000
2005	$24,277,000	-$13,085,000
2004	$23,763,000	-$20,738,000

Curr. Assets:	$40,983,000	Curr. Liab.:	$7,326,000	P/E Ratio:	3.08
Plant, Equip.:	$1,647,000	Total Liab.:	$73,007,000	Indic. Yr. Divd.:	NA
Total Assets:	$50,015,000	Net Worth:	-$22,992,000	Debt/ Equity:	NA

Immtech Pharmaceuticals Inc

Formerly: Immtech International Inc

150 Fairway Dr., Ste. 150, Vernon Hills, IL, 44122; **PH:** 1-847-573-0033; *http://* www.immtech-international.com

General - Incorporation	DE	Stock- Price on:12/24/2007	$8.19
Employees	27	Stock Exchange	AMEX
Auditor	Deloitte & Touche LLP	Ticker Symbol	IMM
Stk Agt	Computershare Investor Services LLC	Outstanding Shares	15,370,000
Counsel	NA	E.P.S.	-$0.902
DUNS No.	NA	Shareholders	NA

Business: The group's principle activities include discover, developing and commercialize oral drugs to treat infectious diseases. The group's pharmaceutical platform develops drugs to treat infections such as fungal diseases, malaria, tuberculosis, hepatitis c and pneumocystis carinii pneumonia and tropical diseases such as trypanosomiasis (african sleeping sickness) and leishmaniasis. Its lead compound db289 has entered human clinical trials including a phase iia trial for the treatment of malaria, a phase iia trial for the treatment of pneumocystis carinii pneumonia and phase iib trial for the treatment of african sleeping sickness. The group also has licensing and exclusive commercialization rights to a dicationic pharmaceutical platform for developing anti-infective oral drugs. The group operates from United States.

Primary SIC and add'l.: 8731 2835

CIK No: 0000882509

Subsidiaries: Immtech Hong Kong Limited, Immtech Pharmaceuticals, Inc.

Officers: Eric L. Sorkin/Chmn., CEO, Lawrence A. Potempa/VP, Daniel M. Schmitt/VP - Licensing, Commercial Development, Wesley K. Clark/Advisor, Cecilia Chan/Executive Dir., Carol Ann Olson/Sr. VP, Chief Medical Officer, Gary C. Parks/CFO, Sec., Treasurer, Norman A. Abood/VP - Discovery Programs, Dorothy S. Zinberg/Advisor, Richard R. Tidwell/Head - Research, Dir. - Research Consortium

Directors: Eric L. Sorkin/Chmn., CEO, David Fleet/Dir., Cecilia Chan/Executive Dir., Judy Lau/Dir., Levi Hong Kaye Lee/Dir., Donald F. Sinex/Dir., David W. Boykin/Member - Scientific Advisory Board, Byron L. Blagburn/Member - Scientific Advisory Board, David W. Wilson/Member - Scientific Advisory Board, John R. Perfect/Member - Scientific Advisory Board, James E. Hall/Member - Scientific Advisory Board, Scott M. Franzblau/Member - Scientific Advisory Board, Christine C. Dykstra/Member - Scientific Advisory Board

Owners: Eric L. Sorkin/2.89%, Levi H.K. Lee/1.94%, Carol Ann Olson, Insiders/9.43%, David M. Fleet, Donald F. Sinex, Cecilia Chan/2.48%, Judy Lau, Gary C. Parks

Financial Data: Fiscal Year End:03/31   Latest Annual Data: 03/31/2007

Year	Sales	Net Income
2007	$4,318,000	-$11,133,000
2006	$3,575,000	-$15,525,000
2005	$5,931,000	-$13,433,000

Curr. Assets:	$14,861,000	Curr. Liab.:	$2,951,000		
Plant, Equip.:	$3,556,000	Total Liab.:	$2,951,000	Indic. Yr. Divd.:	NA
Total Assets:	$18,554,000	Net Worth:	$15,603,000	Debt/ Equity:	NA

Immucell Corp

56 Evergreen Dr, Portland, ME, 04103; **PH:** 1-207-878-2770; *http://* www.immucell.com

General - Incorporation	DE	**Stock**- Price on:12/24/2007	$5.66
Employees	27	Stock Exchange	NDQ
Auditor	Baker Newman & Noyes LLC	Ticker Symbol	ICCC
Stk Agt	American Stock Transfer & Trust Co.	Outstanding Shares	2,900,000
Counsel	Day, Berry & Howard	E.P.S	$0.184
DUNS No.	00-250-7622	Shareholders	NA

Business: The group's principal activity is to develop proprietary products that improve animal health and productivity in the dairy and beef industry. In addition, to this the group also conducts a phase ii clinical trail of diffgam(tm) bovine anti-clostridium difficile immunoglobulins, a human application of its milk derived passive antibody technology. The group has customers in Canada, Australia, New Zealand and Europe. The trademarks of the group are first defense(R), crypto-scan(R), tip-test(R), mastik(R), rpt(tm), accufirm(tm) and rjt(tm).

Primary SIC and add'l.: 2833 8731 2077

CIK No: 0000811641

Officers: Michael F. Brigham/47/Dir., CEO, Pres./$200,350.00, Joseph H. Crabb/53/Dir., VP, Chief Scientific Officer/$116,967.00

Directors: Michael F. Brigham/47/Dir., CEO, Pres., Joseph H. Crabb/53/Dir., VP, Chief Scientific Officer, William H. Maxwell/69/Dir., Linda Rhodes/58/Dir., Jonathan E. Rothschild/54/Dir., Mitchel Sayare/60/Dir., Robert C. Bruce/Dir., David S. Tomsche/51/Dir.

Owners: Michael F. Brigham/6.90%, David S. Tomsche, Joseph H. Crabb/6.40%, Robert C. Bruce/0.20%, Insiders/27.10%, Mitchel Sayare, Jonathan E. Rothschild/13.30%, Linda Rhodes, William H. Maxwell

Financial Data: *Fiscal Year End:*12/31 *Latest Annual Data:* 12/31/2006

Year	Sales	Net Income
2006	$4,801,000	$647,000
2005	$4,983,000	$708,000
2004	$3,696,000	$144,000

Curr. Assets:	$8,351,000	**Curr. Liab.:**	$1,417,000		
Plant, Equip.:	$1,883,000	**Total Liab.:**	$2,032,000	**Indic. Yr. Divd.:**	NA
Total Assets:	$11,364,000	**Net Worth:**	$9,332,000	**Debt/ Equity:**	NA

Immucor Inc

3130 Gateway Dr., Norcross, GA, 30091; *PH:* 1-770-441-2051; *Fax:* 1-770-441-3807; *http://* www.immucor.com

General - Incorporation	GA	**Stock**- Price on:12/24/2007	$29.01
Employees	563	Stock Exchange	NDQ
Auditor	Ernst & Young LLP, Grant Thornton LLP	Ticker Symbol	BLUD
Stk Agt	EquiServe Trust Co N.A	Outstanding Shares	68,880,000
Counsel	Edward L. Gallup & Ralph A. Eatz	E.P.S	$0.92
DUNS No.	06-144-6282	Shareholders	NA

Business: The group's principal activities are to develop, manufacture and market a complete line of reagents and automated systems. These systems are used to detect and identify certain properties of the cell and serum components of human blood prior to blood transfusion. The products are used by hospitals, clinical laboratories and blood donor centers. The products are sold in the United States, Canada, Germany, Portugal, Italy, Spain, France and Belgium. The automated products of the group are abs2000, rosys plato, dias plus, galileo and multi reader plus. The group also distributes laboratory equipment, which are designed to automate certain blood testing procedures and used in conjunction with the group's capture product. The registered trademark of the group is immucor.

Primary SIC and add'l.: 3845

CIK No: 0000736822

Subsidiaries: BCA Acquisition Corporation, Dominion Biologicals Limited, Gamma Biologicals, Inc., Immucor Diagnosticos Medicos Lda., Immucor France EURL, Immucor Gamma Benelux SPRL., Immucor Italia S.r.l., Immucor Medizinische Diagnostik GmbH, Immucor Sales, Inc., Immucor, S.L., Immucor-Kainos, Inc.

Officers: Gioacchino Dechirico/CEO, Pres./$1,080,645.00, Ralph A. Eatz/Chief Scientific Officer, Sr. VP/$842,357.00, Michael C. Poynter/Sr. VP - Sales, Didier L. Lanson/Mgr. - European Operations/$428,322.00, Patrick Waddy/CFO/$436,776.00, Jean-Jacques De Jaegher/VP - International, Philip H. Moise/58/VP

Directors: Edward L. Gallup/Chmn. Emeritus, Joseph E. Rosen/Chmn., Hiroshi Hoketsu/67/Dir., Jack Goldstein/61/Dir., Roswell S. Bowers/59/Dir., Michael S. Goldman/47/Dir., John A. Harris/57/Dir.

Owners: Edward L. Gallup, Roswell S. Bowers, John A. Harris, Insiders/2.60%, Gioacchino De Chirico, Goldman Sachs Asset Management, LP/5.10%, Hiroshi Hoketsu, Ralph A. Eatz/1.10%, Patrick D. Waddy, Jack Goldstein, Joseph E. Rosen, Philip H. Moise, Barclays Global Investors , NA/5.60%, Michael S. Goldman, Didier L. Lanson

Financial Data: *Fiscal Year End:*05/31 *Latest Annual Data:* 05/31/2007

Year	Sales	Net Income
2007	$223,678,000	$60,068,000
2006	$183,506,000	$39,843,000
2005	$144,786,000	$23,910,000

Curr. Assets:	$120,792,000	**Curr. Liab.:**	$27,909,000	**P/E Ratio:**	38.17
Plant, Equip.:	$25,684,000	**Total Liab.:**	$47,816,000	**Indic. Yr. Divd.:**	NA
Total Assets:	$191,687,000	**Net Worth:**	$143,871,000	**Debt/ Equity:**	NA

Immunicon Corp

3401 Masons Mill Rd., Ste. 100, Huntingdon Valley, PA, 19006; *PH:* 1-215-830-0777; *Fax:* 1-215-830-0751; *http://* www.immunicon.com; *Email:* info@immunicon.com

General - Incorporation	DE	**Stock**- Price on:12/24/2007	$2.04
Employees	104	Stock Exchange	NDQ
Auditor	Deloitte & Touche LLP	Ticker Symbol	IMMC
Stk Agt	American Stock Transfer & Trust Co.	Outstanding Shares	27,710,000
Counsel	Morgan, Lewis & Bockius LLP	E.P.S	-$0.73
DUNS No.	NA	Shareholders	NA

Business: The group's principal activity is to develop and commercialize proprietary cell-based research and diagnostic products with an initial focus on cancer. The group's products provides physicians and scientists with clinically meaningful information earlier than current diagnostic methods. Its products can identify, count and characterize the presence and quantity of a small number of tumor cells present in a blood sample. Major brand of the group is celltracks. Its products are based on an integrated system of instruments, reagents and other consumable and ancillary products used to isolate, label, count and analyze tumor cells in the blood, known as circulating tumor cells, or ctcs

Primary SIC and add'l.: 3826 3829

CIK No: 0001083132

Subsidiaries: IMMC Holdings, Inc., Immunicon Europe, Inc., Immunivest Corporation

Officers: Byron D. Hewett/Dir., CEO, Pres./$639,452.00, James G. Murphy/Sr. VP - Finance, Administration, CFO/$386,329.00, Carrie Mulherin/VP - Marketing, John Verrant/VP - Engineering, Peter Scott/VP - Quality Assurance, Regulatory, Affairs, Teresa Lipesey/VP, Corporate Controller, James L. Wilcox/VP, Chief Counsel, Sec./$319,845.00, Michael T. Kagan/VP - Operations/$299,660.00, Mark Connelly/VP - Reagent Development, Leon W.m.m. Terstappen/Sr. VP, Research & Development, Chief Scientific Officer - CSO

Directors: Byron D. Hewett/Dir., CEO, Pres., William J. Freytag/Chmn., Allen J. Lauer/Dir., Jonathan Cool/Dir., Brian Geiger/Dir., Zola P. Horovitz/Dir., Elizabeth E. Tallett/Dir.

Owners: Byron D. Hewett/1.16%, James L. Wilcox, AMVESCAP PLC/5.47%, Elizabeth E. Tallett, Brian J. Geiger, William J. Freytag, Canaan Partners/6.24%, Johnson & Johnson Development Corporation/5.96%, Michael Kagan, Edward L. Erickson/1.73%, Zola P. Horovitz, Insiders/7.20%, Leon W.M.M. Terstappen/1.26%, James G. Murphy/1.07%, Jonathan Cool *(17 Owners included in Index)*

Financial Data: *Fiscal Year End:*12/31 *Latest Annual Data:* 12/31/2006

Year	Sales	Net Income
2006	$8,697,000	-$23,998,000
2005	$4,647,000	-$26,908,000
2004	$1,565,000	-$27,933,000

Curr. Assets:	$58,784,000	**Curr. Liab.:**	$22,346,000		
Plant, Equip.:	$4,011,000	**Total Liab.:**	$45,572,000	**Indic. Yr. Divd.:**	NA
Total Assets:	$65,773,000	**Net Worth:**	$20,201,000	**Debt/ Equity:**	1.4122

ImmunoCellular Therapeutics Ltd

1999 Ave. Of The Stars, 11th Fl. S, Los Angels, CA, 90067; *PH:* 1-310-423-0845

General - Incorporation	DE	**Stock**- Price on:12/24/2007	$1.25
Employees	NA	Stock Exchange	OTC
Auditor	Stonefield Josephson, Inc.	Ticker Symbol	IMUC
Stk Agt	Corporate Transfer Agent	Outstanding Shares	11,780,000
Counsel	NA	E.P.S	-$0.82
DUNS No.	NA	Shareholders	NA

Business: The group was founded in 2004 as Spectral Molecular Imaging, Inc. and changed its name to Optical Molecular Imaging, Inc. in January 2006 and again to ImmunoCellular Therapeutics, Ltd. in November 2006. The group operates from United States.

Primary SIC and add'l.: 5995

CIK No: 0000822411

Officers: David Wohlberg/54/COO, Pres., Kirk C. Peacock/39/Treasurer, CFO, Sanford J. Hillsberg/59/Dir., Sec.

Directors: John S. Yu,/44/Chmn., Manfred Mosk/74/Dir., Sanford J. Hillsberg/59/Dir., Sec., Rudolf Nisi/74/Dir.

Owners: David J. Wohlberg/3.81%, Richard A. Cowell, RAB Special Situations (Master) Fund Limited/9.90%, Sanford J. Hillsberg/13.50%, Jacqueline Brandwynne/1.50%, Robert L. Martuza, Cedars-Sinai Medical Center/5.89%, Insiders/52.29%, Keith Black/11.01%, Manfred Mosk/11.80%, John S. Yu/33.49%

Financial Data: *Fiscal Year End:*12/31 *Latest Annual Data:* 12/31/2006

Year	Sales	Net Income
2006	NA	-$5,153,000

Curr. Assets:	$1,070,000	**Curr. Liab.:**	$103,000		
Plant, Equip.:	NA	**Total Liab.:**	$880,000	**Indic. Yr. Divd.:**	NA
Total Assets:	$1,070,000	**Net Worth:**	$190,000	**Debt/ Equity:**	NA

ImmunoGen Inc

128 Sidney St., Cambridge, MA, 02139; *PH:* 1-617-995-2500; *Fax:* 1-617-995-2510; *http://* www.immunogen.com; *Email:* info@immunogen.com

General - Incorporation	MA	**Stock**- Price on:12/24/2007	$5.98
Employees	192	Stock Exchange	NDQ
Auditor	Ernst & Young LLP	Ticker Symbol	IMGN
Stk Agt	Mellon Investor Services LLC	Outstanding Shares	42,270,000
Counsel	Mintz Levin Cohn Ferris Et Al	E.P.S	-$0.51
DUNS No.	01-199-1874	Shareholders	NA

Business: The group's principal activity is to develop and produce commercial anti-body based cancer therapeutics and other pharmaceuticals based on molecular immunology. A preclinical testing of a second tumor-activated prodrugs candidate, hun901-dm1 is conducted for the treatment of small-cell lung cancer. The product candidates of the group are tumor-activated prodrugs or taps which are based on proprietary technology platform that combines monoclonal antibodies that targets tumor cells and potent drugs.

Primary SIC and add'l.: 6794 2834 8731

CIK No: 0000855654

Subsidiaries: ImmunoGen Europe Limited, ImmunoGen Securities Corp

Officers: Mitchel Sayare/Chmn., CEO, Pres., Daniel M. Junius/CFO, Exec. VP - Finance, John M. Lambert/Sr. VP - Pharmaceutical Development, Craig Barrows/VP, General Counsel, Sec.

Directors: Mitchel Sayare/Chmn., CEO, Pres., Joseph J. Villafranca/Dir., David W. Carter/Dir., Nicole Onetto/Dir., Mark Skaletsky/Dir., Stephen C. McCluski/Dir.

Owners: Stephen C. McCluski, Capital Ventures International/7.30%, Joseph J. Villafranca, Pauline Jen Ryan, John M. Lambert/1.10%, Mark Skaletsky, David W. Carter, Biotechnology Value Fund, L.P./6.60%, Mitchel Sayare/3.40%, Insiders/5.60%, Nicole Onetto, Daniel M. Junius, Walter A. Blttler

Financial Data: *Fiscal Year End:*06/30 *Latest Annual Data:* 6/30/2006

Year	Sales	Net Income
2006	$32,088,000	-$17,834,000
2005	$35,718,000	-$10,951,000
2004	$25,956,000	-$5,917,000

Curr. Assets:	$84,544,000	**Curr. Liab.:**	$10,723,000		
Plant, Equip.:	$9,319,000	**Total Liab.:**	$21,778,000	**Indic. Yr. Divd.:**	NA
Total Assets:	$94,128,000	**Net Worth:**	$72,350,000	**Debt/ Equity:**	NA

Immunomedics Inc

300 American Rd., Morris Plains, NJ, 07950; *PH:* 1-973-605-8200; *Fax:* 1-973-605-8282; *http://* www.immunomedics.com; *Email:* info@immunomedics.com

General - Incorporation .... DE	Stock- Price on:12/24/2007 .... $4.61
Employees 106	Stock Exchange... NDQ
Auditor .... Ernst & Young LLP	Ticker Symbol... IMMU
Stk Agt..... American Stock Transfer & Trust Co.	Outstanding Shares 75,010,000
Counsel .... Warshaw Burstein Cohen Et Al	E.P.S .... -$0.26
DUNS No. 11-535-0605	Shareholders.. NA

Business: The group's principal activity is to develop, manufacture and market monoclonal antibody-based products for the detection and treatment of cancer, autoimmune and other serious diseases. The group has developed a number of advanced technologies to create humanized antibodies that can be either alone in unlabeled form, or conjugated with radioactive isotopes, chemotherapeutics or toxins to create highly targeted agents. The group's product candidates and technologies are protected by a portfolio of intellectual property that includes 90 issued patents in the United States and 250 other issued patents worldwide. The group currently markets cea-scan and leukoscan in the United States, Canada, the European union and Australia.

Primary SIC and add'l.: 2834 3841 8731

CIK No: 0000722830

Subsidiaries: IBC Pharmaceuticals, Inc, Immunomedics GmbH, Immunomedics, B.V.

Officers: Cynthia L. Sullivan/CEO, Pres., David M. Goldenberg/Chmn., Chief Strategic Officer, Gerard G. Gorman/CFO, VP - Finance

Directors: David M. Goldenberg/Chmn., Chief Strategic Officer, Morton Coleman/Dir., Don C. Stark/Dir., Brian A. Markison/Dir., Mary E. Paetzold/Dir., Marvin E. Jaffe/Dir.

Owners: Morton Coleman, Insiders/12.60%, Gerard G. Gorman, Cynthia L. Sullivan/11.20%, David M. Goldenberg/11.10%, Edward T. Wolynic, Don C. Stark, Mary E. Paetzold, Marvin E. Jaffe, FMR Corp./6.60%, Brian A. Markison

Financial Data: Fiscal Year End:06/30 *Latest Annual Data:* 06/30/2007

Year	Sales	Net Income
2007	$8,506,000	-$16,656,000
2006	$4,353,000	-$28,764,000
2005	$3,813,000	-$26,758,000

Curr. Assets:	$44,744,000	Curr. Liab.:	$19,035,000		
Plant, Equip.:	$8,496,000	Total Liab.:	$74,371,000	Indic. Yr. Divd.:	NA
Total Assets:	$55,878,000	Net Worth:	-$18,675,000	Debt/ Equity:	7.2571

Immureboost Inc

Formerly: eSavingsStore.com Inc

1174 Manitou Dr. Nw, Island, WA, 98333; *PH:* 1-253-549-4336; *http://* www.esavingsstore.com

General - Incorporation .... NV	Stock- Price on:12/24/2007 .... $0.6
Employees .... NA	Stock Exchange.. NA
Auditor Child, Van Wagoner & Bradshaw, PLLC	Ticker Symbol.. NA
Stk Agt.. Stalt, Inc.	Outstanding Shares 101,850,000
Counsel .... NA	E.P.S .... NA
DUNS No. .... NA	Shareholders.. NA

Business: The groups principle activities include marketing and selling vacation packages. The group operates from the United States.

Primary SIC and add'l.: 4700

CIK No: 0001309251

Officers: John McLane/Dir., CEO, Pres., Sec., Howard Bouch/60/Dir., CFO

Directors: John McLane/Dir., CEO, Pres., Sec., Howard Bouch/60/Dir., CFO

Owners: Kathy Mowbray/8.80%, Jennie Bouch/9.80%, George Graham/8.80%, Howard Bouch/18.70%, Insiders/18.70%

Curr. Assets:	NA	Curr. Liab.:	$34,000		
Plant, Equip.:	$0	Total Liab.:	$57,000	Indic. Yr. Divd.:	NA
Total Assets:	$33,000	Net Worth:	-$24,000	Debt/ Equity:	NA

Impac Mortgage Holdings Inc

19500 Jamboree Rd., Irvine, CA, 92612; *PH:* 1-949-475-3600; *Fax:* 1-949-475-3969; *http://* www.impaccompanies.com

General - Incorporation .... MD	Stock- Price on:12/24/2007 .... $6.26
Employees 827	Stock Exchange.. NYSE
Auditor .... Ernst & Young LLP	Ticker Symbol.. IMH
Stk Agt...... American Stock Transfer & Trust Co.	Outstanding Shares 76,080,000
Counsel .... NA	E.P.S .... -$3.91
DUNS No. .... NA	Shareholders.. NA

Business: The groups principal activities include acquiring, originating, selling and investing residential mortgages. The group also provides warehouse financing to originators of mortgages. The group operates through four segments namely, long term investment operations, warehouse lending operations, mortgage operations and commercial operations. The group operates from the United States. Of the total assets in the year 2006, the long term investment operations accounted for $21,513,648, warehouse lending operations $1,966,317, mortgage operations $1,631,734 and commercial operations $181,406 (thousands).

Primary SIC and add'l.: 6798

CIK No: 0001000298

Subsidiaries: IMH Assets Corp., Impac Funding Corporation, Impac Warehouse Lending Group, Inc.

Officers: Joseph R. Tomkinson/Chmn., CEO/$1,334,602.00, William S. Ashmore/Dir., Pres./$1,326,275.00, Tania Jernigan/VP - Stockholder Relations, Sheralee Urbano/VP - Human Resources, Richard J. Johnson/COO, Exec. VP/$824,996.00, Gretchen D. Verdugo/CFO, Exec. VP/$991,160.00, Ronald M. Morrison/Exec. VP, General Counsel, Andrew McCormick/47/Exec. VP, Chief Investment Officer - IMH, IFC, Iwlg, Iccc, William D. Endresen/53/Pres. - Iccc

Directors: Joseph R. Tomkinson/Chmn., CEO, William S. Ashmore/Dir., Pres., Leigh J. Abrams/Dir., Frank P. Filipps/Dir., Stephan R. Peers/Dir., William E. Rose/Dir., James Walsh/Dir.

Owners: James Walsh, Insiders/3.10%, Gretchen D. Verdugo, Joseph R. Tomkinson/1.00%, William S. Ashmore, Richard J. Johnson, Stephan R. Peers, Frank P. Filipps, Leigh J. Abrams, Howard Amster/8.70%, William E. Rose

Financial Data: Fiscal Year End:12/31 *Latest Annual Data:* 12/31/2006

Year	Sales	Net Income
2006	$1,558,735,000	-$75,273,000
2005	$1,472,884,000	$270,258,000
2004	$796,392,000	$257,637,000

Curr. Assets:	$295,348,000	Curr. Liab.:	$1,880,395,000		
Plant, Equip.:	$177,064,000	Total Liab.:	$22,589,425,000	Indic. Yr. Divd.:	$0.400
Total Assets:	$23,598,955,000	Net Worth:	$1,009,530,000	Debt/ Equity:	24.5926

Imperial Capital Bancorp Inc

Formerly: ITLA Capital Corp

888 Prospect St., Ste. 110, La Jolla, CA, 92037; *PH:* 1-858-551-0511; *http://* www.itlacapital.com

General - Incorporation .... DE	Stock- Price on:12/24/2007 .... NA
Employees 253	Stock Exchange.. NYSE
Auditor .... Ernst & Young LLP	Ticker Symbol.. IMP
Stk Agt .... Mellon Investor Services, LLC.	Outstanding Shares .... NA
Counsel .... Silver, Freedman & Taff LLP	E.P.S .... NA
DUNS No. 96-876-4019	Shareholders.. NA

Business: The group's principal activity is to originate real estate loans secured by income producing properties. The services provided by the group include accepting of deposits that are used primarily to fund the investment in variable rate commercial and residential real estate loans. The group originates real estate loans through branch offices located in San Francisco, Glendale, Costa Mesa and Del Mar. The group also acquires pools of single family mortgages in the secondary market for investment purposes and accepts deposits insured by FDIC.

Primary SIC and add'l.: 6022 6712

CIK No: 0001000234

Subsidiaries: Imperial Capital Bank, Imperial Capital Real Estate Investment Trust, ITLA Capital Statutory Trust I, ITLA Capital Statutory Trust II, ITLA Capital Statutory Trust III, ITLA Capital Statutory Trust IV, ITLA Capital Statutory Trust V, ITLA Commercial Investment Corporation, ITLA Commercial Warehouse Corporation, ITLA Funding Corporation, ITLA Management Corporation, ITLA Servicing Corporation

Officers: George W. Haligowski/Chmn., CEO, Pres./$1,987,724.00, Norval L. Bruce/Vice Chmn., Chief Credit Officer/$478,850.00, David Hunt/MD - Business Lending Credit, Bradley Satenberg/MD, Anthony A. Rusnak/Deputy MD, General Counsel, Corp. Sec., Lyle C. Lodwick/Exec. MD, COO/$376,198.00, Phillip Lombardi/Sr. MD, Chief - Lending Operations/$268,482.00, Timothy M. Doyle/Exec. MD, CFO/$404,621.00, Scott Wallace/MD - Finance, Treasurer, Brian Benson/Sr. MD, Holly Wilkinson/Investor Relations Contact

Directors: George W. Haligowski/Chmn., CEO, Pres., Norval L. Bruce/Vice Chmn., Chief Credit Officer, Robert R. Reed/Dir., Hirotaka Oribe/Dir., Sandor X. Mayuga/Dir., Preston Martin/84/Dir., Jeffrey L. Lipscomb/Dir.

Owners: Thomson Horstmann & Bryant, Inc./7.44%, Jeffrey L. Lipscomb, Lyle C. Lodwick, Dimensional Fund Advisors, LP/8.75%, Sandor X. Mayuga, Hirotaka Oribe, Timothy M. Doyle/1.66%, Wellington Management Company, LLP/6.84%, Barclays Global Advisors, NA, et al/7.32%, Insiders/9.76%, Norval L. Bruce/1.12%, George W. Haligowski/5.23%, Phillip E. Lombardi, Robert R. Reed, Franklin Mutual Advisers, LLC/8.15%

Curr. Assets:	$51,201,000	Curr. Liab.:	$3,107,573,000		
Plant, Equip.:	$14,580,000	Total Liab.:	$3,194,173,000	Indic. Yr. Divd.:	NA
Total Assets:	$3,415,510,000	Net Worth:	$221,337,000	Debt/ Equity:	NA

Imperial Chemical Industries Plc

10 Finderne Ave., Bridgewater, NJ, 08807; *PH:* 1-908-685-5000; *Fax:* 1-908-685-5005; *http://* www.ici.com; *Email:* ici@ici.com

General - Incorporation .... UK	Stock- Price on:12/24/2007 .... NA
Employees 31,910	Stock Exchange.. OTC
Auditor .... KPMG Audit Plc	Ticker Symbol... ICIYY
Stk Agt .... Morgan ADR Service Center	Outstanding Shares .... NA
Counsel .... NA	E.P.S .... NA
DUNS No. 21-015-2237	Shareholders.. NA

Business: The group's principal activities are research, manufacture and sale of specialty products and paints. The group's businesses comprise national starch, quest, performance specialties and ici paints, which are referred to as the international businesses, and a number of smaller regional and industrial businesses. National starch, includes adhesives, specialty starches, specialty synthetic polymers and electronic and engineering materials. Quest, creates and markets flavours, food ingredients and fragrances. Performance specialties, comprises uniqema - a surfactants and oleochemicals business. Ici paints, concentrates on decorative paint and packaging coatings for food and beverage cans with other businesses. Regional and industrial, includes polyester staple fibre, pure terephthalic acid, soda ash, agrochemicals, pharmaceuticals, nitrocellulose, rubber chemicals and tartaric acid.

Primary SIC and add'l.: 2891 2087 2834 2851 2899 2824

CIK No: 0000049906

Subsidiaries: Deutsche ICI GmbH, ICI American Holdings Inc, ICI Canada Inc, ICI Finance PLC, ICI India Ltd, ICI Pakistan Ltd, Indopco Inc, National Starch and Chemical (Thailand) Ltd, Nippon NSC Ltd, Pakistan PTA Ltd, Quest International Flavours and Fragrances Limited, Quest International Nederland BV, The Glidden Company, Tintas Coral Ltda, Unichema Chemie BV

Officers: John D.G McAdam/CEO, Regina S. Kilfoyle/Dir. - Corporate Communications, John Dawson/VP - Investor Relations, Corporate Communications, Frank Rose/Group VP - Sustainability, Alan Brown/CFO, Rolf Deusinger/Member - Executive Management Team, Andy M. Ransom/Member - Executive Management Team, David Hamill/48/Executive Dir., George St. John Turner/Deputy Company Sec., Beth Horlock/Company Secretariat Mgr.

Directors: Peter Ellwood/Chmn., Lord Butler/Sr. Dir., Joseph T. Gorman/Non Exec. Dir., Baroness Noakes/Non Exec. Dir., David Hamill/48/Executive Dir., Richard N. Haythornthwaite/Non Exec. Dir., Adri Baan/Non Exec. Dir.

Financial Data: Fiscal Year End:12/31 *Latest Annual Data:* 12/31/2005

Year	Sales	Net Income
2005	$10,001,290,000	$357,926,000
2004	$10,858,318,000	$202,293,000
2003	$10,430,903,000	-$295,231,000

Curr. Assets:	$3,918,262,000	Curr. Liab.:	$3,863,196,000		
Plant, Equip.:	$2,751,559,000	Total Liab.:	$9,624,434,000	Indic. Yr. Divd.:	NA
Total Assets:	$13,083,242,000	Net Worth:	$3,458,808,000	Debt/ Equity:	NA

Imperial Consolidated Capital

6075 S E Ave., Ste 1, Las Vegas, NV, 89119; *PH:* 1-702-851-3431;
http:// www.imperialconsolidated.com

General - Incorporation	NV	Stock - Price on:12/24/2007	NA
Employees	NA	Stock Exchange	NA
Auditor	Dohan & Co	Ticker Symbol	NA
Stk Agt	NA	Outstanding Shares	NA
Counsel	NA	E.P.S.	NA
DUNS No.	NA	Shareholders	NA

Business: The group's principal activity is acquiring and exploring for minerals and metals, including gold, silver, zinc and lead. On 15-Aug-2003, the company acquired a 100% undivided mineral interest in the Triune Property, Canada. The Triune Property consists of six mineral claims, the Triune, Enterprise, Silver Chief, Kamloops Fraction, Revenge and Kamloops.

Primary SIC and add'l.: 1000

CIK No: 0001116269

Imperial Industries Inc

3790 Pk. Central Blvd. N, Pompano Beach, FL, 33064; *PH:* 1-954-917-4114; *Fax:* 1-954-970-6565;
http:// www.imperialindustries.com

General - Incorporation	DE	Stock - Price on:12/24/2007	$12.9699
Employees	148	Stock Exchange	NDQ
Auditor	PricewaterhouseCoopers LLP	Ticker Symbol	IPII
Stk Agt	Continental Stock Transfer & Trust Co	Outstanding Shares	2,510,000
Counsel	NA	E.P.S.	$0.37
DUNS No.	04-492-1435	Shareholders	NA

Business: The group's principal activities are to manufacturing and distributing of building materials to dealers and others. The group also involves in the manufacturing and selling of exterior, interior finishing wall coatings and mortar products for the construction industry. The products are marketed to developers, general contractors and subcontractors in the construction or renovation of residential, multi-family and commercial buildings and swimming pools. The group sells products in Florida, Mississippi, Georgia and Alabama and to a lesser extent, other states in the southeastern part of the United States as well as foreign countries. The group manufactures product through its wholly owned subsidiaries, premix-Marbletite manufacturing company and acrocrete inc. The company distributes products through its wholly-owned subsidiary just-rite supply inc. The manufacturing facilities primarily produce and distribute stucco, roof tile mortar and plaster products.

Primary SIC and add'l.: 3253 3251 3272

CIK No: 0000049930

Subsidiaries: DFH, Inc., Just-Rite Supply, Inc., Premix-Marbletite Manufacturing Co., Inc.

Officers: Howard L. Ehler/Dir., CEO, COO, Sec./$354,568.00, Steven M. Healy/CFO/$144,000.00, Stephen C. Brown/Pres. - Just, Rite Supply, Inc, Fred Hansen/Pres. - DFH, Inc/$166,300.00

Directors: Howard L. Ehler/Dir., CEO, COO, Sec., Daniel S. Ponce/Chmn., Nadine Gramling/Dir., Milton J. Wallace/Dir., Morton L. Weinberger/Dir., Lisa M. Brock/Dir.

Owners: Milton J. Wallace/2.00%, Howard L. Ehler/1.40%, Steven Healy/0.20%, Insiders/12.50%, Stephen C. Brown/0.20%, Nadine Gramling/0.10%, Daniel S. Ponce/2.70%, Lisa M. Brock/4.20%, Morton L. Weinberger/1.90%, Fred Hansen/0.20%

*Financial Data: Fiscal Year End:*12/31 *Latest Annual Data:* 12/31/2006

Year	Sales	Net Income
2006	$75,548,000	$2,898,000
2005	$72,254,000	$3,413,000
2004	$55,268,000	$2,466,000

Curr. Assets:	$18,090,000	Curr. Liab.:	$8,065,000	P/E Ratio:	14.96
Plant, Equip.:	$7,064,000	Total Liab.:	$12,596,000	Indic. Yr. Divd.:	NA
Total Assets:	$25,831,000	Net Worth:	$13,235,000	Debt/ Equity:	0.2279

Imperial Oil Ltd

237 4th Ave. SW, Calgary, AB, T2P 3M9; *PH:* 1-800-567-3776; *http://* www.imperialoil.ca

General - Incorporation	Canada	Stock - Price on:12/24/2007	$46.76
Employees	4,900	Stock Exchange	AMEX
Auditor	PricewaterhouseCoopers LLP	Ticker Symbol	IMO
Stk Agt	Mellon Trust Co	Outstanding Shares	939,560,000
Counsel	NA	E.P.S.	$3.30
DUNS No.	20-167-4926	Shareholders	NA

Business: The group's principle activities are to refine petroleum products and produce crude oil and natural gas. The group operates in three segments: natural resources, petroleum products and chemicals. Natural resources include the exploration for and production of crude oil and natural gas. Petroleum products comprise the refining of crude oil into petroleum products and the distribution and marketing of these products. Chemicals include the manufacture and marketing of various hydrocarbon-based chemicals and chemical products. The group's quarterly revenue for September 2007 was 6,430.00 millions of CAD.

Primary SIC and add'l.: 1311 2911 2819 2821

CIK No: 0000049938

Subsidiaries: Imperial Oil Resources Limited, Imperial Oil Resources Ventures Limited, McColl-Frontenac Petroleum Inc.

Officers: T. J. Hearn/Chmn., CEO, Pres., R. L. Broiles/Dir., Sr. VP - Resources Division, P. A. Smith/Dir., Sr. VP, Controller - Finance, Administration

Directors: T. J. Hearn/Chmn., CEO, Pres., P. A. Smith/Dir., Sr. VP, Controller - Finance, Administration, J. M. Mintz/Dir., J. F. Shepard/Dir., R. Phillips/Dir., S. D. Whittaker/Dir., V. L. Young/Dir., R. L. Broiles/Dir., Sr. VP - Resources Division

*Financial Data: Fiscal Year End:*12/31 *Latest Annual Data:* 12/31/2006

Year	Sales	Net Income
2006	$21,270,583,000	$2,612,056,000
2005	$24,207,612,000	$2,230,800,000
2004	$18,648,538,000	$1,703,776,000

Curr. Assets:	$4,555,653,000	Curr. Liab.:	$4,589,119,000	P/E Ratio:	14.99
Plant, Equip.:	$8,973,152,000	Total Liab.:	$7,495,504,000	Indic. Yr. Divd.:	$0.340
Total Assets:	$13,850,592,000	Net Worth:	$6,355,089,000	Debt/ Equity:	NA

Imperial Petroleum Inc

329 Main St., Ste. 801, Evansville, IN, 47725; *PH:* 1-812-867-1433; *http://* www.iptm.net;
Email: investor@iptm.net

General - Incorporation	NV	Stock - Price on:12/24/2007	$0.2
Employees	1	Stock Exchange	OTC
Auditor	Weaver & Tidwell LLP	Ticker Symbol	IPMN
Stk Agt	Interwest Transfer Company, Inc.	Outstanding Shares	11,540,000
Counsel	NA	E.P.S.	-$0.282
DUNS No.	05-895-2656	Shareholders	NA

Business: The group's principal activity is to operate as a diversified energy and mineral mining company. The group has historically been engaged in the production and exploration of crude oil and natural gas. Presently, the group is operating duke gold mine in Utah. It also develops and markets water filtration systems to municipalities through its subsidiary imperial environmental company. The group is in the development stage. On 13-May-2003, the group acquired powder river basin gas corp and on 16-Jan-2004, it acquired the oil and gas assets of warrior resources inc and hillside oil and gas llc.

Primary SIC and add'l.: 1041 1311 3589 1081 1021

CIK No: 0000355356

Subsidiaries: Hoosier Biodiesel Company, I.B. Energy, Inc., Imperial Environmental Company, LaTex Resources International, Premier Operating Company, Ridgepointe Mining Company

Owners: Annalee C. Wilson/6.70%, Taghmen Ventures Ltd/8.20%, RAB Special Situations LP/10.30%, James M. Clements/11.50%, Insiders/24.90%, Aaron M. Wilson/0.30%, Jeffrey T. Wilson/17.90%

*Financial Data: Fiscal Year End:*07/31 *Latest Annual Data:* 7/31/2006

Year	Sales	Net Income
2006	$3,435,000	-$3,427,000
2005	$2,964,000	-$2,696,000
2004	$1,932,000	-$1,171,000

Curr. Assets:	$671,000	Curr. Liab.:	$22,578,000		
Plant, Equip.:	$16,750,000	Total Liab.:	$23,514,000	Indic. Yr. Divd.:	NA
Total Assets:	$18,085,000	Net Worth:	-$5,428,000	Debt/ Equity:	NA

Imperial Sugar Co

8016 Hwy. 90A, Sugar Land, TX, 77487; *PH:* 1-281-491-9181; *Fax:* 1-281-490-9530;
http:// www.imperialsugar.com; *Email:* consumers@imperialsugar.com

General - Incorporation	TX	Stock - Price on:12/24/2007	$29.25
Employees	842	Stock Exchange	NDQ
Auditor	Deloitte & Touche LLP	Ticker Symbol	IPSU
Stk Agt	Bank of New York	Outstanding Shares	11,750,000
Counsel	NA	E.P.S.	$4.83
DUNS No.	00-808-6472	Shareholders	NA

Business: The group is one of the processors and marketers of refined sugar in the United States. The group's customers include retail grocers, foodservice distributors and industrial customers. The group's products include granulated, powdered, liquid and brown sugars marketed in a variety of packaging options. In addition, the group produces selected specialty sugar products, including savannah gold and specialty sugars used in confections and icings. In fiscal 2003 the group discontinued sugar land, Texas sugar refinery operations and the related packaging and distribution operations.

Primary SIC and add'l.: 2063 2062 2035

CIK No: 0000831327

Subsidiaries: Imperial Distributing, Inc., Imperial-Savannah LP, Ragus Holdings, Inc., Savannah Foods & Industries, Inc.

Officers: Robert A. Peiser/Dir., CEO, Pres., Patrick D. Henneberry/Sr. VP - Commodities Management, Kay T. Hastings/Sr. VP - Human Resources, Jack E. Walker/VP - Industrial Sales, Hal P. Mechler/CFO, Sr. VP, Primary Investor Relations Officer, George Muller/CIO, VP, Brian T. Harrison/VP - Operations, William F. Schwer/Sr. VP, Sec., General Counsel, Eric J. Story/VP, Treasurer, John C. Sheptor/COO, Exec. VP, Greig P. Debow/VP - Consumer Sales, Marketing

Directors: Robert A. Peiser/Dir., CEO, Pres., James J. Gaffney/Chmn., John K. Sweeney/Dir., Yves-Andre Istel/Dir., Curtis G. Anderson/Dir., Gaylord O. Coan/Dir., David C. Moran/Dir., Robert S. Kopriva/Dir.

Owners: H. P. Mechler, Insiders/1.84%, Lehman Brothers Holdings Inc./28.10%, Shultze Asset Management, LLC/13.46%, William F. Schwer, John K. Sweeney, John C. Sheptor, Yves-Andre Istel, Curtis G. Anderson, Barclays Global Investors, N.A./11.85%, Goldman Sachs Asset Management, L.P./7.13%, Robert A. Peiser, Gaylord O. Coan, James J. Gaffney, Patrick D. Henneberry *(16 Owners included in Index)*

*Financial Data: Fiscal Year End:*09/30 *Latest Annual Data:* 9/30/2006

Year	Sales	Net Income
2006	$946,823,000	$50,059,000
2005	$803,774,000	-$19,308,000
2004	$963,641,000	$14,964,000

Curr. Assets:	$260,066,000	Curr. Liab.:	$100,453,000	P/E Ratio:	7.10
Plant, Equip.:	$90,449,000	Total Liab.:	$185,258,000	Indic. Yr. Divd.:	$0.280
Total Assets:	$371,143,000	Net Worth:	$185,885,000	Debt/ Equity:	0.0082

Imperial Tobacco Group Plc

PO Box 244, Upton Rd., Bristol, BS99 7UJ; *PH:* 44-1179636636; *http://* www.imperial-tobacco.com

General - Incorporation	England And Wales	Stock - Price on:12/24/2007	$89.73
Employees	14,486	Stock Exchange	NYSE
Auditor	PricewaterhouseCoopers LLP	Ticker Symbol	ITY
Stk Agt	NA	Outstanding Shares	337,300,000
Counsel	Matthew Phillips	E.P.S.	$5.28
DUNS No.	52-531-7137	Shareholders	NA

Business: The group's principal activity is the manufacture, marketing and sale of tobacco and related products. Products include cigarettes, tobacco, rolling papers, and cigars. The group's brands include davidoff, west, drum, rizla, r1, john player, maxim, prima, bastos, regal, capstan, medium navy cut, woodbine, mars, excellence, route 66, lambert & butler, richmond, horizon, cabinet, golden Virginia, embassy, regal, super kings, boss, peter stuyvesant, interval, champion, jp blue, ernte 23, and van nelle.

Primary SIC and add'l.: 2111 5194

CIK No: 0001072670

Subsidiaries: Badische Tabakmanufaktur Roth-Hndle GmbH, Dunkerquoise des Blends S.A.S., Ets. L. Lacroix Fils N.V. (Rizla Belgium N.V.), Imperial Tobacco (Asia) Pte. Ltd., Imperial Tobacco (EFKA) GmbH& Co. KG, Imperial Tobacco Agio GmbH, Imperial Tobacco Australia Limited, Imperial Tobacco CR s.r.o., Imperial Tobacco Finance PLC, Imperial Tobacco France S.A.S., Imperial Tobacco Hellas S.A., Imperial Tobacco Holdings Limited, Imperial Tobacco International Limited, Imperial Tobacco Italy Srl, Imperial Tobacco Limited 37 Subsidiaries included in the Index

Officers: Gareth Davis/58/Dir., CEO, Matthew Phillips/38/Company Sec., Graham Brashill/61/Dir., Dir. - Group Sales, Marketing, Frank Rogerson/55/Dir. - Corporate Affairs, Robert Dyrbus/56/Dir., Dir. - Finance, David Cresswell/64/Dir., Dir. - Manufacturing, Alison Cooper/42/Dir., Dir. - Corporate Development, Kathryn Brown/Group Dir. - Human Resources, Kathryn Turner/Group Dir. - Human Resources, Alex Parsons/Group Mgr. - Media Relations, Simon Evans/Group Press Officer, John Nelson-Smith/Mgr. - Investor Relations, Garry Wilson/Mgr. - Investor Relations, John Jones/Group Treasurer

Directors: Gareth Davis/58/Dir., CEO, Anthony Alexander/70/Vice Chmn., Iain Napier/58/Chmn., Pierre Jungels/64/Dir., Graham Brashill/61/Dir., Dir. - Group Sales, Marketing, Robert Dyrbus/56/Dir., Dir. - Finance, Susan Murray/51/Non - Exec. Dir., Colin Day/52/Non - Exec. Dir., David Cresswell/64/Dir., Dir. - Manufacturing, Charles Knott/53/Non - Exec. Dir., Ken Burnett/56/Non - Exec. Dir., Alison Cooper/42/Dir., Dir. - Corporate Development, Michael Herlihy/55/Non - Exec. Dir., Mark Williamson/Non - Exec. Dir.

Owners: I J G. Napier, Barclays PLC, Lloyds TSB Group plc, Morgan Stanley Investment Management Limited, P. H. Jungels, D. Cresswell, M. R. Phillips, Legal & General Investment Management Limited, G. L. Blashill, Amvescap plc, C. F. Knott, D. C. Bonham, C. R. Day, K. M. Burnett, R. Dyrbus *(24 Owners included in Index)*

Financial Data: *Fiscal Year End:*09/30 *Latest Annual Data:* 9/30/2006

Year	Sales	Net Income
2006	$21,864,478,000	$1,456,883,000
2005	$19,840,314,000	$1,198,704,000
2004	$3,738,759,000	$669,573,000

Curr. Assets:	$4,046,689,000	Curr. Liab.:	$5,621,545,000		
Plant, Equip.:	$1,086,108,000	Total Liab.:	$14,051,990,000	Indic. Yr. Divd.:	$1.660
Total Assets:	$16,902,088,000	Net Worth:	$2,814,518,000	Debt/ Equity:	NA

Implant Sciences Corp

107 Audubon Rd., Ste. 5, Wakefield, MA, 01880; *PH:* 1-781-246-0700; *Fax:* 1-781-246-1167; *http://* www.implantsciences.com; *Email:* info@implantsciences.com

General		Stock	
Incorporation	MA	Price on:12/24/2007	$1.8
Employees	150	Stock Exchange	AMEX
Auditor	BDO Seidman LLP	Ticker Symbol	IMX
Stk Agt	Computershare Trust Co	Outstanding Shares	11,840,000
Counsel	Ellenoff Grossman & Schole LLP	E.P.S.	-$1.04
DUNS No.	14-703-2403	Shareholders	NA

Business: The group's principal activity is to develop products for the medical device and explosives detection industry. These products are developed using ion implantation and thin film coatings of radioactive and non-radioactive materials. The group modifies the surface characteristics of orthopedic joint implants to reduce polyethylene wear and thereby increasing the life of the implant. The group also provides ion implantation of electronic dopants for the semiconductor industry. Ion implantation services are supplied to numerous semiconductor manufacturers, research laboratories and universities. The major customers of the group are howmedica and osteonics division of stryker corporation and biomet incorporated.

Primary SIC and add'l.: 3842 3841 3674

CIK No: 0001068874

Subsidiaries: Core Systems Incorporated (Core), Laurus Master Fund, Ltd. (Laurus).

Officers: Phillip C. Thomas/Dir., CEO, Pres., Walter J. Wriggins/VP - Core Systems Division, Diane J. Ryan/CFO, VP - Finance, Stephen N. Bunker/Dir., VP, Chief Scientist

Directors: Phillip C. Thomas/Dir., CEO, Pres., Anthony J. Armini/Chmn., David B. Eisenhaure/Dir., Michael Szycher/Dir., Stephen N. Bunker/Dir., VP, Chief Scientist, Michael Turmelle/Dir., Joseph Levangie/63/Dir.

Owners: David Eisenhaure/1.00%, Insiders/21.00%, Michael Turmelle, Stephen N. Bunker/6.00%, Michael Szycher/1.00%, Anthony Armini/11.00%, Diane J. Ryan/2.00%, Walter J. Wriggins/1.00%

Financial Data: *Fiscal Year End:*06/30 *Latest Annual Data:* 06/30/2007

Year	Sales	Net Income
2007	$15,432,000	-$10,688,000
2006	$26,391,000	-$7,084,000
2005	$12,286,000	-$7,405,000

Curr. Assets:	$8,201,000	Curr. Liab.:	$5,942,000		
Plant, Equip.:	$8,909,000	Total Liab.:	$8,303,000	Indic. Yr. Divd.:	NA
Total Assets:	$30,799,000	Net Worth:	$19,928,000	Debt/ Equity:	0.0775

Implantable Vision Inc

25730 Lorain Rd., North Olmsted, OH, 44070; *PH:* 1-212-835-6198

General		Stock	
Incorporation	UT	Price on:12/24/2007	$1.3
Employees	4	Stock Exchange	OTC
Auditor	Jaspers & Hall, PC	Ticker Symbol	IMVS
Stk Agt	Stock Transfer & Trust Co.	Outstanding Shares	31,850,000
Counsel	NA	E.P.S.	NA
DUNS No.	NA	Shareholders	NA

Business: The groups principal activities include developing, and commercializing, phakic intraocular lenses. The product of the group is TP.2 Phakic Lens. In December 2005, the group acquired JIGJIG, LLC. The group operates from the United States, Europe, Asia and South America.

Primary SIC and add'l.: 4813

CIK No: 0000352912

Subsidiaries: BT Acquisitions, Inc.

Officers: George Rozakis/53/Dir., CEO, Pres., William Rozakis/29/CFO, Sec., Igor Valyunin/52/Dir., Chief Scientific Officer, Alexander Hatsis/58/Medical Dir.

Directors: George Rozakis/53/Dir., CEO, Pres., Igor Valyunin/52/Dir., Chief Scientific Officer, Jerry Kaeni/56/Dir.

Owners: Kavouria, LLC, Alex Hatsis, The Regency Group, William Rozakis, Igor Valyunin, Rozakis Family, LLC, Rozy Ventures, Insiders, Jerry Kaeni, George Rozakis

Financial Data: *Fiscal Year End:*07/31 *Latest Annual Data:* 7/31/2006

Year	Sales	Net Income
2006	NA	-$935,000
2004	NA	-$150,000
2000	$60,000	-$665,000

Curr. Assets:	$93,000	Curr. Liab.:	$310,000		
Plant, Equip.:	$41,000	Total Liab.:	$310,000	Indic. Yr. Divd.:	NA
Total Assets:	$1,133,000	Net Worth:	$823,000	Debt/ Equity:	NA

Impreso Inc

PO Box 506, Coppell, TX, 75019; *PH:* 1-972-462-0100; *Fax:* 1-800-562-5359; *http://* www.tstimpreso.com; *Email:* service@tstimpreso.com

General		Stock	
Incorporation	DE	Price on:12/24/2007	$2.25
Employees	191	Stock Exchange	OTC
Auditor	Blackman Kallick Bartelstein LLP	Ticker Symbol	ZCOM
Stk Agt	American Stock Transfer & Trust Co.	Outstanding Shares	5,280,000
Counsel	Gardere, Wynne Sewell LLP	E.P.S.	-$0.08
DUNS No.	NA	Shareholders	NA

Business: The group's principal activities are to manufacture and distribute paper and film products. The group's products include continuous computer stock business forms, thermal facsimile paper, cut sheet paper, copying machines and plain paper facsimile machines, digital photo ink jet paper, gloss coated ink jet paper, gloss opaque ink jet film and other products. The products are distributed to dealers and other resellers for commercial and home use in domestic and international markets. Hotsheet.com inc, the company's subsidiary, owns and operates hotsheet.com, an Internet Website directory, specializing in listing popular Web destinations for the general audience.

Primary SIC and add'l.: 2621 2761 2893

CIK No: 0001108345

Subsidiaries: Alexa Springs, Inc., Hotsheet.com, Inc., TST/Impreso of California, Inc., TST/Impreso, Inc.

Financial Data: *Fiscal Year End:*08/31 *Latest Annual Data:* 05/31/2006

Year	Sales	Net Income
2006	NA	NA
2005	$77,728,000	-$2,909,000
2004	$103,989,000	$1,014,000

Curr. Assets:	$29,330,000	Curr. Liab.:	$17,967,000		
Plant, Equip.:	$12,390,000	Total Liab.:	$26,648,000	Indic. Yr. Divd.:	NA
Total Assets:	$41,793,000	Net Worth:	$15,145,000	Debt/ Equity:	0.4932

IMPSAT Fiber Networks Inc

Elvira Rawson De Dellepiane 150, Piso 8, Buenos Aires, C1107BCA; *PH:* 5411-5170-0000; *http://* www.impsat.com

General		Stock	
Incorporation	DE	Price on:12/24/2007	NA
Employees	1,208	Stock Exchange	NA
Auditor	Deloitte & Touche LLP	Ticker Symbol	NA
Stk Agt	Bank of New York	Outstanding Shares	NA
Counsel	Arnold & Porter LLP	E.P.S.	NA
DUNS No.	NA	Shareholders	NA

Business: The groups principle activity is to provide telecommunication network and Internet services to financial institutions, governmental agencies and other customers in Latin America. The group also provides integrated telecommunications solutions with an emphasis on end-to-end broadband data transmission. The group operates from United States.

Primary SIC and add'l.: 4899 7375 6719 4812

CIK No: 0001022329

Subsidiaries: AT&T, Inc, Global Crossing Ltd., global telecommunications operator, Telecomunicaciones Impsat S.A., Telefnica S.A., Telfonos de Mxico S.A. de C.V.

Officers: Ricardo A. Verdaguer/57/CEO, Pres., Guillermo V. Pardo/57/Sr. VP, Hector Alonso/50/CFO, Exec. VP, Marcelo Girotti/43/Exec. VP, Mariano Torre Gomez/56/Exec. VP, Matias Heinrich/42/Exec. VP - Network, Jose R. Torres/49/Sr. VP - Accounting

Directors: Ricardo A. Verdaguer/57/CEO, Pres., Ignacio Troncoso/53/Dir., Thomas Doster/39/Dir., Bryan E. Bloom/49/Dir., Edward T. Dartley/43/Dir.

Owners: Nortel Networks Limited, Marcello Girotti, Ricardo A. Verdaguer, Edward Dartley, Morgan Stanley& Co. Incorporated, Guillermo V. Pardo, Mariano Torre Gmez, Insiders, Ignacio Troncoso, Hector Alonso, James G. Dinan, UBS Securities LLC, SDS Capital Group SPC, Ltd., William R. Huff, Jos R. Torres *(16 Owners included in Index)*

IMS Health Inc

901 Main Ave., Ste. 612, Norwalk, CT, 06851; *PH:* 1-203-845-5200; *Fax:* 1-203-845-5304; *http://* www.imshealth.com

General		Stock	
Incorporation	DE	Price on:12/24/2007	$32.7
Employees	7,400	Stock Exchange	NYSE
Auditor	PricewaterhouseCoopers LLP	Ticker Symbol	RX
Stk Agt	American Stock Transfer & Trust Co.	Outstanding Shares	196,240,000
Counsel	NA	E.P.S.	$1.40
DUNS No.	02-302-0097	Shareholders	NA

Business: The groups principle activity is to provide market intelligence to the pharmaceutical and healthcare industries. The groups information products include sales force effectiveness, portfolio optimization, and launch, brand management and other. The group operates from United States.

Primary SIC and add'l.: 7379 7375

CIK No: 0001058083

Subsidiaries: 949122 Ontario Inc. (medcom), Acceletra Ag, Areks, Areks Japan K.K., Areks US, Inc., Asesorias IMS Health Chile Limitada, Asserta Centroamerica Medicion de Mercados, S.A., Azyx Polska Geopharma Information Services, Sp.z.o.o, Azyx Servicos de Geomarketing Farmaceutico, Ltda., Battaerd Mansley India Private Limited, Battaerd Mansley Pty Ltd., Battaerd Mansley Pty. Ltd., Cambridge Pharma Consultancy, Inc., Cambridge Pharma Consultancy, Ltd., Coordinated Management Systems, Inc. 148 Subsidiaries included in the Index

Officers: David R. Carlucci/Chmn., CEO/$6,985,487.00, Marie B. Sonde/VP - Global Human Resources, John R. Walsh/Sr. VP - Strategy, Business Development, Kevin S. McKay/54/Sr. VP - Customer Delivery, Development, Adel Al-Saleh/Pres. - Europe, Middle East, Africa, Andrew Howden/Pres. - Asia Pacific, William J. Nelligan/Pres. - Americas, Karla L. Packer/Sr. VP - Human

Resources, Gilles V.J. Pajot/COO/$3,942,071.00, Murray L. Aitken/Sr. VP - Healthcare Insight, Bruce F. Boggs/Sr. VP - Marketing, Communications, External Affairs/$1,842,044.00, Tatsuyuki Sacki/Pres. - Japan, Stephen Phua/Pres. - Asia Pacific, Robert H. Steinfeld/Sr. VP, General Counsel, Corp. Sec. - IMS/$2,181,826.00, Jeffrey J. Ford/VP, Treasurer *(17 Officers included in Index)*

Directors: David R. Carlucci/Chmn., CEO, James D. Edwards/Dir., Eugene H. Lockhart/Dir., Bret W. Wise/Dir., Kathryn E. Giusti/Dir., Constantine L. Clemente/Dir., Bernard M. Puckett/Dir., William C. Van Fassen/Dir., Robert J. Kamerschen/Dir., John P. Imlay/Dir.

Owners: Bret W. Wise, Robert H. Steinfeld, FMR Corp., David R. Carlucci, Eugene H. Lockhart, James D. Edwards, Bruce F. Boggs, Gilles V. J. Pajot, David M. Thomas, Kathryn E. Giusti, Constantine L. Clemente, Ariel Capital Management, LLC, Leslye G. Katz, Wellington Management Company, LLP, William C. Van Faasen *(20 Owners included in Index)*

Financial Data: Fiscal Year End:12/31 Latest Annual Data: 12/31/2006

Year	Sales	Net Income
2006	$1,958,588,000	$315,511,000
2005	$1,754,791,000	$284,091,000
2004	$1,569,045,000	$285,422,000

Curr. Assets:	$693,293,000	Curr. Liab.:	$542,874,000		
Plant, Equip.:	$148,190,000	Total Liab.:	$1,772,275,000	Indic. Yr. Divd.:	$0.120
Total Assets:	$1,906,594,000	Net Worth:	$33,909,000	Debt/ Equity:	NA

In Touch Media Group Inc

205 Myrtle Ave., South Clearwater, FL, 33756; *PH:* 1-727-465-0925

General - Incorporation	FL	Stock - Price on:12/24/2007	NA
Employees	NA	Stock Exchange	OTC
Auditor	Kingery & Crouse, P.A.	Ticker Symbol	ITOU
Stk Agt	Florida Atlantic Stock Transfer, Inc.	Outstanding Shares	NA
Counsel	NA	E.P.S.	-$0.19
DUNS No.	NA	Shareholders	NA

Business: The groups principle activity is to provide online marketing and PR firm. The group operates from the United States.

Primary SIC and add'l.: 7379

CIK No: 0001194842

Financial Data: Fiscal Year End:12/31 Latest Annual Data: 12/31/2005

Year	Sales	Net Income
2005	$1,371,000	-$1,795,000
2004	NA	-$522,000
2003	NA	-$319,000

Curr. Assets:	$407,000	Curr. Liab.:	$229,000		
Plant, Equip.:	$63,000	Total Liab.:	$1,983,000	Indic. Yr. Divd.:	NA
Total Assets:	$823,000	Net Worth:	-$1,160,000	Debt/ Equity:	NA

In Veritas Medical Diagnostics Inc

The Green House, Beechwood Business Pk. N, Inverness, IV2 3BL; *PH:* 44-1463667347; *http://* www.ivmd.com; *Email:* info@ivmd.com

General - Incorporation	CO	Stock - Price on:12/24/2007	$0.0035
Employees	NA	Stock Exchange	OTC
Auditor	Cordovano & Honeck LLP	Ticker Symbol	IVME
Stk Agt	Corporate Stock Transfer, Inc.	Outstanding Shares	NA
Counsel	NA	E.P.S.	NA
DUNS No.	NA	Shareholders	NA

Business: The groups principle activity is to develop novel, physical measurement techniques for in vitro diagnostic products. The group operates from United States.

Primary SIC and add'l.: NA

CIK No: 0001142733

Subsidiaries: Hall Effect Medical Products, Inc., Hall Effect Technologies Ltd., Ivmd(uk) Ltd, Jopejo Ltd., Rosti (UK) Ltd.

Officers: Graham Cooper/CEO, Pres., Martin Thorp/CFO, John Fuller/Non Exec. Strategic Advisor, Damian Bond/Commercial Mgr., Patricia Connolly/Dir. - Science, Technology, Nasser Djennati/Member - Science - Clinical, Nigel Simpson/Member - Science - Clinical, James Walker/Professor, Deborah Withington/Professor, Andrew Mitchell/Member - Science - Clinical

Owners: Insiders/25.95%, Brian Cameron/5.44%, Rodney Philip Jackson/5.34%, Martin E. Thorp/3.51%, Triumph Small Cap Fund, Inc./28.43%, John Fuller/6.30%, Rubin Family Irrevocable Stock Trust/3.90%, Abacus Trust Company Limited/16.15%, HEMP Trustees Limited/10.69%

Financial Data: Fiscal Year End:07/31 Latest Annual Data: 07/31/2007

Year	Sales	Net Income
2007	NA	-$3,671,000
2006	$1,271,000	-$1,849,000
2005	$880,000	-$2,451,000

Curr. Assets:	$299,000	Curr. Liab.:	$2,540,000		
Plant, Equip.:	$14,000	Total Liab.:	$5,009,000	Indic. Yr. Divd.:	NA
Total Assets:	$412,000	Net Worth:	-$4,597,000	Debt/ Equity:	NA

Incentra Solutions Inc New

1140 Pearl St., Boulder, CO, 80302; *PH:* 1-303-449-8279; *Fax:* 1-856-439-9960; *http://* www.incentrasolutions.com; *Email:* info@incentrasolutions.com

General - Incorporation	NV	Stock - Price on:12/24/2007	$0.99
Employees	NA	Stock Exchange	OTC
Auditor	GHP Horwath, P.C.	Ticker Symbol	ICNS
Stk Agt	Interwest Transfer Company, Inc.	Outstanding Shares	13,080,000
Counsel	Cashman Sherman & Flynn LLP	E.P.S.	-$0.94
DUNS No.	NA	Shareholders	NA

Business: The groups principle activity is to provider information technology solutions for the enterprises infrastructure and data protection needs. Services of the group include third-party storage, servers, software, networking, security, outsourcing solutions, IT assessments, level 1-3 engineering support, staff augmentation and capital or financing solutions. The group acquired PWI Technologies, Inc. in March 2005, Network Systems Technologies, Inc. in April 2006, Tactix, Inc., for September 2006,

allianceSoft, Inc., in August 2006, and Incentra of CA in August 2006. Specific customers of the group include Cable & Wireless UK, Colt Telecom, Viawest, Network Appliance, Inc., Accenture, American Airlines and Hilton Hotels. The group operates from North America, Europe and Asia. The group's quarterly revenue for September 2007 was 36.36 millions of USD.

Primary SIC and add'l.: 7372 7378 7389 7373 7375 7374 7379 7376 7371

CIK No: 0001025707

Subsidiaries: ManagedStorage International, Inc

Officers: Thomas P. Sweeney/Chmn., CEO, Shawn O'Grady/COO, Pres., Tony Dipaolo/CFO, Matt Richman/Chief Corporate Development Officer, Treasurer, Joe Graziano/Pres. - Midwest, Brian Linse/Pres. - Northwest, Michael Hardy/Pres. - Southwest, Rocky Atkins/MD - Incentra Solutions International, Craig A. Armstong/Sr. VP - Michigan, Chris Wilkes/Sr. VP - South, Suzanne Becker-Gallagher/VP - Marketing, Jill Bertotti/Contact - Investor Relations, Len Hall/Financial Media, John Richardson/Sr. VP - Services, Matt Wight/Sr. VP - Business Development *(16 Officers included in Index)*

Directors: Thomas P. Sweeney/Chmn., CEO, Bobby Kocol/Dir., Tom Hudson/Dir., Carmen Scarpa/Dir., David Weiss/Dir., Jim Wolfinger/Dir., Thomas G. Hudson/61/Dir.

Owners: Thomas P. Sweeney/8.70%, RAB Special Situations (Master) Fund Limited/7.20%, Walter Hinton, Great Hill Equity Partners LP/34.20%, Great Hill Equity Partners LP/24.90%, Thomas P. Sweeney, J.P. Morgan Direct Venture/16.00%, Tudor Investment Corporation/17.50%, Thomas G. Hudson, James Wolfinger/1.40%, Tudor Investment Corporation/40.70%, J.P. Morgan Direct Venture/24.40%, Insiders/12.80%, David E. Weiss, Joseph Graziano/8.00% *(17 Owners included in Index)*

Financial Data: Fiscal Year End:12/31 Latest Annual Data: 12/31/2006

Year	Sales	Net Income
2006	$66,632,000	-$2,833,000
2005	$50,832,000	-$14,226,000
2004	$13,285,000	-$10,438,000

Curr. Assets:	$22,294,000	Curr. Liab.:	$30,224,000		
Plant, Equip.:	$3,064,000	Total Liab.:	$31,206,000	Indic. Yr. Divd.:	NA
Total Assets:	$45,818,000	Net Worth:	-$12,623,000	Debt/ Equity:	NA

Income Opportunity Realty Trust

10670 N Central Expy., Ste. 300, Dallas, TX, 07531; *PH:* 1-214-692-4700

General - Incorporation	CA	Stock - Price on:12/24/2007	$5.01
Employees	NA	Stock Exchange	AMEX
Auditor	NA	Ticker Symbol	IOT
Stk Agt	NA	Outstanding Shares	4,170,000
Counsel	NA	E.P.S.	-$0.23
DUNS No.	NA	Shareholders	NA

Business: The groups principal activities include investing, acquiring and operating real estate properties. The group operates from the United States.

Primary SIC and add'l.: 6798

CIK No: 0000760730

Financial Data: Fiscal Year End:12/31 Latest Annual Data: 12/31/2006

Year	Sales	Net Income
2006	$7,669,000	$172,000
2005	$6,447,000	$1,377,000
2004	$5,905,000	$5,428,000

Curr. Assets:	$45,623,000	Curr. Liab.:	$61,546,000		
Plant, Equip.:	$58,621,000	Total Liab.:	$64,072,000	Indic. Yr. Divd.:	NA
Total Assets:	$108,911,000	Net Worth:	$44,839,000	Debt/ Equity:	NA

IncrediMail Ltd

2 Kaufman St., Tel Aviv, 68012; *PH:* 972-2016898567; *http://* www.incredimail-corp.com

General - Incorporation	Israel	Stock - Price on:12/24/2007	NA
Employees	101	Stock Exchange	NDQ
Auditor	Kost, Forer, Gabbay & Kassierer	Ticker Symbol	MAIL
Stk Agt	American Stock Transfer & Trust Co.	Outstanding Shares	9,400,000
Counsel	NA	E.P.S.	$0.28
DUNS No.	NA	Shareholders	NA

Business: The groups principle activities include designing and marketing customized and entertaining email software products. The products of the group include IncrediMail Xe, IncrediMail Premium, IncrediMail Letter Creator and IncrediMail Super Pack. The group products sold under the trade name INCREDIMAIL. The group operates from the United States. The group's quarterly revenue for September 2007 was 4.60 millions of USD.

Primary SIC and add'l.: 7372

CIK No: 0001338940

Subsidiaries: BizChord Ltd.

Officers: Yaron Adler/Dir., CEO, Ofer Adler/Dir., CPO, Yacov Kaufman/CFO, Gil Pry-Dvash/GM, Jeff Gur Holzmann/Exec. VP - US Office, Dan Blumenfeld/Chief Marketing Officer, Yuval Hamudot/CTO, Nimrod May/VP - Community, Keren Elkin/VP - Human Resources, Administration

Directors: Yaron Adler/Dir., CEO, Tamar Gottlieb/Chmn., Hagay Elyakim/Dir., Elisabeth Demarse/Dir., James H. Lee/Dir., Ofer Adler/Dir., CPO, Yair M. Zadik/Dir., Gittit Guberman/Dir.

Owners: Yaron Adler/14.48%, Longview Fund L.P./8.72%, Ofer Adler/18.09%

Financial Data: Fiscal Year End:12/31 Latest Annual Data: 12/31/2006

Year	Sales	Net Income
2006	$10,851,000	$2,477,000
2005	$7,402,000	$1,149,000
2004	$6,208,000	$2,796,000

Curr. Assets:	$28,604,000	Curr. Liab.:	$7,043,000		
Plant, Equip.:	$877,000	Total Liab.:	$8,847,000	Indic. Yr. Divd.:	NA
Total Assets:	$31,424,000	Net Worth:	$22,577,000	Debt/ Equity:	NA

Incyte Corp

Experimental Sta., Rte. 141 & Henry Clay Rd., Bldg. E336, Wilmington, DE, 19880; *PH:* 1-302-498-6700; *Fax:* 1-302-425-2750; *http://* www.incyte.com; *Email:* investor@incyte.com

General - Incorporation .... DE	Stock- Price on:12/24/2007 ....$6.4
Employees..186	Stock Exchange..NDQ
Auditor .... Ernst & Young LLP	Ticker Symbol..INCY
Stk Agt................Mellon Investor Services LLC	Outstanding Shares 83,990,000
Counsel...NA	E.P.S...-$0.92
DUNS No. 55-696-7347	Shareholders...NA

Business: The group's principal activity is to discover and development of small molecule drugs to treat major medical conditions including HIV, cancer and diabetes. The group's advanced product candidate, reverset(R), is a nucleoside analog reverse transcriptase inhibitor, or nrti, that is being developed as a once-a day oral therapy for use in combination with other antiviral drugs for patients with HIV infections. It also has four internally-generated drug discovery programs underway. The most advanced of these programs is focused on developing antagonists to a key receptor involved in inflammation called the ccr2 receptor. The registered trademarks are incyte, lifeseq, zooseq and bioknowledge. The group operates in the United States and in Austria, Belgium, Canada, France, Denmark, Germany, Israel, Japan, the Netherlands, Sweden, Switzerland, and the United Kingdom. On 19-Feb-2003, the group acquired maxia pharmaceuticals inc.

Primary SIC and add'l.: 8731 7375

CIK No: 0000879169

Subsidiaries: Incyte Asia,Inc., Incyte Corporation Limited, Incyte Dormant Company Limited, Incyte Europe Holdings Limited, Incyte San Diego,Inc., Proteome,Inc.

Officers: Paul A. Friedman/Dir., CEO, Pres./$1,815,056.00, David C. Hastings/CFO, Exec. VP/$828,130.00, Pamela M. Murphy/VP - Investor Relations, Corporate Communications, Dan Maravei/Dir. - Business Development, Patricia A. Schreck/Exec. VP, General Counsel/$790,105.00, Brian W. Metcalf/Exec. VP, Chief Drug Discovery Scientist/$925,089.00, Paula J. Swain/Exec. VP - Human Resources/$780,203.00, John A. Keller/Exec. VP, Chief Business Officer/$936,442.00

Directors: Paul A. Friedman/Dir., CEO, Pres., Richard U. De Schutter/Chmn., Paul A. Brooke/Dir., Matthew W. Emmens/Dir., John F. Niblack/Dir., Julian C. Baker/Dir., Roy A. Whitfield/Dir., Barry M. Ariko/Dir.

Owners: Barry M. Ariko, David C. Hastings, Loomis, Sayles & Co., L.P./7.00%, John A. Keller, Paula J. Swain, Patricia A. Schreck, Brian W. Metcalf, Platinum Asset Management Limited/12.40%, Richard U. De Schutter, Roy A. Whitfield/1.50%, Wellington Management Company, LLP/13.80%, John F. Niblack, Insiders/11.04%, Julian C. Baker/6.00%, T. Rowe Price Associates, Inc./10.30% *(19 Owners included in Index)*

Financial Data: Fiscal Year End:12/31   Latest Annual Data: 12/31/2006

Year	Sales	Net Income
2006	$27,643,000	-$74,166,000
2005	$7,846,000	-$103,043,000
2004	$14,146,000	-$164,817,000

Curr. Assets:	$327,761,000	Curr. Liab.:	$49,340,000		
Plant, Equip.:	$5,890,000	Total Liab.:	$438,511,000	Indic. Yr. Divd.:	NA
Total Assets:	$353,603,000	Net Worth:	-$84,908,000	Debt/ Equity:	NA

Independence Federal Savings Bank

1229 Connecticut Ave. NW, Washington, DC, 20046; *PH:* 1-202-628-5500; *Fax:* 1-202-626-7106; *http://* www.ifsb.com

General - Incorporation .... NY	Stock- Price on:12/24/2007 ....NA
Employees...52	Stock Exchange..NDQ
Auditor ....PricewaterhouseCoopers LLP	Ticker Symbol...IFSB
Stk Agt...... American Stock Transfer & Trust Co.	Outstanding Shares 1,550,000
Counsel.......... Paul, Hastings, Janofsky & Walker LLP	E.P.S...-$1.79
DUNS No. ....NA	Shareholders...NA

Business: The group's principle activities are to provide financial services. The group operates through two segments: bank operations and student loans. The group operates through its two wholly owned subsidiaries: independence financial corporation and cf financial corporation. The financial services provided by the group include originating funds in the form of deposits and investing the same in residential loans, guaranteed student loans, mortgage-backed securities, government securities, consumer loans and commercial loans. The group also provides lockbox services. The sources of funds for the group's lending activities are savings deposits, mortgage-backed securities, federal home loan bank advances, reverse-repurchase agreements and other borrowings. The group operates solely in the domestic market.

Primary SIC and add'l.: 6035 6111

CIK No: 0000846472

Officers: John A. Hall/CEO, Pres., Brenda Watkins Noel/CFO, Jacqueline Daughtry-Miller/Sr. VP - Student Loan Department, Patricia R. Dennison/BSA, Compliance Officer, Sharita Billings/Branch Mgr. - Dupont South, Antonia Palmore/Branch Mgr. - Downtown Branch, Francester Coffee/Branch Mgr. - Friendship Heights, Andrea Couttenye/Corp. Sec., Russell C. Brown/VP - Operations, Darrell T. Holloman/VP - Accounting, Stanley W. Parsons/CIO, VP, Kevin Merrick/Assist. VP - Lending

Directors: Elliott S. Hall/Chmn., Robert B. Isard/Vice Chmn., Morton A. Bender/Dir., Nelson Deckelbaum/Dir., John K. Jenkins/Dir., Douglas D. Grayson/Dir., Lisa E. Gordon-Hagerty/Dir., Arturo Brillembourg/Dir., John Silvanus Wilson/Dir.

Financial Data: Fiscal Year End:12/31   Latest Annual Data: 12/31/2004

Year	Sales	Net Income
2004	$12,468,000	-$2,145,000
2003	$12,673,000	-$2,788,000
2001	$20,761,000	$273,000

Curr. Assets:	$11,054,000	Curr. Liab.:	$158,041,000		
Plant, Equip.:	$1,070,000	Total Liab.:	$160,309,000	Indic. Yr. Divd.:	NA
Total Assets:	$177,305,000	Net Worth:	$16,996,000	Debt/ Equity:	NA

Independence Holding Co

96 Cummings Point Rd., Stamford, CT, 06902; *PH:* 1-203-358-8000; *Fax:* 1-203-348-3103; *http://* www.independenceholding.com; *Email:* info@independenceholding.com

General - Incorporation .... DE	Stock- Price on:12/24/2007 ....$20.13
Employees..652	Stock Exchange...NYSE
Auditor ....KPMG LLP	Ticker Symbol..IHC
Stk Agt........................Registrar & Transfer Co	Outstanding Shares 15,190,000
Counsel...NA	E.P.S..$1.06
DUNS No. 02-660-3407	Shareholders...NA

Business: The group's principal activity is to provide life and health insurance. The operations are carried out through the subsidiaries: standard security life insurance company of New York, madison national life insurance company, inc and independence American insurance company. The group's

principal products include medical stop-loss insurance, short term disability benefit, long term disability benefit, group and individual life and annuity benefit, managed health care and credit life and disability products. The group operates solely in the domestic market. The group acquired 75% interest in majestic underwriters llc in 2004.

Primary SIC and add'l.: 6719 6321 6311

CIK No: 0000701869

Subsidiaries: Community America Insurance Services, Inc., Credico Insurance Services, Inc., Credico Life Insurance Company, G.P. Associates Holding Corp., GroupLink Reinsurance Company, Ltd., GroupLink, Inc., Health Plan Administrators, Inc., HPA Holdings Corp., HPA Marketing, Inc., IAC Holding Corp., IC West Underwriting Services LLC, Independence Capital Corp., Independence Holding LLC, Independence Preferred Trust I, Independence Preferred Trust II 29 Subsidiaries included in the Index

Officers: Roy T.K. Thung/Dir., CEO, Pres./$1,380,976.00, David T. Kettig/Co - COO, Sr. VP/$570,632.00, Brian R. Schlier/VP - Taxation, Larry R. Graber/Dir., Sr. VP - Life, Annuities/$319,771.00, Alex Giordano/VP, Chief Marketing Officer, Henry B. Spencer/VP - Investments, Teresa A. Herbert/CFO, Sr. VP/$490,211.00, Paul R. Janerico/VP - Internal Audit, Mark A. Musser/VP - Strategic Business Development, Scott Wood/Co - COO, Sr. VP/$491,132.00, Winfield C. Swarr/Chief Underwriting Officer, VP, Jeffrey C. Smedsrud/49/Chief Strategic Development Officer, Sr. VP, Bernon R. Erickson/Chief Health Actuary, James Kenneally/VP - Corporate Development, Colleen P. Maggi/VP, Controller *(16 Officers included in Index)*

Directors: Roy T.K. Thung/Dir., CEO, Pres., Edward Netter/Chmn., Larry R. Graber/Dir., Sr. VP - Life, Annuities, Allan C. Kirkman/64/Dir., James G. Tatum/66/Dir., Steven B. Lapin/Dir., Robert P. Ross/Dir., John L. Lahey/61/Dir.

Owners: James G. Tatum, Scott M. Wood/1.38%, Larry R. Graber, Teresa A. Herbert, Geneve Holdings, Inc./53.69%, David T. Kettig, Roy T.K. Thung/4.04%, Allan C. Kirkman, Steven B. Lapin, Insiders/8.52%, John L. Lahey

Financial Data: Fiscal Year End:12/31   Latest Annual Data: 12/31/2006

Year	Sales	Net Income
2006	$364,688,000	$14,061,000
2005	$296,417,000	$17,301,000
2004	$225,669,000	$22,939,000

Curr. Assets:	$232,298,000	Curr. Liab.:	$485,781,000	P/E Ratio:	21.65
Plant, Equip.:	NA	Total Liab.:	$1,028,534,000	Indic. Yr. Divd.:	$0.050
Total Assets:	$1,259,684,000	Net Worth:	$231,150,000	Debt/ Equity:	0.2225

Independence Lead Mines Co

510 Cedar St., Wallace, ID, 83873; *PH:* 1-208-753-2525; *Fax:* 1-208-753-2525; *http://* wallace-id.com; *Email:* info@infomine.com

General - Incorporation .... AZ	Stock- Price on:12/24/2007 ....$4
Employees...NA	Stock Exchange..OTC
Auditor .... Wayne L. Schoonmaker	Ticker Symbol...ILDS
Stk Agt ....OTC Corporate Transfer Service Co	Outstanding Shares 5,260,000
Counsel....................................Boise Idaho	E.P.S...-$0.03
DUNS No. 15-653-0586	Shareholders...NA

Business: The group's principal activity is to own patented & unpatented mining claims. The group owns fifteen patented and seventeen unpatented mining claims. This claim group is situated northwest of hecla mining company's lucky friday mine in the coeur d'alene mining district, shoshone county Idaho. The group is in the exploratory and development stage.

Primary SIC and add'l.: 1031

CIK No: 0000050073

Officers: Bernard C. Lannen/Dir., Pres., Chief Administrative Officer, Wayne L. Schoonmaker/Dir., Sec., Treasurer, Principal Accounting Officer

Directors: Bernard C. Lannen/Dir., Pres., Chief Administrative Officer, Wayne L. Schoonmaker/Dir., Sec., Treasurer, Principal Accounting Officer, Forrest G. Godde/Dir., Robert Bunde/Dir., Gordon Berkhaug/Dir.

Owners: Insiders/13.99%, Bernard C. Lannen/6.34%, Robert Bunde/4.01%, Duff W. Gordon/5.98%, Forrest G. Godde/1.91%, Wayne L. Schoonmaker/0.08%, Gordon Berkhaug/1.65%

Financial Data: Fiscal Year End:12/31   Latest Annual Data: 12/31/2006

Year	Sales	Net Income
2006	NA	-$25,000
2005	NA	-$171,000
2004	NA	-$266,000

Curr. Assets:	$240,000	Curr. Liab.:	$5,000		
Plant, Equip.:	NA	Total Liab.:	$451,000	Indic. Yr. Divd.:	NA
Total Assets:	$240,000	Net Worth:	-$210,000	Debt/ Equity:	NA

Independent Bank Corp

288 Union St., Rockland, MA, 02370; *PH:* 1-781-878-6100; *Fax:* 1-781-982-6130; *http://* www.rocklandtrust.com

General - Incorporation .... MA	Stock- Price on:12/24/2007 ....$30.3
Employees..708	Stock Exchange..NDQ
Auditor ....KPMG LLP	Ticker Symbol..INDB
Stk Agt .... American Stock Transfer & Trust Co.	Outstanding Shares 14,200,000
Counsel...NA	E.P.S..$1.98
DUNS No. 15-216-0768	Shareholders...NA

Business: The group's principal activity is to provide community banking business that includes commercial banking, retail banking and investment management services. The group offers wide range of banking services, including lending activities, acceptance of demand, savings and time deposits, trust and investment management services and mortgage banking income. The group provides loans to individuals and small-to-medium-sized businesses in its market area. It operates through its wholly owned subsidiary, rockland trust company which offers community banking services through its network of 52 banking offices seven commercial lending centers, three investment management offices and three residential lending centers. These banking offices and lending centers are located in the plymouth, norfolk, barnstable and bristol counties of southeastern Massachusetts and cape cod.

Primary SIC and add'l.: 6712 6022

CIK No: 0000776901

Subsidiaries: Independent Capital Trust II, Massachusetts securities corporations, Rockland Trust Community Development Corporation II, Rockland Trust Community Development LLC, Rockland Trust Company, Taunton Avenue Inc

Officers: Michael M. Magee/Dir., CEO, Pres., Ronald L. Long/CEO, Pres. - Independent Bank East Michigan, Edward B. Swanson/CEO, Pres. - Independent Bank South Michigan, Richard E. Butler/Sr. VP - Operations, Independent Bank Corporation, James J. Twarozynski/Sr. VP, Controller, William B. Kessel/COO, Exec. VP, Jane L. Lundquist/54/Exec. VP, Dir. - Retail Banking, Corporate Marketing, Rockland Trust, Denis K. Sheahan/42/CFO, Treasurer/$359,764.00, David C. Reglin/Exec. VP - Retail Banking, Robert N. Shuster/CFO, Exec. VP, Ferdinand T. Kelley/63/Exec. VP - Rockland Trust/$501,068.00, Stefanie M. Kimball/Exec. VP, Chief Lending Officer, Edward F. Jankowski/57/Chief Technology, Operations Officer - Rockland Trust, Edward H. Seksay/50/General Counsel/$302,959.00, Raymond G. Fuerschbach/57/Sr. VP, Dir. - Human Resources, Rockland Trust

Directors: Michael M. Magee/Dir., CEO, Pres., Charles C. Van Loan/Chmn., Terry L. Haske/Dir., Christopher Oddleifson/49/Dir., Charles A. Palmer/Dir., Stephen L. Gulis/Dir., Donna J. Banks/Dir., Jeffrey A. Bratsburg/Dir., Kevin J. Jones/56/Dir., Benjamin A. Gilmore/60/Dir., John H. Spurr/61/Dir., Robert D. Sullivan/65/Dir., Richard H. Sgarzi/65/Dir., Richard S. Anderson/65/Dir., Brian S. Tedeschi/57/Dir. *(24 Directors included in Index)*

Owners: Thomas J. Teuten/2.20%, Robert D. Sullivan, Paul W. Clark, MFC Global Investment Management (US) LLC/5.00%, Eileen C. Miskell, Kevin J. Jones, Donna A. Lopolito, Benjamin A. Gilmore, Insiders/8.48%, Christopher Oddleifson, Edward H. Seksay, Winthrop E. Hall, Richard S. Anderson, Brian S. Tedeschi, John H. Spurr/2.28% *(19 Owners included in Index)*

Financial Data: *Fiscal Year End:*12/31 ***Latest Annual Data:*** 12/31/2006

Year	Sales	Net Income
2006	$197,498,000	$32,851,000
2005	$182,811,000	$33,205,000
2004	$162,968,000	$30,767,000

Curr. Assets:	$140,049,000	**Curr. Liab.:**	$2,503,720,000	**P/E Ratio:**	15.30
Plant, Equip.:	$37,316,000	**Total Liab.:**	$2,599,136,000	**Indic. Yr. Divd.:**	$0.680
Total Assets:	$2,828,919,000	**Net Worth:**	$229,783,000	**Debt/ Equity:**	0.3493

Indevus Pharmaceuticals Inc

33 Hayden Ave., Lexington, MA, 02421; ***PH:*** 1-781-861-8444; ***Fax:*** 1-781-861-3830; ***http://*** www.indevus.com

General - Incorporation	DE	**Stock**- Price on:12/24/2007	$6.85
Employees	158	Stock Exchange	NDQ
Auditor	PricewaterhouseCoopers LLP	Ticker Symbol	IDEV
Stk Agt	American Stock Transfer & Trust Co.	Outstanding Shares	73,980,000
Counsel	Burns & Levinson LLP	E.P.S.	-$1.61
DUNS No.	19-976-9852	Shareholders	NA

Business: The group's principle activities include research, developing and commercializing pharmaceutical compounds and products. The products are used in the treatment of central nervous system disorders and other areas. The group is currently developing pagoclone for panic and generalized anxiety disorders, trospium for overactive bladder, ip 501 for cirrhosis of the liver, citicoline for ischemic stroke, pro 2000 for the prevention of infection by the human immunodeficiency virus and other sexually transmitted pathogens and dersalazine for inflammatory bowel disease. The group operates from United States.

Primary SIC and add'l.: 8731 2834

CIK No: 0000854222

Subsidiaries: CPEC LLC, InterNutria, Inc.

Officers: Glenn L. Cooper/Chmn., CEO, Mark S. Butler/Exec. VP, Chief Administrative Officer, General Counsel, Dale Ritter/Sr. VP - Finance, Bobby W. Sandage/Exec. VP - Research, Development, Chief Scientific Officer, Noah D. Beerman/Exec. VP, Chief Business Officer, Michael W. Rogers/Exec. VP, CFO, Treasurer, Tessa Cooper/Sr. VP - Human Resources, Brooke D. Wagner/VP - Corporate Communications, Thomas F. Farb/COO, Pres., Kurt W. Lewis/Sr. VP - Sales, Marketing, Kevin Pelin/Sr. VP - Operations, GM - Cranbury, NJ, Mark Harnett/Contact - Research, Development, Janice Long/Contact - Sales, Marketing

Directors: Glenn L. Cooper/Chmn., CEO, Michael E. Hanson/Dir., Andrew J. Ferrara/Dir., James C. Gale/Dir., Stephen C. McCluski/Dir., David B. Sharrock/Dir., Cheryl P. Morley/Dir., Malcolm Morville/Dir.

Owners: Wayne P. Rothbaum, Michael E. Hanson, Cheryl P. Morley, Michael W. Rogers, Glenn L. Cooper, OrbiMed Advisors LLC, OrbiMed Capital LLC,, Thomas F. Farb, Joseph Edelman, John H. Tucker, Insiders, Quogue Capital LLC, Wyeth, Mark S. Butler, Stephen C. McCluski, Visium Asset Management, LLC *(19 Owners included in Index)*

Financial Data: *Fiscal Year End:*09/30 ***Latest Annual Data:*** 9/30/2006

Year	Sales	Net Income
2006	$50,452,000	-$50,554,000
2005	$33,336,000	-$53,218,000
2004	$18,726,000	-$68,212,000

Curr. Assets:	$83,202,000	**Curr. Liab.:**	$28,326,000		
Plant, Equip.:	$4,173,000	**Total Liab.:**	$216,511,000	**Indic. Yr. Divd.:**	NA
Total Assets:	$92,307,000	**Net Worth:**	-$124,330,000	**Debt/ Equity:**	NA

India Globalization Capital Inc

4336 Montgomery Ave., Bethesda, MD, 20814; ***PH:*** 1-301-983-0998; ***http://*** www.indiaglobalcap.com; ***Email:*** Inquiries@indiaglobalcap.com

General - Incorporation	MD	**Stock**- Price on:12/24/2007	$5.77
Employees	NA	Stock Exchange	AMEX
Auditor	Goldstein Golub Kessler LLP	Ticker Symbol	IGC
Stk Agt	NA	Outstanding Shares	13,970,000
Counsel	NA	E.P.S.	$0.05
DUNS No.	NA	Shareholders	NA

Business: The groups principal activities include accounting, financing, developing and monitoring networks. The group operates from India and the United States.

Primary SIC and add'l.: 6799

CIK No: 0001326205

Officers: Ram Mukunda/CEO, Pres., Senator Larry Pressler/Special Advisor, P. G. Kakodkar/Special Advisor, Shakti Sinha/Special Advisor, Prabuddha Ganguli/Special Advisor, Anil K. Gupta/Special Advisor, John B. Selvaraj/Treasurer - Principal Financial, Accounting Officer, Howard Gutman/Special Advisor

Directors: Ranga Krishna/Chmn., Sudhakar Shenoy/Dir., Suhail Nathani/Dir., Richard Prins/Dir.

Owners: Shakti Sinha, P. G. Kakodkar, Larry Pressler, Fir Tree, Inc/9.90%, Ram Mukunda/11.99%, Insiders/15.21%, Sudhakar Shenoy, HBK Investments L.P/7.70%, Prabuddha Ganguli, The Baupost Group, L.L.C/7.60%, Ranga Krishna/2.50%, Suhail Nathani, Andrew M. Weiss/7.38%, Anil K. Gupta, D.B. Zwirn & Co., L.P/10.63%

Financial Data: *Fiscal Year End:*03/31 ***Latest Annual Data:*** 03/31/2007

Year	Sales	Net Income
2007	NA	$1,518,000
2006	NA	-$444,000

Curr. Assets:	$70,385,000	**Curr. Liab.:**	$5,000,000		
Plant, Equip.:	NA	**Total Liab.:**	$17,763,000	**Indic. Yr. Divd.:**	NA
Total Assets:	$70,687,000	**Net Worth:**	$52,924,000	**Debt/ Equity:**	NA

Indian Village Bancorp Inc

100 S Walnut St., Gnadenhutten, OH, 44629; ***PH:*** 1-740-254-4313; ***Fax:*** 1-740-254-9555; ***http://*** www.ivcbank.com

General - Incorporation	PA	**Stock**- Price on:12/24/2007	$18.85
Employees	NA	Stock Exchange	OTC
Auditor	NA	Ticker Symbol	IDVB
Stk Agt	Fifth Third Bank	Outstanding Shares	NA
Counsel	NA	E.P.S.	-$0.9
DUNS No.	NA	Shareholders	NA

Business: The groups principal activity is to provide community-banking services. The services of the group include originating loans, business banking, ATM and money debit card, direct deposit, safe deposit boxes, telephone and online banking. The group operates from Ohio in the United States.

Primary SIC and add'l.: 6035 6712

CIK No: 0001081338

Officers: Marty Lindon/COO, Andrea Miley/VP, Controller

Financial Data: *Fiscal Year End:*06/30 ***Latest Annual Data:*** 6/30/2003

Year	Sales	Net Income
2003	$5,734,000	$388,000
2002	$5,462,000	$232,000
2001	$5,387,000	$338,000

Curr. Assets:	$2,725,000	**Curr. Liab.:**	$89,365,000		
Plant, Equip.:	$1,443,000	**Total Liab.:**	$90,027,000	**Indic. Yr. Divd.:**	$0.160
Total Assets:	$98,427,000	**Net Worth:**	$8,400,000	**Debt/ Equity:**	NA

Indiana Business Bancorp

250 E 96th St. Ste. 100, Indianapolis, IN, 46240; ***PH:*** 1-317-218-2180; ***http://*** www.indianabusinessbank.com

General - Incorporation		**Stock**- Price on:12/24/2007	NA
Employees	NA	Stock Exchange	OTC
Auditor	NA	Ticker Symbol	IBBI
Stk Agt	Continental Stock Transfer & Trust Co	Outstanding Shares	NA
Counsel	NA	E.P.S.	NA
DUNS No.	NA	Shareholders	NA

Business: The groups principal activity is to provide banking services. The services of the group include business and personal banking, mortgage lending, and courier direct and online banking. The group operates from the United States.

Primary SIC and add'l.: 6022

CIK No:

Officers: James S. Young/CEO, Pres., Dir. - Indiana Business Bank, James C. Shook/Chmn. - Indiana Business Bank, Murray J. Clark/Dir. - Indiana Business Bank, Patrick J. Early/Dir. - Indiana Business Bank, Kenneth Giffin/Dir. - Indiana Business Bank, Thomas Godby/Dir. - Indiana Business Bank, Thomas Killion/Dir. - Indiana Business Bank, Richard D. Kruse/Dir. - Indiana Business Bank, Brian E. Moore/Dir. - Indiana Business Bank, Vop Osili/Dir. - Indiana Business Bank, Meghan Otis/Dir. - Indiana Business Bank, Carolyn Bickel/Assist. VP - Mortgage Lending, Indiana Business Bank, Matt Foley/Assist. VP, Commerical Portfolio Mgr. - Indiana Business Bank, Angela Jaspers/Bank Officer - Credit Analyst, Indiana Business Bank, Gregory G. Gault/COO, Chief Credit Officer, Dir. - Indiana Business Bank *(27 Officers included in Index)*

Indiana Michigan Power Co

1 Riverside Plz., Columbus, OH, 43215; ***PH:*** 1-614-716-1000; ***Fax:*** 1-614-716-1823; ***http://*** www.indianamichiganpower.com

General - Incorporation	IN	**Stock**- Price on:12/24/2007	$24.37
Employees	2,643	Stock Exchange	NYSE
Auditor	Deloitte & Touche LLP	Ticker Symbol	IJD
Stk Agt	Computershare Ltd.	Outstanding Shares	1,400,000
Counsel	NA	E.P.S.	$66.01
DUNS No.	00-698-5584	Shareholders	NA

Business: The group's principal activities are to generate, purchase, sell, transmit and distribute electric power to 575,000 retail customers in its service territory in northern and eastern Indiana and a portion of southwestern Michigan. The group also sells power on wholesale basis to other electric utility companies, rural electric cooperatives and municipalities. The group serves principal industries such as primary metals, transportation equipment, electrical and electronic machinery, fabricated metal products, rubber and miscellaneous plastic products and chemicals and allied products. The group is a wholly owned subsidiary of American electric power company, which is a public utility electric company.

Primary SIC and add'l.: 4911

CIK No: 0000050172

Subsidiaries: Kentucky Power Company, Ohio Power Company, Public Service Company, Southwestern Electric Power Company

Officers: Michael G. Morris/61/Chmn., CEO, Joseph M. Buonaiuto/Chief Accounting Officer, Controller, David Mayne/Media Contact - Michigan, Jim Riggle/Media Contact - Indiana, Mike Brian/Media Contact - Indiana, Holly K. Koeppel/Dir., CFO, VP, Joann Grevenow/Dir, Dir. - Customer Services, Marketing, Marc Lewis/Dir., VP - External Relations, Susanne Moorman Rowe/Dir., GM - Corporate Communications, Community Relations, Allen R. Glassburn/Dir, Dir. - Business Operations Support, Kent Curry/Dir. - Regulatory Services, Karl G. Boyd/Dir., VP - Distribution Operations, Helen J. Murray/Dir., COO, Pres., Bill Schalk/Media Contact - Michigan

Directors: Michael G. Morris/61/Chmn., CEO, Robert P. Powers/53/Dir., Nicholas K. Akins/Dir., Carl L. English/Dir., Venita McCellon-Allen/48/Dir., Joann Grevenow/Dir, Dir. - Customer Services, Marketing, Marc Lewis/Dir., VP - External Relations, Susanne Moorman Rowe/Dir., GM - Corporate Communications, Community Relations, Allen R. Glassburn/Dir, Dir. - Business Operations Support, Karl G. Boyd/Dir., VP - Distribution Operations, Patrick C. Hale/Dir., Helen J. Murray/Dir., COO, Pres., Susan Tomasky/Dir.

Owners: Insiders, Venita McCellon-Allen, Holly K. Koeppel, Thomas M. Hagan, Stephen P. Smith, Carl L. English, Dennis E. Welch, Susan Tomasky, Nicholas K. Akins, Michael G. Morris, John B. Keane

Financial Data: *Fiscal Year End:*12/31 *Latest Annual Data:* 12/31/2006

Year	Sales	Net Income
2006	$1,976,947,000	$121,168,000
2005	$1,892,602,000	$146,852,000
2004	$1,661,580,000	$133,222,000

Curr. Assets:	$502,124,000	*Curr. Liab.:*	$628,545,000	*P/E Ratio:*	0.37
Plant, Equip.:	$3,312,599,000	*Total Liab.:*	$4,248,916,000	*Indic. Yr. Divd.:*	NA
Total Assets:	$5,546,437,000	*Net Worth:*	$1,297,521,000	*Debt/ Equity:*	1.1600

Indigenous Global Development Corp

100 Bush St., Ste. 600, San Francisco, CA, 94104; *PH:* 1-415-283-4757; *Fax:* 1-415-955-4748; *http://* www.igdc1.com

General - Incorporation	UT	**Stock**- Price on:12/24/2007	$0.0001
Employees	NA	Stock Exchange	OTC
Auditor	Stonefield Josephson, Inc	Ticker Symbol	IGDC
Stk Agt	Transfer Online, Inc.	Outstanding Shares	NA
Counsel	NA	E.P.S.	NA
DUNS No.	NA	Shareholders	NA

Business: The group's principal activity is to provide strategic, financial and investment tools to help deliver economic development, education, empowerment and financial self-sufficiency for native Americans across the United States. The group is focusing on the development of energy merchant power plants, as well as the redevelopment of urban properties.

Primary SIC and add'l.: 6519

CIK No: 0000915461

Financial Data: *Fiscal Year End:*06/30 *Latest Annual Data:* 6/30/2004

Year	Sales	Net Income
2004	NA	-$3,465,000
2001	$81,000	-$1,556,000
2000	NA	-$720,000

Curr. Assets:	$191,000	*Curr. Liab.:*	$1,463,000		
Plant, Equip.:	$30,000	*Total Liab.:*	$1,763,000	*Indic. Yr. Divd.:*	NA
Total Assets:	$332,000	*Net Worth:*	-$1,431,000	*Debt/ Equity:*	NA

Industrial Development Bank Israel Ltd

4 Weizman St., Tel Aviv, 67138; *PH:* 972-36272727; *http://* www.idbi.co.il

General - Incorporation	Israel	**Stock**- Price on:12/24/2007	NA
Employees	NA	Stock Exchange	NA
Auditor	Somekh Chaikin	Ticker Symbol	NA
Stk Agt	JP Morgan Chase Bank, N.A.	Outstanding Shares	NA
Counsel	NA	E.P.S.	NA
DUNS No.	60-001-4146	Shareholders	NA

Business: The groups principle activity is to perform commercial banking operations and other related financial activities; and acts as agent for government in processing applications for grants from government to approved enterprises and makes payment on behalf of the government. The group operates from United States.

Primary SIC and add'l.: 6029

CIK No: 0000050277

Officers: Uri Galili/GM, Rimon Shemaya/Controller, Mgr. Financial Risks, Nathan Dekel/Operations Mgr., Itzhak David/53/Internal Auditor, Michael Warzager/53/General Counsel, Arie Savir/Head - Banking, Credit Division, Natan Atlas/General Sec.

Directors: Ra'anan Cohen/Chmn., Richard Armonn/73/Dep. Chmn., Ben-Zion Dagan/Dir., Avi Olshansky/Dir., Yeheskel Beinisch/66/Dir., Ephrat Bronfeld/Dir., Shulamit Eshbol/42/Dir., Moshe Gavish/59/Dir., Ehud Green/53/Dir., Yacob Aizner/61/Dir., Aharon Hildesheimer/65/Dir.

Owners: Bank HaPoalim B.M. Israel/12.12%, Israel Discount Bank Ltd./10.13%, Bank Leumi le-Israel B.M Israel/20.60%, Bank Hapoalim B.M Israel/6.50%, State of Israel/48.81%

Industrial Distribution Group Inc

950 E Paces Ferry Rd., Ste. 1575, Atlanta, GA, 30326; *PH:* 1-404-949-2100; *Fax:* 1-404-949-2040; *http://* www.idglink.com

General - Incorporation	DE	**Stock**- Price on:12/24/2007	$10.47
Employees	1,300	Stock Exchange	NDQ
Auditor	Ernst & Young LLP	Ticker Symbol	IDGR
Stk Agt	American Stock Transfer & Trust Co.	Outstanding Shares	9,590,000
Counsel	Kilpatrick Stockton	E.P.S.	$0.49
DUNS No.	02-987-0664	Shareholders	NA

Business: The group's principal activity is to supply and distribute flexible procurement solutions for manufacturers and other users of industrial maintenance, repair, operating and production products. The principal products of the group include abrasives, cutting tools, hand and power tools, coolants, lubricants and adhesives. The major customers of the group are general electric company, borg-warner inc, ford motor company, duracell corporation and the boeing company. The group operates in the United States.

Primary SIC and add'l.: 5085 5251

CIK No: 0001042351

Subsidiaries: Idg Usa, LLC, IDG-Mexico, Inc., Memphis Disposition Corp.

Officers: Charles A. Lingenfelter/56/Dir., CEO, Pres./$608,236.00, David K. Barth/63/Dir., Pres., George L. Sachs/65/Dir., Pres., Jack P. Healey/Exec. VP, CFO, Corp. Sec./$499,536.00, Randy Jones/Pres. - Northwest Region, John Kramer/Pres. - Midwest Region, Steve Owings/Pres. - Southern Region, Ed Gerber/Pres. - Northeast Region, Steve Hartkopf/VP - Marketing, Carol L. Marks/Dir. - Business Management Systems, Darrel Wilges/VP - Flexible Procurement Solutions, Laura Wright/VP - Human Resources, Ajita Rajendra/56/Dir., Pres., Kathleen MacIntosh/VP - Finance

Directors: Charles A. Lingenfelter/56/Dir., CEO, Pres., Richard M. Seigel/61/Chmn., William T. Parr/70/Vice Chmn., George L. Sachs/65/Dir., Pres., Ajita Rajendra/56/Dir., Pres., David K. Barth/63/Dir., Pres., William R. Fenoglio/67/Dir.

Owners: Jack P. Healey/1.60%, Michael W. Brice, William T. Parr, William R. Fenoglio, Dalton, Greiner, Hartman, Maher & Co LLC/9.80%, Goldman Capital Management, Inc./9.40%, David K. Barth, Insiders/14.40%, George L. Sachs/1.30%, Charles A. Lingenfelter/3.00%, Richard M. Seigel/1.10%, Dimensional Fund Advisors LP/8.60%, Andrew B. Shearer/5.80%

Financial Data: *Fiscal Year End:*12/31 *Latest Annual Data:* 12/31/2006

Year	Sales	Net Income
2006	$547,874,000	$6,785,000
2005	$538,847,000	$5,421,000
2004	$529,175,000	$7,314,000

Curr. Assets:	$152,528,000	*Curr. Liab.:*	$58,885,000	*P/E Ratio:*	19.39
Plant, Equip.:	$4,928,000	*Total Liab.:*	$83,688,000	*Indic. Yr. Divd.:*	NA
Total Assets:	$160,012,000	*Net Worth:*	$76,324,000	*Debt/ Equity:*	0.3061

Industrial Electrical Services Inc

Ermapao Green Rice Ltd., East Ping Xiang, Zheng Fu Fu, Songyuan City, Jilin, 131108; *PH:* 86-310-441-1888; *http://* www.ies-inc.net

General - Incorporation	FL	**Stock**- Price on:12/24/2007	$1.07
Employees	NA	Stock Exchange	NA
Auditor	Pender Newkirk & Company	Ticker Symbol	NA
Stk Agt	Transfer Online, Inc.	Outstanding Shares	NA
Counsel	NA	E.P.S.	-$0.29
DUNS No.	NA	Shareholders	NA

Business: The groups principal activity is to provide technical and engineering solutions. The services of the group include on-site troubleshooting for equipment, selling and maintaining spare electrical parts for jobs, switchgear maintenance and testing, power delivery equipment installation checkout, industrial power system analysis and studies, electrical protective device setting and testing, and software development. The group operates from the United States.

Primary SIC and add'l.: 1731

CIK No: 0001337826

Subsidiaries: Industrial Electric Services, LLC

Officers: Edward Lynch/56/Dir., CEO, Pres., Huizhi Zhao/Chmn., Pres., Guo Xuefeng/CFO, Byron Lynch/Mgr.

Directors: Edward Lynch/56/Dir., CEO, Pres., Marty Stewart/Owner, Founder

Owners: Simple (Hong Kong) Investment & Management Company Limited/5.60%, Huizhi Xiao/19.60%, Xia Wu/29.10%, Luxesource International Limited/12.00%, China US Bridge Capital Limited/5.30%, Insiders/19.60%, First Capital Limited/5.30%

Financial Data: *Fiscal Year End:*12/31 *Latest Annual Data:* 12/31/2006

Year	Sales	Net Income
2006	$105,000	-$83,000
2005	$329,000	-$149,000
2004	$1,424,100,000	-$124,864,000

Curr. Assets:	$0	*Curr. Liab.:*	$78,000		
Plant, Equip.:	NA	*Total Liab.:*	$78,000	*Indic. Yr. Divd.:*	NA
Total Assets:	$0	*Net Worth:*	-$78,000	*Debt/ Equity:*	NA

Industrial Enterprises of America Inc

711 Third Ave., Ste. 1505, Newyork, NY, 10017; *PH:* 1-212-490-3100

General - Incorporation	NV	**Stock**- Price on:12/24/2007	NA
Employees	NA	Stock Exchange	NDQ
Auditor	Beckstead and Watts, LLP	Ticker Symbol	IEAM
Stk Agt	NA	Outstanding Shares	NA
Counsel	NA	E.P.S.	-$0.71
DUNS No.	NA	Shareholders	NA

Business: The group operates through its subsidiaries whose principle activities include manufacturing, marketing and selling chemicals and additives. The group operates through four segments namely EMC packaging, unifide industries, Todays Way and Spinwell Holding. The group acquired Pitt Penn Group and Spinwell Holding Company, LLC in January 2006, and EMC Packaging, Inc. in June 2005. The group operates from the United States and Canada. The group's quarterly revenue for Mar '07 was 17.62 millions of USD.

Primary SIC and add'l.: 5169

CIK No: 0001059677

Subsidiaries: EMC Packaging, Inc., Spinwell Holding Co., LLC, Todays Way Manufacturing, LLC, Unifide Industries, Limited Liability Company

Owners: Jerome Davis, Robert J. Casper, James W. Margulies/4.10%, JLF Asset Management, L.L.C./5.30%, John Mazzuto/1.70%, Scott L. Margulis/4.04%, Lou Frey, Barry J. Margulis/6.78%, Insiders/15.43%, Jeffrey L. Feinberg/5.30%

Financial Data: *Fiscal Year End:*06/30 *Latest Annual Data:* 6/30/2006

Year	Sales	Net Income
2006	$30,752,000	-$7,176,000
2005	$3,954,000	-$13,922,000
2003	$278,000	-$2,300,000

Curr. Assets:	$15,786,000	*Curr. Liab.:*	$10,170,000		
Plant, Equip.:	$8,095,000	*Total Liab.:*	$21,450,000	*Indic. Yr. Divd.:*	NA
Total Assets:	$32,403,000	*Net Worth:*	$10,953,000	*Debt/ Equity:*	NA

Industrial Minerals Inc

1 Dundas St. W , Ste. 2500, Toronto, ON, M5G 1Z3; *PH:* 1-416-979-4621; *Fax:* 1-416-204-1939; *http://* industrialmineralsinc.com

General - Incorporation	DE	**Stock**- Price on:12/24/2007	$0.18
Employees	NA	Stock Exchange	OTC
Auditor	Toski, Schaefer & Co., P.C.	Ticker Symbol	IDSM
Stk Agt	Fidelity Transfer Co	Outstanding Shares	NA
Counsel	NA	E.P.S.	NA
DUNS No.	NA	Shareholders	NA

Business: The groups principle activities include producing and selling graphite mineral. The group operates from United States.

Primary SIC and add'l.: 1499

CIK No: 0001035422

Subsidiaries: Hi-Plains Energy Corp, Industrial Minerals Canada, Inc.
Officers: David J. Wodar/Pres., Paul K. Cooper/COO, John Carter/Project Dir., Scott W. Old/VP - Marketing, Sales, William Booth/48/VP
Directors: William Thomson/65/Chmn., Dick Van Wyck/Member - Advisory Board, Cam Birge/54/Dir., Robert Dinning/Dir., Bill Booth/Dir., Paul Hynek/Member - Advisory Board, Tony Warner/Member - Advisory Board, Bob Rice/Member - Advisory Board, David Michaud/Member - Advisory Board, Skip Hamilton/Member - Advisory Board
Owners: Patrick Rogers, Thomas S. Bamford, Birge W. Campbell, Insiders/5.20%, Krystar International/17.50%, Larry Van Tol, Stephen W. Weathers, John Melnyk/5.10%
Financial Data: **Fiscal Year End:**12/31 **Latest Annual Data:** 12/31/2006

Year	Sales	Net Income
2006	$3,000	-$1,256,000
2005	$1,000	-$1,844,000
2004	NA	-$561,000

Curr. Assets:	$17,000	**Curr. Liab.:**	$502,000		
Plant, Equip.:	$1,481,000	**Total Liab.:**	$963,000	**Indic. Yr. Divd.:**	NA
Total Assets:	$1,728,000	**Net Worth:**	$765,000	**Debt/ Equity:**	0.5843

Industrial Services of America Inc

7100 Grade Ln., Louisville, KY, 40213; ***PH:*** 1-502-367-7100; ***Fax:*** 1-502-368-1440; ***http://*** www.isa-inc.com; ***Email:*** chulsman@isa-inc.com

General - Incorporation	FL	**Stock**- Price on:12/24/2007	NA
Employees	103	Stock Exchange	NDQ
Auditor	Mountjoy & Bressler LLP	Ticker Symbol	IDSA
Stk Agt	Registrar & Transfer Co	Outstanding Shares	3,640,000
Counsel	NA	E.P.S	$0.71
DUNS No.	11-910-4677	Shareholders	NA

Business: The group's principle activity is to provide waste and recycling management services, scrap processing, brokering and equipment sales and services to commercial, retail and industrial businesses. Computerized waste systems provide waste disposal services including contract negotiation with vendors, centralized billing, invoice auditing and centralized dispatching. The isa recycling segment processes and sells a broad range of materials for recycling. These materials include ferrous and non-ferrous metals, corrugated containers, high-grade paper and plastic. The group's waste equipment sales service segment sells, leases and services waste handling and recycling equipment. The customers of the group are located throughout the United States and Canada. The group operates only in the United States. The group's quarterly revenue for Sep'07 was 17.93 millions of USD.
Primary SIC and add'l.: 7359 4959 8741 8399
CIK No: 0000004187
Subsidiaries: ISA Indiana, Inc, ISA Recycling, LLC
Officers: Brian Donaghy/President, COO, Jim Wiseman/Vice President - ISA Recycling
Owners: David Lester, Roman Epelbaum, Alan Schroering, Albert Cozzi/1.60%, Roberta Kletter/9.90%, Orson Oliver, Insiders/50.50%, K & R, LLC/27.20%, Harry Kletter/37.40%
Financial Data: **Fiscal Year End:**12/31 **Latest Annual Data:** 12/31/2006

Year	Sales	Net Income
2006	$62,082,000	$2,189,000
2005	$117,382,000	$1,102,000
2004	$139,588,000	$1,497,000

Curr. Assets:	$10,032,000	**Curr. Liab.:**	$6,508,000		
Plant, Equip.:	$8,153,000	**Total Liab.:**	$9,585,000	**Indic. Yr. Divd.:**	NA
Total Assets:	$19,332,000	**Net Worth:**	$9,746,000	**Debt/ Equity:**	0.3581

Industrias Bachoco

Avenida Tecnologico No. 401, Cd. Industrial, Celaya, Guanajuato, 38010; ***PH:*** 52-4616183500; ***http://*** www.bachoco.com.mx; ***Email:*** reclutamiento@bachoco.net

General - Incorporation	Mexico	**Stock**- Price on:12/24/2007	$32.98
Employees	20,432	Stock Exchange	NYSE
Auditor	Ernst & Young Global	Ticker Symbol	IBA
Stk Agt	Bank of New York	Outstanding Shares	50,000,000
Counsel	NA	E.P.S	$2.12
DUNS No.	NA	Shareholders	NA

Business: The group's principal activities are breeding, processing and marketing of poultry, eggs, swine products and balanced feed.
Primary SIC and add'l.: 0254 5199 0259
CIK No: 0001044896
Subsidiaries: Acuicola Bachoco, S.A. de C.V., Aviser, S.A. de C.V., Campi Alimentos, S.A. de C.V., Huevo y Derivados, S.A. de C.V., Operadora de Servicios de Personal, S.A. de C.V., Pecuarius Laboratorios, S.A. de C.V., Secba, S.A. de C.V., Sepetec, S. A. de C.V., Servicios de Personal Administrativo, S.A. de C.V.
Officers: Cristobal Mondragon Fragoso/62/CEO, Sec., Alcantar Gutierrez Yolanda/Production, Packing, Transportation Purchases Assist., Barraza Saucedo Roberto/Production, Packing, Transportation Purchases Supervisor, Ambriz Jimenez Xochitl/Domestic Crops Coordinator, Mario Javier Robinson Bours Almada/Proprietary Shareholder Dir., Ricardo Aguirre Borboa/Proprietary Shareholder Dir., David Gastelum Cazares/56/Dir. - Sales, Octavio Robinson Bours Griffith/Proprietary Shareholder Dir., Ricardo Del Castillo/Industrial Purchases, Chickens Packing, Food Processing Equipment Supervisor, Diaz Zavala Rebeca/Importations Coordinator, Figueroa Aguilera Ma. Del Carmen/National raw Materials Assist., Franco Caballero Santiago/Inventories Assist., Garcia Noriega Humberto/National Crops Purchases Mgr., Morales Vargas Vicente/National Crops Mgr., David Campos Orozco/Coordinator, raw Materials Logistic *(26 Officers included in Index)*
Directors: Francisco Javier R. Bours Castelo/Chmn., Enrique Robinson Bours Almada/Honorary Chmn., Humberto Schwarzbeck Noriega/Dir., Guillermo Pineda Cruz/Dir., Jose Eduardo Robinson Bours Castelo/Dir., Ricardo Aguirre Borboa/Proprietary Shareholder Dir., Avelino Fernandez Salido/Dir., Juan Salvador Robinson Bours Martinez/Dir., Jose Francisco Robinson Bours Griffith/Dir.
Financial Data: **Fiscal Year End:**12/31 **Latest Annual Data:** 12/31/2006

Year	Sales	Net Income
2006	$1,390,847,000	$80,098,000
2005	$1,345,340,000	$163,096,000
2004	$1,192,957,000	$66,405,000

Curr. Assets:	$610,771,000	**Curr. Liab.:**	$103,711,000	**P/E Ratio:**	6.88
Plant, Equip.:	$921,738,000	**Total Liab.:**	$312,495,000	**Indic. Yr. Divd.:**	$0.650
Total Assets:	$1,569,388,000	**Net Worth:**	$1,256,894,000	**Debt/ Equity:**	NA

IndyMac Bancorp Inc

888 E Walnut St., Pasadena, CA, 91101; ***PH:*** 1-626-535-5901; ***Fax:*** 1-626-535-8203; ***http://*** www.indymacbank.com

General - Incorporation	DE	**Stock**- Price on:12/24/2007	NA
Employees	6,441	Stock Exchange	NDQ
Auditor	Ernst & Young LLP	Ticker Symbol	NDSN
Stk Agt	Bank of New York	Outstanding Shares	NA
Counsel	NA	E.P.S	-$0.46
DUNS No.	NA	Shareholders	NA

Business: The groups principle activity is to provide home financing products. The group provides mortgage products and services to meet the needs of both consumers and mortgage professionals. The group operates through two segments namely mortgage banking and thrift. The group operates from United States.
Primary SIC and add'l.: 6712 6282 6162 6035
CIK No: 0000773468
Subsidiaries: Financial Freedom Senior Funding Corporation, IndyMac ABS, Inc., IndyMac Bank, F.S.B.
Officers: Patterson R. Jackson/47/CEO - Heloc, Government Lending, Michelle Minier/Vice Chmn., CEO - Financial Freedom Sr. Funding Corporation, Michael W. Perry/Chmn., CEO/$3,968,350.00, Frank M. Sillman/CEO - Indymac Mortgage Bank, James R. Mahoney/Exec. VP, Chmn. - Special Advisor, Financial Freedom/$1,805,091.00, Ruthann K. Melbourne/Exec. VP, Chief Risk Officer, Richard H. Wohl/Dir., Pres. - Indymac Bank/$1,961,682.00, John D. Olinski/Exec. VP, Co - Head - Capital Markets, Scott Keys/CFO, Exec. VP/$1,520,839.00, Meg Wade/Sr. VP, Dir. - Investor Relations, Indymac Bancorp, Inc, Blair S. Abernathy/Exec. VP - Specialty Mortgage Lending, Indymac Bank/$2,066,041.00, Ashwin Adarkar/Exec. VP - New Business Incubation, Organizational Effectiveness, Mergers, Acquisitions, Indymac Bank, Terrence O. Hughes/Exec. VP, General Counsel, Rayman Mathoda/Exec. VP, Chief People Officer, Chief Efficiency Officer - Indymac Bank, Canise Arredondo/Sr. VP, Chief Audit Exec. *(19 Officers included in Index)*
Directors: Michael W. Perry/Chmn., CEO, Gabrielle E. Greene/Dir. - Indymac Bank, Lydia H. Kennard/53/Dir., James R. Ukropina/Dir., Richard H. Wohl/Dir., Pres. - Indymac Bank, Louis E. Caldera/51/Dir., Lyle E. Gramley/81/Dir., Hugh M. Grant/71/Dir., Patrick C. Haden/55/Dir., Terrance G. Hodel/65/Dir., Robert L. Hunt/57/Dir., John Seymour/70/Dir., Bruce G. Willison/59/Dir., Stuart A. Gabriel/54/Dir. - Indymac Bank
Owners: Patrick C. Haden, Hugh M. Grant, Scott A. Keys, Senator John Seymour, Robert L. Hunt, Insiders/7.50%, Lydia H. Kennard, Lyle E. Gramley, Richard H. Wohl/1.40%, Blair S. Abernathy, Bruce G. Willison, James R. Mahoney, Michael W. Perry/3.70%, Louis E. Caldera, Terrance G. Hodel *(18 Owners included in Index)*
Financial Data: **Fiscal Year End:**12/31 **Latest Annual Data:** 12/31/2006

Year	Sales	Net Income
2006	$2,590,991,000	$342,929,000
2005	$1,765,332,000	$300,226,000
2004	$1,211,347,000	$170,522,000

Curr. Assets:	$907,818,000	**Curr. Liab.:**	$21,310,806,000		
Plant, Equip.:	$202,942,000	**Total Liab.:**	$27,467,048,000	**Indic. Yr. Divd.:**	$1.000
Total Assets:	$29,495,316,000	**Net Worth:**	$2,028,268,000	**Debt/ Equity:**	NA

Inergy Holdings LP

2 Brush Creek Blvd., Ste. 200, Kansas City, MO, 64112; ***PH:*** 1-816-446-3749; ***Fax:*** 1-816-842-1904; ***http://*** www.inergypropane.com; ***Email:*** info@inergyservices.com

General - Incorporation	DE	**Stock**- Price on:12/24/2007	$49.93
Employees	2,908	Stock Exchange	NYSE
Auditor	Ernst& Young LLP	Ticker Symbol	NRI
Stk Agt	American Stock Transfer & Trust Co.	Outstanding Shares	20,000,000
Counsel	NA	E.P.S	NA
DUNS No.	NA	Shareholders	NA

Business: The groups principle activity is to acquire retail propane operations. The groups operates through two segments namely propane operations and midstream operations. The group acquired Propane Gas Services, Inc., Delta Gas Company, Homestead Gas Company, Firelands Propane, Deyos Fuel, Country Gas, Inc, Fishers Hoosier Propane in the year 2006 and Atlas Gas Products, Inc, Dowdle Gas, Inc, Graeber Brothers, Inc in the year 2005. The group operates from Alabama, Arkansas, Connecticut, Florida, Georgia, Illinois, Indiana, Kentucky, Maine, Maryland, Massachusetts and Michigan. The group's quarterly revenue for September 2007 was 273.50 millions of USD.
Primary SIC and add'l.: 5984
CIK No: 0001228068
Subsidiaries: Arrow Gas, Atlas Gas, Bastrop Propane, Bayless Gas, Best Butane Co., Blue Flame Gas, Bradley Propane, Burnet Propane, Burnwell Propane, Centex Butane Co., Central New York Oil And Gas, L.L.C., Choctaw Propane, Coleman Propane, Colemans Gas, Country Gas 116 Subsidiaries included in the Index
Officers: John J. Sherman/Dir., CEO, Pres., Phillip L. Elbert/COO, Pres. - Inergy Propane, Brooks R. Sherman/CFO, Exec. VP, Laura L. Ozenberger/Sr. VP, General Counsel, Mike Campbell/Primary Investor Relations Officer, William R. Moler/Sr. VP - Natural GAS Midstream Operations, Carl A. Hughes/Sr. VP - Business Development, Andrew L. Atterbury/Sr. VP - Corporate Development
Directors: John J. Sherman/Dir., CEO, Pres., Warren H. Gfeller/Dir., Arthur B. Krause/Dir., Richard T. OBrien/Dir., Robert A. Pascal/Dir., Robert D. Taylor/Dir.
Owners: Phillip L. Elbert/4.48%, Carl A. Hughes/4.73%, Arthur B. Krause, Laura L. Ozenberger, William C. Gautreaux/5.31%, David G. Dehaemers/5.05%, R. Brooks Sherman/1.97%, John J. Sherman/39.25%, Andrew L. Atterbury/5.34%, Warren H. Gfeller, Robert A. Pascal, Insiders/56.04%

Curr. Assets:	$295,896,000	**Curr. Liab.:**	$308,432,000	**P/E Ratio:**	48.01
Plant, Equip.:	$723,533,000	**Total Liab.:**	$1,665,571,000	**Indic. Yr. Divd.:**	NA
Total Assets:	$1,646,846,000	**Net Worth:**	-$18,725,000	**Debt/ Equity:**	NA

Inergy LP

2 Brush Creek Blvd., Ste. 200, Kansas City, MO, 64112; ***PH:*** 1-816-842-8181; ***Fax:*** 1-816-842-1904; ***http://*** www.inergypropane.com; ***Email:*** info@inergyservices.com

General		Stock	
Incorporation	DE	Price on:12/24/2007	$35.8
Employees	2,908	Stock Exchange	NDQ
Auditor	Ernst& Young LLP	Ticker Symbol	NRGY
Stk Agt	American Stock Transfer & Trust Co.	Outstanding Shares	49,680,000
Counsel	NA	E.P.S.	$0.61
DUNS No.	NA	Shareholders	NA

Business: The groups principle activities include retailing, wholesaling, marketing and distribution propane supply business. The group operates through two segments namely propane operations and midstream operations. The group acquired Propane Gas Services, Inc, Delta Gas Company, Homestead Gas Company, Firelands Propane, Deyos Fuel, Country Gas, Inc, Fishers Hoosier Propane, Bath Storage Facility, Columbus Butane Company, Inc, Hometown Propane, Inc, Mideastern Oil Company, Inc in the year 2006 and Atlas Gas Products, Inc, Dowdle Gas, Inc, Graeber Brothers, Incin the year 2005. The group operates from Wisconsin, Alabama, Georgia, Florida, New York, New Jersey and Texas. The group's quarterly revenue for September 2007 was 273.50 millions of USD.

Primary SIC and add'l.: 5984

CIK No: 0001136352

Subsidiaries: Arrow Gas, Atlas Gas, Bastrop Propane, Bayless Gas, Best Butane Co., Blue Flame Gas, Bradley Propane, Burnet Propane, Burnwell Propane, Centex Butane Co., Central New York Oil And Gas, L.L.C., Choctaw Propane, Coleman Propane, Colemans Gas, Country Gas 109 Subsidiaries included in the Index

Officers: John J. Sherman/Dir., CEO, Pres., Phillip L. Elbert/Dir., Exec. VP - Propane Operations, Brooks R. Sherman/43/CFO, Exec. VP, Laura L. Ozenberger/VP, General Counsel, Sec., Carl A. Hughes/VP - Business Development, Andrew L. Atterbury/Sr. VP - Corporate Development, Mike Campbell/Investor Relations Officer, William R. Moler/Sr. VP - Natural GAS Midstream Operations, Jay Cates/VP - Retail Operations, South, Tom Haiar/VP - Retail Operations, Midwest, Ted Jeffcoat/VP - Retail Operations, East, Tom Wright/Dir. - Fleet Operations, Purchasing, Assets, Joe H. Donnell/Pres. - L&L Transportation, William C. Gautreaux/VP - Supply, Wholesale Marketing, Richard C. Kreul/VP - Inergy Services *(16 Officers included in Index)*

Directors: John J. Sherman/Dir., CEO, Pres., Phillip L. Elbert/Dir., Exec. VP - Propane Operations, Warren H. Gfeller/Dir., Arthur B. Krause/Dir., Robert A. Pascal/Dir., Robert D. Taylor/Dir.

Owners: Warren H. Gfeller/0.10%, Robert D. Taylor, Laura L. Ozenberger, Robert A. Pascal/3.90%, R. Brooks Sherman, Bonavita, Inc./3.90%, Insiders/13.90%, Kayne Anderson MLP Investment Company/7.40%, John J. Sherman/9.60%, Inergy Holdings, L.P./9.50%, Carl A. Hughes/0.20%, Arthur B. Krause

Financial Data: *Fiscal Year End:*09/30 *Latest Annual Data:* 9/30/2006

Year	Sales	Net Income
2006	$1,387,561,000	$9,811,000
2005	$1,050,136,000	$38,637,000
2004	$482,496,000	-$4,596,000

Curr. Assets:	$295,586,000	**Curr. Liab.:**	$308,249,000	**P/E Ratio:**	51.14
Plant, Equip.:	$723,533,000	**Total Liab.:**	$962,883,000	**Indic. Yr. Divd.:**	$2.380
Total Assets:	$1,639,035,000	**Net Worth:**	$676,152,000	**Debt/ Equity:**	0.7416

INfe Human Resources Inc

67 Wall St. Fl 22, New York, NY, 10005; *PH:* 1-212-859-3466; *http://* www.infehumanresources.com; *Email:* info@infehumanresources.com

General		Stock	
Incorporation	NV	Price on:12/24/2007	$0.31
Employees	509	Stock Exchange	OTC
Auditor	Miller, Ellin & Co., LLP	Ticker Symbol	IFHR
Stk Agt	Computershare Trust Co	Outstanding Shares	15,450,000
Counsel	NA	E.P.S.	-$0.08
DUNS No.	NA	Shareholders	NA

Business: The groups principle activity is to provide human resource consulting services to other companies. Services of the group include temporary and permanent staffing for both professional and non-professional employees, payroll and related human resource functions, for client companies.

Primary SIC and add'l.: 8742

CIK No: 0001260376

Subsidiaries: Daniels Corporate Advisory Company, Inc.

Owners: Insiders/64.11%, Arthur Viola/64.11%

Financial Data: *Fiscal Year End:*11/30 *Latest Annual Data:* 11/30/2006

Year	Sales	Net Income
2006	$6,568,000	-$291,000
2005	$6,000	-$479,000
2004	NA	-$18,000

Curr. Assets:	$1,108,000	**Curr. Liab.:**	$926,000		
Plant, Equip.:	$124,000	**Total Liab.:**	$3,223,000	**Indic. Yr. Divd.:**	NA
Total Assets:	$3,474,000	**Net Worth:**	$250,000	**Debt/ Equity:**	12.1005

Infineon Technologies

640 N McCarthy Blvd., Milpitas, CA, 95035; *PH:* 1-408-503-2587; *Fax:* 1-408-503-1587; *http://* www.infineon.com; *Email:* investor.relations@infineon.com

General		Stock	
Incorporation	Germany	Price on:12/24/2007	$16.78
Employees	41,651	Stock Exchange	NYSE
Auditor	KPMG Deutsche Treuhand Gesellschaft	Ticker Symbol	IFX
Stk Agt	Registrar Services GmbH	Outstanding Shares	748,000,000
Counsel	NA	E.P.S.	$0.09
DUNS No.	NA	Shareholders	NA

Business: The group's principal activities are the design, research, development, manufacture and marketing of semiconductors and complete systems solutions used in a variety of micro electrical applications. The group operates through the following divisions: memory products (mainstream drams, high speed graphics, asics with embedded dram, hard drive controllers); wireless communications (radio frequency discretes, ics and modules, bbase banics); wireline communications (codes, slics, transceivers, switching ics, framers, protocol controllers, embedded dsp and embedded dram); automotive & industrial (power semiconductors and controllers with embedded memory); security & chip card ics; opto (security memory ics, security mimicro controllecs, encryption ics, fingertip identification ics, multimediacards).

Primary SIC and add'l.: 3679 5065 3674

CIK No: 0001107457

Subsidiaries: Technologies AG:

Officers: Wolfgang Ziebart/58/Member - Management Board, CEO, Pres., Peter J. Fischl/Member - Management Board, Exec. VP, CFO, Hermann Eul/48/Member - Management Board, Exec. VP, Head - Communication Solutions Business Group, Peter Bauer/48/Member - Management Board, Exec. VP, Head - Automotive, Industrial, Multimarket Business Group, Reinhard Ploss/53/Member - Management Board, Exec. VP, Head - Operations, David Ong/Contact - Media Asia, Infineon Technologies Asia Pacific Pte Ltd, Rachel Loke/Contact - Media Asia, Infineon Technologies Asia Pacific Pte Ltd, Lisa Chen/Contact - Media Asia, Infineon Technologies China Co, Ltd, Prita J. Peter/Contact - Media Asia, Infineon Technologies India Pvt Ltd, Ye Shu Rung/Contact - Media Asia, Infineon Technologies Taiwan Co Ltd, Hirotaka Shiroguchi/Contact - Media Japan, Infineon Technologies Japan KK, Gerhard Zimmermann/Contact - Media North America, Infineon Technologies North America Corp, Agnes Toan/Contact - Media North America, Infineon Technologies North America Corp, Infineon Technologies North America Corp

Directors: Wolfgang Ziebart/58/Member - Management Board, CEO, Pres., Max Dietrich Kley/Chmn. - Supervisory Board, Peter Bauer/48/Member - Management Board, Exec. VP, Head - Automotive, Industrial, Multimarket Business Group, Johannes Feldmayer/Member - Supervisory Board, Renate Kocher/Member - Supervisory Board, Michael Ruth/Member - Supervisory Board, Alfred Eibl/Member - Supervisory Board, Gerd Schmidt/Member - Supervisory Board, Hermann Eul/48/Member - Management Board, Exec. VP, Head - Communication Solutions Business Group, Peter J. Fischl/Member - Management Board, Exec. VP, CFO, Wigand Cramer/Member - Supervisory Board, Alexander Truby/Member - Supervisory Board, Siegfried Luther/Member - Supervisory Board, Doris Schmitt-Landsiedel/Member - Supervisory Board, Martin Winterkorn/Member - Supervisory Board *(21 Directors included in Index)*

Owners: Dodge & Cox Investment Managers/5.10%, Templeton Global Advisors Limited/5.20%, Brandes Investment Partners, L.P./5.10%

Financial Data: *Fiscal Year End:*09/30 *Latest Annual Data:* 9/30/2006

Year	Sales	Net Income
2006	$10,060,315,000	-$340,038,000
2005	$8,143,243,000	-$375,898,000
2004	$8,872,155,000	$75,219,000

Curr. Assets:	$7,208,053,000	**Curr. Liab.:**	$4,193,384,000		
Plant, Equip.:	$4,775,763,000	**Total Liab.:**	$7,447,856,000	**Indic. Yr. Divd.:**	NA
Total Assets:	$14,191,528,000	**Net Worth:**	$6,743,672,000	**Debt/ Equity:**	NA

Infinex Ventures Inc

3914 Seaton Pl, Las Vegas, NV, 89121; *PH:* 1-702-387-4005; *http://* www.infinexventures.com; *Email:* info@infinexventures.com

General		Stock	
Incorporation	NV	Price on:12/24/2007	$0.42
Employees	NA	Stock Exchange	OTC
Auditor	Morgan & Co	Ticker Symbol	INFX
Stk Agt	Pacific Corporate Trust Co	Outstanding Shares	25,350,000
Counsel	NA	E.P.S.	$0.06
DUNS No.	NA	Shareholders	NA

Business: The group's principle activities include acquiring, exploring, and developing mineral properties. It has decided to abandon the business plan relating to its interest in the long canyon property and entered into an agreement to acquire certain nanotechnology patents and related assets. The company is in the development stage. The group operates from United States.

Primary SIC and add'l.: 1031 1099 1044 1021

CIK No: 0001076310

Officers: Michael De Rosa/Dir., CEO, CFO, Pres., Treasurer

Directors: Michael De Rosa/Dir., CEO, CFO, Pres., Treasurer

Owners: Elco Bank & Trust Co./7.59%, CEDE & Co/23.89%, Jorge Lopehandia/23.67%, Carlo Viscardi/6.51%, Insiders/34.75%, Michael De Rosa/34.75%

Financial Data: *Fiscal Year End:*10/31 *Latest Annual Data:* 10/31/2006

Year	Sales	Net Income
2006	NA	-$3,528,000
2005	NA	-$50,000
2004	NA	-$215,000

Curr. Assets:	$1,000	**Curr. Liab.:**	$445,000		
Plant, Equip.:	NA	**Total Liab.:**	$445,000	**Indic. Yr. Divd.:**	NA
Total Assets:	$1,000	**Net Worth:**	-$443,000	**Debt/ Equity:**	NA

Infinite Group Inc

60 Office Pk. Way, Pittsford, NY, 14534; *PH:* 1-585-385-0610; *Fax:* 1-585-385-0614; *http://* www.us-igi.com

General		Stock	
Incorporation	DE	Price on:12/24/2007	$0.6
Employees	75	Stock Exchange	OTC
Auditor	Freed Maxick & Battaglia, CPAs, PC	Ticker Symbol	IMCI
Stk Agt	American Stock Transfer & Trust Co.	Outstanding Shares	23,520,000
Counsel	NA	E.P.S.	-$0.04
DUNS No.	NA	Shareholders	NA

Business: The groups principle activity is to provide information technology solution services. The services of the group include advanced server management, wireless technology, human capital services, enterprise architecture and earned value management. The group operates from the United States.

Primary SIC and add'l.: 7373 7389 7389 7379 7379 7373 7370

CIK No: 0000884650

Officers: Michael S. Smith/53/Chmn., CEO, CFO, Pres., James D. Jim Frost/Chief Operating, Technology Officer, David Slavny/Special Projects, Jim Witzel/Corporate Accountant, Deanna Wohlschlegel/36/Controller, Sec., Michael Tartal/VP - Business Development, Scott Hogan/Practice Dir. - Network Services, Rodney Moore/Practice Dir. - Engineering Services, Michael Amici/Program Mgr. - Human Resources Services, Brian Culbertson/Program Mgr. - Infrastructure, Michael Hill/Project Mgr. - Interoperability, James D. Frost/58/CTO, COO, Lara Milavickas/Dir. - Business Development

Directors: Michael S. Smith/53/Chmn., CEO, CFO, Pres., Paul J. Delmore/51/Dir., Allan M. Robbins/56/Dir.

Owners: James D. Frost/6.20%, Allan M. Robbins/24.30%, David N. Slavny Family Trust/5.60%, Michael Tartal, Paul J. Delmore/15.20%, Northwest Hampton Holdings, LLC/31.50%, Michael S. Smith/4.70%, Insiders/51.50%

Financial Data: *Fiscal Year End:*NA *Latest Annual Data:* 12/31/2006

Year	Sales	Net Income
2006	$6,445,000	-$1,602,000
2005	$8,505,000	$34,000
2004	$5,735,000	$578,000

Curr. Assets:	$605,000	**Curr. Liab.:**	$2,716,000		
Plant, Equip.:	$81,000	**Total Liab.:**	$4,568,000	**Indic. Yr. Divd.:**	NA
Total Assets:	$705,000	**Net Worth:**	-$3,863,000	**Debt/ Equity:**	NA

Infinity Energy Resources Inc

633 17th St., Ste. 1800, Denver, CO, 80202; *PH:* 1-720-932-7800; *Fax:* 1-720-932-5409; *http://* www.infinity-res.com

General - Incorporation .... DE
Employees 16
Auditor ... Ehrhardt Keefe Steiner & Hottman P.C
Stk Agt..... Computershare Investor Services LLC
Counsel .... Davis Graham & Stubbs LLP
DUNS No. 80-981-4635

Stock- Price on:12/24/2007 .... $3.26
Stock Exchange .... NDQ
Ticker Symbol .... IFNY
Outstanding Shares 17,870,000
E.P.S .... NA
Shareholders .... NA

Business: The group's principal activity is to provide oil and gas production enhancement services. The group operates in two segments: oil field services and oil and gas production. The oil field services segment is directed at maintaining and enhancing production obtained from oil and gas wells and currently has operations in Kansas, Oklahoma, and Wyoming. The oil and gas production segment has acquired interest in producing properties in Kansas and undeveloped leasehold in Wyoming of which a portion have been developed into producing properties. The group also operates a wastewater treatment facility on a limited basis. The group provides services associated with drilling and completion of oil and gas wells, including cementing, acidizing, fracturing, nitrogen pumping and water hauling.

Primary SIC and add'l.: 4953 1382 1389 1311

CIK No: 0000822746

Subsidiaries: CIS-Oklahoma, Inc., Consolidated Oil Well Services, Inc., Infinity Oil & Gas of Kansas, Inc., Infinity Oil & Gas of Wyoming, Inc., Infinity Oil and Gas of Texas, Inc.

Officers: Stanton E. Ross/Chmn., CEO/$567,748.00

Directors: Stanton E. Ross/Chmn., CEO, Leroy C. Richie/Dir., Elliot M. Kaplan/Dir., James A. Tuell/Dir., Robert O. Lorenz/Dir.

Owners: Robert O. Lorenz, Dalton, Greiner, Hartman, Maher& Co., LLC/7.50%, Wellington Management Company LLP/8.50%, Stanton E. Ross/6.00%, James A. Tuell/1.30%, Insiders/8.70%, James W. Dean, Elliot M. Kaplan, Leroy C. Richie, Timothy A. Ficker

Financial Data: *Fiscal Year End:*12/31 *Latest Annual Data:* 12/31/2006

Year	Sales	Net Income
2006	$12,292,000	-$12,687,000
2005	$30,775,000	-$13,577,000
2004	$20,988,000	-$4,633,000

Curr. Assets:	$3,711,000	**Curr. Liab.:**	$11,121,000		
Plant, Equip.:	$51,478,000	**Total Liab.:**	$18,687,000	**Indic. Yr. Divd.:**	NA
Total Assets:	$56,304,000	**Net Worth:**	$37,617,000	**Debt/ Equity:**	0.5003

Infinity Pharmaceuticals Inc

Formerly: Discovery Partners International Inc
780 Memorial Dr., Cambridge, MA, 02139; *PH:* 1-617-453-1000; *http://* www.discoverypartners.com

General - Incorporation .... DE
Employees 115
Auditor .... Ernst & Young LLP
Stk Agt...... American Stock Transfer & Trust Co.
Counsel .... Brobeck, Phleger & Harrison
DUNS No. .... NA

Stock- Price on:12/24/2007 .... $10.961
Stock Exchange .... NA
Ticker Symbol .... NA
Outstanding Shares 19,630,000
E.P.S .... -$0.75
Shareholders .... NA

Business: The group's principal activity is to develop and sell instruments and associated consumables to pharmaceutical companies. The group's generates large chemical compounds for drug discovery and provides instrumentation to generate compound libraries. The other services provided by the group include, drug discovery products and services to pharmaceutical and biotechnology companies. The group's main product includes assays, compound libraries, including combinatorial chemistry instruments, parallel synthesis, split-and-pool synthesis. The group's major customers are pfizer, merck, novartis, inspire pharmaceuticals and glaxosmithkline. The trademarks of the group include irori(R), microkan(R), synthesis manager(R), clevap(R), nanokan(R) and xenometrix(r).

Primary SIC and add'l.: 2835 8731 3826

CIK No: 0001113148

Subsidiaries: ChemRx Advanced Technologies, Inc., Discovery Partners International AG, Discovery Partners International GmbH, Discovery Partners International, LLC, Irori Europe, Ltd., Structural Proteomics, Inc., Systems Integration Drug Discovery Company, Inc., Xenometrix, Inc.

Officers: Steven H. Holtzman/54/Chmn., CEO/$1,263,199.00, Julian Adams/53/Pres., Chief Scientific Officer/$956,263.00, Adelene Q. Perkins/48/Exec. VP, Chief Business Officer/$542,000.00

Directors: Steven H. Holtzman/54/Chmn., CEO, Arnold J. Levine/68/Dir., Ronald D. Daniel/78/Dir., Franklin H. Moss/58/Dir., Anthony B. Evnin/67/Dir., Herm Rosenman/60/Dir., Vicki L. Sato/59/Dir., Eric S. Lander/51/Dir., James B. Tananbaum/44/Dir., Patrick Lee/52/Dir., Michael C. Venuti/54/Dir., Harry F. Hixson/69/Dir.

Owners: Vicki L. Sato, Novartis AG/7.35%, Amgen Inc./7.41%, Ronald D. Daniel, Anthony B. Evnin/6.03%, Entities affiliated with Venrock Associates/6.03%, Arnold J. Levine, James B. Tananbaum/7.95%, Entities affiliated with Advent Venture Partners LLP/5.76%, Adelene Q. Perkins, Richard C. Neale, Julian Adams, Franklin H. Moss, Patrick Lee/5.76%, Herm Rosenman *(22 Owners included in Index)*

Financial Data: *Fiscal Year End:*12/31 *Latest Annual Data:* 12/31/2006

Year	Sales	Net Income
2006	$18,495,000	-$28,448,000
2005	$34,837,000	-$14,165,000
2004	$51,564,000	$3,903,000

Curr. Assets:	$146,099,000	**Curr. Liab.:**	$24,834,000		
Plant, Equip.:	$6,540,000	**Total Liab.:**	$92,222,000	**Indic. Yr. Divd.:**	NA
Total Assets:	$154,648,000	**Net Worth:**	$62,425,000	**Debt/ Equity:**	NA

Infinity Property & Casualty Corp

3700 Colonnade Pkwy., Birmingham, AL, 35243; *PH:* 1-205-803-8186; *Fax:* 1-205-803-8186; *http://* ir.ipacc.com; *Email:* investor.relations@infinity-insurance.com

General - Incorporation .... OH
Employees 2,100
Auditor .... Ernst & Young LLP
Stk Agt...... American Stock Transfer & Trust Co.
Counsel .... NA
DUNS No. .... NA

Stock- Price on:12/24/2007 .... $54.19
Stock Exchange .... NDQ
Ticker Symbol .... IPCC
Outstanding Shares 19,390,000
E.P.S $3.74
Shareholders .... NA

Business: The group's principal activity is to provide personal automobile insurance on a national level. The group provides standard and preferred personal auto insurance, non-standard commercial auto insurance and complementary personal lines insurance products. It distributes its products primarily through a network of approximately 14,000 independent agencies. The group operates solely in the domestic market.

Primary SIC and add'l.: 6311 6331 6719

CIK No: 0001195933

Subsidiaries: American Deposit Insurance Company, American Premier Insurance Company, Atlanta Casualty Company, Atlanta Casualty General Agency, Inc., Atlanta Casualty Group, Inc., Atlanta Reserve Insurance Company, Atlanta Specialty Insurance Company, Budget Insurance Premiums, Inc., Casualty Underwriters, Inc., Coventry Insurance Company, Granite Finance Company, Inc., Great Texas County Mutual Insurance Company, Infinity Agency of Texas, Inc., Infinity Insurance Company, Infinity National Insurance Company 28 Subsidiaries included in the Index

Officers: James R. Gober/Chmn., CEO, Pres., Joseph A. Pietrangelo/43/Regional Pres. - East Region, Samuel J. Simon/Dir., Exec. VP, General Counsel, Sec., Roger Smith/Dir., Exec. VP, CFO, John R. Miner/Regional Pres. - Central Region, Glen N. Godwin/50/Regional Pres. - West Region, Scott C. Pitrone/45/Regional Pres. - South Region

Directors: James R. Gober/Chmn., CEO, Pres., Roger Smith/Dir., Exec. VP, CFO, Gregory G. Joseph/Dir., Samuel J. Weinhoff/Dir., Harold E. Layman/Dir., Samuel J. Simon/Dir., Exec. VP, General Counsel, Sec., Jorge G. Castro/Dir., Gregory C. Thomas/Dir., Drayton Nabers/Dir.

Owners: Dimensional Fund Advisors LP/8.41%, Barclays Global Investors NA/5.53%, Roger Smith, Harold E. Layman, Samuel J. Simon, Jorge G. Castro, T. Rowe Price Associates, Inc./12.00%, Samuel J. Weinhoff, Scott C. Pitrone, Drayton Nabers, Joseph A. Pietrangelo, James R. Gober, John R. Miner, Glen N. Godwin, Insiders/1.70% *(17 Owners included in Index)*

Financial Data: *Fiscal Year End:*12/31 *Latest Annual Data:* 12/31/2006

Year	Sales	Net Income
2006	$1,021,349,000	$87,282,000
2005	$1,053,275,000	$106,308,000
2004	$951,763,000	$96,398,000

Curr. Assets:	$522,909,000	**Curr. Liab.:**	$123,995,000	**P/E Ratio:**	13.65
Plant, Equip.:	NA	**Total Liab.:**	$1,349,753,000	**Indic. Yr. Divd.:**	$0.360
Total Assets:	$2,014,354,000	**Net Worth:**	$664,601,000	**Debt/ Equity:**	0.2940

Infitech Ventures Inc

20 Lyall Ave., Toronto, ON, M4E 1V9; *PH:* 1-416-694068; *http://* www.infitechventures.com; *Email:* sales@infitechventures.com

General - Incorporation .... NV
Employees .... NA
Auditor .... Davidson & Co. LLP
Stk Agt. .... NA
Counsel .... NA
DUNS No. .... NA

Stock- Price on:12/24/2007 .... NA
Stock Exchange .... OTC
Ticker Symbol .... IFTV
Outstanding Shares .... NA
E.P.S .... NA
Shareholders .... NA

Business: The group's principal activity is to develop and market a proprietary, patent-pending technology (the "Wax Technology") that uses a molten wax compound consisting of paraffin wax and resins to control, clean and remediate oil and other liquid fuel spills on land and on water. In addition, as part of long-term business plan, the company intend to pursue business opportunities in wastewater treatment solutions. The company is currently a development stage company. The company is seeking exclusive distribution rights from manufacturers of ultraviolet disinfection ,membrane filtration and sequencing batch reactor systems.

Primary SIC and add'l.: 2911

CIK No: 0001129096

Officers: Paul G. Daly/Pres., Sec., Treasurer, Dir., CEO, CFO, William Nelson/Consultant, C. C. Shen/Consultant

Directors: Paul G. Daly/Pres., Sec., Treasurer, Dir., CEO, CFO

Owners: PAUL G. DALY/45.30%

Infocrossing Inc

2 Christie Hts. St., Leonia, NJ, 07605; *PH:* 1-201-840-4700; *http://* www.infocrossing.com

General - Incorporation .... DE
Employees 870
Auditor .... Ernst & Young LLP
Stk Agt............ Continental Stock Transfer & Trust Co
Counsel .... NA
DUNS No. 19-752-2659

Stock- Price on:12/24/2007 .... $17.77
Stock Exchange .... NA
Ticker Symbol .... NA
Outstanding Shares 22,110,000
E.P.S $0.06
Shareholders .... NA

Business: The group's principal activity is to provide information technology outsourcing services. The group provides mainframe outsourcing, midrange systems management including both managed hosting and remote management of IBM as400 and iseries computers. The group provides business process outsourcing, open systems management including hosting and a full suite of managed services for servers running various microsoft and unix operating systems as well as remote systems management for these platforms. The group also provides systems infrastructure and consulting and business continuity solutions. The group's customers include commercial enterprises, institutions and government agencies.group acquired ito acquisition corp in 2004 & on 01-Aug-2004, the group acquired mailwatch service from easylink services corp.

Primary SIC and add'l.: 7371 7372 7374

CIK No: 0000893816

Subsidiaries: Infocrossing EAS Inc., Infocrossing Healthcare Services Inc., Infocrossing Services Inc., Infocrossing Services Southeast Inc., Infocrossing Services West, Infocrossing Southeast Inc., Infocrossing West Inc.

Officers: Zach Lonstein/Chmn., CEO/$721,764.00, Michael Luebke/Pres. - Infocrossing Healthcare Services, Michael Wilczak/Sr. VP - Corporate Development, Robert B. Wallach/COO, Pres./$693,623.00, Garry Lazarewicz/Sr. VP - Research, Development, William McHale/CFO/$329,224.00, Lee C. Fields/Exec. VP - Marketing, Business Development/$466,853.00, Nicholas J. Letizia/Sr. VP, General Counsel/$351,883.00, Michael Jones/Pres. - Information Technology Outsourcing, Art Miller/Pres. - Infocrossing Healthcare Services, Inc

Directors: Zach Lonstein/Chmn., CEO, Peter J. Dapuzzo/Dir., Jeremiah M. Healy/Dir., Kathleen A. Perone/Dir., Howard L. Waltman/Dir.

Owners: Jeremiah M. Healy, Howard L. Waltman, Insiders/17.20%, Nicholas J. Letizia, Kathleen A. Perone, Robert B. Wallach/3.40%, Zach Lonstein/11.70%, Lee C. Fields, Peter J. DaPuzzo, William J. McHale

Financial Data: *Fiscal Year End:*12/31 *Latest Annual Data:* 12/31/2006

Year	Sales	Net Income
2006	$229,207,000	$8,486,000
2005	$148,006,000	$2,573,000
2004	$104,949,000	$19,963,000

Curr. Assets:	$64,960,000	*Curr. Liab.:*	$49,288,000	*P/E Ratio:*	44.43
Plant, Equip.	$45,049,000	*Total Liab.:*	$172,883,000	*Indic. Yr. Divd.:*	NA
Total Assets:	$298,125,000	*Net Worth:*	$125,242,000	*Debt/ Equity:*	0.8938

InFocus Corp

27500 SW Pkwy. Ave., Wilsonville, OR, 97070; *PH:* 1-503-685-8888; *Fax:* 1-503-685-8887; *http://* www.infocus.com; *Email:* sales@infocus.com

General - Incorporation	OR	**Stock**- Price on:12/24/2007	$2.4
Employees	399	Stock Exchange	NDQ
Auditor	KPMG LLP	Ticker Symbol	INFS
Stk Agt	Mellon Investor Services Llc	Outstanding Shares	39,750,000
Counsel	Garvey Schubert & Barer	E.P.S.	-$0.93
DUNS No.	16-151-1795	Shareholders	NA

Business: The group's principal activities are to develop, manufacture and market multimedia projection products and services to present video, audio, graphics and other data. The group has four product platforms for the various projection requirements of its customers. Mobile projectors are used by professionals who place a premium on reduced size and weight. Meeting room projectors are used in conference or training room environments. Installation and integration projectors are placed at large venues and auditorium environments. Home entertainment projectors are used for home theaters, gaming and entertainment environments at home. The group operates in the United States, Europe Asia-Pacific and other countries.

Primary SIC and add'l.: 3577 7379 5043 3724

CIK No: 0000845434

Subsidiaries: ASK AS, InFocus (Shanghai) Co. Ltd., InFocus AG, InFocus AS, InFocus Benelux BV, InFocus GmbH, InFocus International (Cayman) Limited, InFocus International BV, InFocus Norge AS, InFocus SARL, InFocus Sweden AB, InFocus Systems Asia Pte, Ltd., Motif,Inc., Shenzhen South Mountain Technologies Ltd, South Mountain Technologies (Norway), AS 17 Subsidiaries included in the Index

Officers: Robert G. O'Malley/Dir., CEO, Steve Stark/VP - Engineering/$241,034.00, Roger Rowe/47/VP - Finance, Sec./$331,173.00, Joe O'Sullivan/Acting COO, VP - Global Operations, GM - Asia Sales/$395,306.00, Mark Perry/Interim CFO

Directors: Robert G. O'Malley/Dir., CEO, John D. Abouchar/Dir., Peter D. Behrendt/Dir., Michael R. Hallman/Dir., Bruce Berkoff/Dir., Robert B. Ladd/Dir., Bernard T. Marren/Dir.

Owners: Caxton Associates, L.L.C./10.90%, Steve Stark, Dimensional Fund Advisors/7.80%, Scott Ballantyne, Michael R. Hallman, Robert B. Ladd, Renaissance Technologies Corp./5.40%, Svein S. Jacobsen, Kyle C. Ranson/1.40%, Peter D. Behrendt, Duane C. McDougall, Candace Petersen, Insiders/2.90%, Joseph OSullivan, Wells Fargo & Company/5.80% *(16 Owners included in Index)*

Financial Data: *Fiscal Year End:*12/31 *Latest Annual Data:* 12/31/2006

Year	Sales	Net Income
2006	$374,752,000	-$61,920,000
2005	$532,099,000	-$79,794,000
2004	$648,941,000	$7,573,000

Curr. Assets:	$177,106,000	*Curr. Liab.:*	$78,846,000		
Plant, Equip.:	$3,961,000	*Total Liab.:*	$81,993,000	*Indic. Yr. Divd.:*	NA
Total Assets:	$182,256,000	*Net Worth:*	$100,263,000	*Debt/ Equity:*	NA

InfoLogix Inc

101 E County Line Rd., Ste. 210, Hatboro, PA, 19040; *PH:* 1-215-604-0691; *http://* www.infologixsys.com

General - Incorporation	NV	**Stock**- Price on:12/24/2007	$3.7
Employees	81	Stock Exchange	NDQ
Auditor	NA	Ticker Symbol	IFLG
Stk Agt	Registrar & Transfer Co	Outstanding Shares	24,130,000
Counsel	NA	E.P.S.	-$0.19
DUNS No.	NA	Shareholders	NA

Business: The groups principle activity is to provide technology solutions to customers in the healthcare and enterprise sectors. Services of the group include proprietary software and radio frequency identification technologies. In November 2006, the group merged with New Age-DE. The group operates from North America. The group's quarterly revenue for Sep '07 was 20.08 millions of USD.

Primary SIC and add'l.: 7389

CIK No: 0001315320

Subsidiaries: Embedded Technologies, LLC, InfoLogix Systems Corporation, OPT Acquisition LLC

Officers: David T. Gulian/Dir., Co - Founder, CEO, Pres., Richard Hodge/Dir., Exec. VP, Craig Wilensky/Dir., Exec. VP - Enterprise Mobility Division, John A. Roberts/CFO, Thomas Walsh/Primary Investor Relations Officer, Thomas E. Kreuzberger/41/VP

Directors: David T. Gulian/Dir., Co - Founder, CEO, Pres., Warren V. Musser/Chmn., Thomas O. Miller/Dir., Jake Steinfeld/Dir., Richard A. Vermeil/Dir., Wayne D. Hoch/Dir., Richard Hodge/Dir., Exec. VP, Thomas C. Lynch/Dir., Craig Wilensky/Dir., Exec. VP - Enterprise Mobility Division

Owners: Richard A. Vermeil, Jake Steinfeld, David T. Gulian/12.20%, Insiders/42.70%, Wayne D. Hoch, Thomas O. Miller, Richard D. Hodge/10.70%, IL Venture Capital LLC/8.80%, Warren V. Musser/11.20%, Craig A. Wilensky/10.70%, Thomas C. Lynch

Financial Data: *Fiscal Year End:*12/31 *Latest Annual Data:* 12/31/2006

Year	Sales	Net Income
2006	$60,786,000	-$1,869,000

Curr. Assets:	$28,125,000	*Curr. Liab.:*	$14,599,000		
Plant, Equip.:	$1,440,000	*Total Liab.:*	$15,924,000	*Indic. Yr. Divd.:*	NA
Total Assets:	$31,813,000	*Net Worth:*	$15,888,000	*Debt/ Equity:*	0.0762

InfoNow Corp

1875 Lawrence St., Ste. 1100, Denver, CO, 80202; *PH:* 1-303-293-0212; *Fax:* 1-303-293-0213; *http://* www.infonow.com; *Email:* sales_team@infonow.com

General - Incorporation	DE	**Stock**- Price on:12/24/2007	$0.17
Employees	NA	Stock Exchange	OTC
Auditor	Deloitte & Touche LLP	Ticker Symbol	INOW
Stk Agt	Computershare Trust Co	Outstanding Shares	NA
Counsel	NA	E.P.S.	NA
DUNS No.	61-992-6439	Shareholders	NA

Business: The group's principal activities are to provide channel visibility and channel management solutions in the form of software and services to global corporations. The services of the group are provided to global 2000 companies that sell locally through dealers, distributors, resellers or branches, also known as channel partners. The software and services of the group enable large, multi-national companies to utilize the power of the Internet to sell and service end customers in collaboration with their channel partners. The group also offers professional services that include strategic consulting, systems integration and training, managed services including hosting and managing software applications for the client and system management services that include telephone support, a channel partner help desk and support for third-party applications, as needed. The group operates only in the United States of America.

Primary SIC and add'l.: 7375

CIK No: 0000879684

Officers: Mark Geene/Dir., CEO, David Banks/Contact, Harry Philbrick/VP - Operations, Vineet Joshi/VP - Engineering, Brandon Brancato/Dir. - Finance - Administration, David Honan/Dir. - Product Management, Matt Stone/Dir. - Location Insight Operations, Irwin Rosenblum/Dir. - Data, Reporting, Ken Hynes/Dir. - Business Development, John Hulina/Sales Dir.

Directors: Mark Geene/Dir., CEO, Jeffrey Peotter/Chmn., Allan R. Spies/Dir., Ram Velidi/Dir., Tim Conner/Dir.

Financial Data: *Fiscal Year End:*12/31 *Latest Annual Data:* 12/31/2004

Year	Sales	Net Income
2004	$10,879,000	-$686,000
2003	$12,409,000	$499,000
2002	$12,779,000	$1,000

Curr. Assets:	$5,668,000	*Curr. Liab.:*	$2,299,000		
Plant, Equip.:	$457,000	*Total Liab.:*	$2,470,000	*Indic. Yr. Divd.:*	NA
Total Assets:	$6,148,000	*Net Worth:*	$3,678,000	*Debt/ Equity:*	NA

Inform Worldwide Holdings Inc

2501 N Green Valley Pkwy, Ste. 110, Henderson, NV, 89014; *PH:* 1-800-963-6533; *Fax:* 1-702-317-2301; *http://* www.informworldwideholdings.com; *Email:* info@informworldwide.com

General - Incorporation	FL	**Stock**- Price on:12/24/2007	$2.08
Employees	NA	Stock Exchange	OTC
Auditor	Stark Winter Schenkein & Co., LLP	Ticker Symbol	IWWI
Stk Agt	OTC Corporate Transfer Service Co	Outstanding Shares	42,240,000
Counsel	NA	E.P.S.	$0.00
DUNS No.	NA	Shareholders	NA

Business: The group's principle activity is to locate and consummate a business combination or transaction with another entity, which is into a business that, generates revenues, in exchange for its securities. The group currently has no operations and is looking for a prospective merger or acquisition. The group's principle activity was to provide e-commerce service to that of a focused syndicator of l-commerce. L-commerce consists of location - aware Internet applications that deliver location and geographic information for commercial use.

Primary SIC and add'l.: 9999

CIK No: 0001076038

Subsidiaries: Inform Worldwide, Inc

Officers: Ashvin Mascarenhas/39/Chmn., CEO, CFO, Pres., Sec.

Directors: Ashvin Mascarenhas/39/Chmn., CEO, CFO, Pres., Sec.

Owners: Loyola Holdings, Inc, Ashvin Mascarenhas, Insiders

Financial Data: *Fiscal Year End:*06/30 *Latest Annual Data:* 6/30/2006

Year	Sales	Net Income
2006	NA	-$94,000
2005	NA	-$1,718,000
2004	NA	-$177,000

Curr. Assets:	$3,000	*Curr. Liab.:*	$797,000		
Plant, Equip.:	NA	*Total Liab.:*	$797,000	*Indic. Yr. Divd.:*	NA
Total Assets:	$3,000	*Net Worth:*	-$794,000	*Debt/ Equity:*	NA

Informatica Corp

100 Cardinal Way, Redwood City, CA, 94063; *PH:* 1-650-385-5000; *Fax:* 1-650-385-5500; *http://* www.informatica.com; *Email:* ir@informatica.com

General - Incorporation	DE	**Stock**- Price on:12/24/2007	$14.9
Employees	1,221	Stock Exchange	NDQ
Auditor	Ernst & Young LLP	Ticker Symbol	INFA
Stk Agt	American Stock Transfer & Trust Co.	Outstanding Shares	87,320,000
Counsel	Wilson Sonsini Goodrich & Rosati	E.P.S.	$0.51
DUNS No.	NA	Shareholders	NA

Business: The group's principal activities are to provide data integration and business intelligence software. The group provides customers with data integration products, which simplify the process of integrating and analyzing data from multiple systems and complementary analytic application products. Some of the customers of the group include accenture, bea systems, deloitte consulting, hewlett-packard, i2 technologies, IBM, kpmg consulting, mitsubishi electric, peoplesoft, pwc consulting, siebel systems and sybase. The group operates in the United States, Belgium, Canada, France, Germany, the Netherlands, Switzerland and the United Kingdom. On 29-Sep-2003, the group acquired striva corporation.

Primary SIC and add'l.: 7379 7372

CIK No: 0001080099

Subsidiaries: Branch, Informatica Australia PTY Limited, Informatica Belgie N.V., Informatica Business Solutions Private Ltd., Informatica Cayman Ltd., Informatica France S.A.S., Informatica GmbH, Informatica International do Brasil Ltda., Informatica International, Inc Beijing, Informatica International, Inc Informatica, Informatica International, Inc., Informatica International, Inc. Singapore, Informatica Japan KK, Informatica Nederland B.V., Informatica Software (Switzerland) AG 22 Subsidiaries included in the Index

Officers: Sohaib Abbasi/Chmn., CEO, Pres./$3,810,467.00, Paul J. Hoffman/Exec. VP - Worldwide Field Operations/$1,174,303.00, Girish Pancha/Exec. VP - Products/$866,108.00, James Markarian/CTO, Sr. VP, Earl E. Fry/CFO, Exec. VP, Sec./$1,034,960.00, Brian C. Gentile/Exec. VP, Chief Marketing Officer/$756,569.00

Directors: Sohaib Abbasi/Chmn., CEO, Pres., David W. Pidwell/60/Dir., Geoffrey Squire/Dir., Carl J. Yankowski/Dir., Mark A. Bertelsen/Dir., Charles Robel/Dir., Brooke A. Seawell/Dir., Janice D. Chaffin/Dir.

Owners: Insiders/5.90%, Charles J. Robel, Paul Hoffman, Mark A. Bertelsen, Brooke A. Seawell, Brian Gentile, Sohaib Abbasi/2.40%, Carl J. Yankowski, Janice D. Chaffin, Geoffrey W. Squire, David W. Pidwell, Girish Pancha, Earl E. Fry/1.40%, FMR Corp./15.00%

Financial Data: Fiscal Year End:12/31 Latest Annual Data: 12/31/2006

Year	Sales	Net Income
2006	$324,598,000	$36,206,000
2005	$267,431,000	$33,804,000
2004	$219,681,000	-$104,404,000

Curr. Assets:	$476,471,000	**Curr. Liab.:**	$166,522,000
Plant, Equip.:	$14,368,000	**Total Liab.:**	$469,602,000	**Indic. Yr. Divd.:** NA
Total Assets:	$696,765,000	**Net Worth:**	$227,163,000	**Debt/ Equity:** 0.9436

Information Analysis Inc

11240 Waples Mill Rd., Ste. 201, Fairfax, VA, 22030; *PH:* 1-703-383-3000; *Fax:* 1-703-293-7979; *http://* www.infoa.com; *Email:* srosenberg@infoa.com

General - Incorporation	VA	Stock- Price on:12/24/2007	$0.43
Employees	30	Stock Exchange	OTC
Auditor	Reznick Group P.C	Ticker Symbol	IAIC
Stk Agt	American Stock Transfer & Trust Co.	Outstanding Shares	11,200,000
Counsel	Mintz, Levin, Glovsky & Popeo PC	E.P.S.	$0.05
DUNS No.	01-670-0718	Shareholders	NA

Business: The group's principal activities are to develop and market computer application software systems, programming services and related software products and automation systems. The group has developed a series of workbench tools called icons to enhance a programmer's ability to convert code to new platforms and/or computer languages. Icons will facilitate the companies that seek to migrate from mainframe legacy systems to modern environments. The group performed software development and conversion projects for over 100 commercial and government clients including computer sciences corporation, IBM, computer associates, mci, sprint, citibank, U.S. Customsservice, U.S. Department of agriculture, U.S. Department of energy, U.S. Army, U.S. Air force, veterans administration and the federal deposit insurance corporation.

Primary SIC and add'l.: 7372 7371

CIK No: 0000803578

Subsidiaries: International Software Service Corporation

Officers: Sandor Rosenberg/Chmn., CEO, Pres./$140,000.00, Richard Derose/CFO, Sec., Treasurer/$166,520.00, Albert Weisner/Sr. VP, Stanley A. Reese/COO/$144,063.00, Charles Bunce/Sr. VP

Directors: Sandor Rosenberg/Chmn., CEO, Pres., James Wester/Dir., Bonnie Wachtel/Dir., Charles A. May/Dir.

Owners: James D. Wester/1.50%, Stanley A. Reese/1.90%, Bonnie K. Wachtel/1.20%, Traditions LP/8.90%, Sandor Rosenberg/16.40%, Richard S. DeRose/4.00%, Insiders/24.50%, Charles A. May

Financial Data: Fiscal Year End:12/31 Latest Annual Data: 12/31/2006

Year	Sales	Net Income
2006	$9,459,000	$502,000
2005	$10,772,000	$732,000
2004	$9,309,000	$572,000

Curr. Assets:	$3,074,000	**Curr. Liab.:**	$1,475,000
Plant, Equip.:	$67,000	**Total Liab.:**	$1,475,000	**Indic. Yr. Divd.:** NA
Total Assets:	$3,150,000	**Net Worth:**	$1,675,000	**Debt/ Equity:** NA

Information Architects Corp

6500 NW 15th Ave., Ste 300, Ft Lauderdale, FL, 33309; *PH:* 1-954-545-8184; *Fax:* 1-866-550-5254; *http://* www.ia.com

General - Incorporation	NC	Stock - Price on:12/24/2007	NA
Employees	6	Stock Exchange	OTC
Auditor	Jaspers & Hall, P.C	Ticker Symbol	IACH
Stk Agt	Mr. Overhulser	Outstanding Shares	NA
Counsel	NA	E.P.S.	-$0.048
DUNS No.	62-664-4942	Shareholders	NA

Business: The group's principal activity is to develop dynamic content delivery and interchange infrastructure software solutions for corporations and individuals. The aggregation and syndication solutions enable the development and management of global content and functionality syndication from one source to any Web site or Internet accessible device. In may 2003, the group acquired accurate research solutions. In mar 2004 acquired international monetary exchange systems corporation.

Primary SIC and add'l.: 7372

CIK No: 0001018336

Subsidiaries: Accurate Research Solutions, Inc., Daystar Telecom, Inc., Icabs.com, Inc., Information Processing Corporation, International Monetary Exchange Systems Corporation

Officers: Jon Grinter/58/Dir., Pres.

Directors: Jon Grinter/58/Dir., Pres., Alfred Tracy/43/Dir.

Owners: Alfred Tracy, Insiders, Jon Grinter

Financial Data: Fiscal Year End:12/31 Latest Annual Data: 12/31/2006

Year	Sales	Net Income
2006	$503,000	-$620,000
2005	$503,000	-$620,000
2004	$561,000	-$3,193,000

Curr. Assets:	$29,000	**Curr. Liab.:**	$5,401,000
Plant, Equip.:	$1,272,000	**Total Liab.:**	$5,401,000	**Indic. Yr. Divd.:** NA
Total Assets:	$1,827,000	**Net Worth:**	-$3,574,000	**Debt/ Equity:** NA

InforMedix Holdings Inc

5880 Hubbard Dr., Rockville, MD, 20852; *PH:* 1-301-984-1566; *http://* www.informedix.com; *Email:* ServiceInfo@Informedix.com

General - Incorporation	NV	Stock- Price on:12/24/2007	$0.1
Employees	7	Stock Exchange	OTC
Auditor	Bagell, Levine & Company, LLC	Ticker Symbol	IFMX
Stk Agt	InforMedix Holdings, Inc	Outstanding Shares	92,050,000
Counsel	NA	E.P.S.	-$0.063
DUNS No.	NA	Shareholders	NA

Business: The groups principle activity is to develop portable patient monitoring device, hardware, software and networked communications system. Customers of the group include pharmaceutical firms, medical researchers and physicians. The group operates from the United States. The group's quarterly revenue for Sep '07 was 0.06 millions of USD.

Primary SIC and add'l.: 3841

CIK No: 0001123458

Subsidiaries: InforMedix, Inc.

Officers: Bruce A. Kehr/Chmn., CEO, Randy Dulin/VP - Business Developent, Operations, Harry Stokes/CFO, Michael Gavin/VP - Research, Development, Remie J. Smith/Dir. - Software Development, Davison R. Dulin/50/Sr. VP - Operations, Direct Sales, Richard Voss/Sr. VP - Business Development, Marketing, Channel Sales

Directors: Bruce A. Kehr/Chmn., CEO, Harris Kaplan/Dir., Phillip Gross/Dir., Rhonda B. Friedman/Dir., Bruce S. Morra/52/Dir., David B. Nash/Dir.

Owners: Bruce A. Kehr/7.00%, Michael P. Gavin, Rhonda B. Friedman, Phillip Gross, Harry M. Stokes, Davison R. Dulin/0.95%, Insiders/11.70%, David Nash, Bruce S. Morra/1.30%, Harris Kaplan

Financial Data: Fiscal Year End:12/31 Latest Annual Data: 12/31/2006

Year	Sales	Net Income
2006	$103,000	-$3,325,000
2005	$22,000	-$1,986,000
2004	$29,000	-$2,274,000

Curr. Assets:	$814,000	**Curr. Liab.:**	$2,684,000
Plant, Equip.:	$89,000	**Total Liab.:**	$2,684,000	**Indic. Yr. Divd.:** NA
Total Assets:	$903,000	**Net Worth:**	-$1,781,000	**Debt/ Equity:** NA

Inforte Corp

500 N Dearborn St., Ste. 1200, Chicago, IL, 60610; *PH:* 1-312-540-0900; *http://* www.inforte.com

General - Incorporation	DE	Stock- Price on:12/24/2007	$4.17
Employees	253	Stock Exchange	NDQ
Auditor	Grant Thornton LLP	Ticker Symbol	INFT
Stk Agt	American Stock Transfer & Trust Co.	Outstanding Shares	11,600,000
Counsel	Foley & Lardner LLP	E.P.S.	-$0.37
DUNS No.	NA	Shareholders	NA

Business: The group's principal activity is to help clients increase profitability by maximizing the effectiveness of their customer-facing initiatives. Its consultants deliver strategy, process and technology solutions that enhance visibility across our clients' enterprise, making their customer interactions more strategic and lucrative. The group also provides solution expertise to the clients for technology enablement and systems integration. The major clients of the group are: blue cross & blue shield of Illinois, bmc software, bnp paribas, California state automobile association, cuna mutual, dow corning, experian, the hartford, home depot, john h. Harland, lexis-nexis, moore, option one mortgage, prudential, pss world medical, royal automobile club, sabre, sprint, toshiba and wrigley. The group operates in North America and Europe.

Primary SIC and add'l.: 7373 7372 7371

CIK No: 0001099944

Subsidiaries: Inforte Deutschland GmbH, Inforte India Holding Company, Inforte India Private Limited, Inforte Managed Analytics Corp., Inforte SBW Corp.

Officers: Ali Guelerman/Business Development Germany, Allanah Shannon/Recruiting, UK, Greg Mummert/Recruiting, US, Iordan P. Iordanov/Controller, Nicole Kalonda/Recruiting, Germany, Kelly Richards/Marketing, Analyst Relations, Public Relations, Simon Prowse/Contact - Offshore Delivery, Nigel Williams/Business Development United Kingdom

Owners: Stephen Mack/9.40%, Royce & Associates, LLC/9.22%, William Nurthen, Harvey H. Bundy, Thomas E. Hogan, Ray C. Kurzweil, Columbia Management Group, LLC/6.75%, Dimensional Finds Advisors LP/8.61%, Insiders/31.20%, Philip S. Bligh/20.00%, Daniel J. Taylor, Nick Heyes/1.50%

Financial Data: Fiscal Year End:12/31 Latest Annual Data: 12/31/2006

Year	Sales	Net Income
2006	$43,325,000	-$3,560,000
2005	$41,648,000	$537,000
2004	$50,050,000	-$565,000

Curr. Assets:	$38,594,000	**Curr. Liab.:**	$6,378,000
Plant, Equip.:	$1,383,000	**Total Liab.:**	$7,378,000	**Indic. Yr. Divd.:** NA
Total Assets:	$57,050,000	**Net Worth:**	$49,672,000	**Debt/ Equity:** NA

Infosearch Media Inc

4086 Del Rey Ave., Marina Del Rey, CA, 90292; *PH:* 1-310-437-7380; *Fax:* 1-310-919-3072; *http://* www.infosearchmedia.com; *Email:* info@infosearchmedia.com

General - Incorporation	DE	Stock- Price on:12/24/2007	$0.155
Employees	51	Stock Exchange	OTC
Auditor	Singer Lewak Greenbaum & Goldstein	Ticker Symbol	ISHM
Stk Agt	Continental Stock Transfer & Trust Co	Outstanding Shares	52,500,000
Counsel	NA	E.P.S.	-$0.09
DUNS No.	NA	Shareholders	NA

Business: The groups principle activity is to provide search-targeted text and video content for the Internet, designed for publishing and media clients. The group provides text and video content-based Internet marketing solutions. The group operates from United States.

Primary SIC and add'l.: NA

CIK No: 0001164327

Subsidiaries: Trafficlogic Acquisition Corp

Officers: George S. Lichter/Dir., CEO, Frank Knuettel/41/VP, Edan Portaro/40/VP - Sales, David Gagne/34/VP - Technology, Scott Brogi/CFO, Bob Myers/VP - Production, Heather Gore/VP - Product Development, Marketing, David Warthen/CTO, VP, Brinlea Johnson/Investor Contact

Directors: George S. Lichter/Dir., CEO, Claudio A. Pinkus/Dir., Steve Lazuka/34/Founder, John Lavalle/Dir.

Owners: Claudio Pinkus/2.45%, John LaValle, Frank Knuettel, George Lichter/5.21%, Trinad Capital Master Fund, Ltd./14.77%, Edan Portaro, Bruce Galloway/7.66%, Insiders/11.63%, David Warthen/1.76%, Steve Lazuka/8.15%, David Gagne

Financial Data: ***Fiscal Year End:***12/31 ***Latest Annual Data:*** 12/31/2006

Year	Sales		Net Income		
2006	$7,600,000		-$4,040,000		
2005	$9,364,000		$315,000		
2004	$2,800,000		-$4,323,000		
Curr. Assets: $3,197,000	**Curr. Liab.:**	$1,447,000			
Plant, Equip.: $131,000	**Total Liab.:**	$2,843,000	**Indic. Yr. Divd.:**	NA	
Total Assets: $3,680,000	**Net Worth:**	$837,000	**Debt/ Equity:**	NA	

Infosmart Group Inc

Formerly: Cyber Merchants Exchange Inc

600 S Lake Ave, Ste. 405, Pasadena, CA, 91106; ***PH:*** 1-626-793-5000; ***http://*** www.c-me.com

General		**Stock**	
Incorporation	CA	Price on:12/24/2007	$0.3
Employees	NA	Stock Exchange	NA
Auditor	PKF	Ticker Symbol	NA
Stk Agt	U.S. Stock Transfer Corp	Outstanding Shares	NA
Counsel	NA	E.P.S	NA
DUNS No.	NA	Shareholders	NA

Business: The group's principle activity is to provide services related to electronic trading, financing, logistics and trade show organizer targeted at the apparel industry. The company provides its services through four interrelated services: Internet sourcing network, virtual trade show, Web design and hosting and logistics services. The Internet sourcing network is a customized private extranets built and maintained by the company. These networks automate the front-end merchandise sourcing activities and enable retailers and vendors to conduct business privately, using any Internet connection without investing in expensive hardware, software or training. The company also arranges asap show, which is a global apparel and textile sourcing show that brings leading manufacturers from around the world to one venue to meet, greet and sell to buyers. The group operates from United States.

Primary SIC and add'l.: 7389

CIK No: 0001066961

Officers: Frank Yuan/Chmn., CEO, Founder, Howard Moore/Board Adviser, Dir., Jerome Yuan/Contact - Headquarters, Haseeb Alaml/Contact - Bangladesh, Brown Qiu/Contact - Shanghai, Andrew Chung/Contact - Hong Kong, Su Kon Kim/Contact - Korea, Maureen Storch/Dir. - Global, Operations, Deepak Thadhani/Contact - India, Muhammad Ayyob/Contact - Pakistan, Tina Lee/Contact - Philippines, Kevin Chang/Contact - Taiwan, Po Nei Sze/35/Dir., CFO, Treasurer, Sec., Laurie Boon/Dir. - Global Marketing, Donald C. McNabb/Dir., Sr. Board Adviser

Directors: Frank Yuan/Chmn., CEO, Founder, Howard Moore/Board Adviser, Dir., Deborah Shamaley/Dir., Mary McNabb/Dir., Member - Board Adviser, Donald C. McNabb/Dir., Sr. Board Adviser, Philip Hawley/Dir., Po Nei Sze/35/Dir., CFO, Treasurer, Sec., Chung Kwok/41/Dir., Simon Lee/39/Dir., Wai Chuen Leung/43/Dir., Joseph Chang/41/Dir., Chi-man Lam/43/Dir., James L. Vandeberg/Dir., Charles Rice/Dir.

Owners: Po Nei Sze, CIM Dividend Income Investment Fund Limited/10.40%, Andrew Chung Yuen Chang, Sovgem Limited/5.80%, CIM Dividend Income Fund Ltd, Dynamic Decisions Strategic Opportunities/13.40%, Insiders, Prime Corporate Developments Ltd., Chung Kwok, Sau Wan Lui, Platinum Global Dividend Fund Limited/19.40%, CIM Dividend Income Fund Ltd/23.00%

Financial Data: ***Fiscal Year End:***05/31 ***Latest Annual Data:*** 5/31/2006

Year	Sales		Net Income		
2006	NA		-$89,000		
2005	$2,040,000		-$478,000		
Curr. Assets: $64,000	**Curr. Liab.:**	$53,000			
Plant, Equip.: NA	**Total Liab.:**	$53,000	**Indic. Yr. Divd.:**	NA	
Total Assets: $64,000	**Net Worth:**	$11,000	**Debt/ Equity:**	0.2837	

InfoSonics Corp

4350 Executive Dr., Ste. 100, San Diego, CA, 92121; ***PH:*** 1-858-373-1600; ***Fax:*** 1-858-373-1505; ***http://*** www.infosonics.com; ***Email:*** info@infosonics.com

General		**Stock**	
Incorporation	MD	Price on:12/24/2007	$3.29
Employees	52	Stock Exchange	NDQ
Auditor	Singer Lewak Greenbaum & Goldstein	Ticker Symbol	IFON
Stk Agt	Computershare Investor Services LLC	Outstanding Shares	14,500,000
Counsel	NA	E.P.S	$0.05
DUNS No.	NA	Shareholders	NA

Business: The group's principal activity is to distribute wireless handsets and accessories. The group also sells cellular phone subscriptions, cellular phones and accessories. The group operates through two operating segments namely: wireless telecommunication and cellular phone subscriptions. Wireless telecommunications segment distributes wireless handsets and accessories to agents, resellers, distributors, independent dealers and retailers. Cellular phone subscriptions segment sells handsets, accessories and at&t wireless activation directly to end-users. The group operates in the United States of America, Latin America, Asia-pacific and Europe.

Primary SIC and add'l.: 5065 7389

CIK No: 0001274032

Subsidiaries: Axcess Mobile, LLC(CA Limited Liability corporation), InfoSonics de Guatemala S.A. (Guatemala corporation), InfoSonics de Mexico S.A. de C.V. (Mexico corporation), InfoSonics El Salvador S.A. de C.V. (El Salvador corporation), InfoSonics Latin America,Inc. (CA corporation), InfoSonics S.A. (Uruguay corporation)

Officers: Joseph Ram/Founder, CEO, Pres., Jeff Klausner/CFO, John Althoff/Pres. - Latin America Division, Abraham Rosler/Dir., Exec. VP, Joe Murgo/VP - Sales, Marketing, Josh Haims/VP - Finance, Operations, Joseph C. Murgo/VP - Sales, Marketing North America, Christian Camacho/Commercial Dir., Charlie Messman/Investor Relations Officer, Todd Kehrli/Investor Relations Officer, Bonnie McBride/Investor Relations Officer

Directors: Joseph Ram/Founder, CEO, Pres., Kirk A. Waldron/Dir., Randall P. Marx/56/Dir., Abraham Rosler/Dir., Exec. VP, Robert S. Picow/Dir.

Owners: Jeffrey A. Klausner/3.70%, JRC, Inc./11.50%, Randall P. Marx, John Althoff, Robert S. Picow, Joseph C. Murgo, Kirk A. Waldron, Joseph Ram/31.65%, Insiders/40.35%, Abraham G. Rosler/7.46%

Financial Data: ***Fiscal Year End:***12/31 ***Latest Annual Data:*** 12/31/2006

Year	Sales		Net Income		
2006	$240,896,000		$2,539,000		
2005	$145,791,000		$2,707,000		
2004	$73,406,000		$38,000		
Curr. Assets: $81,714,000	**Curr. Liab.:**	$45,028,000	**P/E Ratio:**	65.80	
Plant, Equip.: $615,000	**Total Liab.:**	$45,064,000	**Indic. Yr. Divd.:**	NA	
Total Assets: $82,970,000	**Net Worth:**	$37,907,000	**Debt/ Equity:**	NA	

InfoSpace Inc

601 108th Ave. NE, Ste. 1200, Bellevue, WA, 98004; ***PH:*** 1-425-201-6100; ***Fax:*** 1-425-201-6150; ***http://*** www.infospaceinc.com

General		**Stock**	
Incorporation	DE	Price on:12/24/2007	$22.6
Employees	530	Stock Exchange	NDQ
Auditor	Deloitte & Touche LLP	Ticker Symbol	INSP
Stk Agt	Mellon Investor Services LLC	Outstanding Shares	32,990,000
Counsel	Wilson Sonsini Goodrich & Rosati	E.P.S	-$0.41
DUNS No.	NA	Shareholders	NA

Business: The group's principal activity is to provide Internet and wireless solutions for customers. The group operates in three segments: search and directory, payment solutions and mobile. Search and directory provides Web search and online directory products that help users find the information they need while creating opportunities for merchants. Payment solutions enable merchants to authorize, settle and manage electronic transactions via its ip-based payment gateway, authorize.net. Mobile develops infrastructure, tools and applications that enable carriers and content providers to efficiently develop and deliver mobile data services across multiple devices. The customers of the group range from consumers to merchants to mobile operators, content providers and financial institutions. On 01-Dec-2003, the group acquired moviso llc. At the end of 2003, the group sold all of its non-core services. On 03-Jun-2004, it also acquired switchboard incorporated.

Primary SIC and add'l.: 7319 7375

CIK No: 0001068875

Subsidiaries: elkware GmbH, GSM Information Network B.V. (GIN), InfoSpace Europe Limited, InfoSpace Mobile, Inc., InfoSpace Sales LLC, IOMO Limited, Moviso LLC, a Delaware limited liability company

Officers: Jim Voelkar/Chmn., CEO, Pres., Allen Hsieh/CFO, Brian McManus/Exec. VP - Online, Steve Elfman/Exec. VP - Mobile Division, Stacy Ybarra/Investor Relations Officer, Bruce Easter/Sr. VP, General Counsel, Sec.

Directors: Jim Voelkar/Chmn., CEO, Pres., John E. Cunningham/50/Dir., Richard D. Hearney/Dir., Lewis M. Taffer/60/Dir., George M. Tronsrue/51/Dir., Vanessa A. Wittman/40/Dir., Jules Haimovitz/57/Dir.

Owners: Goldman Sachs Asset Management, L.P./6.20%, Dimensional Fund Advisors LP/7.10%, The Baupost Group, L.L.C./5.50%, Renaissance Technologies Corp./6.10%, George M. Tronsrue, Jules Haimovitz, Stephen J. Davis, Vanessa A. Wittman, Insiders/7.00%, The Sandell Group/8.80%, Lewis M. Taffer, Deutsche Bank AG/5.60%, Brian T. McManus, Edmund O. Belsheim/1.50%, James F. Voelker/5.20% *(19 Owners included in Index)*

Financial Data: ***Fiscal Year End:***12/31 ***Latest Annual Data:*** 12/31/2006

Year	Sales		Net Income		
2006	NA		NA		
2005	NA		NA		
2004	NA		NA		
Curr. Assets: $498,846,000	**Curr. Liab.:**	$80,895,000			
Plant, Equip.: $33,212,000	**Total Liab.:**	$87,274,000	**Indic. Yr. Divd.:**	NA	
Total Assets: $765,839,000	**Net Worth:**	$678,565,000	**Debt/ Equity:**	NA	

Infosys Technologies Ltd

6607 Kaiser Dr., Fremont, CA, 94555; ***PH:*** 1-510-742-3000; ***Fax:*** 1-510-742-3090; ***http://*** www.infosys.com

General		**Stock**	
Incorporation	India	Price on:12/24/2007	$51.9
Employees	72,200	Stock Exchange	NDQ
Auditor	KPMG LLP	Ticker Symbol	INFY
Stk Agt	Karvy Computershare Private Ltd	Outstanding Shares	571,210,000
Counsel	NA	E.P.S	$1.77
DUNS No.	NA	Shareholders	NA

Business: The group's principal activity is to provide information technology services. The group's services include consulting, software development, software re-engineering, systems integration, package evaluation and implementation, software maintenance and business process management. The group provides solutions across software and process life cycles using its global delivery model. The group also provides proprietary software products for the banking industry. The group operates in five segments namely financial services, manufacturing, telecom, retail and others. The group serves customers providing banking, finance, insurance services, manufacturing and telecommunication companies, retail industries, utilities, energy, transport and logistics companies. The group operates in North America, Europe, India and other countries.

Primary SIC and add'l.: 7375 7371 7372 6726

CIK No: 0001067491

Subsidiaries: Infosys China, Infosys Consulting, Infosys Consulting Inc., National Securities Clearing Corporation Limited, Progeon Limited

Officers: S. Gopalakrishnan/MD, CEO, Narayana N.R. Murthy/Chmn., Chief Mentor, V. Balakrishnan/CFO, Shekar Narayanan/Sr. Mgr. - Investor Relations, Sandeep Mahindroo/Sr. Mgr. - Investor Relations, Mohandas T.V. Pai/Dir., Dir. - Human Resources, Srinath Batni/Dir., Group Co - Head - World - Wide Customer Delivery, K. Dinesh/53/Co - Founder, Dir. - Head - Information Systems, Quality, Productivity, Communication Design Group, Parvatheesam Kanchinadham/Company Sec., Compliance Officer, S. D. Shibulal/Dir., COO, T.V. Mohandas Pai/49/Dir., Head - Administration, Human Resources, Education, Research

Directors: Narayana N.R. Murthy/Chief Mentor, Nandan M. Nilekani/Co - Chmn., Marti G. Subrahmanyam/Dir., David L. Boyles/Dir., Deepak M. Satwalekar/Dir., Jeffrey Sean Lehman/Dir., S. D. Shibulal/Dir., COO, Philip Yeo/Dir., Claude Smadja/Dir., Rama Bijapurkar/Dir., K. Dinesh/53/Co - Founder, Dir. - Head - Information Systems, Quality, Productivity, Communication Design Group, Mohandas T.V. Pai/Dir., Dir. - Human Resources, Omkar Goswami/Dir., Sridar Iyengar/Dir., Srinath Batni/Dir., Group Co - Head - World - Wide Customer Delivery

Owners: Narayana N.R. Murthy/5.00%, Mohandas T.V. Pai, V. Balakrishnan, Jeffrey Lehman, David Boyles, Deepak Satwalekar, Marti G. Subrahmanyam, Omkar Goswami, S. D. Shibulal/2.21%, Claude Smadja, Srinath Batni, S. Gopalakrishnan/3.35%, Sridar A. Iyengar, Nandan M. Nilekani/3.46%, Rama Bijapurkar *(16 Owners included in Index)*

Financial Data: *Fiscal Year End:*03/31 *Latest Annual Data:* 3/31/2007

Year	Sales	Net Income
2007	$3,090,000,000	$850,000,000
2006	$2,152,000,000	$555,000,000
2005	$1,592,000,000	$419,000,000

Curr. Assets:	$2,098,000,000	**Curr. Liab.:**	$355,000,000		
Plant, Equip.:	$738,000,000	**Total Liab.:**	$356,000,000	**Indic. Yr. Divd.:**	$0.510
Total Assets:	$3,073,000,000	**Net Worth:**	$2,717,000,000	**Debt/ Equity:**	NA

InfoTech USA Inc

4105 Ohare Dr. , Hoffman Estates, IL, 60195; ***PH:*** 1-847-942-7274; ***Fax:*** 1-847-510-0770; ***http://*** www.infotechusa.com; ***Email:*** info@infotechusainc.com

General - Incorporation	DE	**Stock** - Price on:12/24/2007	$0.21
Employees	25	Stock Exchange	OTC
Auditor	J. H. Cohn LLP	Ticker Symbol	IFTH
Stk Agt	American Stock Transfer & Trust Co.	Outstanding Shares	5,050,000
Counsel	NA	E.P.S	-$0.36
DUNS No.	18-351-0189	Shareholders	NA

Business: The group's principal activity is to provide professional services in the area of systems integration, information technology (IT) procurement and logistics and technology strategy. It also provides integrated ebusiness strategy and technology implementation services on a national and regional basis. The services include technology strategy and due diligence consulting, systems architecture and design, application and technology infrastructure deployment, enterprise security, it product procurement and logistics and provisioning. The group's services are designed to improve a client's competitive and financial position and increase efficiency.

Primary SIC and add'l.: 5045 7379 7373

CIK No: 0001037417

Subsidiaries: Information Technology Services, Inc., InfoTech USA, Inc

Officers: Jonathan F. McKeage/CEO, Pres., Robert J. Patterson/CFO, Joseph Sampson/Dir. - Sales, Guy Miller/Mgr. - Professional Services

Owners: Charles L. Doherty/8.30%, Robert J. Patterson/4.70%, Scott R. Silverman/9.10%, Insiders/23.50%, Jonathan F. McKeage/1.40%, Jeffrey S. Cobb/4.50%

Financial Data: *Fiscal Year End:*09/30 *Latest Annual Data:* 9/30/2006

Year	Sales	Net Income
2006	$16,010,000	-$2,142,000
2005	$16,466,000	-$768,000
2004	$16,684,000	-$2,681,000

Curr. Assets:	$4,038,000	**Curr. Liab.:**	$2,032,000		
Plant, Equip.:	$113,000	**Total Liab.:**	$2,032,000	**Indic. Yr. Divd.:**	NA
Total Assets:	$4,187,000	**Net Worth:**	$2,155,000	**Debt/ Equity:**	NA

infoUSA Inc

5711 S 86th Cir., Omaha, NE, 68127; ***PH:*** 1-402-593-4500; ***Fax:*** 1-402-331-1505; ***http://*** www.infousa.com; ***Email:*** help@infousa.com

General - Incorporation	DE	**Stock** - Price on:12/24/2007	$10.24
Employees	4,089	Stock Exchange	NDQ
Auditor	KPMG LLP	Ticker Symbol	IUSA
Stk Agt	Wells Fargo Bank Minnesota N.A	Outstanding Shares	55,570,000
Counsel	Robins, Kaplan, Miller & Ciresi LLP	E.P.S	$0.63
DUNS No.	06-865-1702	Shareholders	NA

Business: The group's principal activities are to provide business and consumer marketing information products and data processing services in the United States and Canada. The group operates in two business segments: infousa group and donnelley group. The main products of the group include business directories, consumer lists, customized business lists and other information services like on-line and Internet access and CD-ROM directories. The group provides both business and consumer information, offering databases of 200 million individuals, 110 million households in the United States and 14 million businesses in the United States and Canada. In 2003, the group acquired yesmail inc and ltwc corporation. On 09-Jun-2004 onesource information services inc, on 04-Jun-2004 edith roman associates inc, database direct inc and e-post direct inc and 02-Feb-2004, it acquired triplex direct marketing corp.

Primary SIC and add'l.: 7375 7374

CIK No: 0000879437

Subsidiaries: BJ Hunter Information, Inc., City Directories, Inc., Donnelley Marketing, Inc., Edith Roman Holdings, Inc., Hill-Donnelly Corporation, infoUSA Marketing, Inc., infoUSA.com Inc., Millard Group, Inc., OneSource Information Services, Inc., OneSource Information Services, Ltd., Storefront Images USA, Inc., Strategic Information Management, Inc., TGMVC Corporation, Walter Karl, Inc., Yesmail, Inc.

Officers: Vinod Gupta/Founder, Chmn., CEO/$1,936,685.00, D. J. Thayer/Exec. VP - Infousa Group, Rakesh Gupta/Pres. - Enterprise Sales Group, Stormy Dean/CFO/$470,369.00, Fred Vakili/Exec. VP - Administration, Chief Administrative Officer/$825,747.00, Edward C. Mallin/Pres. - Services Group/$1,023,223.00, Gerard Miodus/Pres. - Opinion Research, Greg Mahnke/Pres. - Macro International, John Longwell/General Counsel, Sec.

Directors: Vinod Gupta/Founder, Chmn., CEO, Vasant Raval/Dir., Bill L. Fairfield/Dir., Bernard W. Reznicek/Dir., Dennis P. Walker/Dir., George F. Haddix/Dir., Elliot S. Kaplan/Dir., Anshoo Gupta/Dir.

Owners: Vinod Gupta/40.40%, Cardinal Capital Management, LLC/5.50%, Edward C. Mallin, Bill L. Fairfield, Stormy Dean, Fred Vakili, Bernard W. Reznicek, Monica Messer/1.00%, Vasant H. Raval, Elliot S. Kaplan, George F. Haddix, Insiders/43.10%, Dennis P. Walker

Financial Data: *Fiscal Year End:*12/31 *Latest Annual Data:* 12/31/2006

Year	Sales	Net Income
2006	$434,876,000	$33,300,000
2005	$383,158,000	$31,507,000
2004	$344,859,000	$17,838,000

Curr. Assets:	$187,536,000	**Curr. Liab.:**	$222,485,000	**P/E Ratio:**	16.25
Plant, Equip.:	$61,172,000	**Total Liab.:**	$515,417,000	**Indic. Yr. Divd.:**	$0.250
Total Assets:	$749,575,000	**Net Worth:**	$234,158,000	**Debt/ Equity:**	1.2015

InfoVista

6, Rue De La Terre De Feu, Les Ulis, 91952; ***PH:*** 33-164867900; ***Fax:*** 33-164 867979; ***http://*** www.infovista.com; ***Email:*** sales@infovista.com

General - Incorporation	France	**Stock** - Price on:12/24/2007	NA
Employees	215	Stock Exchange	NA
Auditor	Ernst & Young Audit	Ticker Symbol	NA
Stk Agt	Bank of New York	Outstanding Shares	NA
Counsel	Shearman & Sterling LLP	E.P.S	NA
DUNS No.	NA	Shareholders	NA

Business: The group's principle activity is to provide intelligent performance management software for service providers and large enterprises. Products enable the group's customers to deliver new infrastructure-based services, maximize return on capital investment, optimize the operational expenses, support high levels of customer satisfaction and align infrastructure performance with business operations requirements. The group is operating through the parent company and 6 subsidiaries (usa, Singapore, UK, Germany, Belgium and Spain). Licences accounted for 63% of fiscal 2002 revenues and services, 37%

Primary SIC and add'l.: 3559 8742 7372

CIK No: 0001117064

Subsidiaries: InfoVista (Asia-Pacific) Pte Ltd, InfoVista BNL, InfoVista Corporation, InfoVista GmbH, InfoVista SRL, InfoVista UK Ltd

Officers: Alain Tingaud/Chmn., CEO, Roland Rodriguez/Sr. VP - Worldwide Professional Services, Philippe Ozanian/Pres., Dir., CFO Member, Marc Benrey/Sr. VP - Business Operations, Customer Support, Julien Dahan/Sr. VP - EMEA Operations, Jean-Luc Valente/Sr. VP - Americas Operations, Manuel Stopnicki/CTO, Serge Genetet/Sr. VP - Asia, Pacific Operations, Serge Adda/VP - Research, Development, Ronnie Ray/VP - Strategic Projects, Corporate Marketing, Pete Shah/VP - Sales, Americas, David Forlizzi/VP - Finance, Karena D'Arcy/Mgr. - Investor Relations

Directors: Alain Tingaud/Chmn., CEO, Hubert L. Tardieu/Dir., Jean-Paul Bernardini/Dir., Philippe Ozanian/Pres., Dir., CFO Member, Herbert May/Dir., Philippe Vassor/Dir., Patrick Leleu/Dir.

Infowave Software Inc

4664 Lougheed Hwy, Ste 200, Burnaby, BC, V5C 5T5; ***PH:*** 1-604-473-3600; ***http://*** www.infowave.com; ***Email:*** ir@infowave.com

General - Incorporation	BC	**Stock** - Price on:12/24/2007	$0.4798
Employees	NA	Stock Exchange	OTC
Auditor	KPMG LLP	Ticker Symbol	IWFSF
Stk Agt	Computershare Trust Co of Canada	Outstanding Shares	NA
Counsel	Dorsey & Whitney LLP	E.P.S	NA
DUNS No.	NA	Shareholders	NA

Business: The group's principal activities are to develop, market and sell software solutions for the wireless computing business. The group's software leverages wireless communications networks to enable mobile access to the critical corporate data. This product is called wireless business engine, which provides fast, secure and reliable wireless access to Web-based applications, the Internet, corporate intranets, microsoft exchange and lotus domino. It works across the full spectrum of computing devices from laptop computers and pdas to the newest generation of Web-enabled mobile phones. This engine supports multiple devices, networks, platforms and applications. In addition to this, the group has a desktop solution called symmetry, which is installed on any desktop computer that delivers e-mail, calendar, contacts and task information stored in microsoft outlook to any wireless mobile device capable of receiving text messages, including pagers and digital mobile phones.

Primary SIC and add'l.: 7379 7372 7375

CIK No: 0001074564

Subsidiaries: Infowave USA Inc.

Officers: Paul Townsend/VP - Technology, Product Development, Leonard Cox/Sr. VP, CFO

Directors: Lionel G. Dodd/Chmn., Wayne J. Henderson/Dir., Jerry Trooien/Dir., Al Sello/Dir.

Financial Data: *Fiscal Year End:*12/31 *Latest Annual Data:* 12/31/2005

Year	Sales	Net Income
2005	$1,927,000	-$7,805,000
2004	$4,104,000	-$10,046,000

Curr. Assets:	$4,688,000	**Curr. Liab.:**	$1,216,000		
Plant, Equip.:	$166,000	**Total Liab.:**	$1,216,000	**Indic. Yr. Divd.:**	NA
Total Assets:	$9,656,000	**Net Worth:**	$8,440,000	**Debt/ Equity:**	NA

InfraSource Services Inc

100 W Sixth St., Ste. 300, Media, PA, 19063; ***PH:*** 1-610-480-8000; ***http://*** www.infrasourceinc.com

General - Incorporation	DE	**Stock** - Price on:12/24/2007	$36.7
Employees	4,000	Stock Exchange	NA
Auditor	PricewaterhouseCoopers LLP	Ticker Symbol	NA
Stk Agt	LaSalle Bank N.A	Outstanding Shares	40,490,000
Counsel	NA	E.P.S	$0.56
DUNS No.	12-547-6510	Shareholders	NA

Business: The group's principal activity is to provide contractor services to utility transmission and distribution infrastructure in the United States. The services includes the design, engineering, procurement, construction, testing, maintenance and leasing of utility infrastructure. The customers of the group include electric power utilities, natural gas utilities, government entities and heavy industrial companies, such as petrochemical, processing and refining businesses. On 27-Jan-2004, the group acquired maslonka & associates, inc.

Primary SIC and add'l.: 1623

CIK No: 0001276827

Subsidiaries: Blair Park Services,Inc., Chowns,Inc., Dacon GP LLC, Dacon Ltd, Dashiell Holdings Corporation, Dashiell Ltd, EHV Elecom,Inc., EHV Power USA,Inc., Electric Services,Inc., InfraSource Concrete& Paving Services LLC, InfraSource Corporate Services,Inc., InfraSource Incorporated, InfraSource Maslonka CA,Inc., InfraSource Maslonka LLC, InfraSource Mid-Atlantic Inc. 40 Subsidiaries included in the Index

Officers: Paul Daily/Pres., CEO - Infrasource Underground Services, David R. Helwig/Chmn., CEO, Pres., Larry Coleman/Pres. - Telecom Services, Debbie Lofton/Sr. VP, General Counsel, Barry R. Sauder/VP, Chief Accounting Officer, Doug Chidley/Sr. VP - Engineering, Martha Christinziano/VP - Human Resources, Michael Cicchella/VP, Chief Administrative Officer, Terence R. Montgomery/Sr. VP, CFO, Sec., Peter Walier/Exec. VP - Electric Operations, Steve Hicks/Pres. - Infrasource Dashiell, Damir Novosel/Pres. - Infrasource Technology, Steve Reiten/Pres. - MJ Electric, Doug Link/Sr. VP - Business Development, John Conte/Contact *(17 Officers included in Index)*

Directors: David R. Helwig/Chmn., CEO, Pres., David H. Watts/Dir., John A. Brayman/Dir., Richard S. Siudek/Dir., Michal J. Conaway/Dir., Frederick W. Buckman/Dir., Terry Winter/Dir.

Owners: GLG Partners LP/5.00%, David R. Helwig/1.80%, Terence R. Montgomery, Michal J. Conaway, Terry Winter, Paul M. Daily, Richard S. Siudek, Insiders/3.20%, FMR Corp./13.80%, Barry R. Sauder, John A. Brayman, David H. Watts, Lawrence P. Coleman, Tontine Capital Partners, L.P./8.40%

Financial Data: *Fiscal Year End:*12/31 *Latest Annual Data:* 12/31/2006

Year	Sales	Net Income
2006	$992,305,000	$26,145,000
2005	$865,527,000	$13,729,000
2004	$651,023,000	$9,576,000

Curr. Assets:	$272,775,000	**Curr. Liab.:**	$165,412,000	**P/E Ratio:**	65.54
Plant, Equip.:	$156,432,000	**Total Liab.:**	$242,047,000	**Indic. Yr. Divd.:**	NA
Total Assets:	$581,232,000	**Net Worth:**	$339,185,000	**Debt/ Equity:**	0.1470

InfuSystem Holdings Inc

Formerly: HAPC Inc
1551 E Lincoln Ave., Ste. 200, Madison Heights, MI, 48071; *PH:* 1-248-546-7047;
http:// www.healthcareapc.com

General - Incorporation	DE	**Stock** - Price on:12/24/2007	$5.83
Employees	NA	Stock Exchange	OTC
Auditor	Miller, Ellin & Co., LLP	Ticker Symbol	HAPN
Stk Agt	Stock Transfer Agency	Outstanding Shares	18,630,000
Counsel	NA	E.P.S.	NA
DUNS No.	NA	Shareholders	NA

Business: The groups principal activities include seeking, investigating, and acquiring interest in a business opportunity. The group operates from Delaware in the United States.

Primary SIC and add'l.: 6321
CIK No: 0001337013

Subsidiaries: Iceland Acquisition Inc

Officers: John Voris/Dir., CEO/$2,572,538.00, Pat Lavecchia/Dir., Sec., Erin Enright/CFO, VP/$986,790.00, Steven E. Watkins/Pres., Stephen C. Revere/Controller, Janet L. Skonieczny/VP - Operations, Tony Norkus/VP - Western Regional Sales, Thomas A. Bryniarski/Dir. - Regional Sales

Directors: John Voris/Dir., CEO, Sean McDevitt/Chmn., Pat Lavecchia/Dir., Sec., Jean-Pierre Millon/Dir., Wayne Yetter/Dir.

Owners: Insiders, Fir Tree Recovery Master Fund, L.P., Satellite Asset Management, L.P., Context Advantage Master Fund, L.P., John Voris, Sowood Capital Management LP, FMR Corp., Michael S. Rosen, Sapling, LLC, The Baupost Group, L.L.C., Sean McDevitt, Andrew M. Weiss, Sowood Capital Management LLC, Context Capital Management, LLC, Erin Enright *(22 Owners included in Index)*

Financial Data: *Fiscal Year End:*12/31 *Latest Annual Data:* 12/31/2006

Year	Sales	Net Income
2006	NA	-$7,859,000

Curr. Assets:	$100,298,000	**Curr. Liab.:**	$15,532,000		
Plant, Equip.:	NA	**Total Liab.:**	$35,152,000	**Indic. Yr. Divd.:**	NA
Total Assets:	$100,298,000	**Net Worth:**	$65,146,000	**Debt/ Equity:**	NA

ING Groep

Amstelveenseweg 500, Amsterdam; *PH:* 31-205415411; *Fax:* 31-205415497; *http://* www.ing.com

General - Incorporation	Netherlands	**Stock** - Price on:12/24/2007	$44.96
Employees	NA	Stock Exchange	NYSE
Auditor	Ernst & Young LLP, KPMG LLP	Ticker Symbol	ING
Stk Agt	Morgan ADR Service Center	Outstanding Shares	NA
Counsel	NA	E.P.S.	$6.02
DUNS No.	41-462-0351	Shareholders	NA

Business: The group's principal activity , which was prior to 1995 known as internationale nederlanden groep nv, is the provision of a wide range of insurance and banking services. These include all forms of life and non-life insurance, life reinsurance, funds transfer services, savings plans, investments in securities and other capital market instruments. It has its own establishments in over 60 countries. Banking is dealt with by ing bank and insurance by internationale nederlanden verzekeringen.

Primary SIC and add'l.: 6331 6324 6321 6021 6311
CIK No: 0001039765

Subsidiaries: ING Clarion, ING Insurance

Officers: Eric Bourdais De Charbonniere/69/Member - Exec. Board, Vice Chmn. - Supervisory Board, Cees Maas/61/Vice Chmn., CFO, Jane Park/Mgr. - Investor Relations, Eric Boyer De La Giroday/56/Member - Exec. Board, Tom McInerney/Member - Exec. Board, Koos Timmermans/Member - Exec. Board - CRO, Boris Dunnewijk/Mgr. - Investor Relations, Dorothy Hillenius/Mgr. - Investor Relations, Dick Harryvan/55/Member - Exec. Board, Hans Vander Noordaa/47/Member - Exec. Board, Jacques De Vaucleroy/47/Member - Exec. Board, Nathalie Van Toren/Mgr. - Investor Relations, Bernard Kuiper/Mgr. - Investor Relations, Eli Leenaars/47/Member - Exec. Board, John C.R. Hele/Member - Exec. Board

Directors: Eric Bourdais De Charbonniere/69/Member - Exec. Board, Vice Chmn. - Supervisory Board, Michel Tilmant/56/Chmn., Cor Herkstroter/Chmn. - Supervisory Board, Cees Maas/61/Vice Chmn., CFO, Eric Boyer De La Giroday/56/Member - Exec. Board, Jan H. Hommen/65/Member - Supervisory Board, Luella Gross Goldberg/Member - Supervisory Board, Peter Elverding/Member - Supervisory Board, Piet Hoogendoorn/Member - Supervisory Board, Claus D. Hoffmann/66/Member - Supervisory Board, Henk Breukink/Member - Supervisory Board, Tom McInerney/Member - Exec. Board, Koos Timmermans/Member - Exec. Board - CRO, Paul Van Den Heijden/59/Member - Supervisory Board, Piet C. Klaver/63/Member - Supervisory Board *(23 Directors included in Index)*

Financial Data: *Fiscal Year End:*12/31 *Latest Annual Data:* 12/31/2006

Year	Sales	Net Income
2006	$163,187,760,000	$9,013,688,000
2005	$130,580,100,000	$8,262,374,000
2004	$93,330,418,000	$9,000,947,000

Curr. Assets:	$336,280,410,000	**Curr. Liab.:**	$984,275,729,000		
Plant, Equip.:	$5,316,848,000	**Total Liab.:**	$1,568,835,913,000	**Indic. Yr. Divd.:**	$1.730
Total Assets:	$1,624,882,648,000	**Net Worth:**	$56,046,735,000	**Debt/ Equity:**	NA

ING Life Insurance & Annuity Co

One Orange Way, Windsor, CT, 06095; *PH:* 1-860-723-4646;
http:// www.ingemployeebenefits-us.com

General - Incorporation	CT	**Stock** - Price on:12/24/2007	$45.21
Employees	NA	Stock Exchange	NA
Auditor	Ernst & Young LLP	Ticker Symbol	NA
Stk Agt	American Funds Service Co.	Outstanding Shares	NA
Counsel	NA	E.P.S.	NA
DUNS No.	05-518-1770	Shareholders	NA

Business: The group's principal activity is to offer customers with annuity contracts that offer a variety of funding and payout options for individual and employer sponsored retirement plans qualified and non-qualified annuity contracts. The non-operating segment of the group offers investment advisory services and pension plan administrative services. The products are offered primarily to individuals, pension plans, small businesses and employer-sponsored groups in the health care, government, education and corporate markets. The products are sold through pension professionals, independent agents and brokers, thirdparty administrators, banks, dedicated career agents and financial planners. The group is a wholly owned subsidiary of aetna retirement holdings inc.

Primary SIC and add'l.: 6331 6321 6282
CIK No: 0000837010

Subsidiaries: ING Financial Advisers, LLC, ING Insurance Company of America

Officers: Brian D. Comer/Pres., Kim Smith/Regional Dir. - Houston, Christopher Beck/Regional Mgr. - Detroitmichigan, David Bondeson/Regional Dir. - Mid America, Chip Studer/GM - Mid, Atlantic, Eric Haverkamp/GM - Minneapolis, Darrell Chilton/GM - New Jersey, Mike Fitzpatrick/Assoc. Regional Dir. - Philadelphia, George Sens/Regional Dir. - Phoenix, Randall Wolfe/Regional Dir. - Seattle, David Kath/Regional VP, GM - Southern California, Darrell Smith/Regional Dir. - Tampa, John Breyer/Contact - Association Sales, Joe Beasley/Regional Dir. - Northeast, Bill Mulkeen/Assoc. Regional Dir. - Southeast *(29 Officers included in Index)*

Directors: Thomas J. McInerney/Chmn., Catherine H. Smith/Dir., Robert W. Crispin/Dir., Kathleen A. Murphy/Dir., David A. Wheat/Dir., CFO, Exec. VP

Financial Data: *Fiscal Year End:*12/31 *Latest Annual Data:* 12/31/2006

Year	Sales	Net Income
2006	$163,187,760,000	$9,013,688,000
2005	$130,580,100,000	$8,262,374,000
2004	$93,330,418,000	$9,000,947,000

Curr. Assets:	$336,280,410,000	**Curr. Liab.:**	$984,275,729,000	**P/E Ratio:**	65.54
Plant, Equip.:	$5,316,848,000	**Total Liab.:**	$1,564,942,348,000	**Indic. Yr. Divd.:**	NA
Total Assets:	$1,624,882,648,000	**Net Worth:**	$56,046,735,000	**Debt/ Equity:**	NA

ING USA Annuity & Life Insurance Co

1475 Dunwoody Dr., West Chester, PA, 19380; *PH:* 1-800-325-3792; *Fax:* 1-610-425-3902;
http:// www.ing-usa.com

General - Incorporation	IA	**Stock** - Price on:12/24/2007	$45.19
Employees	NA	Stock Exchange	NA
Auditor	Ernst & Young LLP	Ticker Symbol	NA
Stk Agt	Citibank N.A	Outstanding Shares	NA
Counsel	NA	E.P.S.	NA
DUNS No.	NA	Shareholders	NA

Business: The group's principal activity is to offer a portfolio of variable and fixed insurance products designed to meet customer needs for tax-advantaged saving for retirement and protection from death. The variable and fixed insurance products include goldenselect opportunities, smartdesign multi-rate index annuity and customized solutions-ing focus variable annuity, smartdesign classic flex annuity and smartdesign classic guarantee annuity.

Primary SIC and add'l.: 6311
CIK No: 0000836658

Financial Data: *Fiscal Year End:*12/31 *Latest Annual Data:* 12/31/2006

Year	Sales	Net Income
2006	$163,187,760,000	$9,013,688,000
2005	$130,580,100,000	$8,262,374,000
2004	$93,330,418,000	$9,000,947,000

Curr. Assets:	$336,280,410,000	**Curr. Liab.:**	$984,275,729,000		
Plant, Equip.:	$5,316,848,000	**Total Liab.:**	$1,564,942,348,000	**Indic. Yr. Divd.:**	NA
Total Assets:	$1,624,882,648,000	**Net Worth:**	$56,046,735,000	**Debt/ Equity:**	NA

Ingersoll Rand Co Ltd

PO Box 0445, 155 Chestnut Ridge Rd., Montvale, NJ, 07645; *PH:* 1-201-573-0123;
Fax: 1-201-573-3172; *http://* www.ingersollrand.com; *Email:* seekinfo@irco.com

General - Incorporation	Bermuda	**Stock** - Price on:12/24/2007	$54.75
Employees	43,000	Stock Exchange	NYSE
Auditor	PricewaterhouseCoopers LLP	Ticker Symbol	IR
Stk Agt	Bank of New York	Outstanding Shares	301,630,000
Counsel	NA	E.P.S.	$5.30
DUNS No.	00-136-8026	Shareholders	NA

Business: The group's principal activities are to provide security and safety, climate control, industrial productivity and infrastructure products. The climate control segment markets the required refrigerant-gas compression technology and services & maintains a refrigeration cycle for protecting food and other perishables. The products in this segment include thermo king transport temperature control

units for truck trailers, small trucks and seagoing containers. The industrial solutions segment composes a diverse group of business focused on providing solutions to enhance customers' industrial efficiency. The infrastructure segment supplies products and services for construction projects, industrial and commercial development and golf and utility vehicles. The safety and security segment manufactures and markets architectural hardware and access-control products and services. On 19-Feb-2004, the group sold drilling solutions.

Primary SIC and add'l.: 7382 5049 3531 3511 3499 3463 3585

CIK No: 0001160497

Subsidiaries: A/S Parts Limited, ABG Allgemeine Baumaschinen Gesellschaft mbH, ABG France S.A.R.L., Administradora Lockey CA, Airside Manufacturing Limited, Armoro, Inc., Aro de Venezuela, C.A., Astrum Gesellschaft fur angewandte Informatik mbH, Astrum IT Losungen GmbH, Best Matic Vermogensverwaltungs GmbH, Best-Matic International Limited, Blackrod Europe Limited, Blaw-Knox Company, Blaw-Knox Construction Equipment Corporation, Bobcat Bensheim GmbH & Co. KG 366 Subsidiaries included in the Index

Officers: Herbert L. Henkel/Chmn., CEO, Pres./$18,215,000.00, William B. Gauld/Sr. VP - Enterprise Services, Business Operating System, Barbara A. Santoro/VP - Corporate Governance, Sec., Patricia Nachtigal/Dir., Sr. VP, General Counsel/$3,021,210.00, James R. Bolch/Sr. VP, Pres. Industrial Technologies Sector, Jeff Song/Pres., Investor Relations Officer - China, Timothy E. Scofield/VP, Barbara L. Brasier/VP - Investor Relations, Treasurer, Steven R. Shawley/Sr. VP, Pres. - Climate Control Technologies Sector, Marcia J. Avedon/Sr. VP - Human Resources, Communications, James V. Gelly/Sr. VP, CFO, Patrick Shannon/VP - Strategy - Business Development, John Soriano/VP - Compliance, Deputy General Counsel, Barry Libenson/CIO, VP, Richard F. Pedtke/Sr. VP, Pres. - Compact Vehicle Technologies *(20 Officers included in Index)*

Directors: Herbert L. Henkel/Chmn., CEO, Pres., Ann C. Berzin/Dir., Peter C. Godsoe/Dir., William H. Lichtenberger/Dir., Theodore E. Martin/Dir., Orin R. Smith/Dir., Richard J. Swift/Dir., Tony L. White/Dir., Gary D. Foresee/Dir., Constance Horner/Dir., Patricia Nachtigal/Dir., Sr. VP, General Counsel

Owners: Insiders, P. Nachtigal, H. W. Lichtenberger, H. L. Henkel, O. R. Smith, P. C. Godsoe, T. L. White, R. J. Swift, C. P. Vasiloff, C. J. Horner, T. E. Martin, A. C. Berzin

Financial Data: ***Fiscal Year End:***12/31 ***Latest Annual Data:*** 12/31/2006

Year	Sales	Net Income
2006	$11,409,300,000	$1,032,500,000
2005	$10,546,900,000	$1,054,200,000
2004	$9,393,600,000	$1,218,700,000

Curr. Assets:	$4,095,900,000	**Curr. Liab.:**	$3,613,600,000	**P/E Ratio:**	17.44
Plant, Equip.:	$1,276,300,000	**Total Liab.:**	$6,741,100,000	**Indic. Yr. Divd.:**	$0.720
Total Assets:	$12,145,900,000	**Net Worth:**	$5,404,800,000	**Debt/ Equity:**	0.1676

Ingles Markets Inc

2913 US Hwy. 70 W, Black Mountain, NC, 28711; ***PH:*** 1-828-669-2941; ***Fax:*** 1-828-669-3678; ***http://*** www.ingles-markets.com

General - Incorporation	NC	**Stock**- Price on:12/24/2007	$33.95
Employees	7,728	Stock Exchange	NDQ
Auditor	Ernst & Young LLP	Ticker Symbol	IMKTA
Stk Agt	LaSalle Bank N.A	Outstanding Shares	24,510,000
Counsel	Kritzer & Levick	E.P.S	$1.60
DUNS No.	02-441-8584	Shareholders	NA

Business: The groups principle activity is to operate supermarkets. The groups product line includes grocery, meat and dairy products, pharmacies, health and beauty care products and general merchandise. The group operates through three business segments namely retail grocery sales, shopping center rentals and a fluid dairy processing plant. The group operates from United States.

Primary SIC and add'l.: 6512 5411 2026

CIK No: 0000050493

Subsidiaries: Ingles Markets Investments, Inc, Milkco, Inc., ng Center Financing II, LLC, Shopping Center Financing, LLC, Sky King, Inc

Officers: Robert P. Ingle/74/Dir., CEO, Robert P. Ingle/39/Chmn., VP - Operations, James W. Lanning/48/Dir., COO, Pres., Ronald B. Freeman/50/Dir., CFO, VP - Finance

Directors: Robert P. Ingle/74/Dir., CEO, Robert P. Ingle/39/Chmn., VP - Operations, James W. Lanning/48/Dir., COO, Pres., Charles E. Russell/69/Dir., Ronald B. Freeman/50/Dir., CFO, VP - Finance, Charles L. Gaither/64/Dir., Fred D. Ayers/65/Dir., Laura Ingle Sharp/51/Dir.

Owners: Robert P. Ingle, Laura Ingle Sharp, Robert P. Ingle, Ingles Investment/Profit Sharing Plan, Ingles Investment/Profit Sharing Plan, Insiders, Ronald B. Freeman, Laura Ingle Sharp, Fred D. Ayers, Silver Point Capital, L.P., et al, Charles L. Gaither, Dimensional Fund Advisors, Inc., James W. Lanning, Robert P. Ingle, Ronald B. Freeman *(21 Owners included in Index)*

Financial Data: ***Fiscal Year End:***09/24 ***Latest Annual Data:*** 9/30/2006

Year	Sales	Net Income
2006	$2,612,233,000	$42,582,000
2005	$2,273,941,000	$26,570,000
2004	$2,137,426,000	$28,752,000

Curr. Assets:	$285,818,000	**Curr. Liab.:**	$218,861,000	**P/E Ratio:**	16.64
Plant, Equip.:	$771,628,000	**Total Liab.:**	$770,301,000	**Indic. Yr. Divd.:**	$0.660
Total Assets:	$1,074,974,000	**Net Worth:**	$304,673,000	**Debt/ Equity:**	1.5565

Ingram Micro Inc

1600 E St. Andrew Pl., Santa Ana, CA, 92799; ***PH:*** 1-714-566-1000; ***Fax:*** 1-714-566-7900; ***http://*** www.ingrammicro.com; ***Email:*** investor.relations@ingrammicro.com

General - Incorporation	DE	**Stock**- Price on:12/24/2007	$21.86
Employees	13,700	Stock Exchange	NYSE
Auditor	PricewaterhouseCoopers LLP	Ticker Symbol	IM
Stk Agt	EquiServe Trust Co N.A	Outstanding Shares	170,270,000
Counsel	Davis Polk & Wardwell	E.P.S	$1.44
DUNS No.	00-491-9486	Shareholders	NA

Business: The group's principle activity is to provide sales, marketing and logistic services for IT industry. The group operates from United States.

Primary SIC and add'l.: 5045 7372

CIK No: 0001018003

Subsidiaries: AVAD LLC, Bright Creative Communications BV, CD Access Inc., Chinam Electronics Limited(41), CIM Ventures Inc., Compu-Shack Electronic GmbH, Computek Enterprises (U.S.A.) Inc., Electronic Resources Australia (Qld) Pty Ltd., Electronic Resources Australia (Vic) Pty Ltd., ERIM Sdn Bhd, Export Services Inc., First Tech Pacific Distributors Sdn Bhd, Handelsmaatschappij voor Computers BVBA, Imagineering (NZ)Limited, IMI Washington Inc. 127 Subsidiaries included in the Index

Officers: Gregory M. Spierkel/Dir., CEO/$6,534,128.00, Kevin M. Murai/Dir., COO, Pres./$5,499,767.00, Jay A. Forbes/Exec. VP, Pres. - Designate Ingram Micro EMEA, Shailendra Gupta/Sr. VP - Ingram Micro Inc, Pres. - Ingram Micro Asia, Pacific, William D. Humes/CFO, Exec. VP/$1,406,549.00, Larry C. Boyd/Sr. VP, Sec., General Counsel, Karen Salem/CIO, Sr. VP, Ria M. Carlson/Corporate VP - Strategy, Communications, Matthew A. Sauer/60/Sr. VP - Human Resources, James F. Ricketts/Corporate VP, Treasurer, Keith Bradley/Exec. VP, Pres. - Ingram Micro North America, Alain Maquet/Sr. VP, Pres. - Ingram Micro Latin America, Hans T. Koppen/Exec. VP, Pres. - Ingram Micro Europe/$4,477,425.00, Alain Monie/COO, Pres./$1,975,301.00, Kay Leyba/Primary Investor Relations Officer *(16 Officers included in Index)*

Directors: Gregory M. Spierkel/Dir., CEO, Kent B. Foster/64/Non - Exec. Chmn., Joe B. Wyatt/Dir., Dale R. Laurance/Dir., John R. Ingram/Dir., Leslie S. Heisz/Dir., Michael T. Smith/Dir., Martha R. Ingram/Dir., Howard I. Atkins/Dir., Kevin M. Murai/Dir., COO, Pres., Orrin H. Ingram/Dir., Linda Fayne Levinson/Dir., Gerhard Schulmeyer/Dir.

Owners: Linda Fayne Levinson, Henri T. Koppen, Insiders/19.00%, Gregory M.E. Spierkel, Kent B. Foster/2.30%, John R. Ingram/12.70%, Alain Moni, Kevin M. Murai, Gerhard Schulmeyer, Barclays Global Investors, N.A/15.00%, Michael T. Smith, Dale R. Laurance, Martha R. Ingram/11.70%, William D. Humes, Orrin H. Ingram/12.80% *(19 Owners included in Index)*

Financial Data: ***Fiscal Year End:***12/31 ***Latest Annual Data:*** 12/30/2006

Year	Sales	Net Income
2006	$31,357,477,000	$265,766,000
2005	$28,808,312,000	$216,906,000

Curr. Assets:	$6,071,298,000	**Curr. Liab.:**	$4,105,484,000	**P/E Ratio:**	15.84
Plant, Equip.:	$179,435,000	**Total Liab.:**	$4,596,392,000	**Indic. Yr. Divd.:**	NA
Total Assets:	$7,034,990,000	**Net Worth:**	$2,438,598,000	**Debt/ Equity:**	0.1553

Inhibitex Inc

9005 Westside Pkwy., Alpharetta, GA, 30004; ***PH:*** 1-678-746-1100; ***Fax:*** 1-678-746-1299; ***http://*** www.inhibitex.com; ***Email:*** ir@inhibitex.com

General - Incorporation	DE	**Stock**- Price on:12/24/2007	$1.26
Employees	37	Stock Exchange	NDQ
Auditor	Ernst & Young LLP	Ticker Symbol	INHX
Stk Agt	Computershare Investor Services LLC	Outstanding Shares	30,880,000
Counsel	NA	E.P.S	-$0.72
DUNS No.	NA	Shareholders	NA

Business: The group's principle activities include discover, developing and commercializing novel antibody-based products for the prevention and treatment of serious bacterial and fungal infections in the hospital setting. The group has two product candidates in late-stage clinical development. The veronate product is developed to prevent hospital-associated infections in premature, very low birth weight, infants. Aurexis, another product is developed to treat serious, life-threatening staphylococcus aureus, bloodstream infections in hospitalized patients. In addition, the group has three preclinical product candidates that are being developed to prevent and treat serious infections. The group operates from United States.

Primary SIC and add'l.: NA

CIK No: 0001274913

Officers: Russell H. Plumb/Dir., CEO, CFO, Pres., Sec., Treasurer, Joseph M. Patti/Co - Founder, Chief Scientific Officer, Sr. VP - Research, Development, Samuel J. Michini/VP - Sales, Marketing, Amy M. Morris/VP - Clinical Development, Peter J. Azzarello/VP - Finance, John H. Vernachio/VP - Biology, Jeff T. Hutchins/VP - Preclinical Development, Geoffrey W. Henson/Sr. VP - Drug Development, Maggie Feeney/Dir. - Human Resources, Sarah E. Bates/Intellectual Property Counsel

Directors: Russell H. Plumb/Dir., CEO, CFO, Pres., Sec., Treasurer, Michael A. Henos/Chmn., Louis W. Sullivan/Dir., Carl E. Brooks/Dir., William D. Johnston/Dir., Russell M. Medford/Dir., Robert A. Hamm/Dir., Marc L. Preminger/Dir., James M. Barrett/Dir., Keith A. Willard/Dir.

Owners: Frederick Larcombe, Insiders/34.40%, Chris McGuigan/1.40%, Russell M. Medford, Louis W. Sullivan, Keith A. Willard, Geoffrey W. Henson, QVT Financial L.P./6.40%, Joseph M. Patti, Marc L. Preminger, William D. Johnston/1.40%, John P. Brancaccio, Entities affiliated with New Enterprise Associates/17.30%, Robert A. Hamm, T. Rowe Price Small-Cap Value FundInc./7.50% *(22 Owners included in Index)*

Financial Data: ***Fiscal Year End:***12/31 ***Latest Annual Data:*** 12/31/2006

Year	Sales	Net Income
2006	$846,000	-$31,145,000
2005	$936,000	-$38,575,000
2004	$650,000	-$25,911,000

Curr. Assets:	$62,694,000	**Curr. Liab.:**	$10,015,000		
Plant, Equip.:	$3,531,000	**Total Liab.:**	$13,148,000	**Indic. Yr. Divd.:**	NA
Total Assets:	$66,224,000	**Net Worth:**	$53,077,000	**Debt/ Equity:**	0.0274

InkSure Technologies Inc

1770 NW 64th St., Ste. 350, Fort Lauderdale, FL, 33309; ***PH:*** 1-954-772-8507; ***Fax:*** 1-954-772-8509; ***http://*** www.inksure.com; ***Email:*** info@inksure.com

General - Incorporation	DE	**Stock**- Price on:12/24/2007	$1.9
Employees	22	Stock Exchange	OTC
Auditor	Brightman, Almagor & Co	Ticker Symbol	INKS
Stk Agt	Pacific Stock Transfer Company	Outstanding Shares	15,920,000
Counsel	NA	E.P.S	-$0.2
DUNS No.	NA	Shareholders	NA

Business: The groups principle activities include developing, marketing and selling customized authentication systems used in the security of documents and branded products. The group operates from the United States, Israel and Turkey.

Primary SIC and add'l.: 3829

CIK No: 0001062128

Subsidiaries: InkSure Inc, InkSure Ltd, InkSure RF, Inc., IST Operating Inc.

Officers: Elie Housman/Chmn., CEO - Inksure Technologies Inc./$207,600.00, Yaron Meerfeld/Dir., COO - Inksure Technologies Inc./$264,800.00, Mickey Brandt/CFO - Inksure Technologies/$81,300.00, James R. Assaf/GM - Inksure Inc., Chris Brown/Sr. VP - Sales, Inksure Inc, Don Taylor/VP - Global Marketing, Inksure Inc, Tomer Loiter/VP - Asia - EAS, Inksure Ltd, Ehud Helft/GK Investor Relations Officer, Fiona Darmon/GK Investor Relations Officer

Directors: Elie Housman/Chmn., CEO - Inksure Technologies Inc., Yaron Meerfeld/Dir., COO - Inksure Technologies Inc., Albert Attias/Dir. - Inksure Technologies Inc, David W. Sass/Dir. - Inksure Technologies Inc, Philip M. Getter/Dir. - Inksure Technologies Inc, Pierre L. Schoenheimer/Dir. - Inksure Technologies Inc, Randy F. Rock/Dir. - Inksure Technologies Inc

Owners: Philip M. Getter, Insiders/17.85%, David W. Sass, James E. Lineberger/8.13%, ICTS International N.V./32.33%, Pierre L. Schoenheimer/1.52%, Albert Attias, Yaron Meerfeld/5.32%, Smithfield Fiduciary LLC/9.84%, Elie Housman/8.90%

Financial Data: Fiscal Year End:12/31 Latest Annual Data: 12/31/2006

Year	Sales	Net Income
2006	$2,002,000	-$3,112,000
2005	$1,626,000	-$2,213,000
2004	$955,000	-$2,061,000

Curr. Assets:	$3,599,000	Curr. Liab.:	$564,000		
Plant, Equip.:	$347,000	Total Liab.:	$6,082,000	Indic. Yr. Divd.:	NA
Total Assets:	$4,745,000	Net Worth:	-$1,337,000	Debt/ Equity:	NA

Inland Real Estate Corp

2901 Butterfield Rd., Oak Brook, IL, 60523; *PH:* 1-630-218-8000; *Fax:* 1-630-218-7350; *http://* www.inlandrealestate.com

General - Incorporation	MD	Stock - Price on:12/24/2007	$17.79
Employees	82	Stock Exchange	NYSE
Auditor	KPMG LLP	Ticker Symbol	IRC
Stk Agt	Registrar & Transfer Co	Outstanding Shares	65,200,000
Counsel	Shefsky & Froelich, Ltd.	E.P.S.	$0.71
DUNS No.	NA	Shareholders	NA

Business: The groups principal activities include owning, operating and developing retail shopping centers. In the year 2006, the group acquired eight properties. The group operates from the United States. The groups total assets in the year 2006 were $1,269,161 (thousands).

Primary SIC and add'l.: 6798

CIK No: 0000923284

Subsidiaries: IN RETAIL FUND ALGONQUIN COMMONS LLC, IN RETAIL FUND CHATHAM RIDGE LLC, IN RETAIL FUND COBBLER CROSSING LLC, IN RETAIL FUND FOREST LAKE MARKETPLACE LLC, IN RETAIL FUND GREENTREE LLC, IN RETAIL FUND GREENTREE OUTLOT LLC, IN RETAIL FUND LLC, IN RETAIL FUND MANAGER TEXAS, LLC, IN RETAIL FUND MARKETPLACE AT SIX CORNERS, LLC, IN RETAIL FUND RANDALL SQUARE LLC, IN RETAIL FUND RAVINIA LLC, IN RETAIL FUND SHOPPES OF MILL CREEK LLC, IN RETAIL FUND TEXAS LLC, IN RETAIL FUND THATCHER WOODS LLC, IN RETAIL FUND WOODFIELD COMMONS, LLC 111 Subsidiaries included in the Index

Officers: Robert D. Parks/Dir., CEO, Pres./$50,000.00, Scott D. Carr/Pres. - Property Managment/$268,988.00, Carol L. Adams/Treasurer - Property Management, David J. Kayner/General Counsel, Mark E. Zalatoris/Exec. VP, COO, Treasurer/$370,025.00, Beth Sprecher Brooks/VP, Sec., General Counsel/$203,010.00, Brett A. Brown/CFO/$252,260.00, William W. Anderson/VP - Acquisition, Sales, Kristi A. Rankin/Sr. VP

Directors: Robert D. Parks/Dir., CEO, Pres., Daniel L. Goodwin/Chmn., Joel D. Simmons/Dir., Thomas R. McWilliams/Dir., Roland W. Burris/Dir., Thomas P. D'Arcy/Dir., Joel G. Herter/Dir., Heidi N. Lawton/Dir., Cosenza G. Joseph/Dir., Thomas H. McAuley/Dir.

Owners: FMR Corp./11.40%, Roland W. Burris, Robert D. Parks, Insiders/10.90%, Thomas P. DArcy, Thomas R. McWilliams, Barclays Global Investors, NA, Barclays Global Fund Advisors, Barclays Global Investors, Ltd./6.00%, Beth Sprecher Brooks, Scott D. Carr, Thomas H. McAuley, Joel G. Herter, Brett A. Brown, Joel D. Simmons, Heidi N. Lawton, Mark E. Zalatoris (18 Owners included in Index)

Financial Data: Fiscal Year End:12/31 Latest Annual Data: 12/31/2006

Year	Sales	Net Income
2006	$178,415,000	$45,184,000
2005	$182,715,000	$47,255,000
2004	$187,148,000	$49,373,000

Curr. Assets:	$65,281,000	Curr. Liab.:	$41,337,000	P/E Ratio:	25.06
Plant, Equip.:	$1,045,536,000	Total Liab.:	$892,178,000	Indic. Yr. Divd.:	NA
Total Assets:	$1,269,161,000	Net Worth:	$376,983,000	Debt/ Equity:	2.3909

Inmedica Development Corp

825 N 300 W, Salt Lake City, UT, 84103; *PH:* 1-801-263-9190

General - Incorporation	UT	Stock - Price on:12/24/2007	$0.11
Employees	NA	Stock Exchange	OTC
Auditor	Robison, Hill & Co	Ticker Symbol	IMDD
Stk Agt	Fidelity Transfer Co	Outstanding Shares	18,630,000
Counsel	NA	E.P.S.	-$0.007
DUNS No.	10-688-4075	Shareholders	NA

Business: The group's principal activities are to develop and sale of medical technology. The group develops and markets portable electrocardiograph (ecg) monitor. Other activity of the group is to research and develop a device to measure hematocrit technology. The hematocrit is the percentage of red blood cells in a given volume of blood. The group entered into a development, licensing and manufacturing agreement with chi lin pursuant to which inmedica granted chi lin a worldwide license to develop and manufacture products based on the hematocrit technology.

Primary SIC and add'l.: 8731 3829

CIK No: 0000726037

Subsidiaries: MicroCor, Inc.

Officers: Ralph Henson/63/Dir., CEO, Pres., Richard Bruggeman/53/Dir., CFO, Sec., Treasurer

Directors: Ralph Henson/63/Dir., CEO, Pres., Larry E. Clark/86/Chmn., Sheng Jung Chiang/62/Dir., Mao-Song Lee/60/Dir., Richard Bruggeman/53/Dir., CFO, Sec., Treasurer

Owners: Richard Bruggeman, Insiders/34.80%, Larry E. Clark, Ralph Henson/1.70%

Financial Data: Fiscal Year End:12/31 Latest Annual Data: 12/31/2006

Year	Sales	Net Income
2006	NA	-$116,000
2005	NA	-$294,000
2004	NA	$183,000

Curr. Assets:	$34,000	Curr. Liab.:	$132,000		
Plant, Equip.:	$1,000	Total Liab.:	$239,000	Indic. Yr. Divd.:	NA
Total Assets:	$35,000	Net Worth:	-$111,000	Debt/ Equity:	NA

Inncardio' Inc

C-6f, Huhan Chuangxin Block, Keyuan Rd., Hi-tech Industry Zone, Shenzhen, Guangdong, 518000; *PH:* 86-755-339-65188; *http://* www.inncardio.com

General - Incorporation	UT	Stock - Price on:12/24/2007	NA
Employees	NA	Stock Exchange	NA
Auditor	Kempisty & Co.	Ticker Symbol	NA
Stk Agt	Colonial Stock Transfer Co Inc	Outstanding Shares	NA
Counsel	NA	E.P.S.	NA
DUNS No.	NA	Shareholders	NA

Business: The group's principle activities include researching, developing, manufacturing and marketing mining and excavation equipment. The company develops and markets softwall system and the sacum conveyor system. The softwall system adapts the methods of longwall mining to the conditions found in shallow, soft ore deposits such as those found in the phosphate bearing sands and clays of north central Florida. The sacum conveyor system travels on a roof mounted monorail, which is mounted to the mine roof. It has application for coal and hard rock and any other underground mining, which can use a roof mounted conveyor. The group operates from United States.

Primary SIC and add'l.: 3532

CIK No: 0001082562

Subsidiaries: Cengent Therapeutics Inc.

Officers: Bu Shengfu/41/Chmn., CEO, Pres., Xu Rujiang/45/Dir., COO, Liang Zhu/41/Dir., CFO, Sec., Liu Jingyun/38/CTO, Yin Zhongjun/39/Chief Engineer, Li Xiangdong/43/Principal Controller, Xu Jiafa/45/Principal Production Officer

Directors: Bu Shengfu/41/Chmn., CEO, Pres., Xu Rujiang/45/Dir., COO, Jin Yushan/52/Dir., Chen Dong/46/Dir.

Owners: Barron Partners L.P./9.90%, Vision Opportunity Master Fund, Ltd./9.99%, WestPark Capital, Inc./7.96%, Chen Dong/3.02%, Liang Zhu, MidSouth Investor Fund L.P./13.41%, Liu Jingyun/3.84%, Bu Shengfu/11.69%, Insiders/32.29%, Yin Zhongjun/6.32%, Jin Yushan/6.78%, JCAR Funds, Ltd./6.01%, Shenzhen Chefu Industrial Development Co., Ltd./11.30%

Curr. Assets:	NA	Curr. Liab.:	$3,077,000		
Plant, Equip.:	NA	Total Liab.:	$3,077,000	Indic. Yr. Divd.:	NA
Total Assets:	NA	Net Worth:	-$3,077,000	Debt/ Equity:	NA

Inner Systems Inc

13 Jemez Rd. , Placitas, NM, 87043; *PH:* 1-505-867-0104; *http://* www.keepbreathin.com; *Email:* MA@keepbreathin.com

General - Incorporation	NY	Stock - Price on:12/24/2007	$0.18
Employees	NA	Stock Exchange	OTC
Auditor	Marcum & Kliegman LLP	Ticker Symbol	ISYM
Stk Agt	Liberty Transfer Co	Outstanding Shares	1,000,000
Counsel	NA	E.P.S.	-$0.05
DUNS No.	NA	Shareholders	NA

Business: The groups principle activity is to create bid process for procuring, purchasing and delivering printed product. The product of the group is PPM4. Customers served by the group include advertising, consumer products, publishing and retail industries. The group acquired Applied Graphics, Inc. in October 2006, and Spectrum Printing Systems in March 2007. The group operates from Illinois in the United States.

Primary SIC and add'l.: 5735

CIK No: 0001271551

Officers: John M. Sharpe/55/Dir., CEO, CFO, Pres., Mary Alice Winchell/Hatha Yoga Instructor, Stress Management Consultant, J. Stinson/Human Resources, A. Laurence/Founder - Peoplematter

Directors: John M. Sharpe/55/Dir., CEO, CFO, Pres.

Owners: John M. Sharpe/76.20%, Insiders/76.20%, Pryor & Mandelup/6.50%

Financial Data: Fiscal Year End:12/31 Latest Annual Data: 12/31/2006

Year	Sales	Net Income
2006	NA	-$35,000
2005	NA	-$39,000
2004	NA	-$44,000

Curr. Assets:	$2,000	Curr. Liab.:	$148,000		
Plant, Equip.:	NA	Total Liab.:	$148,000	Indic. Yr. Divd.:	NA
Total Assets:	$2,000	Net Worth:	-$146,000	Debt/ Equity:	NA

InnerWorkings Inc

600 W Chicago Ave., Ste. 850, Chicago, IL, 60610; *PH:* 1-312-642-3700; *Fax:* 1-312-642-3704; *http://* www.iwprint.com; *Email:* info@iwprint.com

General - Incorporation		Stock - Price on:12/24/2007	$15.92
Employees	312	Stock Exchange	NDQ
Auditor	Ernst & Young	Ticker Symbol	INWK
Stk Agt	NA	Outstanding Shares	47,470,000
Counsel	NA	E.P.S.	$0.28
DUNS No.	NA	Shareholders	NA

Business: The groups principle activity is to provide print procurement solutions. The products of the group include direct mail pieces, posters, newsletters, stickers, binders and magazines. The group products sold under the trade name PPM4 (TM). Customers served by the group include commercial printing and business process outsourcing industries. The group acquired Spectrum Printing Servicesin the year 2007 and Applied Graphics, Inc, CoreVision Group, Inc, Graphography Limited LLC in the year 2006. The group operates from the United States. the group's quarterly revenue for September 2007 was 72.15 millions of USD.

Primary SIC and add'l.: 4731 2759 7389

CIK No: 0001350381

Subsidiaries: Applied Graphics, Inc., Graphography Limited LLC, Insight, LLC

Officers: Steven E. Zuccarini/Dir., CEO, Nicholas J. Galassi/CFO, Scott A. Frisoni/Exec. VP - Sales, Eric D. Belcher/COO, Neil P. Graver/CTO

Directors: Steven E. Zuccarini/Dir., CEO, John R. Walter/Non - Exec. Chmn., Sharyar Baradaran/Dir., Peter Barris/Dir., Jack M. Greenberg/Dir., Linda Wolf/Dir.

Owners: Entities affiliated with New Enterprise Associates/17.10%, Jack M. Greenberg, Eric D. Belcher, John R. Walter/2.50%, Richard A. Heise/14.80%, Scott A. Frisoni/1.00%, Nicholas J. Galassi, Neil P. Graver, Steven E. Zuccarini/2.50%, Sharyar Baradaran/1.50%, Old Willow Partners, LLC/8.70%, Insiders/24.20%, Orange Media, LLC/10.40%, Gilder, Gagnon, Howe& Co. LLC/5.90%, Peter J. Barris/17.10%

Financial Data: Fiscal Year End:NA   Latest Annual Data: 12/31/2006

Year	Sales		Net Income
2006		$160,515,000	$8,280,000
Curr. Assets:	$89,539,000	Curr. Liab.:	$31,834,000	P/E Ratio:	56.86
Plant, Equip.:	$2,802,000	Total Liab.:	$32,055,000	Indic. Yr. Divd.:	NA
Total Assets:	$113,510,000	Net Worth:	$81,455,000	Debt/ Equity:	0.0016

Innexus Biotechnology Inc

13208 E Shea Blvd. Ste. 200, The Mayo Clinic MCCRB Bldg., Scottsdale, AZ, 85259;
Fax: 1-425-696-0068; **http://** www.ixsbio.com; **Email:** business@innexusbiotech.com

General - Incorporation	BC	Stock - Price on:12/24/2007	$0.3916
Employees	NA	Stock Exchange	OTC
Auditor	KPMG LLP	Ticker Symbol	IXSBF
Stk Agt	Pacific Corporate Trust Co	Outstanding Shares	NA
Counsel	NA	E.P.S.	NA
DUNS No.	NA	Shareholders	NA

Business: The group's principal activity is to develop an innovative antibody-driven drug on two technology platforms, SuperAntibody and TransMAbs, which improve the potency of existing antibody products and create a novel class of antibody based drugs which penetrate into cells. Antibodies are produced naturally within the body and attack (bind with) diseased cells and either weaken or destroy them, allowing a person to recover from an infection. Monoclonal Antibody technology allows one to isolate and expand individual antibodies for the treatment of numerous diseases, including cancer. Monoclonal Antibodies display qualities unlike any other drug yet discovered in that they are very specific and relatively non-toxic.

Primary SIC and add'l.: 2834
CIK No: 0001278730
Subsidiaries: InNexus Biotechnology International Limited, InNexus Exchange Corp., InNexus Inc., North Bioscience Inc.
Officers: Jeff Morhet/Chmn., CEO, Pres., Wade Brooksby/Dir., CFO, Thomas Kindt/Chief Scientific Officer, Jur Strobos/Chief Medical Officer, Janet Vasquez/Investor Relation Officer, Christine Berni/Investor Relations Officer, Joe Trifunfo/Investor Relations Officer
Directors: Jeff Morhet/Chmn., CEO, Pres., Donald J. Capra/Chmn. - Scientific Advisory Board, Wade Brooksby/Dir., CFO, Gail Thurston/Dir., John D. Minna/Dir., Member - Scientific Advisory Board, Carlos L. Arteaga/Vice Chancellor, Member - Scientific Advisory Board, Ellen S. Vitetta/Dir., Member - Scientific Advisory Board, Martin Weigert/Member - Scientific Advisory Board, Leroy Chiao/Dir., Laurence Luke/Dir., Glenn Williamson/Dir.
Owners: Wade Brooksby/0.22%, Jeff Morhet/0.91%, Gail Thurston/5.70%

Financial Data: Fiscal Year End:06/30   Latest Annual Data: 6/30/2006

Year	Sales		Net Income
2006		$41,000	-$2,433,000
2005		$4,000	-$1,989,000
Curr. Assets:	$646,000	Curr. Liab.:	$211,000		
Plant, Equip.:	$298,000	Total Liab.:	$211,000	Indic. Yr. Divd.:	NA
Total Assets:	$1,038,000	Net Worth:	$827,000	Debt/ Equity:	NA

Innkeepers USA Trust

340 Royal Poinciana Way, Suite, FL, 33480; ; **http://** www.innkeepersusa.com

General - Incorporation	MD	Stock - Price on:12/24/2007	$17.68
Employees	36	Stock Exchange	NA
Auditor	PricewaterhouseCoopers LLP	Ticker Symbol	NA
Stk Agt	Harris Trust And Savings Bank	Outstanding Shares	NA
Counsel	NA	E.P.S.	NA
DUNS No.	NA	Shareholders	NA

Business: The groups principle activities include acquiring and developing premium branded upscale extended stay, mid priced limited service and select service hotels. The group acquired one 83-room Hampton Inn hotel in the year 2005, and one 309 room Hilton hotel and one 230-suite Hilton Suites hotel in the year 2006. The group operates from the United States.

Primary SIC and add'l.: 6798 6798
CIK No: 0000926866
Subsidiaries: Innkeepers Financial Corporation II, Innkeepers Financial Corporation III, Innkeepers Financial Corporation IV, Innkeepers Financial Corporation V, Innkeepers Financing Partnership II, L.P., Innkeepers Financing Partnership III, L.P., Innkeepers Financing Partnership IV, L.P., Innkeepers Financing Partnership, L.P., Innkeepers Morristown, LLC, Innkeepers Optima, S. de R.L. de CV, Innkeepers Residence Addison, Inc., Innkeepers Residence Addison, L.P., Innkeepers Residence Arlington, Inc., Innkeepers Residence Arlington, L.P., Innkeepers Residence Atlanta-Downtown, Inc. 68 Subsidiaries included in the Index
Officers: Tim Walker/CEO, Pres., Jeffrey H. Fisher/Chmn., Pres./$1,632,658.00, Dennis Craven/CFO/$418,054.00, Mark A. Murphy/General Counsel, Sec./$618,131.00, Richard F. Fenton/VP - Financial Planning, Analysis, Linda K. Price/VP, Controller, Bob Martin/VP - Construction - Eastern Region, Michael Nielson/VP - Construction - Western Region
Directors: Jeffrey H. Fisher/Chmn., Pres., Miles Berger/47/Trustee, Randall L. Churchey/47/Trustee, Thomas J. Crocker/54/Trustee, Jack P. Deboer/77/Trustee, Gerald C. Goldsmith/80/Trustee, Rolf E. Ruhfus/63/Trustee, Joel F. Zemans/66/Trustee
Owners: Mark A. Murphy, Randall L. Churchey, Gerald C. Goldsmith, JP Morgan Chase& Co./9.50%, Jack P. DeBoer, Joel F. Zemans, Dennis M. Craven, Rolf E. Ruhfus, Jeffrey H. Fisher/4.20%, The Vanguard Group, Inc./6.00%, Richard A. Mielbye, Barclays Global Investors, NA/6.60%, Miles Berger, Insiders/5.20%, Thomas J. Crocker

Financial Data: Fiscal Year End:12/31   Latest Annual Data: 12/31/2006

Year	Sales		Net Income
2006		$286,713,000	$30,562,000
2005		$247,181,000	$22,659,000
2004		$205,029,000	$14,600,000
Curr. Assets:	$23,540,000	Curr. Liab.:	$40,273,000	P/E Ratio:	25.06
Plant, Equip.:	$1,049,239,000	Total Liab.:	$565,223,000	Indic. Yr. Divd.:	$0.920
Total Assets:	$1,102,006,000	Net Worth:	$517,671,000	Debt/ Equity:	NA

Innocap Inc

5675b Baldwin Ct, Norcross, GA, 30071; **PH:** 1-770-378-4180

General - Incorporation	NV	Stock - Price on:12/24/2007	NA
Employees	NA	Stock Exchange	NA
Auditor	Li & Co., P.C	Ticker Symbol	NA
Stk Agt	NA	Outstanding Shares	NA
Counsel	NA	E.P.S.	NA
DUNS No.	NA	Shareholders	NA

Business: The group's principal activity is to provide investors with the opportunity to participate with a modest amount in venture capital investments that are generally not available to the public and that typically require substantially larger financial commitments. The company also provides professional management and administration that might otherwise be unavailable to investors if they were to engage directly in venture capital investing.

Primary SIC and add'l.: 5810
CIK No: 0001281845
Officers: Alva B. Schoomer/73/Chmn., CFO, Pres.
Directors: Alva B. Schoomer/73/Chmn., CFO, Pres., Stephen B. Schneer/76/Dir.
Owners: Stephen B. Schneer/0.70%, Gary B. Wolff/17.60%, Doyle S. Elliott/14.70%, Insiders/18.40%, GCND,Inc./45.60%, Alva B. Schoomer/17.60%

Innocom Technology Holdings Inc

Rm. 3506 Bank of America Tower, 12 Harcourt Rd., Admiralty; **PH:** 801-450-0716;
Fax: 852-31021932; **http://** www.innocomtechnology.com; **Email:** info@innocomtechnology.com

General - Incorporation	NV	Stock - Price on:12/24/2007	$0.4
Employees	NA	Stock Exchange	OTC
Auditor	NA	Ticker Symbol	INCM
Stk Agt	OTC Stock Transfer, Inc.	Outstanding Shares	NA
Counsel	NA	E.P.S.	NA
DUNS No.	NA	Shareholders	NA

Business: The groups principle activity is to provide musical and performance services for concerts and public events. The group operates from the United States. The group operates from Utah in the United States.

Primary SIC and add'l.: 3661
CIK No: 0001076541
Officers: William Yansui Hui/Chmn., CEO, Davis Jian Li/CEO - Beijing Unismobile Commuciation Technology Company Limited, Roc Sun/VP - Sales, Marketing, Eric Chin Pang Tang/CFO, Cheung Wai Hung/53/Chief Financial Controller
Directors: William Yansui Hui/Chmn., CEO, Eric Yiu Nam Lau/Non Exec. Dir., Fuk Kam Chan/Non Exec. Dir., Tay Siew Leng/40/Non Exec. Dir., Tan Ah Mee/61/Dir., Qian Jian Yu/44/Non Exec. Dir.
Owners: Insiders/60.79%, William Hui Yan Siu/60.97%

Financial Data: Fiscal Year End:09/30   Latest Annual Data: 12/31/2006

Year	Sales		Net Income
2006		$52,723,000	$2,452,000
2005		$1,000	-$7,000
Curr. Assets:	$11,000	Curr. Liab.:	$0		
Plant, Equip.:	NA	Total Liab.:	NA	Indic. Yr. Divd.:	NA
Total Assets:	$11,000	Net Worth:	$11,000	Debt/ Equity:	NA

Innodata Isogen Inc

3 University Plz., Hackensack, NJ, 07601; **PH:** 1-201-371-2828; **Fax:** 1-201-488-9099;
http:// www.innodata-isogen.com; **Email:** info@innodata-isogen.com

General - Incorporation	DE	Stock - Price on:12/24/2007	$3.986
Employees	5,476	Stock Exchange	NDQ
Auditor	Grant Thornton LLP	Ticker Symbol	INOD
Stk Agt	American Stock Transfer & Trust Co.	Outstanding Shares	23,970,000
Counsel	Kramer Levin Naftalis & Frankel LLP	E.P.S.	-$0.56
DUNS No.	NA	Shareholders	NA

Business: The group's principal activities are to deliver content manufacturing and extensible markup language related digital asset services. These services are provided to online information providers and companies in the telecommunications, technology, healthcare, defense and Internet commerce sectors. The group operates through two divisions: content services and professional services. The content services division offers content manufacturing services as a comprehensive outsourcing solution and individually as discrete activities. It also transforms data to extensible markup language (xml). The professional services division offers system design, custom application development, consulting services, systems integration conforming to xml and related standards, a broad range of introductory as well as advanced curricula and training on xml and other knowledge management standards. The group operates in the United States, Europe, Philippines, sri lanka, and India.

Primary SIC and add'l.: 7379 7374
CIK No: 0000903651
Subsidiaries: Content Online Services, Inc., ESS Manufacturing Company, Inc., Innodata Asia Holdings, Limited, Innodata India (Private) Limited, Innodata Lanka (Private) Limited, Innodata XML Content Factory, Inc., Isogen International, LLC
Officers: Jack S. Abuhoff/Chmn., CEO, Pres./$390,114.00, Steven L. Ford/CFO, Exec. VP/$300,000.00, Neelkanth Akhauri/VP - Content Engineering, Klaas Brouwer/VP - Technology, Amy R. Agress/VP, General Counsel, Al Girardi/VP - Marketing, Ashok Kumar Mishra/COO, Exec. VP, Jan Palmen/Sr. VP - Publishing Practice, Renee Swank/VP - Commercial, Advanced Programs, Jurgen Tanpho/VP - Operations, Sunil Jauhar/VP - Project Delivery, Theresa Veloso/VP - Project Delivery, Vincent Henderson/VP - Publishing Practice, Zanetta Hancock/VP - Commercial, Advanced Programs, Sanjay Tangri/VP - Trade, Consumer Publishing *(16 Officers included in Index)*

Directors: Jack S. Abuhoff/Chmn., CEO, Pres., John R. Marozsan/Dir., Haig S. Bagerdjian/Dir., Louise C. Forlenza/Dir., Peter Woodward/Dir.

Owners: George R. Kondrach, Steven L. Ford/1.10%, Louise C. Forlenza, John R. Marozsan, Stephen J. Agress/2.70%, Jack S. Abuhoff/10.60%, Insiders/14.70%, Todd Solomon/9.60%, Haig S. Bagerdjian, Eliot Rose Asset Management/9.10%, Peter Woodward

Financial Data: *Fiscal Year End:* 12/31 *Latest Annual Data:* 12/31/2006

Year	Sales	Net Income
2006	$40,953,000	-$7,323,000
2005	$42,052,000	-$1,651,000
2004	$53,949,000	$7,857,000

Curr. Assets:	$22,922,000	**Curr. Liab.:**	$9,290,000		
Plant, Equip.:	$4,564,000	**Total Liab.:**	$11,320,000	**Indic. Yr. Divd.:**	NA
Total Assets:	$30,329,000	**Net Worth:**	$19,009,000	**Debt/ Equity:**	NA

Innofone.Com Inc

1431 Ocean Ave., Ste. 1500, Santa Monica, CA, 90401; ***PH:*** 1-310-458-3233; ***Fax:*** 1-310-458-2844; ***http://*** www.innofone.com; ***Email:*** info@innofone.com

General - Incorporation	NV	**Stock** - Price on:12/24/2007	NA
Employees	16	Stock Exchange	OTC
Auditor	De Joya Griffith & Co LLC	Ticker Symbol	IMEN
Stk Agt	Interwest Transfer Company, Inc.	Outstanding Shares	NA
Counsel	NA	E.P.S	NA
DUNS No.	NA	Shareholders	NA

Business: The group's principal activity is to operate as holding company for companies that are involved in the procurement, refurbishing and remarketing of used electronic equipment with a focus on used computer equipment. The group is actively seeking new investment opportunities in creating and or acquiring assets involved in this niche market. The group's sole subsidiary, plans to specialize in the disassembly and international distribution of used/refurbished, end of line new personal computers, servers, peripherals and components.

Primary SIC and add'l.: 7378

CIK No: 0001100364

Subsidiaries: IPv6 Summit, Inc.

Officers: Alex Lightman/Chmn., CEO, CFO, Pres., Jim Bacchus/VP - Consulting, Gerard Casale/VP - Business, Legal Affairs, Michael Ambrose/38/Sec.

Directors: Alex Lightman/Chmn., CEO, CFO, Pres., Peter Maddocks/Dir., Irving Aronson/Dir.

Owners: Abbey International Holdings, Ltd./21.78%, Gerard Casale/1.61%, Insiders/40.64%, Paul Shepherd/0.13%, Cogent Capital Investments LLC/9.33%, Alex Lightman/38.57%, Peter Maddocks/0.33%

Curr. Assets:	$344,000	**Curr. Liab.:**	$3,180,000		
Plant, Equip.:	$16,000	**Total Liab.:**	$6,749,000	**Indic. Yr. Divd.:**	NA
Total Assets:	$53,043,000	**Net Worth:**	$46,293,000	**Debt/ Equity:**	NA

Innophos Holdings Inc

259 Prospect Plains Rd., Cranbury, NJ, 08512; ***PH:*** 1-609-495-2495; ***Fax:*** 1-609-860-0138; ***http://*** www.innophos.com; ***Email:*** customerservice@innophos.com

General - Incorporation		**Stock** - Price on:12/24/2007	$14.08
Employees	1,101	Stock Exchange	NDQ
Auditor	Pricewaterhousecoopers LLP	Ticker Symbol	IPHS
Stk Agt	Wells Fargo Bank Minnesota N.A	Outstanding Shares	20,780,000
Counsel	NA	E.P.S	-$0.36
DUNS No.	NA	Shareholders	NA

Business: The groups principal activity is to produce specialty phosphates. The products of the group include Tricalcium Phosphate, Sodium Acid PyroPhosphate, Monocalcium Phosphate and Ammonium Phosphates. Customers served by the group include goods manufacturers, distributors and specialty chemical manufacturers. The group operates through three segments namely the United States, Mexico and Canada. Specific customer of the group is AvGard(TM). The group operates from the United States, Mexico and Canada. Of the net sale in the year 2006, United States accounted for $318,105, Mexico $194,639 and Canada $29,053.

Primary SIC and add'l.: 2819

CIK No: 0001364099

Subsidiaries: Innophos Fosfatados, Innophos Investments Holdings, Inc

Officers: Randy Gress/Chmn., CEO, Pres., Richard Heyse/CFO, VP, Mark Feuerbach/VP - Treasury, Financial Planning, Analysis, William Farran/VP, General Counsel, Tim Treinen/VP - Performance Chemicals, Mark Thurston/VP - Specialties, Louis Calvarin/VP - Operations, Wilma Harris/VP - Human Resources, Joseph Golowski/VP - Sales, Distribution, Charles Brodheim/Corporate Controller, Jose Ramon Gonzalez/General Dir. - Innophos Mexicana SA de CV, Alfredo Celis Toussaint/Dir. - Finance, Innophos Mexicana SA de CV

Directors: Randy Gress/Chmn., CEO, Pres., Gary Cappeline/Dir., Edward Conard/51/Dir., Stephen Zide/Dir., Blair Hendrix/42/Dir., Linda Myrick/Dir., Karen Osar/Dir.

Owners: Bain Capital Investors, LLC/48.60%, Silver Point Capital, L.P./6.00%, Jose Gonzales, Insiders/6.30%, Joseph Golowski, JANA Partners, LLC/5.90%, William N. Farran, Richard Heyse, Ivory Investment Management, L.P./7.20%, Randolph Gress/1.30%

Financial Data: *Fiscal Year End:* NA *Latest Annual Data:* 12/31/2006

Year	Sales	Net Income
2006	$541,797,000	-$32,817,000

Curr. Assets:	$172,297,000	**Curr. Liab.:**	$72,603,000		
Plant, Equip.:	$277,222,000	**Total Liab.:**	$504,608,000	**Indic. Yr. Divd.:**	$0.680
Total Assets:	$565,320,000	**Net Worth:**	$60,712,000	**Debt/ Equity:**	6.9256

Innospec Inc

Formerly: Octel Corp

Innospec Manufacturing Pk., Oil Sites Rd., Ellesmere Port, CH65 4EY; ***PH:*** 44-151-355-3611; ***http://*** www.innospecinc.com

General - Incorporation	DE	**Stock** - Price on:12/24/2007	$59.65
Employees	774	Stock Exchange	NA
Auditor	PricewaterhouseCoopers LLP	Ticker Symbol	NA
Stk Agt	First Chicago Trust Co of New York	Outstanding Shares	12,010,000
Counsel	Kirkland & Ellis LLP	E.P.S	$0.71
DUNS No.	76-935-4276	Shareholders	NA

Business: The group's principal activities are to manufacture and distribute fuel additives and other specialty chemicals. The group operates in two segments : tel (tetraethyl lead) and specialty chemicals. Tel is used for the internal combustion engines to boost octane levels in gasoline and it also acts as a lubricity aid, reducing engine wear. Specialty chemicals comprises of petroleum specialties and performance chemicals. The petroleum specialties business develops, produces and markets a range of specialty products, used as fuel additives, derived from the tel operations. Performance chemicals business develops products for detergent market, personal care, paper and photographics. The manufacturing operations of the group are located at ellesmere port, south wirral, United Kingdom. The products are sold globally and are basically to oil refineries. The group acquired leuna polymer gmbh in 2004. On 26-Aug-2004, the group acquired aroma & fine chemicals ltd.

Primary SIC and add'l.: 5169 2819

CIK No: 0001054905

Subsidiaries: AK Chemie GMBH, Alcor Chemie AG, Alcor Chemie Vertriebs GmbH, Aroma& Fine Chemicals Limited, Associated Octel Company (PTY) Limited, CP35500 International Limited, Finetex Inc., Gamlen Industries SA, Leuna Polymer GmbH, Novoktan GmbH, Octel America Inc, Octel Developments Plc, Octel Environmental Limited, Octel Exhaust Systems Limited, Octel Finance Limited 24 Subsidiaries included in the Index

Officers: Paul W. Jennings/Dir., CEO, Pres./$1,520,952.00, Andrew Hartley/VP, General Counsel, Richard Shone/VP - Safety - Health & Environmental, Patrick S. Williams/Exec. VP, Pres. - Fuel Specialties/$1,036,162.00, Ian Cleminson/CFO, Exec. VP/$329,936.00, Cathy Hessner/Sr. VP - Human Resources/$559,481.00, Ian McRobbie/CTO, Sr. VP/$736,239.00

Directors: Paul W. Jennings/Dir., CEO, Pres., Robert E. Bew/Non Exec. Chmn., Hugh G C Aldous/Non Exec. Dir., Charles M. Hale/Non Exec. Dir., Samuel A. Haubold/Non Exec. Dir., James M C Puckridge/Non Exec. Dir., Martin M. Hale/Non Exec. Dir.

Owners: H. Aldous, I. Cleminson, Tontine Capital Partners, LP/18.22%, J. Puckridge, Barclays Global Investors, NA/5.20%, M. Hale, R. E. Bew, C. Hale/1.04%, FMR Corp./11.51%, Insiders/3.22%, C. Hessner, P. W. Jennings, I. McRobbie, T. Rowe Price Associates, Inc./14.43%, S. Haubold *(16 Owners included in Index)*

Financial Data: *Fiscal Year End:* 12/31 *Latest Annual Data:* 12/31/2006

Year	Sales	Net Income
2006	$532,100,000	$11,400,000
2005	$527,700,000	-$123,700,000
2004	$480,500,000	$6,200,000

Curr. Assets:	$305,300,000	**Curr. Liab.:**	$142,900,000	**P/E Ratio:**	65.55
Plant, Equip.:	$66,500,000	**Total Liab.:**	$344,000,000	**Indic. Yr. Divd.:**	$0.090
Total Assets:	$569,000,000	**Net Worth:**	$225,000,000	**Debt/ Equity:**	0.5911

Innotrac Corp

6655 Sugarloaf Pkwy., Duluth, GA, 30097; ***PH:*** 1-678-584-4000; ***Fax:*** 1-678-475-5840; ***http://*** www.innotrac.com

General - Incorporation	GA	**Stock** - Price on:12/24/2007	$3.94
Employees	1,300	Stock Exchange	NDQ
Auditor	BDO Seidman, LLP	Ticker Symbol	INOC
Stk Agt	Suntrust Bank	Outstanding Shares	12,280,000
Counsel	Kilpatrick Stockton	E.P.S	-$0.19
DUNS No.	12-094-3535	Shareholders	NA

Business: The group's principal activities are to provide technology based marketing services to companies in a variety of industry verticals. The services provided include project management, system integration, electronic data transfer, inventory management, database management, business rules management, order processing, payment processing, product, literature and point-of-purchase fulfillment, kitting and assembly, reverse logistics, and customer care services. The group operates in the United States of America. Major customers include bellsouth corporation, books are fun - a reader's digest company, the coca-cola company, comcast, martha stewart living omnimedia, napa, nordstrom, porsche cars North America, qwest communications, smith and hawken, thane international, wilsonsleather.

Primary SIC and add'l.: 8742

CIK No: 0001051114

Officers: Scott Dorfman/50/Chmn., CEO, Pres./$378,790.00, Jim McMurphy/CIO, Sr. VP/$300,399.00, Larry Hanger/Sr. VP - Client Services/$210,831.00, Robert Toner/Sr. VP - Logistics/$300,797.00, Dena J. Rosenzweig/Sec., General Counsel, Sandy Probst/VP - Sales, Tony Laguna/Sr. Dir. - Call Center Operations, Dan Reeves/Direct Response, Catalog, E, Commerce Markets, Chrissy Herren/Investor Relations Contact, Brooke Thornton/Contact

Directors: Scott Dorfman/50/Chmn., CEO, Pres.

Owners: James R. McMurphy, Thomas J. Marano, Joel E. Marks, Christine A. Herren, Robert J. Toner, Bruce V. Benator/1.10%, Larry C. Hanger/1.40%, Scott D. Dorfman/45.40%, Martin J. Blank/1.20%, IPOF Group/34.00%, Insiders/48.80%

Financial Data: *Fiscal Year End:* 12/31 *Latest Annual Data:* 12/31/2006

Year	Sales	Net Income
2006	$82,343,000	-$5,262,000
2005	$73,892,000	-$4,668,000
2004	$78,322,000	$110,000

Curr. Assets:	$26,770,000	**Curr. Liab.:**	$27,930,000		
Plant, Equip.:	$17,836,000	**Total Liab.:**	$29,506,000	**Indic. Yr. Divd.:**	NA
Total Assets:	$71,540,000	**Net Worth:**	$42,034,000	**Debt/ Equity:**	NA

Innova Pure Water Inc

13130 56th Ct., Ste. 605, Clearwater, FL, 33760; ***PH:*** 1-813-572-1000; ***http://*** www.innovapurewater.com

General - Incorporation	FL	**Stock** - Price on:12/24/2007	$0.06
Employees	NA	Stock Exchange	OTC
Auditor	Turner, Stone & Co. LLP	Ticker Symbol	IPURE
Stk Agt	Continental Stock Transfer & Trust Co	Outstanding Shares	NA
Counsel	Bush, Ross, Gardner, Warren & Rudy	E.P.S	NA
DUNS No.	15-171-4276	Shareholders	NA

Business: The group's principal activity is to design, develop, manufacture and market consumer water filtration and treatment products. The product is of portable nature and consists of a container serving as a water reservoir incorporating water filtering and treatment technology. The water filtration products of the group are designed to provide an improved quality and much better tasting water for the average consumer at an affordable price. The products are primarily designed to treat tap water, reduce chlorine, lead, taste and odor. The customer base for the group's products consists of many major mass merchants, grocery, drug and departmental store retailers as well as hardware and home centers. The products are marketed via television and print media. The group develops filtration products for the removal of biological contaminants including protozoa, cysts and bacteria.

Primary SIC and add'l.: 3589

CIK No: 0000791994

Subsidiaries: DesertView, Numera

Officers: John Thatch/Dir., CEO, Pres.

Directors: John Thatch/Dir., CEO, Pres.

Owners: David Paul Condra, David L. Zich/2.50%, John L. Finan, Jim R. Davisson, John E. Nohren/11.70%, Insiders/24.60%, Randal McClanahan/1.50%, Rose C. Smith/8.40%

Innova Robotics & Automation Inc

15870 Pine Ridge Rd. , Unit 3, Fort Meyers, FL, 33908; *PH:* 1-239-466-0488;
http:// www.innovaholdings.com

General - Incorporation	DE	Stock- Price on:12/24/2007	$0.056
Employees	NA	Stock Exchange	OTC
Auditor	Lopez, Bork & Associates, LLP	Ticker Symbol	INRA
Stk Agt	Continental Stock Transfer & Trust Co	Outstanding Shares	82,510,000
Counsel	NA	E.P.S.	-$0.02
DUNS No.	NA	Shareholders	NA

Business: The groups principal activity is to provide open architecture PC motion control solutions and hardware and software systems based solutions. Customers served by the group include military, service, personal, and industrial robotic companies. The group operates from North America.

Primary SIC and add'l.: 5045

CIK No: 0001156784

Subsidiaries: Innova Robotics, Inc., Robotic Workspace Technologies, Inc.

Officers: Walter K. Weisel/Chmn., CEO, Eugene V. Gartlan/Executive Dir. - Strategic Development, Sheri Aws/VP, Sandra Brooks/Marketing Counsel, Incomm International, Inc

Directors: Walter K. Weisel/Chmn., CEO

Owners: Martin Nielson/4.48%, Eugene V. Gartlan/6.44%, Gary McNear/2.22%, Walter K. Weisel/8.09%, Jerry Horne/7.15%, Insiders/34.13%, Sheri Aws, Lloyd Spencer, Johanna Wynns/3.87%, John Kroon, Chuck House, Craig Conklin/2.75%

Financial Data: *Fiscal Year End:*12/31 *Latest Annual Data:* 12/31/2006

Year	Sales	Net Income
2006	$1,340,000	-$5,607,000
2005	NA	-$1,881,000
2004	NA	-$1,427,000

Curr. Assets:	$736,000	Curr. Liab.:	$5,167,000		
Plant, Equip.:	$156,000	Total Liab.:	$6,276,000	Indic. Yr. Divd.:	NA
Total Assets:	$1,837,000	Net Worth:	-$4,439,000	Debt/ Equity:	NA

Innova Robotics and Automation Inc

Formerly: Innova Holdings Inc
15870 Pine Ridge Rd. , Unit 3, For Mayers, FL, 33908; *PH:* 1-239-466-0488;
http:// www.innovaholdings.com

General - Incorporation	DE	Stock- Price on:12/24/2007	NA
Employees	NA	Stock Exchange	NA
Auditor	Lopez, Blevins, Bork & Assoc. LLP	Ticker Symbol	NA
Stk Agt	Stock Transfer, LLC	Outstanding Shares	NA
Counsel	NA	E.P.S.	-$0.06
DUNS No.	NA	Shareholders	NA

Business: The group's principal activity is to supply computer systems, components and peripherals to computer professionals. The products of the group include desktops, notebooks and servers, computer storage products and computer warranty work. On 28-Apr-2003 the group acquired sanjay haryama.

Primary SIC and add'l.: 7379 3577 5045

CIK No: 0001156784

Subsidiaries: Innova Robotics, Inc, Robotic Workspace Technologies, Inc

Officers: Eugene V. Gartlan/CEO, Sheri Aws/VP, Corp. Sec., Walter K. Weisel/Pres. - Robotic Workspace Technologies, Innova Robotics

Directors: Martin Nielson/Chmn., Sheri Aws/VP, Corp. Sec., Gary F. McNear/63/Dir., Craig W. Conklin/58/Dir., Richard Wynns/62/Dir.

Owners: Lloyd Spencer, Sheri Aws, John Kroon, Craig Conklin/2.75%, Richard K. Wynns/3.87%, Insiders/34.13%, Martin Nielson/4.48%, Gary McNear/2.22%, Eugene V. Gartlan/6.44%, Walter K. Weisel/8.09%, Chuck House, Jerry Horne/7.15%

Financial Data: *Fiscal Year End:*12/31 *Latest Annual Data:* 12/31/2006

Year	Sales	Net Income
2006	$1,340,000	-$5,607,000
2005	NA	-$1,881,000
2004	NA	-$1,427,000

Curr. Assets:	$736,000	Curr. Liab.:	$5,167,000		
Plant, Equip.:	$156,000	Total Liab.:	$6,276,000	Indic. Yr. Divd.:	NA
Total Assets:	$1,837,000	Net Worth:	-$4,439,000	Debt/ Equity:	NA

Innovative Card Technologies Inc

10880 Wilshire Blvd., Ste. 950, Los Angeles, CA, 90024; *PH:* 1-310-312-0700;
Fax: 1-310-312-5367; *http://* www.incardtech.com; *Email:* info@incardtech.com

General - Incorporation	DE	Stock- Price on:12/24/2007	NA
Employees	NA	Stock Exchange	NDQ
Auditor ... Singer Lewak Greenbaum & Goldstein		Ticker Symbol	INVC
Stk Agt	American Stock Transfer & Trust Co.	Outstanding Shares	NA
Counsel	NA	E.P.S.	-$0.43
DUNS No.	NA	Shareholders	NA

Business: The groups principle activities include developing and marketing powered cards for payment, identification, and physical and logical access applications. The product of the group is ICT DisplayCard. The group operates from the United States.

Primary SIC and add'l.: 3674

CIK No: 0001300578

Subsidiaries: LensCard International Limited, LensCard US LLC, PSACo., Inc.

Officers: Steven R. Delcarson/CEO, Pres., Jose Castaneda/Investor Relations Contact, Alan Finkelstein/Founder, Dir., Chief Strategic Officer, Bennet P. Tchaikovsky/CFO

Directors: Donald Joyce/Chmn., George W. Hoover/Dir., John A. Ward/Dir., Alan Finkelstein/Founder, Dir., Chief Strategic Officer, Scott V. Ogilvie/Dir., Robert W. Ramsdell/Dir.

Owners: Robert W. Ramsdell/1.20%, Donald Joyce, nCryptone, S.A./14.70%, Charles Caporale, John A. Ward/1.80%, George Hoover, Insiders/17.00%, Alan Finkelstein/10.50%, Bradley Ross/6.10%, Steven Delcarson/3.40%

Financial Data: *Fiscal Year End:*12/31 *Latest Annual Data:* 12/31/2006

Year	Sales	Net Income
2006	$35,000	-$6,867,000
2005	$21,000	-$2,565,000

Curr. Assets:	$10,626,000	Curr. Liab.:	$2,131,000		
Plant, Equip.:	$361,000	Total Liab.:	$2,131,000	Indic. Yr. Divd.:	NA
Total Assets:	$14,724,000	Net Worth:	$12,593,000	Debt/ Equity:	NA

Innovative Designs Inc

6224 31st St. E., Bradenton, FL, 34203; *PH:* 1-941-752-7779; *Fax:* 1-941-752-7710;
http:// www.innovativedesignsinc.net

General - Incorporation	DE	Stock- Price on:12/24/2007	NA
Employees	4	Stock Exchange	OTC
Auditor	Louis Plung & Co. LLP	Ticker Symbol	IVDNQ
Stk Agt	NA	Outstanding Shares	NA
Counsel	NA	E.P.S.	NA
DUNS No.	NA	Shareholders	NA

Business: The groups principle activities include designing, manufacturing and marketing warmth and comfort products with insulating, windproof and water resistant protection. The groups product line includes Arctic Armor Camo Jacket, Arctic Armor Red Jacket, Arctic Armor Gloves, Arctic Armor Camo Bibs, Arctic Armor Red Bibs, NBU Pants and Tom Nelson Bomber Jacket. The group operates from United States.

Primary SIC and add'l.: NA

CIK No: 0001190370

Officers: Joseph Riccelli/Chmn., CEO, David G. Miller/Sales Representative, Pennsylvania, Chris Chudzy/Sales Representative, Saskatchewan, Manitoba, Canada, Anthony Fonzi/59/Dir., CFO, Joseph A. Riccelli/26/VP, Nathaan Havelaar/Sales Representative - California, John Eigen/Sales Representative - Idaho, Tom Whitehead/Sales Representative - Minnesota, Justin Porlier/Sales Representative - Kentucky, David G. Miller/Sales Representative - Pennsylvania, Ron Steigerwalt/Sales Representative - Pennsylvania, Layton S. Lyon/Sales Representative - Pennsylvania, Kirk Necciai/Sales Representative - Pennsylvania, Joe Miller/Sales Representative - Pennsylvania, Richard Price/Sales Representative - Pennsylvania *(23 Officers included in Index)*

Directors: Joseph Riccelli/Chmn., CEO, Anthony Fonzi/59/Dir., CFO, Dean P. Kolocouris/35/Dir., Robert D. Monsour/53/Dir.

Owners: Gregory P. Domian/0.06%, Insiders/66.25%, Joseph A. Riccelli Trust/1.48%, Joseph Riccelli/59.76%, Anthony Fonzi/0.12%, Dean P. Kolocouris/0.16%, Robert D. Monsour/0.24%

Curr. Assets:	$1,088,000	Curr. Liab.:	$4,822,000		
Plant, Equip.:	$20,000	Total Liab.:	$5,248,000	Indic. Yr. Divd.:	NA
Total Assets:	$1,109,000	Net Worth:	-$4,140,000	Debt/ Equity:	NA

Innovative Solutions & Support Inc

720 Pennsylvania Dr., Exton, PA, 19341; *PH:* 1-610-646-9800; *Fax:* 1-610-646-0149;
http:// www.innovative-ss.com; *Email:* burbanski@innovative-ss.com

General - Incorporation	PA	Stock- Price on:12/24/2007	$24.85
Employees	138	Stock Exchange	NDQ
Auditor	Deloitte & Touche LLP	Ticker Symbol	ISSC
Stk Agt	NA	Outstanding Shares	16,880,000
Counsel	NA	E.P.S.	-$0.34
DUNS No.	NA	Shareholders	NA

Business: The group's principal activities are to design, manufacture and sell avionic electronic products used by various aviation markets during the operation of aircrafts. The products consist of flight information computers, electronic displays and monitoring systems. The group's products are supplied to the military, government, commercial air and corporate aviation market. The engine and fuel data display systems product line is useful to check the fuel and oil levels, engine activities, temperature and liquid oxygen levels. The flat panel display systems product line (the cockpit information portal) displays additional information such as weather radar and ground terrain maps.

Primary SIC and add'l.: 3823 3812

CIK No: 0000836690

Officers: Geoffrey S.M. Hedrick/Chmn., CEO, Shahram Askarpour/VP - Engineering, Brian Urbanski/VP - Quality, James J. Reilly/CFO, Roman G. Ptakowski/Pres., Susan Maggetti/Human Resources Generalist, Farhad Daghigh/Dir. - Military Marketing, Robert M. Hyland/VP - Operations, Fred Phelan/Sales Mgr. Commercial - Air Transport, Peter Robinson/Sales Mgr. - International

Directors: Geoffrey S.M. Hedrick/Chmn., CEO, Raymound J. Wilson/62/Dir.

Owners: Insiders/26.60%, Winston J. Churchill, Robert H. Rau, Glen R. Bressner, James J. Reilly, Roman G. Ptakowski/1.10%, Ivan M. Marks, Geoffrey S. M. Hedrick/23.70%, Robert E. Mittelstaedt, State Teachers Retirement System of Ohio/13.50%, Putnam Investment Management/5.80%, Federated Investors, Inc./15.40%

Financial Data: *Fiscal Year End:*09/30 *Latest Annual Data:* 9/30/2006

Year	Sales	Net Income
2006	$16,722,000	-$2,882,000
2005	$63,264,000	$18,585,000
2004	$46,100,000	$11,932,000

Curr. Assets:	$77,933,000	Curr. Liab.:	$4,181,000			
Plant, Equip.:	$8,970,000	Total Liab.:	$9,032,000	Indic. Yr. Divd.:	NA	
Total Assets:	$87,233,000	Net Worth:	$78,201,000	Debt/ Equity:	0.0572	

Innovex Inc

3033 Campus Dr., Ste. E180, Plymouth, MN, 55441; *PH:* 1-763-383-4000; *Fax:* 1-763-383-4091; *http://* www.innovexinc.com; *Email:* info@innovexinc.com

General - Incorporation	MN	Stock- Price on:12/24/2007	$1.63
Employees	3,582	Stock Exchange	NDQ
Auditor	Grant Thornton LLP	Ticker Symbol	INVX
Stk Agt	Wells Fargo Shareowner Services	Outstanding Shares	19,390,000
Counsel	Lindquist & Vennum PLLP	E.P.S.	-$1.05
DUNS No.	05-709-3734	Shareholders	NA

Business: The group's principal activity is to provide flexible circuit interconnect solutions to original equipment manufacturers (OEMs) in the electronics industry. The group offers customized flexible circuit applications and services from initial design, development and prototype to fabrication, assembly and test on a global basis. These components are used in the computer, data storage, consumer, medical, telecommunications and other electronic industries. Its major customers include maxtor, medtronic, philips, quantum, samsung, seagate, staktek, 3m, dell, hitachi, hp and xerox. The group operates in the United States, Europe and the Pacific Rim.

Primary SIC and add'l.: 3679 3674 3572 5731

CIK No: 0000050601

Subsidiaries: ADFlex Cayman Ltd., ADFlex Mexico S.A. de C.V., ADFlex Solutions Ltd., Iconovex Corporation, Innovex (Thailand) Ltd., Innovex Limited, Innovex Precision Components, Inc., Innovex Southwest, Inc., Mar Engineering, Inc.

Officers: William P. Murnane/46/Chmn., COO, CEO, Pres., C. C. Low/Sales Representative - Singapore, Dave Ring/Sales Representative - Thailand, Lloyd Lo/Sales Representative - Taiwan, Simon Jefferson/Sales Representative - Swindon, Matthew R. Heim/Sales Representative - California, Principal Engineer Mechanical Design - Application Engineering, Ki Lim/Sales Representative - Korea, Alpha Ko/Sales Representative - Hong Kong

Directors: William P. Murnane/46/Chmn., COO, CEO, Pres., Allen D. Andersen/Dir., Robert Buhrmaster/54/Dir., Philip D. Ankeny/45/Dir., Kenneth J. Roering/66/Dir.

Owners: Thomas E. Atchison, Allen D. Andersen, Terry M. Dauenhauer/1.20%, William P. Murnane/1.80%, Kenneth J. Roering, Philip D. Ankeny, Robert C. Buhrmaster, Insiders/6.00%, Keith Foerster, Dimensional Fund Advisors LP/6.50%, Potomac Capital Management, LLC/9.30%, Douglas W. Keller

Financial Data: Fiscal Year End:09/30 Latest Annual Data: 9/30/2006

Year	Sales	Net Income
2006	$173,144,000	-$16,970,000
2005	$200,247,000	-$24,987,000
2004	$155,946,000	-$17,496,000

Curr. Assets:	$38,525,000	Curr. Liab.:	$28,858,000		
Plant, Equip.:	$51,560,000	Total Liab.:	$48,658,000	Indic. Yr. Divd.:	NA
Total Assets:	$94,167,000	Net Worth:	$45,509,000	Debt/ Equity:	0.7404

Innovive Pharmaceuticals Inc

555 Madison Ave. Fl 25, New York, NY, 10022; *PH:* 1-212-716-1810; *http://* www.innovivepharma.com; *Email:* info@innovivepharma.com

General - Incorporation	DE	Stock- Price on:12/24/2007	$3.7
Employees	9	Stock Exchange	OTC
Auditor	J.H. Cohn, LLP	Ticker Symbol	IVPH
Stk Agt	Wells Fargo Shareowner Services	Outstanding Shares	17,660,000
Counsel	NA	E.P.S.	-$2.48
DUNS No.	NA	Shareholders	NA

Business: The group's principal activities include biopharmaceutical development and commercialization of compounds for the treatment of cancer. Its three main business segments: acquire, develop and commercialize novel therapeutics in oncology and hematology. INNO-105 is the first drug in the company's portfolio, it has potential applications in multiple tumor types and believe brings significant advantages above the standard of care for certain cancerous conditions. In December, 2005, the group enrolled the first patients in a Phase I clinical trial of INNO-105 in adult patients with advanced solid malignancies. The objectives of the trial are to determine safety, dose, pharmacokinetic profile and its preliminary efficacy. In addition, the group also intends to leverage the development infrastructure & expect to build during the development of INNO-105 by acquiring and developing additional clinical candidates in the areas of oncology and hematology.

Primary SIC and add'l.: 2834

CIK No: 0001337223

Officers: Steven Kelly/Dir., CEO, Pres., Adam Craig/Chief Medical Officer, VP, Eric E. Poma/VP - Business Development, Gregory J. Jester/CFO, VP

Directors: Steven Kelly/Dir., CEO, Pres., Jay J. Lobell/Dir., Antony Pfaffle/Dir., Angelo De Caro/Dir., Philip Frost/Dir., Neil Herskowitz/Dir., Peter A. Jones/Member - Scientific Advisory Board, Alan F. List/Member - Scientific Advisory Board, Edward A. Sausville/Member - Scientific Advisory Board, Howard I. Scher/Member - Scientific Advisory Board, Daniel D. Von Hoff/Member - Scientific Advisory Board

Owners: Lester Lipschutz/9.56%, Steven Kelly/1.08%, Adam R. Craig, Insiders/3.60%, Lindsay A. Rosenwald/10.19%, Eric Poma, Neil Herskowitz, Jay J. Lobell/1.12%, Angelo De Caro

Financial Data: Fiscal Year End:12/31 Latest Annual Data: 12/31/2006

Year	Sales	Net Income
2006	NA	-$16,690,000

Curr. Assets:	$4,162,000	Curr. Liab.:	$2,832,000		
Plant, Equip.:	$20,000	Total Liab.:	$2,832,000	Indic. Yr. Divd.:	NA
Total Assets:	$4,288,000	Net Worth:	$1,456,000	Debt/ Equity:	NA

InnSuites Hospitality Trust

Innsuites Hotel Ctr., 1625 East Northern Ave., Ste. 102, Phoenix, AZ, 85020; *PH:* 1-602-944-1500; *Fax:* 1-602-678-0281; *http://* www.innSte.strust.com

General - Incorporation	OH	Stock- Price on:12/24/2007	$1.6
Employees	422	Stock Exchange	AMEX
Auditor	Moss Adams LLP	Ticker Symbol	IHT
Stk Agt	NA	Outstanding Shares	9,190,000
Counsel	NA	E.P.S.	$0.10
DUNS No.	NA	Shareholders	NA

Business: The groups principle activities include owning and operating hotel properties. The group operates from the United States. The groups quarterly revenue for September 2007 was 5.51 millions of USD.

Primary SIC and add'l.: 7011

CIK No: 0000082473

Subsidiaries: Albuquerque Suite Hospitality LLC, InnSuites Hotels, Inc, Ontario Hospitality Properties Limited Partnership, RRF Limited Partnership, Tucson Hospitality Properties, Ltd, Tucson St. Marys Suite Hospitality LLC, Yuma Hospitality Properties, Ltd

Officers: James F. Wirth/61/Chmn., CEO, Pres./$146,860.00, Marc E. Berg/55/Trustee, Exec. VP, Sec., Treasurer/$104,674.00, Anthony B. Waters/60/CFO/$157,044.00, James D. Green/Dir. - Operations

Directors: James F. Wirth/61/Chmn., CEO, Pres., Marc E. Berg/55/Trustee, Exec. VP, Sec., Treasurer, Larry Pelegrin/69/Trustee, Steven S. Robson/51/Trustee, Peter A. Thoma/40/Trustee

Owners: Larry Pelegrin, Anthony B. Waters, Insiders/65.10%, Steven S. Robson/2.50%, Marc E. Berg, Peter A. Thoma

Financial Data: Fiscal Year End:01/31 Latest Annual Data: 1/31/2007

Year	Sales	Net Income
2007	$21,791,000	-$46,000
2006	$21,249,000	$542,000
2005	$22,875,000	$240,000

Curr. Assets:	NA	Curr. Liab.:	NA	P/E Ratio:	53.33
Plant, Equip.:	NA	Total Liab.:	NA	Indic. Yr. Divd.:	$0.010
Total Assets:	NA	Net Worth:	NA	Debt/ Equity:	2.6918

Innuity Inc

8644 154th Ave. NE, Redmond, WA, 98052; *PH:* 1-425-497-9909; *Fax:* 1-425-497-0409; *http://* innuity.com

General - Incorporation	UT	Stock- Price on:12/24/2007	$0.3
Employees	170	Stock Exchange	OTC
Auditor	Hansen, Barnett & Maxwell P.C.	Ticker Symbol	INNU
Stk Agt	Standard Registrar & Transfer Co Inc.	Outstanding Shares	29,030,000
Counsel	NA	E.P.S.	-$0.22
DUNS No.	NA	Shareholders	NA

Business: The groups principle activities include designing, acquiring and integrating software applications to deliver solutions for small business. In June 2005, the group acquired 10x Marketing LLC. The group operates through two segments namely promotion and commerce. The group operates from the United States.

Primary SIC and add'l.: 7371 7379 7389 7389 7374 7373 8742 7371 7379 8748 8748 7374 7372 7373 8742

CIK No: 0001103645

Subsidiaries: Jadeon, Inc., Vista.com Inc.

Officers: John Wall/Chmn., CEO, Linden Barney/CFO, John Dennis/Dir., Pres., Marvin Mall/Dir., COO, Shivonne Byrne/Chief Marketing Officer/$389,312.00, Jim Crisera/Pres. - Promotion Division, Doug Merryman/Pres. - Merchant Services Business Line, Stephen Ferrante/Pres. - In, Store Systems Business Line/$279,196.00, Mark Lemay/Exec. VP - Vertical Markets, Robyn Farnsworth/Executive Assist. - Investor Relations

Directors: John Wall/Chmn., CEO, Greg Stevenson/Dir., John Dennis/Dir., Pres., Marvin Mall/Dir., COO, Keith Cannon/Dir., Harold Kawaguchi/Dir.

Owners: Harold H. Kawaguchi/1.30%, Marvin A. Mall/5.60%, Mark A. LeMay/9.90%, Insiders/42.40%, John R. Dennis/6.10%, Greg M. Stevenson, Keith A. Cannon/1.60%

Financial Data: Fiscal Year End:12/31 Latest Annual Data: 12/31/2006

Year	Sales	Net Income
2006	$21,684,000	-$8,474,000
2005	$12,466,000	-$9,366,000
2004	$65,000	$4,000

Curr. Assets:	$2,938,000	Curr. Liab.:	$10,222,000		
Plant, Equip.:	$901,000	Total Liab.:	$10,923,000	Indic. Yr. Divd.:	NA
Total Assets:	$7,343,000	Net Worth:	-$3,580,000	Debt/ Equity:	NA

Inova Technology Inc

Formerly: Edgetech Services Inc
233 Wilshire Blvd., Ste. 400, Santa Monica, CA, 90401; *PH:* 1-800-757-9808; *http://* www.edgetechservices.com

General - Incorporation	NV	Stock- Price on:12/24/2007	NA
Employees	2	Stock Exchange	NA
Auditor	Malone & Bailey, P.C	Ticker Symbol	NA
Stk Agt	Nevada Agency & Trust Company	Outstanding Shares	NA
Counsel	NA	E.P.S.	NA
DUNS No.	NA	Shareholders	NA

Business: The group's principal activity is to provide security services and it solutions and services. The group is a business solutions provider specializing in information technology (IT) security, enterprise resource planning (erp) and knowledge based systems. It security is a complete end-to-end security services offering. It offers detailed security audits to risk analysis and full solutions. Erp provides a variety of services for the global erp market. The group operates principally in Canada.

Primary SIC and add'l.: 7372

CIK No: 0001088211

Subsidiaries: Edgetech Canada

Owners: Paul Aunger, Adam Radly

Inovio Biomedical Corp

11494 Sorrento Valley Rd., San Diego, CA, 92121; *PH:* 1-858-597-6006; *Fax:* 1-858-597-0451; *http://* www.inovio.com; *Email:* human.resources@inovio.com

General - Incorporation	DE
Employees	33
Auditor	Ernst & Young LLP
Stk Agt	Computershare Trust Co
Counsel	NA
DUNS No.	87-916-7674

Stock- Price on:12/24/2007	$2.8
Stock Exchange	AMEX
Ticker Symbol	INO
Outstanding Shares	38,820,000
E.P.S.	-$0.47
Shareholders	NA

Business: The group's principle activtity is to develop drug and gene delivery systems that uses electroporation therapy (ept) to deliver drugs and genes into cells. Ept is the application of brief, pulsed electric fields to cells, which causes tiny pores to temporarily open in the cell membrane. The group operates through two divisions: the drug and gene delivery division and the btx instrument division. The drug and gene delivery division develops drug delivery systems that are designed to use ept to enhance drug or gene delivery in the areas of oncology and gene therapy. The btx instrument division develops manufactures, and markets electroporation instrumentation and accessories used by scientists and researchers to perform genetic engineering techniques. The group sells the majority of its btx products to customers in the United States, Europe, and east Asia. The group's quarterly revenue for Sep'07 was 0.49 millions of USD.

Primary SIC and add'l.: 5912 5047

CIK No: 0001055726

Subsidiaries: Genetronics, Inc., Inovio AS

Officers: Avtar Dhillon/Dir., CEO, Pres./$898,446.00, Paul M. Goldfarb/Department, Surgery, University, California, San Diego, San Diego, CA, Advisor to all Programs, Peter Kies/CFO/$299,257.00, Dietmar Rabussay/VP - Research, Development/$256,315.00, Michael Fons/VP - Corporate Development

Directors: Avtar Dhillon/Dir., CEO, Pres., James L. Heppell/Co - Chmn., Felix Theeuwes/Dir., Bob Rieder/Dir., Robert W. Rieder/61/Dir., Riaz Bandali/Dir., Simon X. Benito/Dir., John Thompson/Member - Scientific Advisory Board, Arlene A. Forastiere/Member - Scientific Advisory Board, Tazdin Esmail/Dir., Daniel Von Hoff/Member - Scientific Advisory Board, Hubert T. Greenway/Member - Scientific Advisory Board, Robert S. Warren/Member - Scientific Advisory Board

Owners: Simon X. Benito, Tazdin Esmail, Insiders/4.39%, Zesiger Capital Group LLC/5.60%, Riaz Bandali, Peter Kies, Newton Investment Management Limited./4.99%, SDS Capital Group SPC, Ltd/7.37%, George McHugh, Felix Theeuwes, Dietmar Rabussa, James L. Heppell, Conus Partners,Inc./5.77%, Robert Goodenow, Avtar Dhillon/2.16%

Financial Data: Fiscal Year End:12/31   Latest Annual Data: 12/31/2006

Year	Sales	Net Income
2006	$3,468,000	-$12,479,000
2005	$5,467,000	-$15,297,000
2004	$1,167,000	-$10,973,000

Curr. Assets:	$24,472,000	Curr. Liab.:	$3,268,000		
Plant, Equip.:	$391,000	Total Liab.:	$8,907,000	Indic. Yr. Divd.:	NA
Total Assets:	$35,950,000	Net Worth:	$21,693,000	Debt/ Equity:	NA

InPhonic Inc

1010 Wisconsin Ave., Ste. 600, Washington, DC, 20007; *PH:* 1-202-333-0001; *Fax:* 1-202-333-5007; *http://* www.inphonic.com; *Email:* investor@inphonic.com

General - Incorporation	DE
Employees	NA
Auditor	Grant Thornton LLP
Stk Agt	American Stock Transfer & Trust Co.
Counsel	NA
DUNS No.	NA

Stock- Price on:12/24/2007	$6.63
Stock Exchange	OTC
Ticker Symbol	INPC
Outstanding Shares	36,960,000
E.P.S.	NA
Shareholders	NA

Business: The groups principle activity is to sale wireless services. The groups services include wireless activation, MVNE and data. The groups operates through three segments namely wireless activation and services, mobile virtual network enabler services, and data services. In the year 2005, the group acquired A1 Wireless USA, Inc and VMC Satellite, Inc. The group operates from the United States. The group's quarterly revenue for September 2007 was 79.42 millions of USD.

Primary SIC and add'l.: 4899 7378 7373 7371 7379 7389 7374 7376 7372 7375

CIK No: 0001133324

Officers: David A. Steinberg/38/Chmn., CEO/$1,980,560.00, Blake Bath/MD, Andy Zeinfeld/48/Pres./$627,701.00, Brian J. Curran/45/COO, Gary J. Smith/CIO, Frank C. Bennett/Chief Strategy Officer, Pres. - Mvno, Brian T. Westrick/Pres. - Wireless Activation, Services/$722,782.00, Michael E. Walden/38/Pres./$639,276.00, Walter W. Leach/Dir., General Counsel, Sec., Kenneth D. Schwarz/CFO, Gregory S. Cole/38/Sr. VP, Corporate Treasurer, George Z. Moratis/42/Exec. VP, Chief Accounting Officer

Directors: David A. Steinberg/38/Chmn., CEO, John Sculley/69/Vice Chmn., Ira Brind/Dir., Laurence E. Harris/72/Dir., Jack F. Kemp/72/Dir., Walter W. Leach/Dir., General Counsel, Sec.

Owners: Ira Brind, Blake Bath, Jack F. Kemp, FMR Corporation/10.60%, Insiders/18.80%, Brian T. Westrick, Thomas Wheeler, Trafelet& Company, LLC/6.90%, Lawrence S. Winkler/1.30%, John Sculley/1.20%, Michael Walden, Andrew B. Zeinfeld/1.10%, Laurence E. Harris, Brian J. Curran, The Goldman Sachs Group, Inc./13.80% *(19 Owners included in Index)*

Financial Data: Fiscal Year End:12/31   Latest Annual Data: 12/31/2006

Year	Sales	Net Income
2006	$369,574,000	-$63,727,000
2005	$320,539,000	-$38,195,000
2004	$204,200,000	-$10,239,000

Curr. Assets:	$186,976,000	Curr. Liab.:	$126,504,000		
Plant, Equip.:	$22,746,000	Total Liab.:	$190,808,000	Indic. Yr. Divd.:	NA
Total Assets:	$264,405,000	Net Worth:	$73,597,000	Debt/ Equity:	0.8672

InQBate Inc

Formerly: Games Inc
425 Walnut St., Ste 2300, Cincinnati, OH, 45202; *PH:* 1-513-721-3900; *Fax:* 1-513-721-6035; *http://* www.gamesinc.net; *Email:* info@sedo.co.uk

General - Incorporation	DE
Employees	16
Auditor	Marcum & Kliegman LLP
Stk Agt	Stock Transfer & Trust Co
Counsel	NA
DUNS No.	NA

Stock- Price on:12/24/2007	$0.1
Stock Exchange	OTC
Ticker Symbol	INQB
Outstanding Shares	3,130,000
E.P.S.	-$4.45
Shareholders	NA

Business: The group's principal activity is to provide subscribers with access to entertaining proprietary content via the Internet. The group's operates in three allied areas of interactive entertainment. The areas include government sponsored lotteries, Internet games and digital greetings. The group owns and operates games and entertainment sites such as cards.com, gameland.com, lottery.com and skillmoney.com.

Primary SIC and add'l.: 7999 7311

CIK No: 0001162093

Subsidiaries: Atari Inc, GameBanc Corporation

Financial Data: Fiscal Year End:06/30   Latest Annual Data: 6/30/2005

Year	Sales	Net Income
2005	$386,000	-$9,511,000
2004	$462,000	-$3,233,000
2003	$218,000	-$2,520,000

Curr. Assets:	$54,000	Curr. Liab.:	$8,318,000		
Plant, Equip.:	$89,000	Total Liab.:	$8,454,000	Indic. Yr. Divd.:	NA
Total Assets:	$335,000	Net Worth:	-$8,119,000	Debt/ Equity:	NA

InRob Tech Ltd

1515 Tropicana Ave., ste 140, Las Vegas, NV, 89119; *PH:* 1-702-795-3601; *Fax:* 1-972-89324334; *http://* www.inrobtech.com

General - Incorporation	NV
Employees	16
Auditor	Spector & Wong, LLP
Stk Agt	Depository Trust Co
Counsel	NA
DUNS No.	17-913-5389

Stock- Price on:12/24/2007	$0.185
Stock Exchange	OTC
Ticker Symbol	IRBL
Outstanding Shares	63,800,000
E.P.S.	-$0.03
Shareholders	NA

Business: The group's principle activity is to seek a new business opportunity through acquisitions or a merger. The group historically disseminated sports and news information directly to customers through band held pagers. On Apr 2001, the group sold its business and is currently seeking business oppturnities. The group operates from United States.

Primary SIC and add'l.: 4899 9999

CIK No: 0000793595

Subsidiaries: Inrob Ltd.

Officers: Ben-Tsur Joseph/48/CEO, CFO, Pres.

Owners: Joseph Ben-Tsur

Financial Data: Fiscal Year End:12/31   Latest Annual Data: 12/31/2006

Year	Sales	Net Income
2006	$1,657,000	-$828,000
2005	NA	-$25,000

Curr. Assets:	$1,000	Curr. Liab.:	$210,000		
Plant, Equip.:	NA	Total Liab.:	$210,000	Indic. Yr. Divd.:	NA
Total Assets:	$1,000	Net Worth:	-$209,000	Debt/ Equity:	NA

INSEQ Corp

One Penn Plaza, Ste. 1612, New York, NY, 10119; *PH:* 1-212-994-5374; *http://* www.inseq.com

General - Incorporation	DE
Employees	133
Auditor	Rosenberg Rich Baker Berman & Co
Stk Agt	Continental Stock Transfer & Trust Co
Counsel	NA
DUNS No.	NA

Stock- Price on:12/24/2007	$0.026
Stock Exchange	NA
Ticker Symbol	NA
Outstanding Shares	184,970,000
E.P.S.	-$0.19
Shareholders	NA

Business: The group's principal activity is to design and market branded and non-branded apparel. The brands offered by the group include m. Sasson(R), home turf and new terrain labels. The product lines offered by the group include sportswear, loungewear, outerwear, as well as accessories such as ties, hats, scarves, gloves, jewellery, backpacks and small leather goods as well as apparel.

Primary SIC and add'l.: 5136 5131 5137 5699

CIK No: 0001127242

Subsidiaries: Air Cycle Corporation, Warnecke Design Services Inc., Warnecke Rentals, LLC

Owners: James Grainer/77.00%, Insiders/100.00%, Kevin Kreisler/100.00%, Kevin Kreisler/100.00%, Insiders/100.00%, Insiders/7.70%

Financial Data: Fiscal Year End:12/31   Latest Annual Data: 12/31/2006

Year	Sales	Net Income
2006	$17,850,000	-$16,333,000
2005	$696,000	$1,947,000
2004	$2,572,000	-$1,678,000

Curr. Assets:	$7,521,000	Curr. Liab.:	$38,336,000		
Plant, Equip.:	$4,043,000	Total Liab.:	$60,689,000	Indic. Yr. Divd.:	NA
Total Assets:	$48,999,000	Net Worth:	-$12,813,000	Debt/ Equity:	NA

Insight Communications Co Inc

126 E 56th St., New York, NY, 10022; *PH:* 1-212-371-2266; *http://* www.insight-com.com

General - Incorporation	DE
Employees	781
Auditor	Ernst & Young LLP
Stk Agt	Bank of New York
Counsel	NA
DUNS No.	NA

Stock- Price on:12/24/2007	NA
Stock Exchange	NA
Ticker Symbol	NA
Outstanding Shares	NA
E.P.S.	NA
Shareholders	NA

Business: The group's principal activity is to own and operate cable television systems in Kentucky, Indiana, Illinois, Ohio, California and Georgia. The group provides a variety of entertainment, information and communications programs through cable television. The group provides interactive digital video, high-speed data access and telephony services. Interactive digital technology significantly enhances and expands the video and service offering that is provided to the customer. High-speed data services are offered for personal computers. Telephony services are provided to local customers under the at&t and digital brand using network infrastructure and at&t broadband's switching and transport facilities.

Primary SIC and add'l.: 4841 4899

CIK No: 0001084421

Subsidiaries: Comcast Cable Holdings, LLC, Insight Communications Company, L.P., Insight Interactive, LLC

Officers: Michael S. Willner/55/Vice Chmn., CEO, Daniel Mannino/Sr. VP, Controller, Hamid Heidary/Exec. VP - Central Operations, Pamela Euler Halling/Sr. VP - Brand, Product Development, Programming, John Abbot/45/CFO, Exec. VP, Paul Meltzer/Sr. VP - Product Management, Jim Morgan/Sr. VP - Human Resources, Sandra D. Colony/Sr. VP - Communications, Scott Cooley/Sr. VP - Operations, West Region, Gregg Graff/Sr. VP - Field Operations, Ohn W. Hutton/Sr. VP - Operations, East Region, Dinni Jain/44/Dir., COO, Pres., Kevin Dowell/Sr. VP - Insight Media, Christopher Slattery/Exec. VP - Field Operations, Charles E. Dietz/Sr. VP - Research, Development, Strategy, CTO *(17 Officers included in Index)*

Directors: Michael S. Willner/55/Vice Chmn., CEO, Sidney R. Knafel/77/Chmn., Geraldine B. Laybourne/60/Dir., Amos B. Hostetter/71/Dir., Stephen C. Gray/49/Dir., William E. Kennard/51/Dir., Michael J. Connelly/56/Dir., James A. Attwood/49/Dir.

Owners: Insiders, Insiders/60.00%, Michael J. Connelly, James A. Attwood, Sidney R. Knafel/47.00%, Andrew G. Knafel/40.00%, William E. Kennard, Michael S. Willner/13.00%, The Carlyle Group affiliates

Insight Enterprises Inc

6820 S Harl Ave., Tempe, AZ, 85283; *PH:* 1-800-467-4448; *Fax:* 1-480-902-1157; *http://* www.insight.com

General - Incorporation	DE	Stock - Price on:12/24/2007	$21.63
Employees	3,967	Stock Exchange	NYSE
Auditor	KPMG LLP	Ticker Symbol	NSR
Stk Agt	Wells Fargo Shareowner Services	Outstanding Shares	49,010,000
Counsel	NA	E.P.S.	$1.45
DUNS No.	87-638-3589	Shareholders	NA

Business: The group's principle activity is to provide business outsourcing and IT services to businesses, government and educational institutions. The group operates from United States, Canada and United Kingdom.

Primary SIC and add'l.: 7379 5045

CIK No: 0000932696

Subsidiaries: 3051918 Nova Scotia Ltd., 3683371 Canada, Inc., Action Computer Supplies Limited, Action Ltd., Computers by Post Limited, Direct Alliance Corporation, Docufile Limited, DSI Data Systems International Limited, Frasier Associates plc, Insight Canada, Inc., Insight Deutschland GmbH & Ko KG, Insight Development Corp Limited, Insight Direct (GB)Limited, Insight Direct (Services) Limited, Insight Direct (UK)Limited 34 Subsidiaries included in the Index

Officers: Richard A. Fennessy/Dir., CEO, Pres., David B. Rice/CIO, Stanley Laybourne/Dir., CFO, Sec., Treasurer, Mark T. McGrath/Pres. - Insight Direct USA, Inc, Catherine Eckstein/Chief Marketing Officer, Carmela Orlando/GM - Insight Canada, Inc, Stuart Fenton/Pres. - Insight EMEA, Gary A. Glandon/Chief People Officer, Karen K. McGinnis/Chief Accounting Officer, Assist. Sec., Cathy Connors/Investor Relations Officer, Steven R. Andrews/55/General Counsel

Directors: Richard A. Fennessy/Dir., CEO, Pres., Timothy A. Crown/Chmn., Robertson C. Jones/Dir., Larry A. Gunning/Dir., Stanley Laybourne/Dir., CFO, Sec., Treasurer, Michael M. Fisher/Dir., Eric J. Crown/Dir., Bennett Dorrance/Dir., Kathleen S. Pushor/Dir., David J. Robino/Dir.

Owners: Bennett Dorrance, Stanley Laybourne, Eric J. Crown/1.08%, Mark T. McGrath, Gary M. Glandon, Robertson C. Jones, Richard A. Fennessy/1.29%, Larry A. Gunning, Prudential Financial, Inc./6.47%, FMR Corp/12.93%, Kathleen S. Pushor, Insiders/4.79%, Timothy A. Crown, Stuart A. Fenton, Barclays Global Investors, N.A. and affiliated entities/9.87% *(18 Owners included in Index)*

Financial Data: *Fiscal Year End:*12/31   *Latest Annual Data:* 12/31/2006

Year	Sales		Net Income
2006	$3,817,085,000		$76,818,000
2005	$3,261,150,000		$54,695,000
2004	$3,082,725,000		$80,528,000
Curr. Assets:	$1,226,394,000	Curr. Liab.: $818,496,000	P/E Ratio: 13.27
Plant, Equip.:	$145,778,000	Total Liab.: $1,083,801,000	Indic. Yr. Divd.: NA
Total Assets:	$1,774,151,000	Net Worth: $690,350,000	Debt/ Equity: NA

Insightful Corp

1700 Westlake Ave. N, Ste. 500, Seattle, WA, 98109; *PH:* 1-206-283-8802; *Fax:* 1-206-283-8691; *http://* www.insightful.com; *Email:* info@insightful.com

General - Incorporation	DE	Stock - Price on:12/24/2007	$2.46
Employees	148	Stock Exchange	NDQ
Auditor	Moss Adams LLP	Ticker Symbol	IFUL
Stk Agt	Mellon Investor Services LLC	Outstanding Shares	12,870,000
Counsel	Orrick, Herrington & Sutcliffe LLP	E.P.S.	NA
DUNS No.	15-068-3779	Shareholders	NA

Business: The group's principal activity is to provide enterprises with scalable data analysis solutions. The solutions help make better decisions faster by revealing patterns, trends and relationships. The group supplies software and services for statistical data mining, business analytics, knowledge management, and information retrieval enabling clients to gain intelligence from numerical data, text and images. The solutions serve industries like financial services, pharmaceuticals and biotechnology, telecommunications, manufacturing, retail and research. The group has its operations in the United Kingdom, Germany, France and Switzerland.

Primary SIC and add'l.: 7372 7374

CIK No: 0000895095

Subsidiaries: Insightful AG, a Swiss subsidiary, Insightful GmbH (i.L.), a German subsidiary, Insightful Limited, a United Kingdom subsidiary, Insightful SAS, a French subsidiary, Statistical Sciences, Inc., a Massachusetts subsidiary

Officers: Jeff Coombs/Dir., CEO, Pres./$716,705.00, Nick Brown/VP - Marketing, Richard Barber/CFO/$315,464.00, Colin Magee/VP - Europe, Giovanni Marchisio/VP - Research, Development, Ann Parker-Way/VP, General Counsel, Corp. Sec., Theresa Smith/Contact - Media Relations, Denise Garcia/Contact - Maintenance Renewals, North America, Benjamin Dupont/Contact - Maintenance Renewals, North America, Songyu He/Contact - Asia Pacific, Latin America Sales, Betty Pan/Contact - Asia Pacific, Latin America Sales

Directors: Jeff Coombs/Dir., CEO, Pres., Samuel Meshberg/Chmn., Sachin Chawla/Dir., Mark Ozur/Dir., Ron Stevens/Dir.

Owners: Mark C. Ozur/1.10%, Ronald M. Stevens, Insiders/30.90%, Jeffrey E. Coombs/4.90%, Richard P. Barber, Samuel R. Meshberg/23.20%, Sachin Chawla

Financial Data: *Fiscal Year End:*12/13   *Latest Annual Data:* 12/31/2006

Year	Sales		Net Income
2006	$24,015,000		$156,000
2005	$22,337,000		$1,982,000
2004	$18,899,000		$2,071,000
Curr. Assets:	$15,143,000	Curr. Liab.: $9,786,000	
Plant, Equip.:	$2,757,000	Total Liab.: $9,786,000	Indic. Yr. Divd.: NA
Total Assets:	$21,196,000	Net Worth: $11,410,000	Debt/ Equity: NA

Insignia Solutions Plc

51 E Campbell Ave., Ste. 130, Campbell, CA, 95008; *PH:* 1-408-874-2600; *http://* www.insignia.com

General - Incorporation	England And Wales	Stock - Price on:12/24/2007	$0.076
Employees	33	Stock Exchange	OTC
Auditor	Burr, Pilger & Mayer LLP	Ticker Symbol	INSGY
Stk Agt	Bank of New York	Outstanding Shares	50,360,000
Counsel	Fenwick & West LLP	E.P.S.	-$0.218
DUNS No.	61-337-6789	Shareholders	NA

Business: The group's principal activities are the development, marketing and support of software technologies that enable mobile operators and phone manufacturers to update the firmware of mobile devices using standard over-the-air data networks. The group's operates as a developer of security system provisioning for the mobile phone and wireless operator industry.

Primary SIC and add'l.: 7372

CIK No: 0001002390

Subsidiaries: Emulation Technologies Inc, Insignia Solutions AB, Insignia Solutions Foreign Sales Inc, Insignia Solutions France SARL, Insignia Solutions Inc, Insignia Solutions International Limited, Jeode Limited, Kenora Ltd., Korrogo Technologies Ltd

Financial Data: *Fiscal Year End:*12/31   *Latest Annual Data:* 12/31/2005

Year	Sales		Net Income
2005	$3,178,000		-$8,362,000
2004	$541,000		-$7,062,000
2003	$710,000		-$4,323,000
Curr. Assets:	$3,129,000	Curr. Liab.: $7,323,000	
Plant, Equip.:	$87,000	Total Liab.: $7,323,000	Indic. Yr. Divd.: NA
Total Assets:	$6,117,000	Net Worth: -$1,206,000	Debt/ Equity: NA

Insignia Systems Inc

6470 Sycamore Ct. N, Maple Grove, MN, 55369; *PH:* 1-763-392-6200; *Fax:* 1-763-392-6222; *http://* www.insigniasystems.com; *Email:* marketing@insigniasystems.com

General - Incorporation	MN	Stock - Price on:12/24/2007	$4.22
Employees	88	Stock Exchange	NDQ
Auditor	Grant Thornton LLP	Ticker Symbol	ISIG
Stk Agt	Wells Fargo Shareowner Services	Outstanding Shares	15,340,000
Counsel	Best & Flanagen LLP	E.P.S.	$0.15
DUNS No.	61-595-4922	Shareholders	NA

Business: The group's principle activity is to market in-store promotional products, programs and services to retailers and consumer packaged goods manufacturers. The group develops turnkey solutions that allow retailers to produce high quality point-of-purchase signs, labels and large sales promotional materials in their stores. The products are marketed internationally through distributors. The products of the group include insignia point-of-purchase services (pops) in-store promotion program, thermal sign card supplies for signright and impulse systems, stylus software and laser printable cardstock and label supplies. Pops enable manufacturers to deliver account-specific promotional messages. The group's quarterly revenue for Sep'07 was 6.46 millions of USD.

Primary SIC and add'l.: 7379 5045

CIK No: 0000875355

Owners: Thomas A. Lucas, Reid V. MacDonald, Insiders/13.90%, Scott J. Simcox, Potomac Capital Management, Inc./6.60%, Scott F. Drill/3.70%, Peter V. Derycz, Gary L. Vars/2.00%, Justin W. Shireman, Perkins Capital Management, Inc./8.70%, Gordon F. Stofer, Robert W. Ramsdell/6.20%, Donald J. Kramer

Financial Data: *Fiscal Year End:*12/31   *Latest Annual Data:* 12/31/2006

Year	Sales		Net Income
2006	$21,894,000		$2,396,000
2005	$19,598,000		-$3,308,000
2004	$20,992,000		-$4,858,000
Curr. Assets:	$8,050,000	Curr. Liab.: $3,033,000	P/E Ratio: 28.13
Plant, Equip.:	$477,000	Total Liab.: $3,721,000	Indic. Yr. Divd.: NA
Total Assets:	$8,583,000	Net Worth: $4,862,000	Debt/ Equity: NA

Insite Vision Inc

965 Atlantic Ave., Alameda, CA, 94501; *PH:* 1-510-865-8800; *Fax:* 1-510-865-5700; *http://* www.insitevision.com

General - Incorporation	DE	Stock - Price on:12/24/2007	$1.48
Employees	40	Stock Exchange	AMEX
Auditor	Burr, Pilger & Mayer LLP	Ticker Symbol	ISV
Stk Agt	Mellon Investor Services LLC	Outstanding Shares	93,820,000
Counsel	Brobeck, Phleger & Harrison	E.P.S.	-$0.07
DUNS No.	15-463-9827	Shareholders	NA

Business: The group's principle activity is to develop ophthalmic pharmaceutical products. The research and development of the company is based on proprietary eye drop-based drug delivery technology. The company has retinal programs, which include a therapeutic agent and a retinal drug delivery technology. The drug delivery technology of the company can be customized to deliver a wide variety of potential drug candidates. The company has also developed a diagnostic/prognostic technology isv-900 that is capable of identifying multiple glaucoma genetic markers from a single sample. The products of the company include ocugene, isv-900, isv-205, isv-401, isv-403, isv-205, aquasite and isv-014. The group operates in the United States and the United Kingdom.

Primary SIC and add'l.: 8731 2834

CIK No: 0000802724

Subsidiaries: Arrow Acquisition Inc., InSite Vision Limited

Officers: Kumar S. Chandrasekaran/65/Chmn., CEO, Pres./$775,518.00, Sandi Heine/VP - Finance, Administration/$197,269.00, David Henigesdavid Heniges/VP, GM - Commercial Opportunities/$289,250.00, Lyle M. Bowman/VP - Development, Operations/$278,737.00, Ronald H. Carlson/54/VP - Regulatory, Quality, Louis Drapeau/CFO, VP

Directors: Kumar S. Chandrasekaran/65/Chmn., CEO, Pres., John L. Mattana/Dir., Mitchell H. Friedlaender/Dir., Jon S. Saxe/Dir., Anders P. Wiklund/Dir., Eric D. Donnenfeld/Member - Scientific Advisory Board, Edward J. Holland/Member - Scientific Advisory Board, Kerry D. Solomon/Member - Scientific Advisory Board

Owners: Kumarv S. Chandrasekaran/2.46%, Mitchell H. Friedlaender, Pinto Technology Ventures, L.P./10.55%, Anders P. Wiklund, Jon S. Saxe, Eli Jacobson/6.27%, Ronald H. Carlson, Sandra C. Heine, Insiders/4.18%, Visium Asset Management LLC/8.65%, Wellington Management/5.48%, David F. Heniges, Lyle M. Bowman, John L. Mattana, Jonathan M. Glaser/5.03%

Financial Data: *Fiscal Year End:*12/31 *Latest Annual Data:* 12/31/2006

Year	Sales	Net Income
2006	$2,000	-$16,611,000
2005	$4,000	-$15,215,000
2004	$542,000	-$5,514,000

Curr. Assets:	$1,878,000	**Curr. Liab.:**	$8,692,000		
Plant, Equip.:	$561,000	**Total Liab.:**	$8,741,000	**Indic. Yr. Divd.:**	NA
Total Assets:	$2,439,000	**Net Worth:**	-$6,302,000	**Debt/ Equity:**	NA

Insituform Technologies Inc

17988 Edison Ave., Chesterfield, MO, 63005; *PH:* 1-636-530-8000; *Fax:* 1-636-519-8010; *http://* www.insituform.com

General - Incorporation	DE	**Stock**- Price on:12/24/2007	$20.67
Employees	2,000	Stock Exchange	NDQ
Auditor	PricewaterhouseCoopers LLP	Ticker Symbol	INSU
Stk Agt	American Stock Transfer & Trust Co.	Outstanding Shares	27,280,000
Counsel	NA	E.P.S	$0.15
DUNS No.	03-940-6616	Shareholders	NA

Business: The group's principal activity is to specialize in the use of trenchless technologies to rehabilitate, replace, maintain and install underground pipes. The insituform cipp process for the rehabilitation of sewers, pipelines and other conduits utilizes a custom-manufactured tube made of a synthetic fiber. Pipebursting is a trenchless method for replacing deteriorated or undersized pipelines. Microtunneling is a trenchless method of drilling a new tunnel from surface operated equipment. Sliplining is a method used to push or pull a new pipeline into an old one. With segmented sliplining, short segments of pipe are joined to form the new pipe. On 01-Jun-2003, the group acquired Sewer Services Ltd.

Primary SIC and add'l.: 9999 1623

CIK No: 0000353020

Subsidiaries: Affholder, Inc., INA Acquisition Corp., Insituform (Netherlands) B.V., Insituform Belgium NV, Insituform France, S.A., Insituform Holdings (UK) Limited, Insituform Linings Plc., Insituform Rioolrenovatietechnieken B.V., Insituform Technologies Iberica SA, Insituform Technologies Limited, Insituform Technologies USA, Inc., Ka-Te Insituform AG, Kinsel Industries, Inc., Video Injection S.A.

Officers: Alfred L. Woods/64/Chmn., Interim CEO, Thomas E. Vossman/46/COO, Sr. VP/$697,249.00, David F. Morris/46/Sr. VP, Chief Administrative Officer, VP., General Counsel, Sec./$507,310.00, David A. Martin/41/CFO, VP, Controller/$305,197.00

Directors: Alfred L. Woods/64/Chmn., Interim CEO, Stephen P. Cortinovis/Dir., Thomas S. Rooney/48/Dir., Sheldon Weinig/Dir., John P. Dubinsky/Dir., Stephanie A. Cuskley/Dir., Juanita H. Hinshaw/Dir., Alfred T. McNeill/Dir.

Owners: AMVESCAP PLC/6.50%, Juanita H. Hinshaw, Barclays Global Investors Japan Limited/5.31%, Stephanie A. Cuskley, David A. Martin, Alfred T. McNeill, Thomas S. Rooney/1.29%, Barrow, Hanley, Mewhinney & Strauss, Inc./6.97%, Sheldon Weinig, Alfred L. Woods, Insiders/2.68%, Stephen P. Cortinovis, T. Rowe Price Associates, Inc./13.68%, David F. Morris, Thomas E. Vossman *(17 Owners included in Index)*

Financial Data: *Fiscal Year End:*12/31 *Latest Annual Data:* 12/31/2006

Year	Sales	Net Income
2006	$596,715,000	$24,678,000
2005	$595,282,000	$13,160,000
2004	$542,598,000	$597,000

Curr. Assets:	$310,364,000	**Curr. Liab.:**	$136,505,000	**P/E Ratio:**	89.87
Plant, Equip.:	$90,453,000	**Total Liab.:**	$209,277,000	**Indic. Yr. Divd.:**	NA
Total Assets:	$550,069,000	**Net Worth:**	$338,611,000	**Debt/ Equity:**	NA

Insmed Inc

8720 Stony Point Pkwy., Ste. 200, Richmond, VA, 23235; *PH:* 1-804-565-3000; *Fax:* 1-804-565-3500; *http://* www.insmed.com

General - Incorporation	VA	**Stock**- Price on:12/24/2007	$0.7111
Employees	157	Stock Exchange	NDQ
Auditor	Ernst & Young LLP	Ticker Symbol	INSM
Stk Agt	Wachovia Bank N.A	Outstanding Shares	101,330,000
Counsel	NA	E.P.S	-$0.35
DUNS No.	NA	Shareholders	NA

Business: The group's principal activity is to develop and market pharmaceutical products for the treatment of metabolic, hormone growth disorders, diabetes and endocrine disorders. The group has two drug candidates, recombinant human insulin-like growth factor-i bound to recombinant human insulin-like growth factor binding protein-3 (rhigf-i) also known as somatokine and rhigfbp-3. These drugs are developed to treat indications in the metabolic and oncology fields. Also correct metabolic defects in the human body by replacing key regulatory molecules in a physiologically relevant fashion.

Primary SIC and add'l.: 2834 8731

CIK No: 0001104506

Subsidiaries: Celtrix Pharmaceuticals

Officers: Geoffrey Allan/Chmn., CEO, Pres./$528,823.00, Ronald D. Gunn/COO, Exec. VP/$329,876.00, Kevin P. Tully/CFO, Exec. VP/$252,375.00, Steve Glover/Pres. - Insmed Therapeutic Proteins, Doug Farrar/VP - Insmed Therapeutic Proteins

Directors: Geoffrey Allan/Chmn., CEO, Pres., Kenneth G. Condon/Dir., Graham K. Crooke/Dir., Steinar J. Engelsen/Dir., Melvin Sharoky/Dir., Randall W. Whitcomb/Dir.

Owners: Randall W. Whitcomb, Geoffrey Allan/1.70%, Andreas Sommer, Graham K. Crooke, Randall W. Whitcomb, Kevin P. Tully, Thomas A. Keuer, Melvin Sharoky, Kenneth G. Condon, Steinar J. Engelsen, Ronald D. Gunn, Philip J. Young

Financial Data: *Fiscal Year End:*12/31 *Latest Annual Data:* 12/31/2006

Year	Sales	Net Income
2006	NA	NA
2005	NA	NA
2004	NA	NA

Curr. Assets:	$25,423,000	**Curr. Liab.:**	$9,681,000		
Plant, Equip.:	$8,000	**Total Liab.:**	$14,468,000	**Indic. Yr. Divd.:**	NA
Total Assets:	$28,348,000	**Net Worth:**	$13,880,000	**Debt/ Equity:**	0.8761

Inspire Pharmaceuticals Inc

4222 Emperor Blvd., Ste. 200, Durham, NC, 27703; *PH:* 1-919-941-9777; *Fax:* 1-919-941-9797; *http://* www.inspirepharm.com; *Email:* info@inspirepharm.com

General - Incorporation	DE	**Stock**- Price on:12/24/2007	$5.64
Employees	170	Stock Exchange	NDQ
Auditor	PricewaterhouseCoopers LLP	Ticker Symbol	ISPH
Stk Agt	Computershare Trust Co	Outstanding Shares	42,400,000
Counsel	Mirco Investors LLC	E.P.S	-$1.45
DUNS No.	NA	Shareholders	NA

Business: The group's principle activities include discovering and developing pharmaceutical products that restore innate defense mechanisms of mucosal hydration and mucociliary clearance, and other non-mucosal disorders. The group is in the development stage. The group's lead products target respiratory and ophthalmic diseases. The group currently has five product candidates in clinical development. The group operates from United States.

Primary SIC and add'l.: 2834 8731

CIK No: 0001040416

Officers: Christy L. Shaffer/Dir., CEO, Pres./$706,077.00, Gerald W. St. Peter/Sr. VP - Sales, Managed Markets, Denise M. Sheehan/VP - Product Planning, Kim R. Brazzell/Sr. VP - Ophthalmic Research, Development, Anita L. Woodring/Sr. Dir. - Regulatory Affairs, Leo A. Trevino/Dir. - Analytical Chemistry, Lynn M. Smiley/Chief Medical Officer, Joseph M. Spagnardi/Sr. VP, General Counsel, Sec./$413,052.00, Brian D. Kaufman/Chief - Quality, Continuous Improvement, Joseph K. Schachle/Exec. VP, Chief - Commercial - Corporate Operations, Donald J. Kellerman/Sr. VP - Development, Benjamin R. Yerxa/Chief Scientific Officer, Exec. VP - Strategic Operations/$403,872.00, Sean K. Blake/Dir. - Information Technology, Vikki A. Brandi/Dir. - Respiratory, Opportunistic Clinical Research, Darrin P. Bryan/Sr. Dir. - Operations, Strategic Markets *(38 Officers included in Index)*

Directors: Christy L. Shaffer/Dir., CEO, Pres., Kenneth B. Lee/Chmn., Nancy J. Hutson/Dir., Jonathan S. Leff/Dir., Kip A. Frey/Dir., Richard S. Kent/Dir., William R. Ringo/Dir.

Owners: Thomas R. Staab, Kenneth B. Lee, William R. Ringo, Warburg Pincus Private Equity IX, L.P./24.80%, Benjamin R. Yerxa, Deerfield Capital, L.P. and related persons/9.30%, Richard S. Kent, Insiders/28.00%, Christy L. Shaffer/1.50%, Kip A. Frey, Bridger Management, LLC and Roberto Mignone/3.80%, Great Point Partners, LLC and Jeffrey Jay/7.60%, T. Rowe Price Associates, Inc./5.50%, Nancy J. Hutson, Jonathan S. Leff/24.90% *(17 Owners included in Index)*

Financial Data: *Fiscal Year End:*12/31 *Latest Annual Data:* 09/30/2007

Year	Sales	Net Income
2007	NA	NA
2006	$37,059,000	-$42,115,000
2005	$23,266,000	-$31,847,000

Curr. Assets:	$107,746,000	**Curr. Liab.:**	$18,091,000		
Plant, Equip.:	$1,754,000	**Total Liab.:**	$38,328,000	**Indic. Yr. Divd.:**	NA
Total Assets:	$116,699,000	**Net Worth:**	$78,371,000	**Debt/ Equity:**	0.2286

Instacare Corp

2660 Townsgate Rd., Ste. 300, Westlake Village, CA, 91361; *PH:* 1-805-446-1973; *Fax:* 1-805-446-1983; *http://* www.instacare.net; *Email:* info@caredecision.net

General - Incorporation	NV	**Stock**- Price on:12/24/2007	$0.17
Employees	6	Stock Exchange	OTC
Auditor	Beckstead & Watts LLP	Ticker Symbol	ISCR
Stk Agt	Pacific Stock Transfer Company	Outstanding Shares	11,030,000
Counsel	NA	E.P.S	NA
DUNS No.	NA	Shareholders	NA

Business: The group's principal activity is to provide enhanced information technology (IT) for physicians. The software allows medical information to be provide at the point of the physician's clinical decision making. The software systems, communication tools and suite of software applications permit the physician to request patient information via the Web on a microsoft windows based personal digital assistant. Utilization of this system by the practicing physician enhances clinical decision-making, improves physician productivity, insures formulary compliance, reduces the cost of healthcare and positively impacts the care provided to the patient. The group operates mainly in the United States of America. On 06-Apr-2004, the group acquired multimedia digital utility services inc.

Primary SIC and add'l.: 7372 7379 8742

CIK No: 0001144225

Subsidiaries: CareGeneration, Inc, CareTechnologies, LLC, Kelly Company World Group, Inc, Medicius, Inc, PDA Services, Inc, Pharma Tech Solutions, Inc

Officers: Robert L. Cox/Dir., CEO, Keith Berman/Dir., CFO, Sec.

Directors: Robert L. Cox/Dir., CEO, Robert Jagunich/Chmn., Keith Berman/Dir., CFO, Sec.

Owners: Pinnacle Investment Partners/7.00%, Insiders/6.00%, Robert Jagunich/2.00%, Mercator Momentum Fund, L.P./10.00%, Keith Berman/4.00%

Financial Data: *Fiscal Year End:*12/31 *Latest Annual Data:* 12/31/2006

Year	Sales	Net Income
2006	$19,220,000	-$2,755,000
2005	$5,614,000	-$4,823,000
2004	$182,000	-$4,551,000

Curr. Assets:	$287,000	**Curr. Liab.:**	$2,605,000		
Plant, Equip.:	$83,000	**Total Liab.:**	$2,605,000	**Indic. Yr. Divd.:**	NA
Total Assets:	$373,000	**Net Worth:**	-$2,232,000	**Debt/ Equity:**	NA

Insteel Industries Inc

1373 Boggs Dr., Mount Airy, NC, 27030; *PH:* 1-336-786-2141; *Fax:* 1-336-786-2144; *http://* www.insteel.com

General - Incorporation	NC	**Stock**- Price on:12/24/2007	$19.17
Employees	621	Stock Exchange	NDQ
Auditor	Grant Thornton LLP	Ticker Symbol	IIIN
Stk Agt.... American Stock Transfer & Trust Co.		Outstanding Shares	18,280,000
Counsel	Womble Carlyle Sandridge & Rice	E.P.S.	$1.57
DUNS No.	00-322-0225	Shareholders	NA

Business: The group's principal activity is to manufacture and market wire products for commercial and industrial applications. The group operates in two business units: concrete reinforcing products and wire products. Concrete reinforcing products consists of the welded wire fabric and PC strand product lines. Wire products consists of industrial wire, nails and tire bead wire product lines. The products of the group are sold to original equipment manufacturers, distributors, wholesalers and retailers located nationwide and also to Canada, Mexico and central and South America.

Primary SIC and add'l.: 3399 3495 3315 1791 3312

CIK No: 0000764401

Subsidiaries: Insteel Wire Products Company, Intercontinental Metals Corporation

Officers: H. O. Woltz/51/Dir., CEO, Pres., James F. Petelle/Insider Ownership, Richard T. Wagner/Insider Ownership

Directors: H. O. Woltz/51/Dir., CEO, Pres., Howard O. Woltz/81/Chmn., Charles B. Newsome/70/Dir., Richard C. Vaughn/67/Dir., Louis E. Hannen/68/Dir., Allen Rogers/Dir., Gary L. Pechota/57/Dir., William J. Shields/74/Dir.

Owners: Royce & Associates LLC/10.30%, Allen W. Rogers, Insiders/9.30%, H. O. Woltz/3.00%, Richard C. Vaughn, James F. Petelle, Lazard Asset Management LLC/10.70%, Howard O. Woltz/3.70%, Michael C. Gazmarian, William J. Shields, Louis E. Hannen, Johnson Concrete Company/6.70%, Gary L. Pechota, Gary D. Kniskern, Charles B. Newsome

Financial Data: *Fiscal Year End:*10/01 *Latest Annual Data:* 9/30/2006

Year	Sales	Net Income
2006	$329,507,000	$33,040,000
2005	$345,536,000	$25,045,000
2004	$332,632,000	$31,489,000

Curr. Assets:	$98,091,000	*Curr. Liab.:*	$41,153,000	*P/E Ratio:*	12.21
Plant, Equip.:	$55,217,000	*Total Liab.:*	$44,158,000	*Indic. Yr. Divd.:*	$0.120
Total Assets:	$166,596,000	*Net Worth:*	$122,438,000	*Debt/ Equity:*	NA

Instinet Group Inc

3 Time Sq., New York, NY, 10022; *PH:* 1-212-310-9500; *http://* www.instinetgroup.com

General - Incorporation	DE	**Stock**- Price on:12/24/2007	NA
Employees	NA	Stock Exchange	NA
Auditor	PricewaterhouseCoopers LLP	Ticker Symbol	NA
Stk Agt.	NA	Outstanding Shares	NA
Counsel	NA	E.P.S.	NA
DUNS No.	NA	Shareholders	NA

Business: The group's principle activities are to provide agency and other brokerage services to brokers, dealers and institutional customers worldwide. The group operates in a financial marketplace where buyers and sellers worldwide can trade securities directly with each other, gain price improvement for their trades and lower their overall trading costs. The customers can also access securities markets throughout the world, including Nasdaq and the nyse stock exchanges in different parts of the world. The group's customers consist of institutional investors such as mutual funds, pension funds, insurance companies, hedge funds and brokers-dealers. The group's revenues consist primarily of transaction fees generated by its securities brokerage and related services.

Primary SIC and add'l.: 6211

CIK No: 0001132327

Subsidiaries: Inet ATS, Inc., Instinet Clearing Services, Inc., Instinet Europe Limited, Instinet Global Services Limited, Instinet Group, Incorporated, Instinet Group, LLC, Instinet International Corporation, Instinet, LLC, Lynch, Jones and Ryan, Inc.

Officers: Edward J. Nicoll/CEO, Joe Marchal/CEO, Pres. - Instinet Asia, Tony MacKay/MD, Pres. - Instinet Europe, Michael Plunkett/Pres. - North America, Mark Dowd/Contact - Media, Alex Goor/Co - Pres., CIO, John F. Fay/Co - CFO, Pres., Cynthia Dansby/Contact - Legal Notices, Cameron Smith/Exec. VP, General Counsel

Insure.com Inc

Formerly: Quotesmith.com Inc
8205 S Cass Ave, Ste. 102, Darien, IL, 60561; ; *http://* www.quotesmith.com

General - Incorporation	DE	**Stock**- Price on:12/24/2007	NA
Employees	99	Stock Exchange	NA
Auditor	Ernst & Young LLP	Ticker Symbol	NA
Stk Agt.	Computershare Investor Services LLC	Outstanding Shares	NA
Counsel	Katten, Muchin, Zavis & Rosenman	E.P.S.	NA
DUNS No.	NA	Shareholders	NA

Business: The group's principal activity is to provide online consumer insurance information services. The group owns and operates a comprehensive online consumer insurance information services, www.insure.com. The insure.com service enables consumers and business owners to obtain instant quotes from over 200 insurance companies for several different life, health, auto and home insurance products.

Primary SIC and add'l.: 7375 6411

CIK No: 0001079996

Subsidiaries: Insure.com, Inc, Life Quotes, Inc, Quotesmith.com, Inc.

Officers: Robert S. Bland/Chmn., CEO, Founder, Pres./$364,656.00, William V. Thoms/Dir., COO, Exec. VP/$331,656.00, Richard C. Claahsen/VP, General Counsel, Corp. Sec./$153,787.00, Phillip A. Perillo/43/CFO, Sr. VP/$350,541.00, John C. McIntyre/42/VP - Sales/$135,981.00, Daniel A. Romito/CIO, VP

Directors: Robert S. Bland/Chmn., CEO, Founder, Pres., Timothy F. Shannon/Dir., William V. Thoms/Dir., COO, Exec. VP, John B. Hopkins/Dir., Jeremiah A. Denton/Dir., Bruce J. Rueben/Dir., Richard F. Gretsch/Dir.

Owners: Timothy F. Shannon, Insiders/40.70%, Bruce J. Rueben, Richard C. Claahsen, Robert S. Bland/29.20%, William V. Thoms/7.80%, John B. Hopkins, Jeremiah A. Denton, Richard F. Gretsch, Zions Bancorporation/31.00%, Daniel A. Romito, Phillip A. Perillo/2.30%

Curr. Assets:	$12,730,000	*Curr. Liab.:*	$1,348,000		
Plant, Equip.:	$334,000	*Total Liab.:*	$1,348,000	*Indic. Yr. Divd.:*	NA
Total Assets:	$20,671,000	*Net Worth:*	$19,324,000	*Debt/ Equity:*	NA

InsWeb Corp

11290 Pyrites Way, Ste. 200, Gold River, CA, 95670; *PH:* 1-916-853-3300; *Fax:* 1-916-853-3325; *http://* www.insweb.com; *Email:* customercare@insweb.com

General - Incorporation	DE	**Stock**- Price on:12/24/2007	$6.9501
Employees	95	Stock Exchange	NDQ
Auditor	Ernst & Young LLP	Ticker Symbol	INSW
Stk Agt .... American Stock Transfer & Trust Co.		Outstanding Shares	4,450,000
Counsel	Shearman & Sterling LLP	E.P.S.	$0.15
DUNS No.	NA	Shareholders	NA

Business: The group's principal activity is to provide a centralized interactive marketplace for insurance information and electronic quotation. The group enables consumers to shop online for a variety of products, including automobile, homeowners, renters and health insurance and obtain insurance company-sponsored quotes for actual coverage. The group's online marketplace also allows consumers to shop for home warranty and motorcycle insurance and critical illness insurance. The group has combined extensive knowledge of insurance and technical expertise and has close relationships with a significant number of insurance companies to develop a sophisticated, integrated online marketplace. The group markets its online marketplace in the United States.

Primary SIC and add'l.: 7372 7375

CIK No: 0001077370

Subsidiaries: Goldrush Insurance Services, Inc., InsWeb Insurance Services, Inc., Strategic Concepts Corporation

Officers: Hussein A. Enan/Chmn., CEO/$319,880.00, Todd R. Ewing/Sr. VP - Agency Operations/$276,488.00, William D. Griffin/CFO/$258,518.00, Eric Loewe/General Counsel, Sec./$229,435.00, James L. Pickles/COO, Pres./$289,414.00, Jaimie Pickles/COO, Pres., John Cadigan/CTO, Sr. VP, Adam Cherubini/Sr. VP - Client Development, Brad Cooper/Sr. VP - Marketing, Advertising, Kiran Rasaretnam/Sr. VP, Steve Yasuda/Chief Accounting Officer

Directors: Hussein A. Enan/Chmn., CEO, James M. Corroon/Dir., Thomas W. Orr/Dir., Robert A. Puccinelli/Dir., Dennis H. Chookaszian/Dir.

Owners: Steven J. Yasuda/1.20%, Kiran Rasaretnam/2.60%, Hassan Elsawaf/11.70%, Thomas W. Orr/1.60%, Dennis H. Chookaszian/2.20%, Insiders/52.50%, Hussein A. Enan/33.90%, Robert A. Puccinelli/1.80%, James L. Pickles/4.10%, Lloyd I. Miller/11.80%, James M. Corroon/1.50%, Eric L. Loewe/3.60%

Financial Data: *Fiscal Year End:*12/31 *Latest Annual Data:* 03/31/2007

Year	Sales	Net Income
2007	$8,110,000	$402,000
2006	$28,501,000	-$3,370,000
2005	$25,015,000	-$5,941,000

Curr. Assets:	$9,952,000	*Curr. Liab.:*	$5,165,000		
Plant, Equip.:	$389,000	*Total Liab.:*	$5,165,000	*Indic. Yr. Divd.:*	NA
Total Assets:	$10,456,000	*Net Worth:*	$5,291,000	*Debt/ Equity:*	NA

Intac International Inc

Unit 6-7, 32/F, Laws Commercial Plaza, 788 Cheung Sha Wan Rd., Kowloon; *PH:* 852-238-58789; *http://* www.intac.com

General - Incorporation	NV	**Stock**- Price on:12/24/2007	$7.01
Employees	183	Stock Exchange	NA
Auditor	KBA Group LLP	Ticker Symbol	NA
Stk Agt	Securities Transfer Corp	Outstanding Shares	22,940,000
Counsel	NA	E.P.S.	-$0.47
DUNS No.	NA	Shareholders	NA

Business: The group's principal activities are carried out through two segments - wireless handset distribution: includes distribution of premium brand wireless handsets from manufacturers and other distributors to network operators, agents, resellers, dealers and retailers. Automobile distribution: includes distribution of automobiles from Europe into mainland China. The group seeks business opportunities in other business segments in China and Asia-pacific. The group has subsidiaries in China, Germany and the United States.

Primary SIC and add'l.: 5012 5065

CIK No: 0001127439

Subsidiaries: Beijing Huana Xinlong Information and Technology Development Co., Ltd, Beijing Intac Media Advertising Company Limited, Beijing Intac Meidi Technology Development Company Limited, Beijing Intac Purun Educational Development Limited, FUTAC Group Limited, Global Creative International Limited, Intac (Tianjin) International Trading Co, INTAC Deutschland GmbH, INTAC Holdco Corp., INTAC International Holdings Limited, INTAC Telecommunications Limited

Officers: Wei Zhou/38/Dir., CEO, Pres., Sec., Principal Executive Officer/$120,000.00, David J. Darnell/62/Sr. VP, CFO, Dir., Principal Financial Officer/$200,000.00

Directors: Wei Zhou/38/Dir., CEO, Pres., Sec., Principal Executive Officer, Heinz-Gerd Stein/67/Dir., Larrie A. Weil/64/Dir., Theodore P. Botts/62/Dir., Kevin Jones/58/Dir., David J. Darnell/62/Sr. VP, CFO, Dir., Principal Financial Officer

Financial Data: *Fiscal Year End:*09/30 *Latest Annual Data:* 9/30/2006

Year	Sales	Net Income
2006	$5,750,000	-$8,142,000
2005	$61,238,000	-$1,466,000
2004	$115,257,000	$5,816,000

Curr. Assets:	$19,198,000	*Curr. Liab.:*	$5,855,000		
Plant, Equip.:	$1,131,000	*Total Liab.:*	$5,855,000	*Indic. Yr. Divd.:*	NA
Total Assets:	$38,578,000	*Net Worth:*	$32,723,000	*Debt/ Equity:*	NA

Integra Bank Corp

21 SE 3rd St., Evansville, IN, 47708; *PH:* 1-812-464-9800; *Fax:* 1-812-464-9825; *http://* www.integrabank.com

General - Incorporation ... IN
Employees ... 802
Auditor ... PricewaterhouseCoopers LLP
Stk Agt ... Integra Bank Trust Department
Counsel ... NA
DUNS No. ... 00-693-6934

Stock- Price on:12/24/2007 ... $22.4
Stock Exchange ... NDQ
Ticker Symbol ... IBNK
Outstanding Shares ... 20,770,000
E.P.S ... $1.15
Shareholders ... NA

Business: The group's principle activity is to provide a wide range of financial services to the communities in Indiana, Kentucky, Illinois and southwestern Ohio. These services include various types of personal and commercial banking services, investment and trust services and selected insurance services. At 31-Dec-2003, the group served its customers through 74 banking centers and 134 automatic teller machines. It serves customers through telephone banking, Web banking and offers a suite of Internet-based products and services. The group operates from United States.

Primary SIC and add'l.: 6712 6021 9999

CIK No: 0000764241

Subsidiaries: IBNK Leasing Corp., Integra Bank NA, Integra Capital Statutory Trust III, Integra Capital Trust II, Integra Illinois Investment Co., LLC, Integra Loan Company, LLC, Integra Reinsurance Company, LTD, Total Title Services, LLC

Officers: Michael T. Vea/Chmn., CEO, Pres. - Integra Bank Corporation/$698,612.00

Directors: Michael T. Vea/Chmn., CEO, Pres. - Integra Bank Corporation, Bradley M. Stevens/56/Dir., Arthur D. Pringle/60/Dir.

Owners: Archie M. Brown, Martin M. Zorn, George D. Martin, Daniel T. Wolfe, Michael T. Vea/2.30%, Robert W. Swan, Insiders, William E. Vieth, Ray H. Hoops, Richard M. Stivers, Thomas W. Miller, Robert D. Vance/4.20%, Roger M. Duncan, Roxy M. Baas, Sandra Clark Berry/3.00% *(16 Owners included in Index)*

Financial Data: *Fiscal Year End:*12/31 *Latest Annual Data:* 12/31/2006

Year	Sales	Net Income
2006	$194,220,000	$19,547,000
2005	$177,589,000	$27,299,000
2004	$165,978,000	-$6,620,000

Curr. Assets:	$69,398,000	**Curr. Liab.:**	$2,171,370,000	**P/E Ratio:**	19.48
Plant, Equip.:	$46,157,000	**Total Liab.:**	$2,449,005,000	**Indic. Yr. Divd.:**	$0.720
Total Assets:	$2,684,479,000	**Net Worth:**	$235,474,000	**Debt/ Equity:**	0.7851

Integra Lifesciences Holdings Corp

311 C Enterprise Dr., Plainsboro, NJ, 08536; *PH:* 1-609-275-0500; *Fax:* 1-609-275-5363; *http://* www.integra-ls.com; *Email:* cehling@integra-ls.com

General - Incorporation ... DE
Employees ... 1,750
Auditor ... PricewaterhouseCoopers LLP
Stk Agt ... American Stock Transfer & Trust Co.
Counsel ... NA
DUNS No. ... 79-016-8090

Stock- Price on:12/24/2007 ... $48.73
Stock Exchange ... NDQ
Ticker Symbol ... IART
Outstanding Shares ... NA
E.P.S ... $1.03
Shareholders ... NA

Business: The group's principal activities are to develop, manufacture and market medical devices, implants and biomaterials for neurosurgery, orthopedics and soft tissue repair. The group operates in two segments: neurosciences and lifesciences. Neurosciences segment provides implants, devices and monitors used in neurosurgery, neurotrauma and related critical care. Lifesciences segment manufactures medical products and devices based on the group's proprietary tissue regeneration technology. Some of the products are camino (R), ventrix (R), integra neurosupplies (TM), vitacuff (R), collacote(R) and biomend(R) membrane. The products of the group are sold in the United States, Canada, the United Kingdom, France, Germany and Asia.

Primary SIC and add'l.: 3842

CIK No: 0000917520

Subsidiaries: Caveangle Limited, GMS mbH, Integra CI, Inc., Integra Clinical Education Institute, Inc., Integra Healthcare Products LLC, Integra LifeSciences (France) LLC, Integra LifeSciences (Ireland) Limited, Integra LifeSciences Corporation, Integra LifeSciences Holdings SAS, Integra LifeSciences Investment Corporation, Integra ME GmbH, Integra NeuroSciences (International), Inc., Integra NeuroSciences (IP), Inc., Integra NeuroSciences Holdings (France) SA, Integra NeuroSciences Holdings B.V. 33 Subsidiaries included in the Index

Officers: Stuart M. Essig/Dir., CEO, Pres./$3,534,840.00, Robert Perrett/CEO, Pres. - Integra Miltex, Howard Jamner/Chmn. - Jarit Surgical Instruments, Maureen B. Bellantoni/CFO, Exec. VP/$648,579.00, Richard D. Gorelick/Sr. VP, General Counsel, David B. Holtz/Sr. VP - Finance/$1,015,824.00, Michael Esch/VP - Product Development, Eric Fourcault/Divisional VP - EMEA, Steven Peltier/VP - Regulatory Affairs, John B. Henneman/Exec. VP, Chief Administrative Officer, Sec./$2,547,119.00, Thomas W. Tarca/VP - Marketing, Reconstructive Surgery, Patrick Sparkes/VP, Chief Administrative Officer - Europe, Mark Spilker/VP - Neurosurgical Marketing, Product Development, Robert Rogowski/Pres. - Jarit Surgical Instruments, Wilma J. Davis/Sr. VP - Human Resources *(34 Officers included in Index)*

Directors: Stuart M. Essig/Dir., CEO, Pres., Richard E. Caruso/Chmn., Keith Bradley/Dir., James M. Sullivan/Dir., Anne M. Vanlent/Dir., Christian S. Schade/Dir., Neal Moszkowski/Dir., Thomas J. Baltimore/Dir.

Owners: Capital Research and Management Company, David B. Holtz, Insiders, Neal Moszkowski, Richard E. Caruso, Stuart M. Essig, T. Rowe Price Associates, Inc., Christian S. Schade, John B. Henneman, Provco Leasing Corporation, Judith E. OGrady, Anne M. VanLent, William Blair & Company, L.L.C, Keith Bradley, TRU ST PARTNERSHIP, L.P. *(17 Owners included in Index)*

Financial Data: *Fiscal Year End:*12/31 *Latest Annual Data:* 12/31/2006

Year	Sales	Net Income
2006	$419,297,000	$29,407,000
2005	$277,935,000	$37,194,000
2004	$229,825,000	$17,197,000

Curr. Assets:	$221,761,000	**Curr. Liab.:**	$274,017,000	**P/E Ratio:**	47.31
Plant, Equip.:	$42,559,000	**Total Liab.:**	$317,456,000	**Indic. Yr. Divd.:**	NA
Total Assets:	$613,618,000	**Net Worth:**	$296,162,000	**Debt/ Equity:**	0.0272

Integral Systems Inc

5000 Philadelphia Way, Lanham, MD, 20706; *PH:* 1-301-731-4233; *Fax:* 1-301-731-9606; *http://* www.integ.com

General - Incorporation ... MD
Employees ... 420
Auditor ... Bernstein & Pinchuk, LLP
Stk Agt ... Registrar & Transfer Co
Counsel ... NA
DUNS No. ... 10-192-5139

Stock- Price on:12/24/2007 ... $24.02
Stock Exchange ... NDQ
Ticker Symbol ... ISYS
Outstanding Shares ... 11,110,000
E.P.S ... $1.17
Shareholders ... NA

Business: The group's principal activities are to build satellite ground systems for command, control, integration, data processing and simulation. The group provides ground systems for over 190 different satellite missions for communications, science, meteorology and earth resource applications. The domestic and international customer base includes government, commercial satellite operators, spacecraft manufactures, payload manufacturers and aerospace systems integrators. The software products include epoch 2000, oasys and abe. Epoch 2000 is used for satellite command and control. Oasys helps in spacecraft orbit determination and control. Abe provides statistical analysis of the information recorded in the real-time epoch archives. The group operates in France, the Netherlands, Thailand and Mexico.

Primary SIC and add'l.: 7373 8711 7372 7374

CIK No: 0000718130

Subsidiaries: Integral Marketing, Inc., Lumistar, Inc, Newpoint Technologies Inc., RT Logic, RT Logic Tract TT2, LLC, SAT Corporation

Officers: Alan W. Baldwin/Dir., CEO, Pres., William M. Bambarger/Exec. VP, CFO, Treasurer, Stuart C. Daughtridge/Exec. VP - Commercial Segment, Elaine M. Brown/Exec. VP - Administration, Sec., Peter J. Gaffney/Exec. VP - New Business, Technology Development, James G. Schuetzle/Exec. VP - Government Division

Directors: Alan W. Baldwin/Dir., CEO, Pres., John M. Albertine/Chmn., Doss R. McComas/Dir., Paul G. Casner/Dir., William F. Harley/Dir., William F. Leimkuhler/Dir.

Owners: Insiders/3.30%, Stuart C. Daughtridge, Patrick R. Woods, Thomas L. Gough/1.40%, Fursa Alternative Strategies, LLC/12.00%, William F. Leimkuhler, Dominic A. Laiti, Gary A. Prince, Ashford Capital Management, Inc./6.70%, Peter J. Gaffney, Doss R. McComas, James G. Schuetzle, Elaine M. Brown, Royce& Associates, LLC/7.10%

Financial Data: *Fiscal Year End:*09/30 *Latest Annual Data:* 9/30/2006

Year	Sales	Net Income
2006	$116,531,000	$12,339,000
2005	$97,725,000	$6,301,000
2004	$90,311,000	$6,761,000

Curr. Assets:	$98,865,000	**Curr. Liab.:**	$24,149,000	**P/E Ratio:**	24.26
Plant, Equip.:	$14,990,000	**Total Liab.:**	$24,149,000	**Indic. Yr. Divd.:**	$0.280
Total Assets:	$166,851,000	**Net Worth:**	$142,702,000	**Debt/ Equity:**	NA

Integral Technologies Inc

805 W Orchard Dr., Ste. 7, Bellingham, WA, 98225; *PH:* 1-360-752-1982; *Fax:* 1-360-752-1983; *http://* www.itkg.net; *Email:* itkgbb@itkg.net

General - Incorporation ... NV
Employees ... 5
Auditor ... Pannell Kerr Forster
Stk Agt ... Corporate Stock Transfer, Inc.
Counsel ... NA
DUNS No. ... NA

Stock- Price on:12/24/2007 ... $1.49
Stock Exchange ... OTC
Ticker Symbol ... ITKG
Outstanding Shares ... 45,490,000
E.P.S ... -$0.14
Shareholders ... NA

Business: The groups principal activities include researching, developing and commercializing ElectriPlast(R) technology. The group operates from the United States.

Primary SIC and add'l.: 3663 3559

CIK No: 0001018281

Subsidiaries: Antek Wireless Inc., Integral Vision Systems, Inc, Plastenna, Inc

Officers: William Robinson/Co - Founder, Chmn., CEO, William Ince/Co - Founder, CFO, Pres., Tom Aisenbrey/GM, VP - Product Development

Directors: William Robinson/Co - Founder, Chmn., CEO, William Ince/Co - Founder, CFO, Pres.

Owners: Wellington Management Company, LLP/9.00%, William S. Robinson/5.10%, Thomas Aisenbrey/5.60%, Insiders/14.70%, William A. Ince/4.60%

Financial Data: *Fiscal Year End:*06/30 *Latest Annual Data:* 6/30/2006

Year	Sales	Net Income
2006	$2,000	-$2,104,000
2005	$67,000	-$1,812,000
2004	$1,000	-$2,544,000

Curr. Assets:	$1,606,000	**Curr. Liab.:**	$688,000		
Plant, Equip.:	NA	**Total Liab.:**	$688,000	**Indic. Yr. Divd.:**	NA
Total Assets:	$1,606,000	**Net Worth:**	$918,000	**Debt/ Equity:**	NA

Integral Vision Inc

49113 Wixom Tech Dr., Wixom, MI, 48393; *PH:* 1-248-668-9230; *Fax:* 1-248-668-9384; *http://* www.iv-usa.com; *Email:* sales@iv-usa.com

General - Incorporation ... MI
Employees ... 18
Auditor ... Rehmann Robson P.C
Stk Agt ... Computershare Investor Services LLC
Counsel ... Warren Cameron Faust & Asciutto
DUNS No. ... 04-928-1215

Stock- Price on:12/24/2007 ... $0.45
Stock Exchange ... OTC
Ticker Symbol ... INVI
Outstanding Shares ... 29,510,000
E.P.S ... -$0.1
Shareholders ... NA

Business: The group's principal activities are to develop, manufacture and market microprocessor-based process monitoring and control systems for industrial manufacturing environments. The group's product is used for optical display inspection (machine vision systems). The machine vision system is used for ensuring a product quality during manufacturing process. The group's machine vision systems automatically identify, gauge or inspect parts with speed and accuracy. The group provides quantitative information about each part is evaluated for functional or cosmetic defects. The systems can be configured to statistically monitor the production process and send data to other equipment in the manufacturing cell. Such data could be used for diverter to send defective parts to a reject bin or by process controllers to automatically adjust process variables. The system is applied to industries like aerospace, medical, textiles and other manufacturing units.

Primary SIC and add'l.: 3829

CIK No: 0000719152

Subsidiaries: Integral Vision LTD

Officers: Charles J. Drake/Chmn., CEO/$174,951.00, Arthur D. Harmala/VP - Marketing/$128,036.00, Mark R. Doede/CFO, COO, Pres./$201,140.00, Vincent Shunsky/Dir., Treasurer, Andrew Blowers/CTO/$205,735.00, Laura Guerrant/Guerrant Assoc.

Directors: Charles J. Drake/Chmn., CEO, Vincent Shunsky/Dir., Treasurer

Owners: Vincent Shunsky, Charles J. Drake/8.29%, Maxco, Inc./8.17%, Mark A. Michniewicz, John R. Kiely/12.25%, J. N. Hunter/9.88%, Samuel O. Mallory, Max A. Coon, Insiders/12.68%, Bonanza Master Fund, LTD/16.24%, Arhur D. Harmala, Austin W. Marxe/19.36%, Andrew Blowers, Mark R. Doede/1.51%

Financial Data: Fiscal Year End:12/31   Latest Annual Data: 12/31/2006

Year	Sales	Net Income
2006	$835,000	-$2,974,000
2005	$686,000	-$2,679,000
2004	$1,542,000	-$2,459,000

Curr. Assets:	$578,000	**Curr. Liab.:**	$923,000		
Plant, Equip.:	$267,000	**Total Liab.:**	$1,301,000	**Indic. Yr. Divd.:**	NA
Total Assets:	$881,000	**Net Worth:**	-$420,000	**Debt/ Equity:**	NA

IntegraMed America

2 Manhattanville Rd., 3rd. Fl., Purchase, NY, 10577; *PH:* 1-914-253-8000; *Fax:* 1-914-253-8008; *http://* www.integramed.com

General - Incorporation	DE	**Stock**- Price on:12/24/2007	$11.17
Employees	849	Stock Exchange	NDQ
Auditor	Pricewaterhousecoopers LLP	Ticker Symbol	INMD
Stk Agt	American Stock Transfer & Trust Co.	Outstanding Shares	8,140,000
Counsel	Dorsey & Whitney LLP	E.P.S.	NA
DUNS No.	15-143-9767	Shareholders	NA

Business: The group's principle activities are to offer products and services to patients, providers, payers and pharmaceutical manufacturers in the fertility industry in 23 major markets. The group has twenty three fertility centers in major markets across the United States. Five of the fertility centers are designated as 'reproductive science centers(r)' that have access to the group's fertilitydirect program. The group is also involved in the additional activities of: (i) administrative services, including accounting and finance, human resource functions and purchasing of supplies and equipment; (ii) access to capital and servicing and financing of patient accounts receivable; (iii) marketing and sales; (iv) integrated information. The group's quarterly revenue for Sep'07 was 40.31 millions of USD.

Primary SIC and add'l.: 8011 8071

CIK No: 0000885988

Subsidiaries: IntegraMed Financial Services, Inc., IntegraMed Pharmaceutical Services, Inc., IntegraMed Reproductive Genetics, Inc, IVF America (NJ), Inc., Reproductive Partners, Inc., Women Medical & Diagnostic Center, Inc.

Officers: Jay Higham/Dir., CEO, Pres./$880,578.00, Donald S. Wood/Sr. VP - Operations Administration/$314,160.00, Claude E. White/VP, General Counsel, Pamela Schumann/Pres. - Consumer Services Division, Scott Soifer/VP - Strategy, Business Development/$239,151.00, John W. Hlywak/CFO, Exec. VP/$382,500.00, Ken Abbott/Internet Product Mgr., Joseph J. Travia/55/Sr. VP - Operations Eastern Region/$287,461.00, Joe Travia/Pres. - Fertility Centers Division

Directors: Jay Higham/Dir., CEO, Pres., Gerardo Canet/Chmn., Sarason D. Liebler/Dir., Wayne R. Moon/Dir., Lawrence J. Stuesser/Dir., Elizabeth E. Tallett/Dir., Yvonne S. Thornton/Dir.

Owners: Scott Soifer, Insiders/6.29%, Austin W. Marxe/7.98%, Peter R. Kellogg/13.44%, Yvonne S. Thornton, Donald S. Wood, Elizabeth E. Tallett, Lawrence J. Stuesser, Gerardo Canet, John W. Hlywak/1.13%, Healthinvest Partners B/9.59%, Sarason D. Liebler, Joseph J. Travia, Jay Higham/1.63%, Wayne R. Moon *(16 Owners included in Index)*

Financial Data: Fiscal Year End:12/31   Latest Annual Data: 12/31/2006

Year	Sales	Net Income
2006	NA	NA
2005	NA	NA
2004	NA	NA

Curr. Assets:	$38,028,000	**Curr. Liab.:**	$25,687,000		
Plant, Equip.:	$13,900,000	**Total Liab.:**	$34,688,000	**Indic. Yr. Divd.:**	NA
Total Assets:	$75,522,000	**Net Worth:**	$40,834,000	**Debt/ Equity:**	0.1661

Integrated BioPharma Inc

225 Long Ave., Hillside, NJ, 07205; *PH:* 1-973-926-0816; *Fax:* 1-973-926-1735; *http://* www.ibiopharma.com

General - Incorporation	DE	**Stock**- Price on:12/24/2007	NA
Employees	156	Stock Exchange	NDQ
Auditor	Amper, Politziner & Mattia P.C	Ticker Symbol	INBP
Stk Agt	Continental Stock Transfer & Trust Co	Outstanding Shares	NA
Counsel	NA	E.P.S.	-$0.45
DUNS No.	05-049-0903	Shareholders	NA

Business: The group's principal activity is to manufacture, market and sell vitamins, nutritional supplements and herbal products. These products are available throughout the United States. The group's subsidiary, manhattan drug company inc, manufactures vitamins and nutritional supplements for sale to distributors and other marketers of their products. The major suppliers of the group include roche vitamins inc, triarco inc and nutrichem resources company. The group also manufactures similar products under its own private brand, 'vitamin factory' which is sold through its own retail outlet or through mail order. It owns the registration in the United States patent and trademark offices for 'oxitiva'. During fiscal 2004, the group acquired nucycle therapy inc, natex georgia llc, paxis pharmaceuticals inc and assets of hauser technical services inc.

Primary SIC and add'l.: 2834

CIK No: 0001016504

Subsidiaries: AgroLabs, Inc, Biotechnologies, Inc., Hauser Pharmaceutical Services, Inc., IHT Health Products, Inc, IHT Properties, Inc, Manhattan Drug Company, Inc, Paxis Pharmaceuticals, Inc., Scientific Sports Nutrition, Inc, Vitamin Factory, Inc.

Officers: Gerald E. Kay/Chmn., CEO - Shareholder, Riva Sheppard/VP - Sales, Manufacturing, Seymour Flug/Sr. Advisor, Christina Kay/VP - Logistics, Dina L. Masi/CFO, Sr. VP, Sec.

Directors: Gerald E. Kay/Chmn., CEO - Shareholder

Owners: Vidadi M. Yusibov, Glenn Chang, Christina Kay/8.40%, Seymour Flug/8.20%, Robert B. Kay/8.50%, Zarko Kraljevic, Riva Sheppard/8.40%, Dina L. Masi, Robert Canarick/1.30%, Carl DeSantis/16.30%, Gerald E. Kay/37.30%, Insiders/69.40%

Financial Data: Fiscal Year End:06/30   Latest Annual Data: 06/30/2007

Year	Sales	Net Income
2007	$60,160,000	-$2,044,000
2006	$57,820,000	$8,432,000
2005	$32,736,000	-$8,580,000

Curr. Assets:	$26,855,000	**Curr. Liab.:**	$15,862,000		
Plant, Equip.:	$4,377,000	**Total Liab.:**	$24,212,000	**Indic. Yr. Divd.:**	NA
Total Assets:	$44,209,000	**Net Worth:**	$19,997,000	**Debt/ Equity:**	NA

Integrated Data Corp

3422 Old Capital Trl., Ste. 741, Wilmington, DE, 19808; *PH:* 1-484-212-4137; *Fax:* 1-484-212-4141; *http://* www.integrateddatacorp.com; *Email:* info@integrateddatacorp.com

General - Incorporation	DE	**Stock**- Price on:12/24/2007	$1.1
Employees	NA	Stock Exchange	OTC
Auditor	Morison Cogen LLP	Ticker Symbol	ITDD
Stk Agt	American Stock Transfer & Trust Co.	Outstanding Shares	NA
Counsel	NA	E.P.S.	NA
DUNS No.	NA	Shareholders	NA

Business: The group's principal activity is to develop a technology for digital transmission of data utilizing radio frequencies transmitted by FM radio stations. The claricast(tm) technology utilizes FM-sca (subsidiary communication authorization) channels from FM radio stations throughout the world. Fm-sca channels do not require new radio frequency spectrum allocation and use the existing transmission infrastructure FM radio station. The technology can be applied for intelligent signage, smart mobile devices, automobile data services and security alert services. The group is developing a wireless voicemail system based on the technology that transmits a message to the owner of a handheld voicemail player, known as a voca(tm), in the actual voice of the person generating the message. On 11-Dec-2002, the group acquired outstanding capital stock of c4 services ltd and on 12-Dec-2002, the group acquired 41% interest in datawave systems inc.

Primary SIC and add'l.: 6719 4813

CIK No: 0000941814

Subsidiaries: C3 Technologies Inc, DataWave International License, DataWave Systems Inc., Integrated Communications Services, Integrated Communications Services Ltd, Integrated Data Technologies Ltd

Officers: Abe Carmel/Dir., CEO, Stuart W. Settle/Dir., Sec., David C. Bryan/Dir., Pres.

Directors: Abe Carmel/Dir., CEO, Ed Will/Dir., Stuart W. Settle/Dir., Sec., Ian Tromans/Dir., David C. Bryan/Dir., Pres.

Owners: David C. Bryan/1.30%, B. Candlin/12.70%, Ian Tromans, I. Hopkins/12.90%, Ansteed Investments Ltd/19.50%, Stuart W. Settle, Eduard Will, Integrated Technologies & Systems Ltd/21.30%, Insiders/2.30%

Financial Data: Fiscal Year End:06/30   Latest Annual Data: 6/30/2006

Year	Sales	Net Income
2006	$73,000	$390,000
2004	$18,174,000	-$2,925,000
2003	$4,017,000	$2,856,000

Curr. Assets:	$79,000	**Curr. Liab.:**	$378,000		
Plant, Equip.:	NA	**Total Liab.:**	$378,000	**Indic. Yr. Divd.:**	NA
Total Assets:	$3,307,000	**Net Worth:**	$2,929,000	**Debt/ Equity:**	0.0285

Integrated Device Technology Inc

6024 Silver Creek Valley Rd., San Jose, CA, 95138; *PH:* 1-408-284-8200; *Fax:* 1-408-284-2775; *http://* www.idt.com; *Email:* ir@idt.com

General - Incorporation	DE	**Stock**- Price on:12/24/2007	$15.11
Employees	2,400	Stock Exchange	NDQ
Auditor	PricewaterhouseCoopers LLP	Ticker Symbol	IDTI
Stk Agt	Computershare Investor Services LLC	Outstanding Shares	197,810,000
Counsel	NA	E.P.S.	-$0.04
DUNS No.	03-814-2600	Shareholders	NA

Business: The group's principle activities include designing, developing, manufacturing and marketing semiconductor products. The applications for these products include data networking and telecommunications equipment, storage area networks, other networked peripherals and servers and personal computers. The group operates in two business segments: communications and high-performance logic and static random access memories. The communications and high-performance logic segment includes fifos and multi-ports. The srams segment consists of high-speed srams. The group markets its products primarily to original equipment manufacturers. The group has operations in Asia-Pacific, Japan and Europe.

Primary SIC and add'l.: 3669 3674

CIK No: 0000703361

Subsidiaries: Baccarat Silicon, Inc., Bay Semiconductor, Inc., Creative Electric, Inc., I.D.T. France S.A.R.L., ICS Technologies, Inc., ICST, Inc., IDT Asia, Limited, IDT Canada Holdings Inc., IDT Canada Inc., IDT Design Australia Pty Ltd., IDT Europe Limited, IDT Foreign Sales Corporation, IDT Integrated Device Technology AB (Sweden), IDT Singapore Pte. Ltd., IDT-Newave Technology (Shanghai) Co. Ltd. 36 Subsidiaries included in the Index

Officers: Greg Lang/Dir., CEO, Pres./$2,632,562.00, Julian Hawkins/VP - World Wide Sales, Jimmy J.M. Lee/Sr. VP, GM - Timing Solutions Group/$1,436,113.00, Clyde Hosein/VP, CFO, Sec./$1,178,070.00, Scott Sarnikowski/VP, GM - IP Co - Processor Division, Thomas Brenner/VP, GM - Flow, Control Management Division, Michael Miller/CTO, Phil Bourekas/VP, GM - PC Audio Operations, Mike Hunter/VP - World Wide Manufacturing/$994,072.00, Chuen-Der Lien/CTO, VP - Process, Circuit Design/$1,016,629.00, Mario Montana/VP, GM - Serial, Switching Division, Chad Taggard/VP - Strategic Planning, Worldwide Marketing

Directors: Greg Lang/Dir., CEO, Pres., Hock E. Tan/Chmn., Ronald Smith/Dir., Lewis Eggebrecht/Dir., John C. Bolger/Dir., John A. Schofield/Dir., John D. Howard/Dir., Kenneth S. Kannappan/Dir., Nam P. Suh/Dir.

Owners: John Howard, Jimmy J.M. Lee, FMR Corp./13.70%, Nam P. Suh, John C. Bolger, Mike Hunter, Perry Corp./5.70%, John Schofield, Clyde R. Hosein, Chuen-Der Lien, Lewis Eggebrecht, Hock Tan, Ken Kannappan, Gregory S. Lang, Ron Smith *(16 Owners included in Index)*

Financial Data: Fiscal Year End:04/02   Latest Annual Data: 4/1/2007

Year	Sales	Net Income
2007	$803,596,000	-$7,578,000
2006	$527,778,000	-$81,708,000
2005	$390,640,000	$13,333,000

Curr. Assets:	$682,804,000	**Curr. Liab.:**	$99,425,000		
Plant, Equip.:	$124,570,000	**Total Liab.:**	$115,024,000	**Indic. Yr. Divd.:**	NA
Total Assets:	$902,140,000	**Net Worth:**	$787,116,000	**Debt/ Equity:**	NA

Integrated Electrical Services Inc

1800 W Loop S., Ste. 500, Houston, TX, 77027; *PH:* 1-713-860-1500; *Fax:* 1-713-860-1599; *http://* www.ies-co.com; *Email:* info@ies-co.com

General - Incorporation	DE	Stock - Price on:12/24/2007	$33.25
Employees	7,183	Stock Exchange	NDQ
Auditor	Ernst & Young LLP	Ticker Symbol	IESC
Stk Agt	Wachovia Bank N.A	Outstanding Shares	15,350,000
Counsel	NA	E.P.S.	$1.88
DUNS No.	83-983-2631	Shareholders	NA

Business: The group's principal activities are to provide electrical contracting services and solutions in the data communications and utilities markets. The group provides services that include designing, building and maintaining electrical, data communications, installation of fire and security alarm systems and utilities systems for commercial, industrial and residential customers. The electrical contracting services include design of the electrical distribution systems within a building or complex, procurement and installation of wiring and connection to power sources and end use equipment and fixtures. The data communication solutions include design and installation of external cables for university and corporate campuses and data centers and switching stations for data communications companies.

Primary SIC and add'l.: 1731

CIK No: 0001048268

Subsidiaries: Aladdin-Ward Electric & Air, Inc., Amber Electric, Inc., ARC Electric, Incorporated, Bachofner Electric, Inc., Bear Acquisition Corporation, Bexar Electric Company, Ltd., Bexar Electric II LLC, Bryant Electric Company, Inc., BW Consolidated, Inc., Bw/bec Ii LLC, BW/BEC, Inc., Bw/bec, LLC, Charles P. Bagby Co., Inc., Collier Electric Company, Inc., Commercial Electrical Contractors, Inc. 133 Subsidiaries included in the Index

Officers: Michael J. Caliel/48/Dir., CEO, Pres., Curt L. Warnock/Sr. VP, General Counsel, Corp. Sec., David A. Miller/Chief Accounting Officer, Sr. VP, Robert B. Callahan/Sr. VP - Human Resources, Raymond K. Guba/48/CFO, Sr. VP

Directors: Michael J. Caliel/48/Dir., CEO, Pres., Michael J. Hall/Chmn., Charles H. Beynon/Dir., Robert W. Butts/Dir., Donald L. Luke/Dir., John E. Welsh/Dir., Joseph V. Lash/Dir.

Owners: Richard C. Humphrey, Michael J. Hall, Jeffrey L. Gendell/34.03%, Robert W. Butts/11.77%, Robert Callahan, Curt L. Warnock, Charles H. Beynon, Donald L. Luke, Insiders/12.67%, John E. Welsh, Michael J. Caliel, Third Point LLC/6.43%, David A. Miller

Financial Data: *Fiscal Year End:*09/30 *Latest Annual Data:* 9/30/2006

Year	Sales	Net Income
2006	$950,234,000	-$383,000
2005	$1,102,814,000	-$129,632,000
2004	$1,424,100,000	-$124,864,000

Curr. Assets:	$286,408,000	Curr. Liab.:	$150,283,000		
Plant, Equip.:	$26,904,000	Total Liab.:	$220,872,000	Indic. Yr. Divd.:	NA
Total Assets:	$375,515,000	Net Worth:	$154,643,000	Debt/ Equity:	0.3821

Integrated Environmental Technologies Ltd

4235 Commerce St., Little River, SC, 29566; *PH:* 1-843-390-2500; *Fax:* 1-843-390-3900; *http://* www.ietltd.net

General - Incorporation		Stock - Price on:12/24/2007	$0.17
Employees	10	Stock Exchange	OTC
Auditor	NA	Ticker Symbol	IEVM
Stk Agt	Nevada Agency & Trust Company	Outstanding Shares	51,190,000
Counsel	NA	E.P.S.	-$0.037
DUNS No.	NA	Shareholders	NA

Business: The groups principle activities include designing, marketing, selling, and assembling equipment, based on EcaFlo technology. The group operates from the United States. The group's quarterly revenue for Sep '07 was 0.21 millions of USD.

Primary SIC and add'l.: 3589

CIK No: 0001340064

Financial Data: *Fiscal Year End:*NA *Latest Annual Data:* 12/31/2006

Year	Sales	Net Income
2006	$434,000	-$1,610,000
2005	$109,000	-$1,449,000
2004	NA	-$1,462,000

Curr. Assets:	$253,000	Curr. Liab.:	$624,000		
Plant, Equip.:	$7,000	Total Liab.:	$663,000	Indic. Yr. Divd.:	NA
Total Assets:	$260,000	Net Worth:	-$402,000	Debt/ Equity:	NA

Integrated Healthcare Holdings Inc

695 Town Ctr Dr., Ste. 260, Costa Mesa, CA, 92705; *PH:* 1-714-953-3652; *Fax:* 1-714-953-3384; *http://* www.ihhioc.com

General - Incorporation	NV	Stock - Price on:12/24/2007	$0.12
Employees	2,775	Stock Exchange	OTC
Auditor	Ramirez International	Ticker Symbol	IHCH
Stk Agt	StockTrans, Inc.	Outstanding Shares	NA
Counsel	NA	E.P.S.	-$0.18
DUNS No.	NA	Shareholders	NA

Business: The group is a development stage company and does not operate any business activities that produce revenues. The company intends to acquire, own and operate hospitals and surgical services throughout the United States. The group's total revenue for year 2007 was 350.67 millions of USD.

Primary SIC and add'l.: 8099

CIK No: 0001051488

Subsidiaries: Hospitals and Mogel Management Group, Inc, WMC-SA, Inc

Officers: Bruce Mogel/CEO/$377,294.00, Daniel Brothman/Sr. VP - Operations/$374,258.00, Larry B. Anderson/Pres./$383,892.00, Shelle Malm/Dir. - Business Development, Western Medical Center Santa Ana, Coastal Communities Hospital, Jodie Wingo/Contact - Western Medical Center Anaheim, Kim Pensenstadler/Chapman Medical Center, Dir. - Business Development, Steve Blake/CFO

Directors: Ajay G. Meka/57/Chmn.

Owners: Robert C. Jameson, Healthcare Financial Management & Acquisitions, Inc., Fernando J. Niebla, Kali P. Chaudhuri, M.D., Medical Provider Financial Corporation III, William E. Thomas, Daniel J. Brothman, Milan Mehta, Larry B. Anderson, Ajay G. Meka, Insiders, Michael Metzler, Bruce Mogel, Network, LLC, Maurice J. DeWald

Financial Data: *Fiscal Year End:*12/31 *Latest Annual Data:* 03/31/2007

Year	Sales	Net Income
2007	$350,672,000	-$20,538,000
2005	$284,314,000	-$44,558,000
2004	NA	-$1,840,000

Curr. Assets:	$74,473,000	Curr. Liab.:	$65,795,000		
Plant, Equip.:	$59,431,000	Total Liab.:	$162,152,000	Indic. Yr. Divd.:	NA
Total Assets:	$135,046,000	Net Worth:	-$30,447,000	Debt/ Equity:	NA

Integrated Management Information Inc

221 Wilcox St. Ste., Castle Rock, CO, 80104; *PH:* 1-303-895-3002; *Fax:* 1-720-221-0411; *http://* imiglobal.com

General - Incorporation	CO	Stock - Price on:12/24/2007	$0.18
Employees	14	Stock Exchange	OTC
Auditor	E. R&all Gruber, Cpa P.C	Ticker Symbol	INMG
Stk Agt	Corporate Stock Transfer, Inc.	Outstanding Shares	19,330,000
Counsel	NA	E.P.S.	-$0.06
DUNS No.	NA	Shareholders	NA

Business: The groups principle activity is to provide information technology and electronic documentation management to the livestock industry. In May 2005, the group acquired Cattlefeeding.com, Inc. The group operates from the United States.

Primary SIC and add'l.: 700

CIK No: 0001360565

Officers: John Saunders/Chmn., CEO, Pres., Mark D. McGregor/CFO, Rob Streight/COO, Leann Saunders/Exec. VP - Quality Services, Cara Gerken/VP - Quality Services, Cory Weaver/VP - Information Technologies, Dusty Markham/Assist. VP - Business Development, Rob Cook/Dir. - Cattlenetworkcom

Directors: John Saunders/Chmn., CEO, Pres., Gary Smith/Dir., Adam Larson/Dir., Pete Lapaseotes/Dir., Robert Van Schoick/Dir.

Owners: Gary Smith, Adam Larson, Cory Weaver, Jay Belk/7.67%, John Saunders/41.27%, Michael D. Smith/5.45%, Cara Gerken, Insiders/55.49%

Financial Data: *Fiscal Year End:*NA *Latest Annual Data:* 03/31/2007

Year	Sales	Net Income
2007	NA	NA
2006	$1,540,000	-$1,559,000

Curr. Assets:	$456,000	Curr. Liab.:	$382,000		
Plant, Equip.:	$32,000	Total Liab.:	$732,000	Indic. Yr. Divd.:	NA
Total Assets:	$1,003,000	Net Worth:	$271,000	Debt/ Equity:	1.2915

Integrated Media Holdings Inc

Formerly: Endavo Media & Communications Inc
10 Glenlake Pkwy., Ste. 130, Atlanta, GA, 30328; *PH:* 1-678-222-3445; *http://* www.endavomedia.com

General - Incorporation	DE	Stock - Price on:12/24/2007	$0.04
Employees	12	Stock Exchange	OTC
Auditor	Ronald N. Silberstein, CPA, PLLC	Ticker Symbol	EDVOE
Stk Agt	Atlas Stock Transfer Corp	Outstanding Shares	17,250,000
Counsel	NA	E.P.S.	-$0.18
DUNS No.	NA	Shareholders	NA

Business: The group's principal activity is to provide telecommunication services using fiber optic cable. These services include local and long distance telephone, video conferencing, and cable television with video on demand, computer email and a host of other related services. The group provides its services to residential, commercial, governmental and educational institutions. The group's product is cerinet ip (Internet protocol) utility network. Cerinet is an ip open standard architecture that integrates software and electronic hardware from ip compliant vendors to handle packets of voice, video and data from origination to termination of that packet.

Primary SIC and add'l.: 4899

CIK No: 0001084507

Subsidiaries: New Planet Resources, Inc., Susquina, Inc.

Officers: Paul D. Hamm/Chmn., CEO, Pres., Peter L. Contardo/VP - Operations, Mario J. Pino/VP - Entertainment, Media, Jorge F. Tomassello/VP - Latin Content

Directors: Paul D. Hamm/Chmn., CEO, Pres., Jerry Dunlap/Dir.

Financial Data: *Fiscal Year End:*12/31 *Latest Annual Data:* 12/31/2006

Year	Sales	Net Income
2006	$1,504,000	-$5,713,000
2005	$432,000	-$4,380,000
2004	$178,000	-$5,303,000

Curr. Assets:	$628,000	Curr. Liab.:	$5,360,000		
Plant, Equip.:	$1,182,000	Total Liab.:	$5,360,000	Indic. Yr. Divd.:	NA
Total Assets:	$5,018,000	Net Worth:	-$342,000	Debt/ Equity:	NA

Integrated Pharmaceuticals Inc

310 Authority Dr., Fitchburg, MA, 01420; *PH:* 1-978-696-0020; *http://* www.intepharm.com; *Email:* investors@intepharm.com

General - Incorporation	ID	Stock - Price on:12/24/2007	$0.2
Employees	6	Stock Exchange	OTC
Auditor	Williams & Webster, P.S	Ticker Symbol	INTP
Stk Agt	Columbia Stock Transfer Co	Outstanding Shares	40,560,000
Counsel	NA	E.P.S.	-$0.07
DUNS No.	NA	Shareholders	NA

Business: The group's principal activity is production of pharmaceuticals and specialty chemicals and compounds. It serves the pharmaceutical, neutraceutical, food and agriculture industries.

Primary SIC and add'l.: 2835

CIK No: 0001265449

Officers: Chinmay Chatterjee/Founder, Dir., CEO, Pres., Richard W. Schoenfeld/VP - Marketing, Business Development, Nilu P. Chatterjee/Founder, VP - Research, Product Development, Dir., Edward D. Furtado/Founder, VP - Operations, Dir.

Directors: Chinmay Chatterjee/Founder, Dir., CEO, Pres., Ken Wlosek/47/Dir., Nilu P. Chatterjee/Founder, VP - Research, Product Development, Dir., Edward D. Furtado/Founder, VP - Operations, Dir.

Owners: Sally Johnson-Chin/2.40%, Ken Wlosek/0.40%, Insiders/38.70%, David H. Smith/19.80%, Chinmay Chatterjee/9.20%, Edward Furtado/3.30%, Nilu P. Chatterjee/3.60%

Financial Data: Fiscal Year End:12/31   Latest Annual Data: 12/31/2006

Year	Sales	Net Income
2006	$61,000	-$2,141,000
2005	$77,000	-$3,855,000

Curr. Assets:	$1,038,000	Curr. Liab.:	$405,000		
Plant, Equip.:	$1,279,000	Total Liab.:	$405,000	Indic. Yr. Divd.:	NA
Total Assets:	$2,429,000	Net Worth:	$2,024,000	Debt/ Equity:	NA

Integrated Security Systems Inc

2009 Chenault Dr., Ste. 114, Carrollton, TX, 75006; *PH:* 1-972-444-8280; *Fax:* 1-972-869-3843; *http://* www.integratedsecurity.com

General - Incorporation	DE	Stock- Price on:12/24/2007	$0.08
Employees	38	Stock Exchange	OTC
Auditor	Weaver & Tidwell LLP	Ticker Symbol	IZZI
Stk Agt	American Stock Transfer & Trust Co.	Outstanding Shares	98,740,000
Counsel	NA	E.P.S.	-$0.05
DUNS No.	80-729-1778	Shareholders	NA

Business: The group's principal activities are to design, develop, manufacture, distribute and service security and traffic control products. It operates through two segments: b&b electromatic, inc. And intelli-site, inc. B&b electromatic, inc. Manufactures and sells road and bridge perimeter security and railroad physical security products such as warning gates, crashbarriers, lane changers, navigational lighting, airport lighting and hydraulic gates. Intelli-site, inc. Develops and markets programmable security systems that integrate multiple security devices and subsystems for governmental, commercial and industrial facilities utilizing the intelli-site(R) software product through systems integrators and original equipment manufacturers to end users. The group operates solely in the domestic market. On 05-Sep-2003, the group acquired armr services corporation.

Primary SIC and add'l.: 3669

CIK No: 0000741114

Subsidiaries: B&b Armr Corporation, B&B Roadway, LLC, DoorTek Corporation, Intelli-Site, Inc.

Officers: Richard B. Powell/Chief Accounting Officer, Controller, Jay Foersterling/Pres., Mohsen Hekmatyar/VP - Sales, Marketing, Service - B, B, Armr Corp, Kristi MacArthur/Controller - B, B, Armr Corp, John Ulibarri/Pres. - Intelli, Site, Inc, Eric Bruening/Customer Service, Marketing, Intelli, Site, Inc, Bob Gardner/Pres. - Doortek Corporation

Directors: C. A. Rundell/Chmn.

Owners: Vernon H. Foersterling, G. M. Ulibarri, US Special Opportunities Trust PLC, William D. Breedlove, Frank R. Marlow, C. A. Rundell, Richard B. Powell, Insiders, Robert M. Galecke, Robert Gardner, Renaissance US Growth Investment Trust PLC, Renaissance Capital Growth & Income Fund III, Inc., Russell Cleveland

Financial Data: Fiscal Year End:06/30   Latest Annual Data: 6/30/2006

Year	Sales	Net Income
2006	$12,278,000	-$4,209,000
2005	$13,479,000	-$4,948,000
2004	$9,827,000	-$3,671,000

Curr. Assets:	$5,006,000	Curr. Liab.:	$6,152,000		
Plant, Equip.:	$494,000	Total Liab.:	$16,906,000	Indic. Yr. Divd.:	NA
Total Assets:	$10,028,000	Net Worth:	-$6,983,000	Debt/ Equity:	NA

Integrated Silicon Solution Inc

1940 Zanker Rd., San Jose, CA, 95112; *PH:* 1-408-969-6600; *Fax:* 1-408-969-7800; *http://* www.issi.com

General - Incorporation	DE	Stock- Price on:12/24/2007	$6.04
Employees	421	Stock Exchange	NDQ
Auditor	Ernst & Young LLP	Ticker Symbol	ISSI
Stk Agt	Mellon Investor Services LLC	Outstanding Shares	37,610,000
Counsel	Wilson Sonsini Goodrich & Rosati	E.P.S.	$0.41
DUNS No.	60-820-8245	Shareholders	NA

Business: The group's principal activity is to design, develop and market high performance memory semiconductors used in Internet access devices, networking equipment, telecom and mobile communications equipment, computer peripherals and other applications. The three products of the group are static random access memory (sram), low and medium density dynamic random access memory (dram) and nonvolatile memory (nvm). The customers of the group are apex, changhong, d-link, samsung, sony, 3com, ambit, askey, cisco, yahoo, bird, ericsson, lg electronics, motorola, nokia, bose, delphi, philips and siemens. The group operates in the United States, China, Hong Kong, Taiwan, Korea, Asia-Pacific, Europe and Canada.

Primary SIC and add'l.: 3674

CIK No: 0000854701

Subsidiaries: Integrated Circuit Solution Inc., Integrated Silicon Solution (Shanghai) Inc., Integrated Silicon Solution (Taiwan) Inc., Integrated Silicon Solution Inc. (Hong Kong) Limited, Signia Technologies Inc., Sofwin, Inc., Winston, Inc.

Officers: Jimmy S.M. Lee/Chmn., CEO, Gary L. Fischer/CFO, Sanjiv Asthana/VP - Sales, Marketing, Henry Pu/GM - Issi, China, Scott D. Howarth/CFO, VP, Chang-Chaio Han/GM - Issi, Taiwan, Sram, Dram Business Division, Kent K.Y. Fu/VP - Quality, Reliability Assurance

Directors: Jimmy S.M. Lee/Chmn., CEO, Kong Yeu Han/Exec. Vice Chmn., Ping K. Ko/57/Dir., Bruce A. Wooley/64/Dir.

Owners: Donald Smith & Co., Inc./9.90%, Dimensional Fund Advisors, Inc./8.40%, Hide L. Tanigami, Kong Yeu Han, Insiders/14.30%, Jimmy S.M. Lee/1.50%, Chang-Chaio Han, Ping K. Ko, Lloyd I. Miller/8.70%, Keith McDonald, Bryant R. Riley/12.10%, Melvin Keating, Scott Howarth, Lip-Bu Tan, Bruce A. Wooley (16 Owners included in Index)

Financial Data: Fiscal Year End:09/30   Latest Annual Data: 9/30/2005

Year	Sales	Net Income
2005	$181,438,000	-$37,892,000
2004	$181,012,000	$3,485,000
2003	$97,660,000	-$28,077,000

Curr. Assets:	$202,455,000	Curr. Liab.:	$54,348,000	P/E Ratio:	604.00
Plant, Equip.:	$21,984,000	Total Liab.:	$56,396,000	Indic. Yr. Divd.:	NA
Total Assets:	$260,278,000	Net Worth:	$203,192,000	Debt/ Equity:	NA

Integrated Surgical Systems Inc

1433 N Market Blvd., Ste. 1, Sacramento, CA, 95834; *PH:* 1-916-285-9943; *Fax:* 1-916-285-9104; *http://* www.robodoc.com; *Email:* issinfo@robodoc.com

General - Incorporation	DE	Stock- Price on:12/24/2007	$0.05
Employees	NA	Stock Exchange	OTC
Auditor	Most & Co., LLP	Ticker Symbol	ISSM
Stk Agt	American Stock Transfer & Trust Co.	Outstanding Shares	NA
Counsel	Snow Becker Krauss P.C.	E.P.S.	$0.90
DUNS No.	62-186-1806	Shareholders	NA

Business: The group's principal activities are to design, manufacture, sell and service image directed computer controlled robotic products for use in orthopedic and neurosurgical procedures. The orthopedic applications products include the robodoc surgical assistant systems, which is a combination of orthodoc presurgical planner and a computer controlled robot, for use in hip and knee replacement surgery. Neurosurgical applications product includes the neuromate system, a computer controlled robotic arm, head stabilizer and presurgical planning workstation, designed to precisely position and hold critical tools during brain surgery. The group also distributes surgical supplies including sterile drapes, bone screws and cutters. The products are marketed in the United States, Europe, Middle East, Africa and Japan.

Primary SIC and add'l.: 3841 7699 7352 5047 7371

CIK No: 0000894871

Subsidiaries: Integrated Surgical Systems, S.A., ISS-SA. In

Owners: Charles J. Novak, Ramesh C. Trivedi/1.63%, Leland W. Witherspoon, Insiders/3.60%, David H. Adams, Michael J. Tomczak, Peter B. Mills

Financial Data: Fiscal Year End:12/31   Latest Annual Data: 12/31/2006

Year	Sales	Net Income
2006	$2,594,000	$1,588,000
2005	$3,430,000	$2,005,000
2004	$2,360,000	-$556,000

Curr. Assets:	$1,902,000	Curr. Liab.:	$1,315,000		
Plant, Equip.:	$9,000	Total Liab.:	$4,015,000	Indic. Yr. Divd.:	NA
Total Assets:	$1,932,000	Net Worth:	-$2,251,000	Debt/ Equity:	NA

Integrative Health

4940 Broadway, Ste.202, San Antineo, TX, 78209; *PH:* 1-210-824-4200; *http://* www.ihtglobal.com

General - Incorporation	DE	Stock- Price on:12/24/2007	NA
Employees	NA	Stock Exchange	NA
Auditor	Traci J. Anderson, CPA	Ticker Symbol	NA
Stk Agt	Interwest Transfer Company, Inc.	Outstanding Shares	NA
Counsel	NA	E.P.S.	$0.04
DUNS No.	NA	Shareholders	NA

Business: The groups principal activities include investing and providing technical and managerial services to support the small growing businesses that are acquired by the BDC as portfolio companies in which the BDC holds varying levels of ownership. In September 2005, the group acquired Emerald Powerboats, Inc. The group operates from the United States.

Primary SIC and add'l.: 8731

CIK No: 0001094788

Officers: Gilbert R. Kaats/Chmn., CEO

Directors: Gilbert R. Kaats/Chmn., CEO, Ovidio Pugnale/Dir., Thomas A. Spalten/Member - Advisory Board, Samuel C. Keith/Member - Advisory Board, Harry G. Preuss/Member - Scientific Advisory Board, Harry A. Croft/Member - Scientific Advisory Board, Larry K. Parker/Member - Scientific Advisory Board, William Squires/Member - Scientific Advisory Board, Dennis Pullin/Hospital Admsinistration Administrative Dir., Member - Advisory Board, Kristi Hobbs/Member - Scientific Advisory Board, Joel Michalek/Member - Advisory Board, Raul Bastarrachea/Member - Advisory Board

Owners: Samuel C. Keith/1.27%, The Gale Trust/20.28%, Gilbert R. Kaats/28.16%, Insiders/36.40%, Shirlie Kaats/12.33%

Financial Data: Fiscal Year End:12/31   Latest Annual Data: 12/31/2006

Year	Sales	Net Income
2006	$370,000	$395,000
2005	NA	-$55,000
2004	NA	-$2,836,000

Curr. Assets:	$8,490,000	Curr. Liab.:	$621,000	P/E Ratio:	0.28
Plant, Equip.:	$19,000	Total Liab.:	$621,000	Indic. Yr. Divd.:	NA
Total Assets:	$9,742,000	Net Worth:	$9,122,000	Debt/ Equity:	NA

Integrative Health Technologies Inc

Formerly: Senticore Inc

4940 Brd.way, Ste. 202, San Antonio, TX, 78209; *PH:* 1-210-824-4200; *http://* www.senticore.com

General - Incorporation	DE	Stock- Price on:12/24/2007	$0.0035
Employees	NA	Stock Exchange	OTC
Auditor	Traci J. Anderson, CPA	Ticker Symbol	SNIOE
Stk Agt	Interwest Transfer Company, Inc.	Outstanding Shares	NA
Counsel	NA	E.P.S.	NA
DUNS No.	NA	Shareholders	NA

Business: The group's principle activity is to seek potential business opportunities and effect a business combination. The company was formed as an Internet professional services firm specializing in high-end Web site development. The company is in the development stage and is yet to commence any planned operations. The group operates from United States.

Primary SIC and add'l.: 7375 7379

CIK No: 0001094788

Subsidiaries: LoboGaming Corporation

Officers: Gilbert R. Kaats/Chmn., CEO, CFO
Directors: Gilbert R. Kaats/Chmn., CEO, CFO, Samuel C. Keith/Dir., Ovidio Pugnale/Dir.
Owners: Gilbert R. Kaats/38.35%, Shirlie Kaats/11.99%, The Gale Trust/9.59%

Integrity Bancshares Inc

11140 State Bridge Rd., Alpharetta, GA, 30022; ***PH:*** 1-770-777-0324;
http:// www.myintegritybank.com

General - Incorporation	GA	**Stock**- Price on:12/24/2007	NA
Employees	NA	Stock Exchange	NDQ
Auditor	Mauldin & Jenkins LLC	Ticker Symbol	ITYC
Stk Agt	Computershare Investor Services LLC	Outstanding Shares	NA
Counsel	Miller & Martin	E.P.S	-$1.736
DUNS No.	NA	Shareholders	NA

Business: The group's principal activities are to accept deposits from the public and invest in loans and other investments. The principal source of funds for integrity bank's loans and investments are demand, time, savings and other deposits (including negotiable orders of withdrawal or now accounts. It also grants loans to residential construction and developmental purposes to customers, borrowers secured by commercial real estate and consumer loans.
Primary SIC and add'l.: 6022 6712
CIK No: 0001103764
Subsidiaries: Integrity (GA) Statutory Trust I, Integrity Bank
Officers: Steven M. Skow/60/Dir., CEO, Pres./$1,839,010.00, Suzanne Long/CFO, Sr. VP, Sec., Treasurer/$272,004.00, Douglas G. Ballard/Exec. VP, Region Pres. - Sr. Lender, Integrity Bank/$847,222.00, Rita B. Gray/Dir., Administrative Sec. - Integrity Bank/$326,191.00, Todd Foster/40/Exec. Officer, Anne Howard/Operations Training Officer - Integrity Bank, Cameron Fausti/VP - Risk Management - Integrity Bank, Charlotte Rountree/Assist. VP - Compliance Officer - Integrity Bank, Debbi Oates/Assist. VP - Administration, Integrity Bank, Debbie Sundal/VP - Human Resources - Integrity Bank, Ellen Doucette/Assist. VP - Loans, Integrity Bank, Ellen Tressler/VP - Risk Management - Integrity Bank, Frank J. Geiss/Sr. VP - Residential Construction Lending - Integrity Bank, Jim Brown/Sr. VP - Loans - Integrity Bank, Mike Dodson/VP - Information Technology - Integrity Bank *(32 Officers included in Index)*
Directors: Steven M. Skow/60/Dir., CEO, Pres., Clinton M. Day/48/Chmn., Richard H. Peden/Dir., Joe Ernest/Dir., Robert S. Wholey/Dir., Gerald O. Reynolds/Dir., Jack S. Murphy/Dir., Don C. Hartsfield/Dir., Charles J. Puckett/75/Dir., Chuck Puckett/Dir.
Owners: Joseph J. Ernest/1.40%, Suzanne Long, Richard H. Peden/3.65%, Rita B. Gray/1.03%, Don C. Hartsfield/2.59%, Todd Foster, Charles J. Puckett/6.29%, Steven M. Skow/5.64%, Clinton M. Day/4.31%, Jack S. Murphy/2.13%, Insiders/29.81%, Robert S. Wholey/1.28%, Gerald O. Reynolds/1.15%, Douglas G. Ballard
Financial Data: ***Fiscal Year End:***12/31 ***Latest Annual Data:*** 12/31/2006

Year	Sales	Net Income
2006	$80,902,000	$10,137,000
2005	$44,918,000	$6,322,000
2004	$23,068,000	$3,012,000

Curr. Assets:	$5,804,000	**Curr. Liab.:**	$930,338,000		
Plant, Equip.:	$15,372,000	**Total Liab.:**	$1,044,449,000	**Indic. Yr. Divd.:**	NA
Total Assets:	$1,124,821,000	**Net Worth:**	$80,372,000	**Debt/ Equity:**	NA

Integrity Mutual Funds Inc

1 Main St. N, Minot, ND, 58703; ***PH:*** 1-701-852-5292; ***Fax:*** 1-701-838-4902;
http:// www.integritymf.com; ***Email:*** info@integritymf.com

General - Incorporation	ND	**Stock**- Price on:12/24/2007	$1
Employees	48	Stock Exchange	OTC
Auditor	Brady, Martz & Assoc. P.C	Ticker Symbol	IMFD
Stk Agt	Integrity Fund Services Inc	Outstanding Shares	14,320,000
Counsel	NA	E.P.S	-$0.02
DUNS No.	61-295-9601	Shareholders	NA

Business: The group's principal activity is to provide investment management, distribution, shareholder services, fund accounting, and other related administrative services to sponsored mutual funds. The group operates through two segments: the mutual fund services and the broker-dealer. The mutual fund services segment acts as investment adviser, distributor and provider of administrative service to sponsored and nonproprietary mutual funds. The broker-dealer segment distributes shares of nonproprietary mutual funds and insurance products. Portfolio of the group consists of one open-end investment company containing six separate portfolios including the Kansas municipal fund, Kansas insured intermediate fund, Nebraska municipal fund, Oklahoma municipal fund, Maine municipal fund, and New Hampshire municipal fund. The group markets its services throughout the midwestern United States and California. On 30-May-2003, the group acquired abbington capital management inc.
Primary SIC and add'l.: 6282 6799 7375 6719
CIK No: 0000944696
Subsidiaries: Capital Financial Services, Inc, Integrity Fund Services, Inc., Integrity Funds Distributor, Inc., Integrity Money Management, Inc.
Officers: Mark R. Anderson/Dir., CEO, Pres., Jerry J. Szilagyi/Sr. VP - Business Development/$347,721.00, Brad Wells/Dir. - Retail Administration, Peter A. Quist/Dir., VP, Jacqueline Case/Corp. Sec., Heather Ackerman/CFO
Directors: Mark R. Anderson/Dir., CEO, Pres., Robert E. Walstad/Founder, Chmn. Emeritus, Jeffrey A. Cummer/Chmn., Myron D. Thompson/Dir., Vance C. Castleman/Dir., Steve Lysne/Dir., Vaune Cripe/Dir., Richard H. Walstad/Dir., Peter A. Quist/Dir., VP
Owners: Steven D. Lysne, Jeffrey A. Cummer/34.30%, Trace Partners, LP/7.10%, Richard H. Walstad/1.10%, Vance A. Castleman/2.50%, Peter A. Quist/2.40%, Myron D. Thompson/2.30%, Jerry J. Szilagyi/19.90%, Robert E. Walstad/17.80%, Mark R. Anderson, Insiders/60.80%
Financial Data: ***Fiscal Year End:***12/31 ***Latest Annual Data:*** 12/31/2006

Year	Sales	Net Income
2006	$26,787,000	-$59,000
2005	$19,441,000	-$332,000
2004	$16,991,000	$135,000

Curr. Assets:	$3,741,000	**Curr. Liab.:**	$2,000,000		
Plant, Equip.:	$1,177,000	**Total Liab.:**	$6,068,000	**Indic. Yr. Divd.:**	NA
Total Assets:	$15,466,000	**Net Worth:**	$9,398,000	**Debt/ Equity:**	0.3923

Intel Corp

2200 Mission College Blvd., Santa Clara, CA, 95054; ***PH:*** 1-408-765-8080; ***Fax:*** 1-408-765-3804;
http:// www.intel.com

General - Incorporation	DE	**Stock**- Price on:12/24/2007	$24.29
Employees	94,100	Stock Exchange	NDQ
Auditor	Ernst & Young LLP	Ticker Symbol	INTC
Stk Agt	Computershare Investor Services LLC	Outstanding Shares	5,810,000,000
Counsel	NA	E.P.S	NA
DUNS No.	04-789-7855	Shareholders	NA

Business: The group's principle activities include designing, developing, manufacturing and marketing computers, networking and communication products. The group's products include processors, motherboard, chipsets, Intel graphics, flash memory, consumer electronics, desktops and software. The group operates from United States.
Primary SIC and add'l.: 3679 9999 7372 3572 3674 7373 7371
CIK No: 0000050863
Subsidiaries: Componentes Intel de Costa Rica, S.A., Intel Americas, Inc., Intel Asia Finance Ltd., Intel Capital Corporation, Intel Copenhagen ApS, Intel Corporation (UK)Ltd., Intel Electronics Finance Limited, Intel Electronics Ltd., Intel Europe, Inc., Intel International, Intel International B.V., Intel Ireland Limited, Intel Israel (74)Limited, Intel Kabushiki Kaisha, Intel Malaysia Sdn. Berhad 26 Subsidiaries included in the Index
Officers: Paul S. Otellini/Dir., CEO, Pres./$9,806,400.00, Arvind Sodhani/Sr. VP, Pres. - Intel Capital, Stephen L. Smith/VP, Dir. - Digital Enterprise Group Operations, William M. Holt/Sr. VP, GM - Technology, Manufacturing Group, Thomas M. Kilroy/VP, GM - Digital Enterprise Group, Patrick P. Gelsinger/Sr. VP, GM - Digital Enterprise Group, Eric B. Kim/Sr. VP, GM - Digital Home Group, Cary I. Klafter/VP - Legal, Government Affairs, Dir. - Corporate Affairs, Corp. Sec., Siva K. Yerramilli/VP - Technology, Manufacturing Group, Dir. - Design, Technology Solutions, Richard L. Coulson/Intel Sr. Fellow, Technology, Manufacturing Group, Dir. - I, O Architecture, Vivek K. De/Intel Fellow, Dir. - Circuit Technology Research, Simcha Gochman/Intel Fellow, Dir. - Future Mobile CPU Architecture, Mario J. Paniccia/Intel Fellow, Dir. - Photonics Technology LAB, Krishnamurthy Soumyanath/Intel Fellow, Dir. - Communications Circuits Research, Robert J. Baker/Sr. VP, GM - Technology, Manufacturing Group/$3,365,200.00 *(177 Officers included in Index)*
Directors: Paul S. Otellini/Dir., CEO, Pres., Craig R. Barrett/Chmn., Susan L. Decker/Dir., Charlene Barshefsky/Dir., James D. Guzy/Dir., James D. Plummer/Dir., Jane E. Shaw/Dir., David B. Yoffie/Dir., Reed E. Hundt/Dir., David S. Pottruck/Dir., John L. Thornton/Dir., Gordon E. Moore/Co - Founder
Owners: James D. Plummer, Jane E. Shaw, Charlene Barshefsky, Paul S. Otellini, James D. Guzy, Sean M. Maloney, Craig R. Barrett, David B. Yoffie, John L. Thornton, Andy D. Bryant, Reed E. Hundt, Insiders, Robert J. Baker, David S. Pottruck
Financial Data: ***Fiscal Year End:***12/31 ***Latest Annual Data:*** 12/30/2006

Year	Sales	Net Income
2006	$35,382,000,000	$5,044,000,000
2005	$38,826,000,000	$8,664,000,000
2004	$34,209,000,000	$7,516,000,000

Curr. Assets:	$21,194,000,000	**Curr. Liab.:**	$9,234,000,000	**P/E Ratio:**	26.69
Plant, Equip.:	$17,111,000,000	**Total Liab.:**	$12,132,000,000	**Indic. Yr. Divd.:**	$0.450
Total Assets:	$48,314,000,000	**Net Worth:**	$36,182,000,000	**Debt/ Equity:**	0.0844

IntelGenx Technologies Corp

6425 rue Abrams, Montral, PQ, H4S 1X9; ***PH:*** 1-514-331-7440; ***Fax:*** 1-514-331-0436;
http:// www.intelgenx.com; ***Email:*** info@intelgenx.com

General - Incorporation	DE	**Stock**- Price on:12/24/2007	$0.85
Employees	NA	Stock Exchange	OTC
Auditor	Rsm Richter LLP	Ticker Symbol	IGXT
Stk Agt	NA	Outstanding Shares	NA
Counsel	NA	E.P.S	NA
DUNS No.	NA	Shareholders	NA

Business: The groups principle activity is to develop oral controlled-release products. The groups products include INT0001/2004, INT0003/2005, INT0004/2006, INT0005/2005, INT0006/2005, INT10/2006 and INT0007/2006. In April 2006, the group acquired IntelGenx Technologies Corp. The group operates from the United States.
Primary SIC and add'l.: 6712
CIK No: 0001098880
Subsidiaries: 6544361 Canada Inc, IntelGenx Corp.
Officers: Horst G. Zerbe/CEO, Pres./$213,918.00, Gino Di Iorio/CFO/$108,227.00, Nadine Paiement/Mgr.
Directors: Bernard J. Boudreau/Dir., David Coffin-Beach/Dir., Reiza Rayman/Dir., Joel Cohen/Dir.
Owners: Reiza Rayman, Bernard J. Boudreau, Joel Cohen/0.10%, Horst Zerbe/30.40%, Ingrid Zerbe/0.30%, Insiders/0.71%, David Coffin-Beach
Financial Data: ***Fiscal Year End:***12/31 ***Latest Annual Data:*** 12/31/2006

Year	Sales	Net Income
2006	$266,000	-$781,000

Curr. Assets:	$489,000	**Curr. Liab.:**	$154,000		
Plant, Equip.:	$162,000	**Total Liab.:**	$323,000	**Indic. Yr. Divd.:**	NA
Total Assets:	$651,000	**Net Worth:**	$328,000	**Debt/ Equity:**	NA

Intelli-Check Inc

246 Crossways Pk. W, Woodbury, NY, 11797; ***PH:*** 1-516-992-1900; ***Fax:*** 1-516-992-1918;
http:// www.intellicheck.com; ***Email:*** investor-relations@intellicheck.com

General - Incorporation	DE	**Stock**- Price on:12/24/2007	$6.3
Employees	21	Stock Exchange	AMEX
Auditor	Amper, Politziner & Mattia P.C	Ticker Symbol	IDN
Stk Agt	Continental Stock Transfer & Trust Co	Outstanding Shares	12,240,000
Counsel	Tenzer Greenblatt	E.P.S	-$0.22
DUNS No.	NA	Shareholders	NA

Business: The group's principal activity is to develop, manufacture and market advanced document verification systems that enable users to detect and alter tampered or fake ids. The verification system enables a retailer to reduce check cashing, credit card and other types of fraud, which principally utilize

fake driver licenses as proof of identity. The system also determines the customer's age and validity of the ID to detect and prevent the use of fraudulent identification for the purchase of alcohol, tobacco and other age-restricted products. This reduces the risk to the retailer of substantial monetary fines, criminal penalties and license revocation for the sale of age-restricted products to minors.

Primary SIC and add'l.: 7372

CIK No: 0001040896

Officers: Frank Mandelbaum/Chmn., CEO/$377,334.00, Edwin Winiarz/Dir., CFO, Sr. Exec. VP/$291,658.00, Russell Embry/CTO, Exec. VP/$168,520.00, Todd Liebman/COO, Sr. VP - Marketing/$487,927.00, Peter Mundy/CFO, VP - Finance, Sec., Treasurer, Lou Gryga/Sr. VP - Marketing, Sales, Operations

Directors: Frank Mandelbaum/Chmn., CEO, Ashok Rao/58/Vice Chmn., Edwin Winiarz/Dir., CFO, Sr. Exec. VP, Arthur L. Money/Dir., Jeffrey Levy/Dir., Guy Smith/Dir., John E. Maxwell/Dir., Robert Blackwell/Dir.

Owners: Jeffrey Levy, Edwin Winiarz/1.80%, John E. Maxwell, Russell T. Embry, Insiders/18.06%, Todd Cohen/5.02%, Ashok Rao/1.21%, Todd Liebman/2.00%, Frank Mandelbaum/11.54%, Arthur L. Money/1.20%, Guy L. Smith

Financial Data: *Fiscal Year End:* 12/31 *Latest Annual Data:* 12/31/2006

Year	Sales	Net Income
2006	$3,162,000	-$2,880,000
2005	$2,384,000	-$3,239,000
2004	$1,119,000	-$6,923,000

Curr. Assets:	$5,505,000	Curr. Liab.:	$1,645,000		
Plant, Equip.:	$86,000	Total Liab.:	$1,718,000	Indic. Yr. Divd.:	NA
Total Assets:	$5,656,000	Net Worth:	$3,937,000	Debt/ Equity:	NA

Intelligent Living Corp

Formerly: Elgrande International Inc
2323 Quebec St., Ste. 221, Vancouver, BC, V5T 4S7; *PH:* 1-604-876-7494;
http:// www.elgrande.com

General - Incorporation	NV	Stock - Price on: 12/24/2007	$0.0029
Employees	NA	Stock Exchange	NA
Auditor	Chisholm, Bierwolf & Nilson, LLC	Ticker Symbol	NA
Stk Agt	Pacific Stock Transfer Company	Outstanding Shares	NA
Counsel	NA	E.P.S.	NA
DUNS No.	NA	Shareholders	NA

Business: The group's principle activities include developing and marketing Internet applications specifically for books, software, audio and video media and computer games. The group operates from United States.

Primary SIC and add'l.: 7372

CIK No: 0001073362

Subsidiaries: Cardinal Points Trading Corporation, Yaletown Marketing Corp.

Officers: Michael F. Holloran/60/Chmn., CEO, Pres., Principal Financial Officer

Directors: Michael F. Holloran/60/Chmn., CEO, Pres., Principal Financial Officer, Murat Erbatur/58/Dir.

Owners: Murat Erbatur/6.00%, Insiders/34.00%, Thomas A. Simons/11.00%, Michael F. Holloran/28.00%

Financial Data: *Fiscal Year End:* 05/31 *Latest Annual Data:* 5/31/2006

Year	Sales	Net Income
2006	$517,000	-$1,234,000
2005	$1,040,000	-$936,000
2004	$1,081,000	-$1,232,000

Curr. Assets:	$350,000	Curr. Liab.:	$2,475,000		
Plant, Equip.:	NA	Total Liab.:	$2,605,000	Indic. Yr. Divd.:	NA
Total Assets:	$484,000	Net Worth:	-$2,122,000	Debt/ Equity:	NA

Intelligent Motor Cars Group Inc

1600 W Sunrise Blvd, Ft Lauderdale, FL, 33311; *PH:* 1-954-462-0500;
http:// www.intelligentmotorcars.com

General - Incorporation	DE	Stock - Price on: 12/24/2007	NA
Employees	NA	Stock Exchange	NA
Auditor	Berkovits, Lago & Co LLP	Ticker Symbol	NA
Stk Agt	American Registrar & Transfer Co	Outstanding Shares	NA
Counsel	NA	E.P.S.	NA
DUNS No.	NA	Shareholders	NA

Business: The group's principle activities are retail auto sales and consumer finance. Its primary services include used auto sales, reconditioning, financing and insurance, warranty services and floor planning (dealer to dealer financing). The other services include acquisition and delivery services for new car sales. The group has three operational locations in the state of Florida, but its channel network covers the southeast United States.

Primary SIC and add'l.: 6141 5599

CIK No: 0001173927

Subsidiaries: IMC

Financial Data: *Fiscal Year End:* 12/31 *Latest Annual Data:* 12/31/2004

Year	Sales	Net Income
2004	$5,835,000	-$338,000
2003	$7,353,000	-$1,009,000

Curr. Assets:	$396,000	Curr. Liab.:	$1,644,000		
Plant, Equip.:	$164,000	Total Liab.:	$1,661,000	Indic. Yr. Divd.:	NA
Total Assets:	$581,000	Net Worth:	-$1,080,000	Debt/ Equity:	NA

Intelligent Systems Corp

4355 Shackleford Rd., Norcross, GA, 30093; *PH:* 1-770-381-2900; *Fax:* 1-770-381-2808;
http:// www.intelsys.com

General - Incorporation	GA	Stock - Price on: 12/24/2007	$3.95
Employees	231	Stock Exchange	AMEX
Auditor	Tauber & Balser, P.C	Ticker Symbol	INS
Stk Agt	American Stock Transfer & Trust Co.	Outstanding Shares	4,480,000
Counsel	Sutherland, Asbill & Brennan	E.P.S.	$1.01
DUNS No.	06-759-6999	Shareholders	NA

Business: The group's principal activity is to help entrepreneurs build valuable companies, by providing operational and strategic management, practical business advice, early stage equity capital, a network of business contacts and a proven incubator program. The group operates in two industry segments: information technology products and services and industrial products. The information technology segment is involved in designing, developing and marketing application software products used by business customers and government agencies. The industrial products segment includes the design, assembly and sale of equipment and associated supplies that are used by commercial, industrial, military and government agencies to maintain and service machinery or vehicles used in their operations. The group's trademarks are smartwasher(R), ozzyjuice(tm), visaer(tm), coreengine(tm) and coreissue (TM).

Primary SIC and add'l.: 7371 7549

CIK No: 0000320340

Subsidiaries: ChemFree Corporation, CoreCard Software, Inc., QS Technologies, Inc., VISaer, Inc.

Officers: Leland J. Strange/Chmn., CEO, Pres./$344,125.00, William J. Goodhew/VP, Bonnie L. Herron/VP, CFO, Sec. - Investor, Media Contact/$197,325.00, Francis A. Marks/VP/$142,950.00

Directors: Leland J. Strange/Chmn., CEO, Pres., James V. Napier/Dir., Parker H. Petit/Dir., John B. Peatman/Dir.

Owners: Parker H. Petit, Wallace R. Weitz & Company/19.70%, John B. Peatman, James V. Napier, Bonnie L. Herron/1.90%, Francis A. Marks/2.40%, Insiders/24.80%

Financial Data: *Fiscal Year End:* 12/31 *Latest Annual Data:* 12/31/2006

Year	Sales	Net Income
2006	$14,460,000	$4,469,000
2005	$16,097,000	-$1,626,000
2004	$22,332,000	$2,563,000

Curr. Assets:	$9,563,000	Curr. Liab.:	$6,714,000	P/E Ratio:	3.91
Plant, Equip.:	$1,009,000	Total Liab.:	$7,070,000	Indic. Yr. Divd.:	NA
Total Assets:	$15,010,000	Net Worth:	$6,424,000	Debt/ Equity:	NA

Intelligroup Inc

499 Thornall St., Edison, NJ, 08837; *PH:* 1-732-590-1600; *Fax:* 1-732-362-2100;
http:// www.intelligroup.com; *Email:* contactus@intelligroup.com

General - Incorporation	NJ	Stock - Price on: 12/24/2007	$1.37
Employees	2,137	Stock Exchange	OTC
Auditor	J. H. Cohn LLP	Ticker Symbol	ITIG
Stk Agt	American Stock Transfer & Trust Co.	Outstanding Shares	41,930,000
Counsel	Buchanan Ingersoll P.C.	E.P.S.	-$0.13
DUNS No.	80-226-5629	Shareholders	NA

Business: The group's principal activity is to develop, implement and support information technology solutions for global corporations and public sector organizations. The group's onsite/offshore delivery model has enabled hundreds of customers to accelerate results and significantly reduce costs. The strategic outsourcing services address the implementation, upgrade, application management and development needs of information technology executives. Provide cost-effective information technology solutions and services. The customers include fortune 2000 companies and large and mid-sized information technology companies. The group's trademarks include intelligroup, myadvisor, assplus, pharma express, contractor express and empower solutions. On 02-04-2003, the group consummated the sale of its Asia-pacific group of subsidiary companies.

Primary SIC and add'l.: 7379 7373 7371 7376

CIK No: 0001016439

Subsidiaries: CPI Consulting Limited, Empower, Inc, Intelligroup Asia Private, Ltd., Intelligroup de Venezuela, Intelligroup Europe Limited, Intelligroup Japan, Ltd, Intelligroup Nordic A/S, Intelligroup Nordic AB

Officers: Vikram Gulati/Dir., CEO, Pres./$753,212.00, Soren Heilskov/MD - Intelligroup Nordic A, S, Sreenivas Unnamatla/MD - Intelligroup, Japan, Satish Subramaniam/MD - Europe, Middle East/$118,304.00, Alok Pant/Sr. VP - Global Marketing, Alliances, Gopal Ramasamy/VP - Outsourcing Services, Pankit Desai/Sr. VP - Sales, North America, Marcelo Casas/Sr. VP - Empower Solutions Division, Ranjit Prithviraj/39/COO - Intelligroup Asia/$196,411.00, Vikram Samant/VP - Strategic Accounting, North America, Alok Bajpai/CFO, Treasurer/$83,962.00, Ramakrishna Karanam/32/Global Controller/$208,499.00, Kalyan Sundaram Mahalingam/COO, Prakash Shah/VP - Client Services, Hiren Bhatt/VP - Global Oracle Practice *(17 Officers included in Index)*

Directors: Vikram Gulati/Dir., CEO, Pres., Sandeep Reddy/Dir., Babar Khan/Dir., Ravi C. Adusumalli/Dir., Srini Raju/Dir., Ajit Isaac/Dir.

Owners: Ajit Isaac, Alok Bajpai, Sandeep Reddy, Ramakrishna Karanam, Satish Subramaniam, Insiders, Vikram Gulati, Ranjit Prithviraj, SB Asia Infrastructure Fund LP, Venture Tech Assets Ltd.

Financial Data: *Fiscal Year End:* 12/31 *Latest Annual Data:* 12/31/2006

Year	Sales	Net Income
2006	$125,309,000	-$3,707,000
2005	$125,326,000	-$6,591,000
2004	$128,903,000	-$866,000

Curr. Assets:	$46,868,000	Curr. Liab.:	$26,810,000		
Plant, Equip.:	$5,472,000	Total Liab.:	$28,149,000	Indic. Yr. Divd.:	NA
Total Assets:	$54,543,000	Net Worth:	$26,394,000	Debt/ Equity:	0.0242

IntelliServices Inc

5620 Paseo Del Norte, Ste 127501, Carlsbad, CA, 92008; *PH:* 1-951-587-3853 ;
http:// www.intelliservices.com

General - Incorporation	DE	Stock - Price on: 12/24/2007	NA
Employees	NA	Stock Exchange	NA
Auditor	NA	Ticker Symbol	NA
Stk Agt	Allied Stock Transfer Inc	Outstanding Shares	NA
Counsel	NA	E.P.S.	NA
DUNS No.	NA	Shareholders	NA

Business: The group's principle activity is to engage in any lawful corporate undertaking. The group has been in the developmental stage since inception and has no operations to date other than issuing shares to its original shareholder for services rendered in connection with the organization of the group. The group operates from United States.

Primary SIC and add'l.: 9995

CIK No: 0001303662

Intellisync Corp

2550 N First St. , Ste. 500, San Jose, CA, 95131; *PH:* 1-408-321-7650; *http://* www.intellisync.com

General - Incorporation	DE	Stock- Price on:12/24/2007	$5.24
Employees	NA	Stock Exchange	NDQ
Auditor	PricewaterhouseCoopers LLP	Ticker Symbol	SYNC
Stk Agt	NA	Outstanding Shares	NA
Counsel	NA	E.P.S.	NA
DUNS No.	NA	Shareholders	NA

Business: The group's principal activities are to develop, market and support synchronization, mobile-application development and mobile-application management or device management software. The software products allow the exchange and synchronization of data across diverse platforms, operating systems and applications. This software enables consumers, business professionals and information technology professionals to extend the capabilities of enterprise groupware and vertical applications, handheld organizers or computers, Web-enabled cellular phones, pagers and other wireless or wireline personal communications platforms. The group offers the products to original equipment manufacturers, enterprise, retail and online markets. During fiscal 2003, the group acquired starfish software, inc and loudfire, inc. On 30-Dec-2003, the group acquired synchrologic inc and on 17-Mar-2004, search software America.

Primary SIC and add'l.: 7379 7372

CIK No: 0001020716

Subsidiaries: Identity Systems Pty. Ltd., Identity Systems,Inc., Intellisync Australia Pty. Ltd., Intellisync Bulgaria Ltd., Intellisync Deutschland GmbH, Intellisync Europe Ltd., Intellisync Identity Systems Ltd., Intellisync Italia S.r.l., Intellisync K.K., Intellisync Romania SRL, NetMind Technologies,Inc., PDA Software (P)Ltd., PDAapps,Inc., Pumatech International, Starfish Software,Inc. 17 Subsidiaries included in the Index

Inter Parfums Inc

551 5th Ave., Ste. 1500, New York, NY, 10176; *PH:* 1-212-983-2640; *Fax:* 1-212-983-4197; *http://* www.interparfumsinc.com

General - Incorporation	DE	Stock- Price on:12/24/2007	$27.8
Employees	235	Stock Exchange	NDQ
Auditor	Mazars LLP	Ticker Symbol	IPAR
Stk Agt	American Stock Transfer & Trust Co.	Outstanding Shares	20,440,000
Counsel	Becker & Poliakoff	E.P.S.	-$0.005
DUNS No.	16-113-5447	Shareholders	NA

Business: The group's principal activity is to manufacture, market and distribute fragrances, cosmetics and personal care products. The group specializes in prestige perfumes, mass market perfumes and cosmetics and health and beauty aids. The group has the rights to manufacture and distribute products namely, Burberry, S.T. Dupont, Paul Smith, Christian Lacroix, Celine, Regine's, Jordache, and Fubu. The products are marketed through major drug chains, mass market merchandisers, supermarkets, wholesalers and other retailers. The group distributes products in Brazil, Mexico, Argentina, Chile, Columbia, Canada, Russia and eastern Europe. On Apr, 2004 the group acquired 67.5% interest in Nickel S.A.

Primary SIC and add'l.: 2844

CIK No: 0000822663

Subsidiaries: Inter Parfums Grand Public, S.A, Inter Parfums Holdings, S.A., Inter Parfums Trademark, S.A, Inter Parfums USA, LLC, Inter Parfums, S.A., Jean Philippe Fragrances, LLC, Nickel USA, Inc., Nickel, S.A.

Officers: Jean Madar/Chmn., CEO, Philippe Benacin/Pres., Vice Chmn./$1,938,981.00, Kiet T. Huynh/VP - Management Information Systems - MIS Department, Han Moon/Contact - MIS Department, Linda Latman/Investor Relation Officer, Nathalie Nunez/Sales Administration, Russell Greenberg/CFO, Exec. VP, Michelle Habert/Contact - Human Resources, Corporate Controller, Stuart Fishel/VP - Retail Sales, Mike Hamerling/Westcoast Regional Sales Mgr., William Dachille/National Accounting Sales Mgr., Eduardo Hermosilla/Mexico, Texas Border Sales Mgr., Michel Bes/Central, South America Regional Sales Mgr., Lynn Konko/Northeast Regional Sales Mgr., Virginie Ejzenbaum/Brand Mgr. - Diane von Furstenberg Beauty, Product Development Mgr. *(21 Officers included in Index)*

Directors: Jean Madar/Chmn., CEO, Philippe Benacin/Pres., Vice Chmn., Hugues De La Chevasnerie/39/Dir., Patrick Choel/Dir.

Owners: Serge Rosinoer, Francois Heilbronn, Philippe Santi, Jean Madar/27.80%, Royce & Associates, LLC12/10.70%, Jean Levy, Philippe Benacin/27.50%, Jean Cailliau, Robert Bensoussan-Torres, Russell Greenberg, Insiders/55.30%, Joseph A. Caccamo, Independence Investments, LLC13/5.90%

Financial Data: *Fiscal Year End:*12/31 *Latest Annual Data:* 06/30/2007

Year	Sales	Net Income
2007	NA	NA
2006	$321,054,000	$17,742,000
2005	$273,533,000	$15,263,000

Curr. Assets:	$262,317,000	Curr. Liab.:	$123,770,000	P/E Ratio:	29.89
Plant, Equip.:	$6,806,000	Total Liab.:	$133,698,000	Indic. Yr. Divd.:	$0.200
Total Assets:	$333,045,000	Net Worth:	$155,272,000	Debt/ Equity:	0.1497

Interactive Brand Development Inc

3275 W Hillsboro Blvd., Ste. 300, Deerfield Beach, FL, 33442; *PH:* 1-954-333-8747; *Fax:* 1-954-333-8679; *http://* www.interactivebranddevelopment.com

General - Incorporation	DE	Stock- Price on:12/24/2007	$0.017
Employees	NA	Stock Exchange	OTC
Auditor	Jewett, Schwartz & Associates	Ticker Symbol	IBDIE
Stk Agt	Executive Registrar & Transfer, Inc.	Outstanding Shares	104,690,000
Counsel	NA	E.P.S.	-$0.279
DUNS No.	NA	Shareholders	NA

Business: The groups principle activity is to provide online entertainment services. In January 2005, the group acquired Media Billing Company LLC and Internet Billing Company LLC. The group operates from the United States.

Primary SIC and add'l.: 6799

CIK No: 0000842927

Subsidiaries: XTV Investments LLC

Officers: Steve Markley/62/Chmn., CEO, Sec., Principal Accounting Officer, Gary Spaniak/44/Dir., Pres.

Directors: Steve Markley/62/Chmn., CEO, Sec., Principal Accounting Officer, Gary Spaniak/44/Dir., Pres., Steve Robinson/59/Dir., Gilbert Singerman/73/Dir., Robert Dolin/87/Dir.

Owners: Insiders/1.00%, Monarch Pointe Fund, LP/8.70%, Granite Management Company, LLC/5.30%, Gary Spaniak, Steven Robinson, Robert Dolin, Gilbert Singerman, Steve Markley, PHSL Worldwide, Inc/28.30%

Financial Data: *Fiscal Year End:*12/31 *Latest Annual Data:* 12/31/2006

Year	Sales	Net Income
2006	$124,000	-$32,913,000
2005	$6,924,000	-$20,199,000
2004	NA	-$3,458,000

Curr. Assets:	$208,000	Curr. Liab.:	$50,329,000		
Plant, Equip.:	$256,000	Total Liab.:	$54,614,000	Indic. Yr. Divd.:	NA
Total Assets:	$21,388,000	Net Worth:	-$33,227,000	Debt/ Equity:	NA

Interactive Data Corp

32 Crosby Dr., Bedford, MA, 01730; *PH:* 1-781-687-8500; *Fax:* 1-781-687-8005; *http://* www.interactivedata.com; *Email:* investorrelations@interactivedata.com

General - Incorporation	DE	Stock- Price on:12/24/2007	$27.83
Employees	2,200	Stock Exchange	NYSE
Auditor	PricewaterhouseCoopers LLP	Ticker Symbol	IDC
Stk Agt	American Stock Transfer & Trust Co.	Outstanding Shares	93,730,000
Counsel	Sullivan & Worcester LLP	E.P.S.	$1.23
DUNS No.	79-283-0184	Shareholders	NA

Business: The group's principal activity is to provide financial and business information to institutional and retail investors. The group operates in two business segments: institutional services and retail investor services. The institutional services segment provides pricing, dividend and corporate information about traded securities. The information is provided to banks, insurance companies, money managers, brokerage firms and mutual fund companies. This segment also provides fixed income portfolio analytics, valuation and consulting services to customers. The retail investor services segment provides financial market information to professional investors, traders and individuals through Internet and broadcast technology. On 28-Feb-2003, the group acquired s&p comstock inc and on 08-Sep-2004, assets of futuresource llc and its subsidiaries.

Primary SIC and add'l.: 7375

CIK No: 0000888165

Subsidiaries: BI Purchasing, Inc., Bonneville Equipment CompanyUtah, Checkrite International, Inc., Checkrite of California, Inc., Checkrite of Kansas City, Inc., Checkrite of Minnesota, Inc., Checkrite of Oklahoma City, Inc., Checkrite of Oregon, Inc., Checkrite, Ltd., Comstock, Inc., CSN, Inc. Utah, Data Broadcasting Corp., Detective Nominees, Inc., eSignal.com, Inc., Exshare Computing Ltd. 48 Subsidiaries included in the Index

Officers: Stuart J. Clark/Dir., CEO, Pres./$2,365,662.00, Stephan Wolf/Chmn. - Interactive Data Managed Solutions, John King/COO/$1,068,709.00, Andrew J. Hajducky/CFO, Exec. VP, Treasurer/$507,429.00, Mark Hepsworth/Pres. - Interactive Data Pricing, Reference Data, Roger Sargeant/MD - Interactive Data Europe, Laurie Adami/Pres. - Interactive Data Fixed Income Analytics, James Farrer/MD - Interactive Data Asia Pacific, Chuck Thompson/Pres. - Esignal, Raymond D'Arcy/Pres. - Sales, Marketing/$1,079,506.00, Andrea H. Loew/Exec. VP, General Counsel/$703,161.00

Directors: Stuart J. Clark/Dir., CEO, Pres., John C. Makinson/53/Chmn., Rona Fairhead/Chmn., Robert C. Lamb/Dir., Carl Spielvogel/Dir., Philip J. Hoffman/Dir., William T. Ethridge/Dir., Donald P. Greenberg/Dir., Myra R. Drucker/Dir., Caspar Hobbs/Dir.

Owners: Pearson DBC Holdings, Inc/61.61%, Stuart J. Clark/1.01%, Insiders/2.35%, Andrew J. Hajducky, Andrea H. Loew, Robert C. Lamb, Raymond L. DArcy, John C. Makinson, Carl Spielvogel, Myra R. Drucker, Donald P. Greenberg, Steven G. Crane, John L. King

Financial Data: *Fiscal Year End:*12/31 *Latest Annual Data:* 12/31/2006

Year	Sales	Net Income
2006	$612,403,000	$93,362,000
2005	$542,867,000	$93,864,000
2004	$484,565,000	$80,271,000

Curr. Assets:	$315,790,000	Curr. Liab.:	$150,381,000	P/E Ratio:	25.07
Plant, Equip.:	$81,988,000	Total Liab.:	$192,219,000	Indic. Yr. Divd.:	$0.500
Total Assets:	$1,103,804,000	Net Worth:	$911,585,000	Debt/ Equity:	NA

Interactive Games Inc

Formerly: Torpedo Sports USA Inc
319 Clematis St., Ste. 703, West Palm Beach, FL, 33401; *PH:* 1-303-796-8940

General - Incorporation	NV	Stock- Price on:12/24/2007	$0.065
Employees	NA	Stock Exchange	NA
Auditor	Hawkins Accounting	Ticker Symbol	NA
Stk Agt	Interwest Transfer Company, Inc.	Outstanding Shares	53,680,000
Counsel	Dewey Ballantine	E.P.S.	-$0.012
DUNS No.	NA	Shareholders	NA

Business: The group's principal activity is to manufacture and distribute outdoor recreational products for children, such as toboggans, baby sleds, snowboards, tricycles, scooters and skateboards. The group operates in Canada and the United States of America.

Primary SIC and add'l.: 5963 7331 5091

CIK No: 0001126411

Subsidiaries: JamDirect, Inc, Torpedo Canada, Torpedo Sports USA, Inc., Torpedo Sports, Inc.

Officers: Henry Fong/73/Dir., CEO, Pres., Barry Hollander/51/CFO, Thomas B. Olson/42/Sec.

Directors: Henry Fong/73/Dir., CEO, Pres., Stephen D. King/52/Dir.

Owners: Thomas B. Olson/1.82%, Barry S. Hollander, Hunter Ridge Partners LLC/5.04%, Stephen D. King, Wayne W. Mills/14.28%, Gulfstream Financial Partners/12.88%, Henry Fong/97.20%, Insiders/97.20%, Michele Friedman/9.82%, Gulfstream Financial Partners/6.74%, Henry Fong/16.48%, Richard W. Perkins/13.22%, Insiders/19.39%

Financial Data: Fiscal Year End:07/31 Latest Annual Data: 7/31/2006

Year	Sales	Net Income
2006	$53,000	-$1,154,000
2005	$77,000	-$429,000
2004	NA	-$2,712,000

Curr. Assets:	$31,000	Curr. Liab.:	$5,169,000		
Plant, Equip.:	$4,000	Total Liab.:	$5,201,000	Indic. Yr. Divd.:	NA
Total Assets:	$91,000	Net Worth:	-$5,111,000	Debt/ Equity:	NA

Interactive Intelligence Inc

7601 Interactive Way, Indianapolis, IN, 46278; *PH:* 1-317-872-3000; *http://* www.inin.com; *Email:* info@inin.com

General		Stock	
Incorporation	IN	Price on:12/24/2007	$19.38
Employees	515	Stock Exchange	NDQ
Auditor	KPMG LLP	Ticker Symbol	ININ
Stk Agt	Computershare Investor Services LLC	Outstanding Shares	17,370,000
Counsel	Woodard Emhardt Naughton Et Al	E.P.S.	$0.41
DUNS No.	NA	Shareholders	NA

Business: The group's principal activity is to provide software applications for contact centers. It also provides mission critical voice over Internet protocol (voip) applications to enterprises. This approach results in lower overall costs for phone devices, system maintenance and customer networking. The applications are pre-integrated to many business applications such as financial, customer relationship management and enterprise resource planning (erp) software, thereby automating and tracking business transactions to customer interactions. The group markets its software applications around the globe both directly to customers and through over 135 value-added resellers. The group's software applications are installed in over 30 countries and are available in 12 languages.

Primary SIC and add'l.: 7372 7378

CIK No: 0001083318

Subsidiaries: ININ (Australia) Pty Ltd., ININ Netherlands B.V., ININ UK Limited, Interactive Intelligence France S.A.R.L., Interactive Intelligence, Inc. International, Interactive Portal, Inc., Vonexus, Inc.

Officers: Donald E. Brown/Chmn., CEO, Pres./$785,834.00, Minda Marshall/VP - Partner Channels, Gary R. Blough/Exec. VP - Worldwide Sales/$568,846.00, Michael D. Gagle/Chief Scientist, Stephen R. Head/CFO, VP - Finance, Sec., Treasurer/$419,716.00, Jeremiah J. Fleming/Pres./$502,214.00, Joseph A. Staples/Sr. VP - Worldwide Marketing/$372,884.00, Pamela J. Hynes/VP - Customer Services

Directors: Donald E. Brown/Chmn., CEO, Pres., Mark E. Hill/Dir., Michael C. Heim/Dir., Edward L. Hamburg/Dir., William E. McWhirter/Dir., Samuel F. Hulbert/Dir., Richard A. Reck/Dir.

Owners: Richard A. Reck, Bares Capital Management, Inc./5.35%, Insiders/28.59%, Samuel F. Hulbert, Donald E. Brown/25.92%, Edward L. Hamburg, Mark E. Hill, Gary R. Blough/1.17%, William E. McWhirter, Jeremiah J. Fleming, Stephen R. Head, Joseph A. Staples, Essex Investment Management Co., LLC/5.38%

Financial Data: Fiscal Year End:12/31 Latest Annual Data: 12/31/2006

Year	Sales	Net Income
2006	$83,220,000	$10,248,000
2005	$62,937,000	$2,108,000
2004	$55,119,000	$1,040,000

Curr. Assets:	$56,946,000	Curr. Liab.:	$42,497,000	P/E Ratio:	30.28
Plant, Equip.:	$5,469,000	Total Liab.:	$42,497,000	Indic. Yr. Divd.:	NA
Total Assets:	$66,775,000	Net Worth:	$24,278,000	Debt/ Equity:	NA

Interactive Motorsports & Entmt Corp

5624 W 73rd St., Indianapolis, IN, 46278; *PH:* 1-317-295-3500; *Fax:* 1-317-298-8924; *http://* www.smsonline.com

General		Stock	
Incorporation	IN	Price on:12/24/2007	$0.0185
Employees	NA	Stock Exchange	OTC
Auditor	HJ & Assoc. LLC	Ticker Symbol	IMTS
Stk Agt	Colonial Stock Transfer Co Inc	Outstanding Shares	96,400,000
Counsel	NA	E.P.S.	-$0.004
DUNS No.	NA	Shareholders	NA

Business: The group owns and operates the chain of officially-licensed, nascar-branded entertainment and retail merchandising stores. The group has a license agreement with nascar for location-based entertainment. The group also has integrated these license agreements with sophisticated proprietary racing simulator technology to create a chain of nascar-themed, family-oriented, racing entertainment and retail merchandise centers. Simulator races take place on famous nascar winston cup racetracks such as daytona international speedway, indianapolis motor speedway, lowe's (charlotte) motor speedway, atlanta motor speedway, bristol motor speedway and richmond international raceway.

Primary SIC and add'l.: 7948 7929

CIK No: 0001115551

Subsidiaries: Perfect Line, Inc., Race Car Simulators, Inc.

Officers: William R. Donaldson/51/Chmn., CEO, Philip E. Langholz/VP, Dir. - Stores, Rick Moncrief/VP - Engineering, CTO, Steve Wagoner/Investor Relations Officer

Directors: William R. Donaldson/51/Chmn., CEO, Cary Agajanian/66/Dir., Carl L. Smith/65/Dir.

Owners: Dolphin Direct Equity Partners, LP/7.41%, Alliance Investment Management, LTD/6.57%, James Matheny/9.02%, William R. Donaldson/18.40%, Insiders/51.88%, Vikki Cook/10.48%

Financial Data: Fiscal Year End:12/31 Latest Annual Data: 03/31/2007

Year	Sales	Net Income
2007	$1,421,000	-$89,000
2006	$5,351,000	-$598,000
2005	$4,839,000	-$1,095,000

Curr. Assets:	$726,000	Curr. Liab.:	$3,843,000		
Plant, Equip.:	$886,000	Total Liab.:	$5,800,000	Indic. Yr. Divd.:	NA
Total Assets:	$1,946,000	Net Worth:	-$3,855,000	Debt/ Equity:	NA

Interactive Systems Worldwide Inc

2 Andrews Dr., 2nd Fl., West Paterson, NJ, 07424; *PH:* 1-973-256-8181; *Fax:* 1-973-256-8211; *http://* www.sportxction.com; *Email:* geninfo@sportxction.com

General		Stock	
Incorporation	DE	Price on:12/24/2007	NA
Employees	18	Stock Exchange	OTC
Auditor	Eisner LLP	Ticker Symbol	ISWI
Stk Agt	American Stock Transfer & Trust Co.	Outstanding Shares	NA
Counsel	NA	E.P.S.	NA
DUNS No.	01-953-1834	Shareholders	NA

Business: The group's principal activity is to design, develop and market an interactive client or server based computer system for purposes of wagering on sporting events. The interactive hardware and software system (the sportxction(TM) system) enables users to wager at fixed prices during the course of a sporting event such as soccer, football, baseball, golf, tennis, cricket and basketball. The sportxction (TM) system accepts bets not only on the outcome of a sporting event, but also on discrete parts of the event and on specific game situations. The sportxction (TM) system software monitors and changes the odds on the contestants in a sporting event to induce the players to wager such that the betting pool for each betting proposition is continuously driven toward a financial balance, to within a pre-set level.

Primary SIC and add'l.: 7373 7999

CIK No: 0001025995

Subsidiaries: Brightform Limited, GIG Operations Limited, Global Interactive Gaming Limited, ISW Acquisition Co., LLC

Officers: Bernard Albanese/Dir., Chmn., CEO, Katrine Winther-Oleson/The Investor Relations Group, Michael Crawford/The Investor Relations Group

Directors: Bernard Albanese/Dir., Chmn., CEO, Bruce Feldman/Dir., Philip Rule/Dir.

Owners: James McDade, Omicron Master Trust/4.90%, Midsummer Investment, Ltd./4.90%, Andrew Harbison, Philip Rule, Insiders/5.00%, The Marie Albanese Trust/2.50%, Bernard Albanese/3.70%, Barry Mindes/24.70%, Mindes Family Limited Partnership/12.30%, Bruce Feldman, Stephen Salmon

Interactive Television Networks Inc

23241 Ventura Blvd., Ste. 101, Woodland Hills, CA, 91364; *PH:* 1-866-988-4988; *Fax:* 1-866-988-4988; *http://* www.itvn.com; *Email:* info@itvn.com

General		Stock	
Incorporation	NV	Price on:12/24/2007	$0.024
Employees	23	Stock Exchange	OTC
Auditor	Lopez, Bork & Associates, LLP	Ticker Symbol	ITTV
Stk Agt	NA	Outstanding Shares	32,570,000
Counsel	NA	E.P.S.	-$0.312
DUNS No.	NA	Shareholders	NA

Business: The groups principal activity is to provide television network services. The group operates from the United States.

Primary SIC and add'l.: 7375 7379

CIK No: 0001174893

Subsidiaries: ITVN, Inc

Officers: Charles Prast/Dir., CEO, Michael Martinez/Chmn., Founder, Pres., David Yohe/VP - Marketing, Business Development

Directors: Charles Prast/Dir., CEO, Michael Martinez/Chmn., Founder, Pres., Joseph Scotti/Dir., Geoff Brown/Dir., John Wirt/Dir.

Owners: XTV Investments LLC/14.11%, Geoff Brown, Monarch Pointe Fund, Ltd/11.19%, Insiders/23.35%, Mercator Momentum Fund, LP/2.61%, Murray Williams/1.98%, Charles Prast/3.46%, John Wirt, Michael Martinez/19.02%, David Koenig/17.87%, Mercator Momentum Fund III, LP/2.80%, Joseph J. Scotti/1.01%, Pentagon Bernini Fund, Ltd./9.99%

Financial Data: Fiscal Year End:12/31 Latest Annual Data: 12/31/2006

Year	Sales	Net Income
2006	$1,045,000	-$7,277,000
2005	NA	-$22,000

Curr. Assets:	$6,000	Curr. Liab.:	$1,000		
Plant, Equip.:	$1,000	Total Liab.:	$1,000	Indic. Yr. Divd.:	NA
Total Assets:	$6,000	Net Worth:	$6,000	Debt/ Equity:	NA

InterActiveCorp

555 W 18th St., New York, NY, 10011; *PH:* 1-212-314-7300; *http://* www.iac.com; *Email:* info@iac.com

General		Stock	
Incorporation	DE	Price on:12/24/2007	$34.75
Employees	16,000	Stock Exchange	NDQ
Auditor	Ernst & Young LLP	Ticker Symbol	IACI
Stk Agt	Bank of NY Stk Trnsfer Div	Outstanding Shares	287,500,000
Counsel	NA	E.P.S.	$0.82
DUNS No.	NA	Shareholders	NA

Business: The groups principle activity is to provide diversified businesses in sectors being transformed by the Internet, online and offline. In the year 2006, the group acquired Shoebuy.com, Inc. The group operates from United States.

Primary SIC and add'l.: 7812 4833 7822 7922 7389 5961

CIK No: 0000891103

Subsidiaries: 4075650 Canada Inc., 8831-8833 Sunset, LLC, Access Direct Telemarketing, Inc., Aqua Acquisition Holdings, LLC, Ask Jeeves (Canada) Inc., Ask Jeeves (Hangzhou) Limited, Ask Jeeves (Jersey) Limited, Ask Jeeves Australia Pty. Ltd., Ask Jeeves B.V., Ask Jeeves Deutschland GmbH, Ask Jeeves Espana S.L., Ask Jeeves Europe Limited, Ask Jeeves International, Inc., Ask Jeeves Internet Limited, Ask Jeeves Italia S.r.l. 262 Subsidiaries included in the Index

Officers: Barry Diller/Chmn., CEO/$17,034,660.00, Terry Barnes/Chmn. - Ticketmaster, IAS Transactions, Craig M. Nash/Memer - Business Management, Michael Jackson/Pres. - Programming, Doug Lebda/COO, Pres./$8,136,350.00, Joanne Hawkins/Sr. VP, Deputy General Counsel, Jay Herratti/Pres. - Citysearch, Michael Schwerdtman/Sr. VP, Controller, Thomas J. McInerney/CFO, Exec. VP/$4,885,832.00, Greg Morrow/Sr. VP - Tax, Jason Stewart/Chief Administrative Officer, Tomo Yebisu/Pres. - Lendingtree Loans, Rich Stalzer/Pres. - IAC Advertising Solutions, Harry Lin/Sr. VP, GM - Evite, Shana Fisher/Sr. VP - Strategy, M, A *(23 Officers included in Index)*

Directors: Barry Diller/Chmn., CEO, Victor A. Kaufman/Vice Chmn., Alan G. Spoon/Dir., Donald R. Keough/Dir., Edgar Bronfman/Dir., Bryan Lourd/Dir., Steven Rattner/Dir., Diane V. Furstenberg/Dir., William H. Berkman/Dir., John C. Malone/Dir., Arthur C. Martinez/Dir., Norman H. Schwarzkopf/Dir.

Owners: Norman H. Schwarzkopf, Legg Mason Capital Management/20.60%, Steven Rattner, Douglas R. Lebda, Diane Von Furstenberg, Victor A. Kaufman, Gregory R. Blatt, Clearbridge Advisors, LLC/6.30%, Capital Research and Management Company/6.50%, Arthur C. Martinez, Liberty Media Corporation/24.10%, Donald R. Keough, Edgar Bronfman, Thomas J. McInerney, Insiders/29.20% *(19 Owners included in Index)*

Financial Data: *Fiscal Year End:*12/31   *Latest Annual Data:* 12/31/2006

Year	Sales	Net Income
2006	$6,277,638,000	$192,635,000
2005	$5,753,671,000	$876,150,000
2004	$4,188,279,000	$164,861,000

Curr. Assets:	$3,812,337,000	**Curr. Liab.:**	$2,253,189,000	**P/E Ratio:**	42.38
Plant, Equip.:	$612,161,000	**Total Liab.:**	$4,400,549,000	**Indic. Yr. Divd.:**	NA
Total Assets:	$13,194,423,000	**Net Worth:**	$8,768,993,000	**Debt/ Equity:**	0.1197

InterCare DX Inc

6080 Ctr. Dr., Ste. 640, Los Angeles, CA, 90045; *PH:* 1-310-242-5634; *Fax:* 1-310-242-5676; *http://* www.intercare.com; *Email:* info@intercare.com

General - Incorporation	CA	**Stock**- Price on:12/24/2007	$0.03
Employees	5	Stock Exchange	OTC
Auditor	Pollard-kelley Auditing Services, Inc	Ticker Symbol	ICCO
Stk Agt	Corporate Stock Transfer of Denver	Outstanding Shares	19,400,000
Counsel	NA	E.P.S	$0.007
DUNS No.	NA	Shareholders	NA

Business: The group's principle activity is to provide healthcare management and information systems solutions through innovative software products and services. The company creates, publishes and markets software products embedded with sound, text and video for the purpose of relaxation training and stress management. It also developed Internet-ready applications for healthcare transactions management as well as medical and health-related content and information targeted toward the education, consumer and healthcare industry markets. It has developed intercare clinical explorer, the latest product designed to integrate virtually all aspects of the health care enterprise, both inpatient and outpatient. The group operates from United States.

Primary SIC and add'l.: 7372

CIK No: 0001103310

Officers: Anthony C. Dike/Chmn., CEO, Pres., Sec.

Directors: Anthony C. Dike/Chmn., CEO, Pres., Sec., Donald Stanford/Dir., Wesley Bradford/Dir., Jude Uwaezooke/Dir., Professor Jeff Raines/Member - Scientific Advisory Board, Wignes Warren/Member - Scientific Advisory Board

Owners: Wesley Bradford/1.40%, Other Public Shareholders/26.00%, Jude Uwaezuoke/1.40%, Insiders/74.00%, Anthony C. Dike/70.00%, Karunyan Arulanantham/0.50%, Donald Stanford/0.50%

Financial Data: *Fiscal Year End:*12/31   *Latest Annual Data:* 12/31/2006

Year	Sales	Net Income
2006	$1,636,000	$130,000
2005	$12,000	-$1,662,000
2004	NA	-$215,000

Curr. Assets:	$59,000	**Curr. Liab.:**	$139,000	**P/E Ratio:**	3.00
Plant, Equip.:	$0	**Total Liab.:**	$139,000	**Indic. Yr. Divd.:**	NA
Total Assets:	$59,000	**Net Worth:**	-$79,000	**Debt/ Equity:**	NA

Intercontinental Exchange Inc

2100 RiverEdge Pkwy., Ste. 500, Atlanta, GA, 30328; *PH:* 1-770-857-4700; *Fax:* 1-770-951-1307; *https://* www.theice.com

General - Incorporation	DE	**Stock**- Price on:12/24/2007	$158.1
Employees	508	Stock Exchange	NYSE
Auditor	Ernst& Young LLP	Ticker Symbol	ICE
Stk Agt	Computershare Investor Services LLC	Outstanding Shares	70,350,000
Counsel	NA	E.P.S	NA
DUNS No.	NA	Shareholders	NA

Business: The groups principle activity is to trade global products. The groups products include sugar, coffee, cocoa, crude and refined oil products, natural gas and power, emissions, and orange juice. The group operates through three segments namely, energy futures and options markets, global OTC markets, and market data. The group operates from the United States. The groups quartely revenue for September 2007 was 151.74 millions of USD.

Primary SIC and add'l.: 6231 6221 5172 4911

CIK No: 0001174746

Subsidiaries: City of New York Board of Trade, Inc., ICE Futures, IntercontinentalExchange Holdings

Officers: Jeffrey C. Sprecher/Chmn., Founder, CEO/$3,965,468.00, Charles A. Vice/COO, Pres./$2,082,886.00, David S. Goone/Sr. VP - Business Development, Sales/$1,627,070.00, Edwin Marcial/CTO/$1,475,001.00, David J. Peniket/COO, Johnathan H. Short/Sr. VP, General Counsel, Corp. Sec., Kelly Loeffler/VP - Investor Relations, Corporate Communications, Thomas W. Farley/COO, Pres., Sarah M. Stashak/Dir. - Investor, Public Relations, Scott A. Hill/CFO

Directors: Jeffrey C. Sprecher/Chmn., Founder, CEO, Richard V. Spencer/Vice Chmn., Charles R. Crisp/Dir., Terrence F. Martell/Dir., Jean-Marc Forneri/Dir., Robert Reid/Dir., Frederic V. Salerno/Dir., Fred W. Schoenhut/Dir., Richard L. Sandor/Dir., Judith A. Sprieser/Dir., Vincent Tese/Dir., Fred W. Hatfield/Dir.

Owners: Delaware Management Holdings/9.20%, Insiders/4.10%, Charles A. Vice, Sands Capital Management, LLC/10.10%, Robert Reid, Richard V. Spencer, Frederic V. Salerno, Terrence F. Martell, Richard L. Sandor, Frederick W. Schoenhut, Charles R. Crisp, Judith A. Sprieser, Vincent Tese, Jeffrey C. Sprecher/3.20%, Jean-Marc Forneri *(17 Owners included in Index)*

Financial Data: *Fiscal Year End:*12/31   *Latest Annual Data:* 12/31/2006

Year	Sales	Net Income
2006	$313,799,000	$143,268,000
2005	$155,865,000	$40,410,000
2004	$108,414,000	$21,949,000

Curr. Assets:	$340,917,000	**Curr. Liab.:**	$37,899,000		
Plant, Equip.:	$26,280,000	**Total Liab.:**	$38,743,000	**Indic. Yr. Divd.:**	NA
Total Assets:	$493,211,000	**Net Worth:**	$454,468,000	**Debt/ Equity:**	0.1713

InterContinental Hotels Group

3 Ravinia Dr., Ste. 100, Atlanta, GA, 30346; *PH:* 1-770-604-2000; *http://* www.ihgplc.com

General - Incorporation	UK	**Stock**- Price on:12/24/2007	$25.9802
Employees	11,456	Stock Exchange	NYSE
Auditor	Ernst & Young LLP	Ticker Symbol	IHG
Stk Agt	Registrar & Transfer Co	Outstanding Shares	354,000,000
Counsel	Richard Winter	E.P.S	$1.65
DUNS No.	NA	Shareholders	NA

Business: The group's principal activities are operation of hotels and distribution and manufacturing of soft drinks. Hotels, owns more than 3,300 owned, leased, managed and franchised hotels in nearly 100 countries and territories. Brands include intercontinental, crowne plaza, holiday inn, express by holiday inn, holiday inn express, staybridge suites and candlewood suites. Soft drinks, manufactures and distributes soft drinks in the United Kingdom. Brands include robinsons, tango, britvic (juice and mixers), r whites and j2o. It also has franchise for the pepsi and 7up brands in great Britain.

Primary SIC and add'l.: NA

CIK No: 0000858446

Subsidiaries: 220 Bloor Street Hotel Inc, 220 Bloor Street West Partnership, Airport Garden Hotel NV, American Commonwealth Assurance Co. Ltd., Arabian Hotel Management Co. LLC, Asia Pacific Holdings Limited, Athenaeum Hotel & Touristic Enterprises S.A., Avendra LLC, B.V. Amstel Maatschappij, Barclay Operating Corp., Barclay Operating Corp. Argentina Branch, BBJV Investments Limited, BCH Hotel Investment, Pte Ltd, BHMC Canada Inc., BHR Holdings B.V. 441 Subsidiaries included in the Index

Officers: Andrew Cosslett/53/Dir., CEO, Graham Pattenden/Sr. VP - Design, Engineering, Asia Pacific, IHG, Jan Smits/COO - Southern Asia, Korea, IHG, Clarence Tan/VP - Business Support, Asia Pacific, Birte Sebastian/Dir. - Corporate Communications, Public Relations, Asia Pacific, Paul Edgecliffe-Johnson/Head - Investor Relations, James Prout/Investor Relation - US Investor, William Morris/Sr. VP - Sales - Marketing EMEA, Heather Wood/Dir. - Investor Relations, Leslie McGibbon/Sr. VP - Global Corporate Affairs, Claire Williams/Dir. - External Communications, Abigail Duncan/Contact - Europe, Middle East, Africa, Interim Communications Dir., Suzanne Seyghal/Contact - Europe, Middle East, Africa, Public Relations Mgr. - EMEA, Jade Adnett/Communications Coordinator, EMEA, Stephanie Yudin/Dir. - Corporate Communications *(66 Officers included in Index)*

Directors: Andrew Cosslett/53/Dir., CEO, David Webster/63/Non Exec. Chmn., Jennifer Laing/Non Exec. Dir., Robert Larson/74/Non Exec. Dir., David Prosser/64/Non Exec. Dir., Ralph Kugler/52/Non Exec. Dir., Stevan Porter/Dir., Pres. - Americas, David Kappler/61/Non Exec. Dir., Jonathan S. Linen/Non Exec. Dir.

Owners: Peter Gowers/0.03%, Richard Hartman/0.02%, Stevan Porter/0.06%, Andrew Cosslett/0.03%, Lloyds TSB Group Plc/3.84%, Jonathan Linen, Richard Winter/0.03%, Ralph Kugler, Robert C. Larson, Patrick Imbardelli/0.03%, Jennifer Laing, Tracy Robbins, Ellerman Corporation Limited/7.13%, David Kappler, Richard Solomons/0.05% *(17 Owners included in Index)*

Financial Data: *Fiscal Year End:*12/31   *Latest Annual Data:* 12/31/2006

Year	Sales	Net Income
2006	$1,880,736,000	$952,123,000
2005	$3,286,728,000	$650,462,000
2004	$4,284,758,000	$655,044,000

Curr. Assets:	$977,591,000	**Curr. Liab.:**	$1,259,701,000		
Plant, Equip.:	$2,601,685,000	**Total Liab.:**	$3,340,266,000	**Indic. Yr. Divd.:**	$0.520
Total Assets:	$6,274,997,000	**Net Worth:**	$2,934,732,000	**Debt/ Equity:**	NA

Intercontinental Resources Inc

Formerly: Anglotajik Minerals Inc
9454 Wilshire Blvd., Ste. 301, Beverly Hills, CA, 90212; *PH:* 1-310-887-4416

General - Incorporation	NV	**Stock**- Price on:12/24/2007	$0.0095
Employees	1	Stock Exchange	OTC
Auditor	Chisholm Bierwolf & Nilson LLC	Ticker Symbol	INCL
Stk Agt	PacWest Transfer LLC	Outstanding Shares	51,820,000
Counsel	NA	E.P.S	-$0.01
DUNS No.	NA	Shareholders	NA

Business: The group's principle activity is to involve in research and exploration, market analysis and other business planning activities. The company is in its development stage. The company intended to create a digital video display jukebox system for distribution in Canada and the United States.

Primary SIC and add'l.: 3651

CIK No: 0001080360

Officers: Matthew Markin/Dir., CEO, CFO, Pres., Randy Miller/Pres.

Directors: Matthew Markin/Dir., CEO, CFO, Pres.

Owners: Randy Miller/5.40%, Matthew Markin/6.40%, Weir & Foulds LLP/5.40%, Insiders/6.40%

Financial Data: *Fiscal Year End:*12/31   *Latest Annual Data:* 12/31/2006

Year	Sales	Net Income
2006	NA	-$401,000
2005	NA	-$331,000
2004	NA	-$413,000

Curr. Assets:	$0	**Curr. Liab.:**	$821,000		
Plant, Equip.:	NA	**Total Liab.:**	$821,000	**Indic. Yr. Divd.:**	NA
Total Assets:	$0	**Net Worth:**	-$821,000	**Debt/ Equity:**	NA

InterDigital Communications Corp

781 3rd Ave., King of Prussia, PA, 19406; *PH:* 1-610-878-7800; *Fax:* 1-610-992-9432; *http://* www.interdigital.com; *Email:* sales@interdigital.com

General - Incorporation	PA	**Stock**- Price on:12/24/2007	NA
Employees	340	Stock Exchange	NDQ
Auditor	PricewaterhouseCoopers LLP	Ticker Symbol	IDCC
Stk Agt	American Stock Transfer & Trust Co.	Outstanding Shares	46,910,000
Counsel	NA	E.P.S	$0.83
DUNS No.	NA	Shareholders	NA

Business: The groups principle activities include designing and developing digital wireless technologies. The products of the group include cellular phones, wireless personal digital assistants and notebook computers, PCMCIA cards. The group products sold under the trade name InterDigital(R). Specific customers of the group include Nokia Corporation, LG Electronics Inc, NEC, Corporation of Japan, Sharp Corporation of Japan and Sony Ericsson Mobile Communications AB. The group operates from the United States, Europe, and Asia.

Primary SIC and add'l.: 6794

CIK No: 0000354913

Subsidiaries: InterDigital Advanced Technologies, Inc., InterDigital Canada Ltee, InterDigital Communications (Europe) Ltd., InterDigital Facility Company, InterDigital Finance Corporation, InterDigital Germany GmbH, InterDigital Technology Corporation, IPR Licensing, Inc., Tantivy Communications, Inc.

Officers: William J. Merritt/Dir., CEO, Pres., Pres. - Interdigital Technology Corporation/$1,024,870.00, Ridgely D. Bolgiano/Dir., VP, Chief Scientist - Interdigital, Janet Point/Investor Relations, Brett Attebery/Technology, Product Inquiries, Bruce G. Bernstein/Chief Intellectual Property, Licensing Officer/$518,941.00, Mark A. Lemmo/Exec. VP - Business Development, Product Management/$552,987.00, Brian G. Kiernan/Exec. VP - Standards, William C. Miller/Exec. VP - Programs, Customer Support, James J. Nolan/Exec. VP - Engineering, Lawrence F. Shay/Chief Legal Officer - Government Affairs/$490,151.00

Directors: William J. Merritt/Dir., CEO, Pres., Pres. - Interdigital Technology Corporation, Harry G. Campagna/Chmn., Ridgely D. Bolgiano/Dir., VP, Chief Scientist - Interdigital, Steven T. Clontz/Dir., Edward B. Kamins/Dir., Robert S. Roath/Dir., Robert W. Shaner/Dir., Alan P. Zabarsky/Dir.

Owners: Alan P. Zabarsky, Ridgely D. Bolgiano, Mark A. Lemmo, Richard J. Fagan, Insiders/4.40%, Harry G. Campagna/1.50%, Bruce G. Bernstein, Robert W. Shaner, Goldman Sachs Asset Management, L.P./6.40%, Steven T. Clontz, Robert S. Roath, William J. Merritt, Heartland Advisors, Inc./6.40%, Edward B. Kamins, Lawrence F. Shay

Financial Data: Fiscal Year End:12/31 Latest Annual Data: 12/31/2006

Year	Sales	Net Income
2006	$480,466,000	$225,222,000
2005	$163,125,000	$54,685,000
2004	$103,685,000	$155,000

Curr. Assets:	$453,802,000	Curr. Liab.:	$121,228,000		
Plant, Equip.:	$16,682,000	Total Liab.:	$288,600,000	Indic. Yr. Divd.:	NA
Total Assets:	$564,076,000	Net Worth:	$275,476,000	Debt/ Equity:	NA

Interdyne Co

503 Industrial Pkwy., Jonesville, MI, 49250; **PH:** 1-517-849-2281; **Fax:** 1-517-849-7557; **http://** www.interdyneinc.com

General - Incorporation	CA	Stock- Price on:12/24/2007	$0.02
Employees	NA	Stock Exchange	OTC
Auditor	Farber Hass Hurley & Mcewen, LLP	Ticker Symbol	ITDN
Stk Agt	OTR Inc	Outstanding Shares	40,000,000
Counsel	NA	E.P.S.	$0.00
DUNS No.	83-757-5174	Shareholders	NA

Business: The group's principle activity is to provide dormant and is looking for new opportunities. The company has made advances to its affiliate and is earning interest from this advance. The group operates from United The group operates from United States..

Primary SIC and add'l.: 9999

CIK No: 0000051011

Owners: Carlee Electronics Pte. Ltd./64.50%

Financial Data: Fiscal Year End:06/30 Latest Annual Data: 06/30/2007

Year	Sales	Net Income
2007	NA	-$1,000
2006	NA	$3,000
2005	NA	$3,000

Curr. Assets:	$250,000	Curr. Liab.:	$15,000		
Plant, Equip.:	NA	Total Liab.:	$15,000	Indic. Yr. Divd.:	NA
Total Assets:	$250,000	Net Worth:	$234,000	Debt/ Equity:	NA

Interep National Radio Sales Inc

100 Pk. Ave., New York, NY, 10017; **PH:** 1-212-916-0700; **Fax:** 1-212-916-0792; **http://** www.interep.com

General - Incorporation	NY	Stock- Price on:12/24/2007	NA
Employees	390	Stock Exchange	OTC
Auditor	BDO Seidman, LLP	Ticker Symbol	IREP
Stk Agt	American Stock Transfer & Trust Co.	Outstanding Shares	11,300,000
Counsel	Salans Herzfeld Heilbronn Et Al	E.P.S.	-$2.13
DUNS No.	NA	Shareholders	NA

Business: The group is an advertising sales and marketing company . The group specializes in radio, the Internet and complementary media. The group is the representation firm for over 1,800 radio stations nationwide. It has 17 offices across the country which enables it to serve radio station clients and advertisers in all 50 states and portions of Mexico and Canada. The group provides national sales representation for clients whose diverse formats include country, rock, sports, hispanic, classical, urban, news, talk, oldies, adult contemporary, jazz, contemporary hits and public radio. The group's quarterly revenue for Sep'07 was 29.23 millions of USD.

Primary SIC and add'l.: 7313

CIK No: 0000796735

Subsidiaries: Allied Radio Partners, Inc., American Radio Sales, Inc., Azteca America Spot Television Sales, Inc., Cybereps, Inc., D&R Radio, Inc., Infinity Radio Sales, Inc., Interactive Video Network, Inc., Interep Interactive, Inc., Interep New Media, Inc., McGavren Guild, Inc., Morrison and Abraham, Inc., Public Radio Network, Inc., SBS/Interep LLC

Officers: Adam Guild/CEO, Pres., Interep Interactive, David Kennedy/Vice Chmn., CEO, Henry Tsu/CIO, Richard Lowden/Sr. VP - Sales, Kay Olin/Regional Sales Exec., Loretta Smith/VP, Dir. - Corporate Events, Tracey Karm/Dir. - Investor Communications, Paul Parzuchowski/Dir. - Benefits, Human Resources, Kevin Garrity/Pres. - ABC Radio Sales, William J. McEntee/CFO, Exec. VP, Kevin Cassidy/Pres. - D&R Radio, Sheila Kirby/Pres. - Strategic Sales Development, Lisa Sirotka-Sonnenklar/Pres. - Mcgavren Guild Radio, Michael Weiss/Pres. - CBS Radio Sales, Bruce Feniger/Pres. - Interep Netsolutions

Directors: David Kennedy/Vice Chmn., CEO, Ralph C. Guild/Chmn., John Palmer/Dir., Howard Brenner/Dir., Arnie Semsky/Dir., Marc G. Guild/Dir.

Financial Data: Fiscal Year End:12/31 Latest Annual Data: 12/31/2006

Year	Sales	Net Income
2006	$81,217,000	-$14,247,000
2005	$100,069,000	-$3,038,000
2004	$102,917,000	-$7,032,000

Curr. Assets:	$50,022,000	Curr. Liab.:	$29,674,000		
Plant, Equip.:	$3,170,000	Total Liab.:	$136,148,000	Indic. Yr. Divd.:	NA
Total Assets:	$73,456,000	Net Worth:	-$62,692,000	Debt/ Equity:	NA

Interface Inc

2859 Paces Ferry Rd., Ste. 2000, Atlanta, GA, 30339; **PH:** 1-770-437-6800; **Fax:** 1-706-882-0500; **http://** www.interfaceinc.com

General - Incorporation	GA	Stock- Price on:12/24/2007	$18.55
Employees	4,873	Stock Exchange	NDQ
Auditor	BDO Seidman LLP	Ticker Symbol	IFSIA
Stk Agt	EquiServe Trust Co N.A	Outstanding Shares	61,270,000
Counsel	Kilpatrick Stockton	E.P.S.	-$0.32
DUNS No.	79-871-1305	Shareholders	NA

Business: The group's principle activity is to manufacturing, marketing and installing carpets, floor covering and related products for commercial and institutional interiors market. The group manufactures modular carpets, panel fabrics for use in open plan office furniture systems and upholstery for officer furniture manufacturers and contract jobbers. The group also provides carpet replacement, installation and maintenance services and produces raised/access flooring systems, antimicrobial additives, adhesives and other specialty chemical compounds and products. The group's products are sold in 100 countries all over the world. The group operates from United States.

Primary SIC and add'l.: 3996 9999 2842 2273 2211 2891 2221

CIK No: 0000715787

Subsidiaries: Bentley Mills, Inc., Bentley Prince Street, Inc., Camborne Holdings Ltd., Interface Americas Holdings, LLC, Interface Americas Re:Source Technologies, LLC, Interface Americas, Inc., Interface Architectural Resources, Inc., Interface Asia-Pacific Hong Kong Ltd., Interface Australia Holdings Pty Ltd., Interface Europe B.V., Interface Europe, Ltd, Interface Fabrics Canada, Inc., Interface Fabrics Elkin, Inc., Interface Fabrics Finishing, Inc., Interface Fabrics Guilford, Inc. 33 Subsidiaries included in the Index

Officers: Daniel T. Hendrix/CEO, Pres./$3,181,905.00, Christopher J. Richard/CEO, Pres. - Interface Fabrics Group Inc, Lindsey K. Parnell/CEO, Pres. - Interface Europe/$1,195,854.00, Robert A. Coombs/CEO, Pres. - Interface Asia Pacific, John R. Wells/CEO, Pres. - Interface Americas, Neel D. Bradham/VP - Business Development, Patrick C. Lynch/CFO/$890,119.00, Michael D. Bertolucci/Sr. VP, Jeff Roman/VP - Information Services, Business Development, Interface Inc, Raymond S. Willoch/Sr. VP - Administration, General Counsel, Corp. Sec. - Interface Inc/$1,271,306.00

Directors: Dianne Dillon-Ridgley/56/Dir., June M. Henton/68/Dir., Christopher G. Kennedy/44/Dir., Thomas R. Oliver/67/Dir., Ray C. Anderson/Founder, Edward C. Callaway/53/Dir., Carl I. Gable/68/Dir., James B. Miller/67/Dir., David K. Kohler/41/Dir., Harold M. Paisner/68/Dir.

Owners: John R. Wells/6.10%, Christopher G. Kennedy, Thomas R. Oliver/1.00%, Edward C. Callaway, John R. Wells/1.00%, Patrick C. Lynch/2.30%, Insiders/75.10%, Carl I. Gable/1.30%, Raymond S. Willoch/2.20%, Thomas R. Oliver, Lindsey K. Parnell/1.40%, Christopher G. Kennedy, James B. Miller, James B. Miller, David K. Kohler (31 Owners included in Index)

Financial Data: Fiscal Year End:01/01 Latest Annual Data: 12/31/2006

Year	Sales	Net Income
2006	$1,075,842,000	$9,992,000
2004	$881,658,000	-$55,402,000

Curr. Assets:	$448,959,000	Curr. Liab.:	$159,606,000		
Plant, Equip.:	$188,725,000	Total Liab.:	$648,440,000	Indic. Yr. Divd.:	$0.060
Total Assets:	$928,340,000	Net Worth:	$274,394,000	Debt/ Equity:	NA

Intergroup Corp

820 Moraga Dr., Los Angeles, CA, 90049; **PH:** 1-310-889-2500; **Fax:** 1-852-237-6044; **http://** www.intergroup.com; **Email:** igfel@intergroup.com

General - Incorporation	DE	Stock- Price on:12/24/2007	$16.3
Employees	11	Stock Exchange	NDQ
Auditor	PricewaterhouseCoopers LLP	Ticker Symbol	INTG
Stk Agt	American Stock Transfer & Trust Co.	Outstanding Shares	2,350,000
Counsel	Christensen, Miller, Fink Et Al	E.P.S.	$0.00
DUNS No.	06-493-0886	Shareholders	NA

Business: The group's principal activity is the ownership and management of multifamily residential properties. The group purchases, develops, operates, rehabilitates and disposes real estate properties and operates in other business and investment activities. The properties include twenty-two apartment complexes, two commercial real estate properties and a single-family house as a strategic investment located throughout the United States. The group also has investments in unimproved real property that is held for sale or development.

Primary SIC and add'l.: 6799 6552

CIK No: 0000069422

Subsidiaries: 11361 Ovada Properties, Inc., 11371 Ovada Properties, Inc., 11378 Ovada Properties, Inc., 11650 Bellagio Properties, Inc., 11680 Bellagio Properties, Inc., 11720 Bellagio Properties, Inc., 2301 Bel-Air Equity, Inc., 614 Acanto Properties, Inc., 636 Acanto Properties, Inc., Bellagio Capital Fund, LLC, Broadview Enterprises, Inc., Golden West Entertainment, Inc., Golden West Television Productions, Inc., Healthy Planet Communications, Inc., Intergroup Arlington Arms, Inc. 36 Subsidiaries included in the Index

Owners: William J. Nance/3.30%, David C. Gonzalez/1.00%, Insiders/70.50%, John V. Winfield/62.60%, Josef A. Grunwald/5.40%, John C. Love/1.20%, Gary N. Jacobs/1.30%

Financial Data: Fiscal Year End:06/30 Latest Annual Data: 06/30/2007

Year	Sales	Net Income
2007	$48,340,000	-$3,592,000
2006	$17,632,000	-$1,923,000
2005	$12,966,000	-$3,128,000

Curr. Assets:	$3,295,000	Curr. Liab.:	$3,405,000		
Plant, Equip.:	$78,916,000	Total Liab.:	$107,973,000	Indic. Yr. Divd.:	NA
Total Assets:	$122,884,000	Net Worth:	$9,243,000	Debt/ Equity:	17.7150

Interim Capital Corp

3960 Howard Hughes Pkwy, Ste. 500, Las Vegas, NV, 89109; *PH:* 1-972-745-3020

General - Incorporation	NV	*Stock* - Price on:12/24/2007	NA
Employees	NA	Stock Exchange	NA
Auditor	Moore & Assoc. Chartered	Ticker Symbol	NA
Stk Agt	Pacific Corporate Trust Co	Outstanding Shares	NA
Counsel	NA	E.P.S.	NA
DUNS No.	NA	Shareholders	NA

Business: The group's principle activity is to identify portfolios or client companies whose shares are capable of being publicly traded and which are at a stage of development. The client companies would benefit from the group's business development, management, support, financing services and market knowledge. The company generally invests in client companies in which they can purchase a large enough stake to enable them to have a significant influence over the management and policies of such client companies, to realize a return to compensate them for their investment in management services provided to it and facilitating the provision of capital. The group operates from United States.

Primary SIC and add'l.: 8742

CIK No: 0001317683

Officers: Mark Lindberg/40/Dir., CEO, CFO, Pres., Jason Freeman/32/Dir., VP

Directors: Mark Lindberg/40/Dir., CEO, CFO, Pres., Jason Freeman/32/Dir., VP

Owners: Mark Lindberg/0.01%, Shocker 200 Index, LP/72.35%, BBX Unit Investment Business Trust/0.95%, Insiders/73.31%

Interleukin Genetics Inc

135 Beaver St., Waltham, MA, 02452; *PH:* 1-781-398-0700; *Fax:* 1-781-398-0720; *http://* www.ilgenetics.com

General - Incorporation	DE	*Stock* - Price on:12/24/2007	$2.05
Employees	27	Stock Exchange	AMEX
Auditor	Grant Thornton LLP	Ticker Symbol	ILI
Stk Agt	U.S. Stock Transfer Corp	Outstanding Shares	27,600,000
Counsel	Fulbright & Jaworski LLP	E.P.S.	-$0.27
DUNS No.	87-422-8000	Shareholders	NA

Business: The group's principal activity is to develop and commercialize genetic diagnostic tests and medical research tools. The group develops and licenses its medical research tools, including biofusion(R) to pharmaceutical companies. The group has agreements with sheffield university, delta dental, kenna technologies, kaiser permanente for product research and development. The group's first genetic susceptibility test, pst, detects a genetic susceptibility to severe gum diseases (periodontitis). The group operates only in the United States.

Primary SIC and add'l.: 3841

CIK No: 0001037649

Subsidiaries: Interleukin Genetics Laboratory Services, Inc

Officers: Timothy J. Richerson/47/CEO/$177,606.00, Thomas R. Curran/Chmn., Interim CEO, John J. McCabe/40/Chief Accounting Officer, Sec./$222,338.00, Gordon Duff/Scientific Advisor, Peter Libby/Scientific Advisor, Kenneth S. Kornman/Dir., Pres., Chief Scientific Officer/$705,626.00, David A. Finkelstein/47/Chief Strategy Officer/$177,606.00, Ramon W. Mohanlal/49/Chief Medical Officer/$372,600.00, Robert Lindsay/Scientific Advisor, Gregory Mundy/Scientific Advisor, Jose Ordovas/Scientific Advisor

Directors: Thomas R. Curran/Chmn., Interim CEO, Dianne E. Bennett/Dir., George D. Calvert/Dir., Kenneth S. Kornman/Dir., Pres., Chief Scientific Officer

Owners: John J. McCabe, Cathy Fine/5.25%, David A. Finkelstein, Pyxis Innovations Inc./58.46%, Jeffrey K. Peterson/7.74%, Philip R. Reilly/2.47%, Timothy J. Richerson, Ramon W. Mohanlal, Insiders/8.06%, Stephen Garofalo/11.71%, Kenneth S. Kornman/5.30%

Financial Data: Fiscal Year End:12/31   Latest Annual Data: 12/31/2006

Year	Sales	Net Income
2006	$4,731,000	-$6,947,000
2005	$23,000	-$6,571,000
2004	$35,000	-$7,246,000

Curr. Assets:	$12,991,000	Curr. Liab.:	$7,388,000		
Plant, Equip.:	$876,000	Total Liab.:	$8,844,000	Indic. Yr. Divd.:	NA
Total Assets:	$22,630,000	Net Worth:	$13,786,000	Debt/ Equity:	NA

Interline Brands Inc

801 W Bay St., Jacksonville, FL, 32204; *PH:* 1-904-421-1400; *Fax:* 1-904-358-2486; *http://* www.interlinebrands.com; *Email:* irinfo@interlinebrands.com

General - Incorporation	NJ	*Stock* - Price on:12/24/2007	$26.18
Employees	3,763	Stock Exchange	NYSE
Auditor	Deloitte& Touche LLP	Ticker Symbol	IBI
Stk Agt	Bank of New York	Outstanding Shares	32,280,000
Counsel	NA	E.P.S.	$0.98
DUNS No.	NA	Shareholders	NA

Business: The groups principle activities include marketing and distributing maintenance, repair and operations, products to the multi-family housing facilities. The groups products category include plumbing, electrical, ventilation, security, appliances, hardware and other. In the year 2005, the group acquired CCS Enterprises, Inc. The group operates from the United States. The group's quarterly revenue for September 2007 was 330.19 millions of USD.

Primary SIC and add'l.: 5074 5251 5075 3585 3088

CIK No: 0001250189

Subsidiaries: Initial Public Offering

Officers: Michael J. Grebe/Chmn., CEO, William E. Sanford/COO, Pres., Fred Bravo/VP - Field Sales, William R. Pray/Sr. VP, Chief Merchandising Officer, Pamela L. Maxwell/VP - Marketing, Thomas J. Tossavainen/CFO, Jim Spahn/VP - Distribution, Annette Ricciuti/VP - Human Resources, Brian Mendelson/VP - Corporate Sales

Directors: Michael J. Grebe/Chmn., CEO, Ernest K. Jacquet/Dir., Charles W. Santoro/Dir., Drew T. Sawyer/Dir., Gideon Argov/Dir., Michael E. Dedomenico/Dir., John J. Gavin/Dir., Barry J. Goldstein/Dir.

Financial Data: Fiscal Year End:12/30   Latest Annual Data: 12/29/2006

Year	Sales	Net Income
2006	$1,067,570,000	$31,185,000
2005	$851,928,000	$28,799,000
2004	$743,905,000	$18,101,000

Curr. Assets:	$346,337,000	Curr. Liab.:	$92,985,000		
Plant, Equip.:	$28,767,000	Total Liab.:	$420,481,000	Indic. Yr. Divd.:	NA
Total Assets:	$673,380,000	Net Worth:	$252,899,000	Debt/ Equity:	NA

Interlink Electronics Inc

546 Flynn Rd., Camarillo, CA, 93012; *PH:* 1-800-340-1331; *Fax:* 1-805-484-8989; *http://* www.interlinkelec.com; *Email:* sales@interlinkelectronics.com

General - Incorporation	DE	*Stock* - Price on:12/24/2007	$1.7
Employees	127	Stock Exchange	OTC
Auditor	BDO Seidman LLP	Ticker Symbol	LINK
Stk Agt	Computershare Trust Co	Outstanding Shares	NA
Counsel	Stoel Rives LLP	E.P.S.	-$0.49
DUNS No.	15-129-6266	Shareholders	NA

Business: The group's principal activity is to develop intuitive interface devices for home and business applications. The products of the group's include interactive remote controls, pen-input pads, wireless keyboards and integrated mouse pointing devices. The group sells interface devices to original equipment manufacturers and through distributors and value-added resellers.

Primary SIC and add'l.: 3861 3679

CIK No: 0000828146

Subsidiaries: Interlink Electronics Asia Pacific Limited, Interlink Electronics, K.K.

Officers: Michael E. Thoben/Chmn., CEO, Pres./$945,162.00, Charles C. Best/CFO, Sec./$321,860.00, Rod Vesling/VP - Sales, Marketing E, Transaction, Specialty Products, David J. Arthur/Sr. VP - Operations, Michael W. Ambrose/Sr. VP - Product Development/$667,201.00, Patrice R. Poleto/VP - Human Resources, Jim Reisteter/VP - Sales, Marketing Business Communications, Home Entertainment, Dave Stallard/VP - Engineering

Directors: Michael E. Thoben/Chmn., CEO, Pres., Eugene F. Hovanec/Dir., John Buckett/Dir., George Gu/Dir., Merritt M. Lutz/Dir., Edward Hamburg/Dir., Tom Thimot/Dir., Lawrence S. Barker/56/Dir.

Owners: Tom Thimot, Insiders/9.30%, Charles C. Best, Steven R. Becker/15.70%, Austin W. Marxe/41.20%, Royce & Associates, LLC/8.00%, Lawrence S. Barker, John A. Buckett, Potomac Capital Management LLC Paul J. Solit/16.70%, George Gu/2.20%, Merritt M. Lutz, Michael W. Ambrose/1.70%, Michael E. Thoben/4.20%, Edward Hamburg

Financial Data: Fiscal Year End:12/31   Latest Annual Data: 12/31/2006

Year	Sales	Net Income
2006	$36,238,000	-$11,756,000
2005	$38,239,000	-$8,305,000
2004	$35,407,000	-$2,284,000

Curr. Assets:	$22,244,000	Curr. Liab.:	$7,491,000		
Plant, Equip.:	$1,594,000	Total Liab.:	$7,491,000	Indic. Yr. Divd.:	NA
Total Assets:	$24,355,000	Net Worth:	$16,864,000	Debt/ Equity:	NA

Intermagnetics General Corp

450 Old Niskayuna Rd. , Latham, NY, 12110; *PH:* 1-518-782-1122; *http://* www.igc.com

General - Incorporation	DE	*Stock* - Price on:12/24/2007	$41.96
Employees	121,732	Stock Exchange	NA
Auditor	PricewaterhouseCoopers LLP	Ticker Symbol	NA
Stk Agt	American Stock Transfer & Trust Co.	Outstanding Shares	1,100,000,000
Counsel	Helfgott & Karas	E.P.S.	$8.72
DUNS No.	05-572-9800	Shareholders	NA

Business: The group's principal activities are to develop and manufacture super conducting materials, electromagnetic components and cryogenic refrigeration systems. The group operates in three segments: magnetic resonance imaging, instrumentation and energy technology. The magnetic resonance imaging segment consists primarily of the manufacture and sale of magnets, radio frequency coils and low temperature super conducting wire. The instrumentation segment consists of refrigeration equipment used primarily in ultra-high vacuum applications, industrial coatings, analytical instruments, medical diagnostics and semiconductor processing and testing. The energy technology segment develops second generation, high temperature super conducting materials. The group exports its products to Netherlands and Japan. On 27th jan 2004, the group acquired invivo corp.

Primary SIC and add'l.: 3643 3812 3585 3845 3357

CIK No: 0000351012

Subsidiaries: Invivo Corporation, Invivo Germany, Invivo Research UK Ltd., SuperPower Inc.

Financial Data: Fiscal Year End:05/28   Latest Annual Data: 12/31/2006

Year	Sales	Net Income
2006	$11,686,620,000	-$762,057,000
2005	$35,999,838,000	$3,396,859,000
2004	$41,367,244,000	$3,869,438,000

Curr. Assets:	$3,469,731,000	Curr. Liab.:	$3,571,884,000		
Plant, Equip.:	$10,433,663,000	Total Liab.:	$7,285,068,000	Indic. Yr. Divd.:	$0.680
Total Assets:	$14,845,994,000	Net Worth:	$7,560,927,000	Debt/ Equity:	NA

Intermec Inc

Formerly: Unova Inc

6001 36th Ave. W, Everett, WA, 98203; *PH:* 1-425-265-2400; *http://* www.unova.com

General - Incorporation	DE	*Stock* - Price on:12/24/2007	$23.84
Employees	2,407	Stock Exchange	NYSE
Auditor	Deloitte & Touche LLP	Ticker Symbol	IN
Stk Agt	Mellon Investor Services LLC	Outstanding Shares	60,590,000
Counsel	NA	E.P.S.	$0.15
DUNS No.	79-924-6558	Shareholders	NA

Business: The group's principal activity is to provide global customers with solutions for improving their efficiency and productivity. It operates in two segments: automated data systems (ads) and industrial automation systems (ias). The ads segment provides mobile computing solutions for the field worker, automated data collection systems for on-premises and site-based workers, wireless network systems for wireless enablement of an enterprise and barcode label and printing solutions. The ias segment is a leading producer of value-added manufacturing products and services spanning the production cycle from process

engineering and design to systems integration including comprehensive life cycle support. Ias serves the global aerospace, automotive, off-road vehicle and diesel engine industries as well as the industrial components, heavy equipment and general job shop markets. In 2003, the group sold substantially all the assets of its lamb body and assembly systems division.

Primary SIC and add'l.: 3571 7371 3545

CIK No: 0001044590

Subsidiaries: Infolink Group Limited, Intermec (South America) Ltda., Intermec AB, Intermec International B.V., Intermec International Inc., Intermec IP Corp., Intermec Label Products B.V., Intermec Printer AB, Intermec Scanner Technology Center S.A.S, Intermec Technologies (S)Pte Ltd, Intermec Technologies A/S, Intermec Technologies AB, Intermec Technologies Australia Pty. Limited, Intermec Technologies Benelux B.V., Intermec Technologies Canada Ltd. 26 Subsidiaries included in the Index

Officers: Patrick J. Byrne/Dir., CEO, Pres., Cohen L. Kenneth/VP - Tax, Treasurer, Sue Y. Taylor/CIO, VP - Human Resources, Douglas Stubsten/VP - Corporate Audit, Janis L. Harwell/Sr. VP, General Counsel, Corp. Sec./$634,181.00, Lanny H. Michael/Sr. VP, CFO/$222,413.00, Kenneth L. Cohen/VP, Treasurer - Tax/$460,753.00, Fredric B. Anderson/VP, Corporate Controller, Michael H. Lanny/Sr. VP, CFO, Anderson B. Fredric/VP, Corporate Controller/$306,391.00

Directors: Patrick J. Byrne/Dir., CEO, Pres., Allen J. Lauer/Chmn., Stephen P. Reynolds/Dir., Claire W. Gargalli/Dir., Gregory K. Hinckley/Dir., Oren G. Shaffer/Dir., Steven B. Sample/Dir., Lydia H. Kennard/Dir., Larry D. Yost/Dir.

Owners: Kenneth L. Cohen, Claire W. Gargalli, Insiders/2.50%, GAMCO Investors, Inc./5.40%, Oren G. Shaffer, Gregory K. Hinckley, Larry D. Brady, Steven J. Winter, Unitrin, Inc./20.93%, Lydia H. Kennard, Lanny H. Michael, Allen J. Lauer, Janis L. Harwell, Fredric B. Anderson, Stephen E. Frank *(21 Owners included in Index)*

Financial Data: Fiscal Year End:12/31   Latest Annual Data: 12/31/2006

Year	Sales		Net Income
2006	$849,969,000		$32,000,000
2005	$875,482,000		$61,792,000
2004	$811,317,000		-$49,129,000
Curr. Assets:	$549,130,000	Curr. Liab.:	$190,236,000	P/E Ratio: 149.00
Plant, Equip.:	$43,453,000	Total Liab.:	$392,738,000	Indic. Yr. Divd.: NA
Total Assets:	$810,340,000	Net Worth:	$417,602,000	Debt/ Equity: 0.2394

Intermost Corp

31st Floor, B31-23 Guomao Bldg., Renmin Rd.S, Shenzhen, 518014; **PH:** 86-755-82210354; **Fax:** 86-755-82210133; **http://** www.intermost.com; **Email:** contact@intermost.com

General - Incorporation	WY	**Stock**- Price on:12/24/2007	$0.16
Employees	NA	Stock Exchange	OTC
Auditor	Samuel H. Wong & Co., LLP	Ticker Symbol	IMOT
Stk Agt	OTC Corporate Transfer Service Co	Outstanding Shares	NA
Counsel	NA	E.P.S.	NA
DUNS No.	NA	Shareholders	NA

Business: The group's principle activity is to provide e-commerce solutions, development of software, provision of consultation services and sales of photographic equipment in China. The group operates in the following segments namely: e-commerce solutions, system sales integration, phone payment, Web advertisement, sales of computer software and photographic business. E-commerce solutions include Web design and development and Web hosting. Photographic business consists of sales of photographic equipment. The group's quarterly revenue for Sep '07 was 0.01 millions of USD.

Primary SIC and add'l.: 7372 7335 7375 7373

CIK No: 0001088312

Subsidiaries: ChinaE.com Information Technology Ltd., ChinaE.com Technology (Shenzhen) Ltd., Golden Anke Technology Ltd, Hainan Concord Financial Products Development Co., Ltd., IMOT Information Technology (Shenzhen) Ltd, Shanghai Newray Photographic Equipment Co. Ltd.

Officers: Rocky Wulianghai/Dir., CEO, Pres., Fred Peck/Dir. - Strategic Planning Advisor, Andy Lin/62/VP, Thomas Lee/Sec. Of Board, CFO

Directors: Rocky Wulianghai/Dir., CEO, Pres., Catalina Chan/Dir., Peter Yang/Dir., Fred Peck/Dir. - Strategic Planning Advisor, Deng Xiang Xiong/Dir., Shim Yang/50/Dir., James Woo/Dir., Xiangxiong Deng/Dir., Wilbert Kam/Dir., Thomas Lee/Sec. Of Board, CFO, Chia Hsun Wu/47/Dir.

Owners: Shim Yang, Magnate Trading Services Ltd./3.10%, Piaster Assets Inc/3.10%, Deng Xiang Xiong, First Federal Holding/18.57%, Grand Grade International Ltd, Catalina Chan, Original Group Holdings Ltd./3.10%, First Core Capital Finance Ltd./10.21%, Allied Point Limited, Alfredo Properties Limited/9.29%, Andy Lin

Financial Data: Fiscal Year End:06/30   Latest Annual Data: 06/30/2007

Year	Sales		Net Income
2007	$4,681,000		-$3,091,000
2006	$12,319,000		-$2,117,000
2005	$16,834,000		$542,000
Curr. Assets:	$12,201,000	Curr. Liab.:	$1,569,000	
Plant, Equip.:	$51,000	Total Liab.:	$1,569,000	Indic. Yr. Divd.: NA
Total Assets:	$17,036,000	Net Worth:	$11,330,000	Debt/ Equity: NA

Intermountain Community Bancorp

231 N Third Ave., Sandpoint, ID, 83864; **PH:** 1-208-263-0505; **http://** www.intermountainbank.com

General - Incorporation	ID	**Stock**- Price on:12/24/2007	$17.3
Employees	415	Stock Exchange	OTC
Auditor	BDO Seidman LLP	Ticker Symbol	IMCB
Stk Agt	American Stock Transfer & Trust Co.	Outstanding Shares	8,190,000
Counsel	NA	E.P.S.	$1.01
DUNS No.	NA	Shareholders	NA

Business: The group's principle activity is to provide forward-looking statements and readers are advised that various factors, including regional and national economic conditions, unfavorable judicial decisions, substantial changes in levels of market interest rates, credit and other risks of lending and investment activities and competitive and regulatory factors could affect the Companys financial performance and could cause the Companys actual results for future periods to differ materially from those anticipated or projected. The group operates from United States.

Primary SIC and add'l.: 6035

CIK No: 0001284506

Subsidiaries: Intermountain Statutory Trust I, Intermountain Statutory Trust II, Panhandle State Bank

Officers: Curt Hecker/Dir., CEO, Pres., Jerrold Smith/Dir., Exec. VP - Imcb, Dale Schuman/Sr. VP - Trust, Wealth Management, Carolyn Gay/Investor Relations Officer, Douglas Wright/CFO, Exec. VP, Pamela Rasmussen/COO, Exec. VP, John Nagel/Exec. VP - Credit Administration, Jerry Smith/Pres. - Panhandle State Bank, Intermountain Community Bank, Jay Vandegriff/Contact - New Accounting, Jim Burnett/VP, Sr. Project Mgr., Debbi Smith/VP, SBA Center Mgr., Michele Groves/SBA Production Assist. - Credit Analyst, Micheal Brown/Business Development Officer, Bonnie Fairfield/Loan Production Assist., Jillian Gulman/Credit Analyst, Loan Production Assist.

Directors: Curt Hecker/Dir., CEO, Pres., James T. Diehl/Vice Chmn., John B. Parker/Chmn., Terry L. Merwin/Dir., Michael J. Romine/Dir., Jerrold Smith/Dir., Exec. VP - Imcb, Ford Elsaesser/Dir., Barbara Strickfaden/Dir., Douglas P. Ward/Dir., Jim Patrick/Dir., Charles L. Bauer/Dir., Maggie Y. Lyons/Dir., Ronald L. Jones/Dir.

Owners: Insiders/24.80%, James Fenton Co./5.70%, Ronald Jones, John B. Parker/1.30%, Terry L. Merwin/1.40%, Barbara Strickfaden, Pamela Rasmussen, Curt Hecker/3.80%, Maggie Y. Lyons, Charles L. Bauer/2.60%, James T. Diehl/2.80%, Wray D. Farmin/5.70%, John Nagel, Jim Patrick, Michael J. Romine/6.40% *(19 Owners included in Index)*

Financial Data: Fiscal Year End:12/31   Latest Annual Data: 12/31/2006

Year	Sales		Net Income
2006	$71,405,000		$9,202,000
2005	$51,311,000		$7,482,000
2004	$34,512,000		$4,346,000
Curr. Assets:	$67,979,000	Curr. Liab.:	$819,184,000	P/E Ratio: 17.13
Plant, Equip.:	$25,444,000	Total Liab.:	$841,786,000	Indic. Yr. Divd.: NA
Total Assets:	$919,866,000	Net Worth:	$78,080,000	Debt/ Equity: 0.3096

Intermountain Refining Co Inc

PO Box 35, Farmington, NM, 87499; **PH:** 1-505-326-2668

General - Incorporation	NM	**Stock**- Price on:12/24/2007	NA
Employees	332	Stock Exchange	OTC
Auditor	Richey, May & Co. LLP	Ticker Symbol	IMNG
Stk Agt	NA	Outstanding Shares	NA
Counsel	NA	E.P.S.	NA
DUNS No.	NA	Shareholders	NA

Business: The group's principal activities are the production of natural gas and manufacture and storage of asphalt paving products. The group also provides management and consulting services, leasing unused space in the group's office building and generation of electric power. The group owns working interests and operates 20 natural gas producing wells located in southwestern Kansas. Natural gas and helium produced are sold under exclusive contract to oneok field services. It also owns petroleum products refinery and asphalt products storage facility in fredonia and Arizona. On 01-Mar-2003, the group acquired a 90% working interest in oil producing properties in kimball county.

Primary SIC and add'l.: 1311 4911 2951 8748

CIK No: 0001084597

Officers: William N. Hagler/75/Chmn., CEO, Pres., Rick L. Hurt/55/Dir., CFO, Controller, Sec., Treasurer

Directors: William N. Hagler/75/Chmn., CEO, Pres., Rick L. Hurt/55/Dir., CFO, Controller, Sec., Treasurer

Owners: William N. Hagler/60.04%, Insiders/60.64%, Rick L. Hurt

InterMune Inc

3280 Bayshore Blvd., Brisbane, CA, 94005; **PH:** 1-415-466-2200; **Fax:** 1-415-466-2300; **http://** www.intermune.com; **Email:** ir@intermune.com

General - Incorporation	DE	**Stock**- Price on:12/24/2007	$25.4
Employees	195	Stock Exchange	NDQ
Auditor	Ernst & Young LLP	Ticker Symbol	ITMN
Stk Agt	Mellon Investor Services LLC	Outstanding Shares	34,530,000
Counsel	Cooley Godward LLP	E.P.S.	-$3.22
DUNS No.	NA	Shareholders	NA

Business: The group's principal activities are to develop and market innovative products for the treatment of serious pulmonary and infectious diseases and cancer. The group marketed three products; actimmune, infergen and amphotec. Actimmune is approved in the United States for two rare congenital disorders. Infergen is marketed in the United States and Canada for the treatment of chronic hepatitis c infections. Amphotec is marketed worldwide for the treatment of invasive aspergillosis. The group has three products in the process of development; actimmune for the treatment of idiopathic pulmonary fibrosis, oritavancin, for the treatment of gram-positive bacterial infections and peg-infergen for the treatment of chronic hepatitis c infections. The major customers of the group include bergen brunswing, cardinal healthcare, caremark, merck medco, mckesson hboc and priority healthcare.

Primary SIC and add'l.: 2833 2834

CIK No: 0001087432

Subsidiaries: InterMune Canada Inc, InterMune Europe Limited

Officers: Daniel G. Welch/Dir., CEO, Pres./$1,107,704.00, Howard Simon/Sr. VP - Human Resources, Corporate Services, Assoc. General Counsel, Chief Compliance Officer, Lawrence Blatt/Chief Science Officer/$1,636,685.00, John Hodgman/Sr. VP, CFO/$313,647.00, Williamson Bradford/VP - Clinical Science, Steven Porter/Chief Medical Officer/$1,285,821.00, Marianne Armstrong/Chief Medical Affairs, Regulatory Officer/$1,298,093.00, Robin Steele/Sr. VP, General Counsel, Corp. Sec., Bruce W. Tomlinson/VP, Controller

Directors: Daniel G. Welch/Dir., CEO, Pres., William Ringo/Chmn., Jonathan Leff/Dir., Michael Smith/Dir., Lars Ekman/Dir., James Healy/Dir., David Kabakoff/Dir., Louis Drapeau/Dir.

Owners: D.E. Shaw& Co., Inc./5.60%, Sectoral Asset Management Inc./9.50%, T. Rowe Price Associates, Inc./7.20%, William R. Ringo, Michael L. Smith, Lawrence M. Blatt, Warburg, Pincus Equity Partners, L.P./21.40%, Citidel Limited Partnership/5.30%, HBK Investments L.P./6.20%, James I. Healy, Jonathan S. Leff/22.00%, Marianne S. Armstrong, Daniel G. Welch, Steven B. Porter, Insiders/27.60%

Financial Data: Fiscal Year End:12/31   Latest Annual Data: 12/31/2006

Year	Sales		Net Income
2006	$90,784,000		-$107,206,000
2005	$110,496,000		-$5,235,000
2004	$150,987,000		-$59,478,000
Curr. Assets:	$242,227,000	Curr. Liab.:	$40,303,000	
Plant, Equip.:	$9,210,000	Total Liab.:	$297,380,000	Indic. Yr. Divd.: NA
Total Assets:	$257,583,000	Net Worth:	-$39,797,000	Debt/ Equity: NA

Internap Network Services Corp

250 Williams St., Atlanta, GA, 30303; *PH:* 1-404-302-9700; *Fax:* 1-404-475-0520; *http://* www.internap.com; *Email:* gen_info@internap.com

General - Incorporation	DE	**Stock**- Price on:12/24/2007	$13.98
Employees	330	Stock Exchange	NDQ
Auditor	PricewaterhouseCoopers LLP	Ticker Symbol	INAP
Stk Agt	American Stock Transfer & Trust Co.	Outstanding Shares	48,920,000
Counsel	Cooley Godward LLP	E.P.S	-$0.19
DUNS No.	NA	Shareholders	NA

Business: The group's principal activity is to provide Internet connectivity solutions to business customers. It delivers these services through its 29 network access points, which feature multiple direct high-speed connections to major Internet networks. In addition to connectivity solutions, the group provides complementary managed Internet services, including content distribution, virtual private networking, managed security, managed storage and video conferencing. The group provides services to customers in various industry verticals, including financial services, media and communications, travel, e-commerce, retail and technology. As of 31-Mar-2004, the group provided its services to over 1,709 customers in the United States and abroad, including approximately 70 customers in the Fortune 1000 companies. The group acquired netvmg inc on 01-Oct-2003 and sockeye networks inc on 15-Oct-2003.

Primary SIC and add'l.: 7375 4813 7372

CIK No: 0001056386

Subsidiaries: CO Space Construction, LLC, CO Space Properties, LLC, CO Space Services, LLC, CO Space, Inc., Internap (Bermuda) Limited, Internap Corporation, Internap Holding Corporation, Internap Network Services (Australia) Ltd., Internap Network Services (HK) Limited, Internap Network Services (Singapore) Pty Limited, Internap Network Services B.V., Internap Network Services U.K. Limited, Internap Technologies (Bermuda) Ltd., Internap Technologies B.V., Internap Technologies, Inc. 18 Subsidiaries included in the Index

Officers: James P. Deblasio/Dir., CEO, Pres./$952,969.00, Eric Klinker/CTO, VP - Engineering/$488,684.00, David A. Buckel/CFO/$796,093.00, Eric Suddith/VP - Human Resources/$436,870.00, David L. Abrahamson/VP - Sales/$1,127,788.00, Andrew S. Albrecht/VP - Corporate Development, Investor Relations, Dorothy An/VP, General Counsel, Alistair A. Sloan/VP - Operations, Vincent J. Molinaro/COO, Tim Sullivan/CTO, Philip N. Kaplan/Chief Strategy Officer, Richard P. Dobb/VP, General Counsel, Corp. Sec., Sarah Willis/Contact - Media Relations

Directors: James P. Deblasio/Dir., CEO, Pres., Eugene Eidenberg/Chmn., Patricia L. Higgins/Vice Chmn., Charles B. Coe/Dir., William J. Harding/Dir., Kevin L. Ober/Dir., Daniel C. Stanzione/Dir.

Owners: Eric Suddith, Kevin L. Ober, Eric Klinker, Patricia L. Higgins, Charles B. Coe, Eugene Eidenberg, David L. Abrahamson, David A. Buckel, Franklin Resources, Inc./9.60%, Daniel C. Stanzione, Insiders/18.90%, William J. Harding, Fredric Harman, James P. DeBlasio, FMR Corp./6.40%

Financial Data: *Fiscal Year End:*12/31 *Latest Annual Data:* 12/31/2006

Year	Sales	Net Income
2006	$181,375,000	$3,657,000
2005	$153,717,000	-$4,964,000
2004	$144,546,000	-$18,062,000

Curr. Assets:	$83,456,000	**Curr. Liab.:**	$26,931,000		
Plant, Equip.:	$47,493,000	**Total Liab.:**	$47,177,000	**Indic. Yr. Divd.:**	NA
Total Assets:	$173,702,000	**Net Worth:**	$126,525,000	**Debt/ Equity:**	0.0095

International Absorbents Inc

6960 Salashan Pkwy., Ferndale, WA, 98248; *PH:* 1-360-734-7415; *Fax:* 1-360-671-1588; *http://* www.absorbent.com; *Email:* absorbs@absorption-corp.com

General - Incorporation	BC	**Stock**- Price on:12/24/2007	$6.4
Employees	137	Stock Exchange	AMEX
Auditor	Moss Adams LLP	Ticker Symbol	IAX
Stk Agt	Pacific Corporate Trust Co	Outstanding Shares	6,410,000
Counsel	NA	E.P.S	$0.18
DUNS No.	24-658-0518	Shareholders	NA

Business: The group's principle activities are to develop, manufacture, and market proprietary, cost-effective absorbent products derived from waste wood fiber (cellulose), a by-product of the pulp and paper manufacturing process. The group operates principally in two business segments: the animal care industry and the industrial products industry primarily in the United States. The group's environmentally-safe, non-toxic, lightweight products are utilized in a broad range of industrial, agricultural, and consumer applications. These applications include commercial/retail animal bedding and litter, oil and hazardous spill cleanup and control, oil/water filtration, and packaging. The group's trademarks are absorbent gp(tm), absorbent w(tm), spillsorb(tm), and spill-dri(tm). The products of the group include carefresh, agrafresh, catworks, ecofresh, spill-dri, and spillsorb, healthypet, ecofresh and hazpak. The group's quarterly revenue for September 2007 was 9.03 millions of USD.

Primary SIC and add'l.: 2621 2899

CIK No: 0000813634

Subsidiaries: Absorption Corp.

Officers: Gordon L. Ellis/Founder, Chmn., CEO, Pres./$196,449.00, David H. Thomspon/Corp. Sec./$240,214.00

Directors: Gordon L. Ellis/Founder, Chmn., CEO, Pres., Michael P. Bentley/45/Dir., John J. Sutherland/58/Dir., Lionel G. Dodd/68/Dir., Daniel J. Whittle/53/Dir.

Owners: Insiders/11.50%, John J. Sutherland, Daniel J. Whittle, David H. Thompson, Gordon L. Ellis/5.70%, Shawn M. Dooley/2.00%, Douglas E. Ellis/2.60%, Praetorian Capital Management LLC/6.10%, Michael P. Bentley, Lionel G. Dodd, First Wilshire Securities Management, Inc./5.20%

Financial Data: *Fiscal Year End:*01/31 *Latest Annual Data:* 1/31/2007

Year	Sales	Net Income
2007	$29,495,000	$701,000
2006	$25,436,000	$655,000
2005	$22,163,000	$1,790,000

Curr. Assets:	$9,329,000	**Curr. Liab.:**	$3,945,000	**P/E Ratio:**	35.56
Plant, Equip.:	$18,096,000	**Total Liab.:**	$12,301,000	**Indic. Yr. Divd.:**	NA
Total Assets:	$27,691,000	**Net Worth:**	$15,390,000	**Debt/ Equity:**	NA

International Aluminum Corp

PO Box 6, Monterey Park, CA, 91754; *PH:* 1-323-264-1670; *http://* www.intlalum.com

General - Incorporation	CA	**Stock**- Price on:12/24/2007	NA
Employees	1,600	Stock Exchange	NA
Auditor	PricewaterhouseCoopers LLP	Ticker Symbol	NA
Stk Agt	Continental Stock Transfer & Trust Co	Outstanding Shares	NA
Counsel	Joel McIntyre	E.P.S	NA
DUNS No.	00-194-7134	Shareholders	NA

Business: The group's principal activity is to manufacture and supply a diversified line of aluminum and vinyl products used in residential and commercial constructions. The group operates in three business segments: commercial products, residential products and aluminum extrusions. Residential products include extensive lines of windows and patio doors manufactured from vinyl and aluminum and wardrobe mirror doors for the residential building and remodeling markets. Commercial products include curtain walls, window walls, slope glazed systems, storefront framing, entrance doors and frames, commercial operable windows, interior office fronts, office partitions and interior doors and frames for the commercial building and tenant improvement markets. Aluminum extrusions include mill finish, anodized, painted and fabricated aluminum extrusions.

Primary SIC and add'l.: 3354

CIK No: 0000051103

Subsidiaries: dba International Window, International Extrusion Corporation, International Extrusion Corporation-Texas, International Window Corporation, International Window-Arizona, Inc., Raco Interior Products, Inc., United States Aluminum Corporation, United States Aluminum Corporation-Carolina, United States Aluminum Corporation-Illinois, United States Aluminum Corporation-Texas, United States Aluminum Of Canada-British Columbia Ltd., United States Aluminum Of Canada-Ontario Ltd.

Owners: Ronald L. Rudy, Cornelius C. Vanderstar/39.90%, John P. Cunningham/3.40%, Alexander L. Dean, Mitchell K. Fogelman, William G. Gainer, Insiders/44.20%

International Assets Holding Corp

220 E Central Pkwy., Ste. 2060, Altamonte Springs, FL, 32701; *PH:* 1-407-741-5300; *Fax:* 1-407-740-0808; *http://* www.intlassets.com

General - Incorporation	DE	**Stock**- Price on:12/24/2007	$23.82
Employees	89	Stock Exchange	NDQ
Auditor	Rothstein, Kass & Co, P.C	Ticker Symbol	IAAC
Stk Agt	Mellon Investor Services LLC	Outstanding Shares	8,230,000
Counsel	Shutts & Bowen	E.P.S	$0.06
DUNS No.	62-079-3877	Shareholders	NA

Business: The group operates as international securities brokerage firm. The group serves as a holding company and operates through its subsidiaries intl trading inc, international asset inc and iahc ltd. Intl trading inc is a wholesale market maker of international securities. International asset inc is involved in international debt transactions and holds the physical assets of the group. Iahc (Bermuda) ltd maintains a proprietary international fixed income securities portfolio managed by the company's fixed income traders.

Primary SIC and add'l.: 6211 6719

CIK No: 0000913760

Subsidiaries: IAHC Bermuda, Ltd., INTL Assets, Inc., INTL Commodities, Inc., INTL Consilium LLC, INTL Global Currencies Limited, INTL Holding (U.K.) Limited, INTL Trading, Inc.

Officers: Sean Oconnor/CEO, Lawrence Steel/Physical Precious Metals, Barry Canham/Head - Trading, Glyn Stevens/Sales, Peter Wallin/Originations, Fabian Jungman/Sales, Michael Lau/Originations, Jeff Rhodes/Chief Executive - Dubai, Jonathan Binder/Asset Management - Fort Lauderdale, Rory Passey/Contact - Asset Management, London, Nora Trotta/Contact - Asset Management, Buenos Aires, Luis Brocardo/Contact - Asset Management, Buenos Aires, Charles Lyon/Head - Trading, Sharon Meeder/Institutional Sales, William Dennis/Domestic Equities *(33 Officers included in Index)*

Directors: Diego Veitia/Chmn., Robert A. Miller/Dir., John Radziwill/Dir., Justin R. Wheeler/Dir., John Fowler/Dir.

Owners: Barbara Branch/4.20%, Insiders/40.00%, Diego J. Veitia/1.80%, Samuel Taub/5.50%, Justin R. Wheeler, Sean M. OConnor/14.10%, Jonathan C. Hinz, Leucadia National Corporation/16.00%, John M. Fowler, St. James Trust/9.00%, Scott J. Branch/12.00%, Brian T. Sephton, Goldcrown Asset Management Ltd./6.60%, John Radziwill/9.60%, Robert A. Miller

Financial Data: *Fiscal Year End:*09/30 *Latest Annual Data:* 9/30/2006

Year	Sales	Net Income
2006	$102,761,000	$3,460,000
2005	$26,229,000	$2,614,000
2004	$22,038,000	-$118,000

Curr. Assets:	$73,037,000	**Curr. Liab.:**	$129,387,000	**P/E Ratio:**	397.00
Plant, Equip.:	$16,017,000	**Total Liab.:**	$165,539,000	**Indic. Yr. Divd.:**	NA
Total Assets:	$199,913,000	**Net Worth:**	$33,943,000	**Debt/ Equity:**	0.6700

International Automated Systems Inc

326 N Sr 198, Salem, UT, 84653; *PH:* 1-801-423-8132; *http://* www.iaus.com; *Email:* contact@iaus.com

General - Incorporation	UT	**Stock**- Price on:12/24/2007	$0.8
Employees	6	Stock Exchange	OTC
Auditor	Mantyla McReynolds, LLC	Ticker Symbol	IAUS
Stk Agt	NA	Outstanding Shares	21,840,000
Counsel	NA	E.P.S	-$0.26
DUNS No.	NA	Shareholders	NA

Business: The groups principle activity is to offer an automated self-service checkout system and management software. Products of the group include Self-Check System, Automatic Fingerprint Identification Machine and Propulsion Steam Turbine. The group operates from Utah in the United States.

Primary SIC and add'l.: 7371

CIK No: 0000820380

Officers: Neldon Johnson/Chmn., CEO, Pres., Randale P. Johnson/39/VP, Sec., Lagrand T. Johnson/42/CFO

Directors: Neldon Johnson/Chmn., CEO, Pres., Bruce Barrett/78/Dir., Blain Phillips/46/Dir.

Owners: Neldon Johnson/4.86%, LaGrand Johnson/1.20%, Directors and Officers as a Group/7.80%, Bruce Barrett, Randale Johnson/1.40%

Financial Data: *Fiscal Year End:*06/30 *Latest Annual Data:* 03/31/2007

Year	Sales	Net Income
2007	NA	NA
2006	NA	-$1,473,000
2005	NA	-$1,443,000

Curr. Assets:	$708,000	Curr. Liab.:	$1,050,000	
Plant, Equip.:	$197,000	Total Liab.:	$1,118,000	Indic. Yr. Divd.: NA
Total Assets:	$1,109,000	Net Worth:	-$10,000	Debt/ Equity: NA

International Bancshares Corp

1200 San Bernardo Ave., Laredo, TX, 78042; *PH:* 1-956-726-6651; *Fax:* 1-956-726-6618;
http:// www.iboc.com

General - Incorporation	TX	**Stock**- Price on:12/24/2007	$26.68
Employees	2,737	Stock Exchange	NDQ
Auditor	KPMG LLP	Ticker Symbol	IBOC
Stk Agt	NA	Outstanding Shares	69,420,000
Counsel	NA	E.P.S.	$1.60
DUNS No.	11-982-2534	Shareholders	NA

Business: The group's principal activities are to provide commercial and retail banking services in south, central and southeast Texas. The group accepts demand and time deposits from individuals, partnerships, corporations and public entities. The loans offered include commercial, real estate, personal, home improvement, automobile and other installment and term loans. The group's international banking business provides letters of credit, commercial and industrial loans and a nominal amount of currency exchange. It also offers credit cards, travelers' checks, safety deposit, collection, notary public, escrow, drive-up and walk-up facilities and other customary banking services. The operations are conducted through 200 ATMs and 100 main banking and branch facilities located in laredo, san antonio, houston, zapata, eagle pass, the rio grande valley of Texas and the coastal bend area of Texas. The group on 21-Jun-2004 acquired local financial corporation.

Primary SIC and add'l.: 6712 6022

CIK No: 0000315709

Subsidiaries: Commerce Bank, Gulfstar Group I, Ltd., Gulfstar Group II, Ltd., Gulfstar Merchant Banking II, Ltd., IBC Capital Corporation, IBC Life Insurance Company, IBC Subsidiary Corporation, IBC Trading Company, International Bank of Commerce

Officers: Fred W. Rusteberg/CEO, Pres. - IBC, Brownsville, David R. Guerra/51/Dir., Pres., CEO - IBC, Mcallen/$338,990.00, Robert B. Barnes/CEO, Pres. - IBC, Austin, Charles R. White/CEO, Pres. - IBC, Corpus Christi, Jay Rogers/CEO, Pres. - IBC, Houston, Hector Cerna/CEO, Pres. - IBC, Eagle Pass, Tom L. Travis/CEO, Pres. - IBC, Oklahoma, Ignacio Urrabazo/CEO, Pres. - Commerce Bank, Laredo, Dennis E. Nixon/Chmn., CEO, Pres./$1,855,117.00, Richard Bothe/CEO, Pres. - IBC, Port Lavaca, Bay City, Renato Ramirez/CEO, Pres. - IBC, Zapata, Steve E. Edlund/CEO, Pres. - IBC, San Antonio, Anselmo Castro/Sr. VP - IBC, Laredo, Guadalupe O. Garcia/Sr. VP - IBC, Laredo, Gerald Schwebel/Exec. VP - International Department *(24 Officers included in Index)*

Directors: David R. Guerra/51/Dir., Pres., CEO - IBC, Mcallen, Dennis E. Nixon/Chmn., CEO, Pres., Antonio R. Sanchez/61/Dir., Imelda Navarro/Dir., CFO, COO, Sr. Exec. VP, Daniel B. Hastings/56/Dir., Lester Avigael/77/Dir., Irving Greenblum/74/Dir., Richard E. Haynes/61/Dir., Sioma Neiman/76/Dir., Peggy J. Newman/72/Dir., Leonardo Salinas/70/Dir.

Owners: A. R. Sanchez/18.73%, Dennis E. Nixon/3.34%, Insiders/26.19%, Imelda Navarro, Richard E. Haynes, Lester Avigael, Sioma Neiman/1.00%, Leonardo Salinas, Irving Greenblum, David R. Guerra, Peggy J. Newman, Daniel B. Hastings

Financial Data: Fiscal Year End:12/31   Latest Annual Data: 12/31/2006

Year	Sales	Net Income
2006	$786,974,000	$117,001,000
2005	$676,108,000	$140,779,000
2004	$487,194,000	$119,032,000

Curr. Assets:	$354,891,000	Curr. Liab.:	$7,696,253,000	P/E Ratio: 16.68
Plant, Equip.:	$390,323,000	Total Liab.:	$10,069,398,000	Indic. Yr. Divd.: $0.640
Total Assets:	$10,911,454,000	Net Worth:	$842,056,000	Debt/ Equity: 2.4267

International Barrier Technology Inc

510 4th St. N., Watkins, MN, 55389; *PH:* 1-320-764-5797; *Fax:* 1-320-764-5799;
http:// www.intlbarrier.com; *Email:* info@intlbarrier.com

General - Incorporation	Canada	**Stock**- Price on:12/24/2007	$0.39
Employees	NA	Stock Exchange	OTC
Auditor	Amisano Hanson	Ticker Symbol	IBTGF
Stk Agt	Pacific Corporate Trust Co	Outstanding Shares	NA
Counsel	NA	E.P.S.	NA
DUNS No.	NA	Shareholders	NA

Business: The groups principle activities include developing, manufacturing and marketing proprietary fire retardant building materials designed to protect people and property from fire. The groups products include blaze quard wood panel and Pyrotite(TM) technology. The group operates from United States.

Primary SIC and add'l.: NA
CIK No: 0000890543
Subsidiaries: Barrier Technology Corporation, Pyrotite Coatings of Canada Inc
Officers: Michael Huddy/Dir., CEO, Pres., David Corcoran/Dir., CFO, Janice B. Loebel/VP, GM - Barrier USA, Todd Lorsung/Financial Services Mgr. - Barrier USA, Melissa McElwee/Mgr. - Investor Relations, International Barrier, Vaughn Zoller/Plant Mgr. - Barrier USA, Lindsey Nauen/56/Corp. Sec.
Directors: Michael Huddy/Dir., CEO, Pres., David Corcoran/Dir., CFO, Victor Yates/Dir., Craig Roberts/Dir.
Owners: Victor A. Yates/2.50%, Michael D. Huddy/5.20%, Carl Marks Group/13.20%, David J. Corcoran/4.90%, Craig Roberts/0.80%, Insiders/13.30%

Financial Data: Fiscal Year End:06/30   Latest Annual Data: 06/30/2007

Year	Sales	Net Income
2007	$6,130,000	-$491,000
2006	$6,604,000	-$212,000
2005	$4,450,000	-$1,116,000

Curr. Assets:	$1,723,000	Curr. Liab.:	$614,000	
Plant, Equip.:	$3,685,000	Total Liab.:	$1,172,000	Indic. Yr. Divd.: NA
Total Assets:	$6,172,000	Net Worth:	$5,000,000	Debt/ Equity: 0.1045

International Broadcasting Corp

5100 N 27th St., Ste. A-2, Lincoln, NE, 68521; *PH:* 1-509-466-3413; *Fax:* 1-509-357-7111;
http:// www.ibcmedia.com; *Email:* office@ibcmedia.com

General - Incorporation	NV	**Stock**- Price on:12/24/2007	$0.002
Employees	NA	Stock Exchange	OTC
Auditor	Sherb & Co. LLP	Ticker Symbol	IBCD
Stk Agt	Patterson Ord Minnette	Outstanding Shares	NA
Counsel	NA	E.P.S.	NA
DUNS No.	NA	Shareholders	NA

Business: The group's principle activity is to provide timely financial news, market commentary and information. The Website provides Internet news service that delivers business, financial news and information focusing on public companies that are quoted on the otc bulletin board. The group sources news and information from television, news wires and the Internet, combined with original editorial commentary. The cult movies online reaches a global audience, and is the first of planned websites designed to capture subscription-based and pay-per-view revenues from the multi-billion dollar Internet broadband market. The corporate reporter advertising section includes brief summaries of companies with business description and summary financial data.

Primary SIC and add'l.: 7389 7375
CIK No: 0001156390
Officers: Darrell W. Nether/Chmn., CEO, Pres., Sandra S. Nether/Dir., Sec., Treasurer, Ted Phillips/Dir., Pres. - Stock Information Systems
Directors: Darrell W. Nether/Chmn., CEO, Pres., Sandra S. Nether/Dir., Sec., Treasurer, Ted Phillips/Dir., Pres. - Stock Information Systems

Financial Data: Fiscal Year End:12/31   Latest Annual Data: 12/31/2004

Year	Sales	Net Income
2004	$106,000	-$218,000
2003	$87,000	-$531,000
2002	$85,000	-$259,000

Curr. Assets:	$120,000	Curr. Liab.:	$311,000	
Plant, Equip.:	$24,000	Total Liab.:	$311,000	Indic. Yr. Divd.: NA
Total Assets:	$144,000	Net Worth:	-$167,000	Debt/ Equity: NA

International Card Establishment Inc

555 Airport Way, Ste. A, Camarillo, CA, 93010; *PH:* 1-805-383-7047; *http://* www.cardnetone.com

General - Incorporation	DE	**Stock**- Price on:12/24/2007	$0.17
Employees	25	Stock Exchange	OTC
Auditor	Mendoza Berger & Co LLP	Ticker Symbol	ICRD
Stk Agt	Pacific Stock Transfer Company	Outstanding Shares	33,950,000
Counsel	NA	E.P.S.	-$0.1
DUNS No.	NA	Shareholders	NA

Business: The group's principal activity is to provide diversified products and services to the electronic transaction processing industry. It offers merchant accounts for the acceptance and processing of credit and debit cards, as well as a proprietary "Smart Card" based gift and loyalty program. The group's merchant card services division, establishes "Merchant Accounts" for businesses that enable those businesses to accept credit cards, debit cards, and other forms of electronic payments from their customers; supplies the necessary card readers and other point-of-sale transaction systems; facilitates processing for the accounts; and, provides e-commerce solutions. Through its worldwide gift and loyalty division, it also markets a proprietary "Smart Card"-based system that enables merchants to economically offer store-branded gift and loyalty cards. On 08-Sep-2004, the group acquired neos merchant solutions inc.

Primary SIC and add'l.: 7389 7375 7372
CIK No: 0001156337
Subsidiaries: GlobalTech Leasing, Inc., International Card Establishment, Inc., Neos Merchant Solutions, Inc.
Officers: William J. Lopshire/44/Dir., CEO, Sec., Kjell Nesen/VP - Operations, Candace Mills/CFO
Directors: William J. Lopshire/44/Dir., CEO, Sec., Hugh Wain Swapp/Dir., Jeff Cox/44/Dir.
Owners: Insiders/5.13%, Randy Simoneaux/6.55%, Charles Salyer/6.63%, William Lopshire/4.71%, Jeff Cox

Financial Data: Fiscal Year End:12/31   Latest Annual Data: 12/31/2006

Year	Sales	Net Income
2006	$10,766,000	-$3,555,000
2005	$6,549,000	-$4,325,000
2004	$14,754,000	-$3,762,000

Curr. Assets:	$690,000	Curr. Liab.:	$1,980,000	
Plant, Equip.:	$860,000	Total Liab.:	$2,446,000	Indic. Yr. Divd.: NA
Total Assets:	$7,041,000	Net Worth:	$4,594,000	Debt/ Equity: 0.1014

International Cellular Accessories

10 Warren Ave., Spring Lake, NJ, 07023; *PH:* 1-703-622-6210

General - Incorporation		**Stock**- Price on:12/24/2007	NA
Employees	NA	Stock Exchange	OTC
Auditor	NA	Ticker Symbol	ICLA
Stk Agt	NA	Outstanding Shares	NA
Counsel	NA	E.P.S.	NA
DUNS No.	NA	Shareholders	NA

Business: The groups principle activity is to provide recruiting services. The groups service area includes the research and development, engineering, marketing, sales, information technology and manufacturing industries. The group operates from United States.

Primary SIC and add'l.: 3670
CIK No:
Officers: Clifford Chapman/39/Pres., Chief Executive, Accounting Officer, Sec., Treasurer, Dir., CFO
Directors: Clifford Chapman/39/Pres., Chief Executive, Accounting Officer, Sec., Treasurer, Dir., CFO
Owners: Insiders/70.20%, Clifford Chapman/70.20%

International Coal Group Inc

300 Corporate Ctr. Dr., Scott Depot, WV, 25560; *PH:* 1-304-760-2400; *http://* www.intlcoal.com; *Email:* contacticg@intlcoal.com

General - Incorporation	DE	Stock- Price on:12/24/2007	$6.17
Employees	2,222	Stock Exchange	NYSE
Auditor	Deloitte & Touche LLP	Ticker Symbol	ICO
Stk Agt	Computershare Trust Co	Outstanding Shares	152,900,000
Counsel	NA	E.P.S.	-$0.13
DUNS No.	NA	Shareholders	NA

Business: The groups principle activities include mining and producing coal. The group operates through three segments namely, Central Appalachian, Northern Appalachian and Illinois Basin. The group operates from the Northern and Central Appalachia.The group's quarterly revenue for September 2007 was 207.83 millions of USD.

Primary SIC and add'l.: 1221 1222

CIK No: 0001320934

Subsidiaries: Anker Coal Group, Inc., Anker Group, Inc., Anker Power Services, Inc., Bronco Mining Company, Inc., CoalQuest Development LLC, Hawthorne Coal Company, Inc., Heather Glen Resources, Inc., Hunter Ridge Coal Company, ICG Addcar Systems, LLC, ICG Beckley, LLC, ICG East Kentucky, LLC, ICG Eastern Land, LLC, ICG Eastern, LLC, ICG Hazard Land, LLC, ICG Hazard, LLC 34 Subsidiaries included in the Index

Officers: Bennett K. Hatfield/Dir., CEO, Pres., Bradley W. Harris/CFO, VP, Charles Snavely/VP - Planning, Acquisitions, William D. Campbell/VP - Accounting, Treasury, Treasurer, Roger L. Nicholson/Sr. VP, General Counsel, Samuel R. Kitts/Sr. VP - West Virginia, Maryland Operations, William Scott Perkins/Sr. VP - Kentucky, Illinois Operations, Michael Hardesty/Sr. VP - Sales, Marketing, Oren Eugene Kitts/Sr. VP - Mining Services, Ira Gamm/VP - Public, Investor Relations, Phillip Michael Hardesty/45/Sr. VP - Sales, Marketing

Directors: Bennett K. Hatfield/Dir., CEO, Pres., Wilbur L. Ross/Non Exec. Chmn., Cynthia B. Bezik/Dir., Maurice E. Carino/Dir., William J. Catacosinos/Dir., Stanley N. Gaines/Dir., Wendy L. Teramoto/Dir.

Owners: Royce& Associates, LLC/5.80%, Samuel R. Kitts, William Scott Perkins, Stanley N. Gaines, Phillip Michael Hardesty, Roger L. Nicholson, WL Ross& Co. LLC/16.05%, Insiders/16.87%, Contrarian Capital Management LLC/7.20%, Wilbur L. Ross/16.05%, Bradley W. Harris, William D. Campbell, Bennett K. Hatfield, Michael A. Roth/7.00%, Oren Eugene Kitts *(17 Owners included in Index)*

Financial Data: Fiscal Year End:12/31 Latest Annual Data: 12/31/2006

Year	Sales		Net Income
2006	$891,594,000		-9,275,000
2005	$647,713,000		$31,825,000
Curr. Assets:	$170,643,000	Curr. Liab.:	$140,140,000	
Plant, Equip.:	$922,196,000	Total Liab.:	$664,099,000 Indic. Yr. Divd.: NA
Total Assets:	$1,321,880,000	Net Worth:	$657,781,000 Debt/ Equity: 0.3312

International Commercial Television Inc

10245 Sunrise Pl NE, Bainbridge Island, WA, 98110; *PH:* 1-206-842-3729; *Fax:* 1-206-842-3678; *http://* www.ictvonline.com; *Email:* info@ictvonline.com

General - Incorporation	NV	Stock- Price on:12/24/2007	$1.9
Employees	3	Stock Exchange	OTC
Auditor	Dohan & Co	Ticker Symbol	ICTL
Stk Agt	Nevada Agency & Trust Company	Outstanding Shares	12,170,000
Counsel	NA	E.P.S.	$0.13
DUNS No.	NA	Shareholders	NA

Business: The group's principal activities are to produce long-form and short-form infomercials and sell proprietary brands of advertised products directly to viewing audience. The short-form infomercial product duration is 30-seconds, 60-seconds or 120-seconds. The short-form infomercial generally feature products that can be explained or demonstrated in two minutes or less. The long-form infomercial product duration is 28 1/2 minute direct response commercial.

Primary SIC and add'l.: 7311

CIK No: 0001076522

Subsidiaries: SMM

Officers: Kelvin Claney/Dir., CEO, Pres., Stephen J. Jarvis/Dir. - Business Development, Kelly Willett/Dir. - International Sales, Packy McFarland/Dir. - Creative, Karl Redekopp/CFO

Directors: Kelvin Claney/Dir., CEO, Pres., William R. Flohr/Dir.

Owners: William Flohr, Insiders, The Better Blocks Trust, Kelvin Claney

Financial Data: Fiscal Year End:12/31 Latest Annual Data: 12/31/2006

Year	Sales		Net Income
2006	$2,977,000		$344,000
2005	$2,415,000		$408,000
2004	$1,126,000		-$98,000
Curr. Assets:	$1,268,000	Curr. Liab.:	$1,171,000 P/E Ratio: 38.00
Plant, Equip.:	$16,000	Total Liab.:	$1,762,000 Indic. Yr. Divd.: NA
Total Assets:	$1,284,000	Net Worth:	-$477,000 Debt/ Equity: NA

International Consolidated Companies Inc

Formerly: Sign Media Systems Inc

2100 19th St., Sarasota, FL, 34234; *PH:* 1-941-330-0336; *http://* www.signmediasystems.com; *Email:* info@signmediasystems.com

General - Incorporation	FL	Stock- Price on:12/24/2007	$0.35
Employees	3	Stock Exchange	NA
Auditor	Bagell, Josephs, Levine & Co. LLC	Ticker Symbol	NA
Stk Agt	NA	Outstanding Shares	11,490,000
Counsel	NA	E.P.S.	NA
DUNS No.	NA	Shareholders	NA

Business: The group's principal activity is developing, manufacturing and marketing mobile billboard mounting systems which are mounted primarily on truck sides, rear panels and breaking panel roll up doors. The company produce digitally created outdoor, full color vinyl images ("graphics") which

are inserted into the mounting systems and displayed primarily on trucks.The company uses HotSwap system which utilizes a break-through framing method for securing photo quality graphic images that are highly durable yet easily replaced. The company has an expanding dealer networks around the United States and internationally.

Primary SIC and add'l.: 7310

CIK No: 0001277859

Officers: Antonio F. Uccello/51/Chmn., CEO, CFO, Pres./$52,921.00, Evelyn P. Silva/40/VP - Operations, Sec., Andrei A. Troubeev/41/VP - Engineering, Stephen R. MacNamara/53/Dir., Sec.

Directors: Antonio F. Uccello/51/Chmn., CEO, CFO, Pres., Stephen R. MacNamara/53/Dir., Sec.

Owners: Nelson J. Martin/0.10%, Nimbus Development Corp./7.00%, Evelyn P. Silva/2.00%, Antonio F. Uccello/66.00%, Phillip C. Asher/11.00%, Dennis D. Derr/2.00%

Financial Data: Fiscal Year End:12/31 Latest Annual Data: 12/31/2006

Year	Sales		Net Income
2006	$727,000		$231,000
Curr. Assets:	$705,000	Curr. Liab.:	$222,000	
Plant, Equip.:	$95,000	Total Liab.:	$222,000 Indic. Yr. Divd.: NA
Total Assets:	$1,217,000	Net Worth:	$995,000 Debt/ Equity: NA

International DisplayWorks Inc

1613 Santa Clara Dr., Ste. 100, Roseville, CA, 95765; *PH:* 1-916-797-6800; *http://* www.idwlcd.com

General - Incorporation	DE	Stock- Price on:12/24/2007	$11.14
Employees	99,000	Stock Exchange	NA
Auditor	Grant Thornton LLP	Ticker Symbol	NA
Stk Agt	Computershare Trust Co	Outstanding Shares	608,650,000
Counsel	NA	E.P.S.	$0.88
DUNS No.	NA	Shareholders	NA

Business: The group's principal activities are to design, manufacture and distribute liquid crystal displays, modules and assemblies for original equipment manufacturers. These products are used in telecommunications, medical equipment, household appliances, utility applications, automotive, retail and office equipment and consumer electronic products. The group operates through its subsidiaries, mulcd microelectronics (shenzhen) co ltd and idw technology (shenzhen) co ltd. The group's products are marketed in the United States, Hong Kong, Asia and Europe.

Primary SIC and add'l.: 3674 3672 3679

CIK No: 0000866415

Subsidiaries: IDW (Beijing) Co., Ltd, IDW Technology (Shenzhen) Co., Ltd, International DisplayWorks (Hong Kong) Limited, International DisplayWorks Ltd, MULCD Microelectronics (Shenzhen) Co., Ltd

Financial Data: Fiscal Year End:10/31 Latest Annual Data: 3/31/2007

Year	Sales		Net Income
2007	$18,853,688,000		$508,638,000
2006	$15,287,976,000		$141,162,000
2005	$15,908,223,000		$339,871,000
Curr. Assets:	$5,591,047,000	Curr. Liab.:	$4,488,068,000 P/E Ratio: 12.66
Plant, Equip.:	$1,998,706,000	Total Liab.:	$6,164,715,000 Indic. Yr. Divd.: NA
Total Assets:	$12,341,374,000	Net Worth:	$6,176,659,000 Debt/ Equity: 0.2418

International Electronics Inc

427 Tpke. St. , Canton, MA, 02072; *PH:* 1-617-821-5566; *http://* www.ieib.com

General - Incorporation	MA	Stock- Price on:12/24/2007	$6.6
Employees	64	Stock Exchange	NDQ
Auditor	Wolf & Co., P.C	Ticker Symbol	IEIB
Stk Agt	American Stock Transfer & Trust Co.	Outstanding Shares	NA
Counsel	Cohan, Rasnick, Myerson	E.P.S.	NA
DUNS No.	09-629-4434	Shareholders	NA

Business: The group's principal activities are to design, manufacture, market and sell electronic products for the security industry and other commercial applications. The group manufactures and markets a line of access control and digital keypad products. The products are sold in a variety of configurations including indoor and outdoor models, with magnetic card readers, proximity readers and keypads. They are sold under the trade names of door-gard tm, secured series tm, powerkey tm, tri-gard(TM) and viper to installers and distributors of alarm security equipment. The group's customers include adi, clark security products and security lock. The group sources most of the components it uses and certain molds from Asia. It sells and markets its products in north and South America, Europe, Asia, South Africa, the Middle East, Australia and New Zealand.

Primary SIC and add'l.: 3669 3699

CIK No: 0000717751

Subsidiaries: Ecco Industries, Inc, International Electronics Europe Limited

Officers: John Waldstein/Chmn., CEO, Pres., Jim Lynch/Dir. - Product Management, Dana Lindsey/Call Center, Inside Sales Mgr., Brad Sampson/Dir. - Business Development, John Lafond/Sales Dir., Peter Demakis/COO, Todd Hammond/Contact - Product Marketing, Bonnie Roberts/Contact - Marketing Coordinator, Stacey Coyne/Contact - Inside Sales, Ken Hall/Sales,Firm Representative, Jacquelyn Baker/Sales,Firm Representative, Brian Kellett/Sales Representative, LRG, North, British Columbia, Alberta, Janet Jones/Sales Representative - LRG, North, Support, Phillip Clement/Sales Representative - LRG, North, Quebec, Ottawa, Robert Stewart/VP - Manufacturing *(55 Officers included in Index)*

Directors: John Waldstein/Chmn., CEO, Pres., Diane Balcom/Dir., Les Charm/Dir., Albert Janjigian/Dir.

Owners: Diane Balcom/0.50%, Insiders/21.30%, Hummingbird Management, LLC/9.60%, Albert Janjigian/1.10%, John Waldstein/14.70%, Peter Demakis/1.70%, Robert Stewart/1.00%, Christopher Hentschel/1.70%, Les Charm/0.60%

Financial Data: Fiscal Year End:08/31 Latest Annual Data: 8/31/2006

Year	Sales		Net Income
2006	$14,121,000		-$407,000
2005	$12,647,000		-$720,000
2004	$11,394,000		-$1,125,000
Curr. Assets:	$4,393,000	Curr. Liab.:	$3,281,000	
Plant, Equip.:	$647,000	Total Liab.:	$3,281,000 Indic. Yr. Divd.: NA
Total Assets:	$5,061,000	Net Worth:	$1,780,000 Debt/ Equity: NA

International Food Products Group Inc

170 Newport Ctr. Dr., Ste. 260, Newport Beach, CA, 92660; *PH:* 1-949-759-7775;
Fax: 1-949-759-5490; *http://* www.goldenchoice.com; *Email:* info@goldenchoice.com

General - Incorporation	NV	Stock- Price on:12/24/2007	$0.0125
Employees	3	Stock Exchange	OTC
Auditor	Gruber & Co., LLC	Ticker Symbol	IFDG
Stk Agt	Colonial Stock Transfer Co Inc	Outstanding Shares	370,590,000
Counsel	NA	E.P.S.	-$0.002
DUNS No.	NA	Shareholders	NA

Business: The group's principle activity is to market and sell snack food products. The company has developed into an international importer and representative for various domestic and foreign product companies. Some of the products represented include premium coffees from columbia, organic vegetables from Asia, breath strips from Japan and upscale potato chips from a U.S. Manufacturer. The group operates from United States.

Primary SIC and add'l.: 2096
CIK No: 0001019216
Officers: Richard Damion/Chmn., CEO, Ketan Mehta/46/Pres.
Directors: Richard Damion/Chmn., CEO
Owners: Insiders/40.00%, Robert George/2.00%, Richard Damion/14.00%, Ketan Mehta/19.00%, Joseph R. Rodriguez/9.00%

Financial Data: *Fiscal Year End:*06/30 *Latest Annual Data:* 06/30/2007

Year	Sales	Net Income
2007	$484,000	-$1,185,000
2006	$839,000	-$1,560,000
2005	$210,000	-$1,388,000

Curr. Assets:	$91,000	Curr. Liab.:	$981,000		
Plant, Equip.:	NA	Total Liab.:	$981,000	Indic. Yr. Divd.:	NA
Total Assets:	$91,000	Net Worth:	-$890,000	Debt/ Equity:	NA

International Freight Logistics Ltd

4 William St., Lynbrook, NY, 11563; *PH:* 1-516-593-1010; *http://* www.intlfreightlogistics.com

General - Incorporation	DE	Stock- Price on:12/24/2007	NA
Employees	NA	Stock Exchange	NA
Auditor	Donahue Assoc. LLC	Ticker Symbol	NA
Stk Agt	NA	Outstanding Shares	NA
Counsel	NA	E.P.S	NA
DUNS No.	NA	Shareholders	NA

Business: The group's principle activity is to provide domestic and international freight forwarding and warehousing company, with a specialty in handling fine art & antiques. The group operates from United States.

Primary SIC and add'l.: 4731
CIK No: 0001180926
Subsidiaries: Pirelli Company.

International Fuel Technology Inc

7777 Bonhomme Ave., Saint Louis, MO, 63105; *PH:* 1-314-727-3333; *http://* www.peerfuel.com

General - Incorporation	NV	Stock- Price on:12/24/2007	$0.4
Employees	8	Stock Exchange	OTC
Auditor	BDO Seidman, LLP	Ticker Symbol	IFUE
Stk Agt	Pacific Stock Transfer Company	Outstanding Shares	84,860,000
Counsel	NA	E.P.S.	-$0.06
DUNS No.	NA	Shareholders	NA

Business: The groups principle activity is to develop fuel additive products used to improve the combustion characteristics of petroleum-based fuels and renewable liquid fuels. Products of the group include DiesoLIFT(TM), GasoLIFT(TM) and KeroLIFT(TM). The group operates from the United States. The group's quarterly revenue for Sep '07 was 0.03 millions of USD.

Primary SIC and add'l.: 2911
CIK No: 0001078723
Officers: Jonathan R. Burst/Chmn., CEO, Gary Kirk/Dir., Dir. - Sales, Marketing Communications, Sergio C. Trindade/Dir. - Science, Technology, Stuart Beath/Investor Relation Officer, Axel Farhi/Dir. - Global Business Development, Thomas M. Powell/Treasurer, Steve Kirkham/Sales, Marketing Mgr. - North America, Paul S. Lee/Assist. Dir. - Sales, Marketing Communications
Directors: Jonathan R. Burst/Chmn., CEO, Gary Kirk/Dir., Dir. - Sales, Marketing Communications
Owners: Gary Kirk/2.35%, Rex Carr/23.05%, Insiders/41.77%, Dion Friedland/7.53%, David B. Norris/1.38%, Jonathan R. Burst/9.93%, Harry F. Demetriou/6.56%, Gary S. Hirstein/1.07%

Financial Data: *Fiscal Year End:*12/31 *Latest Annual Data:* 12/31/2006

Year	Sales	Net Income
2006	$235,000	-$5,243,000
2005	$563,000	-$5,330,000
2004	$24,000	-$4,519,000

Curr. Assets:	$2,682,000	Curr. Liab.:	$593,000		
Plant, Equip.:	$29,000	Total Liab.:	$593,000	Indic. Yr. Divd.:	NA
Total Assets:	$5,090,000	Net Worth:	$4,497,000	Debt/ Equity:	NA

International Game Technology

9295 Prototype Dr., Reno, NV, 89521; *PH:* 1-775-448-7777; *Fax:* 1-775-448-0719;
http:// www.igt.com; *Email:* investor_relations@igt.com

General - Incorporation	NV	Stock- Price on:12/24/2007	$39.18
Employees	5,200	Stock Exchange	NYSE
Auditor	Deloitte & Touche LLP	Ticker Symbol	IGT
Stk Agt	Bank of New York	Outstanding Shares	332,440,000
Counsel	NA	E.P.S.	NA
DUNS No.	NA	Shareholders	NA

Business: The groups principle activity is to designing, manufacturing, and marketing of computerized gaming equipment, systems and services. The group operates through two regional segments namely, North America and international. In the year 2005, the group acquired WagerWorks, Inc. The group operates from the United States, Asia, Australia, Europe, Japan, Latin America, Russia, South Africa, and the United Kingdom. The group's quarterly revenue for September 2007 was 207.83 millions of USD.

Primary SIC and add'l.: 7375 7999 7379 7993
CIK No: 0000353944
Subsidiaries: Acres Gaming Incorporated, I.G.T. (Australia) Pty. Limited, I.G.T. Argentina S.A., IGT, IGT Canada Inc., IGT Europe B.V., IGT Iceland Ltd., IGT Mexicana de Juegos, S. de R.L. de C.V., IGT UK Holdings Limited, IGT Asia, Lda., IGT do Brasil LTDA., IGT Japan, K.K., International Game Technology, International Game Technology Africa (Pty) Ltd., International Game Technology S.R. Ltda. 19 Subsidiaries included in the Index
Officers: Thomas J. Matthews/42/Chmn., CEO, COO, Pres., Anthony Ciorciari/Exec. VP - Operations, Robert A. Bittman/53/Dir., Exec. VP - Product Strategy, Daniel R. Siciliano/Chief Accounting Officer, Treasurer, Principal Financial Officer, David D. Johnson/Exec. VP, General Counsel, Sec., Stephen W. Morro/COO, Richard Pennington/Exec. VP - Corporate Strategy, Connie Jones/Dir. - Responsible Gaming, Rich Newton/Dir. - Supply Chain Management Manufacturing Materials, Mark Demko/Mgr. - Commodity, MRO, Services, Rick Sorensen/Mgr. - Public Relations, Ed Rogich/VP - Marketing
Directors: Thomas J. Matthews/42/Chmn., CEO, COO, Pres., Robert Miller/62/Dir., Leslie S. Heisz/46/Dir., Robert A. Mathewson/43/Dir., Neil Barsky/50/Dir., Robert A. Bittman/53/Dir., Exec. VP - Product Strategy, Richard R. Burt/60/Dir., Patti S. Hart/51/Dir., Frederick B. Rentschler/68/Dir.
Owners: T. Rowe Price Associates, Inc./5.50%, Neil Barsky, Leslie S. Heisz, Stephen Morro, Richard Burt, Robert A. Bittman, Private Capital Management, Inc./9.80%, Thomas J. Matthews, Insiders/2.40%, Frederick B. Rentschler, Robert A. Mathewson, Robert Miller, American Century Companies, Inc./6.10%, Maureen T. Mullarkey, David D. Johnson

Curr. Assets:	$1,375,700,000	Curr. Liab.:	$1,246,600,000		
Plant, Equip.:	$469,800,000	Total Liab.:	$1,860,700,000	Indic. Yr. Divd.:	NA
Total Assets:	$3,902,700,000	Net Worth:	$2,042,000,000	Debt/ Equity:	NA

International Gold Resources Inc

15321 Main St., NE 152, Duvall, WA, 98019; *PH:* 1-425-844-2535; *http://* www.intlgold.com

General - Incorporation	DE	Stock- Price on:12/24/2007	NA
Employees	NA	Stock Exchange	OTC
Auditor	MacKay LLP	Ticker Symbol	IGRU
Stk Agt	Signature Stock Transfer	Outstanding Shares	NA
Counsel	Hogan & Hartson	E.P.S.	-$0.033
DUNS No.	NA	Shareholders	NA

Business: The groups principal activity is to explore minerals. In March 2006 the group acquired Amapa Gold Ltda. The group operates from the United States, Canada and Brazil.

Primary SIC and add'l.: 1040
CIK No: 0001206120
Officers: Tim Acton/CEO, Pres., Rodolfo Michels/Group Controller
Directors: David H. Francisco/Chmn., Lyle Durham/Dir., Lawrence T. Kurlander/Member - Advisory Board
Owners: Roland J. Vetter/1.09%, Lyle Durham/2.79%, Tim Acton, Dave Francisco/2.50%, Bellewood Corporation/5.90%, John Young & Company/6.62%, Diane G. Clifton/7.38%, Insiders/5.62%

Financial Data: *Fiscal Year End:*10/31 *Latest Annual Data:* 10/31/2006

Year	Sales	Net Income
2006	NA	-$9,733,000
2005	NA	-$7,469,000
2004	$8,000	-$13,000

Curr. Assets:	$289,000	Curr. Liab.:	$895,000		
Plant, Equip.:	$77,000	Total Liab.:	$895,000	Indic. Yr. Divd.:	NA
Total Assets:	$716,000	Net Worth:	-$179,000	Debt/ Equity:	NA

International Hi-Tech Industries Inc

1096 W 10th Ave., Vancouver, BC, V6H 1H8; *PH:* 1-604-733-5400; *http://* www.ihiintl.com;
Email: info@ihiintl.com

General - Incorporation	Canada	Stock- Price on:12/24/2007	$0.09
Employees	NA	Stock Exchange	OTC
Auditor	BDO Dunwoody LLP	Ticker Symbol	IHITF
Stk Agt	Computershare Trust Co	Outstanding Shares	NA
Counsel	Lang Michener LLP	E.P.S.	-$0.05
DUNS No.	25-216-0072	Shareholders	NA

Business: The group's principal activity is to develop and commercialize a building technology system which is a construction process that uses completely manufactured prefabricated floor, wall and roof panels in Canada and internationally. The group has the exclusive rights to a revolutionary customized modular technology that brings the power of the computer to the construction industry. Demonstration home shows have been conducted by the group in luxembourg, vancouver and british columbia. The group is ready to begin marketing, manufacturing and constructing hi-rise and low-rise residential and commercial insulated steel and concrete structures for the 178 countries worldwide where the technology is fully patented or protected. This system proves that buildings can be affordable, safe and durable without compromising quality. The subsidiaries of the group are Canadian hi-tech manufacturing ltd. And ihi international holdings ltd.

Primary SIC and add'l.: 1521
CIK No: 0000921887
Subsidiaries: Canadian Hi-Tech Manufacturing Ltd., IHI Construction Ltd., IHI Developments Ltd., IHI International Construction Inc., IHI International Holdings Ltd., IHI Manufacturing Ltd., IHI Planning Ltd., IHI Sales Ltd.
Officers: Roger A. Rached/Pres., Omar Take/Dir., Chief Project Officer
Directors: Omar Take/Dir., Chief Project Officer

Financial Data: *Fiscal Year End:*12/31 *Latest Annual Data:* 12/31/2005

Year	Sales	Net Income
2005	NA	-$9,196,000
2004	$277,000	-$9,441,000
2003	NA	-$4,436,000

Curr. Assets:	$1,769,000	Curr. Liab.:	$4,205,000		
Plant, Equip.:	$14,524,000	Total Liab.:	$14,301,000	Indic. Yr. Divd.:	NA
Total Assets:	$17,874,000	Net Worth:	$3,410,000	Debt/ Equity:	NA

International Imaging Systems Inc

2419 E Commercial Blvd., Ste. 305, Ft. Lauderdale, FL, 33308; PH: 1-954-492-3703;
http:// www.i-i-s-inc.com

General - Incorporation	DE	Stock - Price on:12/24/2007	NA
Employees	NA	Stock Exchange	NA
Auditor	Thomas W. Klash	Ticker Symbol	NA
Stk Agt	Corporate Stock Transfer, Inc.	Outstanding Shares	NA
Counsel	NA	E.P.S.	-$0.59
DUNS No.	NA	Shareholders	NA

Business: The groups principle activities include identifying, investigating, warranting and acquiring other companies. The group operates from the United States.

Primary SIC and add'l.: 5040

CIK No: 0001070045

Subsidiaries: Advanced Staffing International, Inc.

Officers: Gao Xincheng/Chmn., CEO, Pres., Li Gaihong/CFO, Steve Pennington/Contact, Robert Scherne/51/CFO

Directors: Gao Xincheng/Chmn., CEO, Pres., John Vogel/54/Dir., Vincent Finnegan/65/Dir.

Owners: John Vogel, Redsky Group Limited/88.21%, Princeton Capital Group/5.89%

Financial Data: Fiscal Year End:12/31   Latest Annual Data: 12/31/2006

Year	Sales	Net Income
2006	$146,000	-$374,000
2005	$959,000	-$13,000

Curr. Assets:	$78,000	Curr. Liab.:	$14,000		
Plant, Equip.:	NA	Total Liab.:	$14,000	Indic. Yr. Divd.:	NA
Total Assets:	$78,000	Net Worth:	$63,000	Debt/ Equity:	NA

International Isotopes Inc

4137 Commerce Cir., Idaho Falls, ID, 83401; PH: 1-208-524-5300; Fax: 1-208-524-1411;
http:// www.intisoid.com

General - Incorporation	TX	Stock - Price on:12/24/2007	$0.21
Employees	25	Stock Exchange	OTC
Auditor	Hansen, Barnett & Maxwell	Ticker Symbol	INIS
Stk Agt	American Stock Transfer & Trust Co.	Outstanding Shares	NA
Counsel	Locke Purnell Rain Harrell	E.P.S.	-$0.01
DUNS No.	93-315-5509	Shareholders	NA

Business: The group's principal activities are to produce, market and distribute radioisotopes used in diagnostic and therapeutic nuclear medicine, research and industry. The group's products are hsa cobalt, radioisotopes and gemstone processing. The products are used in diverse applications such as hsa cobalt production , which is used primarily in medical devices. The group is also contract manufacturer of flood sources, dose clibrators, rod sources rigid rulers, spot markers and penpoint markers.

Primary SIC and add'l.: 3845

CIK No: 0001038277

Subsidiaries: International Isotopes Fluorine Products Inc., International Isotopes Idaho Inc., International Isotopes Transportation Services Inc.

Officers: Steve Laflin/CEO, Pres./$164,637.00, Lucinda Sherman/Customer Service Representative, John Miller/Radiation, Industrial Safety Officer, Darin Lords/Quality Control, Engineer, Kimmy Jo Daniel/Chief Accountant

Directors: Ralph M. Richart/74/Chmn., Christopher Grosso/40/Dir.

Owners: John M. McCormack/24.10%, Ralph M. Richart/29.10%, William Nicholson/9.60%, Christopher Grosso/5.60%, Insiders/39.30%, Steve T. Laflin/4.60%, Marie C. Keane/7.40%, Walter O'Hearn/6.90%

Financial Data: Fiscal Year End:12/31   Latest Annual Data: 12/31/2006

Year	Sales	Net Income
2006	$4,470,000	-$1,037,000
2005	$2,985,000	-$983,000
2004	$2,849,000	-$845,000

Curr. Assets:	$3,176,000	Curr. Liab.:	$2,410,000		
Plant, Equip.:	$2,176,000	Total Liab.:	$3,379,000	Indic. Yr. Divd.:	NA
Total Assets:	$5,603,000	Net Worth:	$1,374,000	Debt/ Equity:	0.7337

International KRL Resources Corp

Oceanic Plz., 1066 W Hastings St., Ste. 1640, Vancouver, BC, V6E 2X2; PH: 1-604-689-0299;
http:// www.ixsbio.com; Email: info@krl.net

General - Incorporation	BC	Stock - Price on:12/24/2007	$0.199
Employees	NA	Stock Exchange	OTC
Auditor	Manning Elliott LLP	Ticker Symbol	IRKLF
Stk Agt	Computershare Investor Services LLC	Outstanding Shares	NA
Counsel	Miller Thomson LLP	E.P.S.	NA
DUNS No.	NA	Shareholders	NA

Business: The group is engaged in the acquisition, exploration and development of mineral properties throughout Canada. It is an exploration stage company. The group's four main gold and copper mine potential areas where projects are ongoing: Ontario: Copper Hill Gold Project, Saskatchewan: Carswell Uranium Project, Yukon: Nor Uranium, Copper, Gold Project, British Columbia: Bear Gold Project. The group is mainly exploring the majority of its efforts on its Copper Hill Property, which is located in Ontario. The company is a public company listed on the TSX Venture Exchange.

Primary SIC and add'l.: 1400

CIK No: 0001297467

Officers: Seamus Young/Dir., CEO, Pres., Judith T. Mazvihwa/Dir., CFO, Clifford H. Frame/Dir., MD, Michael W. Hibbitts/54/VP-Exploration, Natasha Blackburn/Dir. - Corporate Development

Directors: Seamus Young/Dir., CEO, Pres., Charles F. Vickers/Dir., Judith T. Mazvihwa/Dir., CFO, Mike Muzylowski/Dir., Clifford H. Frame/Dir., MD

Owners: Charles F. Vickers/2.60%, RAB Special Situations LP/6.90%, Insiders/12.58%, Seamus Young/1.60%, Judith T. Mazvihwa/0.01%, Clifford H. Frame/0.97%, Mike Muzylowski/0.50%

International Lease Finance Corp

10250 Constellation Blvd., Ste. 3400, Los Angeles, CA, 90067; PH: 1-310-788-1999;
Fax: 1-310-788-1990; http:// www.ilfc.com; Email: ilfc@ilfc.com

General - Incorporation	CA	Stock - Price on:12/24/2007	$11.85
Employees	NA	Stock Exchange	NA
Auditor	PricewaterhouseCoopers LLP	Ticker Symbol	NA
Stk Agt	NA	Outstanding Shares	NA
Counsel	NA	E.P.S.	NA
DUNS No.	06-622-5574	Shareholders	NA

Business: The group's principle activity is to acquire new and used commercial jet aircraft. The group also leases and sells such aircraft to domestic and foreign airlines; remarkets commercial jet aircraft for its own account, for airlines and for financial institutions; and provides fleet management services for third-party operating lessors. The group operates from United States.

Primary SIC and add'l.: 5088 7359

CIK No: 0000714311

Subsidiaries: American International Group, Inc

Officers: Steven F. Udvar-Hazy/Chmn., CEO, Alan H. Lund/Vice Chmn., CFO, Michael G. Bai/Assist. VP - Marketing, John L. Plueger/Dir., COO, Pres., Julie I. Sackman/Exec. VP, General Counsel, Sec., Chi Yan/Assist. VP - Marketing, Lance Pekala/Assist. VP - Materiel, BFE, Troy Molitor/Assist. VP - Technical, David Johnson/Assist. VP - Marketing, Damon Rideaux/Assist. VP - Finance, Pinella Shapiro/Assist. VP - Information Technology, Housni M. Chraibi/VP - Materiel, BFE, Terry S. Eastley/Sr. VP - Materiel, BFE, Jeanne A. Hillier/Assist. VP - Materiel, BFE, John D. Poerschke/VP - Materiel, BFE (49 Officers included in Index)

Directors: Steven F. Udvar-Hazy/Chmn., CEO, Alan H. Lund/Vice Chmn., CFO, John L. Plueger/Dir., COO, Pres., Louis R. Gonda/Founder, Steven J. Bensinger/Dir., Martin J. Sullivan/Dir., William N. Dooley/Dir., Leslie L. Gonda/Dir.

International Lottery & Totalizator Systems Inc

2310 Cousteau Ct., Vista, CA, 92081; PH: 1-760-598-1655; Fax: 1-760-598-0219;
http:// www.ilts.com; Email: mktg@ilts.com

General - Incorporation	CA	Stock - Price on:12/24/2007	$0.55
Employees	37	Stock Exchange	OTC
Auditor	J. H. Cohn LLP	Ticker Symbol	ITSI
Stk Agt	Mellon Investor Services LLC	Outstanding Shares	12,960,000
Counsel	Lawrence E. Logue	E.P.S.	$0.04
DUNS No.	09-590-0064	Shareholders	NA

Business: The group's principal activity is to design, manufacture, sell, manage, support and service computerized wagering systems and terminals for the global pari-mutuel and on-line lottery industries. The group's technology is used in other transaction-processing applications, such as keno gaming and for toll turnpike systems utilizing automated ticket printer and readers. The registered trademarks of the group include, ilts, datatrak and intertote. The group's services are provided in the United States, India, Malaysia, Singapore, Philippines, Australia, Hong Kong, Sweden, Brazil and other countries.

Primary SIC and add'l.: 6159 8744 3575

CIK No: 0000354813

Subsidiaries: Ilts Australia, Pty. Ltd., Unisyn Solutions, Inc

Officers: Jeffrey M. Johnson/47/CEO, Pres., Millie Kollmyer/Shipping Administrator, Linh T. Nguyen/39/CFO, Corp. Sec.

Directors: Theodore A. Johnson/Chmn., Chan Kien Sing/Dir., Ooi Lee Meng/Dir., Ng Foo Leong/Dir., Martin J. OMeara/Dir., Alain K. Lee/Dir.

Owners: Berjaya Lottery Management H.K. Limited/71.32%, Theodore A. Johnson, Martin J. OMeara, Insiders/1.18%, Jeffrey M. Johnson

Financial Data: Fiscal Year End:04/30   Latest Annual Data: 4/30/2006

Year	Sales	Net Income
2006	$3,445,000	-$2,344,000
2005	$9,666,000	-$1,762,000
2004	$10,777,000	-$1,786,000

Curr. Assets:	$11,161,000	Curr. Liab.:	$10,472,000	P/E Ratio:	13.75
Plant, Equip.:	$436,000	Total Liab.:	$10,472,000	Indic. Yr. Divd.:	NA
Total Assets:	$12,301,000	Net Worth:	$1,829,000	Debt/ Equity:	NA

International Monetary Systems Ltd

16901 W Glendale Dr., New Berlin, WI, 53151; PH: 1-800-559-8515; Fax: 1-262-780-3655;
http:// www.internationalmonetary.com; Email: ir@internationalmonetary.com

General - Incorporation	WI	Stock - Price on:12/24/2007	NA
Employees	NA	Stock Exchange	OTC
Auditor	Webb & Co P.A	Ticker Symbol	INLM
Stk Agt	Registrar & Transfer Co	Outstanding Shares	NA
Counsel	NA	E.P.S.	NA
DUNS No.	NA	Shareholders	NA

Business: The group's principle activities are to acquire, own, manage and operate trade exchanges and other related businesses. Its barter trade exchange business has over 5,000 businesses that regularly trade their goods and services with each other. This business is provided with an effective revenue management tool, which enables them to identify and capture incremental income, liquidate surplus inventories and capitalize on their excess capacity. The barter trade exchange operates in the United States and Canada. On 29-Mar-2004 the group acquired California barter exchange of modesto and on 22-Jul-2004 the group acquired barter network inc.

Primary SIC and add'l.: 7389 2759

CIK No: 0001097430

Subsidiaries: Continental Trade Exchange, Ltd.

Officers: Donald F. Mardak/Chmn., CEO, Pres., John E. Strabley/Dir., Exec. VP, Danny W. Weibling/Treasurer, CFO, Patricia A. Katisch/Sec., Dale L. Mardak/Dir., Sr. VP

Directors: Donald F. Mardak/Chmn., CEO, Pres., Wayne W. Emmer/Dir., Gerald G. Van Dyn Hoven/Dir., Dale L. Mardak/Dir., Sr. VP, John E. Strabley/Dir., Exec. VP, Thomas Delacy/Dir., Wayne Dalin/Dir., Stephen Webster/Dir.

Owners: Patricia Katisch/0.09%, Danny W. Weibling/0.53%, Wayne Emmer/0.46%, Thomas Delacy/1.03%, John E. Strabley/1.21%, Gerald Van Dyn Hoven/0.80%, Donald F. Mardak/33.65%, Wayne R. Dalin/0.38%, Insiders/40.80%, Dale L. Mardak/2.65%

International Paper Co

6400 Poplar Ave., Memphis, TN, 38197; ***PH:*** 1-901-419-9000; ***http://*** www.ipaper.com

General - Incorporation	NY	**Stock**- Price on:12/24/2007	$38.62
Employees	60,600	Stock Exchange	NYSE
Auditor	Deloitte & Touche LLP	Ticker Symbol	IP
Stk Agt	Mellon Investor Services LLC	Outstanding Shares	435,570,000
Counsel	NA	E.P.S	$16.38
DUNS No.	00-131-6561	Shareholders	NA

Business: The groups principle activity is to provide papper,packaging and wood products. The group operates from Europe, Asia and Africa.

Primary SIC and add'l.: 2671 2621 5111 2431 2499 2611 2893

CIK No: 0000051434

Subsidiaries: Federal Forestlands, Inc. (Including subsidiaries), International Paper Do Brasil Ltda., International Paper Investments (France) S.A.S. (Including subsidiaries), IP Pacific Timberlands, Inc. (Including subsidiaries), The Branigar Organization, Inc. (Including subsidiaries)

Officers: John V. Faraci/Chmn., CEO/$13,728,670.00, John N. Balboni/CIO, Sr. VP, Mark S. Sutton/VP - Supply Chain, Tom Cleves/VP - Investor Relations, Wayne H. Brafford/Sr. VP - Printing, Communication Papers, Mary A. Laschinger/Sr. VP - Pres. - IP Europe, Maximo Pacheco/Sr. VP, Pres. - IP do Brasil, Carol L. Roberts/Sr. VP - IP Packaging Solutions, Richard B. Lowe/Sr. VP, Maura Abeln Smith/Sr. VP, General Counsel, Corp. Sec./$3,132,594.00, Thomas G. Kadien/Sr. VP - Pres. - Xpedx, Andrew R. Lessin/Sr. VP - Internal Audit, Michael J. Balduino/Sr. VP, Pres. - Shorewood Packaging, Newland A. Lesko/Exec. VP - Manufacturing, Technology/$4,784,073.00, Richard B. Phillips/Sr. VP - Technology *(23 Officers included in Index)*

Directors: John V. Faraci/Chmn., CEO, Samir G. Gibara/69/Dir., Donald F. McHenry/72/Dir., James A. Henderson/74/Dir., William G. Walter/63/Dir., John F. Turner/66/Dir., Martha F. Brooks/49/Dir., Charles R. Shoemate/53/Dir., Craig W. McClelland/74/Dir., David J. Bronczek/54/Dir., John L. Townsend/52/Dir., Alberto Weisser/53/Dir., Lynn Laverty Elsenhans/52/Dir.

Owners: State Street Bank and Trust Company/6.30%, John V. Faraci, Marianne M. Parrs, Capital Research and Management Company/10.90%, Newland A. Lesko, Maura A. Smith, Donald F. McHenry, David J. Bronczek, Insiders/1.10%, John L. Townsend, Samir G. Gibara, John F. Turner, Morgan Stanley/Van Kampen Asset Management/7.40%, Paul Herbert, Lynn Laverty Elsenhans *(16 Owners included in Index)*

Financial Data: ***Fiscal Year End:***12/31 ***Latest Annual Data:*** 12/31/2006

Year	Sales	Net Income
2006	$21,995,000,000	$1,050,000,000
2005	$24,097,000,000	$1,100,000,000
2004	$25,548,000,000	-$35,000,000

Curr. Assets:	$8,637,000,000	***Curr. Liab.:***	$4,641,000,000	***P/E Ratio:***	2.36
Plant, Equip.:	$10,576,000,000	***Total Liab.:***	$15,858,000,000	***Indic. Yr. Divd.:***	$1.000
Total Assets:	$24,034,000,000	***Net Worth:***	$7,963,000,000	***Debt/ Equity:***	0.8022

International PetroReal Oil Corp

1177 W Hastings, Ste. 1750, Vancouver, BC, V6E 2K3; ***PH:*** 1-604-683-2220; ***http://*** www.petroreal.com; ***Email:*** info@petroreal.com

General - Incorporation	Canada	**Stock**- Price on:12/24/2007	$0.055
Employees	NA	Stock Exchange	NA
Auditor	NA	Ticker Symbol	NA
Stk Agt	Computershare Trust Co	Outstanding Shares	NA
Counsel	NA	E.P.S	NA
DUNS No.	NA	Shareholders	NA

Business: The group's principal activity is oil and natural gas exploration. The group also acquires oil and gas properties to build a first class upstream production company. Effective 01-Jan-2004, the company acquired a 25% interest in the West Bay Oil and Gas Field.

Primary SIC and add'l.: 6199

CIK No: 0001300747

International Power Group Ltd

6 Glory Ln., Sussex, NJ, 07461; ***PH:*** 1-407-566-0318; ***http://*** www.international-power.com; ***Email:*** info@international-power.com

General - Incorporation	DE	**Stock**- Price on:12/24/2007	NA
Employees	2	Stock Exchange	OTC
Auditor	Robert G. Jeffrey, CPA	Ticker Symbol	IPWG
Stk Agt	Routh Stock Transfer	Outstanding Shares	NA
Counsel	NA	E.P.S	-$0.031
DUNS No.	NA	Shareholders	NA

Business: The group's principal activity is to promote energy producing industries and nations. The services provided by the group include waste management, waste reduction, vitification, compaction, shallow burial, remediation and cleanup of radioactive hazardous waste. The group serves the world governments. The group operates in Asia, Central America, and Eastern Europe.

Primary SIC and add'l.: 4950

CIK No: 0001332702

Subsidiaries: IPW Group de Mexico

Officers: Peter Toscano/58/Chmn., CEO, Pres., Principal Financial Officer, Jack Wagenti/Dir., Sec., Jose Garcia/Dir., VP, Salvatore Arnone/Dir., VP - Marketing, Michael Maguire/VP - Engineering, Lennart Strand/Chief Technical Advisor, Louis Garcia/VP - Finance, James W. Fitzgibbons/39/Controller, Chief Accounting Officer

Directors: Peter Toscano/58/Chmn., CEO, Pres., Principal Financial Officer, Jack Wagenti/Dir., Sec., Jose Garcia/Dir., VP, Georgy Grechko/Dir., Robert Astore/Dir., Salvatore Arnone/Dir., VP - Marketing, Walter J. Salvadore/Dir., Sheikh Hani Yamani/Dir., Kenny Tang/Head - Advisory Board, Georgy J. Callegari/Member - Advisory Board, Fergus Reid/Member - Advisory Board

Owners: Walter Salvadore, Peter Toscano/26.35%, Salvatore Arnone, James W. FitzGibbons, Armada Partners, L.P./6.52%, Robert Astore, Sheik Hani A.Z. Yamani, Georgi Grechko, Jack Wagenti/27.71%, Insiders/58.76%, Louis D. Garcia, Jose Garcia

Financial Data: ***Fiscal Year End:***12/31 ***Latest Annual Data:*** 12/31/2006

Year	Sales	Net Income
2006	NA	-$12,831,000
2005	NA	-$3,161,000

Curr. Assets:	$1,665,000	***Curr. Liab.:***	$2,143,000		
Plant, Equip.:	$4,000	***Total Liab.:***	$2,143,000	***Indic. Yr. Divd.:***	NA
Total Assets:	$4,389,000	***Net Worth:***	$2,246,000	***Debt/ Equity:***	NA

International Power Plc

62 Forest St., Ste. 102, Marlborough, MA, 01752; ***PH:*** 1-508-382-9300; ***Fax:*** 1-508-382-9400; ***http://*** www.ipplc.com

General - Incorporation	UK	**Stock**- Price on:12/24/2007	$85.95
Employees	3,671	Stock Exchange	OTC
Auditor	KPMG Audit Plc	Ticker Symbol	IPRPY
Stk Agt	NA	Outstanding Shares	152,170,000
Counsel	NA	E.P.S	NA
DUNS No.	NA	Shareholders	NA

Business: The group's principal activity is the generation of electricity. The group business is primarily focussed on North America, Europe, the Middle East and Australia and has interests in 28 power stations in 12 countries. The group has operating facilities in Australia, the us, the UK, Portugal, Spain, the czech republic, turkey, Malaysia, oman, abu dhabi, pakistan and Thailand.

Primary SIC and add'l.: 4911

CIK No: 0000937293

Subsidiaries: Al Kamil Power Company SAOG, ANP Bellingham Energy Company, LLC, ANP Blackstone Energy Company, LLC, ANP Fundingl, LLC, Canunda Power Pty Limited, Deeside Power Development Company Limited, Electro Metalurgica del Ebro SL, First Hydro Company, First Hydro Finance plc, Gippsland Power Pty Limited, Hays Energy Limited Partnership, Hazelwood Power Partnership, Ibrica de Enrgas SL, International Power (Jersey) Limited, International Power Opatovice A.S. 29 Subsidiaries included in the Index

Officers: Philip Cox/Dir., CEO, Beth Akers/Contact - Media, Gareth Griffiths/Dir. - Global Trading, Peter Barlow/Dir. - Finance, Stephen Riley/Dir., Executive Dir. - Europe, James Flanagan/Investor Relation Officer, Sean Neely/Head - Mergers, Acquisitions, Tony Concannon/44/Dir., Executive Dir. - Australia, Mark Williamson/50/Dir., CFO, Stephen Ramsay/Company Sec., Ken Oakley/Head - Tax, Penny Chalmers/42/Dir. - Global Resources, Bruce Levy/52/Dir., Executive Dir. - North America, Vince Harris/Dir. - Asia, Ed Metcalfe/Dir. - Operations, Engineering

Directors: Philip Cox/Dir., CEO, Neville Simms/Chmn., John Roberts/62/Non Exec. Dir., Mark Williamson/50/Dir., CFO, Tony Concannon/44/Dir., Executive Dir. - Australia, Ranald Spiers/Dir. - Middle East, Africa, Struan Robertson/Non Exec. Dir., Adri Baan/65/Non Exec. Dir., Anthony Concannon/Non Exec. Dir., Alan Murray/Non Exec. Dir.

Financial Data: ***Fiscal Year End:***12/31 ***Latest Annual Data:*** 12/31/2005

Year	Sales	Net Income
2005	$3,326,306,000	$411,271,000
2004	$2,441,002,000	$117,523,000
2003	$2,264,031,000	-$30,235,000

Curr. Assets:	$2,508,926,000	***Curr. Liab.:***	$2,237,040,000		
Plant, Equip.:	$8,068,831,000	***Total Liab.:***	$10,417,723,000	***Indic. Yr. Divd.:***	$1.570
Total Assets:	$14,303,290,000	***Net Worth:***	$3,885,566,000	***Debt/ Equity:***	NA

International Rectifier Corp

233 Kansas St., El Segundo, CA, 90245; ***PH:*** 1-310-252-7105; ***Fax:*** 1-310-252-7903; ***http://*** www.irf.com

General - Incorporation	DE	**Stock**- Price on:12/24/2007	$35.65
Employees	6,300	Stock Exchange	NYSE
Auditor	PricewaterhouseCoopers LLP	Ticker Symbol	IRF
Stk Agt	Mellon Investor Services LLC	Outstanding Shares	72,510,000
Counsel	NA	E.P.S	$0.151
DUNS No.	04-167-4912	Shareholders	NA

Business: The group's principal activities are to design, manufacture and market power semiconductors that convert or regulate electricity at relatively high voltage and current levels. Power semiconductors process electricity into a form more usable by electrical products. Power semiconductors increase system efficiency, allow more compact end products, improve features and functionality and extend battery life. Products offered include analog integrated circuits, advanced circuit devices, power systems and power components. The group caters to customers in North America, Europe and Asia.

Primary SIC and add'l.: 3674

CIK No: 0000316793

Subsidiaries: Advanced Analog, Inc., Electronic Motion Systems, Ltd., Electronic Science & Technology Building, International Rectifier Company (Great Britain) Ltd., International Rectifier Corporation, International Rectifier Corporation Italiana, S.p.A., International Rectifier GmbH, International Rectifier HiRel Products LLC(formerly Omnirel), International Rectifier Hong Kong, Ltd., International Rectifier Japan Company, Ltd., International Rectifier Korea, International Rectifier Southeast Asia Pte. Ltd., IR Epi Services, Inc., IR International Holdings China, Inc., IR International Holdings, Inc. 25 Subsidiaries included in the Index

Officers: Donald R. Dancer/Acting CEO, Michael A. Briere/Exec. VP - Research, Development, CTO, Portia Switzer/VP - Investor Relations, Graham Robertson/Corporate Communications, Linda J. Pahl/Acting CFO

Directors: Eric Lidow/Chmn., Rochus E. Vogt/Dir., Robert S. Attiyeh/Dir., James D. Plummer/Dir., Jack O. Vance/Dir., Philip M. Neches/Dir.

Owners: OppenheimerFunds, Inc./5.36%, Michael P. McGee, Minoru Matsuda, Michael Briere, Eric Lidow/3.10%, Jack O. Vance, Donald R. Dancer, Neuberger Berman LLC/11.26%, Capital Guardian Trust Co./11.02%, Walter Lifsey, Robert S. Attiyeh, Robert Grant, Rochus E. Vogt, James D. Plummer, Alexander Lidow/2.90% *(16 Owners included in Index)*

Financial Data: ***Fiscal Year End:***06/30 ***Latest Annual Data:*** 6/30/2006

Year	Sales	Net Income
2006	$1,171,118,000	$107,156,000
2005	$1,174,424,000	$137,460,000
2004	$1,060,500,000	$89,770,000

Curr. Assets:	$1,075,456,000	***Curr. Liab.:***	$254,650,000	***P/E Ratio:***	15.84
Plant, Equip.:	$576,380,000	***Total Liab.:***	$900,691,000	***Indic. Yr. Divd.:***	NA
Total Assets:	$2,505,023,000	***Net Worth:***	$1,604,332,000	***Debt/ Equity:***	NA

International Securities Exchange Inc

60 Broad St., New York, NY, 10004; *PH:* 1-212-943-2400; *Fax:* 1-212-425-4926;
http:// www.iseoptions.com; *Email:* mail@iseoptions.com

General - Incorporation		Stock - Price on:12/24/2007	$65.14
Employees	216	Stock Exchange	NYSE
Auditor	NA	Ticker Symbol	ISE
Stk Agt	Computershare Trust Co	Outstanding Shares	38,880,000
Counsel	NA	E.P.S	$1.53
DUNS No.	NA	Shareholders	NA

Business: The groups principle activity is to operate an equity options exchange. The group operates from the United States.

Primary SIC and add'l.: 6200

CIK No: 0001178198

Officers: David Krell/CEO, Pres., Gary Katz/COO, Bruce Cooperman/Treasurer, CFO, Michael J. Simon/Sec., General Counsel, Chief Regulatory Officer - International Securities Exchange, LLC, Amit Muni/Principal Accounting Officer, Daniel P. Friel/CIO, Robert J. Cornish/Technology Infrastructure, Development Officer, Jerome Mangano/Technology Operations, Support Officer, Gregory J. Maynard/System, Product Strategy Officer, James O. Sampson/Trading, Marketing Operations Officer, Katherine Simmons/Deputy General Counsel, Legal Officer, Assist. Sec. - International Securities Exchange, LLC, Peter J. Bottini/IndustryDir, Sean Flynn/IndustryDir., Joseph W. Ferraro/Assoc. General Counsel, Legal Officer - International Securities Exchange, LLC, Thomas Gibbons/Investor Relations Officer *(28 Officers included in Index)*

Directors: Frank J. Jones/Chmn., John F. Marshall/Vice Chmn., Barbara B. Diamond/Dir., Sarah A. Miller/Dir., Carelton Day Pearl/Dir., Richard Schmalensee/Dir., Joseph Stefanelli/Dir., Kenneth Vecchione/Dir.

Financial Data: Fiscal Year End:NA   Latest Annual Data: 12/31/2006

Year	Sales	Net Income
2006	$202,081,000	$55,152,000
2005	$155,899,000	$35,347,000
2004	$125,373,000	$26,163,000

Curr. Assets:	$306,979,000	Curr. Liab.:	$47,274,000	P/E Ratio:	42.58
Plant, Equip.:	$29,009,000	Total Liab.:	$101,837,000	Indic. Yr. Divd.:	NA
Total Assets:	$396,425,000	Net Worth:	$258,265,000	Debt/ Equity:	NA

International Shipholding Corp

11 N Water St., Ste. 18290, Mobile, AL, 36602; *PH:* 1-251-243-9150; *http://* www.intship.com;
Email: fli-sales@intship.com

General - Incorporation	DE	Stock - Price on:12/24/2007	$20.29
Employees	581	Stock Exchange	NYSE
Auditor	Ernst & Young LLP	Ticker Symbol	ISH
Stk Agt	American Stock Transfer & Trust Co	Outstanding Shares	6,120,000
Counsel	NA	E.P.S	$3.74
DUNS No.	06-467-1373	Shareholders	NA

Business: The group's principal activity is to operate a diversified fleet of the United States and international flag vessels, which provide domestic and international maritime transportation services. These services are provided to commercial customers and agencies of the United States government primarily under medium to long-term charters or contracts. The group operates in four segments: liner services, time charter contracts, contracts of affreightment and other. It also provides ancillary services such as ship charter brokerage, agency and barge fleeting and other specialized services. The fleet consists of 36 ocean-going vessels, 2 towboats, 7 river barges, 28 special purpose barges and 1,722 lighter aboard ships. The group operates in the United States, gulf, east coast, Middle East, Far East, and northern Europe.

Primary SIC and add'l.: 4499 4449 4424

CIK No: 0000278041

Subsidiaries: Bay Insurance Company Limited, Belden Cement Holding Inc., Belden Management Inc., Belden Shipholding Pte Ltd., Belden Shipping Pte Ltd, Belden Voss Pte Ltd., Cape Holding, Ltd., Central Gulf Lines, Inc., CG Railway, Inc., Dry Bulk Cape Holding, Inc., Dry Bulk Africa, LTD., Dry Bulk Australia, LTD, Echelon Shipping Inc, Emblem Shipping Inc., Enterprise Ship Company, Inc. 30 Subsidiaries included in the Index

Officers: Niels M. Johnsen/Chmn., CEO/$440,567.00, Erik L. Johnsen/Dir., Pres./$385,110.00, Manuel G. Estrada/53/CFO, VP/$210,640.00, Christian R. Johnsen/Sec.

Directors: Niels M. Johnsen/Chmn., CEO, Edwin Lupberger/Dir., Edward K. Trowbridge/Dir., Harold S. Grehan/Dir., Erik F. Johnsen/Dir., Erik L. Johnsen/Dir., Pres., Niels W. Johnsen/Dir., Raymond V. O'Brien/Dir., Merritt H. Lane/Dir.

Owners: Niels M. Johnsen/8.88%, Edward K. Trowbridge, Franklin Resources, Inc./7.76%, Dimensional Fund Advisors LP/5.52%, Raymond V. OBrien, Donald Smith & Co., Inc./8.31%, Harold S. Grehan/1.40%, Erik F. Johnsen/9.08%, Insiders/32.74%, Niels W. Johnsen/14.33%, Edwin Lupberger, Erik L. Johnsen/4.36%, T. Rowe Price Associates, Inc./14.97%

Financial Data: Fiscal Year End:12/31   Latest Annual Data: 12/31/2006

Year	Sales	Net Income
2006	$274,881,000	$17,048,000
2005	$262,156,000	$6,996,000
2004	$263,490,000	$12,785,000

Curr. Assets:	$88,779,000	Curr. Liab.:	$84,668,000	P/E Ratio:	5.43
Plant, Equip.:	$226,937,000	Total Liab.:	$274,306,000	Indic. Yr. Divd.:	NA
Total Assets:	$428,042,000	Net Worth:	$153,736,000	Debt/ Equity:	0.7240

International Smart Sourcing Inc

320 Brd Hollow Rd., Farmingdale, NY, 11735; *PH:* 1-631-293-4796;
http:// www.smart-sourcing.com; *Email:* sales@smart-sourcing.com

General - Incorporation	DE	Stock - Price on:12/24/2007	$0.255
Employees	34	Stock Exchange	OTC
Auditor	Marcum & Kliegman LLP	Ticker Symbol	ISSG
Stk Agt	Continental Stock Transfer & Trust Co	Outstanding Shares	10,970,000
Counsel	NA	E.P.S	-$0.02
DUNS No.	NA	Shareholders	NA

Business: The group's principal activities are to the design, market and manufacture of control knobs used in industrial, consumer and military products. The group also offers molded products and services such as hand painting, pad printing, hot stamping and engraving are provided at a customer's request. The group operates in United States and China through its subsidiaries.

Primary SIC and add'l.: 3089 6719

CIK No: 0001057695

Subsidiaries: Charter Fabrics, Inc, Electronic Hardware Corporation (EHC), SSI

Officers: David Hale/62/Chmn., COO, Pres., Principal Executive Officer, Michael S. Rakusin/52/Dir., CFO, Richard A. Peters/70/Dir., Sec.

Directors: David Hale/62/Chmn., COO, Pres., Principal Executive Officer, Michael S. Rakusin/52/Dir., CFO, Richard A. Peters/70/Dir., Sec.

Owners: H. T. Ardinger/66.73%, Insiders, Donald E. Adams/9.69%, David Hale

Financial Data: Fiscal Year End:12/30   Latest Annual Data: 12/29/2006

Year	Sales	Net Income
2006	$10,698,000	$859,000
2005	$12,188,000	$303,000
2004	$11,500,000	$129,000

Curr. Assets:	$4,089,000	Curr. Liab.:	$2,240,000	P/E Ratio:	3.64
Plant, Equip.:	$241,000	Total Liab.:	$2,407,000	Indic. Yr. Divd.:	NA
Total Assets:	$4,331,000	Net Worth:	$1,924,000	Debt/ Equity:	NA

International Speedway CL B

1801 W.International Speedway Blvd, Daytona Beach, FL, 32114; *PH:* 1-386-254-2700;
http:// www.iscmotorsports.com

General - Incorporation	FL	Stock - Price on:12/24/2007	$53.39
Employees	NA	Stock Exchange	OTC
Auditor	Ernst & Young LLP	Ticker Symbol	ISCB
Stk Agt	Computershare Trust Co	Outstanding Shares	NA
Counsel	NA	E.P.S	NA
DUNS No.	NA	Shareholders	NA

Business: The groups principle activities include promoting motorsports entertainment activities and syndicating numerous racing events and programs. The group operates through two segments namely motorsports event and all other. In October 2005, the group acquired Pikes Peak International Raceway. The group operates from the United States.

Primary SIC and add'l.: 7948

CIK No: 0000051548

Subsidiaries: 380 Development,LLC, Americrown Service Corporation,, ASC Holdings, Inc., ASC Promotions, Inc., Chicago Holdings, Inc., Darlington Raceway of South Carolina, LLC, Daytona International Speedway, LLC, Event Equipment Leasing, Inc., Event Support Corporation, Great Western Sports, Inc., HBP, INC., Homestead-Miami Speedway, LLC, International Speedway, Inc., ISC Properties, Inc. ISC Publications, Inc. 40 Subsidiaries included in the Index

Officers: James C. France/Chmn., CEO, Garrett W. Crotty/Sr. VP, General Counsel, Sec., Susan G. Schandel/Sr. VP, CFO, Treasurer, John E. Graham/VP - Business Affairs, Dan W. Houser/VP, Controller, Chief Accounting Officer, Assist. Treasurer, Grant W. Lynch/Sr. VP - Business Operations, Glenn R. Padgett/VP, Chief Counsel - Operations, Chief Compliance Officer, Assist. Sec., Roger R. Vandersnick/Sr. VP - Marketing, Business Operations, Brian K. Wilson/VP - Corporate Development, Daryl Q. Wolfe/VP, Chief Marketing Officer, Lesa France Kennedy/46/Pres., Sam Cole/Dir. - Marketing Partnerships, Kristie Brown/Mgr. - Marketing Partnerships, Frank Kelleher/Mgr. - Marketing Partnerships, Ryan Mosher/Mgr. - Marketing Partnerships *(17 Officers included in Index)*

Directors: James C. France/Chmn., CEO, Lesa France Kennedy/46/Pres., Morteza Hosseini-Kargar/Dir., Lesa D. Kennedy/Dir., Larry Aiello/Dir., Hyatt J. Brown/Dir., John R. Cooper/Dir., Brian Z. France/Dir., William P. Graves/Dir., Christy F. Harris/Dir., Raymond K. Mason/Dir., Edward H. Rensi/Dir., Lloyd E. Reuss/Dir., Thomas W. Staed/Dir.

Owners: Thomas W. Staed, George S. Leoning, Christy F. Harris, France Family Group, Lesa D. Kennedy, Insiders, Hyatt J. Brown, Raymond K. Mason, John R. Saunders, Edward H. Rensi, Insiders, Edward H. Rensi, Brian Z. France, William P. Graves, Lesa D. Kennedy *(36 Owners included in Index)*

International Speedway Corp

1801 W International Speedway Blvd., Daytona Beach, FL, 32114; *PH:* 1-386-254-2700;
Fax: 1-386-947-6816; *http://* www.iscmotorsports.com

General - Incorporation	FL	Stock - Price on:12/24/2007	$53.08
Employees	1,000	Stock Exchange	NDQ
Auditor	Ernst & Young LLP	Ticker Symbol	ISCA
Stk Agt	Computershare Investor Services LLC	Outstanding Shares	52,970,000
Counsel	NA	E.P.S	$1.35
DUNS No.	04-796-6643	Shareholders	NA

Business: The group's principle activity is to promote motor sports in the United States. These motor sports include 100 stock car, sports car, truck, motorcycle and other racing events. The group owns fourteen motorsports facilities in Florida, Alabama, Arizona, South Carolina, California and other states. The business consists principally of racing events at these major motorsports facilities, which in total have more than 1 million grandstand seats. The group generates revenue primarily from admissions, television, radio and ancillary rights fees, promotion and sponsorship fees, hospitality rentals, advertising revenues, royalties and other. The group's quarterly revenue for Sep'07 was 196.30 millions of USD.

Primary SIC and add'l.: 5812 7948

CIK No: 0000051548

Subsidiaries: 380 Development, LLC, Homestead-Miami Speedway, Kansas Speedway Corporation, Motor Racing Network, Inc, Motorsports Authentics, North Carolina Speedway, Inc, Phoenix Speedway Corp, Speedway Motorsports Incorporated

Officers: James C. France/Vice Chmn., CEO, Susan G. Schandel/CFO, Sr. VP, Treasurer, Garrett W. Crotty/Sr. VP, General Counsel, Sec., John E. Graham/VP - Business Affairs, Grant Lynch/Sr. VP - Business Operations, Lesa D. Kennedy/Dir., Pres., Daniel W. Houser/VP, Controller, Chief Accounting Officer, Assist. Treasurer, Daryl Q. Wolfe/VP, Chief Marketing Officer, Roger Vandersnick/Sr. VP - Marketing, Business Operations, Brian K. Wilson/VP - Corporate Development, John R. Saunders/COO, Exec. VP, Lee H. Combs/54/Sr. VP - Corporate Development, Glenn R. Padgett/VP, Chief Counsel - Operations, Chief Compliance Officer, Assist. Sec.

Directors: James C. France/Vice Chmn., CEO, William C. France/74/Chmn., Brian Z. France/Dir., Lloyd E. Reuss/Dir., Larry Aiello/57/Dir., Lesa D. Kennedy/Dir., Pres., Morteza Hosseini-Kargar/Dir., Christy F. Harris/Dir., Raymond K. Mason/Dir., William P. Graves/Dir., Thomas W. Staed/Dir., Edward H. Rensi/Dir., Gregory W. Penske/45/Dir., John R. Cooper/Dir., Hyatt J. Brown/Dir.

Owners: Lesa D. Kennedy, Betty Jane France, William P. Graves, Hyatt J. Brown, Thomas W. Staed, Lee H. Combs, France Family Group, Edward H. Rensi, Morteza Hosseini-Kargar, Select Equity Group, Inc., Insiders, Raymond K. Mason, Christy F. Harris, Brian Z. France, Insiders *(36 Owners included in Index)*

Financial Data: Fiscal Year End:11/30 **Latest Annual Data:** 11/30/2006

Year	Sales	Net Income
2006	$798,369,000	$116,804,000
2005	$740,129,000	$159,361,000
2004	$647,848,000	$156,318,000

Curr. Assets:	$203,602,000	**Curr. Liab.:**	$196,304,000	**P/E Ratio:**	26.02
Plant, Equip.:	$1,157,313,000	**Total Liab.:**	$766,944,000	**Indic. Yr. Divd.:**	NA
Total Assets:	$1,922,059,000	**Net Worth:**	$1,155,115,000	**Debt/ Equity:**	0.3739

International Star Inc

1818 Marshall St., Shreveport, LA, 71101; **PH:** 1-318-464-8687; **Fax:** 1-318-429-8026; *http://* www.istarnevada.com; **Email:** ir@istarnevada.com

General - Incorporation .... NV	**Stock**- Price on:12/24/2007 ....$0.0175
Employees .... NA	Stock Exchange..OTC
Auditor .... Madsen & Associates, CPA's Inc.	Ticker Symbol...ILST
Stk Agt.. Stalt, Inc.	Outstanding Shares 271,450,000
Counsel .... NA	E.P.S. .... -$0.002
DUNS No. .... NA	Shareholders..NA

Business: The groups principal activities include acquiring and exploring metals mineral properties. The group operates from the United States.

Primary SIC and add'l.: 1000

CIK No: 0001100788

Subsidiaries: Qwik Track, Inc.

Officers: Joseph Therrell/Dir., CEO, Pres., Acting CFO, Jacqulyn B. Wine/Sec., Treasurer

Directors: Joseph Therrell/Dir., CEO, Pres., Acting CFO, Virginia Kilpatrick Shehee/Chmn., Robert M. Glover/Dir., John Tuma/Dir.

Owners: Insiders/23.67%, John Tuma, Jacqulyn B. Wine, Joseph E. Therrell, Kamal Alawas/10.30%, Virginia K. Shehee/21.35%, Denver B. Cashatt, Robert M. Glover/8.35%, Dottie Wommack

Financial Data: Fiscal Year End:12/31 **Latest Annual Data:** 03/31/2007

Year	Sales	Net Income
2007	NA	NA
2006	NA	-$822,000
2005	NA	-$799,000

Curr. Assets:	$3,000	**Curr. Liab.:**	$277,000		
Plant, Equip.:	$29,000	**Total Liab.:**	$277,000	**Indic. Yr. Divd.:**	NA
Total Assets:	$32,000	**Net Worth:**	-$245,000	**Debt/ Equity:**	NA

International Technology Systems Inc

Formerly: International Telecommunication Inc

1140 S Raymond Ave., Fullerton, CA, 92831; **PH:** 1-310-459-1081; *http://* www.itls.tv

General - Incorporation .... NV	**Stock**- Price on:12/24/2007 ....NA
Employees .... NA	Stock Exchange..NA
Auditor ....Chisholm Bierwolf & Nilson LLC	Ticker Symbol..NA
Stk Agt............ Pacific Stock Transfer Company	Outstanding Shares ....NA
Counsel .... NA	E.P.S. ....NA
DUNS No. .... NA	Shareholders..NA

Business: The group's principle activity is to produce television programs for both the Chinese and English media markets. The television programming is directed at the home improvement market in China. The group's assets consist primarily of its library of English and Chinese television programs. It focus as a gateway to China for building material and technology companies with emphasis linked to the 2008 Beijing olympics and the 2010 shanghai world fair. The potential profit centers are TV production and distribution, e-commerce and TV direct sales, media buying and advertising sales.

Primary SIC and add'l.: 7812 4833

CIK No: 0001137117

Subsidiaries: EarthNet Telecom Inc, Millennium Media Internet, Rocket Internetworking Inc

Officers: Alie Chang/Dir., CEO, Pres., Felizian Paul/Chmn., Sec., John Callaci/Dir., CTO, Chief Scientist, Willy Chang/Dir. - Marketing, Shanghai Office, China, Klaus Hilgers/Dir. - Business Management, Hou Haibin/Beijing Office Mgr., Karl Roller/Direct Marketing, Multilevel, Angi Ma/Design, Dir. - Creative, Eric Fu/System Analyst, Michael Spaulding/CFO, Eugene Tseng/Sr. Environmental, Renewable Energy Legal Advisor, James Barber/Sec., Attorney, Gary Petersen/Member - Advisory Board, Sr. Technical Advisor, Robert Sulnick/Member - Advisory Board, Special Renewable Energy Legal Advisor

Directors: Alie Chang/Dir., CEO, Pres., Felizian Paul/Chmn., Sec., John Callaci/Dir., CTO, Chief Scientist, Mary Bradshaw/Member - Advisory Board, Patrick D. Mulcahy/Member - Advisory Board, Holmes Stoner/Member - Advisory Board, David Goddard/Member - Advisory Board, William Chang/Member - Advisory Board, March Fong Eu/Member - Advisory Board, Siro Polo Padolechia/Member - Advisory Board, Gary Petersen/Member - Advisory Board, Sr. Technical Advisor, Robert Sulnick/Member - Advisory Board, Special Renewable Energy Legal Advisor

Curr. Assets:	$47,000	**Curr. Liab.:**	$1,102,000		
Plant, Equip.:	NA	**Total Liab.:**	$1,102,000	**Indic. Yr. Divd.:**	NA
Total Assets:	$50,000	**Net Worth:**	-$1,052,000	**Debt/ Equity:**	NA

International Thoroughbred Breeders Inc

1105 N Market St., Ste. 1300, Wilmington, DE, 19899; **PH:** 1-302-427-7599

General - Incorporation .... DE	**Stock**- Price on:12/24/2007 ....$0.09
Employees 379	Stock Exchange..OTC
Auditor .... Stockton Bates LLP	Ticker Symbol..ITGB
Stk Agt............Computershare Investor Services	Outstanding Shares 11,370,000
Counsel .... NA	E.P.S. ....-$2.17
DUNS No. 01-456-6707	Shareholders..NA

Business: The group's principle activity is to operate the garden state park racetrack and is also involved in the business of purchasing, owning, breeding and selling thoroughbred horses used in thoroughbred (non-harness) racing. The group's racetrack is situated on approximately 280 acres located in cherry hill, New Jersey. Garden state racing dates are primarily nighttime events and include standardbred, thoroughbred and harness racing. The group operates from United States.

Primary SIC and add'l.: 7948 0272

CIK No: 0000320573

Subsidiaries: Atlantic City Harness, Inc., Circa 1850, Inc., Cruise Entertainment, LLC, Garden State Race Track, Inc., GMO Travel, Inc., GSRT, LLC, Holdfree Racing Association, International Thoroughbred Gaming Development Corporation, ITB Management, Inc., ITB Racing, Inc., ITB Realty, Inc., ITG - Brazil, Inc., ITG - Venezuela, Inc., ITG Palm Beach, LLC, ITG Panama, S. A. 26 Subsidiaries included in the Index

Owners: Robert J. Quigley, PDS Gaming Corporation, Francis W. Murray, Insiders, MBC Global 269 Market Square, William H. Warner, Westminster Investments, LLC

Financial Data: Fiscal Year End:12/31 **Latest Annual Data:** 12/31/2006

Year	Sales	Net Income
2006	$30,956,000	-$25,514,000
2005	$32,773,000	-$1,900,000

Curr. Assets:	$5,321,000	**Curr. Liab.:**	$18,405,000		
Plant, Equip.:	$47,617,000	**Total Liab.:**	$53,813,000	**Indic. Yr. Divd.:**	NA
Total Assets:	$83,364,000	**Net Worth:**	$29,550,000	**Debt/ Equity:**	NA

International Tower Hill Mines Ltd

No. 507 837 W Hastings St., Vancouver, BC, V6C 3N6; **PH:** 1-604-683-6332; *http://* www.towerhillmines.com

General - Incorporation ....Canada	**Stock**- Price on:12/24/2007 ....$2.8
Employees .... NA	Stock Exchange..AMEX
Auditor ....MacKay LLP	Ticker Symbol..THM
Stk Agt .... Computershare Investor Services LLC	Outstanding Shares ....NA
Counsel .... NA	E.P.S. .... -$0.273
DUNS No. .... NA	Shareholders..NA

Business: The group's principle activities including acquiring, exploring and evaluating interest in mineral properties. The group operates from United States.

Primary SIC and add'l.: 1061

CIK No: 0001134115

Subsidiaries: Alberta corporation

Officers: Jeffery A. Pontius/CEO, Pres., Quentin Mai/VP - Corporate Communications, Russell Myers/VP - Exploration, Michael Kinley/CFO, Lawrence W. Talbot/VP, General Counsel, Marla K. Ritchie/Corp. Sec.

Directors: Hendrick Van Alphen/Chmn., Benjamin W. Guenther/Dir., Anton J. Drescher/Dir., Rowland Perkins/Dir., Ron Sheardown/Dir., Michael L. Bartlett/67/Dir.

Owners: Lawrence Talbot/1.34%, Quentin Mai/1.59%, Anton J. Drescher/1.82%, Henk Van Alphen/2.73%, Michael Kinley/0.96%, Jeff Pontius/2.29%, Marla Ritchie/0.80%, Ronald Sheardown/0.25%, Rowland Perkins/0.31%, Insiders/12.38%, Russell Myers/0.66%, Michael Bartlett/0.25%

Financial Data: Fiscal Year End:05/31 **Latest Annual Data:** 5/31/2006

Year	Sales	Net Income
2006	NA	-$116,000
2005	NA	-$160,000
2004	$3,000	-$124,000

Curr. Assets:	$19,000	**Curr. Liab.:**	$6,000		
Plant, Equip.:	$169,000	**Total Liab.:**	$6,000	**Indic. Yr. Divd.:**	NA
Total Assets:	$190,000	**Net Worth:**	$184,000	**Debt/ Equity:**	NA

Internet America Inc

PO Box 690753, Houston, TX, 77269; **PH:** 1-713-968-2500; *http://* www.internetamerica.com; **Email:** info@airmail.net

General - Incorporation .... TX	**Stock**- Price on:12/24/2007 ....$0.29
Employees 58	Stock Exchange..OTC
Auditor .... UHY LLP	Ticker Symbol..GEEK
Stk Agt .... Mellon Investor Services LLC	Outstanding Shares 12,510,000
Counsel .... NA	E.P.S. .... -$0.06
DUNS No. 87-803-4487	Shareholders..NA

Business: The group's principal activity is providing the Internet services. Internet services includes broadband and dial-up Internet access, as well as related value-added services. The group also offers dedicated high speed Internet accesses, Web hosting, colocation and other business related services to their subscribers. The operations of the group is carried on in Texas and Louisiana.

Primary SIC and add'l.: 7375

CIK No: 0001001279

Subsidiaries: NeoSoft, Inc., PDQ.Net, Incorporated

Officers: William E. Ladin/Chmn., CEO, Jennifer S. Leblanc/Chief Financial, Accounting Officer, Sec., Mark Ocker/56/Exec. VP

Directors: William E. Ladin/Chmn., CEO, John N. Palmer/Dir., Troy Lemaile-Stoval/Dir., Justin McClure/Dir.

Owners: Justin McClure, John N. Palmer, Sanders Childrens Trust, William E. (Billy) Ladin/7.20%, Justin McClure/3.20%, J.N. Palmer Family Partnership/5.90%, Yvette Sturgis, William E. (Billy) Ladin, George Sturgis, GulfSouth Capital, Inc., Mark Ocker/2.60%, Insiders, Summit Growth Management, LLC, Stuart Sternberg, Jennifer S. LeBlanc *(18 Owners included in Index)*

Financial Data: Fiscal Year End:06/30 **Latest Annual Data:** 06/30/2007

Year	Sales	Net Income
2007	$7,985,000	-$347,000
2006	$9,909,000	-$636,000
2005	$10,647,000	$19,000

Curr. Assets:	$1,638,000	**Curr. Liab.:**	$2,334,000		
Plant, Equip.:	$1,083,000	**Total Liab.:**	$2,677,000	**Indic. Yr. Divd.:**	NA
Total Assets:	$7,533,000	**Net Worth:**	$4,855,000	**Debt/ Equity:**	0.0390

Internet Capital Group Inc

690 Lee Rd., Ste. 310, Wayne, PA, 19087; *PH:* 1-610-727-6900; *Fax:* 1-610-727-6901; *http://* www.internetcapital.com

General - Incorporation............................ DE	**Stock**- Price on:12/24/2007 ....$11.87
Employees 24	Stock Exchange...NDQ
Auditor ....KPMG LLP	Ticker Symbol...ICGE
Stk Agt.................Mellon Investor Services LLC	Outstanding Shares 38,650,000
Counsel.........................Dechert, Price & Rhoads	E.P.S..$0.03
DUNS No. ....NA	Shareholders...NA

Business: The group's principal activity is to provide Internet business-to-business (b2b) e-commerce through a network of partner companies. The group provides software services that facilitate increased efficiency and cost reduction. The services provided spans across three primary sectors of e-commerce - technology infrastructure, horizontal service providers and vertical solutions providers. The horizontal service providers automate and streamline non-core processes and enable the execution of online transactions in credit, logistics and procurement. The vertical solutions providers coordinate, organize and streamline information within specific industry supply chains. The partner companies deliver software and services to help businesses focus on their core competencies. At 31-Dec-2003 the partner company network was comprised of interests in 30 companies b2b e-commerce companies.

Primary SIC and add'l.: 7375 7389 7379

CIK No: 0001085621

Subsidiaries: 1999 Internet Capital (Europe) L.P., Anthem/CIC Ventures Fund L.P., Blackboard, Inc., Captive Capital Corporation, ComputerJobs.com, Inc., CreditTrade Inc., eCredit.com, Inc., Emptoris, Inc., Entegrity Solutions Corporation, epValue.com, Inc., FoodLink Online LLC, Freeborders, Inc., GoIndustry AG, ICG Commerce Germany GmbH, ICG Commerce Holdings, Inc. 41 Subsidiaries included in the Index

Officers: Walter W. Buckley/Co - Founder, Chmn., CEO/$2,314,029.00, Scott Powers/Corporate Counsel, Darren Sandberg/VP - Operations, Karen Greene/VP - Investor Relations, Corporate Communications, Vincent P. Menichelli/VP - Operations, Anthony P. Dolanski/MD - Operations/$1,417,332.00, Kamal Advani/MD - Operations, Philip A. Rooney/VP - Treasury, Tax, Kirk Morgan/CFO/$768,904.00, Michael D. Zisman/MD - Operations/$1,478,375.00, Paul Slaats/MD - Acquisitions, Suzanne Niemeyer/General Counsel, MD, Sec., Doug Alexander/MD - Operations/$2,047,078.00

Directors: Walter W. Buckley/Co - Founder, Chmn., CEO, Michael J. Hagan/Dir., David K. Downes/Dir., Robert E. Keith/Dir., Philip J. Ringo/Dir., Warren Musser/Dir., David Berkman/Dir., Thomas P. Gerrity/Dir., Thomas A. Decker/Dir.

Owners: David J. Berkman, Warren V. Musser, Capital Research and Management Company/8.00%, Douglas A. Alexander/1.00%, Thomas P. Gerrity, Anthony P. Dolanski, Dimensional Fund Advisors LP/8.10%, SMALLCAP World Fund, Inc./6.20%, Michael D. Zisman, Walter W. Buckley/1.80%, Insiders/5.60%, Tontine Capital Partners, L.P./7.60%, Kirk R. Morgan, David K. Downes, Thomas A. Decker *(17 Owners included in Index)*

Financial Data: Fiscal Year End:12/31   Latest Annual Data: 12/31/2006

Year	Sales	Net Income
2006	$64,749,000	$15,624,000
2005	$50,576,000	$72,518,000
2004	$52,400,000	-$135,317,000

Curr. Assets:	$129,671,000	**Curr. Liab.:**	$50,732,000	**P/E Ratio:**	98.92
Plant, Equip.:	$1,847,000	**Total Liab.:**	$51,766,000	**Indic. Yr. Divd.:**	NA
Total Assets:	$354,427,000	**Net Worth:**	$298,538,000	**Debt/ Equity:**	0.0011

Internet Gold-Golden Lines Ltd

1 Alexander Yanai St., Petah Tikva, 49277; *PH:* 972-722003848; *Fax:* 972-39399832; *http://* www.igld.com; *Email:* i.azulay@zahav.net.il,

General - Incorporation..........................Israel	**Stock**- Price on:12/24/2007 ....$12.62
Employees 305	Stock Exchange...NDQ
Auditor ....Somekh Chaikin	Ticker Symbol..IGLD
Stk Agt......American Stock Transfer & Trust Co.	Outstanding Shares 19,660,000
Counsel.......................Carter, Ledyard & Milburn	E.P.S..$0.72
DUNS No. ....NA	Shareholders...NA

Business: The groups principle activity is to provide a wide array of Internet services tailored to meet the needs of our residential and business subscribers, including Internet access and related value-added services. The group operates from United States.

Primary SIC and add'l.: 7375

CIK No: 0001090159

Subsidiaries: Hype Active Media Ltd., Internet Gold International Ltd., MSN Israel Ltd., Nirshamim Lalimudim Ltd., Seret Israel's Movies Portal Ltd., Start Net Ltd., The Money Interactive Ltd., Yahala Internet Solutions Ltd.

Officers: Eli Holtzman/Co - Founder, CEO, Doron Turgeman/Deputy CEO, CFO, Idit Azulay/Mgr. - Investor Relations

Directors: Eli Holtzman/Co - Founder, CEO, Shaul Elovitch/Chmn., Yossef Elovitch/Dir., Anat Winner/Dir., Aliza Schloss/54/Dir., Orly Guy/46/Dir., Ronit Gotliv/54/Dir.

Owners: Insiders/58.80%, Shaul Elovitch/58.01%, Eli Holtzman

Financial Data: Fiscal Year End:12/31   Latest Annual Data: 12/31/2006

Year	Sales	Net Income
2006	$96,944,000	$2,632,000
2005	$65,109,000	$3,998,000
2004	$52,930,000	$4,759,000

Curr. Assets:	$135,950,000	**Curr. Liab.:**	$286,629,000		
Plant, Equip.:	$37,911,000	**Total Liab.:**	$361,914,000	**Indic. Yr. Divd.:**	NA
Total Assets:	$401,666,000	**Net Worth:**	$39,752,000	**Debt/ Equity:**	NA

Internet Infinity Inc

413 Ave. G, No.1, Redondo Beach, CA, 90277; *PH:* 1-800-533-4810; *http://* www.internetinfinity.com

General - Incorporation............................NV	**Stock**- Price on:12/24/2007 ....$0.03
Employees ....NA	Stock Exchange...OTC
Auditor ....Kabani & Co, Inc	Ticker Symbol..ITNF
Stk Agt...NA	Outstanding Shares 28,720,000
Counsel ....NA	E.P.S...-$0.01
DUNS No. ....NA	Shareholders...NA

Business: The group's principle activity is to distribute electronic media duplication services and electronic blank media. The group also distributes prerecorded special interest video programs, Internet Web site and CD authorizing services. The group also operates a business-to-business community Website for direct sales professionals. Electronic media duplication and packaging services include mini-CD business cards, compact disks and videotape. The special interest video programs consist of personal knowledge and skill development; computer, health, medical, sports and exercise training; children's crafts, home and auto repair. The group operates only in domestic market.

Primary SIC and add'l.: 5734 5735 7375

CIK No: 0001020302

Officers: Roger Casas/Dir., CEO, VP, George Morris/Chmn., VP - Marketing, Shirlene Bradshaw/Dir., Corp. Sec.

Directors: Roger Casas/Dir., CEO, VP, George Morris/Chmn., VP - Marketing, Shirlene Bradshaw/Dir., Corp. Sec., Charles Yesson/Dir.

Owners: L&M Media, Inc., Insiders, Roger Casas, Apple Realty, Inc, Shirlene Bradshaw, George Morris

Financial Data: Fiscal Year End:03/31   Latest Annual Data: 03/31/2007

Year	Sales	Net Income
2007	$5,000	-$130,000
2006	$42,000	-$41,000
2005	$25,000	-$118,000

Curr. Assets:	$1,000	**Curr. Liab.:**	$834,000		
Plant, Equip.:	NA	**Total Liab.:**	$834,000	**Indic. Yr. Divd.:**	NA
Total Assets:	$1,000	**Net Worth:**	-$833,000	**Debt/ Equity:**	NA

Internet Initiative Japan Inc

1211 Ave. of the Americas, Ste. 2900, New York, NY, 10036; *PH:* 1-212-440-8080; *http://* www.iij.ad.jp/en/info/management02/index.html; *Email:* info@iij.ad.jp

General - Incorporation ....Japan	**Stock**- Price on:12/24/2007 ....$8.34
Employees 987	Stock Exchange...NDQ
Auditor ....Deloitte Touche Tohmatsu	Ticker Symbol...IIJI
Stk Agt.........Sumitomo Trust & Banking Co Ltd	Outstanding Shares 81,720,000
Counsel..NA	E.P.S..$0.54
DUNS No. ....NA	Shareholders...NA

Business: The group's principle activity is the Internet access services such as dedicated access and dial-up access. The group is also engaged in the systems integration services and Internet data centre services. Koichi suzuki, the president of the group, is the major shareholder with 10.32% of issued stock.

Primary SIC and add'l.: 7379 4822 7373

CIK No: 0001090633

Subsidiaries: atom Co., Ltd., IIJ America Inc., IIJ Financial Systems Inc., IIJ Media Communications Inc., IIJ Technology Inc, Internet Multifeed Co., Internet Revolution Inc., Net Care, Inc.

Officers: Koichi Suzuki/CEO, Representative Dir., Toshiya Asaba/Division Dir. - Network Service Department, Kazuhiro Tokita/Dir., Division Dir. - Solution Department, Masaki Okada/Outside Statutory Auditors, Akihisa Watai/Dir., CFO, Hiroyuki Hisashima/Dir., Division Dir. - Applied Research, Development Department, Hideshi Hojo/Division Dir. - Sales Department, Takamichi Miyoshi/Dir., GM - Strategy Planning Division, Masaaki Koizumi/Outside Statutory Auditors, Hirofumi Takahashi/Statutory Auditor, Yoshiaki Hisamoto/Division Dir. - Administrative Department, Junichi Tate/Outside Statutory Auditors, Junichi Shimagami/Dir., Division Dir. - Network Service Department

Directors: Akihisa Watai/Dir., CFO, Junnosuke Furukawa/Dir., Takashi Hiroi/Dir., Hiroyuki Hisashima/Dir., Division Dir. - Applied Research, Development Department, Takamichi Miyoshi/Dir., GM - Strategy Planning Division, Yasurou Tanahashi/Dir., Kazuhiro Tokita/Dir., Division Dir. - Solution Department, Yoshifumi Nishikawa/Dir., Senji Yamamoto/Dir., Junichi Shimagami/Dir., Division Dir. - Network Service Department

Owners: Nippon Telegraph and Telephone Corporation and affiliates/29.70%, Itochu Corporation/5.10%, Insiders/6.50%, Koichi Suzuki/6.10%

Financial Data: Fiscal Year End:03/31   Latest Annual Data: 3/31/2006

Year	Sales	Net Income
2006	$424,009,000	$40,463,000
2005	$388,944,000	$27,106,000
2004	$372,235,000	-$1,009,000

Curr. Assets:	$236,522,000	**Curr. Liab.:**	$194,915,000	**P/E Ratio:**	14.89
Plant, Equip.:	$87,670,000	**Total Liab.:**	$259,474,000	**Indic. Yr. Divd.:**	NA
Total Assets:	$431,605,000	**Net Worth:**	$172,131,000	**Debt/ Equity:**	NA

Internet Security Systems Inc

6303 Barfield Rd. , Atlanta, GA, 30328; *PH:* 1-678-443-6000; *http://* www.iss.net

General - Incorporation .... DE	**Stock**- Price on:12/24/2007 ....NA
Employees ....NA	Stock Exchange...NA
Auditor ....Ernst & Young LLP	Ticker Symbol..NA
Stk Agt...SunTrust Bank	Outstanding Shares ....NA
Counsel..NA	E.P.S...NA
DUNS No. 00-800-6624	Shareholders...NA

Business: The group's principal activities are to provide security management solutions for protecting digital assets and network security monitoring, detection and response software for protecting the security and integrity of enterprise information systems. The group also provides comprehensive managed security services for organizations to develop an in-house information security solution. The group's customers include public and private sector organizations. The group provides security management solutions in the United States, Canada, Latin America, Europe, Middle East, Africa and Asia/Pacific Rim. As of Dec 31, 2003, the group had more than 11,000 business customers and maintained operations in 22 countries. On 14-Jan-2004, the group acquired cobion ag.

Primary SIC and add'l.: 7372 7378

CIK No: 0001053148

Subsidiaries: Cobion AG, Cobion Corp., Internet Security Systems (Beijing) Co., Ltd., Internet Security Systems (Latin America), Inc., Internet Security Systems BV, Internet Security Systems Gmbh, Internet Security Systems Iberia Sl, Internet Security Systems KK, Internet Security Systems Ltd., Internet Security Systems Ltda., Internet Security Systems Nordic AB, Internet Security Systems NV, Internet Security Systems Pty. Ltd., Internet Security Systems Sarl, Internet Security Systems Srl 27 Subsidiaries included in the Index

Officers: Thomas E. Noonan/Chmn., CEO, Pres., Lawrence A. Costanza/Sr. VP - Americas Sales, Jaap H. Smit/Sr. VP - EMEA Operations, Ja Hong Lin/Pres. - Asia, Pacific Operations, Christopher J. Rouland/CTO, Christopher W. Klaus/Dir., Founder, Chief Security Adviser, Raghavan Rajaji/Sr. VP - Finance, Administration, CFO, Helen Berg/CIO

Directors: Thomas E. Noonan/Chmn., CEO, Pres., Richard S. Bodman/Dir., John P. Imlay/Dir., Senator Sam Nunn/Dir., David N. Strohm/Dir., Robert E. Davoli/Dir., Christopher W. Klaus/Dir., Founder, Chief Security Adviser, Kevin J. O'Connor/Dir.

InternetStudios.com Inc

322 E 50th St., New York, NY, 10022; **PH:** 1-212-489-0645; **Fax:** 1-212-223-7419; http:// www.internetstudios.com

General - Incorporation	NV	**Stock**- Price on:12/24/2007	NA
Employees	NA	Stock Exchange	NA
Auditor	Dale Matheson Carr-Hilton Labonte	Ticker Symbol	NA
Stk Agt	Computershare Trust Co of Canada	Outstanding Shares	NA
Counsel	NA	E.P.S	NA
DUNS No.	NA	Shareholders	NA

Business: The group's principal activity is to produce, distribute and market filmed entertainment products. The group is currently focused on acquiring existing libraries of motion pictures and television programming for film production and DVD distribution. The group's entertainment products include theatrical motion pictures, television programs, home video products, and digitally delivered entertainment and media.

Primary SIC and add'l.: 7812

CIK No: 0001094365

Subsidiaries: International Media Acquisition Group LLC, Montecristo Entertainment LLC

InterOil Corp

25025 I-45 N, Ste. 420, The Woodlands, TX, 77380; **PH:** 1-281-292-1800; **Fax:** 1-281-292-0888; http:// www.interoil.com

General - Incorporation	Canada	**Stock**- Price on:12/24/2007	NA
Employees	295	Stock Exchange	AMEX
Auditor	PricewaterhouseCoopers LLP	Ticker Symbol	IOC
Stk Agt	Computershare Trust Co of Canada	Outstanding Shares	NA
Counsel	NA	E.P.S	NA
DUNS No.	NA	Shareholders	NA

Business: The groups principle activity is to provide oil and gas exploration services. The group operates through four business segments namely exploration and production, refining, marketing and liquefaction, wholesale and retail distribution, and corporate. The group operates from Australia.

Primary SIC and add'l.: 9999

CIK No: 0001221715

Officers: Phil E. Mulacek/Chmn., CEO, Christian M. Vinson/Dir., Exec. VP, Head - Corporate Development, Government Affairs, Peter Diezmann/GM - Downstream, Gerry Gilbert/GM - Upstream Exploration, Anesti Dermedgoglou/VP - Investor - Public Relations, William J. Jasper/COO, Pres., Anthony Poon/GM - Supply, Trading, Risk, Mark Laurie/General Counsel, Corp. Sec., Collin Visaggio/CFO

Directors: Phil E. Mulacek/Chmn., CEO, Gaylen J. Byker/Dir., Edward N. Speal/Dir., Roger N. Grundy/Dir., Christian M. Vinson/Dir., Exec. VP, Head - Corporate Development, Government Affairs, Donald R. Hansen/Dir.

Curr. Assets:	$201,715,000	**Curr. Liab.:**	$146,215,000		
Plant, Equip.:	$280,092,000	**Total Liab.:**	$375,069,000	**Indic. Yr. Divd.:**	NA
Total Assets:	$488,165,000	**Net Worth:**	$113,096,000	**Debt/ Equity:**	NA

Interpharm Holdings Inc

75 Adams Ave., Hauppauge, NY, 11788; **PH:** 1-631-952-0214; **Fax:** 1-631-952-9587; http:// www.interpharminc.com; **Email:** mail@interpharminc.com

General - Incorporation	DE	**Stock**- Price on:12/24/2007	$1.3699
Employees	500	Stock Exchange	AMEX
Auditor	Marcum & Kliegman LLP	Ticker Symbol	IPA
Stk Agt	North American Transfer Co	Outstanding Shares	65,810,000
Counsel	NA	E.P.S	-$0.26
DUNS No.	03-714-6495	Shareholders	NA

Business: The group's principal activities are to develop, manufacture and market generic prescription strength and over-the-counter pharmaceutical products. It currently manufactures and markets nineteen generic drug products in solid dosage form. All of the products that the group manufactures are of solid oral dosage form, consisting of tablets, caplets and capsules. The group sells its products under its own label and also through wholesalers and distributors who sell its products under their own labels. The group operates mostly in the United States of America.

Primary SIC and add'l.: 2834

CIK No: 0000893970

Subsidiaries: Innovative Business Micros, Inc., Interpharm Realty, LLC, Interpharm, Inc., Logix Solutions, Inc., Micro Computer Store, Inc., Saturn Chemical, LLC

Officers: Cameron Reid/CEO, Bhupatlal Sutaria/Pres., Raj M. Sutaria/Exec. VP, Jeffrey Weiss/Exec. VP - Sales, Marketing, Kenneth M. Cappel/Exec. VP, General Counsel, Jonathan Berlent/Sr. VP - Business Development, Peter Giallorenzo/CFO, COO, Exec. VP

Directors: Maganlal K. Sutaria/Chmn., David C. Reback/Dir., Stewart Benjamin/Dir., Kennith C. Johnson/Dir., Richard J. Miller/Dir., Joan P. Neuscheler/Dir.

Owners: David Reback, Maganlal K. Sutaria/1.86%, Kennith C. Johnson, Stewart Benjamin, Jeffrey Weiss, Richard J. Miller, Insiders/22.05%, Tullis Dickerson Capital Focus III, L.P./12.37%, Cameron Reid/4.59%, George Aronson, Peter Giallorenzo, Bhupatlal K. Sutaria/1.20%, Perry Sutaria/66.62%, P&K Holdings, LLC/12.11%, Joan P. Neuscheler/12.40% (20 Owners included in Index)

Financial Data: Fiscal Year End:06/30 Latest Annual Data: 6/30/2006

Year	Sales	Net Income
2006	$63,355,000	-$3,790,000
2005	$39,911,000	-$149,000
2004	$41,100,000	$3,123,000

Curr. Assets:	$26,993,000	**Curr. Liab.:**	$17,735,000		
Plant, Equip.:	$29,069,000	**Total Liab.:**	$31,812,000	**Indic. Yr. Divd.:**	NA
Total Assets:	$62,867,000	**Net Worth:**	$22,830,000	**Debt/ Equity:**	0.6945

Interphase Corp

2901 N Dallas Pkwy., Ste. 200, Plano, TX, 75093; **PH:** 1-214-654-5000; **Fax:** 1-214-654-5500; http:// www.iphase.com; **Email:** fastnet@iphase.com

General - Incorporation	TX	**Stock**- Price on:12/24/2007	$10.2
Employees	132	Stock Exchange	NDQ
Auditor	Grant Thornton LLP	Ticker Symbol	INPH
Stk Agt	Computershare Trust Co	Outstanding Shares	6,190,000
Counsel	Gardere, Wynne Sewell LLP	E.P.S	-$0.01
DUNS No.	07-933-8869	Shareholders	NA

Business: The group's principal activities are to design, develop, manufacture, market and support high-performance connectivity products. The group utilizes advanced technologies for next-generation telecommunication networks and enterprise data/storage networks. Products include telecom server communication controllers, server-based adapter cards, networks operating system device drivers, software development tools and management software applications. The products of the group are sold to OEM's for inclusion in scientific, industrial, medical, printing, graphics, engineering workstations, mini-supercomputer and other computer applications. The group has operations in Europe and Pacific Rim.

Primary SIC and add'l.: 3572 3672 3669

CIK No: 0000728249

Officers: Gregory B. Kalush/50/Chmn., CEO, Pres./$628,870.00, Thomas S. Thawley/66/Vice Chmn., Sec., Marc E. Devinney/VP - Engineering, Jim Gragg/VP - Operations, Fulfillment, Deborah Shute/VP - Human Resources, Administration, Thomas Tipton/CFO, VP - Finance, Treasurer/$390,300.00, Prasad Kallur/VP - Strategic Marketing/$269,750.00, Randall E. McComas/VP - Global Sales/$374,396.00, Don Fenyk/Sales Contact - North Eastern, Mid, Atlantic, Eastern Canada, Jim Bentley/Sales Contact - Western, S Central US, Western Canada, Andrew Treherne/Sales Contact - Asia, The Pac Rim, Harri Rajaniemi/Sales Contact - Northern Europe, William Kerkmeijer/Sales Contact - Central Europe, Patrick Meghnagi/Sales Contact - Southern Europe, Julie Parenzan/Contact - Media Relations, Public Relations (16 Officers included in Index)

Directors: Gregory B. Kalush/50/Chmn., CEO, Pres., Thomas S. Thawley/66/Vice Chmn., Sec., Christopher B. Strunk/59/Dir., Kenneth V. Spenser/58/Dir., Michael J. Myers/60/Dir., Paul N. Hug/63/Dir.

Owners: Randall E. McComas/3.30%, Kenneth V. Spenser, Paul N. Hug, Gregory B. Kalush/9.10%, Thomas N. Tipton, Prasad R. Kallur, Deborah A. Shute/2.50%, Insiders/24.60%, Royce & Associates, LLC/9.20%, James W. Gragg/1.40%, Felix V. Diaz/4.40%, Thomas S. Thawley/4.90%, Michael J. Myers

Financial Data: Fiscal Year End:12/31 Latest Annual Data: 12/31/2006

Year	Sales	Net Income
2006	$33,403,000	$2,086,000
2005	$30,852,000	-$2,299,000
2004	$35,015,000	$1,718,000

Curr. Assets:	$31,573,000	**Curr. Liab.:**	$4,677,000		
Plant, Equip.:	$976,000	**Total Liab.:**	$8,262,000	**Indic. Yr. Divd.:**	NA
Total Assets:	$34,062,000	**Net Worth:**	$25,800,000	**Debt/ Equity:**	NA

Interplay Entertainment Corp

100 N Crescent Dr., Beverly Hills, CA, 90210; **PH:** 1-310-432-1958; http:// www.interplay.com; **Email:** investor-relations@interplay.com

General - Incorporation	DE	**Stock**- Price on:12/24/2007	$0.08
Employees	6	Stock Exchange	OTC
Auditor	Jeffrey S. Gilbert	Ticker Symbol	IPLY
Stk Agt	U.S. Stock Transfer Corp	Outstanding Shares	99,200,000
Counsel	Stubb Alderton & Markiles	E.P.S	$0.06
DUNS No.	13-927-9251	Shareholders	NA

Business: The group's principle activities include developing and publishing interactive entertainment software for core gamers and mass market. The group develops interactive software for personal computers and video game consoles. The group holds licenses to use brands such as advanced dungeons and dragons, matrix, star trek and caesars palace. The products of the group are compatible with microsoft windows for personal computer platform and for video game consoles such as the sony playstation. The group operates from United States.

Primary SIC and add'l.: 7372

CIK No: 0001057232

Subsidiaries: Gamesonline.Com Inc., Interplay Japan K.K., Interplay OEM Inc., Interplay Productions Ltd.

Officers: Herve Caen/CEO, Interim CFO

Directors: Eric Caen/Dir., Michel Welter/Dir.

Owners: Eric Caen, Herve Caen/14.20%, Titus Interactive SA/56.30%, Michel Welter, Insiders/4.70%

Financial Data: Fiscal Year End:12/31 Latest Annual Data: 12/31/2006

Year	Sales	Net Income
2006	$967,000	$3,079,000
2005	$7,158,000	$5,928,000
2004	$13,197,000	-$4,730,000

Curr. Assets:	$312,000	**Curr. Liab.:**	$8,410,000	**P/E Ratio:**	2.00
Plant, Equip.:	$3,000	**Total Liab.:**	$8,410,000	**Indic. Yr. Divd.:**	NA
Total Assets:	$323,000	**Net Worth:**	-$8,087,000	**Debt/ Equity:**	NA

Interpublic Group of Companies Inc

1114 Ave. of the Americas, New York, NY, 10036; **PH:** 1-212-704-1200; **Fax:** 1-212-704-1201; http:// www.interpublic.com

General - Incorporation	DE	**Stock**- Price on:12/24/2007	$11.79
Employees	42,000	Stock Exchange	NYSE
Auditor	PricewaterhouseCoopers LLP	Ticker Symbol	IPG
Stk Agt	Mellon Investor Services LLC	Outstanding Shares	468,890,000
Counsel	NA	E.P.S	$0.10
DUNS No.	00-698-5790	Shareholders	NA

Business: The group's principle activity is to provide advertising, specialized marketing and communication services. The group also provides direct marketing, database and customer relationship management, public relations, sales promotion and event marketing. The group operates from United States.

Primary SIC and add'l.: 7311

CIK No: 0000051644

Subsidiaries: 021 Limited, 10 Media, Ltd., 1995 Ventures Ltd., 20/80 , 3707822 Canada Inc., A.t.m.z. Holding Company Ltd, ACAM, Acclaro International Limited, Acclaro International Sarl, Acts & Artists Entertainment Gmbh, Ad Fabrika Fcb Sp. Zo. O., Adair Greene, Inc., Addition Communications Limited, Addition Marketing Group Limited, Aderal S.a. 1209 Subsidiaries included in the Index

Officers: Michael I. Roth/Chmn., CEO/$7,174,680.00, Marjorie Altschuler/Exec. VP, Chief Growth Officer, Bant Breen/Sr. VP, Dir. - Strategic Development, Innovation, Christopher F. Carroll/Sr. VP, Controller, Chief Accounting Officer, Stephen Gatfield/Exec. VP - Strategy, Network Operations/$2,671,482.00, Frank Mergenthaler/CFO, Exec. VP/$2,854,151.00, Frank Guglielmo/Sr. VP - Leadership, Organizational Development, Nicholas J. Camera/Sr. VP, General Counsel, Sec., Joseph W. Farrelly/CIO, Sr. VP, Richard J. Haray/Sr. VP - Corporate Services, Jerome J. Leshne/Sr. VP - Investor Relations, Terry Peigh/MD, Sr. VP, Ellen T. Johnson/Sr. VP, Treasurer, Jonathan B. Burleigh/Sr. VP - Finance, DevelopmentSr. VP - Finance, Development, Philippe Krakowsky/Exec. VP - Strategy, Corporate Relations/$1,558,842.00 *(22 Officers included in Index)*

Directors: Michael I. Roth/Chmn., CEO, Frank J. Borelli/Dir., Jill M. Considine/Dir., Richard A. Goldstein/Dir., John H. Greeniaus/Dir., Phillip J. Samper/Dir., David M. Thomas/Dir., Jocelyn Carter-Miller/Dir., William T. Kerr/Dir., Reginald K. Brack/Dir.

Owners: Phillip J. Samper, William T. Kerr, Philippe Krakowsky, Jill M. Considine, Lord Abbett & Co. LLC, Reginald K. Brack, Richard A. Goldstein, Frank Mergenthaler, Franklin Resources, Inc., Insiders, John H. Greeniaus, Stephen A. Gatfield, AXA Financial, Inc., ClearBridge Advisors, LLC, David M. Thomas *(22 Owners included in Index)*

Financial Data: **Fiscal Year End:** 12/31 **Latest Annual Data:** 12/31/2006

Year	Sales	Net Income
2006	$6,190,800,000	-$31,700,000
2005	$6,274,300,000	-$262,900,000
2004	$6,387,000,000	-$538,400,000

Curr. Assets:	$7,208,800,000	**Curr. Liab.:**	$6,663,000,000	**P/E Ratio:**	117.90
Plant, Equip.:	$624,000,000	**Total Liab.:**	$9,877,000,000	**Indic. Yr. Divd.:**	NA
Total Assets:	$11,864,100,000	**Net Worth:**	$1,940,600,000	**Debt/ Equity:**	1.0093

Intersections Inc

PO Box 222455, Chantilly, VA, 20153; ***PH:*** 1-703-488-6100; ***Fax:*** 1-703-488-6223; ***http://*** www.intersections.com; ***Email:*** info@intersections.com

General - Incorporation	DE	**Stock** - Price on:12/24/2007	$9.83
Employees	888	Stock Exchange	NDQ
Auditor	Deloitte & Touche LLP	Ticker Symbol	INTX
Stk Agt	American Stock Transfer & Trust Co.	Outstanding Shares	17,120,000
Counsel	NA	E.P.S.	$0.13
DUNS No.	NA	Shareholders	NA

Business: The group's principal activity is to provide identity theft protection and credit management services on a subscription basis to its subscribers. The group's services include daily, monthly or quarterly monitoring of its subscribers' credit files. It also offers credit score analysis tools, credit education, a consumer fraud resource center and identity theft cost coverage. At 31- dec-2003, group had 25 clients, and an additional 39 financial and other companies, offering its services. Company became publicly held on 29-Apr-2004.

Primary SIC and add'l.: 7374

CIK No: 0001095277

Officers: Michael R. Stanfield/Chmn., CEO/$1,205,034.00, George K. Tsantes/CTO, Exec. VP/$511,033.00, Neal Dittersdorf/Exec. VP, Chief Legal Officer/$542,581.00, Tammy Gregory/Executive Assist., Madalyn Behneman/Principal Financial Officer, Sr. VP - Finance, Accounting/$230,282.00, Steven Schwartz/Exec. VP - Endorsed Credit, Security Sales/$312,261.00, John G. Scanlon/Exec. VP - Strategic Growth

Directors: Michael R. Stanfield/Chmn., CEO, Thomas G. Amato/Dir., Thomas L. Kempner/Dir., David A. McGough/Dir., Norman N. Mintz/Dir., Steven F. Piaker/Dir., William J. Wilson/Dir., James L. Kempner/Dir.

Owners: Kenneth D. Schwarz, Insiders, Norman N. Mintz, David A. McGough, Thomas L. Kempner, James L. Kempner, William J. Wilson, Madalyn Behneman, Thomas G. Amato, Conning Capital Partners V, L.P., Steven Schwartz, Neal Dittersdorf, Michael R. Stanfield, Heartland Advisors, Inc., George K. Tsantes *(17 Owners included in Index)*

Financial Data: **Fiscal Year End:** 12/31 **Latest Annual Data:** 12/31/2006

Year	Sales	Net Income
2006	$201,051,000	$9,436,000
2005	$165,171,000	$12,470,000
2004	$152,916,000	$10,945,000

Curr. Assets:	$68,292,000	**Curr. Liab.:**	$41,434,000	**P/E Ratio:**	33.90
Plant, Equip.:	$21,699,000	**Total Liab.:**	$63,441,000	**Indic. Yr. Divd.:**	NA
Total Assets:	$179,467,000	**Net Worth:**	$104,576,000	**Debt/ Equity:**	0.1123

Intersil Corp

1001 Murphy Ranch Rd., Milpitas, CA, 95035; ***PH:*** 1-408-432-8888; ***Fax:*** 1-408-434-5351; ***http://*** www.intersil.com

General - Incorporation	DE	**Stock** - Price on:12/24/2007	$32.22
Employees	1,423	Stock Exchange	NDQ
Auditor	KPMG LLP	Ticker Symbol	ISIL
Stk Agt	American Stock Transfer & Trust Co.	Outstanding Shares	135,140,000
Counsel	NA	E.P.S.	$1.02
DUNS No.	NA	Shareholders	NA

Business: The group's principal activities are to design and manufacture analog integrated circuits. The products are organized into four end market categories: high-end consumer, computing, communications and industrial products. The high-end consumer products include optical storage and video display products and handheld power management products. The computing products include desktop, server and notebook power management, including core power devices and other peripheral applications. The communications products include line drivers and broadband and hot plug power management products. The industrial products include the elantec family of operational amplifiers, bridge driver power management products and other standard analog products. The products are sold in the United States, China, Taiwan, Japan, Germany, Singapore, Korea, Thailand, Malaysia and the United Kingdom. On 28-Aug-2003, the group sold the assets of the wireless networking products group.

Primary SIC and add'l.: 3669 3674 6719 7373

CIK No: 0001096325

Subsidiaries: Analog Integration Partners, LLC, Elantec Semiconductor Malaysia Sdn. Bhd., Elantec Semiconductor U.K. Limited, Elantec Semiconductor, Inc., Intersil (FL), LLC, Intersil Advanced Technology (Labuan) Ltd., Intersil Americas Inc., Intersil China Limited, Intersil Communications, Inc., Intersil Europe Sarl, Intersil GmbH, Intersil Holding GmbH, Intersil Investment Company, Intersil K. K., Intersil Limited 31 Subsidiaries included in the Index

Officers: Rich Beyer/Dir., CEO/$5,023,291.00, Michael Althar/VP, GM, Masato Nozaki/Contact - Public Relations, Japan, Steve Rowley/Contact - Public Relations, Europe, David A. Zinsner/CFO, VP/$1,062,019.00, Rajeeva Lahri/CTO/$1,515,850.00, Vern Kelley/VP - Human Resources, Terry Brophy/VP - Information Technology, Susan Hardman/VP, GM, Peter Oaklander/Sr. VP - Worldwide Sales/$716,027.00, Tom Tokos/VP, General Counsel, Sec./$988,709.00, Davin Lee/VP, GM, Andrew Rhind/VP, GM, Paul Sferrazza/VP, GM, David B. Bell/Dir., COO, Pres. *(20 Officers included in Index)*

Directors: Rich Beyer/Dir., CEO, Gary E. Gist/Chmn., Robert Conn/Dir., Jan Peeters/Dir., James A. Urry/Dir., Greg Lang/Dir., David B. Bell/Dir., COO, Pres., Mercedes Johnson/Dir., Robert Pokelwaldt/Dir., James V. Diller/Dir.

Owners: Insiders/3.30%, T. Rowe Price Associates, Inc./6.10%, James V. Diller, Richard M. Beyer/1.80%, Peter Oaklander, Mercedes Johnson, Rajeeva Lahri, Capital Research and Management Company/8.70%, FMR Corporation/12.80%, Gary Gist, Thomas Tokos, Robert Conn, David Zinsner, Jan Peeters, James A. Urry *(17 Owners included in Index)*

Financial Data: **Fiscal Year End:** 12/30 **Latest Annual Data:** 12/29/2006

Year	Sales	Net Income
2006	$740,597,000	$151,877,000
2005	$600,255,000	$85,877,000
2004	$535,775,000	$40,681,000

Curr. Assets:	$755,192,000	**Curr. Liab.:**	$148,167,000	**P/E Ratio:**	29.56
Plant, Equip.:	$101,354,000	**Total Liab.:**	$148,167,000	**Indic. Yr. Divd.:**	$0.400
Total Assets:	$2,587,570,000	**Net Worth:**	$2,439,403,000	**Debt/ Equity:**	NA

Interstate Hotels & Resorts Inc

4501 N Fairfax Dr., Arlington, VA, 22203; ***PH:*** 1-703-387-3100; ***Fax:*** 1-703-543-0633; ***http://*** www.ihrco.com

General - Incorporation	DE	**Stock** - Price on:12/24/2007	$5.8
Employees	25,500	Stock Exchange	NYSE
Auditor	KPMG LLP	Ticker Symbol	IHR
Stk Agt	Computershare Investor Services LLC	Outstanding Shares	31,650,000
Counsel	NA	E.P.S.	$0.99
DUNS No.	03-550-8816	Shareholders	NA

Business: The group's principal activity is to manage, lease, operate a portfolio of hospitality properties and provide related services in the hotel, corporate housing, resort and golf markets. The group's portfolio is diversified by franchise and brand affiliations. As of Dec 31, 2003, the group managed 295 hotels with 65,250 rooms in 41 states, the district of columbia, Canada and Russia. The group has approximately 2,884 apartments under lease in the United States, Canada, France and the United Kingdom. The group's hotels are operated under nationally recognized brand names such as hilton, sheraton, westin, radisson, marriott, doubletree, embassy suites and holiday inn.

Primary SIC and add'l.: 7011 6519

CIK No: 0001059341

Subsidiaries: AGH Leasing, L.P., Albuquerque Beverage Management, Inc., Anchorage Linen Service, a Joint Venture, Apalachee Bay SAS, Beaumont ABC Corporation, BoyStar Ventures, L.P., BridgeStreet Accommodations, Ltd., BridgeStreet California, LLC, BridgeStreet Canada, LLC, BridgeStreet Colorado, LLC, BridgeStreet Corporate Housing Worldwide, Inc., BridgeStreet London, Ltd., BridgeStreet Maryland, LLC, BridgeStreet Midwest, LLC, BridgeStreet Minneapolis, LLC 137 Subsidiaries included in the Index

Officers: Thomas F. Hewitt/Dir., CEO/$1,271,562.00, Thomas J. Bardenett/Exec. VP - Crossroads, Denis S. McCarthy/Chief Accounting Officer, Evan A. Studer/Exec. VP - Operations Sunstone Hotel Properties, Inc, Bruce Riggins/CFO/$951,212.00, Leslie Ng/Chief Investment Officer, Keith Clampet/Exec. VP - Hotel Operations, Joseph A. Klam/Exec. VP - Finance, Henry L. Ciaffone/Pres. - International Operations, Development, Christopher L. Bennett/Exec. VP, General Counsel/$457,043.00, Samuel E. Knighton/Pres. - Hotel Operations/$603,225.00, C. A. Anderson/Exec. VP - Development, Acquisitions, George J. Brennan/Exec. VP - Sales, Marketing

Directors: Thomas F. Hewitt/Dir., CEO, Paul W. Whetsell/Chmn., Leslie R. Doggett/Dir., John J. Russell/Dir., Ronald W. Allen/Dir., Eric H. Bolton/Dir., James F. Dannhauser/Dir., James B. McCurry/Dir., Joseph J. Flannery/Dir., Karim J. Alibhai/Dir.

Owners: Paul W. Whetsell, Bruce A. Riggins, Dimensional FundAdvisors, Inc./6.56%, John J. Russell, Renaissance Technologies Corp/6.04%, James B. McCurry, Leslie R. Doggett, James F. Dannhauser, American Century Companies/5.16%, Samuel E. Knighton, Christopher L. Bennett, Bear Stearns Asset Management, Inc./6.20%, Insiders/4.19%, Thomas F. Hewitt, Joseph J. Flannery/1.05% *(18 Owners included in Index)*

Financial Data: **Fiscal Year End:** 12/31 **Latest Annual Data:** 12/31/2006

Year	Sales	Net Income
2006	$975,165,000	$29,779,000
2005	$1,116,242,000	$12,877,000
2004	$944,043,000	-$5,663,000

Curr. Assets:	$95,748,000	**Curr. Liab.:**	$84,461,000	**P/E Ratio:**	4.14
Plant, Equip.:	$103,895,000	**Total Liab.:**	$166,478,000	**Indic. Yr. Divd.:**	NA
Total Assets:	$333,690,000	**Net Worth:**	$166,696,000	**Debt/ Equity:**	0.7722

Interstate Power & Light Co

PO Box 77007, Madison, WI, 53707; ***PH:*** 1-319-786-4411; ***Fax:*** 1-608-314-8938; ***http://*** www.alliantenergy.com; ***Email:*** customercare@alliantenergy.com

General - Incorporation	IA	**Stock** - Price on:12/24/2007	$38.72
Employees	5,151	Stock Exchange	NYSE
Auditor	Deloitte & Touche LLP	Ticker Symbol	NA
Stk Agt	Alliant Energy Corp	Outstanding Shares	113,740,000
Counsel	NA	E.P.S.	$3.32
DUNS No.	00-694-0522	Shareholders	NA

Business: The group's principal activities are to generate, transmit, distribute and sell electric energy. The group also purchases, distributes, transmits and sells natural gas and provides steam services in selective markets in Iowa. Operations of the group are divided into three segments: electric utility, gas utility and steam and other utility services. At 31-Dec-2003, the group supplied electric services to 528,977 customers and gas service to 235,812 customers.

Primary SIC and add'l.: 4924 4961 4931

CIK No: 0000052485

Subsidiaries: Alliant Energy Holdings do Brasil Limitada, Alliant Energy International, Inc., Alliant Energy Resources, Inc., Interstate Power and Light Company, Wisconsin Power and Light Company, WPL Transco LLC

Officers: Thomas L. Aller/Pres.

Directors: Michael L. Bennett/54/Dir., Darryl B. Hazel/60/Dir., Singleton B. McAllister/56/Dir., Ann K. Newhall/57/Dir., Dean C. Oestreich/56/Dir., David A. Perdue/58/Dir., Judith D. Pyle/65/Dir., Carol P. Sanders/41/Dir.

Financial Data: *Fiscal Year End:*12/31 *Latest Annual Data:* 12/31/2006

Year	Sales	Net Income
2006	$3,359,400,000	$315,700,000
2005	$3,279,600,000	-$7,700,000
2004	$2,958,700,000	$145,500,000

Curr. Assets:	$1,173,800,000	**Curr. Liab.:**	$1,102,100,000	**P/E Ratio:**	11.88
Plant, Equip.:	$4,944,900,000	**Total Liab.:**	$4,184,100,000	**Indic. Yr. Divd.:**	$1.270
Total Assets:	$7,084,100,000	**Net Worth:**	$2,895,100,000	**Debt/ Equity:**	0.5054

Intertape Polymer Group Inc

3647 Cortez Rd. W, Bradenton, FL, 34210; ***PH:*** 1-941-727-5788; ***Fax:*** 1-941-727-1568; ***http://*** www.intertapepolymer.com; ***Email:*** info@itape.com

General - Incorporation	Canada	**Stock** - Price on:12/24/2007	$4.73
Employees	2,700	Stock Exchange	NYSE
Auditor	Raymond Chabot Grant Thornton LLP	Ticker Symbol	ITP
Stk Agt	Mellon Trust Co	Outstanding Shares	40,990,000
Counsel	Mr. Richards	E.P.S.	-$0.558
DUNS No.	24-902-5305	Shareholders	NA

Business: The group's principle activities include developing, manufacturing, and selling polyolefin plastic, paper packaging products and complementary packaging systems. The products of the company include: intertape, acrylic and natural rubber pressure-sensitive carton sealing tapes, hvac tape and automotive high performance tapes. The other products of the company are: exlfilm, stretchflex, case erectors, shrink packaging, ink jet printers and labeling systems. As at 31-12-2001 the company operates in 23 locations. The group operates from United States.

Primary SIC and add'l.: 2671 2891

CIK No: 0000880224

Subsidiaries: 4273460 Canada Inc., Central Products Company, Fibope Portuguesa-Filmes Biorientados S.A., Flexia Corporation Ltd., Flexia L.P., Intertape Polymer Corp., Intertape Polymer Group Inc., Intertape Polymer Inc., Intertape Polymer US Inc., Intertape Woven Products Services S.A. de C.V., Ipg (us) Holdings Inc., Ipg (us) Inc., IPG Administrative Services Inc., IPG Financial Services Inc., IPG Holding Company of Nova Scotia 18 Subsidiaries included in the Index

Officers: Melbourne F. Yull/Chmn., CEO, Dale H. McSween/Dir., Interim CEO, Sec., Jim Bob Carpenter/Exec. VP - Global Sourcing, Andrew M. Archibald/CFO, Burgess H. Hildreth/VP - Human Resources, Gregory A. Yull/Pres. - Distribution Products, Victor Ditommaso/VP - Finance, Treasurer

Directors: Melbourne F. Yull/Chmn., CEO, Dale H. McSween/Dir., Interim CEO, Sec., Michael L. Richards/Chmn., Ben J. Davenport/Dir., Robbie L. Shaw/Dir., John E. Richardson/Dir., Gordon R. Cunningham/Dir., Thomas E. Costello/Dir.

Financial Data: *Fiscal Year End:*12/31 *Latest Annual Data:* 12/31/2006

Year	Sales	Net Income
2006	$812,285,000	-$166,693,000
2005	$801,844,000	$28,056,000
2004	$692,449,000	$12,739,000

Curr. Assets:	$221,468,000	**Curr. Liab.:**	$101,210,000		
Plant, Equip.:	$322,867,000	**Total Liab.:**	$426,569,000	**Indic. Yr. Divd.:**	NA
Total Assets:	$692,127,000	**Net Worth:**	$265,558,000	**Debt/ Equity:**	NA

Intervest Bancshares Corp

1 Rockefeller Plz., Ste. 400, New York, NY, 10020; ***PH:*** 1-212-218-8383; ***Fax:*** 1-212-218-8390; ***http://*** www.intervestnatbank.com

General - Incorporation	DE	**Stock** - Price on:12/24/2007	$26.07
Employees	72	Stock Exchange	NDQ
Auditor	Hacker, Johnson & Smith P.A, P.C	Ticker Symbol	IBCA
Stk Agt	Bank of New York	Outstanding Shares	8,480,000
Counsel	Emmet, Marvin & Martin	E.P.S.	$2.52
DUNS No.	83-542-9861	Shareholders	NA

Business: The group's principal activities are to provide various banking services to small and medium market businesses and individuals. The operations are conducted through the wholly owned subsidiaries, intervest national bank, intervest mortgage corporation and intervest statutory trust i. The services rendered by the group include acceptance of deposits, lending of loans and provision of Internet banking services. The deposits accepted by the group include certificates of deposit, individual retirement accounts, other time deposits, checking and other demand deposit accounts, now accounts, savings and money market accounts. The loans offered by the group include real estate loans, which primarily includes loans for commercial and multifamily properties and commercial and consumer loans.

Primary SIC and add'l.: 6712 6021

CIK No: 0000927807

Subsidiaries: Intervest Mortgage Corporation, Intervest National Bank, Intervest Securities Corporation, Intervest Statutory Trust I, Intervest Statutory Trust II, Intervest Statutory Trust III, Intervest Statutory Trust IV

Officers: Lowell S. Dansker/57/Chmn., CEO/$720,448.00, Stephen A. Helman/68/Dir., VP, Sec./$210,038.00, John J. Arvonio/45/CFO, Chief Accounting Officer/$209,764.00

Directors: Lowell S. Dansker/57/Chmn., CEO, Lawton Swan/65/Dir., Paul R. Derosa/66/Dir., Stephen A. Helman/68/Dir., VP, Sec., Keith A. Olsen/Dir., Raymond C. Sullivan/Dir., Michael A. Callen/67/Dir., Wayne F. Holly/51/Dir., David J. Willmott/69/Dir., Wesley T. Wood/64/Dir.

Owners: Insiders/14.93%, Insiders, Helene D. Bergman/4.95%, Wesley T. Wood, Thomas E. Willett, Wayne F. Holly, Estate of Jerome Dansker/8.38%, David J. Willmott/1.24%, Lowell S. Dansker, Paul R. DeRosa, Michael A. Callen, Estate of Jerome Dansker, Raymond C. Sullivan, Lowell S. Dansker/11.62%, Lawton Swan *(18 Owners included in Index)*

Financial Data: *Fiscal Year End:*12/31 *Latest Annual Data:* 12/31/2006

Year	Sales	Net Income
2006	$135,460,000	$23,531,000
2005	$104,475,000	$18,184,000
2004	$71,689,000	$11,453,000

Curr. Assets:	$36,178,000	**Curr. Liab.:**	$1,635,253,000	**P/E Ratio:**	10.30
Plant, Equip.:	$6,379,000	**Total Liab.:**	$1,801,707,000	**Indic. Yr. Divd.:**	$0.250
Total Assets:	$1,971,753,000	**Net Worth:**	$170,046,000	**Debt/ Equity:**	0.9571

Intervest Mortgage Corp

1 Rockefeller Plz., Ste. 400, New York, NY, 10020; ***PH:*** 1-212-218-8383; ***Fax:*** 1-212-218-8390; ***http://*** www.intervestnatbank.com

General - Incorporation	NY	**Stock** - Price on:12/24/2007	NA
Employees	69	Stock Exchange	NA
Auditor	Hacker, Johnson & Smith P.A, P.C	Ticker Symbol	NA
Stk Agt	American Stock Transfer & Trust Co.	Outstanding Shares	NA
Counsel	NA	E.P.S.	NA
DUNS No.	NA	Shareholders	NA

Business: The group's principal activity is to provide real estate business including origination and purchase of real estate mortgage loans. Real estate mortgage loans provided by the group include first mortgage, junior mortgage and wraparound mortgage loans. The lending activities of the group are concentrated in the New York city, Connecticut, Florida, New Jersey, Pennsylvania, North Carolina, Washington dc, Georgia and Virginia.

Primary SIC and add'l.: 6162

CIK No: 0000835955

Subsidiaries: Intervest Realty Servicing Corporation

Intervia Inc

3702 S Virginia St., Ste. G12 - 401, Reno, NV, 89502; ***PH:*** 1-702-989-5429

General - Incorporation	NV	**Stock** - Price on:12/24/2007	NA
Employees	NA	Stock Exchange	OTC
Auditor	Dale Matheson Carr-hilton Labonte LLP	Ticker Symbol	ITVA
Stk Agt	NA	Outstanding Shares	NA
Counsel	NA	E.P.S.	NA
DUNS No.	NA	Shareholders	NA

Business: The groups principal activities include developing fuel cell technology and producing fuel cells. The group operates from Canada and the United States.

Primary SIC and add'l.: 7380

CIK No: 0001353633

Officers: Glenn Morimoto/Dir., CEO, CFO, Pres.

Directors: Glenn Morimoto/Dir., CEO, CFO, Pres.

Intervoice Inc

17811 Waterview Pkwy., Dallas, TX, 75252; ***PH:*** 1-972-454-8000; ***Fax:*** 1-972-454-8707; ***http://*** www.intervoice.com

General - Incorporation	TX	**Stock** - Price on:12/24/2007	$7.92
Employees	768	Stock Exchange	NDQ
Auditor	Ernst & Young LLP	Ticker Symbol	INTV
Stk Agt	Computershare Investor Services LLC	Outstanding Shares	38,840,000
Counsel	NA	E.P.S.	-$0.06
DUNS No.	84-800-5518	Shareholders	NA

Business: The group's principal activity is to provide converged voice and data solutions for the telecommunication carrier and enterprise markets. The group offers enterprises and networks carriers a flexible, scalable integration platform, a powerful application development environment and comprehensive services. It has created business solutions that promote customer profitability and satisfaction with demonstrable return on investment. The group also operates a portfolio of operations support services, including maintenance programs, technical support, monitoring and surveillance and disaster recovery services. The operations of the group are carried on in Europe, the Middle East, South America and Asia-Pacific. It has deployed enhanced network systems and services in over 50 countries to over 200 service providers including british telecom (including bt cellnet, now o2), deutsche telecom (Germany), etb (Colombia), ar-tec (U.S.) and others.

Primary SIC and add'l.: 7373

CIK No: 0000764244

Subsidiaries: Brite Voice Systems, Inc, Edify Corporation, Edify EMEA Limited, Edify Holding Corporation, Edify Ireland Limited, Intervoice GP, Inc, Intervoice LP, Inc., Intervoice Ltd.

Officers: Robert E. Ritchey/61/Dir., CEO, Pres./$1,584,149.00, Dean C. Howell/51/Sr. VP, General Counsel, Sec., Don H. Brown/52/Sr. VP - Human Resources, Real Estate, Craig E. Holmes/51/CFO, Exec. VP/$560,745.00, Michael J. Polcyn/50/CTO, Sr. VP - Research, Development, James A. Milton/47/COO, Exec. VP/$735,865.00, Kenneth A. Goldberg/44/Sr. VP - Marketing, Alliances, Corporate Development/$374,434.00, Francis G. Sherlock/47/MD, Sr. VP - EMEA/$473,440.00, Andrea Holko/Sr. VP - Global Consulting, Walter Megura/Sr. VP - America Sales

Directors: Robert E. Ritchey/61/Dir., CEO, Pres., David W. Brandenburg/63/Chmn., Michael J. Willner/50/Vice Chmn., Daniel D. Hammond/56/Vice Chmn., Timothy W. Harris/50/Dir., George C. Platt/67/Dir., Gerald Montry/69/Dir., Don Reed/63/Dir.

Owners: Robert E. Ritchey/2.49%, Kenneth A. Goldberg, George C. Platt, Timothy W. Harris, Craig E. Holmes, BlackRock, Inc/10.43%, David W. Brandenburg/3.68%, James A. Milton, Daniel D. Hammond/1.29%, Master Value Opportunities Trust/8.27%, Francis G. Sherlock, Donald B. Reed, Franklin Resources, Inc/5.93%, Insiders/11.87%, Gerald F. Montry

Financial Data: *Fiscal Year End:*02/28 *Latest Annual Data:* 2/28/2007

Year	Sales	Net Income
2007	$196,345,000	-$1,697,000
2006	$168,103,000	$16,489,000
2005	$183,258,000	$22,510,000

Curr. Assets:	$87,690,000	**Curr. Liab.:**	$65,381,000		
Plant, Equip.:	$34,429,000	**Total Liab.:**	$65,381,000	**Indic. Yr. Divd.:**	NA
Total Assets:	$168,565,000	**Net Worth:**	$103,184,000	**Debt/ Equity:**	NA

Interwoven Inc

160 E Tasman Dr., San Jose, CA, 95134; *PH:* 1-408-774-2000; *Fax:* 1-408-774-2002; *http://* www.interwoven.com; *Email:* info@interwoven.com

General - Incorporation .... DE
Employees 744
Auditor .... Ernst & Young, LLP
Stk Agt...... American Stock Transfer & Trust Co.
Counsel .... Fenwick & West LLP
DUNS No. .... NA

Stock- Price on:12/24/2007 .... $13.66
Stock Exchange .... NDQ
Ticker Symbol .... IWOV
Outstanding Shares 43,580,000
E.P.S $0.37
Shareholders .... NA

Business: The group's principal activities are to provide products and services that automate the process of developing, managing and deploying content used in business applications. The product lines of the group are: content management, featuring teamsite which offers content management solutions; content intelligence, featuring metatagger which offers content intelligence services; content distribution, featuring opendeploy which offers content distribution services; enterprise application connectors suite, featuring teamportal which offers enterprise application connectivity and development suite, featuring teamcode which offers services to integrate interwoven products. The group also provides services, including professional services, maintenance and support.on 27-Jun-2003, the group acquired mediabin inc and in dec 2003, the group acquired component insights India private limited.

Primary SIC and add'l.: 7372 7376 7371 7375

CIK No: 0001042431

Subsidiaries: iManage GmbH, Interwoven AB, Interwoven Australia Pty. Ltd., Interwoven BV, Interwoven Canada Ltd., Interwoven GmbH, Interwoven Hong Kong Ltd., Interwoven Japan KK, Interwoven Korea Inc., Interwoven SARL, Interwoven Software Pte. Ltd., Interwoven Software Services India Private Limited, Interwoven Software SL, Interwoven Srl, Interwoven UK Ltd.

Officers: Joseph L. Cowan/Dir., CEO, David Nelson-Gal/Sr. VP - Engineering, Erik Hansen/Sr. VP, GM - EMEA, Max Carnecchia/Pres., John Calonico/Sr. VP - Finance, CFO, Ben Kiker/Sr. VP, Chief Marketing Officer, Steve Martello/Sr. VP - Client Services, Rafiq Mohammadi/CTO, Brian Andersen/VP - Corporate Development, Primary Investor Relations Officer

Directors: Joseph L. Cowan/Dir., CEO, Bob L. Corey/Chmn., Thomas L. Thomas/Dir., Frank J. Fanzilli/Dir., Ronald E.F. Codd/Dir., Roger J. Sippl/Dir., Charles M. Boesenberg/Dir.

Owners: Dimensional FundAdvisors LP/8.00%, Martin W. Brauns, Goldman Sachs Asset Management, L.P./11.30%, Thomas L. Thomas, David A. Nelson-Gal, Steven J. Martello, Ronald E. F. Codd, Scipio M. Carnecchia, Charles M. Boesenberg, Frank J. Fanzilli, John E. Calonico, Benjamin E. Kiker, Roger J. Sippl, Bob L. Corey, Insiders/4.70%

Financial Data: **Fiscal Year End:**12/31 **Latest Annual Data:** 12/31/2005

Year	Sales	Net Income
2005	$175,037,000	$617,000
2004	$160,388,000	-$23,667,000
2003	$111,512,000	-$47,531,000

Curr. Assets:	$173,934,000	**Curr. Liab.:**	$87,965,000	**P/E Ratio:**	195.14
Plant, Equip.:	$5,044,000	**Total Liab.:**	$100,407,000	**Indic. Yr. Divd.:**	NA
Total Assets:	$398,606,000	**Net Worth:**	$298,199,000	**Debt/ Equity:**	NA

inTEST Corp

7 Esterbrook Ln., Cherry Hill, NJ, 08003; *PH:* 1-856-424-6886; *Fax:* 1-856-751-1222; *http://* www.intest.com; *Email:* info@intest.com

General - Incorporation .... DE
Employees 224
Auditor .... KPMG LLP
Stk Agt .... EquiServe Trust Co N.A
Counsel .... Saul, Ewing, Remick & Saul
DUNS No. 05-151-5203

Stock- Price on:12/24/2007 .... $4.63
Stock Exchange .... NDQ
Ticker Symbol .... INTT
Outstanding Shares 9,410,000
E.P.S .... -$0.27
Shareholders .... NA

Business: The group's principal activities are to design, manufacture and market manipulator and docking hardware products, temperature management systems and tester interface products. The products of the group are used by semiconductor manufacturers in conjunction with automatic test equipment in the testing of integrated circuits. The products of the group are designed to improve the utilization and cost effectiveness of automatic test equipment. The group operates in the United States, the United Kingdom, Germany, Japan and Singapore. The customers of the group include ate manufacturers, agilent technologies, st microelectronics, cascade microtech and analog devices.

Primary SIC and add'l.: 3674 3643

CIK No: 0001036262

Subsidiaries: Temptronic Corporation, TEST GmbH, TEST Kabushiki Kaisha, TEST Limited, Test Pte, Ltd., TEST Silicon Valley Corporation, testlogic GmbH

Officers: Robert E. Matthiessen/Dir., Pres., CEO - Intest Corporation/$412,425.00, Daniel J. Graham/General Mgr. - Manipulator, Docking Product Segment Vice Chmn./$267,041.00, Dale Christman/General Mgr. - Tester Interface Product Segment/$203,909.00, James Pelrin/VP, General Mgr. - Temperature Management Product Segment/$259,717.00, Hugh T. Regan/Treasurer, Sec., CFO/$268,280.00, David Pasquale/Investor Relations Contact

Directors: Robert E. Matthiessen/Dir., Pres., CEO - Intest Corporation, Alyn R. Holt/Chmn., James W. Schwartz/Dir., James J. Greed/Dir., Thomas J. Reilly/Dir., Stuart F. Daniels/Dir.

Owners: FMR Corp./9.70%, Daniel J. Graham/2.20%, Thomas J. Reilly, Rutabaga Capital Management/16.90%, Robert E. Matthiessen/2.40%, James Pelrin, Alyn R. Holt/16.30%, Hugh T. Regan, James W. Schwartz, James J. Greed, Dale E. Christman, Stuart F. Daniels, Wasatch Advisors, Inc./10.50%, Insiders/23.30%

Financial Data: **Fiscal Year End:**12/31 **Latest Annual Data:** 12/31/2006

Year	Sales	Net Income
2006	$62,346,000	$2,871,000
2005	$53,359,000	-$3,620,000
2004	$71,211,000	$1,270,000

Curr. Assets:	$28,803,000	**Curr. Liab.:**	$8,410,000		
Plant, Equip.:	$3,328,000	**Total Liab.:**	$8,937,000	**Indic. Yr. Divd.:**	NA
Total Assets:	$35,759,000	**Net Worth:**	$26,822,000	**Debt/ Equity:**	0.0005

Intevac Inc

3560 Bassett St., Santa Clara, CA, 95054; *PH:* 1-408-986-9888; *Fax:* 1-408-988-8145; *http://* www.intevac.com

General - Incorporation .... CA
Employees 540
Auditor .... Grant Thornton LLP
Stk Agt .... EquiServe Trust Co N.A
Counsel .... Wilson Sonsini Goodrich & Rosati
DUNS No. 62-267-0529

Stock- Price on:12/24/2007 .... $20.08
Stock Exchange .... NDQ
Ticker Symbol .... IVAC
Outstanding Shares 21,390,000
E.P.S $2.34
Shareholders .... NA

Business: The group's principal activities are to design, manufacture and market complex capital equipment and to develop sensitive electro-optical devices and systems. The group operates in three segments: equipment products, photonics technology (ptd) and commercial imaging. Equipment division sells complex capital equipment used in the manufacturing of flat panel displays and thin-film disks and also designs ultra-high vacuum automated equipment for the manufacture of low-cost low-light level cameras. Photonics technology division develops devices and systems utilizing electron sources that permit highly sensitive detection of photons in the visible and the short-wave infrared spectrum. Commercial imaging division develops commercial products based on technology developed by ptd.

Primary SIC and add'l.: 3679 3861 3559

CIK No: 0001001902

Subsidiaries: Intevac Asia Private Limited, Intevac Foreign Sales Corporation, Intevac Limited, Intevac Malaysia Sdn Bhd, Intevac Shenzhen Co. Limited, IRPC, Inc., Lotus Technologies, Inc

Officers: Kevin Fairbairn/Dir., CEO, Pres./$2,142,084.00, Charles B. Eddy/Principal Accounting Officer, Sec., Treasurer, VP - Administration, Finance/$642,694.00, Luke Marusiak/COO/$644,815.00, Michael Barnes/CTO/$1,134,156.00, Ralph Kerns/VP - Business Development, Jeffrey Andreson/CFO, Treasurer, Sec., Joe Pietras/VP, GM - Imaging

Directors: Kevin Fairbairn/Dir., CEO, Pres., Norman H. Pond/Founder, Chmn., Robert Lemos/Dir., David S. Dury/Dir., Stanley J. Hill/Dir., Ping Yang/Dir.

Owners: Arthur L. Money, Ralph Kerns, Barclays Global Investors/5.60%, Robert Lemos, Insiders/6.40%, Norman H. Pond/3.70%, Ping Yang, David S. Dury, Charles B. Eddy, Kevin Fairbairn/1.10%, Michael Barnes, T. Rowe Price Associates, Inc/9.90%, Luke Marusiak, Stanley J. Hill

Financial Data: **Fiscal Year End:**12/31 **Latest Annual Data:** 12/31/2006

Year	Sales	Net Income
2006	$259,875,000	$46,698,000
2005	$137,229,000	$16,151,000
2004	$69,615,000	-$4,344,000

Curr. Assets:	$178,679,000	**Curr. Liab.:**	$60,618,000		
Plant, Equip.:	$13,546,000	**Total Liab.:**	$61,693,000	**Indic. Yr. Divd.:**	NA
Total Assets:	$206,003,000	**Net Worth:**	$144,310,000	**Debt/ Equity:**	NA

Intrado Inc

1601 Dry Creek Dr., Boulder Co, CO, 80503; ; *http://* www.intrado.com

General - Incorporation .... DE
Employees .... NA
Auditor .... PricewaterhouseCoopers LLP
Stk Agt .... Norwest Bank Minnesota, N.A.
Counsel .... NA
DUNS No. 13-086-6551

Stock- Price on:12/24/2007 .... NA
Stock Exchange .... NA
Ticker Symbol .... NA
Outstanding Shares .... NA
E.P.S .... NA
Shareholders .... NA

Business: The group's principal activity is to provide solutions for use by telecommunications providers and public safety organizations. The data managed by the group enables calls to be routed through the appropriate public safety answering point with timely information about the call. The group operates in three segments: wireline, wireless and new markets. The customers of the group include local exchange carriers, competitive local exchange carriers, wireless service providers and a wide variety of state, local, and federal government agencies. The group operates solely in the domestic market. On 20-Feb-2004, the group acquired bmd wireless ag.

Primary SIC and add'l.: 4813 7375

CIK No: 0000924505

Subsidiaries: bmd wireless AG, Intrado (XieAn) Technology (China) Co. Ltd, Intrado Communications Inc., Intrado Communications of Virginia Inc, Intrado International Ltd., Intrado International Singapore Pte. Ltd

Officers: George Heinrichs/Co - Founder, CEO, Pres., Stephen Meer/Co - Founder, CTO, Larry Jennings/COO, Craig W. Donaldson/Sr. VP - Regulatory Affairs, General Counsel, Mary Hester/Sr. VP - Business Operations, Nancy Casey/Corporate Controller, Michael D. Dingman/CFO, Teri Depuy/Sr. VP - Organizational Development, Alexis Braden/Public Relations Contact

Directors: George Heinrichs/Co - Founder, CEO, Pres., Stephen Meer/Co - Founder, CTO

IntraLase Corp

1700 E St. Andrew Pl., Santa Ana, CA, 92705; *PH:* 1-714-247-8200; *https://* www.intralase.com

General - Incorporation .... DE
Employees .... NA
Auditor .... Deloitte& Touche LLP
Stk Agt...... American Stock Transfer & Trust Co.
Counsel .... Meagher & Flom LLP
DUNS No. .... NA

Stock- Price on:12/24/2007 .... NA
Stock Exchange .... NA
Ticker Symbol .... NA
Outstanding Shares .... NA
E.P.S .... NA
Shareholders .... NA

Business: The groups principle activities include designing, developing and ultra-fast laser. The group products sold under the trade names IntraLase(R) FS Laser and IntraLASIK(R) software. The group operates from the United States of America, Asia Pacific, Europe and other.

Primary SIC and add'l.: 3845

CIK No: 0001163848

Subsidiaries: IntraLase Espana S.L.

Officers: Robert J. Palmisano/Dir., CEO, Pres., Charline Gauthier/COO, Exec. VP, Bernard P. Haffey/Exec. VP, Chief Commercial Officer, Shelley B. Thunen/CFO, Exec. VP, James A. Lightman/Sr. VP, General Counsel, Eric Weinberg/Sr. VP - Global Marketing, Greg Anderson/VP - US Sales, Paul Barros/VP - International Business Development, Michael Brownell/VP - Product Development, Michael Clemmons/VP - Business Process Management, Ted Devnew/VP - Corporate Accounting, Melinda Floros/VP - Customer Support, Kevin Harley/VP - Human Resources, Tibor Juhasz/46/CTO, VP, Stephen McCusker/VP - Supply Chain Management *(17 Officers included in Index)*

Directors: Robert J. Palmisano/Dir., CEO, Pres., William J. Link/Chmn., Michael Ball/Dir., Frank M. Fischer/Dir., Jay T. Holmes/Dir., Gilbert H. Kliman/Dir., Thomas S. Porter/Dir.

Owners: Frank M. Fischer, Insiders/17.63%, Waddell & Reed Financial, Inc./11.92%, Jay T. Holmes, Gilbert H. Kliman, Michael Ball, Brentwood Associates IX, L.P./7.12%, James A. Lightman, Shelley B. Thunen, William J. Link/7.66%, Charline Gauthier, Thomas S. Porter, Robert J. Palmisano/4.94%, Bernard P. Haffey

Intraop Medical Corp

570 Del Rey Ave., Sunnyvale, CA, 94086; *PH:* 1-408-636-1020; *http://* www.intraopmedical.com

General - Incorporation .... NV | **Stock**- Price on:12/24/2007 .... $0.27
Employees .... 21 | Stock Exchange .... OTC
Auditor Pohl, McNabola, Berg & Company, LLP | Ticker Symbol .... IOPM
Stk Agt .... Interwest Transfer Company, Inc. | Outstanding Shares 25,780,000
Counsel .... NA | E.P.S. .... -$0.33
DUNS No. .... NA | Shareholders .... NA

Business: The groups principle activities include developing, manufacturing, marketing and servicing the mobile electron beam system designed for intraoperative radiotherapy treatment of cancer, coronary, vascular restenosis and other medical applications. In March 2005, the group acquired Intraop Medical, Inc. The group operates from the United States and Europe.

Primary SIC and add'l.: 3845

CIK No: 0001120817

Subsidiaries: IMS Louisville, LLC, Intraop Medical Services, Inc

Officers: Donald A. Goer/Dir., CEO, Pres., John Powers/47/Dir., CEO, Pres., Howard Solovei/CFO, Richard Belford/VP - Quality Assurance, Regulatory Affairs, Theodore L. Phillips/Dir., Sec., Scott Mestman/VP - Sales, Marketing, Richard Simon/VP - Operations

Directors: Donald A. Goer/Dir., CEO, Pres., John Powers/47/Dir., CEO, Pres., Oliver Janssen/45/Chmn., John P. Matheu/Dir., Theodore L. Phillips/Dir., Sec., Michael Friebe/Dir., Keith Jacobsen/Dir., Stephen L. Kessler/Dir., Greg Koonsman/44/Dir., Rawleigh Ralls/46/Dir.

Owners: Insiders/16.52%, Oliver Janssen/5.01%, Scott J. Mestman/1.21%, Donald A. Goer/2.66%, Keith A. Jacobsen/0.27%, John P. Powers/0.35%, Stephen J. Kessler/0.07%, Greg Koonsman/6.18%, Howard Solovei/0.44%, Richard A. Belford/0.03%, Michael Friebe/0.23%, Richard A. Simon/0.07%

Financial Data: ***Fiscal Year End:***09/30 ***Latest Annual Data:*** 9/30/2006

Year	Sales	Net Income
2006	$5,983,000	-$7,160,000
2005	$3,835,000	-$5,721,000
2004	NA	-$31,000

Curr. Assets:	$7,122,000	**Curr. Liab.:**	$9,750,000		
Plant, Equip.:	$236,000	**Total Liab.:**	$13,063,000	**Indic. Yr. Divd.:**	NA
Total Assets:	$8,926,000	**Net Worth:**	-$4,137,000	**Debt/ Equity:**	NA

Intraware Inc

25 Orinda Way, Ste. 101, Orinda, CA, 94563; *PH:* 1-925-253-4500; *Fax:* 1-925-253-4599; *http://* www.intraware.com; *Email:* sales@intraware.com

General - Incorporation .... DE | **Stock**- Price on:12/24/2007 .... $4.79
Employees .... 47 | Stock Exchange .... NDQ
Auditor .... BDO Seidman, LLP | Ticker Symbol .... ITRA
Stk Agt ..... Computershare Investor Services LLC | Outstanding Shares 6,140,000
Counsel .... Wilson Sonsini Goodrich & Rosati | E.P.S. .... -$0.52
DUNS No. .... NA | Shareholders .... NA

Business: The group's principle activity is to provide electronic software delivery and management (esdm) solutions. These solutions help software publishers to reduce operational and support costs, increase customer satisfaction and retention, accelerate and strengthen software revenue recognition processes, and comply with U.S. Export regulations. It also offers complementary products and services, including enterprise software sales and marketing, and global Web-based content caching and delivery. The group markets its esdm services under the brand name 'subscribenet' to software companies on a subscription basis, charging a one-time implementation fee and a periodic service fee. Its major customers include sun microsystems and software spectrum inc. The group's total revenue for year 2007 was 10.87 millions of USD.

Primary SIC and add'l.: 7389 7372

CIK No: 0001025134

Subsidiaries: Intraware Canada, Inc., Intraware Europe Limited

Officers: Peter H. Jackson/Chmn., CEO, Pres., Founder/$565,920.00, Paul Martinelli/CTO, Co - Founder, Wendy Nieto/CFO, Exec. VP/$400,696.00, Justin Benson/Sr. VP - Business Development, Sales, Marketing/$314,569.00, Roman Reznicek/VP - Finance, Corporate Strategy, Toby Pieper/VP - Engineering, James Brentano/VP - Sales, Lisa Haugh/General Counsel, Roger Johnsen/VP - Information Technology

Directors: Peter H. Jackson/Chmn., CEO, Pres., Founder, Alexander H. Danzberger/Dir., Bradley M. Shuster/Dir., Peter F. Pervere/Dir., Brendan A. McLoughlin/Dir., Raymond L. Ocampo/Dir.

Owners: Insiders/11.70%, Crosslink Capital, Inc./12.60%, Bradley M. Shuster, Paul D. Warenski, Justin M. Benson, Drysdale Partners, Peter F. Pervere, Prescott Group Capital Management, LLC/7.90%, Richard J. Northing, Wendy A. Nieto/1.70%, Digital River, Inc./13.80%, Passport Capital, LLC/7.10%, Peter H. Jackson/8.30%, Raymond L. Ocampo, AWM Investment Company, Inc./12.80% *(16 Owners included in Index)*

Financial Data: ***Fiscal Year End:***02/28 ***Latest Annual Data:*** 2/28/2007

Year	Sales	Net Income
2007	$10,873,000	-$3,159,000
2006	$11,046,000	-$1,666,000
2005	$10,835,000	-$1,858,000

Curr. Assets:	$14,123,000	**Curr. Liab.:**	$4,376,000		
Plant, Equip.:	$587,000	**Total Liab.:**	$5,057,000	**Indic. Yr. Divd.:**	NA
Total Assets:	$15,359,000	**Net Worth:**	$4,152,000	**Debt/ Equity:**	NA

Intrawest Corp

Ste. 800, 200 Burrard St., Vancouver, BC, V6E 4T6; *PH:* 1-604-669-9777; *http://* www.intrawest.com; *Email:* intrainfo@intrawest.com

General - Incorporation .... Canada | **Stock**- Price on:12/24/2007 .... NA
Employees .... NA | Stock Exchange .... NA
Auditor .... KPMG LLP | Ticker Symbol .... NA
Stk Agt .... Mellon Trust Co | Outstanding Shares .... NA
Counsel .... Khaled Sifri | E.P.S. .... NA
DUNS No. .... 24-031-9426 | Shareholders .... NA

Business: The group's principle activity is to develop and operate mountain resorts, village-centered resorts, warm-weather destination resorts and resort club locations which are marketed as timeshare vacation ownership resorts. It provides resort real estate development, retail and equipment rentals, food and beverage, lodging and property management, ski schools, golf courses, athletic centers and sports clubs. There are approximately 730 ski resorts in North America of which 490 are located in the United States and 240 are located in Canada.

Primary SIC and add'l.: 6519 6512 6798

CIK No: 0001035146

Subsidiaries: Nova Scotia Company

Officers: Joe S. Houssian/Chmn., CEO, David Barry/CEO - Alpine Helicopters, Canadian Mountain Holidays, Michael M. Hannan/Pres. - Abercrombie, Kent, Leisure, Travel Group, Stephen K. Rice/Exec. VP, COO - Eastern Region, David B. Brownlie/Exec. VP, COO - Whistler Blackcomb, Panorama Mountain Village, James J. Gibbons/Pres. - Intrawest Resort Club Group, Jeff Stipec/Exec. VP, COO - Lodging, Golf, David Yellowlees/Exec. VP - Marketing, Sales, Catharine Johnston/Exec. VP - Business, Organizational Excellence, Angela Nielsen/Corporate Marketing Mgr. - Media Relations Playground Real Estate Inc, Zandra Wolfgram/Dir. - Marketing, Public Relations, Sandestin, Paul Pinchbeck/Dir. - Marketing, Shannon Ballard/Mgr. Partnerships - Public Relations, Blue Mountain, Marty Von Neudegg/Marketing, General Counsel, Hugh R. Smythe/Pres. - Resort Services *(68 Officers included in Index)*

Directors: Joe S. Houssian/Chmn., CEO, Nicholas C.H. Villiers/Dir., Paul A. Novelly/Dir., Alex Wasilov/Dir., COO, Pres., Khaled C. Sifri/Dir., David A. King/Dir., Bernard A. Roy/Dir., Gordon H. MacDougall/Dir., Paul M. Manheim/Dir., Marti Morfitt/Dir.

Intrepid Holdings Inc

3200 Wilcrest Dr., Ste. 575, Houston, TX, 77042; *PH:* 1-713-278-1990; *Fax:* 1-713-278-1910; *http://* www.intrepidholdings.com

General - Incorporation .... NV | **Stock**- Price on:12/24/2007 .... $0.08
Employees .... 55 | Stock Exchange .... OTC
Auditor .... Ham, Langston & Brezina LLP | Ticker Symbol .... ITPD
Stk Agt .... NA | Outstanding Shares 53,960,000
Counsel .... NA | E.P.S. .... -$0.129
DUNS No. .... NA | Shareholders .... NA

Business: The group's principle activity is to provide third party collection and recovery services to investors, auto loan companies, banks, buy-here-pay-here companies and auto finance related companies who have bad debt account. The company services deficient loan portfolios for lenders nationwide. The loan portfolios are a combination of written off accounts, bankruptcy accounts and other accounts placed for collection. The company currently provides these services on a fee basis. Data storage services are also provided for clients on a long-term agreement basis and reports are generated from this data for clients. The company purchases portfolios from companies that wish to liquidate certain delinquent accounts from their portfolio. The group operates from United States.

Primary SIC and add'l.: 7322

CIK No: 0001125856

Subsidiaries: Rx Fulfillment Services, Inc

Officers: Maurice R. Stone/Chmn., CEO, Toney E. Means/Dir., Pres. - Intrepid Holdings, Inc Pres. - Intrepid Healthcare Group, Harold Woolfolk/GM - Community Allied Development, Kevin Bell/Pres. - Rx Fulfillment Services, Inc, Theodis Ware/Sec., VP - Shareholder - Investor Relations, Natasha Howard/Pres. - My Care Clinic, Inc, My Urban Clinic, Inc

Directors: Maurice R. Stone/Chmn., CEO, Toney E. Means/Dir., Pres. - Intrepid Holdings, Inc Pres. - Intrepid Healthcare Group, James H. Shelton/Dir., Monice Hagler Tate/Dir.

Owners: Insiders/25.34%, James H. Shelton/1.39%, Toney E. Means/4.88%, Monice Hagler-Tate/0.62%, Ernest Carter/2.19%, Maurice R. Stone/13.00%, Theodis Ware/3.26%

Financial Data: ***Fiscal Year End:***12/31 ***Latest Annual Data:*** 12/31/2006

Year	Sales	Net Income
2006	$689,000	-$5,972,000
2005	$39,000	-$1,265,000
2003	NA	-$71,000

Curr. Assets:	$74,000	**Curr. Liab.:**	$2,124,000		
Plant, Equip.:	$307,000	**Total Liab.:**	$2,124,000	**Indic. Yr. Divd.:**	NA
Total Assets:	$508,000	**Net Worth:**	-$1,616,000	**Debt/ Equity:**	NA

Intrepid Technology & Resources Inc

501 W Broadway, Ste. 200, Idaho Falls, ID, 83402; *PH:* 1-208-529-5337; *Fax:* 1-208-529-1014; *http://* www.intrepid21.com; *Email:* sellis@intrepid21.com

General - Incorporation .... ID | **Stock**- Price on:12/24/2007 .... $0.052
Employees .... NA | Stock Exchange .... OTC
Auditor .... Jones Simkins P.C. | Ticker Symbol .... IESV
Stk Agt .... Columbia Stock Transfer Co | Outstanding Shares 317,760,000
Counsel .... NA | E.P.S. .... -$0.008
DUNS No. .... NA | Shareholders .... NA

Business: The group's principal activities are to provide engineering and technology services, produce and market biogas, ethanol and develop mining properties. The group is organsied into three divisions: the science and technology division is a collection of nationally recognized experts in various scientific and engineering disciplines that have consulting arrangements with the company to provide expert advice and service on an as-needed basis, the engineering services provide complete in-house design-build-operate capability and also services a diverse external customer base ranging from the federal government to private commercial and clients and the biofuels division focus on development of integrated, "Self-Contained" biofuels/energy production complexes in which the energy required to support the industrial process is produced on site from renewable sources, thus stabilizing energy costs and greatly enhancing operating margins.

Primary SIC and add'l.: 8711

CIK No: 0001083742

Subsidiaries: Idaho Nano Powders, Intrepid Engineering Services, Inc., Virtual Science Services, Inc., Western Technology and Management, Inc

Officers: Dennis D. Keiser/Dir., CEO, Jacob D. Dustin/Dir., Acting CFO, COO, Pres., Sec., Bradley Frazee/VP - Biomethane Operations, Sec., Donald J. Kenoyer/VP - Biomethane Engineering, Construction Management, Robert V. Searcy/Controller

Directors: Dennis D. Keiser/Dir., CEO, Lynn D. Smith/58/Chmn., John W. Brockage/69/Dir., Mitchell J. Hart/Dir., David Hawk/Dir., William R. Myers/Dir., Steven Whitesides/Dir., Jacob D. Dustin/Dir., Acting CFO, COO, Pres., Sec.

Owners: Dennis D. Keiser/4.20%, Steven Whitesides/2.90%, Donald J. Kenoyer/2.40%, Robert V. Searcy/0.40%, William R. Myers/1.50%, Insiders/17.60%, Lynn D. Smith, Jacob D. Dustin/3.30%, Bradley J. Frazee/2.00%

Financial Data: *Fiscal Year End:* 06/30 *Latest Annual Data:* 06/30/2007

Year	Sales	Net Income
2007	$255,000	-$1,627,000
2006	$447,000	-$1,990,000
2005	$399,000	-$1,471,000

Curr. Assets:	$977,000	**Curr. Liab.:**	$1,014,000		
Plant, Equip.:	$2,218,000	**Total Liab.:**	$1,014,000	**Indic. Yr. Divd.:**	NA
Total Assets:	$3,195,000	**Net Worth:**	$2,181,000	**Debt/ Equity:**	4.0041

Introgen Therapeutics Inc

301 Congress Ave., Ste. 1850, Austin, TX, 78701; *PH:* 1-512-708-9310; *Fax:* 1-512-708-9311; *http://* www.introgen.com

General - Incorporation	DE	**Stock** - Price on:12/24/2007	$3.83
Employees	74	Stock Exchange	NDQ
Auditor	Ernst & Young LLP	Ticker Symbol	INGN
Stk Agt	EquiServe Trust Co N.A	Outstanding Shares	43,730,000
Counsel	Fulbright & Jaworski LLP	E.P.S	-$0.66
DUNS No.	87-897-4153	Shareholders	NA

Business: The group's principal activity is to develop gene therapy products for the treatment of cancer. The group's product, advexin(R) gene therapy combines the p53 gene to protect cells from becoming cancerous. The major products of the group include ingn 241 (mda-7), ingn 251 (pten) and others. The group has conducted a number of studies to establish the safety and evaluate the efficacy of advexin (R), both alone and in combination with radiation therapy, chemotherapy and surgery. The group has also conducted a phase 1 safety study in 53 patients with end-stage nsc lung cancer, who had failed surgery, radiation and chemotherapy.

Primary SIC and add'l.: 2834 8731

CIK No: 0001018710

Subsidiaries: Gendux, AB, Gendux, Inc., Magnum Therapeutics Corporation, TMX Realty Corporation

Officers: David G. Nance/Chmn., CEO, Pres. - Introgen Therapeutics Inc/$2,712,461.00, Sunil Chada/Assoc. VP - Clinical Research, Development, Channing C. Burke/Dir. - Corporate Communications, Rodney Varner/Sec., Robert E. Sobol/Sr. VP - Medical, Scientific Affairs/$616,403.00, Louis A. Zumstein/Assoc. VP - Research, Peter M. Clarke/VP - Production, Technical Processes, David J. Enloe/Sr. VP - Operations/$633,749.00, David L. Parker/VP - Intellectual Property, Max W. Talbott/Sr. VP - Worldwide Commercial Development/$854,636.00, James W. Albrecht/CFO/$547,010.00, Kerstin B. Menander/VP - Clinical Development

Directors: David G. Nance/Chmn., CEO, Pres. - Introgen Therapeutics Inc, Charles E. Long/Dir., Malcolm S. Gillis/Dir., William H. Cunningham/Dir., Peter Barton Hutt/Dir., John N. Kapoor/Dir.

Owners: Malcolm S. Gillis, Insiders/20.57%, SMALLCAP World Fund, Inc./6.13%, FMR Corp./9.98%, James W. Albrecht, David J. Enloe, William H. Cunningham, David L. Parker, David G. Nance/8.10%, Peter Barton Hutt, John N. Kapoor/8.01%, Robert E. Sobol, Charles E. Long, Max W. Talbott, Capital Research and Management Company/9.28% *(16 Owners included in Index)*

Financial Data: *Fiscal Year End:* 12/31 *Latest Annual Data:* 12/31/2006

Year	Sales	Net Income
2006	$1,151,000	-$28,801,000
2005	$1,867,000	-$26,103,000
2004	$1,808,000	-$24,387,000

Curr. Assets:	$48,699,000	**Curr. Liab.:**	$8,742,000		
Plant, Equip.:	$5,172,000	**Total Liab.:**	$17,113,000	**Indic. Yr. Divd.:**	NA
Total Assets:	$54,161,000	**Net Worth:**	$37,048,000	**Debt/ Equity:**	0.1987

Intrusion Inc

1101 E Arapaho Rd., Ste. 200, Richardson, TX, 75081; *PH:* 1-972-234-6400; *Fax:* 1-972-301-3685; *http://* www.intrusion.com; *Email:* sales@intrusion.com

General - Incorporation	DE	**Stock** - Price on:12/24/2007	$0.4
Employees	32	Stock Exchange	OTC
Auditor	KBA Group LLP	Ticker Symbol	INTZ
Stk Agt	Mellon Investor Services LLC	Outstanding Shares	9,220,000
Counsel	Brobeck, Phleger & Harrison	E.P.S	NA
DUNS No.	10-399-1584	Shareholders	NA

Business: The group's principle activity is to develop, market and support a family of security software and appliances that address vital security issues facing organizations deploying business applications over the Internet. The group currently provides network security solutions including intrusion detection systems and virtual private network and firewall appliances. The products are marketed and distributed through a direct sales force to end-users, distributors, system integrators, service providers and value-added resellers. The end user customers include sectors like manufacturing, high technology, telecommunications, retail, transportation, health care, insurance, entertainment, utility and energy companies, government agencies, financial institutions, and academic institutions. The group's quarterly revenue for Sep'07 was 0.92 millions of USD.

Primary SIC and add'l.: 7373

CIK No: 0000736012

Subsidiaries: Intrusion.com GmbH, Intrusion.com Limited, Intrusion.com Ltd., Intrusion.com SARL, Intrusion.com Sdn. Bhd., Intrusion.com, Inc., ODS Investments, Inc., ODS, Inc., Optical Data Systems (Barbados) Ltd., Optical Data Systems - Texas, Inc, Optical Data Systems, Inc., Optical Data Systems, Ltda

Officers: Ward G. Paxton/Co - Founder, Chmn., CEO, Pres./$171,290.00, Michael L. Paxton/CFO, VP/$168,675.00, Garry L. Hemphill/VP - Sales/$155,048.00, Aaron Bawcom/CTO, VP - Engineering/$218,915.00, Joe T. Head/Co - Founder, VP/$225,408.00, Jay Barbour/VP - Marketing

Directors: Ward G. Paxton/Co - Founder, Chmn., CEO, Pres., Donald M. Johnston/Dir., James F. Gero/Dir., Joe T. Head/Co - Founder, VP, Fred J. Bucy/Dir.

Owners: James F. Gero/4.83%, Ward G. Paxton/53.91%, Marshall B. Payne/1.47%, Insiders/77.01%, Aaron M. Bawcom/1.19%, Michael L. Paxton/7.99%, Fred J. Bucy, Joe T. Head/5.86%, Eric H. Gore, Insiders/46.72%, Enable Growth Partners L.P./15.29%, Ward G. Paxton/29.80%, James F. Gero/23.10%, Enable Growth Partners L.P./6.19%, Garry L. Hemphill/0.89% *(17 Owners included in Index)*

Financial Data: *Fiscal Year End:* 12/31 *Latest Annual Data:* 12/31/2006

Year	Sales	Net Income
2006	$5,242,000	-$3,024,000
2005	$5,978,000	-$3,321,000
2004	$6,019,000	-$4,528,000

Curr. Assets:	$2,184,000	**Curr. Liab.:**	$1,666,000		
Plant, Equip.:	$162,000	**Total Liab.:**	$1,666,000	**Indic. Yr. Divd.:**	NA
Total Assets:	$2,387,000	**Net Worth:**	$721,000	**Debt/ Equity:**	NA

Intuit Inc

2632 Marine Way, Mountain View, CA, 94043; *PH:* 1-650-944-6000; *Fax:* 1-650-944-3699; *http://* www.intuit.com

General - Incorporation	DE	**Stock** - Price on:12/24/2007	$29.39
Employees	7,500	Stock Exchange	NDQ
Auditor	Ernst & Young LLP	Ticker Symbol	INTU
Stk Agt	American Stock Transfer & Trust Co.	Outstanding Shares	336,740,000
Counsel	Fenwick & West LLP	E.P.S	$1.35
DUNS No.	55-696-4047	Shareholders	NA

Business: The groups principle activity is to provide business, financial management solutions for small and medium sized businesses, financial institutions, including banks and credit unions. The groups products include QuickBooks, Quicken and TurboTax software. The group operates through six business segments namely quickbooks, payroll and payments, consumer tax, professional tax, financial institutions and other businesses. The group operates from United States.

Primary SIC and add'l.: 7372 7374 7389

CIK No: 0000896878

Subsidiaries: apps.com, Inc., CBS Corporate Services, Inc., CBS Employer Services, Inc., CBS Properties, Inc., Computing Resources, Inc., Dallas Innovative Merchant Solutions, LLC, EmployeeMatters Insurance Agency, Inc., Greenpoint Software, an Intuit company, Innovative Merchant Solutions, LLC, INTU Holdings Ltd., Intuit Administrative Services, Inc., Intuit Canada, Intuit Canada Limited/Ltee, Intuit Do-It-Yourself Payroll, Intuit Limited 33 Subsidiaries included in the Index

Officers: Stephen M. Bennett/Dir., CEO, Pres., Peter J. Karpas/Sr. VP, GM - Quicken Health Group, Alexander M. Lintner/Sr. VP - Strategy, Corporate Development, Brad D. Smith/Sr. VP - Small Business Division, Sasan K. Goodarzi/Sr. VP - Financial Institutions Division, Rick W. Jensen/Sr. VP, Jeffrey P. Hank/VP, Corporate Controller, Laura A. Fennell/Sr. VP, General Counsel, Corp. Sec., Caroline F. Donahue/Sr. VP - Sales, Kiran M. Patel/Sr. VP - Consumer Tax Group, CFO, Mark F. Schar/Sr. VP - CMO

Directors: Stephen M. Bennett/Dir., CEO, Pres., William V. Campbell/Chmn., Jeffrey E. Stiefler/Chmn. - Advisory Board, Financial Institutions Division, Dennis D. Powell/Dir., Christopher W. Brody/Dir., John L. Doerr/Dir., Diane B. Greene/Dir., Michael R. Hallman/Dir., Stratton D. Sclavos/Dir., Suzanne Nora Johnson/Dir., Edward A. Kangas/Dir., Scott D. Cook/Founder, Dir.

Owners: PRIMECAP Management Company/6.50%, L. John Doerr, Barclays Global Investors, NA/8.40%, Edward A. Kangas, Alexander M. Lintner, Stratton D. Sclavos, Jeffrey E. Stiefler, Brad D. Smith, Stephen M. Bennett/1.50%, Scott D. Cook/7.40%, Suzanne Nora Johnson, Dennis D. Powell, Diane B. Greene, Insiders/10.40%, Kiran M. Patel *(19 Owners included in Index)*

Financial Data: *Fiscal Year End:* 07/31 *Latest Annual Data:* 7/31/2006

Year	Sales	Net Income
2006	$2,342,303,000	$416,963,000
2005	$2,037,703,000	$381,627,000
2004	$1,867,663,000	$317,030,000

Curr. Assets:	$1,817,030,000	**Curr. Liab.:**	$1,015,974,000	**P/E Ratio:**	24.09
Plant, Equip.:	$194,434,000	**Total Liab.:**	$1,031,373,000	**Indic. Yr. Divd.:**	NA
Total Assets:	$2,770,027,000	**Net Worth:**	$1,738,086,000	**Debt/ Equity:**	0.5348

Intuitive Surgical Inc

1266 Kifer Rd., Bldg. 101, Sunnyvale, CA, 94086; *PH:* 1-408-523-2100; *Fax:* 1-408-523-1390; *http://* www.intuitivesurgical.com

General - Incorporation	DE	**Stock** - Price on:12/24/2007	$138.98
Employees	563	Stock Exchange	NDQ
Auditor	Ernst & Young LLP	Ticker Symbol	ISRG
Stk Agt	Computershare Trust Co	Outstanding Shares	37,470,000
Counsel	NA	E.P.S	$3.08
DUNS No.	93-864-7021	Shareholders	NA

Business: The group's principal activity is to design, manufacture and market surgical products, which provide flexibility during open surgery while operating through ports. The group conducts research, development, testing and commercialization of its products. The group manufactures da vinci surgical system that consist of information about computer enhanced technology used in the system. This system of translating the surgeon's micro-movements of instruments positioned inside the patient through small puncture incisions or ports enables the surgeon to perform better surgery.

Primary SIC and add'l.: 3845 3841

CIK No: 0001035267

Subsidiaries: Computer Motion, Inc

Officers: Lonnie M. Smith/Chmn., CEO, Pres./$2,277,142.00, Benjamin B. Gong/VP - Finance, Treasurer/$692,486.00, Frank D. Nguyen/VP - Intellectual Property, Licensing, Augusto V. Castello/VP - Manufacturing, Aleks Cukic/VP - Business Development, Strategic Planning, Gary S. Guthart/COO, Pres./$1,623,230.00, Jerry McNamara/Exec. VP - Worldwide Sales, Marketing, Marshall L. Mohr/Sr. VP, CFO, Dave Rosa/VP - Product Development, William C. Nowlin/VP - Research, Product Quality, John F. Runkel/Sr. VP, General Counsel/$1,190,778.00, Jim Alecxih/VP - US Sales, Gene Nagel/VP - Training, Development, Sal Brogna/VP - Engineering, Heather Hand/VP - Human Resources *(17 Officers included in Index)*

Directors: Lonnie M. Smith/Chmn., CEO, Pres., Robert Duggan/Dir., Eric Halvorson/Dir., Richard Kramer/Dir., Alan J. Levy/Dir., Floyd D. Loop/Dir., Keith Grossman/Dir.

Owners: Richard J. Kramer, Robert W. Duggan, Marshall L. Mohr, Alan J. Levy, Jerome J. McNamara, John F. Runkel, Floyd D. Loop, Eric H. Halvorson, Benjamin B. Gong, Insiders/3.00%, Keith D. Grossman, Lonnie M. Smith/1.60%, Gary S. Guthart

Financial Data: *Fiscal Year End:* 12/31 *Latest Annual Data:* 12/31/2006

Year	Sales	Net Income
2006	$372,682,000	$72,044,000
2005	$227,338,000	$94,134,000
2004	$138,803,000	$23,478,000

Curr. Assets:	$374,451,000	Curr. Liab.:	$80,667,000	P/E Ratio:	55.82
Plant, Equip.:	$59,939,000	Total Liab.:	$82,085,000	Indic. Yr. Divd.:	NA
Total Assets:	$671,790,000	Net Worth:	$589,705,000	Debt/ Equity:	0.0039

Invacare Corp

1 Invacare Way, Elyria, OH, 44035; *PH:* 1-440-329-6111; *Fax:* 1-440-366-9008;
http:// www.invacare.com

General - Incorporation ....OH
Employees...6,000
Auditor.................................Ernst & Young LLP
Stk Agt.................................National City Bank
Counsel...NA
DUNS No. 07-691-6246

Stock- Price on:12/24/2007 ....$18.41
Stock Exchange...NYSE
Ticker Symbol..IVC
Outstanding Shares 31,980,000
E.P.S..-$10.79
Shareholders..NA

Business: The group's principal activity is to design, manufacture and distribute an extensive line of health care products. Rehab products of the group include power wheelchairs, custom manual wheelchairs, three and four-wheeled motorized scooters, seat cushions, back supports and accessories. Standard products include manual wheelchairs, personal care, home care beds, low air loss therapy products and patient transport products. Home respiratory products include oxygen concentrators, nebulizer compressors and respiratory disposables, sleep therapy products and portable compressed oxygen systems. Continuing care products include beds and furnishings for the non-acute care markets. The group distributes its products in the United States, Europe, Australia and other countries. On 02-Mar-2004, the group acquired freedom designs, inc and on 09-Sep-2004, wp domus gmbh.

Primary SIC and add'l.: 2599 5712 3842 3841

CIK No: 0000742112

Subsidiaries: 1207273 Alberta ULC, 2083806 Ontario Inc., 6123449 Canada, Inc., Adaptive Switch Laboratories, Inc., Alber GmbH, Wurenlos, Altimate Medical, Inc., Aquatec GmbH, Isny, Aust Healthcare Equipment PTY, Carroll Healthcare, Inc., Carroll Healthcare (USA) Inc., Champion Manufacturing Inc., Dolomite AB, Gislaved, Dolomite Holding AB, Gislaved, Dynamic Controls, Dynamic Europe Ltd 82 Subsidiaries included in the Index

Officers: Malachi A. Mixon/Chmn., CEO/$2,848,465.00, Gregory C. Thompson/Sr. VP, CFO/$875,942.00, Dale Laporte/Sr. VP - Business Development, General Counsel, Bill Corcoran/VP - Financial Services, Louis F. Slangen/Sr. VP - Global Sales, Marketing/$706,531.00, Joe Usaj/Sr. VP - Human Resources, Joseph B. Richey/Dir., Pres. - Invacare Technologies Division, Sr. VP - Electronic, Design Engineering/$476,158.00, Gerald B. Blouch/Dir., COO, Pres./$1,661,336.00, Mary Jo Caserta/Financial Services Mgr., Becky Reaser/Financial Services Mgr., Steve Hubeny/Financial Services Mgr., Michael Grospitch/Financial Services Mgr.

Directors: Malachi A. Mixon/Chmn., CEO, Martin C. Harris/Dir., James L. Jones/Dir., William M. Weber/Dir., Bernadine P. Healy/Dir., James C. Boland/Dir., John S. Kasich/Dir., Michael F. Delaney/Dir., Dan T. Moore/Dir., Joseph B. Richey/Dir., Pres. - Invacare Technologies Division, Sr. VP - Electronic, Design Engineering, Gerald B. Blouch/Dir., COO, Pres.

Owners: Dan T. Moore, John R. Kasich, Louis F.J. Slangen, Bernadine P. Healy, James C. Boland, Lord, Abbett & Co. LLC/5.50%, Malachi C. Mixon/7.70%, Joseph B. Richey/2.70%, Ariel Capital Management, LLC/26.40%, Martin C. Harris, Insiders/97.20%, Malachi A. Mixon/7.70%, Joseph B. Richey/2.70%, Gerald B. Blouch/2.50%, NFJ Investment Group LP/5.90% (*19 Owners included in Index*)

Financial Data: Fiscal Year End:12/31 Latest Annual Data: 12/31/2006

Year	Sales	Net Income
2006	$1,498,035,000	-$317,774,000
2005	$1,529,732,000	$48,852,000
2004	$1,403,327,000	$75,197,000

Curr. Assets:	$655,758,000	Curr. Liab.:	$447,976,000		
Plant, Equip.:	$173,945,000	Total Liab.:	$1,005,087,000	Indic. Yr. Divd.:	$0.050
Total Assets:	$1,490,451,000	Net Worth:	$485,364,000	Debt/ Equity:	NA

INVE$TNet Inc

No. 99 Taibei Rd., Limin Economy And Technology Developing District, Harbin, Heilongjiang, 150025; *PH:* 86-451-57351189; *http://* www.investnnn.com

General - Incorporation ....NV
Employees...NA
Auditor ....Michael T. Studer, Cpa, P.c.
Stk Agt...NA
Counsel.................................Richard Surber
DUNS No. ....NA

Stock- Price on:12/24/2007 ....$0.83
Stock Exchange..NA
Ticker Symbol..NA
Outstanding Shares ....NA
E.P.S..NA
Shareholders..NA

Business: The group's principal activities are the provider of real-time trading solutions, real-time it solutions, real-time it software solutions and system integration and technical consulting services. The real-time trading solutions help to stock, warrant and equity linked trading instruments in Hong Kong stock exchange. The real-time it solutions provide advance switch to handle inbound and outbound calls of public switched telephone network for telecommunications institutions. The real-time it software provides multi-access to production and operation information. The system integration and technical consulting services provide custom made it solutions and integration services to corporate clients. The group is also developing a mobile payment system, which enables uses to conduct money transactions through cellular phones with wap capability. The operations of the group are carried out in Hong Kong and China.

Primary SIC and add'l.: 7372 9999

CIK No: 0001017699

Subsidiaries: China Kangtai Cactus Bio-tech Company Limited, Harbin Hainan Kangda Cacti Hygienical Foods Co., Ltd.

Owners: Insiders/61.30%, Hong Bu/4.20%, Jiping Wang/4.00%, Song Yang/4.10%, Jinjiang Wang/27.10%, Chengzhi Wang/21.90%

Financial Data: Fiscal Year End:12/31 Latest Annual Data: 12/31/2006

Year	Sales	Net Income
2006	$10,385,000	$1,435,000
2005	$8,003,000	$795,000
2004	$149,000	-$4,804,000

Curr. Assets:	$9,638,000	Curr. Liab.:	$1,076,000		
Plant, Equip.:	$3,445,000	Total Liab.:	$1,076,000	Indic. Yr. Divd.:	NA
Total Assets:	$14,971,000	Net Worth:	$13,895,000	Debt/ Equity:	NA

inVentiv Health

Vantage Ct. N, 200 Cottontail Ln., Somerset, NJ, 08873; *PH:* 1-732-537-4800; *Fax:* 1-732-537-4912; *http://* www.ventiv.com; *Email:* corporate@ventiv.com

General - Incorporation ....DE
Employees...5,200
Auditor ....Deloitte & Touche LLP
Stk Agt ..... American Stock Transfer & Trust Co.
Counsel..........................Akerman Senterfitt LLP
DUNS No. ....NA

Stock- Price on:12/24/2007 ....$36.79
Stock Exchange...NDQ
Ticker Symbol..VTIV
Outstanding Shares 31,120,000
E.P.S..$1.69
Shareholders..NA

Business: The group's principle activity is to provide a wide range of integrated services for the pharmaceutical, biotechnology and life sciences industries. The services include consulting, analytics and forecasting; market research and intelligence; strategic and tactical planning; telemarketing and other marketing support; product/brand management; recruitment and training services and sales execution. The customers of the group are boehringer ingleheim, baxter, bayer corporation, bristol-myers squibb, endo pharmaceuticals, merck, novartis, forest laboratories inc, glaxosmithkline and novo nordisk, reliant pharmaceuticals inc. The group's quarterly revenue for September 2007 was 254.91 millions of USD.

Primary SIC and add'l.: 8099 7389

CIK No: 0001089473

Subsidiaries: Adheris, Inc., Anova Clinical Resources, LLC, Blue Diesel, LLC, Cadent Medical Communications LLC, Clinical Communications (UK) Limited, Consultancy Practice Limited, Creative Healthcare Solutions, LLC, Creative Healthcare Solutions, LLCdba Palio Communications, Franklin Pharma Services, LLC, Gerbig, Snell Weisheimer Advertising, LLC, GSW Building Associates, LLC, Halliday Jones Sales Limited, Health Process Management LLC, Health Products Research (UK) Limited, Health Products Research, Inc. 52 Subsidiaries included in the Index

Officers: Thomas A. Hanley/CEO - Smith Hanley Holding Company, Michael Hlinak/Pres., CEO - Ventiv Clinical, Eran Broshy/Chmn., CEO/$7,544,277.00, Terrell Herring/44/Dir., COO/$1,283,267.00, David Bassin/36/CFO, Blane R. Walter/37/Dir., Pres./$390,126.00, William O'Donnell/COO, Pres.

Directors: Eran Broshy/Chmn., CEO, John R. Harris/59/Dir., Terrell Herring/44/Dir., COO, Blane R. Walter/37/Dir., Pres., Clayton A. Perfall/47/Dir., Per G.H. Lofberg/60/Dir., Mark Jennings/44/Dir., Craig Saxton/65/Dir.

Owners: Mark E. Jennings, Insiders/6.20%, John R. Emery, Craig Saxton, Eran Broshy/2.30%, Don Conklin, John R. Harris, Clayton A. Perfall, Terrell G. Herring, Blane R. Walter/2.40%

Financial Data: Fiscal Year End:12/31 Latest Annual Data: 12/31/2006

Year	Sales	Net Income
2006	$766,245,000	$51,235,000
2005	$556,312,000	$43,863,000
2004	$352,184,000	$31,132,000

Curr. Assets:	$289,217,000	Curr. Liab.:	$202,533,000	P/E Ratio:	30.16
Plant, Equip.:	$43,380,000	Total Liab.:	$412,592,000	Indic. Yr. Divd.:	NA
Total Assets:	$771,054,000	Net Worth:	$358,462,000	Debt/ Equity:	0.5153

Inverness Medical Innovations Inc

51 Sawyer Rd., Ste. 200, Waltham, MA, 02453; *PH:* 1-781-647-3900; *Fax:* 1-781-647-3939; *http://* www.invernessmedical.com

General - Incorporation ....DE
Employees...2,561
Auditor ....BDO Seidman LLP
Stk Agt ....EquiServe Trust Co N.A
Counsel......................Goodwin, Procter & Hoar
DUNS No. ....NA

Stock- Price on:12/24/2007 ....$51.97
Stock Exchange..AMEX
Ticker Symbol..IMA
Outstanding Shares 46,580,000
E.P.S..-$4.97
Shareholders..NA

Business: The group's principal activities are to develop, manufacture and market consumer healthcare products. The products include self-test diagnostic products for women's health market, vitamins and nutritional supplements and clinical diagnostic products. Consumer diagnostic products include home pregnancy detection tests and ovulation detection tests. The nutritional and supplement products include multi-vitamin formulas, single-letter vitamins, minerals, herbal and non-herbal supplements. Clinical diagnostics market consists of products designed to assist medical professionals in analyzing human body fluids or other materials for markers of pregnancy or disease or the presence of agents that may signal disease. In 2003, the group acquired ostex international inc and applied biotech inc. On 16-Jun-2004, it also acquired advantage diagnostics corporation.

Primary SIC and add'l.: 2835

CIK No: 0001145460

Subsidiaries: Advantage Diagnostics Corporation, Alpha US Acquisition Corp., Applied Biotech, Inc., Binax Inc., Cambridge Diagnostics Ireland Limited, CLONDIAG chip technologies GmbH, DMD GmbH, Forefront Diagnostics, Inc., Innovations Research, LLC, Inverness Medical (Shanghai) Co., Ltd., Inverness Medical (UK) Holdings, Ltd., Inverness Medical BioStar Inc., Inverness Medical Australia Pty, Ltd., Inverness Medical Benelux BVBA (1), Inverness Medical Canada, Inc. 43 Subsidiaries included in the Index

Officers: Ron Zwanziger/Chmn., CEO, Pres./$1,100,999.00, David Teitel/CFO/$267,534.00, Hilde Eylenbosch/Pres. - Consumer Diagnostics, Paul T. Hempel/Sr. VP - Leadership Development, Special Counsel, Jerry McAleer/Dir., VP - Research, Development/$484,111.00, John Yonkin/Pres. - US Point, Care, David Scott/Dir., Chief Scientific Officer/$556,177.00, Geoffrey Jenkins/VP - Worldwide Operations, David Toohey/Pres. - Professional Diagnostics/$559,058.00, Ellen Chiniara/General Counsel, Assist. Sec., Jon Russell/VP - Finance, Doug Guarino/Spokesman, Steve Ferullo/VP - US Sales, Erik Henau/Dir. - International Consumer Business, Preston Zoller/Dir. - Business Development (*17 Officers included in Index*)

Directors: Ron Zwanziger/Chmn., CEO, Pres., Peter Townsend/Dir., David Scott/Dir., Chief Scientific Officer, John F. Levy/Dir., Robert P. Khederian/Dir., John A. Quelch/Dir., Alfred M. Zeien/Dir., Jerry McAleer/Dir., VP - Research, Development, Carol R. Goldberg/Dir.

Owners: Carol R. Goldberg, David Teitel, David Scott/1.34%, Edward C. Johnson 3d/10.49%, Robert P. Khederian, John F. Levy, Zwanziger Family Ventures, LLC/3.25%, John A. Quelch, Fidelity Management& Research Company/10.05%, David Toohey, Ron Zwanziger/6.04%, Jerry McAleer/1.20%, Christopher J. Lindop, Insiders/10.61%, John Bridgen

Financial Data: Fiscal Year End:12/31 Latest Annual Data: 09/30/2007

Year	Sales	Net Income
2007	$237,636,000	-$180,612,000
2006	$157,008,000	$6,027,000
2005	$421,850,000	-$19,209,000

Curr. Assets:	$275,544,000	Curr. Liab.:	$142,231,000		
Plant, Equip.:	$82,312,000	Total Liab.:	$371,633,000	Indic. Yr. Divd.:	NA
Total Assets:	$1,085,771,000	Net Worth:	$714,138,000	Debt/ Equity:	0.1464

Invesco Plc Llondon

Formerly: AMVESCAP Plc

1360 Peachtree St. Ne, Atlanta, GA, 30309; *PH:* 1-404-892-0896; *http://* www.amvescap.com

General - Incorporation... England And Wales	**Stock** - Price on:12/24/2007 ....NA
Employees..5,798	Stock Exchange...NYSE
Auditor ....Ernst & Young LLP	Ticker Symbol...AVZ
Stk Agt..................American Depositary Shares	Outstanding Shares ....NA
Counsel...NA	E.P.S...NA
DUNS No. 21-027-0765	Shareholders...NA

Business: The group's principal activity is investment management. The group operates primarily under the aim, invesco, and Atlantic trust brands. Aim, manages and distributes mutual funds and related products to retail and institutional investors primarily within North America. Invesco, manages investment products that span a wide range of asset classes from fixed income to value, core, and growth equities to alternative investments such as real estate and private capital. Atlantic trust, provides integrated wealth management services to high net worth individuals and their families. The group provides services to clients in more than 100 countries and manages 1,780 separate institutional accounts and 811 retail funds.

Primary SIC and add'l.: 6722 6282 6726

CIK No: 0000914208

Subsidiaries: AIM Advisors, Inc., AIM Canada Holdings Inc., AIM Capital, Inc., AIM Funds Management, Inc., AIM Management Group Inc., Amvescap Group Services, Inc., Amvescap Inc., AVZ Callco, AVZ Inc., INVESCO Asset Management Limited, INVESCO Fund Managers Limited, INVESCO Institutional (N.A.), Inc., INVESCO International Holdings Limited, INVESCO North American Holdings, Inc., INVESCO Pensions Limited 17 Subsidiaries included in the Index

Officers: Martin L. Flanagan/47/Dir., Pres., CEO - USA, James I. Robertson/50/Sr. MD, Dir. - UK, Bill Hensel/Dir. - Media Relations, Aaron Uhde/Head - Investor Relations, Loren M. Starr/Sr. MD, CFO, Philip A. Taylor/Sr. MD, Robert J. Yerbury/Sr. MD, Michael Perman/Company Sec., Kevin M. Carome/Sr. MD, John S. Markwalter/Sr. MD, Colin D. Meadows/Sr. MD

Directors: Martin L. Flanagan/47/Dir., Pres., CEO - USA, Rex D. Adams/67/Chmn., James I. Robertson/50/Sr. MD, Dir. - UK, John Banham/67/Non Exec. Dir. - UK, Joseph R. Canion/63/Non Exec. Dir. - USA, Edward P. Lawrence/66/Non Exec. Dir. - USA, Denis Kessler/56/Non Exec. Dir. - France, Thomas J. Presby/68/Non Exec. Dir. - USA

Investment Technology Group Inc

380 Madison Ave., New York, NY, 10017; *PH:* 1-917-344-5500; *http://* www.itginc.com

General - Incorporation.............................DE	**Stock** - Price on:12/24/2007 ....$43.84
Employees..1,060	Stock Exchange...NYSE
Auditor ....KPMG LLP	Ticker Symbol...ITG
Stk Agt.....Computershare Investor Services LLC	Outstanding Shares 44,320,000
Counsel..................Cahill Gordon & Reindel LLP	E.P.S..$2.14
DUNS No. 04-310-3340	Shareholders...NA

Business: The group provides equity trading services and transaction research to institutional investors and brokers. The group have two reportable segments: U.S. Operations and international operations. These services help the clients to optimize their portfolio construction and trading strategies, efficiently access liquidity in multiple markets and achieve superior, low-cost trade execution. Its products are posit, triact, electronic trading desk, and the client site. Posit is an electronic stock crossing system. Triact is a continuous intra-day trading vehicle. Electronic trading desk is an agency-only trading desk offering clients the ability to access multiple sources of liquidity. Client-site trading products includes, quantex, triton, itg platform, radical, itg webaccess and smartservers. Geographically the group operates in the United States, Canada, Australia, Europe, Hong Kong and Israel. On 29-Mar-2004, the group acquired radical corporation.

Primary SIC and add'l.: 6231

CIK No: 0000920424

Subsidiaries: AlterNet Securities,Inc., Hoenig (Far East) Limited, Hoenig Group Inc., Hoenig& Company Limited, Investment Technology Group Europe Limited, Investment Technology Group International Limited, Investment Technology Group Limited, ITG Analytics,Inc., ITG Asia Holdings Ltd., ITG Australia Holdings PTY Ltd., ITG Australia Ltd., ITG Canada Corp., ITG Canada Holdings Corp., ITG Capital,Inc., ITG Execution Services 27 Subsidiaries included in the Index

Officers: Ian Domowitz/CEO - ITG Solutions Network, Robert Gasser/Dir., CEO, Pres./$978,057.00, Alasdair Haynes/CEO - International/$1,774,977.00, Nick Thadaney/CEO - ITG Canada Corp, Mark Wright/MD, Andrew Larkin/MD, Maureen Murphy/MD, Alan Herzog/MD, Tony Huck/MD, Anthony J. Huck/43/MD/$2,144,666.00, Stephen Alepa/MD, David L. Meitz/MD, Angelo Bulone/MD, Controller, Chris Heckman/MD/$2,143,196.00, Howard Naphtali/CFO/$2,312,756.00 *(16 Officers included in Index)*

Directors: Robert Gasser/Dir., CEO, Pres., Maureen OHara/Chmn., Kevin J.P. OHara/Dir., William I. Jacobs/Dir., Brian J. Steck/Dir., William J. Burdett/Dir., Timothy L. Jones/Dir., Robert L. King/Dir.

Owners: Brian J. Steck, Christopher J. Heckman, Kevin J.P. OHara, Alasdair Haynes, Maureen OHara, Raymond L. Killian/1.20%, Robert L. King, Howard C. Naphtali, Anthony J. Huck, Timothy L. Jones, Insiders/2.70%

Financial Data: *Fiscal Year End:*12/31 **Latest Annual Data:** 12/31/2006

Year	Sales	Net Income
2006	$599,484,000	$97,923,000
2005	$408,161,000	$67,686,000
2004	$334,486,000	$40,983,000

Curr. Assets:	$924,968,000	**Curr. Liab.:**	$693,378,000	**P/E Ratio:**	20.49
Plant, Equip.:	$34,740,000	**Total Liab.:**	$854,278,000	**Indic. Yr. Divd.:**	NA
Total Assets:	$1,462,312,000	**Net Worth:**	$608,034,000	**Debt/ Equity:**	0.2372

INVESTools Inc

45 Rockefeller Plz., Ste. 2012, New York, NY, 10111 ; ; *http://* www.investools.com

General - Incorporation.............................DE	**Stock** - Price on:12/24/2007 ....NA
Employees..486	Stock Exchange...NDQ
Auditor ....KPMG LLP	Ticker Symbol..SWIM
Stk Agt.......................U.S. Stock Transfer Corp	Outstanding Shares ....NA
Counsel...NA	E.P.S...-$0.16
DUNS No. ....NA	Shareholders...NA

Business: The group's principal activity is to provide investor education products and services, which teaches the investors to achieve their investment goals. The group also provides investment research tools, investment advisory newsletters, customized direct marketing and Web hosting services. The activities are carried out through two segments namely: investor education and publishing and business services. The investor education segment provides instructor-led educational programs and also fulfills the life long educational needs of self directed investors. The publishing and business services include the group's newsletter and other investor education publications. The group also has introduced its lifetime value of the student strategy. On Feb 26, 2004 the group acquired service enhancement systems, inc., a California based direct marketing company operating under the name '360 group'.

Primary SIC and add'l.: 7375

CIK No: 0001145124

Subsidiaries: Entrepreneurs Online, INVESTools Asia Pacific Pte., Limited,), INVESTools Hong Kong Ltd., INVESTools Inc., Investor Education LLC, Memory Improvement Systems, Inc., Online Investors Advantage, Inc., Prophet Financial Systems, Inc., Seminar Marketing Group, Inc., Service Enhancement Systems, Inc., dba 360 Group, Telescan, Inc., ZiaSun Technologies, Inc.

Officers: Lee K. Barba/Chmn., CEO/$1,348,484.00, Dale C. Ainge/Sr. VP/$325,071.00, Ida K. Kane/Sr. VP, CFO/$438,801.00, Paul A. Helbling/Sr. VP, Chief Administrative Officer, Corp. Sec./$316,755.00, Ainslie J. Simmonds/Sr. VP, Chief Marketing, Product Development Officer/$433,067.00

Directors: Lee K. Barba/Chmn., CEO, Hans Von Meiss/Dir., Michael H. Goldsmith/Dir., Douglas T. Tansill/Dir., Warren F. McFarlan/Dir., Lisa Polsky/Dir., Tom Sosnoff/Dir., Scott Sheridan/Dir.

Owners: Lisa Polsky, Hans von Meiss, Tom Sosnoff/6.70%, Paul A. Helbling, Andrew B. Scott, Dale C. Ainge, Warren F. McFarlan, Ainslie J. Simmonds, Insiders/20.20%, TCVV, L.P. and TCV Member Fund, L.P./6.60%, Lee K. Barba/5.60%, Scott D. Sheridan/6.70%, Michael H. Goldsmith, Ida K. Kane, Douglas T. Tansill

Financial Data: *Fiscal Year End:*12/31 **Latest Annual Data:** 12/31/2006

Year	Sales	Net Income
2006	NA	NA
2005	$138,621,000	-$15,742,000
2004	$97,169,000	-$11,727,000

Curr. Assets:	$91,005,000	**Curr. Liab.:**	$155,917,000		
Plant, Equip.:	$5,253,000	**Total Liab.:**	$195,288,000	**Indic. Yr. Divd.:**	NA
Total Assets:	$131,637,000	**Net Worth:**	-$63,651,000	**Debt/ Equity:**	NA

Investors Bancorp Inc

101 Jfk Pk.way, Shorthills, New Jersey, NJ, 07078; *PH:* 1-973-924-5100; *http://* www.investorsbancorp.com

General - Incorporation ....DE	**Stock** - Price on:12/24/2007 ....$13.62
Employees..441	Stock Exchange...NDQ
Auditor ....KPMG LLP	Ticker Symbol..ISBC
Stk Agt.......................Registrar & Transfer Co	Outstanding Shares 112,700,000
Counsel...NA	E.P.S...$0.23
DUNS No. ....NA	Shareholders...NA

Business: The group operates through its subsidiaries whose principle activity is to provide banking and financial services. The products of the group include residential mortgage, home equity, construction, and consumer and other loans. The group operates from the United States. The assets of the group for the year 2006 were $5,497,246 (thousands).

Primary SIC and add'l.: 6712 6022 6035 6036 6712

CIK No: 0001326807

Subsidiaries: Investors Savings Bank, ISB Asset Corporation, ISB Holdings, Inc, ISB Mortgage Company LLC

Officers: Robert M. Cashill/Dir., CEO, Pres., Domenick A. Cama/CFO, Exec. VP, Kevin Cummings/COO, Exec. VP, Diane C. Kraemer/50/Sr. VP - Retail Administration, Susan B. Olson/54/Sr. VP - Accounting, Charles L. Lynch/63/Sr. VP - Residential Lending, Debra A. Richardson/51/Sr. VP - Lending Administration, Richard S. Spengler/46/Sr. VP - Commercial Real Estate Lending, Thomas F. Splaine/43/Sr. VP, Dir. - Financial Reporting, Patricia E. Brown/Corp. Sec.

Directors: Robert M. Cashill/Dir., CEO, Pres., Patrick J. Grant/Chmn., John A. Kirkpatrick/Dir., Joseph H. Shepard/Dir., Doreen R. Byrnes/Dir., Brian D. Dittenhafer/Dir., Rose Sigler/Dir., Stephen J. Szabatin/Dir., Vincent D. Manahan/Dir.

Owners: Insiders/2.60%, John A. Kirkpatrick, Richard S. Spengler, Joseph H. Shepard, Kevin Cummings, Stephen J. Szabatin, Vincent D. Manahan, Robert M. Cashill, Doreen R. Byrnes, Brian D. Dittenhafer, Patrick J. Grant, Investors Bancorp, MHC/57.30%, Advisory Research, Inc./6.00%, Domenick A. Cama, Rose Sigler

Financial Data: *Fiscal Year End:*06/30 **Latest Annual Data:** 6/30/2006

Year	Sales	Net Income
2006	$251,648,000	$15,014,000
2005	$233,587,000	-$3,142,000
2004	$217,558,000	$19,837,000

Curr. Assets:	$60,877,000	**Curr. Liab.:**	$4,547,783,000	**P/E Ratio:**	59.22
Plant, Equip.:	$27,911,000	**Total Liab.:**	$4,597,059,000	**Indic. Yr. Divd.:**	NA
Total Assets:	$5,497,246,000	**Net Worth:**	$900,187,000	**Debt/ Equity:**	1.1463

Investors Capital Holdings Ltd

230 Broadway E., Lynnfield, MA, 01940; *Fax:* 1-781-593-9464; *http://* www.investorscapital.com; *Email:* marketing@investorscapital.com

General - Incorporation ....MA	**Stock** - Price on:12/24/2007 ....$4.72
Employees..83	Stock Exchange...AMEX
Auditor ....UHY LLP	Ticker Symbol...ICH
Stk Agt...........................Brown & Brown LLP	Outstanding Shares 6,160,000
Counsel...NA	E.P.S...-$0.178
DUNS No. ....NA	Shareholders...NA

Business: The group's principal activity is the provision of financial planning services and investment avenues such as mutual funds, individual equities, variable annuities and other insurance products through registered representatives. It makes available multiple investment products, provides support, technology and back-office service to approximately 870 independent registered representative. It also provides portfolio management through the wholly-owned investment adviser. The group with its wholly-owned subsidiaries, investors capital corporation (icc), eastern point advisors, inc. (epa) and icc insurance agency, inc. Are engaged in the financial services industry as general securities brokers and asset managers throughout the United States.

Primary SIC and add'l.: 6282 6719

CIK No: 0001001871

Subsidiaries: Eastern Point Advisors, Inc., ICC Insurance Agency, Inc., Investors Capital Corporation, Investors Capital Holdings Securities Corporation

Officers: Theodore E. Charles/Chmn., CEO, Pres./$1,019,277.00, Steven C. Preskenis/COO/$318,531.00, Timothy B. Murphy/Dir., Exec. VP, Treasurer, CFO/$794,229.00

Directors: Theodore E. Charles/Chmn., CEO, Pres., Robert Martin/Dir., Arthur Stickney/Dir., William J. Atherton/Dir., Timothy B. Murphy/Dir., Exec. VP, Treasurer, CFO

Owners: Timothy B. Murphy/6.05%, Theodore E. Charles/56.09%, Insiders/74.34%, Arthur Stickney, Robino Stortini Holdings, LLC/10.63%, Steven C. Preskenis, Robert Martin, William Atherton

Financial Data: Fiscal Year End:03/31   Latest Annual Data: 03/31/2007

Year	Sales	Net Income
2007	$80,053,000	-$1,084,000
2006	$67,979,000	$450,000
2005	$55,166,000	$619,000

Curr. Assets:	$12,781,000	Curr. Liab.:	$4,740,000		
Plant, Equip.:	$772,000	Total Liab.:	$4,740,000	Indic. Yr. Divd.:	NA
Total Assets:	$15,326,000	Net Worth:	$10,586,000	Debt/ Equity:	NA

Investors Title Co

310 N Westlake Blvd., Westlake Village, CA, 91362; *PH:* 1-805-373-3922; *http://* www.invtitle.com; *Email:* corporate@invtitle.com

General - Incorporation	NC	Stock- Price on:12/24/2007	$49
Employees	229	Stock Exchange	NDQ
Auditor	Dixon Hughes PLLC	Ticker Symbol	ITIC
Stk Agt	First Citizens Bank & Trust Co	Outstanding Shares	2,780,000
Counsel	NA	E.P.S.	$3.73
DUNS No.	02-201-1316	Shareholders	NA

Business: The group's principal activities are to underwrite land title insurance for owners and mortgages as a primary insurer and as reinsurer for other title insurance companies. The operations are carried on through two segments: title insurance and exchange services. The title insurance segment issue title insurance policies through approved attorneys from underwriting offices and through independent issuing agents. Title insurance policies insure titles to residential, institutional, commercial and industrial properties. The exchange services segment acts as an intermediary in tax-free exchanges of property held for productive use in business and investments. This serves as exchange accommodation titleholder, holding property for exchangers in reverse exchange transactions.

Primary SIC and add'l.: 6361 6719

CIK No: 0000720858

Subsidiaries: Investors Capital Management Company, Investors Title Accommodation Corporation, Investors Title Exchange Corporation, Investors Title Management Services, Inc., Investors Trust Company, Northeast Investors Title Company, Title Insurance Company

Owners: Allen J. Fine/7.90%, Insiders/28.73%, Horace R. Johnson, James R. Morton, Loren B. Harrell, James A. Fine/7.20%, Morris W. Fine/7.20%, Markel Corporation/9.30%, Joe H. King, Scott A. Parker/3.30%, David L. Francis/2.00%

Financial Data: Fiscal Year End:12/31   Latest Annual Data: 12/31/2006

Year	Sales	Net Income
2006	$84,662,000	$13,185,000
2005	$87,864,000	$13,293,000
2004	$79,841,000	$10,719,000

Curr. Assets:	$15,838,000	Curr. Liab.:	$11,335,000	P/E Ratio:	9.90
Plant, Equip.:	$6,438,000	Total Liab.:	$48,241,000	Indic. Yr. Divd.:	$0.240
Total Assets:	$143,516,000	Net Worth:	$95,276,000	Debt/ Equity:	NA

Invicta Group Inc

2400 E Coml Blvd., Ste 618, Fort Lauderdale, FL, 33308; *PH:* 1-954-771-0650; *http://* www.invictatravelgroup.com

General - Incorporation	NV	Stock- Price on:12/24/2007	NA
Employees	NA	Stock Exchange	OTC
Auditor	Baum & Co. P.A	Ticker Symbol	IVIT
Stk Agt	Florida Atlantic Stock Transfer, Inc.	Outstanding Shares	NA
Counsel	NA	E.P.S.	-$5.257
DUNS No.	NA	Shareholders	NA

Business: The group's principal activity is to provide on-line travel services. The group offers airline tickets and other travel-related products and services over the telephone and over the Internet. The travel related services include hotel rooms, car rentals, cruises, casino packages and vacation packages. On 09-Jan-2004, the group has acquired isip telecom inc, on 23-Feb-2004, airplan inc and on 14-Jun-2004, Caribbean travel specialists.

Primary SIC and add'l.: 4725 4724 4729

CIK No: 0001212570

Subsidiaries: ISIP Telecom, Inc

Officers: William Forhan/Dir., CEO, Pres., David Scott/CEO, Mercedes Henze/60/Dir., Sec., VP, Richard David Scott/60/Dir., CFO, COO

Directors: William Forhan/Dir., CEO, Pres., Richard David Scott/60/Dir., CFO, COO, Mercedes Henze/60/Dir., Sec., VP, William Kerby/51/Dir.

Owners: William G. Forhan/1.20%, Richard David Scott/0.83%, Mercedes Henze/0.80%, Insiders/2.83%

Financial Data: Fiscal Year End:12/31   Latest Annual Data: 12/31/2006

Year	Sales	Net Income
2006	$402,000	-$470,000
2005	$98,000	-$994,000
2004	$734,000	-$3,293,000

Curr. Assets:	$13,000	Curr. Liab.:	$2,052,000		
Plant, Equip.:	$18,000	Total Liab.:	$2,308,000	Indic. Yr. Divd.:	NA
Total Assets:	$317,000	Net Worth:	-$1,991,000	Debt/ Equity:	NA

INVISA Inc

290 Cocoanut St., Ste. 1A, Sarasota, FL, 34243; *PH:* 1-941-355-9361; *Fax:* 1-941-355-9373; *http://* www.invisa.com

General - Incorporation	NV	Stock- Price on:12/24/2007	$0.025
Employees	2	Stock Exchange	OTC
Auditor	Aidman, Piser & Co. P.A	Ticker Symbol	INSA
Stk Agt	Liberty Transfer Co	Outstanding Shares	25,500,000
Counsel	NA	E.P.S.	-$0.09
DUNS No.	NA	Shareholders	NA

Business: The group's principal activity is to develop, manufacture, market and license presence-sensing products for various applications to improve the safety of powered parking gates. The group's safety system technology and products are automated closure devices, such as parking gates, sliding gates, overhead garage doors and commercial overhead doors. Powered parking gates are motorized barriers used in parking and to control vehicle traffic.

Primary SIC and add'l.: 3679

CIK No: 0001172706

Subsidiaries: RMI, SmartGate, L.C.

Officers: Edmund C. King/73/Dir., CFO, Corp. Sec., Carl Parks/COO, Pres., William Hildebrand/Sr. VP - Sales, Marketing

Directors: Stephen A. Michael/60/Chmn., Gregory J. Newell/Dir., Edmund C. King/73/Dir., CFO, Corp. Sec., John E. Scates/Dir.

Owners: Edmund C. King/3.60%, Samuel S. Duffey/4.90%, William W. Dolan/25.40%, G.M. Capital Partners, Ltd/6.20%, John E. Scates/0.50%, Gregory J. Newell/0.60%, Stephen A. Michael/25.10%, Robert Knight/1.60%, H.R. Williams/6.20%, Joseph F. Movizzo/1.00%

Financial Data: Fiscal Year End:12/31   Latest Annual Data: 12/31/2006

Year	Sales	Net Income
2006	$137,000	-$2,311,000
2005	$197,000	-$3,067,000

Curr. Assets:	$716,000	Curr. Liab.:	$496,000		
Plant, Equip.:	$62,000	Total Liab.:	$796,000	Indic. Yr. Divd.:	NA
Total Assets:	$6,754,000	Net Worth:	$5,958,000	Debt/ Equity:	NA

Invitrogen Corp

1600 Faraday Ave., Carlsbad, CA, 92008; *PH:* 1-760-603-7200; *Fax:* 1-760-602-6500; *http://* www.invitrogen.com; *Email:* ir@invitrogen.com

General - Incorporation	DE	Stock- Price on:12/24/2007	$73.6
Employees	4,835	Stock Exchange	NDQ
Auditor	Ernst & Young LLP	Ticker Symbol	IVGN
Stk Agt	Ernest & Young LLP	Outstanding Shares	46,750,000
Counsel	Blank, Rome, Comisky & McCauley LLP	E.P.S.	$0.03
DUNS No.	NA	Shareholders	NA

Business: The group's principal activity is to develop, manufacture and market research tools in reagent and kit form. The group operates in two segments: the biodiscovery product segment supplies research tools for gene cloning, gene expression, and gene analysis techniques. It also supplies enzymes, nucleic acids, other biochemicals and reagents. The bioproduction segment supplies sera, cell and tissue culture media and reagents for use in research and in processes to grow cells in the laboratory and to produce pharmaceuticals and other materials made by cultured cells. The group operates in the United States, Scotland, New Zealand, Australia, Japan, Brazil, and Israel. It markets its products directly in 24 countries and through distributors or agents in additional 45 countries. The group acquired molecular probes inc on 20-Aug-2003, panvera llc on 28-Mar-2003 and bioreliance corp on 06-Feb-2004 and protometrix inc on 01-Apr-2004.

Primary SIC and add'l.: 2836 2899

CIK No: 0001073431

Subsidiaries: BioReliance (Glasglow) Ltd, BioReliance Biotech Ltd, BioReliance Biotech, Inc., BioReliance Corporation, BioReliance Ltd, BioReliance Manufacturing GmbH, BioReliance UK Holdings Ltd, Biosource B.V., Biosource Europe S.A., Biosource GmbH, BioSource International, Inc., Biosource UK Limited, Caltag Laboratories GmbH, Caltag Laboratories, Inc., Dexter Europe S.A. 74 Subsidiaries included in the Index

Officers: Gregory T. Lucier/Chmn., CEO/$5,403,478.00, Amanda Clardy/VP - Investor Relations, Peter M. Leddy/Sr. VP - Human Resources, John Miller/Sr. VP - Biodiscovery, David F. Hoffmeister/Sr. VP, CFO/$2,628,060.00, John A. Cottingham/Sr. VP, General Counsel, Corp. Sec., Claude D. Benchimol/Sr. VP - Research, Development/$1,719,552.00, Karen S. Gibson/CIO, Sr. VP, Nicolas M. Barthelemy/Sr. VP - Cell Culture Systems, Bernd Brust/Sr. VP - Global Sales, Paul Grossman/Sr. VP - Strategy, Corporate Development, Kelli Richard/VP - Finance, Chief Accounting Officer, Siddhartha C. Kadia/VP - Global Marketing, Ebusiness, Farnaz Khadem/Sr. - Corporate Communications, Revelle Anderson/Public Relations Mgr.

Directors: Gregory T. Lucier/Chmn., CEO, Jay M. Short/Dir., Donald W. Grimm/Dir., Bradley G. Lorimier/Dir., Raymond V. Dittamore/Dir., Ann W. Reynolds/Dir., Per A. Peterson/Dir., David C. U'Prichard/Dir., Balakrishnan S. Iyer/Dir., Ronald A. Matricaria/Dir.

Owners: Ronald A. Matricaria, Per A. Peterson, Raymond V. Dittamore, Balakrishnan S. Iyer, Bradley G. Lorimier, Perry/11.30%, Claude D. Benchimol, David F. Hoffmeister, Benjamin E. Bulkley, Donald W. Grimm, W. Ann Reynolds, John D. Thompson, Jay M. Short, Gregory T. Lucier/1.70%, Insiders/4.20% (16 Owners included in Index)

Financial Data: Fiscal Year End:12/31   Latest Annual Data: 09/30/2007

Year	Sales	Net Income
2007	$314,959,000	$30,996,000
2006	$329,801,000	-$100,154,000
2005	$1,198,452,000	$132,046,000

Curr. Assets:	$797,856,000	Curr. Liab.:	$247,631,000		
Plant, Equip.:	$300,940,000	Total Liab.:	$1,552,448,000	Indic. Yr. Divd.:	NA
Total Assets:	$3,182,875,000	Net Worth:	$1,630,427,000	Debt/ Equity:	0.7064

Inyx Inc

825 3rd Ave., 40th Fl., New York, NY, 10022; *PH:* 1-212-838-1111; *Fax:* 1-212-838-0060; *http://* www.inyxinc.com

General - Incorporation	NV	Stock- Price on:12/24/2007	NA
Employees	572	Stock Exchange	OTC
Auditor	Berkovits, Lago & Co LLP	Ticker Symbol	IYXI
Stk Agt	Securities Transfer Corp	Outstanding Shares	NA
Counsel	Glast, Phillips & Murray	E.P.S.	-$0.789
DUNS No.	NA	Shareholders	NA

Business: The group's principal activities are to develop and manufacture products and technologies for the treatment of respiratory, allergy, dermatological and topical conditions. The group focuses its expertise on development-led contract manufacturing in the sterile pharmaceutical, finished dosage-form,

outsourcing sector. The products of the group include hydrocarbon aerosols, metered dose inhalers, dry powdered inhalers, metered dose pump sprays and saline aerosols. The group offers it products to blue-chip ethical pharmaceutical companies, branded generic firms and biotechnology groups. On 28-Apr-2003, the group acquired inyx pharma ltd and on 07-Mar-2003 inyx pharma ltd acquired pharmaceutical business assets of miza pharmaceuticals (UK) limited.

Primary SIC and add'l.: 7948

CIK No: 0001114241

Subsidiaries: Ashton Pharmaceuticals Ltd, Exaeris Inc, Inyx Canada, Inc., Inyx Europe, Ltd., Inyx Pharma, Ltd., Inyx USA, Ltd

Officers: Jack Kachkar/Chmn., CEO, Colin Hunter/Exec. VP, Chief Scientific Officer, Dir., Rima Goldshmidt/VP, Treasurer, Corp. Sec., Jay M. Green/Exec. VP, Dir. - Corporate Development, Stephen Beckman/VP - Sales, Marketing, Commercial Development, David Zinn/VP - Finance, Marc Couturier/Sr. VP - Global Business Development, Steven J. Handley/Dir., Pres.

Directors: Jack Kachkar/Chmn., CEO, Steven J. Handley/Dir., Pres., Colin Hunter/Exec. VP, Chief Scientific Officer, Dir.

Owners: Rima Goldshmidt/1.00%, David Zinn/0.60%, Duncan McIntyre/0.60%, Potomac Capital Management/6.10%, Viktoria Benkovitch/5.90%, Jack Kachkar/5.90%, Colin Hunter/2.00%, Joseph A. Rotmil/0.80%, Insiders/18.60%, Douglas Brown/2.10%, Larry Stockhamer/17.50%, Steven Handley/4.00%, Stephen Beckman/0.60%, Jay M. Green/3.50%

Financial Data: Fiscal Year End:12/31 Latest Annual Data: 12/31/2005

Year	Sales	Net Income
2005	$49,565,000	-$31,009,000
2004	$15,699,000	-$16,942,000
2003	$13,099,000	-$13,392,000

Curr. Assets:	$34,725,000	Curr. Liab.:	$76,317,000		
Plant, Equip.:	$40,781,000	Total Liab.:	$122,553,000	Indic. Yr. Divd.:	NA
Total Assets:	$92,153,000	Net Worth:	-$30,400,000	Debt/ Equity:	NA

Inzon Corp

238 Ne 1st Ave., Delray Beach, FL, 33444; **PH:** 1-561-279-8200; **Fax:** 1-561-279-8300; http:// www.inzon.net; **Email:** info@inzon.net

General - Incorporation	NV	**Stock** - Price on:12/24/2007	NA
Employees	NA	Stock Exchange	OTC
Auditor	De Joya Griffith & Company LLC	Ticker Symbol	IZON
Stk Agt	Liberty Transfer Co	Outstanding Shares	NA
Counsel	NA	E.P.S.	-$0.05
DUNS No.	NA	Shareholders	NA

Business: The groups principle activity is to provide communication services using VoIP/TDM network. Services of the group include voice over internet protocol technologies and conference call services. The group operates through three divisions telecom, digital media and wireless. The group operates from the United States.

Primary SIC and add'l.: 7372

CIK No: 0000814183

Officers: Sydney D. Camper/Dir., CEO, Richard Dea/57/CFO, Treasurer, Dir., Rodney B. Mikesell/COO, Paul Price/Compliance, Andy Pinkerton/37/Development

Directors: Sydney D. Camper/Dir., CEO, David F. Levy/62/Chmn., Richard Dea/57/CFO, Treasurer, Dir.

Owners: Richard Dea/3.10%, Steel City Ventures, LLC/5.80%, David F. Levy/31.00%, Insiders/66.80%, Philip Loh/1.80%, James B. Smith/30.90%

Financial Data: Fiscal Year End:09/30 Latest Annual Data: 12/31/2006

Year	Sales	Net Income
2006	NA	NA
2005	$556,000	-$1,182,000

Curr. Assets:	$24,000	Curr. Liab.:	$2,606,000		
Plant, Equip.:	$149,000	Total Liab.:	$2,693,000	Indic. Yr. Divd.:	NA
Total Assets:	$1,103,000	Net Worth:	-$1,590,000	Debt/ Equity:	NA

Iomai Corp

20 Firstfield Rd., Ste. 250, Gaithersburg, MD, 20878; **PH:** 1-301-556-4500; **Fax:** 1-301-556-4501; http:// www.iomai.com

General - Incorporation	DE	**Stock** - Price on:12/24/2007	$1.97
Employees	101	Stock Exchange	NDQ
Auditor	Ernst& Young LLP	Ticker Symbol	IOMI
Stk Agt	American Stock Transfer & Trust Co.	Outstanding Shares	25,510,000
Counsel	NA	E.P.S.	-$1.96
DUNS No.	NA	Shareholders	NA

Business: The groups principle activities include discovering, developing and commercializing vaccines and immune system. The group products sold under the trade names Iomai(R), Transcutaneous Immunization(TM), TCI(TM) and Skin Deep(TM). The group operates from the United States. The group's quarterly revenue for September 2007 was 2.95 millions of USD.

Primary SIC and add'l.: 2834 2834

CIK No: 0001125001

Officers: Stanley C. Erck/Dir., CEO, Pres./$1,361,362.00, Kai Chen/VP - Business Development, Jin Sook Chung/VP - Human Resources, Larry Ellingsworth/VP - Research, Sarah A. Frech/VP - Clinical Development, Mervyn L. Hamer/VP - Operations, Kimber L. Poffenberger/VP - Regulatory Affairs, Robert C. Seid/VP - Formulations, Russell P. Wilson/CFO, Sr. VP, General Counsel/$715,540.00, Gregory M. Glenn/Chief Scientific Officer, Sr. VP

Directors: Stanley C. Erck/Dir., CEO, Pres., James M. Barrett/Chmn., Gordon R. Douglas/Dir., Richard Douglas/Dir., Weller F. Meyer/Dir., Thomas Martin Vernon/Dir.

Owners: Thomas M. Vernon, Richard Douglas, Entities affiliated with RA Capital/6.50%, Entities affiliated with New Enterprise Associates/28.30%, R. Gordon Douglas, James M. Barret/28.30%, Stanley C. Erck/2.40%, Jeff Himawan/11.00%, Insiders/41.80%, Gregory M. Glenn/1.90%, F. Weller Meyer, Russell P. Wilson, Essex Woodlands Health Ventures/11.00%

Financial Data: Fiscal Year End:12/31 Latest Annual Data: 12/31/2006

Year	Sales	Net Income
2006	$1,475,000	-$31,785,000
2005	$2,371,000	-$18,030,000
2004	$2,345,000	-$15,080,000

Curr. Assets:	$15,898,000	Curr. Liab.:	$5,497,000		
Plant, Equip.:	$6,736,000	Total Liab.:	$9,050,000	Indic. Yr. Divd.:	NA
Total Assets:	$23,085,000	Net Worth:	$14,035,000	Debt/ Equity:	0.0810

IOMED Inc

3385 W 1820 S, Salt Lake City, UT, 84104; **PH:** 1-801-975-1191; http:// www.iomed.com

General - Incorporation	UT	**Stock** - Price on:12/24/2007	$2.6301
Employees	48	Stock Exchange	AMEX
Auditor	Ernst & Young LLP	Ticker Symbol	IOX
Stk Agt	Computershare Trust Co	Outstanding Shares	7,680,000
Counsel	NA	E.P.S.	-$0.074
DUNS No.	14-475-3514	Shareholders	NA

Business: The group's principal activities are to develop, manufacture and market drug delivery systems employing iontophoresis technology. It currently markets two iontophoretic products, the phoresor (R) and numby stuff (r). The group's products are used in situations when it is advisable to avoid the pain that may accompany needle insertion and drug injection, and/or to minimize the infiltration of carrier fluids, or to avoid the damage caused by needle insertion when tissue is traumatized. Its patented iontophoresis system, the phoresor (R), is designed for clinical use and is comprised of a reusable dose controller and single use, disposable active transdermal patch kits. The dose controller incorporates an advanced microprocessor to precisely control drug dosage through single-use, disposable patch kits, including its iogel(R), transq(R) and anestrode(R) patch kits.

Primary SIC and add'l.: 2834 8731

CIK No: 0001041652

Officers: Robert J. Lollini/Dir., CEO, Pres., Jessica Barrett/Dir. - Sales, Marketing, Brian L. Mower/CFO, Curtis R. Jensen/Dir. - Quality, Regulatory Affairs, Mary A. Crowther/VP - Administrative Services, Sec., James R. Cronkrite/Dir. - Manufacturing, James D. Isaacson/Dir. - Design, Development

Directors: Robert J. Lollini/Dir., CEO, Pres., Peter J. Wardle/Chmn., John W. Fara/Dir., Michael T. Sember/Dir., Warren Wood/Dir., Stephen D. Antion/Dir.

Owners: Insiders/10.90%, Banque Carnegie Luxembourgh S A/8.40%, Robert J. Lollini/3.70%, Ridgestone Corporation/19.60%, Peter J. Wardle/3.90%

Financial Data: Fiscal Year End:06/30 Latest Annual Data: 6/30/2006

Year	Sales	Net Income
2006	$10,843,000	$600,000
2005	$11,426,000	$425,000
2004	$12,189,000	$954,000

Curr. Assets:	$10,882,000	Curr. Liab.:	$1,464,000		
Plant, Equip.:	$750,000	Total Liab.:	$1,857,000	Indic. Yr. Divd.:	NA
Total Assets:	$12,673,000	Net Worth:	$10,816,000	Debt/ Equity:	0.0038

Iomega Corp

10955 Vista Sorrento Pkwy., Ste. 300, San Diego, CA, 92130; **PH:** 1-858-314-7000; **Fax:** 1-858-314-7001; http:// www.iomega.com

General - Incorporation	DE	**Stock** - Price on:12/24/2007	$4.33
Employees	253	Stock Exchange	NYSE
Auditor	BDO Seidman, LLP	Ticker Symbol	IOM
Stk Agt	American Stock Transfer & Trust Co.	Outstanding Shares	54,730,000
Counsel	Hale & Dorr LLP	E.P.S.	$0.15
DUNS No.	02-153-7865	Shareholders	NA

Business: The group's principle activity is to manufacture innovative data management solutions based on removable-media technology for home and office computers. The products are organized into three broad business categories: mobile and desktop storage systems, network storage systems and new technologies. The mobile and desktop storage systems includes magnetic drives and disks marketed under the zip(R) trademark, optical drives marketed under the iomega(R) CD-rw trademark as well as portable and desktop hard disk drives ("Hdd"), iomega(R) mini usb drives and various software titles. The network storage systems include a wide selection of network attached storage ("Nas") servers. The products of the group are sold through computer product and consumer electronic distributors, retailers, value-added resellers (vars) and original equipment manufacturers (OEMs). The group has several sales offices in Europe, Latin America and Asia. The group's quarterly revenue for Sep'07 was 80.67 millions of USD.

Primary SIC and add'l.: 3572

CIK No: 0000352789

Subsidiaries: Iomega Asia Pacific Sdn Bhd, Iomega Canada Development Corporation, Iomega Corporation Australia PTY Ltd., Iomega Gmbh, Iomega Holdings Corporation, Iomega Hong Kong Ltd., Iomega International S.A., Iomega Japan Corporation, Iomega Latin America, Iomega Overseas B.V., Iomega Pacific PTE Ltd., Iomega SARL, Nomai S.A.

Officers: Jonathan S. Huberman/Vice Chmn., CEO, Thomas Kampfer/COO, Pres./$581,861.00, Mike Nikzad/VP - Operations, Customer Satisfaction, Preston Romm/CFO/$299,127.00, Romain Cholat/VP - International Sales, David Griffith/VP - Product Generation REV Solutions, Jamie Stack/VP - Americas Sales, Peter Wharton/VP - Marketing, Ron S. Zollman/General Counsel, Sec.

Directors: Jonathan S. Huberman/Vice Chmn., CEO, Reynolds C. Bish/55/Dir., Daniel R. Maurer/Dir., John E. Nolan/80/Dir., Robert P. Berkowitz/72/Dir., Bruce B. Darling/55/Dir., Stephen N. David/59/Dir., Margaret L. Hardin/35/Dir.

Owners: Lloyd I. Miller/6.30%, Bryant R. Riley/6.80%, Dimensional Fund Advisors Inc./8.20%, 033 Asset Management, LLC/6.40%, John E. Nolan, Thomas D. Kampfer, Insiders, Stephen N. David, Preston S. Romm, Reynolds C. Bish, Jonathan S. Huberman, Robert P. Berkowitz

Financial Data: Fiscal Year End:12/31 Latest Annual Data: 12/31/2006

Year	Sales	Net Income
2006	$229,554,000	-$8,843,000
2005	$264,505,000	-$22,753,000
2004	$328,663,000	-$36,677,000

Curr. Assets:	$147,307,000	Curr. Liab.:	$68,034,000		
Plant, Equip.:	$6,553,000	Total Liab.:	$77,607,000	Indic. Yr. Divd.:	NA
Total Assets:	$167,414,000	Net Worth:	$89,807,000	Debt/ Equity:	NA

ION Geophysical Corp

Formerly: Input Output Inc
2101 Citywest Blvd, Bldg. Iii, Ste. 400, Houston, TX, 77042; **PH:** 1-281-933-3339; http:// www.i-o.com

General - Incorporation .... DE
Employees 1,015
Auditor .... Ernst & Young LLP
Stk Agt.............................OTC Stock Transfer
Counsel.. NA
DUNS No. 04-908-1441

Stock- Price on:12/24/2007 ....$16.67
Stock Exchange..NYSE
Ticker Symbol..NA
Outstanding Shares 80,430,000
E.P.S. $0.31
Shareholders..NA

Business: The group's principal activities are to design, manufacture and market seismic data acquisition products used on land, transition zones and marine environments. Land data acquisition systems include vibrators, remote ground equipment, geophones, application software and reservoir products. Marine data acquisition systems include marine streamers and shipboard electronics that collect and record seismic data in deep-water environment. Other marine products include hydrophones, air guns, data telemetry quality control systems and positioning systems. The group's products are used in the oil and gas industry as an exploration risk management tool and are also employed in field development and reservoir management. The group's operates in Canada and other countries. On 24-Feb-2004, the group acquired concept systems ltd. On 14-Jun-2004, the group acquired gx technology corporation.

Primary SIC and add'l.: 3829

CIK No: 0000866609

Subsidiaries: Cayman Islands, Ltd., Concept Systems Holdings Limited, Concept Systems Limited, Exploration Products (U.K.), Inc., Exploration Products (U.S.A.), Inc., Geophysical Instruments AS, Global Charter S.A., Gmg/axis, Inc., GX Technology Canada, Ltd., GX Technology Corporation, GX Technology de Venezuela C.A., GX Technology EAME. Limited, GX Technology Finance EURL, GX Technology Trinidad, Ltd., HGS (India) Ltd. 28 Subsidiaries included in the Index

Officers: Robert P. Peebler/Dir., CEO, Pres./$1,522,259.00, Charles J. Ledet/Sr. VP - Land Imaging Systems, Jim Hollis/Exec. VP, COO - ION Solutions Division, David Roland/Sr. VP, General Counsel, Corp. Sec./$457,310.00, Marty Williams/Sr. VP - Firefly Solutions, Tim Rigsby/Sr. VP - Seabed Imaging Solutions, Ken Williamson/Sr. VP - GXT Integrated Seismic Solutions, Steve Bate/Sr. VP - Sensor, Brian R. Hanson/CFO, Exec. VP/$651,843.00, Chris M. Friedemann/Sr. VP - Corporate Marketing, VP - Commercial Development/$550,883.00, Michael L. Morrison/VP, Corporate Controller, Kelly Smith/Dir. - Corp Marketing Communications, Koid Tengbeng/Exec. VP, COO - ION Global Business Development, Nick Bernitsas/Sr. VP - GXT Data Processing, Alan Faichney/Sr. VP - Strategic Resources *(16 Officers included in Index)*

Directors: Robert P. Peebler/Dir., CEO, Pres., James M. Lapeyre/Chmn., John N. Seitz/Dir., Sam K. Smith/Dir., Theodore H. Elliott/Dir., Bruce S. Appelbaum/Dir., Franklin Myers/Dir., James S. Nelson/Dir.

Owners: Laitram, L.L.C./9.90%, Theodore H. Elliott, James M. Lapeyre/11.50%, James S. Nelson, Franklin Myers, Michael K. Lambert, Robert P. Peebler/1.90%, Bruce S. Appelbaum, Christopher M. Friedemann, Wells Fargo& Company/5.50%, Insiders/14.20%, Royce& Associates, LLC/5.60%, ClearBridge Advisors, LLC/7.40%, Sam K. Smith, David L. Roland *(16 Owners included in Index)*

Financial Data: Fiscal Year End:12/31 Latest Annual Data: 12/31/2006

Year	Sales	Net Income
2006	$503,556,000	$29,341,000
2005	$362,682,000	$18,779,000
2004	$247,299,000	-$2,979,000

Curr. Assets:	$346,119,000	Curr. Liab.:	$175,777,000	P/E Ratio:	53.77
Plant, Equip.:	$38,129,000	Total Liab.:	$285,468,000	Indic. Yr. Divd.:	NA
Total Assets:	$655,136,000	Net Worth:	$369,668,000	Debt/ Equity:	0.2195

ION Media Networks Inc

Formerly: Paxson Communications Corp
601 Clearwater Pk Rd. , West Palm Beach, FL, 33401; *PH:* 1-561-659-4122; *http://* www.paxson.com

General - Incorporation .... DE
Employees 453
Auditor ....Rachlin Cohen & Holtz, LLP
Stk Agt..... American Stock Transfer & Trust Co
Counsel.........................Holland & Knight LLP
DUNS No. 55-687-4980

Stock- Price on:12/24/2007 ....$1.38
Stock Exchange..AMEX
Ticker Symbol..NA
Outstanding Shares 73,690,000
E.P.S. ....-$0.12
Shareholders..NA

Business: The group's principle activity is to operate as a network television broadcasting company that owns and operates the broadcast television station group in the United States of America. The group currently owns and operates 61 full power broadcast television stations and operates pax TV, which is a network that provides family oriented entertainment programmes. Pax TV's programming consists of shows originally developed by the group and shows that have appeared previously on other broadcast networks that the group has purchased the right to air. The group derives revenue from the sale of network spot advertising time, network long form paid programming and station advertising. The group's quarterly revenue for September 2007 was 56.49 millions of USD.

Primary SIC and add'l.: 4833

CIK No: 0000923877

Subsidiaries: America 51, L.P., Bud Hits, Inc., Bud Songs, Inc., Clearlake Productions, Inc., Flagler Productions, Inc., Iron Mountain Productions, Inc., Ocean State Television, LLC, PAX Hits Publishing, Inc., PAX Internet, Inc., PAX Net Television Productions, Inc., PAX Net, Inc., Paxson Akron License, Inc., Paxson Albany License, Inc., Paxson Albuquerque License, Inc., Paxson Atlanta License, Inc. 158 Subsidiaries included in the Index

Officers: Brandon Burgess/Dir., CEO/$10,542,900.00, Richard Garcia/CFO, Sr. VP/$803,131.00, Adam K. Weinstein/Sr. VP, Sec., Chief Legal Officer/$710,427.00, Steven J. Friedman/Pres., Stephen P. Appel/Pres. - Sales, Marketing/$1,359,181.00, Douglas C. Barker/Pres. - Broadcast Distribution, David A. Glenn/Pres. - Engineering, Emma Cordoba/VP, Dir. - Human Resources/$249,511.00

Directors: Brandon Burgess/Dir., CEO, Lawrence W. Patrick/Chmn., Henry J. Brandon/Dir., Raymond S. Rajewski/Dir., William A. Roskin/Dir., Lucille S. Salhany/Dir., Frederick M.R. Smith/Dir., Todd E. Gjervold/Dir.

Owners: Henry J. Brandon, Ronald W. Wuensch, Raymond S. Rajewski, Steven Robert Zieger, NBC Universal, Inc., Ted S. Lodge, Diane Price Baker, Insiders, Frederick M.R. Smith, Brandon R. Burgess, Lowell W. Paxson, The Goldman Sachs Group, Inc, Citadel Investment Group, L.L.C., Citadel Investment Group, L.L.C./1.57%, William A. Roskin *(19 Owners included in Index)*

Financial Data: Fiscal Year End:12/31 Latest Annual Data: 12/31/2006

Year	Sales	Net Income
2006	$228,896,000	-$173,744,000
2005	$254,176,000	-$235,670,000
2004	$276,630,000	-$187,972,000

Curr. Assets:	$80,866,000	Curr. Liab.:	$687,034,000		
Plant, Equip.:	$76,768,000	Total Liab.:	$2,046,452,000	Indic. Yr. Divd.:	NA
Total Assets:	$1,056,987,000	Net Worth:	-$1,849,871,000	Debt/ Equity:	NA

ION Networks Inc

120 Corporate Blvd., South Plainfield, NJ, 07080; *PH:* 1-908-546-3900;
http:// www.ion-networks.com; *Email:* info@ion-networks.com

General - Incorporation .... DE
Employees 18
Auditor .... Marcum & Kliegman LLP
Stk Agt ....Registrar & Transfer Co
Counsel.. NA
DUNS No. .... NA

Stock- Price on:12/24/2007 ....$0.041
Stock Exchange..OTC
Ticker Symbol...IONN
Outstanding Shares 32,780,000
E.P.S. ....-$0.08
Shareholders..NA

Business: The group's principal activity is to design, develop, manufactures and sells infrastructure security and management products to corporations, service providers and government agencies. These solutions protect a wide variety of infrastructure devices such as firewalls, servers, routers, LAN switches, pbxs and multiplexers from administrator level security threats while maintaining high availability. The solutions of the group include ion secure solutions, on secure priisms centralized management software, 2000, 3000 and 5000 series security appliances and ion secure soft tokens. The group's physical production and shipping facilities are located in the United States.

Primary SIC and add'l.: 3577 7372 7373

CIK No: 0000754813

Subsidiaries: ION Networks Holdings, ION Networks NV, ION Networks, Limited

Officers: Norman E. Corn/CEO, Henry A. Hill/COO, Bill Whitney/CTO, Patrick E. Delaney/CFO

Owners: Insiders/20.37%, Patrick E. Delaney/3.84%, Norman E. Corn/5.25%, Henry A. Hill/2.24%, AWM Investment Company/34.34%, William Whitney/2.25%, Stephen M. Deixler/8.12%, Frank S. Russo/1.06%, Philip Levine/0.25%

Financial Data: Fiscal Year End:12/31 Latest Annual Data: 12/31/2006

Year	Sales	Net Income
2006	$3,380,000	-$753,000
2005	$4,558,000	$182,000
2004	$3,616,000	-$250,000

Curr. Assets:	$1,290,000	Curr. Liab.:	$1,000,000		
Plant, Equip.:	$40,000	Total Liab.:	$1,018,000	Indic. Yr. Divd.:	NA
Total Assets:	$2,589,000	Net Worth:	$1,571,000	Debt/ Equity:	0.0007

IONA Technologies Plc

200 W St., 4th Fl., Waltham, MA, 02451; *PH:* 1-781-902-8000; *Fax:* 1-781-902-8001;
http:// www.iona.com; *Email:* ir@iona.com

General - Incorporation .... Ireland
Employees 351
Auditor .... Ernst & Young LLP
Stk Agt ..... Computershare Inv Srvs (Ireland) Ltd
Counsel.. NA
DUNS No. 98-900-5459

Stock- Price on:12/24/2007 ....$5.25
Stock Exchange...NDQ
Ticker Symbol..IONA
Outstanding Shares 36,070,000
E.P.S. $0.05
Shareholders..NA

Business: The group's principal activity is the provision of standards-based software for the integration of its customers distributed and disparate computer systems. The group's software products enable its customers to build, maintain and scale their disparate computing environments while preserving and extending existing information technology (IT) investments. It also offers professional services, including ongoing customer support and maintenance as well as application design consultation, education and product implementation. The group markets its software and services in Americas, Europe and Asia-Pacific.

Primary SIC and add'l.: 7372 7379

CIK No: 0001032346

Subsidiaries: Genesis Development Corporation, IONA Government Technologies, Inc., IONA Research (Ireland) Limited, IONA Technologies (Belgium) SA, IONA Technologies (Suisse) SA, IONA Technologies China Limited, IONA Technologies Finance, IONA Technologies GmbH, IONA Technologies Italia Srl, IONA Technologies Japan, IONA Technologies Korea Limited, IONA Technologies Netherlands BV, IONA Technologies Pty. Limited, IONA Technologies Sarl, IONA Technologies Singapore 22 Subsidiaries included in the Index

Officers: Peter Zotto/Dir., CEO, Eric Newcomer/CTO, Philip Pender/VP - Human Resources, Andrew O'Sullivan/VP - Services Business Unit, Christopher M. Mirabile/General Counsel, Bill McMurray/VP - Worldwide Sales, Marketing, Stephanos Bacon/VP - Product Development, Sean Baker/Co - Founder, Chief Corporate Scientist, Scott Devens/VP - International Sales, Strategic Alliances, Robert McBride/CFO, Dave Roy/VP - Investor Relations, William McMurray/46/VP - Worldwide Sales, Marketing, Steven Porter/CIO, Larry Alston/VP - Corporate Strategy, Product Management, Pat Walsh/VP - Marketing

Directors: Peter Zotto/Dir., CEO, Kevin Melia/Chmn., Christopher J. Horn/Co - Founder, Vice Chmn., Ivor Kenny/Non Exec. Dir., Sean Baker/Co - Founder, Chief Corporate Scientist, Francesco Violante/Non Exec. Dir., Jim Maikranz/Non Exec. Dir., Bruce Ryan/Non Exec. Dir.

Owners: Kevin C. Melia, Christopher J. Horn/6.53%, William B. McMurray, Peter M. Zotto, John Conroy, Schroder Investment Management International Ltd/7.23%, Peninsula Capital Management, LP/11.81%, Christopher M. Mirabile, Eric A. Newcomer, Christopher J. Horn/6.53%, Francesco Violante, Sean Baker/3.26%, James Maikranz, Christopher J. Horn/6.53%, Ivor Kenny

Financial Data: Fiscal Year End:12/31 Latest Annual Data: 12/31/2006

Year	Sales	Net Income
2006	$77,838,000	$2,520,000
2005	$66,806,000	-$843,000
2004	$68,019,000	$192,000

Curr. Assets:	$82,098,000	Curr. Liab.:	$39,329,000		
Plant, Equip.:	$2,859,000	Total Liab.:	$41,300,000	Indic. Yr. Divd.:	NA
Total Assets:	$85,097,000	Net Worth:	$43,797,000	Debt/ Equity:	NA

Ionatron Inc

3590 E Columbia St., Tucson, AZ, 85714; *PH:* 1-520-628-7415; *Fax:* 1-520-622-3835;
http:// www.ionatron.com; *Email:* ionatron@ionatron.net

General - Incorporation .... DE
Employees 83
Auditor .... BDO Seidman LLP
Stk Agt ....Continental Stock Transfer & Trust Co
Counsel..................................Blank Rome LLP
DUNS No. 11-165-3205

Stock- Price on:12/24/2007 ....$3.95
Stock Exchange...NDQ
Ticker Symbol..IOTN
Outstanding Shares 78,970,000
E.P.S. ....-$0.23
Shareholders..NA

Business: The group's principal activity is to develop and market directed energy weapon technology products for the U.S. Government. It has entered into several contracts with the U.S. Government and cooperative research and development agreements for joint research on laser induced plasma channel (lipc) based directed energy weapons. The lipc technology controls and directs electrical energy between two points. This technology is useful for multiple national security and defense applications as well as for applications in other commercial sectors. On 20-Sep-2004, the group acquired the assets of north star research corporation.

Primary SIC and add'l.: 3524

CIK No: 0000879911

Subsidiaries: Ionatron Technology, Inc., North Star Power Engineering, Inc.

Officers: Dana A. Marshall/Dir., CEO, Pres./$421,793.00, Thomas Q. Donaldson/Sr. VP - Business Development, Government Relations, Bernard Walik/Exec. VP - Operations/$349,177.00, Joseph C. Hayden/Exec. VP - Business Operations/$200,422.00, Stephen W. McCahon/Exec. VP - Technology/$196,712.00, Kenneth M. Wallace/CFO, COO/$615,365.00

Directors: Dana A. Marshall/Dir., CEO, Pres., David C. Hurley/Chmn., George P. Farley/Dir., James K. Harlan/Dir., James A. McDivitt/Dir.

Owners: Insiders/16.50%, James K. Harlan, Dana A. Marshall, Artis Capital Management, L.P./13.00%, Galleon Management L.P./5.10%, Thomas C. Dearmin/9.10%, Stephen W. McCahon/7.40%, George P. Farley, S.A.C. Capital Advisors, LLC/7.90%, Robert Howard/20.40%, James A. McDivitt, Kenneth M. Wallace, David C. Hurley, Joseph C. Hayden/7.50%

Financial Data: Fiscal Year End:12/31   Latest Annual Data: 12/31/2006

Year	Sales	Net Income
2006	$10,030,000	-$17,514,000
2005	$18,876,000	-$3,625,000
2004	$10,931,000	-$3,261,000

Curr. Assets:	$34,739,000	**Curr. Liab.:**	$2,360,000		
Plant, Equip.:	$2,205,000	**Total Liab.:**	$2,504,000	**Indic. Yr. Divd.:**	NA
Total Assets:	$37,153,000	**Net Worth:**	$34,650,000	**Debt/ Equity:**	0.0002

Iowa Telecommunications Services Inc

115 S 2nd Ave. W, Newton, IA, 50208; **PH:** 1-641-787-2000; **Fax:** 1-641-787-2001; **http://** www.iowatelecom.com; **Email:** investorrelations@iowatelecom.com

General - Incorporation	IA	**Stock** - Price on:12/24/2007	$23.39
Employees	644	Stock Exchange	NYSE
Auditor	Deloitte & Touche LLP	Ticker Symbol	IWA
Stk Agt	American Stock Transfer & Trust Co.	Outstanding Shares	31,710,000
Counsel	NA	E.P.S.	$1.01
DUNS No.	NA	Shareholders	NA

Business: The groups principle activity is to provide wireline local exchange telecommunications services to residential and business customers. The group acquired Montezuma Mutual Telephone Company in July 2006 and Baker Communications, Inc. in August 2006. The group operates 228 telephone exchanges in the United States.The group's quarterly revenue for September 2007 was 60.78 in millions of USD.

Primary SIC and add'l.: 7389 4822 4813 4899 7379

CIK No: 0001120462

Subsidiaries: Baker Communications, Inc., Iowa Telecom Communications, Inc., Iowa Telecom Data Services, L.C., Iowa Telecom Technologies, LLC, IT Communications, LLC, IWA Holdings, LLC, IWA Services, LLC, Montezuma Mutual Telephone Company

Officers: Alan L. Wells/Chmn., CEO, Pres./$1,921,368.00, David M. Anderson/VP - External Affairs, Marketing, Charles J. Bruggemann/VP - Operations, Donald G. Henry/VP, General Counsel, Sec./$345,885.00, Lon M. Hopkey/VP - Corporate Development, Dennis R. Kilburg/VP - Engineering/$379,244.00, Craig A. Knock/CFO, VP, Treasurer/$565,116.00, Timothy D. Lockhart/VP - Customer Services, Human Resources, Brian T. Naaden/CIO, VP/$414,390.00, Michael A. Struck/VP - Sales

Directors: Alan L. Wells/Chmn., CEO, Pres., Norman C. Frost/Dir., Brian G. Hart/Dir., Kevin R. Hranicka/Dir., Craig A. Lang/Dir., Kendrik E. Packer/Dir., Lynn H. Horak/62/Dir.

Owners: Brian T. Naaden, NFJ Investment Group L.P./5.67%, Donald G. Henry, Craig A. Knock, Kendrik E. Packer, Alan L. Wells/1.55%, Dennis R. Kilburg, Insiders/2.96%, Brian G. Hart, Norman C. Frost

Financial Data: Fiscal Year End:12/31   Latest Annual Data: 12/31/2006

Year	Sales	Net Income
2006	$234,085,000	$34,043,000
2005	$231,640,000	$46,390,000
2004	$228,119,000	$14,204,000

Curr. Assets:	$40,115,000	**Curr. Liab.:**	$81,060,000	**P/E Ratio:**	23.16
Plant, Equip.:	$298,975,000	**Total Liab.:**	$591,830,000	**Indic. Yr. Divd.:**	$1.620
Total Assets:	$859,529,000	**Net Worth:**	$267,699,000	**Debt/ Equity:**	1.8053

IPALCO Enterprises Inc

1 Monument Cir., Indianapolis, IN, 46206; **PH:** 1-317-261-8261; **Fax:** 1-317-630-5726; **http://** www.ipalco.com; **Email:** CustomerServices@aes.com

General - Incorporation	IN	**Stock** - Price on:12/24/2007	NA
Employees	NA	Stock Exchange	NA
Auditor	Deloitte & Touche LLP	Ticker Symbol	NA
Stk Agt	Deloitte & Touche LLP	Outstanding Shares	NA
Counsel	NA	E.P.S.	NA
DUNS No.	10-222-8590	Shareholders	NA

Business: The group's principle activities of the group are generation, transmission, distribution, production and sale of electric energy and steam in the city of indianapolis and neighboring cities, towns, communities, and adjacent rural areas. The group operates from United States.

Primary SIC and add'l.: 4911 4961

CIK No: 0000728391

Subsidiaries: Indianapolis Power & Light Company, Mid-America Capital Resources, Inc.

Owners: Richard Santoroski, Ann D. Murtlow, Frank P. Marino, The AES Corporation/100.00%, Stephen R. Corwell, Ronald E. Talbot, David Gee, Insiders, James A. Sadtler

iParty Corp

270 Bridge St., Dedham, MA, 02026; **PH:** 1-781-329-3952; **Fax:** 1-781-326-7143; **http://** www.iparty.com; **Email:** customercare@iparty.com

General - Incorporation	DE	**Stock**- Price on:12/24/2007	$0.42
Employees	278	Stock Exchange	AMEX
Auditor	Ernst & Young LLP	Ticker Symbol	IPT
Stk Agt	Continental Stock Transfer & Trust Co	Outstanding Shares	22,620,000
Counsel	Posternak Blankstein & Lund LLP	E.P.S.	NA
DUNS No.	NA	Shareholders	NA

Business: The group's principal activities are to provide retail services for consumers seeking party goods, party planning advice and information. The retail stores feature over 20,000 products including greeting cards, balloons, pinatas, gag gifts, masquerade and hawaiian luau items. In 2003, the group licensed its Internet business to a third party in exchange for royalties under a license agreement. The group operates throughout new England, where 37 of its 41 retail stores are located. The group also has other four stores located in Florida, one of which, in citrus park was opened during the end of the second quarter.

Primary SIC and add'l.: 5947 7375

CIK No: 0001078383

Subsidiaries: iParty Retail Stores Corp

Officers: Sal Perisano/Chmn., CEO/$326,562.00, Dorice Dionne/Sr. VP - Merchandising/$195,938.00, Patrick Farrell/CFO, Pres./$223,485.00

Directors: Sal Perisano/Chmn., CEO, Daniel I. Dewolf/Dir., Christina Weaver-Vest/Dir., Eric Schindler/Dir., Frank Haydu/Dir., Joseph S. Vassalluzzo/Dir., Robert Jevon/Dir.

Owners: HMTF Holdings, Eric Schindler, Robert W. Jevon, Insiders, Roccia Partners, L.P., Naida S. Wharton, Dorice P. Dionne, Robert H. Lessin, Joseph S. Vassalluzzo, Patrick Farrell, Highbridge International LLC, Frank W. Haydu, Christina W. Vest, Sal V. Perisano, Daniel I. De Wolf (17 Owners included in Index)

Financial Data: Fiscal Year End:12/31   Latest Annual Data: 12/30/2006

Year	Sales	Net Income
2006	$78,458,000	$375,000
2005	$72,538,000	-$268,000
2004	$64,276,000	$991,000

Curr. Assets:	$16,397,000	**Curr. Liab.:**	$14,306,000	**P/E Ratio:**	10.50
Plant, Equip.:	$5,187,000	**Total Liab.:**	$15,402,000	**Indic. Yr. Divd.:**	NA
Total Assets:	$21,717,000	**Net Worth:**	$6,316,000	**Debt/ Equity:**	0.5144

iPass Inc

3800 Bridge Pkwy., Redwood Shores, CA, 94065; **PH:** 1-650-232-4100; **Fax:** 1-650-232-4111; **http://** www.ipass.com; **Email:** sales-na@ipass.com

General - Incorporation	DE	**Stock**- Price on:12/24/2007	$5.3
Employees	575	Stock Exchange	NDQ
Auditor	KPMG LLP	Ticker Symbol	IPAS
Stk Agt	ComputerShare Trust Co	Outstanding Shares	63,010,000
Counsel	Cooley Godward LLP	E.P.S.	-$0.12
DUNS No.	NA	Shareholders	NA

Business: The group's principle activity is to provide software-enabled enterprise connectivity services for mobile workers. The primary service offering is designed to enable businesses to provide their employees with secure access from approximately 150 countries to their internal networks through an easy-to-use interface. The software is designed to provide enterprises with a high level of security, the ability to affect and control policy management, and to receive centralized billing and detailed reporting. The group's virtual network aggregates over 18,000 network access points in approximately 150 countries. The group's quarterly revenue in Sep'07 was 47.74 millions of USD.

Primary SIC and add'l.: 7374

CIK No: 0001053374

Subsidiaries: GoRemote Internet Communications, Inc., iPass Asia, Pte., Ltd., iPass France, SAS, iPass Holdings, Pty, Ltd., iPass Japan, K.K., iPass U.K., Limited, iPass, Ltd., Mobile Automation, Inc., Safe3w, Inc.

Officers: Kenneth D. Denman/Chmn., CEO/$859,541.00, Barbara Nelson/VP - Architecture, Design, Sanjeev Malhotra/MD - India, Rene Hendrikse/MD - EMEA, Tim Shanahan/Dir. - Investor Relations, Anurag Lal/Chief Business Development, Sales Officer/$518,552.00, James McGuire/VP - Americas Sales, Loy Chee Leng/MD - Asia Sales, John Cunningham/MD - Australia, New Zealand, Joel Wachtler/VP - Marketing, Strategy, Bruce Posey/Sr. VP, General Counsel, Corp. Sec./$466,506.00, John Charters/COO, Frank E. Verdecanna/CFO, VP/$394,311.00

Directors: Kenneth D. Denman/Chmn., CEO, John D. Beletic/Dir., Gary A. Ames/Dir., Olof Pripp/Dir., Allan R. Spies/Dir., Arthur C. Patterson/Dir., Peter G. Bodine/Dir., Cregg B. Baumbaugh/Dir., Peter C. Clapman/Dir., Michael J. McConnell/Dir.

Owners: Kenneth D. Denman/4.20%, Gary A. Ames, Peter G. Bodine, Royce & Associates LLC/12.70%, Entities affiliated with Shamrock Partners Activist Value Fund, L.L.C./14.30%, Frank Verdecanna, John D. Beletic, Insiders/21.90%, Olof Pripp, Allan R. Spies, Bruce K. Posey, John Charters, Arthur C. Patterson, Anurag Lal, Michael J. McConnell/14.30%

Financial Data: Fiscal Year End:12/31   Latest Annual Data: 12/31/2006

Year	Sales	Net Income
2006	$182,711,000	-$8,089,000
2005	$169,373,000	$12,895,000
2004	$166,319,000	$19,068,000

Curr. Assets:	$142,190,000	**Curr. Liab.:**	$36,723,000		
Plant, Equip.:	$10,519,000	**Total Liab.:**	$40,160,000	**Indic. Yr. Divd.:**	NA
Total Assets:	$263,467,000	**Net Worth:**	$223,307,000	**Debt/ Equity:**	NA

iPayment Inc

40 Burton Hills Blvd., Ste. 415, Nashville, TN, 37215; **PH:** 1-615-665-1858; **Fax:** 1-818-702-2412; **http://** www.ipaymentinc.com; **Email:** merchantsupport@merchant-help.com

General - Incorporation	DE	**Stock**- Price on:12/24/2007	NA
Employees	NA	Stock Exchange	NA
Auditor	Ernst & Young LLP	Ticker Symbol	NA
Stk Agt	Wachovia Bank N.A	Outstanding Shares	NA
Counsel	NA	E.P.S.	NA
DUNS No.	NA	Shareholders	NA

Business: The group's principal activity is to provide credit and debit card-based payment processing to small merchants. Payment processing services enable merchants to process both traditional card-present as well as card not present transactions. The small merchants typically generate less than $250,000 of charge volume per year and have an average transaction of approximately $75. At 31-Dec-2003,the group provided services to approximately 90,000 active small merchants located across the United States. On 05-Aug-2003, the group acquired cardpayment solutions inc and on 15-Sep-2004, it also acquired transaction solutions.

Primary SIC and add'l.: 7389

CIK No: 0001140184

Subsidiaries: 1st National Processing, Inc., CardPayment Solutions, LLC, CardSync Processing, Inc., E-Commerce Exchange, Inc., iPayment Acquisition Sub, LLC, iPayment ICE Holdings, Inc., iPayment ICE of Utah, LLC, iPayment of California, LLC, iPayment of Eureka, Inc., iPayment of Maine, Inc., NPMG Acquisition Sub, LLC, Online Data Corp., PCS Acquisition Sub, LLC, Quad City Acquisition Sub, Inc., TS Acquisition Sub, LLC

Officers: Gregory S. Daily/48/Chmn., CEO, Robert S. Torino/54/Exec. VP, Assist. Sec., Carl A. Grimstad/40/Dir., Pres., Afshin M. Yazdian/35/Exec. VP, General Counsel, Sec., Clay M. Whitson/50/CFO, Treasurer, Nasir Shakouri/Human Resources - Ipayment, Inc

Directors: Gregory S. Daily/48/Chmn., CEO, Carl A. Grimstad/40/Dir., Pres.

IPC Holdings Ltd

29 Richmond Rd. , C/o American International Bldg, Pembroke; **PH:** 441-2985100; **Fax:** 441-2928085; **http://** www.ipcre.bm; **Email:** info@ipcre.bm

General - Incorporation	Bermuda	**Stock**- Price on:12/24/2007	$31.69
Employees	28	Stock Exchange	NDQ
Auditor	KPMG LLP	Ticker Symbol	IPCR
Stk Agt	Computershare Investor Services LLC	Outstanding Shares	63,650,000
Counsel	Sullivan & Cromwell	E.P.S.	NA
DUNS No.	NA	Shareholders	NA

Business: The group's principal activities are to provide property catastrophe reinsurance, casualty and to a limited extent, marine, aviation, property per risk excess and other short-tail property reinsurance through its subsidiaries. The property catastrophe reinsurance covers unpredictable events such as hurricanes, windstorms, hailstorms, earthquakes, volcanic eruptions, fires, freezes, industrial explosions and other man-made or natural disasters. The group is a holding company and operates through the subsidiaries ipcre limited and ipcre underwriting services limited. The operations of the group are carried on throughout the United States, the United Kingdom, Europe, Japan, Australia and New Zealand.

Primary SIC and add'l.: 6719 6399 6331

CIK No: 0000909815

Subsidiaries: IPCRe Europe Limited, IPCRe Limited, IPCRe Underwriting Services Limited

Officers: James P. Bryce/CEO, Pres./$3,348,773.00, Stephen F. Fallon/Sr. VP - Underwriting, North America/$1,651,214.00, John R. Weale/CFO, Sr. VP/$1,321,378.00, Peter J.A. Cozens/Sr. VP - Underwriting, International/$1,771,303.00, Glenn N.B. Clinton/VP - Underwriting, North America, Marco L. Nicolini/VP - Underwriting, International, Robin M. Newman/VP, Controller, Donna Mae Clarke/VP - Accounting, Steven M. Smith/Assist. VP - Underwriting, North America, Judy Gardecki/Assist. VP - Claims, Lori Steinhoff/Assist. VP - Accounting, Joanna Shillington/Assist. VP - Accounting

Directors: Frank Mutch/Chmn., George S. Cubbon/Dep. Chmn., Clarence Eldridge James/Dir., Kenneth L. Hammond/Dir., Antony P.D. Lancaster/Dir., P. S. Christie/Dir.

Owners: Insiders, Stephen F. Fallon, Snow Capital Management, L.P./7.20%, John R. Weale, Pzena Investment Management, LLC/6.40%, James P. Bryce, Frank Mutch, George S. Cubbon, FMR Corp./14.90%, Franklin Resources, Inc./5.90%, Peter J. A. Cozens

iPCS Inc

1901 N Roselle Rd., Ste. 500, Schaumburg, IL, 60195; **PH:** 1-847-885-2833; **Fax:** 1-847-885-7125; **http://** www.ipcswirelessinc.com; **Email:** corporateinquires@ipcswirelessinc.com

General - Incorporation	DE	**Stock**- Price on:12/24/2007	$0.15
Employees	1	Stock Exchange	NDQ
Auditor	Deloitte & Touche LLP	Ticker Symbol	IPCS
Stk Agt	Bank of New York	Outstanding Shares	12,720,000
Counsel	NA	E.P.S.	-$4.56
DUNS No.	NA	Shareholders	NA

Business: The group's principle activity is to provide digital wireless personal communications services pcs). The pcs service packages offered by the company include: third generation services, clear pay/account spending limit & other services like wireless local loop services. Offer national calling plans designed by sprint pcs, as well as local calling plans. The group is a wholly owned subsidiary of airgate pcs inc. The group operates from United States.

Primary SIC and add'l.: 3661 4822 4899

CIK No: 0001108727

Subsidiaries: Bright PCS Holdings, Inc., Bright Personal Communications Services, LLC, Horizon Personal Communications, Inc., iPCS Equipment, Inc., iPCS Wireless, Inc.

Officers: Timothy M. Yager/Dir., CEO, Pres., Patricia M. Greteman/VP, Controller, Craig A. Kinley/Sr. VP, Stebbins B. Chandor/CFO, Exec. VP, John J. Peterman/Sr. VP - Sales, Edmund L. Quatmann/VP, General Counsel, Sec., Lisa Cradit/Financial Dynamics, Conrad J. Hunter/COO, Exec. VP, Michael Polyviou/Investor Contact

Directors: Timothy M. Yager/Dir., CEO, Pres., Robert A. Katz/Chmn., Timothy C. Babich/Dir., Mikal J. Thomsen/Dir., Jeffrey W. Jones/Dir., Ryan L. Langdon/Dir., Timothy G. Biltz/Dir., Kevin M. Roe/Dir., Eric L. Zinterhofer/36/Dir.

Owners: Timothy M. Yager/1.30%, AIG Global Investment Corp./15.80%, Insiders/2.40%, Apollo Management IV, L.P./15.60%, John J. Peterman, Jeffrey W. Jones, Eric L. Zinterhofer, Stebbins B. Chandor, Timothy G. Biltz, Ryan L. Langdon, Kevin M. Roe, The Goldman Sachs Group,Inc. and Goldman, Sachs& Co./5.70%, Edmund L. Quatmann, Greywolf Capital Management LP/6.50%, Silver Point Capital, L.P./17.00%

Financial Data: Fiscal Year End:09/30 Latest Annual Data: 03/31/2007

Year	Sales	Net Income
2007	NA	-$647,000
2006	$492,422,000	-$46,039,000

Curr. Assets:	$184,233,000	Curr. Liab.:	$89,235,000		
Plant, Equip.:	$153,504,000	Total Liab.:	$403,908,000	Indic. Yr. Divd.:	NA
Total Assets:	$673,990,000	Net Worth:	$270,082,000	Debt/ Equity:	NA

IPORussia Inc

12 Tompkins Ave., Jericho, NY, 11753; **PH:** 1-516-937-6600

General - Incorporation	DE	**Stock**- Price on:12/24/2007	$0.115
Employees	NA	Stock Exchange	OTC
Auditor	Aaron Stein CPA	Ticker Symbol	IPOR
Stk Agt	OTC Corporate Transfer Service Co	Outstanding Shares	98,430,000
Counsel	NA	E.P.S.	-$0.042
DUNS No.	NA	Shareholders	NA

Business: The groups principal activity is to offer business advisory services to private companies. Services of the group include providing information for the requirements and procedures of going public, assisting and assembling the team of professionals knowledgeable and experienced, and providing capital rising. The group operates from Russia and the United States.

Primary SIC and add'l.: 8742

CIK No: 0001179090

Subsidiaries: IPOR CAPITAL, LLC.

Officers: Vladimir F. Kuznetsov/58/Dir., CEO, Pres., Mark R. Suroff/34/Exec. VP, Sec., Treasurer

Directors: Richard Bernstein/65/Dir.

Owners: KI Equity Partners VI, LLC/74.72%, Garisch Financial, Inc./7.10%, Kevin R. Keating/2.03%, Insiders/2.03%

Financial Data: Fiscal Year End:12/31 Latest Annual Data: 12/31/2006

Year	Sales	Net Income
2006	NA	-$786,000
2005	NA	-$864,000
2004	NA	-$181,000

Curr. Assets:	$17,000	Curr. Liab.:	$496,000		
Plant, Equip.:	NA	Total Liab.:	$617,000	Indic. Yr. Divd.:	NA
Total Assets:	$17,000	Net Worth:	-$599,000	Debt/ Equity:	NA

IPSCO Inc

650 Warrenville Rd., Ste. 500, Lisle, IL, 60532; **PH:** 1-630-810-4800; **http://** www.ipsco.com

General - Incorporation	Canada	**Stock**- Price on:12/24/2007	$158.56
Employees	4,400	Stock Exchange	NA
Auditor	Ernst & Young LLP	Ticker Symbol	NA
Stk Agt	Computershare Trust Co of Canada	Outstanding Shares	47,220,000
Counsel	Davis Polk & Wardwell	E.P.S.	$12.62
DUNS No.	20-067-5734	Shareholders	NA

Business: The group's principle activities are the production and sale of steel products. The group's business provides a major assist to the environment since virtually all of its raw material is steel scrap. The group operates in two divisions: fabricated products and steel mill products.

Primary SIC and add'l.: 3441 3317 3312 3315 3316

CIK No: 0000879933

Subsidiaries: General Scrap Inc, General Scrap Partnership Saskatchewan General Partnership, IPSCO Construction Inc, IPSCO Direct Inc., IPSCO Enterprises Inc, IPSCO Minnesota Inc, IPSCO Recycling Inc, IPSCO Sales Inc, IPSCO Sales Inc., IPSCO Saskatchewan Inc, IPSCO Steel (Alabama) Inc, IPSCO Steel Inc, IPSCO Texas Inc, IPSCO Tubulars Inc., Western Steel Limited

Officers: Vicki Avril/Sr. VP - Tubular/$1,606,930.00, Phil Marusarz/Controller, Michele Klebuc-Simes/VP, General Counsel, Corp. Sec., Andy Skinner/Works Mgr. - Ipsco Koppel Tubulars Corporation, Koppel, Paul Wilson/Works Mgr. - Ipsco Steel, Alabama Inc, Mobile, David Britten/Sr. VP - Steel/$1,506,898.00, Daniel Miksta/VP, General Sales Mgr. - Steel, Ed Diciccio/Acting Works Mgr. - Ipsco Steel Inc, Montpelier, Doug Dunford/Works Mgr. - Ultra Premium Oilfield Services, Ltd, Odessa Ultra, Harry Lepargneux/Works Mgr. - Ipsco Canada Inc, Red Deer, Dale Rauw/Works Mgr. - Ipsco Saskatchewan Inc, Regina Coil Processing, Olan Smith/Works Mgr. - Ipsco Saskatchewan Inc, Regina Steel, Jeff Clark/Works Mgr. - Ipsco Saskatchewan Inc, Regina Tubular, David Fazekas/Works Mgr. - Ipsco Canada Inc, Surrey, Joseph Folio/Works Mgr. - Ipsco Minnesota Inc, St. Paul (55 Officers included in Index)

Owners: Juanita Hinshaw, Leslie Lederer, Arthur Price, Barclays Global Investors, NA/5.77%, David Sutherland, John Zaozirny, Richard Sim, Harbinger Capital Partners Master Fund I, Ltd./9.92%, Michael Grandin, FMR Corp/9.85%, Allan Olson, John Tulloch, Insiders, Gordon Thiessen, Joseph Russo (26 Owners included in Index)

Financial Data: Fiscal Year End:12/31 Latest Annual Data: 12/31/2006

Year	Sales	Net Income
2006	$3,775,603,000	$643,114,000
2005	$3,032,727,000	$585,816,000
2004	$2,452,675,000	$454,942,000

Curr. Assets:	$1,480,013,000	Curr. Liab.:	$432,586,000	P/E Ratio:	12.56
Plant, Equip.:	$1,313,517,000	Total Liab.:	$1,871,952,000	Indic. Yr. Divd.:	$0.680
Total Assets:	$4,131,753,000	Net Worth:	$2,259,801,000	Debt/ Equity:	0.3661

iQ Power AG

Formerly: iQ Power Technology Inc
BAARERSTR. 137, Zurich, V8 CH-6300; **PH:** 49-89-614-48310; **http://** www.iqpower.com

General - Incorporation	Switzerland	**Stock**- Price on:12/24/2007	NA
Employees	NA	Stock Exchange	OTC
Auditor	Deloitte AG	Ticker Symbol	IQPOF
Stk Agt	Deloitte & Touche LLP	Outstanding Shares	NA
Counsel	NA	E.P.S.	NA
DUNS No.	NA	Shareholders	NA

Business: The groups principle activity is to develop and commercialize electrical power sources and energy management technologies for the automotive, aerospace and defense industry. The group operates from United States.

Primary SIC and add'l.: 3691

CIK No: 0001072667

Subsidiaries: iQ Power Asia Inc., iQ Power Deutschland GmbH, iQ Power Licensing AG

Officers: Charles Robert Sullivan/CEO - Overall Management, Strategy, Sales, Gunther Bauer/CTO, MD - iQ Power Deutschland Gmbh, Peter Krumhoff/CFO - iQ Power Group

Directors: Peter E. Braun/Dir., Hans Ambos/Dir., Raymond Wicki/Dir., Richard Gaul/Dir., Burkhard Goschel/Dir., Thomas Limberger/Dir., Rudiger Wendt/Dir.

Curr. Assets:	$1,630,000	Curr. Liab.:	$803,000		
Plant, Equip.:	$462,000	Total Liab.:	$1,707,000	Indic. Yr. Divd.:	NA
Total Assets:	$2,358,000	Net Worth:	$651,000	Debt/ Equity:	NA

IR BioSciences Holdings Inc

8767 E Via De Ventura, Ste. 190, Scottsdale, AZ, 85258; *PH:* 1-480-922-3926;
Fax: 1-480-922-4781; *http://* www.immuneregen.com; *Email:* info@immuneregen.com

General - Incorporation	DE	**Stock** - Price on:12/24/2007	$0.185
Employees	4	Stock Exchange	OTC
Auditor ... Russell Bedford Stefanou Mirchandani		Ticker Symbol	IRBO
Stk Agt	Continental Stock Transfer & Trust Co	Outstanding Shares	114,320,000
Counsel	NA	E.P.S.	-$0.01
DUNS No.	NA	Shareholders	NA

Business: The group's principal activity is to engage in the research and development of applications utilizing modified substance p, a naturally occurring immunomodulator. Derived from homeostatic substance p, the group has named its proprietary compound 'homspera'. The group's main focus is in the development of several applications for use in improving pulmonary function and stimulating the immune system. On 20-Jul-2003, the group acquired immuneregen biosciences inc.

Primary SIC and add'l.: 8733

CIK No: 0000793043

Subsidiaries: ImmuneRegen Biosciences, Inc.

Officers: Michael K. Wilhelm/Dir., CEO, Pres., John N. Fermanis/CFO, Jason W. Grimley/Contact - Media, Spelling Communications, Bill Lane/In House Investor Relations Officer, Jack Caravelli/Consultant, Michael Caridi/Sr. Advisor, Hal N. Siegel/Dir., Dir. - Product Development, Regulatory Affairs, K.A. Kelly McQueen/Member - Scientific Advisory Board, Consultant, Michelle R. Laroche/Dir. - Operations, Immuneregen Biosciences, Inc

Directors: Michael K. Wilhelm/Dir., CEO, Pres., Theodore E. Staahl/Dir., Asa Hutchinson/Member - Bioterrorism Preparedness Advisory Board, John Kalns/Member - Bioterrorism Preparedness Advisory Board, John Dann/Member - Scientific Advisory Board, Jeffery Friedman/Member - Scientific Advisory Board, Akihiro Shimosaka/Member - Scientific Advisory Board, Frederick M. Burkle/Member - Bioterrorism Preparedness Advisory Board, Paul Carlton/Member - Bioterrorism Preparedness Advisory Board, William Hoehn/Member - Bioterrorism Preparedness Advisory Board, Michael Deutsch/Member - Bioterrorism Preparedness Advisory Board, Kerrie Lindberg/Member - Bioterrorism Preparedness Advisory Board, Hal N. Siegel/Dir., Dir. - Product Development, Regulatory Affairs, Robert J. Hariri/Dir., Lance K. Gordon/Dir. (20 Directors included in Index)

Owners: John N. Fermanis, Mark L. Witten/12.40%, Michael K. Wilhelm/13.70%, Insiders/18.60%, Theodore Staahl/4.70%, Hal N. Siegel

Financial Data: Fiscal Year End:12/31   Latest Annual Data: 12/31/2006

Year	Sales	Net Income
2006	NA	-$1,486,000
2005	NA	-$4,591,000
2004	NA	-$5,305,000

Curr. Assets:	$2,832,000	Curr. Liab.:	$511,000		
Plant, Equip.:	$28,000	Total Liab.:	$511,000	Indic. Yr. Divd.:	NA
Total Assets:	$2,862,000	Net Worth:	$2,351,000	Debt/ Equity:	NA

Ireland Inc

810 Peace Portal Dr., Ste. 201, Blaine, WA, 98230; *PH:* 1-360-318-3020

General - Incorporation	NV	**Stock** - Price on:12/24/2007	$2.915
Employees	NA	Stock Exchange	OTC
Auditor	Telford Sadovnick, PLLC	Ticker Symbol	IREL
Stk Agt	NA	Outstanding Shares	NA
Counsel	NA	E.P.S.	-$0.09
DUNS No.	NA	Shareholders	NA

Business: The groups principal activities include acquiring, exploring and developing mineral properties. The group operates from the United States and Ireland.

Primary SIC and add'l.: 1040

CIK No: 0001166338

Officers: Douglas D.G. Birnie/38/CEO, Pres., Sec., Robert D. McDougal/75/CFO

Directors: Lorrie Ann Archibald/41/Dir.

Owners: Douglas D.G. Birnie/10.10%, Nanominerals Corp./69.70%, Insiders/58.90%, Robert D. McDougal/4.40%, Lorrie Ann Archibald/49.80%

Financial Data: Fiscal Year End:12/31   Latest Annual Data: 12/31/2006

Year	Sales	Net Income
2006	NA	-$95,000

Curr. Assets:	$12,000	Curr. Liab.:	$71,000		
Plant, Equip.:	NA	Total Liab.:	$71,000	Indic. Yr. Divd.:	NA
Total Assets:	$12,000	Net Worth:	-$59,000	Debt/ Equity:	NA

IRIDEX Corp

1212 Terra Bella Ave., Mountain View, CA, 94043; *PH:* 1-650-940-4700; *Fax:* 1-650-940-4710;
http:// www.iridex.com; *Email:* sales@iridex.com

General - Incorporation	DE	**Stock** - Price on:12/24/2007	$5.81
Employees	121	Stock Exchange	NDQ
Auditor	PricewaterhouseCoopers LLP	Ticker Symbol	IRIX
Stk Agt	EquiServe Trust Co N.A	Outstanding Shares	8,170,000
Counsel	Wilson Sonsini Goodrich & Rosati	E.P.S.	NA
DUNS No.	61-292-0785	Shareholders	NA

Business: The group's principal activity is to provide semiconductor-based laser systems, which are used to treat eye diseases in ophthalmology and skin afflictions in dermatology. The ophthalmic products are used to treat eye diseases. The dermatology products treat skin diseases, primarily vascular and pigmented lesions and remove unwanted hair. The group has its operations in the United States, Europe, and rest of America and Asia/Pacific Rim.

Primary SIC and add'l.: 3851 8071 3841

CIK No: 0001006045

Subsidiaries: IRIS Medical Instruments, Inc., Light Solutions Corporation

Officers: Theodore A. Boutacoff/Chmn., CEO, Pres., Larry Tannenbaum/Chief Business Officer, Sr. VP/$256,965.00, James L. Donovan/Dir., VP - Corporate Business Development, Eduardo Arias/Sr. VP - International Sales, Business Development, Timothy Powers/VP - Operations/$221,524.00, Donald J. Todd/Sr. VP - Marketing, Customer Support/$486,248.00, James D. Pardee/Interim CFO

Directors: Theodore A. Boutacoff/Chmn., CEO, Pres., Barry G. Caldwell/57/Dir., Donald L. Hammond/Dir., Robert K. Anderson/72/Dir., James L. Donovan/Dir., VP - Corporate Business Development, Sanford Fitch/Dir., Garrett Garrettson/Dir., William M. Moore/Dir., James B. Hawkins/Dir.

Owners: James L. Donovan/1.45%, Timothy S. Powers/1.55%, Robert K. Anderson/2.21%, Sanford Fitch, Donald L. Hammond, Barry G. Caldwell/1.68%, Garrett A. Garretson, Black River Asset Management LLC/9.31%, Black River Long/Short Fund Ltd./7.32%, Insiders/13.74%, Theodore A. Boutacoff/2.88%, BlueLine Partners, L.L.C./7.77%, 033 Asset Management LLC/7.98%, Donald J. Todd, Eduardo Arias/2.70% (16 Owners included in Index)

Financial Data: Fiscal Year End:12/31   Latest Annual Data: 12/30/2006

Year	Sales	Net Income
2006	$35,904,000	-$5,753,000
2005	$37,029,000	$1,671,000

Curr. Assets:	$38,917,000	Curr. Liab.:	$6,587,000		
Plant, Equip.:	$1,114,000	Total Liab.:	$6,587,000	Indic. Yr. Divd.:	NA
Total Assets:	$41,104,000	Net Worth:	$34,517,000	Debt/ Equity:	NA

IRIS International Inc

9172 Eton Ave., Chatsworth, CA, 91311; *PH:* 1-818-709-1244; *Fax:* 1-818-700-9661;
http:// www.proiris.com

General - Incorporation	DE	**Stock** - Price on:12/24/2007	$15.15
Employees	274	Stock Exchange	NDQ
Auditor	BDO Seidman LLP	Ticker Symbol	IRIS
Stk Agt	Continental Stock Transfer & Trust Co	Outstanding Shares	18,200,000
Counsel	NA	E.P.S.	$0.36
DUNS No.	09-824-0690	Shareholders	NA

Business: The group's principal activity is to design, develop, manufacture, and market invitro diagnostic imaging systems for urinalysis testing. This testing is based on patented and proprietary automated intelligent microscopy technology for automating microscopic procedures performed in clinical laboratories, as well as special purpose centrifuges and other small instruments. The group through its subsidiary manufactures and markets a variety of benchtop centrifuges, small instruments and supplies for the laboratory market. These products are used primarily for manual specimen preparation and dedicated applications in cytology, hematology and urinalysis. The products are sold directly to hospitals, clinical and research laboratories and veterinary and physician offices and also through distributors.

Primary SIC and add'l.: 3845

CIK No: 0000319240

Subsidiaries: AdvancedDigitalImagingResearch,LLC, Iris Deutschland GmbH, Iris Diagnostics France S. A., Iris Global Network, Inc., Poly U/A Systems, Inc., StatSpin, Inc.

Officers: Cesar M. Garcia/Dir., CEO, Pres./$636,234.00, Robert A. Mello/Corporate VP, GM/$317,636.00, Peter Donato/CFO, Corporate VP/$71,115.00, Veronica O. Tarrant/46/Interim CFO, VP - Finance, Corporate Controller, John U. Yi/47/Corporate VP - Operations

Directors: Cesar M. Garcia/Dir., CEO, Pres., Richard H. Williams/Chmn., Richard G. Nadeau/Dir., Steven M. Besbeck/Dir., Michael D. Matte/Dir., Thomas H. Adams/Dir., Stephen E. Wasserman/Dir.

Owners: Csar M. Garca/1.95%, Michael D. Matte, Robert A. Mello, Kopp Investment Advisors LLC/7.76%, Thomas E. Warekois, Thomas H. Adams/1.65%, Richard H. Williams, Steven M. Besbeck, Richard G. Nadeau, Veronica O. Tarrant, Stephen Wasserman, John U. Yi, FMR Corp/8.24%, Insiders/7.37%

Financial Data: Fiscal Year End:12/31   Latest Annual Data: 03/31/2007

Year	Sales	Net Income
2007	NA	NA
2006	$70,494,000	-$175,000
2005	$62,780,000	$6,131,000

Curr. Assets:	$49,011,000	Curr. Liab.:	$11,728,000	P/E Ratio:	47.34
Plant, Equip.:	$7,102,000	Total Liab.:	$11,751,000	Indic. Yr. Divd.:	NA
Total Assets:	$74,317,000	Net Worth:	$62,566,000	Debt/ Equity:	NA

IRobot Corp

63 S Ave., Burlington, MA, 01803; *PH:* 1-781-345-0200; *Fax:* 1-781-345-0201;
http:// www.irobot.com; *Email:* info@irobot.com

General - Incorporation	DE	**Stock** - Price on:12/24/2007	$19.11
Employees	371	Stock Exchange	NDQ
Auditor	PricewaterhouseCoopers LLP	Ticker Symbol	IRBT
Stk Agt	Computershare Trust Co	Outstanding Shares	24,200,000
Counsel	Goodwin Procter LLP	E.P.S.	NA
DUNS No.	NA	Shareholders	NA

Business: The groups principle activity is to provide robots. The products of the group include Home Floor Cleaning Robots, Roomba robots and iRobot Scooba. The group products sold under the trade name iRobot. The groups operates through two segments namely consumer business, and government and industrial business. The group operates from the United States. The group's quarterly revenue for September 2007 was 63.84 millions of USD.

Primary SIC and add'l.: 3635 3639 3634 5088 3795

CIK No: 0001159167

Subsidiaries: iRobot (India) Private Limited, iRobot Holdings LLC., iRobot Securities Corporation, iRobot US Holdings Inc.

Officers: Colin Angle/Co - Founder, CEO/$393,412.00, Rodney Brooks/Co - Founder, CTO, Geoff Clear/CFO/$298,060.00, Joseph W. Dyer/Pres. - Government, Industrial Robots Division/$439,342.00, Glen Weinstein/Sr. VP, General Counsel, Sandra B. Lawrence/Pres., GM - Home Robots Division, Alison Dean/43/VP - Financial Controls, Analysis

Directors: Colin Angle/Co - Founder, CEO, Helen Greiner/Co - Founder, Chmn., Rodney Brooks/Co - Founder, CTO, Ronald Chwang/Dir., George C. McNamee/Dir., Andrea Geisser/Dir., Peter Meekin/Dir., Jacques S. Gansler/Dir., Paul J. Kern/Dir.

Owners: Rodney Brooks/7.00%, Paul J. Kern, Andrea Geisser, Ronald Chwang/7.40%, Geoffrey P. Clear, Colin Angle/7.80%, Joseph W. Dyer, Peter Meekin/7.00%, Insiders/37.50%, Trident Capital/6.90%, Acer Technology Ventures/6.50%, Jacques S. Gansler, Gregory F. White/1.00%, George McNamee, Helen Greiner/6.30%

Financial Data: *Fiscal Year End:* 12/30 *Latest Annual Data:* 12/30/2006

Year	Sales	Net Income
2006	$188,955,000	$3,565,000
2005	$141,968,000	$2,610,000
2004	$95,043,000	$219,000

Curr. Assets:	$117,969,000	**Curr. Liab.:**	$37,379,000	**P/E Ratio:**	477.75
Plant, Equip.:	$6,966,000	**Total Liab.:**	$37,379,000	**Indic. Yr. Divd.:**	NA
Total Assets:	$124,935,000	**Net Worth:**	$87,556,000	**Debt/ Equity:**	NA

Iron & Glass Bancorp Inc

1114 E Carson St., Pittsburgh, PA, 15203; *PH:* 1-412-488-5200; *Fax:* 1-412-488-5224; *http://* www.ironandglassbank.com

General - Incorporation		**Stock** - Price on: 12/24/2007	$50.4
Employees	NA	Stock Exchange	OTC
Auditor	NA	Ticker Symbol	IRGB
Stk Agt	NA	Outstanding Shares	NA
Counsel	NA	E.P.S.	NA
DUNS No.	NA	Shareholders	NA

Business: The groups principal activity is to provide banking services. The services of the group include originating commercial mortgage, residential real estate, and consumer loans, investment securities, deposit services and online banking. The group operates from Pennsylvania in the United States.

Primary SIC and add'l.: 6712 6022

CIK No:

Officers: Michael J. Hagan/Dir., Pres., CEO - Iron, Glass Bank, Karen Joyce/Dir., Exec. VP - Iron, Glass Bank

Directors: Michael J. Hagan/Dir., Pres., CEO - Iron, Glass Bank, Daniel A. Goetz/Chmn., D. W. Swager/Vice Chmn., Thomas M. Colella/Dir., Karen Joyce/Dir., Exec. VP - Iron, Glass Bank, Paul F. Fagan/Dir., Richard L. Anderson/Dir., Joanne Marie Andiorio/Dir., William M. Densmore/Dir., Gregory M. Melvin/Dir., Edward V. Randall/Dir.

Financial Data: *Fiscal Year End:* NA *Latest Annual Data:* 12/31/2002

Year	Sales	Net Income
2002	$18,547,000	$3,245,000
2001	$18,441,000	$2,946,000
2000	$17,427,000	$2,702,000

Curr. Assets:	$58,298,000	**Curr. Liab.:**	$261,510,000		
Plant, Equip.:	$1,781,000	**Total Liab.:**	$274,861,000	**Indic. Yr. Divd.:**	NA
Total Assets:	$302,515,000	**Net Worth:**	$27,654,000	**Debt/ Equity:**	0.3332

Iron Mountain Inc

745 Atlantic Ave., Boston, MA, 02111; ; *http://* www.ironmountain.com

General - Incorporation	DE	**Stock** - Price on: 12/24/2007	$26.01
Employees	10,400	Stock Exchange	NYSE
Auditor	Deloitte & Touche LLP	Ticker Symbol	IRM
Stk Agt	Bank of New York	Outstanding Shares	199,570,000
Counsel	Sullivan & Worcester LLP	E.P.S.	$0.68
DUNS No.	00-291-2111	Shareholders	NA

Business: The groups principle activity is to provide information protection and storage services. The group also provides records management and data protection solutions. In the year 2007 the group acquired Xepa Digital, LLP. The group operates from United States.

Primary SIC and add'l.: 3695 7389 2653 2655 7375 7374

CIK No: 0001020569

Subsidiaries: 397499 British Columbia Ltd., Administradora de Informacion Limitada, Archivage Actif Groupe Iron Mountain SAS, Archive Services Limited, Archivex Box Company Limited, Archivex Limited, Arcus Data Security Limited, Britannia Data Management Limited, COMAC, Inc., Connected G.m.b.H., Custodia SOS Limitada, Datavault Holdings Limited, Datavault Limited, Datavault Northwest Limited, Datavault Southwest Limited 99 Subsidiaries included in the Index

Officers: Richard C. Reese/Chmn., CEO/$2,923,533.00, John Connors/Pres. - Americas/$934,388.00, Bob Brennan/COO, Pres./$1,454,108.00, Marc Duale/Pres. - Iron Mountain Europe/$889,435.00, Ross Engelman/Group Pres. - Iron Mountain Latin America, Harold E. Ebbighausen/Pres. - Global Standards, John F. Kenny/Exec. VP - Corporate Development/$867,351.00, John Clancy/Pres. - Iron Mountain Digital, Joseph Desalvo/Sr. VP, Chief Security Officer, Greg Nicastro/Exec. VP - Integrated Solutions, Development, Linda A. Rossetti/Exec. VP - Human Resources, Administration, Robert G. Miller/Group Pres. - Asia Pacific, Robert T. Brennan/47/COO, Pres., Brian P. McKeon/CFO, Exec. VP

Directors: Richard C. Reese/Chmn., CEO, Clarke H. Bailey/Dir., Michael Lamach/Dir., Laurie Tucker/Dir., Constantin R. Boden/Dir., Kent P. Dauten/Dir., Arthur D. Little/Dir., Vincent J. Ryan/Dir.

Owners: Constantin R. Boden, Morgan Stanley/5.10%, Vincent J. Ryan/8.50%, John J. Connors, Robert T. Brennan, Insiders/11.60%, Clarke H. Bailey, Marc A. Duale, Richard C. Reese/2.60%, Davis Selected Advisers, L.P./20.40%, John F. Kenny, Kent P. Dauten/1.30%, Arthur D. Little

Financial Data: *Fiscal Year End:* 12/31 *Latest Annual Data:* 12/31/2006

Year	Sales	Net Income
2006	$2,350,342,000	$128,863,000
2005	$2,078,155,000	$111,099,000
2004	$1,817,589,000	$94,191,000

Curr. Assets:	$679,721,000	**Curr. Liab.:**	$638,647,000	**P/E Ratio:**	38.25
Plant, Equip.:	$2,015,235,000	**Total Liab.:**	$3,650,958,000	**Indic. Yr. Divd.:**	NA
Total Assets:	$5,209,521,000	**Net Worth:**	$1,553,273,000	**Debt/ Equity:**	1.6331

Iron Star Development Inc

Formerly: Iron Star Development Inc
41-40 Union St., Ste. 6j, Flushing, NY, 11355; *PH:* 1-718-359-2682

General - Incorporation	UT	**Stock** - Price on: 12/24/2007	$0.51
Employees	NA	Stock Exchange	OTC
Auditor	PKF	Ticker Symbol	XNYH
Stk Agt	Atlas Stock Transfer Corp	Outstanding Shares	24,320,000
Counsel	NA	E.P.S.	$0.07
DUNS No.	NA	Shareholders	NA

Business: The group operates through its subsidiaries whose principle activity is to provide printing services. The group provides bank deposit books, deposit receipts, computer bills and other financial notes. The group also provides standard forms, single purpose invoices, passports, and other certificates for banks and insurance companies. The group operates from United States.

Primary SIC and add'l.: 6770

CIK No: 0001307624

Officers: Tian Ling/44/Chmn., CEO, Xie Guihong/45/Dir., VP, Lao Chengxu/36/Dir., Sec., Du Song/61/Dir., CFO

Directors: Tian Ling/44/Chmn., CEO, Xie Guihong/45/Dir., VP, Lao Chengxu/36/Dir., Sec., Du Song/61/Dir., CFO

Owners: Ha Wing Kuen/8.60%, Insiders/27.40%, Du Song, Sun Bao Zhong/7.40%, Xie Guihong, Tian Ling/26.60%

Financial Data: *Fiscal Year End:* 12/31 *Latest Annual Data:* 12/31/2006

Year	Sales	Net Income
2006	$7,810,000	$1,393,000
2005	NA	-$8,000
2004	NA	-$4,000

Curr. Assets:	$4,739,000	**Curr. Liab.:**	$788,000	**P/E Ratio:**	7.29
Plant, Equip.:	$1,833,000	**Total Liab.:**	$1,292,000	**Indic. Yr. Divd.:**	NA
Total Assets:	$7,853,000	**Net Worth:**	$6,561,000	**Debt/ Equity:**	NA

Ironstone Group Inc

539 Bryant St., San Francisco, CA, 94107; *PH:* 1-415-576-3537

General - Incorporation	DE	**Stock** - Price on: 12/24/2007	$1.7
Employees	NA	Stock Exchange	OTC
Auditor	J. H. Cohn LLP	Ticker Symbol	IRNS
Stk Agt	NA	Outstanding Shares	NA
Counsel	NA	E.P.S.	-$0.16
DUNS No.	79-472-4153	Shareholders	NA

Business: The group's principal activities are to provide services on a fee basis to reduce ad valorem taxes assessed to owners of real and personal property in Arizona and California markets. The group is currently reviewing options to invest in new business opportunities.

Primary SIC and add'l.: 8721 8748 7389 7291

CIK No: 0000723269

Subsidiaries: AcadiEnergy, Inc., Belt Perry Associates, Inc., DeMoss Corporation, TaxNet, Inc.

Officers: Robert H. Hambrecht/41/Dir., CEO, Sec., Quock Q. Fong/73/CFO

Directors: Robert H. Hambrecht/41/Dir., CEO, Sec., William R. Hambrecht/72/Dir., Edmund H. Shea/76/Dir.

Owners: Insiders/73.50%, William R. Hambrecht/58.30%, Edmund H. Shea/15.20%

Financial Data: *Fiscal Year End:* 12/31 *Latest Annual Data:* 12/31/2006

Year	Sales	Net Income
2006	NA	-$114,000
2005	$0	-$98,000
2004	$0	-$216,000

Curr. Assets:	$2,090,000	**Curr. Liab.:**	$228,000		
Plant, Equip.:	NA	**Total Liab.:**	$228,000	**Indic. Yr. Divd.:**	NA
Total Assets:	$2,090,000	**Net Worth:**	$1,862,000	**Debt/ Equity:**	NA

IRSA Investments and Representations Inc

Bolivar 108, Buenos Aires; *PH:* 54-1143237400; *Fax:* 54-114323-7480; *http://* www.irsa.com.ar; *Email:* ir@irsa.com.ar

General - Incorporation	AR	**Stock** - Price on: 12/24/2007	$19.56
Employees	NA	Stock Exchange	NYSE
Auditor	Price Waterhouse & Co. S.R.L.	Ticker Symbol	IRS
Stk Agt	Bank of New York	Outstanding Shares	45,360,000
Counsel	Zang Bergel & Vines	E.P.S.	$0.39
DUNS No.	97-076-6523	Shareholders	NA

Business: The group's principal activities are acquisition, development and operation of shopping centers, housing projects, offices, luxury hotels and other properties for lease and acquisition of land reserves held for sale.

Primary SIC and add'l.: 6798 6552 1522 6513 7011

CIK No: 0000933267

Subsidiaries: Abril S.A., APSA, Baldovinos S.A., Buenos Aires Trade& Finance Center S.A., Hoteles Argentinos S.A., Inversora Bolvar, Llao Llao Resorts S.A., Nuevas Fronteras S.A., Palermo Invest, Pereiraola S.A., Ritelco

Officers: Saul Zang/VP, Acting as Pres.

Directors: Mauricio Wior/52/Dir.

Owners: Alejandro G. Elsztain, David A. Perednik, Mario Blejer, Sal Zang, Daniel Ricardo Elsztain, Eduardo S. Elsztain/1.43%, Argentine pension funds in the aggregate/3.90%, Gabriel Blasi, Marcos Fischman, Insiders, Cresud/34.40%, IFISA/1.40%

Financial Data: *Fiscal Year End:* 06/30 *Latest Annual Data:* 6/30/2006

Year	Sales	Net Income
2006	$187,342,000	$29,169,000
2005	$127,871,000	$44,733,000
2004	$88,100,000	$954,000

Curr. Assets:	$156,244,000	**Curr. Liab.:**	$135,956,000		
Plant, Equip.:	$472,850,000	**Total Liab.:**	$323,634,000	**Indic. Yr. Divd.:**	NA
Total Assets:	$814,543,000	**Net Worth:**	$375,657,000	**Debt/ Equity:**	NA

Irvine Sensors Corp

3001 Red Hill Ave., Bldg. 4, Ste. 108, Costa Mesa, CA, 92626; *PH:* 1-714-549-8211;
Fax: 1-714-444-8773; *http://*www.irvine-sensors.com; *Email:* investorrelations@irvine-sensors.com

General - Incorporation	DE	Stock- Price on:12/24/2007	$1.45
Employees	95	Stock Exchange	NDQ
Auditor	Grant Thornton LLP	Ticker Symbol	IRSN
Stk Agt	Mellon Investor Services LLC	Outstanding Shares	25,930,000
Counsel	Brobeck, Phleger & Harrison	E.P.S	-$0.77
DUNS No.	03-805-8038	Shareholders	NA

Business: The group's principal activity is to design, develop and manufacture electronic products, including subsystems and semiconductors. It also develops other products related to miniaturized electronics for defense, security and commercial applications. The group designs and assembles equipment for testing and prototype development. It has developed a family of standard products consisting of stacked memory chips that are used for numerous applications, both governmental and commercial. The group primarily focuses marketing of research and development contracts directly on U.S. Government agencies or contractors to those agencies.

Primary SIC and add'l.: 8732 3674 3679

CIK No: 0000357108

Subsidiaries: iNetWorks Corporation, MicroSensors, Inc., Novalog, Inc., RedHawk Vision, Inc.

Officers: John C. Carson/CEO, Pres., John J. Stuart/Mgr. - Special Projects, Communications, Carolyn Hoffman/Directo, Human Resources, Daryl L. Smetana/56/VP

Directors: Mel R. Brashears/Chmn.

Owners: John C. Carson/16.20%, John J. Stuart/13.30%, Robert G. Richards/1.90%, Insiders/30.00%, Pequot Offshore Private Equity Partners III, L.P./1.20%, Frank Ragano, Wilmington Trust Company/9.40%, Thomas M. Kelly, Daryl L. Smetana, Mel R. Brashears/3.00%, Timothy Looney/9.40%, Clifford Pike, Volkan Ozguz, Marc Dumont, Chris Toffales *(16 Owners included in Index)*

Financial Data: Fiscal Year End:10/02   Latest Annual Data: 10/1/2006

Year	Sales	Net Income
2006	$30,826,000	-$8,482,000
2005	$23,049,000	-$1,797,000
2004	$13,920,000	-$4,167,000

Curr. Assets:	$91,292,000	Curr. Liab.:	$14,561,000		
Plant, Equip.:	$42,928,000	Total Liab.:	$15,957,000	Indic. Yr. Divd.:	NA
Total Assets:	$136,300,000	Net Worth:	$120,343,000	Debt/ Equity:	NA

Irwin Financial Corp

500 Washington St., Columbus, IN, 47202; *PH:* 1-812-376-1909; *http://*www.irwinfinancial.com;
Email: info@irwinfinancial.com

General - Incorporation	IN	Stock - Price on:12/24/2007	$14.75
Employees	1,542	Stock Exchange	NYSE
Auditor	Ernst & Young, LLP	Ticker Symbol	IFC
Stk Agt	National City Bank	Outstanding Shares	29,540,000
Counsel	NA	E.P.S	-$0.37
DUNS No.	07-598-0649	Shareholders	NA

Business: The group's principal activity is to provide financial services to the customers. The operations are carried out in five segments: mortgage banking, commercial banking, home equity lending, equipment leasing and venture capital. The group's lending activities include origination of consumer, mortgage and commercial loan. Other services include personal and commercial checking accounts, savings and time deposit accounts, personal and business loans and credit card services. In addition, the group also provides money transfer services, financial counseling, life and health insurance products, trust services, securities brokerage and safe deposit facilities. The group has operations throughout the United States and Canada.

Primary SIC and add'l.: 6162 7352 6712 6141 6289 6799 6022

CIK No: 0000052617

Subsidiaries: IFC Capital Trust III, IFC Capital Trust IV, IFC Capital Trust V, IFC Capital Trust VI, IFC Capital Trust VIII, IFC Mortgage Corporation, IFC Statutory Trust VII, IHE Funding Corp., IHE Funding Corp. II, Irwin Commercial Finance Canada Corporation, Irwin Commercial Finance Corporation, Irwin Equipment Finance Corporation, Irwin Equipment Lease Funding, LLC, Irwin Franchise Capital Corporation, Irwin FSB Collateral, Inc. 36 Subsidiaries included in the Index

Officers: William I. Miller/Chmn., CEO/$1,601,994.00, Jocelyn Martin-Leano/Pres. - Home Equity, Thomas D. Washburn/Exec. VP/$714,726.00, Gregory F. Ehlinger/Sr. VP, CFO/$528,000.00, Joseph R. Laleggia/Pres. - Commercial Leasing/$599,958.00, Bradley J. Kime/Pres. - Commercial Banking/$553,886.00, Matthew F. Souza/Sr. VP - Ethics, Sec.

Directors: William I. Miller/Chmn., CEO, William H. Kling/Dir., John C. McGinty/Dir., Matthew F. Souza/Sr. VP - Ethics, Sec., David W. Goodrich/Dir., Brenda J. Lauderback/Dir., Marita Zuraitis/Dir., Jocelyn Martin-Leano/Pres. - Home Equity, Dayton H. Molendorp/Dir., Sally A. Dean/Dir., Lance R. Odden/Dir., David R. Hoover/Dir.

Owners: Sally A. Dean, David R. Hoover, William I. Miller/38.10%, Insiders/41.03%, Bradley J. Kime, John C. McGinty, Gregory F. Ehlinger, William H. Kling, Marita Zuraitis, Joseph LaLeggia, Brenda J. Lauderback, Lance R. Odden, Dimensional Fund Advisors LP/8.36%, Thomas D. Washburn, David W. Goodrich *(17 Owners included in Index)*

Financial Data: Fiscal Year End:12/31   Latest Annual Data: 12/31/2006

Year	Sales	Net Income
2006	$547,776,000	$1,727,000
2005	$712,754,000	$18,987,000
2004	$747,449,000	$68,445,000

Curr. Assets:	$444,246,000	Curr. Liab.:	$4,153,959,000		
Plant, Equip.:	$92,784,000	Total Liab.:	$5,707,456,000	Indic. Yr. Divd.:	$0.480
Total Assets:	$6,237,958,000	Net Worth:	$530,502,000	Debt/ Equity:	2.6047

ISA International Inc

46 Dufflaw Rd. , Toronto, ON, M6A 2W1; *PH:* 1-416-782-9100; *Fax:* 1-416-782-7993;
*http://*www.havascat.com; *Email:* isa@havascat.cat

General - Incorporation	DE	Stock- Price on:12/24/2007	$0.35
Employees	2	Stock Exchange	OTC
Auditor	De Joya Griffith & Company LLC	Ticker Symbol	ISAT
Stk Agt	Fidelity Transfer Co	Outstanding Shares	23,990,000
Counsel	NA	E.P.S	-$0.02
DUNS No.	NA	Shareholders	NA

Business: The groups principal activities include purchasing, servicing and collecting charged-off, sub-performing and performing consumer receivables. The group operates from the United States.

Primary SIC and add'l.: 5021

CIK No: 0001095133

Subsidiaries: Internationale Shopping Alliance Incorporated, ISA Acceptance Corporation, ISA Financial Services

Officers: Art Sandler/Pres., Kevin Sandler/VP

Owners: Insiders, Doubletree Capital Partners, Inc., Bernard L. Brodkorb, James S. Dixon, Donald G. Kampmann, Bernard L. Brodkorb

Financial Data: Fiscal Year End:09/30   Latest Annual Data: 12/31/2006

Year	Sales	Net Income
2006	NA	NA

Curr. Assets:	$34,000	Curr. Liab.:	$72,000		
Plant, Equip.:	$5,000	Total Liab.:	$72,000	Indic. Yr. Divd.:	NA
Total Assets:	$430,000	Net Worth:	$357,000	Debt/ Equity:	NA

ISCO International

1001 Cambridge Dr., Elk Grove Village, IL, 60007; *PH:* 1-847-391-9400; *Fax:* 1-847-299-9609;
*http://*www.iscointl.com; *Email:* iscoir@iscointl.com

General - Incorporation	DE	Stock- Price on:12/24/2007	$0.17
Employees	39	Stock Exchange	AMEX
Auditor	Grant Thornton LLP	Ticker Symbol	ISO
Stk Agt	Securities Transfer Corp	Outstanding Shares	190,600,000
Counsel	NA	E.P.S	-$0.03
DUNS No.	62-202-0733	Shareholders	NA

Business: The group's principal activity is to develop and sell solutions designed to optimise the reverse link of wireless networks. The solutions of the group include anf product line, the new rf 2 product line and other solutions and service expertise in improving the reverse link of a wireless system. Its solutions are designed to enhance the quality, capacity, coverage and flexibility of wireless telecommunications services. The group markets its products mainly to cellular, pcs and wireless telecommunications service providers and original equipment manufacturers located in the United States and in international markets.

Primary SIC and add'l.: 3663 3679

CIK No: 0000888693

Subsidiaries: ISCO International, Inc

Officers: John Thode/CEO, Pres./$677,614.00, Neal Campbell/Exec. VP - Strategic Marketing - Next Generation Products, Amr Abdelmonem/CTO/$542,614.00, Frank Cesario/CFO/$239,932.00, Steven Wetterling/Exec. VP - Global Sales, Greg Zaremba/VP - Sales, Business Development

Owners: Elliott International L.P./7.70%, Mike Fenger, Amr Abdelmonem, Frank Cesario, John Thode/1.00%, John Owings, Insiders/1.00%, George Calhoun, Jim Fuentes/7.50%, Alexander Finance L.P./32.30%, Ralph Pini, Elliott Associates L.P./21.30%

Financial Data: Fiscal Year End:12/31   Latest Annual Data: 12/31/2006

Year	Sales	Net Income
2006	$14,997,000	-$4,365,000
2005	$10,264,000	-$2,977,000
2004	$2,622,000	-$6,967,000

Curr. Assets:	$11,979,000	Curr. Liab.:	$13,401,000		
Plant, Equip.:	$523,000	Total Liab.:	$18,711,000	Indic. Yr. Divd.:	NA
Total Assets:	$26,875,000	Net Worth:	$8,164,000	Debt/ Equity:	0.8306

iSECUREtrac Corp

5078 S 111th St., Omaha, NE, 68137; *PH:* 1-402-537-0022; *Fax:* 1-402-537-9847;
*http://*www.isecuretrac.com; *Email:* info@isecuretrac.com

General - Incorporation	DE	Stock- Price on:12/24/2007	$1.46
Employees	82	Stock Exchange	OTC
Auditor	McGladrey & Pullen LLP	Ticker Symbol	ISEC
Stk Agt	McGladrey & Pullen LLP	Outstanding Shares	10,770,000
Counsel	NA	E.P.S	-$0.73
DUNS No.	NA	Shareholders	NA

Business: The group's principal activities are to develop, produce, market and support solutions relating to the wireless electronic tracking. The products are designed to enhance productivity, reduce costs and improve overall response using on-line access to information. The group 's product utilizes wireless communications and proprietary computer software through which the system tracks the geographic location of every offender, reports specific activities and identifies violations against customer-established parameters. The products of the group are primarily for criminal justice applications for electronic monitoring. The group 's products are also used in transportation industry for automatic vehicle tracking and monitoring the status of freight cargo through the installation of tracking units at strategic locations. On 29-Aug-2003, the group acquired tracking systems corporation.

Primary SIC and add'l.: 3823 3669

CIK No: 0001088120

Subsidiaries: iSt Services, Inc., Tracking Systems Corporation

Officers: Peter Michel/Dir., CEO, Pres./$866,842.00, Ron Both/Investor Relations Officer, David G. Sempek/Sr. VP - Technology, CTO/$207,142.00, David G. Vana/CFO, Sec./$205,142.00, Robert Bierman/VP - Sales, Marketing

Directors: Peter Michel/Dir., CEO, Pres., Roger J. Kanne/Chmn., Joseph A. Ethridge/Dir., Bruce Leadbetter/Dir., Ravi Nath/Dir., Robert W. Korba/Dir.

Owners: David Sempek/1.29%, Thomas Wharton/3.25%, Peter A. Michel, Roger Kanne/7.57%, Mykonos 6420, LP/55.98%, Edward Sempek/1.29%, David G. Vana/2.02%, Ken Macke/6.91%, Insiders/15.42%, Ravi Nath, Total Tech LLC/13.20%

Financial Data: Fiscal Year End:12/31   Latest Annual Data: 12/31/2006

Year	Sales	Net Income
2006	$8,064,000	-$5,452,000
2005	$5,590,000	-$3,874,000
2004	$4,679,000	-$9,696,000

Curr. Assets:	$6,761,000	Curr. Liab.:	$2,200,000	
Plant, Equip.:	$3,380,000	Total Liab.:	$8,894,000	Indic. Yr. Divd.: NA
Total Assets:	$12,654,000	Net Worth:	-$6,937,000	Debt/ Equity: NA

Isis Pharmaceuticals Inc

1896 Rutherford Rd., Carlsbad, CA, 92008; *PH:* 1-760-931-9200; *Fax:* 1-760-603-2700; *http://* www.isispharm.com; *Email:* info@isisph.com

General - Incorporation .... DE
Employees 274
Auditor .... Ernst & Young LLP
Stk Agt...... American Stock Transfer & Trust Co.
Counsel.................................. Cooley Godward LLP
DUNS No. 36-194-9092

Stock- Price on:12/24/2007 .... $9.33
Stock Exchange..NDQ
Ticker Symbol..ISIS
Outstanding Shares 82,530,000
E.P.S. .... -$0.64
Shareholders..NA

Business: The group's principal activity is to develop human therapeutic drugs using antisense and combinatorial technology. The antisense technology of the group create inhibitors or oligonucleotides, designed to hybridize or bind with high specificity to their rna target and modulate the production of proteins associated with diseases. It also uses antisense technology in collaborations with pharmaceutical companies to identify and prioritize attractive gene targets for their drug discovery programs. The group used antisense technology to commercialize its first product, vitravene. Vitravene is commerically available in the U.S., Europe, Australia and Brazil. The group uses ibis technology to design small molecule drugs that bind to rna through mechanisms other than hybridization.

Primary SIC and add'l.: 2834 8731

CIK No: 0000874015

Subsidiaries: Isis Pharmaceuticals Singapore Pte Ltd, Isis USA Limited, Orasense, Ltd., PerIsis I Development Corporation

Officers: Stanley T. Crooke/Founder, Chmn., CEO/$1,428,377.00, David J. Ecker/Co - Founder, VP/$638,439.00, Jeffrey M. Jonas/Exec. VP, Rob McKay/Assoc. Dir., Lynne B. Parshall/Dir., Exec. VP, CFO, Sec./$939,217.00, Frank C. Bennett/Sr. VP - Research, Mark K. Wedel/Sr. VP - Development, Chief Medical Officer/$650,179.00, Michael J. Treble/VP/$671,265.00

Directors: Stanley T. Crooke/Founder, Chmn., CEO, Lynne B. Parshall/Dir., Exec. VP, CFO, Sec., David J. Ecker/Co - Founder, VP

Owners: Richard D. DiMarchi, Stanley T. Crooke/1.90%, Federated Investors, Inc./12.40%, Spencer R. Berthelsen, Michael J. Treble, John C. Reed, David J. Ecker, Lynne B. Parshall, Joseph H. Wender, Insiders/3.40%, Mark K. Wedel, Frederick T. Muto, Joseph Klein

Financial Data: *Fiscal Year End:*12/31 *Latest Annual Data:* 12/31/2006

Year	Sales	Net Income
2006	$24,532,000	-$45,903,000
2005	$40,133,000	-$72,401,000
2004	$42,624,000	-$142,503,000

Curr. Assets:	$206,203,000	Curr. Liab.:	$25,139,000	
Plant, Equip.:	$7,157,000	Total Liab.:	$158,005,000	Indic. Yr. Divd.: NA
Total Assets:	$255,907,000	Net Worth:	$68,563,000	Debt/ Equity: 2.9594

Isle of Capri Casinos Inc

600 Emerson Rd., Ste. 300, St. Louis, MO, 63141; *PH:* 1-228-396-7000; *http://* www.isleofcapricasino.com

General - Incorporation .... DE
Employees 8,516
Auditor .... Ernst & Young LLP
Stk Agt...... American Stock Transfer & Trust Co.
Counsel......................................Allan B. Solomon
DUNS No. 79-536-8232

Stock- Price on:12/24/2007 .... $24.51
Stock Exchange..NDQ
Ticker Symbol..ISLE
Outstanding Shares 30,550,000
E.P.S. .... -$1.82
Shareholders..NA

Business: The group's principal activity is to develop, own and operate branded gaming facilities and related lodging and entertainment facilities. The group owns and operates eleven gaming facilities located in lake charles and bossier city, Louisiana; lula, biloxi, vicksburg and natchez, Mississippi; Kansas city and boonville, Missouri; bettendorf, davenport and marquette, Iowa. The group also operates a pari-mutuel harness racing facility in pompano beach, Florida.

Primary SIC and add'l.: 7021 7011 8741 7999

CIK No: 0000863015

Subsidiaries: CCSC/Blackhawk, Inc., Grand Palais Riverboat, Inc, IOC Holdings, LLC, IOC-Boonville, Inc., IOC-Davenport, Inc., IOC-Kansas City, Inc., IOC-Lula, Inc., Isle of Capri Bettendorf, L.C., Isle of Capri Black Hawk, LLC, Isle of Capri Marquette, Inc., Louisiana Riverboat Gaming Partnership, Riverboat Corporation of Mississippi, Riverboat Corporation of Mississippi-Vicksburg, St. Charles Gaming Company, Inc.

Officers: Bernard Goldstein/Chmn., CEO/$1,546,171.00, Robert S. Goldstein/Exec. Vice Chmn., Virginia McDowell/COO, Pres., Jill Haynes/Contact - Investor Relation, Ron Burgess/Sr. VP - Human Resources, Doug Burkhalter/Sr. VP - Marketing, Greg D. Guida/Sr. VP - Development, Legal Affairs, Sec., Robert Griffin/Sr. VP - Operations/$663,872.00, Allan B. Solomon/Exec. VP, General Counsel, Assist. Sec./$1,007,210.00, Donn Mitchell/CFO, Sr. VP, Treasurer/$620,648.00

Directors: Bernard Goldstein/Chmn., CEO, Robert S. Goldstein/Exec. Vice Chmn., Shaun R. Hayes/48/Dir., John G. Brackenbury/72/Dir., Lee S. Wielansky/57/Dir., James B. Perry/58/Dir., Alan J. Glazer/67/Dir., Jeffrey D. Goldstein/55/Dir., Randolph W. Baker/61/Dir.

Owners: Robert S. Goldstein, B.I.J.R.R. Isle, Inc., B.I. Isle Partnership, L.P., Alan J. Glazer, Goldstein Group, Inc., Jeffrey D. Goldstein, Bernard Goldstein, Lee Wielansky, John Brackenbury, James Perry, Emanuel Crystal, Robert F. Griffin, Baron Capital Group, Richard A. Goldstein, Allan B. Solomon (20 Owners included in Index)

Financial Data: *Fiscal Year End:*04/30 *Latest Annual Data:* 04/29/2007

Year	Sales	Net Income
2007	$1,001,394,000	-$4,637,000
2006	$988,020,000	$19,023,000
2005	$1,111,608,000	$18,038,000

Curr. Assets:	$253,698,000	Curr. Liab.:	$223,854,000	
Plant, Equip.:	$1,160,874,000	Total Liab.:	$1,524,566,000	Indic. Yr. Divd.: NA
Total Assets:	$1,833,944,000	Net Worth:	$282,688,000	Debt/ Equity: 4.2075

Isolagen Inc

405 Eagleview Blvd., Exton, PA, 19341; *PH:* 1-484-713-6000; *Fax:* 1-484-713-6001; *http://* www.isolagen.com; *Email:* infouk@isolagen.com

General - Incorporation .... DE
Employees 55
Auditor .... BDO Seidman LLP
Stk Agt ....NA
Counsel ....NA
DUNS No. 93-226-3841

Stock- Price on:12/24/2007 .... $4.43
Stock Exchange...AMEX
Ticker Symbol...ILE
Outstanding Shares 30,380,000
E.P.S. .... -$1.27
Shareholders..NA

Business: The group's principal activity is to develop and commercialize autologous cellular system (acs) for the dermatological and plastic surgery markets. Acs is a process whereby a patient's own (autologous) cells are extracted, reproduced through proprietary process and then reintroduced back into the patient for specific cosmetic and medical applications. The isolagen process is designed to replenish deficiencies caused through the loss of fibroblast cells as the body ages. It reduces dermal depressions and wrinkles by replenishing the area of deficiency with millions of the patient's own new living fibroblast cells. Within weeks after the injection, the millions of new fibroblast cells will produce new collagen and elastin and will help diminish wrinkles. The group is in the development stage.

Primary SIC and add'l.: 2834 8731

CIK No: 0000357097

Subsidiaries: Isolagen Australia Pty Limited, Isolagen Europe Limited, Isolagen International S.A., Isolagen Technologies, Inc.

Officers: Nicholas L. Teti/Chmn., CEO/$1,589,860.00, Christi Chase/Primary Investor Relations Officer, Charlie Huiner/VP - Corporate Development, Sandra Calman/VP - Clinical Development, Chief Medical Officer, Todd J. Greenspan/VP, Corporate Controller/$233,994.00, Declan Daly/CFO, COO/$332,100.00, Steven Trider/Sr. VP - Americas, Sales, Marketing/$240,675.00, Bryant Pearce/Sr. VP - Operations

Directors: Nicholas L. Teti/Chmn., CEO, Henry Y.L. Toh/Dir., Terry Vandewarker/Dir., Steven Morrell/Dir., Ralph V. De Martino/Dir., Marshall G. Webb/Dir.

Owners: Insiders/3.20%, Frank DeLape/4.30%, Todd J. Greenspan/0.01%, Heartland Advisors, Inc/10.50%, Marie Lindner/0.01%, Marshall G. Webb/0.01%, Steven Morrell/0.01%, Martin E. Schmieg/0.01%, Ralph V. DeMartino, Susan S. Ciallella/1.00%, Henry Y.L. Toh/0.01%

Financial Data: *Fiscal Year End:*12/31 *Latest Annual Data:* 12/31/2006

Year	Sales	Net Income
2006	$6,093,000	-$35,821,000
2005	$8,754,000	-$35,778,000
2004	$4,179,000	-$21,474,000

Curr. Assets:	$35,130,000	Curr. Liab.:	$5,642,000	
Plant, Equip.:	$14,835,000	Total Liab.:	$96,806,000	Indic. Yr. Divd.: NA
Total Assets:	$57,287,000	Net Worth:	-$41,624,000	Debt/ Equity: NA

Isonics Corp

5906 McIntyre St., Golden, CO, 80403; *PH:* 1-303-279-7900; *Fax:* 1-303-279-7300; *http://* www.isonics.com; *Email:* info@isonics.com

General - Incorporation .... CA
Employees 561
Auditor .... Hein & Assoc. LLP
Stk Agt ....Continental Stock Transfer & Trust Co
Counsel .... Cooley Godward LLP
DUNS No. 87-670-9619

Stock- Price on:12/24/2007 .... $1.5
Stock Exchange..OTC
Ticker Symbol...ISON
Outstanding Shares 12,640,000
E.P.S. .... -$1.13
Shareholders..NA

Business: The group's principal activities are to develop and market products based on isotopes for applications in the energy, medical research, diagnostic, pharmaceutical and semiconductor industries. The group develops and commercializes products based on enriched stable isotopes and radioactive isotopes. The group's products include cadmium and stable isotope labeled compounds. It currently focuses on two markets, life sciences and semiconductor materials and products. The life science segment sells stable and radioisotopes in elemental and simple compound. The semiconductor materials and products segment sells soi wafers and is involved in several research and development projects including silicon-28 forms for use in life sciences applications. In fiscal 2004 group acquired 85% interest in iut detection technologies inc. The group operates in the United States and Germany.

Primary SIC and add'l.: 2819 3679

CIK No: 0001023966

Subsidiaries: Chemotrade GmbH Dusseldorf, Germany, Isonics Homeland Security and Defense Corporation, Isonics Vancouver, Inc, IUT Detection Technologies, Inc., Protection Plus Security Corporation

Officers: John Sakys/COO, Pres., Interim CEO, Gregory Meadows/VP - Business Operations, Controller, Kenneth J. Deane/CFO, VP

Directors: Christopher Toffales/Chmn., Richard Hagman/Dir., Richard Parker/Dir., Stewart C. Verdery/Dir., Russell W. Weiss/Dir.

Owners: Joanna Lohkamp, Insiders/1.10%, Stewart C. Verdery, Russell W. Weiss, John Sakys, Richard Parker, Richard H. Hagman, Greg Meadows

Financial Data: *Fiscal Year End:*04/30 *Latest Annual Data:* 04/30/2007

Year	Sales	Net Income
2007	$27,731,000	-$13,165,000
2006	$23,716,000	-$32,341,000
2005	$10,105,000	-$15,177,000

Curr. Assets:	$8,306,000	Curr. Liab.:	$15,013,000	
Plant, Equip.:	$4,854,000	Total Liab.:	$15,220,000	Indic. Yr. Divd.: NA
Total Assets:	$17,863,000	Net Worth:	$2,643,000	Debt/ Equity: 5.9422

IsoRay Medical Inc

350 Hills St., Ste 106, Richland, WA, 99354; *PH:* 1-509-375-1202; *Fax:* 1-509-375-3473; *http://* www.isoray.com; *Email:* info@isoray.com

General - Incorporation .... MN
Employees 53
Auditor .... Decoria, Maichel & Teague, P.s.
Stk Agt .... Computershare Trust Co
Counsel ....NA
DUNS No. 10-751-2022

Stock- Price on:12/24/2007 .... NA
Stock Exchange...AMEX
Ticker Symbol..ISR
Outstanding Shares ....NA
E.P.S. .... -$0.447
Shareholders..NA

Business: The group's principle activities include developing, producing and marketing various entertainment properties which include intellectual products of entities engaged in the motion picture, television, and theatrical state productions. At present the company doesn't have any operations and are seeking for a suitable business combination transaction either through acquisition or merger. The group operates from United States.

Primary SIC and add'l.: 7819

CIK No: 0000728387
Subsidiaries: IsoRay Medical, Inc.
Officers: Roger Girard/Chmn., CEO, David Swanberg/Exec. VP - Operations, Jonathan Hunt/CFO, Donald R. Segna/VP - Strategic Planning, Lane Bray/Chief Chemist, Oleg Egorov/Dir. - Research, Development, Lori Woods/VP, Fred Swindler/VP - Quality Assurance, Regulatory Affairs, Eric Knipfer/National Sales Dir.
Directors: Roger Girard/Chmn., CEO
Owners: Robert Kauffman, Roger Girard/3.98%, Stephen Boatwright, Hostetler Living Trust/16.05%, Jamie Granger/17.83%, Aissata Sidibe/33.86%, Thomas LaVoy, Michael Dunlop, David Swanberg/2.21%, Lori Woods, William and Karen Thompson Trust/24.07%, Leslie Fernandez/6.24%, Albert Smith/1.18%, Dwight Babcock, Insiders/11.90%
Financial Data: ***Fiscal Year End:***09/30 ***Latest Annual Data:*** 09/30/2007

Year	Sales	Net Income
2007	NA	NA
2006	NA	NA
2005	NA	-$30,000

Curr. Assets:	$21,730,000	***Curr. Liab.:***	$2,806,000		
Plant, Equip.:	$3,666,000	***Total Liab.:***	$3,360,000	***Indic. Yr. Divd.:***	NA
Total Assets:	$26,076,000	***Net Worth:***	$22,716,000	***Debt/ Equity:***	0.1366

Israel Bank of Agriculture Ltd

83 Hashmonaim St., Tel Aviv;

General - Incorporation	Israel	***Stock***- Price on:12/24/2007	NA
Employees	NA	Stock Exchange	NA
Auditor	Rosenblum-Holtzman	Ticker Symbol	NA
Stk Agt	NA	Outstanding Shares	NA
Counsel	NA	E.P.S	NA
DUNS No.	NA	Shareholders	NA

Business: The groups principle activity is to operate bank that encourages and assists agricultural development in Israel. The group operates from United States.
Primary SIC and add'l.: 6029
CIK No: 0000052723
Officers: Levi Noah/Chief Legal Adviser - Bank, Gelem Avigdor/Mgr. - Information System, Yacov Cohen/CFO, Sec., Dir. - Human Resources, Personnel, Sitton Moshe/Assist. GM, Manager - Credit, Collection, Current Accounting, Patalovsky Lea/GM
Directors: Helmaliah Dorit/Dir., Zibin Nehama/Dir., Cheifetz Avi/Dir., Freeman Menachem/Dir., Navon Erez/Dir.

Isramco Inc

1770 St. James Pl, Ste. 607, Houston, TX, 77056; ***PH:*** 1-713-621-3882

General - Incorporation	DE	***Stock***- Price on:12/24/2007	$45.53
Employees	13	Stock Exchange	NDQ
Auditor	Malone & Bailey, P.C	Ticker Symbol	ISRL
Stk Agt	American Stock Transfer & Trust Co.	Outstanding Shares	2,720,000
Counsel	NA	E.P.S	$0.62
DUNS No.	13-768-7133	Shareholders	NA

Business: The group's principal activity is to acquire, explore, operate and develop oil and gas properties. The group is also involved in the transportation of oil and natural gas. The group is an operator of the offshore preliminary permits. The operator is responsible for directing the oil exploration and drilling activities. The group owns properties in Texas, Louisiana, Oklahoma, Wyoming, New Mexico, the republic of congo, Africa and approximately a 0.5% working interest in various properties located in Israel. The operations are conducted in the United States, Israel and the republic of congo, Africa.the company created isramco oil and gas ltd. (iog) , a wholly-owned subsidiary to act as the general partner for the limited partnership and formed isramco management (1988) ltd., a wholly-owned subsidiary to act as the limited partner and the nominee of limited partnership units held by public investors in Israel.
Primary SIC and add'l.: 1311
CIK No: 0000719209
Subsidiaries: IsramTec Inc.
Officers: Haim Tsuff/51/Chmn., CEO/$240,000.00, Jackob Maimon/52/Dir., Pres./$390,000.00, Yossi Levy/55/Branch Mgr. - Israel Branch
Directors: Haim Tsuff/51/Chmn., CEO, Max Pridgeon/40/Dir., Jackob Maimon/52/Dir., Pres., Donald D. Lovell/75/Dir., Frans Sluiter/40/Dir.
Owners: Insiders/51.25%, Jackob Maimon/1.43%, Haim Tsuff/49.82%
Financial Data: ***Fiscal Year End:***12/31 ***Latest Annual Data:*** 12/31/2006

Year	Sales	Net Income
2006	$12,366,000	$3,842,000
2005	$7,735,000	-$1,132,000
2004	$8,943,000	-$20,000

Curr. Assets:	$28,313,000	***Curr. Liab.:***	$22,561,000	***P/E Ratio:***	73.44
Plant, Equip.:	$12,537,000	***Total Liab.:***	$27,329,000	***Indic. Yr. Divd.:***	NA
Total Assets:	$62,073,000	***Net Worth:***	$34,744,000	***Debt/ Equity:***	NA

ISTA Pharmaceuticals Inc

15295 Alton Pkwy., Irvine, CA, 92618; ***PH:*** 1-949-788-6000; ***Fax:*** 1-949-788-6010; ***http://*** www.istavision.com

General - Incorporation	DE	***Stock***- Price on:12/24/2007	$7.94
Employees	198	Stock Exchange	NDQ
Auditor	Ernst & Young LLP	Ticker Symbol	ISTA
Stk Agt	U.S. Stock Transfer Corp	Outstanding Shares	26,610,000
Counsel	Covington & Burling LLP	E.P.S	-$1.24
DUNS No.	NA	Shareholders	NA

Business: The group's principal activities are to discover, develop and commercialize new remedies for diseases and conditions of the eye. The group develops ophthalmic drugs based on a group of natural enzymes called hyaluronidase that is used to treat diseases and conditions such as vitreous hemorrhage, diabetic retinopathy, corneal opacification and keratoconus. The major products of the group are vitrase, keratase and keraform. Vitrase is a formulation of hyaluronidase used for the treatment of vitreous hemorrhage. Keratase is a formulation of hyaluronidase used for the treatment of corneal opacification. Keraform is used for the treatment of keratoconus, a degenerative corneal disease that impairs vision. The group also develops other late-stage products, including istaloltm (timolol) for the treatment of glaucoma, xibromtm (bromfenac) for the treatment of ocular inflammation, and caprogel(R) (aminocaproic acid) for the treatment of hyphema.
Primary SIC and add'l.: 8731 2834
CIK No: 0000930553
Subsidiaries: ISTA Pharma, Ltd. (United Kingdom), Visionex Pty. Ltd. (Singapore)
Officers: Vicente Anido/Dir., CEO, Pres./$1,102,370.00, Lauren Silvernail/CFO, VP - Corporate Development/$510,102.00, Kirk McMullin/VP - Operations/$394,545.00, Kathleen McGinley/VP - Human Resources, Corporate Services, Marvin J. Garrett/Pres. - Regulatory Affairs, Quality, Compliance/$423,247.00, Lisa R. Grillone/VP - Clinical Research/$444,800.00, Tom Mitro/VP - Sales, Marketing/$500,113.00, Timothy R. McNamara/VP - Clinical Research, Medical Affairs
Directors: Vicente Anido/Dir., CEO, Pres., Richard C. Williams/Chmn., Dean J. Mitchell/Dir., Wayne I. Roe/Dir., Andrew J. Perlman/Dir., Kathleen D. Laporte/Dir., Peter Barton Hutt/Dir., Benjamin F. McGraw/Dir.
Owners: Benjamin F. McGraw, HBK Investments L.P./14.40%, James E. Flynn and Deerfield Investment Entities/11.30%, Kathleen D. LaPorte, Visium Asset Management, LLC/9.30%, Andrew J. Perlman, Insiders/6.80%, Peter Barton Hutt, Richard C. Williams, Mazama Capital Management, Inc./7.00%, Investor AB/8.30%, Marvin J. Garrett, Credit Suisse/22.50%, Thomas A. Mitro, Wayne I. Roe *(20 Owners included in Index)*
Financial Data: ***Fiscal Year End:***12/31 ***Latest Annual Data:*** 12/31/2006

Year	Sales	Net Income
2006	$33,007,000	-$38,419,000
2005	$10,660,000	-$38,480,000
2004	$1,897,000	-$40,424,000

Curr. Assets:	$48,419,000	***Curr. Liab.:***	$20,421,000		
Plant, Equip.:	$3,116,000	***Total Liab.:***	$64,302,000	***Indic. Yr. Divd.:***	NA
Total Assets:	$59,743,000	***Net Worth:***	-$4,559,000	***Debt/ Equity:***	NA

iStar Financial Inc

1114 Ave. of the Americas, 27th Fl., New York, NY, 10036; ***PH:*** 1-212-930-9400; ***Fax:*** 1-212-930-9494; ***http://*** www.istarfinancial.com; ***Email:*** investors@istarfinancial.com

General - Incorporation	MD	***Stock***- Price on:12/24/2007	$46.71
Employees	214	Stock Exchange	NYSE
Auditor	PricewaterhouseCoopers LLP	Ticker Symbol	SFI
Stk Agt	Computershare Trust Co	Outstanding Shares	128,170,000
Counsel	NA	E.P.S	$2.77
DUNS No.	NA	Shareholders	NA

Business: The groups principle activity is to provide financing services to private and corporate owners of real estate. The group operates through two segments namely, real estate lending and corporate tenant leasing. In the year 2005, the group acquired Falcon Financial Investment Trust. The group operates from the United States. The group's quarterly revenue for September 2007 was 419.39 in millions of USD.
Primary SIC and add'l.: 6798
CIK No: 0001095651
Subsidiaries: 100 Riverview Condominium Association Inc., 1001 East Palm, LLC, 300 Riverview Condominium Association Inc., 767 STARS LLC, Acquest Government Holdings II, LLC, Acquest Government Holdings, L.L.C., Acquest Holdings FC, LLC, ACRE CLS, LLC, ACRE HPC, LLC, ACRE IDG Manager, LLC, ACRE IDG, LLC, ACRE Seymour, LLC, ACRE Simon, L.L.C., American Financial Exchange L.L.C., ASTAR ASB AR1, LLC 234 Subsidiaries included in the Index
Officers: Jay Sugarman/Chmn., CEO/$6,600,813.00, Jay Nydick/Pres./$3,175,473.00, Catherine D. Rice/CFO/$2,352,529.00, Timothy J. O'Connor/COO, Exec. VP/$2,008,424.00, Nina B. Matis/Exec. VP, General Counsel, Barbara Rubin/Pres. - Istar Asset Services, Inc., Daniel S. Abrams/Exec. VP, Head - Originations/$2,658,448.00, Steven R. Blomquist/Exec. VP - Investments, Chase S. Curtis/Exec. VP - Credit, Michael R. Dorsch/Exec. VP - Investments, Barclay G. Jones/Exec. VP - Investments, Michelle M. MacKay/Exec. VP - Investments
Directors: Jay Sugarman/Chmn., CEO, Glenn R. August/Dir., Willis Andersen/Dir., Robert W. Holman/Dir., Robin Josephs/Dir., John G. McDonald/Dir., George R. Puskar/Dir., Jeffrey A. Weber/Dir.
Owners: Neuberger Berman Inc./6.05%, John G. McDonald, Robin Josephs, Jay Sugarman/2.64%, Catherine D. Rice, Capital Research and Management Company/13.30%, Robert W. Holman, Jay S. Nydick, Jeffrey A. Weber, Insiders/3.79%, George R. Puskar, Glenn R. August
Financial Data: ***Fiscal Year End:***12/31 ***Latest Annual Data:*** 12/31/2006

Year	Sales	Net Income
2006	$980,193,000	$374,827,000
2005	$798,504,000	$287,913,000
2004	$694,424,000	$260,447,000

Curr. Assets:	$207,891,000	***Curr. Liab.:***	$200,957,000	***P/E Ratio:***	23.16
Plant, Equip.:	$15,042,000	***Total Liab.:***	$8,073,132,000	***Indic. Yr. Divd.:***	$3.300
Total Assets:	$11,059,995,000	***Net Worth:***	$2,986,863,000	***Debt/ Equity:***	NA

IT Group Holdings Inc

Formerly: Green Mountain Capital Inc
1207 Delaware Ave., Ste. 410, Buffalo, NY, 14209; ***PH:*** 1-716-332-6143

General - Incorporation	NV	***Stock***- Price on:12/24/2007	NA
Employees	14	Stock Exchange	NA
Auditor	Marcum & Kliegman, LLP	Ticker Symbol	NA
Stk Agt	American Stock Transfer & Trust Co.	Outstanding Shares	NA
Counsel	NA	E.P.S	NA
DUNS No.	NA	Shareholders	NA

Business: The group's principal activities are to manufacture custom diesel power generating equipment and manage railway traffic, control and public safety. The group buys base system from diesel equipment manufacturers and modifies them to meet custom requirements. It has developed private wireless network system called crosslogixtm. These systems are developed to improve safety at rail crossings, and support various applications like data collection, processing, monitoring and information analysis. The system is composed of five modules: Web sensors, rail sensor processors, digital communications sub-systems, application processor and optical PC based diagnostics and monitoring system. The group operates in the United States and Canada. On 10-Jan-2003, the group sold its wholly-owned subsidiary, t&t diesel power, ltd. On 22-Apr-2003, it acquired majestic refilter ltd and 05-May-2003, hmm capital holdings inc.
Primary SIC and add'l.: 7373 3621

CIK No: 0001081856
Subsidiaries: Vermont Motors Inc.
Officers: Shmuel Shneibalg/38/Dir., CEO, Pres., Charlie Yiasemis/52/CEO, CFO, Pres., Fredrik Verkroost/53/Chmn., Company Sec.
Directors: Shmuel Shneibalg/38/Dir., CEO, Pres., Fredrik Verkroost/53/Chmn., Company Sec., William Malenbaum/78/Dir.
Owners: Demitris Charalambous/33.72%, William Malenbaum/0.26%, Insiders/19.35%, Charlie Yiasemis/14.88%, Fredrik Verkroost/4.55%
Financial Data: Fiscal Year End:01/31   **Latest Annual Data:** 12/31/2006

Year	Sales	Net Income
2006	$22,725,000	-$1,044,000
2005	NA	-$4,158,000

Curr. Assets:	$2,968,000	Curr. Liab.:	$3,114,000		
Plant, Equip.:	$2,015,000	Total Liab.:	$3,171,000	Indic. Yr. Divd.:	NA
Total Assets:	$5,646,000	Net Worth:	$2,475,000	Debt/ Equity:	NA

ITC Deltacom Inc

7037 Old Madison Pike, Huntsville, AL, 35806; **PH:** 1-706-385-8000; **Fax:** 1-706-385-8801; http:// www.deltacom.com

General - Incorporation .... DE	Stock- Price on:12/24/2007 ....$6.25
Employees 1,950	Stock Exchange.............................OTC
Auditor .... BDO Seidman LLP	Ticker Symbol...............................ITCD
Stk Agt............... Mellon Investor Services LLC	Outstanding Shares 18,770,000
Counsel........................... Hogan & Hartson LLP	E.P.S..................................-$9.11
DUNS No. 01-281-1514	Shareholders..................................NA

Business: The group's principal activity is to provide voice and data telecommunications services on a retail basis to businesses and residential customers. The group delivers a comprehensive suite of voice and data communications services, including local exchange, long distance, enhanced data, Internet, colocation and managed services, and sell customer premise equipment to our end-user customers. As of 31-Dec-2003, the group marketed and sold its integrated communications services through 40 branch offices and extended its 10,900 route-mile fiber optic network from New York to Florida and covered portions of its eight-state market. On 06-Oct-2003, the group acquired bti telecom corporation.
Primary SIC and add'l.: 9999 4899 4813 4812
CIK No: 0001041954
Subsidiaries: BTI Telecom Corp, Business Telecom of Virginia, Inc, Business Telecom, Inc, DeltaCom Information Systems, Inc, DeltaCom, Inc, Interstate FiberNet, Inc
Officers: Randall E. Curran/Dir., CEO/$1,809,322.00, Jim O'Brien/Exec. VP - Operations, Richard E. Fish/CFO/$724,094.00, Thomas J. Mullis/General Counsel/$333,061.00, Lee Kimball/VP - Marketing, Sara L. Plunkett/Sr. VP - Finance/$286,437.00, Anthony A. Tomae/Exec. VP - Sales, Marketing Wholesale, Enterprise Markets
Directors: Thomas E. McInerney/Chmn., Campbell B. Lanier/Vice Chmn., Philip M. Tseng/Dir., Michael E. Leitner/Dir., Sanjay Swani/Dir., Clyde A. Heintzelman/Dir., John J. Delucca/Dir., Anthony J. De Nicola/Dir., John Almeida/Dir., Gerald R. McCarley/Dir.
Owners: Campbell B. Lanier/23.70%, Basso Holdings Ltd./5.30%, Welsh, Carson, Anderson& Stowe Group/99.40%, Donald W. Burton/13.20%, Trace Management, LLC and others/6.20%, CT Communications, Inc./7.90%, Basso Multi-Strategy Holdings Fund Ltd./5.30%, Welsh, Carson, Anderson& Stowe Group/72.60%, Smith J. Lanier/13.10%
Financial Data: Fiscal Year End:12/31   **Latest Annual Data:** 12/31/2006

Year	Sales	Net Income
2006	$487,640,000	-$53,459,000
2005	$520,401,000	-$50,849,000
2004	$583,627,000	-$247,228,000

Curr. Assets:	$137,948,000	Curr. Liab.:	$113,939,000		
Plant, Equip.:	$242,519,000	Total Liab.:	$452,451,000	Indic. Yr. Divd.:	NA
Total Assets:	$435,582,000	Net Worth:	-$91,039,000	Debt/ Equity:	NA

ITC Holdings Corp

39500 Orchard Hill Pl., Ste. 200, Novi, MI, 48375; **PH:** 1-248-374-7100; **Fax:** 1-248-374-7140; http:// www.itc-holdings.com; **Email:** lroseland@itctransco.com

General - Incorporation .... MI	Stock- Price on:12/24/2007 ....$43.13
Employees 223	Stock Exchange.............................NYSE
Auditor .... Deloitte & Touche LLP	Ticker Symbol...............................ITC
Stk Agt....................... Computershare Trust Co	Outstanding Shares 42,500,000
Counsel........... Simpson Thacher & Bartlett LLP	E.P.S..................................$1.42
DUNS No. ....NA	Shareholders..................................NA

Business: The groups principle activity is to transmit electricity. In the year 2006, the group acquired Michigan Electric Transmission Company, LLC. The group operates from the United States. The groups quarterly revenue for September 2007 was 109.27 millions of USD.
Primary SIC and add'l.: 4911
CIK No: 0001317630
Subsidiaries: Conjunction LLC., Empire Conjunction LLC., International Transmission Company, ITC Equipment, LLC., ITC Great Plains, LLC., ITC Grid Development, LLC., ITC Midwest, METC GP Holding II, LLC., METC GP Holdings, Inc., METC LP Holding I, LLC., METC LP Holding II, LLC., METC LP Holding III, LLC., METC LP Holding IV, LLC., METC LP Holding V, LLC., Michigan Electric Transmission Company, LLC. 17 Subsidiaries included in the Index
Officers: Joseph L. Welch/Dir., CEO, Pres., Linda H. Blair/Exec. VP, Chief Business Officer, Larry Bruneel/VP - Federal Affairs, Joseph R. Dudak/VP - Major Contracts, Special Projects, Jon E. Jipping/COO, Exec. VP, Daniel J. Oginsky/VP, General Counsel, Edward M. Rahill/CFO, Sr. VP, Richard A. Schultz/64/Sr. VP - Planning, Denis Y. Desrosiers/VP - Information Technology, Facilities, CIO, Joseph E. Fennell/VP, Controller, Elizabeth A. Howell/VP - Operations, Christine Mason Soneral/VP, General Counsel - Utility Operations
Directors: Joseph L. Welch/Dir., CEO, Pres., Edward G. Jepsen/Dir., William J. Museler/Dir., Bennett G. Stewart/Dir., Lee C. Stewart/Dir., Gordon Bennett Stewart/54/Dir., Hazel R. O'Leary/Dir.
Owners: Baron Capital Group, Inc., BAMCO, Inc., Baron Capital Management, Inc/9.00%, Canada Pension Plan Investment Board/5.20%, Edward M. Rahill, Bennett G. Stewart, Edward G. Jepsen, Lewis M. Eisenberg, Insiders/3.40%, Lee C. Stewart, Richard A. Schultz, Jon E. Jipping, Linda H. Blair, Joseph L. Welch/1.80%
Financial Data: Fiscal Year End:12/31   **Latest Annual Data:** 12/31/2006

Year	Sales	Net Income
2006	$223,622,000	$33,223,000
2005	$205,274,000	$34,671,000
2004	$126,449,000	$2,608,000

Curr. Assets:	$109,673,000	Curr. Liab.:	$99,566,000	P/E Ratio:	29.74
Plant, Equip.:	$1,197,862,000	Total Liab.:	$1,596,553,000	Indic. Yr. Divd.:	$1.160
Total Assets:	$2,128,797,000	Net Worth:	$532,244,000	Debt/ Equity:	NA

Iteris Inc

1700 Carnegie Ave., Ste. 100, Santa Ana, CA, 92705; **PH:** 1-949-270-9400; **Fax:** 1-949-270-9401; http:// www.iteris.com

General - Incorporation .... DE	Stock- Price on:12/24/2007 ....$2.5505
Employees 219	Stock Exchange.............................AMEX
Auditor .... McGladrey & Pullen LLP	Ticker Symbol...............................ITI
Stk Agt............................EquiServe,LLP	Outstanding Shares 31,800,000
Counsel.................................NA	E.P.S..................................$0.15
DUNS No. 04-876-5937	Shareholders..................................NA

Business: The group's principal activity is to manufacture and supply products, systems and services that control and manage the use of public roadways and secure the delivery of digital communications. The group operates in two segments: sensors segment includes vantage vehicle detection systems for traffic intersection control and autovue sensors for in vehicle safety . Systems segment includes transportation engineering and consulting activities. The customers of the group include government agencies, television networks and original equipment manufacturers.
Primary SIC and add'l.: 3669 7378 3663 3572 3695
CIK No: 0000350868
Subsidiaries: Iteris Europe GmbH
Officers: Abbas Mohaddes/Dir., CEO, Pres./$321,901.00, Richard D. Crawshaw/VP - Engineering, Francis Memole/Sr. VP, GM - Vehicle Sensors/$236,165.00, Greg McKhann/Sr. VP, GM - Roadway Sensors/$288,590.00, Stephen E. Rowe/Sr. VP, James S. Miele/VP - Finance, CFO/$194,542.00, Ginny Taylor/Primary IR Contact, Alan Clelland/Sr. VP, GM - Transportation Systems
Directors: Abbas Mohaddes/Dir., CEO, Pres., Gregory A. Miner/Chmn., Thomas L. Thomas/Dir., Gary Hernandez/Dir., John W. Seazholtz/Dir., Kevin C. Daly/Dir., Hartmut Marwitz/Dir., Richard Char/Dir., Joel Slutzky/Dir., Paul E. Wright/Dir.
Owners: Austin W. Marxe/13.90%, James S. Miele, Gary Hernandez, Abbas Mohaddes/3.10%, John D. Gruber/8.40%, Paul E. Wright, Richard Char, Bryant R. Riley/10.70%, Francis Memole, Greg McKhann, Jack Johnson/2.70%, Insiders/15.70%, John W. Seazholtz, Clint D. Coghill/5.10%, Thomas L. Thomas (19 Owners included in Index)
Financial Data: Fiscal Year End:03/31   **Latest Annual Data:** 03/31/2007

Year	Sales	Net Income
2007	$58,297,000	$2,918,000
2006	$50,486,000	$80,000
2005	$46,397,000	-$11,328,000

Curr. Assets:	$18,222,000	Curr. Liab.:	$14,929,000	P/E Ratio:	23.19
Plant, Equip.:	$1,783,000	Total Liab.:	$30,998,000	Indic. Yr. Divd.:	NA
Total Assets:	$49,633,000	Net Worth:	$18,635,000	Debt/ Equity:	NA

ITEX Corp

3326 160th Ave. SE, Ste. 100, Bellevue, WA, 98008; **PH:** 1-425-463-4000; **Fax:** 1-425-463-4040; http:// www.itex.com

General - Incorporation .... NV	Stock- Price on:12/24/2007 ....$0.73
Employees 19	Stock Exchange.............................OTC
Auditor ...Ehrhardt Keefe Steiner & Hottman P.A	Ticker Symbol...............................ITEX
Stk Agt..................................OTR Inc	Outstanding Shares 17,970,000
Counsel.................................NA	E.P.S..................................$0.20
DUNS No. 10-287-0508	Shareholders..................................NA

Business: The group's principal activity is to operate a retail trade exchange and to act as a third-party record keeper for transactions between members of the exchanges. The group provides a business-to-business payment system for retail, professional, media and other corporate members. The group's retail trade exchange headquartered in sacramento, California has approximately 14,000 members who, collectively, make up the trade exchange, which operates as an unincorporated association. The group administers the itex exchange and act as a third-party record keeper for transactions entered into by the members. The services are offered through five corporate regional offices and more than sixty independent licensed brokers and franchisees in the United States and Canada.
Primary SIC and add'l.: 7389 6231
CIK No: 0000860518
Subsidiaries: BXI Acquisition Sub, Inc
Officers: Steven White/Chmn., CEO, Interim CFO, Alan Zimmelman/Investor Relations, John A. Wade/Dir., Sec., Treasurer
Directors: Steven White/Chmn., CEO, Interim CFO, John A. Wade/Dir., Sec., Treasurer, Eric Best/Dir.
Owners: Eric Best, Insiders/11.00%, John Wade/1.10%, Steven White/9.50%
Financial Data: Fiscal Year End:07/31   **Latest Annual Data:** 7/31/2006

Year	Sales	Net Income
2006	$14,657,000	$3,433,000
2005	$10,423,000	$3,098,000
2004	$10,283,000	$2,653,000

Curr. Assets:	$2,499,000	Curr. Liab.:	$2,285,000	P/E Ratio:	3.65
Plant, Equip.:	$76,000	Total Liab.:	$2,695,000	Indic. Yr. Divd.:	NA
Total Assets:	$10,663,000	Net Worth:	$7,968,000	Debt/ Equity:	NA

Ithaka Acquisition Corp

100 S Pointe Dr., 23rd Fl., Miami, FL, 33139; **PH:** 1-305-532-3800; http:// www.ithakacorp.com

General - Incorporation....DE
Employees....NA
Auditor....Goldstein Golub Kessler LLP
Stk Agt....Continental Stock Transfer & Trust Co
Counsel....NA
DUNS No....NA

Stock- Price on:12/24/2007....$5.62
Stock Exchange....NDQ
Ticker Symbol....ALUS
Outstanding Shares....10,970,000
E.P.S....-$9.99
Shareholders....NA

Business: The groups principal activity is to operate healthcare industry. The group operates from the United States.

Primary SIC and add'l.: 3841

CIK No: 0001324205

Subsidiaries: Alsius Corporation

Officers: Paul A. Brooke/Chmn., CEO, Eric Hecht/Dir., CFO, Pres., John M. Glazer/Dir., COO, Sec.

Directors: Paul A. Brooke/Chmn., CEO, Eric Hecht/Dir., CFO, Pres., John M. Glazer/Dir., COO, Sec.

Owners: Cheyne Capital Management Limited/6.20%, Insiders/19.40%, Paul A. Brooke/8.70%, Weiss Asset Management, LLC/7.80%, The Baupost Group, L.L.C./9.70%, Fir Tree, Inc/4.90%, John M. Glazer/1.90%, P. Schoenfeld Asset Management LLC/5.50%, Eric Hecht/8.70%

Financial Data: *Fiscal Year End:*12/31 *Latest Annual Data:* 12/31/2006

Year	Sales	Net Income
2006	NA	$207,000
2005	NA	$166,000

Curr. Assets:	$49,470,000	**Curr. Liab.:**	$1,037,000		
Plant, Equip.:	NA	**Total Liab.:**	$10,432,000	**Indic. Yr. Divd.:**	NA
Total Assets:	$49,757,000	**Net Worth:**	$39,325,000	**Debt/ Equity:**	NA

ITIS Holdings Inc

12000 Westheimer, Ste. 340, Houston, TX, 77077; *PH:* 1-281-600-6000; *Fax:* 1-713-462-1950; *http://* www.itisinc.com

General - Incorporation....NV
Employees....3
Auditor....Malone & Bailey, P.C
Stk Agt....Atlas Stock Transfer Corp
Counsel....NA
DUNS No....10-808-2157

Stock- Price on:12/24/2007....$0.024
Stock Exchange....OTC
Ticker Symbol....ITHH
Outstanding Shares....NA
E.P.S....NA
Shareholders....NA

Business: The group's principal activities are to provide automated litigation support services through its subsidiary litidex, pharmacy operations through its subsidiary pharmhouse, and technical support through its subsidiary onpoint solutions. The group provides automated litigation support services related to lawsuits involving stock manipulation of publicly held companies. Using the litidex search engine, millions of documents are processed to create databases that are instantly searchable for data retrieval. The pharmhouse currently operates one pharmacy that focuses primarily on electronic prescription services. The onpoint solutions inc provides technical support for pharmhouse and litidex(R) in the development and operation of the pharmacies of pharmhouse and in software and hardware services for both pharmhouse and litidex (r). The group is temporarily suspended its automated litigation support services as contracts are negotiated.

Primary SIC and add'l.: 7375

CIK No: 0000003959

Subsidiaries: ITIS, Inc., National Law Library, Inc., OnPoint Solutions Inc., PharmHouse Inc.

Officers: Hunter M.A. Carr/Chmn., CEO, Kara Kirker/Sec., Treasurer, Joanna Hoover/CFO, Donald W. Sapaugh/Pres., Dir. - Pharmhouse Inc, Carol A. Wilson/Sec. - Pharmhouse Inc, Kelley V. Kirker/Dir. - Pharmhouse Inc

Directors: Hunter M.A. Carr/Chmn., CEO, George A. Roberts/Dir., Paul Thayer/Dir., Allyn W. Hoaglund/Dir.

Financial Data: *Fiscal Year End:*12/31 *Latest Annual Data:* 12/31/2005

Year	Sales	Net Income
2005	$9,000	-$138,000
2004	NA	-$1,077,000
2003	$824,000	-$5,812,000

Curr. Assets:	$859,000	**Curr. Liab.:**	$3,336,000		
Plant, Equip.:	$8,000	**Total Liab.:**	$7,121,000	**Indic. Yr. Divd.:**	NA
Total Assets:	$869,000	**Net Worth:**	-$6,252,000	**Debt/ Equity:**	NA

Itron Inc

2111 N Molter Rd., Liberty Lake, WA, 99019; *PH:* 1-509-924-9900; *Fax:* 1-509-891-3355; *http://* www.itron.com

General - Incorporation....WA
Employees....2,400
Auditor....Deloitte & Touche LLP
Stk Agt....Mellon Shareholder Services LLC
Counsel....Perkins Coie LLP
DUNS No....09-364-9895

Stock- Price on:12/24/2007....$73.98
Stock Exchange....NDQ
Ticker Symbol....ITRI
Outstanding Shares....30,010,000
E.P.S....-$0.01
Shareholders....NA

Business: The group's principal activity is to provide integrated system solutions for collecting, communicating, analyzing and managing information about electric, gas and water usage. The group provides industry-leading solutions for meter data collection, energy information management, demand side management and response, load forecasting and analysis. The group also provides consulting services and software, transmission and distribution system design and optimization, Web-based workforce automation, commercial and industrial (c&i) customer care and residential energy management. Trademarks of the group include itron(R), linesoft(R), and ert(R), mv-90(R), service-link and "Knowledge To Shape Your Future". On 04-Mar-2003, the group acquired silicon energy corporation. The operations of the group are carried out in the United States, Canada, Australia, Austria, the Netherlands and France.

Primary SIC and add'l.: 3825 7389 3824

CIK No: 0000780571

Subsidiaries: EMD Holding, Inc., Itron Australasia Holdings Pty. Limited, Itron Australasia Technologies Pty. Limited, Itron B.C. Corporation, Itron Brazil I, LLC, Itron Brazil II, LLC, Itron BV, Itron Canada, Inc., Itron Canada, Ltd, Itron Connecticut Finance, Inc., Itron de Mxico, S.A. de C.V, Itron Distribucion, S.A. DE C.V., Itron Electricity Metering, Inc., Itron Engineering Services, Inc., Itron Finance, Inc. 25 Subsidiaries included in the Index

Officers: Leroy D. Nosbaum/61/Chmn., CEO/$1,637,493.00, Doug Staker/VP - International Marketing, Philip Mezey/COO, Sr. VP - North America/$941,373.00, Chuck McAtee/VP - Information Technology, CIO, Steven M. Helmbrecht/Sr. VP, CFO/$901,491.00, Jared Serff/VP - Competitive Resources/$609,050.00, Malcolm Unsworth/Sr. VP - Hardware Solutions/$1,004,508.00, Russell E. Vanos/VP - Marketing, John Holleran/Sr. VP, General Counsel, Corp. Sec., Deloris Duquette/VP - Investor Relations, Corporate Communications

Directors: Leroy D. Nosbaum/61/Chmn., CEO, Gary Pruitt/57/Dir., Michael B. Bracy/66/Dir., Ted C. Demerritt/75/Dir., Kirby A. Dyess/61/Dir., Jon E. Eliassen/60/Dir., Thomas S. Foley/78/Dir., Charles H. Gaylord/62/Dir., Thomas S. Glanville/49/Dir., Sharon L. Nelson/61/Dir., Graham M. Wilson/63/Dir.

Owners: Sharon L. Nelson, Kirby Dyess, Malcolm Unsworth, BlackRock, Inc./9.49%, Jared P. Serff, Insiders/2.04%, Michael B. Bracy, Thomas S. Glanville, Charles H. Gaylord, AXA Financial, Inc./5.77%, Ted C. DeMerritt, Graham M. Wilson, Steven M. Helmbrecht, EARNEST Partners, LLC/5.57%, Gary Pruitt *(19 Owners included in Index)*

Financial Data: *Fiscal Year End:*12/31 *Latest Annual Data:* 12/31/2006

Year	Sales	Net Income
2006	$644,042,000	$33,759,000
2005	$552,690,000	$33,061,000
2004	$399,194,000	-$5,257,000

Curr. Assets:	$596,445,000	**Curr. Liab.:**	$103,584,000		
Plant, Equip.:	$88,689,000	**Total Liab.:**	$597,540,000	**Indic. Yr. Divd.:**	NA
Total Assets:	$988,522,000	**Net Worth:**	$390,982,000	**Debt/ Equity:**	0.7673

Itronics Inc

6490 S McCarran Blvd., Bldg. C, Ste. 23, Reno, NV, 89509; *PH:* 1-775-689-7696; *Fax:* 1-775-689-7691; *http://* www.itronics.com; *Email:* investor@itronics.com

General - Incorporation....TX
Employees....NA
Auditor....Cacciamatta Accountancy Corp
Stk Agt....Securities Transfer Corp
Counsel....Skinner, Sutton & Watson
DUNS No....60-693-0709

Stock- Price on:12/24/2007....$0.017
Stock Exchange....OTC
Ticker Symbol....ITRO
Outstanding Shares....375,420,000
E.P.S....-$0.005
Shareholders....NA

Business: The group's principal activities are to provide mining technical services, developing and implementing photobyproduct recycling, fertilizer manufacturing, precious metals recovery and refining. The group's activities are classified into two segments: photobyproduct fertilizer and mining technical services. Photobyproduct fertilizer segment operates a photobyproduct recycling plant and is developing new silver-gold refining technology. Mining technical services segment provides mining and materials management, geology, engineering and economics consulting. The group also publishes specialized mineral economics and materials financial reports.

Primary SIC and add'l.: 8711 3341 2874

CIK No: 0000825203

Subsidiaries: American Hydromet, Itronics California, Inc., Itronics Metallurgical, Inc, Nevada Hydrometallurgical Project, Whitney & Whitney, Inc

Officers: John W. Whitney/Dir., Pres., Treasurer, Principal Executive Financial Officer, Duane H. Rasmussen/VP, Gregory S. Skinner/Sec., General Counsel, Michael C. Horsley/Principal Accounting Officer, Controller

Directors: John W. Whitney/Dir., Pres., Treasurer, Principal Executive Financial Officer, Howland S. Green/Dir.

Owners: Insiders/13.80%, John W. Whitney/12.10%, Duane H. Rasmussen/1.30%, Howland S. Green

Financial Data: *Fiscal Year End:*12/31 *Latest Annual Data:* 12/31/2006

Year	Sales	Net Income
2006	$1,884,000	-$3,810,000
2005	$1,361,000	-$4,907,000
2004	$1,720,000	-$2,840,000

Curr. Assets:	$902,000	**Curr. Liab.:**	$11,041,000		
Plant, Equip.:	$2,944,000	**Total Liab.:**	$11,695,000	**Indic. Yr. Divd.:**	NA
Total Assets:	$4,266,000	**Net Worth:**	-$7,430,000	**Debt/ Equity:**	NA

ITT Corp

Formerly: ITT Industries Inc
Four W Red Oak Ln., White Plains, NY, 10604; *PH:* 1-914-641-2000; *http://* www.ittind.com

General - Incorporation....IN
Employees....37,500
Auditor....Deloitte & Touche LLP
Stk Agt....The Bank of New York
Counsel....NA
DUNS No....00-121-6845

Stock- Price on:12/24/2007....$68.49
Stock Exchange....NYSE
Ticker Symbol....ITT
Outstanding Shares....181,720,000
E.P.S....$3.44
Shareholders....NA

Business: The groups principle activities include designing and manufacturing engineered products and the provision of related services. In the year 2007, the group acquired International Motion Control. The group operates from United States.

Primary SIC and add'l.: 3812 3728 3443 5084 3678 3663 3561

CIK No: 0000216228

Subsidiaries: 1448170 Ontario Ltd., A.G. Johansons Metallfabrik AB, AC Custom Pumps Division, Admiral Corporation, Advanced Engineering & Sciences Division, AGJ Holding AB, Allen Osbourne Associates, Inc., Anadolu Flygt Pompa Sanayi Ve Ticaret, Avis Werberg GmbH, BEC Acquisition Corporation, Inc., BIW Division, Bolton Insurance Company, Bombas Flygt de Venezuela, Bombas Goulds de Argentina., Bombas Goulds de Mexico S. de R.L. de C.V. 285 Subsidiaries included in the Index

Officers: Steven R. Loranger/Chmn., CEO, Pres./$10,568,450.00, Usha Wright/Sr. Vice Presidant, Dir. - Global Workforce Strategy, Lawrence J. Swire/VP, Assoc. General Counsel, Brenda Reichelderfer/CTO, Sr. VP, William E. Taylor/Pres. - ITT China, Steven F. Gaffney/Sr. VP, Pres. - ITT Defense Electronics, Services/$3,062,005.00, Nicholas P. Hill/Sr. VP, Pres. - ITT Motion, Flow Control, Scott A. Crum/Sr. VP, Dir. - Human Resources, Donald E. Foley/Sr. VP, Treasure, Dir. - Taxes, John P. Williamson/VP, Pres. - ITT Residential, Commercial Water, Thomas R. Martin/54/Sr. VP, Dir. - Corporate Relations, Robert J. Pagano/VP - Finance, Aris Chicles/VP, Dir. - Corporate Strategy, Corporate Development, Henry J. Driesse/Sr. VP - Operations/$3,272,739.00, Kathleen S. Stolar/VP, Corp. Sec., Assoc. General Counsel *(25 Officers included in Index)*

Directors: Steven R. Loranger/Chmn., CEO, Pres., Christina A. Gold/60/Dir., Ralph F. Hake/59/Dir., John J. Hamre/57/Dir., Raymond W. Leboeuf/61/Dir., Frank T. MacInnis/61/Dir., Linda S. Sanford/55/Dir., Markos I. Tambakeras/57/Dir., Curtis J. Crawford/60/Dir.

Owners: John J. Hamre/0.02%, Christina A. Gold/0.02%, Steven F. Gaffney/0.03%, Insiders/0.76%, Linda S. Sanford/0.02%, George E. Minnich/0.02%, Frank T. MacInnis/0.01%, Steven R. Loranger/0.16%, Curtis J. Crawford/0.02%, Raymond W. LeBoeuf/0.02%, Ralph F. Hake/0.01%, Barrow, Hanley, Mewhinney & Strauss, Inc./6.10%, Markos I. Tambakeras/0.01%, Henry J. Driesse/0.07%, Vincent A. Maffeo/0.02%

Financial Data: *Fiscal Year End:*12/31 *Latest Annual Data:* 12/31/2006

Year	Sales	Net Income
2006	$7,807,900,000	$581,100,000
2005	$7,427,300,000	$359,500,000
2004	$6,764,100,000	$432,300,000

Curr. Assets:	$3,347,700,000	Curr. Liab.:	$2,759,400,000	P/E Ratio:	19.91
Plant, Equip.:	$833,000,000	Total Liab.:	$4,565,200,000	Indic. Yr. Divd.:	$0.560
Total Assets:	$7,430,000,000	Net Worth:	$2,864,800,000	Debt/ Equity:	0.1674

ITT Educational Services Inc

13000 N Meridian St., Carmel, IN, 46032; *PH:* 1-317-706-9200; *Fax:* 1-317-706-3040; *http://* www.ittesi.com

General - Incorporation	DE	**Stock**- Price on:12/24/2007	$111.32
Employees	3,500	Stock Exchange	NYSE
Auditor	PricewaterhouseCoopers LLP	Ticker Symbol	ESI
Stk Agt	Bank of New York	Outstanding Shares	40,720,000
Counsel	NA	E.P.S.	$3.28
DUNS No.	05-470-1560	Shareholders	NA

Business: The group's principal activity is to provide technology-oriented postsecondary degree programs in the United States. The group offers associate, bachelor and master degree programs and non-degree diploma programs to more than 37,000 students. Currently, the group has 77 institutes located in 30 states. The group designs its education programs, after consultation with employers, to help graduates prepare for careers in various fields involving technology. The group has provided career-oriented education programs since 1969 under the itt technical institute name and its institutes have graduated over 175,000 students since 1976. As of 31-Dec-2003, we were offering 20 degree programs and several diploma programs in various fields of study. All of the institutes offer degree or diploma programs involving it and electronics and 68 institutes offer a degree or diploma program involving design.

Primary SIC and add'l.: 8221

CIK No: 0000922475

Subsidiaries: ESI Maryland Corp., ESI Service Corp.

Officers: Kevin M. Modany/CEO, Pres./$879,750.00, Nina F. Esbin/51/Sr. VP - Human Resources, Jeffrey R. Cooper/56/Sr. VP, Chief Compliance Officer, Eugene W. Feichtner/52/Sr. VP - Operations/$433,018.00, Clark D. Elwood/47/Sr. VP, General Counsel, Sec./$538,293.00, Daniel M. Fitzpatrick/Sr. VP, CFO/$667,093.00, Glenn E. Tanner/Sr. VP - Marketing, Angela K. Knowlton/VP, Controller, Treasurer, Timothy A. Rauschenbach/VP - Online Operations, Barry S. Simich/VP - Operations, Martin Van Buren/VP - Information Technology

Directors: Rene R. Champagne/66/Chmn., Joanna T. Lau/49/Dir., Samuel L. Odle/58/Dir., John F. Cozzi/46/Dir., John E. Dean/57/Dir., James D. Fowler/63/Dir., Vin Weber/55/Dir., Thomas I. Morgan/54/Dir., John A. Yena/67/Dir.

Owners: Joanna T. Lau, Insiders/3.60%, Warburg Pincus Asset Management, Inc./7.20%, Kevin M. Modany, Columbia Acorn Trust/12.70%, John A. Yena, Clark D. Elwood, Eugene W. Feichtner, John E. Dean, James D. Fowler, The Nuclear Decommissioning Trust of Dominion Nuclear Connecticut, Inc./6.10%, Samuel L. Odle, Vin Weber, Rene R. Champagne/1.80%, Massachusetts Financial Services Company/5.10% (20 Owners included in Index)

Financial Data: *Fiscal Year End:*12/31 *Latest Annual Data:* 12/31/2006

Year	Sales	Net Income
2006	$757,764,000	$118,516,000
2005	$688,003,000	$109,712,000
2004	$617,834,000	$75,263,000

Curr. Assets:	$380,952,000	Curr. Liab.:	$284,505,000	P/E Ratio:	37.74
Plant, Equip.:	$148,411,000	Total Liab.:	$456,375,000	Indic. Yr. Divd.:	NA
Total Assets:	$560,320,000	Net Worth:	$103,945,000	Debt/ Equity:	NA

Ituran Location and Control Ltd

3330 NW 53rd St., Ste. 302, Fort Lauderdale, FL, 33309; *PH:* 1-954-484-3806; *Fax:* 1-866-543-5433; *http://* www.ituran.com

General - Incorporation	Israel	**Stock** - Price on:12/24/2007	$12.61
Employees	800	Stock Exchange	NDQ
Auditor	Fahn Kanne & Co.	Ticker Symbol	ITRN
Stk Agt	American Stock Transfer & Trust Co.	Outstanding Shares	23,320,000
Counsel	NA	E.P.S.	$0.74
DUNS No.	NA	Shareholders	NA

Business: The groups principle activity is to provide location based services and wireless communications products. The groups services include stolen vehicle recovery and fleet management. The products of the group include automatic vehicle location, automatic meter reading and radio frequency identification. The groups operates through two segments namely location based services and wireless communication products. Specific customer of the group is Arad Technologies. The group operates from Israel, Brazil, Argentina, the United States, China and Korea. The group's quarterly revenue for September 2007 was 31.57 millions of USD.

Primary SIC and add'l.: 4899 4789 3799 3812 4812 7382

CIK No: 0001337117

Subsidiaries: Hotas Holding Ltd., Ituran Beheer B.V., Ituran Cellular Communication Ltd., Ituran de Argentina S.A., Ituran Florida Corporation, Ituran License Corp., Ituran NY Corporation, Ituran Sistemas de Monitoramento Ltda., Ituran USA Inc., Telematics Wireless Ltd., Teleran Holding Ltda.

Officers: Nir Sheratzky/36/Dir., Co - CEO, Eddy Kafry/56/Pres., CEO - Telematics Wireless, Guy Aharonov/43/General Counsel, Eli Kamer/42/CFO, Exec. VP - Finance

Directors: Nir Sheratzky/36/Dir., Co - CEO, Izzy Sheratzky/62/Chmn., Co - Founder, Y. Kahane/Dir., Avner Kurtz/Dir., Eyal Sheratzky/Dir., Amos Kurz/52/Dir., Yigal Shani/64/Dir., Gil Sheratzky/31/Dir., Orna Ophir/58/Dir., Israel Baron/55/Dir., Yoav Kahane/34/Dir., Zeev Koren/63/Dir.

Owners: Amos Kurz/6.22%, Yigal Shani/1.69%, Yehuda Kahane/9.20%, Avner Kurz/6.30%, Izzy Sheratzky/24.60%

Financial Data: *Fiscal Year End:*12/31 *Latest Annual Data:* 12/31/2006

Year	Sales	Net Income
2006	$104,052,000	$19,259,000
2005	$90,126,000	$14,375,000
2004	$77,926,000	$11,219,000

Curr. Assets:	$106,836,000	Curr. Liab.:	$33,402,000	P/E Ratio:	477.75
Plant, Equip.:	$19,109,000	Total Liab.:	$47,968,000	Indic. Yr. Divd.:	$0.210
Total Assets:	$144,839,000	Net Worth:	$96,871,000	Debt/ Equity:	NA

Ivanhoe Energy Inc

Ivanhoe Energy Inc., 654 - 999, Vancouver, BC, 93389; *PH:* 1-604-688-8323; *http://* www.ivanhoe-energy.com; *Email:* info@ivanhoemines.com

General - Incorporation	Canada	**Stock**- Price on:12/24/2007	$1.95
Employees	NA	Stock Exchange	NDQ
Auditor	Deloitte & Touche LLP	Ticker Symbol	IVAN
Stk Agt	Mellon Shareholder Services LLC	Outstanding Shares	NA
Counsel	NA	E.P.S.	NA
DUNS No.	NA	Shareholders	NA

Business: The group's principle activities include oil exploration and production and development of gas-to-liquid projects and enhanced oil recovery projects. The operations are currently carried out in the United States and China. Primary oil and gas properties of the company are located in the san joaquin valley area of California. The company also holds interests in exploration and development properties in Texas and Kentucky in the United States and in the hebei province in China. The group operates from United States.

Primary SIC and add'l.: 5172 1382 1311

CIK No: 0001106935

Subsidiaries: EEC Management Corp, EEC Management Corp., Energy Resources Development Japan Corporation, Ensyn Energy Corp., Ensyn Energy Management L.P., Ensyn Petroleum, ITS Ensyn LLC, Ivanhoe Energy (Latin America) Inc, Ivanhoe Energy (Middle East) Inc, Ivanhoe Energy (USA) Inc, Ivanhoe Energy Advisory Inc, Ivanhoe Energy Holdings Inc., Ivanhoe Energy HTL (USA) Inc., Ivanhoe Energy Htl Inc., Ivanhoe Energy International Inc 20 Subsidiaries included in the Index

Officers: Joe Gasca/Dir., CEO, Pres., Gordon W. Lancaster/CFO, Ed Veith/Exec. VP - Upstream, Patrick Chua/Exec. VP - China, Gerald Moench/Exec. VP - China, Ian Barnett/Exec. VP - Finance, Michael Silverman/CTO, Exec. VP

Directors: Joe Gasca/Dir., CEO, Pres., David Martin/Exec. Co - Chmn., Robert Abboud/Co - Chmn., Leon E. Daniel/Dep. Chmn., Robert M. Friedland/Dep. Chmn., Shun-Ichi Shimizu/Dir., Robert Pirraglia/Dir., Brian Downey/Dir., Robert Graham/Dir., Edward R. Flood/62/Dir., Steven J. Rhodes/Dir., Howard Balloch/Dir.

Owners: Steven J. Rhodes, Gerald Moench, Howard R. Balloch, Robert M. Friedland/20.48%, David R. Martin/1.76%, Joseph I. Gasca, Shun-ichi Shimizu, Edward R. Flood, Brian Downey, Robert G. Graham/2.14%, Robert A. Pirraglia, Patrick Chua, Insiders/25.74%, Robert A. Abboud, Leon E. Daniel (17 Owners included in Index)

Financial Data: *Fiscal Year End:*12/31 *Latest Annual Data:* 12/31/2006

Year	Sales	Net Income
2006	$48,524,000	-$42,422,000
2005	$29,939,000	-$14,972,000
2004	$17,997,000	-$20,725,000

Curr. Assets:	$22,087,000	Curr. Liab.:	$18,446,000		
Plant, Equip.:	$89,739,000	Total Liab.:	$26,536,000	Indic. Yr. Divd.:	NA
Total Assets:	$216,365,000	Net Worth:	$189,829,000	Debt/ Equity:	0.0250

Ivanhoe Mines Ltd

999 Canada Pl., Ste. 654, Vancouver, BC, V6C 3E1; *PH:* 1-604-688-5755; *Fax:* 1-604-682-2060; *http://* www.ivanhoe-mines.com; *Email:* info@ivanhoemines.com

General - Incorporation	Canada	**Stock**- Price on:12/24/2007	$14.45
Employees	1,200	Stock Exchange	NYSE
Auditor	Deloitte & Touche LLP	Ticker Symbol	IVN
Stk Agt	Deloitte & Touche LLP	Outstanding Shares	NA
Counsel	NA	E.P.S.	-$0.74
DUNS No.	NA	Shareholders	NA

Business: The groups principle activity is to provide mineral exploration and development services. The group operates from Canada.

Primary SIC and add'l.: 1081

CIK No: 0001158041

Subsidiaries: Ivanhoe Mines Mongolia Inc., Ivanhoe Mines Mongolia Inc. XXK

Officers: Peter Reeve/CEO - Ivanhoe Australia Pty Ltd, John MacKen/Dir., CEO, Pres., Beverly A. Bartlett/VP, Corp. Sec., Bill Trenaman/Investor Relations Officer, Jay Gow/VP - Marketing, Gene Wusaty/Pres. - Coal Division, Garamjav Dondog/Sr. Geologist, Pierre Masse/VP - Finance, Charles Forster/Sr. VP - Oyu Tolgoi Project, Douglas J. Kirwin/Exec. VP - Exploration, Tony Giardini/CFO, Steven Garcia/Exec. VP, David Woodall/Pres. - Ivanhoe's Gold Operations

Directors: John MacKen/Dir., CEO, Pres., Peter Meredith/Dep. Chmn., Robert M. Friedland/Chmn., Robert Hanson/Dir., Marc Faber/Dir., Howard Balloch/Dir., David Korbin/Dir., Edward R. Flood/Dir., Kjeld Thygesen/Dir., Bret K. Clayton/Dir., Tom Albanese/Dir., David Huberman/Dir., John Weatherall/Dir.

Financial Data: *Fiscal Year End:*12/31 *Latest Annual Data:* 12/31/2006

Year	Sales	Net Income
2006	NA	-$198,657,000
2005	NA	-$89,786,000
2004	$44,091,000	-$86,651,000

Curr. Assets:	$401,851,000	Curr. Liab.:	$37,201,000		
Plant, Equip.:	$101,994,000	Total Liab.:	$49,302,000	Indic. Yr. Divd.:	NA
Total Assets:	$703,159,000	Net Worth:	$653,857,000	Debt/ Equity:	NA

IVAX Diagnostics Inc

2140 N Miami Ave., Miami, FL, 33127; *PH:* 1-305-324-2338; *Fax:* 1-305-324-2395; *http://* www.ivaxdiagnostics.com; *Email:* investor_relations@ivaxdiagnostics.com

General - Incorporation	DE
Employees	120
Auditor	Ernst & Young LLP
Stk Agt.	Continental Stock Transfer & Trust Co
Counsel	NA
DUNS No.	NA

Stock - Price on:12/24/2007	$1
Stock Exchange	AMEX
Ticker Symbol	IVD
Outstanding Shares	27,650,000
E.P.S.	-$0.33
Shareholders	NA

Business: The group's principal activity is to develop, manufacture and market diagnostic test kits that are used to aid in the detection of disease markers primarily in the areas of autoimmune and infectious diseases. In addition to diagnostic kits, it also designs and manufactures laboratory instruments that perform the tests and provide results. The group also develops, manufactures and market raw materials, such as antigens used in the production of diagnostic kits. Through its facility in Italy, it develops and manufactures scientific and laboratory instruments, including its proprietary mago(R) instrument, which includes hardware, reagents, and software. The group operates in the United States and Italy.

Primary SIC and add'l.: 3841

CIK No: 0001095858

Subsidiaries: Delta Biologicals, S.r.l., Diamedix Corporation, ImmunoVision, Inc.

Officers: Giorgio Durso/73/CEO, Pres./$348,519.00

Directors: Itzak Krinsky/Chmn.

Owners: Teva Pharmaceutical Industries Limited/72.30%, Jose J. Valdes-Fauli, John B. Harley, Mark S. Deutsch, Glenn L. Halpryn, Insiders/2.70%, Giorgio DUrso/1.20%, Duane M. Steele, Fernando L. Fernandez

Financial Data: Fiscal Year End:12/31　Latest Annual Data: 12/31/2006

Year	Sales	Net Income
2006	$19,523,000	-$2,809,000
2005	$19,762,000	-$510,000
2004	$18,933,000	$152,000

Curr. Assets:	$22,876,000	Curr. Liab.:	$4,511,000		
Plant, Equip.:	$2,688,000	Total Liab.:	$5,969,000	Indic. Yr. Divd.:	NA
Total Assets:	$33,707,000	Net Worth:	$27,738,000	Debt/ Equity:	NA

IVI Communications Inc

555 H St. Ste. H, Eureka, CA, 95501; **PH:** 1-707-444-6617; **http://** www.ivn.net

General - Incorporation	NV
Employees	3
Auditor	Bagell, Levine & Company, LLC
Stk Agt.	Signature Stock Transfer, Inc.
Counsel	NA
DUNS No.	NA

Stock - Price on:12/24/2007	$0.007
Stock Exchange	OTC
Ticker Symbol	IVCM
Outstanding Shares	83,350,000
E.P.S.	-$0.012
Shareholders	NA

Business: The group's principle activities include acquiring dial-up ISP's and aggregating these into regional clusters and developing fixed wireless infrastructure. The group acquired Futura, Inc. in February 2006 and Internet Business Consulting, Inc. and AppState.Net, LLC in January 2005. The group operates from the United States. The group's revenue for Sep '07 was 0.08 millions of USD.

Primary SIC and add'l.: 4813

CIK No: 0001140878

Subsidiaries: Durangonet, Inc., Internet Ventures Oregon, Inc., Internet Ventures, Inc., Northcoast Internet, Inc., Quik Communications, Inc.

Owners: Charles Roodenburg/0.27%, Insiders/24.17%, Nyhl Henson/0.64%, Big Apple Consulting USA, Inc./13.33%, IVI Shareholder Trust/23.26%

Financial Data: Fiscal Year End:03/31　Latest Annual Data: 03/31/2007

Year	Sales	Net Income
2007	$1,860,000	$313,000
2006	$2,681,000	-$4,158,000
2005	$776,000	-$1,588,000

Curr. Assets:	$720,000	Curr. Liab.:	$5,553,000		
Plant, Equip.:	$91,000	Total Liab.:	$6,005,000	Indic. Yr. Divd.:	NA
Total Assets:	$4,931,000	Net Worth:	-$1,074,000	Debt/ Equity:	NA

iVillage Inc

500 7th Ave., 14th Fl., New York, NY, 10018; **PH:** 1-212-600-6000; **Fax:** 1-212-600-6001; **http://** www.ivillage.com; **Email:** iVillage.PR@nbcuni.com

General - Incorporation	DE
Employees	NA
Auditor	PricewaterhouseCoopers LLP
Stk Agt.	Continental Stock Transfer & Trust Co
Counsel	NA
DUNS No.	NA

Stock - Price on:12/24/2007	NA
Stock Exchange	NA
Ticker Symbol	NA
Outstanding Shares	NA
E.P.S.	NA
Shareholders	NA

Business: The group's principle activity is to provide online information about women through its websites ivillage.com, women.com, gurl.com, astrology.com, substance.com and promotions.com. It derives revenues from sponsorship and advertising, astrological charts and related products, advertising placements and other and subscriptions and Internet promotions. It operates through subsidiaries or divisions such as ivillage.com, women.com networks, inc., gurl.com, knowledgeweb, inc., cooperative beauty ventures, llc, ivillage parenting network, inc., public affairs group, inc., promotions.com, inc., ivillage consulting and ivillagesolutions. Its trademarks include ivillage(R), ivillage.com(R), gurl.com(R), deal with it(R) , newborn channel(R), parentsplace.com(R), webstakes.com(R), ivillage consulting(R), ivillage solutions(R), and ivillageaccess(r). The hearst corporation is one of its major customers.

Primary SIC and add'l.: 7319 7375

CIK No: 0001074767

Subsidiaries: NBC Universal, Inc

Ivivi Technologies Inc

224-S Pegasus Ave., Northvale, NJ, 07647; **PH:** 1-201-784-8168; **Fax:** 1-201-784-0620; **http://** www.ivivitechnologies.com; **Email:** info@ivivitechnologies.com

General - Incorporation	NJ
Employees	8
Auditor	NA
Stk Agt.	Computershare Trust Co
Counsel	NA
DUNS No.	NA

Stock - Price on:12/24/2007	$4.45
Stock Exchange	AMEX
Ticker Symbol	II
Outstanding Shares	9,560,000
E.P.S.	-$1.131
Shareholders	NA

Business: The groups principle activity is to provide research and clinical applications. The group operates from United States.

Primary SIC and add'l.: 3845

CIK No: 0001316925

Officers: Andre A. Dimino/Vice Chmn., Co - CEO/$190,601.00, David Saloff/Dir., Co - CEO, Pres./$221,857.00, Edward J. Hammel/Exec. VP/$145,370.00, Alan V. Gallantar/CFO/$146,771.00, Alison Ziegler/Investor Relations Officer

Directors: Andre A. Dimino/Vice Chmn., Co - CEO, David Saloff/Dir., Co - CEO, Pres., Steven M. Gluckstern/Chmn., Louis J. Ignarro/Dir., Kenneth S. Abramowitz/Dir., Pamela J. Newman/Dir., Jeffrey A. Tischler/Dir.

Owners: Insiders/25.80%, Andre A. DiMino/17.50%, Edward J. Hammel/1.30%, Steven M. Gluckstern/7.30%, Sherleigh Associates Defined Benefit Pension Plan/9.90%, Kenneth Abramowitz/1.10%, David Saloff/6.30%, ADM Unlimited, Inc./33.90%, Louis J. Ignarro, ProMed Partners, L.P./6.60%, Pamela J. Newman, Jeffrey A. Tischler

Financial Data: Fiscal Year End:03/31　Latest Annual Data: 03/31/2007

Year	Sales	Net Income
2007	$1,182,000	-$7,779,000
2006	$787,000	-$10,747,000
2005	$329,000	-$2,628,000

Curr. Assets:	$1,019,000	Curr. Liab.:	$3,662,000		
Plant, Equip.:	$341,000	Total Liab.:	$16,921,000	Indic. Yr. Divd.:	NA
Total Assets:	$2,348,000	Net Worth:	-$14,572,000	Debt/ Equity:	NA

iVoice Inc

750 Hwy. 34, Matawan, NJ, 07747; **PH:** 1-732-441-7700; **Fax:** 1-732-441-9895; **http://** www.ivoice.com; **Email:** information@ivoice.com

General - Incorporation	NJ
Employees	2
Auditor	Bagell, Levine & Company, LLC
Stk Agt.	Fidelity Transfer Co
Counsel	NA
DUNS No.	NA

Stock - Price on:12/24/2007	$0.0055
Stock Exchange	OTC
Ticker Symbol	IVOI
Outstanding Shares	85,550,000
E.P.S.	-$0.036
Shareholders	NA

Business: The groups principle activities include distributing shares and acquiring other companies.. In January 2006, the group acquired Thomas Pharmaceuticals Ltd. The group operates from the United States. The group's quarterly revenue for Sep '07 was 0.30 millions of USD.

Primary SIC and add'l.: 7372

CIK No: 0001105064

Subsidiaries: iVoice Innovations, Inc., Thomas Pharmaceuticals, Ltd.

Officers: Jerome Mahoney/Chmn., CEO

Directors: Jerome Mahoney/Chmn., CEO, Frank V. Esser/Dir.

Owners: Insiders, Jerome R. Mahoney, Cornell Capital Partners LLC, Jerome R. Mahoney, Frank V. Esser, Insiders

Financial Data: Fiscal Year End:12/31　Latest Annual Data: 12/31/2006

Year	Sales	Net Income
2006	$316,000	-$3,147,000
2005	$9,000	-$1,266,000
2004	$358,000	-$2,960,000

Curr. Assets:	$11,394,000	Curr. Liab.:	$1,032,000		
Plant, Equip.:	$123,000	Total Liab.:	$8,194,000	Indic. Yr. Divd.:	NA
Total Assets:	$11,854,000	Net Worth:	$3,660,000	Debt/ Equity:	NA

IWI Holding Ltd

P.O. Box 3340, Dawson Bldg., Rd. Town, Tortola;

General - Incorporation	British Virgin Islands
Employees	NA
Auditor	Blackman Kallick Bartelstein LLP
Stk Agt.	NA
Counsel	NA
DUNS No.	88-499-4062

Stock - Price on:12/24/2007	NA
Stock Exchange	OTC
Ticker Symbol	IWIHF
Outstanding Shares	NA
E.P.S.	-$1.46
Shareholders	NA

Business: The group operates through its subsidiary whose principle activities include designing, assembling, merchandising and distribution of jewelry such as rings, pendants, earrings, bracelets, necklaces, pins and brooches made of diamonds, other precious or semi-precious stones, pearls, silver and gold. The group operates from United States.

Primary SIC and add'l.: 6719 5094

CIK No: 0000923168

Subsidiaries: Imperial World, Inc.

Officers: Joseph K. Lau/60/Chmn., CEO, Connie S. Yui/57/Dir., Inventory Mgr., Richard J. Mick/67/Dir., VP - Sales

Directors: Joseph K. Lau/60/Chmn., CEO, Joseph A. Benjamin/65/Dir., Samuel H. Lou/54/Dir., Connie S. Yui/57/Dir., Inventory Mgr., Richard J. Mick/67/Dir., VP - Sales

Owners: Bamberg Company Ltd./35.96%, Joseph K. Lau/0.59%, Insiders/5.58%, Richard J. Mick/4.60%, Bamberg Company Ltd/100.00%, Joseph A. Benjamin/0.39%

Financial Data: Fiscal Year End:12/31　Latest Annual Data: 12/31/2006

Year	Sales	Net Income
2006	$28,944,000	-$127,000
2005	$26,683,000	-$192,000
2004	$28,554,000	$231,000

Curr. Assets:	$19,234,000	Curr. Liab.:	$18,009,000		
Plant, Equip.:	$118,000	Total Liab.:	$18,009,000	Indic. Yr. Divd.:	NA
Total Assets:	$19,352,000	Net Worth:	$1,343,000	Debt/ Equity:	NA

IWT Tesoro Corp

191 Post Rd. W, Ste.10, Westport, CT, 06880; **PH:** 1-203-221-2770; **Fax:** 1-203-221-2797; **http://** www.iwttesoro.com

General - Incorporation.............................NV
Employees 132
Auditor ....McGladrey & Pullen LLP
Stk Agt.............. Florida Atlantic Stock Transfer, Inc.
Counsel...NA
DUNS No. ....NA

Stock - Price on:12/24/2007 ....$0.9
Stock Exchange...OTC
Ticker Symbol..IWTT
Outstanding Shares 14,960,000
E.P.S. ....-$0.9
Shareholders..NA

Business: The groups principle activity is to distribute building materials. The groups building materials include ceramic, porcelain and natural stone floor, wall and decorative tile. The group also provides private label programs for branded retail sales customers, buying groups, large homebuilders and home center store chains. The group operates from United States, Europe, South America, Canada and the Near and Far East.

Primary SIC and add'l.: 6799

CIK No: 0001119190

Subsidiaries: Import Floorig Group Inc, International WholeSale Title Inc, IWT Tesoro International Ltd, IWT Tesoro transport Inc, The Title Club Inc

Officers: Henry J. Boucher/Dir., Principal Executive Officer/$245,417.00, David W. Whitwell/Principal Financial Officer/$24,577.00

Directors: Carl G. Anderson/Dir., Joseph Equale/Dir., Forrest Jordan/Dir., Grey Perna/Dir., James R. Edwards/Dir., Paul F. Boucher/Dir., Allen G. Rosenberg/Dir., Robert Rogers/Dir., Henry J. Boucher/Dir., Principal Executive Officer

Owners: Forrest P. Jordan, Carl G. Anderson, James R. Edwards, Allen G. Rosenberg, Antares Trading Fund/Mercatech SP, Insiders, Robert B. Rogers, David W. Whitwell, Grey Perna, Henry J. Boucher, Joseph A. Equale, Laurus Master Fund, Paul F. Boucher, Global Media Fund, Inc.

Financial Data: Fiscal Year End:12/31 Latest Annual Data: 12/31/2006

Year	Sales	Net Income
2006	$61,607,000	-$3,439,000
2005	$55,589,000	-$4,343,000
2004	$44,925,000	-$1,209,000
Curr. Assets: $40,991,000	**Curr. Liab.:** $46,268,000	
Plant, Equip.: $2,265,000	**Total Liab.:** $48,704,000	**Indic. Yr. Divd.:** NA
Total Assets: $44,272,000	**Net Worth:** -$4,432,000	**Debt/ Equity:** NA

IXI Mobile Inc

Formerly: Israel Technology Acquisition Corp
7 Gush Etzion, 3rd Fl., Givaat Shmuel, 54030; **PH:** 972-353-25918; **http://** www.iaei.org.il

General - Incorporation .... DE
Employees ....NA
Auditor ....Brightman Almagor & Co.
Stk Agt.............. Continental Stock Transfer & Trust Co
Counsel...NA
DUNS No. ....NA

Stock - Price on:12/24/2007 ....$5.7
Stock Exchange...NA
Ticker Symbol...NA
Outstanding Shares ....NA
E.P.S. ....NA
Shareholders..NA

Business: The groups principal activity is to provide services in the Fields of Electronics, communications and information technology. The group operates from Israel.

Primary SIC and add'l.: 4899

CIK No: 0001319644

Subsidiaries: IXI Mobile, Inc

Officers: Israel Frieder/Chmn., CEO, Glen Shear/49/Dir., CFO, Sec., Dael Schnider/34/Dir., Exec. VP, Shlomo B. Waxe/Dir. - General

Directors: Israel Frieder/Chmn., CEO, Glen Shear/49/Dir., CFO, Sec., Dael Schnider/34/Dir., Exec. VP, Victor Halpert/48/Dir., Joseph Ackerman/Dir., David Assia/Dir., Doron Birger/Dir., Yuval Eshel/Dir., Jonathan Levy/Dir., Israel Livnat/Dir., Alex Milner/Dir., David Perlmutter/Dir., Amiram Shore/Dir., Dan Vilenski/Dir.

Owners: Dael Schnider, Southpoint Master Fund LP, Lihi Segal, Gadi Meroz, Glen Shear, Gemini Funds, Amit Haller, Israel Frieder, Yossi Sela, Concord Ventures, Landa, Matthew Hills, Insiders, Gideon Barak

Financial Data: Fiscal Year End:12/31 Latest Annual Data: 12/31/2006

Year	Sales	Net Income
2006	NA	$216,000
2005	NA	$185,000
Curr. Assets: $34,929,000	**Curr. Liab.:** $192,000	
Plant, Equip.: NA	**Total Liab.:** $7,123,000	**Indic. Yr. Divd.:** NA
Total Assets: $34,929,000	**Net Worth:** $27,807,000	**Debt/ Equity:** NA

Ixia

26601 W Agoura Rd., Calabasas, CA, 91302; **PH:** 1-818-871-1800; **Fax:** 1-818-871-1805; **http://** www.ixiacom.com; **Email:** support@ixiacom.com

General - Incorporation .... CA
Employees 750
Auditor ....PricewaterhouseCoopers LLP
Stk Agt.....................U.S. Stock Transfer Corp
Counsel...NA
DUNS No. ....NA

Stock - Price on:12/24/2007 ....$9.46
Stock Exchange..NDQ
Ticker Symbol..XXIA
Outstanding Shares 67,830,000
E.P.S. $0.10
Shareholders..NA

Business: The group's principal activity is to develop, market and sell high-speed, multi-port network performance analysis systems. These systems are used in advanced optical and electrical communications equipment and networks. These products are used throughout the Internet and local, metropolitan wide area networks and includes ixia 1600t, ixia 400t and gigabit ethernet. The products allow customers to generate network and Internet protocol traffic and analyze the performance, accuracy and reliability of equipment and systems. The group's customers include manufacturers of network equipment, Internet and network service providers, communications and chip manufacturers. On 20-Feb-2004, the group acquired g3 nova technology.

Primary SIC and add'l.: 3577 7373

CIK No: 0001120295

Subsidiaries: Calakol Software Development Private Limited, Ixia Europe Limited, Ixia KK, Ixia SRL

Officers: Errol Ginsberg/Dir., CEO, Pres./$634,810.00, Tom Miller/CFO/$383,645.00, Sam Bass/Exec. VP - Operations, David Anderson/Sr. VP - Worldwide Sales, Business Development Operations/$595,248.00, Walker Colston/VP - Engineering Operations, Victor Alston/Sr. VP - Product Development/$466,841.00, Tim Jones/VP - Human Resources, Atul Bhatnagar/COO, Pres.

Directors: Jean-Claude Asscher/Chmn., Jon Rager/Dir., Gail Hamilton/Dir., Massoud Entekhabi/Dir., Jonathan Fram/Dir.

Owners: Franklin Resources, Inc./6.20%, Thomas B. Miller, Massoud Entekhabi, Jonathan Fram, David Anderson, Jean-Claude Asscher, Jon F. Rager, Insiders/10.20%, Errol Ginsberg/7.30%, Gail Hamilton, Victor Alston, Robert W. Bass, Compagnie Fiduciaire Trustees Limited,/35.50%

Financial Data: Fiscal Year End:12/31 Latest Annual Data: 12/31/2006

Year	Sales	Net Income
2006	$180,132,000	$13,481,000
2005	$150,853,000	$28,490,000
2004	$116,978,000	$18,879,000
Curr. Assets: $275,736,000	**Curr. Liab.:** $40,568,000	**P/E Ratio:** 49.79
Plant, Equip.: $22,044,000	**Total Liab.:** $48,270,000	**Indic. Yr. Divd.:** NA
Total Assets: $349,059,000	**Net Worth:** $300,789,000	**Debt/ Equity:** NA

IXYS Corp

3540 Bassett St., Santa Clara, CA, 95054; **PH:** 1-408-982-0700; **Fax:** 1-408-748-9788; **http://** www.ixys.com; **Email:** sales@ixys.net

General - Incorporation .... DE
Employees 1,018
Auditor ....BDO Seidman LLP
Stk Agt.............Mellon Investor Services LLC
Counsel..................Pillsbury, Madison & Sutro
DUNS No. 15-508-9428

Stock - Price on:12/24/2007 ....$9.72
Stock Exchange..NDQ
Ticker Symbol...IXYS
Outstanding Shares 32,540,000
E.P.S. $0.39
Shareholders..NA

Business: The group's principal activities are to design, develop, and market power semiconductors and digital and analog integrated circuits. The power semiconductor products are used primarily to control electricity in power conversion systems, motor drives, medical electronics and renewable energy sources like wind turbines and solar systems. The integrated circuits are used in power management, telecommunications, and display products. The products include power mosfets, insulated gate bipolar transistors (igbts), thyristors and rectifiers. The major customers of the group are abb, astec, delta electronics, eupec, huawei, guidant, medtronics, siemens and still. The products are sold in North America, Europe, the Middle East and Asia. On 05-Sep-2003, the group acquired microwave technology inc.

Primary SIC and add'l.: 5065 3674

CIK No: 0000945699

Subsidiaries: C.P. Clare Electronics GmbH, C.P. Clare Foreign Sales Corporation, C.P. Clare International N.V., C.P. Clare Mexicana S.A. de C.V., Clare Canada, Ltd., Clare Capital, Inc., Clare Components, Inc., Clare Electronics, Inc., Clare France S.A.R.L., Clare Instruments, Inc., Clare Micronix Integrated Systems, Inc., Clare N.V., Clare Services, Inc., Clare Systems, Inc., Clare Technologies (Taiwan), Inc. 32 Subsidiaries included in the Index

Officers: Nathan Zommer/Chmn., CEO, Pres., Founder/$1,285,878.00, Uzi Sasson/VP - Finance, CFO, COO/$607,506.00, Peter H. Ingram/Pres. - European Operations/$331,007.00

Directors: Nathan Zommer/Chmn., CEO, Pres., Founder, Donald L. Feucht/Dir., Joon S. Lee/Dir., Samuel Kory/Dir., David L. Millstein/Dir., James M. Thorburn/Dir., Tim Richardson/Dir.

Owners: Columbia Wagner Asset Management L.P./5.90%, Peter H. Ingram/2.20%, Samuel Kory, Insiders/27.10%, Donald L. Feucht, James M. Thorburn, S. Joon Lee, 6th Avenue Investment Management Company, LLC/10.30%, Uzi Sasson, Nathan Zommer/23.90%

Financial Data: Fiscal Year End:03/31 Latest Annual Data: 06/30/2007

Year	Sales	Net Income
2007	$75,901,000	$7,004,000
2006	$72,274,000	-$106,000
2005	$256,620,000	$16,242,000
Curr. Assets: $200,293,000	**Curr. Liab.:** $57,885,000	
Plant, Equip.: $48,741,000	**Total Liab.:** $92,532,000	**Indic. Yr. Divd.:** NA
Total Assets: $273,641,000	**Net Worth:** $181,109,000	**Debt/ Equity:** 0.0981

J & J Snack Foods Corp

6000 Central Hwy., Pennsauken, NJ, 08109; **PH:** 1-856-665-9533; **Fax:** 1-856-665-6718; **http://** www.jjsnack.com

General - Incorporation .... NJ
Employees 2,300
Auditor ....Grant Thornton LLP
Stk Agt......American Stock Transfer & Trust Co.
Counsel.Blank, Rome, Comisky & McCauley LLP
DUNS No. 05-473-2839

Stock - Price on:12/24/2007 ....$39.24
Stock Exchange..NDQ
Ticker Symbol...JJSF
Outstanding Shares 18,570,000
E.P.S. ....NA
Shareholders..NA

Business: The group's principal activities are to manufacture and market nutritional snack foods and distribute frozen beverages. The group operates in four business segments: food service, retail supermarkets, the restaurant group and frozen beverages. The snack food products include soft pretzels, frozen juice treats, desserts, churros, baked goods and other products. Other products sold by the group include soft drinks, funnel cakes sold under the funnel cake factory brand name, popcorn sold under the airpopt brand name and smaller amounts of various other food products. The group's retail customers are primarily supermarket chains. The restaurant group sells directly to the public through its chain of specialty snack food retail outlets. The group markets frozen beverages to the food service industry, primarily in the United States, Mexico and Canada. On 05-Jan-2004, the group acquired country home bakers inc.

Primary SIC and add'l.: 2086 2051 2087 2024

CIK No: 0000785956

Subsidiaries: Bakers Best Snack Food Corp., Country Home Bakers, Inc., Federal PBC Company, ICEE de Mexico, S.A. De C.V., ICEE-Canada, Inc., J & J Restaurant Group, LLC, J & J Snack Foods Corp. of California, J & J Snack Foods Corp. of Pennsylvania, J & J Snack Foods Corp./Mia, J & J Snack Foods Corp./Midwest, J & J Snack Foods Investment Corp., J & J Snack Foods Sales Corp., J & J Snack Foods Transport Corp., Pretzels, Inc., The ICEE Company

Officers: Gerald B. Shreiber/67/Chmn., CEO, Dennis G. Moore/52/Dir., Sr. VP, CFO, Sec., Treasurer, Robert M. Radano/59/COO, Sr. VP, Daniel Fachner/48/Pres. - Icee Company

Directors: Gerald B. Shreiber/67/Chmn., CEO, Peter G. Stanley/66/Dir., Dennis G. Moore/52/Dir., Sr. VP, CFO, Sec., Treasurer, Leonard M. Lodish/64/Dir., Sidney R. Brown/50/Dir.

Owners: Neuberger Berman LLC/8.00%, Dennis G. Moore, Gerald B. Shreiber/24.00%, Robert M. Radano, Peter G. Stanley, Vincent Melchiorre, Daniel Fachner, Insiders/26.00%, Leonard M. Lodish, Sidney R. Brown, Lord Abbett & Co., L.L.C./8.00%

Financial Data: Fiscal Year End:09/30 Latest Annual Data: 9/30/2006

Year	Sales	Net Income
2006	$514,831,000	$29,450,000
2005	$457,112,000	$26,043,000
2004	$416,588,000	$22,710,000

Curr. Assets:	$172,244,000	Curr. Liab.:	$59,089,000		
Plant, Equip.:	$85,447,000	Total Liab.:	$77,935,000	Indic. Yr. Divd.:	NA
Total Assets:	$340,808,000	Net Worth:	$262,873,000	Debt/ Equity:	NA

J-Pacific Gold Inc

1166 Alberni St. , Ste. 1440, Vancouver, BC, V6E 3Z3; *PH:* 1-604-684-6677; *Fax:* 1-604-684-6678;
http:// www.jpgold.com; *Email:* ir@jpgold.com

General - Incorporation	BC	Stock - Price on:12/24/2007	$0.35
Employees	NA	Stock Exchange	OTC
Auditor	Morgan & Company	Ticker Symbol	JPNJF
Stk Agt	Pacific Stock Transfer Company	Outstanding Shares	NA
Counsel	DuMoulin Black	E.P.S.	NA
DUNS No.	NA	Shareholders	NA

Business: The groups principal activities include acquiring and exploring natural resource properties. The group operates through three segments namely blackdome mine, exploration in Canada and exploration in the United States. The group operates from Canada and the United States.
Primary SIC and add'l.: 1081
CIK No: 0001222758
Subsidiaries: Auric Resources Inc, Equinox Resources (Calif) Inc., Golden Trend Resources Inc.,, No. 75 Corporate Ventures Inc
Officers: Nicholas T. Ferris/Dir., CEO, Pres., Executive Chmn., Ralph Braun/CFO, Cheri Pedersen/Sec., Irwin McCullough O'Connor/Legal Counsel
Directors: Nicholas T. Ferris/Dir., CEO, Pres., Executive Chmn., Martin J. Price/Dir., D'arcy G. Adam/Dir., Kazuo Shuto/Dir., Driffield Cameron/Dir., Jean-Pierre Schumacher/Dir., John D. Anderson/Dir., Manabu Kameda/Dir. - Tokyo
Owners: Ralph Braun, Kazuo Shuto, Nicholas T. Ferris/2.50%, Driffield Cameron, Tamisuke Matsufuji Jipangu Inc/24.50%, Martin Price, Insiders/32.70%, D'Arcy G. Adam/1.20%, John Anderson, Jean-Pierre Schumacher
Financial Data: Fiscal Year End:12/31   Latest Annual Data: 12/31/2006

Year	Sales	Net Income
2006	NA	-$1,875,000
2005	NA	-$1,103,000
2004	NA	-$1,140,000

Curr. Assets:	$3,125,000	Curr. Liab.:	$280,000		
Plant, Equip.:	$2,295,000	Total Liab.:	$280,000	Indic. Yr. Divd.:	NA
Total Assets:	$5,566,000	Net Worth:	$5,285,000	Debt/ Equity:	NA

J. Alexanders Corp

3401 W End Ave., Nashville, TN, 37203; *PH:* 1-615-269-1900; *Fax:* 1-615-269-1999;
http:// www.jalexanders.com

General - Incorporation	TN	Stock - Price on:12/24/2007	$13.04
Employees	2,700	Stock Exchange	AMEX
Auditor	KPMG LLP	Ticker Symbol	JAX
Stk Agt	SunTrust Bank Nashville N.A	Outstanding Shares	6,610,000
Counsel	NA	E.P.S.	$0.79
DUNS No.	05-649-6953	Shareholders	NA

Business: The group's principal activity is to operate 27 j. Alexander's full-service, casual dining restaurants located in Tennessee, Ohio, Florida, Georgia, Kansas, Alabama, Michigan, Illinois, Colorado, Texas, Kentucky and Louisiana. The group is a traditional restaurant with an American menu that features prime rib of beef; hardwood-grilled steaks, seafood and chicken; pasta; salads and soups; assorted sandwiches, appetizers and desserts and a full-service bar.
Primary SIC and add'l.: 5812 6794
CIK No: 0000103884
Subsidiaries: J. Alexander's of Texas, Inc., J. Alexander's Restaurants of Kansas, Inc., J. Alexander's Restaurants, Inc., JAX Real Estate, LLC
Officers: Lonnie J. Stout/Chmn., CEO, Pres.
Directors: Lonnie J. Stout/Chmn., CEO, Pres., Bradbury J. Reed/68/Dir., Brenda B. Rector/60/Dir., Garland G. Fritts/79/Dir., Townes E. Duncan/54/Dir., Joseph N. Steakley/53/Dir.
Owners: Garland G. Fritts, Gregory R. Lewis/2.10%, Joseph N. Steakley, Lonnie J. Stout/7.30%, Insiders/37.80%, Brenda B. Rector, Michael J. Moore/1.10%, Andreeff Equity Advisors, L.L.C./6.60%, Mark A. Parkey, Townes E. Duncan/27.10%, Solidus Company/26.60%, Dimensional Fund Advisors LP/7.20%, Bradbury J. Reed/1.70%, Advisory Research, Inc./8.60%
Financial Data: Fiscal Year End:01/01   Latest Annual Data: 12/31/2006

Year	Sales	Net Income
2006	$137,658,000	$4,717,000
2005	$122,918,000	$4,822,000

Curr. Assets:	$20,530,000	Curr. Liab.:	$13,663,000	P/E Ratio:	16.30
Plant, Equip.:	$71,815,000	Total Liab.:	$41,520,000	Indic. Yr. Divd.:	$0.100
Total Assets:	$99,350,000	Net Worth:	$57,830,000	Debt/ Equity:	0.3684

J. Crew Group Inc

770 Broadway, New York, NY, 10003; *PH:* 1-212-209-2500; *Fax:* 1-212-209-2666;
http:// www.jcrew.com; *Email:* contactus@jcrew.com

General - Incorporation	DE	Stock - Price on:12/24/2007	$54.27
Employees	2,800	Stock Exchange	NYSE
Auditor	KPMG LLP	Ticker Symbol	JCG
Stk Agt	American Stock Transfer & Trust Co.	Outstanding Shares	60,920,000
Counsel	NA	E.P.S.	$1.69
DUNS No.	36-230-8892	Shareholders	NA

Business: The group's principal activities are the retailing of women's and men's apparel, shoes and accessories. The products of the group include basic durables or casual weekend, workwear or casual weekday, swimwear, sport accessories and shoes to meet customers' lifestyle needs. The products are sold under the j. Crew brand name. The group has three major operating divisions j. Crew retail, j. Crew direct and j. Crew factory. The customer base of the group consists primarily of college-educated, professional and upscale customers. On 31-Jul-2004, the group operated 155 retail stores and 42 factory outlet stores in the United States.

Primary SIC and add'l.: 5661 5632 5651 5621 5611
CIK No: 0001051251
Subsidiaries: TPG-MD Investment, LLC
Officers: Millard S. Drexler/Chmn., CEO/$2,264,851.00, Tracy Gardner/Pres. - Jcrew Retail, Direct Divisions/$1,606,884.00, Jeffrey A. Pfeifle/Pres./$1,865,991.00, Arlene S. Hong/Sec., James Scully/CFO, Exec. VP/$1,658,735.00, Allison Malkin/Primary Investor Relations Contact, Chad Jacobs/Primary Investor Relations Contact
Directors: Millard S. Drexler/Chmn., CEO, Mary Ann Casati/Dir., Jonathan Coslet/Dir., James Coulter/Dir., Steven Grand-Jean/Dir., Stuart Sloan/Dir., Josh Weston/Dir., David House/Dir., Heather Reisman/Dir.
Owners: Josh Weston, Millard S. Drexler/14.00%, FMR Corp./11.00%, Jeffrey Pfeifle/2.00%, James Scully, Tracy Gardner, Insiders/35.00%, Steven Grand-Jean, Mary Ann Casati, Stuart Sloan, Richard Boyce, James Coulter/20.00%, TPG Advisors II, L.P./20.00%
Financial Data: Fiscal Year End:01/28   Latest Annual Data: 2/3/2007

Year	Sales	Net Income
2007	$1,152,100,000	$77,782,000
2006	$953,188,000	$3,794,000
2005	$804,216,000	-$100,309,000

Curr. Assets:	$277,098,000	Curr. Liab.:	$159,998,000	P/E Ratio:	32.11
Plant, Equip.:	$121,814,000	Total Liab.:	$422,446,000	Indic. Yr. Divd.:	NA
Total Assets:	$428,066,000	Net Worth:	$5,620,000	Debt/ Equity:	3.8818

J.C. Penney Co Inc

6501 Legacy Dr., Plano, TX, 75024; *PH:* 1-972-431-1000; *Fax:* 1-972-431-9140;
http:// www.jcpenney.com

General - Incorporation	DE	Stock - Price on:12/24/2007	$74.11
Employees	155,000	Stock Exchange	NYSE
Auditor	KPMG LLP	Ticker Symbol	JCP
Stk Agt	Mellon Investor Services LLC	Outstanding Shares	221,490,000
Counsel	NA	E.P.S.	$5.11
DUNS No.	NA	Shareholders	NA

Business: The group's principle activity is to provide merchandise and services to consumers. The groups products include apparel, jewelry, shoes, accessories and home furnishings. The group operates from United States and Brazil.
Primary SIC and add'l.: 7389 6311 5961 6719 5311
CIK No: 0001166126
Subsidiaries: J. C. Penney Corporation, Inc.
Officers: Myron E. Ullman/Chmn., CEO, John W. Irvin/Exec. VP, Pres. - JCP Direct, James W. Labounty/Sr. VP, Dir. - Supply Chain Management, Joanne Bober/Exec. VP, General Counsel, Sec., Michael P. Dastugue/Sr. VP, Dir. - Property Development, Clarence Kelley/Exec. VP, Dir. - Planning, Allocation, Tom Nealon/CIO, Exec. VP, W. J. Alcorn/Sr. VP, Controller, Principal Accounting Officer, Bernard D. Feiwus/COO, Sr. VP, Elizabeth H. Sweney/Exec. VP, General Merchandise Mgr. - Women's Apparel, Lana Cain/Exec. VP, General Merchandise Mgr., Jeffrey J. Allison/Exec. VP, General Merchandise Mgr. - Home Division, Custom Decorating, Michael J. Boylson/Exec. VP, Chief Marketing Officer, Ken C. Hicks/Pres., Chief Merchandising Officer, Thomas A. Clerkin/Sr. VP, Dir. - Finance Stores, Catalog, Internet *(20 Officers included in Index)*
Directors: Myron E. Ullman/Chmn., CEO, Anthony M. Burns/Dir., Gerald R. Turner/Dir., Leonard Roberts/Dir., Maxine K. Clark/Dir., Burl Osborne/Dir., Thomas J. Engibous/Dir., Colleen C. Barrett/Dir., Kent Foster/Dir., Vernon Jordan/Dir., Ann Marie Tallman/Dir., M. E. West/Dir., M. A. Burns/Dir.
Owners: Catherine G. West, Joanne L. Bober, Leonard H. Roberts, Maxine K. Clark, J. C. Penney Corporation, Inc./9.00%, FMR Corp./5.40%, Ken C. Hicks, State Street Bank and Trust Company/13.70%, Myron E. Ullman, Michael T. Theilmann, Thomas J. Engibous, Robert B. Cavanaugh, Colleen C. Barrett, Mary Beth West, Insiders *(21 Owners included in Index)*
Financial Data: Fiscal Year End:01/31   Latest Annual Data: 2/3/2007

Year	Sales	Net Income
2007	$19,903,000,000	$1,153,000,000
2006	$18,781,000,000	$1,088,000,000
2005	$18,424,000,000	$524,000,000

Curr. Assets:	$6,648,000,000	Curr. Liab.:	$3,492,000,000	P/E Ratio:	14.45
Plant, Equip.:	$4,162,000,000	Total Liab.:	$8,385,000,000	Indic. Yr. Divd.:	$0.800
Total Assets:	$12,673,000,000	Net Worth:	$4,288,000,000	Debt/ Equity:	0.8195

J.M. Smucker Co (The)

1 Strawberry Ln., Orrville, OH, 44667; *PH:* 1-330-682-3000; *Fax:* 1-330-684-3370;
http:// www.smucker.com

General - Incorporation	OH	Stock - Price on:12/24/2007	$57.04
Employees	3,500	Stock Exchange	NYSE
Auditor	Ernst & Young LLP	Ticker Symbol	SJM
Stk Agt	Computershare Investor Services LLC	Outstanding Shares	56,620,000
Counsel	NA	E.P.S.	$3.04
DUNS No.	00-446-1406	Shareholders	NA

Business: The groups principle activity is marketing and manufacturing fruit spreads, peanut butter, shortening and oils, ice cream toppings, sweetened condensed milk, and health and natural foods beverages. The groups products are sold under the brand names Smucker's(R), Jif(R) and Crisco(R). The group operates through two business segments namely U.S. retail market and special markets. The group operates from United States.
Primary SIC and add'l.: 2034 2030 2090 2099
CIK No: 0000091419
Subsidiaries: Fantasia Confections, Inc., IMC Bakery International, Inc, IMC North America, Inc., Imc U.s., Inc., Inversiones 91060, C.A., J.M. Smucker (Pennsylvania), Inc., J.M. Smucker de Mexico, S.A. de C.V., J.M. Smucker LLC, JM Smucker (Scotland) Limited, Juice Creations Co., Knudsen & Sons, Inc., Martha White Foods, Inc., Mary Ellen's, Incorporated, RHM Canada LP, RHM Corporation 30 Subsidiaries included in the Index

Directors: Richard K. Smucker/Dir., Co - CEO, Pres., Timothy P. Smucker/Chmn., Co - CEO, Nancy Lopez Knight/Dir., Kathryn W. Dindo/Dir., Vincent C. Byrd/Dir., Sr. VP - Consumer Marketing, William H. Steinbrink/Dir., Charles S. Mechem/Dir. Emeritus, Gary A. Oatey/Dir., Douglas R. Cowan/Dir., Paul J. Dolan/Dir., Elizabeth Valk Long/Dir., Nancy Lopez/Dir.

Owners: Vincent C. Byrd/0.30%, Insiders/8.16%, Mark R. Belgya/0.11%, Nancy Lopez Knight, Richard F. Troyak, Timothy P. Smucker/3.61%, John D. Milliken/0.13%, William H. Steinbrink, Douglas R. Cowan, Barclays Global Investors NA/6.06%, Paul J. Dolan, Ariel Capital Management, LLC/9.94%, Robert E. Ellis, Elizabeth Valk Long, Gary A. Oatey *(17 Owners included in Index)*

Financial Data: Fiscal Year End:04/30   Latest Annual Data: 4/30/2006

Year	Sales	Net Income
2006	$2,154,726,000	$143,354,000
2005	$2,043,877,000	$129,073,000
2004	$1,417,011,000	$111,350,000

Curr. Assets:	$571,495,000	Curr. Liab.:	$235,440,000	P/E Ratio:	19.21
Plant, Equip.:	$527,735,000	Total Liab.:	$921,685,000	Indic. Yr. Divd.:	$1.200
Total Assets:	$2,649,744,000	Net Worth:	$1,728,059,000	Debt/ Equity:	NA

J.P. Morgan Chase & Company

270 Pk. Ave., New York, NY, 10017; *PH:* 1-212-270-6000; *Fax:* 1-212-270-1648; *http://* www.jpmorganchase.com

General - Incorporation	DE	Stock - Price on:12/24/2007	$50.56
Employees	174,360	Stock Exchange	NYSE
Auditor	PricewaterhouseCoopers LLP	Ticker Symbol	JPM
Stk Agt	Mellon Investor Services LLC	Outstanding Shares	3,420,000,000
Counsel	NA	E.P.S.	$4.522
DUNS No.	NA	Shareholders	NA

Business: The groups principle activity is to provide banking services. The group operates through six segments namely, investment bank, retail financial services, card services, commercial banking, treasury and securities services, and asset management. In the year 2006, the group acquired Collegiate Funding Services. The group operates from the United States.

Primary SIC and add'l.: 6162 6722 6289 6211 6282 6159 6221 6799 6726 6371 6712 6733 6141 6021 6099

CIK No: 0000019617

Subsidiaries: Aldermanbury Investments Limited, Banc One Acceptance Corporation, Banc One Arizona Leasing Corporation, Banc One Building Corporation, Banc One Building Management Corporation, Banc One Capital BIDCO-1998, LLC, Banc One Capital Holdings LLC, Banc One Capital Partners BC, LLC, Banc One Capital Partners Holdings, Ltd., Banc One Capital Partners II, LLC, Banc One Capital Partners IV, Ltd., Banc One Capital Partners VI, Ltd., Banc One Capital Partners, LLC, Banc One Community Development Corporation, Banc One Deferred Benefits Corporation 400 Subsidiaries included in the Index

Officers: James Dimon/Chmn., CEO/$39,053,330.00, Steven D. Black/Co - CEO - Investment Bank/$29,635,140.00, Philip F. Bleser/Member - Commercial Bank, Douglas L. Braunstein/Member - Investment Bank, Richard M. Cashin/Member - Private Equity, Louis Rauchenberger/Controller, John F. Bradley/Member - Human Resources, Mark I. Kleinman/Treasury, Anthony J. Horan/Sec., Michael J. Cavanagh/CFO/$7,152,505.00, Blythe S. Masters/Member - Investment Bank, Stephanie B. Mudick/Member - Retail Financial Services, Nicholas P. O'Donohoe/Member - Investment Bank, Daniel E. Pinto/Member - Investment Bank, Gordon A. Smith/Member - Card Services *(47 Officers included in Index)*

Directors: James Dimon/Chmn., CEO, James S. Crown/Dir., Ellen V. Futter/Dir., William H. Gray/Dir., John H. Biggs/Dir., Crandall C. Bowles/Dir., David M. Cote/Dir., Stephen B. Burke/Dir., Laban P. Jackson/Dir., John W. Kessler/Dir., Robert I. Lipp/69/Dir., Sr. Advisor, Richard A. Manoogian/Dir., David C. Novak/Dir., Lee R. Raymond/Dir., William C. Weldon/Dir.

Owners: Lee R. Raymond, James Dimon, James S. Crown, David C. Novak, William H. Gray, William B. Harrison, Robert I. Lipp, Ellen V. Futter, William T. Winters, Laban P. Jackson, Insiders, Steven D. Black, John W. Kessler, Stephen B. Burke, John H. Biggs *(18 Owners included in Index)*

Financial Data: Fiscal Year End:01/01   Latest Annual Data: 12/31/2006

Year	Sales	Net Income
2006	$99,845,000,000	$14,444,000,000
2005	$79,902,000,000	$8,483,000,000
2004	$56,931,000,000	$4,466,000,000

Curr. Assets:	$583,112,000,000	Curr. Liab.:	$889,057,000,000	P/E Ratio:	29.74
Plant, Equip.:	$8,735,000,000	Total Liab.:	$1,235,730,000,000	Indic. Yr. Divd.:	$1.520
Total Assets:	$1,351,520,000,000	Net Worth:	$115,790,000,000	Debt/ Equity:	NA

J.W. Mays Inc

9 Bond St., Brooklyn, NY, 11201; *PH:* 1-718-624-7400; *Fax:* 1-718-935-0378; *http://* www.jwmays.com; *Email:* info@jwmays.com

General - Incorporation	NY	Stock - Price on:12/24/2007	$23
Employees	30	Stock Exchange	NDQ
Auditor	D'arcangelo & Co. LLP	Ticker Symbol	MAYS
Stk Agt	American Stock Transfer & Trust Co.	Outstanding Shares	2,020,000
Counsel	Cullen & Dykman	E.P.S.	NA
DUNS No.	00-697-9140	Shareholders	NA

Business: The group's principal activities are to own, lease and operate commercial real estate properties. The properties are leased to retail tenants and for office space users. The properties of the group are located in brooklyn, jamaica, levittown, fishkill and massapequa in New York and in circleville in Ohio. The group operates solely in the domestic market.

Primary SIC and add'l.: 6519

CIK No: 0000054187

Subsidiaries: Dutchess Mall Sewage Plant, Inc., J. W. M. Realty Corp.

Officers: Lloyd J. Shulman/66/Chmn., Principal Executive Officer, Pres., Principal Operating Officer, CEO, Ward N. Lyke/57/VP, Assist. Treasurer, George Silva/58/VP, Mark Greenblatt/CFO, Salvatore Cappuzzo/Sec.

Directors: Lloyd J. Shulman/66/Chmn., Principal Executive Officer, Pres., Principal Operating Officer, CEO, Sylvia W. Shulman/Dir., Dean L. Ryder/Dir., Jack Schwartz/Dir., Lewis D. Siegel/Dir., Lance D. Myers/Dir.

Owners: Celwyn Company, Inc, Gailoyd Enterprises Corp, Shulman Trustees FBO Lloyd J. Shulman, J. Weinstein Foundation, Inc., Koster Family Partnership L.P. Gail Koster, Shulman Trustees FBO Linda B. Felmus Jessogne, Lloyd J. Shulman, Lloyd J. Shulman, George Orloff, Sylvia W. Shulman, Gail S. Koster, J.W. Acquisitions, LLC, Madeleine L. Orloff, Shulman Trustees FBO Gail S. Koster

Financial Data: Fiscal Year End:07/31   Latest Annual Data: 07/31/2007

Year	Sales	Net Income
2007	$18,159,000	$2,056,000
2006	$13,666,000	$1,433,000
2005	$12,883,000	$348,000

Curr. Assets:	$7,988,000	Curr. Liab.:	$4,584,000	P/E Ratio:	41.82
Plant, Equip.:	$44,970,000	Total Liab.:	$20,466,000	Indic. Yr. Divd.:	NA
Total Assets:	$60,162,000	Net Worth:	$39,697,000	Debt/ Equity:	NA

J2 Global Communications Inc

6922 Hollywood Blvd., Ste. 500, Hollywood, CA, 90028; *PH:* 1-323-860-9200; *Fax:* 1-323-464-1446; *http://* www.j2global.com

General - Incorporation	DE	Stock - Price on:12/24/2007	$35.09
Employees	341	Stock Exchange	NDQ
Auditor	Deloitte & Touche LLP	Ticker Symbol	JCOM
Stk Agt	Computershare Trust Co	Outstanding Shares	49,370,000
Counsel	NA	E.P.S.	$1.12
DUNS No.	NA	Shareholders	NA

Business: The group's principal activities are to provide outsourced, value-added messaging and communications services to individuals and businesses around the world. The services are delivered through its global telephony/Internet protocol network that spans more than 1,300 cities in 20 countries on five continents. The group offers faxing and voicemail solutions, document management solutions, Web-initiated conference calling and unified messaging and communications services. The services are marketed under the brand names efax(R), j2(R), jconnect(R), jfax(R), efax corporate(R), electric mail(R), jblast(R), efax broadcast(tm), papermaster(R), consensus(tm), m4 Internet(R) and protofax(r). On 09-Aug-2004, the group acquired assets of call sciences ltd.

Primary SIC and add'l.: 4899

CIK No: 0001084048

Subsidiaries: Call Sciences Limited, Call Sciences, Inc., Data On Call, Inc., Electric Mail (International) L.P., j2 Global Holdings Limited, j2 Global Ireland Limited, j2 Global UK Limited, Puma Unified Communications Limited, SureTalk.com, Inc., The Electric Mail Company

Officers: Nehemia Zucker/51/COO, Pres./$511,674.00, Scott Turicchi/Pres./$429,339.00, Jeffrey D. Adelman/41/VP, General Counsel, Sec./$246,738.00, Patty Brunton/VP - Human Resources, Doug Chey/VP - Engineering, Tom Dolan/VP - Sales, Ken Ford/VP - Marketing Services, Support, Zohar Loshitzer/Exec. VP - Corporate Strategy, Mike Pugh/VP - Marketing, Ken Truesdale/VP - Product Development, Kathleen M. Griggs/CFO, Alan Alters/VP - Network Operations, Tim McLean/VP - International, David Rolston/Chief Architect

Directors: Richard S. Ressler/Chmn., Douglas Y. Bech/Dir., Robert J. Cresci/63/Dir., John F. Rieley/Co - Founder, Dir., Michael P. Schulhof/Dir., Brian Kretzmer/Dir., Stephen Ross/Dir.

Owners: William Blair & Company, L.L.C./14.18%, Scott R. Turicchi/1.61%, Nehemia Zucker, Robert J. Cresci, Kathleen M. Griggs, Michael P. Schulhof, Stephen Ross, Munder Capital Management/8.46%, John F. Rieley, Jeffrey D. Adelman, Insiders/7.94%, Douglas Y. Bech, Brian W. Kretzmer, FMR Corp./10.26%, Richard S. Ressler/4.74%

Financial Data: Fiscal Year End:12/31   Latest Annual Data: 12/31/2006

Year	Sales	Net Income
2006	$181,079,000	$53,131,000
2005	$143,941,000	$51,258,000
2004	$106,343,000	$31,607,000

Curr. Assets:	$198,514,000	Curr. Liab.:	$33,307,000	P/E Ratio:	29.24
Plant, Equip.:	$18,951,000	Total Liab.:	$33,419,000	Indic. Yr. Divd.:	NA
Total Assets:	$288,160,000	Net Worth:	$254,741,000	Debt/ Equity:	NA

Jabil Circuit Inc

10560 Dr. Martin Luther King Jr. St. N, St. Petersburg, FL, 33716; *PH:* 1-727-577-9749; *Fax:* 1-727-579-8529; *http://* www.jabil.com

General - Incorporation	DE	Stock - Price on:12/24/2007	$20.79
Employees	74,000	Stock Exchange	NYSE
Auditor	KPMG LLP	Ticker Symbol	JBL
Stk Agt	Computershare Investor Services LLC	Outstanding Shares	206,000,000
Counsel	NA	E.P.S.	$0.08
DUNS No.	04-181-0979	Shareholders	NA

Business: The group's principal activity is to design and manufacture electronic circuit board assemblies, subsystems and systems. The products are sold to original equipment manufacturers (OEM) in the networking, telecommunications, computing and storage, instrumentation and medical, computer, peripherals, automotive and consumer products industries. The group's work cell business units provide integrated design and engineering services, component selection, sourcing and procurement, automated assembly and design and implementation of product testing. The customers include cisco systems inc, dell computer corporation, hewlett-packard company, johnson controls inc, intel corporation, valeo, lucent technologies, nokia corporation, marconi communications plc and royal philips electronics. The group operates in Austria, Belgium, Brazil, China, England, France, hungary, India, Ireland, Italy, Malaysia, Mexico, Poland, Scotland and Singapore, besides the United States.

Primary SIC and add'l.: 3672

CIK No: 0000898293

Subsidiaries: Contract Manufacturing Services Singapore Pte. Ltd., Digitek Electronics Ltd., GET Manufacturing Europe S.A., GET Manufacturing USA, Inc., Jabil (Mauritius Holdings Ltd, Jabil (Singapore Pte. Ltd, Jabil Assembly Poland sp. z.o.o., Jabil Circuit (BVI Inc., Jabil Circuit (Guangzhou Ltd, Jabil Circuit (Panyu Ltd, Jabil Circuit (Shanghai Co. Ltd, Jabil Circuit (Shenzhen Ltd, Jabil Circuit (Taiwan Limited, Jabil Circuit (Wuxi Co. Ltd., Jabil Circuit Austria GmbH 68 Subsidiaries included in the Index

Officers: Timothy L. Main/Dir., CEO, Pres., John P. Lovato/Exec. VP, CEO - Consumer Division, William D. Muir/Exec. VP, CEO - EMS Division, William E. Peters/Sr. VP, Regional Pres. - Americas, Courtney J. Ryan/Sr. VP - Global Supply Chain, Anthony Allan/VP - Global Business Units, Brian D. Althaver/VP - Jabil Automotive Group, Steven D. Borges/VP - Business Development, Americas, David Couch/VP - Tools, Systems, Training, CIO, Jace H. Dees/VP - Supply Chain, Americas, Maurice Dunlop/VP - Global Business Units, David S. Emerson/VP - Sales, Marketing The Americas, Patrick A. Evans/VP - Global Business Units, Sirjang L. Tandon/Chief Executive - India Business Ventures, Otto Bik/VP - Finance *(49 Officers included in Index)*

Directors: Timothy L. Main/Dir., CEO, Pres., William D. Morean/Chmn., Thomas A. Sansone/Vice Chmn., Isamu Kamata/Chmn. - Japan Advisory Board, Susumu Miyoshi/Member - Japan Member Advisory Board, Fumiyuki Kobayashi/Member - Japan Member Advisory Board, Takeo Minomiya/Member - Japan Member Advisory Board, Yoshihiro Kawada/Member - Japan Member Advisory Board, Laurence S. Grafstein/Dir., Mel S. Lavitt/Dir., Lawrence J. Murphy/Dir., Frank A. Newman/Dir., Steven A. Raymund/Dir., Kathleen A. Walters/Dir.

Owners: Laurence S. Grafstein, John P. Lovato, Audrey M. Petersen/6.70%, Thomas A. Sansone/1.80%, Steven A. Raymund, FMR Corp./10.40%, William Blair& Company, L.L.C./5.20%, Lawrence J. Murphy, Mark T. Mondello, Insiders/11.80%, Frank A. Newman, Mel S. Lavitt, Capital Group International, Inc./10.90%, Forbes I.J. Alexander, Kathleen A. Walters *(18 Owners included in Index)*

Financial Data: ***Fiscal Year End:***08/31 ***Latest Annual Data:*** 8/31/2006

Year	Sales	Net Income
2006	$10,265,447,000	$164,518,000
2005	$7,524,386,000	$231,847,000
2004	$6,252,897,000	$166,900,000

Curr. Assets:	$3,678,965,000	***Curr. Liab.:***	$2,701,334,000	***P/E Ratio:***	259.88
Plant, Equip.:	$985,262,000	***Total Liab.:***	$3,117,249,000	***Indic. Yr. Divd.:***	$0.280
Total Assets:	$5,411,730,000	***Net Worth:***	$2,294,481,000	***Debt/ Equity:***	0.1306

Jacada Ltd

400 Perimeter Ctr. Ter., Ste. 100, Atlanta, GA, 30346; ***PH:*** 1-770-352-1300; ***Fax:*** 1-770-352-1313; ***http://*** www.jacada.com; ***Email:*** info@jacada.com

General - Incorporation	Israel	***Stock*** - Price on:12/24/2007	$3.45
Employees	159	Stock Exchange	NDQ
Auditor	Kost Forer Gabbay & Kasierer	Ticker Symbol	JCDA
Stk Agt	American Stock Transfer & Trust Co.	Outstanding Shares	20,150,000
Counsel	NA	E.P.S.	-$0.07
DUNS No.	NA	Shareholders	NA

Business: The groups principle activities include developmet, marketing and support of software that enables business to Web-enable, modernize and integrate their existing host-centric software applications to better serve the needs of their users, customers, and partners. The group also provides related professional services including training, consulting, support and maintenance. The group operates from United States.

Primary SIC and add'l.: 7372

CIK No: 0001095747

Subsidiaries: Jacada Inc.

Officers: Gideon Hollander/Founder, Dir., CEO, David Holmes/Exec. VP - Global Marketing, Tzvia Broida/CFO, Paul O'Callaghan/Pres., Oren Shefler/General Counsel, Joe Horne/VP - Sales The Americas, Americas Operations, Steve Woods/VP - Global Corporate Development, Skip Hardin/VP - Field Services Jacada Americas Operations, Steve Herlocher/VP - Product Management, Eyal Shpin/VP - Research, Development, Peter L. Seltzberg/Primary Investor Relations Officer, Janice Warford/Controller, Benny Schlesinger/CTO

Directors: Gideon Hollander/Founder, Dir., CEO, Yossie Hollander/Chmn., Ohad Zuckerman/Dir., Avner Atsmon/Dir., Naomi Atsmon/Dir., Dan Falk/Dir.

Owners: Emancipation Capital, LP/6.55%, Yossie Hollander/11.07%, Gideon Hollander/10.56%

Financial Data: ***Fiscal Year End:***12/31 ***Latest Annual Data:*** 12/31/2006

Year	Sales	Net Income
2006	$20,681,000	-$2,572,000
2005	$19,942,000	-$4,958,000
2004	$19,784,000	-$5,613,000

Curr. Assets:	$19,687,000	***Curr. Liab.:***	$10,529,000		
Plant, Equip.:	$930,000	***Total Liab.:***	$12,315,000	***Indic. Yr. Divd.:***	NA
Total Assets:	$45,710,000	***Net Worth:***	$33,395,000	***Debt/ Equity:***	NA

Jack Henry & Assoc Inc

663 W Hwy. 60, Monett, MO, 65708; ***PH:*** 1-417-235-6652; ***Fax:*** 1-417-235-4281; ***http://*** www.jackhenry.com

General - Incorporation	DE	***Stock*** - Price on:12/24/2007	$25.45
Employees	3,310	Stock Exchange	NDQ
Auditor	Deloitte & Touche LLP	Ticker Symbol	JKHY
Stk Agt	UMB Bank, N.A.	Outstanding Shares	89,670,000
Counsel	NA	E.P.S.	$1.09
DUNS No.	09-826-5341	Shareholders	NA

Business: The group's principal activity is to provide integrated data processing system solution for banks, credit unions and other financial institutions. The group's software applications include Silverlake System(R), CIF 20/20(R) , Core Director(R), Episys(R) and Cruise (TM). The software applications operate on IBM and UNIX/NT operating systems. Key functions of each of the core software applications include deposits, loans, general ledger and customer information file. The group also provides data conversion and hardware and software installation for the implementation of its systems and applications. The group provides outsourcing services through 7 data centers and 17 item-processing centers located across the United States. On 09-Feb-2004, the group acquired Yellow Hammer Software Inc and on 08-Sep-2004, Banc Insurance Service Inc.

Primary SIC and add'l.: 7378 7372 7379 5045

CIK No: 0000779152

Subsidiaries: Banc Insurance Agency, Inc., Banc Insurance Services, Inc., Check Collect, Inc., E-ClassicSystems, Inc., Jack Henry & Associates, Inc., Jack Henry ACH, LP, Jack Henry International, Ltd., Jack Henry Services, L.P., Jack Henry Software/Commlink, L.P., Jack Henry Systems, L.P., Jack Henry, LLC, JHA Synergy, Inc., Optinfo, Inc., Profitstar, Inc., RPM Intelligence, LLC 21 Subsidiaries included in the Index

Officers: John F. Prim/CEO/$657,840.00, Jerry D. Hall/Dir., Exec. VP/$107,400.00, Tony L. Wormington/Pres./$586,067.00, Kevin D. Williams/CFO/$513,433.00, Mark S. Forbis/CTO, VP/$311,333.00

Directors: Michael E. Henry/Chmn., Jerry D. Hall/Dir., Exec. VP, Craig R. Curry/Dir., James J. Ellis/Dir., Wesley A. Brown/Dir., Matthew C. Flanigan/Dir., Marla K. Shepard/Dir.

Owners: Tony L. Wormington, James J. Ellis, FMR Corporation/6.90%, John F. Prim, Kayne Anderson Rudnick/5.90%, Jerry D. Hall/1.80%, T. Rowe Price Associates, Inc/12.90%, Insiders/10.10%, Wesley A. Brown, Craig R. Curry, Insiders/10.10%, Matthew C. Flanigan, Michael E. Henry/6.20%, Kevin D. Williams, Barclays Global Investors UK/5.40% *(17 Owners included in Index)*

Financial Data: ***Fiscal Year End:***06/30 ***Latest Annual Data:*** 6/30/2006

Year	Sales	Net Income
2006	$592,205,000	$89,923,000
2005	$535,863,000	$75,501,000
2004	$467,415,000	$62,315,000

Curr. Assets:	$350,385,000	***Curr. Liab.:***	$330,477,000	***P/E Ratio:***	23.35
Plant, Equip.:	$249,882,000	***Total Liab.:***	$400,975,000	***Indic. Yr. Divd.:***	$0.260
Total Assets:	$999,340,000	***Net Worth:***	$598,365,000	***Debt/ Equity:***	NA

Jack In the Box Inc

9330 Balboa Ave., San Diego, CA, 92123; ***PH:*** 1-858-571-2121; ***Fax:*** 1-858-571-2101; ***http://*** www.jackinthebox.com

General - Incorporation	DE	***Stock*** - Price on:12/24/2007	$74.75
Employees	44,300	Stock Exchange	NYSE
Auditor	KPMG LLP	Ticker Symbol	JBX
Stk Agt	Mellon Investor Services LLC	Outstanding Shares	31,310,000
Counsel	Gray, Cary, Ware & Freidenrich	E.P.S.	$1.88
DUNS No.	04-211-7200	Shareholders	NA

Business: The groups principle activity is to operate restaurants. The groups products include hamburgers, salads, specialty sandwiches, tacos and drinks The group also operates a chain of convenience stores called Quick Stuff. The group operates from United States.

Primary SIC and add'l.: 6794 5812 6799

CIK No: 0000807882

Officers: Gary J. Beisler/51/CEO - Qdoba Restaurant Corporation, Linda A. Lang/Chmn., CEO, Terri F. Graham/Sr. VP, Chief Marketing Officer, David M. Theno/Sr. VP - Quality, Logistics, Paul L. Schultz/COO, Pres., Lawrence E. Schauf/Exec. VP, General Counsel, Sec., Carlo E. Cetti/Sr. VP - Human Resources, Strategic Planning, Phillip H. Rudolph/Sr. VP, General Counsel, Corp. Sec., Jerry P. Rebel/CFO, Exec. VP

Directors: Linda A. Lang/Chmn., CEO, Anne B. Gust/Dir., George Fellows/Dir., Michael E. Alpert/Dir., David M. Tehle/Dir., Alice B. Hayes/Dir., Murray H. Hutchison/Dir., Michael W. Murphy/Dir.

Owners: Alice B. Hayes, Michael W. Murphy, David M. Tehle, Barclays Global Investors, N.A./4.90%, Murray H. Hutchison, Insiders/1.20%, Linda A. Lang, Lawrence E. Schauf, Michael E. Alpert, Paul L. Schultz, George Fellows, Anne B. Gust, David M. Theno, Fidelity Investments/7.70%, Jerry P. Rebel

Financial Data: ***Fiscal Year End:***10/02 ***Latest Annual Data:*** 09/30/2007

Year	Sales	Net Income
2007	$2,875,978,000	$126,304,000
2006	$2,765,649,000	$108,031,000
2005	$2,507,238,000	$91,537,000

Curr. Assets:	$240,155,000	***Curr. Liab.:***	$275,675,000		
Plant, Equip.:	$862,610,000	***Total Liab.:***	$731,943,000	***Indic. Yr. Divd.:***	NA
Total Assets:	$1,285,342,000	***Net Worth:***	$553,399,000	***Debt/ Equity:***	0.9294

Jackson Hewitt Tax Service Inc

3 Sylvan Way, Parsippany, NJ, 07054; ***PH:*** 1-973-630-1040; ***Fax:*** 1-973-496-2785; ***http://*** www.jacksonhewitt.com

General - Incorporation	DE	***Stock*** - Price on:12/24/2007	$28.79
Employees	370	Stock Exchange	NYSE
Auditor	Deloitte & Touche LLP	Ticker Symbol	JTX
Stk Agt	American Stock Transfer & Trust Co.	Outstanding Shares	31,120,000
Counsel	NA	E.P.S.	$1.93
DUNS No.	18-763-1304	Shareholders	NA

Business: The group's principle activity is to prepare tax returns in the United States. It operates through two segments: franchise operations: includes royalty and marketing and advertising revenue, financial product fees, other financial product revenue and other revenue. Company-owned office operations: provides preparation of tax returns and related services. The group operates through its wholly owned subsidiary jackson hewitt inc and provides computerized preparation of federal and state personal income tax returns through a network of franchised and company-owned offices. The products of the group are jackson hewitt cashcard, help, gold guarantee and money now. The group's total revenue for year 2007 was 293.20 millions of USD.

Primary SIC and add'l.: 7291 6719

CIK No: 0001283552

Subsidiaries: Hewfant, Inc., Jackson Hewitt Corporate Services Inc., Jackson Hewitt Inc., Jackson Hewitt Technology Services LLC, Tax Services of America, Inc.

Officers: Michael D. Lister/Chmn., CEO/$2,127,382.00, Steven L. Barnett/Exec. VP, General Counsel, Corp. Sec./$775,504.00, Mark L. Heimbouch/Exec. VP, CFO, Treasurer/$827,190.00, Michael C. Yerington/COO, Pres./$686,165.00, Jeanmarie Cooney/Sr. VP - Strategic Development, Peter N. Karpiak/Sr. VP - Human Resources, Corporate Services, Duane R. Mora/Sr. VP - Franchise Operations, Sales, William Sangiacomo/Group VP - Financial Products, Peter Tahinos/Sr. VP - Marketing, David Kraut/VP - Treasury, Investor Relations, Sheila Cort/VP - Corporate Communications

Directors: Michael D. Lister/Chmn., CEO, Ulysses L. Bridgeman/Dir., Rodman L. Drake/Dir., Louis P. Salvatore/Dir., Margaret Milner Richardson/Dir., James C. Spira/Dir.

Owners: Mark L. Heimbouch, James C. Spira, Steven L. Barnett, Michael D. Lister/2.31%, Louis P. Salvatore, AMVESCAP PLC/15.07%, Ulysses L. Bridgeman, Michael C. Yerington, Rodman L. Drake, Margaret Milner Richardson, Insiders/3.16%, Ziff Asset Management/7.86%

Financial Data: ***Fiscal Year End:***04/30 ***Latest Annual Data:*** 4/30/2006

Year	Sales	Net Income
2006	$275,410,000	$57,961,000
2005	$232,487,000	$49,951,000
2004	$205,615,000	$42,960,000

Curr. Assets:	$53,502,000	***Curr. Liab.:***	$101,279,000	***P/E Ratio:***	14.92
Plant, Equip.:	$35,808,000	***Total Liab.:***	$200,159,000	***Indic. Yr. Divd.:***	$0.720
Total Assets:	$588,082,000	***Net Worth:***	$387,923,000	***Debt/ Equity:***	0.9121

Jacksonville Bancorp Inc FL

100 N Laura St., Ste. 1000, Jacksonville, FL, 32202; **PH:** 1-904-421-3040; **Fax:** 1-904-421-3050; **http://** www.jaxbank.com

General - Incorporation	FL	**Stock**- Price on:12/24/2007	$28.31
Employees	56	Stock Exchange	NDQ
Auditor	Crowe Chizek & Co. LLC	Ticker Symbol	JAXB
Stk Agt	Computershare Investor Services LLC	Outstanding Shares	1,740,000
Counsel	NA	E.P.S	$1.46
DUNS No.	NA	Shareholders	NA

Business: The group's principal activities are to provide community-banking services including Internet banking to businesses and individuals through its three offices in jacksonville, Florida. The group offers a wide range of interest bearing and non interest-bearing deposit accounts, including commercial and retail checking accounts, money market accounts, individual retirement accounts, statement savings accounts and certificates of deposit. The group offers loans including commercial loans and consumer loans, which include collateralized and uncollateralized loans. The group's products include personal online banking, business online banking and sweep accounts tied to goldman sachs proprietary funds.

Primary SIC and add'l.: 6712 6022

CIK No: 0001071264

Subsidiaries: Fountain Financial, Inc, The Jacksonville Bank

Officers: Gilbert J. Pomar/Dir., CEO, Pres./$274,856.00, Luigi Vaccaro/Sr. VP, Business Banking Mgr., Rodney Caccavo/VP, Mortgage Banking Mgr., Kimberly M. Delong/VP, Office Mgr., Cheryl B. Barie/VP, Office Mgr., Rebel D. Wilson/VP, Risk Management Mgr., Valerie A. Kendall/CFO, Exec. VP/$183,489.00, Scott M. Hall/Exec. VP - Commercial Banking, Sr. Loan Officer/$216,293.00, Karen A. Wright/VP - Branch Support, Robert J. Dobbs/Sr. VP - Commercial Banker, Sally A. Blossey/VP, Loan Operations Mgr., Robert B. Main/VP - Business Banker, Nisa M. Roberts/VP, Controller, Michael E. Valley/VP, Finance Mgr., Donna M. Donovan/Sr. VP, Operations Mgr. *(17 Officers included in Index)*

Directors: Gilbert J. Pomar/Dir., CEO, Pres., Price W. Schwenck/Chmn., Gary L. Winfield/Dir., Melvin Gottlieb/Dir., John R. Schultz/Dir., Michael D. Carter/Dir., R. C. Mills/Dir., Bennett A. Tavar/Dir., Donald E. Roller/Dir., James M. Healey/Dir., Charles F. Spencer/Dir., John C. Kowkabany/Dir., John W. Rose/Dir.

Owners: Valerie A. Kendall/0.57%, Michael D. Carter/2.07%, R. C. Mills/5.29%, John W. Rose/4.20%, Insiders/33.37%, Scott M. Hall/1.21%, Price W. Schwenck/1.75%, Bennett A. Tavar/2.34%, James M. Healey/0.50%, John R. Schultz/2.64%, Gilbert J. Pomar/2.69%, John C. Kowkabany/2.27%, Melvin Gottlieb/3.72%, Gary L. Winfield/2.05%, Charles F. Spencer/1.28% *(16 Owners included in Index)*

Financial Data: **Fiscal Year End:**12/31 **Latest Annual Data:** 12/31/2006

Year		Sales			Net Income
2006		$23,073,000			$2,523,000
2005		$16,712,000			$2,173,000
2004		$11,693,000			$1,335,000
Curr. Assets:	$6,585,000	**Curr. Liab.:**	$294,458,000	**P/E Ratio:**	20.08
Plant, Equip.:	$4,616,000	**Total Liab.:**	$302,437,000	**Indic. Yr. Divd.:**	NA
Total Assets:	$325,575,000	**Net Worth:**	$23,138,000	**Debt/ Equity:**	0.2944

Jacksonville Bancorp Inc IL

1211 W Morton Ave., Jacksonville, IL, 62650; **PH:** 1-217-245-4111; **Fax:** 1-217-245-2010; **http://** www.jacksonvillesavings.com; **Email:** info@jacksonvillesavings.com

General - Incorporation	IL	**Stock**- Price on:12/24/2007	$12
Employees	101	Stock Exchange	NDQ
Auditor	BKD, LLP	Ticker Symbol	JXSB
Stk Agt	Suntrust Bank	Outstanding Shares	1,990,000
Counsel	Luse Gorman Pomerenk & Schick	E.P.S	$0.34
DUNS No.	08-209-1422	Shareholders	NA

Business: The group is a community-oriented savings bank holding company offering retail banking services in morgan, macoupin and montgomery counties, Illinois. The group attracts retail deposits from the general public and uses such funds to originate consumer loans and mortgage loans secured by one-to four-family residential real estate. The primary source of funds are deposits, fhlb advances, funds received from the repayment and prepayment of loans and mortgage backed securities, on-going operations and the sale or maturity of investment securities. The group conducts its business from its main office and six branches, located in jacksonville, virden, chapin, concord, litchfield, Illinois.

Primary SIC and add'l.: 6712 6035

CIK No: 0001172097

Subsidiaries: Financial Resources Group, Inc., Jacksonville Savings Bank

Officers: Richard A. Foss/CEO, Pres./$171,385.00, Tom Luber/Contact - Jacksonville Savings Bank, Paul W. Miller/Contact - Chapin State Bank, Diana S. Tone/CFO/$79,818.00, Steve Waltrip/Contact - Jacksonville Savings Bank, Susan L. Wood/Contact - Jacksonville Savings Bank, Jodi Nordwall/Contact - Jacksonville Savings Bank, Ron Norris/Contact - Litchfield Community Savings, Tami Oxley/Contact - Jacksonville Savings Bank, Heidi Potter/Contact - Jacksonville Savings Bank, Angela Retzer/Contact - Jacksonville Savings Bank, Regina Nichols/Contact - Jacksonville Savings Bank, Mikka Dinsmore/Contact - Jacksonville Savings Bank, Linda Watkins/Contact - Jacksonville Savings Bank, Cathy Tolliver/Contact - Jacksonville Savings Bank *(70 Officers included in Index)*

Directors: Dean H. Hess/59/Dir., Harmon B. Deal/47/Dir., John L. Eyth/57/Dir., Michael R. Goldasich/69/Dir.

Owners: Dean H. Hess/1.17%, Insiders/10.62%, Harmon B. Deal, Andrew F. Applebee/3.30%, Harvey D. Scott, Michael R. Goldasich, Emily J. Osburn, John C. Williams, Jacksonville Bancorp, M.H.C/52.81%, John L. Eyth, Richard A. Foss/2.81%

Financial Data: **Fiscal Year End:**12/31 **Latest Annual Data:** 12/31/2006

Year		Sales			Net Income
2006		$16,233,000			$895,000
2005		$14,597,000			$900,000
2004		$14,316,000			$876,000
Curr. Assets:	$11,274,000	**Curr. Liab.:**	$243,030,000	**P/E Ratio:**	35.29
Plant, Equip.:	$6,708,000	**Total Liab.:**	$246,226,000	**Indic. Yr. Divd.:**	$0.300
Total Assets:	$267,372,000	**Net Worth:**	$21,145,000	**Debt/ Equity:**	0.4015

Jaclyn Inc

197 W Spring Valley Ave., Maywood, NJ, 07607; **PH:** 1-201-909-6000; **http://** www.jaclyninc.com

General - Incorporation	DE	**Stock**- Price on:12/24/2007	$11.34
Employees	169	Stock Exchange	AMEX
Auditor	Deloitte & Touche LLP	Ticker Symbol	JLN
Stk Agt	Continental Stock Transfer & Trust Co	Outstanding Shares	2,450,000
Counsel	Jenkens & Gilchrist	E.P.S	NA
DUNS No.	04-319-0511	Shareholders	NA

Business: The group's principle activities are to design, manufacture, distribute and market women's and children's apparel and a variety of vinyl, leather and fabric handbags, travel bags, sport bags and apparel items. The apparel division designs, manufactures and markets a variety of apparel including vests, loungewear, sleepwear, dresses, sportswear, slippers, footwear and lingerie. The apparels of the group are sold under the trade names "Topsville", "I. Appel", "Smart Time", "Emerson Road", "Jordache(Tm)", "Charles Goodnight(Tm)", "Chuckie Goodnight(Tm)" and "Vanity Fair(Tm)". Handbags include denim backpacks, duffels, and quilted, metallic, leather and tapestry bags. The handbag products of the group are sold under the trademarks and trade names of saddle river, shane, aetna, susan gail, robyn lyn and marilyn usa. It markets its products throughout the United States through its own salesmen and independent sales representatives. The group's quarterly revenue for September 2007 was 37.45 millions of USD.

Primary SIC and add'l.: 5137 3199

CIK No: 0000052969

Subsidiaries: Bonnie International (Hong Kong) Ltd., JLN, Inc., Max N. Nitzberg, Inc., The Bag Factory Inc., Topsville, Inc.

Officers: Laura Calabria/Contact

Owners: Insiders/28.90%, Bonnie Sue Levy/9.10%, Howard Ginsburg/7.40%, Robert Chestnov/7.60%, Norman Axelrod, Abe Ginsburg/3.00%, Harold Schechter, Anthony Christon, Martin Brody, Richard Chestnov/2.70%, Allan Ginsburg/8.40%

Financial Data: **Fiscal Year End:**06/30 **Latest Annual Data:** 6/30/2006

Year		Sales			Net Income
2006		$126,601,000			$1,530,000
2005		$126,477,000			$1,049,000
2004		$123,850,000			$1,458,000
Curr. Assets:	$30,167,000	**Curr. Liab.:**	$15,643,000	**P/E Ratio:**	24.71
Plant, Equip.:	$4,278,000	**Total Liab.:**	$18,355,000	**Indic. Yr. Divd.:**	NA
Total Assets:	$38,077,000	**Net Worth:**	$19,274,000	**Debt/ Equity:**	NA

Jaco Electronics Inc

145 Oser Ave., Hauppauge, NY, 11788; **PH:** 1-631-273-5500; **Fax:** 1-631-273-5799; **http://** www.jacoelectronics.com

General - Incorporation	NY	**Stock**- Price on:12/24/2007	$2.3
Employees	205	Stock Exchange	NDQ
Auditor	Grant Thornton LLP	Ticker Symbol	JACO
Stk Agt	Grant Thornton LLP	Outstanding Shares	6,290,000
Counsel	Morrison, Cohen, Singer & Weinstein	E.P.S	-$0.57
DUNS No.	04-585-6879	Shareholders	NA

Business: The group's principal activities are to distribute electronic parts, provide contract manufacturing and value-added services. The group distributes semiconductors, capacitors, resistors, electromechanical devices, flat panel displays, monitors and power supplies. These products are used in the manufacture and assembly of electronic products including telecommunications equipment, medical devices and instrumentation, computers and office equipment, industrial equipment and controls, military and aerospace systems, automotive and consumer electronics. Value-added services include automated inventory management, flat panel systems integration and kitting. Contract manufacturing includes procurement of customer specified components from our network of suppliers and assembly of printed circuit boards and post assembly testing. On 13-Jun-2003, the group acquired assets of the electronics distribution of reptron electronics inc.

Primary SIC and add'l.: 5045 3679 5065

CIK No: 0000052971

Subsidiaries: Interface Electronics Corp., Nexus Custom Electronics, Inc.

Officers: Joel H. Girsky/69/Dir., Chmn., CEO, Pres., Treasurer, Joseph F. Oliveri/59/Vice Chmn., Exec. VP, Charles B. Girsky/74/Dir., Exec. VP, Jeffrey D. Gash/56/CFO, Exec. VP - Finance, Sec., Gary Giordano/51/Exec. VP

Directors: Joel H. Girsky/69/Dir., Chmn., CEO, Pres., Treasurer, Joseph F. Oliveri/59/Vice Chmn., Exec. VP, Charles B. Girsky/74/Dir., Exec. VP, Neil Rappaport/62/Dir., Robert J. Waldman/73/Dir., Don Ackley/55/Dir., Marvin Meirs/70/Dir.

Owners: Charles B. Girsky/7.50%, Joel H. Girsky/16.20%, Jeffrey D. Gash/1.10%, Joseph F. Oliveri, Neil Rappaport, Gary Giordano, Marvin Meirs, Insiders/25.70%, Luis Antonio Hernandez/9.50%, Robert J. Waldman, Dimensional Fund Advisors/6.60%

Financial Data: **Fiscal Year End:**06/30 **Latest Annual Data:** 06/30/2007

Year		Sales			Net Income
2007		$240,232,000			-$3,121,000
2006		$228,521,000			-$6,962,000
2005		$231,825,000			-$4,860,000
Curr. Assets:	$66,684,000	**Curr. Liab.:**	$62,787,000	**P/E Ratio:**	230.00
Plant, Equip.:	$1,433,000	**Total Liab.:**	$63,972,000	**Indic. Yr. Divd.:**	NA
Total Assets:	$96,087,000	**Net Worth:**	$32,115,000	**Debt/ Equity:**	NA

Jacobs Engineering Group Inc

1111 S Arroyo Pkwy., Pasadena, CA, 91105; **PH:** 1-626-578-3500; **Fax:** 1-626-578-6827; **http://** www.jacobs.com; **Email:** contactus@jacobs.com

General - Incorporation	DE	**Stock**- Price on:12/24/2007	$57.74
Employees	43,800	Stock Exchange	NYSE
Auditor	Ernst & Young LLP	Ticker Symbol	JEC
Stk Agt	Wells Fargo Shareowner Services	Outstanding Shares	119,240,000
Counsel	Barton, Klugman & Oetting	E.P.S	$2.35
DUNS No.	07-410-3508	Shareholders	NA

Business: The groups principle activity is to provide technical, professional and construction services. The group also provides project, scientific and consulting services. The group operates from North America, Europe, Asia, and Mexico.

Primary SIC and add'l.: 7389 8711 8741

CIK No: 0000052988

Subsidiaries: Babtie Asia Limited, Babtie Asia Pte Limited, Babtie Asia Technical& Management Consultants Sdn Bhd, Babtie Consultants (India) Private Ltd, Babtie International Limited, Babtie Spol s.r.o, Cell BG, CODE International Assurance Ltd., CRSS International inc., Delta Catalytic Ltd., Delta Catalytic Saudi Arabia Ltd., GIBB Holdings Ltd., GPR Planners Collaborative Inc., HGC Constructors Private Limited., Interhuis SA 81 Subsidiaries included in the Index

Officers: Craig L. Martin/58/Dir., CEO, Pres.

Directors: Craig L. Martin/58/Dir., CEO, Pres., Noel G. Watson/71/Chmn., Dale R. Laurance/61/Dir., John P. Jumper/63/Dir., Benjamin F. Montoya/72/Dir., Robert B. Gwyn/68/Dir., Robert C. Davidson/62/Dir., Thomas M.T. Niles/68/Dir., Linda Fayne Levinson/66/Dir., Joseph R. Bronson/59/Dir., Edward V. Fritzky/57/Dir.

Owners: George A. Kunberger, Robert C. Davidson, Craig L. Martin/0.87%, Thomas R. Hammond/0.20%, Robert B. Gwyn, Barclays Global Investors UK Holdings Limited/6.05%, Insiders/5.52%, Linda Fayne Levinson, Joseph R. Bronson, Dale R. Laurance, Noel G. Watson/1.75%, Thomas MT. Niles, John W. Prosser, Benjamin F. Montoya, FMR LLC/13.66% *(17 Owners included in Index)*

Financial Data: Fiscal Year End:09/30 *Latest Annual Data:* 9/30/2006

Year	Sales	Net Income
2006	$7,421,270,000	$196,883,000
2005	$5,635,001,000	$151,020,000
2004	$4,594,235,000	$128,975,000

Curr. Assets:	$1,817,961,000	**Curr. Liab.:**	$1,041,195,000	**P/E Ratio:**	29.46
Plant, Equip.:	$171,276,000	**Total Liab.:**	$1,423,399,000	**Indic. Yr. Divd.:**	NA
Total Assets:	$2,853,884,000	**Net Worth:**	$1,423,214,000	**Debt/ Equity:**	NA

JAG Media Holdings Inc

6865 SW 18th St., Ste. B-13, Boca Raton, FL, 33433; *PH:* 1-561-892-0821; *Fax:* 1-866-300-7410; *http://* www.jagnotes.com

General - Incorporation	NV	**Stock** - Price on:12/24/2007	NA
Employees	NA	Stock Exchange	OTC
Auditor	J.H. Cohn LLP	Ticker Symbol	JAGH
Stk Agt	Transfer Online, Inc.	Outstanding Shares	NA
Counsel	NA	E.P.S.	-$0.25
DUNS No.	NA	Shareholders	NA

Business: The groups principle activity is to provide financial and investment information within the investment community. Products of the group include JAGNotes and Rumor Room. The group operates from the United States. The group's quarterly revenue for Sep '07 was 0.20 millions of USD.

Primary SIC and add'l.: 2741 6289 7375 7379 4899

CIK No: 0001089029

Subsidiaries: Pixaya (UK) Limited, Pixaya LLC

Officers: Thomas J. Mazzarisi/51/Chmn., CEO, General Counsel, Stephen J. Schoepfer/49/CFO, COO, Pres., Sec.

Directors: Thomas J. Mazzarisi/51/Chmn., CEO, General Counsel

Owners: Insiders/1.80%, Stephen Schoepfer, Thomas Mazzarisi/1.20%

Financial Data: Fiscal Year End:07/31 *Latest Annual Data:* 7/31/2006

Year	Sales	Net Income
2006	$167,000	-$3,637,000
2005	$240,000	-$1,889,000
2003	$386,000	-$2,579,000

Curr. Assets:	$502,000	**Curr. Liab.:**	$3,047,000		
Plant, Equip.:	$77,000	**Total Liab.:**	$5,074,000	**Indic. Yr. Divd.:**	NA
Total Assets:	$578,000	**Net Worth:**	-$4,496,000	**Debt/ Equity:**	NA

Jagged Peak Inc

3140 Venture Dr., Las Vegas, NV, 89101; *PH:* 1-702-735-7575; *http://* www.jaggedpeak.com; *Email:* information@aslg4you.com

General - Incorporation	NV	**Stock** - Price on:12/24/2007	$0.25
Employees	74	Stock Exchange	OTC
Auditor	Pender Newkirk & Co	Ticker Symbol	JGPK
Stk Agt	Pacific Stock Transfer Company	Outstanding Shares	13,950,000
Counsel	NA	E.P.S.	-$0.11
DUNS No.	NA	Shareholders	NA

Business: The group's principle activity is to provide different types of products that are clear, bronze, gray or silver in color with combinations of high-end safety, security and solar control to ensure privacy and protection. The company is in the process of setting up a dealer network to market, sell, distribute, install and represent the full line of its products. The company is currently a development stage company. The group oprates from United States.

Primary SIC and add'l.: 3231

CIK No: 0001121793

Officers: Vince Fabrizzi/Sr. VP, Chief Sales, Marketing Officer

Owners: Scott R. Griffith, Andrew J. Norstrud/2.00%, Insiders/67.00%, Laurus Master Fund, Ltd/11.00%, Jesse B. Shelmire, Vince Fabrizzi/18.00%, Paul Demirdjian/29.00%, George Town/10.00%, Dan Furlong/18.00%

Financial Data: Fiscal Year End:12/30 *Latest Annual Data:* 12/29/2006

Year	Sales	Net Income
2006	$11,462,000	-$1,379,000
2005	$9,682,000	-$730,000
2004	NA	-$1,690,000

Curr. Assets:	$0	**Curr. Liab.:**	$877,000		
Plant, Equip.:	NA	**Total Liab.:**	$877,000	**Indic. Yr. Divd.:**	NA
Total Assets:	$5,000	**Net Worth:**	-$872,000	**Debt/ Equity:**	2.6764

Jaguar Acquisition Corp

1200 River Rd., Ste. 1302, Conshohocken, PA, 19428; *PH:* 1-610-585-0285

General - Incorporation	DE	**Stock** - Price on:12/24/2007	$5.85
Employees	NA	Stock Exchange	OTC
Auditor	BDO Seidman, LLP	Ticker Symbol	JGAC
Stk Agt	Continental Stock Transfer & Trust Co	Outstanding Shares	NA
Counsel	NA	E.P.S.	NA
DUNS No.	NA	Shareholders	NA

Business: The groups principle activity is to provide recruiting services. The groups service area includes the research and development, engineering, marketing, sales, information technology and manufacturing industries. The group operates from United States.

Primary SIC and add'l.: 4841

CIK No: 0001331474

Owners: Globis Overseas Fund, Ltd., Globis Capital Managememt, L.P., Paul Packer, Insiders, Globis Capital Partners, L.P., Mitchell Metzman, Hummingbird Capital, LLC, The Hummingbird Microcap Value Fund, L.P., Hummingbird Management, LLC, Craig Samuels, The Hummingbird Value Fund L.P., Richard C. Corl, Globis Capital, L.L.C., John Hoey, James S. Cassano *(21 Owners included in Index)*

Financial Data: Fiscal Year End:03/31 *Latest Annual Data:* 3/31/2006

Year	Sales	Net Income
2006	NA	-$1,000

Curr. Assets:	$0	**Curr. Liab.:**	$87,000		
Plant, Equip.:	NA	**Total Liab.:**	$87,000	**Indic. Yr. Divd.:**	NA
Total Assets:	$111,000	**Net Worth:**	$24,000	**Debt/ Equity:**	NA

Jakks Pacific Inc

22619 Pacific Coast Hwy., Malibu, CA, 90265; *PH:* 1-310-456-7799; *Fax:* 1-310-317-8527; *http://* www.jakkspacific.com

General - Incorporation	DE	**Stock** - Price on:12/24/2007	$28.43
Employees	702	Stock Exchange	NDQ
Auditor	BDO Seidman, LLP	Ticker Symbol	JAKK
Stk Agt	U.S. Stock Transfer Corp	Outstanding Shares	28,140,000
Counsel	Feder, Kaszovitz, Isaacson Et Al	E.P.S.	$2.48
DUNS No.	92-877-9826	Shareholders	NA

Business: The group's principal activities are to design, develop, produce and market toys and leisure products. The product categories include: action figures, arts and crafts activity kits, stationery, writing instruments, performance kites, water toys, sports activity toys, vehicles, infant/pre-school, plush and dolls. The products are sold under various brand names including flying colors, road champs, remco, child guidance, pentech, trendmasters, toymax, funnoodle, go fly a kite and jpi color workshop. The group also participates in a joint venture with thq inc that has exclusive worldwide rights to publish and market world wrestling entertainment video games. The products are sold in the United States, Europe, Australia, Canada, Latin America and Asia.

Primary SIC and add'l.: 3944 3942

CIK No: 0001009829

Subsidiaries: Arbor Toys Company Limited, Creative Designs International, Ltd., Flying Colors Toys (HK) Ltd., Flying Colors Toys, Inc., Funnoodle (H.K.) Limited, Funnoodle, Inc., Go Fly A Kite (H.K.) Limited, Go Fly A Kite, Inc., JAKKS Pacific (Asia) Limited, JAKKS Pacific (HK) Limited, JAKKS Pacific/Kidz Biz Far East Limited, JAKKS Pacific/Kidz Biz Limited, JP Ferrero Parkway, Inc., JPI ColorWorkshop Limited, JPI ColorWorkshop, Inc. 24 Subsidiaries included in the Index

Officers: Jack Friedman/Chmn., CEO/$3,202,000.00, John Mills/Primary Investor Relations Officer, Joel M. Bennett/CFO, Exec. VP/$674,700.00, Stephen G. Berman/Dir., COO, Pres., Sec./$3,199,500.00

Directors: Jack Friedman/Chmn., CEO, David C. Blatte/Dir., Dan Almagor/54/Dir., Robert E. Glick/63/Dir., Michael G. Miller/Dir., Murray L. Skala/Dir., Stephen G. Berman/Dir., COO, Pres., Sec.

Owners: Jack Friedman/2.40%, AXA Financial, Inc./5.10%, Third Avenue Management LLC/14.20%, David C. Blatte, Dimensional Fund Advisors, Inc./8.30%, Joel M. Bennett, Barclays Global Investors, N.A./8.10%, Stephen G. Berman/2.00%, Insiders/6.30%, FMR Corp./8.10%, Murray L. Skala, Michael G. Miller, Robert E. Glick, Dan Almagor

Financial Data: Fiscal Year End:12/31 *Latest Annual Data:* 12/31/2006

Year	Sales	Net Income
2006	$765,386,000	$72,375,000
2005	$661,536,000	$63,493,000
2004	$574,266,000	$43,559,000

Curr. Assets:	$451,738,000	**Curr. Liab.:**	$171,375,000	**P/E Ratio:**	12.47
Plant, Equip.:	$16,883,000	**Total Liab.:**	$272,606,000	**Indic. Yr. Divd.:**	NA
Total Assets:	$881,894,000	**Net Worth:**	$609,288,000	**Debt/ Equity:**	0.1769

Jamba Inc

6475 Christie Ave., Ste. 150, Emeryville, CA, 94608; *PH:* 1-510-596-0100; *Fax:* 1-510-653-0764; *http://* www.jambajuice.com; *Email:* investors@jambajuice.com

General - Incorporation	DE	**Stock** - Price on:12/24/2007	$9.285
Employees	7,500	Stock Exchange	NDQ
Auditor	Deloitte & Touche	Ticker Symbol	JMBA
Stk Agt	Continental Stock Transfer & Trust Co	Outstanding Shares	NA
Counsel	NA	E.P.S.	NA
DUNS No.	NA	Shareholders	NA

Business: The groups principle activity is to provide blended beverages and healthy snacks. The products of the group include smoothie, boosts, breads, pretzels and packaged snacks and juice. The group products sold under the trade name jamba light(TM) and All Fruit(TM) line, Matcha Green Tea Creations(TM) and Acai Supercharger(TM). In November 29, 2006 the group merged with Jamba Juice Company. The group operates from the United States. The group's quarterly revenue for September 2007 was 83.64 millions of USD.

Primary SIC and add'l.: 5812

CIK No: 0003316898

Subsidiaries: Jamba Juice Company

Officers: Paul E. Clayton/49/Dir., CEO, Pres., Alecia Pulman/Media Inquiries, Don Duffy/Investor Relations, Brian Prenoveau/Investor Relations, Donald D. Breen/49/Sr. VP, CFO, Karen Kelley/42/Sr. VP - Operations, Paul Coletta/44/Sr. VP - Marketing, Russell Testa/51/Sr. VP - Human Resources, William A. Feiler/40/Sr. VP - Development, Michael W. Fox/Sec.

Directors: Paul E. Clayton/49/Dir., CEO, Pres., Steven R. Berrard/Chmn., Thomas C. Byrne/Dir., Richard L. Federico/Dir., Robert C. Kagle/Dir., Ramon Martin-Busutil/Dir., Craig J. Foley/Dir., Brian Swette/Dir.

Owners: Karen Kelley, Soros Strategic Partners LP/5.10%, Donald D. Breen, Ramon Martin-Busutil, Paul E. Clayton, Insiders/11.30%, Richard L. Federico, Brian Swette, Thomas C. Byrne/1.40%, OZ Management, L.L.C./6.40%, Craig J. Foley, Prentice Capital Management, LP/6.40%, Robert C. Kagle/6.70%, Blue Ridge Limited Partnership/11.80%, Steven R. Berrard/2.40% *(16 Owners included in Index)*

Financial Data: Fiscal Year End:12/31   Latest Annual Data: 1/9/2007

Year	Sales	Net Income
2007	$23,115,000	-$59,026,000
2005	$1,454,000	$3,296,000

Curr. Assets:	$1,034,000	Curr. Liab.:	$14,157,000		
Plant, Equip.:	NA	Total Liab.:	$14,157,000	Indic. Yr. Divd.:	NA
Total Assets:	$129,208,000	Net Worth:	$89,809,000	Debt/ Equity:	NA

James Hardie Industries

26300 La Alameda, Ste. 250, Mission Viejo, CA, 92691; *PH:* 1-949-348-1800; *Fax:* 1-949-348-4534; *http://* www.jameshardie.com; *Email:* info@jameshardie.com

General - Incorporation	Netherlands	Stock - Price on:12/24/2007	$40.04
Employees	3,272	Stock Exchange	NYSE
Auditor	PricewaterhouseCoopers LLP	Ticker Symbol	JHX
Stk Agt	Computershare Registry Services	Outstanding Shares	93,460,000
Counsel	NA	E.P.S	$1.64
DUNS No.	NA	Shareholders	NA

Business: The group's principle activity is manufacturing of fibre cement products, such as building & roofing materials. The group has operations in usa, Australia & New Zealand.

Primary SIC and add'l.: 2952 3241 3275

CIK No: 0001159152

Subsidiaries: James Hardie Aust Holdings Pty Ltd., James Hardie Austgroup Pty Ltd., James Hardie Australia Management Pty Ltd., James Hardie Australia Pty Ltd., James Hardie Building Products Inc., James Hardie Europe B.V., James Hardie Fibre Cement Pty Ltd., James Hardie International Finance B.V., James Hardie International Finance Holdings Sub I B.V, James Hardie International Finance Holdings Sub II B.V, James Hardie International Holdings B.V., James Hardie N.V., James Hardie New Zealand Limited, James Hardie Philippines Inc., James Hardie Research (Holdings) Pty Ltd. 18 Subsidiaries included in the Index

Officers: Louis Gries/54/CEO, Timothy Chiu/Contact - Other Enquiries, Russell Chenu/58/Exec Dir., CFO, Benjamin Butterfield/48/General Counsel, Company Sec., Brian Holte/41/VP, GM - Western Division, Joel Rood/51/VP, GM - Southern Division, Steve Ashe/48/VP - Investor Relations, Peter W. Baker/57/Exec. VP - Australia, Jamie Chilcoff/44/VP - International Business, Mark Fisher/37/VP - Research, Development, Grant Gustafson/45/VP - Interiors, Business Development, Nigel Rigby/41/VP, GM - Northern Region, Robert Russell/42/VP - Engineering, Process Development

Directors: Donald Defosset/59/Chmn., Chmn. - Supervisory Board, Donald McGauchie/Dep. Chmn. - Supervisory Board, Brian Anderson/Dir., Member - Supervisory Board, David R. Andrews/66/Dir., Member - Supervisory Board, Michael Hammes/66/Dir., Member - Supervisory Board, James Loudon/65/Dir., Member - Supervisory Board, Rudy Van Der Meer/63/Dir., Member - Supervisory Board, Catherine Walter/56/Dir., Member - Supervisory Board, John D. Barr/61/Dir., Member - Supervisory Board, Russell Chenu/58/Exec Dir., CFO

Owners: John Barr, Robert Russell, James Loudon, Nigel Rigby, Donald DeFosset, Michael Gillfillan, Mark Fisher, Russell Chenu, James Chilcoff, Louis Gries, Meredith Hellicar, Gregory Clark, Benjamin Butterfield, Michael Brown

Financial Data: Fiscal Year End:03/31   Latest Annual Data: 03/31/2007

Year	Sales	Net Income
2007	$1,542,900,000	$151,700,000
2006	$1,488,500,000	-$506,700,000
2005	$1,210,400,000	$126,900,000

Curr. Assets:	$656,800,000	Curr. Liab.:	$506,000,000		
Plant, Equip.:	$775,600,000	Total Liab.:	$1,350,500,000	Indic. Yr. Divd.:	$1.340
Total Assets:	$1,445,400,000	Net Worth:	$94,900,000	Debt/ Equity:	NA

James River Coal Co

901 E Byrd St., Ste. 1600, Richmond, VA, 23219; *PH:* 1-804-780-3000; *Fax:* 1-804-780-0643; *http://* www.jamesrivercoal.com

General - Incorporation	VA	Stock - Price on:12/24/2007	$14.27
Employees	1,742	Stock Exchange	NDQ
Auditor	KPMG LLP	Ticker Symbol	JRCC
Stk Agt	SunTrust Bank	Outstanding Shares	16,670,000
Counsel	NA	E.P.S	-$2.19
DUNS No.	15-338-9283	Shareholders	NA

Business: The group's principal activities are to mine, process and sell bituminous, low sulfur, steam and industrial grade coal primarily to electric utility companies and industrial companies. The mining operations of the group are managed through five operating subsidiaries located throughout eastern Kentucky. The group operates a total of 14 underground mines. It also have rights to another six mines that are typically mined by independent contract mine operators, out of which four are underground mines and two are surface mines. On 25-Mar-2003, the group filed for bankruptcy under chapter 11 and on 06-May-2004, it emerged from bankruptcy proceedings.

Primary SIC and add'l.: 1221

CIK No: 0001297720

Subsidiaries: ZiLOG Asia Ltd., ZiLOG Electronic Philippines,Inc., ZiLOG India Electronics Private Ltd., ZiLOG International Pte. Ltd., ZiLOG Japan K.K., ZiLOG MOD III,Inc, ZiLOG Philippines,Inc., ZiLOG UK, Ltd.

Officers: Peter T. Socha/Chmn., CEO, Pres., Samuel M. Hopkins/VP, Chief Accounting Officer, Coy K. Lane/COO, Sr. VP, Timothy A. Frasure/Pres. - Bledsoe Coal Corporation, Joseph G. Evans/Pres. - Leeco, Inc, Pres. - Blue Diamond Coal Company, Richard L. Douthat/VP - Risk Management, James T. Ketron/VP, General Counsel, Sec., B. J. Reynolds/Pres. - Bell County Coal Corporation, Brian Patton/Pres. - James River Coal Service, Randall K. Taylor/Pres. - Mccoy Elkhorn Coal Corporation, Michael E. Weber/55/Sr. VP, Chief Commercial Officer

Directors: Peter T. Socha/Chmn., CEO, Pres., Alan F. Crown/Dir., Joseph H. Vipperman/Dir., Leonard J. Kujawa/Dir., Ronald J. Florjancic/Dir.

Owners: Millenco, L.L.C./9.08%, Steelhead Partners LLC/9.75%, LaGrange Capital Administration, L.L.C./9.12%, Samuel M. Hopkins, Ronald J. FlorJancic, Pequot Capital Management, Inc./6.65%, Peter T. Socha/1.51%, Alan F. Crown, Michael E. Weber, Joseph H. Vipperman, SouthernSun Asset Management, Inc/11.24%, Coy K. Lane, Douglas W. Blackburn, Leonard J. Kujawa, Insiders/2.91%

Financial Data: Fiscal Year End:12/31   Latest Annual Data: 12/31/2006

Year	Sales	Net Income
2006	$564,791,000	-$26,169,000
2005	$453,999,000	-$12,338,000
2004	$345,647,000	$109,965,000

Curr. Assets:	$71,142,000	Curr. Liab.:	$73,731,000		
Plant, Equip.:	$337,780,000	Total Liab.:	$364,857,000	Indic. Yr. Divd.:	NA
Total Assets:	$451,254,000	Net Worth:	$86,397,000	Debt/ Equity:	2.3532

Janel World Trade Ltd

150-14 132nd Ave., Jamaica, NY, 11434; *PH:* 1-718-527-3800; *Fax:* 1-718-527-1689; *http://* www.janelgroup.net; *Email:* info@janelgroup.net

General - Incorporation	NV	Stock - Price on:12/24/2007	$0.42
Employees	64	Stock Exchange	OTC
Auditor	Paritz & Co P.A	Ticker Symbol	JLWT
Stk Agt	Executive Registrar & Transfer, Inc.	Outstanding Shares	16,990,000
Counsel	Executive Registrar & Transfer Inc	E.P.S	$0.01
DUNS No.	NA	Shareholders	NA

Business: The group's principal activity is to provide logistics services for importers and exporters worldwide. It provides full service cargo transportation logistics management, including freight forwarding through air, ocean and land based carriers, customs brokerage services and warehousing and distribution services. The group also offers related logistics services, such as freight consolidation, insurance, direct computer access interface, logistics planning, landed-cost calculations, in-house computer tracking, product repackaging, online shipment tracking and electronic billing. It conducts business through a network of five company operated facilities and through independent agent relationships in trading countries.

Primary SIC and add'l.: 1796 4731

CIK No: 0001133062

Officers: Linda Bieler/General Inquiries Accounting, New York, Noel R. Jannello/Contact - The Janel Group, New York, William J. Davis/Legal Counsel, Rudy Rufer/General Inquiries Air Import, New York, Denise Rich/Ocean Import, New York, Richard Wolf/Air Export, General Inquiries, New York, Lillian Sheriden/Ocean Export, General Inquiries, New York, Liz Lally/General Inquiries, Import, Chicago, Karin Prince/General Inquiries, Import, Chicago, Al Mondella/General Inquiries, Export, Chicago, Lee Siracusa/General Inquiries Accounting, Chicago, Phil Castagna/General Inquiries, Import, Atlanta, Phil Del Rocco/General Inquiries, Export, Atlanta, Adelaide Grillo/General Inquiries, Import, Los Angeles, Jose Villasenor/General Inquiries, Import, Los Angeles *(20 Officers included in Index)*

Owners: Noel J. Jannello, James N. Jannello/32.27%, William J. Lally/5.87%, Insiders/71.14%, Linda Bieler, Ruth Werra, Stephen P. Cesarski/32.27%

Financial Data: Fiscal Year End:09/30   Latest Annual Data: 9/30/2006

Year	Sales	Net Income
2006	$77,220,000	$57,000
2005	$73,484,000	$430,000
2004	$69,982,000	$264,000

Curr. Assets:	$6,516,000	Curr. Liab.:	$2,907,000	P/E Ratio:	42.00
Plant, Equip.:	$178,000	Total Liab.:	$2,992,000	Indic. Yr. Divd.:	NA
Total Assets:	$6,743,000	Net Worth:	$3,751,000	Debt/ Equity:	0.0009

Janus Capital Group Inc

151 Detroit St., Denver, CO, 80206; *PH:* 1-303-333-3863; *Fax:* 1-303-336-7497; *http://* www.janus.com

General - Incorporation	DE	Stock - Price on:12/24/2007	$28.84
Employees	1,518	Stock Exchange	NYSE
Auditor	Deloitte & Touche LLP	Ticker Symbol	JNS
Stk Agt	Wells Fargo Shareowner Services	Outstanding Shares	185,410,000
Counsel	NA	E.P.S	$0.73
DUNS No.	NA	Shareholders	NA

Business: The group's principal activities are to sponsor, market and provide investment advisory, distribution and administrative services. The group offers these services primarily to mutual funds in both domestic and international markets. As of Dec 31, 2003, the company managed $151.5 billion in assets across multiple investment disciplines.the group acquired capital group partners inc on 01-Dec-2003, 30% interest in perkins, wolf, mcdonnell and company llc in may 2003 and berger financial group llc in feb 2003. The group sold nelson money managers plc in 2003.

Primary SIC and add'l.: 6719 6722 6282

CIK No: 0001065865

Subsidiaries: Bay Isle Financial LLC, Berger Financial Group LLC, Capital Group Partners, Inc.(3), Enhanced Investment Technologies, LLC, Janus Capital Management LLC, Janus Capital Trust Manager Limited, Janus Distributors LLC, Janus Holdings Corporation, Janus International (Asia) Limited, Janus International Holding LLC, Janus International Limited, Janus Management Holdings Corporation, Janus Services LLC, Perkins, Wolf, McDonnell and Company, LLC

Officers: Gary D. Black/Dir., CEO/$14,536,500.00, Gregory A. Frost/Sr. VP, CFO, Robin C. Beery/Chief Marketing Officer, Exec. VP/$3,111,781.00, Dominic Martellaro/Exec. VP, MD - Global Advisory Channel, Jonathan D. Coleman/Co - Chief Investment Officer - Janus Capital Management, Portfolio Mgr./$6,478,571.00, Kelley A. Howes/Sr. VP, General Counsel, Andy Iseman/COO, Sr. VP, Gibson Smith/Co - Chief Investment Officer - Janus Capital Management, Portfolio Mgr.

Directors: Gary D. Black/Dir., CEO, Steven L. Scheid/Chmn., Robert T. Parry/Dir., Andrew Cox/Dir., Richard J. Fredericks/Dir., Jock Patton/Dir., Landon H. Rowland/Dir., Deborah Gatzek/Dir., Robert Skidelsky/Dir., Paul F. Balser/Dir.

Owners: Kelley A. Howes, Gary D. Black, Robert T. Parry, Andrew G. Cox, Dominic C. Martellaro, James P. Craig, Landon H. Rowland/1.24%, Robin C. Beery, Steven L. Scheid, Michael D. Bills, Andrew J. Iseman, Robert Skidelsky, AXA Financial Inc./14.24%, Ariel Capital Management, LLC/15.42%, Insiders/3.27% *(24 Owners included in Index)*

Financial Data: Fiscal Year End:12/31   Latest Annual Data: 12/31/2006

Year	Sales	Net Income
2006	$1,026,700,000	$133,600,000
2005	$953,100,000	$87,800,000
2004	$1,010,800,000	$169,500,000

Curr. Assets:	$925,100,000	Curr. Liab.:	$185,600,000
Plant, Equip.:	$60,300,000	Total Liab.:	$1,213,700,000
Total Assets:	$3,537,900,000	Net Worth:	$2,306,400,000

P/E Ratio: 36.51
Indic. Yr. Divd.: $0.040
Debt/ Equity: 0.2452

Jarden Corp

555 Theodore Fremd Ave., Ste. B-302, Rye, NY, 10580; *PH:* 1-914-967-9400; *Fax:* 1-914-967-9405; *http://* www.jarden.com

General - Incorporation	DE	**Stock**- Price on:12/24/2007	$44.63
Employees	20,000	Stock Exchange	NYSE
Auditor	Ernst & Young LLP	Ticker Symbol	JAH
Stk Agt	National City Bank	Outstanding Shares	71,850,000
Counsel	NA	E.P.S	$1.05
DUNS No.	80-187-5980	Shareholders	NA

Business: The groups principle activity is to sell consumer products. The group is divided into three primary business segments namely Branded Consumables, and Consumer and Outdoor Solutions. The group operates from United States.

Primary SIC and add'l.: 3353 4783 3089 2032 3356

CIK No: 0000895655

Subsidiaries: Alltrista Limited, Alltrista Newco Corporation, Alltrista Plastics Corporation, American Household, Inc., Application des Gaz, S.A.S., Australian Coleman, Inc., Bafiges, S.A.S., Beacon Exports, Inc., Bernardin, Limited, Bicycle Holding, Inc., BRK Brands Europe Limited, BRK Brands Pty. Ltd., BRK Brands, Inc., Camping Gaz CS Spol S.R.O., Camping Gaz International Portugal Ltda. 87 Subsidiaries included in the Index

Officers: Martin E. Franklin/43/Chmn., CEO/$4,991,248.00, Ian G.H. Ashken/47/Vice Chmn., CFO, Corp. Sec./$2,273,832.00, James E. Lillie/46/COO, Pres./$1,632,902.00, David J. Tolbert/47/Sr. VP - Human Resources, Corporate Risk/$949,602.00, Richard T. Sansone/41/Chief Accounting Officer, Sr. VP, John E. Capps/43/Sr. VP, General Counsel, Sec.

Directors: Martin E. Franklin/43/Chmn., CEO, Ian G.H. Ashken/47/Vice Chmn., CFO, Corp. Sec., Richard L. Molen/67/Dir., Douglas W. Huemme/66/Dir., Rene-Pierre Azria/51/Dir., Charles R. Kaye/44/Dir., Irwin D. Simon/49/Dir., Robert L. Wood/52/Dir., Michael S. Gross/45/Dir.

Owners: James E. Lillie, David J. Tolbert, Warburg Pincus Private Equity VIII, L.P./8.50%, Martin E. Franklin/7.70%, Charles R. Kaye/8.50%, Richard L. Molen, Capital Group International, Inc./8.40%, Desiree DeStefano, LMM LLC/6.80%, Ian G.H. Ashken/1.30%, Michael S. Gross, Ren-Pierre Azria, Wellington Management Company, LLP/6.30%, Irwin D. Simon, Douglas W. Huemme *(17 Owners included in Index)*

Financial Data: Fiscal Year End:12/31   Latest Annual Data: 12/31/2006

Year	Sales	Net Income
2006	$3,846,300,000	$106,000,000
2005	$3,189,066,000	$60,716,000
2004	$838,609,000	$42,434,000

Curr. Assets:	$1,563,700,000	Curr. Liab.:	$724,100,000
Plant, Equip.:	$345,800,000	Total Liab.:	$2,625,200,000
Total Assets:	$3,882,600,000	Net Worth:	$1,257,400,000

P/E Ratio: 29.36
Indic. Yr. Divd.: NA
Debt/ Equity: 1.3334

Java Express Inc

5017 Wild Buffalo Ave., Las Vegas, NV, 89131; *PH:* 1-702-839-1098

General - Incorporation	NV	**Stock**- Price on:12/24/2007	$0.3
Employees	NA	Stock Exchange	OTC
Auditor	Madsen & Assoc. CPA's, Inc.	Ticker Symbol	JVEX
Stk Agt	Action Stock Transfer Corp	Outstanding Shares	NA
Counsel	NA	E.P.S	NA
DUNS No.	NA	Shareholders	NA

Business: The group's principal activity is to provide business consulting and coaching service to emerging, developing and growing companies. Its primary services include business plans mapping, consulting and coaching services and bookkeeping services. On 29-Sep-2004, the group acquired K-Com Business Coaching Corp. The group is currently a development stage company. The company had a coffee kiosk business which was abandoned in late 2004.

Primary SIC and add'l.: 5810

CIK No: 0001171838

Subsidiaries: K-Com Business Coaching Corp

Officers: Howard Abrams/48/Chmn., CEO, CFO, Pres., Sec.

Directors: Howard Abrams/48/Chmn., CEO, CFO, Pres., Sec.

Owners: Howard Abrams/17.54%, Wallapha Saipreccha/0.07%, Joshua Musicant/7.02%, John Chris Kirch/9.30%, Jay Kirch/8.77%, Nick Fischella/5.26%, Dominion World Investments/5.26%, Kelly Trimble/16.67%

Javo Beverage Company Inc

1311 Specialty Dr., Vista, CA, 92081; *PH:* 1-760-560-5286; *Fax:* 1-760-560-5287; *http://* www.javobeverage.com; *Email:* sales@javobeverage.com

General - Incorporation	DE	**Stock**- Price on:12/24/2007	$1.4
Employees	46	Stock Exchange	OTC
Auditor	Farber Hass Hurley & McEwen LLP	Ticker Symbol	JAVO
Stk Agt	Corporate Stock Transfer, Inc.	Outstanding Shares	149,500,000
Counsel	NA	E.P.S	$0.05
DUNS No.	NA	Shareholders	NA

Business: The groups principle activity is to manufacturer coffee and tea concentrates, drink mixes, and flavor systems. Customers served by the group include foodservice, food and beverage manufacturing, and retail industries. The group operates from the United States. The group's quarterly revenue for Sep '07 was 3.92 millions of USD.

Primary SIC and add'l.: 2095 5087 5046 2086

CIK No: 0001092302

Officers: Cody C. Ashwell/Chmn., CEO/$180,000.00, Gary Lillian/Pres./$180,000.00, Stephen F. Corey/Sr. VP - Research, Development, Richard A. Gartrell/CFO/$180,000.00, William E. Marshall/General Counsel/$162,750.00

Directors: Cody C. Ashwell/Chmn., CEO, William C. Baker/Dir., Ron S. Beard/Dir., Jerry W. Carlton/Dir., Terry C. Hackett/Dir., James R. Knapp/Dir., Thomas J. Rielly/Dir., Stanley A. Solomon/Dir., Richard B. Specter/Dir.

Owners: Gary A. Lillian, Terry C. Hackett, Thomas J. Rielly/3.30%, Stanley A. Solomon, Richard B. Specter, Richard A. Gartrell, Cody C. Ashwell/6.10%, William C. Baker/4.90%, Insiders/26.70%, Jerry W. Carlton, Curci Investment Co/5.70%, Ronald S. Beard, James P. Knapp/1.50%, William E. Marshall/1.00%

Financial Data: Fiscal Year End:12/31   Latest Annual Data: 12/31/2006

Year	Sales	Net Income
2006	$10,322,000	-$9,926,000
2005	$6,200,000	-$4,844,000
2004	$2,084,000	-$4,855,000

Curr. Assets:	$20,027,000	Curr. Liab.:	$13,431,000
Plant, Equip.:	$881,000	Total Liab.:	$18,133,000
Total Assets:	$21,175,000	Net Worth:	$3,042,000

Indic. Yr. Divd.: NA
Debt/ Equity: NA

Jayhawk Energy Inc

Formerly: Bella Trading Company Inc
370 Interlocken Blvd., Ste. 400, Broomfield, CO, 80021; *PH:* 1-303-327-1571

General - Incorporation	CO	**Stock**- Price on:12/24/2007	NA
Employees	NA	Stock Exchange	NA
Auditor	Meyers Norris Penny LLP	Ticker Symbol	NA
Stk Agt	Corporate Stock Transfer Co.	Outstanding Shares	NA
Counsel	NA	E.P.S	NA
DUNS No.	NA	Shareholders	NA

Business: The groups principle activity is to provide traditional ethnic and contemporary jewelry. The group products include pendants, necklaces, earrings, Gaus, rings, bracelets, chains and brooches. The group operates from Nepal and Thailand and the United States.

Primary SIC and add'l.: 1311

CIK No: 0001308710

Officers: Sara Preston/28/Dir., Pres., Treasurer, CFO, Joseph Young/Pres.

Directors: Sara Preston/28/Dir., Pres., Treasurer, CFO

Owners: Insiders/10.80%, Lindsay E. Gorrill/10.80%

Curr. Assets:	$525,000	Curr. Liab.:	$42,000
Plant, Equip.:	$2,201,000	Total Liab.:	$42,000
Total Assets:	$2,726,000	Net Worth:	$2,684,000

Indic. Yr. Divd.: NA
Debt/ Equity: NA

JDA Software Group Inc

14400 N 87th St., Scottsdale, AZ, 85260; *PH:* 1-480-308-3000; *Fax:* 1-480-308-3001; *http://* www.jda.com; *Email:* info@jda.com

General - Incorporation	DE	**Stock**- Price on:12/24/2007	$19.36
Employees	1,701	Stock Exchange	NDQ
Auditor	Deloitte & Touche LLP	Ticker Symbol	JDAS
Stk Agt	Chase Mellon Shareholder Services	Outstanding Shares	29,610,000
Counsel	Gray, Cary, Ware & Freidenrich	E.P.S	-$0.09
DUNS No.	94-260-3325	Shareholders	NA

Business: The group's principle activity is to provide sophisticated software solutions. The software solutions are enhanced and supported by retail specific professional services. Retail enterprise systems, host systems, analytic applications, in-store systems, collaborative solutions and maintenance & consulting services are its operating segments. The software solutions are designed specifically to address retail demand chain, enhanced decision making and responsiveness to consumer demands, improved inventory management and e-commerce & collaboration capabilities. The company operates in the United States, Asia, Australia, Europe, and Japan. During Aug 2003, the group acquired substantially all assets of engage inc. And during Apr 2003, it acquired all intellectual property and active customer agreements of vista software solutions inc. On 29-Jan-2003, the group acquired intellectual property and certain other assets of timera retail solutions. The group operates from United States.

Primary SIC and add'l.: 8748 7372 8742

CIK No: 0001006892

Subsidiaries: E3 Australia Pty Ltd, JDA Arthur Software Bermuda, Ltd., JDA Asia Pte. Ltd., JDA Chile S.A., JDA Incorporated Software Solutions, S.A., JDA International Limited, JDA Servicios Profesionales, S.A. de C.V., JDA Software Australia Pty Ltd, JDA Software Benelux B.V., JDA Software Brasil Ltda., JDA Software Canada Ltd., JDA Software Danmark ApS, JDA Software de Mexico, S.A. de C.V., JDA Software France SA, JDA Software GmbH 24 Subsidiaries included in the Index

Officers: Hamish Brewer/CEO/$521,147.00, Wayne Usie/Sr. VP - Retail, David King/Sr. VP - Product Development, Chris Koziol/COO/$359,361.00, Arnaud Decarsin/Regional VP - Sales, EMEA, Michael G. Bridge/Sr. VP, General Counsel, Chris Moore/Sr. VP - Customer Support Solutions, Kristen L. Magnuson/CFO, Exec. VP/$342,620.00, Rod Talbot/Regional VP - Asia Pacific, Philip Boland/Sr. VP - Worldwide Consulting Services/$452,396.00, Ronald Kubera/43/Sr. VP - Supply Chain, Jeff Kissling/Sr. VP - Technology Transition/$753,627.00, Tom Dziersk/Sr. VP - Americas/$720,120.00, Brian Boylan/Sr. VP - Human Resources, Larry Ferrere/Sr. VP - Product Management, Chief Marketing Officer *(16 Officers included in Index)*

Directors: James D. Armstrong/Chmn., Douglas Marlin/Dir., Jock Patton/Dir., Orlando Bravo/Dir., Michael J. Gullard/Dir.

Owners: Tom Dziersk, Philip Boland, Kristen L. Magnuson/1.80%, Silver Point Capital, L.P./10.00%, Christopher J. Koziol, Barclays Global Investors NA/5.00%, Thoma Cressey Bravo, Inc./10.90%, Michael J. Gullard, Insiders/12.30%, Dimensional FundAdvisors Inc/8.40%, Jock Patton, Douglas G. Marlin, Goldman Sachs Asset Management, L.P./6.30%, Columbia Wanger Asset Management, L.P./8.80%, James D. Armstrong/6.60% *(18 Owners included in Index)*

Financial Data: Fiscal Year End:12/31   Latest Annual Data: 12/31/2006

Year	Sales	Net Income
2006	$277,467,000	-$446,000
2005	$215,823,000	$6,960,000
2004	$216,874,000	$2,009,000

Curr. Assets:	$166,797,000	Curr. Liab.:	$125,694,000
Plant, Equip.:	$48,391,000	Total Liab.:	$284,392,000
Total Assets:	$624,744,000	Net Worth:	$290,352,000

Indic. Yr. Divd.: NA
Debt/ Equity: 0.4131

JDS Uniphase Corp

430 N McCarthy Blvd., Milpitas, CA, 95035; *PH:* 1-408-546-5000; *Fax:* 1-408-546-4300; *http://* www.jdsu.com; *Email:* investor.relations@jdsu.com

General - Incorporation	DE	**Stock** - Price on:12/24/2007	$13.74
Employees	7,099	Stock Exchange	NDQ
Auditor	Ernst & Young LLP	Ticker Symbol	JDSU
Stk Agt	American Stock Transfer & Trust Co.	Outstanding Shares	211,660,000
Counsel	Morrison & Foerster LLP	E.P.S.	-$0.07
DUNS No.	02-281-0311	Shareholders	NA

Business: The group's principal activities are to design, develop, manufacture and distribute fiber optic components, modules and subsystems for the fiber optic communications industry. These products are deployed in advanced optical communications networks for the telecommunication and cable television industries. The fiber optic communications systems deliver video, audio and text data over fiber optic cables. The group also has optical technology business which incorporate optical technologies to control, enhance and modify the behavior of light utilizing its reflection, absorption and transmission properties to achieve specific effects such as reflectivity, anti-glare and spectral filtering. These products are used in semiconductor and biomedical industries. The group acquired e20 communications, inc and optical communication business from ditech communications, inc in fiscal 2004.

Primary SIC and add'l.: 3674 3663 3823 3825

CIK No: 0000912093

Subsidiaries: Acterna Asia Pacific Pty Ltd., Acterna de Brasil Ltda., Acterna de Mexico S.A. de C.V., Acterna Espana S.A., Acterna France SAS, Acterna Hong Kong Ltd., Acterna Inc., Acterna India Pvt. Ltd., Acterna Investments Ltd., Acterna Italia s.r.l., Acterna Japan K.K., Acterna Korea Ltd., Acterna LLC, Acterna Malaysia Sdn Bhd, Acterna OOO 76 Subsidiaries included in the Index

Officers: Kevin Kennedy/Dir., CEO, Pres./$1,946,649.00, Christopher S. Dewees/Corporate Development, Chief Legal Officer/$1,017,937.00, Judith Kay/Corporate Marketing, Executive Operations, Alan Lowe/Commercial Laser Products Group, Thomas Waechter/Test, Measurement Group, David Vellequette/CFO, Exec. VP/$1,295,732.00, Stan Lumish/CTO, David Gudmundson/Optical Communications Product Group, Alan Etterman/Corporate Services, CIO/$1,353,175.00, Roy Bie/Advanced Optical Technologies Product Group

Directors: Kevin Kennedy/Dir., CEO, Pres., Martin A. Kaplan/Chmn., Casimir S. Skrzypczak/Dir., Richard T. Liebhaber/Dir., Bruce D. Day/Dir., Kevin A. Denuccio/Dir., Richard E. Belluzzo/Dir., Harold L. Covert/Dir., Masood Jabbar/Dir.

Owners: David W. Vellequette, Harold L. Covert, Kevin A. DeNuccio, AXA Financial, Inc./13.30%, Lord, Abbett& Co. LLC/10.97%, Martin A. Kaplan, Insiders, Alan Etterman, Richard T. Liebhaber, Richard E. Belluzzo, Kevin J. Kennedy, Christopher S. Dewees, David Gudmundson, Casimir S. Skrzypczak, Helmut Berg *(18 Owners included in Index)*

Financial Data: *Fiscal Year End:*06/30 *Latest Annual Data:* 06/30/2007

Year		Sales		Net Income
2007		$1,396,800,000		-$26,300,000
2006		$1,204,300,000		-$151,200,000
2005		$712,200,000		-$261,300,000
Curr. Assets:	$1,805,000,000	**Curr. Liab.:**	$422,400,000	
Plant, Equip.:	$201,200,000	**Total Liab.:**	$1,481,500,000	**Indic. Yr. Divd.:** NA
Total Assets:	$3,065,100,000	**Net Worth:**	$1,583,600,000	**Debt/ Equity:** 0.5407

JED Oil Inc

500 - 4th Ave. SW, Ste. 2600, Calgary, AB, T2P 2V6; *PH:* 1-403-537-3250; *http://* www.jedoil.com; *Email:* jedinfo@jedoil.com

General - Incorporation	Canada	**Stock** - Price on:12/24/2007	$1.98
Employees	30	Stock Exchange	AMEX
Auditor	Ernst & Young LLP	Ticker Symbol	JDO
Stk Agt	Ernest & Young LLP	Outstanding Shares	14,970,000
Counsel	NA	E.P.S.	-$5.457
DUNS No.	NA	Shareholders	NA

Business: The group's principle actiivty is to provide oil and gas exploration and production services. The group operates from Canada.

Primary SIC and add'l.: NA

CIK No: 0001258021

Subsidiaries: JED Oil (USA) Inc.

Officers: Thomas J. Jacobsen/Dir., CEO, Linda Latman/Investor Relations Contact, James Rundell/Pres., Richard D. Carmichael/CFO, Raymond Schmidt/VP - Engineering, Marcia L. Johnston/60/VP - Legal, Corporate Affairs

Directors: Thomas J. Jacobsen/Dir., CEO, Justin W. Yorke/Chmn., Ludwig Gierstorfer/Dir., Horst H. Engel/Dir.

Owners: Thomas J. Jacobsen/2.88%, James T. Rundell/0.05%, Marcia L. Johnston/0.11%, Raymond J. Schmidt/0.04%, Richard D. Carmichael/0.04%

Financial Data: *Fiscal Year End:*12/31 *Latest Annual Data:* 12/31/2005

Year		Sales		Net Income
2005		$8,610,000		$1,143,000
2004		$1,707,000		-$8,547,000
Curr. Assets:	$6,041,000	**Curr. Liab.:**	$9,074,000	
Plant, Equip.:	$24,401,000	**Total Liab.:**	$50,292,000	**Indic. Yr. Divd.:** NA
Total Assets:	$36,016,000	**Net Worth:**	-$42,251,000	**Debt/ Equity:** NA

Jefferies Group Inc

520 Madison Ave., 12th Fl., New York, NY, 10022; *PH:* 1-212-284-2300; *Fax:* 1-212-284-2111; *http://* www.jefco.com

General - Incorporation	DE	**Stock** - Price on:12/24/2007	$26.58
Employees	2,254	Stock Exchange	NYSE
Auditor	KPMG LLP	Ticker Symbol	JEF
Stk Agt	American Stock Transfer & Trust Co.	Outstanding Shares	125,430,000
Counsel	Morgan, Lewis & Bockius LLP	E.P.S.	$1.43
DUNS No.	NA	Shareholders	NA

Business: The groups principle activity is to provide investment banking and institutional securities services. The groups services include asset management, and research and analysis services. Customers served by the group include the energy, healthcare and technology industries. The group operates from United States, London, Singapore, China and Paris.

Primary SIC and add'l.: 6211

CIK No: 0001084580

Subsidiaries: Jefferies & Company, Inc., Jefferies (Japan) Limited, Jefferies (Switzerland) Limited, Jefferies Advisers, Inc., Jefferies Asset Management (Zurich), Jefferies Asset Management Japan Limited, Jefferies Asset Management, LLC, Jefferies Capital Management, Inc., Jefferies Execution Services, Inc., Jefferies Financial Products, LLC, Jefferies International (Holdings) Limited, Jefferies International Limited, Jefferies Investment Advisers, LLC, Jefferies Investment Management Limited, Jefferies Pacific Limited

Officers: Richard B. Handler/46/Chmn., CEO/$19,901,790.00, Clifford A. Siegel/50/CEO - Jefferies International Limited, Exec. VP - Jefferies, Company, Inc, Andrew R. Whittake/46/Vice Chmn., Co - Head Investment Banking - Jefferies - Company, Inc, Maxine Syrjamaki/63/Controller/$691,401.00, Joseph A. Schenk/49/CFO, Exec. VP/$2,688,434.00, Jonathan R. Cunningham/45/Exec. VP, Head - Convertible Securities, Jefferies, Company, Inc, Lloyd H. Feller/65/General Counsel, Sec., Exec. VP/$1,624,421.00, Chris M. Kanoff/51/Exec. VP, Co - Head Investment Banking - Jefferies - Company, Inc

Directors: Richard B. Handler/46/Chmn., CEO, Andrew R. Whittake/46/Vice Chmn., Co - Head Investment Banking - Jefferies - Company, Inc, Michael T. O'Kane/62/Dir., Patrick W. Campbell/62/Dir., Robert E. Joyal/63/Dir., Frank J. MacChiarola/66/Dir., Richard G. Dooley/78/Dir., Brian P. Friedman/52/Dir.

Owners: Baron Capital Group, Inc./9.00%, Maxine Syrjamaki, Richard G. Dooley, Lloyd H. Feller, W. Patrick Campbell, Earnest Partners, LLC/9.80%, Frank J. Macchiarola, Richard B. Handler/7.20%, Jefferies Group, Inc./7.70%, Insiders/9.80%, Brian P. Friedman/1.50%, Robert Joyal, Joseph A. Schenk

Financial Data: *Fiscal Year End:*12/31 *Latest Annual Data:* 12/31/2006

Year		Sales		Net Income
2006		$1,963,208,000		$205,750,000
2005		$1,497,873,000		$157,443,000
2004		$1,198,639,000		$131,366,000
Curr. Assets:	$2,211,304,000	**Curr. Liab.:**	$8,098,788,000	**P/E Ratio:** 17.04
Plant, Equip.:	$91,375,000	**Total Liab.:**	$16,161,885,000	**Indic. Yr. Divd.:** $0.500
Total Assets:	$17,899,882,000	**Net Worth:**	$1,581,087,000	**Debt/ Equity:** 5.0997

Jefferson Bancshares Inc

120 Evans Ave., Morristown, TN, 37814; *PH:* 1-423-586-8421; *Fax:* 1-423-587-2605; *http://* www.jeffersonfederal.com; *Email:* custserve@jeffersonfederal.com

General - Incorporation	TN	**Stock** - Price on:12/24/2007	$11.84
Employees	98	Stock Exchange	NDQ
Auditor	Craine, Thompson & Jones P.C	Ticker Symbol	JFBI
Stk Agt	Registrar & Transfer Co	Outstanding Shares	6,440,000
Counsel	NA	E.P.S.	$0.32
DUNS No.	NA	Shareholders	NA

Business: The group's principal activities are to provide of banking services to consumers and businesses in Tennessee. The operations of the group are conducted through its wholly owned subsidiary jefferson federal bank. The group's lending activity consists of origination of mortgage loans one- to four-family home loans, home equity lines of credit, commercial real estate and multi-family loans, construction loans, land loans, commercial business loans, subprime loans and consumer loans. It also offers a variety of deposits consisting of now accounts, money market accounts, regular savings accounts, christmas club savings accounts, certificates of deposit and retirement savings plans.

Primary SIC and add'l.: 6021 6712 6035

CIK No: 0001222915

Subsidiaries: Jefferson Federal Bank, Jefferson Service Corporation of Morristown, Tennessee, Inc.

Officers: Anderson L. Smith/60/Dir., CEO, Pres./$441,459.00, Douglas H. Rouse/55/Sr. VP, Jane P. Hutton/49/CFO, VP/$141,284.00, Eric S. McDaniel/37/VP, Sr. Operations Officer, Janet J. Ketner/55/Exec. VP - Retail Banking/$181,541.00, Anthony J. Carasso/49/Pres. - Knoxville Region/$187,837.00, Stan Greene/Mortgage Team, Sharon Greene/Mortgage Team

Directors: Anderson L. Smith/60/Dir., CEO, Pres., Charles G. Robinette/63/Chmn. - Knoxville Region, John F. McCrary/83/Chmn., William T. Hale/56/Dir., Terry M. Brimer/60/Dir., Scott H. Reams/59/Dir., Jack E. Campbell/69/Dir., William F. Young/68/Dir.

Owners: Insiders/14.74%, William T. Hale/1.15%, Janet Ketner, Jane P. Hutton, Friedlander & Co., Inc./4.46%, Anderson L. Smith/1.80%, Scott H. Reams/2.05%, Charles G. Robinette, Bank of America Corporation/8.36%, Jack E. Campbell/1.39%, Terry M. Brimer/1.96%, William F. Young/1.36%, Anthony J. Carasso, Jefferson Federal Bank/10.37%, John F. McCrary/2.72%

Financial Data: *Fiscal Year End:*06/30 *Latest Annual Data:* 6/30/2006

Year		Sales		Net Income
2006		$19,760,000		$2,330,000
2005		$17,267,000		$3,450,000
2004		$17,134,000		$1,387,000
Curr. Assets:	$13,628,000	**Curr. Liab.:**	$251,299,000	**P/E Ratio:** 53.82
Plant, Equip.:	$12,000,000	**Total Liab.:**	$252,594,000	**Indic. Yr. Divd.:** $0.240
Total Assets:	$327,137,000	**Net Worth:**	$74,543,000	**Debt/ Equity:** NA

Jefferson Security Bank WVA

Washington & Princess St., Shepherdstown, WV, 25443; *PH:* 1-304-876-2501; *http://* www.jeffersonsecuritybank.com

General - Incorporation		**Stock** - Price on:12/24/2007	$123
Employees	NA	Stock Exchange	OTC
Auditor	NA	Ticker Symbol	JFWV
Stk Agt	Registrar and Transfer CO.	Outstanding Shares	NA
Counsel	NA	E.P.S.	NA
DUNS No.	NA	Shareholders	NA

Business: The groups principal activity is to provide banking services. The services of the group include originating loans, deposit account, brokerage and insurance, safe deposit boxes, ATM and debit card, wire transfer, night deposit and online banking. The group operates from the United States.

Primary SIC and add'l.: 6022

CIK No:

Officers: Stephen K. Morris/CEO, Pres., James M. Davis/Sec., Eric J. Lewis/CPA

Directors: William E. Knode/Chmn., Albert F. Kave/Vice Chmn., Monica W. Lingenfelter/Dir., Frederick K. Parsons/Dir., John W. Snyder/Dir., Suellen Myers/Dir.

Jefferson-Pilot Corp

100 N Greene St. , Greensboro, NC, 27401; *PH:* 1-336-691-3000; *http://* www.jpc.com

General - Incorporation	NC	Stock- Price on:12/24/2007	NA
Employees	NA	Stock Exchange	NA
Auditor	Ernst & Young LLP	Ticker Symbol	NA
Stk Agt	Wachovia Bank N.A	Outstanding Shares	NA
Counsel	NA	E.P.S.	NA
DUNS No.	04-635-6358	Shareholders	NA

Business: The group's principal activities are to write life insurance policies, annuity policies, group life, disability income and dental policies and selling other investment products. The group also operates radio and television broadcasting facilities and produces sports programs. The operations are carried out through five segments: life insurance products, annuity and investment products, non medical products, communications & corporate. The life insurance products segment offers a wide array of individual life insurance products including variable life insurance. The annuity and investment products segment offers both fixed and variable annuities and other investment products. Non medical products segment offers products such as term life, disability and dental insurance. Communications segment consists principally of radio and television broadcasting operations. The corporate segment includes activities which are not allocated to other segments.

Primary SIC and add'l.: 6311 6331 4833 4832 6321 6719

CIK No: 0000053347

Subsidiaries: Allied Professional Advisors, Inc., Hampshire Funding Inc., HARCO Capital Corp., Jefferson Pilot Financial Insurance Company, Jefferson Pilot Investment Advisory Corporation, Jefferson Pilot LifeAmerica Insurance Company, Jefferson Pilot Securities Corporation, Jefferson Pilot Variable Corporation, Jefferson Standard Life Insurance Company, Jefferson-Pilot Capital Trust A, Jefferson-Pilot Capital Trust B, Jefferson-Pilot Communications Company, Jefferson-Pilot Communications Company of California, Jefferson-Pilot Communications Company of Colorado, Jefferson-Pilot Communications Company of Florida 30 Subsidiaries included in the Index

Jeffersonville Bancorp

4864 State Rte. 52, Jeffersonville, NY, 12748; *PH:* 1-845-482-4000; *Fax:* 1-845-482-3544; *http://* www.jeffbank.com; *Email:* information@jeffbank.com

General - Incorporation	NY	Stock- Price on:12/24/2007	$18.36
Employees	133	Stock Exchange	NDQ
Auditor	Beard Miller Co. LLP	Ticker Symbol	JFBC
Stk Agt	American Stock Transfer & Trust Co.	Outstanding Shares	4,280,000
Counsel	NA	E.P.S.	$1.20
DUNS No.	78-715-4897	Shareholders	NA

Business: The group's principal activity is to provide a variety of deposit products for both individuals and businesses through its subsidiary, the first national bank of jeffersonville. The group provides depository products including traditional demand deposit accounts, interest bearing transaction accounts and savings account. It originates commercial loans, consumer loans and real estate loans designed to meet the banking needs of individual customers, businesses and municipalities. The group's main office is located in jeffersonville, New York and has nine additional branch offices located in eldred, liberty, loch sheldrake, monticello, livingston manor, narrowsburg, callicoon, wurtsboro and one in a wal*mart store in monticello.

Primary SIC and add'l.: 6712 6021

CIK No: 0000874495

Subsidiaries: The First National Bank of Jeffersonville

Officers: Raymond L. Walter/Dir., CEO, Pres./$437,411.00, Charles E. Burnett/Sr. VP, CFO/$202,601.00, Lorraine Lilholt/Branch Mgr. - Eldred, Deborah Forsblom/Branch Mgr. - Monticelloc, Kerri Jo Nebzydoski/Sales Mgr. - Wal*mart, Rosemarie Finkle/Assist., Branch Mgr. - Liberty, Karen Sayers/Assist. Branch Mgr. - Float, Diane McGrath/Assist. Loan Servicing Mgr., Marisa Heisler/Mgr., Loreen J. Gebelein/VP, Loan Servicing Mgr., Martha Huebsch/AVP, Quality Assurance Officer, John Russell/Auditor, Stacey Stephenson/BSA Officer, Barbara Hahl/Marketing Dir., Ronald Lewis/Accounting Supervisor *(37 Officers included in Index)*

Directors: Raymond L. Walter/Dir., CEO, Pres., Arthur E. Keesler/76/Dir., Edward T. Sykes/Dir., Kenneth C. Klein/47/Dir., Gibson E. McKean/Dir. Emeritus, Earle A. Wilde/Dir., John W. Galligan/Dir., James F. Roche/Dir., John K. Gempler/Dir., Douglas A. Heinle/Dir., Gilbert E. Weiss/Dir. Emeritus, Solomon Katzoff/Dir. Emeritus

Owners: Wayne V. Zanetti/0.26%, Kenneth C. Klein/0.07%, Douglas A. Heinle/1.14%, Edward T. Sykes/0.85%, James F. Roche/2.39%, Insiders/10.63%, Raymond Walter/0.54%, John W. Galligan/0.70%, Arthur E. Keesler/1.49%, Earle A. Wilde/1.52%, Charles E. Burnett/0.01%, John K. Gempler/1.66%

*Financial Data: Fiscal Year End:*12/31 *Latest Annual Data:* 12/31/2006

Year	Sales		Net Income
2006	$27,471,000		$4,943,000
2005	$26,233,000		$5,725,000
2004	$24,692,000		$6,171,000
Curr. Assets:	$14,711,000	Curr. Liab.: $345,976,000	P/E Ratio: 15.30
Plant, Equip.:	$3,040,000	Total Liab.: $356,016,000	Indic. Yr. Divd.: $0.480
Total Assets:	$397,291,000	Net Worth: $41,275,000	Debt/ Equity: NA

Jenex Corp

940 Sheldon Ct., Ste 207, Burlington, ON, L7L 5K6; *PH:* 1-905-632-3830; *http://* www.jenexcorp.com; *Email:* info@jenexcorp.com

General - Incorporation	Canada	Stock- Price on:12/24/2007	$0.29
Employees	NA	Stock Exchange	OTC
Auditor	Sloan Paskowitz Adelmanpartners LLP	Ticker Symbol	JNXCF
Stk Agt	Computershare Trust Co of Canada	Outstanding Shares	NA
Counsel	Heighington Law Firm B & S	E.P.S.	NA
DUNS No.	NA	Shareholders	NA

Business: The group's principal activities are medical device research and development focused on thermal therapy technology. The group operates in the healthcare segment. Therapik, the patented product of the group used for relief of pain and itch caused by insect stings and bites has been approved as a Class II medical device in Canada and the United States. The group's second product InterceptCS has been approved for marketing in Canada with the claim for prevention and relief of the symptoms of herpes labialis (cold sores) such as blistering, lesions, inflammation, and discomfort. Jenex holds the exclusive rights and patents to InterceptCS the hand-held thermal therapy device used for the prevention of cold sores. Worldwide markets including 22 Asian countries where licensing agreement for marketing Therapik has been signed in 2004. Therapik, the first trademarked product of the company is patented in the United States, Canada, Australia and Europe to protect the technology.

Primary SIC and add'l.: 3841

CIK No: 0001309552

Officers: Michael A. Jenkins/48/Dir., CEO, Pres., Sec., Donald F. Felice/60/Dir., VP, CFO, Mike Mayo/Dir. - Sales, Marketing

Directors: Michael A. Jenkins/48/Dir., CEO, Pres., Donald F. Felice/60/Dir., VP, CFO, Francis H. Barker/Dir., Wayne Izumi/Dir.

Jennifer Convertibles Inc

419 Crossways Pk. Dr., Woodbury, NY, 11797; *PH:* 1-516-496-1900; *Fax:* 1-516-496-0008; *http://* www.jenniferfurniture.com

General - Incorporation	DE	Stock- Price on:12/24/2007	$5
Employees	453	Stock Exchange	AMEX
Auditor	Eisner LLP	Ticker Symbol	JEN
Stk Agt	Continental Stock Transfer & Trust Co	Outstanding Shares	6,860,000
Counsel	NA	E.P.S.	$0.50
DUNS No.	15-480-6327	Shareholders	NA

Business: The group's principal activity is to operate sofabed specialty retail stores and leather retail stores. The products marketed in the retail outlets includes complete line of sofas and companion pieces, such as chairs and recliners, loveseats, in both leather and fabric which are designed to suit to a broad range of customers. The group also markets leather living room furniture. The trademarks of the group include, jennifer convertibles, jennifer leather stores under the private label bellissimo collection. At 30-Aug-2003, the group operated 197 jennifer convertibles stores and 17 jennifer leather stores, in which 76 stores are licensed. The group operates solely in the domestic market.

Primary SIC and add'l.: 5712

CIK No: 0000806817

Subsidiaries: Jennifer Chicago, L.P., Jennifer Warehousing, Inc.

Owners: Leslie Falchook/0.40%, Hans J. Klaussner and Klaussner Furniture Industries, Inc./11.80%, Kenneth S. Grossman/5.50%, Edward G. Bohn/1.50%, Nissan Aboodi/8.60%, David A. Belford/5.60%, M. Shanken Communications, Inc./8.30%, Kevin Mattler/0.40%, Jara Enterprises, Inc./1.30%, Harley J. Greenfield/19.10%, Mark Berman/1.40%, Rami Abada/10.60%, Insiders/37.20%, Edward B. Seidner/10.20%, Kevin J. Coyle/1.60% *(16 Owners included in Index)*

*Financial Data: Fiscal Year End:*08/27 *Latest Annual Data:* 8/26/2006

Year	Sales		Net Income
2006	$140,381,000		$5,220,000
2005	$121,907,000		-$3,870,000
2004	$134,170,000		-$4,142,000
Curr. Assets:	$24,352,000	Curr. Liab.: $25,388,000	P/E Ratio: 11.63
Plant, Equip.:	$3,032,000	Total Liab.: $28,708,000	Indic. Yr. Divd.: NA
Total Assets:	$31,522,000	Net Worth: $2,814,000	Debt/ Equity: NA

JER Investors Trust Inc

1650 Tysons Blvd., Ste. 1600, McLean, VA, 22102; *PH:* 1-703-714-8000; *Fax:* 1-703-714-8100; *http://* www.jer.com; *Email:* info@jerinvestors.com

General - Incorporation	MD	Stock- Price on:12/24/2007	$18.3699
Employees	NA	Stock Exchange	NYSE
Auditor	Ernst& Young LLP	Ticker Symbol	JRT
Stk Agt	American Stock Transfer & Trust Co.	Outstanding Shares	25,880,000
Counsel	O'Melveny & Myers LLP	E.P.S.	$1.54
DUNS No.	NA	Shareholders	NA

Business: The groups principle activity is to invest in commercial real estate properties. The group also provides loan services include mezzanine loans, bridge loans and whole mortgage loans. The group operates from the United States. The groups quarterly revenue for September 2007 was 36.16 millions of USD.

Primary SIC and add'l.: 6798

CIK No: 0001294017

Subsidiaries: JER CRE CDO 2005-1 Depositor, LLC, JER CRE CDO 2005-1, Limited, JER CRE CDO 2005-1, LLC, JER CRE CDO 2006-2 Depositor, LLC, JER CRE CDO 2006-2, Limited, JER CRE CDO 2006-2, LLC, JER Investors Trust Finance Company GS, LLC

Officers: Joseph E. Robert/Chmn., CEO, Keith W. Belcher/Vice Chmn., Exec. VP, Mark Weiss/Pres., Tae-Sik Yoon/CFO, Daniel T. Ward/Sec., Kenneth D. Krejca/VP, Michael J. McGillis/VP

Directors: Joseph E. Robert/Chmn., CEO, Keith W. Belcher/Vice Chmn., Exec. VP, Daniel J. Altobello/Dir., Frank Caufield/Dir., James V. Kimsey/Dir., Peter D. Linneman/Dir., Russell W. Ramsey/Dir.

Owners: James V. Kimsey, Daniel T. Ward, DePrince, Race& Zollo, Inc./5.30%, Kenneth D. Krejca, Russell W. Ramsey, Insiders/8.70%, Frank J. Caufield, Peter D. Linneman, Joseph E. Robert/6.70%, Wells Fargo& Company/5.20%, Third Avenue Management LLC/9.30%, Michael J. McGillis, Tae-Sik Yoon, Keith W. Belcher, Dreman Value Management LLC/7.60% *(19 Owners included in Index)*

*Financial Data: Fiscal Year End:*12/31 *Latest Annual Data:* 12/31/2006

Year	Sales		Net Income
2006	$74,010,000		$31,713,000
2005	$36,418,000		$19,560,000
Curr. Assets:	$234,915,000	Curr. Liab.: $21,572,000	P/E Ratio: 13.51
Plant, Equip.:	$38,740,000	Total Liab.: $997,980,000	Indic. Yr. Divd.: $1.800
Total Assets:	$1,367,961,000	Net Worth: $369,981,000	Debt/ Equity: 2.8243

Jersey Central Power & Light Co

76 S Main St., Akron, OH, 44308; *PH:* 1-800-736-3402; *http://* www.firstenergycorp.com

General - Incorporation	NJ	Stock - Price on:12/24/2007	NA
Employees	NA	Stock Exchange	NA
Auditor	PricewaterhouseCoopers LLP	Ticker Symbol	NA
Stk Agt	FirstEnergy Securities Transfer Co	Outstanding Shares	NA
Counsel	NA	E.P.S.	NA
DUNS No.	00-697-3358	Shareholders	NA

Business: The group's principal activity is to provide retail electric energy services in northern, western and east central New Jersey. Firstenergy also holds directly all of the issued and outstanding common shares of Ohio edison company, the cleveland electric illuminating company, the toledo edison company, American transmission systems inc, metropolitan edison company and Pennsylvania electric company. The group distributes and sells electric energy in an area of approximately 3,300 square miles in New Jersey. It also sells, purchases and interchanges electric energy with other electric companies. The area it serves has a population of approximately 2.7 million.

Primary SIC and add'l.: 3568 4911

CIK No: 0000053456

Subsidiaries: American Transmission Systems, Inc, Centerior Service Company, FE Acquisition Corp., FELHC, Inc., FirstEnergy Facilities Services Group, LLC, FirstEnergy Foundation, FirstEnergy Nuclear Generation Corp., FirstEnergy Nuclear Operating Company, FirstEnergy Properties Company, FirstEnergy Securities Transfer Company, FirstEnergy Service Company, FirstEnergy Solutions Corp., FirstEnergy Telecom Services, Inc, FirstEnergy Ventures Corp., GPU Capital, Inc. 26 Subsidiaries included in the Index

Officers: Stephen E. Morgan/57/Pres., Leila L. Vespoli/48/Dir., Sr. VP, General Counsel, J. F. Pearson/53/VP, Treasurer, Donald M. Lynch/Regional Pres., S. E. Morgan/57/Pres. - JCP, L, Harvey L. Wagner/55/VP, Controller, Chief Accounting Officer, Richard H. Marsh/57/Sr. VP, CFO

Directors: Leila L. Vespoli/48/Dir., Sr. VP, General Counsel, Charles E. Jones/Dir., Mark A. Julian/51/Dir., Bradley S. Ewing/47/Dir., Gelorma E. Persson/77/Dir., Stanley C. Van Ness/Dir.

Owners: Bradley S. Ewing, Anthony J. Alexander, Stephen E. Morgan, Donald R. Schneider, Leila L. Vespoli, Jesse T. Williams, Insiders, Mark A. Julian, Richard R. Grigg, Richard H. Marsh

Jet Gold Corp

1102 - 475 Howe St., Vancouver, BC, V6C 2B3; **PH:** 1-604-687-7828; **http://** www.jetgoldcorp.com; **Email:** info@jetgoldcorp.com

General - Incorporation	Canada	Stock - Price on:12/24/2007	$0.3056
Employees	NA	Stock Exchange	OTC
Auditor	Smythe Ratcliffe LLP	Ticker Symbol	JAUGF
Stk Agt	Pacific Corporate Trust Co	Outstanding Shares	NA
Counsel	Tupper Jonsson Yeadon	E.P.S.	NA
DUNS No.	NA	Shareholders	NA

Business: The group is actively engaged in the acquisition and exploration of natural resources and mineral properties in Canada and other global locations. The company has an interest in and holds the minerals rights of gold property in the West Okanagan region of British Columbia in the Similkameen Mining Division. The company's major focus for the near future is the Set Ga Done Project - covering 700 square kilometers of mineral-rich land in North-East Shan State, Myanmar.

Primary SIC and add'l.: 1400

CIK No: 0001318596

Officers: Robert L. Card/70/Dir., CEO, Pres., Lana B. Turner/53/Corp. Sec., Blaine Y. Bailey/CFO, Alex Burton/Consulting Project Geologist, Betty Anne Loy/Corp. Sec.

Directors: Robert L. Card/70/Dir., CEO, Pres., Robert M. Kaplan/Dir., Keith E. Robinson/Dir., Len Harris/Dir., Wayne Waters/Member - Advisory Board, Zigurts Strauss/Dir.

Owners: Leonard Harris/1.48%, Lana Bea Turner, Robert L. Card/11.38%, Insiders/20.93%, Robert Kaplan/4.26%, Keith E. Robinson/1.81%, Zigurts Strauts/1.45%, Blaine Bailey/1.78%

Jetblue Airways Corp

118-29 Queens Blvd., Forest Hills, NY, 11375; **PH:** 1-718-286-7900; **Fax:** 1-718-709-3621; **http://** www.jetblue.com

General - Incorporation	DE	Stock - Price on:12/24/2007	$11.11
Employees	8,393	Stock Exchange	NDQ
Auditor	Ernst & Young LLP	Ticker Symbol	JBLU
Stk Agt	Computershare Trust CO.	Outstanding Shares	178,550,000
Counsel	NA	E.P.S.	$0.21
DUNS No.	NA	Shareholders	NA

Business: The group's principle activity is to provide passenger air transportation service with focus on underserved markets and large metropolitan areas that have high average fares. The revenue of the group is earned from passenger transportation and other components. The passenger air transportation segment provides low-fare passenger air transportation service. The other component derives its revenues from mails, excess baggage charges, commissions from Website travel sales, sale of liquor in-flight, concessions and change in customer's reservations. The group's quarterly revenue for September 2007 was 765.00 millions of USD.

Primary SIC and add'l.: 4512

CIK No: 0001158463

Subsidiaries: BlueBermuda Insurance, LTD., LiveTV International, Inc., LiveTV, LLC

Officers: David Neeleman/Chmn., CEO/$257,672.00, David Barger/Dir., COO, Pres./$521,998.00, Holly Nelson/50/Sr. VP, Controller, Jim Hnat/37/Sr. VP, General Counsel, Assist. Sec., John Harvey/42/CFO, Exec. VP/$539,052.00, Thomas Kelly/55/Exec. VP, Sec., John Owen/52/Exec. VP - Supply Chain, Information Technology/$390,713.00, Russ Chew/COO, Pres., Ed Barnes/Interim CFO, Principal Accounting Officer, Sr. VP - Finance, James Hnat/Exec. VP - Corporate Affairs, General Counsel, Corp. Sec., Trey Urbahn/Exec. VP, Chief Revenue Officer, Rob Maruster/36/Sr. VP - Airports, Operational Planning

Directors: David Neeleman/Chmn., CEO, Joel Peterson/Vice Chmn., Joy Covey/Dir., Frank Sica/Dir., David Checketts/Dir., Kim Clark/Dir., Angela Gittens/Dir., Virginia Gambale/Dir., Neal Moszkowski/Dir., Ann Rhoades/Dir., David Barger/Dir., COO, Pres., Robert Clanin/Dir.

Owners: FMR Corp./14.80%, David Barger, Thomas Anderson, George Soros and related entities/9.50%, Frank Sica, Capital Research and Management Company/8.70%, Angela Gittens, John Owen, Virginia Gambale, Joel Peterson, Wellington Management Company, LLP/7.70%, Neal Moszkowski, John Harvey, Timothy Claydon, Insiders/8.20% (19 Owners included in Index)

Financial Data: Fiscal Year End:12/31   Latest Annual Data: 06/30/2007

Year	Sales	Net Income
2007	NA	NA
2006	NA	NA
2005	$1,701,000,000	-$20,000,000

Curr. Assets:	$927,000,000	**Curr. Liab.:**	$854,000,000	**P/E Ratio:**	222.20
Plant, Equip.:	$3,438,000,000	**Total Liab.:**	$3,891,000,000	**Indic. Yr. Divd.:**	NA
Total Assets:	$4,843,000,000	**Net Worth:**	$952,000,000	**Debt/ Equity:**	2.7968

Jewett-Cameron Trading Co Ltd

PO Box 1010, North Plains, OR, 97133; **PH:** 1-503-647-0110; **Fax:** 1-503-647-2272; **http://** www.jewettcameron.com

General - Incorporation	BC	Stock - Price on:12/24/2007	$7.5401
Employees	59	Stock Exchange	NDQ
Auditor	Davidson & Co LLP	Ticker Symbol	JCTCF
Stk Agt	Computershare Trust Co	Outstanding Shares	2,380,000
Counsel	Richards Buell Sutton	E.P.S.	$0.97
DUNS No.	11-874-5363	Shareholders	NA

Business: The group's principal activity is to operate as a wholesaler of lumber and building materials to home improvement centers located primarily in the pacific and rocky mountain regions of the United States. The group operates as an importer and distributor of pneumatic air tools and industrial clamps throughout the United States. The group is a processor and distributor of agricultural seeds in the United States. The group is also a processor and distributor of industrial wood and other building products to original equipment manufacturers. The group through the subsidiaries operates out of facilities located in north plains, Oregon and ogden, Utah. Major customers of the group are lowes companies, fred meyer inc, the home depot inc, homebase inc and U.S. Marine.

Primary SIC and add'l.: 5211 2079 5085

CIK No: 0000885307

Subsidiaries: JCLC

Officers: Donald M. Boone/68/Dir., CEO, Pres., Treasurer, Jon Lagmay/Contact - Sales, Jason Dovenberg/Contact - Sales, Nunie Salinas/Contact - Sales, Michael C. Nasser/62/Corp. Sec., Terry D. Schumacher/62/CFO

Directors: Donald M. Boone/68/Dir., CEO, Pres., Treasurer, Ted A. Sharp/60/Dir., Richard Y. Cheong/52/Dir., Jeffrey G. Wade/67/Dir.

Owners: Terry D. Schumacher/0.40%, Insiders/50.60%, Michael C. Nasser/9.50%, Donald M. Boone/23.60%, Ted A. Sharp/0.10%, Jewett-Cameron ESOP and Trust/17.00%

Financial Data: Fiscal Year End:08/31   Latest Annual Data: 08/31/2007

Year	Sales	Net Income
2007	$70,516,000	$2,295,000
2006	$76,096,000	$2,339,000
2005	$74,617,000	$931,000

Curr. Assets:	$15,864,000	**Curr. Liab.:**	$4,152,000	**P/E Ratio:**	8.98
Plant, Equip.:	$2,218,000	**Total Liab.:**	$6,234,000	**Indic. Yr. Divd.:**	NA
Total Assets:	$18,225,000	**Net Worth:**	$11,990,000	**Debt/ Equity:**	0.1861

Jilin Chemical Industrial Co Ltd

No. 9 Longtan St., Longtan District, Jilin City; ; **http://** www.jcic.com.cn

General - Incorporation	China	Stock - Price on:12/24/2007	NA
Employees	NA	Stock Exchange	NA
Auditor	PricewaterhouseCoopers LLP	Ticker Symbol	NA
Stk Agt	NA	Outstanding Shares	NA
Counsel	Morrison & Foerster LLP	E.P.S.	NA
DUNS No.	65-371-6118	Shareholders	NA

Business: The group's principal activities are production and sale of petroleum products, petrochemical an organic chemical products, synthetic rubber products, chemical fertilizers and other chemical products and provision of related services. Operations are carried out mainly in the People's Republic of China.

Primary SIC and add'l.: 2869 2822 2911 1479

CIK No: 0000944476

Subsidiaries: Jilin Chemical Group Corporation, Jilin City Songmei Acetic Acid Co.,Ltd, Jilin Jihua Jianxiu Company Limited, Jilin Jihua Jinxiang Pressure Vessel Inspection, Jilin Winsway Chemical Industrial Store and Transport Limited, Jilin Xinhua Nitrochloro-benzene Company Limited

Jingwei International Ltd

Formerly: Neoview Holding Inc
730 W Randolph, Ste. 600, Chicago, IL, 60661; **PH:** 1-312-454-0015

General - Incorporation	NV	Stock - Price on:12/24/2007	NA
Employees	NA	Stock Exchange	NA
Auditor	Amisano Hanson	Ticker Symbol	NA
Stk Agt	Nevada Agency & Trust Company	Outstanding Shares	NA
Counsel	NA	E.P.S.	NA
DUNS No.	NA	Shareholders	NA

Business: The groups principal activities include developing and maintaining an Internet auto parts and tool trade. The group operates from the United States.

Primary SIC and add'l.: 7389

CIK No: 0001314183

Owners: George Du/48.00%, Insiders/48.00%

Financial Data: Fiscal Year End:05/31   Latest Annual Data: 05/31/2006

Year	Sales	Net Income
2006	NA	-$49,000

Curr. Assets:	$0	**Curr. Liab.:**	$5,000		
Plant, Equip.:	NA	**Total Liab.:**	$5,000	**Indic. Yr. Divd.:**	NA
Total Assets:	$0	**Net Worth:**	-$5,000	**Debt/ Equity:**	NA

Jinpan International Ltd

560 Sylvan Ave., 3rd Fl., Englewood Cliffs, NJ, 07632; *PH:* 1-201-227-0680; *Fax:* 1-201-227-0685; *http://* www.ir-site.com

General - Incorporation British Virgin Islands	**Stock**- Price on:12/24/2007 $19.76
Employees 4	Stock Exchange AMEX
Auditor Grant Thornton LLP	Ticker Symbol JST
Stk Agt American Stock Transfer & Trust Co.	Outstanding Shares 7,960,000
Counsel Mr. Burris	E.P.S. $1.62
DUNS No. NA	Shareholders NA

Business: The groups principle activities include designing, manufacturing and selling of cast resin transformers for voltage distribution equipment. The group operates from United States.

Primary SIC and add'l.: 3677

CIK No: 0001053008

Subsidiaries: Hainan Jinpan Electric Company, Ltd, Jinpan International (U.S.A.) Ltd

Officers: Zhiyuan Li/Chmn., CEO, Pres., Xiangsheng Ling/Vice Chmn., VP, Yuqing Jing/Sec., Mark Du/Principal Financial Officer, Rick Wolff/VP - Business Development

Directors: Zhiyuan Li/Chmn., CEO, Pres., Xiangsheng Ling/Vice Chmn., VP, Li-Wen Zhang/53/Dir., Donald S. Burris/64/Dir., Stephan R. Clark/54/Dir.

Owners: Stephan R. Clark, Insiders/34.54%, Li Zhiyuan/22.67%, Jing Yuqing/22.67%, Ling Xiangsheng/11.67%, Li-wen Zhang, Donald S. Burris

Financial Data: *Fiscal Year End:*12/31 *Latest Annual Data:* 12/31/2006

Year	Sales	Net Income
2006	$82,800,000	$7,514,000
2005	$53,945,000	$4,536,000
2004	$42,460,000	$3,489,000

Curr. Assets:	$84,679,000	**Curr. Liab.:**	$26,296,000		
Plant, Equip.:	$5,872,000	**Total Liab.:**	$27,872,000	**Indic. Yr. Divd.:**	$0.240
Total Assets:	$90,652,000	**Net Worth:**	$62,780,000	**Debt/ Equity:**	NA

JLG Industries Inc

1 Jlg Dr., Mcconnellsburg, PA, 17233; *PH:* 1-717-485-5161; *http://* www.jlg.com

General - Incorporation PA	**Stock**- Price on:12/24/2007 NA
Employees 4,088	Stock Exchange NA
Auditor Ernst & Young LLP	Ticker Symbol NA
Stk Agt American Stock Transfer & Trust Co.	Outstanding Shares NA
Counsel NA	E.P.S. NA
DUNS No. 04-388-7728	Shareholders NA

Business: The groups principle activities include manufacturing and marketing access equipment. The groups products include aerial work platforms, excavators, trailers and material handlers. The groups products are sold under the brand names JLG, Manlift, SkyTrak, Lull and Toucan brands. The group operates from United States.

Primary SIC and add'l.: 6159 7359 3535 7353 3531

CIK No: 0000216275

Subsidiaries: Access Financial Solutions, Inc., Fulton International, Inc., JLG Deutschland, GmbH, JLG Equipment Services Ltd., JLG Equipment Services, Inc., JLG Europe BV, JLG France SAS, JLG Industries (Italia) S.r.L, JLG Industries (Norge) AS, JLG Industries (Proprietary) Ltd., JLG Industries (United Kingdom) Ltd., JLG Latino Americana Ltda, JLG Manufacturing Europe BVBA, JLG Manufacturing Services Europe Maatschap, JLG OmniQuip, Inc. 19 Subsidiaries included in the Index

Officers: William M. Lasky/Chmn., CEO, Pres., Thomas D. Singer/Sr. VP, General Counsel, Sec., Phillip H. Rehbein/Sr. VP - Finance, Craig E. Paylor/Sr. VP - Sales, Marketing, Customer Support, Israel Celli/VP - International Sales, Marketing, Customer Support, John F. Louderback/VP - Customer Support Services, Robert E. Cribbs/VP, Treasurer, Wayne P. MacDonald/Sr. VP - Engineering, Peter L. Bonafede/Sr. VP - Manufacturing, James H. Woodward/CFO, Exec. VP, Dale L. Robertson/CIO, VP, Samuel D. Swope/VP - Human Resources, David A. Peacock/VP - Government Products, Programs, Denny Buterbaugh/Dir. - Government Sales

Directors: William M. Lasky/Chmn., CEO, Pres., George R. Kempton/Dir., Thomas C. Wajnert/Dir., James A. Mezera/Dir., Roy V. Armes/Dir., Raymond C. Stark/Dir., Stephen Rabinowitz/Dir., Charles O. Wood/Dir.

JMAR Technologies Inc

10905 Technology Pl., San Diego, CA, 92127; *PH:* 1-858-946-6800; *Fax:* 1-858-946-6899; *http://* www.jmar.com; *Email:* jmarcorporate@jmar.com

General - Incorporation DE	**Stock**- Price on:12/24/2007 NA
Employees 65	Stock Exchange NDQ
Auditor Grant Thornton LLP	Ticker Symbol JMAR
Stk Agt Computershare Trust Co	Outstanding Shares NA
Counsel NA	E.P.S. NA
DUNS No. 18-549-4788	Shareholders NA

Business: The group's principal activities are to develop and manufacture light-based manufacturing systems and specialty semiconductors. The group operates in the three divisions: research, systems and microelectronics. The research division acts as an innovator of laser and laser-produced plasma technologies for the group's cpl source, euv generators and related products such as high-brightness lasers. Systems division encompasses the development of X-ray lithography steppers and the product engineering, production and integration of cpl light sources and complete cpl stepper systems. The microelectronics division provides process integration and maintenance support for the defense microelectronics activity semiconductor fabrication facility.

Primary SIC and add'l.: 9999 8731 3844 3674 3825 3829

CIK No: 0000857953

Officers: Neil C. Beer/CEO, Pres., David L. McCarty/VP - Business Developement, Doug Cheng/VP - Operations, Robert A. Selzer/Sr. VP - Technology, John P. Ricardi/VP - Sensor Products Group, Kathi Kirchmeier/Mgr. - Marketing Communications, Edward C. Hall/CFO

Directors: Barry Ressler/Dir., Paul J. Gilman/Dir., Charles A. Dickinson/Dir., Edward P. O'Sullivan/Dir.

Owners: Charles A. Dickinson, Douglas Cheng, Laurus Master Fund, Ltd./9.99%, Paul J. Gilman, Insiders/3.18%, Barry Ressler, John P. Ricardi, Neil C. Beer, Dennis E. Valentine

Jo-Ann Stores Inc

5555 Darrow Rd., Hudson, OH, 44236; *PH:* 1-330-656-2600; *Fax:* 1-330-463-6675; *http://* www.joann.com

General - Incorporation OH	**Stock**- Price on:12/24/2007 $29.79
Employees 5,570	Stock Exchange NYSE
Auditor Ernst & Young LLP	Ticker Symbol JAS
Stk Agt EquiServe Trust Co N.A	Outstanding Shares 24,960,000
Counsel NA	E.P.S. NA
DUNS No. 00-294-4684	Shareholders NA

Business: The groups principle activity is to operate retail stores. The groups products include a variety of merchandise used in sewing, crafting and home decorating projects, including fabrics, notions, crafts, frames, paper crafting material, artificial and dried flowers, home accents, finished seasonal and home decor merchandise. The group operates from United States.

Primary SIC and add'l.: 5699 5949 5999

CIK No: 0000034151

Subsidiaries: FCA of Ohio, Inc., House of Fabrics, Jo-Ann Stores Asia, Limited, Jo-Ann Stores Supply Chain Management, Inc., Team Jo-Ann, Inc.

Officers: Darrell Webb/Chmn., CEO, Pres./$1,528,838.00, David Holmberg/49/Exec. VP - Operations/$1,332,553.00, James Kerr/CFO, Exec. VP/$659,285.00, Travis Smith/Exec. VP - Merchandising, Marketing/$847,812.00, Kenneth Haverkost/Exec. VP - Store Operations

Directors: Darrell Webb/Chmn., CEO, Pres., Scott Cowen/Dir., Ira J. Gumberg/Dir., Patricia B. Morrison/48/Dir., Frank Newman/59/Dir., Beryl Raff/Dir., Alan Rosskamm/Dir., Gregg Searle/Dir., Tracey T. Travis/Dir.

Owners: Barclays Global Investor, NA and affiliates/5.00%, Insiders/7.70%, James Kerr, Alan Rosskamm/5.66%, Patricia Morrison, Tracey Travis, Travis Smith, Frank Newman, Dimensional Fund Advisors LP/8.13%, Gregg Searle, First Pacific Advisors, LLC/10.51%, Scott Cowen, Beryl Raff, David Holmberg, Ira Gumberg *(16 Owners included in Index)*

Financial Data: *Fiscal Year End:*01/31 *Latest Annual Data:* 2/3/2007

Year	Sales	Net Income
2007	$1,850,600,000	-$1,900,000
2006	$1,882,800,000	-$23,000,000
2005	$1,812,400,000	$46,200,000

Curr. Assets:	$534,200,000	**Curr. Liab.:**	$222,300,000	**P/E Ratio:**	229.15
Plant, Equip.:	$311,800,000	**Total Liab.:**	$446,900,000	**Indic. Yr. Divd.:**	NA
Total Assets:	$856,700,000	**Net Worth:**	$409,800,000	**Debt/ Equity:**	0.4888

Joes Jeans Inc

Formerly: Innovo Group Inc
5901 Se Ave., Commerce, CA, 90040; *PH:* 1-323-837-3700; *http://* www.innovogroup.com

General - Incorporation DE	**Stock**- Price on:12/24/2007 $1.5
Employees 124	Stock Exchange NDQ
Auditor Ernst & Young LLP	Ticker Symbol INNO
Stk Agt Continental Stock Transfer & Trust Co	Outstanding Shares 41,180,000
Counsel NA	E.P.S. -$0.01
DUNS No. 62-644-3204	Shareholders NA

Business: The group's principle activity is to manufacture and distribute various cut and sewn canvas and nylon consumer products, such as tote bags, insulated lunch bags and coolers along with aprons. The group operates in two business segments: crafts and accessories segment and apparel segment. The crafts and accessories segment develops craft canvas, denim totebags, and aprons. The apparel segment incorporates the joe's jeans brand of men and women's denim apparel products and knit shirts and other general apparel items. The group's primary customers include major retailers such as wal-Mart, michael's, hobby lobby, dollar general, goody's and joanne's. The group's sales and marketing offices are located in los angeles, ca and knoxville, tn with showrooms in New York city and los angeles, ca. The group's quarterly revenue for Sep'07 was 15.71 millions of USD.

Primary SIC and add'l.: 2394 2399 2393

CIK No: 0000844143

Subsidiaries: Innovo Azteca Apparel, Inc., Joes Jeans, Inc.

Officers: Marc B. Crossman/CEO, Pres.

Directors: Samuel J. Furrow/Chmn., Samuel J. Furrow/Dir., Kelly Hoffman/Dir., Tom Oriordan/Dir., Suhail Rizvi/Dir., Kent Savage/Dir.

Owners: Tom ORiordan, Windsong DB, LLC/11.75%, BSS-Joes Investors, LLC and Barry S. Sternlicht/11.62%, Samuel J. Furrow/7.32%, Hamish Sandhu, Kelly Hoffman, Azteca Production International,Inc./9.11%, Paul Guez/5.23%, Innavation LLC, Seymour Braun, Yardworth/5.68%, Insiders/11.72%, Marc B. Crossman/3.65%, Suhail R. Rizvi, Kent Savage

Financial Data: *Fiscal Year End:*11/26 *Latest Annual Data:* 11/25/2006

Year	Sales	Net Income
2006	$46,633,000	-$9,293,000
2005	$108,590,000	-$16,433,000
2004	$104,708,000	-$9,576,000

Curr. Assets:	$13,510,000	**Curr. Liab.:**	$9,237,000		
Plant, Equip.:	$270,000	**Total Liab.:**	$17,864,000	**Indic. Yr. Divd.:**	NA
Total Assets:	$38,143,000	**Net Worth:**	$20,279,000	**Debt/ Equity:**	NA

John B Sanfilippo & Son Inc

1703 N Randall Rd., Elgin, IL, 60123; *PH:* 1-847-289-1800; *Fax:* 1-847-289-1843; *http://* www.jbssinc.com

General - Incorporation DE	**Stock**- Price on:12/24/2007 $10.5
Employees 1,800	Stock Exchange NDQ
Auditor PricewaterhouseCoopers LLP	Ticker Symbol JBSS
Stk Agt American Stock Transfer & Trust Co.	Outstanding Shares 10,720,000
Counsel Katz & Karacic	E.P.S. -$1.83
DUNS No. 02-529-3481	Shareholders NA

Business: The group's principal activities are to process, pack, market and distribute shelled and inshell nuts. The products processed include peanuts, pecans, walnuts, cashews, almonds, filberts, pistachios, macadamias, Brazil nuts and pine nuts. The products are sold under various brand names

including fisher, evon's, sunshine country, flavor tree, Texas pride and tom scott. The group also markets and distributes a diverse product line of food and snack items like peanut butter, candy and confectioneries. The products are sold to retail, wholesale, industrial, government and food service customers on a national level. It also manufactures, processes and packs the retail brands of several other snacks food companies.

Primary SIC and add'l.: 0723 2068

CIK No: 0000880117

Subsidiaries: JBSS Properties, LLC

Officers: Jeffrey T. Sanfilippo/45/Dir., CEO, Jasper B. Sanfilippo/40/Dir., COO, Pres., Treasurer, Assist. Sec., Herbert J. Marros/50/Dir. - Financial Reporting, Taxation, Michael J. Valentine/49/Dir., CFO, Group Pres., Sec., Everardo Soria/51/Sr. VP - Pecan Operations, Procurement, Charles M. Nicketta/60/Sr. VP - Manufacturing, William R. Pokrajac/54/VP - Risk Management, Investor Relations, Walter Tankersley/56/Sr. VP - Industrial Sales, James A. Valentine/44/CIO, Michael G. Cannon/55/Sr. VP - Corporate Operations, Frank S. Pellegrino/34/Corporate Controller

Directors: Jeffrey T. Sanfilippo/45/Dir., CEO, Jasper B. Sanfilippo/77/Chmn., Mathias A. Valentine/75/Dir., Michael J. Valentine/49/Dir., CFO, Group Pres., Sec., Timothy R. Donovan/52/Dir., Jasper B. Sanfilippo/40/Dir., COO, Pres., Treasurer, Assist. Sec., Daniel M. Wright/70/Dir., Jim Edgar/62/Dir.

Owners: James J. Sanfilippo, James A. Valentine, Insiders/2.10%, Timothy R. Donovan, Jeffrey T. Sanfilippo, Jasper B. Sanfilippo, Jeffrey T. Sanfilippo, Insiders, Pekin Singer Strauss Asset Mgmt./8.20%, Marian R. Sanfilippo, John E. Sanfilippo, Advisory Research, Inc./5.90%, Daniel M. Wright, Michael J. Valentine, Lisa A. Evon *(25 Owners included in Index)*

Financial Data: ***Fiscal Year End:***06/30 ***Latest Annual Data:*** 6/29/2006

Year	Sales	Net Income
2006	$579,564,000	-$16,721,000
2005	$581,729,000	$14,499,000
2004	$520,811,000	$22,630,000

Curr. Assets:	$261,916,000	***Curr. Liab.:***	$124,152,000		
Plant, Equip.:	$117,769,000	***Total Liab.:***	$198,297,000	***Indic. Yr. Divd.:***	NA
Total Assets:	$394,472,000	***Net Worth:***	$196,175,000	***Debt/ Equity:***	0.1186

John D. Oil & Gas Company

8500 Sta. St., Ste. 345, Mentor, OH, 44060; ***PH:*** 1-440-255-6325; ***Fax:*** 1-440-205-8680; ***http://*** www.johndoilandgas.com

General - Incorporation	MD	***Stock*** - Price on:12/24/2007	$0.45
Employees	10	Stock Exchange	OTC
Auditor	Hausser & Taylor, LLC	Ticker Symbol	JDOG
Stk Agt	Registrar & Transfer Co	Outstanding Shares	9,000,000
Counsel	NA	E.P.S	-$0.22
DUNS No.	NA	Shareholders	NA

Business: The groups principle activity is to explore oil and natural gas. The group operates through two segments namely oil and natural gas and self-storage facilities. The group operates from the United States. The group's quarterly revenue for Sep '07 was 0.73 millions of USD.

Primary SIC and add'l.: 6798 1311

CIK No: 0001086411

Officers: Richard M. Osborne/Dir., Chmn., CEO, Gregory J. Osborne/Dir., COO, Pres., Marc C. Krantz/Dir., Sec., Jean C. Mihitsch/CFO, Assist. Sec., Jeffery J. Heidnik/VP - Operations, Holly Bralley/Executive Assist., Paul Lehtonen/Landowner Relations, Bill Sochor/Title Research, Mike Dinsmore/Geologist, Jessica Dolinar/Accounting Payable Clerk, Erin Steele/Geologist, Tim Reilly/Geologist, Amy Caunter/Title Research

Directors: Richard M. Osborne/Dir., Chmn., CEO, Gregory J. Osborne/Dir., COO, Pres., Marc C. Krantz/Dir., Sec., Steven A. Calabrese/Dir., Terence P. Coyne/Dir., Richard T. Flenner/Dir., Mark D. Grossi/Dir., Thomas J. Smith/Dir., James R. Smail/Dir.

Owners: Richard T. Flenner, Jeffrey J. Heidnik, Steven A. Calabrese/4.90%, Thomas J. Smith, Richard A. Bonner/5.60%, Insiders/55.80%, Gregory J. Osborne/1.70%, Marc C. Krantz, Mark D. Grossi/2.30%, Terence P. Coyne/2.30%, Richard M. Osborne/49.20%, James R. Smail/2.20%

Financial Data: ***Fiscal Year End:***12/31 ***Latest Annual Data:*** 12/31/2006

Year	Sales	Net Income
2006	$1,928,000	-$1,962,000
2005	$550,000	$1,788,000
2004	$501,000	$3,000

Curr. Assets:	$1,257,000	***Curr. Liab.:***	$4,492,000		
Plant, Equip.:	$8,239,000	***Total Liab.:***	$6,647,000	***Indic. Yr. Divd.:***	NA
Total Assets:	$9,543,000	***Net Worth:***	$2,897,000	***Debt/ Equity:***	0.7108

John Wiley & Sons Inc

111 River St., Ste. 2000, Hoboken, NJ, 07030; ***PH:*** 1-201-748-6000; ***Fax:*** 1-201-748-6088; ***http://*** www.wiley.com

General - Incorporation	NY	***Stock*** - Price on:12/24/2007	$47.37
Employees	3,600	Stock Exchange	NYSE
Auditor	KPMG LLP	Ticker Symbol	JW-A
Stk Agt	Registrar & Transfer Co	Outstanding Shares	57,430,000
Counsel	NA	E.P.S	$1.71
DUNS No.	00-151-9248	Shareholders	NA

Business: The group's principal activity is to publish print and electronic products. The group's core businesses include professional and consumer books and subscription services; scientific, technical and medical journals, encyclopedias, books and online products and services and educational materials for undergraduate and graduate students and lifelong learners. The group has publishing, marketing and distribution centers in the United States, Canada, Europe, Asia and Australia.

Primary SIC and add'l.: 2731 7375

CIK No: 0000107140

Subsidiaries: GIT Verlag GmbH & Co. KG, HMI Investment, Inc., John Wiley & Sons (Asia) Pte. Ltd., John Wiley & Sons (HK) Limited, John Wiley & Sons Australia, Ltd., John Wiley & Sons Canada Limited, John Wiley & Sons GmbH, John Wiley & Sons International Rights, Inc., John Wiley & Sons Ltd., Jws Dcm, LLC, Jws Hq, LLC, Wiley Distribution Services Limited, Wiley Europe Investment Holdings Ltd., Wiley Europe Limited, Wiley Heyden Ltd. 24 Subsidiaries included in the Index

Officers: William J. Pesce/Dir., CEO, Pres./$8,111,846.00, Mark Allin/MD - John Wiley, Sons, Asia Pte, Ltd, Singapore, William J. Arlington/Sr. VP - Human Resources, John Jarvis/Sr. VP - Europe, MD - Wiley Europe Limited, Ellis E. Cousens/Exec. VP, Chief Financial, Operations Officer/$2,928,969.00, Warren C. Fristensky/Sr. VP - Information Technology, CIO, Eric A. Swanson/Sr. VP - Wiley, Blackwell/$2,977,700.00, Timothy B. King/Sr. VP - Planning, Development, Peter C. Donoughue/MD - John Wiley, Sons Australia, Ltd, Gary M. Rinck/Sr. VP, General Counsel, Vincent Marzano/VP, Treasurer, Rene Olivieri/COO - Wiley, Blackwell, Deborah E. Wiley/Sr. VP - Corporate Communications, Josephine Bacchi-Mourtziou/VP, Corp. Sec., Steve Smith/COO - UK Publishing, Sr. VP - International Development *(20 Officers included in Index)*

Directors: William J. Pesce/Dir., CEO, Pres., Peter B. Wiley/Chmn., Warren J. Baker/Dir., William B. Plummer/Dir., Matthew S. Kissner/Dir., Bradford Wiley/Dir., Richard M. Hochhauser/Dir., Eduardo Menasce/Dir., Kim Jones/Dir., Raymond W. McDaniel/Dir.

Owners: Insiders/82.80%, Bradford Wiley/27.50%, Raymond W. McDaniel, Peter Booth Wiley/3.00%, Eric A. Swanson, William J. Pesce/3.50%, Ellis E. Cousens/0.50%, Peter Booth Wiley/27.50%, Matthew S. Kissner, Bonnie E. Lieberman/0.60%, Bradford Wiley/2.80%, Stephen A. Kippur/0.80%, Warren J. Baker, Insiders/15.20%, Eric A. Swanson/0.60%

Financial Data: ***Fiscal Year End:***04/30 ***Latest Annual Data:*** 4/30/2006

Year	Sales	Net Income
2006	$1,044,185,000	$110,328,000
2005	$974,048,000	$83,841,000
2004	$922,962,000	$88,840,000

Curr. Assets:	$326,308,000	***Curr. Liab.:***	$362,109,000	***P/E Ratio:***	27.70
Plant, Equip.:	$167,764,000	***Total Liab.:***	$624,169,000	***Indic. Yr. Divd.:***	$0.400
Total Assets:	$1,026,009,000	***Net Worth:***	$401,840,000	***Debt/ Equity:***	0.1630

Johnson & Johnson

1 Johnson & Johnson Plz., New Brunswick, NJ, 08933; ***PH:*** 1-732-524-0400; ***Fax:*** 1-732-214-0332; ***http://*** www.jnj.com

General - Incorporation	NJ	***Stock*** - Price on:12/24/2007	$62.33
Employees	122,200	Stock Exchange	NYSE
Auditor	PricewaterhouseCoopers LLP	Ticker Symbol	JNJ
Stk Agt	Computershare Trust Co	Outstanding Shares	2,900,000,000
Counsel	NA	E.P.S	$3.55
DUNS No.	00-130-7081	Shareholders	NA

Business: The group's principle activity is to manufacture health care products. The group's products include baby, dental and diabetes care, first aid, nutritional, women's health, pain relievers, skin and hair care, and gastro intestinal and medical devices. Customers served by the group include pharmaceutical, medical devices and diagnostics markets. In February 2007, the group acquired Conor Medsystems, Inc. The group operates from United States.

Primary SIC and add'l.: 3841 2841 5122

CIK No: 0000200406

Subsidiaries: Advanced Sterilization Products Services Inc., ALZA Corporation, ALZA Ireland Limited, ALZA Land Management, Inc., Apsis S.A.S., Biosense Webster, Inc., Centocor Biologics (Ireland) Limited, Centocor Biologics,LLC, Centocor Research&Development, Inc., Centocor, Inc., CentocorB.V., Cilag Advanced TechnologiesGmbH, Cilag AG, Cilag de Mexico, S. de R.L. de C.V., Cilag GmbH International 229 Subsidiaries included in the Index

Officers: William C. Weldon/Chmn., CEO/$28,557,750.00, Robert J. Darretta/61/Vice Chmn., CFO/$11,263,530.00, Joseph C. Scodari/Worldwide Chmn. - Pharmaceuticals Group, Russell C. Deyo/58/Dir., Chief Compliance Officer, VP, General Counsel/$8,387,691.00, Dominic J. Caruso/50/Dir., CFO, VP - Finance, Kaye Foster-Cheek/VP - Human Resources, Stephen J. Cosgrove/Corporate Controller

Directors: William C. Weldon/Chmn., CEO, Robert J. Darretta/61/Vice Chmn., CFO, Christine A. Poon/Vice Chmn., Colleen A. Goggins/Worldwide Chmn. - Consumer, Personal Care Group , Michael M.E. Johns/Dir., Nicholas J. Valeriani/51/Dir., Russell C. Deyo/58/Dir., Chief Compliance Officer, VP, General Counsel, Dominic J. Caruso/50/Dir., CFO, VP - Finance, Mary Sue Coleman/Dir., James G. Cullen/Dir., Arnold G. Langbo/Dir., Susan L. Lindquist/Dir., Leo F. Mullin/64/Dir., Charles Prince/Dir., Steven S. Reinemund/58/Dir. *(16 Directors included in Index)*

Owners: Per A. Peterson, Russell C. Deyo, Arnold G. Langbo, Christine A. Poon, Leo F. Mullin, William C. Weldon, David Satcher, Ann Dibble Jordan, Robert J. Darretta, Susan L. Lindquist, Michael M. E. Johns, James G. Cullen, Insiders, Steven S. Reinemund, Charles Prince *(16 Owners included in Index)*

Financial Data: ***Fiscal Year End:***01/01 ***Latest Annual Data:*** 12/31/2006

Year	Sales	Net Income
2006	$53,324,000,000	$11,053,000,000
2005	$47,348,000,000	$8,509,000,000

Curr. Assets:	$22,975,000,000	***Curr. Liab.:***	$19,161,000,000	***P/E Ratio:***	17.27
Plant, Equip.:	$13,044,000,000	***Total Liab.:***	$31,238,000,000	***Indic. Yr. Divd.:***	$1.660
Total Assets:	$70,556,000,000	***Net Worth:***	$39,318,000,000	***Debt/ Equity:***	0.0491

Johnson Controls Inc

5757 N Green Bay Ave., Milwaukee, WI, 53209; ***PH:*** 1-414-524-1200; ***Fax:*** 1-414-524-2077; ***http://*** www.johnsoncontrols.com

General - Incorporation	WI	***Stock*** - Price on:12/24/2007	$114.06
Employees	136,000	Stock Exchange	NYSE
Auditor	PricewaterhouseCoopers LLP	Ticker Symbol	JCI
Stk Agt	Wells Fargo Bank, N.A.	Outstanding Shares	197,300,000
Counsel	NA	E.P.S	NA
DUNS No.	00-609-2860	Shareholders	NA

Business: The group's principle activity is to provide innovative automotive interiors, products and services that optimize energy usage in buildings and batteries for automobiles and hybrid electric vehicles along with systems engineering and service expertise. The group's products include seating, interiors and electronics, buildings automation and control systems, fire life safety products, safety and security products, and refrigeration products. The group's services include consumer research, industrial designing, products and system designing, construction and innovation services. The group operates from United States.

Primary SIC and add'l.: 1796 3822 3691 2531

CIK No: 0000053669

Subsidiaries: Autoseat SA de CV, Beijing Johnson Controls Co. Ltd., Borg Instruments AG, Brookfield LePage Johnson Controls Facility Management Services, Ltd., Building Services S.r.l., Commer 1 S.r.l., Controles Reynosa SA de CV, Cybertron Systems (Pty) Ltd., Enertec Mexico S. de R.L. de C.V., Ensamble de Interiores Automotrices, S. de R.L. de C.V., Erste JCI Holding GmbH, Hoover Universal, Inc., Intertec Systems, LLC, JCI Regelungstechnik GmbH (G), Johnson Control SpA 88 Subsidiaries included in the Index

Officers: Stephen A. Roell/Dir., CEO, Keith E. Wandell/COO, Pres., David C. Myers/VP, Pres. - Building Efficiency, Susan M. Kreh/VP, Corporate Controller, Darryll Fortune/Dir. - Public Relations, Building Efficiency, Kari Pfisterer/Program Mgr. - Public Relations, Stephen Weinstein/Program Mgr. - Public Relations, Rebecca Fitzgerald/Dir. - Global Communications, Jeffrey S. Edwards/VP, GM - Japan, Asia Pacific, Automotive Experience, Jeffrey G. Augustin/VP - Building Efficiency, Alex A. Molinaroli/VP, Pres. - Power Solutions, Frank A. Voltolina/VP, Corporate Treasurer, Susan F. Davis/Exec. VP - Human Resources, Giovanni Fiori/Exec. VP, Pres. - Johnson Controls International, Monica Levy/Exec. Dir. - Branding, Corporate Communication *(22 Officers included in Index)*

Directors: Stephen A. Roell/Dir., CEO, John M. Barth/Chmn., Jeffrey Joerres/Dir., Robert L. Barnett/Dir., Southwood J. Morcott/Dir., Robert A. Cornog/Dir., Richard F. Teerlink/Dir., Dennis Archer/Dir., Paul A. Brunner/Dir., Eugenio C. Reyes-Retana/Dir., Natalie A. Black/Dir., William H. Lacy/Dir.

Owners: Insiders, Capital Research and Management Company, Eugenio Clariond Reyes-Retana, Southwood J. Morcott, William H. Lacy, Bruce R. McDonald, UBS Global Asset Management Americas, Inc, Natalie A. Black, Robert L. Barnett, John M. Barth, Robert A. Cornog, Stephen A. Roell, Paul A. Brunner, Keith E. Wandell, Dennis W. Archer *(18 Owners included in Index)*

Financial Data: ***Fiscal Year End:***09/30 ***Latest Annual Data:*** 9/30/2006

Year	Sales	Net Income
2006	$32,235,000,000	$1,028,000,000
2005	$27,479,400,000	$909,400,000
2004	$26,553,400,000	$817,500,000

Curr. Assets:	$9,264,000,000	**Curr. Liab.:**	$8,146,000,000	**P/E Ratio:**	20.78
Plant, Equip.:	$3,968,000,000	**Total Liab.:**	$14,437,000,000	**Indic. Yr. Divd.:**	$1.320
Total Assets:	$21,921,000,000	**Net Worth:**	$7,355,000,000	**Debt/ Equity:**	0.4560

Johnson Outdoors Inc

555 Main St., Racine, WI, 53403; ***PH:*** 1-262-631-6600; ***Fax:*** 1-262-631-6601; ***http://*** www.johnsonoutdoors.com

General - Incorporation	WI	***Stock***- Price on:12/24/2007	$19.99
Employees	1,300	Stock Exchange	NDQ
Auditor	Reinhart, Boerner,	Ticker Symbol	JOUT
Stk Agt	LaSalle Bank N.A	Outstanding Shares	9,160,000
Counsel	Reinhart, Boerner, Van Deuren sc	E.P.S.	$0.74
DUNS No.	14-474-2129	Shareholders	NA

Business: The group's principal activities are to design, manufacture and market outdoor recreational products. The group operates in four segments: diving, watercraft, outdoor equipment and motors. The diving segment markets underwater diving and snorkeling equipment, stabilizing jackets, tanks, depth gauges, masks, fins and other diving accessories. The watercraft segment manufactures and markets canoes, kayaks, paddles, oars, recreational sailboats and small thermoformed recreational boats. The outdoor equipment segment markets military, commercial and consumer tents and backpacks. The motors segment manufactures battery powered motors used on fishing boats and other boats for quiet trolling power. The group's operations are conducted in the United States, Europe, Canada and the pacific basin. On 06-May-2004, the group acquired techsonic industries inc.

Primary SIC and add'l.: 3732 3792 3953 3949

CIK No: 0000788329

Subsidiaries: Johnson Beteiligungsgesellschaft GmbH, Johnson Outdoors Canada Inc., Johnson Outdoors France, Johnson Outdoors Watercraft Ltd., Johnson Outdoors Watercraft UK, JWA Holding B.V., Leisure Life Limited, Old Town Canoe Company, Scubapro (UK) Ltd.(4), Scubapro Asia Pacific Ltd., Scubapro Asia, Ltd., Scubapro Espana, S.A.(3), Scubapro Eu AG, Scubapro Europe Benelux, S.A., Scubapro Europe S.r.l 23 Subsidiaries included in the Index

Officers: Helen P. Johnson-Leipold/Chmn., CEO, David W. Johnson/CFO, VP, Alisa Swire/VP - Business Development, Legal Affairs, John C. Moon/CIO, VP, Cynthia A. Georgeson/VP - Worldwide Communication, Mark E. Leopold/Group VP - Watercraft, Kelly T. Grindle/Group VP - Marine Electronics, William S. Kelly/Group VP - Outdoor Equipment, Joseph B. Stella/Group VP - Diving, Sarah Vidian/VP - Human Resources

Directors: Helen P. Johnson-Leipold/Chmn., CEO, Thomas Pyle/Vice Chmn., John Fahey/Dir., Terry London/57/Dir., Lee W. McCollum/Dir., Edward Lang/Dir.

Owners: Helen P. Johnson-Leipold/16.70%, Lee W. McCollum, Johnson Bank/33.10%, Insiders/17.80%, John M. Fahey, Fisk H. Johnson, Thomas F. Pyle, Dimensional Fund Advisors Inc./7.20%, Helen P. Johnson-Leipold, Edward F. Lang, TowerView LLC/10.50%, David W. Johnson, Fisk H. Johnson/11.80%, Winifred J. Marquart, Terry E. London *(18 Owners included in Index)*

Financial Data: ***Fiscal Year End:***09/30 ***Latest Annual Data:*** 9/29/2006

Year	Sales	Net Income
2006	$395,790,000	$8,715,000
2005	$380,690,000	$7,101,000
2004	$355,274,000	$8,689,000

Curr. Assets:	$186,035,000	**Curr. Liab.:**	$69,196,000	**P/E Ratio:**	27.01
Plant, Equip.:	$31,393,000	**Total Liab.:**	$116,884,000	**Indic. Yr. Divd.:**	$0.220
Total Assets:	$283,318,000	**Net Worth:**	$166,434,000	**Debt/ Equity:**	NA

Jointland Development Inc

New Henry House, 7th Fl., No.10 Ice House St., Central, Hong Kong; ***PH:*** 852-2824-0008

General - Incorporation	FL	***Stock***- Price on:12/24/2007	NA
Employees	NA	Stock Exchange	OTC
Auditor	Jaspers + Hall, PC	Ticker Symbol	JLDV
Stk Agt	Mountain Share Transfer	Outstanding Shares	NA
Counsel	NA	E.P.S.	NA
DUNS No.	NA	Shareholders	NA

Business: The groups principle activity is to provide recruiting services. The groups service area includes the research and development, engineering, marketing, sales, information technology and manufacturing industries. The group operates from United States.

Primary SIC and add'l.: 9995

CIK No: 0001110283

Officers: Kexi Xu/45/Dir., CEO, Acting CFO, Pres., Wong King/51/Sec., Treasurer

Directors: Kexi Xu/45/Dir., CEO, Acting CFO, Pres., Chen Yurong/29/Dir.

Owners: Shen Tiojuan/10.10%, Insiders/50.50%, Top Harmony Holdings, LTD./7.50%, Madam Yurong Chen/50.50%

Financial Data: ***Fiscal Year End:***12/31 ***Latest Annual Data:*** 12/31/2006

Year	Sales	Net Income
2006	NA	-$42,000
2005	NA	-$110,000
2004	NA	-$556,000

Curr. Assets:	$0	**Curr. Liab.:**	$323,000		
Plant, Equip.:	NA	**Total Liab.:**	$323,000	**Indic. Yr. Divd.:**	NA
Total Assets:	$0	**Net Worth:**	-$323,000	**Debt/ Equity:**	NA

Jones Apparel Group Inc

1411 Broadway, New York, NY, 10018; ***PH:*** 1-212-642-3860; ***Fax:*** 1-215-785-1795; ***http://*** www.jny.com

General - Incorporation	PA	***Stock***- Price on:12/24/2007	$28.24
Employees	10,880	Stock Exchange	NYSE
Auditor	BDO Seidman LLP	Ticker Symbol	JNY
Stk Agt	Bank of New York	Outstanding Shares	108,900,000
Counsel	NA	E.P.S.	-$1.91
DUNS No.	04-006-2168	Shareholders	NA

Business: The group's principle activities include designing, manufacturing and marketing branded apparel, footwear and accessories. The groups products include sportswear, jeanswear, suits, dresses, menswear, shoes, accessories and costume jewelry. The groups products sold under the brand name Kasper, Nine West, Bandolino, Easy Spirit, Napier, Mootsie Tootsies and Jeanstar. The group operates from United States.

Primary SIC and add'l.: 2329 5139 3021 5999 2335 2339 5699

CIK No: 0000874016

Subsidiaries: Apparel Testing Services, Inc., Asia Expert Limited, Barney's, Inc., Barneys Asia Co LLC, Barneys New York, Inc., BNY Licensing Corp., Exportex de Mexico, S.A. de C.V., Greater Durango, S. de R.L. de C.V., Import Technology of Texas, Inc., Jones Apparel Group Canada ULC, Jones Apparel Group Canada, LP, Jones Apparel Group Holdings, Inc., Jones Apparel Group USA, Inc., Jones Apparel of Texas II, Ltd., Jones Canada, Inc. 35 Subsidiaries included in the Index

Officers: Peter Boneparth/48/Dir., CEO, Pres./$4,022,516.00, Lynne F. Cote/CEO - Wholesale Sportswear, Suits, Dresses/$2,479,091.00, Andrew Cohen/CEO - Wholesale Footwear, Accessories, Jack Gross/CEO - Denim, Junior Businesses, Ira M. Dansky/Exec. VP, General Counsel, Sec., Wesley R. Card/CFO, COO/$2,580,828.00, Efthimios P. Sotos/CFO/$1,096,542.00, Patrick M. Farrell/Exec. VP, Corporate Controller, John T. McClain/CFO, Joseph T. Donnalley/Treasurer, Sr. VP - Corporate Taxation, Risk Management

Directors: Peter Boneparth/48/Dir., CEO, Pres., Sidney Kimmel/Chmn., Anthony F. Scarpa/Dir., Ann N. Reese/Dir., Matthew H. Kamens/Dir., Robert J. Kerrey/Dir., Howard Gittis/Dir., Lowell W. Robinson/Dir., Allen I. Questrom/Dir., Gerald C. Crotty/Dir., Frits D. Van Paasschen/Dir.

Owners: Lynne Cote, Efthimios P. Sotos, Howard Gittis, Ann N. Reese, Peter Boneparth/2.20%, Robert J. Kerrey, Matthew H. Kamens, Sidney Kimmel/1.80%, Insiders/5.00%, Rhonda J. Brown, Anthony F. Scarpa, Wesley R. Card

Financial Data: ***Fiscal Year End:***12/31 ***Latest Annual Data:*** 12/31/2006

Year	Sales	Net Income
2006	$4,742,800,000	-$144,100,000
2005	$5,074,200,000	$274,300,000
2004	$4,649,700,000	$301,800,000

Curr. Assets:	$1,278,600,000	**Curr. Liab.:**	$615,400,000		
Plant, Equip.:	$384,800,000	**Total Liab.:**	$1,575,400,000	**Indic. Yr. Divd.:**	$0.560
Total Assets:	$3,787,000,000	**Net Worth:**	$2,211,600,000	**Debt/ Equity:**	0.3447

Jones Lang Lasalle Inc

200 E Randolph Dr., Chicago, IL, 60601; ***PH:*** 1-312-782-5800; ***Fax:*** 1-312-782-4339; ***http://*** www.joneslanglasalle.com

General - Incorporation	MD	***Stock***- Price on:12/24/2007	$114.06
Employees	25,500	Stock Exchange	NYSE
Auditor	KPMG LLP	Ticker Symbol	JLL
Stk Agt	Mellon Investor Services LLC	Outstanding Shares	31,820,000
Counsel	NA	E.P.S.	$6.88
DUNS No.	15-453-7807	Shareholders	NA

Business: The groups principle activity is to provide real estate and money management services. The groups services include agency leasing, property management, project and development, valuations, capital markets, real estate investment banking and merchant banking services. In the year 2007 the group acquired Corporate Realty Advisors and Upstream. The group operates from United States.

Primary SIC and add'l.: 8741 6531

CIK No: 0001037976

Subsidiaries: Abacus Park General Partner Ltd., AMAS Limited, Anderson Wharf General Partner Ltd., Anderson Wharf Nominee Ltd., Beijing Jones Lang LaSalle Property Management Services Co., Ltd., Caledonian LIC II (General Partner) Ltd., Cattleya BV, Chicago Medical Office, LLC, CIN LaSalle Corporation, CIN LaSalle Property Services (London) Ltd., Compass Cayman, CPPI Bridgewater Place General Partner Ltd., Development Partnership No 1 General Partner Ltd., Development Partnership No 1 Nominee Ltd., Easter Development Partnership General Partner Ltd. 242 Subsidiaries included in the Index

Officers: Colin Dyer/Dir., CEO, Pres./$4,636,165.00, Alastair Hughes/CEO - EMEA Jones Lang Lasalle/$2,653,073.00, Peter C. Roberts/CEO - Americas, Jones Lang Lasalle/$2,301,777.00, Peter A. Barge/CEO - Asia Pacific Jones Lang Lasalle/$2,224,247.00, Christian Ulbrich/CEO - Germany, Jeff Jacobson/CEO - Lasalle Investment, Lucy Rumantir/Chmn. - Jones Lang Lasalle, Indonesia, Thierry Delvaux/MD - Jones Lang Lasalle, Hungary, John Moran/Dir. - Capital Markets, K. K. Fung/MD - Jones Lang Lasalle, Hong Kong, Pierre Marin/MD - Italy, Margaret A. Kelly/50/Chief Marketing, Communications Officer, Nick Stanisis/Joint MD, Head - Capital Markets, Andrew Wood/Head - Capital Markets, MD - VIC Jones Lang Lasalle, Benoit Du Passage/MD - France, Southern Europe, Jones Lang Lasalle *(47 Officers included in Index)*

Directors: Colin Dyer/Dir., CEO, Pres., Sheila A. Penrose/Chmn., Derek Higgs/Dir., Henri-Claude De Bettignies/Dir., Lauralee E. Martin/Dir., CFO, COO, Alain Monie/Dir., Sir Derek Higgs/Dir., David B. Rickard/Dir., Darryl Hartley-Leonard/Dir., Thomas C. Theobald/Dir., Vincent H. Querton/Dir.

Owners: Lauralee E. Martin, Insiders, Derek Higgs, Henri-Claude de Bettignies, Alain Moni, Ariel Capital Management, Inc./9.63%, Thomas C. Theobald, Sheila A. Penrose, Peter C. Roberts, FMR Corp./6.03%, Peter A. Barge, Alastair Hughes, Colin Dyer, Lynn C. Thurber, Darryl Hartley-Leonard

Financial Data: Fiscal Year End:12/31 Latest Annual Data: 12/31/2006

Year	Sales	Net Income
2006	$2,013,578,000	$176,401,000
2005	$1,390,610,000	$103,672,000
2004	$1,166,958,000	$64,242,000

Curr. Assets:	$807,445,000	**Curr. Liab.:**	$830,446,000	**P/E Ratio:**	18.10
Plant, Equip.:	$120,376,000	**Total Liab.:**	$979,568,000	**Indic. Yr. Divd.:**	$1.000
Total Assets:	$1,729,948,000	**Net Worth:**	$750,380,000	**Debt/ Equity:**	0.3047

Jones Soda Company

234 9th Ave. N, Seattle, WA, 98109; **PH:** 1-206-624-3357; **Fax:** 1-206-624-6857; http:// www.jonessoda.com

General - Incorporation	WA	**Stock**- Price on:12/24/2007	$15.55
Employees	67	Stock Exchange	NDQ
Auditor	KPMG LLP	Ticker Symbol	JSDA
Stk Agt	Pacific Corporate Trust Co	Outstanding Shares	25,860,000
Counsel	Caircross & Hempelmann,P.S.	E.P.S.	$0.03
DUNS No.	NA	Shareholders	NA

Business: The groups principle activities include producing, marketing and distributing beverages product. The products of the group include soda, organic tea, energy drink, and non carbonated juice and tea. Jones Pure Cane Soda(TM), Jones Organics(TM), Jones Energy(TM), WhoopAss(TM), Jones Naturals(TM) and Jones 24C(TM). The group operates from the United States. The group's quarterly revenue for September 2007 was 11.74 millions of USD.

Primary SIC and add'l.: 2095 2086

CIK No: 0001083522

Subsidiaries: Jones Soda (Canada) Inc, Jones Soda Co. (USA) Inc, Whoopass USA Inc

Officers: Peter Van Stolk/44/Chmn., CEO, Pres./$323,447.00, Hassan N. Natha/49/CFO, Sec./$198,736.00, Lars P. Nilsen/46/Exec. VP - Sales/$194,904.00, Nancy Bucher/Investor Relations Officer/$65,333.00, Erin Kliphardt/Contact - Sale, Northwest, Timothy Aschettino/Contact - Sale, Northern Cali, Mike Ward/Contact - Sale, Midwest, Jim Clemenson/Contact - Sale, Midwest, Chad Kennedy/VP - National Accounting, Jeff Somers/Contact - Arizona, Sin City, Chris Lipka/Contact - Sale, Detroit, Jason Hockney/Contact - Sale, Northwest, Garrett Chu/Contact - Sale, British Columbia, Gilbert Moreno/Contact - Sale, So, Cal, Steve Freant/Contact - Sale, Florida *(47 Officers included in Index)*

Directors: Peter Van Stolk/44/Chmn., CEO, Pres., Rick Eiswirth/Dir., Matthew Kellogg/Dir., Ron B. Anderson/Dir., Michael M. Fleming/Dir., Jack Gallagher/Dir., Al Rossow/Dir., John J. Gallagher/59/Dir., Stephen C. Jones/52/Dir., Steven Jones/Dir.

Owners: Insiders/9.10%, Richard S. Eiswirth, Peter M. van Stolk/8.00%, Hassan N. Natha, John J. Gallagher, Lars P. Nilsen, Michael M. Fleming, Melody Morgan, Sidney H. Ritman/7.90%, Wellington Management Company, LLP/7.90%, Vardon Capital Management, L.L.C./8.20%, Scott Bedbury, Alfred W. Rossow

Financial Data: Fiscal Year End:12/31 Latest Annual Data: 12/31/2006

Year	Sales	Net Income
2006	$39,719,000	$4,574,000
2005	$34,235,000	$1,283,000
2004	$27,450,000	$1,330,000

Curr. Assets:	$45,142,000	**Curr. Liab.:**	$5,668,000		
Plant, Equip.:	$2,171,000	**Total Liab.:**	$5,683,000	**Indic. Yr. Divd.:**	NA
Total Assets:	$47,952,000	**Net Worth:**	$42,269,000	**Debt/ Equity:**	0.0003

Jordan Industries Inc

Arbor Lake Ctr., Ste. 550, 1751 Lake Cook Rd., Deerfield, IL, 60015; **PH:** 1-847-945-5591; **Fax:** 1-847-945-0198; **http://** www.jordanindustries.com; **Email:** info@jordanind.com

General - Incorporation	IL	**Stock**- Price on:12/24/2007	NA
Employees	NA	Stock Exchange	NA
Auditor	Ernst & Young LLP	Ticker Symbol	NA
Stk Agt	NA	Outstanding Shares	NA
Counsel	Sonnenschein Nath & Rosenthal LLP	E.P.S.	NA
DUNS No.	18-915-8736	Shareholders	NA

Business: The group's principal activities are to acquire and operate a diverse group of businesses on a decentralized basis. The group's activities comprises of 21 businesses which are divided into five groups: specialty printing and labeling, jordan specialty plastics, jordan auto aftermarket, motors and gears and consumer and industrial products. The products of the group include promotional and specialty advertising products, specialty plastics products, electronic motors, books and music recordings. The group markets its products in the United States and other foreign countries.

Primary SIC and add'l.: 3356 2741 3679 3678 3084 7379

CIK No: 0000839484

Subsidiaries: ABC Transmission Parts Warehouse, Inc, Alma Products I, Inc, Atco Products, Inc, Beemak Plastics, Inc, DACCO Transmission Parts, DACCO Transmission Parts (NY), Inc, DACCO, Incorporated, DACCO/Detroit of Alabama, Inc., DACCO/Detroit of Arizona, Inc, DACCO/Detroit of Chattanooga, Inc., DACCO/Detroit of Florida, Inc., DACCO/Detroit of Georgia, Inc, DACCO/Detroit of Indiana, Inc, DACCO/Detroit of Kentucky, Inc, DACCO/Detroit of Maryland, Inc 66 Subsidiaries included in the Index

Officers: John W. Jordan/60/Chmn., CEO, Thomas H. Quinn/60/Dir., COO, Pres., Steven L. Rist/49/General Counsel, Assist. Sec., Gordon L. Nelson/50/Sr. VP, Treasurer, Robert G. Fisher/68/Dir., Sec., Lisa M. Ondrula/38/CFO, Sr. VP, Assist. Sec. Pres., Assist. Sec.

Directors: John W. Jordan/60/Chmn., CEO, Thomas H. Quinn/60/Dir., COO, Pres., Joseph S. Steinberg/64/Dir., David W. Zalaznick/52/Dir., Jonathan F. Boucher/Dir., Robert G. Fisher/68/Dir., Sec., Jesse Clyde Nichols/68/Dir.

Owners: John W. Jordan/17.70%, David W. Zalaznick/19.90%, University of Notre Dame/8.50%, Leucadia Investors, Inc./9.90%, Jonathan F. Boucher/5.50%, Robert G. Fisher, Insiders/53.60%

Jos. A. Bank Clothiers Inc

500 Hanover Pike, Hampstead, MD, 21074; **PH:** 1-410-239-2700; **Fax:** 1-410-239-5700; **http://** www.josbank.com; **Email:** service@jos-a-bank.com

General - Incorporation	DE	**Stock**- Price on:12/24/2007	$43.93
Employees	2,646	Stock Exchange	NDQ
Auditor	NA	Ticker Symbol	JOSB
Stk Agt	Continental Stock Transfer & Trust Co	Outstanding Shares	18,090,000
Counsel	NA	E.P.S.	$2.64
DUNS No.	NA	Shareholders	NA

Business: The groups principal activity is to retailing and distributing men's tailored and casual clothing and accessories. The products of the group include suits, dress shirts, neckties, shoes, blazers, sport coats, trousers, sweaters, sport shirts, pants, underwear and formalwear. The group operates from the United States.

Primary SIC and add'l.: 5961 5611

CIK No: 0000814675

Officers: Robert N. Wildrick/CEO, Executive Chmn., Neal R. Black/Pres., Chief Merchandising Officer, Robert B. Hensley/Exec. VP - Store Operations, Real Estate, Human Resources, David E. Ullman/Exec. VP, CFO - Principal Financial, Accounting Officer, Charles D. Frazer/Sr. VP, General Counsel, Sec., Deanna B. Marotz/Chief Compliance Officer

Directors: Robert N. Wildrick/CEO, Executive Chmn., Andrew A. Giordano/Chmn., Gary S. Gladstein/Dir., William E. Herron/Dir., David A. Preiser/Dir., Sidney H. Ritman/Dir.

Financial Data: Fiscal Year End:06/30 Latest Annual Data: 2/3/2007

Year	Sales	Net Income
2007	$546,385,000	$43,222,000
2006	$464,633,000	$35,250,000
2005	$372,500,000	$24,481,000

Curr. Assets.	$250,304,000	**Curr. Liab.:**	$113,742,000	**P/E Ratio:**	17.64
Plant, Equip.:	$117,553,000	**Total Liab.:**	$160,158,000	**Indic. Yr. Divd.:**	NA
Total Assets:	$368,392,000	**Net Worth:**	$208,234,000	**Debt/ Equity:**	0.2034

Journal Communications Inc

333 W State St., Milwaukee, WI, 53203; **PH:** 1-414-224-2000; **Fax:** 1-414-224-2469; **http://** www.jc.com

General - Incorporation	WI	**Stock**- Price on:12/24/2007	$13.33
Employees	3,800	Stock Exchange	NYSE
Auditor	Ernst & Young LLP	Ticker Symbol	JRN
Stk Agt	American Stock Transfer & Trust Co.	Outstanding Shares	68,190,000
Counsel	NA	E.P.S.	$1.77
DUNS No.	NA	Shareholders	NA

Business: The group's principal activity is to provide diversified media and communication services. The group operates through four segments: publishing, broadcasting, telecommunications and printing services. Publishing business consists of the daily newspaper, the milwaukee journal sentinel, and community newspapers and shoppers. Broadcasting business is conducted through the group's wholly-owned subsidiary, which operates 38 radio stations and 6 television stations in 11 states. Telecommunications business provides both wholesale and business-to-business telecommunications services. Printing services business provides electronic publishing, assembly and fulfillment and includes printing scientific, medical and technical journals.

Primary SIC and add'l.: 4813 2711 8748 6719 2759 4832

CIK No: 0001232241

Subsidiaries: IPC Print Services, Inc., Journal Broadcast Corporation, Journal Holdings, Inc., Journal Sentinel Inc., JournalCommunityPublishingGroup, Norlight Telecommunications, Inc., The Journal Company

Officers: Douglas G. Kiel/Pres., CEO - Journal Broadcast Group Inc/$1,071,661.00, Steven J. Smith/Chmn., CEO/$1,372,652.00, Carl D. Gardner/VP - Digital Media, Exec. VP - Television, Radio Operations, Journal Broadcast Group, Elizabeth Brenner/Exec. VP, COO - Publishing Businesses/$640,387.00, Paul E. Kritzer/VP, General Counsel - Media, Corp. Sec., Mark J. Keefe/VP, Pres. - Primenet Marketing Services, Steven H. Wexler/VP, Exec. VP - Journal Broadcast Group, Sara Leuchter Wilkins/VP - Investor Relations, Corporate Communications, James P. Prather/VP, Exec. VP - Television, Radio Operations, Pres. - News, Journal Broadcast Group/$628,580.00, Anne M. Bauer/VP, Corporate Controller, Mary Hill Leahy/Sr. VP, General Counsel, Kenneth L. Kozminski/VP, Pres. - IPC Print Services, Paul M. Bonaiuto/CFO, Exec. VP/$625,400.00, Karen O. Trickle/VP, Treasurer

Directors: Steven J. Smith/Chmn., CEO, Don H. Davis/Dir., David G. Meissner/Dir., Jeanette Tully/Dir., David J. Drury/Dir., Mary Ellen Stanek/Dir., Ellen F. Siminoff/Dir., Owen Sullivan/Dir., Jonathan Newcomb/Dir., Roger D. Peirce/Dir.

Owners: Elizabeth Brenner, James Prather, Douglas G. Kiel, Matex Inc/93.00%, Don H. Davis, David J. Drury, Mary Ellen Stanek, Steven J. Smith, Paul M. Bonaiuto, Insiders, David G. Meissner, Insiders/5.10%, Mary Ellen Stanek, The Journal Company/33.70%, Jeanette Tully *(25 Owners included in Index)*

Financial Data: Fiscal Year End:12/25 Latest Annual Data: 12/31/2006

Year	Sales	Net Income
2006	$671,853,000	$64,373,000
2005	$764,461,000	$66,243,000
2004	$820,761,000	$78,480,000

Curr. Assets.	$222,767,000	**Curr. Liab.:**	$126,841,000	**P/E Ratio:**	7.57
Plant, Equip.:	$223,844,000	**Total Liab.:**	$474,366,000	**Indic. Yr. Divd.:**	$0.300
Total Assets:	$955,258,000	**Net Worth:**	$480,892,000	**Debt/ Equity:**	0.2021

Journal Register Co

790 Township Line Rd., Ste. 300, Yardley, PA, 19067; **PH:** 1-215-504-4200; **http://** www.journalregister.com

General - Incorporation	DE	**Stock**- Price on:12/24/2007	$4.97
Employees	4,500	Stock Exchange	NYSE
Auditor	Ernst & Young LLP, Grant Thornton LLP	Ticker Symbol	JRC
Stk Agt	Bank of New York	Outstanding Shares	39,140,000
Counsel	Edward J. Yocum Jr.	E.P.S	$0.53
DUNS No.	15-411-8400	Shareholders	NA

Business: The group's principal activity is to publish daily and non-daily newspapers. The newspapers of the group focus on the coverage of local news and local sports and offer compelling graphic design in colorful, reader-friendly packages. The group currently owns and operates 23 daily newspapers and 236 non-daily publications in six geographic areas: greater philadelphia, Connecticut, greater cleveland, central new England and the capital-saratoga and mid-hudson regions of New York. It also operates 152 Web sites, which represent each of the group's publications. The group also owns four commercial printing operations that complement and enhance its publishing operations. On 04- apr-2004 the group acquired mohawk valley media. On 13-Aug-2004 the group acquired 21st century newspapers inc.

Primary SIC and add'l.: 2711 7311

CIK No: 0001035815

Subsidiaries: Chanry Media, Inc., INS Holdings, Inc., Journal News, Inc., Journal Register East, Inc., JRC.com, LLC, Register Company, Inc.

Officers: Robert M. Jelenic/Chmn., CEO/$1,458,650.00, Allen J. Mailman/Sr. VP - Technology/$272,275.00, Thomas E. Rice/Sr. VP - Operations/$337,520.00, William J. Higginson/Sr. VP - Production, Joseph A. Lawrence/Dir. - Private Investor, Consultant, Michael Murray/VP - Circulation, James W. Hall/Dir. - Private Investor, Consultant, Julie A. Beck/CFO, Sr. VP/$503,566.00, Edward J. Yocum/Sr. VP, General Counsel, Corp. Sec./$191,462.00, Daryl Hively/VP - Interactive Media, Richard J. Medeiros/VP - Advertising, Scott A. Wright/COO, Pres., Edward S. Condra/Sr. VP - Operations, Judy Brenna/Dir. - Investor Relations

Directors: Robert M. Jelenic/Chmn., CEO, Stephen P. Mumblow/Dir., John L. Vogelstein/Dir., Laurna Godwin Hutchinson/Dir., Joseph A. Lawrence/Dir. - Private Investor, Consultant, James W. Hall/Dir. - Private Investor, Consultant, Burton B. Staniar/Dir.

Owners: Insiders/10.40%, Thomas E. Rice, James W. Hall, Barclays Global Investors, NA/7.40%, Joseph A. Lawrence, T. Rowe Price Associates, Inc./7.00%, Private Management Group, Inc./6.00%, Robert M. Jelenic/6.40%, Burton M. Staniar, Stephen P. Mumblow, Allen J. Mailman, Laurna Godwin-Hutchinson, Ariel Capital Management, LLC/14.90%, John L. Vogelstein/2.50%

Financial Data: *Fiscal Year End:*12/25 *Latest Annual Data:* 12/31/2006

Year	Sales	Net Income
2006	$506,065,000	-$6,238,000
2005	$556,629,000	$46,868,000
2004	$475,727,000	$116,513,000

Curr. Assets:	$89,462,000	**Curr. Liab.:**	$95,362,000	**P/E Ratio:**	9.20
Plant, Equip.:	$161,874,000	**Total Liab.:**	$960,939,000	**Indic. Yr. Divd.:**	$0.080
Total Assets:	$1,160,782,000	**Net Worth:**	$199,843,000	**Debt/ Equity:**	2.8899

Joy Global Inc

100 E Wisconsin Ave., Ste. 2780, Milwaukee, WI, 53202; *PH:* 1-414-319-8500; *Fax:* 1-414-319-8520; *http://* www.joyglobal.com

General - Incorporation	DE	**Stock**- Price on:12/24/2007	$60.63
Employees	8,900	Stock Exchange	NDQ
Auditor	Ernst & Young LLP	Ticker Symbol	JOYG
Stk Agt	American Stock Transfer & Trust Co.	Outstanding Shares	108,620,000
Counsel	NA	E.P.S	$2.51
DUNS No.	NA	Shareholders	NA

Business: The groups principle activity is to manufacture and service mining equipment for the extraction of coal and other minerals and ores. The group operates through two business segments namely underground mining machinery and surface mining equipment. The group operates from United States.

Primary SIC and add'l.: 3532

CIK No: 0000801898

Subsidiaries: Bank of America, LaSalle Bank National Association, Mining Machinery Limited

Officers: Michael W. Sutherlin/Dir., CEO, Pres., Dennis R. Winkleman/Exec. VP - Human Resources, Mark E. Readinger/COO, Pres. - P, H Mining Equipment, Donald C. Roof/Exec. VP, Michael S. Olsen/Chief Accounting Officer, Edward L. Doheny/COO, Pres. - Joy Mining Machinery, Exec. VP, Sean D. Major/Exec. VP, General Counsel, James H. Woodward/CFO, Treasurer, Georganne Palffy/VP - FRB Weber Shandwick

Directors: Michael W. Sutherlin/Dir., CEO, Pres., John Nils Hanson/Chmn., James H. Tate/Dir., Steven L. Gerard/Dir., Eric P. Siegert/Dir., James R. Klauser/Dir., Richard B. Loynd/Dir., Ken C. Johnsen/Dir., Gale E. Klappa/Dir.

Owners: Michael W. Sutherlin, John Nils Hanson/1.10%, FMR Corp./9.90%, Donald C. Roof, Neuberger Berman Inc./7.70%, Dennis R. Winkleman, Mark E. Readinger, Insiders/1.60%

Financial Data: *Fiscal Year End:*10/29 *Latest Annual Data:* 10/26/2007

Year	Sales	Net Income
2007	$2,547,322,000	$279,784,000
2006	$2,401,710,000	$416,421,000
2005	$1,927,474,000	$148,049,000

Curr. Assets:	$992,052,000	**Curr. Liab.:**	$431,852,000	**P/E Ratio:**	17.32
Plant, Equip.:	$207,974,000	**Total Liab.:**	$988,311,000	**Indic. Yr. Divd.:**	$0.600
Total Assets:	$1,440,359,000	**Net Worth:**	$452,048,000	**Debt/ Equity:**	0.8480

Joytoto USA Inc

Formerly: BioStem Inc
3000 Scott Blvd., Ste. 206, Santa Clara, CA, 95054; *PH:* 1-408-970-8050

General - Incorporation	NV	**Stock**- Price on:12/24/2007	$0.34
Employees	8	Stock Exchange	OTC
Auditor	Meyler & Company, LLC	Ticker Symbol	JYTO
Stk Agt	Signature Stock Transfer	Outstanding Shares	175,220,000
Counsel	NA	E.P.S	-$0.01
DUNS No.	NA	Shareholders	NA

Business: The groups principle activity is to provide parking and parking related services. The groups services include valet parking services and immobilization services. The group operates through two segments namely parking and booting. In the year 2005, the group acquired ABS Holding Company, Inc. The group operates from the United States.

Primary SIC and add'l.: 7389

CIK No: 0001178377

Subsidiaries: ABS Holding Company, Inc, BH holding Company Inc, J & K Parking

Officers: Marc Ebersole/50/Dir., CEO, Pres., Treasurer, Sec./$76,208.00, Seongyong Cho/CEO

Directors: Marc Ebersole/50/Dir., CEO, Pres., Treasurer, Sec., Christine Ebersole/38/Dir., Scott Schweber/47/Dir.

Owners: Insiders/74.20%, Christine Ebersole/2.30%, Marc Ebersole/69.60%, Scott Schweber/2.30%

Financial Data: *Fiscal Year End:*12/31 *Latest Annual Data:* 12/31/2006

Year	Sales	Net Income
2006	$1,762,000	-$2,052,000
2005	$1,085,000	-$940,000
2004	$318,000	-$23,000

Curr. Assets:	$66,000	**Curr. Liab.:**	$1,405,000		
Plant, Equip.:	$30,000	**Total Liab.:**	$1,492,000	**Indic. Yr. Divd.:**	NA
Total Assets:	$249,000	**Net Worth:**	-$1,243,000	**Debt/ Equity:**	NA

Jpak Group Inc

Formerly: Rx Staffing Inc New
1718 Fawn Ct., N.w., Gig Harbor, WA, 98332; *PH:* 1-253-720-0022

General - Incorporation	NV	**Stock**- Price on:12/24/2007	NA
Employees	NA	Stock Exchange	NA
Auditor	Bagell, Levine & Company, LLC	Ticker Symbol	NA
Stk Agt	Holladay Stock Transfer, Inc.	Outstanding Shares	NA
Counsel	NA	E.P.S	NA
DUNS No.	NA	Shareholders	NA

Business: The groups principal activity is to provide personnel staffing services to institutions, occupational and alternative site healthcare organizations. The groups organizations consist of three general groups Hospitals and teaching facilities, Clinics and nursing homes and Organizations, such as corporations or schools. The group operates from the United States.

Primary SIC and add'l.: 7363

CIK No: 0001321559

Officers: Shaun M. Jones/40/Dir., CEO, Pres., Principal Financial Officer

Directors: Shaun M. Jones/40/Dir., CEO, Pres., Principal Financial Officer

Owners: QVT Fund LP, Quintessence Fund LP/5.00%, Insiders, Vision Opportunity Master Fund, Quintessence Fund LP, Stewart Shiang Lor, Fabregas Group Limited, QVT Fund LP/45.00%, Joyrich Group Limited, Statepro Investments Ltd., Vision Opportunity Master Fund/50.00%

JPC Capital Partners Inc

555 N Point Ctr E, 4th Fl., Alpharetta, GA, 30022; *PH:* 1-678-366-5019; *http://* www.jpccapital.com; *Email:* info@jpccapital.com

General - Incorporation	DE	**Stock**- Price on:12/24/2007	$0.031
Employees	6	Stock Exchange	OTC
Auditor	Sherb & Co. LLP	Ticker Symbol	JPCI
Stk Agt	Standard Registrar & Transfer Co Inc.	Outstanding Shares	24,800,000
Counsel	NA	E.P.S	$0.007
DUNS No.	NA	Shareholders	NA

Business: The group's principle activity is to provide retail brokerage activities primarily for officers, directors and other related and affiliated parties. The company also provides limited range of other corporate finance functions which include business consulting and merger, acquisition services and retail brokerage services. The group operates from United States.

Primary SIC and add'l.: 6211

CIK No: 0001162867

Officers: John C. Canouse/Chmn., CEO, Jimmie N. Carter/Exec. VP, CFO, Treasurer, Janet L. Thompson/Exec. VP, Chief Compliance Officer

Directors: John C. Canouse/Chmn., CEO, Jimmie N. Carter/Exec. VP, CFO, Treasurer, Janet L. Thompson/Exec. VP, Chief Compliance Officer

Owners: Jimmie N. Carter, John C. Canouse/66.10%, J.P. Carey Asset Management, LLC/9.10%, Insiders/66.40%, Joseph C. Canouse/9.20%, Janet L. Thompson, Cache Capital (USA) L.P.

Financial Data: *Fiscal Year End:*12/31 *Latest Annual Data:* 12/31/2006

Year	Sales	Net Income
2006	$726,000	$16,000
2005	$950,000	-$230,000
2004	$1,454,000	-$277,000

Curr. Assets:	$104,000	**Curr. Liab.:**	$9,000	**P/E Ratio:**	5.17
Plant, Equip.:	$5,000	**Total Liab.:**	$40,000	**Indic. Yr. Divd.:**	NA
Total Assets:	$115,000	**Net Worth:**	$76,000	**Debt/ Equity:**	NA

Juma Technology Corp

Formerly: Elite Cosmetics Inc
154 Toledo St., Farmingdale, NY, 11735; *PH:* 1-631-300-1000; *http://* www.cashin-in.tripod.com

General - Incorporation	DE	**Stock**- Price on:12/24/2007	NA
Employees	NA	Stock Exchange	NA
Auditor	Seligson & Giannattasio, LLP	Ticker Symbol	NA
Stk Agt	Olde Monmouth Stk Trnsfer Co. Inc.	Outstanding Shares	NA
Counsel	NA	E.P.S	NA
DUNS No.	NA	Shareholders	NA

Business: The group's principle activity is to produce cosmetics and creams. The group operates from United States.

Primary SIC and add'l.: 9995

CIK No: 0001309055

Officers: David Giangano/Dir., CEO/$116,260.00, Frances Vinci/56/Dir., Exec. VP - Professional Services/$106,107.00, Joseph Fuccillo/Dir., CTO/$106,107.00, Joseph Cassano/Dir., Exec. VP - Sales/$155,000.00, Anthony Fernandez/Dir., CFO

Directors: Frances Vinci/56/Dir., Exec. VP - Professional Services, Joseph Fuccillo/Dir., CTO, Joseph Cassano/Dir., Exec. VP - Sales, Anthony Fernandez/Dir., CFO
Owners: Frances Vinci/12.00%, Insiders/55.00%, Joseph Cassano/10.00%, Mirus Oportunistic Fund/6.00%, Joseph Fuccillo/14.00%, David Giangano/14.00%, Anthony Fernandez/2.00%

Juniata Valley Financial Corp

Bridge and Main St.s, Mifflintown, PA, 17059; **PH:** 1-717-436-8211; **Fax:** 1-717-436-7551;
http:// www.jvbonline.com

General - Incorporation	PA	Stock - Price on:12/24/2007	$21.15
Employees	125	Stock Exchange	OTC
Auditor	Beard Miller Co. LLP	Ticker Symbol	JUVF
Stk Agt	Registrar & Transfer Co	Outstanding Shares	4,430,000
Counsel	NA	E.P.S	$1.16
DUNS No.	01-516-9170	Shareholders	NA

Business: The group's principal activity is to provide banking and trust services. The group accepts time and demand deposits and offers secured and unsecured commercial and consumer loans, commercial transactions, construction and mortgage loans. The group also administers corporate, pension and personal trust services. These services are provided to individuals, corporations, partnerships, associations, municipalities and other governmental bodies. The group operates 14 offices of commercial banks and savings and loan associations within our market area.
Primary SIC and add'l.: 6712 6022
CIK No: 0000714712
Subsidiaries: Juniata Valley Bank
Officers: Francis J. Evanitsky/Direcotr, Pres. CEO/$313,439.00, Joann N. McMinn/Sr. VP, CFO/$127,623.00, Pamela S. Eberman/Sr. VP - Human Resources, Judy R. Aumiller/Sr. VP - Operations, Technology/$141,462.00, Edward L. Kauffman/Sr. VP - Loans/$120,638.00, Marcie A. Barber/COO, Sr. VP, Lou Ann Wilson/VP, Compliance Officer, William L. Barnett/Sr. VP - Trust, Investment Division Mgr.
Directors: Francis J. Evanitsky/Direcotr, Pres. CEO, Martin L. Dreibelbis/Chmn., Philip E. Gingerich/Vice Chmn., Robert K. Metz/Dir., Jan G. Snedeker/Dir., Jerome A. Cook/Dir., John A. Renninger/Dir., Harold B. Shearer/Dir., Ronald H. Witherite/Dir., Timothy I. Havice/Dir., Joseph E. Benner/Dir., Marshall L. Hartman/Dir., Charles L. Hershberger/Dir., Dale G. Nace/Dir., Richard M. Scanlon/Dir.
Owners: Francis J. Evanitsky, Dale G. Nace, Charles L. Hershberger, Joe E. Benner, Harold B. Shearer, Ronald H. Witherite, Martin L. Dreibelbis, Don E. Haubert, Richard M. Scanlon, Edward L. Kauffman, John A. Renninger, Timothy I. Havice/1.05%, Robert K. Metz, A. Jerome Cook, Jan Snedeker (20 Owners included in Index)
Financial Data: Fiscal Year End:12/31   Latest Annual Data: 12/31/2006

Year	Sales		Net Income
2006	$28,493,000		$5,002,000
2005	$26,030,000		$4,566,000
2004	$25,188,000		$5,829,000
Curr. Assets:	$27,417,000	Curr. Liab.:	$367,218,000	P/E Ratio:	18.72
Plant, Equip.:	$6,542,000	Total Liab.:	$368,145,000	Indic. Yr. Divd.:	$0.720
Total Assets:	$415,931,000	Net Worth:	$47,786,000	Debt/ Equity:	NA

Juniper Group Inc

20283 State Rd. 400, Ste. 400, Boca Raton, FL, 33498; **PH:** 1-561-482-9327;
http:// www.junipergroup.com

General - Incorporation	NV	Stock - Price on:12/24/2007	$0.0099
Employees	5	Stock Exchange	OTC
Auditor	Morgenstern, Svoboda & Baer CPA's PC	Ticker Symbol	JUNI
Stk Agt	NA	Outstanding Shares	15,670,000
Counsel	NA	E.P.S	-$0.043
DUNS No.	80-483-3051	Shareholders	NA

Business: The group's principle activity is to provide entertainment and technology services and healthcare. The group operates in two segments: entertainment and technology services and healthcare.the entertainment segment provides Internet technology services cable companies, DSL, satellite and wireless services providers and also manufactures electronic equipment. Entertainment segment provides Internet and audio streaming, home video, pay-per view, pay television, cable television, networks and independent syndicated television stations. Healthcare segment provides managed care revenue enhancement, comprehensive pricing reviews to newly evolving integrated hospitals and write-off review, appeals of any third party rejections, denials of accounts, including commercial insurance, managed care, medicare and medicaid. The group's quarterly revenue for September 2007 was 0.30 millions of USD.
Primary SIC and add'l.: 7389 8099 7822 8741 7373 7379
CIK No: 0000864921
Subsidiaries: Juniper Services, Inc.
Officers: Vlado P. Hreljanovic/60/Chmn., CEO, CFO, Pres., James A. Calderhead/42/Pres. - Juniper Services
Directors: Vlado P. Hreljanovic/60/Chmn., CEO, CFO, Pres., Barry S. Huston/61/Dir.
Owners: Barry S. Huston/1.30%, James A. Calderhead/7.81%, Vlado P. Hreljanovic/17.65%, Insiders/26.00%
Financial Data: Fiscal Year End:12/31   Latest Annual Data: 12/31/2006

Year	Sales		Net Income
2006	$4,681,000		-$1,736,000
2005	$581,000		-$4,882,000
2004	$1,329,000		-$2,203,000
Curr. Assets:	$966,000	Curr. Liab.:	$2,598,000		
Plant, Equip.:	$400,000	Total Liab.:	$4,728,000	Indic. Yr. Divd.:	NA
Total Assets:	$1,546,000	Net Worth:	-$3,182,000	Debt/ Equity:	NA

Juniper Networks Inc

1194 N Mathilda Ave., Sunnyvale, CA, 94089; **PH:** 1-408-745-2000; **Fax:** 1-408-745-2100;
http:// www.juniper.net

General - Incorporation	DE	Stock - Price on:12/24/2007	$25.31
Employees	4,833	Stock Exchange	NDQ
Auditor	Ernst & Young LLP	Ticker Symbol	JNPR
Stk Agt	Wells Fargo Bank, N.A.	Outstanding Shares	566,300,000
Counsel	Wilson Sonsini Goodrich & Rosati	E.P.S	$0.53
DUNS No.	NA	Shareholders	NA

Business: The groups principle activities include designing products and services for Internet protocol (IP) network solutions. The group operates through three business segments namely infrastructure, SLT and service. The groups products include scalable router products and network security products. The groups services include technical and support services. The group operates from United States.
Primary SIC and add'l.: 7373
CIK No: 0001043604
Subsidiaries: Juniper Networks (Cayman) Ltd., Juniper Networks (US), Inc
Officers: Scott Kriens/Chmn., CEO/$6,522,175.00, Pradeep Sindhu/Vice Chmn., CTO, Founder/$2,124,468.00, Robert R.B. Dykes/58/Exec. VP - Business Operations, CFO/$2,861,075.00, Mitchell Gaynor/General Counsel, Eddie Minshull/Exec. VP - Worldwide Field Operations/$2,130,287.00, Kim Perdikou/Exec. VP, GM - Infrastructure Products Group, Steven Rice/Exec. VP - Human Resources, Spencer Greene/VP - Corporate Development, Penny Still/Contact - Media - EMEA, Ross Inglis/Contact - Media, Apac, Ki-Sung Kim/Contact - Media, Korea, Apac, Robyn Denholm/CFO, Exec. VP, Penny Wilson/Chief Marketing Officer, Queenie Ng/Contact - Media - China, Hong Kong, Taiwan, Apac, Wendy Lang/Contact - Media - Australia, New Zealand, South Asia, Apac (29 Officers included in Index)
Directors: Scott Kriens/Chmn., CEO, Pradeep Sindhu/Vice Chmn., CTO, Founder, Michael J. Lawrie/54/Dir., William R. Hearst/58/Dir., Kenneth Levy/Dir., William R. Stensrud/57/Dir., Stratton Sclavos/46/Dir., Robert M. Calderoni/48/Dir., Kenneth Goldman/58/Dir.
Owners: Robert Sturgeon, Frank Marshall, Michael J. Lawrie, Edward Minshull, Kenneth Levy, Pradeep Sindhu/1.90%, Scott Kriens/2.70%, William R. Stensrud, AXA Financial, Inc./6.50%, Robert Dykes, T. Rowe Price Associates, Inc./12.50%, Stratton Sclavos, Insiders/5.40%, William R. Hearst, FMR Corp./14.90% (17 Owners included in Index)
Financial Data: Fiscal Year End:12/31   Latest Annual Data: 12/31/2006

Year	Sales		Net Income
2006	$2,303,580,000		-$1,001,437,000
2005	$2,063,957,000		$354,029,000
2004	$1,336,019,000		$135,746,000
Curr. Assets:	$2,521,806,000	Curr. Liab.:	$762,617,000	P/E Ratio:	51.65
Plant, Equip.:	$349,930,000	Total Liab.:	$1,253,311,000	Indic. Yr. Divd.:	NA
Total Assets:	$7,368,395,000	Net Worth:	$6,115,084,000	Debt/ Equity:	0.0645

Jupiter Enterprises Inc

No. 24 Xiao Shi Qiao , Jiugulou St., Xicheng District, Beijing, 100009; **PH:** 86-133-41000223

General - Incorporation	NV	Stock - Price on:12/24/2007	$0.07
Employees	NA	Stock Exchange	OTC
Auditor	Killman, Murrell & Co., P.c.	Ticker Symbol	JPTR
Stk Agt	Securities Transfer Corp	Outstanding Shares	NA
Counsel	NA	E.P.S	NA
DUNS No.	NA	Shareholders	NA

Business: The group's principle activity is that of a development stage enterprise. It was formed to be a direct sales marketing company to distribute natural health products via the Internet. The company abandoned this business plan in 2001 without undertaking any operation and its activities have been limited to its formation and the raising of equity capital. Bluesky is a steel fabrication company that fabricates heavy steel girders for hi-rise construction projects, lightweight steel buildings and bridges.
Primary SIC and add'l.: 9999
CIK No: 0001083422
Subsidiaries: Beijing MingHe-Han Science and Technology Co., Ltd
Officers: Chris Harper/59/Dir., CEO, Pres., Sec., Alexander Chen/65/Dir., CFO, Treasurer
Directors: Chris Harper/59/Dir., CEO, Pres., Sec., Alexander Chen/65/Dir., CFO, Treasurer
Owners: Alexander Chen/2.10%, Chris Harper/92.80%, Insiders/94.90%
Financial Data: Fiscal Year End:03/31   Latest Annual Data: 03/31/2007

Year	Sales		Net Income
2007	NA		-$1,000
2006	NA		-$29,000
2005	NA		-$35,000
Curr. Assets:	NA	Curr. Liab.:	$268,000		
Plant, Equip.:	NA	Total Liab.:	$268,000	Indic. Yr. Divd.:	NA
Total Assets:	NA	Net Worth:	-$268,000	Debt/ Equity:	NA

Jupiter Marine International Hldgs Inc

1303 10th St. E, Palmetto, FL, 34221; **PH:** 1-941-729-5000; **Fax:** 1-941-729-5005;
http:// www.jupitermarine.com

General - Incorporation	FL	Stock - Price on:12/24/2007	$0.11
Employees	73	Stock Exchange	OTC
Auditor	Spicer, Jeffries LLP	Ticker Symbol	JMIH
Stk Agt	Florida Atlantic Stock Transfer, Inc.	Outstanding Shares	18,860,000
Counsel	NA	E.P.S	-$0.07
DUNS No.	NA	Shareholders	NA

Business: The group's principal activities are to design, manufacture and market a diverse mix of sportfishing boats under the jupiter name. The outboard product line consists of four outboard powered center console models: 31' open center console, 31' cuddy cabin, 31' forward seating centre, 27' open center console and 27' console-berth model. The inboard models include a completely redesigned 35 foot flybridge convertible as well as a 38 foot flybridge convertible. The inboard boats are primarily used for fishing and fishing related activities and they also serve as cruising vessels. The outboard powered product lines deep-v hulls are specifically designed to perform at high speeds in offshore sea. There is no lean or cavitation in a turn. The group's principal offices and manufacturing facilities are located in port everglades. The boats are sold to authorized dealers in the United States along the east coast and gulf of Mexico, as well as Puerto Rico.

Primary SIC and add'l.: 3732 6719

CIK No: 0001063154

Officers: Carl Herndon/CEO, Pres., Lawrence S. Tierney/62/Dir., CFO, COO, Sec., VP

Directors: Lawrence S. Tierney/62/Dir., CFO, COO, Sec., VP, Kerry Clemmons/63/Dir.

Owners: Insiders/62.00%, Lawrence Tierney/12.50%, Kerry Clemmons/2.50%, Carl Herndon/52.40%, Insiders/62.00%

Financial Data: *Fiscal Year End:*07/30 *Latest Annual Data:* 07/28/2007

Year	Sales	Net Income
2007	$15,225,000	-$1,366,000
2006	$15,150,000	$237,000
2005	$11,463,000	$421,000

Curr. Assets:	$1,796,000	Curr. Liab.:	$1,053,000		
Plant, Equip.:	$904,000	Total Liab.:	$1,509,000	Indic. Yr. Divd.:	NA
Total Assets:	$2,718,000	Net Worth:	$1,209,000	Debt/ Equity:	0.1578

Jupitermedia Corp

23 Old Kings Hwy. S, Darien, CT, 06820; *PH:* 1-203-662-2800; *Fax:* 1-203-655-4686; *http://* www.jupitermedia.com; *Email:* info@jupitermedia.com

General - Incorporation	DE	Stock- Price on:12/24/2007	$7.31
Employees	678	Stock Exchange	NDQ
Auditor	Deloitte & Touche LLP	Ticker Symbol	JUPM
Stk Agt	American Stock Transfer & Trust Co.	Outstanding Shares	35,910,000
Counsel	NA	E.P.S	$0.08
DUNS No.	NA	Shareholders	NA

Business: The group's principal activity is to provide global real-time news, information, research and media resources for information technology, Internet industry and graphics professionals. Jupiterweb, the online division operates five distinct online networks: Internet.com and earthweb.com for it professionals, devx.com for developers, clickz.com for interactive marketers and arttoday.com for graphics professionals. The jupiter research division provides business and technology market research in 18 business areas and 14 vertical markets. In addition, the jupiter events division of the group produces offline conferences and trade shows focused on it and business-specific topics, including wi-fi planet, search engine strategies and Internet planet. On 01-Jul-2003, the group acquired arttoday inc, on 14-Jul-2003, acquired the assets of devx.com, on 11-Dec-2003, the group acquired ppcforhosts.com and on 01-Apr-2004, the group acquired comstock inc.

Primary SIC and add'l.: 7375

CIK No: 0001083712

Subsidiaries: Agence Images S.A.S., asia.internet.com LLC, Australia.internet.com Pty Ltd, Bananastock Limited, Comstock Images Sarl, Creatas, LLC, Dynamic Graphics International, Limited, Dynamic Graphics, Inc., Goodshoot S.A.S., Hemera Technologies Corporation, Hemera Technologies Inc., I-Venture Management LLC, internet.com Canada Corporation, internet.com Limited, IT Stock International Limited 26 Subsidiaries included in the Index

Officers: Alan M. Meckler/Chmn., CEO/$1,577,149.00, Christopher S. Cardell/Dir., COO, Pres./$1,136,977.00, Edward Grossman/Sr. VP, GM - Operations, Marketing, Mitchell S. Eisenberg/Sr. VP, General Counsel, Augustine Venditto/VP, Editor-In-Chief - Jupiteronlinemedia, Mark Labbe/CTO, VP, David M. Arganbright/VP - Business Development, Licensing, Maria Kessler/VP - Creative Business Affairs, Jupiterimages, Mark Nickerson/VP - Image Operations, Jupiterimages, Rick Thompson/VP - Sales, North America, Jupiterimages, Donald J. O'Neill/CFO, VP, Kim Guinta/VP - Human Resources, Administration, Scott Bialous/VP - Group Publisher, Jupiteronlinemedia, Laurel Touby/Sr. VP - Mediabistro, Omer Algar/VP - Operations, Jupiteronlinemedia

Directors: Alan M. Meckler/Chmn., CEO, Christopher S. Cardell/Dir., COO, Pres., Gilbert F. Bach/Dir., Michael J. Davies/Dir., John R. Patrick/Dir., William A. Shutzer/Dir.

Owners: Burgundy Asset Management Ltd./9.00%, Federated Investors, Inc./9.10%, William A. Shutzer/1.20%, Insiders/39.20%, Christopher S. Cardell/3.90%, Christopher J. Baudouin, Transamerica Investment Management, LLC/7.20%, Alan M. Meckler/34.70%, Integral Capital Partners VII, L.P./2.00%, Integral Capital Management VI, LLC/3.10%, Michael J. Davies, Artisan Partners LP/5.30%, John R. Patrick, Gilbert F. Bach, Integral Capital Management VII, LLC/2.00% *(16 Owners included in Index)*

Financial Data: *Fiscal Year End:*12/31 *Latest Annual Data:* 12/31/2006

Year	Sales	Net Income
2006	$137,530,000	$13,124,000
2005	$124,577,000	$78,399,000
2004	$71,888,000	$15,737,000

Curr. Assets:	$40,138,000	Curr. Liab.:	$52,288,000	P/E Ratio:	243.67
Plant, Equip.:	$11,691,000	Total Liab.:	$102,368,000	Indic. Yr. Divd.:	NA
Total Assets:	$332,190,000	Net Worth:	$229,822,000	Debt/ Equity:	0.2076

Jurak Corp World Wide Inc

1181 Grier Dr., Ste. C, Las Vegas, NV, 89119; *PH:* 1-702-914-9688; *http://* www.jurak.com

General - Incorporation	MN	Stock- Price on:12/24/2007	NA
Employees	NA	Stock Exchange	OTC
Auditor	Carver Moquist & O'Connor, LLC	Ticker Symbol	LQWC
Stk Agt	Signature Stock Transfer, Inc.	Outstanding Shares	NA
Counsel	NA	E.P.S	-$0.04
DUNS No.	NA	Shareholders	NA

Business: The groups principle activity is to provide herbal supplement product. The product of the group is Jurak Classic Whole Body Tonic.

Primary SIC and add'l.: 2000

CIK No: 0001060888

Officers: Anthony Carl Jurak/Chmn., CEO, Acting Chief Accounting Officer, Roger Theriault/Pres., Daniel B. Mowrey/Scientific Validation, Maria J. Guedes/39/VP - Operations, Assist. Sec.

Directors: Anthony Carl Jurak/Chmn., CEO, Acting Chief Accounting Officer

Owners: Maria Guedes, Insiders/74.13%, Anthony C. Jurak/66.66%, Roger Theriault/6.91%

Financial Data: *Fiscal Year End:*05/31 *Latest Annual Data:* 5/31/2006

Year	Sales	Net Income
2006	$1,445,000	-$1,088,000
2005	$2,364,000	-$509,000
2004	$2,692,000	-$410,000

Curr. Assets:	$111,000	Curr. Liab.:	$605,000		
Plant, Equip.:	$15,000	Total Liab.:	$606,000	Indic. Yr. Divd.:	NA
Total Assets:	$171,000	Net Worth:	-$435,000	Debt/ Equity:	NA

K Swiss Inc

31248 Oak Crest Dr., Westlake Village, CA, 91361; *PH:* 1-818-706-5100; *Fax:* 1-818-706-5390; *http://* www.kswiss.com; *Email:* kscs@k-swiss.com

General - Incorporation	DE	Stock- Price on:12/24/2007	$28.06
Employees	522	Stock Exchange	NDQ
Auditor	Grant Thornton LLP	Ticker Symbol	KSWS
Stk Agt	Bank of New York	Outstanding Shares	34,650,000
Counsel	NA	E.P.S	$1.62
DUNS No.	04-443-6335	Shareholders	NA

Business: The group's principle activities are to design, develop and market footwear for fitness and casual activities. These products are sold in the United States through independent sales representatives primarily to specialty athletic footwear stores, pro shops, sporting good stores and department stores. The products are manufactured in China and Taiwan and are marketed internationally through a number of foreign distributors. In addition, the group markets a limited line of k-swiss branded apparel and accessories. The group's quarterly revenue for September 2007 was 107.25 millions of USD.

Primary SIC and add'l.: 5139 3149

CIK No: 0000862480

Subsidiaries: 1166789 Ontario Inc., ERE Footwear Inc., ERE Footwear LLC, KSwiss Australia Pty. Ltd., KSwiss Canada Corp., KSwiss Direct Inc., KSwiss International Ltd., KSwiss NS Inc., KSwiss Pacific Inc., KSwiss S.A. de C.V., KSwiss Sales Corp., KS Amsterdam B.V., KS France SAS, KS UK Ltd., KSI Germany GmbH 17 Subsidiaries included in the Index

Officers: George Powlick/63/CFO/$788,820.00

Owners: David Nichols, Insiders/2.50%, David Nichols/1.20%, Lawrence Feldman, Third Avenue Management LLC/8.70%, Royce & Associates, LLC/13.80%, Steven Nichols, George Powlick/0.90%, Insiders, Nichols Family Trust, Barclays Global Investors, NA/10.30%, David Lewin, Lee Green, Lawrence Feldman, Oppenheimer Capital LLC/7.20% *(18 Owners included in Index)*

Financial Data: *Fiscal Year End:*12/31 *Latest Annual Data:* 12/31/2006

Year	Sales	Net Income
2006	$501,148,000	$76,864,000
2005	$508,574,000	$75,248,000
2004	$484,079,000	$71,251,000

Curr. Assets:	$373,440,000	Curr. Liab.:	$49,062,000		
Plant, Equip.:	$15,831,000	Total Liab.:	$58,657,000	Indic. Yr. Divd.:	$0.200
Total Assets:	$404,560,000	Net Worth:	$345,903,000	Debt/ Equity:	NA

K Tel International Inc

2491 Xenium Ln. N, Plymouth, MN, 55441; *PH:* 1-763-559-5566

General - Incorporation	MN	Stock- Price on:12/24/2007	$0.085
Employees	NA	Stock Exchange	OTC
Auditor	Grant Thornton LLP	Ticker Symbol	KTLI
Stk Agt	American Stock Transfer & Trust Co.	Outstanding Shares	NA
Counsel	Briggs & Morgan	E.P.S	NA
DUNS No.	04-670-6594	Shareholders	NA

Business: The group's principal activities are to license its music catalog internationally and market entertainment products through retail and direct response marketing channels in the United States and Europe. It operates through two segments: music and licensing. The music segment consists primarily of the sale of pre-recorded music both from the group's music master catalog and under licenses obtained from other record companies. The group sells compact discs and DVD's directly to retailers, wholesalers and rack service distributors, who stock and manage inventory within music departments for retail stores. In the licensing segment, the group licenses the rights to its master music catalog to third parties worldwide for use in albums, films, television programs and commercials. The customers of the group include retailers, wholesalers and rack service distributors. The group operates in the United States and Europe.

Primary SIC and add'l.: 5941 5735

CIK No: 0000054193

Subsidiaries: Dominion Entertainment, Inc., Dominion Vertriebs GmbH, K-tel (Australia) Pty. Limited, K-tel Direct Limited, K-tel Entertainment (CAN) Inc., K-tel Entertainment (U.K.) Ltd., K-tel Entertainment, Inc., K-tel Services, Inc., K-tel TV, Inc.

Officers: Philip Kives/Chmn., CEO, Kimmy Lockwood/Principal Financial Officer

Directors: Philip Kives/Chmn., CEO

Financial Data: *Fiscal Year End:*06/30 *Latest Annual Data:* 6/30/2006

Year	Sales	Net Income
2006	$4,804,000	-$1,211,000
2005	$6,041,000	-$457,000
2004	$6,679,000	-$87,000

Curr. Assets:	$2,881,000	Curr. Liab.:	$15,254,000		
Plant, Equip.:	$55,000	Total Liab.:	$15,254,000	Indic. Yr. Divd.:	NA
Total Assets:	$3,272,000	Net Worth:	-$11,982,000	Debt/ Equity:	NA

K-Fed Bancorp

1359 N Grand Ave., Covina, CA, 91724; *PH:* 1-626-339-9663; *Fax:* 1-626-858-5745; *http://* www.k-fed.com

General - Incorporation	Federal	Stock- Price on:12/24/2007	$15.91
Employees	94	Stock Exchange	NDQ
Auditor	Crowe Chizek & Co. LLP	Ticker Symbol	KFED
Stk Agt	Registrar & Transfer Co	Outstanding Shares	13,970,000
Counsel	NA	E.P.S	$0.35
DUNS No.	NA	Shareholders	NA

Business: The group's principal activity is to offer a variety of retail and commercial banking services through four branches located in covina, pasadena, fortana and santa clara. The group offers depository products that include savings accounts, money market accounts, demand deposit and time deposit accounts. It originates all types of retail and commercial real estate loans, consumer loans, automobile loans. The group also operates 30 automated teller machines at the kaiser permanente major medical centers located in redwood city, California and south to san diego county.

Primary SIC and add'l.: 6712 6035

CIK No: 0001270985

Subsidiaries: Kaiser Federal Bank

Officers: Kay M. Hoveland/Dir., CEO, Pres., Rita H. Zwern/Dir., Sec., Dustin Luton/CFO

Directors: Kay M. Hoveland/Dir., CEO, Pres., James L. Breeden/Chmn., Gerald A. Murbach/Dir., Robert C. Steinbach/Dir., Frank G. Nicewicz/Dir., Rita H. Zwern/Dir., Sec.

Owners: Laura G. Weisshar, Jeanne R. Thompson, Robert C. Steinbach, K-Fed Mutual Holding Company, Rita H. Zwern, Dustin Luton, James L. Breeden, Insiders, Hovde Capital Advisors LLC, Gerald A. Murbach, Nancy J. Huber, Kay M. Hoveland, K-Fed Mutual Holding Company

Financial Data: Fiscal Year End:06/30   Latest Annual Data: 6/30/2006

Year	Sales	Net Income
2006	$39,835,000	$4,929,000
2005	$31,729,000	$4,997,000
2004	$25,439,000	$3,168,000

Curr. Assets:	$37,356,000	*Curr. Liab.:*	$476,294,000	*P/E Ratio:*	45.46
Plant, Equip.:	$3,416,000	*Total Liab.:*	$646,242,000	*Indic. Yr. Divd.:*	$0.400
Total Assets:	$738,899,000	*Net Worth:*	$92,657,000	*Debt/ Equity:*	1.9634

K-Sea Transportation Partners LP

1 Tower Ctr. Blvd., 17th Fl., East Brunswick, NJ, 10303; *PH:* 1-732-339-6100; *Fax:* 1-732-339-6140; *http://* www.k-sea.com; *Email:* investors@k-sea.com

General - Incorporation	DE	*Stock*- Price on:12/24/2007	$44.35
Employees	690	Stock Exchange	NYSE
Auditor	PricewaterhouseCoopers LLP	Ticker Symbol	KSP
Stk Agt	American Stock Transfer & Trust Co.	Outstanding Shares	9,940,000
Counsel	NA	E.P.S.	$1.55
DUNS No.	NA	Shareholders	NA

Business: The groups principle activity is to provide refined petroleum products marine transportation, distribution and logistics services. The group acquired Sea Coast Transportation LLC, in the year 2005 and ten barges and seven tugboats from Bay Gulf Trading Company, Ltd. The groups specific customers are BP, Chevron, ConocoPhillips, ExxonMobil and Rio Energy. The group operates 61 tank barges, 2 tankers and 41 tugboats in the United States. The groups quarterly revenue for September 2007 was 71.76 millions of USD.

Primary SIC and add'l.: 4424

CIK No: 0001178575

Subsidiaries: Inversiones Kara Sea SRL, K-Sea Acquisition1, LLC, K-Sea Acquisition2, LLC, K-Sea Canada Corp., K-Sea Canada Holdings,Inc., K-Sea OLP GP LLC, K-Sea Operating Partnership L.P., K-Sea Transportation Inc., Norfolk Environmental Services,Inc., Sea Coast Transportation LLC

Officers: Timothy J. Casey/Dir., CEO, Pres., John J. Nicola/CFO, Thomas M. Sullivan/VP - Operations, Richard P. Falcinell/VP - Administration, Sec., Gregory Haslinsky/45/VP - Sales, Marketing, Charles Kauffman/57/VP - Corporate Development

Directors: Timothy J. Casey/Dir., CEO, Pres., James J. Dowling/Chmn., Brian P. Friedman/Dir., Anthony S. Abbate/Dir., Barry J. Alperin/Dir., Frank Salerno/Dir.

Owners: Frank Salerno, Tortoise Energy Infrastructure Corporation/8.10%, Insiders/15.90%, Barry J. Alperin, John J. Nicola, EW Transportation LLC/14.70%, Brian P. Friedman/14.90%, Anthony S. Abbate, Tortoise Capital Advisors, L.L.C./14.10%, Timothy J. Casey, Charles Kauffman, James J. Dowling, Thomas M. Sullivan, Richard P. Falcinelli

Financial Data: Fiscal Year End:06/30   Latest Annual Data: 6/30/2006

Year	Sales	Net Income
2006	$182,768,000	$5,902,000
2005	$121,394,000	$8,136,000
2004	$95,799,000	$21,174,000

Curr. Assets:	$29,901,000	*Curr. Liab.:*	$30,371,000	*P/E Ratio:*	28.61
Plant, Equip.:	$321,689,000	*Total Liab.:*	$219,085,000	*Indic. Yr. Divd.:*	$2.880
Total Assets:	$383,028,000	*Net Worth:*	$163,943,000	*Debt/ Equity:*	1.3931

K-Tron International Inc

Rte. 55 & 553, Pitman, NJ, 08071; *PH:* 1-856-589-0500; *http://* www.ktron.com; *Email:* ktii@ktron.com

General - Incorporation	NJ	*Stock*- Price on:12/24/2007	$102.06
Employees	625	Stock Exchange	NDQ
Auditor	Grant Thornton LLP	Ticker Symbol	KTII
Stk Agt	American Stock Transfer & Trust Co.	Outstanding Shares	2,680,000
Counsel	Morgan, Lewis & Bockius LLP	E.P.S.	$6.851
DUNS No.	04-327-9504	Shareholders	NA

Business: The group's principal activities are to design, manufacture, market and service gravimetric and volumetric feeders, pneumatic conveying systems and related equipments. These equipments are used for handling bulk solids in industries such as plastics, food, chemical, pharmaceutical, cement and other manufacturing industries. The group operates through two business units: feeder group and pneumatic conveying group. The feeder group produces feeders that control the flow of materials into a manufacturing process by mass or weight (gravimetric) or by volume (volumetric feeding). The pneumatic conveying group integrates two brand names, pcs and colormax and the manufacturing of hurricane product line into one business group. The group operates in United States, Canada, Europe, the Middle East, Africa and Asia. On 02-Jan-2003, the group acquired Pennsylvania Crusher Corporation & Jeffrey Specialty Equipment Corporation.

Primary SIC and add'l.: 3823 3559

CIK No: 0000000020

Subsidiaries: Colormax Limited, Gundlach Equipment Corporation, Jeffrey Specialty Equipment Corporation, K-Tron (Schweiz) AG, K-Tron America, Inc., K-Tron Asia Pte Ltd, K-Tron China Limited, K-Tron Deutschland GmbH, K-Tron France S.a.r.l., K-Tron Great Britain Ltd., K-Tron Investment Co., K-Tron Technologies, Inc., Pennsylvania Crusher Corporation, Pneumatic Conveying Systems Limited

Officers: Edward B. Cloues/Chmn., CEO/$1,212,879.00, Donald W. Melchiorre/Sr. VP - Size Reduction Group/$510,231.00, Kevin C. Bowen/Sr. VP - K, Tron Process Group/$547,434.00, Lukas Guenthardt/Sr. VP - Corporate Development/$472,802.00, Ronald R. Remick/Sr. VP, CFO, Treasurer/$523,768.00

Directors: Edward B. Cloues/Chmn., CEO, Richard J. Pinola/Dir., Edward T. Hurd/Dir., Robert A. Engel/Dir., Norman Cohen/Dir.

Owners: Lukas Guenthardt/2.12%, Robert E. Robotti/9.28%, Insiders/18.38%, Donald W. Melchiorre, T. Rowe Price Associates, Inc./9.58%, Robert A. Engel, Richard J. Pinola, Edward B. Cloues/10.62%, Edward T. Hurd, Royce & Associates, LLC/5.58%, Kevin C. Bowen/2.37%, Ronald R. Remick/2.06%, Norman Cohen

Financial Data: Fiscal Year End:12/31   Latest Annual Data: 12/30/2006

Year	Sales	Net Income
2006	$148,127,000	$12,872,000
2005	$118,940,000	$7,282,000

Curr. Assets:	$51,506,000	*Curr. Liab.:*	$25,941,000		
Plant, Equip.:	$22,271,000	*Total Liab.:*	$39,590,000	*Indic. Yr. Divd.:*	NA
Total Assets:	$89,110,000	*Net Worth:*	$49,520,000	*Debt/ Equity:*	0.4366

K-Tronik International Corp

144 Front St., Ste. 700, Toronto, ON, M5J 2L7; *PH:* 1-416-477-2303

General - Incorporation	NV	*Stock*- Price on:12/24/2007	$0.05
Employees	NA	Stock Exchange	NA
Auditor	Rotenberg & Co., LLP	Ticker Symbol	NA
Stk Agt	Pacific Corporate Trust Co	Outstanding Shares	NA
Counsel	NA	E.P.S.	NA
DUNS No.	NA	Shareholders	NA

Business: The group's principal activity is to design, market and distribute electronic stabilizers and illuminator ballasts for florescent lighting fixtures. A ballast is a device in lighting systems that operates fluorescent lights. The group manufactures and distributes only electronic ballasts. The group has a number of product lines including its new mvp multi-voltage product line. This product line is designed to cater to the growing market demand for multi-voltage electronic ballast products. The operations of the group are conducted primarily in the United States and minimally in Asia.

Primary SIC and add'l.: 3612

CIK No: 0001125053

Officers: John Simmonds/Dir., CEO, Pres.

Directors: John Simmonds/Dir., CEO, Pres.

Owners: Jason R. Moretto/3.00%, Insiders/3.00%, Foundation Venture Leasing Inc., in trust/42.20%, ETIFF Holdings, LLC/5.00%, Foundation Opportunities Inc./6.00%

Financial Data: Fiscal Year End:09/30   Latest Annual Data: 9/30/2006

Year	Sales	Net Income
2006	$116,000	-$60,000
2005	NA	$806,000
2004	$5,531,000	-$1,261,000

Curr. Assets:	$33,000	*Curr. Liab.:*	$188,000		
Plant, Equip.:	NA	*Total Liab.:*	$188,000	*Indic. Yr. Divd.:*	NA
Total Assets:	$1,350,000	*Net Worth:*	$1,162,000	*Debt/ Equity:*	NA

K-V Pharmaceutical Co

2503 S Hanley Rd. , St Louis, MO, 63144; *PH:* 1-314-645-6600; *http://* www.kvpharma.com

General - Incorporation	DE	*Stock*- Price on:12/24/2007	$27.24
Employees	1,145	Stock Exchange	NYSE
Auditor	KPMG LLP	Ticker Symbol	KV-A
Stk Agt	United Missouri Bank	Outstanding Shares	49,530,000
Counsel	Gallop, Johnson & Neuman LC	E.P.S.	NA
DUNS No.	00-629-1405	Shareholders	NA

Business: The group's principal activities are to develop, acquire, manufacture and market technologically distinguished branded and generic prescription pharmaceutical products. The group also develops, manufactures and markets raw material products for pharmaceutical, nutritional, personal care, food and other markets. The operations of the group are carried out through its three wholly owned subsidiaries: the branded pharmaceutical operations are conducted through ther-rx corporation. The generic pharmaceutical operations are conducted through ethex corporation with emphasis on the cardiovascular, women's health, pain management and respiratory areas. Particle dynamics, inc. Focus on development, manufacture and marketing of technologically advanced, value-added raw material products.

Primary SIC and add'l.: 2834 6794

CIK No: 0000057055

Subsidiaries: DrugTech Corporation, DrugTech, sarl, ETHEX Corporation, FP1096, Inc., KV Pharmaceutical Company Limited, Particle Dynamics, Inc., Ther-Rx Corporation

Officers: Richard H. Chibnall/52/VP - Finance, Catherine M. Biffignani/VP - Investor Relations

Financial Data: Fiscal Year End:03/31   Latest Annual Data: 3/31/2006

Year	Sales	Net Income
2006	$367,618,000	$15,787,000
2005	$303,493,000	$33,269,000
2004	$283,941,000	$45,848,000

Curr. Assets:	$347,990,000	*Curr. Liab.:*	$36,756,000	*P/E Ratio:*	29.93
Plant, Equip.:	$178,042,000	*Total Liab.:*	$308,738,000	*Indic. Yr. Divd.:*	NA
Total Assets:	$618,013,000	*Net Worth:*	$309,275,000	*Debt/ Equity:*	0.7527

K2 Inc

5818 El Camino Real, Carlsbad, CA, 92008; *PH:* 1-760-494-1000; *http://* www.k2inc.net

General - Incorporation	DE	*Stock*- Price on:12/24/2007	$15.42
Employees	5,000	Stock Exchange	NA
Auditor	Ernst & Young LLP	Ticker Symbol	NA
Stk Agt	Computershare Trust Co	Outstanding Shares	49,460,000
Counsel	Gibson, Dunn & Crutcher LLP	E.P.S.	NA
DUNS No.	00-691-4253	Shareholders	NA

Business: The group's principal activities are to design, manufacture and market sporting goods, recreational products and selected industrial products. The group offers a diverse portfolio of products used primarily in individual sports activities such as alpine skiing, snowboarding, in-line skates, snowboards, mountain and bmx biking, fishing and watersport activities. The industrial products consist primarily of shakespeare monofilament line used in weed trimmers, paper mills, shakespeare fiberglass,

composite marine antennas and composite utility and decorative light pole. The group acquired rawlings sporting goods company, inc, worth, inc, brass eagle, inc, fotoball usa, inc and certain assets and liabilities of winterquest llc in 2003 and volkl sports holding ag, the marker group, marmot mountain ltd and ex officio in 2004.

Primary SIC and add'l.: 3949 2329 2339 3663

CIK No: 0000006720

Subsidiaries: BIL Grudstucksverwaltungs-GmbH& Co. WEDA KG, Brass Eagle LLC, Carve Inc., Cavoma LP, Cavoma Ltd., Clarance S.a.r.l., Earth Products Inc., Ex Officio Internet Company LLC, Ex Officio LLC, Expandpermit Limited, Hilton Corporate Casuals LLC, JRC Products Limited, JT Protective Gear LLC, Jt Usa LLC, K-2 Corporation 78 Subsidiaries included in the Index

Officers: Wayne J. Merck/Dir., CEO, Pres./$1,381,145.00, David Y. Satoda/VP - Taxes, Thomas R. Hillebrandt/Corporate Controller, Dudley W. Mendenhall/Sr. VP, CFO/$522,090.00, John J. Rangel/Pres./$723,448.00, Monte H. Baier/VP, General Counsel, Sec.

Directors: Richard J. Heckmann/64/Chmn., Edward F. Ryan/51/Dir., Wilford D. Godbold/69/Dir., Brian R. Anderson/Dir. - Business Development, Dan Quayle/60/Dir., Lou L. Holtz/71/Dir., Alfred E. Osborne/63/Dir., Ann Meyers/53/Dir., Robin E. Hernreich/63/Dir., Christopher C. Ames/53/Dir.

Owners: Goldman Sachs & Co. and The Goldman Sachs Group, Inc./5.60%, J. Wayne Merck, Dimensional Fund Advisors LP/8.50%, Dudley W. Mendenhall, Alfred E. Osborne, Robert Marcovitch, Ann Meyers, Richard J. Heckmann/1.60%, ICM Asset Management, Inc./5.00%, Insiders/4.40%, Lou L. Holtz, John J. Rangel, Robin E. Hernreich, Dan Quayle, Wilford D. Godbold *(17 Owners included in Index)*

Financial Data: Fiscal Year End:12/31   Latest Annual Data: 12/31/2006

Year	Sales	Net Income
2006	$1,394,656,000	$37,688,000
2005	$1,313,598,000	-$211,561,000
2004	$1,200,727,000	$38,941,000

Curr. Assets:	$844,218,000	Curr. Liab.:	$283,542,000	P/E Ratio: 20.56
Plant, Equip.:	$143,350,000	Total Liab.:	$695,817,000	Indic. Yr. Divd.: NA
Total Assets:	$1,235,454,000	Net Worth:	$539,637,000	Debt/ Equity: 0.6970

Kadant Inc

1 Technology Pk. Dr., Westford, MA, 01886; **PH:** 1-978-776-2000; **Fax:** 1-978-635-1593; *http://* www.kadant.com

General - Incorporation	DE	Stock - Price on:12/24/2007	$29.65
Employees	2,000	Stock Exchange	NYSE
Auditor	Ernst & Young LLP	Ticker Symbol	KAI
Stk Agt	American Stock Transfer & Trust Co.	Outstanding Shares	13,940,000
Counsel	NA	E.P.S.	$1.32
DUNS No.	61-734-9139	Shareholders	NA

Business: The group's principal activity is to manufacture and market custom-engineered systems and equipment, accessory equipment and related consumables. The group operates in two segments: pulp and papermaking equipment and systems and composite and fiber-based products. The pulp and papermaking equipment and systems segment develops, manufactures and markets a range of equipment and products for the domestic and international papermaking and paper recycling industries. The composite and fiber-based products segment manufactures and markets fiber-based composite products for the building industry and manufactures and sells agricultural carriers derived from cellulose fiber.

Primary SIC and add'l.: 3555 3554

CIK No: 0000886346

Subsidiaries: ArcLine Products, Inc., D.S.T. Pattern Engineering Company Limited, Fibergen Securities Corporation, Fiberprep Inc., Fiberprep Securities Corporation, Fibertek U.K. Limited, Johnson Acquisition Corp., Johnson Australia Pty., Ltd., Johnson Corp. Asia Pacific Pty., Ltd., Johnson Corporation (JoCo) Limited, Johnson Diagnosys Ltd., Johnson Nederland B.V., Johnson Norway AS, Johnson Services Wisconsin Corp., Johnson-Fluiten S.r.l. 69 Subsidiaries included in the Index

Officers: William A. Rainville/Chmn., CEO, Pres./$1,960,163.00, Edward J. Sindoni/COO, Exec. VP/$549,032.00, Thomas M. Obrien/CFO, Exec. VP/$580,200.00, Michael J. McKenney/VP - Finance, Chief Accounting Officer, Sandra L. Lambert/VP, General Counsel, Sec., Daniel J. Walsh/Treasurer, Edwin D. Healy/VP/$404,968.00, Jonathan W. Painter/Exec. VP/$454,906.00, Eric T. Langevin/Sr. VP, Wesley A. Martz/VP - Marketing

Directors: William A. Rainville/Chmn., CEO, Pres., John M. Albertine/Dir., Thomas C. Leonard/Dir., John K. Allen/Dir., Francis L. McKone/Dir.

Owners: Jonathan W. Painter, Wachovia Corporation/7.90%, William A. Rainville/3.90%, Edward J. Sindoni, Thomas C. Leonard, John K. Allen, John M. Albertine, NWQ Investment Management Co LLC/6.20%, Insiders/7.10%, Thomas M. OBrien, Edwin D. Healy, Dimensional Fund Advisors LP/8.50%, Francis L. McKone

Financial Data: Fiscal Year End:12/31   Latest Annual Data: 06/30/2007

Year	Sales	Net Income
2007	$89,107,000	$4,914,000
2006	$341,613,000	$17,097,000
2005	$243,713,000	$6,877,000

Curr. Assets:	$155,361,000	Curr. Liab.:	$79,915,000	P/E Ratio: 22.63
Plant, Equip.:	$32,907,000	Total Liab.:	$147,141,000	Indic. Yr. Divd.: NA
Total Assets:	$355,811,000	Net Worth:	$207,625,000	Debt/ Equity: 0.1762

Kahiki Foods Inc

1100 Morrison Rd., Gahanna, OH, 43230; **PH:** 1-614-322-3180; *http://* www.kahiki.com

General - Incorporation	OH	Stock - Price on:12/24/2007	NA
Employees	NA	Stock Exchange	NA
Auditor	Plante & Moran, PLLC	Ticker Symbol	NA
Stk Agt	Fifth Third Bank	Outstanding Shares	NA
Counsel	NA	E.P.S.	-$0.08
DUNS No.	NA	Shareholders	NA

Business: The groups principle activity is to manufacture frozen food. Products of the group include egg rolls, appetizers, single serve entrees, family meal entrees, sauces, and similar products. Customers served by the group include retail food stores, membership warehouse clubs and foodservice operators. The group operates from the United States, Canada and Mexico.

Primary SIC and add'l.: 2035 2038 5142

CIK No: 0001283928

Officers: Alan Hoover/52/CEO, Pres., Fred Niebauer/CFO, Mark Novak/53/VP - Manufacturing, Logistics, Tim Tsao/VP - Sales, Marketing, Gil Wilson/48/VP - Strategic Accounting

Financial Data: Fiscal Year End:03/31   Latest Annual Data: 03/31/2006

Year	Sales	Net Income
2006	$22,652,000	$565,000
2005	$18,499,000	$64,000

Curr. Assets:	$5,387,000	Curr. Liab.:	$11,621,000	
Plant, Equip.:	$12,211,000	Total Liab.:	$12,071,000	Indic. Yr. Divd.: NA
Total Assets:	$18,184,000	Net Worth:	$6,114,000	Debt/ Equity: 0.0694

Kaire Holdings Inc

7700 Irvine Ctr. Dr., Ste. 870, Irvine, CA, 92618; **PH:** 1-949-861-3560; *http://* www.imt-ltd.com

General - Incorporation	DE	Stock - Price on:12/24/2007	$0.015
Employees	8	Stock Exchange	OTC
Auditor	PMB Helin Donovan, LLP	Ticker Symbol	KAIH
Stk Agt	Jersey Transfer & Trust Co	Outstanding Shares	NA
Counsel	NA	E.P.S.	NA
DUNS No.	62-308-4993	Shareholders	NA

Business: The group's principal activity is to provide specialized pharmacy services and products to defined markets that include HIV patients and seniors. The group's subsidiary, classic care, inc. Operates as an agency distributor of pharmaceutical products, via a unique prescription packaging system for consumers at senior assisted living and retirement centers in the los angeles area. Classic care purchases prescription drugs in bulk and fills prescriptions for individuals. The yesrx health advocate program (hap) provides medication compliance programs to HIV/aids, diabetic and senior health communities. The hap provides specialized pharmacy care, health and disease information and education and individual patient counseling along with customizable medication compliance program for HIV patients.the group acquired sespe pharmacy and entremetrix in 2003 and the group discontinued the operation of entremetrix in Feb,2004.

Primary SIC and add'l.: 2836 2835 8071

CIK No: 0000822997

Subsidiaries: Effective Health, Inc.

Owners: Steve Westlund, Alpha Capital Aktiengesellschaft, Bi Coastal Consulting Group, Longview Intl Equity Fund, LP, Insiders, Longview Fund, LP, Longview Equity Fund, LP

Financial Data: Fiscal Year End:12/31   Latest Annual Data: 12/31/2006

Year	Sales	Net Income
2006	NA	-$1,314,000
2005	$1,253,000	-$2,160,000
2004	$2,218,000	-$976,000

Curr. Assets:	NA	Curr. Liab.:	$5,022,000	
Plant, Equip.:	NA	Total Liab.:	$5,022,000	Indic. Yr. Divd.: NA
Total Assets:	$7,000	Net Worth:	-$5,015,000	Debt/ Equity: NA

Kaiser Aluminum & Chemical Corp

27422 Portola Pk.way, Ste. 350, Foothill Ranch, CA, 92610; **PH:** 1-949-614-1740; *http://* www.kaiseral.com

General - Incorporation	DE	Stock - Price on:12/24/2007	NA
Employees	2,400	Stock Exchange	NA
Auditor	Deloitte & Touche LLP	Ticker Symbol	NA
Stk Agt	NA	Outstanding Shares	NA
Counsel	NA	E.P.S.	NA
DUNS No.	00-916-1191	Shareholders	NA

Business: The group's principal activities are mining and refining of bauxite into alumina, production of primary aluminum and manufacture of fabricated aluminum products. The group operates in three operating segments of aluminum industry and commodities marketing and corporate segments. The aluminum industry segments include: alumina and bauxite, primary aluminum and fabricated products. The alumina and bauxite business unit's products are smelter grade alumina and chemical grade alumina hydrate. The primary aluminum business unit produces commodity grade products as well as value-added products such as rod and billet. The fabricated products group sells value-added products such as heat treat aluminum sheet and plate used in the aerospace and general engineering markets. The commodities marketing segment includes the results of the company's alumina and aluminum hedging activities.

Primary SIC and add'l.: 2819 1099 3334 3354

CIK No: 0000054291

Subsidiaries: Anglesey Aluminium Limited, Kaiser Aluminium International, Inc, Kaiser Aluminum & Chemical of Canada Limited, Kaiser Bellwood Corporation

Officers: Jack A. Hockema/Dir., CEO, Pres., David Conrow/Operations Mgr., John Barneson/Sr. VP, Chief Administrative Officer, Peter Bunin/VP, GM - Raw Materials Engineered Products, Keith Harvey/VP - Sales, Marketing, Aerospace, General Engineering Products, Doug Richman/VP - Engineering, Technology, Ted Diguiseppe/VP, GM - Automotive, Industrial Products, John M. Donnan/VP, Sec., General Counsel, Joseph P. Bellino/CFO, Exec. VP, James McAuliffe/VP - Human Resources, Daniel J. Rinkenberger/VP, Treasurer, Tom Gannon/VP - Marketing, Aerospace, Distribution Products, Ray Parkinson/VP - Research, Development, Engineering, Lynton J. Rowsell/Chief Accounting Officer, Martin Carter/VP, GM - Common Alloy Products

Directors: Jack A. Hockema/Dir., CEO, Pres., Carolyn Bartholomew/Chmn., Brett Wilcox/Dir., Jack Quinn/Dir., Thomas M. Vanleeuwen/Dir., Carl B. Frankel/Dir., Teresa A. Hopp/Dir., William F. Murdy/Dir., Alfred E. Osborne/Dir., Georganne C. Proctor/Dir.

Kaiser Aluminum Corp

27422 Portola Pkwy., Ste. 350, Foothill Ranch, CA, 92610; **PH:** 1-949-614-1740; **Fax:** 1-949-614-1930; *http://* www.kaiseral.com; **Email:** kinfo@kaiseraluminum.com

General - Incorporation	DE	Stock - Price on:12/24/2007	$79.45
Employees	2,425	Stock Exchange	NDQ
Auditor	Deloitte & Touche LLP	Ticker Symbol	KALU
Stk Agt	NA	Outstanding Shares	20,580,000
Counsel	NA	E.P.S.	$159.93
DUNS No.	17-776-2192	Shareholders	NA

Business: The group's principal activities are that of an aluminum industry. The operations of the group are carried out in five segments: alumina and bauxite, engineered products, primary aluminum, flat-rolled products and commodities marketing. Alumina and bauxite segment produces smelter grade alumina and chemical grade alumina hydrate. Engineered products business unit serves a wide range of

industrial segments including the automotive, distribution, aerospace and general engineering markets. Primary aluminum segment produces commodity grade products and value-added products such as rod and billet. Flat-rolled products segment produces and markets heat treat aluminum sheet and plate, which are used in the aerospace and general engineering markets. The operations of the group are located in many foreign countries, including Australia, Canada, ghana, jamaica, and the United Kingdom.

Primary SIC and add'l.: 1099 3354 3334 3353

CIK No: 0000811596

Subsidiaries: Anglesey Aluminium Limited, Kaiser Aluminium International, Inc., Kaiser Aluminum & Chemical Corporation, Kaiser Aluminum & Chemical of Canada Limited, Kaiser Bellwood Corporation

Officers: Jack A. Hockema/Chmn., CEO, Pres./$5,054,056.00, John Barneson/Sr. VP, Chief Administrative Officer/$1,368,253.00, Joseph P. Bellino/CFO, Exec. VP/$653,529.00, Peter Bunin/VP, GM, David Conrow/VP - Kaiser Production System, Ted Diguiseppe/VP, GM - Automotive, Industrial Products, Tom Gannon/VP - Marketing, Aerospace, Distribution Products, Keith Harvey/VP - Sales, Marketing, Doug Richman/VP - Engineering, Technology, Lynton J. Rowsell/Chief Accounting Officer, Martin Carter/VP, GM, Ray Parkinson/VP - Research, Development, Engineering, Daniel J. Rinkenberger/VP, Treasurer, John M. Donnan/VP, Sec., General Counsel/$916,096.00, James McAuliffe/VP - Human Resources

Directors: Jack A. Hockema/Chmn., CEO, Pres., William F. Murdy/Dir., Alfred E. Osborne/Dir., Georganne C. Proctor/Dir., Jack Quinn/Dir., Thomas M. Van Leeuwen/Dir., Brett Wilcox/Dir., Carolyn Bartholomew/Dir., Carl B. Frankel/Dir., Teresa A. Hopp/Dir.

Owners: Daniel J. Rinkenberger, Brett E. Wilcox, Jack Quinn, Insiders/1.80%, Carl B. Frankel, Joseph P. Bellino, Daniel D. Maddox, Georganne C. Proctor, Union VEBA Trust/26.60%, John Barneson, Charles H. Witmer/5.34%, William F. Murdy, Witmer Asset Management/5.20%, Meryl B. Witmer/5.29%, Jack A. Hockema (20 Owners included in Index)

Financial Data: Fiscal Year End:12/31 **Latest Annual Data:** 12/31/2006

Year	Sales	Net Income
2006	$1,357,300,000	$3,167,400,000
2005	$1,089,700,000	-$753,700,000
2004	$942,400,000	-$746,800,000

Curr. Assets:	$384,900,000	Curr. Liab.:	$176,400,000	P/E Ratio:	1.25
Plant, Equip.:	$170,300,000	Total Liab.:	$284,700,000	Indic. Yr. Divd.:	$0.180
Total Assets:	$655,400,000	Net Worth:	$370,700,000	Debt/ Equity:	NA

Kaman Corp

1332 Blue Hills Ave., Bloomfield, CT, 06002; **PH:** 1-860-243-7100; **Fax:** 1-860-243-6365; **http://** www.kaman.com

General - Incorporation	CT	**Stock**- Price on:12/24/2007	$31.72
Employees	3,906	Stock Exchange	NDQ
Auditor	KPMG LLP	Ticker Symbol	KAMN
Stk Agt	Mellon Investor Services LLC	Outstanding Shares	24,350,000
Counsel	Murtha Cullina	E.P.S.	$1.67
DUNS No.	00-115-5225	Shareholders	NA

Business: The group's principal activities are carried out through three segments namely, industrial distribution, aerospace and music distribution. The industrial distribution provides industrial replacement parts like power transmission components, motion control, materials handling, electrical components and wide range of bearings. The aerospace manufactures self-lubricating bearings and driveline couplings for aircraft applications, sh-2g maritime helicopter, k-max aerial truck helicopter and subcontract work of aircraft structures. The music distribution provides domestic and foreign markets with music instruments and accessories and manufactures guitars and other music products. The group's trademarks include adamas, applause, hamer, kaflex, karon, k-max, magic lantern, ovation, lp and latin percussion. In 2003, the group acquired industrial supplies inc.

Primary SIC and add'l.: 3931 3728 3568 3724 5085 5084

CIK No: 0000054381

Subsidiaries: B & J Music Ltd., Delamac de Mexico, S.A. de C.V., Genz Benz Enclosures, Inc., K-MAX Corporation, Kaman Aerospace Corporation, Kaman Aerospace Group, Inc., Kaman Aerospace International Corporation, Kaman Dayron, Inc., Kaman Industrial Technologies Corporation, Kaman Industrial Technologies, Ltd., Kaman Music Corporation, Kaman PlasticFab Group, Inc., Kaman X Corporation, Kamatics Corporation, KMI Europe, Inc. 18 Subsidiaries included in the Index

Officers: Paul R. Kuhn/66/Dir., CEO, Pres./$4,778,605.00, Ronald M. Galla/56/CIO, Sr. VP/$836,379.00, Robert M. Garneau/63/CFO, Exec. VP/$2,780,841.00, John C. Kornegay/58/Pres. - Kamatics Corporation, Lowell J. Hill/VP - Human Resources, Candace A. Clark/53/Sr. VP, Chief Legal Officer, Sec./$1,092,282.00, Michael J. Morneau/VP, Controller, Jack T. Cahill/59/Pres. - Kaman Industrial Technologies Corporation/$1,261,711.00, John B. Lockwood/VP - Tax, Glenn M. Messemer/VP, General Counsel, Edward G. Miller/61/Pres. - Kaman Music Corporation, Gary L. Tong/Assist. VP - Corporate Risk, Safety, Environmental Management, Russell H. Jones/63/Sr. VP, Chief Investment Officer, Treasurer, John J. Tedone/VP - Finance, Patricia C. Goldenberg/Assist. VP, Assistant Treasurer (17 Officers included in Index)

Directors: Paul R. Kuhn/66/Dir., CEO, Pres., Brian E. Barents/64/Dir., Robert Alvine/69/Dir., Reeves E. Callaway/60/Dir., Karen M. Garrison/59/Dir., Richard J. Swift/63/Dir., Edwin A. Huston/69/Dir., Neal J. Keating/52/Dir., COO, Pres., John A. Dibiaggio/75/Dir., Eileen S. Kraus/69/Dir.

Owners: Jack T. Cahill, Ronald M. Galla, Reeves E. Callaway, John A. DiBiaggio, Robert M. Garneau, Karen M. Garrison, Robert Alvine, Insiders/3.10%, Paul R. Kuhn, Richard J. Swift, Brian E. Barents, Candace A. Clark, Eileen S. Kraus, Edwin A. Huston

Financial Data: Fiscal Year End:12/31 **Latest Annual Data:** 12/31/2006

Year	Sales	Net Income
2006	$1,206,154,000	$31,786,000
2005	$1,101,196,000	$13,028,000
2004	$995,192,000	-$11,822,000

Curr. Assets:	$477,920,000	Curr. Liab.:	$198,337,000	P/E Ratio:	21.58
Plant, Equip.:	$54,165,000	Total Liab.:	$333,852,000	Indic. Yr. Divd.:	$0.560
Total Assets:	$630,413,000	Net Worth:	$296,561,000	Debt/ Equity:	NA

Kana Software Inc

181 Constitution Dr., Menlo Park, CA, 94025; **PH:** 1-650-614-8300; **Fax:** 1-650-614-8301; **http://** www.kana.com

General - Incorporation	DE	**Stock**- Price on:12/24/2007	$3.005
Employees	181	Stock Exchange	OTC
Auditor	Burr, Pilger & Mayer, LLP	Ticker Symbol	KANA
Stk Agt	Mellon Investor Services	Outstanding Shares	36,210,000
Counsel	NA	E.P.S.	-$0.148
DUNS No.	NA	Shareholders	NA

Business: The group's principal activity is to provide enterprise customer relationship management software solutions. The group's kana icare application suite is a flexible and scalable, Web-architected solution, integrated on a single platform, that supports multiple customer communication channels. The products of the kana icare application are kana contact center, kana iq, kana response, kana response iq, kana connect and kana marketing. The group also offers optimized versions of icare application software for several specific industries including healthcare, financial services, high technology manufacturing, and telecommunications. The consulting services provided by the group includes business and technical expertise to support the partners and customers, technical support providing multi-channel global support to customers and education services relating to training programs and materials for customers and partners. On 10-Feb-2004, the group acquired hipbone(R) inc.

Primary SIC and add'l.: 7372 5734 7373 7379

CIK No: 0001089907

Subsidiaries: Broadbase Software Gmbh, Broadbase Software, Inc., Foundation Cv, Kana Communications Europe Ltd, Kana Communications Pty Ltd., Kana Software Ab, Kana Software Austria Gmbh, Kana Software B.v., Kana Software Bvba, Kana Software Canada Ltd., Kana Software Gmbh, Kana Software Hong Kong Limited, Kana Software India, Kana Software International Ltd., Kana Software Kk 19 Subsidiaries included in the Index

Officers: Michael S. Fields/Chmn., CEO/$3,065,192.00, John Thompson/CFO, Exec. VP/$576,146.00, Jay Jones/Chief Administrative Officer/$435,512.00, Charlie Isaacs/CTO, Marchai Bruchey/Chief Marketing Officer, Will Bose/General Counsel/$406,847.00, Mark Angel/Sr. VP - Corporate Development, Strategy, Daniel Turano/Sr. VP - Worldwide Field Operations, Sham Chotai/Sr. VP - Engineering

Directors: Michael S. Fields/Chmn., CEO, Jerry R. Batt/Dir., Stephanie Vinella/Dir., Mike Shannahan/Dir., William T. Clifford/Dir., John Nemelka/Dir.

Owners: Empire Overseas Funds / Charter Oak Funds/4.30%, Michael S. Fields/2.30%, William A. Bose, William T. Clifford, John F. Nemelka/21.90%, Michael J. Shannahan, Insiders/25.40%, Jerry R. Batt, Empire Capital Partners, L.P./4.10%, Stephanie Vinella, Jay A. Jones, John M. Thompson, NightWatch Capital Management, LLC/21.90%, William Rowe

Financial Data: Fiscal Year End:12/31 **Latest Annual Data:** 12/31/2006

Year	Sales	Net Income
2006	$54,030,000	-$2,426,000
2005	$43,128,000	-$17,966,000
2004	$48,900,000	-$21,768,000

Curr. Assets:	$16,516,000	Curr. Liab.:	$27,560,000		
Plant, Equip.:	$1,221,000	Total Liab.:	$33,467,000	Indic. Yr. Divd.:	NA
Total Assets:	$30,335,000	Net Worth:	-$3,132,000	Debt/ Equity:	NA

Kanbay International Inc

6400 Shafer Ct., Ste. 100, Rosemont, IL, 60018; **PH:** 1-847-384-6100; **http://** www.kanbay.com

General - Incorporation	DE	**Stock**- Price on:12/24/2007	NA
Employees	5,242	Stock Exchange	NA
Auditor	Ernst & Young LLP	Ticker Symbol	NA
Stk Agt	American Stock Transfer & Trust Co.	Outstanding Shares	NA
Counsel	NA	E.P.S.	NA
DUNS No.	NA	Shareholders	NA

Business: The group's principal activity is to provide information technology services and solutions focused on the financial services industry that combines their industry expertise and technology capabilities. It offer services like business process and technology advice, software package selection and integration, application development, maintenance and support, network and system security and specialized services. The group serves its clients through three-tier global delivery model which combines a relationship management team at the client's location, an offsite team of technology and industry experts at one of their regional delivery centers and an application development, maintenance and support team at one of their delivery centers in India. The group operates in Australia, Hong Kong, India, Japan, Singapore, Canada, United Kingdom and United States.

Primary SIC and add'l.: 7379

CIK No: 0001125011

Subsidiaries: Accurum India Private Limited, Accurum, Inc., Adjoined Consulting LLC, Kanbay (Asia) Limited, Kanbay (HK) Ltd., Kanbay (Japan) Incorporated, Kanbay (Singapore) Pte Ltd., Kanbay Australia Pty Ltd., Kanbay Canada, Inc., Kanbay Europe Limited, Kanbay Global Services, Inc., Kanbay Incorporated, Kanbay Limited, Kanbay Managed Solutions Canada, Inc., Kanbay Managed Solutions, Inc. 18 Subsidiaries included in the Index

Owners: Wasatch Advisors,Inc./7.40%, Donald R. Caldwell/6.00%, Douglas B. Morriss/2.10%, William F. Weissman, Insiders/16.50%, FMR Corp./10.30%, Raymond J. Spencer/5.00%, Cyprian DSouza, Michael E. Mikolajczyk, Harry C. Gambill, Household Investment Funding,Inc./12.70%, William Blair& Company, L.L.C./10.20%, Kenneth M. Harvey, Jean A. Cholka, Roy K. Stansbury

Kandi Technologies Corp

Formerly: Stone Mountain Resources Inc
701 N Green Valley Pk.way, Ste. 200, Henderson, NV, 89074; **PH:** 1-702-990-3489

General - Incorporation	DE	**Stock**- Price on:12/24/2007	$0.51
Employees	NA	Stock Exchange	NA
Auditor	Gately & Associates, LLC	Ticker Symbol	NA
Stk Agt	Corporate Stock Transfer	Outstanding Shares	19,960,000
Counsel	NA	E.P.S.	NA
DUNS No.	NA	Shareholders	NA

Business: The groups principal activity is gold exploration that will be exploring Nevada mineral properties. The group operates from the United States.

Primary SIC and add'l.: 1041

CIK No: 0001316517

Officers: Peter Dodge/54/Dir., CEO, CFO, Pres., Treasurer

Directors: Peter Dodge/54/Dir., CEO, CFO, Pres., Treasurer

Owners: Peter Dodge/15.03%, Excelvantage Group Limited/60.12%

Kansas City Life Insurance Co

3520 Broadway, Kansas City, MO, 64111; *PH:* 1-816-753-7000; *Fax:* 1-816-753-0138; *http://* www.kclife.com

General - Incorporation	MO	Stock- Price on:12/24/2007	$44.96
Employees	537	Stock Exchange	NDQ
Auditor	KPMG LLP	Ticker Symbol	KCLI
Stk Agt	Cheryl Keefer	Outstanding Shares	11,860,000
Counsel	NA	E.P.S.	$3.32
DUNS No.	00-696-5834	Shareholders	NA

Business: The group's principal activity is to provide a diversified portfolio of individual insurance, annuity and group products. The group operates in four business segments: the Kansas city life - individual, the Kansas city life - group, sunset life and the old American. The Kansas city life - individual segment markets variable life and annuities, interest sensitive products and traditional life insurance products. The Kansas city life - group markets group life, disability and dental products and administrative services. The sunset life segment markets interest sensitive and traditional products. The old American segment markets whole life final expense products to seniors. In addition, the group provides interest sensitive and variable products. The operations are carried on in the United States. The group acquired guideone life insurance company in 2003.

Primary SIC and add'l.: 6311 6321

CIK No: 0000054473

Subsidiaries: Old American Insurance Company, Sunset Life Insurance Company of America

Officers: William A. Schalekamp/Sr. VP, General Counsel, Sec.

Owners: Mark A. Milton, Daryl D. Jensen, Tracy W. Knapp, Donald E. Krebs, William R. Blessing, Mark A. Milton, Warren J. Hunzicker, Bradford T. Nordholm, Lee M. Vogel, Walter E. Bixby, Richard L. Finn, Larry E. Winn, Insiders, Cecil R. Miller, JRB Interests, Ltd. *(23 Owners included in Index)*

Financial Data: Fiscal Year End:12/31 Latest Annual Data: 12/31/2006

Year	Sales	Net Income
2006	$448,404,000	$36,918,000
2005	$450,072,000	$36,184,000
2004	$502,473,000	$57,687,000

Curr. Assets:	$203,210,000	Curr. Liab.:	$35,319,000	P/E Ratio:	14.05
Plant, Equip.:	$29,364,000	Total Liab.:	$3,776,118,000	Indic. Yr. Divd.:	$1.080
Total Assets:	$4,460,422,000	Net Worth:	$684,304,000	Debt/ Equity:	NA

Kansas City Power & Light Co

1201 Walnut St., Kansas, MO, 64106; *PH:* 1-816-556-2200; *http://* www.greatplainsenergy.com

General - Incorporation	MO	Stock- Price on:12/24/2007	$29.3
Employees	2,470	Stock Exchange	NA
Auditor	Deloitte & Touche LLP	Ticker Symbol	NA
Stk Agt	UMB Bank, N.A.	Outstanding Shares	86,000,000
Counsel	NA	E.P.S.	$1.67
DUNS No.	00-696-5842	Shareholders	NA

Business: The group's principle activities are to generate, transmit, distribute and sell electricity through its subsidiaries. The subsidiaries of the group are Kansas city power and light company, klt inc and great plains power inc. Kansas city power and light company provides low-cost electricity to retail customers. Klt inc is an investment company that holds interests in unregulated energy-related businesses. Great plains power inc focuses on development, production and trading of wholesale electric capacity and energy.

Primary SIC and add'l.: 4911 4924 6719

CIK No: 0000054476

Subsidiaries: Custom Energy Holdings, LLC, Innovative Energy Consultants Inc., Kansas City Power & Light Company, KLT Energy Services Inc., KLT Inc., Strategic Energy, LLC

Officers: William H. Downey/CEO, Pres., Kevin Bryant/VP - Energy Solutions, Lora Cheatum/VP - Administrative Services, Dana Crawford/VP - Plant Operations, Terry Bassham/CFO, Principal Financial Officer, David Price/VP - Construction, Lori A. Wright/45/Controller, Richard A. Spring/VP - Transmission Services, Stephen T. Easley/Sr. VP - Supply, Chris B. Giles/VP - Regulatory Affairs, William P. Herdegen/VP - Customer Operations, John Marshall/Sr. VP - Delivery, William G. Riggins/VP - Legal, Environmental Affairs, General Counsel, Marvin L. Rollison/VP - Corporate Culture, Community Strategy, Barbara B. Curry/53/Sec. *(17 Officers included in Index)*

Directors: Michael J. Chesser/59/Chmn., Mark A. Ernst/Dir., Randall C. Ferguson/Dir., Luis A. Jimenez/Dir., James A. Mitchell/66/Dir., William C. Nelson/Dir., Linda H. Talbott/Dir., David L. Bodde/65/Dir.

Financial Data: Fiscal Year End:12/31 Latest Annual Data: 12/31/2006

Year	Sales	Net Income
2006	$2,675,349,000	$127,630,000
2005	$2,604,882,000	$162,310,000
2004	$2,464,018,000	$180,811,000

Curr. Assets:	$570,782,000	Curr. Liab.:	$1,202,993,000	P/E Ratio:	17.54
Plant, Equip.:	$3,066,201,000	Total Liab.:	$2,954,744,000	Indic. Yr. Divd.:	$1.660
Total Assets:	$4,335,660,000	Net Worth:	$1,380,916,000	Debt/ Equity:	0.9098

Kansas City Southern

427 W 12th St., Kansas City, MO, 64105; *PH:* 1-816-983-1303; *Fax:* 1-816-983-1108; *http://* www.kcsi.com

General - Incorporation	DE	Stock- Price on:12/24/2007	$39.31
Employees	6,470	Stock Exchange	NYSE
Auditor	KPMG LLP	Ticker Symbol	KSU
Stk Agt	UMB Bank, N.A.	Outstanding Shares	76,810,000
Counsel	NA	E.P.S.	$1.16
DUNS No.	00-194-2218	Shareholders	NA

Business: The groups principle activity is to provide transportation solutions. The group operates from United States.

Primary SIC and add'l.: 6719 4011

CIK No: 0000054480

Subsidiaries: Arrendadora TFM, S.A. de C.V., Canama Transportation, Caymex Transportation, Inc., Gateway Eastern Railway Company, Grupo Transportacion Ferroviaria Mexicana, S.A. de C.V., Joplin Union Depot, Kansas City Southern de Mexico, S.A. de C.V., Kansas City Southern International, Inc, KARA Sub, Inc., KC Terminal Railway, KCS Investment I, Ltd., KCSRC y Compania, S, de N.C. de C.V., Merician Speedway, LLC, Mexrail, Inc., NAFTA Rail, S.A. de C.V. 30 Subsidiaries included in the Index

Officers: Michael R. Haverty/Chmn., CEO/$2,315,352.00, Larry M. Lawrence/Exec. VP, Assist. to The Chmn., Paul J. Weyandt/Sr. VP - Finance, Treasurer, Warren K. Erdman/Exec. VP - Corporate Affairs, Richard M. Zuza/Sr. VP - International Purchasing - Materials/$647,198.00, Arthur L. Shoener/Dir., COO, Exec. VP/$1,344,006.00, Patrick J. Ottensmeyer/CFO, Exec. VP/$560,527.00, Daniel W. Avramovich/Exec. VP - Sales, Marketing/$617,584.00, Scott E. Arvidson/CIO, Exec. VP, Michael K. Borrows/Chief Accounting Officer, Sr. VP, William J. Wochner/Sr. VP, Chief Legal Officer

Directors: Michael R. Haverty/Chmn., CEO, James R. Jones/Dir., Thomas A. McDonnell/Dir., Arthur L. Shoener/Dir., COO, Exec. VP, Robert J. Druten/Dir., Edward A. Allinson/Dir., Karen L. Pletz/60/Dir., Rodney E. Slater/Dir., Terrence P. Dunn/Dir.

Owners: Terrence P. Dunn, Insiders/5.93%, Highbridge Capital Management LLC/6.90%, Patrick J. Ottensmeyer, Arthur L. Shoener, Neuberger Berman, Inc./9.80%, Janus Capital Management LLC/5.40%, Ronald G. Russ, Thomas A. McDonnell, Mac-Per-Wolf Company/5.70%, Daniel W. Avramovich, Michael R. Haverty/3.57%, James R. Jones, Richard M. Zuza, Karen L. Pletz *(19 Owners included in Index)*

Financial Data: Fiscal Year End:12/31 Latest Annual Data: 3/31/2007

Year	Sales	Net Income
2007	NA	$144,500,000
2006	NA	$100,200,000
2005	$1,352,000,000	$100,900,000

Curr. Assets:	$606,000,000	Curr. Liab.:	$637,400,000		
Plant, Equip.:	$2,452,200,000	Total Liab.:	$2,954,600,000	Indic. Yr. Divd.:	NA
Total Assets:	$4,637,300,000	Net Worth:	$1,582,400,000	Debt/ Equity:	1.0055

Kansas City Southern de Mexico, S.A. de C.V.

Formerly: TFM
Av. Perifrico Sur No. 4829, 4to Piso, Col. Parques Del Pedregal, Mexico City, 14010; *PH:* 52-5554475800; *http://* www.tfm.com.mx; *Email:* tfm@tfm.com.mx

General - Incorporation	Mexico	Stock- Price on:12/24/2007	NA
Employees	NA	Stock Exchange	NA
Auditor	PricewaterhouseCoopers, S.C	Ticker Symbol	NA
Stk Agt	NA	Outstanding Shares	NA
Counsel	NA	E.P.S.	NA
DUNS No.	NA	Shareholders	NA

Business: The groups principle activity is to provide freight transportation for the transferring ownership of the concession and related assets to the winning bidder in the government privatization auction. The group operates from United States.

Primary SIC and add'l.: 4011

CIK No: 0001055294

Subsidiaries: Arrendadora TFM S.A. de C.V, Kansas City Southern de Mxico, S. A. de C. V., Mexrail, Inc., Texas Mexican Railway Company

Officers: Michael R. Haverty/Chmn., CEO, Larry M. Lawrence/Exec. VP, Mgr., Paul J. Weyandt/Sr. VP - Finance, Treasurer, Daniel W. Avramovich/Exec. VP - Sales, Marketing, Warren K. Erdman/Exec. VP - Corporate Affairs, Patrick J. Ottensmeyer/CFO, Exec. VP, Michael K. Borrows/Chief Accounting Officer, Sr. VP, William J. Wochner/Sr. VP, Chief Legal Officer, Richard M. Zuza/Sr. VP - International Purchasing, Materials, James R. Jones/Dir., Mgr., Scott E. Arvidson/CIO, Exec. VP, Arthur L. Shoener/Dir., COO, Exec. VP

Directors: Michael R. Haverty/Chmn., CEO, Robert J. Druten/Dir., Terrence P. Dunn/Dir., Thomas A. McDonnell/Dir., Larry M. Lawrence/Dir., Karen L. Pletz/Dir., Rodney E. Slater/Dir., James R. Jones/Dir., Mgr., Arthur L. Shoener/Dir., COO, Exec. VP

Owners: KCS Investment I, Ltd./24.97%, Caymex Transportation, Inc./1.04%, Nafta Rail, S.A. de C.V./49.00%, Kara Sub, Inc./24.97%, KCSM Holdings LLC/0.02%, Insiders/100.00%

Kansas Gas & Electric Co

818 S Kansas Ave., Topeka, KS, 66612; *PH:* 1-785-575-6300; *Fax:* 1-785-575-1796; *http://* www.westarenergy.com

General - Incorporation	KS	Stock- Price on:12/24/2007	$24.76
Employees	2,223	Stock Exchange	NA
Auditor	Deloitte & Touche LLP	Ticker Symbol	NA
Stk Agt	NA	Outstanding Shares	88,850,000
Counsel	NA	E.P.S.	$1.86
DUNS No.	00-694-4151	Shareholders	NA

Business: The group's principle activities include generating, transmiting, distributing and selling electricity in southeastern Kansas. The group operates from United States.

Primary SIC and add'l.: 4911

CIK No: 0000054496

Subsidiaries: Westar Energy, Inc

Officers: William B. Moore/Dir., CEO, Pres., Mark A. Ruelle/CFO, Exec. VP, James Ludwig/Exec. VP - Public Affairs, Consumer Services, Bruce Akin/VP - Operations Strategy, Support, Jeff Beasley/VP - Corporate Compliance, Internal Audit, Greg A. Greenwood/VP - Generation Construction, Kelly B. Harrison/VP - Transmission Operations, Environmental Services, Larry Irick/VP, General Counsel, Corp. Sec., Caroline A. Williams/VP - Distribution Power Delivery, Tony Somma/Treasurer, Leroy P. Wages/VP, Controller, Karla Olsen/Dir. - Corporate Communications, Gina Penzig/Sr. Representative, Communications Media, Erin Dehn/Representative, Communications, Nick Bundy/Representative, Web Content *(19 Officers included in Index)*

Directors: William B. Moore/Dir., CEO, Pres., Charles Q. Chandler/Chmn., Mollie Hale Carter/Dir., R. A. Edwards/Dir., Jerry B. Farley/Dir., Sandra A.J. Lawrence/Dir., Anthony Isaac/Dir., Arthur Krause/Dir., Michael Morrissey/Dir., John C. Nettels/Dir.

Financial Data: Fiscal Year End:12/31 Latest Annual Data: 12/31/2006

Year	Sales	Net Income
2006	$1,605,743,000	$165,309,000
2005	$1,583,278,000	$135,610,000
2004	$1,464,489,000	$178,870,000

Curr. Assets:	$536,720,000	**Curr. Liab.:**	$663,176,000	**P/E Ratio:** 13.03
Plant, Equip.:	$4,071,607,000	**Total Liab.:**	$3,894,280,000	**Indic. Yr. Divd.:** $1.080
Total Assets:	$5,455,175,000	**Net Worth:**	$1,560,895,000	**Debt/ Equity:** 0.9885

Karma Media Inc

4606 Fm 1960 W, Ste. 443, Houston, TX, 77069; *PH:* 1-281-315-8895; *http://* www.karmamedia.com

General - Incorporation	NV	**Stock**- Price on:12/24/2007	NA
Employees	NA	Stock Exchange	OTC
Auditor	Bagell, Josephs, Levine & Co. LLC	Ticker Symbol	GAGI
Stk Agt	Holladay Stock Transfer, Inc.	Outstanding Shares	NA
Counsel	NA	E.P.S.	$0.034
DUNS No.	NA	Shareholders	NA

Business: The group's principle activity is to provide Internet marketing campaigns to socially responsible merchants that market products and services over the Web to like-minded consumers who support the advancement of nonprofit and charitable causes. It matches merchant clients with consumers desiring to support charitable organizations through online purchases. Participating merchants systematically donate a portion of all sales generated through the network of karma media affinity partners to a designated charity. The customers include the special wish foundation, 5-time nba champion dennis rodman, immunocorp and xtrax.

Primary SIC and add'l.: 7375 7379

CIK No: 0001171326

Officers: Claude Eldridge/47/Chmn., CEO, Estelle Reyna/Chmn. - Spokesperson, Jonathan Marshall/National Sales Dir.

Directors: Estelle Reyna/Chmn. - Spokesperson

Financial Data: Fiscal Year End:12/31   Latest Annual Data: 12/31/2006

Year	Sales	Net Income
2006	NA	-$379,000
2005	$230,000	-$939,000
2004	$732,000	-$899,000

Curr. Assets:	$0	**Curr. Liab.:**	$190,000	
Plant, Equip.:	NA	**Total Liab.:**	$190,000	**Indic. Yr. Divd.:** NA
Total Assets:	$50,000	**Net Worth:**	-$139,000	**Debt/ Equity:** NA

Karver International Inc

601 Key Brickell Dr. Ste. 9, Miami, FL, 33131; *PH:* 1-305-350-3996; *http://* www.karverint.com; *Email:* info@karverint.com

General - Incorporation	NY	**Stock**- Price on:12/24/2007	$0.62
Employees	3	Stock Exchange	OTC
Auditor	Berkovits, Lago & Company, LLP	Ticker Symbol	KRVR
Stk Agt	StockTrans, Inc.	Outstanding Shares	13,640,000
Counsel	NA	E.P.S.	-$0.06
DUNS No.	NA	Shareholders	NA

Business: The groups principal activity is to provide health and pharmaceutical services. The group operates from the United States.

Primary SIC and add'l.: 8099

CIK No: 0001124813

Subsidiaries: MDRX, Inc.

Owners: Viktoria Benkovitch/7.89%, First Jemini Trust/37.29%, Karver Holdings, Ltd./17.13%

Financial Data: Fiscal Year End:12/31   Latest Annual Data: 12/31/2006

Year	Sales	Net Income
2006	NA	-$439,000
2005	NA	-$286,000
2004	NA	-$325,000

Curr. Assets:	$42,000	**Curr. Liab.:**	$980,000	
Plant, Equip.:	$38,000	**Total Liab.:**	$980,000	**Indic. Yr. Divd.:** NA
Total Assets:	$108,000	**Net Worth:**	-$872,000	**Debt/ Equity:** NA

Katahdin Bankshares Corp

17 Main St., Ashland, ME, 04732; *PH:* 1-207-435-6461; *Fax:* 1-207-435-6894; *http://* www.katahdintrust.com

General - Incorporation		**Stock**- Price on:12/24/2007	$21
Employees	NA	Stock Exchange	OTC
Auditor	NA	Ticker Symbol	KTHN
Stk Agt	NA	Outstanding Shares	3,010,000
Counsel	NA	E.P.S.	NA
DUNS No.	NA	Shareholders	NA

Business: The groups principal activity is to provide personal and business online banking. The services of the group include checking and saving account, originating loans, mortgages, night depository, safe deposit boxes, merchant credit and debit card services, FICA and withholding tax payment, wire transfer and payroll services. The group operates from the United States.

Primary SIC and add'l.: 6022

CIK No:

Officers: Jon J. Prescott/CEO, Pres., Janet Jandreau/Branch Mgr., Kevin Mirise/VP, Jeffrey Chapman/Financial Consultant, Karen Chapman/VP, Branch Mgr., Carrie Hull/Branch Mgr., Susan Fitzherbert/Branch Mgr., Annette Beaton/VP, Branch Mgr., Emily Hosford/Branch Mgr., Rena Bouchard/VP, Branch Mgr., Linda Delong/AVP, Branch Mgr., Debra Schillinger/Branch Mgr., Diane Green/AVP, Branch Mgr., Peggy Bugbee/Branch Mgr.

Katy Industries Inc

2461 S Clark St., Ste. 630, Arlington, VA, 22202; *PH:* 1-703-236-4300; *Fax:* 1-703-236-3170; *http://* www.katyindustries.com

General - Incorporation	DE	**Stock**- Price on:12/24/2007	NA
Employees	1,544	Stock Exchange	OTC
Auditor	PricewaterhouseCoopers LLP	Ticker Symbol	KATY
Stk Agt	LaSalle Bank N.A	Outstanding Shares	NA
Counsel	Sesco	E.P.S.	-$0.69
DUNS No.	04-463-8369	Shareholders	NA

Business: The group's principal activities are to manufacture and distribute industrial and consumer products. The group operates in two segments: maintenance products group and electrical/electronics group. The maintenance product group manufactures and distributes sanitary maintenance supplies, professional cleaning products, consumer products, abrasives and stains. The electrical/electronics group manufactures and distributes consumer electric corded products, electrical and electronic accessories and components, nonpowered hand tools and specialty metals. The group has international operations in Canada, Mexico, Europe and the Far East countries. On 02-Apr-2003, the group acquired spraychem limited.

Primary SIC and add'l.: 3291 2842 3639 3699 3679

CIK No: 0000054681

Subsidiaries: American Gage & Machine Company, Ashford Holding Corp., CEH Limited, Chatham Resource Recovery Systems, Inc., Contico Europe Limited, Contico Manufacturing Limited, Continental Commercial Products, LLC, DBPI, Inc, GCW, Inc., Glit/Gemtex, Ltd., Hermann Lowenstein, Inc., HPMI, Inc., K-S Energy Corp., Katy International, Inc., Katy Teweh Inc. 26 Subsidiaries included in the Index

Officers: Anthony T. Castor/Dir., CEO, Pres./$1,230,223.00, Keith R. Mills/VP - Sales/$301,983.00, Amir Rosenthal/VP, CFO, General Counsel, Sec./$425,673.00, Philip D. Reinkemeyer/Dir. - Financial Reporting, Treasurer, Robert A. Gail/Pres. - Continental Commercial Products, Douglas A. Brady/VP - Operations/$383,903.00, Joseph E. Mata/VP - Human Resources, David C. Cooksey/Corporate Controller, Assist. Treasurer

Directors: Anthony T. Castor/Dir., CEO, Pres., William F. Andrews/Chmn., Wallace E. Carroll/Dir., Daniel D. Carroll/Dir., Christopher Lacovara/43/Dir., Samuel P. Frieder/Dir., Robert M. Baratta/78/Dir., Christopher Anderson/Dir., Shant Mardirossian/Dir.

Owners: Robert M. Baratta, William F. Andrews, David C. Cooksey, Daniel B. Carroll, Philip D. Reinkemeyer, Wallace E. Carroll, Jr. and the WEC Jr. Trusts/39.10%, Joseph E. Mata, Gabelli Funds, LLC, GAMCO Asset Management Inc.,/22.40%, Keith Mills, Dimensional Fund Advisors, LP/5.60%, Douglas A. Brady, Amelia M. Carroll and the WEC Jr. Trusts/39.40%, Anthony T. Castor/6.00%, Insiders/46.00%, Amir Rosenthal/3.20% (16 Owners included in Index)

Financial Data: Fiscal Year End:12/31   Latest Annual Data: 12/31/2006

Year	Sales	Net Income
2006	$396,166,000	-$12,379,000
2005	$455,197,000	-$13,157,000
2004	$457,642,000	-$36,121,000

Curr. Assets:	$124,860,000	**Curr. Liab.:**	$120,393,000	
Plant, Equip.:	$41,744,000	**Total Liab.:**	$140,662,000	**Indic. Yr. Divd.:** NA
Total Assets:	$182,694,000	**Net Worth:**	$42,032,000	**Debt/ Equity:** NA

Kaydon Corp

315 E Eisenhower Pkwy., Ste. 300, Ann Arbor, MI, 48108; *PH:* 1-734-747-7025; *Fax:* 1-734-747-6565; *http://* www.kaydon.com

General - Incorporation	DE	**Stock**- Price on:12/24/2007	$52.59
Employees	1,900	Stock Exchange	NYSE
Auditor	Ernst & Young LLP	Ticker Symbol	KDN
Stk Agt	Bank of New York	Outstanding Shares	28,290,000
Counsel	NA	E.P.S.	$2.27
DUNS No.	10-163-3782	Shareholders	NA

Business: The group's principal activity is to manufacture bearing systems and components and filters and filter housings. The products also include custom rings, shaft seals, specialty retaining rings, specialty balls, slip-rings, industrial presses, metal alloys and linear deceleration products. These products are used by customers in a wide variety of medical, instrumentation, material handling, machine tool positioning, aerospace, defense, construction, electronic, marine and other industrial applications.

Primary SIC and add'l.: 3592 3593 3569 3562

CIK No: 0000740694

Subsidiaries: ACE Controls International, Inc., ACE Controls, Inc., ACE Japan, LLC, ACE Stossdaempfer, GmbH, Canfield Technologies, Inc., Cooper Geteilte Rollenlager GmbH, Cooper Roller Bearing Company Limited, Cooper Split Roller Bearing Corp., Indiana Precision, Inc., Industrial Tectonics Inc, ITI Japan Trading Company, Kaydon Acquisition XI, Inc., Kaydon Acquisition XII, Inc., Kaydon Custom Filtration Corporation, Kaydon Ring and Seal, Inc. 19 Subsidiaries included in the Index

Officers: Brian P. Campbell/Chmn., CEO, CFO, Pres./$2,812,165.00, Kenneth W. Crawford/50/VP, Corporate Controller, Treasurer/$650,418.00, Peter C. Dechants/VP - Corporate Development, Treasurer/$835,846.00, John F. Brocci/VP - Administration, Sec./$831,493.00

Directors: Brian P. Campbell/Chmn., CEO, CFO, Pres., David A. Brandon/55/Dir., Timothy J. Odonovan/62/Dir., James Oleary/45/Dir., Thomas C. Sullivan/70/Dir.

Owners: John R. Emling, Cramer Rosenthal McGlynn, LLC/7.15%, Peter C. DeChants, Brian P. Campbell/1.07%, Kenneth W. Crawford, James OLeary, David A. Brandon, John F. Brocci, Thomas C. Sullivan, Timothy J. ODonovan, Fenimore Asset Management, Inc./5.13%, Barclays Global Investors, NA/5.11%, Insiders/1.99%, Barrow, Hanley, Mewhinney& Strauss, Inc./5.12%

Financial Data: Fiscal Year End:12/31   Latest Annual Data: 12/31/2006

Year	Sales	Net Income
2006	$403,992,000	$69,508,000
2005	$354,558,000	$73,889,000
2004	$333,811,000	$38,358,000

Curr. Assets:	$497,910,000	**Curr. Liab.:**	$51,632,000	**P/E Ratio:** 23.17
Plant, Equip.:	$95,280,000	**Total Liab.:**	$304,376,000	**Indic. Yr. Divd.:** $0.600
Total Assets:	$737,556,000	**Net Worth:**	$433,180,000	**Debt/ Equity:** 0.4483

Kayenta Kreations Inc

311 S State St., Ste. 460, Salt Lake City, UT, 84111; *PH:* 1-801-364-9262

General - Incorporation	NV	**Stock**- Price on:12/24/2007	$1.15
Employees	NA	Stock Exchange	OTC
Auditor	Pritchett Siler & Hardy P.C	Ticker Symbol	KKRI
Stk Agt	American Registrar & Transfer Co	Outstanding Shares	1,320,000
Counsel	NA	E.P.S.	-$0.01
DUNS No.	93-760-8644	Shareholders	NA

Business: The group's principle activities include producing and marketing specialty children's coloring art books and art coloring pencils. The company discontinued this activity and is currently seeking potential acquisitions. The company is a development stage company. The group operates from United States.

Primary SIC and add'l.: 2731 3952

CIK No: 0001011395

Officers: Brenda White/48/Chmn., CEO, CFO, Pres., Sec., Treasurer

Directors: Brenda White/48/Chmn., CEO, CFO, Pres., Sec., Treasurer

Owners: Lynn Dixon/43.90%, Insiders, Thomas G. Kimble/38.00%, Brenda White

Financial Data: Fiscal Year End:12/31 **Latest Annual Data:** 12/31/2006

Year	Sales	Net Income
2006	NA	-$10,000
2005	NA	-$8,000
2004	NA	-$8,000

Curr. Assets:	NA	Curr. Liab.:	$1,000		
Plant, Equip.:	NA	Total Liab.:	$1,000	Indic. Yr. Divd.:	NA
Total Assets:	NA	Net Worth:	-$1,000	Debt/ Equity:	NA

Kayne Anderson Energy Development Company

717 Texas Ave., Ste.3100, Houston, TX, 77002; *PH:* 1-888-533-1232; *http://* www.kaynebdc.com; *Email:* info@kaynecapital.com

General - Incorporation	MD	Stock- Price on:12/24/2007	$25.92
Employees	NA	Stock Exchange	NYSE
Auditor	PricewaterhouseCoopers LLP	Ticker Symbol	KED
Stk Agt	American Stock Transfer & Trust Co.	Outstanding Shares	NA
Counsel	NA	E.P.S.	NA
DUNS No.	NA	Shareholders	NA

Business: The groups principle activity is to generate current income and capital appreciation primarily through debt and equity investments. The group operates from the United States and Canada. The groups quarterly revenue for September 2007 was 2.82 miilions of USD.

Primary SIC and add'l.: 6726

CIK No: 0001363890

Officers: Kevin McCarthy/Dir., CEO, Pres., David Shladovsky/Chief Compliance Officer, Sec., Ian Sinnott/Research Analyst, Marc Minikes/Research Analyst, David Schumacher/Research Analyst, Justin Campeau/Analyst, Terry Hart/CFO, Treasurer, J. C. Frey/VP, Assist. Sec., Assist. Treasurer, Sr. MD, Portfolio Mgr., Ron Logan/VP, Jim Baker/VP, John Riley/Controller, Jody Meraz/VP - Kayne Anderson Capital Advisors, Ryan Scott/Assoc. - Kayne Anderson Capital Advisors, David Labonte/Head - Energy Research, Michael Schimmel/Research Analyst, Kayne Anderson Capital Advisors *(18 Officers included in Index)*

Directors: Kevin McCarthy/Dir., CEO, Pres., Robert V. Sinnott/Dir., Keith B. Forman/Dir., Barry R. Pearl/Dir., Albert L. Richey/Dir., William L. Thacker/Dir.

Owners: Terry A. Hart, J. C. Frey, Kevin S. McCarthy, Albert L. Richey, William L. Thacker, Keith B. Forman, Ron M. Logan, Barry R. Pearl, David J. Shladovsky, Robert V. Sinnott, Insiders, James C. Baker

Financial Data: Fiscal Year End:11/30 **Latest Annual Data:** 11/30/2006

Year	Sales	Net Income
2006	$2,047,000	$8,688,000

Curr. Assets:	$136,832,000	Curr. Liab.:	$1,690,000		
Plant, Equip.:	NA	Total Liab.:	$1,690,000	Indic. Yr. Divd.:	NA
Total Assets:	$243,604,000	Net Worth:	$241,914,000	Debt/ Equity:	NA

KB Home

10990 Wilshire Blvd., 7th Fl., Los Angeles, CA, 90024; *PH:* 1-310-231-4000; *Fax:* 1-310-231-4222; *http://* www.kbhome.com; *Email:* investorrelations@kbhome.com

General - Incorporation	DE	Stock- Price on:12/24/2007	$42
Employees	5,100	Stock Exchange	NYSE
Auditor	Ernst & Young LLP	Ticker Symbol	KBH
Stk Agt	Mellon Investor Services LLC	Outstanding Shares	89,330,000
Counsel	NA	E.P.S.	-$0.23
DUNS No.	06-446-4621	Shareholders	NA

Business: The groups principle activity is to provide construction of homes. The group operates through two segments namely construction operation and mortgage banking. The group operates from United States.

Primary SIC and add'l.: 6162 1521 1542

CIK No: 0000795266

Subsidiaries: Branching Tree Corp., City Ranch, LLC, Clear Brook Crossing Development LP, Clear Brook Crossing Inc., Colony Homes LLC, Custom Decor, Inc., e.KB,Inc., Estes Homebuilding Co., Fgmc, Inc., General Homes Corporation, General Homes Development LLC, Gie KB, Hallmark Residential Group, Inc., HomeSafe Company, HomeSafe Escrow Company 116 Subsidiaries included in the Index

Officers: Jeffrey T. Mezger/CEO, Pres., William A. Richelieu/Assist. Corp. Sec., Wendy Marlett/Sr. VP - Sales, Marketing, Glen Barnard/Sr. VP - Kbnxt Group, Kelly Masuda/Sr. VP, Treasurer, William R. Hollinger/Chief Accounting Officer, Sr. VP, Lisa M. Kalmbach/Sr. VP - Studios, Cory F. Cohen/Sr. VP - Tax, Robert Freed/51/Sr. VP - Investment, John Staines/Sr. VP - Human Resources, Wendy C. Shiba/Exec. VP, General Counsel, Corp. Sec., Katoiya Marshall/Primary Investor Relations Officer, Anna Levin/Primary Investor Relations Officer, Dom Cecere/CFO, Sr. VP

Directors: Stephen F. Bollenbach/Chmn., Leslie Moonves/Dir., Luis G. Nogales/Dir., Ron Burkle/Dir., Timothy W. Finchem/59/Dir., Ray R. Irani/73/Dir., Kenneth M. Jastrow/Dir., James A. Johnson/64/Dir., Terrence J. Lanni/Dir., Melissa Lora/Dir., Michael G. McCaffery/54/Dir.

Owners: Jeffrey L. Gendell/6.80%, Marsico Capital Management, LLC/9.20%, Jeffrey T. Mezger, William R. Hollinger, Melissa Lora, Luis G. Nogales, Domenico Cecere, Ronald W. Burkle, KBHome Grantor Stock Ownership Trust./13.80%, Bruce Karatz, Ray R. Irani, Robert Freed, FMR Corp./7.80%, Insiders, Kelly Masuda

Financial Data: Fiscal Year End:11/30 **Latest Annual Data:** 11/30/2006

Year	Sales	Net Income
2006	$11,003,792,000	$482,351,000
2005	$9,441,650,000	$842,421,000
2004	$7,052,684,000	$480,902,000

Curr. Assets:	$7,768,903,000	Curr. Liab.:	$2,777,555,000		
Plant, Equip.:	$62,700,000	Total Liab.:	$5,903,358,000	Indic. Yr. Divd.:	$1.000
Total Assets:	$9,014,464,000	Net Worth:	$2,922,748,000	Debt/ Equity:	1.0803

KBR Inc

601 Jefferson St., Ste. 3400, Houston, TX, 77002; *PH:* 1-713-753-5082; *Fax:* 1-713-753-5353; *http://* www.kbr.com; *Email:* investors@kbr.com

General - Incorporation	DE	Stock- Price on:12/24/2007	$27.69
Employees	56,000	Stock Exchange	NYSE
Auditor	KPMG LLP	Ticker Symbol	KBR
Stk Agt	Mellon Investor Services LLC	Outstanding Shares	168,780,000
Counsel	NA	E.P.S.	$1.66
DUNS No.	NA	Shareholders	NA

Business: The groups principle activities include designing and constructing energy and petrochemical projects. The group operates through two segments namely, government and infrastructure, and energy and chemicals. The group operates from the United States. The group's quarterly revenue for September 2007 was 2,177.00 millions of USD.

Primary SIC and add'l.: 8744 1623 8741 1542 8711 1541 1629

CIK No: 0001357615

Subsidiaries: KBR Holdings, LLC

Officers: William P. Utt/Chmn., CEO, Pres./$1,384,946.00, Heather L. Browne/Dir. - Corporate Communications, Media Inquiries, Matthew Carmichael/Sr. Mgr. - External Communications, Media Inquiries, Cedric W. Burgher/CFO, Sr. VP/$670,051.00, John L. Rose/Exec. VP/$620,280.00, Bruce A. Stanski/Pres./$1,092,338.00, Andrew D. Farley/Sr. VP, General Counsel, Klaudia J. Brace/Sr. VP - Administration, John W. Gann/50/VP, Chief Accounting Officer/$513,168.00, Rob Kukla/Dir. - Investor Relations, David Zimmerman/Pres. - Services, Timothy B. Challand/Pres. - Technology, John Quinn/Pres. - Downstream, Dennis Calton/Sr. VP - Project Management Oversight, Controls, Tom Mumford/Sr. VP - Business Development Oversight

Directors: William P. Utt/Chmn., CEO, Pres., Albert O. Cornelison/58/Dir., Christopher C. Gaut/51/Dir., Andrew R. Lane/48/Dir., Mark A. McCollum/48/Dir., Richard J. Slater/Dir., Jeffrey E. Curtiss/Dir., Frank W. Blount/Dir., Loren K. Carroll/Dir., John R. Huff/Dir.

Owners: Insiders, Cedric W. Burgher, Capital Research and Management Company/12.20%, Frank w. Blount, Loren K. Carroll, John L. Rose, Jeffrey E. Curtiss, John W. Gann, Bruce A. Stanski, John R. Huff, Richard J. Slater, Tontine Management, L.L.C. and affiliates/11.20%, William P. Utt

Financial Data: Fiscal Year End:12/31 **Latest Annual Data:** 12/31/2006

Year	Sales	Net Income
2006	$9,633,000,000	$168,000,000

Curr. Assets:	$3,898,000,000	Curr. Liab.:	$2,983,000,000	P/E Ratio:	24.10
Plant, Equip.:	$492,000,000	Total Liab.:	$3,620,000,000	Indic. Yr. Divd.:	NA
Total Assets:	$5,407,000,000	Net Worth:	$1,787,000,000	Debt/ Equity:	0.0005

KBW Inc

The Equitable Bldg., 787 7th Ave., 4th Fl., New York, NY, 10019; *PH:* 1-212-887-7777; *Fax:* 1-212-541-6668; *http://* www.kbw.com

General - Incorporation	DE	Stock- Price on:12/24/2007	$31.08
Employees	455	Stock Exchange	NYSE
Auditor	KPMG LLP	Ticker Symbol	KBW
Stk Agt	NA	Outstanding Shares	29,270,000
Counsel	NA	E.P.S.	$1.59
DUNS No.	NA	Shareholders	NA

Business: The groups principle activities include investment banking, equity and fixed income sales and trading, and research. In the year 2005, the group merged with KBWI Acquisition Corp. The group operates from the United States. The groups quarterly revenue for September 2007 was 101.14 millions of USD.

Primary SIC and add'l.: 6211 6289 6282 6722

CIK No: 0001063494

Subsidiaries: KBW Asset Management, Inc., KBW Ventures, Inc, Keefe, Bruyette & Woods Limited, Keefe, Bruyette & Woods, Inc.

Officers: John G. Duffy/Chmn., CEO/$3,371,324.00, Thomas B. Michaud/Vice Chmn., Pres./$3,398,070.00, Andrew M. Senchak/Vice Chmn., Pres./$3,365,744.00, Catherine R. Kinne/Pres., COO - Nyse

Directors: John G. Duffy/Chmn., CEO, Thomas B. Michaud/Vice Chmn., Pres., Andrew M. Senchak/Vice Chmn., Pres.

Owners: Insiders/10.81%, Andrew M. Senchak/3.21%, Thomas B. Michaud/2.87%, Christopher M. Condron, Mitchell B. Kleinman, John G. Duffy/3.20%, Daniel M. Healy, Robert Giambrone

Financial Data: Fiscal Year End:12/31 **Latest Annual Data:** 12/31/2006

Year	Sales	Net Income
2006	$406,586,000	$53,284,000
2005	$307,866,000	$17,407,000
2004	$300,298,000	$31,273,000

Curr. Assets:	$439,418,000	Curr. Liab.:	$407,451,000	P/E Ratio:	24.10
Plant, Equip.:	$22,151,000	Total Liab.:	$407,451,000	Indic. Yr. Divd.:	NA
Total Assets:	$804,211,000	Net Worth:	$396,760,000	Debt/ Equity:	NA

KCS Energy Inc

5555 San Felipe Rd., Ste. 1200, Houston, TX, 77056; *PH:* 1-713-877-8006; *http://* www.petrohawk.com

General - Incorporation	DE	Stock- Price on:12/24/2007	NA
Employees	154	Stock Exchange	NA
Auditor	Ernst & Young LLP	Ticker Symbol	NA
Stk Agt	American Stock Transfer & Trust Co.	Outstanding Shares	NA
Counsel	NA	E.P.S.	$0.62
DUNS No.	19-407-7335	Shareholders	NA

Business: The group's principal activities are to acquire, explore and produce natural gas and crude oil with operations predominately in the mid-continent and gulf coast regions. The group purchases reserves (priority rights to future delivery of oil and gas) through its volumetric production payment (vpp) program. The drilling programs of the group are concentrated predominately in the mid-continent and gulf coast regions. In the mid-continent region, the group explores in Oklahoma (anadarko and arkoma basins), north Louisiana, west Texas and Michigan.

Primary SIC and add'l.: 1311 1381 4923

CIK No: 0000832820

Subsidiaries: KCS Energy Services, Inc., KCS Resources, Inc., Medallion California Properties Company, Proliq, Inc.

Officers: James W. Christmas/Chmn., CEO, Weldon H. Holcombe/Exec. VP - Mid Continent Region

Directors: James W. Christmas/Chmn., CEO, Christopher A. Viggiano/Dir., Robert G. Raynolds/Dir., Gary A. Merriman/Dir.

Financial Data: ***Fiscal Year End:***12/31 ***Latest Annual Data:*** 12/31/2006

Year	Sales	Net Income
2006	$587,762,000	$116,563,000
2005	$258,039,000	-$16,634,000
2004	$33,577,000	$8,117,000

Curr. Assets:	$246,712,000	***Curr. Liab.:***	$332,019,000		
Plant, Equip.:	$3,066,043,000	***Total Liab.:***	$2,351,312,000	***Indic. Yr. Divd.:***	NA
Total Assets:	$4,279,656,000	***Net Worth:***	$1,928,344,000	***Debt/ Equity:***	0.7559

Kearny Financial Corp

120 Passaic Ave., Fairfield, NJ, 07004; ***PH:*** 1-973-244-4500; ***Fax:*** 1-800-273-3406; ***https://*** www.kearnyfederalsavings.com; ***Email:*** info@kearnyfederalsavings.net

General - Incorporation	USA	***Stock***- Price on:12/24/2007	$13.56
Employees	268	Stock Exchange	NDQ
Auditor	Beard Miller Company, LLP	Ticker Symbol	KRNY
Stk Agt	Registrar & Transfer Co	Outstanding Shares	71,600,000
Counsel	NA	E.P.S.	$0.05
DUNS No.	NA	Shareholders	NA

Business: The groups principal activity is to provide banking and financial services. The products of the group include home equity, consumer, commercial mortgage and construction loans. The group operates from the United States. The assets of the group for the year 2006 were $2,007,525 (thousands).

Primary SIC and add'l.: 6712 6035

CIK No: 0001295664

Subsidiaries: Kearny Federal Investment Corp., Kearny Financial Securities, Inc., Kearny Federal Savings Bank, KFS Financial Services, Inc.

Officers: John N. Hopkins/Dir., CEO, Pres./$2,647,933.00, Patrick M. Joyce/Chief Lending Officer, Sr. VP/$612,602.00, Allan Beardslee/Sr. VP - Information Technology, Kearny Federal Savings, Sharon Jones/Sr. VP, Corp. Sec., Albert E. Gossweiler/Sr. VP, Chief Investment Officer, Treasurer/$642,745.00, William C. Ledgerwood/CFO, Sr. VP/$641,929.00, Erika Sacher Parisi/Sr. VP, Branch Administrator/$574,783.00, Craig L. Montanaro/Sr. VP, Dir. - Strategic Planning

Directors: John N. Hopkins/Dir., CEO, Pres., John J. Mazur/Chmn., Matthew T. McClane/Dir., Leopold W. Montanaro/Dir., John F. Regan/Dir., Theodore J. Aanensen/Dir., Joseph P. Mazza/Dir., John F. McGovern/Dir., Henry S. Parow/Dir.

Owners: Matthew T. McClane, Henry S. Parow, Leopold W. Montanaro, Albert E. Gossweiler, John N. Hopkins, Erika Parisi, John F. McGovern, Patrick M. Joyce, John J. Mazur, John F. Regan, William C. Ledgerwood, Craig L. Montanaro, Joseph P. Mazza, Theodore J. Aanensen, Sharon Jones

Financial Data: ***Fiscal Year End:***06/30 ***Latest Annual Data:*** 6/30/2006

Year	Sales	Net Income
2006	$92,648,000	$9,608,000
2005	$91,944,000	$18,898,000
2004	$80,214,000	$12,897,000

Curr. Assets:	$239,115,000	***Curr. Liab.:***	$1,504,843,000	***P/E Ratio:***	271.20
Plant, Equip.:	$35,941,000	***Total Liab.:***	$1,516,639,000	***Indic. Yr. Divd.:***	$0.200
Total Assets:	$2,007,525,000	***Net Worth:***	$490,886,000	***Debt/ Equity:***	NA

Keewatin Windpower Corp

666 Burrard St., Ste. 617, Vancouver, BC, V6C 3P6; ***PH:*** 1-604-818-4100

General - Incorporation	NV	***Stock***- Price on:12/24/2007	$1.6
Employees	NA	Stock Exchange	OTC
Auditor	Chang G. Park, CPA	Ticker Symbol	KWPW
Stk Agt	Empire Stock Transfer Inc.	Outstanding Shares	NA
Counsel	NA	E.P.S.	NA
DUNS No.	NA	Shareholders	NA

Business: The groups principal activities include exploring and developing wind power projects to generate electricity. The group operates from Canada.

Primary SIC and add'l.: 4911

CIK No: 0001332445

Officers: Chris Craddock/49/Dir., CEO, Pres., Sec., Victor S. Dusik/58/Dir., CFO, Exec. VP

Directors: Chris Craddock/49/Dir., CEO, Pres., Sec., William Iny/57/Dir., Greg Yanke/37/Dir., Victor S. Dusik/58/Dir., CFO, Exec. VP

Owners: Greg Yanke/16.90%, Victor S. Dusik, William Iny/16.80%, Chris Craddock/16.52%, Insiders/51.99%

Financial Data: ***Fiscal Year End:***05/31 ***Latest Annual Data:*** 05/31/2007

Year	Sales	Net Income
2007	NA	-$435,000
2006	NA	-$58,000

Curr. Assets:	$4,000	***Curr. Liab.:***	$40,000		
Plant, Equip.:	$20,000	***Total Liab.:***	$40,000	***Indic. Yr. Divd.:***	NA
Total Assets:	$24,000	***Net Worth:***	-$15,000	***Debt/ Equity:***	NA

Keithley Instruments Inc

28775 Aurora Rd., Solon, OH, 44139; ***PH:*** 1-440-248-0400; ***Fax:*** 1-440-248-6168; ***http://*** www.keithley.com; ***Email:*** info@keithley.com

General - Incorporation	OH	***Stock***- Price on:12/24/2007	$12.72
Employees	673	Stock Exchange	NYSE
Auditor	PricewaterhouseCoopers LLP	Ticker Symbol	KEI
Stk Agt	National City Bank	Outstanding Shares	16,250,000
Counsel	James B. Griswold	E.P.S.	-$0.02
DUNS No.	00-419-0419	Shareholders	NA

Business: The group's principle activities are to design, develop, manufacture and market complex electronic instruments and systems. The products of the group include integrated systems solutions, along with instruments and PC plug-in boards that can be used as system components or stand-alone solutions. These products are used to test, measure and analyze electrical, radio frequency, optical or physical properties. The products cater to the specialized needs of electronics manufacturers for high-performance production testing, process monitoring, product development and research. The customers of the group include engineers, technicians and scientists in a range of industries. The products of the group are sold in over 70 countries throughout the world. The group has sales offices located in great Britain, Germany, France, the Netherlands, Italy, Japan, Belgium, Finland, Sweden, China, Korea, Taiwan, India and Singapore. The group's total revenue for year 2007 was 143.66 millions of USD.

Primary SIC and add'l.: 3829 7372 3674 3825 5065

CIK No: 0000054991

Subsidiaries: Keithley Instruments BV, Keithley Instruments GmbH, Keithley Instruments International Corporation, Keithley Instruments KK, Keithley Instruments Ltd, Keithley Instruments S.A., Keithley Instruments SARL, Keithley Instruments Sdn Bhd, Keithley Instruments SRL

Officers: Joseph P. Keithley/Chmn., CEO, Pres. - Keithley Instruments, Inc, Elton R. White/Dir. - Private Investor, Debra Sibila/Corporate Controller, Brian R. Bachman/Dir. - Private Investor, Mark J. Plush/CFO, VP, James B. Griswold/Dir. - Private Investor, Linda C. Rae/COO, Exec. VP, John A. Pesec/VP - Worldwide Sales, Larry L. Pendergrass/VP - New Product Development, Philip R. Etsler/VP - Human Resources, Mark A. Hoersten/VP - Business Management, Alan S. Gaffney/VP - Commercial Marketing, Information Systems, Thomas A. Saponas/Dir. - Private Investor, Stephen A. Chipchase/VP - Operations, Suzanne Schulze Taylor/VP, General Counsel, Chief Compliance Officer

Directors: Joseph P. Keithley/Chmn., CEO, Pres. - Keithley Instruments, Inc, Brian R. Bachman/Dir. - Private Investor, Elton R. White/Dir. - Private Investor, James B. Griswold/Dir. - Private Investor, Brian J. Jackman/Dir., Leon J. Hendrix/Dir., James T. Bartlett/Dir., Mohan N. Reddy/Dir., Thomas A. Saponas/Dir. - Private Investor, Barbara V. Scherer/Dir.

Owners: Barbara V. Scherer, John A. Pesec/1.00%, Thomas A. Saponas, Mohan N. Reddy, Mark J. Plush/1.50%, Insiders/13.70%, Linda C. Rae/1.20%, Leon J. Hendrix, Brian R. Bachman, Mark A. Hoersten, Joseph P. Keithley/3.90%, Brian J. Jackman, Insiders/99.10%, James B. Griswold, Joseph P. Keithley/99.10% *(18 Owners included in Index)*

Financial Data: ***Fiscal Year End:***09/30 ***Latest Annual Data:*** 9/30/2006

Year	Sales	Net Income
2006	$155,212,000	$8,361,000
2005	$141,552,000	$10,128,000
2004	$140,248,000	$11,381,000

Curr. Assets:	$94,640,000	***Curr. Liab.:***	$22,597,000		
Plant, Equip.:	$14,425,000	***Total Liab.:***	$32,389,000	***Indic. Yr. Divd.:***	NA
Total Assets:	$148,892,000	***Net Worth:***	$116,503,000	***Debt/ Equity:***	NA

Kellogg Co

1 Kellogg Sq., Battle Creek, MI, 49016; ***PH:*** 1-269-961-2000; ***Fax:*** 1-269-961-2871; ***http://*** www.kelloggs.com; ***Email:*** investor.relations@kellogg.com

General - Incorporation	DE	***Stock***- Price on:12/24/2007	$51.83
Employees	25,856	Stock Exchange	NYSE
Auditor	PricewaterhouseCoopers LLP	Ticker Symbol	K
Stk Agt	Wells Fargo Shareowner Services	Outstanding Shares	397,610,000
Counsel	NA	E.P.S.	$2.76
DUNS No.	00-535-6209	Shareholders	NA

Business: The groups principle activities include manufacturing and marketing ready-to-eat cereal and convenience food products. The groups products include froot loops,apple jacks, and icecream corns. The groups products are sold under the brand names Nutri-Grain(R), Rice Krispies(R), All-Bran(R), Special K(R), Mini-Wheats(R), and Chips Deluxe(R). The group operates from United States.

Primary SIC and add'l.: 2064 2043 2038

CIK No: 0000055067

Subsidiaries: 3112111 Nova Scotia Company, Alimentos Kellogg, S.A., Alimentos Kellogg, S.A. Subsidiaries, AQFTM, Inc., Argkel Servicios, S.C., Argkel, Inc., Asia-Pacific Kellogg Company Subsidiaries, Austin Quality Foods, Inc., Austin Quality Foods, Inc. Subsidiaries:, Barbara Dee Cookie Company, LLC, BDH, Inc.- Delaware, Canada Holding LLC, Cary Land Corporation, Celnasa (la Compania De Cereales Nacionales S.a.), Day Dawn Pty Ltd. 165 Subsidiaries included in the Index

Officers: David A.F. MacKay/Dir., CEO, Pres./$13,233,090.00, Jeffrey M. Boromisa/53/Sr. VP - Kellogg Company, Exec. VP - Kellogg International, Pres. - Kellogg Asia Pacific/$3,433,346.00, Nikki Gentles/Contact - Kellogg Canada, Benjamin S. Carson/Dir., Dir. - Pediatric Neurosurgery, Gary H. Pilnick/44/Sr. VP - General Counsel - Corporate Development, Sec. - Kellogg Company, Alan R. Andrews/Officer, Donna J. Banks/52/Sr. VP - Global Supply Chain, Celeste A. Clark/43/Sr. VP - Global Nutrition, Corporate Affairs, Kellogg Company, Annuciata Cerioli/Officer, John A. Bryant/43/CFO, Exec. VP, Kellogg Company Pres. - Kellogg North America/$4,404,123.00, Jeffrey W. Montie/Exec. VP - Kellogg Company, Pres./$4,662,221.00, Ruth E. Bruch/55/CIO, Sr. VP - Kellogg Company, Bradford J. Davidson/47/Sr. VP - Kellogg Company, Pres. - US Snacks, Timothy P. Mobsby/53/VP - Kellogg Company, Exec. VP - Kellogg International, Pres. - Kellogg Europe, Kathleen Wilson-Thompson/Sr. VP - Global Human Resources *(23 Officers included in Index)*

Directors: David A.F. MacKay/Dir., CEO, Pres., James M. Jenness/62/Chmn., Ann McLaughlin Korologos/Dir., Claudio X. Gonzalez/Dir., Daniel L. Jorndt/66/Dir., Benjamin S. Carson/Dir., Dir. - Pediatric Neurosurgery, Sterling Speirn/Dir., Robert A. Steele/Dir., Dorothy A. Johnson/Dir., William D. Perez/Dir., John T. Dillon/Dir., John L. Zabriskie/Dir., Gordon Gund/Dir.

Owners: Insiders/1.60%, W. C. Richardson, J. M. Boromisa, A. F. Harris, G. Gund, A. M. Korologos, KeyCorp/8.00%, J. W. Montie, J. A. Bryant, C. X. Gonzalez, B. S. Carson, L. D. Jorndt, J. T. Dillon, George GundIII/8.50%, W. K. Kellogg Foundation Trust/23.60% *(17 Owners included in Index)*

Financial Data: ***Fiscal Year End:***01/01 ***Latest Annual Data:*** 12/30/2006

Year	Sales	Net Income
2006	$10,906,700,000	$1,004,100,000
2005	$10,177,200,000	$980,400,000

Curr. Assets:	$2,196,500,000	***Curr. Liab.:***	$3,162,800,000	***P/E Ratio:***	19.71
Plant, Equip.:	$2,648,400,000	***Total Liab.:***	$8,290,800,000	***Indic. Yr. Divd.:***	$1.240
Total Assets:	$10,574,500,000	***Net Worth:***	$2,283,700,000	***Debt/ Equity:***	NA

Kellwood Co

600 Kellwood Pkwy., Chesterfield, MO, 63017; *PH:* 1-314-576-3100; *Fax:* 1-314-576-3460; *http://* www.kwdco.com; *Email:* corp_communications@kellwood.com

General - Incorporation ..... DE
Employees 30,000
Auditor ..... PricewaterhouseCoopers LLP
Stk Agt..... American Stock Transfer & Trust Co.
Counsel ..... NA
DUNS No. 00-512-0431

Stock- Price on:12/24/2007 ..... $28.78
Stock Exchange ..... NYSE
Ticker Symbol ..... KWD
Outstanding Shares 25,860,000
E.P.S. $1.14
Shareholders ..... NA

Business: The groups principle activity is to market apparel and consumer soft goods. The group markets branded, including private-label products. In the year 2007 the group acquired Hanna Andersson Corporation. The group operates from United States.

Primary SIC and add'l.: 2321 2389 2329 2361 2331

CIK No: 0000055080

Subsidiaries: Academy Broadway, Briggs New York Corp., Dorby Frocks, Ltd., Fritzi California, Gerber Childrenswear, Inc., Group B Clothing Co., Inc. q, Koret, Inc., Phat Fashions, LLC/Phat Licensing, LLC, Romance Du Jour, Inc.

Officers: Robert C. Skinner/Chmn., CEO, Pres./$1,869,942.00, Richard J. Klimberg/CEO - Briggs New York, Inc, Rea L. Laccone/CEO - Vince, Inc, Phil Iosca/CEO, Pres. - Hanna Andersson Corporation, Stephen F. Powers/CEO, Pres. - Koret, California, Inc, Gary F. Simmons/CEO, Pres. - Gerber Childrenswear, Inc, Jesse C.P. Zee/Chmn. - Smart Shirts, Ltd, Margie Greenlees/Pres. - Phat Fashions LLC, George J. Grabner/Pres. - American Recreation Products, Inc, Fran Boland/Pres. - Prophecy, Sag Harbor, Gerald K. Rhoads/MD - Smart Shirts, Ltd, Debra S. Garcia/Pres. - Kellwood Retail Group, Inc, Christopher J. Lapolice/Pres. - Vince, Inc, Kimora Lee Simmons/Dir. - Creative, Phat Fashions LLC, John V. Windham/COO, Pres. - Briggs New York, Inc *(39 Officers included in Index)*

Directors: Robert C. Skinner/Chmn., CEO, Pres., Janice E. Page/Dir., Ben B. Blount/Dir., Larry R. Katzen/Dir., Harvey A. Weinberg/Dir., Kitty G. Dickerson/Dir., Jerry M. Hunter/Dir., Philip B. Miller/Dir.

Owners: Barclays Global Investors NA/ CA //5.24%, Roger D. Joseph, Dimensional Fund Advisors LP/8.89%, LSV Asset Management/5.19%, Artisan Partners Limited Partnership/6.70%, Larry R. Katzen, Insiders, Gregory W. Kleffner, Franklin Resources, Inc./7.10%, Snow Capital Management, L.P./7.62%, Thomas H. Pollihan, Harvey A. Weinberg, Goldman Sachs Asset Management, L.P./12.00%, Janice E. Page, Donna B. Weaver *(20 Owners included in Index)*

Financial Data: ***Fiscal Year End:***01/28 ***Latest Annual Data:*** 2/3/2007

Year	Sales	Net Income
2007	$1,961,750,000	$31,402,000
2006	$2,062,144,000	-$38,413,000
2005	$2,555,704,000	$66,336,000

Curr. Assets:	$972,562,000	**Curr. Liab.:**	$330,110,000	**P/E Ratio:**	25.25
Plant, Equip.:	$75,997,000	**Total Liab.:**	$879,450,000	**Indic. Yr. Divd.:**	$0.640
Total Assets:	$1,514,576,000	**Net Worth:**	$635,126,000	**Debt/ Equity:**	NA

Kelly Services Inc

999 W Big BeAve.r Rd., Troy, MI, 48084; *PH:* 1-248-362-4444; *Fax:* 1-248-244-4360; *http://* www.kellyservices.com

General - Incorporation ..... DE
Employees 8,800
Auditor ..... PricewaterhouseCoopers LLP
Stk Agt ..... Mellon Investor Services LLC
Counsel ..... NA
DUNS No. 00-695-8318

Stock- Price on:12/24/2007 ..... $27.33
Stock Exchange ..... NDQ
Ticker Symbol ..... KELYA
Outstanding Shares 36,630,000
E.P.S. $1.89
Shareholders ..... NA

Business: The group's principle activity is to provide staffing services to a diversified group of customers. The group operates through three segments: U.S. Commercial staffing segment offers employees for administrative services, call centers, technical support hotlines, telemarketing units, supply qualified substitute teachers, provide support staff, technicians and staff experienced in facilities management and materials handling. It also gives its customers and employees an opportunity to evaluate before making a fulltime employment decision. Professional, technical and staffing alternatives segment provides a number of industry-specific services relating to scientific, healthcare, home care, financial, law registry, it resources, automotive and engineering. It also includes staff leasing, management services, vendor management solutions and hr consulting. International segment provides personnel assessment techniques and recruiting and human resources services. The group's quarterly revenue for September 2007 was 1,425.30 millions of USD.

Primary SIC and add'l.: 7363

CIK No: 0000055135

Subsidiaries: Agensi Pekerjaan BTI Consultants SDN. BHD., BTI Consultants (India) Private Limited, BTI Consultants Hong Kong Limited, BTI Consultants Pte. Ltd., BTI Executive Placement (Thailand) Co. Ltd., Competences RH, Kelly Administratiekantoor B.V., Kelly Home Care Services, Inc., Kelly Managed Services (Nederland) B.V., Kelly Management Services, Srl., Kelly Payroll Services Limited, Kelly Properties, Inc., Kelly Receivables Services, LLC, Kelly Services (Australia), Ltd., Kelly Services (Canada), Ltd. 52 Subsidiaries included in the Index

Officers: Carl T. Camden/Dir., CEO, Pres./$2,794,969.00, James H. Bradley/Sr. VP - Administration, Michael S. Webster/Exec. VP - Global, Sales, Service, Marketing, Allison M. Everett/Sr. VP - Information Technology, Michael S. Morrow/Sr. VP - Marketing, Daniel T. Lis/Sr. VP, General Counsel, Corp. Sec./$779,714.00, Michael E. Debs/Sr. VP, Corporate Controller, Chief Accounting Officer, Nina M. Ramsey/Sr. VP - Human Resources, Steve S. Armstrong/Sr. VP - Technical Services Group, Pamela M. Berklich/Sr. VP - Global Staffing Alternatives, Dana Curtis/Sr. VP - Service, Shaun C. Fracassi/Sr. VP, GM - Metro Markets, Jonathan D. Means/Sr. VP, GM - Major Markets, Edward W. Meisenheimer/Sr. VP, GM - Middle Markets, Dhiren Shantilal/Sr. VP *(22 Officers included in Index)*

Directors: Carl T. Camden/Dir., CEO, Pres., Terence E. Adderley/Chmn., Verne G. Istock/Dir., Jane E. Dutton/Dir., Maureen A. Fay/Dir., Donald R. Parfet/Dir., Joseph B. White/Dir.

Owners: M. A. Fay, D. T. Lis, D. R. Parfet, V. G. Istock, B. J. White, J. E. Dutton, V. G. Istock, C. T. Camden, Terence E. Adderley/92.90%, M. L. Durik, D. T. Lis, M. A. Fay, Insiders/92.90%, C. T. Camden, Insiders/30.50% *(22 Owners included in Index)*

Financial Data: ***Fiscal Year End:***01/01 ***Latest Annual Data:*** 12/31/2006

Year	Sales	Net Income
2006	$5,605,752,000	$63,491,000
2005	$4,984,051,000	$21,211,000

Curr. Assets:	$1,031,533,000	**Curr. Liab.:**	$568,277,000	**P/E Ratio:**	14.93
Plant, Equip.:	$170,288,000	**Total Liab.:**	$710,867,000	**Indic. Yr. Divd.:**	NA
Total Assets:	$1,469,424,000	**Net Worth:**	$758,557,000	**Debt/ Equity:**	NA

Kemet Corp

2835 KEMET Way, Simpsonville, SC, 29681; *PH:* 1-864-963-6300; *http://* www.kemet.com

General - Incorporation ..... DE
Employees 9,100
Auditor ..... KPMG LLP
Stk Agt ..... EquiServe Trust Co N.A
Counsel ..... NA
DUNS No. 78-842-1808

Stock- Price on:12/24/2007 ..... $7.44
Stock Exchange ..... NYSE
Ticker Symbol ..... KEM
Outstanding Shares 83,860,000
E.P.S. $0.20
Shareholders ..... NA

Business: The group's principal activity is to manufacture and sell solid tantalum, multilayer ceramic and solid aluminum. The products of the group are used in communication systems, data processing equipment, personal computers, cellular phones, automotive electronic systems, military and aerospace systems, and consumer electronics. The customers of the group include alcatel, arrow electronics, avnet, celestica, compaq, dell, delphi, flextronics, hewlett-packard, IBM, intel, jabil, jaco, lucent technologies, motorola, nokia, pioneer, qualcomm, sanmina/sci, siemens, solectron, tti, and visteon.on 30-Jun-2003, the group acquired the assets of greatbatch technologies inc and on 17-Dec-2003, the group acquired forest electronic company.

Primary SIC and add'l.: 3675

CIK No: 0000887730

Subsidiaries: KEMET de Mexico, S.A. de C.V., KEMET Electronics (Canada) Limited, KEMET Electronics (Shanghai) Co., Ltd., KEMET Electronics (Suzhou) Co., Ltd., KEMET Electronics Asia Limited, KEMET Electronics Asia Pacific Pte Ltd., KEMET Electronics Corporation, KEMET Electronics GMBH, KEMET Electronics Greater China Limited, KEMET Electronics Japan Co., Ltd., KEMET Electronics Ltd., KEMET Electronics Marketing (S)Pte Ltd., KEMET Electronics Pty Ltd., KEMET Electronics SARL, KEMET Electronics, S.A. 19 Subsidiaries included in the Index

Officers: Per-Olof Loof/Dir., CEO/$2,382,817.00, John E. Schneider/53/VP - Sales, Asia, Pacific, Dennis Constantine/Sr. VP, Chief - Staff/$826,384.00, Conrado Hinojosa/43/VP - Tantalum Business Unit, Charles C. Meeks/47/VP - Ceramics Business Unit, Marc Kotelon/44/VP - Sales, EMEA, David E. Gable/Sr. VP, CFO, Investor Relations Officer/$630,050.00, Kirk D. Shockley/49/VP - Business Integration, Daniel F. Persico/VP - Strategic Marketing, Business Development, John Drabik/VP - Sales, Americas, Philip M. Lessner/CTO, VP, James P. McClintock/COO, Pres., Daniel E. Lamorte/CIO, VP, Larry C. McAdams/VP - Human Resources/$445,853.00

Directors: Per-Olof Loof/Dir., CEO, Robert G. Paul/66/Dir.

Owners: Sprucegrove Investment Management Ltd./7.60%, Brandes Investment Partners, L.P./5.80%, Dennis R. Constantine, Per-Olof Loof, Maureen E. Grzelakowski, Insiders, Erwin E. Maddrey, Robert G. Paul, Gurminder S. Bedi, Frank G. Brandenberg, Dimensional Fund Advisors Inc./8.80%, Kelly J. Vogt, Joseph D. Swann, David E. Gable, Larry C. McAdams

Financial Data: ***Fiscal Year End:***03/31 ***Latest Annual Data:*** 3/31/2007

Year	Sales	Net Income
2007	$658,714,000	$6,897,000
2006	$490,106,000	$375,000
2005	$425,338,000	-$174,094,000

Curr. Assets:	$486,897,000	**Curr. Liab.:**	$147,801,000	**P/E Ratio:**	46.50
Plant, Equip.:	$352,821,000	**Total Liab.:**	$407,768,000	**Indic. Yr. Divd.:**	NA
Total Assets:	$943,526,000	**Net Worth:**	$535,758,000	**Debt/ Equity:**	0.4735

Kendle International Inc

1200 Carew Tower, 441 Vine St., Cincinnati, OH, 45202; *PH:* 1-513-381-5550; *Fax:* 1-513-381-5870; *http://* www.kendle.com

General - Incorporation ..... OH
Employees 3,050
Auditor ..... Deloitte & Touche LLP
Stk Agt ..... LaSalle Bank N.A
Counsel ..... Keating, Muething & Klekamp
DUNS No. 01-696-8919

Stock- Price on:12/24/2007 ..... $35.81
Stock Exchange ..... NDQ
Ticker Symbol ..... KNDL
Outstanding Shares 14,460,000
E.P.S. $0.52
Shareholders ..... NA

Business: The group's principal activity is to provide integrated clinical research services to the pharmaceutical and biotechnology industries. The group offers quality, value added clinical research services and proprietary information technology, designed to reduce drug development time and expense. The contract research services group conducts clinical trial management, clinical data management, statistical analysis, medical writing and regulatory consulting and representation. The medical communications group provides organizational, meeting management, and publication services to professional associations and pharmaceutical companies. The group has operations in North America, Europe, Asia and Australia. On 01-Oct-2003, the group acquired Mexican cro estadisticos y clinicos asociados sa.

Primary SIC and add'l.: 8071 8733 7374 8748

CIK No: 0001039151

Subsidiaries: AAC Consulting Group, Inc., Acer/excel Inc., Kendle Americas Holding Inc., Kendle Americas Investment Inc., Kendle Americas Management Inc., Kendle Branches Limited, Kendle Canada Inc., Kendle CTA Limited, Kendle GmbH, Kendle India Private Limited, Kendle International B.V., Kendle International CPU LLC, Kendle International Holdings Limited, Kendle International Holdings Pty Limited, Kendle International Limited 29 Subsidiaries included in the Index

Officers: Candace Kendle/Chmn., CEO/$541,459.00, Christopher C. Bergen/Dir., COO, Pres./$444,936.00, Patty Frank/Dir. - Investor Relations, Mary Briggs/Sr. Dir. - Strategic Accounting, William K. Sietsema/VP - Clinical Regulatory Strategic Planning, Sylva H. Collins/VP - Global Biometrics, Deborah Covington/Dir. - Registries, Epidemiology, Karen L. Crone/VP - Global Human Resources, Karl Brenkert/Sr. VP, CFO, Sec./$307,455.00, Simon S. Higginbotham/VP, Chief Marketing Officer/$316,997.00, Martha R. Feller/Sr. VP - Global Clinical Development, Melanie A. Bruno/VP - Global Regulatory Affairs, Quality, Anthony L. Forcellini/VP - Strategic Development, Corporate Treasurer, Dennis P. Hurley/VP - Global Clinical Development, Latin America, Gary M. Wedig/CIO, VP *(22 Officers included in Index)*

Directors: Candace Kendle/Chmn., CEO, Christopher C. Bergen/Dir., COO, Pres., Frederick A. Russ/Dir., Timothy E. Johnson/Dir., Donald C. Harrison/Dir., Robert R. Buck/Dir., Steven G. Geis/Dir.

Owners: Robert C. Simpson, Donald C. Harrison, Frederick A. Russ, Steven G. Geis, Robert R. Buck, Candace Kendle/6.55%, Insiders/13.52%, Simon S. Higginbotham, Thompson, Siegel & Walms ley, Inc/5.49%, Independence Investments LLC/6.49%, Karl Brenkert, Christopher C. Bergen/5.33%, Timothy E. Johnson, Nicholas Applegate Capital Management LLC/5.00%

Financial Data: *Fiscal Year End:*12/31 *Latest Annual Data:* 12/31/2006

Year	Sales	Net Income
2006	$373,936,000	$8,530,000
2005	$250,639,000	$10,674,000
2004	$215,868,000	$3,572,000

Curr. Assets:	$166,676,000	*Curr. Liab.:*	$110,272,000	*P/E Ratio:*	67.57
Plant, Equip.:	$23,024,000	*Total Liab.:*	$314,960,000	*Indic. Yr. Divd.:*	NA
Total Assets:	$455,072,000	*Net Worth:*	$140,112,000	*Debt/ Equity:*	1.4003

Kenexa Corp

650 E Swedesford Rd., 2nd Fl., Wayne, PA, 19087; *PH:* 1-877-971-9171; *Fax:* 1-610-971-9181; *http://* www.kenexa.com; *Email:* contactus@kenexa.com

General - Incorporation	PA	**Stock**- Price on:12/24/2007	$36.76
Employees	636	Stock Exchange	NDQ
Auditor	BDO Seidman, LLP	Ticker Symbol	KNXA
Stk Agt	StockTrans, Inc.	Outstanding Shares	25,270,000
Counsel	NA	E.P.S.	$0.94
DUNS No.	NA	Shareholders	NA

Business: The groups principle activity is to provide software services. The group products sold under the trade names Kenexa Recruiter(R), Kenexa Recruiter(R) BrassRing and Kenexa StoreFront(TM). In the year 2006, the group acquired Webhire, Inc, Knowledge Workers, Inc, Gantz-Wiley Research Consulting Group, Inc, BrassRing Inc and Psychometric Services Limited. The group operates from the United States, Europe, Middle East and Africa, Canada, and other. The group's quarterly revenue for September 2007 was 46.80 millions of USD.

Primary SIC and add'l.: 7361 7372 8742

CIK No: 0001114714

Subsidiaries: BrassRing Asia Pacific Limited, BrassRing BV, BrassRing Canada, Inc., BrassRing GmgH Messeveranstalter und Medienagentur, BrassRing Holdings BV, BrassRing Limited, Devon Royce, Inc., Kenexa BrassRing, Inc., Kenexa Care, Inc., Kenexa Government Solutions, Inc., Kenexa Limited, Kenexa Puerto Rico Inc., Kenexa Recruiter, Inc., Kenexa Technologies Private Limited, Kenexa Technology Canada Inc. 18 Subsidiaries included in the Index

Officers: Nooruddin S. Karsan/Chmn., CEO/$1,028,750.00, Troy A. Kanter/Dir., COO, Pres./$716,250.00, Sarah M. Teten/Chief Marketing Officer/$263,500.00, Donald F. Volk/CFO/$726,475.00, Archie L. Jones/35/VP - Business Development/$303,750.00

Directors: Nooruddin S. Karsan/Chmn., CEO, Barry M. Abelson/Dir., Troy A. Kanter/Dir., COO, Pres., Joseph A. Konen/Dir., John A. Nies/Dir., Richard J. Pinola/Dir., Renee B. Booth/Dir., Rebecca Maddox/Dir.

Owners: Barry M. Abelson, Joseph A. Konen, Elliot H. Clark, Rebecca J. Maddox, John A. Nies, Insiders/7.50%, Nooruddin S. Karsan/5.60%, Sarah M. Teten, Richard J. Pinola, Donald F. Volk, FMR Corp./12.70%, Renee B. Booth, Archie L. Jones, Troy A. Kanter/1.10%

Financial Data: *Fiscal Year End:*12/31 *Latest Annual Data:* 06/30/2007

Year	Sales	Net Income
2007	NA	NA
2006	$112,107,000	$15,893,000
2005	$65,641,000	$6,091,000

Curr. Assets:	$86,671,000	*Curr. Liab.:*	$74,928,000	*P/E Ratio:*	42.74
Plant, Equip.:	$8,469,000	*Total Liab.:*	$120,298,000	*Indic. Yr. Divd.:*	NA
Total Assets:	$267,459,000	*Net Worth:*	$147,161,000	*Debt/ Equity:*	0.0007

Kennametal Inc

1600 Technology Way, Latrobe, PA, 15650; *PH:* 1-724-539-5000; *Fax:* 1-724-539-6657; *http://* www.kennametal.com; *Email:* investor.relations@kennametal.com

General - Incorporation	PA	**Stock**- Price on:12/24/2007	$82.36
Employees	13,282	Stock Exchange	NYSE
Auditor	PricewaterhouseCoopers LLP	Ticker Symbol	KMT
Stk Agt	Mellon Investor Services LLC	Outstanding Shares	38,860,000
Counsel	NA	E.P.S.	$2.27
DUNS No.	00-439-7659	Shareholders	NA

Business: The groups principle activity is to supply tooling, engineered components and advanced materials consumed in production processes. The groups products include wear components and metalworking products. Customers served by the group include the aerospace, automotive, machine tool, light machinery and heavy machinery industries. The group operates from United States.

Primary SIC and add'l.: 3545 3531

CIK No: 0000055242

Subsidiaries: Carbidie Asia Pacific Pte. Ltd, CIRBO Limited, Cleveland Twist Drill de Mexico, S.A. de C.V., Extrude Hone (Ireland) Ltd, Extrude Hone (U.K.) Ltd., Extrude Hone Corporation, Extrude Hone France S.A., Extrude Hone GmbH, Extrude Hone Holding GmbH, Extrude Hone KK, Extrude Hone Korea Co. Ltd., Extrude Hone Ltd, Extrude Hone Participacoes Ltda., Extrude Hone Shanghai, Co. Ltd., Extrude Hone Spain 107 Subsidiaries included in the Index

Officers: Carlos M. Cardoso/Dir., CEO, Pres./$3,575,832.00, David W. Greenfield/VP, Sec., General Counsel, Kevin R. Walling/VP, Chief Human Resources Officer, Philip H. Weihl/VP - Kvbs - Lean Enterprise, Stanley B. Duzy/VP, Chief Administrative Officer/$1,653,920.00, Ragesh Datt/42/CIO, VP, Frank P. Simpkins/CFO, VP/$868,905.00, John H. Jacko/VP - Corporate Strategy - Mssg Global Marketing, Gary W. Weismann/VP, Pres. - Advanced Materials Solutions Group, Lawrence J. Lanza/VP, Treasurer, Wayne D. Moser/VP - Finance, Corporate Controller, Daniel R. Bagley/VP - Corporate Strategy, Mssg Global Marketing, James E. Morrison/VP - Mergers, Acquisitions, James R. Breisinger/VP, Pres. - Advanced Components Group, William Y. Hsu/CTO, VP/$1,284,399.00

Directors: Carlos M. Cardoso/Dir., CEO, Pres., Larry D. Yost/Chmn., Timothy R. McLevish/Dir., William R. Newlin/Dir., Peter A. Held/Dir., Ronald M. Defeo/Dir., Lawrence W. Stranghoener/Dir., Philip A. Dur/Dir., Steven H. Wunning/Dir.

Owners: Philip A. Dur, William R. Newlin, Stanley B. Duzy, Carlos M. Cardoso, Insiders, Frank P. Simpkins, Steven H. Wunning, Transamerica Investment Management LLC/5.41%, Peter A. Held, Ronald C. Keating, Ronald M. DeFeo, Wellington Management Company LLP/5.01%, Larry D. Yost, Timothy R. McLevish, William Y. Hsu *(16 Owners included in Index)*

Financial Data: *Fiscal Year End:*06/30 *Latest Annual Data:* 06/30/2007

Year	Sales	Net Income
2007	$2,385,493,000	$174,243,000
2006	$2,329,628,000	$256,283,000
2005	$2,304,167,000	$119,291,000

Curr. Assets:	$1,086,857,000	*Curr. Liab.:*	$462,199,000	*P/E Ratio:*	11.73
Plant, Equip.:	$530,379,000	*Total Liab.:*	$1,125,281,000	*Indic. Yr. Divd.:*	$0.840
Total Assets:	$2,435,272,000	*Net Worth:*	$1,295,365,000	*Debt/ Equity:*	NA

Kenneth Cole Productions Inc

603 W 50th St., New York, NY, 10019; *PH:* 1-212-265-1500; *Fax:* 1-866-741-5753; *http://* www.kennethcole.com

General - Incorporation	NY	**Stock**- Price on:12/24/2007	$24.57
Employees	1,900	Stock Exchange	NYSE
Auditor	Ernst & Young LLP	Ticker Symbol	KCP
Stk Agt	Bank of New York	Outstanding Shares	15,600,000
Counsel	NA	E.P.S.	$0.89
DUNS No.	07-644-8257	Shareholders	NA

Business: The group's principal activities are to design, source and market footwear and handbags, men's and women's apparel and accessories. Consumer catalogues are distributed under the kenneth cole New York, reaction kenneth cole and unlisted brand names. The group markets the products to more than 7,500 department and specialty store locations through its consumer direct business. Consumer direct business includes an expanding base of retail and outlet stores, consumer catalogs and interactive websites, including on-line e-commerce. The group's international markets include Canada, United Kingdom, Mexico, venezuela, Ecuador, Costa Rica, Peru, panama, aruba, bahamas, curacao, Colombia, Dominican Republic, El Salvador, Guatemala, haiti, Honduras, jamaica, st. Croix, Hong Kong, Japan, Taiwan, the Philippines and Singapore.

Primary SIC and add'l.: 2389 5139 9651

CIK No: 0000921691

Subsidiaries: Cole 57th. St., LLC, Cole Amsterdam, B.V., Cole Amsterdam, Inc., Cole Broadway, Inc., Cole Clinton, Inc., Cole Dawsonville, Inc., Cole Fashion Valley, Inc., Cole Forum, Inc., Cole Garden State, Inc., Cole Georgetown, Inc., Cole Grand Central, Inc., Cole Grant, Inc., Cole Las Vegas, Inc., Cole Michigan Avenue, Inc., Cole New Orleans, Inc. 41 Subsidiaries included in the Index

Officers: Kenneth D. Cole/Chmn., CEO/$4,124,045.00, Michael F. Colosi/Corporate VP, General Counsel, David P. Edelman/CFO, Treasurer/$799,954.00, Harry M. Kubetz/Sr. VP - Operations/$774,945.00, Michael Devirgilio/Exec. VP - Business Development/$824,715.00, Richard S. Olicker/Pres. - Wholesale Division, Exec. VP/$702,126.00, Doug Jakubowski/Pres. - Kenneth Cole Reaction, Henrik Madsen/Sr. VP, GM - International Operations, Linda Nash Merker/Sr. VP - Human Resources, Jeff Cohen/Divisional Pres. - Company Stores, Marty Nealon/Divisional Pres. - Full, Priced Retail Stores, Kyle Andrew/Sr. VP - Marketing, Advertising, Joshua Schulman/36/Pres. - Kenneth Cole New York Brand

Directors: Kenneth D. Cole/Chmn., CEO, Philip R. Peller/Dir., Denis F. Kelly/Dir., Robert C. Grayson/Dir., Martin E. Franklin/Dir.

Owners: Kenneth D. Cole/46.80%, Michael DeVirgilio, Kenneth D. Cole/100.00%, Insiders/100.00%, Robert C. Grayson, Richard S. Olicker, Philip R. Peller, Harry Kubetz, Insiders/48.40%, Denis F. Kelly, Martin E. Franklin, David P. Edelman

Financial Data: *Fiscal Year End:*12/31 *Latest Annual Data:* 12/31/2006

Year	Sales	Net Income
2006	$536,499,000	$26,765,000
2005	$518,043,000	$33,526,000
2004	$516,201,000	$35,852,000

Curr. Assets:	$224,660,000	*Curr. Liab.:*	$54,798,000	*P/E Ratio:*	21.00
Plant, Equip.:	$72,141,000	*Total Liab.:*	$103,437,000	*Indic. Yr. Divd.:*	$0.720
Total Assets:	$361,113,000	*Net Worth:*	$257,676,000	*Debt/ Equity:*	NA

Kensey Nash Corp

735 Pennsylvania Dr., Exton, PA, 19341; *PH:* 1-484-713-2100; *Fax:* 1-484-713-2900; *http://* www.kenseynash.com

General - Incorporation	DE	**Stock**- Price on:12/24/2007	$25.5
Employees	356	Stock Exchange	NDQ
Auditor	Deloitte & Touche LLP	Ticker Symbol	KNSY
Stk Agt	Computershare Trust Co	Outstanding Shares	11,930,000
Counsel	NA	E.P.S.	$0.16
DUNS No.	13-110-7757	Shareholders	NA

Business: The group's principal activity is to design and develop absorbable biomaterial products for the orthopaedic, cardiology, drug and biologics delivery and wound care markets. The group has developed the triactiv(tm) balloon protected flush extraction system, a device designed to provide distal protection during saphenous vein graft treatment. The group has also developed the angio-seal(R) vascular closure device, which is used in sealing arterial punctures created during common cardiovascular catheterization procedures such as diagnostic angiography, balloon angioplasty and stenting. Angio-seal(R) vascular closure device is currently marketed, manufactured and distributed by st. Jude medical under a license agreement.

Primary SIC and add'l.: 3841 8731

CIK No: 0001002811

Subsidiaries: ILT Acquisition Sub, Inc., Kensey Nash Europe GmbH, Kensey Nash Holding Company

Officers: Joseph W. Kaufmann/Dir., CEO, Pres., Wendy F. Dicicco/CFO, Douglas G. Evans/Dir., COO, John E. Nash/Dir., Co - Founder, VP - New Technology, Kevin M. Carouge/VP - Biomaterials Marketing Development, Donald L. Daveler/VP - Quality Assurance, Quality Control, Todd M. Dewitt/VP - Biomaterials, Guenter Ernst/VP - European Sales, Robin M. Fatzinger/VP - Clinical, Regulatory Affairs, Holly C. Harrity/VP - Business Development, Russell T. Kronengold/VP - Biomaterials Research, James Rauth/VP - Operations, June E. Sheets/VP - Human Resources, Gregory A. Walters/VP - Product Development

Directors: Joseph W. Kaufmann/Dir., CEO, Pres., Walter R. Maupay/69/Chmn., Jeffrey C. Smith/36/Dir., Ceasar N. Anquillare/52/Dir., Steven J. Lee/Dir., Harold N. Chefitz/Dir., Mccollister C. Evarts/Dir., Robert J. Bobb/Dir., Douglas G. Evans/Dir., COO, Kim D. Rosenberg/Dir., John E. Nash/Dir., Co - Founder, VP - New Technology

Owners: Insiders/15.80%, Wendy F. DiCicco, John E. Nash/2.50%, Steven J. Lee, Walter R. Maupay, Joseph W. Kaufmann/5.80%, Robert J. Bobb, Ramius Capital Group LLC/20.30%, McCollister C. Evarts, Lord, Abbett and Co., LLC/8.10%, Wellington Management Company, LLP/10.40%, United States Trust Company, N.A./7.40%, Barclays Global Investors/5.00%, Kim D. Rosenberg, Harold N. Chefitz *(18 Owners included in Index)*

Financial Data: *Fiscal Year End:*06/30 *Latest Annual Data:* 06/30/2007

Year	Sales	Net Income
2007	$69,494,000	$3,633,000
2006	$60,397,000	$3,718,000
2005	$61,376,000	$12,931,000

Curr. Assets:	$51,942,000	**Curr. Liab.:**	$7,594,000	**P/E Ratio:**	39.84
Plant, Equip.:	$63,251,000	**Total Liab.:**	$16,999,000	**Indic. Yr. Divd.:**	NA
Total Assets:	$130,191,000	**Net Worth:**	$113,192,000	**Debt/ Equity:**	0.0639

Kent Financial Services Inc

PO Box 97, 211 Pennbrook Rd., Far Hills, NJ, 07931; ***PH:*** 1-908-604-2181; ***Fax:*** 1-908-926-2562; ***http://*** www.kentfinancialservices.com

General - Incorporation	DE	**Stock**- Price on:12/24/2007	$2.09
Employees	NA	Stock Exchange	NDQ
Auditor	Paritz & Co., P.A.	Ticker Symbol	KENT
Stk Agt	American Stock Transfer & Trust Co.	Outstanding Shares	2,800,000
Counsel	NA	E.P.S	-$0.15
DUNS No.	02-193-1498	Shareholders	NA

Business: The group's principal activities are to buy and sell securities, provide investment advisory and management services. The group operates through its subsidiary t.r. Winston and company, a securities broker-dealer licensed in all states except in Alaska. Winston conducts retail securities brokerage, trading and investment banking activities.

Primary SIC and add'l.: 6719 6211

CIK No: 0000316028

Subsidiaries: Asset Value Holdings, Inc., Asset Value Management, Inc., Cortech, Inc., Kent Educational Services, Inc., The Academy for Teaching and Leadership, Inc.

Officers: Paul O. Koether/72/Chmn., CEO/$297,653.00, Sue Ann Merrill/Principal Financial, Accounting Officer/$46,909.00, Qun Yi Zheng/Pres./$268,983.00, Bryan P. Healey/CFO/$97,323.00

Directors: Paul O. Koether/72/Chmn., CEO, William Mahomes/Dir., Casey K. Tjang/Dir., Michael M. Witte/Dir.

Owners: Michael M. Witte, Marital Trust u/w/o Natalie I. Koether/16.12%, Bryan P. Healey, Insiders/56.07%, Paul O. Koether/55.18%

Financial Data: ***Fiscal Year End:***12/31 ***Latest Annual Data:*** 12/31/2006

Year	Sales	Net Income
2006	$1,135,000	-$546,000
2005	$894,000	-$181,000
2004	$1,930,000	$949,000

Curr. Assets:	$13,324,000	**Curr. Liab.:**	$388,000		
Plant, Equip.:	$35,000	**Total Liab.:**	$1,032,000	**Indic. Yr. Divd.:**	NA
Total Assets:	$13,505,000	**Net Worth:**	$7,240,000	**Debt/ Equity:**	NA

Kent International Holdings Inc

Formerly: Cortech Inc

211 Pennbrook Rd., Far Hills, NJ, 07931; ***PH:*** 1-908-766-7222; ***http://*** www.cortechcrtq.com

General - Incorporation	DE	**Stock**- Price on:12/24/2007	$2.81
Employees	NA	Stock Exchange	NA
Auditor	Paritz & Co., P.A.	Ticker Symbol	NA
Stk Agt	Computershare Investor Services LLC	Outstanding Shares	3,570,000
Counsel	NA	E.P.S	-$0.06
DUNS No.	10-905-6051	Shareholders	NA

Business: The group's principle activity is to research and develop novel therapeutics for the treatment of inflammatory disorders. The company uses its collaborative partners to conduct and fund on-going research and development on those components of its portfolio that had not been out licensed. The company undertakes clinical trials to develop protease inhibitors and bradykinin antagonists in treatment of acute respiratory distress and brain injury. The company in response to disappointing test results and its loss of collaborative partner support discontinued all research and development activities. The company also decommissioned its laboratories and sold all of its remaining scientific, technical and office equipment. The company's strategy is to seek collaborative partners to conduct and fund future research and development on the components of its portfolio. The group operates from United States.

Primary SIC and add'l.: 9999

CIK No: 0000728478

Subsidiaries: Kent Financial Services, Inc

Officers: Paul O. Koether/Chmn., CEO, Qun Y. Zheng/Dir., Pres./$233,495.00, Bryan P. Healey/CFO, Treasurer, Sec.

Directors: Paul O. Koether/Chmn., CEO, Rocco Mastrodomenico/Dir., James L. Bicksler/Dir., Qun Y. Zheng/Dir., Pres., Diarmuid F. Boran/Dir.

Owners: Paul O. Koether, Bryan P. Healey, Biotechnology Value Fund, Kent Financial Services, Inc., James L. Bicksler, Insiders

Financial Data: ***Fiscal Year End:***12/31 ***Latest Annual Data:*** 12/31/2006

Year	Sales	Net Income
2006	$564,000	-$212,000
2005	$337,000	-$84,000
2004	$140,000	-$306,000

Curr. Assets:	$10,909,000	**Curr. Liab.:**	$74,000		
Plant, Equip.:	$34,000	**Total Liab.:**	$74,000	**Indic. Yr. Divd.:**	NA
Total Assets:	$10,948,000	**Net Worth:**	$10,874,000	**Debt/ Equity:**	NA

Kentucky Bancshares Inc

PO Box 157, Paris, KY, 40362; ***PH:*** 1-859-987-1795; ***http://*** www.kybank.com

General - Incorporation	KY	**Stock**- Price on:12/24/2007	$30.25
Employees	203	Stock Exchange	OTC
Auditor	Crowe Chizek & Co. LLC	Ticker Symbol	KTYB
Stk Agt	Kentucky Bank Trust Department	Outstanding Shares	NA
Counsel	NA	E.P.S	$2.41
DUNS No.	NA	Shareholders	NA

Business: The group's principal activity is offering loans and other banking services through its wholly owned subsidiary, the Kentucky bank. The group accepts checking, savings, club and money market accounts and certificates of deposits and offers commercial, agricultural and real estate loans to small to medium sized industrial and agricultural businesses. It also offers residential mortgage, installment and other loans to individual and non-commercial customers. Other services include credit cards and other consumer oriented financial services. Through its wealth management department, the group also provides brokerage services, annuities, life and long term care insurance, personal trust and agency services and corporate trust services. The group also offers Internet banking services. The group's offices are located in the bourbon, clark, scott, jessamine and harrison counties of the state of Kentucky. On 07-Nov-2003, the group acquired Kentucky first bancorp, inc.

Primary SIC and add'l.: 6022 6712

CIK No: 0001000232

Subsidiaries: Kentucky Bank

Officers: Louis Prichard/54/Dir., CEO, Pres., Allyson Eads/Dir. - Bourbon Country, Lonnie Conley/Dir. - Bourbon Country, Rodes Shackelford Parrish/Dir. - Bourbon County, Mary Beth Hendricks/Dir. - Clark County, Edwin S. Saunier/Dir, Dir. - Clark County, Donald Pace/Dir. - Clark County, John G. Roche/Dir. - Clark County, Bruce K. Florence/Dir. - Harrison County, Joel Techau/Dir. - Harrison County, Gerry Whalen/Dir. - Harrison County, Brad Marshall/Dir. - Harrison County, William M. Arvin/67/Dir., Dir - Jessamine County, Dan Brewer/Dir. - Jessamine County, Tom Buford/Dir. - Jessamine County *(35 Officers included in Index)*

Directors: Louis Prichard/54/Dir., CEO, Pres., Buckner Woodford/63/Chmn., Edwin S. Saunier/Dir, Dir. - Clark County, William M. Arvin/67/Dir., Dir - Jessamine County, Woodford Van Meter/54/Dir., Robert G. Thompson/58/Dir., Theodore Kuster/64/Dir., Betty J. Long/60/Dir., Dir - Harrison County, Proctor B. Caudill/Dir., Special Project Mgr., Ted McClain/56/Dir., Henry Hinkle/56/Dir.

Owners: Edwin S. Saunier, Ted McClain, Norman J. Fryman, Proctor B. Caudill/6.00%, Betty J. Long, Darren M. Henry, Theodore Kuster, Gregory J. Dawson, Henry Hinkle/1.30%, Insiders/19.70%, Woodford Van Meter/1.10%, Louis Prichard, Robert G. Thompson, Buckner Woodford/8.50%, William Arvin/1.00%

Financial Data: ***Fiscal Year End:***12/31 ***Latest Annual Data:*** 12/31/2006

Year	Sales	Net Income
2006	$42,829,000	$6,486,000
2005	$35,646,000	$5,820,000
2004	$32,642,000	$5,762,000

Curr. Assets:	$24,666,000	**Curr. Liab.:**	$563,848,000		
Plant, Equip.:	$14,327,000	**Total Liab.:**	$574,262,000	**Indic. Yr. Divd.:**	$1.080
Total Assets:	$629,542,000	**Net Worth:**	$55,281,000	**Debt/ Equity:**	0.1286

Kentucky First Federal Bancorp

479 Main St., Hazard, KY, 41702; ***PH:*** 1-502-223-1638; ***http://*** www.ffbankky.com

General - Incorporation	USA	**Stock**- Price on:12/24/2007	$10.1
Employees	40	Stock Exchange	NDQ
Auditor	Grant Thornton, LLP	Ticker Symbol	KFFB
Stk Agt	Illinois Stock Transfer Co	Outstanding Shares	8,350,000
Counsel	NA	E.P.S	$0.10
DUNS No.	NA	Shareholders	NA

Business: The group operates through its subsidiaries whose principle activity is to provide banking and financial services. The products of the group include consumer lending, construction, multi family and non residential, and residential mortgage loans. The group operates from the United States. The assets of the group for the year 2006 were $261.9 (million).

Primary SIC and add'l.: 6035 6035

CIK No: 0001297341

Subsidiaries: First Federal Savings and Loan Association of Hazard, First Federal Savings Bank of Frankfort, Frankfort First Bancorp, Inc., Main Street Financial Services, Inc.

Officers: Tony D. Whitaker/61/Chmn., CEO, Louis Prichard/Dir., CEO, Pres. - Kentucky Bank, William M. Arvin/Dir., Regional Dir. - Jessamine County, Rocky Adkins/Regional Dir. - Elliott, Rowan Counties, Donald Pace/Regional Dir. - Clark County, Allyson Eads/Regional Dir. - Bourbon County, Lonnie Conley/Regional Dir. - Bourbon County, Rodes Shackelford Parrish/Regional Dir. - Bourbon County, Mary Beth Hendricks/Regional Dir. - Clark County, Robert Richardson/Regional Dir. - Woodford County, Tod Barhorst/Regional Dir. - Elliott, Rowan Counties, Madonna Weathers/Regional Dir. - Elliott, Rowan Counties, G. R. Jones/Regional Dir. - Elliott, Rowan Counties, Edwin S. Saunier/Dir., Regional Dir. - Clark County, Betty J. Long/Dir., Regional Dir. - Harrison County *(34 Officers included in Index)*

Directors: Louis Prichard/Dir., CEO, Pres. - Kentucky Bank, Tony D. Whitaker/61/Chmn., CEO, Buckner Woodford/Chmn. - Kentucky Bank, Don D. Jennings/43/Dir., COO, Pres., Proctor B. Caudill/Dir., Stephen G. Barker/54/Dir., William D. Gorman/84/Dir., Herman D. Regan/79/Dir., Walter G. Ecton/54/Dir., William M. Arvin/Dir., Regional Dir. - Jessamine County, Edwin S. Saunier/Dir., Regional Dir. - Clark County, Henry Hinkle/Dir., Theodore Kuster/Dir., Betty J. Long/Dir., Regional Dir. - Harrison County, Ted McClain/Dir. *(18 Directors included in Index)*

Owners: Walter G. Ecton, First Federal MHC/57.50%, William D. Gorman, Don D. Jennings, Insiders/3.60%, David R. Harrod, Herman D. Regan, Stephen G. Barker, Tony D. Whitaker

Financial Data: ***Fiscal Year End:***06/30 ***Latest Annual Data:*** 6/30/2006

Year	Sales	Net Income
2006	$12,925,000	$1,588,000
2005	$8,425,000	$1,629,000

Curr. Assets:	$3,162,000	**Curr. Liab.:**	$196,340,000	**P/E Ratio:**	84.17
Plant, Equip.:	$2,908,000	**Total Liab.:**	$198,060,000	**Indic. Yr. Divd.:**	$0.400
Total Assets:	$261,941,000	**Net Worth:**	$63,881,000	**Debt/ Equity:**	NA

Kentucky Investors Inc

200 Capital Ave., Frankfort, KY, 40601; ***PH:*** 1-502-223-2361; ***Fax:*** 1-502-875-7084; ***http://*** www.investorsheritage.com; ***Email:*** ihlic@ihlic.com

General - Incorporation	KY	**Stock**- Price on:12/24/2007	$25
Employees	86	Stock Exchange	OTC
Auditor	Ernst & Young LLP	Ticker Symbol	KINV
Stk Agt	Investors Heritage Life Insurance Co	Outstanding Shares	1,110,000
Counsel	NA	E.P.S	$1.30
DUNS No.	05-427-2489	Shareholders	NA

Business: The group's principal activity is to provide insurance and annuity products including accident, health and group insurance. The insurance and annuity products include participating, non-participating, whole life, limited pay, universal life, annuity contracts, credit life, credit accident and health and group insurance policies. The group markets its products in the commonwealths of Kentucky and Virginia, and the states of North Carolina, South Carolina, Georgia, Ohio, Indiana, Florida, Tennessee, Illinois, west Virginia, Arizona, Michigan, Mississippi and Texas.

Primary SIC and add'l.: 6311 6321 6719

CIK No: 0000055362

Subsidiaries: Heritage Financial Services Group, Inc., Heritage Life Insurance Company, Heritage Printing, Inc., Underwriters, Inc.

Officers: Harry Lee Waterfield/64/Chmn., CEO, Pres./$515,647.00, Raymond L. Carr/59/CFO, VP/$312,750.00, Jane S. Jackson/53/Sec., Jimmy R. McIver/56/Treasurer, Robert M. Hardy/50/Dir., VP, General Counsel/$222,658.00

Directors: Harry Lee Waterfield/64/Chmn., CEO, Pres., Michael F. Dudgeon/46/Dir., Harold G. Doran/54/Dir., Helen S. Wagner/71/Dir., Howard L. Graham/73/Dir., Robert M. Hardy/50/Dir., VP, General Counsel, Jerry F. Howell/66/Dir., Gordon C. Duke/62/Dir., David W. Reed/53/Dir.

Owners: David W. Reed/2.00%, Robert M. Hardy/1.40%, Michael F. Dudgeon, Raymond L. Carr/1.90%, Gordon C. Duke, Harold G. Doran/1.10%, Insiders/59.50%, Jerry F. Howell, Howard L. Graham/2.00%, Helen S. Wagner/2.40%, Harry Lee Waterfield/46.00%

Financial Data: Fiscal Year End:12/31   Latest Annual Data: 12/31/2006

Year	Sales	Net Income
2006	$54,384,000	$1,234,000
2005	$55,462,000	$2,230,000
2004	$56,825,000	$2,156,000

Curr. Assets:	$59,436,000	Curr. Liab.:	$6,578,000	P/E Ratio:	17.01
Plant, Equip.:	$2,016,000	Total Liab.:	$374,059,000	Indic. Yr. Divd.:	NA
Total Assets:	$415,229,000	Net Worth:	$41,170,000	Debt/ Equity:	0.4427

Kentucky Power Co

1701 Central Ave., Ashland, KY, 41101; *PH:* 1-614-716-2663; *http://* www.kentuckypower.com

General - Incorporation	KY	Stock- Price on:12/24/2007	NA
Employees	NA	Stock Exchange	NA
Auditor	Deloitte & Touche LLP	Ticker Symbol	NA
Stk Agt	Medallion Program	Outstanding Shares	NA
Counsel	NA	E.P.S.	NA
DUNS No.	00-698-6277	Shareholders	NA

Business: The group's principle activities include generating, purchasing, selling, transmiting and distributing electric power. The company is a wholly owned subsidiary of American electric power company, inc. It provides services to 174,000 retail customers in eastern Kentucky and does business as American electric power. It also sells wholesale power to the aep system power pool and municipalities. As a member of the aep system, the company operates in conjunction with the facilities of certain other aep affiliated utilities as an integrated utility system. The group operates from United States.

Primary SIC and add'l.: 4911
CIK No: 0000055373
Subsidiaries: American Electric Power Company, Inc.
Officers: Michael G. Morris/61/Chmn., CEO, Joseph M. Buonaiuto/Controller, Chief Accounting Officer, Holly K. Koeppel/49/Dir., CFO, VP, Timothy C. Mosher/COO, Pres.
Directors: Michael G. Morris/61/Chmn., CEO, John B. Keane/61/Dir., Keane /Dir., Nicholas K. Akins/47/Dir., Susan Tomasky/54/Dir., Carl L. English/61/Dir., Holly K. Koeppel/49/Dir., CFO, VP, Dennis E. Welch/56/Dir., Donald G. Smith/46/Dir., Robert P. Powers/53/Dir.
Owners: Nicholas K. Akins, John B. Keane, Carl L. English, Michael G. Morris, Holly K. Koeppel, Susan Tomasky, Stephen P. Smith, Thomas M. Hagan, Dennis E. Welch, Insiders, Venita McCellon-Allen

Kentucky Utilities Co

One Quality St., Lexington, KY, 40507; *PH:* 1-859-255-2100; *http://* www.eon-us.com

General - Incorporation	KY	Stock- Price on:12/24/2007	NA
Employees	NA	Stock Exchange	NA
Auditor	PricewaterhouseCoopers LLP	Ticker Symbol	NA
Stk Agt.	Illinois Stock Transfer Co	Outstanding Shares	NA
Counsel	NA	E.P.S.	NA
DUNS No.	00-694-4938	Shareholders	NA

Business: The group's principle activities include generating, transmiting and selling electric energy. The group operates from United States.
Primary SIC and add'l.: 4911
CIK No: 0000055387
Subsidiaries: Louisville Gas and Electric Company
Officers: Victor A. Staffier/Chmn., CEO, Pres. - EON US, Michael S. Beer/VP - Federal Regulation, Policy, EON, Ralph D. Bowling/VP - Power Operations, EON, Martyn Gallus/Sr. VP - Energy Marketing, EON, Bradford S. Rives/CFO - EON, Chris Hermann/Dir., Sr. VP - Energy Delivery, John R. McCall/Exec. VP, General Counsel, Corp. Sec. EON, Paul W. Thompson/Dir., Sr. VP - Energy Services, EON, Chip R.W. Keeling/VP - Communications, EON, Paula Pottinger/Sr. VP - Human Resources, EON, George R. Siemens/VP - External Affairs, EON, John N. Voyles/VP - Regulated Generation, EON, Wendy C. Welsh/Sr. VP - Information Technology, EON, Kiran Bhojani/Exec. VP - Investor Relations, EON US, Peter Blankenhorn/Mgr. - Investor Relations, EON US (22 Officers included in Index)
Directors: Victor A. Staffier/Chmn., CEO, Pres. - EON US, Paul W. Thompson/Dir., Sr. VP - Energy Services, EON, Chris Hermann/Dir., Sr. VP - Energy Delivery, John R. McCall/Exec. VP, General Counsel, Corp. Sec. EON

Keryx Biopharmaceuticals Inc

750 Lexington Ave., 20th Fl., New York, NY, 10022; *PH:* 1-212-531-5965; *Fax:* 1-212-531-5961; *http://* www.keryx.com; *Email:* ir@keryx.com

General - Incorporation	DE	Stock- Price on:12/24/2007	NA
Employees	40	Stock Exchange	NDQ
Auditor	KPMG LLP	Ticker Symbol	KERX
Stk Agt.	American Stock Transfer & Trust Co.	Outstanding Shares	43,570,000
Counsel	Hale & Dorr LLP	E.P.S.	-$1.82
DUNS No.	NA	Shareholders	NA

Business: The group's principal activities are to acquire, develop and commercialize novel pharmaceutical products for the treatment of life-threatening diseases including diabetes and cancer. It has two product candidates, krx-101 and krx-0401 in late-stage clinical development. Krx-101 (sulodexide) is a novel oral heparinoid compound for the treatment of diabetic nephropathy, a kidney

disease caused by diabetes. Krx-0401 (perifosine) is the prototype of a new group of anti-cancer drugs. Additionally, the group is developing three clinical stage oncology compounds namely: krx-0401, krx-0402 and krx-0403. It also has an active in-licensing and acquisition program designed to identify and acquire clinical-stage drug candidates. On 06-Feb-2004, the group acquired access oncology inc.

Primary SIC and add'l.: 8731 2834
CIK No: 0001114220
Subsidiaries: ACCESS Oncology, Inc., Accumin Diagnostics, Inc., AOI Pharma, Inc., AOI Pharmaceuticals, Inc., Keryx (Israel) Ltd., Keryx Biomedical Technologies Ltd., Neryx Biopharmaceuticals, Inc., Online Collaborative Oncology Group, Inc.
Officers: Michael S. Weiss/41/Chmn., CEO/$8,773,304.00, Craig I. Henderson/Dir., Pres./$2,063,326.00, Beth F. Levine/Sr. VP, General Counsel, Chief Compliance Officer, Corp. Sec., Mark Stier/VP, Chief Accounting Officer
Directors: Michael S. Weiss/41/Chmn., CEO, Craig I. Henderson/Dir., Pres., Malcolm Hoenlein/63/Dir., Eric Rose/57/Dir., Kevin J. Cameron/39/Dir., Wyche Fowler/Dir., Jack Kaye/Dir., Michael P. Tarnok/Dir.
Owners: Ronald C. Renaud, Franklin Resources, Inc./8.30%, Chilton Investment Company, LLC/5.20%, Malcolm Hoenlein, Craig I. Henderson/1.30%, College Retirement Equities Fund/10.10%, Eric Rose, Insiders/12.00%, Ron Bentsur, Michael S. Weiss/9.80%

Financial Data: Fiscal Year End:12/31   Latest Annual Data: 06/30/2007

Year	Sales	Net Income
2007	$50,000	-$19,460,000
2006	$534,000	-$73,764,000
2005	$574,000	-$26,895,000

Curr. Assets:	$114,968,000	Curr. Liab.:	$12,194,000		
Plant, Equip.:	$8,489,000	Total Liab.:	$16,492,000	Indic. Yr. Divd.:	$0.110
Total Assets:	$140,313,000	Net Worth:	$123,821,000	Debt/ Equity:	NA

Kerzner International Ltd

Coral Towers, Paradise Island; ; *http://* www.eurodisney.com

General - Incorporation	Bahamas	Stock- Price on:12/24/2007	NA
Employees	NA	Stock Exchange	NA
Auditor	Deloitte & Touche LLP	Ticker Symbol	NA
Stk Agt	Registrar & Transfer Co	Outstanding Shares	NA
Counsel	Cravath, Swaine & Moore LLP	E.P.S.	NA
DUNS No.	87-504-1006	Shareholders	NA

Business: The group operates through its subsidiaries whose principle activity is to develop, operate and manage premier resort and casino properties. The group operates from United States.
Primary SIC and add'l.: 7011 6719
CIK No: 0000914444
Subsidiaries: Kerzner International Bahamas Limited, Kerzner International Management Limited, Kerzner International North America, Inc, One&Only (Indian Ocean) Management Limited
Officers: Meagan McCutcheon/Contact

Kewaunee Scientific Corp

2700 W Front St., Statesville, NC, 28677; *PH:* 1-704-873-7202; *Fax:* 1-704-873-1275; *http://* www.kewaunee.com

General - Incorporation	DE	Stock- Price on:12/24/2007	$11.7
Employees	566	Stock Exchange	NDQ
Auditor	Pricewaterhousecoopers LLP	Ticker Symbol	KEQU
Stk Agt	Mellon Investor Services LLC	Outstanding Shares	2,490,000
Counsel	NA	E.P.S.	$1.08
DUNS No.	00-503-6330	Shareholders	NA

Business: The group's principal activity is to design, manufacture and install scientific and technical furniture. The group operates in two units: laboratory products and technical products. Laboratory products include both steel and wood cabinetry, fume hoods, flexible systems and worksurfaces. Technical furniture products include workstations, workbenches, computer enclosures and network storage systems. These products are sold to pharmaceutical, biotechnology, industrial, chemical and commercial research laboratories, educational institutions, health care institutions and governmental entities. Technical products segment manufactures and sells technical furniture including network storage systems, workstations, workbenches, computer enclosures and related accessories. Technical products are sold to manufacturing facilities and users of computer and networking furniture. The group has operations in the United States, Singapore and India.
Primary SIC and add'l.: 2599 3821
CIK No: 0000055529
Subsidiaries: Kewaunee Labway Asia Pte. Ltd.
Officers: William A. Shumaker/CEO, Pres./$413,195.00, Dana L. Dahlgren/VP - Sales, Marketing Laboratory Products Group, Bain K. Black/VP, GM - Technical Furniture Group, Keith D. Smith/VP - Manufacturing/$169,676.00, Kurt P. Rindoks/VP - Engineering, Product Development/$193,689.00, Sudhir K. Vadehra/VP - International Operations/$208,868.00, Michael D. Parker/Sr. VP - Finance, CFO, Treasurer, Sec./$263,490.00, David M. Rausch/VP - Construction Services
Directors: Silas Keehn/Dir., John C. Campbell/65/Dir., James T. Rhind/86/Dir., Wiley N. Caldwell/81/Dir., Eli Manchester/77/Dir., Margaret B. Pyle/56/Dir.
Owners: Laura Campbell Rhind/15.60%, Ernest and Patricia R. Ohnell/6.60%, Eli Manchester/5.00%, Margaret B. Pyle/2.20%, Wiley N. Caldwell, James T. Rhind/15.60%, William A. Shumaker/2.80%, Michael D. Parker/1.60%, Keith D. Smith, John C. Campbell/1.70%, Insiders/29.30%, Kurt P. Rindoks, Dimensional Fund Advisors LP/5.00%, Elizabeth B. Gardner/8.50%, Silas Keehn

Financial Data: Fiscal Year End:04/30   Latest Annual Data: 04/30/2007

Year	Sales	Net Income
2007	$81,441,000	$1,540,000
2006	$84,071,000	$193,000
2005	$73,481,000	-$147,000

Curr. Assets:	$28,514,000	Curr. Liab.:	$16,183,000	P/E Ratio:	37.74
Plant, Equip.:	$11,255,000	Total Liab.:	$20,010,000	Indic. Yr. Divd.:	$0.280
Total Assets:	$45,240,000	Net Worth:	$24,048,000	Debt/ Equity:	NA

Key Corp

127 Public Sq., Cleveland, OH, 44114; *PH:* 1-216-689-6300; *http://* www.keybank.com

General - Incorporation	OH	**Stock**- Price on:12/24/2007	$36.33
Employees	20,006	Stock Exchange	NYSE
Auditor	Ernst & Young LLP	Ticker Symbol	KEY
Stk Agt	Computershare Investor Services LLC	Outstanding Shares	392,300,000
Counsel	NA	E.P.S	$2.60
DUNS No.	00-294-5293	Shareholders	NA

Business: The groups principle activity is to provide financial services. The groups services include commercial banking, commercial leasing, investment management, consumer finance and investment banking. The group operates from United States.

Primary SIC and add'l.: 6021 6712

CIK No: 0000091576

Subsidiaries: KeyBank National Association

Officers: Henry L. Meyer/Chmn., CEO, Pres./$12,024,790.00, Thomas C. Stevens/Vice Chmn., Chief Administrative Officer/$3,352,188.00, Michael P. Barnum/Exec. VP, Beth E. Mooney/Member - Exec. Counsel/$3,383,322.00, Christopher Gorman/Member - Exec. Counsel, Thomas E. Helfrich/Chief Human Resources Officer, Jeffrey B. Weeden/CFO, Sr. Exec. VP/$3,011,914.00, Bruce D. Murphy/Pres. - Community Development Banking, Stephen E. Yates/CIO, Exec. VP, Robert L. Morris/Chief Accounting Officer, Vernon L. Patterson/Exec. VP, E. J. Burke/Exec. VP, Michael J. Monroe/Exec. VP, Chief Communications Officer, Amy K. Carlson/Mgr., Sr. VP, Paul A. Larkins/Member - Exec. Counsel *(32 Officers included in Index)*

Directors: Henry L. Meyer/Chmn., CEO, Pres., Thomas C. Stevens/Vice Chmn., Chief Administrative Officer, Thomas W. Bunn/Vice Chmn., Alexander M. Cutler/56/Dir., Bill R. Sanford/63/Dir., Edward P. Campbell/58/Dir., Margot J. Copeland/Dir., Exec. VP, Ralph Alvarez/52/Dir., William G. Bares/66/Dir., Carol A. Cartwright/66/Dir., Eduardo R. Menasce/62/Dir., Peter G. Ten Eyck/69/Dir., James H. Dallas/49/Dir., Charles R. Hogan/70/Dir., Lauralee E. Martin/57/Dir.

Owners: Beth E. Mooney, Thomas C. Stevens, Carol A. Cartwright, Charles R. Hogan, William G. Bares, Edward P. Campbell, Lauralee E. Martin, Thomas W. Bunn, Jeffrey B. Weeden, Eduardo R. Menasc, Peter G. TenEyck, Alexander M. Cutler, Ralph Alvarez, James H. Dallas, Henry L. Meyer *(17 Owners included in Index)*

Financial Data: *Fiscal Year End:*12/31 *Latest Annual Data:* 12/31/2006

Year	Sales	Net Income
2006	$7,507,000,000	$1,055,000,000
2005	$6,695,000,000	$1,129,000,000
2004	$5,564,000,000	$954,000,000

Curr. Assets:	$3,671,000,000	**Curr. Liab.:**	$67,987,000,000	**P/E Ratio:**	12.88
Plant, Equip.:	$1,719,000,000	**Total Liab.:**	$84,634,000,000	**Indic. Yr. Divd.:**	$1.460
Total Assets:	$92,337,000,000	**Net Worth:**	$7,703,000,000	**Debt/ Equity:**	1.8047

Key Hospitality Acquisition Corp

4 Becker Farm Rd., Roseland, NJ, 07068; *PH:* 1-973-992-3707

General - Incorporation	DE	**Stock**- Price on:12/24/2007	$7.49
Employees	NA	Stock Exchange	OTC
Auditor	Rothstein, Kass & Company, P.C.	Ticker Symbol	KHPA
Stk Agt	Continental Stock Transfer & Trust Co	Outstanding Shares	NA
Counsel	NA	E.P.S	NA
DUNS No.	NA	Shareholders	NA

Business: The groups principle activity is to provide recruiting services. The groups service area includes the research and development, engineering, marketing, sales, information technology and manufacturing industries. The group operates from United States.

Primary SIC and add'l.: 6770

CIK No: 0001326959

Officers: Jeffrey S. Davidson/48/Co - Chmn., CEO, Udi Toledano/57/Dir., Pres., Glyn F. Aeppel/48/Dir., Sec.

Directors: Jeffrey S. Davidson/48/Co - Chmn., CEO, Thomas W. Parrington/62/Co - Chmn., Udi Toledano/57/Dir., Pres., Stephen B. Siegel/63/Dir., Glyn F. Aeppel/48/Dir., Sec.

Owners: Weiss Asset Management, LLC/15.80%, The Baupost Group, L.L.C./9.10%, Insiders/15.40%, Fir Tree, Inc./9.80%, Glyn F. Aeppel/1.60%, Thomas W. Parrington/2.10%, Udi Toledano/4.70%, Jeffrey S. Davidson/6.10%, Stephen B. Siegel/1.30%

Financial Data: *Fiscal Year End:*12/31 *Latest Annual Data:* 12/31/2006

Year	Sales	Net Income
2006	$4,841,000	$3,832,000
2005	$306,000	$127,000

Curr. Assets:	$690,000	**Curr. Liab.:**	$3,049,000		
Plant, Equip.:	NA	**Total Liab.:**	$12,783,000	**Indic. Yr. Divd.:**	NA
Total Assets:	$49,448,000	**Net Worth:**	$36,665,000	**Debt/ Equity:**	NA

Key Technology Inc

150 Ave.ry St., Walla Walla, WA, 99362; *PH:* 1-509-529-2161; *Fax:* 1-509-527-1331; *http://* www.keyww.com; *Email:* contact@keytechinc.com

General - Incorporation	OR	**Stock**- Price on:12/24/2007	$21.4
Employees	486	Stock Exchange	NDQ
Auditor	Grant Thornton, LLP	Ticker Symbol	KTEC
Stk Agt	Deloitte & Touche LLP	Outstanding Shares	5,430,000
Counsel	Tonkon Torp LLP	E.P.S	$0.37
DUNS No.	07-782-9695	Shareholders	NA

Business: The group's principal activities are to design, manufacture, sell and service process automation systems for food processing industry. The group's products include automated inspection systems, specialized conveying systems, processing and preparation systems and service/contracts and parts. Automated inspection systems are used in the processing application to detect and eliminate defects during raw product processing. Specialized conveying systems are utilized in the food industry and other industries to move large quantities of products within a processing plant. The group designs and manufactures raw food preparation systems to prepare vegetables prior to freezing, canning or other processing.

Primary SIC and add'l.: 3556

CIK No: 0000906193

Subsidiaries: Freshline Machines Pty. Ltd., Key Technology AMVC LLC, Key Technology Australia Pty. Ltd, Key Technology B.V., Key Technology Holdings USA LLC, Productos Key Mexicana S. de R.L. de C.V, Suplusco Holding B.V.

Officers: David M. Camp/Dir., CEO, Pres., James D. Ruff/43/MD - Key Technology BV, Ronald W. Burgess/59/CFO, Sr. VP, John C. Boutsikaris/Sr. VP - Sales, Marketing, Craig T.J. Miller/Sr. VP, GM - Aftermarket Business, Gordon Wicher/Sr. VP, GM - Americas, Asia

Directors: David M. Camp/Dir., CEO, Pres., Charles H. Stonecipher/Chmn., Donald A. Washburn/Dir., Michael L. Shannon/Dir., John E. Pelo/Dir.

Owners: David M. Camp, Thomas C. Madsen/8.30%, John C. Boutsikaris, Ronald W. Burgess, Royce & Associates, LLC/10.50%, Charles H. Stonecipher, Insiders/19.40%, John E. Pelo, Craig T. J. Miller, Kirk W. Morton, Richard L. Scott/8.50%, Gordon Wicher/3.90%, Bank of America/11.20%, Donald A. Washburn, Michael L. Shannon/3.70%

Financial Data: *Fiscal Year End:*09/30 *Latest Annual Data:* 9/30/2006

Year	Sales	Net Income
2006	$84,840,000	-$793,000
2005	$80,322,000	$2,691,000
2004	$80,610,000	$3,684,000

Curr. Assets:	$46,101,000	**Curr. Liab.:**	$16,044,000	**P/E Ratio:**	25.18
Plant, Equip.:	$4,275,000	**Total Liab.:**	$16,686,000	**Indic. Yr. Divd.:**	NA
Total Assets:	$57,938,000	**Net Worth:**	$41,252,000	**Debt/ Equity:**	NA

Key Tronic Corp

N 4424 Sullivan Rd., Spokane, WA, 99216; *PH:* 1-509-928-8000; *Fax:* 1-509-927-5383; *http://* www.keytronic.com; *Email:* investorinfo@keytronic.com

General - Incorporation	WA	**Stock**- Price on:12/24/2007	$4.75
Employees	2,840	Stock Exchange	NDQ
Auditor	BDO Seidman LLP	Ticker Symbol	KTCC
Stk Agt	Mellon Investor Services LLC	Outstanding Shares	9,920,000
Counsel	NA	E.P.S	$0.39
DUNS No.	04-844-0424	Shareholders	NA

Business: The group's principal activity is to provide electronic manufacturing services for original equipment manufacturers and manufacturing of keyboards for personal computers, terminals and workstations. The electronic manufacturing services provided by the group include product design, tool making, precision molding, prototype design, liquid plastic injection molding, printed circuit based assembly, full box build and screened silver flexible circuit membranes. The major customers of the group are hewlett packard, lexmark and clorox products manufacturing company. The trademark of the group is keytronicems. The group sells its products in the United States, China, Ireland and Mexico.

Primary SIC and add'l.: 3575 3577

CIK No: 0000719733

Subsidiaries: Key Tronic China LTD, Key Tronic Computer Peripherals (Shanghai) Co. LTD, Key Tronic Europe, LTD, Key Tronic Juarez, SA de CV, Key Tronic Reynosa, S.A. de CV, KT Services, Inc., KTI Limited

Officers: Jack W. Oehlke/62/Dir., CEO, Pres./$576,637.00, Craig D. Gates/49/Exec. VP, GM/$394,652.00, Ronald F. Klawitter/56/Exec. VP - Administration, CFO, Treasurer/$354,819.00, Efren R. Perez/68/VP - Southwest Operations/$281,858.00, George R. Alford/55/VP - Materials/$242,578.00, Michael Newman/Contact - Investor Relations, Kathleen L. Nemeth/Sec.

Directors: Jack W. Oehlke/62/Dir., CEO, Pres., Dale F. Pilz/82/Chmn., Yacov A. Shamash/58/Dir., Patrick Sweeney/73/Dir., James R. Bean/58/Dir.

Owners: Craig D. Gates/2.90%, Jack W. Oehlke/4.30%, Tieton Capital Management/6.60%, Patrick Sweeney, Dale F. Pilz, Citigroup Investment Research/5.40%, Yacov A. Shamash, Efren R. Perez/1.60%, Ronald F. Klawitter/3.10%, Signia Capital Management LLC/13.90%, Dimensional Fund Advisors, Inc./8.20%, Insiders/12.80%

Financial Data: *Fiscal Year End:*07/02 *Latest Annual Data:* 6/30/2007

Year	Sales	Net Income
2007	$201,712,000	$5,230,000
2006	$187,699,000	$9,753,000
2005	$202,877,000	$4,376,000

Curr. Assets:	$54,720,000	**Curr. Liab.:**	$31,252,000	**P/E Ratio:**	5.05
Plant, Equip.:	$11,131,000	**Total Liab.:**	$44,704,000	**Indic. Yr. Divd.:**	NA
Total Assets:	$67,938,000	**Net Worth:**	$23,234,000	**Debt/ Equity:**	NA

Keynote Systems Inc

777 Mariners Island Blvd., San Mateo, CA, 94404; *PH:* 1-650-403-2400; *Fax:* 1-650-403-5500; *http://* www.keynote.com; *Email:* info@keynote.com

General - Incorporation	DE	**Stock**- Price on:12/24/2007	$15.29
Employees	270	Stock Exchange	NDQ
Auditor	Deloitte & Touche, LLP	Ticker Symbol	KEYN
Stk Agt	American Stock Transfer & Trust Co.	Outstanding Shares	17,450,000
Counsel	Brobeck, Phleger & Harrison	E.P.S	-$0.27
DUNS No.	NA	Shareholders	NA

Business: The group's principal activity is to provide Internet performance services that enable companies to benchmark, test, manage, and improve their e-business Web sites. The Web performance benchmarking and application performance measurement services rendered by the group enable the customers to measure and improve their e-business quality services from multiple points on the Internet. The customers of the group include American express, at&t wireless, cable & wireless, hewlett-packard, IBM, intermedia communications/digex, microsoft, overture services, sbc communications and sprint. As of 30-Sep-2003, the group had 1,750 measurement computers deployed in 50 cities and in over 120 locations. On 06-Apr-2004, the group acquired netraker. On 16-Sep-2004, the group, acquired vividence corporation.

Primary SIC and add'l.: 7375 7379

CIK No: 0001032761

Subsidiaries: Big Red Acquisition Corporation, Envision Acquisition Corporation, Hudson Williams, Inc, Keynote Canada, Keynote Europe Limited, NetMechanic, Inc, NetRaker Corporation, OnDevice Acquisition Corporation, Velogic, Inc, Vividence Corporation

Officers: Umang Gupta/Chmn., CEO, Andrew Hamer/VP - Finance, CFO, Jeff Kraatz/VP - Sales, Americas, Asia Pacific, Krishna Khadloya/VP - Engineering, Donald Aoki/Sr. VP, GM - Customer Experience Management, Haran Sold/VP, MD - Europe, Middle East, Africa, Eric Stokesberry/VP - Operations, Vik Chaudhary/VP - Marketing, Corporate Development, Drew Hamer/CFO, VP, Anshu Agarwal/Executive Dir. - Marketing, Dan Berkowitz/Sr. Dir. - Corporatecommunications, Josh Danson/Sr. Mgr. - Public Relations

Directors: Umang Gupta/Chmn., CEO, Raymond L. Ocampo/Dir., Jennifer Bolt/Dir., David Cowan/Dir., Deborah Rieman/Dir., Mohan Gyani/Dir., Charles Boesenberg/Dir.

Owners: Jennifer Bolt, Krishna Khadloya, S Squared Technology/8.26%, David Cowan, Jeffrey Kraatz, Mohan Gyani, Umang Gupta/20.10%, Geoffrey Penney, Insiders/28.39%, Raymond L. Ocampo, Dimensional Fund Advisors, Inc./5.73%, David J. Greene & Co/8.73%, Andrew Hamer, Royal Capital Management, LLC/6.41%, Deborah Rieman *(16 Owners included in Index)*

Financial Data: *Fiscal Year End:*09/30   *Latest Annual Data:* 09/30/2007

Year	Sales	Net Income
2007	$67,754,000	-$4,691,000
2006	$55,508,000	-$7,534,000
2005	$53,692,000	$7,365,000

Curr. Assets:	$102,793,000	*Curr. Liab.:*	$22,028,000		
Plant, Equip.:	$34,464,000	*Total Liab.:*	$25,763,000	*Indic. Yr. Divd.:*	NA
Total Assets:	$199,152,000	*Net Worth:*	$173,389,000	*Debt/ Equity:*	0.0002

Keyspan Corp

175 E Old Country Rd., Hicksville, NY, 11801; *PH:* 1-516-755-6650;
http:// www.keyspanenergy.com

General - Incorporation	NY	Stock- Price on:12/24/2007	$41.83
Employees	9,594	Stock Exchange	NA
Auditor	Deloitte & Touche LLP	Ticker Symbol	NA
Stk Agt	Computershare Trust Co	Outstanding Shares	175,760,000
Counsel	NA	E.P.S.	$2.503
DUNS No.	96-140-7665	Shareholders	NA

Business: The groups principle activities include gas distribution, electric and energy services, gas exploration and production, energy investments and installation and management services. The group operates from United States.

Primary SIC and add'l.: 4922 1311 4911 6719 4925

CIK No: 0001062379

Subsidiaries: Adrian Associates L.P., Alberta Northeast Gas Ltd., Arlington Associates LP, Bard, Rao + Athanas Consulting Engineers, LLC, Boston Gas Company, Broken Bridge Corp., Colonial Gas Company, Eastern Rivermoor Company, Inc., EnergyNorth Natural Gas, Inc., Enporian, Inc., Essex Gas Company, Fritze KeySpan, LLC, Honeoye Storage Corporation, Iroquois Gas Transmission System LP, Iroquois Pipeline Operating Company 84 Subsidiaries included in the Index

Officers: Robert B. Catell/71/Chmn., CEO, Michael A. Walker/51/VP, Deputy General Counsel, Michael J. Taunton/Sr. VP, Treasurer, Chief Risk Officer, John F. Haran/57/Sr. VP - Keyspan Energy Delivery, Chief Gas Engineer, Nickolas Stavropoulos/48/Exec. VP - Keyspan Energy, John J. Bishar/58/Exec. VP, General Counsel, Chief Governance Officer, Sec., John A. Caroselli/Chief Strategy Officer, Exec. VP, David J. Manning/57/Exec. VP - Corporate Affairs, Chief Environmental Officer, Robert J. Fani/53/Dir., COO, Pres., Elaine Weinstein/60/Sr. VP - Human Resources, Chief Diversity Officer, Theresa A. Balog/VP, Chief Accounting Officer, Coleen A. Ceriello/49/Sr. VP - Shared Services, Anthony Nozzolillo/59/Exec. VP - Electric Operations, Joseph E. Hajjar/55/VP, Controller, Joseph F. Bodanza/60/VP - Regulatory Affairs Asset Optimization *(19 Officers included in Index)*

Directors: Robert B. Catell/71/Chmn., CEO, Andrea S. Christensen/68/Dir., Edward D. Miller/66/Dir., Vikki L. Pryor/54/Dir., Robert J. Fani/53/Dir., COO, Pres., James L. Larocca/64/Dir., Gloria C. Larson/57/Dir., Stephen W. McKessy/70/Dir., Alan H. Fishman/61/Dir., James R. Jones/68/Dir.

Owners: J. L. Larocca, G. Luterman, S. W. McKessy, R. J. Fani, J. R. Jones, A. S. Christensen, R. B. Catell/1.40%, G. C. Larson, W. P. Parker, A. H. Fishman, E. D. Miller, S. L. Zelkowitz, Insiders

Financial Data: *Fiscal Year End:*12/31   *Latest Annual Data:* 12/31/2006

Year	Sales	Net Income
2006	$7,181,600,000	$434,200,000
2005	$7,662,000,000	$390,200,000
2004	$6,650,466,000	$463,665,000

Curr. Assets:	$2,787,000,000	*Curr. Liab.:*	$1,708,000,000	*P/E Ratio:*	16.71
Plant, Equip.:	$7,578,300,000	*Total Liab.:*	$9,903,000,000	*Indic. Yr. Divd.:*	$1.900
Total Assets:	$14,437,500,000	*Net Worth:*	$4,518,800,000	*Debt/ Equity:*	0.9161

Keystone Automotive Industries Inc

700 E Bonita Ave., Pomona, CA, 91767; *PH:* 1-909-624-8041; *Fax:* 1-909-624-9136;
http:// www.keystone-auto.com

General - Incorporation	CA	Stock- Price on:12/24/2007	$40.79
Employees	3,778	Stock Exchange	NDQ
Auditor	Ernst & Young LLP	Ticker Symbol	KEYS
Stk Agt	U.S. Stock Transfer Corp	Outstanding Shares	16,520,000
Counsel	NA	E.P.S.	NA
DUNS No.	05-923-0151	Shareholders	NA

Business: The group's principal activity is to distribute after market collision replacement parts produced by independent manufacturers for automobiles and light trucks. The group also recycles and produces chrome plated and plastic bumpers and remanufactures alloy wheels. The group's principal product lines consist of automotive body parts, bumpers and remanufactured alloy wheels and other materials used in repairing a damaged vehicle. The group operates a distribution system consisting of 125 distribution centers and 15 depots, located in 38 states throughout the United States, as well as in the provinces of ontario, quebec and british columbia in Canada. In addition, the group operates nine wheel remanufacturing facilities and 42 plastic and steel bumper recycling facilities. On 12-Aug-2003, the group acquired multipro auto body parts, inc and quinte bumper and fender inc on 13-Jan-2004.

Primary SIC and add'l.: 5013

CIK No: 0001012393

Subsidiaries: Keystone Automotive Industries BC Inc., Keystone Automotive Industries CDN, Inc., Keystone Automotive Industries FL, Inc., Keystone Automotive Industries MN, Inc., Keystone Automotive Industries OH, Inc., Keystone Automotive Industries ON, Inc., Keystone Automotive Industries QC, Inc., Keystone Automotive Industries Resources, Inc., Keystone Automotive Industries TN, Inc.

Officers: Richard L. Keister/Dir., CEO, Pres./$2,015,674.00, John G. Arena/37/VP, General Counsel, Sec., James M. Pundt/41/VP - Operations

Directors: Richard L. Keister/Dir., CEO, Pres., Ronald G. Foster/Chmn., Timothy C. McQuay/Dir., John R. Moore/Dir., John G. Arena/37/VP, General Counsel, Sec., James Robert Gerrity/Dir., Keith M. Thompson/Dir., Stephen A. Rhodes/Dir.

Owners: Wasatch Advisors, Inc./6.05%, Ronald G. Foster, Stephen A. Rhodes, Carl F. Hartman, James R. Gerrity, Timothy C. McQuay, Richard L. Keister, Christopher N. Northrup, John R. Moore, T. Rowe Price Associates, Inc./6.93%, Jeffrey T. Gray, Wells Fargo Company/6.06%, Insiders/2.39%, Currey D. Hall, Keith M. Thompson

Financial Data: *Fiscal Year End:*03/31   *Latest Annual Data:* 3/30/2007

Year	Sales	Net Income
2007	$713,955,000	$30,324,000
2006	$628,328,000	$22,258,000
2005	$557,705,000	$14,260,000

Curr. Assets:	$185,470,000	*Curr. Liab.:*	$40,224,000		
Plant, Equip.:	$31,079,000	*Total Liab.:*	$42,807,000	*Indic. Yr. Divd.:*	NA
Total Assets:	$234,584,000	*Net Worth:*	$191,777,000	*Debt/ Equity:*	0.0141

Keystone Consolidated Industries Inc

5430 Lbj Fwy., Ste. 1740, Three Lincoln Ctr., Dallas, TX, 75240; *PH:* 1-972-458-0028

General - Incorporation	DE	Stock- Price on:12/24/2007	$20
Employees	1,100	Stock Exchange	OTC
Auditor	PricewaterhouseCoopers LLP	Ticker Symbol	KYCN
Stk Agt	NA	Outstanding Shares	10,000,000
Counsel	NA	E.P.S.	NA
DUNS No.	NA	Shareholders	NA

Business: The groups principle activity is to manufacture steel fabricated wire products, welded wire reinforcement, coiled rebar, industrial wire and wire rod. The group operates through three segments namely keystone steel and wire, engineered wire products and keystone wire products. In the year 2005, the group acquired CaluMetals, Inc. The group operates from the United States, Canada, Great Britain, Australia and Ireland. Of the total sales in the year 2006, keystone steel and wire accounted for 47%, engineered wire products 49% and keystone wire products 28%.

Primary SIC and add'l.: 3312 3315 3496

CIK No: 0000055604

Subsidiaries: Engineered Wire Products, Inc., FV Steel and Wire Company, Keystone Energy Resources, LLC, Keystone Wire Products, Inc.

Owners: Contran Corporation/51.00%, Annette C. Simmons, Third Point LLC/9.90%, KCI Liquidating Trust/9.10%

Financial Data: *Fiscal Year End:*12/31   *Latest Annual Data:* 12/31/2006

Year	Sales	Net Income
2006	$440,540,000	$57,732,000
2005	$367,545,000	$39,232,000
2002	$372,819,000	$38,420,000

Curr. Assets:	$110,158,000	*Curr. Liab.:*	$78,382,000		
Plant, Equip.:	$88,695,000	*Total Liab.:*	$360,274,000	*Indic. Yr. Divd.:*	NA
Total Assets:	$763,936,000	*Net Worth:*	$403,662,000	*Debt/ Equity:*	0.0660

Kforce Inc

1001 E Palm Ave., Tampa, FL, 33605; *PH:* 1-813-552-5000; *Fax:* 1-866-894-6799;
http:// www.kforce.com; *Email:* kforce@kforce.com

General - Incorporation	FL	Stock- Price on:12/24/2007	$15.87
Employees	2,160	Stock Exchange	NDQ
Auditor	Deloitte & Touche LLP	Ticker Symbol	KFRC
Stk Agt	EquiServe Trust Co N.A	Outstanding Shares	41,110,000
Counsel	Holland & Knight LLP	E.P.S.	$0.94
DUNS No.	05-828-7814	Shareholders	NA

Business: The group's principal activity is to provide professional and technical specialty staffing services. The group operates in three segments: information technology segment focus on systems/applications programmers, systems analysts, e-business and networking technicians relating to information technology. Finance and accounting segment provides both temporary staffing and permanent placement services to our clients in areas such as taxation, budget preparation and analysis, financial reporting, cost analysis, accounts payable, accounts receivable, credit and collections, general accounting and audit services. Health and life sciences consists of skilled professionals and technical services in the pharmaceutical, health care and scientific fields. On 07-Jun-2004, the group acquired hall kinion.

Primary SIC and add'l.: 7361 7363

CIK No: 0000930420

Subsidiaries: Cayman company, H.I.G. Pinkerton, Inc, Kinion and Associates Inc, PCCI Holdings, Inc, Trevose Acquisition Corporation

Officers: Patrick Moneymaker/CEO - Kforce Government Holdings Inc, David L. Dunkel/Chmn., CEO/$1,891,583.00, Howard W. Sutter/Vice Chmn., VP - Mergers, Acquisitions, Joseph J. Liberatore/CFO/$1,005,143.00, Mike Ettore/Chief Services Officer/$596,646.00, William L. Sanders/Pres./$1,553,614.00, Steve McMahan/Chief Sales Officer/$590,481.00, Randy Marmon/Pres. - East, Jeffrey Neal/Pres. - West, Peter M. Alonso/Pres. - Health, Life Sciences, David Kelly/VP - Finance, Michael R. Blackman/Sr. VP - Investor Relations, Andy Thomas/Sr. VP - National Champions, Product Management

Directors: David L. Dunkel/Chmn., CEO, Howard W. Sutter/Vice Chmn., VP - Mergers, Acquisitions, Richard M. Cocchiaro/Vice Chmn., John Allred/Dir., Elaine D. Rosen/Dir., Gordon Tunstall/Dir., Mark Furlong/Dir., Ralph E. Struzziero/Dir., W. R. Carey/Dir.

Owners: William L. Sanders/2.31%, Insiders/21.16%, Ralph E. Struzziero, Gordon A. Tunstall, David L. Dunkel/7.96%, Elaine D. Rosen, Michael L. Ettore, Howard W. Sutter/4.50%, Richard M. Cocchiaro/4.42%, Mark F. Furlong, Strong Capital Management Inc./6.34%, Stephen McMahan, William Blair & Company, L.L.C./7.78%, John N. Allred, Joseph J. Liberatore/1.22% *(17 Owners included in Index)*

Financial Data: *Fiscal Year End:*12/31   *Latest Annual Data:* 06/30/2007

Year	Sales	Net Income
2007	NA	NA
2006	$938,448,000	$32,519,000
2005	$802,265,000	$22,321,000

Curr. Assets:	$150,454,000	*Curr. Liab.:*	$86,029,000	*P/E Ratio:*	17.83
Plant, Equip.:	$12,610,000	*Total Liab.:*	$180,693,000	*Indic. Yr. Divd.:*	NA
Total Assets:	$442,618,000	*Net Worth:*	$261,925,000	*Debt/ Equity:*	0.2756

KHD Humboldt Wedag International Ltd

Formerly: MFC Bancorp Ltd
Ste. 702, 7th Fl., Ruttonjee House, Ruttonjee Centre, Ruttonjee Ctr., Hong Kong Sar; ;
http:// www.khdhumboldt.com

Kilroy Realty Corp (continued / left column top)

General - Incorporation	Canada	Stock - Price on:12/24/2007	NA
Employees	1,235	Stock Exchange	NA
Auditor	BDO Dunwoody LLP	Ticker Symbol	NA
Stk Agt	Mellon Investor Services LLC	Outstanding Shares	NA
Counsel	NA	E.P.S.	$2.86
DUNS No.	NA	Shareholders	NA

Business: The group's principal activity is to provide specialized banking and corporate finance services internationally with a focus on merchant banking. The group advises clients on corporate strategy and structure including mergers and acquisitions and capital raising. The group also invests its own capital in promising enterprises whose intrinsic value is not properly reflected in their share value. In addition, the group also offers interim finance to business enterprises pending reorganization or going public to generate fee income. The operations of the group are carried on in Europe, Canada and the United States. In Oct 2001, the group expanded the merchant banking operations by acquiring prada holdings, ltd., an austrian trading group and approximately 53% of trimble resources corporation. As on 08-Aug-2002 the group acquired 85.3% of banff resources ltd.

Primary SIC and add'l.: 6799 8742 6159

CIK No: 0000016859

Subsidiaries: Altmark Industriepark AG, Humboldt Wedag Inc., Humboldt Wedag India Ltd., KHD Humboldt Wedag GmbH, KHD Humboldt Wedag International GmbH, KHD Humboldt Wedag International Holdings GmbH, MFC Commodities AG, MFC Industrial Holdings AG, MFC Merchant Bank S.A., Robabond Holding AG, Sasamat Capital Corporation, ZAB Industrietechnik& Service GmbH, Zementanlagenbau Dessau GmbH

Officers: James B. Busche/CEO, Pres., Michael J. Smith/Chmn., CFO, Sec., George Zimmerman/Sr. VP, Rudolf Pich/VP - Sales, Marketing, Herman Krager/VP - Engineering, Joseph Allen/Investor

Directors: Michael J. Smith/Chmn., CFO, Sec., Shuming Zhao/53/Dir., Silke Brossmann/Dir., Kelvin K. Yao/54/Dir., Indrajit Chatterjee/61/Dir.

Owners: Mass Financial Corp./5.30%, Michael J. Smith, FMR Corp./6.90%, Peter Kellogg/21.30%

Financial Data: Fiscal Year End:12/31 Latest Annual Data: 12/31/2006

Year	Sales	Net Income
2006	$401,238,000	$25,720,000
2005	$820,257,000	$21,719,000
2004	$579,353,000	$30,699,000

Curr. Assets:	$440,237,000	Curr. Liab.:	$271,229,000
Plant, Equip.:	$50,884,000	Total Liab.:	$368,612,000	Indic. Yr. Divd.: NA
Total Assets:	$634,721,000	Net Worth:	$266,109,000	Debt/ Equity: NA

Kid Castle Educational Corp

8th Floor, No. 98 Min Chuan Rd, Hsien Tien, Taipei; PH: 886-222185996; http:// www.kidcastle.com

General - Incorporation	FL	Stock - Price on:12/24/2007	$0.2
Employees	NA	Stock Exchange	OTC
Auditor	PricewaterhouseCoopers LLP	Ticker Symbol	KDCE
Stk Agt	Securities Transfer Corp	Outstanding Shares	NA
Counsel	NA	E.P.S.	NA
DUNS No.	NA	Shareholders	NA

Business: The group's principal activities are to publish, distribute and sell books, magazines, audio and video tapes and compact discs related to English language instruction and educational services. The group also sells merchandise through franchise stores. The group's products serve children whose primary language is Chinese. The operations of the group are conducted through over 2,800 franchises and cooperative schools serving more than 323,000 thousand students using the teaching materials. The group operates in Taiwan and the Peoples Republic of China. The group has three main operations: franchise, publishing & Internet/computer education. The group currently has 300 Kid Castle franchisees, 2,000 cooperating schools and 500 care taking schools.

Primary SIC and add'l.: 3652 2731

CIK No: 0001049011

Subsidiaries: Higoal Developments Limited, Kid Castle Educational Software Development Company Limited (KCES), Kid Castle Internet Technologies Limited (KCIT, Millennia, Inc, PRC

Officers: Min-Tan Yang/42/Dir., CEO, Suang-Yi Pai/47/Chmn., Acting CFO

Directors: Min-Tan Yang/42/Dir., CEO, Suang-Yi Pai/47/Chmn., Acting CFO, Robert Theng/46/Dir., Ming-Tsung Shih/39/Dir.

Owners: Chin-Chen Huang/0.02%, Min-Tang Yang/36.66%, Suang-Yi Pai/19.36%, Insiders/56.02%

Financial Data: Fiscal Year End:12/31 Latest Annual Data: 12/31/2006

Year	Sales	Net Income
2006	$9,712,000	-$46,000
2005	$10,232,000	-$1,698,000
2004	$9,729,000	-$1,255,000

Curr. Assets:	$5,937,000	Curr. Liab.:	$6,745,000
Plant, Equip.:	$1,756,000	Total Liab.:	$10,008,000	Indic. Yr. Divd.: NA
Total Assets:	$9,373,000	Net Worth:	-$635,000	Debt/ Equity: NA

Kiewit Royalty Trust

1700 Farnam St., Omaha, NE, 68102; PH: 1-402-348-6000

General - Incorporation	NE	Stock - Price on:12/24/2007	NA
Employees	NA	Stock Exchange	OTC
Auditor	KPMG LLP	Ticker Symbol	KIRY
Stk Agt		Outstanding Shares	NA
Counsel	NA	E.P.S.	$0.28
DUNS No.	NA	Shareholders	NA

Business: The groups principal activity is to explore minerals. The group operates from the United States.

Primary SIC and add'l.: 6733

CIK No: 0000711477

Officers: Ted L. Hall/52/VP, Trust Officer

Financial Data: Fiscal Year End:12/31 Latest Annual Data: 12/31/2006

Year	Sales	Net Income
2006	$3,414,000	$3,330,000
2005	$3,953,000	$4,636,000
2004	$3,973,000	$3,884,000

Curr. Assets:	$136,000	Curr. Liab.:	$136,000		
Plant, Equip.:	NA	Total Liab.:	$136,000	Indic. Yr. Divd.:	NA
Total Assets:	$159,000	Net Worth:	$23,000	Debt/ Equity:	NA

KIK Technology International Inc

590 Airport Rd., Oceanside, CA, 92054; PH: 1-760-967-2777; Fax: 1-760-967-4071; http:// www.kiktire.com

General - Incorporation	CA	Stock - Price on:12/24/2007	NA
Employees	15	Stock Exchange	OTC
Auditor	S. W. Hatfield, CPA	Ticker Symbol	KKTI
Stk Agt	American Registrar & Transfer Co	Outstanding Shares	NA
Counsel	NA	E.P.S.	-$0.024
DUNS No.	NA	Shareholders	NA

Business: The group's principal activity is to manufacture and market micro-cellular polyurethane tires. The industries served by the group include lawn and garden, health and wellness, industrial, and sports and recreation. The group manufactures polyurethane tires by blending hydrocarbon-based quality isocyanate intermediates with glycol-based polyols and other chemicals. The resulting compound makes a light but tough tire. The group also manufactures non-tire urethane products, for non-tire customers.

Primary SIC and add'l.: 3011

CIK No: 0001109662

Subsidiaries: KIK Technology, Inc.

Officers: William M. Knooihuizen/CEO, Pres., Kuldip C. Baid/60/Dir., CFO

Directors: Donald P. Dean/72/Chmn., Kuldip C. Baid/60/Dir., CFO

Owners: Donald P. Dean/0.99%, KIK Polymers, Inc./65.95%, William M. Knooihuizen/0.99%, Kuldip C. Baid/0.99%, Insiders/68.91%

Financial Data: Fiscal Year End:01/31 Latest Annual Data: 01/31/2007

Year	Sales	Net Income
2007	$1,858,000	-$442,000
2006	$1,947,000	-$381,000
2005	$2,463,000	-$435,000

Curr. Assets:	$369,000	Curr. Liab.:	$1,308,000	
Plant, Equip.:	$82,000	Total Liab.:	$1,308,000	Indic. Yr. Divd.: NA
Total Assets:	$509,000	Net Worth:	-$799,000	Debt/ Equity: NA

Killbuck Bancshares Inc

165 N Main St., Killbuck, OH, 44637; PH: 1-330-276-2771; Fax: 1-330-276-0216; http:// www.killbuckbank.com

General - Incorporation	OH	Stock - Price on:12/24/2007	$109
Employees	101	Stock Exchange	OTC
Auditor	S R Snodgrass, A.C	Ticker Symbol	KLIB
Stk Agt	NA	Outstanding Shares	NA
Counsel	NA	E.P.S.	$7.86
DUNS No.	NA	Shareholders	NA

Business: The group's principal activity is to provide a wide range of retail banking services to individuals and small to medium-sized businesses through eight full service offices. The group, through its subsidiary, the killbuck savings bank company, conducts the business of a commercial banking organization. These services include a variety of deposit products, business and personal loans, credit cards, residential mortgage loans, home equity loans, Internet banking, bill payment and other consumer oriented financial services including ira accounts, safe deposit and night depository facilities. The bank also has automatic teller machines located at all locations that provide 24 hour banking service to customers. The bank belongs to mac, a national ATM network with thousands of locations nationwide.

Primary SIC and add'l.: 6712 6022

CIK No: 0001060455

Subsidiaries: The Killbuck Savings Bank Company

Officers: Luther E. Proper/58/Vice Chmn., CEO, Pres./$262,491.00, Diane S. Knowles/45/CFO, VP, Sec./$149,379.00, Craig A. Lawhead/50/VP, Treasurer/$157,166.00

Directors: Luther E. Proper/58/Vice Chmn., CEO, Pres., Allan R. Mast/58/Chmn., Ted Bratton/47/Dir., John W. Baker/63/Dir., Max A. Miller/52/Dir., Dean J. Mullet/56/Dir., Kenneth E. Taylor/55/Dir., Michael S. Yoder/65/Dir.

Owners: Thomas D. Gindlesberger/5.49%, The Holmes Limestone Co./7.07%

Financial Data: Fiscal Year End:12/31 Latest Annual Data: 12/31/2006

Year	Sales	Net Income
2006	$21,345,000	$5,223,000
2005	$17,883,000	$4,211,000
2004	$15,048,000	$3,419,000

Curr. Assets:	$44,101,000	Curr. Liab.:	$274,073,000	P/E Ratio: 13.34
Plant, Equip.:	$5,714,000	Total Liab.:	$274,073,000	Indic. Yr. Divd.: $2.800
Total Assets:	$313,205,000	Net Worth:	$39,134,000	Debt/ Equity: NA

Kilroy Realty Corp

12200 W Olympic Blvd., Ste. 200, Los Angeles, CA, 90064; PH: 1-310-481-8400; Fax: 1-310-481-6580; http:// www.kilroyrealty.com; Email: investorrelations@kilroyreality.com

General - Incorporation	MD	Stock - Price on:12/24/2007	$72.38
Employees	143	Stock Exchange	NYSE
Auditor	Deloitte & Touche LLP	Ticker Symbol	KRC
Stk Agt	Mellon Investor Services LLC	Outstanding Shares	32,700,000
Counsel	NA	E.P.S.	$1.47
DUNS No.	NA	Shareholders	NA

Business: The groups principle activities include owning, operating, developing and acquiring real estate properties. The group operates through two segments namely, office properties and industrial properties. In the year 2005, the group acquired one industrial building. The group operates from the United States.The group's quarterly revenue for September 2007 was 67.64 millions of USD.

Primary SIC and add'l.: 6798

CIK No: 0001025996

Subsidiaries: Kilroy RB II, LLC, Kilroy Realty Finance Partnership, L.P., Kilroy Realty Finance, Inc., Kilroy Realty Partners, L.P., Kilroy Realty TRS, Inc., Kilroy Realty, L.P., Kilroy Services, LLC

Officers: John B. Kilroy/Dir., CEO, Pres./$6,627,208.00, Jeffrey C. Hawken/COO, Exec. VP/$2,435,304.00, Richard E. Moran/CFO, Exec. VP/$1,781,858.00, Conan C. Cotrell/Sr. VP - Marketing, Leasing, John T. Fucci/Sr. VP - Asset Management, Tyler H. Rose/Sr. VP, Treasurer/$864,122.00, Heidi Roth/Sr. VP, Controller, Steven R. Scott/Sr. VP - San Diego/$1,043,403.00, Justin W. Smart/Sr. VP - Los Angeles, Joseph Hanen/VP - Acqusitions, Dispositions

Directors: John B. Kilroy/Dir., CEO, Pres., John B. Kilroy/Chmn., Edward F. Brennan/Dir., William P. Dickey/Dir., Matthew J. Hart/Dir., Dale F. Kinsella/Dir., Scott Ingraham/Dir.

Owners: Richard E. Moran, William P. Dickey, Jeffrey C. Hawken, John B. Kilroy/3.60%, Cohen & Steers Capital Management, Inc./8.80%, Stichting Pensioenfonds ABP/6.90%, Edward F. Brennan, John B. Kilroy/2.00%, John R. DEathe, Dale F. Kinsella, Steven R. Scott, Tyler H. Rose, Matthew J. Hart, The Vanguard Group, Inc./5.80%, T. Rowe Price Associates, Inc./7.80%

Financial Data: *Fiscal Year End:*12/31 *Latest Annual Data:* 12/31/2006

Year	Sales	Net Income
2006	$251,244,000	$81,864,000
2005	$241,715,000	$33,819,000
2004	$218,549,000	$33,541,000

Curr. Assets:	$80,261,000	**Curr. Liab.:**	$87,339,000	**P/E Ratio:**	24.10
Plant, Equip.:	$1,601,466,000	**Total Liab.:**	$1,125,056,000	**Indic. Yr. Divd.:**	$2.220
Total Assets:	$1,799,352,000	**Net Worth:**	$674,296,000	**Debt/ Equity:**	NA

Kimball International Inc

1600 Royal St., Jasper, IN, 47549; ***PH:*** 1-812-482-1600; ***Fax:*** 1-812-482-8300; ***http://*** www.kimball.com

General		**Stock**	
Incorporation	IN	Price on:12/24/2007	$13.33
Employees	7,512	Stock Exchange	NDQ
Auditor	Deloitte & Touche LLP	Ticker Symbol	KBALB
Stk Agt	National City Bank	Outstanding Shares	38,800,000
Counsel	NA	E.P.S.	$0.56
DUNS No.	00-636-5803	Shareholders	NA

Business: The group's principal activity is to manufacture and sell furniture and related components and electronic assemblies, serving customers around the world. The group operates through two business segments: furniture and cabinets segment and the electronic contract assemblies segment. The furniture and cabinets segment provides furniture for the office, residential, lodging and healthcare industries. The other products include television cabinets and stands, residential furniture retail infrastructure products, and forest products. The electronic contract assemblies segment provides engineering and manufacturing services. Production occurs in group's-owned or leased facilities located in the United States, Mexico, Thailand and Poland. In the United States, the group has facilities and showrooms in 13 states and the district of columbia.

Primary SIC and add'l.: 3674 2435 2511 2517 2426 3672

CIK No: 0000055772

Subsidiaries: CODE International Assurance Ltd., Jacobs Constructors, Jacobs Consultancy Inc., Jacobs Engineering Company, Jacobs Engineering Espana, Jacobs Engineering Group of Ohio Inc., Jacobs Engineering Inc., Jacobs Field Services North America, Jacobs Government Services Company, Jacobs Industrial Maintenance Company LLC., Jacobs Maintenance, JE Remediation Technologies

Officers: James C. Thyen/Dir., CEO, Pres./$2,623,471.00, Donald W. Vanwinkle/VP, GM - National Office Furniture, Kevin R. Smith/VP - North American Operations, Kimball Electronics Group, David E. White/VP, GM - Kimball Office, Zygmunt Witort/VP - European Operations, Kimball Electronics Group, Jeffrey L. Fenwick/VP - Marketing, Kimball Office, Kevin B. Stokes/VP - Global Technical Services, Kimball Electronics Group, Stanley C. Sapp/VP, GM - Kimball Hospitality, Paul J. Plante/VP - Medical Industry Solution, Kimball Electronics Group, Gary W. Schwartz/CIO, Exec. VP, Robert F. Schneider/CFO, Exec. VP/$819,604.00, Dean M. Vonderheide/VP - Human Resources, John H. Kahle/Exec. VP, General Counsel, Sec., Donald D. Charron/Exec. VP/$818,938.00, Daniel P. Miller/Exec. VP, Pres. - Furniture/$1,009,595.00 *(26 Officers included in Index)*

Directors: James C. Thyen/Dir., CEO, Pres., Douglas A. Habig/Chmn., Gary P. Critser/Dir., Christine M. Vujovich/Dir., John B. Habig/Dir., Jack R. Wentworth/Dir., John T. Thyen/Dir., Polly B. Kawalek/Dir., Harry W. Bowman/Dir., Gregory R. Kincer/Dir., VP - Business Development, Treasurer, Ronald J. Thyen/Dir., Geoffrey L. Stringer/Dir.

Owners: A. C. Sermersheim Family Limited Partnership/7.00%, John B. Habig/2.00%, Insiders/32.40%, John B. Habig/15.10%, James C. Thyen/4.80%, John T. Thyen/3.60%, John T. Thyen, Douglas A. Habig/1.70%, Insiders/6.50%, James C. Thyen/1.60%, Ronald J. Thyen/3.10%, Ronald J. Thyen/1.40%, Douglas A. Habig/17.10%, A. C. Sermersheim Family Limited Partnership

Financial Data: *Fiscal Year End:*06/30 *Latest Annual Data:* 06/30/2007

Year	Sales	Net Income
2007	$1,286,930,000	$19,152,000
2006	$1,142,581,000	$15,362,000
2005	$1,124,212,000	$16,588,000

Curr. Assets:	$447,848,000	**Curr. Liab.:**	$249,237,000	**P/E Ratio:**	20.83
Plant, Equip.:	$173,800,000	**Total Liab.:**	$267,293,000	**Indic. Yr. Divd.:**	$0.640
Total Assets:	$694,741,000	**Net Worth:**	$427,448,000	**Debt/ Equity:**	NA

Kimber Resources Inc

800 W Pender St., Ste. 215, Vancouver, BC, V6C 2V6; ***PH:*** 1-604-669-2251; ***Fax:*** 1-604-669-8577; ***http://*** www.kimberresources.com; ***Email:*** info@kimberresources.com

General		**Stock**	
Incorporation	BC	Price on:12/24/2007	NA
Employees	NA	Stock Exchange	AMEX
Auditor	D&H Group LLP	Ticker Symbol	KBX
Stk Agt	Computershare Investor Services	Outstanding Shares	NA
Counsel	NA	E.P.S.	NA
DUNS No.	NA	Shareholders	NA

Business: The group's principle activity is to develop and exploration of gold and silver properties. The group controls 28,000 hectares in Chihuahua State. The company has been active on the property for four years after first acquiring an option to purchase 100% ownership of the original concessions, free of any royalty. The group's current project is Monterde property, which is currently being developed and a pre-feasibility study expected in 2006. The deposit is open to the northeast, southeast, and at depth with further exploration and development drilling is ongoing. The group had shifted a major part of its drilling budget to the search for additional deposits on the Monterde. The group's additional exploration targets have been identified but not yet named and will be subject to further mapping, sampling and trenching. The group operates from United States.

Primary SIC and add'l.: 1400

CIK No: 0001294662

Subsidiaries: Kimber Resources de Mexico S.A. de C.V., Minera Monterde, S. de R.L. de C.V., Minera Pericones S.A. de C.V.

Officers: Robert Longe/Dir., CEO, Pres., Gordon Cummings/CFO, Michael Hoole/VP, Sec., Byron J. Richards/VP - Engineering, Abraham Urias/Mexican Legal Adviser

Directors: Robert Longe/Dir., CEO, Pres., Larry Bell/Chmn., James Puplava/Dir., Dennis R. Bergen/Dir., Leanne Baker/Dir., Keith Barron/Dir., Peter Nixon/Dir., Stephen Quin/Dir.

Owners: Sprott Asset Management Inc./13.90%, James J. Puplava/10.80%, Sun Valley Gold LLC/6.00%

Kimberly Clark Corp

351 Phelps Dr., Irving, TX, 75038; ***PH:*** 1-972-281-1200; ***Fax:*** 1-972-281-1490; ***http://*** www.kimberly-clark.com

General		**Stock**	
Incorporation	DE	Price on:12/24/2007	$67.58
Employees	55,000	Stock Exchange	NYSE
Auditor	Deloitte & Touche LLP	Ticker Symbol	KMB
Stk Agt	EquiServe Trust Co.	Outstanding Shares	456,130,000
Counsel	NA	E.P.S.	$4.07
DUNS No.	00-607-2136	Shareholders	NA

Business: The groups principle activities include manufacturing and marketing of a range of health and hygiene products. The group operates through four segments namely personal care, consumer tissue, k-c professional & other, and health care. The group operates from United States.

Primary SIC and add'l.: 2389 2676 2621 2679

CIK No: 0000055785

Subsidiaries: 1194127 Ontario Inc., Avent de Honduras S.A. de C.V., Avent Holdings LLC, Avent Inc., Avent S.R.L., Avent Slovakia Inc., Avent Slovakia s.r.o., Ballard Medical Products, Ballard Medical Products (Canada) Inc., Balmoral Participacoes Ltda., Beco Inc., Delaware Overseas Finance Inc., Durafab Inc., Elfi Papier GmbH, Excell Paper Sales Co. 178 Subsidiaries included in the Index

Officers: Thomas J. Falk/50/Chmn., CEO/$10,685,910.00, Mark A. Buthman/CFO, Sr. VP/$2,604,666.00, Joanne Bauer/Pres. - Kimberly, Clarks Health Care Business, Jan B. Spencer/Pres. - Kimberly, Clark Professional, North Atlantic, Robert W. Black/Sr. VP, Chief Strategy Officer, Michael D. Masseth/VP - Investor Relations, Paul J. Alexander/Dir. - Investor Relations, Randy J. Vest/VP, Controller, Principal Accounting Officer, Lizanne C. Gottung/Sr. VP - Human Resources, Steven R. Kalmanson/Group Pres. - North Atlantic Consumer Products/$3,173,076.00, Robert E. Abernathy/Group Pres. - Developing, Emerging Markets/$2,852,441.00

Directors: Thomas J. Falk/50/Chmn., CEO, John R. Alm/Dir., Dennis R. Beresford/Dir., Craig G. Sullivan/Dir., James M. Jenness/Dir., Ian C. Read/Dir., Pastora San Juan Cafferty/Dir., G. Craig Sullivan/Dir., John F. Bergstrom/Dir., Abelardo E. Bru/Dir., Robert W. Decherd/Dir., Claudio X. Gonzalez/Dir., Mae C. Jemison/Dir., Linda Johnson Rice/Dir., Marc J. Shapiro/Dir.

Owners: Mark A. Buthman, Ronald D. Mc Cray, Insiders, Robert E. Abernathy, John F. Bergstrom, Dennis R. Beresford, Craig G. Sullivan, Steven R. Kalmanson, Pastora SanJuan Cafferty, John R. Alm, Thomas J. Falk, James M. Jenness, Claudio X. Gonzalez, Marc J. Shapiro, Mae C. Jemison *(18 Owners included in Index)*

Financial Data: *Fiscal Year End:*12/31 *Latest Annual Data:* 12/31/2006

Year	Sales	Net Income
2006	$16,746,900,000	$1,499,500,000
2005	$15,902,600,000	$1,568,300,000
2004	$15,083,200,000	$1,800,200,000

Curr. Assets:	$5,269,700,000	**Curr. Liab.:**	$5,015,800,000	**P/E Ratio:**	18.57
Plant, Equip.:	$7,684,800,000	**Total Liab.:**	$9,753,600,000	**Indic. Yr. Divd.:**	$2.120
Total Assets:	$17,067,000,000	**Net Worth:**	$6,097,400,000	**Debt/ Equity:**	NA

Kimco Realty Corp

3333 New Hyde Pk. Rd., New Hyde Park, NY, 11042; ***PH:*** 1-516-869-9000; ***Fax:*** 1-516-869-9001; ***http://*** www.kimcorealty.com

General		**Stock**	
Incorporation	MD	Price on:12/24/2007	$42.56
Employees	632	Stock Exchange	NYSE
Auditor	PricewaterhouseCoopers LLP	Ticker Symbol	KIM
Stk Agt	Bank of New York	Outstanding Shares	252,010,000
Counsel	Goodwin Procter LLP	E.P.S.	$1.87
DUNS No.	NA	Shareholders	NA

Business: The groups principle activities include owning and operating community shopping centers. In the year 2006, the group acquired 40 operating properties. The group operates from the United States. The groups quarterly revenue for September 2007 was 173.71millions of USD.

Primary SIC and add'l.: 6798

CIK No: 0000879101

Subsidiaries: 44 Plaza, Inc., Auk Realty Corporation, BKS Realty Inc., Brenda Properties, Inc., Cherry Hillview, INC., East End Operating Corp., Easton 257, INC., GC Acquisition Corp., Hamburg Wellness Partners, Harvest Properties Corp., K & W Investors, Inc., KB Birmingham 1035, Inc., KCH Acquisition, INC., KCHGC, Inc., KD Hazel Dell 1031, INC. 470 Subsidiaries included in the Index

Officers: Milton Cooper/Chmn., CEO/$2,886,569.00, David B. Henry/Vice Chmn., Chief Investment Officer/$1,707,597.00, Michael J. Flynn/Vice Chmn., COO, Pres./$2,928,603.00, Michael V. Pappagallo/CFO, Exec. VP/$1,275,678.00, Anne Lang/Investor Relations Assoc., Bruce M. Kauderer/Sec., Jerald Friedman/Exec. VP/$1,682,577.00, Scott Onufrey/Dir. - Investor Relations

Directors: Milton Cooper/Chmn., CEO, David B. Henry/Vice Chmn., Chief Investment Officer, Michael J. Flynn/Vice Chmn., COO, Pres., Martin S. Kimmel/Chmn. Emeritus, Richard B. Saltzman/Dir., Richard G. Dooley/Dir., Patrick F. Hughes/Dir., Joe Grills/Dir., Frank Lourenso/Dir.

Owners: Richard G. Dooley, Michael J. Flynn, Martin S. Kimmel/3.40%, David B. Henry, Frank Lourenso, Joe Grills, Richard Saltzman, Vanguard Group Inc./6.10%, Stichting Pensioenfonds ABP/5.20%, Michael V. Pappagallo, Insiders/11.10%, Milton Cooper/5.90%, Jerald Friedman, Patrick F. Hughes

Financial Data: *Fiscal Year End:*12/31 *Latest Annual Data:* 12/31/2006

Year	Sales	Net Income
2006	$653,380,000	$428,259,000
2005	$522,545,000	$363,628,000
2004	$587,571,000	$297,137,000

Curr. Assets:	$428,483,000	**Curr. Liab.:**	$350,112,000	**P/E Ratio:**	22.52
Plant, Equip.:	$5,646,380,000	**Total Liab.:**	$4,502,321,000	**Indic. Yr. Divd.:**	$1.600
Total Assets:	$7,869,280,000	**Net Worth:**	$3,366,959,000	**Debt/ Equity:**	NA

Kinder Morgan Energy Partners LP

500 Dallas St., Ste. 1000, Houston, TX, 77002; ***PH:*** 1-713-369-9000; ***Fax:*** 1-713-369-9410; ***http://*** www.kindermorgan.com

General - Incorporation .... DE
Employees .... NA
Auditor .... PricewaterhouseCoopers LLP
Stk Agt........ EquiServe Trust Co N.A
Counsel .... NA
DUNS No. .... NA

Stock- Price on:12/24/2007 .... $54.5207
Stock Exchange .... NYSE
Ticker Symbol .... KMP
Outstanding Shares 231,490,000
E.P.S .... -$0.12
Shareholders .... NA

Business: The group's principal activity is to own and manage diversified portfolio of midstream energy assets that provide fee-based services to customers. The operations are carried out through limited partnerships. The group operates in four business segments. Natural gas pipelines segment consist of a 6,700-mile natural gas pipeline, including the pony express pipeline extending from northwestern Wyoming east into Nebraska, Missouri, Colorado and Kansas. Product pipelines segment transports refined petroleum products such as gasoline, diesel and jet fuel. Bulk terminals segment operates in coal, petroleum coke and other products. Co2 pipelines segment consist of the kinder morgan co2 company, l.p., which produces and transports carbon dioxide for use in enhanced oil recovery operations. On 31-Aug-2004, the group acquired kaston pipeline company l.p.

Primary SIC and add'l.: 1321 4922 4613

CIK No: 0000888228

Subsidiaries: Agnes B Crane, LLC, Arrow Terminals B.V., Arrow Terminals Canada B. V., Arrow Terminals Canada Company, Calnev Pipe Line LLC, Carbon Exchange LLC, Central Florida Pipeline LLC, CGT Trailblazer, LLC, CIG Trailblazer Gas Company, LLC, Colton Processing Facility, Dakota Bulk Terminal, Inc., Delta Terminal Services LLC, Elizabeth River Terminals LLC, Emory B Crane, LLC, Entrega Gas Pipeline LLC 123 Subsidiaries included in the Index

Officers: Richard D. Kinder/Chmn., CEO, Garner W. Dotson/VP - Internal Audit, Park C. Shaper/Pres., Debra M. Witges/VP, Controller, Larry S. Pierce/VP - Corporate Communications, Steven J. Kean/COO, Exec. VP, Jordan H. Mintz/Chief Tax Officer, VP, Richard T. Bradley/52/Pres., VP, Tim R. Bradley/Pres. - CO2, Thomas A. Bannigan/Pres. - Products Pipelines, Jeffrey R. Armstrong/Pres. - Terminals, David D. Kinder/VP - Corporate Development, Treasurer, Scott Parker/Pres. - Natural Gas Pipelines, James E. Street/VP - Human Resources, Administration, Information Technology, Joseph Listengart/VP, General Counsel *(17 Officers included in Index)*

Directors: Richard D. Kinder/Chmn., CEO, Gary Hultquist/64/Dir., Edward O. Gaylord/76/Dir., Perry M. Waughtal/72/Dir.

Owners: David D. Kinder, Richard D. Kinder, Gary L. Hultquist, Joseph Listengart, Insiders, Kimberly A. Dang, Jeffrey R. Armstrong, Kinder Morgan, Inc./100.00%, Kinder Morgan, Inc./8.90%, Park C. Shaper, Perry M. Waughtal, Edward O. Gaylord

Financial Data: ***Fiscal Year End:***12/31 ***Latest Annual Data:*** 12/31/2006

Year	Sales	Net Income
2006	$8,954,583,000	$972,143,000
2005	$9,787,128,000	$812,227,000
2004	$7,932,861,000	$831,578,000

Curr. Assets:	$1,036,745,000	**Curr. Liab.:**	$2,885,699,000		
Plant, Equip.:	$9,445,471,000	**Total Liab.:**	$8,174,142,000	**Indic. Yr. Divd.:**	$3.520
Total Assets:	$12,246,394,000	**Net Worth:**	$4,021,653,000	**Debt/ Equity:**	1.3832

Kinder Morgan Inc

500 Dallas St., Ste. 1000, Houston, TX, 77002; ***PH:*** 1-713-369-9000; ***http://*** www.kindermorgan.com

General - Incorporation .... KS
Employees 8,481
Auditor .... PricewaterhouseCoopers LLP
Stk Agt........ EquiServe Trust Co N.A
Counsel .... NA
DUNS No. 00-694-3500

Stock- Price on:12/24/2007 .... NA
Stock Exchange .... NA
Ticker Symbol .... NA
Outstanding Shares .... NA
E.P.S .... NA
Shareholders .... NA

Business: The group's principle activity is to provide pipeline transportation and energy storage services. Customers served by the group include KM Canada, KM power company and KM Co2 company. The group operartes from United States.

Primary SIC and add'l.: 4939 4924 4922 1321

CIK No: 0000054502

Subsidiaries: 0731297 B.c. Ltd., 1197774 Alberta ULC, 1197779 Alberta ULC, Administracion y Operacion de Infraestructura, S.A. de C.V., Canyon Creek Compression Company, Cogeneration Holdings LLC, Cogeneration LLC, Gas Natural del Noroeste, S.A. de C.V., GNN Servicios, S. de R.L. de C.V., Kinder Morgan (Delaware), Inc., Kinder Morgan Canada Inc., Kinder Morgan Finance Company, ULC, Kinder Morgan Foundation A21, Kinder Morgan Ft. Lupton Operator LLC, Kinder Morgan G.P., Inc. 57 Subsidiaries included in the Index

Officers: Richard D. Kinder/Chmn., CEO, Park C. Shaper/Pres., Henry W. Neumann/CIO, VP, David D. Kinder/VP - Corporate Development, Treasurer, Steven J. Kean/COO, Exec. VP, Ian Anderson/Pres. - Kinder Morgan Canada, Scott Parker/Pres. - Natural Gas Pipelines, Paul Steinway/Pres. - Power, Richard L. Bullock/VP - TAX, Kinder Morgan Interstate GAS Transmission, LLC, Kimberly Allen Dang/CFO, VP - Investor Relations, Garner W. Dotson/VP - Internal Audit, Joseph Listengart/VP, General Counsel, Sec., Larry S. Pierce/VP - Corporate Communications, James E. Street/VP - Human Resources, Administration, Information Technology, Debra M. Witges/VP, Controller *(31 Officers included in Index)*

Directors: Richard D. Kinder/Chmn., CEO, Perry M. Waughtal/Dir. - Kinder Morgan Management, LLC, Edward H. Austin/66/Dir., William J. Hybl/65/Dir., Ted A. Gardner/50/Dir., Charles W. Battey/76/Dir., H. A. True/65/Dir., Fayez S. Sarofim/79/Dir., James M. Stanford/70/Dir., Michael C. Morgan/39/Dir., Stewart A. Bliss/74/Dir., Edward Randall/81/Dir., Douglas W.G. Whitehead/61/Dir., Gary Hultquist/Dir. - Kinder Morgan Management, LLC, Edward O. Gaylord/Dir. - Kinder Morgan Management, LLC

Kinder Morgan Management LLC

500 Dallas St., Ste. 1000, Houston, TX, 77002; ***PH:*** 1-713-369-9000; ***Fax:*** 1-713-495-2817; ***http://*** www.kindermorgan.com; ***Email:*** kmp_ir@kindermorgan.com

General - Incorporation .... DE
Employees .... NA
Auditor .... PricewaterhouseCoopers LLP
Stk Agt........ Computershare Trust Co
Counsel .... NA
DUNS No. .... NA

Stock- Price on:12/24/2007 .... $52
Stock Exchange .... NYSE
Ticker Symbol .... KMR
Outstanding Shares 64,310,000
E.P.S $1.14
Shareholders .... NA

Business: The groups principle activities include owning and operating natural gas properties. The group operates through four segment namely, product pipelines, natural gas pipelines, carbon dioxide and terminals. In the year 2006, the group acquired Transload Services, Inc., Devco USA L.L.C. and 24 terminals. The group operates from United States.

Primary SIC and add'l.: 4619 4922 1241 4925 4612 4923 4613

CIK No: 0001135017

Subsidiaries: Kinder Morgan Energy Partners, L.P, Kinder Morgan G.P., Inc, Kinder Morgan Services LLC

Officers: Richard D. Kinder/Chmn., CEO, Debra M. Witges/VP, Controller, Ian Anderson/Pres. - Kinder Morgan, Inc. Canada, Paul Steinway/Pres. - Power, James Brett/Contact - Trailblazer, Canyon Creek, Randy Holstlaw/Contact - Transcolorado, Gary Lamphier/Contact - Kinder Morgan Texas Pipeline LLC, Peter Barbour/Contact - Natural Gas Gathering, Processing, Ken Kemp/Contact - Natural Gas Liquids, Dan Rial/Contact - Transcolorado, Jim Kehlet/Contact - Pacific Operations, Mark Evans/Contact - Plantation Pipe Line, Kinder Morgan Southeast Terminals, Jim Lelio/Contact - Central Florida Pipeline, Pete Dito/Contact - Products Pipelines Tariffs, John Schlosser/Contact - Kinder Morgan Terminals *(29 Officers included in Index)*

Directors: Richard D. Kinder/Chmn., CEO, Edward O. Gaylord/Dir., Gary Hultquist/Dir., Perry M. Waughtal/Dir., Park C. Shaper/Dir., Pres.

Owners: David D. Kinder, Kinder Morgan, Inc./15.53%, Richard D. Kinder, Kimberly A. Dang, Park C. Shaper, Advisors, L.P./10.79%, Perry M. Waughtal, OppenheimerFunds, Inc./8.40%, Insiders, Tortoise Capital Advisors,L.L.C./6.50%

Financial Data: ***Fiscal Year End:***12/31 ***Latest Annual Data:*** 12/31/2006

Year	Sales	Net Income
2006	NA	$78,990,000
2005	NA	$56,324,000
2004	NA	$75,122,000

Curr. Assets:	$18,724,000	**Curr. Liab.:**	$18,648,000	**P/E Ratio:**	45.61
Plant, Equip.:	NA	**Total Liab.:**	$125,277,000	**Indic. Yr. Divd.:**	$3.320
Total Assets:	$1,699,971,000	**Net Worth:**	$1,574,694,000	**Debt/ Equity:**	NA

Kindred Healthcare Inc

680 S 4th St., Louisville, KY, 40202; ***PH:*** 1-502-596-7300; ***Fax:*** 1-502-596-4170; ***http://*** www.kindredhealthcare.com

General - Incorporation .... DE
Employees 40,800
Auditor .... PricewaterhouseCoopers LLP
Stk Agt........ National City Bank
Counsel .... NA
DUNS No. 83-982-4406

Stock- Price on:12/24/2007 .... $32.1
Stock Exchange .... NYSE
Ticker Symbol .... KND
Outstanding Shares 40,490,000
E.P.S .... -$1.05
Shareholders .... NA

Business: The group operates through its subsidiaries whose principle activity is to operate hospitals, nursing centers and a contract rehabilitation services business. The group operates in three segments include health services, hospital and pharmacy. The health services division provides a full range of pharmacy, medical and clinical services and routine services, including daily dietary, social and recreational and rehabilitation services. The group operates from United States.

Primary SIC and add'l.: 8069 5912 8093 8099 8051

CIK No: 0001060009

Subsidiaries: Advanced Infusion Systems Inc., Avery Manor Nursing LLC, Braintree Nursing LLC, Caribbean Behavioral Health Systems Inc., Cornerstone Insurance Company, Country Estates Nursing LLC, Courtland Gardens Health Center Inc., Foothill Nursing Company Partnership, Forestview Nursing LLC, Fox Hill Village Partnership, Goddard Nursing LLC, Harborlights Nursing LLC, Helian ASC of Northridge Inc., Helian Health Group Inc., Helian Recovery Corporation 144 Subsidiaries included in the Index

Officers: Paul J. Diaz/Dir., CEO, Pres./$6,376,489.00, Edward L. Kuntz/Exec. Chmn./$2,124,681.00, Joseph L. Landenwich/Sr. VP - Corporate Legal Affairs, Corp. Sec., Richard A. Lechleiter/CFO, Exec. VP/$1,956,699.00, Benjamin A. Breier/Pres. - Peoplefirst Rehabilitation Division, Frank J. Battafarano/Exec. VP, Pres. - Hospital Division/$2,062,833.00, Mark A. McCullough/46/Pres. - Pharmacy Division, William M. Altman/Sr. VP - Compliance, Government Programs, Richard E. Chapman/Exec. VP, Chief Administrative, Information Officer/$1,739,398.00, Suzanne M. Riedman/Sr. VP, General Counsel, Lane M. Bowen/Exec. VP, Pres. - Health Services Division, Gregory C. Miller/Sr. VP - Corporate Development, Financial Planning, John J. Lucchese/Sr. VP, Corporate Controller

Directors: Paul J. Diaz/Dir., CEO, Pres., Edward L. Kuntz/Exec. Chmn., John H. Klein/Dir., Eddy J. Rogers/Dir., Isaac Kaufman/Dir., Michael J. Embler/Dir., Garry N. Garrison/Dir., Thomas P. Cooper/Dir., Ann C. Berzin/Dir.

Owners: John H. Klein, Insiders/24.20%, Richard A. Lechleiter, Thomas P. Cooper, Frank J. Battafarano, Eddy J. Rogers, Michael J. Embler/19.00%, Richard E. Chapman, Dimensional Fund Advisors LP/7.00%, Edward L. Kuntz, Garry N. Garrison, Paul J. Diaz/2.30%, Franklin Mutual Advisers, LLC/19.00%, Isaac Kaufman

Financial Data: ***Fiscal Year End:***12/31 ***Latest Annual Data:*** 12/31/2006

Year	Sales	Net Income
2006	$4,266,661,000	$78,711,000
2005	$3,923,999,000	$144,909,000
2004	$3,531,223,000	$70,580,000

Curr. Assets:	$1,002,561,000	**Curr. Liab.:**	$606,998,000		
Plant, Equip.:	$551,230,000	**Total Liab.:**	$1,020,549,000	**Indic. Yr. Divd.:**	NA
Total Assets:	$2,016,127,000	**Net Worth:**	$995,578,000	**Debt/ Equity:**	0.1126

Kinetic Concepts Inc

8023 Vantage Dr., San Antonio, TX, 78230; ***PH:*** 1-210-524-9000; ***Fax:*** 1-210-255-6998; ***http://*** www.kci1.com

General - Incorporation	TX
Employees	8,300
Auditor	Ernst& Young LLP
Stk Agt.	NA
Counsel	NA
DUNS No.	NA

Stock- Price on:12/24/2007	$50
Stock Exchange	NYSE
Ticker Symbol	KCI
Outstanding Shares	71,260,000
E.P.S.	$2.78
Shareholders	NA

Business: The groups principle activities include designing, manufacturing, marketing and servicing proprietary products. The group operates through two geographic segments namely, USA and international. The group operates from the United States and other international countries.

Primary SIC and add'l.: 3845 3841 3842 3845 2590 3842 3841

CIK No: 0000831967

Subsidiaries: Alliance Investments Limited, BioMonde GmbH, Equi-Tron Manufacturing, Inc., European Medical Distributors LP, International Medical Distributors LP, KCI (Bermuda) Holding Ltd., KCI APAC Holdings Ltd, KCI Austria GmbH, KCI Clinic Spain S.L., KCI Equitron, Inc., KCI Ethos Clinic Limited, KCI Ethos Medical Products Limited, KCI Europe Holding B.V., KCI Holding Co., Inc., KCI International Holdings Company, Inc. 46 Subsidiaries included in the Index

Officers: Catherine M. Burzik/Dir., CEO, Pres./$898,352.00, David H. Ramsey/CIO, Sr. VP, Rohit Kashyap/Sr. VP - Corporate Development, Lynne Sly/Pres. - Global Therapeutic Surfaces, Nterim Pres. - KCI International, Martin J. Landon/Sr. VP, CFO/$1,018,863.00, Stephen D. Seidel/Sr. VP, General Counsel, Sec./$1,008,460.00, Todd M. Fruchterman/CTO, Sr. VP, James R. Cravens/Sr. VP - Human Resources, Linwood A. Staub/Pres. - Global VAC Therapy, Michael Schneider/Sr. VP - Manufacturing, Operations, Daniel G. Ciaburri/Sr. VP, Chief Medical Officer

Directors: Catherine M. Burzik/Dir., CEO, Pres., Ronald W. Dollens/Chmn., James R. Leininger/Dir., John P. Byrnes/Dir., Woodrin Grossman/Dir., Harry R. Jacobson/Dir., Colin N. Lind/Dir., David J. Simpson/Dir., Thomas C. Smith/Dir., Donald E. Steen/Dir.

Owners: Steven J. Hartpence, David J. Simpson, Lynne D. Sly, Todd M. Fruchterman, Ronald W. Dollens, AMVESCAP PLC and related parties/19.12%, John P. Byrnes, Catherine M. Burzik, Blum Capital Partners, L.P. and related parties/7.18%, Martin J. Landon, James R. Cravens, Michael J. Burke, Christopher M. Fashek, Donald E. Steen, Woodrin Grossman *(24 Owners included in Index)*

Financial Data: *Fiscal Year End:*12/31 *Latest Annual Data:* 12/31/2006

Year	Sales	Net Income
2006	$1,371,636,000	$195,468,000
2005	$1,208,556,000	$122,155,000
2004	$992,636,000	$96,488,000

Curr. Assets:	$531,788,000	Curr. Liab.:	$250,848,000	P/E Ratio:	45.61
Plant, Equip.:	$230,931,000	Total Liab.:	$486,229,000	Indic. Yr. Divd.:	NA
Total Assets:	$842,442,000	Net Worth:	$356,213,000	Debt/ Equity:	NA

King Pharmaceuticals Inc

501 5th St., Bristol, TN, 37620; *PH:* 1-423-989-8000; *Fax:* 1-423-274-8677; *http://* www.kingpharm.com

General - Incorporation	TN
Employees	2,800
Auditor	PricewaterhouseCoopers LLP
Stk Agt.	American Stock Transfer & Trust Co.
Counsel	NA
DUNS No.	80-958-7413

Stock- Price on:12/24/2007	$20.34
Stock Exchange	NYSE
Ticker Symbol	KG
Outstanding Shares	243,660,000
E.P.S.	$0.73
Shareholders	NA

Business: The groups principle activities include developing, manufacturing, marketing and selling branded prescription pharmaceutical products. The groups products include Avinza(R), Thrombin-JMI(R) and Levoxyl(R). The group operates from United States.

Primary SIC and add'l.: 2834

CIK No: 0001047699

Subsidiaries: King Pharmaceuticals of Nevada, Inc., King Pharmaceuticals Research and Development, Inc, Meridian Medical Technologies, Inc., Monarch Pharmaceuticals Ireland Limited, Monarch Pharmaceuticals, Inc., Parkedale Pharmaceuticals, Inc.

Officers: Brian A. Markison/CEO, Pres./$4,992,474.00, Joseph Squicciarino/CFO/$2,072,462.00, James W. Elrod/Acting General Counsel/$1,163,654.00, Frederick Brouillette/57/Corporate Compliance Officer, Stephen J. Andrzejewski/42/Chief Commercial Officer/$1,642,728.00, James E. Green/48/Exec. VP - Corporate Affairs, Eric J. Bruce/Chief Technical Operations Officer/$1,279,280.00, Eric G. Carter/56/Chief Science Officer, Rick Brouillette/Corporate Compliance Officer

Directors: Greg D. Rooker/60/Dir., Elizabeth M. Greetham/58/Dir., Gregory D. Jordan/56/Dir., Charles R. Moyer/62/Dir., Ted G. Wood/70/Dir., Earnest W. Deavenport/70/Dir., Philip A. Incarnati/54/Dir.

Owners: Elizabeth M. Greetham, Joseph Squicciarino, Greg D. Rooker, Stephen J. Andrzejewski, Ted G. Wood, Charles R. Moyer, Earnest W. Deavenport, James W. Elrod, Eric J. Bruce, Eric G. Carter, James E. Green, Insiders, Frederick Brouillette, Barclays Global Investors, NA./12.16%, Gregory D. Jordan *(17 Owners included in Index)*

Financial Data: *Fiscal Year End:*12/31 *Latest Annual Data:* 12/31/2006

Year	Sales	Net Income
2006	$1,988,500,000	$288,949,000
2005	$1,772,881,000	$117,833,000
2004	$1,304,364,000	-$160,288,000

Curr. Assets:	$1,673,473,000	Curr. Liab.:	$617,796,000	P/E Ratio:	16.02
Plant, Equip.:	$307,036,000	Total Liab.:	$1,040,925,000	Indic. Yr. Divd.:	NA
Total Assets:	$3,329,531,000	Net Worth:	$2,288,606,000	Debt/ Equity:	0.1659

Kings Road Entertainment Inc

447 B Doheny Dr., Beverly Hills, CA, 90210; *PH:* 1-310-278-9975

General - Incorporation	DE
Employees	NA
Auditor	HJ Assoc. & Consultants LLP
Stk Agt.	Mellon Trust Co
Counsel	NA
DUNS No.	04-679-8435

Stock- Price on:12/24/2007	$0.08
Stock Exchange	OTC
Ticker Symbol	KREN
Outstanding Shares	NA
E.P.S.	NA
Shareholders	NA

Business: The group's principal activities are to develop, finance and produce motion pictures for distribution in theaters, pay network and syndicated television, home video and in other ancillary media. The operations of the group are carried out in the United States and all other countries and territories of the world.

Primary SIC and add'l.: 5961 7812

CIK No: 0000773588

Subsidiaries: Animal Town, Inc, Kings Road Productions (Europe), Gmbh, KRTR, Inc., Ticker, Inc.

Financial Data: *Fiscal Year End:*04/30 *Latest Annual Data:* 4/30/2005

Year	Sales	Net Income
2005	$242,000	-$496,000
2004	$378,000	-$294,000
2000	$661,000	-$2,172,000

Curr. Assets:	$242,000	Curr. Liab.:	$706,000		
Plant, Equip.:	NA	Total Liab.:	$706,000	Indic. Yr. Divd.:	NA
Total Assets:	$295,000	Net Worth:	-$411,000	Debt/ Equity:	NA

Kingsway Financial Services Inc

7120 Hurontario St., Ste 800, Mississauga, ON, L5W 0A9; *PH:* 1-905-677-8889; *Fax:* 1-905-677-5008; *http://* www.kingsway-financial.com; *Email:* ir@kingsway-financial.com

General - Incorporation	ON
Employees	2,440
Auditor	KPMG LLP
Stk Agt	Computershare Investor Services LLC
Counsel	Fogler, Rubinoff
DUNS No.	NA

Stock- Price on:12/24/2007	$18.86
Stock Exchange	NYSE
Ticker Symbol	KFS
Outstanding Shares	55,580,000
E.P.S.	$1.81
Shareholders	NA

Business: The group's principle activities of the group are underwriting of property and casualty insurance in Canada and the North America. The group's primary business is the insuring of automobile risks for drivers who do not meet the criteria for coverage by standard automobile insurers. The group also operates standard automobile, property, motorcycle and other niche markets. The group's quarterly revenue for September 2007 was 528.08 millions of USD.

Primary SIC and add'l.: 6331 6282

CIK No: 0001072627

Subsidiaries: American Country Financial Services Corp., American Country Holdings Inc., American Country Insurance Company, American Country Professional Services Corp., American Country Underwriting Agency Inc., American Service Insurance Company, Inc, American Service Insurance Company, Inc., American Service Investment Corporation, AOA Payment Plan Inc., Appco Finance Corporation, ARK Insurance Agency Inc., Auto Body Tech Inc., Avalon Risk Management, Inc., Funding Plus of America, Hamilton Risk Management Company 38 Subsidiaries included in the Index

Officers: Tom Ossmann/Pres., CEO - American Service Insurance Company Inc, Roger T. Beck/Dir., Pres., CEO - American Country Insurance Company, Rob Zieper/Pres., CEO - Mendota, William G. Star/Dir., CEO, Pres., John McGlynn/Pres., CEO - Kingsway General Insurance Company, Paul Iacono/Dir. - Kingsway General Insurance Company, York Fire, Casualty Insurance Company, Azmin Daya/VP, CFO, Sec., Treasurer - Kingsway General Insurance Company, Linda Paccanaro/VP - Claims, Kingsway General Insurance Company, Tom Mallozzi/VP - Underwriting, Lili Pacevicius/VP - Commercial Lines, Kingsway General Insurance Company, Ralph Golberg/VP - Kingsway General Insurance Company, Colin Simpson/VP, COO - York Fire, Casualty Insurance Company, Katherine Evans/VP, CFO, Sec. Treasurer - York Fire, Casualty Insurance Company, Mike Tolan/VP - Claims, York Fire, Casualty Insurance Company, Jean Lariviere/Dir. - Jevco Insurance Company *(75 Officers included in Index)*

Directors: William G. Star/Dir., CEO, Pres., John L. Beamish/Dir., Walter Farnam/Dir., Brian J. Reeve/Dir., Thomas Di Giacomo/Dir., Michael F. Walsh/Dir., Robert T.E. Gillespie/Dir., David H. Atkins/Dir., Jack Sullivan/Dir.

Financial Data: *Fiscal Year End:*12/31 *Latest Annual Data:* 12/31/2006

Year	Sales	Net Income
2006	$1,916,355,000	$123,309,000
2005	$1,923,217,000	$135,008,000
2004	$2,023,599,000	$109,639,000

Curr. Assets:	$658,145,000	Curr. Liab.:	$124,760,000		
Plant, Equip.:	$108,149,000	Total Liab.:	$3,147,376,000	Indic. Yr. Divd.:	$0.300
Total Assets:	$4,063,597,000	Net Worth:	$916,221,000	Debt/ Equity:	NA

Kingthomason Group Inc

309 Ave. H, Ste C, Redondo Beach, CA, 90277; *PH:* 1-877-540-5484; *http://* www.kgth.com

General - Incorporation	NV
Employees	1
Auditor	Kabani & Co, Inc
Stk Agt	Securities Transfer Corp
Counsel	NA
DUNS No.	NA

Stock- Price on:12/24/2007	$0.015
Stock Exchange	OTC
Ticker Symbol	KGTH
Outstanding Shares	23,770,000
E.P.S.	-$0.003
Shareholders	NA

Business: The group's principle activity is to create, develop and market high margin, proprietary, insurance and financial service products. The operations are conducted through two principal divisions. Kingthomason credit card services, contracts with physicians and hospitals to convert their outstanding patient-pay account receivable into performing credit card assets. It offers a national medical bill consolidation program that allows credit-counseling agencies manage their client's medical bills and credit. Kingthomason spectraone basic major medical plan provides a basic major medical plan to an underserved market of uninsured or underinsured people. The insurance operations operate much as an insurance company without involving itself directly in the adjudication of claims or issuance of policies. The group distributes its insurance products through marsh mcclennan, aon employee benefits and arthur j gallagher & co.

Primary SIC and add'l.: 6799 7389 6399

CIK No: 0001133116

Subsidiaries: King Thomason, Inc.

Officers: Thomas E. King/39/Chmn., CEO, CFO, Pres., Sec.

Directors: Thomas E. King/39/Chmn., CEO, CFO, Pres., Sec., William T. Walker/70/Dir., T. E. King/Dir.

Owners: Insiders/54.90%, T. E. King/29.40%, William T. Walker/4.00%, Hume A. Thomason/26.60%, Ralph Mele/7.00%, T. E. King/5.50%

Financial Data: *Fiscal Year End:*12/31 *Latest Annual Data:* 06/30/2007

Year	Sales	Net Income
2007	NA	NA
2006	NA	NA
2005	$58,000	-$757,000

Curr. Assets:	$5,000	**Curr. Liab.:**	$1,106,000		
Plant, Equip.:	$0	**Total Liab.:**	$1,106,000	**Indic. Yr. Divd.:**	NA
Total Assets:	$6,000	**Net Worth:**	-$1,101,000	**Debt/ Equity:**	NA

Kintera Inc

9605 Scranton Rd., Ste. 240, San Diego, CA, 92121; ***PH:*** 1-858-795-3000; ***Fax:*** 1-858-795-3010; ***http://*** www.kintera.com; ***Email:*** info@kintera.com

General - Incorporation: DE
Employees: 366
Auditor: Ernst & Young LLP
Stk Agt: U.S. Stock Transfer Corp
Counsel: NA
DUNS No.: NA

Stock - Price on:12/24/2007: $1.82
Stock Exchange: NDQ
Ticker Symbol: KNTA
Outstanding Shares: 40,120,000
E.P.S: -$0.5
Shareholders: NA

Business: The group's principle activities are to provide online enterprise-level software and related services to non-profit organization to use the Internet to increase awareness, commitment and donations. The product of the group include kintera sphere which is managed as a single system and services accessed with a Web browser. The kintera sphere software system includes content management, contact management, communication, commerce, community and reporting. The customers of the group include nonprofit organization's employees, volunteers and donors. The group operates solely in the United States of America. The group's quarterly revenue for September 2007 was 11.94 millions of USD.

Primary SIC and add'l.: 7372

CIK No: 0001117119

Officers: Richard Labarbera/Dir., CEO, Pres., William H. Hewit/Sr. Sales Executive - Donor Advised Funds, Scott Crowder/CTO, Dennis N. Berman/57/Dir., Exec. VP - Corporate Development/$462,142.00, Jeane Chen/Exec. VP - Engineering, David Lawson/GM - Prospect Relationship Management, Alex Fitzpatrick/General Counsel, Erin Leventhal/Dir. - Public Relations, Richard Davidson/CFO/$439,981.00, Darryl Gordon/VP - Marketing, Ephraim Feig/CTO

Directors: Richard Labarbera/Dir., CEO, Pres., Alfred R. Berkeley/Chmn., Philip Heasley/Dir., Harry E. Gruber/Co - Founder, Hector Garcia-Molina/Dir., Mitch Tuchman/Dir., Deborah D. Rieman/Dir., Robert J. Korzeniewski/Dir., Mitchell Tuchman/51/Dir., Dennis N. Berman/57/Dir., Exec. VP - Corporate Development

Owners: Alfred R. Berkeley, Philip Heasley, Dennis N. Berman/8.30%, Financial & Investment Management Group, Ltd./9.10%, Hector Garcia-Molina, Robert J. Korzeniewski, Coghill Capital Management, LLC/10.00%, Allen B. Gruber/8.80%, Diker Management, LLC/9.20%, Insiders/30.00%, Magnetar Capital Partners LLC/10.30%, Deborah D. Rieman, Richard LaBarbera, Richard R. Davidson, Harry E. Gruber/10.60%

Financial Data: *Fiscal Year End:*12/31 *Latest Annual Data:* 12/31/2006

Year	Sales	Net Income
2006	$41,103,000	-$33,123,000
2005	$40,924,000	-$41,904,000
2004	$23,717,000	-$19,237,000

Curr. Assets:	$41,949,000	**Curr. Liab.:**	$39,110,000		
Plant, Equip.:	$1,818,000	**Total Liab.:**	$39,619,000	**Indic. Yr. Divd.:**	NA
Total Assets:	$65,221,000	**Net Worth:**	$25,602,000	**Debt/ Equity:**	NA

Kirby Corp

55 Waugh Dr., Ste. 1000, Houston, TX, 77007; ***PH:*** 1-713-435-1000; ***Fax:*** 1-713-435-1011; ***http://*** www.kirbycorp.com

General - Incorporation: NV
Employees: 3,000
Auditor: KPMG LLP
Stk Agt: Computershare Investor Services LLC
Counsel: NA
DUNS No.: NA

Stock - Price on:12/24/2007: $38.46
Stock Exchange: NYSE
Ticker Symbol: KEX
Outstanding Shares: 53,300,000
E.P.S: $2.10
Shareholders: NA

Business: The groups principle activities include oil and gas exploration and production, marine transportation and property and casualty insurance. The groups products include black oil products, refined petroleum products and agricultural chemicals. The group operates through two segments namely, marine transportation and diesel engine services. The group operates from the United States. The group's quarterly revenue for Sept 2007 was 302.56 millions of USD.

Primary SIC and add'l.: 4449 4491

CIK No: 0000056047

Subsidiaries: AFRAM Carriers, Inc., Dixie Carriers, Inc., Dixie Offshore Transportation Company, Engine Systems, Inc., KIM Holdings, Inc., KIM Partners, LLC, Kirby Corporate Services, LLC, Kirby Engine Systems, Inc., Kirby Inland Marine, LP, Kirby Tankships, Inc., Kirby Terminals, Inc., Marine Highways, LLC, Marine Systems, Inc., Mariner Reinsurance Company Limited, Matagorda Terminals, Ltd. 18 Subsidiaries included in the Index

Officers: Joseph H. Pyne/60/Dir., CEO, Pres./$3,206,679.00, Norman W. Nolen/CFO, Exec. VP, Treasurer/$1,090,412.00, Steven P. Valerius/Pres. - Kirby Inland Marine, LP/$1,266,341.00, Dorman L. Strahan/Pres. - Kirby Engine Systems, Inc/$601,999.00, Thomas G. Adler/Sec., Mark R. Buese/Sr. VP - Administration, Ronald A. Dragg/VP, Controller, Stephen G. Holcomb/VP - Investor Relations, David R. Mosley/CIO, VP, Jack M. Sims/VP - Human Resources, James F. Farley/Exec. VP - Operations, Kirby Inland Marine, LP, William G. Ivey/Exec. VP - Marketing, Kirby Inland Marine, LP, Mel R. Jodeit/Sr. VP - Sales, Kirby Inland Marine, LP, John E. Russell/Sr. VP - Sales, Kirby Inland Marine, LP, David L. Shaw/Sr. VP - Vessel Operations, Kirby Inland Marine, LP *(41 Officers included in Index)*

Directors: Joseph H. Pyne/60/Dir., CEO, Pres., George A. Peterkin/80/Chmn. Emeritus, Berdon C. Lawrence/65/Chmn., Bob G. Gower/70/Dir., Monte J. Miller/64/Dir., Sean C. Day/58/Dir., William M. Lamont/59/Dir., Walter E. Johnson/71/Dir., David L. Lemmon/Dir.

Owners: Steven P. Valerius, Berdon C. Lawrence/5.50%, George A. Peterkin, Dorman L. Strahan, William M. Lamont, Bob G. Gower, David L. Lemmon, Joseph H. Pyne/1.10%, Walter E. Johnson, Sean C. Day, Monte J. Miller, Insiders/8.80%, Norman W. Nolen

Financial Data: *Fiscal Year End:*12/31 *Latest Annual Data:* 12/31/2006

Year	Sales	Net Income
2006	$984,218,000	$95,451,000
2005	$795,722,000	$68,781,000
2004	$675,319,000	$49,544,000

Curr. Assets:	$249,592,000	**Curr. Liab.:**	$166,867,000		
Plant, Equip.:	$766,606,000	**Total Liab.:**	$639,124,000	**Indic. Yr. Divd.:**	NA
Total Assets:	$1,271,119,000	**Net Worth:**	$631,995,000	**Debt/ Equity:**	0.5440

Kirkland S Inc

805 N Pkwy., Jackson, TN, 38305; ***PH:*** 1-731-668-2444; ***Fax:*** 1-731-664-9345; ***http://*** www.kirklands.com

General - Incorporation: TN
Employees: 4,312
Auditor: Ernst & Young, LLP
Stk Agt: StockTrans, Inc.
Counsel: Pepper Hamilton LLP
DUNS No.: NA

Stock - Price on:12/24/2007: $4.05
Stock Exchange: NDQ
Ticker Symbol: KIRK
Outstanding Shares: 19,650,000
E.P.S: NA
Shareholders: NA

Business: The group's principal activity is retailing home decor products in the United States. As of 31-Jul-2004, the group operated 289 stores in 36 states. The products of the group include broad selection of distinctive merchandise, including framed art, mirrors, candles, lamps, picture frames, accent rugs, garden accessories and artificial floral products. The stores also offer holiday merchandise, as well as items carried throughout the year suitable for giving as gifts. The group also provides female customers a shopping experience characterized by a diverse, ever-changing merchandise selection at surprisingly attractive prices. The group operates in major metropolitan markets such as houston, Texas, atlanta and Georgia, middle markets such as birmingham, Alabama and buffalo, New York and smaller markets such as appleton, Wisconsin and panama city, Florida.

Primary SIC and add'l.: 5947

CIK No: 0001056285

Subsidiaries: Kirklands Stores, Inc, Kirklands.com, Inc.

Officers: Robert E. Alderson/Dir., CEO/$1,230,260.00, Todd A. Weier/Sr. VP - Logistics, Rob Janes/VP - Information Services, CIO, Catherine David/COO, Pres./$869,053.00, Michelle R. Graul/VP - Human Resources, Michael W. Madden/VP - Finance, CFO/$295,298.00, Roland L. MacKie/Sr. VP - Real Estate, Lowell E. Pugh/VP, General Counsel, Sec.

Directors: Robert E. Alderson/Dir., CEO, Wilson R. Orr/Chmn., Gabriel Gomez/Dir., Murray M. Spain/Dir., Steven J. Collins/Dir., Carl Kirkland/Dir., David M. Mussafer/Dir., Ralph T. Parks/Dir.

Owners: Reynolds C. Faulkner, Michael W. Madden, Gabriel Gomez, Insiders, Catherine A. David, Ralph T. Parks, Endowment Capital, Wilson R. Orr, David M. Mussafer, Carl Kirkland, Steven J. Collins, Vardon Capital, Advent International Group, Murray M. Spain, Robert E. Alderson *(16 Owners included in Index)*

Financial Data: *Fiscal Year End:*01/28 *Latest Annual Data:* 2/3/2007

Year	Sales	Net Income
2007	$446,828,000	-$140,000
2006	$415,092,000	$229,000
2005	$394,429,000	$6,589,000

Curr. Assets:	$78,220,000	**Curr. Liab.:**	$47,364,000		
Plant, Equip.:	$71,314,000	**Total Liab.:**	$83,484,000	**Indic. Yr. Divd.:**	NA
Total Assets:	$151,466,000	**Net Worth:**	$67,982,000	**Debt/ Equity:**	NA

Kite Realty Group Trust

30 S Meridian St., Ste. 1100, Indianapolis, IN, 46204; ***PH:*** 1-317-577-5600; ***Fax:*** 1-317-577-5605; ***http://*** www.kiterealty.com

General - Incorporation: MD
Employees: 109
Auditor: Ernst& Young LLP
Stk Agt: LaSalle Bank N.A
Counsel: NA
DUNS No.: NA

Stock - Price on:12/24/2007: $19.5
Stock Exchange: NYSE
Ticker Symbol: KRG
Outstanding Shares: NA
E.P.S: $0.41
Shareholders: NA

Business: The groups principle activities include oil and gas exploration and production, marine transportation and property and casualty insurance. The groups products include black oil products, refined petroleum products and agricultural chemicals. The group operates through two segments namely, marine transportation and diesel engine services. The group operates from the United States. The group's quarterly revenue for September 2007 was 302.56 millions of USD.

Primary SIC and add'l.: 6798

CIK No: 0001286043

Subsidiaries: 116 & Olio, LLC, 176th & Meridian, LLC, 50th & 12th, LLC, 82 & Otty, LLC, Brentwood Land Partners, LLC, Centre Associates, LP, Cornelius Adair, LLC, Corner Associates, LP, Eagle Plaza II, LLC, Estero Town Commons Property Owners Association, Inc., Fishers Station Development Company, Glendale Centre, LLC, International Speedway Square, Ltd., Jefferson Morton, LLC, Kite Acworth, LLC 130 Subsidiaries included in the Index

Officers: John A. Kite/Trustees, CEO, Pres., Thomas K. McGowan/Exec. VP - Development, COO, Daniel R. Sink/Sr. VP, CFO, Adam Chavers/Mgr. - Investor Relations, Dame Prout/Sec.

Directors: John A. Kite/Trustees, CEO, Pres., Alvin E. Kite/Chmn., Richard A. Cosier/Trustee, Michael L. Smith/Trustee, William E. Bindley/Trustee, Eugene Golub/Trustee, Gerald L. Moss/Trustee

Owners: William E. Bindley, Michael L. Smith, Thomas K. McGowan/5.26%, T. Rowe Price Associates, Inc./7.25%, Gerald L. Moss, Richard A. Cosier, Stichting Pensioenfonds ABP/6.93%, Insiders/22.09%, Columbia Wanger Asset Management, L.P/8.68%, John A. Kite/7.61%, Franklin Resources, Inc./6.14%, Paul W. Kite, Eugene Golub, Daniel R. Sink, Alvin E. Kite/11.51%

Financial Data: *Fiscal Year End:*12/31 *Latest Annual Data:* 12/31/2006

Year	Sales	Net Income
2006	$131,928,000	$10,180,000
2005	$99,365,000	$13,436,000
2004	$49,098,000	-$525,000

Curr. Assets:	$57,416,000	**Curr. Liab.:**	$40,104,000		
Plant, Equip.:	$892,625,000	**Total Liab.:**	$713,247,000	**Indic. Yr. Divd.:**	$0.820
Total Assets:	$983,161,000	**Net Worth:**	$269,914,000	**Debt/ Equity:**	NA

Kitty Hawk Inc

1515 W 20th St., Dallas Fort Worth Airport, TX, 75261; ***PH:*** 1-972-456-2200; ***Fax:*** 1-972-456-2490; ***http://*** www.kittyhawkcompanies.com

General - Incorporation: DE
Employees: 849
Auditor: Grant Thornton LLP
Stk Agt: American Stock Transfer & Trust Co.
Counsel: NA
DUNS No.: NA

Stock - Price on:12/24/2007: $0.265
Stock Exchange: OTC
Ticker Symbol: KHKH
Outstanding Shares: 53,530,000
E.P.S: -$0.347
Shareholders: NA

Business: The group's principle activities are to provide airfreight services to freight forwarders who transport the freight to and from our cargo facilities in the origin and destination cities through its wholly owned subsidiaries. The group also arranges for the pick up from shippers and final delivery to recipients. Through kitty hawk cargo, inc., the group operates independent city-to-city expedited scheduled freight network in 50 cities in the United States and one city in Canada providing next-morning, two-day and three-day delivery services. Through kitty hawk aircargo, inc., the group provides airfreight transportation services in North America using owned or leased boeing 727-200 freighter aircraft. These services are provided under contractual arrangements. The group's quarterly revenue for June 2007 was 44.42 millions of USD.

Primary SIC and add'l.: 4581 4512 4731

CIK No: 0000932110

Subsidiaries: Kitty Hawk Aircargo., Kitty Hawk Cargo

Officers: Steven Markhoff/COO, Sr. VP, Corp. Sec., Helen Manning/Corporate Contact, Danny K. Clifton/VP, Dir. - Flight Operations, James Kupferschmid/CFO, Principal Executive Officer, VP, Jessica L. Wilson/Chief Accounting Officer, Gary Jensen/COO, VP - Kitty Hawk Ground, Inc, Robbie Barron/COO, VP - Kitty Hawk Aircargo, Inc, Brad Eagelston/VP, Chief Human Resources Officer

Directors: Gerald L. Gitner/Chmn., Laurie M. Shahon/Dir., Melvin L. Keating/Dir., Bryant Riley/Dir., Robert Zoller/Dir., Joseph D. Ruffolo/Dir., Myron Kaplan/Dir., Raymond Greer/Dir., Alan Howe/Dir.

Owners: Bryant R. Riley/17.20%, Bonanza Master Fund, Ltd./8.90%, Insiders/21.70%, Robert Barron, Lloyd I. Miller/21.60%, Paul J. Solit/9.00%, Alan Howe, Robert W. Zoller/2.10%, Steven E. Markhoff, Resurgence Asset Management, L.L.C./8.00%, James R. Kupferschmid, Laurus Master Fund, Ltd./9.00%, Gary Jensen, Dane Andreeff/11.10%, Joseph D. Ruffolo *(17 Owners included in Index)*

Financial Data: ***Fiscal Year End:***12/31 ***Latest Annual Data:*** 12/31/2006

Year	Sales	Net Income
2006	$229,642,000	-$14,433,000
2005	$156,637,000	-$8,510,000
2004	$158,497,000	$6,530,000

Curr. Assets:	$43,516,000	***Curr. Liab.:***	$26,648,000		
Plant, Equip.:	$7,411,000	***Total Liab.:***	$26,783,000	***Indic. Yr. Divd.:***	NA
Total Assets:	$53,823,000	***Net Worth:***	$14,898,000	***Debt/ Equity:***	NA

Kiwa Bio-Tech Products Group Corp

415 W.Foothill Blvd, Ste. 206, Claremont, CA, 91711; ***PH:*** 1-909-626-2358; ***Fax:*** 1-909-626-2306; ***http://*** www.kiwabiotech.com; ***Email:*** kiwabiotech@kiwabiotech.com

General - Incorporation	DE	**Stock**- Price on:12/24/2007	$0.1
Employees	81	Stock Exchange	OTC
Auditor	Grobstein, Horwath & Company, LLP	Ticker Symbol	KWBT
Stk Agt	Fidelity Transfer Co	Outstanding Shares	73,720,000
Counsel	NA	E.P.S	-$0.04
DUNS No.	NA	Shareholders	NA

Business: The groups principle activities include developing, manufacturing, distributing and marketing bio-technological products for agriculture. Products of the group include bio-fertilizer, livestock feed, and animal drugs and disinfectants. The group operates through three segments namely bio-fertilizer, livestock feed and urea entrepot trade. The group operates from the United States and China.

Primary SIC and add'l.: 2040

CIK No: 0001159275

Subsidiaries: Kiwa Bio-Tech Products (Shandong) Co., Ltd., Kiwa Bio-Tech Products Group Ltd., Tianjin Kiwa Feed Co., Ltd.

Officers: Wei Li/Chmn., CEO, Pres./$19,257.00, Robert Schechter/Investor Relations Officer - Consultant, Qi Wang/Vice Dir. - Research Center, Chen Guisheng/Chief Scientist, Johnson Shun-pong Lau/COO, Lianjun Luo/38/Dir., CFO, Yvonne Wang/Sec., Xiaonan Wu/VP, Wenbin Li/VP - Marketing

Directors: Wei Li/Chmn., CEO, Pres., Yunlong Zhang/44/Dir., Dachang Ju/68/Dir., Lianjun Luo/38/Dir., CFO

Owners: Insiders/33.25%, All Star Technology Inc./16.60%, Lianjun Luo/1.75%, Dachang Ju/13.52%, Yunlong Zhang, InvestLink (China) Limited/13.52%, Wei Li/17.56%

Financial Data: ***Fiscal Year End:***12/31 ***Latest Annual Data:*** 12/31/2006

Year	Sales	Net Income
2006	$3,307,000	-$2,284,000
2005	$632,000	-$1,328,000
2004	$1,300,000	-$2,729,000

Curr. Assets:	$2,328,000	***Curr. Liab.:***	$1,853,000		
Plant, Equip.:	$1,515,000	***Total Liab.:***	$4,425,000	***Indic. Yr. Divd.:***	NA
Total Assets:	$4,518,000	***Net Worth:***	$93,000	***Debt/ Equity:***	NA

KKR Financial Corp

555 California St., 50th Fl., San Francisco, CA, 94104; ***PH:*** 1-415-315-3620; ***Fax:*** 1-415-391-3077; ***http://*** www.kkrfinancial.com; ***Email:*** kfninfo@kkr.com

General - Incorporation	MD	**Stock**- Price on:12/24/2007	$26.66
Employees	55	Stock Exchange	NYSE
Auditor	Deloitte & Touche LLP	Ticker Symbol	KFN
Stk Agt	American Stock Transfer & Trust Co.	Outstanding Shares	80,460,000
Counsel	NA	E.P.S	NA
DUNS No.	NA	Shareholders	NA

Business: The groups principal activity is to provide financial services. The group operates from the United States.

Primary SIC and add'l.: 6798

CIK No: 0001301508

Subsidiaries: Gre Ocns Holdings, KFN Pei I, LLC, KFN Pei II, LLC, KFN Pei III, LLC, KFN Pei IV, LLC, KFN Pei V, LLC, KFN Pei VI, LLC, KFN Pei VII, LLC, KFN Pei VIII, LLC, KKR Atlantic Funding Depositor Corporation, KKR Atlantic Funding Trust, KKR Financial Capital Trust I, KKR Financial Capital Trust II, KKR Financial Capital Trust IIII, KKR Financial Capital Trust IV 27 Subsidiaries included in the Index

Officers: Saturnino S. Fanlo/47/Dir., CEO, Founder Partner, Laurie Poggi/Dir. - Investor Relations, Human Resources, Administration, William B. Fisher/Chief Investment Operations Officer, Geoffrey M. Jones/General Counsel, Michael McFerran/CFO, Chief Accounting Officer - KFL, Jeffery L. Power/Treasurer, Andrew J. Sossen/General Counsel, Jeffrey B. Van Horn/47/CFO, David A. Netjes/Co - Founder Partner, COO, Derek M. Larson/MD, Christopher A. Sheldon/MD - Credit Professional

Directors: Saturnino S. Fanlo/47/Dir., CEO, Founder Partner, Paul M. Hazen/Chmn., William F. Aldinger/Dir., Ryan J. Marshall/Partner, Mark D. Lerdal/Partner, Tracy Collins/Dir., Willy Strothotte/Dir., David A. Netjes/Co - Founder Partner, COO, Kenneth M. Deregt/Dir., Vincent Paul Finigan/Dir., Glenn R. Hubbard/Dir., Ross J. Kari/Dir., Ely L. Licht/Dir., Deborah H. McAneny/Dir., Scott C. Nuttall/Dir. *(20 Directors included in Index)*

Owners: David A. Netjes/4.10%, Ely L. Licht, Scott C. Nuttall/3.60%, Jeffrey B. Van Horn, Saturnino S. Fanlo/4.30%, Marsico Capital Management, LLC/9.80%, William F. Aldinger, Paul M. Hazen/3.90%, Kenneth M. deRegt, R. Glenn Hubbard, Ross J. Kari, Wellington Management Company, LLP/5.40%, Vincent Paul Finigan, Deborah H. McAneny, Insiders/5.30%

KLA-Tencor Corp

160 Rio Robles, San Jose, CA, 95134; ***PH:*** 1-408-875-3000; ***Fax:*** 1-408-875-4144; ***http://*** www.kla-tencor.com; ***Email:*** info@kla-tencor.com

General - Incorporation	DE	**Stock**- Price on:12/24/2007	$55.86
Employees	5,900	Stock Exchange	NDQ
Auditor	PricewaterhouseCoopers LLP	Ticker Symbol	KLAC
Stk Agt	EquiServe Trust Co N.A	Outstanding Shares	191,620,000
Counsel	Wilson Sonsini Goodrich & Rosati	E.P.S	$2.61
DUNS No.	01-093-6193	Shareholders	NA

Business: The groups principal activity is to provide inspection and diagnostic tools including process control expertise and practice know-how for the semiconductor industry. The groups services include global, and learning and knowledge services. The group operates from United States.

Primary SIC and add'l.: 7372 3827 3826 3829 7389

CIK No: 0000319201

Subsidiaries: Blue 29 Corporation, Candela Instruments, International Sales & Business, Inc., KLA Instruments S.A., KLA-Tencor (Cayman) Limited IV, KLA-Tencor (Malaysia) Sdn Bhd, KLA-Tencor (Services) Limited, KLA-Tencor (Singapore) PTE, Ltd., KLA-Tencor (Thailand) Ltd., KLA-Tencor Asia-Pac Distribution Corporation, KLA-Tencor Building Corporation, KLA-Tencor China Corporation, KLA-Tencor Corporation (Cayman) Limited, I, KLA-Tencor Corporation (Cayman) Limited, II, KLA-Tencor Corporation (Cayman) Limited, III 37 Subsidiaries included in the Index

Officers: Richard P. Wallace/Dir., CEO, John Kispert/COO, Pres., Jeffrey Hall/CFO, Chris Brocoum/Mgr. - Investor Relations, Charles Lewis/Dir. - Global Public Relations, Jorge Luis Titinger/Sr. VP - Global Operations, Corporate Support Groups, Bin-Ming Benjamin Tsai/50/CTO, Exec. VP, Brian M. Martin/46/Sr. VP, General Counsel, Robert Dellacamera/Sr. Mgr. - Corporate Communications

Directors: Richard P. Wallace/Dir., CEO, Edward W. Barnholt/Dir., Robert T. Bond/Dir., Lida Urbanek/Dir., Raymond H. Bingham/Dir., Stephen P. Kaufman/Dir., David C. Wang/Dir., John Dickson/Dir., Kevin Kennedy/Dir., Robert M. Calderoni/Dir.

Owners: Raymond H. Bingham, Edward W. Barnholt, Capital Group International, Inc./15.60%, John H. Kispert, John T. Dickson, Kevin J. Kennedy, Capital Research & Management Co./9.50%, Capital Guardian Trust Company/6.80%, Robert T. Bond, Richard P. Wallace, Jeffrey L. Hall, Insiders/1.20%, Stephen P. Kaufman, Bin-ming Benjamin Tsai, The Growth Fund of America, Inc./7.00% *(19 Owners included in Index)*

Financial Data: ***Fiscal Year End:***06/30 ***Latest Annual Data:*** 6/30/2006

Year	Sales	Net Income
2006	$2,070,627,000	$380,452,000
2005	$2,085,153,000	$466,695,000
2004	$1,496,718,000	$243,701,000

Curr. Assets:	$3,543,243,000	***Curr. Liab.:***	$1,002,481,000	***P/E Ratio:***	21.40
Plant, Equip.:	$395,412,000	***Total Liab.:***	$1,002,481,000	***Indic. Yr. Divd.:***	$0.600
Total Assets:	$4,575,911,000	***Net Worth:***	$3,567,991,000	***Debt/ Equity:***	NA

Klondike Star Mineral Corp

2009 Iron St., Bellingham, WA, 98225; ***PH:*** 1-360-647-3170; ***http://*** www.klondikestar.com; ***Email:*** information@klondikestar.com

General - Incorporation	DE	**Stock**- Price on:12/24/2007	$1.02
Employees	NA	Stock Exchange	OTC
Auditor	Williams & Webster, P.S	Ticker Symbol	KDSM
Stk Agt	Signature Stock Transfer, Inc.	Outstanding Shares	NA
Counsel	NA	E.P.S	NA
DUNS No.	NA	Shareholders	NA

Business: The group is a development stage company engaged in developing, owning and operating a Web-site designed to meet the needs and tastes of the afro-american consumer. The Web-site, urbanfind.com, is a search portal (a search engine driven Web-site) designed to generate revenue in form of a percentage fee for sales generated by a click-through. The Web-site uses the 20 most popular search engines on its home page and some links to Web-sites that offer news, business, sports, travel, weather, entertainment and shopping. All links are geared to the interests of the afro-american consumer. The company maintains offices in bellevue, Washington, vancouver and british columbia.

Primary SIC and add'l.: 7375 7372

CIK No: 0001083321

Subsidiaries: Klondike Source Limited

Officers: Hans Boge/Chmn., CEO, Pres., Principal Financial Officer, Don Flinn/Dir., VP - Operations, James B. Parsons/Legal Counsel, Lead Corporate, US Counsel, Colin Young/43/Controller, Barbara Stevenson/60/Assist. Corp. Sec., Rodney A. Snow/Legal Counsel, Canadian Counsel

Directors: Hans Boge/Chmn., CEO, Pres., Principal Financial Officer, Don Flinn/Dir., VP - Operations, Sergei Doodchenko/Dir., Albert Khelfa/Dir., Ayman Shahin/Dir.

Owners: Ceylon Enterprises Incorporated/4.60%, Single shareholder within Cede and Co./11.10%, Balance of Cede and Co./21.00%, PanAmerica Capital Group Inc./7.40%, ARY Traders & Company/12.10%, Tuthill Network Assets Inc./7.30%, Swisspulse Corporate Investment AG/5.50%, Rene Hussey/6.40%, Insiders/0.03%, Top-Gold AG MVK/4.70%, Lantz Financial Inc./6.70%

Financial Data: ***Fiscal Year End:***02/28 ***Latest Annual Data:*** 02/28/2007

Year	Sales	Net Income
2007	NA	-$10,044,000
2006	NA	-$8,742,000
2005	NA	-$2,953,000

Curr. Assets:	$2,860,000	**Curr. Liab.:**	$817,000		
Plant, Equip.:	$2,228,000	**Total Liab.:**	$817,000	**Indic. Yr. Divd.:**	NA
Total Assets:	$5,088,000	**Net Worth:**	$4,271,000	**Debt/ Equity:**	NA

KMA Global Solutions International Inc

5570A Kennedy Rd., Mississauga, ON, L4Z-2A9; *PH:* 1-905-568-5220; *Fax:* 1-905-568-4446; *http://* www.kmaglobalsolutions.com

General - Incorporation	NV	**Stock**- Price on:12/24/2007	$1.32
Employees	NA	Stock Exchange	OTC
Auditor	Mcgovern, Hurley, Cunningham, LLP	Ticker Symbol	KMAG
Stk Agt	American Registrar & Transfer Co	Outstanding Shares	NA
Counsel	NA	E.P.S	NA
DUNS No.	NA	Shareholders	NA

Business: The groups principle activity is to manufacture branded apparel and sport specific gloves. The groups products include hang tags, wraps, dual tags, nexttags and grocery products. The group operates from United States.

Primary SIC and add'l.: 7380

CIK No: 0001357585

Officers: Jeffrey D. Reid/Chmn., CEO, Robert Miller/VP - Sales, Laura Wilkes/Pres. - KMA, Asia, Scott Dixon/Pres., Norm Nowlan/VP - Operations, William Randal Fisher/48/Sec., Treasurer

Directors: Jeffrey D. Reid/Chmn., CEO, Michael McBride/Dir., Michael J. Riley/Dir., Daniel K. Foster/56/Dir.

Owners: Michael McBride, Insiders/28.97%, Daniel K. Foster, KMA Global Solutions, LLC/28.97%, Scott Dixon, Jeffrey D. Reid/28.85%

Financial Data: *Fiscal Year End:*NA *Latest Annual Data:* 1/31/2007

Year	Sales	Net Income
2007	$6,631,000	-$736,000

Curr. Assets:	$954,000	**Curr. Liab.:**	$1,118,000		
Plant, Equip.:	$579,000	**Total Liab.:**	$1,205,000	**Indic. Yr. Divd.:**	NA
Total Assets:	$2,201,000	**Net Worth:**	$995,000	**Debt/ Equity:**	NA

KMG America Corp

12600 Whitewater Dr., Ste. 150, Minnetonka, MN, 55343; *PH:* 1-952-930-4800; *Fax:* 1-952-930-4802; *http://* www.kmgamerica.com; *Email:* customerservice@kanawha.com

General - Incorporation	VA	**Stock**- Price on:12/24/2007	$5.37
Employees	505	Stock Exchange	NA
Auditor	Ernst& Young LLP	Ticker Symbol	NA
Stk Agt	American Stock Transfer & Trust Co.	Outstanding Shares	22,330,000
Counsel	NA	E.P.S	-$0.32
DUNS No.	NA	Shareholders	NA

Business: The group is the holding company operates through its subsidiaries whose principle activity is to provide life and accident and health insurance. The group operates through three segments namely, worksite insurance business, senior market insurance business and third-party administration business. The group operates from the United States.

Primary SIC and add'l.: 6311 7389 6321

CIK No: 0001299210

Subsidiaries: Kanawha HealthCare Solutions, Inc., Kanawha Insurance Company, Kanawha Marketing Group, Inc., KMG America Corporation

Officers: Kenneth U. Kuk/Chmn., CEO, Pres./$808,266.00, Lorrinda Lattimore/Sales Dir., Vanessa Breslow/Sales Dir., Dan Oftedahl/Regional Dir., Mark Weibel/Sales Dir., Jon Harts/Sales Dir. - Eastern Wisconsin, David Braxton/Regional Dir., Jack Femrite/Regional Dir., Dan Gechter/Regional Dir., Anne Swain/Regional Dir., Andrew Godfried/Sales Dir., Dale R. Vaughan/Pres., COO - Kanawha Insurance Company, Scott H. Delong/Dir., Sr. VP, CFO/$428,503.00, Paul F. Kraemer/Sr. VP - Sales/$522,799.00, Paul P. Moore/Sr. VP - Sales/$519,824.00 *(22 Officers included in Index)*

Directors: Kenneth U. Kuk/Chmn., CEO, Pres., Stanley D. Johnson/Dir., Scott H. Delong/Dir., Sr. VP, CFO, John H. Flittie/Dir., Robert L. Laszewski/Dir., Dennis M. Mathisen/Dir., James J. Ritchie/Dir.

Owners: Paul P. Moore, Dennis M. Mathisen, Robert L. Laszewski, Wells Fargo & Company/11.90%, John H. Flittie, Hotchkis and Wiley Capital/6.60%, Insiders/3.30%, Scott H. DeLong, Corbyn Investment Management, Inc./5.40%, Paul F. Kraemer, Security Management Company, LLC/6.15%, James J. Ritchie, Thomas D. Sass, Kenneth U. Kuk/1.60%

Financial Data: *Fiscal Year End:*12/31 *Latest Annual Data:* 12/31/2006

Year	Sales	Net Income
2006	$181,110,000	$7,219,000
2005	$153,423,000	$4,660,000
2004	$18,000	-$176,000

Curr. Assets:	$118,853,000	**Curr. Liab.:**	$26,109,000		
Plant, Equip.:	$15,069,000	**Total Liab.:**	$639,662,000	**Indic. Yr. Divd.:**	NA
Total Assets:	$831,714,000	**Net Worth:**	$192,051,000	**Debt/ Equity:**	NA

KMG Chemicals Inc

10611 Harwin Dr., Ste. 402, Houston, TX, 77036; *PH:* 1-713-988-9252; *Fax:* 1-713-988-9298; *http://* www.kmgb.com; *Email:* info@kmgchemicals.com

General - Incorporation	TX	**Stock**- Price on:12/24/2007	$23.15
Employees	110	Stock Exchange	NDQ
Auditor	UHY LLP	Ticker Symbol	KMGB
Stk Agt	Securities Transfer Corp	Outstanding Shares	10,580,000
Counsel	Woods & Jackson	E.P.S	$0.80
DUNS No.	00-974-1745	Shareholders	NA

Business: The group's principal activities are to manufacture and distribute specialty chemicals. The group sells three wood preserving chemicals products such as pentachlorophenol ('penta'), creosote and sodium pentachlorophenate ('sodium penta') to extend life of wood products. Wood preserving chemicals are sold to industrial customers principally in the railroad, utility and construction industries. The group sells a herbicide product consisting of monosodium and disodium methanearsonic acids ('msma'). Msma is sold in the United States as bueno 6a to protect cotton crops from weed growth and as ansar 6.6a for highway weed control. The group also sells tetrachlorvinphos a pesticide product to domestic livestock and poultry growers. It is sold as rabon to protect animals from flies and other pests. On 05-Dec-2003, the group acquired the assets of wood protection products inc.

Primary SIC and add'l.: 2491 2861 2879

CIK No: 0001028215

Subsidiaries: KMG de Mexico, SA de CV, KMG-Bernuth, Inc.

Officers: David L. Hatcher/Chmn., CEO, John V. Sobchak/CFO, Investor Relations Officer, Thomas H. Mitchell/VP - KMG, Bernuth, Roger C. Jackson/General Counsel, Sec., Neal J. Butler/COO, Pres., Randy Berry/Rabon Product Mgr. - Contact

Directors: David L. Hatcher/Chmn., CEO, Fred C. Leonard/Dir., Charles L. Mears/Dir., Charles M. Neff/Dir., Richard L. Urbanowski/Dir., George W. Gilman/Dir., Stephen A. Thorington/52/Dir.

Owners: Tontine Capital Partners, L.P./9.40%, George W. Gilman, David L. Hatcher/37.70%, Charles L. Mears, Insiders/45.80%, Fred C. Leonard/6.60%, Charles M. Neff, Valves Incorporated of Texas/6.10%, Austin W. Marxe and David Greenhouse/5.60%, Stephen A. Thorington, Richard L. Urbanowski

Financial Data: *Fiscal Year End:*07/31 *Latest Annual Data:* 07/31/2007

Year	Sales	Net Income
2007	$89,785,000	$8,849,000
2006	$71,016,000	$3,776,000
2005	$59,168,000	$3,052,000

Curr. Assets:	$31,004,000	**Curr. Liab.:**	$11,381,000	**P/E Ratio:**	34.04
Plant, Equip.:	$9,149,000	**Total Liab.:**	$25,784,000	**Indic. Yr. Divd.:**	$0.080
Total Assets:	$72,702,000	**Net Worth:**	$46,918,000	**Debt/ Equity:**	0.2380

Knape & Vogt Manufacturing Co

2700 Oak Industrial Dr., NE, Grand Rapids, MI, 49505; *PH:* 1-616-459-3311; *http://* www.kv.com

General - Incorporation	MI	**Stock**- Price on:12/24/2007	NA
Employees	NA	Stock Exchange	NA
Auditor	Deloitte & Touche LLP	Ticker Symbol	NA
Stk Agt	Computershare Investor Services LLC	Outstanding Shares	NA
Counsel	Varnum Riddering S & H LLP	E.P.S	NA
DUNS No.	00-602-4699	Shareholders	NA

Business: The group's principle activities are to design, manufacture and distribute functional hardware, kitchen and bath storage solutions and office products for original equipment manufacturers, specialty distributors, hardware chains and major home centers. The group operates through two segments: office products and home and commercial products. The office products segment develops, markets and distributes hardware and idea@work brand of ergonomic products to office furniture OEMs and office furniture dealers. The home and commercial products segment develops, markets and distributes hardware, kitchen and storage solutions to retailers, specialty distributors and kitchen OEM's. The products are sold through the group's own sales personnel and independent sales representatives.

Primary SIC and add'l.: 9999 3429 2542

CIK No: 0000056362

Subsidiaries: Feeny Manufacturing Company, Knape & Vogt Canada, Inc.

Officers: Peter Martin/CEO, Pres., Jack Master/VP - Business Products, Dan Pickett/VP - Home, Commercial Products, Leslie J. Cummings/CFO, Treasurer, Sec., Gordon Kirsch/VP - Operations

KNBT Bancorp Inc

90 Highland Ave., Bethlehem, PA, 18017; *PH:* 1-610-861-5000; *Fax:* 1-610-861-5727; *http://* www.knbt.com

General - Incorporation	PA	**Stock**- Price on:12/24/2007	$14.97
Employees	700	Stock Exchange	NDQ
Auditor	Grant Thornton LLP	Ticker Symbol	KNBT
Stk Agt	Registrar & Transfer Co	Outstanding Shares	27,590,000
Counsel	NA	E.P.S	$0.88
DUNS No.	NA	Shareholders	NA

Business: The group's principal activity is that of a community savings bank. The group provides a range of financial services to individual and corporate customers through its branches in the greater lehigh valley area of Pennsylvania. The lending activity is concentrated primarily on residential first mortgage and equity loans secured by real estate. The group was formed in may 2003 on conversion of keystone savings bank from mutual savings bank to stock savings bank. Immediately after conversion, the group completed its merger with first colonial group, inc., the holding company for nazareth national bank and trust company which was then merged with the bank. The group became publicly held in Oct 2003. On 28-Sep-2004, the group acquired oakwood financial corp.

Primary SIC and add'l.: 6035

CIK No: 0001236964

Subsidiaries: Abstractors, Inc., Caruso Benefits Group, Higgins Insurance Associates, Inc., KLVI, Inc., KNBT Inv. I, KNBT Inv. II, KNBT Securities., NEP Capital Trust I, NEP Capital Trust II, NEPF, Traditions Settlement Services LLC

Officers: Scott V. Fainor/Dir., CEO, Pres./$887,631.00, David B. Kennedy/Exec. VP, Regional Pres. - Greater Lehigh Valley Region/$281,411.00, Eugene T. Sobol/Sr. Exec. VP, CFO, Treasurer/$903,311.00, Allen G. Weiss/Exec. VP, Pres. - Wealth Management Group, Keystone Nazareth Bank, Trust, Carl F. Kovacs/CIO, Exec. VP, Sandra L. Bodnyk/Sr. Exec. VP, Chief Risk Officer/$356,538.00, John T. Andreacio/Exec. VP, Regional Pres. - Northeast Pennsylvania Region/$290,973.00, Deborah R. Goldsmith/Exec. VP - Retail Lending, Administration/$301,676.00, Michele A. Linsky/Corp. Sec., Joseph F. McDonald/54/Sr. VP

Directors: Scott V. Fainor/Dir., CEO, Pres., Jeffrey P. Feather/Chmn., Charles J. Peischl/Dir., Christian F. Martin/Dir., Thomas L. Kennedy/Dir., Charles R. Stehly/Dir., Chadwick R. Paul/Dir., Kenneth R. Smith/Dir., Richard Stevens/Dir., Michael J. Gausling/Dir., Paul R. Chadwick/Dir., Maria Zumas Thulin/Dir., Donna D. Holton/Dir.

Owners: Insiders/7.50%, Chadwick R. Paul, Sandra L. Bodnyk, Thomas L. Kennedy, John T. Andreacio, Maria Z. Thulin, Keystone Nazareth Charitable Foundation/5.50%, Michael J. Gausling, Richard Stevens, Jeffrey P. Feather/1.30%, Dimensional Fund Advisors LP/8.20%, Charles R. Stehly, David P. Kennedy, Christian F. Martin, Deborah R. Goldsmith *(20 Owners included in Index)*

Financial Data: *Fiscal Year End:*12/31 *Latest Annual Data:* 12/31/2006

Year	Sales	Net Income
2006	$190,492,000	$23,603,000
2005	$158,653,000	$20,826,000
2004	$112,725,000	$17,606,000

Curr. Assets:	$70,466,000	Curr. Liab.:	$2,483,928,000		
Plant, Equip.:	$48,228,000	Total Liab.:	$2,542,801,000	Indic. Yr. Divd.:	$0.400
Total Assets:	$2,898,827,000	Net Worth:	$356,026,000	Debt/ Equity:	1.3724

Knewtrino Inc

601 Union St., Two Union Sq., 42nd Fl., Seattle Washington, WA, 98101; *PH:* 1-206-652-3246;
http:// www.knewtrino.com

General - Incorporation	NV	*Stock*- Price on:12/24/2007	$0.505
Employees	1	Stock Exchange	NA
Auditor	Moore & Assoc., Chartered	Ticker Symbol	NA
Stk Agt	Pacific Stock Transfer Company	Outstanding Shares	76,020,000
Counsel	NA	E.P.S	-$0.006
DUNS No.	NA	Shareholders	NA

Business: The groups principal activities include refining and marketing instant messaging and information delivery services for next-generation smartphones and mobile devices. In May 2006, the group acquired Wirefree, Inc. The group operates from the United States.

Primary SIC and add'l.: 4899

CIK No: 0001279620

Officers: Vladimir Fedyunin/CEO, Pres., Dir. - Principal Financial, Accounting Officer, John W. Maddry/Consultant

Directors: Andrew Bowering/Dir., Harshawardan Shetty/Dir.

Owners: Insiders/7.85%, Ivan Bebek/7.85%

Financial Data: Fiscal Year End:12/31 *Latest Annual Data:* 12/31/2006

Year	Sales	Net Income
2006	NA	-$356,000
2005	NA	-$86,000

Curr. Assets:	$298,000	Curr. Liab.:	$24,000		
Plant, Equip.:	$12,000	Total Liab.:	$24,000	Indic. Yr. Divd.:	NA
Total Assets:	$356,000	Net Worth:	$332,000	Debt/ Equity:	NA

Knight Capital Group Inc

Formerly: Knight Trading Group Inc
545 Washington Blvd., Jersey City, NJ, 07310; *PH:* 1-201-222-9400; *http://* www.knight.com

General - Incorporation	DE	*Stock*- Price on:12/24/2007	$17.39
Employees	844	Stock Exchange	NYSE
Auditor	PricewaterhouseCoopers LLP	Ticker Symbol	NJR
Stk Agt	Mellon Investor Services LLC	Outstanding Shares	103,860,000
Counsel	Skadden, Meagher & Flom LLP	E.P.S	$1.16
DUNS No.	01-820-3229	Shareholders	NA

Business: The group's principal activities are securities market-making and asset management. The group operates in three segments: equity markets, derivative market and asset management. Equity market provides trade execution services to institutions and broker-dealers in cash equities and options. The institutional clients include mutual funds, hedge funds, pension plans, plan sponsors, trusts and endowments. The broker-dealer clients include global, national and regional broker-dealers and on-line brokers. Derivative markets provides comprehensive trade execution services to institutions and broker-dealers across a significant number of U.S. Option products. Asset management provides investment management services to institutions, trusts and individuals. In 2004, the group acquired ownership interests of the minority owners of krel.

Primary SIC and add'l.: 6719 6211

CIK No: 0001060749

Subsidiaries: Deephaven Capital Management LLC, Direct Edge ECN LLC, Direct Trading Institutional, L.P., DT Holdings (GP) LLC, DT Holdings (LP) LLC, DTI Acquisition LLC, KFP Holdings I LLC, Knight Capital Group, Inc., Knight Capital Markets LLC, Knight Equity Markets, L.P., Knight Securities General, Inc., Knight Securities Operations, Inc., Knight/Trimark, Inc.

Officers: Thomas M. Joyce/Chmn., CEO/$9,346,906.00, Colin J. Smith/CEO, Chief Investment Officer - Deephaven Capital Management, James P. Smyth/Exec. VP, Head - Broker, Dealer Client Group/$3,114,727.00, Leonard J. Amoruso/Sr. MD, General Counsel, Thomas M. Merritt/Corp. Sec., Margaret E. Wyrwas/Sr. MD - Corporate Communications, Investor Relations, Gregory C. Voetsch/Exec. VP, Head - Institutional Client Group/$4,349,056.00, John B. Howard/38/Sr. MD, CFO/$1,899,888.00, Bronwen Bastone/MD - Human Resources, Steven J. Sadoff/Sr. MD, CIO/$1,993,434.00, Michael Williams/Sr. MD, Head - Hotspot FX, Jonathan Mairs/VP - Corporate Communications, Investor Relations

Directors: Thomas M. Joyce/Chmn., CEO, Gary R. Griffith/68/Dir., Thomas C. Lockburner/68/Dir., William L. Bolster/64/Dir., Robert M. Lazarowitz/51/Dir., James T. Milde/47/Dir., Rodger O. Riney/62/Dir., Laurie M. Shahon/56/Dir.

Owners: Steven J. Sadoff, James T. Milde, John B. Howard, Royce & Associates, LLC/12.80%, Gregory C. Voetsch, James P. Smyth, Thomas C. Lockburner, Gary R. Griffith, Rodger O. Riney/1.63%, Insiders/7.19%, Thomas M. Joyce/1.64%, William L. Bolster, Robert M. Lazarowitz/2.58%, Charles V. Doherty

Financial Data: Fiscal Year End:12/31 *Latest Annual Data:* 12/31/2006

Year	Sales	Net Income
2006	$951,210,000	$158,346,000
2005	$634,623,000	$66,361,000
2004	$625,750,000	$91,132,000

Curr. Assets:	$699,861,000	Curr. Liab.:	$1,065,727,000	P/E Ratio:	13.59
Plant, Equip.:	$66,450,000	Total Liab.:	$1,065,727,000	Indic. Yr. Divd.:	NA
Total Assets:	$2,028,214,000	Net Worth:	$962,487,000	Debt/ Equity:	NA

Knight Resources Ltd

605 Robson St., Ste 1360, Vancouver, BC, V6B 5J3; *PH:* 1-604-684-6535;
http:// www.knightresources.ca; *Email:* knight@bed-rock.com

General - Incorporation	Canada	*Stock*- Price on:12/24/2007	$0.27
Employees	NA	Stock Exchange	OTC
Auditor	KPMG LLP	Ticker Symbol	KNPRF
Stk Agt	NA	Outstanding Shares	NA
Counsel	NA	E.P.S	NA
DUNS No.	NA	Shareholders	NA

Business: The groups' principal activity is to acquire and explore natural resource properties. The group has a Board Of Directors and management team well suited to the exploration of nickel and to operating in the junior capital markets. The group's corporate office is at Vancouver, Canada. The group also has Anglo American Exploration Canada Limited (AAEC) as their operator and partner in the West Raglan Project. AAEC is a wholly owned subsidiary of Anglo American Plc, one of the world's largest mining companies. The Anglo American group is geographically diverse, with operations and projects in Africa, Europe, South America, North America and Australia.

Primary SIC and add'l.: 1000

CIK No: 0001278466

Officers: Harvey Keats/Dir., CEO, David Patterson/Dir., CFO, Robin Adair/Dir., VP - Exploration

Directors: Harvey Keats/Dir., CEO, David Patterson/Dir., CFO, Laurie Sadler/Dir., Kerry Sparkes/Dir., Robin Adair/Dir., VP - Exploration

Knight Ridder Inc

50 W San Fernando St. , Ste. 1500, San Jose, CA, 95113; *PH:* 1-408-938-7700;
http:// www.mcclatchy.com

General - Incorporation	FL	*Stock*- Price on:12/24/2007	$26.33
Employees	15,250	Stock Exchange	NDQ
Auditor	Ernst & Young LLP	Ticker Symbol	MNKD
Stk Agt	Mellon Investor Services LLC	Outstanding Shares	82,020,000
Counsel	NA	E.P.S	-$2.23
DUNS No.	00-416-4026	Shareholders	NA

Business: The group's principle activity is to publish daily and non-daily newspapers. The group has two operating segments: newspapers and online. Newspapers include advertising and newspaper sales. Advertising includes retail, national and classified. Newspaper advertising volume is categorized as either rop or preprint. The group publishes 31 daily newspapers and 37 nondaily newspapers in 28 U.S. Markets, with a readership of 8.7 million daily and 12.6 million on sunday. Online consists primarily of online recruitment and other classified advertising, Web banner advertising and revenue from content syndication.

Primary SIC and add'l.: 2731 7375 4841 4833 2711

CIK No: 0000205520

Subsidiaries: Aberdeen News Company, Aboard Publishing, Inc., Bellingham Herald Publishing, LLC, Belton Publishing Company, Inc., Biscayne Bay Publishing, Inc., Cass County Publishing Company, Inc., Circom Corporation, Columbia State, Inc., Columbus Ledger-Enquirer, Inc., Consumer & Community Publishing, Inc., Contra Costa Newspapers, Inc., Cypress Media, Inc., Cypress Media, LLC, Dagren, Inc., Double A Publishing, Inc. 71 Subsidiaries included in the Index

Financial Data: Fiscal Year End:12/25 *Latest Annual Data:* 12/31/2006

Year	Sales	Net Income
2006	$1,675,190,000	-$155,577,000
2005	$1,186,115,000	$160,519,000
2004	$1,163,376,000	$155,876,000

Curr. Assets:	$1,575,339,000	Curr. Liab.:	$1,112,114,000		
Plant, Equip.:	$975,976,000	Total Liab.:	$4,951,086,000	Indic. Yr. Divd.:	$0.720
Total Assets:	$8,054,710,000	Net Worth:	$3,103,624,000	Debt/ Equity:	0.8759

Knight Transportation Inc

5601 W Buckeye Rd., Phoenix, AZ, 85043; *PH:* 1-602-269-2000; *Fax:* 1-602-269-8409;
http:// www.knighttrans.com

General - Incorporation	AZ	*Stock*- Price on:12/24/2007	$19.81
Employees	4,176	Stock Exchange	NYSE
Auditor	Deloitte& Touche LLP	Ticker Symbol	KNX
Stk Agt	Mellon Investor Services LLC	Outstanding Shares	86,280,000
Counsel	NA	E.P.S	$0.85
DUNS No.	NA	Shareholders	NA

Business: The groups principal activity is to provide dry van truckload and temperature controlled truckload carrier services. The group operates through two segments namely, truckload transportation and brokerage. The group acquired Edwards Bros., Inc. in the year 2005 and Roads West Transportation, Inc. in the year 2006. The group operates from the United States.

Primary SIC and add'l.: 4231 4731 4213

CIK No: 0000929452

Subsidiaries: Knight Brokerage LLC, Knight Management Services Inc., Knight Refrigerated LLC, Knight Transportation Services Inc., Knight Transportation South Central L.P, Knight Truck & Trailer Sales LLC, Quad-K Leasing Inc., The New Roads West LLC

Officers: Kevin P. Knight/Chmn., CEO/$1,329,777.00, Timothy M. Kohl/60/Pres., Sec./$714,513.00, Keith T. Knight/53/COO/$552,001.00, David A. Jackson/32/CFO, Treasurer/$227,493.00

Directors: Kevin P. Knight/Chmn., CEO, Gary J. Knight/56/Vice Chmn., G. D. Madden/68/Dir., Kathryn L. Munro/59/Dir., Richard J. Lehmann/64/Dir., Donald A. Bliss/75/Dir., Mark Scudder/45/Dir., Randy Knight/59/Dir., Michael Garnreiter/56/Dir., Casey Comen/59/Dir.

Owners: Casey Comen, Gary J. Knight/8.40%, David A. Jackson, Keith T. Knight/8.20%, Randy Knight/8.00%, Richard J. Lehmann, Ruane, Cunniff & Goldfarb, Inc./16.30%, Donald A. Bliss, Michael Garnreiter, G. D. Madden, Wasatch Advisors, Inc./10.50%, Kathryn L. Munro, Wellington Management Company, LLP/10.10%, Mark Scudder, Kevin P. Knight/8.50% (*17 Owners included in Index*)

Financial Data: Fiscal Year End:12/31 *Latest Annual Data:* 12/31/2006

Year	Sales	Net Income
2006	$664,407,000	$72,966,000
2005	$566,813,000	$61,714,000
2004	$442,288,000	$47,860,000

Curr. Assets:	$120,987,000	Curr. Liab.:	$61,598,000	P/E Ratio:	23.31
Plant, Equip.:	$433,828,000	Total Liab.:	$144,124,000	Indic. Yr. Divd.:	$0.120
Total Assets:	$570,219,000	Net Worth:	$426,095,000	Debt/ Equity:	NA

Knightsbridge Fine Wines Inc

25200 Arnold Dr., Sonoma, CA, 95476; *PH:* 1-707-934-4039

General - Incorporation	NV	Stock- Price on:12/24/2007	NA
Employees	89	Stock Exchange	NA
Auditor	David S. Hall P.C., Lopez, Blevins	Ticker Symbol	NA
Stk Agt	Pacific Stock Transfer Company	Outstanding Shares	NA
Counsel	NA	E.P.S.	NA
DUNS No.	NA	Shareholders	NA

Business: The group's principle activities are to market and distribute wines produced by third parties under its own label or of the third party producers. It also develops and finances the growth of a diversified international wine company consisting of estate vineyards and brands from various wine growing regions of the world operating a winery in Argentina and also sales and marketing business in Australia. The products are sold through direct sales, independent distributors and the group's own customer list in 50 states, the district of columbia and Puerto Rico and internationally, in the Caribbean islands and Canada such as the global collection of guy buffet, kirkland ranch estate wines, kirkland ranch, jamieson canyon, alexander park, vinus and saddle mountain.

Primary SIC and add'l.: 5182

CIK No: 0001124019

Subsidiaries: 360 Global Wine Company, 360 Viansa LLC, Dominion Wines International Ltd, KFWBA Acquisition Corporation, KKLLC, Knightsbridge Torrique, Viansa

Officers: John A.A. Bryan/51/CEO, Chief Restructuring Officer - Principal Financial, Accounting Officer, Joel A. Shapiro/36/Dir., Pres., Lynn K. Fetterman/COO

Directors: Anthony J.A. Bryan/83/Non Exec. Chmn., Joel A. Shapiro/36/Dir., Pres., Michael L. Jeub/63/Dir.

Owners: Anthony J. A. Bryan/4.13%, John A. Bryan/5.45%, Laurus Master Fund, Ltd./4.99%, The Watley Group LLC/5.45%, Insiders/25.09%, Joel A. Shapiro/15.50%, Wynthrop Barrington Inc./6.17%

Knightsbridge Tankers Ltd

Par-La-Ville Pl, 14 Par-La-Ville Rd., Hamilton; *PH:* 1-441-2950182; *Fax:* 1-441-2953494; *http://* www.knightbridgetankers.com

General - Incorporation	Bermuda	Stock- Price on:12/24/2007	$31.47
Employees	NA	Stock Exchange	NDQ
Auditor	Moore Stephens, P.C	Ticker Symbol	VLCCF
Stk Agt	Mellon Investor Services LLC	Outstanding Shares	17,100,000
Counsel	NA	E.P.S.	$1.97
DUNS No.	NA	Shareholders	NA

Business: The group operates through its subsidiaries whose principle activity is to lease and charter crude oil carriers. The group operates from United States.

Primary SIC and add'l.: 4499 6719

CIK No: 0001029145

Subsidiaries: Cedarhurst Tankers LDC, Hewlett Tankers LDC, Inwood Tankers LDC, KTL Camden, Inc., KTL Chelsea, Inc., KTL Hampstead, Inc., KTL Kensington, Inc., KTL Mayfair, Inc., Lawrence Tankers LDC, Woodmere Tankers LDC

Officers: Tor Olav Troim/Vice Chmn., CEO, Bjorn Sjaastad/50/CEO - Frontline Management, Georgina E. Sousa/58/Company Sec., Kate Blankenship/CFO

Directors: Tor Olav Troim/Vice Chmn., CEO, Inger M. Klemp/Vice Chmn., Ola Lorentzon/Chmn., Douglas C. Wolcott/Dir., Timothy J. Counsell/Dir., David M. White/Dir., Graham Baker/48/Dir.

Financial Data: *Fiscal Year End:* 12/31 *Latest Annual Data:* 12/31/2006

Year	Sales	Net Income
2006	$105,728,000	$45,717,000
2005	$100,179,000	$43,967,000
2004	$135,695,000	$85,839,000

Curr. Assets:	$33,261,000	Curr. Liab.:	$24,309,000		
Plant, Equip.:	$267,949,000	Total Liab.:	$122,309,000	Indic. Yr. Divd.:	$2.000
Total Assets:	$301,499,000	Net Worth:	$179,190,000	Debt/ Equity:	NA

Knobias Inc

875 NPk. Dr., Bldg. 2, Ste. 500, Ridgeland, MS, 39157; *PH:* 1-601-978-3399; *Fax:* 1-601-978-3675; *http://* www.knobias.com; *Email:* info@knobias.com

General - Incorporation	DE	Stock- Price on:12/24/2007	$0.02
Employees	33	Stock Exchange	OTC
Auditor	KMJ Corbin & Co. LLP	Ticker Symbol	KBAS
Stk Agt	Continental Stock Transfer & Trust Co	Outstanding Shares	53,040,000
Counsel	NA	E.P.S.	-$0.04
DUNS No.	NA	Shareholders	NA

Business: The groups principle activity is to provide financial information services. Customers served by the group include investors, day-traders, financial oriented websites, public issuers, brokers, professional traders and institutional investors. The group operates from the United States. The group's quarterly revenue for Sep '07 was 0.48 millions of USD.

Primary SIC and add'l.: 7379 4899 7375

CIK No: 0001161979

Subsidiaries: Knobias Holdings, Inc., Knobias.com, LLC, Kollage, LLC

Officers: Steve Lord/39/Inside Dir., CEO, Key E. Ramsey/47/Chmn., Pres., Gregory E. Ballard/41/VP, Dir., COO, Robert L. Atkins/48/Dir., Sec., Danny M. Dunnaway/59/Dir., Private Investor, Ken Ivey/Exec. VP, GM, Susan R. Walker/39/CFO

Directors: Steve Lord/39/Inside Dir., CEO, Key E. Ramsey/47/Chmn., Pres., Gregory E. Ballard/41/VP, Dir., COO, Robert L. Atkins/48/Dir., Sec., Timothy J. Aylor/43/Dir., John S. Gross/57/Dir., Danny M. Dunnaway/59/Dir., Private Investor, Joseph L. Stephens/50/Dir.

Owners: Key E. Ramsey/9.80%, E. Key Ramsey/1.50%, Duncan Capital Group, LLC/1.40%, CAMOFI Master LDC/38.80%, CAMOFI Master LDC/15.40%, Gregory E. Ballard/1.50%, Gamma Opportunity Capital Partners, LP/1.00%, Bushido Capital Partners, Ltd./38.50%, Bushido Capital Partners, Ltd./55.60%, Danny M. Dunnaway/5.80%, Duncan Capital Group, LLC/18.40%, Duncan Capital Group, LLC/46.10%, Gregory E. Ballard/9.90%

Financial Data: *Fiscal Year End:* 12/31 *Latest Annual Data:* 12/31/2006

Year	Sales	Net Income
2006	$2,266,000	-$2,260,000
2005	$2,125,000	-$2,643,000
2004	$1,972,000	-$2,811,000

Curr. Assets:	$217,000	Curr. Liab.:	$4,954,000		
Plant, Equip.:	$147,000	Total Liab.:	$4,954,000	Indic. Yr. Divd.:	NA
Total Assets:	$372,000	Net Worth:	-$4,582,000	Debt/ Equity:	NA

Knockout Holdings Inc

Formerly: United Network Marketing Services Inc
100 W Whitehall Ave., Northlake, IL, 60164; *PH:* 1-708-273-6900

General - Incorporation	DE	Stock- Price on:12/24/2007	NA
Employees	3	Stock Exchange	NA
Auditor	BDO Seidman LLP	Ticker Symbol	NA
Stk Agt	Continental Stock Transfer & Trust Co	Outstanding Shares	NA
Counsel	NA	E.P.S.	-$1.34
DUNS No.	NA	Shareholders	NA

Business: The group's principle activities include developing and marketing Internet content for consumer based websites. The company currently owns a fifty-percent interest in accessnewage corporation, which owns and operates an Internet Website. There are no operations or material business interests independent of accessnewage. The Website, offers a large selection of new age information products and services that are holistic, esoteric, spiritual, metaphysical and philosophical in character. The company is a development stage company. The group operates from United States.

Primary SIC and add'l.: 7375 7372

CIK No: 0001128008

Subsidiaries: Access: New Age Corp., The Knockout Group, Inc.

Officers: John Bellamy/Founder, Chmn., CEO, Katie Green/VP - Administration, Dali E. Pollard/Executive Liaison, Business Development, Technology, Sr. Project Management Support

Directors: John Bellamy/Founder, Chmn., CEO, Robert Smith/Dir., Isaac Horton/Dir.

Financial Data: *Fiscal Year End:* 12/31 *Latest Annual Data:* 12/31/2005

Year	Sales	Net Income
2005	$1,883,000	-$17,410,000
2004	$679,000	-$12,575,000
2003	NA	-$66,000

Curr. Assets:	$1,298,000	Curr. Liab.:	$5,167,000		
Plant, Equip.:	$217,000	Total Liab.:	$5,167,000	Indic. Yr. Divd.:	NA
Total Assets:	$1,668,000	Net Worth:	-$3,499,000	Debt/ Equity:	NA

Knoll Inc

1235 Water St., East Greenville, PA, 18041; *PH:* 1-215-679-7991; *Fax:* 1-215-679-1755; *http://* www.knoll.com; *Email:* info@knoll.com

General - Incorporation	DE	Stock- Price on:12/24/2007	$23.97
Employees	4,224	Stock Exchange	NYSE
Auditor	Ernst& Young LLP	Ticker Symbol	KNL
Stk Agt	Bank of New York	Outstanding Shares	49,680,000
Counsel	NA	E.P.S.	$1.40
DUNS No.	NA	Shareholders	NA

Business: The groups principle activities include designing and manufacturing office furniture products and textiles. The groups products include side chairs, sofas, desks, desk components, tables and data systems. The groups products marketed under the brand names LIFE(TM), Knoll Textiles(TM), Spinneybecj(R) and AutoStrada(R).The group's quarterly revenue for September 2007 was 253.96 millions of USD.

Primary SIC and add'l.: 2522 5021 3372 2521 2541 2599 2542 2531

CIK No: 0001011570

Subsidiaries: Spinneybeck Enterprises, Inc

Officers: Andrew B. Cogan/Dir., CEO/$2,311,218.00, Kathleen G. Bradley/Dir., CEO, Pres. - Knoll North America/$1,934,476.00, Stephen A. Grover/55/Sr. VP - Operations/$887,321.00, Barry L. McCabe/61/CFO, Sr. VP/$944,468.00, Benjamin A. Pardo/46/Sr. VP, Dir. - Design, Michael A. Pollner/35/VP, General Counsel, Sec., Marcia A. Thompson/51/VP - Human Resources, David L. Schutte/43/Sr. VP, Chief Marketing Officer, Ed Godwin/VP - Knoll International, David E. Bright/VP - Communications, Lavinia Galieti/Contact - Europe, Laura Colombo/Contact - Europe, Laura Silvi/Contact - Europe, Arthur C. Graves/Sr. VP - Sales, Distribution

Directors: Andrew B. Cogan/Dir., CEO, Kathleen G. Bradley/Dir., CEO, Pres. - Knoll North America, Burton B. Staniar/Chmn., Stephen F. Fisher/Dir., Jeffrey A. Harris/Dir., Sidney Lapidus/Dir., Kewsong Lee/Dir., John F. Maypole/Dir., Sarah E. Nash/Dir., Anthony P. Terracciano/Dir.

Owners: Systematic Financial Management, L.P./7.50%, Mazama Capital Management, Inc./11.40%, Stephen A. Grover, Jeffrey A. Harris, Barry L. McCabe, Andrew B. Cogan/1.50%, AXA and related companies/6.00%, Arthur C. Graves, Burton B. Staniar/1.10%, Insiders/6.00%, FMR Corp./16.10%, Kathleen G. Bradley/2.20%, Anthony P. Terracciano, Sidney Lapidus, Stephen F. Fisher (16 Owners included in Index)

Financial Data: *Fiscal Year End:* 12/31 *Latest Annual Data:* 12/31/2006

Year	Sales	Net Income
2006	$982,152,000	$58,633,000
2005	$807,960,000	$35,909,000
2004	$706,390,000	$26,744,000

Curr. Assets:	$248,384,000	Curr. Liab.:	$171,214,000	P/E Ratio:	17.89
Plant, Equip.:	$137,729,000	Total Liab.:	$627,753,000	Indic. Yr. Divd.:	$0.480
Total Assets:	$632,137,000	Net Worth:	$4,384,000	Debt/ Equity:	17.8279

Knology Inc

1241 O. G. Skinner Dr., West Point, GA, 31833; *PH:* 1-706-645-8553; *Fax:* 1-706-645-0148; *http://* www.knology.com

General - Incorporation	DE	Stock- Price on:12/24/2007	$17.34
Employees	1,365	Stock Exchange	NDQ
Auditor	BDO Seidman, LLP	Ticker Symbol	KNOL
Stk Agt	American Stock Transfer & Trust Co.	Outstanding Shares	35,040,000
Counsel	NA	E.P.S.	-$1.34
DUNS No.	09-801-3613	Shareholders	NA

Business: The group's principal activity is to provide cable television, local and long-distance telephone and high-speed Internet access services to residential and business customers in southeastern United States. It also provides advanced communications services, such as video-on-demand, subscriber

video-on-demand, digital video recording, interactive television, ip centrex services and passive optical network services. As of 31-Dec-2003, the group had 382,000 connections for video, voice and data services. It provides the services through their wholly owned, fully upgraded 750 mhz interactive broadband network.

Primary SIC and add'l.: 4841

CIK No: 0001096788

Subsidiaries: Globe Telecommunications, Inc., Interstate Telephone Company, ITC Globe, Inc., Knology Broadband of California, Inc., Knology Broadband of Florida, Inc., Knology Broadband, Inc., Knology New Media, Inc., Knology of Alabama, Inc., Knology of Augusta, Inc., Knology of Charleston, Inc., Knology of Columbus, Inc., Knology of Florida, Inc., Knology of Georgia, Inc., Knology of Huntsville, Inc., Knology of Kentucky, Inc. 23 Subsidiaries included in the Index

Officers: Rodger L. Johnson/Dir., CEO, Pres./$1,222,178.00, Allan H. Goodson/VP - Regional Operations, Richard D. Perkins/VP - Information Technology, Billing, Richard Luke/CTO, Todd M. Holt/CFO, Treasurer/$378,258.00, Marcus R. Luke/CTO, Chad S. Wachter/VP, General Counsel, Sec./$354,604.00, Bret T. McCants/Sr. VP - Operations/$417,464.00, Michael B. Roddy/VP - Marketing/$373,216.00, Felix L. Boccucci/VP - New Business Development, Andrew M. Sivell/VP - Network Operations, Brad M. Vanacore/VP - Human Resources, Anthony J. Palermo/VP - Marketing, Ronald Johnson/VP - Business Sales

Directors: Rodger L. Johnson/Dir., CEO, Pres., Campbell B. Lanier/Chmn., Alan A. Burgess/Dir., Donald W. Burton/Dir., Eugene I. Davis/Dir., Gene O. Gabbard/Dir., William H. Scott/Dir.

Owners: Allan H. Goodson, Bret T. McCants, Gilder, Gagnon, Howe& Co., LLC/14.20%, Andrew M. Sivell, Bear Stearns Asset Management, Inc./6.20%, Felix L. Boccucci, Alan A. Burgess, Brad M. Vanacore, Donald W. Burton/9.00%, Eugene I. Davis, Marcus R. Luke, Chad S. Wachter, Farallon Capital Management, LLC/7.20%, William H. Scott, Rodger L. Johnson/1.90% *(22 Owners included in Index)*

Financial Data: Fiscal Year End:12/31 **Latest Annual Data:** 12/31/2006

Year	Sales	Net Income
2006	$258,991,000	-$38,758,000
2005	$230,857,000	-$54,814,000
2004	$211,458,000	-$75,564,000

Curr. Assets:	$38,217,000	**Curr. Liab.:**	$47,887,000		
Plant, Equip.:	$243,831,000	**Total Liab.:**	$319,188,000	**Indic. Yr. Divd.:**	NA
Total Assets:	$336,561,000	**Net Worth:**	$17,373,000	**Debt/ Equity:**	NA

Knot Inc

462 Broadway, 6th Fl., New York, NY, 10013; **PH:** 1-212-219-8555; **Fax:** 1-212-219-1929; **http://** www.theknot.com

General - Incorporation	DE	**Stock**- Price on:12/24/2007	$20.42
Employees	367	Stock Exchange	NDQ
Auditor	Ernst & Young LLP	Ticker Symbol	KNOT
Stk Agt	American Stock Transfer & Trust Co.	Outstanding Shares	31,280,000
Counsel	Proskauer Rose LLP	E.P.S.	$0.73
DUNS No.	NA	Shareholders	NA

Business: The group's principal activity is to provide products and services to couples to plan their wedding. The group's Website, www.theknot.com offers online comprehensive content, wedding related shopping, wedding gift registry and an active community. The knot wedding gowns, is an extensive magazine providing essential information regarding wedding gowns from the top designers of the world. The group through its subsidiary, wedding pages, inc. Publishes regional wedding magazines and also authors a series of books on wedding plans, gift book, wedding flowers, honeymoon booking and other travel services.

Primary SIC and add'l.: 7375 2741 7389

CIK No: 0001062292

Subsidiaries: Click Trips, Inc, Weddingpages, Inc

Officers: David Liu/Chmn., CEO, Pres./$778,446.00, Sandra Stiles/Dir., COO, Assist. Sec./$653,323.00, Carley Roney/Editor in Chief, Co - Founder, Richard Szefc/CFO, Treasurer, Sec./$643,483.00, Armando Cardenas-Nolazco/CTO/$320,802.00, Rob Fassino/VP - Business Integration, Co - Founder, Melissa Bauer/Contact - Press

Directors: David Liu/Chmn., CEO, Pres., Carley Roney/Editor in Chief, Co - Founder, Sandra Stiles/Dir., COO, Assist. Sec., Lanny Baker/Dir., Randy Ronning/Dir., Rob Fassino/VP - Business Integration, Co - Founder, Lisa Gersh/49/Dir., Ira Carlin/Dir., Eileen Naughton/Dir.

Owners: Armando Cardenas-Nolazco, Ira Carlin, Insiders/6.70%, Charles Baker, David Liu/2.90%, Federated Department Stores, Inc./11.70%, Richard Szefc/2.00%, Rainier Investment Management, Inc./5.00%, Lisa Gersh, AXA Financial, Inc./5.90%, Eileen Naughton, Tracer Capital Management, Inc./5.80%, Sandra Stiles/1.70%

Financial Data: Fiscal Year End:12/31 **Latest Annual Data:** 06/30/2007

Year	Sales	Net Income
2007	NA	NA
2006	$72,679,000	$23,427,000
2005	$51,409,000	$3,952,000

Curr. Assets:	$102,174,000	**Curr. Liab.:**	$18,209,000	**P/E Ratio:**	26.87
Plant, Equip.:	$9,376,000	**Total Liab.:**	$33,826,000	**Indic. Yr. Divd.:**	NA
Total Assets:	$204,251,000	**Net Worth:**	$170,424,000	**Debt/ Equity:**	0.0003

Knova Software Inc

10201 Torre Ave., Ste. 350, Cupertino, CA, 95014; **PH:** 1-408-863-5800; **http://** www.knova.com

General - Incorporation	DE	**Stock** - Price on:12/24/2007	NA
Employees	95	Stock Exchange	NA
Auditor	PricewaterhouseCoopers LLP	Ticker Symbol	NA
Stk Agt	American Stock Transfer & Trust Co.	Outstanding Shares	NA
Counsel	Hastings, Janofsky & Walker	E.P.S.	NA
DUNS No.	NA	Shareholders	NA

Business: The group's principle activity is to provide enterprise knowledge management solutions. The product of the group includes serviceware enterprise, which include serviceware self-service, serviceware professional and serviceware architect software products. The group also provides installation, training, consulting, and customer support services. The software solutions of the group enable organizations to easily provide customers, partners, suppliers and employees with fast, accurate answers to inquiries across various communication channels including the phone, e-mail, chat and the Web. The products are marketed through a direct sales force and indirect sales channels throughout North America and the United Kingdom. The customers of the group include eds, h&r block, at&t wireless, cingular wireless, fifth third bancorp, green mountain energy, reuters, stream international and qualcomm.

Primary SIC and add'l.: 7379 7372

CIK No: 0001062606

Subsidiaries: Kanisa Inc.

Officers: Bruce Armstrong/Dir., CEO, Pres.

Directors: Bruce Armstrong/Dir., CEO, Pres., Kent Heyman/Chmn., Thomas I. Unterberg/Dir., Thomas P. Shanahan/Dir., Tim Wallace/Dir., Ram Gupta/Dir.

Owners: Insiders/12.80%, Mark Angel/1.90%, Meritech Capital Partners II, L.P. and affiliates/6.30%, Bruce Armstrong/3.40%, Ram Gupta, Richard Nieset, Thomas I. Unterberg/3.80%, Needham Capital Management, LLC and affiliates/20.40%, Timothy Wallace/1.00%, Frank Lauletta, Sierra Ventures and affiliates/5.50%, C.E. Unterberg, Towbin Holdings, Inc. and affiliates/19.70%, Kent Heyman/2.50%, Thomas Muise

Knowledge Transfer Systems Inc

201 S Biscayne Blvd., 28th Fl. Miami Ctr., Miami, FL, 33131; **PH:** 1-800-936-3204

General - Incorporation	NV	**Stock**- Price on:12/24/2007	$0.03
Employees	3	Stock Exchange	NA
Auditor	Robison, Hill & Co	Ticker Symbol	NA
Stk Agt	Securities Transfer Corp	Outstanding Shares	53,040,000
Counsel	NA	E.P.S.	-$0.095
DUNS No.	NA	Shareholders	NA

Business: The group's principal activity is to design, produce and market e-learning courses and solutions. The group develops courses that map to the respective industry certifications in the information technology sector. The courses include desktop applications and operating system. The application courses include microsoft office xp, microsoft office 2000, 1998, and 1997. The operating system courses include microsoft windows 2000, microsoft windows nt 4.0, microsoft windows 98 and 95. It also offers it certification courses such as cisco ccna, java, mcse certification and oracle. The customers of the group include publishers, multiple resellers, integrators and e-learning companies. The group solely operates in the United States of America. On 15-Sep-2003, the group discontinued the operations of kt solutions inc.

Primary SIC and add'l.: 7375

CIK No: 0001092455

Subsidiaries: enSurge, Inc., GoThink!.com, Inc., H7 Security Systems, Inc., KT Solutions, Inc.

Officers: Shmuel Shneibalg/37/Dir., CEO, Pres., Sec. - Principal Executive, Financial Officer

Directors: Shmuel Shneibalg/37/Dir., CEO, Pres., Sec. - Principal Executive, Financial Officer

Owners: Greene Spring Company/14.50%, Shmuel Shneibalg/5.60%

Financial Data: Fiscal Year End:12/31 **Latest Annual Data:** 12/31/2006

Year	Sales	Net Income
2006	NA	-$4,092,000
2005	NA	-$3,324,000
2004	NA	$1,046,000

Curr. Assets:	$25,000	**Curr. Liab.:**	$617,000		
Plant, Equip.:	NA	**Total Liab.:**	$617,000	**Indic. Yr. Divd.:**	NA
Total Assets:	$25,000	**Net Worth:**	-$592,000	**Debt/ Equity:**	NA

Kodiak Energy Inc

734 7 Ave. SW, Ste. 460, Calgary, AB, T2P 3P8; **PH:** 1-403-262-8044; **Fax:** 1-403-513-2670; **http://** www.kodiakpetroleum.com; **Email:** KodiakEnergy@Gmail.com

General - Incorporation	DE	**Stock**- Price on:12/24/2007	NA
Employees	NA	Stock Exchange	OTC
Auditor	Meyers Norris Penny LLP	Ticker Symbol	KDKN
Stk Agt	NA	Outstanding Shares	NA
Counsel	Borden Ladner Gervais	E.P.S.	-$0.04
DUNS No.	NA	Shareholders	NA

Business: The groups principle activity is to explore oil and natural gas. The group operates from the United States and Canada.

Primary SIC and add'l.: 1311

CIK No: 0001109553

Subsidiaries: Kodiak Petroleum (Montana), Inc.,, Kodiak Petroleum (Utah), Inc.,, Kodiak Petroleum ULC

Officers: Mark Hlady/Dir., Chmn., CEO/$67,081.00, Wm S. Tighe/Dir., COO, Pres., Glenn Watt/Dir., VP - Operations, William E. Brimacombe/CFO, Borden Ladner Gervais/Legal Counsel/$29,508.00

Directors: Mark Hlady/Dir., Chmn., CEO, Wm S. Tighe/Dir., COO, Pres., Glenn Watt/Dir., VP - Operations, Peter A. Schriber/Dir., Marvin J. Jones/Dir., Peter Gross/Member - Advisory Board, Peter Boyd/Member - Advisory Board, Greg Cave/Member - Advisory Board

Owners: Glenn Watt/9.65%, William Tighe/13.83%, 1164572 Alberta Limited/5.46%, Marvin Jones, Peter Schriber/3.22%, Insiders/30.74%, Mark Hlady/3.64%

Financial Data: Fiscal Year End:12/31 **Latest Annual Data:** 12/31/2006

Year	Sales	Net Income
2006	$27,000	$18,000
2005	NA	$858,660,000
2004	NA	-$63,000

Curr. Assets:	$1,331,000	**Curr. Liab.:**	$859,000		
Plant, Equip.:	$1,326,000	**Total Liab.:**	$950,000	**Indic. Yr. Divd.:**	NA
Total Assets:	$2,707,000	**Net Worth:**	$1,757,000	**Debt/ Equity:**	NA

Kodiak Oil & Gas Corp

1625 Broadway, Ste. 330, Denver, CO, 80202; **PH:** 1-303-592-8075; **Fax:** 1-303-592-8071; **http://** www.kodiakog.com

General - Incorporation	YT	**Stock**- Price on:12/24/2007	$6.15
Employees	12	Stock Exchange	AMEX
Auditor	Hein & Associates LLP	Ticker Symbol	KOG
Stk Agt	Mellon Trust Co	Outstanding Shares	87,570,000
Counsel	NA	E.P.S.	-$0.45
DUNS No.	NA	Shareholders	NA

Business: The groups principle activities include exploitation, acquisition and production of natural gas and crude oil. The customers of the group include Eighty Eight Oil LLC, Duke Energy Field Services and Questar Gas Marketing. The group operates from the United States and Canada. The group's quarterly revenue for September 2007 was 2.51 millions of USD.

Primary SIC and add'l.: 1311

CIK No: 0001322866

Subsidiaries: Kodiak Oil and Gas (USA), Inc

Officers: Lynn A. Peterson/55/Dir., CEO, Pres., James E. Catlin/61/Chmn., Sec., COO, Russ D. Cunningham/Sr. Staff Officer, David G. Majewski/Sr. Staff Officer, Primary Responsibility/Sr. Staff Officer, James P. Henderson/43/CFO, VP

Directors: Lynn A. Peterson/55/Dir., CEO, Pres., James E. Catlin/61/Chmn., Sec., COO, Rodney D. Knutson/64/Dir., Hugh J. Graham/Dir., Herrick K. Lidstone/57/Dir., Don McDonald/Dir.

Owners: Satellite Overseas Fund IX, Ltd., Satellite Overseas Fund VII, Ltd., Satellite Overseas Fund VI, Ltd., Satellite Fund IV, L.P., The Apogee Fund, Ltd., Satellite Overseas Fund V, Ltd., Satellite Fund II, L.P., Satellite Overseas Fund VIII, Ltd., David Charles, Insiders, Satellite Overseas Fund, Ltd.

Financial Data: Fiscal Year End:12/31   Latest Annual Data: 12/31/2006

Year	Sales			Net Income
2006		$4,965,000		-$2,786,000
2005		$453,000		-$2,005,000
Curr. Assets:	$61,117,000	Curr. Liab.:	$9,879,000	
Plant, Equip.:	$52,432,000	Total Liab.:	$10,129,000	Indic. Yr. Divd.: NA
Total Assets:	$113,774,000	Net Worth:	$103,645,000	Debt/ Equity: NA

Kohl's Corp

N56 W17000 Ridgewood Dr., Menomonee Falls, WI, 53051; *PH:* 1-262-703-7000; *Fax:* 1-262-703-6143; *http://* www.kohls.com

General - Incorporation	WI	Stock - Price on:12/24/2007	$70.45
Employees	23,000	Stock Exchange	NYSE
Auditor	Ernst & Young LLP	Ticker Symbol	KSS
Stk Agt	Bank of New York	Outstanding Shares	322,630,000
Counsel	Godfrey & Kahn	E.P.S	$3.49
DUNS No.	15-420-2360	Shareholders	NA

Business: The groups principle activity is to operate specialty departmental stores. The groups products include kids, food fancy and gift cards. The group products are sold under the brand names Candies(R), Kitchen air(R) and Dockers(R). The group operates from United States.

Primary SIC and add'l.: 5311

CIK No: 0000885639

Subsidiaries: Kohls Department Stores, Inc., Kohls Illinois, Inc., Kohls Indiana, Inc., Kohls Indiana, L.P., Kohls Investment Corporation, Kohls Michigan, L.P., Kohls New York DC, Inc., Kohls Pennsylvania, Inc., Kohls Texas Limited Partner, LLC, Kohls Texas, L.P., Kohls Texas, LLC

Officers: Lawrence R. Montgomery/59/Chmn., CEO/$4,218,153.00, Wesley S. McDonald/45/CFO, Exec. VP/$2,095,653.00, Richard D. Schepp/Sec., Kevin Mansell/Dir., Pres./$3,527,451.00, Thomas Kingsbury/Sr. Exec. VP/$2,818,845.00

Directors: Lawrence R. Montgomery/59/Chmn., CEO, Kevin Mansell/Dir., Pres., Wayne Embry/71/Dir., John F. Herma/Dir., Stephen E. Watson/Dir., Elton R. White/Dir., William S. Kellogg/Dir., Steven A. Burd/58/Dir., James D. Ericson/72/Dir., Frank V. Sica/57/Dir., Peter M. Sommerhauser/Dir.

Owners: Peter M. Sommerhauser/6.10%, Stephen E. Watson, AXA Financial, Inc./7.30%, Arlene Meier, John F. Herma/2.40%, William S. Kellogg/3.70%, Wayne Embry, Kevin Mansell, Elton R. White, Capital Research and Management Co./7.20%, Frank V. Sica, Lawrence R. Montgomery, Insiders/8.90%, Thomas Kingsbury, Steven A. Burd (18 Owners included in Index)

Financial Data: Fiscal Year End:01/28   Latest Annual Data: 2/3/2007

Year	Sales			Net Income
2007		$15,544,184,000		$1,108,681,000
2006		$13,402,217,000		$841,960,000
2005		$11,700,619,000		$730,380,000
Curr. Assets:	$3,401,040,000	Curr. Liab.:	$1,918,658,000	P/E Ratio: 20.19
Plant, Equip.:	$5,352,974,000	Total Liab.:	$3,437,782,000	Indic. Yr. Divd.: NA
Total Assets:	$9,041,177,000	Net Worth:	$5,603,395,000	Debt/ Equity: 0.1761

Kolorfusion International Inc

16075 E 32nd Ave., Unit A, Aurora, CO, 80011; *PH:* 1-303-340-9993; *Fax:* 1-303-340-9982; *http://* www.kolorfusion.com; *Email:* customerservice@kolorfusion.com

General - Incorporation	CO	Stock - Price on:12/24/2007	$0.1
Employees	9	Stock Exchange	OTC
Auditor	Carver Moquist & OConnor, LLC	Ticker Symbol	KOLR
Stk Agt	Computershare Trust Co	Outstanding Shares	24,310,000
Counsel	NA	E.P.S	$0.02
DUNS No.	NA	Shareholders	NA

Business: The groups principle activities include developing and providing technology, products and services for surface enhancement to manufacturers. The group operates from the United States. The group's quarterly revenue for Sep '07 was 0.54 millions of USD.

Primary SIC and add'l.: 2759 6794

CIK No: 0001059397

Officers: Steve Nagel/CEO, CFO, Pres., Kevin Geraghty/National Sales Mgr., Joe Brisson/Design, Equipment Fabrication Development, Kenneth Bradley/60/Sec.

Directors: Thomas Gerschman/Chmn., Thomas Lefort/39/Dir.

Owners: Stephen Nagel, Philippe Nordman, Thomas LeFort, Thomas Gerschman

Financial Data: Fiscal Year End:06/30   Latest Annual Data: 06/30/2007

Year	Sales			Net Income
2007		$1,562,000		$472,000
2006		$2,087,000		-$292,000
2005		$2,344,000		-$572,000
Curr. Assets:	$374,000	Curr. Liab.:	$1,093,000	
Plant, Equip.:	$360,000	Total Liab.:	$1,319,000	Indic. Yr. Divd.: NA
Total Assets:	$1,008,000	Net Worth:	-$312,000	Debt/ Equity: NA

Komatsu Ltd

2-3-6 Akasaka Minato-Ku, Tokyo; *PH:* 81-3-55612752; *http://* www.komatsu.com

General - Incorporation	Japan	Stock - Price on:12/24/2007	$29.5
Employees	NA	Stock Exchange	OTC
Auditor	KPMG Azsa & Co	Ticker Symbol	KMTUF
Stk Agt	Mitsubishi UFJ Trust & Banking Corp	Outstanding Shares	NA
Counsel	NA	E.P.S.	NA
DUNS No.	69-054-1560	Shareholders	NA

Business: The group's principal activities are manufacturing and marketing various types of construction and mining equipments. The group operates through three segments: construction and mining equipment, industrial machinery, vehicles & others and electronics. The products of the construction and mining equipment includes excavating equipment, loading, grading, roadbed preparation equipment, hauling equipment, tunneling machines, recycling equipment, engines, components, casting products and other equipment. The electronic segment manufactures semiconductor materials and manufacturing equipment, which includes electronic materials, communications equipment, control equipment and temperature control equipment. The products classified as other include metal forging, stamping presses, sheet-metal machines, machine tools, industrial vehicles, logistics and defense systems. In fiscal 2004, the group acquired partek forest ab and partek forest holdings llc.

Primary SIC and add'l.: 3531 3545 3679 3549 3552

CIK No: 0000056594

Subsidiaries: Bangkok Komatsu Co. Ltd., Bangkok Komatsu Co., Ltd., Formosa Komatsu Silicon Corporation, Hensley Industries, Inc., Komatsu (Changzhou) Construction Machinery Corp., Komatsu (Changzhou) Foundry Corporation, Komatsu (China) Ltd., Komatsu America Corp, Komatsu America Corp., Komatsu Asia& Pacific Pte Ltd., Komatsu Australia Pty. Ltd., Komatsu Castex Ltd., Komatsu Chugoku Ltd., Komatsu Cummins Engine Co., Ltd., Komatsu do Brasil Ltda. 44 Subsidiaries included in the Index

Officers: Kunio Noji/Dir., CEO, Pres., Tadashi Okada/Executive Officer, Masao Fuchigami/Sr. Executive Officer, Susumu Isoda/Dir., Sr. Executive Officer, Mamoru Hironaka/Sr. Executive Officer, Taizo Kayata/Sr. Executive Officer, Mikio Fujitsuka/Executive Officer, Deputy GM - Corporate Planning, Ichirou Sasaki/Executive Officer, Osaka Plant Mgr. Production Division, Fujitoshi Takamura/Executive Officer, GM - Construction Equipment Technical Center 1, Development Division, Yoshisada Takahashi/Executive Officer, Amazu Plant Mgr. Production Division, Hiroyuki Kamano/Outside Corporate Auditor, Mitsuru Ueno/Executive Officer, Kazunori Kuromoto/Executive Officer, Masahiro Uegaki/Executive Officer, Masafumi Kanemoto/Corporate Auditor (30 Officers included in Index)

Directors: Kunio Noji/Dir., CEO, Pres., Masahiro Sakane/Chmn., Masahiro Yoneyama/Dir., Sr. Executive Officer, Kenji Kinoshita/Dir., Sr. Executive Officer, Hajime Sasaki/Dir., Morio Ikeda/Dir., Toshio Morikawa/Dir., Yoshinori Komamura/Dir., Sr. Executive Officer, Yasuo Suzuki/Dir., Sr. Executive Officer

Owners: Japan Trustee Services Bank, Ltd./1.56%, NATS CUMCO/1.34%, Masahiro Sakane, Makoto Nakamura, State Street Bank and Trust Company/2.08%, NIPPONKOA Insurance Co., Ltd./1.39%, Susumu Isoda, Trust & Custody Services Bank, Ltd./1.30%, Masafumi Kanemoto, Yasuo Suzuki, Hiroyuki Kamano, Nippon Life Insurance Co./3.18%, Yoshinori Komamura, Masahiro Yoneyama, Toshio Morikawa (23 Owners included in Index)

Komodo Inc

No. 1820 - 1111 W Georgia St., Vancouver, BC, V6E4M3; *PH:* 1-604-689-9417; *Fax:* 1-604-689-9413; *http://* www.kmdo.com

General - Incorporation	NV	Stock - Price on:12/24/2007	$0.024
Employees	NA	Stock Exchange	OTC
Auditor	Chisholm, Bierwolf & Nilson, LLC	Ticker Symbol	KMDO
Stk Agt	Signature Stock Transfer, Inc.	Outstanding Shares	NA
Counsel	NA	E.P.S.	NA
DUNS No.	NA	Shareholders	NA

Business: The groups principal activities include refining secure email messaging and operating environment used to eliminate viruses, spam, and other potential online threats. Products of the group include KOGO and SPC 1. The group operates from the United States.

Primary SIC and add'l.: 1000

CIK No: 0000786129

Owners: Insiders/88.00%, Penny Perfect/39.00%, Gordon Muir/39.00%, Insiders/78.00%

Financial Data: Fiscal Year End:03/31   Latest Annual Data: 03/31/2007

Year	Sales			Net Income
2007		$11,000		-$1,649,000
2006		NA		-$2,259,000
2005		NA		-$812,000
Curr. Assets:	$1,000	Curr. Liab.:	$245,000	
Plant, Equip.:	$137,000	Total Liab.:	$245,000	Indic. Yr. Divd.: NA
Total Assets:	$138,000	Net Worth:	-$107,000	Debt/ Equity: NA

Kona Grill Inc

7150 E Camelback Rd., Ste. 220, Scottsdale, AZ, 85251; *PH:* 1-480-922-8100; *Fax:* 1-480-991-6811; *http://* www.konagrill.com; *Email:* information@konagrill.com

General - Incorporation	DE	Stock - Price on:12/24/2007	$19.11
Employees	1,761	Stock Exchange	NDQ
Auditor	Ernst& Young LLP	Ticker Symbol	KONA
Stk Agt	Continental Stock Transfer & Trust Co	Outstanding Shares	5,860,000
Counsel	Greenberg Traurig, LL Phoenix,	E.P.S.	-$0.15
DUNS No.	NA	Shareholders	NA

Business: The groups principle activity is to provide restaurants services. The groups services include lunch and dinner. The products of the group include appetizers, pizzas, sandwiches, salads, noodle dishes, signature entrees, and desserts. The group products sold under the trade name Kona Grill. The group operates from the United States. The group's quarterly revenue for September 2007 was 19.21 millions of USD.

Primary SIC and add'l.: 5812

CIK No: 0001265572

Subsidiaries: Kona Macadamia, Inc., Kona Restaurant Holdings, Inc., Kona Sushi, Inc., Kona Texas Restaurants, Inc.

Officers: Marcus E. Jundt/Chmn., CEO, Pres./$640,050.00, Jason J. Merritt/COO, Exec. VP/$408,375.00, Mark S. Robinow/CFO, Exec. VP, Sec./$371,625.00

Directors: Marcus E. Jundt/Chmn., CEO, Pres., Richard J. Hauser/Dir., Kirk W. Patterson/Dir., Anthony L. Winczewski/Dir., Mark L. Bartholomay/48/Dir., Douglas G. Hipskind/Dir., Kent D. Carlson/Dir., Mark Zesbaugh/Dir.

Owners: James R. Jundt/5.20%, Jason J. Merritt/1.80%, William Blair & Company, L.L.C./14.60%, Marcus E. Jundt/18.20%, Douglas G. Hipskind, Anthony L. Winczewski, Cortina Asset Management, LLC/6.20%, Kirk W. Patterson, Kona MN, LLC/6.60%, Mark L. Bartholomay, Richard J. Hauser/9.70%, Kent D. Carlson, Insiders/24.40%, Mark S. Robinow/1.40%

Financial Data: Fiscal Year End:12/31 Latest Annual Data: 12/31/2006

Year	Sales	Net Income
2006	$50,693,000	-$2,744,000
2005	$36,828,000	-$383,000
2004	$25,050,000	$276,000

Curr. Assets:	$17,873,000	Curr. Liab.:	$8,731,000	
Plant, Equip.:	$40,516,000	Total Liab.:	$22,974,000	Indic. Yr. Divd.: NA
Total Assets:	$58,796,000	Net Worth:	$35,822,000	Debt/ Equity: 0.0715

Konami Corp

1400 Bridge Pkwy. , Ste. 101, Redwood City, CA, 94065; **PH:** 1-888-212-0573; **Fax:** 1-650-654-5690; **http://** www.konami.co.jp

General - Incorporation	Japan	Stock- Price on:12/24/2007	$24.17
Employees	5,127	Stock Exchange	NYSE
Auditor	KPMG Azsa & Co	Ticker Symbol	KNM
Stk Agt	Sumitomo Trust & Banking Co Ltd	Outstanding Shares	137,250,000
Counsel	NA	E.P.S.	$1.11
DUNS No.	NA	Shareholders	NA

Business: The group's principle activities are the research, development, manufacture and marketing of software and hardware for electronic equipment. The group's products include amusement equipment and software for personal computers, gameboys, PC engines and megadrives. The operations are carried out through the following divisions: game software, which produces and sales of computer/video game software. The health and fitness division operates health and fitness clubs and toys & hobby division deals with card games and character goods. The amusement division deals with amusement arcade video games and token-operated games and casino deals with pachinko systems and gaming machines (coin games). The others division operates amusement facility and real estate management services.

Primary SIC and add'l.: 3999 7999 7372 3679 6159 7991 7993

CIK No: 0001191141

Subsidiaries: Hudson Entertainment, Inc., Hudson Soft Co., Ltd., Internet Revolution Inc., Konami Australia Pty Ltd, Konami Career Management, Inc., Konami Corporation of America, Konami Digital Entertainment B.V., Konami Digital Entertainment Co., Ltd., Konami Digital Entertainment GmbH, Konami Digital Entertainment Limited, Konami Digital Entertainment, Inc., Konami Gaming, Inc., Konami Logistics& Service, Inc., Konami Real Estate, Inc., Konami School, Inc. 19 Subsidiaries included in the Index

Officers: Kagemasa Kozuki/Dir., CEO, Pres., Satoshi Sakamoto/Corp. Officer - Gaming, System Business, Fumiaki Tanaka/Corp. Officer, Executive Officer - Japan, Minoru Nagaoka/84/Corporate Auditor, Toshimitsu Oishi/Corp. Officer - Health, Fitness Business, Shuji Kido/Corp. Officer - New Business, Tachio Ohori/Corporate Auditor, Masaru Mizuno/Corporate Auditor, Shogo Sasabe/Corporate Auditor, Akihiko Nagata/49/Executive Corp. Officer - Asia, Kimihiko Higashio/Dir., Chief Administrative Officer, Shigeo Niwa/Corp. Officer - Legal Affairs, Intellectual Property, Akira Tamai/Corp. Officer - Finance, Accounting, Masataka Imaizumi/Corporate Auditor, Noboru Onuma/60/Standing Corporate Auditor (19 Officers included in Index)

Directors: Kagemasa Kozuki/Dir., CEO, Pres., Kagehiko Kozuki/Dir., Hiroyuki Mizuno/Dir. - External, Tomokazu Godai/69/Dir. - External, Kimihiko Higashio/Dir., Chief Administrative Officer, Akira Gemma/74/Dir. - External, Tsutomu Takeda/71/Dir., Noriaki Yamaguchi/64/VP, Dir., CFO

Owners: Kozuki Holding B.V./9.86%, Kozuki Capital Corporation/5.13%, Kozuki Foundation For Sports, Athletes and Higher Education/10.44%, Kagemasa Kozuki/25.51%

Financial Data: Fiscal Year End:03/31 Latest Annual Data: 03/31/2007

Year	Sales	Net Income
2007	$2,374,240,000	$137,323,000
2006	$2,231,523,000	$195,863,000
2005	$2,427,517,000	$97,644,000

Curr. Assets:	$1,507,943,000	Curr. Liab.:	$929,574,000	
Plant, Equip.:	$433,886,000	Total Liab.:	$1,848,068,000	Indic. Yr. Divd.: $0.420
Total Assets:	$2,833,793,000	Net Worth:	$985,725,000	Debt/ Equity: NA

KongZhong Corp

35th Floor, Tengda Plz., No. 168 Xizhimenwai St, Beijing, Haidian District, 100044; **PH:** 86-1088576000; **http://** phx.corporate-ir.net; **Email:** ir@kongzhong.com

General - Incorporation	Cayman Islands	Stock- Price on:12/24/2007	$4.9601
Employees	798	Stock Exchange	NDQ
Auditor	Deloitte Touche Tohmatsu CPA Ltd	Ticker Symbol	KONG
Stk Agt	NA	Outstanding Shares	35,580,000
Counsel	Prc Legal System	E.P.S.	$0.49
DUNS No.	NA	Shareholders	NA

Business: The groups principle activity is to provide advanced second-generation wireless interactive entertainment, media, and community services, in terms of revenue, to customers of China Mobile Communications Corporation. The group operates from United States.

Primary SIC and add'l.: NA

CIK No: 0001285137

Subsidiaries: Anjian Xingye Technology (Beijing) Company Limited, Beijing AirInbox Information Technologies Co., Ltd., Beijing Boya Wuji Technologies Co., Ltd., Beijing Wireless Interactive Network Technologies Co., Ltd., Beijing Xinrui Network Technology Company Limited, KongZhong China, KongZhong Information Technologies (Beijing) Co., Ltd., Sharp Edge Group Limited, Tianjin Mammoth Technology Co., Ltd., Wuhan Chengxitong Information Technology Company Limited

Officers: Yunfan Zhou/Chmn., CEO, Hanhui Sun/CFO, Nick Yang/Pres., CTO

Directors: Yunfan Zhou/Chmn., CEO, Charlie Y. Shi/Dir., Hui Zhang/Dir., Hope Ni/Dir.

Owners: Fu Lam Wu/5.10%, Samuel Shin Fang/5.40%, Timothy C. Draper/9.20%, John H.N. Fisher/6.00%, Draper Fisher Jurvetson ePlanet Ventures L.P./5.80%, Asad Jamal/5.90%, Draper Fisher Jurvetson ePlanet Partners, Ltd./5.80%, Stephen T. Jurvetson/6.00%, Nick Yang/18.00%, Yunfan Zhou/18.00%

Financial Data: Fiscal Year End:12/31 Latest Annual Data: 12/31/2005

Year	Sales		Net Income
2005	$77,753,000		$22,174,000
2004	$47,969,000		$20,369,000
2003	$7,807,000		$2,408,000

Curr. Assets:	$145,346,000	Curr. Liab.:	$10,822,000	P/E Ratio: 10.12
Plant, Equip.:	$3,101,000	Total Liab.:	$10,964,000	Indic. Yr. Divd.: NA
Total Assets:	$166,741,000	Net Worth:	$155,777,000	Debt/ Equity: NA

Koninklijke Ahold N.V.

Piet Heinkade 167 - 173, 1019 GM, Amsterdam, 1019; **PH:** 31-20 509 51 00; **Fax:** 31-20 509 51 10; **http://** www.ahold.com

General - Incorporation	CA	Stock- Price on:12/24/2007	$13.04
Employees	NA	Stock Exchange	NA
Auditor	NA	Ticker Symbol	NA
Stk Agt	Bank of New York	Outstanding Shares	1,560,000,000
Counsel	NA	E.P.S.	$0.77
DUNS No.	NA	Shareholders	NA

Business: The groups principle activity is to provide food services. The group operates from the United States and Europe.

Primary SIC and add'l.: 5411

CIK No: 0000854499

Officers: John Rishton/CEO, Pres., Peter Wakkie/Exec. VP, Chief Corporate Governance Counsel, Dick Boer/51/Exec. VP, COO - Europe, Henk Jan Ten Brinke/VP - Investor Relations, Sjoerd Holleman/Analyst Investor Relations, Caro Bamforth/Dir. - International Media Relations, Enrique Boerboom/Corp. Sec., Marielle Reints/Deputy Corp. Sec., Friso Coppes/VP - Corporate Affairs, Kerry Underhill/Sr. VP - Communications, Barry F. Scher/VP - Public Affairs, Communications, Ahold USA, Kimberly Ross/CFO

Directors: Rene Dahan/Chmn., Tom De Swaan/67/Vice Chmn., Judith Sprieser/55/Dir., Karen M.A De Segundo/62/Dir., Derk C. Doijer/59/Dir., Stephanie M. Shern/60/Dir.

Financial Data: Fiscal Year End:12/31 Latest Annual Data: 12/31/2006

Year	Sales		Net Income
2006	$59,244,502,000		$1,284,652,000
2005	$70,543,200,000		$149,226,000

Curr. Assets:	$8,787,917,000	Curr. Liab.:	$7,685,466,000	P/E Ratio: 17.89
Plant, Equip.:	$9,421,661,000	Total Liab.:	$17,390,992,000	Indic. Yr. Divd.: NA
Total Assets:	$31,259,423,000	Net Worth:	$13,551,559,000	Debt/ Equity: NA

Koninklijke Kpn

Maanplein 55, The Hague; **PH:** 070-3434343; **http://** www.kpn.com

General - Incorporation	Netherlands	Stock- Price on:12/24/2007	$16.35
Employees	NA	Stock Exchange	OTC
Auditor	PricewaterhouseCoopers Accountants	Ticker Symbol	KKPNF
Stk Agt	NA	Outstanding Shares	NA
Counsel	Allen & Overy	E.P.S.	NA
DUNS No.	NA	Shareholders	NA

Business: The group's principal activity is providing telecommunication services to consumers and businesses. The group operates under four divisions fixed network services, mobile communications, business solutions and other activities. Fixed network services: comprises of domestic telephone traffic, fixed-to-mobile traffic and outbound international traffic; mobile communications: comprises of mobile activities in the Netherlands, Germany and Belgium; business solutions: comprises of transmission services, ip services, integrated solutions and managed application services; other activities: comprises of business communication solutions and retail distribution channel.

Primary SIC and add'l.: 1731 4812 4813 4822

CIK No: 0001001474

Subsidiaries: E-Plus Mobilfunk GmbH& Co.KG, EuroWeb International Corp., GMI Mobilfunk Beteiligungen GmbH, Infonet Nederland B.V., KPN Consumer Internet and Media Services B.V., KPN EuroRings B.V., KPN Eurovoice Holding B.V., KPN HotSpots B.V., KPN Mobile Holding B.V.:, KPN Mobile International B.V., KPN Mobile N.V.:, KPN Mobile The Netherlands B.V., KPN Telecom B.V.:, KPN Telecom Retail B.V., KPN Telecommerce B.V.: 18 Subsidiaries included in the Index

Officers: A. J. Scheepbouwer/64/Chmn., CEO, E. Blok/51/Dir., MD Business Marketing, Marcel H. Smits/47/Dir., CFO, Stan P. Miller/50/Dir., MD Mobile Division, J.B. P. Coopmans/Dir., MD Consumer Marketing

Directors: A. J. Scheepbouwer/64/Chmn., CEO, A. H.J. Risseeuw/72/Chmn. - Supervisory Board, D. G. Eustace/72/Vice Chmn. - The Member - Supervisory Board, Marcel H. Smits/47/Dir., CFO, Stan P. Miller/50/Dir., MD Mobile Division, D. I. Jager/65/Member - Supervisory Board, E. Blok/51/Dir., MD Business Marketing, J.B. P. Coopmans/Dir., MD Consumer Marketing, Ir M.E. Van Lier Lels/49/Member - Supervisory Board, J.B. M. Streppel/59/Member - Supervisory Board, V. Halberstadt/69/Member - Supervisory Board, M. Bischoff/66/Member - Supervisory Board, C. M. Colijn-Hooijmans/Member - Supervisory Board

Koninklijke Philips Electronics

Amstelplein 2, Breitner Ctr., MX, Amsterdam, 1070; **PH:** 31-402791111; **http://** www.philips.nl

General - Incorporation	Netherlands	Stock- Price on:12/24/2007	NA
Employees	121,732	Stock Exchange	NYSE
Auditor	KPMG Accountants N.V	Ticker Symbol	PHG
Stk Agt	Citibank N.A	Outstanding Shares	1,100,000,000
Counsel	Eric Poelman	E.P.S.	$4.57
DUNS No.	40-045-5344	Shareholders	NA

Business: The group's principal activity is the development and manufacture of electronic and electrical products through the following divisions: consumer electronics: video, audio and personal communication products, PC peripherals and remote control systems; lighting: lamps (incandescent and halogen, automotive, high-intensity gas-discharge and ql induction) fixtures, ballasts, lighting electronics and batteries; semiconductors: integrated circuits and discrete semiconductors; medical systems: systems for diagnostic imaging and the provision of services to the healthcare sector; dap: domestic appliances and personal care.

Primary SIC and add'l.: 3674 3841 3645 3641 3675 3679 3651

CIK No: 0000313216

Subsidiaries: Compagnie Franaise Philips, Suresnes, Philips Beteiligungs-GmbH, Philips Electronics China B.V. Eindhoven, Philips Electronics Nederland B.V, Philips Electronics North America Corporation, Philips UK Limited, Croydon

Officers: Rudy Provoost/Dir., CEO, Exec. VP, Daniel Hartert/CEO, Exec. VP - Imaging Systems, Theo Van Deursen/Dir., CEO, Exec. VP - Philips Lighting, Pierre-Jean Sivignon/Dir., CFO, Exec. VP, Gottfried Dutine/Dir., Exec. VP - Royal Philips Electronics, Gerard Kleisterlee/Dir., CFO, Pres., Exec. VP - Royal Philips, Barbara Kux/Chief Procurement Officer - Royal Philips Electronics, Andrea Ragnetti/Dir., Exec. VP, Chief Marketing Officer, Rick Harwig/CTO - Royal Philips Electronics, Steve Kelly/Sr. Public Relations Mgr. - Philips Medical Systems, Gert Van Santen/Dir. - Healthcare Communications EMEA, Royal Philips Electronics, Radhika Choksey/Regional Dir. - Public Relations, Royal Philips Electronics, Asia, Tessa Yau/Marketing Support Specialist - Philips Medical Systems, Asia, Alan S. Cathcart/Sr. VP - Investor Relations, Raymond Schras/Mgr. - Investor Relations *(20 Officers included in Index)*

Directors: Rudy Provoost/Dir., CEO, Exec. VP, Theo Van Deursen/Dir., CEO, Exec. VP - Philips Lighting, W. De Kleuver/Chmn. - Supervisory Board, Von H. Prondzynski/Member - Supervisory Board, Richard Greenbury/Member - Supervisory Board, Andrea Ragnetti/Dir., Exec. VP, Chief Marketing Officer, Steve Rusckowski/Dir., Gottfried Dutine/Dir., Exec. VP - Royal Philips Electronics, Gerard Kleisterlee/Dir., CFO, Pres., Exec. VP - Royal Philips, J. M. Thompson/Member - Supervisory Board, Wong Ngit Liong/Member - Supervisory Board, E. Kist/Member - Supervisory Board, J-M Hessels/Member - Supervisory Board, C. J.A Van Lede/Member - Supervisory Board, Pierre-Jean Sivignon/Dir., CFO, Exec. VP *(18 Directors included in Index)*

Financial Data: *Fiscal Year End:*12/31 *Latest Annual Data:* 12/31/2006

Year	Sales	Net Income
2006	$11,686,620,000	-$762,057,000
2005	$35,999,838,000	$3,396,859,000
2004	$41,367,244,000	$3,869,438,000

Curr. Assets:	$3,469,731,000	**Curr. Liab.:**	$3,571,884,000	**P/E Ratio:**	10.12
Plant, Equip.:	$10,433,663,000	**Total Liab.:**	$7,285,067,000	**Indic. Yr. Divd.:**	$0.680
Total Assets:	$14,845,994,000	**Net Worth:**	$7,560,927,000	**Debt/ Equity:**	NA

Kookmin Bank

565 Fifth Ave., 24th Fl., New York, NY, 10017; ***PH:*** 1-212-697-6100; ***Fax:*** 1-212-697-1456; ***http://*** inf.kbstar.com

General - Incorporation	Korea	**Stock**- Price on:12/24/2007	$96.45
Employees	43,281	Stock Exchange	NYSE
Auditor	Deloitte Anjin LLC	Ticker Symbol	KB
Stk Agt	Kookmin Bank	Outstanding Shares	336,380,000
Counsel	NA	E.P.S	$7.24
DUNS No.	NA	Shareholders	NA

Business: The group's principal activity is the provision of commercial banking services which include remittances, deposits, foreign investments, corporate financing, financial advisory and mid-long term funding.

Primary SIC and add'l.: 6021

CIK No: 0001143680

Subsidiaries: Kookmin Bank Hong Kong Ltd., Kookmin Bank International Ltd.

Officers: Chung Won Kang/58/CEO, Pres., Kap Joe Song/Information Technology Group, Yong Kook Oh/Corporate Banking Group, Ki Hong Kim/51/Sr. Exec. VP, Young Han Choi/Capital Markets, Treasury Group, Dong Won Kim/Human Resources Group, Jung Min Kim/Sales Supporting Group, Hyo Sung Won/Credit Card Group, De Oak Shin/Contact - Private Banking Group, Dal Soo Lee/Marketing, Product Group, Won Sik Yeo/Consumer Banking Group I, Jacques P.M. Kemp/Non Exec. Dir., Dong Su Yeo/Consumer Banking Group II, Hyeog Kwan Kwon/Consumer Banking Group III, Kyung Woo Woo/Trust, NHF Management Group *(20 Officers included in Index)*

Directors: Dam Cho/56/Non Exec. Dir., Kee Young Chung/60/Non Exec. Dir., Bo Kyung Byun/55/Non Exec. Dir., Baek In Cha/50/Non Exec. Dir., Dong Soo Chung/63/Non Exec. Dir., Nobuya Takasugi/66/Non Exec. Dir., Chang Kyu Lee/58/Non Exec. Dir.

Owners: Citibank N.A., Euro-Pacific Growth Fund

Financial Data: *Fiscal Year End:*12/31 *Latest Annual Data:* 12/31/2006

Year	Sales	Net Income
2006	$15,359,744,000	$3,323,189,000
2005	$13,501,982,000	$2,716,197,000
2004	$14,386,331,000	$996,766,000

Curr. Assets:	$15,461,517,000	**Curr. Liab.:**	$144,114,179,000	**P/E Ratio:**	10.12
Plant, Equip.:	$1,733,311,000	**Total Liab.:**	$191,619,430,000	**Indic. Yr. Divd.:**	NA
Total Assets:	$207,503,489,000	**Net Worth:**	$15,884,059,000	**Debt/ Equity:**	NA

Koor Industries Ltd

Azrieli Ctr., Triangle Tower, 43rd Fl., Tel Aviv, 67023; ***PH:*** 972-36075111; ***Fax:*** 972-36075110; ***http://*** www.koor.com; ***Email:*** info@koor.com

General - Incorporation	Israel	**Stock**- Price on:12/24/2007	NA
Employees	2,318	Stock Exchange	OTC
Auditor	Somekh Chaikin	Ticker Symbol	KORIY
Stk Agt	Bank of New York	Outstanding Shares	NA
Counsel	Herzog Fox & Neeman, Skadden Arps	E.P.S	NA
DUNS No.	60-001-6810	Shareholders	NA

Business: The group's principal activities are the development, manufacture and marketing of telecommunication equipment, defense electronics, agrochemicals and other chemicals, building and infrastructure materials and other. The group operates mainly through its subsidiaries. Its shares are traded on the Tel Aviv and the New York stock exchanges.

Primary SIC and add'l.: 4899 3669 6719 8741 2879 6799 3679

CIK No: 0000791531

Subsidiaries: ECI Telecom Ltd., Koor Corporate Venture Capital, Makhteshim-Agan Industries Ltd., Telrad Networks Ltd.

Officers: Raanan Cohen/CEO, David Paz/Exec. VP, Oren Hillinger/Dir. - Finance, Ehud Helft/GK Investor Relations, Kenny Green/GK Investor Relations, Shlomo Heller/General Counsel, Corp. Sec., Michal Yageel/Corporate Controller

Directors: Jonathan Kolber/Chmn., Avraham Asheri/Dir., Shlomo Reizman/Dir., Mark Shimmel/Dir., Nochi Dankner/Dir., Isaac Manor/Dir., Zvika Livnat/Dir., Avi Fischer/Dir., Rafi Bisker/Dir., Gideon Lahav/Dir., Haim Gavrieli/Dir., Ayelet Ben Ezer/Dir.

Owners: Discount Investment Corporation Ltd./42.12%, IDB Development Corporation Ltd./9.86%

Financial Data: *Fiscal Year End:*12/31 *Latest Annual Data:* 12/31/2006

Year	Sales	Net Income
2006	$154,526,000	-$44,453,000
2005	$344,479,000	$76,864,000
2004	$2,134,592,000	$25,807,000

Curr. Assets:	$294,395,000	**Curr. Liab.:**	$81,854,000		
Plant, Equip.:	$190,293,000	**Total Liab.:**	$785,990,000	**Indic. Yr. Divd.:**	NA
Total Assets:	$1,292,441,000	**Net Worth:**	$487,796,000	**Debt/ Equity:**	NA

Kopin Corp

200 John Hancock Rd., Taunton, MA, 02780; ***PH:*** 1-508-824-6696; ***Fax:*** 1-508-824-6958; ***http://*** www.kopin.com; ***Email:*** info@kopin.com

General - Incorporation	DE	**Stock**- Price on:12/24/2007	$4.03
Employees	313	Stock Exchange	NDQ
Auditor	Deloitte & Touche LLP	Ticker Symbol	KOPN
Stk Agt	Boston EquiServe Shareholder Services	Outstanding Shares	67,880,000
Counsel	Bingham Dana Ltd	E.P.S	$0.15
DUNS No.	14-412-3528	Shareholders	NA

Business: The group's principal activity is to develop, manufacture and sell gallium arsenide-based hbt transistor wafers and other commercial semiconductor products that use indium phosphide, gallium nitride, and gallium arsenide-based substrates. Major products of the group are iii-v products and miniature flat panel displays. It also been also been developing light emitting diodes (leds) grown on sapphire substrates which are called cyberlitestm. Hbt transistor wafers are customer-specific arrays of vertically oriented transistors used primarily to produce high performance integrated circuits for wireless communications products. Cyberdisplay products are miniature, high performance, high resolution, low cost displays designed for consumer electronics and next generation mobile communications devices. The customers of the group are victor company of Japan ltd (jvc), skyworks solutions inc and samsung electronics co ltd.

Primary SIC and add'l.: 3674 3577 8733

CIK No: 0000771266

Subsidiaries: Jacobs Constructors, Jacobs Consultancy Inc., Jacobs Engineering Company, Jacobs Engineering Group of Ohio Inc., Jacobs Engineering Inc., Jacobs Field Services North America, Jacobs Government Services Company, Jacobs Industrial Maintenance Company LLC., Jacobs Maintenance, JE Remediation Technologies

Officers: John C.C. Fan/Chmn., CEO, Daily S. Hill/Sr. VP - Gallium Arsenide Operations, David E. Brook/Dir. - Secretory, Hong Choi/CTO, Richard Sneider/Treasurer, CFO, Bor-Yeu Tsaur/Exec. VP - Display Operations, Michael Presz/VP - Government Programs, Special Projects

Directors: John C.C. Fan/Chmn., CEO, David E. Brook/Dir. - Secretory, Andrew H. Chapman/Dir., Chi Chia Hsieh/Dir., Morton Collins/Dir., James K. Brewington/Dir., Michael J. Landine/Dir.

Financial Data: *Fiscal Year End:*12/31 *Latest Annual Data:* 12/31/2005

Year	Sales	Net Income
2005	$90,296,000	$11,671,000
2004	$87,281,000	-$13,832,000
2003	$76,552,000	-$6,878,000

Curr. Assets:	$143,929,000	**Curr. Liab.:**	$14,794,000	**P/E Ratio:**	26.87
Plant, Equip.:	$11,250,000	**Total Liab.:**	$15,534,000	**Indic. Yr. Divd.:**	NA
Total Assets:	$166,332,000	**Net Worth:**	$146,460,000	**Debt/ Equity:**	NA

Koppers Inc

436 Seventh Ave., Pittsburgh, PA, 15219; ***PH:*** 1-412-227-2001; ***http://*** www.koppers.com

General - Incorporation	PA	**Stock**- Price on:12/24/2007	NA
Employees	2,026	Stock Exchange	NA
Auditor	Ernst & Young LLP	Ticker Symbol	NA
Stk Agt	Mellon Investor Services LLC	Outstanding Shares	NA
Counsel	NA	E.P.S	NA
DUNS No.	19-699-1582	Shareholders	NA

Business: The group's principal activity is to produce carbon compounds and treated wood products for use in a variety of markets including the railroad, aluminum, chemical, utility and steel industries. The group has two segments namely carbon materials and chemicals and railroad and utility products. The carbon materials and chemicals division manufactures carbon pitch, phthalic anhydride, creosote, carbon black and furnace coke. The railroad and utility products division provides various products and services to railroads, including crossties, track and switch pre-assemblies and disposal services. This segment supplies treated wood poles to electric and telephone utilities and provides wood treating services for vineyards, construction and commercial applications. The group operates 37 facilities in the United States, Australia, New Zealand, Europe and South Africa.

Primary SIC and add'l.: 2861 2895 2899

CIK No: 0000916075

Subsidiaries: Concrete Partners, Inc., Continental Carbon Australia Pty. Ltd., Koppers (China) Carbon& Chemical Company Limited, Koppers Arch Chemicals (M)Sdn Bhd, Koppers Arch International Pty Limited, Koppers Arch Investments Pty Limited, Koppers Arch Wood Protection (Aust) Pty Limited, Koppers Arch Wood Protection (Fiji) Limited, Koppers Arch Wood Protection (M)Sdn Bhd, Koppers Arch Wood Protection (NZ) Limited, Koppers Arch Wood Protection (SA) (Proprietary) Limited, Koppers Assurance, Inc., Koppers Australia Holding Company Pty Limited, Koppers Australia Pty. Limited, Koppers Carbon Materials& Chemicals Pty. Ltd. 36 Subsidiaries included in the Index

Officers: Walter W. Turner/Dir., CEO, Pres., Randall D. Collins/VP - Safety Health & Environmental Affairs, David T. Bryce/VP, GM - Utility Poles, Piling, Thomas D. Loadman/VP, GM - Railroad Products, Services, Steven R. Lacy/Sr. VP - Administration, General Counsel, Sec., Leslie S. Hyde/VP - Safety, Environmental Affairs, Claire M. Schaming/Treasurer, Assist. Sec., Rebecca R. Duke/Dir. - Communications, Development, Compensation, Ernest S. Bryon/VP - Business Development, Asia, David Whittle/VP, GM - Carbon Materials, Chemicals, European Operations, Richard Bennett/Business Mgr. - Takura Qld, Greg Horvath/Plant Mgr. - New South Wales, Robert H. Wombles/VP - Technology, Brian H. McCurrie/CFO, VP, Kevin J. Fitzgerald/Sr. VP - Global Carbon Materials, Chemicals *(46 Officers included in Index)*

Directors: Walter W. Turner/Dir., CEO, Pres., Robert Cizik/Chmn., Michael T. Young/Dir., Rebecca R. Duke/Dir. - Communications, Development, Compensation, James C. Stalder/Dir., David M. Hillenbrand/Dir., Christian L. Oberbeck/Dir., Clayton A. Sweeney/Dir.

Kore Holdings Inc

8905 Fairview Rd., Ste. 600, Silver Spring, MD, 20910; *PH:* 1-559-692-2474;
http:// www.koreholdings.com

General - Incorporation		NV	Stock- Price on:12/24/2007		$0.2
Employees		NA	Stock Exchange		OTC
Auditor	Bagell, Josephs, Levine & Co. LLC		Ticker Symbol		KORH
Stk Agt.	Florida Atlantic Stock Transfer, Inc.		Outstanding Shares		NA
Counsel		NA	E.P.S.		NA
DUNS No.		NA	Shareholders		NA

Business: The group's principal activity is to provide alternative back-up power and financial services. The alternative back-up power provided by the group includes wind and hydro electricity. The group manufactures and markets energy products designed to provide electricity during power failure, blackouts and low voltage distribution from the power grid. It also provides financial services such as real estate mortgages and other financial products. The group has acquired yosemite brokerage, inc. And wolverine power corporation in fiscal 2003.

Primary SIC and add'l.: 6162 4931

CIK No: 0001101137

Subsidiaries: First Washington Financial Corporation, Mortgage American Bankers, LLC, Opportunity Knocks, LLC, Sun Electronics, Inc., Sun Volt, Inc

Officers: Robert F. Rood/Chmn., CEO, Pres., Sec.

Directors: Robert F. Rood/Chmn., CEO, Pres., Sec., James A. Sharon/Dir., Bruce Persson/Dir.

*Financial Data: Fiscal Year End:*09/30   *Latest Annual Data:* 9/30/2005

Year		Sales		Net Income
2005		$1,814,000		-$120,000
2004		$2,608,000		$81,000
2003		$2,042,000		-$74,000
Curr. Assets:	$459,000	Curr. Liab.:	$242,000	
Plant, Equip.:	$19,767,000	Total Liab.:	$242,000	Indic. Yr. Divd.: NA
Total Assets:	$23,362,000	Net Worth:	$23,119,000	Debt/ Equity: NA

Korea Electric Power Corp

400 Kelby St., Parker Plz. 16th Fl., Fort Lee, NJ, 07024; *PH:* 1-201-541-4007; *Fax:* 1-201-613-4009;
http:// www.kepco.co.kr

General - Incorporation	Korea	Stock- Price on:12/24/2007	$22.39
Employees	36,853	Stock Exchange	NYSE
Auditor	Deloitte Anjin LLC	Ticker Symbol	KEP
Stk Agt.	Kookmin Bank	Outstanding Shares	NA
Counsel	NA	E.P.S.	$1.80
DUNS No.	68-781-8906	Shareholders	NA

Business: The group's principal activities are the transmission and distribution of electricity to industrial, general and residential sectors. It operates 1 head office.

Primary SIC and add'l.: 4911 7375 1241 6159 1094

CIK No: 0000887225

Subsidiaries: Jiaozuo KEPCO Power Company Ltd., KEPCO Asia International Ltd., KEPCO China International Ltd., KEPCO Gansu International Ltd., KEPCO Ilijan Corporation, KEPCO International Hong Kong Ltd., KEPCO International Philippines Inc., KEPCO Nuclear Fuel Co., Ltd., KEPCO Philippines Corporation, KEPCO Philippines Holdings Inc., KEPCO Salcon Power Corporation, Korea East-West Power Co., Ltd., Korea Electric Power Data Network Co., Ltd., Korea Hydro& Nuclear Power Co., Ltd., Korea Midland Power Co., Ltd. 20 Subsidiaries included in the Index

Officers: Won-Gul Lee/59/Dir., CEO, Pres., Tae-Wook Huh/Mgr., Seong-Hee Yang/Assist. Mgr., Seung Bum Kim/Mgr., Ho Moon/57/Dir., VP, Dir. General - Planning, Coordination Division, Jong-Hwak Park/58/Standing Dir., Sr. VP - Marketing, Service Division, Myeong-Chul Chang/57/Dir., Sr. VP - Overseas Business Division, Gang Byun/59/Dir., Sr. VP - Transmission Division, Oh-Hyung Kwon/57/Dir., Sr. VP - Management Support Division, Kim Myung-Whan/Genenral Mgr., Ji Changyoung/Mgr., Cecilia (hyang-Joo) Cecilia (hyang-Joo)/Mgr.

Directors: Won-Gul Lee/59/Dir., CEO, Pres., Ho Moon/57/Dir., VP, Dir. General - Planning, Coordination Division, Jong-Hwak Park/58/Standing Dir., Sr. VP - Marketing, Service Division, Myeong-Chul Chang/57/Dir., Sr. VP - Overseas Business Division, Jae-Kyu Kim/59/Non - Standing Dir., Chung-Boo Park/66/Non - Standing Dir., Gang Byun/59/Dir., Sr. VP - Transmission Division, Oh-Hyung Kwon/57/Dir., Sr. VP - Management Support Division, Oh-Sung Kwon/46/Non - Standing Dir., Eung-Seon Kang/58/Non - Standing Dir., Ju-Sub Kim/57/Non - Standing Dir., Jae-Hyun Shin/61/Non - Standing Dir., Jong-Geol Yoo/60/Non - Standing Dir., Bae-Hee Kwak/62/Non - Standing Dir.

Owners: Korea Development Bank/29.95%, Resolution & Finance Corporation/5.02%, KEPCO/3.19%, National Pension Corporation/2.75%, Government/21.12%

*Financial Data: Fiscal Year End:*12/31   *Latest Annual Data:* 12/31/2006

Year		Sales		Net Income
2006		$29,471,842,000		$2,844,289,000
2005		$25,192,779,000		$2,940,569,000
2004		$23,143,331,000		$3,414,688,000
Curr. Assets:	$10,467,371,000	Curr. Liab.:	$9,269,545,000	P/E Ratio: 10.12
Plant, Equip.:	$60,224,583,000	Total Liab.:	$35,264,954,000	Indic. Yr. Divd.: NA
Total Assets:	$76,030,198,000	Net Worth:	$40,765,244,000	Debt/ Equity: NA

Korea Thrunet Co Ltd

1337-20, Seocho-2dong, Seoul; *PH:* 82-62667114; *http://* www.thrunet.com;
Email: ircontact@corp.thrunet.com

General - Incorporation	Korea	Stock- Price on:12/24/2007	NA
Employees	NA	Stock Exchange	NA
Auditor	Samil PricewaterhouseCoopers	Ticker Symbol	NA
Stk Agt.	Bank of New York	Outstanding Shares	NA
Counsel	NA	E.P.S.	NA
DUNS No.	NA	Shareholders	NA

Business: The groups principle activity is to provide provision of high-speed cable, modem-based Internet services to residential customers and small- and medium- sized business. The group operates from United States.

Primary SIC and add'l.: 7374 7375 4813

CIK No: 0001097714

Subsidiaries: Korea.com Communications Co., Ltd., Multiplus Limited

Korn Ferry International

1900 Ave. of the Stars, Ste. 2600, Los Angeles, CA, 90067; *PH:* 1-310-552-1834;
Fax: 1-310-553-6452; *http://* www.kornferry.com; *Email:* global.marketing@kornferry.com

General - Incorporation	DE	Stock- Price on:12/24/2007	$26.52
Employees	1,401	Stock Exchange	NYSE
Auditor	Ernst & Young LLP	Ticker Symbol	KFY
Stk Agt	Chase Mellon Shareholder Services LLC	Outstanding Shares	47,170,000
Counsel	Sullivan & Cromwell	E.P.S.	$1.36
DUNS No.	05-223-9530	Shareholders	NA

Business: The group's principal activity is to provide recruitment and leadership development services. The group operates in two segments, namely executive recruitment and future step. The executive recruitment segment offers recruitment services at board level and for chief executive and other senior executive positions. These services are offered to clients in the advanced technology, consumer goods, industrial, financial services, healthcare and professional services industries. The middle-management recruitment segment named futurestep, offers services for middle and lowers management positions with annual compensation between $75,000 to $150,000. It also offers project recruitment and managed services. In addition to these, the group provides management assessment and executive coaching services. It operates in North America, Europe, Asia/pacific and South America.

Primary SIC and add'l.: 8742 7361

CIK No: 0000056679

Subsidiaries: Agensi Pekerjaan Futurestep Worldwide (M) Sdn. Bhd., Agensi Pekerjaan Korn/Ferry International (Malaysia) Sdn. Bhd., Avery & Associates, Inc., Carre, Orban & Partners Ltd., Carre, Orban & Partners Two Ltd., Continental American Management Corp., Futurestep (Australia) Pty Ltd, Futurestep (Hong Kong) Ltd, Futurestep (Japan) K.K., Futurestep (New Zealand) Ltd, Futurestep (Singapore) Pte Ltd, Futurestep (UK) Limited, Gabriele 7 Vermgensberatungs GmbH, Hofman, Herbold & Partner Management Beratung, Hofmann, Herbold & Partners Beteiligungs GmbH 81 Subsidiaries included in the Index

Officers: Cheryl Buxton/CEO - Service Consultant, Princeton, John Johnson/CEO - Service Consultant, Cleveland, Charles King/CEO - Service Consultant, New York, Nels Olson/CEO - Service Consultant - Washington, DC, Tierney Remick/CEO - Service Consultant, Chicago, Scott Kingdom/CEO - Service Consultant, Chicago, Jeff Rosin/CEO - Service Consultant, Toronto, Michael Rottblatt/CEO - Service Consultant, Stamford, Marti Smye/CEO - Service Consultant, Toronto, Marketing Leader - Coaching, Development, Leadership Development Solutions, New York, Richard Spitz/CEO - Service Consultant, Los Angeles, Charles Wardell/CEO - Service Consultant, New York, Paul C. Reilly/Chmn., CEO/$6,528,320.00, Don Spetner/Exec. VP - Corporate Affairs, CEO Service Consultant - Los Angeles, Robert McNabb/CEO, Exec. VP - Futurestep/$1,376,648.00, Alan Choi/CEO - Service Consultant , Hong Kong (99 Officers included in Index)

Directors: Paul C. Reilly/Chmn., CEO, Ihno Schneevoigt/Dir., Gary D. Burnison/Dir., CFO, COO, Exec. VP, Edward D. Miller/Dir., Frank V. Cahouet/Dir., Harry L. You/Dir., James E. Barlett/Dir., Patti S. Hart/Dir., Gerhard Schulmeyer/Dir., Ken Whipple/Dir.

Owners: Gary C. Hourihan, David L. Lowe, Frank V. Cahouet, Gary D. Burnison, Edward D. Miller, Kenneth Whipple, Gerhard Schulmeyer, Sakie T. Fukushima, Credit Suisse First Boston International/10.70%, Insiders/2.63%, James E. Barlett, Barclays Global Investors/6.60%, Paul C. Reilly, Robert H. McNabb, Royce & Associates, LLC/5.00% (19 Owners included in Index)

*Financial Data: Fiscal Year End:*04/30   *Latest Annual Data:* 04/30/2007

Year		Sales		Net Income
2007		$689,201,000		$55,498,000
2006		$551,769,000		$59,430,000
2005		$476,377,000		$38,620,000
Curr. Assets:	$464,760,000	Curr. Liab.:	$229,489,000	P/E Ratio: 21.39
Plant, Equip.:	$25,999,000	Total Liab.:	$328,536,000	Indic. Yr. Divd.: NA
Total Assets:	$761,491,000	Net Worth:	$432,955,000	Debt/ Equity: NA

Kosan Biosciences Inc

3832 Bay Ctr. Pl., Hayward, CA, 94545; *PH:* 1-510-732-8400; *Fax:* 1-510-732-8401;
http:// www.kosan.com; *Email:* info@kosan.com

General - Incorporation	DE	Stock- Price on:12/24/2007	$5.96
Employees	82	Stock Exchange	NDQ
Auditor	Ernst & Young LLP	Ticker Symbol	KOSN
Stk Agt	Mellon Investor Services LLC	Outstanding Shares	42,520,000
Counsel	Wilson Sonsini Goodrich & Rosati	E.P.S.	-$0.6
DUNS No.	NA	Shareholders	NA

Business: The group's principle activity is to develop drug candidates from natural product compounds known as polyketides. Polyketides are naturally made in very small amounts in certain microorganisms and are difficult to make or modify chemically. The company develops polyketides for infectious diseases like gastrointestinal motility disorders, mucus hypersecretion, cancer, immunosuppression and nerve regeneration. The group has collaborative arrangements with hoffman-la roche, inc. And f. Hoffman-la roche ltd., johnson & johnson pharmaceutical research and development, llc, a subsidiary of ortho-mcneil pharmaceutical, inc. And several other research groups, including sloan-kettering institute for cancer research and the national cancer institute.The group operates from United States.

Primary SIC and add'l.: 8731 2834

CIK No: 0001110206

Officers: Robert G. Johnson/Dir., CEO, Pres./$786,205.00, Pieter B.M.W.M. Timmermans/Sr. VP - Drug Discovery, Preclinical Development/$422,098.00, Margaret A. Horn/58/Sr. VP - Legal, Corporate Development, General Counsel, Sec., Jane M. Green/VP - Corporate Communications, Robert De Jager/66/Sr. VP - Clinical Development, Chief Medical Officer, Gary S. Titus/Sr. VP, CFO/$186,093.00, Peter J. Licari/Sr. VP - Manufacturing, Operations/$408,270.00, Gary W. Ashley/VP - Exploratory Research, Kosan Fellow, Albert L. Kraus/VP - Regulatory Affairs

Directors: Robert G. Johnson/Dir., CEO, Pres., Peter Davis/Chmn., Jean Deleage/Dir., Kevan Clemens/Dir., Charles Homcy/Dir., Christopher Walsh/Dir., Chaitan Khosla/Dir., Bruce A. Chabner/Dir., Paul S. Anderson/Member - Scientific Advisory Board, Samuel J. Danishefsky/Member - Scientific Advisory Board, David A. Hopwood/Member - Scientific Advisory Board, Neal Rosen/Member - Scientific Advisory Board, Edward Sausville/Member - Scientific Advisory Board

Owners: Robert G. Johnson/1.30%, Charles J. Homcy, Bruce A. Chabner, OppenheimerFunds, Inc./7.70%, Gary S. Titus, Wellington Management Company, LLP/5.40%, Great Point Partners, LLC/6.40%, Peter J. Licari, Peter Davis, Chaitan S. Khosla/3.80%, Federated Investors, Inc./9.40%, Margaret A. Horn, Christopher T. Walsh, Daniel V. Santi/6.10%, Pieter B. Timmermans (18 Owners included in Index)

Financial Data: *Fiscal Year End:*12/31 *Latest Annual Data:* 12/31/2006

Year	Sales	Net Income
2006	$13,506,000	-$29,469,000
2005	$13,410,000	-$29,637,000
2004	$22,892,000	-$22,126,000

Curr. Assets:	$65,197,000	**Curr. Liab.:**	$22,935,000		
Plant, Equip.:	$4,801,000	**Total Liab.:**	$29,433,000	**Indic. Yr. Divd.:**	NA
Total Assets:	$71,187,000	**Net Worth:**	$41,754,000	**Debt/ Equity:**	0.0133

Koss Corp

4129 N Port Washington Ave., Milwaukee, WI, 53212; *PH:* 1-414-964-5000; *Fax:* 1-414-964-8615; *http://* www.koss.com; *Email:* customersupport@koss.com

General - Incorporation .... DE
Employees 115
Auditor .... Grant Thornton LLP
Stk Agt...... American Stock Transfer & Trust Co.
Counsel .... Hughes & Luce LLP
DUNS No. 00-128-6020

Stock- Price on:12/24/2007 .... $19.15
Stock Exchange .... NDQ
Ticker Symbol .... KOSS
Outstanding Shares 3,680,000
E.P.S $1.29
Shareholders .... NA

Business: The group's principle activities are to design, manufacture and sell stereo headphones and related accessory products in the audio/video industry segment of the home entertainment industry. The group's products are sold through audio specialty stores, catalog showrooms, regional department store chains, military exchanges and national retailers under the "Koss" name and dual label. Domestic sales representatives serve the group's international markets, which utilizes independent distributors. The group's products are marketed to approximately 2,000 customers worldwide. The group's total revenue for year 2007 was 46.20 millions of USD.

Primary SIC and add'l.: 3651

CIK No: 0000056701

Subsidiaries: Bi-Audio, Koss Classics

Owners: Koss Employee Stock Ownership Trust, Cheryl Mike, Sujata Sachdeva, Lenore E. Lillie, Koss Family Voting Trust, Royce and Associates, LLC, John Koss, Declan Hanley, Insiders, John C. Koss, Michael J. Koss, Theodore H. Nixon, John J. Stollenwerk

Financial Data: *Fiscal Year End:*06/30 *Latest Annual Data:* 06/30/2007

Year	Sales	Net Income
2007	$46,202,000	$5,157,000
2006	$50,892,000	$6,222,000
2005	$40,287,000	$4,494,000

Curr. Assets:	$23,870,000	**Curr. Liab.:**	$4,130,000	**P/E Ratio:**	14.40
Plant, Equip.:	$2,567,000	**Total Liab.:**	$5,244,000	**Indic. Yr. Divd.:**	$0.520
Total Assets:	$29,174,000	**Net Worth:**	$23,930,000	**Debt/ Equity:**	0.0054

Kraft Foods Inc

3 Lakes Dr., Northfield, IL, 60093; *PH:* 1-847-646-2000; *Fax:* 1-847-646-6005; *http://* www.kraft.com

General - Incorporation .... VA
Employees 90,000
Auditor .... PricewaterhouseCoopers LLP
Stk Agt.......... Wells Fargo Shareowner Services
Counsel .... Hunton & Williams LLP
DUNS No. .... NA

Stock- Price on:12/24/2007 .... $34.46
Stock Exchange .... NYSE
Ticker Symbol .... KFT
Outstanding Shares 1,600,000,000
E.P.S $1.63
Shareholders .... NA

Business: The group's principal activity is to manufacture and market packaged retail food products. It operates through its subsidiaries, kraft foods North America inc and kraft foods international inc. The group's brands span five consumer sectors: snacks, beverages, cheese, grocery and convenient meals. Products include cookies, crackers, confectionery, coffee, aseptic juice drinks, powdered beverages, natural, processed and cream cheese, ready-to-eat cereals, enhancers and desserts and convenient meals such as frozen pizza, packaged dinners, lunch combinations and processed meats. The group's main brands include kraft, jacobs, philadelphia, maxwell house, nabisco, oscar mayer and post. The group has operations in 68 countries with products sold in over 150 countries. On 29-Mar-2004, the group acquired veryfine products inc.

Primary SIC and add'l.: 2099 2022 2043 2095 2052 5147 2066

CIK No: 0001103982

Subsidiaries: 152999 CanadaInc., 3072440 Nova Scotia Company, AB Kraft Foods Lietuva, Aberdare DevelopmentsLtd., Aberdare Two DevelopmentsLtd., AGF Pack,Inc., AGF SP, Inc, Airco IHC,Inc., Ajinomoto General Foods,Inc., Alimentos Especiales, Sociedad Anonima, Balance Bar Company, Beijing Nabisco Food CompanyLtd., Boca Foods Company, Cafe Grand Mere S.A.S., Callard& Bowser-Suchard,Inc. 183 Subsidiaries included in the Index

Officers: Irene B. Rosenfeld/55/Chmn., CEO/$8,958,736.00, James P. Dollive/56/Exec. VP/$2,287,715.00, Karen J. May/Exec. VP - Global Human Resources, Perry Yeatman/VP - Global External Communications, Nancy Daigler/VP - Corporate, Government Affairs, Kraft North America Commercial, Laurie Guzzinati/Sr. Mgr. - Corporate, Government Affairs, United States, Renee Zahery/Sr. Dir. - Corporate, Government Affairs, United States, Elisabeth Wenner/Assoc. Dir. - Corporate, Government Affairs, United States, Jeri B. Finard/48/Exec. VP, Chief Marketing Officer, Richard G. Searer/Exec. VP, Pres. - North America Commercial/$2,865,918.00, Franz-Josef Vogelsang/Exec. VP - Global Supply Chain/$5,009,410.00, David Brearton/Exec. VP - Global Business Services, Strategy, Hugh H. Roberts/Exec. VP, Pres. - International Commercial/$4,107,164.00, Marc Firestone/Exec. VP - Corporate, Legal Affairs, General Counsel, Jean Spence/Exec. VP - Global Technology, Quality *(52 Officers included in Index)*

Directors: Irene B. Rosenfeld/55/Chmn., CEO, Louis C. Camilleri/Dir., John C. Pope/Dir., Mary L. Schapiro/Dir., Donna Hrinak/Dir. - Corporate, Government Affairs, Latin America Region, Ajay Banga/Dir., Jan Bennink/Dir., Richard A. Lerner/Dir., Deborah C. Wright/Dir.

Owners: Jan Bennink, Richard A. Lerner, Dinyar S. Devitre, Insiders, John C. Pope, Lord, Abbett & Co. LLC/7.40%, Franz-Josef Vogelsang, Deborah C. Wright, Irene B. Rosenfeld, Charles R. Wall, James P. Dollive, Mary L. Schapiro, Louis C. Camilleri, Richard G. Searer

Financial Data: *Fiscal Year End:*12/31 *Latest Annual Data:* 12/31/2006

Year	Sales	Net Income
2006	$34,356,000,000	$3,060,000,000
2005	$34,113,000,000	$2,632,000,000
2004	$32,168,000,000	$2,665,000,000

Curr. Assets:	$8,254,000,000	**Curr. Liab.:**	$10,473,000,000	**P/E Ratio:**	20.63
Plant, Equip.:	$9,693,000,000	**Total Liab.:**	$27,019,000,000	**Indic. Yr. Divd.:**	$1.080
Total Assets:	$55,574,000,000	**Net Worth:**	$28,555,000,000	**Debt/ Equity:**	0.2464

Kratos Defense & Security Solutions

Formerly: Wireless Facilities Inc
4810 Egate Mall, San Diego, CA, 92121; *PH:* 1-858-228-2000; *http://* www.wfinet.com

General - Incorporation .... DE
Employees 2,300
Auditor .... KPMG LLP
Stk Agt.......... Wells Fargo Shareowner Services
Counsel .... Morrison Foerster LLP
DUNS No. .... NA

Stock- Price on:12/24/2007 .... $1.7001
Stock Exchange .... NA
Ticker Symbol .... NA
Outstanding Shares 73,880,000
E.P.S .... -$0.15
Shareholders .... NA

Business: The group's principal activity is to provide outsource services for wireless carriers and equipment vendors. The services include project planning, design, deployment and management wireless telecommunication networks. The group also provides network management services, which involve day-to-day optimization and maintenance of wireless networks. The major customers include at&t wireless, bechtel, cingular, ericsson, nextel, siemens, triton pcs, telecorp pcs, telcel and verizon. The group's international operations are carried out in Europe, Middle East, Africa and Latin America. In 2003, the group acquired two privately held companies. On 06-Jan-2004, the group acquired high technology solutions, inc and defense systems inc on 04-Aug-2004.

Primary SIC and add'l.: 7379 7372 8742 4812

CIK No: 0001069258

Subsidiaries: Questus GmbH, Questus Ltd., Questus Scandinavia AB, WFI Asesoria En Administracion SC, WFI Asesoria En Telecommunicaciones SC, WFI de Mexico S. de R.L. de C.V., WFI FSC Inc., WFI India Pvt. Ltd., WFI Network Management Services Corp., WFI NMC Corp., Wfi Nmc Lp, WFI Scandinavia AB, WFI Services de Mexico S.A. de C.V., WFI Spain SL, WFI Telekomunikasyon Servis Ltd. 22 Subsidiaries included in the Index

Officers: Eric M. Demarco/Dir., CEO, Pres., Jim Edward/Sr. VP, General Counsel, Sec., Deanna Lund/Sr. VP, CFO, Laura L. Siegal/45/VP, Corporate Controller, Principal Accounting Officer, Robin Mickle/Pres., Claudia Angelone/Sr. VP, GM - Kratos Government Solutions, Inc, Sam Liberatore/Sr. VP, Eneral Mgr. - Kratos Government Solutions, Inc, Bob Stewart/Sr. VP, GM - Kratos Government Solutions, Inc, Jim Savage/Sr. VP - Business Development, Kratos Government Solutions, Inc, Fred Thomas/Sr. VP, GM - Kratos Defense, Security Solutions, Inc, Mike Matte/Sr. VP, GM - Kratos Defense, Security Solutions, Inc, Steve Cory/Sr. VP, GM - Kratos Defense, Security Solutions, Inc, Chris Caulson/VP - Finance, Kratos Defense, Security Solutions, Inc

Directors: Eric M. Demarco/Dir., CEO, Pres., Bandel Carano/Dir., William Hoglund/Dir., Scot Jarvis/Dir., Scott Anderson/Dir.

Owners: Scott I. Anderson, Insiders/22.69%, William A. Hoglund, Bandel L. Carano/7.46%, Scot B. Jarvis, Rowe T. Price/8.10%, Deanna Lund, Robin D. Mickle, ICMAssetManagement/5.02%, James R. Edwards, State of Wisconsin Investment Board/7.41%, Masood Tayebi/8.73%, Eric M. DeMarco/2.67%, Dariush G. Alipanah

Financial Data: *Fiscal Year End:*12/30 *Latest Annual Data:* 12/31/2005

Year	Sales	Net Income
2005	$375,300,000	$3,700,000
2004	$397,000,000	$5,000,000
2003	$261,000,000	$9,500,000

Curr. Assets:	$176,500,000	**Curr. Liab.:**	$102,800,000		
Plant, Equip.:	$14,600,000	**Total Liab.:**	$106,000,000	**Indic. Yr. Divd.:**	NA
Total Assets:	$336,300,000	**Net Worth:**	$230,300,000	**Debt/ Equity:**	0.0008

Kreido Biofuels Inc

1140 Ave.nida Acaso, Camarillo, CA, 93012; *PH:* 1-604-738-0540; *Fax:* 1-805-384-0989; *http://* www.kreido.com; *Email:* info@kreido.com

General - Incorporation .... NV
Employees 14
Auditor .... Vasquez & Co. LLP
Stk Agt............ Transfer Online, Inc.
Counsel .... NA
DUNS No. .... NA

Stock- Price on:12/24/2007 .... $0.9
Stock Exchange .... OTC
Ticker Symbol .... KRBF
Outstanding Shares 52,530,000
E.P.S .... -$0.09
Shareholders .... NA

Business: The groups principal activity is to manufacture chemicals and biodiesel. The product of the group is biodiesel. The group operates from the United States.

Primary SIC and add'l.: 2860

CIK No: 0001342219

Subsidiaries: Kreido Laboratories

Officers: Joel A. Balbien/53/Dir., CEO, Pres., Philip L. Lichtenberger/COO, Alan McGrevy/VP - Engineering, Denica Gordon/Public Relations Contact, Ina McGuinness/Investor Relations Contact, John Mills/Investor Relations Contact, Larry Sullivan/CTO, John Philpott/CFO

Directors: Joel A. Balbien/53/Dir., CEO, Pres., Betsy Wood Knapp/Chmn., G. A. Ben Binninger/59/Dir., David Mandel/Advisory Dir., Richard A. Redoglia/Dir., Murli Tolaney/Dir.

Owners: Ben Binninger, Insiders/12.00%, Larry Sullivan, Joel A. Balbien, Alan McGrevy/1.00%, Smart Technology Ventures and affiliates/27.80%, Betsy Wood Knapp/9.10%, John M. Philpott, David R. Fuchs/8.00%, David Mandel/7.10%, Wellington Management Company, LLP/17.70%, Philip Lichtenberger/1.30%

Financial Data: *Fiscal Year End:*09/30 *Latest Annual Data:* 12/31/2006

Year	Sales	Net Income
2006	NA	-$3,268,000

Curr. Assets:	$59,000	**Curr. Liab.:**	$6,984,000		
Plant, Equip.:	$322,000	**Total Liab.:**	$7,050,000	**Indic. Yr. Divd.:**	NA
Total Assets:	$1,190,000	**Net Worth:**	-$19,499,000	**Debt/ Equity:**	NA

Kreisler Manufacturing Corp

180 Van Riper Ave., Elmwood Park, NJ, 07407; *PH:* 1-201-791-0700; *Fax:* 1-201-791-8015; *http://* www.kreisler-ind.com; *Email:* kreisler@kreisler-ind.com

General - Incorporation .... DE
Employees 151
Auditor .... Gregory, Sharer & Stuart Pa
Stk Agt...... American Stock Transfer & Trust Co.
CounselBlank, Rome, Comisky & McCauley LLP
DUNS No. 00-131-9003

Stock- Price on:12/24/2007 .... $16.43
Stock Exchange .... NDQ
Ticker Symbol .... KRSL
Outstanding Shares 1,860,000
E.P.S $1.09
Shareholders .... NA

Business: The group's principal activities are manufacturing of precision metal components and assemblies for military and commercial aircraft engines and for industrial gas turbines. The products of the group include tube assemblies of multiple sizes and configuration, vane inserts and blade locks. The main function of the group's tubular products is to transport fluids, including air, oil and gas to various parts of the aircraft, aircraft engine and industrial gas turbine.

Primary SIC and add'l.: 3724 3728

CIK No: 0000056806

Subsidiaries: Kreisler Industrial Corporation, Kreisler Polska, Sp. z o.o.

Officers: Michael D. Stern/42/Dir., CEO, Co - Pres., Edward A. Stern/47/CFO, Co - Pres., Sec., Treasurer

Directors: Michael D. Stern/42/Dir., CEO, Co - Pres., Wallace N. Kelly/69/Chmn., Ronald L. Nussle/45/Dir., John W. Poling/63/Dir., Richard T. Swope/66/Dir.

Owners: Insiders/40.50%, Michael D. Stern/1.70%, Wallace N. Kelly/37.20%, Edward A. Stern/1.70%

Financial Data: *Fiscal Year End:*06/30 *Latest Annual Data:* 03/31/2007

Year	Sales	Net Income
2007	NA	NA
2006	$19,723,000	$1,163,000
2005	$14,448,000	$170,000

Curr. Assets:	$13,694,000	**Curr. Liab.:**	$2,415,000	**P/E Ratio:**	19.56
Plant, Equip.:	$2,425,000	**Total Liab.:**	$3,099,000	**Indic. Yr. Divd.:**	NA
Total Assets:	$16,243,000	**Net Worth:**	$13,143,000	**Debt/ Equity:**	NA

Krispy Kreme Doughnuts Inc

370 Knollwood St., Ste. 500, Winston-Salem, NC, 27102; *PH:* 1-336-725-2981; *Fax:* 1-336-733-3791; *http://* www.krispykreme.com

General - Incorporation	NC	**Stock**- Price on:12/24/2007	$8.5
Employees	3,875	Stock Exchange	NYSE
Auditor	PricewaterhouseCoopers LLP	Ticker Symbol	KKD
Stk Agt	Branch Banking & Trust Co	Outstanding Shares	64,750,000
Counsel	NA	E.P.S.	-$0.94
DUNS No.	NA	Shareholders	NA

Business: The groups principle activities include retailing and wholesaling doughnuts. The groups products marketed under the brand names Hot Original Glazed(TM). The group operates through three segments namely, company stores, franchisee and KKM&D. The group acquired Montana Mills in the year 2005 and Krispy Kreme Doughnut Corporation in the year 2006. The group operates 402 stores in the United States, Canada, Australia, Mexico, South Korea and the United Kingdom.The group's quarterly revenue for September 2007 was 103.36 millions of USD.

Primary SIC and add'l.: 5812 2051

CIK No: 0001100270

Subsidiaries: Gazed Investments, LLC, Golden Gate Doughnuts, LLC, HD Capital Corporation, HDN Development Corporation, Hot Doughnuts Now International Ltd., Java Joes Public Market Roastery, Inc., KK Canada Holdings, Inc., Krispy K Canada Company, Krispy Kreme Brand FundCorporation, Krispy Kreme Canada, Inc., Krispy Kreme Distributing Company, Incorporated, Krispy Kreme Doughnut Corporation, Krispy Kreme International Ltd., Krispy Kreme ManagementI, LLC, Krispy Kreme ManagementII, LLC 47 Subsidiaries included in the Index

Officers: Daryl G. Brewster/Dir., CEO, Pres./$2,647,838.00, Jeffrey L. Jervik/51/Exec. VP - Operations/$618,954.00, Douglas R. Muir/CFO, Exec. VP/$408,079.00, Kenneth J. Hudson/Sr. VP - Human Resources, Organizational Development, Krispy Kreme Doughnut Corporation, Stanley L. Parker/Sr. VP - Strategic Marketing, Krispy Kreme Doughnut Corporation, Bradley M. Wall/Sr. VP - Supply Chain, Krispy Kreme Doughnut Corporation, Jeffrey B. Welch/Sr. VP, GM - Global Franchise Operations, Development, Krispy Kreme Doughnut Corporation, Brian K. Little/Dir. - Corporate Communications, Sandra K. Michel/Exec. VP, General Counsel, Steven A. Lineberger/Sr. VP, GM - US Company Operations, Krispy Kreme Doughnut Corporation, Thomas C. McNeil/Sr. VP - Safety, Risk Management, Krispy Kreme Doughnut Corporation, Wesley M. Suttle/Sec.

Directors: Daryl G. Brewster/Dir., CEO, Pres., James H. Morgan/Chmn., Robert S. McCoy/Dir., Charles A. Blixt/Dir., Andrew J. Schindler/Dir., Michael H. Sutton/Dir., Lizanne Thomas/Dir., Togo D. West/Dir., Lynn Crump-Caine/Dir., Stephen C. Lynn/Dir.

Owners: Jefferies Asset Management, LLC/5.60%, Courage Capital Management, LLC/6.70%, Mohamed Abdulmohsin Al Kharafi & Sons W.L.L./9.50%, Schultze Master Fund, Ltd./5.70%, Morgan Stanley/5.20%

Financial Data: *Fiscal Year End:*01/29 *Latest Annual Data:* 10/29/2006

Year	Sales	Net Income
2006	$117,107,000	-$7,201,000

Curr. Assets:	$119,363,000	**Curr. Liab.:**	$117,635,000	**P/E Ratio:**	17.89
Plant, Equip.:	$309,214,000	**Total Liab.:**	$239,335,000	**Indic. Yr. Divd.:**	NA
Total Assets:	$480,278,000	**Net Worth:**	$240,943,000	**Debt/ Equity:**	NA

Kroger Co

1014 Vine St., Cincinnati, OH, 45202; *PH:* 1-513-762-4000; *Fax:* 1-513-762-1160; *http://* www.kroger.com; *Email:* kroger.investors@kroger.com

General - Incorporation	OH	**Stock**- Price on:12/24/2007	$30.09
Employees	310,000	Stock Exchange	NYSE
Auditor	PricewaterhouseCoopers LLP	Ticker Symbol	KR
Stk Agt	Bank of New York	Outstanding Shares	709,560,000
Counsel	NA	E.P.S.	$1.76
DUNS No.	00-699-9528	Shareholders	NA

Business: The group's principle activity is to operate grocery and multi-department, convenience and mall jewelry stores. The groups also distribute and merchandise food, pharmacy, health and personal care items, seasonal merchandise, and related products and services. The group operates from United States.

Primary SIC and add'l.: 5912 5411 5311 5944

CIK No: 0000056873

Subsidiaries: Agri-Products, Inc., Alpha Beta Company(Subsidiary of Food 4 Less of Southern California, Inc.), Americas Beverage Company, Bakers Supermarkets, Barclay Jewelers, Bay Area Warehouse Stores, Inc.(Subsidiary of Cala Co.), Bell Markets, Inc.(Subsidiary of Cala Co.), Bi-Lo Discount Foods, Bluefield Beverage Company, Cala Co.(Subsidiary of Ralphs Grocery Company), Cala Foods, Inc.(Subsidiary of Cala Co.), CB&S Advertising Agency, Inc.(Subsidiary of Fred Meyer Stores, Inc.), Chefs Choice Catering, City Market, Country Oven Bakery 141 Subsidiaries included in the Index

Officers: David B. Dillon/57/Chmn., CEO/$8,254,537.00, Lynn Marmer/55/Group VP - Corporate Affairs, Denise Thomas/Dir. - Corporate Supplier Diversity, Christopher T. Hjelm/46/CIO, Sr. VP, Elizabeth M. Van Oflen/50/VP, Controller, John Bays/Operating Unit Head - Dillon Stores, Donna Giordano/Operating Unit Head - QFC, Phyllis Norris/Operating Unit Head - City Marketing, Michael L. Ellis/Operating Unit Head - Fred Meyer Stores, Paul W. Heldman/56/Exec. VP, Sec., General Counsel, Donald E. Becker/59/Exec. VP/$3,251,364.00, William T. Boehm/60/Sr. VP, Pres. - Manufacturing, Paul J. Scutt/59/Sr. VP - Retail Operations, Michael J. Schlotman/50/CFO, Sr. VP/$1,859,658.00, Scott M. Henderson/52/VP, Treasurer *(44 Officers included in Index)*

Directors: David B. Dillon/57/Chmn., CEO, Rodney W. McMullen/47/Vice Chmn., John L. Clendenin/73/Dir., Robert D. Beyer/48/Dir., Steven R. Rogel/65/Dir., Bobby S. Shackouls/57/Dir., Reuben V. Anderson/65/Dir., Jorge P. Montoya/61/Dir., James A. Runde/61/Dir., Ronald L. Sargent/52/Dir., Katherine D. Ortega/73/Dir., Don W. McGeorge/53/Dir., COO, Pres., Susan M. Phillips/63/Dir., John T. Lamacchia/66/Dir., Clyde R. Moore/54/Dir. *(16 Directors included in Index)*

Owners: Steven R. Rogel, Rodney W. McMullen, Lord, Abbett & Co. LLC/6.50%, James A. Runde, Reuben V. Anderson, David B. Lewis, Clyde R. Moore, Ronald L. Sargent, David B. Dillon, Robert D. Beyer, Michael J. Schlotman, Donald E. Becker, Don W. McGeorge, Susan M. Phillips, John T. LaMacchia *(21 Owners included in Index)*

Financial Data: *Fiscal Year End:*01/28 *Latest Annual Data:* 2/3/2007

Year	Sales	Net Income
2007	$66,111,000,000	$1,115,000,000
2006	$60,553,000,000	$958,000,000
2005	$56,434,000,000	-$100,000,000

Curr. Assets:	$6,755,000,000	**Curr. Liab.:**	$7,581,000,000	**P/E Ratio:**	19.54
Plant, Equip.:	$11,779,000,000	**Total Liab.:**	$16,292,000,000	**Indic. Yr. Divd.:**	$0.300
Total Assets:	$21,215,000,000	**Net Worth:**	$4,923,000,000	**Debt/ Equity:**	NA

Kronos Advanced Technologies Inc

464 Common St., Ste. 301, Belmont, MA, 02478; *PH:* 1-617-993-9965; *http://* www.kronosati.com; *Email:* info@kronosati.com

General - Incorporation	NV	**Stock**- Price on:12/24/2007	$0.025
Employees	12	Stock Exchange	OTC
Auditor	Sherb & Co. LLP	Ticker Symbol	KNOS
Stk Agt	American Stock Transfer & Trust Co.	Outstanding Shares	242,340,000
Counsel	Kirkpatrick & Lockhart	E.P.S.	-$0.023
DUNS No.	NA	Shareholders	NA

Business: The group's principal activity is to develop and commercialize new, proprietary air movement and purification technology known as kronos (TM) devices. The product has the ability to provide silent, energy efficient, clean air to applications ranging from standalone consumer devices, to havoc systems, to industrial scrubbers. The group's activity is divided into six distinct market segments such as air movement and purification, air purification for unique spaces, specialized military, embedded cooling and cleaning, industrial scrubbing and hazardous gas destruction. Air movement and purification segments includes health care, hospitality, residential and commercial facilities. Air purification for unique spaces includes clean rooms, automotive, cruise ships and airplanes. Specialized military segment includes naval vessels, closed vehicles and environmental devices. Embedded cooling and cleaning includes electronic devices and medical equipment.

Primary SIC and add'l.: 3569

CIK No: 0001108248

Subsidiaries: Kronos Air Technologies, Inc.

Officers: Daniel R. Dwight/Dir., CEO, Pres., Richard F. Tusing/Dir., COO, Igor Krichtafovitch/CTO, Karl Winkler/VP - General Manger Engineering, Product Development

Directors: Daniel R. Dwight/Dir., CEO, Pres., Richard F. Tusing/Dir., COO, Charles D. Strang/Member - Advisory Board, William Poster/Member - Advisory Board, M. J. Segal/Dir., James P. McDermott/Dir.

Owners: James P. McDermott, Daniel R. Dwight, AirWorks Funding LLLP, Hilltop Holding LP, Richard F. Tusing, Milton M. Segal, Insiders

Financial Data: *Fiscal Year End:*06/30 *Latest Annual Data:* 6/30/2006

Year	Sales	Net Income
2006	$219,000	-$4,000,000
2005	$430,000	-$7,094,000
2004	$533,000	-$2,495,000

Curr. Assets:	$381,000	**Curr. Liab.:**	$1,589,000		
Plant, Equip.:	$7,000	**Total Liab.:**	$1,823,000	**Indic. Yr. Divd.:**	NA
Total Assets:	$2,111,000	**Net Worth:**	$287,000	**Debt/ Equity:**	NA

Kronos Worldwide Inc

5430 LBJ Fwy., Ste. 1700, Dallas, TX, 75240; *PH:* 1-972-233-1700; *Fax:* 1-972-448-1445; *http://* www.kronostio2.com

General - Incorporation	DE	**Stock**- Price on:12/24/2007	$27.78
Employees	2,450	Stock Exchange	NYSE
Auditor	PricewaterhouseCoopers LLP	Ticker Symbol	KRO
Stk Agt	Deutsche Bank Luxembourg S.A.	Outstanding Shares	48,950,000
Counsel	NA	E.P.S.	$1.62
DUNS No.	NA	Shareholders	NA

Business: The group's principle activity is to produce and market tio2 - titanium dioxide pigments that are used for imparting whiteness, brightness and opacity to a range of products including paints, plastics, paper fibers and ceramics. The group produces over 40 different tio2 grades, which is sold under kronos trademark. Tio2 is produced in two forms : rutile and anatase. Rutile tio2 is used in plastics, coatings and inks. Anatase tio2 is used in paper, ceramics, rubber and man-made fibers. The group's manufacturing facilities are located in United States, Germany, Canada, Belgium, Norway and Europe. The group is also engaged in the mining and sale of ilmenite. The group is also engaged in the manufacture and sales of iron-based water treatment chemicals used as conditioning agents for industrial effluents and in the manufacture of iron pigments. The group's quarterly revenue for September 2007 was 343.30 millions of USD.

Primary SIC and add'l.: 2819 2816 1479

CIK No: 0001257640

Officers: Harold C. Simmons/76/Chmn., CEO, Gregory M. Swalwell/51/CFO, VP - Finance, Robert D. Graham/52/VP, General Counsel, Kelly D. Luttmer/44/VP, Dir. - Tax, Douglas C. Weaver/66/Sr. VP - Development, Ulfert Fiand/59/Pres. - Manufacturing, Technology, Joseph H. Maas/56/Pres. - Sales, Marketing, John A. St Wrba/51/VP, Treasurer, Tim C. Hafer/46/VP, Controller

Directors: Harold C. Simmons/76/Chmn., CEO, Steven L. Watson/57/Vice Chmn., Gerald R. Turner/62/Dir., George E. Poston/72/Dir., Keith R. Coogan/55/Dir., Cecil H. Moore/68/Dir., Glenn R. Simmons/80/Dir.

Owners: Insiders/95.10%, TIMET Finance Management Company, Cecil H. Moore, Valhi, Inc./59.20%, Steven L. Watson, NL Industries, Inc/35.80%, George E. Poston, Harold C. Simmons, Glenn R. Simmons, Gerald R. Turner, Keith R. Coogan, Annette C. Simmons

Financial Data: *Fiscal Year End:*12/31 *Latest Annual Data:* 12/31/2006

Year	Sales	Net Income
2006	$1,279,447,000	$81,969,000
2005	$1,196,729,000	$71,006,000
2004	$1,128,600,000	$314,853,000

Curr. Assets:	$562,889,000	**Curr. Liab.:**	$179,457,000	**P/E Ratio:**	17.15
Plant, Equip.:	$462,003,000	**Total Liab.:**	$973,076,000	**Indic. Yr. Divd.:**	$1.000
Total Assets:	$1,421,516,000	**Net Worth:**	$448,399,000	**Debt/ Equity:**	1.2517

KSW Inc

37-16 23rd St., Long Island City, NY, 11101; *PH:* 1-718-361-6500

General		**Stock**	
Incorporation	DE	Price on:12/24/2007	$7.16
Employees	45	Stock Exchange	NDQ
Auditor	Marden, Harrison & Kreuter P.C	Ticker Symbol	KSW
Stk Agt	Depository Trust Co	Outstanding Shares	6,130,000
Counsel	Weil, Gotshal & Manges LLP	E.P.S	$0.54
DUNS No.	82-489-8118	Shareholders	NA

Business: The group's principal activities are to furnish and install heating, ventilating and air conditioning systems and processing piping systems. The operations of the group are carried out through its wholly owned subsidiary, ksw mechanical services inc. The equipments furnished are catered for institutional, industrial, commercial, high-rise residential and public works projects. The group provides these contracting services primarily in the state of New York. The group also serves as a mechanical trade manager, performing project management services relating to the mechanical trades. The major customers of the group are bovis lend lease inc, glenwood management corporation and newmark construction services llc and related entities.

Primary SIC and add'l.: 8711 8742 8748

CIK No: 0001004125

Subsidiaries: KSW Mechanical Services, Inc.

Owners: Richard W. Lucas, Insiders/15.90%, Nicusa Capital Partners, LP/6.70%, Innis O Rourke, Floyd Warkol/14.60%, Vincent Terraferma, Microcapital LLC/6.50%, Allen & Company/5.10%, John Cavanagh, Stanley Kreitman

Financial Data: *Fiscal Year End:*12/31 *Latest Annual Data:* 12/31/2006

Year	Sales	Net Income
2006	$77,128,000	$2,765,000
2005	$53,378,000	$2,711,000
2004	$26,281,000	-$1,280,000

Curr. Assets:	$34,783,000	**Curr. Liab.:**	$22,422,000	**P/E Ratio:**	13.51
Plant, Equip.:	$256,000	**Total Liab.:**	$22,422,000	**Indic. Yr. Divd.:**	$1.960
Total Assets:	$35,545,000	**Net Worth:**	$13,123,000	**Debt/ Equity:**	NA

KT Corp

206 Jung Ta Dong Bunn Dong Gu, Sungnam, Gyunggi-do, 463711; *PH:* 82-25207800;
http:// www.kt.co.kr

General		**Stock**	
Incorporation	Korea	Price on:12/24/2007	$23.98
Employees	43,970	Stock Exchange	NYSE
Auditor	KPMG Samjong Accounting Corp	Ticker Symbol	KTC
Stk Agt	Kookmin Bank	Outstanding Shares	NA
Counsel	NA	E.P.S	$2.82
DUNS No.	68-783-4424	Shareholders	NA

Business: The group's principal activities is the provision of wired telecommunication services such as Internet, telegram/telex, local service, domestic long distance and customer service charter.

Primary SIC and add'l.: 4822 7359 3661 4812 4813

CIK No: 0000892450

Subsidiaries: Korea Telecom America, Inc., Korea Telecom Japan Co., Ltd., Korea Telecom Philippines, Inc., KT China Co., Ltd., KT Commerce Inc., KT Freetel Co., Ltd., KT Hitel Co., Ltd., KT Internal Venture Fund No.1, KT Internal Venture Fund No.2, KT Linkus Co., Ltd., KT Networks Corporation, KT Powertel Co. Ltd., KT Submarine Co., Ltd., KT Telecom Venture Fund No.1, KTF Technologies Inc. 17 Subsidiaries included in the Index

Officers: Joong Soo Nam/CEO, Pres., Dong-Hoon Han/48/VP - Technology Support Business Unit, Tae-Yol Yoo/48/VP - Management Research Laboratory, Seok-Kuen Oh/46/VP - Corporate Relations Support Office, Ouk-Jung Hwang/53/VP - Real Assets Management Office, Yi Ki-Won/Contact - Overseas Information Technology Business Department, Shin Hyeon-Deuk/Contact - Global Business Department, Ahn Ki-Hwan/Contact - Overseas Investment Strategy Department, Gil-Joo Lee/52/VP - Public Relations Office, Yoon-Hak Bang/50/VP - Network Technology Laboratory, Kil-Ho Song/55/VP - Future Technology Laboratory, Tae-Poong Kang/53/VP - Metropolitan North Regional Business Unit, Gwang-Ju Seo/51/Sr. VP - Network Group, Dong-Myun Lee/45/VP - BcN Business Unit, Sang-Heon Song/49/VP - Chungbuk Regional Business Unit *(74 Officers included in Index)*

Directors: Jeong-Ro Yoon/53/Dir., Kook-Hyun Moon/59/Dir., Jong-Kyoo Yoon/52/Dir., Paul Chang Yi/41/Dir., Thae-Surn Khwarg/49/Dir., Do-Hwan Kim/49/Dir., Jong-Lok Yoon/50/Standing Dir., Sr. Exec. VP, Kon-Sik Kim/53/Dir., Stuart B. Solomon/58/Dir., Jeong-Soo Suh/50/Dir., Exec. VP

Owners: Insiders/100.00%, NTT DoCoMo Inc/10.31%, Microsoft Corp./1.04%, Others/34.20%, Qualcomm Incorporated/2.26%, KT Corporation/52.19%

Financial Data: *Fiscal Year End:*12/31 *Latest Annual Data:* 12/31/2006

Year	Sales	Net Income
2006	$15,496,512,000	$1,462,277,000
2005	$12,327,563,000	$1,148,534,000
2004	$17,068,371,000	$1,404,616,000

Curr. Assets:	$6,578,429,000	**Curr. Liab.:**	$5,964,297,000	**P/E Ratio:**	10.12
Plant, Equip.:	$16,352,951,000	**Total Liab.:**	$17,403,073,000	**Indic. Yr. Divd.:**	NA
Total Assets:	$26,244,865,000	**Net Worth:**	$8,841,792,000	**Debt/ Equity:**	NA

Kubota Corp

3401 Del Amo Blvd, Torrance, CA, 90503; *PH:* 1-310-370-3370; *Fax:* 1-310-370-2370;
http:// www.kubota.co.jp

General		**Stock**	
Incorporation	Japan	Price on:12/24/2007	$41.5032
Employees	NA	Stock Exchange	NYSE
Auditor	Deloitte Touche Tohmatsu	Ticker Symbol	KUB
Stk Agt	Chuo Mitsui Trust & Banking Co Ltd	Outstanding Shares	258,300,000
Counsel	NA	E.P.S	$2.66
DUNS No.	69-055-5149	Shareholders	NA

Business: The group's principal activity is manufacturing internal combustion engines and machinery, including farm equipment, construction machinery and industrial products. The group operates in the following five segments: internal combustion engines and machinery; industrial products and engineering, environmental engineering, building materials and housing and others.

Primary SIC and add'l.: 3259 3498 3519 3523 3589

CIK No: 0000109821

Subsidiaries: Kubota Baumaschinen GmbH, Kubota Construction Co., Ltd., Kubota Credit Co., Ltd., Kubota Credit Corporation, U.S.A., Kubota Engine America Corporation, Kubota Environmental Service Co., Ltd., Kubota Europe S.A.S., Kubota Maison Co., Ltd., Kubota Manufacturing of America Corporation, Kubota Metal Corporation, Kubota Tractor Corporation, Kubota-C.I. Co., Ltd.

Officers: Toshihiro Fukuda/Exec. MD, Eisaku Shinohara/MD, Morimitsu Katayama/Dir., MD, Nobuyuki Toshikuni/Dir., MD, Yuzuru Mizuno/Dir., Corporate Auditor, Moriya Hayashi/Representative Dir., Exec. VP, Masanobu Wakabayashi/Dir., Corporate Auditor, Junichi Maeda/Dir., Corporate Auditor, Yoshio Suekawa/Dir., Corporate Auditor, Yasuo Masumoto/Exec. MD, Yoshiharu Nishiguchi/Dir., Corporate Auditors, Daisuke Hatakake/Representative Dir., Pres., Kazunobu Ueta/Dir., MD, Yoshihiko Tabata/Dir., MD, Hirokazu Nara/Dir., Principal Financial Officer, MD

Directors: Morimitsu Katayama/Dir., MD, Nobuyuki Toshikuni/Dir., MD, Yuzuru Mizuno/Dir., Corporate Auditor, Moriya Hayashi/Representative Dir., Exec. VP, Nobuyo Shioji/Dir., Takeshi Torigoe/Dir., Satoru Sakamoto/Dir., Hideki Iwabu/Dir., Kohkichi Uji/Dir., Toshihiro Kubo/Dir., Kenshiro Ogawa/Dir., Masanobu Wakabayashi/Dir., Corporate Auditor, Takashi Yoshii/Dir., Junichi Maeda/Dir., Corporate Auditor, Yoshio Suekawa/Dir., Corporate Auditor *(24 Directors included in Index)*

Owners: Trust& Custody Services Bank, Ltd./1.90%, Japan Trustee Services Bank, Ltd./8.03%, Sumitomo Mitsui Banking Corporation/3.48%, The Dai-ichi Mutual Life Insurance Company/3.66%, The Chase Manhattan Bank N.A. London/3.11%, Mizuho Corporate Bank, Ltd./3.16%, Nippon Life Insurance Company/6.86%, The Master Trust Bank of Japan, Ltd./7.97%, Mizuho Bank, Ltd./2.19%, Insiders/0.00%, Meiji Yasuda Life Insurance Company/5.12%

Financial Data: *Fiscal Year End:*03/31 *Latest Annual Data:* 3/31/2006

Year	Sales	Net Income
2006	$8,983,248,000	$692,598,000
2005	$9,189,028,000	$1,101,879,000
2004	$8,775,821,000	$110,377,000

Curr. Assets:	$6,480,547,000	**Curr. Liab.:**	$4,414,000,000	**P/E Ratio:**	10.12
Plant, Equip.:	$1,934,804,000	**Total Liab.:**	$6,828,359,000	**Indic. Yr. Divd.:**	$0.260
Total Assets:	$12,011,983,000	**Net Worth:**	$5,183,624,000	**Debt/ Equity:**	NA

Kuhlman Co Inc

Formerly: Gaming Venture Corp USA
701 N Third St., Ste. B-1, Minneapolis, MN, 55401; *PH:* 1-612-338-5752;
http:// www.gamingventurecorp.com

General		**Stock**	
Incorporation	NV	Price on:12/24/2007	NA
Employees	NA	Stock Exchange	NA
Auditor	Schechter Dokken Kanter	Ticker Symbol	NA
Stk Agt	Florida Atlantic Stock Transfer, Inc.	Outstanding Shares	NA
Counsel	NA	E.P.S	NA
DUNS No.	NA	Shareholders	NA

Business: The groups principle activity is to provide mens and womens shirts, pants and accessories. The group's products sold under the brand name Kuhlman. The group operates from United States.

Primary SIC and add'l.: NA

CIK No: 0001219641

Subsidiaries: A3 LLC, SK2, Inc.

Officers: Alan Woinski/Chmn., CEO, Pres., Kim Santangelo-Woinski/VP, Dir. - Gaming USA

Directors: Alan Woinski/Chmn., CEO, Pres., Kim Santangelo-Woinski/VP, Dir. - Gaming USA

Owners: Susan Kuhlman/10.60%, Charles Walensky/1.20%, Insiders/11.40%, David Ferris, Greg Griffith, Jon Sabes/12.80%, Jon Gangelhoff/1.10%, Scott J. Kuhlman/10.60%, Chris Larson, Luis A. Padilla/2.40%

Kuhlman Company Inc

701 N 3rd St. Ste. B1, Minneapolis, MN, 55401; *PH:* 1-612-338-5752;
http:// www.kuhlmancompany.com

General		**Stock**	
Incorporation	NV	Price on:12/24/2007	NA
Employees	NA	Stock Exchange	OTC
Auditor	Schechter Dokken Kanter	Ticker Symbol	KUHM
Stk Agt	Florida Atlantic Stock Transfer, Inc.	Outstanding Shares	NA
Counsel	NA	E.P.S	NA
DUNS No.	NA	Shareholders	NA

Business: The groups principle activity is to provide apparel and accessories. The group markets its products under the brand name Kuhlman. The group operates from the United States.

Primary SIC and add'l.: 5651

CIK No: 0001219641

Subsidiaries: A3 LLC, SK2, Inc

Owners: Greg Griffith, Luis A. Padilla/2.40%, Jon Sabes/12.80%, Chris Larson, Jon Gangelhoff/1.10%, Charles Walensky/1.20%, David Ferris, Insiders/11.40%, Scott J. Kuhlman/10.60%

Curr. Assets:	$6,447,000	**Curr. Liab.:**	$5,254,000		
Plant, Equip.:	$2,311,000	**Total Liab.:**	$5,531,000	**Indic. Yr. Divd.:**	NA
Total Assets:	$9,073,000	**Net Worth:**	$3,542,000	**Debt/ Equity:**	NA

Kulicke & Soffa Industries Inc

1005 Virginia Dr., Fort Washington, PA, 19034; **PH:** 1-215-784-6000; **Fax:** 1-215-784-6001; **http://** www.kns.com; **Email:** investors@kns.com

General - Incorporation ... PA
Employees ... 2,454
Auditor ... PricewaterhouseCoopers LLP
Stk Agt... American Stock Transfer & Trust Co.
Counsel ... Drinker Biddle & Reath LLP
DUNS No. ... 00-235-1203

Stock- Price on:12/24/2007 ... $10.95
Stock Exchange ... NDQ
Ticker Symbol ... KLIC
Outstanding Shares ... 57,820,000
E.P.S ... $0.47
Shareholders ... NA

Business: The group's principal activity is to design, manufacture and market capital equipment, packaging materials and test interconnect solutions and services. The group manufactures a line of bonding wire and wire bonders that are used on an integrated circuit package. It also manufactures fixtures that are used for connecting automatic test equipment to the semiconductor device under test during wafer fabrication. The group's flip chip business unit licenses its flip chip technology and provides flip chip bumping and wafer level packaging services. The group caters to the companies that manufacture and assemble semiconductor devices. Major customers include advanced micro devices, advanced semiconductor engineering, chippac, general dynamics and other semiconductor manufacturers that primarily operate in the Asia/pacific.

Primary SIC and add'l.: 3565 3559 3674

CIK No: 0000056978

Subsidiaries: AFWH Sub, Inc., American Fine Wire Corporation Alabama, American Fine Wire, Limited Cayman Islands, Dr. Muller Feindraht AG Switzerland, Flip Chip Technologies, LLC Delaware, Flip ChipTechnologies, LLC, K&S Interconnect, Inc. Delaware, Kulicke & Soffa (Asia) Limited Hong Kong, Kulicke & Soffa Singapore, Inc. Delaware, Kulicke and Soffa (Israel) Ltd. Israel, Kulicke and Soffa (Japan) Ltd. Japan and Delaware, Kulicke and Soffa (Suzhou) Limited China, Kulicke and Soffa AG Switzerland, Kulicke and Soffa Investments, Inc. Delaware, Kulicke and Soffa Pte, Limited Singapore 17 Subsidiaries included in the Index

Officers: Scott C. Kulicke/Chmn., CEO/$1,430,051.00, Christian Rheault/VP - Equipment Segment, David Anderson/VP, General Counsel, Mike Lutz/VP, Chief Human Resources Officer, Maurice Carson/CFO/$823,893.00, Charles Salmons/Sr. VP/$735,792.00, Jack G. Belani/Sr. VP - Wire Bonding, Corporate Marketing/$667,228.00, Bruce Griffing/VP - Engineering/$492,063.00, Shay Torton/VP - WW Operations

Directors: Scott C. Kulicke/Chmn., CEO, Brian R. Bachman/Dir., Macdonell Roehm/Dir., William C. Zadel/Dir., John A. O'Steen/Dir., Garrett E. Pierce/Dir., Barry Waite/Dir.

Owners: Jagdish Belani, Brian R. Bachman, Maurice E. Carson, Bruce Griffing, Insiders/4.50%, Garrett E. Pierce, MacDonell Roehm, Barry Waite, William C. Zadel, Charles Salmons, John A. OSteen, Scott C. Kulicke/2.60%

Financial Data: ***Fiscal Year End:***09/30 ***Latest Annual Data:*** 9/30/2006

Year	Sales	Net Income
2006	$696,311,000	$52,170,000
2005	$561,274,000	-$104,082,000
2004	$717,811,000	$55,880,000

Curr. Assets:	$344,068,000	**Curr. Liab.:**	$95,090,000	**P/E Ratio:**	23.30
Plant, Equip.:	$28,487,000	**Total Liab.:**	$326,195,000	**Indic. Yr. Divd.:**	NA
Total Assets:	$405,501,000	**Net Worth:**	$79,306,000	**Debt/ Equity:**	NA

KVH Industries Inc

50 Enterprise Ctr., Middletown, RI, 02842; **PH:** 1-401-847-3327; **Fax:** 1-401-849-0045; **http://** www.kvh.com

General - Incorporation ... DE
Employees ... 311
Auditor ... KPMG LLP
Stk Agt... EquiServe Trust Co N.A
Counsel ... NA
DUNS No. ... 09-320-7215

Stock- Price on:12/24/2007 ... $9
Stock Exchange ... NDQ
Ticker Symbol ... KVHI
Outstanding Shares ... 15,000,000
E.P.S ... $0.11
Shareholders ... NA

Business: The group's principal activities are to develop, manufacture and market satellite communications products for the automotive, recreational vehicle and marine markets, and navigation, guidance and stabilization products for defense markets. The products enable customers to receive live digital television, telephone and Internet services in their automobiles, recreational vehicles and marine vessels while in motion. The defense products include tactical navigation systems that provide uninterrupted navigation and pointing information in a broad range of military vehicles, including humvees and light armored vehicles. The group also offer precision fiber optic gyro-based systems that help stabilize platforms such as gun turrets and radar units and also provide guidance for munitions. The proucts of the group are tacnav(tm),tracvision(R) and tracphone(r). The products are sold in the United States, Canada and European countries.

Primary SIC and add'l.: 3812 4810 3660 3663

CIK No: 0001007587

Subsidiaries: KVH Europe A/S

Officers: Martin A. Kits Van Heyningen/Chmn., CEO, Pres./$631,894.00, Daniel R. Conway/VP - Business Development, Patrick J. Spratt/CFO/$420,294.00, Robert W.B. Kits Van Heyningen/Dir., VP - Research, Development/$289,145.00, Jeffrey Brunner/VP - Operations, Military, Fiber Optic Products, Ian C. Palmer/Exec. VP - Satellite Sales/$300,488.00, Robert Balog/VP - Engineering, Satellite Products/$339,831.00, James S. Dodez/VP - Marketing, Strategic Planning, Kalyan Ganesan/VP - Engineering, Defense Products, Arent H. Kits Van Heyningen/Chief Scientist/$284,785.00, Mads E. Bjerre-Petersen/MD - KVH Europe A, S, Jeffrey Greer/VP - Operations, Satellite Products

Directors: Martin A. Kits Van Heyningen/Chmn., CEO, Pres., Charles R. Trimble/Dir., Bruce J. Ryan/Dir., Robert W.B. Kits Van Heyningen/Dir., VP - Research, Development, Stanley K. Honey/Dir., Mark S. Ain/Dir.

Owners: State of Wisconsin Investment Board/7.20%, Charles R. Trimble, Stanley K. Honey, Insiders/11.00%, Royce & Associates, LLC/11.90%, Ian C. Palmer, Systematic Financial Management, L.P./8.70%, Robert W.B. Kits van Heyningen, Mark S. Ain, Arent H. Kits van Heyningen/3.80%, Cortina Asset Management, LLC/6.80%, Martin A. Kits van Heyningen/2.40%, Patrick J. Spratt, Arbor Capital Management, LLC/6.30%, Bruce J. Ryan *(16 Owners included in Index)*

Financial Data: ***Fiscal Year End:***12/31 ***Latest Annual Data:*** 12/31/2006

Year	Sales	Net Income
2006	$78,973,000	$3,675,000
2005	$71,258,000	$2,931,000
2004	$62,303,000	-$6,147,000

Curr. Assets:	$75,367,000	**Curr. Liab.:**	$8,244,000	**P/E Ratio:**	60.00
Plant, Equip.:	$9,569,000	**Total Liab.:**	$10,629,000	**Indic. Yr. Divd.:**	NA
Total Assets:	$88,424,000	**Net Worth:**	$77,795,000	**Debt/ Equity:**	0.0277

Kyocera Corp

8611 Balboa Ave., San Diego, CA, 92123; **PH:** 1-858-576-2600; **Fax:** 1-858-492-1456; **http://** www.kyocera.co.jp

General - Incorporation ... Japan
Employees ... 61,468
Auditor ... Misuzu Pricewaterhousecoopers
Stk Agt ... Daiko Clearing Services Corp
Counsel ... NA
DUNS No. ... 69-055-7624

Stock- Price on:12/24/2007 ... $103.74
Stock Exchange ... NYSE
Ticker Symbol ... KYO
Outstanding Shares ... NA
E.P.S ... $5.01
Shareholders ... NA

Business: The group's principal activities are the manufacture and marketing of electronic components, semiconductor parts and telecommunications equipment. The group's activities are carried out through four divisions: fine ceramics group, electronic device group, equipment group and other. Fine ceramics group contains fine ceramic parts, semiconductor parts, cutting tools, jewelry, solar energy products and applied ceramic products. The electronic device group contains electronic components and thin-film products. The equipment group consists of telecommunications equipment, information equipment and optical instruments. The other consist of telecommunication network systems, financial services such as leasing, credit financing, office rental services and other services.

Primary SIC and add'l.: 3699 5043 3827 7389 3670 4899

CIK No: 0000057083

Subsidiaries: AVX Corporation, Kyocera Leasing Co., Ltd

Officers: Makoto Kawamura/Pres.

Directors: Noboru Nakamura/Chmn., Kazuo Inamori/Founder, Chmn. Emeritus

Owners: Kazuo Inamori/3.56%, State Street Bank and Trust Company/4.15%, Mitsubishi UFJ Financial Group, Inc./5.53%, Japan Trustee Services Bank, Ltd./1.63%, The Bank of Tokyo-Mitsubishi UFJ, Ltd./2.65%, BNP Paribas Securities (Japan) Limited/1.90%, The Inamori Foundation/2.45%, Japan Trustee Services Bank, Ltd./5.79%, The Bank of Kyoto, Ltd./3.77%, KI Enterprise Co., Ltd./1.86%, The Master Trust Bank of Japan, Ltd./5.70%

Financial Data: ***Fiscal Year End:***03/31 ***Latest Annual Data:*** 03/31/2007

Year	Sales	Net Income
2007	$10,880,483,000	$902,576,000
2006	$10,098,197,000	$595,692,000
2005	$11,034,159,000	$429,047,000

Curr. Assets:	$8,868,568,000	**Curr. Liab.:**	$2,594,814,000	**P/E Ratio:**	10.12
Plant, Equip.:	$2,380,559,000	**Total Liab.:**	$5,219,525,000	**Indic. Yr. Divd.:**	$0.790
Total Assets:	$18,054,780,000	**Net Worth:**	$12,835,255,000	**Debt/ Equity:**	NA

Kyphon Inc

1221 Crossman Ave., Sunnyvale, CA, 94089; **PH:** 1-408-548-6500; **Fax:** 1-408-548-6501; **http://** www.kyphon.com

General - Incorporation ... DE
Employees ... 1,090
Auditor ... PricewaterhouseCoopers LLP
Stk Agt ... U.S. Stock Transfer Corp
Counsel ... NA
DUNS No. ... NA

Stock- Price on:12/24/2007 ... $47.98
Stock Exchange ... NDQ
Ticker Symbol ... KYPH
Outstanding Shares ... 45,560,000
E.P.S ... $0.19
Shareholders ... NA

Business: The group's principal activity is to develop medical devices to restore spinal anatomy using minimally invasive technology. The group's products include bone access systems, inflatable bone tamp, inflation syringe, bone filler device, bone biopsy device and curette. The group's products are primarily used by surgeons to repair compression fractures of the spine caused by osteoporosis and cancer. The group markets its instruments to physicians who perform spine surgery, including orthopedic spine surgeons and neurosurgeons in the United States, Europe, South Korea and China. As of 31-Dec-2003, the group has trained 3,900 physicians in the use of its kyphx instruments and these physicians have used these instruments in over 60,000 spine surgeries. The group acquired sanatis gmbh in feb 2003.

Primary SIC and add'l.: 3842 3841

CIK No: 0001123313

Subsidiaries: Kyphon Australia Pty Ltd, Kyphon Austria GmbH, Kyphon Canada Inc., Kyphon Cayman Ltd., Kyphon Deutschland GmbH, Kyphon Europe B.V.B.A., Kyphon France SARL, Kyphon Iberica S.L., Kyphon Ireland Ltd., Kyphon Ireland Research Holding Ltd., Kyphon Italia S.R.L., Kyphon Nippon K.K., Kyphon UK Ltd., Sanatis GmbH

Officers: Richard W. Mott/49/Dir., CEO, Pres./$3,050,298.00, Arthur T. Taylor/51/COO, VP, CFO, Treasurer/$1,478,712.00, Robert A. Vandervelde/45/Pres. - International, David M. Shaw/41/VP - Legal Affairs, General Counsel, Sec./$1,175,414.00, Bradley W. Paddock/34/VP - US Sales, Karen D. Talmadge/55/Dir., Exec. VP, Co - Founder, Chief Science Officer, Maureen L. Lamb/46/CFO, VP, Treasurer/$319,975.00

Directors: Richard W. Mott/49/Dir., CEO, Pres., James T. Treace/62/Dir., Elizabeth H. Weatherman/48/Dir., Karen D. Talmadge/55/Dir., Exec. VP, Co - Founder, Chief Science Officer, Louis J. Lavigne/59/Dir., Frank M. Phillips/47/Dir.

Financial Data: ***Fiscal Year End:***12/31 ***Latest Annual Data:*** 12/31/2006

Year	Sales	Net Income
2006	$407,790,000	$39,732,000
2005	$306,082,000	$29,836,000
2004	$213,414,000	$21,717,000

Curr. Assets:	$301,473,000	**Curr. Liab.:**	$73,427,000	**P/E Ratio:**	252.53
Plant, Equip.:	$27,590,000	**Total Liab.:**	$83,906,000	**Indic. Yr. Divd.:**	NA
Total Assets:	$428,606,000	**Net Worth:**	$344,700,000	**Debt/ Equity:**	1.5016

Kyto BioPharma Inc

41A Ave. Rd., York Sq., Toronto, ON, M5R 2G3; ; **http://** www.kytobiopharma.com

General - Incorporation ... FL
Employees ... NA
Auditor ... Jewett, Schwartz & Associates
Stk Agt ... OTC Stock Transfer, Inc.
Counsel ... NA
DUNS No. ... NA

Stock- Price on:12/24/2007 ... $0.4
Stock Exchange ... OTC
Ticker Symbol ... KBPH
Outstanding Shares ... NA
E.P.S ... NA
Shareholders ... NA

Business: The groups principal activity is to develop potential targeted biologic treatment including cytotoxic drugs to cancer cells, therapeutic effect of vitamin B12 depletion by receptor modulators and monoclonal antibodies to block the vitamin B12 uptake by cancer. The group operates from the United States and Canada.

Primary SIC and add'l.: 2834

CIK No: 0001164888

Subsidiaries: B Twelve Limited

Officers: Georges Benarroch/Dir., CEO, Acting CFO, Pres., Uri Sagman/Dir. - Special Consultant, Robert Graziano/Assoc. - Project Team, Kenneth P. Pritzker/Assoc. - Project Team, Edward Quadros/Assoc. - Project Team

Directors: Georges Benarroch/Dir., CEO, Acting CFO, Pres., Uri Sagman/Dir. - Special Consultant, Jean-Luc Berger/Dir., Donald MacAdam/Dir.

Owners: Don MacAdam/0.30%, Jean-Luc Berger/4.40%, Credifinance Capital Corp./73.60%, Delaware, United States Medarex Inc./10.80%, Georges Benarroch/0.30%, Uri Sagman/7.50%

Financial Data: *Fiscal Year End:*03/31 *Latest Annual Data:* 03/31/2007

Year	Sales	Net Income
2007	NA	-$4,149,000
2006	NA	-$3,535,000
2005	NA	-$1,964,000

Curr. Assets:	$41,000	**Curr. Liab.:**	$273,000		
Plant, Equip.:	$0	**Total Liab.:**	$273,000	**Indic. Yr. Divd.:**	NA
Total Assets:	$41,000	**Net Worth:**	-$231,000	**Debt/ Equity:**	NA

L Q Corp Inc

888 Seventh Ave., New York, NY, 10019; *PH:* 1-212-974-5730

General - Incorporation	DE	**Stock**- Price on:12/24/2007	$0.95
Employees	23	Stock Exchange	NA
Auditor	Rothstein, Kass & Co, P.C	Ticker Symbol	NA
Stk Agt	Mellon Investor Services LLC	Outstanding Shares	3,210,000
Counsel	NA	E.P.S	-$0.51
DUNS No.	NA	Shareholders	NA

Business: The group's principal activity is to provide an open platform that enables the digital delivery of music over the Internet. The software products and services of the group gives artists, record companies, Web-sites and retailers, the ability to create, syndicate and sell recorded music with copy protection and copyright management. The group's main products and services are liquifier pro, encoding services, liquid server, liquid hosting services, liquid music network, kiosks, liquid player, liquid muze previews and liquid promotions. The major customers of the group are cyber music entertainment and liquid audio greater China.

Primary SIC and add'l.: 7379 7372 7389

CIK No: 0001016613

Subsidiaries: SES Resources International,, Inc, Sielox, LLC

Officers: Sebastian Cassetta/Dir., CEO, Pres., Melvyn Brunt/63/CFO, Sec.

Directors: Sebastian Cassetta/Dir., CEO, Pres., Steven Berns/42/Chmn., Stephen Liguori/50/Dir., Michael A. McManus/63/Dir., Dianne McKeever/Dir.

Owners: Sebastian E. Cassetta, James Mitarotonda/11.03%, Insiders/12.53%, Lloyd I. Miller/12.00%, Jay Gottlieb/8.44%, Rory J. Cowan, Barington Capital Group, L.P./11.03%, Raymond Steele, Melvyn Brunt

Financial Data: *Fiscal Year End:*12/31 *Latest Annual Data:* 12/31/2006

Year	Sales	Net Income
2006	$6,399,000	-$1,914,000
2005	NA	-$757,000
2004	NA	-$847,000

Curr. Assets:	$4,113,000	**Curr. Liab.:**	$1,518,000		
Plant, Equip.:	$237,000	**Total Liab.:**	$1,559,000	**Indic. Yr. Divd.:**	NA
Total Assets:	$5,296,000	**Net Worth:**	$3,737,000	**Debt/ Equity:**	0.0105

L-3 Communications Holdings Inc

600 3rd Ave., New York, NY, 10016; *PH:* 1-212-697-1111; *Fax:* 1-212-867-5249; *http://* www.l-3com.com

General - Incorporation	DE	**Stock**- Price on:12/24/2007	$99.46
Employees	63,700	Stock Exchange	NYSE
Auditor	PricewaterhouseCoopers LLP	Ticker Symbol	LLL
Stk Agt	First Chicago Trust	Outstanding Shares	125,150,000
Counsel	NA	E.P.S	$5.46
DUNS No.	00-889-8843	Shareholders	NA

Business: The group's principle activity is to provide communication systems, aviation products and support services. The group operates through four segments namely command, control, communications, intelligence, surveillance and reconnaissance. In the year 2007, the group acquired Geneva Aerospace, Inc. The group operates from United States.

Primary SIC and add'l.: 3669 3812 3663 9999 3728

CIK No: 0001056239

Subsidiaries: 6292151 Canada Inc., Apcom, Inc., Aydin Foreign Sales Limited, Broadcast Sports Inc., D.P. Associates Inc., Datron / Trans World Communications Intl. Ltd., ELAC Nautik Unterstützungskae GmbH, Electrodynamics, Inc., Electronic Space Systems International Corp., EuroAtlas Gesellschaft fr Leistungselektronik mbH, Henschel Inc., Horizons Technology International, Ltd., Hygienetics Environmental Services, Inc., Intelligence Data Systems, Inc., Interstate Electronics Corporation 106 Subsidiaries included in the Index

Officers: Michael T. Strianese/Dir., CEO, Pres./$3,693,950.00, Kenneth R. Goldstein/62/VP - Tax Counsel, David T. Butler/Sr. VP - Business Operations, Carl E. Vuono/Sr. VP, Pres. - L, 3 Services Group/$5,985,173.00, John S. Mega/VP, Pres. - Microwave Group, Charles J. Schafer/Sr. VP, Pres. - Products Group, R. L. Denino/VP - Procurement, Stephen M. Souza/VP, Treasurer, Michael A. Andrews/CTO, VP, Jill J. Wittels/VP - Business Development, Christopher C. Cambria/Sr. VP - Sr. Counsel Mergers, Acquisitions, Steve Kantor/VP, Pres. - Power, Control Systems Group, David M. Reilly/VP, Assist. Sec., Assist. General Counsel, Cynthia Swain/VP - Corporate Communications, Ralph G. D'Ambrosio/CFO, VP *(133 Officers included in Index)*

Directors: Michael T. Strianese/Dir., CEO, Pres., Robert B. Millard/57/Non - Exec. Chmn., Peter A. Cohen/61/Dir., Arthur L. Simon/76/Dir., John M. Shalikashvili/71/Dir., John P. White/71/Dir., Thomas A. Corcoran/63/Dir., Alan H. Washkowitz/67/Dir., Claude R. Canizares/62/Dir.

Owners: Thomas A. Corcoran, Robert B. Millard, James W. Dunn, Michael T. Strianese, Alan H. Washkowitz, Clearbridge Advisors, LLC/11.60%, John M. Shalikashvili, Claude R. Canizares, John P. White, Insiders/1.10%, Carl E. Vuono, Robert W. Drewes, Arthur L. Simon, Peter A. Cohen

Financial Data: *Fiscal Year End:*12/31 *Latest Annual Data:* 12/31/2006

Year	Sales	Net Income
2006	$12,476,900,000	$526,100,000
2005	$9,444,700,000	$508,500,000
2004	$6,896,997,000	$381,880,000

Curr. Assets:	$3,929,800,000	**Curr. Liab.:**	$2,376,400,000	**P/E Ratio:**	18.22
Plant, Equip.:	$736,100,000	**Total Liab.:**	$7,896,500,000	**Indic. Yr. Divd.:**	$1.000
Total Assets:	$13,286,700,000	**Net Worth:**	$5,305,900,000	**Debt/ Equity:**	0.8606

L. B. Foster Co

415 Holiday Dr., Pittsburgh, PA, 15220; *PH:* 1-412-928-3417; *Fax:* 1-412-928-7891; *http://* www.lbfoster.com; *Email:* investors@lbfosterco.com

General - Incorporation	PA	**Stock**- Price on:12/24/2007	$26.81
Employees	665	Stock Exchange	NDQ
Auditor	Ernst & Young LLP	Ticker Symbol	FSTR
Stk Agt	American Stock Transfer & Trust Co.	Outstanding Shares	10,570,000
Counsel	NA	E.P.S	$1.52
DUNS No.	00-439-2619	Shareholders	NA

Business: The group's principal activities are to manufacture, fabricate and distribute products that serve the nation's surface transportation infrastructure. The group classifies its activities into three segments: rail products, construction products and tubular products. The rail products include heavy and light rail, relay rail, concrete ties, insulated rail joints, rail accessories and transit products. The construction products consist of sheet, pipe and bearing piling, fabricated highway products, and precast concrete buildings. The tubular products of the group include fusion bond and other coatings for corrosion protection on oil, gas and other pipelines. In 2003, the group disposed of all the assets of rail signaling and communication device business.

Primary SIC and add'l.: 3353 3312 3531

CIK No: 0000352825

Subsidiaries: Foster Technologies

Officers: Stan L. Hasselbusch/Dir., CEO, Pres./$873,978.00, David L. Voltz/VP, General Counsel, Sec., Tim Chiasson/Operations Mgr., Gregory W. Lippard/VP - Rail Product Sales, Donald L. Foster/Sr. VP - Construction Products Piling Products/$406,500.00, Merry L. Brumbaugh/VP - Tubular Products, Linda K. Patterson/Controller, David J. Russo/CFO, Sr. VP, Treasurer/$403,865.00, John F. Kasel/Sr. VP - Operations, Manufacturing/$417,304.00, Samuel K. Fisher/Sr. VP - Rail Products/$327,278.00, Brian H. Kelly/VP - Human Resources, Michelle Chapin/Customer Service Mgr., Beth Kotsenas/Customer Service Representative, Brad Porter/Customer Service Representative, Sidney A. Shue/GM - Engineered Products *(75 Officers included in Index)*

Directors: Stan L. Hasselbusch/Dir., CEO, Pres., Lee B. Foster/Chmn., Diane B. Owen/52/Dir., William H. Rackoff/59/Dir., John W. Puth/79/Dir., Henry J. Massman/45/Dir., Thomas G. McKane/64/Dir.

Owners: Lee B. Foster/3.01%, Stan L. Hasselbusch/2.17%, Tontine Management, L.L.C., Tontine Partners, L.P./6.42%, Keely Asset Management Corp./16.00%, David J. Russo, Diane B. Owen, Keely Small Cap Fund/8.78%, John W. Puth, Henry J. Massman, Insiders/8.50%, Donald L. Foster, William H. Rackoff, Thomas G. McKane, John F. Kasel, Jeffrey L. Gendell/12.59% *(16 Owners included in Index)*

Financial Data: *Fiscal Year End:*12/31 *Latest Annual Data:* 12/31/2006

Year	Sales	Net Income
2006	$389,788,000	$13,530,000
2005	$353,484,000	$5,434,000
2004	$297,866,000	$1,480,000

Curr. Assets:	$167,284,000	**Curr. Liab.:**	$75,822,000	**P/E Ratio:**	22.91
Plant, Equip.:	$49,919,000	**Total Liab.:**	$137,800,000	**Indic. Yr. Divd.:**	NA
Total Assets:	$235,833,000	**Net Worth:**	$98,033,000	**Debt/ Equity:**	NA

L.S. Starrett Co (The)

L. S Starrett Company Limited, Oxnam Rd., Jedburgh, TD8 6LR; *PH:* 440-1835-863501; *Fax:* 440-1835-863018; *http://* www.starrett.co.uk

General - Incorporation	MA	**Stock**- Price on:12/24/2007	$17.42
Employees	2,129	Stock Exchange	NYSE
Auditor	Deloitte & Touche LLP	Ticker Symbol	SCX
Stk Agt	Mellon Investor Services LLC	Outstanding Shares	6,620,000
Counsel	Ropes & Gray LLP	E.P.S	$1.32
DUNS No.	00-112-5681	Shareholders	NA

Business: The group's principal activities are to manufacture and market hand measuring tools and precision equipment. The products of the group include precision tools, tape measures, levels, electronic gages, dial indicators, gage blocks, digital readout measuring tools, granite surface plates, optical measuring projectors, coordinate measuring machines, vises, m1 lubricant, hacksaw blades, hole saws, band saw blades, jig saw blades, reciprocating saw blades, and precision ground flat stock. The customers of the group include metalworking industry, automotive, aviation, marine and farm equipment shops, builders, carpenters, plumbers and electricians. The group operates in the United States, Canada, Scotland, Brazil, China, Mexico and Australia.

Primary SIC and add'l.: 3545 3553 3999 3829

CIK No: 0000093676

Subsidiaries: E-r Rule Company Of Puerto Rico, Inc., Evans Rule Company, Inc, Evans Rule Company, Inc., L.s.starrett Co. Of The Dominican Republic, Starrett (new Zealand) Limited, Starrett Gmbh, Starrett Industria E Commercio Ltd, Starrett Precision Optical Limited, Starrett Securities Corporation, Starrett Tools (Shanghai) Co. Ltd (warehouse And Distribution), Starrett Tools (Suzhou) Co. Ltd (saw And Tool Mfg), Taylor Investments, Inc., The L. S. Starrett Co. Of Canada Limited, The L. S. Starrett Company, The L. S. Starrett Company Limited 17 Subsidiaries included in the Index

Officers: Douglas A. Starrett/56/Dir., CEO, Pres./$413,021.00, Stephen F. Walsh/62/Dir., Sr. VP - Operations/$212,606.00, Randall J. Hylek/CFO, Treasurer/$168,242.00, Anthony M. Aspin/55/VP - Sales/$162,761.00

Directors: Douglas A. Starrett/56/Dir., CEO, Pres., Antony McLaughlin/79/Dir., Terry A. Piper/63/Dir., Ralph G. Lawrence/65/Dir., Richard B. Kennedy/65/Dir., Stephen F. Walsh/62/Dir., Sr. VP - Operations, Robert L. Montgomery/70/Dir.

Owners: Ralph G. Lawrence, Robert L. Montgomery, Stephen F. Walsh, Insiders, Richard B. Kennedy, Antony McLaughlin, Anthony M. Aspin, Anthony M. Aspin, Terry A. Piper, Douglas A. Starrett/4.59%, Stephen F. Walsh, Insiders/5.09%, Randall J. Hylek, Douglas A. Starrett

Financial Data: Fiscal Year End:06/25 Latest Annual Data: 6/24/2006

Year	Sales	Net Income
2006	$200,916,000	-$3,782,000
2005	$195,909,000	$4,029,000
2004	$179,996,000	-$2,352,000

Curr. Assets:	$122,751,000	Curr. Liab.:	$22,682,000	P/E Ratio: 56.19
Plant, Equip.:	$62,859,000	Total Liab.:	$56,641,000	Indic. Yr. Divd.: $0.400
Total Assets:	$218,924,000	Net Worth:	$162,283,000	Debt/ Equity: NA

La Jolla Pharmaceutical Co

6455 Nancy Ridge Dr., San Diego, CA, 92121; **PH:** 1-858-452-6600; **Fax:** 1-858-626-2851; http:// www.ljpc.com

General - Incorporation	DE	Stock - Price on:12/24/2007	$4.49
Employees	84	Stock Exchange	NDQ
Auditor	Ernst & Young LLP	Ticker Symbol	LJPC
Stk Agt	American Stock Transfer & Trust Co.	Outstanding Shares	39,540,000
Counsel	Goodwin Procter LLP	E.P.S.	-$1.37
DUNS No.	61-354-1192	Shareholders	NA

Business: The group's principal activity is to conduct research and development of therapeutics for the treatment of certain life-threatening antibody-mediated diseases. The diseases include autoimmune conditions such as systemic lupus erythematosus and antibody-mediated stroke that are caused by abnormal b cell production of antibodies that attach healthy tissues. The current therapies for these autoimmune disorders target the symptoms of the diseases or nonspecifically suppress the normal operation of the immune system. The group's strategy is to collaborate with pharmaceutical companies to access their research, drug development, manufacturing, marketing and financial resources.

Primary SIC and add'l.: 8731 2834

CIK No: 0000920465

Subsidiaries: La Jolla Limited

Officers: Deirdre Y. Gillespie/Dir., CEO, Pres./$1,263,681.00, Michael Tansey/Chief Medical Officer, Exec. VP, Lisa Koch Hulle/VP - Regulatory Affairs, Luke Seikkula/VP - Manufacturing, Andrew Wiseman/Sr. Dir. - Investor Relations, Matthew D. Linnik/Chief Scientific Officer, Exec. VP/$950,048.00, Gail A. Sloan/VP - Finance, Sec./$571,713.00, Josefina T. Elchico/VP - Quality Operations/$486,443.00, Niv E. Caviar/Exec. VP, Chief Business, Financial Officer, Peter Potgieter/VP, Medical Dir., Vickie Motte/Sr. Dir. - Human Resources

Directors: Deirdre Y. Gillespie/Dir., CEO, Pres., Craig R. Smith/Chmn., Stephen M. Martin/Dir., Thomas H. Adams/Dir., Robert A. Fildes/Dir., James N. Topper/Dir., Frank E. Young/76/Dir., Martin Sutter/Dir., Nader J. Naini/Dir.

Owners: Craig R. Smith, Robert A. Fildes, Essex Woodlands Health Ventures Fund VI LP, Frazier Healthcare V L.P, Theodora Reilly, James N. Topper, Alejandro Gonzalez, Josefina T. Elchico, Stephen M. Martin, Steven Engle, Paul C. Jenn, Bruce K. Bennett, Martin P. Sutter, Thomas H. Adams, Nader J. Naini (20 Owners included in Index)

Financial Data: Fiscal Year End:12/31 Latest Annual Data: 12/31/2006

Year	Sales	Net Income
2006	NA	-$39,445,000
2005	NA	-$27,363,000
2004	NA	-$40,544,000

Curr. Assets:	$43,913,000	Curr. Liab.:	$6,240,000	
Plant, Equip.:	$2,333,000	Total Liab.:	$6,436,000	Indic. Yr. Divd.: NA
Total Assets:	$49,525,000	Net Worth:	$43,089,000	Debt/ Equity: 0.0053

La Quinta Corp

909 Hidden Ridge, Ste. 600, Irving, TX, 75038; **PH:** 1-214-492-6600; http:// www.laquinta.com

General - Incorporation	DE	Stock - Price on:12/24/2007	NA
Employees	NA	Stock Exchange	NA
Auditor	Ernst & Young LLP	Ticker Symbol	NA
Stk Agt.	EquiServe Trust Co N.A	Outstanding Shares	NA
Counsel	Goodwin, Procter & Hoar	E.P.S.	NA
DUNS No.	03-718-5329	Shareholders	NA

Business: The group's principal activity is to own and operate hotels. The group design hotels that attract both business and leisure travellers. The group operates in two segments: lodging and all other. The lodging segment represents a network of owned and franchised hotels operated under the la quinta inn and la quinta inn & suites trademarks. The all other segment represents the remaining assets of our healthcare real estate financing business. As of 31-Dec-2003, the group owned and operated 276 hotels, 36,000 rooms in 28 states. The hotels are concentrated in the western and southern regions of the United States. The group conducts its business in ten markets that include Dallas/ft worth, houston, san antonio, denver, austin, new orleans, phoenix, miami/ft lauderdale, orlando and atlanta. The group operates and manages hotel properties that it leases from its controlled subsidiary, lq properties inc.

Primary SIC and add'l.: 7011

CIK No: 0000313749

Subsidiaries: Baymont Franchising LLC, Baymont Licensing Corporation, Baymont Management Services LLC, Baymont Properties LLC, Budgetel Franchising LLC, Budgetel Inns LLC, Budgetel Licensing Corporation, La Quinta Arlington Beverage Services, Inc., La Quinta Beverage Services, Inc., La Quinta Development Partners, L.P., La Quinta Franchise, LLC, La Quinta Franchising LLC, La Quinta Inns de Mexico S.A. de C.V., La Quinta Inns, Inc., La Quinta Investments, Inc. 47 Subsidiaries included in the Index

Officers: Wayne B. Goldberg/CEO, Pres., Angelo J. Lombardi/COO, Exec. VP, Robert M. Harshbarger/CFO, Exec. VP, Julie M. Cary/Exec. VP, Chief Marketing Officer, Murry J. Cathlina/Exec. VP - Design, Construction, Mark M. Chloupek/Exec. VP - Legal, General Counsel, Feliz P. Jarvis/Exec. VP - Sales, Jeffrey M. Schagren/Exec. VP - Human Resources, Corporate Counsel, Rajiv K. Trivedi/Exec. VP - Franchising, Temple H. Weiss/Exec. VP - Acquisitions, Development, Teresa Ferguson/Dir. - Communications, Public Relations

La Z Boy Inc

1284 N Telegraph Rd., Monroe, MI, 48162; **PH:** 1-734-242-1444; **Fax:** 1-734-457-2005; http:// www.lazyboy.com; **Email:** investorrelations@la-z-boy.com

General - Incorporation	MI	Stock - Price on:12/24/2007	$11.99
Employees	13,404	Stock Exchange	NYSE
Auditor	PricewaterhouseCoopers LLP	Ticker Symbol	LZB
Stk Agt	American Stock Transfer & Trust Co.	Outstanding Shares	51,370,000
Counsel	NA	E.P.S.	-$0.37
DUNS No.	00-504-2841	Shareholders	NA

Business: The groups principle activity is to produce residential furniture for the hospitality, health care and assisted-living industries. The groups products include reclining chairs and upholstered furniture. The group operates from United States.

Primary SIC and add'l.: 2521 2512 2599 2511

CIK No: 0000057131

Subsidiaries: Alexvale Furniture, Inc., American Furniture Company, Incorporated, Bauhaus U.S.A., Inc., Centurion Furniture plc, Clayton-Marcus Company, Inc., England, Inc., Kincaid Furniture Company, Incorporated, La-Z-Boy (Thailand) Ltd., La-Z-Boy Canada Limited, La-Z-Boy Europe B.V., La-Z-Boy Germany GmbH, La-Z-Boy Global Limited, La-Z-Boy Greensboro, Inc., La-Z-Boy Import Sourcing, Inc., La-Z-Boy Logistics, Inc. 39 Subsidiaries included in the Index

Officers: Kurt L. Darrow/53/Dir., CEO, Pres./$1,343,791.00, Rodney D. England/Sr. VP, Pres. - Non Branded Upholstered Product/$696,171.00, Steven M. Kincaid/Sr. VP, Pres. - Casegoods Product/$704,095.00, Louis M. Riccio/CFO, Sr. VP/$430,603.00, Otis S. Sawyer/Sr. VP - Corporate Operations/$430,616.00

Directors: Kurt L. Darrow/53/Dir., CEO, Pres., James W. Johnston/69/Chmn., Jack L. Thompson/69/Dir., David K. Hehl/61/Dir., Rocque E. Lipford/69/Dir., John H. Foss/65/Dir., Richard M. Gabrys/66/Dir., Nido R. Qubein/59/Dir., George H. Levy/58/Dir., Alan W. McCollough/58/Dir.

Owners: Otis S. Sawyer, Royce& Associates, LLC/7.90%, Steven M. Kincaid, Patrick H. Norton, W. Alan McCollough, FMR Corp. and related person/14.90%, Jack L. Thompson, David K. Hehl, Kurt L. Darrow, John H. Foss, James W. Johnston/2.80%, Rodney D. England, Louis M. Riccio, David M. Risley, H. George Levy (23 Owners included in Index)

Financial Data: Fiscal Year End:04/30 Latest Annual Data: 04/28/2007

Year	Sales	Net Income
2007	$1,617,302,000	$4,139,000
2006	$1,916,777,000	-$3,041,000
2005	$2,048,381,000	$37,185,000

Curr. Assets:	$638,365,000	Curr. Liab.:	$228,724,000	
Plant, Equip.:	$210,565,000	Total Liab.:	$499,071,000	Indic. Yr. Divd.: $0.480
Total Assets:	$1,026,357,000	Net Worth:	$527,286,000	Debt/ Equity: NA

Labarge Inc

9900 Clayton Rd., St. Louis, MO, 63124; **PH:** 1-314-997-0800; **Fax:** 1-314-812-9438; http:// www.labarge.com

General - Incorporation	DE	Stock - Price on:12/24/2007	$12.39
Employees	1,200	Stock Exchange	AMEX
Auditor	KPMG LLP	Ticker Symbol	LB
Stk Agt	Registrar & Transfer Co	Outstanding Shares	15,300,000
Counsel	NA	E.P.S.	$0.713
DUNS No.	00-721-7805	Shareholders	NA

Business: The group's principal activities are to manufacture and design high-performance electronics and interconnect systems for customers in diverse technology-driven markets. It also designs and markets proprietary cellular and network communication systems products and Internet services. These are used in monitoring and controlling of remote industrial equipment. The group through its manufacturing services group designs and manufactures high performance electronics, electro-mechanical assemblies and interconnect systems for specialized applications. The group's engineering and manufacturing facilities are located in Arkansas, Missouri, Oklahoma and Texas. The group's major three customers are l-3 communications, schlumberger and lockheed martin. The group's main trademark is scadanet network. It serves the customers in the defense, aerospace, oil and gas, railroad and other commercial markets. On 18-Feb-2004, the group acquired pinnacle electronics llc.

Primary SIC and add'l.: 3812 3674

CIK No: 0000057139

Subsidiaries: LaBarge Electronics, Inc., LaBarge Properties, Inc., LaBarge-OCS, Inc., LaBarge/STC, Inc.

Officers: Craig E. Labarge/Dir., CEO, Pres., Terry Geisz/GM - Joplin, Missouri, Craig McCartney/Plant Mgr. - Berryville, Arkansas, Teresa K. Huber/VP - Operations, Pittsburgh, Pennsylvania, John R. Parmley/VP - Sales, Marketing Joplin, Missouri, William Bitner/VP - Operations, Tulsa, Oklahoma, Melanie Keenan/Dir. - Finance, Administration, Pittsburgh, Pennsylvania, Gregg Mozdy/Dir. - Business Development, Pittsburgh, Pennsylvania, Weems Turner/GM - Houston, Texas, Robert Mihalco/Dir. - Human Resources, Ron Falk/GM - Tulsa, Oklahoma, Scott Gustafson/GM - Pittsburgh, Pennsylvania, Donald Nonnenkamp/VP, CFO - St. Louis, Missouri, Jim Key/Dir. - Supply Chain Management, Tulsa, Oklahoma, Rick Parmley/VP - Sales, Marketing, Joplin, Missouri (21 Officers included in Index)

Directors: Craig E. Labarge/Dir., CEO, Pres., Robert G. Clark/Dir., Jack E. Thomas/Dir., Thomas A. Corcoran/Dir., John G. Helmkamp/Dir., Lawrence J. Legrand/Dir.

Owners: Insiders/26.90%, Lawrence J. LeGrand/7.10%, Robert G. Clark, Thomas A. Corcoran, Jack E. Thomas, Donald H. Nonnenkamp/3.20%, Craig E. LaBarge/12.40%, Randy L. Buschling/2.30%, Leo V. Garvin/7.10%, John G. Helmkamp/2.10%, Sanfurd G. Bluestein/9.50%, John R. Parmley/1.30%, Wentworth Hauser & Violich, Inc./5.00%, Teresa K. Huber, Joanne V. Lockard/7.10%

Financial Data: Fiscal Year End:07/03 Latest Annual Data: 7/2/2006

Year	Sales	Net Income
2006	$190,089,000	$9,708,000
2005	$182,294,000	$10,870,000
2004	$131,510,000	$6,869,000

Curr. Assets:	$67,894,000	Curr. Liab.:	$39,902,000	P/E Ratio: 17.70
Plant, Equip.:	$18,849,000	Total Liab.:	$66,107,000	Indic. Yr. Divd.: NA
Total Assets:	$119,937,000	Net Worth:	$53,830,000	Debt/ Equity: NA

Labopharm Inc

480 Armand-Frappier Blvd., Laval, QC, H7V 4B4; **PH:** 1-450-686-1017; http:// www.labopharm.com; **Email:** info@labopharm.com

General - Incorporation AB
Employees NA
Auditor NA
Stk Agt Computershare Trust Co
Counsel NA
DUNS No. NA

Stock- Price on:12/24/2007 $3.3101
Stock Exchange NDQ
Ticker Symbol DDSS
Outstanding Shares 56,780,000
E.P.S -$0.6
Shareholders NA

Business: The groups principal activity is to provide pharmaceutical product. The products of the group include Tramadol, Betahistine, DDS-2001 and Trazodone. The group products sold under the trade name Contramid(R). The group operates from the United States and Europe.

Primary SIC and add'l.: 2834

CIK No: 0001284519

Subsidiaries: Kearny Federal Savings Bank, Labopharm (Barbados) Limited, Labopharm Cyprus Limited, Labopharm Europe Limited

Officers: James R. Howard -Tripp/Dir., CEO, Pres., Sylvie Bouchard/VP - Clinical Development, Regulatory Affairs, Lynda Covello/General Counsel, Corp. Sec., Damon Smith/VP - Research, Development, Mark D'Souza/CFO, Jason Hogan/Media Contact, Uwe Erbrich/VP - Global Quality Assurance, Mary Anne Heino/VP - Sales, Marketing

Directors: James R. Howard -Tripp/Dir., CEO, Pres., Santo J. Costa/Chmn., Richard J. MacKay/Dir., Julia Brown/Dir., Anthony C. Playle/Dir., Frederic Porte/Dir., Jacques Roy/Dir., James S. Scibetta/Dir., Lawrence E. Posner/Dir.

Owners: James R. Howard-Tripp, Anthony C. Playle, James S. Scibetta, Frdric Porte, Richard J. MacKay

Financial Data: *Fiscal Year End:*12/31 *Latest Annual Data:* 12/31/2006

Year	Sales	Net Income
2006	$13,621,000	-$20,442,000

Curr. Assets:	$2,863,000	**Curr. Liab.:**	$2,987,000		
Plant, Equip.:	$188,000	**Total Liab.:**	$37,649,000	**Indic. Yr. Divd.:**	NA
Total Assets:	$5,410,000	**Net Worth:**	$3,725,000	**Debt/ Equity:**	NA

Labor Ready Inc

1015 A St., Tacoma, WA, 98402; *PH:* 1-253-383-9101; *http://* www.laborready.com

General - Incorporation WA
Employees 3,500
Auditor PricewaterhouseCoopers LLP
Stk Agt ComputerShare Trust Co
Counsel Preston Gates & Ellis
DUNS No. 14-440-6014

Stock- Price on:12/24/2007 $22.72
Stock Exchange NYSE
Ticker Symbol LRW
Outstanding Shares 46,420,000
E.P.S $1.52
Shareholders NA

Business: The group's principal activity is to provide temporary workers for manual labor jobs. The customers of the group consist of businesses in freight handling, warehousing, landscaping, construction and light manufacturing industries. These businesses typically require workers for lifting, hauling, cleaning, assembling, digging, painting and other types of manual or unskilled work. The group provides services through 779 dispatch offices located in the United States, Canada, the United Kingdom and Puerto Rico. On 05-Apr-2004, the group acquired spartan staffing, inc.

Primary SIC and add'l.: 7363 7361

CIK No: 0000768899

Subsidiaries: CLP Holdings Corp, CLP Resources, Inc., Contractors Labor Pool, Inc., Labor Ready Asset Acquisition Sub., Inc., Labor Ready Assurance Co., Labor Ready Central II, LLC, Labor Ready Central III, LP, Labor Ready Central, Inc., Labor Ready Franchise Development Corp. Inc., Labor Ready Funding Corporation, Labor Ready GP Co., Inc., Labor Ready Holdings, Inc., Labor Ready Leasing, Inc., Labor Ready Mid-Atlantic, Inc., Labor Ready Midwest, Inc. 26 Subsidiaries included in the Index

Officers: Steven C. Cooper/Dir., CEO, Robert P. Breen/43/VP - Strategic Planning, Financial Analysis, Derrek Gafford/CFO/$546,852.00, Billie R. Otto/41/CIO, VP, Chris Burger/Regional VP - Operations/$471,320.00, Jim E. Defebaugh/VP, General Counsel/$539,765.00, Wayne Larkin/Regional VP - Operations/$477,704.00, Richard L. Mercuri/61/VP - Human Resources, Organizational Development/$504,904.00, Edward B. Nubel/57/VP - Sales, Marketing

Directors: Steven C. Cooper/Dir., CEO, Robert J. Sullivan/Chmn., Craig Tall/Dir., Thomas E. McChesney/Dir., Joseph P. Sambataro/Dir., Keith D. Grinstein/Dir., William W. Steele/Dir., Gates McKibbin/Dir.

Owners: Derrek L. Gafford, Craig E. Tall, Wayne W. Larkin, Richard L. Mercuri, Robert J. Sullivan, Barclays Global Investors, NA./5.17%, Royce & Associates, LLC/5.64%, Noel S. Wheeler, Steven C. Cooper, Insiders/1.80%, Joseph P. Sambataro, Putnam, LLC./5.00%, Thomas E. McChesney, Keith D. Grinstein, William W. Steele *(18 Owners included in Index)*

Financial Data: *Fiscal Year End:*12/30 *Latest Annual Data:* 12/29/2006

Year	Sales	Net Income
2006	$1,349,118,000	$76,472,000
2005	$1,236,070,000	$62,021,000
2004	$1,044,236,000	$36,313,000

Curr. Assets:	$261,058,000	**Curr. Liab.:**	$76,508,000	**P/E Ratio:**	14.95
Plant, Equip.:	$25,174,000	**Total Liab.:**	$241,713,000	**Indic. Yr. Divd.:**	NA
Total Assets:	$444,107,000	**Net Worth:**	$202,394,000	**Debt/ Equity:**	NA

Laboratory Corp of America Holdings

358 S Main St., Burlington, NC, 27215; *PH:* 1-336-229-1127; *Fax:* 1-336-436-1205; *http://* www.labcorp.com

General - Incorporation DE
Employees 25,000
Auditor PricewaterhouseCoopers LLP
Stk Agt American Stock Transfer & Trust Co.
Counsel NA
DUNS No. 86-142-2434

Stock- Price on:12/24/2007 $79.45
Stock Exchange NYSE
Ticker Symbol LH
Outstanding Shares 117,600,000
E.P.S $3.75
Shareholders NA

Business: The groups principle activity is to provide clinical laboratory services. The groups services include ambulatory monitoring, bone marrow and paternity services. The group operates from United States.

Primary SIC and add'l.: 6719 8071

CIK No: 0000920148

Subsidiaries: 1004679 Ontario Limited, 3024539 Nova Scotia Company, 3065619 Nova Scotia Co., 3901858 Canada Inc., 563911 Ontario Limited, 591893 Alberta Ltd., 794475 Ontario Inc., 829318 Ontario Limited, 854512 Ontario Limited, 879606 Ontario Limited, 896988 Ontario Inc., 900747 Ontario Ltd., 925893 Ontario Limited, 925893 Ontario Ltd., 942487 Ontario Ltd. 91 Subsidiaries included in the Index

Officers: David King/Dir., CEO, Pres./$2,626,343.00, Bradford T. Smith/Vice Chmn., Exec. VP - Corporate Affairs, Chief Legal Officer, Sec./$3,524,327.00, Richard L. Novak/Exec. VP - Strategic Planning/$7,763,617.00, William Hayes/CFO, Exec. VP, Treasurer/$2,004,576.00, Benjamin Miller/45/Exec. VP - Sales, Marketing, Managed Care, William B. Haas/43/Exec. VP - Esoteric Business, Myla P. Lai-Goldman/50/Exec. VP, Chief Scientific Officer, Dir. - Medical, Don Hardison/COO, Exec. VP, Eric Lindblom/Sr. VP - Investor, Media Relations, Woodrow L. Cook/54/Exec. VP - Eastern Operations, Allen W. Troub/49/Exec. VP - Western Operations, Andrew S. Walton/41/Exec. VP - Strategic Planning, CIO

Directors: David King/Dir., CEO, Pres., Bradford T. Smith/Vice Chmn., Exec. VP - Corporate Affairs, Chief Legal Officer, Sec., Thomas MacMahon/Chmn., Arthur H. Rubenstein/70/Dir., Robert E. Mittelstaedt/64/Dir., Kerrii B. Anderson/50/Dir., Jean-Luc Belingard/59/Dir., Wendy E. Lane/56/Dir., Keith M. Weikel/70/Dir., Sanders R. Williams/59/Dir.

Owners: M. Keith Weikel, Bradford T. Smith, Arthur H. Rubenstein, Longview Asset Management, LLC/6.30%, Kerrii B. Anderson, Andrew G. Wallace, Richard L. Novak, William B. Hayes, Jean-Luc Blingard, Janus Capital Management LLC/6.00%, Chieftain Capital Management, Inc./6.10%, Wendy E. Lane, Robert E. Mittelstaedt, David P. King, Thomas P. Mac Mahon/1.40% *(16 Owners included in Index)*

Financial Data: *Fiscal Year End:*12/31 *Latest Annual Data:* 12/31/2006

Year	Sales	Net Income
2006	$3,590,800,000	$431,600,000
2005	$3,327,600,000	$386,200,000
2004	$3,084,800,000	$363,000,000

Curr. Assets:	$887,000,000	**Curr. Liab.:**	$930,900,000		
Plant, Equip.:	$393,200,000	**Total Liab.:**	$2,023,700,000	**Indic. Yr. Divd.:**	NA
Total Assets:	$4,000,800,000	**Net Worth:**	$1,977,100,000	**Debt/ Equity:**	0.3373

Labranche & Co Inc

1 Exchange Plz., 25th Fl., New York, NY, 10006; *PH:* 1-212-425-1144; *Fax:* 1-212-344-1469; *http://* www.labranche.com; *Email:* main@labranche.com

General - Incorporation DE
Employees 429
Auditor KPMG LLP
Stk Agt Mellon Investor Services LLC
Counsel Fulbright & Jaworski LLP
DUNS No. NA

Stock- Price on:12/24/2007 $7.55
Stock Exchange NYSE
Ticker Symbol LAB
Outstanding Shares 61,470,000
E.P.S $0.31
Shareholders NA

Business: The group's principal activity is to provide brokerage and dealership services to individual and institutional customers. The group operates through its subsidiaries in two segments: specialist and execution and clearing. The specialist segment includes labranche and co llc (labranche) and labranche structured products llc. The segment provides specialist services in equity securities and options listed on the New York stock exchange (nyse) and the American stock exchange (amex). Labranche and co bv is a dutch subsidiary that provides client services to labranche's European listed companies. The execution and clearing segment consists of the operations of labranche financial services inc, a member of the nyse. It provides securities clearing and execution, direct-access floor brokerage and other services.

Primary SIC and add'l.: 6719 6211

CIK No: 0001089044

Subsidiaries: LABDR Services, Inc., LaBranche & Co. B.V., LaBranche & Co. LLC, LaBranche Financial Services, Inc., LaBranche Structured Holdings, Inc., LaBranche Structured Products Europe Limited, LaBranche Structured Products Hong Kong Limited, LaBranche Structured Products LLC, LaBranche Structured Products Specialists, LLC

Officers: Michael Labranche/Chmn., CEO, Pres./$1,008,704.00, Thomas L. Patterson/CEO - Labranche Financial Services, Inc, Stephen H. Gray/Corp. Sec., General Counsel/$511,608.00, Jeffrey A. McCutcheon/CFO/$640,420.00, William J. Burke/COO/$759,844.00, Alfred O. Hayward/Dir., Exec. VP/$858,704.00, John Longobardi/Dir. - Business Development

Directors: Michael Labranche/Chmn., CEO, Pres., Alfred O. Hayward/Dir., Exec. VP, Donald E. Kiernan/Dir., Robert E. Torray/Dir., Katherine Dietze Courage/Dir., Stuart M. Robbins/Dir.

Owners: William J. Burke/1.00%, Jeffrey A. McCutcheon, Horizon Asset Management, Inc./27.70%, George M.L. LaBranche/6.80%, Donald E. Kiernan, Robert E. Torray/3.60%, Stephen H. Gray, Insiders/14.20%, Dimensional Fund Advisors LP/5.30%, Torray LLC/4.90%, Kinetics Asset Management, Inc./16.70%, Alfred O. Hayward/2.60%

Financial Data: *Fiscal Year End:*12/31 *Latest Annual Data:* 12/31/2006

Year	Sales	Net Income
2006	$673,994,000	$136,804,000
2005	$340,190,000	$37,521,000
2004	$319,047,000	-$43,780,000

Curr. Assets:	$693,408,000	**Curr. Liab.:**	$3,762,407,000		
Plant, Equip.:	$18,069,000	**Total Liab.:**	$4,500,182,000	**Indic. Yr. Divd.:**	NA
Total Assets:	$5,374,889,000	**Net Worth:**	$874,707,000	**Debt/ Equity:**	0.5345

Laclede Group Inc

720 Olive St., St. Louis, MO, 63101; *PH:* 1-314-342-0500; *Fax:* 1-314-421-1979; *http://* www.thelacledegroup.com; *Email:* investorservices@lacledegas.com

General - Incorporation MO
Employees 3,849
Auditor Deloitte& Touche LLP
Stk Agt Computershare Trust CO.
Counsel NA
DUNS No. NA

Stock- Price on:12/24/2007 $32.1
Stock Exchange NYSE
Ticker Symbol LG
Outstanding Shares 21,600,000
E.P.S NA
Shareholders NA

Business: The groups principle activity is to provide natural gas services through its regulated core utility operations. The group operates through three segments namely, regulated gas distribution, non-regulated services and non-regulated gas marketing. In the year 2006, the group acquired Reliant Services, LLC. The group operates from the United States. The group's quarterly revenue for September 2007 was 323.27millions of USD.

Primary SIC and add'l.: 4923 1623 4925 4924 1542 4613 6552 5172

CIK No: 0001126956

Subsidiaries: Laclede Development Company, Laclede Energy Resources, Inc., Laclede Gas Company, Laclede Gas Family Services, Inc., Laclede Investment LLC, Laclede Pipeline Company, Laclede Venture Corp, SM&P Utility Resources, Inc.

Officers: Douglas H. Yaeger/Chmn., CEO, Pres., James A. Muhl/Treasurer, Assist. Sec. - SM, P Utility Resources, Anthony Sincere/VP - Business Development, SM, P Utility Resources, Ryan Hyman/VP - Emerging Enterprise Development, SM, P Utility Resources, Kevin F. Beauchamp/CFO - SM&P Utility Resources, John Gilbert/VP - Operations, SM, P Utility Resources, Gwen Kibbe/VP - Quality Management, Operations Compliance, SM, P Utility Resources, Timothy M. Seelig/VP - Sales, Marketing, SM, P Utility Resources, Mark C. Darrell/General Counsel, Mary Caola Kullman/Chief Governance Officer, Corp. Sec., Michael C. Geiselhart/VP - Strategic Development, Planning, Lynn D. Rawlings/Treasurer, Assist. Sec., Robert E. Shively/Pres. - Business, Services Development, SM, P Utility Resources, Craig R. Hoeferlin/VP - Operations, Laclede Gas Company, Richard A. Skau/Sr. VP - Human Resources, Laclede Gas Company (27 Officers included in Index)

Directors: Douglas H. Yaeger/Chmn., CEO, Pres., Edward L. Glotzbach/Dir., Stephen W. Maritz/Dir., Brenda D. Newberry/Dir., Arnold W. Donald/Dir., Anthony V. Leness/Dir., William E. Nasser/Dir., John P. Stupp/Dir., Mary Ann Van Lokeren/Dir.

Owners: Insiders/7.00%, B. D. Newberry, M. C. Geiselhart, D. H. Yaeger, Ameriprise Financial, Inc./8.10%, Advisors/Barclays Global Investors Ltd./6.80%, R. E. Shively, W. E. Nasser, Stupp Bros., Inc./5.30%, B. C. Cooper, E. L. Glotzbach, W. S. Maritz, A. W. Donald, K. J. Neises, A. V. Leness (16 Owners included in Index)

Curr. Assets:	$459,846,000	Curr. Liab.:	$430,882,000	P/E Ratio:	28.61
Plant, Equip.:	$777,189,000	Total Liab.:	$1,166,736,000	Indic. Yr. Divd.:	NA
Total Assets:	$1,570,160,000	Net Worth:	$403,424,000	Debt/ Equity:	NA

Lacrosse Footwear Inc

17634 NE Airport Way, Portland, OR, 97230; *PH:* 1-503-262-0110; *Fax:* 1-503-262-0115; *http://* www.lacrossefootwear.com

General - Incorporation	WI	Stock - Price on:12/24/2007	$18.109
Employees	303	Stock Exchange	NDQ
Auditor	McGladrey & Pullen LLP	Ticker Symbol	BOOT
Stk Agt.	Wells Fargo Shareowner Services	Outstanding Shares	6,070,000
Counsel	Foley & Lardner LLP	E.P.S.	$1.13
DUNS No.	11-622-7315	Shareholders	NA

Business: The group's principal activities are to design, manufacture and market branded, premium and innovative footwear and apparel for the sporting, occupational and recreational users. The products are marketed under the lacrosse(R), red ball(R), rainfair(R) and danner(R) brands through selected distributors and independent representatives. The customers include workers in law enforcement, agriculture, firefighting, construction, industry, military services and people active in hunting, fishing, camping and other outdoor activities.

Primary SIC and add'l.: 3021 3142 3144 3069 3143

CIK No: 0000919443

Subsidiaries: Danner, Inc., LaCrosse International, Inc

Officers: Joseph P. Schneider/Dir., CEO, Pres./$998,341.00, David P. Carlson/CFO, Exec. VP, Sec./$613,891.00, Gary J. Rebello/VP - Human Resources/$240,457.00, Robert G. Rinehart/VP - Product/$222,577.00, Erron S. Sorensen/38/VP - Marketing/$200,013.00, Craig P. Cohen/VP - Demand, Supply Planning, C. Kirk Layton/Corporate Controller, Kirk S. Nichols/VP - Sales, Michael Newman/Investor Relations Officer

Directors: Joseph P. Schneider/Dir., CEO, Pres., Richard A. Rosenthal/Chmn., Charles W. Smith/Dir., Stephen F. Loughlin/Dir., William H. Williams/Dir., Luke E. Sims/Dir., John D. Whitcombe/Dir.

Owners: John D. Whitcombe, William H. Williams, Joseph P. Schneider/5.50%, George W. and Virginia F. Schneider Trust U/A/17.80%, Insiders/9.90%, David P. Carlson/1.30%, David M. Strouse, Gary J. Rebello, Robert G. Rinehart, Charles W. Smith, Virginia F. Schneider/18.60%, Royce & Associates, LLC/7.10%, Richard A. Rosenthal, Stephen F. Loughlin, Erron S. Sorensen (16 Owners included in Index)

Financial Data: *Fiscal Year End:*12/31 *Latest Annual Data:* 12/31/2006

Year	Sales	Net Income
2006	$107,798,000	$6,344,000
2005	$99,378,000	$5,234,000
2004	$105,470,000	$6,973,000

Curr. Assets:	$56,862,000	Curr. Liab.:	$10,185,000	P/E Ratio:	17.89
Plant, Equip.:	$5,442,000	Total Liab.:	$16,189,000	Indic. Yr. Divd.:	$0.150
Total Assets:	$73,533,000	Net Worth:	$57,344,000	Debt/ Equity:	0.0081

Ladenburg Thalmann Financial Svcs Inc

4400 Biscayne Blvd., 12th Fl., Miami, FL, 33137; *PH:* 1-305-572-4100; *Fax:* 1-305-572-4199; *http://* www.gbicapital.com

General - Incorporation	FL	Stock - Price on:12/24/2007	$2.6
Employees	172	Stock Exchange	AMEX
Auditor	Eisner LLP	Ticker Symbol	LTS
Stk Agt.	American Stock Transfer & Trust Co.	Outstanding Shares	157,200,000
Counsel	Graubard Miller	E.P.S.	$0.00
DUNS No.	NA	Shareholders	NA

Business: The group's principle activities are to provide retail and institutional securities brokerage, investment banking and research services. The services are provided through its principal operating subsidiaries, ladenburg thalmann and co. Inc. And ladenburg capital management inc. The group provides services for middle market, emerging growth companies and high net worth individuals through a coordinated effort among corporate finance, research, capital markets, investment management, brokerage and trading professionals. The activities also consist of retail sales and trading of exchange listed and over-the-counter equity securities, options and mutual funds and investment banking and research services. The group's quarterly revenue for September 2007 was 10.45 millions of USD.

Primary SIC and add'l.: 6211 6719

CIK No: 0001029730

Subsidiaries: Ladenburg Thalmann & Co. Inc., Ladenburg Thalmann Asset Management Inc.

Officers: Richard Lampen/Dir., CEO, Pres./$77,201.00, Richard Rosenstock/Financial Consultant - Melville, NY, Mark Klein/Financial Consultant - NEW York City, NY/$2,272,192.00, Mark Coe/Financial Consultant - Lincolnshire, IL, Mark Zeitchick/43/Financial Consultant - Miami, FL/$648,525.00, Joe Angelone/Financial Consultant - Princeton, NJ, David Antelo/Financial Consultant - Boca Raton, FL, Jason Baker/Financial Consultant - Lincolnshire, IL, Ross Barish/Financial Consultant - NEW York City, NY, Alex Barrios/Financial Consultant - NEW York

City, NY, Joe Berland/Financial Consultant - Melville, NY, Marc Bernstein/Financial Consultant - Melville, NY, Philip Blancato/Financial Consultant - NEW York City, NY, Alex Breslin/Financial Consultant - Melville, NY, Richard Klein/Financial Consultant - Melville, NY (73 Officers included in Index)

Directors: Phillip Frost/Chmn., Howard Lorber/Vice Chmn.

Owners: Diane Chillemi, Richard J. Rosenstock/2.63%, Jeffrey S. Podell, New Valley LLC/8.68%, Robert J. Eide, Mark Zeitchick/1.25%, Phillip Frost/30.51%, Insiders/37.62%, Mark D. Klein/1.08%, Henry C. Beinstein, Saul Gilinski, Howard M. Lorber/2.08%, Richard J. Lampen, Richard M. Krasno, Brian S. Genson

Financial Data: *Fiscal Year End:*12/31 *Latest Annual Data:* 12/31/2006

Year	Sales	Net Income
2006	$46,858,000	$4,659,000
2005	$30,690,000	-$25,971,000
2004	$38,441,000	-$9,854,000

Curr. Assets:	$36,287,000	Curr. Liab.:	$12,457,000	P/E Ratio:	260.00
Plant, Equip.:	$706,000	Total Liab.:	$19,009,000	Indic. Yr. Divd.:	NA
Total Assets:	$47,343,000	Net Worth:	$28,334,000	Debt/ Equity:	0.1607

Ladish Co Inc

5481 S Packard Ave., Cudahy, WI, 53110; *PH:* 1-414-747-2611; *Fax:* 1-414-747-2963; *http://* www.ladishco.com

General - Incorporation	WI	Stock - Price on:12/24/2007	$40.47
Employees	1,900	Stock Exchange	NDQ
Auditor	KPMG LLP	Ticker Symbol	LDSH
Stk Agt	American Stock Transfer & Trust CO.	Outstanding Shares	14,510,000
Counsel	NA	E.P.S.	$2.00
DUNS No.	00-608-5401	Shareholders	NA

Business: The group's principal activity is to engineer, produce and market high-strength and high technology forged and cast metal components for load-bearing and fatigue-resisting applications used in the jet engine, aerospace and industrial markets. The group markets its products to manufacturers of jet engines, commercial business and defense aircraft, helicopters, satellites, heavy-duty off-road vehicles and industrial and marine turbines. The group's customers include rolls-royce, united technologies, general electric, caterpillar, volvo, techspace aero and snecma.

Primary SIC and add'l.: 3724 3462

CIK No: 0000814250

Subsidiaries: Metallum Corporation, Pacific Cast Technologies, Inc., Stowe Machine Co., Inc., Valley Machining, Inc., Zaklad Kuznia Matrycowa

Officers: Kerry L. Woody/CEO, Pres./$887,959.00, Randy Turner/Pres. - Pacific Cast Technologies/$357,554.00, Wayne E. Larsen/VP, VP - Law, Finance, Sec./$558,838.00, Gary Vroman/VP - Sales, Marketing/$423,468.00, Gene E. Bunge/62/VP - Engineering, George Groppi/59/VP - Quality - Metallurgy, David Provan/58/VP - Materials Management, Lawrence Hammond/60/VP - Human Resources/$388,945.00, Josef Burdzy/Pres. - Management Board, General Dir. ZKM Forging, John Delaney/Pres. - Stowe Machine

Directors: Lawrence W. Bianchi/66/Dir., James C. Hill/59/Dir., Leon A. Kranz/68/Dir., Robert J. Peart/45/Dir., John W. Splude/62/Dir.

Owners: Insiders, Luther King Capital Management Corp./5.20%, Provident Investment Counsel, Inc./5.80%, James C. Hill, Wayne E. Larsen, Kerry L. Woody, Lazard Asset Management LLC/5.20%, Tygh Capital Management, Inc./5.20%

Financial Data: *Fiscal Year End:*12/31 *Latest Annual Data:* 06/30/2007

Year	Sales	Net Income
2007	NA	NA
2006	$369,290,000	$28,481,000
2005	$266,841,000	$13,715,000

Curr. Assets:	$183,753,000	Curr. Liab.:	$59,989,000	P/E Ratio:	20.13
Plant, Equip.:	$112,096,000	Total Liab.:	$175,301,000	Indic. Yr. Divd.:	NA
Total Assets:	$328,606,000	Net Worth:	$152,670,000	Debt/ Equity:	0.2708

Lafarge

61, Rue Des Belles Feuilles, Paris, 75116; *PH:* 33-144341111; *http://* www.lafarge.com; *Email:* info.cement@lafarge.com

General - Incorporation	France	Stock - Price on:12/24/2007	$44.96
Employees	82,734	Stock Exchange	NA
Auditor	Deloitte & Assoc.	Ticker Symbol	NA
Stk Agt	Morgan ADR Service Center	Outstanding Shares	707,340,000
Counsel	NA	E.P.S.	$3.34
DUNS No.	NA	Shareholders	NA

Business: The group's principal activity is to produce construction materials. The group's operations are organized into four divisions: cement, aggregates & concrete, roofing and plaster. The cement segment produces and sells a wide range of cement and hydraulic binders adapted to the needs of the construction industry. The concrete and aggregates segment produces and sells construction aggregates, ready mix concrete and other concrete products. The roofing segment produces and sells roof tiles, roofing accessories and chimney systems. The plaster segment mainly produces and sells drywall for the commercial and residential construction sectors. The group has operations in France, the United Kingdom, Spain, Greece, North America, Canada, the United States, South Africa, Brazil, Chile, Malaysia, Singapore, turkey and etc. In aug 2003, the group acquired limay grinding mill corporation and in oct 2003, acquired 75% of interest in ural cement.

Primary SIC and add'l.: 1742 1761 3273 3274 3241 2952 3272

CIK No: 0000913785

Subsidiaries: Lafarge North America Inc

Officers: Bruno Lafont/Dir., Group CEO, Jean-Charles Blatz/64/Group Exec. VP - Aggregates, Concrete, Ulrich Glaunach/52/Group Exec. VP - Cement, Jean-Jacques Gauthier/49/Exec. VP - Finance, Christian Herrault/57/Exec. VP - Gypsum, Isidoro Miranda/49/Exec. VP - Cement, Michel Rose/65/Group COO - Cement, Pierre Juston/Contact - Research, Development, Jean-Carlos Angulo/59/Exec. VP - Cement Business, Francois Redron/Contact - Research & Development, Nouveaux Produits, Thomas Farrell/Exec. VP - Aggregates, Concrete, Gerard Kuperfarb/47/Exec. VP - Aggregates, Concrete, Eric Olsen/Exec. VP - Organization, Human Resources, Stephanie Tessier/VP - Group External Communications, Lucy Wadge/Head - Media Relations (19 Officers included in Index)

Directors: Bruno Lafont/Dir., Group CEO, Bertrand Collomb/62/Chmn., Oscar Fanjul/58/Non Exec. Vice Chmn., Guilherme Frering/49/Dir., Juan Gallardo/60/Dir., Alain Joly/69/Dir., Jacques Lefevre/69/Dir., Michael Blakenham/70/Dir., Jean-Pierre Boisivon/67/Dir., Michel Bon/64/Dir., Bernard Kasriel/61/Dir., Pierre De Lafarge/61/Dir., Philippe Charrier/53/Dir., Qin Xiao/Member - International Advisory Board, Titus Naikuni/Member - International Advisory Board *(28 Directors included in Index)*

Owners: Groupe Bruxelles Lambert/15.90%, Treasury shares/0.80%, Insiders/100.00%, Other institutional shareholders/69.10%, Capital Group International Inc./3.20%, Individual shareholders/11.00%

Financial Data: Fiscal Year End:12/31   Latest Annual Data: 12/31/2006

Year	Sales	Net Income
2006	$22,324,953,000	$1,715,070,000
2005	$18,913,684,000	$1,299,287,000
2004	$19,696,478,000	$1,346,663,000

Curr. Assets:	$12,367,250,000	**Curr. Liab.:**	$8,134,368,000		
Plant, Equip.:	$14,764,915,000	**Total Liab.:**	$23,791,805,000	**Indic. Yr. Divd.:**	$0.760
Total Assets:	$39,504,696,000	**Net Worth:**	$13,876,353,000	**Debt/ Equity:**	NA

Lake Shore Bancorp Inc

125 E 4th St., Dunkirk, NY, 14048; **PH:** 1-716-366-4070; **Fax:** 1-716-366-3010; *http://* www.lakeshoresavings.com

General - Incorporation	USA	**Stock** - Price on:12/24/2007	$12.2
Employees	82	Stock Exchange	NDQ
Auditor	Beard Miller Company LLP	Ticker Symbol	LSBK
Stk Agt	Registrar & Transfer Co	Outstanding Shares	6,610,000
Counsel	NA	E.P.S.	$0.21
DUNS No.	NA	Shareholders	NA

Business: The group operates through its subsidiaries whose principle activity is to provide financial services. The financial products of the group include Mortgage, Commercial and Consumer loan. The group operates from the United States. The assets of the group for the year 2006 were $354,237 (thousands).

Primary SIC and add'l.: 6712 6036

CIK No: 0001341318

Subsidiaries: Lake Shore Savings

Officers: David C. Mancuso/Dir., CEO, Pres., Rachel A. Foley/CFO, Beverley J. Mulkin/Sec., Treasurer, Branch Mgr., Janinne Fiegl Dugan/Human Resources Officer, Brian D. Lydic/VP, Commercial Loan Officer, Sally Pyne/Assist. VP, Branch Mgr., Lou Dipalma/VP, Reginald S. Corsi/Exec. VP, Chief Operating, Commercial Officer, Katherine A. Kaus/Sr. VP, Mortgage Lending Officer, Community Reinvestment Officer, Beverly Sutton/Internal Auditor, Nicole Rybij/Compliance Officer, John Huber/VP, Branch Mgr., Nancy March/Assist. VP, Branch Mgr.

Directors: David C. Mancuso/Dir., CEO, Pres., Michael E. Brunecz/Chmn., Daniel P. Reininga/Vice Chmn., James P. Foley/Dir., Thomas E. Reed/Dir., Nancy L. Brumfield-Yocum/Dir., Sharon E. Brautigam/Dir., Gary W. Winger/Dir.

Owners: Lake Shore, MHC/55.00%, Michael E. Brunecz, Thomas E. Reed, PL Capital, LLC/5.50%, Rachel A. Foley, Reginald S. Corsi, Daniel P. Reininga, Sharon E. Brautigam, Gary W. Winger, Nancy L. Yocum, David C. Mancuso, Insiders/5.80%, James P. Foley

Financial Data: Fiscal Year End:12/31   Latest Annual Data: 12/31/2006

Year	Sales	Net Income
2006	$19,579,000	$1,819,000
2005	$17,803,000	$2,054,000

Curr. Assets:	$20,086,000	**Curr. Liab.:**	$260,242,000	**P/E Ratio:**	45.19
Plant, Equip.:	$7,234,000	**Total Liab.:**	$300,490,000	**Indic. Yr. Divd.:**	$0.160
Total Assets:	$354,237,000	**Net Worth:**	$53,747,000	**Debt/ Equity:**	0.6093

Lakeland Bancorp Inc

250 Oak Ridge Rd., Oak Ridge, NJ, 07438; **PH:** 1-973-697-2000; **Fax:** 1-973-697-8385; *http://* www.lakelandbank.com

General - Incorporation	NJ	**Stock** - Price on:12/24/2007	$13.64
Employees	538	Stock Exchange	NDQ
Auditor	Grant Thornton LLP	Ticker Symbol	LBAI
Stk Agt	American Stock Transfer & Trust Co.	Outstanding Shares	22,110,000
Counsel	Lowenstein Sandler PC	E.P.S.	$0.77
DUNS No.	80-876-7933	Shareholders	NA

Business: The group's principal activities are to provide a range of lending, depository and related financial services to individuals and small to medium sized businesses in northern New Jersey. The deposits of the group include checking accounts, savings accounts, now accounts, money market accounts and certificates of deposit. The group offers short and medium term loans, lines of credit, letters of credit, inventory and account receivable financing. The other services offered include securities brokerage services, mutual funds and variable annuities. The group operates through 38 branch offices located in Passaic, Morris, Sussex, Bergen and Essex counties of New Jersey. On 25-Aug-2003, the group acquired CSB Financial Corp.

Primary SIC and add'l.: 6712 6022

CIK No: 0000846901

Subsidiaries: Lakeland Bancorp Capital Trust I, Lakeland Bancorp Capital Trust II, Lakeland Bancorp Capital Trust III, Lakeland Bank, Lakeland Investment Corporation, Lakeland NJ Investment Corporation

Officers: Roger Bosma/65/Dir., CEO, Pres./$882,088.00, Joseph F. Hurley/CFO, Exec. VP/$323,961.00, Robert A. Vandenbergh/Sr. Exec. VP, Chief Loan Officer/$351,662.00, Louis Luddecke/COO, Exec. VP/$288,852.00, Stephen Schachtel/Pres. - Lakeland Bank Equipment Leasing Division, Jeffrey J. Buonforte/Exec. VP, Chief Retail Officer/$288,667.00, James R. Noonan/Exec. VP, Chief Credit Officer

Directors: Roger Bosma/65/Dir., CEO, Pres., John W. Fredericks/Chmn., Arthur L. Zande/Vice Chmn., John Pier/Dir. Emeritus, Stephen Tilton/Dir., Paul G. Viall/Dir., Robert E. McCracken/Dir., Robert Nicholson/Dir. Emeritus, Joseph P. O'Dowd/Dir., Charles L. Tice/Dir. Emeritus, Bruce G. Bohuny/Dir. Emeritus, Paul P. Lubertazzi/Dir. Emeritus, Mary A. Deacon/Dir., Mark J. Fredericks/Dir., George H. Guptill/Dir. *(17 Directors included in Index)*

Owners: Insiders/16.90%, Paul G. Viall, Arthur L. Zande/0.30%, Robert E. McCracken/0.50%, Janeth C. Hendershot/0.30%, Steven Schachtel/0.20%, Roger Bosma/1.50%, Mark J. Fredericks/1.70%, Joseph P. ODowd/0.20%, Louis E. Luddecke/0.40%, George H. Guptill/3.00%, Stephen R. Tilton/3.00%, Robert A. Vandenbergh/0.50%, John W. Fredericks/2.70%, Robert B. Nicholson *(19 Owners included in Index)*

Financial Data: Fiscal Year End:12/31   Latest Annual Data: 12/31/2006

Year	Sales	Net Income
2006	$136,983,000	$16,977,000
2005	$118,967,000	$20,221,000
2004	$96,718,000	$16,495,000

Curr. Assets:	$88,473,000	**Curr. Liab.:**	$1,901,688,000	**P/E Ratio:**	17.71
Plant, Equip.:	$32,072,000	**Total Liab.:**	$2,064,073,000	**Indic. Yr. Divd.:**	$0.400
Total Assets:	$2,263,573,000	**Net Worth:**	$199,500,000	**Debt/ Equity:**	0.7439

Lakeland Financial Corp

202 E Ctr. St., Warsaw, IN, 46581; **PH:** 1-574-267-6144; **Fax:** 1-574-267-6063; *http://* www.lakecitybank.com

General - Incorporation	IN	**Stock** - Price on:12/24/2007	$22.45
Employees	449	Stock Exchange	NDQ
Auditor	Crowe Chizek & Co. LLC	Ticker Symbol	LKFN
Stk Agt	American Stock Transfer & Trust Co.	Outstanding Shares	12,190,000
Counsel	NA	E.P.S.	$1.52
DUNS No.	10-235-6003	Shareholders	NA

Business: The group's principal activity is to provide commercial banking services through its wholly owned subsidiary, lake city bank. The group's primary deposit products are checking accounts, savings accounts and term certificate accounts. Lending products include commercial loans, agricultural loans, direct and indirect customer lending and real estate mortgage lending. In addition, the group also provides safe deposit box services and trust and brokerage services. The group operates through forty three branch offices in twelve counties in northern Indiana.

Primary SIC and add'l.: 6712 6022

CIK No: 0000721994

Subsidiaries: Lake City Bank

Officers: Michael L. Kubacki/Chmn., CEO, Pres./$563,597.00, David M. Findlay/CFO, Exec. VP/$334,800.00, Charles D. Smith/Exec. VP/$286,185.00, Kevin L. Deardorff/Exec. VP/$231,053.00, Robert C. Condon/67/Exec. VP, Teresa A. Bartman/VP, Controller, James D. Westerfield/50/Sr. VP, Trust Officer/$206,637.00, James J. Nowak/VP, Treasurer, Jill A. Debatty/Sr. VP - Human Resources, Training, Michael E. Gavin/Sr. VP - Commercial, Betty L. McHenry/Sr. VP, H. A. Meyer/Sr. VP - Commercial, Frank A. Soltis/Sr. VP - Operations

Directors: Michael L. Kubacki/Chmn., CEO, Pres., Terry L. Tucker/Dir., Richard L. Pletcher/Dir., Craig L. Fulmer/Dir., Emily E. Pichon/Dir., Steven D. Ross/Dir., Donald B. Steininger/Dir., Robert E. Bartels/Dir., Allan J. Ludwig/Dir., George B. Huber/50/Dir., Charles E. Niemier/Dir., Scott M. Welch/Dir., Thomas A. Hiatt/Dir.

Owners: Lakeland Financial Corporation 401(k) Plan/8.20%, Michael L. Kubacki/1.47%, James D. Westerfield, M. Scott Welch, Kevin L. Deardorff, Charles D. Smith, Thomas A. Hiatt, Richard L. Pletcher, David M. Findlay, Robert E. Bartels, Donald B. Steininger, L. Craig Fulmer, Terry L. Tucker, Charles E. Niemier, Emily E. Pichon *(19 Owners included in Index)*

Financial Data: Fiscal Year End:12/31   Latest Annual Data: 12/31/2006

Year	Sales	Net Income
2006	$123,883,000	$18,721,000
2005	$98,396,000	$17,958,000
2004	$76,563,000	$14,545,000

Curr. Assets:	$128,419,000	**Curr. Liab.:**	$1,675,208,000	**P/E Ratio:**	14.77
Plant, Equip.:	$25,177,000	**Total Liab.:**	$1,706,519,000	**Indic. Yr. Divd.:**	$0.560
Total Assets:	$1,836,706,000	**Net Worth:**	$130,187,000	**Debt/ Equity:**	NA

Lakeland Industries Inc

701 Koehler Ave., Ste. 7, Ronkonkoma, NY, 11779; **PH:** 1-631-981-9700; **Fax:** 1-631-981-9751; *http://* www.lakeland.com; **Email:** info@lakeland.com

General - Incorporation	DE	**Stock** - Price on:12/24/2007	$13.99
Employees	1,667	Stock Exchange	NDQ
Auditor	Pricewaterhousecoopers LLP	Ticker Symbol	LAKE
Stk Agt	Registrar & Transfer Co	Outstanding Shares	5,520,000
Counsel	NA	E.P.S.	$0.76
DUNS No.	05-588-3458	Shareholders	NA

Business: The group's principle activity is to manufacture and sell a comprehensive line of safety garments and accessories for the industrial protective clothing market. The products include limited or disposable protective clothing, high-end chemical protective suits, fire fighting and heat protective apparel, gloves and arm guards and reusable woven garments. The group sells these products through its in-house sales force and independent sales representatives to a network of over 500 safety and mill supply distributors. These distributors in turn supply end user industrial customers such as chemical/petrochemical, automobile, steel, glass, construction, smelting, janitorial, pharmaceutical and high technology electronics manufacturers, as well as hospitals and laboratories. The group has manufacturing operations in the United States, Mexico and China. The group's total revenue for year 2007 was 100.17 millions of USD.

Primary SIC and add'l.: 2261 3842 2326 2389 2253 6719 2262

CIK No: 0000798081

Subsidiaries: Laidlaw, Adams & Peck, Inc., Lakeland de Mexico S.A. de C.V., Lakeland Industries Europe Ltd., Lakeland Protective Wear, Inc., Mifflin Valley, Inc., Qing Dao Maytung Healthcare Co., RFB Lakeland Industries Private, Ltd, Weifang Lakeland Safety Products Co., Ltd.

Officers: Christopher J. Ryan/CEO, Pres./$1,324,065.00, Gary Pokrassa/CFO/$220,735.00

Owners: Michael E. Cirenza, Stephen M. Bachelder, Paul C. Smith, Raymond J. Smith/9.55%, Robeco Investment Management, Inc./6.37%, Christopher J. Ryan/6.63%, John J. Collins/2.09%, John Kreft, Eric O. Hallman, Seymour Holtzman/7.13%, Gary Pokrassa, Insiders/19.40%

Financial Data: Fiscal Year End:01/31   Latest Annual Data: 1/31/2007

Year	Sales	Net Income
2007	$100,171,000	$5,104,000
2006	$98,740,000	$6,329,000
2005	$95,320,000	$5,016,000

Curr. Assets:	$62,114,000	**Curr. Liab.:**	$4,326,000	**P/E Ratio:**	18.41
Plant, Equip.:	$11,084,000	**Total Liab.:**	$8,139,000	**Indic. Yr. Divd.:**	NA
Total Assets:	$74,198,000	**Net Worth:**	$66,059,000	**Debt/ Equity:**	0.0616

Lakes Entertainment Inc

130 Cheshire Ln., Ste. 101, Minnetonka, MN, 55305; *PH:* 1-952-449-9092; *Fax:* 1-952-449-9353; *http://* www.lakesgaming.com

General - Incorporation	MN	*Stock*- Price on:12/24/2007	$11.77
Employees	140	Stock Exchange	NDQ
Auditor	Piercy Bowler Taylor& Kern	Ticker Symbol	LACO
Stk Agt	Registar and Transfer Co.	Outstanding Shares	24,330,000
Counsel	NA	E.P.S.	-$0.16
DUNS No.	NA	Shareholders	NA

Business: The groups principle activities include developing, financing and managing Indian owned casino properties. The products of the group include electronic and wireless entertainment, DVD, home entertainment, casino games, and giftware. The group products sold under the trade names FOUR THE MONEY(TM) and CARLOS SOPRANOS(TM). The group operates through three segments namely casino projects, world poker, and corporate and eliminations. The group operates from the United States. The group's quarterly revenue for September 2007 was 7.01 millions of USD.

Primary SIC and add'l.: 8999 7812 7999

CIK No: 0001071255

Subsidiaries: Borders Land Company, LLC, Grand Casinos Nevada 1, Inc., Grand Casinos of Louisiana, LLC Tunica-Biloxi, Grand Casinos Pechanga, Inc., Grand Casinos Washington, Inc., Grand Media & Electronics Distributing, Inc., Great Lakes Gaming of Michigan, LLC, Lakes California Land Development, Inc., Lakes Cloverdale, LLC, Lakes Game Development, LLC, Lakes Gaming & Resorts, LLC, Lakes Gaming Mississippi, LLC, Lakes Gaming of Louisiana, LLC, Lakes Iowa Consulting, LLC, Lakes Iowa Management, LLC 31 Subsidiaries included in the Index

Officers: Lyle Berman/66/Chmn., CEO/$878,779.00, Timothy J. Cope/56/Dir., CFO, Pres./$520,864.00, Janice Saeugling/Primary Investor Relations Officer, Robert Wyre/Sr. VP - Operations/$308,800.00, Richard Bienapfl/VP - Development/$278,800.00, Mark Sicilia/VP - Food, Beverage/$288,800.00

Directors: Lyle Berman/66/Chmn., CEO, Timothy J. Cope/56/Dir., CFO, Pres., Morris Goldfarb/Dir., Ray Moberg/59/Dir., Neil I. Sell/66/Dir., Larry Barenbaum/66/Dir., Richard White/Dir.

Owners: Morris Goldfarb, Ray M. Moberg, Larry C. Barenbaum, Neil I. Sell/8.90%, Lyle Berman/21.90%, Dreman Value Management, LLC/6.10%, Timothy J. Cope/2.60%, Wells Fargo& Company/7.60%, Insiders/32.80%

*Financial Data: Fiscal Year End:*01/01 *Latest Annual Data:* 12/31/2006

Year	Sales	Net Income
2006	$81,596,000	$19,840,000
2005	$17,557,000	-$4,041,000

Curr. Assets:	$88,029,000	*Curr. Liab.:*	$29,349,000		
Plant, Equip.:	$34,250,000	*Total Liab.:*	$156,400,000	*Indic. Yr. Divd.:*	NA
Total Assets:	$361,176,000	*Net Worth:*	$204,776,000	*Debt/ Equity:*	NA

Lakeside Mortgage Fund LLC

443 Redcliff Dr., Ste 240, Redding, CA, 96002; *PH:* 1-530-226-5850; *http://* www.lakesidefinancial.com; *Email:* info@lakesidefinancial.com

General - Incorporation	CA	*Stock*- Price on:12/24/2007	NA
Employees	NA	Stock Exchange	NA
Auditor	Armanino Mckenna LLP	Ticker Symbol	NA
Stk Agt	NA	Outstanding Shares	NA
Counsel	NA	E.P.S.	NA
DUNS No.	NA	Shareholders	NA

Business: The group's principle activity is to invest in trust deeds secured by commercial real property. The group is engaged in making loans to owners and developers real property who seek an alternative from traditional mortgage lenders for their financing needs. The group operates from United States.

Primary SIC and add'l.: 6162

CIK No: 0001299919

Officers: William F. Webster/48/Dir., CEO, Pres., Sec., Placido H. Canta/55/CFO, Richard A. Nelson/68/VP

Directors: William F. Webster/48/Dir., CEO, Pres., Sec., James S. Koenig/55/Dir., Gary Armitage/58/Dir., Jeffery Guidi/52/Dir.

Owners: Jeffery Guidi/23.50%, James S. Koenig/47.00%, Gary Armitage/23.50%, Gary Armitage/6.00%, Insiders/100.00%

Lam Research Corp

4650 Cushing Pkwy., Fremont, CA, 94538; *PH:* 1-510-572-0200; *Fax:* 1-510-572-2935; *http://* www.lamrc.com

General - Incorporation	DE	*Stock*- Price on:12/24/2007	$52.85
Employees	2,430	Stock Exchange	NDQ
Auditor	Ernst & Young LLP	Ticker Symbol	LRCX
Stk Agt	Mellon Investor Services LLC	Outstanding Shares	135,070,000
Counsel. Heller Ehrman White & McAuliffe LLP		E.P.S.	$4.41
DUNS No.	03-813-7956	Shareholders	NA

Business: The group's principle activities are to design, manufacture, market and service semiconductor processing equipment used in the fabrication of integrated circuits. The products include single wafer plasma etch systems with a wide range of applications, chemical mechanical planarization (cmp) and post-cmp wafer cleaning systems as well as post-sale services and support for these systems. Etch and cmp products selectively remove portions of various films from the wafer to create an integrated circuit. The group's customers consist of semiconductor manufacturers in the United States, Europe, Japan and Asia-Pacific. The group's quarterly revenue for March 2007 was 650.27 millions of USD.

Primary SIC and add'l.: 3674

CIK No: 0000707549

Subsidiaries: Lam Research (Ireland) Limited, Lam Research (Israel) Ltd., Lam Research (Shanghai) Co., Ltd., LAM Research B.V., Lam Research Co., Ltd., Lam Research Corporation, Lam Research GmbH, Lam Research International B.V., Lam Research International Sarl, Lam Research Korea Limited, Lam Research Ltd., Lam Research S.r.l., Lam Research SAS, Lam Research Service Co., Ltd., Lam Research Singapore Pte Ltd 16 Subsidiaries included in the Index

Officers: James W. Bagley/Exec. Chmn., Martin Anstice/Sr. Dir., Operations Controller, Stephen G. Newberry/Dir., COO, Exec. VP

Directors: James W. Bagley/Exec. Chmn., David G. Arscott/Dir., Robert M. Berdahl/Dir., Grant Inman/Dir., Seiichi Watanabe/Dir., Jack R. Harris/Dir., Stephen G. Newberry/Dir., COO, Exec. VP, Richard J. Elkus/Dir., Catherine Lego/Dir., Patricia S. Wolpert/Dir.

Owners: Martin B. Anstice, Nicolas J. Bright, Richard J. Elkus, Fidelity Management & Research Company/7.84%, Jack R. Harris, Insiders, Stephen G. Newberry, Barclays Global Investors, NA/11.84%, Robert M. Berdahl, David G. Arscott, Wellington Management Company LLP/7.99%, Grant M. Inman, James W. Bagley, Ernest E. Maddock

*Financial Data: Fiscal Year End:*06/26 *Latest Annual Data:* 6/25/2006

Year	Sales	Net Income
2006	$1,642,171,000	$335,755,000
2005	$1,502,453,000	$299,341,000
2004	$935,946,000	$82,988,000

Curr. Assets:	$896,388,000	*Curr. Liab.:*	$376,606,000	*P/E Ratio:*	11.98
Plant, Equip.:	$42,444,000	*Total Liab.:*	$386,160,000	*Indic. Yr. Divd.:*	NA
Total Assets:	$1,198,626,000	*Net Worth:*	$812,466,000	*Debt/ Equity:*	NA

Lamar Advertising Company

5551 Corporate Blvd., Ste 2-A, Baton Rouge, LA, 70808; *PH:* 1-225-926-1000; *Fax:* 1-225-926-1005; *http://* www.lamar.com

General - Incorporation	DE	*Stock*- Price on:12/24/2007	$63.38
Employees	NA	Stock Exchange	NDQ
Auditor	KPMG LLP	Ticker Symbol	LAMR
Stk Agt	American Stock Transfer & Trust Co.	Outstanding Shares	98,100,000
Counsel	NA	E.P.S.	$0.49
DUNS No.	NA	Shareholders	NA

Business: The groups principle activity is to provide outdoor advertising services. The products of the group include billboards, logo signs and transit advertising displays. Customers served by the group include restaurants, retailers, health care and hotels and motels. The group operates from the United States and Canada. The group's quarterly revenue for September 2007 was 314.25 millions of USD.

Primary SIC and add'l.: 7319 7312

CIK No: 0001090425

Subsidiaries: American Signs, Inc., Canadian TODS Limited, Colorado Logos, Inc., Delaware Logos, L.L.C., Florida Logos, Inc., Georgia Logos, L.L.C., Interstate Logos, L.L.C., Kansas Logos, Inc., Kentucky Logos, LLC, Lamar Advantage GP Company, LLC, Lamar Advantage Holding Company, Lamar Advantage LP Company, LLC, Lamar Advantage Outdoor Company, L.P., Lamar Advertising Company, Lamar Advertising of Colorado Springs, Inc. 77 Subsidiaries included in the Index

Officers: Kevin P. Reilly/Chmn., CEO, Pres./$3,681,329.00, Keith A. Istre/CFO/$2,221,187.00, Jim McIlwain/General Counsel, Rachel Tempanaro/GM, Theresa Doran/General Information, Sean Reilly/COO, Pres. - Outdoor Division/$3,190,720.00, Brent McCoy/Exec. VP, James R. McIlwain/Sec., General Counsel, Everett Stewart/Pres. - Interstate Logos, Robert B. Switzer/VP - Operations, Thomas F. Teepell/Chief Marketing Officer, John M. Miller/VP, Dir. - National Sales, Hal Kilshaw/VP - Governmental Relations, Tammy Duncan/VP - Human Resources, Scott Butterfield/Mgr. - Northwest Region *(24 Officers included in Index)*

Directors: Kevin P. Reilly/Chmn., CEO, Pres., John Maxwell Hamilton/Dir., Robert M. Jelenic/Dir., Stephen P. Mumblow/Dir., Thomas V. Reifenheiser/Dir., Wendell Reilly/Dir., Anna Reilly Cullinan/Dir.

Owners: Charles W. Lamar, Scout Capital, Keith A. Istre, Thomas V. Reifenheiser, Wendell Reilly, Anna Reilly, Stephen P. Mumblow, Sean E. Reilly, Wendell Reilly, Insiders, Janus Capital Management LLC, The Reilly Family Limited Partnership, SPO Advisory Corp., Anna Reilly, Kevin P. Reilly *(21 Owners included in Index)*

*Financial Data: Fiscal Year End:*12/31 *Latest Annual Data:* 3/31/2007

Year	Sales	Net Income
2007	NA	NA
2006	NA	NA
2005	$1,021,656,000	$41,779,000

Curr. Assets:	$230,770,000	*Curr. Liab.:*	$110,979,000		
Plant, Equip.:	$1,405,948,000	*Total Liab.:*	$2,385,695,000	*Indic. Yr. Divd.:*	NA
Total Assets:	$3,924,228,000	*Net Worth:*	$1,538,533,000	*Debt/ Equity:*	NA

Lamperd Less Lethal Inc

1200 Michener Rd., Sarnia, ON, N7T 7H8; *PH:* 1-519-344-4445; *http://* www.lamperdlesslethal.com; *Email:* info@lamperdlesslethal.com

General - Incorporation	NV	*Stock*- Price on:12/24/2007	$0.085
Employees	NA	Stock Exchange	OTC
Auditor	Mintz & Partners LLP	Ticker Symbol	LLLI
Stk Agt	Nevada Agency & Trust Company	Outstanding Shares	NA
Counsel	NA	E.P.S.	NA
DUNS No.	NA	Shareholders	NA

Business: The groups principle activities include developing and manufacturing civil defense products. Products of the group include shields, service equipment, training gear and accessories. In April 2005, the group acquired Ontario Limited. The group operates from North America.

Primary SIC and add'l.: 3480

CIK No: 0001169394

Officers: Barry Lamperd/Dir., CEO, Pres., Sharon Scott/54/COO

Directors: Barry Lamperd/Dir., CEO, Pres., Ed Ferguson/Dir., Sandy Glenn/Dir., Domenic Dicarlo/Dir., Alexander Purvis Glenn/61/Dir., R. Nicholls/Dir., Terry Smith/55/Dir., D'arcy David William Bell/54/Dir.

Owners: Dominic Dicarlo/5.29%, Bruce Strebinger/5.56%, Insiders/27.69%, D'Arcy David William Bell/10.66%, Barry Lamperd/11.28%, Edward Ferguson, 1109630 Ontario Limited/2.07%, Ernie Taglione/5.29%, Mercer Investments Inc/5.56%

*Financial Data: Fiscal Year End:*12/31 *Latest Annual Data:* 12/31/2006

Year	Sales	Net Income
2006	$316,000	-$723,000
2005	$242,000	-$944,000
2004	NA	-$11,000

Curr. Assets:	$170,000	*Curr. Liab.:*	$418,000		
Plant, Equip.:	$219,000	*Total Liab.:*	$418,000	*Indic. Yr. Divd.:*	NA
Total Assets:	$418,000	*Net Worth:*	$1,000	*Debt/ Equity:*	NA

Lamson & Sessions Co (The)

25701 Science Pk. Dr, Cleveland, OH, 44122; **PH:** 1-216-464-3400;
http:// www.lamson-sessions.com

General - Incorporation	OH	**Stock**- Price on:12/24/2007	$25.94
Employees	1,281	Stock Exchange	NYSE
Auditor	Ernst & Young LLP	Ticker Symbol	LMS
Stk Agt	National City Bank	Outstanding Shares	15,850,000
Counsel	Jones Day	E.P.S.	$1.83
DUNS No.	00-419-6556	Shareholders	NA

Business: The group's principal activities are to manufacture and distribute a broad range of thermoplastic electrical, telecommunications and engineered sewer products. The group operates in three segments, carlon, lamson home products and pvc pipe. The products sold by carlon segment include electrical and telecommunications raceway systems and electrical outlet boxes and fittings. The products of lamson home products segment include liquidtight conduit, electrical fittings, door chimes and lighting controls. The products of pvc pipe segment include electrical, power and communications conduit. The customers of the group are electrical contractors and distributors, original equipment manufacturers, electric power utilities, cable television (catv), telecommunications companies, home centers and mass merchandisers.

Primary SIC and add'l.: 3643 3644 3084 3645

CIK No: 0000057497

Subsidiaries: Jacobs Engineering Company, Jacobs Engineering Group of Ohio Inc., Jacobs Field Services North America, Jacobs Government Services Company, JE Remediation Technologies

Officers: Michael J. Merriman/Dir., CEO, Pres., James A. Rajecki/VP - Operations, Aileen Liebertz/Mgr. - Investor Relations, Jones Day/Corporate Counsel, William H. Coquillette/Assist. Sec., Dir., Donald A. Gutierrez/Sr. VP, Eileen E. Clancy/VP, Lori L. Spencer/VP, Controller, Norman P. Sutterer/Sr. VP, James J. Abel/Dir., Exec. VP, Sec., Treasurer, CFO, Andrew J. Patterson/CIO, VP, Michael R. Pearch/VP - Supply Chain

Directors: Michael J. Merriman/Dir., CEO, Pres., John B. Schulze/Non Exec. Chmn., George R. Hill/Dir., William H. Coquillette/Assist. Sec., Dir., John C. Dannemiller/Dir., Malachi A. Mixon/Dir., James J. Abel/Dir., Exec. VP, Sec., Treasurer, CFO, James T. Bartlett/Dir., Van D. Skilling/Dir., William E. MacDonald/Dir.

Owners: Michael J. Merriman, Donald A. Gutierrez, Malachi A. Mixon, Norman P. Sutterer, John C. Dannemiller, Starboard Value and Opportunity Master FundLtd. et al./9.99%, James T. Bartlett, William E. MacDonald, Van D. Skilling, Barclays Global Investors, NA/3.01%, Thompson, Siegel& Walmsley, Inc./6.16%, James J. Abel/3.50%, George R. Hill, Farhad Fred Ebrahimi/8.90%, William H. Coquillette *(19 Owners included in Index)*

Financial Data: *Fiscal Year End:*12/31   *Latest Annual Data:* 12/30/2006

Year	Sales	Net Income
2006	$561,270,000	$39,143,000
2005	$494,195,000	$27,395,000

Curr. Assets:	$129,197,000	**Curr. Liab.:**	$71,978,000	**P/E Ratio:**	12.18
Plant, Equip.:	$48,833,000	**Total Liab.:**	$149,708,000	**Indic. Yr. Divd.:**	NA
Total Assets:	$240,007,000	**Net Worth:**	$90,299,000	**Debt/ Equity:**	0.0523

Lan Airlines

1960 E Grand Ave., Ste. 530., El Segundo, CA, 90245; **PH:** 1-310-416-9061; **Fax:** 1-310-416-9864;
http:// www.7.lan.com

General - Incorporation	Chile	**Stock**- Price on:12/24/2007	$82.58
Employees	15,099	Stock Exchange	NYSE
Auditor	PricewaterhouseCoopers LLP	Ticker Symbol	LFL
Stk Agt	NA	Outstanding Shares	63,780,000
Counsel	NA	E.P.S.	$0.84
DUNS No.	NA	Shareholders	NA

Business: The group's principal activity is the operation of domestic and international passenger and cargo air carrier in Chile. It serves destinations in Chile, Peru, Latin America, North America and South Pacific.

Primary SIC and add'l.: 4491 4512 4731

CIK No: 0001047716

Subsidiaries: Aircraft International Leasing Limited, Bluebird Leasing LLC, Inmobiliaria Aeronutica S.A., Inversiones Lan S.A., Lan Cargo Overseas Services Limited, Lan Cargo S.A., Lan Logistics Corp., Lan Pax Group S.A., Lan Per S.A., Seagull Leasing LLC, South Florida Air Cargo, Transporte Areo S.A.

Officers: Armando Valdivieso Montes/CEO - Passenger, Enrique Cueto Plaza/VP - Exec., CEO, Cristian Ureta Larrain/CEO - Cargo, Jorge Awad Mehech/Chmn., Pres., Alejandro De La Fuente Goic/CFO, Ignacio Cueto Plaza/COO, Pres., Enrique Elsaca Hirmas/Sr. VP - Strateic Planning, Carlos Prado Canepa/Sr. VP - Corporate Investment, Marco Jofre Marin/Sr. VP - Operations - Engineering, Maintanance, Emilio Delreal Sota/Sr. VP - Human Resources

Directors: Jorge Awad Mehech/Chmn., Pres., Juan Jose Cueto Plaza/Dir., Jose Cox Donoso/Dir., Juan Cueto Sierra/Dir., Andres Navarro Haeussler/Dir., Dario Calderon Gonzalez/Dir., Bernardo Fontaine Talavera/Dir., Ramon Eblen Kadis/Dir.

Owners: Axxion S.A./20.64%, Principal Shareholder/9.96%, Inversiones Costa Verde Limitada y Compaa en Comandita por Acciones/27.01%, Inversiones Santa Cecilia S.A./7.34%

Financial Data: *Fiscal Year End:*12/31   *Latest Annual Data:* 12/31/2006

Year	Sales	Net Income
2006	$3,033,960,000	$209,730,000
2005	$2,506,353,000	$154,970,000
2004	$2,092,945,000	$160,703,000

Curr. Assets:	$706,308,000	**Curr. Liab.:**	$876,283,000		
Plant, Equip.:	$1,876,455,000	**Total Liab.:**	$2,316,965,000	**Indic. Yr. Divd.:**	$0.860
Total Assets:	$2,931,284,000	**Net Worth:**	$614,319,000	**Debt/ Equity:**	NA

Lanbo Financial Group Inc

C/o W Windsor Professional Ctr, 51 Everett Dr., Ste. A-20, West Windsor, NJ, 08550;
PH: 1-609-799-1889; *http://* www.lbfi.cc

General - Incorporation	NV	**Stock**- Price on:12/24/2007	$0.055
Employees	NA	Stock Exchange	OTC
Auditor	LL Bradford & Co	Ticker Symbol	LNBO
Stk Agt	Interwest Transfer Company, Inc.	Outstanding Shares	NA
Counsel	NA	E.P.S.	NA
DUNS No.	NA	Shareholders	NA

Business: The group's principle activity is to provide technology to develop processes at lower the costs of production of printed circuit boards. The company manufactures and markets circuit boards. Licensed and proprietary technology are used by the company to develop direct electronic imaging, plating and etching workstations for high density interconnects and a prototype production facility to manufacture printed circuit boards. The company operates as a development stage company. The group operates from United States.

Primary SIC and add'l.: 3678

CIK No: 0001061819

Subsidiaries: New Star Real Estate Development Co.

Officers: Genxiang Xiao/41/CEO, Pres., Yulong Wan/42/CFO, Zhiyong Shi/47/VP

Directors: Genxiang Xiao/41/CEO, Pres., Pingji Lu/55/Chmn., Xiaohong Feng/41/Dir.

Financial Data: *Fiscal Year End:*12/31   *Latest Annual Data:* 09/30/2005

Year	Sales	Net Income
2005	NA	NA
2004	$40,258,000	$4,525,000
2003	NA	$216,000

Curr. Assets:	$11,475,000	**Curr. Liab.:**	$32,811,000		
Plant, Equip.:	$30,117,000	**Total Liab.:**	$37,046,000	**Indic. Yr. Divd.:**	NA
Total Assets:	$44,192,000	**Net Worth:**	$7,146,000	**Debt/ Equity:**	0.5137

Lancaster Colony Corp

37 W Broad St., Columbus, OH, 43215; **PH:** 1-614-224-7141; **Fax:** 1-614-469-8219;
http:// www.lancastercolony.com

General - Incorporation	OH	**Stock**- Price on:12/24/2007	$41.79
Employees	5,600	Stock Exchange	NDQ
Auditor	Deloitte & Touche LLP	Ticker Symbol	LANC
Stk Agt	American Stock Transfer & Trust Co.	Outstanding Shares	31,280,000
Counsel	Squire, Sanders & Dempsey LLP	E.P.S.	$1.52
DUNS No.	00-192-8035	Shareholders	NA

Business: The group's principal activities are to manufacture and market specialty foods, glassware, candles and automotive accessories. The specialty food segment manufactures and sells a family of pourable and refrigerated produce salad dressings, croutons, sauces, refrigerated produce vegetable and fruit dips. It also includes dry and frozen egg noodles, caviar, frozen ready-to-bake pies, frozen hearth-baked breads and frozen yeast rolls for the retail and food service markets under the brand names of marzetti, pfeiffer, sister schubert's and others. The glassware and candles segment sells table and giftware consisting of domestic and imported glassware; candles in popular sizes, shapes and scents; industrial glass and lighting components and glass floral containers. The automotive segment manufactures and sells rubber, vinyl and carpet-on-rubber car mats for original equipment manufacturers, truck and trailer splashguards and aluminum running boards for trucks and vans.

Primary SIC and add'l.: 3069 3229 3999 2098 2051 2053 2035

CIK No: 0000057515

Subsidiaries: Dee Zee, Inc., E. O. Brody Company, Indiana Glass Company, Jackson Plastics Operations, Inc., Koneta, Inc., LaGrange Molded Products, Inc., Lancaster Colony Commercial Products, Inc., Lancaster Glass Corporation, Marzetti Frozen Pasta, Inc. (FKA Reames Foods, Inc.), New York Frozen Foods, Inc., Pretty Products, Inc., Sister Schuberts Homemade Rolls, Inc., T. Marzetti Company, The Quality Bakery Company, Inc.

Officers: John B. Gerlach/Chmn., CEO, Pres., Bruce L. Rosa/VP - Development, John L. Boylan/VP, CFO, Treasurer, Assist. Sec., Dir., David M. Segal/Corp. Sec., Corporate Counsel, Matthew R. Shurte/Assist. Sec., Corporate Counsel

Directors: John B. Gerlach/Chmn., CEO, Pres., James B. Bachmann/65/Dir., Henry M. O'Neill/73/Dir., John L. Boylan/VP, CFO, Treasurer, Assist. Sec., Dir., Neeli Bendapudi/45/Dir., Robert S. Hamilton/80/Dir., Robert L. Fox/59/Dir., Edward H. Jennings/71/Dir., Zuheir Sofia/64/Dir.

Owners: Bruce L. Rosa, Barington Companies Equity/5.61%, Zuheir Sofia, Insiders/29.51%, Dareth A. Gerlach/19.67%, Henry M. ONeill, John L. Boylan, Edward H. Jennings, Neeli Bendapudi, Robert S. Hamilton, James B. Bachmann, Robert L. Fox/3.62%, John B. Gerlach/27.43%

Financial Data: *Fiscal Year End:*06/30   *Latest Annual Data:* 6/30/2006

Year	Sales	Net Income
2006	$1,175,260,000	$82,954,000
2005	$1,131,466,000	$93,088,000
2004	$1,096,953,000	$80,002,000

Curr. Assets:	$278,911,000	**Curr. Liab.:**	$141,790,000	**P/E Ratio:**	28.82
Plant, Equip.:	$208,431,000	**Total Liab.:**	$154,188,000	**Indic. Yr. Divd.:**	$1.080
Total Assets:	$598,497,000	**Net Worth:**	$444,309,000	**Debt/ Equity:**	NA

Lance Inc

8600 S Blvd., Charlotte, NC, 28273; **PH:** 1-704-554-1421; **Fax:** 1-704-554-5562;
http:// www.lance.com

General - Incorporation	NC	**Stock**- Price on:12/24/2007	$24.01
Employees	4,800	Stock Exchange	NDQ
Auditor	KPMG LLP	Ticker Symbol	LNCE
Stk Agt	First Union Nat'l Bank	Outstanding Shares	30,990,000
Counsel	NA	E.P.S.	$0.90
DUNS No.	00-315-9100	Shareholders	NA

Business: The group's principal activity is to manufacture, market and distribute branded and un-branded snack food products. The products include sandwich crackers and cookies, crackers, cookies, potato chips, nuts, cakes and other salty snacks. The brands, under which these products are sold includes, lance, cape cod potato chips, toastchee, toasty, nekot, nipchee, choc-o-lunch, van-o-lunch, gold-n-chees, captain's wafers, thunder, rj munchers, bloops, outpost, vista and jodan. The group distributes its products through its direct-store delivery system or by direct shipments. The customer base for the products include grocery stores, convenience stores, food service brokers and institutions, mass merchandisers, drug stores, vending operators, schools, military and government facilities and outlets such as recreational facilities, offices, and independent retailers. The products are distributed throughout the United States, parts of Canada and Europe.

Primary SIC and add'l.: 5461 2051 2052

CIK No: 0000057528

Subsidiaries: Cape Cod Potato Chip Company Inc., Caronuts, Inc., Columbus Capital Acquisitions, Inc., Fresno Ventures, Inc., Lance Mfg. LLC, Lanfin Investments Inc., Lanhold Investments, Inc., Tamming Foods Ltd., Vista Bakery, Inc.

Officers: David V. Singer/Dir., CEO, Pres./$2,389,051.00, Earl D. Leake/VP - Human Resources/$552,007.00, Margaret E. Wicklund/Controller, Principal Accounting Officer, Assist. Sec., Frank I. Lewis/VP - Sales/$589,681.00, Dean H. Fields/VP, Rick D. Puckett/Exec. VP, CFO, Treasurer, Sec./$930,680.00, Blake Thompson/VP - Supply Chain/$719,058.00, Glenn Patcha/Sr. VP - Sales, Marketing

Directors: David V. Singer/Dir., CEO, Pres., W. J. Prezzano/Chmn., Robert V. Sisk/Dir., Dan C. Swander/Dir., Barbara R. Allen/Dir., Jeffrey A. Atkins/Dir., J. P. Bolduc/Dir., William R. Holland/Dir., Isaiah Tidwell/Dir., Lance S. Van Every/Dir.

Owners: Earl D. Leake, Frank I. Lewis, William R. Holland, Robert V. Sisk, Wellington Management/12.68%, Barbara R. Allen, Isaiah Tidwell, J. P. Bolduc, Barclays Global Investors, NA/5.41%, W. J. Prezzano, S. Lance Van Every/1.30%, Insiders/2.40%, David L. Burner, Jeffrey A. Atkins, Nan D. Van Every/5.38% *(19 Owners included in Index)*

Financial Data: Fiscal Year End:12/31   Latest Annual Data: 12/30/2006

Year	Sales	Net Income
2006	$730,116,000	$18,478,000
2005	$679,257,000	$18,470,000
2004	$600,455,000	$24,855,000

Curr. Assets:	$119,625,000	Curr. Liab.:	$116,050,000	P/E Ratio:	29.28
Plant, Equip.:	$186,093,000	Total Liab.:	$167,370,000	Indic. Yr. Divd.:	$0.640
Total Assets:	$369,079,000	Net Worth:	$201,709,000	Debt/ Equity:	NA

Lancer Corp TX

6655 Lancer Blvd., San Antonio, TX, 78219; **PH:** 1-210-310-7000; *http://* www.lancercorp.com

General - Incorporation	TX	Stock - Price on:12/24/2007	$22
Employees	NA	Stock Exchange	AMEX
Auditor	BDO Seidman LLP	Ticker Symbol	LAN
Stk Agt	Bank of New York	Outstanding Shares	NA
Counsel	Lang Ladon Green Coghlan Fisher	E.P.S.	NA
DUNS No.	04-701-3412	Shareholders	NA

Business: The group's principal activity is to design, engineer, manufacture and market fountain soft drink, beer and citrus beverage dispensing systems, and other equipment. The products are divided into four categories: soft drink, citrus, and frozen beverage dispensers category manufactures and sells a broad range of mechanically cooled and ice cooled soft drink and citrus dispensing systems. Post-mix dispensing valves category manufactures and sells post-mix dispensing valves. Beer dispensing systems category manufactures and markets beer dispensing equipment and related accessories. Other related products and services category remanufacture various dispensing systems and sells replacement parts. The customers include soft drink companies, bottlers, equipment distributors, beer breweries and food service chains. The group manufactures products in Australia and Mexico, and operates warehouses in Belgium, Ecuador, New Zealand, and the United Kingdom.

Primary SIC and add'l.: 3585 3556

CIK No: 0000768162

Subsidiaries: Advanced Beverage Solutions, LLC, Industrias Lancermex, S.A. de C.V., Lancer Capital Corporation, Lancer de Mexico, S.A. de C.V., Lancer do Brasil, Industria e Comercio Ltda., Lancer Europe, S.A., Lancer FBD Partnership, Ltd., Lancer Frank Corporation, Lancer GB, LLP, Lancer Ice Link, LLC, Lancer International Sales, Inc., Lancer Investment Corporation, Lancer Pacific, Ltd., Lancer Pacific, Pty. Ltd., Lancer Partnership, Ltd. 17 Subsidiaries included in the Index

Officers: Elsayed Moniem/Regional Mgr. - Egypt, Middle East, Patrick Co/Dir. Asia - Authorized Distributors, Carlos Robles/Authorized Distributor - Mexico, Luciano Lopez/Authorized Distributor - Las Acacias, Rafael Mendoza/Authorized Distributor, SA, Argentina, Fabio Queiroz/Authorized Distributor - Brasil, Heriberto Concha/Authorized Distributor - Chile, Shabbir Shafiqui/Area Mgr. - India, Sub, Continent

Landauer Inc

2 Science Rd., Glenwood, IL, 60425; **PH:** 1-708-755-7000; **Fax:** 1-708-755-7016; *http://* www.landauerinc.com; **Email:** custserv@landauerinc.com

General - Incorporation	DE	Stock - Price on:12/24/2007	$48.09
Employees	420	Stock Exchange	NYSE
Auditor	PricewaterhouseCoopers LLP	Ticker Symbol	LDR
Stk Agt	American Stock Transfer & Trust Co.	Outstanding Shares	9,190,000
Counsel	Sidley, Austin, Brown & Wood	E.P.S.	$2.25
DUNS No.	18-980-7159	Shareholders	NA

Business: The group's principal activity is to provide services for monitoring radiation. The service offered relates to measuring of dosages of X-ray, gamma radiation and other penetrating ionizing radiations to which the client has been exposed. It is measured primarily through optically stimulated luminescent badges worn by the client. The technology is marketed under the trade name 'luxel'. The other services of the group include the detection of radon gas and radiation monitoring. The group also operates a crystal manufacturing facility. The services of the group are marketed in the United States, Japan, Brazil, China, the United Kingdom and France.

Primary SIC and add'l.: 8071 8734

CIK No: 0000825410

Subsidiaries: Beijing-Landauer, Ltd., HomeBuyers Preferred, Inc., LCIE-Landauer, Ltd., Nagase-Landauer, Ltd., SAPRA-Landauer, Ltda.

Officers: Jonathon M. Singer/Sr. VP, Treasurer, Sec., CFO, Gerard P. Bilek/46/VP, Controller, Richard E. Bailey/Sr. VP - Operations

Owners: NFJ Investment Group L.P./5.80%, Eaton Vance Management/7.30%, Stephen C. Mitchell, Craig R. Yoder, Robert M. Greaney, Gary D. Eppen, Robert J. Cronin, Gail E. de Planque, Royce & Associates, LLC/6.10%, Richard E. Bailey, Richard R. Risk, T. Rowe Price Associates, Inc./9.30%, William E. Saxelby, Insiders/2.70%, Michael D. Winfield *(17 Owners included in Index)*

Financial Data: Fiscal Year End:09/30   Latest Annual Data: 9/30/2006

Year	Sales	Net Income
2006	$79,043,000	$19,046,000
2005	$75,221,000	$17,208,000
2004	$69,809,000	$17,770,000

Curr. Assets:	$50,505,000	Curr. Liab.:	$27,967,000	P/E Ratio:	22.79
Plant, Equip.:	$16,654,000	Total Liab.:	$37,542,000	Indic. Yr. Divd.:	$1.900
Total Assets:	$97,340,000	Net Worth:	$59,510,000	Debt/ Equity:	NA

Landec Corp

3603 HAve.n Ave., Menlo Park, CA, 94025; **PH:** 1-650-306-1650; **Fax:** 1-650-368-9818; *http://* www.landec.com

General - Incorporation	CA	Stock - Price on:12/24/2007	$12.67
Employees	186	Stock Exchange	NDQ
Auditor	Ernst & Young LLP	Ticker Symbol	LNDC
Stk Agt	U.S. Stock Transfer Corp	Outstanding Shares	25,590,000
Counsel	Orrick, Herrington & Sutcliffe LLP	E.P.S.	$1.16
DUNS No.	17-707-0794	Shareholders	NA

Business: The group's principal activities are to design, develop, manufacture and sell temperature-activated and other specialty polymer products. It operates in two business segments: food products technology segment markets and packs produce and specialty packaged fresh-cut vegetables that incorporate the intelimer packaging technology for the fresh-cut produce industry. Agricultural seed technology segment markets and distributes hybrid seed corn to the farming industry and is developing seed coatings using the proprietary intelimer(R) polymers. The group also operates a technology licensing/research and development business that licenses products outside its business to leading industries.

Primary SIC and add'l.: 8731 8734 2823

CIK No: 0001005286

Subsidiaries: Apio, Inc., Landec Ag, Inc

Owners: Robert Tobin, Nicholas Tompkins/4.56%, Richard S. Schneider, Stephen E. Halprin, Steven P. Bitler, Kenneth E. Jones/3.13%, David D. Taft, Insiders/15.87%, Wynnefield Partners Small Cap Value, L.P./5.84%, Duke K. Bristow, Gary T. Steele/2.82%, Gregory S. Skinner/1.33%, Frederick Frank/2.31%

Financial Data: Fiscal Year End:05/28   Latest Annual Data: 05/27/2007

Year	Sales	Net Income
2007	$210,498,000	$29,189,000
2006	$231,953,000	$8,651,000
2005	$205,230,000	$5,402,000

Curr. Assets:	$36,011,000	Curr. Liab.:	$27,095,000	P/E Ratio:	11.84
Plant, Equip.:	$18,341,000	Total Liab.:	$29,906,000	Indic. Yr. Divd.:	NA
Total Assets:	$93,007,000	Net Worth:	$61,549,000	Debt/ Equity:	NA

Landmark Bancorp Inc

701 Poyntz Ave., Manhattan, KS, 66505; **PH:** 1-785-565-2000; **Fax:** 1-785-537-0619; *http://* www.banklandmark.com

General - Incorporation	DE	Stock - Price on:12/24/2007	$28
Employees	194	Stock Exchange	NDQ
Auditor	KPMG LLP	Ticker Symbol	LARK
Stk Agt	Registrar & Transfer Co	Outstanding Shares	2,330,000
Counsel	NA	E.P.S.	$2.26
DUNS No.	87-298-8118	Shareholders	NA

Business: The group's principal activities are to accept deposits from the general public and use these deposits to originate consumer, commercial, multi-family, and one-to-four family residential mortgage loans in Kansas. Commercial lending includes loans to service, retail, wholesale and light manufacturing businesses including agricultural operations. Consumer lending includes automobile, boat, student loans, home improvement and home equity loans. The group also purchases mortgage-backed securities and investment securities. The group operates through its branch offices in manhattan, auburn, dodge city, garden city, great bend, hoisington, lacrosse, topeka, osage city and wamego, Kansas and the surrounding communities in riley, barton, finney, ford, pottawatomie, rush, shawnee and osage counties in Kansas. On 01-Apr-2004, the group acquired first Kansas financial corporation.

Primary SIC and add'l.: 6712 6035

CIK No: 0001141688

Subsidiaries: Landmark Capital Trust I, Landmark Capital Trust II, Landmark National Bank

Owners: Insiders/26.30%, Richard A. Ball/1.70%, Larry R. Heyka, Jim W. Lewis/2.30%, Joseph L. Downey, Michael E. Scheopner/1.90%, Patrick L. Alexander/4.30%, Mark A. Herpich/1.60%, C. Duane Ross/1.90%, Jerry R. Pettle, Brent A. Bowman, Mark J. Oliphant, Dean R. Thibault, Larry L. Schugart/5.00%, First Manhattan Co./5.40% *(17 Owners included in Index)*

Financial Data: Fiscal Year End:12/31   Latest Annual Data: 12/31/2006

Year	Sales	Net Income
2006	$41,608,000	$6,010,000
2005	$27,181,000	$3,897,000
2004	$25,075,000	$4,251,000

Curr. Assets:	$22,044,000	Curr. Liab.:	$512,836,000	P/E Ratio:	11.29
Plant, Equip.:	$13,767,000	Total Liab.:	$541,332,000	Indic. Yr. Divd.:	$0.760
Total Assets:	$590,568,000	Net Worth:	$49,236,000	Debt/ Equity:	0.5686

Landmark National Bank CA

937 Lomas Santa Fe Dr., Solana Beach, CA , 92075; **PH:** 1-858-509-2700; **Fax:** 1-858-509-0898; *http://* www.landmarknb.com; **Email:** Info@LandmarkNationalBank.com

General - Incorporation		Stock - Price on:12/24/2007	$11.47
Employees	NA	Stock Exchange	NA
Auditor	NA	Ticker Symbol	NA
Stk Agt	NA	Outstanding Shares	1,920,000
Counsel	NA	E.P.S.	NA
DUNS No.	NA	Shareholders	NA

Business: The groups principal activity is to provide banking service. The services of the group include personal account, business account, originating loans, deposit, wire transfer, safe deposit boxes, automatic teller machine, direct deposit, night depository, payroll services, merchant teller booth and phone and online banking. The group operates from California in the United States.

Primary SIC and add'l.: 6021

CIK No:

Officers: Rick Mandelbaum/Dir., CEO, COO, Pres., Founder, James A. Boyce/Exec. VP - Solana Beach, Philip Chapman/Sr. VP, Chief Credit Officer, Tony Divita/Sr. VP, Chief Banking Officer, Steven Bechen/VP, Commercial Loan Officer, Relationship Mgr., Jack Clemmer/VP - Lending, Jim Healy/VP - Lending, Catherine Anthony/VP, Administrative Officer, Jane Guthrie/VP, Dir. - Human Resources, Joe Snyder/VP, Client Services Mgr., Karen Vold/VP, Loan Officer

Directors: Rick Mandelbaum/Dir., CEO, COO, Pres., Founder, James J. Schmid/Chmn., Vincent E. Benstead/Vice Chmn., Martin C. Dickinson/Founder, Vice Chmn., Ronald J. Carlson/Founder, Dir., Michael McCafferty/Founder, Edward Richard/Founder, Larry G. Showley/Dir., Edward J. Osuna/Founder, Dir., Marshal A. Scarr/Dir., Orrin L. Gabsch/Founder, Dir., David B. Goodell/Founder, Dir., Christopher Scripps McKellar/Dir., Anne C. Taubman/Dir., Christopher Weil/Dir. *(21 Directors included in Index)*

Landrys Restaurants Inc

1510 W Loop S, Houston, TX, 77027; *PH:* 1-713-850-1010; *Fax:* 1-713-850-7205; *http://* www.landrysseafood.com

General - Incorporation	DE	**Stock**- Price on:12/24/2007	$30.24
Employees	31,245	Stock Exchange	NYSE
Auditor	Grant Thornton LLP	Ticker Symbol	LNY
Stk Agt	American Stock Transfer & Trust Co.	Outstanding Shares	22,020,000
Counsel	NA	E.P.S.	$0.79
DUNS No.	10-266-4935	Shareholders	NA

Business: The group's principal activity is the ownership and operation of full-service, casual dining restaurants. The restaurants are run under the names of joe's crab snack, landry's seafood house, the crab house, charley's crab, the chart house, saltgrass steak house and rainforest cafe. The restaurants offer a wide variety of broiled, grilled and fried seafood items with a choice of unique seasonings, stuffing and toppings. The restaurant menu also includes side dishes, salads, garlic bread, appetizers and desserts. On 31-Dec-2003, the group operates 286 full service restaurants. The group operates eight franchised international units of rainforest cafes in the United Kingdom, Japan, France and Mexico and one company owned and operated unit in toronto, Canada.

Primary SIC and add'l.: 5812 5813

CIK No: 0000908652

Subsidiaries: C. A. Muer Corporation, Capt. Crabs Take-Away of 79th Street, Inc., CHLN, Inc., CHLN-Idaho, Inc., CHLN-Maryland, Inc., Crab Addison, Inc., Crab House, Inc., Cryo Realty Corp., FSI Devco, Inc., FSI Restaurant Development Limited, Gnl, Corp., Gnlv, Corp., Golden Nugget Experience, LLC, Golden Nugget, Inc., Hospitality Headquarters, Inc. 106 Subsidiaries included in the Index

Officers: Tilman J. Fertitta/Chmn., CEO, Pres./$15,328,910.00, Richard H. Liem/54/CFO, Exec. VP/$1,041,865.00, Steven L. Scheinthal/46/Dir., Exec. VP, General Counsel, Sec./$1,657,101.00, Jeffrey L. Cantwell/43/Sr. VP - Development/$587,999.00, Kelly K. Roberts/Chief Administration Officer - Hospitality, Gaming Division/$440,236.00

Directors: Tilman J. Fertitta/Chmn., CEO, Pres., Steven L. Scheinthal/46/Dir., Exec. VP, General Counsel, Sec., Michael S. Chadwick/56/Dir., Michael Richmond/60/Dir., Joe Max Taylor/75/Dir., Kenneth Brimmer/53/Dir.

Owners: Michael Richmond, Tilman J. Fertitta/34.60%, Michael S. Chadwick, Kelly K. Roberts, Steven L. Scheinthal/1.00%, Richard H. Liem, Jeffrey L. Cantwell, Kenneth Brimmer, Deutsche Bank AG/10.50%, Insiders/35.80%, Joe Max Taylor, Dimensional Fund Advisors Inc/11.00%

Financial Data: *Fiscal Year End:*12/31 *Latest Annual Data:* 12/31/2006

Year	Sales	Net Income
2006	$1,134,301,000	-$21,770,000
2005	$1,254,806,000	$44,815,000
2004	$1,167,475,000	$66,522,000
Curr. Assets: $147,655,000	**Curr. Liab.:** $214,839,000	
Plant, Equip.: $1,215,626,000	**Total Liab.:** $970,204,000	**Indic. Yr. Divd.:** $0.200
Total Assets: $1,464,912,000	**Net Worth:** $494,707,000	**Debt/ Equity:** 1.7076

Landstar System Inc

13410 Sutton Pk. Dr. S, Jacksonville, FL, 32224; *PH:* 1-904-398-9400; *Fax:* 1-904-390-1437; *http://* www.landstar.com

General - Incorporation	DE	**Stock**- Price on:12/24/2007	$46.75
Employees	1,298	Stock Exchange	NDQ
Auditor	KPMG LLP	Ticker Symbol	LSTR
Stk Agt	Bank of New York	Outstanding Shares	55,560,000
Counsel	NA	E.P.S.	$1.94
DUNS No.	19-466-0387	Shareholders	NA

Business: The groups principle activity is to provide transportation and logistics solutions. Customers served by the group include the iron and steel, automotive products, paper, lumber and building products, retail and electronics industries. The group operates through three business segments namely carrier, global logistics and insurance. The group operates from United States.

Primary SIC and add'l.: 4213 4522 6410

CIK No: 0000853816

Subsidiaries: Also d/b/a Gemini Transportation Services of Greensburg, Also d/b/a GTSI Transportation Services in Ontario, Also d/b/a Independent Freightways, Inc., Also d/b/a Inway Nationwide Transportation Services, Also d/b/a Landstar Less Than Truck Load, Also d/b/a Landstar LTL, Also d/b/a Ligon Contract Services in Kentucky, Also d/b/a Ranger/Landstar, Inc. in South Carolina, Also d/b/a RMCS, Inc. in Alabama and California, Landstar Carrier Services, Inc., Landstar Contractor Financing, Inc., Landstar Express America, Inc., Landstar Global Logistics, Inc., Landstar Inway, Inc., Landstar Ligon, Inc. 22 Subsidiaries included in the Index

Officers: Henry H. Gerkens/Dir., CEO, Pres./$5,334,480.00, Michael Kneller/VP, General Counsel, Sec., Ronald G. Stanley/57/COO, VP/$1,303,922.00, Larry S. Thomas/CIO, VP/$1,251,925.00, Robert C. Larose/53/Exec. VP, Co - CFO/$2,808,073.00, Jim M. Handoush/Pres. - Landstar Global Logistics, Inc, Jeff L. Pundt/Pres. - Landstar Carrier Group/$1,322,889.00, Joe Beacom/VP, Chief Compliance - Security, Safety Officer, James B. Gattoni/VP, Co - CFO, Ginger Whitcher/Mgr. - Corporate Communications, Patty McMenamin/VP - Corporate Communications

Directors: Henry H. Gerkens/Dir., CEO, Pres., Jeffrey C. Crowe/Chmn., William S. Elston/Dir., Ronald W. Drucker/Dir., Diana M. Murphy/Dir., David G. Bannister/Dir., Michael A. Henning/Dir.

Owners: Wellington Management Company, LLP/10.50%, Jim M. Handoush, Insiders/2.60%, Jeffrey C. Crowe, James B. Gattoni, Ronald G. Stanley, Merritt J. Mott, FMR Corp./11.80%, Barclays Global Investors, NA./5.40%, Larry S. Thomas, T. Rowe Price Associates, Inc./8.00%, Henry H. Gerkens, Jeffrey L. Pundt, Scout Capital Management, LLC/5.10%, Diana M. Murphy *(21 Owners included in Index)*

Financial Data: *Fiscal Year End:*12/30 *Latest Annual Data:* 12/30/2006

Year	Sales	Net Income
2006	$2,518,006,000	$113,085,000
2005	$2,520,523,000	$119,956,000
2004	$2,021,282,000	$71,872,000

Curr. Assets: $613,801,000	**Curr. Liab.:** $299,496,000	**P/E Ratio:** 24.10
Plant, Equip.: $89,131,000	**Total Liab.:** $510,125,000	**Indic. Yr. Divd.:** $0.150
Total Assets: $762,760,000	**Net Worth:** $252,635,000	**Debt/ Equity:** 0.3395

Langer Inc

450 Commack Rd., Deer Park, NY, 11729; *PH:* 1-631-667-1200; *Fax:* 1-631-667-1203; *http://* www.langerbiomechanics.com; *Email:* info@langerinc.com

General - Incorporation	DE	**Stock**- Price on:12/24/2007	$5.15
Employees	574	Stock Exchange	NDQ
Auditor	BDO Seidman, LLP	Ticker Symbol	GAIT
Stk Agt	Registrar & Transfer Co	Outstanding Shares	11,470,000
Counsel	Kane Kessler P.C	E.P.S.	-$0.43
DUNS No.	06-595-5049	Shareholders	NA

Business: The group's principal activity is to design, manufacture and market foot and gait-related biomechanical products. The group applies scientific and quantitative methods for the diagnosis and treatment of foot and gait-related problems. The core product of the group is a custom-made, prescription orthotic device known as foot orthoses. They are placed inside the patients' shoes to correct the abnormalities in their gait and relieve symptoms associated with foot or postural malalignment. The other products of the group include ppt products and pediatric counter rotation system. Ppt is a medical grade soft tissue cushioning material. It provides protection against forces of pressure, shock and shear. In 2003, the group acquired all the capital stock of bi-op laboratories inc.

Primary SIC and add'l.: 3842

CIK No: 0000725460

Subsidiaries: Langer Biomechanics Group (UK) Limited, Langer Canada Inc, Langer Distribution Services, Inc, Silipos, Inc.

Officers: Kathryn P. Kehoe/Sr. VP/$302,000.00, Gray W. Hudkins/Dir., COO, Kathleen P. Bloch/CFO, VP

Directors: Warren B. Kanders/Chmn., Stephen M. Brecher/Dir., Burtt R. Ehrlich/Dir., Stuart P. Greenspon/Dir., Gray W. Hudkins/Dir., COO, Peter A. Asch/Dir.

Owners: Millennium Partners, L.P./7.00%, Warren B. Kanders/23.50%, Burtt R. Ehrlich/2.20%, Arthur Goldstein/1.30%, Peter A. Asch/5.30%, Stuart P. Greenspon/1.70%, Ashford Capital Management, Inc./17.80%, Stephen M. Brecher, Kathryn P. Kehoe, Gray W. Hudkins/3.10%, Kennedy Capital Management, Inc./5.70%, David M. Knott/13.00%, Bank of America Corporation/5.10%, Insiders/34.90%

Financial Data: *Fiscal Year End:*12/31 *Latest Annual Data:* 12/31/2006

Year	Sales	Net Income
2006	$35,236,000	-$4,853,000
2005	$40,141,000	-$4,557,000
2004	$30,127,000	$375,000
Curr. Assets: $38,535,000	**Curr. Liab.:** $5,223,000	
Plant, Equip.: $8,245,000	**Total Liab.:** $39,832,000	**Indic. Yr. Divd.:** NA
Total Assets: $68,849,000	**Net Worth:** $29,017,000	**Debt/ Equity:** NA

Lannett Co Inc

9000 State Rd., Philadelphia, PA, 19136; *PH:* 1-215-333-9000; *Fax:* 1-215-333-9004; *http://* www.lannett.com

General - Incorporation	DE	**Stock**- Price on:12/24/2007	$5.92
Employees	193	Stock Exchange	AMEX
Auditor	Grant Thornton LLP	Ticker Symbol	LCI
Stk Agt	Registrar & Transfer Co	Outstanding Shares	24,170,000
Counsel	NA	E.P.S.	-$0.35
DUNS No.	00-227-7481	Shareholders	NA

Business: The group's principal activities are to develop, manufacture, package, market and distribute pharmaceutical products. It also provides contract manufacturing and packaging services for pharmaceutical products for other companies. The group manufactures and sells a line of both prescription and over-the-counter drug products. As of 30-Jun-2003, it manufactured or distributed 23 products, all of which are either tablets, or capsules and sold generically to the drug distribution industry. They include fiorinal(R), lanoxin(R), mysoline(R), bentyl(R), diamox(R), lomotil(R), and unithroid(R). These are used in the treatment of migraine headaches, heart failure, epilepsy, glaucoma, diarrhea, tuberculosis, thyroid deficiency and allergies. The group sells its pharmaceutical products primarily to wholesalers, distributors, warehousing chains, retail chains and other pharmaceutical companies.

Primary SIC and add'l.: 2834

CIK No: 0000057725

Subsidiaries: Astrochem Corporation, Lannett Holdings, Inc.

Officers: Arthur P. Bedrosian/Dir., CEO, Pres., Bernard Sandiford/Pres. - Operations, William Schreck/VP - Logistics, Brian J. Kearns/VP - Finance, Treasurer, Sec., CFO, Kevin Smith/VP - Sales, Marketing

Directors: Arthur P. Bedrosian/Dir., CEO, Pres., Garnet Peck/Dir., Kenneth Sinclair/Dir., Jeffrey Farber/Dir., Albert I. Wertheimer/Dir., Ronald A. West/Dir., William R. Farber/Dir., Myron R. Winkelman/Dir.

Owners: Jeffrey Farber/0.71%, Arthur Bedrosian/2.69%, Bernard Sandiford/0.21%, Albert Wertheimer/0.09%, Insiders/60.09%, William Schreck/0.12%, William Farber/55.27%, Ronald A. West/0.24%, Brian Kearns/0.29%, Kevin Smith/0.34%, Myron Winkelman/0.15%

Financial Data: *Fiscal Year End:*06/30 *Latest Annual Data:* 6/30/2006

Year	Sales	Net Income
2006	$64,060,000	$4,969,000
2005	$44,902,000	-$32,780,000
2004	$63,781,000	$13,215,000
Curr. Assets: $44,285,000	**Curr. Liab.:** $22,250,000	**P/E Ratio:** 39.47
Plant, Equip.: $27,619,000	**Total Liab.:** $34,473,000	**Indic. Yr. Divd.:** NA
Total Assets: $104,656,000	**Net Worth:** $70,183,000	**Debt/ Equity:** NA

LanOptics Ltd

PO Box 527, Yokneam, 20692; *PH:* 972-49596666; *Fax:* 972-49594166; *http://* www.lanoptics.com; *Email:* info@ezchip.com

General - Incorporation	Israel
Employees	100
Auditor	Kost Forer Gabbay & Kasierer
Stk Agt	American Stock Transfer & Trust Co.
Counsel	Carter Ledyard & Milburn LLP
DUNS No.	60-017-7158

Stock - Price on:12/24/2007	$14.6999
Stock Exchange	NDQ
Ticker Symbol	LNOP
Outstanding Shares	15,750,000
E.P.S.	-$0.58
Shareholders	NA

Business: The group's principle activity is to develop of high performance networks processors for 10/40 gigabit networking equipment. The group operates from United States.

Primary SIC and add'l.: 7373

CIK No: 0000892534

Subsidiaries: EZchip

Officers: Eli Fruchter/52/Chmn., Principal Executive Officer, Dror Israel/CFO, Guy Koren/VP - Technology, CTO - Ezchip, Amir Eyal/VP - Business Development, Ezchip, Rob O'Hara/VP - Sales, Ezchip, Eyal Choresh/VP - Research & Development, Ezchip, Patrick Bisson/VP - Technology Applications, Ezchip, Doron Vertesh/VP - Operations, Ezchip

Directors: Eli Fruchter/52/Chmn., Principal Executive Officer, David Schlachet/62/Dir., Karen Sarid/57/Dir., Ran Giladi/53/Dir., Shai Saul/45/Dir.

Owners: Insiders/3.48%, Star Ventures Management/8.23%, Nokia Venture Partners/6.68%, Eli Fruchter/3.38%

Financial Data: Fiscal Year End:12/31 **Latest Annual Data:** 12/31/2006

Year	Sales	Net Income
2006	$8,469,000	-$12,317,000
2005	$5,848,000	-$10,347,000
2004	$4,746,000	-$9,154,000

Curr. Assets:	$23,536,000	Curr. Liab.:	$4,109,000		
Plant, Equip.:	$352,000	Total Liab.:	$34,237,000	Indic. Yr. Divd.:	NA
Total Assets:	$66,293,000	Net Worth:	$32,056,000	Debt/ Equity:	NA

Lantronix Inc

15353 Barranca Pkwy., Irvine, CA, 92618; *PH:* 1-949-453-3990; *Fax:* 1-949-450-7249; *http://* www.lantronix.com; *Email:* sales@lantronix.com

General - Incorporation	DE
Employees	157
Auditor	Ernst & Young LLP
Stk Agt	Mellon Investor Services
Counsel	NA
DUNS No.	NA

Stock - Price on:12/24/2007	$1.24
Stock Exchange	NDQ
Ticker Symbol	LTRX
Outstanding Shares	59,880,000
E.P.S.	$0.00
Shareholders	NA

Business: The group's principal activity is to design, develop and market devices and software solutions that make it possible to access, manage, control and configure almost any electronic product over the Internet or other networks. It provides three broad categories of products: device networking solutions, it management solutions and software solutions. Device networking solutions enable almost any electronic product to be connected to a network. It management solutions enable multiple pieces of hardware, usually it-related network hardware such as servers, outers, switches, and similar pieces of equipment to be managed over a network. Software solutions is either embedded in the hardware devices or stand-alone application software. The major customers of the group include ingram micro, inc., tech data corporation, atlantik systems gmbh, astradis elecktronik gmbh and lightwave communications gmbh.

Primary SIC and add'l.: 3577 3679

CIK No: 0001114925

Subsidiaries: Japan Lantronix K.K., Lantonix Deutschland GmbH, Lantronix Australia Pty. Ltd., Lantronix Europe GmbH, Lantronix France, SARL, Lantronix Hong Kong Ltd., Lantronix International AG Switzerland, Lantronix Netherlands B.V., Lantronix UK Ltd., Stallion Inc., Stallion Pty, United States Software Corporation

Officers: Reagan Y. Sakai/CEO, CFO, Mark Prowten/VP - Marketing, Brad Painter/VP - Worldwide Channel Sales, Brian H. Campbell/Sr. VP - Worldwide Operations, Daryl Miller/VP - Engineering

Directors: H. K. Desai/Chmn., Thomas Burton/Dir., Howard Slayen/Dir., Kathryn Braun Lewis/Dir., Curt Brown/Dir., Bernhard Bruscha/Dir., Thomas M. Wittenschlaeger/Dir.

Owners: Howard T. Slayen, Marc H. Nussbaum/1.80%, Bernhard Bruscha/33.80%, James W. Kerrigan/1.00%, Reagan Y. Sakai, Thomas W. Burton, Empire Capital Management, LLC/10.60%, Kathryn Braun Lewis, H. K. Desai, Insiders/37.80%, Heartland Advisors, Inc/9.50%

Financial Data: Fiscal Year End:06/30 **Latest Annual Data:** 06/30/2007

Year	Sales	Net Income
2007	$55,306,000	-$1,723,000
2006	$51,943,000	-$3,045,000
2005	$48,502,000	-$7,004,000

Curr. Assets:	$35,968,000	Curr. Liab.:	$30,596,000		
Plant, Equip.:	$1,589,000	Total Liab.:	$31,037,000	Indic. Yr. Divd.:	NA
Total Assets:	$47,815,000	Net Worth:	$16,778,000	Debt/ Equity:	0.0069

Lanvision Systems Inc

10200 Alliance Rd., Ste. 200, Cincinnati, OH, 45242; *PH:* 1-513-794-7100; *http://* www.streamlinehealth.net

General - Incorporation	DE
Employees	105
Auditor	Ernst & Young LLP
Stk Agt	Fifth Third Bank
Counsel	NA
DUNS No.	62-282-5412

Stock - Price on:12/24/2007	$3.85
Stock Exchange	NDQ
Ticker Symbol	STRM
Outstanding Shares	9,210,000
E.P.S.	-$0.03
Shareholders	NA

Business: The group's principal activities are to provide healthcare information access system through an electronic medical record solutions in the United States. The solution uses application-hosting services as an application service provider. This solution connects hospitals, physicians and patients through Internet/intranet. The system enables to access electronically both structured and unstructured patient data and various forms of healthcare information such as clinician's handwritten notes, lab reports, photographs and insurance cards. The products enable to capture, store, manage, route, retrieve and process clinical and financial patient information.

Primary SIC and add'l.: 7375 7373 7372

CIK No: 0001008586

Subsidiaries: Lakeland Bank

Officers: Brian J. Patsy/56/Co - Founder, Chmn., CEO, Pres./$299,260.00, Joe Brown/Contact - Hosting Services, Melissa Vincent/Contact - Business Partnerships, William A. Geers/COO, VP - Product Development/$241,483.00, Donald E. Vick/44/Controller, Assist. Treasurer, Assist. Sec./$116,925.00, Paul W. Bridge/CFO, Treasurer/$200,049.00, Gretchen Brown/Contact - Sales

Directors: Brian J. Patsy/56/Co - Founder, Chmn., CEO, Pres., Richard C. Levy/61/Dir., Jonathan R. Phillips/35/Dir., Edward J. Vonderbrink/63/Dir., Andrew L. Turner/61/Dir.

Owners: Sharon B. Patsy/11.30%, Richard C. Levy, Insiders/15.40%, Paul W. Bridge/1.60%, William A. Geers, Andrew L. Turner, Eric S. Lombardo/20.10%, Donald E. Vick, Jonathan R. Phillips, Edward J. VonderBrink, Brian J. Patsy/12.20%, The HillStreet Fund, L.P./7.50%

Financial Data: Fiscal Year End:01/31 **Latest Annual Data:** 1/31/2007

Year	Sales	Net Income
2007	$15,867,000	$96,000
2006	$16,127,000	$2,551,000
2005	$12,751,000	$558,000

Curr. Assets:	$8,126,000	Curr. Liab.:	$5,378,000		
Plant, Equip.:	$1,577,000	Total Liab.:	$6,656,000	Indic. Yr. Divd.:	NA
Total Assets:	$15,301,000	Net Worth:	$8,644,000	Debt/ Equity:	0.0038

Lapis Technologies Inc

19 W 34th St., Ste. 1008, New York, NY, 10001; *PH:* 1-212-937-3580

General - Incorporation	DE
Employees	62
Auditor	Gvilli & Co
Stk Agt	Transfer & Trust Co
Counsel	NA
DUNS No.	NA

Stock - Price on:12/24/2007	$1.1
Stock Exchange	OTC
Ticker Symbol	LPST
Outstanding Shares	5,480,000
E.P.S.	$0.02
Shareholders	NA

Business: The groups principle activities include manufacturing, distributing and marketing electronic components. The group provides products relating to automatic test equipment, simulators, and various military and airborne systems, power supplies, converters, and related power conversion products. The group also provides test systems, airborne, ship borne, land electronic equipment, and various military systems. The group operates from United States.

Primary SIC and add'l.: NA

CIK No: 0000854800

Subsidiaries: Enertec Electronics Limited, Enertec Systems 2001 LTD

Owners: Insiders/73.44%, Harry Mund/73.30%, Miron Markovitz, Zvi Avni/15.40%

Financial Data: Fiscal Year End:12/31 **Latest Annual Data:** 12/31/2006

Year	Sales	Net Income
2006	$7,839,000	-$115,000
2005	$7,269,000	-$48,000
2004	$6,176,000	$343,000

Curr. Assets:	$8,047,000	Curr. Liab.:	$6,737,000		
Plant, Equip.:	$299,000	Total Liab.:	$7,139,000	Indic. Yr. Divd.:	NA
Total Assets:	$8,368,000	Net Worth:	$896,000	Debt/ Equity:	0.4493

LaPolla Industries Inc

15402 Vantage Pkwy. E, Ste. 322, Houston, TX, 77032; *PH:* 1-281-219-4100; *Fax:* 1-281-219-4102; *http://* www.lapollaindustries.com; *Email:* info@lapollacoatings.com

General - Incorporation	DE
Employees	48
Auditor	Baum & Co. P.A
Stk Agt	Continental Stock Transfer & Trust Co
Counsel	NA
DUNS No.	NA

Stock - Price on:12/24/2007	$0.68
Stock Exchange	AMEX
Ticker Symbol	LPA
Outstanding Shares	53,580,000
E.P.S.	-$0.08
Shareholders	NA

Business: The group's principal activities are to develop and market spray applied elastomeric coatings to the waterproofing, corrosion, roofing and construction industries. It also develops, manufactures and markets coatings, paints and sealants to the construction, paint, roofing and waterproofing industries. The group offers three series of products, which include rsm seriestm, spectrum series tm, and infiniti series tm. Rsm seriestm is comprised of two series, rsm hundred seriestm and rsm thousand seriestm products, which consists of coatings made from three component rsmtm formula. Spectrum seriestm is comprised of high performance primers, urethanes, acrylics, hybrids and polyureas suitable for use for a variety of industrial and commercial applications. The infiniti seriestm is comprised of roof coatings, paints and sealants.

Primary SIC and add'l.: 2851 2952 6794

CIK No: 0000875296

Subsidiaries: IFT Corporation, Infiniti, LaPolla, RSM Technologies, Inc

Officers: Douglas J. Kramer/Dir., CEO, Pres./$460,872.00, John A. Campbell/42/Treasurer/$112,619.00, Timothy J. Novak/CFO, Treasurer

Directors: Douglas J. Kramer/Dir., CEO, Pres., Richard J. Kurtz/Chmn., Arthur J. Gregg/Dir., Michael T. Adams/Dir., Jay C. Nadel/Dir., Augustus J. Larson/Dir., Howard L. Brown/Dir.

Owners: Insiders/60.40%, Michael T. Adams/2.08%, John A. Campbell/0.00%, Richard J. Kurtz/58.11%, Douglas J. Kramer/0.10%, Arthur J. Gregg/0.11%

Financial Data: Fiscal Year End:12/31 **Latest Annual Data:** 12/31/2006

Year	Sales	Net Income
2006	$30,315,000	-$3,014,000
2005	$20,179,000	-$1,525,000
2004	$2,564,000	-$5,769,000

Curr. Assets:	$8,336,000	Curr. Liab.:	$7,499,000		
Plant, Equip.:	$1,490,000	Total Liab.:	$7,806,000	Indic. Yr. Divd.:	NA
Total Assets:	$12,091,000	Net Worth:	$4,286,000	Debt/ Equity:	0.5252

Large Scale Biology Corp

3333 Vaca Valley Pkwy., Vacaville, CA, 95688; *PH:* 1-707-446-5501; *http://* www.lsbc.com; *Email:* irinfo@lsbc.com

General - Incorporation DE | Employees 78 | Auditor Deloitte & Touche LLP | Stk Agt American Stock Transfer & Trust Co. | Counsel Cahill Gordon & Reindel LLP | DUNS No. NA

Stock- Price on:12/24/2007 $0.425 | Stock Exchange OTC | Ticker Symbol LSBC | Outstanding Shares 6,450,000 | E.P.S -$2.602 | Shareholders NA

Business: The group's principal activity is to develop therapeutic products for treatment of cancer and prevention of infectious diseases. The product categories include vaccines for the treatment of cancer and the treatment and prevention of infectious diseases and complex proteins for therapeutic product applications. It applies proprietary proteomics, functional genomics, and biomanufacturing technologies to develop and manufacture drugs and vaccines for effective treatment of diseases. The corporate office and genomics research facility is located in vacaville, California. The group's biomanufacturing plant is located in owensboro, Kentucky, and the proteomics research facility is located in germantown, Maryland.

Primary SIC and add'l.: 2834

CIK No: 0001108951

Subsidiaries: Biosource Genetics Corporation, Biosource Technologies,Inc., Large Scale Bioprocessing,Inc., Large Scale Proteomics Corporation, Predictive Diagnostics,Inc., Sunrise Biosystems,Inc.

Officers: Kevin J. Ryan/CEO, Pres., Greg Pogue/VP, Executive Program Mgr., Ronald J. Artale/Sr. VP, CFO, COO, Sec., Stephen J. Garger/Exec. VP - Biomanufacturing, Daniel Tuse/VP - Business Development, Michael D. Centron/VP, Treasurer, Laurence K. Grill/Sr. VP - Research, Chief Scientific Officer

Directors: Robert L. Erwin/Chmn.

Financial Data: **Fiscal Year End:**12/31 **Latest Annual Data:** 12/31/2004

Year	Sales	Net Income
2004	$1,767,000	-$17,425,000
2003	$3,570,000	-$25,293,000
2002	$2,622,000	-$33,184,000

Curr. Assets:	$1,766,000	**Curr. Liab.:**	$1,130,000		
Plant, Equip.:	$7,798,000	**Total Liab.:**	$3,364,000	**Indic. Yr. Divd.:**	NA
Total Assets:	$12,795,000	**Net Worth:**	$9,431,000	**Debt/ Equity:**	NA

Largo Vista Group Ltd

4570 Campus Dr., Newport Beach, CA, 92660; ***PH:*** 1-949-252-2180; ***Fax:*** 1-949-252-2181; ***http://*** www.largovista.com; ***Email:*** ir@largovista.com

General - Incorporation NV | Employees 15 | Auditor Russell Bedford Stefanou Mirchandani | Stk Agt OTR Transfer Agency | Counsel NA | DUNS No. NA

Stock- Price on:12/24/2007 $0.015 | Stock Exchange OTC | Ticker Symbol LGOV | Outstanding Shares 291,740,000 | E.P.S -$0.001 | Shareholders NA

Business: The groups principle activities include purchasing and reselling liquid petroleum gas. The group operates from the United States. The group's quarterly revenue for Sep '07 was 0.09 million of USD.

Primary SIC and add'l.: 5984 1321

CIK No: 0000915471

Subsidiaries: Largo Vista Construction Inc., Largo Vista International Corp., Largo Vista, Inc

Officers: Deng Shan/Chmn., Interim CEO, Albert N. Figueroa/Dir., Sec., Denise Deng/CFO

Directors: Deng Shan/Chmn., Interim CEO, Albert N. Figueroa/Dir., Sec.

Owners: Albert Figueroa/1.36%, Deng Shan/27.80%, Insiders/29.16%

Financial Data: **Fiscal Year End:**12/31 **Latest Annual Data:** 12/31/2006

Year	Sales	Net Income
2006	$702,000	-$241,000
2005	$367,000	-$345,000
2004	$439,000	-$277,000

Curr. Assets:	$285,000	**Curr. Liab.:**	$1,334,000		
Plant, Equip.:	$1,000	**Total Liab.:**	$1,334,000	**Indic. Yr. Divd.:**	NA
Total Assets:	$288,000	**Net Worth:**	-$1,047,000	**Debt/ Equity:**	NA

Larrea Biosciences Corp

4119 Montrose Blvd, Ste. 230, Houston, TX, 77006; ***PH:*** 1-832-695-0096; ***Fax:*** 1-713-807-7743; ***http://*** www.labsci.com; ***Email:*** customersupport@larrearx.com

General - Incorporation NV | Employees NA | Auditor R. E. Bassie & Co. | Stk Agt Pacific Stock Transfer Company | Counsel NA | DUNS No. NA

Stock- Price on:12/24/2007 NA | Stock Exchange OTC | Ticker Symbol LRRA | Outstanding Shares NA | E.P.S -$0.01 | Shareholders NA

Business: The groups principle activities include creating, developing and distributing proprietary formulations of natural products. The group markets its products under the trade names LarreaRx(TM) and Shegoi(TM). The group operates from the United States and Canada.

Primary SIC and add'l.: 2834

CIK No: 0001175594

Subsidiaries: Global Botanics, Inc., LarreaRx Strategies, Inc., LarreaRx, Inc.

Officers: Peter P. Smetek/64/Chmn., CEO, CFO

Directors: Peter P. Smetek/64/Chmn., CEO, CFO

Owners: Peter P. Smetek/2.20%, Insiders/27.89%, A & S Holdings Management, Ltd./51.39%, Robert Sinnott/15.78%

Financial Data: **Fiscal Year End:**04/30 **Latest Annual Data:** 4/30/2006

Year	Sales	Net Income
2006	$458,000	-$664,000
2005	$514,000	-$2,065,000
2004	NA	-$113,000

Curr. Assets:	$4,000	**Curr. Liab.:**	$1,072,000		
Plant, Equip.:	NA	**Total Liab.:**	$1,072,000	**Indic. Yr. Divd.:**	NA
Total Assets:	$18,000	**Net Worth:**	-$1,053,000	**Debt/ Equity:**	NA

Las Vegas From Home Com Entertainmnt Inc

1255 W Pender St., Ste. 100, Vancouver, BC, V6E 2V1; ***PH:*** 1-604-680204; ***http://*** www.lasvegasfromhome.com; ***Email:*** info@lvfh.com

General - Incorporation BC | Employees NA | Auditor Smythe Ratcliffe LLP | Stk Agt Computershare Trust Co | Counsel Anfield Sujir Kennedy & Durno | DUNS No. NA

Stock- Price on:12/24/2007 $0.14 | Stock Exchange OTC | Ticker Symbol LVFHF | Outstanding Shares NA | E.P.S NA | Shareholders NA

Business: The group's principle activities include acquiring, exploring and developing mineral properties. The group operates from United States.

Primary SIC and add'l.: 1099

CIK No: 0001061612

Subsidiaries: 4010493 Canada Inc., Action Commerce Limited, Action Poker Gaming Inc., APG Enterprises Limited., Guardian Commerce Ltd

Officers: Jake H. Kalpakian/Dir., CEO, Pres., Penilla Klomp/Corp. Sec., David A. Shore/CFO

Directors: Jake H. Kalpakian/Dir., CEO, Pres., Bedo H. Kalpakian/Chmn., Gregory T. McFarlane/Dir., Neil Spellman/Dir.

Owners: Neil Spellman, Gregory T. McFarlane, CDS & Co., Jacob H. Kalpakian, Penilla Klomp, Bedo H. Kalpakian

Financial Data: **Fiscal Year End:**12/31 **Latest Annual Data:** 12/31/2006

Year	Sales	Net Income
2006	$736,000	-$3,942,000
2005	$10,057,000	$934,000
2004	$1,647,000	-$4,439,000

Curr. Assets:	$7,477,000	**Curr. Liab.:**	$411,000		
Plant, Equip.:	$448,000	**Total Liab.:**	$411,000	**Indic. Yr. Divd.:**	NA
Total Assets:	$8,253,000	**Net Worth:**	$7,842,000	**Debt/ Equity:**	NA

Las Vegas Gaming Inc

4000 W Ali Baba, Ste. D, Las Vegas, NV, 89118; ***PH:*** 1-702-877-8111; ***http://*** www.lvgi.com; ***Email:*** info@lvgi.com

General - Incorporation NV | Employees NA | Auditor Piercy, Bowler, Taylor & Kern | Stk Agt NA | Counsel NA | DUNS No. NA

Stock- Price on:12/24/2007 NA | Stock Exchange NA | Ticker Symbol NA | Outstanding Shares NA | E.P.S NA | Shareholders NA

Business: The group's principle activities include developing, marketing and distributing casino games and selling gaming supplies and keno equipment, and providing various related services to the gaming industry. The company conducts its operations through two primary business segments, casino games unit and other products and services unit. The company has the rights to a keno-style game (Nevada numbers 0 and linked, progressive 10-spot game know as million dollar ticket) and bingo (Nevada bingo 0 and super bonanza). The other products unit designs, markets, installs, and maintains keno systems for the casino industries. In 2003, the company acquired imagineering systems inc (isi) and triple win in Nevada (twin). The group operates from United States.

Primary SIC and add'l.: 7999 7993

CIK No: 0001103993

Subsidiaries: Imagineering Gaming, Inc.

Officers: Russell Roth/Chmn., CEO, Zak Khal/COO, Bruce Shepard/CFO, John English/Sr. VP - Business, Creative Development, Karen Fisher/VP - Marketing, Business Development

Directors: Russell Roth/Chmn., CEO, Stephen A. Crystal/Dir., Kylene Cane/Dir., Richard H. Irvine/Dir., Terry L. Caudill/Dir., Robert B. Washington/65/Dir., Jon Berkley/Dir., Robert McMonigle/Dir.

Owners: Richard H. Irvine/1.22%, Stephen A. Crystal/3.96%, Zak Khal/4.00%, Jon D. Berkley/0.81%, Kyleen E. Cane, Bruce A. Shepard/2.14%, Insiders/22.25%, Russell R. Roth/10.18%, Terry L. Caudill/0.90%, Robert M. McMonigle/0.08%

Las Vegas Sands Corp

3355 Las Vegas Blvd. S, Las Vegas, NV, 89109; ***PH:*** 1-702-414-1000; ***Fax:*** 1-702-414-4884; ***http://*** www.lasvegassands.com

General - Incorporation NV | Employees 15,280 | Auditor PricewaterhouseCoopers LLP | Stk Agt American Stock Transfer & Trust Co. | Counsel NA | DUNS No. NA

Stock- Price on:12/24/2007 $76.06 | Stock Exchange NYSE | Ticker Symbol LVS | Outstanding Shares 354,810,000 | E.P.S $0.53 | Shareholders NA

Business: The groups principle activity is to operate casino. The group also develops resorts and properties. The group operates through two geographic segments namely, Las Vegas and Macao. The group operates from the United States. The group's quarterly revenue in Sptember 2007 was 660.95 millions of USD.

Primary SIC and add'l.: 5812 7999 5813 7011

CIK No: 0001300514

Subsidiaries: Grand Canal Shops Mall MM Subsidiary, Inc., Interface Employee Leasing, LLC, Interface Group-Nevada, Inc., Las Vegas Sands (Ibrox) Limited, Las Vegas Sands (Sheffield) Limited, Las Vegas Sands (UK)Limited, Las Vegas Sands, LLC, Lido Casino Resort Holding Company, LLC, Lido Casino Resort, LLC, Lido Intermediate Holding Company, LLC, Mall Intermediate Holding Company, LLC, Marina Bay Sands Pte. Ltd., Phase II Mall Holding, LLC, Phase II Mall Subsidiary, LLC, Sands Bethworks Gaming, LLC 43 Subsidiaries included in the Index

Officers: Sheldon G. Adelson/Chmn., CEO, William P. Weidner/Dir., COO, Pres., Robert P. Rozek/CFO, Sr. VP, Bradley H. Stone/Exec. VP, Robert G. Goldstein/Sr. VP, Scott D. Henry/Sr. VP - Finance

Directors: Sheldon G. Adelson/Chmn., CEO, William P. Weidner/Dir., COO, Pres., Irwin Chafetz/Dir., Charles D. Forman/Dir., Andrew R. Heyer/Dir., Michael A. Leven/Dir., James L. Purcell/Dir., Irwin A. Siegel/Dir.

Owners: 2002 Remainder Trust, Michael A. Leven, Charles D. Forman, Robert P. Rozek, Marsico Capital Management, LLC, William P. Weidner, Sheldon G. Adelson 2004 Remainder Trust, Bradley H. Stone, Insiders, Sheldon G. Adelson 2005 Family Trust, Irwin A. Siegel, Robert G. Goldstein, Irwin Chafetz, Scott D. Henry, James L. Purcell *(16 Owners included in Index)*

Financial Data: Fiscal Year End:12/31   Latest Annual Data: 12/31/2006

Year	Sales	Net Income
2006	$2,236,859,000	$442,003,000
2005	$1,740,912,000	$283,686,000
2004	$1,197,056,000	$495,183,000

Curr. Assets:	$1,093,557,000	**Curr. Liab.:**	$734,648,000		
Plant, Equip.:	$4,582,325,000	**Total Liab.:**	$5,051,304,000	**Indic. Yr. Divd.:**	NA
Total Assets:	$7,126,458,000	**Net Worth:**	$2,075,154,000	**Debt/ Equity:**	1.9931

Lasalle Brands Corp

Formerly: Creative Eateries Corp
7702 E Doubletree Ranch, Ste. 300, Scottsdale, AZ, 85258; *PH:* 1-480-905-5550;
http:// www.creativeeateries.com

General - Incorporation	NV	**Stock** - Price on:12/24/2007	NA
Employees	7	Stock Exchange	NA
Auditor	Epstein Weber & Conover, PLC	Ticker Symbol	NA
Stk Agt	Nevada Agency & Trust Company	Outstanding Shares	NA
Counsel	NA	E.P.S.	NA
DUNS No.	NA	Shareholders	NA

Business: The group's principle activities include manufacturing and marketing state-of-the-art ultraviolet disinfection systems for wastewater and sewage effluent treatment. The group operates from United States.

Primary SIC and add'l.: 6719 3559

CIK No: 0001014989

Officers: Scott Campbell/48/Dir., CFO, Pres.

Directors: Frank Holdraker/63/Chmn., Erin Strench/Dir., John R. Gaetz/Dir., Kenneth E. Fielding/Dir., Scott Campbell/48/Dir., CFO, Pres.

Owners: Oak Point Partners, Inc./13.80%, 659999 BC Ltd/6.30%, American Restaurant Development/9.80%, Erin Strench/0.01%, Insiders/29.10%, Ken Fielding/18.20%, John Gaetz/10.30%, Frank Holdraker/0.50%

LaSalle Hotel Properties

3 Bethesda Metro Ctr., Ste. 1200, Bethesda, MD, 20814; *PH:* 1-301-941-1500; *Fax:* 1-301-941-1553;
http:// www.lasallehotels.com

General - Incorporation	MD	**Stock** - Price on:12/24/2007	$44.29
Employees	31	Stock Exchange	NYSE
Auditor	KPMG LLP	Ticker Symbol	LHO
Stk Agt	LaSalle Bank N.A	Outstanding Shares	40,100,000
Counsel	NA	E.P.S.	$1.39
DUNS No.	NA	Shareholders	NA

Business: The groups principle activities include owning and leasing luxury full-service hotels. The group operates 32 hotels in 11 states and the District of Columbia. The group's quarterly revenue for September 2007 was 182.74 millions of USD.

Primary SIC and add'l.: 6798 7011

CIK No: 0001053532

Subsidiaries: I&G Capital, LLC, LaSalle Hotel Lessee, Inc., LaSalle Hotel Operating Partnership, LaSalle Hotel Properties, LaSalle Washington Four Lessee, Inc, LaSalle Washington One Lessee, Inc, LaSalle Washington Three Lessee, Inc, LaSalle Washington Two Lessee, Inc, LHO Alexandria One Lessee, LLC, LHO Alexandria One, LLC, LHO Alexis Hotel, LLC, LHO Alexis Lessee, LLC, LHO Backstreets Lessee, LLC, LHO Backstreets, LLC, LHO Badlands Lessee, LLC 71 Subsidiaries included in the Index

Officers: Jon E. Bortz/Chmn., CEO, Pres., Michael D. Barnello/COO, Exec. VP - Acquisitions, Hans S. Weger/CFO, Treasurer, Exec. VP, Sec.

Directors: Jon E. Bortz/Chmn., CEO, Pres., Darryl Hartley-Leonard/Trustee, Kelly L. Kuhn/Trustee, William S. McCalmont/Trustee, Donald S. Perkins/Trustee, Stuart L. Scott/Trustee, Donald A. Washburn/Trustee

Owners: Barclays Global Investors, NA and affiliates/6.21%, Michael D. Barnello, T. Rowe Price Associates, Inc./8.70%, Jon E. Bortz, Hans S. Weger, The Vanguard Group, Inc./5.97%, Insiders/1.10%

Financial Data: Fiscal Year End:12/31   Latest Annual Data: 12/31/2006

Year	Sales	Net Income
2006	$626,853,000	$99,060,000
2005	$394,613,000	$35,396,000
2004	$280,617,000	$23,223,000

Curr. Assets:	$108,329,000	**Curr. Liab.:**	$105,294,000	**P/E Ratio:**	31.86
Plant, Equip.:	$1,992,690,000	**Total Liab.:**	$915,271,000	**Indic. Yr. Divd.:**	NA
Total Assets:	$2,151,451,000	**Net Worth:**	$1,145,066,000	**Debt/ Equity:**	0.7972

Laser Master International Inc

1000 1st St., Harrison, NJ, 07029; *PH:* 1-973-482-7200; *Fax:* 1-973-482-9254;
http:// www.flexocraft.com

General - Incorporation	NY	**Stock** - Price on:12/24/2007	$0.31
Employees	NA	Stock Exchange	OTC
Auditor	Lazar Levine & Felix LLP	Ticker Symbol	LMTI
Stk Agt	American Stock Transfer & Trust Co.	Outstanding Shares	NA
Counsel	Baratta & Goldstein	E.P.S.	NA
DUNS No.	02-606-2554	Shareholders	NA

Business: The group's principle activity is to print an extensive line of patterns and designs for the textile and gift wrap paper industry. In addition the group has a real estate subsidiary harrison first realty corp. Which owns a factory building in harrison, New Jersey. Flexo-craft prints inc. Is the printing subsidiary that uses computerized laser system to accomplish flexographic printing for industrial and commercial printing and engraving. The products are sold through direct sales force and resellers in the United States.

Primary SIC and add'l.: 6519 2754

CIK No: 0000700892

Subsidiaries: Flexo-Crafts Prints Inc., Harrison First Realty Corp, Passport Papers Inc. & East River Arts Inc.

Financial Data: Fiscal Year End:11/30   Latest Annual Data: 11/30/2004

Year	Sales	Net Income
2004	$21,882,000	$160,000
2002	$13,267,000	$297,000
2001	$12,618,000	-$2,695,000

Curr. Assets:	$12,577,000	**Curr. Liab.:**	$8,239,000		
Plant, Equip.:	$7,983,000	**Total Liab.:**	$12,614,000	**Indic. Yr. Divd.:**	NA
Total Assets:	$20,648,000	**Net Worth:**	$8,034,000	**Debt/ Equity:**	NA

LaserCard Corp

1875 N Shoreline Blvd., Mountain View, CA, 94043; *PH:* 1-650-969-4428; *Fax:* 1-650-969-3140;
http:// www.lasercard.com; *Email:* sales@lasercard.com

General - Incorporation	DE	**Stock** - Price on:12/24/2007	$11.27
Employees	299	Stock Exchange	NDQ
Auditor	Odenberg, Muranishi & Co. LLP	Ticker Symbol	LCRD
Stk Agt	Mellon Investor Services LLC	Outstanding Shares	11,880,000
Counsel	Rosenblum, Parish & Isaacs	E.P.S.	-$1.05
DUNS No.	04-649-0652	Shareholders	NA

Business: The group's principle activity is to develop, manufacture and market optical data storage products. It operates in two segments: optical memory cards and optical card drives. Product line consists of lasercard optical memory cards, optical card read/write drives, optical card systems and chip-ready hybrid cards. Other products include optical card-related software and third-party peripherals, such as fingerprint sensor units and digital video cameras. Trademarks include lasercard(R) and drexon(r). The group's largest customer is anteon international corporation, which is the government contractor for lasercard product sales to the us department of homeland security, us department of state, us department of defense, the government of Canada and other foreign governments. The group operates in the United States, Germany, Italy, Canada, Asia, Middle East and Africa. The group's total revenue for year 2007 was 32.27 millions of USD.

Primary SIC and add'l.: 3572 7372 3695 6794

CIK No: 0000030140

Subsidiaries: Challenge Card Design Plastikkarten GmbH, LaserCard Corporation

Officers: Richard M. Haddock/56/Dir., CEO, Pres./$587,728.00, Steven G. Larson/58/VP - Finance, Treasurer/$407,630.00, Stephen M. Wurzburg/Sec., Christopher J. Dyball/57/Dir., COO/$494,913.00, Stephen D. Price-Francis/61/VP - Business Development/$294,979.00

Directors: Richard M. Haddock/56/Dir., CEO, Pres., Christopher J. Dyball/57/Dir., COO, Walter F. Walker/53/Dir., Bernard C. Bailey/54/Dir., Donald E. Mattson/75/Dir., Arthur H. Hausman/84/Dir., Dan Maydan/72/Dir., Albert J. Moyer/64/Dir.

Owners: Dan Maydan/0.30%, Walter F. Walker/1.30%, Christopher J. Dyball/2.10%, Steven G. Larson/1.30%, Albert J. Moyer/0.20%, Stephen D. Price-Francis, Insiders/8.20%

Financial Data: Fiscal Year End:03/31   Latest Annual Data: 3/31/2007

Year	Sales	Net Income
2007	$32,270,000	-$12,371,000
2006	$39,857,000	$794,000
2005	$28,544,000	-$8,901,000

Curr. Assets:	$37,304,000	**Curr. Liab.:**	$9,083,000		
Plant, Equip.:	$19,328,000	**Total Liab.:**	$35,501,000	**Indic. Yr. Divd.:**	NA
Total Assets:	$58,100,000	**Net Worth:**	$22,599,000	**Debt/ Equity:**	NA

Laserlock Technologies Inc

837 Lindy Ln., Bala Cynwyd, PA, 19004; *PH:* 1-610-668-1952; *Fax:* 1-610-668-2771;
http:// www.laserlocktech.com; *Email:* invest@laserlocktech.com

General - Incorporation	NV	**Stock** - Price on:12/24/2007	$0.012
Employees	1	Stock Exchange	OTC
Auditor	Morison Cogen LLP	Ticker Symbol	LLTI
Stk Agt	Interwest Transfer Company, Inc.	Outstanding Shares	73,440,000
Counsel	NA	E.P.S.	-$0.016
DUNS No.	NA	Shareholders	NA

Business: The group's principal activity is to utilize a technology that allows for non-intrusive document and product authentication that can reduce losses caused by fraudulent document reproduction and by product counterfeiting and/or diversion. The technology involves utilization of an ink activating system, which is completely compatible with currently used printing systems. The group's document authentication technologies are useful to businesses desiring to authenticate a wide variety of printed materials and products. The printed materials and products include a technology with the ability to print invisibly in specific areas of a document that can then be activated or revealed by use of an inexpensive laser light when authentication is required. The technology also allows certain code, message or emblem to self-reveal when rubbed. The group is in the development stage.

Primary SIC and add'l.: 2759

CIK No: 0001104038

Subsidiaries: EDS Marketing, Inc., LL Security Products, Inc

Officers: Norman A. Gardner/Chmn., CEO, Harvey Goldberg/Business Advisor, Edward H. Bell/Dir. - Research, Development, Michael J. Prevot/Dir., VP, Howard Goldberg/Acting COO

Directors: Norman A. Gardner/Chmn., CEO, Michael J. Prevot/Dir., VP, Mark Juliano/Member - Advisory Board

Owners: Norman A. Gardner/10.39%, Insiders/11.14%, Howard Goldberg/8.21%, Michael J. Prevot/0.86%, Californian Securities S.A./23.65%, Pacific Continental Securities/24.23%

Financial Data: Fiscal Year End:12/31   Latest Annual Data: 12/31/2006

Year	Sales	Net Income
2006	$123,000	-$1,607,000
2005	$209,000	-$1,267,000
2004	$108,000	-$1,407,000

Curr. Assets:	$192,000	**Curr. Liab.:**	$1,194,000		
Plant, Equip.:	$14,000	**Total Liab.:**	$1,194,000	**Indic. Yr. Divd.:**	NA
Total Assets:	$346,000	**Net Worth:**	-$848,000	**Debt/ Equity:**	NA

Laserscope

3070 Orchard Dr., San Jose, CA, 95134; *PH:* 1-408-943-0636; *http://* www.laserscope.com

General - Incorporation	CA	*Stock*- Price on:12/24/2007	NA
Employees	NA	Stock Exchange	NA
Auditor	PricewaterhouseCoopers LLP	Ticker Symbol	NA
Stk Agt	American Stock Transfer & Trust Co.	Outstanding Shares	NA
Counsel	Orrick, Herrington & Sutcliffe LLP	E.P.S	NA
DUNS No.	06-471-5188	Shareholders	NA

Business: The group's principal activities are to design, manufacture and market an advanced line of medical laser systems and related energy devices for the medical office, outpatient surgical center and hospital markets. The product portfolio of the group consists of 150 products, which includes ktp/532, nd: yag, er:yag, dye medical laser systems and related energy delivery devices. The primary medical markets include dermatology, aesthetic surgery and urology. The secondary markets include ear, nose and throat surgery, general surgery, gynecology, photo-dynamic therapy and other surgical specialties. The products are marketed in Europe, the Middle East, Latin America, Asia and Pacific Rim.

Primary SIC and add'l.: 3845 3842 3841

CIK No: 0000851737

Subsidiaries: Laserscope (UK) Ltd., Laserscope France S.A., Laserscope International, Inc.

Officers: Eric M. Reuter/CEO, Pres., Robert L. Mathews/Group VP - Operations, Product Development, Ken Arnold/VP - Research, Development, A. Van Frazier/VP - Quality Assurance, Regulatory Affairs, Dennis Lalumandiere/VP - Human Resources, Organizational Development, Robert Mann/VP - Global Sales, Marketing, Surgical, Peter Hadrovic/VP - Legal Affairs, General Counsel, Sec., Kester Nahen/VP - Application Research, Derek Bertocci/VP - Finance, CFO, Lloyd Diamond/VP - Marketing, Urology

Lasersight Inc

6848 Stapoint Ct, Winter Park, FL, 32792; *PH:* 1-407-678-9900; *http://* www.lasetech.com; *Email:* sales@lase.com

General - Incorporation	DE	*Stock*- Price on:12/24/2007	$0.05
Employees	20	Stock Exchange	OTC
Auditor	Moore Stephens Lovelace P.A	Ticker Symbol	LRST
Stk Agt	American Stock Transfer & Trust Co.	Outstanding Shares	10,000,000
Counsel	Lowenbaum Partnership	E.P.S	-$0.07
DUNS No.	78-320-4662	Shareholders	NA

Business: The group's principle activities are to develop, manufacture and market quality product technologies for laser refractive surgery and other areas of vision correction. The products of the group include precision microspot scanning excimer laser systems, software for custom ablation planning and programming, keratome systems, keratome blades, diagnostic and other products. The group operates in two major operating segments: refractive products and patent services. Refractive product segment develops, manufactures and markets ophthalmic lasers and related devices. Patent services involve the revenues and expenses generated from the ownership of certain refractive laser procedure patents.

Primary SIC and add'l.: 3827 6794

CIK No: 0000879301

Subsidiaries: LaserSight Patents, Inc, LaserSight Technologies, Inc

Financial Data: Fiscal Year End:12/31   *Latest Annual Data:* 12/31/2005

Year	Sales	Net Income
2005	$6,322,000	$486,000
2004	$7,912,000	$14,690,000
2003	$6,437,000	-$23,516,000

Curr. Assets:	$3,400,000	*Curr. Liab.:*	$2,365,000		
Plant, Equip.:	$89,000	*Total Liab.:*	$7,306,000	*Indic. Yr. Divd.:*	NA
Total Assets:	$4,264,000	*Net Worth:*	-$3,043,000	*Debt/ Equity:*	NA

Latin American Export Bank

50th St. and Aquilino De La Guardia, Panama; *PH:* 1-507-210-8500; *Fax:* 1-507-269-6333; *http://* www.blx.com

General - Incorporation	Panama	*Stock*- Price on:12/24/2007	$19.47
Employees	169	Stock Exchange	NYSE
Auditor	KPMG LLP	Ticker Symbol	BLX
Stk Agt	Bank of New York	Outstanding Shares	36,330,000
Counsel	NA	E.P.S	$2.10
DUNS No.	85-367-2954	Shareholders	NA

Business: The groups principle activity is to provide commercial banking operations and other related financial activities. The group operates from United States.

Primary SIC and add'l.: 6029

CIK No: 0000890541

Officers: Jaime Rivera/Dir., CEO, Rubens V. Amaral/Exec. VP - Commercial, Tesyla Guanti/VP, Elsa Crespo/VP, Ernesto A. Bruggia/COO, Gregory D. Testerman/Sr. VP - Treasury, Eliseo Sanchez-Lucca/VP, Miguel Moreno/COO, Luisa De Polo/Mgr. - Shareholder Relations, Ana Maria M. De Arias/Sr. VP - Human Resources, Administration, Carlos S. Yap/Sr. VP, CFO, Roberto Teixeira Dacosta/Dir., Advisory Counsel Member, Carlos Martabit/Advisory Counsel, Alberto C. Motta/VP, Member - Advisory Counsel, Eucadis De Molina/Assist. VP *(81 Officers included in Index)*

Directors: Jaime Rivera/Dir., CEO, Nicolas Ardito Barleta/Honorary Chmn., Gonzalo Menendez Duque/Chmn., Santiago Perdomo Maldonado/Dir., Maria Dagraca Franca/Dir., Roberto R. Aleman/Dir., Roberto Teixeira Dacosta/Dir., Advisory Counsel Member, Alberto C. Motta/VP, Member - Advisory Counsel, William D. Hayes/Dir., Herminio A. Blanco/Dir., Guillermo Guemez Garcia/Dir., Jose Maria Rabelo/Dir., Mario Covo/Dir., Will Wood/Dir.

Owners: Banco do Brasil/15.40%, Brandes Investment Partners, LP/11.50%, Porter Orlin LLC/7.40%, Banco de Comercio Exterior de Colombia/7.70%, Capital Research and Management Co/5.40%, Mondrian Investment Partners Ltd/9.60%, Oppenheimer Funds Inc/14.80%, Arnhold & S. Bleichroeder Advisers, LLC/9.40%, Banco de la Nacin Argentina/16.50%, Banco de la Provincia de Buenos Aires/32.50%, Banco Central del Paraguay/6.90%, Banco Central del Ecuador/6.80%, Banco de la Nacin/7.00%, Banco de la Nacin Argentina/10.90%, Franklin Resources Inc/9.60% *(17 Owners included in Index)*

Financial Data: Fiscal Year End:12/31   *Latest Annual Data:* 12/31/2006

Year	Sales	Net Income
2006	$243,668,000	$57,902,000
2005	$135,405,000	$80,101,000
2004	$86,003,000	$141,730,000

Curr. Assets:	$563,485,000	*Curr. Liab.:*	$2,781,139,000		
Plant, Equip.:	$11,136,000	*Total Liab.:*	$3,394,442,000	*Indic. Yr. Divd.:*	$0.880
Total Assets:	$3,978,337,000	*Net Worth:*	$583,895,000	*Debt/ Equity:*	NA

Latin Television Inc

Formerly: Communications Research Inc

3764 Nw 124th Ave., Coral Springs, FL, 33065; *PH:* 1-516-214-5565; *http://* www.vistele.com

General - Incorporation	NJ	*Stock*- Price on:12/24/2007	NA
Employees	3	Stock Exchange	NA
Auditor	Chisholm Bierwolf & Nilson LLC	Ticker Symbol	NA
Stk Agt	NA	Outstanding Shares	NA
Counsel	Farber & Klein	E.P.S	NA
DUNS No.	NA	Shareholders	NA

Business: The group's principal activity is to design, develop, install and support communication systems that process and transmit video, audio and data. The group also manufactures and sells fully integrated, PC based and full motion video conferencing systems. The group operates under two segments - systems integration division and special systems consulting division. The systems integration division designs, develops and installs sophisticated data, audio and video networks. The special systems consulting division provides clients with design, development, bid specifications, cost consulting and project management of audio, video, data and communication systems.

Primary SIC and add'l.: 3663 7372

CIK No: 0001122686

Subsidiaries: TeleWRITER CORPORATION, INC, Visual Telephone International, Visual Telephone of New Jersey, Inc

Officers: Carl R. Ceragno/61/Founder, Dir., CEO, CFO, Pres., Treasurer, Lawrence S. Hartman/42/Dir., VP, Almajean O'Connor/58/Sec.

Directors: Carl R. Ceragno/61/Founder, Dir., CEO, CFO, Pres., Treasurer, Lawrence S. Hartman/42/Dir., VP

Owners: Lawrence S. Hartman/1.25%, Carl R. Ceragno/100.00%, Carl R. Ceragno/5.50%, Almajean O Connor/1.40%, Insiders/8.25%

Financial Data: Fiscal Year End:12/31   *Latest Annual Data:* 12/31/2006

Year	Sales	Net Income
2006	$44,000	-$1,408,000
2005	$77,000	-$411,000
2004	$149,000	-$478,000

Curr. Assets:	$1,000	*Curr. Liab.:*	$194,000		
Plant, Equip.:	NA	*Total Liab.:*	$194,000	*Indic. Yr. Divd.:*	NA
Total Assets:	$1,000	*Net Worth:*	-$192,000	*Debt/ Equity:*	NA

Lattice Inc

Formerly: Science Dynamics Corp

1919 Springdale Rd. , Cherry Hill, NJ, 08003; *PH:* 1-856-424-0068; *http://* www.scidyn.com

General - Incorporation	DE	*Stock*- Price on:12/24/2007	NA
Employees	27	Stock Exchange	OTC
Auditor	Peter C. Cosmas Co., Cpas	Ticker Symbol	LTTC
Stk Agt	Peter C. Cosmas Co	Outstanding Shares	NA
Counsel	Stephen M. Robinson	E.P.S	$0.01
DUNS No.	08-571-0986	Shareholders	NA

Business: The group's principal activities are to develop, design and market a variety of telecommunication systems. The group provides intelligent call processing platforms, which include telecommunication service capabilities to the public switched telephone network. These platforms are sophisticated software based systems that satisfy a wide range of computer telephony integration applications. The group has focused its strategy to be a provider of key enabling technologies required for the convergence of traditional and new communications media and infrastructure. The group's products include ip telephony, video over frame relay, voice response system and commander inmate telephone control system.

Primary SIC and add'l.: 7373

CIK No: 0000350644

Subsidiaries: M3 Acquisition Corp, SciDyn Corporation, Systems Management Engineering, Inc

Officers: Paul Burgess/Pres., CEO - Contact - Investor Relations, Joe Noto/CFO, Thomas R. Spadaro/VP - Engineering, Eric D. Zelsdorf/41/CTO, Michael Ricciardi/48/COO

Directors: Paul Burgess/Pres., CEO - Contact - Investor Relations, Robert E. Galbraith/63/Dir., Jeannemarie Devolites Davis/51/Dir., Thomas F. Gillett/61/Dir., Donald Upson/53/Dir.

Owners: Joe Noto, Burlington Assembly of God/5.70%, Dragonfly Capital Partners, LLC/5.60%, Marie Ricciardi/21.40%, Paul Burgess/4.60%, Insiders/30.00%, Michael Ricciardi/21.40%, Eric D. Zelsdorf/3.30%, Alan Bashforth/9.50%, Robert Galbraith

Financial Data: Fiscal Year End:12/31   *Latest Annual Data:* 12/31/2006

Year	Sales	Net Income
2006	$7,495,000	-$15,551,000
2005	$4,235,000	-$863,000
2004	$1,610,000	-$481,000

Curr. Assets:	$3,567,000	*Curr. Liab.:*	$24,579,000		
Plant, Equip.:	$37,000	*Total Liab.:*	$24,985,000	*Indic. Yr. Divd.:*	NA
Total Assets:	$13,620,000	*Net Worth:*	-$11,501,000	*Debt/ Equity:*	NA

Lattice Semiconductor Corp

5555 NE Moore Ct., Hillsboro, OR, 97124; *PH:* 1-503-268-8000; *Fax:* 1-503-268-8347; *http://* www.latticesemi.com; *Email:* lic_admn@latticesemi.com

General - Incorporation	DE	*Stock*- Price on:12/24/2007	$5.96
Employees	960	Stock Exchange	NDQ
Auditor	PricewaterhouseCoopers LLP	Ticker Symbol	LSCC
Stk Agt	Mellon Investor Services LLC	Outstanding Shares	114,770,000
Counsel	Wilson Sonsini Goodrich & Rosati	E.P.S	-$0.08
DUNS No.	10-301-7299	Shareholders	NA

Business: The group's principal activity is to design, develop and market high performance programmable logic devices and related software. Programmable logic devices are widely-used semiconductor components that can be configured by end customers as specific logic circuits and thus enable shorter design cycle times and reduced development costs. The group pioneered the development of in-system programmability (isp). Isp devices can be configured and reconfigured by a system designer without being removed from the printed circuit board. The end customers of the group are primarily original equipment manufacturers in the communications, computing, industrial, automotive, medical, consumer and military end markets.

Primary SIC and add'l.: 3674

CIK No: 0000855658

Subsidiaries: Lattice Semiconducteurs SARL, Lattice Semiconductor (Shanghai) Co. Ltd., Lattice Semiconductor AB, Lattice Semiconductor Asia Limited, Lattice Semiconductor Canada Corporation, Lattice Semiconductor GmbH, Lattice Semiconductor International Corporation, Lattice Semiconductor KK, Lattice Semiconductor SRL, Lattice Semiconductor UK Limited

Officers: Stephen A. Skaggs/Dir., CEO, Pres./$1,192,917.00, Martin R. Baker/Corporate VP, General Counsel, Sec./$370,524.00, Stephen M. Donovan/Corporate VP - Sales/$393,243.00, Jan Johannessen/CFO, Sr. VP/$500,965.00

Directors: Stephen A. Skaggs/Dir., CEO, Pres., Patrick S. Jones/Chmn., Harry A. Merlo/Dir., David E. Coreson/Dir., Daniel S. Hauer/Dir., Balaji Krishnamurthy/Dir., Gerhard H. Parker/Dir.

Owners: Balaji Krishnamurthy, Harry A. Merlo, Dimensional Fund Advisors L.P./8.40%, Patrick S. Jones, Gerhard Parker, Stephen A. Skaggs/1.40%, Soo Boon Koh, Frank J. Barone, Martin R. Baker, Insiders/3.20%, Mazama Capital Management Inc./19.60%, David E. Coreson, Jan Johannessen, Daniel S. Hauer, Mark O. Hatfield *(16 Owners included in Index)*

Financial Data: **Fiscal Year End:** 12/31 **Latest Annual Data:** 12/30/2006

Year	Sales	Net Income
2006	$245,459,000	$3,093,000
2005	$211,060,000	-$49,119,000

Curr. Assets:	$340,964,000	**Curr. Liab.:**	$63,887,000		
Plant, Equip.:	$45,450,000	**Total Liab.:**	$217,773,000	**Indic. Yr. Divd.:**	NA
Total Assets:	$715,857,000	**Net Worth:**	$498,084,000	**Debt/ Equity:**	0.1547

Laureate Education Inc

1001 Fleet St., Baltimore, MD, 21202; ***PH:*** 1-410-843-6100; ***http://*** www.laureate-inc.com

General - Incorporation	MD	**Stock**- Price on:12/24/2007	$61.36
Employees	12,000	Stock Exchange	NA
Auditor	Ernst & Young LLP	Ticker Symbol	NA
Stk Agt	American Stock Transfer & Trust Co.	Outstanding Shares	51,580,000
Counsel	NA	E.P.S.	$0.15
DUNS No.	NA	Shareholders	NA

Business: The group's principal activity is to provide higher educational services. It also offers working-adult students the convenience and flexibility of distance learning to pursue undergraduate, master's and pH.d. Degree programs in the fields of engineering, education, business, and healthcare. It provides the services through global network of accredited campus based and online universities and other higher education institutions. The group operates through two segments: campus based higher education institution segment owns and maintains controlling interests in nine separately accredited higher education institutions. The online higher education segment provides career-oriented degree programs to working-adult students through canter and associates, walden e-learning, inc. And national technological university, inc. On 30-Jun-2003, the group sold the operations of its k-12 segment. On 16-Sep-2004 the group acquired remaining 49% interest in walden university.

Primary SIC and add'l.: NA

CIK No: 0000912766

Subsidiaries: A.S. Cyprus College Ltd., Administradora del Valle de Texoco, Administradora del Valle de Toluca, Administradora del Valle del Centro, CAMPVS Mater, SA, Canter and Associates, Inc., Centro de Formacion Tecnica Instituto AIEP Regional SA, Centro de Formacion Tecnica Instituto AIEP SA, Corporacion Universidad Nacional Andres Bello, Desarrollo de la Educacion Superior SA, Desarrollo del Conocimiento, SA, Ecole Centrale des Techniques de lEnvironement Industriel SA, Ecole Superior du Commerce Exterieur, Escuela Superior de Alta Gestion de Hotel, SL, Estrategia Educativa y Cultural de Tabasco, SC 51 Subsidiaries included in the Index

Officers: Paula R. Singer/Pres., CEO - Laureate Online Education, Douglas L. Becker/Chmn., CEO, Daniel M. Nickel/Exec. VP - Corporate Operations, Robert W. Zentz/Sr. VP, General Counsel, Joseph D. Duffey/Sr. VP, William C. Dennis/Pres. - Latin America Operations, Rosemarie Mecca/CFO, Exec. VP, Raph Appadoo/Pres.

Directors: Douglas L. Becker/Chmn., CEO, Christopher R. Hoehn-Saric/Dir., John A. Miller/Dir., William R. Pollock/Dir., Richard W. Riley/Dir., James H. McGuire/Dir., Isabel Aguilera/Dir., Wolf H. Hengst/Dir., David A. Wilson/Dir., Todd E. Benson/Dir., Brian F. Carroll/Dir., Yves De Balmann/Dir., Jonathan D. Smidt/Dir., Ian K. Snow/Dir., Steven M. Taslitz/Dir. *(16 Directors included in Index)*

Owners: Paula R. Singer/0.16%, Citigroup Private Equity LP/0.06%, Insiders/8.65%, Douglas L. Becker/3.79%, Steven M. Taslitz/0.52%, William Blair & Company, LLC/6.94%, Yves de Balmann, T. Rowe Price Mutual Funds/8.16%, William C. Dennis, Rosemarie Mecca/0.17%, Christopher R. Hoehn-Saric/2.61%, Select Equity Group/9.74%, Sigma Capital Associates, LLC/0.08%, Daniel M. Nickel/0.11%, Raph Appadoo/1.07%

Financial Data: **Fiscal Year End:** 12/31 **Latest Annual Data:** 12/31/2006

Year	Sales	Net Income
2006	$1,145,761,000	$105,623,000
2005	$875,376,000	$75,183,000
2004	$648,019,000	$63,011,000

Curr. Assets:	$435,387,000	**Curr. Liab.:**	$609,354,000	**P/E Ratio:**	41.46
Plant, Equip.:	$729,312,000	**Total Liab.:**	$1,026,894,000	**Indic. Yr. Divd.:**	NA
Total Assets:	$2,203,013,000	**Net Worth:**	$1,130,695,000	**Debt/ Equity:**	0.3687

Laurier International Inc

101-1870 Pk.inson Way, Kelowna, BC, V1Y 8C9; ***PH:*** 1-250-712-9354

General - Incorporation	DE	**Stock**- Price on:12/24/2007	NA
Employees	NA	Stock Exchange	OTC
Auditor	Chang G. Park, CPA	Ticker Symbol	LRNL
Stk Agt	NA	Outstanding Shares	NA
Counsel	NA	E.P.S.	NA
DUNS No.	NA	Shareholders	NA

Business: The groups principle activity is to provide recruiting services. The groups service area includes the research and development, engineering, marketing, sales, information technology and manufacturing industries. The group operates from United States.

Primary SIC and add'l.: 6712

CIK No: 0001195116

Subsidiaries: Geotheatre Productions, Inc.

Officers: John Bracey/60/Dir., CEO, CFO, Pres., Treasurer, Principal Accounting Officer, Sec.

Directors: John Bracey/60/Dir., CEO, CFO, Pres., Treasurer, Principal Accounting Officer, Sec., Katherine E. Bracey/52/Dir.

Owners: La Pergola Investments Limited/14.54%, Fountainhead Capital Management Limited/82.37%

Law Enforcement Assoc Corp

100 Hunter Pl., Youngsville, NC, 27596; ***PH:*** 1-919-554-4700; ***Fax:*** 1-919-556-6240; ***http://*** www.leacorp.com

General - Incorporation	NV	**Stock**- Price on:12/24/2007	$0.72
Employees	35	Stock Exchange	AMEX
Auditor	Baum & Co. P.A	Ticker Symbol	AID
Stk Agt	Computershare Investor Services LLC	Outstanding Shares	25,250,000
Counsel	NA	E.P.S.	-$0.004
DUNS No.	NA	Shareholders	NA

Business: The group's principal activities are to manufacture and distribute undercover surveillance products including a complete line of audio surveillance equipment. The products are marketed under brand names such as the bloodhound global positioning tracking system (bgpts) and the under vehicle inspection system (uvis). The bgpts is a global positioning system receiver combined with a cellular telephone that allows undercover surveillance agents to monitor the movements of a vehicle. The uvis is used to view the underside of vehicles entering and exiting secure areas or facilities for explosive devices and other contraband. The products are sold primarily to military, law enforcement, security and corrections personnel throughout the world, as well as governmental agencies and other organizations.

Primary SIC and add'l.: 3823

CIK No: 0001165921

Subsidiaries: Law Enforcement Associates, Inc.

Officers: Paul Feldman/Dir., CEO, CFO, Pres., Geoff High/Contact - Primary Investor Relations

Directors: Paul Feldman/Dir., CEO, CFO, Pres., Anthony Rand/Dir., Martin Perry/Dir., James J. Lindsay/Dir., Joseph A. Jordan/Dir.

Owners: Martin L. Perry/0.44%, Anthony Rand/0.50%, John H. Carrington/57.44%, Insiders/3.11%, James J. Lindsay/0.21%, Paul Feldman/1.95%, Joseph Jordan/0.00%

Financial Data: **Fiscal Year End:** 12/31 **Latest Annual Data:** 12/31/2006

Year	Sales	Net Income
2006	$7,547,000	-$3,000
2005	$8,157,000	-$282,000
2004	$6,236,000	-$177,000

Curr. Assets:	$3,004,000	**Curr. Liab.:**	$631,000		
Plant, Equip.:	$309,000	**Total Liab.:**	$631,000	**Indic. Yr. Divd.:**	NA
Total Assets:	$6,028,000	**Net Worth:**	$5,397,000	**Debt/ Equity:**	NA

Lawson Products Inc

1666 E Touhy Ave., Des Plaines, IL, 60018; ***PH:*** 1-847-827-9666; ***http://*** www.lawsonproducts.com; ***Email:*** info@lawsonproducts.com

General - Incorporation	DE	**Stock**- Price on:12/24/2007	$35.45
Employees	1,540	Stock Exchange	NDQ
Auditor	Ernst & Young LLP	Ticker Symbol	LAWS
Stk Agt	EquiServe Trust Co N.A	Outstanding Shares	8,520,000
Counsel	McDermott Will & Emery	E.P.S.	NA
DUNS No.	00-543-8890	Shareholders	NA

Business: The group's principal activity is the distribution of expendable parts and supplies for maintenance, repair and operation of equipment. These products can be divided into three broad categories: fasteners, fittings and related parts, industrial supplies and automotive and equipment maintenance parts. Fasteners, fittings and related parts include screws, nuts, rivets and other fasteners. Industrial supplies include hoses and hose fittings, lubricants, cleansers, adhesives and other chemicals, as well as files, drills, welding products and other shop supplies. Automotive and equipment maintenance parts include primary wiring, connectors and other electrical supplies, exhaust and other automotive parts.

Primary SIC and add'l.: 5065 5013 5072 5085

CIK No: 0000703604

Subsidiaries: Assembly Component Systems, Inc., Automatic Screw Machine Products Company, Inc.1, C.B. Lynn Company, Cronatron Welding Systems, Inc., Drummond American Corporation, Lawson Products de Mexico S. de RL. de C.v., Lawson Products, Inc., Lawson Products, Inc. (Ontario), LP Industrial Products Company, LP Service Co., LPI Holdings, Inc., Rutland Tool & Supply Co.

Officers: Thomas Neri/CEO, Pres./$500,342.00, Neil E. Jenkins/Exec. VP, Sec., General Counsel, Rick L. Considine/VP - Business Development, William Holmes/VP, Treasurer, Tom Pavlick/VP, GM - Kent Automotive, Peter A. Alsberg/CIO, Sr. VP, Michael Ruprich/Group Pres. - MRO, Joseph L. Pawlick/Sr. VP - Accounting, James W. Degnan/Pres. - Lawson MRO, Warren Ludvigsen/VP - Spectrum Industrial Solutions, Stewart Howley/Sr. VP, Chief Marketing Officer, Michelle Russell/VP - Corporate Affairs, Chief Ethics Officer, Richard Schwind/Sr. VP - Corporate Procurement, Global Accounting Development, Lisa Kaplan/VP - Corporate Marketing, Susan Collins/Pres. - Cronatron Welding Systems INC *(39 Officers included in Index)*

Directors: Ronald B. Port/Chmn., Sidney L. Port/Vice Chmn., Wilma J. Smelcer/Dir., Thomas S. Postek/Dir., Lee S. Hillman/52/Dir., James S. Errant/59/Dir., Mitchell H. Saranow/Dir.

Owners: Roger F. Cannon, Royce & Associates LLC/11.10%, Roberta Port Washlow/35.60%, Mitchell H. Saranow, James T. Brophy, Thomas S. Postek, Insiders/50.90%, Lee S. Hillman, Wilma J. Smelcer, Sidney L. Port/13.70%, Robert G. Rettig, Jeffrey B. Belford, Ronald B. Port/35.60%, James S. Errant, Robert J. Washlow

Financial Data: **Fiscal Year End:** 12/31 **Latest Annual Data:** 06/30/2007

Year	Sales	Net Income
2007	$127,721,000	-$349,000
2006	$126,187,000	$1,344,000
2005	$450,185,000	$26,738,000

Curr. Assets:	$165,197,000	Curr. Liab.:	$63,427,000	P/E Ratio:	25.50
Plant, Equip.:	$42,664,000	Total Liab.:	$108,566,000	Indic. Yr. Divd.:	$0.800
Total Assets:	$278,883,000	Net Worth:	$170,317,000	Debt/ Equity:	NA

Lawson Software Inc

380 St. Peter St., St. Paul, MN, 55102; *PH:* 1-651-767-7000; *http://* www.lawson.com

General - Incorporation	DE	Stock- Price on:12/24/2007	$9.81
Employees	3,400	Stock Exchange	NDQ
Auditor	PricewaterhouseCoopers LLP	Ticker Symbol	LWSN
Stk Agt	Mellon Investor Services LLC	Outstanding Shares	187,670,000
Counsel	NA	E.P.S.	$0.00
DUNS No.	NA	Shareholders	NA

Business: The group's principle activities are to design, develop and market enterprise software solutions. The group's software solutions automate and integrate critical business processes, facilitating collaboration among customers, partners, suppliers, employees and professional services. The group also offers comprehensive financial management, human resources, professional service automation, procurement, distribution and customer relationship management solutions. The customers include healthcare, retail, professional services, financial services and public sector industries. The group has its operations in the United States, Canada, the United Kingdom, Germany, France and the Netherlands. The group's total revenue for year 2007 was 750.39 millions of USD.

Primary SIC and add'l.: 7372 7379 7371

CIK No: 0001141517

Subsidiaries: Account4,Inc., Apexion Technologies,Inc., Closedloop Solutions,Inc., Keyola Corporation, Lawson Software Benelux, B.V., Lawson Software France SARL, Lawson Software GmbH, Lawson Software Limited, Lawson Software USA,Inc., Lawson Technologies,Inc., Numbercraft Limited

Officers: Harry Debes/Dir., CEO, Pres., Dean Hager/Sr. VP - Product Management, Ana Paula Horemans/Contact - Brazil, Jaap Van Den Akker/Country Mgr. - Belgium, Lut Verschueren/Public Relations, Communications, Belgium, David Grooten/Mgr. - Marketing, Belgium, Hanneli Avingu/Business Consultant - Estonia, Kevin Dix/MD, Financial Mgr. - South Africa, Lorraine Coetzee/Implex Responsible, South Africa, Eduardo Sanchez/Exec. VP - Global Sales, Travis White/Sr. VP - Marketing, Trygve Slette/Services Dir. - Indonesia, Regional Dir. - South East Asia, Edwin Chow/GM - Philippines, Jorge Zambrano/Contact - Mexico, Yvonne Sanderson/Human Resources - Belgium *(28 Officers included in Index)*

Directors: Harry Debes/Dir., CEO, Pres., Richard H. Lawson/Chmn., Romesh Wadhwani/Chmn., Steven C. Chang/Dir., Peter Gyenes/Dir., Michael A. Rocca/Dir., David Hubers/Dir., David J. Eskra/66/Dir., Paul Wahl/Dir.

Financial Data: *Fiscal Year End:*05/31   *Latest Annual Data:* 05/31/2007

Year	Sales	Net Income
2007	$750,388,000	-$20,937,000
2006	$390,776,000	$15,959,000

Curr. Assets:	$514,562,000	Curr. Liab.:	$346,361,000		
Plant, Equip.:	$26,189,000	Total Liab.:	$378,993,000	Indic. Yr. Divd.:	NA
Total Assets:	$1,170,652,000	Net Worth:	$791,659,000	Debt/ Equity:	0.0067

Laycor Ventures Corp

1128 Quebec St., Ste. 407, Vancouver, BC, V6A 4E1; *PH:* 1-604-689-1453

General - Incorporation	NV	Stock- Price on:12/24/2007	$0.7
Employees	NA	Stock Exchange	OTC
Auditor	Telford Sadovnick, PLLC	Ticker Symbol	LYVN
Stk Agt	Pacific Stock Transfer Company	Outstanding Shares	NA
Counsel	NA	E.P.S.	NA
DUNS No.	NA	Shareholders	NA

Business: The groups principal activities include acquiring and exploring mining properties. The group operates from the United States.

Primary SIC and add'l.: 1040

CIK No: 0001292518

Officers: Robert Wayne Morgan/55/Dir., Pres., Principal Executive Officer, Treasurer, Principal Financial Officer

Directors: Robert Wayne Morgan/55/Dir., Pres., Principal Executive Officer, Treasurer, Principal Financial Officer

Owners: Robert Wayne Morgan/62.41%, Insiders/62.41%

Financial Data: *Fiscal Year End:*03/31   *Latest Annual Data:* 03/31/2007

Year	Sales	Net Income
2007	NA	-$28,000
2006	NA	-$66,000

Curr. Assets:	$32,000	Curr. Liab.:	$8,000		
Plant, Equip.:	NA	Total Liab.:	$8,000	Indic. Yr. Divd.:	NA
Total Assets:	$32,000	Net Worth:	$25,000	Debt/ Equity:	NA

Layne Christensen Co

1900 Shawnee Mission Pkwy., Mission Woods, KS, 66205; *PH:* 1-913-362-0510; *Fax:* 1-913-362-0133; *http://* www.laynechristensen.com; *Email:* dademeese@laynechristensen.com

General - Incorporation	DE	Stock- Price on:12/24/2007	$43.17
Employees	3,919	Stock Exchange	NDQ
Auditor	Deloitte & Touche LLP	Ticker Symbol	LAYN
Stk Agt	National City Bank	Outstanding Shares	15,520,000
Counsel	NA	E.P.S.	$2.12
DUNS No.	00-696-5917	Shareholders	NA

Business: The group's principle activity is to provide drilling and related services. The group operates through four segments: water resources, mineral exploration, geoconstruction services and energy services. Water resources include hydrological studies and related engineering services, water well design and drilling, pump sales, installation, repair and maintenance. Mineral exploration drilling helps to identify, define and develops mineral deposits. Geoconstruction services are used to modify weak and unstable soils, decrease water flow in bedrock and provide support and groundwater control. Energy operations offer drilling services to the shallow, unconventional oil and gas market, conventional oil field fishing services, coil tubing fishing services. The group's customers include municipalities, industrial companies, mining companies, consulting and engineering firms and oil and gas companies. The group's total revenue for year 2007 was 722.77 millions of USD.

Primary SIC and add'l.: 1781 1771 1381 1481

CIK No: 0000888504

Subsidiaries: Ausdrill Burkina SARL, Boyles Bros. Drilling Company, Camken-Reynolds, LLC, Cherryvale Pipeline, LLC, Christensen Boyles Corporation, ESEMES (Mauritius) Limited, G&K Properties Pty Ltd, Inliner Technologies, LLC, International Directional Services of Canada Ltd., International Directional Services, LLC, International Mining Services Pty Ltd, Investments (Pvt) Ltd, Layne Christensen Australia Pty Limited, Layne Christensen Canada Limited, Layne de Bolivia S.R.L. 56 Subsidiaries included in the Index

Officers: Andrew B. Schmitt/Dir., CEO, Pres./$2,048,458.00, Jeffrey J. Reynolds/Dir., Sr. VP/$603,607.00, Steven F. Crooke/VP, General Counsel, Sec., Peter L. Iovino/Pres. - Geoconstruction Services Division, Colin B. Kinley/Pres. - Energy Services, Production Division/$698,539.00, Gregory F. Aluce/Pres. - Water Resources Division, Jerry W. Fanska/VP - Finance, Treasurer/$433,701.00, Eric R. Despain/Pres. - Mineral Exploration Division/$508,540.00

Directors: Andrew B. Schmitt/Dir., CEO, Pres., David A.B. Brown/Chmn., Samuel J. Butler/Dir., Anthony B. Helfet/Dir., Donald K. Miller/Dir., Nelson Obus/Dir., John J. /Dir.

Owners: Anthony B. Helfet, John J. Quicke, Andrew B. Schmitt/1.50%, Jerry W. Fanska, Donald K. Miller, Colin B. Kinley, Insiders/12.20%, PowerShares Capital Management LLC/8.80%, Samuel J. Butler, Nelson Obus/3.90%, Jeffrey J. Reynolds/5.30%, David A. B. Brown, Eric R. Despain

Financial Data: *Fiscal Year End:*01/31   *Latest Annual Data:* 1/31/2007

Year	Sales	Net Income
2007	$722,768,000	$26,252,000
2006	$463,015,000	$14,681,000
2005	$343,462,000	$9,754,000

Curr. Assets:	$223,208,000	Curr. Liab.:	$156,219,000	P/E Ratio:	22.72
Plant, Equip.:	$214,517,000	Total Liab.:	$342,130,000	Indic. Yr. Divd.:	NA
Total Assets:	$547,164,000	Net Worth:	$205,034,000	Debt/ Equity:	0.7573

Lazard Ltd

30 Rockefeller Plz., New York, NY, 10020; *PH:* 1-212-632-6000; *Fax:* 1-212-632-6060; *http://* www.lazard.com

General - Incorporation	Bermuda	Stock- Price on:12/24/2007	$46.81
Employees	2,200	Stock Exchange	NYSE
Auditor	Deloitte & Touche LLP	Ticker Symbol	LAZ
Stk Agt	Bank of New York	Outstanding Shares	51,440,000
Counsel	NA	E.P.S.	$2.50
DUNS No.	NA	Shareholders	NA

Business: The groups principle activity is to provide financial advisory and asset management. The group operates through two segments namely, financial advisory and asset management. The group operates from the United States, Europe, North America, Asia, Australia and South America.The group's quarterly revenue for September 2007 was 580.12 millions of USD.

Primary SIC and add'l.: 6282 6799 6726 6211 6221

CIK No: 0001311370

Subsidiaries: Lazard & Co. Srl*, Lazard & Co., Holdings Limited, Lazard & Co., Limited, Lazard Asset Management LLC, Lazard Frres & Co. LLC, Lazard Frres Banque SA, Lazard Frres Gestion, Lazard Frres SAS, Lazard Funding Limited LLC, Lazard Group LLC, Maison Lazard SAS

Officers: Bruce Wasserstein/60/Chmn., CEO/$7,039,967.00, Charles G. Ward/Pres., Chmn. - Asset Management Group/$3,113,652.00, Scott D. Hoffman/General Counsel/$2,462,735.00, Michael J. Castellano/CFO/$2,122,137.00, Judi Frost MacKey/Media Contact, Richard Creswell/Media Contact, Jean Greene/Investor Contact, Lisa Henkoff/Contact - Financial Advisory, Cathy Mignone/Contact - Financial Advisory, Anna Woodward/Contact - Financial Advisory, Tony Tang/Contact

Directors: Bruce Wasserstein/60/Chmn., CEO, Steven J. Golub/Vice Chmn., Chmn. - Financial Advisory Group, Charles G. Ward/Pres., Chmn. - Asset Management Group, John K. Shank/Dir., Michael J. Turner/Dir., Ronald J. Doerfler/Dir., Steven J. Heyer/55/Dir., Sylvia Jay/Dir., Ellis Jones/54/Dir., Vernon E. Jordan/72/Dir., Anthony Orsatelli/56/Dir., Hal S. Scott/Dir.

Owners: Bruce Wasserstein/3.80%, Anthony Orsatelli/3.90%, AXA Financial, Inc./9.30%, IXIS/3.90%, FMR Corp./14.20%

Financial Data: *Fiscal Year End:*12/31   *Latest Annual Data:* 12/31/2006

Year	Sales	Net Income
2006	$1,597,809,000	$92,985,000
2005	$1,379,807,000	$143,486,000
2004	$1,328,180,000	$246,974,000

Curr. Assets:	$2,220,402,000	Curr. Liab.:	$1,871,033,000	P/E Ratio:	21.69
Plant, Equip.:	$168,310,000	Total Liab.:	$3,449,018,000	Indic. Yr. Divd.:	$0.360
Total Assets:	$3,208,665,000	Net Worth:	-$240,353,000	Debt/ Equity:	NA

Lazare Kaplan International Inc

19 W 44th St., New York, NY, 10036; *PH:* 1-212-972-9700; *Fax:* 1-212-972-8561; *http://* lazarediamonds.com

General - Incorporation	DE	Stock- Price on:12/24/2007	$8.45
Employees	223	Stock Exchange	AMEX
Auditor	BDO Seidman LLP	Ticker Symbol	LKI
Stk Agt	Mellon Investor Services LLC	Outstanding Shares	8,200,000
Counsel	Warshaw Burstein Cohen Et Al	E.P.S.	-$0.09
DUNS No.	05-667-7925	Shareholders	NA

Business: The group's principal activity is to cut, polish and sell ideally proportioned diamonds under the brand name lazare diamonds'r'. Non-ideal cut (commercial) diamonds are also cut, polished and then sold under the bellataire diamonds brand name. These stones are sold through wholesalers, distributors and retail jewelers. The group also buys and sells uncut rough diamonds. The manufacturing facilities are located in Puerto Rico and Russia. The polished diamonds are marketed to customers in the United States, South America, the Far East and Europe. The rough diamond trading markets are primarily located in Belgium, India and Israel.

Primary SIC and add'l.: 3915 5094

CIK No: 0000202375

Subsidiaries: Bellataire Inc., Lazare Kaplan Africa Inc., Lazare Kaplan Belgium, N.V., Lazare Kaplan Europe Inc., Lazare Kaplan Japan Inc., Pegasus Overseas LLC, Pegasus Overseas Ltd., POCL Bvba, POCL, N.V

Officers: Leon Tempelsman/52/Vice Chmn., CEO, Pres./$525,899.00, William H. Moryto/50/CFO, VP/$381,442.00

Directors: Leon Tempelsman/52/Vice Chmn., CEO, Pres., Maurice Tempelsman/79/Chmn., Lucien Burstein/Dir., Robert A. Del Genio/Dir., Richard A. Berenson/Dir.

Owners: William H. Moryto, Dimensional Fund Advisors Inc., Leon Tempelsman, Maurice Tempelsman, Richard A. Berenson, Lucien Burstein, Robert A. Del Genio, Insiders, Fifth Avenue Group LLC

Financial Data: *Fiscal Year End:*05/31 *Latest Annual Data:* 5/31/2006

Year	Sales	Net Income
2006	$528,045,000	$1,528,000
2005	$421,411,000	$5,230,000
2004	$235,775,000	$2,399,000

Curr. Assets:	$247,464,000	**Curr. Liab.:**	$103,740,000		
Plant, Equip.:	$8,318,000	**Total Liab.:**	$167,916,000	**Indic. Yr. Divd.:**	NA
Total Assets:	$263,712,000	**Net Worth:**	$95,796,000	**Debt/ Equity:**	NA

LCA-Vision Inc

7840 Montgomery Rd., Cincinnati, OH, 45236; *PH:* 1-513-792-9292; *http://* www.lca-vision.com

General - Incorporation	DE	**Stock**- Price on:12/24/2007	$46.06
Employees	614	Stock Exchange	NDQ
Auditor	Ernst & Young LLP	Ticker Symbol	LCAV
Stk Agt	LCA Vision Inc	Outstanding Shares	20,070,000
Counsel	Dinsmore & Shohl	E.P.S.	$1.67
DUNS No.	16-107-7169	Shareholders	NA

Business: The group's principal activity is to develop and operate value-priced laser vision correction centers. These centers provide facilities, equipment and support services for performing vision correction procedures using state-of-the-art laser technologies to correct nearsightedness, farsightedness and astigmatism. The group currently utilizes three excimer lasers: the bausch and lomb technolas 217, the visx star s2/s3 and the alcon ladarvision. Laser vision correction procedures are designed to reshape the outer layers of the cornea to correct refractive vision disorders by changing its curvature with an excimer laser. As of 31-Dec-2003, the group operates 40 lasikplus laser vision correction centers, 36 of which are located in metropolitan markets throughout the United States, three in Canada and one in Europe.

Primary SIC and add'l.: 8062

CIK No: 0001003130

Subsidiaries: Lasik Insurance Company, Ltd., Lasik M.D. Toronto Inc., LCA-Vision (Canada) Inc., LCA-Vision (Ohio) Inc., The Baltimore Laser Sight Center, Ltd., The Toronto Laservision Centre (1992)Inc.

Officers: Steven C. Straus/CEO/$79,445.00, James H. Brenner/Chief Marketing Officer, Michael J. Celebrezze/Sr. VP - Finance, Treasurer, Stephen M. Jones/Sr. VP - Human Resources, Alan H. Buckey/CFO, Exec. VP - Finance/$705,450.00, Craig P.R. Joffe/Non - Dir., General Counsel, Sec./$763,485.00, Kevin M. Hassey/Pres./$322,011.00, Patricia Forsythe/VP - Investor Relations

Directors: Anthony E. Woods/Chmn., William F. Bahl/Dir., Craig P.R. Joffe/Non - Dir., General Counsel, Sec., John C. Hassan/Dir., Thomas G. Cody/Dir., John H. Gutfreund/Dir., David W. Whiting/Dir.

Owners: Alan H. Buckey, Thomas G. Cody, William F. Bahl, Insiders/1.40%, The Guardian Life Insurance Company of America/7.50%, Columbia Wanger Asset Management, L.P./8.00%, Tremblant Capital Group/7.80%, HWP Capital PartnersII L.P./6.50%, Barclays Global Investors, NA/10.20%, Ziff Asset Management L.P./6.20%, Anthony E. Woods, John C. Hassan, Lord Abbett& Co., LLC/8.50%, John H. Gutfreund, David W. Whiting

Financial Data: *Fiscal Year End:*12/31 *Latest Annual Data:* 12/31/2006

Year	Sales	Net Income
2006	$238,925,000	$28,370,000
2005	$192,397,000	$31,653,000
2004	$127,122,000	$32,029,000

Curr. Assets:	$134,981,000	**Curr. Liab.:**	$39,969,000	**P/E Ratio:**	32.44
Plant, Equip.:	$30,924,000	**Total Liab.:**	$80,307,000	**Indic. Yr. Divd.:**	$0.720
Total Assets:	$189,470,000	**Net Worth:**	$109,116,000	**Debt/ Equity:**	0.0164

LCC International Inc

7900 W Pk. Dr., Ste. A-315, McLean, VA, 22102; *PH:* 1-703-873-2000; *Fax:* 1-703-873-2100; *http://* www.lcc.com

General - Incorporation	DE	**Stock**- Price on:12/24/2007	$4.37
Employees	977	Stock Exchange	NDQ
Auditor	KPMG LLP	Ticker Symbol	LCCI
Stk Agt	American Stock Transfer & Trust Co.	Outstanding Shares	25,640,000
Counsel	Hogan & Hartson LLP	E.P.S.	-$0.32
DUNS No.	93-991-4909	Shareholders	NA

Business: The group's principal activities are to provide wireless network and infrastructure services. The services include planning, design and deployment of the networks and their ongoing operations and maintenance. The group provides integrated end-to-end solutions for wireless voice and data communications networks with offerings ranging from high level technical consulting. The products cater to wireless carriers, satellite service providers, telecommunication equipment vendors, tower companies and Internet content providers. The major customers include at&t wireless services, ericsson, h3g, nextel, o2, sprint, t-mobile and U.S. Cellular. The group has operations in the United States, the United Kingdom, the Netherlands, Italy, algeria and Asia-Pacific.

Primary SIC and add'l.: 7371 4812 8711 3669

CIK No: 0001016229

Subsidiaries: Beijing LCC Bright Oceans Communication Consultants Co., Ltd., Detron LCC Network Services, B.V., Koll Telecommunications Services, LLC, LCC Algeria LLP, LCC Asia Pacific LTD PTE, LCC China Services, LLC, LCC Deployment Services UK, Limited, LCC Design and Deployment Services. Ltd., LCC Design Services, LLC, LCC do Brazil Ltda., LCC Egypt, LCC Espana, LCC Europe AS, LCC India, Private Limited, LCC International Consulting (Shanghai) Ltd. 26 Subsidiaries included in the Index

Officers: Carlo Baravalle/Exec. VP - Europe, Middle East, Africa, Central, South Americas, Asia Pacific, Peter Deliso/Sr. VP - Corporate Affairs, General Counsel, Sec., Dean Douglas/Dir., Pres., Chief Excecutive Officer, Louis Salamone/CFO, Exec. VP, Kenneth Young/Sr. VP, Chief Marketing Officer, Pres. - Americas, John Buckholz/VP - Information Technology, Ananth Velupillai/Sr. VP - Operations, Americas, Fabio D'Emilio/Sr. VP - Middle East, Africa, Nancy O. Feeney/Dir. - Marketing Communications, External Relations

Directors: Julie A. Dobson/Chmn., Neera Singh/Co - Founder, Dir., Susan Ness/Dir., Mark D. Ein/Dir., Dean Douglas/Dir., Pres., Chief Excecutive Officer, Rajendra Singh/Co - Founder, Richard J. Lombardi/Dir.

Owners: Neera Singh/14.53%, Richard J. Lombardi, Julie A. Dobson, Peter A. Deliso, Riley Investment Partners Master Fund, L.P/12.96%, Louis Salamone, Susan Ness, Carlo Baravalle/1.25%, Dimensional FundAdvisors, Inc./5.58%, Rajendra Singh/14.53%, SACC Partners/8.27%, Kenneth M. Young, Dean J. Douglas/2.26%, Insiders/19.39%

Financial Data: *Fiscal Year End:*12/31 *Latest Annual Data:* 12/31/2005

Year	Sales	Net Income
2005	$193,973,000	-$12,527,000
2004	$193,158,000	-$6,311,000
2003	$108,439,000	-$6,523,000

Curr. Assets:	$101,784,000	**Curr. Liab.:**	$64,014,000		
Plant, Equip.:	$3,642,000	**Total Liab.:**	$65,202,000	**Indic. Yr. Divd.:**	NA
Total Assets:	$118,953,000	**Net Worth:**	$53,751,000	**Debt/ Equity:**	NA

LCNB Corp

2 N Broadway, Lebanon, OH, 45036; *PH:* 1-513-932-1414; *Fax:* 1-513-933-5262; *http://* www.lcnb.com

General - Incorporation	OH	**Stock**- Price on:12/24/2007	$14
Employees	226	Stock Exchange	OTC
Auditor	J. D. Cloud & Co. LLP	Ticker Symbol	LCNB
Stk Agt	Registrar & Transfer Co	Outstanding Shares	6,370,000
Counsel	NA	E.P.S.	$0.98
DUNS No.	NA	Shareholders	NA

Business: The group's principal activities are to provide full banking services, including trust services to customers. The group operates through 17 branch offices located in warren, butler, clinton, clermont, and hamilton counties, Ohio. The group offers a wide range of commercial and personal services, which includes commercial loans, consumer loans, credit cards and commercial leases. The group's other services include safe deposit boxes, night depositories, U.S. Savings bonds, travelers' checks and money orders. The group operates 29 automated teller machines in its market area.

Primary SIC and add'l.: 6712 6021

CIK No: 0001074902

Subsidiaries: Dakin Insurance Agency, Inc., Lebanon Citizens National Bank

Officers: Stephen P. Wilson/Chmn., Pres., CEO/$360,260.00, Kathleen Porter Stolle/Dir., Sec., Eric J. Meilstrup/Exec. VP - Cashier, Bernard H. Wright/Exec. VP, Trust Officer/$171,595.00, Benjamin D.J. Jackson/Sr. Lending Officer, Exec. VP/$194,118.00, Patti Partch/Assist. Cashier, Fairfield, Kim Johnson/Assist. VP - Goshen, Mike Lavatori/Investment Rep - Goshen, Lebanon Main Office, Dave Theiss/Assist. VP - Hamilton, Mary Jane Mayer/Assist. Cashier, Hamilton, Tammy Murray/Assist. Cashier, Joyce Search/Investment Rep, Harry Campbell/Assist. VP - Loveland, Karen Cramer/Assist. VP - Maineville, Kimberli Layer/Assist. VP - Mason *(35 Officers included in Index)*

Directors: Stephen P. Wilson/Chmn., Pres., CEO, George L. Leasure/Dir., Rick L. Blossom/Dir., Kathleen Porter Stolle/Dir., Sec., Spencer S. Cropper/Dir., William H. Kaufman/Dir., David S. Beckett/Dir., Joseph W. Schwarz/Dir., Steve P. Foster/Dir., Exec. VP, CFO

Owners: James A. Markley/1.64%, Robin Maas/7.60%, John S. Calhoun/8.20%, William A. Huddleson/7.93%, Insiders/26.21%, Russell D. Korman/2.84%, William F. Meyers/5.22%, William F. Stautberg/1.84%, John A. Rost/1.24%, Don Ottke/2.54%, Robert J. Stautberg/6.02%

Financial Data: *Fiscal Year End:*12/31 *Latest Annual Data:* 12/31/2006

Year	Sales	Net Income
2006	$38,905,000	$6,514,000
2005	$35,535,000	$6,705,000
2004	$33,307,000	$6,596,000

Curr. Assets:	$15,505,000	**Curr. Liab.:**	$497,216,000	**P/E Ratio:**	14.29
Plant, Equip.:	$12,090,000	**Total Liab.:**	$497,216,000	**Indic. Yr. Divd.:**	$0.620
Total Assets:	$548,215,000	**Net Worth:**	$50,999,000	**Debt/ Equity:**	0.0973

Leading Brands Inc

1500 W Georgia St., Ste. 1800, Vancouver, BC, V6G 2Z6; *PH:* 1-604-685-5200; *Fax:* 1-604-685-5249; *http://* www.lbix.com; *Email:* info@lbix.com

General - Incorporation	BC	**Stock**- Price on:12/24/2007	$4.46
Employees	179	Stock Exchange	NDQ
Auditor	BDO Dunwoody LLP	Ticker Symbol	LBIX
Stk Agt	Pacific Corporate Trust Co	Outstanding Shares	16,420,000
Counsel	NA	E.P.S.	-$0.23
DUNS No.	24-897-7100	Shareholders	NA

Business: The group's principal activities are to package, distribute, sell, merchandise juices, water, soft drinks, new age beverages, snack food and confectionery items across Canada. The group is also into brand management. Some of the beverage brands include caesar's bloody caesar, caesar's caesar cocktail, coocanadian, premium spring water, country harvest, natural juices and johnny's roadside, lemonade and iced teas, fiji natural artesian water, hansen's, signature sodas and functional beverages and stewart's fountain classics. The group provides private label juices and snacks for every major grocery chains in western Canada.

Primary SIC and add'l.: 2064 5149 2086

CIK No: 0000884247

Subsidiaries: Brio Snack Distributors Inc., Kert Technologies, Inc., LBI Brands, Inc., Leading Brands of America, Inc, Leading Brands of Canada, Inc., Leading Brands USA, Inc, Quick, Inc.

Officers: Ralph D. McRae/Chmn., CEO, Pres., Bill Franklin/Sr. VP, Donna Higgins/CFO, Jody Christopherson/VP - Sales, Western Canada, Sinan Alzubaidi/VP - Bottling Operations, Patrick Wilson/Sr. VP - Sales, Pres. - Leading Brands USA, Inc, Robert Mockford/VP - Operations, Dave Read/Pres., Johanna Duprey/VP - Marketing, Michel Houle/VP - Sales, Quebec, Cindy Krenn/VP - Sales, Western Canada, Donna Louis/Corporate Treasurer, Craig Thibodeau/VP - Sales, Grocery, Brenda Williams/VP - Brand Development

Directors: Ralph D. McRae/Chmn., CEO, Pres., Douglas Carlson/Dir., Peter Buckley/Dir., Thomas R. Gaglardi/Dir., Jonathan D. Merriman/Dir., David Bowra/Dir., Iain J. Harris/Dir.

Owners: Fort Mason Partners, LP/0.40%, Freestone Capital Partners LP/0.80%, Freestone Capital Qualified Partners/1.20%, Investcorp Interlachen Multi-Strategy/5.00%, Vision Opportunity Master Fund, Ltd./2.80%, Fort Mason Master, LP/6.30%

Financial Data: *Fiscal Year End:*02/28 *Latest Annual Data:* 2/28/2007

Year	Sales	Net Income
2007	$45,758,000	-$3,489,000
2006	$36,759,000	-$1,230,000
2005	$33,566,000	$783,000

Curr. Assets:	$9,939,000	Curr. Liab.:	$10,536,000		
Plant, Equip.:	$7,175,000	Total Liab.:	$14,436,000	Indic. Yr. Divd.:	NA
Total Assets:	$23,874,000	Net Worth:	$9,438,000	Debt/ Equity:	0.4561

Leadis Technology Inc

800 W California Ave., Ste. 200, Sunnyvale, CA, 94086; *PH:* 1-408-331-8600;
Fax: 1-408-331-8601; *http://* www.leadis.com

General - Incorporation	DE	Stock- Price on:12/24/2007	$3.51
Employees	141	Stock Exchange	NDQ
Auditor	PricewaterhouseCoopers LLP	Ticker Symbol	LDIS
Stk Agt	Mellon Investor Services LLC	Outstanding Shares	29,720,000
Counsel	NA	E.P.S.	-$0.79
DUNS No.	NA	Shareholders	NA

Business: The group's principal activity is to design, develop and market mixed-signal semiconductors that enable and enhance the features and capabilities of small panel displays.

Primary SIC and add'l.: 3674

CIK No: 0001130626

Subsidiaries: Leadis International Limited, Leadis Technology Korea, Inc, Leadis Technology, Ltd.

Officers: Antonio Alvarez/51/Dir., CEO, Pres./$350,552.00, John Allen/CFO, Corp. Sec., Ken Lee/Dir., Exec. VP, COO/$349,265.00, Jose Arreola/Exec. VP - Engineering/$479,497.00, Paul Novell/VP - Sales, Marketing

Directors: Antonio Alvarez/51/Dir., CEO, Pres., Ken Lee/Dir., Exec. VP, COO, Byron Bynum/Dir., Alden Chauvin/Dir., James Plummer/Dir., Kenneth Goldman/Dir., Doug McBurnie/Dir., Jack Saltich/Dir.

Owners: Jose Arreola, James Plummer, Sung Tae/8.20%, George S. Sarlo/5.00%, Byron Bynum, Jack Saltich, Insiders/8.80%, Alden Chauvin, Ken Lee/4.90%, Antonio Alvarez/1.31%, Kenneth Goldman, Victor Lee/1.50%, Douglas McBurnie

Financial Data: *Fiscal Year End:*12/31 *Latest Annual Data:* 12/31/2006

Year	Sales	Net Income
2006	$101,208,000	-$11,911,000
2005	$64,182,000	-$11,350,000
2004	$150,250,000	$17,593,000

Curr. Assets:	$135,463,000	Curr. Liab.:	$26,153,000		
Plant, Equip.:	$4,160,000	Total Liab.:	$26,692,000	Indic. Yr. Divd.:	NA
Total Assets:	$140,729,000	Net Worth:	$114,037,000	Debt/ Equity:	NA

Leap Technology Inc

5601 N Dixie Hwy, Ste 411, Fort Lauderdale, FL, 33334; *PH:* 1-919-929-8814;
http:// www.leap-tech.com; *Email:* info@leaptech.com

General - Incorporation	DE	Stock- Price on:12/24/2007	$0.8
Employees	2	Stock Exchange	OTC
Auditor	Berkowitz Dick Pollack & Brant LLP	Ticker Symbol	LPTC
Stk Agt	Registrar & Transfer Co	Outstanding Shares	65,220,000
Counsel	Proskauer Rose Goetz & Mendelsohn	E.P.S.	-$0.02
DUNS No.	07-220-7376	Shareholders	NA

Business: The group's principal activities are to acquire and invest in companies providing services in healthcare and life sciences. The group seeks to expand its participation in Internet, business-to-business and e-commerce. The group intends to utilize the healthcare skills, experience and industry contacts of its management and board of directors in the development of a network of investment and partner companies. The group will also make other acquisitions or investments outside of its normal business plan.

Primary SIC and add'l.: 6712 6324

CIK No: 0000110027

Subsidiaries: Caribe Company, Corpus Company, First Seal, Inc., Parkson Property LLC, Primary Care Medical Centers of America, Inc., Seal (GP), Inc., Seal Offshore, Inc., Seal Properties, Inc., Sealcraft Operators, Inc., South Corporation

Officers: Donald J. Ciappenelli/Chmn., CEO, Pres., Mary E. Thomas/Dir., Acting Principal Financial Officer, Lenny Kubiak/Dir. - Sales, Local Sales Representative, Michael Sabatino/District Sales Mgr., John Celani/Local Sales Representative, Glen Cook/Local Sales Represanative, Ian Hilton/Local Sales Representative, Carlos Perez/Local Sales Representative, Scott Donenfeld/Local Sales Representative, Wes Moyers/District Sales Mgr. - West Coast, Ed Dietz/Local Sales Representative, Joe Wiegel/Local Sales Representative, Tony D'Antico/Local Sales Representative, Bob Nesman/Local Sales Representative, Carl Chatfield/Local Sales Representative *(17 Officers included in Index)*

Directors: Donald J. Ciappenelli/Chmn., CEO, Pres., Mayra V. Diaz/Dir., Mary E. Thomas/Dir., Acting Principal Financial Officer, Timothy C. Lincoln/Dir., Jerome Fields/Dir.

Owners: Lee M. Pearce, Jerome Fields, Donald J. Ciappenelli, Insiders, Howard Benjamin, Timothy C. Lincoln, Lee M. Pearce, Mary E. Thomas, Lee M. Pearce

Financial Data: *Fiscal Year End:*12/31 *Latest Annual Data:* 12/31/2006

Year	Sales	Net Income
2006	NA	-$532,000
2005	NA	$2,986,000
2004	NA	-$471,000

Curr. Assets:	$3,010,000	Curr. Liab.:	$190,000		
Plant, Equip.:	$513,000	Total Liab.:	$784,000	Indic. Yr. Divd.:	NA
Total Assets:	$3,524,000	Net Worth:	$2,740,000	Debt/ Equity:	NA

Leap Wireless International Inc

10307 Pacific Ctr. Ct., San Diego, CA, 92121; *PH:* 1-858-882-6000; *Fax:* 1-858-882-6010;
http:// www.leapwireless.com

General - Incorporation	DE	Stock- Price on:12/24/2007	$84.39
Employees	2,034	Stock Exchange	NDQ
Auditor	PricewaterhouseCoopers LLP	Ticker Symbol	LEAP
Stk Agt	Mellon Investor Services LLC	Outstanding Shares	68,090,000
Counsel	Latham & Watkins	E.P.S.	-$0.53
DUNS No.	NA	Shareholders	NA

Business: The group's principal activity is to provide digital wireless services. It offers wireless services under the brand name cricket. Cricket is a simple and affordable wireless solution alternative to traditional landline service offering unlimited anytime minutes within a cricket calling area over a high-quality and all-digital cdma network. As of 30-Jun-2004, the group had approximately 1,547,000 customers located in 39 markets throughout the United States. On 13-Apr-2003, the group filed a voluntary petition for relief under chapter 11 of the United States bankruptcy code. On 17-Aug-2004, the group emerged from chapter 11 proceedings.

Primary SIC and add'l.: 4812 7372

CIK No: 0001065049

Subsidiaries: Backwire.com, Inc., Chasetel Licensee Corp., Chasetel Real Estate Holding Company, Inc., Cricket Alabama Property Company, Cricket Arizona Property Company, Cricket Arkansas Property Company, Cricket California Property Company, Cricket Communications, Inc., Cricket Holdings Dayton, Inc., Cricket Licensee (Albany), Inc., Cricket Licensee (Columbus), Inc., Cricket Licensee (Denver) Inc., Cricket Licensee (Lakeland) Inc., Cricket Licensee (Macon), Inc., Cricket Licensee (North Carolina) Inc. 38 Subsidiaries included in the Index

Officers: Douglas S. Hutcheson/Dir., CEO, Pres./$3,232,021.00, Robert Irving/Sr. VP, General Counsel, David Davis/Sr. VP - Operations, Launch, Glenn Umetsu/CTO, Exec. VP/$2,059,516.00, Linda K. Wokoun/Sr. VP - Marketing, Customer Care, Albin Moschner/Exec. VP, Chief Marketing Officer/$2,029,730.00, Leonard Stephens/Sr. VP - Human Resources/$1,187,092.00, Grant A. Burton/VP, Chief Accounting Officer, Controller, Scott T. Edwards/Sr. VP - Marketing, John Sedej/Sr. VP - Procurement

Directors: Douglas S. Hutcheson/Dir., CEO, Pres., Mark H. Rachesky/Chmn., Michael B. Targoff/Dir., John D. Harkey/Dir., Robert V. Lapenta/Dir.

Owners: Michael B. Targoff, Douglas S. Hutcheson, MHR Institutional PartnersII LP/4.90%, Insiders/25.10%, Robert V. LaPenta, Amin I. Khalifa, MHR Institutional PartnersIIA LP/12.40%, John D. Harkey, Albin F. Moschner, Glenn T. Umetsu, Entities affiliated with Highland Capital Management, L.P./6.90%, T. Rowe Price Associates, Inc./5.50%, James D. Dondero/6.90%, Mark H. Rachesky/17.30%, Leonard C. Stephens

Financial Data: *Fiscal Year End:*12/31 *Latest Annual Data:* 12/31/2006

Year	Sales	Net Income
2006	$1,136,700,000	-$4,139,000
2005	$914,663,000	$29,966,000
2004	$344,360,000	-$8,629,000

Curr. Assets:	$595,959,000	Curr. Liab.:	$410,768,000		
Plant, Equip.:	$1,086,591,000	Total Liab.:	$2,283,211,000	Indic. Yr. Divd.:	NA
Total Assets:	$4,084,947,000	Net Worth:	$1,771,793,000	Debt/ Equity:	0.9338

LeapFrog Enterprises Inc

6401 Hollis St., Emeryville, CA, 94608; *PH:* 1-510-420-5000; *Fax:* 1-510-420-5001;
http:// www.leapfrog.com

General - Incorporation	DE	Stock- Price on:12/24/2007	$10.27
Employees	916	Stock Exchange	NYSE
Auditor	Ernst & Young LLP	Ticker Symbol	LF
Stk Agt	Continental Stock Transfer & Trust Co	Outstanding Shares	90,910,000
Counsel	Cooley Godward LLP	E.P.S.	-$1.81
DUNS No.	NA	Shareholders	NA

Business: The group's principle activities are to design, develop and market innovative, technology based educational products and related proprietary content. These products are used by eighth grade school children. The products are used in different subject matters like phonics, reading, mathematics, spelling, science, geography, history and music. The group operates in three segment based on the customers they cater: the us consumer segment markets and sells products directly to national and regional mass-Market; the education and training segment targets the school market in the United States, including sales directly to educational institutions, teachers and educators. The international segment sells products outside the United States directly to overseas retailers. The group has international operations in the United Kingdom, Hong Kong, Canada and France. The group's quarterly revenue for September 2007 was 144.04 millions of USD.

Primary SIC and add'l.: 3944

CIK No: 0001138951

Subsidiaries: Leap Frog Toys (UK) Limited, Leapfrog (H.K.) Limited, LeapFrog Canada, Inc., LeapFrog International Research Company, LeapFrog Mexico S.A. de C.V., LF France, SAS, LF Macao Commercial Offshore Limited

Officers: Jeffrey G. Katz/Dir., CEO, Pres./$1,932,841.00, Michael J. Dodd/Sr. VP - Supply Chain, Operations/$558,636.00, Peter M.O. Wong/General Counsel, Corp. Sec., Nancy C. MacIntyre/Exec. VP - Product, Innovation, Marketing, Martin A. Pidel/Exec. VP - International, Michael J. Lorion/Pres. - Leapfrog Schoolhouse, William K. Campbell/Sr. VP - US Consumer Sales, Hilda S. West/Sr. VP - Human Resources, Robert L. Moon/CIO, Sr. VP, William B. Chiasson/CFO, Principal Financial Officer, Principal Accounting Officer/$761,877.00

Directors: Jeffrey G. Katz/Dir., CEO, Pres., Steven B. Fink/Chmn., Thomas J. Kalinske/Vice Chmn., Stanley E. Maron/Dir., Stanton E. Mckee/Dir., David C. Nagel/Dir., Ralph R. Smith/Dir., Caden Wang/Dir.

Owners: Insiders/3.70%, Michael J. Dodd, Jerome Perez, Vardon Capital Management/7.20%, Michael R. Milken/4.50%, Lowell J. Milken, Lowell J. Milken/1.30%, Steven B. Fink, Michael R. Milken, Timothy M. Bender, Insiders, Lawrence J. Ellison, Stanley E. Maron, Thomas J. Kalinske/2.00%, Franklin Resources, Inc./9.90% *(26 Owners included in Index)*

Financial Data: *Fiscal Year End:*12/31 *Latest Annual Data:* 06/30/2007

Year	Sales	Net Income
2007	NA	NA
2006	$502,255,000	-$145,092,000
2005	$649,757,000	$17,500,000

Curr. Assets:	$387,429,000	Curr. Liab.:	$97,445,000		
Plant, Equip.:	$27,794,000	Total Liab.:	$116,479,000	Indic. Yr. Divd.:	NA
Total Assets:	$450,441,000	Net Worth:	$333,962,000	Debt/ Equity:	NA

Lear Corp

21557 Telegraph Rd., Southfield, MI, 48034; *PH:* 1-248-447-1500; *Fax:* 1-248-447-1772;
http:// www.lear.com

General - Incorporation .... DE
Employees 104,276
Auditor .... Ernst & Young LLP
Stk Agt .... Bank of New York
Counsel .... NA
DUNS No. 96-055-8948

Stock- Price on:12/24/2007 .... $36.5
Stock Exchange .... NYSE
Ticker Symbol .... LEA
Outstanding Shares 76,670,000
E.P.S .... -$7.45
Shareholders .... NA

Business: The group's principle activity is to provide automotive products. The groups products include instrument panels and cockpit systems, headliners and overhead systems, door panels and flooring, and acoustic systems. The group operates from United States.

Primary SIC and add'l.: 3714

CIK No: 0000842162

Subsidiaries: Alfombras San Luis S.A., Amtex, Inc., Asia Pacific Components Co., Ltd., Automotivos Ltda., Beijing Lear Dymos Automotive Seating and Interior Co., Ltd., Chongqing Lear Chang'an Automotive Interior Trim Co., Ltd., CL Automotive, LLC, Consorcio Industrial Mexicanos de Autopartes, S.A. de C.V., Dong Kwang Lear Yuhan Hoesa, General Seating of America, Inc., General Seating of Canada, Ltd., General Seating of Thailand Corp. Ltd., GHW Engineering GmbH, Grote & Hartmann Automotive de Mexico S.A. de C.V., Grote & Hartmann de Mexico S.A. de C.V. 148 Subsidiaries included in the Index

Officers: Robert E. Rossiter/Chmn., CEO, Pres., Douglas G. Delgrosso/46/COO, Pres., Andrea Puchalsky/Dir. - Corporate Communications, Matthew J. Simoncini/CFO, Sr. VP, Shari L. Burgess/49/VP, Treasurer, Roger A. Jackson/61/Sr. VP - Human Resources, James L. Murawski/56/VP, Corporate Controller, Daniel A. Ninivaggi/43/Exec. VP, Sec., General Counsel, Raymond E. Scott/42/Sr. VP, Pres. - North American Seating Systems Group, James M. Brackenbury/49/Sr. VP, Pres. - European Operations

Directors: Robert E. Rossiter/Chmn., CEO, Pres., James H. Vandenberghe/Vice Chmn., James A. Stern/Dir., David E. Fry/Dir., Roy E. Parrott/Dir., Henry D.G. Wallace/Dir., Larry W. McCurdy/Dir., David P. Spalding/Dir., Conrad L. Mallett/Dir., Richard F. Wallman/Dir., Vincent J. Intrieri/Dir.

Owners: Raymond E. Scott, David E. Fry, Conrad L. Mallett, Daniel A. Ninivaggi, David C. Wajsgras, James A. Stern, Pzena Investment Management, LLC/8.84%, Richard F. Wallman, Merrill Lynch& Co., Inc./8.39%, Roy E. Parrott, James H. Vandenberghe, Carl C. Icahn and affiliated companies/15.64%, Henry D.G. Wallace, Vanguard Windsor Funds/8.05%, David P. Spalding *(19 Owners included in Index)*

Financial Data: *Fiscal Year End:*12/31 *Latest Annual Data:* 12/31/2006

Year	Sales	Net Income
2006	$17,838,900,000	-$707,500,000
2005	$17,089,200,000	-$1,381,500,000
2004	$16,960,000,000	$422,200,000

Curr. Assets:	$3,890,300,000	**Curr. Liab.:**	$3,887,300,000		
Plant, Equip.:	$1,471,700,000	**Total Liab.:**	$7,248,500,000	**Indic. Yr. Divd.:**	NA
Total Assets:	$7,850,500,000	**Net Worth:**	$602,000,000	**Debt/ Equity:**	3.5116

Learning Care Group Inc

21333 Haggerty Rd., Ste. 300, Novi, MI, 48375; ***PH:*** 1-248-697-9000;
http:// www.learningcaregroup.com

General - Incorporation .... MI
Employees .... NA
Auditor .... Deloitte & Touche LLP
Stk Agt..... Computershare Investor Services LLC
Counsel .... NA
DUNS No. .... NA

Stock- Price on:12/24/2007 .... NA
Stock Exchange .... NA
Ticker Symbol .... NA
Outstanding Shares .... NA
E.P.S .... NA
Shareholders .... NA

Business: The group's principle activity is to provide childcare and preschool educational services. The group provides childcare and preschool education, five days a week throughout the year to children between the ages of six weeks and twelve years. The classrooms are organized in seven levels following the sequential process of growth and impart the creative curriculum(R) for early childhood, a nationally recognized educational curriculum. The group operates in three segments: childtime, tutor time and franchise opers. Under the childtime and tutor time segments, the group operates child care centers and under the franchise opers segment it licenses and provides developmental and administrative support to franchises operating under the tutor time brand.

Primary SIC and add'l.: 8351 7299

CIK No: 0001003648

Subsidiaries: Childtime Childcare, Inc., Tutor Time Franchise, LLC, Tutor Time Learning Centers International, Inc., Tutor Time Learning Centers, LLC

Officers: William D. Davis/CEO, Pres., Kathryn Winkelhaus/COO, Ira Young/General Counsel, Corp. Sec., Frank M. Jerneycic/CFO, Scott W. Smith/Chief Human Resources Officer, Joann Johnson/VP - Corporate Operations

Learning Quest Technologies Inc

875 E 400 S, Springville, UT, 84663; ***PH:*** 1-800-358-8591; ***http://*** www.learning-quest.com;
Email: info@learning-quest.com

General - Incorporation .... NV
Employees .... NA
Auditor .... HJ & Assoc. LLC
Stk Agt .... NA
Counsel .... NA
DUNS No. .... NA

Stock- Price on:12/24/2007 .... NA
Stock Exchange .... NA
Ticker Symbol .... NA
Outstanding Shares .... NA
E.P.S .... NA
Shareholders .... NA

Business: The group's activity is to or develop, license and market elearning educational products and services. The services provided by the group include educational tools and solutions for creating, authoring, publishing, presenting and selling training materials and content via the Internet, online professional development planning services and videoconference professional development sessions.

Primary SIC and add'l.: 6770

CIK No: 0001311369

Officers: Fred Hall/41/Dir., CEO, CFO, Pres.

Directors: Fred Hall/41/Dir., CEO, CFO, Pres.

Owners: Fred Hall/86.00%

Learning Tree International Inc

1805 Library St., Reston, VA, 20190; ***PH:*** 1-703-709-9119; ***Fax:*** 1-703-709-6405;
http:// www.learningtree.com; ***Email:*** uscourses@learningtree.com

General - Incorporation .... DE
Employees 481
Auditor .... BDO Seidman, LLP
Stk Agt .... Computershare Trust Co
Counsel .... Guth Christopher
DUNS No. 09-946-4729

Stock- Price on:12/24/2007 .... $13.41
Stock Exchange .... NDQ
Ticker Symbol .... LTRE
Outstanding Shares 16,500,000
E.P.S .... -$0.19
Shareholders .... NA

Business: The group's principal activity is to develop, market and deliver advanced technology training courses to meet the needs of professionals in business and government organizations. The group's course materials cover topics on information technology such as client/server systems, intranet/Internet technologies, computer networks, operating systems, programming languages, databases, object-oriented technology, it management and related topics. On Sept 2003, the group was offering a library of four- and five-day instructor-led courses, comprising 152 different course titles representing over 3,800 hours of training. The classroom courses are delivered through the group's learning tree education centers located in the United States, the United Kingdom, France, Canada, Sweden and Japan. The courses are also conducted in hotel and conference facilities and at customers' sites throughout the world.

Primary SIC and add'l.: 8748 8299

CIK No: 0001002037

Subsidiaries: Advanced Technology Marketing, Inc., Learning Tree International AB, Learning Tree International Inc., Learning Tree International Ltd., Learning Tree International S.A., Learning Tree International USA, Inc., Learning Tree International, K.K., Learning Tree Limited, Learning Tree Publishing AB, System for Business and Industry, Inc., Technology For Business & Industry, Inc.

Officers: Nicholas R. Schacht/Dir., CEO, Pres., Howard A. Bain/Dir. - Consultant, Mary C. Adams/51/Chief Administrative Officer, Sec., Lemoyne T. Zacherl/54/Chief Accounting Officer, Magnus Nylund/CIO, Charles R. Waldron/CFO, George T. Robson/Dir., Consultant, Stefan C. Riesenfeld/Dir., Consultant

Directors: Nicholas R. Schacht/Dir., CEO, Pres., David C. Collins/Vice Chmn., Eric R. Garen/Chmn., Mathew W. Juechter/Dir., Howard A. Bain/Dir. - Consultant, Curtis A. Hessler/Dir., George T. Robson/Dir., Consultant

Owners: Mary C. Adams/25.60%, Howard A. Bain, Insiders/47.50%, Eric R. Garen/20.50%, Epoch Investment Partners, Inc./5.70%, Nicholas R. Schacht, LeMoyne T. Zacherl, Curtis A. Hessler, Hawkshaw Capital Management LLC/5.30%, Mathew W. Juechter, David C. Collins/25.60%, Magnus Nylund, Theodore E. Guth/7.00%

Financial Data: *Fiscal Year End:*09/30 *Latest Annual Data:* 9/29/2006

Year	Sales	Net Income
2006	$154,049,000	-$3,122,000
2005	$151,558,000	-$708,000
2004	$152,058,000	$569,000

Curr. Assets:	$98,937,000	**Curr. Liab.:**	$64,020,000		
Plant, Equip.:	$21,683,000	**Total Liab.:**	$70,969,000	**Indic. Yr. Divd.:**	NA
Total Assets:	$131,978,000	**Net Worth:**	$61,009,000	**Debt/ Equity:**	NA

Lecg Corp

2000 Powell St., Ste. 600, Emeryville, CA, 94608; ***PH:*** 1-510-985-6700; ***Fax:*** 1-510-653-9898;
http:// www.lecg.com

General - Incorporation .... DE
Employees 1,196
Auditor .... Deloitte & Touche LLP
Stk Agt .... LaSalle Bank N.A
Counsel .... NA
DUNS No. 55-747-3295

Stock- Price on:12/24/2007 .... $15.02
Stock Exchange .... NDQ
Ticker Symbol .... XPRT
Outstanding Shares 25,250,000
E.P.S $0.76
Shareholders .... NA

Business: The group's principal activity is to provide expert services to public and private enterprises. The group conducts economic and financial analysis and provides independent expert testimony, litigation support and strategic management consulting. The services also include data collection, factual and statistical analyses and report preparation. The group experts consist of academics, former senior government officials, experienced industry leaders and seasoned consultants. The group's customers are fortune global 500 corporations, major law firms and local, state and federal governments and agencies in the United States and certain other countries. The international offices are located in Argentina, Australia, Canada, New Zealand, South Korea and the United Kingdom. In mar 2004 the group acquired economic analysis llc and low rosen taylor soriano and in aug 2004 the group acquired silicon valley expert witness group inc.

Primary SIC and add'l.: 7389 8742

CIK No: 0001192305

Subsidiaries: LECG Canada Holding, Inc., LECG Canada Ltd, LECG Consulting Belgium, NC, LECG Consulting France, SAS, LECG Consulting Italy, SrL, LECG Consulting Spain, SL, LECG Holding Company (UK) Ltd, LECG Limited New Zealand, LECG Limited UK, LECG, LLC, Silicon Valley Expert Witness Group, Inc.

Officers: David J. Teece/Vice Chmn. - Emeryville, David Evans/Vice Chmn. - Lecg Europe, Cambridge, London, Guy F. Erb/Dir. - New York, Cherie Fieri/Principal, Nashville, William Fitzsimmons/MD - Emeryville, Jonathan Flaum/Dir. - Chicago Office, Michael Flynn/Principal, Emeryville, Bruce Fortenbaugh/Principal, San Francisco, Paula Frederick/Principal, Toronto, Ken Froese/Dir. - Toronto, Robert Frosch/Dir. - Washington DC, Daniel Garcia-Swartz/Sr. Managing Economist, Chicago, A. J. Gravel/Dir. - Washington DC, Kevin Green/Dir. - Los Angeles, Quintin Gregor/Principal, Atlanta Office *(294 Officers included in Index)*

Directors: Garrett F. Bouton/Dir., William W. Liebeck/Dir., Walter H. Vandaele/63/Dir., Michael J. Jeffery/Dir., COO, Ruth M. Richardson/Dir., William J. Spencer/Dir.

Owners: Insiders/9.70%, John C. Burke, Michael R. Gaulke, David J.Teece/7.00%, T. Rowe Price Associates, Inc./7.50%, Royce & Associates/10.10%, Ruth M. Richardson, Walter H.A. Vandaele/1.60%, Marvin A. Tenenbaum, Gary S. Yellin, Mellon Financial Corporation/5.10%, Franklin Resources, Inc./6.40%, Endowment Capital, L.P./5.40%

Financial Data: *Fiscal Year End:*12/31 *Latest Annual Data:* 12/31/2006

Year	Sales	Net Income
2006	$353,850,000	$21,467,000
2005	$286,656,000	$22,376,000
2004	$216,555,000	$17,104,000

Curr. Assets:	$160,563,000	**Curr. Liab.:**	$72,722,000	**P/E Ratio:**	19.76
Plant, Equip.:	$13,701,000	**Total Liab.:**	$96,039,000	**Indic. Yr. Divd.:**	NA
Total Assets:	$327,153,000	**Net Worth:**	$231,114,000	**Debt/ Equity:**	NA

Lecroy Corp

700 Chestnut Ridge Rd., Chestnut Ridge, NY, 10977; ***PH:*** 1-845-425-2000; ***Fax:*** 1-845-425-8967;
http:// www.lecroy.com; ***Email:*** contact.corp@lecroy.com

General - Incorporation	DE	**Stock**- Price on:12/24/2007	$9.26
Employees	458	Stock Exchange	NDQ
Auditor	KPMG LLP	Ticker Symbol	LCRY
Stk Agt	The First National Bank	Outstanding Shares	12,250,000
Counsel	NA	E.P.S	-$1.14
DUNS No.	00-163-6950	Shareholders	NA

Business: The group's principal activity is to develop, manufacture, sell and license signal acquisition and analysis products.the principal product line consists of a family of high-performance digital oscilloscopes. It is used primarily by electrical design engineers in various markets, including computer and semiconductor, data storage, communications and power measurement. The products include the wavemaster, wavepro and waverunner families of digital oscilloscopes. The group's products also include modular digitizers, probing and accessory products, and other electronic components. In addition, the group offers a full range of aftermarket service and support for all of its products. The products are marketed in the United States, Europe, Japan, China, South Korea and Singapore.

Primary SIC and add'l.: 3826 8742 3825

CIK No: 0000943580

Subsidiaries: Computer Access Technology Corporation., LeCroy AB, LeCroy Japan Corporation., LeCroy Korea, Ltd., LeCroy Lightspeed Corporation., LeCroy, GmbH, LeCroy, Hong Kong, Ltd. ., LeCroy, Ltd., LeCroy, Pte. Ltd. ., LeCroy, S.A., LeCroy, S.A.R.L., LeCroy, S.R.L.

Officers: Thomas H. Reslewic/Dir., CEO, Pres., Sean B. O'Connor/CFO, VP - Finance, Sec., Treasurer, Roberto Petrillo/VP - Sales Americas, Europe, Middle East, Africa, Corey Hirsch/CIO, Conrad Fernandes/VP, GM - Oscilloscope Division, Carmine J. Napolitano/VP, GM - Protocol Solutions Group, David C. Graef/CTO, VP

Directors: Thomas H. Reslewic/Dir., CEO, Pres., Charles A. Dickinson/Chmn., Walter O. Lecroy/Founder, Robert E. Anderson/Dir., William G. Scheerer/Dir., Allyn C. Woodward/Dir., Norman R. Robertson/Dir.

Owners: Dimensional Fund Advisors LP/8.40%, Millennium Management L.L.C./8.70%, Royce & Associates, LLC/7.20%, Norman R. Robertson, Barclays Global Investors, N.A. and certain affiliates/5.70%, Allyn C. Woodward, State of Wisconsin Investment Board/10.00%, Bank of America Corporation/5.90%, Walter O. LeCroy/2.20%, The TCW Group, Inc. and its direct and indirect subsidiaries/7.10%, Carmine J. Napolitano/1.50%, Conrad J. Fernandes, Kennedy Capital Management, Inc./6.30%, Charles A. Dickinson, David C. Graef/1.00% *(19 Owners included in Index)*

Financial Data: *Fiscal Year End:*06/30 *Latest Annual Data:* 6/30/2006

Year			Sales		Net Income
2006			$160,536,000		$6,573,000
2005			$164,978,000		$2,143,000
2004			$124,940,000		$8,044,000
Curr. Assets:	$93,117,000	**Curr. Liab.:**	$46,120,000		
Plant, Equip.:	$20,359,000	**Total Liab.:**	$72,271,000	**Indic. Yr. Divd.:**	NA
Total Assets:	$201,974,000	**Net Worth:**	$129,703,000	**Debt/ Equity:**	NA

Lectec Corp

5610 Lincoln Dr., Edina, MN, 55346; *PH:* 1-952-933-2291; *Fax:* 1-952-942-5369; *http://* www.lectec.com

General - Incorporation	MN	**Stock**- Price on:12/24/2007	$3.25
Employees	1	Stock Exchange	OTC
Auditor	Lurie Besikof Lapidus & Co. LLP	Ticker Symbol	LECT
Stk Agt	Wells Fargo Shareowner Services	Outstanding Shares	4,150,000
Counsel	Dorsey & Whitney LLP	E.P.S	-$0.1
DUNS No.	08-611-3925	Shareholders	NA

Business: The group's principal activities are to develop, design, manufacture and market skin care ingredients and therapeutic consumer products. The analgesic and anti-itch products are marketed under the brand name therapatch(r). The acne treatment patches of the group are marketed by johnson & johnson consumer products under the brand names neutrogena(R), on-the-spot(R) acne patch and clean & clear(R) brand names. Novartis and johnson & johnson are the major customers of the group. The products of the group are sold in Europe, Middle East, Latin America, Canada, Asia and other countries.

Primary SIC and add'l.: 3842 3845 2834

CIK No: 0000805928

Officers: Judd M. Berlin/Chmn., CEO, CFO, Bill Johnson/Controller

Directors: Judd M. Berlin/Chmn., CEO, CFO, Andrew C. Rollwagen/Dir., Daniel C. Sigg/Dir.

Owners: Insiders/3.30%, Lee M. Berlin/9.88%, Alan C. Hymes/9.73%, Judd A. Berlin/3.29%

Financial Data: *Fiscal Year End:*12/31 *Latest Annual Data:* 12/31/2006

Year			Sales		Net Income
2006			$127,000		-$367,000
2005			$443,000		-$531,000
2004			$1,065,000		$2,297,000
Curr. Assets:	$1,348,000	**Curr. Liab.:**	$218,000		
Plant, Equip.:	NA	**Total Liab.:**	$218,000	**Indic. Yr. Divd.:**	NA
Total Assets:	$1,515,000	**Net Worth:**	$1,297,000	**Debt/ Equity:**	NA

Lee Enterprises Inc

201 N Harrison St., Ste. 600, Davenport, IA, 52801; *PH:* 1-563-383-2100; *Fax:* 1-563-323-9609; *http://* www.lee.net; *Email:* information@lee.net

General - Incorporation	DE	**Stock**- Price on:12/24/2007	$21.47
Employees	9,400	Stock Exchange	NYSE
Auditor	Deloitte & Touche LLP	Ticker Symbol	LEE
Stk Agt	Wells Fargo Bank Minnesota N.A	Outstanding Shares	46,050,000
Counsel	Lane & Waterman	E.P.S	$1.77
DUNS No.	00-526-4064	Shareholders	NA

Business: The group's principal activity is to publish daily newspapers. The group publishes 44 daily newspapers in 18 states and 200 other weekly. Publication include classified and specialty publications. Others services provided by the group include associated online services. The group provides retail, national and classified advertising services. Online activities of the group comprise of maintaining websites that support each of its daily newspapers and other publications.

Primary SIC and add'l.: 7319 2711 2759

CIK No: 0000058361

Subsidiaries: Accudata, Inc., Fairgrove LLC, Flagstaff Publishing Co., Hanford Sentinel, Inc., Homechoice, LLC, HSTAR LLC, INN Partners, L.C. d/b/a TownNews.com, Journal-Star Printing Co., K. Falls Basin Publishing, Inc., Kauai Publishing Co., Lee Charitable Foundation, Lee Consolidated Holdings Co., Lee Enterprises, Incorporated, Lee Procurement Solutions Co., Lee Publications, Inc. 41 Subsidiaries included in the Index

Officers: Mary E. Junck/Chmn., CEO, Pres., Carl G. Schmidt/CFO, VP, Treasurer, Michael R. Gulledge/VP - Publishing, Brian E. Kardell/VP - Production, CIO, Joyce Dehli/VP - News, Karen J. Guest/VP, Chief Legal Officer, C. D. Waterman/Sec., Paul M. Farrell/VP - Sales, Marketing, Gregory P. Schermer/Dir., VP - Interactive Media, Corporate Counsel, Linda R. Lindus/VP - Publishing, Daniel K. Hayes/VP - Corporate Communications, Kevin D. Mowbray/VP, Nancy L. Green/VP - Circulation, Greg R. Veon/VP - Publishing, Vytenis P. Kuraitis/VP - Human Resources *(16 Officers included in Index)*

Directors: Mary E. Junck/Chmn., CEO, Pres., Andrew E. Newman/Dir., Gordon D. Prichett/Dir., Mark Vittert/Dir., Nancy S. Donovan/Dir., Herbert W. Moloney/Dir., Gregory P. Schermer/Dir., VP - Interactive Media, Corporate Counsel, William E. Mayer/Dir., Richard R. Cole/Dir.

Owners: Lee Endowment Foundation/8.10%, Grant E. Schermer, Betty A. Schermer/6.40%, Lloyd G. Schermer/8.20%, Gregory P. Schermer, Carl G. Schmidt, Insiders/8.40%, Herbert W. Moloney, Nancy S. Donovan, Gregory P. Schermer/8.30%, Gordon D. Prichett, Ariel Capital Management, LLC/20.90%, Richard R. Cole, William E. Mayer, Cedar Rock Capital Limited/9.00% *(27 Owners included in Index)*

Financial Data: *Fiscal Year End:*09/30 *Latest Annual Data:* 9/30/2006

Year			Sales		Net Income
2006			$1,128,648,000		$70,832,000
2005			$860,859,000		$76,878,000
2004			$683,324,000		$86,071,000
Curr. Assets:	$184,412,000	**Curr. Liab.:**	$200,323,000		
Plant, Equip.:	$327,252,000	**Total Liab.:**	$2,332,910,000	**Indic. Yr. Divd.:**	$0.720
Total Assets:	$3,329,809,000	**Net Worth:**	$990,625,000	**Debt/ Equity:**	NA

Leesport Financial Corp

1240 Broadcasting Rd., Wyomissing, PA, 19610; *PH:* 1-610-208-0966; *Fax:* 1-610-926-9824; *http://* www.leesportbank.com

General - Incorporation	PA	**Stock**- Price on:12/24/2007	$21.5
Employees	216	Stock Exchange	NDQ
Auditor	Beard Miller Co. LLP	Ticker Symbol	FLPB
Stk Agt	American Stock Transfer & Trust CO.	Outstanding Shares	5,740,000
Counsel	NA	E.P.S	$1.37
DUNS No.	16-099-3218	Shareholders	NA

Business: The group's principal activity is to provide commercial and consumer banking services. The services include accepting of deposits and originating secured and unsecured commercial and consumer loans. Deposits are mainly time deposits and savings account. Time deposits include certificates of deposit, individual retirement accounts, roth ira accounts and club accounts. The savings accounts include money market accounts, now accounts and traditional savings accounts. The group originates both secured and unsecured commercial and consumer loans and finances commercial transactions. The group also provides equipment lease and accounts receivable financing. The group operates through eleven full service offices in Pennsylvania.

Primary SIC and add'l.: 6712 6021

CIK No: 0000775662

Subsidiaries: Essick & Barr Insurance, LLC, First Leesport Capital Trust I, Leesport Bank, Leesport Capital Trust II, Leesport Mortgage Holdings, LLC, Leesport Realty Solutions, LLC, Madison Financial Advisors, LLC, Madison Statutory Trust I

Officers: Robert D. Davis/60/Dir., CEO, Pres./$440,619.00, Diane L. Herbein/Accounting, Essick, Barr Insurance, Cynthia L. Morgan/Accounting Representative, Essick, Barr Insurance, Carl Raring/Sales Exec. - Essick, Barr Insurance, Lynne K. Titus/Client Administrator - Group, Individual Insurance, Essick, Barr Insurance, David J. Greif/VP - Group, Individual Insurance, Essick, Barr Insurance, Christopher D. Kline/Dept Mgr. - Personal Insurance, Essick, Barr Insurance, Donna J. Meyer/Accounting Representative, Personal Insurance, Essick, Barr Insurance, Edward C. Barrett/CFO, Exec. VP/$241,626.00, Jenette L. Eck/45/Sec., Charles J. Hopkins/Pres. - Essick, Barr Insurance/$434,519.00, James E. Kirkpatrick/46/Exec. VP - Leesport Bank/$163,910.00, Christina S. McDonald/42/Exec. VP - Leesport Bank/$132,894.00, Robert J. Miranda/Registered Investment Advisor, Esther Ganas-Miranda/Client Services Mgr., Registered Assist. *(33 Officers included in Index)*

Directors: Robert D. Davis/60/Dir., CEO, Pres., James H. Burton/51/Dir., Andrew J. Kuzneski/67/Dir., Michael J. O'Donoghue/65/Dir., Patrick J. Callahan/49/Dir., Philip E. Hughes/58/Dir., Domer M. Leibensperger/67/Dir., Frank C. Milewski/57/Dir., Harry J. O'Neill/58/Dir., Karen A. Rightmire/60/Dir., Michael L. Shor/48/Dir., Alfred J. Weber/55/Dir., Vito A. Delisi/59/Dir.

Owners: Edward C. Barrett, Alfred J. Weber, Karen A. Rightmire, Michael J. ODonoghue, Vito A. DeLisi, James H. Burton, Charles J. Hopkins, Andrew J. Kuzneski/2.57%, Frank C. Milewski, Andrew J. Kuzneski, Alfred J. Weber, Karen A. Rightmire, Patrick J. Callahan, Michael L. Shor, Insiders *(39 Owners included in Index)*

Financial Data: *Fiscal Year End:*12/31 *Latest Annual Data:* 12/31/2006

Year			Sales		Net Income
2006			$82,835,000		$9,153,000
2005			$74,518,000		$8,731,000
2004			$51,280,000		$5,416,000
Curr. Assets:	$21,835,000	**Curr. Liab.:**	$875,931,000	**P/E Ratio:**	15.69
Plant, Equip.:	$6,941,000	**Total Liab.:**	$939,502,000	**Indic. Yr. Divd.:**	$0.760
Total Assets:	$1,041,632,000	**Net Worth:**	$102,130,000	**Debt/ Equity:**	0.3664

Left Behind Games

Formerly: Bonanza Gold Inc

PO Box 110, 25060 Hancock Ave., Ste. 103, Murrieta, CA, 92562; *PH:* 1-951-894-6597

General - Incorporation	WA	**Stock**- Price on:12/24/2007	NA
Employees	27	Stock Exchange	NA
Auditor	KMJ Corbin & Co. LLP	Ticker Symbol	NA
Stk Agt	Columbia Stock Transfer Co	Outstanding Shares	NA
Counsel	NA	E.P.S	-$0.311
DUNS No.	NA	Shareholders	NA

Business: The group's principal activity is exploring, acquiring and developing mineral properties with a potential for production. The company had been involved in the acquisition and exploration of various mining properties, located in the states of Alaska, Montana and Idaho. Exploration efforts were unsuccessful and none of these mining properties produced any commercial ore. It intends to acquire or merge with another company.

Primary SIC and add'l.: 1040

CIK No: 0000013055

Subsidiaries: Left Behind Games Inc.

Officers: Troy A. Lyndon/Chmn., CEO, Robilyn J. Lyndon/Co - Founder, Exec. VP, Kevin Hoekman/Sr. Producer, Martin Colby/Advisor, James Alan Cook/Advisor, James B. Frakes/CFO

Directors: Troy A. Lyndon/Chmn., CEO, Jeffrey S. Frichner/50/Dir., Thomas H. Axelson/64/Dir., Robilyn J. Lyndon/Co - Founder, Exec. VP, Paul Danchik/Member - Advisory Board, Helmut Teichert/Member - Advisory Board, Ray Dixon/55/Dir.

Owners: Jeffrey S. Frichner/8.50%, Troy A. Lyndon/7.90%, Southpointe Financial/3.00%, James B. Frakes, Thomas H. Axelson/2.20%, Insiders/22.00%

Financial Data: Fiscal Year End:03/31 Latest Annual Data: 3/31/2006

Year	Sales	Net Income
2006	NA	-$8,609,000
2005	NA	-$21,000

Curr. Assets:	$4,163,000	Curr. Liab.:	$1,143,000		
Plant, Equip.:	$42,000	Total Liab.:	$1,143,000	Indic. Yr. Divd.:	$0.870
Total Assets:	$4,245,000	Net Worth:	$3,102,000	Debt/ Equity:	NA

Left Behind Games Inc

25060 Hancock Ave., Murrieta, CA, 92562; **PH:** 1-951-894-6597; *http://* www.leftbehindgames.com

General - Incorporation	WA	**Stock**- Price on:12/24/2007	$0.29
Employees	27	Stock Exchange	OTC
Auditor	Corbin & CO., LLP	Ticker Symbol	LFBG
Stk Agt	Colonial Stock Transfer Co Inc	Outstanding Shares	25,620,000
Counsel	NA	E.P.S.	-$0.311
DUNS No.	NA	Shareholders	NA

Business: The groups principal activities include developing and publishing video game products based on Left Behind series of novels. The group merged with Bonanza Gold, Inc. in January 2006, and acquired Left Behind Games Inc. in February 2006. The group operates from the United States.

Primary SIC and add'l.: 5092

CIK No: 0000013055

Officers: Troy A. Lyndon/Co - Founder, Chmn., CEO, James B. Frakes/CFO, Robilyn J. Lyndon/Co - Founder, Exec. VP, Kevin Hoekman/Sr. Producer, Jerome Mikulich/Executive Dir. - Outreach, Sales

Directors: Troy A. Lyndon/Co - Founder, Chmn., CEO, Jeffrey S. Frichner/50/Dir., Robilyn J. Lyndon/Co - Founder, Exec. VP, Martin Colby/Member - Advisory Board, James Alan Cook/Member - Advisory Board, Paul Danchik/Member - Advisory Board, Helmut Teichert/Member - Advisory Board, Thomas H. Axelson/64/Dir., Ray Dixon/55/Dir.

Owners: Thomas H. Axelson/2.20%, Troy A. Lyndon/7.90%, Insiders/22.00%, James B. Frakes, Southpointe Financial/3.00%, Jeffrey S. Frichner/8.50%

Financial Data: Fiscal Year End:03/31 Latest Annual Data: 03/31/2007

Year	Sales	Net Income
2007	$768,000	-$26,084,000
2006	NA	-$8,609,000
2005	NA	-$21,000

Curr. Assets:	$4,163,000	Curr. Liab.:	$1,143,000		
Plant, Equip.:	$42,000	Total Liab.:	$1,143,000	Indic. Yr. Divd.:	NA
Total Assets:	$4,245,000	Net Worth:	$3,102,000	Debt/ Equity:	NA

Left Right Marketing Technology Inc

2580 Anthem Village Dr., Henderson, NV, 89052; **PH:** 1-702-563-1600

General - Incorporation	DE	**Stock**- Price on:12/24/2007	$3.15
Employees	NA	Stock Exchange	NA
Auditor	Beadle, McBride, Evans & Reeves LLP	Ticker Symbol	NA
Stk Agt	NA	Outstanding Shares	8,850,000
Counsel	NA	E.P.S.	-$0.38
DUNS No.	07-399-4931	Shareholders	NA

Business: The group's principal activity was to market electronic gaming devices and coinless games of chance. With the acquisition of lrmt on 29-Sep-2003, the group intends to own and operate the Website www.crazygrazer.com, an online shopping mall. On 29-Sep-2003, the group acquired left right marketing & technology inc which was accounted as a reverse acquisition. On 26-Apr-2004, the group acquired crazy grazer which was accounted as a reverse merger.

Primary SIC and add'l.: 5092

CIK No: 0000278165

Subsidiaries: CrazyGrazer.com, SGI, Ultimate Poker League, Inc.

Owners: Matthew S. Schultz/36.80%, Jason F. Griffith/9.00%, Insiders/75.10%, Lawrence S. Schroeder/29.30%

Financial Data: Fiscal Year End:12/31 Latest Annual Data: 12/31/2006

Year	Sales	Net Income
2006	NA	-$298,000
2005	NA	-$136,000
2004	NA	-$2,744,000

Curr. Assets:	$25,000	Curr. Liab.:	$862,000		
Plant, Equip.:	NA	Total Liab.:	$862,000	Indic. Yr. Divd.:	NA
Total Assets:	$37,000	Net Worth:	-$825,000	Debt/ Equity:	NA

Legacy Bancorp Inc

99 N St., Pittsfield, MA, 01202; **PH:** 1-413-443-4421; **Fax:** 1-413-442-8155; *http://* www.legacy-banks.com

General - Incorporation	DE	**Stock**- Price on:12/24/2007	$15
Employees	160	Stock Exchange	NDQ
Auditor	Wolf & Company, P.C.	Ticker Symbol	LEGC
Stk Agt	American Stock Transfer & Trust Co.	Outstanding Shares	10,240,000
Counsel	NA	E.P.S.	$0.21
DUNS No.	NA	Shareholders	NA

Business: The groups principal activity is to provide financial products and services. The groups service is online banking. The products of the group include mortgage, residential, commercial and consumer loans, and debit and credit card. The group operates from the United States. The assets of the group for the year 2006 were $150,008.

Primary SIC and add'l.: 6036 6712

CIK No: 0001332199

Subsidiaries: CSB Service Corporation, LB Funding Corporation, Legacy Banks, Legacy Insurance Service of the Berkshires, Legacy Securities Corporation

Officers: Williar J. Dunlaevy/Chmn., CEO/$626,447.00, Michael A. Christopher/COO, Pres./$404,690.00, Lori Gazzillo/Mgr. - Advertising, Public Relations, Paul Bruce/Sr. VP, Investor Relations Officer, Richard M. Sullivan/Sr. VP/$258,770.00, Steven F. Pierce/56/Exec. VP/$251,035.00, Stephen M. Conley/59/CFO, Sr. VP, Treasurer/$223,514.00, Kimberly A. Mathews/Corp. Sec.

Directors: Williar J. Dunlaevy/Chmn., CEO, Eugene A. Dellea/Dir., Gary A. Lopenzina/Dir., Robert B. Trask/Dir., David L. Klausmeyer/Dir., Anne W. Pasko/Dir., Dorothy B. Winsor/Dir.

Owners: Eugene A. Dellea, First Bankers Trust Services, Inc./8.00%, Michael A. Christopher, Richard M. Sullivan, David L. Klausmeyer, Williar J. Dunlaevy/1.34%, Stephen M. Conley, Robert B. Trask, Wellington Management Company, LLP/5.37%, Gary A. Lopenzina, Steven F. Pierce, The Legacy Banks Foundation/7.40%, Insiders/5.33%, Anne W. Pasko, Dorothy Winsor

Financial Data: Fiscal Year End:12/31 Latest Annual Data: 12/31/2006

Year	Sales	Net Income
2006	$49,103,000	$2,806,000
2005	$42,955,000	-$2,235,000

Curr. Assets:	$25,196,000	Curr. Liab.:	$657,377,000	P/E Ratio:	71.43
Plant, Equip.:	$15,416,000	Total Liab.:	$658,321,000	Indic. Yr. Divd.:	$0.160
Total Assets:	$808,318,000	Net Worth:	$149,997,000	Debt/ Equity:	0.0079

Legacy Bank NA CA

125 E Campbell Ave., Campbell, CA, 95008; **PH:** 1-408-341-1000; *http://* www.legacybankna.com; **Email:** legacybankna@legacybankna.com

General - Incorporation		**Stock**- Price on:12/24/2007	NA
Employees	NA	Stock Exchange	NA
Auditor	NA	Ticker Symbol	NA
Stk Agt	NA	Outstanding Shares	NA
Counsel	NA	E.P.S.	NA
DUNS No.	NA	Shareholders	NA

Business: The groups principal activity is to provide commercial banking services. The services of the group include consumer and business banking, insurance, investment, originating loans, deposit and lending services. The group operates from the United States.

Primary SIC and add'l.: 6029

CIK No:

Officers: Thomas E. Ray/Chmn., CEO, Kevin Gilday/Dir. - Management Consultant, Rene A. Kakebeen/Exec. VP, Chief Banking Officer, Michael T. Namba/Exec. VP, CFO, Investor Relations Officer, Lane S. Lawson/Exec. VP, Commercial Lending Mgr., David Clower/Sr. VP, Real Estate Division Mgr., Brad Lebsack/Sr. VP, Mgr. - SBA Lending Division, Larry Buyers/VP - SBA Lending Division

Directors: Thomas E. Ray/Chmn., CEO, Martha Sanford/Dir., Gerald McIntyre/Dir., Joseph Petkewich/Dir., Kevin Gilday/Dir. - Management Consultant, Donald Gootee/Dir., Jerry Greer/Dir., Gary L. Hong/Dir., Oneal Sutton/Dir., Les Workman/Dir., Samson Zarnegar/Dir.

Legacy Communications Corp

4955 Peoria St., Ste. A, Denver, Colorado, 80239; **PH:** 1-303-799-3933; **Fax:** 1-303-799-9612; *http://* www.legacycomm.com

General - Incorporation	NV	**Stock**- Price on:12/24/2007	$0.34
Employees	3	Stock Exchange	OTC
Auditor	HJ & Associates, LLC	Ticker Symbol	LGCC
Stk Agt	Pacific Stock Transfer Company	Outstanding Shares	17,340,000
Counsel	NA	E.P.S.	$0.01
DUNS No.	NA	Shareholders	NA

Business: The groups principle activities include purchasing, developing and reselling AM and FM radiobroadcast facilities. The group operates from the United States.

Primary SIC and add'l.: 4832

CIK No: 0001124127

Subsidiaries: AM Radio 1370, Inc, AM Radio 1440, Inc, AM Radio 1470, Inc, AM Radio 1490, Inc, AM Radio 790, Inc, Americast Media Corporation, Diamond Broadcasting Corporation, Diamond Media, LLC, Sunset Communications Corporation, Tri-State Media Corporation

Officers: Morgan E. Skinner/67/Dir., CEO, Pres., Lavon Randall/65/Dir., Sec., Michael R. Bull/59/Principal Accounting Officer

Directors: Morgan E. Skinner/67/Dir., CEO, Pres., Lavon Randall/65/Dir., Sec., Jeffrey B. Bate/44/Dir.

Owners: Insiders/77.31%, Michael R. Bull/4.54%, Lavon Randall/33.53%, Morgan E. Skinner/37.22%, Jeffrey B. Bate/2.02%

Financial Data: Fiscal Year End:12/31 Latest Annual Data: 12/31/2006

Year	Sales	Net Income
2006	$889,000	$197,000

Curr. Assets:	$263,000	Curr. Liab.:	$6,212,000		
Plant, Equip.:	$1,347,000	Total Liab.:	$6,222,000	Indic. Yr. Divd.:	NA
Total Assets:	$2,950,000	Net Worth:	-$3,273,000	Debt/ Equity:	NA

Legacy Vulcan Corp

Formerly: Vulcan Materials Co
1200 Urban Ctr. Dr., Birmingham, AL, 35242; *PH:* 1-205-298-3000; *Fax:* 1-205-298-2960;
http:// www.vulcanmaterials.com; *Email:* media@vmcmail.com

General - Incorporation	NJ	Stock - Price on:12/24/2007	$118.3
Employees	7,983	Stock Exchange	NYSE
Auditor	Deloitte & Touche LLP	Ticker Symbol	VMC
Stk Agt	Bank of New York	Outstanding Shares	95,290,000
Counsel	Bradley, Arant, Rose & White	E.P.S.	$4.89
DUNS No.	00-339-6025	Shareholders	NA

Business: The groups principle activity is to produce construction aggregates including primarily crushed stone, sand and gravel. In November 2007, Vulcan acquired Florida Rock Industries, Inc., a producer of construction aggregates, cement, concrete and concrete products. The group operates from United States.

Primary SIC and add'l.: 1442 2812 1422 1429

CIK No: 0000103973

Subsidiaries: Atlantic Granite Company, Azusa Rock, Inc., BHJ Chemical Company, LLC, Calizas Industriales del Carmen, S.A. de C.V., CalMat Co., CalMat Leasing Co., MedTex Lands, Inc., Nolichuckey Sand Co., Inc., Palomar Transit Mix Co., Rancho Piedra Caliza, S.A. de C.V., Rapica Servicios Tecnicos Y Administrativos, S.A. de C.V., RECO Transportation, LLC, Servicios Integrales, Gestoria Y Administracion, S.A. de C.V., Soportes Tecnicos Y Administrativos, S.A. de C.V., Southwest Gulf Railroad Company 28 Subsidiaries included in the Index

Officers: Donald M. James/57/Chmn., CEO/$16,022,490.00, Wayne J. Houston/Sr. VP - Human Resources, James W. O'Brien/VP - Tax, Assist. Treasurer, Bradley C. Rosenwald/VP - Safety, Health and Environment, Ejaz A. Khan/VP, Controller, CIO, Philip J. Alford/Treasurer, Daniel F. Sansone/CFO, Sr. VP/$2,097,695.00, Robert A. Wason/Sr. VP - Corporate Development, Danny R. Shepherd/Sr. VP - Construction Materials, East, Guy M. Badgett/Sr. VP - Construction Materials Group/$2,334,936.00, Ronald G. McAbee/Sr. VP - Construction Materials, West, Jerry F. Perkins/Sec., Mark Warren/Investor Relations Officer, Norman Jetmundsen/Assist. General Counsel, Assist. Sec., Harri Haikala/Assist. General Counsel, Assist. Sec. (16 Officers included in Index)

Directors: Donald M. James/57/Chmn., CEO, Phillip W. Farmer/67/Dir., Vincent J. Trosino/65/Dir., Allen H. Franklin/61/Dir., James V. Napier/69/Dir., Donald B. Rice/66/Dir., Orin R. Smith/70/Dir., Ann McLaughlin Korologos/66/Dir., Douglas J. McGregor/65/Dir., Philip J. Carroll/68/Dir.

Owners: James W. Smack, Insiders/3.50%, Ronald G. McAbee, Donald M. James/1.70%, Davis Selected Advisors, L.P./8.72%, Guy M. Badgett, James V. Napier, Daniel F. Sansone, Vincent J. Trosino, Allen H. Franklin, State Farm Mutual Automobile Insurance/11.72%, Orin R. Smith, Douglas J. McGregor, Regions Financial Corporation/6.11%, Phillip W. Farmer (18 Owners included in Index)

Financial Data: Fiscal Year End:12/31 Latest Annual Data: 12/31/2006

Year	Sales	Net Income
2006	$3,342,475,000	$467,534,000
2005	$2,895,327,000	$388,757,000
2004	$2,454,335,000	$287,385,000

Curr. Assets:	$731,379,000	Curr. Liab.:	$493,687,000	P/E Ratio: 24.19
Plant, Equip.:	$1,869,114,000	Total Liab.:	$1,423,114,000	Indic. Yr. Divd.: $1.840
Total Assets:	$3,424,225,000	Net Worth:	$2,001,111,000	Debt/ Equity: 0.1534

Legal Access Technologies Inc

3275 E Warm Springs Rd. , Las Vegas, NV, 89120; *PH:* 1-702-949-6115;
http:// www.legalaccesstech.com

General - Incorporation	NV	Stock - Price on:12/24/2007	$0.035
Employees	1	Stock Exchange	OTC
Auditor	Piercy, Bowler, Taylor & Kern	Ticker Symbol	LGAL
Stk Agt	National Stock Transfer, Inc.	Outstanding Shares	NA
Counsel	NA	E.P.S.	NA
DUNS No.	NA	Shareholders	NA

Business: The group's principal activity is to provide phone and Web based technical services to legal service organizations such as legal aids, state and local bar associations, federal, state and local courts, and government agencies. In the process, the group enters into strategic partnerships with these organizations for the creation of statewide consumer hubs and a virtual law office environment for attorneys. The services offered by the group include legal services network, serving legal aid organizations, virtual law office, serving bar associations and their member attorneys, court services network, serving the courts and administrative agencies and Internet law center, serving consumers.

Primary SIC and add'l.: 8111

CIK No: 0000878146

Subsidiaries: Las Vegas, Tele-Lawyer, Inc, WEC Acquisition Sub, Inc

Financial Data: Fiscal Year End:04/30 Latest Annual Data: 4/30/2005

Year	Sales	Net Income
2005	NA	-$469,000
2004	$154,000	-$891,000
2003	$583,000	-$2,238,000

Curr. Assets:	$0	Curr. Liab.:	$381,000	
Plant, Equip.:	NA	Total Liab.:	$381,000	Indic. Yr. Divd.: NA
Total Assets:	$0	Net Worth:	-$381,000	Debt/ Equity: NA

Legend International Holdings Inc

Level 8, 580 St Kilda Rd., Melbourne, Victoria, 3004; *PH:* 61-385322866; *Fax:* 61-385322805;
http:// www.lgdi.net; *Email:* lgdi@axisc.com.au

General - Incorporation	DE	Stock - Price on:12/24/2007	$0.11
Employees	NA	Stock Exchange	OTC
Auditor	PKF Witt Mares, PLC	Ticker Symbol	NA
Stk Agt	Holladay Stock Transfer, Inc.	Outstanding Shares	NA
Counsel	NA	E.P.S.	NA
DUNS No.	NA	Shareholders	NA

Business: The groups principle activity is to explore phosphate, diamond and base metals. The group operates from United States.

Primary SIC and add'l.: 1040

CIK No: 0001132143

Subsidiaries: Legend Consolidated Group, Inc.

Officers: Joseph I. Gutnick/Chmn., CEO, Pres., Peter J. Lee/CFO, Sec., James Wright/Sr. Exploration Geologist, Craig Michael/Chief Project Mgr.

Directors: Joseph I. Gutnick/Chmn., CEO, Pres., David S. Tyrwhitt/Non Exec., Dir.

Owners: Insiders/53.57%, Joseph Stera Gutnick/53.42%, Peter Lee

Financial Data: Fiscal Year End:12/31 Latest Annual Data: 12/31/2006

Year	Sales	Net Income
2006	NA	-$414,000
2005	NA	-$1,295,000
2004	NA	-$1,691,000

Curr. Assets:	$27,000	Curr. Liab.:	$157,000	
Plant, Equip.:	$4,000	Total Liab.:	$157,000	Indic. Yr. Divd.: NA
Total Assets:	$31,000	Net Worth:	-$126,000	Debt/ Equity: NA

Legend Mobile Inc

244 Fifth Ave., Ste. P203, New York, NY, 10001; *PH:* 1-212-252-2459; *http://* www.legendm.com;
Email: investors@legendm.com

General - Incorporation	DE	Stock - Price on:12/24/2007	$0.018
Employees		Stock Exchange	OTC
Auditor	Gruber & Co., LLC	Ticker Symbol	LGMB
Stk Agt	Corporate Stock Transfer, Inc.	Outstanding Shares	25,300,000
Counsel	NA	E.P.S.	-$0.025
DUNS No.	NA	Shareholders	NA

Business: The group's principal activities are to develop and market mobile accessories such as faceplates for cellular phones, mobile data services and mobile applications. The group has licensing agreements with nelly, christina aguilera, playboy enterprises, rusty wallace and the arena football league. The group sells java based application for mobile phones called 'christina everywhere'. The group has supply and distribution agreement with motorola inc to supply mobile accessories and mobile applications using our rights to christina aguilera. The products of the group include mobile covers, mobile games like 'rapstar featuring nelly' and 'on tour with christina aguilera' and java based applications for mobile phones called 'christina everywhere'. The group operates only in the domestic market.

Primary SIC and add'l.: 3669 3679

CIK No: 0001061169

Subsidiaries: Legend Credit, Inc.

Officers: Peter Klamka/39/Chmn., CEO, Pres., Treasurer, Sec.

Directors: Peter Klamka/39/Chmn., CEO, Pres., Treasurer, Sec.

Owners: Peter Klamka/100.00%, Peter Klamka/100.00%, Peter Klamka/1.90%, Peter Klamka/100.00%, Barton PK, LLC/6.20%

Financial Data: Fiscal Year End:12/31 Latest Annual Data: 12/31/2006

Year	Sales	Net Income
2006	$0	-$633,000
2005	$2,000	-$742,000
2004	$18,000	-$1,416,000

Curr. Assets:	$20,000	Curr. Liab.:	$3,746,000	
Plant, Equip.:	$1,000	Total Liab.:	$3,746,000	Indic. Yr. Divd.: NA
Total Assets:	$22,000	Net Worth:	-$3,725,000	Debt/ Equity: NA

Legg Mason Inc

100 Light St., Baltimore, MD, 21202; *PH:* 1-410-539-0000; *Fax:* 1-410-454-4923;
http:// www.leggmason.com; *Email:* webinquiries@leggmason.com

General - Incorporation	MD	Stock - Price on:12/24/2007	$100.75
Employees	3,820	Stock Exchange	NYSE
Auditor	PricewaterhouseCoopers LLP	Ticker Symbol	LM
Stk Agt	Wachovia Bank	Outstanding Shares	133,850,000
Counsel	NA	E.P.S.	NA
DUNS No.	00-695-0141	Shareholders	NA

Business: The groups principle activity is to provide investment management and related services to institutional and individual clients. The group operates through three business segments namely managed investments, institutional and wealth management. The group operates from United States.

Primary SIC and add'l.: 6211 6282 6531

CIK No: 0000704051

Subsidiaries: 3040692 Nova Scotia Company, Barrett Associates, Inc., Bartlett & Co., Bartlett Real Estate, Inc., Batterymarch Financial Management, Inc., Berkshire Asset Management, Inc., Brandywine Global Investment Management, LLC, CAM North America, LLC, Carnes Capital Corporation, Citicorp Investment Management (Luxembourg) S.A, Citicorp Investment Management Luxembourg S.A., CitiMoney S.A., Legg Mason & Co., LLC, Legg Mason Asset Management Asia Pte Ltd, Legg Mason Canada Holdings Ltd. 50 Subsidiaries included in the Index

Officers: Raymond A. Mason/Chmn., CEO, Peter L. Bain/Sr. Exec. VP/$4,124,068.00, James W. Hirschmann/47/COO, Pres., Robert F. Price/Sec., Barry F. Bilson/Sr. VP, Charles J. Daley/CFO, Sr. VP, Treasurer/$2,210,098.00, Mark R. Fetting/Sr. Exec. VP/$5,121,402.00, Elisabeth N. Spector/60/Sr. VP, Mary Athridge/Contact - Corporate Communications, Maria Rosati/Contact - Corporate Communications, Deepak Chowdhury/49/Sr. VP

Directors: Raymond A. Mason/Chmn., CEO, James E. Ukrop/Dir., John E. Koerner/Dir., Cheryl Gordon Krongard/Dir., Harold L. Adams/Dir., Carl Bildt/Dir., Margaret Milner Richardson/Dir., Roger W. Schipke/Dir., Dennis R. Beresford/Dir., Kurt L. Schmoke/Dir., Nicholas J. St George/Dir., Allen W. Reed/Dir., Edward I. O'Brien/Dir., Robert Angelica/Dir.

Owners: Mark R. Fetting, Peter L. Bain, Nicholas J. George, Allen W. Reed, Kurt L. Schmoke, Timothy C. Scheve, Cheryl Gordon Krongard, Charles J. Daley, Raymond A. Mason/2.17%, John E. Koerner, Insiders/3.65%, Dennis R. Beresford, Edward I. OBrien, AXA Financial, Inc./14.00%, T. Rowe Price Associates, Inc./6.66% (20 Owners included in Index)

Financial Data: Fiscal Year End:03/31 Latest Annual Data: 3/31/2007

Year	Sales	Net Income
2007	$4,343,675,000	$646,818,000
2006	$2,645,212,000	$1,144,168,000
2005	$2,489,552,000	$408,431,000

Curr. Assets:	$2,391,507,000	Curr. Liab.:	$1,312,061,000	P/E Ratio: 21.35
Plant, Equip.:	$219,437,000	Total Liab.:	$3,062,998,000	Indic. Yr. Divd.: $0.960
Total Assets:	$9,604,488,000	Net Worth:	$6,541,490,000	Debt/ Equity: NA

Leggett & Platt Inc

No. 1 Leggett Rd., Carthage, MO, 64836; ***PH:*** 1-417-358-8131; ***Fax:*** 1-417-358-5840; ***http://*** www.leggett.com; ***Email:*** invest@leggett.com

General - Incorporation	MO	**Stock**- Price on:12/24/2007	$23.57
Employees	32,828	Stock Exchange	NYSE
Auditor	PricewaterhouseCoopers LLP	Ticker Symbol	LEG
Stk Agt	UMB Bank, N.A.	Outstanding Shares	177,140,000
Counsel	NA	E.P.S	$1.49
DUNS No.	00-714-0064	Shareholders	NA

Business: The group's principle activities include designing and manufacturing engineered components and products. The group operates through five segments include residential furnishings, commercial furnishings, aluminum products, industrial materials and specialized products. The groups products sold under the brand names include Semi-Flex, Lok-Fast, Schukra, Patternlink, and Masterack. The group operates from United States, Canada, Europe and Mexico.

Primary SIC and add'l.: 2542 3363 2514 2515 3714 3315

CIK No: 0000058492

Subsidiaries: Administradora Soal S.A. de C.V., Americas Body Company Holdings, Inc., Americas Body Company, Inc., American Commercial Truck Equipment, Inc., Askona Block LLC, Bentley Sales Unlimited, LLC, Bergen Cable Technology, LLC, Block Russian Holdings, Inc., Buffalo Batt& Felt, LLC, Cable Bergen de Mexico, S.A. de C.V., Changsha Pangeo Cable Industries, Ltd., Collier-Keyworth, LLC, Consorcio Industrial Serrano, S.A. de C.V., Craftmatic/Contour Organization, Inc., Crest-Foam Corp. 196 Subsidiaries included in the Index

Officers: David S. Haffner/Dir., CEO, Pres./$2,233,607.00, Paul R. Hauser/56/Sr. VP, Pres. - Residential Furnishings/$612,074.00, Karl G. Glassman/Dir., COO, Exec. VP/$1,464,547.00, Ernest C. Jett/Sr. VP, General Counsel, Sec., William S. Weil/VP, Corporate Controller, Robert G. Griffin/55/Sr. VP, Pres. - Fixture, Display Group, Jack D. Crusa/Sr. VP, Pres. - Specialized Products Segment, Matthew C. Flanigan/CFO, Sr. VP/$679,488.00, Dennis S. Park/Sr. VP, Pres. - Commercial Fixturing, Components, Michael W. Blinzler/Information Technology, Raymond J. Cavanaugh/Internal Audit, Peter W. Connelly/Corporate Procurement, John M. Desonier/Strategy, Investor Relations, John A. Hale/Human Resources, James L. Hess/Operations Services *(51 Officers included in Index)*

Directors: David S. Haffner/Dir., CEO, Pres., Felix E. Wright/Chmn., Raymond F. Bentele/71/Dir., Joseph W. McClanathan/Dir., Maurice E. Purnell/Dir., Richard T. Fisher/Dir., Harry M. Cornell/Dir., Karl G. Glassman/Dir., COO, Exec. VP, Ralph W. Clark/Dir., Phoebe A. Wood/Dir., Ted R. Enloe/Dir., Judy C. Odom/Dir., Robert Ted Enloe/69/Dir.

Owners: Capital Group International, Inc./5.90%, Joseph W. McClanathan, Harry M. Cornell, Insiders, Richard T. Fisher, Robert Ted Enloe, Ralph W. Clark, Raymond F. Bentele, Matthew C. Flanigan, Felix E. Wright, David S. Haffner, Phoebe A. Wood, Paul R. Hauser, Judy C. Odom, Maurice E. Purnell *(17 Owners included in Index)*

Financial Data: ***Fiscal Year End:***12/31 ***Latest Annual Data:*** 12/31/2006

Year		*Sales*		*Net Income*	
2006		$5,505,400,000		$300,300,000	
2005		$5,299,300,000		$251,300,000	
2004		$5,085,500,000		$285,400,000	
Curr. Assets:	$1,894,100,000	***Curr. Liab.:***	$691,200,000	***P/E Ratio:***	15.01
Plant, Equip.:	$962,800,000	***Total Liab.:***	$1,914,200,000	***Indic. Yr. Divd.:***	$1.000
Total Assets:	$4,265,300,000	***Net Worth:***	$2,351,100,000	***Debt/ Equity:***	NA

Legrand

128, Ave. Mar Chal Du Lattre Tassigny, 8700 Limoges, Limoges, 8700; ***PH:*** 33-555068787; ***http://*** www.legrandelectric.com

General - Incorporation	France	**Stock**- Price on:12/24/2007	NA
Employees	NA	Stock Exchange	NA
Auditor	PricewaterhouseCoopers LLP	Ticker Symbol	NA
Stk Agt	American Registrar & Transfer Co	Outstanding Shares	NA
Counsel	NA	E.P.S	NA
DUNS No.	38-209-2732	Shareholders	NA

Business: The groups principle activity is to provide production of low voltage fittings and accessories. The groups products include circuit breakers, earth leakage protection devices, distribution cabinets and enclosures, patch panels; switching and connection, sockets, switches, dimmers, timers. The group operates from United States.

Primary SIC and add'l.: 3645 3613 3612 3629 3643 3699

CIK No: 0001231859

Subsidiaries: BTicino., Legrand SA, Legrand SAS

Lehman Brothers Holdings Inc

745 Seventh Ave., New York, NY, 10019; ***PH:*** 1-212-526-7000; ***http://*** www.lehman.com

General - Incorporation	DE	**Stock**- Price on:12/24/2007	$81.65
Employees	25,900	Stock Exchange	NYSE
Auditor	Ernst & Young LLP	Ticker Symbol	LEH
Stk Agt	Bank of New York	Outstanding Shares	530,200,000
Counsel	NA	E.P.S	$7.46
DUNS No.	00-891-7783	Shareholders	NA

Business: The group's principle activity is to provide financial services including equity and fixed income sales, trading and research, investment banking services, and investment management and advisory services. The group operates from United States.

Primary SIC and add'l.: 6719 6282 6211

CIK No: 0000806085

Subsidiaries: 314 Commonwealth Ave. Inc., Aurora Loan Services LLC, Banque Lehman Brothers S.A., Blixen U.S.A. Inc., Blue Way Finance Corporation U.A., BNC Mortgage Inc., Brasstown Entrada I SCA, Brasstown LLC, Brasstown Mansfield I SCA, Capital Analytics II, LP, Cohort Investments Limited, e-Valuate, LP, Entrada II Sarl, Executive Monetary Management, Inc., Furno & Del Castano Capital Partners LLP 139 Subsidiaries included in the Index

Officers: Jasjit S. Bhattal/CEO - Lehman Brothers Asia, Pacific, Jeremy M. Isaacs/CEO - Lehman Brothers Europe, Middle East, Asia, Pacific, Thomas Wind/Co - CEO - Lehman Brothers Bank, Richard S. Fuld/Chmn., CEO, Vincent Primiano/Co - CEO - Lehman Brothers Bank, Thomas A. Russo/Vice Chmn., Chief Legal Officer, Christopher M. O'Meara/CFO, Scott J. Freidheim/Co - Chief Administrative Officer, Stephen M. Lessing/Head - Client Relationship Management, Ian T. Lowitt/Co - Chief Administrative Officer, Herbert H. McDade/Global Head - Equities, Theodore P. Janulis/Global Head - Mortgage Capital, Dir. - Lehman Brothers Bank, Lana Franks/Dir. - Lehman Brothers Bank, Paolo Tonucci/Dir. - Lehman Brothers Bank, George H. Walker/Global Head - Investment Management *(20 Officers included in Index)*

Directors: Richard S. Fuld/Chmn., CEO, Marsha Johnson Evans/Dir., Henry Kaufman/Dir., John F. Akers/Dir., Roland A. Hernandez/Dir., John D. MacOmber/Dir., Michael L. Ainslie/Dir., Christopher Gent/Dir., Roger S. Berlind/Dir., Thomas H. Cruikshank/Dir.

Owners: Joseph M. Gregory/1.33%, David Goldfarb, Thomas H. Cruikshank, Insiders/4.48%, Marsico Capital Management, LLC/5.33%, Thomas A. Russo, Marsha Johnson Evans, ClearBridge Advisors, LLC/5.30%, Michael L. Ainslie, Henry Kaufman, Roland A. Hernandez, John D. Macomber, John F. Akers, Christopher M. OMeara, Scott J. Freidheim *(18 Owners included in Index)*

Financial Data: ***Fiscal Year End:***11/30 ***Latest Annual Data:*** 11/30/2006

Year		*Sales*		*Net Income*	
2006		$46,709,000,000		$4,007,000,000	
2005		$32,420,000,000		$3,260,000,000	
2004		$21,250,000,000		$2,369,000,000	
Curr. Assets:	$40,049,000,000	***Curr. Liab.:***	$360,166,000,000	***P/E Ratio:***	10.92
Plant, Equip.:	$3,269,000,000	***Total Liab.:***	$484,354,000,000	***Indic. Yr. Divd.:***	$0.600
Total Assets:	$503,545,000,000	***Net Worth:***	$18,096,000,000	***Debt/ Equity:***	13.8972

Leisure Direct Inc

1070 Commerce Dr., Perrysburg, OH, 43551; ***PH:*** 1-419-873-1111; ***http://*** www.leisuredirectinc.net

General - Incorporation	NV	**Stock**- Price on:12/24/2007	$0.06
Employees	3	Stock Exchange	OTC
Auditor	Rosenberg Rich Baker Berman & Co	Ticker Symbol	LDTI
Stk Agt	Olde Monmouth Stk Trnsfer Co. Inc.	Outstanding Shares	13,190,000
Counsel	NA	E.P.S	-$0.054
DUNS No.	NA	Shareholders	NA

Business: The groups principle activity is to sell wood and steer swimming pools. The group operates from United States.

Primary SIC and add'l.: NA

CIK No: 0001131089

Subsidiaries: Olympic Manufacturing Company, LLC, Uranium Strategies, Inc.

Officers: John R. Ayling/Chmn., CEO, Robert Dapper/Pres., Ernie Stevens/VP - Operations, Paul M. Hoag/51/Pres., David Clark/VP - Business Development

Directors: John R. Ayling/Chmn., CEO

Owners: DABE Inc/9.50%, Olympic Pools, Inc./10.40%, John R. Ayling, John R. Ayling/19.90%, Michael D. Slates/2.90%, Capital First Corporation, LLC, Paul M. Hoag/8.00%, Insiders/20.70%

Financial Data: ***Fiscal Year End:***12/31 ***Latest Annual Data:*** 12/31/2006

Year		*Sales*		*Net Income*	
2006		NA		-$1,063,000	
2005		$93,000		-$3,020,000	
2004		$359,000		-$874,000	
Curr. Assets:	NA	***Curr. Liab.:***	$2,381,000		
Plant, Equip.:	$113,000	***Total Liab.:***	$2,381,000	***Indic. Yr. Divd.:***	NA
Total Assets:	$113,000	***Net Worth:***	-$2,268,000	***Debt/ Equity:***	NA

LeMaitre Vascular Inc

63 2nd Ave., Burlington, MA, 01803; ***PH:*** 1-781-221-2266; ***Fax:*** 1-781-425-5049; ***http://*** www.lemaitre.com

General - Incorporation		**Stock**- Price on:12/24/2007	$6.32
Employees	218	Stock Exchange	NDQ
Auditor	Ernst& Young LLP	Ticker Symbol	LMAT
Stk Agt	Mellon Investor Services LLC	Outstanding Shares	15,360,000
Counsel	NA	E.P.S	-$0.2
DUNS No.	NA	Shareholders	NA

Business: The groups principal activity is to provide medical devices. The products of the group include endovascular and dialysis access, vascular and general surgery. In the year 2005, the group acquired Endomed, Inc. The group operates from the United States, the Europe and Japan. The net sale of the group for the year 2006 was $34,628 (thousands).

Primary SIC and add'l.: 3841

CIK No: 0001158895

Subsidiaries: LeMaitre UK Acquisition LLC, LeMaitre Vascular GmbH, LeMaitre Vascular KK, LeMaitre Vascular LLC, Vascutech Acquisition LLC

Officers: George W. Lemaitre/Chmn., CEO, Pres./$372,789.00, David B. Roberts/Dir., CFO/$382,865.00, Ryan H. Connelly/30/Dir. - Research, Development, Cornelia A. Lemaitre/Dir., VP - Human Resources, Kimberly L. Cieslak/VP - Marketing, Peter R. Gebauer/Pres. - International Operations/$466,175.00, Aaron M. Grossman/VP, General Counsel - Security, Maik D. Helmers/VP - Central Europe, Sales, Trent G. Kamke/Sr. VP - Operations, Kevin D. Kelly/VP - North American Sales/$280,863.00, Jonathan W. Ngau/VP - Information Technology, Joseph P. Pellegrino/CFO/$256,698.00, Nobuhiro Okabe/Country Mgr.

Directors: George W. Lemaitre/Chmn., CEO, Pres., George D. Lemaitre/Dir., Chmn. - Scientific Advisory Board, Lawrence Jasinski/Dir., Cornelia A. Lemaitre/Dir., VP - Human Resources, Duane M. Desisto/Dir., David N. Gill/Dir., Virginia S. Newman/Member - Scientific Advisory Board, Michael C. Jackson/Dir., Guido J. Neels/59/Dir., David B. Roberts/Dir., CFO, Frank J. Criado/Member - Scientific Advisory Board, Alan Dardik/Member - Scientific Advisory Board, Herbert Dardik/Member - Scientific Advisory Board, William D. Jordan/Member - Scientific Advisory Board, Steven Anthony Kagan/Member - Scientific Advisory Board *(16 Directors included in Index)*

Owners: Insiders/50.20%, Michael C. Jackson/9.10%, Duane M. Desisto, Cornelia W. LeMaitre/3.60%, Guido J. Neels, Lawrence J. Jasinski, George W. LeMaitre/29.30%, David N. Gill, Housatonic Partners/9.10%, George D. LeMaitre/4.00%, David B. Roberts/2.50%, Kevin D. Kelly, Peter R. Gebauer/2.50%, The Guardian Life Insurance Company of America/7.60%, Joseph P. Pellegrino

Financial Data: ***Fiscal Year End:***NA ***Latest Annual Data:*** 12/31/2006

Year	*Sales*	*Net Income*
2006	$34,628,000	-$1,172,000
2005	$30,727,000	$55,000
2004	$26,183,000	$927,000

Curr. Assets:	$43,641,000	Curr. Liab.:	$5,378,000		
Plant, Equip.:	$2,389,000	Total Liab.:	$6,264,000	Indic. Yr. Divd.:	NA
Total Assets:	$56,963,000	Net Worth:	$50,699,000	Debt/ Equity:	NA

Lennar Corp

700 NW 107th Ave., Ste. 400, Miami, FL, 33172; PH: 1-305-559-4000; Fax: 1-305-229-6453; http:// www.lennar.com

General - Incorporation............... DE	Stock- Price on:12/24/2007 ....$40.29
Employees..12,605	Stock Exchange...NYSE
Auditor ....Deloitte & Touche LLP	Ticker Symbol...LEN
Stk Agt........................Computershare Trust Co	Outstanding Shares ....NA
Counsel................................Clifford Chance	E.P.S...NA
DUNS No. 03-249-7497	Shareholders...NA

Business: The groups principle activity is to provide home building services. The group operates through three segments namely homebuilding east, homebuilding central and homebuilding west. The group operates from United States.

Primary SIC and add'l.: 6361 6411 1531 6162 7375 6311 7382

CIK No: 0000920760

Subsidiaries: Acme Water Supply& Management Company, Admiral Homes SPE, LLC, Admiral SPE 2-4, LLC, Ahdg Spe 2-4, LLC, Ahdg Spe, LLC, Ahdg Spe-3, LLC, Alabama Property Ventures, LLC, American Hotel Lofts - Greystone, LLC, AmeriStar Financial Services, Inc., Aquaterra Utilities, Inc., Arbor Club, LLC, Arbor West, LLC, Arboretum - Pcc Iii, LLC, Arboretum Holdings, LLC, Arborwest-int-strawberry Court, LLC 431 Subsidiaries included in the Index

Officers: Stuart A. Miller/Dir., CEO, Pres., Allan J. Pekor/Chmn. - Lennar Financial Services, LLC, Linda Reed/Exec. VP - Lennar Financial Services, LLC, Larry Somma/Treasurer, Kay L. Howard/Dir. - Communications, Rick Beckwitt/Exec. VP, Marshall Ames/VP, Jonathan M. Jaffe/COO, VP, Jeff Roos/Regional Pres. - Lennar Land, Homebuilding, Diane J. Bessette/VP, Controller, Sam B. Crimaldi/Regional Pres. - Lennar Land, Homebuilding, Craig M. Johnson/Regional Pres. - Lennar Land, Homebuilding, Marc Chasman/Regional Pres. - Lennar Land, Homebuilding, Mark Sustana/Sec., General Counsel, Bruce E. Gross/CFO, VP *(24 Officers included in Index)*

Directors: Stuart A. Miller/Dir., CEO, Pres., Steven L. Gerard/Dir., Kirk R. Landon/Dir., Irving Bolotin/Dir., Sidney Lapidus/Dir., Donna E. Shalala/Dir., Jeffrey Sonnenfeld/Dir.

Owners: Insiders/3.50%, Steven L. Gerard, Donna Shalala, Hotchkis& Wiley Capital Management, LLC/10.20%, Bruce E. Gross, Insiders/69.10%, Richard Beckwitt, Steven L. Gerard, Irving Bolotin, Jeffrey Sonnenfeld, Stuart A. Miller/68.50%, Irving Bolotin, Marsico Capital Management, LLC/15.40%, Stuart A. Miller/1.60%, Diane J. Bessette *(28 Owners included in Index)*

Financial Data: Fiscal Year End:11/30 Latest Annual Data: 11/30/2006

Year	Sales	Net Income
2006	$16,266,662,000	$593,869,000
2005	$13,866,971,000	$1,355,155,000
2004	$10,504,899,000	$945,619,000

Curr. Assets:	$9,426,645,000	Curr. Liab.:	$1,093,793,000		
Plant, Equip.:	NA	Total Liab.:	$6,651,501,000	Indic. Yr. Divd.:	NA
Total Assets:	$12,408,266,000	Net Worth:	$5,701,372,000	Debt/ Equity:	0.6025

Lennox International Inc

2140 Lake Pk. Blvd., Richardson, TX, 75080; PH: 1-972-497-5000; Fax: 1-972-497-5299; http:// www.lennoxinternational.com

General - Incorporation............... DE	Stock- Price on:12/24/2007 ....$34.78
Employees..16,000	Stock Exchange...NYSE
Auditor ....KPMG LLP	Ticker Symbol...LII
Stk Agt..................Mellon Investor Services	Outstanding Shares 68,260,000
Counsel...NA	E.P.S...$2.04
DUNS No. ....NA	Shareholders...NA

Business: The group's principle activity is to design and manufacture products for the heating, ventilation, air conditioning and refrigeration markets. The group operates through four business segments: north American residential market, north American retail service market, commercial air-conditioning and commercial refrigeration. The products include furnaces, heat pumps, residential and commercial air conditioning equipment, heating and cooling systems, pre-fabricated fireplaces, stoves, chillers, condensing units, fluid coolers and other products. The group also provides installation, maintenance and repair services. The products are sold under the brand names of lennox, armstrong air, ducane, bohn, larkin, advanced distributor products, heatcraft, service experts and others. The group's quarterly revenue for September 2007 was 1,029.80 millions of USD.

Primary SIC and add'l.: 3585 7623 3677

CIK No: 0001069202

Subsidiaries: A. Frank Woods and Sons LLC, Ac/dac, LLC, Advanced Distributor Products LLC, Advanced Heat Transfer LLC, Air Experts LLC, Air Safe Pty Limited, Aire-Tech LLC, AL GL Pty Ltd, Aldo Marine, Allbritten Plumbing, Heating and Air Conditioning Service, Inc., Alliance Compressor LLC, Alliance Mechanical Heating and Air Conditioning, Inc., Allied Air Enterprises Inc., Andros Refrigeration LLC, Armstrong Air Conditioning Inc. 214 Subsidiaries included in the Index

Officers: Todd M. Bluedorn/Dir., CEO, Mark Hogan/Exec. VP - Engineering, Scott J. Boxer/COO, Pres. - Service Experts/$2,885,753.00, Mary Joyce/Investor Relations Assist., Daniel M. Sessa/Chief Human Resources Officer, Harry J. Bizios/COO, Pres. - LII Commercial Heating, Cooling, Douglas L. Young/COO, Pres. - LII Residential Heating, Cooling, Karen Fugate/VP - Investor Relations, Roy A. Rumbough/52/VP, Controller, Chief Accounting Officer, Susan K. Carter/CFO/$2,693,946.00, Harry J. Ashenhurst/59/Exec. VP, Chief Administrative Officer/$3,584,323.00, William F. Stoll/Chief Legal Officer, Corp. Sec., Linda A. Goodspeed/Exec. VP - Information Technology, Business Development/$2,527,751.00, David W. Moon/COO, Pres. - Worldwide Refrigeration, Bill Moltner/VP - Investor Relations

Directors: Todd M. Bluedorn/Dir., CEO, Richard L. Thompson/Chmn., Steven R. Booth/Dir., John E. Major/Dir., Janet K. Cooper/Dir., James J. Byrne/Dir., Terry D. Stinson/Dir., Thomas W. Booth/Dir., Jeffrey D. Storey/Dir., Linda G. Alvarado/Dir., John W. Norris/Dir., Paul W. Schmidt/Dir., C. L. Henry/Dir.

Owners: Richard L. Thompson, Janet K. Cooper, Linda A. Goodspeed, Paul W. Schmidt, Jeffrey D. Storey, John W. Norris/6.61%, Harry J. Ashenhurst, Linda G. Alvarado, Robert E. Schjerven/2.77%, Insiders/12.83%, Scott J. Boxer, John W. Norris, James J. Byrne, John E. Major, Thomas W. Booth/4.22% *(19 Owners included in Index)*

Financial Data: Fiscal Year End:12/31 Latest Annual Data: 12/31/2006

Year	Sales		Net Income
2006	$3,671,100,000		$166,000,000
2005	$3,366,200,000		$150,700,000
2004	$2,982,700,000		-$134,400,000

Curr. Assets:	$1,018,400,000	Curr. Liab.:	$651,100,000	P/E Ratio:	17.05
Plant, Equip.:	$288,200,000	Total Liab.:	$915,400,000	Indic. Yr. Divd.:	$0.520
Total Assets:	$1,719,800,000	Net Worth:	$804,400,000	Debt/ Equity:	0.1590

Lescarden Inc

420 Lexington Ave., Ste. 212, New York, NY, 10170; PH: 1-212-687-1050; Fax: 1-212-687-1051; http:// www.catrix.com

General - Incorporation ....NY	Stock- Price on:12/24/2007 ....$0.13
Employees...3	Stock Exchange...OTC
Auditor ....Goldstein Golub Kessler LLP	Ticker Symbol...LCAR
Stk Agt.......................Registrar & Transfer Co	Outstanding Shares 31,060,000
Counsel...NA	E.P.S...$0.01
DUNS No. 00-118-5792	Shareholders...NA

Business: The group's principle activity is to research, test and develop medications for the control and cure of various diseases and the licensing of its technologies for commercialization by other companies. The company has discovered and is primarily investigating catrix(R), a complex of mucopolysaccharides derived from bovine cartilage. The products sold by the company include its proprietary bovine cartilage material, bio-cartilage(R), as a food supplement, and direct sales to consumers of a line of cosmetic products. Additionally, the company has pursued a program to establish the clinical efficacy of its poly-nag(R) material as an anti-arthritic. The group's total revenue for year 2007 was 1.06 millions of USD.

Primary SIC and add'l.: 8731 9651 2834

CIK No: 0000058822

Officers: William E. Luther/48/Dir., CEO, CFO, Pres.

Directors: William E. Luther/48/Dir., CEO, CFO, Pres., Xavier Gras Balaguer/55/Dir., George E. Ehrlich/79/Dir., Charles T. Maxwell/76/Dir., Russell O. Wiese/42/Dir.

Owners: Insiders/48.92%, Russel O. Wiese/6.44%, Charles T. Maxwell/41.00%, William Luther/0.99%, Xavier Gras Balaguer/0.48%, George Ehrlich/0.48%

Financial Data: Fiscal Year End:05/31 Latest Annual Data: 05/31/2007

Year	Sales	Net Income
2007	$1,063,000	$138,000
2006	$1,571,000	$68,000
2005	$2,432,000	$394,000

Curr. Assets:	$724,000	Curr. Liab.:	$46,000		
Plant, Equip.:	NA	Total Liab.:	$467,000	Indic. Yr. Divd.:	NA
Total Assets:	$724,000	Net Worth:	$257,000	Debt/ Equity:	NA

Leslies Poolmart Inc

3925 E Brdway Rd. , Ste 100, Phoenix, AZ, 85040; PH: 1-602-366-3999; http:// www.lesliespool.com

General - Incorporation ....DE	Stock- Price on:12/24/2007 ....NA
Employees...NA	Stock Exchange...NA
Auditor ....Ernst & Young LLP	Ticker Symbol...NA
Stk Agt...NA	Outstanding Shares ....NA
Counsel...NA	E.P.S...NA
DUNS No. 05-010-6095	Shareholders...NA

Business: The group's principle activity is to provide retails swimming pool and related products, including maintenance items, such as chemicals, equipment, pool covers and recreational items such as games, fins and snorkels, through retail stores and mail order catalogs. The group operates from United States.

Primary SIC and add'l.: 5961 5999

CIK No: 0000866048

Subsidiaries: Blackwood & Simmons, Inc., LPM Manufacturing Inc, Sandys Pool Supply, Inc

Officers: Lawrence H. Hayward/Chmn., CEO, Michael L. Hatch/COO, Pres., Steven L. Ortega/Dir., CFO, Exec. VP, Janet I. McDonald/CIO, Sr. VP, Brian Agnew/Sr. VP - Store Operations, Rick D. Carlson/Sr. VP - Commercial, Service, Logistics

Directors: Lawrence H. Hayward/Chmn., CEO, Steven L. Ortega/Dir., CFO, Exec. VP

Owners: Michael L. Hatch, Leslies Coinvestment, LLC, Steven L. Ortega, GCP California Fund, L.P., Michael J. Fourticq, Lawrence H. Hayward, Rick D. Carlson, Insiders, John G. Danhakl, Janet I. McDonald, John M. Baumer

Leucadia National Corp

315 Pk. Ave. S, New York, NY, 10010; PH: 1-212-460-1900; Fax: 1-212-598-4869; http:// www.leucadia.com

General - Incorporation ....NY	Stock- Price on:12/24/2007 ....$36.55
Employees.......................................1,323	Stock Exchange...NYSE
Auditor ....PricewaterhouseCoopers LLP	Ticker Symbol...LUK
Stk Agt.....American Stock Transfer & Trust Co.	Outstanding Shares 216,580,000
Counsel................Weil, Gotshal & Manges LLP	E.P.S...$0.51
DUNS No. 00-192-1543	Shareholders...NA

Business: The group's principal activities include telecommunication, healthcare services, banking and lending, manufacturing, winery operations, real estate activities and development of copper mine. The group owns or leases and operates a nationwide inter-city fiber-optic network to provide Internet, data, voice and video services. The banking and lending operations consists of making instalment loans to niche markets primarily funded by customer banking deposits. The healthcare services include the provision of physical, occupational, speech and respiratory therapies. The group manufactures and markets proprietary lightweight plastic netting products. The real estate operations include a mixture of commercial properties, residential land development projects and other unimproved land. Other operations primarily consist of winery operations and developments of copper mine. On 05-Nov-2003, the group acquired wiltel communications group inc.

Primary SIC and add'l.: 1021 3089 2084 8099 4813 6159 6512

CIK No: 0000096223

Subsidiaries: AC (Barbados) IBC, Inc., AIC Financial Corporation, Alumni Forest Products, LLC, American Investment Company, American Investment Holdings, LLC, Antilles Crossing (St. Lucia) Limited, Antilles Crossing - St. Croix, Inc., Antilles Crossing Holding Company (St. Lucia) Limited, Antilles Crossing International, LP, Antilles Crossing, LP, ATX Communications, Inc., ATX Licensing, Inc., ATX Telecommunications Services of Virginia, LLC, Aviation Leasing Company, LLC, Baldwin Aircraft Leasing, LLC 169 Subsidiaries included in the Index

Officers: Ian M. Cumming/Chmn., CEO/$7,896,730.00, Joseph S. Steinberg/Pres./$7,916,645.00, Thomas E. Mara/Exec. VP, Treasurer/$1,584,930.00, Joseph A. Orlando/CFO, VP/$1,344,259.00

Directors: Ian M. Cumming/Chmn., CEO, Jesse Clyde Nichols/68/Dir., Jeffrey C. Keil/64/Dir., Paul M. Dougan/70/Dir., Lawrence D. Glaubinger/82/Dir., Alan J. Hirschfield/72/Dir., James E. Jordan/64/Dir.

Owners: Thomas E . Mara, Joseph A . Orlando, Insiders/25.00%, Cumming Foundation, Jeffrey C . Keil, Alan J . Hirschfield, Horizon Asset Management Inc/6.80%, James E . Jordan, Ian M . Cumming/11.70%, Lawrence D . Glaubinger, Paul M . Dougan, Joseph S . Steinberg/12.90%, H. E. Scruggs, Jesse Clyde Nichols

Financial Data: ***Fiscal Year End:***12/31 ***Latest Annual Data:*** 12/31/2006

Year	Sales	Net Income
2006	$862,672,000	$189,399,000
2005	$1,041,147,000	$1,636,041,000
2004	$2,262,111,000	$145,500,000

Curr. Assets:	$1,366,209,000	***Curr. Liab.:***	$326,653,000	***P/E Ratio:***	71.67
Plant, Equip.:	$410,944,000	***Total Liab.:***	$1,391,567,000	***Indic. Yr. Divd.:***	$0.250
Total Assets:	$5,303,824,000	***Net Worth:***	$3,893,275,000	***Debt/ Equity:***	0.3671

Lev Pharmaceuticals Inc

675 3rd Ave., Ste. 2200, New York, NY, 10017; ***PH:*** 1-212-682-3096; ***Fax:*** 1-212-682-2559; ***http://*** www.levpharma.com

General - Incorporation	DE	***Stock***- Price on:12/24/2007	$1.9
Employees	17	Stock Exchange	OTC
Auditor	Eisner LLP	Ticker Symbol	LEVP
Stk Agt	Securities Transfer Corp	Outstanding Shares	114,110,000
Counsel	NA	E.P.S	-$0.217
DUNS No.	NA	Shareholders	NA

Business: The group's principle activity is to manufacture plain and flavored popcorn and distribute food products in Nevada. It distributes over 400 other snack food products including cheese sauces, potato chips, nuts, snow cone syrups, candy, cookies and beverages. In connection with its popcorn sales, the company offers popcorn machines and nacho cheese machines to its customers free of charge. The customers include hotels, school, casino, supermarkets, prisons and concessionaires. The company has trademarked its 'players choice' and 'sunburst' brand names for popcorn and cookies. On 30-Sep-2003, the company discontinued all its operations.

Primary SIC and add'l.: 2082 2096

CIK No: 0001144062

Subsidiaries: Lev Development Corp.

Officers: Joshua D. Schein/Dir., CEO, Judson Cooper/Chmn., Exec. VP, Sec., Douglas J. Beck/CFO, Jason Bablak/VP - Regulatory Affairs, Joseph Truitt/VP - Sales, Marketing, Jason Tuthill/Contact, Dov Elefant/40/Corporate Controller

Directors: Joshua D. Schein/Dir., CEO, Judson Cooper/Chmn., Exec. VP, Sec., Eric I. Richman/Dir., Thomas Lanier/Dir., Scott Eagle/Dir.

Owners: Joshua D. Schein, Hound Partners, LLC, Southpoint Capital Advisors, LP, Scott Eagle, Douglas J. Beck, Alexandra Global Master Fund, Ltd., Insiders, Thomas Lanier, Prism Ventures, LLC, Emigrant Capital Corp., Eric I. Richman, Judson Cooper, Richard Stone

Financial Data: ***Fiscal Year End:***12/31 ***Latest Annual Data:*** 12/31/2006

Year	Sales	Net Income
2006	NA	-$11,767,000
2005	NA	-$6,308,000
2004	NA	-$4,622,000

Curr. Assets:	$18,348,000	***Curr. Liab.:***	$3,157,000		
Plant, Equip.:	$131,000	***Total Liab.:***	$4,961,000	***Indic. Yr. Divd.:***	NA
Total Assets:	$18,573,000	***Net Worth:***	$13,612,000	***Debt/ Equity:***	0.1325

Levcor International Inc

1065 Ave. Of The Americas, New York, NY, 10018; ***PH:*** 1-212-354-8500

General - Incorporation	DE	***Stock***- Price on:12/24/2007	$0.3
Employees	118	Stock Exchange	OTC
Auditor	Friedman LLP	Ticker Symbol	LEVC
Stk Agt	OTC Corporate Transfer Service Co	Outstanding Shares	5,330,000
Counsel	NA	E.P.S	$0.04
DUNS No.	05-983-1016	Shareholders	NA

Business: The group's principle activities are to convert woven textile fabrics and processing knit textile fabrics sold for production principally to domestic manufacturers of women's apparel. The textile fabric converting process consists of (i) designing fabrics (ii) purchasing yarns both dyed and undyed and commissioning knitting mills to knit the yarns into greige fabric according to the group's specifications and (iii) commissioning fabric finishers to finish the fabrics through a process of washing, bleaching, dyeing and applying certain chemical finishes to greige fabric according to the specifications. The finished apparel fabric is cut and sewn into garments. The group contracts with commercial transporters to deliver greige fabric from textile mills to the fabric finish. The group places orders for the sale of finished fabrics through its sales personnel and independent commission agents.

Primary SIC and add'l.: 2261

CIK No: 0000076094

Subsidiaries: Blumenthal/Lansing Company, LLC, Carlyle Manufacturing Company, Inc.

Owners: Insiders/37.50%, Robert A. Levinson/30.81%, Giandomenico Picco, Insiders/98.30%, Edward H. Cohen, Roger L. Hueglin/5.04%, John McConnaughy/1.13%, GAMCO Investors, Inc./5.49%, Robert A. Levinson/98.30%, Edward F. Cooke/4.90%

Financial Data: ***Fiscal Year End:***12/31 ***Latest Annual Data:*** 12/31/2006

Year	Sales	Net Income
2006	$21,936,000	$1,626,000
2005	$29,401,000	-$8,304,000
2004	$33,736,000	$659,000

Curr. Assets:	$8,444,000	***Curr. Liab.:***	$8,571,000	***P/E Ratio:***	1.15
Plant, Equip.:	$1,917,000	***Total Liab.:***	$17,932,000	***Indic. Yr. Divd.:***	NA
Total Assets:	$13,185,000	***Net Worth:***	-$9,587,000	***Debt/ Equity:***	NA

Level 3 Communications Inc

1025 Eldorado Blvd., Broomfield, CO, 80021; ***PH:*** 1-720-888-1000; ***Fax:*** 1-720-888-5085; ***http://*** www.level3.com; ***Email:*** investor.relations@level3.com

General - Incorporation	DE	***Stock***- Price on:12/24/2007	$5.54
Employees	NA	Stock Exchange	NDQ
Auditor	KPMG LLP	Ticker Symbol	LVLT
Stk Agt	Wells Fargo Shareowner Services	Outstanding Shares	1,530,000,000
Counsel	NA	E.P.S	NA
DUNS No.	NA	Shareholders	NA

Business: The groups principle activity is to provide communications services. The groups services include customer focused organization, switched service, level 3 voice termination, level 3 local inbound and level 3 voip enhanced local. Specific customers of the group include Wholesale Markets Group, Business Markets Group and Content Markets Group. The group acquired Broadwing Corporation in the year 2007 and ICG Communications, Inc, TelCove, Inc, Looking Glass Networks Holding Co., Inc in the year 2006 and WilTel Communications Group, LLC in the year 2005. The group operates from North America, Europe and Asia. The group's quarterly revenue for September is 1,061.00 millions of USD.

Primary SIC and add'l.: 4899 4899 5045 4813 7379 7389 4822 4813 5045 7379 4822 7389

CIK No: 0000794323

Subsidiaries: BTE Equipment, LLC, Eldorado Acquisition Three, LLC, KCP,Inc, Level 3 Communications GmbH (Germany), Level 3 Communications Limited (UK), Level 3 Communications, LLC, Level 3 Communications,Inc., Level 3 Financing,Inc., Level 3 Holdings, B.V., Level 3 Holdings,Inc., Level 3 International,Inc., WilTel Communications Group, LLC, WilTel Communications, LLC

Officers: James Q. Crowe/Dir., CEO/$8,737,825.00, Keith R. Coogan/CEO - Software Spectrum/$4,428,301.00, Charles C. Miller/Vice Chmn., Exec. VP/$3,763,372.00, John Neil Hobbs/48/Pres. - Global Network Services, Chris Hardman/VP - Corporate Communications, Jennifer Daumler/Dir. - Public Relations, Sunit Patel/CFO, Group VP/$3,405,154.00, Sureel Choksi/Pres. - Wholesale Markets, Donald H. Gips/Group VP - Corporate Strategy, Robin E. Grey/Treasurer, Sr. VP, James Heard/MD - European Markets, Meg Porfido/Chief Officer - Human Resources, Jack Waters/CTO, Exec. VP, Kevin J. O'Hara/COO, Pres./$5,236,569.00, Eric J. Mortensen/49/Sr. VP, Controller *(23 Officers included in Index)*

Directors: James Q. Crowe/Dir., CEO, Charles C. Miller/Vice Chmn., Exec. VP, Walter Scott/Chmn., Richard R. Jaros/Dir., Michael J. Mahoney/Dir., Robert E. Julian/Dir., Arun Netravali/Dir., John T. Reed/Dir., Michael B. Yanney/Dir., Albert C. Yates/Dir., James O. Ellis/Dir., Douglas C. Eby/Dir.

Owners: Southeastern Asset Management, Inc./22.40%, Thomas C. Stortz, John T. Reed, Albert C. Yates, FMR Corp. and Edward C. Johnson 3d/11.70%, Robert E. Julian, AXA Financial, Inc./8.30%, James Q. Crowe, Insiders/3.20%, Richard R. Jaros, Walter Scott/1.90%, Legg Mason/8.80%, Sunit S. Patel, Kevin J. OHara, James O. Ellis *(18 Owners included in Index)*

Curr. Assets:	$2,389,000,000	***Curr. Liab.:***	$929,000,000		
Plant, Equip.:	$6,468,000,000	***Total Liab.:***	$9,620,000,000	***Indic. Yr. Divd.:***	NA
Total Assets:	$9,994,000,000	***Net Worth:***	$374,000,000	***Debt/ Equity:***	4.8253

Level 8 Systems Inc

1433 State Hwy. 34, Bldg. C, Farmingdale, NJ, 07727; ***PH:*** 1-732-919-3150; ***http://*** www.level8.com

General - Incorporation	DE	***Stock***- Price on:12/24/2007	NA
Employees	NA	Stock Exchange	OTC
Auditor	Margolis & Co P.C	Ticker Symbol	CICN
Stk Agt	American Stock Transfer & Trust Co.	Outstanding Shares	NA
Counsel	NA	E.P.S	-$0.34
DUNS No.	78-161-4979	Shareholders	NA

Business: The group's principal activity is to provide business integration software that enables organizations to integrate new and existing information and processes at the desktop. The group operates through two segments: desktop integration products and messaging and application engineering products. Desktop integration includes cicero, which maximizes end-user productivity and integrates disparate systems and applications. Messaging and application engineering product include geneva integration broker.

Primary SIC and add'l.: 7379 7378 7371 6719 7372

CIK No: 0000945384

Subsidiaries: 3020126 Canada, Inc. , Cicero Technologies, Inc, Level 8 Benelux B.V, Level 8 Canada, Inc, Level 8 Europe (Deutschland) GmbH, Level 8 FSC, Inc, Level 8 Ireland Limited, Level 8 Italia S.R.L., Level 8 Systems Australia Pty Ltd, Level 8 Systems Nordic AB, Level 8 Technologies, Inc., Level 8 Worldwide Holdings Ltd, Seer Korea Co., Limited, Seer Technologies de Argentina S.A, Seer Technologies do Brasil Ltd. 21 Subsidiaries included in the Index

Officers: John P. Broderick/Dir., CEO, CFO, Neil Crane/Dir. - Product Development, Clint Babcock/Dir. - Professional Services, Keith Anderson/Dir. - Client Services

Directors: John P. Broderick/Dir., CEO, CFO, John Steffens/Chmn., John Atherton/Dir., Don Peppers/Dir., Mark Landis/Dir., Anthony C. Pizi/Dir., Bruce W. Hasenyager/Dir., Jay R. Kingley/Dir., Charles B. Porciello/Dir., Bruce Miller/Dir., Bruce A. Percelay/Dir.

Owners: Charles Porciello, Anthony C. Pizi/4.00%, Insiders/24.80%, Carolyn P. Landis/13.80%, Bruce W. Hasenyager, QueeQueg Partners, L.P./12.20%, Queequeg Ltd./5.00%, John P. Broderick, John W. Atherton, Bruce Miller/3.80%, Jay R. Kingley, Bruce Percelay/2.90%

Financial Data: ***Fiscal Year End:***12/31 ***Latest Annual Data:*** 12/31/2006

Year	Sales	Net Income
2006	$972,000	-$2,997,000
2005	$785,000	-$3,681,000
2004	$775,000	-$9,761,000

Curr. Assets:	$582,000	***Curr. Liab.:***	$8,476,000		
Plant, Equip.:	$15,000	***Total Liab.:***	$8,509,000	***Indic. Yr. Divd.:***	NA
Total Assets:	$597,000	***Net Worth:***	-$7,912,000	***Debt/ Equity:***	NA

Levi Strauss & Co

1155 Battery St., San Francisco, CA, 94111; ***PH:*** 1-415-501-3380; ***http://*** www.levistrauss.com; ***Email:*** newsmediarequests@levi.com

General - Incorporation	DE	**Stock**- Price on:12/24/2007	NA
Employees	NA	Stock Exchange	NA
Auditor	KPMG LLP	Ticker Symbol	NA
Stk Agt	NA	Outstanding Shares	NA
Counsel	NA	E.P.S	NA
DUNS No.	00-910-9273	Shareholders	NA

Business: The groups principle activities include designing and marketing jeans and jeans related pants, casual and dress pants, tops, jackets and related accessories. The groups products sold under the brand name Levis. The group operates from United States.

Primary SIC and add'l.: 2389

CIK No: 0000094845

Subsidiaries: Battery Street Enterprises, Inc., Casualwear Direct B.V., Dockers Europe B.V., Dongguan Levi Apparel Company Limited, Hartwell Commodities Group, Levi Strauss & Co. (Canada) Inc., Levi Strauss & Co. Europe SCA, Levi Strauss (Australia) Pty. Ltd., Levi Strauss (Hong Kong) Limited, Levi Strauss (India) Private Limited, Levi Strauss (Malaysia) Sdn. Bhd., Levi Strauss (New Zealand) Limited, Levi Strauss (Phil.) Inc. II, Levi Strauss (Philippines) Inc., Levi Strauss (Suisse) SA 60 Subsidiaries included in the Index

Officers: John Anderson/CEO, Pres., Armin Broger/Pres. - Levi Strauss, Europe, Alan Hed/Pres. - Asia Pacific Division, David Love/Sr. VP - Global Sourcing, David Bergen/CIO, Sr. VP, Hans Ploos/CFO, John Goodman/Pres. - US Dockers Brand, Robert Hanson/Pres. - Levi Strauss North America, Hilary K. Krane/Sr. VP, General Counsel, Larry Ruff/Global Marketing Officer, Sr. VP - Strategy, Worldwide Marketing, Mike Mecham/Event Mgr. - Sales Operations, Kristy Atkins/Designer, Dockers Brand, Narc Jagroop/Controller

Directors: Bob Haas/Chmn., Patricia Salas Pineda/56/Dir., Peter A. Georgescu/68/Dir., Peter E. Haas/Dir., Warren F. Hellman/73/Dir., Patricia A. House/53/Dir., Leon J. Level/67/Dir., Gary T. Rogers/65/Dir.

Owners: Margaret E. Haas/7.47%, Miriam L. Haas/17.56%, Insiders/39.84%, Warren F. Hellman/1.92%, Peter E. Haas/27.31%, Robert D. Haas/10.61%

Levitt Corp

2200 W Cypress Creek Rd., Fort Lauderdale, FL, 33309; ***PH:*** 1-954-958-1800; ***Fax:*** 1-954-958-1966; ***http://*** www.levittcorporation.com; ***Email:*** corporatecommunications@levittcorporation.com

General - Incorporation	FL	**Stock**- Price on:12/24/2007	$9.32
Employees	666	Stock Exchange	NYSE
Auditor	PricewaterhouseCoopers LLP	Ticker Symbol	LEV
Stk Agt	American Stock Transfer & Trust Co.	Outstanding Shares	19,830,000
Counsel	NA	E.P.S	-$0.38
DUNS No.	NA	Shareholders	NA

Business: The group's principal activity is to develop single-family home and master-planned communities. The group operates through the subsidiaries levitt and sons, llc, core communities, llc and levitt commercial, llc. The properties developed include commercial and industrial properties and multi-family complexes. The group acquires raw land, obtains appropriate entitlements and develops roads and other infrastructure before building homes on the finished parcels. On 28-Apr- 2004, the group acquired bowden building corporation.

Primary SIC and add'l.: 6531 1521

CIK No: 0001218320

Subsidiaries: BankAtlantic Venture Partners 1, LLC, BankAtlantic Venture Partners 10, Inc., BankAtlantic Venture Partners 14, Inc., BankAtlantic Venture Partners 15, Inc., BankAtlantic Venture Partners 2, LLC, BankAtlantic Venture Partners 3, LLC, BankAtlantic Venture Partners 4, LLC, BankAtlantic Venture Partners 7, Inc., BankAtlantic Venture Partners 8, Inc., BankAtlantic Venture Partners 9, Inc., Core Communities, LLC, Cypress Creek Holding, LLC, Levitt and Sons, LLC, Levitt Commercial Andrews, LLC, Levitt Commercial Boynton Commerce Center, LLC 23 Subsidiaries included in the Index

Officers: Alan B. Levan/Chmn., CEO/$753,430.00, George Scanlon/CFO, Exec. VP/$527,673.00, Elliott Wiener/Pres. - Levitt, Sons, LLC/$797,650.00, Seth M. Wise/Pres., Paul J. Hegener/Pres. - Core Communities, LLC/$592,835.00, John Laguardia/Sr. VP - Corporate Acquisitions, Susan McGregor/Exec. VP - Human Resources, Leo Hinkley/Investor Relations Officer

Directors: Alan B. Levan/Chmn., CEO, John E. Abdo/Vice Chmn., Joel Levy/Dir., Lawrence S. Kahn/Dir., William R. Scherer/Dir., Darwin C. Dornbush/Dir., James J. Blosser/Dir., William R. Nicholson/Dir., Alan Levy/Dir.

Owners: Lawrence S. Kahn, Insiders/100.00%, William R. Scherer, John E. Abdo, James J. Blosser, Advisory Research, Inc./18.83%, Pennant Capital Management, LLC/5.09%, Alan B. Levan, Alan Levy, Tradewinds Global Advisors, LLC/24.93%, Paul J. Hegener, Insiders/12.38%, Darwin C. Dornbush, Capital Research & Management Co./5.37%, Barclays Global Investors N.A./5.04% *(20 Owners included in Index)*

Financial Data: ***Fiscal Year End:***12/31 ***Latest Annual Data:*** 12/31/2006

Year	Sales	Net Income
2006	$575,327,000	-$9,164,000
2005	$561,862,000	$54,911,000
2004	$554,450,000	$57,415,000

Curr. Assets:	$871,828,000	**Curr. Liab.:**	$653,283,000		
Plant, Equip.:	$78,675,000	**Total Liab.:**	$747,427,000	**Indic. Yr. Divd.:**	$0.080
Total Assets:	$1,090,666,000	**Net Worth:**	$343,239,000	**Debt/ Equity:**	1.9484

Lexar Media Inc

47300 Bayside Pk.way, Fremont, CA, 94538; ***PH:*** 1-510-413-1200; ***http://*** www.lexarmedia.com

General - Incorporation	DE	**Stock**- Price on:12/24/2007	$12.91
Employees	21,100	Stock Exchange	NYSE
Auditor	PricewaterhouseCoopers LLP	Ticker Symbol	MUR
Stk Agt	Lexar Shareholder Services	Outstanding Shares	NA
Counsel	Fenwick & West LLP	E.P.S	-$0.13
DUNS No.	NA	Shareholders	NA

Business: The group's principal activities are to design, develop and market high-performance flash-cards and connectivity products. The products are marketed as 'digital film' to the digital photography market and other markets utilizing portable digital storage media. It offers flash cards in the five primary media formats: compactflash, memory stick, smartmedia, secure digital card and multimedia card, jumpdrive tm, a new, high-speed portable universal serial bus (usb) flash drive for consumer applications. The group offer connectivity, software and other products that facilitate the transfer of digital images to personal computers and other devices without a direct connection to the digital camera. The group offer software products,like image rescue 2.0 software, that recovers lost or deleted image files (jpeg, tiff and raw) from a compactflash card. The group markets its products in the United States, Asia, Europe and other parts of the world.

Primary SIC and add'l.: 3861 7384 7372

CIK No: 0001058289

Subsidiaries: Lexar (Shanghai) Electronics Company Limited, Lexar Hong Kong Limited, Lexar Media (Europe) Limited, Lexar Media International Limited, Lexar Media K.K., Lexar Media Pty Ltd., Lexar Singapore Pte. Ltd.

Officers: Eric Stang/Chmn., CEO, Pres., Petro Estakhri/CTO, Exec. VP - Engineering, Farhad Tabrizi/VP - Business Development, Strategic Alliances, Eric Whitaker/Exec. VP - Corporate Strategy, General Counsel, Sec., Tim Sullivan/Exec. VP - Worldwide Sales, Michael Scarpelli/CFO, Mark Adams/COO, Leslie Adams/VP - Consumer, Retail Marketing

Directors: Eric Stang/Chmn., CEO, Pres., Brian Jacobs/Dir., Mary Tripsas/Dir., William T. Dodds/Dir., Charles Levine/Dir., Robert Hinckley/Dir.

Financial Data: ***Fiscal Year End:***12/31 ***Latest Annual Data:*** 8/31/2006

Year	Sales	Net Income
2006	$5,272,000,000	$408,000,000
2005	$4,880,200,000	$188,000,000
2004	$4,404,200,000	$157,200,000

Curr. Assets:	$2,638,700,000	**Curr. Liab.:**	$972,100,000		
Plant, Equip.:	$4,712,700,000	**Total Liab.:**	$2,145,200,000	**Indic. Yr. Divd.:**	NA
Total Assets:	$7,760,000,000	**Net Worth:**	$5,614,800,000	**Debt/ Equity:**	0.0774

Lexaria Corp

700 Pender St. W , Ste. 604, Vancouver, BC, V6C 1G8; ***PH:*** 1-604-602-1675; ***Fax:*** 1-604-602-1625; ***http://*** www.lexariaenergy.com; ***Email:*** info@lexariaenergy.com

General - Incorporation	NV	**Stock**- Price on:12/24/2007	$0.85
Employees	NA	Stock Exchange	OTC
Auditor	Vellmer & Chang	Ticker Symbol	LXRA
Stk Agt	Nevada Agency & Trust Company	Outstanding Shares	NA
Counsel	NA	E.P.S	NA
DUNS No.	NA	Shareholders	NA

Business: The groups principle activity is to explore petroleum and natural gas. The group operates from North America.

Primary SIC and add'l.: 1382

CIK No: 0001348362

Officers: Chris Bunka/Chmn., CEO, Pres., Leonard MacMillan/Dir., VP, William K. Griffin/Pres. - Griffin, Griffin, John Andrew Griffin/VP - Exploration - Griffin, Griffin, Raymond Lewand/Sr. Geologist, Pittman S. Calhoun/Chief Geophysist, Bob Boyett/Drilling Mgr. - Joint Operations

Directors: Chris Bunka/Chmn., CEO, Pres., Leonard MacMillan/Dir., VP, Peter Philipchuk/Member - Advisory Board, Thomas Ihrke/Member - Advisory Board, Todd McMahon/Member - Advisory Board, Ken Brooks/Member - Advisory Board

Owners: Garth Braun/5.07%, Insiders/16.82%, Christopher Bunka/14.92%, Stewart Gray/7.60%, Lanesborough Balfour Trust/8.45%, Venture Capital Asset Management Ltd./6.89%, Ben Jenks/9.85%, Leonard MacMillan/1.90%

Financial Data: ***Fiscal Year End:***10/31 ***Latest Annual Data:*** 10/31/2006

Year	Sales	Net Income
2006	$20,000	-$508,000

Curr. Assets:	$1,299,000	**Curr. Liab.:**	$2,015,000		
Plant, Equip.:	$1,420,000	**Total Liab.:**	$2,015,000	**Indic. Yr. Divd.:**	NA
Total Assets:	$2,719,000	**Net Worth:**	$705,000	**Debt/ Equity:**	NA

Lexicon Pharmaceuticals Inc

Formerly: Lexicon Genetics Inc

8800 Technology Forest Pl., The Woodlands, TX, 77381; ***PH:*** 1-281-863-3000; ***http://*** www.lexgen.com

General - Incorporation	DE	**Stock**- Price on:12/24/2007	$22.29
Employees	755	Stock Exchange	NDQ
Auditor	Ernst & Young LLP	Ticker Symbol	LXRX
Stk Agt	Mellon Investor Services LLC	Outstanding Shares	NA
Counsel	Andrews & Kurch LLP	E.P.S	-$0.72
DUNS No.	NA	Shareholders	NA

Business: The group's principal activity is to conduct research, develop and market products and services for the treatment of human diseases. The group uses the gene knockout technology to systematically discover the functions and pharmaceutical utility of genes in living mammals. The technology is applicable to therapeutic discovery programs in diabetes, obesity, cardiovascular disease, immune disorders, neurological disease and cancer. It alters the dna of genes in a special variety of mouse cells, called embryonic stem cells, which can be cloned and used to generate mice with the altered gene. Using this technology, the group discovers thousands of genes and expands its omnibank library of 200,000 frozen gene knockout es cell clones, each identified by dna sequence in a relational database. The omnibank library currently contains gene knockout clones for more than half of all genes in the mammalian genome.

Primary SIC and add'l.: 8731 2835

CIK No: 0001062822

Subsidiaries: Lexicon Pharmaceuticals ,Inc

Officers: Arthur T. Sands/Dir., CEO, Pres./$1,938,733.00, Jeffrey L. Wade/Exec. VP, General Counsel/$668,595.00, Philip M. Brown/VP - Clinical Development, Brian P. Zambrowicz/Chief Scientific Officer, Exec. VP/$800,384.00, James R. Piggott/Sr. VP - Pharmaceutical Biology, Alan J. Main/Exec. VP - Pharmaceutical Research/$628,052.00, Julia P. Gregory/CFO, Exec. VP/$747,142.00, Lance K. Ishimoto/Sr. VP - Intellectual Property, Sapna Srivastava/Analyst Coverage, Morgan Stanley, Piper Jaffray/Analyst Coverage, Edward Tenthoff, Tamar D. Howson/Exec. VP - Business Development, Arti Allam/Contact - Investor Relations, William Sargent/Analyst Coverage, Bank, America, Sharon Seiler/Analyst Coverage, Punk, Ziegel, Company, Jason Kantor/Analyst Coverage, RBC Capital Markets

Directors: Arthur T. Sands/Dir., CEO, Pres., Barry Mills/Dir., Clayton S. Rose/Dir., Samuel L. Barker/Dir., Philippe J. Amouyal/Dir., Raymond Debbane/Dir., Christopher J. Sobecki/Dir., Judith L. Swain/Dir., Kathleen M. Wiltsey/Dir., Robert J. Lefkowitz/Dir., Frank P. Palantoni/Dir., Alan S. Nies/Dir.

Owners: Alan S. Nies, Insiders/5.90%, Julia P. Gregory, Brian P. Zambrowicz, Arthur T. Sands/2.70%, Barry Mills, Clayton S. Rose, Alan J. Main, Samuel L. Barker, Kathleen M. Wiltsey, Robert J. Lefkowitz, Jeffrey L. Wade, Frank P. Palantoni

Financial Data: *Fiscal Year End:* 12/31 *Latest Annual Data:* 12/31/2006

Year	Sales		Net Income
2006	$72,798,000		-$54,311,000
2005	$75,680,000		-$36,315,000
2004	$61,740,000		-$47,172,000
Curr. Assets:	$85,552,000	**Curr. Liab.:**	$45,966,000	
Plant, Equip.:	$78,192,000	**Total Liab.:**	$104,765,000	**Indic. Yr. Divd.:** NA
Total Assets:	$190,266,000	**Net Worth:**	$85,501,000	**Debt/ Equity:** NA

Lexington Energyservices Inc

Formerly: Lexington Energy Services Inc
207 W Hastings St., Ste. 1209, Vancouver, BC, V6B 1H7; *PH:* 1-604-899-4550;
http:// www.lexingtonenergyservices.com

General - Incorporation	NV	**Stock** - Price on:12/24/2007	$0.45
Employees	NA	Stock Exchange	OTC
Auditor	Amisano Hanson	Ticker Symbol	LXES
Stk Agt	Island Stock Transfer	Outstanding Shares	NA
Counsel	NA	E.P.S.	NA
DUNS No.	NA	Shareholders	NA

Business: The groups principle activities include providing, manufacturing and leasing oilfield service equipment to oil and gas and oil field service companies. The products of the group include nitrogen generation unit, mobile well production testing units coring units. The group operates from the United States and Canada.

Primary SIC and add'l.: 3533
CIK No: 0001357335
Subsidiaries: Lexcore Services Inc.
Officers: Larry Kristof/37/Dir., CEO, CFO, Pres., Sec., Treasurer, Principal Accounting Officer, Brent Nimeck/Sr. VP - Operations, Interim Pres., CEO - Lexington Energy Services, Pres. - Lexcore Services, Dan Nanninga/VP - Operations, Lexcore Services, Maribel Jordan/Controller
Directors: Larry Kristof/37/Dir., CEO, CFO, Pres., Sec., Treasurer, Principal Accounting Officer, Elston Johnston/Dir.
Owners: Larry Kristof/18.60%, Brent Nimeck/20.70%, Elston Johnston/5.70%, Insiders/26.40%
Financial Data: *Fiscal Year End:* 11/30 *Latest Annual Data:* 11/30/2006

Year	Sales		Net Income
2006	NA		-$1,971,000
Curr. Assets:	$917,000	**Curr. Liab.:**	$1,247,000	
Plant, Equip.:	$3,250,000	**Total Liab.:**	$1,247,000	**Indic. Yr. Divd.:** NA
Total Assets:	$5,741,000	**Net Worth:**	$4,494,000	**Debt/ Equity:** NA

Lexington Precision Corp

800 3rd Ave., New York, NY, 10022; *PH:* 1-212-319-4657; *Fax:* 1-212-319-4659;
http:// www.lexingtonprecision.com

General - Incorporation	DE	**Stock** - Price on:12/24/2007	NA
Employees	797	Stock Exchange	OTC
Auditor	Ernst & Young LLP	Ticker Symbol	LEXP
Stk Agt	Wells Fargo Bank Minnesota N.A	Outstanding Shares	NA
Counsel	Nixon Peabody	E.P.S.	NA
DUNS No.	04-543-3307	Shareholders	NA

Business: The group's principal activity is carried out through two core business segments, rubber group and metal group. The rubber group produces seals used in automotive wiring systems, insulators for automotive ignition wire sets, components for medical devices and molds used to produce components for the group's customers. The metals group manufactures aluminum die castings and machine components from aluminum, brass and steel bars. These products are sold primarily to automotive suppliers, industrial equipment manufacturers and manufacturers of computer and office equipment. The rubber group and the metals group conduct substantially all of their business in the continental United States.

Primary SIC and add'l.: 3061 3429 3364 3363 6719
CIK No: 0000012570
Subsidiaries: Lexington Rubber Group, Inc.
Officers: Michael A. Lubin/58/Chmn., Co - Principal Executive Officer, Dennis J. Welhouse/59/CFO, Sr. VP, Sec.
Directors: Michael A. Lubin/58/Chmn., Co - Principal Executive Officer, Kenneth I. Greenstein/78/Dir., William B. Conner/75/Dir., Warren Delano/57/Dir., Joseph A. Pardo/74/Dir., Elizabeth H. Ruml/55/Dir.
Owners: Kenneth I. Greenstein, Joseph A. Pardo, Michael A. Lubin/33.50%, Insiders/70.10%, Warren Delano/28.00%, William B. Conner/7.30%, Dennis J. Welhouse/1.90%

Curr. Assets:	$20,222,000	**Curr. Liab.:**	$82,211,000	
Plant, Equip.:	$24,226,000	**Total Liab.:**	$83,431,000	**Indic. Yr. Divd.:** NA
Total Assets:	$54,440,000	**Net Worth:**	-$28,991,000	**Debt/ Equity:** NA

Lexington Realty Trust

Formerly: Lexington Corporate Properties Trust
One Penn Plz., Ste.4015, New York, NY, 10119; *PH:* 1-212-692-7200; *http://* www.lxp.com

General - Incorporation	MD	**Stock** - Price on:12/24/2007	$20.93
Employees	56	Stock Exchange	NA
Auditor	Janofsky & Walker LLP	Ticker Symbol	NA
Stk Agt	Mellon Investor Services LLC	Outstanding Shares	66,170,000
Counsel	NA	E.P.S.	$0.25
DUNS No.	NA	Shareholders	NA

Business: The groups principle activities include acquiring, owning and management leased offices, industrial and retail properties. In the year 2005, the group acquired AT&T Wireless Services, Inc. The group operates 365 properties from the United States and Netherlands. The groups quarterly revenue for September 2007 was 105.52 millions of USD.

Primary SIC and add'l.: 6512
CIK No: 0000910108

Subsidiaries: 111 Debt Acquisition LLC, 111 Debt Acquisition MEZZ LLC, 111 Debt Acquisition-TWO LLC, 1701 MARKET ASSOCIATES L.P., 1701 MARKET GP LLC, ACQUIPORT 550 MANAGER LLC, ACQUIPORT 600 MANAGER LLC, ACQUIPORT ARLINGTON MANAGER LLC, ACQUIPORT BREA L.P., ACQUIPORT BREA MANAGER LLC, ACQUIPORT COLORADO SPRINGS LLC, ACQUIPORT COLORADO SPRINGS MANAGER LLC, ACQUIPORT INTL PARKWAY L.P., ACQUIPORT INTL PARKWAY MANAGER LLC, ACQUIPORT ISSAQUAH LLC 655 Subsidiaries included in the Index
Officers: Wilson T. Eglin/43/Dir., CEO, COO, Trustee, Pres./$6,174,005.00, Richard J. Rouse/62/Trustees, Co - Vice Chmn., Chief Investment Officer/$5,071,799.00, Michael L. Ashner/55/Executive Chmn., Trustee, Dir. - Strategic Acquisitions, Robert E. Roskind/62/Trustee, Co - Vice Chmn./$5,641,937.00, Patrick Carroll/44/CFO, Exec. VP, Treasurer/$3,898,019.00, John B. Vander Zwaag/50/Exec. VP/$2,180,152.00, Paul R. Wood/47/VP, Chief Accounting Officer, Sec., Lara Sweeney Johnson/Exec. VP - Strategic Acquisitions, Carol Merriman/Investor Relations Contact
Directors: Wilson T. Eglin/43/Dir., CEO, COO, Trustee, Pres., Richard J. Rouse/62/Trustees, Co - Vice Chmn., Chief Investment Officer, Michael L. Ashner/55/Executive Chmn., Trustee, Dir. - Strategic Acquisitions, Robert E. Roskind/62/Trustee, Co - Vice Chmn., William J. Borruso/61/Trustee, Dir., Clifford Broser/46/Trustee, Dir., Geoffrey Dohrmann/Trustee, Dir., Richard Frary/60/Trustee, Dir., Carl D. Glickman/Trustee, Dir., James Grosfield/Trustee, Dir., Kevin W. Lynch/Trustee, Dir.
Owners: Barclays Global Investors, NA, et. al./6.70%, Vornado Realty Trust/10.70%, Michael L. Ashner/1.60%, Patrick Carroll, Clifford Broser, Kevin W. Lynch, Insiders/7.30%, Robert E. Roskind/3.40%, Wilson T. Eglin, Richard J. Rouse, Geoffrey Dohrmann, John B. VanderZwaag, James Grosfeld, Carl D. Glickman, William J. Borruso (19 Owners included in Index)
Financial Data: *Fiscal Year End:* 12/31 *Latest Annual Data:* 12/31/2006

Year	Sales		Net Income
2006	$54,162,000		-$6,249,000
2005	NA		$61,372,000
2004	NA		$56,759,000
Curr. Assets:	$231,235,000	**Curr. Liab.:**	$107,619,000	**P/E Ratio:** 21.69
Plant, Equip.:	$3,540,639,000	**Total Liab.:**	$3,502,413,000	**Indic. Yr. Divd.:** $1.500
Total Assets:	$4,624,857,000	**Net Worth:**	$1,122,444,000	**Debt/ Equity:** NA

Lexington Resources Inc

7473 W Lake Mead Rd., Las Vegas, TX, 89128 ; *PH:* 1-702-382-5139;
http:// www.lexingtonresources.com; *Email:* info@lexingtonresources.com

General - Incorporation	NV	**Stock** - Price on:12/24/2007	NA
Employees	NA	Stock Exchange	OTC
Auditor	Whitley Penn LLP	Ticker Symbol	LXRS
Stk Agt	Transfer Online, Inc.	Outstanding Shares	NA
Counsel	NA	E.P.S.	-$0.427
DUNS No.	NA	Shareholders	NA

Business: The groups principle activities include acquiring and developing oil and gas properties. In January 2006, the group acquired Oak Hills Drilling and Operating International, Inc. the group operates from the United States.

Primary SIC and add'l.: 2741
CIK No: 0001060791
Subsidiaries: Lexington Oil & Gas Ltd. Co.
Owners: Insiders/6.84%, Touradji Global Resources Master Fund, Ltd./9.29%, Douglas Humphreys/5.80%, Steve Jewett, Touradji Deep Rock Master Fund, Ltd./6.19%, Longfellow Industries (B.C.) Ltd./7.74%, Alexander Cox/13.30%, Norman J. R. MacKinnon, Eastern Capital Corp./5.44%, Grant R. Atkins, Newport Capital Corp/5.64%
Financial Data: *Fiscal Year End:* 12/31 *Latest Annual Data:* 12/31/2006

Year	Sales		Net Income
2006	$2,337,000		-$10,577,000
2005	$694,000		-$8,539,000
2004	$472,000		-$6,093,000
Curr. Assets:	$1,628,000	**Curr. Liab.:**	$9,863,000	
Plant, Equip.:	$16,804,000	**Total Liab.:**	$12,698,000	**Indic. Yr. Divd.:** NA
Total Assets:	$18,433,000	**Net Worth:**	$5,735,000	**Debt/ Equity:** NA

Lexmark International Inc

One Lexmark Ctr. Dr., 740 W New Cir. Rd., Lexington, KY, 40550; *PH:* 1-859-232-2000;
Fax: 1-859-232-2403; *http://* www.lexmark.com

General - Incorporation	DE	**Stock** - Price on:12/24/2007	$50.7
Employees	14,900	Stock Exchange	NYSE
Auditor	PricewaterhouseCoopers LLP	Ticker Symbol	LXK
Stk Agt	Bank of New York	Outstanding Shares	94,570,000
Counsel	NA	E.P.S.	$3.02
DUNS No.	NA	Shareholders	NA

Business: The group's principle activities include developing, manufacturing and supplying printing instruments. The groups products include laser, all-in-one inkjet printers and mono lazer printer. The group operates from United States, Europe, the Middle East, Africa, Asia, the Pacific Rim and the Caribbean.

Primary SIC and add'l.: 3577 3579
CIK No: 0001001288
Subsidiaries: Blue Mark International SA, Lexington Tooling Corporation, Lexmark (Schweiz) AG, Lexmark Asia Pacific Corporation, Inc., Lexmark Canada, Inc., Lexmark Deutschland GmbH, Lexmark Espana, LLC, Lexmark Espana, LLC & Cia, S.R.C., Lexmark Europe Holding Company I, LLC, Lexmark Europe Holding Company, II, LLC, Lexmark Europe S.A.R.L., Lexmark Europe Trading Corporation, Inc., Lexmark Handelsgesellshaft m.b.H., Lexmark Internacional Mexicana S. De R.L. de C. V., Lexmark Internacional Servicios, S. de R.L. de S.A. 63 Subsidiaries included in the Index
Officers: Paul J. Curlander/55/Chmn., CEO, Najib Bahous/VP - Lexmark, Pres. - Consumer Printer Division, Daniel P. Bork/VP - Tax, Vincent J. Cole/VP, General Counsel, Sec., John W. Gamble/CFO, Exec. VP, David Goodnight/VP - Asia Pacific, Latin America, Richard A. Pelini/VP, Treasurer, Paul A. Rooke/Exec. VP - Lexmark, Pres. - Printing Solutions, Services Division, Gary Stromquist/VP, Corporate Controller, Jeri Stromquist/VP - Human Resources, Marty Canning/VP - Lexmark, Pres. - Printing Solutions, Services Division, Jeri Isbell/VP - Human Resources

Directors: Paul J. Curlander/55/Chmn., CEO, Martin D. Walker/75/Dir., Marvin L. Mann/74/Dir., Michael J. Maples/65/Dir., Ralph E. Gomory/78/Dir., Charles B. Ames/82/Dir., Teresa Beck/53/Dir., William R. Fields/58/Dir., Stephen R. Hardis/72/Dir., James F. Hardymon/73/Dir., Robert Holland/67/Dir., Kathi P. Seifert/59/Dir., Jean-Paul L. Montupet/60/Dir.

Owners: Stephen R. Hardis, Vincent J. Cole, James F. Hardymon, Kathi P. Seifert, Robert Holland, State Street Bank and Trust Company/7.49%, Charles B. Ames, Goldman Sachs Asset Management, L.P./10.20%, Najib Bahous, Martin D. Walker, Ralph E. Gomory, Jean-Paul L. Montupet, William R. Fields, John W. Gamble, Teresa Beck *(21 Owners included in Index)*

Financial Data: *Fiscal Year End:*12/31   *Latest Annual Data:* 12/31/2006

Year		Sales		Net Income
2006		$5,108,100,000		$338,400,000
2005		$5,221,500,000		$356,300,000
2004		$5,313,800,000		$568,700,000
Curr. Assets:	$1,830,000,000	Curr. Liab.:	$1,324,000,000	P/E Ratio: 15.00
Plant, Equip.:	$846,800,000	Total Liab.:	$1,813,800,000	Indic. Yr. Divd.: NA
Total Assets:	$2,849,000,000	Net Worth:	$1,035,200,000	Debt/ Equity: 0.1502

Lexon Technologies Inc

8 Corporate Pk., Irvine, CA, 92606; *PH:* 1-949-477-4000; *http://* www.lexontech.com; *Email:* info3@lexontech.com

General - Incorporation	DE	Stock- Price on:12/24/2007	NA
Employees	NA	Stock Exchange	OTC
Auditor	Chisholm, Bierwolf & Nilson, LLC	Ticker Symbol	LEXO
Stk Agt	Fidelity Transfer Co	Outstanding Shares	NA
Counsel	Taylor & Associates	E.P.S.	NA
DUNS No.	NA	Shareholders	NA

Business: The groups principle activities include designing, developing, manufacturing, selling and supporting high performance, Low Temperature Cofired Ceramic components. Specific customers served by the group include Yulim, and Samsung Electronics Co. The group operates from the United States.

Primary SIC and add'l.: 3290

CIK No: 0001065189

Subsidiaries: Techone Co. Ltd

Officers: Hyung Soon Lee/56/Dir., CEO, CFO, Mary Park/Investor Relations Officer

Directors: Hyung Soon Lee/56/Dir., CEO, CFO, Joon Ho Chang/63/Chmn.

Owners: Kyoung Ho Lim/11.70%, Kenneth Eaken/7.54%, Kyu Hong Hwang/14.42%, Ben Hwang/6.92%, Insiders/31.41%, Jehy J. Lah/9.45%

Curr. Assets:	$0	Curr. Liab.:	$2,780,000	
Plant, Equip.:	NA	Total Liab.:	$3,055,000	Indic. Yr. Divd.: NA
Total Assets:	$112,000	Net Worth:	-$2,943,000	Debt/ Equity: NA

LG Philips LCD Co Ltd

150 E Brokaw Rd., San Jose, CA, 95112; *PH:* 1-408-350-7723; *http://* www.lgphilips-lcd.com

General - Incorporation	Korea	Stock- Price on:12/24/2007	$23.38
Employees	23,639	Stock Exchange	NYSE
Auditor	Samil PricewaterhouseCoopers	Ticker Symbol	LPL
Stk Agt	Jae Man Song Sec Agent Srvcs Dept	Outstanding Shares	715,630,000
Counsel	NA	E.P.S.	-$1.37
DUNS No.	NA	Shareholders	NA

Business: The groups principle activities include manufacturing and developing TFT-LCD panels for televisions and monitors. The groups products include televisions, monitors and note book PCs. The group operates from United States.

Primary SIC and add'l.: NA

CIK No: 0001290109

Subsidiaries: LG.Philips LCD, LG.Philips LCD America, Inc., LG.Philips LCD Germany GmbH, LG.Philips LCD Hong Kong Co., Ltd., LG.Philips LCD Japan Co., Ltd., LG.Philips LCD Nanjing Co., Ltd., LG.Philips LCD Poland Sp.z o.o., LG.Philips LCD Taiwan Co., Ltd.

Officers: Young Soo Kwon/Joint Representative Dir., CEO, Pres., Jong Sik Kim/Exec. VP - CPO, Hyun He Ha/Exec. VP, Head - Small, Medium Displays Business Unit, Soo Youle Cha/VP, Head - Panel Center, Jae Geol Ju/Exec. VP, Head - Japan Service Center, Sang Deog Yeo/Exec. VP, Head - TV Business Unit, Budiman Sastra/CTO, Exec. VP, Ron H. Wirahadiraksa/CFO, Pres., Joint Representative Dir., Bock Kwon/Exec. VP, Head - Overseas Marketing Center, Sang Beom Han/Exec. VP, Head - Panel Center, In-Jae Chung/CTO, Exec. VP

Directors: Young Soo Kwon/Joint Representative Dir., CEO, Pres., Rudy Provoost/Chmn., Bart Van Halder/Dir., Bongsung Oum/Dir., Dong Woo Chun/Dir., Ingoo Han/Dir., Doug J. Dunn/Dir., Hee Gook Lee/Dir., Ron H. Wirahadiraksa/CFO, Pres., Joint Representative Dir.

Owners: Citibank, N.A./7.80%, LG Electronics/37.90%, Philips Electronics/32.90%

Financial Data: *Fiscal Year End:*12/31   *Latest Annual Data:* 12/31/2006

Year		Sales		Net Income
2006		$11,423,871,000		-$744,923,000
2005		$9,975,822,000		$536,287,000
2004		$8,042,502,000		$1,645,915,000
Curr. Assets:	$3,391,721,000	Curr. Liab.:	$3,491,577,000	
Plant, Equip.:	$10,199,084,000	Total Liab.:	$7,121,277,000	Indic. Yr. Divd.: NA
Total Assets:	$14,512,213,000	Net Worth:	$7,390,936,000	Debt/ Equity: 0.3985

LGA Holdings Inc

Formerly: LGA Inc
3380 N El Paso St., Ste G, Colorado Springs, CO, 80907; *PH:* 1-719-630-3800; *http://* www.letsgoaero.com

General - Incorporation	UT	Stock- Price on:12/24/2007	NA
Employees	NA	Stock Exchange	NA
Auditor	Cordovano & Honeck P.C	Ticker Symbol	NA
Stk Agt	Interwest Transfer Company, Inc.	Outstanding Shares	NA
Counsel	NA	E.P.S.	-$0.08
DUNS No.	10-839-4479	Shareholders	NA

Business: The group's principal activities are to design and market computer-based medical and health information systems related primarily to the emergency departments in the hospitals throughout the United States. It has designed an integrated information management, patient tracking system called ednet. The ednet patient tracking module replaces the grease board, chalk board, magnets and markers with an on-screen display, continuously updated and distributed throughout the emergency department. During fiscal 2003, the group discontinued consulting division and ednet product lines.

Primary SIC and add'l.: 6794 7373 7372

CIK No: 0000845696

Subsidiaries: Aero inc., LGA Holdings Inc.

Officers: Marty Williams/48/Dir., CEO, Pres., Sara Williams/39/Dir., Sec., Treasurer, Principal Financial Officer, Matthew Drabczyk/49/Dir., VP - Engineering

Directors: Marty Williams/48/Dir., CEO, Pres., Sara Williams/39/Dir., Sec., Treasurer, Principal Financial Officer, Eric Nickerson/57/Dir., Matthew Drabczyk/49/Dir., VP - Engineering

Owners: Eric J. Nickerson, Marty Williams, Matthew Drabczyk, Floyd Murray, Sara Williams, Insiders

Financial Data: *Fiscal Year End:*06/30   *Latest Annual Data:* 06/30/2006

Year		Sales		Net Income
2006		$337,000		-$261,000
2005		$286,000		-$590,000
2004		$188,000		$496,000
Curr. Assets:	$196,000	Curr. Liab.:	$219,000	
Plant, Equip.:	$136,000	Total Liab.:	$279,000	Indic. Yr. Divd.: NA
Total Assets:	$432,000	Net Worth:	$152,000	Debt/ Equity: NA

LGL Group Inc

Formerly: Lynch Corp
140 Greenwich Ave, 4th Fl., Greenwich, CT, 06830; *PH:* 1-203-622-1150

General - Incorporation	IN	Stock- Price on:12/24/2007	$12.794
Employees	386	Stock Exchange	AMEX
Auditor	Ernst & Young LLP	Ticker Symbol	NA
Stk Agt	Mellon Investor Services LLC	Outstanding Shares	2,150,000
Counsel	NA	E.P.S.	-$1.331
DUNS No.	04-468-7424	Shareholders	NA

Business: The group's principal activities are to design, develop, manufacture and market manufacturing equipment for the electronic display and consumer glass industries. The group also produces replacement parts for various types of packaging and glass container-making machines. The group operates through two segments: lynch systems and M-Tron. Lynch systems, the glass manufacturing equipment segment designs, develops, manufactures and markets manufacturing equipment for the electronic display and consumer glass industries. M-Tron, the frequency control devices segment manufactures and markets electronic components to control the frequency of electronic signals in communications equipment.

Primary SIC and add'l.: 3565 7389 3679 6719 2891 4813 5084

CIK No: 0000061004

Subsidiaries: Lynch Systems, Inc, M-tron Industries, Inc, M-tron Industries, Limited, Piezo Technology, Inc

Officers: Jeremiah M. Healy/CEO, Pres./$142,780.00, Steve Pegg/CFO

Directors: Marc Gabelli/Chmn., Val E. Cerutti/67/Dir., Avrum Gray/72/Dir., Anthony R. Pustorino/82/Dir., Peter Dapuzzo/68/Dir., Timothy Foufas/39/Dir., Patrick J. Guarino/65/Dir., Kuni Nakamura/39/Dir., Javier Romero/35/Dir.

Owners: Insiders/27.30%, Kuni Nakamura, Marc Gabelli/24.50%, Robert R. Zylstra, Patrick J. Guarino, Peter DaPuzzo, Avrum Gray, Jeremiah M. Healy, Steve Pegg, Val E. Cerutti, Anthony R. Pustorino, Bulldog Investors, Phillip Goldstein and Andrew Dakos/6.60%, Mario J. Gabelli/17.00%

Financial Data: *Fiscal Year End:*12/31   *Latest Annual Data:* 12/31/2006

Year		Sales		Net Income
2006		$49,300,000		$865,000
2005		$46,183,000		$1,210,000
2004		$33,834,000		-$3,326,000
Curr. Assets:	$23,613,000	Curr. Liab.:	$11,150,000	P/E Ratio: 28.43
Plant, Equip.:	$6,765,000	Total Liab.:	$14,250,000	Indic. Yr. Divd.: NA
Total Assets:	$30,957,000	Net Worth:	$16,707,000	Debt/ Equity: 0.1916

LHC Group Inc

Formerly: LHC Group
420 W Pinhook Rd., Ste. a, Lafayette, LA, 70503; *PH:* 1-337-233-1307; *http://* www.lhcgroup.com

General - Incorporation	DE	Stock- Price on:12/24/2007	$25.91
Employees	2,478	Stock Exchange	NDQ
Auditor	Ernst & Young LLP	Ticker Symbol	LHCG
Stk Agt	SunTrust Bank	Outstanding Shares	18,000,000
Counsel	NA	E.P.S.	$1.36
DUNS No.	NA	Shareholders	NA

Business: The groups principle activity is to provide post acute healthcare services. The groups services include skilled nursing, nursing, physical, occupational, and speech therapy. The groups operates through two segments namely home based services and facility based services. Customers served by the group include nursing agencies and hospitals. The group operates from the United States. The group's quarterly revenue for September 2007 was 77.50 millions of USD.

Primary SIC and add'l.: 8059 8099 8082 8062

CIK No: 0001303313

Subsidiaries: Able Home Health, Inc., Acadian Home Health Care Services, LLC, Acadian HomeCare, LLC, Acadian Premiere Regional Nursing, LLC, AHCG Management, LLC, Alabama Health Care Group, LLC, Arkansas Health Care Group, LLC, Arkansas HomeCare of Hot Springs, LLC, Baton Rouge HomeCare, LLC, Bienville Medical Center, Clay County Hospital HomeCare, LLC, D. W. McMillan Memorial Hospital, Dallas County Medical Center HomeCare, LLC, Diabetes Self-Management Center, Inc., Eureka Springs Hospital Home Care, LLC 85 Subsidiaries included in the Index

Officers: Keith G. Myers/Chmn., CEO, Joey Benoit/Payroll Mgr., Aline Voorhies/Legal Department Mgr., Blaine Williams/VP - Marketing, John L. Indest/Dir., Sec., COO, Pres., Daryl Doise/Sr. VP - Corporate Development, Don Stelly/Sr. VP - Operations, Randy Smith/VP - Corporate

Development, Liz Regard/Mgr. - Area Operations, Peter J. Roman/CFO, Sr. VP, Denise H. Romano/Chief Compliance Officer, Morris Sanford/CIO, VP, Albert Simien/VP - Procurement, Liz Starr/VP - Operations, Sr. Analyst, Home Based Services, Jimmy Steinocher/Dir. - Customer Service, Employee Retention *(40 Officers included in Index)*

Directors: Keith G. Myers/Chmn., CEO, John L. Indest/Dir., Sec., COO, Pres., Monica Azare/Dir., Nancy G. Brinker/61/Dir., W. J. Tauzin/Dir., John B. Breaux/Dir., Dan S. Wilford/Dir., George A. Lewis/Dir., Ted W. Hoyt/Dir., Ronald T. Nixon/Dir.

Owners: Fidelity Management & Research/7.40%, John B. Breaux, Keith G. Myers/17.50%, Ronald T. Nixon, John L. Indest, W.J. Tauzin, Daryl J. Doise, Donald D. Stelly, Nancy G. Brinker, George A. Lewis, Dan S. Wilford, Richard A. MacMillan, AllianceBernstein L.P./6.30%, Insiders/19.40%, Barry E. Stewart *(16 Owners included in Index)*

Financial Data: Fiscal Year End:12/31 Latest Annual Data: 12/31/2006

Year	Sales	Net Income
2006	$215,248,000	$20,594,000
2005	$162,549,000	$10,102,000
2004	$122,980,000	$9,313,000

Curr. Assets:	$90,051,000	Curr. Liab.:	$21,607,000	P/E Ratio:	19.63
Plant, Equip.:	$11,705,000	Total Liab.:	$30,805,000	Indic. Yr. Divd.:	NA
Total Assets:	$152,694,000	Net Worth:	$121,889,000	Debt/ Equity:	0.0244

Libbey Inc

300 Madison Ave., Toledo, OH, 43604; **PH:** 1-419-325-2100; **Fax:** 1-419-325-2117; **http://** www.libbey.com; **Email:** info@libbey.com

General - Incorporation	DE	Stock - Price on:12/24/2007	$22.65
Employees	7,150	Stock Exchange	NYSE
Auditor	Ernst & Young LLP	Ticker Symbol	LBY
Stk Agt	Bank of New York	Outstanding Shares	14,400,000
Counsel	NA	E.P.S.	-$0.41
DUNS No.	15-284-5202	Shareholders	NA

Business: The group's principal activities are to manufacture, design and market machine-made glass tableware, ceramic dinnerware and metal flatware. Glass tableware products include tumblers, stemware, mugs, plates, bowls, ashtrays, bud vases, salt and pepper shakers, canisters, candle holders and various other items. Ceramic dinnerware products include plates, bowls, platters, cups, saucers and other tableware accessories. Metal flatware products include knives, forks, spoons and serving utensils. The group also imports and sells flatware, hollowware and ceramic dinnerware through its subsidiary world tableware. It conducts its operations in the United States and Canada. The products are sold to a broad range of customers in the food service, retail and industrial and premium sectors and exported to more than seventy-five countries.

Primary SIC and add'l.: 3229

CIK No: 0000902274

Subsidiaries: B.V. Koninklijke Nederlandsche Glasfabriek Leerdam, B.V. Leerdam Crystal, Crisal Cristalaria Automatica, S.A., LGA3 Corp., LGA4 Corp., LGAC LLC, LGC Corp., LGFS Inc., Libbey Asia Limited, Libbey Canada Inc., Libbey Europe B.V., Libbey Glass Inc., Libbey Glassware (China) Co., Ltd., Libbey.com LLC, Syracuse China Company 18 Subsidiaries included in the Index

Officers: John F. Meier/Chmn., CEO/$1,290,923.00, Richard I. Reynolds/Dir., Exec. VP, COO/$819,436.00, Jonathan S. Freeman/VP - Global Supply Chain, Gregory T. Geswein/CFO, VP

Directors: John F. Meier/Chmn., CEO, Carlos V. Duno/Dir., William A. Foley/Dir., Peter C. Howell/Dir., Richard I. Reynolds/Dir., Exec. VP, COO, Deborah G. Miller/Dir., Carol B. Moerdyk/Dir., Terence P. Stewart/Dir., Gary L. Moreau/Dir., Jean-Rene Gougelet/Dir.

Owners: William A. Foley, Insiders/6.30%, Terence P. Stewart, John F. Meier/1.90%, Daniel P. Ibele, Peter C. McC. Howell, Gary L. Moreau, FMR Corp./9.82%, Carol B. Moerdyk, Dimensional Fund Advisors LP/7.08%, Scott M. Sellick, Carlos V. Duno, Kenneth G. Wilkes, Deborah G. Miller, Zesiger Capital Group LLC/13.90% *(16 Owners included in Index)*

Financial Data: Fiscal Year End:12/31 Latest Annual Data: 12/31/2006

Year	Sales	Net Income
2006	$692,401,000	-$20,899,000
2005	$570,065,000	-$19,355,000
2004	$546,797,000	$8,252,000

Curr. Assets:	$320,844,000	Curr. Liab.:	$153,587,000		
Plant, Equip.:	$321,520,000	Total Liab.:	$790,281,000	Indic. Yr. Divd.:	$0.100
Total Assets:	$878,131,000	Net Worth:	$87,850,000	Debt/ Equity:	5.6182

Liberate Technologies

310 University Ave., Ste. 201, Palo Alto, CA, 94301; **PH:** 1-650-330-8960; **http://** www.liberate.com

General - Incorporation	DE	Stock - Price on:12/24/2007	$0.059
Employees	NA	Stock Exchange	OTC
Auditor	PricewaterhouseCoopers LLP	Ticker Symbol	LBTE
Stk Agt	NA	Outstanding Shares	NA
Counsel	Skadden, Meagher & Flom LLP	E.P.S.	NA
DUNS No.	NA	Shareholders	NA

Business: The group's principal activity is to provide digital infrastructure software and services for cable networks. The group's open-platform software for digital services automation allows network operators to manage video, voice and data on high-capacity digital networks. Its software also supports services such as interactive and enhanced TV, on-demand video, service management and provisioning of voice and high-speed data communications. The group's software platforms are used by network operators such as cable and satellite television operators and telecommunications companies, broadcasters, content providers and manufacturers of information-oriented consumer devices. Customers include ntl, telewest, aol, comcast, cogeco cable, essent kabelcom and others. The group operates through offices located in the United States, Canada, Europe, Asia and Australia. In fiscal 2003, the group sold bill-care, a business unit of sigma systems.

Primary SIC and add'l.: 7372 7371

CIK No: 0001085776

Subsidiaries: Liberate Technologies B.V., Liberate Technologies Canada Ltd, Liberate Technologies LLC

Financial Data: Fiscal Year End:05/31 Latest Annual Data: 5/31/2005

Year	Sales	Net Income
2005	$2,344,000	$46,940,000
2002	$80,323,000	-$325,011,000
2001	$51,709,000	-$306,438,000

Curr. Assets:	$54,958,000	Curr. Liab.:	$16,146,000		
Plant, Equip.:	$422,000	Total Liab.:	$43,789,000	Indic. Yr. Divd.:	NA
Total Assets:	$59,739,000	Net Worth:	$15,950,000	Debt/ Equity:	NA

Liberty Bancorp Inc

16 W Franklin St., Liberty, MO, 64068; **PH:** 1-816-781-4822; **Fax:** 1-816-781-6851; **http://** www.libertysb.com

General - Incorporation	MO	Stock - Price on:12/24/2007	$11.38
Employees	NA	Stock Exchange	NDQ
Auditor	Michael Trokey & Company, P.C.	Ticker Symbol	LBCP
Stk Agt	Liberty Transfer Co	Outstanding Shares	NA
Counsel	Muldoon Murphy & Aguggia LLP	E.P.S.	$0.42
DUNS No.	NA	Shareholders	NA

Business: The groups principal activity is to provide banking services. The products of the group include commercial, consumer, construction, single-family residential real estate lending. The group operates from the United States.

Primary SIC and add'l.: 6712 6035

CIK No: 0001353268

Subsidiaries: BankLiberty

Officers: Brent M. Giles/40/Dir., CEO, Pres., Steven K. Havens/57/Dir., Sec., Treasurer, James Shevling/VP - Commercial Lending, Gary Shriver/Assist. VP - Commercial Lending, Bankliberty, Dan Gutshall/VP - Commercial Lending, Imelda MacKen/Assist. VP, Gladstone Branch Mgr. - Bankliberty, Marc Weishaar/Sr. VP, CFO, Martin Weishaar/Sr. VP, General Counsel, Ken Honeck/Sr. VP - Retail Banking, Joe Pickett/VP, Liberty Area Mgr., Tara Wehri/Assist. VP, Platte City Branch Mgr. - Bankliberty, Susan Tolle/Assist. VP, Plattsburg Branch Mgr. - Bankliberty, Shawna Croucher/Assist. VP, Independence Branch Mgr. - Bankliberty, Debbie Kincaid/Assist. VP, Boardwalk Branch Mgr. - Bankliberty, Mark Hecker/Sr. VP, Chief Lending Officer - Bankliberty *(19 Officers included in Index)*

Directors: Brent M. Giles/40/Dir., CEO, Pres., Daniel G. Odell/53/Chmn., Steven K. Havens/57/Dir., Sec., Treasurer, Marvin J. Weishaar/75/Dir. Emeritus, Robert T. Sevier/67/Dir., Ralph W. Brant/60/Dir.

Owners: Robert T. Sevier/4.30%, Amended and Restated Liberty Savings Bank/6.30%, Brent M. Giles/2.40%, Ralph W. Brant/2.80%, Mark E. Hecker, Marc J. Weishaar, Daniel G. ODell/5.40%, Marvin J. Weishaar/1.70%, Steven K. Havens/3.30%, Insiders/27.20%

Financial Data: Fiscal Year End:09/30 Latest Annual Data: 09/30/2007

Year	Sales	Net Income
2007	$22,041,000	$1,944,000
2006	$17,901,000	$1,463,000

Curr. Assets:	$14,890,000	Curr. Liab.:	$236,396,000		
Plant, Equip.:	$8,280,000	Total Liab.:	$238,580,000	Indic. Yr. Divd.:	NA
Total Assets:	$287,561,000	Net Worth:	$48,982,000	Debt/ Equity:	NA

Liberty Bancorp Inc CA

500 Linden Ave., South San Francisco, CA, 94080; **PH:** 1-650-871-2400; **Fax:** 1-650-871-0345; **http://** www.libertybk.com; **Email:** support@libertybk.com

General - Incorporation	NA	Stock - Price on:12/24/2007	$36.85
Employees	NA	Stock Exchange	OTC
Auditor	NA	Ticker Symbol	LIBC
Stk Agt	Mellon Investor Services LLC	Outstanding Shares	NA
Counsel	NA	E.P.S.	NA
DUNS No.	NA	Shareholders	NA

Business: The groups principal activity is to provide banking service. The services of the group include personal account, business account, originating loans, deposit, wire transfer, safe deposit boxes, automatic teller machine, direct deposit, night depository, payroll services, merchant teller booth and phone and online banking. The group operates from the United States.

Primary SIC and add'l.: 6022 6162

CIK No:

Officers: Larry W. Woods/Dir., CEO, Pres., Lowell G. Hallock/Exec. VP, Chief Lending Officer, Thomas M. Amendola/Sr. VP, CFO, Lety Delgadillo/Accounting Representative, South San Francisco, Frances Holbrook/Accounting Representative, Boulder Creek, Mimi Tawasha/Accounting Representative, Palo Alto, Karen Edwards/Operations Mgr., Vanessa A. Slagboom/VP, Administrative Officer, Lynn S. Francisco/VP, Information Technology Mgr., Barbara E. Ziegler/VP, Central Operations Support Mgr., Debra R. Watkins/Assist. VP - Business Development, Romel Carsola/VP, Sr. Operations Officer, Ariella Fioranelli/Assist. VP, Controller, Kathleen Aschero Aronson/Corp. Sec., Jackie Mar/Loans Operations Officer *(23 Officers included in Index)*

Directors: Larry W. Woods/Dir., CEO, Pres., John M. Cullison/Chmn., John B. De Nault/Vice Chmn., John B. De Nault/Dir., Kenneth J. De Nault/Dir., Joel P. Michel/Dir., Stephanie Uccelli-Menner/Dir., Robert E. Locatelli/Dir., Michael Scarborough/Dir.

Liberty Bell Bank NJ

2099 Rte. 70 E, Cherry Hill, NJ, 08003; **PH:** 1-856-489-8401; **Fax:** 1-856-489-8405; **http://** www.libertybellbank.com

General - Incorporation	NA	Stock - Price on:12/24/2007	$6
Employees	NA	Stock Exchange	NDQ
Auditor	NA	Ticker Symbol	LBBB
Stk Agt	StockTrans, Inc.	Outstanding Shares	2,690,000
Counsel	NA	E.P.S.	NA
DUNS No.	NA	Shareholders	NA

Business: The groups principal activity is to provide banking services. The groups services include checking, money market, savings account and certificates of deposit. The group operates from the United States.

Primary SIC and add'l.: 6022

CIK No:

Officers: Kevin Kutcher/Dir., CEO, Pres., Arthur Olson/Chief Lending Officer, Exec. VP, Silvana Milelli/Deposit, Retail Operations, Sr. VP, Brian Schaeffer/CTO, Sr. VP, John Herring/Sr. Lending Officer, Sr. VP

Directors: Kevin Kutcher/Dir., CEO, Pres., William Dunkelberg/Chmn., Jeff Altman/Dir., Roy Fazio/Dir., Vito Germinario/Dir., Dean Kaplan/Dir., Rita Kaplan/Dir., Joyce Petrini/Dir., Michael Ruccolo/Dir., James Tamburro/Dir., Ronald Henkel/Dir.

Liberty Diversified Holdings Inc

2100 N Orange Mall, Orange, CA, 92865; *PH:* 1-949-376-4846;
http:// www.libertydiversifiedholdings.com; *Email:* info@libertydiversifiedholdings.com

General - Incorporation	NV	Stock- Price on:12/24/2007	NA
Employees	NA	Stock Exchange	OTC
Auditor	Chisholm Bierwolf & Nilson, LLC	Ticker Symbol	LDHG
Stk Agt	NA	Outstanding Shares	NA
Counsel	NA	E.P.S.	NA
DUNS No.	NA	Shareholders	NA

Business: The groups principle activities include acquiring and developing subsidiaries. In December 2005, the group acquired MCR Printing and Packaging Corporation. The group operates from the United States.

Primary SIC and add'l.: 2752

CIK No: 0000355168

Subsidiaries: MCR Printing and Packaging Corporation, Packaging City, Inc.

Officers: Ronald C. Touchard/Co - Chmn., CEO, Wayne Bailey/CFO, Michael Brown/Pres.

Directors: Ronald C. Touchard/Co - Chmn., CEO

Owners: Insiders/35.80%, Ronald C. Touchard/3.50%, Ronald C. Touchard/46.90%, Wayne Bailey/47.30%, Michael Brown/3.20%, Wayne Bailey/10.70%, Insiders/9.90%, Insiders/47.30%, Michael Brown/18.70%, Wayne Bailey/3.20%

Financial Data: Fiscal Year End:12/31 Latest Annual Data: 12/31/2006

Year	Sales	Net Income
2006	$1,000	-$14,419,000
2005	$484,000	-$3,937,000
2004	$1,314,000	-$2,993,000

Curr. Assets:	$102,000	Curr. Liab.:	$389,000		
Plant, Equip.:	$107,000	Total Liab.:	$597,000	Indic. Yr. Divd.:	NA
Total Assets:	$362,000	Net Worth:	-$236,000	Debt/ Equity:	NA

Liberty Global Inc

12300 Liberty Blvd., Englewood, CO, 80112; *PH:* 1-303-220-6600; *Fax:* 1-303-220-6601;
http:// www.lgi.com; *Email:* info@lgi.com

General - Incorporation	DE	Stock- Price on:12/24/2007	$40.47
Employees	20,500	Stock Exchange	NDQ
Auditor	KPMG LLP	Ticker Symbol	LBTYA
Stk Agt	Computershare Trust Co	Outstanding Shares	383,940,000
Counsel	NA	E.P.S.	$0.74
DUNS No.	NA	Shareholders	NA

Business: The groups principle activity is to provide broadband communications services. The groups services include video, voice and broadband Internet access. In the year 205, the group acquires Cablecom, Astral Telecom SA, NTL Ireland, Austar United. The group operates from Netherlands, Austria, Switzerland, Ireland, Belgium, Hungary, Romania, Poland and Slovenia. The groups operates through three segments namely Western Europe, Central and Eastern Europe, and Central and corporate operations. The group's quarterly revenue for September 2007 was 2,255.30 millions of USD.

Primary SIC and add'l.: 4899 7389 4841 4813

CIK No: 0001316631

Subsidiaries: @NetHome Co., Ltd., Artson System Pty Ltd., Asia Television Advertising LLC, Asia Television Communications International LLC, Associated SMR, Inc., At Media Sp. z o.o., Austar Entertainment Pty Ltd., Austar Satellite Pty Ltd., Austar Satellite Ventures Pty Ltd., Austar Services Pty Ltd., Austar United Broadband Pty Ltd., Austar United Communications Ltd., Austar United Holdcol Pty Ltd., Austar United Licenceco Pty Ltd., Austar United Mobility Pty Ltd. 331 Subsidiaries included in the Index

Officers: Michael T. Fries/Dir., CEO, Pres., Mauricio Ramos/CEO - VTR Global Com SA, Pres. - Liberty Global Latin America, Frederick G. Westerman/Sr. VP - Investor Relations, Corporate Communications, Bob Leighton/Sr. VP - Programming, Balan Nair/CTO, Sr. VP, Amy M. Blair/Sr. VP - Global Human Resources, Charles H.R. Bracken/Co - CFO, Principal Financial Officer, Sr. VP, Miranda Curtis/Pres. - Liberty Global Japan, Bernard G. Dvorak/Co - CFO, Principal Accounting Officer, Sr. VP, Elizabeth M. Markowski/Sr. VP, Sec., General Counsel, Gene M. Musselman/COO, Pres. - UPC Broadband, Shane O'Neill/Chief Strategy Officer, Pres. - Chellomedia, Sr. VP

Directors: Michael T. Fries/Dir., CEO, Pres., John C. Malone/Chmn., John P. Cole/Dir., John W. Dick/Dir., Paul A. Gould/Dir., David E. Rapley/Dir., Larry E. Romrell/Dir., Gene W. Schneider/Dir., J. C. Sparkman/Dir., David J. Wargo/Dir.

Owners: Larry E. Romrell, John C. Malone, Michael T. Fries, John P. Cole, Shane O'Neill, Insiders/2.50%, Gene W. Musselman, J. C. Sparkman, John W. Dick, Janus Capital Management LLC/1.90%, Michael T. Fries, Paul A. Gould, David E. Rapley, Insiders/6.60%, Gene W. Schneider *(37 Owners included in Index)*

Financial Data: Fiscal Year End:12/31 Latest Annual Data: 12/31/2006

Year	Sales	Net Income
2006	$6,487,500,000	$706,200,000
2005	$5,151,332,000	-$80,097,000

Curr. Assets:	$3,562,500,000	Curr. Liab.:	$3,744,700,000	P/E Ratio:	109.38
Plant, Equip.:	$8,136,900,000	Total Liab.:	$16,410,700,000	Indic. Yr. Divd.:	NA
Total Assets:	$25,569,300,000	Net Worth:	$7,247,100,000	Debt/ Equity:	1.8067

Liberty Media LLC

Formerly: Liberty Media Corp
12300 Liberty Blvd., Englewood, CO, 80112; *PH:* 1-720-875-5400; *http://* www.libertymedia.com

General - Incorporation	DE	Stock- Price on:12/24/2007	NA
Employees	NA	Stock Exchange	NDQ
Auditor	KPMG LLP	Ticker Symbol	LCAPA
Stk Agt	Computershare Investor Services LLC	Outstanding Shares	NA
Counsel	NA	E.P.S.	NA
DUNS No.	NA	Shareholders	NA

Business: The groups principle activity is to provide electronic retailing, video programming, broadband distribution and other communication services. The group operates from United States, Europe and South America.

Primary SIC and add'l.: 7372 4833 4841 4899 4832 6719

CIK No: 0001082114

Subsidiaries: 1227844 Ontario Ltd., 4G Media Ltd., ACTV Entertainment,Inc., ACTV Intellocity GmbH, ACTV International BV, ACTV,Inc., Advision, LLC, AEI Music Network,Inc., Affiliate Investment,Inc., Affiliate Marks Investments,Inc., Affiliate Relations Holdings,Inc., Affiliate Sales& Marketing,Inc., Aries Pictures LLC, Ascent Entertainment Group,Inc., Associated Information Services Corporation 353 Subsidiaries included in the Index

Officers: Gregory B. Maffei/Dir., CEO, Pres., Christopher W. Shean/Sr. VP, Controller, David J.A. Flowers/Sr. VP, Treasurer, Charles Y. Tanabe/Exec. VP, Sec., General Counsel

Directors: Gregory B. Maffei/Dir., CEO, Pres., John C. Malone/Chmn., Robert R. Bennett/Dir., Donne F. Fisher/Dir., David E. Rapley/Dir., Lavoy M. Robison/Dir., Larry E. Romrell/Dir., Paul A. Gould/Dir.

Liberty Mint Ltd

378 N, Ste. 124, Layton, UT, 84061; *PH:* 1-801-497-9075; *http://* www.akesis.com

General - Incorporation	NV	Stock- Price on:12/24/2007	$0.47
Employees	2	Stock Exchange	NA
Auditor	Swenson Advisors LLP	Ticker Symbol	NA
Stk Agt	Colorado to Interwest Trnsfer Co	Outstanding Shares	22,580,000
Counsel	NA	E.P.S.	-$0.08
DUNS No.	NA	Shareholders	NA

Business: The group's principle activity is to seek new business opportunity. It is reviewing various business plans to merge with or acquire. The company previously operated through two subsidiaries, gwm and sccs. Gwm provided custom minting services for corporations, associations, government agencies and other organizations. Sccs created and marketed licensed entertainment and sports related collectibles. On 31-Dec-2001, the company disposed these subsidiaries. The group operates from United States.

Primary SIC and add'l.: 5094

CIK No: 0001042420

Subsidiaries: Liberty Mint Marketing, Inc, Liberty Mint, Inc, Liberty Mint, Ltd, The Great Western Mint, Inc

Officers: Jay Lichter/Dir., CEO, Pres./$481,927.00, John T. Hendrick/CFO/$167,538.00

Directors: Jay Lichter/Dir., CEO, Pres., Kevin R. Sayer/Dir., John F. Steel/Dir., Kevin J. Kinsella/Dir., Chris Orvig/Member - Scientific Advisory Board, John H. McNeill/Member - Scientific Advisory Board, Michael C. Scaife/Member - Scientific Advisory Board

Owners: Insiders, Gary R. Keeling, Kevin J. Kinsella, Avalon Ventures VII, L.P., Kevin R. Sayer, Jay B. Lichter, John F. Steel, John T. Hendrick, Edward B. Wilson, SFLL Fine Family Investments Partnership, L.P., Kelly Joy

Financial Data: Fiscal Year End:12/31 Latest Annual Data: 12/31/2006

Year	Sales	Net Income
2006	NA	-$1,358,000
2005	NA	-$3,106,000
2004	NA	-$1,526,000

Curr. Assets:	$4,114,000	Curr. Liab.:	$140,000		
Plant, Equip.:	NA	Total Liab.:	$140,000	Indic. Yr. Divd.:	NA
Total Assets:	$4,199,000	Net Worth:	$4,059,000	Debt/ Equity:	NA

Liberty Property Trust

500 Chesterfield Pkwy., Malvern, PA, 19355; *PH:* 1-610-648-1700; *Fax:* 1-610-644-4129;
http:// www.libertyproperty.com

General - Incorporation	MD	Stock- Price on:12/24/2007	$43.34
Employees	474	Stock Exchange	NYSE
Auditor	Ernst & Young LLP	Ticker Symbol	LRY
Stk Agt	Wells Fargo Bank, N.A.	Outstanding Shares	91,960,000
Counsel	NA	E.P.S.	$2.37
DUNS No.	NA	Shareholders	NA

Business: The groups principle activity is to provide leasing, property management, development, acquisition and other tenant-related services for the properties in operation. The group operates through geographic segments. In the year 2006, the group acquired 23 properties. The group operates from the United States and the United Kingdom. The group's quarterly revenue for September 2007 was 177.82 millions of USD.

Primary SIC and add'l.: 6798

CIK No: 0000921112

Subsidiaries: 9755 Patuxent Woods Drive Trust, Beaufighter Unit Trust, Cambridge Medipark Limited, Hurricane Unit Trust, iCo Didsbury Limited, Kings Hill Estate Management Company Limited, Kings Hill Property Management Limited, Kings Hill Residential Estate Management Company Limited, Kings Hill Unit Trust, L/S 4775 League Island Blvd., LLC, L/S 4775 League Island Blvd., LP, L/S One Crescent Drive, LLC, L/S One Crescent Drive, LP, Land Holdings Realty LLC, Liberty 600 Industrial, G.P. 57 Subsidiaries included in the Index

Officers: William P. Hankowsky/Trustee, Chmn., CEO, Pres./$1,637,507.00, Claire Cahill/CEO, Pres., Exec. Assist. to Chmn., Joe Denny/Sr. Advisor to Chmn., Joseph P. Denny/Sr. Advisor to Chmn., John N. Divall/Sr. VP, City Mgr., Massie Flippin/VP, City Mgr., John Gattuso/Sr. VP, Dir. - National, Urban Development, Laurie Brown/Sr. VP, Shelby Christensen/Sr. VP, National Dir. - Property Management, Nicholas Condon/Project Dir., Craig Cope/VP, City Mgr., Lawrence D. Gildea/Sr. VP, Regional Dir. - Tampa, Mark Goldstein/VP, City Mgr., Michael Heise/VP, City Mgr. *(434 Officers included in Index)*

Directors: William P. Hankowsky/Trustee, Chmn., CEO, Pres., Willard G. Rouse/Founder, Chmn., Daniel P. Garton/Trustee, Stephen B. Siegel/Trustee, David L. Lingerfelt/Trustee, John A. Miller/Trustee, Jose A. Mejia/Trustee, Anthony J. Hayden/Trustee, Leanne M. Lachman/Trustee, Frederick F. Buchholz/Trustee, Thomas C. Deloach/Trustee

Owners: George J. Alburger, Robert E. Fenza, Leanne M. Lachman, The Vanguard Group, Inc./5.40%, Morgan Stanley/5.50%, ING Groep N.V./9.30%, Michael T. Hagan, Cohen& Steers, Inc./14.20%, David L. Lingerfelt, Frederick F. Buchholz, Thomas C. DeLoach, Anthony J. Hayden, Daniel P. Garton, Barclays Global Investors, NA/5.70%, John A. Miller *(20 Owners included in Index)*

Financial Data: Fiscal Year End:12/31 Latest Annual Data: 12/31/2006

Year	Sales	Net Income
2006	$666,719,000	$266,574,000
2005	$680,730,000	$249,351,000
2004	$655,355,000	$161,443,000

Curr. Assets:	$133,217,000	**Curr. Liab.:**	$135,891,000	**P/E Ratio:**	18.29
Plant, Equip.:	$4,460,553,000	**Total Liab.:**	$3,039,307,000	**Indic. Yr. Divd.:**	$2.480
Total Assets:	$4,910,911,000	**Net Worth:**	$1,871,604,000	**Debt/ Equity:**	1.3484

Liberty Star Uranium & Metals Corp

Formerly: Liberty Star Gold Corp
3024 E Ft. Lowell Rd., Tucson, AZ, 85716; ***PH:*** 1-520-731-8786; ***http://*** www.libertystargold.com

General - Incorporation .... NV
Employees .... NA
Auditor .... Semple, Marchal & Cooper, LLP
Stk Agt............ Nevada Agency & Trust Company
Counsel .... NA
DUNS No. .... NA

Stock- Price on:12/24/2007 .... NA
Stock Exchange .... NA
Ticker Symbol .... NA
Outstanding Shares .... NA
E.P.S .... -$0.116
Shareholders .... NA

Business: The groups principal activities include acquiring and exploring mineral properties. The group operates from the United States.

Primary SIC and add'l.: 1000

CIK No: 0001172178

Subsidiaries: Big Chunk Corp

Officers: James A. Briscoe/Chmn., CEO, Pres., Jon Young/Dir., CFO, Gary Musil/Sec.

Directors: James A. Briscoe/Chmn., CEO, Pres., Jon Young/Dir., CFO, John M. Guilbert/Dir., Member - Technical Advisory Board, Jan Klein/Member - Technical Advisory Board, Shea Clark Smith/Member - Technical Advisory Board, Michael J. Schaefer/Member - Technical Advisory Board, Karen Wenrich/Member - Technical Advisory Board, Philip George/49/Dir.

Owners: Platinum Partners Long Term Growth VI, Bridgepointe Master Fund, Ltd., Gary Musil, Cede & Co., Alpha Capital Anstalt, Jon Young, James Briscoe, John Guilbert, Insiders

Financial Data: *Fiscal Year End:*01/31 *Latest Annual Data:* 1/31/2007

Year	Sales	Net Income
2007	NA	-$3,268,000
2006	NA	-$4,628,000
2005	NA	-$18,392,000

Curr. Assets:	$750,000	**Curr. Liab.:**	$146,000		
Plant, Equip.:	$347,000	**Total Liab.:**	$197,000	**Indic. Yr. Divd.:**	NA
Total Assets:	$1,100,000	**Net Worth:**	$903,000	**Debt/ Equity:**	NA

Life Medical Sciences Inc

200 Middlesex Essex Tpke., Ste. 210, Iselin, NJ, 08830; ***PH:*** 1-732-404-1117

General - Incorporation .... DE
Employees 4
Auditor .... Eisner LLP
Stk Agt..... Computershare Investor Services LLC
Counsel....Rubin Baum Levin Constant Friedman
DUNS No. 80-305-0384

Stock- Price on:12/24/2007 .... $0.88
Stock Exchange .... NA
Ticker Symbol .... NA
Outstanding Shares 83,760,000
E.P.S .... -$0.05
Shareholders .... NA

Business: The group's principle activities include developing and marketing medical products for therapeutic applications. The products of the company are designed to prevent or reduce the formation of adhesions (scar tissue) following a broad range of surgical procedures. These products are targeted to various segments in the medical community, including physicians, surgeons, and other care providers. The products repel, repel-cv, resolve and relieve are in various stages of development and prevent open heart, gynecological, orthopaedic and spinal surgeries. The group operates from United States.

Primary SIC and add'l.: 2834 3841 3842

CIK No: 0000889428

Subsidiaries: Dimotech Ltd., Technion Research and Development Foundation Ltd

Officers: Robert P. Hickey/62/Dir., CEO, CFO, Pres./$654,800.00, Eli Pines/VP, Chief Scientific Officer/$464,000.00

Directors: Robert P. Hickey/62/Dir., CEO, CFO, Pres., Richard L. Franklin/62/Chmn., Barry R. Frankel/57/Dir., David G.P. Allan/66/Dir., Edward A. Celano/Dir., Walter R. Maupay/68/Dir.

Owners: Eli Pines/2.30%, Walter R. Maupay/1.10%, Robert P. Hickey/4.40%, Richard L. Franklin/3.70%, Insiders/18.30%, Barry R. Frankel/0.40%, Edward A. Celano/0.80%, Joerg Gruber/6.80%, David G. P. Allan/1.00%

Financial Data: *Fiscal Year End:*12/31 *Latest Annual Data:* 12/31/2006

Year	Sales	Net Income
2006	$142,000	-$3,895,000
2005	NA	-$2,148,000
2004	$23,000	-$1,841,000

Curr. Assets:	$3,923,000	**Curr. Liab.:**	$851,000		
Plant, Equip.:	$166,000	**Total Liab.:**	$851,000	**Indic. Yr. Divd.:**	NA
Total Assets:	$4,178,000	**Net Worth:**	$3,327,000	**Debt/ Equity:**	NA

Life Partners Holdings Inc

204 Woodhew, Waco, TX, 76712; ***PH:*** 1-254-751-7797; ***Fax:*** 1-254-751-1025; ***http://*** www.lphi.net; ***Email:*** questions@lifepartnersinc.com

General - Incorporation .... TX
Employees 37
Auditor ..... Murrell, Hall, McIntosh & Co., PLLP
Stk Agt..... American Stock Transfer & Trust CO.
Counsel .... NA
DUNS No. 09-286-4719

Stock- Price on:12/24/2007 .... $34.58
Stock Exchange .... NDQ
Ticker Symbol .... LPHI
Outstanding Shares 9,590,000
E.P.S $1.01
Shareholders .... NA

Business: The group's principal activity is to match viators with viatical settlement purchasers. The group also undertakes senior life settlement transactions. A viatical settlement is the sale of a life insurance policy by a terminally ill person to another party. By selling the policy, the insured (a viator) receives an immediate cash payment to use as he or she wishes. The purchaser takes an ownership interest in the policy at a discount to its face value and receives the death benefit under the policy when the viator dies. In the senior life settlement transactions the group assists elderly individuals to reallocate their assets from insurance policies into assets used for long-term care coverage, annuities and investments.

Primary SIC and add'l.: 6411

CIK No: 0000049534

Subsidiaries: Life Partners, Inc., LPHI Portfolio Management Services, LLC, LPHI Preferred Private Issue Series I, LLC

Officers: Brian D. Pardo/64/CEO/$550,233.00, Scott R. Peden/44/General Counsel, Sec./$167,956.00, Mark Embry/51/COO, CIO - Life Partners, Inc/$152,610.00, Kurt D. Carr/38/VP - Policy Administration, Life Partners, Inc, Nina Piper/CFO, Treasurer

Directors: Tad M. Ballantyne/53/Dir., Fred Dewald/63/Dir., Harold E. Rafuse/66/Dir.

Owners: Pardo Family Holdings, Ltd, Brian D. Pardo, Insiders, Fred Dewald, Scott R. Peden

Financial Data: *Fiscal Year End:*02/28 *Latest Annual Data:* 2/28/2007

Year	Sales	Net Income
2007	$29,795,000	$3,641,000
2006	$20,084,000	$1,144,000
2005	$18,746,000	$2,683,000

Curr. Assets:	$12,702,000	**Curr. Liab.:**	$8,544,000	**P/E Ratio:**	46.11
Plant, Equip.:	$1,303,000	**Total Liab.:**	$8,894,000	**Indic. Yr. Divd.:**	$0.250
Total Assets:	$16,599,000	**Net Worth:**	$7,706,000	**Debt/ Equity:**	NA

Life Time Fitness Inc

6442 City W Pkwy., Eden Prairie, MN, 55344; ***PH:*** 1-952-947-0000; ***Fax:*** 1-952-947-9137; ***http://*** www.lifetimefitness.com

General - Incorporation .... MN
Employees 4,400
Auditor .... Deloitte & Touche LLP
Stk Agt .... Wells Fargo Bank, N.A.
Counsel .... NA
DUNS No. .... NA

Stock- Price on:12/24/2007 .... $55.2435
Stock Exchange .... NYSE
Ticker Symbol .... LTM
Outstanding Shares 37,080,000
E.P.S $1.69
Shareholders .... NA

Business: The group's principal activity is to operate sports, athletic, fitness and family recreation centers. It designs and develops centers and provides customers with products and in the areas of exercise, education and nutrition. In addition to traditional health club offerings, the centers also include swimming pools with water slides, basketball and racquet courts, interactive and entertaining child centers, full-service spas, dining services, climbing walls and outdoor swimming pools. The group operates under the life time fitness(R) brand. As of Jun 5, 2004, the group operated 34 centers primarily in suburban locations across eight states in the United States.

Primary SIC and add'l.: 7997

CIK No: 0001076195

Subsidiaries: Bloomingdale LIFE TIME Fitness, LLC, FCA Construction Company, LLC, FCA Real Estate Holdings, LLC, FCA Restaurant Company, LLC, Life Time Fitness Foundation, LTF Club Management Company, LLC, LTF Club Operations Company, Inc., LTF Michigan Real Estate Company, LLC, LTF Minnesota Real Estate Company, LLC, LTF Operations Holdings, Inc., LTF Real Estate Company, Inc., LTF Real Estate Holdings, LLC, Ltf Tiaa Real Estate Holdings, LLC, LTF USA Real Estate Company, LLC, Ltfmf Az Real Estate, LLC 17 Subsidiaries included in the Index

Officers: Bahram Akradi/Founder, Chmn., CEO, Pres./$4,169,868.00, Eric J. Buss/Exec. VP, General Counsel, Sec./$628,086.00, Michael R. Robinson/CFO, Exec. VP/$941,046.00, Michael J. Gerend/COO, Exec. VP/$889,255.00, Mark L. Zaebst/Exec. VP - Real Estate Development/$663,043.00

Directors: Bahram Akradi/Founder, Chmn., CEO, Pres., Stephen R. Sefton/Dir., Giles H. Bateman/Dir., James F. Halpin/Dir., Guy C. Jackson/Dir., John B. Richards/Dir., Joseph S. Vassalluzzo/Dir.

Owners: Mark L. Zaebst, Michael J. Gerend, Giles H. Bateman, Guy C. Jackson, Stephen F. Rowland/1.50%, U.S. Trust Corporation/6.50%, Insiders/15.40%, Michael R. Robinson, John B. Richards, James F. Halpin, Stephen R. Sefton/1.20%, Joseph S. Vassalluzzo, Eric J. Buss, William Blair & Company, L.L.C/5.90%, Bahram Akradi/11.60%

Financial Data: *Fiscal Year End:*12/31 *Latest Annual Data:* 12/31/2006

Year	Sales	Net Income
2006	$511,897,000	$50,565,000
2005	$390,116,000	$41,213,000
2004	$312,033,000	$28,908,000

Curr. Assets:	$39,846,000	**Curr. Liab.:**	$140,355,000	**P/E Ratio:**	34.96
Plant, Equip.:	$907,777,000	**Total Liab.:**	$595,163,000	**Indic. Yr. Divd.:**	NA
Total Assets:	$987,676,000	**Net Worth:**	$392,513,000	**Debt/ Equity:**	1.0230

Lifecell Corp

1 Millennium Way, Branchburg, NJ, 08876; ***PH:*** 1-908-947-1100; ***Fax:*** 1-908-947-1200; ***http://*** www.lifecell.com

General - Incorporation .... DE
Employees 335
Auditor .... PricewaterhouseCoopers LLP
Stk Agt .... Computershare Investor Services LLC
Counsel .... NA
DUNS No. 15-722-4205

Stock- Price on:12/24/2007 .... $31.32
Stock Exchange .... NDQ
Ticker Symbol .... LIFC
Outstanding Shares 33,840,000
E.P.S $0.74
Shareholders .... NA

Business: The group's principle activities include developing and marketing biologically based solutions for the repair and replacement of damaged or inadequate human tissues in different clinical applications. The company's tissue matrix technology removes all cells from the tissue and preserves the tissue without damaging the essential biochemical and structural components necessary for normal tissue regeneration. The products of the company include: alloderm(R) for plastic reconstructive, burn and periodontal procedures; cymetra(tm) for non-surgical correction of soft tissue defects; repliform(tm) for urology and gynecology procedures; cryopreserved allograft skin for use as a temporary wound dressing in the treatment of burns; cymetra (R), a version of alloderm in particulate form; repliform(R) for urogynecologic procedures; graft jacket(R) for orthopedic applications and allocrat f (TM) dbm for bone grafting. The group operates from United States.

Primary SIC and add'l.: 8731 2836

CIK No: 0000849448

Officers: Paul G. Thomas/Chmn., CEO, Pres./$3,093,769.00, Lisa N. Colleran/Sr. VP - Commercial Operations/$1,246,281.00, Steven T. Sobieski/CFO, VP - Finance, Administration/$838,403.00, Bruce Lamb/Sr. VP - Development, Regulatory Affairs, Quality/$552,795.00, Bradly C. Tyler/Controller

Directors: Paul G. Thomas/Chmn., CEO, Pres., Michael E. Cahr/Dir., David Fitzgerald/Dir., James G. Foster/Dir., Michael R. Minogue/Dir., Robert P. Roche/Dir., Martin P. Sutter/Dir.

Owners: David Fitzgerald, Lisa N. Colleran, Robert P. Roche, Michael E. Cahr, Paul G. Thomas/1.30%, Insiders/3.50%, Samuel D. Isaly/10.10%, Michael R. Minogue, Steven T. Sobieski, James G. Foster, Martin P. Sutter, Eaton Vance Management/6.80%, Bruce Lamb

Financial Data: **Fiscal Year End:**12/31 **Latest Annual Data:** 12/31/2006

Year	Sales	Net Income
2006	$141,680,000	$20,469,000
2005	$94,398,000	$12,044,000
2004	$61,127,000	$7,184,000

Curr. Assets:	$122,533,000	**Curr. Liab.:**	$27,822,000		
Plant, Equip.:	$19,914,000	**Total Liab.:**	$27,822,000	**Indic. Yr. Divd.:**	NA
Total Assets:	$157,121,000	**Net Worth:**	$129,299,000	**Debt/ Equity:**	NA

Lifecore Biomedical Inc

3515 Lyman Blvd., Chaska, MN, 55318; ***PH:*** 1-952-368-4300; ***Fax:*** 1-952-368-3411; ***http://*** www.lifecore.com; ***Email:*** info@lifecore.com

General - Incorporation	MN	**Stock**- Price on:12/24/2007	$16.11
Employees	216	Stock Exchange	NDQ
Auditor	Grant Thornton LLP	Ticker Symbol	LCBM
Stk Agt	Wells Fargo Bank Minnesota N.A	Outstanding Shares	13,410,000
Counsel	Dorsey & Whitney LLP	E.P.S	$0.57
DUNS No.	08-535-8869	Shareholders	NA

Business: The group's principle activities are to manufacture biomaterials and medical devices for use in various surgical markets and to provide related specialized contract aseptic manufacturing services. The group operates in two divisions: the hyaluronan division and the oral restorative division. The hyaluronan division develops and manufactures products utilizing hyaluronan, a naturally occurring carbohydrate that moisturizes the body tissues. The products are marketed through OEM and contract manufacturing alliances in gynecologic and ophthalmologic surgery and veterinary medicine. The oral restorative division develops and markets precision surgical and prosthetic devices for the restoration of damaged dentition and associated support tissues and markets its products through direct sales in the United States, Italy, Germany, Sweden and through distributors in other foreign countries. The group's total revenue for year 2007 was 69.63 millions of USD.

Primary SIC and add'l.: 3841 3843 3842

CIK No: 0000028626

Subsidiaries: Implant Support Systems, Inc., Lifecore Biomedical GmbH, Lifecore Biomedical SpA, Lifecore Biomedical, AB, Lifecore Biomedical, SAS, Sustain, Inc.

Officers: Dennis J. Allingham/Dir., CEO, Pres., Sec., Larry D. Hiebert/VP, GM - Hyaluronan Division, David M. Noel/VP - Finance, CFO, Kipling Thacker/VP - New Business Development, James G. Hall/VP - Technical Operations

Directors: Dennis J. Allingham/Dir., CEO, Pres., Sec., John E. Runnells/Dir., Orwin L. Carter/Dir., Martin J. Emerson/Dir., Thomas H. Garrett/Dir., Luther T. Griffith/Dir., Richard W. Perkins/Dir.

Owners: John E. Runnells, Bank of America Corporation/5.10%, Richard W. Perkins/1.20%, The Vertical Group, L.P./6.60%, David M. Noel, Thomas H. Garrett, Martin J. Emerson, Dennis J. Allingham/2.30%, William Blair & Company, L.L.C./9.60%, Orwin L. Carter, Carnegie Investment Bank AB/7.90%, Kipling Thacker, Luther T. Griffith, James G. Hall, Larry D. Hiebert *(18 Owners included in Index)*

Financial Data: **Fiscal Year End:**06/30 **Latest Annual Data:** 6/30/2006

Year	Sales	Net Income
2006	$63,097,000	$7,040,000
2005	$55,221,000	$17,511,000
2004	$47,036,000	$707,000

Curr. Assets:	$71,937,000	**Curr. Liab.:**	$7,323,000		
Plant, Equip.:	$24,596,000	**Total Liab.:**	$12,801,000	**Indic. Yr. Divd.:**	NA
Total Assets:	$102,271,000	**Net Worth:**	$89,470,000	**Debt/ Equity:**	NA

Lifepoint Hospitals Inc

103 Powell Ct., Ste. 200, Brentwood, TN, 37027; ***PH:*** 1-615-372-8500; ***Fax:*** 1-615-372-8575; ***http://*** www.lifepointhospitals.com; ***Email:*** general.information@lifepointhospitals.com

General - Incorporation	DE	**Stock**- Price on:12/24/2007	$38.5
Employees	14,800	Stock Exchange	NDQ
Auditor	Ernst & Young LLP	Ticker Symbol	LPNT
Stk Agt	National City Bank	Outstanding Shares	57,730,000
Counsel	NA	E.P.S	$1.93
DUNS No.	NA	Shareholders	NA

Business: The groups principle activity is to provide healthcare services. The group operates from United States.

Primary SIC and add'l.: 6324 8062

CIK No: 0001074772

Subsidiaries: America Group Offices, LLC, America Management Companies, LLC, AMG - Crockett, LLC, AMG - Hilcrest, LLC, AMG - Hillside, LLC, AMG - Livingston, LLC, AMG - Logan, LLC, AMG - Southern Tennessee, LLC, AMG - Trinity, LLC, Ashley Valley Medical Center, LLC, Ashley Valley Physician Practice, LLC, Athens Physician Practice, LLC, Athens Regional Medical Center, LLC, Barrow Medical Center, LLC, Bartow General Partner, LLC 118 Subsidiaries included in the Index

Officers: William F. Carpenter/Dir., CEO, Pres., William M. Gracey/COO, Penny Brake/Investor Relations Officer, Todd Wiltsie/Contact - Physician Recruitment, David M. Dill/CFO, Melissa Clontz/Contact - Corporate, Exec. Recruitment

Directors: William F. Carpenter/Dir., CEO, Pres., Owen G. Shell/Chmn., John E. Maupin/Dir., Richard H. Evans/Dir., Dewitt Ezell/Dir., Michael P. Haley/Dir., William V. Lapham/Dir., Marguerite W. Kondracke/Dir.

Financial Data: **Fiscal Year End:**12/31 **Latest Annual Data:** 12/31/2006

Year	Sales	Net Income
2006	$2,439,700,000	$146,200,000
2005	$1,855,100,000	$72,900,000
2004	$996,900,000	$85,700,000

Curr. Assets:	$614,200,000	**Curr. Liab.:**	$303,100,000	**P/E Ratio:**	18.78
Plant, Equip.:	$1,373,600,000	**Total Liab.:**	$2,175,500,000	**Indic. Yr. Divd.:**	NA
Total Assets:	$3,638,400,000	**Net Worth:**	$1,450,000,000	**Debt/ Equity:**	1.1142

LifeSpan Inc

27 Oakmont Dr., Rancho Mirage, CA, 92270; ***PH:*** 1-866-883-9971; ***http://*** www.lifespanservices.org; ***Email:*** contactus@lifespanservices.org

General - Incorporation		**Stock**- Price on:12/24/2007	NA
Employees	NA	Stock Exchange	OTC
Auditor	P.Caob	Ticker Symbol	LSPN
Stk Agt	Liberty Transfer Co	Outstanding Shares	NA
Counsel	NA	E.P.S	-$0.01
DUNS No.	NA	Shareholders	NA

Business: The groups principle activity is to evaluate health care programs, products and systems. The group operates from the United States.

Primary SIC and add'l.: 8099 8090 8099

CIK No: 0001040839

Officers: Stuart Brame/61/Dir., CEO, Terrie Lee/Contact - Developmental Disabilities or Lifespan, Leigh Derby/Dir., Pres., Ralph Adams/Dir., CFO, Mitch Jackson/Boards Of Visitors - Mecklenburg County, Dana Hay/Boards Of Visitors - Mecklenburg County, Leigh Dyer/Boards Of Visitors - Mecklenburg County, John Cervantes/Boards Of Visitors - Mecklenburg County, Jennifer Frey Sternlieb/Contact - Lifespan at Joshua's Farm, Frances Gill/Contact - Lifespan Employment High Point, Merrill Lynch/Stock Donations, Brokerage, Rick Werner/Mecklenburg County, Boards Of Visitors, Michele Pfaff/Boards Of Visitors - Mecklenburg County, Kari Lawson/Boards Of Visitors - Mecklenburg County, Jeff Katz/Boards Of Visitors - Mecklenburg County *(52 Officers included in Index)*

Directors: Stuart Brame/61/Dir., CEO, Mary Lynne Calhoun/Chmn., Steve Byrum/Vice Chmn., Rhonda Kontos/Chmn. - Board Of Visitor, Iredell County, Doug Draughn/Chmn. - Board Of Visitor - Surry County, Suzanne Bowman/Member - Board Of Visitor, Surry County, Marcus Wever/Member - Board Of Visitor, Iredell County, Laura E. Wyly/Member - Board Of Visitor, Iredell County, Barry A. Lippard/Member - Board Of Visitor, Iredell County, Betty Marion/Member - Board Of Visitor, Iredell County, David Pressly/Member - Board Of Visitor, Iredell County, Shannon Sherfey/Member - Board Of Visitor, Iredell County, Carolyn Comer/Member - Board Of Visitor, Surry County, Ted Creed/Member - Board Of Visitor, Surry County, Jan Critz/Member - Board Of Visitor, Surry County *(84 Directors included in Index)*

Owners: Karl Harz/1.83%, Albert Cook/0.60%, William Blase/0.81%, Insiders/3.25%

Financial Data: **Fiscal Year End:**12/31 **Latest Annual Data:** 12/31/2006

Year	Sales	Net Income
2006	$3,000	-$588,000
2005	NA	-$324,000
2004	NA	-$1,075,000

Curr. Assets:	$0	**Curr. Liab.:**	$25,000		
Plant, Equip.:	NA	**Total Liab.:**	$25,000	**Indic. Yr. Divd.:**	NA
Total Assets:	$0	**Net Worth:**	-$25,000	**Debt/ Equity:**	NA

Lifestyle Innovations Inc

4700 Lakeshore Ct, Colleyville, TX, 76034; ***PH:*** 1-817-294-4000; ***http://*** www.lifestech.com

General - Incorporation	NV	**Stock**- Price on:12/24/2007	$0.004
Employees	NA	Stock Exchange	OTC
Auditor	Guest & Co. P.C	Ticker Symbol	LFSI
Stk Agt	Olde Monmouth Stk Trnsfer Co. Inc.	Outstanding Shares	29,160,000
Counsel	NA	E.P.S	-$0.036
DUNS No.	10-637-7989	Shareholders	NA

Business: The group's principal activity is to design and install the wiring and hardware system. It is a source for the builders for all their entertainment, security and home technology solution for their projects. The group is a home entertainment and technology company that provides builders and homeowners with a single source for their audio/video, home theater, security, telephone, and home automation needs. It operates in United States. As on 01-Mar-2004 the group discontinued its operations located in atlanta.

Primary SIC and add'l.: 3699

CIK No: 0000080327

Subsidiaries: Brittany Enterprises, Inc., FutureSmart Systems, Inc., Lauraan Corp., LFSI Acquisition, Inc., Lifestyle Integrators, Inc., Lifestyle Security Inc, Lifestyle Technologies, Lifestyle Technologies Atlanta, Inc., Lifestyle Technologies Charlotte, Inc., Lifestyle Technologies Franchising Corp., LST Integrators, Inc., LST of Baltimore, Inc., Princeton Mining Company, Syslync - Colorado, Inc.

Financial Data: **Fiscal Year End:**06/30 **Latest Annual Data:** 6/30/2005

Year	Sales	Net Income
2005	NA	-$1,184,000
2004	$138,000	-$6,994,000
2003	$2,206,000	-$6,094,000

Curr. Assets:	$5,000	**Curr. Liab.:**	$5,889,000		
Plant, Equip.:	NA	**Total Liab.:**	$6,039,000	**Indic. Yr. Divd.:**	NA
Total Assets:	$39,000	**Net Worth:**	-$6,000,000	**Debt/ Equity:**	NA

Lifetime Brands Inc

Formerly: Lifetime Hoan Corp
1000 Stewart Ave., Garden City, NY, 11530; ***PH:*** 1-516-683-6000; ***http://*** www.lifetime.hoan.com

General - Incorporation	DE	**Stock**- Price on:12/24/2007	$21.47
Employees	1,199	Stock Exchange	NDQ
Auditor	Ernst & Young LLP	Ticker Symbol	NA
Stk Agt	Wells Fargo Bank, N.A.	Outstanding Shares	13,290,000
Counsel	Morgan, Lewis & Bockius LLP	E.P.S	$0.97
DUNS No.	11-521-3613	Shareholders	NA

Business: The group's principal activities are to design, market and distribute a broad range of household cutlery, kitchenware, cutting boards, pantryware, decorative bath accessories and bakeware products. The group owned trade names include hoffritz (R), prestige (R), tristar (R), old homestead (R), roshco (R), baker's advantage (R), kamenstein(R) and hoan (r). Licensed trade names include farberware (R), kitchenaid(R) and various names under license from the pillsbury company. The group's products are sold primarily in the United States to approximately 700 customers including national retailers, department store chains, mass merchant retail and discount stores, supermarket chains, warehouse clubs, direct marketing companies and specialty chains and through other channels of distribution. It also operates 62 retail outlet stores in 30 states. On oct-2003, it acquired the business and certain assets of use(tm) and on nov-2003, acquired assets of gemco ware, inc.

Primary SIC and add'l.: 3421 5719 3365

CIK No: 0000874396

Subsidiaries: Luxury Tabletop, Inc., M. Kamenstein Corp., Outlet Retail Stores, Inc, Pfaltzgraff Factory Stores, Inc., Roshco, Inc, The Pfaltzgraff Co.

Officers: Jeffrey Siegel/Chmn., CEO, Pres./$2,937,902.00, Ronald Shiftan/Vice Chmn., COO/$648,439.00, Craig Phillips/Dir., Sec., Sr. VP - Distribution, Evan Miller/Exec. VP, Pres. - Sales/$790,128.00, Robert McNally/61/VP - Finance, Treasurer/$366,685.00, Robert Reichenbach/Exec. VP, Group Pres. - Cutlery, Cutting Boards, Bakeware, Larry Sklute/Group Pres. - Kitchenware, Christian G. Kasper/Sr. VP - Strategy, Corporate Development, Laurence Winoker/Sr. VP - Finance, Treasurer, CFO, Sara Shindel/Assoc. General Counsel

Directors: Jeffrey Siegel/Chmn., CEO, Pres., Ronald Shiftan/Vice Chmn., COO, Howard Bernstein/87/Dir., Michael Jeary/Dir., Sheldon Misher/Dir., William Westerfield/Dir., Craig Phillips/Dir., Sec., Sr. VP - Distribution, Cherrie Nanninga/59/Dir., David Dangoor/Dir., Fiona P. Dias/Dir.

Owners: Craig Phillips/6.31%, Evan Miller, Larry Sklute, Milton L. Cohen/7.59%, Michael Jeary, Jove Partners, LP/5.27%, Schwartz Investment Counsel, Inc/7.51%, Laura Miller/5.28%, Robert McNally, Jeffrey Siegel/9.79%, Ronald Shiftan/3.33%, Jodie Glickman/5.15%, Fiona Dias, Sheldon Misher, Insiders/21.73% (20 Owners included in Index)

Financial Data: Fiscal Year End:12/31   Latest Annual Data: 12/31/2006

Year	Sales	Net Income
2006	$457,400,000	$15,532,000
2005	$307,897,000	$14,109,000
2004	$189,458,000	$8,472,000

Curr. Assets:	$231,633,000	Curr. Liab.:	$89,727,000	P/E Ratio: 22.36
Plant, Equip.:	$42,722,000	Total Liab.:	$181,453,000	Indic. Yr. Divd.: $0.250
Total Assets:	$343,064,000	Net Worth:	$161,611,000	Debt/ Equity: 0.4996

Lifevantage Corp

Formerly: Lifeline Therapeutics Inc
6400 S Fiddler, Ste. 1970, Greenwood Village, CO, 80111; **PH:** 1-720-488-1711;
http:// www.lifelinetherapeutics.com

General - Incorporation	CO	Stock - Price on:12/24/2007	NA
Employees	11	Stock Exchange	OTC
Auditor	Gordon, Hughes & Banks LLP	Ticker Symbol	LFVN
Stk Agt	Computershare Investor Services LLC	Outstanding Shares	NA
Counsel	NA	E.P.S.	-$0.14
DUNS No.	82-741-9250	Shareholders	NA

Business: The group's principal activity is to seek business combinations with one or more existing private business enterprises. The group was in the business of mining of gold, other precious and base metal. Its efforts to pursue as a mining industry failed and the group resolved to sell its mining properties. The group is in development stage.

Primary SIC and add'l.: 9999

CIK No: 0000849146

Subsidiaries: Lifeline Nutraceuticals Corporation, Lifeline Nutraceuticals, Inc

Officers: James Krejci/CEO, Vice Chmn., Joe McCord/Dir. - Science, Bradford Amman/Dir. - Finance, Sec., Anthony Del Vicario/VP - Strategic Sales - Marketing

Directors: James Krejci/CEO, Vice Chmn., John B. Van Heuvelen/Chmn., Jack R. Thompson/Dir., James Crapo/Dir.

Owners: Insiders/12.20%, Paul R. Myhill/10.60%, Joe M. McCord/7.60%, Daniel W. Streets/12.20%, Bradford K. Amman, William J. Driscoll/9.60%, Jack R. Thompson, James D. Crapo/3.30%

Financial Data: Fiscal Year End:06/30   Latest Annual Data: 06/30/2007

Year	Sales	Net Income
2007	$5,051,000	-$3,694,000
2006	$7,166,000	-$2,735,000
2005	$2,354,000	-$5,822,000

Curr. Assets:	$2,000	Curr. Liab.:	$14,000	
Plant, Equip.:	NA	Total Liab.:	$14,000	Indic. Yr. Divd.: NA
Total Assets:	$38,000	Net Worth:	$23,000	Debt/ Equity: NA

Lifeway Foods Inc

6431 W Oakton St., Morton Grove, IL, 60053; **PH:** 1-847-967-1010; **Fax:** 1-847-967-6558;
http:// lifeway.net; **Email:** info@lifeway.net

General - Incorporation	IL	Stock - Price on:12/24/2007	$10.37
Employees	120	Stock Exchange	NDQ
Auditor	Plante & Moran, PLLC	Ticker Symbol	LWAY
Stk Agt	Computershare Trust Co	Outstanding Shares	16,890,000
Counsel	Futro & Travernicht	E.P.S.	$0.17
DUNS No.	15-303-2214	Shareholders	NA

Business: The group's principal activity is to produce and market dairy products, soy-based products and vegetable-based seasoning. The group's primary product is kefir, a drinkable product in several flavors. The other products are plain farmer's cheeses, fruit sugar-flavored products which are dairy based beverage. These are sold under the names Lifeway Kefir, Farmers Cheese, Sweet Kiss, Basics Plus, Elita, Kwashenka, Kefir Starter. The group also produces several soy-based products named soy treat and a vegetable-based seasoning named Golden Zesta. The group operates a restaurant/supper club, through a wholly owned subsidiary LFI Enterprises, Inc. The products of the group are marketed through out the United States, Canada, Russia and Ukraine. The group currently sells the products to various retail establishments including supermarkets, grocery stores, gourmet shops, delicatessens and convenience stores.

Primary SIC and add'l.: 2022 2023

CIK No: 0000814586

Subsidiaries: LFI Enterprises, Inc., Lifeway Foods Canada, LLC

Officers: Julie Smolyansky/CEO, Pres./$207,700.00, Sarah Ryser/Public Relations, Media Relations, Lisa Kornblatt/Public Relations, Media Relations

Directors: Mike Smolyansky/Founder - Lifeway Foods

Owners: Val Nikolenko, Edward Smolyansky/2.50%, Julie Smolyansky/3.10%, Ludmila Smolyansky/45.00%, Renzo Bernardi, Insiders/50.70%, DS Waters, LP/20.40%, Pol Sikar

Financial Data: Fiscal Year End:12/31   Latest Annual Data: 12/31/2006

Year	Sales	Net Income
2006	$27,721,000	$2,896,000
2005	$20,132,000	$2,548,000
2004	$16,319,000	$2,052,000

Curr. Assets:	$16,887,000	Curr. Liab.:	$3,074,000	P/E Ratio: 61.00
Plant, Equip.:	$8,581,000	Total Liab.:	$9,271,000	Indic. Yr. Divd.: NA
Total Assets:	$32,999,000	Net Worth:	$23,728,000	Debt/ Equity: 0.2091

Ligand Pharmaceuticals Inc

10275 Science Ctr. Dr., San Diego, CA, 92121; **PH:** 1-858-550-7500; **Fax:** 1-858-550-7506;
http:// www.ligand.com; **Email:** investors@ligand.com

General - Incorporation	DE	Stock - Price on:12/24/2007	$7.15
Employees	122	Stock Exchange	NDQ
Auditor	BDO Seidman LLP	Ticker Symbol	LGND
Stk Agt	Mellon Investor Services LLC	Outstanding Shares	101,100,000
Counsel	Clifford Chance	E.P.S.	$4.37
DUNS No.	18-410-5260	Shareholders	NA

Business: The group's principal activities are to discover, develop and market drugs for the treatment of cancer, men's and women's health, skin diseases, osteoporosis, and metabolic, cardiovascular and inflammatory diseases. The group's drug discovery and development programs are based on proprietary gene transcription technology related to intracellular receptors, signal transducers and activators of transcription. The four oncology products marketed in the United States include panretin(R) gel, ontak(R) and targretin(R) capsules and targretin(R) gel. The major customers include eli lilly and company, cardinal health and bergen brunswig drug company.

Primary SIC and add'l.: 8731 2834 2835

CIK No: 0000886163

Subsidiaries: Ligand Pharmaceuticals Incorporated, Ligand Pharmaceuticals International, Inc, Nexus Equity VI LLC, Seragen, Inc

Officers: John L. Higgins/Dir., CEO, Pres., Syed Kazmi/VP - Business Development, Strategic Planning, John P. Sharp/VP - Finance, CFO, Charles Berkman/VP, General Counsel, Sec., Audrey Warfield-Graham/Dir. - Human Resources, Kenneth Kaushansky/Scientific Advisor, Ronald M. Evans/Scientific Advisor, Erika Luib/Contact - Investor Relations, Martin D. Meglasson/VP - Discovery Research/$684,137.00, Tod G. Mertes/43/VP, Interim CFO, Zofia E. Dziewanowska/VP - Clinical Research, Development

Directors: John L. Higgins/Dir., CEO, Pres., John W. Kozarich/57/Chmn., Elizabeth M. Greetham/Dir., David M. Knott/Dir., Alexander D. Cross/75/Dir., Jeffrey R. Perry/Dir., Michael A. Rocca/63/Dir., Jason Aryeh/Dir., Todd C. Davis/Dir.

Owners: David M. Knott/8.37%, Andres F. Negro-Vilar, John L. Higgins, Henry F. Blissenbach, Martin D. Meglasson, Warner R. Broaddus, Jeffrey R. Perry, Glenview Capital Management LLC/7.24%, Michael A. Rocca, Harvest Management, LLC/5.34%, OZ Management, LLC/5.14%, Insiders/10.84%, Jason M. Aryeh/1.62%, John W. Kozarich, Paul V. Maier

Financial Data: Fiscal Year End:12/31   Latest Annual Data: 12/31/2006

Year	Sales	Net Income
2006	$140,960,000	-$31,743,000
2005	$176,608,000	-$36,399,000
2004	$163,512,000	-$45,141,000

Curr. Assets:	$235,557,000	Curr. Liab.:	$170,810,000	P/E Ratio: 1.64
Plant, Equip.:	$5,551,000	Total Liab.:	$286,356,000	Indic. Yr. Divd.: NA
Total Assets:	$326,053,000	Net Worth:	$27,352,000	Debt/ Equity: 0.0285

Light Sciences Oncology Inc

34931 SE Douglas St., Ste. 250, Snoqualmie, WA, 98065; **PH:** 1-425-957-8900;
Fax: 1-425-957-8999; **http://** www.lsoncology.com; **Email:** info@lsoncology.com

General - Incorporation	WA	Stock - Price on:12/24/2007	NA
Employees	NA	Stock Exchange	NA
Auditor	NA	Ticker Symbol	NA
Stk Agt	Mellon Investor Services LLC	Outstanding Shares	NA
Counsel	NA	E.P.S.	NA
DUNS No.	NA	Shareholders	NA

Business: The groups principal activity is to develop light infusion therapy. The groups product is Litx(TM) system. The group operates from the United States.

Primary SIC and add'l.: 3841 3841 2836 3845 2899 2834 2834 2836 3845 2899

CIK No: 0001342272

Officers: Llew Keltner/Dir., CEO, Pres., Jay Winship/COO, Chief Medical Officer, Robert Littauer/CFO, VP, Sy-Shi Wang/VP - Clinical Development, Erik Hagstrom/VP - Engineering, James C. Chen/Chief Scientific Officer

Directors: Llew Keltner/Dir., CEO, Pres., Jeff Himawan/Chmn., Vincent T. Devita/Chmn. - Scientific Advisory Board, Peter S. Edelstein/Member - Scientific Advisory Board, Craig Watjen/Dir., Rich Whitney/Dir., Martin Olin Andersen/Dir., Ulrik Spork/Dir., Philip J. Johnson/Member - Scientific Advisory Board, Robert Lustig/Member - Scientific Advisory Board, Alan P. Venook/Member - Scientific Advisory Board, Daniel Von Hoff/Member - Scientific Advisory Board, Terry Gould/Dir.

Lightbridge Inc

30 Corporate Dr., Burlington, MA, 01803; **PH:** 1-781-359-4000; **http://** www.lightbridge.com

General - Incorporation	DE	Stock - Price on:12/24/2007	NA
Employees	593	Stock Exchange	NA
Auditor	Deloitte & Touche LLP	Ticker Symbol	NA
Stk Agt	American Stock Transfer & Trust Co.	Outstanding Shares	NA
Counsel	Foley, Hoag & Eliot LLP	E.P.S.	$0.91
DUNS No.	61-032-3966	Shareholders	NA

Business: The group's principal activities are to develop, market and support a network of products and services for communication providers. It also offers on-line, real-time transaction processing and call center services to aid communications as well as software-based point-of-sale support services. It operates in four segments: transaction, software license, consulting and services and hardware. The group's products and services include credit decision system, retail management system and lightbridge consulting services. The customers of the group include sprint spectrum lp and at&t wireless services, inc. The group operates only in the United States. On 31-Mar-2004 the group acquired authorize.net corporation.

Primary SIC and add'l.: 7373 7375 7372

CIK No: 0001017172

Subsidiaries: Authorize.Net Corporation, Credit Technologies, Inc

Officers: Robert Donahue/Dir., CEO, Pres./$2,484,499.00, Roy Banks/Pres. - Authorizenet/$681,929.00, Eugene J. Didonato/VP, General Counsel/$537,467.00, Timothy C. Obrien/CFO/$1,022,092.00, Kathleen A. Harris/VP - Human Resources, David Schwartz/Dir. - Marketing

Directors: Robert Donahue/Dir., CEO, Pres., Gary Haroian/Chmn., Kevin C. Melia/Chmn., Andrew G. Mills/Dir., Rachelle B. Chong/Dir.

Owners: Wells Fargo& Company/15.18%, Barclays Global Investors, NA/7.33%, Robert E. Donahue/2.14%, Andrew G. Mills, Roy Banks, Dimensional FundAdvisors, Inc./4.89%, Eugene J. DiDonato, Kevin C. Melia, Timothy C. OBrien, Insiders/4.09%, Rachelle B. Chong, Gary E. Haroian

Financial Data: Fiscal Year End:12/31   Latest Annual Data: 12/31/2006

Year	Sales	Net Income
2006	$95,646,000	$24,758,000
2005	$108,278,000	$19,012,000
2004	$133,055,000	-$15,405,000

Curr. Assets:	$127,743,000	Curr. Liab.:	$23,777,000		
Plant, Equip.:	$4,907,000	Total Liab.:	$32,159,000	Indic. Yr. Divd.:	NA
Total Assets:	$222,474,000	Net Worth:	$190,315,000	Debt/ Equity:	NA

Lighting Science Group Corp

2100 Mckinney Ave., Ste. 1555, Dallas, TX, 75201; **PH:** 1-214-382-3630

General - Incorporation	DE	Stock - Price on:12/24/2007	$0.44
Employees	13	Stock Exchange	OTC
Auditor	R. E. Bassie & Co.	Ticker Symbol	LSGP
Stk Agt	American Stock Transfer & Trust Co.	Outstanding Shares	112,090,000
Counsel	NA	E.P.S.	-$0.2
DUNS No.	NA	Shareholders	NA

Business: The groups principle activities include designing and developing power management lighting products utilizing light emitting diodes as the source of light. The products of the group include flashlights, cabinet lighting, floodlights, parking garage lighting and outdoor lighting. The group operates from the United States and Canada. The group's revenue for Sep '07 was 0.45 millions of USD.

Primary SIC and add'l.: 3641 3699 3644 3643 3648

CIK No: 0000866970

Subsidiaries: Lighting Science, Inc.

Officers: Robert H. Warshauer/50/Pres.

Owners: Daryl N. Snadon, Insiders/4.50%, Don R. Harkleroad, Robert E. Bachman, Kenneth Honeycutt/1.10%, LED Holdings, LLC/75.50%, Ronald E. Lusk/1.60%, Fredric S. Maxik

Financial Data: Fiscal Year End:12/31   Latest Annual Data: 12/31/2006

Year	Sales	Net Income
2006	$436,000	-$9,753,000
2005	$73,000	-$3,105,000
2004	$3,000	-$3,771,000

Curr. Assets:	$1,763,000	Curr. Liab.:	$2,796,000		
Plant, Equip.:	$360,000	Total Liab.:	$11,322,000	Indic. Yr. Divd.:	NA
Total Assets:	$6,267,000	Net Worth:	-$5,055,000	Debt/ Equity:	NA

Lightpath Technologies Inc

2603 Challenger Tech Ct., Ste. 100, Orlando, FL, 32826; **PH:** 1-407-382-4003; **Fax:** 1-407-382-4007; **http://** www.lightpath.com

General - Incorporation	DE	Stock - Price on:12/24/2007	$5.09
Employees	149	Stock Exchange	NDQ
Auditor	KPMG LLP	Ticker Symbol	LPTH
Stk Agt	Registrar & Transfer CO.	Outstanding Shares	4,510,000
Counsel	NA	E.P.S.	-$0.48
DUNS No.	17-495-6839	Shareholders	NA

Business: The group's principal activities are to design, develop, manufacture and distribute optical components and assemblies utilizing optical manufacturing process. The group operates through two business segments: optical lens and laser components. Optical lens segment provides precision molded optics, gradium(R) glass lenses and collimator products. Laser components segment provides isolators, custom modules and assemblies. Molded aspheres are used in telecom applications to couple laser to fiber, fiber to fiber and fiber to other optical devices. Collimators are assemblies that are used to straighten and make parallel diverging light as it exits a fiber. Isolators are used throughout fiber optic systems whenever light must enter or exit the fiber. The major customers of the group include finisar corp, agere systems, inc and lucent, inc.

Primary SIC and add'l.: 8731 3827 3851

CIK No: 0000889971

Subsidiaries: Geltech, Inc.

Officers: Joseph Gaynor/Interim CEO, Corporate VP - Operations, Zhouling Wu/Corp VP - GM, Pres. China, James Magos/57/Corporate VP - Sales - Marketing, Dorothy Cipolla/52/CFO, Corp VP, Zhouling Wu Wu/Corp VP - GM, Pres. China, Jim Magos/Corporate VP - Sales - Marketing

Directors: Robert Ripp/Chmn., Robert Bruggeworth/Dir., Steven Brueck/Dir., Gary Silverman/Dir., Louis Leeburg/Dir., Sohail Khan/Dir.

Owners: Insiders/10.60%, Dorothy Cipolla, Gary Silverman, Sohail Khan, Robert Ripp/5.61%, Kenneth Brizel/1.40%, Steve Brueck, Robert Bruggeworth, Zhouling Wu, James J. Gaynor, Edward Patton, James Magos, Louis Leeburg, Carl E. Berg/13.63%

Financial Data: Fiscal Year End:06/30   Latest Annual Data: 6/30/2006

Year	Sales	Net Income
2006	$12,173,000	-$3,369,000
2005	$11,754,000	-$3,480,000
2004	$8,332,000	-$5,598,000

Curr. Assets:	$7,676,000	Curr. Liab.:	$2,705,000		
Plant, Equip.:	$1,173,000	Total Liab.:	$2,745,000	Indic. Yr. Divd.:	NA
Total Assets:	$9,174,000	Net Worth:	$6,430,000	Debt/ Equity:	0.0644

Lightspace Corp

529 Main St. Ste. 330, Boston, MA, 02129; **PH:** 1-617-868-1700; **http://** www.lightspacecorp.com; **Email:** info@lightspacecorp.com

General - Incorporation	DE	Stock - Price on:12/24/2007	$1.1
Employees	14	Stock Exchange	OTC
Auditor	Miller Wachman LLP	Ticker Symbol	LGTS
Stk Agt	Continental Stock Transfer & Trust Co	Outstanding Shares	15,280,000
Counsel	NA	E.P.S.	-$0.34
DUNS No.	NA	Shareholders	NA

Business: The groups principle activities include researching, designing, developing, marketing and selling lightspace systems, consist of patent pending hardware and software technologies designed to integrate light, sound and movement. The group operates from the United States.

Primary SIC and add'l.: 7929

CIK No: 0001311318

Officers: Gary Florindo/Chmn., CEO, Pres., Chris Cantone/Sr. VP - Sales - Marketing, Brian Batease/VP, COO, Louis P. Nunes/CFO, VP, David J. Hoch/Co - Founder, Chief Scientist, Rich Leitermann/VP - Engineering, Derek Hunter/VP - International Business Development

Directors: Gary Florindo/Chmn., CEO, Pres., David J. Hoch/Co - Founder, Chief Scientist, Joe Parkinson/Dir., Rob Giannini/Dir.

Owners: Robert Giannini/6.36%, Ganot Corporation/1.34%, South Ferry Building Company/5.55%, Cam-Elm Company, LLC/1.67%, Ellis International LP/0.67%, Asia Marketing Limited/3.31%, AME Capital Group/1.67%, LaPlace Group/3.31%, Adrian Stecyk/2.18%, Paul Packer/0.67%

Financial Data: Fiscal Year End:12/31   Latest Annual Data: 12/31/2006

Year	Sales	Net Income
2006	$848,000	-$2,708,000

Curr. Assets:	$1,291,000	Curr. Liab.:	$1,273,000		
Plant, Equip.:	$82,000	Total Liab.:	$1,273,000	Indic. Yr. Divd.:	NA
Total Assets:	$1,570,000	Net Worth:	$297,000	Debt/ Equity:	NA

Lihir Gold Ltd

Level 7, Pacific Pl, Cnr Champion Parade and musgrave St, Port Moresby; **PH:** 675-3217711; **Fax:** 675-3214705; **http://** www.lihir.com.pg

General - Incorporation	Papua New Guinea	Stock - Price on:12/24/2007	$26.03
Employees	1,127	Stock Exchange	NDQ
Auditor	PricewaterhouseCoopers LLP	Ticker Symbol	LIHR
Stk Agt	Computershare Investor Services	Outstanding Shares	1,400,000,000
Counsel	NA	E.P.S.	-$0.01
DUNS No.	NA	Shareholders	NA

Business: The group's principal activity is the exploration of gold and other minerals.

Primary SIC and add'l.: 1041 1099

CIK No: 0001000300

Subsidiaries: Lihir Business Development Limited, Lihir Management Company Limited, Lihir Services Australia Pty Limited, Niugini Mining (Australia) Pty Limited, Niugini Mining Limited

Officers: Arthur Hood/Dir., CEO, Paul Fulton/CFO, Murray Eagle/GM - External Affairs, Sustainable Development, Joe Dowling/GM - Corporate Affairs, Graham Folland/GM - Corporate Development, Noel Foley/Executive GM - Operations, Ron Yung/GM - Organisation Performance, Stuart MacKenzie/Group Sec., General Counsel, Wojciech Ozga/GM - Ballarat Gold, Richard Laufmann/Executive GM Australian Operations - Business Development, Joseph Daimol/GM - Corporate Affairs

Directors: Arthur Hood/Dir., CEO, Ross Garnaut/Chmn., Peter Cassidy/Dir., Geoff Loudon/Dir., Bruce Brook/52/Dir., Alister Maitland/Dir., Mike Etheridge/Dir., Winifred Kamit/Dir.

Owners: Nuveen Investments Inc./15.34%, BlackRock Inc./10.07%

Financial Data: Fiscal Year End:12/31   Latest Annual Data: 12/31/2006

Year	Sales	Net Income
2006	$310,454,000	$36,279,000
2005	$224,871,000	$21,845,000
2004	$234,668,000	$141,614,000

Curr. Assets:	$132,751,000	Curr. Liab.:	$177,386,000		
Plant, Equip.:	$765,501,000	Total Liab.:	$684,181,000	Indic. Yr. Divd.:	NA
Total Assets:	$1,185,022,000	Net Worth:	$500,841,000	Debt/ Equity:	NA

Lime Energy Co

Formerly: Electric City Corp

1280 Landmeier Rd., Elk Grove, IL, 60007; **PH:** 1-847-437-1666; **http://** www.elccorp.com

General - Incorporation	DE	Stock - Price on:12/24/2007	$11.4
Employees	NA	Stock Exchange	NA
Auditor	BDO Seidman LLP	Ticker Symbol	NA
Stk Agt	Computershare Trust Co	Outstanding Shares	NA
Counsel	NA	E.P.S.	NA
DUNS No.	NA	Shareholders	NA

Business: The group's principal activities are to develop, manufacture and integrate energy saving technologies and custom electric switchgear. The group operates in three segments: the energy technology segment designs, manufactures and markets energy saving technologies primarily to commercial and industrial customers. The energy saving product is the energysaver(tm) system, which reduces energy consumed by lighting, typically by 20% to 30%, with minimal lighting level reduction. This technology has applications in commercial buildings, factories and office structures, as well as street lighting and parking lot lighting. The power management segment designs, manufactures and markets a wide range of commercial and industrial switch gear and distribution panels for use in telecommunication and Internet network centers. The building control and automation segment provides integration of building and environmental control systems for commercial and industrial customers.

Primary SIC and add'l.: 3625 3613

CIK No: 0001065860

Subsidiaries: Elc Vnpp Sub I, LLC, Elc Vnpp Sub Ii, LLC, Great Lakes Controlled Energy Corporation, Maximum Performance Group, Inc

Officers: David R. Asplund/CEO/$2,351,317.00, Jeffrey R. Mistarz/CFO/$618,577.00, Glen Akselrod/Investor Relation Officer, Daniel W. Parke/Dir., COO, Pres./$484,346.00, Leonard Pisano/Exec. VP - Business Development/$826,390.00, Pradeep Kapadia/Pres. - Engineering Services, David R. Krueger/Sr. VP - Western Region, Joseph A. Barnes/VP - Midwest Region, Robert Meier/VP - Engineering Services, Daniel Newman/Sr. VP - Eastern Region, Brad Boyett/Sr. VP - Southwest Region, Chris Barbary/VP - Technology

Directors: Richard P. Kiphart/Chmn., Daniel W. Parke/Dir., COO, Pres., David W. Valentine/Dir., Gerald A. Pientka/Dir., Gregory T. Barnum/Dir., William R. Carey/Dir., Joseph F. Desmond/Dir.

Owners: David Asplund/8.68%, Leaf Mountain Company/6.15%, Insiders/47.94%, Daniel R. Parke/10.07%, SF Capital Partners Ltd./7.95%, David W. Valentine, Richard P. Kiphart/29.05%, Leonard Pisano/1.77%, Jeffrey R. Mistarz/1.36%, Gregory Barnum, William Carey, Joseph Desmond, Duke Investments, LLC/5.84%

Limelight Media Group Inc

1300 N Nlake Way, Seattle, WA, 98103; *PH:* 1-206-633-1852; *http://* www.llmt.net

General - Incorporation	NV	**Stock**- Price on:12/24/2007	$0.5
Employees	58	Stock Exchange	OTC
Auditor	Peterson Sullivan PLLC	Ticker Symbol	IMMG
Stk Agt	First American Stock Transfer, Inc.	Outstanding Shares	23,960,000
Counsel	NA	E.P.S	-$0.55
DUNS No.	NA	Shareholders	NA

Business: The group's principle activity is to provide video-streaming technology to consumers and the entertainment industry. It is a development stage company which intends to develop the necessary structure to deliver the video-streaming technology for profitable commercialization through internal development and licensing agreements with other companies. The company will then market and deploy products and services resulting from the company's technology applications. On 01-Sep-2002, the company acquired uniguest of Tennessee, inc. The group operates from United States.

Primary SIC and add'l.: 7379

CIK No: 0001104161

Subsidiaries: Impart Media Advertising, Inc., Impart, Inc.

Officers: Joe F. Martinez/Dir., CEO, Pres./$720,089.00, Laird Laabs/Dir., Co - Founder, Pres. - Impart Asia, Pacific/$119,940.00, Todd Weaver/CTO/$254,738.00, Michael Medico/Pres. - Impart Media Advertising, Inc/$118,145.00, Steve Corey/Co - Founder - Strategic Advisor/$90,850.00, Stephen Wilson/CFO, Scott J. Campbell/Chief Creative Officer/$234,738.00, Chickie Bucco/Strategic Member - Advisory Board

Directors: Joe F. Martinez/Dir., CEO, Pres., Ron Elgin/Chmn., Joachim Kempin/Dir., Laird Laabs/Dir., Co - Founder, Pres. - Impart Asia, Pacific, Steve Corey/Co - Founder - Strategic Advisor, John H. Bauer/Member - Strategic Advisory Board, Stan Golden/Member - Strategic Advisory Board, Larry D. Calkins/Dir., Jim Haworth/Member - Strategic Advisory Board

Owners: Laird Laabs/11.00%, Joseph F. Martinez/4.40%, Scott J. Campbell, Ronald Elgin, Steven Corey/13.20%, Todd Weaver, Michael Medico/3.90%, Joachim Kempin, Insiders/37.40%, Larry Calkins, Thomas C. Muniz/4.00%

Financial Data: ***Fiscal Year End:***12/31 ***Latest Annual Data:*** 12/31/2006

Year		**Sales**		**Net Income**	
2006		$6,595,000		-$10,097,000	
2005		$4,945,000		-$2,420,000	
2004		$19,000		-$4,473,000	
Curr. Assets:	$6,749,000	**Curr. Liab.:**	$10,425,000		
Plant, Equip.:	$1,309,000	**Total Liab.:**	$10,650,000	**Indic. Yr. Divd.:**	NA
Total Assets:	$15,097,000	**Net Worth:**	$4,448,000	**Debt/ Equity:**	NA

Limited Brands Inc

3 Limited Pkwy., Columbus, OH, 43230; *PH:* 1-614-415-7000; *Fax:* 1-614-415-7440; *http://* www.limitedbrands.com

General - Incorporation	DE	**Stock**- Price on:12/24/2007	$26.39
Employees	20,400	Stock Exchange	NYSE
Auditor	Ernst & Young LLP	Ticker Symbol	LTD
Stk Agt	Bank of New York	Outstanding Shares	397,940,000
Counsel	NA	E.P.S	NA
DUNS No.	80-533-8449	Shareholders	NA

Business: The groups principle activity is to provide womens intimate apparel, personal care and beauty products. The group operates through three segments namely victorias secret, bath and body works and apparel. In the year 2007, the group acquired La Senza Corporation. The group operates from United States.

Primary SIC and add'l.: 5632 5621 5611

CIK No: 0000701985

Subsidiaries: Bath& Body Works, Inc, beautyAvenues, Inc., Express, LLC, Henri Bendel, Inc., Intimate Brands, Inc., Limited Brands Store Operations, Inc., Limited Logistics Services, Inc., Limited Service Corporation, Mast Industries (Far East) Limited, Mast Industries, Inc., The Limited Stores, Inc., Victorias Secret Direct, LLC, Victorias Secret Stores Brand Management, Inc., Victorias Secret Stores, LLC

Officers: Leslie H. Wexner/Chmn., CEO/$9,379,185.00, Sharen Jester Turney/CEO, Pres. - Victoria's Secret Megabrand, Intimate Apparel/$2,322,345.00, Jay M. Margolis/59/Group Pres. - Apparel/$4,691,127.00, Jane L. Ramsey/Exec. VP - Human Resources, William R. Loomis/Investor, Dir., Mark A. Giresi/Exec. VP - International, Thomas J. Katzenmeyer/Sr. VP - Investor, Media, Community Relations, Limited Brands, Martyn R. Redgrave/Exec. VP, Chief Administrative Officer, CFO/$3,206,806.00, Abigail S. Wexner/Dir., Attorney at Law

Directors: Leslie H. Wexner/Chmn., CEO, Amie Preston/Trustee, Bruce A. Soll/Trustee, Leonard A. Schlesinger/55/Dir., Eugene M. Freedman/Dir., Gordon E. Gee/Dir., James L. Heskett/Dir., Donna A. James/Dir., David T. Kollat/Dir., William R. Loomis/Investor, Dir., Jeffrey B. Swartz/Dir., Allan R. Tessler/Dir., Abigail S. Wexner/Dir., Attorney at Law, Raymond Zimmerman/Dir., Dennis S. Hersch/Dir. *(17 Directors included in Index)*

Owners: Allan R. Tessler, William R. Loomis, Donna A. James, James L. Heskett, Dennis S. Hersch, Jeffrey H. Miro, Leonard A. Schlesinger, Abigail S. Wexner/2.20%, Sharen J. Turney, Gordon E. Gee, Capital Research and Management Company/18.80%, AXA Assurances I.A.R.D. Mutuelle/6.00%, Jeffrey B. Swartz, Eugene M. Freedman, Leslie H. Wexner/12.80% *(22 Owners included in Index)*

Financial Data: ***Fiscal Year End:***01/28 ***Latest Annual Data:*** 2/3/2007

Year		**Sales**		**Net Income**	
2007		$10,671,000,000		$676,000,000	
2006		$9,699,000,000		$683,000,000	
2005		$9,408,000,000		$705,000,000	
Curr. Assets:	$2,771,000,000	**Curr. Liab.:**	$1,709,000,000	**P/E Ratio:**	16.92
Plant, Equip.:	$1,862,000,000	**Total Liab.:**	$4,067,000,000	**Indic. Yr. Divd.:**	$0.600
Total Assets:	$7,093,000,000	**Net Worth:**	$2,955,000,000	**Debt/ Equity:**	0.5529

Lin Television Corp

4 Richmond Sq., Ste. 200, Providence, RI, 02906; *PH:* 1-401-454-2880; *Fax:* 1-401-454-0089; *http://* www.lintv.com

General - Incorporation	DE	**Stock**- Price on:12/24/2007	$19.3
Employees	2,119	Stock Exchange	NYSE
Auditor	PricewaterhouseCoopers LLP	Ticker Symbol	NA
Stk Agt	Bank of New York	Outstanding Shares	50,770,000
Counsel	NA	E.P.S	$0.80
DUNS No.	79-143-1067	Shareholders	NA

Business: The group owns and operates 24 television stations, operate two television stations under local marketing agreements and provide management or sales services to four television stations, in the United States and Puerto Rico.

Primary SIC and add'l.: 4833

CIK No: 0000931058

Subsidiaries: Airwaves, Inc., Indiana Broadcasting LLC, KXAN, Inc., KXTX Holdings, Inc., LIN Airtime, LLC, LIN of Alabama, LLC, LIN of Colorado, LLC, LIN of New Mexico, LLC, LIN of Wisconsin, LLC, LIN Sports, Inc., LIN Television Corporation, LIN Television of San Juan, Inc., LIN Television of Texas, Inc., LIN Television of Texas, L.P., LIN TV Corp. 34 Subsidiaries included in the Index

Officers: Vincent L. Sadusky/Dir., Pres., CEO - LIN TV Corp, Gregory M. Schmidt/Exec. VP - Digital Media, Scott M. Blumenthal/Exec. VP - Television, Ed Munson/VP - Sales, Denise M. Parent/VP, Deputy General Counsel, Courtney Guertin/Public Relations Specialist, Bart W. Catalene/Sr. VP, CFO, William A. Cunningham/VP, Controller, Principal Accounting Officer

Directors: Vincent L. Sadusky/Dir., Pres., CEO - LIN TV Corp, Royal W. Carson/Dir., William S. Banowsky/Dir., William H. Cunningham/Dir., Peter S. Brodsky/Dir., Michael A. Pausic/Dir., Douglas W. McCormick/Dir., Patti S. Hart/Dir., Mitchell Stern/Dir.

Owners: GAMCO/15.45%, MJG Associates, Gabelli Funds/2.22%

Financial Data: ***Fiscal Year End:***12/31 ***Latest Annual Data:*** 12/31/2006

Year		**Sales**		**Net Income**	
2006		$426,100,000		-$234,500,000	
2003		$349,529,000		-$90,390,000	
2002		$349,594,000		-$47,215,000	
Curr. Assets:	$137,939,000	**Curr. Liab.:**	$104,347,000	**P/E Ratio:**	24.13
Plant, Equip.:	$305,143,000	**Total Liab.:**	$1,527,094,000	**Indic. Yr. Divd.:**	NA
Total Assets:	$2,125,846,000	**Net Worth:**	$588,721,000	**Debt/ Equity:**	1.4027

Lin Tv Corp

1 Richmond Sq., Ste. 230E, Providence, RI, 02906; *PH:* 1-401-454-2880; *Fax:* 1-401-454-6990; *http://* www.lintv.com

General - Incorporation	DE	**Stock**- Price on:12/24/2007	$19.29
Employees	2,119	Stock Exchange	NYSE
Auditor	PricewaterhouseCoopers LLP	Ticker Symbol	TVL
Stk Agt	Bank of New York	Outstanding Shares	50,770,000
Counsel	NA	E.P.S	$0.80
DUNS No.	NA	Shareholders	NA

Business: The group's principle activity is to own and operate television stations in the United States and Puerto Rico. The group combines strong network-affiliated programming with local news and a multi-channel strategy which enables it to increase audience share by operating multiple stations in the same market. The group's local sales force has capitalized on the strong local presence to increase the revenues from local advertising. The group has also identified and implemented innovative business strategies, including pioneering the multi-channel strategy by extending it on a regional basis. The group's quarterly revenue for September 2007 was 93.74 millions of USD.

Primary SIC and add'l.: 4833

CIK No: 0001166789

Subsidiaries: Airwaves, Inc., Indiana Broadcasting LLC, KXAN, Inc., KXTX Holdings, Inc., LIN Airtime, LLC, LIN of Alabama, LLC, LIN of Colorado, LLC, LIN of New Mexico, LLC, LIN of Wisconsin, LLC, LIN Sports, Inc., LIN Television Corporation, LIN Television of San Juan, Inc., LIN Television of Texas, Inc., LIN Television of Texas, L.P., LIN TV Corp. 34 Subsidiaries included in the Index

Officers: Vincent L. Sadusky/Dir., CEO, Pres./$2,076,662.00, Gregory M. Schmidt/Exec. VP - Digital Media/$1,394,191.00, Scott M. Blumenthal/VP - Television/$1,098,288.00, Denise M. Parent/44/VP - General Counsel, Sec./$883,581.00, William A. Cunningham/50/VP, Controller, Bart W. Catalane/Sr. VP, CFO/$42,451.00, Robert S. Richter/VP - Internet, Courtney Guertin/Public Relations Specialist

Directors: Vincent L. Sadusky/Dir., CEO, Pres., Douglas W. McCormick/Chmn., Patti S. Hart/Dir., William H. Cunningham/Dir., Michael A. Pausic/Dir., Peter S. Brodsky/Dir., Royal W. Carson/Dir., William S. Banowsky/Dir., Mitchell Stern/Dir.

Owners: Scott Blumenthal, Peter S. Brodsky, Peter S. Brodsky, Denise M. Parent, HM Entities, Wellington Management Company LLP/10.90%, William H. Cunningham, Mellon Financial Corporation/5.10%, Michael A. Pausic, Royal W. Carson/1.20%, Insiders/100.00%, Scott Blumenthal, Peter S. Brodsky/50.00%, Insiders, Michael A. Pausic *(34 Owners included in Index)*

Financial Data: ***Fiscal Year End:***12/31 ***Latest Annual Data:*** 12/31/2006

Year		**Sales**		**Net Income**	
2006		$426,100,000		-$234,500,000	
2003		$349,529,000		-$90,390,000	
2002		$349,594,000		-$47,215,000	
Curr. Assets:	$137,939,000	**Curr. Liab.:**	$104,347,000		
Plant, Equip.:	$305,143,000	**Total Liab.:**	$1,527,094,000	**Indic. Yr. Divd.:**	NA
Total Assets:	$2,125,846,000	**Net Worth:**	$588,721,000	**Debt/ Equity:**	NA

Lincare Holdings Inc

19387 US 19 N, Clearwater, FL, 33764; *PH:* 1-727-530-7700; *Fax:* 1-727-532-9692; *http://* www.lincare.com

General - Incorporation	DE	**Stock**- Price on:12/24/2007	$39.75
Employees	9,070	Stock Exchange	NDQ
Auditor	KPMG LLP	Ticker Symbol	LNCR
Stk Agt	Bank of America, N.A	Outstanding Shares	83,840,000
Counsel	NA	E.P.S	$2.38
DUNS No.	08-642-1534	Shareholders	NA

Business: The group's principal activity is to provide oxygen, respiratory therapy services, infusion therapy services and home medical equipment such as hospital beds, wheelchairs and other medical supplies to the home health care market. The group provides services to patients suffering from chronic obstructive pulmonary diseases such as emphysema and chronic bronchitis or asthma. These patients require supplemental oxygen or other respiratory therapy services in order to alleviate the symptoms and discomfort of respiratory dysfunction. As of 31-Dec-2003, the group served over 480,000 customers in 47 states through 727 operating centers.

Primary SIC and add'l.: 8082 5047

CIK No: 0000882235

Subsidiaries: Alpha Respiratory Inc, ConvaCare Services Inc., Gamma Acquisition Inc, HCS Lancaster LLC, Health Care Solutions at Home Inc, Healthlink Medical Equipment LLC, Home-Care Equipment Network Inc, Kappa Corporation, Lincare Inc, Lincare Licensing Inc, Lincare of New York Inc, Lincare Pharmacy Services Inc., Lincare Procurement Inc, Med 4 Home Inc., Parma Hospital Home Medical LLC

Officers: John P. Byrnes/Chmn., CEO/$6,728,745.00, Shawn Schabel/COO, Pres./$4,573,165.00, Paul G. Gabos/CFO, Sec./$3,342,515.00

Directors: John P. Byrnes/Chmn., CEO, Chester B. Black/62/Dir., Stuart H. Altman/70/Dir., Frank D. Byrne/55/Dir., William F. Miller/58/Dir.

Owners: FMR Corp./13.50%, Paul G. Gabos/1.50%, GE Asset Management Incorporated/8.30%, Shawn S. Schabel/1.60%, John P. Byrnes/3.40%, William F. Miller, Stuart H. Altman, Frank D. Byrne, Insiders/7.20%, Barclays Global Investors/5.20%, Chester B. Black

Financial Data: Fiscal Year End:12/31   **Latest Annual Data:** 12/31/2006

Year	Sales	Net Income
2006	$1,409,795,000	$212,981,000
2005	$1,266,627,000	$213,696,000
2004	$1,268,531,000	$273,428,000

Curr. Assets:	$242,279,000	**Curr. Liab.:**	$189,464,000	**P/E Ratio:**	16.70
Plant, Equip.:	$321,325,000	**Total Liab.:**	$664,733,000	**Indic. Yr. Divd.:**	NA
Total Assets:	$1,775,310,000	**Net Worth:**	$1,110,577,000	**Debt/ Equity:**	0.3068

Lincoln Bancorp

905 Sfield Dr., Plainfield, IN, 46168; **PH:** 1-317-839-6539; **Fax:** 1-317-837-3928; **http://** www.lincolnbankonline.com; **Email:** Sfield@lincolnbank.biz

General - Incorporation	IN	**Stock** - Price on:12/24/2007	$18.5
Employees	224	Stock Exchange	NDQ
Auditor	BKD LLP	Ticker Symbol	LNCB
Stk Agt	Computershare Investor Services LLC	Outstanding Shares	5,360,000
Counsel	Barnes & Thornburg	E.P.S.	$0.27
DUNS No.	NA	Shareholders	NA

Business: The group's principal activity is to provide banking services. It is a holding company and operates its activities though it's subsidiary, lincoln bank. The bank offers business consists of attracting deposits from the general public and originating fixed-rate and adjustable-rate loans secured primarily by first mortgage liens on one- to four-family residential real estate. The group accepts savings accounts, checking accounts, now accounts, certificates of deposit and money market demand accounts. It conducts its business through nine full service offices located in hendricks, montgomery, clinton, johnson and morgan counties, Indiana with the main office located in plainfield.

Primary SIC and add'l.: 6712 6035

CIK No: 0001070259

Subsidiaries: Citizens Loan and Service Corporation, LF Portfolio Services, Inc., LF Service Corporation, Lincoln Bank

Officers: Jerry R. Engle/Chmn., CEO, Pres./$346,516.00, John B. Ditmars/VP/$200,683.00, Jonathan D. Slaughter/VP/$162,252.00, John M. Baer/Sec., Treasurer/$176,403.00, Susan Haines/Internal Auditor

Directors: Jerry R. Engle/Chmn., CEO, Pres., Lester N. Bergum/Dir., Dennis W. Dawes/Dir., Thomas W. Harmon/Dir., Jerry R. Holifield/Dir., R. J. McConnell/Dir., David E. Mansfield/Dir., Patrick A. Sherman/Dir.

Owners: Dennis W. Dawes/0.50%, David E. Mansfield/0.80%, John L. Wyatt/0.90%, Lester N. Bergum/1.00%, John B. Ditmars/1.10%, Jerry R. Holifield/1.20%, John M. Baer/2.40%, Thomas W. Harmon/1.40%, Lincoln Bank Employee Stock Ownership and 401(k) Savings Plan/9.30%, Jonathan D. Slaughter/0.30%, Insiders/14.00%, R. J. McConnell, John C. Milholland/1.50%, Patrick A. Sherman/0.70%, Tim T. Unger/5.00% (16 Owners included in Index)

Financial Data: Fiscal Year End:12/31   **Latest Annual Data:** 06/30/2007

Year	Sales	Net Income
2007	NA	NA
2006	$56,648,000	$2,900,000
2005	$49,046,000	$1,199,000

Curr. Assets:	$23,195,000	**Curr. Liab.:**	$674,988,000	**P/E Ratio:**	56.06
Plant, Equip.:	$14,297,000	**Total Liab.:**	$784,242,000	**Indic. Yr. Divd.:**	$0.560
Total Assets:	$883,543,000	**Net Worth:**	$99,300,000	**Debt/ Equity:**	0.8769

Lincoln Educational Services Corp

200 Executive Dr., Ste. 340, West Orange, NJ, 07052; **PH:** 1-973-736-9340; **Fax:** 1-973-736-1750; **http://** www.lincolneducationalservices.com

General - Incorporation	NJ	**Stock** - Price on:12/24/2007	$15.09
Employees	2,462	Stock Exchange	NDQ
Auditor	Deloitte & Touche LLP	Ticker Symbol	LINC
Stk Agt	Continental Stock Transfer & Trust Co	Outstanding Shares	25,470,000
Counsel	Shearman & Sterling LLP	E.P.S.	$0.32
DUNS No.	NA	Shareholders	NA

Business: The groups principle activity is to provide career oriented post secondary education. The groups provide their services in automotive technology, health sciences, skilled trades, spa and culinary and business and information technology area. The group provides their services under the trade names Lincoln College of Technology, Lincoln Technical Institute Nashville Auto-Diesel College, Southwestern College, and Euphoria Institute of Beauty Arts and Sciences. The group acquired New England Technical Institute in the year 2006 and Euphoria Institute LLC in the year 2005. The group operates from the United States, England and New York. The group's quarterly revenue for September 2007 was 86.57 millions of USD.

Primary SIC and add'l.: 8249 8299 8331 8244

CIK No: 0001286613

Subsidiaries: ComTech Services Group Inc., Euphoria Acquisition, LLC, Florida Acquisition, LLC, Lincoln Technical Institute, Inc., Nashville Acquisition, LLC, New England Acquisition LLC, New England Institute of Technology at Palm Beach, Inc., Southwestern Acquisition LLC

Officers: David F. Carney/Chmn., CEO/$517,462.00, Shaun McAlmont/COO, Pres./$527,802.00, Scott M. Shaw/Exec. VP - Strategic Planning, Development/$389,502.00, Cesar Ribeiro/Sr. VP, CFO, Treasurer/$467,889.00, Thomas McHugh/Sr. VP, Chief Compliance Officer, Deborah Ramentol/Pres. - Lincoln Tech Group, Edward B. Abrams/Pres. - Lincoln Educational Group

Directors: David F. Carney/Chmn., CEO, Lawrence E. Brown/Vice Chmn., Celia Currin/Dir., Alexis P. Michas/Dir., James J. Burke/Dir., Steven W. Hart/Dir., Jerry G. Rubenstein/Dir., Paul Glaske/Dir., Peter S. Burgess/Dir., Barry J. Morrow/Dir.

Owners: Peter S. Burgess, Steven W. Hart, Celia Currin, Insiders, Alexis P. Michas, Shaun E. McAlmont, Paul E. Glaske, Cesar Ribeiro, David F. Carney, Scott M. Shaw, Back to School Acquisition L.L.C., Lawrence E. Brown, Barry J. Morrow, Jerry G. Rubenstein, James J. Burke (16 Owners included in Index)

Financial Data: Fiscal Year End:12/31   **Latest Annual Data:** 12/31/2006

Year	Sales	Net Income
2006	$321,506,000	$15,552,000
2005	$299,221,000	$18,709,000
2004	$261,275,000	$12,978,000

Curr. Assets:	$38,168,000	**Curr. Liab.:**	$59,111,000		
Plant, Equip.:	$94,368,000	**Total Liab.:**	$74,433,000	**Indic. Yr. Divd.:**	NA
Total Assets:	$226,216,000	**Net Worth:**	$151,783,000	**Debt/ Equity:**	0.1510

Lincoln Electric Holdings Inc

22801 St. Clair Ave., Cleveland, OH, 44117; **PH:** 1-216-481-8100; **Fax:** 1-216-486-1751; **http://** www.lincolnelectric.com

General - Incorporation	OH	**Stock** - Price on:12/24/2007	$74.88
Employees	8,430	Stock Exchange	NDQ
Auditor	Ernst & Young LLP	Ticker Symbol	LECO
Stk Agt	National City Bank	Outstanding Shares	42,880,000
Counsel	NA	E.P.S.	$4.73
DUNS No.	00-419-9048	Shareholders	NA

Business: The groups principle activity is to provide welding and cutting solutions. The groups products include welding power sources, wire feeding systems, robotic welding packages, fume extraction equipment, regulators and torches used in oxy-fuel welding and cutting. In the year 2007 the group acquired Vernon Tool Company Ltd. The group operates from United States.

Primary SIC and add'l.: 7692 3625 2899

CIK No: 0000059527

Subsidiaries: A. B. Arriendos S.A., Autobraze Inc., Bester S.A., C.i.f.e. S.r.l., Electrodos Oerlikon de Colombia Limitada, Harris Calorific GmbH, Harris Calorific Limited, Harris Calorific S.r.l., Harris Calorific, Inc., Harris Corporation, S. de R.L. de C.V., Harris-Euro S.L., Inversiones LyL S.A., J.W. Harris Co., Inc., Kaynak Teknigi Sanayi ve Ticaret A.S., Kuang Tai Metal Industrial Co., Ltd. 51 Subsidiaries included in the Index

Officers: John M. Stropki/Chmn., CEO, Pres./$3,901,351.00, Joseph G. Doria/VP, Pres. - Lincoln Electric Canada, Richard J. Seif/Sr. VP - Sales, Marketing, Sr. VP - Middle East, Africa, George D. Blankenship/Sr. VP - Global Engineering, US Operations, Frederick G. Stueber/Sr. VP, General Counsel, Sec./$1,357,709.00, Gabriel Bruno/VP, Corporate Controller, Robert K. Gudbranson/VP - Strategic Planning, Acquisitions, Michele R. Kuhrt/VP - Corporate Tax, Ronald A. Nelson/VP - Machine Division, David J. Nangle/VP, Group Pres. - Brazing, Cutting, Retail Subsidiaries, Vinod K. Kapoor/VP - Global Operations Development, Ralph C. Fernandez/VP, Pres. - Lincoln Electric Latin America/$1,671,491.00, Thomas A. Flohn/VP, Pres. - Lincoln Electric Asia Pacific, Vincent K. Petrella/CFO, Sr. VP, Treasurer/$1,037,563.00, David M. Leblanc/VP, Pres. - Lincoln Electric Europe/$821,739.00 (16 Officers included in Index)

Directors: John M. Stropki/Chmn., CEO, Pres., Kathryn Jo Lincoln/Dir., Harold L. Adams/Dir., David H. Gunning/Dir., William E. MacDonald/Dir., Russell G. Lincoln/Dir., George H. Walls/Dir., Robert J. Knoll/Dir., Stephen G. Hanks/Dir., Hellene S. Runtagh/Dir.

Owners: Harold L. Adams, David H. Gunning, George H. Walls, Ralph C. Fernandez, Russell G. Lincoln, Stephen G. Hanks, Kathryn Jo Lincoln/1.23%, John M. Stropki, Robert J. Knoll, Frederick G. Stueber, Hellene S. Runtagh, David M. LeBlanc, Vincent K. Petrella, Insiders/3.27%

Financial Data: Fiscal Year End:12/31   **Latest Annual Data:** 12/31/2006

Year	Sales	Net Income
2006	$1,971,915,000	$175,008,000
2005	$1,601,190,000	$122,306,000
2004	$1,333,675,000	$80,596,000

Curr. Assets:	$829,410,000	**Curr. Liab.:**	$338,288,000	**P/E Ratio:**	17.37
Plant, Equip.:	$389,518,000	**Total Liab.:**	$541,603,000	**Indic. Yr. Divd.:**	$0.880
Total Assets:	$1,394,579,000	**Net Worth:**	$852,976,000	**Debt/ Equity:**	NA

Lincoln Gold Corp

885 Dunsmuir St., Ste. 350, Vancouver, BC, N6C 1N5; **PH:** 1-604-688-7377; **http://** www.lincolngold.com; **Email:** info@lincolngold.com

General - Incorporation	NV	**Stock** - Price on:12/24/2007	$0.11
Employees	NA	Stock Exchange	OTC
Auditor	Manning Elliott LLP	Ticker Symbol	LGCP
Stk Agt	Pacific Stock Transfer	Outstanding Shares	NA
Counsel	Lang Michener	E.P.S.	NA
DUNS No.	NA	Shareholders	NA

Business: The groups principal activities include acquiring and exploring mineral properties. The group operates from Nevada in the United States.

Primary SIC and add'l.: 1000

CIK No: 0001080535

Officers: Paul F. Saxton/60/Dir., CEO, CFO, COO, Pres., Jeffrey Wilson/58/VP - Exploration

Directors: Paul F. Saxton/60/Dir., CEO, CFO, COO, Pres., Andrew F.B. Milligan/84/Chmn., James Chapman/53/Dir., Andrew Bowering/47/Dir., Steven Chi/68/Dir.

Owners: Andrew F.B. Milligan/3.70%, Sprott Asset Management Inc./7.20%, Insiders/22.10%, Joe Eberhard/6.40%, James Chapman/2.00%, Paul F. Saxton/12.40%, Andrew Bowering, Jeffrey Wilson/2.40%, Michael Baybak/6.70%

Financial Data: Fiscal Year End:12/31   **Latest Annual Data:** 12/31/2006

Year	Sales	Net Income
2006	NA	-$414,000
2005	NA	-$1,295,000
2004	NA	-$1,691,000

Curr. Assets:	$27,000	Curr. Liab.:	$157,000		
Plant, Equip.:	$4,000	Total Liab.:	$157,000	Indic. Yr. Divd.:	NA
Total Assets:	$31,000	Net Worth:	-$126,000	Debt/ Equity:	NA

Lincoln International Corp

12a Block, Xinhe Rd., Xinqiao No. 3, Industrial Zone, Shaijing District, Baoan Town, Shenzen, 150090; *PH:* 86-075-529-758811

General - Incorporation	DE	Stock- Price on:12/24/2007	NA
Employees	NA	Stock Exchange	NA
Auditor	Sherb & Co. LLP	Ticker Symbol	NA
Stk Agt	NA	Outstanding Shares	NA
Counsel	Pedley, Zielke & Gardiner	E.P.S	NA
DUNS No.	04-573-1841	Shareholders	NA

Business: The group's principal activity is to provide bookkeeping and payroll services through its accounting usa business division. These services are provided for small to medium sized businesses primarily in the metropolitan area of louisville Kentucky. The core services provided are: accounts payable; accounts receivable; job cost; bank reconciliation; time and billing and financial statements. The group also provided rental of commercial office property located in louisville, Kentucky but sold this property and is no longer in the commercial real estate business.

Primary SIC and add'l.: 8721 7359

CIK No: 0000059544

Officers: Lawrence Kwok-Yan Chan/Chmn., CEO, Samir N. Masri/63/Dir., CFO, Treasurer, Assist., Sec.

Directors: Lawrence Kwok-Yan Chan/Chmn., CEO, Samir N. Masri/63/Dir., CFO, Treasurer, Assist., Sec.

Owners: Hong Liang/3.70%, Lawrence Kwok Yan Chan/50.30%, Insiders/54.00%

Lincoln National Corp

1500 Market St., Ste. 3900, Philadelphia, PA, 19102; *PH:* 1-215-448-1400; *Fax:* 1-215-448-3962; *http://* www.lfg.com; *Email:* contact@lincolnfinancialfield.com

General - Incorporation	IN	Stock- Price on:12/24/2007	$71.39
Employees	10,744	Stock Exchange	NYSE
Auditor	Ernst & Young LLP	Ticker Symbol	LNC
Stk Agt	Mellon Investor Services LLC	Outstanding Shares	270,770,000
Counsel	NA	E.P.S	$5.36
DUNS No.	00-693-7163	Shareholders	NA

Business: The groups principle activity is to provide insurance and investment management services. The group operates through four segments namely lincoln retirement, life insurance, investment management and lincoln UK. The group operates from United States and United Kingdom.

Primary SIC and add'l.: 6719 6371 6282 6311

CIK No: 0000059558

Subsidiaries: AMG Service Corp., AnnuityNet Insurance Agency, Inc., Bamwood Property Group Limited, Bamwood Property Limited, California Fringe Benefit and Insurance Marketing Corporation, Chapel Ash Financial Services Ltd., City Financial Limited, Consumers Financial Education Company Limited, Corporate Benefit Systems, Inc., Delaware Distributors, L.P., Delaware General Management, Inc., Delaware Investments U.S., Inc, Delaware Management Business Trust, Delaware management company, Inc ., Delaware Management Holdings, Inc . 73 Subsidiaries included in the Index

Officers: Jon A. Boscia/55/Chmn., CEO/$18,128,900.00, Frederick J. Crawford/CFO, Sr. VP/$3,131,687.00, Dennis R. Glass/Dir., COO, Pres./$5,208,904.00, Charles C. Cornelio/Sr. VP - Shared Services, CIO, Robert W. Dineen/Pres. - Lincoln Financial Advisors, Mark E. Konen/Pres., Head Retail Markets, Barbara S. Kowalczyk/56/Sr. VP - Corporate Development, Lincoln Financial Group, Elizabeth L. Reeves/Human Resources, Sr. VP, Chief Human Resources Officer, Dennis L. Schoff/Sr. VP, General Counsel, Westley V. Thompson/Heads The Employer Markets Area, Lincoln Financial Group/$4,500,991.00, Suzanne C. Womack/Sec., Douglas N. Miller/VP, Chief Accounting Officer, Heather C. Dzielak/39/VP - Lincoln National Life Insurance Company

Directors: Jon A. Boscia/55/Chmn., CEO, Jill S. Ruckelshaus/Dir., Leanne M. Lachman/Dir., Patrick J. Barrett/Dir., William J. Avery/Dir., William H. Cunningham/Dir., Dennis R. Glass/Dir., COO, Pres., George W. Henderson/Dir., Eric G. Johnson/Dir., Michael F. Mee/Dir., William Porter Payne/Dir., Patrick S. Pittard/Dir., David A. Stonecipher/Dir., Isaiah Tidwell/Dir., Glenn F. Tilton/Dir.

Owners: George W. Henderson, Eric G. Johnson, William J. Avery, David A. Stonecipher, Jill S. Ruckelshaus, Frederick J. Crawford, Jon A. Boscia, Patrick S. Pittard, Patrick J. Barrett, Leanne M. Lachman, Insiders/2.55%, William P. Payne, William H. Cunningham, Dennis R. Glass, Patrick P. Coyne (21 Owners included in Index)

Financial Data: *Fiscal Year End:*12/31   *Latest Annual Data:* 12/31/2006

Year	Sales	Net Income
2006	$9,063,000,000	$1,316,000,000
2005	$5,487,938,000	$831,055,000
2004	$5,371,274,000	$707,009,000

Curr. Assets:	$12,952,000,000	Curr. Liab.:	$658,000,000	P/E Ratio:	13.47
Plant, Equip.:	NA	Total Liab.:	$166,293,000,000	Indic. Yr. Divd.:	$1.660
Total Assets:	$178,494,000,000	Net Worth:	$12,201,000,000	Debt/ Equity:	NA

Lincoln Park Bancorp

31 Boonton Tpke, Lincoln Park, NJ, 07035; *PH:* 1-973-694-0330; *http://* www.lincolnparksavings.com; *Email:* info@lincolnparksavings.com

General - Incorporation	Federal	Stock- Price on:12/24/2007	$8.5
Employees	12	Stock Exchange	OTC
Auditor	Beard Miller Company LLP	Ticker Symbol	LPBC
Stk Agt	Registrar & Transfer Co	Outstanding Shares	1,850,000
Counsel	NA	E.P.S	$0.08
DUNS No.	NA	Shareholders	NA

Business: The groups principle activity is to provide banking services. Services of the group include originating mortgage loans and consumer loans, mortgage-backed and investment securities, demand deposits, savings and club accounts, and certificates of deposit. The group operates from the United States.

Primary SIC and add'l.: 6036

CIK No: 0001294206

Subsidiaries: Lincoln Park Savings Bank, LPS Investment Company

Officers: David G. Baker/Dir., Pres., CEO - Lincoln Park Saving Bank/$63,230.00, Stanford Stoller/Chmn. - Lincoln Park Saving Bank, John F. Feeney/Dir. - Lincoln Park Saving Bank, Edith Perrotti/Dir. - Lincoln Park Saving Bank/$59,202.00, Nancy M. Shaw/VP, Sec., Investor Relations Officer - Lincoln Park Saving Bank, Nandini S. Mallya/VP, CFO - Lincoln Park Saving Bank, Francesca D'Ambrosia/Assist. VP - Lincoln Park Saving Bank, Henry Fitschen/Dir. - Lincoln Park Saving Bank, Lincoln Park Saving Bank, Mary Baumiller/Investor Relations Officer - Lincoln Park Saving Bank

Directors: William H. Weisbrod/Member - Advisory Board

Owners: Lincoln Park Bancorp, MHC/54.00%, Insiders/2.80%

Financial Data: *Fiscal Year End:*12/31   *Latest Annual Data:* 12/31/2006

Year	Sales	Net Income
2006	$5,099,000	$314,000
2005	$4,525,000	$576,000
2004	$3,831,000	$405,000

Curr. Assets:	$3,279,000	Curr. Liab.:	$79,822,000	P/E Ratio:	56.67
Plant, Equip.:	$851,000	Total Liab.:	$80,726,000	Indic. Yr. Divd.:	NA
Total Assets:	$93,970,000	Net Worth:	$13,244,000	Debt/ Equity:	NA

Lindsay Corp

Formerly: Lindsay Manufacturing Co

2707 N 108th St., Ste. 102, Omaha, NE, 68164; *PH:* 1-402-428-2131; *http://* www.zimmatic.com

General - Incorporation	DE	Stock- Price on:12/24/2007	$44.28
Employees	763	Stock Exchange	NYSE
Auditor	KPMG LLP	Ticker Symbol	LNN
Stk Agt	Wells Fargo Bank Minnesota N.A	Outstanding Shares	11,640,000
Counsel	NA	E.P.S	$1.17
DUNS No.	06-864-5696	Shareholders	NA

Business: The group's principal activities are to design and manufacture self-propelled center pivot and lateral move irrigation systems. The group operates in two segments: irrigation equipment and diversified products. Irrigation equipment segment manufactures and markets center pivot, lateral move and hose reel irrigation systems. Diversified products segment produces and sells large diameter thin wall steel tubing and also provide manufacturing services such as welding, machining, painting, punching, forming, galvanizing and hydraulic, electrical and mechanical assembly. The products of the group are sold under the trademarks, zimmatic, greenfield and glowsmart. The group has international operations in Europe, Africa, the Middle East, Mexico, Latin America and other foreign countries.

Primary SIC and add'l.: 3479 3523 3317 3443

CIK No: 0000836157

Subsidiaries: Barrier Systems, Inc., Irrigation Specialists, Inc., Lindsay America do Sul Ltda., Lindsay Europe SAS, Lindsay Manufacturing Africa (PTY) Ltd, Lindsay Transportation, Inc.

Officers: Richard W. Parod/Dir., CEO, Pres., David B. Downing/VP, CFO, Sec., Treasurer, Matthew T. Cahill/VP - Manufacturing, Robert S. Snoozy/VP - Domestic Sales, Gary E. Kaplan/VP - Marketing Services, Dirk A. Lenie/VP - Marketing, Charles H. Meis/VP - Engineering, Timothy J. Paymal/Corporate Controller, Randall S. Hester/VP - Human Resources, Sam Haidar/VP - International, Barry A. Ruffalo/38/Pres. - North American Irrigation, Mark A. Roth/34/VP - Corporate Development, Douglas A. Taylor/45/CIO, VP

Directors: Richard W. Parod/Dir., CEO, Pres., Michael N. Christodolou/Chmn., Howard G. Buffett/Dir., Larry H. Cunningham/Dir., David J. McIntosh/Dir., Michael C. Nahl/Dir., William F. Welsh/Dir.

Owners: Mellon Capital Management/5.50%, Barry A. Ruffalo, David J. McIntosh, Owen S. Denman, Powershares Capital Management, LLC/9.20%, Richard W. Parod/2.90%, Michael N. Christodolou, Samir A. Haidar, Michael C. Nahl, Larry H. Cunningham, Howard G. Buffett, David B. Downing, Insiders/5.50%, Gary D. Parker/5.20%, Pictet Asset Management SA/8.90% (19 Owners included in Index)

Financial Data: *Fiscal Year End:*08/31   *Latest Annual Data:* 8/31/2006

Year	Sales	Net Income
2006	$226,001,000	$11,700,000
2005	$177,271,000	$4,838,000
2004	$196,696,000	$9,286,000

Curr. Assets:	$149,778,000	Curr. Liab.:	$51,502,000	P/E Ratio:	35.42
Plant, Equip.:	$44,292,000	Total Liab.:	$101,177,000	Indic. Yr. Divd.:	$0.260
Total Assets:	$242,205,000	Net Worth:	$141,028,000	Debt/ Equity:	NA

Linear Technology Corp

1630 McCarthy Blvd., Milpitas, CA, 95035; *PH:* 1-408-432-1900; *Fax:* 1-408-434-0507; *http://* www.linear.com

General - Incorporation	DE	Stock- Price on:12/24/2007	$35.5
Employees	3,755	Stock Exchange	NDQ
Auditor	Ernst & Young LLP	Ticker Symbol	LLTC
Stk Agt	EquiServe Trust Co N.A	Outstanding Shares	253,830,000
Counsel	NA	E.P.S	$1.39
DUNS No.	03-253-3788	Shareholders	NA

Business: The group's principle activities are to design, manufacture and market a broad line of standard high performance linear integrated circuits. The products are used in the following applications: telecommunications, cellular telephones, networking products and satellite systems, notebook and desktop computers, computer peripherals, video/multimedia, industrial instrumentation, automotive electronics, factory automation, process control and military and space systems. The principal product categories that utilize the manufactured integrated circuits are amplifiers, high-speed amplifiers, voltage regulators, voltage references, interface circuits, data converters and other linear circuits. It markets the products worldwide, through direct sales staff, electronics distributors and a small network of independent sales representatives. The products are marketed to a broad range of customers in diverse industries. The group's total revenue for September 2007 was 1,083.08 millions of USD.

Primary SIC and add'l.: 3679 3674 3672

CIK No: 0000791907

Subsidiaries: Linear Semiconductor Sdn Bhd, Linear Technology (Taiwan) Corporation, Linear Technology (U.K.) Limited, Linear Technology A.B. (Sweden), Linear Technology Corporation Limited (Hong Kong), Linear Technology Foreign Sales Corporation, Linear Technology GmbH, Linear Technology KK, Linear Technology Korea, Linear Technology PTE, Linear Technology S.A.R.L., Linear Technology S.r.l. (Italy)

Owners: Donald E. Paulus, Robert C. Dobkin, Paul Coghlan, Lothar Maier, Richard M. Moley, Capital Research and Management Company/23.30%, Insiders/3.20%, Goldman Sachs Group Inc./7.40%, Robert H. Swanson, David S. Lee, Thomas S. Volpe, State Farm Insurance Companies/7.00%

Financial Data: *Fiscal Year End:*07/03   *Latest Annual Data:* 04/01/2007

Year	Sales	Net Income
2007	$254,992,000	$98,550,000
2006	$1,092,977,000	$428,680,000
2005	$1,049,694,000	$433,974,000

Curr. Assets:	$2,007,309,000	**Curr. Liab.:**	$207,739,000	**P/E Ratio:**	25.54
Plant, Equip.:	$221,028,000	**Total Liab.:**	$279,200,000	**Indic. Yr. Divd.:**	NA
Total Assets:	$2,286,234,000	**Net Worth:**	$2,007,034,000	**Debt/ Equity:**	NA

Linens N Things Inc

6 Brighton Rd. , Clifton, NJ, 07015; *PH:* 1-973-778-1300; *http://* www.lnthings.com; *Email:* investor@LNT.com

General - Incorporation	DE	**Stock**- Price on:12/24/2007	NA
Employees	NA	Stock Exchange	NA
Auditor	KPMG LLP	Ticker Symbol	NA
Stk Agt	EquiServe Trust Co N.A	Outstanding Shares	NA
Counsel	Pitney, Hardin,Kipp & Search	E.P.S.	NA
DUNS No.	01-094-8586	Shareholders	NA

Business: The groups principle activity is to operate retail stores. The groups products include home textiles, housewares and decorative home accessories. The group operates from United States.

Primary SIC and add'l.: 7213 5023 5719

CIK No: 0001023052

Subsidiaries: Bloomington MN, L.T., Inc., Citadel LNT LLC, Linens 'n Things Canada Corp., Linens 'n Things Canada Limited Partnership, Linens 'n Things Center, Inc., Linens 'n Things Investment Canada I Company, Linens 'n Things Investment Canada II Company, LNT Leasing II LLC, LNT Leasing III LLC, LNT Leasing LLC, LNT Merchandising Company, LLC, LNT Services, Inc., LNT Virginia LLC, LNT West, Inc., LNT, Inc.

Officers: Robert J. Dinicola/60/Chmn., CEO, Pres., Francis M. Rowan/45/CFO, Sr. VP, Barbara L. Smith/VP, Treasurer, Primary Investor Relations Officer, David F. Coder/50/Sr. VP - Store Operations, Robert Homler/62/Exec. VP - Merchandising

Directors: Robert J. Dinicola/60/Chmn., CEO, Pres., Joyce F. Brown/61/Dir., Peter P. Copses/49/Dir., Michael A. Gatto/40/Dir., George G. Golleher/60/Dir., Damian J. Giangiacomo/31/Dir., Andrew S. Jhawar/36/Dir., Lee S. Neibart/57/Dir., Brian H. Pall/48/Dir.

Owners: Damian J. Giangiacomo, Linens Investors, LLC, Michael A. Gatto, Robert Homler, Insiders, Francis M. Rowan, Andrew S. Jhawar, Robert J. DiNicola, George G. Golleher, Peter P. Copses, David F. Coder, Joyce F. Brown, Brian H. Pall, Lee S. Neibart

Lingo Media Inc

151 Bloor St. W, Ste. 703, Toronto, ON, M5S 1S4; *PH:* 1-416-927-7000; *http://* www.lingomedia.com; *Email:* info@lingomedia.com

General - Incorporation	Canada	**Stock**- Price on:12/24/2007	NA
Employees	NA	Stock Exchange	OTC
Auditor	KPMG LLP	Ticker Symbol	LNGMF
Stk Agt	Computershare Trust Co	Outstanding Shares	NA
Counsel	NA	E.P.S.	NA
DUNS No.	NA	Shareholders	NA

Business: The groups principle activities include developing, publishing, distributing and licensing books, audio and video cassettes, compact discs-based products and supplemental products for learning English. The group operates through two business segments namely English language learning and early childhood development. The group operates from Canada.

Primary SIC and add'l.: 9999

CIK No: 0001177167

Subsidiaries: Lingo Group Limited, Lingo Media International Inc, Lingo Media Ltd.

Officers: Michael P. Kraft/Dir., CEO, Pres., Jessica Zhang/VP - Corporate Development, China, Daniel Wiseman/VP - Corporate Development, Khurram R. Qureshi/Dir., CFO, Colin MacLennan/Contact - China Office, Michael Williams/VP - China Operations, Jenny Bao/Marketing Dir., Krishna Bala/Contact Person, Katherine Du/Contact Person, Angela Yang/Contact - China Administration, Imran Atique/31/Sec., Treasurer

Directors: Michael P. Kraft/Dir., CEO, Pres., Khurram R. Qureshi/Dir., CFO, Nereida Flannery/Dir., Bailing Xia/Dir., Scott Remborg/Dir., Richard J.G. Boxer/Dir., John P. Schram/Dir.

Owners: Buckingham Group Ltd/8.31%, Nereida Flannery, John Schram, Imran Atique, Khurram Qureshi/2.34%, Bailing Xia, Scott Remborg/Dir., Michael P. Kraft/16.60%, Insiders/21.28%

Financial Data: *Fiscal Year End:*12/31   *Latest Annual Data:* 12/31/2006

Year	Sales	Net Income
2006	$1,351,000	-$543,000
2004	$490,000	-$355,000
2003	$786,000	-$97,000

Curr. Assets:	$622,000	**Curr. Liab.:**	$397,000		
Plant, Equip.:	$45,000	**Total Liab.:**	$397,000	**Indic. Yr. Divd.:**	NA
Total Assets:	$798,000	**Net Worth:**	$400,000	**Debt/ Equity:**	NA

Link Group Inc

Ste. 950 - 789, West Pender St., Vancouver, BC, M4W 2J4; *PH:* 1-604-689-4407; *http://* www.linuxgoldcorp.com

General - Incorporation	CO	**Stock**- Price on:12/24/2007	$0.004
Employees	NA	Stock Exchange	OTC
Auditor	Amisano Hanson	Ticker Symbol	LNKG
Stk Agt	Mountain Share Transfer	Outstanding Shares	NA
Counsel	NA	E.P.S.	NA
DUNS No.	NA	Shareholders	NA

Business: The group's principal activities are to develop and market computer hardware, Web-based surveillance monitoring and control systems. The group also provides data acquisition systems, Internet services and wireless communication systems. The products of the group include video and audio monitoring systems used for security surveillance, remote business management, monitoring of unmanned premises and equipment and traffic control. These products enable users to observe and monitor through personal computers what is happening in remote sites via phone lines, isdn, gsm, intranet and Internet. The products of the group are marketed under the brand name geniuseye. The operations of the group are carried outside the United States. In 2002, the group acquired protect serve pacific limited which is accounted as a reverse acquisition.

Primary SIC and add'l.: 7389

CIK No: 0001145237

Financial Data: *Fiscal Year End:*12/31   *Latest Annual Data:* 12/31/2002

Year	Sales	Net Income
2002	$364,000	-$1,521,000
2001	NA	$2,000

Curr. Assets:	$340,000	**Curr. Liab.:**	$148,000		
Plant, Equip.:	$339,000	**Total Liab.:**	$1,214,000	**Indic. Yr. Divd.:**	NA
Total Assets:	$1,158,000	**Net Worth:**	-$56,000	**Debt/ Equity:**	NA

Linktone Ltd

12F,Cross Tower, No.318 Fu Zhou Rd, Shanghai, 200001; *PH:* 86-2133184900; *Fax:* 86-2163611550; *http://* www.linktone.com; *Email:* info@linktone.com

General - Incorporation	Cayman Islands	**Stock**- Price on:12/24/2007	NA
Employees	832	Stock Exchange	NDQ
Auditor	PricewaterhouseCoopers	Ticker Symbol	LTON
Stk Agt	Dexia Corporate Srvcs Hong Kong Ltd.	Outstanding Shares	23,920,000
Counsel	Morrison & Foerster LLP	E.P.S.	$0.04
DUNS No.	NA	Shareholders	NA

Business: The groups principle activity is to provide wireless value-added services. The groups services include media, games and information. The group operates from United States.

Primary SIC and add'l.: NA

CIK No: 0001270532

Subsidiaries: Beijing Cosmos Digital Technology Co., Ltd., Beijing Lian Fei Wireless Communications Technology Co., Ltd., Beijing Ojava Wuxian Co., Ltd., Beijing RuiDa Internet Technology Co., Ltd., Brilliant Concept Investments Ltd., Hainan Zhong Tong Computer Network Co., Ltd., Linktone Software Co., Ltd., Ojava Overseas Ltd., Shanghai Huitong Information Co., Ltd., Shanghai Linktone Consulting Co., Ltd., Shanghai Linktone Internet Technology Co., Ltd., Shanghai Qimingxing E-commerce Co., Ltd., Shanghai Unilink Computer Co., Ltd., Shanghai Weilan Computer Co., Ltd., Shenzhen Yuan Hang Technology Co., Ltd. 16 Subsidiaries included in the Index

Officers: Michael Li/Dir., CEO, Edward Liu/Contact - Investor Relations, Colin Sung/Dir., CFO, Maggie Su/Exec. VP, Harry Liu/Exec. VP

Directors: Michael Li/Dir., CEO, Elaine La Roche/58/Chmn., Thomas Hubbs/Dir., Jun Wu/Dir., Mark Begert/36/Dir., Colin Sung/Dir., CFO, Allan Kwan/Dir.

Owners: Farallon Capital Partners, L.P./5.50%, Mark Begert/2.00%, Michael Guangxin Li, Insiders/15.71%, Jun Wu/12.72%, Merry Asia Limited/12.59%, Elaine La Roche, Thomas Hubbs, Colin Sung

Financial Data: *Fiscal Year End:*12/31   *Latest Annual Data:* 12/31/2005

Year	Sales	Net Income
2005	$70,487,000	$12,449,000
2004	$48,084,000	$12,510,000
2003	$16,601,000	$3,616,000

Curr. Assets:	$70,448,000	**Curr. Liab.:**	$8,945,000		
Plant, Equip.:	$2,853,000	**Total Liab.:**	$9,000,000	**Indic. Yr. Divd.:**	NA
Total Assets:	$98,149,000	**Net Worth:**	$89,149,000	**Debt/ Equity:**	NA

Linkwell Corp

No. 476 Hutai Br. Rd., Baoshan District, Shanghai, 200436; *PH:* 86-215-668-9332; *http://* www.linkwell.us

General - Incorporation	FL	**Stock**- Price on:12/24/2007	$0.189
Employees	NA	Stock Exchange	OTC
Auditor	Sherb & Co., LLP	Ticker Symbol	LWLL
Stk Agt	Corporate Stock Transfer, Inc.	Outstanding Shares	NA
Counsel	NA	E.P.S.	NA
DUNS No.	NA	Shareholders	NA

Business: The groups principle activities include developing, manufacturing, selling and distributing disinfectant health care products. Products of the group include liquids-gel, tablets-powder, aerosol, chemical indicator, disinfectant appliance and liquids-foam. The group operates through two segments namely disinfectant products and import and export business. The group operates from the United States and China. The group's quarterly revenue for Sep '07 was 3.37 millions of USD.

Primary SIC and add'l.: 2842 2841 3291 2843 2899

CIK No: 0001042463

Subsidiaries: Aerisys Incorporated, Linkwell Tech Group, Inc., Shanghai Likang Disinfectant High-Tech Company, Limited

Officers: Xuelian Bian/Chmn., CEO, Pres., Wei Guan/Dir., VP, Sec., Gendi Li/Controller, Guoqiang Fan/44/GM - Marketing, Wensheng Sun/40/GM - Production

Directors: Xuelian Bian/Chmn., CEO, Pres., Wei Guan/Dir., VP, Sec.

Owners: Xue Lian Bian/25.20%, Wei Guan/19.80%, Insiders/44.90%

Financial Data: *Fiscal Year End:*12/31   *Latest Annual Data:* 12/31/2006

Year	Sales	Net Income
2006	$7,745,000	$568,000
2005	$5,466,000	$544,000
2004	$79,000	-$29,000

Curr. Assets:	$6,170,000	Curr. Liab.:	$2,605,000		
Plant, Equip.:	$775,000	Total Liab.:	$3,000,000	Indic. Yr. Divd.:	NA
Total Assets:	$6,944,000	Net Worth:	$3,945,000	Debt/ Equity:	NA

Linn Energy LLC

J P Morgan Chase Tower, 600 Travis, Ste. 7000, Houston, TX, 77002; **PH:** 1-281-605-4100; **Fax:** 1-281-605-4104; **http://** www.linnenergy.com; **Email:** ir@linnenergy.com

General - Incorporation	DE	**Stock** - Price on:12/24/2007	$34.59
Employees	220	Stock Exchange	NDQ
Auditor	KPMG LLP	Ticker Symbol	LINE
Stk Agt.	Computershare Trust Co	Outstanding Shares	57,800,000
Counsel	NA	E.P.S.	-$2.98
DUNS No.	NA	Shareholders	NA

Business: The group operates through its subsidiaries whose principle activities including developing and acquiring oil and gas properties. The groups services include drilling and gathering. Specific customers of the group include Dominion Resources, Inc and ConocoPhillips. The group operates from the United States. The group's quarterly revenue for September 2007 was 18.48 millions of USD.

Primary SIC and add'l.: 1311

CIK No: 0001326428

Subsidiaries: inn Energy Holdings, LLC

Officers: Michael C. Linn/Chmn., CEO, Pres./$14,220,010.00, Kolja Rockov/CFO, Exec. VP/$7,578,620.00, Mark E. Ellis/COO, Exec. VP/$3,561,419.00, Thomas A. Lopus/Sr. VP - Eastern Operations/$403,946.00, Roland P. Keddie/Sr. VP - Administration, Lisa D. Anderson/Chief Accounting Officer, Sr. VP/$520,992.00, Arden L. Walker/Sr. VP - Western Operations, Charlene A. Ripley/Sr. VP, General Counsel, Corp. Sec.

Directors: George A. Alcorn/Dir., Terrence S. Jacobs/Dir., Jeffrey C. Swoveland/Dir., Joseph P. McCoy/Dir.

Owners: Insiders, George A. Alcorn, Michael C. Linn, Lisa D. Anderson, Mark E. Ellis, Thomas A. Lopus, Alan L. Smith, Terrence S. Jacobs, Kolja Rockov

Financial Data: Fiscal Year End:12/31 Latest Annual Data: 12/31/2006

Year	Sales	Net Income
2006	$191,058,000	$79,185,000
2005	$49,713,000	-$56,351,000
2004	$21,912,000	-$3,978,000

Curr. Assets:	$69,676,000	Curr. Liab.:	$18,017,000		
Plant, Equip.:	$754,043,000	Total Liab.:	$465,354,000	Indic. Yr. Divd.:	$2.280
Total Assets:	$916,308,000	Net Worth:	$450,954,000	Debt/ Equity:	0.9716

Linux Gold Corp

1103-11871 Horseshoe Way, Richmond, BC, V7A 5H5; **PH:** 1-604-278-5996; **http://** www.linuxgoldcorp.com; **Email:** info@linuxgoldcorp.com

General - Incorporation	BC	**Stock** - Price on:12/24/2007	$0.165
Employees	NA	Stock Exchange	OTC
Auditor	Smythe Ratcliffe LLP	Ticker Symbol	LNXGF
Stk Agt.	Computershare Trust Co	Outstanding Shares	NA
Counsel	NA	E.P.S.	NA
DUNS No.	NA	Shareholders	NA

Business: The groups principle activity is to provide mineral property exploration services. The group operates from Canada.

Primary SIC and add'l.: 6799

CIK No: 0001088158

Officers: John Robertson/Chmn., CEO, Pres., Jennifer Lorette/Dir., VP, Sec., Robert Murray/Registered Professional Geologist, Jeff Keener/Geological Consultant

Directors: John Robertson/Chmn., CEO, Pres., Susanne Robertson/Dir., Jennifer Lorette/Dir., VP, Sec., Monique Van Oord/Dir.

Owners: Susanne Robertson/9.35%, Jennifer Lorette, John G. Robertson/3.31%, Monique van Oord

Financial Data: Fiscal Year End:02/28 Latest Annual Data: 02/28/2007

Year	Sales	Net Income
2007	NA	-$3,358,000
2006	NA	-$724,000
2005	NA	-$680,000

Curr. Assets:	$204,000	Curr. Liab.:	$306,000		
Plant, Equip.:	$4,000	Total Liab.:	$306,000	Indic. Yr. Divd.:	NA
Total Assets:	$209,000	Net Worth:	-$97,000	Debt/ Equity:	NA

Lion Capital Holdings Inc

6836 Bee CAve. Rd. , Ste 242, Austin, TX, 78746; **PH:** 1-512-617-6351; **http://** www.lioncapitalholdings.com

General - Incorporation	DE	**Stock** - Price on:12/24/2007	NA
Employees	1	Stock Exchange	OTC
Auditor	Chisholm Bierwolf & Nilson LLC	Ticker Symbol	LCHI
Stk Agt.	NA	Outstanding Shares	NA
Counsel	NA	E.P.S.	$0.001
DUNS No.	NA	Shareholders	NA

Business: The group's principal activity was the manufacturing of copper and fiber optic specialty custom cabling for the data and telecommunications industries in Mexico for distribution in the United States and Mexico. In mid-2003, the group changed its business focus from a cable assembly house and operates as a boutique consulting firm engaged in assisting private micro-cap companies in the transition to publicly traded status. The group also operates as a consultant and facilitator to undervalued, micro to mid-cap private companies focused on transitioning themselves to fully reporting public company status with publicly listed and traded common stock.

Primary SIC and add'l.: 3357

CIK No: 0001109219

Subsidiaries: Capital Cable and Wire, Inc.

Officers: Timothy T. Page/Chmn., CEO, Pres.

Directors: Timothy T. Page/Chmn., CEO, Pres., Martin Cantu/Dir.

Owners: Timothy T. Page/75.94%, Martin Cantu/1.43%, Jesus Aguirre/6.55%, Insiders/77.37%

Financial Data: Fiscal Year End:12/31 Latest Annual Data: 12/31/2006

Year	Sales	Net Income
2006	$117,000	$33,000
2005	$221,000	$137,000
2004	NA	-$356,000

Curr. Assets:	$241,000	Curr. Liab.:	$1,709,000		
Plant, Equip.:	NA	Total Liab.:	$1,709,000	Indic. Yr. Divd.:	NA
Total Assets:	$241,000	Net Worth:	-$1,468,000	Debt/ Equity:	NA

Lion Inc

4700-42nd Ave. Sw, Ste. 430, Seattle, WA, 98116; **PH:** 1-206-577-1440

General - Incorporation	WA	**Stock** - Price on:12/24/2007	$0.15
Employees	108	Stock Exchange	OTC
Auditor	Grant Thornton LLP	Ticker Symbol	LINN
Stk Agt	Computershare Investor Services LLC	Outstanding Shares	38,620,000
Counsel	NA	E.P.S.	-$0.03
DUNS No.	NA	Shareholders	NA

Business: The groups principle activities include providing online mortgage leads and business solutions to streamline the mortgage loan fulfillment process in the mortgage industry. The group operates from the United States. The group operates through two segments namely LION and TRMS. The group's quarterly revenue for Sep '07 was 1.01millions of USD.

Primary SIC and add'l.: 6162 4899 6163 7375

CIK No: 0000941179

Subsidiaries: Tuttle Risk Management Services LLC

Officers: David Stedman/58/Pres./$210,006.00, Steve Thomson/55/CFO, Corp. Sec., Treasurer/$167,698.00

Directors: John A. McMillan/76/Dir., Griffith J. Straw/59/Dir., James Russo/61/Dir., David Stedman/58/Pres., J. C. Marshall/62/Dir., Sam Ringer/48/Dir.

Owners: David Stedman/3.10%, Sam Ringer/5.04%, Insiders/19.74%, Randall D. Miles/1.70%, James Russo, Steve Thomson/2.83%, Griffith J. Straw, J. C. Marshall/1.73%, Continental Advisors LLC/11.16%, John A. McMillan/5.10%

Financial Data: Fiscal Year End:12/31 Latest Annual Data: 12/31/2006

Year	Sales	Net Income
2006	$13,702,000	-$1,320,000
2005	$15,789,000	-$102,000
2004	$15,192,000	$616,000

Curr. Assets:	$5,118,000	Curr. Liab.:	$2,745,000		
Plant, Equip.:	$555,000	Total Liab.:	$2,753,000	Indic. Yr. Divd.:	NA
Total Assets:	$8,487,000	Net Worth:	$5,734,000	Debt/ Equity:	0.0013

Lion-Gri International Inc

1809 E Brd.way St. , Ste. 346, Oviedo, FL, 32765; ; **http://** www.lion-gri.com

General - Incorporation	CO	**Stock** - Price on:12/24/2007	NA
Employees	NA	Stock Exchange	NA
Auditor	Wiener, Goodman & Co., P.c.	Ticker Symbol	NA
Stk Agt	Pacific Stock Transfer Company	Outstanding Shares	NA
Counsel	NA	E.P.S.	NA
DUNS No.	NA	Shareholders	NA

Business: The group's principal activity is to manufacture and distribute wine. The group markets and sells over 120 varieties of wine including red and white varietals, cognac, champagne, and desert wine in Russia and western Europe. The group's operation are conducted in the republic of moldova. On 22-Jul-2003, the group acquired lion- gri srl.

Primary SIC and add'l.: 9999

CIK No: 0001093800

Subsidiaries: Lion-Gri S.R.L., Napoli Resources (USA)

Owners: Maria Gracia Roasales/28.00%, Ramon Rosales/7.00%, Maria Fernanda Rosales/25.00%

Lionbridge Technologies Inc

1050 Winter St., Ste. 2300, Waltham, MA, 02451; **PH:** 1-781-434-6000; **Fax:** 1-781-434-6034; **http://** www.lionbridge.com

General - Incorporation	DE	**Stock** - Price on:12/24/2007	$5.99
Employees	4,295	Stock Exchange	NDQ
Auditor	PricewaterhouseCoopers LLP	Ticker Symbol	LIOX
Stk Agt	American Stock Transfer & Trust Co.	Outstanding Shares	60,510,000
Counsel	Testa, Hurwitz & Thibeault	E.P.S.	-$0.11
DUNS No.	NA	Shareholders	NA

Business: The group's principle activities is to provide outsourced globalization and testing services that enable clients to develop, release, manage and maintain their enterprise content and technology applications. The group's activities include product and content globalization, multilingual application development and maintenance, software and hardware testing and product certification and competitive analysis. The group operates in two business segments: globalization segment provides product localization and content globalization services that enable simultaneous worldwide release and ongoing maintenance of products and related technical support, training materials, and sales and marketing information in multiple languages. Testing segment provides comprehensive testing of software, hardware and Web sites, as well as product certification programs. The group's quarterly revenue for September 2007 was 111.54 millions of USD.

Primary SIC and add'l.: 7379 7375

CIK No: 0001058299

Subsidiaries: Huanqui Tonglian WFOE, Lionbridge (Canada) Inc., Lionbridge (UK) Ltd, Lionbridge Belgium bvba/sprl, Lionbridge Chile Tracciones Limitada, Lionbridge Denmark A/S, Lionbridge Deutschland GmbH, Lionbridge Espana, Lionbridge France SAS, Lionbridge Global Solutions BV, Lionbridge Global Solutions Companies, Inc., Lionbridge Global Solutions Federal, Inc., Lionbridge Global Solutions Holdings (Netherlands) B.V., Lionbridge Global Solutions II, Inc., Lionbridge Holding GmbH 41 Subsidiaries included in the Index

Officers: Rory J. Cowan/Chmn., CEO, Pres./$2,117,329.00, Satish Maripuri/COO/$688,615.00, Dave Flanagan/CTO, CIO, Eileen Sweeney/Sr. VP - Human Resources, Paula Shannon/Chief Sales Officer, Sr. VP/$567,749.00, Kevin Bolen/Chief Marketing Officer, Henri Brockmate/Sr. VP - Global Client Services/$457,805.00, Stephen J. Lifshatz/49/Sr. VP/$728,730.00, Peggy Shukur/VP, General Counsel, Sec., Sara Buda/VP - Investor Relations, Corporate Development, Donald Muir/CFO, Aaron Dun/Dir. - Corporate Marketing Communications, Ketan Pote/Mgr. - Public Relations, India Media

Directors: Rory J. Cowan/Chmn., CEO, Pres., Edward A. Blechschmidt/Dir., Guy L. De Chazal/Dir., Jeff Goodman/Dir., Paul A. Kavanagh/Dir., Claude P. Sheer/Dir.

Owners: Wells Fargo& Company/8.51%, Guy L. de Chazal, Paul Kavanagh, FMR Corp./9.98%, Edward A. Blechschmidt, Jeffrey H. Goodman, Rory J. Cowan/6.48%, Stephen J. Lifshatz, Claude P. Sheer, Satish Maripuri, Independence Investments LLC/5.37%, Insiders/9.24%, Paula Shannon, Henri Brockmate

Financial Data: Fiscal Year End:12/31 Latest Annual Data: 12/31/2006

Year	Sales	Net Income
2006	$418,884,000	-$4,902,000
2005	$236,262,000	-$3,913,000
2004	$154,101,000	$7,140,000

Curr. Assets:	$136,758,000	Curr. Liab.:	$75,865,000		
Plant, Equip.:	$13,032,000	Total Liab.:	$164,812,000	Indic. Yr. Divd.:	NA
Total Assets:	$321,500,000	Net Worth:	$156,688,000	Debt/ Equity:	0.4777

Lions Gate Entertainment Corp

2700 Colorado Ave., Santa Monica, CA, 90404; **PH:** 1-604-983-5555; **http://** www.lionsgate-ent.com

General - Incorporation	BC	Stock - Price on:12/24/2007	NA
Employees	354	Stock Exchange	NYSE
Auditor	Ernst & Young LLP	Ticker Symbol	LGF
Stk Agt	Mellon Trust Co	Outstanding Shares	NA
Counsel	NA	E.P.S	-$0.56
DUNS No.	25-505-3878	Shareholders	NA

Business: The group's principal activities are the development and distribution of feature films. The group provides development, production and distribution of feature films, television series, television movies, mini-series, non-fiction programs and animated programs. The group also provides management services.

Primary SIC and add'l.: 7812 7822 7922 7829 7819

CIK No: 0000929351

Subsidiaries: 3 Wise Guys Productions, 3191451 Canada Inc. (Marco Polo), 3349217 Canada Inc. (Kit & Kaboodle), 3583848 Canada Inc. (Kids from Room402), 3583856 Canada Inc. (Wilderness Station), 3584305 Canada Inc. (Bad Dog II), 3600793 Canada Inc. (Wounchpounch), 3600807 Canada Inc. (Lions of Oz), 3600815 Canada Inc. (Mega Babies), 3611587 Canada Inc. (Emma), 3687295 Canada Inc., 3711561 Canada Inc. (WWA), 3734994 Canada Inc. , 3735010 Canada Inc. (Daft Planet I, II), 3851923 Canada Inc. (Big Wolf II) 138 Subsidiaries included in the Index

Officers: Jon Feltheimer/Co - Chmn., CEO/$3,297,740.00, Joe Drake/CEO - Mandate Pictures, Co - COO, Pres. - Lionsgate Motion Picture Group, Steve Beeks/COO, Pres./$3,146,577.00, Wilkes Handles/Contact - Corporate Media, Jim Keegan/CFO/$559,288.00, Peter D. Wilkes/Contact - Investor, Media Inquiries, Wayne Levin/45/General Counsel, Exec. VP - Corporate Operations/$782,321.00

Directors: Jon Feltheimer/Co - Chmn., CEO, Mark Amin/58/Vice Chmn., Michael Burns/Vice Chmn., Scott G. Paterson/44/Dir., Morley Koffman/78/Dir., Norman Bacal/52/Dir., Arthur Evrensel/50/Dir., Harald Ludwig/53/Dir., Brian V. Tobin/53/Dir., Daryl Simm/47/Dir., Hardwick Simmons/68/Dir., Laurie May/41/Dir.

Owners: Steinberg Asset Management, LLC/5.40%, Daryl Sim, Michael Burns/1.20%, James Keegan, Arthur Evrensel, Mark H. Rachesky/10.90%, Kornitzer Capital Management, Inc/10.10%, Brian V. Tobin, Laurie May, Harald Ludwig, Hardwick Simmons, Great Plains TrustCompany/4.80%, Norman Bacal, Mark Amin/1.40%, Scott Paterson (22 Owners included in Index)

Financial Data: Fiscal Year End:03/31 Latest Annual Data: 03/31/2007

Year	Sales	Net Income
2007	$976,740,000	$27,479,000
2006	$951,228,000	$6,096,000
2005	$842,586,000	$20,281,000

Curr. Assets:	$186,908,000	Curr. Liab.:	$155,617,000		
Plant, Equip.:	$13,095,000	Total Liab.:	$889,205,000	Indic. Yr. Divd.:	NA
Total Assets:	$1,137,095,000	Net Worth:	$247,890,000	Debt/ Equity:	NA

Lions Petroleum Inc

Formerly: Energy Ventures Inc
600 - 17th St., Ste. 2800, South Denver, CO, 80202; **PH:** 1-720-359-1604

General - Incorporation	DE	Stock - Price on:12/24/2007	$0.355
Employees	NA	Stock Exchange	OTC
Auditor	Chisholm, Bierwolf & Nilson, LLC	Ticker Symbol	LPET
Stk Agt	Equity Transfer Services Inc	Outstanding Shares	NA
Counsel	Cassels Brock & Blackwell LLP	E.P.S	NA
DUNS No.	NA	Shareholders	NA

Business: The group's principal activities are the research and development of technology used to manufacture fuel cells and batteries. A fuel cell is a device that combines hydrogen and oxygen to generate electricity through an electrochemical reaction. The group has proprietary interests in technology relating to direct methanol fuel cells (dmfc's) and lithium ion, nickel zinc and zinc carbon (bromine complex) rechargeable batteries. Currently, the group is focusing its efforts primarily in two areas: the development of its proprietary dmfc's and the commercialization of its nickel zinc technology. In oct-2003, the group acquired 49.6% shareholding in pure energy inc.

Primary SIC and add'l.: 8731 3691 8733

CIK No: 0001048407

Subsidiaries: Energy Visions Inc.

Officers: Gordon L. Wiltse/41/Dir., CEO, CFO, VP, Sec.

Directors: Gordon L. Wiltse/41/Dir., CEO, CFO, VP, Sec., Duane D. Fadness/59/Dir., Dale M. Paulson/46/Dir., Eric H. Olsen/56/Dir.

Owners: Duane D. Fadness/1.50%, Dale M. Paulson/39.60%, Gordon L. Wiltse/39.70%, Eric H. Olsen, Insiders/79.70%

Lipid Sciences Inc

7068 Koll Ctr. Pkwy., Ste. 401, Pleasanton, CA, 94566; **PH:** 1-925-249-4000; **Fax:** 1-925-249-4040; **http://** www.lipidsciences.com; **Email:** info@lipidsciences.com

General - Incorporation	DE	Stock - Price on:12/24/2007	$1.57
Employees	18	Stock Exchange	NDQ
Auditor	Deloitte & Touche LLP	Ticker Symbol	LIPD
Stk Agt	Bank of New York	Outstanding Shares	37,120,000
Counsel	NA	E.P.S	-$0.31
DUNS No.	06-108-4240	Shareholders	NA

Business: The group's principal activities are to conduct research and develop products and processes intended to treat major medical conditions in which lipids, or fat components, play a key role. Its technologies are based on a patented process that selectively removes lipids from proteins. This unique delipidation process has the potential for far-reaching implications for human health. It may provide an effective therapeutic effect on many infectious agents, including the viruses that cause aids, hepatitis b and c, as well as reverse cardio and cerebrovascular disease.

Primary SIC and add'l.: 8731

CIK No: 0000071478

Subsidiaries: Bridge Financial Corporation, Lipid Sciences, Pty. Ltd., NZ Corporation, NZ Development Corporation, NZ Properties, Inc., NZU Inc.

Officers: Lewis S. Meyer/Dir., CEO, Pres./$426,177.00, Bryan H. Brewer/Vice Chmn., Chief Scientific Dir., Jo-Ann Maltais/VP - Scientific Affairs/$236,046.00, Sandra A. Gardiner/CFO/$301,730.00, Deborah S. Lorenz/VP - Investor Relations, Corporate Communications, Dale L. Richardson/VP - Business Development/$327,409.00, Petar Alaupovic/Member - Scientific Advisory Board

Directors: Lewis S. Meyer/Dir., CEO, Pres., Bryan H. Brewer/Vice Chmn., Chief Scientific Dir., Frank M. Placenti/Dir., Bosko Djordjevic/Dir., Gary S. Roubin/Dir., John E. Crawford/Dir., Aftab A. Ansari/Member - Viral Advisory Board, Susan B. Zolla-Pazner/Member - Viral Advisory Board, James E.K. Hildreth/Member - Viral Advisory Board, Howard N. Hodis/Member - Scientific Advisory Board, Frank M. Sacks/Member - Scientific Advisory Board, George A. Bray/Member - Scientific Advisory Board, Gerhard M. Kostner/Member - Scientific Advisory Board, Stephen E. Renneckar/Dir., John J.P. /Member - Scientific Advisory Board

Owners: Bosko Djordjevic/4.10%, Dale L. Richardson, Lewis S. Meyer/3.00%, Sandra Gardiner, Bryan H. Brewer/2.00%, Stephen E. Renneckar, Jo-Ann Maltais, Frank M. Placenti, Robert E.& Margaret M. Petersen Living Trust/5.70%, Insiders/12.50%, John E. Crawford, KAI International, LLC/5.40%, Diker Management, LLC/6.20%, Lenny K. Dykstra/6.60%, RA Capital Management, LLC/10.00% (19 Owners included in Index)

Financial Data: Fiscal Year End:12/31 Latest Annual Data: 12/31/2006

Year	Sales	Net Income
2006	$59,000	-$11,177,000
2005	$9,000	-$10,214,000
2004	$32,000	-$11,642,000

Curr. Assets:	$17,043,000	Curr. Liab.:	$2,441,000		
Plant, Equip.:	$374,000	Total Liab.:	$2,457,000	Indic. Yr. Divd.:	NA
Total Assets:	$17,436,000	Net Worth:	$14,979,000	Debt/ Equity:	NA

LipidViro Tech Inc

1338 Foothill Blvd. 126, Salt Lake City, UT, 84108; **PH:** 1-801-583-9900; **http://** www.lipidvirotech.com; **Email:** PR@lipidvirotech.com

General - Incorporation	NV	Stock- Price on:12/24/2007	$0.35
Employees	NA	Stock Exchange	OTC
Auditor	Pritchett, Siler & Hardy, P.C.	Ticker Symbol	LPVT
Stk Agt	Atlas Stock Transfer Corp	Outstanding Shares	17,880,000
Counsel	NA	E.P.S	-$0.17
DUNS No.	NA	Shareholders	NA

Business: The groups principal activities include researching and commercializing the development of d-OSAB therapy and PathPure. The group operates from the United States.

Primary SIC and add'l.: 8731

CIK No: 0000006732

Officers: Kenneth P. Hamik/47/Dir., CEO, Pres.

Directors: Kenneth P. Hamik/47/Dir., CEO, Pres., Steven Keyser/Chmn., Linda Sharkus/Dir.

Owners: Benedente Holdings, LLC/14.40%, Ariannus Limitada/7.78%, Kenneth P. Hamik/1.15%, Linda Sharkus

Financial Data: Fiscal Year End:12/31 Latest Annual Data: 12/31/2005

Year	Sales	Net Income
2005	NA	-$172,000
2004	NA	-$249,000
2003	NA	-$22,000

Curr. Assets:	NA	Curr. Liab.:	$505,000		
Plant, Equip.:	$2,000	Total Liab.:	$1,113,000	Indic. Yr. Divd.:	NA
Total Assets:	$325,000	Net Worth:	-$788,000	Debt/ Equity:	NA

Lipman Electronic Engineering Ltd

11 Haamal St., Pk. Afek, Rosh Haayin, 48092; ; **http://** www.lipman.co.il

General - Incorporation	Israel	Stock- Price on:12/24/2007	$36.45
Employees	1,306	Stock Exchange	NA
Auditor	Kost Forer Gabbay & Kasierer	Ticker Symbol	NA
Stk Agt	American Stk Trnsfer & Trust Co	Outstanding Shares	82,970,000
Counsel	Fulbright & Jaworski LLP	E.P.S	$0.62
DUNS No.	NA	Shareholders	NA

Business: The groups principle activity is to provide transaction systems and solutions for the payment industry. The groups products include wireless point-of-sale, terminals, personal identification number (PIN) pads and electronic cash registers. The group operates from United States.

Primary SIC and add'l.: NA

CIK No: 0001270484

Subsidiaries: Dione Ltd., Lipman do Brazil Ltda., Lipman Elektronik ve Danismanlik Ltd, Lipman U.S.A., Inc.

Financial Data: Fiscal Year End:12/31 Latest Annual Data: 10/31/2006

Year	Sales	Net Income
2006	$581,070,000	$59,511,000
2005	$485,367,000	$33,239,000
2004	$390,088,000	$5,606,000

Curr. Assets:	$319,244,000	Curr. Liab.:	$152,668,000	P/E Ratio:	58.79
Plant, Equip.:	$7,300,000	Total Liab.:	$354,204,000	Indic. Yr. Divd.:	NA
Total Assets:	$452,945,000	Net Worth:	$98,741,000	Debt/ Equity:	0.8619

Liquidgolf Holding Corp

2203 N Lois Ave., Ste. 929, Tampa, FL, 33607; **PH:** 1-813-600-4081

General - Incorporation .... DE	Stock - Price on:12/24/2007 ....NA
Employees 2	Stock Exchange.......................................NA
Auditor .....Tedder, James, Worden & Assoc. P.A	Ticker Symbol...NA
Stk Agt...NA	Outstanding Shares ....NA
Counsel..NA	E.P.S ....-$0.083
DUNS No. ....NA	Shareholders...NA

Business: The group's principal business activity consisted of developing mobile applications to improve customer productivity and responsiveness through the use of the latest mobile and collaborative technologies. During 2002 the group has acquired omnitrix technologies, inc.

Primary SIC and add'l.: 7372 6719

CIK No: 0001062720

Subsidiaries: LiquidGolf Corporation, Nomadic Collaboration International, Inc

Officers: Chris Trina/CEO, Charles Wernicke/40/CTO, Dir., Steven Weldon/32/CFO

Directors: Charles Wernicke/40/CTO, Dir., William Parsons/59/Dir., Dwight Day/43/Dir.

Owners: Charles Wenicke/3.72%, Insiders/4.71%, Burns Administrative Trust/56.00%, William Parsons, Dwight Day

Financial Data: Fiscal Year End:12/31   **Latest Annual Data:** 12/31/2005

Year	Sales	Net Income
2005	$33,000	-$1,404,000
2004	$909,000	-$3,101,000
2003	$781,000	-$1,759,000

Curr. Assets:	$189,000	Curr. Liab.:	$435,000		
Plant, Equip.:	NA	Total Liab.:	$435,000	Indic. Yr. Divd.:	NA
Total Assets:	$189,000	Net Worth:	-$246,000	Debt/ Equity:	NA

Liquidity Services Inc

1920 L St. NW, 6th Fl., Washington, DC, 20036; **PH:** 1-202-467-6868; **Fax:** 1-202-467-5475; **http://** www.liquidityservicesinc.com; **Email:** sales@liquidityservicesinc.com

General - Incorporation .... DE	Stock- Price on:12/24/2007 ....$18.22
Employees 410	Stock Exchange.....................................NDQ
Auditor ....Ernst & Young, LLP	Ticker Symbol.......................................LQDT
Stk Agt.........Computershare Shareholder Ser Inc	Outstanding Shares 27,850,000
Counsel..NA	E.P.S $0.39
DUNS No. ....NA	Shareholders...NA

Business: The groups principle activity is to provide online auction services. The groups services include key word advertising, sponsorship, seller directory, classified ads, industry news and wholesale auctions. The group acquired STR, Inc. in the year 2006 and Aldnet Media Group, LLC in the year 2005. The group operates from the United States. The group's quarterly revenue for September 2007 was 51.67 millions of USD.

Primary SIC and add'l.: 7389 9999

CIK No: 0001235468

Subsidiaries: DOD Surplus LLC, Government Liquidation.com, LLC, Liquidity (Shanghai) Business Services Co., Ltd., Liquidity Services Asia Limited, Liquidity Services Limited, Liquidity Services, GmbH, Surplus Acquisition Venture, LLC

Officers: William P. Angrick/Co - Founder, Chmn., CEO, Jaime Mateus-Tique/Co - Founder, Pres., Dir., COO, Benjamin R. Brown/Co - Founder, CTO - Government Liquidation, LLC, James M. Rallo/Treasurer, CFO, Thomas B. Burton/Pres., COO - Government Liquidation, LLC, James E. Williams/VP, General Counsel, Corp. Sec., Holger Schwarz/Exec. VP - Europe, GM, Julie Davis/Corporate Communications Dir.

Directors: William P. Angrick/Co - Founder, Chmn., CEO, Jaime Mateus-Tique/Co - Founder, Pres., Dir., COO, Phillip A. Clough/Dir., Patrick W. Gross/Dir., Franklin D. Kramer/Dir., David F. Fowler/Dir.

Owners: Patrick W. Gross, Jaime Mateus-Tique/14.00%, Thomas B. Burton, Entities affiliated with ABS Capital Partners/11.70%, Benjamin R. Brown/2.20%, Insiders/61.30%, Franklin D. Kramer, James M. Rallo, William P. Angrick/31.00%, Phillip A. Clough/11.70%

Financial Data: Fiscal Year End:09/30   **Latest Annual Data:** 9/30/2006

Year	Sales	Net Income
2006	$147,813,000	$7,981,000
2005	$89,415,000	$4,122,000
2004	$75,869,000	$5,269,000

Curr. Assets:	$75,911,000	Curr. Liab.:	$21,829,000	P/E Ratio:	55.21
Plant, Equip.:	$2,362,000	Total Liab.:	$22,286,000	Indic. Yr. Divd.:	NA
Total Assets:	$88,038,000	Net Worth:	$65,752,000	Debt/ Equity:	0.0004

Liquidmetal Technologies Inc

25800 CommerCtr. Dr., Ste. 100, Lake Forest, CA, 92630; **PH:** 1-949-206-8000; **Fax:** 1-949-206-8008; **http://** www.liquidmetal.com; **Email:** information@liquidmetal.com

General - Incorporation .... DE	Stock - Price on:12/24/2007 ....$0.9
Employees 636	Stock Exchange.......................................OTC
Auditor ....Choi, Kim & Park, LLP	Ticker Symbol.......................................LQMT
Stk Agt..... American Stock Transfer & Trust Co.	Outstanding Shares 44,630,000
Counsel...............................Foley & Lardner LLP	E.P.S ....-$0.11
DUNS No. ....NA	Shareholders...NA

Business: The group's principal activity is to develop, manufacture and market products made from amorphous alloys. The group operates in two segments namely, bulk alloys and industrial coatings. The bulk alloys segment manufactures the liquidmetal(R) family of alloys is used in different applications including industrial coatings, defense, electronic casing, medical devices and sporting goods. The segment also produces casings for cellular phones and other electronic products. The alloys are used to produce skis, baseball bats, ice skates, bicycles and solar wind collector tiles. The industrial coatings segment manufactures protective coatings for industrial machinery and equipment. The group has operations in the United States and South Korea. The major customers of the group are samsung electronics company, grant prideco and growell metal inc.

Primary SIC and add'l.: 3313 3499

CIK No: 0001141240

Subsidiaries: Liquidmetal Golf, Liquidmetal Korea Co., Ltd

Officers: John Kang/Chmn., CEO, Pres., Larry E. Buffington/CEO, Pres.

Directors: John Kang/Chmn., CEO, Pres., William Johnson/Dir., Dean G. Tanella/47/Dir., C. K. Cho/Dir., Robert J. Biehl/Dir., William D. Nix/Dir., Michael Ashby/Member - Advisory Board, Merton C. Flemings/Member - Advisory Board, Patrick P. Caruana/Dir.

Owners: Tjoa Thian Song/9.00%, James KangHyundai/14.00%, Robert Biehl, Insiders/17.00%, CK Cho/2.00%, John Kang/11.00%, Dean Tanella, William Johnson/3.00%, Jack Chitayat/12.00%, Won Chung, Patrick Caruana

Financial Data: Fiscal Year End:12/31   **Latest Annual Data:** 03/31/2007

Year	Sales	Net Income
2007	NA	NA
2006	NA	NA
2005	$16,365,000	-$7,053,000

Curr. Assets:	$8,673,000	Curr. Liab.:	$31,830,000		
Plant, Equip.:	$12,289,000	Total Liab.:	$32,607,000	Indic. Yr. Divd.:	NA
Total Assets:	$22,244,000	Net Worth:	-$10,363,000	Debt/ Equity:	NA

Liska Biometry Inc

100 Main St., Ste. 230 , Dover, NH, 03820; **PH:** 1-44-877-775-4752; **http://** www.liskabiometry.com

General - Incorporation .... FL	Stock - Price on:12/24/2007 ....NA
Employees ....NA	Stock Exchange.......................................OTC
Auditor ....Liska Biometry, Inc.	Ticker Symbol.....................................LSKAE
Stk Agt .... Securities Transfer Corp	Outstanding Shares ....NA
Counsel..NA	E.P.S ....NA
DUNS No. ....NA	Shareholders...NA

Business: The groups principal activity is to develop fingerprint biometric solutions. Services of the group include individual authentication, precise identification searches, and cross-platform data interoperability. Customers served by the group include federal, state, and local government agencies. The group operates from the United States and Canada.

Primary SIC and add'l.: 9995

CIK No: 0001102065

Subsidiaries: Liska Biometry (Canada) Inc.

Officers: Charles Benz/59/Chmn., CEO, Christopher J. Leclerc/Co - Founder, Dir., CFO, Pres., Brian F. Hynes/Dir., Corp Sec., Virginia K. Sourlis/Legal Counsel

Directors: Charles Benz/59/Chmn., CEO, Bryan G. Thomas/Dir., Javaid I. Sheikh/Dir., Brian F. Hynes/Dir., Corp Sec., Christopher J. Leclerc/Co - Founder, Dir., CFO, Pres.

Owners: Christopher J. LeClerc/6.18%, Javaid Sheikh, Bryan G. Thomas, Bryan Hynes, Charles Benz/11.45%, Insiders/19.68%

LiteWave Corp

1620 W 8th Ave., Ste. 300, Vancouver, BC, V6J 1V4; **PH:** 1-604-675-7637; **Fax:** 1-604-736-5004; **http://** www.litewavecorp.com; **Email:** info@litewavecorp.com

General - Incorporation .... NV	Stock - Price on:12/24/2007 ....$0.09
Employees ....NA	Stock Exchange.......................................OTC
Auditor .... Telford Sadovnick, PLLC	Ticker Symbol.......................................LTWV
Stk Agt .... Pacific Stock Transfer Company	Outstanding Shares ....NA
Counsel..NA	E.P.S ....NA
DUNS No. ....NA	Shareholders...NA

Business: The groups principal activity is to explore oil and natural gas. The group operates from the United States.

Primary SIC and add'l.: 1311

CIK No: 0001096264

Officers: Ian D. Lambert/61/Dir., CEO, Pres., Bob Cairns/Dir., COO, Harvey M.J. Lawson/59/Dir., CFO, Sec., Jim Newton/VP - Corporate Development, Doug McGown/Project Operator, Robert Cairns/66/Dir., COO

Directors: Ian D. Lambert/61/Dir., CEO, Pres., Bob Cairns/Dir., COO, Harvey M.J. Lawson/59/Dir., CFO, Sec., Edward D. Duncan/72/Dir.

Owners: Insiders/12.80%, Robert Cairns/1.40%, Edward Duncan/1.20%, Ian Lambert/8.30%, Harvey Lawson/1.90%

Financial Data: Fiscal Year End:12/31   **Latest Annual Data:** 12/31/2006

Year	Sales	Net Income
2006	NA	-$2,415,000
2005	NA	-$197,000
2004	NA	-$107,000

Curr. Assets:	$201,000	Curr. Liab.:	$1,309,000		
Plant, Equip.:	$1,223,000	Total Liab.:	$1,309,000	Indic. Yr. Divd.:	NA
Total Assets:	$1,423,000	Net Worth:	$114,000	Debt/ Equity:	NA

LitFunding Corp

6375 S Pecos Rd. Ste. 217, Las Vegas, NV, 89120; **PH:** 1-702-898-8388; **http://** www.litfunding.com

General - Incorporation .... NV	Stock - Price on:12/24/2007 ....$0.14
Employees 8	Stock Exchange.......................................NA
Auditor ....Lawrence Scharfman CPA	Ticker Symbol...NA
Stk Agt ....Colonial Stock Transfer Co Inc	Outstanding Shares 79,390,000
Counsel..NA	E.P.S ....-$0.03
DUNS No. ....NA	Shareholders...NA

Business: The groups principle activity is to investigate in litigation recoveries. The group operates from the United States.

Primary SIC and add'l.: 6153

CIK No: 0001142488

Subsidiaries: LFC 100, LLC., LFC 101, LLC., LFC 102, LLC., LFC 103, LLC., LFC 104, LLC., LitFunding USA

Officers: Morton Reed/CEO - Litfunding Corp, Jackelyn Giroux/Pres., CEO - Global Universal Film Group, Inc, Gary A. Rasmussen/Chmn. - Consultant, Global Universal Film Group, Inc, Virginia Perfili/Dir. - Business Consultant, Edward N. Jones/CFO - Global Universal Film Group, Inc, Robert P. Amira/Exec. VP, Terry Gabby/CFO, Treasurer, Stanley B. Weiner/Dir., VP - Finance, Peter Foldy/Member - Advisory Board, Global Universal Film Group - Inc, Peter Liapis/Member - Advisory Board, Global Universal Film Group - Inc, Luciano Lisi/Member - Advisory Board, Global Universal Film Group - Inc, Melvin Pearl/Member - Advisory Board, Global Universal Film Group - Inc, Joseph Weaver/Member - Advisory Board, Global Universal Film Group - Inc, Natalie Pokorny/Dir. - Shareholder Relations

Directors: Gary A. Rasmussen/Chmn. - Consultant, Global Universal Film Group, Inc, Virginia Perfili/Dir. - Business Consultant, Stanley B. Weiner/Dir., VP - Finance, Donald Hejmanowski/Dir., Dennis H. Johnston/54/Dir.

Owners: Rochester Capital Partners, LP, Gary Rasmussen, Insiders, Donald Hejmanowski, Terry Gabby, Stanley Weiner, Morton Reed

Financial Data: Fiscal Year End:12/31 **Latest Annual Data:** 12/31/2006

Year	Sales	Net Income
2006	$644,000	-$1,028,000
2005	$355,000	-$3,972,000
2004	$1,879,000	$13,206,000

Curr. Assets:	$702,000	Curr. Liab.:	$3,331,000		
Plant, Equip.:	$230,000	Total Liab.:	$3,521,000	Indic. Yr. Divd.:	NA
Total Assets:	$1,142,000	Net Worth:	-$2,378,000	Debt/ Equity:	NA

Lithia Motors Inc

360 E Jackson St., Medford, OR, 97501; *PH:* 1-541-776-6899; *Fax:* 1-541-774-7617; *http://* www.lithia.com

General - Incorporation	OR	Stock- Price on:12/24/2007	$26.83
Employees	6,261	Stock Exchange	NYSE
Auditor	KPMG LLP	Ticker Symbol	LAD
Stk Agt	Computershare Investor Services LLC	Outstanding Shares	19,640,000
Counsel	Foster, Pepper & Shefelman Et Al	E.P.S.	$1.52
DUNS No.	05-221-3907	Shareholders	NA

Business: The groups principle activity is to operate automotive franchises. The group sells new and used cars, light truck and sport utility vehicles. The groups services include vehicle maintenance, warranty, paint and repair services. The group operates from United States.

Primary SIC and add'l.: 6410 5511 5521 5599

CIK No: 0001023128

Subsidiaries: Camp Automotive, Inc., Hutchins Eugene Nissan, Inc., Hutchins Imported Motors, Inc., LGPAC, Inc., Lithia Automotive, Inc., Lithia BC, Inc., Lithia BNM, Inc., Lithia CB, Inc., Lithia CCTF, Inc., Lithia CDH, Inc., Lithia Centennial Chrysler Plymouth Jeep, Inc., Lithia Cherry Creek Dodge, Inc., Lithia Chrysler Jeep of Anchorage, Inc., Lithia CIMR, Inc., Lithia CJD of Omaha, Inc. 91 Subsidiaries included in the Index

Officers: Sidney B. Deboer/Chmn., CEO, Sec./$1,470,838.00, Bryan B. Deboer/COO, Pres./$1,092,372.00, Don Jones/Sr. VP - Retail Operations/$976,579.00, Jeffrey B. Deboer/CFO, Sr. VP/$755,597.00, Bradford R. Gray/Dir., Exec. VP/$999,356.00, Linda A. Ganim/VP, Chief Accounting Officer, Principal Accounting Officer

Directors: Sidney B. Deboer/Chmn., CEO, Sec., M. L. Dick Heimann/Vice Chmn., Thomas Becker/Dir., Bradford R. Gray/Dir., Exec. VP, William J. Young/Dir., Maryann N. Keller/Dir., Gerald F. Taylor/Dir.

Owners: Sidney B. DeBoer, Lithia Holding Company, LLC, Maryann N. Keller, Sidney B. DeBoer/1.40%, Morgan Stanley/5.50%, Gerald F. Taylor, William J. Young, FMR Corp./15.00%, Dick M.L Heimann/1.70%, Insiders, Bradford R. Gray, Thomas Becker, Jeffrey B. DeBoer, Bryan B. DeBoer, Insiders/5.10% (18 Owners included in Index)

Financial Data: Fiscal Year End:12/31 **Latest Annual Data:** 12/31/2006

Year	Sales	Net Income
2006	$3,172,894,000	$37,304,000
2005	$2,935,419,000	$53,627,000
2004	$2,745,787,000	$42,671,000

Curr. Assets:	$779,640,000	Curr. Liab.:	$629,939,000		
Plant, Equip.:	$417,103,000	Total Liab.:	$1,085,964,000	Indic. Yr. Divd.:	$0.560
Total Assets:	$1,579,357,000	Net Worth:	$493,393,000	Debt/ Equity:	0.8069

Lithium Technology Corp

5115 Campus Dr., Plymouth Meeting, PA, 19462; *PH:* 1-610-940-6090; *Fax:* 1-610-940-6091; *http://* www.lithiumtech.com; *Email:* info@lithiumtech.com

General - Incorporation	DE	Stock- Price on:12/24/2007	$0.1
Employees	71	Stock Exchange	OTC
Auditor	BDO Seidman LLP	Ticker Symbol	LTHU
Stk Agt	StockTrans, Inc.	Outstanding Shares	387,400,000
Counsel	NA	E.P.S.	-$0.071
DUNS No.	61-296-3637	Shareholders	NA

Business: The group's principal activity is to develop and produce large format lithium-ion rechargeable batteries. The batteries are used in the national security systems, automotive and stationary power markets. The group's manufacturing and marketing activities are focused to develop innovative lithium polymer batteries primarily for the automotive battery applications, including hybrid electric vehicle. In the past, it has worked closely with selected portable electronics original equipment manufacturers exploring various notebook computer, personal digital assistant and wireless handset applications. The group also holds various patents relating to such batteries.

Primary SIC and add'l.: 3691

CIK No: 0000804154

Subsidiaries: DILO Trading AG, GAIA Advanced Lithium Battery Systems Europe GmbH, GAIA Akkumulatorenwerke GmbH, GAIA Holding B.V., Lithion Corporation, Lithiontech B.V., Lithiontech Licensing B.V.

Officers: Klaus Brandt/Dir., CEO, Amir Elbaz/CFO, Exec. VP, Ken Rudisuela/COO, Exec. VP

Directors: Klaus Brandt/Dir., CEO

Financial Data: Fiscal Year End:12/31 **Latest Annual Data:** 12/31/2005

Year	Sales	Net Income
2005	$1,803,000	-$21,972,000
2004	$766,000	-$14,751,000
2003	$229,000	-$10,191,000

Curr. Assets:	$1,344,000	Curr. Liab.:	$8,065,000		
Plant, Equip.:	$5,419,000	Total Liab.:	$15,285,000	Indic. Yr. Divd.:	NA
Total Assets:	$14,342,000	Net Worth:	-$943,000	Debt/ Equity:	NA

Littelfuse Inc

800 E N W Hwy., Des Plaines, IL, 60016; *PH:* 1-847-824-1188; *Fax:* 1-847-391-0894; *http://* www.littelfuse.com

General - Incorporation	DE	Stock- Price on:12/24/2007	$36.78
Employees	6,550	Stock Exchange	NDQ
Auditor	Ernst & Young LLP	Ticker Symbol	LFUS
Stk Agt	LaSalle Bank N.A	Outstanding Shares	22,230,000
Counsel	Chapman & Cutler	E.P.S.	$1.50
DUNS No.	00-521-2246	Shareholders	NA

Business: The group's principal activities are to design, manufacture and supply fuses and other circuit protection devices. The group operates in three segments: electronic segment includes electronic circuit protection products used to protect circuits in electronic systems. Automotive segment include fuses for automobiles, trucks, buses and off-road equipment to protect electrical circuits and wires that supply electrical power to operate lights, heating, air conditioning and other controls. The electrical segment includes low-voltage circuit protection products to electrical distributors, OEMs and the industrial maintenance and repair operations market. The customers of the group include compaq, dell computer, ge, intel, motorola, nokia, palm, panasonic, samsung and sony.

Primary SIC and add'l.: 3679 3613

CIK No: 0000889331

Subsidiaries: Dongguan EFEN Electrical Products Co., Dongguan Wickmann Electrical Products Co., EFEN Gmbh, EFEN Kasposvar Hungaria, EFEN Polska Sp. Z.o.o., H.I. Immobilien Management GmbH, H.I. Verwaltungs GmbH, Heinrich Industrie, A.G., Littelfuse Beteiligungs, GmbH, Littelfuse da Amazonia, Ltda., Littelfuse do Brasil Ltda., Littelfuse Europe Holding, B.V., Littelfuse Far East Pte Ltd., Littelfuse GmbH, Littelfuse GP, Inc. 43 Subsidiaries included in the Index

Officers: Gordon Hunter/56/Chmn., CEO/$2,242,232.00, Philip G. Franklin/VP - Operations Support, CFO/$1,230,747.00, Dieter Roeder/VP, GM - Automotive Business Unit, Jan Lahayne/CIO, VP, Dal Ferbert/VP, GM - Electrical Business Unit/$746,585.00, Mary S. Muchoney/Corp. Sec., David Heinzmann/VP - Global Operations/$657,597.00, David Samyn/VP, GM - Electronics Business Unit/$726,511.00, Paul Dickinson/VP - Corporate Development, Treasurer, Ryan Stafford/General Counsel, VP - Human Resources

Directors: Gordon Hunter/56/Chmn., CEO, John P. Driscoll/72/Dir., Anthony Grillo/52/Dir., Bruce A. Karsh/Dir., John E. Major/62/Dir., Ronald L. Schubel/64/Dir., William P. Noglows/50/Dir.

Owners: Columbia Wanger Asset Management, L.P./6.00%, Gordon Hunter, Anthony Grillo, Philip G. Franklin, T. Rowe Price Associates, Inc./9.70%, Ronald L. Schubel, Ariel Capital Management, Inc/10.50%, Barclays Global Investors, NA/6.60%, Dal Ferbert, John E. Major, John P. Driscoll, David W. Heinzmann, Bruce A. Karsh, Barrow, Hanley, Mewhinney & Strauss, Inc./6.40%, Insiders/3.00% (16 Owners included in Index)

Financial Data: Fiscal Year End:12/31 **Latest Annual Data:** 06/30/2007

Year	Sales	Net Income
2007	NA	$143,000
2006	$534,859,000	$23,824,000
2005	$467,089,000	$17,710,000

Curr. Assets:	$203,169,000	Curr. Liab.:	$99,916,000	P/E Ratio:	28.73
Plant, Equip.:	$125,493,000	Total Liab.:	$126,721,000	Indic. Yr. Divd.:	NA
Total Assets:	$403,931,000	Net Worth:	$277,066,000	Debt/ Equity:	0.0051

Little Bank (The)

804 Carey Rd., Kinston, NC, 28501; *PH:* 1-252-939-9990; *Fax:* 1-252-939-1255; *http://* www.thelittlebank.com

General - Incorporation	NA	Stock- Price on:12/24/2007	$20.6
Employees	NA	Stock Exchange	OTC
Auditor	NA	Ticker Symbol	LTLB
Stk Agt	NA	Outstanding Shares	NA
Counsel	NA	E.P.S.	NA
DUNS No.	NA	Shareholders	NA

Business: The groups principal activity is to provide banking services. The services of the group include originating loans, mortgage loans, checking and saving account, CDs and IRAs, cash management, deposit, wire transfer, safe deposit boxes, automatic teller machine, direct deposit, night depository, payroll services, merchant teller booth and phone and online banking. The group operates from the United States.

Primary SIC and add'l.: 6029

CIK No:

Officers: Vincent Robert Jones/Dir., CEO - Greenville, North Carolina, Lee Burrows/Chmn. - Atlanta, Georgia, Stuart D. Lindley/Exec. VP, Chief Credit Officer, Susan Barrett/Sr. VP, Operations Officer, Scott Newton/Sr. VP - City Executive, Kinston, NC, Roy J. Parker/Sr. VP - City Executive, Goldsboro, NC, Vivian Sutton/VP - City Executive, La Grange, NC, Chris Moncourtois/Sr. VP - City Executive, Jacksonville, NC

Directors: Vincent Robert Jones/Dir., CEO - Greenville, North Carolina, Felix C. Harvey/Dir. - Kinston, North Carolina, Marty Beam/Dir. - Kinston, North Carolina, Kelly Barnhill/Dir. - Greenville, North Carolina, Oscar Greene/Dir. - Kinston, North Carolina, James T. Hill/Dir. - Kinston, North Carolina, Dwight C. Howard/Dir. - Kinston, North Carolina, Cam McRae/Dir. - Kinston, North Carolina, David Weil/Dir. - Goldsboro, North Carolina

Little Squaw Gold Mining Co

3412 S Lincoln Dr., Spokane, WA, 99203; *PH:* 1-509-624-5831; *http://* www.littlesquawgold.com; *Email:* ir@littlesquawgold.com

General - Incorporation	AK	Stock- Price on:12/24/2007	$1.01
Employees	3	Stock Exchange	OTC
Auditor	Decoria, Maichel & Teague, P.S	Ticker Symbol	LITS
Stk Agt	Columbia Stock Transfer Co	Outstanding Shares	35,930,000
Counsel	NA	E.P.S	-$0.12
DUNS No.	02-024-5148	Shareholders	NA

Business: The group's principal activity is to acquire, explore and develop mineral properties, primarily those containing gold and associated base and precious metals. The group is the owner in fee of 426.5 acres of patented federal mining claims consisting of 21 lode claims, one placer claim and one millsite. The group controls an additional 8,127 acres of unpatented state of Alaska mining claims consisting of 81 claims. The group is considered to be in the development stage, as only nominal operations have occurred to date. Planned principal operations include lode mining of claims. The group operates in one reportable segment: mining operations.

Primary SIC and add'l.: 6794 1041

CIK No: 0000059860

Officers: Richard R. Walters/63/Dir., CEO, Pres./$77,225.00, Ted R. Sharp/51/CFO, Sec., Treasurer/$95,100.00, Robert G. Pate/56/VP - Operations/$111,275.00, Susan J. Schenk/55/Mgr. - Investor Relations, Rodney A. Blakestad/59/VP - Exploration, James C. Barker/Management Consultant

Directors: Richard R. Walters/63/Dir., CEO, Pres., William V. Schara/51/Chmn., William Orchow/63/Dir., David S. Atkinson/39/Dir., James K. Duff/62/Dir., Charles G. Bigelow/76/Dir., Kenneth S. Eickerman/50/Dir., James A. Fish/77/Dir.

Owners: James A. Fish, Ted R. Sharp, Charles G. Bigelow, Forza Partners, L.P./0.17%, Nicholas Gallagher/0.10%, Kenneth S. Eickerman, RAB Special Situations (Master) Fund Limited/0.10%, Robert G. Pate, Richard R. Walters/0.02%, William V. Schara, James K. Duff, Insiders/0.05%, Wilbur G. Hallauer/0.06%, William Orchow

Financial Data: *Fiscal Year End:*12/31 *Latest Annual Data:* 12/31/2006

Year	Sales	Net Income
2006	NA	-$2,004,000
2005	NA	-$386,000
2004	NA	-$553,000

Curr. Assets:	$4,131,000	**Curr. Liab.:**	$300,000		
Plant, Equip.:	$678,000	**Total Liab.:**	$1,174,000	**Indic. Yr. Divd.:**	NA
Total Assets:	$4,933,000	**Net Worth:**	$3,759,000	**Debt/ Equity:**	NA

Littlefield Corp

2501 N Lamar Blvd., Austin, TX, 78705; *PH:* 1-512-476-5141; *Fax:* 1-512-476-5680; *http://* www.littlefield.com

General - Incorporation	DE	Stock- Price on:12/24/2007	$1.16
Employees	142	Stock Exchange	OTC
Auditor	Sprouse & Anderson LLP	Ticker Symbol	LTFD
Stk Agt	American Stock Transfer & Trust Co.	Outstanding Shares	11,220,000
Counsel	NA	E.P.S	$0.05
DUNS No.	92-665-7529	Shareholders	NA

Business: The group's principal activities are to develop, own and operate charitable bingo halls, gaming and amusement arcades and party rental and catering companies. The group operates in three business segments: entertainment, amusements and hospitality. The entertainment segment consists of management of charitable bingo halls. The hospitality segment offers catering services, installation of tents for events, parties, weddings, festivals as well as event planning. The group owns and operates 28 charitable bingo businesses in Texas, Alabama, and South Carolina. As on 31-Jan-2003 the group discontinued littlefield amusements.

Primary SIC and add'l.: 7999 7389 7993

CIK No: 0000931683

Subsidiaries: Aiken Bingo Inc, Columbia One Inc, Conway Bingo Inc

Officers: Jeffrey L. Minch/Dir., CEO, Pres./$297,580.00, Michael J. Lindley/Sr. VP - Acquisitions, Institutional, Investor Relations Officer, Richard Chilinski/CFO, Cecil Whitmore/Investor Relations Officer

Directors: Jeffrey L. Minch/Dir., CEO, Pres., Carlton R. Williams/Chmn., Michael L. Wilfley/Dir., Alfred T. Stanley/Dir., Lanny Chiu/30/Dir.

Owners: Alfred T. Stanley, Value Fund Advisors, LLC/3.60%, Jeffrey L. Minch/31.90%, Insiders/36.80%, Michael L. Wilfley, Carlton Williams/1.10%

Financial Data: *Fiscal Year End:*12/31 *Latest Annual Data:* 12/31/2006

Year	Sales	Net Income
2006	$13,401,000	$786,000
2005	$11,331,000	$1,037,000
2004	$9,928,000	-$1,097,000

Curr. Assets:	$4,267,000	**Curr. Liab.:**	$2,104,000	**P/E Ratio:**	23.20
Plant, Equip.:	$6,057,000	**Total Liab.:**	$6,777,000	**Indic. Yr. Divd.:**	NA
Total Assets:	$16,054,000	**Net Worth:**	$9,276,000	**Debt/ Equity:**	0.4545

Livedeal Inc

Formerly: YP Corp

4840 E Jasmine St., Ste. 105, Mesa, AZ, 85205; *PH:* 1-480-654-9646; *http://* www.ypcorp.com

General - Incorporation	NV	Stock- Price on:12/24/2007	$0.74
Employees	76	Stock Exchange	NA
Auditor	Mayer Hoffman Mccann, P.C	Ticker Symbol	NA
Stk Agt	Registrar and Transfer Co.	Outstanding Shares	50,120,000
Counsel	NA	E.P.S	$0.33
DUNS No.	NA	Shareholders	NA

Business: The groups principle activities include publishing basic directory listings on the Internet free of charge, which contains the business name, address and telephone number. The group operates from the United States.

Primary SIC and add'l.: 5499

CIK No: 0001045742

Subsidiaries: Telco Billing, Inc.,, Telco of Canada, Inc

Officers: Daniel L. Coury/Chmn., CEO, John Raven/COO, Gary L. Perschbacher/CFO, John Clay Evans/COO

Directors: Daniel L. Coury/Chmn., CEO, Joseph F. Cunningham/Dir., Benjamin Milk/Dir., Richard Butler/Dir., Elizabeth Demarse/Dir.

Owners: Endurance Partners, L.P/2.60%, Rajesh Navar/12.30%, Ewing Asset Management, LLC/8.70%, Elisabeth DeMarse, Torstar Corporation/7.20%, Joseph Cunningham, Benjamin Milk, Richard Butler, Endurance General Partners, L.P/8.70%, Ewing & Partners/8.70%, Endurance Partners (Q.P.), L.P/6.10%, Gary Perschbacher, Daniel L. Coury/2.70%, Rajesh Navar and Arati Navar Co-Trustees of the Rajesh & Arati Navar Living Trust/10.10%, Timothy Ewing/8.70% *(18 Owners included in Index)*

Financial Data: *Fiscal Year End:*09/30 *Latest Annual Data:* 9/30/2006

Year	Sales	Net Income
2006	$36,881,000	-$1,051,000
2005	$25,205,000	-$618,000
2004	$57,168,000	$8,961,000

Curr. Assets:	$18,259,000	**Curr. Liab.:**	$4,351,000	**P/E Ratio:**	123.33
Plant, Equip.:	$179,000	**Total Liab.:**	$4,351,000	**Indic. Yr. Divd.:**	NA
Total Assets:	$26,727,000	**Net Worth:**	$22,376,000	**Debt/ Equity:**	NA

Liveperson Inc

462 7th Ave., 3rd Fl., New York, NY, 10018; *PH:* 1-212-609-4200; *Fax:* 1-212-609-4201; *http://* www.liveperson.com

General - Incorporation	DE	Stock- Price on:12/24/2007	$6.47
Employees	178	Stock Exchange	NDQ
Auditor	BDO Seidman, LLP	Ticker Symbol	LPSN
Stk Agt	American Stock Transfer & Trust Co.	Outstanding Shares	42,980,000
Counsel	Proskauer Rose	E.P.S	$0.10
DUNS No.	NA	Shareholders	NA

Business: The group's principle activity is to provide technology to facilitate real-time sales and customer service for companies doing business on the Internet. The group is an application service provider offering proprietary real-time interaction technologies as outsourced services. Its services include liveperson chat and liveperson exchange. Liveperson chat allows real-time text-based interaction between the client's operators and Internet users. Liveperson exchange integrates a faq service with secure e-mail and document management. These services are sold via telephone, through the group's interactive chat service or via direct automated download from the Internet. The group's services are provided to online retailers, financial service providers and offline businesses with a Web presence. Its clients include ameritrade, bell Canada, computer associates, ebay and microsoft. The group's quarterly revenue for September 2007 was 12.82 millions of USD.

Primary SIC and add'l.: 7375 7372

CIK No: 0001102993

Subsidiaries: HumanClick Ltd

Officers: Robert Locascio/Chmn., CEO/$509,811.00, Philippe Lang/GM - SMB, Tim Bixby/CFO, Pres./$498,979.00, Eli Campo/Exec. VP, GM - Tel Aviv Office, Jim Dicso/Sr. VP - Sales, Tal Goldberg/Co - CTO, Kevin Kohn/Exec. VP - Marketing, Eyal Halahmi/Co - CTO, Jackson Wilson/Sr. VP - Product Marketing

Directors: Robert Locascio/Chmn., CEO, Tim Bixby/CFO, Pres.

Owners: Insiders/17.50%, Timothy E. Bixby/3.00%, Steven Berns, Gilder, Gagnon, Howe & Co. LLC/9.10%, Robert P. LoCascio/12.00%, Janus Capital Management LLC/8.10%, Kevin C. Lavan, William G. Wesemann, Emmanuel Gill/2.70%

Financial Data: *Fiscal Year End:*12/31 *Latest Annual Data:* 12/31/2006

Year	Sales	Net Income
2006	NA	NA
2005	NA	NA
2004	NA	NA

Curr. Assets:	$27,315,000	**Curr. Liab.:**	$8,082,000	**P/E Ratio:**	107.83
Plant, Equip.:	$1,124,000	**Total Liab.:**	$8,766,000	**Indic. Yr. Divd.:**	NA
Total Assets:	$43,315,000	**Net Worth:**	$34,549,000	**Debt/ Equity:**	NA

LiveReel Media Corp

3400 One First Canadian Pl., Toronto, ON, M5X 1A4;

General - Incorporation	Canada	Stock- Price on:12/24/2007	$0.08
Employees	NA	Stock Exchange	OTC
Auditor	Schwartz Levitsky Feldman LLP	Ticker Symbol	LVRLF
Stk Agt	NA	Outstanding Shares	NA
Counsel	NA	E.P.S	NA
DUNS No.	NA	Shareholders	NA

Business: The groups principle activities include licensing, developing, producing and distributing films and television programs. The group operates through three segments namely licensing, production and distribution. The group operates from Canada.

Primary SIC and add'l.: 7812

CIK No: 0001168981

Subsidiaries: LiveReel Productions Corporation

Officers: Damian Lee/CEO, Pres., Kam Shah/CFO, Lowell Conn/VP

Owners: Gregg Goldstein/20.00%, Crystal Star Productions Limited/15.00%, Snapper Inc./6.00%, Sui & Company in trust/33.00%

Financial Data: *Fiscal Year End:*06/30 *Latest Annual Data:* 06/30/2006

Year	Sales	Net Income
2006	$6,000	-$579,000
2005	$4,000	-$211,000

Curr. Assets:	$2,337,000	**Curr. Liab.:**	$104,000		
Plant, Equip.:	NA	**Total Liab.:**	$104,000	**Indic. Yr. Divd.:**	NA
Total Assets:	$2,359,000	**Net Worth:**	$2,255,000	**Debt/ Equity:**	NA

Lixte Biotechnology Holdings Inc

Formerly: SRKP 7 Inc

248 Rte. 25a, No. 2, East Setauket, NY, 11733; *PH:* 1-631-942-7959

General - Incorporation	DE	Stock- Price on:12/24/2007	NA
Employees	NA	Stock Exchange	NA
Auditor	Aj. Robbins, P.C	Ticker Symbol	NA
Stk Agt	NA	Outstanding Shares	NA
Counsel	NA	E.P.S	NA
DUNS No.	NA	Shareholders	NA

Business: The groups principle activity is to develop low cost, specific, and sensitive tests for the early detection of cancers. The group also develops new treatments for brain cancer and gliobastoma multiforme. The groups markets include improved cancer treatments, diagnostic assays, estimation of prognosis and assessment of therapeutic effectiveness. The group operates from United States.

Primary SIC and add'l.: 6770

CIK No: 0001335105

Officers: John S. Kovach/Chmn., CFO, CEO

Directors: John S. Kovach/Chmn., CFO, CEO, Philip F. Palmedo/73/Dir.

Owners: John S. Kovach/64.03%, Insiders/64.37%, Richard Rappaport/5.85%, Philip F. Palmedo/0.96%

Liz Claiborne Inc

1441 Broadway, New York, NY, 10018; *PH:* 1-212-354-4900; *Fax:* 1-212-626-3416; *http://* www.lizclaiborne.com

General - Incorporation		Stock- Price on:12/24/2007	$38.06
Employees	17,000	Stock Exchange	NYSE
Auditor	NA	Ticker Symbol	LIZ
Stk Agt	Bank of New York	Outstanding Shares	104,530,000
Counsel	NA	E.P.S.	$1.33
DUNS No.	NA	Shareholders	NA

Business: The groups principle activities include designing and marketing womens and mens apparel, accessories and fragrance products. In the year 2006, the group acquired Westcoast Contempo Fashions Limited, Mac & Jav Holdings Limited and Kate Spade LLC. The group operates from the United States. The groups quarterly revenue for September 2007 was 253.96 millions of USD.

Primary SIC and add'l.: 2389 2385 2325 2337 2321 5136 2251 5621 2326 3171 3142 2387 2342 5999 2341 5699 3144 2339 2331 2335 2384 5137 2329

CIK No: 0001170403

Officers: William L. McComb/45/Dir., CEO, Michael Scarpa/COO, Tim Gunn/Chief Creative Officer, Lawrence D. McClure/Sr. VP - Human Resources, Roberta Schuhalter Karp/Sr. VP - Business Development, Legal, Corporate Affairs, Elaine H. Goodell/VP, Corporate Controller, Chief Accounting Officer, Jill Granoff/Exec. VP - Direct Brands, Dave McTague/Exec. VP - Partnered Brands, Andrew Warren/CFO, Nick Rubino/VP, General Counsel, Corp. Sec., Robert Vill/VP - Finance, Treasurer

Directors: William L. McComb/45/Dir., CEO, Kay Koplovitz/62/Chmn., Kenneth P. Kopelman/56/Dir., Arthur C. Martinez/68/Dir., Bernard W. Aronson/61/Dir., Daniel A. Carp/59/Dir., Raul J. Fernandez/41/Dir., Nancy J. Karch/60/Dir., Oliver R. Sockwell/64/Dir., Paul E. Tierney/65/Dir.

Financial Data: *Fiscal Year End:*12/31 *Latest Annual Data:* 12/30/2006

Year		Sales			Net Income
2006		$4,994,318,000			$254,685,000
2005		$4,847,753,000			$317,366,000
Curr. Assets:	$1,456,537,000	Curr. Liab.:	$607,739,000	P/E Ratio:	19.72
Plant, Equip.:	$494,693,000	Total Liab.:	$1,149,330,000	Indic. Yr. Divd.:	$0.230
Total Assets:	$3,152,036,000	Net Worth:	$2,002,706,000	Debt/ Equity:	0.3333

LJ International Inc

Unit No. 12, 12/f, Block A, Focal Industrial Ctr., 21 Man Lok St., Hung Hom, Kowloon; *PH:* 852-27643622; *Fax:* 852-27643783; *http://* www.ljintl.com; *Email:* ir@ljintl.com

General - Incorporation. British Virgin Islands		Stock- Price on:12/24/2007	$11.48
Employees	2,800	Stock Exchange	NDQ
Auditor	Moores Rowland Mazars	Ticker Symbol	JADE
Stk Agt	American Securities T & T Inc.	Outstanding Shares	18,940,000
Counsel	Andrew N. Bernstein	E.P.S.	$0.30
DUNS No.	68-686-7482	Shareholders	NA

Business: The group operates through its subsidiaries whose principle activity is to produce finished gemstones and fine quality gemstone jewelry; manufacture, market and distribute gem set jewelry to fine jewelers, department stores, national jewelry chains and electronic and specialty retailers. The group operates from United States.

Primary SIC and add'l.: 6719 3911

CIK No: 0001046692

Subsidiaries: Enzo (Shenzhen) Co., Ltd, Enzo Ltd., Goldleaves Gems (Shenzhen) Co., Ltd, Lorenzo (Shenzhen) Co., Ltd., Lorenzo Crystal Ltd., Lorenzo Jewellery (Shenzhen) Co, Lorenzo Jewelry Limited, Shenzhen PGS Jewelry Mfg

Officers: Yu Chuan Yih/Chmn., CEO, Danie Tangchai/Sr. VP - Sales, Marketing, Ringo Ng/48/Dir., CFO, Alfonsa Au/COO

Directors: Yu Chuan Yih/Chmn., CEO, Ringo Ng/48/Dir., CFO

Owners: Insiders/24.40%, Yu Chuan Yih/22.50%, Po Yee Elsa Yue, Ka Man Au/1.30%, Hon Tak Ringo Ng, Andrew N. Bernstein

Financial Data: *Fiscal Year End:*12/31 *Latest Annual Data:* 12/31/2005

Year		Sales			Net Income
2005		$99,646,000			$4,351,000
2004		$77,379,000			$2,687,000
2003		$58,167,000			$1,813,000
Curr. Assets:	$98,604,000	Curr. Liab.:	$63,050,000	P/E Ratio:	58.79
Plant, Equip.:	$7,621,000	Total Liab.:	$63,222,000	Indic. Yr. Divd.:	NA
Total Assets:	$108,230,000	Net Worth:	$45,008,000	Debt/ Equity:	0.0009

LKA International Inc

3724 47th St. Ct. N.W., Gig Harbor, WA, 98335; *PH:* 1-253-851-7486; *Fax:* 1-253-851-5449; *http://* www.lkaintl.com; *Email:* info@lkaintl.com

General - Incorporation	DE	Stock- Price on:12/24/2007	$0.8
Employees	1	Stock Exchange	OTC
Auditor	HJ & Associates, LLC	Ticker Symbol	LKAI
Stk Agt	Interwest Transfer Company, Inc.	Outstanding Shares	12,840,000
Counsel	NA	E.P.S.	-$0.03
DUNS No.	NA	Shareholders	NA

Business: The groups principle activities include acquiring and exploring gold properties. The group operates from the United States.

Primary SIC and add'l.: 1400

CIK No: 0000831355

Subsidiaries: LKA International, Inc

Officers: Kye A. Abraham/Chmn., Pres., Branden Burningham/Lkai Counsel, Nanette Abraham/Dir., Sec., Treasurer

Directors: Kye A. Abraham/Chmn., Pres., Nanette Abraham/Dir., Sec., Treasurer

Owners: Kye Abraham/60.20%

Financial Data: *Fiscal Year End:*12/31 *Latest Annual Data:* 12/31/2006

Year		Sales			Net Income
2006		$822,000			$56,000
2005		$888,000			$312,000
2004		$266,000			$25,000
Curr. Assets:	$1,929,000	Curr. Liab.:	$258,000		
Plant, Equip.:	$453,000	Total Liab.:	$320,000	Indic. Yr. Divd.:	NA
Total Assets:	$2,451,000	Net Worth:	$2,131,000	Debt/ Equity:	NA

LKQ Corp

120 N LaSalle St., Ste. 3300, Chicago, IL, 60602; *PH:* 1-312-621-1950; *Fax:* 1-312-621-1969; *http://* www.lkqcorp.com

General - Incorporation	DE	Stock- Price on:12/24/2007	$24.18
Employees	4,100	Stock Exchange	NDQ
Auditor	Deloitte & Touche LLP	Ticker Symbol	LKQX
Stk Agt	NA	Outstanding Shares	53,480,000
Counsel	Davis Polk & Wardwell	E.P.S.	$0.48
DUNS No.	NA	Shareholders	NA

Business: The group's principal activity is to provide recycled original equipment manufacturers automated products and related services. The group procures salvage vehicles at auctions and obtains some vehicles directly from insurance companies, automobile manufacturers and other suppliers. After getting the proper title of vehicles, which assures that the vehicles have not been stolen, it will be sent for recycling. The products include engines, transmissions, front-ends, doors and trunk-lids. These products are sold to collision repair shops, mechanical repair shops and indirectly to insurance companies and warranty companies.

Primary SIC and add'l.: 5015

CIK No: 0001065696

Subsidiaries: A-Reliable Auto Parts & Wreckers, Inc., Accu-Parts LLC, Akron Airport Properties, Inc., B&D Automotive International, Inc., Black Horse Auto Parts, Inc., Bodymaster Auto Parts Supply, Inc., Bodymaster Auto Parts, Inc., Bumper Parts LLC, Damron Holding Company, LLC, DAP Trucking, Inc., DAP Trucking, LLC, Distribuidora Hermanos Copher Internacional, SA, Double R Auto Sales, Inc., Etirtif Body Parts LLC, Fit-Master Body Parts LLC 83 Subsidiaries included in the Index

Officers: Joseph M. Holsten/Dir., CEO, Pres./$1,837,397.00, Victor M. Casini/VP, General Counsel, Sec., Frank P. Erlain/VP - Finance, Controller, Leonard A. Damron/Sr. VP - Southeast Region/$499,556.00, Mark T. Spears/Sr. VP, CFO/$1,038,124.00, Bradley H. Willen/VP - Procurement, Product Pricing, Midwest Region, Robert L. Wagman/VP - Insurance Services, Aftermarket Operations

Directors: Joseph M. Holsten/Dir., CEO, Pres., Donald F. Flynn/Chmn., Clinton A. Allen/Dir., Robert M. Devlin/Dir., Paul M. Meister/Dir., John F. O'Brien/Dir., William M. Webster/Dir.

Owners: Robert M. Devlin, Mark T. Spears/1.70%, Walter P. Hanley, Joseph M. Holsten/2.12%, Insiders/20.73%, John F. OBrien, Clinton A. Allen, Donald F. Flynn/7.26%, Paul M. Meister, William M. Webster, Leonard A. Damron/5.95%, Steven H. Jones, Waddell& Reed Financial,Inc./6.22%, AXA Financial,Inc./6.06%

Financial Data: *Fiscal Year End:*12/31 *Latest Annual Data:* 12/31/2006

Year		Sales			Net Income
2006		$789,381,000			$44,395,000
2005		$547,392,000			$30,887,000
2004		$424,756,000			$20,573,000
Curr. Assets:	$183,814,000	Curr. Liab.:	$61,394,000	P/E Ratio:	26.87
Plant, Equip.:	$127,084,000	Total Liab.:	$162,536,000	Indic. Yr. Divd.:	NA
Total Assets:	$564,355,000	Net Worth:	$401,202,000	Debt/ Equity:	0.2553

LL&E Royalty Trust

919 Congress Ave., Austin, TX, 78701;

General - Incorporation	TX	Stock- Price on:12/24/2007	$1.52
Employees	NA	Stock Exchange	NYSE
Auditor	KPMG LLP	Ticker Symbol	LRT
Stk Agt	JP Morgan Chase Bank, N.A.	Outstanding Shares	18,990,000
Counsel	The Bank of New York Trust Co.,	E.P.S.	$0.09
DUNS No.	NA	Shareholders	NA

Business: The groups principle activity is to invest in oil and gas properties. In the year 2006, the group acquired Burlington Resources Inc. The group operates from the United States. The groups quarterly revenue for Septembre 2007 was 0.16 million of USD.

Primary SIC and add'l.: 6792

CIK No: 0000721765

Officers: Mike Ulrich/VP, Robert J. Oberst/Sr. VP - PE, Carl D. Richard/Sr. VP - PE, Gary W. Priddy/Engineer PE

Financial Data: *Fiscal Year End:*12/31 *Latest Annual Data:* 12/31/2006

Year		Sales			Net Income
2006		$3,069,000			$2,094,000
2005		$7,355,000			$6,587,000
2004		$10,858,000			$10,179,000
Curr. Assets:	$848,000	Curr. Liab.:	NA	P/E Ratio:	19.72
Plant, Equip.:	NA	Total Liab.:	NA	Indic. Yr. Divd.:	$0.400
Total Assets:	$2,616,000	Net Worth:	$2,616,000	Debt/ Equity:	NA

Lloyds TSB Group Plc

25 Gresham St., London, EC2V 7HN; *PH:* 020-76261500; *http://* www.lloydstsbgroup.co.uk

General - Incorporation: Scotland
Employees: 76,092
Auditor: PricewaterhouseCoopers LLP
Stk Agt: Bank of New York
Counsel: NA
DUNS No.: NA

Stock - Price on:12/24/2007: $46.23
Stock Exchange: NYSE
Ticker Symbol: LYG
Outstanding Shares: 1,430,000,000
E.P.S: $4.37
Shareholders: NA

Business: The group's principal activities are organised into three businesses: UK retail banking and mortgages, insurance and investments, wholesale and international banking. Retail banking and mortgages encompass the provision of banking and other financial services, private banking, stockbroking and mortgages to personal customers. Insurance and investments offers life assurance, pensions and savings products, general insurance and fund management services. Wholesale and international banking provides banking and related services for major UK and multinational companies, banks and financial institutions, and small and medium-sized UK businesses. It also provides asset finance to personal and corporate customers; manages the group's activities in financial markets through its treasury function and provides banking and financial services overseas.

Primary SIC and add'l.: 6411 6311 6021

CIK No: 0001160106

Subsidiaries: Abbey Life Assurance, Black Horse Limited, Cheltenham & Gloucester plc, Company Limited, Lloyds TSB Asset Finance Division Limited, Lloyds TSB Bank plc, Lloyds TSB Commercial Finance Limited, Lloyds TSB General Insurance Limited, Lloyds TSB Insurance Services Limited, Lloyds TSB Leasing Limited, Lloyds TSB Offshore Limited, Lloyds TSB Private Banking Limited, Lloyds TSB Scotland plc, Scottish Widows Annuities Limited, Scottish Widows Investment Partnership Group Limited 17 Subsidiaries included in the Index

Officers: Michael E. Fairey/60/Executive Dir., Deputy Group Chief Executive, Truett G. Tate/58/Group Executive Dir. - Wholesale, International Banking, Amy Mankelow/Mgr. - Media Relations, Eleanor Ross/Mgr. - Media Relations, Eve Speight/Press Officer, Amanda Glover/Press Officer, Glen McGill/Press Office Contact - Lloyds TSB Scotland, Sara Brown/Press Office Contact - Lloyds TSB Foundation, Melissa Russell/Press Office Contact - Cheltenham, Gloucester, Paula Sutherland/Press Office Contact - Scottish Widows, Terri A. Dial/58/Group Executive Dir. - UK Retail Banking, Eric J. Daniels/57/Dir., Group Chief Executive, Helen A. Weir/46/Executive Dir., Group Dir. - Finance, Archie G. Kane/56/Group Executive Dir. - Insurance, Investments, Michael Oliver/Dir. - Investor Relations *(19 Officers included in Index)*

Directors: Victor Blank/66/Chmn., Wolfgang C.G. Berndt/66/Non Exec. Dir., Helen A. Weir/46/Executive Dir., Group Dir. - Finance, Archie G. Kane/56/Group Executive Dir. - Insurance, Investments, Michael E. Fairey/60/Executive Dir., Deputy Group Chief Executive, Truett G. Tate/58/Group Executive Dir. - Wholesale, International Banking, Terri A. Dial/58/Group Executive Dir. - UK Retail Banking, Eric J. Daniels/57/Dir., Group Chief Executive, Ewan Brown/66/Non Exec. Dir., Jan P. Du Plessis/54/Non Exec. Dir., Gavin J.N. Gemmell/66/Dir., Julian Horn-Smith/59/Non Exec. Dir., Lord Leitch/61/Non Exec. Dir., Philip N. Green/55/Non Exec. Dir.

Financial Data: **Fiscal Year End:** 12/31 **Latest Annual Data:** 12/31/2006

Year	Sales	Net Income
2006	$57,397,712,000	$5,695,104,000
2005	$46,625,076,000	$2,324,801,000
2004	$42,889,969,000	$2,905,313,000

Curr. Assets:	$17,798,424,000	**Curr. Liab.:**	$345,884,983,000	**P/E Ratio:**	58.79
Plant, Equip.:	$17,614,268,000	**Total Liab.:**	$651,289,081,000	**Indic. Yr. Divd.:**	$2.780
Total Assets:	$673,142,842,000	**Net Worth:**	$21,853,761,000	**Debt/ Equity:**	NA

LM Ericsson Telephone Co

6300 Legacy Dr., Plano, TX, 75024; *PH:* 1-972-583-0000; *http://* www.ericsson.com

General - Incorporation: Sweden
Employees: 63,781
Auditor: PricewaterhouseCoopers AB
Stk Agt: Citibank Shareholder Services
Counsel: NA
DUNS No.: 35-406-2143

Stock - Price on:12/24/2007: $39.56
Stock Exchange: NDQ
Ticker Symbol: ERIC
Outstanding Shares: 1,590,000,000
E.P.S: $2.56
Shareholders: NA

Business: The group's principal activity is to develop and supply advanced systems and services for mobile and fixed line communications to network operators. The group operates through three business divisions: systems, phones and other operations. Systems division offers solutions to operators for both mobile systems and wireline multi-service networks. The group's solutions include telecommunication and data communication products which provides end-to-end solutions, systems and service that enable mobile and fixed-line networks to transmit voice, data and multimedia communication. Phones division offers mobile handsets, including handsets supporting multi-media applications and other personal communication devices. Other operations consist of technology licensing, business innovation and enterprise systems. The group has operations in Europe, Middle East, Africa, Asia-Pacific, North America and Latin America.

Primary SIC and add'l.: 3663 3661

CIK No: 0000717826

Subsidiaries: Ericsson Radio Systems AB, Ericsson Telecom AB

Officers: Carl-Henric Svanberg/56/Dir., CEO, Pres., Hakan Eriksson/47/CTO, Sr. VP, Head - Group Function Technology, Bjorn Olsson/52/Exec. VP, GM - Business Unit Systems, Bert Nordberg/52/Exec. VP - Group Function Sales, Marketing, Carl Olof Blomqvist/57/Sr. VP, General Counsel, Head - Group Function Legal Affairs, Henry Stenson/53/Sr. VP - Group Function Communications, Roland Hagman/VP - Group Function Financial Control, Hans Vestberg/43/Exec. VP, CFO, Head - Business Unit Global Services, Bo Hjalmarsson/Statutory Auditors, Thomas Thiel/Statutory Auditors, Jeanette Skoglund/Deputy Auditors, Robert Barnden/Deputy Auditor, Sivert Bergman/62/Sr. VP, Head - Business Unit Broadband Networks, Stefan Holmstrom/Deputy Auditor, Peter Clemedtson/Statutory Auditors *(21 Officers included in Index)*

Directors: Carl-Henric Svanberg/56/Dir., CEO, Pres., Michael Treschow/65/Chmn., Sverker Martin-Lof/65/Dep. Chmn., Marcus Wallenberg/52/Dep. Chmn., Nancy McKinstry/49/Dir., Peter L. Bonfield/64/Dir., Ulf J. Johansson/63/Dir., Monica Bergstrom/47/Dir., Jan Hedlund/62/Dir., Borje Ekholm/45/Dir., Katherine M. Hudson/61/Dir., Anders Nyren/55/Dir., Kristina Davidsson/53/Dir., Torbjorn Nyman/47/Dir., Anna Guldstrand/44/Dir.

Owners: Livfrs. AB Skandia/0.47%, SHB/SPP fonder/1.87%, SEB fonder/1.26%, SHB/SPP fonder/0.07%, Frsta AP-fonden/0.57%, Alecta/1.62%, Tredje AP-fonden/0.94%, of which Barclays/2.00%, Nordea fonder/1.29%, AB Industrivrden/28.42%, Fjrde AP-fonden/0.88%, AMF Pension/1.70%, of which Fidelity/1.72%, Alecta/1.53%, Nordea fonder/0.15% *(37 Owners included in Index)*

Financial Data: **Fiscal Year End:** 12/31 **Latest Annual Data:** 12/31/2006

Year	Sales	Net Income
2006	$25,974,096,000	$3,810,288,000
2005	$19,083,900,000	$3,079,022,000
2004	$19,980,561,000	$2,178,040,000

Curr. Assets:	$22,143,939,000	**Curr. Liab.:**	$10,273,898,000		
Plant, Equip.:	$1,123,509,000	**Total Liab.:**	$13,899,662,000	**Indic. Yr. Divd.:**	NA
Total Assets:	$31,708,960,000	**Net Worth:**	$17,809,298,000	**Debt/ Equity:**	NA

LMI Aerospace Inc

411 Fountain Lakes Blvd., St. Charles, MO, 63301; *PH:* 1-636-946-6525; *Fax:* 1-636-949-1576; *http://* www.lmiaerospace.com

General - Incorporation: MO
Employees: 839
Auditor: BDO Seidman LLP
Stk Agt: NA
Counsel: NA
DUNS No.: NA

Stock - Price on:12/24/2007: $25
Stock Exchange: NDQ
Ticker Symbol: LMIA
Outstanding Shares: 11,210,000
E.P.S: $1.07
Shareholders: NA

Business: The group's principal activity is to fabricate machines and integrates formed, close tolerance aluminum and specialty alloy components. The group operates through two segments: sheet metal and machining and technology. The sheet metal segment fabricates, finishes, and integrates close tolerance aluminum and specialty alloy components primarily for the aerospace industry. The machining and technology segment integrates the close tolerance aluminum and specialty alloy components for the aerospace, semiconductor, and medical products industries. Components manufactured by the group include edge wing slats, flap and lens assemblies, cockpit window frame assemblies, fuselage skins and supports and cargo doorframes and supports. The group provides value-added services, including engineered tool design, production and repairs, heat treating, chemical milling, assembly and metal finishing processes.

Primary SIC and add'l.: 4581

CIK No: 0001059562

Subsidiaries: Leonards Metal, Inc., LMI Finishing, Inc., LMI Services, Inc., Lmi-tca, Inc., Precise Machine Company, Precise Machine Partners, LLP, Tempco Engineering, Inc., Versaform Corporation

Officers: Ronald S. Saks/Dir., CEO, Pres./$341,201.00, Phil Lajeunesse/GM - Savannah, Ed Campbell/GM - San Diego, Sanford S. Neuman/Dir., Assist. Sec., Robert Grah/VP - Central Region, Michael J. Biffignani/CIO, Lawrence E. Dickinson/CFO, Sec., Darrel E. Keesling/COO, Marc Arnold/Dir. - Materiel, Jim Ward/Purchasing Mgr., Corporate Purchasing Mgr. Raw Materials, Debbie Lajeunesse/Purchasing Agent, Corporate Contracting Extrusion, Steel Materials, Tina Riefer/Purchasing Agent, Corporate Contracting Sheet Metal, Carla Behme/Purchasing Agent, Corporate Contracting Sheet Metal, Mark Dorlaque/Corporate Supervisor Supplier Management, Procurement, Melanie Busse/Purchasing Agent, Corporate Subcontracting Parts *(23 Officers included in Index)*

Directors: Ronald S. Saks/Dir., CEO, Pres., Joseph Burstein/Chmn., John M. Roeder/Dir., Thomas G. Unger/Dir., Brian D. Geary/Dir., Sanford S. Neuman/Dir., Assist. Sec., John S. Eulich/Dir., Judith W. Northup/Dir.

Owners: Thomas G. Unger, Joseph Burstein/4.60%, Michael J. Biffignani, Robert T. Grah, John M. Roeder, BlackRock, Inc./5.50%, Ronald S. Saks/20.60%, Insiders/29.30%, Sanford S. Neuman/2.10%, FMR Corp./10.00%, Lawrence E. Dickinson, Brian D. Geary, John S. Eulich, Judith W. Northup

Financial Data: **Fiscal Year End:** 12/31 **Latest Annual Data:** 12/31/2006

Year	Sales	Net Income
2006	$122,993,000	$10,675,000
2005	$101,073,000	$5,151,000
2004	$85,908,000	$430,000

Curr. Assets:	$79,470,000	**Curr. Liab.:**	$14,059,000	**P/E Ratio:**	26.60
Plant, Equip.:	$19,514,000	**Total Liab.:**	$18,100,000	**Indic. Yr. Divd.:**	NA
Total Assets:	$108,610,000	**Net Worth:**	$90,510,000	**Debt/ Equity:**	0.0090

LML Payment Systems Inc

1140 W Pender St., Ste. 1680, Vancouver, BC, V6E 4G1; *PH:* 1-604-689-4440; *Fax:* 1-604-689-4413; *http://* www.lmlpayment.com; *Email:* info@lmlpayment.com

General - Incorporation: Canada
Employees: 51
Auditor: Grant Thornton LLP
Stk Agt: Computershare Investor Services LLC
Counsel: Kirkland & Ellis LLP
DUNS No.: 24-034-3939

Stock - Price on:12/24/2007: $4.33
Stock Exchange: NDQ
Ticker Symbol: LMLP
Outstanding Shares: 20,210,000
E.P.S: -$0.07
Shareholders: NA

Business: The group's principle activities are to provide electronic payment services employed primarily at the retail point-of-sale. The group focuses on providing electronic check authorization services, including check verification, check conversion and check recovery solutions to supermarkets, grocery stores, multi-lane retailers and convenience stores. Through its subsidiary IHTW Properties Inc, the group owns and operates an adult styled residential community in Wildwood, Florida. Operations include the sale of manufactured homes and lots. The group's quarterly revenue for September 2007 was 3.18 millions of USD.

Primary SIC and add'l.: 6531 7389 6099

CIK No: 0000781891

Subsidiaries: Legacy Promotions Inc., LHTW Properties Inc., LML Corp, LML Patent Corp., LML Payment Systems Corp.

Officers: Patrick H. Gaines/Chmn., CEO, Pres./$266,797.00, Pete Stenhjem/VP, Shawn Ratcliffe/VP, Clark Wilson/Canadian Legal Counsel, Carolyn Gaines/Corp. Sec., Richard R. Schulz/Controller, Chief Accounting Officer - Principal Financial, Accounting Officer/$242,107.00, Jutta Beekmann/Dir. - Electronic Checking, Robert E. Peyton/Exec. VP - Information Technology/$186,591.00, Mccarthy Tetrault/Canadian Legal Counsel

Directors: Patrick H. Gaines/Chmn., CEO, Pres., William L. Seidman/Dir., Greg MacRae/Dir., Jacqueline Pace/Dir.

Owners: William L. Seidman, The Estate of Robert E. Moore/24.90%, Robert E. Peyton/3.50%, Richard R. Schulz, Patrick H. Gaines/3.90%, Greg A. MacRae, Insiders/10.30%, Jacqueline Pace

Financial Data: **Fiscal Year End:** 03/31 **Latest Annual Data:** 3/31/2007

Year	Sales	Net Income
2007	$6,554,000	-$1,073,000
2006	$5,458,000	-$4,647,000
2005	$6,658,000	-$4,150,000

Curr. Assets:	$11,148,000	**Curr. Liab.:**	$2,860,000		
Plant, Equip.:	$1,362,000	**Total Liab.:**	$9,447,000	**Indic. Yr. Divd.:**	NA
Total Assets:	$13,679,000	**Net Worth:**	$4,232,000	**Debt/ Equity:**	0.1717

LMS Medical Systems Inc

LMS Medical Systems (USA) Inc., 575 Madison Ave., 10th Fl., New York, NY, 10022;
PH: 1-410-349-4634; *Fax:* 1-410-349-4635; *http://* www.lmsmedical.com;
Email: investor@lmsmedical.com

General - Incorporation	Canada	*Stock* - Price on:12/24/2007	$1.79
Employees	57	Stock Exchange	AMEX
Auditor	Ernst & Young LLP	Ticker Symbol	LMZ
Stk Agt	U.S. Co-Transfer Agent	Outstanding Shares	21,230,000
Counsel	NA	E.P.S.	-$0.54
DUNS No.	NA	Shareholders	NA

Business: The group's principle activity is to develop and market software based products that are focused in the area of obstetrics. These products specifically deal with the labor and delivery process. The core technology used is Computer Assisted Labor Management. In year 2003, the group's product offering was increased by adding remote decision assistance which effectively allows outlying hospitals to consult in real time with specialists at large delivery facilities throughout the delivery process using the internet. Products include CALM(TM) Patterns, which identifies and labels fetal heart rate patterns. In addition, development continues on CALM(TM) ANNi, a product which uses neural network techniques to recognize certain forms in fetal heart rate recordings and to estimate the risk of brain damage during birth. Prior to March 31, 2004, the group was known as Trophy Capital Inc. The group operates from United States.

Primary SIC and add'l.: 3829

CIK No: 0001286455

Subsidiaries: LMS Medical Systems (Canada) Ltd., LMS Medical Systems (USA) Inc

Officers: Diane Cote/Dir., CEO, Pres., David Gordon/Investor Relations Officer, Grant Howard/Investor Relations Officer, Yves Grou/CFO, Emily Hamilton/Founder, VP - Medical Research, Bruno Bendavid/Product Development, Pamela Haswell/Quality Assurance, Regulatory Affairs, Isabelle Lafortune/Marketing, Dennis McClinton/Contact - Sales, J. D. Miller/Corporate Development, Andrea Miller/Investor Relations Officer

Directors: Diane Cote/Dir., CEO, Pres., Benoit La Salle/Chmn., Elaine Beaudoin/Dir., Emily Hamilton/Founder, VP - Medical Research, Terrance H. Gregg/Dir., Harry G. Hohn/Dir., Michael Maher/Dir., Arthur T. Porter/Dir., Marilyn Sue Bogner/Member - Risk, Patient Safety Advisory Board, Thomas J. Garite/Member - Risk, Patient Safety Advisory Board, Eric Knox/Member - Risk, Patient Safety Advisory Board, Catherine Rommal/Member - Risk, Patient Safety Advisory Board, Andre Lalonde/Member - Scientific Advisory Board, Michele Lauria/Member - Scientific Advisory Board, James Low/Member - Scientific Advisory Board *(16 Directors included in Index)*

Financial Data: Fiscal Year End:03/31   Latest Annual Data: 3/31/2006

Year	Sales	Net Income
2006	$1,356,000	-$8,041,000
2005	$872,000	-$7,610,000

Curr. Assets:	$5,535,000	Curr. Liab.:	$2,105,000	P/E Ratio:	6.88
Plant, Equip.:	$464,000	Total Liab.:	$2,147,000	Indic. Yr. Divd.:	NA
Total Assets:	$6,248,000	Net Worth:	$4,100,000	Debt/ Equity:	NA

LNB Bancorp Inc

457 Broadway, Lorain, OH, 44052; *PH:* 1-440-244-6000; *Fax:* 1-440-244-4815;
http:// www.4lnb.com

General - Incorporation	OH	*Stock* - Price on:12/24/2007	$15.46
Employees	243	Stock Exchange	NDQ
Auditor	Plant & Moran, PLLC	Ticker Symbol	LNBB
Stk Agt	Registrar & Transfer Co	Outstanding Shares	6,440,000
Counsel	NA	E.P.S.	$0.86
DUNS No.	11-814-0037	Shareholders	NA

Business: The group's principal activity is to provide a range of banking services through its subsidiary, lorain national bank. These services include a wide range of loans, deposits and other services including, safe deposit boxes, night depository, u. S. Savings bonds, travelers' checks, money orders, cashiers checks, bank-by-mail, automatic teller machine, debit cards and wire transfers. In addition, the group performs trust administrative functions and offers agency and trust services and mutual investment products. The group operates 20 retail branches and 23 ATM's in the nine communities of lorain, elyria, amherst, avon lake, lagrange, oberlin, olmsted township, vermilion and westlake.

Primary SIC and add'l.: 6712 6021

CIK No: 0000737210

Subsidiaries: Charleston Insurance Agency, Inc, Charleston Title Agency, LLC, LNB Mortgage, LLC, North Coast Community Development Corporation, The Lorain National Bank

Owners: John W. Schaeffer, AMG Investments, LLC/7.70%, James F. Kidd/1.10%, The Lorain National Bank/6.52%, Daniel P. Batista, James R. Herrick, Bank Funds V, VI and VII, L.P./5.92%, Daniel E. Klimas, Jeffrey F. Riddell/1.75%, Donald F. Zwilling, Terry D. Goode, Terry M. White, Frank A. Soltis, Martin J. Erbaugh/1.41%, Kevin C. Martin *(21 Owners included in Index)*

Financial Data: Fiscal Year End:12/31   Latest Annual Data: 12/31/2006

Year	Sales	Net Income
2006	$58,993,000	$5,424,000
2005	$53,829,000	$6,413,000
2004	$48,443,000	$7,475,000

Curr. Assets:	$33,061,000	Curr. Liab.:	$782,401,000	P/E Ratio:	17.98
Plant, Equip.:	$13,888,000	Total Liab.:	$782,401,000	Indic. Yr. Divd.:	$0.720
Total Assets:	$851,098,000	Net Worth:	$68,697,000	Debt/ Equity:	NA

Local.com Corp

1 Technology Dr., Bldg. G, Irvine, CA, 92618; *PH:* 1-949-784-0800; *Fax:* 1-949-784-0880;
http:// corporate.local.com

General - Incorporation	DE	*Stock* - Price on:12/24/2007	$4.06
Employees	58	Stock Exchange	NDQ
Auditor	Rutan & Tucker, LLP	Ticker Symbol	LOCM
Stk Agt	U.S. Stock Transfer Corp	Outstanding Shares	9,300,000
Counsel	NA	E.P.S.	-$1.82
DUNS No.	NA	Shareholders	NA

Business: The groups principle activity is to provide paid search advertising services. The groups services include local search and national search. Specific customers of the group include LookSmart, Ltd and Yahoo! Inc. The group operates from the United States and Europe. The group's quarterly revenue for September 2007 was 5.61 millions of USD.

Primary SIC and add'l.: 8748 7319 7379 7375

CIK No: 0001259550

Subsidiaries: Interchange Europe Holding Corporation

Officers: Heath Clarke/Chmn., CEO, Pres./$274,950.00, Bruce Crair/COO, Pres., Douglas Norman/CFO/$441,755.00, Jennifer Black/VP - Marketing, Heather Dilley/VP - Human Resources, Peter Hutto/VP - Business Development, Sales, Ralph Kravitz/VP - Operations, Lee Siegfried/VP - Engineering, Kim Lafleur/VP - Product Management, Malcolm Lewis/VP, GM - Private Label, Cameron Triebwasser/Contact - Public Relations

Directors: Heath Clarke/Chmn., CEO, Pres., Philip Fricke/Dir., Theodore Lavoie/Dir., Norman Farra/Dir., John Rehfeld/Dir.

Owners: Douglas S. Norman/1.90%, John E. Rehfeld/0.60%, Heath B. Clarke/12.80%, Norman K. Farra, Hearst Communications, Inc./13.70%, Theodore E. Lavoie/0.60%, Stanley B. Crair/1.20%, Insiders/16.90%, Steven R. Becker/5.00%, Philip K. Fricke/0.60%

Financial Data: Fiscal Year End:12/31   Latest Annual Data: 12/31/2006

Year	Sales	Net Income
2006	$14,213,000	-$13,286,000
2005	$18,139,000	-$6,502,000
2004	$19,072,000	$1,536,000

Curr. Assets:	$7,670,000	Curr. Liab.:	$4,293,000		
Plant, Equip.:	$2,028,000	Total Liab.:	$4,293,000	Indic. Yr. Divd.:	NA
Total Assets:	$24,891,000	Net Worth:	$20,598,000	Debt/ Equity:	NA

Locateplus Holdings Corp

100 Cummings Ctr., Ste. 235M, Beverly, MA, 01915; *PH:* 1-978-921-2727; *Fax:* 1-978-524-8767;
https:// www.locateplus.com; *Email:* customerservice@locateplus.com

General - Incorporation	DE	*Stock*- Price on:12/24/2007	NA
Employees	95	Stock Exchange	OTC
Auditor	Carlin, Charron & Rosen, LLP	Ticker Symbol	LPHC
Stk Agt	Transfer Online, Inc.	Outstanding Shares	NA
Counsel	Kirkpatrick & Lockhart	E.P.S.	NA
DUNS No.	NA	Shareholders	NA

Business: The group's principal activity is to provide business-to-business and business-to-government public information via data integration solutions. The group operates in two segments: information segment and engineering services. Information segment includes CD rom, online, wireless and channel partner services. The CD rom segment provides information on motor vehicles and drivers' licenses, contained on compact disks. Online segment provides information on individuals throughout the United States of America through the company's Website. Engineering services include software and integration services provided to a third party database provider. The group acquired entersect corporation on 02-Oct-2003 and voice power technology on 04-Nov-2003.

Primary SIC and add'l.: 7372 7375

CIK No: 0001160084

Subsidiaries: Certifion Corporation, Dataphant, Inc, LocatePLUS Corporation, Metrigenics, Inc., Worldwide Information, Inc

Officers: Jon R. Latorella/43/Chmn., CEO, Pres., Geoffrey Chalmers/Contact - Legal, James Fields/VP - Finance, Treasurer Sec., Acting CFO, Mark Ettinger/VP - Sales, Marketing

Directors: Jon R. Latorella/43/Chmn., CEO, Pres., Sonia P. Bejjani/Dir., David Skerrett/57/Dir., Chris Romeo/44/Dir., Ralph Carusso/57/Dir., Mike Ryan/48/Dir., Peter Zekos/45/Dir.

Owners: Jon R. Latorella/9.13%, Sonia P. Bejjani, David Skerrett, Peter Zekos, Cornell Capital Partners, L.P./57.40%, James C. Fields, Special Situation Funds/13.21%, Ralph Caruso

Curr. Assets:	$1,576,000	Curr. Liab.:	$6,164,000		
Plant, Equip.:	$1,942,000	Total Liab.:	$6,174,000	Indic. Yr. Divd.:	NA
Total Assets:	$5,671,000	Net Worth:	-$503,000	Debt/ Equity:	NA

Lockheed Martin Corp

6801 Rockledge Dr., Bethesda, MD, 20817; *PH:* 1-301-897-6000; *Fax:* 1-301-897-6704;
http:// www.lockheedmartin.com; *Email:* investor.relations@lmco.com

General - Incorporation	MD	*Stock*- Price on:12/24/2007	$96.19
Employees	140,000	Stock Exchange	NYSE
Auditor	Ernst & Young LLP	Ticker Symbol	LMT
Stk Agt	Computershare Investor Services LLC	Outstanding Shares	417,300,000
Counsel	NA	E.P.S.	$6.89
DUNS No.	78-766-1875	Shareholders	NA

Business: The group's principle activities include research, designing, development, manufacturing and integration of advanced technology systems, products and services. The group's products include acoustic arrays, active matrix liquid crystal display monitor, advanced gunnery training system, aegis weapon system, composite liquid oxygen tank, defense message system and message switching system. The group operates from United States.

Primary SIC and add'l.: 3721 3812 8731 3728 3761 9999

CIK No: 0000936468

Subsidiaries: DoE and Sandia Corporation, Lockheed Martin Investment Management Company, Sandia Corporation

Officers: Robert J. Stevens/Chmn., CEO, Pres./$18,603,520.00, Lynn Fisher/Contact - Media, Space Systems Business Area, Steve Tatum/Contact - Media, Space Systems Business Area, Joan Underwood/Contact - Media, Space Systems Business Area, Gary Napier/Contact - Media, Space Systems Business Area, Dee Valleras/Contact - Media, Space Systems Business Area, Kate Dunlap/Contact - Media, Electronic Systems Business Area, Craig Quigley/Contact - Media, Electronic Systems Business Area, Pete Harrigan/Contact - Media, Electronic Systems Business Area, Jennifer Allen/Contact - Media, Electronic Systems Business Area, James Gring/Contact - Media, Electronic Systems Business Area, Ellen Mitchell/Contact - Media, Electronic Systems Business Area, Ken Ross/Contact - Media, Electronic Systems Business Area, Tierney Helmers/Contact - Media, Electronic Systems Business Area, Jack Papp/Contact - Media, Electronic Systems Business Area *(64 Officers included in Index)*

Directors: Robert J. Stevens/Chmn., CEO, Pres., E. C. Aldridge/Dir., Nolan D. Archibald/Dir., Marcus C. Bennett/Dir., James O. Ellis/Dir., Gwendolyn S. King/Dir., James M. Loy/Dir., Douglas H. McCorkindale/Dir., Eugene F. Murphy/Dir., Joseph W. Ralston/Dir., Frank Savage/Dir., James M. Schneider/Dir., Anne Stevens/Dir., James R. Ukropina/Dir., Douglas C. Yearley/Dir.

Owners: Douglas H. McCorkindale, Ralph D. Heath, Douglas C. Yearley, Eugene F. Murphy, James M. Schneider, Robert B. Coutts, Insiders, Marcus C. Bennett, U.S. Trust Company, N.A., State Street Bank and Trust Company, Gwendolyn S. King, James R. Ukropina, Michael F. Camardo, Stanton D. Sloane, Barclays Global Investors, N.A *(18 Owners included in Index)*

Financial Data: ***Fiscal Year End:***12/31 ***Latest Annual Data:*** 12/31/2006

Year	Sales	Net Income
2006	$39,620,000,000	$2,529,000,000
2005	$37,213,000,000	$1,825,000,000
2004	$35,526,000,000	$1,266,000,000

Curr. Assets:	$10,164,000,000	***Curr. Liab.:***	$9,553,000,000	***P/E Ratio:***	15.90
Plant, Equip.:	$4,056,000,000	***Total Liab.:***	$21,347,000,000	***Indic. Yr. Divd.:***	$1.680
Total Assets:	$28,231,000,000	***Net Worth:***	$6,884,000,000	***Debt/ Equity:***	0.6267

Lodgenet Entertainment Corp

3900 W Innovation St., Sioux Falls, SD, 57107; ***PH:*** 1-605-988-1000; ***Fax:*** 1-605-988-1511;
http:// www.lodgenet.com; ***Email:*** investors@lodgenet.com

General - Incorporation	DE	***Stock***- Price on:12/24/2007	$34.31
Employees	803	Stock Exchange	NDQ
Auditor	PricewaterhouseCoopers LLP	Ticker Symbol	LNET
Stk Agt	Computershare Trust Co	Outstanding Shares	22,720,000
Counsel	NA	E.P.S	-$2.2
DUNS No.	10-229-2851	Shareholders	NA

Business: The group's principal activities are to provide interactive television systems and broadband services to hotels, resorts and casinos. The group's services are categorized into guest pay interactive services and free-to-guest and other services. Guest pay interactive services include on-demand movies, network-based video games, music services and Internet-enhanced television. Free-to-guest and other services include cable television programming and sale of system equipment. As of 31-Dec-2003, the group provided interactive television services to approximately 5,800 hotel properties. The group's services are provided throughout the United States, Canada and selected international markets to hotel chains like baymont inns and suites, delta hotels, doubletree and embassy suites and reits and management companies like felcor, flagstone, interstate, kimpton,prime and westcoast hospitality.

Primary SIC and add'l.: 7359 7999 4841 5065

CIK No: 0000911002

Subsidiaries: LodgeNet Entertainment (Canada) Corporation

Officers: Scott C. Petersen/Chmn., CEO, Pres./$1,188,886.00, Gary H. Ritondaro/Sr. VP, CFO/$718,885.00, David M. Bankers/Sr. VP - Product, Technology Development/$552,292.00, Steven R. Pofahl/Sr. VP - Technical Operations/$471,185.00, James G. Naro/Sr. VP, General Counsel, Sec., Scott E. Young/Sr. VP, Chief Marketing Officer

Directors: Scott C. Petersen/Chmn., CEO, Pres., Douglas R. Bradbury/Dir., Rodney F. Leyendecker/Dir., Vikki I. Pachera/Dir., Scott H. Shlecter/Dir.

Owners: Stephen D. McCarty, Richard R. Hylland, R. F. Leyendecker, Insiders/8.62%, Gary H. Ritondaro, Steven R. Pofahl, PAR Investment Partners, L.P/6.00%, David M. Bankers/1.10%, Federated Investors Inc./5.92%, Reed Conner& Birdwell LLC/7.39%, Scott C. Petersen/3.40%, Douglas R. Bradbury, Scott H. Shlecter, Barclays Global Investors NA/7.05%, Wellington Management Company LLP/8.40% *(16 Owners included in Index)*

Financial Data: ***Fiscal Year End:***12/31 ***Latest Annual Data:*** 12/31/2006

Year	Sales	Net Income
2006	$288,213,000	$1,841,000
2005	$275,771,000	-$6,959,000
2004	$266,441,000	-$20,781,000

Curr. Assets:	$67,488,000	***Curr. Liab.:***	$47,970,000		
Plant, Equip.:	$185,770,000	***Total Liab.:***	$321,331,000	***Indic. Yr. Divd.:***	NA
Total Assets:	$263,209,000	***Net Worth:***	-$58,122,000	***Debt/ Equity:***	NA

Lodgian Inc

3445 Peachtree Rd. NE, Ste. 700, Atlanta, GA, 30326; ***PH:*** 1-404-364-9400; ***Fax:*** 1-404-364-0088;
http:// www.lodgian.com; ***Email:*** headquarters@lodgian.com

General - Incorporation	DE	***Stock***- Price on:12/24/2007	$14.92
Employees	3,534	Stock Exchange	AMEX
Auditor	Deloitte & Touche LLP	Ticker Symbol	LGN
Stk Agt	American Stock Transfer & Trust Co.	Outstanding Shares	24,670,000
Counsel	Cadwalader, Wickersham & Taft LLP	E.P.S	-$0.86
DUNS No.	NA	Shareholders	NA

Business: The group's principal activity is to own and operate full-service hotels. The group provides lodging services, food and beverage services, banquet and meeting space facilities through 88 hotels containing 16,627 rooms, located in 30 states and Canada. Of the group's 88 hotels, 78 hotels, with an aggregate of 14,348 rooms, are part of our continuing operations, while 10 hotels, with an aggregate of 2,279 rooms, are held for sale. The group operates substantially all of its hotels under nationally recognized brands, such as crowne plaza, holiday inn and marriott.

Primary SIC and add'l.: 7011

CIK No: 0001066138

Subsidiaries: 1075 Hospitality, LP, 12801 Nwf Beverage Management, Inc., Albany Hotel, Inc., AMI Operating Partners, L.P., AMIOP Acquisition General Partner SPE Corp., Apico Hills. Inc., Apico Inns of Greentree, Inc., Apico Inns of Pennsylvania, Inc., Apico Inns of Pittsburgh, Inc., Apico Management Corp., Atlanta-Boston Holdings, LLC, Atlanta-Boston Lodging, LLC, Atlanta-Boston SPE, Inc., Brunswick Motel Enterprises, Inc., Courtyard Club 155 Subsidiaries included in the Index

Officers: Edward J. Rohling/Dir., CEO, Pres./$1,304,005.00, Deborah N. Ethridge/VP - Finance, Investor Relations, James A. MacLennan/CFO, Exec. VP/$432,072.00, Daniel E. Ellis/39/Sr. VP, General Counsel, Sec./$511,696.00, Mark D. Linch/51/Sr. VP - Capital Investment/$184,418.00, Carol L. Mayne/VP - Human Resources, Kevin B. Richards/VP - Asset Management, Donna B. Cohen/VP, Controller, Susan King/VP - Franchise Communications, Daniel Webber/VP - Information Technology

Directors: Edward J. Rohling/Dir., CEO, Pres., Russel S. Bernard/Chmn., Sheryl E. Kimes/Dir., Kevin C. McTavish/50/Dir., Stewart J. Brown/Dir., Stephen P. Grathwohl/Dir., Alex R. Lieblong/Dir., Peter T. Cyrus/Dir., Paul J. Garity/Dir., Michael J. Grondahl/Dir.

Owners: Oaktree Capital Management, LLC/11.40%, Kevin C. McTavish, Michael J. Grondahl/11.70%, Key Colony Fund, LP/11.70%, James A. MacLennan, Stewart J. Brown, BRE/HY Funding LLC/5.40%, Donald Smith & Co., Inc./9.90%, Insiders/12.80%, Dimensional Fund Advisors LP/8.40%, Stephen P. Grathwohl, Mark D. Linch, Daniel E. Ellis, Alex R. Lieblong/11.70%, Sean F. Armstrong *(19 Owners included in Index)*

Financial Data: ***Fiscal Year End:***12/31 ***Latest Annual Data:*** 12/31/2006

Year	Sales	Net Income
2006	$261,785,000	-$15,176,000
2005	$319,264,000	$12,301,000
2004	$322,109,000	-$31,834,000

Curr. Assets:	$186,510,000	***Curr. Liab.:***	$153,821,000		
Plant, Equip.:	$487,694,000	***Total Liab.:***	$446,122,000	***Indic. Yr. Divd.:***	NA
Total Assets:	$699,158,000	***Net Worth:***	$242,114,000	***Debt/ Equity:***	NA

Loews Corp

667 Madison Ave., New York, NY, 10021; ***PH:*** 1-212-521-2000; ***Fax:*** 1-212-521-2525;
http:// www.loews.com; ***Email:*** ir@loews.com

General - Incorporation	DE	***Stock***- Price on:12/24/2007	$52.43
Employees	21,600	Stock Exchange	NYSE
Auditor	Deloitte & Touche LLP	Ticker Symbol	LTR
Stk Agt	Mellon Investor Services LLC	Outstanding Shares	537,030,000
Counsel	NA	E.P.S	$4.04
DUNS No.	00-166-7237	Shareholders	NA

Business: The group's principle activities are: property, casualty and life insurance; operation of hotels; operation of offshore oil and gas drilling rigs and distribution and sale of watches and clocks. The group's subsidiary, cna financial corporation, provides property, casualty, life, accident, health insurance, retirement products and annuities. The services include risk management, information services, health care management and employee leasing/payroll processing. Loews hotels holding corporation owns and operates 20 hotels. Bulova corporation distributes and sells watches and clocks. Diamond offshore drilling inc, owns and operates drilling rigs that are used in the drilling of offshore oil and gas wells. The group's quarterly revenue for September 2007 was 4,653.30 millions of USD.

Primary SIC and add'l.: 2111

CIK No: 0000060086

Subsidiaries: CNA Casualty of California, CNA Financial Corporation, CNA National Warranty Corporation, CNA Surety Corporation, Commercial Insurance Company of Newark, New Jersey, Continental Assurance Company, Continental Casualty Company, Diamond Offshore Drilling, Inc, Firemens Insurance Company of Newark, New Jersey, First Insurance Company of Hawaii, Lorillard Tobacco Company, Lorillard, Inc., National Ben Franklin Insurance Company of Illinois, Pacific Insurance Company, The Buckeye Union Insurance Company 19 Subsidiaries included in the Index

Officers: James S. Tisch/Dir., CEO, Pres./$5,043,405.00, Herbert C. Hofmann/65/Sr. VP, Arthur L. Rebell/Sr. VP/$3,952,468.00, David B. Edelson/48/Sr. VP, Peter W. Keegan/63/CFO, Sr. VP/$2,629,198.00, Mark S. Schwartz/Controller, Gary W. Garson/61/Sr. VP, General Counsel, Sec.

Directors: James S. Tisch/Dir., CEO, Pres., Jonathan M. Tisch/Co - Chmn., Andrew H. Tisch/Co - Chmn., Ann E. Berman/Dir., Philip A. Laskawy/Dir., Joseph L. Bower/Dir., Paul J. Fribourg/Dir., Gloria R. Scott/Dir., Walter L. Harris/Dir., Charles M. Diker/Dir.

Owners: FMR Corp/5.40%, Joseph L. Bower, Paul J. Fribourg, James S. Tisch/2.40%, Philip A. Laskawy, Davis Selected Advisers, L.P/8.60%, Walter L. Harris, Jonathan M. Tisch, Peter W. Keegan, Joan H. Tisch/9.80%, Insiders/5.60%, Ann E. Berman, Arthur L. Rebell, Gloria R. Scott, Charles M. Diker *(17 Owners included in Index)*

Financial Data: ***Fiscal Year End:***12/31 ***Latest Annual Data:*** 12/31/2006

Year	Sales	Net Income
2006	$17,911,000,000	$2,491,300,000
2005	$16,017,800,000	$1,211,600,000
2004	$15,248,500,000	$1,235,300,000

Curr. Assets:	$25,983,500,000	***Curr. Liab.:***	$543,700,000	***P/E Ratio:***	12.48
Plant, Equip.:	$5,501,300,000	***Total Liab.:***	$57,482,800,000	***Indic. Yr. Divd.:***	$0.250
Total Assets:	$76,880,900,000	***Net Worth:***	$16,501,800,000	***Debt/ Equity:***	NA

Logan Resources Ltd

789 Pender St. W, Ste. 570, Vancouver, BC, V6C 1H2; ***PH:*** 1-604-689-0299; ***Fax:*** 1-604-689-0288;
http:// www.loganresources.ca; ***Email:*** info@loganresources.ca

General - Incorporation	BC	***Stock***- Price on:12/24/2007	$0.241
Employees	NA	Stock Exchange	OTC
Auditor	Manning Elliott LLP	Ticker Symbol	LGREF
Stk Agt	Computershare Investor Services LLC	Outstanding Shares	NA
Counsel	NA	E.P.S	NA
DUNS No.	NA	Shareholders	NA

Business: The group's principle activity is to engage in the acquisition and exploration of mineral resource properties. The group has interests in five mineral properties in British Columbia and the Yukon Territory, respectively: Albert Creek, Antler Creek, Redford, and Shell Creek and Heidi properties. During Fiscal 2005, ended 3/31/2005 and the first three months of Fiscal 2006, the group expended $488,999 and $210,114, respectively, on property acquisition/exploration. The group operates from United States.

Primary SIC and add'l.: 1000

CIK No: 0001288268

Officers: Seamus Young/Dir., CEO, Pres., Clifford Frame/Dir., MD, Judith T. Mazvihwa/Dir., CFO, Natasha Blackburn/Dir. - Corporate Development

Directors: Seamus Young/Dir., CEO, Pres., Clifford Frame/Dir., MD, Charles F. Vickers/Dir., Peter F. Cummings/Dir., Judith T. Mazvihwa/Dir., CFO

Owners: Clifford H. Frame/1.59%, Charles F. Vickers/7.24%, Insiders/15.49%, Seamus Young/6.22%, Judith Mazvihwa/0.18%, Peter Cummings/0.25%

Logic Devices Inc

1375 Geneva Dr., Sunnyvale, CA, 94089; ***PH:*** 1-408-542-5400; ***Fax:*** 1-408-542-0080;
http:// www.logicdevices.com; ***Email:*** sales@logicdevices.com

General - Incorporation	CA	***Stock***- Price on:12/24/2007	$2.33
Employees	18	Stock Exchange	NDQ
Auditor	Hein & Assoc., LLP	Ticker Symbol	LOGC
Stk Agt	Computershare Investor Services LLC	Outstanding Shares	6,800,000
Counsel	Barack Ferrazzano Kirschbaum Et Al	E.P.S	-$0.22
DUNS No.	10-210-0203	Shareholders	NA

Business: The group's principle activities are to develop and market digital integrated circuits for the requirements of original equipment manufacturers. The products of the group include digital signal processing chips that are used in digital communications, broadcast and medical imaging processing applications, instrumentation and smart weapons systems. The customers include sony, teradyne, pinnacle microsystems, lockheed martin, ge medical, phillips, acuson, and honeywell. Sales representatives and

distributors conduct international sales in Belgium, Canada, Denmark, England, Finland, France, Germany, Hong Kong, Israel, Italy, Japan, Korea, the Netherlands, Spain, Sweden and Taiwan. Taiwan semiconductor manufacturing company is the primary wafer supplier to the group. The group's total revenue for year 2007 was 4.69 millions of USD.

Primary SIC and add'l.: 3674

CIK No: 0000802851

Officers: William J. Volz/60/Dir., Pres., Principal Executive Officer, Kimiko Milheim/37/CFO, Sec., Adesh Sidhu/43/VP - Worldwide Sales

Directors: Howard L. Farkas/83/Chmn., William J. Volz/60/Dir., Pres., Principal Executive Officer, Brian P. Cardozo/49/Dir., Albert Morrison/Dir., Steven R. Settles/49/Dir.

Owners: William J. Volz/10.70%, Brian P. Cardozo, Howard L. Farkas/3.70%, Insiders/22.30%, Hummingbird Management, LLC/5.10%, Steven R. Settles/7.10%, Steven J. Revenig/9.20%

Financial Data: Fiscal Year End:09/30 Latest Annual Data: 9/30/2006

Year	Sales	Net Income
2006	$4,641,000	$129,000
2005	$3,509,000	-$1,363,000
2004	$4,415,000	-$1,472,000

Curr. Assets:	$8,197,000	Curr. Liab.:	$300,000		
Plant, Equip.:	$1,101,000	Total Liab.:	$320,000	Indic. Yr. Divd.:	NA
Total Assets:	$9,717,000	Net Worth:	$9,397,000	Debt/ Equity:	NA

Logica Holdings Inc

Formerly: Maximum Awards Inc
326 Old Cleveland Rd., Coorparoo Queensland, Cen, 4151; *PH:* 61-7331-93110;
http:// www.maximumawards.com.au

General - Incorporation	NV	Stock - Price on:12/24/2007	NA
Employees	NA	Stock Exchange	NA
Auditor	Sf Partnership, LLP	Ticker Symbol	NA
Stk Agt	Nevada Agency & Trust Company	Outstanding Shares	NA
Counsel	NA	E.P.S	NA
DUNS No.	NA	Shareholders	NA

Business: The group's principal activities are operating a loyalty and rewards program known as Maximum Awards. Under the Maximum Awards program, consumers earn points by purchasing products and services offered by the company and its program partners. Accumulated points then can be redeemed in order to acquire additional desired products or services from the same list of such items offered by the company. The company operates its program in Australia.

Primary SIC and add'l.: 7200

CIK No: 0001282224

Subsidiaries: Easy Shopper Direct, Global Business, Travel Easy Holidays

Officers: Maxwell Thomas/46/Dir., CEO, CFO

Directors: Maxwell Thomas/46/Dir., CEO, CFO, Enzo Taddei/33/Dir.

Owners: Insiders/25.90%, Maxwell A. Thomas/25.90%, Winterman Group/11.10%, Cutan Trust/9.40%, Lorraine Krueger/4.70%, Vieles Geld Trust/25.90%, Maxjam Pty Ltd/7.10%, Michael Sullivan/1.30%

Financial Data: Fiscal Year End:12/31 Latest Annual Data: 12/31/2006

Year	Sales	Net Income
2006	$495,000	-$869,000

Curr. Assets:	$138,000	Curr. Liab.:	$1,148,000		
Plant, Equip.:	$22,000	Total Liab.:	$1,148,000	Indic. Yr. Divd.:	NA
Total Assets:	$160,000	Net Worth:	-$988,000	Debt/ Equity:	NA

Logicvision Inc

25 Metro Dr., 3rd Fl., San Jose, CA, 95110; *PH:* 1-408-453-0146; *Fax:* 1-408-573-7640;
http:// www.logicvision.com; *Email:* info@logicvision.com

General - Incorporation	DE	Stock - Price on:12/24/2007	$0.94
Employees	59	Stock Exchange	NDQ
Auditor	Burr, Pilger & Mayer, LLP	Ticker Symbol	LGVN
Stk Agt	Mellon Investor Services LLC	Outstanding Shares	24,120,000
Counsel	Pillsbury Winthrop LLP	E.P.S	-$0.19
DUNS No.	NA	Shareholders	NA

Business: The group's principal activity is to provide proprietary technologies for embedded test that enables the design and manufacture of complex semiconductors. The embedded test solution allows integrated circuit designers to embed into a semiconductor design test functionality that can be used during semiconductor production and throughout the useful life of the chip. The technology also allows testing of integrated circuits after they have been assembled onto boards and systems. The group's products include chip test assembly, ic memory bist, logic bist, embedded logic test, ic memory bist with bira, pll bist, programmable ic memory bist and programmable external memory test. The customers of the group include integrated device manufacturers, fabless semiconductor companies and integrated circuit designers in system companies.

Primary SIC and add'l.: 7372

CIK No: 0001041418

Subsidiaries: LogicVision (Canada) Inc., LogicVision Europe Limited, LogicVision India Private Limited, LogicVision International, Inc., LogicVision Japan KK

Officers: James T. Healy/Dir., CEO, Pres./$340,432.00, Bruce M. Jaffe/VP - Finance, CFO, Investor Contact - Sec./$236,061.00, Ron H. Mabry/VP - Field Operations, Applications Engineering/$255,854.00, Farhad Hayat/VP - Marketing/$115,105.00, Fadi Maamari/VP - Engineering/$187,028.00, Benoit Nadeau-Dostie/Chief Scientist

Directors: James T. Healy/Dir., CEO, Pres., Gregg Adkin/Chmn., Richard C. Black/39/Dir., Randall A. Hughes/Dir., Matthew Raggett/Dir., Richard Yonker/Dir., James D. Guzy/Dir.

Owners: Insiders/11.56%, Austin W. Marxe/6.40%, Fadi Maamari, Farhad Hayat, Pacific Asset Partners/5.02%, Randall A. Hughes, Ronald H. Mabry, Lewis Asset Management, Corp./5.75%, Richard C. Yonker, Bruce M. Jaffe, Gregg E. Adkin/9.69%, Valley Ventures II, L.P./9.53%, MicroCapital LLC/14.21%, Mathew Raggett, James T. Healy

Financial Data: Fiscal Year End:12/31 Latest Annual Data: 12/31/2006

Year	Sales	Net Income
2006	$10,517,000	-$7,087,000
2005	$10,882,000	-$9,973,000
2004	$10,094,000	-$8,388,000

Curr. Assets:	$11,083,000	Curr. Liab.:	$7,405,000		
Plant, Equip.:	$743,000	Total Liab.:	$7,690,000	Indic. Yr. Divd.:	NA
Total Assets:	$19,491,000	Net Worth:	$11,801,000	Debt/ Equity:	NA

Logility Inc

470 E Paces Ferry Rd. NE, Atlanta, GA, 30305; *PH:* 1-404-261-9777; *Fax:* 1-404-264-5206;
http:// www.logility.com

General - Incorporation	GA	Stock - Price on:12/24/2007	$10.1
Employees	139	Stock Exchange	NDQ
Auditor	KPMG LLP	Ticker Symbol	LGTY
Stk Agt	First Union Nat'l Bank	Outstanding Shares	12,900,000
Counsel	NA	E.P.S	NA
DUNS No.	17-183-4203	Shareholders	NA

Business: The group's principle activity is to develop, market and support an integrated suite of business-to-business collaborative commerce software products. The products are designed to manage the flow of information and products along the entire value chain of an enterprise. Logility voyager solutions(TM) consists of an Internet and client or server based, integrated software suite that provides advanced supply chain management including collaborative planning, strategic network design, optimized supply sourcing, production management, warehouse management and collaborative logistics capabilities. The software is designed to increase revenues, reduce inventory costs, improve forecast accuracy, optimize production scheduling, reduce transportation costs and improve customer service. The consumers of the group include suppliers, manufacturers, distributors and retailers. The group's total revenue for year 2007 was 43.76 millions of USD.

Primary SIC and add'l.: 7379 7372

CIK No: 0001043915

Subsidiaries: Demand Management, Inc

Officers: Michael J. Edenfield/Dir., CEO, Pres./$819,556.00, Vincent C. Klinges/CFO, VP - Finance/$301,526.00, Allan H. Dow/Exec. VP - Worldwide Sales, Marketing/$370,810.00, Donald L. Thomas/VP - Customer Service/$206,306.00, Pat McManus/Investor Contact, James R. McGuone/Sec., Karin L. Bursa/VP - Marketing at Logility, Mark A. Balte/VP - Research, Development, Leonard G. Sherwinski/VP - Professional Services

Directors: Michael J. Edenfield/Dir., CEO, Pres., James C. Edenfield/73/Chmn., Frederick E. Cooper/Dir., Parker H. Petit/Dir., John A. White/Dir.

Owners: American Software, Inc., Frederick E. Cooper, Vincent C. Klinges, Thomas L. Newberry, J. Michael Edenfield, Donald L. Thomas, James C. Edenfield, John A. White, H. Allan Dow, Insiders, Parker H. Petit

Financial Data: Fiscal Year End:04/30 Latest Annual Data: 04/30/2007

Year	Sales	Net Income
2007	$43,763,000	$5,994,000
2006	$37,303,000	$8,013,000
2005	$24,876,000	-$606,000

Curr. Assets:	$38,140,000	Curr. Liab.:	$17,510,000	P/E Ratio:	24.63
Plant, Equip.:	$457,000	Total Liab.:	$19,184,000	Indic. Yr. Divd.:	NA
Total Assets:	$53,074,000	Net Worth:	$33,890,000	Debt/ Equity:	NA

Logistical Support Inc

19734 Dearborn St., Chatsworth, CA, 91311; *PH:* 1-818-885-0300;
http:// www.logistical-support.com

General - Incorporation	UT	Stock - Price on:12/24/2007	$0.18
Employees	28	Stock Exchange	OTC
Auditor	A.J. Robbins P.C.	Ticker Symbol	LGSL
Stk Agt	Interwest Transfer Company, Inc.	Outstanding Shares	78,850,000
Counsel	Richardson & Patel LLP	E.P.S	$0.00
DUNS No.	NA	Shareholders	NA

Business: The groups principle activity is to provide aerospace and defense contracts. The group operates from the United States. The group's quarterly revenue for Sep '07 was 1.29 millions of USD.

Primary SIC and add'l.: 3728

CIK No: 0001158486

Subsidiaries: Hill Aerospace & Defense, LLC, Logistical Support, LLC

Officers: Bruce Littell/Chmn., CEO - Contact - Investor Relations, Joe Lucan/VP - Engineering, Jerry Hill/VP - Operations, Contact - Repair, Overhaul, Agnes Houng/Contact - International Customers, Lisa Higgins/42/VP - Finance

Directors: Bruce Littell/Chmn., CEO - Contact - Investor Relations

Owners: Harry Lebovitz/33.79%, Absolute Return Europe Fund/7.62%, Insiders/34.87%, Scott G. Littell/22.96%, Bruce Littell/10.90%, Joseph Lucan/3.94%, European Catalyst Fund/14.73%

Financial Data: Fiscal Year End:12/31 Latest Annual Data: 12/31/2006

Year	Sales	Net Income
2006	$6,219,000	$136,000
2005	$5,318,000	-$1,835,000
2004	$5,669,000	-$72,000

Curr. Assets:	$3,403,000	Curr. Liab.:	$2,241,000		
Plant, Equip.:	$484,000	Total Liab.:	$2,549,000	Indic. Yr. Divd.:	NA
Total Assets:	$3,887,000	Net Worth:	$1,338,000	Debt/ Equity:	NA

Logitech International SA

Taikoo Pl., 979 Kings Rd., Quarry Bay, 94555; *PH:* 1-852-2821-5900; *Fax:* 1-852-2520-2230;
http:// www.logitech.com

General - Incorporation	Switzerland	Stock - Price on:12/24/2007	$27.58
Employees	7,431	Stock Exchange	NDQ
Auditor	PricewaterhouseCoopers LLP	Ticker Symbol	LOGI
Stk Agt	Bank of New York	Outstanding Shares	182,240,000
Counsel	NA	E.P.S	$0.99
DUNS No.	02-423-7877	Shareholders	NA

Business: The group's principal activities are to design, develop, produce and market personal interface products. It also develops supporting software that serve as the primary physical interface between people and their personal computers and other digital platforms. Products of the group include

input and pointing devices such as corded and cordless mice, trackballs, and keyboards, interactive gaming devices for entertainment such as joysticks, gamepads and steering wheels, multimedia speakers and Internet video cameras. The group markets its products mainly in North America, Europe, Asia-pacific, Latin America, the Middle East and Africa.

Primary SIC and add'l.: 7371 3572 3577 5063 5045

CIK No: 0001032975

Subsidiaries: 3Dconnexion (U.K.) Limited, 3Dconnexion France SARL, 3Dconnexion GmbH, 3Dconnexion Holding S.A., 3Dconnexion Inc., 3Dconnexion Polaska Sp z.o.o, Labtec Europe S.A., Labtec Inc., Logi (U.K.) Ltd., Logi-Computer Hungary Trading and Services Limited Liability Company, LogiCool Co. Ltd., Logitech (Intrigue) Inc., Logitech (Jersey) Ltd., Logitech 3D Holding GmbH, Logitech Asia Logistic Ltd. 44 Subsidiaries included in the Index

Officers: Guerrino De Luca/Dir., CEO, Pres., Junien Labrousse/Exec. VP - Products, Joseph L. Sullivan/Sr. VP - Worldwide Operations, David Henry/Sr. VP - Customer Experience, Chief Marketing Officer, Mark J. Hawkins/Sr. VP - Finance, Information Technology, CFO, Gerald P. Quindlen/Sr. VP - Worldwide Sales, Marketing, Joe Greenhalgh/VP - Investor Relations - Corporate Finance, Andre Jaekel/Mgr. - Investor Relations, Europe, Heather Brandon/Investor Relations Specialist

Directors: Guerrino De Luca/Dir., CEO, Pres., Daniel Borel/Chmn., Co - Founder, Gary F. Bengier/Dir., Erh-Hsun Chang/58/Dir., Sally Davis/Dir., Robert Malcom/Dir., Monika Ribar/Dir., Kee-Lock Chua/Dir., Matthew Bousquette/Dir.

Owners: Daniel Borel/5.70%

Financial Data: Fiscal Year End:03/31   Latest Annual Data: 03/31/2007

Year	Sales	Net Income
2007	$2,066,569,000	$229,848,000
2006	$1,796,715,000	$181,105,000
2005	$1,482,626,000	$149,266,000

Curr. Assets:	$1,007,420,000	Curr. Liab.:	$465,065,000	P/E Ratio:	24.63
Plant, Equip.:	$87,054,000	Total Liab.:	$482,939,000	Indic. Yr. Divd.:	NA
Total Assets:	$1,327,463,000	Net Worth:	$844,524,000	Debt/ Equity:	NA

LoJack Corp

200 Lowder Brook Dr., Ste. 1000, Westwood, MA, 02090; *PH:* 1-781-251-4700; *Fax:* 1-781-251-4649; *http://* www.lojack.com

General - Incorporation	MA	Stock - Price on:12/24/2007	$22.56
Employees	913	Stock Exchange	NDQ
Auditor	Deloitte & Touche LLP	Ticker Symbol	LOJN
Stk Agt	American Stock Transfer & Trust Co.	Outstanding Shares	18,740,000
Counsel	Sullivan & Worcester LLP	E.P.S.	$1.10
DUNS No.	04-893-0218	Shareholders	NA

Business: The group's principle activities are to develop and market the lojack system, which is a unique patented system designed to assist law enforcement personnel in locating, tracking and recovering stolen vehicles. The lojack system comprises of a registration system maintained and operated by the company; a sector activation system and police tracking computers operated by law enforcement officials and the lojack unit, a VHF (very high frequency) transponder sold to consumers. The group has also introduced lojack early warning(tm) recovery system for stolen vehicle recovery. It also licenses the use of its stolen vehicle recovery system technology in selected international markets. The group markets through national sales force that routinely visits franchised new car dealers to educate and train dealership personnel on the benefits of the lojack system. The group's quarterly revenue for September 2007 was 55.10 millions of USD.

Primary SIC and add'l.: 3669

CIK No: 0000355777

Subsidiaries: An Jie China Holdings Limited, Boomerang Tracking Inc., LJPR, Inc, LoJack de Mexico, S. de R.L. de CV, LoJack do Brasil LTDA, LoJack Exchangeco Canada Inc., LoJack Global LLC, LoJack International Corporation, LoJack Italia Network S.r.l., LoJack Italia S.r.l., LoJack Operating Company, L.P.

Officers: Richard T. Riley/Chmn., CEO, William R. Duvall/CTO, Exec. VP, Thomas M. Camp/Sr. VP, GM - International, Thomas Wooters/Exec. VP, General Counsel, Kevin M. Mullins/Sr. VP, GM - US Automotive, Michael Umana/Sr. VP, CFO/$407,461.00, Ronald V. Waters/Dir., COO, Pres., John Swanson/Investor Relation Officer

Directors: Richard T. Riley/Chmn., CEO, Robert L. Rewey/Dir., John H. MacKinnon/Dir., Harvey Rosenthal/Dir., Robert J. Murray/Dir., Maria Renna Sharpe/Dir., Ronald V. Waters/Dir., COO, Pres., Rory J. Cowan/Dir.

Owners: Keith Farris, Michael Umana, Insiders/5.63%, Maria Renna Sharpe, Ronald V. Waters, Joseph F. Abely, Thomas M. Camp, Richard T. Riley, Wellington Management Company, LLP/5.65%, Barclays Global Investors, NA./5.27%, William R. Duvall/1.13%, Thomas A. Wooters, Robert J. Murray, Harvey Rosenthal, Kevin M. Mullins (18 Owners included in Index)

Financial Data: Fiscal Year End:12/31   Latest Annual Data: 12/31/2006

Year	Sales	Net Income
2006	$213,288,000	$16,507,000
2005	$190,726,000	$18,439,000
2004	$145,691,000	$10,400,000

Curr. Assets:	$111,861,000	Curr. Liab.:	$50,464,000	P/E Ratio:	21.90
Plant, Equip.:	$21,571,000	Total Liab.:	$92,020,000	Indic. Yr. Divd.:	NA
Total Assets:	$202,020,000	Net Worth:	$110,000,000	Debt/ Equity:	NA

Lone Star Steakhouse & Saloon Inc

224 E Douglas, Ste. 700, Wichita, KS, 67202; *PH:* 1-316-264-8899; *http://* www.lonestarsteakhouse.com

General - Incorporation	DE	Stock - Price on:12/24/2007	$16.7
Employees	19,750	Stock Exchange	NDQ
Auditor	Ernst & Young LLP	Ticker Symbol	NA
Stk Agt	American Stock Transfer & Trust Co.	Outstanding Shares	62,420,000
Counsel	Olshan Grundman Frome Et Al	E.P.S.	$0.11
DUNS No.	78-618-1792	Shareholders	NA

Business: The group's principal activity is to own and operate a chain of mid-priced full service and casual-dining restaurants. The restaurants provide mesquite-grilled steaks, prime rib, ribs, chicken, fish, king crab, shrimp, salad, bread, baked potato, baked sweet potato, steak fries, steamed vegetables or Texas rice, hamburgers, chicken sandwiches and soups. As of 15-Jun-2004, the group owned and operated 251

restaurants in the United States. During 2003, the group discontinued its operations in Australia. The restaurants are operated under the trade names lone star steakhouse & saloon (R), lone star cafe (R), del frisco's (R), double eagle steak house(R) and sullivan's steakhouse (r). On 28-Jan-2004, the group acquired txcc.

Primary SIC and add'l.: 5813 5812

CIK No: 0000883670

Subsidiaries: Big Guns, Inc., Bridgewater Properties, Inc., California Sullivan's, Inc., Carolina, Inc., CGB Delaware, Inc., Colorado Sullivan's, Inc., Crockett Beverage Corp. (Ft. Worth) CWA Delaware, Inc., Del Frisco's of Colorado, Inc., Del Frisco's of Illinois, Inc., Del Frisco's of Nevada, Inc., Del Frisco's of New York, Inc., Del Frisco's of North Carolina, Inc., Del Frisco's of Philadelphia, Inc., Del Frisco's of Washington, D.C., Inc. 127 Subsidiaries included in the Index

Officers: Jamie B. Coulter/CEO, Fred B. Chaney/Chmn. - Business Consultant, John D. White/Dir., CFO, Exec. VP, Treasurer, Gerald T. Aaron/Sr. VP - Counsel, Sec., Pat Barth/Regional VP, Robert R. Crawford/VP - Taxes, Scottie Cronin/VP - Quality Assurance, Ryan Franklin/Regional VP, Jon Howie/Chief Accounting Officer, Mark Mednansky/COO

Directors: Fred B. Chaney/Chmn. - Business Consultant, Clark R. Mandigo/Dir., Thomas C. Lasorda/Dir., William B. Greene/Dir., Michael A. Ledeen/Dir., Mark G. Saltzgaber/Dir., Anthony Bergamo/Dir., John D. White/Dir., CFO, Exec. VP, Treasurer

Owners: William B. Greene, Barington Companies Equity Partners, L.P./9.30%, Wachovia Corporation/6.70%, Insiders/19.70%, Jamie B. Coulter/15.80%, Clark R. Mandigo, Deutsche Bank AG/9.80%, Millenium Management, L.L.C/5.00%, Gerald T. Aaron/1.00%, Mark Mednansky, Michael Ledeen, Anthony Bergamo, Fred B. Chaney, Pioneer Global Asset Management/6.10%, Deidra Lincoln (20 Owners included in Index)

Financial Data: Fiscal Year End:12/27   Latest Annual Data: 12/31/2006

Year	Sales	Net Income
2006	$94,350,000	$3,642,000
2005	$59,660,000	$904,000

Curr. Assets:	$91,544,000	Curr. Liab.:	$72,239,000	P/E Ratio:	151.82
Plant, Equip.:	$10,839,000	Total Liab.:	$79,508,000	Indic. Yr. Divd.:	NA
Total Assets:	$104,267,000	Net Worth:	-$105,511,000	Debt/ Equity:	NA

Lone Star Technologies Inc

15660 N Dallas Pk.way, Ste. 500, Dallas, TX, 75248; *PH:* 1-972-770-6401; *http://* www.lonestartech.com

General - Incorporation	DE	Stock - Price on:12/24/2007	NA
Employees	2,699	Stock Exchange	NA
Auditor	Deloitte & Touche LLP	Ticker Symbol	NA
Stk Agt	American Stock Transfer & Trust Co.	Outstanding Shares	NA
Counsel	NA	E.P.S.	NA
DUNS No.	00-750-5464	Shareholders	NA

Business: The group's principal activity is to manufacture and market steel tubular products which is used in the completion and production of oil and gas wells. The group also manufactures line pipe used to gather and transmit oil and natural gas. The group operates in three segments: oilfield products, specialty tubing products and flat rolled steel and other products. Oilfield products include casing, production tubing and line pipe. Specialty tubing products include precision mechanical and as-welded tubing. Flat rolled steel and other include products secondary to the manufacture of oilfield and specialty tubing products. On 02-Jun-2003, the group acquired frank's tubular international.

Primary SIC and add'l.: 1389 6719 3317 3312

CIK No: 0000791348

Subsidiaries: Aletas y Birlos Mexicana, S.A. de C.V., Aletas y Birlos, S.A. de C.V., Bellville Tube Company, L.P., Delta Tubular International, L.P., Delta Tubular Processing, L.P., Environmental Holdings, Inc., Fintube (Thailand) Ltd., Fintube Canada, Inc., Fintube Technologies, Inc., Lone Star Logistics, Inc., Lone Star ST Holdings, Inc., Lone Star Steel Company, Lone Star Steel International de Mexico, Lone Star Steel International, L.P., Lone Star Steel Mexico, LLC 24 Subsidiaries included in the Index

Officers: Dan O. Dinges/54/Chmn., CEO, Pres., Robert F. Spears/64/VP, General Counsel, Sec./$546,842.00, Charles J. Keszler/45/CFO, VP/$586,316.00, Joseph Alvarado/55/COO, Pres./$1,199,704.00

Directors: Dan O. Dinges/54/Chmn., CEO, Pres., Frederick B. Hegi/64/Dir., Jerry E. Ryan/65/Dir., Rhys J. Best/61/Dir., Robert Kelley/62/Dir., Joseph M. McHugh/70/Dir., Alfred M. Micallef/65/Dir., David A. Reed/60/Dir.

Owners: Frederick B. Hegi, David A. Reed, Dan O. Dinges, Joseph M. McHugh, TIAA-CREF Investment Management, LLC/7.44%, Joseph Alvarado, Barclays Global Investors, NA/6.89%, Rhys J. Best/1.54%, Byron W. Dunn, Insiders/3.18%, Charles J. Keszler, Robert F. Spears, Alfred M. Micallef, Robert Kelley, Robert L. Keiser (17 Owners included in Index)

Longfoot Communications Corp

914 Wwood Blvd. No.809, Los Angeles, CA, 90024; *PH:* 1-310-385-9631

General - Incorporation	DE	Stock - Price on:12/24/2007	$1.05
Employees	NA	Stock Exchange	OTC
Auditor	Farber Hass Hurley & McEwen LLP	Ticker Symbol	LGFC
Stk Agt	Holladay Stock Transfer, Inc.	Outstanding Shares	4,370,000
Counsel	NA	E.P.S.	-$0.07
DUNS No.	NA	Shareholders	NA

Business: The groups principal activities include constructing, developing, managing and operating Low Power Television stations and AM and FM radio stations. The group operates from the United States.

Primary SIC and add'l.: 4832

CIK No: 0001345721

Subsidiaries: Village Broadcasting Corp

Officers: Arthur Lyons/62/Chmn., CEO, Pres., Jack Brehm/80/Dir., CFO, Sec.

Directors: Arthur Lyons/62/Chmn., CEO, Pres., Jack Brehm/80/Dir., CFO, Sec., Aaron A. Grunfeld/61/Dir.

Owners: Jack Brehm/2.00%, Andrew Limpert/5.00%, Aaron A. Grunfeld/2.00%, 32 Mayall, LLC/22.00%, Insiders/24.60%, Arthur Lyons, Gusmail, LLC/18.30%, PP60, LLC/36.00%

Financial Data: Fiscal Year End:09/30   Latest Annual Data: 09/30/2006

Year	Sales	Net Income
2006	NA	-$176,000

Curr. Assets:	$73,000	Curr. Liab.:	$7,000		
Plant, Equip.:	$34,000	Total Liab.:	$7,000	Indic. Yr. Divd.:	NA
Total Assets:	$127,000	Net Worth:	$120,000	Debt/ Equity:	NA

Longport Inc

Spring Valley Business Pk., 2 Braxton Way, Ste. 111, Glen Mills, PA, 19342; *PH:* 1-610-675-0090; *Fax:* 1-610-675-0630; *http://* www.longportinc.com; *Email:* info@longportinc.com

General - Incorporation	DE	**Stock**- Price on:12/24/2007	$0.035
Employees	NA	Stock Exchange	OTC
Auditor	Mayer Hoffman Mccann, P.C	Ticker Symbol	LPTI
Stk Agt	Corporate Stock Transfer, Inc.	Outstanding Shares	NA
Counsel	NA	E.P.S.	NA
DUNS No.	80-883-9476	Shareholders	NA

Business: The group's principal activity is to develop and market soft tissue ultrasound scanner that is used for wound care and other medical applications. Ultrasound scanner produces an image of the skin and underlying tissue. These images can be printed, stored as bitmap files or e-mailed to an off-site diagnostic center for interpretation or archiving. The scanner system is comprised of a desktop PC like housing, which includes a proprietary board, a separate monitor, keyboard and interchangeable hand-held probes. The scanner technology has applications in wound detection, burn assessment, product testing, dermatology and women's health. The group takes patents in the United States, Australia and South Africa.

Primary SIC and add'l.: 8099 3845

CIK No: 0000919043

Subsidiaries: Longport International, Inc, Longport International, Ltd., Longport Medical, Inc

Officers: Michael C. Boyd/Dir., CEO, Paul D. Wilson/Dir., Pres., Mary Dyson/Exec. VP, Brian Nedbalski/Dir. - Operations, Kathy Solari/Clinical Support, Theresa Boyle/Executive Assist.

Directors: Michael C. Boyd/Dir., CEO, Michie Proctor/Dir., Paul R. Quintavalle/Dir., Paul D. Wilson/Dir., Pres., Brian W. Clymer/Dir.

Financial Data: *Fiscal Year End:*12/31   *Latest Annual Data:* 12/31/2004

Year	Sales	Net Income
2004	$2,458,000	-$634,000
2003	$500,000	-$928,000
2002	$444,000	-$826,000

Curr. Assets:	$2,445,000	**Curr. Liab.:**	$1,793,000		
Plant, Equip.:	$240,000	**Total Liab.:**	$1,793,000	**Indic. Yr. Divd.:**	NA
Total Assets:	$2,697,000	**Net Worth:**	$904,000	**Debt/ Equity:**	NA

Longs Drug Stores Corp

141 N Civic Dr., Walnut Creek, CA, 94596; *PH:* 1-925-937-1170; *Fax:* 1-925-210-6886; *http://* www.longs.com

General - Incorporation	MD	**Stock**- Price on:12/24/2007	$52.37
Employees	9,855	Stock Exchange	NYSE
Auditor	Deloitte & Touche LLP	Ticker Symbol	LDG
Stk Agt	Wells Fargo Shareowner Services	Outstanding Shares	38,090,000
Counsel	Latham & Watkins	E.P.S.	$2.08
DUNS No.	00-691-0004	Shareholders	NA

Business: The group operates through its subsidiaries whose principle activity is to operate retail drug stores. The group operates from United States.

Primary SIC and add'l.: 5912

CIK No: 0000764762

Subsidiaries: LDG Property Company, Inc., LDG Property Company, LLC, Longs Drug Stores California, Inc., RxAmerica LLC

Officers: Warren F. Bryant/Chmn., CEO, Pres./$5,821,990.00, Farra Levin/Contact - Media, Todd J. Vasos/Sr. VP, Chief Merchandising Officer/$1,578,608.00, Linda M. Watt/Sr. VP - Human Resources, Michael M. Laddon/CIO, Sr. VP, Steve McCann/CFO, Exec. VP/$2,098,085.00, Bruce E. Schwallie/Exec. VP - Business Development - Managed Care/$2,060,642.00, Karen Stout/COO, Exec. VP, Roger Chelemedos/Sr. VP - Finance, Controller, Treasurer, William J. Rainey/Sr. VP, General Counsel, Sec./$1,556,768.00, Phyllis J. Proffer/Investor Relations Officer

Directors: Warren F. Bryant/Chmn., CEO, Pres., Murray H. Dashe/Dir., Harold R. Somerset/Dir., Anthony G. Wagner/Dir., Mary S. Metz/Dir., Leroy T. Barnes/Dir., Lisa M. Harper/Dir., Donna A. Tanoue/Dir., Evelyn S. Dilsaver/Dir.

Owners: Robert M. Long/4.16%, Todd J. Vasos, Warren F. Bryant, J.M. Long Foundation/1.29%, William J. Rainey, Leroy T. Barnes, Goldman Sachs Asset Management, L.P./6.13%, Advisory Research, Inc./8.60%, AXA Financial, Inc./5.93%, Steven F. McCann, Harold R. Somerset, Mary S. Metz, Employee Savings and Profit Sharing Plan/13.48%, Murray H. Dashe, Donna A. Tanoue (22 Owners included in Index)

Financial Data: *Fiscal Year End:*01/26   *Latest Annual Data:* 1/25/2007

Year	Sales	Net Income
2007	$5,097,052,000	$74,461,000
2006	$4,670,303,000	$73,884,000
2005	$4,607,873,000	$36,560,000

Curr. Assets:	$700,579,000	**Curr. Liab.:**	$465,040,000	**P/E Ratio:**	25.18
Plant, Equip.:	$618,354,000	**Total Liab.:**	$684,026,000	**Indic. Yr. Divd.:**	$0.560
Total Assets:	$1,411,163,000	**Net Worth:**	$727,137,000	**Debt/ Equity:**	0.1337

Longview Fibre Co

300 Fibre Way, Longview, WA, 98632; *PH:* 1-360-425-1550; *http://* www.longviewfibre.com

General - Incorporation	WA	**Stock**- Price on:12/24/2007	NA
Employees	NA	Stock Exchange	NA
Auditor	PricewaterhouseCoopers LLP	Ticker Symbol	NA
Stk Agt	Mellon Investor Services LLC	Outstanding Shares	NA
Counsel	NA	E.P.S.	NA
DUNS No.	00-904-1443	Shareholders	NA

Business: The group's principal activities are to own, manage and operate timberlands, pulp and paper mill and converting plants. The group operates in three business segments: timber, paper and paperboard and converted products. The timber segment owns and manages timberlands in Oregon and Washington, which produces logs for sale. The paper and paperboard segment includes the operation of pulp and paper mill that produces kraft paper and paperboard. The converted products segment produces finished products such as corrugated containers, specialty packaging, creative point-of-purchase displays, handle shopping bags and merchandise bags. The group sells its paper and paperboard products to a number of domestic and export customers. The group exports its products to customers in Japan, China and southeast Asia.

Primary SIC and add'l.: 2631 2652 2671 2621 2411

CIK No: 0000060302

Subsidiaries: Longtimber Company of Oregon, Longview Fibre Paper and Packaging, Inc.

Officers: Steven J. Buhaly/50/CFO, Sr. VP - Finance, Sec., Treasurer, Frank V. McShane/55/COO, Sr. VP, Blake S. Rowe/51/Sr. VP - Timber

Directors: R. L. Bentzinger/Dir., C. M. Stevens/Dir., M. A. Dow/Dir.

Owners: Richard H. Wollenberg/3.72%, Kenneth D. Gettman, Lisa J. McLaughlin, Dimensional Fund Advisors LP/7.95%, David L. Bowden, Insiders/4.07%, Alexis M. Dow, John R. Kretchmer, David A. Wollenberg/3.22%, Barclays Global Investors, NA, et al./5.36%, Blake S. Rowe, Richard J. Parker, Michael C. Henderson, Robert B. Arkell, Robert A. Kirchner

Looksmart Ltd

625 2nd St., San Francisco, CA, 94107; *PH:* 1-415-348-7000; *Fax:* 1-415-348-7050; *http://* www.looksmart.com

General - Incorporation	DE	**Stock**- Price on:12/24/2007	$3.9
Employees	120	Stock Exchange	NDQ
Auditor	PricewaterhouseCoopers LLP	Ticker Symbol	LOOK
Stk Agt	Chase Mellon Shareholder Services LLC	Outstanding Shares	22,900,000
Counsel	Gibson, Dunn & Crutcher LLP	E.P.S.	-$0.47
DUNS No.	NA	Shareholders	NA

Business: The group's principle activities are to provide Internet search-targeted marketing solutions for online businesses globally. The group operates through two business segments: listing and licensing. The listing product segment provides businesses of all sizes to include listings for their company and product pages in relevant search results. The products include both inclusion-targeted listings and keyword-targeted listings and are sold directly to advertisers or indirectly through advertising agencies. The licensing business segment revenues are derived from licensing the database content to the group's partners that include microsoft. The group's quarterly revenue for September 2007 was 12.63 millions of USD.

Primary SIC and add'l.: 6794 7373 7375

CIK No: 0001077866

Subsidiaries: BTLookSmart Pty Ltd., LookSmart (Barbados), Inc., LookSmart Germany GmbH, LookSmart Holdings (Delaware), Ltd., LookSmart International Pty Ltd., LookSmart Netherlands B.V., LookSmart United Kingdom Ltd., WiseNut, Inc.

Officers: David B. Hills/52/Dir., CEO, Pres./$1,192,069.00, Stacey Giamalis/Sr. VP - Legal - Human Resources, General Counsel, Sec./$325,378.00, Michael Grubb/42/CTO, Sr. VP/$338,724.00, John Simonelli/CFO, COO/$492,071.00, Thomas J. Kelly/36/VP - Marketing, Michael Schoen/36/VP - Product, Technology/$281,396.00, Jonathan Ewert/GM - Advertising Networks, Ari Kaufman/GM - Publisher Services, Bert Knorr/VP - Technology, Brian McAllister/VP - Business Analytics, Allyson Pooley/Integrated Corporate Relations, Yolanda Loh Berry/34/VP - Ad Sales

Directors: David B. Hills/52/Dir., CEO, Pres., Edward F. West/Chmn., Anthony Castagna/Dir., Teresa Dial/Dir., Mark Sanders/Dir., Timothy J. Wright/Dir., Jean-Yves Dexmier/Dir.

Owners: S Squared Technology LLC/6.50%, Michael Grubb, Deborah Richman, Mark Sanders, David B. Hills/1.60%, Insiders/4.87%, Bryan Everett, Edward F. West, Michael Schoen, Anthony Castagna, T. Rowe Price Associates, Inc./5.50%, Sidus Investment Management LLC/9.90%, Timothy J. Wright, Stacey Giamalis, John Simonelli (16 Owners included in Index)

Financial Data: *Fiscal Year End:*12/31   *Latest Annual Data:* 12/31/2006

Year	Sales	Net Income
2006	$48,673,000	-$13,666,000
2005	$41,359,000	-$17,797,000
2004	$76,996,000	-$9,638,000

Curr. Assets:	$45,652,000	**Curr. Liab.:**	$12,132,000		
Plant, Equip.:	$4,588,000	**Total Liab.:**	$15,008,000	**Indic. Yr. Divd.:**	NA
Total Assets:	$72,557,000	**Net Worth:**	$57,549,000	**Debt/ Equity:**	0.0462

LoopNet Inc

185 Berry St., Ste. 4000, San Francisco, CA, 94107; *PH:* 1-415-243-4200; *Fax:* 1-415-764-1622; *http://* www.loopnet.com; *Email:* salesteam@loopnet.com

General - Incorporation		**Stock**- Price on:12/24/2007	$22.92
Employees	198	Stock Exchange	NDQ
Auditor	NA	Ticker Symbol	LOOP
Stk Agt	Computershare Trust Co	Outstanding Shares	38,400,000
Counsel	NA	E.P.S.	$0.41
DUNS No.	NA	Shareholders	NA

Business: The groups principle activity is to provide online marketplace services for commercial real estate. The group products sold under the trade name LoopNet, BizBuySell and LoopLink. The groups services include basic and premium membership, property listing, myloopnet, enhanced listing exposure, prospectlist, marketing exposure statistics, controlled access marketing and property searching. The group operates from the United States. The group's quarterly revenue for September 2007 was 18.63 millions of USD.

Primary SIC and add'l.: 7375

CIK No: 0001353209

Officers: Richard Boyle/Chmn., CEO, Pres., Brent Stumme/CFO, Sr. VP - Finance, Administration, Wayne Warthen/CTO, Sr. VP - Information Technology, Jason Greenman/Chief Product Officer, Sr. VP - Business, Product Development, Thomas Byrne/Chief Marketing Officer, Sr. VP - Marketing, Sales

Directors: Richard Boyle/Chmn., CEO, Pres., Jeffrey D. Brody/48/Dir., William Byrnes/Dir., Dennis Chookaszian/Dir., Noel Fenton/Dir., Scott Ingraham/Dir., Thomas E. Unterman/Dir., William A. Millichap/64/Dir.

Owners: Scott Ingraham, Thomas E. Unterman/8.40%, Jeffrey Brody/7.80%, Wayne Warthen/1.40%, Dennis Chookaszian, William Millichap, FMR Corp./12.80%, Brent Stumme/1.50%, Jason Greenman/1.50%, Rustic Canyon Ventures, L.P./8.40%, Insiders/29.40%, Brentwood Associates IX, LP/7.60%, Thomas Byrne/1.40%, Noel Fenton/2.80%, STFIII, LP/7.10% (17 Owners included in Index)

Financial Data: *Fiscal Year End:*NA   *Latest Annual Data:* 12/31/2006

Year	Sales	Net Income
2006	$48,411,000	$15,495,000
2005	$30,977,000	$18,936,000
2004	$17,036,000	$3,720,000

Curr. Assets:	$92,086,000	**Curr. Liab.:**	$10,202,000		
Plant, Equip.:	$1,020,000	**Total Liab.:**	$10,202,000	**Indic. Yr. Divd.:**	NA
Total Assets:	$100,205,000	**Net Worth:**	$90,003,000	**Debt/ Equity:**	NA

Loral Space & Communications Ltd

600 Third Ave, New York, NY, 10016; *PH:* 1-212-697-1105; *http://* www.ssloral.com

General - Incorporation	DE	*Stock* - Price on:12/24/2007	$49.12
Employees	2,100	Stock Exchange	NDQ
Auditor	Deloitte & Touche LLP	Ticker Symbol	LORL
Stk Agt	Registrar & Transfer Co	Outstanding Shares	20,070,000
Counsel	Willkie Farr & Gallagher LLP	E.P.S.	-$0.3
DUNS No.	94-681-6212	Shareholders	NA

Business: The group's principal activities are to design and manufacture satellites and satellite systems for commercial and government applications. The group also provides satellite services, television broadcasting, direct-to-home television services, broadband communications, military communications, wireless telephony, digital satellite radio, weather monitoring and air traffic management. The group operates through two business segments: satellite services and satellite manufacturing. Satellite services include leasing transponder capacity to customers for distribution of network and cable television programming, direct-to-home video transmission and live video feeds from breaking news and sporting events and broadband data distribution. Satellite manufacturing designs, manufactures and integrates satellites and space systems. The customers of the group include the United States, Asia, Europe and Mexico.

Primary SIC and add'l.: 4899 4812 3663

CIK No: 0001006269

Subsidiaries: Cosmotech, CyberStar, LLC, Earth Station Ecuador CIA Ltda., International Space Technology, Inc4, LAD Telecommunications GmbH, LGP (Bermuda) Ltd., Loral Asia Pacific Satellite (HK) Limited, Loral Communications Services, Inc., Loral CyberStar de Argentina SRL, Loral CyberStar GmbH3, Loral CyberStar Holdings, LLC, Loral CyberStar International, Inc., Loral CyberStar Services, Inc., Loral CyberStar, LLC, Loral General Partner, Inc. 37 Subsidiaries included in the Index

Officers: Michael B. Targoff/Vice Chmn., CEO/$2,652,778.00, Eric J. Zahler/COO, Pres./$2,599,868.00, Laurence D. Atlas/VP - Government Relations, Telecommunications, Richard P. Mastoloni/VP, Treasurer, Barry J. Sitler/VP - Tax, John Stack/Assist. Treasurer, John Celli/Pres., COO - Space Systems, Loral, Arnold Friedman/Sr. VP - Worldwide Marketing, Sales, Chris Hoeber/Sr. VP - Program Management, Systems Engineering, Space Systems, Loral, Inc, Ron Haley/Sr. VP, CFO - Finance, Contracts Engineering, Space Systems, Loral, Inc, Chris Goodman/Sr. VP - Engineering, Manufacturing, Test Operations, Space Systems, Loral, Inc, Patrick K. Brant/VP, Pres. - Loral Skynet, John McCarthy/Sr. Dir. - Communications, Investor Relations, Janet T. Yeung/VP, Deputy General Counsel, Assist. Sec., Avi Katz/VP, General Counsel, Sec./$948,633.00 *(21 Officers included in Index)*

Directors: Michael B. Targoff/Vice Chmn., CEO, Arthur L. Simon/76/Dir., Mark H. Rachesky/49/Dir., Sai Devabhaktuni/36/Dir., Hal Goldstein/42/Dir., John D. Harkey/47/Dir., Dean Olmstead/52/Dir., John P. Stenbit/68/Dir.

Owners: Mark H. Rachesky, EchoStar Communications Corporation, Avi Katz, Eric J. Zahler, Arthur L. Simon, Richard J. Townsend, BlackRock, Inc., MHR Fund Management LLC/100.00%, Michael B. Targoff, Insiders, MHR Fund Management LLC and Mark H. Rachesky, MHR Fund Management LLC/100.00%, Highland Capital Management, L.P. and James Dondero

Financial Data: Fiscal Year End:12/31   *Latest Annual Data:* 12/31/2006

Year	Sales	Net Income
2006	$797,333,000	-$22,720,000
2005	$626,348,000	$1,029,588,000
2004	$522,127,000	-$176,695,000

Curr. Assets:	$547,700,000	*Curr. Liab.:*	$419,554,000		
Plant, Equip.:	$558,879,000	*Total Liab.:*	$868,653,000	*Indic. Yr. Divd.:*	NA
Total Assets:	$1,729,911,000	*Net Worth:*	$647,002,000	*Debt/ Equity:*	0.1414

Lorus Therapeutics Inc

2 Meridian Rd., Toronto, ON, M9W 4Z7; *PH:* 1-416-798-1200; *http://* www.lorusthera.com; *Email:* info@lorusthera.com

General - Incorporation	ON	*Stock* - Price on:12/24/2007	$0.24
Employees	NA	Stock Exchange	AMEX
Auditor	KPMG LLP	Ticker Symbol	LRP
Stk Agt	Computershare Trust Co	Outstanding Shares	211,280,000
Counsel	Torys LLP	E.P.S.	-$0.01
DUNS No.	24-664-3910	Shareholders	NA

Business: The group's principle activities include researching, developing and commercializing pharmaceutical products and technologies for the management of cancer. The group discovers, research and development of cancer therapies. The group's three products are in the clinical trial stage of development. The group operates from United States.

Primary SIC and add'l.: 2833 2834 8731

CIK No: 0000882361

Subsidiaries: GeneSense Technologies Inc

Officers: Aiping H. Young/Director, CEO, Pres., Mace L. Rothenberg/Medical Advisor

Directors: Aiping H. Young/Director, CEO, Pres., Louis Siminovitch/Chmn. - Medical, Member - Scientific Advisory Board, Denis R. Burger/Chmn., Susan Koppy/Dir., Mark Vincent/Dir., George R. Stark/Member - Medical Scientific Advisory Board, Georg Ludwig/Dir., Herbert Abramson/Dir., Jim A. Wright/Dir., Alan A. Steigrod/Dir., Kevin J. Buchi/Dir., Donald P. Braun/Member - Medical Scientific Advisory Board, Jaime G. De La Garza Salazar/Member - Medical Scientific Advisory Board, Robert Kerbel/Member - Medical Scientific Advisory Board, Bishnu D. Sanwal/Member - Medical Scientific Advisory Board

Owners: Graham Strachan, Elizabeth Williams, Kevin Buchi, Insiders/16.14%, Jim A. Wright/2.12%, Aiping H. Young, Donald Paterson, Georg Ludwig/13.92%

Financial Data: Fiscal Year End:05/31   *Latest Annual Data:* 05/31/2007

Year	Sales	Net Income
2007	$100,000	-$8,527,000
2006	$24,000	-$14,874,000
2005	$5,000	-$16,161,000

Curr. Assets:	$8,018,000	*Curr. Liab.:*	$2,736,000		
Plant, Equip.:	$803,000	*Total Liab.:*	$15,680,000	*Indic. Yr. Divd.:*	NA
Total Assets:	$10,551,000	*Net Worth:*	-$5,130,000	*Debt/ Equity:*	NA

Lotus Capital Corp

Ste. 501, Bank Of America Tower, 12 Harcourt Rd., Central; *PH:* 852-252-10373

General - Incorporation	NV	*Stock* - Price on:12/24/2007	NA
Employees	NA	Stock Exchange	NA
Auditor	Kempisty & Co	Ticker Symbol	NA
Stk Agt	NA	Outstanding Shares	NA
Counsel	NA	E.P.S.	NA
DUNS No.	NA	Shareholders	NA

Business: The group's principle activity is to provide financial services. The group operates from United States.

Primary SIC and add'l.: 9995

CIK No: 0000734543

Subsidiaries: AL Marine

Officers: Andrew Liu Fu Kang/46/Chmn., CEO, Pres., Yip Kam Ming/38/CFO, Sec.

Directors: Andrew Liu Fu Kang/46/Chmn., CEO, Pres., John Liu Shou Kang/47/Dir.

Owners: Andrew Liu/62.04%, Insiders/87.58%, John Liu/25.54%

Loud Technologies Inc

16220 Wood-Red Rd. NE, Woodinville, WA, 98072; *PH:* 1-425-892-6500; *Fax:* 1-425-487-4337; *http://* www.loud-technologies.com

General - Incorporation	WA	*Stock* - Price on:12/24/2007	$5.5
Employees	704	Stock Exchange	NDQ
Auditor	KPMG LLP	Ticker Symbol	LTEC
Stk Agt	Mellon Investor Services LLC	Outstanding Shares	4,620,000
Counsel	NA	E.P.S.	-$2.31
DUNS No.	NA	Shareholders	NA

Business: The group's principal activities are to develop, manufacture, market and support professional audio equipment. The products include analog and digital mixers, mixer-related products, recorders, amplifiers, loudspeakers and loudspeaker components. These products are used in a variety of sound applications including home and commercial recording studios, multimedia and video production, compact disc, read-only memory (CD-ROM) authoring, live performances and public address systems. The customers of the group include musicians, sound installation contractors and broadcast professionals in recordings, live presentations systems and installed sound systems. The group distributes its products through a network of over 1,500 retail dealers of professional audio equipment. Internationally products are provided through its subsidiaries in Italy, France, Germany, the United Kingdom and China.the group discontinued its operation at mackie Italy during 2003.

Primary SIC and add'l.: 3651

CIK No: 0000946815

Subsidiaries: LOUD Technologies (Europe) Plc., LOUD Technologies Canada Inc., Mackie Designs Inc., SIA Software Company, Inc., St. Louis Music, Inc.

Officers: Jamie T. Engen/44/Chmn., CEO, Pres./$400,017.00, Kevin J. Calhoun/47/Dir., VP, Shawn Powers/Sr. VP - Operations/$208,377.00, Lynn Skillen/51/Dir., VP, Scott T. King/55/Dir., VP, Jason Neimark/36/Dir., VP, Gary Reilly/Sr. VP - Engineering, Clarence E. Terry/60/Dir., VP, Case Kuehn/55/Dir., VP, Gerry Ng/Sr. VP, CFO

Directors: Jamie T. Engen/44/Chmn., CEO, Pres., Jon W. Gacek/45/Dir., George R. Rea/69/Dir., Lynn Skillen/51/Dir., VP, Scott T. King/55/Dir., VP, Jason Neimark/36/Dir., VP, Clarence E. Terry/60/Dir., VP, Daryl C. Hollis/63/Dir., Kevin J. Calhoun/47/Dir., VP, Case Kuehn/55/Dir., VP, Thomas V. Taylor/42/Dir.

Owners: Timothy P. ONeil, Frank J. Loyko, James T. Engen, Insiders, Rodger R. Krouse, Marc J. Leder, Sun Mackie, LLC, Shawn C. Powers

Financial Data: Fiscal Year End:12/31   *Latest Annual Data:* 12/31/2006

Year	Sales	Net Income
2006	$215,033,000	$625,000
2005	$204,328,000	$3,757,000
2004	$123,276,000	-$2,291,000

Curr. Assets:	$82,889,000	*Curr. Liab.:*	$55,341,000		
Plant, Equip.:	$6,543,000	*Total Liab.:*	$95,551,000	*Indic. Yr. Divd.:*	NA
Total Assets:	$105,756,000	*Net Worth:*	$10,205,000	*Debt/ Equity:*	3.9299

Loudeye Corp

1130 Rainier Ave. S, Seattle, WA, 98144; *PH:* 1-206-832-4000; *http://* www.loudeye.com

General - Incorporation	DE	*Stock* - Price on:12/24/2007	$28.71
Employees	68,483	Stock Exchange	NDQ
Auditor	Moss Adams LLP	Ticker Symbol	NOOF
Stk Agt	Mellon Investor Services LLC	Outstanding Shares	3,920,000,000
Counsel	Robinson & Cole	E.P.S.	$2.00
DUNS No.	NA	Shareholders	NA

Business: The group's principal activity is to provide enterprise webcasting, related digital media services and media restoration services. The group operates in two segments: digital media services and media restoration services. Digital media services enable enhanced enterprise communication, digital media management and distribution via the Internet and other emerging technologies. Media restoration services include restoration and migration of legacy media archive collections to current media formats. Its customers include the coca cola company, microsoft amazon, America online, universal music group and barnesandnoble.com. The group conducts its business in the United States, Canada and Europe. On 2-Mar-2004, the group acquired overpeer inc. On 22-Jun-2004, the group acquired on demand distribution ltd and sold media restoration business on 30-Jan-2004.

Primary SIC and add'l.: 7371 7379 7372

CIK No: 0001064648

Subsidiaries: Demand Distribution SAS, Loudeye Enterprise Communications, Inc., Privateer Acquisition Corp, VMRLE Co., Inc.

Financial Data: Fiscal Year End:12/31   *Latest Annual Data:* 12/31/2006

Year	Sales	Net Income
2006	$54,292,056,000	$5,644,283,000
2005	$40,495,820,000	$4,242,521,000
2004	$39,931,895,000	$4,561,189,000

Curr. Assets:	$24,539,096,000	*Curr. Liab.:*	$13,415,568,000		
Plant, Equip.:	$1,980,450,000	*Total Liab.:*	$13,938,408,000	*Indic. Yr. Divd.:*	NA
Total Assets:	$30,051,348,000	*Net Worth:*	$15,991,474,000	*Debt/ Equity:*	NA

Louisiana Pacific Corp

414 Union St., Ste. 2000, Nashville, TN, 37219; *PH:* 1-615-986-5600; *Fax:* 1-615-986-5666;
http:// www.lpcorp.com

General - Incorporation		*Stock*- Price on:12/24/2007	
Employees	5,600	Stock Exchange	NYSE
Auditor	Deloitte & Touche LLP	Ticker Symbol	LPX
Stk Agt	EquiServe Trust Co N.A	Outstanding Shares	104,320,000
Counsel	Jones Day	E.P.S.	-$1.47
DUNS No.	06-150-0534	Shareholders	NA

Business: The group's principle activity is to manufacture and distribute building products. The group's products are used in new home construction, repair and remodeling, and manufactured housing. The group operates from United States.

Primary SIC and add'l.: 2421 3089 5211 2439 2411

CIK No: 0000060519

Subsidiaries: 3047525 Nova Scotia Company, 3047526 Nova Scotia Company, Abitibi - LP Engineered Wood II Inc., AbitibiLP Engineered Wood,Inc., Canfor - LP OSB (G.P.) Corp., Canfor - LP OSB Limited Partnership, GreenStone Industries,Inc., Ketchikan Pulp Company, L-p Spv2, LLC, L-PSPV,Inc, Louisiana Pacific de Mexico, S.A. de C.V., Louisiana-Pacific Canada Pulp Co., Louisiana-Pacific CanadaLtd., Louisiana-Pacific Chile S.A., Louisiana-Pacific International,Inc. 24 Subsidiaries included in the Index

Officers: Richard W. Frost/57/Dir., CEO/$3,584,101.00, Mike Blosser/VP - Environmental, Health, Safety, Mike Kinney/Investor Relations Officer, Jamey Barnes/VP - Oriented Strand Board - OSB Manufacturing, Anton C. Kirchhof/Sec., Richard S. Olszewski/Exec. VP - Specialty Products, Sales, Marketing/$130,198.00, Mary Cohn/Contact - Media Relations, Becky Barckley/Investor Relations Officer, Mark Fuchs/VP, General Counsel, Ann Harris/VP - Human Resources, Brian Luoma/VP, GM Engineered Wood Products, John Neilson/VP - Marketing, Neil Sherman/VP - Procurement - Logistics, Supply Management, Mike Sims/VP - Sales, John Sooker/GM *(20 Officers included in Index)*

Directors: Richard W. Frost/57/Dir., CEO, Gary E. Cook/63/Chmn., Daniel K. Frierson/64/Dir., Archie W. Dunham/67/Dir., Paul W. Hansen/56/Dir., Lizanne C. Gottung/Dir., Dustan E. McCoy/59/Dir., Colin D. Watson/67/Dir., Kurt M. Landgraf/61/Dir.

Owners: Paul W. Hansen, Colin D. Watson, Dustan E. McCoy, John C. Kerr, Lizanne C. Gottung, Barclays Global Investors, N.A./9.84%, Gary E. Cook, Richard S. Olszewski, Insiders/0.95%, Harold N. Stanton, Archie W. Dunham, Highland Capital Management, L.P./6.42%, Daniel K. Frierson, Richard W. Frost/0.38%, Kurt M. Landgraf *(18 Owners included in Index)*

Financial Data: Fiscal Year End:12/31   Latest Annual Data: 12/31/2006

Year	Sales	Net Income
2006	$2,235,100,000	$123,700,000
2005	$2,598,900,000	$455,500,000
2004	$2,849,400,000	$420,700,000

Curr. Assets:	$1,504,000,000	*Curr. Liab.:*	$264,900,000	*P/E Ratio:*	664.67
Plant, Equip.:	$990,400,000	*Total Liab.:*	$1,369,000,000	*Indic. Yr. Divd.:*	$0.600
Total Assets:	$3,436,400,000	*Net Worth:*	$2,067,400,000	*Debt/ Equity:*	NA

Louisville Gas & Electric Co

220 W Main St. , Louisville, KY, 40232; *PH:* 1-502-627-2000

General - Incorporation	KY	*Stock*- Price on:12/24/2007	NA
Employees	NA	Stock Exchange	NA
Auditor	Deloitte & Touche, LLP	Ticker Symbol	NA
Stk Agt	NA	Outstanding Shares	NA
Counsel	NA	E.P.S.	NA
DUNS No.	00-694-5505	Shareholders	NA

Business: The group's principal activity is to supply natural gas and electricity to louisville and adjacent areas in Kentucky. The group is a wholly owned subsidiary of powergen limited. It supplies natural gas to approximately 312,000 customers and electricity to approximately 384,000 customers in louisville and adjacent areas in Kentucky. The group also provides limited gas service in additional areas of Kentucky. The group generates electricity by coal-fired plants and a hydroelectric power plant with combustion turbines.

Primary SIC and add'l.: 4923 4931

CIK No: 0000060549

Subsidiaries: Kentucky Utilities Company, Louisville Gas and Electric Company

Officers: Victor A. Staffieri/52/Chmn., CEO, Pres., Michael S. Beer/49/VP - Federal Regulation, Policy, George R. Siemens/58/VP - External Affairs, Martyn Gallus/43/Sr. VP - Energy Marketing, Daniel K. Arbough/46/Treasurer, John N. Voyles/53/VP - Regulated Generation, Paula H. Pottinger/51/Sr. VP - Human Resources, Chris Hermann/60/Sr. VP - Energy Delivery, Bradford S. Rives/49/CFO, Paul W. Thompson/51/Sr. VP - Energy Services, John R. McCall/64/Exec. VP, General Counsel, Corp. Sec., Valerie L. Scott/51/Controller, Chip R.W. Keeling/51/VP - Communications, Ralph D. Bowling/50/VP - Power Operations WKE, Wendy C. Welsh/54/Sr. VP - Information Technology

Directors: Victor A. Staffieri/52/Chmn., CEO, Pres.

Lounsberry Holdings III Inc

24a Jefferson Plz., Princeton, NJ, 08540;

General - Incorporation	DE	*Stock*- Price on:12/24/2007	$2.94
Employees	105	Stock Exchange	OTC
Auditor	Moore Stephens Wurth F & T LLP	Ticker Symbol	CHME
Stk Agt	Continental Stock T & T Co.	Outstanding Shares	12,760,000
Counsel	NA	E.P.S.	$0.58
DUNS No.	NA	Shareholders	NA

Business: The group's principal activities are obtaining initial financing and seeking the acquisition of, or merger with an existing company. The group was formed as a vehicle to pursue a business combination and has neither conducted negotiations nor entered into a letter of intent concerning a target business so far.

Primary SIC and add'l.: 6770

CIK No: 0001328790

Subsidiaries: Guangzhou Konzern Medicine Co., Ltd.

Officers: Senshan Yang/47/Dir., CEO, Lin Li/38/VP, Sec., Minhua Liu/40/Dir., Exec. VP, Huizhen Yu/28/CFO, Meiyi Xia/57/VP

Directors: Senshan Yang/47/Dir., CEO, Minhua Liu/40/Dir., Exec. VP, Robert Adler/73/Dir., Rachel Gong/40/Dir., Yanfang Chen/44/Dir.

Owners: Rachel Gong/0.30%, Junhua Liu/6.40%, Insiders/69.00%, Lin Li/4.80%, Minhua Liu/25.50%, Senshan Yang/31.90%, Yanfang Chen/0.30%, Meiyi Xia/7.00%, Robert Adler/0.30%, Barron Partners L.P./10.70%

Financial Data: Fiscal Year End:12/31   Latest Annual Data: 12/31/2006

Year	Sales	Net Income
2006	$23,992,000	$4,788,000

Curr. Assets:	$13,426,000	*Curr. Liab.:*	$600,000	*P/E Ratio:*	5.07
Plant, Equip.:	$1,215,000	*Total Liab.:*	$1,509,000	*Indic. Yr. Divd.:*	NA
Total Assets:	$14,642,000	*Net Worth:*	$13,134,000	*Debt/ Equity:*	NA

Lowe's Cos Inc

1000 Lowe's Blvd., Mooresville, NC, 28117; *PH:* 1-704-758-1000; *Fax:* 1-336-658-4766; *http://* www.lowes.com; *Email:* investorrelations@lowes.com

General - Incorporation	NC	*Stock*- Price on:12/24/2007	$31.9
Employees	157,000	Stock Exchange	NYSE
Auditor	Deloitte & Touche LLP	Ticker Symbol	NA
Stk Agt	Computershare Trust Co	Outstanding Shares	1,510,000,000
Counsel	William C. Warden, Jr.	E.P.S.	NA
DUNS No.	00-699-7142	Shareholders	NA

Business: The group's principle activity is to provide products and services for home decoration, maintenance, repair, remodeling and property maintenance. The group's services include installation, credit, gift cards, in-store and protection plan services. The group's products include appliances, indoor and outdoor, tools and building products. The group operates from United States.

Primary SIC and add'l.: 5231 5722 5261 5211 5251

CIK No: 0000060667

Subsidiaries: Lowes HIW, Inc., Lowes Home Centers, Inc.

Officers: Robert A. Niblock/Chmn., CEO/$6,600,370.00, Steven M. Stone/CIO, Sr. VP, Marshall A. Croom/Sr. VP - Merchandising, Store Support, Michael K. Brown/Exec. VP - Store Operations, Joseph M. Mabry/Exec. VP - Logistics, Distribution, Larry D. Stone/COO, Pres./$4,351,360.00, Rick D. Damron/Sr. VP - Store Operations, Northeast, Charles W. Canter/Exec. VP - Merchandising/$1,862,710.00, Robert F. Wagner/Sr. VP - Store Operations, West, David J. Steed/Sr. VP, General Merchandising Mgr. - Building Products, James M. Frasso/Sr. VP - Store Operations, Southeast, Gregory M. Bridgeford/Exec. VP - Business Development/$2,504,012.00, John L. Kasberger/Sr. VP, General Merchandising Mgr. - Kitchen, Bath, Eric D. Sowder/Sr. VP - Logistics, Robert J. Gfeller/Sr. VP - Marketing, Advertising *(32 Officers included in Index)*

Directors: Robert A. Niblock/Chmn., CEO, Temple O. Sloan/Dir., Peter C. Browning/Dir., Dawn E. Hudson/Dir., Robert L. Johnson/Dir., Richard K. Lochridge/Dir., Leonard L. Berry/Dir., Robert A. Ingram/Dir., Marshall O. Larsen/Dir., Stephen F. Page/Dir., David W. Bernauer/Dir.

Owners: Larry D. Stone, Robert A. Ingram, State Street Bank and Trust Company, Trustee/7.10%, Robert L. Johnson, Robert A. Niblock, Charles W. Canter, Gregory M. Bridgeford, Capital Research and Management Company/20.90%, Insiders, Dawn E. Hudson, David W. Bernauer, Richard K. Lochridge, Peter C. Browning, Stephen F. Page, Paul Fulton *(19 Owners included in Index)*

Financial Data: Fiscal Year End:02/03   Latest Annual Data: 2/2/2007

Year	Sales	Net Income
2007	$46,927,000,000	$3,105,000,000
2006	$43,243,000,000	$2,765,000,000
2005	$36,464,000,000	$2,176,000,000

Curr. Assets:	$7,788,000,000	*Curr. Liab.:*	$5,832,000,000		
Plant, Equip.:	$16,354,000,000	*Total Liab.:*	$10,343,000,000	*Indic. Yr. Divd.:*	NA
Total Assets:	$24,639,000,000	*Net Worth:*	$14,296,000,000	*Debt/ Equity:*	NA

Lowrance Electronics Inc

12000 E Skelly Dr, Tulsa, OK, 74128; *PH:* 1-918-437-6881; *http://* www.lowrance.com

General - Incorporation	DE	*Stock*- Price on:12/24/2007	$22.29
Employees	NA	Stock Exchange	NA
Auditor	Deloitte & Touche LLP	Ticker Symbol	NA
Stk Agt	Chase Mellon Shareholder Services LLC	Outstanding Shares	NA
Counsel	Doerner, Saunders, Daniel & Anderson	E.P.S.	NA
DUNS No.	00-713-9199	Shareholders	NA

Business: The group's principal activities are to design, manufacture, market and distribute sound navigation and ranging system (sonar), global positioning system (gps), navigational equipment and other marine electronic products and various related accessories. The group's sound navigation and ranging systems, known as depth-sounders and fish-finders are used by sports fishermen for detecting the presence of fish and by sports fishermen and boaters as navigational and safety devices for determining bottom depth in lakes, rivers and coastal waters. The gps receivers are used in a variety of marine and non-Marine applications including aviation, hunting, hiking and backpacking. The trademarks used by the group are lowrance and eagle.

Primary SIC and add'l.: 3824 3812

CIK No: 0000804073

Subsidiaries: Electronica Lowrance, LEI Extras, Inc.

Officers: Darrell J. Lowrance/CEO, Pres.

LP Innovations

66 B St. , Needham, MA, 02494; ; *http://* www.lpinnovations.com; *Email:* sales@lpinnovations.com

General - Incorporation	NV	*Stock*- Price on:12/24/2007	NA
Employees	NA	Stock Exchange	NA
Auditor	NA	Ticker Symbol	NA
Stk Agt	NA	Outstanding Shares	NA
Counsel	NA	E.P.S.	NA
DUNS No.	NA	Shareholders	NA

Business: The group's principle activity is to provide loss prevention services and system solutions with comprehensive loss preventing programs aimed at reducing costs, increasing quality and lowering shrink. The company's loss prevention services include in-store audits,employee investigations, employee

training and awareness, and specially designed software. Through LPI's subsidiary, Securex LLC, the company also sells and installs security equipment and alarm and security central monitoring, allowingthe company to provide a comprehensive loss prevention solution to its clients.The area of loaction includes throughout the United States.

Primary SIC and add'l.: 8742

CIK No: 0001207856

Officers: Steven May/CEO, Pres., John Fice/COO, Kevin Ricci/CFO, Rubin Press/VP - Sales, Marketing

Lpath Inc

6335 Ferris Sq Ste. A, San Diego, CA, 92121; ***PH:*** 1-858-678-0800; ***http://*** www.lpath.com; ***Email:*** info@lpath.com

General		***Stock***	
Incorporation	NV	Price on:12/24/2007	$1.63
Employees	18	Stock Exchange	OTC
Auditor	Levitz, Zacks & Ciceric	Ticker Symbol	LPTN
Stk Agt	Nevada Agency & Trust Company	Outstanding Shares	39,580,000
Counsel	NA	E.P.S.	-$0.37
DUNS No.	NA	Shareholders	NA

Business: The groups principle activity is to produce bioactive signaling lipids used for treating and diagnosing human diseases. Products of the group include Sphingomab(TM), Lpathomab(TM), nSMase inhibitor, SphingoTest(TM) and ELISA-based assay. In November 2005, the group merged with Neighborhood Connections, Inc. The group operates from the United States.

Primary SIC and add'l.: 2836

CIK No: 0001251769

Subsidiaries: Lpath Therapeutics Inc.

Officers: Scott Pancoast/Dir., CEO, Pres./$663,482.00, Roger Sabbadini/Founder, Dir., VP, Chief Scientific Officer, William Garland/VP - Drug Development/$273,279.00, Gary Atkinson/CFO, VP/$255,332.00, Genevieve Hansen/VP - Research, Glenn Stoller/Head - Lpath Ocular

Directors: Scott Pancoast/Dir., CEO, Pres., Charles Mathews/Dir., Jason Slakter/Member - Ocular Advisory Board, Richard Spaide/Member - Ocular Advisory Board, Nabil Hanna/Member - Scientific Advisory Board, Brad Cunningham/Member - Scientific Advisory Board, Donald Swortwood/Dir., Roger Sabbadini/Founder, Dir., VP, Chief Scientific Officer, Gordon Mills/Member - Scientific Advisory Board, Bart Barlogie/Member - Scientific Advisory Board, Douglas Mann/Member - Scientific Advisory Board, Judith Varner/Member - Scientific Advisory Board, Edward Dennis/Member - Scientific Advisory Board, Joseph Witztum/Member - Scientific Advisory Board, Robert Engler/Member - Scientific Advisory Board *(21 Directors included in Index)*

Owners: Donald R. Swortwood/12.80%, Scott Pancoast/1.90%, William Garland, Letitia H. Swortwood/12.80%, Eugene McColley/9.10%, Charles Mathews, Genevieve Hansen, Insiders/18.10%, Charles Polsky/13.60%, Brian E. Peierls/6.30%, Roger Sabbadini/2.80%, LB I Group Inc/23.70%, Gary J.G. Atkinson, Jeffrey E. Peierls/7.60%

Financial Data: ***Fiscal Year End:***12/31 ***Latest Annual Data:*** 12/31/2006

Year	Sales	Net Income
2006	$512,000	-$5,605,000
2005	$743,000	-$2,797,000

Curr. Assets:	$1,681,000	***Curr. Liab.:***	$795,000		
Plant, Equip.:	$259,000	***Total Liab.:***	$795,000	***Indic. Yr. Divd.:***	NA
Total Assets:	$2,354,000	***Net Worth:***	$1,559,000	***Debt/ Equity:***	NA

LSB Bancshares Inc

One Lsb Plz, Lexington, NC, 27292; ***PH:*** 1-336-248-6500; ***http://*** www.lsbbancshares.com

General		***Stock***	
Incorporation	NC	Price on:12/24/2007	$13.66
Employees	407	Stock Exchange	NA
Auditor	Turlington And Co LLP	Ticker Symbol	NA
Stk Agt	EquiServe Trust Co N.A	Outstanding Shares	8,410,000
Counsel	NA	E.P.S.	$0.71
DUNS No.	10-348-6486	Shareholders	NA

Business: The group's principal activity is to provide banking and other financial services in the United States. The operations are conducted through its subsidiary bank and two non-bank subsidiaries. The group provides commercial banking services including accepting deposits, corporate cash management, discount brokerage, ira plans, secured and unsecured loans and trust management functions through its subsidiary bank. The trust management functions of the group include providing estate planning, estate and trust administration, ira trusts, personal investment accounts and pension and profit sharing trusts. The group offers secured and unsecured loans, uninsured, non-deposit investment products, including mutual funds, annuities, stocks and bonds through its non-bank subsidiaries. The group operates twenty-six offices and ten off-premises automated teller locations.

Primary SIC and add'l.: 6712 6022

CIK No: 0000714530

Subsidiaries: LSB Financial Services, Peoples Finance Company of Lexington

Officers: Robert F. Lowe/Chmn., CEO, Denise Barnhardt/Investor Relations Officer, Monty J. Oliver/Exec. VP - Finance, Pressley A. Ridgill/Pres., Michael W. Shelton/Exec. VP, CFO, Treasurer, Robin A. Huneycutt/Exec. VP, Sec.

Directors: Robert F. Lowe/Chmn., CEO, Alfred G. Webster/59/Dir., David Branch/61/Dir., Mary E. Rittling/58/Dir.

Owners: David A. Smith, Mary E. Rittling, David J. Branch, Samuel R. Harris, Burr W. Sullivan, Insiders/5.59%, Monty J. Oliver, Wellington Management Company, LLP/5.51%, Franklin H. Sherron, John W. Thomas, Robert C. Clark, John F. Watts, Julius S. Young, Robert F. Lowe/1.64%, Leonard H. Beck *(19 Owners included in Index)*

Financial Data: ***Fiscal Year End:***12/31 ***Latest Annual Data:*** 12/31/2006

Year	Sales	Net Income
2006	$81,613,000	$6,000,000
2005	$74,217,000	$9,637,000
2004	$63,382,000	$8,380,000

Curr. Assets:	$53,339,000	***Curr. Liab.:***	$891,631,000	***P/E Ratio:***	19.24
Plant, Equip.:	$19,848,000	***Total Liab.:***	$898,437,000	***Indic. Yr. Divd.:***	$0.680
Total Assets:	$987,746,000	***Net Worth:***	$89,309,000	***Debt/ Equity:***	NA

LSB Corp

30 Massachusetts Ave., North Andover, MA, 01845; ***PH:*** 1-978-725-7500; ***Fax:*** 1-978-725-7593; ***http://*** www.riverbk.com

General		***Stock***	
Incorporation	MA	Price on:12/24/2007	$16.38
Employees	101	Stock Exchange	NDQ
Auditor	KPMG LLP	Ticker Symbol	LSBX
Stk Agt	Computershare Trust Co	Outstanding Shares	4,600,000
Counsel	Goulston & Storrs	E.P.S.	$0.14
DUNS No.	NA	Shareholders	NA

Business: The group's principal activities are to provide financial services to the general public including loans for different purposes. The types of loans provided include commercial real estate, commercial business, construction, residential mortgage, home equity and consumer loans. The group also offers deposits such as savings, checking, money market and certificates of deposit and individual retirement accounts. The group operates through four wholly owned subsidiaries. The group operates through banking offices in andover, lawrence, methuen, north andover and Massachusetts.

Primary SIC and add'l.: 6712 6036

CIK No: 0001143848

Subsidiaries: Lawrence Savings Bank, Pemberton Corporation, Shawsheen Security Corporation, Shawsheen Security Corporation II, Spruce Wood Realty Trust

Officers: Gerald T. Mulligan/62/Dir., CEO, Pres./$419,440.00, Thomas J. Burke/67/Chmn. - Attorney, Marsha A. McDonough/64/Dir. - Education Consultant, Teresa K. Flynn/49/Sr. VP - Human Resources, Bank, Joseph Corcoran/Branch Mgr., Linda Firth/Branch Mgr., Johanny Guillermo/Assist. VP, Branch Mgr., Linda Buell/VP, Branch Mgr., Veronica Calixto/Assist. VP, Branch Mgr., Rachel Oliveri/Assist. VP, Branch Mgr., Jack Teoli/Contact - Lending, Chris Kuchar/Contact - Lending, Gayle Fili/Contact - Lending, Karen Dussault/Contact - Deposit Servicing, Carmela Cutuli/Contact - Retirement Services *(28 Officers included in Index)*

Directors: Gerald T. Mulligan/62/Dir., CEO, Pres., Thomas J. Burke/67/Chmn. - Attorney, Kathleen Boshar Reynolds/52/Dir. - Real Estate Management Consultant, Eugene A. Beliveau/77/Dir., Byron R. Cleveland/76/Dir., Robert F. Hatem/72/Dir., Malcolm W. Brawn/68/Dir., Richard Hart Harrington/71/Dir.

Owners: Thomas J. Burke, Richard Hart Harrington, Insiders/3.59%, Michael J. Ecker, Robert F. Hatem, Kathleen Boshar Reynolds, Malcolm W. Brawn, Jacob Kojalo, Eugene A. Beliveau, Stephen B. Jones, Diane L. Walker, Gerald T. Mulligan, Paul A. Miller/1.65%, First Manhattan Co./6.07%, John Sheldon Clark/6.14% *(18 Owners included in Index)*

Financial Data: ***Fiscal Year End:***12/31 ***Latest Annual Data:*** 12/31/2006

Year	Sales	Net Income
2006	$30,968,000	$126,000
2005	$29,346,000	$4,157,000
2004	$26,164,000	$4,680,000

Curr. Assets:	$21,383,000	***Curr. Liab.:***	$439,181,000	***P/E Ratio:***	117.00
Plant, Equip.:	$3,807,000	***Total Liab.:***	$484,434,000	***Indic. Yr. Divd.:***	$0.560
Total Assets:	$542,965,000	***Net Worth:***	$58,531,000	***Debt/ Equity:***	3.1946

LSB Financial Corp

101 Main St., Lafayette, IN, 47901; ***PH:*** 1-765-742-1064; ***Fax:*** 1-765-742-1507; ***http://*** www.lsbank.com

General		***Stock***	
Incorporation	IN	Price on:12/24/2007	$25
Employees	89	Stock Exchange	NDQ
Auditor	BKD LLP, Crowe Chizek & Co. LLC	Ticker Symbol	LSBI
Stk Agt	Computershare Trust Co	Outstanding Shares	1,600,000
Counsel	Stuart & Branigin	E.P.S.	$1.68
DUNS No.	83-592-3269	Shareholders	NA

Business: The group's principal activities are attracting retail deposits from the general public and investing those funds in loans. These loans are primarily first mortgage loans secured by owner-occupied one-to-four-family residences. The categories of deposits accepted by the group include now and savings accounts. The group offers commercial, consumer and real estate loans. The operations of the group are conducted in tippecanoe county, Indiana and its surrounding counties through five retail banking offices.

Primary SIC and add'l.: 6712 6035

CIK No: 0000930405

Subsidiaries: L.S.B. Service Corporation, Lafayette Insurance and Investments, Inc., Lafayette Savings Bank, FSB

Officers: Randolph F. Williams/59/Dir., CEO, Pres./$283,572.00, Diana Cook/Member - Consumer Lending Team, Gail Jackson/Member - Consumer Lending Team, Jessica Jackson/Member - Consumer Lending Team, Jeri Cain/Member - Consumer Lending Team, Tammy Wilson/Member - Consumer Lending Team, Greg Bonner/Assist. VP - Loan, Tom Murtaugh/Loan Specialist, Greg Eller/VP - Loan, Keven Jennings/VP - Loan, Jim Allen/Contact - Health Savings Accounting, Mary Jo David/58/Dir., CFO, VP, Sec., Treasurer/$122,874.00, Harry A. Dunwoody/61/Dir., Sr. VP, John Clark/Loan Specialist, Cecilia Kaczmarek/Loan Specialist *(16 Officers included in Index)*

Directors: Randolph F. Williams/59/Dir., CEO, Pres., Mariellen M. Neudeck/66/Chmn., Jeffrey A. Poxon/61/Dir., Peter Neisel/69/Dir., Charles W. Shook/52/Dir., James A. Andrew/58/Dir., Kenneth P. Burns/63/Dir., Philip W. Kemmer/64/Dir., Mary Jo David/58/Dir., CFO, VP, Sec., Treasurer, Harry A. Dunwoody/61/Dir., Sr. VP, Thomas R. McCully/67/Dir.

Owners: Harry A. Dunwoody/1.90%, Kenneth P. Burns/0.30%, Thomas R. McCully/1.50%, First Bankers Trust Services, Inc/6.70%, Randolph F. Williams/2.10%, Peter Neisel/1.70%, Philip W. Kemmer/0.20%, James A. Andrew/2.80%, John C. Shen/5.20%, Jeffrey A. Poxon/1.70%, Mary Jo David/1.60%, Mariellen M. Neudeck/1.70%, Charles W. Shook/0.20%, Insiders/15.40%, Morris Propp/5.20%

Financial Data: ***Fiscal Year End:***12/31 ***Latest Annual Data:*** 12/31/2006

Year	Sales	Net Income
2006	$26,101,000	$3,350,000
2005	$24,007,000	$3,268,000
2004	$21,526,000	$3,264,000

Curr. Assets:	$18,415,000	***Curr. Liab.:***	$333,560,000	***P/E Ratio:***	14.12
Plant, Equip.:	$6,600,000	***Total Liab.:***	$333,560,000	***Indic. Yr. Divd.:***	$1.000
Total Assets:	$368,400,000	***Net Worth:***	$34,840,000	***Debt/ Equity:***	NA

LSB Industries Inc

16 S Pennsylvania Ave., Oklahoma City, OK, 73107; ***PH:*** 1-405-235-4546; ***Fax:*** 1-405-235-5067; ***http://*** www.lsbindustries.com; ***Email:*** info@lsb-okc.com

General - Incorporation DE
Employees 1,565
Auditor Ernst & Young LLP
Stk Agt UMB Bank, N.A.
Counsel NA
DUNS No. 04-686-0979

Stock- Price on:12/24/2007 $22.98
Stock Exchange AMEX
Ticker Symbol LXU
Outstanding Shares 19,660,000
E.P.S $1.82
Shareholders NA

Business: The group's principal activity is to manufacture and sell chemical products for agricultural, mining and industrial acid markets. The group operates in two segments: chemical and climate control. Chemical segment manufactures explosives for agricultural and industrial acids market. The facilities of chemical segment are located at El Dorado, Arkansas, Cherokee and Alabama. The other manufacturing operations are located in the Hallowell, Kansas, Wilmington, North Carolina, and Baytown, Texas. Climate control segment manufactures and sells hydronic fan coils and water source heat pumps as well as other products used in commercial and residential air conditioning systems. Climate control products are used in buildings, such as: hotels, motels, office buildings, schools, universities, apartments, hospitals, industrial and high tech manufacturing facilities.

Primary SIC and add'l.: 6719 3541 3822 2873

CIK No: 0000060714

Subsidiaries: ACP International Limited, CEPOLK Holdings, Inc, Chemex I Corp., Chemex II Corp, Cherokee Nitrogen Company, Cherokee Nitrogen Holdings, Inc, ClimaCool Corp., Climate Master, Inc., Climate Mate, Inc., ClimateCraft Technologies, Inc., ClimateCraft, Inc., Clipmate Corporation, DSN Corporation, El Dorado Acid II, LLC, El Dorado Acid, LLC 34 Subsidiaries included in the Index

Officers: Linda Latman/Investor Relations, Michael Marchisi/Member - American Stock Exchange Located in New York, Donald Vaneck/Member - American Stock Exchange Located in New York

Owners: Jim D. Jones, David M. Shear, Paul J. Denby/6.50%, Jack E. Golsen/18.80%, Raymond B. Ackerman, Horace G. Rhodes, David R. Goss/1.30%, Insiders, Insiders/27.20%, Grant J. Donovan, Kent C. McCarthy& affiliates/16.80%, Jack E. Golsen and certain members of his family, Jack E. Golsen, Charles A. Burtch, Tony M. Shelby/1.60% *(22 Owners included in Index)*

Financial Data: **Fiscal Year End:**12/31 **Latest Annual Data:** 12/31/2006

Year	Sales	Net Income
2006	$491,952,000	$15,515,000
2005	$396,722,000	$5,102,000
2004	$363,608,000	$1,370,000

Curr. Assets:	$132,495,000	**Curr. Liab.:**	$84,251,000	**P/E Ratio:**	25.25
Plant, Equip.:	$76,404,000	**Total Liab.:**	$176,293,000	**Indic. Yr. Divd.:**	NA
Total Assets:	$219,927,000	**Net Worth:**	$43,634,000	**Debt/ Equity:**	NA

LSI Corp

Formerly: LSI Logic Corp
1621 Barber Ln., Milpitas, CA, 95035; ***PH:*** 1-408-433-8000; ***http://*** www.lsilogic.com

General - Incorporation DE
Employees 4,010
Auditor PricewaterhouseCoopers LLP
Stk Agt EquiServe Trust Co N.A
Counsel Wilson Sonsini Goodrich & Rosati
DUNS No. 01-244-4253

Stock- Price on:12/24/2007 $8.17
Stock Exchange NYSE
Ticker Symbol NA
Outstanding Shares 767,900,000
E.P.S -$0.5
Shareholders NA

Business: The groups principle activity is to provide silicon, systems and software technologies that enable products to bring people, information and digital content together. The groups products include ICs, adapters, systems and software. The group operates in two business segments namely the semiconductor and storage systems segment. The group operates from United States.

Primary SIC and add'l.: 3674 7371 3679 3572

CIK No: 0000703360

Subsidiaries: Accerant Inc., C-Cube International Limited, C-Cube Microsystems (Asia Pacific) Ltd., C-Cube Microsystems (Canada) Ltd., C-Cube Microsystems International Ltd., C-Cube Technology Limited, C-Cube US, Inc., Engenio Enterprises, Inc., Engenio Holdings, Ltd., Engenio Information Technologies Europe Limited, Engenio Information Technologies GmbH, Engenio Information Technologies International Services, Inc., Engenio Information Technologies Limited, Engenio Information Technologies, Inc., Engenio Information Technologies, SAS 44 Subsidiaries included in the Index

Officers: Abhijit Y. Talwalkar/Dir., CEO, Pres./$6,358,822.00, Bryon Look/CFO, Exec. VP/$1,474,549.00, Jeff Richardson/Exec. VP - Network, Storage Products Group/$1,640,180.00, Flavio Santoni/Exec. VP - Server, Storage Customer Sales/$1,192,082.00, Ruediger Stroh/Exec. VP - Storage Peripherals Group, Phil Brace/Sr. VP - Corporate Planning, Marketing, Phil Bullinger/Sr. VP - Engenio Storage Group, Umesh Padval/50/Exec. VP - Consumer Products Group/$1,339,969.00, Jon Gibson/VP - Human Resources, Andrew Hughes/42/VP, General Counsel, Corp. Sec., William J. Wuertz/50/Sr. VP - Storage Components Group, Jeff Hoogenboom/Exec. VP - Networking, Storage Peripheral, Consumer Sales, Andrew Micallef/Exec. VP - Worldwide Manufacturing Operations, Jean F. Rankin/Exec. VP, General Counsel, Sec., Denis Regimbal/Exec. VP - Mobility Group *(17 Officers included in Index)*

Directors: Abhijit Y. Talwalkar/Dir., CEO, Pres., James H. Keyes/Chmn., Charles A. Haggerty/Dir., Timothy Y. Chen/51/Dir., Malcolm R. Currie/80/Dir., John H.F. Miner/Dir., Douglas R. Norby/Dir., Gregorio Reyes/Dir., Richard S. Hill/Dir., Matthew O'Rourke/Dir., Michael J. Mancuso/Dir., Arun Netravali/Dir.

Owners: Joseph M. Zelayeta, Malcolm R. Currie, Insiders/1.80%, John H. F. Miner, Umesh Padval, Arun Netravali, Abhijit Y. Talwalkar, Jeffrey D. Richardson, Bryon Look, Charles A. Haggerty, Gregorio Reyes, Paulsen & Co., Inc./5.90%, Richard S. Hill, Black Rock, Inc./11.80%, Flavio Santoni *(20 Owners included in Index)*

Financial Data: **Fiscal Year End:**12/31 **Latest Annual Data:** 12/31/2006

Year	Sales	Net Income
2006	$1,982,148,000	$169,638,000
2005	$1,919,250,000	-$5,623,000
2004	$1,700,164,000	-$463,531,000

Curr. Assets:	$1,635,737,000	**Curr. Liab.:**	$526,771,000	**P/E Ratio:**	17.76
Plant, Equip.:	$86,045,000	**Total Liab.:**	$956,171,000	**Indic. Yr. Divd.:**	NA
Total Assets:	$2,852,144,000	**Net Worth:**	$1,895,738,000	**Debt/ Equity:**	NA

LSI Industries Inc

10000 Alliance Rd., Cincinnati, OH, 45242; ***PH:*** 1-513-793-3200; ***Fax:*** 1-513-984-1335; ***http://*** www.lsi-industries.com

General - Incorporation OH
Employees 1,440
Auditor Grant Thornton LLP
Stk Agt. Computershare Trust Co
Counsel Keating, Muething & Klekamp
DUNS No. 08-093-4375

Stock- Price on:12/24/2007 $15.3
Stock Exchange NDQ
Ticker Symbol LYTS
Outstanding Shares 21,490,000
E.P.S $1.01
Shareholders NA

Business: The group's principal activity is to provide corporate visual image solutions through a combination of screen and digital graphics capabilities, indoor and outdoor lighting products, and related professional services. The group operates through two segments: lighting segment and graphics segment. The lighting segment manufactures and markets outdoor, indoor, and landscape lighting for the commercial, industrial and multi-site retail markets, including the petroleum / convenience store market. The graphics segment manufactures and sells exterior and interior visual image elements related to graphics, and menu board systems. The group primarily operates in the United States of America.

Primary SIC and add'l.: 2796 3646 2752 2754 3648

CIK No: 0000763532

Subsidiaries: GradyMcCauleyInc., GreenleeIncorporated, GreenleeLightingInc., GreenleeLightingL.P., LSI Adapt Inc., LSI Integrated Graphic Systems LLC, LSI Kentucky LLC, LSI Lightron Inc., LSI Marcole Inc., LSI MidWest Lighting Inc., LSIPartnershipHoldingLLC, LSIRetailGraphicsInc.

Officers: Robert J. Ready/65/Chmn., CEO, Pres./$1,048,417.00, Fred D. Jalbout/Pres. - LSI Technology Solutions Plus, David W. McCauley/Pres. - LSI Graphic Solutions Plus/$457,967.00, James P. Sferra/68/Dir., Exec. VP - Manufacturing/$828,830.00, Ronald S. Stowell/CFO, VP, Treasurer/$551,916.00, Scott D. Ready/Pres. - LSI Lighting Solutions Plus/$446,424.00

Directors: Robert J. Ready/65/Chmn., CEO, Pres., Wilfred T. O'Gara/50/Dir., Dennis B. Meyer/73/Dir., James P. Sferra/68/Dir., Exec. VP - Manufacturing, Gary P. Kreider/69/Dir., Mark A. Serrianne/60/Dir.

Owners: Columbia Management Group, Inc./8.82%, Royce & Associates LLC/5.89%, Wells Capital Management, Inc./5.12%

Financial Data: **Fiscal Year End:**06/30 **Latest Annual Data:** 6/30/2007

Year	Sales	Net Income
2007	$337,453,000	$20,789,000
2006	$280,470,000	$14,443,000
2005	$282,440,000	$14,636,000

Curr. Assets:	$123,358,000	**Curr. Liab.:**	$54,961,000	**P/E Ratio:**	18.00
Plant, Equip.:	$47,558,000	**Total Liab.:**	$57,551,000	**Indic. Yr. Divd.:**	$0.600
Total Assets:	$233,612,000	**Net Worth:**	$176,061,000	**Debt/ Equity:**	NA

LTC Properties Inc

31365 Oak Crest Dr., Ste. 200, Westlake Village, CA, 91361; ***PH:*** 1-805-981-8655; ***Fax:*** 1-805-981-8663; ***http://*** www.ltcproperties.com

General - Incorporation MD
Employees 12
Auditor Ernst& Young LLP
Stk Agt..... Computershare Investor Services LLC
Counsel NA
DUNS No. NA

Stock- Price on:12/24/2007 $23.63
Stock Exchange NYSE
Ticker Symbol LTC
Outstanding Shares 23,660,000
E.P.S $1.35
Shareholders NA

Business: The groups principle activity is to invest in health related properties through mortgage loans, property lease transactions and other investments. In the year 2006, the group acquired five skilled nursing properties. The group operates from the United States. The group's quarterly revenue for September 2007 was18.25 millions of USD.

Primary SIC and add'l.: 6798

CIK No: 0000887905

Subsidiaries: Albuquerque Real Estate Investments, Inc., Bakersfield-LTC, Inc., Beaumont Real Estate Investments, LP, BV Holding-LTC, Inc., Coronado Corporation, East New Mexico, Inc., Education Property Investors, Inc., Florida-LTC, Inc., Kansas-LTC Corporation, L-Tex GP, Inc., L-Tex L.P. Corporation, LTC GP I, Inc., LTC GP II, Inc., LTC GP III, Inc., LTC GP IV, Inc. 47 Subsidiaries included in the Index

Officers: Wendy L. Simpson/Dir., CEO, Pres./$600,586.00, Andre C. Dimitriadis/Executive Chmn./$777,209.00

Directors: Wendy L. Simpson/Dir., CEO, Pres., Andre C. Dimitriadis/Executive Chmn., Boyd W. Hendrickson/Dir., Edmund C. King/Dir., Timothy J. Triche/Dir.

Owners: Insiders/5.20%, Deutsche Bank AG/10.80%, Pamela Shelley Kessler, Wendy L. Simpson/1.40%, Sam Yellen, Barclays Global Investors, NA/7.60%, National Health Investors,Inc./10.50%, Andre C. Dimitriadis/3.00%, Edmund C. King, Boyd W. Hendrickson, Timothy J. Triche, Peter Lyew, Clint Malin, David J. Dunn/7.00%

Financial Data: **Fiscal Year End:**12/31 **Latest Annual Data:** 12/31/2006

Year	Sales	Net Income
2006	$73,163,000	$78,788,000
2005	$72,992,000	$52,709,000
2004	$66,917,000	$36,388,000

Curr. Assets:	$33,057,000	**Curr. Liab.:**	$10,004,000	**P/E Ratio:**	19.72
Plant, Equip.:	$386,196,000	**Total Liab.:**	$67,333,000	**Indic. Yr. Divd.:**	$1.500
Total Assets:	$567,767,000	**Net Worth:**	$500,434,000	**Debt/ Equity:**	NA

LTX Corp

825 University Ave., Norwood, MA, 02062; ***PH:*** 1-781-461-1000; ***Fax:*** 1-781-461-0993; ***http://*** www.ltx.com

General - Incorporation MA
Employees 418
Auditor Ernst & Young LLP
Stk Agt..... Computershare Investor Services LLC
Counsel Bingham McCutchen
DUNS No. 08-003-1917

Stock- Price on:12/24/2007 $5.7
Stock Exchange NDQ
Ticker Symbol LTXX
Outstanding Shares 62,350,000
E.P.S -$0.25
Shareholders NA

Business: The group's principle activity is to design, manufacture, market and service semiconductor test solutions. It has introduced the ltx fusion test platform, which is used to test system-on-a-chip devices in a single step. The products of the group are used to test analog, digital and mixed signal integrated circuits. It also provides test systems, global applications consulting, repair services and operational support to its customers in over fifteen countries. The customers of the group include semiconductor

designers and manufacturers such as analog devices, infineon technologies, national semiconductor, philips semiconductor, stmicroelectronics and Texas instruments who use semiconductor test equipment to test devices at two different stages during the manufacturing process.it operates in Taiwan, Japan, Singapore beside United States. The group's total revenue for year 2007 was 147.64 millions of USD.

Primary SIC and add'l.: 3825 3826

CIK No: 0000357020

Subsidiaries: LTX (Deutschland) GmBH, LTX (Europe) Limited, LTX (Foreign Sales Corporation) B.V., LTX (Italia) S.r., LTX (Malaysia) SDN.BHD, LTX Asia International, Inc., LTX France S.A., LTX International Inc., Domestic International Sales Corporation (DISC), LTX Israel Limited, LTX LLC, LTX Test Systems Corporation

Officers: David G. Tacelli/Dir., CEO, Pres., Daniel Wallace/VP, Corporate Controller, Mark J. Gallenberger/CFO, Treasurer, Richard L. Bove/VP, Peter S. Rood/VP, Thomas J. Young/VP, Joseph A. Hedal/General Counsel, Sec., Bruce R. MacDonald/VP

Directors: David G. Tacelli/Dir., CEO, Pres., Roger W. Blethen/Chmn., Robert E. Moore/Dir., Roger J. Maggs/Dir., Mark S. Ain/Dir., Stephen M. Jennings/Dir., Samuel Rubinovitz/Dir., Patrick J. Spratt/Dir.

Owners: FMR Corp./14.70%, Robert E. Moore, Patrick J. Spratt, Stephen M. Jennings, Roger W. Blethen/2.80%, Insiders/6.00%, Barclays Global Investors, Ltd./8.20%, Samuel Rubinovitz, Roger J. Maggs, State of Wisconsin Investment Board/12.70%, David G. Tacelli/1.50%, Artisan Partners Limited Partnership/10.80%, Peter S. Rood, Mark S. Ain, Renaissance Technology Corp/5.60% *(16 Owners included in Index)*

Financial Data: Fiscal Year End:07/31   Latest Annual Data: 7/31/2006

Year	Sales	Net Income
2006	$216,503,000	$12,241,000
2005	$134,531,000	-$132,726,000
2004	$255,801,000	$1,961,000

Curr. Assets:	$270,197,000	**Curr. Liab.:**	$126,910,000	**P/E Ratio:**	47.50
Plant, Equip.:	$37,633,000	**Total Liab.:**	$210,051,000	**Indic. Yr. Divd.:**	NA
Total Assets:	$327,690,000	**Net Worth:**	$117,639,000	**Debt/ Equity:**	NA

Lubrizol Corp (The)

29400 Lakeland Blvd, Wickliffe, OH, 44092; *PH:* 1-440-943-4200; *http://* www.lubrizol.com

General - Incorporation	OH	Stock - Price on:12/24/2007	$65.57
Employees	6,700	Stock Exchange	NYSE
Auditor	Deloitte & Touche LLP	Ticker Symbol	LZ
Stk Agt	American Stock Transfer & Trust Co.	Outstanding Shares	NA
Counsel	NA	E.P.S.	$3.49
DUNS No.	00-417-2565	Shareholders	NA

Business: The groups principle activity is to develop chemicals and additives. The group operates through two segments include Lubrizol Advanced Materials and Lubrizol additives. The groups servicing areas include transportation, industrial and consumer markets. The group operates from United States.

Primary SIC and add'l.: 2899 2992

CIK No: 0000060751

Subsidiaries: 1500 West Elizabeth Corporation, Cosmetochem U.S.A., Inc., CPI Engineering Services, Inc., Engine Control Systems Ltd., FCC Acquisition Corp., Freedom Chemical Diamalt Beteiligungs GmbH, Gateway Additive Company, Gemoplast SA, Indiamalt Private Limited, Lanzhou Lubrizol Lanlian Additive Co. Ltd., Lubricant Investments, Inc., Lubrizol (Gibraltar) Limited, Lubrizol (Gibraltar) Limited Luxembourg SCS, Lubrizol (Gibraltar) Minority Limited, Lubrizol (Gibraltar) Two Limited 106 Subsidiaries included in the Index

Officers: James L. Hambrick/53/Chmn., CEO, Pres./$15,058,950.00, Gregory D. Taylor/49/VP - Corporate Planning, Development, Communications, Stephen F. Kirk/58/Sr. VP, Pres. - Lubricant Additives/$3,343,078.00, Donald W. Bogus/60/Sr. VP, Pres. - Lubrizol Advanced Materials/$2,759,462.00, Joanne Wanstreet/56/VP - Investor Relations, Scott W. Emerick/43/Corporate Controller, Leslie M. Reynolds/47/Corp. Sec., Mark W. Meister/53/VP, Chief Ethics Officer, Jeffrey A. Vavruska/47/Chief Tax Officer, Joseph W. Bauer/54/VP, General Counsel/$2,112,714.00, Patrick Saunier/52/VP - Information Systems, Karen Lerchbacher/Contact - Foundation, Charles P. Cooley/52/Sr. VP - Treasure, CFO/$3,270,423.00

Directors: James L. Hambrick/53/Chmn., CEO, Pres., Daniel E. Somers/Dir., William P. Madar/68/Dir., Peggy Gordon Miller/Dir., Victoria F. Haynes/60/Dir., Robert E. Abernathy/53/Dir., Gordon D. Harnett/65/Dir., James E. Sweetnam/55/Dir., Harriett Tee Taggart/59/Dir., Dominic J. Pileggi/56/Dir., Forest J. Farmer/67/Dir., Jerald A. Blumberg/68/Dir.

Owners: Charles P. Cooley, Daniel E. Somers, Victoria F. Haynes, Joseph W. Bauer, Forest J. Farmer, Insiders, Gordon D. Harnett, James L. Hambrick, Peggy Gordon Miller, Robert E. Abernathy, William P. Madar, Barclays Global Investors Japan Trust and Banking Company Limited/5.72%, Alliance Capital Management L.P./6.60%, Dominic J. Pileggi, Stephen F. Kirk

Financial Data: Fiscal Year End:12/31   Latest Annual Data: 12/31/2006

Year	Sales	Net Income
2006	$4,040,800,000	$105,600,000
2005	$4,042,700,000	$189,300,000
2004	$3,159,500,000	$93,500,000

Curr. Assets:	$1,836,300,000	**Curr. Liab.:**	$632,000,000		
Plant, Equip.:	$1,081,300,000	**Total Liab.:**	$2,626,100,000	**Indic. Yr. Divd.:**	$1.200
Total Assets:	$4,386,200,000	**Net Worth:**	$1,707,400,000	**Debt/ Equity:**	NA

Luby's Inc

13111 NW Fwy., Ste. 600, Houston, TX, 77040; *PH:* 1-713-329-6800; *Fax:* 1-713-329-6809; *http://* www.lubys.com; *Email:* investors@lubys.com

General - Incorporation	DE	Stock - Price on:12/24/2007	$9.84
Employees	8,210	Stock Exchange	NYSE
Auditor	Grant Thornton, LLP	Ticker Symbol	LUB
Stk Agt	American Stock Transfer & Trust Co.	Outstanding Shares	26,150,000
Counsel	HSF & Beiter Inc	E.P.S.	$0.50
DUNS No.	02-701-4984	Shareholders	NA

Business: The group's principal activity is to own and operate cafeteria-style restaurants. The group's restaurants are operated under the name luby's. These restaurants are situated in close proximity to retail centers, business developments and residential areas and cater primarily to shoppers, store and office personnel at lunch and to families at dinner. Each of the group's restaurants offers 12 to 14 entrees, 12 to 14 vegetable dishes, 12 to 16 salads and 15 to 18 desserts. As of 07-Jun-2004, the group owned and operated 139 restaurants located in Arizona, Arkansas, Louisiana, Oklahoma, Tennessee and Texas.

Primary SIC and add'l.: 5812

CIK No: 0000016099

Officers: Scott K. Gray/Sr. VP, CFO, Paulette Gerukos/VP - Human Resources

Owners: Judith B. Craven, Harris J. Pappas/12.18%, Insiders/25.19%, Ramius Capital Group, L.L.C./6.56%, Dimensional Fund Advisors, LP/5.99%, Gasper Mir, Frank Markantonis, Arthur R. Emerson, Peter Tropoli, Scott K. Gray, Joe C. McKinney, Christopher J. Pappas/12.18%, Jim W. Woliver, Jill Griffin, Deutsche Bank Aktiengesellschaft/5.02% *(16 Owners included in Index)*

Financial Data: Fiscal Year End:08/31   Latest Annual Data: 8/30/2006

Year	Sales	Net Income
2006	$324,640,000	$19,561,000
2005	$322,151,000	$3,448,000
2004	$308,817,000	-$5,978,000

Curr. Assets:	$9,326,000	**Curr. Liab.:**	$35,479,000	**P/E Ratio:**	15.14
Plant, Equip.:	$195,355,000	**Total Liab.:**	$61,928,000	**Indic. Yr. Divd.:**	NA
Total Assets:	$206,214,000	**Net Worth:**	$144,286,000	**Debt/ Equity:**	NA

Lucas Energy Inc

3000 Richmond Ave., Ste. 400, Houston, TX, 77098; *PH:* 1-604-618-2419; *Fax:* 1-604-738-4080; *http://* www.lucasenergy.com; *Email:* Info@lucasenergy.com

General - Incorporation	NV	Stock - Price on:12/24/2007	$2.45
Employees	NA	Stock Exchange	OTC
Auditor	Malone & Bailey, P.C	Ticker Symbol	LUCE
Stk Agt	Empire Stock Transfer Inc.	Outstanding Shares	29,450,000
Counsel	NA	E.P.S.	$0.01
DUNS No.	NA	Shareholders	NA

Business: The groups principal activity is to supply giftware and specialty items. The group operates from the North America.

Primary SIC and add'l.: 1311

CIK No: 0001309082

Officers: James J. Cerna/39/Chmn., CEO, William A. Sawyer/59/Dir., COO, Malek A. Bohsali/CFO

Directors: James J. Cerna/39/Chmn., CEO, William A. Sawyer/59/Dir., COO, Eric Wold/Dir., Rick Schmid/Dir., Peter Grunebaum/74/Dir.

Owners: William A. Sawyer/3.57%, James J. Cerna/11.34%, Eric Wold, LGA, Inc./19.88%, Insiders/16.66%, Malek A. Bohsali, Rick Schmid, Peter Grunebaum

Financial Data: Fiscal Year End:11/30   Latest Annual Data: 03/31/2007

Year	Sales	Net Income
2007	$1,330,000	$322,000
2005	NA	-$23,000

Curr. Assets:	$27,000	**Curr. Liab.:**	$5,000		
Plant, Equip.:	NA	**Total Liab.:**	$5,000	**Indic. Yr. Divd.:**	NA
Total Assets:	$27,000	**Net Worth:**	$22,000	**Debt/ Equity:**	NA

Lucille Farms Inc

12 Jonergin Dr., Swanton, VT, 05488; *PH:* 1-802-868-7301; *http://* www.lucille-farms.com; *Email:* orders@lucille-farms.com

General - Incorporation	DE	Stock - Price on:12/24/2007	$0.04
Employees	NA	Stock Exchange	OTC
Auditor	Reslow & Walker, LLP	Ticker Symbol	LUCY
Stk Agt	Continental Stock Transfer & Trust Co	Outstanding Shares	NA
Counsel	Breslow & Walker LLP	E.P.S.	NA
DUNS No.	00-394-8528	Shareholders	NA

Business: The group's principal activities are to manufacture, process and market low moisture mozzarella cheese, reduced fat and non-fat low moisture mozzarella cheese, pizza cheese and other cheese blends. The products include conventional cheese products, nutritional products and whey. Conventional products consist of conventional mozzarella, provolone and feta. Nutritional products consist of organic cheese like shredded mozzarella and the cheddar and monterey jack varieties, sold under the brand names of mozzi-rite(tm), tasty-lite cheese(tm) fat free and tasty-lite cheese(tm) light. Other products include popcorn whey, a dried and milled form of whey to be used in animal feed. The products are sold through a network of brokers to pizza chains, restaurants, health care facilities and other institutions.

Primary SIC and add'l.: 2048 2022

CIK No: 0000908179

Financial Data: Fiscal Year End:03/31   Latest Annual Data: 3/31/2005

Year	Sales	Net Income
2005	$47,802,000	-$3,269,000
2004	$42,174,000	$209,000
2003	$36,691,000	-$847,000

Curr. Assets:	$8,664,000	**Curr. Liab.:**	$5,057,000		
Plant, Equip.:	$9,206,000	**Total Liab.:**	$18,823,000	**Indic. Yr. Divd.:**	NA
Total Assets:	$18,561,000	**Net Worth:**	-$262,000	**Debt/ Equity:**	NA

Lucy's Cafe Inc

2685 Pk. Ctr. Dr., Bldg. A, Simi Valley, CA, 93065; *PH:* 1-805-433-8000; *http://* www.intermetro.net; *Email:* info@intermetro.net

General - Incorporation	NV	Stock - Price on:12/24/2007	NA
Employees	NA	Stock Exchange	NA
Auditor	Mayer Hoffman Mccann, P.C	Ticker Symbol	NA
Stk Agt	Interwest Transfer Company, Inc.	Outstanding Shares	NA
Counsel	NA	E.P.S.	NA
DUNS No.	NA	Shareholders	NA

Business: The group's principle activities include acquiring and operating restaurant. Customers served by the group include office workers, professionals, and government employees. The group operates from the United States.

Primary SIC and add'l.: 4813

CIK No: 0001160142

Officers: Charles Rice/44/Chmn., CEO, Pres./$290,259.00, Jon Deong/34/CTO, Dir./$244,313.00, Vincent Arena/38/Dir., CFO/$218,640.00

Directors: Charles Rice/44/Chmn., CEO, Pres., Jon Deong/34/CTO, Dir.

Owners: Jon deOng/4.50%, Robert Grden, Charles Rice/55.00%, Douglas Benson/6.70%, Vincent Arena/4.10%, Mitchell Pindus/5.10%, Joshua Touber/1.80%, Hunter World Markets, Inc./7.50%, Insiders/62.20%, David Marshall/10.40%

Curr. Assets:	$11,970,000	**Curr. Liab.:**	$20,542,000		
Plant, Equip.:	$1,637,000	**Total Liab.:**	$20,637,000	**Indic. Yr. Divd.:**	NA
Total Assets:	$15,567,000	**Net Worth:**	-$5,070,000	**Debt/ Equity:**	NA

Lufkin Industries Inc

601 S Raguet, Lufkin, TX, 75904; ***PH:*** 1-936-634-2211; ***Fax:*** 1-936-637-5272; ***http://*** www.lufkin.com

General - Incorporation	TX	**Stock**- Price on:12/24/2007	$66.14
Employees	3,000	Stock Exchange	NDQ
Auditor	Deloitte & Touche LLP	Ticker Symbol	LUFK
Stk Agt	Computershare Investor Services LLC	Outstanding Shares	15,050,000
Counsel	NA	E.P.S	$5.10
DUNS No.	00-809-0375	Shareholders	NA

Business: The group's principal activities are to manufacture, design, distribute and provide services for various types of oil field pumping units, power transmission products and highway trailers. The group operates under three segments: oil field, power transmission and trailer. The oil field segment manufactures four basic types of pump units: an air-balanced unit; a beam-balanced unit; a crank-balanced unit and a mark ii unitorque unit. Power transmission segment manufacturers mechanical power transmission equipment used in industrial application. Trailer products and services segment produces vans, floats, dumps trailers and related services. The group operates in the United States, Canada, Latin America, Europe and Japan. In 2003, it acquired the remaining shares of lufkin Argentina sa and operating assets of basin technical services.

Primary SIC and add'l.: 3537 3612 3533 3531

CIK No: 0000060849

Subsidiaries: Lufkin Argentina, S.A., Lufkin France, EURL, Lufkin Industries Canada, Ltd., Lufkin Industries FSC, Corp, Lufkin Japan, L. L. C., Lufkin Middle East, P. T. Lufkin Indonesia

Officers: Douglas V. Smith/Chmn., CEO, Pres./$3,015,263.00, L. M. Hoes/Exec. VP, Special Assist. to The Pres./$813,088.00, S. H. Semlinger/VP - Manufacturing Technology, J. F. Glick/Dir., VP, GM - Power Transmission Division/$574,667.00, Paul G. Perez/VP, General Counsel, Sec./$579,960.00, R. D. Leslie/VP, Treasurer, CFO/$626,454.00, T. L. Orr/VP - Power Transmission Division

Directors: Douglas V. Smith/Chmn., CEO, Pres., J. F. Glick/Dir., VP, GM - Power Transmission Division, S. V. Baer/Dir., J. H. Lollar/Dir., James T. Jongebloed/Dir., S. W. Henderson/Dir., H. J. Trout/Dir., J. F. Anderson/Dir., B. H. O'Neal/Dir., T. E. Wiener/Dir.

Owners: John F. Anderson, Bob H. ONeal, John H. Lollar, Suzanne V. Baer, Paul G. Perez, H. J. Trout/2.60%, James T. Jongebloed, Barclays Global Investors, NA/5.11%, Simon W. Henderson/1.60%, Douglas V. Smith/1.00%, Insiders/6.70%, Larry M. Hoes, John F. Glick, Thomas E. Wiener, Robert D. Leslie

Financial Data: ***Fiscal Year End:***12/31 ***Latest Annual Data:*** 06/30/2007

Year	Sales	Net Income
2007	NA	NA
2006	$605,492,000	$72,994,000
2005	$492,167,000	$44,544,000

Curr. Assets:	$243,452,000	**Curr. Liab.:**	$61,495,000	**P/E Ratio:**	13.25
Plant, Equip.:	$113,081,000	**Total Liab.:**	$100,929,000	**Indic. Yr. Divd.:**	$0.920
Total Assets:	$429,069,000	**Net Worth:**	$328,140,000	**Debt/ Equity:**	NA

Luke Energy Ltd

520 - 5th Ave. S.w., Ste. 1200, Calgary, AB, T2P 3R7; ; ***http://*** www.connacheroil.com

General - Incorporation	Canada	**Stock**- Price on:12/24/2007	NA
Employees	NA	Stock Exchange	NA
Auditor	KPMG LLP	Ticker Symbol	NA
Stk Agt	Computershare Investor Services	Outstanding Shares	NA
Counsel	NA	E.P.S	NA
DUNS No.	NA	Shareholders	NA

Business: The groups principle activities include acquiring, exploring, developing, producing and marketing oil and natural gas. The group operates from Canada.

Primary SIC and add'l.: NA

CIK No: 0001268947

Lumera Corp

19910 N Creek Pkwy., Bothell, WA, 98011; ***PH:*** 1-425-415-6900; ***Fax:*** 1-425-398-6599; ***http://*** www.lumera.com

General - Incorporation	DE	**Stock**- Price on:12/24/2007	$4.65
Employees	56	Stock Exchange	NDQ
Auditor	PricewaterhouseCoopers LLP	Ticker Symbol	LMRA
Stk Agt	American Stock Transfer & Trust Co.	Outstanding Shares	20,060,000
Counsel	Ropes & Gray LLP	E.P.S	-$0.71
DUNS No.	12-769-3146	Shareholders	NA

Business: The group's principle activities include developing, manufacturing and marketing devices using proprietary polymer materials. The company's key products consist of wireless antennas and systems, biotechnology disposables, electro-optic devices and polymer-based products for government applications. The customers of the company include original equipment manufacturers of mobile computing and communications equipment, municipal communication systems, defense battlefield networks, bioassay and pharmaceuticals companies, diagnostic laboratories, government and academic laboratories, telecommunications component and systems manufacturers, networking and switching suppliers, semiconductor companies, aerospace companies and government agencies. The group operates from United States.

Primary SIC and add'l.: 3679 3663

CIK No: 0001137399

Officers: Thomas D. Mino/61/Dir., CEO, Pres./$581,413.00, Peter Biere/CFO, VP, Treasurer/$442,464.00, Daniel C. Lykken/VP - Sales, Marketing/$360,199.00, Helene F. Jaillet/Dir. - Investor Relations, Corporate Communications, Raluca Dinu/VP - Electro, Optics

Directors: Thomas D. Mino/61/Dir., CEO, Pres., James C. Judson/Chmn., Sanjiv Sam Gambhir/Dir., Joseph J. Vallner/Dir., Charles T. Campbell/Member - Scientific Advisory Board, Robert A. Ratliffe/Dir., Fraser Black/Dir., Donald Guthrie/Dir., Larry R. Dalton/Member - Scientific Advisory Board, Leroy Hood/Member - Scientific Advisory Board, Alex Jen/Member - Scientific Advisory Board, Joshua Labaer/Member - Scientific Advisory Board, Seth Marder/Member - Scientific Advisory Board, William H. Steier/Member - Scientific Advisory Board, Kimberly D.C. Trapp/Dir.

Owners: Fraser Black, Sanjiv Sam Gambhir, James C. Judson, Insiders/5.56%, Joseph Vallner, Daniel C. Lykken, Peter J. Biere, Paulson Investment Company/4.48%, Donald Guthrie, Kimberly D.C. Trapp, Chester L.F. Paulson and Jaqueline M. Paulson/5.38%, Thomas O. Mino/2.48%, Robert A. Ratliffe

Financial Data: ***Fiscal Year End:***12/31 ***Latest Annual Data:*** 12/31/2006

Year	Sales	Net Income
2006	NA	NA
2005	NA	NA
2004	NA	NA

Curr. Assets:	$27,627,000	**Curr. Liab.:**	$1,832,000		
Plant, Equip.:	$2,759,000	**Total Liab.:**	$2,239,000	**Indic. Yr. Divd.:**	NA
Total Assets:	$31,132,000	**Net Worth:**	$28,893,000	**Debt/ Equity:**	NA

Luminent Mortgage Capital Inc

101 California St., Ste. 1350, San Francisco, CA, 94111; ***PH:*** 1-415-217-4500; ***Fax:*** 1-415-217-4518; ***http://*** www.luminentcapital.com; ***Email:*** ir@luminentcapital.com

General - Incorporation	MD	**Stock**- Price on:12/24/2007	$9.47
Employees	32	Stock Exchange	NYSE
Auditor	Deloitte & Touche LLP	Ticker Symbol	LUM
Stk Agt	Mellon Investor Services LLC	Outstanding Shares	46,820,000
Counsel	NA	E.P.S	-$10.584
DUNS No.	NA	Shareholders	NA

Business: The groups principle activity is to invest in residential mortgage loans. The group operates from the United States. The group's quarterly revenue for Sept 2007 was 133.99 millions of USD.

Primary SIC and add'l.: 6798

CIK No: 0001236309

Officers: Trezevant S. Moore/Dir., CEO, Pres., Christopher J. Zyda/Sr. VP, CFO, Francesco Piovanetti/Dir., Pres.

Directors: Trezevant S. Moore/Dir., CEO, Pres., Gail P. Seneca/55/Chmn., Bruce A. Miller/Dir., Leonard Auerbach/61/Dir., Robert B. Goldstein/Dir., Donald H. Putnam/56/Dir., Joseph E. Whitters/Dir., Frank L. Raiter/Dir., Zachary H. Pashel/Dir., Francesco Piovanetti/Dir., Pres., Jay A. Johnston/Dir., Craig Cohen/Dir.

Owners: Leonard Auerbach, Eleanor Cornfeld Melton, Ronald Viera, Trezevant S. Moore, Joseph E. Whitters, Donald H. Putnam, Bruce A. Miller, Frank L. Raiter, Robert B. Goldstein, Gail P. Seneca/1.10%, Insiders/2.90%, Christopher J. Zyda

Financial Data: ***Fiscal Year End:***12/31 ***Latest Annual Data:*** 12/31/2006

Year	Sales	Net Income
2006	$365,866,000	$46,797,000
2005	$181,421,000	-$82,991,000
2004	$124,824,000	$57,112,000

Curr. Assets:	$51,165,000	**Curr. Liab.:**	$2,741,321,000	**P/E Ratio:**	9.38
Plant, Equip.:	NA	**Total Liab.:**	$8,142,240,000	**Indic. Yr. Divd.:**	$1.280
Total Assets:	$8,613,795,000	**Net Worth:**	$471,555,000	**Debt/ Equity:**	NA

Luminex Corp

12212 Technology Blvd., Austin, TX, 78727; ***PH:*** 1-512-219-8020; ***Fax:*** 1-512-219-5195; ***http://*** www.luminexcorp.com; ***Email:*** info@luminexcorp.com

General - Incorporation	DE	**Stock**- Price on:12/24/2007	$12.04
Employees	209	Stock Exchange	NDQ
Auditor	Ernst & Young LLP	Ticker Symbol	LMNX
Stk Agt	Mellon Investor Services LLC	Outstanding Shares	35,830,000
Counsel	Thompson & Knight	E.P.S	-$0.39
DUNS No.	NA	Shareholders	NA

Business: The group's principal activities are to manufacture and market products incorporating a proprietary technology that advances and simplifies biological testing for the life sciences industry. The group's xmap technology allows the luminex 100 system to simultaneously perform up to 100 bioassays on a single drop of fluid by reading biological tests taking place on the surface of microscopic polystyrene beads called microspheres. The xmap technology is currently being used within the various segments of the life sciences industry in the fields of drug discovery, clinical diagnostics, genetic analysis and biomedical research.

Primary SIC and add'l.: 3841 8731

CIK No: 0001033905

Subsidiaries: Dutch Private Limited Liability Company, Luminex B.V., Luminex International, Inc., Luminex Project, Inc.

Officers: Patrick J. Balthrop/Dir., CEO, Pres., James W. Jacobson/Chmn. - Scientific Advisory Board, VP - Research Development, Chief Scientific Officer, Ronald Bowsher/VP, Chief Scientific Officer - Linco Diagnostic Services, Inc, Oliver H. Meek/VP - Quality Assurance, Regulatory Affairs, David S. Reiter/VP, General Counsel, Corp. Sec./$677,737.00, Jeremy Bridge-Cook/VP - Luminex Molecular Diagnostics, Gregory J. Gosch/VP - Marketing, Sales, Douglas C. Bryant/COO, Exec. VP, Russell W. Bradley/VP - Business Development, Strategic Planning, John C. Carrano/VP - Research, Development, Harriss T. Currie/CFO, VP - Finance, Treasurer/$699,839.00, Randel S. Marfin/VP - Luminex Bioscience Group/$570,992.00

Directors: Patrick J. Balthrop/Dir., CEO, Pres., Walter G. Loewenbaum/64/Chmn., James W. Jacobson/Chmn. - Scientific Advisory Board, VP - Research Development, Chief Scientific Officer, Stark J. Thompson/67/Dir., Gerard Vaillant/67/Dir., Robert J. Cresci/64/Dir., Thomas W. Erickson/57/Dir., Fred C. Goad/68/Dir., Jay B. Johnston/65/Dir., Jim D. Kever/56/Dir., Kevin M. McNamara/52/Dir.

Owners: Kevin M. McNamara, Denis J. Villere & Company, LLC/14.30%, Fred C. Goad, David S. Reiter, Randel S. Marfin, Walter G. Loewenbaum/5.10%, Robert J. Cresci, Jim D. Kever, Thomas W. Erickson, Jay Johnston, Gerard Vaillant, Insiders/13.50%, Patrick J. Balthrop/2.00%, Barclays Global Investors, N.A./5.60%, Harriss T. Currie *(17 Owners included in Index)*

Financial Data: ***Fiscal Year End:***12/31 ***Latest Annual Data:*** 12/31/2006

Year	Sales	Net Income
2006	$52,989,000	$1,507,000
2005	$42,313,000	-$2,666,000
2004	$35,880,000	-$3,605,000

Curr. Assets:	$53,095,000	Curr. Liab.:	$8,916,000		
Plant, Equip.:	$4,985,000	Total Liab.:	$12,537,000	Indic. Yr. Divd.:	NA
Total Assets:	$66,696,000	Net Worth:	$54,159,000	Debt/ Equity:	0.0338

Lumonall Inc

Formerly: Midland International Corp
12650 Jane St., King City, On, L7B 1A3; **PH:** 1-905-833-9845

General - Incorporation	NV	Stock - Price on:12/24/2007	$0.06
Employees	NA	Stock Exchange	OTC
Auditor	Rotenberg & Co., LLP	Ticker Symbol	LUMN
Stk Agt	Interwest Transfer Company, Inc.	Outstanding Shares	NA
Counsel	NA	E.P.S.	NA
DUNS No.	NA	Shareholders	NA

Business: The groups principle activity is to market wireless devices including cellular phones. The group operates from the United States.
Primary SIC and add'l.: 2810
CIK No: 0001099561
Officers: John G. Simmonds/57/Chmn., CEO, Pres., Gary Hokkanen/CFO, Carrie J. Weiler/49/Dir., Corp. Sec.
Directors: John G. Simmonds/57/Chmn., CEO, Pres., Carrie J. Weiler/49/Dir., Corp. Sec.
Owners: Insiders/9.40%, Prolink Holdings AS/20.30%, Carrie J. Weiler/2.00%, John G. Simmonds/7.40%
Financial Data: Fiscal Year End:03/31   Latest Annual Data: 03/31/2007

Year	Sales	Net Income
2007	NA	-$315,000
2006	$60,000	-$895,000
2005	NA	-$558,000

Curr. Assets:	NA	Curr. Liab.:	$791,000		
Plant, Equip.:	NA	Total Liab.:	$791,000	Indic. Yr. Divd.:	NA
Total Assets:	NA	Net Worth:	-$791,000	Debt/ Equity:	NA

Luna Innovations Inc

1703 S Jefferson St. SW, Ste. 400, Roanoke, VA, 24016; **PH:** 1-540-769-8400;
Fax: 1-540-769-8401; **http://** www.lunainnovations.com; **Email:** solutions@lunainnovations.com

General - Incorporation	193	Stock - Price on:12/24/2007	$5.05
Employees	193	Stock Exchange	NDQ
Auditor	Grant Thornton LLP	Ticker Symbol	LUNA
Stk Agt	American Stock Transfer & Trust Co.	Outstanding Shares	10,040,000
Counsel	Wilson Sonsini Goodrich & Rosati, PC	E.P.S.	-$1.08
DUNS No.	NA	Shareholders	NA

Business: The groups principle activities include researching, developing and commercializing technologies. The products of the group include optical vector analyzer, optical backscattering reflectometer and distributed sensing. The groups product is EDAC(TM) QUANTIFIER. The groups operates through two segments namely technology development and product and licensing. Specific customers of the group include United States Government and Non Government. The group operates from the United States. The group's quarterly revenue for September 2007 was 8.82 millions of USD.
Primary SIC and add'l.: 8734 8731
CIK No: 0001239819
Subsidiaries: Luna Technologies, Inc.
Officers: Kent A. Murphy/Chmn., CEO, Pres., Sec., Treasurer, Dale Messick/CFO, John T. Goehrke/COO, Scott A. Graeff/Chief Commercialization Officer, Scott A. Meller/Pres. - Technology Development Division, Ken Ferris/Pres. - Products Group, Robert Lenk/Pres. - Luna Nanoworks Division, Sally Beerbower/Primary Investor Relations Officer
Directors: Kent A. Murphy/Chmn., CEO, Pres., Sec., Treasurer, Leigh N. Anderson/Dir., John C. Backus/Dir., Bobbie Kilberg/Dir., Edward G. Murphy/Dir., Richard W. Roedel/Dir., Paul E. Torgersen/76/Dir., Mike Daniels/Dir.
Owners: Insiders, John C. Backus, Leigh N. Anderson, Paul E. Torgersen, Richard W. Roedel, Robert P. Lenk, Dale E. Messick, Bobbie Kilberg, Wasatch Advisors, Inc., Kent A. Murphy, Magnetar Investment Management, Inc. and affiliates, Kenneth D. Ferris, Edward G. Murphy, Carilion Clinic, Scott A. Graeff (16 Owners included in Index)
Financial Data: Fiscal Year End:12/31   Latest Annual Data: 12/31/2006

Year	Sales	Net Income
2006	$23,546,000	-$9,438,000
2005	$16,454,000	-$1,994,000
2004	$22,587,000	$4,056,000

Curr. Assets:	$26,843,000	Curr. Liab.:	$7,560,000		
Plant, Equip.:	$5,730,000	Total Liab.:	$13,142,000	Indic. Yr. Divd.:	NA
Total Assets:	$35,217,000	Net Worth:	$22,075,000	Debt/ Equity:	0.2277

Luna Technologies International Inc

445 Pk. Ave. Fl 9, New York, NY, 10022; **PH:** 1-888-955-8883; **http://** www.lunaplast.com

General - Incorporation	DE	Stock - Price on:12/24/2007	NA
Employees	NA	Stock Exchange	OTC
Auditor	Dale Matheson Carr-Hilton LaBonte LLP	Ticker Symbol	LTII
Stk Agt	Corporate Stock Transfer, Inc.	Outstanding Shares	NA
Counsel	NA	E.P.S.	NA
DUNS No.	NA	Shareholders	NA

Business: The groups principle activities include developing, manufacturing and selling photoluminescent products. The products of the group include adhesive vinyl tapes, rigid polyvinyl chloride marker strips, and silk-screened plastic signage. The group operates from the United States and Canada.
Primary SIC and add'l.: 7379
CIK No: 0001085217
Subsidiaries: Luna Technologies (Canada) Ltd.
Officers: Robert Kaul/Dir. - Operations, Satish Lal/Production Mgr., Shannon Barrows/Office Administrator, John Kuehne/Investor Relations Contact
Financial Data: Fiscal Year End:12/31   Latest Annual Data: 12/31/2005

Year	Sales	Net Income
2005	$674,000	-$1,771,000
2004	$657,000	-$671,000
2003	$482,000	-$612,000

Curr. Assets:	$242,000	Curr. Liab.:	$402,000		
Plant, Equip.:	$9,000	Total Liab.:	$819,000	Indic. Yr. Divd.:	NA
Total Assets:	$252,000	Net Worth:	-$567,000	Debt/ Equity:	NA

Lund Gold Ltd

1055 W Hastings St., Ste. 2000 Guinness Tower, Vancouver, BC, V6E 2E9; **PH:** 1-604-338772;
http:// www.lundgold.com; **Email:** info@lundgold.com

General - Incorporation	BC	Stock - Price on:12/24/2007	$0.3584
Employees	NA	Stock Exchange	OTC
Auditor	Davidson & Co LLP	Ticker Symbol	LGDOF
Stk Agt	PricewaterhouseCoopers LLP	Outstanding Shares	NA
Counsel	NA	E.P.S.	NA
DUNS No.	NA	Shareholders	NA

Business: The group's principle activities include acquiring and exploring oil and gas and gold, silver and other mineral producing properties. Oil and gas exploration activities are in the pre-production stage. The group operates from United States.
Primary SIC and add'l.: 1041 1044 1382
CIK No: 0001075756
Officers: Naomi Corrigan/Consultant, Ian Brown/60/CFO
Directors: Max Fugman/Dir., David Mallo/Dir., Chet Idziszek/Dir., James G. Stewart/Dir., Douglas J. Brown/Dir.
Owners: Insiders/14.90%, Max Fugman/2.70%, Naples Gold LLC/6.70%, J. G. Stewart/2.70%, Chet Idziszek/7.40%, Douglas J. Brown/1.40%
Financial Data: Fiscal Year End:06/30   Latest Annual Data: 06/30/2007

Year	Sales	Net Income
2007	NA	-$1,118,000
2006	NA	-$397,000
2005	NA	-$1,280,000

Curr. Assets:	$857,000	Curr. Liab.:	$32,000		
Plant, Equip.:	$63,000	Total Liab.:	$32,000	Indic. Yr. Divd.:	NA
Total Assets:	$935,000	Net Worth:	$903,000	Debt/ Equity:	NA

Luxottica Group SpA

Via C. Cant 2, Milan, 20123; ; **http://** www.luxottica.it

General - Incorporation	Italy	Stock - Price on:12/24/2007	$37.78
Employees	49,325	Stock Exchange	NYSE
Auditor	Deloitte & Touche S.P.A	Ticker Symbol	LUX
Stk Agt	Bank of New York	Outstanding Shares	454,760,000
Counsel	NA	E.P.S.	$1.58
DUNS No.	43-682-5376	Shareholders	NA

Business: The group's principal activities are to design, manufacture and distribute prescription frames and sunglasses in the mid and premium priced categories. The group's products are primarily manufactured in Italy and are marketed in 115 countries worldwide under a variety of well-known brand names. The house brands include Ray-Ban, Revo, Luxottica and Sferoflex. The designer lines include Giorgio Armani, Emporio Armani, Genny, Salvatore Ferragamo, Anne Klein, Bulgari and Moschino. The group's customers include retailers of mid and premium priced eyewear, such as independent opticians, optical and sunglass chains, optical superstores, sunglass specialty stores and duty-free shops. The group's subsidiaries are located in the United States, the United Kingdom, Canada, Brasil, Belgium, Sweden, Netherlands, Australia, Norway, Singapore, India and Argentina.
Primary SIC and add'l.: 3851 5995 5048
CIK No: 0000857471
Subsidiaries: 198 North Terrace Pty, AIR SUN, Arnette Optic Illusions Inc., Arrap Finance Holdings Pty Ltd, Avant Garde Optics LLC, Budget Eyewear Australia Ptyltd, Budget Specs (franchising) Ptyltd, C&M OPTICAL COMPANY LTD, Centre Professionel De Vision Ussc Inc, Cole National Corporation, Cole National Group, Inc., Cole Vision Canada Inc., Cole Vision Corporation, Cole Vision Ipa LLC, Cole Vision Services Inc. 34 Subsidiaries included in the Index
Officers: Andrea Guerra/42/Dir., CEO, Fabio Dangelantonio/38/Head - Group Marketing, Garland Gunter/57/CIO - Retail NA, Valerio Giacobbi/43/Exec. VP - Retail N. A., Enrico Cavatorta/46/Dir., Group CFO, Umberto Soccal/57/Group Chief Information Technology Officer, Frank Baynham/54/Exec. VP - Stores, Retail NA, Roberto Chemello/53/Dir., Head - Group Operations, Antonio Miyakawa/41/Head - Wholesale, Group Marketing, Giuseppe La Boria/49/Head - Wholesale Europe, South, Kerry Bradley/51/COO - Retail NA, Mildred Curtis/51/Sr. VP - Human Resources, Marco Vendramini/37/Group CAO, Nicola Pela/45/Head - Group Human Resources, Mario Pacifico/45/Head - Group Internal Auditing (16 Officers included in Index)
Directors: Andrea Guerra/42/Dir., CEO, Leonardo Del Vecchio/72/Chmn., Luigi Francavilla/70/Dep. Chmn., Lucio Rondelli/Dir., Mario Cattaneo/77/Dir., Roger Abravanel/61/Dir., Claudio Costamagna/52/Dir., Gianni Mion/62/Dir., Roberto Chemello/53/Dir., Head - Group Operations, Sabina Grossi/42/Dir., Sergio Erede/67/Dir., Enrico Cavatorta/46/Dir., Group CFO, Tancredi Bianchi/79/Dir., Claudio Del Vecchio/50/Dir.
Owners: Leonardo Del Vecchio/68.23%, Insiders/1.72%
Financial Data: Fiscal Year End:12/31   Latest Annual Data: 12/31/2006

Year	Sales	Net Income
2006	$6,171,123,000	$559,930,000
2005	$5,175,835,000	$405,345,000
2004	$4,407,025,000	$388,371,000

Curr. Assets:	$1,959,512,000	Curr. Liab.:	$1,880,938,000	P/E Ratio:	58.79
Plant, Equip.:	$1,038,869,000	Total Liab.:	$3,562,103,000	Indic. Yr. Divd.:	$0.680
Total Assets:	$6,486,359,000	Net Worth:	$2,924,256,000	Debt/ Equity:	NA

Luzerne NATL BK Corp

118 Main St., Luzerne, PA, 18709; **PH:** 1-570-288-4511; **http://** www.luzernenational.com;
Email: info@luzernebank.com

General - Incorporation
Employees ... NA
Auditor ... NA
Stk Agt ... NA
Counsel ... NA
DUNS No. ... NA

Stock- Price on:12/24/2007 ... $42.5
Stock Exchange ... OTC
Ticker Symbol ... LUZR
Outstanding Shares ... NA
E.P.S ... NA
Shareholders ... NA

Business: The groups principle activity is to provide banking services and products. The groups services include Telephone Transfer, Travelers Checks, Safe Deposit Boxes, Night Depository, Coupon Collection, Club Account, Certified Check, Cashier's Check and Account Research. The group operates from United States.

Primary SIC and add'l.: 6021

CIK No:

Officers: Robert C. Snyder/Dir., CEO, Pres. - Luzerne Bank, Robert Neher/Mgr. - Wilkes, Barre Office, Luzerne Bank, Peggy Walsh/Mgr. - Wyoming Office, Luzerne Bank, Jack Jones/Mgr. - Luzerne Bank, Pamela Bonomo/Mgr. - Dallas Office, Luzerne Bank, Mary Miller/Mgr. - Plains Office, Luzerne Bank, Maureen Sambo/Mgr. - Swoyersville Office, Luzerne Bank

Lydall Inc

1 Colonial Rd., Manchester, CT, 06040; *PH:* 1-860-646-1233; *Fax:* 1-860-646-4917; *http://* www.lydall.com; *Email:* info@lydall.com

General - Incorporation ... DE
Employees ... 1,400
Auditor ... PricewaterhouseCoopers LLP
Stk Agt ... American Stock Transfer & Trust Co.
Counsel ... NA
DUNS No. ... 00-113-9963

Stock- Price on:12/24/2007 ... $14.17
Stock Exchange ... NYSE
Ticker Symbol ... LDL
Outstanding Shares ... 16,420,000
E.P.S ... $0.54
Shareholders ... NA

Business: The group's principal activities are to develop and manufacture specialty engineered air and liquid filtration media, automotive thermal and acoustical barriers. The group operates in two segments: thermal/acoustical and filtration/separation. Thermal/acoustical segment includes thermal and acoustical barriers, organic and inorganic fiber composites and fiber and metal combinations. Filtration/separation segment includes air and liquid filtration products for industrial and consumer applications, vital fluids management systems for medial and biopharmaceutical applications. The group's other products and services include transport, distribution, warehousing business, electrical insulation, assorted specialty products and battery separator materials. In the first quarter of 2004, the group began the process of closing the columbus, Ohio operation and consolidating its operations into the other domestic automotive operations.

Primary SIC and add'l.: 5113 3086 3714 3496 3053

CIK No: 0000060977

Subsidiaries: Affinity Industries Asia LLC, Charter Medical, Ltd., Lydall Deutschland Holding GmbH, Lydall Distribution Services, Inc., Lydall Express, LLC, Lydall Filtration/Separation S.A.S., Lydall Filtration/Separation, Inc., Lydall Finance, Inc., Lydall France S.A.S., Lydall FSC, Limited, Lydall Gerhardi GmbH& Co. KG, Lydall Gerhardi Verwaltungs GmbH, Lydall Industrial Thermal Sales/Service, LLC, Lydall Industrial Thermal Solutions, Inc., Lydall International, Inc. 21 Subsidiaries included in the Index

Officers: David Freeman/Dir., CEO, Pres./$821,750.00, Thomas P. Smith/CFO, VP, Treasurer/$329,277.00, Mona G. Estey/VP - Human Resources, Mary A. Tremblay/VP, General Counsel, Daniel J. Collett/VP - Operations Finance, Bertrand Ploquin/MD/$460,827.00, John F. Tattersall/VP - Marketing, Sales, Green Island Operation/$370,041.00

Directors: David Freeman/Dir., CEO, Pres., Leslie W. Duffy/Chmn., Matthew T. Farrell/51/Dir., Kathleen Burdett/Dir., William D. Gurley/Dir., Lee A. Asseo/Dir., Carl S. Soderstrom/Dir., Suzanne Hammett/52/Dir.

Owners: Thomas P. Smith, Kathleen Burdett, Matthew T. Farrell, William D. Gurley, T. Rowe Price Associates, Inc./8.20%, Reich& Tang Asset Management, LLC/6.00%, Dimensional Fund Advisors LP/8.50%, AXA Assurances I.A.R.D. Mutuelle/5.10%, Carl S. Soderstrom, Royce& Associates, LLC/6.30%, John F. Tattersall, Insiders/4.80%, Bertrand Ploquin, David Freeman/1.00%, Suzanne Hammett *(18 Owners included in Index)*

Financial Data: ***Fiscal Year End:***12/31 ***Latest Annual Data:*** 12/31/2006

Year	Sales	Net Income
2006	$326,358,000	$10,228,000
2005	$306,485,000	$5,101,000
2004	$292,437,000	-$537,000

Curr. Assets:	$94,327,000	***Curr. Liab.:***	$43,717,000	***P/E Ratio:***	24.02
Plant, Equip.:	$103,469,000	***Total Liab.:***	$79,956,000	***Indic. Yr. Divd.:***	NA
Total Assets:	$241,173,000	***Net Worth:***	$161,217,000	***Debt/ Equity:***	NA

Lynch Interactive Corp

401 Theordore Fremd Ave., Rye, NY, 10580; *PH:* 1-914-921-8821; *http://* www.lynchcorp.com

General - Incorporation ... DE
Employees ... NA
Auditor ... Deloitte & Touche LLP
Stk Agt ... Mellon Investor Services LLC
Counsel ... NA
DUNS No. ... NA

Stock- Price on:12/24/2007 ... NA
Stock Exchange ... OTC
Ticker Symbol ... LICT
Outstanding Shares ... NA
E.P.S ... NA
Shareholders ... NA

Business: The group's principal activity is to provide multimedia operations. The multimedia operations of the group include telecommunications, television broadcasting and personal communication services. The telecommunication services of the group are divided into four major categories namely local network, network access, long distance services and other services like long distance and Internet services. The group provides licenses for personal communication and broadcasts. At Dec 31, 2003, Internet access customers totaled are 19,184 and 6,712 alarm customers.

Primary SIC and add'l.: 4899 4830 4810 6719

CIK No: 0001088771

Subsidiaries: Alpha Enterprises Limited, Bear Lake Communications, Inc., Belmont Telephone Company, Bretton Woods Telephone Company, Brighton Communications Corporation, Cache Valley Wireless, LC, Cassadaga Telephone Company, Central Scott Telephone Company ., Central Telecom Services, LLC, Central Utah Telephone, Inc., CLR Video, LLC, Comantel, Inc., CS Technologies, Inc., CST Communications Inc., Cuba City Telephone Exchange Company 70 Subsidiaries included in the Index

Financial Data: ***Fiscal Year End:***12/31 ***Latest Annual Data:*** 12/31/2004

Year	Sales	Net Income
2004	$87,794,000	$4,466,000
2003	$87,453,000	$7,390,000
2002	$86,304,000	$1,873,000

Curr. Assets:	$39,438,000	***Curr. Liab.:***	$35,546,000		
Plant, Equip.:	$120,328,000	***Total Liab.:***	$210,965,000	***Indic. Yr. Divd.:***	NA
Total Assets:	$257,080,000	***Net Worth:***	$34,572,000	***Debt/ Equity:***	NA

Lyndonbank VT

NA, NA, Na, AK, 11111; ; *http://* www.lyndonbank.com

General - Incorporation
Employees ... NA
Auditor ... NA
Stk Agt ... NA
Counsel ... NA
DUNS No. ... NA

Stock- Price on:12/24/2007 ... $19
Stock Exchange ... OTC
Ticker Symbol ... LYSB
Outstanding Shares ... NA
E.P.S ... NA
Shareholders ... NA

Business: The groups principal activity is to provide banking services. The services of the group include personal banking, business banking, mortgages, lending activities and online banking. The group operates from the United States.

Primary SIC and add'l.: 6799

CIK No:

Officers: Charles W. Bucknam/Dir., CEO, Pres., Robert J. Richardson/VP, Commercial Loan Officer, Jay E. Dudley/VP, Loan Review Officer, Mark C. Belanger/Assist. VP, Commercial Loan Officer, Tammi L. Stahler/Assist. VP, Loan Administration Mgr., Kara L. Coons/Assist. Treasurer, Branch Operations Mgr., Mary J. Marceau/Assist. Treasurer, Assist. Human Resources Mgr., Penny Johnson/Assist. Treasurer, Loan Officer, Jean Begnoche/Mortgage Contact - Franklin, Addison Counties, Patsy French/Contact - Lamoille County, Elaine A. Smith/Sr. VP, Sec., Treasurer, CFO, Compliance Officer, Eileen D. Beliveau/VP, Information Technology Officer, Bonnie B. Norway/VP, Retail Services Officer, Patrick J. Calecas/VP, Sr. Loan Officer, Larry D. Sharer/VP, Commercial Loan Officer, Marketing Officer *(19 Officers included in Index)*

Directors: Charles W. Bucknam/Dir., CEO, Pres., Charles C. Howe/Chmn., Val Bonk/Member - Northern Advisory Board, Dena L. Gray/Member - Northern Advisory Board, Judy Desorcie/Member - Northern Advisory Board, Jean Lamphere/Member - Northern Advisory Board, Cheryl Boissoneault/Member - Northern Advisory Board, Timothy Bates/Member - Agricultural Advisory Board, Vernon Hurd/Member - Agricultural Advisory Board, Kent Henderson/Member - Agricultural Advisory Board, David Allard/Dir., Constance Houston/Dir., Jacques Parent/Dir., Member - Agricultural Advisory Board, Jeffrey Poulin/Dir., David Stahler/Dir.

Lyondell Chemical Co

1221 McKinney St., Ste. 700, Houston, TX, 77010; *PH:* 1-713-652-7200; *http://* www.lyondell.com

General - Incorporation ... DE
Employees ... 10,905
Auditor ... PricewaterhouseCoopers LLP
Stk Agt ... American Stock Transfer & Trust Co.
Counsel ... NA
DUNS No. ... 19-412-3154

Stock- Price on:12/24/2007 ... $38.84
Stock Exchange ... NYSE
Ticker Symbol ... LYO
Outstanding Shares ... 252,890,000
E.P.S ... -$0.27
Shareholders ... NA

Business: The groups principle activity is to manufacture chemicals. The group also provides high sulfer cruid oil and fuel products. The group's products include Benzene, Ethylene and propylene. The group operates from United States.

Primary SIC and add'l.: 2999 2992 2869 2911

CIK No: 0000842635

Subsidiaries: Anatase Limited, Ashco, Inc., CUE Insurance Limited, DR Insurance Company, Equistar Bayport, LLC, Equistar Chemicals de Mexico, Inc., Equistar Chemicals, LP, Equistar Funding Corporation, Equistar Mont Belvieu Corporation, Equistar Olefins G.P., LLC, Equistar Olefins Offtake G.P., LLC, Equistar Olefins Offtake, LP, Equistar Polyproylene, LLC, Equistar Receivables II, LLC, Equistar Receivables, LLC 170 Subsidiaries included in the Index

Officers: Dan F. Smith/Chmn., CEO, Pres./$15,618,200.00, Charles C. Yang/VP, Chmn., Pres. - Lyondell, Asia Pacific, Karen A. Twitchell/VP, Treasurer, Dale Young/VP - Supply Chain, Douglas Pike/Investor Relations Officer, Charles W. Graham/VP, Exec. VP - Lyondell Asia Pacific, Allen C. Holmes/VP - Tax, Real Estate, Gerald O'Brien/VP, Deputy General Counsel, David J. Prilutski/VP, Pres. - Lyondell Europe, James W. Bayer/Sr. VP - Manufacturing, Health, Safety, Environment, Morris Gelb/COO, Exec. VP/$8,928,574.00, Kevin T. Denicola/CFO, Sr. VP/$3,549,717.00, Edward J. Dineen/Sr. VP - Chemicals, Polymers/$3,278,639.00, Bart De Jong/VP - Technology, Norman W. Phillips/Sr. VP - Fuels, Pipelines *(24 Officers included in Index)*

Directors: Dan F. Smith/Chmn., CEO, Pres., Susan K. Carter/Dir., Travis Engen/Dir., Danny W. Huff/Dir., Carol A. Anderson/Dir., Paul S. Halata/Dir., David J. Lesar/Dir., Daniel J. Murphy/Dir., David J.P. Meachin/Dir., William R. Spivey/Dir., Stephen I. Chazen/Dir.

Owners: Dan F. Smith, Travis Engen, Danny W. Huff, Stephen I. Chazen, William R. Spivey, Carol A. Anderson, Occidental Petroleum Corporation/8.50%, Barclays Global Investors, NA and certain affiliates/9.64%, David J.P. Meachin, Edward J. Dineen, Kevin T. DeNicola, Insiders, David J. Lesar, Morris Gelb, Paul S. Halata *(20 Owners included in Index)*

Financial Data: ***Fiscal Year End:***12/31 ***Latest Annual Data:*** 12/31/2006

Year	Sales	Net Income
2006	$22,228,000,000	$186,000,000
2005	$18,606,000,000	$531,000,000
2004	$5,968,000,000	$54,000,000

Curr. Assets:	$5,146,000,000	***Curr. Liab.:***	$3,207,000,000		
Plant, Equip.:	$9,191,000,000	***Total Liab.:***	$14,484,000,000	***Indic. Yr. Divd.:***	$0.900
Total Assets:	$17,846,000,000	***Net Worth:***	$3,188,000,000	***Debt/ Equity:***	2.4399

Lyons Bancorp Inc

35 William St., Lyons, NY, 14489; *PH:* 1-315-946-4871; *Fax:* 1-315-946-6215; *http://* www.lyonsbancorp.com

General - Incorporation ... NY
Employees ... NA
Auditor ... NA
Stk Agt ... NA
Counsel ... NA
DUNS No. ... NA

Stock- Price on:12/24/2007 ... $33.1
Stock Exchange ... OTC
Ticker Symbol ... LYBC
Outstanding Shares ... NA
E.P.S ... NA
Shareholders ... NA

Business: The group operates through its subsdiary whose principle activity is to provide commercial banking and real estate services. The group operates from United States.

Primary SIC and add'l.: 6712 6021

CIK No: 0000816332

Officers: Robert A. Schick/Dir., CEO, Pres., Carol A. Snook/Dir. - Corporate, Executive Sec.

Directors: Robert A. Schick/Dir., CEO, Pres., David J. Breen/Dir., Clair J. Britt/Dir., Andrew F. Fredericksen/Dir., Theodore J. Marshall/Dir., Thomas L. Kime/Dir., James A. Homburger/Dir., Dale H. Hemminger/Dir., James E. Santelli/Dir., John J. Werner/Dir., Carol A. Snook/Dir. - Corporate, Executive Sec.

Financial Data: Fiscal Year End:NA Latest Annual Data: 12/31/2002

Year	Sales	Net Income
2002	$10,978,000	$1,370,000
2001	$10,051,000	$979,000
2000	$9,000,000	$807,000

Curr. Assets:	$6,733,000	**Curr. Liab.:**	$164,608,000		
Plant, Equip.:	$2,928,000	**Total Liab.:**	$175,644,000	**Indic. Yr. Divd.:**	NA
Total Assets:	$187,723,000	**Net Worth:**	$12,079,000	**Debt/ Equity:**	0.4943

Lyris Inc

Formerly: JL Halsey Corp

103 Foulk Rd. , Ste. 205q, Wilmington, DE, 19803; *PH:* 1-302-691-6189; *http://* www.jlhalsey.com

General - Incorporation	DE	**Stock** - Price on:12/24/2007	$0.86
Employees	113	Stock Exchange	NA
Auditor	Burr, Pilger & Mayer, LLP	Ticker Symbol	NA
Stk Agt	Mailengine	Outstanding Shares	98,330,000
Counsel	NA	E.P.S	$0.00
DUNS No.	04-840-9353	Shareholders	NA

Business: The group's principle activities are to resolve its outstanding liabilities and realize its remaining assets. The group provided physical rehabilitation services and employee services prior to the sale of its three operating segments: long-term care services, outpatient services and employee services. Long-term care services included rehabilitation and healthcare consulting services on a contract basis to health care institutions. Outpatient services included orthotic, prosthetic, physical rehabilitation and occupational health rehabilitation services. Employee services included integrated outsourcing solutions to human resource issues such as payroll management, workers' compensation, risk management, benefits administration, unemployment services and human resource consulting services for small and medium-sized businesses. The group's total revenue for year 2007 was 39.01 millions of USD.

Primary SIC and add'l.: 9999

CIK No: 0001166220

Subsidiaries: Admiral Holdings, Inc., Admiral Management Company, ClickTracks Analytics, Inc., Commodore Resources, Inc., Hot Banana Software, Inc., Lyris Technologies, Inc., NC Holdings, Inc., Uptilt, Inc.

Officers: Richard McDonald/Investor Relations Officer, Neal Rosen/Investor Relations Officer, Peter Biro/COO, Loren T. McDonald/VP - Corporate Communications, Luis A. Rivera/Dir., COO, Joseph Lambert/CFO, Robb Wilson/VP - Technology, Sean Ryan/VP - Engineering, Krista Lariviere/GM - Hot Banana, Jason Han/VP - Sales, Sylvie Moreau/VP - Business Development, Dave Dabbah/Sr. Dir. - Marketing, Anne Gerow/Dir. - Operations

Directors: William T. Comfort/Chmn., Luis A. Rivera/Dir., COO, Andrew Richard Blair/Dir., Nicolas De Santis Cuadra/Dir., James A. Urry/Dir.

Owners: Andrew Richard Blair/1.00%, Insiders/48.70%, Loren McDonald, Peter Biro, David R. Burt/8.30%, Nicolas De Santis Cuadra, Jason Han, Joseph Lambert, LDN Stuyvie Partnership/32.80%, William T. Comfort/37.20%, Luis A. Rivera/2.40%, Robb Wilson

Financial Data: Fiscal Year End:06/30 Latest Annual Data: 6/30/2006

Year	Sales	Net Income
2006	$24,353,000	$2,566,000
2005	$2,207,000	-$230,000
2004	NA	$2,755,000

Curr. Assets:	$7,109,000	**Curr. Liab.:**	$15,870,000		
Plant, Equip.:	$1,675,000	**Total Liab.:**	$27,653,000	**Indic. Yr. Divd.:**	NA
Total Assets:	$57,719,000	**Net Worth:**	$30,066,000	**Debt/ Equity:**	0.3258

M & F Worldwide Corp

35 E 62nd St., New York, NY, 10021; *PH:* 1-212-572-8600; *Fax:* 1-212-572-8650; *http://* www.mandfworldwide.com

General - Incorporation	DE	**Stock** - Price on:12/24/2007	$67.62
Employees	212	Stock Exchange	NYSE
Auditor	Ernst & Young LLP	Ticker Symbol	MFW
Stk Agt	American Stock Transfer & Trust Co.	Outstanding Shares	20,730,000
Counsel	NA	E.P.S	-$0.44
DUNS No.	88-398-3413	Shareholders	NA

Business: The group's principal activity is to produce licorice flavors for sale to the tobacco, spice, pharmaceutical and health food industries. The licorice flavours are used by flavouring and moistening agents in the manufacture of American blend cigarettes, moist snuff, chewing tobacco and pipe tobacco. The group sells licorice to worldwide confectioners, food processors and pharmaceutical manufacturers for use as flavoring or masking agents. The group licorice rootresidue as garden mulch under the name right dress. The group manufactures and sells other flavor products and plant products which include natural roots, spices and botanicals.

Primary SIC and add'l.: 3861 2087 7359 7819

CIK No: 0000945235

Subsidiaries: B(2)Direct, Inc., Checks in the Mail, Inc., Clarke American Checks, Inc., Clarke American Corp., Concord Pacific Corporation (50% owned), Core Skills Inc., EVD Holdings Inc., EVD Holdings S.A.S., Extraits Vegetaux Et Derives, S.A.S., Flavors Holdings, Inc., Jensen Kelly Corporation, Mafco Shanghai Corporation, Mafco Weihai Green Industry of Science and Technology Co. Ltd, Mafco Worldwide Corporation, PCT International Holdings, Inc. 20 Subsidiaries included in the Index

Officers: Howard Gittis/74/Chmn., CEO, Pres., Stephen G. Taub/Dir., Pres., CEO - Mafco Worldwide/$1,964,709.00, Jeffrey D. Heggedahl/Pres., CEO - Scantron, John E. Omalley/Pres., CEO - Harland Financial Solutions, Christine M. Taylor/Sr. VP - Corporate Communications, Barry F. Schwartz/Exec. VP, General Counsel, Paul G. Savas/CFO, Exec. VP

Directors: Howard Gittis/74/Chmn., CEO, Pres., Stephen G. Taub/Dir., Pres., CEO - Mafco Worldwide, Bruce Slovin/Dir., Paul M. Meister/Dir., Ronald O. Perelman/Dir., Philip E. Beekman/Dir., Jaymie A. Durnan/Dir., Theo W. Folz/Dir., Charles T. Dawson/Dir., Martha L. Byorum/Dir., Viet D. Dinh/Dir., Carl B. Webb/Dir.

Owners: Dimensional Fund Advisors Inc./8.38%, Bay Harbour Management, L.C./5.10%, Mafco Consolidated Group Inc./37.10%, Ronald O. Perelman, Stephen G. Taub/1.90%, Bruce Slovin, Carl Webb, Paul M. Meister, Philip E. Beekman, Theo W. Folz, Howard Gittis, Jaymie A. Durnan, Barry F. Schwartz, Insiders/41.51%

Financial Data: Fiscal Year End:12/31 Latest Annual Data: 12/31/2006

Year	Sales	Net Income
2006	$722,000,000	$36,200,000
2005	$121,400,000	$24,000,000
2004	$93,400,000	$25,200,000

Curr. Assets:	$219,600,000	**Curr. Liab.:**	$129,900,000		
Plant, Equip.:	$106,100,000	**Total Liab.:**	$1,049,400,000	**Indic. Yr. Divd.:**	NA
Total Assets:	$1,459,900,000	**Net Worth:**	$410,500,000	**Debt/ Equity:**	1.5712

M 2003 Plc

8 Salisbury Sq., London, EC4Y 8BB;

General - Incorporation	England and Wales	**Stock** - Price on:12/24/2007	NA
Employees	NA	Stock Exchange	OTC
Auditor	Deloitte & Touche LLP	Ticker Symbol	MTWOY
Stk Agt	NA	Outstanding Shares	NA
Counsel	NA	E.P.S	NA
DUNS No.	NA	Shareholders	NA

Business: The groups principal activities include developing, manufacturing, selling and supporting optical networks, transmission systems and network management software and providing support services to the communications industry. The group operates through three segments namely network equipment, network services and other. The group operates from the United States, Europe, Middle East and Africa, Central and Latin America, and the Asia Pacific.

Primary SIC and add'l.: 3661

CIK No: 0001122133

Financial Data: Fiscal Year End:03/31 Latest Annual Data: 03/31/2006

Year	Sales	Net Income
2006	NA	-$448,000
2005	NA	-$2,039,000
2004	$309,000,000	$4,188,000,000

Curr. Assets:	$13,298,000	**Curr. Liab.:**	$162,000	**P/E Ratio:**	70.00
Plant, Equip.:	NA	**Total Liab.:**	$162,000	**Indic. Yr. Divd.:**	NA
Total Assets:	$13,298,000	**Net Worth:**	$13,136,000	**Debt/ Equity:**	NA

M&F Bancorp Inc

2634 Durham Chapel Hill Blvd., Durham, NC, 27707; *PH:* 1-919-683-1521; *Fax:* 1-919-687-7807; *http://* www.mfbonline.com

General - Incorporation	NC	**Stock** - Price on:12/24/2007	$9.25
Employees	87	Stock Exchange	OTC
Auditor	Mcgladrey & Pullen, LLP	Ticker Symbol	MFBP
Stk Agt	American Stock Transfer & Trust Co.	Outstanding Shares	1,690,000
Counsel	NA	E.P.S	$0.76
DUNS No.	NA	Shareholders	NA

Business: The group operates through its subsidiary whose principle activity is to provide banking services. The Services of the group include lending activities, deposits, borrowing and providing loans. The group operates from the United States.

Primary SIC and add'l.: 6022 6712

CIK No: 0001094738

Subsidiaries: Mechanics and Farmers Bank

Officers: Jonathan Sears Woodall/Sr. VP, CFO/$123,067.00, Valerie Quiett/Assist., Corp. Sec., E. Elaine Small/VP, Assist. Corp. Sec., Soberina Traywick/Sec. - Raleigh, City Advisory Boards, Bruce Osterhout/Sec. - Charlotte, Genevia Gee Fulbright/Dir., VP - Fulbright, Fulbright, CPA, PA, Queron Smith/Member - City Advisory Boards, Sec.

Directors: James A. Stewart/Chmn., Connie J. White/Vice Chmn., Lem Long/Chmn. - Charlotte, Walter S. Tucker/Member - City Advisory Boards, Charlotte, Jewett L. Walker/Member - City Advisory Boards, Charlotte, Anthony V. Hunt/Member - City Advisory Boards, Charlotte, Marie P. Tann/Member - City Advisory Boards, Charlotte, Terrance A. Hawkins/Member - City Advisory Boards, Charlotte, Kim D. Saunders/Dir. - M&F Bank, Soberina Traywick/Sec. - Raleigh, City Advisory Boards, Dexter V. Perry/Member - City Advisory Boards, Raleigh, Martel A. Perry/Member - City Advisory Boards, Raleigh, Paul L. Anderson/Member - City Advisory Boards, Raleigh, Helen Calloway/Member - City Advisory Boards, Raleigh, Portia H. Brandon/Member - City Advisory Boards, Raleigh (29 Directors included in Index)

Owners: Aaron L. Spaulding/3.50%, Vivian M. Sansom/10.73%, Ronald Wiley, J. C. Scarborough, Genevia Gee Fulbright, Joseph M. Sansom, Selena W. Wheeler/9.68%, Jonathan Sears Woodall, Connie J. White, Michael L. Lawrence, Willie T. Closs, Cedric L. Russell, Insiders/6.48%, James A. Stewart/1.55%, Maceo K. Sloan (16 Owners included in Index)

Financial Data: Fiscal Year End:12/31 Latest Annual Data: 12/31/2006

Year	Sales	Net Income
2006	$18,073,000	$1,786,000
2005	$16,538,000	$772,000
2004	$15,396,000	$1,139,000

Curr. Assets:	$39,035,000	**Curr. Liab.:**	$228,430,000	**P/E Ratio:**	10.28
Plant, Equip.:	$5,880,000	**Total Liab.:**	$246,246,000	**Indic. Yr. Divd.:**	$0.200
Total Assets:	$268,008,000	**Net Worth:**	$21,762,000	**Debt/ Equity:**	0.8107

M&T Bank Corp

1 M&T Plz., Buffalo, NY, 14203; *PH:* 1-716-842-4470; *Fax:* 1-716-842-5839; *http://* www.mandtbank.com; *Email:* ir@mandtbank.com

General - Incorporation .... NY
Employees 11,904
Auditor .... PricewaterhouseCoopers LLP
Stk Agt .... Registrar & Transfer Co
Counsel .... NA
DUNS No. 07-279-6022

Stock- Price on:12/24/2007 .... $108.52
Stock Exchange .... NYSE
Ticker Symbol .... MTD
Outstanding Shares 108,240,000
E.P.S $7.22
Shareholders .... NA

Business: The group's principle activity is to provide commercial and retail banking services. The groups services include trust, mortgage banking, asset management, insurance and other financial services. The group provides commercial and residential mortgage loans secured by income producing properties. The group operates from United States.

Primary SIC and add'l.: 6021 6712

CIK No: 0000036270

Subsidiaries: M&T Bank, National Association (M&T Bank, N.A.).

Officers: Robert G. Wilmers/Chmn., CEO/$1,374,972.00, Atwood Collins/Exec. VP/$1,958,190.00, James J. Beardi/Exec. VP, Gregory L. Ford/Exec. VP, Brian E. Hickey/Exec. VP, Rene F. Jones/CFO, Exec. VP, Adam C. Kugler/Exec. VP, Treasurer, Kevin J. Pearson/Exec. VP, Kathleen M. Dewyea/Assist. VP, Amie M. Lograsso/Shareholder Relations Administrator, Melinda R. Rich/Dir. - Manufacturers, Traders Trust Company, Emerson L. Brumback/Exec. VP, Mark J. Czarnecki/Dir., Pres./$1,698,902.00, Stephen J. Braunscheidel/Exec. VP, Robert J. Bojdak/Exec. VP, Chief Credit Officer *(47 Officers included in Index)*

Directors: Robert G. Wilmers/Chmn., CEO, Robert E. Sadler/Vice Chmn., Jorge G. Pereira/Vice Chmn., Michael P. Pinto/Vice Chmn., Stephen G. Sheetz/Dir., Daniel R. Hawbaker/Dir., Herbert L. Washington/Dir., Angela C. Bontempo/Dir., Richard G. King/Dir., Robert J. Bennett/Dir., Eugene J. Sheehy/Dir., Michael D. Buckley/Dir., Reginald B. Newman/Dir., Brent D. Baird/Dir., Robert T. Brady/Dir. *(20 Directors included in Index)*

Owners: R.I. REM Investments S.A./4.12%, St. Simon Charitable, Roche Foundation, Berkshire Hathaway Inc./6.12%, West Ferry Foundation, Robert G. Wilmers/4.62%, Elisabeth Roche Wilmers, Interlaken Foundation

Financial Data: *Fiscal Year End:*12/31 *Latest Annual Data:* 12/31/2006

Year	Sales	Net Income
2006	$4,359,945,000	$839,189,000
2005	$3,766,545,000	$782,183,000
2004	$3,241,701,000	$722,521,000

Curr. Assets:	$4,021,868,000	**Curr. Liab.:**	$43,893,069,000	**P/E Ratio:**	15.16
Plant, Equip.:	$335,008,000	**Total Liab.:**	$50,783,810,000	**Indic. Yr. Divd.:**	$2.800
Total Assets:	$57,064,905,000	**Net Worth:**	$6,281,095,000	**Debt/ Equity:**	NA

M-Wave Inc

11533 Franklin Ave, Franklin Park, IL, 60106; *PH:* 1-630-562-5550; *http://* www.mwav.com

General - Incorporation .... DE
Employees 21
Auditor .... McGladrey & Pullen LLP
Stk Agt..... Computershare Investor Services LLC
Counsel...... Sonnenschein Nath & Rosenthal LLP
DUNS No. 78-727-6575

Stock- Price on:12/24/2007 .... $2.96
Stock Exchange .... NDQ
Ticker Symbol .... NA
Outstanding Shares 1,790,000
E.P.S .... -$1.13
Shareholders .... NA

Business: The group is a value-added service provider of high performance printed circuit boards used in a variety of digital and high frequency applications. The group also produces customer specified bonded assemblies consisting of a printed circuit board bonded in some manner to a metal carrier or pallet and microwave systems. The printed circuit boards and bonded assemblies are used in printed circuit boards and bonded assemblies are used in a variety of telecommunications and industrial electronic applications. The group also provides services to broadband access suppliers. The customers of the group are westell, celestica and remec.

Primary SIC and add'l.: 3679 3672

CIK No: 0000883842

Subsidiaries: Enhance Interactive, Inc.

Officers: Jim Mayer/57/Interim CEO, Joseph A. Turek/50/Chmn., COO, Pres., Jeff Figlewicz/CFO, Robert Duke/Pres. - EMG Division

Directors: Joseph A. Turek/50/Chmn., COO, Pres., Gary L. Castagna/45/Dir., Bruce K. Nelson/53/Dir., Glenn A. Norem/55/Dir.

Owners: Jeff Figlewicz/1.38%, Glenn Norem/2.02%, Joseph A. Turek/21.77%, Jim Mayer/5.50%, Asset Managers International Limited/10.93%, Gary L. Castagna/2.42%, Insiders/35.47%, M.A.G. Capital, LLC/19.29%, Bruce Nelson/2.37%

Financial Data: *Fiscal Year End:*12/31 *Latest Annual Data:* 12/31/2006

Year	Sales	Net Income
2006	$9,762,000	-$3,217,000
2005	$16,605,000	-$5,409,000
2004	$17,462,000	-$335,000

Curr. Assets:	$4,256,000	**Curr. Liab.:**	$1,785,000		
Plant, Equip.:	$289,000	**Total Liab.:**	$1,785,000	**Indic. Yr. Divd.:**	NA
Total Assets:	$4,545,000	**Net Worth:**	$2,760,000	**Debt/ Equity:**	NA

M-WISE Inc

3 Sapir St., Hertzelya, 46733; ; *http://* www.m-wise.com; *Email:* sales@m-wise.com

General - Incorporation .... DE
Employees .... NA
Auditor .... SF Partnership, LLP
Stk Agt............ Manhattan Transfer Registrar Co
Counsel .... NA
DUNS No. .... NA

Stock- Price on:12/24/2007 .... $0.105
Stock Exchange .... OTC
Ticker Symbol .... MWIS
Outstanding Shares .... NA
E.P.S .... NA
Shareholders .... NA

Business: The groups principle activities include developing, manufacturing, marketing and supporting software and hardware based content and service delivery platform. Products of the group include servers, network switches and digital storage devices. The group operates from America, Europe and Far East. Of the total sales in the year 2006, America accounted for 75%, Europe 17% and Far East 8%. The group's quarterly revenue for Sep '07 was 0.54 millions of USD.

Primary SIC and add'l.: 4812

CIK No: 0001242047

Subsidiaries: m-Wise Ltd, m-Wise s.a.r.l, m-Wise S.r.l, m-Wise Spain, S.L

Officers: Mati Broudo/48/Co - Founder, CEO, Asaf Lewin/CTO, Zach Sivan/VP - Sales, Marketing, Gabriel Kabazo/CFO

Directors: Mati Broudo/48/Co - Founder, CEO, Shay Ben-Asulin/Co - Founder, Chmn.

Owners: DEP Technology Holdings Ltd./8.50%, Inter-content Development for the Internet Ltd./6.20%, Mordechai Broudo/13.00%, Syntek capital AG, Insiders/34.10%, Miretzky Holdings Ltd./17.60%, Gabriel Kabazo/3.70%, Shay Ben-Asulin/13.70%, Asaf Lewin/3.70%

Financial Data: *Fiscal Year End:*12/31 *Latest Annual Data:* 12/31/2006

Year	Sales	Net Income
2006	$2,230,000	-$197,000
2005	$2,168,000	-$645,000
2004	$1,361,000	-$513,000

Curr. Assets:	$647,000	**Curr. Liab.:**	$1,389,000		
Plant, Equip.:	$111,000	**Total Liab.:**	$1,425,000	**Indic. Yr. Divd.:**	NA
Total Assets:	$790,000	**Net Worth:**	-$635,000	**Debt/ Equity:**	NA

M.D.C Holdings Inc

4350 S Monaco St., Denver, CO, 80237; *PH:* 1-303-773-1100; *Fax:* 1-720-977-3204; *http://* www.richmondamerican.com; *Email:* communications@mdch.com

General - Incorporation .... DE
Employees 3,200
Auditor .... Ernst & Young LLP
Stk Agt .... Continental Stock Transfer & Trust Co
Counsel .... NA
DUNS No. 06-970-2181

Stock- Price on:12/24/2007 .... $50.23
Stock Exchange .... NYSE
Ticker Symbol .... MDC
Outstanding Shares 45,720,000
E.P.S .... -$3.49
Shareholders .... NA

Business: The group's principle activities include owning, managing, building and sell homes. The group also originates mortgage loans and provides insurance and title agency services. The groups homebuilding division designs, builds and markets single-family homes. The financial services provide mortgage loans primarily to the group's homebuyers. The group operates from United States.

Primary SIC and add'l.: 6162 6163 1521 1522

CIK No: 0000773141

Subsidiaries: Aht Reinsurance, Inc., Allegiant Insurance Company, Inc., A Risk Retention Group, American Home Insurance Agency, Inc, American Home Title And Escrow Company, Asfc-w, Inc., Asw Finance Company, Enerwest, Inc., Financial Asset Management Corporation, Homeamerican Mortgage Corporation, Lion Insurance Company, Lion Warranty Corporation, M.d.c. Acceptance Corporation, M.d.c. Home Finance Corporation, M.d.c. Land Corporation, M.d.c. Residual Holdings, Inc. 48 Subsidiaries included in the Index

Officers: Larry A. Mizel/Chmn., CEO/$15,343,630.00, Paris G. Reece/CFO, Exec. VP/$2,825,792.00, Jody Longfellow/Media Mgr., Michael Touff/Sr. VP, General Counsel/$1,366,996.00, David D. Mandarich/Dir., COO, Pres./$14,867,590.00, Rob Hathaway/Pres. - Home American Mortgage Corporation, Patrick Rice/Pres. - American Home Title, Escrow, Joelle Lipski-Rockwood/Dir. - National Marketing, Communications, John J. Heaney/Sr. VP, Treasurer, Kirby Slunaker/CIO, VP, Shelley Casagrande/VP - Internal Audit, James L. Yates/VP - Division Finance, Marilyn Gardner/VP - National Sales, Joseph H. Fretz/Sec., Corporate Counsel, Doug Moran/Regional Pres. - Florida Region *(32 Officers included in Index)*

Directors: Larry A. Mizel/Chmn., CEO, Michael A. Berman/Dir., David E. Blackford/Dir., Steven J. Borick/Dir., David D. Mandarich/Dir., COO, Pres., William B. Kemper/Dir., Gilbert Goldstein/Dir., Herbert T. Buchwald/Dir.

Owners: Michael Touff, Paris G. Reece/1.00%, Insiders/26.40%, Franklin Resources, Inc./7.80%, Ziff Asset Management, L.P./9.40%, Greenlight Capital, L.L.C. and affiliates/9.70%

Financial Data: *Fiscal Year End:*12/31 *Latest Annual Data:* 12/31/2006

Year	Sales	Net Income
2006	$4,801,742,000	$214,253,000
2005	$4,884,160,000	$505,723,000
2004	$4,009,072,000	$391,165,000

Curr. Assets:	$3,408,353,000	**Curr. Liab.:**	$619,144,000		
Plant, Equip.:	$44,606,000	**Total Liab.:**	$1,747,993,000	**Indic. Yr. Divd.:**	$1.000
Total Assets:	$3,909,875,000	**Net Worth:**	$2,161,882,000	**Debt/ Equity:**	0.5213

M/I Homes Inc

3 Eon Oval, Ste. 500, Columbus, OH, 43219; *PH:* 1-614-418-8000; *Fax:* 1-614-418-8080; *http://* www.mihomes.com; *Email:* cgates@mihomes.com

General - Incorporation .... OH
Employees 1,018
Auditor .... Deloitte & Touche LLP
Stk Agt .... Computershare Trust Co
Counsel .... NA
DUNS No. 07-164-9743

Stock- Price on:12/24/2007 .... $27.02
Stock Exchange .... NYSE
Ticker Symbol .... MHO
Outstanding Shares 14,040,000
E.P.S .... -$2.6
Shareholders .... NA

Business: The group's principal activity is to construct and sell single family homes. The group operates under two product segments: homebuilding and financial services. Homebuilding operations include the development and sale of land and the construction and sale of single-family attached and detached homes in columbus and cincinnati, Ohio; tampa, orlando and palm beach county, Florida; charlotte and raleigh, North Carolina; indianapolis, Indiana; and the Virginia and Maryland suburbs of Washington, d.c. The financial services segment provides mortgage financing services through m/i financial corp and title-related services through affiliated entities.

Primary SIC and add'l.: 6162 1521

CIK No: 0000799292

Subsidiaries: Etowah, LLC, K-Tampa, LLC, M/I Financial Corp, M/I Homes First Indiana LLC, M/I Homes of Central Ohio, LLC, M/I Homes of Charlotte, M/I Homes of Cincinnati, LLC, M/I Homes of DC, LLC, M/I Homes of Florida, LLC, M/I Homes of Lake County, LLC, M/I Homes of Raleigh, LLC, M/I Homes of Tampa, LLC, M/I Homes of West Palm Beach, LLC, M/I Homes Second Indiana LLC, M/I Homes Service Corp 26 Subsidiaries included in the Index

Officers: Robert H. Schottenstein/55/Chmn., CEO, Pres./$2,092,897.00, Thomas J. Mason/50/Dir., Sec./$482,746.00, Phillip G. Creek/Investor Relations Officer/$900,546.00, Dinah King/Sales Inquiries, Charlotte, Jodi Kern/Sales Inquiries, Cincinnati, Jill Cuthbert/Sales Inquiries, Columbus, Wendi Smith/Sales Inquiries, Indianapolis, Kathy Pritchard/Sales Inquiries, Maryland, Delaware, Erin Baker/Sales Inquiries, Orlando, Mike Lindsay/Sales Inquiries, Raleigh, Kristin Akrouche/Sales Inquiries, Showcase Homes, Pamela Galati/Sales Inquiries, Tampa, Karen Katnich/Sales Inquiries, Virginia, Suzanne Bates/Sales Inquiries, West Palm Beach, Ann Marie Hunker/Investor Relations Officer

Directors: Robert H. Schottenstein/55/Chmn., CEO, Pres., Thomas J. Mason/50/Dir., Sec., Jeffrey H. Miro/65/Dir., Thomas D. Igoe/76/Dir., Friedrich K.M. Bohm/66/Dir., Joseph A. Alutto/66/Dir., Norman L. Traeger/68/Dir., Yvette Mcgee Brown/46/Dir.

Owners: Joseph A. Alutto, Phillip G. Creek, Robert H. Schottenstein/6.20%, Barclays Global Investors, NA./5.30%, Dimensional Fund Advisors LP/8.00%, Jeffrey H. Miro, Yvette McGee Brown, Norman L. Traeger, Franklin Resources, Inc./10.70%, Friedrich K. M. Bhm, Thomas J. Mason, Steven Schottenstein/6.60%, Jeffrey L. Gendell/6.40%, Basswood Capital Management, LLC/6.10%, Insiders/7.40% *(18 Owners included in Index)*

Financial Data: Fiscal Year End:12/31 **Latest Annual Data:** 12/31/2006

Year	Sales	Net Income
2006	$1,359,293,000	$38,875,000
2005	$1,347,646,000	$100,785,000
2004	$1,174,635,000	$91,534,000

Curr. Assets:	$1,196,074,000	**Curr. Liab.:**	$123,391,000		
Plant, Equip.:	$36,258,000	**Total Liab.:**	$860,027,000	**Indic. Yr. Divd.:**	$0.100
Total Assets:	$1,477,079,000	**Net Worth:**	$617,052,000	**Debt/ Equity:**	0.7179

M45 Mining Resources Inc

Formerly: Quantitative Methods Corp
1212 Redpath Cres., Montreal, QC, H3G-2K1; **PH:** 1-514-288-8494

General - Incorporation	NV	Stock - Price on:12/24/2007	NA
Employees	NA	Stock Exchange	NA
Auditor Child, Van Wagoner & Bradshaw, PLLC		Ticker Symbol	NA
Stk Agt	National Stock Transfer, Inc.	Outstanding Shares	NA
Counsel	NA	E.P.S.	NA
DUNS No.	NA	Shareholders	NA

Business: The groups principal activity is the development and potential marketing of micromanagement hardware and software solutions in vehicle fleet operation management. In the year 2005, the group acquired Roadvision Technologies Inc. The group operates from the United States.

Primary SIC and add'l.: 6770

CIK No: 0000894561

Subsidiaries: Softguard Enterprises Inc

Officers: Andrea M. Cortellazzi/53/Dir., CEO, Craig A. Perry/Dir., Pres., Gilles Ouellette/Dir., Sec., Treasurer, Principal Financial Officer

Directors: Andrea M. Cortellazzi/53/Dir., CEO, Helga Leuthe/Dir., Pierre C. Miron/Dir., Michel Roy/Dir., Craig A. Perry/Dir., Pres., Gilles Ouellette/Dir., Sec., Treasurer, Principal Financial Officer

Owners: MacGuyver Enterprises Ltd., E.A.S. Mcquiston Holdings Ltd., 55566779, Euro Holdings, Inc./46.90%, Insiders/56.00%, Prestige International Growth Fund Ltd.

Financial Data: Fiscal Year End:03/31 **Latest Annual Data:** 12/31/2004

Year	Sales	Net Income
2004	NA	-$20,000
2003	NA	-$15,000

Curr. Assets:	$110,000	**Curr. Liab.:**	$227,000		
Plant, Equip.:	$1,000	**Total Liab.:**	$227,000	**Indic. Yr. Divd.:**	NA
Total Assets:	$111,000	**Net Worth:**	-$116,000	**Debt/ Equity:**	NA

Mac Gray Corp

404 Wyman St., Ste. 400, Waltham, MA, 02451; **PH:** 1-781-487-7600; **Fax:** 1-781-487-7601; http:// www.mac-gray.com

General - Incorporation	DE	Stock - Price on:12/24/2007	$15
Employees	737	Stock Exchange	NYSE
Auditor	PricewaterhouseCoopers LLP	Ticker Symbol	TUC
Stk Agt	American Stock Transfer & Trust CO.	Outstanding Shares	13,180,000
Counsel	NA	E.P.S.	$0.56
DUNS No.	01-930-0060	Shareholders	NA

Business: The group's principal activities are to provide card and coin-operated laundry services to multiple housing facilities such as apartment buildings, colleges and universities and public housing complexes. The group operates in two business segments: laundry and reprographics and microfridge(R) services. Laundry and reprographics operates laundry rooms, under long-term leases & also provides card and coin-operated reprographics equipment. The microfridge(R) services segment offers sale and rental of a family of patented combination refrigerator, freezer, microwave ovens to colleges, universities, military bases, the hotel and motel market. The group owns and operates card and coin-operated washers and dryers in more than 34,000 multiple housing laundry rooms located in 27 states. The group operates in the United States of America.

Primary SIC and add'l.: 7215 5078

CIK No: 0001038280

Officers: Stewart Gray MacDonald/Chmn., CEO/$1,140,505.00, Neil F. MacLellan/COO, Exec. VP/$602,845.00, Michael J. Shea/Exec. VP, CFO, Treasurer, Sec./$687,178.00, Robert J. Tuttle/55/CIO, CTO/$318,995.00, Linda Serafini/VP, General Counsel, Sec., Todd O. Burger/Exec. VP - Operations

Directors: Stewart Gray MacDonald/Chmn., CEO, Jerry A. Schiller/Dir., Thomas E. Bullock/Dir., David W. Bryan/Dir., Edward F. McCauley/Dir., Christopher T. Jenney/Dir., William F. Meagher/Dir., Mary Ann Tocio/Dir.

Owners: Stewart G. MacDonald, Neil F. MacLellan, Insiders, Sandra E. MacDonald, Polaris Capital Management, Inc., Thomas E. Bullock, Daniel W. MacDonald, Dimensional Fund Advisors LP, Edward F. McCauley, Todd O. Burger, Insiders, R. Robert Woodburn, Fairview Capital Investment Management, Robert J. Tuttle, Cynthia V. Doggett *(25 Owners included in Index)*

Financial Data: Fiscal Year End:12/31 **Latest Annual Data:** 12/31/2006

Year	Sales	Net Income
2006	$279,327,000	$856,000
2005	$260,623,000	$12,052,000
2004	$182,694,000	$5,263,000

Curr. Assets:	$42,319,000	**Curr. Liab.:**	$40,255,000	**P/E Ratio:**	500.00
Plant, Equip.:	$118,654,000	**Total Liab.:**	$247,364,000	**Indic. Yr. Divd.:**	NA
Total Assets:	$339,004,000	**Net Worth:**	$91,640,000	**Debt/ Equity:**	1.8642

Macatawa Bank Corp

10753 Macatawa Dr., Holland, MI, 49424; **PH:** 1-616-820-1444; **Fax:** 1-616-494-7644; http:// www.macatawabank.com

General - Incorporation	MI	Stock - Price on:12/24/2007	$15.74
Employees	357	Stock Exchange	NDQ
Auditor	Grant Thornton, LLP	Ticker Symbol	MCBC
Stk Agt	Registrar & Transfer Co	Outstanding Shares	17,230,000
Counsel	NA	E.P.S.	$1.05
DUNS No.	96-953-5152	Shareholders	NA

Business: The group's principal activity is to provide banking services. The group is a holding company with the operations being conducted by two wholly owned subsidiaries, macatawa bank and grand bank. It offers checking and savings accounts, safe deposit boxes, travelers checks, money orders, trust services and provision of real estate commercial and residential loans, mortgage loans and consumer loans. The operations are carried out through a network of 20 full service branches located in ottawa county, northern allegan county and southwestern kent county in Michigan.

Primary SIC and add'l.: 6022 6712

CIK No: 0001053584

Subsidiaries: Macatawa Bank, Macatawa Bank Mortgage Company, Macatawa Investment Services, Inc., Macatawa Statutory Trust I, Macatawa Statutory Trust II

Officers: Philip J. Koning/Dir., Pres., CEO - Macatawa Bank/$427,743.00, Benj A. Smith/Chmn. - Macatawa Bank, CEO - Macatawa Bank Corporation/$215,720.00, Renae Eckland/VP, Dir. - Technology, Ray D. Tooker/Sr. VP - Loan Administration/$229,594.00, Amy Ziel/VP, Dir. - Human Resources, Lee Pankratz/Sr. VP, Sr. Credit Officer, Thomas R. Hilliker/Sr. VP, Trust Services Dir., Ronald L. Haan/Exec. VP/$576,902.00, Jill A. Walcott/Sr. VP, Sr Retail Banking Officer, Christine M. Bart/VP, Dir. - Marketing, Jon W. Swets/Sr. VP, CFO/$236,039.00, Vicki K. Denboer/Sr. VP, Dir. - Retail Lending, Richard D. Wieringa/Sr. VP - Commercial Loans, John Groothuis/Community Bank Pres. - Grand Haven

Directors: Philip J. Koning/Dir., Pres., CEO - Macatawa Bank, Benj A. Smith/Chmn. - Macatawa Bank, CEO - Macatawa Bank Corporation, Thomas G. Boylan/Member - Bank Board, Robert Den Herder/Member - Bank Board, Douglas B. Padnos/Member - Bank Board, Birgit M. Klohs/Member - Bank Board, Arend D. Lubbers/Dir., Member - Bank Board, Wayne J. Elhart/Member - Bank Board, Robert D. Denherder/53/Dir., Thomas J. Wesholski/Member - Bank Board, John F. Koetje/Dir., Member - Bank Board

Owners: Arend D. Lubbers, John F. Koetje/1.90%, Robert E. DenHerder/1.90%, Philip J. Koning, Thomas G. Boylan/2.00%, Benj A. Smith/2.70%

Financial Data: Fiscal Year End:12/31 **Latest Annual Data:** 12/31/2006

Year	Sales	Net Income
2006	$147,683,000	$19,831,000
2005	$118,399,000	$20,889,000
2004	$88,371,000	$12,776,000

Curr. Assets:	$51,115,000	**Curr. Liab.:**	$1,684,711,000	**P/E Ratio:**	14.05
Plant, Equip.:	$60,731,000	**Total Liab.:**	$1,917,967,000	**Indic. Yr. Divd.:**	$0.520
Total Assets:	$2,074,816,000	**Net Worth:**	$156,849,000	**Debt/ Equity:**	1.4871

MACC Private Equities Inc

101 Second St. Se, Ste. 800, Cedar Rapids, Iowa, IA, 52401; **PH:** 1-319-363-8249

General - Incorporation	DE	Stock - Price on:12/24/2007	$2.44
Employees	NA	Stock Exchange	NDQ
Auditor	KPMG LLP	Ticker Symbol	MACC
Stk Agt	Mellon Investor Services LLC	Outstanding Shares	2,460,000
Counsel	NA	E.P.S.	-$0.04
DUNS No.	NA	Shareholders	NA

Business: The group's principal activity is to invest in portfolio companies to achieve capital appreciation and to realize gains in the portfolio. The group operates from the United States. The assets of the group for the year 2006 were $22.8 (millions).

Primary SIC and add'l.: 6726 6799

CIK No: 0000923808

Subsidiaries: MorAmerica Capital Corporation

Officers: David R. Schroder/64/Pres., Sec., Robert A. Comey/CFO, Exec. VP, Chief Compliance Officer, Treasurer, Assist. Sec., Kevin F. Mullane/52/Sr. VP, Michael H. Reynoldson/42/VP

Directors: Geoffrey T. Woolley/48/Chmn., Benjamin Jiaravanon/37/Dir., Gordon J. Roth/53/Dir., Jasja Kotterman/38/Dir., Michael W. Dunn/58/Dir.

Owners: Michael W. Dunn, Benjamin Jiaravanon, Insiders, Kevin F. Mullane, Gordon J. Roth, Jasja Kotterman, Robert A. Comey, David R. Schroder, Atlas Management Partners, LLC, Bridgewater International Group, LLC, Timothy A. Bridgewater, Geoffrey T. Woolley

Financial Data: Fiscal Year End:09/30 **Latest Annual Data:** 9/30/2006

Year	Sales	Net Income
2006	$1,194,000	-$2,047,000
2005	$6,936,000	$2,588,000
2004	$2,610,000	-$2,008,000

Curr. Assets:	$2,680,000	**Curr. Liab.:**	$422,000	**P/E Ratio:**	7.63
Plant, Equip.:	NA	**Total Liab.:**	$11,212,000	**Indic. Yr. Divd.:**	NA
Total Assets:	$22,830,000	**Net Worth:**	$11,618,000	**Debt/ Equity:**	0.9069

Macdermid Inc

1401 Blake St., Denver, CO, 80202; **PH:** 1-720-479-3060; http:// www.macdermid.com

General - Incorporation	CT	Stock - Price on:12/24/2007	NA
Employees	2,800	Stock Exchange	NYSE
Auditor	KPMG LLP	Ticker Symbol	MRH
Stk Agt	Bank of New York	Outstanding Shares	NA
Counsel	NA	E.P.S.	NA
DUNS No.	00-116-4599	Shareholders	NA

Business: The group's principal activities are to develop, produce and market specialty chemical products. The group operates in two segments: advanced surface finishing and printing solutions. Advanced surface finishing segment supplies chemicals used for finishing metals and non-metallic surfaces, electro-plating metal surfaces, etching, imaging, offshore fluids and cleaning. Printing solutions segment supplies chemicals for use in the production of offset blankets, printing plates and textile blankets. The group's products are used in metal and plastic finishing, electronics, graphic arts, offshore lubricants, printing plates, offset and textile blankets and photo-polymer printing industries. The group operates in the United States, Europe and Asia-Pacific.

Primary SIC and add'l.: 3559 2899

CIK No: 0000061138

Subsidiaries: Autotype Americas, Inc., Autotype Holdings, Inc., Autotype International (Asia) Pte Ltd., Autotype International Ltd., Autotype Italia SRL, CPS Chemical Products & Services, Jager Jeune, S.A., Letcombe Investments Ltd., MacDermid Asia, Ltd, MacDermid Benelux BV, MacDermid Canning, MacDermid Canning, ltd, MacDermid Chemicals, Inc., MacDermid Colorspan, Inc., MacDermid Equipment GmbH 40 Subsidiaries included in the Index

Officers: Daniel H. Leever/Chmn., CEO, John Cordani/General Counsel, Sindy Chui/Contact - Asia, Pacific, Macdermid Hong Kong Ltd, Alan Hanson/Contact - Macdermid England, Anne Watkowski/Contact - Macdermid Americas, Lisa Guerrera/Contact - Worldwide Marketing, Innovation, Mark Baker/Contact - Macdermid England, Hazel Edah/Contact - Worldwide Marketing, Innovation

Directors: Daniel H. Leever/Chmn., CEO

Owners: Bank of America Corporation/6.10%, GAMCO Investors,Inc./8.40%, Michael Siegmund, MacDermid Employees Profit Sharing, Pension and Stock Ownership Plans; MacDermid Equipment,Inc./7.70%, Daniel H. Leever/7.30%, Robert L. Ecklin, PRIMECAP Management Company/5.50%, Gregory M. Bolingbroke, Insiders/10.60%, John L. Cordani, Frank J. Monteiro, Quinn T. Spitzer, Joseph M. Silvestri, Donald G. Ogilvie, James C. Smith (*18 Owners included in Index*)

Mace Security International Inc

401 E Las Olas Blvd., Ste. 1570, Fort Lauderdale, FL, 33301; *PH:* 1-954-449-1300; *Fax:* 1-954-522-5432; *http://* www.mace.com

General - Incorporation	DE	Stock - Price on:12/24/2007	$2.47
Employees	1,428	Stock Exchange	NDQ
Auditor	Grant Thornton LLP	Ticker Symbol	MACE
Stk Agt	American Stock Transfer & Trust CO.	Outstanding Shares	15,280,000
Counsel	NA	E.P.S.	-$0.384
DUNS No.	18-576-9312	Shareholders	NA

Business: The group's principal activities are to operate a full car wash facilities and market consumer safety and security products. Car and truck wash facilities provide washing and waxing services for fleet transport vehicles. Cars are moved through the car wash tunnel by a conveyor system where automatic equipment cleans the vehicle. Additional services, including wheel cleaning, fragrance and rust protection treatment, interior and wheel treatments, waxing and shampooing, are also offered at the locations. The security products division designs markets and sells consumer products for use in protection of the home and automobile, for personal and child protection. These products include a line of defense sprays, two personal alarms, whistles, and window and door lock alarms. The defense sprays include tear gas sprays, pepper sprays and sprays with both tear gas and pepper solution.

Primary SIC and add'l.: 7538 7549 7542 5983

CIK No: 0000912607

Subsidiaries: 50's Classic Car Wash of Lubbock, Inc., Car Care, Inc., Care Investment, Inc., Colonial Full Service Car Wash, Inc., CRCD, Inc., Crystal Falls Car Wash, Inc., Eager Beaver Car Wash, Inc., F.E.D. Properties, Inc., Mace Car Wash - Arizona, Inc., Mace Car Wash, Inc., Mace Security Centers, Inc., Mace Security International, Inc., Mace Security Products, Inc., Mace Texas I, Inc., Mace Texas II, Inc. 20 Subsidiaries included in the Index

Officers: Louis D. Paolino/Chmn., CEO, Pres., Mark S. Alsentzer/Chmn., CEO, Pres., Matthew Paolino/Dir., VP, Constantine Papadakis/Dir., Pres., Robert M. Kramer/General Counsel, Sec., Exec. VP, COO, Gregory M. Krzemien/CFO, Treasurer

Directors: Louis D. Paolino/Chmn., CEO, Pres., Mark S. Alsentzer/Chmn., CEO, Pres., Matthew Paolino/Dir., VP, Constantine Papadakis/Dir., Pres., Burton Segal/Dir.

Owners: Constantine N. Papadakis, Burton Segal, Insiders/23.60%, Lawndale Capital Management, LLC/9.60%, Ancora Capital, Inc./8.00%, Gregory M. Krzemien/2.60%, Louis D. Paolino/13.50%, Matthew J. Paolino/1.90%, Robert M. Kramer/3.60%, Mark S. Alsentzer/3.70%

Financial Data: *Fiscal Year End:*12/31   *Latest Annual Data:* 12/31/2006

Year	Sales	Net Income
2006	$49,215,000	-$6,782,000
2005	$68,242,000	-$5,020,000
2004	$57,647,000	-$6,410,000

Curr. Assets:	$44,561,000	Curr. Liab.:	$18,005,000		
Plant, Equip.:	$38,307,000	Total Liab.:	$31,092,000	Indic. Yr. Divd.:	NA
Total Assets:	$87,598,000	Net Worth:	$56,506,000	Debt/ Equity:	0.2374

Macerich Company (The)

401 Wilshire Blvd., Ste. 700, Santa Monica, CA, 90401; *PH:* 1-310-394-6000; *Fax:* 1-310-395-2791; *http://* www.macerich.com

General - Incorporation	MD	Stock - Price on:12/24/2007	$84.11
Employees	3,036	Stock Exchange	NYSE
Auditor	Deloitte & Touche LLP	Ticker Symbol	MAC
Stk Agt	Computershare Trust Co	Outstanding Shares	71,680,000
Counsel	NA	E.P.S.	$2.30
DUNS No.	NA	Shareholders	NA

Business: The groups principle activities include acquiring, owning, developing, redeveloping, management and leasing of regional and community shopping centers. In the year 2006, the group acquired Valley River Center and Deptford Mall. The group operates from the United States.

Primary SIC and add'l.: 6798

CIK No: 0000912242

Subsidiaries: , ARROWHEAD FESTIVAL L.L.C., BILTMORE SHOPPING CENTER PARTNERS LLC, BROAD RAFAEL ASSOCIATES (LIMITED PARTNERSHIP), BROAD RAFAEL PROPERTIES CORP., CAMELBACK COLONNADE ASSOCIATES LIMITED PARTNERSHIP, CAMELBACK COLONNADE PARTNERS, CAMELBACK COLONNADE SPE LLC, CAMELBACK SHOPPING CENTER LIMITED PARTNERSHIP, CHANDLER FESTIVAL SPE LLC, CHANDLER GATEWAY PARTNERS LLC, CHANDLER GATEWAY SPE LLC, CHANDLER VILLAGE CENTER LLC, CHRIS-TOWN VILLAGE ASSOCIATES, COOLIDGE HOLDING LLC 338 Subsidiaries included in the Index

Officers: Arthur M. Coppola/Dir., CEO, Pres./$4,823,005.00, Jerry Anderson/VP - Leasing Northern California, Mark Strain/VP - Leasing Southern California - Pacific Northwest, Doug Healey/Sr. VP - Leasing, Mark Klein/VP - Leasing Central, Mike Nevins/VP - Leasing East - Phoenix, Erin McCormick/Sr. Leasing Mgr., Jeff Labarba/Sr. Leasing Mgr., Jim Varsamis/Leasing Mgr., Lauren Gausden/Leasing Associate, Edward C. Coppola/Dir., Sr. Exec. VP, Chief Investment Officer/$2,239,480.00, Tony Grossi/Dir., Exec. VP, COO, Richard A. Bayer/Dir., Exec. VP, Chief Legal Officer, Sec./$1,601,501.00, Thomas E. O'Hern/Dir., Exec. VP, CFO, Treasurer/$1,823,633.00, Larry E. Sidwell/Dir., Exec. VP - Real Estate (*51 Officers included in Index*)

Directors: Arthur M. Coppola/Dir., CEO, Pres., Mace Siegel/Chmn., Dana K. Anderson/Vice Chmn., Edward C. Coppola/Dir., Sr. Exec. VP, Chief Investment Officer, Tony Grossi/Dir., Exec. VP, COO, James S. Cownie/Dir., Fred S. Hubbell/Dir., Diana M. Laing/Dir., Stanley A. Moore/Dir., William P. Sexton/Dir., Richard A. Bayer/Dir., Exec. VP, Chief Legal Officer, Sec., Thomas E. O'Hern/Dir., Exec. VP, CFO, Treasurer, Larry E. Sidwell/Dir., Exec. VP - Real Estate

Owners: Oz Special Funding (OZMD) LP, Goldman Sachs & Co. Profit Sharing, Linden Capital LP, D.E. Shaw Valence Portfolios, L.L.C., Akanthos Arbitrage Master Fund L.P., Banc of America Securities LLC

Financial Data: *Fiscal Year End:*12/31   *Latest Annual Data:* 12/31/2006

Year	Sales	Net Income
2006	$829,656,000	$252,358,000
2005	$767,385,000	$71,686,000
2004	$547,268,000	$91,633,000

Curr. Assets:	$457,948,000	Curr. Liab.:	$304,575,000	P/E Ratio:	30.70
Plant, Equip.:	$5,755,283,000	Total Liab.:	$5,920,924,000	Indic. Yr. Divd.:	$3.200
Total Assets:	$7,562,163,000	Net Worth:	$1,542,305,000	Debt/ Equity:	3.5931

MachineTalker Inc

513 De La Vina St., Santa Barbara, CA, 93101; *PH:* 1-805-957-1680; *http://* www.machinetalker.com; *Email:* info@machinetalker.com

General - Incorporation	DE	Stock - Price on:12/24/2007	$0.075
Employees	5	Stock Exchange	OTC
Auditor	Hj Assoc. & Consultants, LLP	Ticker Symbol	MTKN
Stk Agt	HJ Associates & Consultants, LLP	Outstanding Shares	162,440,000
Counsel	NA	E.P.S.	-$0.01
DUNS No.	NA	Shareholders	NA

Business: The groups principle activity is to provide security network components and wireless security systems. The products of the group include MACHINETALKER(R), MINITALKER(R), TAGTALKER(TM), TOUGHTALKER(TM), CONTAINERTRACKER(TM) and ASSETTRACKER(TM). The group operates from the United States.

Primary SIC and add'l.: 3823

CIK No: 0001172631

Officers: Roland F. Bryan/Chmn., CEO, CFO, Pres., Gerald A. Nadler/66/Chief Scientist, Christopher S. Outwater/Dir. - New Business Development, Gerry Nadler/Principal Scientist

Directors: Roland F. Bryan/Chmn., CEO, CFO, Pres.

Owners: Insiders/24.45%, Roland F. Bryan/24.45%, CHRISTOPHER T. KLEVELAND/14.54%, JULIE OREAR/8.20%, WINGS FUND, INC./6.37%, MARK P. Harris/14.54%

Financial Data: *Fiscal Year End:*12/31   *Latest Annual Data:* 12/31/2006

Year	Sales	Net Income
2006	$553,000	-$612,000
2005	$225,000	-$1,068,000

Curr. Assets:	$103,000	Curr. Liab.:	$394,000		
Plant, Equip.:	$31,000	Total Liab.:	$908,000	Indic. Yr. Divd.:	NA
Total Assets:	$137,000	Net Worth:	-$771,000	Debt/ Equity:	NA

Mackinac Financial Corp

130 S Cedar St., Manistique, MI, 49854; *PH:* 1-906-341-8401; *Fax:* 1-906-341-8578; *http://* www.northcountrybank.com

General - Incorporation	MI	Stock - Price on:12/24/2007	$9.25
Employees	105	Stock Exchange	NDQ
Auditor	Plante & Moran, PLLC	Ticker Symbol	MFNC
Stk Agt	Registrar & Transfer Co	Outstanding Shares	3,430,000
Counsel	NA	E.P.S.	$2.91
DUNS No.	01-028-7548	Shareholders	NA

Business: The group's principal activity is to provide general commercial banking services. It operates through its banking subsidiary, north country bank and trust. The group renders customary retail and commercial banking services including checking and savings accounts, time deposits and interest bearing transaction accounts through 22 branch offices in the peninsula of Michigan. The services include safe deposit facilities, real estate mortgage lending, commercial lending, commercial and governmental lease financing and indirect consumer financing. Through its non-banking subsidiaries, the group sells annuities as well as life and health insurance, provides relending services to nonprofit organizations, brokers loans and leases including tax-exempt lease/purchase financing to municipalities.

Primary SIC and add'l.: 6712 6022

CIK No: 0000036506

Subsidiaries: American Financial Mortgage Corporation, First Manistique Agency Inc, First Rural Relending Company, mBank, mBank Employee Services, LLC, mBank Mortgage Company LLC, NCB Real Estate Company, North Country Capital Trust

Officers: Paul D. Tobias/Chmn., CEO - Mbank/$365,394.00, Kelly George/Pres., CEO - CLO, Mbank/$227,163.00, Ernie Krueger/Sr. VP, CFO - Mbank/$187,070.00, Julie Bosanic/Branch Mgr. Mortgage Lender - Mbank, Eliot R. Stark/Dir., Exec. VP, Business Development Officer - Mbank/$293,501.00, Barbara Parrett/Branch Mgr. Mortgage Lender - Stephenson, Mbank, Jeremy Flodin/Commercial Lending Officer - Mbank, Janet M. Willbee/Assist. VP - Mortgage Lender - Mbank, David Crimmins/Regional Pres. - Commercial Lending, Mbank, Tim Timmer/VP - Commercial Lender - Gaylord, Mbank, Clarice Ghiardi/VP - Consumer Loan Sales Mgr. - Banker, Marquette, Mbank, Sue Preiss/Branch Mgr. Mortgage Lender - Mbank, Dave Thomas/Commercial Lender, Mbank, Andy Sabatine/Regional Pres. Commercial Banking Mgr. - Mbank, Theresa Zednicek/Branch Mgr. Mortgage Lender - Mbank (*19 Officers included in Index*)

Directors: Paul D. Tobias/Chmn., CEO - Mbank, Dennis B. Bittner/Dir. - Mbank, Joe Garea/Dir. - Mbank, Brooks L. Patterson/Dir. - Mbank, Randolph C. Paschke/Dir. - Mbank, Eliot R. Stark/Dir., Exec. VP, Business Development Officer - Mbank, Walter J. Aspatore/Dir. - Mbank, Robert H. Orley/Dir. - Mbank

Owners: Financial Stocks Capital/9.92%, Raymond Garea/6.74%, Joseph D. Garea/1.22%, Kelly W. George, Eliot R. Stark/2.12%, Insiders/8.30%, Wellington Management Company LLP/6.20%, Ernie R. Krueger, Hot Creek Ventures 2, LP/8.75%, Randolph C. Paschke, Paul D. Tobias/3.39%, Walter J. Aspatore, Dennis B. Bittner, Brooks L. Patterson, Robert H. Orley (*17 Owners included in Index*)

Financial Data: *Fiscal Year End:*12/31   *Latest Annual Data:* 12/31/2006

Year	Sales	Net Income
2006	$25,036,000	$1,716,000
2005	$18,087,000	-$7,364,000
2004	$27,395,000	-$1,595,000

Curr. Assets:	$11,562,000	Curr. Liab.:	$312,421,000	P/E Ratio:	14.02
Plant, Equip.:	$12,479,000	Total Liab.:	$354,001,000	Indic. Yr. Divd.:	NA
Total Assets:	$382,791,000	Net Worth:	$28,790,000	Debt/ Equity:	1.2798

Macquarie Infrastructure Company Trust

125 W 55th St., 22nd Fl., New York, NY, 10019; *PH:* 1-212-231-1000; *Fax:* 1-212-231-1010; *http://* www.macquarie.com

General - Incorporation	DE	Stock - Price on:12/24/2007	$44.3
Employees	2,728	Stock Exchange	NDQ
Auditor	KPMG LLP	Ticker Symbol	MICC
Stk Agt	Bank of New York	Outstanding Shares	37,560,000
Counsel	NA	E.P.S.	$0.20
DUNS No.	NA	Shareholders	NA

Business: The groups principle activity is to provide everyday services. The groups services include parking, roads and water. The group also operates infrastructure business. The group operates through four segments namely, airport services business, airport parking business, district energy, and the gas production and distribution. The group operates from the United States.

Primary SIC and add'l.: 4924 4581 4789 8741 4581 7521 5984 8741 5984 4924 4789 5172 7521

CIK No: 0001289788

Subsidiaries: AAC Subsidiary, LLC, Airport Parking Management Inc., Atlantic Aviation Corporation, Atlantic Aviation FBO, Inc., Atlantic Aviation Flight Support, Inc., Atlantic Aviation Holding Corporation, Atlantic Aviation Philadelphia, Inc., Atlantic SMO GP LLC, Atlantic SMO Holdings LLC, BASI Holdings, LLC, Brainard Airport Services, Inc, Bridgeport Airport Services, Inc, BTV Avcenter, Inc., Charter Oak Aviation, Inc., COAI Holdings, LLC 76 Subsidiaries included in the Index

Officers: Grant MacKenzie/CEO - Macquarie Financial, Peter Stokes/CEO, Frank Joyce/CFO, David Morrissey/COO - Macquarie Financial, Heidi Mortensen/General Counsel, Corp. Sec.

Directors: Shemara Wikramanayake/Alternate Chmn., John Roberts/Chmn., Norman H. Brown/Dir., George W. Carmany/Dir., William H. Webb/Dir.

Owners: Norman H. Brown, Insiders/7.60%, George W. Carmany, Peter Stokes/7.00%, Shemara Wikramanayake/7.30%, William H. Webb, Macquarie Infrastructure Management (USA) Inc./6.90%, BlackRock, Inc./6.90%, John Roberts/7.10%

Financial Data: Fiscal Year End:12/31 Latest Annual Data: 12/31/2006

Year	Sales	Net Income
2006	$520,251,000	$49,918,000
2005	$304,743,000	$15,196,000

Curr. Assets:	$230,966,000	Curr. Liab.:	$72,139,000	P/E Ratio:	30.70
Plant, Equip.:	$522,759,000	Total Liab.:	$1,224,927,000	Indic. Yr. Divd.:	$2.480
Total Assets:	$2,097,533,000	Net Worth:	$864,425,000	Debt/ Equity:	NA

Macreport Net Inc

150 Brdhollow Rd. , Ste Ph11, Melville, NY, 11747; *PH:* 1-631-423-4222; *http://* www.macreport.net; *Email:* clientservices@macreport.net

General - Incorporation	DE	Stock - Price on:12/24/2007	NA
Employees	20	Stock Exchange	OTC
Auditor	Holtz Rubenstein Reminick LLP	Ticker Symbol	MRPT
Stk Agt	Continental Stock Transfer & Trust Co	Outstanding Shares	NA
Counsel	NA	E.P.S.	-$0.07
DUNS No.	NA	Shareholders	NA

Business: The groups principle activity is to provide web based financial information. The group provides information about textual information, such as news, trade press, SEC filings, executive biographies, and analyst reports; and numeric information. The group operates from United States.

Primary SIC and add'l.: NA

CIK No: 0001143994

Subsidiaries: JA Spa, LLC, Macnetworks, Inc, Michael Adams Securities, Inc., SpringBay Oil Company, Inc, The Marcellus Group, LLC

Officers: William V. Lucchetti/Chmn., CEO, Pres., Adam J. Reznikoff/Dir., Exec. VP, Stephen Czarnik/Special Counsel

Directors: William V. Lucchetti/Chmn., CEO, Pres., Adam J. Reznikoff/Dir., Exec. VP, Kenneth T. Hutchinson/Dir.

Financial Data: Fiscal Year End:11/30 Latest Annual Data: 11/30/2005

Year	Sales	Net Income
2005	$1,639,000	-$1,831,000
2004	$2,122,000	$1,245,000
2003	$391,000	-$1,037,000

Curr. Assets:	$745,000	Curr. Liab.:	$1,860,000		
Plant, Equip.:	$2,233,000	Total Liab.:	$2,147,000	Indic. Yr. Divd.:	NA
Total Assets:	$3,062,000	Net Worth:	$915,000	Debt/ Equity:	NA

Macrochem Corp

40 Washington St., Ste. 220, Wellesley Hills, MA, 02481; *PH:* 1-781-489-7310; *Fax:* 1-781-489-7311; *http://* www.macrochem.com; *Email:* info@macrochem.com

General - Incorporation	DE	Stock - Price on:12/24/2007	$0.96
Employees	5	Stock Exchange	OTC
Auditor	Vitale, Caturano & Co., Ltd.	Ticker Symbol	MACM
Stk Agt	American Stock Transfer & Trust Co.	Outstanding Shares	3,190,000
Counsel	NA	E.P.S.	$0.27
DUNS No.	11-885-2862	Shareholders	NA

Business: The group's principle activities include developing and licensing transdermal drug delivery compounds and systems intended to promote the delivery of drugs from the surface of the skin into the skin or the bloodstream. It develops pharmaceutical products for commercial use by applying sepa(R) (soft enhancer of percutaneous absorption), one of its patented topical drug delivery systems. It has also developed a series of new low molecular weight polymers for cosmetic use and topical delivery. The company operates only in domestic market. The group operates from United States.

Primary SIC and add'l.: 8731 2834

CIK No: 0000743884

Officers: Robert J. Deluccia/Vice Chmn., CEO, Pres./$689,954.00, Bernard R. Patriacca/CFO, VP, Treasurer/$371,539.00, Jordan Silverstein/Investor Relations Officer, Christine Berni/Investor Relations Officer, Bill Douglass/Contact - Media, Rachel Anscher/Contact - Media

Directors: Robert J. Deluccia/Vice Chmn., CEO, Pres., Thomas C. Chan/Chmn. - Scientific Advisory Board, John L. Zabriskie/Chmn., Jeffrey B. Davis/Dir., Michael A. Davis/Dir., Paul S. Echenberg/Dir., Peter G. Martin/Dir., Mark J. Alvino/Dir.

Owners: Paul S. Echenberg, FSS Franklin Biotechnology Discovery Fund/12.64%, Robert J. DeLuccia/1.08%, Michael A. Davis, Bernard R. Patriacca, Peter G. Martin, Jeffrey B. Davis/4.95%, Glenn E. Deegan, John L. Zabriskie, Joseph Edelman/10.56%, Whalehaven Capital Fund Limited/5.23%, Insiders/9.99%, Mark J. Alvino, Stephen S. Rouhandeh/52.21%

Financial Data: Fiscal Year End:12/31 Latest Annual Data: 12/31/2006

Year	Sales	Net Income
2006	NA	$1,951,000
2005	NA	-$5,760,000
2004	NA	-$8,275,000

Curr. Assets:	$5,049,000	Curr. Liab.:	$269,000		
Plant, Equip.:	$37,000	Total Liab.:	$1,473,000	Indic. Yr. Divd.:	NA
Total Assets:	$5,654,000	Net Worth:	$4,181,000	Debt/ Equity:	NA

Macromedia Inc

601 Townsend St., San Francisco, CA, 94103; *PH:* 1-415-832-2000; *http://* www.adobe.com

General - Incorporation	DE	Stock - Price on:12/24/2007	$41.53
Employees	6,082	Stock Exchange	NA
Auditor	KPMG LLP	Ticker Symbol	NA
Stk Agt	Computershare Investor Services LLC	Outstanding Shares	587,930,000
Counsel	Fenwick & West LLP	E.P.S.	$0.95
DUNS No.	17-481-3634	Shareholders	NA

Business: The group's principal activity is to provide software solutions that enable development of websites and other Internet applications. The Internet solutions include websites,media content and Internet applications across multiple platforms and devices. The products of the group include client software and development tools. The client software serves macromedia flash player, macromedia shockwave player, macromedia mx product family, macromedia coldfusion mx and macromedia jrun server. The development tool serves macromedia dreamweaver mx, macromedia flash mx director shockwave studio. The group has international operations in the Netherlands, France, Germany, Sweden, Belgium, Italy, Brazil, Australia, Hong Kong, Singapore, Canada and the republic of Korea. On 19-Dec-2003, the group acquired ehelp corporation.

Primary SIC and add'l.: 7371 7372

CIK No: 0000913949

Subsidiaries: Allaire Corporation, Allaire Europe Holdings B.V., Allaire GmbH, Allaire International, Inc., Allaire Securities Corporation, Animoi Oy, Bright Tiger Technologies, Inc., Live Software, Inc., Macromedia Asia Pacific Pty, Ltd., Macromedia Belgium BVBA, Macromedia Brasil Ltda., Macromedia Canada Ltd., Macromedia Europe Ltd., Macromedia GmbH, Macromedia Hong Kong Ltd. 31 Subsidiaries included in the Index

Financial Data: Fiscal Year End:03/31 Latest Annual Data: 12/1/2006

Year	Sales	Net Income
2006	$2,575,300,000	$505,809,000
2005	$1,966,321,000	$602,839,000
2004	$1,666,581,000	$450,398,000

Curr. Assets:	$1,551,029,000	Curr. Liab.:	$451,408,000	P/E Ratio:	43.72
Plant, Equip.:	$99,675,000	Total Liab.:	$535,155,000	Indic. Yr. Divd.:	NA
Total Assets:	$1,958,632,000	Net Worth:	$1,423,477,000	Debt/ Equity:	NA

Macronix International Co Ltd

680 N McCarthy Blvd., Milpitas, CA, 95035; *PH:* 1-408-262-8887; *Fax:* 1-408-262-8810; *http://* www.macronix.com

General - Incorporation	China	Stock - Price on:12/24/2007	$4.17
Employees	3,591	Stock Exchange	AMEX
Auditor	Diwan, Ernst & Young	Ticker Symbol	MXM
Stk Agt	NA	Outstanding Shares	2,910,000,000
Counsel	NA	E.P.S.	$0.039
DUNS No.	65-600-3282	Shareholders	NA

Business: The groups principle activities include designing, manufacturing and salling of integrated circuits and memory chips. The group also provides development and consultation services, import, and export trading. The groups products include flash products, mask rom, memory card, digital voice recorder, polyphonic sound generator, digital answering machine, micro controller unit, digital still camera and flat panel display. The group operates from United States.

Primary SIC and add'l.: 3674

CIK No: 0001009680

Subsidiaries: Biomorphic Microsystems Corporation, Hui Ying Investment Ltd., Joyteck Co., Ltd., Kang Bao Investment Ltd., Macronix (B.V.I.) Co., Ltd., Macronix (Hong Kong) Co., Ltd., Macronix America, Inc., Macronix Europe N.V., Macronix Japan, Macronix Microelectronics (Suzhou) Co., Ltd, Macronix Pte Ltd., MaxNova Inc., New Trend Technology Inc., Run Hong Investment Ltd., Wedgewood International Ltd.

Officers: Miin Wu/Chmn., CEO, Chih-Yuan Lu/Pres., Tom Yiu/Sr. VP, Chief Marketing Officer, W. S. Pan/51/Dir., VP, F. L. Ni/49/Dir., VP, Gueimin Lee/Supervisor

Directors: Miin Wu/Chmn., CEO, W. S. Pan/51/Dir., VP, F. L. Ni/49/Dir., VP

Owners: Akira Takata/2.40%, C. Y. Lu, Kuo Hwa Life Insurance Co., Ltd./1.74%, F. L. Ni, Cheng Yi Fang/0.02%, Paul Yeh/0.12%, Powerchip Semiconductor Corp/6.04%, Raymond S. Mak/0.14%, Ping Tien Wu, J. D. Lee/2.40%, National Stabilization Fund/1.14%, Dang-Hsing Yiu/0.35%, Rich Liu/0.01%, W. S. Pan, Shun Yin Investment Co., Ltd./2.40% *(22 Owners included in Index)*

Financial Data: Fiscal Year End:12/31 Latest Annual Data: 12/31/2006

Year	Sales	Net Income
2006	$721,503,000	$19,515,000
2005	$574,807,000	-$140,921,000
2004	$736,602,000	-$13,509,000

Curr. Assets:	$673,062,000	**Curr. Liab.:**	$215,582,000	**P/E Ratio:**	58.79
Plant, Equip.:	$435,379,000	**Total Liab.:**	$337,340,000	**Indic. Yr. Divd.:**	NA
Total Assets:	$1,247,779,000	**Net Worth:**	$909,916,000	**Debt/ Equity:**	NA

Macrovision Corp

2830 De La Cruz Blvd., Santa Clara, CA, 95050; *PH:* 1-408-562-8400; *Fax:* 1-408-567-1800; *http://* www.macrovision.com

General - Incorporation .... DE
Employees 784
Auditor .... KPMG LLP
Stk Agt...... American Stock Transfer & Trust Co.
Counsel............ Manatt, Phelps & Phillips LLP
DUNS No. 11-329-4870

Stock- Price on:12/24/2007 .... $29.75
Stock Exchange .... NDQ
Ticker Symbol .... MVSN
Outstanding Shares 53,030,000
E.P.S $0.72
Shareholders .... NA

Business: The group's principal activity is to develop and license rights management and copy protection technologies. It operates in two segments: entertainment technologies group and the software technologies group. The entertainment technologies group develops and licenses copy protection and rights management for videos, music cds and PC games. The software technologies group provides electronic license management software to hardware and software manufacturers and enterprise end-users. The group's include major hollywood studios, independent video producers, hardware and software vendors, music labels, consumer electronic, PC and digital set-top box manufacturers and digital pay-per-view ("Ppv") and video-on-demand ("Vod") network operators.

Primary SIC and add'l.: 7389 3861 7372

CIK No: 0001027443

Subsidiaries: Deterrence Acquisition Ltd., Macrovision Europe Limited, Macrovision International Holding Limited Partnership, Macrovision Israel, Ltd., Macrovision Japan and Asia KK, Macrovision Japan and Asia YK, Macrovision Korea Co., Ltd., Macrovision Licensing& Holding B.V., Macrovision Limited, Macrovision Service LLC, Macrovision Taiwan Ltd., Macrovision UK Limited, Trymedia Systems S.L., Trymedia Systems, Inc., Zero G Software, Inc.

Officers: Alfred J. Amoroso/Dir., CEO, Pres./$2,972,673.00, Mark Bishof/Exec. VP, GM - Software/$933,088.00, Eric Free/Exec. VP, GM - Embedded Solutions, Jim Ryan/Sr. VP, GM - EMEA, James Budge/CFO, Exec. VP/$1,070,030.00, Eric Rodli/Exec. VP, GM - Entertainment, Eileen Schloss/Exec. VP - Human Resources, David Rowley/Sr. VP, GM - Asia, Pacific, Jim Wickett/Exec. VP - Corporate Development/$981,172.00, Stephen Yu/Exec. VP, General Counsel, Sec., Michael Buchheim/Exec. VP, GM - Distribution, Commerce, Robert Doyle/Sr. VP - Engineering, Corey Ferengul/Exec. VP - Marketing, Solutions

Directors: Alfred J. Amoroso/Dir., CEO, Pres., John O. Ryan/Chmn., Co - Founder, Steven G. Blank/Dir., William N. Stirlen/Dir., Donna S. Birks/Dir., Andrew K. Ludwick/Dir., Robert J. Majteles/Dir.

Owners: William Krepick/1.46%, Insiders/3.69%, Lord, Abbett& Co., LLC/5.04%, Loren Hillberg, Transamerica Investment Management, LLC/5.24%, Unicredito Italiano S.p.A./5.68%, James Wickett, Blum Capital Partners, LP/5.41%, PRIMECAP Management Company/9.77%, Mark Bishof, Robert J. Majteles, Steven G. Blank, John O. Ryan/1.66%, Alfred J. Amoroso, James Budge *(19 Owners included in Index)*

Financial Data: **Fiscal Year End:**12/31 **Latest Annual Data:** 12/31/2006

Year	Sales	Net Income
2006	$247,590,000	$33,043,000
2005	$203,230,000	$22,115,000
2004	$182,099,000	$36,730,000

Curr. Assets:	$402,591,000	**Curr. Liab.:**	$109,914,000	**P/E Ratio:**	49.58
Plant, Equip.:	$21,818,000	**Total Liab.:**	$353,473,000	**Indic. Yr. Divd.:**	NA
Total Assets:	$819,615,000	**Net Worth:**	$466,142,000	**Debt/ Equity:**	0.5509

Macys Inc

Formerly: Federated Department Stores Inc
7 W Seventh St., Cincinnati, OH, 45202; *PH:* 1-212-705-2000; *http://* www.federated-fds.com

General - Incorporation .... DE
Employees 232,000
Auditor .... KPMG LLP
Stk Agt............ Bank of New York
Counsel .... NA
DUNS No. 80-029-9976

Stock- Price on:12/24/2007 .... NA
Stock Exchange .... NA
Ticker Symbol .... NA
Outstanding Shares .... NA
E.P.S .... NA
Shareholders .... NA

Business: The group's principle activity is to provide retail stores that sells a wide range of merchandise including men's, women's and children's apparel and accessories, cosmetics, home furnishings and various consumer goods. The group operates from United States.

Primary SIC and add'l.: 5961 7375 5311

CIK No: 0000794367

Subsidiaries: Advertex Communications, Inc., After Hours Formalwear, Inc., Bloomingdales By Mail Ltd., Bloomingdales, Inc., Bloomingdales.com, Inc., Davids Bridal, Inc., FACS Group, Inc., FACS Insurance Agency, Inc., FDS Bank, FDS Thrift Holding Co., Inc., Federated Brands, Inc., Federated Corporate Services, Inc., Federated Department Stores Insurance Company, Inc., Federated Department Stores Insurance Company, Ltd. (99.99% ownership), Federated Retail Holdings, Inc. 29 Subsidiaries included in the Index

Officers: Terry J. Lundgren/Chmn., CEO, Pres./$15,647,120.00, Thomas L. Cole/Vice Chmn., Exec. Officer/$4,995,089.00, Janet E. Grove/Vice Chmn., Exec. Officer/$4,908,573.00, Susan D. Kronick/Vice Chmn., Exec. Officer/$5,740,196.00, Thomas G. Cody/Vice Chmn., Exec. Officer, Michael Zorn/VP - Employee Relations, Jessica Light/Assoc. Mgr. - Supplier Diversity, Howard Thompson/OVP, Corp. Dir. - Supplier Diversity, Gary J. Nay/VP - Real Estate, James A. Sluzewski/VP - Corporate Communications, External Affairs, Cynthia Ray Walker/VP - Area Research, Felicia Williams/VP - Internal Audit, Karen M. Hoguet/CFO, Exec. VP/$3,980,332.00, David W. Clark/Sr. VP - Human Resources, William L. Hawthorne/Chief Diversity Officer - Legal Affairs *(25 Officers included in Index)*

Directors: Terry J. Lundgren/Chmn., CEO, Pres., Thomas G. Cody/Vice Chmn., Exec. Officer, Thomas L. Cole/Vice Chmn., Exec. Officer, Janet E. Grove/Vice Chmn., Exec. Officer, Susan D. Kronick/Vice Chmn., Exec. Officer, Stephen F. Bollenbach/Dir., Meyer Feldberg/Dir., Craig E. Weatherup/Dir., Joyce M. Roche/Dir., Karl M. Von Der Heyden/Dir., Joseph Neubauer/Dir., Sara Levinson/Dir., Marna C. Whittington/Dir., Joseph A. Pichler/Dir.

Owners: Karl M. von der Heyden, Terry J. Lundgren, Thomas L. Cole, Sara Levinson, Joseph A. Pichler, Karen M. Hoguet, Insiders/1.50%, Joyce M. Roch, Susan D. Kronick, FMR Corp./5.60%, Thomas G. Cody, Marna C. Whittington, Meyer Feldberg, William P. Stiritz, Joseph Neubauer *(18 Owners included in Index)*

Mad Catz Interactive Inc

7480 Mission Valley Rd., Ste. 101, San Diego, CA, 92108; *PH:* 1-619-683-9830; *Fax:* 1-619-683-9839; *http://* www.madcatz.com

General - Incorporation .... Canada
Employees 138
Auditor .... KPMG LLP
Stk Agt .... Computershare Investor Services LLC
Counsel .... Lang Michener
DUNS No. .... NA

Stock- Price on:12/24/2007 .... $1.49
Stock Exchange .... AMEX
Ticker Symbol .... MCZ
Outstanding Shares 54,240,000
E.P.S $0.09
Shareholders .... NA

Business: The group's principle activities are to design, manufacture and market accessories for video game consoles and PC gaming systems. The product lines include previously played and republished video games for Ninetendo, Sega and Sony Game Systems. The products are represented internationally with sales to Europe, South America, Canada, Australia and New Zealand. The group's total revenue for year 2007 was 99.72 millions of USD.

Primary SIC and add'l.: 7372 6719

CIK No: 0001088162

Subsidiaries: 1328158 Ontario Inc., FX Unlimited Inc., Mad Catz (Asia) Limited, Mad Catz Europe, Limited, Mad Catz Interactive Asia Limited, Mad Catz Limited, Mad Catz, Inc., Singapore Holdings Inc., Xencet USA, Inc.

Officers: Darren Richardson/Dir., CEO, Pres., COO/$737,331.00, Jon Middleton/VP - Business Development/$367,727.00, Whitney Peterson/VP - Corporate Development, General Counsel - Mad Catz, Inc/$369,097.00

Directors: Darren Richardson/Dir., CEO, Pres., COO, Geofrey Myers/Interim Chmn., Thomas R. Brown/Dir., Robert J. Molyneux/Dir., William Woodward/Dir.

Owners: William Woodward, Thomas R. Brown, Darren Richardson/1.60%, Robert J. Molyneux, Insiders/2.90%, Whitney Peterson, Gruber& McBaine Capital Management Group, LLC/6.00%, Stewart Halpern, Geofrey Myers

Financial Data: **Fiscal Year End:**03/31 **Latest Annual Data:** 03/31/2007

Year	Sales	Net Income
2007	$99,721,000	$3,705,000
2006	$100,768,000	-$6,653,000
2005	$112,071,000	$4,326,000

Curr. Assets:	$37,972,000	**Curr. Liab.:**	$31,883,000	**P/E Ratio:**	18.63
Plant, Equip.:	$2,427,000	**Total Liab.:**	$31,883,000	**Indic. Yr. Divd.:**	NA
Total Assets:	$68,735,000	**Net Worth:**	$36,852,000	**Debt/ Equity:**	NA

Madeco

Ureta Cox 930, San Miguel, Santiago; *PH:* 56-25201000; *Fax:* 56-25201140; *http://* www.madeco.cl; *Email:* ir@madeco.cl

General - Incorporation .... Chile
Employees 2,858
Auditor .... Ernst & Young LTDA.
Stk Agt .... NA
Counsel............ Enrique Sotomayor
DUNS No. 98-000-1440

Stock- Price on:12/24/2007 .... $14.02
Stock Exchange .... NYSE
Ticker Symbol .... NA
Outstanding Shares 55,410,000
E.P.S $0.67
Shareholders .... NA

Business: The group's principle activities are the manufacturing of copper-and-aluminum based products carried out in four divisions: wires & cables which includes the production and sale of multi-strand copper and fiber optic telecommunications cables, building wire, copper and aluminum power cables and magnet wire; brass mills which includes the manufacturing and sale of a wide range of tubes, sheets, coils, brass bars and coin blanks; flexible packaging which includes the manufacturing and sale of flexible packaging and aluminum foil principally for manufacturers of food products; and aluminum profiles which includes the manufacturing and sale of aluminum profiles used in housing construction and industrial sectors. Its brand portfolio includes madeco, ficap, optel, indeco, decker, cotelsa, indelqui, alusa, alufoil, aluflex and indalum. The group's quarterly revenue for Sep '07 was 488,551.67 millions of CLP.

Primary SIC and add'l.: 3497 3353 3351 3316 3354 3357

CIK No: 0000899296

Subsidiaries: Aluflex S.A., Alufoil S.A., Alumco S.A., Alusa Overseas, Alusa S.A., Armat S.A., Cobrecon S.A., Colada Continua Chilena S.A., Comercial Madeco S.A., Cotelsa S.A., Decker Indelqui S.A., Distribuidora Boliviana Indalum S.A., Ficap S.A., H.B. San Luis S.A., Indalum S.A. 32 Subsidiaries included in the Index

Officers: Juan E. Rivera/CEO - Indeco, Jorge O. Tagle/CEO - Alusa, Sady Herrera/CEO - Decker, Indelqui, Mario Puentes/CEO - Indalum, Agilio Leao De MacEdo Filho/CEO - Ficap, Tiberio Dall'Olio/CEO, Eduardo Calvo/CEO - Aluflex, Jorge Uribe/CEO - Cedsa, Manuel Jose Noguera Eyzaguirre/Advisor, Cristian L. Montes/CFO, Julio Cordoba/Dir. - Operations Madeco, Enrique Sotomayor Arangua/Legal Counsel

Directors: Jean P. Luksic/Vice Chmn., Guillermo Luksic/Chmn., Oscar Ruiz-Tagle/Honorary Chmn., Eugenio Valck/Dir., Francisco Perez/Dir., Alessandro Bizzarri Carvallo/47/Dir., Hernan Buchi/Dir., Andronico Luksic/Dir., Felipe Joannon/Dir.

Owners: Insiders/1.50%, Quienco S.A. and subsidiaries/46.15%, The Bank of New York/5.70%, AFP Habitat S.A./6.52%, AFP Bansander S.A./5.77%

Financial Data: **Fiscal Year End:**12/31 **Latest Annual Data:** 12/31/2006

Year	Sales	Net Income
2006	$1,062,369,000	$64,678,000
2005	$694,426,000	$26,734,000
2004	$583,263,000	$17,243,000

Curr. Assets:	$441,339,000	**Curr. Liab.:**	$152,463,000	**P/E Ratio:**	58.79
Plant, Equip.:	$280,550,000	**Total Liab.:**	$335,031,000	**Indic. Yr. Divd.:**	NA
Total Assets:	$795,471,000	**Net Worth:**	$460,440,000	**Debt/ Equity:**	NA

Madison Ave Holdings Inc

428 S Atlantic Blvd., Ste. 328, Monterey Park, CA, 91754;

General - Incorporation	DE	Stock - Price on:12/24/2007	NA
Employees	NA	Stock Exchange	NA
Auditor	Michael T. Studer CPA P.C	Ticker Symbol	NA
Stk Agt.	Fidelity Transfer Co.	Outstanding Shares	NA
Counsel	NA	E.P.S.	NA
DUNS No.	NA	Shareholders	NA

Business: The group's principal activities are to engage in any lawful corporate undertaking, including, but not limited to, selected mergers and acquisitions. The company was incorporated on February 27, 2004 under the laws of the State of Delaware. The company is in developmental stage since inception and its operations to date have been limited to issuing shares to its original shareholders.

Primary SIC and add'l.: 6770

CIK No: 0001284196

Officers: Alex Kam/54/Dir., CEO, Pres., Chief Financial, Officer, Sec., Pan-Rong Liu/50/CFO

Directors: Alex Kam/54/Dir., CEO, Pres., Chief Financial, Officer, Sec.

Owners: Pan-Rong Liu, Acer Limited, Seung Chi Tang, Cesar Villavicencio, Alex Kam

Madison Explorations Inc

525 Seymour St., Ste 807, Vancouver, BC, V6B 3H7; *PH:* 1-604-974-0568;
http:// www.madisonexploration.com; *Email:* info@madisonexploration.com

General - Incorporation	NV	Stock - Price on:12/24/2007	$0.035
Employees	NA	Stock Exchange	OTC
Auditor	Kyle L. Tingle, Cpa LLC	Ticker Symbol	MDEX
Stk Agt.	NA	Outstanding Shares	NA
Counsel	NA	E.P.S.	NA
DUNS No.	NA	Shareholders	NA

Business: The group's principal activity is diamond exploration in the southern area of the province of Province of Saskatchewan, Canada. The group has incorporated one wholly owned subsidiary named Scout Resources, Inc. to conduct our Canadian exploration activities and for us to be in compliance with local law that requires a domestic Canadian corporation to conduct local exploration activities. Through Scout Resources Inc., the group is party to an agreement to acquire an 80% interest in the claims.

Primary SIC and add'l.: 1400

CIK No: 0001318268

Subsidiaries: Scout Resources, Inc.

Officers: Joseph Gallo/CEO, Steven Cozine/CFO, Kevin M. Stunder/39/Dir., Pres., Joel Haskins/37/Dir., Sec., Treasurer

Directors: Kevin M. Stunder/39/Dir., Pres., Joel Haskins/37/Dir., Sec., Treasurer

Owners: Kevin M. Stunder/28.14%, Insiders/56.28%, Joel Haskins/28.14%

Financial Data: Fiscal Year End:12/31 Latest Annual Data: 12/31/2006

Year	Sales		Net Income
2006	$94,000		-$39,000
2005	NA		-$49,000
Curr. Assets:	$26,000	**Curr. Liab.:**	$110,000
Plant, Equip.:	NA	**Total Liab.:**	$110,000	**Indic. Yr. Divd.:** NA
Total Assets:	$26,000	**Net Worth:**	-$85,000	**Debt/ Equity:** NA

Madison Minerals Ltd

Formerly: Madison Enterprises Corp
Guinness Tower, Ste. 2000, 1055 W Hastings St., Vancouver, BC, V6E 2E9; *PH:* 1-604-331-8772;
Fax: 1-604-331-8773; *http://* www.madison-enterprises.com

General - Incorporation	BC	Stock - Price on:12/24/2007	$0.39
Employees	NA	Stock Exchange	OTC
Auditor	Davidson & Co LLP	Ticker Symbol	MMRSF
Stk Agt.	Pacific Corporate Trust Co.	Outstanding Shares	NA
Counsel	NA	E.P.S.	NA
DUNS No.	25-313-2096	Shareholders	NA

Business: The group's principal activities are to acquire, explore and develop mineral properties located principally in papua new guinea and panama. The group has interests in the following mineral properties: mt. Kare property and belencillo property located in papua new guinea and is in the exploration stage. The subsidiaries of the group are madison enterprises (Latin America) s.a., madison enterprises (bvi) inc., madison enterprises (png) ltd., frontier mining exploration nl, oakland limited and matu mining limited.

Primary SIC and add'l.: 1499 1481

CIK No: 0001038621

Subsidiaries: A Panamanian corporation, Madison Enterprises (Latin American) S.A, Madison Enterprises (Nevada) Inc

Officers: Chet Idziszek/Chmn., CEO, Pres., James G. Stewart/Dir., General Counsel, Sec., Naomi Corrigan/CFO, David Mallo/VP - Exploration, Minerals, David J. Scott/Investor Relations Officer, Contact - Marketing

Directors: Chet Idziszek/Chmn., CEO, Pres., Donald W. Kohls/Member - Advisory Board, Robert Sibthorpe/Dir., Nell M. Dragovan/Dir., James G. Stewart/Dir., General Counsel, Sec., Martha F. Deacon/Dir., Henry Ewanchuk/Member - Advisory Board, Edward Yurkowski/Member - Advisory Board

Owners: Longview Strategies Inc./6.00%, Chet Idziszek/5.00%, Nell Dragovan/4.20%, Insiders/11.70%, J. G. Stewart/1.30%

Financial Data: Fiscal Year End:10/31 Latest Annual Data: 10/31/2006

Year	Sales		Net Income
2006	NA		-$2,019,000
2005	NA		-$2,001,000
2004	NA		-$13,278,000
Curr. Assets:	$6,295,000	**Curr. Liab.:**	$449,000
Plant, Equip.:	$284,000	**Total Liab.:**	$449,000	**Indic. Yr. Divd.:** NA
Total Assets:	$6,578,000	**Net Worth:**	$6,129,000	**Debt/ Equity:** NA

Magal Security Systems Ltd

43180 Osgood Rd., Fremont, CA, 94539; *PH:* 1-510-440-1000; *Fax:* 1-510-440-8686;
http:// www.magal-ssl.com; *Email:* contact@magal-ssl.com

General - Incorporation	Israel	Stock - Price on:12/24/2007	$10.32
Employees	309	Stock Exchange	NDQ
Auditor	Kost Forer Gabbay & Kasierer	Ticker Symbol	MAGS
Stk Agt.	American Stock Transfer & Trust Co.	Outstanding Shares	10,390,000
Counsel	NA	E.P.S.	-$0.12
DUNS No.	60-001-8626	Shareholders	NA

Business: The groups principle activities include development, manufacturing and marketing of computerized security systems that automatically detect, locate and identify the nature of intrusions and automatically detect, locate and identify explosive devices in luggage, packages and other parcels. The group operates from United States.

Primary SIC and add'l.: 3669

CIK No: 0000896494

Subsidiaries: E.S.E. Ltd., Kobb Inc., Magal B.V., Magal Security Sisteme S.R.L, Magal Security Systems Poland, Magal Senstar Inc., Senstar GmbH, Senstar-Stellar Corporation, Senstar-Stellar Latin America S.A. de C.V., Senstar-Stellar Limited, Smart Interactive Systems, Inc.

Officers: Izhar Dekel/Dir., CEO, Pres., Dany Pizen/VP - Marketing, East Europe - CIS, Galit Betzalel/Marcom Mgr., Ofer Katz/VP - Aviation Security, Effi Gutman/Purchasing, Import Mgr., Raffi Netzer/VP - Marketing, Africa, Latin America, Raya Asher/CFO, VP - Finance, Sec., Moshe Zilbershtein/CTO, Adam Rosenberg/Sales Mgr. - Dreambox Division, Yehezkel Farber/VP - Operations, Zvi Dank/VP - Research, Development, Yehonatan Ben Hamozeg/VP - Integrated Systems Development, Asaf Even-Ezra/VP - Marketing, Israel, West Europe

Directors: Izhar Dekel/Dir., CEO, Pres., Jacob Even-Ezra/Chmn., Jacob Perry/Dir., Anat Winner/Dir., Nathan Kirsh/Dir., Zeev Livne/Dir., Shaul Kobrinsky/Dir., Jacob Nuss/Dir.

Owners: Izhar Dekel/1.47%, Jacob Even-Ezra/3.32%, Insiders/24.82%, Asaf Even-Ezra/1.16%, Nathan Kirsh/17.63%

Financial Data: Fiscal Year End:12/31 Latest Annual Data: 12/31/2006

Year	Sales		Net Income
2006	$66,958,000		$810,000
2005	$61,282,000		-$3,211,000
2004	$60,974,000		$1,053,000
Curr. Assets:	$75,147,000	**Curr. Liab.:**	$35,430,000	**P/E Ratio:** 58.79
Plant, Equip.:	$14,366,000	**Total Liab.:**	$45,531,000	**Indic. Yr. Divd.:** NA
Total Assets:	$103,681,000	**Net Worth:**	$58,150,000	**Debt/ Equity:** NA

Magellan Health Services Inc

55 Nod Rd., Avon, CT, 06001; *PH:* 1-860-507-1900; *Fax:* 1-860-507-1990;
http:// www.magellanhealth.com

General - Incorporation	DE	Stock - Price on:12/24/2007	$18.5
Employees	NA	Stock Exchange	OTC
Auditor	Ernst & Young LLP	Ticker Symbol	MGLNW
Stk Agt.	Wachovia Bank N.A	Outstanding Shares	NA
Counsel	King & Spalding LLP	E.P.S.	$2.16
DUNS No.	04-969-3732	Shareholders	NA

Business: The group's principle activity is to provide healthcare services. The group's services include beahavioral care management and conditional care management services. The group operates from United States.

Primary SIC and add'l.: 8093 8049 8063 8011 8082 8099 6371

CIK No: 0000019411

Subsidiaries: Advantage Behavioral Systems,Inc., AdvoCare of Tennessee,Inc., AGCA New York,Inc., AGCA,Inc., Alliance Health Systems,Inc., Arizona Biodyne,Inc., Ceres Behavioral Healthcare Systems, LLC, Charter Alvarado Behavioral Health System,Inc., Charter Bay Harbor Behavioral Health System,Inc., Charter Behavioral Health System at Fair Oaks,Inc., Charter Behavioral Health System at Hidden Brook,Inc., Charter Behavioral Health System at Potomac Ridge,Inc., Charter Behavioral Health System of Dallas,Inc., Charter Behavioral Health System of Delmarva,Inc., Charter Behavioral Health System of Lafayette,Inc. 100 Subsidiaries included in the Index

Officers: Eric Reimer/CEO - National Imaging Associates, Steven J. Shulman/Chmn., CEO/$8,326,050.00, Michael Majerik/Chief Sales, Marketing Officer/$951,507.00, Mark S. Demilio/CFO/$2,825,879.00, Daniel N. Gregoire/General Counsel, Sec./$987,993.00, Caskie Lewis-Clapper/Chief Human Resources Officer, Rene Lerer/Dir., COO, Pres./$4,350,829.00, Anthony M. Kotin/Chief Clinical Officer, Raju L. Mantena/Pres. - Icore Healthcare, LLC, Russell C. Petrella/Pres. - Behavioral Health, Jeffrey N. West/Sr. VP, Controller

Directors: Steven J. Shulman/Chmn., CEO, Michael P. Ressner/Dir., Robert M. Le Blanc/Dir., Michael Diament/Dir., Saul E. Burian/Dir., William J. McBride/Dir., Barry M. Smith/Dir., Rene Lerer/Dir., COO, Pres., Allen F. Wise/Dir., Nancy L. Johnson/Dir., William D. Forrest/Dir.

Owners: Insiders/3.20%, Mark Demilio, Robert M. Le Blanc, Allen F. Wise, Daniel N. Gregoire, Barry M. Smith, Steven J. Shulman/2.50%, Saul E. Burian, William J. McBride, Ren Lerer, Michael P. Ressner, Guardian Investor Services LLC/7.30%, TimesSquare Capital Management, LLC/6.90%, Michael Diament

Financial Data: Fiscal Year End:12/31 Latest Annual Data: 12/31/2006

Year	Sales		Net Income
2006	$1,690,270,000		$86,262,000
2005	$1,808,003,000		$130,589,000
2004	$1,795,402,000		$88,372,000
Curr. Assets:	$535,574,000	**Curr. Liab.:**	$321,073,000	**P/E Ratio:** 24.25
Plant, Equip.:	$100,255,000	**Total Liab.:**	$443,779,000	**Indic. Yr. Divd.:** NA
Total Assets:	$1,207,520,000	**Net Worth:**	$763,567,000	**Debt/ Equity:** NA

Magellan Midstream Partners LP

1 Williams Ctr., Tulsa, OK, 74172; *PH:* 1-918-574-7000; *Fax:* 1-918-573-6714;
http:// www.magellanlp.com

General - Incorporation	MD	Stock - Price on:12/24/2007	$43.95
Employees	NA	Stock Exchange	NYSE
Auditor	Ernst& Young LLP	Ticker Symbol	MMP
Stk Agt.	Computershare Trust CO.	Outstanding Shares	66,550,000
Counsel	NA	E.P.S.	$2.28
DUNS No.	NA	Shareholders	NA

Business: The groups principle activities include transportation and distribution of petroleum products, oil refineries and gasoline products. The group operates through three segments namely, petroleum products pipeline system, petroleum products terminals and ammonia pipeline system. In the year 2005, the group acquired marine terminal in Wilmington. The group operates from the United States. Of the total revenue in the year 2006, petroleum products pipeline system segment accounted for $580,482, petroleum products terminals $102,121 and ammonia pipeline system $13,922 (thousands).

Primary SIC and add'l.: 4613

CIK No: 0001126975

Subsidiaries: Magellan Ammonia Pipeline, L.P.,, Magellan Asset Services, L.P.,, Magellan GP, LLC,, Magellan Midstream Partners, L.P.,, Magellan NGL, LLC,, Magellan OLP, L.P.,, Magellan Operating GP, LLC,, Magellan Pipeline Company, L.P.,, Magellan Pipeline GP, LLC,, Magellan Pipeline Terminals, L.P.,, Magellan Pipelines Holdings, L.P.,, Magellan Terminals Holdings, L.P.,

Officers: Don R. Wellendorf/Chmn., CEO, Pres./$1,723,342.00, John D. Chandler/Sr. VP, CFO, Treasurer/$914,111.00, Lisa J. Korner/VP - Human Resources, Administration, Michael N. Mears/Sr. VP - Transportation, Terminals/$821,815.00, Richard A. Olson/Sr. VP - Operations, Technical Services/$825,631.00, Brett C. Riley/Sr. VP - Business Development, Lonny E. Townsend/Sr. VP, General Counsel - Compliance, Ethics Officer, Assist. Sec./$824,432.00, Paula Farrell/Investor Contact, Suzanne H. Costin/Sec., Bruce Heine/Operations Media Contact

Directors: Don R. Wellendorf/Chmn., CEO, Pres., Thomas S. Souleles/Dir., Thomas T. MacEjko/Dir., John P. Desbarres/Dir., Patrick C. Eilers/Dir., James R. Montague/Dir., George A. O'Brien/Dir.

Owners: George A. OBrien, Richard A. Olson, Tortoise Capital Advisors, L.L.C./5.60%, John P. DesBarres, Lonny E. Townsend/6.10%, Don R. Wellendorf, Kayne Anderson Capital Advisors, L.P./7.30%, John D. Chandler/18.30%, Lonny E. Townsend, John D. Chandler, James R. Montague, Insiders/87.40%, Michael N. Mears/18.30%, Michael N. Mears, Don R. Wellendorf/26.30% *(16 Owners included in Index)*

Financial Data: Fiscal Year End:12/31 **Latest Annual Data:** 06/30/2007

Year	Sales	Net Income
2007	NA	NA
2006	$1,223,560,000	$192,728,000
2005	$1,137,072,000	$159,483,000

Curr. Assets:	$177,018,000	**Curr. Liab.:**	$518,389,000	**P/E Ratio:**	19.28
Plant, Equip.:	$1,702,739,000	**Total Liab.:**	$1,146,167,000	**Indic. Yr. Divd.:**	$2.580
Total Assets:	$1,952,649,000	**Net Worth:**	$806,482,000	**Debt/ Equity:**	1.0565

Magellan Petroleum Corp

10 Columbus Blvd., Hartford, CT, 06106; **PH:** 1-860-293-2006; **Fax:** 1-860-293-2349; *http://* www.magpet.com

General - Incorporation	DE	**Stock**- Price on:12/24/2007	$1.55
Employees	29	Stock Exchange	AMEX
Auditor	Deloitte & Touche LLP	Ticker Symbol	MPN-PC
Stk Agt	American Stock Transfer & Trust Co.	Outstanding Shares	41,500,000
Counsel	NA	E.P.S.	-$0.004
DUNS No.	05-253-7644	Shareholders	NA

Business: The group's principal activities are to explore, develop and sell oil and gas reserves in Canada, Australia, New Zealand, the United Kingdom and the United States. The major assets of the group are two petroleum production leases covering the mereenie oil and gas field (35% working interest) and one petroleum production lease covering the palm valley gas field (52% working interest). Both the fields are located in the amadeus basin in the northern territory of Australia. The group also has a direct carried interest in the kotaneelee gas field in the yukon territory of Canada.

Primary SIC and add'l.: 1382

CIK No: 0000061398

Subsidiaries: Jarl Pty. Ltd., Magellan Petroleum (Belize) Limited, Magellan Petroleum (Eastern) Pty. Ltd., Magellan Petroleum (N.T.) Pty. Ltd., Magellan Petroleum (NZ)Limited, Magellan Petroleum (Southern) Pty. Ltd., Magellan Petroleum (Ventures) Pty Ltd., Magellan Petroleum (W.A.) Pty. Ltd., Magellan Petroleum Australia Limited, Paroo Petroleum (Holdings), Inc., Paroo Petroleum (USA), Inc., Paroo Petroleum Pty. Ltd.

Officers: Daniel J. Samela/CEO, Pres., Chief Financial, Accounting Officer, Edward B. Whittemore/Sec.

Directors: Walter McCann/Chmn., Ronald P. Pettirossi/Dir., Donald V. Basso/Dir., Timothy L. Largay/Dir., Robert Mollah/Dir.

Owners: Timothy L. Largay, Walter McCann, Insiders, Donald Basso, Ronald P. Pettirossi

Financial Data: Fiscal Year End:06/30 **Latest Annual Data:** 6/30/2006

Year	Sales	Net Income
2006	$26,562,000	$749,000
2005	$21,871,000	$87,000
2004	$20,524,000	$350,000

Curr. Assets:	$37,570,000	**Curr. Liab.:**	$8,566,000	**P/E Ratio:**	38.75
Plant, Equip.:	$40,321,000	**Total Liab.:**	$21,642,000	**Indic. Yr. Divd.:**	NA
Total Assets:	$85,616,000	**Net Worth:**	$63,975,000	**Debt/ Equity:**	NA

Magic Communications Inc

5 W Main St., Elmsford, NY, 10523; **PH:** 1-914-391-5549; *http://* magiccomm.com

General - Incorporation	DE	**Stock**- Price on:12/24/2007	$0.65
Employees	NA	Stock Exchange	NA
Auditor	NA	Ticker Symbol	NA
Stk Agt	Continental Stock Transfer & Trust Co	Outstanding Shares	NA
Counsel	NA	E.P.S.	NA
DUNS No.	NA	Shareholders	NA

Business: The groups principle activities include owning and operating pay phones. The group operates from New York in the United States.

Primary SIC and add'l.: 7373

CIK No: 0001205332

Officers: Stephen D. Rogers/57/Dir., CEO, CFO, Pres., Maureen Rogers/51/Dir., VP

Directors: Stephen D. Rogers/57/Dir., CEO, CFO, Pres., Maureen Rogers/51/Dir., VP

Owners: John Hohman/37.10%, Insiders/76.90%, Kelly T. Hickel/2.20%, Edward Hohman/37.10%

Financial Data: Fiscal Year End:12/31 **Latest Annual Data:** 12/31/2006

Year	Sales	Net Income
2006	$53,000	-$58,000

Curr. Assets:	$1,000	**Curr. Liab.:**	$195,000		
Plant, Equip.:	NA	**Total Liab.:**	$195,000	**Indic. Yr. Divd.:**	NA
Total Assets:	$4,000	**Net Worth:**	-$190,000	**Debt/ Equity:**	NA

Magic Lantern Group. Inc

1385 Brdway, New York, NY, 10018; **PH:** 1-905-827-2755; *http://* www.magiclantern.ca; **Email:** info@magiclantern.ca

General - Incorporation	NY	**Stock**- Price on:12/24/2007	$73.1
Employees	NA	Stock Exchange	OTC
Auditor	Mahoney Cohen & Co. CPA, P.C	Ticker Symbol	GMLI
Stk Agt	First Montauk Securities Corp	Outstanding Shares	NA
Counsel	Hodgson Russ	E.P.S.	NA
DUNS No.	02-128-0060	Shareholders	NA

Business: The group's principal activity is to sell and distribute educational and learning content in video and other electronic formats. The group also designs and distributes casual apparel for men and boys. The group's library includes content from numerous producers, including disney educational, annenbreg/cpb and ctv television. The group's tutorbuddy is an Internet-enabled provider of content and related educational services on demand to students, teachers and parents. The group's catalogue consists of more than 10,000 video titles covering all subject areas from pre-school through high school, post-secondary and general interest, with distribution agreements with more than 200 producers and suppliers. The group's customers includes educational institutions and libraries in Canada.

Primary SIC and add'l.: 5136 5735

CIK No: 0000811933

Subsidiaries: Magic Lantern Communications, Ltd., Magic Vision Digital Media Inc, Sonoptic Technologies, Inc

Curr. Assets:	$767,000	**Curr. Liab.:**	$6,797,000	**P/E Ratio:**	58.79
Plant, Equip.:	$589,000	**Total Liab.:**	$7,013,000	**Indic. Yr. Divd.:**	NA
Total Assets:	$8,124,000	**Net Worth:**	$1,111,000	**Debt/ Equity:**	NA

Magic Software Enterprises Ltd

23046 Ave.nida de la Carlota, Ste. 300, Laguna Hills, CA, 92653; **PH:** 1-949-250-1718; **Fax:** 1-949-250-7404; *http://* www.magicsoftware.com; **Email:** sales@magicsoftware.com

General - Incorporation	Israel	**Stock**- Price on:12/24/2007	$2.35
Employees	567	Stock Exchange	NDQ
Auditor	Kost Forer Gabbay & Kasierer	Ticker Symbol	MGIC
Stk Agt	American Stock Transfer & Trust Co.	Outstanding Shares	31,310,000
Counsel	Pelles, Eiss, Moser Efrima Sherman	E.P.S.	$0.08
DUNS No.	60-005-2146	Shareholders	NA

Business: The group's principle activities are the development, marketing and support of its software and user technology, which is based on visual table-driven computer programming methods. The table-driven technology enables enterprises to accelerate the process of building and deploying business software applications that can be customized and integrated within existing systems. The company also sells applications developed using the table-driven technology which are designed for e-business, customer relations management and other enterprise uses. The company also provides maintenance and technical support as well as consulting and project management services for its products. The group's quarterly revenue for Sep '07 was 17.63 millions of USD.

Primary SIC and add'l.: 7376 7373 7371

CIK No: 0000876779

Subsidiaries: Advanced Answers on Demand Holding Corporation

Officers: Eitan Naor/Dir., CEO, Pres., Oren Inbar/VP - MSE Ltd, CEO, Pres. - Magic Inc, Udi Ertel/CEO - Magic Israel, Member - MSE Management, Ziv Zviel/VP - Finance - Operations, Avikam Perry/CTO, VP - Research, Development, Regev Yativ/VP - International Sales, Avigdor Luttinger/VP - Corporate Strategy, Ayelet Regev/Investor Relations Officer, Amit Ben-Zvi/VP - Magic Software, Amit Birk/General Counsel, VP - M, A, David Zigdon/CFO, Arita Mattsoff/VP - Global Marketing

Directors: Eitan Naor/Dir., CEO, Pres., Guy Bernstein/Chmn., Eli Reifman/Dir., Itiel Efrat/Dir., Hadas Gazit Kaiser/Dir., David Assia/56/Dir., Gad Goldstein/Dir., Naamit Salomon/Dir., Yehezkel Zeira/Dir., Elan Penn/Dir.

Owners: Ziv Zviel, Insiders/4.57%, Elan Penn, Yehezkel Zeira, David Assia/4.36%

Financial Data: Fiscal Year End:12/31 **Latest Annual Data:** 12/31/2006

Year	Sales	Net Income
2006	$61,725,000	-$5,006,000
2005	$60,990,000	-$4,607,000
2004	$65,167,000	$4,090,000

Curr. Assets:	$28,045,000	**Curr. Liab.:**	$19,404,000	**P/E Ratio:**	58.79
Plant, Equip.:	$6,414,000	**Total Liab.:**	$22,267,000	**Indic. Yr. Divd.:**	NA
Total Assets:	$69,911,000	**Net Worth:**	$47,644,000	**Debt/ Equity:**	NA

Magma Design Automation Inc

1650 Technology Dr., San Jose, CA, 95110; **PH:** 1-408-565-7500; **Fax:** 1-408-565-7501; *http://* www.magma-da.com; **Email:** info@magma-da.com

General - Incorporation	DE	**Stock**- Price on:12/24/2007	$14.77
Employees	843	Stock Exchange	NDQ
Auditor	Grant Thornton LLP	Ticker Symbol	LAVA
Stk Agt	Mellon Investor Services LLC	Outstanding Shares	39,780,000
Counsel	Fenwick & West LLP	E.P.S.	-$1.67
DUNS No.	NA	Shareholders	NA

Business: The group's principal activity is to provide design and implementation software. Its products include blast fusion, blast chip, blast plan, blast noise and diamond si. These products are designed to reduce the timing closure iterations caused by separate front-end and back-end processes. The group also provides consulting, training and chip design services. Its customers include broadcom, infineon, nec, nokia, Texas instruments, renesas technology, toshiba and vitesse. During fiscal 2004, the group acquired the following business: aplus design technologies, inc, silicon metrics corporation, random logic, inc, siliconcraft, inc and in fiscal 2005 it acquired lemmatis, inc and mojave, inc.

Primary SIC and add'l.: 7379 7372

CIK No: 0001065034

Subsidiaries: Beijing Magma Design Automation, Inc., Magma Design Automation BV, Magma Design Automation Cayman Ltd., Magma Design Automation Corp., Magma Design Automation India Private Limited, Magma Design Automation K.K., Magma Design Automation Limited GmbH, Magma Design Automation Ltd., Magma Design Automation SARL, Magma Design Automation, Inc. Taiwan Ltd., Magma Korea d/b/a Silicon Craft, Inc., Magma Services, Inc., MDA Netherlands, C.V.

Officers: Rajeev Madhavan/Chmn., CEO/$1,343,542.00, Roy E. Jewell/Dir., COO, Pres./$1,499,084.00, Premal Buch/GM, VP - Product Development, Design Implementation Business Unit, Kam Kittrell/GM, VP - Design Implementation Business Unit, John Lee/GM, VP - Physical Verification Business Unit, Vivek Raghavan/GM, VP - Product Development, Physical Verification Business Unit, Anirudh Devgan/GM, VP - Product Development, Custom Design Business Unit, David Stanley/Corporate VP - Corporate Affairs/$607,692.00, Peter S. Teshima/Corporate VP - Finance, CFO/$673,663.00, Milan G. Lazich/VP - Corporate Marketing, Camellia Ngo/VP - Human Resources, Suk Lee/GM, VP - Custom Design Business Unit, Heidi Flannery/Investor Relations Consultant, Heidi Flannery - Ficomm/Investor Relations Consultant, Saeid Ghafouri/Corporate VP - Field Operations

Directors: Rajeev Madhavan/Chmn., CEO, Roy E. Jewell/Dir., COO, Pres., Timothy J. Ng/Dir., Chet Silvestri/Dir., Susumu Kohyama/Dir., Kevin C. Eichler/Dir., Thomas Rohrs/Dir.

Owners: Thomas M. Rohrs, Rajeev Madhavan/5.10%, Insiders/9.70%, Timothy J. Ng, Roy E. Jewell/2.00%, David H. Stanley, Federated Investors, Inc./12.90%, Andreas Bechtolsheim/8.30%, Chester J. Silvestri, Gregory C. Walker, Susumu Kohyama, Kevin C. Eichler, Peter S. Teshima, Third Avenue Management LLC/5.90%, Saeid Ghafouri

Financial Data: Fiscal Year End:04/02 Latest Annual Data: 4/1/2007

Year	Sales	Net Income
2007	$178,153,000	-$61,185,000
2006	$164,044,000	-$20,937,000
2005	$145,941,000	-$8,581,000

Curr. Assets:	$135,161,000	Curr. Liab.:	$58,934,000		
Plant, Equip.:	$20,062,000	Total Liab.:	$170,161,000	Indic. Yr. Divd.:	NA
Total Assets:	$284,064,000	Net Worth:	$113,903,000	Debt/ Equity:	0.7983

Magna Entertainment Corp

337 Magna Dr., Aurora, ON, L4G 7K1; *PH:* 1-905-726-2462; *http://* www.magnaent.com; *Email:* mec.investors@magnaent.com

General - Incorporation	DE	Stock- Price on:12/24/2007	$3.1418
Employees	5,300	Stock Exchange	NDQ
Auditor	Ernst & Young LLP	Ticker Symbol	MECA
Stk Agt.	Computershare Trust CO.	Outstanding Shares	107,670,000
Counsel	NA	E.P.S.	-$0.81
DUNS No.	NA	Shareholders	NA

Business: The group's principal activity is to acquire, develop and operate horse racetracks and related wagering operations. Currently, the group operates in twelve thoroughbred racetracks, two standardbred racetrack and one greyhound racetrack. The group also operates simulcast-wagering venues across the United States, Canada, Mexico, the Caribbean region, United Kingdom and Australia. The racetrack facilities include dirt track, seating facilities, and turf course, parking, clubhouse and food and beverage facilities. The real estate operations of the group include a portfolio of undeveloped land and land under various stages of development including gated residential community and golf courses in the United States, Canada, and Austria.

Primary SIC and add'l.: 7999 6512 7997 6513 6552 7948

CIK No: 0001093273

Subsidiaries: 20002DelawareInc., 20004Maryland,Inc., Adena Meadows II Limited, Allegheny Harness Racing Association,Inc., Allegheny Thoroughbred Racing Association,Inc., Aurora Hospitality Services,Inc., Bay Meadows Catering Company, Bay Meadows Operating Company,LLC, DLR,Inc., FEX KO-FaserverarbeitungsGmbH, Fex Straw ManufacturingInc., Fontana Beteiligungs AG, GPRA Commercial Enterprises,Inc., GPRA Thoroughbred Training Center,Inc., Gulfstream Park Racing Association,Inc. 69 Subsidiaries included in the Index

Officers: Frank Stronach/Chmn., Interim CEO, Blake Tohana/CFO, Exec. VP, Frank Demarco/VP - Regulatory Affairs, Mary Lyn Seymour/VP, Controller, Joe De Francis/Exec. VP, William G. Ford/Sec., Brant Latta/Sr. VP - Operations, James Bromby/Sr. VP - Operations

Directors: Frank Stronach/Chmn., Interim CEO, William J. Menear/Dir., Jerry D. Campbell/Dir., Ron Charles/Dir., Charlie J. Williams/Dir., Frank Vasilkioti/Dir., Jennifer Jackson/Dir.

Financial Data: Fiscal Year End:12/31 Latest Annual Data: 12/31/2006

Year	Sales	Net Income
2006	$702,139,000	-$87,351,000
2005	$624,655,000	-$105,293,000
2004	$731,577,000	-$95,636,000

Curr. Assets:	$150,930,000	Curr. Liab.:	$245,131,000		
Plant, Equip.:	$939,035,000	Total Liab.:	$846,267,000	Indic. Yr. Divd.:	NA
Total Assets:	$1,246,885,000	Net Worth:	$400,618,000	Debt/ Equity:	1.1236

Magna International Inc

600 Wilshire Dr., Troy, MI, 48084; *PH:* 1-248-729-2400; *Fax:* 1-248-729-2410; *http://* www.magnaint.com; *Email:* magnaint_productinfo@magna.on.ca

General - Incorporation	Canada	Stock- Price on:12/24/2007	$91.51
Employees	83,000	Stock Exchange	NYSE
Auditor	Ernst & Young LLP	Ticker Symbol	MGA
Stk Agt.	Computershare Trust Co of Canada	Outstanding Shares	109,960,000
Counsel	NA	E.P.S.	$5.44
DUNS No.	20-151-6002	Shareholders	NA

Business: The group's principle activities are manufacturing of vehicles and systems integration. The company designs, engineers, manufactures and supplies components, modules and systems primarily for original equipment manufacturers. The company also manufactures and supplies plastics and metallic exterior components and systems, complete seat systems, seat tracks, seat frames, integrated child safety seats and other seating components. The company supplies instrument panels, cockpit modules, consoles, glove boxes, package trays, overhead systems, door panels, automotive carpets, interior panels and other interior components. The company acquires, develops and operates horse racetracks and related pari-mutual wagering operations.

Primary SIC and add'l.: 2273 3711 3465 3647

CIK No: 0000749098

Officers: Siegfried Wolf/50/Dir., Co - CEO, Donald J. Walker/51/Dir., Co - CEO, Belinda Stronach/42/Executive Vice Chmn., Bassem Shakeel/Assist. Sec., Michael G.R. Sinnaeve/VP - Operational Improvement, Quality, The Americas, Paul Brock/Treasurer, Herbert Demel/COO - Vehicles, Powertrain, Peter N. Corcoran/Exec. VP, Alon Ossip/Exec. VP, Robert D. Merkley/VP - Internal Audit, Peter Koob/Exec. VP - Corporate Development, Vincent J. Galifi/CFO, Exec. VP, Mark T. Hogan/Pres., Gerd R. Brusius/VP - Operational Improvement, Quality, Europe, Hubert Hodl/VP - Marketing, New Business Development, Europe (25 Officers included in Index)

Directors: Siegfried Wolf/50/Dir., Co - CEO, Donald J. Walker/51/Dir., Co - CEO, Belinda Stronach/42/Executive Vice Chmn., Frank Stronach/75/Chmn., Louis E. Lataif/69/Dir., Gregory C. Wilkins/52/Dir., James D. Wolfensohn/74/Dir., Donald Resnick/80/Dir., Lawrence D. Worrall/64/Dir., Lady Barbara Thomas Judge/61/Dir., Klaus Mangold/64/Dir., Franz Vranitzky/70/Dir., Michael D. Harris/63/Dir.

Financial Data: Fiscal Year End:12/31 Latest Annual Data: 12/31/2006

Year	Sales	Net Income
2006	$24,180,000,000	$548,000,000
2005	$22,811,000,000	$639,000,000
2004	$20,653,000,000	$668,000,000

Curr. Assets:	$7,060,000,000	Curr. Liab.:	$4,858,000,000		
Plant, Equip.:	$4,097,000,000	Total Liab.:	$6,118,000,000	Indic. Yr. Divd.:	$0.960
Total Assets:	$13,175,000,000	Net Worth:	$7,057,000,000	Debt/ Equity:	NA

Magna Lab Inc

6800 Jericho Tpke., Ste 120w, Syosset, NY, 11791; *PH:* 1-516-393-5874; *http://* www.magna-lab.com

General - Incorporation	NY	Stock- Price on:12/24/2007	NA
Employees	NA	Stock Exchange	OTC
Auditor	Rothstein, Kass & Co, P.C	Ticker Symbol	MAGAA
Stk Agt.	American Stock Transfer & Trust Co.	Outstanding Shares	NA
Counsel	NA	E.P.S.	-$0.12
DUNS No.	78-756-9912	Shareholders	NA

Business: The group's principal activity is to enter into a arrangement in order to complete commercialization of its illuminator products and development of its artery view product. The group is also seeking other means to realize value through sale, license or otherwise or merging the group with an unrelated business. The group was in development and commercialization of disposable medical services designed to enhance the effectiveness of magnetic resonance imaging in detection and diagnosis of coronary heart disease.

Primary SIC and add'l.: 6719 3845

CIK No: 0000895464

Subsidiaries: Cardiac MRI, Inc.

Officers: Lawrence A. Minkoff/58/Chmn., Principal Executive Officer, Chief Scientific Officer, Pres., Kenneth C. Riscica/54/Principal Financial Officer, Treasurer, Sec., J. M. Feldman/63/Dir., VP

Directors: Lawrence A. Minkoff/58/Chmn., Principal Executive Officer, Chief Scientific Officer, Pres., Jonathan Adereth/61/Dir., J. M. Feldman/63/Dir., VP, Joel S. Kanter/51/Dir., Seymour Kessler/76/Dir.

Owners: Jonathan Adereth/0.20%, Magna Acquisition LLC/55.10%, Lawrence A. Minkoff, Seymour Kessler/0.10%, Insiders, Insiders, J. M. Feldman, Lawrence A. Minkoff, Kenneth C. Riscica/1.90%, Joel Kanter/0.30%

Financial Data: Fiscal Year End:02/28 Latest Annual Data: 2/28/2007

Year	Sales	Net Income
2007	NA	-$114,000
2006	NA	-$90,000
2005	NA	-$101,000

Curr. Assets:	$10,000	Curr. Liab.:	$318,000		
Plant, Equip.:	NA	Total Liab.:	$318,000	Indic. Yr. Divd.:	NA
Total Assets:	$10,000	Net Worth:	-$308,000	Debt/ Equity:	NA

Magnetek Inc

N49 W13650 Campbell Dr., Menomonee Falls, WI, 53051; *PH:* 1-262-783-3500; *Fax:* 1-262-783-3510; *http://* www.magnetek.com; *Email:* productinfo@magnetek.com

General - Incorporation	DE	Stock- Price on:12/24/2007	$5
Employees	300	Stock Exchange	NYSE
Auditor	Ernst & Young LLP	Ticker Symbol	MAG
Stk Agt.	Mellon Investor Services	Outstanding Shares	29,850,000
Counsel	NA	E.P.S.	-$1.68
DUNS No.	11-753-1954	Shareholders	NA

Business: The group's principal activity is to supply digital power-electronic products for use in information technology and in industrial, communications, consumer and other markets. The group operates in a single segment, digital power products, which includes two product lines, components and systems. Components include: ac-to-dc switching power supplies, ac-to-dc rectifiers/battery chargers, dc-to-dc power converters, dc-to-ac power inverters and peripheral component interconnects (pcis). Major customers include merloni, IBM, siemens, motorola, alcatel and ericsson. Magnetek's systems consist of programmable motion control, power conditioning systems, verizon, nortel, U.S. Cellular and t-mobile. The group acquired mxt holdings, inc on 30-Dec-2002.

Primary SIC and add'l.: 3677 3674

CIK No: 0000751085

Subsidiaries: Magnetek ADS Power,Inc., Magnetek Alternative Energy,Inc., Magnetek Electronics Co., Ltd., Magnetek Industrial Controls (U.K.) Limited, Magnetek Kft, Magnetek Mondel Holding,Inc., Magnetek S.p.A, Magnetek Vertriebsgesellschaft m.b.H., Mondel ULC

Officers: David P. Reiland/Dir., Exec. VP/$629,747.00, Peter M. McCormick/Exec. VP - Power Control Systems/$480,269.00, Robert Murray/VP - Communications, Investor Relations, Lynn Bostrom Lynn Bostrom/Mgr. - Marketing Communications, Marty J. Schwenner/CFO, VP/$447,087.00, Jolene Shellman/VP - Legal Affairs, Corp. Sec./$119,456.00, Ryan Gile/VP, Controller/$185,996.00

Directors: Yon Yoon Jorden/53/Dir., David P. Reiland/Dir., Exec. VP, Mitchell I. Quain/Dir., Dewain K. Cross/Dir.

Owners: Robert E. Wycoff, Marty J. Schwenner, Renaissance Technologies Corp./5.56%, Pete McCormick, Ryan D. Gile, David P. Reiland/2.82%, Dimensional Fund Advisors, L.P./7.88%, Andrew G. Galef/5.73%, Alexander Levran/1.08%, Dewain K. Cross, Yon Yoon Jorden, Thomas G. Boren/1.83%, Paul J. Kofmehl, Insiders/15.00%, Mitchell I. Quain (16 Owners included in Index)

Financial Data: Fiscal Year End:07/03 Latest Annual Data: 7/2/2006

Year	Sales	Net Income
2006	$83,102,000	-$46,849,000
2005	$242,389,000	-$26,870,000
2004	$242,834,000	-$11,471,000

Curr. Assets:	$121,266,000	**Curr. Liab.:**	$75,527,000		
Plant, Equip.:	$31,939,000	**Total Liab.:**	$183,626,000	**Indic. Yr. Divd.:**	NA
Total Assets:	$229,180,000	**Net Worth:**	$45,554,000	**Debt/ Equity:**	NA

Magnitude Information Systems Inc

1250 Rte. 28, Ste. 309, Branchburg, NJ, 08876; ***PH:*** 1-908-879-2722; ***Fax:*** 1-908-879-7006; ***http://*** www.magnitude.com; ***Email:*** info@magnitude.com

General - Incorporation: DE
Employees: 4
Auditor: Rosenberg Rich Baker Berman & Co
Stk Agt: Securities Transfer Corp
Counsel: NA
DUNS No.: 17-190-6951

Stock - Price on:12/24/2007: $0.055
Stock Exchange: OTC
Ticker Symbol: MAGY
Outstanding Shares: 229,050,000
E.P.S.: -$0.026
Shareholders: NA

Business: The group's principal activities are developing, marketing and licensing risk aversion and productivity enhancement software products for computerized workplace environment. The group's primary product is an integrated suite of proprietary software modules marketed under the name ergomanagertm. These are designed to help individual computer users and businesses increase productivity and reduce the risk of potentially preventable repetitive stress injury (rsi). These software modules can be applied individually or together in a comprehensive ergonomic and early intervention program. The modules seek to modify a user's behavior by monitoring computer usage patterns over time and warning the user when to break a dangerous trend in repetitive usage of an input device, such as a keyboard or mouse. The group operates primarily in the United States of America.

Primary SIC and add'l.: 7372 3577

CIK No: 0000838796

Subsidiaries: Magnitude, Inc.

Officers: Edward L. Marney/Dir., CEO, Pres./$92,488.00, Joerg H. Klaube/66/Dir., CFO, Sr. VP, Sec.

Directors: Edward L. Marney/Dir., CEO, Pres., Steven L. Gray/59/Chmn., Joseph J. Tomasek/61/Dir., Joerg H. Klaube/66/Dir., CFO, Sr. VP, Sec.

Owners: Insiders/4.32%, Steven L. Gray/2.46%, 33 Group LLC/5.70%, Steven D. Rudnik/10.30%, Azzurri Group, LLC/5.70%, Joerg H. Klaube/0.62%, Michael G. Martin/5.70%, Joseph J. Tomasek/1.25%

Financial Data: ***Fiscal Year End:***12/31 ***Latest Annual Data:*** 12/31/2006

Year	Sales	Net Income
2006	$48,000	-$3,895,000
2005	$190,000	-$2,218,000
2004	$122,000	-$2,309,000

Curr. Assets:	$121,000	**Curr. Liab.:**	$2,675,000		
Plant, Equip.:	$10,000	**Total Liab.:**	$2,675,000	**Indic. Yr. Divd.:**	NA
Total Assets:	$169,000	**Net Worth:**	-$2,505,000	**Debt/ Equity:**	NA

Magnum d'Or Resources Inc

1108 W Valley Blvd., Ste. 6-399, Alhambra, CA, 91803; ***PH:*** 1-626-407-2618; ***http://*** www.magnumexploration.com; ***Email:*** info@magnumexploration.com

General - Incorporation: NV
Employees: 2
Auditor: Murrell, Hall, Mcintosh & Co., PLLP
Stk Agt: Holladay Stock Transfer, Inc.
Counsel: NA
DUNS No.: NA

Stock - Price on:12/24/2007: $0.32
Stock Exchange: OTC
Ticker Symbol: MDOR
Outstanding Shares: 5,790,000
E.P.S.: -$0.08
Shareholders: NA

Business: The group's principal activities are to invest and develop resource properties. In Apr 2003, the group spun off its wholly-owned subsidiary progolftournaments.com inc. The group acquired an option to earn a 100% interest in the shandi gold-copper property located in southeastern mongolia and in the khol morit porphyry-copper gold property located west of ivanhoe mine's turquoise hill project in south-eastern mongolia.

Primary SIC and add'l.: 9999

CIK No: 0001099963

Subsidiaries: Sunrise Mining Corporation

Officers: Chad Curtis/31/Dir., CEO, Pres., Treasurer, Shao Jun Sun/34/Dir., Sec., CFO, VP/$30,000.00

Directors: Chad Curtis/31/Dir., CEO, Pres., Treasurer, John K. Yee/62/Dir., Shao Jun Sun/34/Dir., Sec., CFO, VP, Ka Suen Chau/59/Dir.

Owners: Shaojun Sun/10.60%, Sunrise Lighting Holdings Limited/4.80%, Insiders/10.60%, Chad Curtis/100.00%, Insiders/100.00%

Financial Data: ***Fiscal Year End:***09/30 ***Latest Annual Data:*** 9/30/2006

Year	Sales	Net Income
2006	NA	-$118,000
2005	NA	-$2,074,000
2004	NA	-$1,513,000

Curr. Assets:	$7,000	**Curr. Liab.:**	$3,000		
Plant, Equip.:	NA	**Total Liab.:**	$3,000	**Indic. Yr. Divd.:**	NA
Total Assets:	$7,000	**Net Worth:**	$4,000	**Debt/ Equity:**	NA

Magnus International Resources Inc

1055 Hastings St. W , Ste. 550, Vancouver, BC, V6E 2E9; ***PH:*** 1-604-694-1432; ***Fax:*** 1-604-602-1499; ***http://*** www.magnusresources.com; ***Email:*** info@magnusresources.com

General - Incorporation: NV
Employees: 4
Auditor: Schumacher & Associates, Inc.
Stk Agt: Pacific Stock Transfer Company
Counsel: NA
DUNS No.: NA

Stock - Price on:12/24/2007: $0.15
Stock Exchange: OTC
Ticker Symbol: MGNU
Outstanding Shares: 38,790,000
E.P.S.: NA
Shareholders: NA

Business: The groups principal activities include acquiring, exploring and developing metal properties. In November 2005, the group acquired Golden River. The group operates from the United States, Canada, China and the United Kingdom.

Primary SIC and add'l.: 1041

CIK No: 0001163003

Subsidiaries: Golden River Resources Corp., Gravity Spin Event Marketing, Inc, Magnus International Holdings (BVI) Inc., Magnus International Resources Inc(Magnus BVI), Magnus Resources (HK) Limited (Magnus HK), Qinghai Minerals(Nevis)Inc, Yunnan Long Tenge Mining (BVI) Inc, Yunnan Long Tenge MiningLtd, Yunnan Western MiningLtd

Officers: Graham Taylor/Founder, Dir., CEO, CFO, Pres., Treasurer, Sec., Anthony Tam/Consultant, Ruben Verzosa/Sr. Geologist, Leon Ma/Member - Geologist, Rui Zhang/Member - Geological Data Information Coordinator

Directors: Graham Taylor/Founder, Dir., CEO, CFO, Pres., Treasurer, Sec., Stephen Tan/Dir., Steven Tan/73/Dir.

Owners: Insiders/35.72%, Anthony Tam/4.00%, Emerson Capital Corp./16.16%, Gavin Conway, Genesio Circosta, Steven Tan, Graham Taylor/3.20%, Excel Capital Corp./16.16%

Magstar Technologies Inc

410 11th Ave. S, Hopkins, MN, 55343; ***PH:*** 1-952-935-6921; ***http://*** www.magstar.com; ***Email:*** info@magstar.com

General - Incorporation: MN
Employees: 59
Auditor: Virchow, Krause & Co. LLP
Stk Agt: American Stock Transfer & Trust Co.
Counsel: NA
DUNS No.: 00-624-8256

Stock - Price on:12/24/2007: $0.37
Stock Exchange: OTC
Ticker Symbol: MGST
Outstanding Shares: 9,140,000
E.P.S.: $0.02
Shareholders: NA

Business: The group's principle activity is to manufacture precision-machined components and devices for medical, magnetic, motion control and industrial original equipment manufacturers. The group manufactures close tolerance bearing-related assemblies for the medical device industry. It also manufactures and sells self-powered oil centrifuges and hydraulic actuators, under the name reuter (r). The medical devices manufactured by the group include production of blood centrifuges, blood analyzers, thrombectomy proximal motors, organic chemical synthesizers and valves for medical oxygen delivery. It operates in domestic market only. The group also contract manufactures biometric identification assemblies, spindles, precision slides and complex magnetic assemblies. The group operates from United States.

Primary SIC and add'l.: 3544

CIK No: 0000083490

Subsidiaries: Activar Properties, Inc.

Officers: Jon L. Reissner/CEO, Pres./$229,648.00, Bob Robinson/Contact - Eastern Regional Sales Mgr. - East, USA, Canada, Doug Bren/Contact - Quality Mgr., Josh Krause/Contact - Engineering Mgr., Todd Tevogt/Contact - Regional Sales Mgr. - Motion Control, Contract Manufacturing, Vernae Esler/Contact - Customer Service, Sales Coordinator, Jackie Mitchell/Contact - Accounting, Controller, Gary Vasey/Contact - Western Regional Sales Mgr., Mike Sidor/Contact - WA, OR, ID, AZ, NM, UT, Mexico, Western Canada, Pres., Randy Getz/Contact - Cymatix, Inc, California, Emmett M. Day/Contact - Central Territory, Sales, Marketing Mgr., Scott Sorensen/Contact - MN, West WI, ND, SD, Automation Inc, VP, Paul Fagerberg/Product Mgr., Andrew J. Thompson/Contact - Integrated Machinery Inc, Southern Ontario, Quebec Canada, Barry Link/Contact - Aptek, Inc, Michigan *(17 Officers included in Index)*

Owners: Robert Stehlik/0.30%, Duane R. Bryngelson/1.60%, James L. Reissner/10.40%, Insiders/51.60%, James R. Zavoral/0.30%, Theodore A. Colvin/0.20%, Jon L. Reissner/2.10%, Michael J. Tate/7.60%, Perkins Capital Management, Inc./5.80%, Richard F. McNamara/26.90%, Joseph A. Petrich/1.80%

Financial Data: ***Fiscal Year End:***12/31 ***Latest Annual Data:*** 12/31/2006

Year	Sales	Net Income
2006	$9,983,000	$814,000
2005	$8,105,000	$193,000
2004	$7,350,000	-$213,000

Curr. Assets:	$1,969,000	**Curr. Liab.:**	$1,382,000	**P/E Ratio:**	18.50
Plant, Equip.:	$184,000	**Total Liab.:**	$4,746,000	**Indic. Yr. Divd.:**	NA
Total Assets:	$2,187,000	**Net Worth:**	-$2,559,000	**Debt/ Equity:**	NA

Maguire Properties Inc

355 S Grand Ave., Ste. 300, Los Angeles, CA, 90071; ***PH:*** 1-213-626-3300; ***Fax:*** 1-310-857-1198; ***http://*** www.maguirepartners.com

General - Incorporation: MD
Employees: 170
Auditor: KPMG LLP
Stk Agt: Continental Stock Transfer & Trust Co
Counsel: NA
DUNS No.: NA

Stock - Price on:12/24/2007: $34.26
Stock Exchange: AMEX
Ticker Symbol: MPP
Outstanding Shares: 47,000,000
E.P.S.: $0.77
Shareholders: NA

Business: The groups principle activities include owning, acquiring, manage, leasing and developing real estate properties. The group operates through two segments namely, hotel and office. The group operates from the United States.

Primary SIC and add'l.: 6798 6512

CIK No: 0001204560

Subsidiaries: Bunker Hill Junior Mezzanine, LLC, Bunker Hill Senior Mezzanine, LLC, Library Square Associates, LLC, Maguire Partners - 355 S. Grand, LLC, Maguire Partners - Plaza Las Fuentes, LLC, Maguire Properties - 17885 Von Karman, LLC, Maguire Properties - 207 Goode, LLC, Maguire Properties - 2385 Northside, LLC, Maguire Properties - 3030 Olympic, LLC, Maguire Properties - 3121 Michelson, LLC, Maguire Properties - 3161 Michelson, LLC, Maguire Properties - 3301 Exposition, LLC, Maguire Properties - 350 S. Figueroa Mezzanine, LLC, Maguire Properties - 350 S. Figueroa, LLC, Maguire Properties - 555 W. Fifth Mezzanine, LLC 65 Subsidiaries included in the Index

Officers: Robert F. Maguire/Chmn., CEO, William H. Flaherty/Sr. VP - Marketing, Mark T. Lammas/Exec. VP - Development, Javier F. Bitar/Sr. VP - Finance, Sr. Investment Officer, Robert P. Goodwin/Sr. VP - Construction, Development, Ted Bischak/Sr. VP - Asset Management, Paul S. Rutter/Exec. VP - Major Transactions, Martin Griffiths/CFO, Exec. VP, Peter K. Johnston/Sr. VP - Leasing, Peggy Moretti/Sr. VP - Investor Relations, Jonathan Abrams/Sr. VP, General Counsel

Directors: Robert F. Maguire/Chmn., CEO, Lawrence S. Kaplan/Dir., Caroline S. McBride/54/Dir., Andrea L. Van De Kamp/Dir., Walter L. Weisman/Dir., Lewis Wolff/72/Dir., George A. Vandeman/Dir.

Owners: Insiders/20.26%, Dallas E. Lucas, Andrea L. Vande Kamp, Caroline S. McBride, Paul S. Rutter, Lewis N. Wolff, Robert F. Maguire/18.83%, Cohen & Steers Capital Management, Inc/11.34%, Neuberger Berman, Inc/6.96%, Martin A. Griffiths, Mark T. Lammas, Peter K. Johnston, ING Groep N.V./13.77%, The Vanguard Group, Inc/5.43%, Walter L. Weisman *(16 Owners included in Index)*

Financial Data: Fiscal Year End:12/31 Latest Annual Data: 12/31/2006

Year	Sales	Net Income
2006	$462,206,000	$70,326,000
2005	$487,207,000	-$23,818,000
2004	$326,714,000	$33,467,000

Curr. Assets:	$228,256,000	Curr. Liab.:	$177,980,000		
Plant, Equip.:	$3,017,249,000	Total Liab.:	$3,079,817,000	Indic. Yr. Divd.:	$1.600
Total Assets:	$3,511,729,000	Net Worth:	$431,912,000	Debt/ Equity:	6.4836

Magyar Bancorp Inc

400 Somerset St., New Brunswick, NJ, 08903; **PH:** 1-732-342-7600; **http://** www.magbank.com; **Email:** customerservice@magbank.com

General - Incorporation.................DE	Stock- Price on:12/24/2007 ....$14.5
Employees.................................89	Stock Exchange.............................NDQ
Auditor.............................Grant Thornton LLP	Ticker Symbol.............................MGYR
Stk Agt..... American Stock Transfer & Trust CO.	Outstanding Shares 5,920,000
Counsel...NA	E.P.S...$0.12
DUNS No...NA	Shareholders.....................................NA

Business: The groups principal activity is to provide banking and financial services. The products of the group include commercial, real estate, Construction, Home equity lines of credit and residential loan. The group operates from the United States. The assets of the group for the year 2006 were $434.2 (million).

Primary SIC and add'l.: 6036 6712
CIK No: 0001337068
Subsidiaries: Magbank Investment Company, Magyar Bank, Magyar Service Corp
Officers: Elizabeth E. Hance/Dir., CEO, Pres., Jon R. Ansari/CFO, Sr. VP, John S. Fitzgerald/Exec. VP, Chief Lending Officer, Karen Leblon/Corp. Sec., John Reissner/Investor Relations Contact
Directors: Elizabeth E. Hance/Dir., CEO, Pres., Joseph J. Lukacs/Chmn., Thomas Lankey/Vice Chmn., Andrew G. Hodulik/Dir., Martin A. Lukacs/Dir., Salvatore J. Romano/Dir., Edward C. Stokes/Dir., Joseph A. Yelencsics/Dir.
Owners: Andrew G. Hodulik, Edward C. Stokes, John S. Fitzgerald, Joseph J. Lukacs, Salvatore J. Romano, Joseph A. Yelencsics, PL Capital Group, Thomas Lankey, Jon R. Ansari, Martin A. Lukacs, Magyar Bancorp, MHC, Elizabeth E. Hance, Insiders

Financial Data: Fiscal Year End:09/30 Latest Annual Data: 9/30/2006

Year	Sales	Net Income
2006	$24,677,000	$5,000
2005	$19,167,000	$1,560,000

Curr. Assets:	$8,235,000	Curr. Liab.:	$384,834,000		
Plant, Equip.:	$21,690,000	Total Liab.:	$385,992,000	Indic. Yr. Divd.:	NA
Total Assets:	$434,204,000	Net Worth:	$48,212,000	Debt/ Equity:	0.0206

Magyar Telekom Telecommunications Co Ltd

Krisztina Krt 55, Budapest, 1013; ; **http://** www.magyartelekom.hu

General - Incorporation..............Hungary	Stock- Price on:12/24/2007 ....NA
Employees.................................12,341	Stock Exchange.........................NYSE
Auditor.................PricewaterhouseCoopers LLP	Ticker Symbol.................................NA
Stk Agt...................Morgan ADR Service Center	Outstanding Shares 208,550,000
Counsel...NA	E.P.S...$2.08
DUNS No...NA	Shareholders.....................................NA

Business: The group's principal activity is the telecom services in hungary. The company provides a broad range of service including telephony, data transmission, value-added services as well as mobile services and Internet access. In 2003 the company had total number of 2,830,841 fixed lines; 4,289,938 mobile phone customers, 259,720 Internet customers and 362,366 cabel TV customers.

Primary SIC and add'l.: 4812 4813 1731 5065 4822
CIK No: 0001047564
Officers: Christopher Mattheisen/46/Chmn., CEO - Magyar Telekom Plc, Janos Winkler/54/COO - Mobile Services LoB, Thilo Kusch/43/CFO, Zoltan Tanko/51/COO - Business Services LoB, Gyorgy Simo/41/COO - Wireline Services LoB
Directors: Christopher Mattheisen/46/Chmn., CEO - Magyar Telekom Plc, Gerhard Viktor Mischke/49/Dir., Michael Gunther/63/Dir., Istvan Foldesi/59/Dir., Geza Bohm/56/Member - Supervisory Board, Attila Csizmadia/58/Member - Supervisory Board, Gellert Kadlot/59/Member - Supervisory Board, Laszlo Pap/65/Member - Supervisory Board, Peter Vermes/61/Member - Supervisory Board, Adam Farkas/40/Member - Supervisory Board, Gyorgy Varju/61/Member - Supervisory Board, Thomas Knoll/42/Member - Supervisory Board, Horst Hermann/53/Dir., Ralph Rentschler/48/Dir.
Owners: MagyarCom/59.21%

Financial Data: Fiscal Year End:12/31 Latest Annual Data: 12/31/2006

Year	Sales	Net Income
2006	$3,557,339,000	$378,849,000
2005	$2,937,190,000	$378,082,000
2004	$3,368,053,000	$222,236,000

Curr. Assets:	$1,105,410,000	Curr. Liab.:	$1,667,263,000	P/E Ratio:	24.03
Plant, Equip.:	$2,919,770,000	Total Liab.:	$3,213,745,000	Indic. Yr. Divd.:	$3.730
Total Assets:	$6,066,152,000	Net Worth:	$2,852,407,000	Debt/ Equity:	NA

Mahanagar Telephone Nigam Ltd

12th Fl., Jeevan Bharati Tower-1, 124 Connaught Cir., New Delhi, Delhi, 110 001; ; **http://** www.mtnl.net.in/directors.htm; **Email:** feedback.delhi@bol.net.in

General - Incorporation ....India	Stock- Price on:12/24/2007 ....$7.58
Employees.................................51,221	Stock Exchange.............................NYSE
Auditor..............Price Waterhouse & Co. S.R.L.	Ticker Symbol.................................MTG
Stk Agt.................................Bank of New York	Outstanding Shares 314,520,000
Counsel...NA	E.P.S...$0.88
DUNS No...NA	Shareholders.....................................NA

Business: The group's principal activity is to provide telecommunication services including telephone, mobile radio telephone and telex services. The group also provides other services such as radio paging, call waiting, automatic morning alarm, Internet access, abbreviated dialing, voice mail, call transfer, computerized inquiry and an all India telex directory inquiry and telephone directory services both in hindi and English.

Primary SIC and add'l.: 4812 4822 4813
CIK No: 0001160262
Subsidiaries: Mahanagar Telephone Mauritius Limited, Maharashtra Krishna Valley Development Corporation, Mauritius, Millennium Telecom Limited, MTNL
Officers: R.S. P. Sinha/Chmn., MD, A. K. Arora/Executive Dir. - Mtnl, Delhi, Anita Soni/Dir., Dir. - Finance, Kuldeep Singh/Dir., Dir. - Technical, M. Sahu/Dir., Jt Sec. - DOT, I. C. Srivastava/PGM, D, S. L. Winston/PGM, S, V. Shivkumar/Dir., Dir. - Human Resources, K. C. Gupta/59/Executive Dir. - Operation, J. Gopal/Dir., Executive Dir. - Mtnl Mumbai, S. R. Sayal/Dir., Company Sec., G. D. Gaiha/Dir. - Tech, K. C. Saha/PGM, CVO, K. H. Khan/CGM, Mtnl Delhi, N. K. Gupta/PGM, D *(17 Officers included in Index)*
Directors: R.S. P. Sinha/Chmn., MD, M. S. Rana/Dir., S. Balasubramanian/Dir., J. Gopal/Dir., Executive Dir. - Mtnl Mumbai, M. Sahu/Dir., Jt Sec. - DOT, V. Shivkumar/Dir., Dir. - Human Resources, Anita Soni/Dir., Dir. - Finance, Kuldeep Singh/Dir., Dir. - Technical, A. S. Bhola/Dir., S. R. Sayal/Dir., Company Sec.
Owners: Life Insurance Corporation of India/17.50%, The Bank of New York/5.09%, Government of India/56.25%

Financial Data: Fiscal Year End:03/31 Latest Annual Data: 03/31/2007

Year	Sales	Net Income
2007	$1,055,000,000	$262,000,000
2006	$1,049,000,000	$24,000,000
2005	$1,150,000,000	$77,000,000

Curr. Assets:	$1,096,000,000	Curr. Liab.:	$894,000,000	P/E Ratio:	58.79
Plant, Equip.:	$1,820,000,000	Total Liab.:	$2,016,000,000	Indic. Yr. Divd.:	$0.090
Total Assets:	$3,825,000,000	Net Worth:	$1,809,000,000	Debt/ Equity:	NA

MAI Systems Corp

26110 Enterprise Way, Lake Forest, CA, 92630; **PH:** 1-714-598-6000; **http://** www.maisystems.com

General - Incorporation ....DE	Stock- Price on:12/24/2007 ....NA
Employees.....................................NA	Stock Exchange.................................NA
Auditor.............................BDO Seidman LLP	Ticker Symbol.................................NA
Stk Agt...............Mellon Investor Services LLC	Outstanding Shares ....NA
Counsel...NA	E.P.S...NA
DUNS No.............................12-084-8312	Shareholders.....................................NA

Business: The group's principal activities are to design, implement, install and support total information technology solutions. The solutions of the group include applications software, computer hardware, peripherals and wide and local area network. The group also provides on-site and off-site service and support to users of network and systems hardware. The solutions are provided to the hospitality, resort and destination industries. The group operates in the United States, Canada, the United Kingdom, Hong Kong, Singapore, Mexico, the People's Republic of China and Malaysia.

Primary SIC and add'l.: 7373 7379 7372
CIK No: 0000760436
Subsidiaries: Boss Solutions Limited, CLS Software International,Inc., Hospitality Services and Solutions, Hotel Information Solutions Limited, Hotel Information Systems Asia, Pte. Limited, Hotel Information Systems Ltd., Mai Systems Corporation

Maidenform Brands Inc

154 Ave. E, Bayonne, NJ, 07002; **PH:** 1-201-436-9200; **Fax:** 1-201-436-8322; **http://** www.maidenform.com; **Email:** ir@maidenform.com

General - Incorporation ....DE	Stock- Price on:12/24/2007 ....$21.15
Employees.................................1,300	Stock Exchange.............................NYSE
Auditor.................PricewaterhouseCoopers LLP	Ticker Symbol.................................MFB
Stk Agt...............Continental Stock Transfer & Trust Co	Outstanding Shares 22,980,000
Counsel...NA	E.P.S...$1.29
DUNS No...NA	Shareholders.....................................NA

Business: The groups principle activities include designing, sourcing and marketing intimate apparel products. The groups products include bras, panties and shapewear. The group operates through two segments namely, wholesale and retail. The groups customers include Federated, JCPenney, Sears, Target, Wal-Mart and Castco. The group operates from the United States and Canada.

Primary SIC and add'l.: 2342 5632 5999 5699
CIK No: 0001323531
Subsidiaries: Creaciones Textiles de Merida, S.A. de C.V., Maidenform (Indonesia) Ltd., Maidenform Asia Limited, Maidenform International Ltd., Maidenform Online,Inc., Maidenform,Inc., MF Retail,Inc., NCC Industries,Inc.
Officers: Thomas J. Ward/61/Dir., CEO, Maurice Reznik/Pres., Dorvin Lively/CFO, Exec. VP, Steven Masket/Exec. VP, General Counsel, Sec., Manette Scheininger/Sr. VP - Merchandising, Design, Research, Development, Gayle Weibley/Sr. VP - Human Resources, Steven Nelson/Sr. VP - Finance, Mitch Kauffman/Sr. VP - Sales, Virginia Vallorani/VP - Retail, Felise Glantz Kissell/VP - Investor Relations
Directors: Thomas J. Ward/61/Dir., CEO, David B. Kaplan/Chmn., Norman Axelrod/Dir., Harold Compton/Dir., Barbara Eisenberg/Dir., Karen Rose/Dir., Adam Stein/Dir.
Owners: Barclays Global Investors, NA./6.80%, Harold F. Compton, Ares Corporate Opportunities Fund, L.P./16.30%, Insiders/6.60%, Karen Rose, Maurice S. Reznik/1.20%, Steven N. Masket, Barbara Eisenberg, Norman Axelrod, Putnam, LLC/5.20%, Dorvin D. Lively, Thomas J. Ward/4.20%

Financial Data: *Fiscal Year End:*12/30 *Latest Annual Data:* 12/30/2006

Year	Sales	Net Income
2006	$416,835,000	$27,762,000
2005	$382,169,000	$8,940,000

Curr. Assets:	$117,185,000	*Curr. Liab.:*	$37,465,000	
Plant, Equip.:	$18,230,000	*Total Liab.:*	$194,645,000	*Indic. Yr. Divd.:* NA
Total Assets:	$247,348,000	*Net Worth:*	$52,703,000	*Debt/ Equity:* 1.3001

MailTec Inc

4105 E Florida Ave., Denver, CO, 80222; *PH:* 1-303-753-6512; *http://* www.mailtecinc.com

General - Incorporation ....NV	*Stock*- Price on:12/24/2007 ....$1.01
Employees..1	Stock Exchange...................................OTC
Auditor ....Jaspers & Hall, P.C.	Ticker Symbol...................................MTLE
Stk Agt................Corporate Stock Transfer, Inc.	Outstanding Shares 1,650,000
Counsel..NA	E.P.S...-$0.08
DUNS No..NA	Shareholders.......................................NA

Business: The groups principal activity is to provide bulk mail expediting to the established businesses that utilize bulk mailings in their operations. Services of the group include flat mail, bound printed matter irregulars. Customers served by the group include financial institutions, health organizations and government. The group operates from the United States.

Primary SIC and add'l.: 4215

CIK No: 0001335493

Officers: Jeff A. Hanks/42/Dir., CEO, CFO, Pres.

Directors: Jeff A. Hanks/42/Dir., CEO, CFO, Pres.

Owners: Venture Resources, Inc./87.50%

Financial Data: *Fiscal Year End:*03/31 *Latest Annual Data:* 3/31/2006

Year	Sales	Net Income
2006	NA	-$125,000

Curr. Assets:	$41,000	*Curr. Liab.:*	$44,000	
Plant, Equip.:	$3,000	*Total Liab.:*	$215,000	*Indic. Yr. Divd.:* NA
Total Assets:	$45,000	*Net Worth:*	-$170,000	*Debt/ Equity:* NA

Main Street Restaurant Group Inc

5050 N 40th St., Ste 200, Phoenix, AZ, 85018; *PH:* 1-602-852-9000; *http://* www.mainandmain.com; *Email:* guestrelations@mstreetinc.com

General - Incorporation ....DE	*Stock*- Price on:12/24/2007 ....NA
Employees..399	Stock Exchange...................................NDQ
Auditor ....Mayer Hoffman Mccann, P.C	Ticker Symbol......................................NA
Stk Agt..NA	Outstanding Shares ....NA
Counsel..NA	E.P.S..NA
DUNS No..NA	Shareholders.......................................NA

Business: The group's principal activities are to acquire, develop and operate restaurants featuring a wide selection of high quality and freshly prepared popular foods. The group is a franchisee of tgi friday's restaurants. It currently owns 56 tgi friday's restaurants and also owns and operates five redfish and five bamboo club restaurants. The restaurants provide quick, efficient and friendly table service designed to minimize customer-waiting time and facilitate table turnover. The operations of the group are carried on in the United States.

Primary SIC and add'l.: 5812

CIK No: 0000847466

Subsidiaries: Bamboo Club, Inc., Cornerstone Productions, Inc., Main St. California, Inc., Main St. Midwest, Inc., Redfish America, LLC, Redfish Cleveland, Inc.

Main Street Trust Inc

100 W University Ave., Champaign, IL, 61820; *PH:* 1-217-351-6500; *http://* www.bankillinois.com

General - Incorporation IL	*Stock*- Price on:12/24/2007 ....$30.54
Employees..399	Stock Exchange.....................................NA
Auditor ....McGladrey & Pullen LLP	Ticker Symbol......................................NA
Stk Agt..NA	Outstanding Shares 10,040,000
Counsel..NA	E.P.S...$1.89
DUNS No......................................82-504-6857	Shareholders.......................................NA

Business: The group's principle activity is to provide consumer and commercial banking and trust services and retail payment processing. The bank offers a full range of financial services including demand, savings, time and individual retirement accounts; commercial, consumer, agricultural and real estate lending; safe deposit and night depository services; farm management. The trust services include investment management, acting as a trustee, serving a guardian, executor or agent. It provides remittance services to electric, water and gas utilities, telecommunication companies, cable television firms and charitable organizations: retail lockbox processing of payments delivered by mail on behalf of the biller, processing of payments delivered by customers to pay agents such as grocery stores, convenience stores. It operates through its subsidiaries, bankillinois, the first national bank of decatur and firsttech, inc. The group operates from United States.

Primary SIC and add'l.: 6712 6021

CIK No: 0001099777

Subsidiaries: FirsTech, Inc., Main Street Bank & Trust

Officers: A. Van Dukeman/CEO, Pres., Robert F. Plecki/Pres. - Champaign, Christopher M. Shroyer/Pres. - Decatur, David B. White/CFO, Exec. VP, Donna R. Greene/Pres. - Main Street Wealth Management, Mark J. Wisniewski/Exec. VP, Scott R. Tapley/VP, Darold D. Sage/VP, Chief Investment Officer, Paul E. Donohue/Exec. VP - Sales, Marketing, Howard F. Mooney/43/Exec. VP, Monya Russell/Assist. VP, Employee Benefits Specialist, Charlee Seaton/Employee Benefits Specialist, Kyle Wetters/Financial Planning Specialist, Officer, Nicholas John Waddock/Exec. VP, Chief Credit Officer, Leanne C. Heacock/Exec. VP - MIS *(30 Officers included in Index)*

Directors: A. Van Dukeman/CEO, Pres., Gregory B. Lykins/60/Chmn., David J. Downey/66/Dir., Larry D. Haab/70/Dir., Frederic L. Kenney/Dir., August C. Meyer/70/Dir., George T. Shapland/77/Dir., Thomas G. Sloan/Dir., Gale H. Zacheis/69/Dir.

Owners: Van A. Dukeman/1.60%, August C. Meyer/1.00%, Paul E. Donohue, Donna R. Greene, David J. Downey/2.70%, Larry D. Haab, Thomas G. Sloan/1.10%, Gale H. Zacheis, Gregory B. Lykins/21.50%, Frederic L. Kenney, Insiders/35.00%, George T. Shapland/3.80%, David B. White

Financial Data: *Fiscal Year End:*12/31 *Latest Annual Data:* 12/31/2006

Year	Sales	Net Income
2006	$113,342,000	$19,237,000
2005	$98,055,000	$18,308,000
2004	$74,652,000	$14,778,000

Curr. Assets:	$71,048,000	*Curr. Liab.:*	$1,371,474,000	*P/E Ratio:* 16.16
Plant, Equip.:	$22,447,000	*Total Liab.:*	$1,386,246,000	*Indic. Yr. Divd.:* $1.000
Total Assets:	$1,536,601,000	*Net Worth:*	$150,355,000	*Debt/ Equity:* NA

Maine & Maritimes Corp

209 State St., Presque Isle, ME, 04769; *PH:* 1-207-760-2499; *Fax:* 1-207-760-2419; *http://* www.maineandmaritimes.com; *Email:* investor@maineandmaritimes.com

General - Incorporation ....MN	*Stock*- Price on:12/24/2007 ....$25.07
Employees..218	Stock Exchange...................................AMEX
Auditor ....Vitale, Caturano & Co. Ltd	Ticker Symbol......................................MAM
Stk Agt ....Computershare Investor Services LLC	Outstanding Shares 1,680,000
Counsel..NA	E.P.S...-$3.13
DUNS No..NA	Shareholders.......................................NA

Business: The group's principal activity is to transmit and distribute electricity. It supplies electricity to retail and wholesale customers in northern Maine. The group continues to provide transmission services to former wholesale energy customers and transmission and distribution services to retail customers in the service territory. The service area features agricultural and wood product customers. Potato growing and processing, as well as the manufacturing of wood products, principally lumber, continues to be the dominant economic forces in the service area. The major customers of the group are commercial users, lumber and wood-chip producers. On 01-Dec-2003, the group acquired eastcan consultants, inc and on 01-Jun-2004, the group acquired morris & richard consulting engineers limited. On 17-Jun-2004, the group acquired res engineering, inc.

Primary SIC and add'l.: 6719 4911

CIK No: 0001222497

Subsidiaries: Cornwallis Court Developments Ltd, Maine & New Brunswick Electrical Power Co, Ltd, Maine Public Service Company, Maricor Properties Ltd, Maricor Technologies, Inc, Mecel Properties Ltd, The Maricor Group, The Maricor Group New England, The Maricor Group, Canada Ltd

Officers: Brent M. Boyles/49/Dir., Pres., CEO - Maine, Maritimes Corporation, Maine Public Service Company, Patrick C. Cannon/36/VP, General Counsel, Sec., Clerk/$191,335.00, Michael A. Eaton/44/VP - Information, Technology Management, Tim D. Brown/48/VP - Engineering, Operations, Michael I. Williams/40/Dir., CFO, Interim COO, Sr. VP, VP, Assist. Sec./$132,674.00, Randi J. Arthurs/28/VP - Accounting, Controller, Assist. Treasurer/$115,679.00

Directors: Brent M. Boyles/49/Dir., Pres., CEO - Maine, Maritimes Corporation, Maine Public Service Company, Nathan L. Grass/69/Vice Chmn., Robert E. Anderson/70/Chmn., Deborah L. Gallant/55/Dir., Brian N. Hamel/50/Dir., James D. Daigle/72/Dir., David N. Felch/64/Dir., Lance A. Smith/56/Dir., Richard G. Daigle/60/Dir., Michael W. Caron/59/Dir., Michael I. Williams/40/Dir., CFO, Interim COO, Sr. VP, VP, Assist. Sec.

Owners: James D. Daigle, Robert E. Anderson, Richard G. Daigle, Nicholas J. Bayne, Insiders, Lance A. Smith, Deborah L. Gallant, David N. Felch, Michael W. Caron, Nathan L. Grass, GAMCO Investors./6.92%, FMR Corp./6.89%, Brian N. Hamel

Financial Data: *Fiscal Year End:*12/31 *Latest Annual Data:* 12/31/2006

Year	Sales	Net Income
2006	$35,601,000	-$5,921,000
2005	$39,974,000	-$220,000
2004	$37,138,000	$1,318,000

Curr. Assets:	$13,527,000	*Curr. Liab.:*	$24,713,000	
Plant, Equip.:	$60,146,000	*Total Liab.:*	$106,720,000	*Indic. Yr. Divd.:* NA
Total Assets:	$148,247,000	*Net Worth:*	$41,527,000	*Debt/ Equity:* 0.8667

Mainsource Financial Group Inc

201 N Broadway, Greensburg, IN, 47240; *PH:* 1-812-663-0157; *Fax:* 1-812-663-4812; *http://* www.mainsourcefinancial.com

General - Incorporation ....IN	*Stock*- Price on:12/24/2007 ....$17.05
Employees..829	Stock Exchange...................................NDQ
Auditor ....Crowe Chizek & Co. LLC	Ticker Symbol......................................MSFT
Stk Agt ....Registrar & Transfer Co	Outstanding Shares 18,730,000
Counsel..NA	E.P.S...$1.24
DUNS No.....................................15-060-3892	Shareholders.......................................NA

Business: The group's principal activity is to provide financial services through the offices located in Indiana, Illinois and Kentucky. The group accepts deposits inclusive of checking accounts, savings and term certificate accounts. The various kinds of loans offered by the group include residential mortgage, commercial and installment loans. The other services offered by the group include issuing credit cards, renting safe deposit facilities, provision of general agency personal and business insurance services including letter of credit and repurchase agreements. The operations are conducted through 58 offices located in Indiana and Illinois and five insurance offices in Indiana and one in Kentucky. In 8-Jun-2004, the group acquired peoples financial corp.

Primary SIC and add'l.: 6035 6712

CIK No: 0000720002

Subsidiaries: IUB Reinsurance Co., Ltd., MainSource Bank, MainSource Bank of Illinois, MainSource Insurance, LLC, MainSource Mortgage, LLC, MainSource Statutory Trust I, MainSource Statutory Trust II, MainSource Statutory Trust III, MainSource Title, LLC, MSB Holdings of Nevada, Inc., MSB Investments of Nevada, Inc., MSB of Nevada, LLC, MSB Realty, Inc.

Officers: James L. Saner/CEO, Pres./$430,049.00

Owners: James L. Saner, James M. Anderson, Robert E. Hoptry/1.00%, Douglas I. Kunkel, Rick S. Hartman/1.50%, Philip A. Frantz, Robert S. Dunevant/5.00%, D. J. Hines, Insiders/7.10%, John C. Parker, Brian J. Crall, Daryl R. Tressler, William G. Barron/2.70%

Financial Data: *Fiscal Year End:*12/31 *Latest Annual Data:* 12/31/2006

Year	Sales	Net Income
2006	$143,770,000	$22,241,000
2005	$99,986,000	$16,192,000
2004	$91,385,000	$16,793,000

Curr. Assets:	$141,005,000	*Curr. Liab.:*	$2,068,132,000	*P/E Ratio:* 13.64
Plant, Equip.:	$40,370,000	*Total Liab.:*	$2,176,526,000	*Indic. Yr. Divd.:* $0.560
Total Assets:	$2,429,773,000	*Net Worth:*	$253,247,000	*Debt/ Equity:* NA

Mainstreet Bankshares Inc

730 E Church St., Ste. 30, Martinsville, VA, 24112; *PH:* 1-276-632-8054; *Fax:* 1-276-632-8043; *http://* www.mainSt.bankshares.com; *Email:* shareholder@msbsinc.com

General - Incorporation	VA	Stock- Price on:12/24/2007	NA
Employees	NA	Stock Exchange	OTC
Auditor	Brown, Edwards & Co LLP	Ticker Symbol	MREE
Stk Agt	Mainstreet Bankshares Inc	Outstanding Shares	NA
Counsel	NA	E.P.S	NA
DUNS No.	NA	Shareholders	NA

Business: The group operates through its subsdiary whose principle activity is to provide comercial banking operations and other related financial activities. The group operates from United States.

Primary SIC and add'l.: 6712 6021

CIK No: 0001094742

Subsidiaries: Franklin Community Bank, N.A., Rocky Mount

Officers: Larry A. Heaton/Dir., CEO, Pres./$279,553.50, Christopher A. Ames/Assist. VP, Information Technology Officer, Brenda H. Smith/Exec. VP, CFO, Corp. Sec./$123,140.40, Sonya B. Smith/Assist. VP, Compliance Officer, Judy H. McNeely/Assist., Corp. Sec., Catherine M. Frazier/Loan Operations Officer, Lisa J. Correll/Assist. VP, Accounting Officer, Edward L. Arrington/Sr. VP, Operations Officer

Directors: Larry A. Heaton/Dir., CEO, Pres., Joel R. Shepherd/Chmn., Joseph F. Clark/Dir., Morton W. Lester/Dir., Charles Laine Dalton/Dir., Danny M. Perdue/Dir., Michael A. Turner/Dir., Milford A. Weaver/Dir., Mac J. Deekens/Dir., Laine C. Dalton/44/Dir.

Owners: Milford A. Weaver/0.50%, Charles L. Dalton/0.30%, Joel R. Shepherd/5.40%, Insiders/22.40%, William L. Cooper, John M. Deekens/0.30%, Morton W. Lester/3.40%, TCF Financial Corporation, Inc./7.50%, Michael A. Turner/1.70%, Joseph F. Clark/0.30%, Danny M. Perdue/2.30%, C. R. McCullar/2.20%, Larry A. Heaton/3.90%, Brenda H. Smith/2.00%

Mair Holdings Inc

150 S 5th St., Ste. 1360, Minneapolis, MN, 55402; *PH:* 1-612-333-0021; *Fax:* 1-612-337-0355; *http://* www.mairholdings.com

General - Incorporation	MN	Stock- Price on:12/24/2007	$6.77
Employees	2,598	Stock Exchange	NDQ
Auditor	Deloitte & Touche LLP	Ticker Symbol	MAIR
Stk Agt	Wells Fargo shareowner Services	Outstanding Shares	20,590,000
Counsel	NA	E.P.S	NA
DUNS No.	09-905-1047	Shareholders	NA

Business: The group's principal activity is to provide regional scheduled passenger services. The group is a holding company for mesaba aviation, inc. The group has an airlines services agreement with northwest airlines, inc. With this agreement, the schedules are coordinated with those of northwest to facilitate interline connections at the minneapolis/st. Paul international airport, detroit metropolitan airport and the memphis international airport. The group provides its services under the name 'mesaba airlines/northwest airlink' or 'mesaba airlines/northwest jet airlink'. The group operated flights to 106 cities in United States and Canada from northwest's hub airports. As of 30-Apr-2004, the group's aircraft fleet comprised 35 avro rj85 and 64 saab 340 aircraft.

Primary SIC and add'l.: 4522 4731 4512

CIK No: 0000835768

Subsidiaries: Compass Airlines, Inc., Mesaba Aviation, Inc.

Officers: Paul F. Foley/Dir., CEO, CFO, Pres./$1,070,241.00, Ruth M. Timm/VP, General Counsel, Sec./$239,932.00, Robert E. Weil/43/CFO, VP, Treasurer/$438,809.00, Fred L. Deleeuw/Pres. - Big Sky/$192,250.00, John Spanjers/Pres., COO - Mesaba/$197,217.00

Directors: Paul F. Foley/Dir., CEO, CFO, Pres., James A. Lee/Dir., Robert C. Pohlad/Dir., Donald E. Benson/Dir., Pierson M. Grieve/Dir., Carl R. Pohlad/92/Dir., Raymond W. Zehr/Dir., John J. Ahn/Dir.

Owners: Robert E. Weil/1.15%, Schultze Asset Management, LLC/5.91%, Lloyd I. Miller/6.35%, Paul F. Foley/3.87%, Donald Smith & Co./13.59%, Donald E. Benson, John G. Spanjers, Pierson M. Grieve, Dimensional Fund Advisors Inc./10.24%, Insiders/19.44%, Riley Investment Management LLC/6.41%, Raymond W. Zehr, Carl R. Pohlad/13.44%, FMR Corp./13.33%, Aegis Financial Corporation/8.78% (18 Owners included in Index)

Financial Data: Fiscal Year End:03/31 Latest Annual Data: 03/31/2007

Year	Sales	Net Income
2007	$23,932,000	-$7,405,000
2006	$256,279,000	-$82,848,000
2005	$456,067,000	$7,355,000

Curr. Assets:	$98,436,000	Curr. Liab.:	$12,571,000	P/E Ratio:	84.63
Plant, Equip.:	$1,423,000	Total Liab.:	$13,343,000	Indic. Yr. Divd.:	NA
Total Assets:	$121,942,000	Net Worth:	$108,599,000	Debt/ Equity:	NA

Majesco Entertainment Co

Formerly: Majesco Holdings Inc
160 Raritan Ctr. Pk.way, Edison, NJ, 08837; *PH:* 1-732-225-8910; *http://* www.majescogames.com

General - Incorporation	DE	Stock- Price on:12/24/2007	$1.5794
Employees	70	Stock Exchange	NDQ
Auditor	Goldstein Golub Kessler LLP	Ticker Symbol	COOL
Stk Agt	American Stock Transfer & Trust Co.	Outstanding Shares	23,860,000
Counsel	NA	E.P.S	-$0.28
DUNS No.	NA	Shareholders	NA

Business: The group's principle activity is to develop, publish and market interactive entertainment software. It also manufactures number of accessories licensed by nintendo. The group's customers include wal-Mart, target, toys "R" us, best buy, electronics boutique, gamestop and other national and regional retailers. The group's products are targeted to a wide demographic, from children to active teens and the old, mass market consumer. The group operates through subsidiary in United Kingdom besides United States. The group's quarterly revenue for July 2007 was 10.01 millions of USD.

Primary SIC and add'l.: 8748 9999

CIK No: 0001076682

Subsidiaries: Majesco Europe Limited

Officers: Jesse Sutton/Interim Dir., CEO, Kevin Ray/CTO, Adam Sultan/General Counsel, Sr. VP - Business - Legal Affairs, Sec., Gui Karyo/Exec. VP - Operations, Ken Gold/VP - Marketing, Joseph Sutton/Exec. VP - Research, Development, Jason Dutton/VP - Europe, John Gross/CFO

Directors: Jesse Sutton/Interim Dir., CEO, Louis Lipschitz/Dir., Laurence Aronson/Dir., Stephen Wilson/Dir., Mark Stewart/Dir., Allan Grafman/Dir.

Owners: Laurence Aronson, Mark Stewart, Jesse Sutton/9.37%, Robert S. Ellin/12.84%, Royce & Associates, LLC/9.02%, Joseph Sutton/9.44%, Jesse M. Sutton Foundation, Dick Wnuk, Stephen Wilson, Allan Grafman, Adam Sutton/8.20%, Morris Sutton/3.59%, Gui Karyo/1.26%, John Gross, Louis Lipschitz (16 Owners included in Index)

Financial Data: Fiscal Year End:10/31 Latest Annual Data: 10/31/2006

Year	Sales	Net Income
2006	$66,683,000	-$5,366,000
2005	$59,716,000	-$70,900,000
2004	$120,984,000	-$11,186,000

Curr. Assets:	$14,239,000	Curr. Liab.:	$13,262,000		
Plant, Equip.:	$701,000	Total Liab.:	$13,262,000	Indic. Yr. Divd.:	NA
Total Assets:	$15,011,000	Net Worth:	$1,749,000	Debt/ Equity:	NA

Majestic Oil & Gas Inc

33 1st Ave. S, Cut Bank, MT, 59427; *PH:* 1-406-873-5580; *http://* www.majesticoilandgas.com

General - Incorporation	NV	Stock- Price on:12/24/2007	$0.4
Employees	NA	Stock Exchange	OTC
Auditor	Gordon, Hughes & Banks, LLP	Ticker Symbol	MJOG
Stk Agt	Transfer Online, Inc.	Outstanding Shares	6,240,000
Counsel	NA	E.P.S	-$0.01
DUNS No.	NA	Shareholders	NA

Business: The groups principle activities include exploring, developing, acquiring and operating gas properties. The group operates from the United States.

Primary SIC and add'l.: 4932

CIK No: 0001334741

Subsidiaries: Grizzly Energy, Inc.,

Officers: Patrick M. Montalban/Chmn., CEO, Pres., Danny M. Mitchell/VP, Dir.

Directors: Danny M. Mitchell/VP, Dir.

Owners: Patrick M. Montalban/73.70%, Danny Mitchell, Insiders/74.40%

Financial Data: Fiscal Year End:12/31 Latest Annual Data: 12/31/2006

Year	Sales	Net Income
2006	$49,000	-$20,000

Curr. Assets:	$198,000	Curr. Liab.:	$16,000		
Plant, Equip.:	$142,000	Total Liab.:	$16,000	Indic. Yr. Divd.:	NA
Total Assets:	$339,000	Net Worth:	$324,000	Debt/ Equity:	NA

Makemusic Inc

7615 Golden Triangle Dr., Ste. M, Eden Prairie, MN, 55344; *PH:* 1-952-937-9611; *Fax:* 1-952-937-9760; *http://* www.makemusic.com; *Email:* investorrelations@makemusic.com

General - Incorporation	MN	Stock- Price on:12/24/2007	$6.09
Employees	79	Stock Exchange	NDQ
Auditor	McGladrey & Pullen LLP	Ticker Symbol	MMUS
Stk Agt	Wells Fargo Shareowner Services	Outstanding Shares	4,090,000
Counsel	NA	E.P.S	$0.12
DUNS No.	78-105-0828	Shareholders	NA

Business: The group's principal activities are to develop and market proprietary music technology products that enhance music learning and composition. The products include smartmusic studio, finale notation family and intonation trainer. The customers include music educators, music makers and the music publishing industry. The products of the group are marketed through traditional distribution channels and its websites. The group's product offerings are sold in North America, Europe and other countries.

Primary SIC and add'l.: 7373 7372

CIK No: 0000920707

Officers: John W. Paulson/Dir., CEO/$306,785.00, Ronald B. Raup/Dir., Chief Marketing Officer/$226,600.00, Mark E. Dunn/CTO, Karen L. Vanderbosch/Sec., Treasurer, CFO/$20,636.00, Mary Schneider/Chief Marketing Officer

Directors: John W. Paulson/Dir., CEO, Jeffrey A. Koch/Chmn., John Whisnant/Dir., Ronald B. Raup/Dir., Chief Marketing Officer, Graham Richmond/Dir., Larry Morton/Dir., Keith Fenhaus/Dir., Robert Morrison/Dir., Michael Skinner/Dir.

Owners: William R. Wolff/3.40%, Alan G. Shuler, Walrus Partners, L.L.C/8.70%, Jeffrey A. Koch/27.40%, Graham Richmond, Keith A. Fenhaus, Insiders/34.00%, Karen L. VanDerBosch, LaunchEquity Entities/27.40%, Ronald B. Raup, Norman H. Pessin/5.10%, Michael Skinner, John W. Paulson/2.60%, Lawrence M. Morton

Financial Data: Fiscal Year End:12/31 Latest Annual Data: 06/30/2007

Year	Sales	Net Income
2007	$2,403,000	-$705,000
2006	$12,978,000	$255,000
2005	$11,817,000	-$498,000

Curr. Assets:	$5,340,000	Curr. Liab.:	$3,671,000	P/E Ratio:	67.67
Plant, Equip.:	$663,000	Total Liab.:	$3,782,000	Indic. Yr. Divd.:	NA
Total Assets:	$10,626,000	Net Worth:	$6,844,000	Debt/ Equity:	0.0018

MakeUp.com Ltd

3388 Via Lido, 4th Fl., Newport Beach, CA, 92663; *PH:* 1-604-306-2525; *Fax:* 1-866-347-5058; *http://* www.makeup.com; *Email:* info@makeupinvestor.com

General - Incorporation	NV	Stock- Price on:12/24/2007	$0.12
Employees	NA	Stock Exchange	OTC
Auditor	Mendoza Berger & Co., LLP	Ticker Symbol	MAKU
Stk Agt	NA	Outstanding Shares	NA
Counsel	NA	E.P.S	NA
DUNS No.	NA	Shareholders	NA

Business: The groups principle activity is to market custom embroidery products and services via the Internet. The group operates from the United States.

Primary SIC and add'l.: 5912

CIK No: 0001281198

Officers: Robert E. Rook/CEO, Pres., Munjit S. Johal/CFO, Treasurer

Owners: Robert E. Rook/2.90%, Silver Road Corporation/7.10%, Fete Enterprises S.A/9.90%, Insiders/4.90%, Ulex Holdings S.A/8.50%, Munjit Johal/2.00%, Susan Jeffs/7.50%, Manhattan Assets Corp/29.80%

Financial Data: Fiscal Year End:12/31 Latest Annual Data: 12/31/2006

Year	Sales	Net Income
2006	$247,000	-$1,084,000
2005	$7,000	-$38,000

Curr. Assets:	$434,000	Curr. Liab.:	$3,204,000		
Plant, Equip.:	$115,000	Total Liab.:	$3,204,000	Indic. Yr. Divd.:	NA
Total Assets:	$952,000	Net Worth:	-$2,252,000	Debt/ Equity:	NA

Makita Corp

14930 Nam St., La Mirada, CA, 90638; *PH:* 1-714-522-8088; *Fax:* 1-714-522-8133; *http://* www.makita.co.jp

General - Incorporation ....Japan	Stock- Price on:12/24/2007 ....$43.79
Employees............................9,062	Stock Exchange...........................NDQ
Auditor .... KPMG Azsa & Co	Ticker Symbol............................MKTY
Stk Agt...... Chuo Mitsui Trust & Banking Co Ltd	Outstanding Shares 143,700,000
Counsel.............................. NA	E.P.S....................................$2.88
DUNS No. 69-053-8780	Shareholders...............................NA

Business: The group's principal activity is to manufacture portable electric power tools. The group operates in five divisions: portable woodworking tools, portable general tools, stationary woodwork, part and repairs and others. Portable woodworking tools consist of saws, planers, routers and trackers. Portable general purpose tools include drills, hammer drills, rotary hammers, electric breakers, grinders, sanders, screwdrivers and impact wrenches. Stationary woodwork machines include planer-jointers, wood surfacers, band saws and table saws. Part repairs and accessories include parts for the group's products and also providing services. Other products include chain saws, hand held vacuum cleaners, submersible pumps and garden tools.

Primary SIC and add'l.: 3629 3553 3699 3546

CIK No: 0000202467

Subsidiaries: Makita EU S.R.L. in Romania

Officers: Hiromichi Murase/Statutory Auditor, Masami Tsuruta/MD, Kazuya Nakamura/60/Dir., GM - International Sales Headquarters, Asia, Oceania Area, Shoichi Hase/Statutory Auditor, Masahiko Goto/Pres., Representative Dir., Keiichi Usui/Outside Statutory Auditor, Yasuhiko Kanzaki/MD, Kenichiro Nakai/Dir., GM - Administration Headquarters, Akio Kondo/Statutory Auditor, Masafumi Nakamura/Statutory Auditor

Directors: Kazuya Nakamura/60/Dir., GM - International Sales Headquarters, Asia, Oceania Area, Shiro Hori/Dir., Masahiko Goto/Pres., Representative Dir., Tadashi Asanuma/Dir., Zenji Mashiko/Dir., Motohiko Yokoyama/Dir., Hisayoshi Niwa/Dir., Masahiro Yamaguchi/Dir., Tadayoshi Torii/Dir., Tomoyasu Kato/Dir., Kenichiro Nakai/Dir., GM - Administration Headquarters, Toshio Hyuga/Dir., Shinichiro Tomita/Dir., Tetsuhisa Kaneko/Dir.

Owners: Masami Tsuruta, Silchester International Investors Limited, Goldman Sachs International, Goldman Sachs International, Masahiko Goto, Tadayoshi Torii, Zenji Mashiko, Shiro Hori, Keiichi Usui, Silchester International Investors Limited, Nippon Life Insurance Company, Nippon Life Insurance Company, Barclays Global Investors, N.A., Mitsubishi UFJ Financial Group, Silchester International Investors Limited *(38 Owners included in Index)*

Financial Data: Fiscal Year End:03/31 Latest Annual Data: 3/31/2006

Year	Sales	Net Income
2006	$1,957,906,000	$345,393,000
2005	$1,819,972,000	$206,879,000
2004	$1,770,356,000	$73,952,000

Curr. Assets:	$1,946,744,000	Curr. Liab.:	$392,830,000	P/E Ratio:	58.79
Plant, Equip.:	$506,009,000	Total Liab.:	$508,154,000	Indic. Yr. Divd.:	$0.670
Total Assets:	$2,786,650,000	Net Worth:	$2,278,496,000	Debt/ Equity:	NA

Malaga Financial Corp

2514 Via Tejon, Pls Vrds Pnsl, CA, 90274; *PH:* 1-310-375-9000; *http://* www.malagabank.com

General - Incorporation	Stock- Price on:12/24/2007 ....$10.3
Employees.............................. NA	Stock Exchange...........................OTC
Auditor .... NA	Ticker Symbol............................MLGF
Stk Agt............................. NA	Outstanding Shares ....NA
Counsel.............................. NA	E.P.S.....................................NA
DUNS No. .... NA	Shareholders...............................NA

Business: The groups principle activity is to provide recruiting services. The groups service area includes the research and development, engineering, marketing, sales, information technology and manufacturing industries. The group operates from United States.

Primary SIC and add'l.: 6036

CIK No:

Officers: Randy C. Bowers/CEO, Pres., Steven P.L. Sheng/Dir., Corp. Sec., Debbie J. Richardson/Exec. VP, Susanne M. Chandler/Sr. VP, Mary Roberts/Sr. VP, CFO, Mel Hashimoto/VP, Controller - Malaga Bank, Gayle Cdebaca/Assist. VP - Project Coordinator, Malaga Bank, Mark Bustamante/Sr. VP - Income Property Lending, Malaga Bank, Kenneth A. Johnson/VP, Income Property Loan Officer - Malaga Bank, John W. Turner/VP, Business Banking Mgr. - Malaga Bank, Bonnie Shaw/VP, Loan Operations Mgr. - Malaga Bank, Nina Brister/Assist. VP - Loan Service Supervisor, Malaga Bank, Cathy Jaramillo/Assist. VP, Assistant Loan Operations Mgr., Assist. VP, Assistant Loan Operations Mgr., Aaron Aalcides/Sr. VP - Branch Banking Executive, Malaga Bank, Kristy M. Smith/Sr. VP, Dir. - Branch Operations, Malaga Bank *(20 Officers included in Index)*

Directors: Robert E. Kershaw/Chmn., Steven P.L. Sheng/Dir., Corp. Sec., Raymond L. Craemer/Dir., Jerry A. Donahue/Dir., Leo K.C. Lee/Dir., Richard A. Oas/Dir.

Financial Data: Fiscal Year End:NA Latest Annual Data: 12/31/2002

Year	Sales	Net Income
2002	$5,585,000	$1,275,000
2001	$6,024,000	$1,183,000
2000	$5,959,000	$934,000

Curr. Assets:	$33,274,000	Curr. Liab.:	$309,823,000		
Plant, Equip.:	$270,000	Total Liab.:	$310,535,000	Indic. Yr. Divd.:	NA
Total Assets:	$337,385,000	Net Worth:	$26,850,000	Debt/ Equity:	0.0074

Malex Inc

730 W Randolph, 6th Fl., Chicago, IL, 60661; *PH:* 1-312-454-0015

General - Incorporation ....DE	Stock- Price on:12/24/2007 ....$0.37
Employees.............................. NA	Stock Exchange...........................OTC
Auditor ....Comiskey & Company	Ticker Symbol............................MLEX
Stk Agt .... Empire Stock Transfer	Outstanding Shares 8,420,000
Counsel.............................. NA	E.P.S....................................$0.00
DUNS No. .... NA	Shareholders...............................NA

Business: The groups principle activity is to provide recruiting services. The groups service area includes the research and development, engineering, marketing, sales, information technology and manufacturing industries. The group operates from United States.

Primary SIC and add'l.: 7381

CIK No: 0000819926

Officers: Bartly J. Loethen/Chmn., Principal Executive Officer, CFO, Pres., VP, Sec., Treasurer

Owners: Insiders/93.00%, Synergy Business Consulting, LLC/93.00%

Financial Data: Fiscal Year End:04/30 Latest Annual Data: 04/30/2007

Year	Sales	Net Income
2007	NA	-$16,000
2006	NA	-$2,000
2005	NA	-$1,000

Curr. Assets:	NA	Curr. Liab.:	$13,000		
Plant, Equip.:	NA	Total Liab.:	$13,000	Indic. Yr. Divd.:	NA
Total Assets:	NA	Net Worth:	-$13,000	Debt/ Equity:	NA

Mammatech Corp

930 NW 8th Ave., Gainesville, FL, 32601; *PH:* 1-352-375-0607; *http://* www.mammacare.com; *Email:* info@mammacare.com

General - Incorporation ....FL	Stock- Price on:12/24/2007 ....$0.072
Employees.............................. NA	Stock Exchange...........................OTC
Auditor ....Stark Winter Schenkein & Co. LLP	Ticker Symbol............................MAMM
Stk Agt ....Manhattan Transfer Registrar Co	Outstanding Shares 5,120,000
Counsel.............................. NA	E.P.S....................................-$0.034
DUNS No. 07-695-3827	Shareholders...............................NA

Business: The group's principal activity is to market breast tumor detection training systems. The training system is known by the brand name mammacare system. Mammacare system is designed to train individuals to perform effective manual breast examination, which would help in the early detection of breast tumor. It also markets an integrated training system known as the mammacare learning system to the health care providers. It provides the mammacare clinical learning system, which trains physicians and other professional health care providers to conduct clinical breast examinations. The customers of the group include health care providers who use the group's system to detect breast tumors in their patients. It operates a mammacare center at gainesville, Florida for selling and providing training on its systems. It also provides specialized training and products to medical personnel from military facilities.

Primary SIC and add'l.: 5047

CIK No: 0000704366

Officers: Fran Robinson/National Dir. - Training, Mammacare, Nancy Homler/National Dir. - Training, Mammacare, Lucille Little/National Dir. - Training, Mammacare, Henry Pennypacker/Pres.

Directors: Mark Goldstein/Chmn.

Owners: Insiders/52.70%, Mark Kane Goldstein/23.90%, Henry S. Pennypacker/26.60%, Mary Bailey Sellers/2.20%

Financial Data: Fiscal Year End:08/31 Latest Annual Data: 8/31/2006

Year	Sales	Net Income
2006	$343,000	-$185,000
2005	$293,000	-$139,000
2004	$341,000	-$245,000

Curr. Assets:	$437,000	Curr. Liab.:	$1,080,000		
Plant, Equip.:	$270,000	Total Liab.:	$1,080,000	Indic. Yr. Divd.:	NA
Total Assets:	$929,000	Net Worth:	-$150,000	Debt/ Equity:	NA

Man Sang Holdings Inc

21st Floor, Railway Plz., 39 Chatham Rd. S, Tsimshatsui, Kowloon; *PH:* 852-23175300; *Fax:* 852-2317-5243; *http://* www.man-sang.com; *Email:* pearl@man-sang.com

General - Incorporation ....NV	Stock- Price on:12/24/2007 ....$8.7
Employees............................1,030	Stock Exchange...........................NYSE
Auditor ....Deloitte Touche Tohmatsu	Ticker Symbol............................MHK
Stk Agt .... American Stock Transfer & Trust Co.	Outstanding Shares 6,380,000
Counsel........... Paul, Hastings, Janofsky & Walker LLP	E.P.S....................................$0.624
DUNS No. .... NA	Shareholders...............................NA

Business: The group operates through its subsidiaries whose principle activity is to purchase, process, assemble and distribute pearls and pearl products; including assembled necklaces, earrings, rings, pendants, brooches, bracelets and watches; and manage and lease commercial real estate. The group operates from United States.

Primary SIC and add'l.: 6719 6512 5094

CIK No: 0000807630

Subsidiaries: 4376zone.com Limited, Arcadia Jewellery Limited, Asean Gold Limited, Cyber Bizport Limited, Damei Pearls Jewellery Goods (Shenzhen) Co. Ltd., Excel Access Limited, Hong Kong Man Sang Investments Limited, M.S. Collections Limited, M.S. Electronic Emporium Limited, Man Hing Industry Development (Shenzhen) Co., Ltd., Man Sang China Investment Limited, Man Sang Development Company Limited, Man Sang Enterprise Ltd., Man Sang Innovations Limited, Man Sang International (B.V.I.) Limited 21 Subsidiaries included in the Index

Officers: Francis King Chung Tsui/Non Exec. Dir., Martin Wai Keung Pak/44/Group Financial Controller, Company Sec., Sai Cheng/51/Deputy GM - Man Hing Industry Development, Shenzhen Co, Ltd

Directors: Sonny Kwok Wing Hung/44/Dir., Matthew Chau Ming Lai/Non Exec. Dir., Henry Gee Hang Wong/Non Exec. Dir., Francis King Chung Tsui/Non Exec. Dir.

Owners: Cheng Tai Po, Insiders, Cheng Chung Hing Ricky, Cafoong Limited, Insiders, Cheng Chung Hing Ricky, Cafoong Limited, Cheng Tai Po

Financial Data: Fiscal Year End:03/31 Latest Annual Data: 03/31/2007

Year	Sales	Net Income
2007	$51,061,000	$3,585,000
2006	$48,931,000	$2,258,000
2005	$53,450,000	$3,451,000

Curr. Assets:	$56,528,000	Curr. Liab.:	$4,597,000	P/E Ratio:	13.94
Plant, Equip.:	$21,171,000	Total Liab.:	$4,857,000	Indic. Yr. Divd.:	NA
Total Assets:	$78,047,000	Net Worth:	$37,294,000	Debt/ Equity:	NA

Management Network Group Inc

7300 College Blvd., Ste. 302, Overland Park, KS, 66210; *PH:* 1-913-345-9315;
Fax: 1-913-451-1845; *http://* www.tmng.com

General - Incorporation........................ DE
Employees...148
Auditor ....Deloitte & Touche LLP
Stk Agt................. Continental Stock T & T Co.
Counsel.................Shughart, Thomson & Kilroy
DUNS No. ....NA

Stock- Price on:12/24/2007 ....$2.35
Stock Exchange..................................NDQ
Ticker Symbol.....................................TMNG
Outstanding Shares 35,800,000
E.P.S...-$0.35
Shareholders......................................NA

Business: The group's principle activity is to provide management consulting services to the global communications and e-business industries in North America, western Europe, Latin America and Asia. Management consulting services provided by the group include business strategy and planning, marketing and customer relationship management, operating system support, revenue assurance, corporate investment services, networks and business model transformation. The group provides services to approximately 600 domestic and international customers, primarily communication services providers and technology and application firms. The group's quarterly revenue for September 2007 was 20.81 millions of USD.

Primary SIC and add'l.: 8742
CIK No: 0001094814
Subsidiaries: The Management Network Group Canada Ltd, The Management Network Group Europe, TMNG Strategy, Inc, TMNG.com, Inc.
Officers: Richard P. Nespola/Chmn., CEO/$1,041,029.00, Donald E. Klumb/45/VP, CFO - Partner/$398,510.00, Micky K. Woo/COO, Pres./$614,427.00, Ronald Angner/Principal, Sr. VP - Operations, Ned Feldman/Principal, VP - Business Development, Janet Hall/Chief Marketing Officer, Nancy Morrow/VP - Human Resources, Tom Murphy/VP - Business Development, Kirk Odegaard/VP, GM - Europe, Bill Opet/Sr. VP, Joe Sharkey/Principal, VP, Susan Simmons/VP - Boston, William Tyson/Principal, VP - Business Operations, Thurston Cromwell/Corporate Counsel, Don Zurawski/VP *(34 Officers included in Index)*
Directors: Richard P. Nespola/Chmn., CEO, Andrew D. Lipman/Dir., Robert J. Currey/Dir., Frank M. Siskowski/Dir., Roy A. Wilkens/Dir.
Owners: William M. Matthes, Potomac Capital Management LLC, Roy A. Wilkens, Grant G. Behrman, Richard P. Nespola, Frank M. Siskowski, Andrew D. Lipman, Behrman Capital II L.P., Micky K. Woo, Robert J. Currey, Donald E. Klumb, Insiders

Financial Data: *Fiscal Year End:*12/31 **Latest Annual Data:** 12/30/2006

Year	Sales	Net Income
2006	$34,013,000	-$12,370,000
2005	$30,378,000	-$2,420,000

Curr. Assets:	$57,179,000	Curr. Liab.:	$4,682,000		
Plant, Equip.:	$900,000	Total Liab.:	$7,501,000	Indic. Yr. Divd.:	NA
Total Assets:	$73,549,000	Net Worth:	$66,048,000	Debt/ Equity:	0.0372

Manakoa Services Corp

7203 W Deschutes Ave., Kennewick, WA, 99336; *PH:* 1-509-736-7000; *http://* www.manakoa.com

General - Incorporation.............................NV
Employees...NA
Auditor ....Cordovano and Honeck, LLP
Stk Agt...... American Stock Transfer & Trust Co.
Counsel..NA
DUNS No. ....NA

Stock- Price on:12/24/2007 ....NA
Stock Exchange..................................OTC
Ticker Symbol.....................................MKOS
Outstanding Shares ....NA
E.P.S...-$0.039
Shareholders......................................NA

Business: The groups principle activity is to provide vertical security and risk management solutions for organizations. In July 2005 the group acquired Vigilant Network Technologies, Inc. The group operates from the United States, European Union, Japan, the United Kingdom and Canada.

Primary SIC and add'l.: 7374
CIK No: 0001091967
Subsidiaries: Advanced Cyber Security, Inc
Officers: James C. Katzaroff/Dir., CEO, Paul Reep/Pres., Debra S. Kasparek/Interim CFO, Administrative Services Mgr., Robert A. Papke/Dir., COO, Exec. VP, John Barnett/New Business Development Consultant
Directors: James C. Katzaroff/Dir., CEO, Stuart Platt/Chmn., Ken Hatch/Dir., Robert A. Papke/Dir., COO, Exec. VP
Owners: Robert A. Papke/5.50%, James C. Katzaroff/19.00%, Kenneth L. Hatch/5.60%, Insiders/45.70%, Debra S. Kasparek/1.40%, Kenin M. Spivak/5.10%, Stuart Platt/5.70%, Robert G. Williams/10.30%, Utek Corporation/13.70%

Financial Data: *Fiscal Year End:*12/31 **Latest Annual Data:** 12/31/2006

Year	Sales	Net Income
2006	$8,000	-$2,186,000
2005	$22,000	-$3,426,000
2004	NA	-$4,526,000

Curr. Assets:	NA	Curr. Liab.:	$1,728,000		
Plant, Equip.:	$1,000	Total Liab.:	$1,728,000	Indic. Yr. Divd.:	NA
Total Assets:	$4,000	Net Worth:	$112,195,000	Debt/ Equity:	NA

Manaris Corp

1155 Rene-Levesque W, Ste. 2720, Montreal, PQ, H3B 2K8; *PH:* 1-514-337-2447;
Fax: 1-514-337-0985; *http://* www.manariscorp.com; *Email:* info@manariscorp.com

General - Incorporation ....NV
Employees...NA
Auditor ...Raymond Chabot Grant Thornton, LLP
Stk Agt............. Pacific Stock Transfer Company
Counsel............................Anna Pennino
DUNS No. ....NA

Stock- Price on:12/24/2007 ....$0.087
Stock Exchange..................................OTC
Ticker Symbol...................................MANSE
Outstanding Shares ....NA
E.P.S...NA
Shareholders......................................NA

Business: The group's principal activity is to develop and market products and provide services, which uses integrated wireless communications technology, transaction processing, software applications and the Internet and global positioning system (gps) technology to enable users to efficiently access, control and manage remote assets. The products and services are designed to allow the customers to use the Website to remotely access, control, locate and monitor different types of equipment or services. The group has targeted their products and services to the large automotive sector, but their basic technology has applications to a variety of assets which span several business sectors including industrial equipment, office equipment and consumer electronic products. On 07-Jan-2003, acquired all assets and intellectual property related to the the c-chip technology from capex investments limited ("Capex") and on 23-Feb-2004, acquired Canadian security agency inc.

Primary SIC and add'l.: 3669
CIK No: 0001125051
Subsidiaries: Avensys Inc., C-Chip Technologies Corporation
Officers: John G. Fraser/Dir., CEO, Pres., Truc N. Nguyen/Investor Relations Officer, Sherine Attia/In House Legal Counsel, Tony J. Giuliano/CFO, Hassan Kassi/GM - Avensys Tech, Pres. - Avensys Inc, Marie-Annick Riel/Pres. - C, Chip Technologies, North America
Directors: John G. Fraser/Dir., CEO, Pres., John H. Simons/Chmn., Jos J. Wintermans/Dir., Bernard Bougie/Dir.
Owners: Jos J. Wintermans, Tony Giuliano, Bernard Bougie, John H. Simons, Insiders/1.69%, John Fraser/1.28%

Financial Data: *Fiscal Year End:*06/30 **Latest Annual Data:** 6/30/2006

Year	Sales	Net Income
2006	$10,499,000	-$11,902,000
2005	$7,021,000	-$6,231,000
2004	$1,041,000	-$4,591,000

Curr. Assets:	$6,072,000	Curr. Liab.:	$7,730,000		
Plant, Equip.:	$3,082,000	Total Liab.:	$9,913,000	Indic. Yr. Divd.:	NA
Total Assets:	$17,143,000	Net Worth:	$7,206,000	Debt/ Equity:	0.3737

Manatron Inc

510 E Milham Ave., Portage, MI, 49002; *PH:* 1-269-567-2900; *Fax:* 1-269-567-2930;
http:// www.manatron.com; *Email:* info@manatron.com

General - Incorporation ....MI
Employees...359
Auditor .... Ernst & Young LLP
Stk Agt.....................Registrar & Transfer Co
Counsel.................Warner, Norcross & Judd
DUNS No. 07-927-8305

Stock- Price on:12/24/2007 ....$9.26
Stock Exchange..................................NDQ
Ticker Symbol....................................MANA
Outstanding Shares 5,080,000
E.P.S...$0.25
Shareholders......................................NA

Business: The group's principal activity is to design, develop, market and support a family of Web-based and client/server application software products for county, city and township governments. The services rendered include mass appraisal services for assessment of residential, commercial and other types of properties. Its products support the back-office processes for government agencies and also facilitate the 'virtual courthouse' by providing Internet access to information for industry professionals and the public or by processing transactions over the Internet such as the payment of property taxes. The group's suite of products include manatron grm, manatron tax, manatron cama, manatron egovernment. At 30-04-2004, the company served approximately 1,700 customers in 24 states and three Canadian provinces.

Primary SIC and add'l.: 7372 8742 7373 7379
CIK No: 0000798736
Subsidiaries: ASIX Inc.
Officers: Paul R. Sylvester/Dir., CEO/$277,956.00, Krista L. Inosencio/CFO, VP - Finance/$232,877.00, Early L. Stephens/Chief Technology, Marketing Officer/$256,573.00, Marty A. Ulanski/Exec. VP - Sales, Business Development/$257,895.00, Mary Nestell Gephart/VP - Human Resources, Administation, William G. McKinzie/COO, Pres./$296,803.00, Kurt Wagner/Pres. - Asix Division, Matthew Hayden/Investor Relations Officer, Jane M. Rix/Sec., Bob Brower/Regional VP - Sales, South Central Region, Woody Carter/Regional VP - Sales, Northern Region, John Walters/Regional VP - Sales, Western Region
Directors: Paul R. Sylvester/Dir., CEO, Randall L. Peat/Chmn., Stephen C. Waterbury/Dir., Gene Bledsoe/Dir., Richard J. Holloman/Dir., Scott W. Baker/Dir.
Owners: Eliot Rose Asset Management LLC/15.60%, Paul R. Sylvester/2.80%, Scott w. Baker, Stephen C. Waterbury, William G. McKinzie/2.20%, Randall L. Peat/7.90%, Richard J. Holloman/3.40%, Marty A. Ulanski/1.40%, Gene Bledsoe, Early L. Stephens/1.90%, Insiders/24.90%, Krista L. Inosencio/1.20%

Financial Data: *Fiscal Year End:*04/30 **Latest Annual Data:** 04/30/2007

Year	Sales	Net Income
2007	$41,796,000	$946,000
2006	$36,324,000	-$4,317,000
2005	$40,155,000	$2,366,000

Curr. Assets:	$23,442,000	Curr. Liab.:	$18,760,000	P/E Ratio:	48.74
Plant, Equip.:	$2,619,000	Total Liab.:	$21,379,000	Indic. Yr. Divd.:	NA
Total Assets:	$44,422,000	Net Worth:	$23,043,000	Debt/ Equity:	NA

Manchester Inc

100 Crescent Ct., Ste. 7061, Dallas, TX, 75201; *PH:* 1-214-459-3230; *http://* www.manchesterinc.net

General - Incorporation ....NV
Employees...2
Auditor ....Rodefer Moss & Co, PLLC
Stk Agt.......... Nevada Agency & Trust Company
Counsel..NA
DUNS No. ....NA

Stock- Price on:12/24/2007 ....$1.8
Stock Exchange..................................OTC
Ticker Symbol...................................MNCS
Outstanding Shares 34,280,000
E.P.S...-$0.19
Shareholders......................................NA

Business: The group's principle activity is to operate Buy-Here or Pay-Here used car sales enterprises. The group acquired Nice Cars, Inc. and Nice Cars Capital Acceptance Corporation in October 2006, and F.S. English, Inc. in December 2006. The group operates from the United States.

Primary SIC and add'l.: 5500

CIK No: 0001214933

Subsidiaries: Nice Cars Acceptance AcquisitionCo, Inc., Nice Cars Capital Acceptance Corporation, Nice Cars Funding LLC, Nice Cars Operations AcquisitionCo, Inc., Nice Cars, Inc.

Officers: Raymond Lyle/60/Pres., CEO - Nice Cars, Inc, Nice Cars Capital Acceptance Corporation, Richard Gaines/63/Dir., Corp. Sec., Victoria E. Lyle/59/Treasurer - Nice Cars, Inc, Nice Cars Capital Acceptance Corporation Nice Cars, Inc, Nice Cars Capital Acceptance Corp, Chantelle Hardy/Dir. - Communications

Directors: Richard Gaines/63/Dir., Corp. Sec.

Owners: Richard Gaines, Insiders, Raymond Lyle/9.02%, Victoria E. Lyle/9.02%

Financial Data: *Fiscal Year End:* 11/30 *Latest Annual Data:* 11/30/2006

Year	Sales	Net Income
2006	$17,256,000	-$3,333,000
2005	NA	-$70,000
2004	NA	-$51,000

Curr. Assets:	$67,996,000	**Curr. Liab.:**	$1,162,000		
Plant, Equip.:	$914,000	**Total Liab.:**	$78,915,000	**Indic. Yr. Divd.:**	NA
Total Assets:	$93,052,000	**Net Worth:**	$14,136,000	**Debt/ Equity:**	5.2913

Mangosoft Inc

1500 W Pk. Dr., Ste 190, Westborough, MA, 01581; *PH:* 1-603-324-0400; *http://* www.mangosoft.com

General		**Stock**	
Incorporation	NV	Price on:12/24/2007	$1.15
Employees	1	Stock Exchange	OTC
Auditor	Stowe & Degon	Ticker Symbol	MGOF
Stk Agt	Interwest Transfer Company, Inc.	Outstanding Shares	3,410,000
Counsel	NA	E.P.S.	-$0.06
DUNS No.	10-839-8801	Shareholders	NA

Business: The group's principal activity is to develop Internet software and services that improve the utility and effectiveness of Internet-based business applications. It develops, markets and supports software solutions to address the networking needs of small businesses, workgroups and large enterprises. The group has its patented technology known as 'pooling' to develop software solutions. Mangomind is a multi-user, business-oriented, peer-to-peer file sharing system, allowing individual users to collaborate over the Internet across organizational boundaries in a secure manner. The group's filetrust is an online data storage service, which helps the user to access their stored files from any Internet-connected system. Cachelink is a software-based Web-caching product that increases the delivery speed of Internet and intranet content to end-users. The group operates in the United States.

Primary SIC and add'l.: 7372 7379

CIK No: 0000947969

Subsidiaries: MangoMerger Corp.

Officers: Dale Vincent/61/Dir., CEO, Pres.

Directors: Dale Vincent/61/Dir., CEO, Pres.

Owners: Selig Zises/11.80%, Jay Zises/11.60%, Dale Vincent/7.00%, Insiders/7.00%

Financial Data: *Fiscal Year End:* 12/31 *Latest Annual Data:* 03/31/2007

Year	Sales	Net Income
2007	NA	NA
2006	$275,000	$126,000
2005	$337,000	-$347,000

Curr. Assets:	$146,000	**Curr. Liab.:**	$114,000	**P/E Ratio:**	19.17
Plant, Equip.:	NA	**Total Liab.:**	$364,000	**Indic. Yr. Divd.:**	NA
Total Assets:	$146,000	**Net Worth:**	-$218,000	**Debt/ Equity:**	NA

Manhattan Assoc Inc

2300 Windy Ridge Pkwy., Ste. 700, Atlanta, GA, 30339; *PH:* 1-770-955-7070; *Fax:* 1-770-955-0302; *http://* www.manhattanassoicates.com; *Email:* info@manh.com

General		**Stock**	
Incorporation	GA	Price on:12/24/2007	$27.17
Employees	1,965	Stock Exchange	NDQ
Auditor	Ernst & Young LLP	Ticker Symbol	MANH
Stk Agt	Suntrust Bank	Outstanding Shares	26,960,000
Counsel	Morris, Manning & Martin	E.P.S.	$0.97
DUNS No.	78-548-4387	Shareholders	NA

Business: The group's principal activity is to provide technology-based solutions to improve supply chain effectiveness and efficiencies. The group's solutions, which consist of software, services and hardware, enhance distribution and transportation efficiencies through the real-time integration of supply chain constituents. The solutions are provided to the manufacturers, distributors, retailers and transportation providers primarily in the following markets: retail, consumer goods, food and grocery, third-party logistics, industrial and wholesale, electronics, healthcare and government. The group also markets hardware products manufactured by third party. On 23-Jan-2004, the group acquired avere inc.

Primary SIC and add'l.: 5072 8999 7372

CIK No: 0001056696

Subsidiaries: Manhattan Associates (India) Development Centre Private Limited, Manhattan Associates Europe B.V., Manhattan Associates France SARL, Manhattan Associates GmbH, Manhattan Associates KK, Manhattan Associates Limited, Manhattan Associates Pty Ltd., Manhattan Associates Software (Shanghai), Co. Ltd., Manhattan Associates Software Pte Ltd.

Officers: Pete Sinisgalli/Dir., CEO, Pres./$1,363,688.00, Diane Tuccito/VP - Global Human Resources, David Dabbiere/Sr. VP, Chief Legal Officer, Eddie Capel/Sr. VP - Product Management, Customer Relations, Jeff Cashman/Sr. VP - Business Development, Pervinder Johar/CTO, Sr. VP/$764,353.00, Jeff Baum/Sr. VP - International/$270,450.00, Jeff Mitchell/Exec. VP - Americas/$540,007.00, Dennis Story/Sr. VP, CFO/$2,426,794.00, Steve Smith/VP - Europe, Middle East, Africa, EMEA, Terrie O'Hanlon/VP, Chief Marketing Officer

Directors: Pete Sinisgalli/Dir., CEO, Pres., John J. Huntz/Chmn., Brian J. Cassidy/Dir., Paul R. Goodwin/Dir., Deepak Raghavan/Dir., Thomas E. Noonan/Dir.

Owners: Dennis B. Story, Thomas E. Noonan, Deepak Raghavan, Peter F. Sinisgalli/2.20%, Barclays Global Investors NA/8.45%, Brian J. Cassidy, Insiders/7.94%, Kornitzer Capital Management, Inc./6.09%, Pervinder Johar, U.S. Trust Corporation/5.47%, Artisan Partners Limited Partnership/8.20%, Jeffrey S. Mitchell/1.55%, John J. Huntz, Paul R. Goodwin, David K. Dabbiere

Financial Data: *Fiscal Year End:* 12/31 *Latest Annual Data:* 12/31/2006

Year	Sales	Net Income
2006	$288,868,000	$19,331,000
2005	$246,404,000	$18,635,000
2004	$214,919,000	$21,634,000

Curr. Assets:	$187,103,000	**Curr. Liab.:**	$76,072,000	**P/E Ratio:**	31.23
Plant, Equip.:	$15,850,000	**Total Liab.:**	$77,753,000	**Indic. Yr. Divd.:**	NA
Total Assets:	$314,893,000	**Net Worth:**	$237,140,000	**Debt/ Equity:**	NA

Manhattan Pharmaceuticals Inc

810 7th Ave., 4th Fl., New York, NY, 10019; *PH:* 1-212-582-3950; *Fax:* 1-212-582-3957; *http://* www.manhattanpharma.com; *Email:* info@manhattanpharma.com

General		**Stock**	
Incorporation	DE	Price on:12/24/2007	$0.84
Employees	8	Stock Exchange	NDQ
Auditor	J. H. Cohn LLP	Ticker Symbol	MHA
Stk Agt	Continental Stock Transfer & Trust Co	Outstanding Shares	70,470,000
Counsel	NA	E.P.S.	-$0.2
DUNS No.	NA	Shareholders	NA

Business: The group's principal activity is to develop and market early-stage technologies. The activities include identifying development-stage biomedical, pharmaceutical, medical devices or other technologies that are commercially viable. The group intends to acquire proprietary rights to these technologies, fund its research and development and bring these technologies to market. The group has developed a technology that can be used in treating pain and inflammation. The group and its operating subsidiaries are in the development stage, concentrating on performing research and development activities. The group is developing its proprietary compound ct-3, a patented synthetic derivative of carboxylic tetrahydrocannabinol (thc-7c), as an alternative to nonsteroidal anti-inflammatory drugs, such as aspirin and ibuprofen. During the year 2003, the group completed a reverse acquisition of privately held manhattan research development inc.

Primary SIC and add'l.: 8731 2834 8734

CIK No: 0001001316

Subsidiaries: Tarpan Therapeutics, Inc.

Officers: Douglas Abel/CEO, Pres./$1,748,841.00, Michael McGuinness/CFO/$181,851.00, Alan G. Harris/Chief Medical Officer/$467,220.00, Louis Aronne/Member - Scientific Advisory Board, Stanley Heshka/Member - Scientific Advisory Board, Larry J. Jameson/Member - Scientific Advisory Board, Michelle Carroll/Contact - Corporate Communications, Investor Relations

Directors: Timothy McInerney/Dir., Richard I. Steinhart/Dir., Neil Herskowitz/Dir., Malcolm Hoenlein/Dir., Michael Weiser/Dir., Joan P. Gimbert/58/Dir., Joseph R. Vasselli/Member - Scientific Advisory Board

Owners: Neil Herskowitz, Lindsay A. Rosenwald/5.70%, Alan G. Harris, Oleoylestrone Developments, SL/5.60%, Malcolm Hoenlien, Michael Weiser/3.50%, Joan Pons Gimbert/5.80%, Lester E. Lipschutz/12.70%, Douglas Abel/2.70%, Insiders/13.60%, Richard I. Steinhart, Timothy McInerney/1.20%

Financial Data: *Fiscal Year End:* 12/31 *Latest Annual Data:* 12/31/2006

Year	Sales	Net Income
2006	NA	-$9,695,000
2005	NA	-$19,141,000
2004	NA	-$5,896,000

Curr. Assets:	$3,294,000	**Curr. Liab.:**	$1,943,000		
Plant, Equip.:	$84,000	**Total Liab.:**	$1,943,000	**Indic. Yr. Divd.:**	NA
Total Assets:	$3,448,000	**Net Worth:**	$1,505,000	**Debt/ Equity:**	NA

Manhattan Scientifics Inc

405 Lexington Ave., 32nd Fl., New York, NY, 10174; *PH:* 1-212-550-5577; *http://* www.mhtx.com

General		**Stock**	
Incorporation	DE	Price on:12/24/2007	NA
Employees	2	Stock Exchange	OTC
Auditor	Eisner LLP	Ticker Symbol	MHTX
Stk Agt	Interwest Transfer Company, Inc.	Outstanding Shares	NA
Counsel	Bach & Associates	E.P.S.	-$0.006
DUNS No.	NA	Shareholders	NA

Business: The group's principal activity is to acquire, develop and commercialize technologies in the areas of alternative energy, consumer and commercial electronics. The group is currently working to develop and commercialize three technologies; micro fuel cell technology, which is designed to become an ultra efficient miniature electricity generator that converts hydrogen into electricity by chemical means, for portable electronic devices, including cellular telephones; mid-range fuel cell technology, which is an ultra efficient medium-size electricity generating device that converts hydrogen into electricity, with potential applications for personal transportation cordless appliances, power tools, wheelchairs, bicycles, boats and emergency home generators; haptics touch and feel computer applications, which is a technology that allows computer users to be able to touch and feel any objects they see on their computer screen with the aid of special mouse.

Primary SIC and add'l.: 8732 3621 9999 3691 6794

CIK No: 0001099132

Subsidiaries: Grand Subsidiary, Inc., Tamarack Storage Devices, Inc

Officers: Marvin Maslow/Chmn., CEO, Pres., Robert E. Hermes/Sr. Staff Scientist, Unit Leader, Scott L. Bach/General Counsel, Corp. Sec., Tom Anderson/Unit Leader, Jack Harrod/COO, Arthur Koschany/Unit Leader, David A. Teich/Dir., Controller, Robert G. Hockaday/Unit Leader

Directors: Marvin Maslow/Chmn., CEO, Pres., Arthur Lipper/Member - Science, Business Advisory Board, Martin Cooper/Member - Science, Business Advisory Board, Donald J. Sandstrom/Member - Science, Business Advisory Board, Ralph J. Anderson/Dir., Larry Schatz/Dir., George A. Cowan/Member - Science, Business Advisory Board, David A. Teich/Dir., Controller

Owners: David A. Teich/4.00%, Insiders/17.54%, Marvin Maslow/13.54%, Lancer Funds/21.46%, Saraklis Inc./5.78%

Financial Data: *Fiscal Year End:* 12/31 *Latest Annual Data:* 12/31/2005

Year	Sales	Net Income
2005	NA	-$219,000
2004	$150,000	-$1,517,000
2001	NA	-$6,662,000

Curr. Assets:	$513,000	**Curr. Liab.:**	$2,832,000		
Plant, Equip.:	$43,000	**Total Liab.:**	$2,832,000	**Indic. Yr. Divd.:**	NA
Total Assets:	$1,170,000	**Net Worth:**	-$1,662,000	**Debt/ Equity:**	NA

Manitowoc Co Inc

2400 S 44th St., Manitowoc, WI, 54221; *PH:* 1-920-684-4410; *Fax:* 1-920-652-9778; *http://* www.manitowoc.com; *Email:* info@manitowoc.com

General - Incorporation WI
Employees 9,500
Auditor PricewaterhouseCoopers LLP
Stk Agt Computershare Trust Co
Counsel Quarles & Brady LLP
DUNS No. 00-607-3183

Stock- Price on:12/24/2007 $82.57
Stock Exchange NDQ
Ticker Symbol MTXX
Outstanding Shares 62,360,000
E.P.S $2.22
Shareholders NA

Business: The groups principle activity is to manufacture cranes and related products, food service and marine. The groups products include mobile telescopic cranes, tower cranes, walk-in and reach-in refrigerators and freezers, and fountain beverage delivery systems. The groups services include construction, shiprepair and maintenance services for freshwater and saltwater vessels. The group operates from United States.

Primary SIC and add'l.: 3585 3536 3537 3731 3531

CIK No: 0000061986

Subsidiaries: Axiome de Re SA, BPGR Sarl, Brunello Holding Co., LLC, Cadillon GmbH, Deutsche Grove GmbH, Diversified Refrigeration, LLC, DRI Holding Company LP, Environmental Rehab, Inc., Femco Machine Company, Inc., Grove Australia Pty. Ltd., Grove Cranes Limited, Grove Cranes S.L., Grove Europe Pension Trustees Limited, Grove U.S. LLC, Grove Worldwide Holdings Germany AG 79 Subsidiaries included in the Index

Officers: Glen E. Tellock/47/CEO, Pres., Sr. VP/$1,655,160.00, Mary Ellen Bowers/VP - Corporate Development, Dennis E. McCloskey/65/VP - Global Procurement, Dean J. Nolden/39/VP - Finance, Controller, Thomas G. Musial/56/Sr. VP - Human Resources, Administration/$1,364,058.00, Robert P. Herre/55/Sr. VP, Carl J. Laurino/46/CFO, Sr. VP/$927,515.00, Maurice D. Jones/48/Sr. VP, General Counsel, Sec., Eric Etchart/52/Sr. VP, Michael J. Kachmer/49/Sr. VP

Directors: Terry D. Growcock/62/Chmn., Robert S. Throop/Dir., Daniel W. Duval/70/Dir., Dean H. Anderson/66/Dir., Robert C. Stift/65/Dir., Kenneth W. Krueger/50/Dir., Keith D. Nosbusch/56/Dir., Virgis W. Colbert/69/Dir., James L. Packard/64/Dir.

Owners: Carl J. Laurino, Robert S. Throop, Insiders, Timothy J. Kraus, James L. Packard, Robert C. Stift, Terry D. Growcock, Daniel W. Duval, Keith D. Nosbusch, FMR Corp./12.37%, Glen E. Tellock, Virgis W. Colbert, Kenneth W. Krueger, Thomas G. Musial, Dean H. Anderson

Financial Data: **Fiscal Year End:**12/31 **Latest Annual Data:** 12/31/2006

Year	Sales	Net Income
2006	$2,933,300,000	$166,200,000
2005	$2,254,097,000	$65,800,000
2004	$1,964,101,000	$39,138,000

Curr. Assets:	$1,142,700,000	**Curr. Liab.:**	$935,400,000	**P/E Ratio:**	25.97
Plant, Equip.:	$398,900,000	**Total Liab.:**	$1,445,000,000	**Indic. Yr. Divd.:**	$0.080
Total Assets:	$2,219,500,000	**Net Worth:**	$774,500,000	**Debt/ Equity:**	NA

Mannatech Inc

600 S Royal Ln., Ste. 200, Coppell, TX, 75019; ***PH:*** 1-972-471-7400; ***Fax:*** 1-972-471-8135; ***http://*** www.mannatech.com; ***Email:*** ir@mannatech.com

General - Incorporation TX
Employees 564
Auditor Grant Thornton LLP
Stk Agt PricewaterhouseCoopers LLP
Counsel Lerach Coughlin Stoia Geller R & R
DUNS No. NA

Stock- Price on:12/24/2007 $15.45
Stock Exchange NYSE
Ticker Symbol MTH
Outstanding Shares 26,430,000
E.P.S -$1.45
Shareholders NA

Business: The group's principal activity is to develop and market proprietary nutritional supplements, topical products and weight-management products. These products are sold through a global network-marketing system throughout the United States, Canada, Australia, the United Kingdom, Japan and New Zealand. The products are designed to support various systems and functions of the human body such as cell-to-cell communication and optimal health, sports performance, skin care and weight management. The products of the group includes ambrotose(R), bulk ambrotose(R), plus, glycentials(R) vitamin, ambroglycintmmineral, antioxidant formula, ambrostart(R), phytaaloe(R), bulk phytaloe(R), gi-protm, gi-zymetm, immunostarttm, manna-ctm, mannatonintm, sport, bulkempact(R) and mannabartm vanilla yogurt-coated apple-crunch.

Primary SIC and add'l.: 2833 2834 5963

CIK No: 0001056358

Subsidiaries: Internet Health Group, Inc., Mannatech (International) Limited, Mannatech Australia Pty Limited, Mannatech Foreign Sales Corporation, Mannatech Japan, Inc., Mannatech Korea, Ltd., Mannatech Limited, Mannatech Payment Services Incorporated, Mannatech Products Company, Inc., Mannatech Taiwan Corporation, Mannatech Taiwan Corporation Taiwan Branch

Officers: Samuel L. Caster/57/Chmn., CEO/$976,295.00, Stephen D. Fenstermacher/CFO, Sr. VP/$350,631.00, Linda Padilla/VP - Global Marketing, Robert A. Sinnott/Chief Science Officer, Sr. VP/$386,641.00, Terry L. Persinger/Dir., COO, Pres./$434,608.00, Cindy L. Tysinger/CIO, Sr. VP, Terry O'Day/COO, Exec. VP

Directors: Samuel L. Caster/57/Chmn., CEO, Robert C. Blattberg/Dir., Alan D. Kennedy/Dir., Marlin Ray Robbins/Dir., Gerald E. Gilbert/Dir., Terry L. Persinger/Dir., COO, Pres., John Stewart Axford/Dir., Stanley J. Fredrick/Dir., Larry A. Jobe/Dir., Patricia A. Wier/Dir.

Owners: John S. Axford, Terry L. Persinger/0.80%, Stephen D. Fenstermacher/0.90%, Stanley J. Fredrick/11.90%, Larry A. Jobe/0.10%, Robert A. Sinnott, Patricia A. Wier/0.10%, Samuel L. Caster/21.20%, Marlin Ray Robbins/7.70%, Alan D. Kennedy/0.20%, John W. Price, Cynthia L. Tysinger/0.20%, Gerald E. Gilbert/0.20%, Insiders/43.50%

Financial Data: **Fiscal Year End:**12/31 **Latest Annual Data:** 12/31/2006

Year	Sales	Net Income
2006	$410,069,000	$32,390,000
2005	$389,383,000	$28,647,000
2004	$294,508,000	$19,552,000

Curr. Assets:	$80,830,000	**Curr. Liab.:**	$52,036,000	**P/E Ratio:**	15.93
Plant, Equip.:	$41,248,000	**Total Liab.:**	$63,438,000	**Indic. Yr. Divd.:**	$0.360
Total Assets:	$152,235,000	**Net Worth:**	$88,797,000	**Debt/ Equity:**	0.0297

MannKind Corp

28903 N Ave. Paine, Valencia, CA, 91355; ***PH:*** 1-661-775-5300; ***Fax:*** 1-661-775-2080; ***http://*** www.mannkindcorp.com; ***Email:*** ir@mannkindcorp.com

General - Incorporation DE
Employees 545
Auditor Deloitte& Touche LLP
Stk Agt Mellon Investor Services LLC
Counsel Cooley Godward LLP
DUNS No. NA

Stock- Price on:12/24/2007 $13.02
Stock Exchange NDQ
Ticker Symbol MNRK
Outstanding Shares 73,420,000
E.P.S -$4.21
Shareholders NA

Business: The groups principle activities include discovering, developing and commercializing therapeutic products. The products of the group include Sulfonylureas, Meglitinides, Biguanides and Incretin mimetics. The group products sold under the trade names Humalog(R) Prandin(R) and Starlix(R) Glucotrol(R), Diabeta(R), Glynase(R), Micronase(R) and Amaryl(R). The group operates from the United States.

Primary SIC and add'l.: 8731 7374 8734 2834

CIK No: 0000899460

Subsidiaries: Pharmaceutical Discovery Corp.

Officers: Alfred E. Mann/Chmn., CEO/$4,228,596.00, Hakan S. Edstrom/Dir., COO, Pres./$3,073,253.00, Alexander Fleming/Dir. - Scientific Advisor, Martin Kast/Dir. - Scientific Advisor, Thomas Kundig/Dir. - Scientific Advisor, Harold E. Lebovitz/Dir. - Scientific Advisor, Frederick Levy/Dir. - Scientific Advisor, Robert Morgan/Dir. - Scientific Advisor, Robert Ozols/Dir. - Scientific Advisors, Daniel Porte/Dir. - Scientific Advisors, Philip Raskin/Dir. - Scientific Advisor, Julio Rosenstock/Dir. - Scientific Advisors, Jesse Roth/Dir. - Scientific Advisor, Jay S. Skyler/Dir. - Scientific Advisor, Rolf Zinkernagel/Dir. - Scientific Advisor *(24 Officers included in Index)*

Directors: Alfred E. Mann/Chmn., CEO, Hakan S. Edstrom/Dir., COO, Pres., Barry E. Cohen/Dir., Heather Hay Murren/41/Dir., Kathleen Connell/60/Dir., Ronald Consiglio/Dir., Michael Friedman/Dir., Llew Keltner/58/Dir., Kent Kresa/Dir., David H. MacCallum/Dir., Henry Nordhoff/Dir.

Owners: Insiders/43.20%, Henry L. Nordhoff, Hakan S. Edstrom, Ronald Consiglio, Kathleen Connell, FMR Corp./15.10%, Kent Kresa, LMM LLC/10.90%, Llew Keltner, David H. MacCallum, Michael Friedman, David Thomson, Alfred E. Mann/41.70%, Diane M. Palumbo, Richard L. Anderson

Financial Data: **Fiscal Year End:**12/31 **Latest Annual Data:** 03/31/2007

Year	Sales	Net Income
2007	NA	NA
2006	$100,000	-$230,548,000
2005	NA	-$114,338,000

Curr. Assets:	$449,547,000	**Curr. Liab.:**	$44,959,000		
Plant, Equip.:	$88,328,000	**Total Liab.:**	$156,250,000	**Indic. Yr. Divd.:**	NA
Total Assets:	$539,737,000	**Net Worth:**	$383,487,000	**Debt/ Equity:**	0.2901

Manor Care Inc

333 N Summit St., Toledo, OH, 43604; ***PH:*** 1-419-252-5500; ***Fax:*** 1-419-252-5554; ***http://*** www.hcr-manorcare.com; ***Email:*** info@hcr-manorcare.com

General - Incorporation DE
Employees 59,500
Auditor Ernst & Young LLP
Stk Agt National City Bank
Counsel NA
DUNS No. 00-790-3347

Stock- Price on:12/24/2007 $64.75
Stock Exchange NYSE
Ticker Symbol HCR
Outstanding Shares 73,170,000
E.P.S NA
Shareholders NA

Business: The groups principle activity is to provide short-term post-acute medical care and rehabilitation, and long-term skilled nursing care services. The group operates from United States.

Primary SIC and add'l.: 8062 8082 8051 8059

CIK No: 0000878736

Subsidiaries: Four Seasons Nursing Centers, Inc., HCR Home Health Care and Hospice, Inc., HCR Information Corporation, Health Care and Retirement Corporation of America, an Ohio, Heartland Rehabilitation Services, Inc., In Home Health, Inc., ManorCare Health Services, Inc., MileStone Healthcare, Inc., MNR Finance Corp.

Officers: Paul A. Ormond/Chmn., CEO, Pres./$17,250,300.00, Stephen L. Guillard/COO, Exec. VP/$2,295,695.00, Steven M. Cavanaugh/CFO, VP/$870,085.00, Richard A. Parr/VP, General Counsel, Sec./$532,923.00, Nancy A. Edwards/57/VP, GM - Central Division, Jeffrey A. Grillo/49/VP, GM - Mid, Atlantic Division, Lynn M. Hood/46/VP, GM - Southeast Division, Larry C. Lester/65/VP, GM - Midwest Division, Dir. - Marketing, Spencer C. Moler/60/VP, Controller, Susan E. Morey/55/VP, GM - Eastern Division, Michael J. Reed/56/VP, GM - Assisted Living Division, Joseph F. Schmitt/59/VP, GM - West Division

Directors: Paul A. Ormond/Chmn., CEO, Pres., Mary Taylor Behrens/47/Dir., Joseph F. Damico/54/Dir., John T. Schwieters/68/Dir., Richard C. Tuttle/52/Dir., Thomas L. Young/64/Dir., William H. Longfield/69/Dir., Gail R. Wilensky/64/Dir.

Owners: Ronald Baron/8.30%, Stephen L. Guillard, Wellington Management Company, LLP/5.70%, Gail R. Wilensky, T. Rowe Price Associates, Inc./8.60%, Paul A. Ormond/4.90%, John K. Graham, Jeffrey R. Bixler, Richard C. Tuttle, Insiders/8.40%, Janus Capital Management LLC/12.30%, John T. Schwieters, Thomas L. Young, Steven M. Cavanaugh, William H. Longfield *(19 Owners included in Index)*

Financial Data: **Fiscal Year End:**12/31 **Latest Annual Data:** 12/31/2006

Year	Sales	Net Income
2006	$3,613,185,000	$167,084,000
2005	$3,417,290,000	$160,955,000
2004	$3,208,867,000	$168,222,000

Curr. Assets:	$619,194,000	**Curr. Liab.:**	$523,629,000		
Plant, Equip.:	$1,493,576,000	**Total Liab.:**	$1,825,284,000	**Indic. Yr. Divd.:**	$0.680
Total Assets:	$2,398,477,000	**Net Worth:**	$573,193,000	**Debt/ Equity:**	1.3333

Manpower Inc

100 Manpower Pl., Milwaukee, WI, 53212; ***PH:*** 1-414-961-1000; ***Fax:*** 1-414-906-7985; ***http://*** www.manpower.com

General - Incorporation WI
Employees 30,000
Auditor Deloitte & Touche, LLP
Stk Agt Mellon Investor Services LLC
Counsel NA
DUNS No. 00-607-3068

Stock- Price on:12/24/2007 $93.16
Stock Exchange NYSE
Ticker Symbol MAN
Outstanding Shares 84,530,000
E.P.S $5.60
Shareholders NA

Business: The group's principle activity is to deliver staffing and workforce management solutions. The group provides human resource services including permanent, temporary, and contract recruitment, employee assessment, training, internal audit, accounting, technology and tax services and organizational consulting services. The group has a comprehensive system of assessment, selection, training and quality assurance used by its temporary staffing operations. The operations are carried out through branch offices and franchise offices in the United States, Canada, France, Europe, Middle East and Africa. Manpower (R), ultraskill(R) and skillware(R) are the trademarks of the group. The group's quarterly revenue for September 2007 was 5,295.40 millions of USD.

Primary SIC and add'l.: 8742 8331 7363 7389

CIK No: 0000871763

Subsidiaries: Adam Ltd., Adgrams, Inc., Adi Ltd., Adservice GmbH, Agensi Pekerjaan Manpower Recruitment Sdn Bhd, Aide Temporaire SARL, Alisia SARL, Allegra Finanz AG, Alternative International Limited, Ambridge Group GmbH, Ambridge Professional Services GmbH, AMFO Members Insurance Company, Ltd., Apel Servis d.o.o., Aris Sociedad Anonima, Atlas Group Holdings Limited 340 Subsidiaries included in the Index

Officers: Jeffrey A. Joerres/Chmn., CEO, Pres./$8,377,551.00, Owen Sullivan/CEO, Exec. VP - Right Management, Jefferson Wells/$1,565,486.00, Tammy Johns/Sr. VP - Workforce Strategy, Yoav Michaely/51/Exec. VP - Global Operational/$1,854,576.00, Rick Davidson/Sr. VP, Global CIO, Jonas Prising/Exec. VP, Pres. - US, Canadian Operations/$1,382,359.00, Mara Swan/Sr. VP - Global Human Resources, Michael J. Van Handel/48/CFO, Exec. VP, Sec./$3,113,467.00, Barbara J. Beck/Exec. VP, Pres. - EMEA/$2,354,163.00, Darryl Green/Exec. VP, Pres. - Asia Pacific , Francoise Gri/Exec. VP, Pres. - France, Tracy Shilobrit/Dir. - Global Communications, David Arkless/Sr. VP - Corporate Affairs

Directors: Jeffrey A. Joerres/Chmn., CEO, Pres., Thomas J. Bouchard/Dir., Ulice Payne/Dir., Dennis Stevenson/Dir., Edward J. Zore/Dir., Marc J. Bolland/Dir., Terry A. Huenecke/Dir., Stephanie A. Burns/Dir., Willie D. Davis/Dir., Jack M. Greenberg/Dir., Rozanne L. Ridgway/Dir., John R. Walter/Dir., Gina Boswell/Dir., Cari Dominguez/Dir.

Owners: Jonas Prising, Yoav Michaely, John R. Walter, Marc J. Bolland, Insiders/2.00%, Willie D. Davis, Jeffrey A. Joerres, Jack M. Greenberg, T. Rowe Price Associates, Inc./5.80%, Stephanie A. Burns, Thomas J. Bouchard, Owen J. Sullivan, Edward J. Zore, Rozanne L. Ridgway, Barbara J. Beck *(20 Owners included in Index)*

Financial Data: **Fiscal Year End:**12/31 **Latest Annual Data:** 12/31/2006

Year	Sales	Net Income
2006	$17,562,500,000	$398,000,000
2005	$16,080,400,000	$260,100,000
2004	$14,930,000,000	$245,700,000

Curr. Assets:	$4,682,000,000	**Curr. Liab.:**	$2,881,600,000	**P/E Ratio:**	16.64
Plant, Equip.:	$202,100,000	**Total Liab.:**	$4,039,900,000	**Indic. Yr. Divd.:**	$0.640
Total Assets:	$6,514,100,000	**Net Worth:**	$2,474,200,000	**Debt/ Equity:**	0.3201

Mantech International Corp

12015 Lee Jackson Hwy., Fairfax, VA, 22033; *PH:* 1-703-218-6000; *Fax:* 1-703-218-8296; *http://* www.mantech.com

General - Incorporation	DE	**Stock**- Price on:12/24/2007	$31.63
Employees	5,600	Stock Exchange	NDQ
Auditor	Deloitte & Touche LLP	Ticker Symbol	MANT
Stk Agt	American Stock Transfer & Trust Co.	Outstanding Shares	34,020,000
Counsel	NA	E.P.S.	$1.74
DUNS No.	05-351-8312	Shareholders	NA

Business: The group's principal activity is to provide innovative technologies and solutions for mission-critical national security programs for the intelligence community, the department of defense and other U.S. Federal government customers. The group's expertise includes software development, enterprise security architecture, information assurance, intelligence operations support, network and critical infrastructure protection, information technology, communications integration and engineering support. It provides information technology and technical services solutions through three principal areas of expertise: secure systems and infrastructure, information technology solutions and systems engineering solutions. On 28-Feb-2003, it acquired integrated data systems corporation and on 05-Mar-2003, msm security services inc. In Feb 2003, it sold its australian-based software solutions business. In 2004, it acquired certain assets from affiliated computer services inc.

Primary SIC and add'l.: 8741 7372

CIK No: 0000892537

Subsidiaries: DB Data Systems LLC, Field Support Services Muhendislik Ltd., Gray Hawk Technology Solutions LLC, Hawkeye Systems LLC, ManTech Advanced Development Group Inc., ManTech Advanced Recognition Limited, ManTech Advanced Systems International Inc., ManTech Australia International Inc., ManTech Australia Pty. Ltd., ManTech Colombia S.A., ManTech Command Control Systems Corporation, ManTech Database Services Europe Limited, ManTech Environmental Corporation, ManTech Environmental Research Services Corporation, ManTech Europe Ltd. 36 Subsidiaries included in the Index

Officers: George J. Pedersen/72/Chmn., CEO/$2,158,751.00, Gary A. Dorland/Pres./$667,136.00, Kevin M. Phillips/CFO/$671,502.00, Eugene C. Renzi/Sr. Exec. VP/$1,628,746.00, Robert A. Coleman/COO, Pres./$1,907,217.00, Kenneth J. Farquhar/Pres., Joseph R. Fox/Pres., Jay W. Kelley/Pres., Kurt J. Snapper/CTO, Sr. Corporate VP, John J. Fitzgerald/Sr. VP - Finance, Controller, Principal Accounting Officer

Directors: George J. Pedersen/72/Chmn., CEO, David E. Jeremiah/Dir., Richard L. Armitage/Dir., Kenneth A. Minihan/Dir., Richard J. Kerr/Dir., Stephen W. Porter/Dir., Walter R. Fatzinger/65/Dir., Barry G. Campbell/Dir., Mary K. Bush/Dir.

Owners: Richard J. Kerr, Walter R. Fatzinger, Richard L. Armitage, Robert A. Coleman, Gary A. Dorland, Stephen W. Porter, Eugene C. Renzi, David E. Jeremiah, Kevin M. Phillips, Paul G. Stern, Insiders/1.90%, George J. Pedersen/100.00%, Mary K. Bush, Barclays Global Investors, NA/0.60%, Royce & Associates, LLC/1.00% *(17 Owners included in Index)*

Financial Data: **Fiscal Year End:**12/31 **Latest Annual Data:** 12/31/2006

Year	Sales	Net Income
2006	$1,137,178,000	$50,701,000
2005	$980,290,000	$44,193,000
2004	$842,422,000	$24,707,000

Curr. Assets:	$294,910,000	**Curr. Liab.:**	$126,749,000	**P/E Ratio:**	19.77
Plant, Equip.:	$13,881,000	**Total Liab.:**	$154,253,000	**Indic. Yr. Divd.:**	NA
Total Assets:	$613,252,000	**Net Worth:**	$458,999,000	**Debt/ Equity:**	NA

Manulife Financial Corp

200 Bloor St. E, NT 11, Toronto, ON, M4W 1E5; *PH:* 1-416-926-3000; *http://* www.manulife.com; *Email:* corporate_communications@manulife.com

General - Incorporation	Canada	**Stock**- Price on:12/24/2007	$36.61
Employees	20,000	Stock Exchange	NYSE
Auditor	Ernst & Young LLP	Ticker Symbol	MFC
Stk Agt	Ernest & Young LLP	Outstanding Shares	1,540,000,000
Counsel	NA	E.P.S.	$2.76
DUNS No.	25-101-7042	Shareholders	NA

Business: The group's principle activity is to provides a wide range of financial products and services, including individual life insurance, group life and health insurance, pension products, annuities and mutual funds to individual and group customers in Canada, the United States and Asia. The group also offers reinsurance services, primarily life and accident and health reinsurance, and provides investment management services with respect to the group's general fund assets, segregated fund assets and mutual funds and, in Canada, to institutional customers. The group's quarterly revenue for September 2007 was 9,358.00 millions of USD.

Primary SIC and add'l.: 6321 6371 6311 6282 6719

CIK No: 0001086888

Subsidiaries: Declaration Management & Research LLC, Elliott & Page Limited, First North American Insurance Company, First Signature Bank & Trust Company, FNA Financial Inc., Hancock Natural Resource Group Inc., Independence Declaration Holdings LLC, Independence Investment LLC, Independence Management Holdings LLC, John Hancock Canadian Holdings Limited, John Hancock Financial Network, Inc., John Hancock Financial Services, Inc., John Hancock Funds LLC, John Hancock Holdings (Delaware) LLC, John Hancock International Holdings, Inc. 60 Subsidiaries included in the Index

Officers: Paul L. Rooney/Pres., CEO - Manulife Canada, Roy J. Firth/Exec. VP - Individual Wealth Management, Canadian Division, Chmn., CEO - Elliott, Page Limited, John D. Desprez/Pres., CEO - John Hancock Financial Services, Inc, Dominic Dalessandro/Dir., CEO, Pres., Jean-Paul Bisnaire/Sr. Exec. VP - Business Development, General Counsel, John Mather/Sr. Exec. VP, Chief Administrative Officer, Angela K. Shaffer/VP, Corp. Sec., Simon Curtis/Exec. VP, Chief Actuary, Marianne Harrison/Exec. VP, Controller, Robert A. Cook/Sr. Exec. VP, GM - Asia, Joseph Cooper/CIO, Exec. VP, Diane Bean/Exec. VP - Corporate Affairs, Human Resources, Bruce Gordon/Sr. Exec. VP, GM - Canada, Beverly S. Margolian/Exec. VP, Chief Risk Officer - Corporate Finance, Peter Rubenovitch/Sr. Exec. VP, CFO *(18 Officers included in Index)*

Directors: Dominic Dalessandro/Dir., CEO, Pres., Arthur R. Sawchuk/Chmn., John M. Cassaday/Dir., Gail C.A. Cook-Bennett/Dir., Thomas E. Kierans/Dir., Lorna R. Marsden/Dir., Hugh W. Sloan/Dir., Gordon G. Thiessen/Dir., Lino J. Celeste/Dir., Thomas P. Daquino/Dir., Richard B. Dewolfe/Dir., Robert E. Dineen/Dir., Pierre Y. Ducros/Dir., Allister P. Graham/Dir.

Financial Data: **Fiscal Year End:**12/31 **Latest Annual Data:** 12/31/2006

Year	Sales	Net Income
2006	$24,636,909,000	$2,720,177,000
2005	$24,052,314,000	$2,954,952,000
2004	$18,553,884,000	$2,179,538,000

Curr. Assets:	$9,265,764,000	**Curr. Liab.:**	$6,731,795,000	**P/E Ratio:**	54.05
Plant, Equip.:	NA	**Total Liab.:**	$303,347,789,000	**Indic. Yr. Divd.:**	$0.970
Total Assets:	$328,728,671,000	**Net Worth:**	$25,380,882,000	**Debt/ Equity:**	NA

Mapinfo Corp

One Global View, Troy, NY, 12180; *PH:* 1-518-285-6000; *http://* www.mapinfo.com

General - Incorporation	DE	**Stock**- Price on:12/24/2007	NA
Employees	NA	Stock Exchange	NA
Auditor	PricewaterhouseCoopers LLP	Ticker Symbol	NA
Stk Agt	Computershare Investor Services LLC	Outstanding Shares	NA
Counsel	Wilmer Cutler Pickering H & D LLP	E.P.S.	NA
DUNS No.	15-144-4767	Shareholders	NA

Business: The group's principal activities are to design, develop, market, license and support software and data products, application development tools and industry-focused solutions. It also provides consulting, training and technical support services. The group's software and data products include MapInfo Professional (R), MapInfo(R) Mapxtreme&Trade, MapInfo(R) Mapmarker(R) J Server and MapInfo(R) routing J Server. Software-based applications of the group designed for enterprise-wide implementations to solve specific industry problems include MapInfo(R) Callingareainfo&Trade, MapInfo(R) Miaware&Trade, MapInfo(R) Targetpro(R) and MapInfo(R) Branch Manager&Trade. The group markets its products worldwide including North America, the United Kingdom, Germany, Japan and Australia. On 06-Jan-2003, the group acquired Thompson Associates. On 08-Sep-2004, the group acquired Southbank Systems Limited.

Primary SIC and add'l.: 7372 7375

CIK No: 0000916238

Subsidiaries: GeoBusiness Solutions Limited, MapInfo Australia Pty. Limited, MapInfo Canada Inc., MapInfo GmbH, MapInfo Limited, MapInfo Realty LLC, MapInfo UK Limited, Moleseye Limited, Southbank Systems Limited

Officers: Mark Cattini/CEO, Pres., Michael Hickey/Pres. - Pitney Bowes Software, Jim Scott/VP - Engineering, John Renehan/VP - Operations, Marilyn Otto/VP - Global Data Development, Doug Gordon/MD - Strategy, Industry Management, Kurt Hasbrouck/VP, GM - Location Intelligence, Reid Hislop/VP - Global Marketing, Robert Pipe/VP - Product Management, Product Marketing, Location Intelligence, Alan Slater/VP, GM - Customer Communications Management, Ben Semmes/Sr. VP - Global Services, Jay Bourland/VP, GM - Customer Data Quality, Data Integration, Scott Landers/VP - Global Finance, Michael Cooper/VP, GM - Mailing Efficiency, Elizabeth Walter/Exec. VP - International Field Operations *(17 Officers included in Index)*

Owners: Cannell Capital LLC/6.20%, Westport Asset Management, Inc./Westport Advisors LLC/5.30%, Joni Kahn, George C. Moon, John C. Cavalier, Thomas L. Massie, Michael J. Hickey, Wayne K. McDougall, Simon J. Orebi Gann, Mark P. Cattini/1.80%, Kopp Investment Advisors LLC/7.90%, Insiders/5.80%, Robert P. Schechter

Maple Mountain Explorations Inc

1313 E Maple St., Ste. 507, Ste. 201, Bellingham, WA, 98225; *PH:* 1-306-824-6463

General - Incorporation	NV	**Stock**- Price on:12/24/2007	NA
Employees	NA	Stock Exchange	OTC
Auditor	George Stewart, Cpa	Ticker Symbol	MPXP
Stk Agt	Holladay Stock Transfer, Inc.	Outstanding Shares	NA
Counsel	NA	E.P.S.	NA
DUNS No.	NA	Shareholders	NA

Business: The groups principle activity is to provide recruiting services. The groups service area includes the research and development, engineering, marketing, sales, information technology and manufacturing industries. The group operates from United States.

Primary SIC and add'l.: 1081

CIK No: 0001363254

Officers: Marvin Wosk/76/Dir., Pres., Sec., Treasurer, CFO, CEO

Directors: Marvin Wosk/76/Dir., Pres., Sec., Treasurer, CFO, CEO, Pacharee Soonthornsawad/32/Dir., David Moss/38/Dir., Alan Gelfand/48/Dir.

Owners: Insiders/29.00%, Marvin Wosk/29.00%

Curr. Assets:	$44,000	**Curr. Liab.:**	NA		
Plant, Equip.:	NA	**Total Liab.:**	NA	**Indic. Yr. Divd.:**	NA
Total Assets:	$44,000	**Net Worth:**	$44,000	**Debt/ Equity:**	NA

Marathon Oil Corp

5555 San Felipe Rd., Houston, TX, 77056; ***PH:*** 1-713-629-6600; ***Fax:*** 1-713-296-2952; ***http://*** www.marathon.com

General - Incorporation .... DE
Employees 28,195
Auditor .... PricewaterhouseCoopers LLP
Stk Agt .... National City Bank Corp Trust Ops
Counsel .... NA
DUNS No. 00-202-8801

Stock- Price on:12/24/2007 .... $64.63
Stock Exchange .... NYSE
Ticker Symbol .... MRO
Outstanding Shares 342,980,000
E.P.S $6.30
Shareholders .... NA

Business: The group's principle activity is to apply innovative technologies to discover and develop valuable energy resources for providing products to marketplace. The group operates from United States.

Primary SIC and add'l.: 4922 1321 5171 2911 1311

CIK No: 0000101778

Subsidiaries: Alaska Transportation Service Company, Alba Associates LLC, Alba Equatorial Guinea Partnership, L.P., Alba Plant LLC, Alvheim AS, Amethyst Calypso Pipeline LLC, AMPCO Marketing, LLC, AMPCO Services, LLC, Arctic Sun Shipping Company, Ltd., Beluga Pipe Line Company, Brae Gas Marketing Company Limited, Caprock Investment Corporation, Catlettsburg Refining, LLC, E.G. Global LNG Services, Ltd., Equatorial Guinea LNG Company, S.A. 138 Subsidiaries included in the Index

Officers: Clarence P. Cazalot/57/Dir., CEO, Pres./$21,371,380.00, Michael A. Peak/VP - Risk Management, Trading, Marathon Petroleum Company LLC, Mary Ellen Peters/Sr. VP - Marketing, Marathon Petroleum Company LLC, Michael J. Wilder/General Counsel, Sec. - Marathon Petroleum Company LLC, Rodney P. Nichols/VP - Human Resources, Administrative Services, Marathon Petroleum Company LLC, Randy K. Lohoff/VP - Corporate Responsibility, Marathon Petroleum Company LLC, Jerry C. Welch/VP - Refining, Marathon Petroleum Company LLC, Jerry Howard/Sr. VP - Corporate Affairs, Kenneth L. Matheny/VP - Investor Relations, Public Affairs, Alard Kaplan/VP - Major Projects, Steven B. Hinchman/Sr. VP - Worldwide Production/$4,969,179.00, William F. Schwind/VP, General Counsel, Sec., Paul C. Reinbolt/VP - Finance, Treasurer, Janet F. Clark/CFO, Exec. VP/$3,572,565.00, Anthony R. Kenney/Pres. - Speedway Superamerica LLC *(31 Officers included in Index)*

Directors: Clarence P. Cazalot/57/Dir., CEO, Pres., Thomas J. Usher/65/Chmn., William L. Davis/64/Dir., Philip Lader/61/Dir., Seth E. Schofield/68/Dir., David A. Daberko/62/Dir., Shirley Ann Jackson/61/Dir., Charles F. Bolden/61/Dir., Charles R. Lee/67/Dir., Dennis H. Reilley/54/Dir., Douglas C. Yearley/72/Dir., John W. Snow/68/Dir.

Owners: Shirley Ann Jackson, William L. Davis, Barclays Global Investors, NA/8.48%, David A. Daberko, John W. Snow, Gary R. Heminger, Philip G. Behrman, Charles F. Bolden, Clarence P. Cazalot, Charles R. Lee, Thomas J. Usher, Douglas C. Yearley, Capital Research and Management Company/10.00%, Insiders, Dennis H. Reilley *(19 Owners included in Index)*

Financial Data: ***Fiscal Year End:***12/31 ***Latest Annual Data:*** 12/31/2006

Year	Sales	Net Income
2006	$65,449,000,000	$5,234,000,000
2005	$63,673,000,000	$3,032,000,000
2004	$49,907,000,000	$1,261,000,000

Curr. Assets:	$10,096,000,000	**Curr. Liab.:**	$8,061,000,000	**P/E Ratio:**	9.12
Plant, Equip.:	$16,653,000,000	**Total Liab.:**	$15,706,000,000	**Indic. Yr. Divd.:**	$0.960
Total Assets:	$30,831,000,000	**Net Worth:**	$14,607,000,000	**Debt/ Equity:**	0.1798

Marchex Inc

413 Pine St., Ste. 500, Seattle, WA, 98101; ***PH:*** 1-206-331-3300; ***Fax:*** 1-206-331-3695; ***http://*** www.marchex.com; ***Email:*** info@marchex.com

General - Incorporation .... DE
Employees 283
Auditor .... KPMG LLP
Stk Agt .... Mellon Investor Services LLC
Counsel .... NA
DUNS No. .... NA

Stock- Price on:12/24/2007 .... $14.93
Stock Exchange .... NDQ
Ticker Symbol .... MCHX
Outstanding Shares 42,010,000
E.P.S $0.02
Shareholders .... NA

Business: The group's principal activity is to provide technology-based services to merchants engaged in online transactions. The group also provides performance-based advertising and search marketing industries, which is focused on helping merchants market and sell products and services via the Internet. The group provides these services through its wholly owned operating subsidiaries, enhance interactive and trafficleader. On 27-Jul-2004, the group acquired goclick.com inc.

Primary SIC and add'l.: 7379

CIK No: 0001224133

Subsidiaries: eFamily.com, Inc., Enhance Interactive, Inc., goClick.com, Inc., IndustryBrains, LLC, Marchex Paymaster, LLC, MDNH CA Corporation, Mdnh Cah, Inc., MDNH International, Ltd., MDNH, Inc., TrafficLeader, Inc.

Officers: Russell C. Horowitz/Chmn., CEO, Peter Christothoulou/Chief Strategy Officer, John Keister/Dir., COO, Pres., Ethan Caldwell/Chief Administrative Officer, General Counsel, Michael Arends/CFO, Cameron Ferroni/CTO, Mark S. Peterson/VP - Public Relations, Media Inquiries, Trevor Caldwell/Chief Administrative Officer, General Counsel, Bill Day/Chief Media Officer

Directors: Russell C. Horowitz/Chmn., CEO, Jonathan Fram/Dir., Dennis Cline/Dir., John Keister/Dir., COO, Pres., Anne Devereux/Dir.

Owners: SMALLCAP World Fund, Inc./7.10%, FMR Corporation/6.50%, Jonathan Fram, Mazama Capital Management, Inc./11.90%, Cameron Ferroni, Insiders/9.80%, Russell C. Horowitz/68.20%, Capital Research and Management Company/9.90%, Insiders/96.10%, Michael A. Arends/1.70%, Russell C. Horowitz/4.80%, John Keister/2.20%, Dennis Cline, John Keister/17.20%, Wells Fargo & Company/7.40%

Financial Data: ***Fiscal Year End:***12/31 ***Latest Annual Data:*** 12/31/2006

Year	Sales	Net Income
2006	$127,759,000	-$444,000
2005	$94,996,000	$3,908,000
2004	$43,804,000	-$733,000

Curr. Assets:	$72,871,000	**Curr. Liab.:**	$16,083,000		
Plant, Equip.:	$7,280,000	**Total Liab.:**	$16,175,000	**Indic. Yr. Divd.:**	$0.080
Total Assets:	$333,388,000	**Net Worth:**	$317,213,000	**Debt/ Equity:**	NA

Marco Community Bancorp Inc

1770 San Marco Rd., Marco Island, FL, 34145; ***PH:*** 1-239-389-5200; ***Fax:*** 1-239-389-5273; ***http://*** www.marcocommunitybank.com; ***Email:*** customerservice@mcbfl.com

General - Incorporation .... FL
Employees 36
Auditor .... Hacker, Johnson & Smith PA
Stk Agt .... NA
Counsel .... NA
DUNS No. .... NA

Stock- Price on:12/24/2007 .... $17.5
Stock Exchange .... OTC
Ticker Symbol .... MCBN
Outstanding Shares 3,160,000
E.P.S .... -$0.8
Shareholders .... NA

Business: The groups principle activity is to provide banking services. Services of the group include mortgage loans, consumer loan, and deposit services. The group operates from the United States.

Primary SIC and add'l.: 6035

CIK No: 0001221354

Subsidiaries: Commercial Lending Capital Corp, Marco Community Bank

Officers: Richard Storm/Chmn., CEO, Stephen A. McLaughlin/Vice Chmn., Pres./$8,700.00, Jamie B. Greusel/44/Dir., Assist. Corp. Sec., Bruce G. Fedor/70/Dir., Corp. Sec., Thomas M. Whelan/56/Sr. VP, CFO/$133,777.00, Howard B. Montgomery/59/Pres./$140,854.00

Directors: Richard Storm/Chmn., CEO, Stephen A. McLaughlin/Vice Chmn., Pres., Robert A. Marks/74/Dir., Joel M. Cox/67/Dir., Jamie B. Greusel/44/Dir., Assist. Corp. Sec., John V. Cofer/62/Dir., Bruce G. Fedor/70/Dir., Corp. Sec., Terry E. Skone/65/Dir.

Owners: Stephen A. McLaughlin/7.34%, Jamie B. Greusel/2.44%, Joel M. Cox/2.18%, Robert A. Marks/1.93%, Thomas M. Whelan, Melanie J. Hanson/6.51%, Terry E. Skone/5.77%, Insiders/39.51%, Richard Storm/11.50%, Bruce G. Fedor, John V. Cofer/1.82%

Financial Data: ***Fiscal Year End:***12/31 ***Latest Annual Data:*** 12/31/2006

Year	Sales	Net Income
2006	$12,653,000	$1,854,000
2005	$9,404,000	$1,589,000

Curr. Assets:	$27,792,000	**Curr. Liab.:**	$143,322,000		
Plant, Equip.:	$3,590,000	**Total Liab.:**	$143,322,000	**Indic. Yr. Divd.:**	NA
Total Assets:	$166,000,000	**Net Worth:**	$22,678,000	**Debt/ Equity:**	NA

Marconi Corp Plc

New Century Pk., Coventry, CV3 1HJ; ; ***http://*** www.marconi.com

General - Incorporation .... UK
Employees .... NA
Auditor .... Deloitte & Touche LLP
Stk Agt .... HSBC Bank PLC
Counsel .... NA
DUNS No. .... NA

Stock- Price on:12/24/2007 .... $9.92
Stock Exchange .... NA
Ticker Symbol .... NA
Outstanding Shares .... NA
E.P.S .... NA
Shareholders .... NA

Business: The group's principal activity is the provision of telecommunications equipment and services together with associated support applications. The group operates in the United Kingdom, the Americas, rest of Europe, Africa, Asia and australasia. During 2004, the group disposed its interest in easynet group plc and the north American business.

Primary SIC and add'l.: NA

CIK No: 0001122135

Subsidiaries: Marconi Communications GmbH, Marconi Communications Limited, Marconi Communications S.p.A, Marconi Communications, Inc

Officers: Carl-Henric Svanberg/56/Dir., CEO, Pres., Hans Vestberg/43/Exec. VP, CFO, Head - Business Unit Global Services, Kurt Jofs/50/Exec. VP, Head - Business Unit Networks, Bert Nordberg/52/Exec. VP, Head - Group Function Sales, Marketing, Since 2004, Bjorn Olsson/52/Exec. VP, Deputy Head - Business Unit Networks, Carl Olof Blomqvist/57/Sr. VP, General Counsel, Head - Group Function Legal Affairs, Hakan Eriksson/CTO, Sr. VP, Head - Group Function Technology, Since 2004, Marita Hellberg/53/Sr. VP, Head - Group Function Human Resources, Organization, Since 2003, Henry Stenson/53/Sr. VP, Head - Group Function Communications, Since 2002, Joakim Westh/47/Sr. VP, Head - Group Function Operational Excellence, Since 2004, Karin Aberg/49/Dir. - Deputy Employee Representative, Anna Guldstrand/44/Dir. - Deputy Employee Representative, Kristina Davidsson/53/Dir. - Deputy Employee Representative

Directors: Carl-Henric Svanberg/56/Dir., CEO, Pres., Michael Treschow/65/Chmn., Marcus Wallenberg/52/Dep. Chmn., Sverker Martin-Lof/65/Dep. Chmn., Peter L. Bonfield/64/Dir., Borje Ekholm/45/Dir., Katherine M. Hudson/61/Dir., Ulf J. Johansson/63/Dir., Nancy McKinstry/49/Dir., Anders Nyren/54/Dir., Jan Hedlund/62/Dir., Monica Bergstrom/47/Dir., Torbjorn Nyman/47/Dir., Karin Aberg/49/Dir. - Deputy Employee Representative, Anna Guldstrand/44/Dir. - Deputy Employee Representative *(16 Directors included in Index)*

Financial Data: ***Fiscal Year End:***03/31 ***Latest Annual Data:*** 3/31/2005

Year	Sales	Net Income
2005	$2,386,330,000	$219,843,000
2004	$2,674,000,000	$5,088,000,000

Curr. Assets:	$1,668,552,000	**Curr. Liab.:**	$952,653,000		
Plant, Equip.:	$217,964,000	**Total Liab.:**	$1,625,335,000	**Indic. Yr. Divd.:**	NA
Total Assets:	$2,882,386,000	**Net Worth:**	$1,257,051,000	**Debt/ Equity:**	NA

Marcus Corp (The)

100 E Wisconsin Ave., Ste 1900, Milwaukee, WI, 53202; ***PH:*** 1-414-905-1000; ***http://*** www.marcuscorp.com; ***Email:*** joanvoelzke@marcuscorp.com

General - Incorporation .... WI
Employees 2,650
Auditor .... Ernst & Young LLP
Stk Agt .... LaSalle Bank N.A
Counsel .... Foley & Lardner LLP
DUNS No. 05-874-2347

Stock- Price on:12/24/2007 .... $24.03
Stock Exchange .... NYSE
Ticker Symbol .... MCS
Outstanding Shares 30,540,000
E.P.S $0.99
Shareholders .... NA

Business: The group's principal activities are to operate limited-service lodges, movie theatres and hotels and resorts. The group operates in three segments. The limited-service lodging business segment operates and franchises lodging facilities primarily in the eastern half of the United States under the names Baymont Inns, Baymont Inns & Suites and Woodfield Suites. The theatres segment operates multiscreen motion picture theatres in Wisconsin, Illinois, Ohio and Minnesota and a family entertainment center in Wisconsin. The hotels and resorts segment owns, operates and manages full service hotels and resorts in Wisconsin, Missouri and California and also operates a vacation ownership development in Wisconsin. As of 27-May-2004, the group operated 185 limited-service facilities, 46 movie theatres, owned and operated six hotels and managed five hotels.

Primary SIC and add'l.: 7999 7933 5812 7011 7832

CIK No: 0000062234

Subsidiaries: 802-California-Ontario, LLC, B&G Realty, LLC, Baymont Erlanger, LLC, Cafe Refreshments, Inc., Captains-Kenosha, Inc., Colony Inns Restaurant Corporation, Family Entertainment, LLC, First American Finance Corporation, Grand Geneva, LLC, Marcs Carryout Corporation, Marcus BIS Franchises International, LLC, Marcus BIS Hospitality, LLC, Marcus BIS Partners, LLC, Marcus BIS, LLC, Marcus Cinemas of Minnesota and Illinois, Inc. 38 Subsidiaries included in the Index

Officers: Stephen H. Marcus/Chmn., CEO, Pres./$1,012,752.00, Douglas A. Neis/CFO, Treasurer/$459,220.00, Gregory S. Marcus/Sr. VP - Corporate Development/$503,893.00, Jane Durment/CIO, William J. Otto/Pres. - Marcus Hotels, Resorts/$514,361.00, Thomas F. Kissinger/VP, General Counsel, Sec./$463,473.00, Bruce J. Olson/Dir., Sr. VP, Pres. - Marcus Theatres Corporation/$705,019.00

Directors: Stephen H. Marcus/Chmn., CEO, Pres., Allan H. Selig/Dir., Diane Marcus Gershowitz/Dir., Daniel F. McKeithan/Dir., Bruce J. Olson/Dir., Sr. VP, Pres. - Marcus Theatres Corporation, Timothy E. Hoeksema/Dir., Philip L. Milstein/Dir., Bronson J. Haase/Dir., James D. Ericson/Dir.

Owners: Barclays Global Investors, NA/6.00%, William J. Otto, Advisory Research, Inc./10.50%, Douglas A. Neis, Private Capital Management, L.P./21.60%, Insiders/94.80%, Stephen H. Marcus/45.50%, Gregory S. Marcus/3.00%, Insiders/3.50%, Allan H. Selig, James D. Ericson, Thomas F. Kissinger, Timothy E. Hoeksema, Bronson J. Haase, Philip L. Milstein *(21 Owners included in Index)*

Financial Data: ***Fiscal Year End:***05/25 ***Latest Annual Data:*** 5/25/2006

Year		*Sales*		*Net Income*
2006		$289,244,000		$28,271,000
2005		$272,707,000		$99,221,000
2004		$409,207,000		$24,611,000

Curr. Assets:	$59,353,000	***Curr. Liab.:***	$127,143,000	***P/E Ratio:***	24.27
Plant, Equip.:	$559,785,000	***Total Liab.:***	$378,874,000	***Indic. Yr. Divd.:***	$0.340
Total Assets:	$698,383,000	***Net Worth:***	$319,509,000	***Debt/ Equity:***	NA

Margo Caribe Inc

Rd. 690, Kilometer 5.8, Vega Alta, 00692; ***PH:*** 787-883-2570; ***http://*** www.margocaribe.com

General - Incorporation	PR	***Stock***- Price on:12/24/2007	$4.8
Employees	101	Stock Exchange	OTC
Auditor	Deloitte & Touche LLP	Ticker Symbol	MRGO
Stk Agt	Mellon Investor Services LLC	Outstanding Shares	2,860,000
Counsel	Simmons Hart & Sheehe	E.P.S	-$0.79
DUNS No.	07-113-3417	Shareholders	NA

Business: The group's principal activity is to produce and distribute a wide range of tropical plants. The tropical plants are targeted at the interior and exterior landscapers, wholesalers and retailers located in Puerto Rico and the Caribbean. The group also manufactures and distributes planting media, sells and distributes lawn and garden products, provides landscaping design installation and maintenance services. The operations are conducted at a 92 acre nursery farm in vega alta, Puerto Rico, approximately 25 miles west of san juan. The group's trademarks are 'margo farms', 'margo farms del caribe' and 'rain forest'.

Primary SIC and add'l.: 0181 5193 0781

CIK No: 0000808493

Subsidiaries: Garrochales Construction and Development Corporation, Margo Development Corporation, Margo Flora, Inc., Margo Garden Products, Inc., Margo Landscaping and Design, Inc., Margo Nursery Farms, Inc., Margo State Line, Inc., Rain Forest Products Group, Inc.

Officers: John Upchurch/Sr. VP, CFO, Alison Witkovich/CFO, VP

Owners: Michael J. Spector, Margaret D. Spector, Bls Ferraiuoli, Evan H. Berger, Insiders, Ramn L. Domnguez, Morton J. Davis, Michael A. Rubin

Financial Data: ***Fiscal Year End:***12/31 ***Latest Annual Data:*** 12/31/2005

Year		*Sales*		*Net Income*
2005		$9,669,000		-$2,203,000
2004		$8,423,000		-$617,000
2003		$8,433,000		-$1,492,000

Curr. Assets:	$5,702,000	***Curr. Liab.:***	$1,864,000		
Plant, Equip.:	$5,384,000	***Total Liab.:***	$10,419,000	***Indic. Yr. Divd.:***	NA
Total Assets:	$12,924,000	***Net Worth:***	$2,505,000	***Debt/ Equity:***	NA

Marine Products Corp

2801 Buford Hwy., Ste. 520, Atlanta, GA, 30329; ***PH:*** 1-404-321-7910; ***Fax:*** 1-404-321-5483; ***http://*** www.marineproductscorp.com

General - Incorporation	DE	***Stock***- Price on:12/24/2007	$7.85
Employees	1,100	Stock Exchange	NYSE
Auditor	Grant Thornton LLP	Ticker Symbol	MPX
Stk Agt	Suntrust Bank	Outstanding Shares	37,990,000
Counsel	NA	E.P.S	$0.42
DUNS No.	NA	Shareholders	NA

Business: The group's principal activity is to design, manufacture and sell recreational fiberglass powerboats in the sportboat, deckboat and cruiser markets. It distributes four lines of powerboats through a network of domestic and foreign independent authorized dealers. The products of the group are chaparral sterndrive and inboard pleasure boats and robalo outboard offshore sport fishing boats. The group's operations are based in the United States.

Primary SIC and add'l.: 3732

CIK No: 0001129155

Subsidiaries: Chaparral Boats, Inc, Chaparral Marine Inc., Marine Products Investment Company, LLC, Robalo Acquisition Company, LLC

Officers: Richard A. Hubbell/63/Dir., CEO, Pres./$682,400.00, James A. Lane/64/Dir., Exec. VP/$4,374,332.00, Ben M. Palmer/47/CFO, VP, Treasurer/$345,930.00, Linda H. Graham/71/Dir., VP, Sec./$197,290.00, Jim Landers/VP - Corporate Finance, Natasha Coleman/Investor Relations, Corporate Mgr. - Communications

Directors: Richard A. Hubbell/63/Dir., CEO, Pres., Randall R. Rollins/76/Chmn., Gary W. Rollins/63/Dir., James A. Lane/64/Dir., Exec. VP, James B. Williams/Dir., Henry B. Tippie/80/Dir., Wilton Looney/Dir., Bill J. Dismuke/Dir., Linda H. Graham/71/Dir., VP, Sec.

Owners: Ben M. Palmer, FMR Corporation, Insiders, Henry B. Tippie, Linda H. Graham, James B. Williams, Gary W. Rollins, Richard A. Hubbell, Wilton Looney, Bill J. Dismuke, R. Randall Rollins, James A. Lane

Financial Data: ***Fiscal Year End:***12/31 ***Latest Annual Data:*** 12/31/2006

Year		*Sales*		*Net Income*
2006		$261,378,000		$20,314,000
2005		$272,057,000		$26,223,000
2004		$252,418,000		$23,743,000

Curr. Assets:	$93,595,000	***Curr. Liab.:***	$17,089,000	***P/E Ratio:***	16.70
Plant, Equip.:	$16,641,000	***Total Liab.:***	$22,778,000	***Indic. Yr. Divd.:***	$0.240
Total Assets:	$124,179,000	***Net Worth:***	$101,401,000	***Debt/ Equity:***	NA

Marinemax Inc

18167 US Hwy. 19 N, Ste. 300, Clearwater, FL, 33764; ***PH:*** 1-727-531-1700; ***Fax:*** 1-727-532-8367; ***http://*** www.marinemax.com

General - Incorporation	DE	***Stock***- Price on:12/24/2007	$21.51
Employees	2,182	Stock Exchange	NYSE
Auditor	Ernst & Young LLP	Ticker Symbol	HZO
Stk Agt	American Stock Transfer & Trust Co.	Outstanding Shares	18,700,000
Counsel	Greenberg Traurig	E.P.S	$1.58
DUNS No.	00-292-9946	Shareholders	NA

Business: The group's principal activities are to sell and provide service to new and used boats, motors, trailers, marine parts and accessories. The group provides boat financing, insurance and extended service contracts. It also provides repair and maintenance services, boat, yacht brokerage services. The marine parts and accessories include life jackets, inflatables, wakeboards, various oils, lubricants, steering, control systems, corrosion control products, shirts, caps and floor mats. The boats are marketed under product lines motor yachts, convertibles, pleasure and fishing boat. The operations are carried out through 66 retail locations in Arizona, California, Delaware, Florida, Georgia, Minnesota, Nevada, New Jersey, North Carolina, Ohio, South Carolina, Texas and Utah. During fiscal 2003, the group acquired killinger marine center of Alabama, inc and killinger marine center inc. During fiscal 2004, the group acquired emarine international inc and steven myers inc.

Primary SIC and add'l.: 5561 5551

CIK No: 0001057060

Subsidiaries: 11502 Dumas, Inc., Bassett Boat Company, Bassett Realty, LLC, Boating Gear Center, Inc., C & N Marine Realty, LLC, Delaware Avlease, LLC, Dumas GP, Inc., Dumas GP, LLC, Gulfwind South Realty, LLC, Harrisons Realty California, LLC, Harrisons Realty, LLC, Marina Drive Realty I, LLC, Marina Drive Realty II, LLC, MarineMax International, LLC, MarineMax MidAtlantic, LP 43 Subsidiaries included in the Index

Officers: William H. McGill/Chmn., CEO, Pres., Michael H. McLamb/Dir., Exec. VP, CFO, Sec., Edward A. Russell/VP - Operations, Kurt M. Frahn/VP - Finance, Treasurer, Anthony M. Aisquith/Regional Pres. - Central Region, Jack P. Ezzell/VP, Chief Accounting Officer, Michael J. Aiello/Regional Pres. - Northeast Region

Directors: William H. McGill/Chmn., CEO, Pres., Robert S. Kant/Dir., Michael H. McLamb/Dir., Exec. VP, CFO, Sec., Dean S. Woodman/Dir., Joseph A. Watters/Dir., Robert D. Basham/59/Dir., Hilliard M. Eure/Dir., John B. Furman/Dir.

Owners: Dean S. Woodman, Hilliard M. Eure, Joseph A. Watters, BAMCO, Inc./8.10%, Robert D. Basham, Robert S. Kant, Insiders/12.60%, Anthony M. Aisquith, John B. Furman, Michael J. Aiello, Michael H. McLamb/1.60%, Edward A. Russell, FMR Corp./9.60%, T. Rowe Price Associates, Inc./10.30%, William H. McGill/8.70% *(16 Owners included in Index)*

Financial Data: ***Fiscal Year End:***09/30 ***Latest Annual Data:*** 9/30/2006

Year		*Sales*		*Net Income*
2006		$1,213,541,000		$39,382,000
2005		$947,347,000		$33,826,000
2004		$762,009,000		$26,298,000

Curr. Assets:	$558,480,000	***Curr. Liab.:***	$407,383,000	***P/E Ratio:***	15.70
Plant, Equip.:	$122,215,000	***Total Liab.:***	$451,676,000	***Indic. Yr. Divd.:***	NA
Total Assets:	$801,563,000	***Net Worth:***	$349,887,000	***Debt/ Equity:***	0.0853

Mariner Energy Inc

2000 W Sam Houston Pkwy. S, 1 BriarLake Plz., Ste. 2000, Houston, TX, 77042; ***PH:*** 1-713-954-5500; ***Fax:*** 1-713-265-5555; ***http://*** www.mariner-energy.com

General - Incorporation	DE	***Stock***- Price on:12/24/2007	$25.11
Employees	217	Stock Exchange	NYSE
Auditor	Deloitte & Touche LLP	Ticker Symbol	ME
Stk Agt	Continental Stock Transfer & Trust Co	Outstanding Shares	87,130,000
Counsel	NA	E.P.S	$1.59
DUNS No.	NA	Shareholders	NA

Business: The groups principle activities include oil and gas exploration, development and production. The group operates through three geographic segments. In the year 2006, the group acquired Forest Oil Corporation. The group operates from the United States and Gulf of Mexico.

Primary SIC and add'l.: 1311 1321

CIK No: 0001022345

Subsidiaries: Mariner Energy Resources, Inc, Mariner Energy Texas LP, Mariner LP LLC

Officers: Scott D. Josey/Chmn., CEO, Pres./$3,903,599.00, Dalton F. Polasek/COO/$2,013,252.00, John H. Karnes/Sr. VP, CFO, Treasurer/$233,038.00, Jesus G. Melendrez/Sr. VP - Corporate Development, Michiel C. Van Den Bold/Sr. VP, Chief Exploration Officer/$1,542,105.00, Teresa G. Bushman/Sr. VP, General Counsel, Sec., Judd A. Hansen/Sr. VP - Shelf, Onshore/$1,292,262.00, Cory L. Loegering/VP - Deepwater, Richard A. Molohon/VP - Reservoir Engineering

Directors: Scott D. Josey/Chmn., CEO, Pres., Jonathan Ginns/Dir., Bernard Aronson/Dir., Alan R. Crain/Dir., John F. Greene/Dir., Clayton H. Peterson/Dir., John L. Schwager/Dir.

Owners: Philip F. Anschutz/7.40%, Alan R. Crain, Scott D. Josey, Jonathan Ginns, Rick G. Lester, Mike C. van den Bold, John H. Karnes, Artisan Partners Limited Partnership/6.60%, John F. Greene, Dalton F. Polasek, Judd A. Hansen, Clayton H. Peterson, Bernard Aronson, FMR Corp./15.00%, First Manhattan Co./5.70% *(18 Owners included in Index)*

Financial Data: ***Fiscal Year End:***12/31 ***Latest Annual Data:*** 12/31/2006

Year		*Sales*		*Net Income*
2006		$659,505,000		$121,462,000
2005		$199,710,000		$40,481,000

Curr. Assets:	$308,441,000	***Curr. Liab.:***	$239,727,000		
Plant, Equip.:	$2,012,062,000	***Total Liab.:***	$1,377,562,000	***Indic. Yr. Divd.:***	NA
Total Assets:	$2,680,153,000	***Net Worth:***	$1,302,591,000	***Debt/ Equity:***	0.5020

Marisa Christina Inc

1924 Pearman Dairy Rd., Anderson, SC, 29625; *PH:* 1-864-231-1200; *Fax:* 1-864-231-1201; *http://* www.marisachristina.com

General - Incorporation	DE	Stock - Price on:12/24/2007	NA
Employees	370	Stock Exchange	NA
Auditor	KPMG LLP	Ticker Symbol	NA
Stk Agt	Continental Stock Transfer & Trust Co	Outstanding Shares	NA
Counsel	Pryor Cashman Sherman & Flynn LLP	E.P.S.	$0.62
DUNS No.	00-170-9252	Shareholders	NA

Business: The group's principal activity is design, manufacture, source and market a broad line of high quality clothing for women primarily under the marisa christina(tm) label. The group's products include sweaters and a selection of other "Classic Look" garments encompassing knitted and casual sportswear and complementary pieces such as skirts, slacks and jackets. Its products are marketed under three primary labels: marisa christina, christina rotelli and claire murray.management of the group believes that raw materials to be readily available and can be provided from a number of alternative suppliers. In addition, group has arrangements with independent distributors in Canada that sell to various accounts outside the United States on a royalty basis and a licensing arrangement in Japan. The group uses a centralized distribution system, under which all merchandise is received, processed, and distributed through the company's distribution facility.

Primary SIC and add'l.: 2369 2253

CIK No: 0000923149

Financial Data: Fiscal Year End:12/31 Latest Annual Data: 12/31/2005

Year	Sales	Net Income
2005	$324,281,000	$11,414,000
2004	$301,999,000	$13,725,000
2003	$292,651,000	$5,627,000

Curr. Assets:	$129,255,000	Curr. Liab.:	$36,525,000		
Plant, Equip.:	$2,056,000	Total Liab.:	$39,549,000	Indic. Yr. Divd.:	NA
Total Assets:	$142,514,000	Net Worth:	$102,965,000	Debt/ Equity:	0.0004

Maritrans Inc

Two Harbour Pl., 302 Knights Run Ave., Tampa, FL, 33602; *PH:* 1-813-209-0600; *http://* www.maritrans.com

General - Incorporation	DE	Stock - Price on:12/24/2007	$80.19
Employees	3,980	Stock Exchange	NA
Auditor	Ernst & Young LLP	Ticker Symbol	NA
Stk Agt	American Stock Transfer & Trust Co.	Outstanding Shares	33,220,000
Counsel	NA	E.P.S.	NA
DUNS No.	17-420-1277	Shareholders	NA

Business: The group's principal activity is to own and operate oil tankers, tugboats and oceangoing petroleum tank barges principally used in the transportation of oil and related products along the gulf and Atlantic coast. The operations of the group are primarily in the gulf of Mexico and along the coastal waters of the northeastern United States, particularly the Delaware bay. The group provides marine transportation services primarily to integrated oil companies, independent oil companies, petroleum trading companies and petroleum distributors in the southern and eastern United States. The group owns a fleet of 27 vessels, of which 4 are oil tankers, 11 are barges and 12 are tugboats.

Primary SIC and add'l.: 4449

CIK No: 0000810113

Subsidiaries: Maritrans 192 Co., Maritrans 193 Co., Maritrans 196 Co., Maritrans 210 Co., Maritrans 211 Co., Maritrans 215 Co., Maritrans 244 Co., Maritrans 250 Co., Maritrans 252 Co., Maritrans 300 Co., Maritrans 400 Co., Maritrans Allegiance Co., Maritrans Barge Co., Maritrans Business Services Co. Inc., Maritrans Columbia Co. 34 Subsidiaries included in the Index

Financial Data: Fiscal Year End:12/31 Latest Annual Data: 12/31/2006

Year	Sales	Net Income
2006	$1,047,403,000	$392,660,000
2005	$1,000,303,000	$464,829,000
2004	$810,835,000	$401,236,000

Curr. Assets:	$845,521,000	Curr. Liab.:	$227,576,000		
Plant, Equip.:	$2,532,596,000	Total Liab.:	$2,023,358,000	Indic. Yr. Divd.:	$1.250
Total Assets:	$4,230,669,000	Net Worth:	$2,207,311,000	Debt/ Equity:	0.5053

Markel Corp

4521 Highwoods Pkwy., Glen Allen, VA, 23060; *PH:* 1-804-747-0136; *Fax:* 1-804-965-1600; *http://* www.markelcorp.com; *Email:* information@markelcorp.com

General - Incorporation	VA	Stock - Price on:12/24/2007	$480.51
Employees	1,897	Stock Exchange	NYSE
Auditor	KPMG LLP	Ticker Symbol	MKL
Stk Agt	American Stock Transfer & Trust Co.	Outstanding Shares	9,960,000
Counsel	McGuire-Woods	E.P.S.	$43.45
DUNS No.	00-313-4582	Shareholders	NA

Business: The groups principle activity is to market and underwrite specialty insurance products and programs. The groups products include casualty, property, inland and ocean marine, and specialty accident and medical. The group operates from United States.

Primary SIC and add'l.: 6351 6361

CIK No: 0001096343

Subsidiaries: Associated International Insurance Company, Deerfield Insurance Company, Essex Insurance Company, Evanston Insurance Company, Gryphon Holding Inc., Markel American Insurance Company, Markel Capital Limited, Markel Insurance Company, Markel International Insurance Company Limited, Markel International Limited, Shand/Evanston Group, Inc., Terra Nova (Bermuda) Holdings Ltd.

Officers: Alan I. Kirshner/Chmn., CEO/$1,250,543.00, Michael D. Jones/Sec., Thomas S. Gayner/Chief Investment Officer, Exec. VP/$1,478,002.00, Paul W. Springman/Exec. VP/$1,515,523.00, Anthony F. Markel/Dir., COO, Pres./$1,187,843.00, Richard R. Whitt/CFO, Sr. VP/$1,236,732.00, Bruce Kay/VP - Investor Relations

Directors: Alan I. Kirshner/Chmn., CEO, Steven A. Markel/Vice Chmn., Anthony F. Markel/Dir., COO, Pres., Lemuel E. Lewis/Dir., Jay M. Weinberg/Dir., Leslie A. Grandis/Dir., Douglas C. Eby/Dir., Alfred J. Broaddus/Dir., Stewart M. Kasen/Dir.

Owners: Alfred J. Broaddus, Douglas C. Eby, Insiders/8.54%, Anthony F. Markel/2.89%, Jay M. Weinberg, Richard R. Whitt, Stewart M. Kasen, Paul W. Springman, Thomas S. Gayner, Leslie A. Grandis, Steven A. Markel/4.17%, Alan I. Kirshner

Financial Data: Fiscal Year End:12/31 Latest Annual Data: 12/31/2006

Year	Sales	Net Income
2006	$2,519,005,000	$392,502,000
2005	$2,200,148,000	$147,915,000
2004	$2,262,058,000	$165,412,000

Curr. Assets:	$2,497,941,000	Curr. Liab.:	$58,880,000	P/E Ratio:	11.54
Plant, Equip.:	$45,967,000	Total Liab.:	$7,791,738,000	Indic. Yr. Divd.:	$1.880
Total Assets:	$10,088,131,000	Net Worth:	$2,296,393,000	Debt/ Equity:	NA

Market Central Inc

6701 Carmel Rd., Ste. 205, Charlotte, NC, 28266; *PH:* 1-704-837-0500

General - Incorporation	DE	Stock - Price on:12/24/2007	NA
Employees	21	Stock Exchange	OTC
Auditor	Russell Bedford Stefanou Mirchandani	Ticker Symbol	SCNG
Stk Agt	RBSM LLP	Outstanding Shares	NA
Counsel	NA	E.P.S.	$1.04
DUNS No.	15-049-2429	Shareholders	NA

Business: The group's principle activity is to provide customer relationship management solutions through its customer contact center in jacksonville. The group performs these activities through its wholly owned subsidiary ecommerce support centers inc(ecom) and u.s.convergion inc. Ecom provides outsourced contact centers and customer relationship management solutions that include proprietary, patented software for data capture, cleansing, mining, integration, search and document recognition. Convergion provides systems design, integration, sales and service of internal contact centers and is a reseller for microsoft's ms crm solution. Combined, the subsidiaries provide inbound technical support, sales, and customer service.

Primary SIC and add'l.: 7379 7372

CIK No: 0001043933

Subsidiaries: Convey Systems International, Inc., Tigo Search, Inc

Financial Data: Fiscal Year End:08/31 Latest Annual Data: 08/31/2005

Year	Sales	Net Income
2005	$32,000	-$11,190,000
2004	$7,732,000	-$7,683,000
2003	$11,721,000	-$3,679,000

Curr. Assets:	$2,718,000	Curr. Liab.:	$2,670,000		
Plant, Equip.:	$135,000	Total Liab.:	$4,820,000	Indic. Yr. Divd.:	NA
Total Assets:	$3,633,000	Net Worth:	-$1,186,000	Debt/ Equity:	NA

MarketAxess Holdings Inc

140 Broadway, 42nd Fl., New York, NY, 10005; *PH:* 1-212-813-6000; *Fax:* 1-212-813-6390; *http://* www.marketaxess.com; *Email:* uscs@marketaxess.com

General - Incorporation	DE	Stock - Price on:12/24/2007	$17.01
Employees	176	Stock Exchange	NDQ
Auditor	PricewaterhouseCoopers LLP	Ticker Symbol	MKTX
Stk Agt	Wachovia Bank N.A	Outstanding Shares	33,630,000
Counsel	NA	E.P.S.	$0.31
DUNS No.	NA	Shareholders	NA

Business: The groups principle activity is to provide electronic trading of corporate bonds and other securities services. The group products sold under the trade name DealerAxess(R). The group operates from Brazil, Colombia, Mexico, Peru, the Philippines, Russia, Turkey and Venezuela. The group's quarterly revenue for September 2007 was 22.20 millions of USD.

Primary SIC and add'l.: 6221 6211

CIK No: 0001278021

Subsidiaries: MarketAxess Canada Limited, MarketAxess Corporation, MarketAxess Europe Limited

Officers: Richard M. McVey/Chmn., CEO, Kelley Millet/Dir., Pres., James N.B. Rucker/CFO, Nicholas Themelis/CIO, Cordelia Boise/Head - Human Resources, Charles R. Hood/General Counsel, Richard J. Schiffman/Head - Business Development, Strategy, Stephen Gallagher/Head - Dealer Services, Stephen Davidson/Investor Relations

Directors: Richard M. McVey/Chmn., CEO, Kelley Millet/Dir., Pres., Stephen P. Casper/Dir., David G. Gomach/Dir., Carlos Hernandez/Dir., Ronald M. Hersch/Dir., Wayne D. Lyski/Dir., Jerome S. Markowitz/Dir., Nicolas S. Rohatyn/Dir., John Steinhardt/Dir.

Owners: Insiders/11.04%, John Steinhardt, Stephen P. Casper, UBS AG/7.18%, James N.B. Rucker, Wayne D. Lyski, J.P.Morgan Partners (23A SBIC), L.P./3.51%, Jerome S. Markowitz, Nicolas S. Rohatyn, Richard McVey/8.65%, David G. Gomach, Kelley T. Millet, Janus Capital Management LLC/6.42%, Nicholas Themelis, Royce& Associates, L.L.C./7.20% (20 Owners included in Index)

Financial Data: Fiscal Year End:12/31 Latest Annual Data: 12/31/2006

Year	Sales	Net Income
2006	$83,316,000	$5,421,000
2005	$78,560,000	$8,142,000
2004	$75,797,000	$57,587,000

Curr. Assets:	$99,429,000	Curr. Liab.:	$18,136,000	P/E Ratio:	85.05
Plant, Equip.:	$4,304,000	Total Liab.:	$18,993,000	Indic. Yr. Divd.:	NA
Total Assets:	$204,278,000	Net Worth:	$185,285,000	Debt/ Equity:	NA

Marketing Acquisition Corp

211 W Wall St., Midland, TX, 79701; *PH:* 1-432-682-1761

General - Incorporation	NV	Stock - Price on:12/24/2007	NA
Employees	NA	Stock Exchange	OTC
Auditor	S. W. Hatfield, CPA	Ticker Symbol	MAQC
Stk Agt	Securities Transfer Corp	Outstanding Shares	NA
Counsel	NA	E.P.S.	-$0.01
DUNS No.	NA	Shareholders	NA

Business: The groups principle activity is to provide recruiting services. The groups service area includes the research and development, engineering, marketing, sales, information technology and manufacturing industries. The group operates from United States.

Primary SIC and add'l.: 6770

CIK No: 0001363343

Officers: Glenn A. Little/54/Chmn., CEO, CFO, Pres.

Directors: Glenn A. Little/54/Chmn., CEO, CFO, Pres.

Owners: Timothy P. Halter, Halter Financial Investments, L.P., Insiders

Financial Data: ***Fiscal Year End:***12/31 ***Latest Annual Data:*** 12/31/2006

Year	Sales	Net Income
2006	NA	-$15,000

Curr. Assets:	$7,000	***Curr. Liab.:***	$0		
Plant, Equip.:	NA	***Total Liab.:***	$10,000	***Indic. Yr. Divd.:***	NA
Total Assets:	$7,000	***Net Worth:***	-$3,000	***Debt/ Equity:***	NA

Marketing Educational Corp

211 W Wall St., Midland, TX, 79701; ***PH:*** 1-432-682-1761

General - Incorporation	FL	***Stock***- Price on:12/24/2007	NA
Employees	NA	Stock Exchange	NA
Auditor	S. W. Hatfield, CPA	Ticker Symbol	NA
Stk Agt.	Fidelity Transfer Co.	Outstanding Shares	NA
Counsel	Joshua C. Nathan	E.P.S.	NA
DUNS No.	NA	Shareholders	NA

Business: The group's principle activity is to seek a suitable reverse acquisition candidate through acquisition, merger or other suitable business combination method. The group operates from United States.

Primary SIC and add'l.: 5960

CIK No: 0000869708

Marketing Worldwide Corp

2212 Grand Commerce Dr., Howell, MI, 48855; ***PH:*** 1-517-540-0045

General - Incorporation	DE	***Stock***- Price on:12/24/2007	$0.5
Employees	18	Stock Exchange	OTC
Auditor	Russell Bedford Stefanou Mirchandani	Ticker Symbol	MWWC
Stk Agt	Continental Stock Transfer & Trust Co	Outstanding Shares	11,360,000
Counsel	NA	E.P.S.	$0.03
DUNS No.	NA	Shareholders	NA

Business: The group's principle activities include designing, manufacturing and wholesale supplier of original equipment manufacturer components in the automotive accessory aftermarket. The group operates from United States.

Primary SIC and add'l.: 5013

CIK No: 0001278363

Subsidiaries: KIA Motors Corporation of Seoul, Marketing Worldwide LLC, Toyota Motor Corporation, Worldwide Corporation

Officers: Michael Winzkowski/57/Dir., CEO, Pres., Sec., James C. Marvin/52/Dir., CFO, COO, Gregory G. Green/51/Mgr. - Sales

Directors: Michael Winzkowski/57/Dir., CEO, Pres., Sec., James C. Marvin/52/Dir., CFO, COO

Owners: Insiders/95.94%, Greg Green/4.70%, James C. Marvin/45.62%, Michael Winzkowski/45.62%

Financial Data: ***Fiscal Year End:***09/30 ***Latest Annual Data:*** 9/30/2006

Year	Sales	Net Income
2006	$9,476,000	$306,000

Curr. Assets:	$3,441,000	***Curr. Liab.:***	$2,774,000	***P/E Ratio:***	16.67
Plant, Equip.:	$2,132,000	***Total Liab.:***	$4,347,000	***Indic. Yr. Divd.:***	NA
Total Assets:	$6,114,000	***Net Worth:***	$1,551,000	***Debt/ Equity:***	0.8947

Markland Technologies Inc

222 Metro Ctr. Blvd., Warwick, RI, 02886; ***PH:*** 1-617-973-5104; ***http://*** www.marklandtech.com; ***Email:*** markland@marklandtech.com

General - Incorporation	FL	***Stock***- Price on:12/24/2007	$0.0066
Employees	196	Stock Exchange	OTC
Auditor	Wolf & Co. P.C	Ticker Symbol	MRKL
Stk Agt.	Florida Atlantic Stock Transfer, Inc.	Outstanding Shares	350,450,000
Counsel	NA	E.P.S.	-$0.278
DUNS No.	NA	Shareholders	NA

Business: The group's principal activity is to provide integrated security solutions to the homeland security marketplace. It provides certain emerging technology services and products to protect the country's borders, infrastructure assets and personnel. The emerging technologies include automatic detection of explosives and illicit materials and cryptographic systems for secure communications. The group's principal end customer is the United States government. The group acquired ergo systems inc in 2003, science and technology research corporation inc and e-oir technologies inc in 2004.

Primary SIC and add'l.: 7389 7372

CIK No: 0001102833

Subsidiaries: Ergo Systems, Inc., Science & Technology Research, Inc., Technest Holdings, Inc.

Officers: Joe MacKin/Dir., CEO - Eoir Technologies Inc, Robert Tarini/Dir., CEO, Diane Deterline/Dir. - Software Research & Development, Eoir Technologies Inc, David Bonzo/Dir. - Tactical Sensors Support, Eoir Technologies Inc, Larry Bramlette/COO - Eoir Technologies Inc, Michael Curran/CTO, Gino Pereira/CFO, Larry Fillian/Exec. VP - Eoir Technologies Inc, Pres. - STR, Mark Coleman/Dir. - Business Developmen, Eoir Technologies Inc, Diana Durbin/Exec. VP - Eoir Technologies Inc, Richard Robison/Program Mgr. - Eoir Technologies Inc

Directors: Joe MacKin/Dir., CEO - Eoir Technologies Inc, Robert Tarini/Dir., CEO

Owners: Deer Creek Fund LLC/5.90%, James LLC/10.00%, Southridge Partners LP/10.00%

Financial Data: ***Fiscal Year End:***06/30 ***Latest Annual Data:*** 6/30/2005

Year	Sales	Net Income
2005	$66,695,000	-$30,700,000
2004	$6,014,000	-$10,511,000
2003	$659,000	-$2,837,000

Curr. Assets:	$15,421,000	***Curr. Liab.:***	$18,043,000		
Plant, Equip.:	$908,000	***Total Liab.:***	$25,677,000	***Indic. Yr. Divd.:***	NA
Total Assets:	$43,939,000	***Net Worth:***	$13,106,000	***Debt/ Equity:***	NA

MarkWest Energy Partners LP

1515 Arapahoe St., Tower 2, Ste. 700, Denver, CO, 80202; ***PH:*** 1-303-290-8700; ***Fax:*** 1-303-290-8769; ***http://*** www.markwest.com; ***Email:*** investorrelations@markwest.com

General - Incorporation	DE	***Stock***- Price on:12/24/2007	$34.3
Employees	NA	Stock Exchange	NYSE
Auditor	Deloitte & Touche LLP	Ticker Symbol	MWE
Stk Agt	Computershare Trust Co	Outstanding Shares	37,700,000
Counsel	NA	E.P.S.	$1.28
DUNS No.	NA	Shareholders	NA

Business: The groups principle activities include gathering, processing and transmission of natural gas and crude oil. In the year 2005, the group acquired Javelina Company, Javelina Pipeline Company and Javelina Land Company. Specific customers of the group include ONEOK Inc. and Targa Resources Partners, L.P. The group's quarterly revenue for September 2007 was 167.06 millions of USD.

Primary SIC and add'l.: 4923 4613 4922 4612 4925

CIK No: 0001166036

Subsidiaries: Basin Pipeline L.L.C., Bright Star Gathering, Inc., MarkWest Blackhawk, L.P., MarkWest Energy Appalachia, L.L.C., MarkWest Energy East Texas Gas Company, L.P., MarkWest Energy Finance Corporation, MarkWest Energy Operating Company, L.L.C., MarkWest Javelina Company, MarkWest Javelina Holding Company, L.P., MarkWest Javelina Pipeline Company, MarkWest Javelina Pipeline Holding, L.P., MarkWest Michigan Pipeline Company, L.L.C., MarkWest New Mexico, L.P., MarkWest Pinnacle L.P., MarkWest Pipeline Company, L.P. 27 Subsidiaries included in the Index

Officers: Frank M. Semple/Dir., CEO, Pres., Nancy K. Buese/Sr. VP, CFO, Andrew L. Schroeder/VP - Finance, Treasurer, Assist. Sec., Bert Dillman/VP - Business Development, Jim Bryant/Dir. - Business Development, Scott Garner/Dir. - Corporate Development, Roxanne Fowles/Mgr. - Business Development, Lenice Stanford/Gas Supply Representative, Business Development, Dale Zimmerman/Natural Gas Business Development, Consultant, Tamara Stockin/NGL Scheduler, John C. Mollenkopf/COO, Sr. VP, Randy S. Nickerson/Sr. VP, Chief Commercial Officer, Brett Snyder/Dir. - NGL Marketing Services, Diana Finley/NGL Marketer, Russ Moran/Dir. - Natural Gas Marketing *(20 Officers included in Index)*

Directors: Frank M. Semple/Dir., CEO, Pres., John M. Fox/Chmn., Keith E. Bailey/Dir., Charles K. Dempster/Dir., Donald C. Heppermann/Dir., William A. Kellstrom/Dir., William P. Nicoletti/Dir.

Owners: Keith E. Bailey, John M. Fox/15.50%, Insiders/16.00%, Corwin C. Bromley, Frank M. Semple, Charles K. Dempster, John C. Mollenkopf, Kayne Anderson Capital Advisors, L.P./8.70%, William P. Nicoletti, Randy S. Nickerson, William A. Kellstrom, Tortoise Capital Advisors, L.L.C./9.70%, Tortoise Energy Infrastructure Corporation/6.40%, MarkWest Hydrocarbon,Inc./15.20%, Nancy K. Buese *(17 Owners included in Index)*

Financial Data: ***Fiscal Year End:***12/31 ***Latest Annual Data:*** 12/31/2006

Year	Sales	Net Income
2006	$629,911,000	$70,084,000
2005	$499,084,000	$2,355,000
2004	$301,314,000	$9,962,000

Curr. Assets:	$136,033,000	***Curr. Liab.:***	$131,775,000		
Plant, Equip.:	$550,886,000	***Total Liab.:***	$662,131,000	***Indic. Yr. Divd.:***	$2.200
Total Assets:	$1,114,780,000	***Net Worth:***	$452,649,000	***Debt/ Equity:***	NA

Markwest Hydrocarbon Inc

1515 Arapahoe St., Tower 2, Ste. 700, Denver, CO, 80202; ***PH:*** 1-303-925-9200; ***Fax:*** 1-303-290-8769; ***http://*** www.markwest.com

General - Incorporation	DE	***Stock***- Price on:12/24/2007	$56.52
Employees	318	Stock Exchange	AMEX
Auditor	Deloitte & Touche LLP	Ticker Symbol	MWP
Stk Agt	Computershare Trust Co	Outstanding Shares	11,990,000
Counsel	NA	E.P.S.	-$1.25
DUNS No.	18-835-4799	Shareholders	NA

Business: The group's principal activities are to provide natural gas processing and related services. The activities include gathering, treatment and natural gas liquids (ngls) extraction services for natural gas producers and pipeline companies and fractionation of ngls into marketable products. The group also purchases, stores and markets natural gas and ngls. The operations are concentrated in four core areas: the southern appalachian region of eastern Kentucky, southern west Virginia, and southern Ohio; Michigan; the rocky mountains of Colorado and New Mexico; and alberta, Canada. In 2003, the group acquired pinnacle natural gas company, pinnacle pipeline company, png transmission company, png utility company, bright star gathering inc, western Oklahoma gas company l.l.c, Michigan crude pipeline, lukbbok pipeline & southwest lateral pipeline.

Primary SIC and add'l.: 1321 1389 1382

CIK No: 0001019756

Subsidiaries: Basin Pipeline, LLC, MarkWest Blackhawk, L.P., MarkWest Energy Appalachia, LLC, MarkWest Energy East Texas Gas Company, L.P., MarkWest Energy GP, LLC, MarkWest Energy Operating Company, LLC, MarkWest Energy Partners, L.P., MarkWest Javelina Company, MarkWest Javelina Holding Company, L.P., MarkWest Javelina Pipeline Company, MarkWest Javelina Pipeline Holding, L.P., MarkWest Michigan Pipeline Company, LLC, MarkWest Michigan, Inc., MarkWest New Mexico, L.P., MarkWest Pinnacle L.P. 25 Subsidiaries included in the Index

Officers: Frank M. Semple/Dir., CEO, Pres./$7,739,493.00, Randy S. Nickerson/Sr. VP, Chief Commercial Officer/$5,446,981.00, Corwin C. Bromley/Sr. VP, General Counsel, Sec./$1,535,655.00, Andrew L. Schroeder/VP - Finance, Treasurer, Assist. Sec., John C. Mollenkopf/COO, Sr. VP/$5,350,012.00

Directors: Frank M. Semple/Dir., CEO, Pres., John M. Fox/Chmn., Donald C. Heppermann/Dir., Michael L. Beatty/Dir., William A. Kellstrom/Dir., Anne E. Mounsey/Dir., Karen L. Rogers/Dir., William F. Wallace/Dir., Donald D. Wolf/Dir.

Owners: Michael L. Beatty, Randy S. Nickerson, Nancy K. Buese, Anne E. Mounsey, Kayne Anderson Capital Advisors, L.P/7.50%, William F. Wallace, Donald D. Wolf, William A. Kellstrom, Karen L. Rogers, Corwin C. Bromley, Insiders/46.40%, John M. Fox/44.60%, Frank M. Semple, John C. Mollenkopf, Donald C. Heppermann *(16 Owners included in Index)*

Financial Data: ***Fiscal Year End:***12/31 ***Latest Annual Data:*** 12/31/2006

Year	Sales	Net Income
2006	$785,722,000	$9,537,000
2005	$714,177,000	-$6,802,000
2004	$460,113,000	-$903,000

Curr. Assets:	$218,136,000	**Curr. Liab.:**	$152,106,000	**P/E Ratio:**	269.14
Plant, Equip.:	$554,335,000	**Total Liab.:**	$720,180,000	**Indic. Yr. Divd.:**	$1.440
Total Assets:	$1,203,241,000	**Net Worth:**	$41,489,000	**Debt/ Equity:**	14.8315

Marlin Business Services Corp

300 Fellowship Rd., Mt. Laurel, NJ, 08054; ***PH:*** 1-856-359-9111; ***Fax:*** 1-888-479-1100; ***http://*** www.marlincorp.com; ***Email:*** investorrelations@marlincorp.com

General - Incorporation.....PA
Employees.....314
Auditor.....Deloitte & Touche, LLP
Stk Agt.....StockTrans, Inc.
Counsel.....NA
DUNS No.....13-838-8793

Stock- Price on:12/24/2007.....$20.21
Stock Exchange.....NDQ
Ticker Symbol.....MRLN
Outstanding Shares.....12,260,000
E.P.S.....$1.53
Shareholders.....NA

Business: The group's principle activity is to provide equipment leasing solutions primarily to small businesses nationwide in a segment of the equipment leasing market. The company finances over 60 categories of commercial equipment important to its end user customers including copiers, telephone systems, computers and certain commercial and industrial equipment. The company operates through its network of over 7,700 independent equipment dealers. The group operates from United States.

Primary SIC and add'l.: 7377

CIK No: 0001260968

Subsidiaries: AssuranceOne, Ltd., Marlin Business Bank, Marlin Leasing Corporation, Marlin Leasing Receivables Corp. IV, Marlin Leasing Receivables Corp. IX, Marlin Leasing Receivables Corp. VII, Marlin Leasing Receivables Corp. VIII, Marlin Leasing Receivables Corp.II, Marlin Leasing Receivables IX LLC, Marlin Leasing Receivables VII LLC, Marlin Leasing Receivables VIII LLC, Marlin Leasing ReceivablesII LLC, Marlin Leasing ReceivablesIV LLC

Officers: Daniel P. Dyer/Chmn., CEO, Treasurer, Gary R. Shivers/Dir., Pres., George D. Pelose/Exec. VP, General Counsel, Sec., Lynne C. Wilson/Sr. VP, CFO

Directors: Daniel P. Dyer/Chmn., CEO, Treasurer, Lawrence J. Deangelo/Dir., John J. Calamari/Dir., Kevin J. McGinty/Dir., Gary R. Shivers/Dir., Pres., Edward Grzedzinski/Dir., James W. Wert/Dir.

Owners: Edward Grzedzinski, Gary R. Shivers/2.80%, William Blair& Company/8.46%, Lynne C. Wilson, Lawrence J. DeAngelo, Peachtree Equity Investment Management/19.60%, George D. Pelose/1.60%, Bruce E. Sickel, JP Morgan Chase& Co./8.50%, Pequot Capital Management/5.50%, Daniel P. Dyer/2.40%, The Northwestern Mutual Life Insurance Company/5.30%, Kevin J. McGinty, James W. Wert, John J. Calamari *(18 Owners included in Index)*

Financial Data: ***Fiscal Year End:***12/31 ***Latest Annual Data:*** 12/31/2006

Year	Sales	Net Income
2006	$103,456,000	$18,634,000
2005	$90,211,000	$16,248,000
2004	$75,551,000	$13,459,000

Curr. Assets:	$89,072,000	**Curr. Liab.:**	$20,303,000	**P/E Ratio:**	13.21
Plant, Equip.:	$3,430,000	**Total Liab.:**	$661,163,000	**Indic. Yr. Divd.:**	NA
Total Assets:	$795,452,000	**Net Worth:**	$134,289,000	**Debt/ Equity:**	4.5032

Marmion Industries Corp

9103 Emmott Rd. Ste. 6, Houston, TX, 77040; ***PH:*** 1-713-466-6585; ***http://*** marmionind.com

General - Incorporation.....NV
Employees.....10
Auditor.....Sherb & Co., LLP
Stk Agt.....American Registrar & Transfer Co
Counsel.....NA
DUNS No.....NA

Stock- Price on:12/24/2007.....$0.0084
Stock Exchange.....OTC
Ticker Symbol.....MMIO
Outstanding Shares.....73,610,000
E.P.S.....-$0.209
Shareholders.....NA

Business: The groups principle activities include manufacturing and marketing explosion-proof air conditioners, refrigeration systems, chemical filtration systems and building pressurize air condition and services for the commercial sector. The specific customer of the group is Marmion Air. The group operates from the United States. The group's quarterly revenue for Sep '07 was 1.59 millions of USD.

Primary SIC and add'l.: 1711

CIK No: 0001123195

Subsidiaries: Marmion Investments, Inc

Officers: Wilbert H. Marmion/50/Dir., CEO, Ellen Raidl/41/Dir., Sec., Treasurer, Bill Marmion/Pres.

Directors: Wilbert H. Marmion/50/Dir., CEO, Ellen Raidl/41/Dir., Sec., Treasurer

Owners: Wilbert H. Marmion/90.00%, Insiders/90.00%

Financial Data: ***Fiscal Year End:***12/31 ***Latest Annual Data:*** 12/31/2006

Year	Sales	Net Income
2006	$4,613,000	-$6,955,000
2005	$2,492,000	-$2,276,000
2004	$1,090,000	-$3,101,000

Curr. Assets:	$1,425,000	**Curr. Liab.:**	$2,146,000		
Plant, Equip.:	$100,000	**Total Liab.:**	$2,179,000	**Indic. Yr. Divd.:**	NA
Total Assets:	$1,526,000	**Net Worth:**	-$654,000	**Debt/ Equity:**	NA

Marriott International Inc

10400 Fernwood Rd., Bethesda, MD, 20817; ***PH:*** 1-301-380-3000; ***Fax:*** 1-301-380-3969; ***http://*** www.marriott.com

General - Incorporation.....DE
Employees.....150,600
Auditor.....Ernst & Young LLP
Stk Agt.....Ernest & Young LLP
Counsel.....NA
DUNS No.....15-650-6446

Stock- Price on:12/24/2007.....$46.02
Stock Exchange.....NYSE
Ticker Symbol.....MAR
Outstanding Shares.....386,340,000
E.P.S.....$1.81
Shareholders.....NA

Business: The group's principle activity is to provide franchise hotels and related lodging facilities. The group operates through five business segments namely full service lodging, select service lodging, extended stay lodging, timeshare and synthetic fuel. The group operates from United States.

Primary SIC and add'l.: 1389 7011

CIK No: 0001048286

Subsidiaries: 158 Ferny Avenue Pty Limited, 30 Pitt Street Pty Limited , 515 Queen Street PTY LTD, Adamar (Turks & Caicos) Ltd., Adamar Amsterdam Hotel B.V., Adamar Beteiligungs GmbH, Adamar Garni Franchise Systems, Inc., Adamar Hotelbesitz Dusseldorf GmbH & Co. KG, Adamar Hotels International B.V., Adamar Hotels Netherlands B.V., Adamar International Lodging, Ltd., Adamar International Management Company B.V., Adamar International Management Company B.V. (Australian Branch), Adamar Netherlands Antilles N.V., Addison SHS, LLC 693 Subsidiaries included in the Index

Officers: J. W. Marriott/76/Chmn., CEO/$12,596,810.00, Thomas E. Ladd/Sr. VP - Government Affairs, Edwin D. Fuller/MD, Pres., Stephen P. Joyce/Exec. VP - Owner, Franchise Services And North American Full Service Development, Bradford A. Bryan/Exec. VP - Architecture, Construction, Simon F. Cooper/COO, Pres. - Ritz, Carlton Hotel Company, LLC, Robin J. Uler/Sr. VP - Operations Planning, Support, Terri L. Turner/Sec., Bancroft Gordon/VP, Corp. Sec. - Sr. Counsel, Deborah Marriott Harrison/VP - Government Affairs, Kathleen Matthews/Exec. VP - Global Communications, Public Affairs, Richard S. Hoffman/Exec. VP - Mergers, Acquisitions, Development Planning, Michael E. Jannini/Exec. VP, GM - Global Brand Strategy, Innovation, Joel M. Eisemann/Exec. VP - Owner, Franchise Services, Carolyn B. Handlon/Exec. VP - Finance, Global Treasurer *(43 Officers included in Index)*

Directors: J. W. Marriott/76/Chmn., CEO, John W. Marriott/47/Vice Chmn., William J. Shaw/62/Dir., COO, Pres., Floretta D. McKenzie/72/Dir., Lawrence M. Small/66/Dir., Harry J. Pearce/65/Dir., Richard S. Braddock/66/Dir., George Munoz/56/Dir., William R. Tiefel/Dir., Steven S. Reinemund/59/Dir., Lawrence W. Kellner/49/Dir., Debra L. Lee/53/Dir., Sterling D. Colton/Dir. Emeritus

Owners: Harry J. Pearce, James M. Sullivan, Richard E. Marriott/12.70%, Lawrence M. Small, Insiders/17.90%, JWM Family Enterprises, Inc./6.20%, Richard S. Braddock, Stephen G. Marriott/9.60%, Deborah M. Harrison/6.80%, William J. Shaw, Lawrence W. Kellner, Robert J. McCarthy, J. W. Marriott/15.60%, JWM Family Enterprises, L.P./6.20%, George Munoz *(21 Owners included in Index)*

Financial Data: ***Fiscal Year End:***12/30 ***Latest Annual Data:*** 12/29/2006

Year	Sales	Net Income
2006	$12,160,000,000	$608,000,000
2005	$11,550,000,000	$669,000,000
2004	$10,099,000,000	$596,000,000

Curr. Assets:	$1,946,000,000	**Curr. Liab.:**	$2,356,000,000	**P/E Ratio:**	25.43
Plant, Equip.:	$2,389,000,000	**Total Liab.:**	$4,575,000,000	**Indic. Yr. Divd.:**	$0.300
Total Assets:	$8,668,000,000	**Net Worth:**	$4,081,000,000	**Debt/ Equity:**	1.0400

Marsh & McLennan Cos Inc

1166 Ave. of the Americas, New York, NY, 10036; ***PH:*** 1-212-345-5000; ***http://*** www.marshmac.com

General - Incorporation.....DE
Employees.....55,200
Auditor.....Deloitte & Touche LLP
Stk Agt.....PFTC
Counsel.....NA
DUNS No.....04-156-4378

Stock- Price on:12/24/2007.....$32.17
Stock Exchange.....AMEX
Ticker Symbol.....MMK
Outstanding Shares.....555,420,000
E.P.S.....$4.69
Shareholders.....NA

Business: The groups principle activity is to provide consulting, insurance, and reinsurance broking services. The group operates through three segments three segments namely risk and insurance services, investment management and consulting. The group operates from United States.

Primary SIC and add'l.: 6282 6411 8742

CIK No: 0000062709

Subsidiaries: 1302318 Ontario Inc., 600 North Pearl Inc., 964886 Ontario, Inc., A. Constantinidi & CIA. S.C., ACTU Insurance Broking Pty Limited, Administradora de Inmuebles Fin, S.A. de C.V., Admiral Holdings Limited, Admiral Underwriting Agencies Limited, AFCO Premium Acceptance Inc., AFCO Premium Credit LLC, Affinity Financial Incorporated, Aldgate Investments Limited, Aldgate US Investments, Alfram Consultores S.A.C., All Asia Sedgwick Insurance Brokers Corporation 773 Subsidiaries included in the Index

Officers: Simon Freakley/46/CEO, Pres. - Kroll Inc, Brian M. Storms/53/Chmn., CEO - Marsh Inc, Michael G. Cherkasky/58/Dir., CEO, Pres., Member - International Advisory Board, John Drzik/45/CEO, Pres. - Mercer Specialty Consulting, David Nadler/59/Vice Chmn., CEO, Member - International Advisory Board, Michele M. Burns/50/Chairwoman, CEO - Mercer Human Resources Consulting, Mathis Cabiallavetta/63/Vice Chmn., CEO, Charles E. Haldeman/59/CEO, Pres. - Putnam Investments, Robert J. Rapport/VP, Controller, Chief Accounting Officer, Scott E. Gilbert/52/Sr. VP, Chief Compliance Officer, Luciana Fato/Corp. Sec., Matthew B. Bartley/51/CFO, Michael A. Beber/48/Sr. VP, Chief Strategic Development Officer, Michael A. Petrullo/40/Sr. VP, Chief Administrative Officer, Peter J. Beshar/46/Exec. VP, General Counsel

Directors: Brian M. Storms/53/Chmn., CEO - Marsh Inc, Michael G. Cherkasky/58/Dir., CEO, Pres., Member - International Advisory Board, Michele M. Burns/50/Chairwoman, CEO - Mercer Human Resources Consulting, Mathis Cabiallavetta/63/Vice Chmn., CEO, David Nadler/59/Vice Chmn., CEO, Member - International Advisory Board, Stephen R. Hardis/71/Non - Exec. Chmn., Marc D. Oken/59/Dir., Leslie M. Baker/65/Dir., Oscar Fanjul/58/Dir., Member - International Advisory Board, Abdlatif Y. Al-Hamad/Member - International Advisory Board, Gwendolyn S. King/66/Dir., Zachary W. Carter/57/Dir., Morton O. Schapiro/53/Dir., Adele Simmons/66/Dir., David A. Olsen/69/Dir. *(27 Directors included in Index)*

Owners: Marc D. Oken, Charles E. Haldeman, David A. Olsen, Matthew B. Bartley, Gwendolyn S. King, Lord Lang, Morton O. Schapiro, Brian M. Storms, Insiders, Adele Simmons, Lewis W. Bernard, T. Rowe Price Associates, Inc./6.80%, Zachary W. Carter, Michael G. Cherkasky, Sandra S. Wijnberg *(21 Owners included in Index)*

Financial Data: ***Fiscal Year End:***12/31 ***Latest Annual Data:*** 12/31/2006

Year	Sales	Net Income
2006	$11,921,000,000	$990,000,000
2005	$11,652,000,000	$404,000,000
2004	$12,159,000,000	$176,000,000

Curr. Assets:	$5,834,000,000	**Curr. Liab.:**	$5,549,000,000	**P/E Ratio:**	21.74
Plant, Equip.:	$1,043,000,000	**Total Liab.:**	$12,318,000,000	**Indic. Yr. Divd.:**	$0.760
Total Assets:	$18,137,000,000	**Net Worth:**	$5,819,000,000	**Debt/ Equity:**	NA

Marsh Supermarkets Inc

9800 Crosspoint Blvd., Indianapolis, IN, 46256; ***PH:*** 1-317-594-2100; ***http://*** www.marsh.net

General - Incorporation ....IN
Employees...NA
Auditor ....Ernst & Young LLP
Stk Agt....................................National City Bank
Counsel...NA
DUNS No..00-694-0282

Stock - Price on:12/24/2007 ....NA
Stock Exchange...NA
Ticker Symbol...NA
Outstanding Shares ....NA
E.P.S..NA
Shareholders...NA

Business: The groups principle activity is to operate grocery stores. The group also provides cafeteria management, catering, and concession services for clients. The group operates from United States.

Primary SIC and add'l.: 5411

CIK No: 0000062737

Subsidiaries: BF Property, LLC, Butterfield Foods, LLC, CF Property, LLC, Contract Transport, Inc., Contract Transport, LLC, Crystal Caf Management Group, LLC, Crystal Food Management Services, LLC, Crystal Food Services, LLC, CSD Property, LLC, Floral Fashions, LLC, Floral Property, LLC, LB Property, LLC, Limited Holdings, Inc., LoBill Foods, LLC, Mar Properties, Inc. 35 Subsidiaries included in the Index

Marshall & Ilsley Corp

770 N Water St., Milwaukee, WI, 53202; *PH:* 1-414-765-7700; *Fax:* 1-414-298-2921;
http:// www.micorp.com

General - Incorporation ....WI
Employees...14,699
Auditor ....Deloitte & Touche LLP
Stk Agt.............Continental Stock Transfer & Trust Co
Counsel...NA
DUNS No...00-794-6981

Stock - Price on:12/24/2007 ....$48.78
Stock Exchange...NYSE
Ticker Symbol..MIC
Outstanding Shares 259,110,000
E.P.S...$3.28
Shareholders...NA

Business: The group's principle activity is to provide diversified financial services, comprehensive financial products and services, and unparalleled customer service to personal, business, corporate and institutional customers nationwide. The group operates from United States.

Primary SIC and add'l.: 6021 7374 6712

CIK No: 0000062741

Subsidiaries: 6027580 Canada, Inc., AdminiSource Communications, L.P., AdminiSource Holdings, Inc., Advanced Financial Solutions LLC, Advanced Financial Solutions, Inc., Brasfield Technology LLC, Endpoint Exchange LLC, Everlink Payment Services, Inc., GHR Systems Canada, Inc., GHR Systems, Inc., Kirchman Company LLC, Kirchman Corporation, Link2Gov Corp., Loansoft, Inc., Louisville Realty Company 77 Subsidiaries included in the Index

Officers: Dennis J. Kuester/65/Chmn., CEO/$8,085,707.00, Thomas R. Ellis/Sr. VP, John L. Roberts/Sr. VP, Kenneth C. Krei/Sr. VP, Mark R. Hogan/Sr. VP, Chief Credit Officer, Frank R. Martire/Sr. VP/$2,836,248.00, Patricia R. Justiliano/Sr. VP, Corporate Controller, Mark F. Furlong/50/Dir., Pres./$4,215,096.00, Thomas A. Root/Sr. VP, Audit Dir., Ryan R. Deneen/Sr. VP, Dir. - Corporate Tax, Beth D. Knickerbocker/Sr. VP, Chief Risk Officer, Randall J. Erickson/Sr. VP, General Counsel, Chief Administrative Officer, Paul J. Renard/Sr. VP, Dir. - Human Resources, Gregory A. Smith/CFO, Sr. VP/$907,318.00, Brent J. Kelly/Sr. VP, Dir. - Corporate Marketing *(19 Officers included in Index)*

Directors: Dennis J. Kuester/65/Chmn., CEO, Burleigh E. Jacobs/Dir. Emeriti, Andrew N. Baur/Dir., James B. Wigdale/Dir., Mark F. Furlong/50/Dir., Pres., John S. Shiely/Dir., Jon F. Chait/Dir., George E. Wardeberg/Dir., John W. Daniels/Dir., Debra S. Waller/Dir., John A. Mellowes/Dir., Katharine C. Lyall/Dir., Ted D. Kellner/Dir., Malcolm M. Aslin/Dir., San W. Orr/Dir. *(26 Directors included in Index)*

Owners: Edward L. Meyer, Frank R. Martire, Ted D. Kellner, James B. Wigdale, Malcolm M. Aslin, Peter M. Platten, Andrew N. Baur, San W. Orr, Marshall& Ilsley Corporation/6.30%, John W. Daniels, Jon F. Chait, John M. Presley, Katharine C. Lyall, Michael D. Hayford, John S. Shiely *(26 Owners included in Index)*

Financial Data: Fiscal Year End:12/31   Latest Annual Data: 12/31/2006

Year	Sales	Net Income
2006	$5,146,370,000	$807,838,000
2005	$3,962,890,000	$727,469,000
2004	$3,112,285,000	$627,086,000

Curr. Assets:	$3,277,936,000	**Curr. Liab.:**	$42,052,731,000	**P/E Ratio:**	14.87
Plant, Equip.:	$571,637,000	**Total Liab.:**	$50,078,886,000	**Indic. Yr. Divd.:**	$1.240
Total Assets:	$56,230,257,000	**Net Worth:**	$6,151,371,000	**Debt/ Equity:**	NA

Marshall Edwards Inc

140 Wicks Rd. , North Ryde, NSW, 2113; ; *http://* www.marshalledwardsinc.com;
Email: meiinformation@marshalledwardsinc.com

General - Incorporation ....DE
Employees...NA
Auditor ....Marshall Edwards, Inc
Stk Agt.....Computershare Investor Services LLC
Counsel..............................Pepper Hamilton LLP
DUNS No..NA

Stock - Price on:12/24/2007 ....$3.2
Stock Exchange...NDQ
Ticker Symbol...MSHL
Outstanding Shares 63,390,000
E.P.S..-$0.2
Shareholders...NA

Business: The group's principal activities are to develop and commercialize drugs for the treatment of cancer. The group is presently involved in the clinical developments of the anti-cancer drug phenoxodiol. The group has been formed to commercialize new family of chemicals known as multiple signal transduction regulators (mstrs). The group is in its development stage and phase ii trials of the drug phenoxodiol. The phenoxodiol appears to target a number of key components involved in cancer cell survival and proliferation with little or no effect on normal cells based on the emerging field of signal transduction regulation, which is the regulation of the chemical signals within cells that control specific cell functions. It has spun off from novogen limited its parent company.

Primary SIC and add'l.: 8731 2834

CIK No: 0001262104

Subsidiaries: Marshall Edwards Pty, Limited

Officers: Christopher Naughton/Dir., CEO, Pres., David R. Seaton/Dir., Company Sec., CFO

Directors: Christopher Naughton/Dir., CEO, Pres., Bryan R.G. Williams/Non Exec. Chmn., William D. Rueckert/Non Exec. Dir., Paul J. Nestel/Non Exec. Dir., Stephen Breckenridge/Non Exec. Dir., Philip A. Johnston/Non Exec. Dir., David R. Seaton/Dir., Company Sec., CFO

Owners: Novogen Limited/71.90%, Insiders, William D. Rueckert, Josiah T. Austin/6.20%

Financial Data: Fiscal Year End:06/30   Latest Annual Data: 6/30/2006

Year	Sales	Net Income
2006	$446,000	-$7,386,000
2005	$308,000	-$6,421,000
2004	$193,000	-$8,538,000

Curr. Assets:	$10,395,000	**Curr. Liab.:**	$1,260,000		
Plant, Equip.:	NA	**Total Liab.:**	$1,260,000	**Indic. Yr. Divd.:**	NA
Total Assets:	$10,395,000	**Net Worth:**	$9,135,000	**Debt/ Equity:**	NA

Marshall Holdings International Inc

Formerly: Gateway Distributors Ltd
2555 E Washburn Rd., North Las Vegas, NA, 89081; *PH:* 1-702-317-2400

General - Incorporation ....NV
Employees...NA
Auditor ....Madsen & Assoc. CPA's, Inc.
Stk Agt........OTC Corporate Transfer Service Co
Counsel...NA
DUNS No...NA

Stock - Price on:12/24/2007 ....$0.0045
Stock Exchange..OTC
Ticker Symbol..MHII
Outstanding Shares ....NA
E.P.S..$0.00
Shareholders...NA

Business: The group's principal activity is to distribute whole food nutrition, health and dietary supplements and environmental solutions. The group markets and distributes eighteen different nutritional and health products under the trademark of the right solution. The products are intended to provide nutritional supplements to the users and are not intended to diagnose, treat, cure or prevent any disease. The products are marketed through a network marketing system within the United States and wholesale personal imports outside the United States. The group also sells its products in Canada and Japan. Fulvic factor, body gard with lactoferrin, lifetonic, master formula, natural immunity, new life corrective a, superfood are some the products distributed by the group.

Primary SIC and add'l.: 5122

CIK No: 0001062760

Subsidiaries: Gateway Corporate Administration, Inc., Gateway Distributors, Ltd., Gateway Venture Holdings, Inc., The Right Solution Gateway

Officers: Jamie W. Plante/39/CFO

Owners: Insiders/100.00%, Richard A. Bailey/46.97%, Richard A. Bailey, Florian Ternes, Insiders, Florian Ternes/63.03%

Financial Data: Fiscal Year End:12/31   Latest Annual Data: 12/31/2006

Year	Sales	Net Income
2006	$3,757,000	-$3,735,000
2005	$770,000	-$904,000
2004	$1,154,000	-$8,677,000

Curr. Assets:	$2,968,000	**Curr. Liab.:**	$10,031,000		
Plant, Equip.:	$3,151,000	**Total Liab.:**	$12,047,000	**Indic. Yr. Divd.:**	NA
Total Assets:	$12,434,000	**Net Worth:**	$387,000	**Debt/ Equity:**	1.3515

Marsulex Inc

111 Gordon Baker Rd., Ste 300, Toronto, ON, M2H 3R1; *PH:* 1-416-496-9655;
http:// www.marsulex.com; *Email:* investor@marsulex.com

General - Incorporation ....Canada
Employees...NA
Auditor ....KPMG LLP
Stk Agt .... Computershare Investor Services LLC
Counsel...NA
DUNS No...NA

Stock - Price on:12/24/2007 ....$12.56
Stock Exchange..OTC
Ticker Symbol...MRLXF
Outstanding Shares ....NA
E.P.S..NA
Shareholders...NA

Business: The group's principle activity is to provide outsourced compliance solutions, environmental services and environmental removal services. The group operates under three segments: refinery services, power generation and western markets. Refinery services segment provides outsourced compliance solutions to major oil refinery customers in the United States and Canada. Power generation segment provides outsourced environmental services, primarily air quality compliance, to customers in the power generation industry. The segment also provides services to the cement industry. Western markets segment provides environmental removal services and chemical products to customers in western Canada. The group's quarterly revenue for September 2007 was 68.68 millions of CAD.

Primary SIC and add'l.: 2819 7389

CIK No: 0000852600

Subsidiaries: BCT Chemtrade Corporation, ICI plc, IT Holding, Inc.

Officers: Laurie Tugman/CEO, Pres., Peter Stott/Dir. - Risk Management, Regulatory, Brian Stasiewicz/VP - Refinery Services, Doug Osborne/VP - Western Markets, David Horsley/Dir. - Operations, Engineering, Robert McComb/VP - Human Resources, Robert Cardell/VP, GM - Power Generation, William E. Martin/CFO, Lucio Milanovich/Dir. - Finance

Directors: William C. Stevens/Chmn., Ian M. Matheson/Dir., Lee C. Stewart/Dir., Robert L. Yohe/Dir., William A. Lambert/Dir., Roderick F. Barrett/Dir., John A. Rogers/Dir.

Financial Data: Fiscal Year End:12/31   Latest Annual Data: 12/31/2005

Year	Sales	Net Income
2005	$142,819,000	$2,673,000
2004	$113,769,000	$4,086,000

Curr. Assets:	$49,730,000	**Curr. Liab.:**	$36,938,000	**P/E Ratio:**	169.33
Plant, Equip.:	$177,017,000	**Total Liab.:**	$229,523,000	**Indic. Yr. Divd.:**	NA
Total Assets:	$317,235,000	**Net Worth:**	$87,712,000	**Debt/ Equity:**	NA

Martek Biosciences Corp

6480 Dobbin Rd., Columbia, MD, 21045; *PH:* 1-410-740-0081; *Fax:* 1-410-740-2985;
http:// www.martekbio.com; *Email:* contactus@martekbio.com

General - Incorporation ....DE
Employees...506
Auditor ....Ernst & Young LLP
Stk Agt ....Registrar & Transfer Co
Counsel...............................Hogan & Hartson LLP
DUNS No...13-148-0451

Stock - Price on:12/24/2007 ....$24.37
Stock Exchange..NDQ
Ticker Symbol...MATK
Outstanding Shares 32,270,000
E.P.S..$0.98
Shareholders...NA

Business: The group's principal activities are to develop, manufacture and sell products derived from microalgae. These products include specialty, nutritional oils for infant formula; nutritional supplements and food ingredients to promote mental and cardiovascular health; fluorescent markers for diagnostics, rapid miniaturized screening and gene and protein detection. The group also develops new fluorescent detection products from microalgae that connect fluorescent algal proteins to antibodies. The trademarks of the group include neuromins (R), dha gold (R), dhasco (R), and arasco (r).

Primary SIC and add'l.: 2834 2833 2835

CIK No: 0000892025

Subsidiaries: Martek Biosciences Boulder Corporation, Martek Biosciences Kingstree Corporation

Officers: Steve Dubin/Dir., CEO, Peter L. Buzy/CFO, Treasurer, Exec. VP - Finance - Administration, David Abramson/Sr. VP - Business Development, James H. Flatt/48/Sr. VP - Research, Peter A. Nitze/COO, Sr. VP, Barney Easterling/Sr. VP - Manufacturing, David M. Feitel/Sr. VP, General Counsel, Sec., Tim Fealey/Sr. VP, Chief Innovation Officer

Directors: Steve Dubin/Dir., CEO, Robert J. Flanagan/Chmn., John H. Mahar/73/Dir., Henry Linsert/67/Dir., Jerome C. Keller/Dir., Eugene H. Rotberg/Dir., James R. Beery/Dir., Douglas J. MacMaster/Dir., Polly B. Kawalek/Dir., Harry D'Andrea/Dir.

Owners: T. Rowe Price Associates, Inc./7.13%, Insiders/6.37%, Peter L. Buzy, Robert J. Flanagan/1.14%, Insiders/6.37%, Douglas J. MacMaster, Jerome C. Keller, David M. Abramson, James R. Beery, Henry Linsert/1.63%, Capital Research and Management Company/12.29%, Steve Dubin, Eugene H. Rotberg, George P. Barker, John H. Mahar *(17 Owners included in Index)*

Financial Data: *Fiscal Year End:*10/31 *Latest Annual Data:* 10/31/2007

Year	Sales	Net Income
2007	$306,813,000	$32,013,000
2006	$270,654,000	$14,938,000
2005	$217,852,000	$15,284,000

Curr. Assets:	$195,486,000	**Curr. Liab.:**	$46,141,000	**P/E Ratio:**	64.13
Plant, Equip.:	$277,915,000	**Total Liab.:**	$64,968,000	**Indic. Yr. Divd.:**	NA
Total Assets:	$596,695,000	**Net Worth:**	$531,727,000	**Debt/ Equity:**	0.0809

Marten Transport Ltd

129 Marten St., Mondovi, WI, 54755; *PH:* 1-715-926-4216; *Fax:* 1-715-926-5609;
http:// www.marten.com

General - Incorporation	DE	**Stock**- Price on:12/24/2007	$18.82
Employees	2,727	Stock Exchange	NDQ
Auditor	KPMG LLP	Ticker Symbol	MRTN
Stk Agt	Mellon Investor Services LLC	Outstanding Shares	21,780,000
Counsel	Oppenheimer Wolff & Donnelly	E.P.S	$0.95
DUNS No.	00-486-6257	Shareholders	NA

Business: The group's principle activity is to provide long-haul truckload carriage. It specializes in carriages providing protective service transportation of time and temperature sensitive materials and general commodities to customers in the United States and Canada. Through protective service transportation, the company provides temperature controlled or insulated carriage of temperature sensitive materials and commodities. It also provides dry freight carriage. As of 31-Dec-2003, it operated a fleet of 2,181 tractors and 2,835 trailers. The customers of the company include procter & gamble company, kraft inc and general mills inc.The group operates from United States.

Primary SIC and add'l.: 4213

CIK No: 0000799167

Officers: Randolph L. Marten/Chmn., CEO, Pres./$510,872.00, James J. Hinnendael/CFO/$294,389.00, Tom Letscher/Sec., Robert G. Smith/COO/$273,983.00, Donald J. Hinson/VP - Operations/$194,237.00, Timothy P. Nash/Exec. VP - Sales, Marketing/$246,332.00

Directors: Randolph L. Marten/Chmn., CEO, Pres., Larry B. Hagness/Dir., Christine K. Marten/Dir., Roger Marten/Founder, Thomas J. Winkel/Dir., Jerry M. Bauer/Dir.

Owners: Jerry M. Bauer, Insiders/30.80%, Donald J. Hinson, Randolph L. Marten/23.50%, Thomas J. Winkel, Robert G. Smith, NWQ Investment Management Company, LLC/10.70%, James J. Hinnendael, Timothy P. Nash, Christine K. Marten/6.80%, Larry B. Hagness, FMR Corp/5.90%, Dimensional Fund Advisors LP/5.00%

Financial Data: *Fiscal Year End:*12/31 *Latest Annual Data:* 12/31/2006

Year	Sales	Net Income
2006	$518,890,000	$24,518,000
2005	$460,202,000	$25,061,000
2004	$380,048,000	$17,536,000

Curr. Assets:	$76,510,000	**Curr. Liab.:**	$59,422,000	**P/E Ratio:**	19.81
Plant, Equip.:	$329,888,000	**Total Liab.:**	$188,916,000	**Indic. Yr. Divd.:**	NA
Total Assets:	$410,822,000	**Net Worth:**	$220,993,000	**Debt/ Equity:**	0.2881

Martha Stewart Living Omnimedia Inc

11 W 42nd St., New York, NY, 10036; *PH:* 1-212-827-8000; *Fax:* 1-212-827-8204;
http:// www.marthastewart.com

General - Incorporation	DE	**Stock**- Price on:12/24/2007	$17.53
Employees	755	Stock Exchange	NYSE
Auditor	Ernst & Young LLP	Ticker Symbol	NA
Stk Agt	Mellon Investor Services LLC	Outstanding Shares	53,350,000
Counsel	NA	E.P.S	-$0.13
DUNS No.	NA	Shareholders	NA

Business: The group's principal activities are to provide content and domestic merchandise related to home, cooking and entertainment, gardening, crafts, holidays, keeping, and kids. The group operates in four segments: publishing, television, merchandising and Internet/direct commerce. Publishing segment includes operations related to magazines, books, radio, newspapers and music. Television segment includes production of new television programming and its distribution. Merchandising segment includes the design of merchandise and related packaging, promotional and advertising materials. Internet/direct commerce segment include operations related to Internet and catalog business. The products of the group are marketed under the 'martha stewart' brand name.

Primary SIC and add'l.: 2721 2731 7375 7812 5961 5994 7379

CIK No: 0001091801

Subsidiaries: Body & Soul Omnimedia, Inc., Martha Stewart, Inc., MSLO Productions EDF, Inc., MSLO Productions Home, Inc., MSLO Productions, Inc., MSO IP Holdings, Inc., MSO Productions, Inc., MSX UK Limited

Officers: Susan Lyne/58/Dir., CEO, Pres./$4,405,782.00, Holly Brown/41/Pres. - Internet, Carolyn Licata/Sales Planner, Midwest, Kyle Wenzel/Sales Associate, West Coast, Jennifer Cernitz/Sales Associate, Northeast, David Lamarca/Sales Associate, Southeast, Wendy Robbins/Sales Dir. - Midwest, Gina Johnson/Sales Mgr. - Midwest, Mark Burnett/Executive Producer, Sarah Carey/Depty Food Editor, Margaret Roach/Editorial Dir., Bernie Young/Co - Executive Producer, Katie Spear/Contact - Digital Advertising Sales, Marketing Inquiries, Rhonda Bitterman/Sales Dir. - Northeast, Viktoria Degtar/Sales Dir. - Southeast *(22 Officers included in Index)*

Directors: Susan Lyne/58/Dir., CEO, Pres., Charles A. Koppelman/68/Chmn., Michael Goldstein/66/Dir., Thomas C. Siekman/67/Dir., Bradley E. Singer/42/Dir., Martha Stewart/Founder, Rick Boyko/59/Dir., Jill A. Greenthal/Dir.

Owners: Susan Lyne/1.70%, Sheraton Kalouria, Insiders/7.10%, Robin Marino, Rick Boyko, Michael Goldstein, Howard Hochhauser, FMR Corporation/5.70%, Lauren Stanich, Martha Stewart/53.90%, Charles A. Koppelman/3.00%, Thomas C. Siekman, Bradley E. Singer, Wenda Harris Millard, Jill A. Greenthal *(17 Owners included in Index)*

Financial Data: *Fiscal Year End:*12/31 *Latest Annual Data:* 03/31/2007

Year	Sales	Net Income
2007	NA	NA
2006	$288,341,000	-$16,995,000
2005	$209,462,000	-$75,789,000

Curr. Assets:	$147,564,000	**Curr. Liab.:**	$74,753,000		
Plant, Equip.:	$19,616,000	**Total Liab.:**	$97,090,000	**Indic. Yr. Divd.:**	NA
Total Assets:	$228,047,000	**Net Worth:**	$130,957,000	**Debt/ Equity:**	NA

Martin Marietta Materials Inc

2710 Wycliff Rd., Raleigh, NC, 27607; *PH:* 1-919-781-4550; *Fax:* 1-919-783-4695;
http:// www.martinmarietta.com

General - Incorporation	NC	**Stock**- Price on:12/24/2007	$168.77
Employees	5,500	Stock Exchange	AMEX
Auditor	Ernst & Young LLP	Ticker Symbol	MLP
Stk Agt	American Stock Transfer & Trust Co.	Outstanding Shares	NA
Counsel	NA	E.P.S	$6.08
DUNS No.	19-649-7184	Shareholders	NA

Business: The groups principle activity is to produce construction aggregates including crushed stone, sand and gravel to build roads, sidewalks and foundations. The groups products include asphalt and concrete, and composite materials. The group operates from United States.

Primary SIC and add'l.: 1442 1423 3297 1422

CIK No: 0000916076

Subsidiaries: Alamo Gulf Coast Railroad Company, a Texas corporation, Alamo North Texas Railroad Company, a Texas corporation, American Aggregates Corporation, a Delaware corporation, American Stone Company, a North Carolina corporation, Bahama Rock Limited, a Bahamas corporation, Central Rock Company, a North Carolina corporation, City Wide Rock & Excavating Co., a Nebraska corporation, Fredonia Valley Railroad, Inc., a Delaware corporation, Granite Canyon Quarry, a Wyoming joint venture, Harding Street Corporation, a Delaware corporation, Hunt Martin Materials, LLC, a Delaware limited liability company, J.W. Jones Materials, LLC, a Delaware limited liability company, Martin Marietta Composites, Inc., a Delaware corporation

Officers: Stephen P. Zelnak/Chmn., CEO/$9,474,537.00, Daniel G. Shephard/Exec. VP/$1,289,121.00, Anne H. Lloyd/CFO, Sr. VP, Treasurer/$1,142,183.00, Jonathan T. Stewart/Sr. VP - Human Resources, Philip J. Sipling/Exec. VP/$2,026,135.00, Roselyn R. Bar/Sr. VP, General Counsel, Corp. Sec., Howard C. Nye/COO, Pres., Michael J. Pertsch/Sr. VP, George S. Seamen/VP - Operations, Donald M. Moe/Sr. VP/$2,126,921.00, Bruce A. Vaio/Exec. VP/$1,192,353.00, Dana F. Guzzo/Chief Accounting Officer, VP, Controller

Directors: Stephen P. Zelnak/Chmn., CEO, Richard A. Vinroot/Dir., David G. Maffucci/Dir., Frank H. Menaker/Dir., Marcus C. Bennett/Dir., Laree E. Perez/Dir., Sue W. Cole/Dir., William E. McDonald/Dir., Dennis L. Rediker/Dir.

Owners: Philip J. Sipling, Davis Selected Advisers, L.P/6.80%, Daniel G. Shephard, Frank H. Menaker, Insiders, William E. McDonald, Davis Selected Advisers, L.P/14.40%, Dennis L. Rediker, Bruce A. Vaio, Sue W. Cole, David G. Maffucci, Laree E. Perez, Marcus C. Bennett, Stephen P. Zelnak, Richard A. Vinroot *(18 Owners included in Index)*

Financial Data: *Fiscal Year End:*12/31 *Latest Annual Data:* 12/31/2006

Year	Sales	Net Income
2006	$2,206,401,000	$245,422,000
2005	$2,004,243,000	$192,666,000
2004	$1,759,613,000	$129,163,000

Curr. Assets:	$592,354,000	**Curr. Liab.:**	$315,072,000	**P/E Ratio:**	29.92
Plant, Equip.:	$1,295,491,000	**Total Liab.:**	$1,252,449,000	**Indic. Yr. Divd.:**	$1.380
Total Assets:	$2,506,421,000	**Net Worth:**	$1,253,972,000	**Debt/ Equity:**	0.5780

Martin Midstream Partners LP

4200 Stone Rd., Kilgore, TX, 75662; *PH:* 1-903-983-6200; *Fax:* 1-903-983-6262;
http:// www.martinmidstream.com; *Email:* info@martinmidstream.com

General - Incorporation	DE	**Stock**- Price on:12/24/2007	$40.8399
Employees	NA	Stock Exchange	NYSE
Auditor	KPMG LLP	Ticker Symbol	MMP
Stk Agt	Mellon Investor Services LLC	Outstanding Shares	13,160,000
Counsel	NA	E.P.S	$1.773
DUNS No.	NA	Shareholders	NA

Business: The groups principal activities include collecting, transporting, storing and distributing petroleum products. The groups operates through five segments namely erminalling and storage, natural gas services, marine transportation, sulfur and fertilizer. The group acquired Gulf States Asphalt Company LP and Prime Materials and Supply Corporation in the year 2006 and Prism Gas in the year 2005. The group operates from the United States. The groups operates through five segments namely terminalling and storage $24,182, natural gas services $389,735, marine transportation $47,835, sulfur $61,271and fertilizer $41,326 (thousands).

Primary SIC and add'l.: 2874 5984 2873 5171

CIK No: 0001176334

Subsidiaries: Martin Operating GP LLC, Martin Operating Partnership L.P., McLeod Gas Gathering and Processing Company, L.L.C., Prism Gas Systems GP, L.L.C., Prism Gas Systems I, L.P., Prism Gulf Coast Systems, L.L.C.

Officers: Ruben S. Martin/Chmn., CEO, Pres., Scott D. Martin/Dir., Exec. VP, Jeff Posey/Sales Mgr. - Southern Region, Ken Mull/Contact - Agricultural Sales, Robert D. Bondurant/CFO, Exec. VP, Donald R. Neumeyer/COO, Exec. VP, Wesley M. Skelton/Exec. VP, Controller, Chief Administrative

Officer, Chris Booth/38/VP, General Counsel, Sec., Tom Redd/VP - LPG Sales, Muggs Athey/Propane Sales Mgr., Linda Dougan/Distribution, Exchange Coordinator, Jimmie Grant/South Texas Sales Mgr., John Edwards/Arkansas, Louisiana Sales Mgr., W. H. Wofford/Mgr. - Sales, AL, FL, NC, SC, TN, George Moon/Mississippi, Alabama Sales Mgr. *(23 Officers included in Index)*

Directors: Ruben S. Martin/Chmn., CEO, Pres., Scott D. Martin/Dir., Exec. VP, John P. Gaylord/Dir., Scott C. Massey/Dir., Howard Hackney/Dir.

Owners: Scott D. Martin, Martin Product Sales LLC, Donald R. Neumeyer, Midstream Fuel Service LLC, Kayne Anderson Capital Advisors,L.P., Wesley M. Skelton, Scott C. Massey, Insiders, Martin Resource LLC, Robert D. Bondurant, Martin Resource Management Corporation, Howard Hackney, Chris Booth, John P. Gaylord, Ruben S. Martin

Financial Data: Fiscal Year End:12/31 **Latest Annual Data:** 12/31/2006

Year	Sales	Net Income
2006	$576,384,000	$22,243,000
2005	$438,443,000	$13,880,000
2004	$294,144,000	$12,326,000

Curr. Assets:	$103,853,000	**Curr. Liab.:**	$82,697,000	**P/E Ratio:**	22.94
Plant, Equip.:	$247,845,000	**Total Liab.:**	$258,936,000	**Indic. Yr. Divd.:**	$2.560
Total Assets:	$457,461,000	**Net Worth:**	$198,525,000	**Debt/ Equity:**	0.9755

Marvel Entertainment Inc

417 5th Ave., 11th Fl., New York, NY, 10016; **PH:** 1-212-576-4000; **Fax:** 1-212-576-8517; *http://* www.marvel.com

General - Incorporation	DE	**Stock**- Price on:12/24/2007	NA
Employees	255	Stock Exchange	NYSE
Auditor	PricewaterhouseCoopers LLP	Ticker Symbol	MVL
Stk Agt	American Stock Transfer & Trust Co.	Outstanding Shares	85,290,000
Counsel	NA	E.P.S.	$1.47
DUNS No.	18-582-5569	Shareholders	NA

Business: The group's principal activities are to license comic characters, publish comic books and develop and market toys. It has a proprietary library of over 4,700 characters. The group's operations are carried out through three business segments: toy biz, licensing and publishing. Toy biz designs, develops, markets and distributes a limited line of toys to the worldwide marketplace. Toy biz's products are based upon movies and television shows featuring spider-man and produced by sony pictures and upon the movie trilogy lord of the rings. Licensing division licenses the company's characters for use in a wide variety of products, including toys, electronic games, apparel, accessories, footwear, collectibles and novelties. Publishing division of the group publishes comic books. On 18-Dec-2003, the group acquired cover concepts.

Primary SIC and add'l.: 2731 3942 3944

CIK No: 0000933730

Subsidiaries: Marvel Characters, Inc., Marvel Entertainment International Limited, Marvel Entertainment Japan Limited, Marvel Property, Inc., Marvel Publishing, Inc., Marvel Studios, Inc., Marvel Toys Limited, MRV, Inc., MVL Film Finance LLC, MVL Productions LLC, MVL Rights LLC, Spider-Man Merchandising L.P., Toy Biz International Limited

Officers: Alan Fine/CEO - Publishing, Toy Divisions, Exec. VP/$1,181,351.00, Isaac Perlmutter/Vice Chmn., CEO/$3,371,176.00, John N. Turitzin/Exec. VP - Office, Chief Executive/$1,523,296.00, David Maisel/Exec. VP - Office, Chief Executive/$5,247,923.00, Kenneth West/CFO, Exec. VP/$607,612.00, Jeff Klein/Exec. VP - Media Relation, Benjamin Dean/Sec., Dan Klores/Communications, Media Relations

Directors: Isaac Perlmutter/Vice Chmn., CEO, Peter F. Cuneo/Vice Chmn., Morton E. Handel/Chmn., James F. Halpin/Dir., Sid Ganis/Dir., Richard L. Solar/Dir., Jim Breyer/Dir., Laurence N. Charney/Dir.

Owners: David Maisel, John Turitzin, Kenneth P. West, James W. Breyer, Alan Fine, James F. Halpin, Morton E. Handel, Insiders/35.70%, Isaac Perlmutter/34.00%, Timothy Rothwell, Sid Ganis, Artisan Partners Limited Partnership/5.70%, Goldman Sachs Asset Management, L.P./6.20%, Avi Arad/2.00%, Richard L. Solar *(17 Owners included in Index)*

Financial Data: Fiscal Year End:12/31 **Latest Annual Data:** 05/27/2007

Year	Sales	Net Income
2007	$5,567,100,000	$201,400,000
2006	$351,798,000	$58,704,000
2005	$390,507,000	$102,819,000

Curr. Assets:	$193,987,000	**Curr. Liab.:**	$252,546,000		
Plant, Equip.:	$4,444,000	**Total Liab.:**	$368,974,000	**Indic. Yr. Divd.:**	NA
Total Assets:	$623,865,000	**Net Worth:**	$254,891,000	**Debt/ Equity:**	NA

Marvell Technology Group Ltd

5488 Marvell Ln., Santa Clara, CA, 95054; *PH:* 1-408-222-2500; *http://* www.marvell.com

General - Incorporation	Bermuda	**Stock**- Price on:12/24/2007	$17.64
Employees	2,500	Stock Exchange	AMEX
Auditor	PricewaterhouseCoopers LLP	Ticker Symbol	MRY
Stk Agt	NA	Outstanding Shares	585,200,000
Counsel	Sullivan & Cromwell	E.P.S.	-$0.44
DUNS No.	NA	Shareholders	NA

Business: The group's principal activity is to design, develop and market integrated circuits for communication-related markets. The group operates through two segments: storage product and broadband communication products. Storage product consists of read channel, system-on-chip and preamplifier products. Broadband communication products consist of transceiver products, switching products, internetworking products and wireless LAN products. The products of the group provide critical interface between analog signals and the digital information used in computing and communication systems. The group operates in Bermuda, Israel, the United States and other countries. On 27-Jun-2003, the group acquired radlan computer communications ltd.

Primary SIC and add'l.: 3679 3674

CIK No: 0001058057

Subsidiaries: Marvell Asia Pte Ltd, Marvell GmbH, Marvell Hong Kong Limited, Marvell India Private Limited, Marvell International Ltd., Marvell Italia S.r.l., Marvell Japan K.K., Marvell Semiconductor Israel Ltd., Marvell Semiconductor Korea, Ltd., Marvell Semiconductor,Inc., Marvell Switzerland S.A.R.L., Marvell T.I. Ltd., Marvell Taiwan Ltd., Marvell Technology (Beijing) Ltd., Marvell Technology Japan Y.K. 23 Subsidiaries included in the Index

Officers: Sehat Sutardja/Chmn., CEO, Pres./$10,286,260.00, Gani Jusuf/VP - Product Development, Communications, Consumer Business Group, Hoo Kuong/VP, GM - Marvell Asia Pte, Ltd, Eliaz Lavi/VP, GM - Marvell Semiconductor Israel Ltd, Communications, Consumer Business Group, Bouchung Lin/VP, GM - Marvell Taiwan Ltd, Communications, Consumer Business Group,

Simon Milner/VP, GM - Enterprise Business Unit, Communications, Consumer Business Group, Partho Mishra/VP - Software Engineering, Communications, Consumer Business Group, Michelle Oakes/VP - Worldwide Human Resources, General Employment Counsel, Thomas Ruf/VP - Product Development, Syskonnect Gmbh, Communications, Consumer Business Group, Lawrence Tse/VP - Engineering, Wireless Products, Communications, Consumer Business Group, Albert Wu/VP - Operations, David Y. Young/VP, GM - Connectivity Business Unit, Communications, Consumer Business Group, Michael Rashkin/Interim CFO, VP - Strategic Development, VP - Taxes, Sam Azimi/VP - System, On, Chip Development, Storage Business Group, Yuval Cohen/VP, GM - Marvell Software Solutions Israel *(24 Officers included in Index)*

Directors: Sehat Sutardja/Chmn., CEO, Pres., Arturo Krueger/Dir., Mike Sophie/Dir., Juergen W. Gromer/Dir., Pantas Sutardja/Dir., CTO, Paul R. Gray/Dir., Kuo Wei Chang/Dir.

Owners: Pantas Sutardja/6.90%, Sehat Sutardja/12.70%, Weili Dai/12.70%, Insiders/19.90%, T. Rowe Price Associates, Inc/10.70%, Prudential Financial, Inc./6.10%, FMR Corp/15.00%, Arturo Krueger, George Hervey, Kuo Wei Chang, Douglas King, Paul R. Gray

Financial Data: Fiscal Year End:01/28 **Latest Annual Data:** 01/27/2007

Year	Sales	Net Income
2007	$2,237,553,000	-$12,095,000
2006	$1,670,266,000	$331,363,000
2005	$1,224,580,000	$141,661,000

Curr. Assets:	$1,499,874,000	**Curr. Liab.:**	$332,748,000		
Plant, Equip.:	$260,921,000	**Total Liab.:**	$467,192,000	**Indic. Yr. Divd.:**	NA
Total Assets:	$3,513,289,000	**Net Worth:**	$3,046,097,000	**Debt/ Equity:**	0.0071

Marwich II Ltd

203 N Lasalle St., Ste. 2100, Chicago, IL, 60601; **PH:** 1-312-264-2682

General - Incorporation	CO	**Stock**- Price on:12/24/2007	$13
Employees	2	Stock Exchange	OTC
Auditor	Marwich Ii, Ltd.	Ticker Symbol	MWII
Stk Agt	NA	Outstanding Shares	3,790,000
Counsel	Mr. Weiss	E.P.S.	-$0.03
DUNS No.	NA	Shareholders	NA

Business: The groups principle activity is to provide acquisition of assets and properties. The group operates from United States.

Primary SIC and add'l.: 6531

CIK No: 0000738214

Officers: Eric A. McAfee/44/Dir., CEO, Pres., William J. Maender/61/Dir., CFO, Sec.

Directors: Eric A. McAfee/44/Dir., CEO, Pres., William J. Maender/61/Dir., CFO, Sec.

Owners: American Ethanol, Inc./88.30%

Financial Data: Fiscal Year End:01/31 **Latest Annual Data:** 1/31/2007

Year	Sales	Net Income
2007	NA	-$104,000
2006	$13,310,869,000	$2,117,471,000
2005	$10,893,508,000	$1,987,239,000

Curr. Assets:	NA	**Curr. Liab.:**	$91,000		
Plant, Equip.:	NA	**Total Liab.:**	$91,000	**Indic. Yr. Divd.:**	NA
Total Assets:	NA	**Net Worth:**	-$91,000	**Debt/ Equity:**	NA

Masco Corp

21001 Van Born Rd., Taylor, MI, 48180; **PH:** 1-313-274-7400; **Fax:** 1-313-792-6135; *http://* www.masco.com

General - Incorporation	DE	**Stock**- Price on:12/24/2007	$28.71
Employees	57,000	Stock Exchange	NYSE
Auditor	PricewaterhouseCoopers LLP	Ticker Symbol	MAS
Stk Agt	Bank of New York	Outstanding Shares	377,700,000
Counsel	NA	E.P.S.	$0.92
DUNS No.	00-532-0924	Shareholders	NA

Business: The group's principle activities include manufacturing, distributing and installing home improvement and building products. The group operates through five segments namely cabinet and related, plumbing, installation and other services, decorative architectural and specialty products. In the year 2007the group acquired Erickson Construction Company and Guy Evans, Inc. The group operates from United States.

Primary SIC and add'l.: 3399 2514 3432 1796 2434 3088 2851

CIK No: 0000062996

Subsidiaries: Airex, LLC, Alsons Corporation, American Shower & Bath Corporation, Aqua Glass Corporation, Aran World, Inc., Arrow Fastener Co., Inc., Beacon Hill Fine Art Corporation, Behr Holdings Corporation, Behr Paint Corp., Behr Paints It!, Inc., Behr Process Canada Ltd., Behr Process Corporation, BPC Realty LLC, Brass-Craft Manufacturing Company, Brasstech de Mexico, S.A. DE C.V. 30 Subsidiaries included in the Index

Officers: Richard A. Manoogian/Chmn., CEO/$17,293,100.00, John R. Leekley/64/Sr. VP, General Counsel/$2,716,051.00, Daniel R. Foley/VP - Human Resources/$2,234,283.00, Eugene A. Gargaro/65/VP, Sec., John G. Sznewajs/40/VP - Corporate Development, Treasurer, Alan H. Barry/65/COO, Pres./$6,798,260.00, Timothy Wadhams/59/CFO, Sr. VP/$2,356,118.00

Directors: Richard A. Manoogian/Chmn., CEO, Thomas G. Denomme/68/Dir., Mary Ann Van Lokeren/60/Dir., Dennis W. Archer/66/Dir., Peter A. Dow/74/Dir., Anthony F. Earley/58/Dir., Verne G. Istock/67/Dir., David L. Johnston/66/Dir., Michael J. Losh/61/Dir., Lisa A. Payne/49/Dir.

Owners: UBS AG/13.80%, Michael J. Losh, Lisa A. Payne, Verne G. Istock, David L. Johnston, Peter A. Dow, David A. Doran, Massachusetts Financial Services Company/6.80%, Timothy Wadhams, John R. Leekley, Richard A. Manoogian/2.90%, Dodge& Cox/6.40%, Thomas G. Denomme, Dennis W. Archer, Alan H. Barry *(19 Owners included in Index)*

Financial Data: Fiscal Year End:12/31 **Latest Annual Data:** 12/31/2006

Year	Sales	Net Income
2006	$12,778,000,000	$488,000,000
2005	$12,642,000,000	$940,000,000
2004	$12,074,000,000	$893,000,000

Curr. Assets:	$5,115,000,000	**Curr. Liab.:**	$3,389,000,000	**P/E Ratio:**	26.58
Plant, Equip.:	$2,363,000,000	**Total Liab.:**	$7,854,000,000	**Indic. Yr. Divd.:**	$0.920
Total Assets:	$12,325,000,000	**Net Worth:**	$4,471,000,000	**Debt/ Equity:**	0.7902

Masisa

Av. Apoquindo 3650, Piso 10, Las Condes, Santiago; *PH:* 56-27078800; *http://* www.masisa.com; *Email:* info@masisa.com.ar

General - Incorporation	Chile	Stock - Price on:12/24/2007	$13.6993
Employees	4,782	Stock Exchange	NYSE
Auditor	PricewaterhouseCoopers LLP	Ticker Symbol	MYS
Stk Agt	The Bank Of Nova Scotia	Outstanding Shares	107,870,000
Counsel	NA	E.P.S.	$0.30
DUNS No.	98-019-6075	Shareholders	NA

Business: The group's principal activities are investments; and manufacture and sale of raw, melamine laminated and wood veneered particle board, medium density fiberboard and wood doors for residential and commercial applications, for sale principally in Chile, Argentina and Brazil. It exports its goods in North America, central and South America, Asia and Europe.

Primary SIC and add'l.: 2493 2499 2448 0811 5031

CIK No: 0000900335

Subsidiaries: Forestal Argentina S.A., Forestal Ro Calle-Calle S.A., Forestal Tornagaleones S.A., Inversiones Coige Dos S.A., Inversiones Coronel Ltda, Maderas y Sintticos de Mexico, S.A. de C.V., Maderas y Sintticos del Per S.A.C, Masisa Argentina, Masisa Brazil, Masisa Concepcin Ltda., Masisa do Brasil Ltda., Masisa Ecuador S.A., Masisa Inversiones Ltda., Masisa Mexico, Masisa Overseas Ltd 18 Subsidiaries included in the Index

Officers: Enrique B. Cibie/CEO, Jaime F. Valenzuela/Chief Officer - Boards, Patricio U. Reyes/General Counsel, Alejandro B. Droste/COO - Retail, Maria Emilia Correa/Chief, Sustainable Development Officer, Jorge D. Correa/Chief Officer - Forestry Division, Ronald Jean Degen/Dir., VP, Julio Moura/Dir., Pres., Claudio H. Cerda/Chief Officer - Solid Wood Division, Eugenio I. Arteaga/CFO, Ana Maria Rabagliati/Chief Human Resources Officer, Matias G.H. MacKenna/Corporate Development Officer, Rosangela Mac Cord Faria/Corporate Governance Mgr. - Auditoria, Luis W. Zuniga/Chief Audit Executive

Directors: Enrique Seguel/Dir., Antonio Tuset/Dir., Ronald Jean Degen/Dir., VP, Julio Moura/Dir., Pres., Patrick Nielson/Dir., Juan Carlos Mendez/Dir., Jorge Carey/Dir.

Financial Data: Fiscal Year End: 12/31   *Latest Annual Data:* 12/31/2006

Year	Sales	Net Income
2006	$886,507,000	$24,539,000
2004	$397,312,000	$41,304,000
2003	$281,826,000	$11,095,000
Curr. Assets:	$466,528,000	Curr. Liab.:	$258,525,000		
Plant, Equip.:	$1,358,041,000	Total Liab.:	$821,156,000	Indic. Yr. Divd.:	$0.070
Total Assets:	$1,758,751,000	Net Worth:	$937,595,000	Debt/ Equity:	NA

Mass Megawatts Wind Power Inc

PO Box 60398, Worcester, MA, 01606; *PH:* 1-508-755-4432; *http://* www.massmegawatts.com; *Email:* info@massmegawatts.com

General - Incorporation	MA	Stock - Price on:12/24/2007	$0.73
Employees	NA	Stock Exchange	OTC
Auditor	Malone & Bailey, P.C	Ticker Symbol	MMGW
Stk Agt	OTC Corporate Transfer Service Co	Outstanding Shares	3,770,000
Counsel	NA	E.P.S.	-$0.08
DUNS No.	NA	Shareholders	NA

Business: The group's principle activities include building and operating wind energy power plants and sell the electricity to the electric power exchange. Multiaxis turbosystem, product of the company provides free, clean, inexhaustible power source to convert wind energy into electricity. The company has got exclusive license to market multiaxis turbosystem (mat) and any associated technology relative to wind velocity augmentation in Massachusetts, New York, New Jersey, Pennsylvania, California, Illinois, Kansas, Michigan, Minnesota, Nebraska, North Dakota, South Dakota, Texas, Vermont, Washington, and Wisconsin. The group operates from United States.

Primary SIC and add'l.: 3511

CIK No: 0001117228

Officers: Jonathan Ricker/Chmn., CEO, Adrian Price/Principal Mechanical Engineer, Michael A. Cook/Consultant, Project Finance Advisor, Thomas M. Dill/Consulting Dir. - Corporate Services, Thomas McBride/COO

Directors: Jonathan Ricker/Chmn., CEO

Owners: Insiders, Jonathan Ricker, Jodi A. Vizzo, Thomas Weisz, Allison Gray

Financial Data: Fiscal Year End: 04/30   *Latest Annual Data:* 04/30/2007

Year	Sales	Net Income
2007	NA	-$328,000
2006	NA	-$317,000
2005	NA	-$696,000
Curr. Assets:	$20,000	Curr. Liab.:	$206,000		
Plant, Equip.:	$10,000	Total Liab.:	$206,000	Indic. Yr. Divd.:	NA
Total Assets:	$30,000	Net Worth:	-$176,000	Debt/ Equity:	NA

Massbank Corp

123 HAve.n St., Reading, MA, 01867; *PH:* 1-781-662-0100; *Fax:* 1-781-942-8194; *http://* www.massbank.com

General - Incorporation	DE	Stock - Price on:12/24/2007	$32.79
Employees	107	Stock Exchange	NDQ
Auditor	Parent, McLaughlin & Nangle	Ticker Symbol	MASB
Stk Agt	American Stock Transfer & Trust CO.	Outstanding Shares	4,340,000
Counsel	Goodwin, Procter & Hoar	E.P.S.	$1.60
DUNS No.	01-976-1188	Shareholders	NA

Business: The group's principal activity is to attract deposits from the general public through fifteen full service banking offices. The services provided by the group include originating residential and commercial real estate mortgages, construction loans and variety of consumer loans. The group also provides a variety of investment, trust and estate planning services and serves as trustee, executor and executor agent for bank customers. The group offers its services in reading, chelmsford, dracut, everett, lowell, medford, melrose, stoneham, tewksbury, westford and wilmington located in Massachusetts.

Primary SIC and add'l.: 6712 6022

CIK No: 0000799166

Subsidiaries: Melbank Investment Corporation, Readibank Investment Corporation, Readibank Properties, Inc.

Officers: Gerard H. Brandi/59/Chmn., CEO, Pres./$784,855.00, Robert S. Cummings/Sec., Reginald E. Cormier/59/CFO, Sr. VP, Treasurer/$219,669.00, Donna H. West/62/Assist. Sec./$281,396.00

Directors: Gerard H. Brandi/59/Chmn., CEO, Pres., William F. Rucci/48/Dir., Allan S. Bufferd/70/Dir., Kathleen M. Camilli/49/Dir., Stephen W. Carr/65/Dir., Alexander S. Costello/54/Dir., Bradley O. Latham/67/Dir., Stephen E. Marshall/69/Dir., Nancy L. Pettinelli/61/Dir., Paul J. McCarthy/Dir., Nalin M. Mistry/65/Dir.

Owners: Bradley O. Latham, Alexander S. Costello, Dimensional FundAdvisors LP/6.20%, Kathleen M. Camilli, Private Capital Management, L.P./9.10%, Mathias B. Bedell, Stephen E. Marshall, James L. Milinazzo, Nancy L. Pettinelli, William F. Rucci, Reginald E. Cormier/1.60%, Gerard H. Brandi/6.10%, Stephen W. Carr, Insiders/11.40%, Allan S. Bufferd (17 Owners included in Index)

Financial Data: Fiscal Year End: 12/31   *Latest Annual Data:* 12/31/2006

Year	Sales	Net Income
2006	$42,144,000	$7,027,000
2005	$38,665,000	$7,323,000
2004	$36,199,000	$7,380,000
Curr. Assets:	$195,992,000	Curr. Liab.:	$724,338,000	P/E Ratio:	20.49
Plant, Equip.:	$7,510,000	Total Liab.:	$736,637,000	Indic. Yr. Divd.:	$1.120
Total Assets:	$843,522,000	Net Worth:	$106,885,000	Debt/ Equity:	0.0123

Massey Energy Co

4 N 4th St., Richmond, VA, 23219; *PH:* 1-804-788-1800; *Fax:* 1-804-788-1870; *http://* www.masseycoal.com

General - Incorporation	DE	Stock - Price on:12/24/2007	$27.84
Employees	5,517	Stock Exchange	NYSE
Auditor	Ernst & Young LLP	Ticker Symbol	MEE
Stk Agt	Wells Fargo Shareowner Services	Outstanding Shares	81,100,000
Counsel	NA	E.P.S.	$1.20
DUNS No.	00-690-7190	Shareholders	NA

Business: The groups principle activities include producing, processing and selling bituminous coal of steam and metallurgical grades. The group operates from United States.

Primary SIC and add'l.: 1241 1222 1221

CIK No: 0000037748

Subsidiaries: A. T. Massey Coal Company, Inc., Alex Energy, Inc., Aracoma Coal Company, Inc., Bandmill Coal Corporation, Bandytown Coal Company, Barnabus Land Company, Belfry Coal Corporation, Ben Creek Coal Company, Big Bear Mining Company, Big Sandy Venture Capital Corp., Black King Mine Development Co., Blue Ridge Venture Capital Corp., Boone East Development Co., Boone Energy Company, Boone West Development Co. 111 Subsidiaries included in the Index

Officers: Don L. Blankenship/57/Chmn., CEO, Pres/$5,328,422.00, John M. Poma/42/VP - Human Resources, Christopher J. Adkins/43/COO, Sr. VP, Drexel H. Short/51/Sr. VP - Group Operations, Richard R. Grinnan/39/VP, Corp. Sec., John Parker/Sr. VP - Massey Utility Sales Company, Michael Allen/Pres. - Massey Metallurgical Coal, Steve Sears/Pres. - Massey Industrial Sales Company, Gary Smith/VP - Massey Industrial Sales Company, Gary Temple/Sales Representative - Massey Industrial Sales Company, Tom Kielty/VP - Massey Traffic, Distribution, J. C. Adkins/COO, Sr. VP/$1,098,027.00, Philip W. Nichols/Treasurer - Massey Energy, Michael D. Bauersachs/42/VP - Planning, Shane M. Harvey/VP, Assist. General Counsel (22 Officers included in Index)

Directors: Don L. Blankenship/57/Chmn., CEO, Pres., Robert H. Foglesong/61/Dir., Richard M. Gabrys/63/Dir., Baxter F. Phillips/61/Dir., Exec. VP, Chief Administrative Officer, Bobby R. Inman/75/Dir., James B. Crawford/64/Dir., William R. Grant/Dir., Martha R. Seger/Dir., Gordon E. Gee/63/Dir., Daniel S. Loeb/46/Dir., Dan R. Moore/66/Dir., Todd Q. Swanson/33/Dir.

Owners: Christopher J. Adkins, Franklin Mutual Advisers, LLC/6.00%, Third Point LLC/6.00%, Robert H. Foglesong, Schneider Capital Management Corporation/5.00%, Drexel H. Short, BlackRock, Inc./14.00%, Lazard Asset Management, LLC/14.00%, Eric B. Tolbert, FMR Corp./11.00%, Bobby R. Inman, Insiders/7.00%

Financial Data: Fiscal Year End: 12/31   *Latest Annual Data:* 12/31/2006

Year	Sales	Net Income
2006	$2,219,854,000	$40,977,000
2005	$2,204,258,000	-$101,638,000
2004	$1,766,644,000	$13,852,000
Curr. Assets:	$799,728,000	Curr. Liab.:	$354,537,000	P/E Ratio:	33.14
Plant, Equip.:	$1,776,781,000	Total Liab.:	$2,043,405,000	Indic. Yr. Divd.:	$0.200
Total Assets:	$2,740,696,000	Net Worth:	$697,291,000	Debt/ Equity:	NA

Mastec Inc

800 Douglas Rd., 12th Fl., Coral Gables, FL, 33134; *PH:* 1-305-599-1800; *Fax:* 1-305-406-1960; *http://* www.mastec.com; *Email:* services@mastec.com

General - Incorporation	FL	Stock - Price on:12/24/2007	$15.39
Employees	9,260	Stock Exchange	NYSE
Auditor	BDO Seidman, LLP	Ticker Symbol	MU
Stk Agt	American Stock Transfer & Trust Co.	Outstanding Shares	65,610,000
Counsel	NA	E.P.S.	-$0.45
DUNS No.	00-692-4385	Shareholders	NA

Business: The group's principal activity is to provide end-to-end communication, broadband and energy infrastructure services for clients in North America and Brazil. The group designs, builds, installs, maintains, upgrades and monitors internal and external networks and other facilities for its clients. The group also provides services related to the installation of integrated voice, data and video local and wide area networks within office buildings and underground locating, construction and maintenance services to utilities. These services are provided primarily to incumbent local exchange carriers, cable television operators, long distance carriers, wireless service providers, government agencies, public and private energy companies and financial institutions. The group's clients include adelphia communications corporation, bellsouth corporation, carolina power and light company, comcast corporation, time warner inc and sprint corp.

Primary SIC and add'l.: 1623 7379 1731

CIK No: 0000015615

Subsidiaries: Acietel Mexicana, S.A., Aidco de Mexico, S.A. de C.V., Burntel Telecommunications, C.A., Church & Tower, Inc., CIDE Engenharia, Ltda., Direct Star TV LLC, f/k/a Central America Construction, Inc., Globetec Construction, LLC, Integral Power & Telecommunications Incorporated, MasTec Asset Management Company, Inc., MasTec Brasil S/A, MasTec Brazil II, Inc., MasTec Brazil, Inc., MasTec Contracting Company, Inc., MasTec FC, Inc. 33 Subsidiaries included in the Index

Officers: Jose R. Mas/Dir., CEO, Pres./$481,380.00, Bob Apple/COO, Barry J. Batson/VP - Business Development Electric Utility, Ramon Mas/Sr. VP - Business Development, Larry Burch/VP - Government Services, Chris Brown/Operations Mgr. - Florida, Malek Rais/Operations Mgr. - Georgia, Oscar Pena/Operations Mgr. - Georgia, Bryan Westerman/Group Pres. - Communications, Jerry Martin/Operations Mgr. - Georgia, Wanzel Jessie/Region VP - Georgia, Paul Zucha/Operations Mgr. - NEW Mexico, Patrick Thompson/Operations Mgr. - North Carolina, Eddie Phillips/Operations Mgr. - North Carolina, Joe Parsons/Operations Mgr. - Texas (28 Officers included in Index)

Directors: Jose R. Mas/Dir., CEO, Pres., Jorge Mas/Chmn., Austin Shanfelter/Dir., Ernst N. Csiszar/Dir., Robert J. Dwyer/Dir., Carlos M. De Cespedes/Dir., Julia L. Johnson/Dir., Jose S. Sorzano/Dir., John Van Heuvelen/Dir., Frank E. Jaumot/Dir.

Owners: Austin Shanfelter/1.61%, John Van Heuvelen, Jorge Mas/29.86%, Jose R. Mas/3.82%, Julia L. Johnson, Jose S. Sorzano, C. Robert Campbell, Robert J. Dwyer, Alberto de Cardenas, FMR Corp./11.81%, Carlos M. de Cespedes, Robert Apple, Insiders/35.31%, Ernst N. Csiszar, Frank E. Jaumot

Financial Data: Fiscal Year End:12/31 Latest Annual Data: 12/31/2006

Year	Sales	Net Income
2006	$945,806,000	-$50,348,000
2005	$848,046,000	-$14,616,000
2004	$913,795,000	-$49,437,000

Curr. Assets:	$339,920,000	Curr. Liab.:	$175,878,000		
Plant, Equip.:	$61,470,000	Total Liab.:	$339,097,000	Indic. Yr. Divd.:	NA
Total Assets:	$646,113,000	Net Worth:	$304,711,000	Debt/ Equity:	NA

Mastercard Inc

2000 Purchase St., Purchase, NY, 10577; **PH:** 1-914-249-2000; **Fax:** 1-914-249-4206; **http://** www.mastercard.com; **Email:** customerservicecenter@mastercard.com

General - Incorporation	DE	Stock- Price on:12/24/2007	$168.8
Employees	4,600	Stock Exchange	NYSE
Auditor	PricewaterhouseCoopers LLP	Ticker Symbol	MA
Stk Agt	Continental Stock T & T Co.	Outstanding Shares	135,090,000
Counsel	NA	E.P.S.	$6.03
DUNS No.	NA	Shareholders	NA

Business: The groups principle activity is to provide services in support of the credit, debit and related payment programs. The group also provides payment solutions, process payment transactions and consulting services. The groups services marketed under the brand names include MasterCard(R), MasterCard Electronic(TM), Maestro(R) and Cirrus(R). The group operates from the United States.

Primary SIC and add'l.: 7322 7375 7389 7374

CIK No: 0001141391

Subsidiaries: Bright Skies LLC, Cirrus System, LLC, Clear Skies LLC, EMVCo, LLC, euro travellers cheque International S.A., Eurocard Limited, EUROCARD U.S.A., Inc., European Payment Systems Services sprl, GVP Holding Incorporated, JNS Corporation Yugen Kaisha, Maestro Asia/Pacific Ltd., Maestro Canada, Inc., Maestro International Incorporated, Maestro Latin America, Inc., Maestro Middle East/Africa, Inc. 89 Subsidiaries included in the Index

Officers: Robert W. Selander/Dir., CEO, Pres./$15,328,760.00, Alan J. Heuer/Vice Chmn., COO/$10,271,540.00, Chris A. McWilton/Pres. - Global Accounting/$2,798,202.00, Walt M. MacNee/Pres. - Global Markets, Michael W. Michl/62/Chief Administrative Officer/$4,560,418.00, Roy W. Dunbar/Pres. - Global Technology, Operations/$5,216,498.00, Gary Flood/Exec. VP - Global Accounting Management, Noah J. Hanft/General Counsel, Corp. Sec./$3,462,450.00, Martina Hund-Mejean/CFO, Diane Dann/Deputy Chief Compliance Officer, Tara Maguire/Corporate Controller

Directors: Robert W. Selander/Dir., CEO, Pres., Richard Haythornthwaite/50/Chmn., Alan J. Heuer/Vice Chmn., COO, David R. Carlucci/52/Dir., Manoel Luiz Ferrao De Amorim/Dir., Steven J. Freiberg/50/Dir., Bernard S.Y. Fung/53/Dir., Norman C. McLuskie/Dir., Marc Olivie/53/Dir., Mark Schwartz/52/Dir., Edward Su-Ning Tian/44/Dir., Nancy J. Karch/60/Dir., Tan Teong Hean/64/Dir.

Owners: HSBC Holdings plc/5.56%, Chris A. McWilton, FMR Corp./6.48%, Christopher D. Thom, JPMorganChase&Co./9.96%, Viking Global/5.08%, Bank of America Corporation/5.50%, Robert W. Selander, Atticus Capital LP/9.25%, The MasterCard Foundation/17.00%, Michael Michl, Citigroup, Inc./9.29%, Insiders, Marsico Capital Management, LLC/13.63%, Lone Pine Capital LLC/6.11% (18 Owners included in Index)

Financial Data: Fiscal Year End:12/31 Latest Annual Data: 12/31/2006

Year	Sales	Net Income
2006	$3,326,074,000	$50,190,000
2005	$2,937,628,000	$266,719,000
2004	$2,593,330,000	$238,060,000

Curr. Assets:	$3,577,229,000	Curr. Liab.:	$1,811,590,000	P/E Ratio:	32.84
Plant, Equip.:	$252,731,000	Total Liab.:	$2,718,111,000	Indic. Yr. Divd.:	$0.600
Total Assets:	$5,082,470,000	Net Worth:	$2,364,359,000	Debt/ Equity:	0.0882

Matav-Cable Systems Media Ltd

42 Pinkas St., N Ind. Pk., Netanya, 42134; ; **http://** www.hot.net.il

General - Incorporation	Israel	Stock- Price on:12/24/2007	NA
Employees	NA	Stock Exchange	NA
Auditor	Kost Forer Gabbay & Kasierer	Ticker Symbol	NA
Stk Agt	Puglisi & Associates	Outstanding Shares	NA
Counsel	NA	E.P.S.	NA
DUNS No.	60-008-1863	Shareholders	NA

Business: The group's principal activity is the provision of broadband cable television services in Israel. It owns substantially all of its cable television network infrastructure and provides cable television services to approximately 26.4% of all cable television subscribers in Israel. The exclusive franchises cover four operating areas, three of which include the major metropolitan areas of bat-yam - holon, haifa, netanya - hadera and one of which serves the less densely populated area of the galilee. Other group's activities include the provision of access to high speed Internet over cable and investment in telecommunications companies.

Primary SIC and add'l.: 4841

CIK No: 0001014925

Subsidiaries: Cable Systems Media Haifa-Hadera Ltd., Matav Infrastructure 2001 L.P., Matav Investments Ltd.

Material Sciences Corp

2200 E Pratt Blvd., Elk Grove Village, IL, 60007; **PH:** 1-847-439-2210; **Fax:** 1-847-439-0737; **http://** www.matsci.com

General - Incorporation	DE	Stock- Price on:12/24/2007	$12.5
Employees	583	Stock Exchange	NYSE
Auditor	Deloitte & Touche LLP	Ticker Symbol	NA
Stk Agt	Mellon Investor Services LLC	Outstanding Shares	14,620,000
Counsel	Kirkland & Ellis LLP	E.P.S.	$0.419
DUNS No.	06-457-2563	Shareholders	NA

Business: The group's principal activity is to provide materials-based solutions for electronic, acoustical or thermal and coated metal applications. The majority of these materials are used in the automotive, building and construction, electronics, lighting and appliance markets. The electronic materials-based solutions consist of coated and laminated noise reducing materials used in the electronics market. The acoustical or thermal materials-based solutions consist of layers of metal and other materials used to manage noise and thermal energy for the automotive, lighting and appliance markets. The coated metal materials-based solutions include coil coated and electrogalvanized products primarily used in the automotive, building and construction, appliance and lighting markets. The group's products and services are sold through independent distributors, agents and licensees.

Primary SIC and add'l.: 3479 3399 3559

CIK No: 0000755003

Subsidiaries: Material Sciences Corporation, Engineered Materials and Solutions Group, Inc., Material Sciences Foreign Sales Corporation, MSC Europe Beteiligungs GmbH, MSC Europe GmbH & Co, KG, MSC Europe Holding GmbH, MSC Holland Holding Company, MSC Laminates and Composites (EGV) Inc., MSC Laminates and Composites Inc., MSC Pre Finish Metals (EGV) Inc., MSC Pre Finish Metals (MT) Inc., MSC Pre Finish Metals (MV) Inc., MSC Pre Finish Metals (PP) Inc., MSC Richmond Holding Company, MSC San Diego Holding Company Inc., MSC Walbridge Coatings Inc. 16 Subsidiaries included in the Index

Officers: Clifford D. Nastas/45/Dir., CEO/$441,842.00, James M. Froisland/Sr. VP, CFO, CIO, Corp. Sec./$257,447.00, Kevin R. Williams/37/VP - Operations/$230,029.00, Mark J. Gresser/VP - Sales, Mkt/$299,267.00, Linda Koester/Contact - Automotive, Philipp Wagner/Contact - Quiet Steel Body, Powertrain, Marco Benetazzo/Contact - Quiet Steel Brakes, Jeff Vellines/Contact - Consumer, Industrial, Electronic, Electrical, John Klepper/VP - Human Resources, Robert R. Rogowski/49/VP, Corporate Controller

Directors: Clifford D. Nastas/45/Dir., CEO, Ronald A. Mitsch/73/Non Exec. Chmn., Sam Licavoli/67/Dir., Avrum Gray/72/Dir., Frank L. Hohmann/62/Dir., John Reilly/64/Dir., Dominick Schiano/53/Dir., Patrick J. McDonnell/Dir.

Owners: Frank L. Hohmann/12.30%, Dimensional Fund Advisors LP/7.70%, Kevin Williams, Jeffrey J. Siemers, John M. Klepper, Wells Fargo& Company/6.80%, Ronald A. Mitsch, James M. Froisland, Clifford D. Nastas, Wellington Management Company, LLP/7.40%, T. Rowe Price Associates, Inc./11.50%, Curtis G. Solsvig, Mark J. Gresser, Insiders/13.10%, Avrum Gray (16 Owners included in Index)

Financial Data: Fiscal Year End:02/28 Latest Annual Data: 2/28/2007

Year	Sales	Net Income
2007	$262,627,000	$6,124,000
2006	$286,614,000	$5,204,000
2005	$264,853,000	-$320,000

Curr. Assets:	$106,999,000	Curr. Liab.:	$51,845,000	P/E Ratio:	50.00
Plant, Equip.:	$74,904,000	Total Liab.:	$61,036,000	Indic. Yr. Divd.:	NA
Total Assets:	$187,369,000	Net Worth:	$126,333,000	Debt/ Equity:	NA

Material Technologies Inc

11661 San Vicente Blvd., Ste. 707, Los Angeles, CA, 90049; **PH:** 1-310-208-5589; **Fax:** 1-310-473-3177; **http://** www.matechcorp.com; **Email:** ir@matechcorp.com

General - Incorporation	DE	Stock- Price on:12/24/2007	$1.06
Employees	3	Stock Exchange	OTC
Auditor	Corbin & Co LLP	Ticker Symbol	MTTG
Stk Agt	Interwest Transfer Co.	Outstanding Shares	106,830,000
Counsel	NA	E.P.S.	-$0.61
DUNS No.	17-553-8164	Shareholders	NA

Business: The group's principle activities include research and development of comprehensive system of monitoring devices for metal fatigue measurement. The first product, fatigue fuse, developed by the company is a small, extremely simple device that continuously integrates the effect of fatigue loading in a structural member. The second product is an instrument that is intended to measure the amount of fatigue life remaining in an existing structural member. The company is a development stage company doing business as tensiodyne scientific corporation. The group operates from United States.

Primary SIC and add'l.: 3829 8732

CIK No: 0001036668

Officers: Robert M. Bernstein/Chmn., CEO, Marybeth Miceli/COO, Nick Simionescu/Advisor, William L. Berks/Project Mgr., Samuel I. Schwartz/Advisor, Brent M. Phares/Chief Engineer, Henryka Manes/Advisor, Campbell Laird/Advisors

Directors: Robert M. Bernstein/Chmn., CEO

Owners: Robert M. Bernstein/36.60%, William Berks/1.50%, Insiders/42.40%, Barry Mitchell/6.50%, Joel R. Freedman/4.30%, UTEK Corporation/13.90%, John Goodman/1.40%, Robert M. Bernstein/100.00%

Financial Data: Fiscal Year End:12/31 Latest Annual Data: 03/31/2007

Year	Sales	Net Income
2007	$44,000	-$4,863,000
2006	$127,000	-$4,981,000
2005	$139,000	-$20,749,000

Curr. Assets:	$421,000	Curr. Liab.:	$543,000		
Plant, Equip.:	$5,000	Total Liab.:	$4,414,000	Indic. Yr. Divd.:	$0.300
Total Assets:	$433,000	Net Worth:	-$3,982,000	Debt/ Equity:	NA

MathStar Inc

19075 NW Tanasbourne Dr., Ste. 200, Hillsboro, OR, 97124; **PH:** 1-503-726-5500; **Fax:** 1-503-726-5501; **http://** www.mathstar.com; **Email:** info@mathstar.com

General - Incorporation	DE	Stock- Price on:12/24/2007	$1.6
Employees	63	Stock Exchange	NDQ
Auditor	PricewaterhouseCoopers LLP	Ticker Symbol	MATH
Stk Agt	Wells Fargo Shareowner Services	Outstanding Shares	20,940,000
Counsel	NA	E.P.S	NA
DUNS No.	NA	Shareholders	NA

Business: The groups principle activities include designing, developing and marketing semiconductor integrated circuit. The group operates from the United States. The group's quarterly revenue for September 2007 was 0.06 millions of USD.

Primary SIC and add'l.: 7372 3674

CIK No: 0001118037

Officers: Douglas M. Pihl/Chmn., CEO, Pres./$274,866.00, Ronald K. Bell/CTO/$392,174.00, Daniel J. Sweeney/COO/$642,125.00, James W. Cruckshank/CFO/$590,808.00, Timothy A. Teckman/VP - Engineering/$644,561.00, Sean P. Riley/VP - Marketing, Sales/$621,502.00, Glen R. Wiley/57/VP - Sales/$575,327.00, Dyne A. Mark/Contact - Sales, Alabama, Mike Henson/Contact - Sales, Arkansas, Elena Meyers/Area Sales Mgr. - Colorado, Richard Hoge/Area Sales Mgr. - Alaska, Richard Bethell/Contact - Sales, United Kingdom, Ireland, Joe D'Elia/Dir. - European Sales, EMEA, India, Pakistan, Tim Rainear/Sales Mgr. - Northeast USA, Canada

Directors: Douglas M. Pihl/Chmn., CEO, Pres., Benno G. Sand/Dir., Merrill A. McPeak/Dir., Morris Goodwin/Dir., Mike Maerz/Dir.

Owners: James W. Cruckshank, Glen R. Wiley, Timothy A. Teckman, Merrill A. McPeak, Morris Goodwin, Benno G. Sand, Michael O. Maerz, Insiders/11.80%, Douglas M. Pihl/6.70%, Sean P. Riley, Daniel J. Sweeney, Ronald K. Bell

Financial Data: *Fiscal Year End:*12/31 *Latest Annual Data:* 12/31/2006

Year	Sales	Net Income
2006	$53,000	-$22,643,000
2005	$134,000	-$18,935,000
2004	$130,000	-$8,749,000

Curr. Assets:	$14,849,000	**Curr. Liab.:**	$2,997,000		
Plant, Equip.:	$621,000	**Total Liab.:**	$2,997,000	**Indic. Yr. Divd.:**	NA
Total Assets:	$15,614,000	**Net Worth:**	$12,617,000	**Debt/ Equity:**	NA

Matria Healthcare Inc

1850 Pkwy. Pl., Marietta, GA, 30067; *PH:* 1-770-767-4500; *Fax:* 1-770-767-8849; *http://* www.matria.com; *Email:* investor_relations@matria.com

General - Incorporation	DE	Stock- Price on:12/24/2007	$30.02
Employees	1,704	Stock Exchange	NDQ
Auditor	KPMG LLP	Ticker Symbol	MATR
Stk Agt	SunTrust Bank	Outstanding Shares	21,330,000
Counsel	NA	E.P.S	$2.42
DUNS No.	NA	Shareholders	NA

Business: The groups principle activity is to provide wellness programs. The groups service is Health Enhancement. The group acquired CorSolutions Medical, Inc in the year 2006 and Miavita LLC and WinningHabits, Inc, in the year 2005. The group operates from the United States. The group's quarterly revenue for September 2007 was 89.60 millions of USD.

Primary SIC and add'l.: 8082 8099

CIK No: 0001007228

Subsidiaries: CorSolutions Medical, Inc., CorSolutions, Inc., Diabetes Acquisition, Inc., Health and Productivity Corporation of America, Inc., Matria Case Management, Inc., Matria Health Enhancement Company, Matria Healthcare of Illinois, Inc., Matria of New York, Inc., Matria Womens and Childrens Health, LLC, MHI Insurance Ltd., Miavita, Inc., Quality Oncology, Inc., WinningHabits GP, Inc., WinningHabits LP, Inc., WinningHabits, Inc. 16 Subsidiaries included in the Index

Officers: Parker H. Petit/Chmn., CEO/$2,477,238.00, Jeffrey L. Hinton/Sr. VP, CFO/$430,101.00, Roberta L. McCaw/Sr. VP, General Counsel, Sec./$598,100.00, Thornton A. Kuntz/Sr. VP, Chief Administrative Officer, Yvonne V. Scoggins/Sr. VP - Business Analysis/$632,674.00, Martin L. Olson/Sr. VP - Research, Development, Informatics, Donald E. Fetterolf/Corporate VP - Health Intelligence, Ronald A. Lyon/VP - Commercialized Informatics, Kenneth P. Yale/VP - Government Programs, Joseph A. Blankenship/VP, Corporate Controller, Richard A. Cockrell/VP - Investor Relations, Scott J. McClintock/Chief Marketing Officer, Earl P. Rousseau/Pres. - Health Enhancement, Kathryn H. Creech/Sr. VP - Health Enhancement Product Management, Patrick F. Cua/Exec. VP - Sales Health Enhancement *(25 Officers included in Index)*

Directors: Parker H. Petit/Chmn., CEO, Joseph G. Bleser/Dir., Frederick P. Zuspan/Dir. Emeritus, Terry J. Dewberry/Dir., Richard M. Hassett/Dir., COO, Pres., Donald J. Lothrop/Dir., Myldred H. Mangum/Dir., Guy W. Millner/Dir., Carl E. Sanders/Dir., Kaaren J. Street/Dir., Thomas S. Stribling/Dir., Wayne P. Yetter/Dir.

Owners: Yvonne V. Scoggins, EARNEST Partners, LLC/12.90%, Wayne P. Yetter, Joseph G. Bleser, UBS Global Asset Management (Americas) Inc./5.00%, Richard M. Hassett, Jeffrey L. Hinton, Insiders/9.70%, Kaaren J. Street, TimesSquare Capital Management, LLC/5.60%, Myldred H. Mangum, Donald J. Lothrop, Terry J. Dewberry, Guy W. Millner, Thomas S. Stribling *(18 Owners included in Index)*

Financial Data: *Fiscal Year End:*12/31 *Latest Annual Data:* 12/31/2006

Year	Sales	Net Income
2006	$336,139,000	$52,690,000
2005	$179,231,000	$13,963,000
2004	$294,382,000	$27,066,000

Curr. Assets:	$96,517,000	**Curr. Liab.:**	$108,420,000	**P/E Ratio:**	12.40
Plant, Equip.:	$38,950,000	**Total Liab.:**	$392,397,000	**Indic. Yr. Divd.:**	NA
Total Assets:	$711,373,000	**Net Worth:**	$318,976,000	**Debt/ Equity:**	0.8149

Matritech Inc

330 Nevada St., Newton, MA, 02460; *PH:* 1-617-928-0820; *Fax:* 1-617-928-0821; *http://* www.matritech.com

General - Incorporation	DE	Stock- Price on:12/24/2007	$0.35
Employees	75	Stock Exchange	AMEX
Auditor	PricewaterhouseCoopers LLP	Ticker Symbol	NA
Stk Agt	Registrar & Transfer Co	Outstanding Shares	60,130,000
Counsel	Testa, Hurwitz & Thibeault	E.P.S	-$0.242
DUNS No.	18-422-6918	Shareholders	NA

Business: The group's principal activity is to develop, produce and distribute products for the diagnosis and potential treatment of cancer. The products are based on proprietary nuclear matrix protein technology. The group has developed minimally invasive cancer diagnostic tests for bladder and colon cancer, cervical cancer, breast cancer and prostrate cancer, using proprietary technology and expertise. The group's products include NMP221 test kit for bladder cancer, NMP179 for cervical cancer and nmp66 for breast cancer. The major customers of the group include Institut Fur Klinische and Fisher.

Primary SIC and add'l.: 8731 2835

CIK No: 0000884847

Subsidiaries: Matritech GmbH

Officers: Stephen D. Chubb/Chmn., CEO/$318,650.00, Melodie R. Domurad/VP - Clinical, Regulatory Affairs/$243,926.00, David G. Kolasinski/VP - Sales, Richard A. Sandberg/65/Dir., VP - Finance, CFO, Treasurer, Assist. Sec./$185,661.00, Gary Fagan/VP - Research, Development, John E. Quigley/VP - Sales, Marketing, Patricia Randall/VP, General Counsel, David L. Corbet/Dir., COO, Pres./$255,919.00, Franz Maier/Pres. - Matritech Gmbh

Directors: Stephen D. Chubb/Chmn., CEO, Richard A. Sandberg/65/Dir., VP - Finance, CFO, Treasurer, Assist. Sec., Stephen T. Thompson/Dir., William C. Zadel/Dir., Walter O. Fredericks/Dir., Jonathan M. Niloff/Dir., Judith Kurland/Dir., David L. Corbet/Dir., COO, Pres., Bruce Lehman/Dir., David B. Musket/Dir., Robert J. Rosenthal/Dir.

Owners: Insiders/7.50%, Judith Kurland, SDS Capital Group SPC, Ltd./11.40%, Stephen D. Chubb/1.70%, Jonathan M. Niloff, H&Q Life Science Investors/12.10%, David B. Musket/2.80%, ProMed Offshore FundII, Ltd./8.90%, Walter O. Fredericks, Stephen T. Thompson, Richard A. Sandberg, David L. Corbet, Robert J. Rosenthal, William C. Zadel, Bruce Lehman *(17 Owners included in Index)*

Financial Data: *Fiscal Year End:*12/31 *Latest Annual Data:* 12/31/2006

Year	Sales	Net Income
2006	$12,195,000	-$11,935,000
2005	$10,415,000	-$7,865,000
2004	$7,483,000	-$11,123,000

Curr. Assets:	NA	**Curr. Liab.:**	NA		
Plant, Equip.:	NA	**Total Liab.:**	NA	**Indic. Yr. Divd.:**	NA
Total Assets:	NA	**Net Worth:**	NA	**Debt/ Equity:**	NA

Matrix Bancorp Inc

700 17th St., Ste. 2100, Denver, CO, 80202; *PH:* 1-303-595-9898; *http://* www.matrixcap.com

General - Incorporation	CO	Stock- Price on:12/24/2007	$25.14
Employees	282	Stock Exchange	NA
Auditor	KPMG LLP, McGladrey & Pullen LLP	Ticker Symbol	NA
Stk Agt	Computershare Trust Co	Outstanding Shares	7,260,000
Counsel	NA	E.P.S	$1.49
DUNS No.	82-636-7948	Shareholders	NA

Business: The group's principal activities are to provide traditional banking, mortgage banking, trust and clearing activities and other fee-based service and lending activities through seven operating subsidiaries. Traditional banking activities include originating and servicing residential, commercial and consumer loans and depository services. Mortgage banking activities consist of purchasing and selling residential mortgage loans; offering brokerage, consulting and analytical services to financial services companies and financial institutions; servicing residential mortgage portfolios for investors and providing real estate management and disposition services. Trust and clearing activities offer specialized custody and clearing services. Other fee-based service and lending activities include providing outsourced business services, such as budgeting, governmental reporting, accounts payable, payroll, facility and safety management and comprehensive insurance programs.

Primary SIC and add'l.: 6712 6035

CIK No: 0000944725

Subsidiaries: Matrix Bancorp Trading, Matrix Bank, Matrix Tower Holdings, LLC

Officers: Scot T. Wetzel/Dir., CEO, Pres./$873,042.00, William D. Snider/Vice Chmn., CFO/$497,144.00, Michael J. McCloskey/COO/$574,692.00, Benjamin C. Hirsh/Chief Accounting Officer/$378,214.00, Linda Selub/Investor Relations, VP - Corporate Affairs, Jeffrey R. Leventhal/General Counsel, Sr. VP, Sec., Susan J. Lewis/Investor Relations Officer

Directors: Scot T. Wetzel/Dir., CEO, Pres., William D. Snider/Vice Chmn., CFO, Guy A. Gibson/Chmn., Lester Ravitz/Dir., James H. Bullock/Dir., Jeffrey R. Leeds/Dir., Robert T. Slezak/Dir.

Owners: Michael J. McCloskey, Jonathan Starr/Flagg Street Capital, LLC/9.99%, FrontPoint Partners LLC/6.15%, James H. Bullock, William D. Snider, Jeffrey R. Leeds, Robert T. Slezak, Magnetar Capital Master Fund, Ltd./9.63%, Lester Ravitz, Diaco Investments LP/7.54%, Benjamin C. Hirsh, Wasatch Advisors, Inc./10.77%, Insiders/18.67%, Guy A. Gibson/17.88%, Scot T. Wetzel *(16 Owners included in Index)*

Financial Data: *Fiscal Year End:*12/31 *Latest Annual Data:* 12/31/2006

Year	Sales	Net Income
2006	$144,315,000	$11,656,000
2005	$128,173,000	$1,558,000
2004	$162,853,000	$21,897,000

Curr. Assets:	$52,262,000	**Curr. Liab.:**	$1,865,228,000		
Plant, Equip.:	$13,994,000	**Total Liab.:**	$2,048,795,000	**Indic. Yr. Divd.:**	$0.240
Total Assets:	$2,156,548,000	**Net Worth:**	$107,753,000	**Debt/ Equity:**	1.7514

Matrix Energy Services Corp

378 N Main, No. 124, Layton, UT, 84041; *PH:* 1-801-497-9075; *http://* www.matrixenergycorp.com

General - Incorporation	NV	Stock- Price on:12/24/2007	$0.0057
Employees	NA	Stock Exchange	OTC
Auditor	Killman, Murrell & Co. P.C	Ticker Symbol	MXSV
Stk Agt	Securities Transfer Corp	Outstanding Shares	92,670,000
Counsel	NA	E.P.S	$0.13
DUNS No.	NA	Shareholders	NA

Business: The group's principal activities are to explore and develop oil and gas properties. In addition to exploration and development of new properties, the group redevelops producing oil and gas fields. The group focuses its exploration efforts on its holdings in Texas. It has leasehold interests in the corsicana field, located in south central Texas. The corsicana field is comprised of 875 existing wells on 67 leases, of which the group has a leasehold interest of approximately 8,000 acres in the underground minerals. Of these wells, there were only 215 active wells as of Sept 30, 2003. Of the 215 active wells, not all are regularly producing wells. The group also redevelops existing fields in and around corsicana, Texas and other areas of the region where fields have been partially depleted by conventional production methods, but where significant, proven reserves of oil and gas still remain.

Primary SIC and add'l.: 1311

CIK No: 0000316621
Subsidiaries: Spartan Resources Partners, G.P.
Officers: James Anderson/49/Dir., CEO, Pres.
Directors: James Anderson/49/Dir., CEO, Pres.
Owners: Portsmith Partners of Nevada/53.00%
Financial Data: Fiscal Year End:09/30 **Latest Annual Data:** 9/30/2006

Year	Sales	Net Income
2006	NA	-$77,000
2005	NA	-$5,261,000
2004	$158,000	-$1,237,000

Curr. Assets:	NA	Curr. Liab.:	$468,000	P/E Ratio:	0.04
Plant, Equip.:	NA	Total Liab.:	$468,000	Indic. Yr. Divd.:	NA
Total Assets:	NA	Net Worth:	-$468,000	Debt/ Equity:	NA

Matrix Service Co

10701 E Ute St., Tulsa, OK, 74116; **PH:** 1-918-838-8822; **Fax:** 1-918-838-8810;
http:// www.matrixservice.com

General - Incorporation	DE	Stock- Price on:12/24/2007	$25.9501
Employees	2,092	Stock Exchange	NDQ
Auditor	Deloitte & Touche LLP	Ticker Symbol	MTRX
Stk Agt	UMB Bank, N.A.	Outstanding Shares	24,270,000
Counsel	NA	E.P.S.	$0.808
DUNS No.	11-510-5827	Shareholders	NA

Business: The group's principal activity is to provide construction and repair and maintenance services. The services are provided to the petroleum, power, petrochemical, terminal, pipeline, manufacturing and industrial gas industries. The group operates in two segments: construction services and repair and maintenance services. The construction services include turnkey/grassroots projects, plant expansions/relocations, terminals/bulk storage facilities, new tank construction, heavy hauling, asme code work/welding, rigging, and millwrighting. The repair and maintenance services include plant maintenance, turnaround services, outages, industrial cleaning, hydroblasting, substation, and aboveground storage tank repair/maintenance. The group also provides bundled services where both business segments combine to provide a complete service. On 07-Mar-2003, the group acquired hake group, inc.
Primary SIC and add'l.: 1791 6719 7699 1629 1389 1623
CIK No: 0000866273
Subsidiaries: Bish Investments, Inc., Bogan, Inc., Hake Group, Inc., Hake, LLC, Hover Systems, Inc., I & S Joint Venture, LLC, I & S, Inc, Matrix Service Inc, Matrix Service Inc. Canada, Matrix Service Industrial Contractors Canada, Inc, Matrix Service Industrial Contractors ULC, Matrix Service Industrial Contractors, Inc, Matrix Service Specialized Transport, Inc, McBish Management, Inc., Mechanical Construction, Inc 17 Subsidiaries included in the Index
Officers: Michael J. Bradley/Dir., CEO, Pres./$1,684,219.00, Vance R. Davis/VP - AST Services, Kevin S. Cavanah/43/VP - Accounting, Financial Reporting, Philip C. Chappelle/49/VP - Risk Management, George L. Austin/42/VP - Finance, CFO/$485,847.00, Albert D. Fosbenner/VP - Accounting, Administration, East Coast, John S. Newmeister/VP - Marketing, Business Development/$325,435.00, James A. Bogan/Pres. Matrix Service Industrial Contractors - Inc, Nancy E. Downs/VP - Human Resources, James P. Ryan/Pres. - Matrix Service Inc/$461,077.00, Bradley J. Rinehart/VP - Midwestern Operations, Matrix Service Inc/$338,691.00
Directors: Michael J. Bradley/Dir., CEO, Pres., Michael J. Hall/Chmn., Paul K. Lackey/Dir., Tom E. Maxwell/Dir., David J. Tippeconnic/Dir., Edgar I. Hendrix/Dir.
Owners: Tom E. Maxwell, George L. Austin, James P. Ryan, Bear Stearns Asset Management Inc./9.40%, Tontine Capital Partners, LP, et. al./12.40%, Barclays Global Fund Advisors, et. al./5.10%, Bradley J. Rinehart, Michael J. Hall, Insiders/1.40%, Paul K. Lackey, John S. Newmeister, Edgar I. Hendrix, Michael J. Bradley, David J. Tippeconnic
Financial Data: Fiscal Year End:05/31 **Latest Annual Data:** 5/31/2006

Year	Sales	Net Income
2006	$493,927,000	$7,653,000
2005	$439,138,000	-$38,830,000
2004	$608,761,000	$9,542,000

Curr. Assets:	$122,915,000	Curr. Liab.:	$80,259,000	P/E Ratio:	36.04
Plant, Equip.:	$37,440,000	Total Liab.:	$111,877,000	Indic. Yr. Divd.:	NA
Total Assets:	$188,276,000	Net Worth:	$76,399,000	Debt/ Equity:	0.1461

Matrix Ventures Inc

2640 Tempe Knoll Dr., North Vancouver, BC, V7N 4K6; **PH:** 1-604-986-9633

General - Incorporation	NV	Stock- Price on:12/24/2007	NA
Employees	NA	Stock Exchange	OTC
Auditor	Manning Elliott LLP	Ticker Symbol	FSON
Stk Agt	Empire Stock Transfer Inc.	Outstanding Shares	NA
Counsel	NA	E.P.S.	NA
DUNS No.	NA	Shareholders	NA

Business: The groups principal activities include acquiring and exploring mineral properties. The group operates from the United States and Canada.
Primary SIC and add'l.: 8712
CIK No: 0001305451
Financial Data: Fiscal Year End:06/30 **Latest Annual Data:** 6/30/2006

Year	Sales	Net Income
2006	NA	-$27,000

Curr. Assets:	$5,000	Curr. Liab.:	$42,000		
Plant, Equip.:	NA	Total Liab.:	$42,000	Indic. Yr. Divd.:	NA
Total Assets:	$5,000	Net Worth:	-$37,000	Debt/ Equity:	NA

Matrixx Initiatives Inc

4742 N 24th St., Ste. 455, Phoenix, AZ, 85016; **PH:** 1-602-385-8888; **Fax:** 1-602-387-4112;
http:// www.matrixxinc.com

General - Incorporation	DE	Stock- Price on:12/24/2007	$20.6
Employees	31	Stock Exchange	NDQ
Auditor	Mayer Hoffman Mccann, P.C	Ticker Symbol	NA
Stk Agt	Corporate Stock Transfer, Inc.	Outstanding Shares	10,000,000
Counsel	Snell & Wilmer LLP	E.P.S.	$0.65
DUNS No.	79-003-7253	Shareholders	NA

Business: The group's principal activity is to develop, produce, market and sell innovative over-the-counter pharmaceutical products with an emphasis on those which utilize unique or novel delivery systems. The group through its subsidiary zicam llc produces, markets and sells 10 different products under the zicam(R) brand. The group's products include zicam cold remedy nasal gel, zicam cold remedy swabs and zicam cold remedy swabs-kids size, zicam cold remedy chewables, zicam cold remedy rapidmelts, zicam cold remedy oral mist, zicam allergy relief, zicam extreme congestion relief, zicam sinus relief and zicam nasal moisturizer. The group has two patents from the us patent and trademark office for the zicam cold remedy nasal technology. The group markets its products directly to major food, drug, mass market and wholesale warehouse retailers throughout the United States and to distributors that sell to smaller retail establishments.
Primary SIC and add'l.: 2834
CIK No: 0001006195
Subsidiaries: Gum Tech International, Inc., Zicam, LLC
Officers: Carl J. Johnson/57/CEO, Pres./$583,129.00, Lynn Romero/VP - Administration, Timothy L. Clarot/VP - Research, Development, James A. Marini/VP - Sales, William J. Hemelt/CFO, Exec. VP, Treasurer, Sec.
Directors: Edward E. Faber/Chmn., Michael A. Zeher/Dir., Samuel C. Cowley/Dir., William C. Egan/Dir., Lori H. Bush/Dir., White L. Matthews/Dir., John M. Clayton/Dir.
Owners: John M. Clayton, Timothy Clarot/1.30%, William C. Egan, Edward E. Faber, Kennedy Capital Management, Inc./6.40%, Segall, Bryant & Hamill Investment Counsel/6.70%, Edward J. Walsh, William Hemelt/1.20%, Carl J. Johnson/2.30%, Jove Partners, LP/5.00%, James Marini, Samuel C. Cowley, MFC Global Investment Management (US) LLC/5.50%, L. White Matthews, Michael A. Zeher **(19 Owners included in Index)**
Financial Data: Fiscal Year End:12/31 **Latest Annual Data:** 3/31/2007

Year	Sales	Net Income
2007	$19,046,000	$1,709,000
2006	$96,231,000	$4,927,000
2005	$90,461,000	$3,078,000

Curr. Assets:	$62,012,000	Curr. Liab.:	$25,929,000	P/E Ratio:	28.22
Plant, Equip.:	$5,527,000	Total Liab.:	$27,020,000	Indic. Yr. Divd.:	NA
Total Assets:	$85,107,000	Net Worth:	$58,087,000	Debt/ Equity:	NA

Matrixx Resource Holdings Inc

11601 Wilshire Blvd., Ste. 500, Los Angeles, CA, 90025; **PH:** 1-310-235-1479;
Fax: 1-310-456-3199; *http://* www.mrhi.net; **Email:** info@mrhi.net

General - Incorporation	DE	Stock- Price on:12/24/2007	$0.004
Employees	1	Stock Exchange	OTC
Auditor	Lucas, Murphy & Pindroh, LLP	Ticker Symbol	MXXR
Stk Agt	Standard Registrar & Transfer Co Inc.	Outstanding Shares	278,180,000
Counsel	NA	E.P.S.	NA
DUNS No.	NA	Shareholders	NA

Business: The groups principal activity is to explore natural resources. The group operates from the United States and Canada.
Primary SIC and add'l.: 1311
CIK No: 0000030966
Subsidiaries: Visual Interviews
Officers: Konstantine Tsakumis/Contact - Investor Relations, Catherine Thompson/Dir., CFO
Directors: Catherine Thompson/Dir., CFO
Owners: Catherine Thompson/2.86%, Insiders/2.89%, Michael Avatar, GarcyCo Capital Corp./59.16%

Matsushita Electric Industrial Co Ltd

1 Panasonic Way, Secaucus, NJ, 07094; **PH:** 1-201-348-7000; **Fax:** 1-201-348-7016;
http:// www.matsushita.co.jp

General - Incorporation	Japan	Stock- Price on:12/24/2007	$20.39
Employees	328,645	Stock Exchange	NYSE
Auditor	KPMG Azsa & Co	Ticker Symbol	MC
Stk Agt	Che Chuo Mitsui Trust & Banking Co	Outstanding Shares	2,150,000,000
Counsel	NA	E.P.S.	$0.88
DUNS No.	69-053-6552	Shareholders	NA

Business: The group's principal activities are manufacturing of consumer electric and electronic products. The group's operations are carried out through the following divisions: avc network: includes video, audio equipment and information and communication equipment; home appliances: includes televisions, vcrs and camcorders, DVD players and disks, audio equipment, refrigerators, washing machines, vacuum cleaners, microwave ovens and air conditioners; industrial equipment includes pcs and related equipment, communications and networking equipment; components and devices: includes display devices, electric motors and batteries.
Primary SIC and add'l.: 3639 3679 3651 3669
CIK No: 0000063271
Subsidiaries: Healthcare Business Company, Lighting Company, Matsushita Battery Industrial Co., Ltd., Matsushita Ecology Systems Co., Ltd., Matsushita Electric Works, Ltd., Matsushita Home Appliances Company, Matsushita Plasma Display Panel Co., Ltd., Matsushita Refrigeration Company, Motor Company, PanaHome Corporation, Panasonic Asia Pacific Pte. Ltd., Panasonic Automotive Systems Company, Panasonic AVC Networks Company, Panasonic AVC Networks Czech, s.r.o., Panasonic AVC Networks Singapore Pte. Ltd. 29 Subsidiaries included in the Index
Officers: Takahiro Mori/MD, Hiroyuki Takahashi/Corporate Auditor, Hideo Kawasaki/Exec. Officer, Shigeru Omori/Exec. Officer, Takumi Kajisha/Exec. Officer, Masaaki Fujita/Exec. Officer, Kazunori Takami/Exec. Officer, Yoshihisa Fukushima/Exec. Officer, Toshiro Kisaka/Exec. Officer, Jun Ishii/Exec. Officer, Takashi Toyama/Exec. Officer, Yoshiiku Miyata/Exec. Officer, Joseph Taylor/Exec. Officer, Toshiaki Kobayashi/Exec. Officer, Osamu Waki/Exec. Officer **(47 Officers included in Index)**
Directors: Kunio Nakamura/69/Chmn., Masayuki Matsushita/Vice Chmn., Ikuo Uno/Dir., Makoto Uenoyama/Dir., Hidetsugu Otsuru/Dir., Yoshihumi Nishikawa/70/Dir.

Owners: Japan Trustee Services Bank, Ltd./3.42%, Matsushita Electric Employee Shareholding Association/1.37%, State Street Bank and Trust Co./2.78%, Nippon Life Insurance Co./2.73%, Japan Trustee Services Bank, Ltd./1.33%, The Master Trust Bank of Japan, Ltd./5.13%, Sumitomo Mitsui Banking Corporation/2.35%, Mitsui Sumitomo Insurance Co., Ltd./1.43%, Moxley & Co./7.71%, Sumitomo Life Insurance Co./1.44%

Financial Data: ***Fiscal Year End:***03/31 ***Latest Annual Data:*** 3/31/2006

Year	Sales	Net Income
2006	$75,601,797,000	$1,312,485,000
2005	$81,036,815,000	$543,873,000
2004	$72,547,273,000	$400,378,000

Curr. Assets:	$35,690,217,000	**Curr. Liab.:**	$23,305,870,000		
Plant, Equip.:	$13,959,491,000	**Total Liab.:**	$33,831,845,000	**Indic. Yr. Divd.:**	$0.230
Total Assets:	$67,124,143,000	**Net Worth:**	$33,292,299,000	**Debt/ Equity:**	NA

Mattel Inc

333 Continental Blvd., El Segundo, CA, 90245; ***PH:*** 1-310-252-2000; ***Fax:*** 1-310-252-2179; ***http://*** www.mattel.com

General - Incorporation	DE	***Stock*** - Price on:12/24/2007	$25.58
Employees	32,000	Stock Exchange	NYSE
Auditor	PricewaterhouseCoopers LLP	Ticker Symbol	MAT
Stk Agt	Computershare Trust Co	Outstanding Shares	393,340,000
Counsel	NA	E.P.S	$1.42
DUNS No.	00-828-6643	Shareholders	NA

Business: The group's principle activities include designing, manufacturing and marketing toy products. The groups product lines include fashion dolls, accessories, games and puzzles. The groups products sold under the brand names Barney(TM), Disney(R), Pixter(TM), Kelly(TM), Max Steel(TM) and Othello(TM). The group operates from United States.

Primary SIC and add'l.: 2721 3942 3944

CIK No: 0000063276

Subsidiaries: American Girl, Inc., Mattel Asia Pacific Sourcing Limited, Mattel Europa B.V., Mattel Europe Holdings B.V., Mattel Europe Marketing B.V., Mattel Factoring, Inc., Mattel Finance, Inc., Mattel Foreign Holdings Ltd., Mattel International Finance B.V., Mattel International Holdings B.V., Mattel Investment, Inc., Mattel Marketing Holdings Pte. Ltd., Mattel Overseas Operations Ltd., Mattel Overseas, Inc., Mattel Sales Corp.

Officers: Robert A. Eckert/Chmn., CEO/$5,994,559.00, Alan Kaye/Sr. VP - Human Resources, Neil Friedman/Pres. - Mattel Brands/$3,926,446.00, Thomas A. Debrowski/Exec. VP - Worldwide Operations/$2,056,513.00, Ellen L. Brothers/52/Exec. VP, Pres. - American Girl Brands, Bryan G. Stockton/Exec. VP - International/$1,735,983.00, Robert Normile/48/Sr. VP, General Counsel, Sec., Michael A. Salop/43/Sr. VP - External Affairs, Treasurer, Kevin Farr/CFO/$1,687,898.00, Matthew C. Bousquette/Pres. - Mattel Brands, Bob Normile/Sr. VP, General Counsel, Sec., Scott H. Topham/47/Sr. VP, Corporate Controller, Joleen Jackson/Dir. - Investor Relations, Securities Analyst

Directors: Robert A. Eckert/Chmn., CEO, Craig G. Sullivan/Dir., Frances D. Fergusson/63/Dir., Dean A. Scarborough/52/Dir., Andrea L. Rich/Dir., Eugene P. Beard/Dir., Michael J. Dolan/Dir., Tully M. Friedman/Dir., Dominic Ng/Dir., Ronald L. Sargent/Dir., Chistopher A. Sinclair/Dir., John L. Vogelstein/Dir., Kathy Brittain White/Dir.

Owners: Kevin M. Farr, Insiders, T. Rowe Price Associates, Inc./5.00%, Kathy Brittain White, John L. Vogelstein, Tully M. Friedman, Eugene P. Beard, Craig G. Sullivan, Thomas A. Debrowski, Frances D. Fergusson, Barclays Global Investors, N.A./10.53%, Neil B. Friedman, Christopher A. Sinclair, Insiders, Ronald L. Sargent *(20 Owners included in Index)*

Financial Data: ***Fiscal Year End:***12/31 ***Latest Annual Data:*** 12/31/2006

Year	Sales	Net Income
2006	$5,650,156,000	$592,927,000
2005	$5,179,016,000	$417,019,000
2004	$5,102,786,000	$572,723,000

Curr. Assets:	$2,850,138,000	**Curr. Liab.:**	$1,582,520,000	**P/E Ratio:**	17.28
Plant, Equip.:	$536,749,000	**Total Liab.:**	$2,522,910,000	**Indic. Yr. Divd.:**	$0.750
Total Assets:	$4,955,884,000	**Net Worth:**	$2,432,974,000	**Debt/ Equity:**	NA

Matthews International Corp

Two NShore Ctr., Ste. 200, Pittsburgh, PA, 15212; ***PH:*** 1-412-442-8200; ***Fax:*** 1-412-442-8290; ***http://*** www.matthewsinternational.com

General - Incorporation	PA	***Stock*** - Price on:12/24/2007	$43.43
Employees	3,900	Stock Exchange	NDQ
Auditor	PricewaterhouseCoopers LLP	Ticker Symbol	MATW
Stk Agt	Computershare Investor Services LLC	Outstanding Shares	31,590,000
Counsel	NA	E.P.S	$2.04
DUNS No.	00-434-1533	Shareholders	NA

Business: The group's principal activity is to manufacture and market memorialization products and caskets for the cemetery and funeral home industries. It operates in five segments: bronze, graphics imaging, marking products, york casket and cremation. The bronze segment manufactures cast bronze memorials and other memorialization products. The graphics imaging segment manufactures and provides printing plates, pre-press and imaging services for corrugated and packaging industries. The marking products segment manufactures marking equipment and consumables to identify consumer and industrial products, components and packaging containers. The york casket segment produces two types of caskets: metal and wood. The cremation segment manufactures cremation equipment and cremation caskets. The group operates in Germany, Austria, Denmark, hungary, Brussels and Switzerland. The group cloverleaf group in fiscal 2004. On 30-Aug-2004, it acquired the intouch group plc.

Primary SIC and add'l.: 3364 3953

CIK No: 0000063296

Subsidiaries: Center Point Mortgage, Inc., Centre Point Title Services, Inc., Computer Dynamics Group, Inc., EFS Financial Services, Inc., EFS Service Corporation, Equitable Finance Corp., MAF Bancorp Capital Trust I, MAF Bancorp Capital Trust II, MAF Developments, Inc., MAF Realty Co., LLC III, MAF Realty Co., LLC IV, Mid America Bank, fsb, Mid America Finance Corporation, Mid America Insurance Agency, Inc., Mid America Investment Services, Inc. 24 Subsidiaries included in the Index

Officers: Joseph C. Bartolacci/47/Dir., CEO, Pres., Martin J. Beck/Pres. - Brand Solutions, Paul F. Rahill/51/Pres. - Cremation Division, Steven F. Nicola/48/CFO, Sec., Treasurer, Harry A. Pontone/Pres. - Casket Division, David F. Beck/56/Controller, Franz J. Schwarz/60/Pres. - Graphics Europe, Timothy S. Obrien/44/Pres. - Bronze Division, Brian J. Dunn/51/Group Pres. - Graphics, Marking Products, James P. Doyle/57/Group Pres. - Memorialization

Directors: Joseph C. Bartolacci/47/Dir., CEO, Pres., David J. Decarlo/62/Vice Chmn., David M. Kelly/65/Chmn., John P. O'Leary/61/Dir., John D. Turner/61/Dir., Robert G. Neubert/65/Dir., William J. Stallkamp/68/Dir., Glenn R. Mahone/62/Dir.

Owners: T. Rowe Price Associates, Inc./8.60%, M. J. Beck, J. C. Bartolacci, J. P. OLeary, D. M. Kelly/1.30%, Insiders/3.00%, Neuberger Berman, L.P./14.50%, D. J. DeCarlo, J. D. Turner, R. J. Kavanaugh, Ariel Capital Management, Inc./9.10%, G. R. Mahone, W. J. Stallkamp, R. G. Neubert

Financial Data: ***Fiscal Year End:***09/30 ***Latest Annual Data:*** 9/30/2006

Year	Sales	Net Income
2006	$715,891,000	$66,444,000
2005	$639,822,000	$59,824,000
2004	$508,801,000	$56,195,000

Curr. Assets:	$242,843,000	**Curr. Liab.:**	$137,209,000	**P/E Ratio:**	20.11
Plant, Equip.:	$88,099,000	**Total Liab.:**	$323,665,000	**Indic. Yr. Divd.:**	$0.220
Total Assets:	$716,090,000	**Net Worth:**	$392,425,000	**Debt/ Equity:**	NA

Mattmar Minerals Inc

828 Harbourside Dr., Ste. 208, North Vancouver, BC, V7P 3R9; ***PH:*** 1-604-696-2026

General - Incorporation	NV	***Stock*** - Price on:12/24/2007	NA
Employees	NA	Stock Exchange	OTC
Auditor	De Joya Griffith & Co., LLC	Ticker Symbol	MTTM
Stk Agt	Holladay Stock Transfer, Inc.	Outstanding Shares	NA
Counsel	NA	E.P.S	NA
DUNS No.	NA	Shareholders	NA

Business: The groups principle activity is to provide recruiting services. The groups service area includes the research and development, engineering, marketing, sales, information technology and manufacturing industries. The group operates from United States.

Primary SIC and add'l.: 1000

CIK No: 0001366317

Officers: Sean Mitchell/41/Dir., Pres., Sec., Treasurer, CFO, CEO

Directors: Sean Mitchell/41/Dir., Pres., Sec., Treasurer, CFO, CEO

Owners: Sean Mitchell/77.00%, Insiders/77.00%

Mattson Technology Inc

47131 Bayside Pkwy., Fremont, CA, 94538; ***PH:*** 1-510-657-5900; ***Fax:*** 1-510-492-5911; ***http://*** www.mattson.com; ***Email:*** info@mattson.com

General - Incorporation	DE	***Stock*** - Price on:12/24/2007	$10.1
Employees	614	Stock Exchange	NYSE
Auditor	PricewaterhouseCoopers LLP	Ticker Symbol	MTU
Stk Agt	Mellon Investor Services LLC	Outstanding Shares	52,680,000
Counsel	NA	E.P.S	$0.50
DUNS No.	60-605-4476	Shareholders	NA

Business: The group's principle activities are to design, manufacture and market semiconductor wafer processing equipment for use in front-end fabrication of integrated circuits. The group also offers products for back-end of line processing. The products of the group include dry strip equipment, rapid thermal processing equipment, wet surface preparation equipment and plasma-enhanced chemical vapor deposition equipment. The group's manufacturing operations are located in the United States and Europe. It sells its products worldwide through sales support offices located in France, Germany, Italy, Japan, Korea, Singapore, Taiwan and the United Kingdom. Major customers of the group include hewlett packard, infineon, IBM microelectronics, promos technologies, samsung, silicon integrated systems, Texas instruments and sony. The group's quarterly revenue for September 2007 was 58.48 millions of USD.

Primary SIC and add'l.: 3674 3559

CIK No: 0000928421

Subsidiaries: Mattson International France SARL, Mattson International GmbH, Mattson International Korea Co., Mattson International,Inc., Mattson InternationalInc. (Taiwan Branch), Mattson Technology CanadaInc., Mattson Technology Cayman Holdings,Ltd., Mattson Technology Center KK, Mattson Technology Holding GmbH, Mattson Technology IsraelLtd., Mattson Technology LLC, Mattson Technology of Singapore Pte.Ltd., Mattson Technology Srl, Mattson Technology UKLtd., Mattson Thermal Products, GmbH 21 Subsidiaries included in the Index

Officers: David L. Dutton/Dir., CEO/$812,934.00, Robert B. MacKnight/COO, Pres./$684,805.00, William I. Turner/CFO/$290,757.00

Directors: David L. Dutton/Dir., CEO, Jochen Melchior/Chmn., John C. Bolger/Dir., Shigeru Nakayama/Dir., Kenneth Smith/Dir., Kenneth Kannappan/Dir., Hans-Georg Betz/61/Dir.

Owners: David L. Dutton/1.40%, Ludger H. Viefhues/1.10%, Insiders/4.40%, Rainier Investment Management, Inc./5.30%, William I. Turner, NWQ Investment Management Company, LLC/17.20%, Kenneth Kannappan, Kenneth G. Smith, Jochen Melchior, Shigeru Nakayama, The TCW Group, Inc., on behalf of the TCW Business Unit/10.90%, Robert B. MacKnight/1.10%, Hans-Georg Betz

Financial Data: ***Fiscal Year End:***12/31 ***Latest Annual Data:*** 12/31/2006

Year	Sales	Net Income
2006	$281,781,000	$17,114,000
2005	$209,379,000	$11,299,000
2004	$252,761,000	$36,525,000

Curr. Assets:	$258,825,000	**Curr. Liab.:**	$77,422,000	**P/E Ratio:**	19.80
Plant, Equip.:	$27,838,000	**Total Liab.:**	$77,822,000	**Indic. Yr. Divd.:**	NA
Total Assets:	$316,752,000	**Net Worth:**	$238,930,000	**Debt/ Equity:**	0.0375

Maui General Store Inc

PO Box 297, Hana Maui, HI, 96713; ***PH:*** 1-212-935-1781; ***http://*** www.mauigeneralstore.com

General - Incorporation	NY	***Stock*** - Price on:12/24/2007	$0.024
Employees	NA	Stock Exchange	OTC
Auditor	Webb & Co P.A	Ticker Symbol	MAUG
Stk Agt	American Stock Transfer & Trust Co.	Outstanding Shares	140,000,000
Counsel	NA	E.P.S	$0.00
DUNS No.	NA	Shareholders	NA

Business: The group is in development stage. The group was formerly known as Kelly Green Products, Inc. in year 2001. The group operates from United States.

Primary SIC and add'l.: NA

CIK No: 0000928835

Subsidiaries: Hana Pearl, LLC, Trinity Biogenics, Inc

Officers: Richard H. Miller/62/Chmn., CEO, CFO, Pres.

Directors: Richard H. Miller/62/Chmn., CEO, CFO, Pres.

Owners: Richard H. Miller/80.20%, Insiders/80.20%

Financial Data: Fiscal Year End:12/31 Latest Annual Data: 12/31/2006

Year	Sales	Net Income
2006	NA	-$39,000
2005	NA	-$16,000
2004	$36,000	-$42,000

Curr. Assets:	$0	Curr. Liab.:	$7,000		
Plant, Equip.:	NA	Total Liab.:	$7,000	Indic. Yr. Divd.:	NA
Total Assets:	$0	Net Worth:	-$7,000	Debt/ Equity:	NA

Maui Land & Pineapple Co Inc

120 Kane St., Kahului, HI, 96733; *PH:* 1-808-877-3351; *Fax:* 1-808-871-0953;
http:// www.mauiland.com; *Email:* communications@mlpmaui.com

General - Incorporation	HI	**Stock**- Price on:12/24/2007	$36.24
Employees	855	Stock Exchange	AMEX
Auditor	Deloitte & Touche LLP	Ticker Symbol	
Stk Agt	Mellon Investor Services LLC	Outstanding Shares	8,130,000
Counsel	NA	E.P.S.	$1.38
DUNS No.	00-913-2184	Shareholders	NA

Business: The group's principle activities include pineapple business, development and sale of resort and commercial and property business. The group operates through three segments: pineapple, resort and commercial and property. The pineapple segment includes growing pineapple, canning pineapple in tinplated steel containers, production of pineapple juice and fresh cut pineapple products and marketing of canned pineapple products, pineapple juice products and fresh whole and fresh cut pineapple products. The resort segment includes the development and sale of resort real estate, property management and the operation of recreational and retail facilities and utility companies at kapalua, maui. The commercial and property segment includes the group's investment in kaahumanu center associates, the napili plaza shopping center, and non-resort real estate development, rentals and sales. The group's quarterly revenue for September 2007 was 28.49 millions of USD.

Primary SIC and add'l.: 0179 6531 7011 9999

CIK No: 0000063330

Subsidiaries: Honolua Plantation Land Company, Ltd., Kapalua Advertising Company, Ltd., Kapalua Bay Holdings, LLC, Kapalua Bay, LLC, Kapalua Land Company, Ltd., Kapalua Realty Company, Ltd., Kapalua Waste Treatment Company, Ltd., Kapalua Water Company, Ltd., Maui Pineapple Company, Ltd., Royal Coast Tropical Fruit Company,Inc.

Officers: David C. Cole/Chmn., CEO, Pres./$1,515,009.00

Directors: David C. Cole/Chmn., CEO, Pres.

Owners: John H. Agee, David C. Cole/5.60%, Mary C. Stanford/8.50%, Fred E. Trotter, Robert I. Webber, Stephen M. Case Revocable Trust/45.50%, Insiders/7.50%, David A. Heenan, Duncan MacNaughton, Brian C. Nishida, Walter A. Dods, Robert M. McNatt, Kent T. Lucien, Fred W. Rickert, Thomas M. Gottlieb (16 Owners included in Index)

Financial Data: Fiscal Year End:12/31 Latest Annual Data: 12/31/2006

Year	Sales	Net Income
2006	$178,897,000	$7,225,000
2005	$186,680,000	$14,569,000
2004	$153,249,000	-$383,000

Curr. Assets:	$46,420,000	Curr. Liab.:	$27,417,000	P/E Ratio:	29.23
Plant, Equip.:	$129,849,000	Total Liab.:	$119,292,000	Indic. Yr. Divd.:	NA
Total Assets:	$220,199,000	Net Worth:	$100,369,000	Debt/ Equity:	NA

Maverick Minerals Corp

2501 Lansdowne Ave., Saskatoon, SK, S7J 1H3; *PH:* 1-306-343-5799

General - Incorporation	NV	**Stock**- Price on:12/24/2007	$0.03
Employees	NA	Stock Exchange	OTC
Auditor	Moen & Co LLP	Ticker Symbol	MVRM
Stk Agt	Pacific Corporate Trust Co	Outstanding Shares	NA
Counsel	NA	E.P.S.	NA
DUNS No.	NA	Shareholders	NA

Business: The group's principal activity is to focus in the surface reclamation only of a closed coal mining operation and this is by way of a lease on the property. The group changed their name to maverick minerals corporation on may 23, 2003 to reflect acquisition of the keno hill mining camp on Nov 6th 2001.on Apr 9, 2003 it entered into an agreement of purchase and sale for 100% of the shares of uco energy corp to enter the coal recovery business.

Primary SIC and add'l.: 5052

CIK No: 0001074929

Subsidiaries: Eskota Energy Corporation, Inc., UCO Energy Corp.

Financial Data: Fiscal Year End:12/31 Latest Annual Data: 12/31/2005

Year	Sales	Net Income
2005	$33,000	-$1,186,000
2004	$1,000	$1,024,000
2003	$692,000	-$1,396,000

Curr. Assets:	$8,000	Curr. Liab.:	$1,747,000		
Plant, Equip.:	NA	Total Liab.:	$2,447,000	Indic. Yr. Divd.:	NA
Total Assets:	$1,083,000	Net Worth:	-$1,364,000	Debt/ Equity:	NA

Maverick Oil & Gas Inc

16415 Addison Rd. Ste. 850, Addison, TX, 75001; *PH:* 1-214-239-4333; *Fax:* 1-214-239-4334;
http:// www.maverickoilandgas.com

General - Incorporation	NV	**Stock** - Price on:12/24/2007	$0.05
Employees	12	Stock Exchange	OTC
Auditor	Malone & Bailey, PC	Ticker Symbol	MVOG
Stk Agt	StockTrans, Inc.	Outstanding Shares	108,430,000
Counsel	NA	E.P.S.	-$0.02
DUNS No.	NA	Shareholders	NA

Business: The groups principle activities include finding and developing oil and gas reserves. In March 2005, the group acquired Hurricane Energy, LLC. The group operates from the United States. The group's quarterly revenue for Aug '07 was 0.02 millions of USD.

Primary SIC and add'l.: 1382

CIK No: 0001193159

Subsidiaries: Maverick Basin Exploration, LLC, Maverick Operating, LLC, Maverick Turner Escalera, LLC, Maverick Whitewater, LLC, Maverick Woodruff County, LLC, Maverick Zapata County, LLC, RBE, LLC

Officers: James A. Watt/57/CEO

Owners: Andrej Rucigaj, John A. Ruddy/1.40%, Insiders/2.30%, Matthew Fitzgerald, Continental Capital, SPC/5.80%, M.V. Oil and Gas Company/16.10%, Lance E. Johnson, Line Trust Corporation Limited/18.20%, Stephen M. Cohen, David Preng

Financial Data: Fiscal Year End:08/31 Latest Annual Data: 8/31/2006

Year	Sales	Net Income
2006	$2,500,000	-$21,529,000
2005	$284,000	-$29,142,000
2004	NA	-$156,000

Curr. Assets:	$4,440,000	Curr. Liab.:	$36,714,000		
Plant, Equip.:	$33,488,000	Total Liab.:	$38,130,000	Indic. Yr. Divd.:	NA
Total Assets:	$40,898,000	Net Worth:	$2,768,000	Debt/ Equity:	NA

Maverick Tube Corp

16401 Swingley Ridge Rd. , 7th Fl., Chesterfield, MO, 63017; *PH:* 1-636-733-1600;
http:// www.maverick-tube.com

General - Incorporation	DE	**Stock**- Price on:12/24/2007	NA
Employees	2,057	Stock Exchange	NDQ
Auditor	Ernst & Young LLP	Ticker Symbol	MVSN
Stk Agt	Computershare Investor Services LLC	Outstanding Shares	NA
Counsel	Gallop, Johnson & Neuman LC	E.P.S.	NA
DUNS No.	08-691-8398	Shareholders	NA

Business: The group's principal activity is to produce welded tubular steel products for use in energy and industrial applications. It manufactures structural tubing products, electrical conduit, standard pipe and piling products. The group operates in two segments: energy products and industrial products. The energy product line includes line pipe and oil country tubular goods such as drill pipe, production casing, surface casing and production. These products are sold to distributors throughout the United States and Canada who then resell to oil and natural gas production companies. The industrial product line includes structural tubing products, standard pipe and piling products. These products are sold to distributors and to end users in construction, transportation, agriculture and other industries. On 28-Feb-2003, the group acquired seacat corporation. On 23-Apr-2004, the group acquired the assets and certain liabilities of Texas arai.

Primary SIC and add'l.: 3317 3312

CIK No: 0000869087

Subsidiaries: Advance Tubular de Ecuador S.A., Advance Tubular de Venezuela ATV, C.A., AdvanceCo LP, Consorcio Metalrgico Nacional Ltda., Hickman Pipe Coating, LLC, International Growth Investors Ltd., International Growth Partners S. de R.L., Maverick C&P, Inc., Maverick GP, LLC, Maverick Investment, LLC, Maverick Tube Canada GP Ltd., Maverick Tube Canada LP, Maverick Tube Canada ULC, Maverick Tube International Holdings, Inc., Maverick Tube Latino America, SRL 33 Subsidiaries included in the Index

Officers: German Cura/Chmn., CEO, Pres., Milton Brice/Dir., CFO

Directors: Milton Brice/Dir., CFO, Roland Balkenende/Dir., Ricardo Soler/Dir., Cecilia Bilesio/Dir.

Max & Ermas Restaurants Inc

4849 Evanswood Dr., Columbus, OH, 43229; *PH:* 1-614 431-5800; *http://* www.maxandermas.com

General - Incorporation	DE	**Stock**- Price on:12/24/2007	$8.8
Employees	2,057	Stock Exchange	NDQ
Auditor	Deloitte & Touche LLP	Ticker Symbol	MAXE
Stk Agt	National City Bank	Outstanding Shares	2,550,000
Counsel	Porter Wright Morris & Arthur LLP	E.P.S.	-$0.02
DUNS No.	00-119-5833	Shareholders	NA

Business: The group's principal activity is to operate a chain of restaurants. The restaurants offer gourmet burgers, overstuffed sandwiches, homemade pasta dishes, chargrilled steak and chicken specialties, super salads and taste-tempting munchies. In addition, the restaurants offer a full complement of alcoholic and non-alcoholic beverages. The group owns and operates restaurants under the trade name max and erma's - neighborhood gatheringplace. As on 26-Oct-2003, the group owned 73 restaurants and 16 franchises.

Primary SIC and add'l.: 5812 6794 5813

CIK No: 0000706471

Officers: Todd B. Barnum/65/Chmn., CEO, William C. Niegsch/55/Exec. VP, CFO, Treasurer, Sec., Robert A. Lindeman/39/Pres., James Howenstein/36/COO

Directors: Todd B. Barnum/65/Chmn., CEO, Jay B. Barney/53/Dir., Donal H. Malenick/69/Dir., Mark F. Emerson/60/Dir., Michael G. Giulioli/55/Dir.

Owners: Mark F. Emerson/10.10%, James Howenstein/1.10%, Roger D. Blackwell/16.60%, Todd B. Barnum/14.80%, Donal H. Malenick/3.00%, Insiders/34.00%, William C. Niegsch/5.70%, Robert A. Lindeman/0.80%

Financial Data: Fiscal Year End:10/31 Latest Annual Data: 10/29/2006

Year	Sales	Net Income
2006	$180,290,000	-$579,000
2005	$183,705,000	-$1,315,000
2004	$182,959,000	$1,097,000

Curr. Assets:	$6,430,000	Curr. Liab.:	$15,998,000		
Plant, Equip.:	$55,350,000	Total Liab.:	$57,051,000	Indic. Yr. Divd.:	NA
Total Assets:	$71,107,000	Net Worth:	$14,056,000	Debt/ Equity:	NA

Max Capital Group Ltd

Formerly: Max Re Capital Ltd

Max House, 2 Front St., Hamilton, HM 11; *PH:* 809-441-295-8800; *http://* www.maxre.bm

General - Incorporation: Bermuda; Employees: 82; Auditor: KPMG LLP; Stk Agt: Mellon Investor Services LLC; Counsel: Mr. Minton; DUNS No.: NA

Stock - Price on:12/24/2007: NA; Stock Exchange: NDQ; Ticker Symbol: MXGL; Outstanding Shares: NA; E.P.S: $5.29; Shareholders: NA

Business: The groups principle activity is to provide reinsurance for both the life and annuity and property and casualty insurance markets. The group operates from United States.

Primary SIC and add'l.: 6331 6351

CIK No: 0001141719

Subsidiaries: Max Europe Holdings Limited, Max Insurance Europe Limited, Max Re Diversified Strategies Ltd, Max Re Europe, Max Re Ltd, Max Re Managers Ltd.

Officers: Marston W. Becker/Chmn., CEO/$2,067,057.00, Angelo M. Guagliano/54/Chief Underwriting Officer/$2,105,750.00, Clark A. Hontz/Exec. VP - Exposure Management, Ceded Reinsurance, Peter A. Minton/Dir., COO, Exec. VP, Chief Risk Officer/$2,562,065.00, James N. Tees/Exec. VP - CRO, Joseph W. Roberts/37/Exec. VP, Controller/$1,040,123.00, Sarene A. Bourdages/Exec. VP, General Counsel, Jim Tees/Exec. VP, Chief Risk Officer

Directors: Marston W. Becker/Chmn., CEO, William H. Heyman/Dir., Willis T. King/Dir., Steven M. Skala/Dir., Gordon F. Cheesbrough/55/Dir., Bruce K. Connell/55/Dir., Peter A. Minton/Dir., COO, Exec. VP, Chief Risk Officer, Zack H. Bacon/Dir., Mario P. Torsiello/Dir., James L. Zech/Dir., William Kronenberg/56/Dir.

Owners: FRM Corp./8.50%, Keith S. Hynes, Bruce K. Connell, Peter A. Minton, William Kronenberg, James L. Zech, Zack H. Bacon, Insiders/3.40%, Robert J. Cooney/2.60%, T. Rowe Price Associates, Inc./5.30%, Entities affiliated with Moore Capital/3.80%, Louis Moore Bacon/17.00%, Steven M. Skala, Joseph W. Roberts, Marston W. Becker *(20 Owners included in Index)*

Financial Data: **Fiscal Year End:**12/31 **Latest Annual Data:** 12/31/2006

Year	Sales	Net Income
2006	$895,011,000	$216,888,000
2005	$1,204,111,000	$9,505,000
2004	$1,097,574,000	$133,725,000

Curr. Assets:	$1,514,158,000	**Curr. Liab.:**	$641,778,000		
Plant, Equip.:	NA	**Total Liab.:**	$4,458,923,000	**Indic. Yr. Divd.:**	$0.360
Total Assets:	$5,848,984,000	**Net Worth:**	$1,390,061,000	**Debt/ Equity:**	NA

MAX Resource Corp

400 Burrard St., Ste. 1400, Vancouver, BC, V6C 3G2; ; ***http://*** www.maxresource.com

General - Incorporation: AB; Employees: NA; Auditor: Dale Matheson Carr-Hilton LaBonte LLP; Stk Agt: Pacific Stock Transfer Company; Counsel: NA; DUNS No.: NA

Stock - Price on:12/24/2007: $1.15; Stock Exchange: OTC; Ticker Symbol: MXROF; Outstanding Shares: NA; E.P.S: NA; Shareholders: NA

Business: The groups principal activities include exploring and developing mineral properties. The group operates from the United States and Canada.

Primary SIC and add'l.: 1000

CIK No: 0001116548

Subsidiaries: MAX Resources, Inc.

Officers: Stuart Rogers/Dir., CEO, Pres., David Pearce/Sec., Dir., CFO, Leonard MacMillan/Contact - Corporate Communications, Clancy Wendt/VP - Exploration

Directors: Stuart Rogers/Dir., CEO, Pres., Paul John/Dir., David Pearce/Sec., Dir., CFO, Daniel T. MacInnis/Dir., Tim Coupland/Dir.

Owners: Paul John/2.01%, David Pearce/2.85%, Stuart Rogers/1.77%, Tim Coupland, Clancy Wendt/2.32%

Financial Data: **Fiscal Year End:**12/31 **Latest Annual Data:** 12/31/2006

Year	Sales	Net Income
2006	NA	-$677,000
2005	NA	-$934,000
2004	NA	-$576,000

Curr. Assets:	$776,000	**Curr. Liab.:**	$50,000		
Plant, Equip.:	$0	**Total Liab.:**	$56,000	**Indic. Yr. Divd.:**	NA
Total Assets:	$776,000	**Net Worth:**	$721,000	**Debt/ Equity:**	NA

Maxco Inc

1005 Charlevoix Dr., Grand Ledge, MI, 48837; ***PH:*** 1-517-627-1734; ***Fax:*** 1-517-627-4951; ***http://*** www.maxc.com

General - Incorporation: MI; Employees: 260; Auditor: Rehmann Robson P.C; Stk Agt: Computershare Investor Services LLC; Counsel: Warren Cameron Faust & Asciutto; DUNS No.: 05-062-0129

Stock - Price on:12/24/2007: NA; Stock Exchange: OTC; Ticker Symbol: MAXC; Outstanding Shares: NA; E.P.S: $0.06; Shareholders: NA

Business: The group's principle activity is the heat-treating through its subsidiary, atmosphere annealing inc., a production metal heat-treating service company. The group provides metal heat treating, phosphate coating, bar shearing and sawing services to the cold forming, stamping, forging and casting industries. Its services are sold through atmosphere's own sales personnel and outside sales representatives, primarily to automotive companies and automotive suppliers. Its facilities are located in lansing, Michigan; canton, Ohio; and north vernon, Indiana. The group also investments in real estate and investments representing less than majority interest.

Primary SIC and add'l.: 3479 3398

CIK No: 0000078966

Subsidiaries: Atmosphere Annealing, Inc., Ledges Commerce Park, Inc.

Officers: Max A. Coon/73/Chmn., CEO, Pres., Eric L. Cross/64/Exec. VP, Sec., Lawrence O. Fields/54/CFO, Treasurer

Directors: Max A. Coon/73/Chmn., CEO, Pres., Sanjeev Deshpande/49/Dir., David R. Layton/67/Dir., Samuel O. Mallory/75/Dir., Joel I. Ferguson/69/Dir.

Owners: Lawrence O. Fields, Samuel O. Mallory, Insiders/37.50%, Daryle L. Doden/10.70%, Max A. Coon/28.60%, Sanjeev Deshpande/1.30%, Eric L. Cross/6.90%, ROI Capital Management, Inc/27.40%

Financial Data: **Fiscal Year End:**03/31 **Latest Annual Data:** 03/31/2006

Year	Sales	Net Income
2006	$46,564,000	$14,000
2005	$45,364,000	$134,000
2004	$40,798,000	-$1,531,000

Curr. Assets:	$9,500,000	**Curr. Liab.:**	$17,197,000		
Plant, Equip.:	$20,686,000	**Total Liab.:**	$24,328,000	**Indic. Yr. Divd.:**	NA
Total Assets:	$34,125,000	**Net Worth:**	$9,797,000	**Debt/ Equity:**	NA

Maxicare Health Plans Inc

14241 E Firestone Blvd, Los Angeles, CA, 90638; ***PH:*** 1-562-293-4074; ***http://*** www.maxicare.com

General - Incorporation: DE; Employees: NA; Auditor: Ernst & Young LLP; Stk Agt: American Stock Transfer & Trust Co.; Counsel: NA; DUNS No.: 06-459-2710

Stock - Price on:12/24/2007: NA; Stock Exchange: OTC; Ticker Symbol: MAXI; Outstanding Shares: NA; E.P.S: -$0.028; Shareholders: NA

Business: The group's principal activity is to evaluate the disposition of its surviving subsidiaries. On 25-May-2001, the group's wholly-owned subsidiary in California, operating health maintenance organizations, filed for relief under chapter 11 bankruptcy proceedings. As of 15-Mar-2002, the group terminated all its operations. Previously, it managed health care services and operated health maintenance organizations in California and Indiana. The group, through a subsidiary, also served as administrator of the California access for infants and mothers program. In addition, it also owned and operated an insurance company and a health assurance company.

Primary SIC and add'l.: 6324

CIK No: 0000722573

Subsidiaries: HealthCare Assurance Company, LTD., Maxicare Indiana, Inc., Maxicare Life And Health Insurance Company

Owners: George H. Bigelow, Paul R. Dupee/2.80%, John H. Gutfreund, Joseph W. White, Insiders/3.00%, Simon J. Whitmey

Financial Data: **Fiscal Year End:**12/31 **Latest Annual Data:** 12/31/2005

Year	Sales	Net Income
2005	$74,000	-$676,000
2004	$48,000	-$1,231,000
2003	$3,504,000	$2,742,000

Curr. Assets:	$2,137,000	**Curr. Liab.:**	$6,752,000		
Plant, Equip.:	NA	**Total Liab.:**	$7,501,000	**Indic. Yr. Divd.:**	NA
Total Assets:	$2,137,000	**Net Worth:**	-$5,364,000	**Debt/ Equity:**	NA

Maxim Integrated Products Inc

120 San Gabriel Dr., Sunnyvale, CA, 94086; ***PH:*** 1-408-737-7600; ***Fax:*** 1-408-737-7194; ***http://*** www.maxim-ic.com; ***Email:*** info2@maxim-ic.com

General - Incorporation: DE; Employees: NA; Auditor: Deloitte & Touche LLP; Stk Agt: EquiServe Trust Co N.A; Counsel: Morrison & Foerster LLP; DUNS No.: 10-211-2489

Stock - Price on:12/24/2007: $32.57; Stock Exchange: OTC; Ticker Symbol: MXIM; Outstanding Shares: 320,070,000; E.P.S: NA; Shareholders: NA

Business: The groups principle activity is to provide analog and mixed-signal engineering solutions. The groups products include data converters, interface circuits, microprocessor supervisors, operational amplifiers and power supplies. In the year 2007 the group acquired Storage Products Business of Vitesse Semiconductor Corporation. The group operates from United States.

Primary SIC and add'l.: 3674

CIK No: 0000743316

Subsidiaries: Chartec Laboratories A/S, Chartec Laboratories Holding ApS, Dallas Semiconductor Asia Limited, Dallas Semiconductor Corporation, Dallas Semiconductor Corporation (Taiwan), Dallas Semiconductor Philippines, Inc., Maxim Dallas/Direct, Inc., Maxim GmbH, Maxim India Integrated Circuit Design Private Limited, Maxim Integrated Products (Thailand) Co., Ltd., Maxim Integrated Products Korea, Inc., Maxim Integrated Products Switzerland AG, Maxim Integrated Products UK Limited, Maxim Japan Co., Ltd., Maxim Nordic ApS 20 Subsidiaries included in the Index

Officers: Charles G. Rigg/General Counsel, Drew Ehrlich/Sr. Public Relations Specialist, Kohei Shimooka/Mgr. - Marketing Communications Japan, Sunny Nam/Sr. Marketing Communications Specialist

Financial Data: **Fiscal Year End:**06/25 **Latest Annual Data:** 6/25/2005

Year	Sales	Net Income
2005	$1,671,713,000	$540,837,000
2004	$1,439,263,000	$419,752,000
2003	$1,153,219,000	$309,601,000

Curr. Assets:	$1,564,642,000	**Curr. Liab.:**	$215,917,000		
Plant, Equip.:	$769,885,000	**Total Liab.:**	$297,550,000	**Indic. Yr. Divd.:**	$0.620
Total Assets:	$2,367,962,000	**Net Worth:**	$2,070,412,000	**Debt/ Equity:**	NA

Maxim Pharmaceuticals Inc

8899 University Ctr. Ln., Ste. 400, San Diego, CA, 92122; ***PH:*** 1-858-453-4040; ***http://*** www.maxim.com

General - Incorporation: DE; Employees: 34; Auditor: KPMG LLP; Stk Agt: American Stock Transfer & Trust Co.; Counsel: Harry Kanner Esq; DUNS No.: 05-951-8019

Stock - Price on:12/24/2007: $2.63; Stock Exchange: NA; Ticker Symbol: NA; Outstanding Shares: 32,400,000; E.P.S: -$0.88; Shareholders: NA

Business: The group's principal activity is to develop and offer drug candidates for life-threatening cancers, hepatitis c and other chronic liver diseases. The group's leading drug candidate is ceplene(TM) designed to prevent or reverse damage associated with oxidative stress, thereby protecting immune cells and other critical cells and tissue. Clinical trials of ceplene have been conducted for advanced metastatic melanoma, acute myelogenous leukemia, renal cell carcinoma and hepatitis c. The group has also developed and is employing a proprietary high-throughput screening system to identify compounds that

modulate programmed cell death, or apoptosis. The group research, clinical trials and other product development activities through a combination of efforts by our internal personnel and collaborative programs with universities and other clinical research sites, contract research organizations and other similar service providers and persons.

Primary SIC and add'l.: 8731 2834 2833

CIK No: 0001013351

Subsidiaries: EpiCept, Magazine Acquisition Corp, Odyssey Pharmaceuticals, Inc

Financial Data: Fiscal Year End:09/30 Latest Annual Data: 12/31/2006

Year	Sales	Net Income
2006	$2,095,000	-$65,453,000
2005	$829,000	-$7,215,000

Curr. Assets:	$15,264,000	Curr. Liab.:	$19,746,000		
Plant, Equip.:	$1,316,000	Total Liab.:	$27,800,000	Indic. Yr. Divd.:	NA
Total Assets:	$18,426,000	Net Worth:	-$9,373,000	Debt/ Equity:	NA

Maximus Inc

11419 Sunset Hills Rd., Reston, VA, 20190; *PH:* 1-703-251-8500; *Fax:* 1-703-251-8240; *http://* www.maximus.com; *Email:* info@maximus.com

General		Stock	
Incorporation	VA	Price on:12/24/2007	$43.58
Employees	5,735	Stock Exchange	NYSE
Auditor	Ernst & Young LLP	Ticker Symbol	MMS
Stk Agt.	American Stock Transfer & Trust Co.	Outstanding Shares	21,880,000
Counsel	Palmer & Dodge LLP	E.P.S.	-$0.38
DUNS No.	08-234-7477	Shareholders	NA

Business: The group's principal activities are to provide program management, consulting services and systems solutions to state and local government agencies throughout the United States. The group's operations are conducted through four segments: consulting segment, health service segment, human service segment and systems segment. The consulting segment comprises of financial services and management services. The health service segment administers and directs managed care enrollment programs. The human service segment administers and manages state and local government human service programs on a fully-outsourced basis. The systems segment provides government agencies with systems design and implementation to improve efficiency and cost-effectiveness of their program administration.

Primary SIC and add'l.: 8742 7379 8399

CIK No: 0001032220

Subsidiaries: Acn 083 406 795 Pty Limited, Israel Workforce Solutions Ltd, LGA Recruitment Plus Pty Limited, MAXIMUS Brazil, Ltda., MAXIMUS Canada,Inc., MAXIMUS Federal Services,Inc., MAXIMUS Government Services,Inc., MAXIMUS International, LLC, MAXIMUS Properties LLC, MAXNetwork Pty Limited, Unison Maximus,inc.

Officers: Richard A. Montoni/Dir., CEO, Pres., Paul Mack/Chief Administrative Officer, Special Assist., CEO, David N. Walker/CFO, David Casey/Pres., Chief Marketing Officer, Mark Andrekovich/Chief - Human Capital, Robert B. Sullivan/Pres. - Consulting, Andrew Cramer/Pres. - Enterprise Systems, Michael Plymack/53/Pres. - Health, Human Services Systems, Adelaide K. Mayhew/Chief Compliance Officer, David Francis/General Counsel, Sec., Rachael Rowland/VP - Government, Public Relations, Jonathan Ross/Acting Chief - Quality, Risk Management, John F. Boyer/Pres. - Federal Services, Bruce L. Caswell/Pres. - Operations Segment, Akbar Piloti/Pres. - Human Services Segment *(17 Officers included in Index)*

Directors: Richard A. Montoni/Dir., CEO, Pres., Peter B. Pond/Chmn., Raymond Ruddy/Dir., Paul R. Lederer/Dir., Russell A. Beliveau/Dir., Wellington E. Webb/Dir., John J. Haley/Dir., Marilyn R. Seymann/Dir., James R. Thompson/Dir.

Owners: Raymond B. Ruddy/1.00%, John F. Boyer, Russell A. Beliveau, Paul R. Lederer, JANA Partners LLC/14.60%, Bruce L. Caswell, Morgan Stanley/8.20%, Royce & Associates, LLC/7.90%, John J. Haley, Richard A. Montoni, Wellington E. Webb, Michael Plymack, Peter B. Pond, Wellington Management Company, LLP/7.60%, James R. Thompson *(20 Owners included in Index)*

Financial Data: Fiscal Year End:09/30 Latest Annual Data: 9/30/2006

Year	Sales	Net Income
2006	$700,894,000	$2,460,000
2005	$647,538,000	$36,069,000
2004	$603,774,000	$38,774,000

Curr. Assets:	$383,680,000	Curr. Liab.:	$136,614,000		
Plant, Equip.:	$33,429,000	Total Liab.:	$153,602,000	Indic. Yr. Divd.:	$0.400
Total Assets:	$558,501,000	Net Worth:	$404,899,000	Debt/ Equity:	0.0041

Maxus Realty Trust Inc

104 Armour Rd., North Kansas, MO, 64116; *PH:* 1-816-303-4500

General		Stock	
Incorporation	MO	Price on:12/24/2007	$12
Employees	NA	Stock Exchange	NDQ
Auditor	KPMG LLP	Ticker Symbol	MRVC
Stk Agt.	American Stock Transfer & Trust Co.	Outstanding Shares	1,400,000
Counsel	NA	E.P.S.	$1.23
DUNS No.	NA	Shareholders	NA

Business: The groups principal activity is to makes equity investments in real estate properties. The groups operates through two segments namely apartments and commercial. The group acquired Highland Pointe Apartments in the year 2007, Northtown Business Center in the year 2006 and Bicycle Club Apartments in the year 2005. The group operates from the United States.

Primary SIC and add'l.: 6798

CIK No: 0000748580

Subsidiaries: ACI Financing, LLC, Arbor Gate Acquisition, L.L.C., Barrington Hills Acquisition, L.L.C., Bicycle Club, L.L.C., Chalet I Acquisition, L.L.C., Chalet II Acquisition, L.L.C., Highland Pointe Acquisition, L.L.C., Kings Court/Terrace Acquisition L.L.C., Landings Acquisition, L.L.C., Maxus Operating Limited Partnership, Maxus Realty G.P., Inc., North Winn Acquisition, L.L.C., Northtown Business Center, L.L.C, Waverly Acquisition, L.L.C., West OKC HighlandPointe Associates L.L.C.

Owners: Mercury Real Estate/7.30%, Christopher J. Garlich/5.50%, David R. Jarvis/7.30%, Robert W. Kohorst/2.90%, Jose L. Evans/2.10%, MacKenzie Patterson/7.10%, Mercury Special Situations/5.10%, Insiders/35.30%, John W. Alvey/4.00%, Monte McDowell/1.60%, Malcolm F. MacLean/7.30%, Danley K. Sheldon/1.60%, David L. Johnson/13.70%, Kevan D. Acord/4.40%

Financial Data: Fiscal Year End:12/31 Latest Annual Data: 12/31/2006

Year	Sales	Net Income
2006	$8,208,000	$2,140,000
2005	$7,896,000	-$1,091,000
2004	$5,980,000	$1,493,000

Curr. Assets:	$8,589,000	Curr. Liab.:	$1,745,000	P/E Ratio:	9.76
Plant, Equip.:	$43,100,000	Total Liab.:	$41,783,000	Indic. Yr. Divd.:	$0.800
Total Assets:	$54,234,000	Net Worth:	$12,451,000	Debt/ Equity:	4.4085

Maxus Technology Corp

890 Service St., San Jose, CA, 95112; *PH:* 1-408-956-8888; *http://* www.maxustechnology.com

General		Stock	
Incorporation	DE	Price on:12/24/2007	$0.005
Employees	NA	Stock Exchange	OTC
Auditor	Schwartz Levitsky Feldman LLP	Ticker Symbol	MXUS
Stk Agt	American Stock Transfer & Trust Co.	Outstanding Shares	NA
Counsel	NA	E.P.S.	-$1.2
DUNS No.	NA	Shareholders	NA

Business: The group's principle activity is to distribute new and used telecommunications and information technology equipment and recycling ewaste through its subsidiaries, maxus technology inc. And triple-too communications inc. It operates under four segments: broker sales, equipment resales, consignment sales and other sales. Broker sales consists of transactions whereby the equipment is procured and sold. Equipment resales consists of sales of equipment stored at the group's warehouse. Consignment sales involve contracts that result in end of life and surplus equipment being delivered to on consignment for potential sale. Other sales mainly consists of revenues generated from recycling business.

Primary SIC and add'l.: 3661

CIK No: 0001054709

Subsidiaries: 901133 Alberta Ltd., Maxus (Nova Scotia) Company, Maxus Holdings, Inc., Maxus Technology, Inc., MAXUS Technology, S. DE R.L. DE C.V., Triple-Too Communications, Inc.

Financial Data: Fiscal Year End:11/30 Latest Annual Data: 11/30/2004

Year	Sales	Net Income
2004	$6,189,000	-$4,486,000
2003	$3,583,000	-$805,000
2002	NA	-$1,788,000

Curr. Assets:	$81,000	Curr. Liab.:	$39,000		
Plant, Equip.:	NA	Total Liab.:	$3,104,000	Indic. Yr. Divd.:	NA
Total Assets:	$81,000	Net Worth:	-$3,023,000	Debt/ Equity:	NA

Maxwell Technologies Inc

9244 Balboa Ave., San Diego, CA, 92123; *PH:* 1-858-503-3300; *Fax:* 1-858-503-3301; *http://* www.maxwell.com; *Email:* info@maxwell.com

General		Stock	
Incorporation	DE	Price on:12/24/2007	$13.63
Employees	278	Stock Exchange	NDQ
Auditor	McGladrey & Pullen LLP	Ticker Symbol	NA
Stk Agt	Mellon Investor Services LLC	Outstanding Shares	17,390,000
Counsel	NA	E.P.S.	-$0.97
DUNS No.	00-956-7942	Shareholders	NA

Business: The group's principal activities are to develop, manufacture and market electronic components and power and computing systems. The components developed are used in transportation, telecommunications, consumer and industrial electronics, medical and aerospace industries. The products of the group include ultracapacitors, high-voltage capacitors and radiation-mitigated microelectronics products. The group operates in the United States of America and Switzerland.

Primary SIC and add'l.: 3679 3589 3675 7372 3571

CIK No: 0000319815

Subsidiaries: I-Bus/Phoenix, Inc., Maxwell Technologies SA, Maxwell Technologies Systems Division, Inc., Maxwell Technologies, Inc., PurePulse Technologies, Inc

Owners: Jos L. Cortes/11.95%, Royce & Associates, LLC/5.09%, Insiders/17.37%, AMVESCAP PLC, U.K., dba Powerhares Capital Mgt., LLC/10.42%, Mark Rossi, Thomas Ringer, Burkhard Goeschel, Van Den Berg Management/9.99%, Edward Caudill, Montena, SA/11.79%, Robert Guyett, Jean Lavigne, Kingdon Capital Mgt, LLC/5.81%, Richard D. Balanson/2.91%, Tim T. Hart *(18 Owners included in Index)*

Financial Data: Fiscal Year End:12/31 Latest Annual Data: 12/31/2006

Year	Sales	Net Income
2006	$53,885,000	-$16,495,000
2005	$45,437,000	-$6,294,000
2004	$32,212,000	-$9,075,000

Curr. Assets:	$37,626,000	Curr. Liab.:	$18,864,000		
Plant, Equip.:	$13,621,000	Total Liab.:	$45,786,000	Indic. Yr. Divd.:	NA
Total Assets:	$91,669,000	Net Worth:	$45,883,000	Debt/ Equity:	0.4544

Maxxam Inc

1330 Post Oak Blvd., Ste. 2000, Houston, TX, 77056; *PH:* 1-713-975-7600; *Fax:* 1-713-267-3701; *http://* www.maxxaminc.com

General		Stock	
Incorporation	DE	Price on:12/24/2007	$28
Employees	1,570	Stock Exchange	AMEX
Auditor	Deloitte & Touche LLP	Ticker Symbol	MXM
Stk Agt	Bank of New York	Outstanding Shares	5,250,000
Counsel	NA	E.P.S.	-$9.98
DUNS No.	00-129-4230	Shareholders	NA

Business: The group's principal activity is to operate through four divisions: aluminum industry, division is into mining, production and manufacture of fabricated and semi-fabricated aluminum products. Forest product division grows and harvests redwood and douglas-fir timber, the milling of logs into lumber and the manufacture of lumber into a variety of finished products. Real estate division is into residential and commercial real estate investment and development primarily in Puerto Rico, Arizona, California and Texas. Racing division owns and operates a class 1 pari-mutuel horseracing facility in the greater houston metropolitan area and a pari-mutuel greyhound racing facility in harlingen, Texas.

Primary SIC and add'l.: 7948 2819 6552 3354 2421 1099

CIK No: 0000063814

Subsidiaries: Beltway Assets LLC, Britt Lumber Co., Inc., EN LLC, FireRock, LLC, Lakepointe Assets LLC, Laredo Race Park LLC, M-Six Penvest II Business Trust, MAXXAM Group Holdings Inc., MAXXAM Group Inc., MAXXAM Property Company, MCO Mirada LLC, MCO Properties Inc., MCO Properties LP, MCO Realty, Inc., Palmas Country Club, Inc. 20 Subsidiaries included in the Index

Officers: Charles E. Hurwitz/Chmn. CEO, Pres./$2,781,607.00

Directors: Charles E. Hurwitz/Chmn. CEO, Pres.

Owners: Stanley D. Rosenberg, The Stockholder Group, Insiders, The Stockholder Group, Charles E. Hurwitz, Michael J. Rosenthal, Kent J. Friedman, Gilda Investments, LLC, Ezra G. Levin, Robert J. Cruikshank, Christian Leone, Charles E. Hurwitz, Dimensional Fund Advisors Inc., Shawn M. Hurwitz, M. Emily Madison *(17 Owners included in Index)*

Financial Data: Fiscal Year End:12/31 **Latest Annual Data:** 12/31/2006

Year	Sales	Net Income
2006	$291,500,000	$374,400,000
2005	$406,400,000	-$4,000,000
2004	$347,500,000	-$46,600,000

Curr. Assets:	$287,500,000	Curr. Liab.:	$259,600,000	P/E Ratio:	0.46
Plant, Equip.:	$583,300,000	Total Liab.:	$1,221,700,000	Indic. Yr. Divd.:	NA
Total Assets:	$1,009,900,000	Net Worth:	-$211,800,000	Debt/ Equity:	NA

Maxxon Inc

2073 Shell Ring Cir., Mt. Pleasant, SC, 29466; **PH:** 1-843-971-4848; **http://** www.maxxoninc.com

General - Incorporation	NV	**Stock**- Price on:12/24/2007	NA
Employees	NA	Stock Exchange	OTC
Auditor	Sutton Robinson Freeman & Co. P.C	Ticker Symbol	RMCP
Stk Agt	Nevada Agency & Trust Company	Outstanding Shares	NA
Counsel	NA	E.P.S.	NA
DUNS No.	NA	Shareholders	NA

Business: The group's principle activities include developing and marketing commercially viable hypodermic syringe that reduces the risk of accidental needle injuries. The syringe uses a proprietary and patented technology whereby a vacuum causes the needle to retract into the barrel of the syringe after an injection is given. The company is in the development stage and also plans to develop a prototype of a blood extraction device. The company will target clinics, hospitals, doctors' office, laboratories, public health departments, medical research facilities, medical schools and retail purchaser of syringes for diabetes to market the syringe. The group operates from United States.

Primary SIC and add'l.: 3841

CIK No: 0001041009

Officers: Rondald L. Wheet/43/Chmn., CEO

Directors: Rondald L. Wheet/43/Chmn., CEO, Thomas M. Beahm/57/Dir., Thomas O'Brien/60/Dir.

Owners: Thomas Beahm/10.41%, Rondald L. Wheet/14.64%, Insiders/36.34%, Thomas O'Brien/11.29%

Curr. Assets:	$4,000	Curr. Liab.:	$1,425,000		
Plant, Equip.:	NA	Total Liab.:	$1,425,000	Indic. Yr. Divd.:	NA
Total Assets:	$4,000	Net Worth:	-$1,420,000	Debt/ Equity:	NA

Maxygen Inc

515 Galveston Dr., Redwood City, CA, 94063; **PH:** 1-650-298-5300; **Fax:** 1-650-364-2715; http:// www.maxygen.com

General - Incorporation	DE	**Stock**- Price on:12/24/2007	$8.81
Employees	151	Stock Exchange	NDQ
Auditor	Ernst & Young LLP	Ticker Symbol	MAXY
Stk Agt	Computershare Investor Services LLC	Outstanding Shares	36,790,000
Counsel	NA	E.P.S.	-$0.81
DUNS No.	16-200-9690	Shareholders	NA

Business: The group's principal activities are to develop therapeutic and industrial products using proprietary directed molecular evolution technologies. The group operates in three segments: human therapeutics, agriculture and chemicals. Human therapeutics provides protein pharmaceuticals and preventative and therapeutic vaccines. Agriculture segment provides solutions to commercial problems in plant-based businesses through the application of advanced dna breeding methods. Chemicals segment provides biologically-based process solutions for the discovery and manufacture of bulk, specialty and fine chemicals, including pharmaceutical intermediates. The group has collaborations with companies such as Delta and Pine Land Company, Aventis Pasteur and Pfizer inc. The group operates in the United States, Denmark, the United Kingdom and France.

Primary SIC and add'l.: 2834 8731

CIK No: 0001068796

Subsidiaries: Maxygen ApS, Maxygen Holdings Ltd.

Officers: Russell J. Howard/CEO/$829,571.00, Lawrence W. Briscoe/CFO, Sr. VP/$504,879.00, Michael Rabson/General Counsel, Sr. VP/$530,006.00, Elliot Goldstein/COO/$1,146,815.00, Santosh Vetticaden/Chief Medical Officer, Grant Yonehiro/Sr. VP - Global Business Development, US Operations, Michele Boudreau/Dir. - Investor, Public Relations

Directors: Isaac Stein/Chmn., Gordon Ringold/Dir., M. R.C. Greenwood/Dir./James R. Sulat/Dir., Louis G. Lange/Dir., Ernest Mario/Dir., Alejandro C. Zaffaroni/Co - Founder - Maxygen, Member - Scientific Advisory Board, Baruch S. Blumberg/Member - Scientific Advisory Board, Arthur Kornberg/Member - Scientific Advisory Board, Joshua Lederberg/Member - Scientific Advisory Board

Owners: Dimensional FundAdvisors LP/5.80%, Ernest Mario, Isaac Stein/2.00%, M.R.C. Greenwood, HBK Investments L.P./5.30%, Gordon Ringold/1.30%, R.A. Investment Group/5.90%, Louis G. Lange, Michael Rabson/2.50%, Insiders/14.30%, Russell J. Howard/5.50%, GlaxoSmithKline plc/17.90%, Elliot Goldstein/1.20%, Lawrence W. Briscoe/2.60%, James R. Sulat

Financial Data: Fiscal Year End:12/31 **Latest Annual Data:** 12/31/2006

Year	Sales	Net Income
2006	$25,021,000	-$16,482,000
2005	$14,501,000	-$18,436,000
2004	$16,275,000	$9,342,000

Curr. Assets:	$187,120,000	Curr. Liab.:	$11,764,000		
Plant, Equip.:	$3,262,000	Total Liab.:	$15,848,000	Indic. Yr. Divd.:	NA
Total Assets:	$205,647,000	Net Worth:	$189,799,000	Debt/ Equity:	NA

Maytag Corp

403 W 4th St. N, Newton, IA, 50208; **PH:** 1-641-792-7000; **http://** www.whirlpoolcorp.com

General - Incorporation	DE	**Stock**- Price on:12/24/2007	NA
Employees	NA	Stock Exchange	NA
Auditor	Ernst & Young LLP	Ticker Symbol	NA
Stk Agt	Computershare Investor Services LLC	Outstanding Shares	NA
Counsel	NA	E.P.S.	NA
DUNS No.	00-528-5689	Shareholders	NA

Business: The group's principal activity is to manufacture home and commercial appliances. The home appliances segment manufactures laundry products, dishwashers, refrigerators, cooking appliances and floor care products. The brands under this segment include maytag, amana, hoover, jenn-air and magic chef. The home appliance products are sold to national retailers and independent retail dealers in North America and targeted international markets. The commercial appliances segment manufactures commercial cooking and vending equipment. The brands under this segment include dixie-narco, blodgett and pitco frialator. The commercial appliance products are sold to distributors, soft drink bottles, restaurant chains and dealers in North America and international markets.

Primary SIC and add'l.: 3635 3633 3581 3632 3589 3631 3639

CIK No: 0000063541

Subsidiaries: Amana Financial Services, Inc., Anvil Technologies LLC, Dixie-Narco, Inc., Hoover Company I LP, Hoover Holdings Inc., Jade Products Company, Juver Industrial S.A. de C.V., Maharashtra Investment, Inc., Maytag (Australia) Pty., Ltd., Maytag Comercial, S.de R.L. de C.V., Maytag Europe Ltd., Maytag Holdings, Inc., Maytag International Investments, Inc., Maytag International, Inc., Maytag Limited 24 Subsidiaries included in the Index

MB Financial Inc MD

800 W Madison St., Chicago, IL, 60607; **PH:** 1-312-421-7600; **http://** www.mbfinancial.com

General - Incorporation	MD	**Stock**- Price on:12/24/2007	$35.4
Employees	1,380	Stock Exchange	NDQ
Auditor	McGladrey & Pullen LLP, KPMG LLP	Ticker Symbol	MBFI
Stk Agt	LaSalle Bank N.A	Outstanding Shares	36,490,000
Counsel	NA	E.P.S.	$2.05
DUNS No.	NA	Shareholders	NA

Business: The group's principal activity is to provide commercial, retail, insurance, investment, trust and executive banking services. It provides commercial banking services to privately-owned companies run by entrepreneurs and selected types of service companies. In addition, the group provides lease banking services to small and medium size equipment leasing companies. The group's other customers include individuals, small and middle market businesses, real estate operators, investors and home developers. It operates thirty-six banking offices in Chicago metropolitan area and five in Oklahoma city metropolitan area. On 07-Feb-2003, the group acquired south Holland bancorp inc and on 28-May-2004, the group acquired first securityfed financial inc.

Primary SIC and add'l.: 6021 6712

CIK No: 0001139812

Subsidiaries: Ashland Management Agency, Inc., Coal City Capital Trust I, LaSalle Business Solutions, LLC, LaSalle Systems Leasing, Inc., MB Deferred Exchange Corporation, MB Financial Bank, N.A., MB Financial Capital Trust I, MB Financial Capital Trust II, MB Financial Center Land Owner, LLC, MB Financial Center, LLC, MB Financial Community Development Corporation, MB Real Estate Holdings, LLC, MB1200 Corporation, MBRE Holdings, LLC, Melrose Equipment Company, LLC 19 Subsidiaries included in the Index

Officers: Mitchell Feiger/Dir., CEO, Pres./$1,520,105.00, Thomas D. Panos/Pres., Chief Commercial Banking Officer - MB Financial Bank, Rosemarie Bouman/Exec. VP, Chief Administrative Officer - MB Financial Bank, Susan Peterson/58/Chief Retail Banking Officer - MB Financial Bank, Brian Wildman/Sr. VP - Wealth Management, MB Financial Bank, Jill E. York/CFO, VP/$622,117.00, Ronald D. Santo/VP/$699,342.00, Thomas P. Fitzgibbon/Exec. VP - MB Financial Bank, Burton J. Field/VP, Larry Kallembach/Sr. VP, CIO - MB Financial Bank

Directors: Mitchell Feiger/Dir., CEO, Pres., Thomas H. Harvey/Chmn., James N. Hallene/Vice Chmn., Charles J. Gries/Dir., Robert S. Engelman/Dir., Richard J. Holmstrom/Dir., Patrick Henry/Dir., Karen J. May/Dir., David P. Bolger/Dir.

Owners: Richard J. Holmstrom, Thomas H. Harvey/1.58%, Insiders/9.99%, Ronald D. Santo, Mitchell Feiger/1.50%, David P. Bolger, Jill E. York, Thomas D. Panos, Robert S. Engelman, Karen J. May, James N. Hallene, Charles J. Gries, Richard M. Rieser/1.51%, Patrick Henry/2.97%

Financial Data: Fiscal Year End:12/31 **Latest Annual Data:** 12/31/2006

Year	Sales	Net Income
2006	$471,909,000	$67,114,000
2005	$357,864,000	$66,368,000
2004	$295,136,000	$64,429,000

Curr. Assets:	$160,050,000	Curr. Liab.:	$6,693,745,000	P/E Ratio:	17.52
Plant, Equip.:	$197,619,000	Total Liab.:	$7,131,346,000	Indic. Yr. Divd.:	$0.720
Total Assets:	$7,978,298,000	Net Worth:	$846,952,000	Debt/ Equity:	0.4276

MB Software Corp

777 Main St., Ste. 3100, Fort, TX, 76102;

General - Incorporation	TX	**Stock**- Price on:12/24/2007	$0.25
Employees	3	Stock Exchange	OTC
Auditor	Clancy & Co. PLLC	Ticker Symbol	MBSB
Stk Agt	Continental Stock Transfer & Trust Co	Outstanding Shares	16,150,000
Counsel	NA	E.P.S.	-$0.03
DUNS No.	80-704-3914	Shareholders	NA

Business: The group's principal activity is to provide prescription drug monitoring services to healthcare professionals and regulatory agencies. Veriscrip is currently the group's only product offering. Veriscrip allows physicians to electronically write scripts via any windows(R) or palm(R) compatible device, complete with payor-specific drug formulary information and electronically send prescriptions to any pharmacy. The group acquired, mb holding corporation on 10-Nov-2003.

Primary SIC and add'l.: 8099

CIK No: 0000714256

Subsidiaries: Wound Care Innovations, LLC

Owners: Araldo A. Cossutta/33.00%, Applied Nutritionals/6.00%, Scott A. Haire/54.00%, Gilbert Valdez, Steven W. Evans/7.00%, Insiders/83.50%

Financial Data: Fiscal Year End:12/31 **Latest Annual Data:** 12/31/2006

Year	Sales	Net Income
2006	$190,000	-$624,000
2005	$211,000	-$758,000
2004	$174,000	-$1,876,000

Curr. Assets:	$439,000	Curr. Liab.:	$1,767,000		
Plant, Equip.:	$43,000	Total Liab.:	$1,767,000	Indic. Yr. Divd.:	NA
Total Assets:	$496,000	Net Worth:	-$1,271,000	Debt/ Equity:	NA

MB Tech Inc

Ste 5408, Dongseoul College, Bokjeong-Dong, Seongnam City, Sujeong-Gu; *PH:* 82-313816666; *http://* www.mbtech.co.kr; *Email:* mbir@mbtech.co.kr

General - Incorporation ...... NV	Stock - Price on:12/24/2007 ...... $0.001
Employees ...... NA	Stock Exchange ...... OTC
Auditor ...... SF Partnership LLP	Ticker Symbol ...... MBTT
Stk Agt ...... Stalt, Inc.	Outstanding Shares ...... NA
Counsel ...... NA	E.P.S. ...... NA
DUNS No. ...... NA	Shareholders ...... NA

Business: The group's principal activity is to manufacture and distribute electronic components. It manufactures products for the dbs satellite industry and state of the art rf microwave and communications technologies with consumer and military applications. The group serves satellite television market as a provider of hardware and bundled solutions. The group also develops flat antenna with an automatic satellite tracking system. The antenna is ideal for the yet to be tapped apartment, condominium and office building market as well as all other portable use solutions including boats in marinas and recreational vehicles or summer homes.

Primary SIC and add'l.: 3679 7375

CIK No: 0001085819

Subsidiaries: Faserwave Inc.

Financial Data: Fiscal Year End:12/31   Latest Annual Data: 12/31/2005

Year	Sales	Net Income
2005	$40,000	-$855,000
2004	$249,000	-$1,065,000
2003	$404,000	-$999,000

Curr. Assets:	$25,000	Curr. Liab.:	$408,000		
Plant, Equip.:	$60,000	Total Liab.:	$955,000	Indic. Yr. Divd.:	NA
Total Assets:	$568,000	Net Worth:	-$388,000	Debt/ Equity:	NA

MBA Holdings Inc

9419 E San Salvador Dr., Ste. 105, Scottsdale, AZ, 85258; *PH:* 1-480-860-2288; *Fax:* 1-480-860-0867; *http://* www.biker247.com; *Email:* custsvc@mbadirect.com

General - Incorporation ...... NV	Stock - Price on:12/24/2007 ...... $0.0012
Employees 21	Stock Exchange ...... OTC
Auditor ...... Semple & Cooper LLP	Ticker Symbol ...... MBAH
Stk Agt ...... Holladay Stock Transfer, Inc.	Outstanding Shares 217,690,000
Counsel ...... NA	E.P.S. ...... -$0.028
DUNS No. ...... NA	Shareholders ...... NA

Business: The group's principle activity is to provide vehicle service contracts and extended warranties.The group opreates from Unitred States.

Primary SIC and add'l.: 6719 6411

CIK No: 0001097273

Subsidiaries: Mechanical Breakdown Administrators, Inc., National Motorcycle Dealers Association, LLC, Rent2Ride Nationwide, LLC, WorldWide Rentals, LLC

Financial Data: Fiscal Year End:10/31   Latest Annual Data: 10/31/2005

Year	Sales	Net Income
2005	$4,887,000	-$7,855,000
2004	$5,744,000	-$1,209,000
2003	$5,628,000	-$1,785,000

Curr. Assets:	$3,383,000	Curr. Liab.:	$4,733,000		
Plant, Equip.:	$533,000	Total Liab.:	$8,594,000	Indic. Yr. Divd.:	NA
Total Assets:	$6,842,000	Net Worth:	-$1,752,000	Debt/ Equity:	NA

MBI Mortgage Services Ltd

Formerly: Local Telecom Systems Inc
1845 Woodall Rodgers, No. 1225, Dallas, TX, 75201; *PH:* 1-214-468-0000

General - Incorporation ...... NV	Stock - Price on:12/24/2007 ...... $0.55
Employees 92	Stock Exchange ...... NA
Auditor ...... Ernst & young LLP	Ticker Symbol ...... NA
Stk Agt ...... Karen Lee	Outstanding Shares 15,320,000
Counsel ...... NA	E.P.S. ...... -$0.96
DUNS No. ...... NA	Shareholders ...... NA

Business: The group's principal activity is to provide local and long distance telecom service on a prepaid basis. The local services include a 'bare bones' product providing unlimited local dial tone and 911 emergency access with the option of several custom calling features, for additional fees, including call waiting, caller ID, call forwarding and speed dialing. These features can be purchased individually or in a package at reduced rates. The group purchases phone services from the incumbent local exchange carrier (ilec) and resells the services on a prepaid basis at a premium, with attractive profit margins. The markets are households without phone service. The group is a flat rate service provider with a customer base in Texas, New Mexico and Arizona as of Sept 30, 2003. The services are not measured on a per call or minute basis.

Primary SIC and add'l.: 4899 1389

CIK No: 0000051511

Subsidiaries: MBI Mortgage, Inc

Officers: Patrick A. McGeeney/Dir., CEO, John M. Farkas/Pres. - MBI Mortgage, Greg Block/CIO, Exec. VP, Eric C. Conner/VP - Sales, Marketing, Keith Morgan/Dir. - Sales, Brett Faryniarz/Dir. - Sales, Rey Lerma/Dir. - Sales, Seamus Donohoe/Dir. - Sales, Larry D. Weisinger/Dir. - Sales, Bob Currier/CFO, Paul Bennett/VP - Corporate Development, William Marshall/Dir. - Sales

Directors: Patrick A. McGeeney/Dir., CEO, William R. Miertschin/Chmn., Richard M. Hewitt/Dir., Bruce A. Hall/Dir.

Owners: Bobby Lutz/7.00%, Brett Faryniarz/11.00%, William Miertschin/11.40%, Richard M. Hewitt/0.60%, Kelly Bergstrom/5.30%, William Scott Sears/6.40%, Insiders/3.10%, William R. Miertschin/11.40%, Ray W. Washburne/6.40%

Financial Data: Fiscal Year End:09/30   Latest Annual Data: 9/30/2006

Year	Sales	Net Income
2006	$6,994,000	-$12,205,000
2005	$1,082,000	-$1,755,000
2004	NA	-$553,000

Curr. Assets:	$3,573,000	Curr. Liab.:	$7,925,000		
Plant, Equip.:	$363,000	Total Liab.:	$8,776,000	Indic. Yr. Divd.:	NA
Total Assets:	$10,908,000	Net Worth:	$2,132,000	Debt/ Equity:	NA

Mbia Inc

113 King St., Armonk, NY, 10504; *PH:* 1-914-273-4545; *Fax:* 1-914-765-3163; *http://* www.mbia.com

General - Incorporation ...... CT	Stock - Price on:12/24/2007 ...... $64.11
Employees 492	Stock Exchange ...... NYSE
Auditor ...... PricewaterhouseCoopers LLP	Ticker Symbol ...... MBI
Stk Agt ...... Wells Fargo Shareowner Services	Outstanding Shares 130,800,000
Counsel ...... NA	E.P.S. $5.98
DUNS No. 11-278-6512	Shareholders ...... NA

Business: The group's principle activity is to operate through three segments, insurance, investment management services and municipal services. The operations are conducted through its wholly owned subsidiary, mbia insurance corporation. The insurance segment provides an unconditional and irrevocable guarantee of the payment of principal and interest on insured obligations when due. The investment management services segment provides an array of products and services to the public and not-for-profit sectors. These include local government investment pools, investment agreements and discretionary and non-discretionary portfolio management services. The municipal services segment provides revenue enhancement services and products to public-sector clients nationwide. The group's quarterly revenue for September 2007 was 436.40 millions of USD.

Primary SIC and add'l.: 6282 6351 6719

CIK No: 0000814585

Subsidiaries: 1838 Delaware Holding, LLC, Allen W. Charkow, Inc., Asia Credit Services Ltd., Asian Securitization& Infrastructure Assurance Ltd., Assurance Funding Limited, Capital Asset Holdings GP, Inc., Capital Asset Holdings, Ltd. ., Capital Markets Assurance Corporation, CapMAC Asia Ltd., CapMAC Financial Services, Inc., CapMAC Holdings Inc., CapMAC Investment Management, Inc., Colorado Investor Services Corporation, Euro Asset Acquisition Limited, John T. Austin, Inc. 41 Subsidiaries included in the Index

Officers: Gary C. Dunton/Chmn., CEO, Pres./$14,291,950.00, Edward C. Chaplin/Vice Chmn., CFO/$2,042,049.00, Mitchell I. Sonkin/Head - Insured Portfolio Management, Government Relations, Tom McLoughlin/Head - Global Public Finance, Ram D. Wertheim/General Counsel, Ruth M. Whaley/Chief Risk Officer, Clifford D. Corso/Chief Investment Officer, Douglas C. Hamilton/Assist. VP, Controller, Greg Diamond/Dir. - Investor Relations, Iain Barbour/MD, Kevin D. Silva/Chief Administrative Officer, William C. Fallon/Head - Corporate Strategy, Christopher E. Weeks/Head - International

Directors: Gary C. Dunton/Chmn., CEO, Pres., Joseph W. Brown/Chmn., Edward C. Chaplin/Vice Chmn., CFO, Laurence Meyer/Dir., Richard H. Walker/Dir., John A. Rolls/Dir., Debra J. Perry/Dir., David C. Clapp/Dir., Claire L. Gaudiani/Dir., Jeffery W. Yabuki/Dir., Daniel P. Kearney/Dir., David M. Moffett/56/Dir., Richard C. Vaughan/58/Dir.

Owners: Wellington Management Company, LLP/12.45%, Goldman Sachs/8.40%, AXA Financial, Inc./7.60%

Financial Data: Fiscal Year End:12/31   Latest Annual Data: 06/30/2007

Year	Sales	Net Income
2007	NA	NA
2006	NA	NA
2005	$2,300,507,000	$710,986,000

Curr. Assets:	$3,717,597,000	Curr. Liab.:	$536,940,000	P/E Ratio:	10.69
Plant, Equip.:	$105,950,000	Total Liab.:	$32,558,776,000	Indic. Yr. Divd.:	$1.360
Total Assets:	$39,763,030,000	Net Worth:	$7,204,254,000	Debt/ Equity:	2.3394

MBT Financial Corp

102 E Front St., Monroe, MI, 48161; *PH:* 1-734-241-3431; *Fax:* 1-734-384-8230; *http://* www.mbandt.com

General - Incorporation ...... MI	Stock - Price on:12/24/2007 ...... $13.9
Employees 402	Stock Exchange ...... NDQ
Auditor ...... Plante & Moran, PLLC	Ticker Symbol ...... MBTF
Stk Agt ...... American Stock Transfer & Trust Co.	Outstanding Shares 16,610,000
Counsel ...... NA	E.P.S. $0.85
DUNS No. ...... NA	Shareholders ...... NA

Business: The group's principle activities are to provide customary retail and commercial banking and trust services to its customers. The group offers commercial loans, personal loans, real estate mortgage loans, installment loans, iras, ATM and night depository facilities. It also provides treasury management services, telephone and Internet banking, personal trust, employee benefit and investment management services. The operations of the group are conducted through its subsidiary monroe bank & trust. The group offers a variety of deposits consisting of checking and savings accounts, time deposits, safe deposit facilities. The group operates its business from its main office complex and 23 full service branches in the counties of monroe and wayne, Michigan.

Primary SIC and add'l.: 6712 6022

CIK No: 0001118237

Subsidiaries: MB&T Financial Services, Inc., MBT Credit Company, Inc., Monroe Bank & Trust

Officers: Douglas H. Chaffin/Dir., CEO, Pres./$421,522.00, Tracy Oberleiter/Sr. VP, Sr. Mgr. - Business Development, Barbara B. Klemans/Sr. VP, Mgr. - Human Resources, Scott McKelvey/Exec. VP, Sr. Wealth Management Officer, Herbert J. Lock/Sr. VP, Chief Investment Officer, John L. Skibski/43/CFO, Exec. VP/$189,464.00, Donald M. Lieto/Exec. VP, Sr. Administration Mgr./$182,739.00, James E. Morr/Exec. VP, General Counsel/$190,617.00, Thomas G. Myers/Exec. VP, Chief Lending Mgr./$199,803.00, Mary Jane Town/VP, Dir. - Marketing, Barbara McMillen/Sr. VP, Mgr. - Retail Administration, Diane Kamprath/Sr. VP, Mgr. - Wealth Administration, Jerry Griffith/Sr. VP, MBT Downriver Community Pres., Mary Delk/VP, Audit Mgr.

Directors: Douglas H. Chaffin/Dir., CEO, Pres., William D. McIntyre/Chmn., Joseph S. Daly/Dir., Philip P. Swy/Dir., Karen M. Wilson/Dir., Michael James Miller/Dir., Thomas M. Huner/Dir., Rocque E. Lipford/Dir., Peter H. Carlton/Dir., Debra J. Shah/Dir.

Owners: Douglas H. Chaffin, Thomas G. Myers, James E. Morr, John F. Weaver/5.40%, Karen M. Wilson, Peter H. Carlton, Insiders/3.30%, Philip P. Swy, Donald M. Lieto, Joseph S. Daly, William D. McIntyre, John L. Skibski, Debra J. Shah, Thomas M. Huner, Monroe Bank & Trust/11.70% *(17 Owners included in Index)*

Financial Data: Fiscal Year End:12/31 **Latest Annual Data:** 12/31/2006

Year	Sales	Net Income
2006	$110,522,000	$3,773,000
2005	$104,144,000	$17,979,000
2004	$93,479,000	$22,599,000

Curr. Assets:	$55,864,000	Curr. Liab.:	$1,430,757,000	P/E Ratio:	86.88
Plant, Equip.:	$33,979,000	Total Liab.:	$1,430,757,000	Indic. Yr. Divd.:	$0.720
Total Assets:	$1,566,819,000	Net Worth:	$136,062,000	Debt/ Equity:	NA

MC Shipping Inc

Richmond House, 12 Par-la-ville Rd., Hamilton, HM CX; **PH:** 44-129-57933; *http://* www.mcshipping.com

General - Incorporation	Liberia	Stock - Price on:12/24/2007	$11.91
Employees	9	Stock Exchange	NA
Auditor	Moore Stephens Hays LLP	Ticker Symbol	NA
Stk Agt.	Mellon Investor Services LLC	Outstanding Shares	9,510,000
Counsel	Milbank, Tweed Hadley & McCoy	E.P.S.	$1.00
DUNS No.	87-564-1045	Shareholders	NA

Business: The group operates through its subsidiaries whose principle activity is to operate and charter second-hand vessels including multi-purpose carriers, feeder containerships, a product tanker, liquiq petroleum gas carriers, and scariver carriers. The group operates from United States.

Primary SIC and add'l.: 6719 4412

CIK No: 0000847831

Subsidiaries: International Consulting and Management Limited, MC Chantilly Limited, MC Cormorant Shipping Limited, MC Egret Shipping Limited, MC Eid Shipping Limited, MC Heron Shipping Limited, MC Ibis Shipping Limited, MC Link Shipping Limited, MC Pelerin Shipping Limited, MC Shipping S.A.M., MC Shrike Shipping Limited, MC Tercel Shipping Limited, Sphinx Limited

Officers: Antony S. Crawford/CEO, Alexander Gorchakov/Chief Investment Officer, Louis Carrel/CTO, Mark Jewell/MD

Owners: Insiders/3.70%, Horst Schomburg, Anton Pardini, Antony Crawford/1.70%, Weco-Rederi Holding A/S/8.90%, Graham Pimblett, Charles B. Longbottom, Navalmar Transportes Maritimos LDA/44.40%, Dominique Sergent, John H. Blankley

Financial Data: Fiscal Year End:12/31 **Latest Annual Data:** 12/31/2006

Year	Sales	Net Income
2006	$52,417,000	$10,149,000
2005	$35,397,000	$10,769,000
2004	$31,895,000	$1,112,000

Curr. Assets:	$12,034,000	Curr. Liab.:	$39,243,000	P/E Ratio:	12.41
Plant, Equip.:	$191,216,000	Total Liab.:	$173,083,000	Indic. Yr. Divd.:	$0.250
Total Assets:	$221,329,000	Net Worth:	$48,247,000	Debt/ Equity:	2.5496

McAfee Inc

3965 Freedom Cir., Santa Clara, CA, 95054; **PH:** 1-408-988-3832; **Fax:** 1-408-970-9727; *http://* www.mcafee.com

General - Incorporation	DE	Stock - Price on:12/24/2007	$35.2
Employees	3,290	Stock Exchange	NYSE
Auditor	Deloitte & Touche LLP	Ticker Symbol	MFE
Stk Agt.	Mellon Investor Services LLC	Outstanding Shares	159,800,000
Counsel	NA	E.P.S.	$1.15
DUNS No.	NA	Shareholders	NA

Business: The group's principal activities are to develop, market, distribute and support network security and network management software products. The group offers two types of products, namely, mcafee system protection solutions and mcafee network protection solutions. The group markets computer security, management and availability software and hardware for corporate, government and institutional users, resellers and distributors. It also offers managed security and availability applications to corporations and governments on the Internet. The group operates in the United States, Canada, Latin America, Europe and Asia-pacific. On 14-May-2003, the group acquired intruvert networks inc and on 30-Apr-2003, entercept security technologies inc.

Primary SIC and add'l.: 7373 7372

CIK No: 0000890801

Subsidiaries: CoreKT Security Systems, Inc., Entercept Security Technologies Europe Ltd., Inversiones NAI Guatemala S.A., McAfee (Hong Kong) Ltd., McAfee A.G., McAfee Consolidated, Inc., McAfee Software de Mexico S.A. de C.V., McAfee, GmbH, McAfee, S.r.l, McAfee.com Holdings Corporation, McAfee.com Limited, MyCIO.com, Inc., NA NetTools Holding Company, NAI International Holdings Corp., Network Associates Holding Company, Inc. 16 Subsidiaries included in the Index

Officers: David Dewalt/Dir., CEO, Pres., David Milam/Chief Marketing Officer, George Kurtz/Sr. VP - Enterprise Business, James Lewandowski/Exec. VP - North American Sales, Mark Cochran/Exec. VP, General Counsel, Michael Decesare/Exec. VP - Worldwide Sales, Joseph Gabbert/Exec. VP - Human Resources, David Welsh/Exec. VP - Corporate Strategy, Business Development, Christopher Bolin/CTO, Exec. VP, Lawrence Wee/Pres. - Asiapacific Region, Mike Dalton/Pres. - Europe, Middle East, Africa, EMEA Region, Eric F. Brown/CFO, COO, Dennis Omanoff/Sr. VP - Worldwide Manufacturing, Takahiro Kato/Pres. - Japan Region, Richard J. Decker/CIO, Sr. VP *(21 Officers included in Index)*

Directors: David Dewalt/Dir., CEO, Pres., Chuck Robel/Chmn., Robert B. Bucknam/Dir., Robert Pangia/Dir., Liane Wilson/Dir., Leslie G. Denend/Dir., Denis J. Oleary/Dir.

Owners: Lord, Abbett& Co. LLC/8.00%, Eric Brown, Christopher Bolin, Leslie Denend, J&W Seligman& Co. LLC/8.00%, Wellington Management Company, LLP, Insiders

Financial Data: Fiscal Year End:12/31 **Latest Annual Data:** 12/31/2005

Year	Sales	Net Income
2005	$987,299,000	$138,828,000
2004	$910,542,000	$225,065,000
2003	$936,336,000	$70,242,000

Curr. Assets:	$1,567,661,000	Curr. Liab.:	$868,991,000	P/E Ratio:	35.56
Plant, Equip.:	$85,641,000	Total Liab.:	$1,187,591,000	Indic. Yr. Divd.:	NA
Total Assets:	$2,642,624,000	Net Worth:	$1,455,033,000	Debt/ Equity:	0.1114

McClatchy Co

2100 Q St., Sacramento, CA, 95816; **PH:** 1-916-321-1846; **Fax:** 1-916-321-1964; *http://* www.mcclatchy.com

General - Incorporation	DE	Stock - Price on:12/24/2007	$25.8
Employees	15,250	Stock Exchange	NYSE
Auditor	Deloitte & Touche LLP	Ticker Symbol	MNI
Stk Agt.	Wells Fargo Shareowner Services	Outstanding Shares	82,020,000
Counsel	Banc of America Securities LLC	E.P.S.	-$19.23
DUNS No.	01-655-3971	Shareholders	NA

Business: The groups principle activity is to publish newspapers. The groups papers include Miami Herald, The Sacramento Bee, the (Fort Worth) Star-Telegram, The Kansas City Star and The Charlotte Observer. The group operates from United States.

Primary SIC and add'l.: 2711 7375

CIK No: 0001056087

Subsidiaries: Newsprint Ventures, Inc.

Officers: Gary B. Pruitt/Chmn., CEO, Pres./$5,601,811.00, Lynn Dickerson/VP - Operations, Robert J. Weil/VP - Operations, Frank Whittaker/VP - Operations, Patrick J. Talamantes/CFO, VP - Finance, Howard C. Weaver/VP - News, Elaine Lintecum/Treasurer, Christian A. Hendricks/VP - Interactive Media, Heather L. Fagundes/VP - Human Resources, Karole Morgan-Prager/VP, General Counsel, Corp. Sec./$954,970.00

Directors: Gary B. Pruitt/Chmn., CEO, Pres., Donley S. Ritchey/Dir., Maggie Wilderotter/53/Dir., Frederick R. Ruiz/Dir., Elizabeth A. Ballantine/Dir., Leroy Barnes/Dir., William K. Coblentz/Dir., Molly Maloney Evangelisti/Dir., Kathleen Foley Feldstein/Dir., Larry Jinks/Dir., Joan F. Lane/Dir., Brown McClatchy Maloney/Dir., Kevin S. McClatchy/Dir., William McClatchy/Dir., Theodore R. Mitchell/Dir. *(16 Directors included in Index)*

Owners: Robert J. Weil, William K. Coblentz/21.00%, Patrick J. Talamantes, Insiders/30.60%, Leroy Barnes, William Ellery McClatchy/18.80%, Frank R.J. Whittaker, JPMorgan Chase& Co./5.40%, Gardner Russo& Gardner/5.30%, Maggie Wilderotter, Frederick R. Ruiz, James B. McClatchy, Ariel Capital Management, LLC/14.70%, William McClatchy/18.30%, Private Capital Management/17.90% *(28 Owners included in Index)*

Financial Data: Fiscal Year End:12/25 **Latest Annual Data:** 12/31/2006

Year	Sales	Net Income
2006	$1,675,190,000	-$155,577,000
2005	$1,186,115,000	$160,519,000
2004	$1,163,376,000	$155,876,000

Curr. Assets:	$1,575,339,000	Curr. Liab.:	$1,112,114,000		
Plant, Equip.:	$975,976,000	Total Liab.:	$4,951,086,000	Indic. Yr. Divd.:	$0.720
Total Assets:	$8,054,710,000	Net Worth:	$3,103,624,000	Debt/ Equity:	0.8759

McCormick & Co Inc

18 Loveton Cir., Sparks, MD, 21152; **PH:** 1-410-771-7301; **Fax:** 1-410-771-7462; *http://* www.mccormick.com

General - Incorporation	MD	Stock - Price on:12/24/2007	$37.41
Employees	7,500	Stock Exchange	NDQ
Auditor	Ernst & Young LLP	Ticker Symbol	MKSI
Stk Agt.	Wells Fargo Bank, N.A.	Outstanding Shares	130,660,000
Counsel	NA	E.P.S.	$1.58
DUNS No.	04-361-4130	Shareholders	NA

Business: The groups principle activities include manufacturing, marketing and distributing spices, seasonings and flavors to the food industry. The groups products are sold under the brand names McCormick, Zatarain's, Simply Asia and Thai Kitchens. The group operates through two business segments namely consumer and industrial. The group operates from United States.

Primary SIC and add'l.: 2087 5149 2099

CIK No: 0000063754

Subsidiaries: Dessert Products International S.A.S., La Cie McCormick Canada Co., McCormick (Guangzhou) Food Company Limited, McCormick (U.K.) Ltd., McCormick Cyprus Limited, McCormick de Centro America, S.A. de C.V., McCormick Europe, Ltd., McCormick Foods Australia Pty. Ltd., McCormick France Holdings S.A.S., McCormick France, S.A.S., McCormick Global Ingredients Limited, McCormick Ingredients Southeast Asia Private Limited, McCormick International Holdings Ltd., McCormick Netherlands Holdings B.V., McCormick Pesa, S.A. de C.V. 21 Subsidiaries included in the Index

Officers: Robert J. Lawless/61/Chmn., CEO, Karen D. Weatherholtz/57/Sr. VP - Human Relations, Kenneth A. Kelly/VP, Controller, Lawrence E. Kurzius/Pres. - Europe, Africa, Middle East, Mark T. Timbie/Pres., Alan D. Wilson/COO, Pres., Paul C. Beard/VP - Finance, Treasurer, Francis A. Contino/62/Dir., CFO, Exec. VP, Charles T. Langmead/Pres. - U S Industrial Group, Robert W. Skelton/Sr. VP, General Counsel, Sec., Joyce Brooks/Assist. Treasurer - Financial Services, Dorothy H. Powe/Mgr. - Investor Relations, Cecile K. Perich/VP - Human Relations

Directors: Robert J. Lawless/61/Chmn., CEO, James T. Brady/67/Dir., Freeman A. Hrabowski/57/Dir., John P. Bilbrey/51/Dir., William E. Stevens/65/Dir., Margaret M.V. Preston/50/Dir., Michael J. Fitzpatrick/61/Dir., Francis A. Contino/62/Dir., CFO, Exec. VP, Michael D. Mangan/Dir., George A. Roche/66/Dir.

Owners: Margaret M.V. Preston, James T. Brady, Robert J. Lawless/9.20%, John P. Bilbrey, Insiders/21.40%, Freeman A. Hrabowski, Francis A. Contino/2.70%, William E. Stevens, Michael J. Fitzpatrick

Financial Data: Fiscal Year End:11/30 **Latest Annual Data:** 11/30/2006

Year	Sales	Net Income
2006	$2,716,400,000	$202,200,000
2005	$2,592,000,000	$214,900,000
2004	$2,526,200,000	$214,500,000

Curr. Assets:	$899,400,000	Curr. Liab.:	$780,500,000	P/E Ratio:	21.75
Plant, Equip.:	$469,500,000	Total Liab.:	$1,631,100,000	Indic. Yr. Divd.:	$0.800
Total Assets:	$2,568,000,000	Net Worth:	$933,300,000	Debt/ Equity:	0.4235

McCormick & Schmicks Seafood Restrnt Inc

720 SW Washington St., Ste. 550, Portland, OR, 97205; ***PH:*** 1-503-226-3440; ***Fax:*** 1-503-228-5074; ***http://*** www.mccormickandschmicks.com

General - Incorporation	DE	**Stock**- Price on:12/24/2007	$25.12
Employees	5,866	Stock Exchange	NDQ
Auditor	PricewaterhouseCoopers LLP	Ticker Symbol	MSSR
Stk Agt	Computershare Ltd.	Outstanding Shares	14,640,000
Counsel	NA	E.P.S	$0.98
DUNS No.	NA	Shareholders	NA

Business: The group's principal activity is to operate seafood restaurant. Its daily printed menu typically contains 85 and 110 made-to-order dishes including international, national, regional and local species of seafood which containes 30 to 40 varieties of fresh seafood, based on product availability, price and customer preferences. The group has 51 restaurants in 22 states.

Primary SIC and add'l.: 5812

CIK No: 0001288741

Subsidiaries: McCormick& Schmick Acquisition Corp., McCormick& Schmick Acquisition Corp. II, McCormick& Schmick Acquisition I Texas,Inc., McCormick& Schmick Acquisition II Texas,Inc., McCormick& Schmick Acquisition III Texas,Inc., McCormick& Schmick Acquisition Texas, LP, McCormick& Schmick Austin Liquor,Inc., McCormick& Schmick Austin, LP, McCormick& Schmick Dallas Liquor,Inc., McCormick& Schmick Dallas, LP, McCormick& Schmick Maryland Liquor,Inc., McCormick& Schmick Orlando, LLC, McCormick& Schmick Restaurant Corp., McCormick& Schmicks Atlanta II, LLC, McCormick& Schmicks Hackensack, LLC

Officers: Douglas L. Schmick/Co - Founder, Chmn., CEO, Emanuel N. Hilario/CFO, VP - Finance, Michael B. Liedberg/VP - Operations, John Flanagan/Contact - Business, Financial Media, David E. Jenkins/VP - Operations, Jerry R. Kelso/Chief Internal Auditor, Compliance Officer, Jeffrey H. Skeele/VP - Operations, Raymond E. Bean/Chief Accounting Officer, Controller

Directors: Douglas L. Schmick/Co - Founder, Chmn., CEO, Elliott H. Jurgensen/Dir., Rice J. Edmonds/Dir., David B. Pittaway/Dir., Harold O. Rosser/59/Dir., Justin B. Wender/38/Dir., Lee M. Cohn/61/Dir., Fortunato N. Valenti/60/Dir., James R. Parish/Dir.

Owners: Jeffrey D. Klein, FMR Corp/14.60%, Wellington Management Company, LLP/5.10%, Emanuel N. Hilario, Systematic Financial Management, L.P./7.20%, Fortunato N. Valenti, David B. Pittaway, Insiders/1.40%, Douglas L. Schmick, Arbor Capital Management, LLC/5.40%, David E. Jenkins, Rice J. Edmonds, Jeffrey H. Skeele

Financial Data: ***Fiscal Year End:***12/31 ***Latest Annual Data:*** 12/30/2006

Year	Sales	Net Income
2006	$308,323,000	$13,348,000
2005	$278,813,000	$11,008,000
2004	$238,757,000	$703,000

Curr. Assets:	$25,791,000	***Curr. Liab.:***	$32,769,000	***P/E Ratio:***	25.63
Plant, Equip.:	$104,727,000	***Total Liab.:***	$60,707,000	***Indic. Yr. Divd.:***	NA
Total Assets:	$204,160,000	***Net Worth:***	$143,453,000	***Debt/ Equity:***	0.0538

McData Corp

380 Interlocken Cres., Broomfield, CO, 80021; ***PH:*** 1-303-460-9200; ***http://*** www.mcdata.com

General - Incorporation	DE	**Stock**- Price on:12/24/2007	NA
Employees	1,447	Stock Exchange	NA
Auditor	Deloitte & Touche LLP	Ticker Symbol	NA
Stk Agt	Bank of New York	Outstanding Shares	NA
Counsel	NA	E.P.S	NA
DUNS No.	NA	Shareholders	NA

Business: The group's principal activities are to design, develop, manufacture and sell open storage networking solutions and provides highly available, scalable and centrally managed storage area networks. The storage area networks address enterprise-wise storage problems. The group's enterprise solutions consist of hardware products, software products and professional services. Its main products include san directors, fabricenter (TM) cabinet, epoch(tm) software architecture and the sanavigator(tm) software. The group also provides services for emc corporation's proprietary mainframe protocol (escon) switch business. The group sells its products, software, services and solutions through original equipment manufacturers (OEMs) and resellers. The customers of the group include emc corporation, hewlett-packard company, IBM corporation, hitachi data systems and compaq corporation. In 2003, the group acquired nishan systems inc and sanera systems inc.

Primary SIC and add'l.: 7371 3572

CIK No: 0000731502

Subsidiaries: Articulent, Inc., Inrange Global Consulting, Inc., Inrange Technologies Canada, Inc., Inrange Technologies Corporation, McDATA A.G., McDATA Australia Pty Limited, McDATA Belgium S.A., McDATA Deutschland GmbH, McDATA France S.A.S., McDATA GmbH, McDATA Hong Kong Limited, McDATA International ltd., McDATA Italia Srl., McDATA Japan K.K., McDATA Services Corporation 21 Subsidiaries included in the Index

Owners: Insiders/10.04%, Laurence G. Walker, S.A.C. Capital Advisors, LLC/6.30%, Thomas Hudson/1.70%, Todd Oseth, Renato DiPentima, John A. Kelley/3.36%, Michael J. Sophie, Renato DiPentima, Insiders/1.70%, Van D. Skilling, Black River Asset Management/7.35%, Thomas O. McGimpsey, Laurence G. Walker, Gary M. Gysin *(26 Owners included in Index)*

McDermott International Inc

777 N ElDr.idge Pkwy., Houston, TX, 77079; ***PH:*** 1-281-870-5000; ***Fax:*** 1-281-870-5095; ***http://*** www.mcdermott.com; ***Email:*** mdrinvestorrelations@mcdermott.com

General - Incorporation	Panama	**Stock**- Price on:12/24/2007	$84.12
Employees	27,800	Stock Exchange	NYSE
Auditor	PricewaterhouseCoopers LLP	Ticker Symbol	MDR
Stk Agt	Computershare Trust Co	Outstanding Shares	111,280,000
Counsel	NA	E.P.S	$2.56
DUNS No.	04-775-8503	Shareholders	NA

Business: The group's principal activities are carried out through two business segments: marine construction services, which include the design, engineering, fabrication and installation of offshore drilling and production facilities. It also includes other specialized structures, modular facilities, marine pipelines and subsea production systems, management and engineering services and procurement activities. Government operations supply nuclear components to the us navy. It also provides uranium processing, environmental site restoration services and management and operating services for various us government-owned facilities. Government operations also includes contract research activities. Customers include us government, oil and gas companies and foreign government owned companies. The group operates in the us gulf of Mexico, Mexico, South America, the Middle East, India, the caspian sea and Asia-Pacific. On 29-Aug-2003, it discontinued operations of menck gmbh.

Primary SIC and add'l.: 8711 3731 3621

CIK No: 0000708819

Subsidiaries: Babcock & Wilcox Investment Company, BWX Technologies, Inc., J. Ray McDermott Eastern Hemisphere Limited, J. Ray McDermott Holdings, Inc., J. Ray McDermott International, Inc., J. Ray McDermott Middle East, Inc., J. Ray McDermott, S.A., McDermott Caspian Contractors, Inc., McDermott Far East, Inc., McDermott Incorporated, P. T. McDermott Indonesia

Officers: Robert A. Deason/CEO - J Ray Mcdermott, SA/$1,765,153.00, John A. Fees/CEO - Babcock, Wilcox/$2,436,644.00, Bruce W. Wilkinson/Chmn., CEO, David S. Black/VP, Controller - Babcock, Wilcox Companies, Robert S. Cochran/Pres. - Bwxt Services, Inc, BWX Technologies, Winfred D. Nash/Pres. - Nuclear Operations Division, BWX Technologies, John T. Nesser/Exec. VP, Chief Administrative, Legal Officer/$1,697,847.00, Francis S. Kalman/Exec. VP/$2,215,942.00, Thomas A. Henzler/VP, Corporate Compliance Officer, Louis J. Sannino/Exec. VP - Human Resources, Health, Safety, Environmental, Dennis S. Baldwin/VP, Chief Accounting Officer, Paul M. Garner/CIO, VP, Jay Roueche/VP - Investor Relations, Corporate Communications, Robby Bellamy/Mgr. - Investor Relations, Corporate Communications, James R. Easter/VP - Corporate Development, Strategic Planning *(35 Officers included in Index)*

Directors: Bruce W. Wilkinson/Chmn., CEO, Bradley D. McWilliams/Dir., Thomas C. Schievelbein/Dir., Bruce Demars/Dir., Robert L. Howard/Dir., Robert W. Goldman/Dir., Ronald C. Cambre/Dir., Roger A. Brown/Dir., Oliver D. Kingsley/Dir., John F. Bookout/Dir.

Owners: Oliver D. Kingsley, FMR Corp., Ronald C. Cambre, John F. Bookout, Robert W. Goldman, Roger A. Brown, John A. Fees, John T. Nesser, Insiders, Francis S. Kalman, Robert A. Deason, D.Bradley McWilliams, Robert L. Howard, Thomas C. Schievelbein, Bruce W. Wilkinson *(17 Owners included in Index)*

Financial Data: ***Fiscal Year End:***12/31 ***Latest Annual Data:*** 06/30/2007

Year	Sales	Net Income
2007	NA	NA
2006	$4,120,141,000	$342,299,000
2005	$1,856,311,000	$197,977,000

Curr. Assets:	$2,140,478,000	***Curr. Liab.:***	$2,479,581,000	***P/E Ratio:***	21.57
Plant, Equip.:	$513,494,000	***Total Liab.:***	$3,205,807,000	***Indic. Yr. Divd.:***	NA
Total Assets:	$3,594,187,000	***Net Worth:***	$388,380,000	***Debt/ Equity:***	NA

McDonald's Corp

McDonald's Plz., Oak Brook, IL, 60523; ***PH:*** 1-630-623-3000; ***Fax:*** 1-630-623-5004; ***http://*** www.mcdonalds.com

General - Incorporation	DE	**Stock**- Price on:12/24/2007	$52.4
Employees	465,000	Stock Exchange	NYSE
Auditor	Ernst & Young LLP	Ticker Symbol	MCD
Stk Agt	EquiServe Trust Co N.A	Outstanding Shares	1,190,000,000
Counsel	NA	E.P.S	$1.93
DUNS No.	01-187-9665	Shareholders	NA

Business: The group's principle activity is to provide food service through retailers and restaurants. The group operates from United States.

Primary SIC and add'l.: 5812 6794

CIK No: 0000063908

Subsidiaries: Arras Comercio de Alimentos Ltda., Boston Market Corporation, Chipotle Mexican Grill, Inc., Franchise Realty Investment Trust - Illinois, Golden Arches Limited Partnership, McDonalds AMEA, LLC, McDonalds Australia Holding Limited, McDonalds Australia Limited, McDonalds Comercia de Alimentos Ltda., McDonalds Danmark A/S, McDonalds Deutschland, Inc., McDonalds Development Italy, Inc., McDonalds Europe, Inc., McDonalds France, S.A., McDonalds GmbH 37 Subsidiaries included in the Index

Officers: James A. Skinner/Vice Chmn., CEO, David M. Pojman/48/Corporate Sr. VP, Controller, Jim Johannesen/Central Division Pres. - Mcdonald's USA, Gloria Santona/Exec. VP, General Counsel, Sec., Jeff Stratton/Corporate Exec. VP, Chief Restaurant Officer, Denis Hennequin/Pres. - Mcdonald's Europe/$3,815,147.00, Janice L. Fields/COO, Exec. VP - Mcdonalds USA, Mary Dillon/Exec. VP, Global Chief Marketing Officer, Timothy J. Fenton/50/Pres. - Mcdonalds Asia, Pacific, Middle East, Africa, Peter J. Bensen/45/Corporate Sr. VP, Controller, Jose Armario/Pres. - Mcdonalds Latin America, Karen King/Pres. - East Division, Matthew H. Paull/CFO, Sr. Exec. VP/$4,816,472.00, Richard Floersch/Exec. VP - Human Resources, Tim Fenton/Pres. - Asia, Pacific, Middle East, Africa/$3,568,936.00 *(18 Officers included in Index)*

Directors: James A. Skinner/Vice Chmn., CEO, Andrew J. McKenna/75/Chmn., Hall Adams/74/Dir., Richard H. Lenny/56/Dir., John W. Rogers/50/Dir., Fred L. Turner/Trustee, Jeanne P. Jackson/56/Dir., Roger W. Stone/73/Dir., Enrique Hernandez/52/Dir., Walter E. Massey/69/Dir., Cary D. McMillan/50/Dir., Sheila Penrose/62/Dir., Edward A. Brennan/74/Dir., Robert A. Eckert/53/Dir.

Owners: Insiders, AXA/5.70%, Dodge & Cox/5.50%, John W. Rogers, Cary D. McMillan, Michael J. Roberts, Jeanne P. Jackson, Edward A. Brennan, Matthew H. Paull, Robert A. Eckert, Ralph Alvarez, Roger W. Stone, Timothy J. Fenton, Denis Hennequin, Hall Adams *(21 Owners included in Index)*

Financial Data: ***Fiscal Year End:***12/31 ***Latest Annual Data:*** 12/31/2006

Year	Sales	Net Income
2006	$21,586,400,000	$3,544,200,000
2005	$20,460,200,000	$2,602,200,000
2004	$19,064,700,000	$2,278,500,000

Curr. Assets:	$3,625,300,000	***Curr. Liab.:***	$3,008,100,000	***P/E Ratio:***	17.64
Plant, Equip.:	$20,845,700,000	***Total Liab.:***	$13,565,500,000	***Indic. Yr. Divd.:***	$1.500
Total Assets:	$29,023,800,000	***Net Worth:***	$15,458,300,000	***Debt/ Equity:***	NA

MCF Corp

600 California St., 9th Fl., San Francisco, CA, 94108; ***PH:*** 1-415-248-5600; ***Fax:*** 1-415-274-5651; ***http://*** www.merrimanco.com

General - Incorporation	DE	**Stock**- Price on:12/24/2007	$5.91
Employees	166	Stock Exchange	AMEX
Auditor	Ernst & Young LLP	Ticker Symbol	MEM
Stk Agt	OTC Stock Transfer, Inc.	Outstanding Shares	12,180,000
Counsel	NA	E.P.S	-$0.322
DUNS No.	NA	Shareholders	NA

Business: The group's principle activity is to provide brokerage services through its subsidiary, rtx securities corporation. It offers sales and trading services to institutions and private clients, as well as advisory and investment banking services to its corporate clients. Proprietary ratexchange trading software (rts) of the group enables market participants to buy and sell fiber optic, Internet and satellite bandwidth capacity globally. The rts serves not only as a platform for bandwidth trading, but for the aggregation of data from third parties as well. Through its emerging commodities division, the group provides valuable and marketable information to rtx securities. The group also provides a wide range of consulting services to existing and prospective market participants through this division. The group's quarterly revenue for September 2007 was 17.66 millions of USD.

Primary SIC and add'l.: 6211 6799

CIK No: 0000826683

Subsidiaries: MCF Asset Management, LLC, MCF Wealth Management, LLC, Merriman Curhan Ford & Co.

Officers: Jonathan D. Merriman/Chmn., CEO/$370,211.00, Robert E. Ford/COO, Pres./$383,578.00, John D. Hiestand/CFO/$336,358.00, Christopher L. Aguilar/General Counsel/$329,421.00, Gregory Curhan/Exec. VP

Directors: Jonathan D. Merriman/Chmn., CEO, Patrick H. Arbor/Dir., Anthony B. Helfet/Dir., Raymond J. Minehan/Dir., Scott Potter/Dir., Dennis G. Schmal/Dir., Ronald E. Spears/Dir., Steven W. Town/Dir., William J. Febbo/Dir.

Owners: Jonathan D. Merriman/13.30%, Gregory S. Curhan/5.50%, Robert E. Ford/3.00%, Anthony B. Helfet/1.10%, Steven W. Town, Raymond J. Minehan, Dennis G. Schmal, Christopher L. Aguilar, Insiders/25.30%, John D. Hiestand, Ronald E. Spears, Brock Ganeles/2.80%, Scott Potter, Patrick Arbor, Highfields Capital Management L.P./9.99% *(16 Owners included in Index)*

Financial Data: *Fiscal Year End:*12/31 *Latest Annual Data:* 12/31/2006

Year	Sales	Net Income
2006	$51,819,000	-$8,220,000
2005	$43,839,000	-$1,514,000
2004	$38,368,000	$1,874,000

Curr. Assets:	$17,643,000	**Curr. Liab.:**	$12,665,000		
Plant, Equip.:	$1,587,000	**Total Liab.:**	$14,283,000	**Indic. Yr. Divd.:**	NA
Total Assets:	$30,498,000	**Net Worth:**	$16,215,000	**Debt/ Equity:**	NA

MCG Capital Corp

1100 Wilson Blvd., Ste. 3000, Arlington, VA, 22209; *PH:* 1-703-247-7500; *Fax:* 1-703-247-7500; *http://* www.mcgcapital.com

General - Incorporation	DE	**Stock**- Price on:12/24/2007	$17.062
Employees	85	Stock Exchange	NDQ
Auditor	Ernst & Young LLP	Ticker Symbol	MCGC
Stk Agt	American Stock Transfer & Trust Co.	Outstanding Shares	62,480,000
Counsel	Fried Frank Harris Shriver & Jacobson	E.P.S	$2.10
DUNS No.	NA	Shareholders	NA

Business: The group's principal activity is to operate as a closed-end investment company. The group provides financing and advisory services to small and medium-sized companies. It provides services to companies in the communications, information services, media and technology-enabled transactions processing industry sectors in the United States.

Primary SIC and add'l.: 6159 6162

CIK No: 0001141299

Subsidiaries: Crystal Media Network, Inc., IH ETC, Inc., IH Sunshine, Inc., MCG Capital Advisory Services, Inc., MCG Credit Corporation, MCG Finance I, LLC, MCG Finance II, LLC, MCG Finance III, LLC, MCG Finance IV, LLC, MCG Finance V, LLC, MCG Finance VI, MCG Finance VII, LLC, MCG IH Holdings, Inc., MCG-Kagan Research, Inc., Solutions Capital GP, LLC 16 Subsidiaries included in the Index

Officers: Steven F. Tunney/Dir., CEO, Pres./$3,137,277.00, Robert J. Merrick/Dir., Chief Investment Officer/$1,163,829.00, Miriam G. Krieger/Sr. VP, Chief Compliance Officer, Samuel G. Rubenstein/General Counsel, Exec. VP, Corp. Sec., Hagen B. Saville/Dir., Exec. VP/$2,780,258.00, Rick Cravey/MD, Charlie E. Booth/VP - Risk Management, Underwriting, Robert S. Grazioli/CIO, Exec. VP, Michael R. McDonnell/CFO, COO/$3,646,377.00, William B. Ford/MD, Douglas H. Gilbert/MD, Andrew J. Jacobson/MD, Peter E. Malekian/MD, Robert L. Marcotte/MD/$1,270,422.00, Michael S. McHugh/MD *(19 Officers included in Index)*

Directors: Steven F. Tunney/Dir., CEO, Pres., Jeffrey M. Bucher/Chmn., Kim D. Kelly/Dir., Edward S. Civera/Dir., Hagen B. Saville/Dir., Exec. VP, Kenneth J. O'Keefe/Dir., Wallace B. Millner/Dir., Robert J. Merrick/Dir., Chief Investment Officer

Owners: Jeffrey M. Bucher, Edward S. Civera, Hagen B. Saville, Robert J. Merrick, Insiders/3.30%, Dimensional Fund Advisors LP/6.10%, Robert L. Marcotte, Samuel G. Rubenstein, Kenneth J. OKeefe, U.S. Trust Corporation/6.70%, Michael R. McDonnell, Wallace B. Millner, Steven F. Tunney, Kim D. Kelly

Financial Data: *Fiscal Year End:*12/31 *Latest Annual Data:* 12/31/2006

Year	Sales	Net Income
2006	$154,393,000	$100,949,000
2005	$119,545,000	$68,193,000
2004	$103,924,000	$47,647,000

Curr. Assets:	$50,660,000	**Curr. Liab.:**	$29,850,000	**P/E Ratio:**	9.02
Plant, Equip.:	NA	**Total Liab.:**	$566,131,000	**Indic. Yr. Divd.:**	$1.760
Total Assets:	$1,319,268,000	**Net Worth:**	$753,137,000	**Debt/ Equity:**	0.5251

McGrath Rentcorp

5700 Las Positas Rd., Livermore, CA, 94551; *PH:* 1-925-606-9200; *Fax:* 1-925-453-3200; *http://* www.mgrc.com; *Email:* information@mgrc.com

General - Incorporation	CA	**Stock**- Price on:12/24/2007	$31.45
Employees	603	Stock Exchange	NDQ
Auditor	Grant Thornton LLP	Ticker Symbol	MGRC
Stk Agt	Computershare Trust CO.	Outstanding Shares	25,190,000
Counsel	Christoher Ream	E.P.S	$1.70
DUNS No.	09-622-6253	Shareholders	NA

Business: The group's principal activities are to manufacture, rent and sell relocatable modular offices and classrooms. The group's operations are comprised of three segments: mobile modular management corporation ('mmmc'), rentelco and enviroplex. Mmmc rents and sells modular buildings and related accessories to address customer's temporary and permanent space needs in California and Texas. Mmmc also serves classroom and specialty space needs from pre-school to post secondary grade levels. Rentelco rents and sells electronic test equipment to engineers, scientists, technicians and field-service personnel. Enviroplex manufactures moment-resistant, rigid steel framed portable classrooms and sells directly to California public school districts. The group's manufacturing facility is located in stockton, California.

Primary SIC and add'l.: 7359

CIK No: 0000752714

Subsidiaries: Enviroplex, Inc., Mobile Modular Management Corporation, TRS-RenTelco Inc.

Officers: Dennis C. Kakures/Dir., CEO, Pres./$1,193,646.00, Randle F. Rose/Sr. VP, Chief Administrative Officer, Sec./$393,780.00, Joseph F. Hanna/COO, Sr. VP/$579,253.00, Richard G. Brown/VP, Division Mgr. - Mobile Modular/$414,084.00, Keith E. Pratt/Sr. VP, CFO/$576,427.00, David M. Whitney/VP, Principal Accounting Officer, Corporate Controller

Directors: Dennis C. Kakures/Dir., CEO, Pres., Robert P. McGrath/Chmn., Founder, Robert C. Hood/Dir., Dennis P. Stradford/Dir., Ronald H. Zech/Dir., Joan M. McGrath/Dir., William J. Dawson/Dir.

Owners: Ronald H. Zech, Insiders/9.60%, Richard Brown, Dennis C. Kakures/2.10%, William J. Dawson, T. Rowe Price Associates, Inc./11.80%, Robert P. McGrath/5.70%, Dennis P. Stradford, Randle F. Rose, Joseph Hanna, Robert C. Hood, Columbia Wanger Asset Management, L.P./6.60%, Keith E. Pratt

Financial Data: *Fiscal Year End:*12/31 *Latest Annual Data:* 12/31/2006

Year	Sales	Net Income
2006	$267,066,000	$41,078,000
2005	$272,180,000	$40,819,000
2004	$202,520,000	$29,997,000

Curr. Assets:	$60,183,000	**Curr. Liab.:**	$55,509,000	**P/E Ratio:**	18.61
Plant, Equip.:	$509,488,000	**Total Liab.:**	$351,271,000	**Indic. Yr. Divd.:**	$0.720
Total Assets:	$585,542,000	**Net Worth:**	$230,792,000	**Debt/ Equity:**	NA

McGraw-Hill Companies Inc

1221 Ave. of the Americas, New York, NY, 10020; *PH:* 1-212-512-2000; *Fax:* 1-212-512-3840; *http://* www.mcgraw-hill.com; *Email:* customer.service@mcgraw-hill.com

General - Incorporation	NY	**Stock**- Price on:12/24/2007	$69.96
Employees	20,214	Stock Exchange	NYSE
Auditor	Ernst & Young LLP	Ticker Symbol	MHS
Stk Agt	Bank of New York	Outstanding Shares	343,200,000
Counsel	NA	E.P.S	$3.05
DUNS No.	00-121-3206	Shareholders	NA

Business: The group's principle activity is to provide to provide information products and services. The group operates through three segments namely education, financial, and information and media service segments. The group operates from United States.

Primary SIC and add'l.: 6282 4833 8732 2741 2731 2721

CIK No: 0000064040

Subsidiaries: Beijing Business E-win Information & Consultant Co., BizNet.TV, Inc., Capital IQ Information Systems (India) Pvt. Ltd., Capital IQ, Inc., CapitalKey Advisors (Europe) Limited, Carringbush Publications Pty Ltd., CRISIL Ltd., CTB/McGraw-Hill LLC, Dragon Media International Pty Ltd., Editora McGraw-Hill de Portugal, Ltda., Editorial Interamericana, S.A., Grow.net, Inc., Grupo McGraw-Hill, S.A. de C.V., Grupo Standard & Poors, S.A. de C.V., International Advertising/McGraw-Hill, Inc. 86 Subsidiaries included in the Index

Officers: Harold McGraw/58/Chmn., CEO, Pres./$19,884,770.00, David B. Stafford/CEO, Sr. VP - Corporate Affairs, Assist. to The Chmn., Bruce D. Marcus/CIO, Exec. VP/$1,239,883.00, Henry Hirschberg/Pres. - Mcgraw, Hill Education, Glenn S. Goldberg/Pres. - Information, Media, David L. Murphy/Exec. VP - Human Resources/$3,037,721.00, Robert J. Bahash/CFO, Exec. VP/$5,191,745.00, Kenneth M. Vittor/Exec. VP, General Counsel/$2,190,282.00, Talia M. Griep/Corporate Controller, Sr. VP - Global Business Services, Financial Planning, Peter C. Davis/Exec. VP - Global Strategy

Directors: Harold McGraw/58/Chmn., CEO, Pres., Pedro Aspe/56/Dir., Linda Koch Lorimer/55/Dir., James H. Ross/68/Dir., Robert P. McGraw/53/Dir., Douglas N. Daft/64/Dir., Edward B. Rust/56/Dir., Winfried Bischoff/65/Dir., Hilda Ochoa-Brillembourg/62/Dir., Kurt L. Schmoke/58/Dir., Sidney Taurel/58/Dir., Harold W. McGraw/Dir.

Owners: FMR Corp./5.54%, James H. Ross, Pedro Aspe, Douglas N. Daft, Linda Koch Lorimer, Bruce D. Marcus, Hilda Ochoa-Brillembourg, Harold McGraw/2.10%, Robert J. Bahash, Deven Sharma, Robert P. McGraw, Kurt L. Schmoke, Kenneth M. Vittor, Insiders/2.70%, David L. Murphy *(19 Owners included in Index)*

Financial Data: *Fiscal Year End:*12/31 *Latest Annual Data:* 12/31/2006

Year	Sales	Net Income
2006	$6,255,138,000	$882,231,000
2005	$6,003,642,000	$844,306,000
2004	$5,250,538,000	$755,823,000

Curr. Assets:	$2,257,938,000	**Curr. Liab.:**	$2,468,016,000	**P/E Ratio:**	26.70
Plant, Equip.:	$542,219,000	**Total Liab.:**	$3,363,272,000	**Indic. Yr. Divd.:**	$0.820
Total Assets:	$6,042,890,000	**Net Worth:**	$2,679,618,000	**Debt/ Equity:**	NA

McKesson Corp

1 Post St., San Francisco, CA, 94104; *PH:* 1-415-983-8300; *Fax:* 1-415-983-7160; *http://* www.mckesson.com; *Email:* community.relations@mckesson.com

General - Incorporation	DE	**Stock**- Price on:12/24/2007	$58.99
Employees	26,400	Stock Exchange	NYSE
Auditor	Deloitte & Touche LLP	Ticker Symbol	MCK
Stk Agt	Bank of New York	Outstanding Shares	297,200,000
Counsel	NA	E.P.S	$2.99
DUNS No.	17-766-7227	Shareholders	NA

Business: The group's principle activity is to distribute medicines used in North America. The group also provides decision support software, develop and install electronic systems, and prevent medication errors every week through bar-code scanning technology. In February 2007, the group acquired Physician Micro Systems, Inc. The group operates from United States.

Primary SIC and add'l.: 7372 5122 7375 5047

CIK No: 0000927653

Subsidiaries: McKesson Information Solutions Holdings Limited

Officers: John H. Hammergren/49/Chmn., CEO, Pres./$30,973,170.00, Marc E. Owen/Exec. VP - Corporate Strategy, Business Development/$4,496,177.00, Jeffrey C. Campbell/CFO, Exec. VP/$7,465,070.00, Laureen E. Seeger/Exec. VP, General Counsel, Sec., Randall N. Spratt/CIO, Exec.

VP, Pamela J. Pure/Exec. VP, Pres. - Mckesson Technology Solutions/$6,114,594.00, Paul C. Julian/Exec. VP, Group Pres. - Mckesson Distribution Solutions/$12,283,140.00, Paul E. Kirincic/Exec. VP - Human Resources, Nigel A. Rees/VP, Controller, Nicholas A. Loiacono/VP, Treasurer

Directors: John H. Hammergren/49/Chmn., CEO, Pres., Wayne A. Budd/66/Dir., Jane E. Shaw/69/Dir., Marie L. Knowles/61/Dir., Christine M. Jacobs/57/Dir., Alton F. Irby/67/Dir., David M. Lawrence/67/Dir., James V. Napier/71/Dir.

Owners: Wayne A. Budd, John H. Hammergren/1.80%, James V. Napier, Paul C. Julian, Robert W. Matschullat, Capital Research and Management Company/5.00%, Insiders/3.00%, Christine M. Jacobs, Wellington Management Company, LLP/12.38%, Pamela J. Pure, Vanguard Specialized Funds Vanguard Health Care Fund/5.00%, David M. Lawrence, Marie L. Knowles, Jeffrey C. Campbell, Marc E. Owen *(17 Owners included in Index)*

Financial Data: Fiscal Year End:03/31 Latest Annual Data: 3/31/2007

Year	Sales	Net Income
2007	$92,977,000,000	$913,000,000
2006	$88,050,000,000	$751,000,000
2005	$80,514,600,000	-$156,700,000

Curr. Assets:	$16,919,000,000	**Curr. Liab.:**	$13,515,000,000		
Plant, Equip.:	$671,000,000	**Total Liab.:**	$15,068,000,000	**Indic. Yr. Divd.:**	$0.240
Total Assets:	$20,975,000,000	**Net Worth:**	$5,907,000,000	**Debt/ Equity:**	0.2874

McLeodUSA Inc

One Martha's Way, Hiawatha, IA, 52233; *PH:* 1-319-790-7800; *http://* www.mcleodusa.com

General - Incorporation	DE	**Stock** - Price on:12/24/2007	NA
Employees	NA	Stock Exchange	NA
Auditor	Deloitte & Touche LLP	Ticker Symbol	NA
Stk Agt	Wells Fargo Shareowner Services	Outstanding Shares	NA
Counsel	NA	E.P.S.	NA
DUNS No.	80-886-2957	Shareholders	NA

Business: The group's principal activity is to provide integrated communications services to small and medium-sized business and residential customers. The services provided by the group include telecommunications and related services such as local, long distance, voice mail and Internet access services. It also markets end-to-end data communications and telecommunications network equipment. The group operates solely in the domestic market.

Primary SIC and add'l.: 4813

CIK No: 0000919943

Subsidiaries: CapRock Communications Corp., CapRock Design Services, L.P., CapRock Fiber Network, Ltd., CapRock Network Services, L.P., CapRock Telecommunications Corp., CapRock Telecommunications Leasing Corp., Devise Associates, Inc., Intelispan, Inc., JPMorgan Chase Bank, McLeodUSA Holdings, Inc., McLeodUSA Information Services, Inc., McLeodUSA Integrated Business Systems, Inc, McLeodUSA Market Response, Inc., McLeodUSA Network Services, Inc., McLeodUSA Purchasing, LLC 18 Subsidiaries included in the Index

Officers: Royce J. Holland/Dir., CEO, Chris MacFarland/CTO, Group VP, John Dumbleton/Group VP - Wholesale Services, Indirect Channels, Bernie Zuroff/Group VP, General Counsel, Sec., Tim Naramore/Group VP, CIO, Catherine Weekley/Chief - Staff, VP - Corporate Communications, Richard J. Buyens/Exec. VP - Sales, Joseph H. Ceryanec/Group VP, CFO, Chris J. Ryan/Group VP - Customer Services, Michael F. Edl/Group VP - Network Operations

Directors: Royce J. Holland/Dir., CEO, John Hank Bonde/Dir., Donald C. Campion/Dir., Eugene Davis/Dir., John D. McEvoy/Dir., Alex Stadler/Dir., Craig D. Young/Dir.

McMoran Exploration Co

1615 Poydras St., New Orleans, LA, 70112; *PH:* 1-504-582-4000; *Fax:* 1-504-582-1662; *http://* www.mcmoran.com

General - Incorporation	DE	**Stock** - Price on:12/24/2007	$15.05
Employees	37	Stock Exchange	NYSE
Auditor	Ernst & Young LLP	Ticker Symbol	MMR
Stk Agt	Mellon Investor Services LLC	Outstanding Shares	28,470,000
Counsel	NA	E.P.S.	-$3.48
DUNS No.	05-084-8092	Shareholders	NA

Business: The group's principal activity is to explore, develop and produce oil and gas offshore in the gulf of Mexico and onshore in the gulf coast region. The oil and gas operations include oil and gas exploration, development and production principally in the gulf of Mexico and the gulf coast region. As of 01-Jan-2004, the group owned or controlled interests in 52 oil and gas leases in the gulf of Mexico and onshore Louisiana and Texas covering approximately 201,000 gross acres. The group operates only in the United States.

Primary SIC and add'l.: 1479 1311

CIK No: 0000064279

Subsidiaries: Freeport-McMoRan Energy LLC, McMoRan Oil & Gas LLC

Officers: Glenn A. Kleinert/CEO, Pres./$1,755,278.00, Morrison C. Bethea/Advisory Dir., Gabrielle K. McDonald/Advisory Dir., Nancy D. Parmelee/Sr. VP, CFO, Sec./$819,655.00, Howard C. Murrish/67/Exec. VP/$1,725,779.00

Directors: Richard C. Adkerson/Co - Chmn., B. M. Rankin/Vice Chmn. - Board, James R. Moffett/Dir., Taylor J. Wharton/Dir., Suzanne T. Mestayer/55/Dir., Gerald J. Ford/Dir., Devon H. Graham/Dir., Robert A. Day/Dir.

Owners: Unicredito Italiano S.p.A./6.00%, FMR Corp./7.50%, Columbia Wanger Asset Management, L.P./5.60%, Wells Fargo& Company/12.20%, k1 Ventures Limited/14.60%, Alpine Capital, L.P./17.10%

Financial Data: Fiscal Year End:12/31 Latest Annual Data: 12/31/2006

Year	Sales	Net Income
2006	$209,738,000	-$47,654,000
2005	$130,127,000	-$39,712,000
2004	$29,849,000	-$51,671,000

Curr. Assets:	$117,112,000	**Curr. Liab.:**	$143,018,000		
Plant, Equip.:	$282,538,000	**Total Liab.:**	$448,077,000	**Indic. Yr. Divd.:**	NA
Total Assets:	$408,677,000	**Net Worth:**	-$68,443,000	**Debt/ Equity:**	NA

McNab Creek Gold Corp

11850 S Hwy. 191, Unit B-9, Moab, UT, 84532; *PH:* 1-435-259-0460

General - Incorporation	NV	**Stock** - Price on:12/24/2007	$1.36
Employees	NA	Stock Exchange	OTC
Auditor	Dale Matheson Carr-hilton Labonte LLP	Ticker Symbol	MCNB
Stk Agt	Computershare Investor Services LLC	Outstanding Shares	NA
Counsel	NA	E.P.S.	NA
DUNS No.	NA	Shareholders	NA

Business: The group's principle activities include mining and exploration of minerals. The group operates from United States.

Primary SIC and add'l.: 1040

CIK No: 0001295190

Officers: Peter Dickie/44/Dir., Pres., Christopher J. Turley/39/CFO

Directors: Christopher R. Verrico/50/Dir., Peter Dickie/44/Dir., Pres., Michael H. Sandidge/51/Dir., Donald O. Miller/57/Dir.

Owners: Michael Sandidge/0.00%, James Zaniol/0.06%, Kenneth Townsend/0.53%, Richard Luxford/0.06%, Peter Dickie/0.00%, Christopher Verrico/0.00%, Spectre Investments Inc./0.09%

McRae Industries Inc

400 N Main St., Mt. Gilead, NC, 27306; *PH:* 1-910-439-6147; *Fax:* 1-910-439-9596; *http://* www.mcraeindustries.com

General - Incorporation	DE	**Stock** - Price on:12/24/2007	$12.75
Employees	NA	Stock Exchange	OTC
Auditor	Grant Thornton LLP	Ticker Symbol	MRINB
Stk Agt	Wachovia Bank N.A	Outstanding Shares	2,570,000
Counsel Kennedy Covington Lobdell & Hickman		E.P.S.	NA
DUNS No.	00-316-5941	Shareholders	NA

Business: The group's principal activities are to manufacture and sell bar code reading and related printing devices; manufacture and sell military combat boots, western and work boots and selling, leasing and servicing office equipment. The bar code unit manufactures and sells bar code reading and printing devices and other item related to optical data collection, including licensing and selling computer software. The footwear segment manufactures western and work boots and combat boots. The office products segment sells, maintains and leases toshiba photocopiers and facsimile machines and riso digital/duplicators through its subsidiary, mcrae office solutions, inc.

Primary SIC and add'l.: 3861 3577 7389 3143 3144 2752 7377

CIK No: 0000729284

Subsidiaries: Compsee, Inc, Dan Post Boot Company, DataScan Corporation, Hoke Development Company, Inc., McRae Boot, Inc., System Integrators Plus, Inc

MD Technologies Inc

620 Florida St., Ste 200, Baton Rouge, LA, 70801; *PH:* 1-225-343-7169; *http://* www.mdtechnologies.com; *Email:* sales@mdtechnologiesinc.com

General - Incorporation	DE	**Stock** - Price on:12/24/2007	NA
Employees	82	Stock Exchange	OTC
Auditor	Comiskey & Co. P.C	Ticker Symbol	MDTO
Stk Agt	Corporate Stock Transfer, Inc.	Outstanding Shares	NA
Counsel	NA	E.P.S.	-$0.8
DUNS No.	NA	Shareholders	NA

Business: The group's principal activities are to provide Internet-based solutions to the healthcare industry, including practice management, e-commerce, and patient interactivity applications. The software tools and services allow physicians to access data and to provide patients with the means of accessing data using the Internet. The medtopia suite of products and services consist of medtopia manager, mymedtopia, medtopia mobile and medtopia expert billing and accounts receivable management. The group's customers are located throughout the continental United States and consist of physicians, hospitals, health clinics, and other healthcare providers. In may 2003 the group acquired listech, inc.

Primary SIC and add'l.: 7389 7372 7375

CIK No: 0001260465

Subsidiaries: Medical Consultants Inc., Medical Group Services, Inc.

Officers: William Eglin/32/CEO, Pres., Jose S. Canseco/47/Dir., VP - Mergers, Acquisitions, William C. Ellison/47/Dir., Sec., General Counsel, Joseph Palazzo/COO, Anthony Maniscalco/54/VP - RCM Services, Jon Trezona/VP - Development, Jerry Leblanc/33/Operations Mgr., Amy Dixon/Dir., Medtopia Mgr. Support, Sean Marchiafava/36/CIO, VP - Research & Development, Brina Cabrera/VP - RCM Services, Jonathan Stuckey/Controller

Directors: William D. Davis/Chmn., Jose S. Canseco/47/Dir., VP - Mergers, Acquisitions, William C. Ellison/47/Dir., Sec., General Counsel

Owners: Ricardo Marcos/10.10%, Commonwealth Advisors, Inc./22.00%, Jose S. Canseco/12.50%, William D. Eglin/0.80%, Insiders/48.40%, William D. Davis/19.60%, Anthony F. Maniscalco/3.60%, Brina Cabrera/0.40%

Financial Data: Fiscal Year End:12/31 Latest Annual Data: 12/31/2006

Year	Sales	Net Income
2006	$6,472,000	-$3,297,000
2005	$1,378,000	-$1,788,000
2004	$646,000	-$1,288,000

Curr. Assets:	$951,000	**Curr. Liab.:**	$862,000		
Plant, Equip.:	$664,000	**Total Liab.:**	$8,331,000	**Indic. Yr. Divd.:**	NA
Total Assets:	$6,000,000	**Net Worth:**	-$2,331,000	**Debt/ Equity:**	NA

MDC Partners Inc

45 Hazelton Ave., Toronto, ON, M5R 2E3; *PH:* 1-416-960-9000; *http://* www.mdccorp.com; *Email:* mnadal@mdc-partners.com

General - Incorporation	Canada	**Stock** - Price on:12/24/2007	$8.16
Employees	4,994	Stock Exchange	NDQ
Auditor	BDO Seidman, LLP	Ticker Symbol	MDCA
Stk Agt	Mellon Trust Co	Outstanding Shares	25,100,000
Counsel	Fogler, Rubinoff	E.P.S.	-$0.946
DUNS No.	NA	Shareholders	NA

Business: The group's principle activities include personalized transaction products such as personal and business cheques; electronic transactions such as credit, debit, telephone and smart cards; secure ticketing products such as airline, transit and event tickets; stamps, both postal and excise and a comprehensive range of communication services that includes advertising, direct marketing, database management, sales promotion, public relations, investor relations, research and consulting, corporate identity, branding and interactive marketing.

Primary SIC and add'l.: 8742 2782 2754 2752

CIK No: 0000876883

Subsidiaries: 656712 Ontario Limited , 939 GP Inc., Accent Marketing Services, LLC, Accumark Communications Inc., ACLC Inc., Allard Johnson Communications Inc., Ashton-Potter (USA) Ltd., Ashton-Potter Canada Inc., Ashton-Potter Canada Ltd., Banjo Strategic Entertainment, LLC, Bratskeir& Company,Inc., Bruce Mau Design Inc., Bryan Mills Group Ltd., Chinnici Direct,Inc., Cliff Freeman and Partners LLC 43 Subsidiaries included in the Index

Officers: Miles S. Nadal/Chmn., CEO/$4,872,855.00, Brandon Berger/Dir. - Digital Innovation, Graham L. Rosenberg/MD/$704,170.00, Mitchell Gendel/General Counsel, Corp. Sec., Charles K. Porter/Chief Strategist, Glenn W. Gibson/CFO - Financial Marketing Communications, Thomas Boyle/Corporate Controller, Ray Forzley/Dir. - Corporate Development, Steven Berns/43/Dir., CFO, Pres./$1,623,114.00, Gavin Swartzman/MD/$666,373.00, Robert E. Dickson/MD/$885,037.00, Michael Sabatino/Chief Accounting Officer, Robert B. Van Horn/Exec. Dir. - Partner Development, Katie Kempner/Dir. - Corporate Communication, Donna Granato/Dir. - Finance, Investor Relation

Directors: Miles S. Nadal/Chmn., CEO, Richard R. Hylland/Dir., Stephen M. Pustil/Dir., Steven Berns/43/Dir., CFO, Pres., Michael J.L. Kirby/Dir., Sanator Michael J.l. Kirby/Dir., Jeffery E. Epstien/Dir., Clare Copeland/Dir., Francois R. Roy/Dir., Robert Kamerschen/Dir., Thomas E. Weigman/Dir., Scott L. Kauffman/Dir., Thomas N. Davidson/Dir.

Owners: Franois R. Roy, Weiss Peck & Greer Investments, a division of Robeco USA, LLC/6.65%, Alex A. Porter/5.61%, Thomas N. Davidson, Steven Berns, Thomas E. Weigman, Robert Kamerschen, Wellington Management Company, LLP/12.71%, Goldman Capital Management Inc./5.15%, Cardinal Capital Management, LLC/9.25%, Richard R. Hylland, Gavin Swartzman, Stephen M. Pustil, Miles S. Nadal/8.97%, Robert Dickson *(21 Owners included in Index)*

Financial Data: *Fiscal Year End:*12/31 *Latest Annual Data:* 12/31/2006

Year	Sales	Net Income
2006	$423,671,000	-$33,539,000
2005	$443,462,000	-$7,949,000
2004	$316,812,000	-$2,157,000

Curr. Assets:	$166,476,000	**Curr. Liab.:**	$271,515,000		
Plant, Equip.:	$44,425,000	**Total Liab.:**	$369,087,000	**Indic. Yr. Divd.:**	NA
Total Assets:	$493,501,000	**Net Worth:**	$124,414,000	**Debt/ Equity:**	0.3771

MDI Inc

10226 San PeDr.o Ave., Ste. 200, San Antonio, TX, 78216; ***PH:*** 1-210-582-2664; ***Fax:*** 1-210-477-5401; ***http://*** www.mdisecure.com; ***Email:*** sales@mdisecure.com

General - Incorporation	DE	**Stock**- Price on:12/24/2007	$1.23
Employees	59	Stock Exchange	NDQ
Auditor	PMB Helin Donovan, LLP	Ticker Symbol	MDII
Stk Agt	Securities Transfer Corp	Outstanding Shares	32,090,000
Counsel	NA	E.P.S	-$0.28
DUNS No.	NA	Shareholders	NA

Business: The group's principle activities are to design, market, sell and service niche security products for use in industrial, governmental and consumer surveillance markets worldwide. The group operates through two segments: professional security group (psg): whose primary focus is access control products and the diversified sales group (dsg): which markets products to the consumer/do-it-yourself business as well as its industrial video and alarm management businesses. The corporate segment provides human resources, legal, financial, information technologies, accounting and reporting functions for the entire business. The group's quarterly revenue for September 2007 was 1.84 millions of USD.

Primary SIC and add'l.: 7382 3663

CIK No: 0000318259

Subsidiaries: ABC Merger Corp, ABM Data SystemsInc., Diamond Electronics, Digitel Inc, Lenel Systems International Inc, Monitor Dynamics Inc.a California corporation, Security Procurement B.V., Security Procurement France S.A., Security Warranty BVI Ltd., Security Warranty Inc., Ultrak (Asia Pacific) Pty. Ltd., Ultrak (Asia) Pte. Ltd., Ultrak (SA) (Proprietary) Limited , Ultrak (Switzerland) S.A., Ultrak (UK) Limited 26 Subsidiaries included in the Index

Officers: James Collier Sparks/Dir., CEO, Pres./$347,345.00, Michael Sweet/CFO, COO/$170,968.00, Darwin Valentine/Regional Sales Mgr. - International, Chuck Adams/Regional Sales Mgr. - West, Scott Lawson/Subsidiary Contact - ABM Data Systems, Dir., Christopher Davila/Customer Service Mgr. - Subsidiary Contact - Mobile Video Products, Sales Mgr., Kevin Caufield/Regional Sales Mgr. - Eastern, Peter Tran/Subsidiary Contact - OEM, Dealer & Distributor Sales, ABM Data Systems, Tim Rohrbach/CIO, VP, CTO, Robert A. Schorr/Distribution Sales Mgr., Michael M. Garcia/VP - Marketing, Sr. VP/$166,740.00, Richard A. Larsen/Sr. VP, General Counsel, Sec./$222,711.00, Harold Haug/57/Sr. VP - Sales, Marketing/$230,928.00, Jim Pierre/Pres. - MDI Federal Systems Division

Directors: James Collier Sparks/Dir., CEO, Pres., James W. Power/78/Chmn., Peter B. Knepper/Dir., Robert E. McCann/Dir., James M. Vandevere/46/Dir., Carlo R. Loi/Dir.

Owners: Robert McCann, Richard Larsen/2.40%, Michael Garcia/1.00%, Victoria & Eagle Strategic Fund, Ltd./7.10%, Michael Sweet/1.70%, Peter Knepper, Insiders/14.90%, Carlo Loi/1.50%, James Power/1.10%, Stratis Authority/17.90%, Collier Sparks/4.00%, Fursa Alternative Strategies LLC/5.30%, Harold Haug/1.70%, James Vandevere, Victoria & Eagle Strategic Fund, Ltd./100.00%

Financial Data: *Fiscal Year End:*12/31 *Latest Annual Data:* 12/31/2006

Year	Sales	Net Income
2006	$8,720,000	-$6,984,000
2005	$8,797,000	-$5,645,000
2004	$14,245,000	-$7,811,000

Curr. Assets:	$2,570,000	**Curr. Liab.:**	$3,037,000		
Plant, Equip.:	$225,000	**Total Liab.:**	$3,037,000	**Indic. Yr. Divd.:**	NA
Total Assets:	$7,798,000	**Net Worth:**	$4,761,000	**Debt/ Equity:**	NA

MDI Technologies Inc

940 W Port Plz., Ste. 100, St. Louis, MO, 63146; ***PH:*** 1-314-439-6400; ***Fax:*** 1-314-317-9710; ***http://*** www.mditech.com; ***Email:*** info@mditech.com

General - Incorporation	DE	**Stock**- Price on:12/24/2007	NA
Employees	NA	Stock Exchange	NA
Auditor	Rubin, Brown, Gornstein & Co. LLP	Ticker Symbol	NA
Stk Agt	Pacific Corporate Trust Co	Outstanding Shares	NA
Counsel	NA	E.P.S	NA
DUNS No.	NA	Shareholders	NA

Business: The group's principal activity is to provide software and support services to the healthcare industry over the Internet using ultra-thin client technologies. It provides an accounting software package to the skilled care industry and a standard clinical package to provide a complete solution for skilled nursing organizations. The group's product on-line advantage enables smooth transfer of data into the various clinical, accounting, admissions and marketing modules from a single data entry format. It includes software like medical records, quick admit/ marketing, accounts receivable and payables, pay roll, human resources, touch time, etc. The two major segments of the market are the freestanding skilled nursing centers and freestanding assisted living facilities. Currently, the group serves over 1300 facilities.

Primary SIC and add'l.: 7372 7374

CIK No: 0001082575

Subsidiaries: Management-Data, Inc.

Officers: Anne Sherrod/Member - Sales Team - Midwestern US, Angie Clifton/Member - MDI Sales Team - Sales Coordinator, Jane Sullivan/Member - MDI Sales Team - Northwestern US, Carrie Price/e-Charting Specialist, Polly Kirkwood/Dir. - Sales, Marketing, Bob Skinner/Member - MDI Sales Team - Ohio Valley - New England, Mark Herbert/Member - MDI Sales Team - Southeastern US, Brian Weck/Member - MDI Sales Team - Ohio Valley - Midwestern US, Kathy Munie/Implementation Specialist, Doc Devore/Dir. - Research & Development, Tami Peters/Client Relations Mgr., Dennis Huebner/Dir. - Client Services, Hillary Devisser/Install, Training Coordinator

MDS Inc

2700 Matheson Blvd. E, Ste. 300, W Tower, Mississauga, ON, L4W 4V9; ***PH:*** 1-416-675-6777; ***http://*** www.mdsinc.com

General - Incorporation	Canada	**Stock**- Price on:12/24/2007	$20.43
Employees	5,600	Stock Exchange	NYSE
Auditor	Ernst & Young LLP	Ticker Symbol	MDZ
Stk Agt	CIBC Mellon Trust CO.	Outstanding Shares	122,290,000
Counsel	Fasken Martineau Dumoulin	E.P.S	$5.85
DUNS No.	NA	Shareholders	NA

Business: The group operates in three segments: life sciences, health and proteomics. Life sciences segment consists of supplying pharmaceuticals, medical devices and supplies. The products and services offered in this segment include advanced analytical equipment, medical isotopes and pharmaceutical contract research services. In the health segment, the group provides health care services to consumers. The services offered in this segment include clinical laboratory testing and distribution of medical products. In the proteomics segment, the group focuses on research and development of proteomic-enabled drug discovery. Customers include manufacturers of medical products and health care institutions. The company operates in Canada, the United States, Europe and Asia. The services offered in this segment include capabilities in proteomics systems, technology, drug design and screening. The group's quarterly revenue for September 2007 was 338.00 millions of USD.

Primary SIC and add'l.: 8731 8082 2819 8071

CIK No: 0001057698

Subsidiaries: MDS (Canada) Inc, MDS Laboratory Services Inc., MDS Life Sciences (Singapore) Pte. Lte, MDS Nordion Europe SA (NESA), MDS Pharma Services (Taiwan), Ltd, MDS Pharma Services (U.S.) Inc, MDS Pharma Services Central Lab GmbH, MDS Pharma Services Central Lab S.A.S, MDS Pharma Services Espana, S.A, MDS Pharma Services France S.A.S., MDS Pharma Services G.B. Limited, MDS Pharma Services SA, MDS Pharma Services Switzerland AG

Officers: Stephen P. Defalco/46/Dir., CEO, Pres., James M. Reid/Exec. VP - Global Human Resources, Hans K. Thunem/Pres., Steven M. West/Pres. - MDS Nordion, Thomas E. Gernon/CIO, Jim A.H. Garner/CFO, Exec. VP, Kenneth L. Horton/Exec. VP - Corporate Development, General Counsel, Sharon M. Mathers/Sr. VP - Investor Relations, External Communications, David Spaight/Pres. - MDS Pharma Services, Catherine Melville/Dir. - External Communications, Charlene McGrady/Dir. - Communications, Douglas S. Prince/CFO, Exec. VP - Finance, Kim Lee/Mgr. - Investor Relations, Andrew W. Boorn/Pres. - MDS Analytical Technologies

Directors: Stephen P. Defalco/46/Dir., CEO, Pres., John T. Mayberry/63/Chmn., John T. Mayberr/Dir., Mary Mogford/63/Dir., William Anderson/58/Dir., Richard H. McCoy/65/Dir., Robert W. Luba/65/Dir., Nelson M. Sims/60/Dir., Kathleen M. Oneill/54/Dir., William A. Etherington/66/Dir., Paul S. Anderson/69/Dir., James S.A MacDonald/62/Dir.

Financial Data: *Fiscal Year End:*10/31 *Latest Annual Data:* 10/31/2006

Year	Sales	Net Income
2006	$1,017,222,000	$123,137,000
2005	$1,265,799,000	$26,353,000
2004	$1,448,068,000	$22,164,000

Curr. Assets:	$1,085,037,000	**Curr. Liab.:**	$473,811,000		
Plant, Equip.:	$339,966,000	**Total Liab.:**	$970,822,000	**Indic. Yr. Divd.:**	$0.110
Total Assets:	$2,389,579,000	**Net Worth:**	$1,418,757,000	**Debt/ Equity:**	NA

MDU Communications (USA) Inc

60 -D Commerce Way, Totowa, NJ, 07512; ***PH:*** 1-973-237-9499; ***http://*** www.mduc.com

General - Incorporation	DE	**Stock**- Price on:12/24/2007	NA
Employees	107	Stock Exchange	OTC
Auditor	J. H. Cohn LLP	Ticker Symbol	MDTV
Stk Agt	NA	Outstanding Shares	NA
Counsel	NA	E.P.S	-$0.15
DUNS No.	NA	Shareholders	NA

Business: The group's principal activities are to provide digital satellite television programming and high-speed (broadband) Internet service to residents of multi-dwelling unit properties (mdus) in the United States. The properties include apartment buildings, condominiums, gated communities, hotels and universities. The group has two types of digital satellite television service: digital broadcast service (dbs), which uses an in-suite set-top digital box and private cable service, where digital satellite television programming can be tailored to the needs of an individual property. On 01-Jun-2004 the group acquired direct satellite inc.

Primary SIC and add'l.: 4841 7379

CIK No: 0001086139

Subsidiaries: Liberty Media Corporation (NYSE: L, LMCb)., MDU Communications International, Inc.

Officers: Sheldon B. Nelson/46/Chmn., CEO, Pres., Brad Holmstrom/42/General Counsel, Steve Moore/GM - Midwest, Rich Dibello/Dir. - Sales, North East Regional Office, Michael Stanway/VP - Operations, Product Planning, Engineering, Carmen Ragusa/VP - Finance, Administration, Patrick Cunningham/38/VP - Marketing, Business Development, Tom Tracey/COO, Pres., Joe Nassau/VP - Customer Service, Operations, John Silvers/GM - Northeast, Mid Atlantic, Mark Mayhook/Southeast GM, Rick Erikson/GM - South East Regional, Cory Washburn/Sales Mgr. - South East

Directors: Sheldon B. Nelson/46/Chmn., CEO, Pres., Douglas G. Hooper/47/Dir., John Edward Boyle/61/Dir., Carolyn C. Howard/44/Dir.

Owners: Michael Stanway, Fuller & Thaler/3.60%, Brad Holmstrom/0.80%, Carmen Ragusa, SC Fundamental/5.70%, Steve Cox, Insiders/8.10%, Capital Group International, Inc. and Capital Guardian Trust Co./15.00%, J. E. Boyle, Joe Nassau, Patrick Cunningham/1.00%, John Silvers, Douglas Hooper, Carolyn Howard/0.50%, Tom Tracey *(16 Owners included in Index)*

Financial Data: *Fiscal Year End:*09/30 *Latest Annual Data:* 09/30/2006

Year	Sales	Net Income
2006	$13,366,000	-$8,011,000
2005	$9,142,000	-$4,680,000
2004	$4,490,000	-$8,941,000

Curr. Assets:	$5,269,000	**Curr. Liab.:**	$3,206,000		
Plant, Equip.:	$19,626,000	**Total Liab.:**	$7,252,000	**Indic. Yr. Divd.:**	NA
Total Assets:	$27,169,000	**Net Worth:**	$19,918,000	**Debt/ Equity:**	NA

MDU Resources Group Inc

1200 W Century Ave., Bismarck, ND, 58506; *PH:* 1-701-530-1000; *Fax:* 1-701-530-1698; *http://* www.mdu.com; *Email:* investor@mduresources.com

General - Incorporation	DE	**Stock**- Price on:12/24/2007	$28.82
Employees	11,526	Stock Exchange	NYSE
Auditor	Deloitte & Touche LLP	Ticker Symbol	MDU
Stk Agt	Wells Fargo Bank, N.A.	Outstanding Shares	181,830,000
Counsel	Thelen Reid & Priest LLP	E.P.S.	$2.30
DUNS No.	00-696-2286	Shareholders	NA

Business: The group's principle activities include generating, transmitting and distributing electricity. The group provides services include construction materials and mining, construction services, electric and natural gas utilities, natural gas pipeline and energy services, and natural gas and oil production. The groups construction services include electrical line construction, pipeline construction, inside electrical wiring and cabling, mechanical services and the manufacture and distribution of specialty equipment. The group operates from United States.

Primary SIC and add'l.: 4924 1382 4925 4922 5082 1389 4939

CIK No: 0000067716

Subsidiaries: Alaska Basic Industries, Inc., Anchorage Sand and Gravel Company, Inc., Aquifirst, Inc., Baldwin Contracting Company, Inc., Bauerly Brothers, Inc., BEH Electric Holdings, LLC, Bell Electrical Contractors, Inc., Bitter Creek Pipelines, LLC, BIV Generation Company, LLC, BMH Mechanical Holdings, LLC, Bombard Electric, LLC, Bombard Mechanical, LLC, Brush Generation Company, LLC, Brush Power, LLC, Buffalo Bituminous, Inc. 104 Subsidiaries included in the Index

Officers: Terry D. Hildestad/Dir., CEO, Pres./$2,731,925.00, William E. Schneider/CEO, Pres. - Knife River Corporation/$1,635,147.00, John G. Harp/CEO, Pres. - MDU Construction Services Group, Inc/$2,074,089.00, John K. Castleberry/53/Exec. VP - Administration/$985,241.00, Paul K. Sandness/53/General Counsel, Sec., Arlene Stillwell/Investor Relations Officer, Nicole A. Kivisto/34/Controller, Vernon A. Raile/63/CFO, Exec. VP, Treasurer/$1,355,184.00, Cindy C. Redding/49/VP - Human Resources, Doran N. Schwartz/38/VP, Chief Accounting Officer

Directors: Terry D. Hildestad/Dir., CEO, Pres., Harry J. Pearce/65/Chmn., John K. Wilson/53/Dir., Thomas Everist/58/Dir., John L. Olson/68/Dir., Sister T. Welder/67/Dir., Dennis W. Johnson/58/Dir., Richard H. Lewis/58/Dir., Karen B. Fagg/54/Dir., Patricia L. Moss/54/Dir.

Owners: John G. Harp, Richard H. Lewis, Patricia L. Moss, John K. Wilson, Warren L. Robinson, Harry J. Pearce, John K. Castleberry, Karen B. Fagg, Vernon A. Raile, Sister Thomas Welder, Thomas Everist/1.90%, Martin A. White, John L. Olson, New York Life Trust Company/6.36%, Terry D. Hildestad *(18 Owners included in Index)*

Financial Data: *Fiscal Year End:*12/31 *Latest Annual Data:* 12/31/2006

Year	Sales	Net Income
2006	$4,070,684,000	$315,757,000
2005	$3,455,414,000	$275,083,000
2004	$2,719,257,000	$207,067,000

Curr. Assets:	$993,735,000	**Curr. Liab.:**	$653,962,000	**P/E Ratio:**	16.95
Plant, Equip.:	$3,398,962,000	**Total Liab.:**	$2,738,561,000	**Indic. Yr. Divd.:**	$0.580
Total Assets:	$4,903,474,000	**Net Worth:**	$2,164,913,000	**Debt/ Equity:**	NA

MDwerks Inc

1020 Nw 6th St. Windolph, Deerfield Beach, FL, 33442; *PH:* 1-954-389-8300; *http://* www.mdwerks.com; *Email:* info@mdwerks.com

General - Incorporation	DE	**Stock**- Price on:12/24/2007	$1.04
Employees	18	Stock Exchange	OTC
Auditor	Sherb & Co., LLP	Ticker Symbol	MDWK
Stk Agt	Corporate Stock Transfer, Inc.	Outstanding Shares	12,580,000
Counsel	NA	E.P.S.	-$0.899
DUNS No.	NA	Shareholders	NA

Business: The groups principle activities include processing, funding and collecting solutions to the healthcare provider industry. Services of the group include CLAIMwerks(TM) solutions, Billing, Lending and Consulting. Customers served by the group include doctors, hospital based practices, and healthcare providers. The group acquired MDwerks Global Holdings, Inc. in October 2005, and Xeni Companies in June 2005. The group operates from the United States.

Primary SIC and add'l.: 6411

CIK No: 0001295514

Subsidiaries: MDwerks Global Holdings, Inc, Xeni Financial Services, Corporation, Xeni Medical Billing, Corp., Xeni Medical Systems, Inc.

Officers: Howard B. Katz/Chmn., CEO, Adam Prior/Investor Relations Contact, Solon L. Kandel/Dir., Pres., Vincent Colangelo/CFO, Lila Sobel/49/COO, Gerard Maresca/VP - Business Development, Stephen M. Weiss/COO

Directors: Howard B. Katz/Chmn., CEO, Solon L. Kandel/Dir., Pres., David M. Barnes/65/Dir., Peter Dunne/50/Dir., Paul Kushner/61/Dir.

Owners: Howard B. Katz/11.50%, Lila Sobel/0.10%, MEDwerks.com Corp/17.00%, Solon Kandel/9.20%, Insiders/24.70%, David M. Barnes/0.40%, Gerard Maresca/1.20%, Paul Kushner/1.20%, AJMN Partnership/5.60%, Vincent Colangelo/0.90%, Jacob Nudel/3.40%, AJKN Partnership/5.60%, Peter Dunne/0.50%, AJLN Partnership/5.60%, Stephen Weiss/0.70%

Financial Data: *Fiscal Year End:*12/31 *Latest Annual Data:* 12/31/2006

Year	Sales	Net Income
2006	$428,000	-$9,675,000
2005	$58,000	-$2,577,000
2004	NA	-$62,000

Curr. Assets:	$3,750,000	**Curr. Liab.:**	$1,367,000		
Plant, Equip.:	$156,000	**Total Liab.:**	$2,096,000	**Indic. Yr. Divd.:**	NA
Total Assets:	$4,408,000	**Net Worth:**	$2,311,000	**Debt/ Equity:**	0.6185

Meade Instruments Corp

6001 Oak Canyon, Irvine, CA, 92618; *PH:* 1-949-451-1450; *Fax:* 1-949-451-1460; *http://* www.meade.com

General - Incorporation	DE	**Stock**- Price on:12/24/2007	$2.27
Employees	308	Stock Exchange	NDQ
Auditor	PricewaterhouseCoopers LLP	Ticker Symbol	MEAD
Stk Agt	Computershare Trust CO.	Outstanding Shares	20,090,000
Counsel	O'melveny & Myers	E.P.S.	-$0.91
DUNS No.	06-763-4956	Shareholders	NA

Business: The group's principal activities are to design, manufacture, import and distribute telescopes, telescope accessories, binoculars, riflescopes microscopes and other optical and digital imaging products. The products of the group include advanced astronomical telescopes, entry-level telescopes, binoculars, rifle and pistol scopes and accessories. The products are sold under the brand names simmons (R), weaver(R) and redfield (r). The customers include: discovery channel stores, wal-Mart, aldi, mic international corp., sam's club and jerry's sport center. The group has operations in the United States, Germany and Mexico.

Primary SIC and add'l.: 3827

CIK No: 0001032067

Subsidiaries: Coronado Instruments, Inc., Meade Instruments (Guangzhou) Co., Ltd., Meade Instruments Europe GmbH and Co. KG, Meade Instruments Mexico, S. de R.L. de C.V., Meade Instruments Verwaltungs GmbH, Simmons Outdoor Corp

Officers: Steven L. Muellner/58/Dir., CEO, Pres./$565,184.00, Robert L. Davis/41/Sr. VP - Sales/$688,320.00, Donald Finkle/50/Sr. VP - Operations/$167,827.00, Paul Ross/Sr. VP - Finance, CFO, Paul E. Ross/Sr. VP - Finance, CFO

Directors: Steven L. Muellner/58/Dir., CEO, Pres., Harry L. Casari/72/Chmn., Timothy C. McQuay/Dir., Steven G. Murdock/55/Dir., Frederick H. Schneider/Dir., Paul D. Sonkin/Dir., James M. Chadwick/Dir.

Owners: Mark D. Peterson/1.43%, Timothy C. McQuay, Steven G. Murdock/5.93%, Paul E. Ross, Dimensional Fund Advisors, Inc./7.44%, Steven L. Muellner, Brent W. Christensen/1.49%, Meade Instruments Corp. Employee Stock Ownership Plan/4.78%, Insiders/27.13%, Harry L. Casari, Paul D. Sonkin/15.74%, Austin N. Marxe/9.08%, Wells Fargo & Company/5.64%, Robert L. Davis, Frederick H. Schneider *(18 Owners included in Index)*

Financial Data: *Fiscal Year End:*02/28 *Latest Annual Data:* 2/28/2007

Year	Sales	Net Income
2007	$101,535,000	-$19,182,000
2006	$119,835,000	-$13,980,000
2005	$111,799,000	-$875,000

Curr. Assets:	$42,225,000	**Curr. Liab.:**	$17,836,000		
Plant, Equip.:	$4,851,000	**Total Liab.:**	$20,653,000	**Indic. Yr. Divd.:**	NA
Total Assets:	$55,129,000	**Net Worth:**	$34,476,000	**Debt/ Equity:**	0.0344

Meadow Valley Corp

4602 E Thomas Rd., Phoenix, AZ, 85018; *PH:* 1-602-437-5400; *Fax:* 1-602-437-1681; *http://* www.meadowvalley.com; *Email:* info@meadowvalley.com

General - Incorporation	NV	**Stock**- Price on:12/24/2007	$13.55
Employees	483	Stock Exchange	NDQ
Auditor	Semple, Marchal & Cooper, LLP	Ticker Symbol	MVIS
Stk Agt	Corporate Stock Transfer, Inc.	Outstanding Shares	5,130,000
Counsel	NA	E.P.S.	$0.76
DUNS No.	10-685-7154	Shareholders	NA

Business: The group's principal activity is to operate as a heavy construction contractor and to manufacture and distribute ready mix concrete. The group operates as a holding entity of meadow valley contractors, inc (mvci) and ready mix, inc (rmi). Mvci is a general contractor, primarily engaged in the construction of structural concrete highway bridges and overpasses and the paving of highways and airport runways in the states of Nevada, Arizona, and Utah. Rmi manufactures and distributes ready mix concrete in the las vegas and phoenix metropolitan areas. Rmi primarily targets prospective customers such as concrete subcontractors, prime contractors, homebuilders, commercial and industrial property developers, pool builders and homeowners. Rmi owns and operates 4 ready mix concrete batch plants and 120 ready mix trucks as well as a small fleet of aggregate hauling tractors and trailers.

Primary SIC and add'l.: 1622 1629 1611

CIK No: 0000934749

Subsidiaries: MVCI, Ready Mix, Inc., RMI

Officers: Bradley E. Larson/CEO, Pres./$677,774.00, David Doty/Principal Accounting Officer/$412,264.00, Alan Terril/VP, COO/$439,435.00, Kenneth D. Nelson/VP, Chief Administrative Officer/$419,639.00, Robert Terril/Area Pres., Robert Bottcher/Area Pres.

Directors: Charles E. Cowan/61/Dir., Charles R. Norton/66/Dir., Don A. Patterson/54/Dir.

Owners: Don A. Patterson, North Atlantic Value LLP/7.60%, Kenneth D. Nelson/2.70%, Hoak Public Equities, LP/5.20%, Kim A. Lewis/7.50%, Insiders/5.90%, Charles R. Norton, Bradley E. Larson/2.80%, Tontine Capital Partners, LP/6.60%, Praesidium Investment Management Company, LLC/6.20%, David D. Doty, Cyrus W. Spurlino/9.50%, CD Capital Management LLC/4.90%

Financial Data: *Fiscal Year End:*12/31 *Latest Annual Data:* 12/31/2006

Year	Sales	Net Income
2006	$195,522,000	$4,166,000
2005	$183,873,000	$4,204,000
2004	$166,832,000	$600,000

Curr. Assets:	$62,060,000	Curr. Liab.:	$34,805,000	P/E Ratio:	17.83
Plant, Equip.:	$35,553,000	Total Liab.:	$51,776,000	Indic. Yr. Divd.:	NA
Total Assets:	$102,106,000	Net Worth:	$31,341,000	Debt/ Equity:	0.4699

Meadowbrook Insurance Group Inc

26255 American Dr., Southfield, MI, 48034; **PH:** 1-248-358-1100; **Fax:** 1-248-358-1614;
http:// www.meadowbrookinsgrp.com; **Email:** ecommerce.feedback@meadowbrook.com

General - Incorporation	MI	**Stock**- Price on:12/24/2007	$10.08
Employees	648	Stock Exchange	NDQ
Auditor	Ernst & Young LLP	Ticker Symbol	MIG
Stk Agt.	LaSalle Bank N.A	Outstanding Shares	30,450,000
Counsel	Howard & Howard Attorneys PC	E.P.S.	$0.85
DUNS No.	07-424-8923	Shareholders	NA

Business: The group's principal activities are to develop and manage alternative market risk management programs for defined client groups and their members. The services are also provided including reinsurance brokering, risk management consulting, claims handling, administrative services, along with various types of property and casualty insurance coverage including workers' compensation, general liability and commercial multiple peril. The group operates insurance agencies for commercial insurance as well as personal property, casualty, life and accident and health insurance with multiple insurance carriers.

Primary SIC and add'l.: 6351 6331

CIK No: 0000949156

Subsidiaries: American Highway Carriers Association, Ameritrust Insurance Corporation, Case Management Resources, Inc., Commercial Carriers Insurance Agency, Inc., Crest Financial Corporation, Florida Preferred Administrators,inc, Interline Insurance Services,Inc., Liberty Premium Finance,inc, Market Place Resources, Inc., Meadowbrook Capital Trust I, Meadowbrook Capital Trust II, Meadowbrook Insurance Agency, Inc., Meadowbrook Insurance Group, Inc., Meadowbrook Insurance, Inc., Meadowbrook Intermediaries, Inc 31 Subsidiaries included in the Index

Officers: Robert Samuel Cubbin/Dir., CEO, Pres./$1,664,632.00, Gregory L. Wilde/Exec. VP/$610,335.00, Karen Marwell Spaun/Sr. VP, CFO/$553,054.00, Michael G. Costello/General Counsel, Sec., Sr. VP/$589,710.00, Holly Moltane/Dir. - External Financial Reporting, Randolph Fort/Sr. VP - Corporate Claims, Stephen A. Belden/52/Sr. VP, Chief Actuary, Robert Christopher Spring/54/Sr. VP - Business Operations, Archie S. McIntyre/42/Sr. VP - Business Development, Kenn R. Allen/59/Sr. VP, James M. Mahoney/Sr. VP - Field Operations, Joseph E. Mattingly/Sr. VP - Insurance Operations

Directors: Robert Samuel Cubbin/Dir., CEO, Pres., Merton J. Segal/Chmn., Robert W. Sturgis/Dir., Robert H. Naftaly/Dir., Herbert Tyner/Dir., Joseph S. Dresner/Dir., David K. Page/Dir., Florine Mark/Dir., Bruce E. Thal/Dir., Hugh W. Greenberg/Dir.

Owners: Michael G. Costello, Robert S. Cubbin/1.30%, Robert H. Naftaly, Dimensional Fund Advisors, Inc./8.10%, Bruce E. Thal, Herbert Tyner, Joseph E. Mattingly, Insiders/12.10%, James M. Mahoney, Florine Mark, Karen M. Spaun, Merton J. Segal/8.00%, Robert C. Spring, David K. Page, Joseph S. Dresner *(21 Owners included in Index)*

Financial Data: Fiscal Year End:12/31 Latest Annual Data: 12/31/2006

Year	Sales	Net Income
2006	$318,236,000	$22,034,000
2005	$304,017,000	$17,910,000
2004	$270,278,000	$14,061,000

Curr. Assets:	$351,558,000	Curr. Liab.:	$30,826,000	P/E Ratio:	12.44
Plant, Equip.:	NA	Total Liab.:	$767,307,000	Indic. Yr. Divd.:	NA
Total Assets:	$969,000,000	Net Worth:	$201,693,000	Debt/ Equity:	0.3198

Meadwestvaco Corp

11013 W Broad St., Glen Allen, VA, 23060; **PH:** 1-804-327-5200; **Fax:** 1-404-897-6383;
http:// www.meadwestvaco.com

General - Incorporation	DE	**Stock**- Price on:12/24/2007	$35.32
Employees	24,000	Stock Exchange	NYSE
Auditor	PricewaterhouseCoopers LLP	Ticker Symbol	NA
Stk Agt	Bank of New York	Outstanding Shares	184,440,000
Counsel	NA	E.P.S.	$0.62
DUNS No.	00-423-1445	Shareholders	NA

Business: The groups principle activity is to produce packaging systems, paper, consumer and office products and specialty chemicals. The groups products include paperboard, coated natural kraft paperboard, linerboard and saturating kraft. The group operates from United States, Canada, and Latin America.

Primary SIC and add'l.: 2895 2677 2671 2621

CIK No: 0001159297

Subsidiaries: AGI Media Packaging Ltd., Alfred Wall GmbH, MeadWestvaco Coated Board, Inc., MeadWestvaco Consumer Packaging Group, LLC, MeadWestvaco Forestry, LLC, MeadWestvaco South Carolina, LLC, MeadWestvaco Spain S.L., MeadWestvaco Virginia Corporation, Rigesa, Celulose, Papel E. Embalagens Ltda.

Officers: John A. Luke/59/Chmn., CEO/$6,158,083.00, Bruce V. Thomas/51/Sr. VP - Global Marketing Strategy, Emerging Markets, Mark V. Gulling/55/Pres. - Global Business Services, Dirk Krouskop/53/VP, Ned W. Massee/58/VP, Jack C. Goldfrank/65/Pres. - Center Packaging Innovation, Mark S. Cross/51/Sr. VP, Mark E. Rajkowski/47/CFO, Sr. VP/$2,474,327.00, John E. Banu/60/Controller, Donna Owens Cox/44/VP, Mark T. Watkins/54/Sr. VP/$1,510,175.00, Linda V. Schreiner/49/Sr. VP, Wendell L. Willkie/56/Sr. VP, General Counsel, Sec./$1,471,239.00, Marvin E. Hundley/54/Pres. - Forestry Division, Robert E. Birkenholz/47/Treasurer *(23 Officers included in Index)*

Directors: John A. Luke/59/Chmn., CEO, Michael E. Campbell/Dir., Richard B. Kelson/Dir., Jane L. Warner/Dir., Susan J. Kropf/Dir., Douglas S. Luke/Dir., John A. Krol/Dir., Thomas W. Cole/Dir., Robert C. McCormack/Dir., Timothy H. Powers/Dir., Edward M. Straw/Dir., James M. Kilts/Dir., James G. Kaiser/Dir.

Owners: Jane L. Warner, John A. Krol, James G. Kaiser, Timothy H. Powers, John A. Luke, Robert C. McCormack, Insiders/1.50%, Mark E. Rajkowski, Thomas W. Cole, Douglas S. Luke, Edward M. Straw, Wendell L. Willkie, Mark T. Watkins, Richard B. Kelson, James A. Buzzard *(17 Owners included in Index)*

Financial Data: Fiscal Year End:12/31 Latest Annual Data: 12/31/2006

Year	Sales	Net Income
2006	$6,530,000,000	$93,000,000
2005	$6,170,000,000	$28,000,000
2004	$8,227,000,000	-$349,000,000

Curr. Assets:	$2,015,000,000	Curr. Liab.:	$1,465,000,000	P/E Ratio:	86.15
Plant, Equip.:	$4,523,000,000	Total Liab.:	$5,752,000,000	Indic. Yr. Divd.:	$0.920
Total Assets:	$9,285,000,000	Net Worth:	$3,533,000,000	Debt/ Equity:	0.6702

Measurement Specialties Inc

1000 Lucas Way, Hampton, VA, 23666; **PH:** 1-757-766-1500; **Fax:** 1-757-766-4347;
http:// www.meas-spec.com

General - Incorporation	NJ	**Stock**- Price on:12/24/2007	$22.09
Employees	2,191	Stock Exchange	NDQ
Auditor	KPMG LLP	Ticker Symbol	MEAS
Stk Agt.	American Stock Transfer & Trust Co.	Outstanding Shares	14,290,000
Counsel	McCorter & English LLP	E.P.S.	$1.08
DUNS No.	02-935-1079	Shareholders	NA

Business: The group's principal activity is to design, manufacture and market sensors and sensor-based products. These sensors measure precise ranges of physical characteristics, including pressure, motion, force, displacement, angle, flow and distance. The group has two businesses: consumer products business and sensors business. The consumer products business manufactures and markets sensor-based consumer products which include bathroom and kitchen scales, tire pressure gauges and distance estimators. The group's sensors business designs, manufactures and markets sensors for original equipment manufacturer applications. These products include pressure sensors, custom microstructures, accelerometers, tilt/angle sensors and displacement sensors for electronic, automotive, military and industrial applications. On 24-Jun-2004, the group acquired elekon industries usa inc and on 16-Jul-2004 it acquired entran inc and encoder devices llc.

Primary SIC and add'l.: 3822 3823 3829 3824

CIK No: 0000778734

Subsidiaries: Acalon Holding Limited, ATEX, Elekon Industries USA Inc, Entran Devices LLC, Entran Limited, Entran SA, Entran Sensoren GmbH, HL Planartechnik GmbH, Humirel SA, I C Sensors Inc, Kenabell Holding Limited, Measurement Specialties Foreign Holding Corporation, MSI Sensor (Asia)Limited, MSI Sensor (China)Limited, MWS Sonsorik GmbH

Officers: Frank D. Guidone/43/Dir., CEO, Pres./$895,000.00, Victor J. Chatigny/57/Group VP - Position, Vibration, Piezo/$255,284.00, Jean-Francois Allier/54/Group VP - Humidity, Chemical, Gas, Glen MacGibbon/46/Group VP - Pressure, Force, Steven Smith/59/VP, GM - Asia/$543,478.00, Terence Monaghan/45/Group VP - Temperature, Optical/$358,170.00, Mark Thomson/40/CFO, Sec.

Directors: Frank D. Guidone/43/Dir., CEO, Pres., Morton L. Topfer/71/Chmn., Satish Rishi/48/Dir., Barry R. Uber/63/Dir., John D. Arnold/53/Dir., Kenneth E. Thompson/48/Dir.

Owners: Kenneth E. Thompson, R. Barry Uber, Steven Smith, John D. Arnold, Insiders/8.85%, Victor J. Chatigny, Terence Monaghan, Satish Rishi, Frank D. Guidone, Morton L. Topfer/5.86%

Financial Data: Fiscal Year End:03/31 Latest Annual Data: 3/31/2007

Year	Sales	Net Income
2007	$200,250,000	$14,234,000
2006	$121,417,000	$24,534,000
2005	$140,941,000	$14,826,000

Curr. Assets:	$91,830,000	Curr. Liab.:	$40,895,000	P/E Ratio:	20.45
Plant, Equip.:	$27,559,000	Total Liab.:	$102,426,000	Indic. Yr. Divd.:	NA
Total Assets:	$224,691,000	Net Worth:	$120,637,000	Debt/ Equity:	NA

Mechanical Technology Inc

431 New Karner Rd., Albany, NY, 12205; **PH:** 1-518-533-2200; **Fax:** 1-518-533-2201;
http:// www.mechtech.com; **Email:** contact@mechtech.com

General - Incorporation	NY	**Stock**- Price on:12/24/2007	$1.31
Employees	132	Stock Exchange	NDQ
Auditor	PricewaterhouseCoopers LLP	Ticker Symbol	MLAN
Stk Agt.	American Stock Transfer & Trust Co.	Outstanding Shares	38,070,000
Counsel	NA	E.P.S.	-$0.31
DUNS No.	00-206-9409	Shareholders	NA

Business: The group's principal activities are to develop and commercialize the direct methanol micro fuel cells and high performance test and measurement instruments and systems. The group operates in two segments: new energy technologies and test and measurement instrumentation. The new energy technologies segment develops and markets direct methanol fuel cells, an alternative form of energy to conventional power sources, for use in handheld portable electronics and military applications. The test and measurement instrumentation segment develops, manufactures and sells portable engine balancing systems for the aircraft industry, non-contact measurement probes and electronics and metrology tools for the semiconductor industry. These products are sold to customers in the computer, electronic, semiconductor, automotive, aerospace, aircraft and bioengineering industries.

Primary SIC and add'l.: 3812 3829 8731 3663 3699 3826

CIK No: 0000064463

Subsidiaries: Embedded Power LLC, MTI Instruments, Inc., MTI International, Inc, MTI MicroFuel Cells Inc., Turbonetics Energy, Inc.

Officers: Peng K. Lim/Dir., CEO/$1,048,804.00, George Relan/VP - Corporate Development, Alan Soucy/Consultant, Chief Corporate Strategist, Cynthia A. Scheuer/VP, CFO, Sec./$362,557.00, Shimshon Gottesfeld/67/Sr. Technical Advisor, MTI Microfuel Cells Inc/$277,004.00, Juan J. Becerra/47/VP - Marketing, Business Development/$402,452.00, Robert J. Kot/57/VP, GM - MTI Instruments, Inc/$201,658.00, William P. Acker/Advisor/$385,394.00

Directors: Peng K. Lim/Dir., CEO, Steven N. Fischer/Chmn., Thomas J. Marusak/Dir., Walter L. Robb/Dir., William P. Phelan/Dir., Dennis E. O'Connor/Dir.

Owners: Shimshon Gottesfeld, Heights Capital Management, Inc./5.64%, William P. Acker/1.26%, Robert J. Kot, William P. Phelan, Insiders/5.95%, Steven N. Fischer/1.44%, Juan J. Becerra, Russel H. Marvin, Cynthia A. Scheuer, Peng K. Lim, Thomas J. Marusak, Walter L. Robb/1.41%, Dennis E. OConnor/1.07%

Financial Data: Fiscal Year End:12/31 Latest Annual Data: 12/31/2006

Year	Sales	Net Income
2006	$8,156,000	-$13,667,000
2005	$7,841,000	-$15,094,000
2004	$8,570,000	-$4,191,000

Curr. Assets:	$27,891,000	Curr. Liab.:	$7,071,000		
Plant, Equip.:	$2,926,000	Total Liab.:	$10,735,000	Indic. Yr. Divd.:	NA
Total Assets:	$33,811,000	Net Worth:	$22,871,000	Debt/ Equity:	NA

Mechanics Bank CA

3170 Hilltop Mall Rd., Richmond, CA, 94806; *PH:* 1-510-262-7980; *Fax:* 1-510-262-7941;
http:// www.mechbank.com

General - Incorporation		Stock - Price on:12/24/2007	$19600
Employees	NA	Stock Exchange	OTC
Auditor	NA	Ticker Symbol	MCHB
Stk Agt	NA	Outstanding Shares	NA
Counsel	NA	E.P.S.	$1,367.66
DUNS No.	NA	Shareholders	NA

Business: The groups principal activity is to provide community-banking services. The services of the group include personal banking, business banking, loans, mortgage, safe deposit boxes, wire transfer, and fax boxes, ATM and debit card, and ACH direct deposit. The group operates from the United States.

Primary SIC and add'l.: 6712 6022

CIK No:

Officers: Steven K. Buster/Dir., CEO, Pres., Raulin J. Butler/Sr. VP, Retail Banking Mgr., Steven I. Barlow/COO, Exec. VP, Thomas N. Brennan/Sr. VP, Mgr. - Consumer Lending, Michael Frith/Office Mgr. - El Sobrante, Thomas Bennett/Office Mgr. - Hilltop, Sharon Camandona/Office Mgr. - Sacramento, Jennifer Ballard/VP, Loan Services Mgr., Sterling Burnett/Office Mgr. - Albany, Raudel Wilson/Office Mgr. - Berkeley, Jessica Smith/Customer Service Officer - West Berkeley, Linda Morris/Office Mgr. - Concord, Patti Barsotti/Office Mgr. - Danville, Nancy McCarthy/Office Mgr. - El Cerrito, Susan Hamlin/Office Mgr. - El Dorado Hills *(56 Officers included in Index)*

Directors: Steven K. Buster/Dir., CEO, Pres., Dianne D. Felton/Vice Chmn., Edward M. Downer/Chmn., Deborah Downer Abono/Dir., John Bryan/Dir. Emeritus, Daniel W. Albert/Dir., Michael Downer/Dir., Robert W. Snelling/Dir. Emeritus, Mark Wilson/Dir., Martin McNair/Dir., John R. Segerstrom/Dir., William S. Oliver/Dir. Emeritus, Donald E. Pryde/Dir. Emeritus, James Staes/Dir., Daniel M. Daiss/Dir. *(18 Directors included in Index)*

Financial Data: Fiscal Year End:NA Latest Annual Data: 12/31/2002

Year	Sales	Net Income
2002	$140,017,000	$26,615,000
2001	$144,158,000	$22,165,000
2000	$135,077,000	$20,281,000

Curr. Assets:	$173,618,000	Curr. Liab.:	$1,802,137,000	P/E Ratio:	14.33
Plant, Equip.:	$14,885,000	Total Liab.:	$1,879,932,000	Indic. Yr. Divd.$340.000
Total Assets:	$2,087,848,000	Net Worth:	$207,916,000	Debt/ Equity:	0.2490

Mechel OAO

Formerly: Mechel Steel Group OAO
1, Krasnoarmeyskaya, Ul, 125993; *PH:* 44-74952218888; *http://* www.mechel.com;
Email: career@mechel.com

General - Incorporation .... Russian Federation	Stock - Price on:12/24/2007	$38.5
Employees	NA	Stock Exchange	NDQ
Auditor	Ernst & Young LLP	Ticker Symbol	MTLK
Stk Agt	NA	Outstanding Shares	135,510,000
Counsel	NA	E.P.S.	$6.75
DUNS No.	NA	Shareholders	NA

Business: The groups principle activity is to operate mining and steel properties. The group operates through two segments namely, mining and steel. In the year 2006, the group acquired Mechel Recycling. The group operates from the Russia.

Primary SIC and add'l.: 3312

CIK No: 0001302362

Subsidiaries: Beloretsk Metallurgical Plant (BMP), Chelyabinsk Metallurgical Plant (CMP), Izhstal, Kaslinsky Architectural Art Casting Plant, Korshunov Mining Plant (KMP), Krasnogorsk Open Pit Mine (KOPM), Kuzbass Central Processing Plant (KCPP), Lenin Mine (LM), Mechel Campia Turzii SA, Mechel Coal Resources (MCR), Mechel International Holdings AG, Mechel Metal Supply AG (MMS), Mechel Nemunas (MN), Mechel Targoviste SA, Mechel Trading House (MTH) 29 Subsidiaries included in the Index

Officers: Igor V. Zyuzin/Dir., CEO, Alexey G. Ivanushkin/Dir., COO, Anton V. Vishanenko/29/CFO, Boris G. Nikishichev/Sr. VP - Mining, Victor A. Trigubko/Sr. VP - Government Relations, Stanislav A. Ploschenko/Acting CFO, Alexander Tolkach/Head - International Relations, Affairs Relations

Directors: Igor V. Zyuzin/Dir., CEO, Valentin V. Proskurnya/Chmn., Serafim V. Kolpakov/Dir., Alexander E. Yevtushenko/Dir., Alex Polevoy/Dir., Alexey G. Ivanushkin/Dir., COO, Roger I. Gale/Dir., David A. Johnson/Dir., Vladimir A. Polin/Dir.

Owners: Igor V. Zyuzin/68.30%, Insiders/100.00%, Free float/31.70%

Financial Data: Fiscal Year End:12/31 Latest Annual Data: 12/31/2006

Year	Sales	Net Income
2006	$4,397,811,000	$603,249,000
2005	$3,804,995,000	$381,180,000
2004	$3,635,955,000	$1,342,706,000

Curr. Assets:	$1,635,030,000	Curr. Liab.:	$755,367,000	P/E Ratio:	32.84
Plant, Equip.:	$2,012,828,000	Total Liab.:	$1,584,095,000	Indic. Yr. Divd.:	NA
Total Assets:	$4,449,058,000	Net Worth:	$2,864,963,000	Debt/ Equity:	NA

Med Gen Inc

7284 W Palmetto Pk. Rd., Ste. 207, Boca Raton, FL, 33433; *PH:* 1-561-750-1100;
Fax: 1-561-750-4623; *http://* www.medgen.com; *Email:* customerservice@medgen.com

General - Incorporation	NV	Stock - Price on:12/24/2007	$0.0017
Employees	8	Stock Exchange	OTC
Auditor	Stark Winter Schenkein & Co. LLP	Ticker Symbol	MGEN
Stk Agt	Liberty Transfer Co	Outstanding Shares	393,010,000
Counsel	NA	E.P.S.	$0.009
DUNS No.	NA	Shareholders	NA

Business: The group's principle activities include manufacturing, marketing and licensing healthcare products, specifically to the market for alternative therapies (health self-care). The products of the company are snorenz (TM), good nights sleep (TM), 4-in-1 (TM), snore quell (TM) and comfortcare (TM). The company's flagship product has been snorenz, a throat spray which reduces or eliminates the sounds ordinarily associated with snoring. Snorenz is currently sold through a number of fortune 100 retailers representing a marketing network in excess of 30,000 stores nationwide. The company's customers include wal-Mart, walgreens and eckerd. The company sells its products through Internet in Canada, the United Kingdom, Germany, France, Switzerland, Portugal, turkey, Australia, New Zealand, Japan, China and Korea. The group operates from United States.

Primary SIC and add'l.: 2834

CIK No: 0001045707

Officers: Paul B. Kravitz/Chmn., CEO, Sec., Paul S. Mitchell/55/Dir., Pres., Treasurer, COO

Directors: Paul B. Kravitz/Chmn., CEO, Sec., Paul S. Mitchell/55/Dir., Pres., Treasurer, COO

Owners: Paul B. Kravitz/0.06%

Financial Data: Fiscal Year End:09/30 Latest Annual Data: 9/30/2006

Year	Sales	Net Income
2006	$271,000	-$7,907,000
2005	$802,000	-$12,215,000
2004	$1,043,000	-$9,171,000

Curr. Assets:	$1,487,000	Curr. Liab.:	$1,745,000		
Plant, Equip.:	$37,000	Total Liab.:	$8,734,000	Indic. Yr. Divd.:	NA
Total Assets:	$1,884,000	Net Worth:	-$6,850,000	Debt/ Equity:	NA

Med-Emerg International Inc

6711 Mississauga Rd., Ste. 404, Mississauga, ON, L5N 2W3; *PH:* 1-905-858-1368;
Fax: 1-905-858-1399; *http://* www.med-emerg.com

General - Incorporation	Canada	Stock - Price on:12/24/2007	$0.15
Employees	109	Stock Exchange	OTC
Auditor	Grant Thornton, LLP	Ticker Symbol	MDER
Stk Agt	Continental Stock Transfer & Trust Co	Outstanding Shares	58,280,000
Counsel	NA	E.P.S.	-$0.02
DUNS No.	24-484-0781	Shareholders	NA

Business: The group's principle activity is to provide integrated healthcare management services. The group specializes in the coordination and staffing of emergency physicians for hospitals and clinics. The group's operations are divided into five divisions: hospital staffing, medical clinics, department of national defence, pharmaceutical support and long-term care. The group's quarterly revenue for September 2007 was 5.76 millions of USD.

Primary SIC and add'l.: 8011

CIK No: 0001030179

Subsidiaries: 927563 Ontario Inc., 927564 Ontario Inc., CPM Health Centres Inc., Doctors on Call Ltd., Med-Emerg Health Centres Inc., Med-Emerg Inc., OPA Locum Direct Inc., YFMC Healthcare (Alberta) Inc., YFMC Heathcare Inc.

Officers: Ramesh Zacharias/Founder, CEO, Executive Medical Dir., William J. Danis/52/CFO, Corp. Sec., Donald Ross/VP - Business Development, Jackie Benoit/Business Mgr., Paul Lee/Information Technology

Directors: Ramesh Zacharias/Founder, CEO, Executive Medical Dir., Michael Sinclair/65/Chmn., Sidney Braun/48/Dir., John Yarnell/79/Dir., Lewis MacKenzie/70/Dir., Jacob Ofek/50/Dir.

Owners: Calian Technologies/11.50%, The Sinclair Montrose Trust/9.80%, 1245841 Ontario Inc./8.70%, David Kassie/6.90%, Koby Ofek/24.60%, H. T. Ardinger/7.00%, Insiders/53.20%, BXR1 Holdings Inc./10.30%, Walt & Co. Inc./6.90%

Financial Data: Fiscal Year End:12/31 Latest Annual Data: 12/31/2006

Year	Sales	Net Income
2006	$17,717,000	$872,000
2005	$14,393,000	-$857,000
2004	$48,448,000	-$1,341,000

Curr. Assets:	$7,066,000	Curr. Liab.:	$3,153,000		
Plant, Equip.:	$598,000	Total Liab.:	$3,887,000	Indic. Yr. Divd.:	NA
Total Assets:	$7,901,000	Net Worth:	$907,000	Debt/ Equity:	NA

Med-Tech Solutions Inc

1825 W Walnut Hill Ln., Irving, Texas, 75038; *PH:* 1-866-970-6262;
http:// www.med-tech-solutions.net/About%20Us.htm; *Email:* support.us@2x.com

General - Incorporation		Stock - Price on:12/24/2007	NA
Employees	NA	Stock Exchange	OTC
Auditor	NA	Ticker Symbol	MDTU
Stk Agt	Pacific Stock Transfer Company	Outstanding Shares	NA
Counsel	NA	E.P.S.	NA
DUNS No.	NA	Shareholders	NA

Business: The groups principal activity is to provide the networking components. The products of the group include NEC Telecommunication System, InstaGate EX2, AT&T Solution Provider, Microsoft Certified Partners and 2X Partners. The group operates from the United States.

Primary SIC and add'l.: 7389

CIK No:

Officers: Edgar Strange/Founder, Pres.

Directors: Edgar Strange/Founder, Pres.

Financial Data: Fiscal Year End:NA Latest Annual Data: 10/31/2006

Year	Sales	Net Income
2006	NA	-$58,000
2005	NA	-$71,000

Curr. Assets:	$3,000	Curr. Liab.:	$36,000		
Plant, Equip.:	NA	Total Liab.:	$36,000	Indic. Yr. Divd.:	NA
Total Assets:	$3,000	Net Worth:	-$33,000	Debt/ Equity:	NA

Med-Zone Biotechnologies Acquisition Inc

28w 38th St., Ste. 8w, New York, NY, 10018; *PH:* 1-212-398-2880

General - Incorporation	DE	Stock- Price on:12/24/2007	NA
Employees	NA	Stock Exchange	NA
Auditor	Gately & Assoc. LLC	Ticker Symbol	NA
Stk Agt.	NA	Outstanding Shares	NA
Counsel	NA	E.P.S.	NA
DUNS No.	NA	Shareholders	NA

Business: The group's activity is to form acquisitions and mergers. The group is in the developmental stage since inception and has no operations to date.

Primary SIC and add'l.: 9995

CIK No: 0001294604

Officers: Dennis Chen/Dir., CEO, CFO, Pres.

Directors: Dennis Chen/Dir., CEO, CFO, Pres.

MedAire Inc

80 E Rio Salado Pkwy., Ste. 610, Tempe, AZ, 85281; **PH:** 1-480-333-3700; **Fax:** 1-480-333-3592; http:// www.medaire.com; **Email:** info@medairinc.com

General - Incorporation	NV	Stock- Price on:12/24/2007	$0.865
Employees	NA	Stock Exchange	OTC
Auditor	Moss Adams LLP	Ticker Symbol	MEDRF
Stk Agt.	NA	Outstanding Shares	NA
Counsel	Coppersmith Gordon Schermer O & N Plc	E.P.S.	NA
DUNS No.	NA	Shareholders	NA

Business: The group's primary activity is providing fully integrated medical and health services to remote travelers all over the world. The company also provides medical assistance to the aviation and maritime industries, and runs a network of international medical clinics. The company is a single source emergency information and real-time assistance provider - in the air, on land or at sea. The company's capabilities include: 24-hour remote emergency assistance through a 24/7, state-of-the-art Global Response Center; Advanced training programs; Life-saving equipment (vital sign monitors, medical kits and defibrillators) and International network of medical clinics (Global Doctor). The company caters to the aviation and maritime industries as well as corporate business travelers.

Primary SIC and add'l.: 8093 8299 8099

CIK No: 0001337301

Subsidiaries: MedAire Limited., MedSpace, Inc

Officers: James A. Williams/Dir., CEO

Directors: James A. Williams/Dir., CEO, Joan Sullivan Garrett/Founder, Chmn., Terry D. Giles/Dir., Gregory J. Bell/Dir., Neil Warren Hickson/Dir., John Jessup/Dir., Sandra Wilkenfeld Wadsworth/Dir., Roy A. Herberger/Dir.

Owners: ANZ Nominees Limited, Joan Sullivan Garrett, Procuro, Inc., Insiders, Roger Sandeen, James Allen Williams, Terry Giles, Janis Straty, Roy Herberger, Heidi Giles

Financial Data: Fiscal Year End:12/31 Latest Annual Data: 12/31/2006

Year	Sales		Net Income
2006	$30,149,000		-$1,600,000
Curr. Assets:	$11,206,000	Curr. Liab.:	$10,865,000
Plant, Equip.:	$1,652,000	Total Liab.:	$12,122,000	Indic. Yr. Divd.: NA
Total Assets:	$13,992,000	Net Worth:	$1,870,000	Debt/ Equity: 0.1434

Medallion Financial Corp

437 Madison Ave., 38th Fl., New York, NY, 10022; **PH:** 1-212-328-2100; **Fax:** 1-212-328-2121; http:// www.medallionfinancial.com

General - Incorporation	DE	Stock- Price on:12/24/2007	$11.72
Employees	111	Stock Exchange	NDQ
Auditor	Weiser LLP	Ticker Symbol	TAXI
Stk Agt.	American Stock Transfer & Trust Co.	Outstanding Shares	17,480,000
Counsel	NA	E.P.S.	$0.98
DUNS No.	NA	Shareholders	NA

Business: The groups principle activities include originating, acquiring, and servicing loans. The groups operates through two segments namely lending and taxicab rooftop advertising. The group operates from the United States and Japan. The group's quarterly revenue for September 2007 was 13.55 millions of USD.

Primary SIC and add'l.: 6153 6159

CIK No: 0001000209

Subsidiaries: Freshstart Venture Capital Corp., Generation Outdoor, Inc, Medallion Bank, Medallion Business Credit, LLC, Medallion Capital, Inc., Medallion Funding Corp., Medallion Hamptons Holding LLC, Taxi Medallion Loan Trust I, Taxi Medallion Loan Trust II

Officers: Alvin Murstein/Chmn., CEO/$830,385.00, John M. Taggart/Pres., CEO - Medallion Bank, Connie Mitchko/Sr. VP - Medallion Business Credit, LLC, Paul Meyering/Pres. - Medallion Capital, Inc, Dean R. Pickerell/Exeurtive VP - Medallion Capital, Inc, Stephen A. Lewis/Sr. VP - Medallion Capital, Inc, Andrew M. Murstein/Dir., Pres./$1,502,644.00, Brian S. O'Leary/COO, Chief Credit Officer/$336,375.00, Larry D. Hall/CFO/$286,597.00, Michael J. Kowalsky/Exec. VP/$354,034.00, Marie Russo/Sr. VP, Sec., Jeffrey Yin/Chief Compliance Officer, General Counsel, Gerald Grossman/Pres. - Medallion Business Credit, LLC

Directors: Alvin Murstein/Chmn., CEO, Andrew M. Murstein/Dir., Pres., Mario M. Cuomo/Dir., Stanley Kreitman/Dir., David L. Rudnick/Dir., Henry D. Jackson/Dir., Frederick A. Menowitz/Dir., Henry L. Aaron/Dir., Lowell P. Weicker/Dir.

Owners: Frederick A. Menowitz, Mario M. Cuomo, Michael J. Kowalsky, Lowell P. Weicker, Henry L. Aaron, Alvin Murstein/9.26%, Dimensional Fund Advisors LP/8.41%, River Road Asset Management, LLC/7.81%, Larry D. Hall, Insiders/20.27%, Andrew M. Murstein/9.29%, David L. Rudnick, Stanley Kreitman, Brian S. OLeary, Henry D. Jackson

Financial Data: Fiscal Year End:12/31 Latest Annual Data: 12/31/2006

Year	Sales		Net Income
2006	$52,816,000		$13,108,000
2005	$61,054,000		$6,862,000
2004	$59,709,000		$22,512,000
Curr. Assets:	$17,577,000	Curr. Liab.:	$6,840,000
Plant, Equip.:	$525,000	Total Liab.:	$461,977,000	Indic. Yr. Divd.: $0.760
Total Assets:	$631,605,000	Net Worth:	$169,628,000	Debt/ Equity: 0.4537

Medarex Inc

707 State Rd., Princeton, NJ, 08540; **PH:** 1-609-430-2880; **Fax:** 1-609-430-2850; http:// www.medarex.com; **Email:** information@medarex.com

General - Incorporation	NJ	Stock- Price on:12/24/2007	$14.72
Employees	492	Stock Exchange	NDQ
Auditor	Ernst & Young LLP	Ticker Symbol	MEDX
Stk Agt.	Continental Stock Transfer & Trust Co	Outstanding Shares	125,950,000
Counsel	Satterlee Stephens Burke & Burke LLP	E.P.S.	-$0.25
DUNS No.	19-045-2631	Shareholders	NA

Business: The group's principal activities are to discover and develop human antibody-based therapeutic products. The group uses its proprietary technology platform, the ultimab human antibody development system to rapidly create and develop therapeutic products for the treatment of cancer, inflammation, auto-immune disease and other life-threatening and debilitating diseases. The group's therapeutic product candidates are currently under development and include mdx-33, mdx-010, humax(tm)-CD4, humax-il15, centocor/j&j antibody and mdx-070. As of 01-Aug-2003, the group had licensing and collaborative partnerships with more than 45 pharmaceutical and biotechnology companies either to jointly develop and commercialize products or use the group's proprietary technology in the development of new therapeutic products.

Primary SIC and add'l.: 2834 8731

CIK No: 0000874255

Subsidiaries: GenPharm International, Inc.

Officers: Howard H. Pien/Dir., CEO, Pres., Geoffrey M. Nichol/Sr. VP - Product Development/$642,781.00, Ursula B. Bartels/Sr. VP, General Counsel, Sec., Christian S. Schade/CFO, Sr. VP - Finance, Administration/$811,468.00, Ronald A. Pepin/Sr. VP - Business Development, Bradford W. Middlekauff/Sr. VP, General Counsel, Sec./$638,317.00, Nils Lonberg/Sr. VP, Dir. - Scientific/$692,904.00

Directors: Howard H. Pien/Dir., CEO, Pres., Irwin Lerner/Chmn., Charles R. Schaller/Founder, Chmn., Ronald J. Saldarini/Dir., Patricia M. Danzon/Dir., Julius A. Vida/Dir., Robert C. Dinerstein/Dir., Abhijeet J. Lele/Dir., Marc Rubin/Dir.

Owners: Nils Lonberg, Christian S. Schade, Bradford W. Middlekauff, Irwin Lerner, Insiders/3.80%, Julius A. Vida, Ronald A. Pepin, Robert C. Dinerstein, Patricia M. Danzon, Charles R. Schaller, Ronald J. Saldarini, FMR Corp./14.60%, Geoffrey M. Nichol, Donald L. Drakeman, Abhijeet J. Lele *(16 Owners included in Index)*

Financial Data: Fiscal Year End:12/31 Latest Annual Data: 12/31/2006

Year	Sales		Net Income
2006	$48,646,000		-$181,701,000
2005	$51,455,000		-$148,012,000
2004	$12,474,000		-$186,509,000
Curr. Assets:	$511,765,000	Curr. Liab.:	$70,436,000
Plant, Equip.:	$84,341,000	Total Liab.:	$309,821,000	Indic. Yr. Divd.: NA
Total Assets:	$954,693,000	Net Worth:	$640,173,000	Debt/ Equity: 0.2549

Medarts Medical System Inc

Formerly: Along Mobile Technology Inc
6/f E Yang International Mansion No.27, Science & Technology Rd., Xian, 710075; **PH:** 86-29-88319908

General - Incorporation	DE	Stock- Price on:12/24/2007	NA
Employees	NA	Stock Exchange	OTC
Auditor	Gately & Assoc. LLC	Ticker Symbol	AGMB
Stk Agt.	Pacific Stock Transfer Company	Outstanding Shares	NA
Counsel	NA	E.P.S.	NA
DUNS No.	NA	Shareholders	NA

Business: The groups principle activity is to engage in lawful corporate undertaking, including, but not limited to, selected mergers and acquisitions. The group also sets up a system to locate and negotiate with business entities for meeting targets. The group operates from United States.

Primary SIC and add'l.: 9995

CIK No: 0001309054

Officers: Jianwei Lee/Co - Founder, CEO, Pres., CTO, Zhen Wang/CFO, Xiaomeng Ma/COO, Dir., Don D. Meyers/Assoc.

Directors: Jianwei Lee/Co - Founder, CEO, Pres., CTO, Xiaomeng Ma/COO, Dir.

Financial Data: Fiscal Year End:10/31 Latest Annual Data: 12/31/2006

Year	Sales		Net Income
2006	$6,428,000		$3,258,000
2005	$4,515,000		$677,000
2003	NA		-$5,153,000
Curr. Assets:	$9,443,000	Curr. Liab.:	$2,195,000
Plant, Equip.:	$4,186,000	Total Liab.:	$2,195,000	Indic. Yr. Divd.: NA
Total Assets:	$15,748,000	Net Worth:	$13,553,000	Debt/ Equity: NA

MedaSorb Technologies Corp

7 Deer Pk. Dr., Ste. K, Monmouth Junction, NJ, 08852; **PH:** 1-732-329-8885; **Fax:** 1-732-329-8650; http:// www.medasorb.com; **Email:** info@medasorb.com

General - Incorporation	NV	Stock- Price on:12/24/2007	$0.6
Employees	8	Stock Exchange	OTC
Auditor	BDO Dunwoody LLP	Ticker Symbol	MSBT
Stk Agt.	Pacific Stock Transfer Company	Outstanding Shares	24,690,000
Counsel	NA	E.P.S.	-$0.18
DUNS No.	NA	Shareholders	NA

Business: The groups principal activity is to develop medical devices. Products of the group include CytoSorb(TM) and BetaSorb(TM). In June 2006, the group acquired MedaSorb Technologies, Inc. and MedaSorb Acquisition Inc. The group operates from North America, Europe, Latin America and the Asia Pacific.

Primary SIC and add'l.: 3841

CIK No: 0001175151

Subsidiaries: MedaSorb Acquisition Inc.,

Officers: Al Kraus/Dir., CEO, Pres., Vincent Capponi/COO, David Lamadrid/CFO, James Winchester/Chief Medical Officer, Jean Futrell/Scientific Advisor, Vadim A. Davankov/Scientific Advisor, Hans Dietrich Polascheg/Scientific Advisors, Robert Albright/Scientific Advisor, John

Kellum/Medical Advisor, Severe Sepsis, Inflammatory Disease, Michael Pinsky/Medical Advisor, Severe Sepsis, Inflammatory Disease, Claudio Ronco/Medical Advisor, Severe Sepsis, Inflammatory Disease, Chronic, Acute Kidney Failure, Joe Carcillo/Medical Advisor, Severe Sepsis, Inflammatory Disease, Juan Ochoa/Medical Advisor, Severe Sepsis, Inflammatory Disease, Patrick Murray/Medical Advisor, Severe Sepsis, Inflammatory Disease, Thomas Stewart/Medical Advisor, Severe Sepsis, Inflammatory Disease *(18 Officers included in Index)*

Directors: Al Kraus/Dir., CEO, Pres., William R. Miller/Chmn., Martin F. Whalen/Dir., Edward R. Jones/Dir., Joseph Rubin/Dir., Kurt Katz/Dir.

Owners: Guillermina Montiel/20.50%, Robert Shipley/5.80%, Margery Germain/8.10%, William R. Miller, Vince Capponi/1.80%, Joseph Rubin/1.60%, David Lamadrid/2.30%, James Winchester, Insiders/15.00%, Al Kraus/8.70%, Margie Chassman/25.10%, Kurt Katz

Financial Data: *Fiscal Year End:*05/31   *Latest Annual Data:* 12/31/2006

Year	Sales	Net Income
2006	NA	-$7,672,000
2005	$12,000	-$78,000

Curr. Assets:	$2,898,000	**Curr. Liab.:**	$1,082,000		
Plant, Equip.:	$304,000	**Total Liab.:**	$1,082,000	**Indic. Yr. Divd.:**	NA
Total Assets:	$3,445,000	**Net Worth:**	$2,363,000	**Debt/ Equity:**	NA

MedAvant Healthcare Solutions

Formerly: Proxymed Inc
1854 Shackleford Ct., Ste. 200, Norcross, GA, 30093; *PH:* 1-770-806-9918;
http:// www.proxymed.com

General - Incorporation	FL	**Stock**- Price on:12/24/2007	$2.2
Employees	336	Stock Exchange	NDQ
Auditor	Deloitte & Touche LLP	Ticker Symbol	PILL
Stk Agt	Registrar & Transfer Co	Outstanding Shares	13,210,000
Counsel	NA	E.P.S.	-$2.48
DUNS No.	78-747-7462	Shareholders	NA

Business: The group's principal activities are to provide connectivity services and related value-added products to physician offices, payers, medical laboratories, pharmacies and other healthcare institutions. Its customers include pharmacies, commercial and hospital laboratories, insurance companies, managed care organizations and nursing homes. Its operating facilities are located in fort lauderdale, florida; santa ana, California; and new albany, Indiana. Electronic transaction processing services support a broad range of financial and clinical transactions. The group operates a proprietary national electronic information network known as phoenix. The healthcare industry offers services like new prescription orders, refill authorizations, laboratory orders and results and medical insurance claims. In Mar 2004, the group acquired planvista corporation.

Primary SIC and add'l.: 7374 7373
CIK No: 0000906337
Subsidiaries: National Network Services, LLC, PlanVista Corporation, PlanVista Solutions, Inc, ProxyMed Lab Services, LLC, ProxyMed Transaction Services, Inc
Officers: John G. Lettko/CEO/$550,754.00, Lonnie W. Hardin/Exec. VP - Business Operations/$334,825.00, Teresa D. Stubbs/Exec. VP - Marketing, Corporate Communications, Gerard M. Hayden/CFO, Douglas J. O'Dowd/42/CFO, Exec. VP, Treasurer/$229,717.00, Eric D. Arnson/Exec. VP - Product Management/$235,717.00, Peter E. Fleming/Exec. VP, General Counsel/$273,112.00, Adnane Khalil/Exec. VP - Information Technology, Allison W. Myers/Exec. VP - Human Resources, Emily J. Pietrzak/Exec. VP - Sales, Accounting Management
Directors: Eugene R. Terry/69/Dir., Edwin M. Cooperman/64/Dir., James B. Hudak/Dir., Samuel R. Schwartz/58/Dir.
Owners: Lonnie Hardin, Insiders/5.98%, Peter E. Fleming, Samuel R. Schwartz, Eric Arnson, Eugene R. Terry, James B. Hudak, Douglas J. ODowd, Galleon Management/14.76%, John G. Lettko/3.44%, General Atlantic LLC/24.54%, Laurus Master Fund/5.30%, Edwin M. Cooperman

Financial Data: *Fiscal Year End:*12/31   *Latest Annual Data:* 12/31/2006

Year	Sales	Net Income
2006	$65,462,000	-$6,610,000
2005	$77,519,000	-$105,294,000
2004	$90,246,000	-$3,800,000

Curr. Assets:	$17,872,000	**Curr. Liab.:**	$25,508,000		
Plant, Equip.:	$5,555,000	**Total Liab.:**	$44,816,000	**Indic. Yr. Divd.:**	NA
Total Assets:	$72,240,000	**Net Worth:**	$27,424,000	**Debt/ Equity:**	3.2248

Medcath Corp

10720 Sikes Pl., Ste. 300, Charlotte, NC, 28277; *PH:* 1-704-708-6600; *Fax:* 1-704-708-5035;
http:// www.medcath.com

General - Incorporation	DE	**Stock**- Price on:12/24/2007	$33.41
Employees	2,712	Stock Exchange	NDQ
Auditor	Deloitte & Touche LLP	Ticker Symbol	MDTH
Stk Agt	Wachovia Bank N.A	Outstanding Shares	21,200,000
Counsel	Moore & Van Allen	E.P.S.	$0.54
DUNS No.	NA	Shareholders	NA

Business: The group's principal activities are to design, develop, own and operate heart hospitals. The group operates in three divisions: hospital division, diagnostics division and cardiology consulting and management division (ccm) . Hospital division owns and operates heart hospitals in partnership with cardiologists and cardiovascular surgeons. Diagnostics division provides cardiovascular care services in diagnostic and therapeutic facilities and through mobile cardiac catheterization laboratories.Ccm provides consulting and management services to cardiologists and cardiovascular surgeons. The group increased in holding in heart hospital of New Mexico from 69% to 72% on 1-Apr-2003.

Primary SIC and add'l.: 8069
CIK No: 0001139463
Subsidiaries: AHH Management, Inc., Arizona Heart Hospital, LLC, Austin MOB, Inc., Blue Ridge Cardiology Services, LLC, Brighton Center for Sleep Disorders, LLC, Caldwell Cardiology Services, LLC, Cape Cod Cardiology Services, LLC, Center for Cardiac Sleep Medicine, LLC, Central Park Medical Office Building, LP, Central Texas Cardiovascular Sleep Institute, LP, Colorado Springs Cardiology Services, LLC, DTO Management, Inc., El Paso Cardiovascular Institute, LP, El Paso Holdings, Inc., EP Cardiovascular Institute Management, Inc. 60 Subsidiaries included in the Index
Officers: Edwin O. French/CEO, Pres., Phil Mazzuca/COO, Joan McCanless/Sr. VP, Chief Clinical, Compliance Officer, Arthur J. Parker/Sr. VP, Treasurer, James E. Harris/CFO, Exec. VP, Sec.

Owners: Edwin O. French/2.40%, Adam C. Clammer, Dimensional FundAdvisors, Inc./5.60%, Phillip J. Mazzuca/1.40%, Thomas K. Hearn, Nierenberg Investment Management Company, Inc./8.20%, Welsh, Carson, Anderson& StoweVII, L.P./16.80%, Joan McCanless, Paul B. Queally/17.00%, James E. Harris/1.10%, Insiders/23.70%, John B. McKinnon, Robert S. McCoy, John T. Casey, MedCath 1998 LLC/18.80% *(18 Owners included in Index)*

Financial Data: *Fiscal Year End:*09/30   *Latest Annual Data:* 06/30/2007

Year	Sales	Net Income
2007	$192,279,000	$9,265,000
2006	$706,374,000	$12,576,000
2005	$758,560,000	$8,791,000

Curr. Assets:	$332,976,000	**Curr. Liab.:**	$135,701,000	**P/E Ratio:**	40.74
Plant, Equip.:	$338,152,000	**Total Liab.:**	$442,381,000	**Indic. Yr. Divd.:**	NA
Total Assets:	$785,849,000	**Net Worth:**	$317,660,000	**Debt/ Equity:**	0.5697

Medco Health Solutions Inc

100 Parsons Pond Dr., Franklin Lakes, NJ, 07417; *PH:* 1-201-269-3400; *Fax:* 1-201-269-1109;
http:// www.medco.com

General - Incorporation	DE	**Stock**- Price on:12/24/2007	$78.65
Employees	15,200	Stock Exchange	NYSE
Auditor	PricewaterhouseCoopers LLP	Ticker Symbol	MHS
Stk Agt	Bank of New York	Outstanding Shares	280,140,000
Counsel	NA	E.P.S.	$3.10
DUNS No.	NA	Shareholders	NA

Business: The group's principle activity is to provide traditional and specialty prescription drug benefit programs and services. The group operates from United States.

Primary SIC and add'l.: 6324 5912
CIK No: 0001170650
Subsidiaries: Accredo Health Group, Inc., Accredo Health Resources, Inc. (New York), Accredo Health Services (Infusion), Inc., Accredo Health, Incorporated, AHG of New York, Inc., BioPartners In Care, Inc., Bravell, Inc., Clinical Business Solutions, Inc., Hemophilia Resources of America, Inc., Home Healthcare Resources, Inc., Home Healthcare Resources, Limited, HRA Holding Corp., Medco at Home, LLC, Medco Containment Insurance Company of New Jersey, Medco Containment Insurance Company of New York 50 Subsidiaries included in the Index
Officers: Timothy C. Wentworth/CEO, Pres. - Accredo Health Group, Inc, David B. Snow/52/Chmn., CEO, Karin Princivalle/Sr. VP - Human Resources, Robert S. Epstein/51/Sr. VP - Medical, Analytical Affairs, Chief Medical Officer, Glenn C. Taylor/55/Group Pres. - Key Accounting, Joann A. Reed/51/CFO, Sr. VP - Finance, Brian T. Griffin/48/Group Pres. - Health Plans, John P. Driscoll/Pres. - Insured, Emerging Markets, Richard J. Rubino/50/Sr. VP, Controller, Chief Accounting Officer, David S. MacHlowitz/53/Sr. VP, General Counsel, Sec., Kenneth O. Klepper/53/COO, Pres., Arthur H. Nardin/48/Sr. VP - Pharmaceutical Contracting, Bryan D. Birch/41/Group Pres. - Employer Accounting, Jack A. Smith/59/Sr. VP, Chief Marketing Officer, Laizer Kornwasser/Sr. VP - Channel, Generic Strategy
Directors: David B. Snow/52/Chmn., CEO, Howard W. Barker/Dir., Charles M. Lillis/66/Dir., Edward H. Shortliffe/Dir., John L. Cassis/Dir., Lawrence S. Lewin/Dir., David D. Stevens/Dir., Michael Goldstein/66/Dir., Blenda J. Wilson/Dir.
Owners: Charles M. Lillis, Howard W. Barker, John L. Cassis, Insiders/1.02%, JoAnn A. Reed, Bryan Birch, Kenneth O. Klepper, John P. Driscoll, Blenda J. Wilson, UBS AG/5.80%, Edward H. Shortliffe, Michael Goldstein, David D. Stevens, Lawrence S. Lewin, David B. Snow

Financial Data: *Fiscal Year End:*12/29   *Latest Annual Data:* 12/30/2006

Year	Sales	Net Income
2006	$42,543,700,000	$630,200,000
2005	$37,870,900,000	$602,000,000
2004	$35,351,900,000	$481,600,000

Curr. Assets:	$5,060,900,000	**Curr. Liab.:**	$3,760,800,000	**P/E Ratio:**	27.21
Plant, Equip.:	$672,300,000	**Total Liab.:**	$5,978,800,000	**Indic. Yr. Divd.:**	NA
Total Assets:	$13,703,000,000	**Net Worth:**	$7,724,200,000	**Debt/ Equity:**	0.1184

Medcom USA Inc

7975 N Hayden, Ste. D-333, Scottsdale, AZ, 85258; *PH:* 1-480-675-8865; *Fax:* 1-480-945-1909;
http:// www.medcomusa.com; *Email:* info@medcomusa.com

General - Incorporation	DE	**Stock**- Price on:12/24/2007	$0.37
Employees	37	Stock Exchange	OTC
Auditor	Jewett, Schwartz, Wolfe & Assoc.	Ticker Symbol	EMED
Stk Agt	Corporate Stock Transfer, Inc.	Outstanding Shares	70,320,000
Counsel	Hart & Trinen LLP	E.P.S.	-$0.025
DUNS No.	60-252-6758	Shareholders	NA

Business: The group's principle activity is to provide electronic medical transaction processing services. It utilizes the medcard system, which provides innovative technology-based solutions for the healthcare industry, which enables users to efficiently collect, utilize, analyze and disseminate data from payers, health care providers and patients. The medcard system operates through a point-of-sale terminal and an on-line enabled personal computer. The revenue form the medical transaction processing segment includes revenues from the medcard system, including the sale of terminals, processing fees and billing service revenue and the licensing, sales and services related to the group's one medical services network. The customers of the group include health care providers, primarily medical doctors' offices. It operates solely in the domestic market. The group's total revenue for year 2007 was 4.00 millions of USD.

Primary SIC and add'l.: 7374 7359
CIK No: 0000907127
Subsidiaries: Card Activations
Officers: William P. Williams/55/Chmn., CEO, CFO, Pres., Kent Barghols/Investors Contact, Anthony Pizzolo/Executive Contact - Exec. VP - Medcard Division, Michael Malet/Executive Contact - Exec. VP
Directors: William P. Williams/55/Chmn., CEO, CFO, Pres.
Owners: American Nortel Communications/22.00%, William P. Williams/8.00%

Financial Data: *Fiscal Year End:*06/30   *Latest Annual Data:* 06/30/2007

Year	Sales	Net Income
2007	$4,005,000	-$2,554,000
2006	$6,000,000	-$6,339,000
2005	$2,747,000	-$7,115,000

Curr. Assets:	$1,001,000	**Curr. Liab.:**	$3,395,000		
Plant, Equip.:	$1,307,000	**Total Liab.:**	$10,516,000	**Indic. Yr. Divd.:**	NA
Total Assets:	$3,681,000	**Net Worth:**	-$6,835,000	**Debt/ Equity:**	NA

Media General Inc

333 E Franklin St., Richmond, VA, 23219; *PH:* 1-804-649-6000; *Fax:* 1-804-649-6066; *http://* www.media-general.com

General - Incorporation ... VA
Employees ... 7,200
Auditor ... Ernst & Young LLP
Stk Agt... American Stock Transfer & Trust Co.
Counsel ... NA
DUNS No. ... 04-833-1490

Stock - Price on:12/24/2007 ... $34.32
Stock Exchange ... NYSE
Ticker Symbol ... MEG
Outstanding Shares ... 22,630,000
E.P.S. ... $2.16
Shareholders ... NA

Business: The group's principal activities are to publish newspapers, operate broadcast television stations and provide interactive media services. The group operates in three segments: publishing, broadcast and interactive media. Publishing segment publishes 25 daily newspapers and nearly 100 weekly newspapers and other publications in Virginia, Florida, North Carolina, South Carolina and Alabama. Broadcast segment includes the operations of 26 network-affiliated broadcast television stations. This segment also provides equipment and studio design services. Interactive media segment provides online news, information and entertainment to its customers without geographic restrictions. In 2003, the group sold media general financial services inc, a component of its interactive media division.

Primary SIC and add'l.: 4833 2621 2711 7375

CIK No: 0000216539

Subsidiaries: Blockdot, Inc., Media General Broadcasting of South Carolina Holdings, Inc., Media General Communications, Inc., Media General Operations, Inc., NES II, Inc., Professional Communications Systems, Inc., SP Newsprint Company (Partnership), The Tribune Company Holdings, Inc., Virginia Paper Manufacturing Corp.

Officers: Marshall N. Morton/Dir., CEO, Pres./$3,282,114.00, Reid O. Ashe/Dir., Exec. VP, COO/$2,522,189.00, Graham H. Woodlief/VP/$1,719,646.00, James A. Zimmerman/VP, Pres. - Broadcast Division, Neal F. Fondren/VP, Pres. - Interactive Media Division, Stephen Y. Dickinson/Controller, George L. Mahoney/VP, General Counsel, Sec., Lou Anne J. Nabhan/VP, Dir. - Corporate Communications, John A. Schauss/VP - Finance, CFO/$878,207.00, James F. Woodward/VP - Human Resources, Kirk C. Read/VP, Pres. - Interactive Media Division

Directors: Marshall N. Morton/Dir., CEO, Pres., Stewart J. Bryan/Chmn., Walter E. Williams/Dir., Thompson L. Rankin/Dir., Charles A. Davis/Dir., Reid O. Ashe/Dir., Exec. VP, COO, Coleman Wortham/Dir., Diana F. Cantor/Dir., Rodney A. Smolla/Dir.

Owners: John A. Schauss, Private Capital Management, L.P./12.40%, Fidelity Investments Institutional/7.50%, Jane Bryan Brockenbrough/10.00%, Rodney A. Smolla, Insiders/83.80%, Thompson L. Rankin, Marshall N. Morton/1.10%, Walter E. Williams, Diana F. Cantor, Charles A. Davis, Stewart J. Bryan/83.80%, Graham H. Woodlief, Mario J. Gabelli/20.40%, Barclays Global Investors, NA/5.00% *(19 Owners included in Index)*

Financial Data: **Fiscal Year End:**12/31 **Latest Annual Data:** 12/31/2006

Year	Sales	Net Income
2006	$983,189,000	$79,042,000
2005	$917,937,000	-$243,042,000
2004	$900,420,000	$80,185,000

Curr. Assets:	$202,748,000	**Curr. Liab.:**	$131,520,000	**P/E Ratio:**	15.89
Plant, Equip.:	$490,049,000	**Total Liab.:**	$1,567,868,000	**Indic. Yr. Divd.:**	$0.920
Total Assets:	$2,505,228,000	**Net Worth:**	$937,360,000	**Debt/ Equity:**	1.0078

Media Sciences International Inc

8 Allerman Rd., Oakland, NJ, 07463; *PH:* 1-201-677-9311; *Fax:* 1-201-677-1440; *http://* www.mediasciences.com; *Email:* support@mediasciences.com

General - Incorporation ... DE
Employees ... 61
Auditor ... J. H. Cohn LLP
Stk Agt... Continental Stock Transfer & Trust Co
Counsel ... NA
DUNS No. ... NA

Stock - Price on:12/24/2007 ... $6.04
Stock Exchange ... NDQ
Ticker Symbol ... NA
Outstanding Shares ... 11,420,000
E.P.S. ... $0.00
Shareholders ... NA

Business: The group's principal activity is to manufacture supplies for digital workgroup color printers. The group's wholly owned subsidiary, media sciences, inc., manufactures and distributes color printer supplies, including solid ink sticks and color toner cartridges for use in xerox and other color printers. These products are distributed internationally through a network of dealers and distributors. The group's another wholly owned subsidiary, cadapult graphic systems, inc., sells supplies directly to certain end users through no-cap color program.

Primary SIC and add'l.: 2893

CIK No: 0001024022

Subsidiaries: Cadapult Graphic Systems, Inc, Media Sciences UK Limited, Media Sciences, Inc.

Officers: Michael W. Levin/Chmn., CEO, Pres., Denise Hawkins/VP, Controller, Sec., Frances K. Blanco/VP - Marketing, Lawrence L. Anderson/COO, Sr. VP, Kevan D. Bloomgren/CFO

Directors: Michael W. Levin/Chmn., CEO, Pres., Edwin Ruzinsky/Dir., Henry Royer/Dir., Alan Bazaar/Dir., Paul C. Baker/Dir., Dennis Ridgeway/Dir., Willem Van Rijn/Dir., Frank J. Tanki/Dir.

Owners: Paul Baker/1.50%, Kevan D. Bloomgren, Lawrence Anderson, Michael W. Levin/12.90%, Alan L. Bazaar/8.80%, Henry Royer, Insiders/25.20%, Edwin Ruzinsky, Denise Hawkins

Financial Data: **Fiscal Year End:**06/30 **Latest Annual Data:** 06/30/2007

Year	Sales	Net Income
2007	$22,517,000	$777,000
2006	$21,273,000	$2,128,000
2005	$17,879,000	-$83,000

Curr. Assets:	$8,972,000	**Curr. Liab.:**	$3,865,000	**P/E Ratio:**	28.76
Plant, Equip.:	$2,580,000	**Total Liab.:**	$5,191,000	**Indic. Yr. Divd.:**	NA
Total Assets:	$15,215,000	**Net Worth:**	$10,024,000	**Debt/ Equity:**	0.0334

Mediabay Inc

2 Ridgedale Ave., Cedar Knolls, NJ, 07927; *PH:* 1-973-539-9528; *Fax:* 1-973-539-1273; *http://* www.mediabay.com; *Email:* investor.relations@mbayinc.com

General - Incorporation ... FL
Employees ... 27
Auditor ... Amper, Politziner & Mattia P.C
Stk Agt... Continental Stock Transfer & Trust Co
Counsel ... NA
DUNS No. ... 87-812-7703

Stock - Price on:12/24/2007 ... $0.065
Stock Exchange ... OTC
Ticker Symbol ... MBAY
Outstanding Shares ... 10,520,000
E.P.S. ... -$2.22
Shareholders ... NA

Business: The group's principal activities are to market spoken audio and nostalgia products, including audiobooks and old-time radio shows. These products are sold through direct response, retail and Internet channels. The content and products are sold both in secure digital download format as well as in physical formats like cassette and compact disc. The group operates through four business segments: corporate, audio book club, radio spirits and mediabay.com. Audio book club is a membership-based club. Radio spirits markets old-time radio and classic video programs. Mediabay.com is a content-rich media portal. Radio classics distributes national classic radio programs, which are been collectively heard on more than 500 traditional radio stations.

Primary SIC and add'l.: 5961

CIK No: 0001040973

Financial Data: **Fiscal Year End:**12/31 **Latest Annual Data:** 12/31/2005

Year	Sales	Net Income
2005	$8,955,000	-$11,444,000
2004	$18,831,000	-$30,113,000
2003	$36,617,000	-$6,623,000

Curr. Assets:	$10,684,000	**Curr. Liab.:**	$5,320,000		
Plant, Equip.:	$1,785,000	**Total Liab.:**	$5,928,000	**Indic. Yr. Divd.:**	NA
Total Assets:	$18,667,000	**Net Worth:**	$12,739,000	**Debt/ Equity:**	NA

Mediacom Communications Corp

100 Crystal Run Rd., Middletown, NY, 10941; *PH:* 1-845-695-2600; *Fax:* 1-845-695-2699; *http://* www.mediacomcc.com

General - Incorporation ... DE
Employees ... 4,295
Auditor ... PricewaterhouseCoopers LLP
Stk Agt... Mellon Investor Services LLC
Counsel... Sonnenschein Nath & Rosenthal LLP
DUNS No. ... NA

Stock - Price on:12/24/2007 ... $9.5
Stock Exchange ... NDQ
Ticker Symbol ... MCCC
Outstanding Shares ... 109,910,000
E.P.S. ... -$0.57
Shareholders ... NA

Business: The group's principal activities are to acquire and develop cable television systems serving smaller cities and towns in the United States. Through these cable television systems, the group provides entertainment, information and telecommunications services including traditional video services, digital television and high-speed Internet access to its subscribers. As of 31-Dec-2003, the group had acquired and operated cable systems in 23 states, principally Alabama, California, Delaware, Florida, Georgia, Illinois, Indiana, Iowa, Kentucky, Minnesota, Missouri, North Carolina and South Dakota.

Primary SIC and add'l.: 4841

CIK No: 0001098659

Subsidiaries: Illini Cable Holding, Inc., Illini Cablevision of Illinois, Inc., MCC Georgia LLC, MCC Illinois LLC, MCC Iowa LLC, MCC Missouri LLC, Mediacom Arizona LLC, Mediacom Broadband Corporation, Mediacom Broadband LLC, Mediacom California LLC, Mediacom Capital Corporation, Mediacom Delaware LLC, Mediacom Illinois LLC, Mediacom Indiana Holdings, L.P., Mediacom Indiana LLC 22 Subsidiaries included in the Index

Officers: Rocco B. Commisso/Chmn., CEO/$2,972,736.00, Mark E. Stephan/Dir., CFO, Exec. VP/$727,564.00, Matt Derdeyn/Group VP - Corporate Finance, Treasurer, John G. Pascarelli/Exec. VP - Operations/$700,431.00, Michael Rahimi/Sr. VP - Marketing, Consumer Services, Bruce Gluckman/Legal Department, Phyllis Peters/Sr. Mgr. - Communications, Charles J. Bartolotta/Sr. VP - Customer Operations, Calvin G. Craib/Sr. VP - Business Development, Brian M. Walsh/Sr. VP, Corporate Controller, Italia Commisso Weinand/Sr. VP - Programming, Human Resources/$546,831.00, Joseph E. Young/Sr. VP, General Counsel, Sec./$592,259.00

Directors: Rocco B. Commisso/Chmn., CEO, Mark E. Stephan/Dir., CFO, Exec. VP, Thomas V. Reifenheiser/Dir., Craig S. Mitchell/Dir., Natale S. Ricciardi/Dir., Robert L. Winikoff/Dir., William S. Morris/Dir.

Owners: Insiders/35.60%, Craig S. Mitchell/34.30%, Insiders/100.00%, John G. Pascarelli, Joseph E. Young, Italia Commisso Weinand, Rocco B. Commisso, Thomas V. Reifenheiser, Rocco B. Commisso/100.00%, William S. Morris/34.20%, Robert L. Winikoff, Natale S. Ricciardi, Mark E. Stephan, Mark E. Stephan

Financial Data: **Fiscal Year End:**12/31 **Latest Annual Data:** 12/31/2006

Year	Sales	Net Income
2006	$1,210,400,000	-$124,922,000
2005	$1,098,822,000	-$222,228,000
2004	$1,057,226,000	$13,552,000

Curr. Assets:	$131,822,000	**Curr. Liab.:**	$397,467,000		
Plant, Equip.:	$1,451,134,000	**Total Liab.:**	$3,747,164,000	**Indic. Yr. Divd.:**	NA
Total Assets:	$3,652,350,000	**Net Worth:**	-$94,814,000	**Debt/ Equity:**	NA

Medialink Worldwide Inc

708 3rd Ave., New York, NY, 10017; *PH:* 1-212-682-8300; *Fax:* 1-212-682-5260; *http://* www.medialink.com; *Email:* ir@medialink.com

General - Incorporation ... DE
Employees ... 126
Auditor ... KPMG LLP
Stk Agt... Mellon Shareholder Services LLC
Counsel... Tashlik, Goldwyn & Crandell P.C.
DUNS No. ... 17-726-6970

Stock - Price on:12/24/2007 ... $4.78
Stock Exchange ... NDQ
Ticker Symbol ... MDLK
Outstanding Shares ... 6,410,000
E.P.S. ... NA
Shareholders ... NA

Business: The group's principal activity is to provide media communication services. The group provides worldwide video and audio production and distribution services and public relations research services for businesses and other organizations. These services help the businesses to communicate and evaluate their news through television, radio, the Internet and other media. The group specializes in working with clients to create and produce video news segments. The group produces these news segments on behalf of more than 1,500 clients and provides them to television newsrooms, be they network or local, domestic or foreign, for their free and unrestricted use. The clients include corporations and other organizations seeking to communicate their messages through the news media, primarily television, to the audience worldwide.

Primary SIC and add'l.: 4899 7812

CIK No: 0000812890

Subsidiaries: Medialink UK Limited, Ttx (us) LLC, TTX Limited

Officers: Laurence Moskowitz/Chmn., CEO, Pres./$1,048,504.00, Kenneth G. Torosian/CFO/$453,101.00, James J. O'Neill/Dir. - Private Financial Consultant, Lucy Hadfield/MD, Andy Nobbs/Pres. - Teletrax, Mary C. Buhay/Sr. VP - Corporate Communications, Larry Thomas/COO Strategic Planning - Development, Donald M. Michels/CTO, Scott Michaeloff/Sr. VP - Executive Producer, Michele Wallace/Sr. VP - Client Solutions

Directors: Laurence Moskowitz/Chmn., CEO, Pres., Theodore W. Tashlik/Dir., Bruce Bishop/Dir., Douglas S. Knopper/Dir., James J. O'Neill/Dir. - Private Financial Consultant, Catherine Lugbauer/Dir., Harold Finelt/Dir., John M. Greening/Dir.

Owners: Gotham Holdings, LP/7.26%, Laurence Moskowitz/7.25%, Dimensional Fund Advisors LP/7.31%, Theodore Wm. Tashlik/1.53%, William McCarren, Lawrence Thomas, Insiders/13.26%, Bruce E. Bishop, Harold Finelt/1.63%, Donald Kimelman, James J. O'Neill, Catherine Lugbauer, AMH Equity LLC/5.20%, Kenneth G. Torosian, Douglas S. Knopper *(18 Owners included in Index)*

Mediamax Technology Corp

5355 Capital Ct., Ste. 108, Reno, NV, 89502; ; *http://*www.mediamaxtech.com

General - Incorporation	NV	Stock - Price on:12/24/2007	NA
Employees	2	Stock Exchange	OTC
Auditor	Semple & Cooper LLP	Ticker Symbol	MMXT
Stk Agt	NA	Outstanding Shares	NA
Counsel	NA	E.P.S.	NA
DUNS No.	60-665-3525	Shareholders	NA

Business: The group's principal activity is to produce methodologies that are designed to thwart illegal copying or ripping of optical media that complies to iec 90608 redbook standards. These methodologies are meant to work toward defeating the various software products currently available on the market today that are used for the purpose of making illegal copies of cds or of individual audio tracks. The group operates solely in the domestic market.

Primary SIC and add'l.: 7372

CIK No: 0001057024

Subsidiaries: SunnComm International, Inc

Officers: Scott S. Stoegbauer/Pres.

Financial Data: Fiscal Year End:12/31   Latest Annual Data: 12/31/2005

Year	Sales	Net Income
2005	$231,000	-$3,586,000
2004	$106,000	-$1,541,000

Curr. Assets:	$92,000	Curr. Liab.:	$1,122,000		
Plant, Equip.:	$7,000	Total Liab.:	$1,122,000	Indic. Yr. Divd.:	NA
Total Assets:	$962,000	Net Worth:	-$160,000	Debt/ Equity:	NA

Medianet Group Technologies Inc

5100 W Copans Rd. , Ste 710, Margate, FL, 33063; *PH:* 1-954-974-5818; *http://*www.medianetgroup.com; *Email:* shareholder@medianetgroup.com

General - Incorporation	NV	Stock - Price on:12/24/2007	$0.19
Employees	8	Stock Exchange	OTC
Auditor Child, Van Wagoner & Bradshaw, PLLC		Ticker Symbol	MEDG
Stk Agt. Executive Registrar & Transfer, Inc.		Outstanding Shares	11,960,000
Counsel	NA	E.P.S.	-$0.072
DUNS No.	NA	Shareholders	NA

Business: The group's principal activity is to provide online, business to business and business to consumer community portal to a variety of industries. The group brings a variety of interests to the portal to assist users in communicating with each other and to gather and supply information to users. The group has developed brand-a-port software, a brandable and customizable full portal application with many of the features and functions of yahoo, msn and aol. The group also provides bsp rewards program, which offers members up to 10% rewards, added to any rewards already associated with their credit cards and memory lane syndications, which is the epicenter for our media business. The customers include small, medium and large sized companies and organizations. The operations are carried on in the United States. On 31-Mar-2003, the group acquired shutterport inc.

Primary SIC and add'l.: 7372 7375

CIK No: 0001097792

Subsidiaries: Brand-A-Port, Inc, BSP Rewards, Inc, Memory Lane Syndication Inc., Nevada corporation

Officers: Martin A. Berns/Chmn., CEO, James Dyas/58/Dir., CFO, Treasurer, Larry Lipman/Dir., Dir. - Business Development, Tom Hill/Dir., Dir. - Operations, BSP Rewards, James Yagielo/Dir. - Technical Services

Directors: Martin A. Berns/Chmn., CEO, Brad A. Moss/Member - Advisory Board, James Dyas/58/Dir., CFO, Treasurer, Dennis Lane/Member - Advisory Board, Larry Lipman/Dir., Dir. - Business Development, Tom Hill/Dir., Dir. - Operations, BSP Rewards, Joseph Porrello/Member - Advisory Board, William D. Stimack/Member - Advisory Board, Eugene H. Berns/Dir., Gary Serota/Member - Advisory Board, Gary Serota, Jeffrey W. Meshel/Dir., Bruce L. Hollander/Dir., Robert Hussey/59/Dir.

Owners: Jeffrey Meshel/1.10%, Insiders/33.10%, Gregory Fortunoff/5.30%, Lawrence Lipman/0.60%, Martin A. Berns/22.10%, James Dyas/0.20%, Sandra F. Pessin/5.00%, Robert Hussey/0.80%, Norman H. Pessin/17.50%, Eugene H. Berns/4.10%, Ivan L. Bial/4.30%, Thomas C. Hill/0.70%

Financial Data: Fiscal Year End:12/31   Latest Annual Data: 12/31/2006

Year	Sales	Net Income
2006	$434,000	-$1,120,000
2005	$177,000	-$1,073,000
2004	$112,000	-$336,000

Curr. Assets:	$236,000	Curr. Liab.:	$167,000		
Plant, Equip.:	$3,000	Total Liab.:	$167,000	Indic. Yr. Divd.:	NA
Total Assets:	$343,000	Net Worth:	$175,000	Debt/ Equity:	NA

Medianews Group Inc

1560 Brdway, Ste. 2100, Denver, CO, 80202; *PH:* 1-303-563-6360; *http://*www.medianewsgroup.com

General - Incorporation	DE	Stock - Price on:12/24/2007	NA
Employees	NA	Stock Exchange	NA
Auditor	Ernst & Young LLP	Ticker Symbol	NA
Stk Agt	NA	Outstanding Shares	NA
Counsel	Hughes Hubbard & Reed LLP	E.P.S.	NA
DUNS No.	NA	Shareholders	NA

Business: The group operates thorugh its subsdiary whose principle activity is to publish daily and non-daily newspaper serving markets in ten states; and owns four radio stations and one television station. The group operates from United States.

Primary SIC and add'l.: 6719 6794 2711

CIK No: 0000918944

Subsidiaries: Alaska Broadcasting Company, Inc., (Northern Television, Inc. KTVA)., California Newspapers Limited Partnership, California Newspapers Partnership, Charleston Publishing Company, Clock Tower Condominium Association, Connecticut Newspapers Publishing Company, (Connecticut Post), Eastern Colorado Publishing Company, Graham Newspapers, Inc.,), Kearns-Tribune, LLC, (The Salt Lake Tribune), Long Beach Publishing Company, (Press-Telegram), Los Angeles Daily News Publishing Company, (Daily News), Lowell Internet Media Publishing Company, Inc., Lowell Publishing Company, (The Sun), MediaNews Group Interactive, Inc., MediaNews Services, Inc. 29 Subsidiaries included in the Index

Officers: William Dean Singleton/Vice Chmn., CEO, James McDougald/Treasurer, Joseph J. Lodovic/Pres., Steven B. Rossi/COO, Exec. VP, Steven M. Barkmeier/VP - Tax, Michael J. Koren/VP, Controller, Anthony F. Tierno/Sr. VP - Operations, Ronald A. Mayo/CFO, VP, Liz Gaier/Sr. VP - New Business Development, Charles Kamen/VP - Human Resources, Steve Barkmeier/VP - Tax, David Bessen/CIO, VP, Pat Robinson/Sec., Elizabeth A. Gaier/43/Sr. VP - New Business Development, Howell E. Begle/64/Dir., Assist. Sec. - General *(20 Officers included in Index)*

Directors: William Dean Singleton/Vice Chmn., CEO, Richard B. Scudder/95/Chmn., Jean L. Scudder/54/Dir., Howell E. Begle/64/Dir., Assist. Sec. - General

MediaREADY Inc

888 E Las Olas Blvd., Ste. 710, Fort Lauderdale, FL, 33301; *PH:* 1-954-527-7780; *Fax:* 1-954-527-7772; *http://*www.mediareadyinc.com; *Email:* Media@MediaREADYInc.com

General - Incorporation	FL	Stock - Price on:12/24/2007	$0.063
Employees	9	Stock Exchange	OTC
Auditor	Baum & Company, P.A.	Ticker Symbol	MRED
Stk Agt	Interwest Transfer Company, Inc.	Outstanding Shares	122,410,000
Counsel	NA	E.P.S.	-$0.01
DUNS No.	NA	Shareholders	NA

Business: The groups principle activity is to supply broadband products, services and content including digital video and web interactivity. The products of the group include MediaREADY(TM) 4000, MediaREADY(TM) 5000, MediaREADY(TM) Flyboy and MediaREADY(TM) CoPilot. The group operates from the United States.

Primary SIC and add'l.: 7389

CIK No: 0001123493

Officers: Jeffrey V. Harrell/42/Chmn., Pres. - Principal Executive, Financial, Accounting Officer, Sec., Canny Gau/Dir., Dir. - Product Engineering, Manufacturing, Terry Glatt/CTO, Dir., David Novak/Exec. VP - Sales, Marketing, Dir.

Directors: Jeffrey V. Harrell/42/Chmn., Pres. - Principal Executive, Financial, Accounting Officer, Sec., Canny Gau/Dir., Dir. - Product Engineering, Manufacturing, Terry Glatt/CTO, Dir., David Novak/Exec. VP - Sales, Marketing, Dir.

Owners: Jeffrey V. Harrell/2.00%

Financial Data: Fiscal Year End:12/31   Latest Annual Data: 12/31/2006

Year	Sales	Net Income
2006	$1,212,000	-$3,405,000
2005	$181,000	-$2,463,000
2004	$14,000	-$2,986,000

Curr. Assets:	$823,000	Curr. Liab.:	$9,366,000		
Plant, Equip.:	$12,000	Total Liab.:	$9,366,000	Indic. Yr. Divd.:	NA
Total Assets:	$848,000	Net Worth:	-$8,518,000	Debt/ Equity:	NA

Medical Action Industries Inc

800 Prime Pl., Hauppauge, NY, 11788; *PH:* 1-631-231-4600; *Fax:* 1-631-231-3075; *http://*www.medical-action.com; *Email:* mdci@medical-action.com

General - Incorporation	DE	Stock - Price on:12/24/2007	NA
Employees	NA	Stock Exchange	NDQ
Auditor	Grant Thornton LLP	Ticker Symbol	MDCI
Stk Agt	American Stock Transfer & Trust Co.	Outstanding Shares	15,820,000
Counsel	NA	E.P.S.	$0.87
DUNS No.	09-236-4462	Shareholders	NA

Business: The group's principle activity is to develop, manufacture and market disposable surgical-related products. The company's products are divided into four categories namely collection systems for the containment of medical waste, minor procedure kits and trays, operating room disposables and sterilization products and dressings and surgical sponges. The products include laparotomy sponges, sterile operating room towels, medical pouches, burn dressings, suture removal trays, surgical start kits, autoclave bags and others. The company also manufactures products under private label programs with other distributors and medical suppliers. The products are marketed through a network of independent distributors, direct sales personnel and manufacturers' representatives. The customers include acute care facilities in domestic and certain international markets, as well as physician, dental and veterinary offices. The group's total revenue for year 2007 was 217.33 millions of USD.

Primary SIC and add'l.: 3841 3842

CIK No: 0000748270

Officers: Paul D. Meringolo/Chmn., CEO, Pres./$1,115,251.00, Manuel B. Losada/VP - Sales, Marketing/$610,752.00, Victor Bacchioni/Corporate Controller, David Dahle/Dir. - Corporate Accounting, Steven Carlson/Dir. - North American Manufacturing Operations, Richard G. Satin/Dir., VP - Operations, General Counsel/$591,665.00, Carmine Morello/VP - Information Technology, Eric Liu/VP - International Operations, Global Development/$515,551.00, Anthony Gadzinski/Dir. - Alternate Care, Laurie Darnaby/Dir. - Human Resources, Richard Pohland/GM - Clarksburg Facility, John Kringel/Dir. - Marketing, Peter Meringolo/Dir. - International Marketing, Adnan Syed/Dir. - E-Commerce, System Development

Directors: Paul D. Meringolo/Chmn., CEO, Pres., William W. Burke/Dir., Henry A. Berling/Dir., Thomas A. Nicosia/Dir., Bernard Wengrover/Dir., Richard G. Satin/Dir., VP - Operations, General Counsel, Philip F. Corso/Dir.

Owners: FMR Corp/15.00%, Insiders/11.50%, Richard G. Satin/2.10%, Bernard Wengrover, Royce & Associates, LLC/5.40%, Eric Liu/3.10%, William W. Burke, Philip F. Corso, Manuel B. Losada, Paul D. Meringolo/5.20%, Henry A. Berling, Barclays Global Investments, N.A./7.30%, Kenneth R. Newsome, Vaughan Nelson Investment Management, LP/6.40%

Financial Data: Fiscal Year End:03/31   Latest Annual Data: 3/31/2007

Year	Sales	Net Income
2007	$217,328,000	$12,969,000
2006	$150,942,000	$11,461,000
2005	$141,423,000	$10,682,000

Curr. Assets:	$58,553,000	Curr. Liab.:	$40,833,000		
Plant, Equip.:	$32,553,000	Total Liab.:	$94,306,000	Indic. Yr. Divd.:	NA
Total Assets:	$192,670,000	Net Worth:	$98,364,000	Debt/ Equity:	NA

Medical Connections Holdings Inc

Formerly: Webb Mortgage Depot Inc
2300 Glades Rd., Ste. 202(e), Boca Raton, FL, 33431; **PH:** 1-561-353-1110;
http:// www.webbmortgage.com

General - Incorporation	FL	Stock- Price on:12/24/2007	$2
Employees	30	Stock Exchange	OTC
Auditor	Bagell, Josephs, Levine & Co. LLC	Ticker Symbol	MCTH
Stk Agt	Interwest Transfer Company, Inc.	Outstanding Shares	10,260,000
Counsel	NA	E.P.S.	-$1.14
DUNS No.	NA	Shareholders	NA

Business: The group's principal activity is to originate and process mortgage loans that are funded by third parties. It offers a full range of loan products, including adjustable rate mortgages, fifteen-year and thirty-year fixed rate loans and balloon loans with a variety of maturities. In addition it also offers refinancing, construction loans, second mortgages, debt consolidation and home equity loans. The services provided by the group include data entry, compilation of personal financing and other materials including appraisals, titles, credit reports, employment verification and underwriting. The group provides both on line and traditional mortgage services through mortgage brokers who are independent contractors.

Primary SIC and add'l.: 6163 6531 6162

CIK No: 0001140303

Subsidiaries: Medical Connections Inc, Omega Capital Solutions, Inc.

Officers: Joseph Azzata/47/Dir., CEO, Anthony Nicolosi/37/Dir., Pres., Daniel L. Cammarano/46/CFO, Luke Jansen/43/VP

Directors: Joseph Azzata/47/Dir., CEO, Anthony Nicolosi/37/Dir., Pres.

Owners: Anthony Nicolosi/32.40%, Luke Jansen/1.70%, Joseph Azzata/32.40%

Financial Data: Fiscal Year End:12/31   Latest Annual Data: 12/31/2006

Year	Sales	Net Income
2006	$2,215,000	-$2,648,000
2005	$516,000	-$2,148,000
2004	$462,000	$101,000

Curr. Assets:	$335,000	Curr. Liab.:	$1,643,000		
Plant, Equip.:	$772,000	Total Liab.:	$2,103,000	Indic. Yr. Divd.:	NA
Total Assets:	$1,136,000	Net Worth:	-$967,000	Debt/ Equity:	NA

Medical Discoveries Inc

1338 S Foothill Dr., No. 266, Salt Lake City, UT, 84108; **PH:** 1-800-582-9583;
http:// www.medicaldiscoveries.com; **Email:** info@medicaldiscoveries.com

General - Incorporation	UT	Stock- Price on:12/24/2007	NA
Employees	2	Stock Exchange	OTC
Auditor	Hansen, Barnett & Maxwell	Ticker Symbol	MLSC
Stk Agt	Colonial Stock Transfer Co Inc	Outstanding Shares	NA
Counsel	Stephen R. Drake Epstein B & G	E.P.S.	$0.00
DUNS No.	80-953-7251	Shareholders	NA

Business: The group's principal activity is to do research, develop and validate a new class of drugs based upon it's patented and proprietary electrolysis technologies. The group is developing active anti-viral, anti-bacterial and anti-fungal agents for a variety of applications. Mdi-p is a product developed by the group to destroy certain viruses, bacteria, pathogenic fungi, parasites and other infectious agents. The product may be used as a sterilizing agent for medical and dental instruments. Mdi-p may also potentially be used to remove or inactivate infectious agents in human and animal blood-derived products such as plasma and gamma globulin. The group is in the development stage.

Primary SIC and add'l.: 5912

CIK No: 0000748790

Subsidiaries: MDI Oncology, Inc.

Officers: Judy M. Robinett/48/Dir., CEO, Investor Contact, David R. Walker/Chmn., Treasurer, Richard Palmer/Dir., COO, Pres., Stephen R. Drake/Corporate Counsel, Eric J. Melvin/Dir., Sec.

Directors: Judy M. Robinett/48/Dir., CEO, Investor Contact, David R. Walker/Chmn., Treasurer, Richard Palmer/Dir., COO, Pres., Eric J. Melvin/Dir., Sec., Martin Schroeder/Dir.

Owners: David Firestone, David R. Walker, Richard Palmer, Judy M. Robinett, Eric J. Melvin, Monarch Pointe Fund, Ltd., Insiders, Mobius Risk Group, LLC, Mercator Momentum Fund, LP, Martin Schroeder, Mercator Momentum Fund III, LP

Financial Data: Fiscal Year End:12/31   Latest Annual Data: 12/31/2005

Year	Sales	Net Income
2005	NA	-$1,487,000
2004	NA	-$3,731,000
2003	NA	-$952,000

Curr. Assets:	$654,000	Curr. Liab.:	$6,548,000		
Plant, Equip.:	$81,000	Total Liab.:	$6,548,000	Indic. Yr. Divd.:	NA
Total Assets:	$1,031,000	Net Worth:	-$5,516,000	Debt/ Equity:	NA

Medical Information Technology Inc

MEDITECH Cir., Westwood, MA, 02090; **PH:** 1-781-821-3000; **Fax:** 1-781-821-2199;
http:// www.meditech.com; **Email:** info@meditech.com

General - Incorporation	MA	Stock- Price on:12/24/2007	NA
Employees	NA	Stock Exchange	NA
Auditor	Ernst & Young LLP	Ticker Symbol	NA
Stk Agt:	NA	Outstanding Shares	NA
Counsel	NA	E.P.S.	NA
DUNS No.	06-515-2530	Shareholders	NA

Business: The group's principle activities are to develop and market information system software for the hospital industry. The company has developed a hospital information system, which is a cohesive set of software products designed to work in conjunction with the overall operation of the hospital, while also minimizing the need for specialized interfaces. The company has also developed a hospital billing and accounts receivable product and various other general accounting products. The company's customers include hca-the healthcare company, which represented 9% of the company's revenues. The principal market for the company's products consists of health care providers primarily located in the United States and Canada.

Primary SIC and add'l.: 7372 7379

CIK No: 0001011452

Officers: Neil A. Pappalardo/Chmn., CEO, Michelle O'Connor/VP - Product Development, Christopher Anschuetz/55/VP - Technology, Howard Messing/COO, Pres./$967,948.00, Hoda Sayed-Friel/VP - Marketing, Barbara Manzolillo/CFO, Treasurer/$731,948.00, Robert Gale/VP - Product Development, Joanne Wood/VP - Client Services, Chris Anschuetz/VP - System Technology, Stu Lefthes/VP - Sales/$745,948.00, Steven Koretz/VP - Implementation

Directors: Neil A. Pappalardo/Chmn., CEO, Lawrence Polimeno/Vice Chmn., Roland L. Driscoll/79/Dir., Edward B. Roberts/72/Dir., Morton E. Ruderman/71/Dir., L. P. Dan Valente/77/Dir.

Owners: Barbara A. Manzolillo/0.62%, Dan L.P. Valente/0.24%, Grossman Group/5.82%, Roland L. Driscoll/1.49%, Lawrence A. Polimeno/2.95%, Morton E. Ruderman/14.10%, Curtis W. Marble/9.89%, Neil A. Pappalardo/38.04%, Stuart N. Lefthes/0.21%, Insiders/62.22%, MEDITECH Profit Sharing Trust/11.80%, Howard Messing/0.97%, Edward B. Roberts/2.68%

Medical International Technology Inc

1872 Beaulac, Ville Saint-Laurent, Toronto, PQ, HR4 2E7; **PH:** 1-514-339-9355;
http:// www.mitcanada.ca; **Email:** marketing@mitcanada.ca

General - Incorporation	CO	Stock- Price on:12/24/2007	NA
Employees	19	Stock Exchange	OTC
Auditor	PS Stephenson & Co., P.C.	Ticker Symbol	MDLH
Stk Agt	Corporate Stock Transfer, Inc.	Outstanding Shares	NA
Counsel	NA	E.P.S.	NA
DUNS No.	NA	Shareholders	NA

Business: The group's principal activity is to specialize in the research, development, marketing and sale of needle-free jet injector technology and products for humans and animals, for single and mass injections. The group intends to concentrate its activities in the medical and para-medical sectors, in particular, in the field of instrumentation. The first product that the group intends to market is the agro-jet. The agro-jet is a high performance, semi-automatic needle-free injector, intended for general use of live stock market. Med-jet gun-type is a product intended to be marketed in the very short term for other animal markets and for which, like the agro-jet, there is a substantial potential for use in cattle, poultry, horse, sheep and other livestock. Pro-jet is a variation of the med-jet products and intended for use in the human sector.

Primary SIC and add'l.: 5047

CIK No: 0001112372

Subsidiaries: Medical International Technologies (MIT Canada) Canada, Inc

Officers: Karim Menassa/56/Chmn., Principal Executive Officer, Pres., Michel Bayouk/61/Dir., Sec., Principal Accounting Officer

Directors: Karim Menassa/56/Chmn., Principal Executive Officer, Pres., Michel Bayouk/61/Dir., Sec., Principal Accounting Officer

Owners: 2845351 Canada, Inc./7.40%, Michel Bayouk/12.10%, Karim Menassa/53.70%, Insiders/65.80%

Financial Data: Fiscal Year End:09/30   Latest Annual Data: 09/30/2005

Year	Sales	Net Income
2005	$354,000	-$734,000
2004	$196,000	-$1,415,000
2003	$347,000	-$1,696,000

Curr. Assets:	$334,000	Curr. Liab.:	$1,103,000		
Plant, Equip.:	$127,000	Total Liab.:	$1,103,000	Indic. Yr. Divd.:	NA
Total Assets:	$463,000	Net Worth:	-$641,000	Debt/ Equity:	NA

Medical Makeover Corp of America

500 Australian Ave. S, Ste. 700, West Palm Beach, FL, 33401; **PH:** 1-561-514-0196

General - Incorporation	DE	Stock- Price on:12/24/2007	$0.0099
Employees	1	Stock Exchange	OTC
Auditor	Lawrence Scharfman, CPA	Ticker Symbol	MMAM
Stk Agt	Florida Atlantic Stock Transfer, Inc.	Outstanding Shares	65,100,000
Counsel	NA	E.P.S.	-$0.001
DUNS No.	NA	Shareholders	NA

Business: The group is a development stage company, does not have significant operations. It intends to acquire or merge with operating business entities. Previously, the company focused on operating in the medical makeover/anti-aging business. Medical Makeover Corporation was founded in 1999. It was formerly known as Cactus New Media I, Inc. and changed its name to Medical Makeover Corporation of America in 2004. The company is based in West Palm Beach, Florida. The group operates from United States.

Primary SIC and add'l.: 8099

CIK No: 0001083944

Subsidiaries: Aventura Makeover Corporation, Aventura Electrolysis and Skin Care Center, Inc, Garden of Eden, Inc, R&I Salon Incorporated

Officers: Douglas Martin/43/Dir., Chmn., Pres., Robert Rudman/60/CFO, Sec., Treasurer

Owners: Gala Enterprises Ltd/19.87%, Douglas Martin/2.71%, Randy Baker/6.10%

Financial Data: Fiscal Year End:12/31   Latest Annual Data: 12/31/2006

Year	Sales	Net Income
2006	NA	-$69,000
2005	$4,000	-$694,000
2004	$4,000	-$354,000

Curr. Assets:	NA	Curr. Liab.:	$353,000	
Plant, Equip.:	NA	Total Liab.:	$353,000	Indic. Yr. Divd.: NA
Total Assets:	NA	Net Worth:	-$353,000	Debt/ Equity: NA

Medical Nutrition USA Inc

10 W Forest Ave., Englewood, NJ, 07631; *PH:* 1-800-220-3308; *http://* www.mdnu.com;
Email: info@pro-stat.com

General - Incorporation .... DE	Stock- Price on:12/24/2007 ....NA
Employees 24	Stock Exchange.............................NDQ
Auditor .... Goldstein & Ganz, CPA's P.C	Ticker Symbol............................MDNU
Stk Agt..... American Stock Transfer & Trust Co.	Outstanding Shares ....NA
Counsel ....NA	E.P.S.................................$0.16
DUNS No. 06-757-7742	Shareholders.............................NA

Business: The group's principal activities are to develop and distribute nutritional and health products. The group develops and distributes targeted, uniquely engineered, nutrition-medicine products for the anti-aging, weight loss and elder care markets within the medical, institutional and mass-Market communities. The trademarks of the group include pro-stat(tm), nutrition support system(tm), the healthy nut(tm).

Primary SIC and add'l.: 2834 8099
CIK No: 0000722617
Subsidiaries: Gender Sciences, Inc.
Officers: Frank A. Newman/58/Chmn., CEO/$350,688.00, Arnold M. Gans/Founder, Chief Science Officer/$306,127.00, Myra D. Gans/Exec. VP/$236,716.00, Jeffrey M. Janco/COO, Sr. VP/$193,508.00, Nancy Collins/Medical, Clinical Advisor, Mary Ellen Posthauer/Medical, Clinical Advisor, Brenda Richardson/Medical, Clinical Advisor, Alan Levy/46/VP - Finance, CFO, Treasurer, Sec. - Principal Financial, Accounting Officer/$78,596.00, David Shapiro/46/VP - Sales/$38,607.00, Linda Roberts/Medical, Clinical Advisor
Directors: Frank A. Newman/58/Chmn., CEO, Mark H. Rosenberg/Dir., Andrew Horowitz/Dir., Bernard J. Korman/Dir., Arnold M. Gans/Founder, Chief Science Officer
Owners: Mark Rosenberg/0.40%, Bernard Korman/2.00%, Andrew Horowitz/1.90%, Richard Ullman/16.50%, Jeffrey Janco/1.90%, Arnold Gans/7.40%, Myra Gans/7.40%, Insiders/27.60%, Mark Rachesky/26.90%, Francis Newman/16.10%

Financial Data: Fiscal Year End:01/31 Latest Annual Data: 1/31/2007

Year	Sales	Net Income
2007	$10,531,000	-$294,000
2006	$7,311,000	-$177,000
2005	$4,727,000	-$332,000

Curr. Assets:	$9,958,000	Curr. Liab.:	$1,024,000	
Plant, Equip.:	$163,000	Total Liab.:	$1,024,000	Indic. Yr. Divd.: NA
Total Assets:	$11,944,000	Net Worth:	$10,920,000	Debt/ Equity: NA

Medical Properties Trust Inc

1000 Urban Ctr. Dr., Ste. 501, Birmingham, AL, 35242; *PH:* 1-205-969-3755; *Fax:* 1-205-969-3756; *http://* www.medicalpropertiestrust.com; *Email:* info@medicalpropertiestrust.com

General - Incorporation .... MD	Stock- Price on:12/24/2007 ....$13.39
Employees 20	Stock Exchange.............................NYSE
Auditor ....KPMG LLP	Ticker Symbol............................MPW
Stk Agt..... American Stock Transfer & Trust Co.	Outstanding Shares 48,970,000
Counsel........... Baker, Caldwell & Berkowitz, Pc	E.P.S.................................$0.80
DUNS No. ....NA	Shareholders.............................NA

Business: The groups principle activities include acquiring, developing, leasing and making healthcare service properties. In the year 2006, the group acquired 18 healthcare facilities. The group operates from the United States. The group's quarterly revenuefor sept 2007 was 25.68millions of USD.

Primary SIC and add'l.: 6798
CIK No: 0001287865
Subsidiaries: 1300 Campbell Lane, LLC, 4499 Acushnet Avenue, LLC, 7173 North Sharon Avenue, LLC, 8451 Pearl Street, LLC, 92 Brick Road, LLC, Medical Properties Trust, LLC, MPT Development Services, Inc., MPT Finance Company, LLC, MPT of Bloomington, LLC, MPT of Bucks County, L.P., MPT of Bucks County, LLC, MPT of California, LLC, MPT of Centinela, L.P., MPT of Centinela, LLC, MPT of Chino, LLC 47 Subsidiaries included in the Index
Officers: Edward K. Aldag/Chmn., CEO, Pres., William G. McKenzie/Vice Chmn., VP, Steven R. Hamner/Dir., CFO, Exec. VP, Emmett E. McLean/Exec. VP, COO, Treasurer, Assist. Sec., Michael G. Stewart/Exec. VP, General Counsel, Sec., Thomas W. Schultz/Dir. - Asset Management, Charles Lambert/Dir. - Finance
Directors: Edward K. Aldag/Chmn., CEO, Pres., William G. McKenzie/Vice Chmn., VP, Steven R. Hamner/Dir., CFO, Exec. VP, Steven G. Dawson/Dir., Robert E. Holmes/Dir., Virginia A. Clarke/Dir., Glenn L. Orr/Dir., Sherry A. Kellett/63/Dir.
Owners: Steven R. Hamner, Steven G. Dawson, Sherry A. Kellett, AXA Assurances I.A.R.D. Mutuelle/4.21%, Robert E. Holmes, Edward K. Aldag/1.15%, Glenn L. Orr, Michael G. Stewart, Insiders/3.03%, William G. McKenzie, Emmett E. McLean, Virginia A. Clarke, The Vanguard Group, Inc./4.72%

Financial Data: Fiscal Year End:12/31 Latest Annual Data: 12/31/2006

Year	Sales	Net Income
2006	$50,471,000	$30,160,000
2005	$31,549,000	$19,640,000
2004	$10,893,000	$4,576,000

Curr. Assets:	$28,683,000	Curr. Liab.:	$30,046,000	P/E Ratio: 15.94
Plant, Equip.:	$651,068,000	Total Liab.:	$401,036,000	Indic. Yr. Divd.: $1.080
Total Assets:	$744,757,000	Net Worth:	$343,721,000	Debt/ Equity: 0.5739

Medical Solutions Management Inc

Formerly: Metaphor Corp
237 Cedar Hill St., Marlboro, MA, 01752; *PH:* 1-508-597-6300

General - Incorporation .... NV	Stock- Price on:12/24/2007 ....$3.5
Employees 24	Stock Exchange.............................OTC
Auditor............................Michael F. Cronin	Ticker Symbol............................MSMT
Stk Agt............... Action Stock Transfer Corp	Outstanding Shares 20,450,000
Counsel ....NA	E.P.S.................................-$5.13
DUNS No. ....NA	Shareholders.............................NA

Business: The group's principal activities are to design, develop, market and manufacture skateboards, wakeboards, snowboards, related clothing and accessories to specialty retail outlets. The group manufactures and/or assembles its products from components acquired from suppliers in North America. Products are marketed with the group's own trade names, such as, thruster, revelation, human, republic and enemy. The products are sold to specialty retail outlets in the United States and in 13 foreign countries.

Primary SIC and add'l.: 9999
CIK No: 0000104401
Subsidiaries: China Media Networks International, Inc., CMNW Acquisition Corporation, Thunderbird Global Corporation
Officers: Brian Lesperance/55/Dir., Pres., Treasurer, Principal Executive Officer, Robert G. Coffill/50/Dir., Sr. VP - Field Operations, Sec., Kenneth Fischer/55/CFO, Ross Fine/46/VP - Sales, Marketing
Directors: Brian Lesperance/55/Dir., Pres., Treasurer, Principal Executive Officer, Robert G. Coffill/50/Dir., Sr. VP - Field Operations, Sec., Marshall Sterman/76/Dir.
Owners: Patricia Jenkins, Vicis Capital Master Fund, Insiders, Brian Lesperance, Robert G. Coffill, Marshall Sterman, John Hallal

Financial Data: Fiscal Year End:12/31 Latest Annual Data: 12/31/2006

Year	Sales	Net Income
2006	$1,014,000	-$3,958,000
2005	$460,000	-$778,000
2004	NA	-$76,000

Curr. Assets:	$1,120,000	Curr. Liab.:	$1,390,000	
Plant, Equip.:	$103,000	Total Liab.:	$2,389,000	Indic. Yr. Divd.: NA
Total Assets:	$1,223,000	Net Worth:	-$1,166,000	Debt/ Equity: NA

Medical Staffing Network Holdings Inc

901 Yamato Rd., Ste. 110, Boca Raton, FL, 33431; *PH:* 1-561-322-1300; *Fax:* 1-561-322-1200; *http://* www.msnhealth.com; *Email:* webinfo@msnhealth.com

General - Incorporation .... DE	Stock- Price on:12/24/2007 ....$6.08
Employees 1,000	Stock Exchange.............................NYSE
Auditor .... Ernst & Young LLP	Ticker Symbol............................MRN
Stk Agt ..... American Stock Transfer & Trust Co.	Outstanding Shares 30,260,000
Counsel .... Willkie Farr & Gallagher LLP	E.P.S.................................-$0.729
DUNS No. ....NA	Shareholders.............................NA

Business: The group's principal activity is to provide medical staffing services to hospitals and other healthcare facilities in the United States. These services are provided through four divisions. The per diem nurse staffing division provides nurses for duration lesser than thirteen weeks across all specialties including pediatric, geriatric, intensive care and cardiovascular. The allied staffing division provides allied professionals to hospitals, nursing homes, clinics, surgical and ambulatory care centers, both on a per diem and a travel basis. The travel nursing operations provide hospitals with nurses and surgical technicians for assignments lasting over thirteen weeks. The physician staffing division provides certified radiologists, anesthesiologists and psychiatrists. In Mar 2003 the group acquired saber-salisbury group. The group discontinued physician staffing services in 2003.

Primary SIC and add'l.: 7363
CIK No: 0001163958
Subsidiaries: Medical Staffing Network Assets, LLC, Medical Staffing Network, Inc, MSN-Illinois Holdings, Inc
Officers: Robert J. Adamson/Chmn., CEO, Kevin S. Little/Pres., Patricia Donohoe/Chief Nursing Officer, COO, Jeffrey Yesner/Primary IR Contact - Medical Staffing Network
Directors: Robert J. Adamson/Chmn., CEO, Philip A. Incarnati/Dir., David Wester/Dir., Anne Boykin/Dir., David J. Wenstrup/Dir., Joel Ackerman/Dir., Daryl C. Hollis/Dir., Edward J. Robinson/Dir.
Owners: Daryl C. Hollis, Edward Robinson, Patricia G. Donohoe, Robert J. Adamson, Insiders, David J. Wenstrup, Warburg Pincus Private Equity VIII, L.P., Artisan Partners Limited Partnership, Kevin S. Little, Anne Boykin, Joel Ackerman, Nautic Partners V, LP, Dimensional Fund Advisors, Inc.

Financial Data: Fiscal Year End:12/25 Latest Annual Data: 12/31/2006

Year	Sales	Net Income
2006	$385,450,000	-$26,997,000
2005	$402,507,000	-$799,000
2004	$417,058,000	-$1,326,000

Curr. Assets:	$62,291,000	Curr. Liab.:	$26,072,000	
Plant, Equip.:	$7,691,000	Total Liab.:	$48,824,000	Indic. Yr. Divd.: NA
Total Assets:	$171,151,000	Net Worth:	$122,327,000	Debt/ Equity: 0.1503

Medical Staffing Solutions Inc

8150 Leesburg Pike, Ste 1200, Vienna, VA, 22182; *PH:* 1-703-641-8890; *http://* www.telescience.com; *Email:* investmentrelations@telescience.com

General - Incorporation .... NV	Stock- Price on:12/24/2007 ....$0.0017
Employees 178	Stock Exchange.............................OTC
Auditor .... Bagell, Josephs, Levine & Co. LLC	Ticker Symbol............................MSSIE
Stk Agt .... Holladay Stock Transfer, Inc.	Outstanding Shares 182,200,000
Counsel ....Dr. Jacobsen	E.P.S.................................-$0.008
DUNS No. ....NA	Shareholders.............................NA

Business: The group's principal activity is to provide staffing services to institutions, occupational and alternate site healthcare organizations. The group provides staffing needs for the following categories of healthcare professionals: registered nurses, licensed practical nurses, physical, speech and occupational therapists, certified nursing assistants, medical assistants and medical technologists. On 08-Oct-2003, the group acquired telescience international, inc.

Primary SIC and add'l.: 7361
CIK No: 0001160437
Subsidiaries: Nurses Onsite Corp., Nurses PRN Acquisition Corp., SYSTRAN Financial Service Corporation, TeleScience International, Inc
Officers: B. B. Sahay/Chmn., CEO, Christopher Wallace/VP - Medical Systems Division, Reeba Magulick/VP - Operations Nurses PRN
Directors: B. B. Sahay/Chmn., CEO
Owners: Brajnandan B. Sahay/25.99%
Financial Data: Fiscal Year End:12/31 Latest Annual Data: 12/31/2006

Year	Sales	Net Income
2006	$18,849,000	-$3,950,000
2005	$12,346,000	-$1,827,000
2004	$6,735,000	-$2,112,000

Curr. Assets:	$3,508,000	Curr. Liab.:	$9,995,000
Plant, Equip.:	$100,000	Total Liab.:	$9,995,000	Indic. Yr. Divd.: NA
Total Assets:	$4,679,000	Net Worth:	-$5,315,000	Debt/ Equity: NA

Medicalcv Inc

9725 S Robert Trl., Inver Grove Heights, MN, 55077; *PH:* 1-651-452-3000; *Fax:* 1-651-452-4948; *http://* www.medcvinc.com

General - Incorporation............................MN
Employees..23
Auditor ....Lurie Besikof Lapidus & Co. LLP
Stk Agt.............PricewaterhouseCoopers LLP
Counsel...................................Briggs & Morgan
DUNS No...NA

Stock- Price on:12/24/2007 ....$5.4
Stock Exchange..OTC
Ticker Symbol..MCVI
Outstanding Shares 9,840,000
E.P.S..-$1.42
Shareholders...NA

Business: The group's principle activities include designing, manufacturing and marketing mechanical heart valves known as theomnicarbon series 3000 and series 4000, which are used to treat heart valve failure caused by heart disease, natural aging, prosthetic heart valve failure and congenital defects. The group operates from United States.

Primary SIC and add'l.: 3842
CIK No: 0001144284

Officers: Marc P. Flores/Dir., CEO, Pres./$1,171,174.00, Dennis E. Steger/VP - Regulatory Affairs, Quality Assurance, Robert W. Clapp/VP - Operations/$393,025.00, Adam L. Berman/VP - Research, Development/$404,714.00, Gary O. Tegan/VP - Marketing, Eapen Chacko/VP - Finance, CFO, Traci Christensen/Primary Investor Relations Officer

Directors: Marc P. Flores/Dir., CEO, Pres., Susan L. Critzer/Chmn., Lonnie L. Whiddon/Member - Scientific Advisory Board, Larry G. Haimovitch/Dir., David B. Kaysen/Dir., Robert J. Paulson/Dir., David A. Chazanovitz/Dir., Richard J. Faleschini/Dir., Patrick M. McCarthy/Member - Scientific Advisory Board, Paul K. Miller/Dir., Lishan Aklog/Member - Scientific Advisory Board, Michael P. Caskey/Member - Scientific Advisory Board, Marc Gerdisch/Member - Scientific Advisory Board, Baron L. Hamman/Member - Scientific Advisory Board, Ralph Lazzara/Member - Scientific Advisory Board (25 Directors included in Index)

Owners: Robert J. Paulson, Whitebox Advisors, LLC, Millennium Partners, L.P., Marc P. Flores, Adam L. Berman, Peter L. Hauser, Susan L. Critzer, David A. Chazanovitz, Larry G. Haimovitch, MedCap Partners, L.P., Robert W. Clapp, Paul K. Miller Irrevocable Trust, David B. Kaysen, Perkins Capital Management,Inc., MedCap Master Fund, L.P. (21 Owners included in Index)

Financial Data: Fiscal Year End:04/30 Latest Annual Data: 04/30/2007

Year	Sales	Net Income
2007	$32,000	-$12,716,000
2006	NA	$9,232,000
2005	NA	-$19,095,000

Curr. Assets:	$11,713,000	Curr. Liab.:	$1,092,000
Plant, Equip.:	$828,000	Total Liab.:	$31,910,000	Indic. Yr. Divd.: NA
Total Assets:	$12,998,000	Net Worth:	-$18,912,000	Debt/ Equity: 1.4960

Medicines Co

8 Campus Dr., Parsippany, NJ, 07054; *PH:* 1-973-656-1616; *Fax:* 1-973-656-9898; *http://* www.themedicinescompany.com; *Email:* medical.director@themedco.com

General - Incorporation............................DE
Employees...289
Auditor ....Ernst & Young LLP
Stk Agt......American Stock Transfer & Trust Co.
Counsel....................................WilmerHale
DUNS No...NA

Stock- Price on:12/24/2007 ....$17.66
Stock Exchange..NDQ
Ticker Symbol..MDCO
Outstanding Shares 51,720,000
E.P.S..$0.67
Shareholders...NA

Business: The group's principal activities are to acquire, develop and commercialize the acute care hospital products. The group's products are angiomax, also is in the process of developing late stage pharmaceutical products are cleveloxtm and cangrelor. Angiomax is used as an anticoagulant in combination with aspirin in patients with unstable angina undergoing coronary angioplasty. Cleveloxtm is used for short -term control of blood pressure in patients undergoing for cardiac surgery. Cangelor is used for an anticoagulant that prevents platelet clotting in patients undergoing for coronary angioplasty and cardiac surgery. The group operates in the United States.

Primary SIC and add'l.: 2834 8731
CIK No: 0001113481

Officers: Clive A. Meanwell/Chmn., CEO/$1,466,580.00, Glenn Sblendorio/CFO, Exec. VP/$1,152,554.00, Paul M. Antinori/Sr. VP, General Counsel, Sec./$625,117.00, John P. Kelley/COO, Pres./$1,145,353.00, Catharine Newberry/Sr. VP, Chief Human Strategy Officer/$717,945.00

Directors: Clive A. Meanwell/Chmn., CEO, Armin M. Kessler/Dir., Scott T. Johnson/Dir., Robert J. Hugin/Dir., Robert G. Savage/Dir., Melvin K. Spigelman/Dir., William W. Crouse/Dir., Elizabeth H.S. Wyatt/Dir., Hiroaki Shigeta/Dir.

Owners: Armin M. Kessler, Federated Investors,Inc./5.60%, Wellington Management Company, LLP/12.00%, Clive A. Meanwell/1.70%, Melvin K. Spigelman, Glenn Sblendorio, Robert J. Hugin, John Kelley, Robert G. Savage, T. Rowe Price Associates, Inc./6.50%, Catharine Newberry, Paul M. Antinori, Sectoral Asset Management,Inc/5.00%, D.E. Shaw& Co, L.P./6.40%, Scott T. Johnson (19 Owners included in Index)

Financial Data: Fiscal Year End:12/31 Latest Annual Data: 12/31/2006

Year	Sales	Net Income
2006	$213,952,000	$63,726,000
2005	$150,207,000	-$7,753,000
2004	$144,251,000	$16,999,000

Curr. Assets:	$274,326,000	Curr. Liab.:	$45,803,000	P/E Ratio: 11.62
Plant, Equip.:	$3,071,000	Total Liab.:	$48,617,000	Indic. Yr. Divd.: NA
Total Assets:	$318,568,000	Net Worth:	$269,951,000	Debt/ Equity: NA

MediciNova Inc

4350 La Jolla Village Dr., San Diego, CA, 92122; *PH:* 1-858-373-1500; *http://* www.medicinova.com; *Email:* info@medicinova.com

General - Incorporation ....DE
Employees..27
Auditor ....Ernst& Young LLP
Stk Agt......American Stock Transfer & Trust Co.
Counsel...NA
DUNS No...NA

Stock- Price on:12/24/2007 ....$8.68
Stock Exchange..NDQ
Ticker Symbol..MNOV
Outstanding Shares 11,620,000
E.P.S..-$4.11
Shareholders...NA

Business: The groups principle activities include acquiring and developing novel, small molecule therapeutics. Specific customers of the group include Kissei Pharmaceutical, Kyorin Pharmaceutical, Mitsubishi Pharma Corporation and Meiji Seika Kaisha, Ltd. The products of the group include inhaled corticosteroids, bronchodilators and leukotriene antagonists. The group products sold under the trade names Flovent(R), Vanceril(R) and Singulair(R). The group operates from the United States.

Primary SIC and add'l.: 8731
CIK No: 0001226616
Subsidiaries: MediciNova (Europe) Ltd.

Officers: Yuichi Iwaki/CEO, Pres., Founder/$3,090,882.00, Richard E. Gammans/Chief Development Officer/$1,833,162.00, Kenneth Locke/Chief Scientific Officer/$1,522,730.00, Shintaro Asako/CFO, VP/$1,189,399.00, Masatsune Okajima/VP, Head - Japanese Office/$1,207,116.00, Kale Ruby/Dir. - Quality Assurance, Maria Feldman/Dir. - Regulatory Affairs

Directors: Yuichi Iwaki/CEO, Pres., Founder, Jeff Himawan/Chmn., Arlene M. Morris/Dir., Alan W. Dunton/Dir., Hideki Nagao/Dir., John K.A. Prendergast/Dir., Daniel Vapnek/Dir.

Owners: Insiders/18.90%, Jeff Himawan/10.20%, John K.A. Prendergast, Shintaro Asako, Hideki Nagao, Kenneth W. Locke, Yuichi Iwaki/6.10%, Arlene Morris, Richard E. Gammans, Essex Woodland Health Ventures Fund VI, L.P./10.20%, Daniel Vapnek, Masatsune Okajima, Alan Dunton

Financial Data: Fiscal Year End:12/31 Latest Annual Data: 12/31/2006

Year	Sales	Net Income
2006	$264,000	-$35,690,000
2005	$804,000	-$25,692,000
2004	$490,000	-$48,273,000

Curr. Assets:	$110,670,000	Curr. Liab.:	$10,569,000
Plant, Equip.:	$871,000	Total Liab.:	$10,610,000	Indic. Yr. Divd.: NA
Total Assets:	$111,591,000	Net Worth:	$100,981,000	Debt/ Equity: NA

Medicis Pharmaceutical Corp

8125 N Hayden Rd., Scottsdale, AZ, 85258; *PH:* 1-602-808-8800; *Fax:* 1-602-808-0822; *http://* www.medicis.com; *Email:* investor_relations@medicis.com

General - Incorporation ....DE
Employees...391
Auditor ....Ernst & Young LLP
Stk Agt........... Wells Fargo Shareowner Services
Counsel...NA
DUNS No.............................18-283-7492

Stock- Price on:12/24/2007 ....$31.11
Stock Exchange..NYSE
Ticker Symbol..MRX
Outstanding Shares 55,840,000
E.P.S..$0.40
Shareholders...NA

Business: The group's principal activity is to focus primarily on the treatment of dermatological and podiatric conditions, and aesthetics medicine. The group has branded prescription products in a number of therapeutic categories, including acne, asthma, eczema, fungal infections, psoriasis, rosacea, seborrheic dermatitis and skin and skin-structure infections. Its products include the prescription brands restylane(R), dynacin(R), loprox(R), omnicef(R), plexion(R), triaz(R), lidex(R), and synalar(R), the over-the-counter brand esoterica(R) and buphenyl(R), a prescription product indicated in the treatment of urea cycle disorder. The products are sold primarily to pharmaceutical distributors and retail pharmacy chains. Customers include cardinal health inc, mckesson corp, quality king distributors and amerisourcebergen corp.

Primary SIC and add'l.: 2844 2834
CIK No: 0000859368

Subsidiaries: Dermavest Swedish Holdings AB, Dermavest, Inc., GenDerm Corporation, HA North American Sales AB, Masterpiece Acquisition Corporation, Medicis Aesthetics Canada Ltd., Medicis Aesthetics Holdings Inc., Medicis Aesthetics Inc., Medicis Canada Ltd., Medicis Manufacturing Corporation, Medicis Pediatrics, Inc., Medicis, The Dermatology Company, Ucyclyd Pharma, Inc.

Officers: Jonah Shacknai/Chmn., CEO/$5,255,296.00, Joseph P. Cooper/Exec. VP - Corporate, Product Development/$1,471,779.00, Richard J. Havens/Exec. VP - Sales, Marketing/$1,535,592.00, Mark A. Prygocki/Exec. VP, CFO, Corp. Sec., Treasurer/$1,846,688.00, Mitchell S. Wortzman/Chief Scientific Officer, Exec. VP/$1,418,799.00, Kara J. Stancell/Dir. - Investor Relations, Corporate Communications

Directors: Jonah Shacknai/Chmn., CEO, Spencer Davidson/65/Dir., Lottie H. Shackelford/Dir., Peter S. Knight/Dir., Stuart Diamond/Dir., Arthur G. Altschul/43/Dir., Philip S. Schein/68/Dir., Michael A. Pietrangelo/65/Dir.

Owners: Michael A. Pietrangelo, Capital Research & Management Co./13.30%, Richard J. Havens, Philip S. Schein, Arthur G. Altschul, FMR Corp./7.30%, Lottie H. Shackelford, Insiders/7.90%, Stuart Diamond, Spencer Davidson, Mitchell S. Wortzman, Joseph P. Cooper, Merrill Lynch & Co., Inc./5.90%, Peter S. Knight, Legg Mason Capital Management, Inc./10.50% (18 Owners included in Index)

Financial Data: Fiscal Year End:06/30 Latest Annual Data: 12/31/2006

Year	Sales	Net Income
2006	$349,242,000	-$75,849,000
2005	$376,899,000	$64,990,000

Curr. Assets:	$698,925,000	Curr. Liab.:	$98,854,000	
Plant, Equip.:	$6,143,000	Total Liab.:	$556,905,000	Indic. Yr. Divd.: $0.120
Total Assets:	$1,043,251,000	Net Worth:	$486,346,000	Debt/ Equity: 0.8498

Medicor Ltd

4560 S Decatur Blvd, Ste 300, Las Vegas, NV, 89103; *PH:* 1-702-932-4560; *http://* www.medicorltd.com; *Email:* info@medicorltd.com

General - Incorporation ....DE
Employees...410
Auditor........................Greenberg & Co. LLC
Stk Agt.............U.S. Stock Transfer Corp
Counsel...NA
DUNS No...NA

Stock- Price on:12/24/2007 ....NA
Stock Exchange..OTC
Ticker Symbol..MDCR
Outstanding Shares ....NA
E.P.S..-$1.246
Shareholders...NA

Business: The group's principle activities are to develop, manufacture and market products for medical specialties in aesthetic, plastic and reconstructive surgery and dermatology markets. The group products include surgically implantable prostheses for aesthetic, plastic and reconstructive surgery and scar management products. The group products are sold to hospitals, surgery centers and physicians through various distributors and direct sales personnel. The group sells products in approximately 50 countries worldwide.

Primary SIC and add'l.: 3841 7372

CIK No: 0001143799

Subsidiaries: Biosil Limited, Dermatological Medical Products and Specialties, S.A. de C.V., ES Holdings S.A.S., Eurosilicone S.A.S., HPL Biomedical, Inc. d/b/a Biodermis, III Acquisition Corporation d/b/a PIP.America, Intellectual Property International Inc., International Integrated U.S.A. Incorporated, MediCor Aesthetics, MediCor Deutschland G.m.b.H., MediCor Development Company, MediCor Latin America S.A. de C.V., MediCor Management, Inc., MediCor Services Company S.A. de C.V., Nagor Limited

Officers: Theodore R. Maloney/46/Dir., CEO, Jim J. McGhan/54/Dir., COO, Marc S. Sperberg/45/Exec. VP, Sec., Paul R. Kimmel/CFO, Edward V. Lower/VP - Corporate Development

Directors: Theodore R. Maloney/46/Dir., CEO, Donald K. McGhan/73/Chmn., Samuel Clay Rogers/Dir., Jim J. McGhan/54/Dir., COO, Thomas Y. Hartley/74/Dir., Mark E. Brown/47/Dir., Ikram U. Khan/Dir., Eugene I. Davis/52/Dir., Robert L. Forbuss/Dir.

Owners: 1999 III Equity Performance II, LP/5.49%, Samuel Clay Rogers/3.69%, Marc S. Sperberg/1.26%, Mark E. Brown, Eugene I. Davis, Paul R. Kimmel, Ikram U. Khan, Robert L. Forbuss, Donald K. McGhan/36.91%, Insiders/57.38%, Nikki M. Pomeroy/7.00%, Thomas Y. Hartley, Theodore R. Maloney/2.49%, Jim J. McGhan/11.62%

Financial Data: **Fiscal Year End:**06/30   **Latest Annual Data:** 06/30/2006

Year	Sales	Net Income
2006	$31,383,000	-$17,945,000
2005	$26,959,000	-$15,897,000
2004	$1,422,000	-$16,448,000

Curr. Assets:	$36,216,000	Curr. Liab.:	$25,700,000		
Plant, Equip.:	$8,135,000	Total Liab.:	$119,164,000	Indic. Yr. Divd.:	NA
Total Assets:	$129,115,000	Net Worth:	$3,141,000	Debt/ Equity:	NA

Medicure Inc

4 - 1200 WAve.rley St., Winnipeg, MB, R3T 0P4; **PH:** 1-204-487-7412; **Fax:** 1-204-488-9823; *http://* www.medicureinc.com; **Email:** info@medicure.com

General - Incorporation	Canada	Stock - Price on:12/24/2007	$1.3
Employees	NA	Stock Exchange	AMEX
Auditor	KPMG LLP	Ticker Symbol	MCU
Stk Agt	Computershare Investor Services LLC	Outstanding Shares	116,260,000
Counsel	NA	E.P.S.	-$0.4
DUNS No.	NA	Shareholders	NA

Business: The groups principle activity is to develop therapeutics for unmet needs in the field of cardiovascular medicine. The groups products include MC-4232 and Aggrastat(R). The group operates from Canada.

Primary SIC and add'l.: 9999

CIK No: 0001133519

Subsidiaries: American Cardio Therapeutics Inc., Medicur Pharma Inc., Medicure Europe Limited, Medicure International Inc.

Officers: Albert D. Friesen/Chmn., CEO, Pres., Deborah Douglas/Dir. - Physiology, Derek G. Reimer/CFO, Karl-Gunnar Hidinger/VP - Clinical Development, Jim Diakur/Dir. - Chemistry, Hogan Mullally/Mgr. - Investor, Public Relations, Wasimul Haque/Dir. - Chemistry, Jan-Ake Westin/VP - Clinical Development, Charles Gluchowski/VP - Research, Development, Brian Best/VP - Marketing, Ahmad Khalil/Medical Dir., Moray Merchant/VP - Marketing, Business Development, Dawson J. Reimer/VP - Operations

Directors: Albert D. Friesen/Chmn., CEO, Pres., Paul Armstrong/Chmn. - Supervisory Board, Morris Karmazyn/Member - Scientific Advisory Board, Stephen Hanessian/Member - Scientific Advisory Board, Jeffrey Weitz/Member - Scientific Advisory Board, Trevor Hassell/Member - Scientific Advisory Board, Kishore Kapoor/Dir., Peter Quick/Dir., Michael A. Lincoff/Member - Scientific Advisory Board, John McNeill/Member - Scientific Advisory Board, Eldon Smith/Member - Scientific Advisory Board, Arnold Naimark/Dir., Pierre Theroux/Member - Scientific Advisory Board, Gerald P. McDole/Dir.

Owners: Derek G. Reimer, Albert D. Friesen/6.46%, Dawson Reimer, Jan-Ake Westin, Gerald P. McDole

Financial Data: **Fiscal Year End:**05/31   **Latest Annual Data:** 05/31/2007

Year	Sales	Net Income
2007	$5,540,000	-$29,928,000
2006	$272,000	-$12,866,000
2005	$366,000	-$12,123,000

Curr. Assets:	$32,530,000	Curr. Liab.:	$1,492,000	P/E Ratio:	21.78
Plant, Equip.:	$46,000	Total Liab.:	$1,492,000	Indic. Yr. Divd.:	NA
Total Assets:	$35,228,000	Net Worth:	$33,735,000	Debt/ Equity:	NA

Medifast Inc

11445 Cronhill Dr., Owings Mills, MD, 21117; **PH:** 1-410-581-8042; **Fax:** 1-410-581-8070; *http://* www.medifast.net; **Email:** success@medifastdiet.com

General - Incorporation	DE	Stock - Price on:12/24/2007	$8.87
Employees	265	Stock Exchange	NYSE
Auditor	Bagell, Josephs, Levine & Co., L.l.c.	Ticker Symbol	MED
Stk Agt	American Stock Transfer & Trust Co.	Outstanding Shares	NA
Counsel	Micheal Tanczyn	E.P.S.	$0.26
DUNS No.	82-463-1725	Shareholders	NA

Business: The group's principal activity is to manufacture, distribute and sell weight and disease management products and other consumable health and diet products. The products of the group include weight and disease management, meal replacement and sports nutrition products. These products are sold through physicians, supported by the Internet, diet centers and other licensed, qualified medical practitioners including qualified health advisors. The group offers a variety of products under the brand name medifast(R) and for select private label customers. Medifast(R) products are being used in clinical studies conducted by the U.S. Government and major hospitals.

Primary SIC and add'l.: 5499 5912 5122

CIK No: 0000910329

Subsidiaries: Jason Enterprises, Inc.

Officers: Bradley T. MacDonald/Chmn., CEO/$331,600.00, Leo V. Williams/Exec. VP/$128,800.00, Richard Law/Corporate VP - Infrastructure, Development, Brendan Connors/VP - Finance/$132,400.00, Margaret MacDonald/30/Exec. VP - Operations/$324,400.00, Michael S. McDevitt/29/CFO, Pres.

Directors: Bradley T. MacDonald/Chmn., CEO, Donald Francis Reilly/Dir., Mary T. Travis/Dir., Michael J. McDevitt/Dir., Joseph D. Calderone/Dir., Michael C. MacDonald/Dir., George Lavin/Dir., Charles P. Connolly/59/Dir., Dennis M. McCarthy/63/Dir., Richard T. Aab/59/Dir.

Owners: Joseph D. Calderone, Michael J. McDevitt, Mary Travis, Michael S. McDevitt/1.94%, Donald F. Reilly, Insiders/10.76%, Bjurman, Barry & Associates/5.40%, George Lavin, Charles P. Connolly, Leo Williams, Brendan N. Connors, Bradley T. MacDonald/6.09%, Margaret MacDonald/1.03%, Dennis M. McCarthy, Michael C. MacDonald

Financial Data: **Fiscal Year End:**12/31   **Latest Annual Data:** 12/31/2006

Year	Sales	Net Income
2006	$74,086,000	$5,156,000
2005	$40,129,000	$2,403,000
2004	$27,340,000	$1,747,000

Curr. Assets:	$14,864,000	Curr. Liab.:	$5,252,000	P/E Ratio:	30.59
Plant, Equip.:	$14,020,000	Total Liab.:	$8,761,000	Indic. Yr. Divd.:	NA
Total Assets:	$36,677,000	Net Worth:	$27,916,000	Debt/ Equity:	0.1146

Medimmune Inc

One Medimmune Way, Gaithersburg, MD, 20878; **PH:** 1-301-398-0000; *http://* www.medimmune.com

General - Incorporation	DE	Stock - Price on:12/24/2007	NA
Employees	2,059	Stock Exchange	NA
Auditor	PricewaterhouseCoopers LLP	Ticker Symbol	NA
Stk Agt	American Stock Transfer & Trust Co.	Outstanding Shares	NA
Counsel	Dewey Ballantine	E.P.S.	NA
DUNS No.	19-063-9906	Shareholders	NA

Business: The group's principal activity is to discover, develop, manufacture and market products for treatment and prevention of infectious diseases, immune system disorders and cancer. The products of the group include synagis, flumist and ethyol. Synagis is a humanized monoclonal antibody for the prevention of respiratory tract disease caused by respiratory syncytial virus in pediatric patients. Ethyol is used to prevent certain unwanted side effects of specific types of chemo and radiotherapies that are used to treat cancer. Flumist is a vaccine for the prevention of disease caused by influenza a and b viruses. The other products of the group are cytogam, neutrexin, and respigam. These products are used for prevention of disease associated with kidney, liver or heart transplantation, for the treatment of aids patients and for the treatment of respiratory virus disease in children. The group operates five facilities in the United States and Europe.

Primary SIC and add'l.: 2836

CIK No: 0000873591

Subsidiaries: Cellective Therapeutics, Inc, MedImmune Distribution Holdings, Inc., MedImmune Distribution LLC, MedImmune Finance, Inc., MedImmune Oncology, Inc, MedImmune Pharma B.V., MedImmune U.K. Ltd., MedImmune Vaccines, MedImmune Ventures, Inc., MedImmune West, Inc

Officers: David M. Mott/Dir., CEO, Pres., Bernardus N.M. MacHielse/Exec. VP - Operations, Edward T. Mathers/Dir., Exec. VP - Corporate Development, Venture, Linda J. Peters/Sr. VP - Regulatory Affairs, Edward M. Connor/Chief Medical Officer, Exec. VP, James F. Young/Pres. - Research, Development, Lota S. Zoth/Sr. VP, CFO, Gail Folena-Wasserman/Sr. VP - Development, Christine A. Dingivan/Sr. VP - Clinical Development, Operations, Frank Malinoski/Sr. VP - Medical, Scientific Affairs, Peter A. Kiener/Sr. VP - Research, William C. Bertrand/Sr. VP - Legal Affairs, General Counsel, Corporate Compliance Officer, Peter Greenleaf/Sr. VP - Marketing, Sales, Pamela J. Lupien/Sr. VP - Human Resources

Directors: David M. Mott/Dir., CEO, Pres., David R. Brennan/Dir., David V. Elkins/Dir., John Patterson/Dir., Lynn Tetrault/Dir.

Medina International Corp

37 Inbar St. , Caesarea, 30889; **PH:** 972-463-60297

General - Incorporation	NV	Stock - Price on:12/24/2007	$0.43
Employees	NA	Stock Exchange	OTC
Auditor	Somekh Chaikin	Ticker Symbol	ACRI
Stk Agt	Signature Stock Transfer, Inc.	Outstanding Shares	NA
Counsel	NA	E.P.S.	NA
DUNS No.	NA	Shareholders	NA

Business: The group's principal activity is to provide professional consulting services for the technical and economic evaluation and prospect generation of petroleum and natural gas resources worldwide. The group also provides regulatory support, drilling, production and construction management, wellsite consultants, equipment verification and onsite quality surveillance to the oil and gas industry. The company provides services to petroleum and natural gas companies, oil service companies, utilities and manufacturing companies with petroleum and/or natural gas interests, institutional and individual investors, banks, independent power developers, drilling and producing property income funds and various agencies within domestic and foreign governments.

Primary SIC and add'l.: 8742

CIK No: 0001228386

Officers: Gadi Aner/54/Chmn., Interim CEO, Jacob Bar Shalom/41/Acting CFO, Treasurer

Directors: Gadi Aner/54/Chmn., Interim CEO, Ehud Keinan/60/Dir., Dan Elnathan/53/Dir., Ehud Barak/Member - Advisory Board, Richard A. Lerner/Member - Advisory Board, Barry K. Sharpless/Member - Advisory Board

Owners: Insiders/37.90%, Ehud Keinan/30.38%, Gadi Aner/7.60%, Zeev Bronfeld/8.90%

Financial Data: **Fiscal Year End:**12/31   **Latest Annual Data:** 12/31/2006

Year	Sales	Net Income
2006	NA	-$1,352,000
2005	NA	-$158,000
2004	NA	-$21,000

Curr. Assets:	$384,000	Curr. Liab.:	$141,000		
Plant, Equip.:	$76,000	Total Liab.:	$148,000	Indic. Yr. Divd.:	NA
Total Assets:	$581,000	Net Worth:	$433,000	Debt/ Equity:	NA

Medis Technologies Ltd

805 3rd Ave., 15th Fl., New York, NY, 10022; *PH:* 1-212-935-8484; *Fax:* 1-212-935-9216; *http://* www.medisel.com; *Email:* medistechnologies@broadviewnet.net

General - Incorporation	DE	**Stock**- Price on:12/24/2007	$14
Employees	152	Stock Exchange	NDQ
Auditor	Kost Forer Gabbay & Kasierer	Ticker Symbol	MDTL
Stk Agt	Registrar & Transfer Co	Outstanding Shares	34,950,000
Counsel	Sonnenschein Nath & Rosenthal LLP	E.P.S.	-$1.07
DUNS No.	NA	Shareholders	NA

Business: The group's principal activities are the development, manufacturing, marketing and distribution of direct liquid cell products for portable electronic devices, for the consumer (personal and professional) and military markets. The group's other technologies, include cellscan, inherently conductive polymers, stirling cycle system, toroidal technologies and rankin cycle liner compressor. The group's products include cell phones, digital cameras, pdas, mp3 players, hand-held video games and other devices with similar power requirements.

Primary SIC and add'l.: 3629 8731 3692 6719

CIK No: 0001090507

Subsidiaries: Medis El Ltd., More Energy Ltd.

Officers: Robert K. Lifton/Chmn., CEO/$661,000.00, Asaf Ben - Arye/CEO - Cell Kinetics Ltd, Howard Weingrow/Dep. Chmn., COO/$636,000.00, Michael S. Resnick/Sr. VP, Controller, Michelle Rush/VP - Marketing, Jacob S. Weiss/Dir., Pres./$635,000.00, Israel Fisher/Sr. VP - Finance, CFO/$403,000.00, Gennadi Finkelshtain/GM - More Energy, CTO New Energies

Directors: Robert K. Lifton/Chmn., CEO, Howard Weingrow/Dep. Chmn., COO, Zeev Nahmoni/Dir., Jacob E. Goldman/Dir., Mitchell H. Freeman/Dir., Jacob S. Weiss/Dir., Pres., Amos Eiran/Dir., Philip Weisser/Dir., Steve M. Barnett/Dir., Daniel Luchansky/Dir.

Owners: Robert K. Lifton/12.00%, Howard Weingrow/9.70%, Jacob E. Goldman, Zeev Nahmoni, Israel Aerospace Industries Ltd./15.80%, CVF, LLC/6.60%, Insiders/19.60%, Israel Fisher, Jacob S. Weiss, Mitchell H. Freeman, BlackRock, Inc./13.90%, Steve M. Barnett, Amos Eiran, Philip Weisser

Financial Data: *Fiscal Year End:*12/31　*Latest Annual Data:* 12/31/2006

Year	Sales	Net Income
2006	$150,000	-$33,047,000
2005	$425,000	-$18,550,000
2004	NA	-$15,662,000

Curr. Assets:	$90,564,000	**Curr. Liab.:**	$11,917,000		
Plant, Equip.:	$27,318,000	**Total Liab.:**	$67,172,000	**Indic. Yr. Divd.:**	NA
Total Assets:	$177,608,000	**Net Worth:**	$110,436,000	**Debt/ Equity:**	NA

Mediscience Technology Corp

1235 Folkestone Wy, Cherry Hill, NJ, 08034; *PH:* 1-856-428-7952; *http://* www.medisciencetech.com; *Email:* info@medisciencetech.com

General - Incorporation	NJ	**Stock**- Price on:12/24/2007	$0.1
Employees	5	Stock Exchange	OTC
Auditor	Morison Cogen LLP	Ticker Symbol	MDSC
Stk Agt	Registrar & Transfer Co	Outstanding Shares	65,460,000
Counsel	NA	E.P.S.	-$0.03
DUNS No.	10-721-7788	Shareholders	NA

Business: The group's principle activities include designing and develops medical diagnostic instruments which detect cancer, based upon differentiations in amounts of light re-emitted from malignant and benign tissue. The group operates from United States.

Primary SIC and add'l.: 3845

CIK No: 0000064647

Subsidiaries: MEDI, Medi-Photonics Development LLC

Officers: Peter Katevatis/Co - Founder, Chmn. CEO, Robert R. Alfano/Co - Founder, Chmn., Chief Scientific Advisor, Stephene Lubicz/Chief Medical Operating Officer, Frank D. Benick/CFO, John M. Kennedy/Dir., VP, Sec.

Directors: Peter Katevatis/Co - Founder, Chmn. CEO, Robert R. Alfano/Co - Founder, Chmn., Chief Scientific Advisor, John M. Kennedy/Dir., VP, Sec., Stimson Pryor Schantz/Member - Strategic Advisory Board, William W. Armstrong/Dir., Michael N. Kouvatas/Dir.

Owners: John M. Kennedy/3.87%, Michael N. Kouvatas, Insiders/20.10%, William W. Armstrong, Peter Katevatis/14.98%

Financial Data: *Fiscal Year End:*02/28　*Latest Annual Data:* 02/28/2007

Year	Sales	Net Income
2007	NA	-$1,413,000
2006	NA	-$2,199,000
2005	NA	-$2,361,000

Curr. Assets:	$164,000	**Curr. Liab.:**	$3,568,000		
Plant, Equip.:	$1,000	**Total Liab.:**	$3,568,000	**Indic. Yr. Divd.:**	NA
Total Assets:	$918,000	**Net Worth:**	-$2,650,000	**Debt/ Equity:**	NA

MediStem Laboratories Inc

2027 E Cedar St. Ste. 102, Tempe, AZ, 85281; *PH:* 1-954-727-3662; *http://* www.medisteminc.com

General - Incorporation	NV	**Stock**- Price on:12/24/2007	$0.16
Employees	5	Stock Exchange	OTC
Auditor	Malone & Bailey, P.C	Ticker Symbol	MDSM
Stk Agt	Holladay Stock Transfer, Inc.	Outstanding Shares	131,410,000
Counsel	NA	E.P.S.	-$0.02
DUNS No.	NA	Shareholders	NA

Business: The groups principle activities include creating and commercializing medical therapies based on non-controversial adult stem cells. The group operates from the United States.

Primary SIC and add'l.: 6794

CIK No: 0001186519

Officers: Neil Riordan/Chmn., Pres., Chief Executive, Roger M. Nocera/Dir., Exec. VP, Chief Medical Officer, Chris McGuinn/VP, COO, Steven M. Rivers/CFO, VP, Thomas Ichim/Chief - Scientific Development, Fabio Solano/Medical Dir. - ICM, Eduardo Glenn Calvo/Laboratory Dir. - ICM

Directors: Neil Riordan/Chmn., Pres., Chief Executive, Roger M. Nocera/Dir., Exec. VP, Chief Medical Officer, John Peterson/Dir.

Owners: John Peterson, Roger Nocera/2.30%, Insiders/77.80%, Neil H. Riordan/76.50%

Financial Data: *Fiscal Year End:*12/31　*Latest Annual Data:* 12/31/2006

Year	Sales	Net Income
2006	$319,000	-$3,793,000
2005	NA	-$2,892,000
2004	NA	-$12,000

Curr. Assets:	$1,030,000	**Curr. Liab.:**	$255,000		
Plant, Equip.:	$657,000	**Total Liab.:**	$255,000	**Indic. Yr. Divd.:**	NA
Total Assets:	$1,777,000	**Net Worth:**	$1,522,000	**Debt/ Equity:**	NA

Medivation Inc

55 Hawthorne St., Ste. 610, San Francisco, CA, 94105; *PH:* 1-415-543-3470; *Fax:* 1-415-543-3411; *http://* www.medivation.net; *Email:* info@medivation.com

General - Incorporation	DE	**Stock**- Price on:12/24/2007	NA
Employees	NA	Stock Exchange	NDQ
Auditor	Singer Lewak Greenbaum & Goldstein	Ticker Symbol	MDVN
Stk Agt	American Stock Transfer & Trust Co.	Outstanding Shares	NA
Counsel	NA	E.P.S.	-$1.03
DUNS No.	NA	Shareholders	NA

Business: The groups principal activities include acquire, research and development of promising medical technologies. The group marketed its products under the trade name Dimebon (TM). The groups products include Dimebon and MDV3100. The group operates from the United States.

Primary SIC and add'l.: 8731

CIK No: 0001011835

Subsidiaries: Medivation Neurology, Inc, Medivation Prostate Therapeutics, Inc., Medivation Technologies, Inc.

Officers: David T. Hung/Dir., CEO, Pres./$442,563.00, Patrick C. MacHado/CFO, Sr. VP/$387,813.00, Lynn Seely/Chief Medical Officer/$640,313.00, Andrew A. Protter/VP - Preclinical Development, Sue Wollowitz/VP - Chemistry, Manufacturing, Lisa Taylor/VP - Commercial Development, Paul Aisen/Scientific, Clinical Advisors, Sergey Bachurin/Scientific, Clinical Advisors, Rachelle Doody/Scientific, Clinical Advisors, Michael E. Jung/Scientific, Clinical Advisor, Benjamin Lewin/Scientific, Clinical Advisors, Marc A. Shuman/Scientific, Clinical Advisor, Roger Tung/Scientific, Clinical Advisors, Michael W. Hall/Corp. Sec., Sarvajit Chakravarty/VP - Medicinal Chemistry

Directors: David T. Hung/Dir., CEO, Pres., Kim D. Blickenstaff/Chmn., Gregory H. Bailey/Dir., Daniel D. Adams/Dir., Anthony W. Vernon/Dir.

Owners: David T. Hung/6.19%, Selena Pharmaceuticals, Inc./7.96%, Lynn Seely/1.26%, Entities affiliated with Knoll Capital Management, LP/12.82%, Gregory Bailey/2.02%, Patrick C. Machado/1.76%, Anthony W. Vernon, Daniel Adams, Kim D. Blickenstaff, Entities affiliated with Austin Marxe and David Greenhouse/10.87%, Insiders/12.31%

Financial Data: *Fiscal Year End:*12/31　*Latest Annual Data:* 12/31/2006

Year	Sales	Net Income
2006	NA	-$15,363,000

Curr. Assets:	$47,506,000	**Curr. Liab.:**	$1,740,000		
Plant, Equip.:	$7,000	**Total Liab.:**	$1,740,000	**Indic. Yr. Divd.:**	NA
Total Assets:	$47,612,000	**Net Worth:**	$45,873,000	**Debt/ Equity:**	NA

Mediware Information Systems Inc

11711 W 79th St., Lenexa, KS, 66214; *PH:* 1-913-307-1000; *Fax:* 1-913-307-1111; *http://* www.mediware.com

General - Incorporation	NY	**Stock**- Price on:12/24/2007	$7.35
Employees	202	Stock Exchange	NDQ
Auditor	Eisner LLP	Ticker Symbol	MEDW
Stk Agt	American Stock Transfer & Trust Co.	Outstanding Shares	8,150,000
Counsel	NA	E.P.S.	$0.29
DUNS No.	17-724-0249	Shareholders	NA

Business: The group's principal activities are to develop, implement and support clinical management information systems to the healthcare industry. The products are marketed in three lines: pharmacy systems, blood bank systems and operating room systems. The blood bank division includes hemocare (TM) products, lifetrak (TM) products, lifeline (TM) products and starpath (TM) products. The group licensed the surgiwaretm system for use in surgical suites. Surgiwarea is a comprehensive information system for managing the human resources, facilities, equipment and supplies. The pharmacy division includes worxa drug therapy management system and worxa universal. The customers of the group are research institutions such as university of California medical center, university of Kansas medical center and hospitals.

Primary SIC and add'l.: 7373 7379 3845

CIK No: 0000874733

Subsidiaries: Digimedics Corporation, Informedics Inc., JAC Computer Services Ltd.

Officers: Thomas K. Mann/CEO, John Damgaard/39/COO, Sr. VP, Robert C. Weber/37/Sr. VP, Chief Legal Officer, General Counsel, Sec., Mark B. Williams/38/CFO, Principal Accounting Officer

Directors: Lawrence Auriana/64/Chmn., John Gorman/Dir., Ira Nordlicht/Dir., Roger Clark/74/Dir., Robert F. Sanville/65/Dir., Joseph Delario/75/Dir., Richard Greco/39/Dir.

Owners: Robert C. Weber/1.10%, Ira S. Nordlicht, Robert Tysall-Blay, John Gorman/1.00%, Roger Clark, Bank of America Corporation/5.50%, Lawrence Auriana/29.40%, Bares Capital Management, Inc/9.20%, Insiders/37.20%, Peninsula Master Capital Management, LP/20.30%, Robert F. Sanville, John Damgaard/1.20%, Thomas Mann/1.40%, Joseph Delario/3.50%, Mark Williams/1.00%

Financial Data: *Fiscal Year End:*06/30　*Latest Annual Data:* 03/31/2007

Year	Sales	Net Income
2007	$11,057,000	$831,000
2006	$37,871,000	$2,328,000
2005	$36,559,000	$2,936,000

Curr. Assets:	$29,131,000	**Curr. Liab.:**	$11,036,000	**P/E Ratio:**	25.34
Plant, Equip.:	$1,220,000	**Total Liab.:**	$15,222,000	**Indic. Yr. Divd.:**	NA
Total Assets:	$53,723,000	**Net Worth:**	$38,501,000	**Debt/ Equity:**	NA

Medizone International Inc

PO Box 742, Stinson Beach, CA, 94970; *PH:* 1-415-868-0300; *http://* www.medizoneint.com; *Email:* Operations@MedizoneInt.com

General - Incorporation	NV	**Stock** - Price on:12/24/2007	NA
Employees	I	Stock Exchange	OTC
Auditor	HJ Assoc. & Consultants LLP	Ticker Symbol	MZEI
Stk Agt	Colonial Stock Transfer Co Inc	Outstanding Shares	NA
Counsel	NA	E.P.S.	-$0.002
DUNS No.	16-163-9265	Shareholders	NA

Business: The group's principal activity is to develop, promote and distribute ozone-generating equipment and related products for medical applications. As on 31-Dec-2003, the group's activity is in the development stage. The group is seeking regulatory approval for the drug called medizone(R), which is a precise mixture of ozone and oxygen. The drug can be used as a therapeutic drug in humans to inactivate certain viruses and to treat certain viral diseases including aids-related virus, hepatitis b, hepatitis c, epstein-barr, herpes, cytomegalovirus and to decontaminate blood and blood products. The group owns two patents for process and equipment that includes ozone decontamination of blood and blood products, approaches for the control generation and administration of ozone and external application of ozone/oxygen for external applications.

Primary SIC and add'l.: 2834

CIK No: 0000753772

Officers: Edwin G. Marshall/65/Chmn., CEO, Steve M. Hanni/40/CFO

Directors: Edwin G. Marshall/65/Chmn., CEO

Financial Data: Fiscal Year End:12/31 Latest Annual Data: 12/31/2005

Year	Sales	Net Income
2005	NA	-$326,000
2004	NA	-$371,000
2003	NA	-$523,000

Curr. Assets:	NA	Curr. Liab.:	$2,991,000		
Plant, Equip.:	NA	Total Liab.:	$2,991,000	Indic. Yr. Divd.:	NA
Total Assets:	NA	Net Worth:	-$2,991,000	Debt/ Equity:	NA

MedLink International Inc

11 Oval Dr., Ste. 200B, Islandia, NY, 11749; *PH:* 1-631-342-8800; *Fax:* 1-631-342-8819; *http://* www.medlinkus.com; *Email:* info@medlinkus.com

General - Incorporation	DE	**Stock** - Price on:12/24/2007	$1.35
Employees	11	Stock Exchange	OTC
Auditor	Jewett, Schwartz & Associates	Ticker Symbol	MLKNA
Stk Agt	Computershare Trust Co	Outstanding Shares	20,530,000
Counsel	NA	E.P.S.	-$0.13
DUNS No.	NA	Shareholders	NA

Business: The groups principle activities include selling, implementing and supporting software solutions and hardware to healthcare providers for secure access to clinical, administrative and financial data in real time. Specific customers of the group include New Island Hospital, UCLA, Miracle Mile Medical Center and select radiology groups. The group operates from the United States.

Primary SIC and add'l.: 7371 7373 8099 7389 7374 7372

CIK No: 0000225501

Subsidiaries: CNI Medical Coding & Recovery, Inc, KRad Konsulting, LLC, MedLink FE, Inc, MedLink USA, Inc, MedLink VPN, Inc, Norika USA, Inc, Western Media Acquisition Corp, Western Media Publishing Corporation

Officers: Ray Vuono/Chmn., CEO, Pres., Jameson Rose/CFO, Exec. VP, Konrad Kim/Dir., CTO, James Decker/43/Exec. VP - Sales

Directors: Ray Vuono/Chmn., CEO, Pres., Konrad Kim/Dir., CTO, Michael Carvo/Dir.

Owners: Konrad Kim/5.16%, Michael Carvo/2.84%, Jerry Bermensolo/21.76%, Ray Vuono/29.42%, Jameson Rose/16.72%

Financial Data: Fiscal Year End:12/31 Latest Annual Data: 12/31/2006

Year	Sales	Net Income
2006	$11,000	-$1,589,000
2005	NA	-$957,000
2004	NA	-$1,627,000

Curr. Assets:	NA	Curr. Liab.:	$450,000		
Plant, Equip.:	$57,000	Total Liab.:	$450,000	Indic. Yr. Divd.:	NA
Total Assets:	$62,000	Net Worth:	-$388,000	Debt/ Equity:	NA

Medsolutions Inc

12750 Merit Dr. Pk. Cental Vii, Ste 770, Dallas, TX, 75251; *PH:* 1-972-931-2374; *http://* www.medsolutions.net; *Email:* information@medsolutions.com

General - Incorporation	TX	**Stock** - Price on:12/24/2007	NA
Employees	NA	Stock Exchange	NA
Auditor	Marcum & Kliegman LLP	Ticker Symbol	NA
Stk Agt	NA	Outstanding Shares	NA
Counsel	NA	E.P.S.	NA
DUNS No.	NA	Shareholders	NA

Business: The group's principal activities are to design, develop, manufacture and market solid waste treatment technology systems for destruction of regulated medical and other specialized waste streams generated by the medical, industrial and commercial business communities in an environmentally sound manner. The group also provides regulated medical waste management services that include collection, transportation, treatment and disposal of regulated medical waste from a variety of healthcare customers. These customers include hospitals, clinics, doctors' offices and a variety of other regulated medical waste generators.

Primary SIC and add'l.: 4953

CIK No: 0001144870

Subsidiaries: EnviroClean Management Services, Inc, SharpsSolutions, Inc, ShredSolutions, Inc, Waste Servicing, Inc

Officers: Matthew H. Fleeger/Founder, CEO, Pres., Steven Evans/VP - Finance, James M. Treat/VP - Business Development, Lonnie Cole/Sr. VP - Sales, Alan Larosse/VP - Operations, Beverly L. Fleeger/VP, Corp. Sec.

Directors: Matthew H. Fleeger/Founder, CEO, Pres., Winship B. Moody/Chmn., Mark M. Altenau/Dir., Steven R. Block/52/Dir.

Medtox Scientific Inc

402 W County Rd. D, St. Paul, MN, 55112; *PH:* 1-651-636-7466; *Fax:* 1-651-636-5351; *http://* www.medtox.com; *Email:* investors@medtox.com

General - Incorporation	DE	**Stock** - Price on:12/24/2007	$27.6301
Employees	460	Stock Exchange	NDQ
Auditor	Deloitte & Touche LLP	Ticker Symbol	MTRX
Stk Agt	American Stock Transfer & Trust Co.	Outstanding Shares	8,220,000
Counsel	Hinshaw & Culbertson	E.P.S.	$0.66
DUNS No.	11-505-8828	Shareholders	NA

Business: The group's principal activities are to manufacture and distribute diagnostic devices and forensic and clinical laboratory services. The group operates through two subsidiaries, medtox laboratories, inc. And medtox diagnostics, inc. The group's laboratory provides services like forensic toxicology, clinical toxicology and heavy metal analyses. It also provides logistics, data management and program management services. The group's diagnostics segment develops, manufactures and markets products based on immunoassay technology for the detection of antibiotic residues, mycotoxins, drugs of abuse and other hazardous substances. It also distributes agridiagnostic and food safety testing products. The group's products and services include profile-ii test system, for detection of drugs of abuse in human urine, ez-screen breath control alcohol test system and verdict-ii on site screening devices.

Primary SIC and add'l.: 8071 2836

CIK No: 0000739944

Subsidiaries: MEDTOX Diagnostics, Inc, MEDTOX Laboratories, Inc., New Brighton Business Center, LLC.

Officers: Richard J. Braun/Chmn., CEO, Pres./$1,366,874.00, Susan E. Puskas/VP - Quality, Regulatory Affairs, H, R/$488,828.00, James A. Schoonover/VP - CMO, Sales, Marketing/$512,828.00, Kevin J. Wiersma/VP, CFO - Medtox Scientific, Inc, COO - Laboratory Division/$464,828.00, Mitchell B. Owens/VP, COO Medtox Diagnostics - Inc/$437,953.00, Jennifer A. Collins/Dir. - Forensic Laboratory, Karla J. Walker/Dir. - Clinical Toxicology

Directors: Richard J. Braun/Chmn., CEO, Pres., Brian P. Johnson/Dir., Samuel C. Powell/Dir., Robert A. Rudell/Dir., Robert J. Marzec/Dir.

Owners: Susan E. Puskas/1.42%, Heartland Advisors, Inc./9.17%, Perkins Capital Management, Inc/4.97%, Richard J. Braun/6.66%, Dimensional Fund Advisors LP/7.38%, Samuel C. Powell/3.66%, Insiders/18.72%, Mitchell B. Owens/2.24%, Kevin J. Wiersma/2.26%, James A. Schoonover/2.43%, Brian P. Johnson, Robert J. Marzec, Robert A. Rudell, Rutabaga Capital Management/6.54%

Financial Data: Fiscal Year End:12/31 Latest Annual Data: 12/31/2006

Year	Sales	Net Income
2006	$69,804,000	$4,548,000
2005	$63,047,000	$3,318,000
2004	$56,736,000	$1,821,000

Curr. Assets:	$18,707,000	Curr. Liab.:	$8,892,000	P/E Ratio:	41.86
Plant, Equip.:	$19,572,000	Total Liab.:	$11,930,000	Indic. Yr. Divd.:	NA
Total Assets:	$59,874,000	Net Worth:	$47,944,000	Debt/ Equity:	0.0304

Medtronic Inc

710 Medtronic Pkwy., Minneapolis, MN, 55432; *PH:* 1-763-514-4000; *Fax:* 1-763-514-4879; *http://* www.medtronic.com

General - Incorporation	MN	**Stock** - Price on:12/24/2007	$51.79
Employees	36,000	Stock Exchange	NYSE
Auditor	PricewaterhouseCoopers LLP	Ticker Symbol	MDT
Stk Agt	Wells Fargo Bank Minnesota N.A	Outstanding Shares	1,150,000,000
Counsel	NA	E.P.S.	$2.48
DUNS No.	00-626-1481	Shareholders	NA

Business: The groups principle activity is to provide medical technology, alleviating pain, restoring health, and extending life for people around the world. In the year 2007, the group acquired Kyphon Inc. The group operates from United States.

Primary SIC and add'l.: 3845

CIK No: 0000064670

Subsidiaries: Arterial Vascular Engineering Canada, Company, Arterial Vascular Engineering Netherlands Holding, Arterial Vascular Engineering UK Limited, AVE Ireland Limited, AVECOR Cardiovascular Limited, B.V. Medtronic FSC, Cardiotron G.m.b.H., IGN AB, IGN GmbH, India Medtronic Private Limited, Magnolia Medical LLC, Medical Education K.K., Medtronic (Africa) (Proprietary) Limited, Medtronic (Schweiz) A.G. / Medtronic (Suisse) S.A., Medtronic (Shanghai) Ltd. 143 Subsidiaries included in the Index

Officers: Stephen N. Oesterle/Sr. VP - Medicine, Technology, Scott R. Ward/Sr. VP, Pres. - Cardiovascular, Michael F. Demane/52/COO/$4,581,891.00, Stephen H. Mahle/Exec. VP - Sr. Healthcare Policy Advisor/$3,936,710.00, Jean-Luc Butel/Sr. VP, Pres. - Asia Pacific, Susan Alpert/VP, Chief Quality, Regulatory Officer, William A. Hawkins/54/Dir., COO, Pres./$4,412,312.00, James H. Dallas/CIO, Sr. VP, Richard Kuntz/Sr. VP, Pres. - Neuromodulation, Peter L. Wehrly/Sr. VP, Pres. - Spinal, Biologics, Pat MacKin/Sr. VP, Pres. - Cardiac Rhythm Disease Management, Christopher J. OConnell/Sr. VP, Pres. - Diabetes, Carol McCormick/Sr. VP - Human Resources, Terrance L. Carlson/Sr. VP, General Counsel, Corp. Sec., Barry W. Wilson/64/Sr. VP - International Affairs *(17 Officers included in Index)*

Directors: Arthur D. Collins/60/Chmn., Jean Pierre Rosso/Dir., Richard H. Anderson/Dir., David L. Calhoun/Dir., James T. Lenehan/Dir., Kendall J. Powell/Dir., Denise M. O'Leary/Dir., William A. Hawkins/54/Dir., COO, Pres., Robert C. Pozen/Dir., Jack W. Schuler/Dir., Shirley Ann Jackson/Dir.

Owners: Gordon M. Sprenger, Richard H. Anderson, Michael R. Bonsignore, Michael F. DeMane, Insiders, Robert C. Pozen, Wellington Management Company, LLP/6.80%, Denise M. OLeary, Stephen H. Mahle, Gary L. Ellis, Kendall J. Powell, William A. Hawkins, Capital Research and Management Company/10.40%, Shirley Ann Jackson, James T. Lenehan *(20 Owners included in Index)*

Financial Data: Fiscal Year End:04/28 Latest Annual Data: 04/27/2007

Year	Sales	Net Income
2007	$12,299,000,000	$2,802,000,000
2006	$11,292,000,000	$2,546,700,000
2005	$10,054,600,000	$1,803,900,000

Curr. Assets:	$5,312,700,000	Curr. Liab.:	$4,240,600,000	P/E Ratio:	21.49
Plant, Equip.:	$1,708,300,000	Total Liab.:	$5,033,800,000	Indic. Yr. Divd.:	$0.440
Total Assets:	$14,110,800,000	Net Worth:	$9,077,000,000	Debt/ Equity:	NA

Medusa Style Corp

4128 Colfax Ave., Studio City, CA, 91604; *PH:* 1-818-985-2417

General - Incorporation	NV	Stock- Price on:12/24/2007	$0.65
Employees	NA	Stock Exchange	OTC
Auditor	Vellmer & Chang	Ticker Symbol	ENGO
Stk Agt	Signature Stock Transfer, Inc.	Outstanding Shares	NA
Counsel	NA	E.P.S.	NA
DUNS No.		Shareholders	NA

Business: The groups principal activity is to distribute products to the professional salon industry through the Internet. The products of the group include shampoo, conditioners, hairsprays, gels, mousse, pomades, permanent hair dyes, curling irons, clippers, foil and rollers. The group operates from the United States.

Primary SIC and add'l.: 5190

CIK No: 0001200528

Officers: Paul E. Fishkin/65/CEO, Pres., CFO, Sec., Treasurer, Dir.

Directors: Paul E. Fishkin/65/CEO, Pres., CFO, Sec., Treasurer, Dir., Tolga F. Katas/42/Dir.

Owners: Insiders/53.30%, Tolga F. Katas/27.30%, Paul E. Fishkin/27.30%, Kevin R. Griffith/25.80%

Medwave Inc

4382 Round Lake Rd. W, St. Paul, MA, 55112; *PH:* 1-651-639-1227; *Fax:* 1-651-639-1338; *http://* www.mdwv.com; *Email:* info@mdwv.com

General - Incorporation	DE	Stock- Price on:12/24/2007	$0.2805
Employees	22	Stock Exchange	OTC
Auditor	Carlin, Charron & Rosen LLP	Ticker Symbol	MDWV
Stk Agt	Wells Fargo Shareowner Services	Outstanding Shares	13,100,000
Counsel	NA	E.P.S.	-$0.434
DUNS No.	15-696-5428	Shareholders	NA

Business: The group's principal activity is to develop, manufacture and distribute non-invasive blood pressure products. Vasotrac(R) hand held monitor, the vasotrac(R) apm205a nibp monitor and the mj23 OEM module are the new approaches to non-invasive blood pressure monitoring. Vasotrac(R) system monitors blood pressure continuously and provides new readings approximately for every fifteen heart beats which has helped the group to provide with the most advanced monitoring system. The customers include physicians and hospitals. The trademarks include medwave (R), vasotrac (R), vasotrax (r). It also provides on-call technical support and equipment services. The group markets its technology in Europe, Asia and the United States.

Primary SIC and add'l.: 3841

CIK No: 0000876043

Officers: Frank A. Katarow/Dir., CEO, Principal Executive Officer, Donna R. Lunak/VP, GM, Ramon L. Burton/CFO - Principal Financial, Accounting Officer

Directors: Frank A. Katarow/Dir., CEO, Principal Executive Officer, William D. Corneliuson/Chmn., Solomon Aronson/50/Dir., James C. Hawley/Dir.

Owners: Donna R. Lunak, James C. Hawley, Insiders/10.40%, William D. Corneliuson/8.90%, Hambrecht & Quist Capital Management LLC/12.20%, Frank A. Katarow, Solomon Aronson

Financial Data: Fiscal Year End:09/30 Latest Annual Data: 9/30/2006

Year	Sales		Net Income
2006		$1,117,000	-$5,804,000
2005		$1,172,000	-$4,148,000
2004		$864,000	-$2,831,000
Curr. Assets:	$5,826,000	Curr. Liab.:	$1,572,000
Plant, Equip.:	$451,000	Total Liab.:	$1,572,000	Indic. Yr. Divd.:	NA
Total Assets:	$6,276,000	Net Worth:	$4,705,000	Debt/ Equity:	NA

Mega Media Group Inc

Formerly: Family Healthcare Solutions Inc
598 Broadway Way, 3rd Fl., New York, NY, 10012; *PH:* 1-646-839-5500

General - Incorporation	NV	Stock- Price on:12/24/2007	$0.3
Employees	NA	Stock Exchange	OTC
Auditor	Teodoro F. Franco L	Ticker Symbol	MMDA
Stk Agt	Madison Stock Transfer, Inc.	Outstanding Shares	33,960,000
Counsel	NA	E.P.S.	-$0.02
DUNS No.	NA	Shareholders	NA

Business: The group's principle activity is to produce film and video for theatrical, cable and televised releases. Currently, the group is in the development stage and has limited operations, assets and liabilities. The group produced one full-length movie entitled 'the blood game', intended for adult video and cable release. Due to the distribution problems encountered with the movie and due to the recent changes in the entertainment industry regarding the technological demands of producing, the officers and directors of the group have reviewed and analyzed the current business plan of producing low budget movies. The group has expanded the scope of its business to include and emphasize direct-response retailing production. The group operates from United States.

Primary SIC and add'l.: 7812

CIK No: 0001063262

Officers: Cynthia Robinson/Founder, CEO, Pres., Teodoro F. Franco/Dir., Sole Officer, Lynne Powers/Partner, VP

Directors: Cynthia Robinson/Founder, CEO, Pres., Teodoro F. Franco/Dir., Sole Officer

Owners: Lev Paukman/10.77%, Eric Schwartz/7.63%, Aleksandr Shvarts/12.46%, Gennady Pomeranets CPA/1.74%, David Kokakis, Esq./5.30%, Elan Kaufman/13.88%, Insiders/51.78%

Financial Data: Fiscal Year End:09/30 Latest Annual Data: 9/30/2006

Year	Sales		Net Income
2006		NA	-$316,000
2005		NA	-$29,000
2004		NA	-$81,000
Curr. Assets:	NA	Curr. Liab.:	$69,000
Plant, Equip.:	NA	Total Liab.:	$69,000	Indic. Yr. Divd.:	NA
Total Assets:	NA	Net Worth:	-$69,000	Debt/ Equity:	NA

Megadata Corp

47 Arch St., Greenwich, CT, 06830; *PH:* 1-203-622-4086; *Fax:* 1-203-629-2970; *http://* www.passur.com

General - Incorporation	NY	Stock- Price on:12/24/2007	$2.75
Employees	17	Stock Exchange	OTC
Auditor	BDO Seidman LLP	Ticker Symbol	MDTA
Stk Agt	Continental Stock Transfer & Trust Co	Outstanding Shares	4,090,000
Counsel	NA	E.P.S.	$0.10
DUNS No.	04-919-7361	Shareholders	NA

Business: The group's principal activity is to supply information, data services and software to satisfy the needs of the aviation industry, primarily airlines, airports and other aviation related companies. It delivers data and software by subscription from its passur (passive secondary surveillance radar) network of flight tracking systems. Passur is the engine that drives all present and future data, information, and solution products sold by the group. The group provides information services, solution services and maintenance services. Information services provide airline and airport customers with specific and timely information. Solution services include a series of decision support tools and software solutions and maintenance services are provided pursuant to contractual arrangements.

Primary SIC and add'l.: 7371 3661 8999 7372

CIK No: 0000225628

Officers: James T. Barry/45/Dir., CEO, Pres., Matthew H. Marcella/VP - Software Development, John R. Keller/66/Dir., Exec. VP, James A. Cole/Sr. VP - Research, Development, Jeffrey P. Devaney/CFO, Treasurer, Sec., Ron Dunsky/VP - Marketing

Directors: James T. Barry/45/Dir., CEO, Pres., Beckwith G.S. Gilbert/66/Chmn., Paul L. Graziani/50/Dir., James J. Morgan/65/Dir., Richard R. Schilling/82/Dir., John R. Keller/66/Dir., Exec. VP, Bruce N. Whitman/73/Dir.

Owners: Insiders, Matthew H. Marcella, Ron A. Dunsky, Paul L. Graziani, Beckwith G.S. Gilbert, Bruce N. Whitman, James T. Barry, Richard R. Schilling, John R. Keller, James J. Morgan, Jeffrey P. Devaney, James A. Cole

Financial Data: Fiscal Year End:10/31 Latest Annual Data: 04/30/2007

Year	Sales		Net Income
2007		$1,392,000	$115,000
2006		$4,314,000	$103,000
2005		$3,809,000	-$924,000
Curr. Assets:	$1,788,000	Curr. Liab.:	$2,066,000	P/E Ratio:	30.56
Plant, Equip.:	$145,000	Total Liab.:	$13,322,000	Indic. Yr. Divd.:	NA
Total Assets:	$6,029,000	Net Worth:	-$7,294,000	Debt/ Equity:	NA

Megawest Energy Corp

Formerly: Brockton Capital Corp
926 - 5th Ave. Sw, Ste. 800, Calgary, AB, T2P 0N7;

General - Incorporation	BC	Stock- Price on:12/24/2007	NA
Employees	NA	Stock Exchange	NA
Auditor	KPMG LLP	Ticker Symbol	NA
Stk Agt	Pacific Corporate Trust Co	Outstanding Shares	NA
Counsel	NA	E.P.S.	NA
DUNS No.	NA	Shareholders	NA

Business: The groups principal activity is to exploration of minerals. The group operates from the United States and Canada.

Primary SIC and add'l.: 6799

CIK No: 0001172298

Subsidiaries: MegaWest Energy

Officers: George T. Stapleton/54/Chmn., CEO, Pres., George Orr/47/CFO, Treasurer, William R. Thornton/52/COO, Gerry Hampshire/VP - Exploitation, Wayne E. Sampson/VP - Land, David Sealock/VP - Corporate Services, Corp. Sec., Kelly Sledz/Finance Mgr., Controller

Directors: George T. Stapleton/54/Chmn., CEO, Pres., Brad Kitchen/45/Dir., Terry M. Amisano/51/Dir., Kevin R. Hanson/50/Dir., Brian J. Evans/Dir., Gail Bloomer/73/Dir.

Owners: FireBird Global Master Fund II LTD & LTD/6.00%, Gundyco I/T/F Pinetree Resource Partnership/5.70%, Brad Kitchen, William R. Thornton/3.40%, Brian J. Evans, George T. Stapleton/2.40%, Cushing MLP Opportunity Fund I LP/5.50%

Financial Data: Fiscal Year End:04/30 Latest Annual Data: 3/26/2007

Year	Sales		Net Income
2007		NA	-$192,000
2006		NA	-$200,000
2005		NA	-$49,000
Curr. Assets:	$26,394,000	Curr. Liab.:	$1,166,000
Plant, Equip.:	$38,268,000	Total Liab.:	$4,011,000	Indic. Yr. Divd.:	NA
Total Assets:	$66,628,000	Net Worth:	$62,617,000	Debt/ Equity:	NA

Megola Inc

446 Lyndock St., Ste 102, Corunna, ON, N0N 1G0; *PH:* 1-519-480628; *http://* www.megola.com; *Email:* megola@megola.com

General - Incorporation	NV	Stock- Price on:12/24/2007	NA
Employees	NA	Stock Exchange	OTC
Auditor	Malone & Bailey, P.C	Ticker Symbol	MGOA
Stk Agt	Pacific Stock Transfer Company	Outstanding Shares	NA
Counsel	NA	E.P.S.	NA
DUNS No.	NA	Shareholders	NA

Business: The group's principal activities are to franchise and support third party carpet cleaning operations. The group markets its products in the United States, China and Canada.

Primary SIC and add'l.: 7217

CIK No: 0001144392

Officers: Joel Gardner/CEO, Pres., Daniel Gardner/GM, Treasurer, Michael Gardner/Environmental Scientist, Aldo Rotondi/Dir. - Business Development, T. A. McGill/CFO

Directors: Sufan Siauw/Dir., William De Waal/Member - Megola Advisory Board, Todd Clark/Member - Megola Advisory Board, Don Greer/Member - Megola Advisory Board, Willard Brown/Dir., Bill Weaver/Member - Megola Advisory Board

Owners: Don Greer, Joel Gardner/9.00%, Todd Clark/5.40%

Curr. Assets:	$357,000	**Curr. Liab.:**	$531,000		
Plant, Equip.:	$12,000	**Total Liab.:**	$531,000	**Indic. Yr. Divd.:**	NA
Total Assets:	$369,000	**Net Worth:**	-$162,000	**Debt/ Equity:**	NA

Melo Biotechnology Holdings Inc

Formerly: MIAD Systems Ltd
Rm. 1411, W Tower, Shuntak Center, 168-200 Connaught Rd., Central; ; *http://* www.miad.com

General - Incorporation	Canada	**Stock**- Price on:12/24/2007	$1.25
Employees	NA	Stock Exchange	NA
Auditor	Schwartz Levitsky Feldman LLP	Ticker Symbol	NA
Stk Agt	Manhattan Transfer Registrar Co	Outstanding Shares	NA
Counsel	NA	E.P.S.	NA
DUNS No.	NA	Shareholders	NA

Business: The group's principle activity is to supply business computer systems, maintenance, installation and networking services. The group operates from United States.

Primary SIC and add'l.: 7373 3577

CIK No: 0001081568

Officers: Fung Ming/Dir., CFO, Pres.

Directors: Fung Ming/Dir., CFO, Pres.

Owners: Michael A.S. Green/61.97%

Financial Data: ***Fiscal Year End:***09/30 ***Latest Annual Data:*** 9/30/2006

Year	Sales	Net Income
2006	$7,921,000	-$126,000
2005	$7,108,000	$24,000
2004	$5,501,000	-$198,000

Curr. Assets:	$1,249,000	**Curr. Liab.:**	$1,648,000		
Plant, Equip.:	$131,000	**Total Liab.:**	$1,648,000	**Indic. Yr. Divd.:**	NA
Total Assets:	$1,380,000	**Net Worth:**	-$268,000	**Debt/ Equity:**	NA

Melt Inc

22912 Mill Creek Dr., Ste. D, Laguna Hills, CA, 92653; ***PH:*** 1-949-707-0456; ***Fax:*** 1-949-707-0457; *http://* www.meltgelato.com; ***Email:*** alincruz@meltgelato.com

General - Incorporation	NV	**Stock**- Price on:12/24/2007	$0.4
Employees	12	Stock Exchange	OTC
Auditor	HJ Associates & Consultants, LLP	Ticker Symbol	MLTC
Stk Agt	Nevada Agency & Trust Company	Outstanding Shares	21,290,000
Counsel	NA	E.P.S.	-$0.11
DUNS No.	NA	Shareholders	NA

Business: The groups principle activity is to franchise retail gelato bars and coffee shops under the name Melt-gelato italiano and Melt gelato & crepe caf. The group operates from the United States.

Primary SIC and add'l.: 5143

CIK No: 0001267612

Subsidiaries: Melt (California) Inc., Melt Franchising LLC.

Officers: Clive Barwin/Dir., Sec., CEO, Pres., Scott Miller/CFO, Exec. VP, Brandon Barwin/Dir., VP - Operations

Directors: Clive Barwin/Dir., Sec., CEO, Pres., Brandon Barwin/Dir., VP - Operations

Owners: Glynis Sive/9.34%, Insiders/27.41%, Clive Barwin/22.92%, The Norwood Trust/8.49%, Brandon Barwin/4.48%

Financial Data: ***Fiscal Year End:***12/31 ***Latest Annual Data:*** 12/31/2006

Year	Sales	Net Income
2006	$3,815,000	-$1,101,000
2005	$1,740,000	-$207,000

Curr. Assets:	$2,104,000	**Curr. Liab.:**	$2,409,000		
Plant, Equip.:	$52,000	**Total Liab.:**	$2,409,000	**Indic. Yr. Divd.:**	NA
Total Assets:	$2,354,000	**Net Worth:**	-$55,000	**Debt/ Equity:**	NA

MEMC Electronic Materials Inc

501 Pearl Dr., St. Peters, MO, 63376; ***PH:*** 1-636-474-5000; ***Fax:*** 1-636-474-5158; *http://* www.memc.com

General - Incorporation	DE	**Stock**- Price on:12/24/2007	$57.8
Employees	5,000	Stock Exchange	NYSE
Auditor	KPMG LLP	Ticker Symbol	WFR
Stk Agt	Computershare Investor Services LLC	Outstanding Shares	224,390,000
Counsel	NA	E.P.S.	$2.50
DUNS No.	36-183-4617	Shareholders	NA

Business: The group's principal activities are to design, manufacture and sell electronic grade wafers for the semiconductor industry. The products include three general categories of wafers: prime polished wafers, epitaxial and test/monitor wafers. Prime polished wafers are pure wafer with an ultraflat and ultraclean surface. The epitaxial wafer consists of a thin single-crystal silicon layer grown on the polished surface of the wafer. The test/monitor wafers are used for testing semiconductor fabrication lines and processes. The group's products are sold to memory, microprocessor and application specific integrated circuit (asic) manufacturers and foundries. The group operates manufacturing facilities including Europe, Malaysia, Japan, South Korea and the United States and through a joint venture in Taiwan.

Primary SIC and add'l.: 3674

CIK No: 0000945436

Subsidiaries: MEMC Electronic Materials (UK) Ltd., MEMC Electronic Materials France Sarl, MEMC Electronic Materials Sales, Sdn. Bhd., MEMC Electronic Materials, GmbH, MEMC Electronic Materials, S.p.A., MEMC Electronic Materials, Sdn. Bhd., MEMC Holding B.V., MEMC Holdings Corporation, MEMC International, Inc., MEMC Japan Ltd., MEMC Korea Company, MEMC Kulim Electronic Materials, Sdn. Bhd., MEMC Pasadena, Inc., Taisil Electronic Materials Corporation

Officers: Nabeel Gareeb/Dir., CEO, Pres./$6,490,776.00, Shaker Sadasivam/Sr. VP - Research, Development/$985,935.00, Sean Hunkler/Sr. VP - Manufacturing/$1,938,277.00, John Kauffmann/Sr. VP - Sales, Customer Service, Marketing/$1,254,769.00, Brad Kohn/VP, General Counsel/$1,389,115.00, Ken Hannah/Sr. VP, CFO/$2,686,123.00, Bill Michalek/Dir. - Investor Relations, Brett W. Avants/Dir. - Global Communicatons, Mike Cheles/VP - Information Technology, CIO, Mignon Cabrera/Sr. VP - Human Resources

Directors: Nabeel Gareeb/Dir., CEO, Pres., John Marren/Chmn., William Stevens/Dir., Robert Boehlke/Dir., Peter Blackmore/Dir., Douglas C. Marsh/Dir., James B. Williams/Dir., Marshall Turner/Dir.

Owners: Douglas C. Marsh, Thomas E. Linnen, TPG Wafer Partners LLC, Shaker Sadasivam, T(3) Advisors, Inc., GEI Capital III, LLC, T(3) Advisors II, Inc., William E. Stevens, Green Equity Investors Side III, L.P., TCW/Crescent Mezzanine Partners III Netherlands, L.P., TCW/Crescent Mezzanine Partners III, L.P., Leonard Green& Partners, L.P., James B. Williams, Robert J. Boehlke, John Marren *(25 Owners included in Index)*

Financial Data: ***Fiscal Year End:***12/31 ***Latest Annual Data:*** 12/31/2006

Year	Sales	Net Income
2006	$1,540,584,000	$369,288,000
2005	$1,107,379,000	$249,353,000
2004	$1,027,958,000	$226,201,000

Curr. Assets:	$899,514,000	**Curr. Liab.:**	$257,818,000	**P/E Ratio:**	25.80
Plant, Equip.:	$603,509,000	**Total Liab.:**	$560,069,000	**Indic. Yr. Divd.:**	NA
Total Assets:	$1,765,524,000	**Net Worth:**	$1,166,893,000	**Debt/ Equity:**	0.0221

Memory Pharmaceuticals Corp

100 Philips Pkwy., Montvale, NJ, 07645; ***PH:*** 1-201-802-7100; ***Fax:*** 1-201-802-7190; *http://* www.memorypharma.com; ***Email:*** info@memorypharma.com

General - Incorporation	DE	**Stock**- Price on:12/24/2007	$2.52
Employees	61	Stock Exchange	NDQ
Auditor	KPMG LLP	Ticker Symbol	MEMY
Stk Agt	American Stock Transfer & Trust Co.	Outstanding Shares	71,860,000
Counsel	NA	E.P.S.	-$0.58
DUNS No.	NA	Shareholders	NA

Business: The group's principle activities include research and developing innovative drug candidates. Innovative drug candidates are used for the treatment of central nervous system conditions that exhibit impairment of memory and other cognitive functions. The central nervous system therapies are designed to address biological targets within the cellular pathways. These are involved in memory formation and other cognitive functions. It currently has four clinical and preclinical drug candidates and also multiple drug discovery programs in development. The company operates in the domestic market. The group operates from United States.

Primary SIC and add'l.: 2834

CIK No: 0001062216

Officers: James R. Sulat/Dir., CEO, Pres., Principal Financial Officer/$851,288.00, Stephen Murray/Chief Medical Officer/$382,697.00, David A. Lowe/Dir., Chief Scientific Officer/$855,263.00, Jzaneen Lalani/General Counsel/$490,093.00, Michael P. Smith/VP - Business Development, Joseph M. Donabauer/VP, Controller/$305,425.00

Directors: James R. Sulat/Dir., CEO, Pres., Principal Financial Officer, Jonathan J. Fleming/Co - Founder, Chmn., Anthony B. Evnin/Dir., Peter F. Young/Dir., Robert I. Kriebel/Dir., Michael E. Meyers/Dir., David A. Lowe/Dir., Chief Scientific Officer, Walter Gilbert/Co - Founder, Dir., Member - Scientific Advisory Board, Eric R. Kandel/Member - Scientific Advisory Board, Rene Hen/Member - Scientific Advisory Board, Hans-Jurgen Hess/Member - Scientific Advisory Board, Richard P. Mayeux/Member - Scientific Advisory Board, Steven Siegelbaum/Member - Scientific Advisory Board, Scott Small/Member - Scientific Advisory Board, Larry R. Squire/Member - Scientific Advisory Board *(16 Directors included in Index)*

Owners: Insiders/35.08%, Michael E. Meyers, Vaughn Kailian/19.82%, Anthony B. Evnin/5.34%, Stephen R. Murray, MPM Entities/19.82%, Walter Gilbert, Tony Scullion/1.06%, David A. Lowe, Robert I. Kriebel, Jzaneen Lalani, Joseph M. Donabauer, Jonathan J. Fleming/8.41%, Peter F. Young, Aletheia Research and Management, Inc./5.26% *(17 Owners included in Index)*

Financial Data: ***Fiscal Year End:***12/31 ***Latest Annual Data:*** 12/31/2006

Year	Sales	Net Income
2006	$9,322,000	-$31,107,000
2005	$11,111,000	-$31,686,000
2004	$9,780,000	-$24,096,000

Curr. Assets:	$52,720,000	**Curr. Liab.:**	$14,465,000		
Plant, Equip.:	$7,413,000	**Total Liab.:**	$37,440,000	**Indic. Yr. Divd.:**	NA
Total Assets:	$60,642,000	**Net Worth:**	$23,202,000	**Debt/ Equity:**	NA

Memry Corp

3 Berkshire Blvd., Bethel, CT, 06801; ***PH:*** 1-203-739-1100; ***Fax:*** 1-203-798-6511; *http://* www.memry.com; ***Email:*** info@memry.com

General - Incorporation	DE	**Stock**- Price on:12/24/2007	$1.7
Employees	340	Stock Exchange	AMEX
Auditor	Deloitte & Touche LLP	Ticker Symbol	MRY
Stk Agt	American Stock Transfer & Trust Co.	Outstanding Shares	29,850,000
Counsel	Finn Dixon & Herling LLP	E.P.S.	-$0.009
DUNS No.	05-711-4506	Shareholders	NA

Business: The group's principal activities are to develop, manufacture and market formed components and value-added sub-assembled products. The group produces both the wire and tubing that is used to fabricate guidewire, catheters and stents and also provides completed stent structures to medical device companies, as well as other surgical and diagnostic instrument assemblies. The group also serves non-medical industry sectors such as telecommunications, aerospace, defense and automotive industries. These products include sealing devices, actuators, fasteners and cellular phone antennae. The group conducts its operations from its two operating facilities located in bethel, Connecticut and menlo park, California.

Primary SIC and add'l.: 8731 3841 3545

CIK No: 0000720896

Subsidiaries: Putnam Plastics Company LLC

Officers: Robert Belcher/CEO, Vice Chmn., Marcy MacDonald/VP - Human Resources, Dean J. Tulumaris/COO, Pres., Philippe Poncet/VP - Business Development, Richard F. Sowerby/CFO, Treasurer

Directors: Robert Belcher/CEO, Vice Chmn., Edwin Snape/Chmn., Kempton J. Coady/60/Dir., Andrew W. Krusen/60/Dir., Francois Marchal/64/Dir., Michel De Beaumont/66/Dir., Carmen L. Diersen/48/Dir., James V. Dandeneau/50/Dir.

Owners: Dean J. Tulumaris, New England Partners Capital, L.P./7.90%, Richard F. Sowerby, Francois Marchal/1.40%, Signia Capital Management, LLC/10.60%, Carmen L. Diersen, Edwin Snape/8.00%, Michel de Beaumont, Marcy F. Macdonald, James V. Dandeneau/9.60%, Robert P. Belcher/2.00%, Andrew W. Krusen/2.60%, Kempton J. Coady, Insiders/24.50%

Financial Data: ***Fiscal Year End:***06/30 ***Latest Annual Data:*** 6/30/2007

Year	Sales	Net Income
2007	$51,677,000	$317,000
2006	$52,588,000	$2,673,000
2005	$45,008,000	$2,725,000

Curr. Assets:	$16,861,000	**Curr. Liab.:**	$6,626,000	**P/E Ratio:**	15.45
Plant, Equip.:	$8,817,000	**Total Liab.:**	$7,396,000	**Indic. Yr. Divd.:**	NA
Total Assets:	$48,746,000	**Net Worth:**	$41,350,000	**Debt/ Equity:**	NA

Men's Wearhouse Inc

5803 Glenmont Dr., Houston, TX, 77081; ***PH:*** 1-713-592-7200; ***Fax:*** 1-713-664-1957; ***http://*** www.menswearhouse.com

General - Incorporation .... TX
Employees 10,700
Auditor .... Deloitte & Touche LLP
Stk Agt...... American Stock Transfer & Trust Co.
Counsel............ Fulbright & Jaworski LLP
DUNS No. 06-510-1974

Stock- Price on:12/24/2007 .... $51.44
Stock Exchange .... NDQ
Ticker Symbol .... MWAV
Outstanding Shares 53,790,000
E.P.S $2.93
Shareholders .... NA

Business: The groups principle activity is to operate retail apparel stores. The groups products include designer, brand name and private-label mens business attire, including basic suits, navy blazers and tuxedos. The group operates from United States.

Primary SIC and add'l.: 5611

CIK No: 0000884217

Subsidiaries: 5507 Renwick, Inc., Golden Brand Clothing (Canada) Ltd, K&G Mens Company Inc., Moores Retail Group Inc., Moores The Suit People Inc., MWDC Holding Inc., MWDC Texas Inc., Renwick Technologies, Inc., The Mens Wearhouse of Michigan, Inc., The Mens Wearhouse of Texas LP, TMW Marketing Company, Inc, TMW Merchants LLC, TMW Purchasing LLC, TMW Realty Inc., TMW Texas General LLC 16 Subsidiaries included in the Index

Officers: George Zimmer/Chmn., CEO, Founder/$1,376,824.00, William C. Silveira/50/Exec. VP - Manufacturing, Charles Bresler/Pres./$572,447.00, Carole L. Souvenir/47/Chief Legal Officer, Exec. VP - Employee Relations, Michael W. Conlon/Sec., Neill P. Davis/CFO, Exec. VP, Treasurer, Principal Financial Officer/$511,279.00, Douglas S. Ewert/COO, Exec. VP/$923,186.00, Gary G. Ckodre/58/Sr. VP, Chief Compliance Officer, James E. Zimmer/56/Sr. VP - Merchandising, Diana M. Wilson/60/Sr. VP, Chief Accounting Officer, Principal Accounting Officer, Pasquale De Marco/47/Pres. - Moores Retail Group Inc/$429,335.00, Christopher M. Zender/44/Pres. - K, G Mens Company

Directors: George Zimmer/Chmn., CEO, Founder, David H. Edwab/Vice Chmn., Rinaldo S. Brutoco/Dir., Larry R. Katzen/62/Dir., Michael L. Ray/Dir., Sheldon I. Stein/Dir., Kathleen Mason/Dir., Deepak Chopra/Dir., William B. Sechrest/Dir.

Owners: Pasquale De Marco, Neill P. Davis, Insiders/9.00%, Larry R. Katzen, Kathleen Mason, Rinaldo S. Brutoco, William B. Sechrest, George Zimmer/7.10%, PRIMECAP Management Company/8.60%, Deepak Chopra, Sheldon I. Stein, Vanguard HorizonFunds-Vanguard Capital Opportunity Fund/6.70%, Charles Bresler, Douglas S. Ewert, Michael L. Ray *(16 Owners included in Index)*

Financial Data: **Fiscal Year End:**01/28 **Latest Annual Data:** 2/3/2007

Year	Sales	Net Income
2007	$1,882,064,000	$148,575,000
2006	$1,724,898,000	$103,903,000
2005	$1,546,679,000	$71,356,000

Curr. Assets:	$680,829,000	**Curr. Liab.:**	$226,138,000	**P/E Ratio:**	17.56
Plant, Equip.:	$289,640,000	**Total Liab.:**	$343,180,000	**Indic. Yr. Divd.:**	$0.240
Total Assets:	$1,096,952,000	**Net Worth:**	$753,772,000	**Debt/ Equity:**	0.0998

Mendocino Brewing Co Inc

1601 Airport Rd., Ukiah, CA, 95482; ***PH:*** 1-707-463-6610; ***http://*** www.mendobrew.com; ***Email:*** questions@mendobrew.com

General - Incorporation .... CA
Employees 54
Auditor .... Moss Adams LLP
Stk Agt............ EquiServe Trust Co N.A
Counsel............ NA
DUNS No. 10-293-9048

Stock- Price on:12/24/2007 .... $0.4
Stock Exchange .... OTC
Ticker Symbol .... MENB
Outstanding Shares 11,990,000
E.P.S .... -$0.06
Shareholders .... NA

Business: The group's principal activities are to produce beer and malt beverages for the specialty craft segment of the beer market. The products of the group include ale, stout and craft beer. The products are sold under the brands including red tail ale, blue heron pale ale, black hawk stout, peregrine golden ale, yuletide porter, frolic shipwreck ale, carmel wheat beer, olde saratoga root beer and carmel pale ale. The group also operates a retail outlet which sells the off-sale packages of the group's brews and merchandise such as hand-screened label t-shirts, posters, engraved glasses and mugs, logo caps, books about brewing, gift packs and other brewery-related articles.

Primary SIC and add'l.: 5813 2082 5181 5921 5947

CIK No: 0000919134

Subsidiaries: Releta Brewing Company, LLC

Officers: Yashpal Singh/Dir., CEO, Pres./$215,906.00, Keith Stevenson/Advertising Mgr., David Boone/Central Coast Area Mgr., Steve Miller/Area Sales Mgr., Mahadevan Narayanan/Dir., CFO, Sec./$104,319.00, Tim Howard/North Bay Area Mgr., Matt Gaskill/California Chain Accounting Mgr., Victor Bacerra/Sales, Marketing Mgr., Barry Siegel/Area Sales Mgr., Don Barkley/Master Brewer, John Scahill/Project, Maintenance Mgr., Don Tubbs/Brewing Supervisor, Nigel Swinney/Packaging Supervisor, Sharon Cline/Sales Coordinator, A, C Receivables, Carlos Swinney/System Administrator - Webmaster *(21 Officers included in Index)*

Directors: Yashpal Singh/Dir., CEO, Pres., Vijay Mallya/Chmn., Scott R. Heldfond/Dir., Michael H. Laybourn/Dir., Jerome G. Merchant/47/Dir., Sury R. Palamand/Dir., Kent D. Price/Dir., Mahadevan Narayanan/Dir., CFO, Sec.

Owners: Scott R. Heldfond, H. Michael Laybourn/2.70%, Inversiones Mirabel S.A., Insiders, Sury Rao Palamand, Insiders/2.70%, Kent D. Price, United Breweries (Holdings) Limited., United Breweries of America, Inc., Jerome G. Merchant, Vijay Mallya, H. Michael Laybourn

Financial Data: **Fiscal Year End:**12/31 **Latest Annual Data:** 12/31/2006

Year	Sales	Net Income
2006	$32,275,000	-$1,431,000
2005	$31,292,000	-$1,315,000
2004	$31,506,000	-$469,000

Curr. Assets:	$10,250,000	**Curr. Liab.:**	$12,933,000		
Plant, Equip.:	$13,446,000	**Total Liab.:**	$20,546,000	**Indic. Yr. Divd.:**	NA
Total Assets:	$24,052,000	**Net Worth:**	$3,506,000	**Debt/ Equity:**	2.0603

Mentor Corp Minn

201 Mentor Dr, Santa Barbara, CA, 93111; ***PH:*** 1-805-879-6000; ***http://*** www.mentorcorp.com

General - Incorporation .... MN
Employees 950
Auditor .... Ernst & Young LLP
Stk Agt...... American Stock Transfer & Trust Co.
Counsel............ Brobeck, Phleger & Harrison
DUNS No. 04-671-2931

Stock- Price on:12/24/2007 .... $42.44
Stock Exchange .... NDQ
Ticker Symbol .... MNTG
Outstanding Shares 39,730,000
E.P.S $5.99
Shareholders .... NA

Business: The group's principal activities are to develop, manufacture and market products for use in aesthetic and general surgery and urology. The group operates in three segments: aesthetic and general surgery, surgical urology and clinical and consumer healthcare. Aesthetic and general surgery products include surgically implantable prostheses for plastic and reconstructive surgery. Surgical urology products include surgically implantable prostheses to treat impotence. Clinical and consumer healthcare include catheters and other products for urinary incontinence and retention. The products are sold in the United States, Canada, western Europe, Japan, and Australia. In fiscal 2003, the group acquired mills biopharmaceuticals inc and assets of urology and ostomy businesses of portex ltd. The group acquired a-life ltd. On 25-Aug-2003, the group acquired a-life limited and inform solutions inc on 29-Oct-2003.

Primary SIC and add'l.: 3845 3842 3841

CIK No: 0000064892

Subsidiaries: Biopolymers (Scotland) Limited, Byron Medical, Inc., Inform Solutions Inc., MDI Company Ltd., Melene Corporation, Mentor Aesthetics B.V., Mentor Benelux B.V., Mentor Biologics, Inc., Mentor Biopharmaceuticals, Inc., Mentor Biopolymers Limited, Mentor Deutschland GmbH, Mentor International Holdings Alpha, Inc., Mentor International Holdings Beta, Inc., Mentor International Holdings Camda, Inc., Mentor International Holdings Delta, Inc. 27 Subsidiaries included in the Index

Officers: Joshua H. Levine/Dir., CEO, Pres., Dir. - Employee/$4,105,939.00, Clarke L. Scherff/VP - Regulatory Compliance, Quality Assurance, Compliance Officer, Loren L. McFarland/CFO, VP, Treasurer/$1,537,741.00, Cathryn S. Ullery/VP - Human Resources, Joseph A. Newcomb/VP, General Counsel, Sec./$1,674,523.00, Edward S. Northup/VP, COO, Thomas Garcia/Assist. Sec.

Directors: Joshua H. Levine/Dir., CEO, Pres., Dir. - Employee, Joseph E. Whitters/50/Chmn., Michael L. Emmons/Dir., Walter W. Faster/Dir., Ronald J. Rossi/Dir., Margaret H. Jordan/Dir., Katherine S. Napier/Dir., Burt Rosen/Dir.

Owners: Joseph A. Newcomb, Katherine S. Napier, Insiders/2.66%, Michael L. Emmons, Capital Research and Management Company/9.23%, Joseph E. Whitters, Neuberger Berman, LLC/10.78%, Joshua H. Levine/1.08%, Loren L. McFarland, Walter W. Faster, Margaret H. Jordan, Ronald J. Rossi, FMR Corp./17.57%

Financial Data: **Fiscal Year End:**03/31 **Latest Annual Data:** 3/31/2007

Year	Sales	Net Income
2007	$301,974,000	$290,614,000
2006	$268,272,000	$62,357,000
2005	$483,397,000	$54,881,000

Curr. Assets:	$637,380,000	**Curr. Liab.:**	$112,731,000	**P/E Ratio:**	7.09
Plant, Equip.:	$34,683,000	**Total Liab.:**	$274,900,000	**Indic. Yr. Divd.:**	$0.800
Total Assets:	$709,768,000	**Net Worth:**	$434,868,000	**Debt/ Equity:**	NA

Mentor Graphics Corp

8005 SW Boeckman Rd., Wilsonville, OR, 97070; ***PH:*** 1-503-685-7000; ***Fax:*** 1-503-685-7704; ***http://*** www.mentor.com

General - Incorporation .... OR
Employees 4,230
Auditor .... KPMG LLP
Stk Agt...... American Stock Transfer & Trust Co.
Counsel............ NA
DUNS No. 03-137-4879

Stock- Price on:12/24/2007 .... $13.39
Stock Exchange .... NDQ
Ticker Symbol .... MENT
Outstanding Shares .... NA
E.P.S $0.33
Shareholders .... NA

Business: The group's principal activity is to develop, manufacture, market and support electronic design automation (eda) products and related services. The products enable engineers to design, analyze, simulate, model, implement and verify the components of electronic systems. The group markets its products and services to communications, computer, consumer electronics, semiconductor, aerospace, networking, multimedia and transportation industries. The products are used in designing automotive electronics, video game consoles, telephone-switching systems, cellular handsets, hubs and routers, personal computers, video conferencing equipment, 3-D graphics boards, digital audio broadcast radios and smart cards. The group sells and licenses its products in North America, Europe, Japan and Pacific Rim. In 2003, the group acquired first earth limited, translogic polska sp z o o, mentor italia s r l and the business and technology of dde-eda a/s.

Primary SIC and add'l.: 7372 7373 7378 3825

CIK No: 0000701811

Subsidiaries: 0-In Design Automation, 0-In Design Automation K.K., Accelerated Technology (PVTD) Ltd., Accelerated Technology Sarl, Anacad Electrical Engineering Ltd., Descon Management GmbH, First Earth, Limited, Harness Software Limited, HSL Holdings Limited, IKOS Systems Limited, Ikos Systems, Inc., Innoveda GmbH, Innoveda Korean Holdings, Inc., Innoveda Limited, Mentor Design Systems Pte. Ltd. 62 Subsidiaries included in the Index

Officers: Walden C. Rhines/Chmn., CEO/$2,952,342.00, Larry Toda/Contact - Scalable Verification, Intellectual Property, James Price/Contact - Cabling, Wire Harness, Nathan James/Contact - ESL, C, Based Design, Design Test, DFT, Paul Hofstadler/VP - Worldwide Consulting, Monte Koller/Contact - Investor Relations, Ry Schwark/Dir. - Public, Investor Relations, Ethan Manuel/Corporate Treasurer, Sonia Harrison/Sr. Public Relations Mgr., Suzanne Graham/Sr. Public Relations Mgr., Sarah Bartash/Public Relations Coordinator, Carole Thurman/Contact - Design, to, Silicon, DFM, Deep Submicron, Analog, Digital, Mixed Signal, Jennifer Tanveer/Contact - Embedded Software, Brian Derrick/VP - Corporate Marketing, Hanns Windele/VP - Europe *(29 Officers included in Index)*

Directors: Walden C. Rhines/Chmn., CEO, Fontaine K. Richardson/Dir., Kevin McDonough/Dir., Patrick B. McManus/Dir., Gregory K. Hinckley/Dirctor, Pres., Exec. VP, COO, d CFO, Peter Bonfield/Dir., Marsha B. Congdon/Dir., James R. Fiebiger/Dir.

Owners: Don L. Maulsby, Insiders/5.60%, Goldman Sachs Asset Management, L.P./10.20%, Joseph D. Sawicki, Walden C. Rhines/2.10%, Barclays Global Investors, N.A./5.50%, Walter H. Potts, Gregory K. Hinckley/1.30%, Renaissance Technologies Corp./5.30%, Private Capital Management, L.P./11.80%, Capital Research and Management Company/5.00%

Financial Data: *Fiscal Year End:* 12/31 *Latest Annual Data:* 12/31/2006

Year	Sales	Net Income
2006	$791,583,000	$27,204,000
2005	$705,249,000	$5,807,000
2004	$710,956,000	-$20,550,000

Curr. Assets:	$435,211,000	*Curr. Liab.:*	$329,008,000	*P/E Ratio:*	40.58
Plant, Equip.:	$86,100,000	*Total Liab.:*	$593,172,000	*Indic. Yr. Divd:*	NA
Total Assets:	$1,126,239,000	*Net Worth:*	$533,067,000	*Debt/ Equity:*	0.4668

Mer Telemanagement Solutions Ltd

12015 115th Ave. NE, Ste. E-215, Kirkland, WA, 98034; *PH:* 1-800-745-8725; *Fax:* 1-425-896-4002; *http://* www.mtsint.com; *Email:* mts@mtsint.com

General - Incorporation	Israel	**Stock** - Price on:12/24/2007	$1.36
Employees	104	Stock Exchange	NDQ
Auditor	Kost Forer Gabbay & Kasierer	Ticker Symbol	MTSX
Stk Agt	American Stock Transfer & Trust Co.	Outstanding Shares	5,770,000
Counsel	Ms. Dora Mer	E.P.S.	-$0.99
DUNS No.	51-464-7239	Shareholders	NA

Business: The groups principle activities include designing, development, marketing and support of comprehensive line of telecommunication management solutions which enable business organizations and other enterprises to effectively manage their communication resources. The group operates from United States.

Primary SIC and add'l.: 7372 7373 3661

CIK No: 0001025561

Subsidiaries: Bohera B.V., Jaraga B.V., Jusan S.A., MER Fifth Avenue Realty Inc., MTS Asia Ltd., MTS IntegraTRAK Inc., TABS Brazil Ltd, Telegent Ltd., Verdura B.V., Voltera Technologies V.O.F.

Officers: Eytan Bar/CEO, Pres., Shlomi Hagai/Corporate COO, Hanoch Magid/GM - MTS Asia, VP - International Sales - Marketing, Europe, Middle East, Africa, Eric Fay/VP - North America - Enterprise, Channel Sales, Marketing, Dani Paroz/VP - Business Development, Strategic Marketing, Omer Gotlieb/VP - Products - Enterprise Solutions Division, Alon Mualem/CFO

Directors: Chaim Mer/60/Chmn., Alon Aginsky/45/Dir., Isaac Ben-Bassat/54/Dir., Orna Berry/58/Dir., Yehoshua Gleitman/58/Dir., Steven J. Glusband/61/Dir., Yaacov Goldman/53/Dir.

Owners: Eytan Bar/3.80%, Chaim Mer/35.05%, Steven J. Glusband, Alon Aginsky, Hanoch Magid, Shlomi Hagai, Isaac Ben-Bassat/11.94%

Financial Data: *Fiscal Year End:* 12/31 *Latest Annual Data:* 12/31/2006

Year	Sales	Net Income
2006	$10,484,000	-$2,246,000
2005	$11,563,000	-$4,216,000
2004	$9,413,000	-$4,127,000

Curr. Assets:	$5,169,000	*Curr. Liab.:*	$4,983,000		
Plant, Equip.:	$439,000	*Total Liab.:*	$6,512,000	*Indic. Yr. Divd:*	NA
Total Assets:	$14,054,000	*Net Worth:*	$7,542,000	*Debt/ Equity:*	NA

Mera Pharmaceuticals Inc

73-4460 Queen Ka'ahumanu Hwy., Ste. 110, Kailua-Kona, HI, 96740; *PH:* 1-808-326-9301; *Fax:* 1-808-326-9401; *http://* www.merapharma.com; *Email:* info@merapharma.com

General - Incorporation	DE	**Stock** - Price on:12/24/2007	$0.007
Employees	5	Stock Exchange	OTC
Auditor	Buttke, Bersch & Wanzek P.C	Ticker Symbol	MRPI
Stk Agt	American Securities T & T Inc.	Outstanding Shares	510,370,000
Counsel	NA	E.P.S.	-$0.001
DUNS No.	94-133-5549	Shareholders	NA

Business: The group's principal activities are to develop and commercialize natural products from microalgae using the large-scale photobioreactor technology known as mera growth module (mgm). The group uses its photobioreactor technology in the production and marketing of its first commercial product, astafactor(R), a nutraceutical and source of natural astaxanthin. The microalgae are a group of over 30,000 species of microscopic plants that have a wide range of physiological and biochemical characteristics. The microalgae are known to contain valuable substances that have existing and potential commercial applications in fields such as animal and human nutrition, food colorings, cosmetics, diagnostic products, pharmaceuticals, research grade chemicals, pigments and dyes. The group operates only in the United States.

Primary SIC and add'l.: 8731 2834 8999

CIK No: 0000837490

Officers: Gregory Kowal/Dir., CEO, Daniel Beharry/55/Pres. - Research Division, Kenneth Crowder/69/Dir., COO - Consumer Products Division, Anthony Applebaum/Principal Financial, Accounting Officer, Sonolynne Flores/VP, GM - Operations, Production Facility, Melanie Kelekolio/Research Mgr.

Directors: Gregory Kowal/Dir., CEO, Kenneth Crowder/69/Dir., COO - Consumer Products Division

Owners: Daniel P. Beharry, Kenneth Crowder/1.27%, Gregory F. Kowal/8.12%

Financial Data: *Fiscal Year End:* 10/31 *Latest Annual Data:* 10/31/2006

Year	Sales	Net Income
2006	$387,000	-$508,000
2005	$388,000	-$1,306,000
2004	$910,000	-$1,105,000

Curr. Assets:	$42,000	*Curr. Liab.:*	$438,000		
Plant, Equip.:	$2,372,000	*Total Liab.:*	$438,000	*Indic. Yr. Divd:*	NA
Total Assets:	$2,433,000	*Net Worth:*	$1,995,000	*Debt/ Equity:*	NA

Mercantile Bancorp Inc

440 Maine St., Quincy, IL, 62301; *PH:* 1-217-223-7300; *Fax:* 1-217-223-7340; *http://* www.mercbanx.com; *Email:* info@mercbanx.com

General - Incorporation	DE	**Stock** - Price on:12/24/2007	$22.5
Employees	358	Stock Exchange	AMEX
Auditor	BKD LLP	Ticker Symbol	MBR
Stk Agt	Illinois Stock Transfer Co.	Outstanding Shares	5,830,000
Counsel	NA	E.P.S.	$1.75
DUNS No.	NA	Shareholders	NA

Business: The group's principle activity is to bring together the resources of proven community banks in order to provide its markets the very best financial products, services, and technologies combined with superior community bank service. The group is a diversified financial services company engaged in retail, commercial, and agricultural banking serving all personal, business, and civic financial needs. The group's affiliate banks collectively offer everything from a full line of FDIC-insured deposit services including checking accounts, savings accounts, money market accounts, certificates of deposit, and individual retirement accounts, to a complete line of lending services: consumer loans, credit cards, mortgage loans, home equity lines of credit, and commercial and agricultural loans and lines of credit. Additional services include asset management services: trusts, estate planning, investment services and farm management. The group operates from United States.

Primary SIC and add'l.: 6021

CIK No: 0001289701

Subsidiaries: bank holding company, Heartland Bank

Officers: Ted T. Awerkamp/Dir., CEO, Pres., Michael P. McGrath/Exec. VP, Treasurer, Sec., CFO, Daniel J. Cook/CIO, Exec. VP

Directors: Ted T. Awerkamp/Dir., CEO, Pres., Dan S. Dugan/Chmn., William G. Keller/Dir., Frank H. Musholt/Dir., Walter D. Stevenson/Dir., Michael J. Foster/Dir., Dennis M. Prock/Dir., James W. Tracy/Dir.

Owners: Mercantile Trust & Savings Bank/6.68%, Michael J. Foster, Dan S. Dugan, Insiders/10.92%, Ted T. Awerkamp, Daniel J. Cook, Michael P. McGrath, William G. Keller, Dennis M. Prock/6.32%, Dean R. Phillips/15.04%, Frank H. Musholt

Financial Data: *Fiscal Year End:* 12/31 *Latest Annual Data:* 12/31/2006

Year	Sales	Net Income
2006	$90,080,000	$10,319,000
2005	$68,327,000	$9,504,000
2004	$57,647,000	$8,318,000

Curr. Assets:	$109,424,000	*Curr. Liab.:*	$1,199,191,000	*P/E Ratio:*	12.86
Plant, Equip.:	$25,984,000	*Total Liab.:*	$1,322,169,000	*Indic. Yr. Divd:*	$0.360
Total Assets:	$1,422,827,000	*Net Worth:*	$100,658,000	*Debt/ Equity:*	1.0232

Mercantile Bank Corp

310 Leonard St. NW, Grand Rapids, MI, 49504; *PH:* 1-616-406-3000; *http://* www.mercbank.com

General - Incorporation	MI	**Stock** - Price on:12/24/2007	$28.12
Employees	256	Stock Exchange	NDQ
Auditor	Crowe Chizek & Co. LLC	Ticker Symbol	MBWM
Stk Agt	Hub International	Outstanding Shares	8,480,000
Counsel	Dickinson, Wright	E.P.S.	$1.92
DUNS No.	36-429-3415	Shareholders	NA

Business: The group's principal activity is to provide commercial and retail banking services through its subsidiaries. The services are provided primarily to small to medium-sized businesses based in and around grand rapids. The group accepts demand deposits, checking accounts, savings deposits, money market accounts, certificates of deposits and time deposits. It lends secured and unsecured commercial loans, construction loans, residential mortgage loans, commercial mortgage loans, residential real estate loans, home equity loans, construction loans and consumer loans. Also owns four automated teller machines that participate in the mac, nyce and plus regional network systems, as well as other ATM networks throughout the country. The other services provided by the group are financial planning, retail brokerage, equity research, insurance and annuities, retirement planning, trust services and estate planning to its customers.

Primary SIC and add'l.: 6022 6712

CIK No: 0001042729

Subsidiaries: Mercantile Bank Capital Trust I, Mercantile Bank Mortgage Company, LLC, Mercantile Bank of Michigan, Mercantile Bank Real Estate Co., LLC, Mercantile Insurance Center, Inc, Michigan banking corporation, Michigan limited liability company

Officers: Gerald Johnson/61/Chmn., CEO/$543,899.00, Renee Frazier/Branch Mgr. - Alpine, Erica Morris/Assist. Branch Mgr. - Alpine, Melanie Salamone/Branch Mgr. - Downtown, Reyna Van Kuiken/Assist. Branch Mgr. - Downtown, Dan Poskey/Assist. Branch Mgr. - Downtown, Maurice Groce/Branch Mgr. - Kentwood, Shelvy Griffin/Assist. Branch Mgr. - Kentwood, Cathy Calveneau/Branch Mgr. - Knapp's Corner, Amy Derry/Assist. Branch Mgr. - Knapp's Corner, Cris Hugmeyer/Branch Mgr. - Wyoming, Wanda Martinez/Assist. Branch Mgr. - Wyoming, Claire Rotman/Branch Mgr. - Holland, Howard Haas/City Pres. - Lansing, Cassy Puskala/Branch Mgr. - Lansing *(25 Officers included in Index)*

Directors: Gerald Johnson/61/Chmn., CEO, Doyle Hayes/Dir., Susan Jones/Dir., Donald Williams/Dir., Lawrence Larsen/Dir., John Gill/Dir., Peter Cordes/Dir., Edward Clark/Dir., Merle Prins/Dir., David Cassard/Dir., Dale Visser/Dir.

Owners: Robert B. Kaminski, Calvin D. Murdock, John C. Gill, Peter A. Cordes, David M. Hecht/1.50%, Michael H. Price, Insiders/10.20%, Edward J. Clark, Charles E. Christmas, Susan K. Jones, Gerald R. Johnson/1.90%, Betty S. Burton, JPMorgan Chase& Co/5.00%, Dale J. Visser/3.20%, Donald Williams *(19 Owners included in Index)*

Financial Data: *Fiscal Year End:* 12/31 *Latest Annual Data:* 12/31/2006

Year	Sales	Net Income
2006	$142,521,000	$19,847,000
2005	$107,791,000	$17,901,000
2004	$73,324,000	$13,721,000

Curr. Assets:	$61,667,000	*Curr. Liab.:*	$1,859,047,000	*P/E Ratio:*	14.65
Plant, Equip.:	$33,539,000	*Total Liab.:*	$1,895,353,000	*Indic. Yr. Divd:*	$0.560
Total Assets:	$2,067,268,000	*Net Worth:*	$171,915,000	*Debt/ Equity:*	0.2078

Mercer Insurance Group Inc

10 N Hwy. 31, Pennington, NJ, 08534; *PH:* 1-609-737-0426; *Fax:* 1-609-737-8719; *http://* www.franklininsurance.com; *Email:* contact@mercerins.com

General - Incorporation	PA
Employees	214
Auditor	KPMG LLP
Stk Agt.	Registrar & Transfer Co
Counsel	NA
DUNS No.	NA

Stock - Price on:12/24/2007	$19.98
Stock Exchange	NDQ
Ticker Symbol	NA
Outstanding Shares	6,560,000
E.P.S.	$2.26
Shareholders	NA

Business: The group's principal activity is to provide a wide array of property and casualty insurance products to consumers, small and medium-sized businesses throughout New Jersey and Pennsylvania. The group operates in three segments: commercial lines insurance, personal lines insurance and investment function. The insurance products include homeowners, commercial multi-peril, other liability, personal automobile, workers compensation, fire and inland marine and commercial automobile coverages. The products are marketed through a network of over 300 independent producers in New Jersey and Pennsylvania. In 2003, the group acquired franklin holding company, inc.

Primary SIC and add'l.: 6331

CIK No: 0001050690

Subsidiaries: BICUS Services Corporation, Financial Pacific Insurance Company, Franklin Insurance Company, Mercer Insurance Company, Mercer Insurance Company of New Jersey, Inc., Queenstown Holding Company, Inc.

Officers: Andrew R. Speaker/45/Dir., CEO, Pres./$1,140,504.00, Roland D. Boehm/70/Dir. - Self, Employed Business Consultant, David B. Merclean/57/Sr. VP, CFO/$500,793.00, Paul D. Ehrhardt/50/Corp. Sec./$650,226.00, Debbie Johnstone/Marketing Mgr.

Directors: Andrew R. Speaker/45/Dir., CEO, Pres., William C. Hart/74/Dir., Roland D. Boehm/70/Dir. - Self, Employed Business Consultant, Samuel J. Malizia/53/Dir., George T. Hornyak/58/Dir., Thomas H. Davis/59/Dir., William V.R. Fogler/63/Dir., Richard G. Van Noy/Dir.

Owners: Insiders/15.40%, Richard G. Van Noy, Andrew R. Speaker/2.50%, William V. R. Fogler, William C. Hart, Samuel J. Malizia, Thomas H. Davis/5.60%, Dimensional Fund Advisors LP/7.70%, Paul D. Ehrhardt/1.00%, Mercer Insurance Group, Inc./9.70%, David B. Merclean, Roland D. Boehm, Richard U. Niedt, George T. Hornyak/2.80%

Financial Data: Fiscal Year End:12/31   Latest Annual Data: 12/31/2006

Year	Sales		Net Income
2006	$149,929,000		$10,635,000
2005	$81,266,000		$7,020,000
2004	$59,467,000		$3,264,000
Curr. Assets:	$167,710,000	Curr. Liab.: $38,030,000	P/E Ratio: 11.89
Plant, Equip.:	$11,936,000	Total Liab.: $391,128,000	Indic. Yr. Divd.: $0.200
Total Assets:	$506,967,000	Net Worth: $115,839,000	Debt/Equity: 0.1557

Mercer International Inc

14900 Interurban Ave. S, Ste 282, Seattle, WA, 98168; **PH:** 1-206-674-4639; **http://** www.mercerinternational.com; **Email:** info@mercerint.com

General - Incorporation	WA
Employees	1,469
Auditor	Deloitte & Touche LLP
Stk Agt.	Mellon Investor Srvcs LLC
Counsel	Sangra Moller LLP
DUNS No.	NA

Stock - Price on:12/24/2007	$9.95
Stock Exchange	NDQ
Ticker Symbol	MERC
Outstanding Shares	36,250,000
E.P.S.	$1.33
Shareholders	NA

Business: The group's principal activity is to produce and market pulp and paper products. The group is based in zurich, Switzerland has its operations primarily in Germany. The group's pulp operations are conducted through spezialpapierfabrik blankenstein gmbh and its paper operations are conducted through dresden papier gmbh and its affiliates, all of which are wholly-owned subsidiaries of the group. It manufactures and markets softwood kraft pulp and two primary classes of paper products. The group's products are produced from both virgin fibre, being wood chips, pulpwood and chemical woodfree pulp, and recycled fibre, being waste paper. The manufacturing plants are located in Germany in the states of saxony and thuringia and in graubunden, Switzerland.

Primary SIC and add'l.: 4731 2621 2611

CIK No: 0000075659

Subsidiaries: Dresden Papier GmbH, Zellstoff Celgar Limited, Zellstoff Stendal GmbH, Zellstoff-und Papierfabrik Rosenthal GmbH & Co. KG

Officers: Jimmy S.H Lee/Chmn., CEO, Trustee, Pres., David M. Gandossi/CFO, Exec. VP, Sec., Eric Lauritzen/Dir., Trustee, Independent Consultant, David Cooper/VP - Sales, Marketing Europe, Eric Heine/VP - Sales, Marketing North America, Asia, Werner Stuber/VP - Technical Support, Pulp Operations, Leonhard Nossol/MD, Claes-Inge Isacson/COO, David Ure/VP, Controller, Genevieve Stannus/Treasurer, Jochen Riepl/MD - Stendal, Alan Hitzroth/General Mill Mgr. - Celgar, Eric Boyriven/Contact - Investor, Media, Wolfram Ridder/VP - Business Development

Directors: Jimmy S.H Lee/Chmn., CEO, Trustee, Pres., Eric Lauritzen/Dir., Trustee, Independent Consultant, Guy W. Adams/Dir., Kenneth A. Shields/Dir., Graeme A. Witts/Dir., Trustee, William D. McCartney/Dir., Trustee, George Malpass/Dir.

Financial Data: Fiscal Year End:12/31   Latest Annual Data: 12/31/2006

Year	Sales		Net Income
2006	$823,837,000		$83,456,000
2005	$608,673,000		-$138,748,000
Curr. Assets:	$292,843,000	Curr. Liab.: $158,439,000	P/E Ratio: 5.96
Plant, Equip.:	$1,283,520,000	Total Liab.: $1,430,932,000	Indic. Yr. Divd.: NA
Total Assets:	$1,719,815,000	Net Worth: $288,883,000	Debt/Equity: NA

Merchants & Manufacturers Bancorp Inc

5445 S Westridge Dr., New Berlin, WI, 53151; **PH:** 1-262-827-6700; **Fax:** 1-262-796-8158; **http://** www.mmbancorp.com; **Email:** mmbancorpir@cfg-mail.com

General - Incorporation	WI
Employees	454
Auditor	McGladrey & Pullen LLP
Stk Agt.	American Stock Transfer & Trust Co.
Counsel	NA
DUNS No.	11-411-0992

Stock - Price on:12/24/2007	$26.5
Stock Exchange	OTC
Ticker Symbol	MMBI
Outstanding Shares	3,660,000
E.P.S.	$1.15
Shareholders	NA

Business: The group provides community-oriented, commercial and retail banking services to individuals and small to mid-size businesses. The group also redevelops and rejuvenates certain areas located on the near south side of milwaukee. The services offered include acceptance of demand, savings and time deposits, including regular checking, now accounts, money market, certificates of deposit, individual retirement and club accounts. The lending activities of the group include secured and unsecured

commercial loans, mortgage loans, construction and consumer term loans. The operations are conducted through 34 banking facilities in Wisconsin, Iowa and Minnesota. In 2003, the group acquired integrated financial services inc., keith c. Winters & associates ltd and reedsburg bancorporation inc and on 12-Aug -2004, random lake bancorp limited.

Primary SIC and add'l.: 6022 6712

CIK No: 0000753682

Subsidiaries: CBOC Investments, Inc., Community Bank Financial, Community Financial Group Financial Services, Inc., Community Financial Group Mortgage, Inc., Community Financial Group, Inc., Community Financial Services, LLC., Fortress Bank, Fortress Bank Minnesota, Fortress Bank of Cresco, Franklin State Bank, Grafton State Bank, GSB Investments, Inc., Keith C. Winters & Associates, LTD., Lincoln Neighborhood Redevelopment Corporation, Lincoln State Bank 23 Subsidiaries included in the Index

Officers: Michael J. Murry/Chmn., CEO/$359,639.00, James F. Bomberg/EPres., Community Financial Group/$302,050.00, James C. Mroczkowski/COO, Exec. VP, Conrad C. Kaminski/73/Pres./$252,880.00, John M. Krawczyk/Exec. VP, General Counsel, Edward H. Cichurski/Pres. - CFG Financial Services, Inc/$201,520.00, Frederick R. Klug/CFO, Exec. VP - Investor Relations Contact/$176,800.00, Charles P. Heffernan/50/COO, Exec. VP

Directors: Michael J. Murry/Chmn., CEO, Thomas J. Sheehan/Vice Chmn., Michael J. Bartels/Dir., Nicholas S. Logarakis/Dir., James A. Sass/Dir., Rodney T. Goodell/Dir., William L. Adamany/Dir., Steven R. Blakeslee/Dir., Donald A. Zellmer/Dir., Joel Read/Dir., Richard C. Bemis/Dir., Sister Joel Read/82/Dir.

Owners: Rodney Goodell/1.60%, Tontine Financial Partners, L.P./9.00%, Thomas Sheehan, Steven Blakeslee, James Sass, Conrad Kaminski/1.40%, Michael Murry, Edward Cichurski, Richard C. Bemis, Insiders/13.40%, Nicholas Logarakis, James Bomberg, Donald Zellmer, Frederick Klug, Michael J. Bartels/1.20% (16 Owners included in Index)

Financial Data: Fiscal Year End:12/31   Latest Annual Data: 12/31/2006

Year	Sales		Net Income
2006	$105,661,000		$3,996,000
2005	$91,457,000		$5,098,000
2004	$73,525,000		$4,002,000
Curr. Assets:	$51,226,000	Curr. Liab.: $1,229,412,000	P/E Ratio: 23.04
Plant, Equip.:	$35,197,000	Total Liab.: $1,411,643,000	Indic. Yr. Divd.: $0.720
Total Assets:	$1,505,940,000	Net Worth: $94,297,000	Debt/Equity: 1.8718

Merchants Bancshares Inc

275 Kennedy Dr., South Burlington, VT, 05403; **PH:** 1-802-658-3400; **Fax:** 1-802-865-1874; **http://** www.mbvt.com

General - Incorporation	DE
Employees	259
Auditor	KPMG LLP
Stk Agt.	American Stock Transfer & Trust Co.
Counsel	NA
DUNS No.	14-451-1839

Stock - Price on:12/24/2007	$22.7845
Stock Exchange	NDQ
Ticker Symbol	MBVT
Outstanding Shares	6,180,000
E.P.S.	$1.74
Shareholders	NA

Business: The group's principal activities are to provide a full range of deposit, loan, cash management and trust services through 35 branch offices and with 41 ATMs in the state of Vermont. The group's retail products include interest bearing and non-interest bearing checking accounts, money market accounts, club accounts and short-term and long-term certificates of deposit. It lends consumer loans, real estate loans and commercial loans. It also provides services such as customary check collection services, wire transfers, safe deposit box rentals, automated teller machine (ATM) cards and services. Credit programs include secured and unsecured installment lending, credit cards, home equity lines of credit and home mortgages.

Primary SIC and add'l.: 6712 6022

CIK No: 0000726517

Subsidiaries: MBVT Statutory Trust I, Merchants Bank, Merchants Properties, Inc., Merchants Trust Company

Officers: Michael R. Tuttle/52/Dir., CEO, Pres./$209,611.00, Thomas R. Havers/Sr. VP - Operating, Administrative Division Mgr. - Merchants Bank/$166,447.00, Thomas S. Leavitt/Exec. VP - Community Banking, Trust, Merchants Bank/$155,953.00, Janet P. Spitler/Treasurer, CFO, Sr. VP - Merchants Bank/$156,295.00, Zoe P. Erdman/Sr. VP, Credit Division Mgr. - Merchants Bank, Geoffrey R. Hesslink/Sr. VP - Sr. Lender, Merchants Bank/$185,384.00

Directors: Michael R. Tuttle/52/Dir., CEO, Pres., Raymond C. Pecor/69/Chmn., Patrick S. Robins/69/Dir., Peter A. Bouyea/60/Dir., Charles A. Davis/58/Dir., Jeffrey L. Davis/55/Dir., Bruce M. Lisman/61/Dir., Michael G. Furlong/57/Dir., Robert A. Skiff/66/Dir., Lorilee A. Lawton/61/Dir., John A. Kane/55/Dir.

Owners: Janet P. Spitler/6.00%, Carole A. Ziter, Patrick S. Robins/1.00%, Insiders/33.00%, Bruce M. Lisman, Charles A. Davis/7.00%, Robert A. Skiff, Geoffrey R. Hesslink/7.00%, Michael G. Furlong, Michael R. Tuttle/1.00%, Jeffrey L. Davis/1.00%, Zoe P. Erdman, Thomas S. Leavitt/1.00%, Scott F. Boardman, Merchants Bank 401/8.00% (22 Owners included in Index)

Financial Data: Fiscal Year End:12/31   Latest Annual Data: 12/31/2006

Year	Sales		Net Income
2006	$71,508,000		$10,871,000
2005	$62,792,000		$11,902,000
2004	$56,418,000		$11,933,000
Curr. Assets:	$78,706,000	Curr. Liab.: $967,899,000	P/E Ratio: 13.27
Plant, Equip.:	$12,538,000	Total Liab.: $1,067,261,000	Indic. Yr. Divd.: $1.120
Total Assets:	$1,136,958,000	Net Worth: $69,697,000	Debt/Equity: NA

Merchants Group Inc

250 Main St. , Buffalo, NY, 14202; **PH:** 1-716-849-3333; **http://** www.merchantsgroup.com

General - Incorporation	DE
Employees	NA
Auditor	PricewaterhouseCoopers LLP
Stk Agt.	Continental Stock Transfer & Trust Co
Counsel	Jaeckle Fleischmann & Mugel
DUNS No.	13-168-7519

Stock - Price on:12/24/2007	NA
Stock Exchange	NDQ
Ticker Symbol	MGP
Outstanding Shares	NA
E.P.S.	NA
Shareholders	NA

Business: The group's principal activity is to provide property and casualty insurance to individuals and small to medium sized business in the northeastern United States. The group operates through its wholly owned subsidiary merchants insurance company. The group is licensed to underwrite major lines

of property and casualty insurance. The products are marketed through approximately 485 independent agents. The commercial line of business is primarily retail and mercantile in nature and generally consists of small to medium sized, low hazard commercial risks. The personal line of business offers personal automobile and homeowners' insurance to preferred risk individuals.

Primary SIC and add'l.: 6719 6331

CIK No: 0000803027

Subsidiaries: Merchants Insurance Company of New Hampshire, Inc.

Officers: Robert M. Zak/50/CEO, COO, Sr. VP, Kenneth J. Wilson/60/CFO, VP, Treasurer, Sec., Samuel Guarnieri/Regional Mgr. - Midlantic Strategic Business Center, Charlie Makey/Regional Mgr. - Central States Strategic Business Center, Marge Kafka/VP - Corporate Services, Tina Schaedler/Mgr. - Western Regional, Cammy Belser/Regional Mgr. - Eastern Strategic Business Center, Tom Wallace/Regional Mgr. - Hudson Valley Strategic Business Center, Edward M. Murphy/57/VP, Chief Investment Officer, Assist. Sec.

Directors: Thomas E. Kahn/55/Chmn., Henry P. Semmelhack/71/Dir., Andrew A. Alberti/62/Dir., Frank J. Colantuono/59/Dir., Brent D. Baird/69/Dir.

Owners: Henry P. Semmelhack, Kahn Brothers & Co., Inc./5.20%, John D. Weil/11.90%, Brent D. Baird/10.80%, Brent D. Baird and others/10.80%, Kenneth J. Wilson, Insiders/12.00%, Franklin Resources, Inc./7.30%, Merchants Mutual Insurance Company/11.90%, Dimensional Fund Advisors, Inc./5.20%, Robert M. Zak/1.00%, Frank J. Colantuono

Merci Inc

645 5 St. Ste. 403, New York, NY, 10022;

General - Incorporation	DE	***Stock***- Price on:12/24/2007	NA
Employees	NA	Stock Exchange	NA
Auditor	Child, Sullivan & Co	Ticker Symbol	NA
Stk Agt	Manhattan Transfer Registrar Co	Outstanding Shares	NA
Counsel	NA	E.P.S.	NA
DUNS No.	NA	Shareholders	NA

Business: The groups principle activity is to provide auto cars. The group markets Toyota, Honda, and Suzuki manufacturers cars. The group operates from United States.

Primary SIC and add'l.: 9995

CIK No: 0001112551

Merck & Co Inc

1 Merck Dr., Whitehouse Station, NJ, 08889; ***PH:*** 1-908-423-1000; ***Fax:*** 1-908-735-1253; ***http://*** www.merck.com

General - Incorporation	NJ	***Stock***- Price on:12/24/2007	$49.3
Employees	60,000	Stock Exchange	NYSE
Auditor	Jewett, Schwartz, Wolfe & Assoc.	Ticker Symbol	MRK
Stk Agt	Wells Fargo Bank Minnesota N.A	Outstanding Shares	2,170,000,000
Counsel	NA	E.P.S.	$2.46
DUNS No.	00-131-7064	Shareholders	NA

Business: The groups principle activities include discovering, developing, manufactureing and marketing vaccines and medicines to address unmet medical needs. The group's products include Aldomet, Aldoril and Aramine injection. The group operates from United States.

Primary SIC and add'l.: 2834

CIK No: 0000064978

Subsidiaries: AMRAD Pharmaceuticals Pty. Ltd., Aton Pharma, Inc., Banyu Pharmaceutical Company, Ltd., Blue Jay Investments C.V., BRC Ltd, Charles E. Frosst (U.K.) Limited, Chibret A/S, Chibret Pharmazeutische GmbH, China-MSD HIV/AIDS Public Private Partnership, Inc., Chippewa Holdings LLC, Cloverleaf International Holdings S.A., CM Delaware LLC, Comsort, Inc., Coophavet S.A.S. 1, Coordinated Patient Care Scandinavia AS 230 Subsidiaries included in the Index

Officers: Richard T. Clark/Chmn., CEO, Pres./$10,236,740.00, Raymond V. Gilmartin/63/Chmn., CEO, Pres., Mirian Graddick-Weir/Sr. VP - Human Resources, Peter H. Loescher/Pres. - Global Human Health/$3,651,597.00, Chris J. Scalet/Sr. VP - Global Process, Services, CIO, Robert H. Boisclair/56/Acting Pres. - Merck Manufacturing Division, J. Saltzman/Sr. Dir. - Applied Computer Sciences, Mathematics, J. Pearson/Sr. Dir. - Scientific Staff, Epidemiology, N. Santanello/Exec. Dir. - Epidemiology, P. Dephillips/Assoc. Dir. - Bioprocess Research, Development, J. Gimenez/Dir. - Bioprocess Research, Development, A. Howard/Distinguished Sr. Investigator, Metabolic Disorders, Diabetes, M. Kloss/Sr. Dir. - Regulatory Affairs, J. Lin/Exec. Dir. - Drug Metabolism, K. Petrukhin/Sr. Research Fellow, Project Leader - Ophthalmic Genetics *(54 Officers included in Index)*

Directors: Richard T. Clark/Chmn., CEO, Pres., Raymond V. Gilmartin/63/Chmn., CEO, Pres., Thomas E. Shenk/Dir., Anne M. Tatlock/Dir., Samuel O. Thier/Dir., Wendell P. Weeks/Dir., Peter C. Wendell/Dir., Steven F. Goldstone/Dir., Johnnetta B. Cole/Dir., William B. Harrison/Dir., William G. Bowen/Dir., William N. Kelley/Dir., Rochelle B. Lazarus/Dir.

Owners: Rochelle B. Lazarus, Capital Research/5.40%, Fidelity/5.30%, Per Wold-Olsen, Richard T. Clark, Samuel O. Thier, William G. Bowen, Peter C. Wendell, Johnnetta B. Cole, Lawrence A. Bossidy, Insiders, Judy C. Lewent, William N. Kelley, Thomas E. Shenk, David W. Anstice *(19 Owners included in Index)*

Financial Data: ***Fiscal Year End:***12/31 ***Latest Annual Data:*** 12/31/2006

Year	*Sales*	*Net Income*
2006	$22,636,000,000	$4,433,800,000
2005	$22,011,900,000	$4,631,300,000
2004	$22,938,600,000	$5,813,400,000

Curr. Assets:	$15,230,200,000	***Curr. Liab.:***	$12,722,700,000	***P/E Ratio:***	23.36
Plant, Equip.:	$13,194,100,000	***Total Liab.:***	$24,604,000,000	***Indic. Yr. Divd.:***	$1.520
Total Assets:	$44,569,800,000	***Net Worth:***	$17,559,700,000	***Debt/ Equity:***	NA

Mercury Computer Systems Inc

199 Riverneck Rd., Chelmsford, MA, 01824; ***PH:*** 1-978-256-1300; ***Fax:*** 1-978-256-3599; ***http://*** www.mc.com

General - Incorporation	MA	***Stock***- Price on:12/24/2007	$12.21
Employees	836	Stock Exchange	NDQ
Auditor	KPMG LLP	Ticker Symbol	MRGE
Stk Agt	EquiServe Trust Co N.A	Outstanding Shares	22,220,000
Counsel	Hitchins, Wheeler & Dittmar	E.P.S.	-$1.78
DUNS No.	10-676-0549	Shareholders	NA

Business: The group's principal activities are to design, manufacture and market real-time digital signal and image processing computer systems. The group operates in defense electronics, medical imaging and OEM solution segments. The products under defense electronics segment are digital signal and image processing computer systems that are embedded into air, sea and land-based platforms for processing radar, sonar and sigint data. The products under medical imaging segment are mri, digital X-ray, pet, single photon emission computed tomography and ultrasound devices. Oem segment products are the semiconductors imaging equipment and the high-end airport baggage scanning equipment. The group's software products include mc/os multicomputing environment and scientific algorithm library. On 07-May-2004, the group acquired tgs group.

Primary SIC and add'l.: 3571 3674 4899 3845

CIK No: 0001049521

Subsidiaries: 191 Riverneck, LLC, 199 Riverneck, LLC, Advanced Radio Corporation, Echotek Corporation, Mercury Computer International Sales LLC, Mercury Computer Securities Corporation, Mercury Computer System SAS, Mercury Computer Systems GmbH (Berlin), Mercury Computer Systems GmbH (Fuerth), Mercury Computer Systems Ltd., Mercury Computer Systems N.V., Mercury Computer Systems SAS, Mercury Modular Products and Services, Inc., Nihon Mercury Computer Systems K.K., Radin GmbH 17 Subsidiaries included in the Index

Officers: James R. Bertelli/Chmn., Co - Founder, CEO, Pres., Russell K. Johnsen/Dir., Pres., Anthony J. Medaglia/Sec., Terry M. Ryan/Sr. VP, GM - Federal Government Businesses, Didier M.C. Thibaud/Sr. VP - Advanced Computing Solutions, Mark F. Skalabrin/Sr. VP - Advanced Computing Solutions, Joel B. Radford/VP - Strategic Marketing, Alliances, Craig Lund/CTO, VP, Albert P. Belle Isle/Dir., Independent Investor, Douglas F. Flood/VP - Corporate Development, Alex N. Braverman/VP, Controller, Chief Accounting Officer, Craig Barrows/VP, General Counsel, Craig A. Saline/Sr. VP - Organization Development, Human Resources, Robert E. Hult/Sr. VP, CFO

Directors: James R. Bertelli/Chmn., Co - Founder, CEO, Pres., George W. Chamillard/Dir., Russell K. Johnsen/Dir., Pres., Sherman N. Mullin/Dir., Vincent Vitto/Dir., Richard P. Wishner/Dir., Gordon B. Baty/Dir., Lee C. Steele/Dir., Albert P. Belle Isle/Dir., Independent Investor

Owners: Robert E. Hult, Gordon B. Baty, Russell K. Johnsen, Renaissance Technologies Corp./5.30%, James R. Bertelli/5.10%, Richard P. Wishner, Marcelo G. Lima, George W. Chamillard, Mark F. Skalabrin, Lee C. Steele, Wells Fargo& Company/8.60%, Vincent Vitto, Barrow, Hanley, Mewhinney& Strauss, Inc./8.20%, Insiders/10.20%, Royce& Associates, LLC/9.90% *(19 Owners included in Index)*

Financial Data: ***Fiscal Year End:***06/30 ***Latest Annual Data:*** 6/30/2006

Year	*Sales*	*Net Income*
2006	$236,117,000	-$16,168,000
2005	$250,172,000	$30,186,000
2004	$185,595,000	$22,885,000

Curr. Assets:	$201,149,000	***Curr. Liab.:***	$57,736,000		
Plant, Equip.:	$32,091,000	***Total Liab.:***	$194,457,000	***Indic. Yr. Divd.:***	NA
Total Assets:	$386,446,000	***Net Worth:***	$191,989,000	***Debt/ Equity:***	0.6742

Mercury General Corp

4484 Wilshire Blvd., Los Angeles, CA, 90010; ***PH:*** 1-323-937-1060; ***Fax:*** 1-323-857-7116; ***http://*** www.mercuryinsurance.com

General - Incorporation	CA	***Stock***- Price on:12/24/2007	$54.08
Employees	5,100	Stock Exchange	NYSE
Auditor	KPMG LLP	Ticker Symbol	MCY
Stk Agt	Bank of New York	Outstanding Shares	54,680,000
Counsel	Latham & Watkins	E.P.S.	$4.44
DUNS No.	07-530-0004	Shareholders	NA

Business: The groups principle activity is writing automobile insurances. The groups coverage to automobile policyholders including bodily injury liability, underinsured and uninsured motorist, personal injury protection, property damage liability, comprehensive, collision and other hazards. The group also writes homeowners, mechanical breakdown, commercial and dwelling fire, and commercial property insurances. The group operates from United States.

Primary SIC and add'l.: 6712 6331

CIK No: 0000064996

Subsidiaries: American Mercury Insurance Company (AMI), American Mercury Lloyds Insurance Company (AML), California Automobile Insurance Company (CAIC), Mercury Casualty Company (MCC), Mercury County Mutual Insurance Company (MCM), Mercury Indemnity Company of America (MIDAM), Mercury Indemnity Company of Georgia (MID GA), Mercury Insurance Company (MIC), Mercury Insurance Company of Florida (MIC FL), Mercury Insurance Company of Georgia (MIC GA), Mercury Insurance Company of Illinois (MIC IL), Mercury National Insurance Company (MNIC)

Officers: Gabriel Tirador/43/Dir., CEO, Pres./$1,473,110.00, Theodore R. Stalick/CFO, VP/$596,381.00, Michael D. Curtius/57/Dir. - Exec. Consultant, Joanna Y. Moore/Sr. VP, Chief Claims Officer/$618,734.00, Christopher Graves/VP, Chief Investment Officer/$574,466.00, Judy A. Walters/VP - Corporate Affairs, Sec., Charles Toney/VP, Chief Actuary, Bruce E. Norman/Sr. VP - Marketing, Kenneth G. Kitzmiller/VP - Underwriting, Rick McCathron/36/VP - West Region, Peter Simon/48/Pres., CTO, Kenneth Van Wagner/VP - North East Region, Ronald Deep/VP - South East Region, Randy Farner/CIO, VP

Directors: Gabriel Tirador/43/Dir., CEO, Pres., George Joseph/Chmn., Founder, Richard E. Grayson/78/Dir., Nathan Bessin/82/Dir., Bruce A. Bunner/74/Dir., Charles E. McClung/93/Dir., Donald R. Spuehler/73/Dir., Michael D. Curtius/57/Dir. - Exec. Consultant, Donald P. Newell/70/Dir.

Owners: Donald R. Spuehler, Charles E. McClung, Gloria Joseph/16.80%, Michael D. Curtius, Joanna Y. Moore, Bruce A. Bunner, Theodore Stalick, Nathan Bessin, Donald P. Newell, Christopher Graves, Gabriel Tirador, George Joseph/34.40%, Insiders/34.87%

Financial Data: ***Fiscal Year End:***12/31 ***Latest Annual Data:*** 12/31/2006

Year	*Sales*	*Net Income*
2006	$3,168,743,000	$214,817,000
2005	$2,991,913,000	$253,259,000
2004	$2,668,157,000	$286,208,000

Curr. Assets:	$668,378,000	***Curr. Liab.:***	$155,435,000	***P/E Ratio:***	13.80
Plant, Equip.:	$152,260,000	***Total Liab.:***	$2,576,932,000	***Indic. Yr. Divd.:***	$2.080
Total Assets:	$4,301,062,000	***Net Worth:***	$1,724,130,000	***Debt/ Equity:***	NA

Meredith Corp

1716 Locust St., Des Moines, IA, 50309; ***PH:*** 1-515-284-3000; ***Fax:*** 1-515-284-2700; ***http://*** www.meredith.com

General - Incorporation	IA	**Stock**- Price on:12/24/2007	$63.18
Employees	3,030	Stock Exchange	NYSE
Auditor	KPMG LLP	Ticker Symbol	MDP
Stk Agt	Wells Fargo Bank Minnesota N.A	Outstanding Shares	48,090,000
Counsel	NA	E.P.S	$3.37
DUNS No.	00-527-9138	Shareholders	NA

Business: The group's principle activities are magazine publishing and television broadcasting. The group operates in two segments namely, publishing and broadcasting. The publishing segment includes magazine and book publishing, integrated marketing, interactive media, database-related activities, brand licensing and other related operations. The segment includes 17 magazine brands, approximately 160 special interest publications and 300 books in print. The magazine brands include better homes and gardens, ladies' home journal, country home, traditional home and successful farming. The broadcasting segment includes the operations of 11 network-affiliated television stations. The stations include wgcl-TV, kpho-TV, kptv, kpdx-TV, wfsb-TV, wsmv-TV, kctv and kfxo-TV. In fiscal 2003, the group acquired American baby magazine and related assets from primedia inc. The group's largest source of revenue is magazine and television advertising. The group's total revenue for year 2007 was 1,615.98 millions of USD.

Primary SIC and add'l.: 4833 2721 2731

CIK No: 0000065011

Subsidiaries: Metcare MIS, Inc., Metcare Pharmacy Group, Inc.

Officers: Stephen M. Lacy/Dir., CEO, Pres./$4,775,383.00, Jack Griffin/Pres. - Meredith Publishing Group, Jennifer Harken/Contact - Broadcasting, Amy Nichols/Contact - Book, Steven M. Cappaert/Corporate Controller, Suku V. Radia/CFO, VP, Acting Treasurer/$2,007,057.00, John S. Zieser/Chief Development Officer, General Counsel, Sec./$2,005,498.00, Paul Karpowicz/Pres. - Meredith Broadcasting Group/$2,070,495.00, Mike Lovell/Investor Relations Officer

Directors: Stephen M. Lacy/Dir., CEO, Pres., William T. Kerr/Chmn., James R. Craigie/Dir., Joel W. Johnson/Dir., Robert E. Lee/Dir., Alfred H. Drewes/Dir., David Londoner/Dir., Frederick B. Henry/Dir., Mary Sue Coleman/Dir., Philip A. Marineau/Dir., Mell Meredith D. Frazier/Dir., Herbert M. Baum/Dir.

Owners: E. T. Meredith/24.18%, Insiders/11.62%, John S. Zieser, Katherine C. Meredith/49.29%, Philip A. Marineau, John H. Griffin, Charles D. Peebler, Herbert M. Baum, David J. Londoner, Paul A. Karpowicz, Mary Sue Coleman, Mell Meredith D. Frazier/23.33%, William T. Kerr/2.68%, James R. Craigie, Suku V. Radia *(24 Owners included in Index)*

Financial Data: *Fiscal Year End:*06/30 *Latest Annual Data:* 6/30/2007

Year	Sales	Net Income
2007	$1,615,985,000	$162,346,000
2006	$1,597,564,000	$144,792,000
2005	$1,221,289,000	$129,042,000

Curr. Assets:	$431,520,000	**Curr. Liab.:**	$463,946,000	**P/E Ratio:**	19.56
Plant, Equip.:	$194,798,000	**Total Liab.:**	$1,342,571,000	**Indic. Yr. Divd.:**	$0.740
Total Assets:	$2,040,675,000	**Net Worth:**	$698,104,000	**Debt/ Equity:**	0.5148

Merge Technologies Inc

6737 W Washington St., Ste. 2250, Milwaukee, WI, 53214; ***PH:*** 1-414-977-4000; ***Fax:*** 1-414-977-4200; ***http://*** www.merge.com

General - Incorporation	WI	**Stock**- Price on:12/24/2007	$6.67
Employees	450	Stock Exchange	NYSE
Auditor	KPMG LLP	Ticker Symbol	MRK
Stk Agt	American Stock Transfer & Trust Co.	Outstanding Shares	32,200,000
Counsel	NA	E.P.S	-$1.85
DUNS No.	18-111-6013	Shareholders	NA

Business: The group's principal activity is to integrate radiology images and information into healthcare enterprise networks. The group's products and services enhance the quality of healthcare provided to patients because they improve radiology workflow efficiencies, reduce healthcare operating costs and improve clinical decision making processes. The group delivers healthcare facilities of all sizes, specifically targeting small to medium size hospitals, multi-hospital groups, clinics and diagnostic imaging centers by working with its customers to offer modular, cost effective solutions to solve their image and information management and radiology workflow needs. It acquired ris logic on 17-Jul-2003. The group has its operations in Canada, Netherlands and the United States of America. The group's trademarks are efilm workstation, fusion & viewcheck.

Primary SIC and add'l.: 7376 7378 7375 7374

CIK No: 0000944765

Subsidiaries: Cedara Software (Shanghai) Co. Ltd., Cedara Software (USA) Ltd., Cedara Software Corp., Cedara Software Limited, Cedara Software SARL, eFilm Medical, Inc., Merge Cedara Exchange Co. Limited, Merge eMed, Inc., Merge Technologies Holdings Co., Merge Technologies, K.K.

Officers: Kenneth D. Rardin/Dir., CEO, Pres./$840,717.00, Steven M. Oreskovich/Chief Accounting Officer, Interim Treasurer, Principal Financial Officer/$422,390.00, Jacques F. Cornet/Pres. - Merge Healthcare EMEA Division/$425,257.00, Loris Sartor/Sr. VP, Cedara Pres./$383,915.00, Gary D. Bowers/Pres. - Merge Healthcare North America/$245,533.00, Steven R. Norton/46/Exec. VP, CFO, Treasurer

Directors: Kenneth D. Rardin/Dir., CEO, Pres., Richard Reck/Dir., Dennis Brown/Dir., Ian R. Lennox/Dir., Robert A. Barish/Dir., Robert T. Geras/Dir., Michael D. Dunham/Dir., Anna M. Hajek/Dir., Kevin G. Quinn/Dir., Ram Ramkumar/Dir., Kevin E. Moley/Dir.

Owners: Gary D. Bowers, Robert T. Geras, Brian E. Pedlar, Insiders/3.34%, Kenneth D. Rardin, William C. Mortimore, Silver Point Capital, L. P./5.12%, Kevin E. Moley, Dennis Brown, Loris Sartor, Glenhill Advisors, LLC/5.60%, Robert J. White, Steven M. Oreskovich, Michael D. Dunham, R. Ian Lennox *(24 Owners included in Index)*

Financial Data: *Fiscal Year End:*12/31 *Latest Annual Data:* 12/31/2006

Year	Sales	Net Income
2006	$74,322,000	-$258,923,000
2005	$82,601,000	-$2,657,000
2004	$37,005,000	$7,467,000

Curr. Assets:	$67,204,000	**Curr. Liab.:**	$40,103,000		
Plant, Equip.:	$3,940,000	**Total Liab.:**	$44,950,000	**Indic. Yr. Divd.:**	NA
Total Assets:	$234,875,000	**Net Worth:**	$189,925,000	**Debt/ Equity:**	NA

Meridian Bioscience Inc

3471 River Hills Dr., Cincinnati, OH, 45244; ***PH:*** 1-513-271-3700; ***Fax:*** 1-513-271-3762; ***http://*** www.meridianbioscience.com

General - Incorporation	OH	**Stock**- Price on:12/24/2007	$21.67
Employees	402	Stock Exchange	NDQ
Auditor	Grant Thornton, LLP	Ticker Symbol	VIVO
Stk Agt	Computershare Investor Services LLC	Outstanding Shares	39,720,000
Counsel	Keating, Muething & Klekamp	E.P.S	$0.62
DUNS No.	09-281-5364	Shareholders	NA

Business: The group's principal activity is to develop, manufacture and market disposable diagnostic test kits for rapid diagnosis of infectious diseases. The group's operating segments are classified as, us diagnostics, European diagnostics and life science. The us diagnostics segment focuses on the development, manufacture and distribution of diagnostic test kits, primarily for certain respiratory, gastrointestinal, viral and parasitic infectious diseases. The European diagnostics segment focuses on the sale and distribution of diagnostic test kits, manufactured by the us diagnostics operating segment and others manufactured by third-party vendors. The life science segment focuses on the development, manufacture, sale and distribution of bulk antigens and reagents used by researchers and other diagnostic companies, as well as the contract manufacturing of proteins and other biologicals used by biopharmaceutical and biotechnology companies.

Primary SIC and add'l.: 5047 3841

CIK No: 0000794172

Subsidiaries: Gull Europe S.A. Holding, Meridian Bioscience Corporation, Meridian Bioscience Europe B.V., Meridian Bioscience Europe S.A., Meridian Bioscience Europe, s.r.l., Meridian Bioscience FSC, Inc., Meridian Life Science, Inc., Omega Technologies, Inc., Viral Antigens, Inc.

Officers: William J. Motto/Chmn., CEO, Susan D. Rolih/VP - Regulatory Affairs, Quality Systems, Lawrence J. Baldini/Exec. VP - Operations, Information Systems, Antonio A. Interno/Sr. VP, Pres., MD - Meridian Bioscience Europe, John A. Kraeutler/Dir., COO, Pres., Todd W. Motto/VP - Sales, Marketing, Melissa A. Lueke/CFO, VP, Richard L. Eberly/Exec. VP, Pres. - Meridian Life Science, Grady Barnes/VP - Research - Product Development

Directors: William J. Motto/Chmn., CEO, David C. Philips/Dir., John A. Kraeutler/Dir., COO, Pres., James A. Buzard/Dir., Gary P. Kreider/Dir., Robert J. Ready/Dir.

Owners: Melissa A. Lueke, Richard L. Eberly, David C. Phillips, Antonio A. Interno, James A. Buzard, Susan A. Rolih, Insiders/5.50%, Gary P. Kreider, William J. Motto/1.00%, Robert J. Ready, Todd W. Motto/2.20%, John A. Kraeutler/1.00%, Lawrence J. Baldini

Financial Data: *Fiscal Year End:*09/30 *Latest Annual Data:* 9/30/2006

Year	Sales	Net Income
2006	$108,413,000	$18,325,000
2005	$92,965,000	$12,565,000
2004	$79,606,000	$9,185,000

Curr. Assets:	$93,745,000	**Curr. Liab.:**	$17,067,000	**P/E Ratio:**	34.95
Plant, Equip.:	$18,311,000	**Total Liab.:**	$19,750,000	**Indic. Yr. Divd.:**	$0.430
Total Assets:	$132,698,000	**Net Worth:**	$112,948,000	**Debt/ Equity:**	NA

Meridian Company Ltd

3f, Poonglim Tech-one B/d, 273-10, Seongsu-dong 2ga, Seongdong-gu, Seoul; ***PH:*** 82-221-033300; ***http://*** www.meridian.co.kr

General - Incorporation	Republic of Korea	**Stock**- Price on:12/24/2007	$0.715
Employees	NA	Stock Exchange	OTC
Auditor	Choi, Kim & Park LLP	Ticker Symbol	MRDAF
Stk Agt	Pacific Corporate Trust Co	Outstanding Shares	NA
Counsel	NA	E.P.S	NA
DUNS No.	NA	Shareholders	NA

Business: The groups principle activities include researching, developing, manufacturing, and marketing integrative medical devices in the healthcare industry. Products of the group include Meridian-II, ABR-2000, Lapex2000, Digital Pulse Analyzer and Venus 21C. for Sep 2005, the group acquired Rapha & Health Co., Ltd. The group operates from the United States, South Asia and China.

Primary SIC and add'l.: 3841

CIK No: 0001135174

Subsidiaries: Meridian America Medicals, Inc, Rapha & Health Co., Ltd

Officers: Hyeon-Seong Myeong/Dir., CEO, Pres., In Beom Park/Dir., Sec.

Directors: Hyeon-Seong Myeong/Dir., CEO, Pres., In Beom Park/Dir., Sec., Soon Woon Jang/Dir.

Owners: Insiders/2.94%, Hyeong-seong Myeong/2.94%

Financial Data: *Fiscal Year End:*12/31 *Latest Annual Data:* 12/31/2006

Year	Sales	Net Income
2006	$1,642,000	-$349,000
2005	$1,420,000	-$3,316,000
2004	$2,129,000	-$1,986,000

Curr. Assets:	$913,000	**Curr. Liab.:**	$5,468,000		
Plant, Equip.:	$18,000	**Total Liab.:**	$9,752,000	**Indic. Yr. Divd.:**	NA
Total Assets:	$1,043,000	**Net Worth:**	-$8,709,000	**Debt/ Equity:**	NA

Meridian Gold Inc

9670 Gateway Dr., Ste. 200, Reno, NV, 89521; ***PH:*** 1-775-850-3777; ***Fax:*** 1-775-850-3733; ***http://*** www.meridiangold.com

General - Incorporation	Canada	**Stock**- Price on:12/24/2007	$25.78
Employees	282	Stock Exchange	NYSE
Auditor	KPMG LLP	Ticker Symbol	MDG
Stk Agt	Computershare Trust Co of Canada	Outstanding Shares	101,150,000
Counsel	NA	E.P.S	$0.55
DUNS No.	NA	Shareholders	NA

Business: The groups principle activities include operating and exploring gold and precious metals. The group operates from United States and China.

Primary SIC and add'l.: 1040

CIK No: 0001016888

Subsidiaries: Brancote Holdings PLC, Emerald Limited, Meridian Beartrack Company, Meridian Gold (Barbados) Limited, Meridian Gold Company, Meridian Gold Holdings (Cayman) Limited, Meridian Gold Holdings (Mexico) SADCV, Meridian Gold Holdings II (Cayman) Limited, Meridian Jerritt Canyon Corporation, Meridian Minerals Corporation, Meridian Rossi Corporation, Meridian Subco I Limited, Meridian Subco II Limited, Meridian Subco V (Argentina) Limited, Minera El Desquite S.A. 24 Subsidiaries included in the Index

Officers: Edward C. Dowling/Dir., CEO, Pres., Howard Stevenson/VP - Business Development, Darrin L. Rohr/VP, Chief People Officer, Edgar A. Smith/VP - Operations, Darcy E. Marud/VP - Exploration, Curtis K. Turner/Corporate Controller

Directors: Edward C. Dowling/Dir., CEO, Pres., Brian J. Kennedy/Chmn., Christopher R. Lattanzi/Dir. - Meridian Gold Inc, Malcolm W. MacNaught/Dir., Carl L. Renzoni/Dir., Richard P. Graff/Dir., Gerard E. Munera/Dir., Robert A. Horn/Dir.

Financial Data: Fiscal Year End:12/31 **Latest Annual Data:** 12/31/2006

Year	Sales	Net Income
2006	$240,000,000	$49,200,000
2005	$131,800,000	-$345,800,000
2004	$127,100,000	$37,200,000

Curr. Assets:	$220,000,000	**Curr. Liab.:**	$45,500,000	**P/E Ratio:**	12.86
Plant, Equip.:	$276,100,000	**Total Liab.:**	$167,100,000	**Indic. Yr. Divd.:**	NA
Total Assets:	$528,000,000	**Net Worth:**	$345,600,000	**Debt/ Equity:**	NA

Meridian Holdings Inc

6201 Bristol Pkwy., Culver City, CA, 90230; **PH:** 1-213-627-8878; **Fax:** 1-310-743-0581; **http://** www.meho.com; **Email:** info@meho.com

General - Incorporation	CO	**Stock**- Price on:12/24/2007	$0.028
Employees	14	Stock Exchange	OTC
Auditor	Madsen & Assoc. CPAs, Inc	Ticker Symbol	MRDH
Stk Agt	Depository Trust Co	Outstanding Shares	18,120,000
Counsel	NA	E.P.S.	-$0.075
DUNS No.	NA	Shareholders	NA

Business: The group operates thorugh its subsdiary whose principle activity is to provide healthcare and technology services, the company's network of affiliated companies is designed to encourage maximum leverage of information technology, operational excellence, industry expertise, and synergistic business opportunities. The group operates from United States.

Primary SIC and add'l.: 8099 7389

CIK No: 0001071758

Subsidiaries: CGI Communications Services, Inc, Meridian Energy Corporation

Officers: Anthony C. Dike/Chmn., CEO, Wesley G. Bradford/Chief Medical Officer

Directors: Anthony C. Dike/Chmn., CEO, Ludlow Creary/Dir., James W. Truher/Dir., Marcellina Offoha/Dir., Andrew M. Smith/Dir.

Financial Data: Fiscal Year End:12/31 **Latest Annual Data:** 12/31/2005

Year	Sales	Net Income
2005	$1,771,000	-$1,363,000
2004	$2,365,000	-$522,000
2003	$2,624,000	$139,000

Curr. Assets:	$2,288,000	**Curr. Liab.:**	$711,000		
Plant, Equip.:	$16,000	**Total Liab.:**	$807,000	**Indic. Yr. Divd.:**	NA
Total Assets:	$4,304,000	**Net Worth:**	$3,497,000	**Debt/ Equity:**	0.0466

Meridian Resource Corp

1401 EnclAve. Pkwy., Ste. 300, Houston, TX, 77077; **PH:** 1-281-597-7000; **Fax:** 1-281-597-8880; **http://** www.tmrc.com

General - Incorporation	TX	**Stock**- Price on:12/24/2007	$3.07
Employees	95	Stock Exchange	NYSE
Auditor	BDO Seidman LLP	Ticker Symbol	TMR
Stk Agt	American Stock Transfer & Trust Co.	Outstanding Shares	89,360,000
Counsel	Fulbright & Jaworski LLP	E.P.S.	-$0.9
DUNS No.	79-131-2358	Shareholders	NA

Business: The group's principal activities are to explore, acquire and develop oil and natural gas properties utilizing 3-D seismic technology. The group uses 3-D seismic technology to analyze prospects, define risk and target high-potential wells for exploration and development. The group focuses its operations on the onshore oil and gas regions in south Louisiana, the Texas gulf coast and offshore in the gulf of Mexico. As of 31-Dec-2003, the group had interests in 280,000 gross acres including 18 fields and 91 wells. The group markets its production to third parties. The customers of the group include Louisiana intrastate gas, superior natural gas and conoco inc.

Primary SIC and add'l.: 1311

CIK No: 0000869369

Subsidiaries: Cairn Energy USA, Inc., FBB Anadarko Corporation, Louisiana Onshore Properties LLC, Sundance Acquisition Corporation, TE TMR Corporation, The Meridian Production Corporation, The Meridian Resource & Exploration LLC, The Meridian Resource Corporation

Officers: Joseph A. Reeves/61/Chmn., CEO/$1,855,244.00, Lloyd V. Delano/Chief Accounting Officer, Sr. VP/$994,645.00, Lance Weaver/Dir. - Investor Relations, Bill Bishop/VP - Land, Dale Breaux/VP - Operations, Thomas J. Tourek/Sr. VP - Exploration/$740,619.00, Alan S. Pennington/VP - New Ventures, Business Development/$1,000,151.00, Michael J. Mayell/60/Dir., COO, Pres./$1,855,244.00, Steven G. Ives/VP - Finance, Larry Sheppard/VP - Business Development

Directors: Joseph A. Reeves/61/Chmn., CEO, E. L. Henry/72/Dir., John B. Simmons/55/Dir., David W. Tauber/58/Dir., Joe E. Kares/64/Dir., Gary A. Messersmith/59/Dir., Fenner R. Weller/56/Dir., Michael J. Mayell/60/Dir., COO, Pres., Mark C. Pearson/53/Dir.

Owners: Joe E. Kares, Insiders/11.00%, Fenner R. Weller, Joseph A. Reeves/5.80%, Lloyd V. DeLano, John B. Simmons, David W. Tauber, Alan S. Pennington, Gary A. Messersmith, Donald Smith & Co/9.70%, Barclays Global Investors, NA/6.90%, Michael J. Mayell/5.50%, E. L. Henry, Dimensional Fund Advisors Inc./7.30%, Thomas J. Tourek

Financial Data: Fiscal Year End:12/31 **Latest Annual Data:** 12/31/2006

Year	Sales	Net Income
2006	$190,957,000	-$73,884,000
2005	$195,696,000	$28,751,000
2004	$203,118,000	$33,125,000

Curr. Assets:	$69,086,000	**Curr. Liab.:**	$50,539,000		
Plant, Equip.:	$397,883,000	**Total Liab.:**	$147,098,000	**Indic. Yr. Divd.:**	NA
Total Assets:	$467,895,000	**Net Worth:**	$320,797,000	**Debt/ Equity:**	0.2348

Merisel Inc

127 W 30th St., 5th Fl., New York, NY, 10001; **PH:** 1-212-594-4800; **Fax:** 1-212-594-4488; **http://** www.merisel.com; **Email:** corp@merisel.com

General - Incorporation	DE	**Stock**- Price on:12/24/2007	$5.25
Employees	501	Stock Exchange	OTC
Auditor	BDO Seidman LLP	Ticker Symbol	MSEL
Stk Agt	U.S. Stock Transfer Corp	Outstanding Shares	8,010,000
Counsel	NA	E.P.S.	$0.62
DUNS No.	03-818-1483	Shareholders	NA

Business: The group's principal activity is to license software products. The group's software licensing business provides customers with nearly 20,000 licensing products from various manufacturers. The software licensing products offered by the group fall mainly in the categories of anti-virus, desktop applications, graphics, it management, security, storage and storage management, system utilities, system applications and Web-based solutions products. It also provides e-business solutions. The group operates solely in the domestic market.

Primary SIC and add'l.: 5045

CIK No: 0000724941

Subsidiaries: Color Edge Visual, LLC, Color Edge, LLC, Comp 24, LLC, Crush Creative, LLC, Merisel Americas, Inc., Merisel Properties, Inc

Officers: Donald R. Uzzi/Chmn., CEO, Pres., John J. Sheehan/Exec. VP - Sales - Marketing, Guy Claudy/Exec. VP, Kenneth Wasserman/Pres. - Comp24, Jon H. Peterson/CFO, Exec. VP

Directors: Donald R. Uzzi/Chmn., CEO, Pres., Bradley J. Hoecker/Dir., Albert J. Fitzgibbons/Dir., Ronald P. Badie/Dir., Lawrence J. Schoenberg/Dir., Edward A. Grant/Dir.

Owners: Jon H. Peterson, Albert J. Fitzgibbons, John J. Sheehan, Ronald P. Badie, Bradley J. Hoecker, Kenneth Wasserman, Gary Furukawa/7.79%, Phoenix Acquisition Company II, L.L.C./65.97%, Donald R. Uzzi/5.35%, Insiders/6.93%, Lawrence J. Schoenberg, Edward Grant

Financial Data: Fiscal Year End:12/31 **Latest Annual Data:** 12/31/2006

Year	Sales	Net Income
2006	$84,720,000	$7,055,000
2005	$63,009,000	$10,835,000
2004	NA	-$793,000

Curr. Assets:	$34,894,000	**Curr. Liab.:**	$11,408,000	**P/E Ratio:**	7.09
Plant, Equip.:	$8,355,000	**Total Liab.:**	$21,900,000	**Indic. Yr. Divd.:**	NA
Total Assets:	$84,580,000	**Net Worth:**	$62,680,000	**Debt/ Equity:**	NA

Merit Medical Systems Inc

1600 W Merit Pkwy., South Jordan, UT, 84095; **PH:** 1-801-253-1600; **Fax:** 1-801-253-1687; **http://** www.merit.com

General - Incorporation	UT	**Stock**- Price on:12/24/2007	$11.75
Employees	1,709	Stock Exchange	NYSE
Auditor	Deloitte & Touche LLP	Ticker Symbol	MNC
Stk Agt	Zions First National Bank	Outstanding Shares	27,380,000
Counsel	Parr Waddups Brown Gee & Loveless	E.P.S.	$0.45
DUNS No.	18-476-3290	Shareholders	NA

Business: The group's principal activities are to develop, manufacture and market disposable medical products primarily for use in the diagnosis and treatment of cardiovascular disease. The products are manufactured at facilities located in south jordan, Utah; santa clara, California; galway, Ireland; angleton, Texas and murray, Utah. The products are designed to provide physicians and other health care professionals with devices that enable them to perform interventional and diagnostic procedures safely and effectively. The group serves hospital-based cardiologists, radiologists, anesthesiologists, physiatrists (pain management), neurologists, technicians and nurses.

Primary SIC and add'l.: 3841

CIK No: 0000856982

Subsidiaries: MCTec B.V., MCTec Holding B.V., Merit Holdings,Inc., Merit Medical Belgium B.V.B.A., Merit Medical France SAS, Merit Medical Germany GmbH, Merit Medical International,Inc., Merit Medical Ireland Limited, Merit Medical Nederland B.V., Merit Medical Services, L.P., Merit Medical UK Limited, Merit Sensor Systems,Inc., Merit Services,Inc.

Officers: Fred P. Lampropoulos/Chmn., CEO, Pres./$838,155.00, Joe Wright/VP - International Sales, Martin R. Stephens/VP - Sales/$368,149.00, Kent W. Stanger/Dir., Co - Founder, CFO, Sec., Treasurer/$390,504.00, Anne Marie Wright/VP - Corporate Communications, Gregory L. Barnett/46/Chief Accounting Officer/$263,082.00, Arlin D. Nelson/67/COO/$251,706.00

Directors: Fred P. Lampropoulos/Chmn., CEO, Pres., Franklin J. Miller/Dir., Kent W. Stanger/Dir., Co - Founder, CFO, Sec., Treasurer, Richard W. Edelman/Dir., Rex C. Bean/Dir., James J. Ellis/Dir., Michael E. Stillabower/Dir.

Owners: Gregory L. Barnett, Fred P. Lampropoulos/5.00%, Frank J. Miller, Insiders/11.70%, Arlin D. Nelson, Michael E. Stillabower, Rex C. Bean/1.30%, Kent W. Stanger/3.40%, Richard W. Edelman, Martin R. Stephens, James J. Ellis, FMR Corp./15.00%, B. Leigh Weintraub

Financial Data: Fiscal Year End:12/31 **Latest Annual Data:** 12/31/2006

Year	Sales	Net Income
2006	$190,674,000	$12,301,000
2005	$166,585,000	$15,778,000
2004	$151,398,000	$17,932,000

Curr. Assets:	$75,646,000	**Curr. Liab.:**	$20,674,000	**P/E Ratio:**	26.11
Plant, Equip.:	$92,383,000	**Total Liab.:**	$31,456,000	**Indic. Yr. Divd.:**	NA
Total Assets:	$182,668,000	**Net Worth:**	$151,212,000	**Debt/ Equity:**	0.0011

Meritage Homes Corp

17851 N 85th St., Ste. 300, Scottsdale, AZ, 85255; **PH:** 1-480-515-8100; **Fax:** 1-480-998-9162; **http://** www.meritagehomes.com

General - Incorporation	MD	**Stock**- Price on:12/24/2007	$29.18
Employees	1,950	Stock Exchange	NDQ
Auditor	Deloitte & Touche LLP	Ticker Symbol	MTLG
Stk Agt	Mellon Investor Services LLC	Outstanding Shares	26,230,000
Counsel	NA	E.P.S.	$6.01
DUNS No.	NA	Shareholders	NA

Business: The groups principle activities include designing and building homes. The group operates from United States.

Primary SIC and add'l.: 1521

CIK No: 0000833079

Subsidiaries: California Urban Builders,Inc., California Urban Homes, LLC, Greater Homes,Inc., Hulen Park Venture, LLC, Meritage Holdings, LLC, Meritage Homes Construction,Inc., Meritage Homes of Arizona,Inc., Meritage Homes of California,Inc., Meritage Homes of Colorado,Inc., Meritage Homes of Florida,Inc., Meritage Homes of Nevada,Inc., Meritage Homes of Texas GP,Inc., Meritage Homes of Texas LP Holding,Inc., Meritage Homes of Texas, L.P., Meritage Homes Operating Company, L.P. 19 Subsidiaries included in the Index

Officers: Steven J. Hilton/46/Chmn., CEO/$9,740,205.00, Larry W. Seay/52/CFO, Exec. VP/$2,578,567.00, Timothy C. White/Exec. VP, General Counsel, Sec./$1,424,838.00, Sandra R.A. Karrmann/Chief Human Resources Officer, Exec. VP/$860,146.00, Steven M. Davis/Exec. VP - National Homebuilding Operations/$530,384.00

Directors: Steven J. Hilton/46/Chmn., CEO, Raymond Oppel/51/Dir., Peter L. Ax/49/Dir., Gerald W. Haddock/60/Dir., Robert G. Sarver/46/Dir., Richard T. Burke/64/Dir.

Owners: Steven J. Hilton/7.80%, John R. Landon/4.20%, Raymond Oppel, Robert G. Sarver/1.90%, Peter L. Ax, Larry W. Seay, Richard T. Burke, William G. Campbell, Sandra R.A Karrmann, Gerald W. Haddock, Insiders/10.90%, C. Timothy White

Financial Data: ***Fiscal Year End:***12/31 ***Latest Annual Data:*** 06/30/2007

Year	Sales	Net Income
2007	$568,667,000	-$56,576,000
2006	$821,193,000	$9,024,000
2005	$3,001,102,000	$255,665,000

Curr. Assets:	$125,435,000	***Curr. Liab.:***	$430,417,000	***P/E Ratio:***	4.86
Plant, Equip.:	$1,576,583,000	***Total Liab.:***	$1,163,693,000	***Indic. Yr. Divd.:***	NA
Total Assets:	$2,170,525,000	***Net Worth:***	$1,006,832,000	***Debt/ Equity:***	0.7920

Meritage Hospitality Group Inc

1971 E Beltline Ne, Ste. 200, Grand Rapids, MI, 49525; ***PH:*** 1-616-776-2600; ***http://*** www.meritagehospitality.com

General - Incorporation	MI	***Stock***- Price on:12/24/2007	NA
Employees	NA	Stock Exchange	OTC
Auditor	Ernst & Young LLP	Ticker Symbol	MHGU
Stk Agt	LaSalle Bank N.A	Outstanding Shares	NA
Counsel	Dykema Gossett	E.P.S	-$0.76
DUNS No.	94-191-2917	Shareholders	NA

Business: The group's principal activity is to operate 48 wendy's restaurants in western and southern Michigan. The restaurants of the group are operated under a franchise agreement with wendy's international inc, the franchiser of quick-service restaurant system that operates under the wendy's brand name. The restaurants offer food items that include hamburgers, chicken sandwiches, baked and French fried potatoes, salads, soft drinks, desserts and children's meals. The group's restaurants are located in the Michigan counties of allegan, calhoun, ionia, kalamazoo, kent, muskegon, newaygo, ottawa and van buren.

Primary SIC and add'l.: 7011 5812

CIK No: 0000808219

Subsidiaries: Michigan limited

Officers: Robert E. Schermer/Dir., CEO, Pres., Robert H. Potts/VP - Real Estate, Gary A. Rose/VP, CFO, COO, James R. Saalfeld/VP, Chief Administrative Officer, General Counsel

Directors: Robert E. Schermer/Dir., CEO, Pres., James P. Bishop/Dir., Brian N. McMahon/Dir., Duane Kluting/Dir., Joseph L. Maggini/Dir.

Financial Data: ***Fiscal Year End:***11/27 ***Latest Annual Data:*** 11/27/2005

Year	Sales	Net Income
2005	$56,037,000	-$4,858,000
2004	$53,303,000	-$489,000
2003	$48,513,000	$740,000

Curr. Assets:	$1,251,000	***Curr. Liab.:***	$4,497,000		
Plant, Equip.:	$41,558,000	***Total Liab.:***	$41,657,000	***Indic. Yr. Divd.:***	NA
Total Assets:	$50,030,000	***Net Worth:***	$8,374,000	***Debt/ Equity:***	NA

Merix Corp

1521 Poplar Ln., Forest Grove, OR, 97116; ***PH:*** 1-503-359-9300; ***Fax:*** 1-503-357-9755; ***http://*** www.merix.com; ***Email:*** info@merix.com

General - Incorporation	OR	***Stock***- Price on:12/24/2007	$8.11
Employees	4,225	Stock Exchange	NDQ
Auditor	Grant Thornton, LLP	Ticker Symbol	MERX
Stk Agt	PricewaterhouseCoopers LLP	Outstanding Shares	20,660,000
Counsel	Perkins Coie LLP	E.P.S	-$3.89
DUNS No.	82-619-6388	Shareholders	NA

Business: The group's principle activity is to manufacture technologically advanced electronic interconnect solutions for use in electronic equipment. The products of the company include complex multi layer printed circuit boards used to interconnect microprocessors, integrated circuits and other components that are essential to the operation of electronic products and systems. In addition, it provides design assistance and engineering services in the early stages of product development. Customers of the company include original equipment manufacturers and contract manufacturers within selected high growth segments of the electronics industry, including communications, high-end computing, and test and measurement. The group operates from United States.

Primary SIC and add'l.: 3672

CIK No: 0000921365

Subsidiaries: Eastern Pacific Circuits Limited, Merix Asia, Merix San Jose, Inc

Officers: Michael D. Burger/Dir., CEO, Pres./$831,951.00, Thomas R. Ingham/Exec. VP - Global Sales, Marketing, Kelly E. Lang/CFO, Exec. VP - Finance/$550,540.00, Steven R. Robinson/Exec. VP - Global Operations/$480,841.00, Linda V. Moore/Exec. VP - Global Human Resources, General Counsel

Directors: Michael D. Burger/Dir., CEO, Pres., William C. McCormick/Chmn., William W. Lattin/Dir., Robert C. Strandberg/Dir., Chee W. Chung/Dir., Kirby A. Dyess/Dir., Donald D. Jobe/Dir., George H. Kerckhove/Dir.

Owners: Donald D. Jobe, Kirby A. Dyess, Steven R. Robinson, Michael D. Burger, Daniel T. Olson, Royce & Associates LLC/6.02%, Chee W. Cheung, William W. Lattin, Robert C. Strandberg, Mark R. Hollinger, William C. McCormick, Dimensional Fund Advisors, Inc./8.04%, Paradigm Capital Management, Inc./6.73%, 6th Avenue Investment Management Co. LLC/10.73%, Chris L. Remy *(21 Owners included in Index)*

Financial Data: ***Fiscal Year End:***05/28 ***Latest Annual Data:*** 5/27/2006

Year	Sales	Net Income
2006	$308,982,000	$1,432,000
2005	$186,994,000	-$2,610,000
2004	$156,400,000	$28,000

Curr. Assets:	$165,515,000	***Curr. Liab.:***	$26,398,000		
Plant, Equip.:	$84,021,000	***Total Liab.:***	$51,766,000	***Indic. Yr. Divd.:***	NA
Total Assets:	$250,181,000	***Net Worth:***	$198,415,000	***Debt/ Equity:***	0.3522

Merrill Lynch & Co Inc

4 World Financial Ctr., 250 Vesey St., New York, NY, 10080; ***PH:*** 1-212-449-1000; ***Fax:*** 1-212-449-9418; ***http://*** www.merrilllynch.com

General - Incorporation	DE	***Stock***- Price on:12/24/2007	$87.3
Employees	56,300	Stock Exchange	NYSE
Auditor	Deloitte & Touche LLP	Ticker Symbol	MER
Stk Agt	Citibank, N.A	Outstanding Shares	870,800,000
Counsel	NA	E.P.S	$10.09
DUNS No.	00-892-0951	Shareholders	NA

Business: The group's principle activity is to provide a wide range of services to private clients, small business, and institutions and corporations, organizing its activities into two interrelated business segments including global markets and investment banking group and global wealth management. The group operates from United States.

Primary SIC and add'l.: 6282 6289 6211 6221 6159

CIK No: 0000065100

Subsidiaries: Advest Insurance Agency, Inc., Advest, Inc., Balanced Capital Services, Inc., Banco Merrill Lynch de Investimentos S.A., Berndale Securities Limited, del Risparmio S.p.A., Equity Margins Ltd., FAM Distributors, Inc., Financial Data Services, Inc., Fund Asset Management, L.P., GPC Securities, Inc., Herzog, Heine, Geduld, LLC, Institucion Financiera Externa Merrill Lynch Bank (Uruguay) S.A., Investor Protection Insurance Company, IQ Investment Advisors LLC 147 Subsidiaries included in the Index

Officers: Stanley E. ONeal/55/Chmn., CEO/$91,375,380.00, Stan ONeal/Chmn., CEO, Pres., Harry McMahon/Vice Chmn., Member - Exec. Client Coverage Group, Rosemary T. Berkery/Vice Chmn., General Counsel, Gregg Seibert/Vice Chmn., Member - Exec. Client Coverage Group, Brian P. Hull/Vice Chmn., Member - Exec. Client Coverage Group, Thomas A. Petrie/Vice Chmn., Member - Exec. Client Coverage Group, Gregg Siebert/Vice Chmn., Member - Exec. Client Coverage Group, Jerome P. Kenney/Vice Chmn., Member - Exec. Client Coverage Group, Samuel R. Chapin/Vice Chmn. - Exec. Client Coverage Group, William J. McDonough/Vice Chmn. - Special Advisor, Hugh Sullivan/Vice Chmn. - Executive Client Coverage Group, Andrea Orcel/Sr. VP, Head - Global Origination, Pres. - EMEA Global Markets, Investment Banking, Gardner H. McIntyre/Sr. VP, Head - Americas Region, Global Wealth Management Group, The Global Bank Group, Gregory J. Fleming/Exec. VP/$33,883,120.00 *(39 Officers included in Index)*

Directors: Stanley E. ONeal/55/Chmn., CEO, Stan ONeal/Chmn., CEO, Pres., Gregg Seibert/Vice Chmn., Member - Exec. Client Coverage Group, Brian P. Hull/Vice Chmn., Member - Exec. Client Coverage Group, Richard McCormack/Vice Chmn., Harold E. Ford/Vice Chmn., Thomas A. Petrie/Vice Chmn., Member - Exec. Client Coverage Group, Gregg Siebert/Vice Chmn., Member - Exec. Client Coverage Group, James B. Quigley/Vice Chmn., Jerome P. Kenney/Vice Chmn., Member - Exec. Client Coverage Group, Rosemary T. Berkery/Vice Chmn., General Counsel, Harry McMahon/Vice Chmn., Member - Exec. Client Coverage Group, David K. Newbigging/Dir., Alberto Cribiore/61/Dir., Charles O. Rossotti/66/Dir. *(24 Directors included in Index)*

Owners: Joseph W. Prueher, Dow Kim, Aulana L. Peters, Jill K. Conway, Robert J. McCann, Charles O. Rossotti, Jeffrey N. Edwards, State Street Bank and Trust Com- Merrill Lynch Employee Stock Ownership Plan/2.55%, AXA and certain related parties, including AXA Financial, Inc./7.18%, State Street Bank and Trust Com- discretionary advisor for certain unaffiliated accounts & collecti/2.75%, Ahmass L. Fakahany, Ann N. Reese, Stanley E. ONeal, Insiders, State Street Bank and Trust Com- Merrill Lynch employee benefit plans/3.46% *(19 Owners included in Index)*

Financial Data: ***Fiscal Year End:***12/30 ***Latest Annual Data:*** 12/29/2006

Year	Sales	Net Income
2006	$70,591,000,000	$7,499,000,000
2005	$47,783,000,000	$5,116,000,000
2004	$32,467,000,000	$4,436,000,000

Curr. Assets:	$339,665,000,000	***Curr. Liab.:***	$348,182,000,000	***P/E Ratio:***	9.23
Plant, Equip.:	$2,508,000,000	***Total Liab.:***	$616,689,000,000	***Indic. Yr. Divd.:***	$1.400
Total Assets:	$648,059,000,000	***Net Worth:***	$31,370,000,000	***Debt/ Equity:***	6.5685

Merrill Lynch Life Insurance Co

1300 Merrill Lynch Dr., Pennington, NJ, 08534; ***PH:*** 1-609-274-6900

General - Incorporation	AR	***Stock***- Price on:12/24/2007	$90.17
Employees	56,300	Stock Exchange	NA
Auditor	Deloitte & Touche LLP	Ticker Symbol	NA
Stk Agt	NA	Outstanding Shares	870,800,000
Counsel	NA	E.P.S	NA
DUNS No.	78-656-6075	Shareholders	NA

Business: The group's principle activity is to provide non-participating life insurance and annuity products such as variable life insurance, variable annuities, market value adjusted annuities and immediate annuities. The company is a wholly owned subsidiary of merrill lynch insurance group. The licensed agents, career life insurance agents and financial consultants sell the company's insurance products. The company is currently licensed in 49 states, the district of columbia, Puerto Rico, the U.S. Virgin islands and guam. In 2003, the company discontinued manufacturing single premium variable life insurance product. The group operates from United States.

Primary SIC and add'l.: 6311

CIK No: 0000845091

Subsidiaries: Merrill Lynch & Co, Merrill Lynch & Co., Inc, Merrill Lynch Insurance Group, Merrill Lynch Insurance Group, Inc.)

Officers: Deborah J. Adler/Chmn., CEO, Pres., Chief Actuary, John C. Carroll/Dir., Sr. VP, Joseph E. Justice/Dir., CFO, Sr. VP, Treasurer, Barry G. Skolnick/Dir., Sr. VP, General Counsel, Paul Michalowski/Dir., VP, Elizabeth Garrison/VP, Controller

Directors: Deborah J. Adler/Chmn., CEO, Pres., Chief Actuary, John C. Carroll/Dir., Sr. VP, Joseph E. Justice/Dir., CFO, Sr. VP, Treasurer, Barry G. Skolnick/Dir., Sr. VP, General Counsel, Paul Michalowski/Dir., VP

Financial Data: ***Fiscal Year End:***12/31 ***Latest Annual Data:*** 06/29/2007

Year	Sales	Net Income
2007	$23,806,000,000	$2,139,000,000
2006	$18,993,000,000	$2,346,000,000
2005	$47,783,000,000	$5,116,000,000

Curr. Assets:	$339,665,000,000	Curr. Liab.:	$348,182,000,000	P/E Ratio:	9.53
Plant, Equip.:	$2,508,000,000	Total Liab.:	$616,689,000,000	Indic. Yr. Divd.:	$1.400
Total Assets:	$648,059,000,000	Net Worth:	$31,370,000,000	Debt/ Equity:	6.5685

Merrill Merchants Bancshares Inc

201 Main St. , Bangor, ME, 04401; PH: 1-207-942-4800; http:// www.merrillmerchants.com

General - Incorporation ....ME	Stock - Price on:12/24/2007 ....NA
Employees.....................137	Stock Exchange..........................NA
Auditor ....Berry, Dunn, Mcneil & Parker	Ticker Symbol........................NA
Stk Agt........................Registrar & Transfer Co	Outstanding Shares ....NA
Counsel...................................NA	E.P.S ....NA
DUNS No..................................NA	Shareholders.......................NA

Business: The group's principal activity is to provide a wide range of consumer, commercial, trust and investment services through its branch offices located in central and eastern Maine. The bank is a holding company of merrill merchants bank and Maine acceptance corporation. The group also grants single and multi-family residential, commercial real estate and a variety of consumer loans. Maine acceptance corporation is a finance company providing a variety of loans including personal, unsecured, recreational vehicle, automobile, home and equity loans.

Primary SIC and add'l.: 6712 6022

CIK No: 0000913072

Subsidiaries: Merrill Merchants Bank

Officers: Edwin N. Clift/68/Chmn., CEO, William P. Lucy/49/Pres., Deborah A. Jordan/41/Exec. VP, Alena Sibley/Mgr. - Main Office, Kelly Shorey/Branch Supervisor, Milford, Kevin McKaig/Mgr. - Bangor, Margie Downing/Mgr. - Newport, Stacie Buzzell/Bangor, Mgr., Brent Folster/Orono, Mgr., Don Smith/Branch Mgr. - Brewer, Ron Landry/Branch Mgr. - Orrington, Andy Reed/Mgr. - Pittsfield, Lucille Zelenkewich/Mgr. - Waterville, Chip Applegate/Mgr. - Waterville

Directors: Edwin N. Clift/68/Chmn., CEO, Perry B. Hansen/60/Dir., John R. Graham/70/Dir., Michael T. Shea/58/Dir., Joseph H. Cyr/67/Dir., Frederick A. Oldenburg/60/Dir., William C. Bullock/71/Dir., Dennis L. Shubert/60/Dir.

Owners: Frederick A. Oldenburg/1.57%, Deborah A. Jordan/0.59%, Joseph H. Cyr/4.95%, William P. Lucy/0.56%, The Bullock Family Trust/6.03%, Perry B. Hansen/10.34%, John R. Graham/1.82%, Dennis L. Shubert/1.90%, Edwin N. Clift/2.03%, Insiders/29.79%

Merrimac Industries Inc

41 Fairfield Pl., West Caldwell, NJ, 07006; PH: 1-973-575-1300; Fax: 1-973-882-5990; http:// www.merrimacind.com

General - Incorporation ....DE	Stock - Price on:12/24/2007 ....$9.78
Employees.....................230	Stock Exchange..........................NYSE
Auditor ....Grant Thornton, LLP	Ticker Symbol........................MRO
Stk Agt...............Mellon Investor Services LLC	Outstanding Shares 2,910,000
Counsel...................Kmz Rosenman	E.P.S ....-$2.74
DUNS No..................00-215-3914	Shareholders.......................NA

Business: The group's principal activity is to design and manufacture passive rf and microwave components for industry, government and science. The group's operations are conducted primarily through two segments: electronic components and microwave micro-circuitry. The electronic components segment designs, manufactures and sells electronic component devices offering extremely broad frequency coverage and high performance characteristics. The microwave micro-circuitry segment designs, manufactures and sells microstrip, bonded stripline and thick metal-backed teflon(R) (ptfe) and mixed dielectric multilayer circuits. These products are used for communications, defense and aerospace applications. The group's customers are primarily major industrial corporations that integrate the group's products into a wide variety of defense and commercial systems.

Primary SIC and add'l.: 3669

CIK No: 0000706864

Subsidiaries: 508790 N.b. Inc., Filtran Microcircuits Inc., Multi-Mix Microtechnology

Officers: Mason N. Carter/Chmn., CEO/$373,752.00, Annette Malins/International Representative - England, Yvonne Brooks/International Representative - England, Andy Cackett/International Representative - England, Louise Roughneed/International Representative - England, Terry Gamblin/International Representative - England, Hans Brunner/International Representative - Germany, Hans Boogaard/International Representative - Holland, Robert Verschuur/International Representative - Holland, Stella Beemer/International Representative - Holland, Mary Watanyar/International Representative - India, Pakistan, Turkey, Scott Watanyar/International Representative - India, Pakistan, Turkey, Franco Cugusi/International Representative - Italy, Renato Clerici/International Representative - Italy, Marco Del Viscio/International Representative - Italy (67 Officers included in Index)

Directors: Mason N. Carter/Chmn., CEO

Owners: Edward H. Cohen, Insiders/26.80%, Albert H. Cohen, David B. Miller, Lior Bregman/10.78%, Arthur A. Oliner/6.55%, Fernando L. Fernandez, Mason N. Carter/1.73%, Harold J. Ravech, Ludwig G. Kuttner/10.31%, E.I. DuPont de Nemours and Company/18.17%, Dimensional Fund Advisors Inc./5.06%, Robert V. Condon, Neuberger Berman, LLC/8.76%, Joel H. Goldberg/2.51% (18 Owners included in Index)

Financial Data: Fiscal Year End:12/31 **Latest Annual Data:** 12/30/2006

Year	Sales	Net Income
2006	$27,421,000	-$2,225,000
2005	$29,719,000	$761,000

Curr. Assets:	$14,352,000	Curr. Liab.:	$4,498,000		
Plant, Equip.:	$13,973,000	Total Liab.:	$6,731,000	Indic. Yr. Divd.:	NA
Total Assets:	$34,422,000	Net Worth:	$27,690,000	Debt/ Equity:	NA

Mesa Air Group Inc

410 N 44th St., Ste. 100, Phoenix, AZ, 85008; PH: 1-602-685-4000; Fax: 1-602-685-4350; http:// www.mesa-air.com; Email: corpcomm@mesa-air.com

General - Incorporation ....NV	Stock - Price on:12/24/2007 ....$7.09
Employees.....................5,200	Stock Exchange..........................NDQ
Auditor ....Deloitte & Touche LLP	Ticker Symbol........................MESA
Stk Agt.................Computershare Trust Co	Outstanding Shares 31,410,000
Counsel...................Chapman & Cutler	E.P.S $0.73
DUNS No..................05-815-3370	Shareholders.......................NA

Business: The group's principal activity is to operate as regional air carriers providing scheduled passenger and airfreight services. It also carries freight and express packages and has contract with U.S. Postal service for carriage of mail. The group also has code share agreements with America west, midwest express airlines, frontier airlines and us airways. These code-share agreements allow use of the code-share partner's reservation system and flight designator code to identify flights and fares in computer reservation systems, permit use of logos, service marks, aircraft paint schemes and uniforms similar to the code-share partners and provide coordinated schedules and joint advertising. The group serves 163 cities in 40 states, the district of columbia, Canada and Mexico. As of 30-Sep-2003, the group operated a fleet of 150 aircraft and had approximately 943 daily departures. On 19-Dec-2003, it acquired assets of midway airlines corporation.

Primary SIC and add'l.: 4512 4522

CIK No: 0000810332

Subsidiaries: Air Midwest, Inc., Freedom Airlines, Inc, MAGI Insurance, Ltd., Mesa Airlnes, Inc., MPD, Inc., Regional Aircraft Services, Inc., Ritz Hotel Management, Inc.

Officers: Jonathan G. Ornstein/Chmn., CEO, Michael Ferverda/COO - Kunpeng Airlines, Brian Davis/VP - Technical Operations, Mesa Airlines, Inc, Pete Hayes/Pres. - Mesa Pilot Development, Inc, Carter Leake/Sr. VP - Planning, Corporate Development, Kristen Brookshire/VP - Inflight Services, Rodena T. Bojorquez/VP - Contract Management, Mesa Airlines, Inc, Robert Hornberg/CIO, VP - Mesa Air Group, Inc, Scott Lyon/VP - Human Resources, Allan Lowery/VP - Training, Mesa Airlines, Inc, Charles Kettler/VP - Purchasing, Technical Services, Mesa Airlines, Inc, Eric Gust/VP - Safety, Regulatory Compliance, Mesa Airlines, Inc, George P. Murnane/CFO, Exec. VP, Brian S. Gillman/VP, General Counsel, Sec., Michael J. Lotz/COO, Pres. (53 Officers included in Index)

Directors: Jonathan G. Ornstein/Chmn., CEO, Maurice A. Parker/Dir., Robert Beleson/Dir., Joseph L. Manson/Dir., Daniel J. Altobello/Dir., Peter F. Nostrand/Dir., Carlos E. Bonilla/Dir., Richard R. Thayer/Dir.

Owners: Dimensional FundAdvisors Inc./5.40%, Daniel J. Altobello, Michael J. Lotz/1.70%, Maurice A. Parker, Robert Beleson, Barclays Global/10.80%, Brian S. Gillman, Michael Ferverda, George Murnane, Joseph L. Manson, Carlos Bonilla, Peter F. Nostrand, Richard R. Thayer, Insiders/8.10%, Jonathan G. Ornstein/5.10% (16 Owners included in Index)

Financial Data: Fiscal Year End:09/30 **Latest Annual Data:** 9/30/2006

Year	Sales	Net Income
2006	$1,337,197,000	$33,967,000
2005	$1,136,268,000	$56,867,000
2004	$896,812,000	$26,282,000

Curr. Assets:	$458,770,000	Curr. Liab.:	$263,063,000		
Plant, Equip.:	$669,912,000	Total Liab.:	$974,003,000	Indic. Yr. Divd.:	NA
Total Assets:	$1,238,213,000	Net Worth:	$264,210,000	Debt/ Equity:	NA

Mesa Laboratories Inc

12100 W 6th Ave., Lakewood, CO, 80228; PH: 1-303-987-8000; Fax: 1-303-987-8989; http:// www.mesalabs.com; Email: investorrelations@mesalabs.com

General - Incorporation ....CO	Stock - Price on:12/24/2007 ....$23
Employees.....................51	Stock Exchange..........................NDQ
Auditor ...Ehrhardt Keefe Steiner & Hottman P.C	Ticker Symbol........................MLAB
Stk Agt.................Computershare Trust Co	Outstanding Shares 3,180,000
Counsel...................Andrew N. Bernstein	E.P.S $1.22
DUNS No..................10-253-0326	Shareholders.......................NA

Business: The group's principle activities include designing, developing, acquiring, manufacturing and marketing electronic instruments and systems for industrial applications and hemodialysis therapy. The product line includes data logging, tracers, fluid measurements, flow meters and concentration analyzers, instruments for hemodialysis therapy, western meters and dialyzer reprocessor. The company markets reuse data management system. The system consists of custom database management software package, computer system, barcode scanner and label printer. The company has international operations in the South America, Asia, Europe and in other geographical locations. The group operates from United States.

Primary SIC and add'l.: 3825 3823

CIK No: 0000724004

Officers: Luke R. Schmieder/65/Chmn., CEO, Treasurer, Steven W. Peterson/CFO, VP - Finance, Chief Accounting Officer, Sec., John J. Sullivan/COO, Pres.

Directors: Luke R. Schmieder/65/Chmn., CEO, Treasurer, Paul D. Duke/66/Dir., Stuart H. Campbell/78/Dir., Michael T. Brooks/59/Dir., Robert V. Dwyer/67/Dir.

Owners: Robert V. Dwyer/5.80%, Michael T. Brooks/1.10%, Steven W. Peterson/2.20%, Luke R. Schmieder/10.60%, Stuart H. Campbell/3.00%, Insiders/26.10%, FMR Corp./7.30%, John J. Sullivan, Paul D. Duke/3.00%

Financial Data: Fiscal Year End:03/31 **Latest Annual Data:** 3/31/2007

Year	Sales	Net Income
2007	$17,242,000	$3,958,000
2006	$11,583,000	$2,805,000
2005	$10,041,000	$2,312,000

Curr. Assets:	$10,842,000	Curr. Liab.:	$1,469,000	P/E Ratio:	18.85
Plant, Equip.:	$3,521,000	Total Liab.:	$1,631,000	Indic. Yr. Divd.:	$0.400
Total Assets:	$22,354,000	Net Worth:	$20,723,000	Debt/ Equity:	NA

Mesa Offshore Trust

919 Congress Ave., Austin, TX, 78701; PH: 1-800-852-1422

General - Incorporation ....TX	Stock - Price on:12/24/2007 ....$0.076
Employees.....................NA	Stock Exchange..........................OTC
Auditor ....KPMG LLP	Ticker Symbol........................MOSH
Stk Agt ....Computershare Investor Services LLC	Outstanding Shares 71,980,000
Counsel...................................NA	E.P.S $0.00
DUNS No..................................NA	Shareholders.......................NA

Business: The groups principle activity is to provide recruiting services. The groups service area includes the research and development, engineering, marketing, sales, information technology and manufacturing industries. The group operates from United States.

Primary SIC and add'l.: 6733
CIK No: 0000711303
Officers: Mike Ulrich/VP, Trust Officer
Owners: MOSH Holding, L.P/10.20%
Financial Data: Fiscal Year End:12/31 Latest Annual Data: 12/31/2006

Year	Sales	Net Income
2006	$175,000	NA
2005	$2,293,000	NA
2004	NA	NA

Curr. Assets:	$800,000	**Curr. Liab.:**	$800,000		
Plant, Equip.:	NA	**Total Liab.:**	$800,000	**Indic. Yr. Divd.:**	NA
Total Assets:	$803,000	**Net Worth:**	$3,000	**Debt/ Equity:**	NA

Mesa Royalty Trust

919 Congress Ave., Austin, TX, 78701; **PH:** 1-800-852-1422

General - Incorporation	TX	Stock - Price on:12/24/2007	$59.79
Employees	NA	Stock Exchange	NYSE
Auditor	KPMG LLP	Ticker Symbol	MTS
Stk Agt.	KPMG LLP	Outstanding Shares	1,860,000
Counsel	NA	E.P.S.	$5.44
DUNS No.	NA	Shareholders	NA

Business: The groups principal activities include producing and selling natural gas. The group operates from the United States.
Primary SIC and add'l.: 6792
CIK No: 0000313364
Officers: Mike Ulrich/VP, Trust Officer, Paul McDonald/VP - Domestic Reservoir Engineering
Financial Data: Fiscal Year End:12/31 Latest Annual Data: 12/31/2006

Year	Sales	Net Income
2006	$9,839,000	$9,771,000
2005	$10,586,000	$10,523,000
2004	$8,866,000	$8,814,000

Curr. Assets:	$1,733,000	**Curr. Liab.:**	$1,732,000	**P/E Ratio:**	15.94
Plant, Equip.:	NA	**Total Liab.:**	$1,732,000	**Indic. Yr. Divd.:**	$6.490
Total Assets:	$9,835,000	**Net Worth:**	$8,103,000	**Debt/ Equity:**	NA

Mesabi Trust

60 Wall St., 27th fl., New York, NY, 10005; **PH:** 1-615-835-2749

General - Incorporation	NY	Stock - Price on:12/24/2007	$22.32
Employees	NA	Stock Exchange	NYSE
Auditor	Gordon, Hughes & Banks, LLP	Ticker Symbol	NA
Stk Agt.	Deutsche Bank Trust Co America	Outstanding Shares	13,120,000
Counsel	Wolff & Donnelly LLP	E.P.S.	$1.14
DUNS No.	NA	Shareholders	NA

Business: The groups principal activity is to operate mining properties. The group operates from the United States.
Primary SIC and add'l.: 1011
CIK No: 0000065172
Owners: Insiders, Richard G. Lareau, David J. Hoffman, Jeffrey L. Gendell, Tontine Capital Partners, L.P/0.07%, James A. Ehrenberg, Norman F. Sprague.
Financial Data: Fiscal Year End:12/31 Latest Annual Data: 01/31/2007

Year	Sales	Net Income
2007	$17,903,000	$17,147,000
2006	$666,700,000	$45,300,000
2005	$715,400,000	$24,400,000

Curr. Assets:	$4,668,000	**Curr. Liab.:**	$4,275,000	**P/E Ratio:**	15.94
Plant, Equip.:	NA	**Total Liab.:**	$5,415,000	**Indic. Yr. Divd.:**	$0.680
Total Assets:	$5,415,000	**Net Worth:**	$0	**Debt/ Equity:**	NA

Mestek Inc

260 N Elm St., Westfield, MA, 01085; **PH:** 1-413-568-9571; **http://** www.mestek.com

General - Incorporation	PA	Stock - Price on:12/24/2007	$13.75
Employees	2,584	Stock Exchange	OTC
Auditor	Vitale, Caturano & Co. Ltd	Ticker Symbol	MCCK
Stk Agt.	Computershare Shareholder Ser Inc	Outstanding Shares	8,730,000
Counsel	Baker & McKenzie LLP	E.P.S.	$1.07
DUNS No.	00-432-8225	Shareholders	NA

Business: The group's principal activities are to manufacture and sell heating, ventilating and air conditioning equipment (hvac) and metal forming equipment. The hvac segment provides heating, cooling, ventilating, or some combination thereof, for a wide range of residential, commercial and industrial applications. It is comprised of three interrelated hvac product groups: hydronic products, gas and industrial products and air distribution and cooling products. The metal forming segment, operating under the umbrella name 'formtek,' comprises of closely related entities, all manufacturers, remanufacturers or distributors of equipment used in the metal forming industry. The technologies of the metal forming segment include processing of equipment for roll forming, coil processing, metal duct fabrication and tube and pipe systems. The products of the group are sold in the United States, Canada and other foreign countries.
Primary SIC and add'l.: 3549 3585
CIK No: 0000065195
Subsidiaries: 1470604 Ontario, Inc., Advanced Thermal Hydronics, Inc., Axon Electric, LLC, Boyertown Foundry Company, Deltex Partners, Inc., Embassy Manufacturing, Inc., Engel Industries, Inc., Formtek Machinery (Beijing) Co., Ltd, Formtek Metal Forming, Inc, Formtek Metal Processing, Inc., Formtek, Inc., Gentex Partners, Inc., Keyser Properties, Inc., Mestek Canada, Inc., Mestex, Ltd. (Texas limited partnership) 19 Subsidiaries included in the Index
Officers: John E. Reed/Chmn., CEO, Robert P. Kandel/VP - OEM, National Accounting, Edward L. Graham/VP - Industrial Products, Timothy P. Scanlan/Assist., Sec., Nicholas J. Filler/Sr. VP - Corporate, Legal Affairs, Sec., Bruce R. Dewey/COO, Pres., Phil K. Larosa/VP - Distributor

Development, Dave Debell/VP - Human Resources, James A. Burk/VP, James Monahan/VP - Manufacturing Services, Richard E. Kessler/VP - Materials Management, William S. Rafferty/Exec. VP, Stephen M. Shea/Sr. VP - Finance, Treasurer, Stephen M. Schwaber/Sr. VP - Distributor Products, John W. Kaddaras/VP
Directors: John E. Reed/Chmn., CEO, David M. Kelly/Dir., William J. Coad/Dir., Stewart B. Reed/Dir., Edward J. Trainor/Dir., Winston R. Hindle/Dir., David W. Hunter/Dir., George F. King/Dir.
Financial Data: Fiscal Year End:12/31 Latest Annual Data: 12/31/2005

Year	Sales	Net Income
2005	$372,295,000	$7,452,000
2004	$404,863,000	$21,534,000
2003	$366,513,000	-$43,165,000

Curr. Assets:	$138,906,000	**Curr. Liab.:**	$93,924,000	**P/E Ratio:**	22.54
Plant, Equip.:	$52,913,000	**Total Liab.:**	$122,853,000	**Indic. Yr. Divd.:**	NA
Total Assets:	$228,573,000	**Net Worth:**	$104,910,000	**Debt/ Equity:**	NA

Met Pro Corp

160 Cassell Rd., Harleysville, PA, 19438; **PH:** 1-215-723-6751; **Fax:** 1-215-723-6758;
http:// www.met-pro.com; **Email:** mpr@met-pro.com

General - Incorporation	PA	Stock - Price on:12/24/2007	$16.28
Employees	365	Stock Exchange	NYSE
Auditor	Margolis & Co P.C	Ticker Symbol	MPW
Stk Agt.	American Stock Transfer & Trust Co.	Outstanding Shares	NA
Counsel	Jeffrey H. Nicholas Esq	E.P.S.	$0.86
DUNS No.	00-234-9280	Shareholders	NA

Business: The group's principal activities are to manufacture and market product recovery/pollution control equipment and fluid handling equipment for corrosive, abrasive and high temperature liquids. The group operates through two segments: product recovery/pollution control equipment and fluid handling equipment. The product recovery/pollution control equipment segment consists of seven divisions. These divisions supply product recovery and dry particulate collectors used for manufacturing food products and pharmaceuticals. The fluid handling equipment segment consists of four divisions. These divisions design and manufacture filter systems utilizing horizontal disc technology for superior performance. The group operates in the United States, Canada, Europe, Asia and other countries.
Primary SIC and add'l.: 3569 3589
CIK No: 0000065201
Subsidiaries: Flex-Kleen Canada Inc, Mefiag (Guangzhou) Filter Systems Ltd., Mefiag B.V., Met-Pro (Hong Kong) Company Limited, MPC Inc., Pristine Water Solutions Inc., Strobic Air Corporation
Officers: Raymond J. De Hont/54/Chmn., CEO, Pres./$449,352.00, Gary J. Morgan/Dir., Sr. VP - Finance, CFO - Investor Relations/$309,141.00, Vincent J. Verdone/VP, Lew Osterhoudt/VP, GM Keystone Filter Division, Robert P. Replogle/VP, Assist. to The Pres., Hans J.D. Huizinga/MD, Gregory C. Kimmer/VP - General Manager Duall Division/$229,401.00, Paul A. Tetley/Exec. VP Product Recovery, Pollution Control Technologies/$219,177.00, William L. Kacin/76/Dir., Pres., James G. Board/Exec. VP, GM/$234,759.00, Jeffrey H. Nicholas/General Counsel
Directors: Raymond J. De Hont/54/Chmn., CEO, Pres., Gary J. Morgan/Dir., Sr. VP - Finance, CFO - Investor Relations, Alan Lawley/74/Dir., George H. Glatfelter/56/Dir., Nicholas Debenedictis/62/Dir., William L. Kacin/76/Dir., Pres., Michael J. Morris/73/Dir., Constantine N. Papadakis/62/Dir.
Owners: Raymond J. De Hont/1.40%, Alan Lawley, Gregory C. Kimmer, William L. Kacin/1.20%, George H. Glatfelter, Nicholas DeBenedictis, Michael J. Morris, Insiders/8.00%, Gary J. Morgan, Paul A. Tetley, James G. Board
Financial Data: Fiscal Year End:01/31 Latest Annual Data: 1/31/2007

Year	Sales	Net Income
2007	$91,411,000	$7,191,000
2006	$85,116,000	$7,313,000
2005	$72,116,000	$4,815,000

Curr. Assets:	$59,228,000	**Curr. Liab.:**	$14,525,000		
Plant, Equip.:	$16,833,000	**Total Liab.:**	$24,590,000	**Indic. Yr. Divd.:**	$0.220
Total Assets:	$97,167,000	**Net Worth:**	$72,577,000	**Debt/ Equity:**	NA

Meta Financial Group Inc

121 E 5th St., Storm Lake, IA, 50588; **PH:** 1-712-732-4117; **Fax:** 1-712-732-7105;
http:// www.metacash.com; **Email:** contact@metabankonline.com

General - Incorporation	DE	Stock - Price on:12/24/2007	$37.33
Employees	229	Stock Exchange	NDQ
Auditor	McGladrey & Pullen LLP	Ticker Symbol	CASH
Stk Agt.	Registrar & Transfer Co	Outstanding Shares	2,570,000
Counsel	Mack, Harsen, Gadd, Armstrong & Brown	E.P.S.	$0.45
DUNS No.	82-735-0943	Shareholders	NA

Business: The group's principal activities are to provide a range of financial services, which include accepting retail deposits from the general public and investing these funds in one to four family residential mortgage loans. The funds are also invested in commercial and multi-family real estate, agricultural real estate, construction, consumer and commercial business loans. The group is a community oriented savings and loan holding bank, which operates, through first federal savings bank of the midwest and security state bank. The operations are conducted through branch offices located in storm lake, des moines, lake view, laurens, odebolt, sac city, Iowa and South Dakota.
Primary SIC and add'l.: 6035 6712
CIK No: 0000907471
Subsidiaries: Brookings Service Corporation, First Midwest Financial Capital Trust I, First Services Financial Limited, Meta Trust Company, MetaBank, MetaBank West Central
Officers: Tyler J. Haahr/Dir., CEO, Pres., Kathy Thorson/Pres. - Sioux Empire Marketing, Lisa Binder/VP - Marketing, Sales, Sandra K. Hegland/Sr. VP - Human Resources, Tim D. Harvey/Pres. - Brookings Marketing, Brad C. Hanson/Dir., Exec. VP, Ben Guenther/Pres. - Northwest Iowa Marketing, David W. Leedom/Acting CFO, Sr. VP, Brian R. Bond/Chief Lending Officer, Sr. VP, Ron Butterfield/Sr. VP - Meta Payment Systems, Raymond J. Frohnapfel/CIO, Sr. VP, John Hagy/VP, Chief Risk Officer, General Counsel, Barb Koopman/VP - Operations, Troy Moore/COO, Exec. VP, Eugene I. Richardson/Pres. - Central Iowa Marketing, Metabank West Central Marketing
Directors: Tyler J. Haahr/Dir., CEO, Pres., James S. Haahr/Chmn., Rodney G. Muilenburg/Dir., Brad C. Hanson/Dir., Exec. VP, Wayne E. Cooley/Dir., Thurman E. Gaskill/Dir., Frederick V. Moore/Dir.

Owners: Troy Moore/2.88%, Jonathan M. Gaiser, Tontine Financial Partners, L.P./8.63%, James S. Haahr/9.64%, Frederick V. Moore, Insiders/30.78%, Rodney G. Muilenburg/4.17%, Tyler J. Haahr/7.55%, Jeanne Partlow, Thurman E. Gaskill/1.98%, Bradley C. Hanson/1.23%, Meta Financial Group, Inc. Employee Plans/15.19%, Wayne E. Cooley/3.01%

Financial Data: *Fiscal Year End:*09/30 *Latest Annual Data:* 03/31/2007

Year	Sales	Net Income
2007	NA	NA
2006	$53,986,000	$3,921,000
2005	$44,843,000	-$924,000

Curr. Assets:	$119,623,000	**Curr. Liab.:**	$685,969,000	**P/E Ratio:**	219.59
Plant, Equip.:	$17,673,000	**Total Liab.:**	$695,800,000	**Indic. Yr. Divd.:**	$0.520
Total Assets:	$741,132,000	**Net Worth:**	$45,332,000	**Debt/ Equity:**	0.2305

Metabasis Therapeutics Inc

11119 N Torrey Pines Rd., La Jolla, CA, 92037; *PH:* 1-858-587-2770; *Fax:* 1-858-458-3504; *http://* www.mbasis.com

General - Incorporation .... DE | **Stock**- Price on:12/24/2007 .... $8.24
Employees .... 127 | Stock Exchange .... NDQ
Auditor .... Ernst & Young LLP | Ticker Symbol .... MBRX
Stk Agt...... American Stock Transfer & Trust Co. | Outstanding Shares 30,520,000
Counsel .... NA | E.P.S .... -$1.33
DUNS No. .... NA | Shareholders .... NA

Business: The group's principal activity is to discover, develop and commercialize novel small molecule drugs principally to treat metabolic diseases. The diseases treated are diabetes, hyperlipidemia, cholesterol, and obesity. The product candidates in clinical trials are cs-917, remofovir and mb07133, indicated for the treatment of type 2 diabetes, hepatitis b and primary liver cancer, respectively. The group also have research programs focused on metabolic diseases linked to pathways in the liver such as type 2 diabetes, hyperlipidemia and obesity, as well as liver diseases such as hepatitis c and liver fibrosis.

Primary SIC and add'l.: 2834

CIK No: 0001053221

Subsidiaries: Aramed, Inc.

Officers: Paul K. Laikind/52/Dir., CEO, Pres./$863,181.00, John W. Beck/CFO, Sr. VP - Finance/$478,857.00, Edgardo Baracchini/Sr. VP - Business Development/$566,864.00, Mark D. Erion/Dir., Exec. VP - Research, Development, Chief Scientific Officer/$656,976.00, Constance C. Bienfait/VP - Investor Relations, Corporate Communications, Howard L. Foyt/VP - Clinical Development/$419,418.00, Wayne R. Frost/VP - Regulatory Affairs, Quality Assurance

Directors: Paul K. Laikind/52/Dir., CEO, Pres., David F. Hale/Chmn., Arnold L. Oronsky/Dir., William R. Rohn/Dir., George F. Schreiner/Dir., Montgomery D. Bissell/Member - Scientific Advisory Board, Alan P. Venook/Member - Scientific Advisory Board, Daniel D. Burgess/Dir., Gerald I. Shulman/Member - Scientific Advisory Board, Anna Mae Diehl/Member - Scientific Advisory Board, Jules Dienstag/Member - Scientific Advisory Board, Alan Cherrington/Member - Scientific Advisory Board, Luke B. Evnin/Dir., Heinz W. Gschwend/Dir., Mark D. Erion/Dir., Exec. VP - Research, Development, Chief Scientific Officer *(16 Directors included in Index)*

Owners: Insiders, William R. Rohn, Luke B. Evnin, Howard Foyt, Federated Investors, Inc., David F. Hale, Sicor Inc., Paul K. Laikind, Felix J. Baker, Arnold L. Oronsky, Credit Suisse/Sprout Group, Mark D. Erion, InterWest Management Partners VII, LLC, MPM Capital L.P., Edgardo Baracchini *(18 Owners included in Index)*

Financial Data: *Fiscal Year End:*12/31 *Latest Annual Data:* 12/31/2006

Year	Sales	Net Income
2006	$4,386,000	-$33,268,000
2005	$3,771,000	-$23,580,000
2004	$6,837,000	-$14,972,000

Curr. Assets:	$79,413,000	**Curr. Liab.:**	$10,025,000		
Plant, Equip.:	$6,263,000	**Total Liab.:**	$17,717,000	**Indic. Yr. Divd.:**	NA
Total Assets:	$85,855,000	**Net Worth:**	$68,138,000	**Debt/ Equity:**	0.0584

Metabolic Research Inc

Formerly: Datastand Technologies Inc
8333 Won Rd., Ste. 106, Woodbridge, ON, L4L 8E2; *PH:* 1-416-626-5346

General - Incorporation .... IN | **Stock**- Price on:12/24/2007 .... NA
Employees .... NA | Stock Exchange .... NA
Auditor .... Sherb & Co., LLP | Ticker Symbol .... NA
Stk Agt........ Signature Stock Transfer, Inc. | Outstanding Shares .... NA
Counsel .... NA | E.P.S .... NA
DUNS No. .... NA | Shareholders .... NA

Business: The group's principal activities are to provide customer-oriented information research and document delivery services. The group provides up-to-date and focused information to businesses to meet their business needs, develops Internet software and publishes financial data. The operations are carried on through two divisions: business to business division, which provides financial data to websites; and business to consumer division, which operates a financial network. The group's first database is a proprietary financial database which contains fundamental corporate data on 3000 companies quoted on the otc- bb. This database is updated daily to reflect the numerous changes, additions and deletions on otc- bb issues. In addition, the group provides 28 distinct fields of data on over 2700 otc-bb quoted companies.

Primary SIC and add'l.: 7375

CIK No: 0001081369

Officers: Nick Montesano/37/Chmn., CEO, David P. Summers/COO, Pres., Robert Shorr/Scientific Team, Tianna W. Owen/CFO, COO, Mike King/Contact - Investor Relations

Directors: Nick Montesano/37/Chmn., CEO

Owners: T. W. Owen/19.50%, Insiders/21.40%, David P. Summers/19.50%, Nick Montesano/1.90%

Financial Data: *Fiscal Year End:*12/31 *Latest Annual Data:* 12/31/2006

Year	Sales	Net Income
2006	$18,000	-$13,000
2005	$19,000	-$6,000
2004	$19,000	-$10,000

Curr. Assets:	$2,000	**Curr. Liab.:**	$27,000		
Plant, Equip.:	$2,000	**Total Liab.:**	$27,000	**Indic. Yr. Divd.:**	NA
Total Assets:	$4,000	**Net Worth:**	-$24,000	**Debt/ Equity:**	NA

Metabolix Inc

21 Erie St., Cambridge, MA, 02139; *PH:* 1-617-583-1700; *Fax:* 1-617-583-1768; *http://* www.metabolix.com; *Email:* info@metabolix.com

General - Incorporation .... DE | **Stock**- Price on:12/24/2007 .... $21.8
Employees .... 59 | Stock Exchange .... NDQ
Auditor .... NA | Ticker Symbol .... MBLX
Stk Agt ..... American Stock Transfer & Trust Co. | Outstanding Shares 21,620,000
Counsel .... NA | E.P.S .... -$2.03
DUNS No. .... NA | Shareholders .... NA

Business: The groups principle activities include developing and planning for commercialize environmentally sustainable, economically attractive alternatives to petrochemical based plastics, fuels and chemicals. The product of the group is Natural Plastic. The group products sold under the trade names Mirel(TM) and Telles(TM). The group operates from the United States. The group's quarterly revenue for September 2007 was 0.18 millions of USD.

Primary SIC and add'l.: 2869 2821 2823

CIK No: 0001121702

Subsidiaries: Metabolix Securities Corp.

Officers: Jay Kouba/Chmn., CEO, Pres., Oliver P. Peoples/Dir., Chief Scientific Officer, VP - Research & Development/$522,305.00, James J. Barber/Dir., Pres./$1,160,180.00, Kathleen Heaney/Investor Relations Officer, Johan Van Walsem/VP - Manufacturing, Development, Operations/$364,105.00, Thomas G. Auchincloss/Head - Business Development, New Technologies/$364,105.00, Robert C. Findlen/VP - Sales, Marketing/$382,246.00, Brian Igoe/VP, Chief Brand Officer, Robert Whitehouse/Dir. - Applications Development, Dan Gilliland/Dir. - Business Development, Ben Locke/Dir. - Government Programs, Kristi Snell/Team Leader - Plant Metabolic Engineering, Tom M. Ramseier/Assoc. Dir. - Microbial Development, Frank Skraly/Team Leader - Microbial Metabolic Engineering, Yossef Shabtai/Sr. Fermentation Scientist *(18 Officers included in Index)*

Directors: Jay Kouba/Chmn., CEO, Pres., Edward Giles/Dir., Jack W. Lasersohn/Dir., Robert L. Van Nostrand/Dir., Edward M. Muller/Dir., James J. Barber/Dir., Pres., Peter N. Kellogg/Dir., Oliver P. Peoples/Dir., Chief Scientific Officer, VP - Research & Development, Anthony J. Sinskey/Dir., Matthew Strobeck/Dir.

Owners: The Vertical Group, L.P./7.57%, Jack W. Lasersohn/7.65%, Matthew Strobeck/2.68%, State Farm Mutual Automobile Insurance Co./10.88%, Insiders/28.50%, Jay Kouba, Robert C. Findlen, Archer Daniels Midland Company/5.78%, Thomas G. Auchincloss, Oliver P. Peoples/3.02%, Edward M. Muller/5.51%, James J. Barber/1.80%, Robert L. Van Nostrand, Edward M. Giles/4.82%, Mazama Capital Management,Inc./5.65% *(18 Owners included in Index)*

Financial Data: *Fiscal Year End:*12/31 *Latest Annual Data:* 12/31/2006

Year	Sales	Net Income
2006	$4,590,000	-$16,062,000
2005	$2,781,000	-$7,625,000
2004	$3,678,000	-$5,055,000

Curr. Assets:	$123,400,000	**Curr. Liab.:**	$3,221,000		
Plant, Equip.:	$3,673,000	**Total Liab.:**	$18,008,000	**Indic. Yr. Divd.:**	NA
Total Assets:	$127,596,000	**Net Worth:**	$109,588,000	**Debt/ Equity:**	NA

Metairie BK & TR Co LA

3344 Metairie Rd., Metairie, LA, 70001; *PH:* 1-504-834-6330; *http://* www.metairiebank.com; *Email:* info@metairiebank.com

General - Incorporation .... | **Stock**- Price on:12/24/2007 .... $34
Employees .... NA | Stock Exchange .... OTC
Auditor .... NA | Ticker Symbol .... MBKL
Stk Agt .... NA | Outstanding Shares .... NA
Counsel .... NA | E.P.S .... NA
DUNS No. .... NA | Shareholders .... NA

Business: The groups principal activity is to provide personal banking, business banking, professional banking, consumer lending, home mortgage lending, commercial lending and online banking services. The group operates from the United States.

Primary SIC and add'l.: 6021

CIK No:

Officers: Reginald Smith/CEO, Pres., William F. Haacke/CFO, Ray Markase/Dir. - Human Resources, Scott A. Schellhaas/Mortgage Lending Specialist, Elaine White/Mortgage Lending Specialist, Ed Vollenweider/Mortgage Lending Specialist, Leroy James/Assist. VP - New Vehicles, Beverly Nauck/Assist. VP - Used Vehicles, Bruce Chapman/Assist. VP - Home Equity Loans, Sandra Sanders/Banking Officer, Jack Blanke/Contact - Loan Specialist, Ron Cunningham/Contact - Loan Specialist, Paul A. Myers/Contact - Loan Specialist

Metal Management Inc

500 N Dearborn St., Ste. 405, Chicago, IL, 60610; *PH:* 1-312-645-0700; *Fax:* 1-312-645-0714; *http://* www.mtlm.com

General - Incorporation .... DE | **Stock**- Price on:12/24/2007 .... $45.69
Employees .... 1,829 | Stock Exchange .... NYSE
Auditor .... PricewaterhouseCoopers LLP | Ticker Symbol .... MM
Stk Agt .... Mellon Investor Services LLC | Outstanding Shares 25,610,000
Counsel .... NA | E.P.S $3.21
DUNS No. .... NA | Shareholders .... NA

Business: The groups principal activity is to provide metals recyclers services. The products of the group include scrap metals. Customers served by the group include manufacturers scrap sources and producers of electricity, telecommunication service. In March 31, 2006 the group acquired Morris Recycling, Inc. The group operates from the United States. The net sale of the group for the year 2006 was $1,589,126 (thousands).

Primary SIC and add'l.: 5093

CIK No: 0000795665

Subsidiaries: CIM Trucking, Inc, Metal Management Aerospace, Inc, Metal Management Alabama, Inc, Metal Management Arizona, LLC, Metal Management Connecticut, Inc, Metal Management Indiana, Inc, Metal Management Jackson, LLC, Metal Management Memphis, LLC, Metal Management Midwest, Inc, Metal Management Mississippi, Inc, Metal Management Nashville, LLC,, Metal Management New Haven, Inc, Metal Management Northeast, Inc, Metal Management Ohio, Inc, Metal Management Pittsburgh, Inc 26 Subsidiaries included in the Index

Officers: Daniel W. Dienst/Chmn., CEO, Pres./$4,642,934.00, Robert C. Larry/CFO, Exec. VP - Finance, Treasurer/$1,153,842.00, Amit N. Patel/VP - Finance, Controller, Principal Accounting Officer, Christopher Dandrow/Pres. - Metal Management Midwest, Inc/$1,148,540.00, Larry S. Snyder/Exec. VP - Non - Ferrous/$944,809.00, Kenneth P. Mueller/Pres. - Metal Management Arizona, LLC/$755,576.00, Alan D. Ratner/Pres. - Metal Management Northeast, Inc., Thomas O. Whitman/Pres. - Metal Management Mississippi, Inc.

Directors: Daniel W. Dienst/Chmn., CEO, Pres., Norman R. Bobins/Dir., John T. Dilacqua/Dir., Robert Lewon/Dir., Gerald E. Morris/Dir.

Owners: Royce & Associates, LLC/14.70%, Daniel W. Dienst/3.50%, CCM Master Qualified Fund, Ltd./5.10%, Robert Lewon, Insiders/5.00%, Gerald E. Morris, Larry S. Snyder, Norman R. Bobins, T. Rowe Price Associates, Inc./5.30%, Robert C. Larry, Alan D. Ratner, John T. DiLacqua

Financial Data: *Fiscal Year End:* 03/31 *Latest Annual Data:* 3/31/2007

Year	Sales	Net Income
2007	$2,229,012,000	$116,405,000
2006	$1,589,126,000	$60,264,000
2005	$1,701,958,000	$92,250,000

Curr. Assets:	$445,728,000	**Curr. Liab.:**	$225,546,000	**P/E Ratio:**	12.62
Plant, Equip.:	$187,124,000	**Total Liab.:**	$230,693,000	**Indic. Yr. Divd.:**	$0.300
Total Assets:	$695,523,000	**Net Worth:**	$464,830,000	**Debt/ Equity:**	0.0045

Metal Mgmt Inc

500 N Dearborn St., Ste. 405, Chicago, IL, 60610; *PH:* 1-312-645-0700; *Fax:* 1-312-645-0714; *http://* www.mtlm.com

General - Incorporation	DE	**Stock**- Price on:12/24/2007	$45.76
Employees	1,829	Stock Exchange	NYSE
Auditor	PricewaterhouseCoopers LLP	Ticker Symbol	MMA
Stk Agt	LaSalle Bank N.A	Outstanding Shares	25,610,000
Counsel	NA	E.P.S	$4.43
DUNS No.	10-296-2370	Shareholders	NA

Business: The group's principal activity is to collect and process ferrous and non-ferrous metals. The group collects industrial scrap and obsolete scrap, processes it into reusable forms and supplies the recycled metals to its customers, including electric arc furnace mills, integrated steel mills, foundries, secondary smelters and metals brokers. These services are provided through the recycling facilities located in 13 states. The ferrous products primarily include shredded, sheared, cold briquetted, bundled scrap, turnings and broken furnace iron. The group also processes non-ferrous metals, including aluminum, stainless steel, copper, brass, titanium and high-temperature alloys, using similar techniques and through application of certain of the proprietary technologies.

Primary SIC and add'l.: 5093

CIK No: 0000795665

Subsidiaries: CIM Trucking, Inc, Metal Management Aerospace, Inc, Metal Management Alabama, Inc, Metal Management Arizona, LLC, Metal Management Connecticut, Inc, Metal Management Indiana, Inc, Metal Management Jackson, LLC, Metal Management Memphis, LLC, Metal Management Midwest, Inc, Metal Management Mississippi, Inc, Metal Management Nashville, LLC, Metal Management New Haven, Inc, Metal Management Northeast, Inc, Metal Management Ohio, Inc, Metal Management Pittsburgh, Inc 26 Subsidiaries included in the Index

Officers: Daniel W. Dienst/Chmn., CEO, Pres./$4,642,934.00, Robert C. Larry/CFO, Exec. VP - Finance, Treasurer/$1,153,842.00, Christopher Dandrow/Pres. - Metal Management Midwest, Inc, Kenneth P. Mueller/Pres. - Metal Management Arizona, LLC, Thomas O. Whitman/Pres. - Metal Management Mississippi, Inc

Directors: Daniel W. Dienst/Chmn., CEO, Pres., John T. Dilacqua/Dir., Robert Lewon/Dir., Norman R. Bobins/Dir., Gerald E. Morris/Dir.

Owners: John T. DiLacqua, Robert C. Larry, Robert Lewon, Daniel W. Dienst/3.50%, Gerald E. Morris, T. Rowe Price Associates, Inc./5.30%, CCM Master Qualified Fund, Ltd./5.10%, Norman R. Bobins, Royce& Associates, LLC/14.70%, Larry S. Snyder, Alan D. Ratner, Insiders/5.00%

Financial Data: *Fiscal Year End:* 03/31 *Latest Annual Data:* 3/31/2007

Year	Sales	Net Income
2007	$2,229,012,000	$116,405,000
2006	$1,589,126,000	$60,264,000
2005	$1,701,958,000	$92,250,000

Curr. Assets:	$445,728,000	**Curr. Liab.:**	$225,546,000	**P/E Ratio:**	12.64
Plant, Equip.:	$187,124,000	**Total Liab.:**	$230,693,000	**Indic. Yr. Divd.:**	$0.300
Total Assets:	$695,523,000	**Net Worth:**	$464,830,000	**Debt/ Equity:**	NA

Metal Storm Ltd

4350 N Fairfax Dr., Ste. 810, Arlington, VA, 22203; *PH:* 1-703-248-8218; *Fax:* 1-703-248-8263; *http://* www.metalstorm.com

General - Incorporation	Australia	**Stock**- Price on:12/24/2007	$2.35
Employees	25	Stock Exchange	NYSE
Auditor	Ernst & Young LLP	Ticker Symbol	MTW
Stk Agt	Bank of New York	Outstanding Shares	27,630,000
Counsel	NA	E.P.S	-$0.42
DUNS No.	NA	Shareholders	NA

Business: The group's principle activity is the research and development of electronic ballistics technology. It offers applications across a broad range of defence and commercial end uses. It has offices in Australia and the United States.

Primary SIC and add'l.: 8731

CIK No: 0001119775

Subsidiaries: Metal Storm Inc., Metal Storm U.S.A. Limited, ProCam Machine LLC

Officers: Lee Finniear/CEO, Peter Faulkner/Sr. VP - Dir., US Operations, Arthur Schatz/VP - Business Development, Peter Pursey/Program Development Mgr., Joe Cronin/Managing Engineer, Peter R. Wetzig/Company Sec.

Directors: Terence James O'Dwyer/Chmn., James Michael Crunk/Non Exec. Dir., Peter Jonson/Non Exec. Dir., John Nicholls/Non Exec. Dir.

Owners: J. M. Crunk, T. J. ODwyer, P. R. Wetzig, P. D. Jonson, James Michael ODwyer

Financial Data: *Fiscal Year End:* 12/31 *Latest Annual Data:* 12/31/2006

Year	Sales	Net Income
2006	$1,846,000	-$8,754,000
2005	$606,000	-$8,773,000
2004	$3,885,000	-$9,652,000

Curr. Assets:	$21,000,000	**Curr. Liab.:**	$19,810,000		
Plant, Equip.:	$496,000	**Total Liab.:**	$20,444,000	**Indic. Yr. Divd.:**	NA
Total Assets:	$26,988,000	**Net Worth:**	$6,544,000	**Debt/ Equity:**	NA

Metaldyne Corp

47603 Halyard Dr., Plymouth, MI, 48170; *PH:* 1-734-207-6200; *Fax:* 1-734-207-6500; *http://* www.metaldyne.com

General - Incorporation	DE	**Stock**- Price on:12/24/2007	NA
Employees	NA	Stock Exchange	NA
Auditor	KPMG LLP	Ticker Symbol	NA
Stk Agt	NA	Outstanding Shares	NA
Counsel	NA	E.P.S	NA
DUNS No.	11-926-9827	Shareholders	NA

Business: The group's principle activity is to provides metal forming, precision casting, machining and modular assembly capabilities. The group operates from United States.

Primary SIC and add'l.: 3313 3312

CIK No: 0000745448

Subsidiaries: Metaldyne Company LLC, Metaldyne Precision Forming

Officers: Timothy D. Leuliette/Chmn., CEO, Pres., Jeff Stafeil/CFO, Exec. VP, Joe Nowak/Pres. - Chassis Group, Kimberly A. Kovac/Exec. VP - Human Resources, Metaldyne University, Linda Theisen/VP - Global Purchasing, Powertrain Sales, Steve Dickerson/VP - Quality, Advanced Manufacturing, James Hudak/MD - Asia Pacific, Tammera Hallums/Mgr. - Global Corporate Communications, Thomas A. Amato/Exec. VP - Corporate Development, Chief Integration Officer, Tom Chambers/COO, Pres., Logan Robinson/Exec. VP, General Counsel - Government Relations, Sec., Marjorie Sorge/VP - Corporate Communications, Daniel J. Brinker/VP - Sales, Engineering, Chassis Group, Jeff Beringer/CIO, VP, Jim Hudak/MD - Metaldyne Asia Pacific *(18 Officers included in Index)*

Directors: Timothy D. Leuliette/Chmn., CEO, Pres.

Owners: Insiders, Masco Corporation/5.82%, Heartland Industrial Associates, L.L.C./50.04%, Joseph Nowak, Credit Suisse Entities/24.60%, Thomas A. Amato

Metalico Inc

186 N Ave. E, Cranford, NJ, 07016; *PH:* 1-908-497-9610; *Fax:* 1-908-497-1097; *http://* www.metalico.com; *Email:* info@metalico.com

General - Incorporation	DE	**Stock**- Price on:12/24/2007	$8.3999
Employees	391	Stock Exchange	AMEX
Auditor	McGladrey & Pullen LLP	Ticker Symbol	MEA
Stk Agt	Corporate Stock Transfer, Inc.	Outstanding Shares	15,240,000
Counsel	NA	E.P.S	$0.42
DUNS No.	NA	Shareholders	NA

Business: The group operates in twelve locations through eight operating subsidiaries in two distinct business segments: (a) ferrous and non-ferrous scrap metal recycling and lead metal product manufacturing, fabricating, and smelting. The group operates from United States.

Primary SIC and add'l.: 3330

CIK No: 0001048685

Subsidiaries: Buffalo Hauling Corp, General Smelting and Refining, Inc., Gulf Coast Recycling, Inc., HHP Corporation, Lake Erie Recycling Corp, Mayco Industries, Inc., Metalico Alabama Realty, Inc, Metalico Aluminum Recovery, Inc, Metalico Niagara, Inc, Metalico Rochester, Inc, Metalico Syracuse, Inc., Metalico-College Grove, Inc., Metalico-Evans, Inc, Metalico-Granite City, Inc, Santa Rosa Lead Products, Inc. 16 Subsidiaries included in the Index

Officers: Carlos E. Aguero/Chmn., CEO, Pres./$424,320.00, Michael J. Drury/Dir., Exec. VP/$302,265.00, Peter Boykin/Contact - West Coast Shot, Inc, Robyn Richardson/Contact - Granite City Shot, Brandon Stetser/Contact - Tranzact Corporation, Bill Lowery/Contact - Metalico Annaco, Arnold S. Graber/Exec. VP, General Counsel, Sec./$278,073.00, Eric W. Finlayson/Sr. VP, CFO/$200,313.00, Jesse Swartz/Ferrous Contact - Metalico Annaco, Brian Carlone/Non - Ferrous Contact - Metalico Annaco, Kurt Ellis/Contact - Federal Autocat Recycling, Gerry Smith/Contact - Hypercat ACP, Warren Jennings/VP - Operations/$239,794.00, David J. Delbianco/VP - Business Development, Kevin R. Whalen/VP, Corporate Controller *(26 Officers included in Index)*

Directors: Carlos E. Aguero/Chmn., CEO, Pres., Walter H. Barandiaran/Dir., Earl B. Cornette/Dir., Michael J. Drury/Dir., Exec. VP, Paul A. Garrett/Dir., Bret R. Maxwell/Dir.

Owners: Argentum Capital Partners II, L.P., Kitty Hawk Capital Limited Partnership IV, Kitty Hawk Capital Limited Partnership IV, Earl B. Cornette/1.40%, Arnold S. Graber, Walter H. Barandiaran, Carlos E. Agero, Michael J. Drury, Insiders, Argentum Capital Partners II, L.P./3.40%, Paul A. Garrett, Eric W. Finlayson, Apex Strategic Partners, LLC, RFE Investment Partners V, L.P./3.80%, RFE Investment Partners V, L.P. *(24 Owners included in Index)*

Financial Data: *Fiscal Year End:* 12/31 *Latest Annual Data:* 12/31/2006

Year	Sales	Net Income
2006	$207,655,000	$10,328,000
2005	$164,292,000	$5,589,000
2004	$115,363,000	$6,664,000

Curr. Assets:	$45,967,000	**Curr. Liab.:**	$22,072,000	**P/E Ratio:**	20.00
Plant, Equip.:	$29,425,000	**Total Liab.:**	$44,694,000	**Indic. Yr. Divd.:**	NA
Total Assets:	$118,407,000	**Net Worth:**	$73,713,000	**Debt/ Equity:**	0.1883

Metaline Contact Mines

PO Box 387, Murray, ID, 83874; *PH:* 1-920-987-5317; *Fax:* 1-920-987-5317; *http://* www.metalinecontactmines.com; *Email:* info@metalinecontactmines.com

General - Incorporation	WA	**Stock**- Price on:12/24/2007	NA
Employees	NA	Stock Exchange	OTC
Auditor	Williams & Webster, P.S	Ticker Symbol	MTLI
Stk Agt	Columbia Stock Transfer Co	Outstanding Shares	NA
Counsel	Michael C. Ormsby	E.P.S	$0.00
DUNS No.	NA	Shareholders	NA

Business: The group's principle activities include acquiring, leasing, exploring and to developing and mining mineral resource properties. The company acquires non-patented zinc-lead mining claims and other mineral rights in the metaline district, pend oreille county in the state of Washington. These non-patented mining claims are claims in which an individual, corporation or other legal entity has

obtained a right to remove and extract minerals from the land but full title of the land has not been acquired from the United States government. The company leases its mineral rights and properties to cominco American incorporated. Cominco is currently exploring for zinc and lead ores on the company's mineral rights. The group operates from United States.

Primary SIC and add'l.: 1481

CIK No: 0001113006

Subsidiaries: Gulf Resources & Chemical

Officers: Michael C. Ormsby/Legal Counsel

Directors: Ed Pommerening/Dir., David O. Baldwin/Dir., John W. Beasley/Dir., Jack W. Kendrick/Dir., Richard L. Howell/Dir.

Financial Data: Fiscal Year End: 12/31   **Latest Annual Data:** 12/31/2005

Year	Sales	Net Income
2005	$67,000	$22,000
2004	$26,000	-$69,000
2003	$16,000	-$17,000

Curr. Assets:	$85,000	Curr. Liab.:	$4,000		
Plant, Equip.:	$250,000	Total Liab.:	$4,000	Indic. Yr. Divd.:	NA
Total Assets:	$509,000	Net Worth:	$505,000	Debt/ Equity:	NA

Metalink Ltd

105 Lake Forest Way, Folsom, CA, 95630; **PH:** 1-916-355-1580; **Fax:** 1-916-355-1585; http:// www.metalinkltd.com; **Email:** sales_info@metalinkbb.com

General - Incorporation	Israel	**Stock** - Price on:12/24/2007	$5.4
Employees	162	Stock Exchange	NDQ
Auditor	Brightman Almagor & Co	Ticker Symbol	NA
Stk Agt.	NA	Outstanding Shares	19,880,000
Counsel	Goldfarb, Levy, Eran & Co	E.P.S.	-$0.97
DUNS No.	NA	Shareholders	NA

Business: The groups principle activities include designing, development and marketing of digital subscriber line chip sets used by manufacturers of telecommunications equipment. The group operates from United States.

Primary SIC and add'l.: 3674

CIK No: 0001098462

Subsidiaries: Metalink Asia Pacific Ltd., Metalink Inc, Metalink International Ltd., Metalink Japan K.K.

Officers: Tzvika Shukhman/Chmn., Founder, CEO, Barry Volinskey/VP - Wireless LAN Marketing, David Pereg/VP - Corporate Development, Yuval Ruhama/CFO, Liat Hortig/VP - Human Resources, Itzik Ben-Bassat/COO, Bentsi Algazi/VP - Operations, Yaron Ashri/VP - Engineering, Wireless

Directors: Tzvika Shukhman/Chmn., Founder, CEO, Naama Zeldis/45/Dir.

Owners: Uzi Rozenberg/24.00%, Tzvi Shukhman/28.80%

Financial Data: Fiscal Year End: 12/31   **Latest Annual Data:** 12/31/2006

Year	Sales	Net Income
2006	$14,476,000	-$16,220,000
2005	$14,529,000	-$16,288,000
2004	$22,112,000	-$12,931,000

Curr. Assets:	$29,294,000	Curr. Liab.:	$6,338,000		
Plant, Equip.:	$3,517,000	Total Liab.:	$9,403,000	Indic. Yr. Divd.:	NA
Total Assets:	$40,286,000	Net Worth:	$30,883,000	Debt/ Equity:	NA

Metallic Ventures Gold Inc

40 King St. W., Ste. 2100, Toronto, ON, M5H 3Y2; **PH:** 1-775-826-7567; http:// www.metallicventuresgold.com; **Email:** mvg@metallicventuresgold.com

General - Incorporation	Canada	**Stock** - Price on:12/24/2007	NA
Employees	NA	Stock Exchange	AMEX
Auditor	NA	Ticker Symbol	NA
Stk Agt.	NA	Outstanding Shares	NA
Counsel	NA	E.P.S.	NA
DUNS No.	NA	Shareholders	NA

Business: The group's principle activity is to operate mineral exploration with an inventory of gold assets primarily within the State of Nevada. Metallic controls two pre-feasibility projects, Converse and Goldfield, and eight exploration projects. The group's current combined resource base is 5.96 million measured and indicated ounces of gold, 0.84 million inferred ounces of gold and 17 million ounces of silver. Metallic is well funded and currently focused on advancing Converse and Goldfield through scoping and feasibility studies and seek joint venture partners. The exploration projects are located within prolific Nevada trends and have the potential for new gold discoveries. Metallic has entered into Exploration and Option Agreements with Geologix (U.S.) Inc. on the Scraper Springs Project, and with Royal Standard Minerals, Inc. on the Mustang Canyon Project.

Primary SIC and add'l.: 1040

CIK No: 0001253882

Subsidiaries: etallic Ventures (U.S.)Inc., Metallic GoldfieldInc., Metallic NevadaInc.

Officers: Jeffrey R. Ward/Chmn., CEO, Robert Bennett/VP - Exploration, Miles Bachman/CFO, Terra Andromeda/Controller

Directors: Jeffrey R. Ward/Chmn., CEO, Rand A. Lomas/Dir., Norman F. Findlay/Dir., Timothy J. Ryan/Dir., Richard D. McNeely/Dir., William R. Blundell/Dir.

Curr. Assets:	$3,378,000	Curr. Liab.:	$301,000		
Plant, Equip.:	$27,000	Total Liab.:	$301,000	Indic. Yr. Divd.:	NA
Total Assets:	$7,612,000	Net Worth:	$7,311,000	Debt/ Equity:	NA

Metallica Resources Inc

12200 E Briarwood Ave., Ste. 165, Centennial, CO, 80112; **PH:** 1-303-796-0229; http:// www.metal-res.com; **Email:** metallica@metal-res.com

General - Incorporation	Canada	**Stock** - Price on:12/24/2007	$4.55
Employees	85	Stock Exchange	NDQ
Auditor	PricewaterhouseCoopers LLP	Ticker Symbol	MRBK
Stk Agt.	Equity Transfer Services Inc	Outstanding Shares	NA
Counsel	Beach, Hepburn	E.P.S.	-$0.07
DUNS No.	96-745-4463	Shareholders	NA

Business: The group's principle activity is precious metals exploration and acquisition of mineral deposits principally in Mexico and South America. The company is advancing a mine development project in Mexico in conjunction with glamis gold ltd. The company is also pursuing various exploration projects in north and South America. The group operates from United States.

Primary SIC and add'l.: 1041

CIK No: 0000927993

Subsidiaries: Datawave Sciences Inc., De Re Holdings Inc., Metallica (Barbados) Inc., Metallica Management Inc., Minera Metallica Ltda., Minera San Xavier, S.A. de C.V., MMM Exploraciones S.A. de C.V., Raleigh Mining International Ltd., Servicios del Plata y Oro, S.A. de C.V.

Officers: Richard J. Hall/Dir., CEO, Pres., Brad Blacketor/VP, CFO, Sec., Troy J. Fierro/VP - Operations, Bradley J. Blacketor/49/VP, CFO, Sec., Mark A. Petersen/VP - Exploration

Directors: Richard J. Hall/Dir., CEO, Pres., Craig J. Nelsen/56/Chmn., Oliver Lennox-King/58/Dir., Amjad J. Ali/64/Dir., Ian A. Shaw/68/Dir., Alan J. Spence/Dir., Robert Martinez/61/Dir., Jorge Mendizabal/Dir.

Owners: Oliver Lennox-King, Alan J. Spence, Jorge Mendizabal, Bradley J. Blacketor, Xstrata PLC, Royce & Associates, LLC, Ian A. Shaw, Craig J. Nelsen, Troy J. Fierro, Richard J. Hall, Mark A. Petersen

Financial Data: Fiscal Year End: 12/31   **Latest Annual Data:** 12/31/2006

Year	Sales	Net Income
2006	$1,216,000	-$4,734,000
2005	$9,386,000	$7,453,000
2004	$1,225,000	$954,000

Curr. Assets:	$47,886,000	Curr. Liab.:	$5,790,000		
Plant, Equip.:	$72,666,000	Total Liab.:	$6,958,000	Indic. Yr. Divd.:	NA
Total Assets:	$120,792,000	Net Worth:	$113,834,000	Debt/ Equity:	NA

Metalline Mining Company

1330 E Margaret Ave., Coeur D Alene, ID, 83815; **PH:** 1-208-665-2002; **Fax:** 1-202-665-0041; http:// www.metalin.com; **Email:** metalin@attglobal.net

General - Incorporation	NV	**Stock** - Price on:12/24/2007	$4.0801
Employees	4	Stock Exchange	NDQ
Auditor	Williams & Webster, P.S.	Ticker Symbol	MMLP
Stk Agt.	Idaho Stock Transfer Co.,	Outstanding Shares	36,820,000
Counsel	NA	E.P.S.	-$0.383
DUNS No.	NA	Shareholders	NA

Business: The groups principle activity is exploration of minerals. The group operates from the United States and Canada. The groups principle activities include acquiring and leasing hotel properties. The group acquired the Crowne Plaza Jacksonville in 2005 and Louisville Ramada Riverfront Inn in the year 2006. The group operates from United States.

Primary SIC and add'l.: 1081

CIK No: 0001031093

Subsidiaries: Contratistas de Sierra Mojada S.A. de C.V., Minera Metalin S.A. de C.V.

Officers: Merlin Bingham/Chmn., CEO, Pres., Roger Kolvoord/Dir., Exec. VP, Terry Brown/VP - Operations, Wayne Schoonmaker/Treasurer, Sec., Robert J. Devers/CFO

Directors: Merlin Bingham/Chmn., CEO, Pres., Roger Kolvoord/Dir., Exec. VP, Wesley Pomeroy/Dir., Robert Kramer/Dir., Gregory A. Hahn/Dir.

Owners: Roger Kolvoord/2.80%, Duncan Hsia/6.90%, Merlin D. Bingham/5.90%, Insiders/11.80%, Terry Brown, Wesley Pomeroy/1.40%, Robert Kramer/1.40%, Lazarus Investment Partners LLP/7.80%, John C. Barrett/8.80%, Steven Carlitz/6.70%

Financial Data: Fiscal Year End: 10/31   **Latest Annual Data:** 10/31/2006

Year	Sales	Net Income
2006	NA	-$11,193,000
2005	NA	-$3,302,000
2004	NA	-$5,037,000

Curr. Assets:	$6,665,000	Curr. Liab.:	$490,000		
Plant, Equip.:	$612,000	Total Liab.:	$490,000	Indic. Yr. Divd.:	NA
Total Assets:	$11,612,000	Net Worth:	$11,122,000	Debt/ Equity:	NA

Metallurg Holdings Inc

435 Devon Pk. Dr., Bldg 400, Wayne, PA, 19087; **PH:** 1-212-835-0200; http:// www.metallurg.com

General - Incorporation	DE	**Stock** - Price on:12/24/2007	NA
Employees	NA	Stock Exchange	NA
Auditor	PricewaterhouseCoopers LLP	Ticker Symbol	NA
Stk Agt.	NA	Outstanding Shares	NA
Counsel	NA	E.P.S.	NA
DUNS No.	NA	Shareholders	NA

Business: The group operates through its subsdiary whose principle actvitis include producing and selling high-quality specialty metals, alloys and metallic chemicals, which are essential to the production of high-performance aluminum and titanium alloys, superalloys, steel and certain non-metallic materials for various applications in the aerospace, power supply, automotive, petrochemical processing and telecommunications industries to customers worldwide. The group operates from United States.

Primary SIC and add'l.: 6719 8734 3325

CIK No: 0001067054

Subsidiaries: Companhia Industrial Fluminense, London & Scandinavian Metallurgical Co Limited, Metallurg Acquisition Corp., Metallurg Holdings Corporation, Metallurg International Resources, LLC, Metallurg Services, Inc., Metallurg, Inc., MIR (China), Inc., SMC

Officers: Heinz C. Schimmelbusch/Chmn., CEO, Eric E. Jackson/COO, Pres., William J. Levy/Sr. VP, CFO

Directors: Heinz C. Schimmelbusch/Chmn., CEO, Arthur R. Spector/Vice Chmn., Nils A. Kindwall/Dir., Samuel A. Plum/Dir., Michael J. Emmi/Dir., Michael D. Winfield/Dir.

Metals USA Inc

One Riverway, Ste 1100, Houston, TX, 77056; **PH:** 1-713-965-0990; http:// www.metalsusa.com

General - Incorporation .... DE
Employees .... NA
Auditor .... Deloitte & Touche LLP
Stk Agt .... EquiServe Trust Co N.A
Counsel .... Fullbright & Jaworski LLP
DUNS No. 15-780-8379

Stock- Price on:12/24/2007 .... NA
Stock Exchange .... NDQ
Ticker Symbol .... MVCO
Outstanding Shares .... NA
E.P.S .... NA
Shareholders .... NA

Business: The group's principle activity is to provide value-added processed steel, aluminum and specialty metals, as well as manufactured metal components. The group operates through three segments. Plates and shapes includes carbon steel and specialty metal products such as structural plate, beams, aluminum, magnesium, stainless steel and ductile iron. The flat rolled group includes cold rolled and hot rolled steel products as well as nonferrous flat rolled products. The building products group includes aluminum and steel building products such as covered canopies and walkways, awnings, sunrooms and solariums. The products are sold to the furniture, construction, consumer durables and machinery and equipment manufacturing industries. The group operates principally in the United States.

Primary SIC and add'l.: 3499 3399 5051 5211

CIK No: 0001038363

Subsidiaries: Metal Management, Inc

Officers: Lourenco C. Goncalves/Chmn., CEO, Pres., Joe Longo/Pres. - Plates, Shapes Group, East, Robert T. Reilley/Pres. - i, Solutions Group, Keith Koci/Sr. VP - Business Development, John A. Hageman/Sr. VP, Chief Legal, Administrative Officer, Sec., Roger Krohn/Pres. - Flat Rolled Group, Non - Ferrous Group, Samuel Sciple/VP, Dir. - Internal Audit, Sharon Romere/VP - Human Resources, David Martens/Pres. - Plates, Shapes Group, West, Dan Henneke/VP, Corporate Controller, Pete Lent/VP - Flat Rolled Group, Mike Cooney/VP - Non - Ferrous Products, Chuck Stipanovich/VP - Plates, Shapes Ohio Valley, Gary Shiner/Contact - Flat Rolled, Wichita, Bob Skinner/Contact - Flat Rolled, Jeffersonville *(28 Officers included in Index)*

Directors: Lourenco C. Goncalves/Chmn., CEO, Pres., Josh J. Harris/Dir., Marc E. Becker/Dir., Eric L. Press/Dir., Ali Rashid/Dir., John T. Baldwin/Dir.

Owners: Insiders/3.30%, M. Ali Rashid, Marc E. Becker, Eric L. Press, Robert C. McPherson, John A. Hageman, Keith A. Koci, Lourenco C. Goncalves/2.00%, Joe Longo, John T. Baldwin, David A. Martens, Roger Krohn, Joshua J. Harris, Apollo Management V, L.P./96.80%

MetaMorphix Inc

8000 Virginia Manor Rd., Ste 140, Beltsville, MD, 20705; ***PH:*** 1-301-617-9080; ***http://*** www.metamorphixinc.com; ***Email:*** info@metamorphixinc.com

General - Incorporation .... DE
Employees .... NA
Auditor .... Deloitte & Touche LLP
Stk Agt .... NA
Counsel .... NA
DUNS No. .... NA

Stock- Price on:12/24/2007 .... NA
Stock Exchange .... NA
Ticker Symbol .... NA
Outstanding Shares .... NA
E.P.S .... NA
Shareholders .... NA

Business: The group's principal activity is to discover and develop life sciences products. The products provided by the group includes livestock products, animal and human health products. The services provided by the group include DNA genotyping services. The group serves the livestock, animal and the human health industries.

Primary SIC and add'l.: 2834

CIK No: 0001289370

Subsidiaries: Genetics Institute, Inc., MetaMorphix Canada, Inc., MMI Genomics, Inc., PE Corporation

Officers: Edwin C. Quattlebaum/Co - Chmn., CEO, Pres., Thomas P. Russo/CFO, Exec. VP, Ronald L. Stotish/Exec. VP - Research, Development, Linda Yaswen-Corkery/Chief Compliance Officer, Dennis Fantin/Exec. VP - Operations, Victoria M. Geis/VP - Human Relation, Sue Denise/VP - Genomic Research, Development, Li-Fang Liang/Dir. - Molecular Biology Discovery, David Rosenfeld/Dir. - Software Development, Tom Holm/Mgr. - Business Development, Mary Ellen Defrancesco/Contact - Media, Michael Thomas/Investor Relations Officer, Bridger Feuz/Contact - Technical, Roni Sue K. Denise/52/VP - Genomic Research, Development

Directors: Edwin C. Quattlebaum/Co - Chmn., CEO, Pres., Peter A. Meyer/Co - Chmn., John Block/Dir., Victor M. Casini/Dir., Peter Drake/Dir., William Buckner/Dir., Howard L. Minigh/59/Dir., Clifton Baile/Dir., Victoria M. Geis/VP - Human Relation, Edward T. Shonsey/Dir.

Owners: Raynemark Investments LLC/7.70%, Kevin F. Flynn/9.20%, Theodore Swindells/5.70%, Biostar, Inc./6.50%, Applera Corporation/8.70%, Samuel R. Dunlap/5.90%, Clifton Baile/1.30%, Insiders/18.20%, John R. Block, Howard Minigh, Peter F. Drake, New Frontiers Capital LLC/27.50%, Victor M. Casini, Peter A. Meyer/4.10%, Paul Moore/7.60% *(16 Owners included in Index)*

Methanex Corp

1800 Waterfront Ctr., 200 Burrard St., Vancouver, BC, V6C 3M1; ***PH:*** 1-604-661-2600; ***Fax:*** 1-604-661-2676; ***http://*** www.methanex.com; ***Email:*** publicaffairs@methanex.com

General - Incorporation .... Canada
Employees 818
Auditor .... KPMG LLP
Stk Agt .... Mellon Trust Co
Counsel .... NA
DUNS No. 20-635-4367

Stock- Price on:12/24/2007 .... $26.44
Stock Exchange .... NDQ
Ticker Symbol .... MEOH
Outstanding Shares 103,210,000
E.P.S $3.62
Shareholders .... NA

Business: The group's principle activity is to produce and market methanol. Methanol is produced from natural gas and is used to produce formaldehyde, acetic acid and a variety of other chemical intermediates. The group operates from United States.

Primary SIC and add'l.: 2819 2911 5983 2861

CIK No: 0000886977

Officers: Bruce Aitken/Dir., CEO, Pres., John K. Gordon/Sr. VP - Corporate Resources, Ian Cameron/Sr. VP - Finance, CFO, John Floren/Sr. VP - Global Marketing, Logistics, Jason Chesko/Dir. - Investor Relations, Andrew Browning/Government Relations Activities, Gerry Kennedy/Public Affairs Mgr., David Chen/Sr. Marketing Mgr. - China, Ho Song/Sr. Marketing Mgr. - Korea, Jun Yoshimatsu/Sr. Marketing Mgr., Freddye Weigel/Marketing, Logistics, North America, Amparo Cornejo/Mgr. - Public Affairs, CSR, Mark Scott/Contact, Julie Doherty/Contact Information, Deborah Samaru/Contact Information *(21 Officers included in Index)*

Directors: Bruce Aitken/Dir., CEO, Pres., Pierre Choquette/Chmn., Monica Sloan/Dir., Howard Balloch/Dir., Phillip H. Cook/Dir., Douglas W. Mahaffy/Dir., Terence A. Poole/Dir., Janice G. Rennie/Dir., John Reid/Dir., Graham Sweeney/Dir.

Financial Data: ***Fiscal Year End:*** 12/31 ***Latest Annual Data:*** 12/31/2006

Year	Sales	Net Income
2006	$2,108,250,000	$481,225,000
2005	$1,658,120,000	$164,299,000
2004	$1,719,484,000	$229,940,000

Curr. Assets:	$990,254,000	**Curr. Liab.:**	$340,620,000		
Plant, Equip.:	$1,389,031,000	**Total Liab.:**	$1,252,524,000	**Indic. Yr. Divd.:**	$0.560
Total Assets:	$2,472,326,000	**Net Worth:**	$1,219,802,000	**Debt/ Equity:**	NA

Methode Electronics Inc

7401 W Wilson Ave., Chicago, IL, 60706; ***PH:*** 1-708-867-6777; ***Fax:*** 1-708-867-6999; ***http://*** www.methode.com; ***Email:*** info@methode.com

General - Incorporation .... DE
Employees 3,535
Auditor .... Ernst& Young LLP
Stk Agt .... Chase Mellon Shareholder Services LLC
Counsel .... NA
DUNS No. .... NA

Stock- Price on:12/24/2007 .... $15.79
Stock Exchange .... NYSE
Ticker Symbol .... MEI
Outstanding Shares 36,560,000
E.P.S $0.91
Shareholders .... NA

Business: The groups principle activity is to manufacture component devices. The products of the group include bus devices, cabling systems, electronic and electromechanical devices, copper and fiber optic, sensing dynamic and static torque. The groups operates through four segments namely automotive, interconnect, power distribution and other. The group's quarterly revenue for September 2007 was 133.77 millions of USD. The group operates from the United States, Asia Pacific, Malta and Europe. In March 2005, the group acquired Cableco Technologies Corporation.

Primary SIC and add'l.: 3674 3629 3679 3678 8734

CIK No: 0000065270

Subsidiaries: ABAS, Inc., Automotive Safety Technologies, Inc., Cableco Technologies, Inc., Contech-Europe Ltd., Duel Systems, Inc., KBA, Inc., Magna-lastic Devices, Inc., Methode Delaware Holdings, Inc. (2), Methode Development Company, Methode Electronics (Shanghai) Co. Ltd., Methode Electronics China PTE, Ltd., Methode Electronics Connectivity Technologies, Inc., Methode Electronics Europe, Ltd., Methode Electronics Far East Pte., Ltd., Methode Electronics Foreign Sales Corporation 23 Subsidiaries included in the Index

Officers: Donald W. Duda/Dir., CEO, Pres./$2,911,005.00, Theodore P. Kill/VP - Global Sales, Paul E. Whybrow/VP - Interconnect Group, Timothy R. Glandon/VP, GM - North American Automotive Operations/$477,584.00, Douglas A. Koman/VP - Corporate Finance, CFO/$856,147.00, Thomas D. Reynolds/Sr. VP - Global Automotive Operations/$1,077,075.00, Joey Iske/Dir. - Investor Relations, Shahanas Ahmad/Sales Mgr. - Methode Electronics Far East, Pte Ltd

Directors: Donald W. Duda/Dir., CEO, Pres., Warren L. Batts/Chmn., Darren M. Dawson/Dir., Isabelle C. Goossen/Dir., Paul G. Shelton/Dir., George S. Spindler/Dir., Edward J. Colgate/Dir., Christopher J. Hornung/Dir., Lawrence B. Skatoff/Dir.

Owners: Paul G. Shelton, Robert J. Kuehnau, Lawrence B. Skatoff, Royce & Associates, LLC/6.60%, Warren L. Batts, Edward J. Colgate, Isabelle C. Goossen, George S. Spindler, T. Rowe Price Associates, Inc./6.30%, Darren M. Dawson, Donald W. Duda/1.50%, Timothy R. Glandon, Christopher J. Hornung, Barclays Global Investors, N.A/9.90%, Douglas A. Koman *(18 Owners included in Index)*

Financial Data: ***Fiscal Year End:*** 04/30 ***Latest Annual Data:*** 04/28/2007

Year	Sales	Net Income
2007	$450,023,000	$26,084,000
2006	$422,689,000	$17,049,000
2005	$394,445,000	$25,533,000

Curr. Assets:	$221,272,000	**Curr. Liab.:**	$74,203,000	**P/E Ratio:**	31.58
Plant, Equip.:	$90,497,000	**Total Liab.:**	$82,874,000	**Indic. Yr. Divd.:**	$0.200
Total Assets:	$374,583,000	**Net Worth:**	$291,709,000	**Debt/ Equity:**	NA

Metlife Inc

200 Pk. Ave., New York, NY, 10166; ***PH:*** 1-212-578-2211; ***Fax:*** 1-212-578-3320; ***http://*** www.metlife.com

General - Incorporation .... DE
Employees 47,000
Auditor .... Deloitte & Touche LLP
Stk Agt .... Mellon Investor Services LLC
Counsel .... NA
DUNS No. .... NA

Stock- Price on:12/24/2007 .... $64.27
Stock Exchange .... NYSE
Ticker Symbol .... MET
Outstanding Shares 741,610,000
E.P.S $8.06
Shareholders .... NA

Business: The group's principle activity is to provide life insurance, annuities, automobile and homeowners insurance, retail banking and various financial services to individuals, group insurance and reinsurance, retirement and savings product, and corporations and various institutions. The group operates from United States.

Primary SIC and add'l.: 6719 6331 7389 6311

CIK No: 0001099219

Subsidiaries: 190 S. Lasalle Associates LLC, 23RD Street Iinvestments, Inc., 334 Madison Avenue Btp-d Holdings, LLC, 334 Madison Avenue Btp-e Holdings, LLC, 334 Madison Euro Investments, Inc., 440 South Lasalle LLC, 500 Grant Street Associates Limited Partnership, 500 Grant Street Gp LLC, Alternative Fuel I, LLC, Best Market S.a., Bond Trust Account A, Cdmk, Inc., Citicorp Life Insurance Company, Citistreet Associates Insurance Agency Of Massachusetts LLC, Citistreet Associates LLC 235 Subsidiaries included in the Index

Officers: Robert C. Henrikson/61/Chmn., CEO, Pres./$18,889,570.00, Catherine A. Rein/65/Chief Administrative Officer, Sr. Exec. VP/$5,929,661.00, William J. Toppeta/59/Pres. - International/$8,006,233.00, Lisa M. Weber/45/Pres. - Individual Business/$4,637,197.00, William J. Mullaney/47/Pres. - Institutional Business, James L. Lipscomb/61/Exec. VP, General Counsel, William J. Wheeler/46/CFO, Exec. VP/$3,899,966.00, Steven A. Kandarian/56/Exec. VP, Chief Investment Officer

Directors: Robert C. Henrikson/61/Chmn., CEO, Pres., Cheryl W. Grise/56/Dir., Sylvia Mathews Burwell/43/Dir., Curtis H. Barnette/73/Dir., James R. Houghton/72/Dir., John M. Keane/65/Dir., William C. Steere/72/Dir., Glenn R. Hubbard/50/Dir., Helene L. Kaplan/75/Dir., David Satcher/Dir., Harry P. Kamen/75/Dir., Hugh B. Price/66/Dir., Kenton J. Sicchitano/63/Dir., James M. Kilts/60/Dir., Charles M. Leighton/73/Dir. *(16 Directors included in Index)*

Owners: Charles M. Leighton, Barclays Global Investors, NA/5.14%, Kenton J. Sicchitano, Robert C. Henrikson, Sylvia M. Burwell, David Satcher, Insiders, Helene L. Kaplan, William J. Wheeler/36.30%, Curtis H. Barnette, James M. Kilts, Lisa M. Weber, Glenn R. Hubbard, Hugh B. Price, Cheryl W. Grise *(27 Owners included in Index)*

Financial Data: ***Fiscal Year End:*** 12/31 ***Latest Annual Data:*** 12/31/2006

Year	Sales	Net Income
2006	$48,396,000,000	$6,293,000,000
2005	$44,776,000,000	$4,714,000,000
2004	$39,014,000,000	$2,758,000,000

Curr. Assets:	$25,065,000,000	Curr. Liab.:	$49,720,000,000	P/E Ratio:	7.12
Plant, Equip.:	$7,000,000	Total Liab.:	$493,639,000,000	Indic. Yr. Divd.:	$0.590
Total Assets:	$527,715,000,000	Net Worth:	$33,798,000,000	Debt/ Equity:	1.8274

MetLife Insurance Co of Connecticut

Formerly: Travelers Insurance Co
One Citypl., Hartford, CT, 06103; *PH:* 1-860-308-1000; *http://* www.stpaultravelers.com

General - Incorporation	CT	*Stock*- Price on:12/24/2007	NA
Employees	NA	Stock Exchange	NA
Auditor	Deloitte & Touche LLP	Ticker Symbol	NA
Stk Agt	Mellon Investor Services, L.L.C.	Outstanding Shares	NA
Counsel	NA	E.P.S.	NA
DUNS No.	00-691-7413	Shareholders	NA

Business: The groups principle activity is to provide property and casualty insurance products. The group operates from United Kingdom, Ireland and Canada.

Primary SIC and add'l.: 6311 6321

CIK No: 0000733076

Subsidiaries: Annuity Company, Travelers Life

Officers: Stanley J. Talbi/CFO, Exec. VP, Joseph J. Prochaska/Chief Accounting Officer, Exec. VP

Directors: Lisa M. Weber/45/Dir., William J. Mullaney/Dir.

Metris Companies Inc

2700 Sanders Rd., Prospect Heights, IL, 60070; *PH:* 1-847-564-5000;
http:// www.metriscompanies.com

General - Incorporation	DE	*Stock*- Price on:12/24/2007	NA
Employees	NA	Stock Exchange	NYSE
Auditor	KPMG LLP	Ticker Symbol	NA
Stk Agt	Computershare Investor Services LLC	Outstanding Shares	NA
Counsel	NA	E.P.S.	NA
DUNS No.	61-521-8781	Shareholders	NA

Business: The group's principal activity is to provide financial products and services in the United States. The products offered include unsecured credit cards including the direct merchants bank mastercard (R), visa (r). It also offers co-branded credit cards through partnerships with other companies. The products also include credit protection and insurance products. The group operates through its subsidiaries direct merchants credit card bank, national association, metris direct, inc. And metris receivables, inc.

Primary SIC and add'l.: 6141

CIK No: 0001021061

Subsidiaries: ICOM Limited, magnUS Services, Inc., MES Insurance Agency, LLC, Metris Asset Funding Co., Metris Card Services, LLC, Metris Credit Card Services, Inc., Metris Direct, Metris Direct, Inc., Metris Funding Co., Metris Receivables, Inc., Metris Warranty Services, Metris Warranty Services, Inc.

Metro One Telecommunications Inc

11200 Murray Scholls Pl., Beaverton, OR, 97007; *PH:* 1-503-643-9500; *Fax:* 1-503-643-9600;
http:// www.metro1.com; *Email:* info@metro1.com

General - Incorporation	OR	*Stock*- Price on:12/24/2007	$2.16
Employees	560	Stock Exchange	NDQ
Auditor	BDO Seidman, LLP	Ticker Symbol	INFO
Stk Agt	Mellon Investor Services LLC	Outstanding Shares	6,230,000
Counsel	Heller Ehrman White & McAuliffe LLP	E.P.S.	-$2.45
DUNS No.	60-511-4867	Shareholders	NA

Business: The group's principle activity is to provide enhanced directory assistance and information services for the wireless telecommunications industry. It delivers a wide variety of information, which includes directory assistance, restaurant reservations etc. The customers of the company include sprint pcs, at&t wireless services, nextel communications and alltel communications. The company has expanded into the landline telecommunications market and provides services to gst communications, a regional competitive local exchange carrier. It operates 31 call centers located in strategic local markets throughout the United States. The group operates from United States.

Primary SIC and add'l.: 7389

CIK No: 0000920990

Officers: Gary E. Henry/51/Dir., CEO, Pres., Sec./$267,071.00, Karen L. Johnson/58/Sr. VP - Corporate Development/$206,303.00, Duane C. Fromhart/53/Sr. VP, CFO/$200,243.00, Lynne L. Michaelson/Sr. VP - Human Resources/$190,892.00, Philip A. Ljubicich/Pres. - M1 Data, Analytics/$161,163.00

Directors: Gary E. Henry/51/Dir., CEO, Pres., Sec., William D. Rutherford/Chmn., Murray L. Swanson/67/Dir., James M. Usdan/58/Dir., Elchanan Maoz/41/Dir., Mary H. Oldshue/56/Dir.

Owners: Elchanan Maoz/8.20%, James M. Usdan/1.30%, Insiders/24.00%, Strategic Turnaround Equity Partners, L.P./11.70%, Insiders/100.00%, Phillip Ljubicich, Lynn Michaelson, Gary E. Henry/1.40%, Mary H. Oldshue, Kenneth D. Peterson/12.40%, Kenneth D. Peterson/80.00%, Elchanan Maoz/20.00%, Karen L. Johnson

Financial Data: Fiscal Year End:12/31   Latest Annual Data: 12/31/2006

Year	Sales	Net Income
2006	$30,339,000	-$19,221,000
2005	$77,810,000	-$39,759,000
2004	$140,369,000	-$63,166,000

Curr. Assets:	$19,846,000	Curr. Liab.:	$6,566,000		
Plant, Equip.:	$3,014,000	Total Liab.:	$7,036,000	Indic. Yr. Divd.:	NA
Total Assets:	$27,612,000	Net Worth:	$20,576,000	Debt/ Equity:	NA

Metrocorp Bancshares Inc

9600 Bellaire Blvd., Ste. 252, Houston, TX, 77036; *PH:* 1-713-776-3876; *Fax:* 1-713-414-3575;
http:// www.metrobank-na.com; *Email:* metrobank@metrobank-na.com

General - Incorporation	TX	*Stock*- Price on:12/24/2007	$21.25
Employees	350	Stock Exchange	NDQ
Auditor	PricewaterhouseCoopers LLP	Ticker Symbol	MCBI
Stk Agt	American Stock Transfer & Trust Co.	Outstanding Shares	10,960,000
Counsel	Bracewell & Giuliani	E.P.S.	$1.14
DUNS No.	01-197-4057	Shareholders	NA

Business: The group's principal activity is to provide general, commercial and mortgage banking services. It provides a variety of loans including commercial and industrial loans, commercial and residential mortgage loans, construction loans, residential mortgage brokerage and lending, government guaranteed small business lending, trade finance, automobile loans, lines of credit and other personal loans. The deposit products and services include checking and savings accounts, money market accounts, time deposits, ATM cards, debit cards and online banking. The group serves through fourteen branch offices located in houston, Dallas and Texas. It is a holding bank for metro bank, national association.

Primary SIC and add'l.: 6712 6022

CIK No: 0001068300

Subsidiaries: AFC-Metro Corporation, First United Bank, MC Bancshares of Delaware, Inc., MCBI Statutory Trust I, MetroBank, N.A.

Officers: George M. Lee/Dir., Executive Vice Chmn., CEO, Pres./$647,355.00, David C. Choi/CFO, Exec. VP/$294,041.00, Mitchell Kitayama/Exec. VP/$274,375.00, David Tai/Dir., Exec. VP, Sec./$335,194.00

Directors: George M. Lee/Dir., Executive Vice Chmn., CEO, Pres., Don J. Wang/Chmn., Edward A. Monto/Dir., Tommy F. Chen/Dir., Helen F. Chen/Dir., May P. Chu/Dir., Charles L. Roff/Dir., Tiong L. Ang/Dir., Joe Ting/Dir., John Lee/Dir., Shirley Liu Clayton/Dir., David Tai/Dir., Exec. VP, Sec., Robert W. Hsueh/Dir.

Owners: David Choi, Wellington Management Company, LLP/5.33%, David Tai/3.73%, May P. Chu/1.28%, Tommy F. Chen/2.97%, Shirley L. Clayton, Charles L. Roff, Edward A. Monto, Mitchell Kitayama, Tiong Loi Ang/1.51%, John E. Peterson, Terrance J. Tangen, Siah Chin Leong/6.30%, Daniel B. Wright, Leslie Looi Meng/5.29% *(22 Owners included in Index)*

Financial Data: Fiscal Year End:12/31   Latest Annual Data: 12/31/2006

Year	Sales	Net Income
2006	$94,602,000	$13,504,000
2005	$67,165,000	$10,780,000
2004	$54,380,000	$8,594,000

Curr. Assets:	$164,892,000	Curr. Liab.:	$1,091,179,000	P/E Ratio:	18.16
Plant, Equip.:	$10,332,000	Total Liab.:	$1,162,486,000	Indic. Yr. Divd.:	$0.160
Total Assets:	$1,268,434,000	Net Worth:	$105,948,000	Debt/ Equity:	0.5658

Metrogas Inc

Gregorio Aranoz De LamaDr.id 1360, C 1267 AAB, Buenos Aires; *PH:* 54-1143091000;
http:// www.metrogas.com.ar; *Email:* info@metrogas.com.ar

General - Incorporation	AR	*Stock*- Price on:12/24/2007	NA
Employees	1,019	Stock Exchange	AMEX
Auditor	PricewaterhouseCoopers LLP	Ticker Symbol	MGT
Stk Agt	Bank of New York	Outstanding Shares	56,920,000
Counsel	NA	E.P.S.	$23,727.54
DUNS No.	97-093-5474	Shareholders	NA

Business: The groups principle activities include storage, transportation and distribution of natural gas, compressed natural gas and processed natural gas. Customers served by the group include power plants, residential, commercial, governmental and industrial users. The group operates from United States.

Primary SIC and add'l.: 4922 1311 4923 4924

CIK No: 0000931069

Officers: Juan Pablo Mirazon/Dir. - Internal Audit, Vito Sergio Camporeale/VP, Eduardo Villegas Contte/Dir. - Administration, Finance, Magdalena Gonzalez Garano/Dir. - Legal, Regulatory Affairs, Valeria Soifer/Corporate Controller, Fernando Aceiro/Dir., Commercial Dir., Enrique Barruti/Dir. - Human Resources, Patricia Carcagno/45/Dir., Operations Dir., Pablo Boselli/Finance Mgr., Lucia Domville/Contact - New York, Eugenia Gatti/Investor Relation, Roberto Granero/Contact, Daniel Infer/Contact

Directors: Carolina Fino/39/Dir., Juan Carlos Fronza/72/Dir., Victor Jose Sardella/57/Dir., Luis Augusto Domenech/Dir., Cristian Marcaida/40/Dir., Cynthia Gimenez Arrillaga/41/Dir., Jorge Alberto Depino/Dir., Luis Chaparro/41/Dir., Roberto Brandt/Dir., Fernando Aceiro/Dir., Commercial Dir., Patricia Carcagno/45/Dir., Operations Dir., Jorge Emilio Verruno/59/Dir., Andres Cordero Gimenez/62/Dir., Gonzalo Lopez Fanjul/Dir., Paul John Jordan/51/Dir. *(19 Directors included in Index)*

Owners: Private Investors/13.20%, PPP/10.00%, British Gas International B.V./6.80%, Gas Argentino/19.00%, Gas Argentino/51.00%

Financial Data: Fiscal Year End:12/31   Latest Annual Data: 12/31/2006

Year	Sales	Net Income
2006	$285,239,000	$35,619,000
2005	$430,052,000	$86,653,000
2004	$274,017,000	-$33,332,000

Curr. Assets:	$591,454,000	Curr. Liab.:	$1,757,094,000		
Plant, Equip.:	$1,725,038,000	Total Liab.:	$1,772,040,000	Indic. Yr. Divd.:	NA
Total Assets:	$2,511,441,000	Net Worth:	$739,394,000	Debt/ Equity:	NA

Metrologic Instruments Inc

90 Coles Rd. At Rte, Blackwood, NJ, 08012; *PH:* 1-856-228-8100; *http://* www.metrologic.com

General - Incorporation	NJ	*Stock*- Price on:12/24/2007	NA
Employees	1,400	Stock Exchange	NA
Auditor	Ernst & Young LLP	Ticker Symbol	NA
Stk Agt	StockTrans, Inc.	Outstanding Shares	NA
Counsel	NA	E.P.S.	NA
DUNS No.	04-862-0462	Shareholders	NA

Business: The group's principal activities are to design, manufacture and market bar code scanning and high-speed automated data capture solutions using laser, holographic and vision-based technologies. These scanners rapidly and efficiently read and decode all widely used bar codes and provide an efficient means for data capture and automated data entry into computerized systems. The group's principal laser scanner products include hand-held scanners, fixed projection scanners, in-counter scanners and industrial scanners. The automatic identification products serve customers in retail, commercial, manufacturing, transportation and logistics, and postal and parcel delivery industries. It sells its products through distributors, value added resellers, OEMs and directly to end-users located through out the world. On 27-Sep-2004, the group acquired omniplanar inc.

Primary SIC and add'l.: 3575 3577

CIK No: 0000815910

Subsidiaries: Adaptive Optics Associates, Inc.

Officers: Darius Adamczyk/Dir., CEO, Bruce Harrison/VP, General Counsel, Michael R. Coluzzi/CFO, VP, Treasurer, Mark Ryan/VP - EMEA, Dale M. Fischer/VP - Asia Pacific, Mark C. Schmidt/Marketing, Product Management, VP, Joseph Sawitsky/VP - Operations, Greg T. Dinoia/VP - Americas

Directors: Darius Adamczyk/Dir., CEO, Dipanjan Deb/Dir., David Ibnale/Dir., Andrew Kowal/Dir., Jesse A. Cohn/Dir.

Owners: Dale M. Fischer, John H. Mathias, Reich& Tang Asset Management, LLC, Insiders, Richard C. Close, Mark Schmidt, Hsu Jau Nan, William Rulon-Miller, Harry C. Knowles, Elliott Associates, L.P., Gregory DiNoia, Burgundy Asset Management Ltd., Joseph Sawitsky, Elliott International, L.P., Mark Ryan *(20 Owners included in Index)*

MetroPacific Bank CA

18831 Von Karman Ave., Ste 101, Irvine, CA, 92612; ***PH:*** 1-949-477-1200;
http:// www.metropacificbank.com

General - Incorporation		***Stock***- Price on:12/24/2007	$14.25
Employees	NA	Stock Exchange	OTC
Auditor	NA	Ticker Symbol	MPBK
Stk Agt	NA	Outstanding Shares	NA
Counsel	NA	E.P.S	NA
DUNS No.	NA	Shareholders	NA

Business: The groups principal activity is to provide banking services. The services of the group include personal banking, business banking, loans and online banking. The group operates from the Canada.

Primary SIC and add'l.: 6029

CIK No:

Metropolitan Edison Co

76 S Main St., Akron, OH, 44308; ***PH:*** 1-800-736-3402; ***http://*** www.firstenergycorp.com

General - Incorporation	PA	***Stock***- Price on:12/24/2007	NA
Employees	NA	Stock Exchange	NA
Auditor	PricewaterhouseCoopers LLP	Ticker Symbol	NA
Stk Agt	Medallion Program	Outstanding Shares	NA
Counsel	NA	E.P.S	NA
DUNS No.	00-791-6836	Shareholders	NA

Business: The group's principle activities are the distribution and sale of electric energy in an area of approximately 3,300 square miles in eastern Pennsylvania. The group also sells, purchases and interchanges electric energy with other electric companies. The group's retail customers are metered on a cycle basis. Revenue is recognized for unbilled electric service through the end of the year. The group is a wholly owned electric utility operating subsidiary of firstenergy corp.

Primary SIC and add'l.: 4911

CIK No: 0000065350

Subsidiaries: American Transmission Systems, Inc., Centerior Service Company, FE Acquisition Corp, FELHC, Inc, FirstEnergy Facilities Services Group, LLC, FirstEnergy Foundation, FirstEnergy Nuclear Generation Corp., FirstEnergy Nuclear Operating Company, FirstEnergy Properties Company, FirstEnergy Securities Transfer Company, FirstEnergy Service Company, FirstEnergy Solutions Corp., FirstEnergy Telecom Services, Inc., FirstEnergy Ventures Corp., GPU Capital, Inc. 26 Subsidiaries included in the Index

Officers: K. W. Dindo/58/VP, Chief Risk Officer, A. Jamshidi/53/VP - Commodity Operations, FES, C. D. Lasky/45/VP - Fossil Operations, FES, G. R. Leidich/57/Pres., Chief Nuclear Officer - Fenoc, D. C. Luff/60/Sr. VP - Governmental Affairs, G. L. Pipitone/57/Pres. - FES, T. M. Welsh/58/Sr. VP - External Affairs, D. R. Schneider/46/VP - Energy Delivery, C. B. Snyder/62/Sr. VP, L. M. Cavalier/56/Sr. VP - Human Resources, M. T. Clark/57/Sr. VP - Strategic Planning, Operations

Metropolitan Health Networks Inc

250 Australian Ave. S, Ste. 400, West Palm Beach, FL, 33401; ***PH:*** 1-561-805-8500;
Fax: 1-561-805-8501; ***http://*** www.metcare.com

General - Incorporation	FL	***Stock***- Price on:12/24/2007	$1.82
Employees	204	Stock Exchange	AMEX
Auditor	Grant Thornton, LLP	Ticker Symbol	MDF
Stk Agt	Atlantic Stock Transfer	Outstanding Shares	50,270,000
Counsel	NA	E.P.S	$0.01
DUNS No.	86-930-4022	Shareholders	NA

Business: The group's principal activities is to provide heath care benefits to managed care companies on a full risk basis. The group operates in two segments: managed care and direct medical services (psn) and pharmacy. Managed care provides network management services. The group provides services to patients through a network of primary care physicians, specialists, hospitals and ancillary facilities. The operations of the group serve a variety of at risk mco's including medical groups and clinics, managed care health plans, HIV clinics and long-term care facilities. The group's pharmacy operations has been discontinued.

Primary SIC and add'l.: 8011 8099

CIK No: 0001009379

Subsidiaries: Ben-Tal Pharmacy Services, Inc., METCARE Health Plans, Inc., MetCare IV, Inc., Metcare MIS, Inc., MetCare of Florida, Inc., Metcare Pharmacy Group, Inc., MetCare Rx, (FL) Inc., Metcare Rx, (MD) Inc., MetCare VIII, Inc., MetCare X, Inc., Metlabs, Inc., R&K Pharmacy Services, Inc., West Palm Beach

Officers: Michael M. Earley/Chmn., CEO/$421,697.00, Roberto L. Palenzuela/General Counsel, Chief Compliance Officer, Sec./$306,500.00, Roman G. Fisher/CIO, Sr. VP, Hymin Zucker/Chief Medical Officer - Metcare, Florida, Inc, Sharon Munroe/VP - Human Resources, Maria A. Xirau/VP - Operations, Brenton R. Hood/VP - Network Development, Lucille Soltesz/VP - Clinical Affairs, Quality, Gary Baine/VP - Health Services, Robert J. Sabo/CFO/$54,550.00, Jose A. Guethon/Chief Medical Officer - Advantagecare, Britt Travis/Sr. VP - Sales, Marketing

Directors: Michael M. Earley/Chmn., CEO, David A. Florman/55/Dir., Martin W. Harrison/55/Dir., Eric Haskell/61/Dir., Karl M. Sachs/71/Dir., Robert E. Shields/60/Dir., Barry T. Zeman/62/Dir.

Owners: Robert E. Shields, David S. Gartner, Karl M. Sachs/1.50%, Pequot Capital Management/5.50%, Norman Pessin/5.30%, Jose A. Guethon, Nicusa Capital Partners, L.P./5.20%, Eric Haskell, Debra A. Finnel/3.00%, Roberto L. Palenzuela, Michael M. Earley/1.30%, Barry T. Zeman, David A. Florman, Insiders/16.60%, Fundamental Management Corporation/5.00% *(16 Owners included in Index)*

Financial Data: ***Fiscal Year End:***12/31 ***Latest Annual Data:*** 12/31/2006

Year	***Sales***	***Net Income***
2006	$228,216,000	$473,000
2005	$183,765,000	$2,382,000
2004	$158,070,000	$18,823,000

Curr. Assets:	$30,465,000	***Curr. Liab.:***	$10,912,000	***P/E Ratio:***	62.76
Plant, Equip.:	$2,275,000	***Total Liab.:***	$10,912,000	***Indic. Yr. Divd.:***	NA
Total Assets:	$41,841,000	***Net Worth:***	$30,929,000	***Debt/ Equity:***	NA

Metso Corp

2900 Courtyards Dr., Norcross, GA, 30071; ***PH:*** 1-770-263-7863; ***Fax:*** 1-770-441-9652;
http:// www.metso.com

General - Incorporation	Finland	***Stock***- Price on:12/24/2007	$59.22
Employees	25,678	Stock Exchange	NA
Auditor	PricewaterhouseCoopers LLP	Ticker Symbol	NA
Stk Agt	Metso USA Inc	Outstanding Shares	141,490,000
Counsel	NA	E.P.S	$3.54
DUNS No.	NA	Shareholders	NA

Business: The group's principal activity is to supply process industry machinery and systems. It operates in four segments: paper, minerals, automaton and ventures. The paper segment provides paper machines, tissue machines, board machines, paper finishing systems, equipment and machinery for mechanical and chemical pulp production, know-how and aftermarket services. The minerals segment provides equipment and solutions for crushing, grinding, screening and transport of rock and minerals. The automation segment provides automation and field systems applications for the pulp, paper, power and process industries. The ventures segment provides machines and equipment for the manufacture of panelboard, solutions for mechanical power transmission, materials technologies and contract manufacture of specialty cars. The group operates in nordic countries, north and South America, Asia-Pacific and other countries.

Primary SIC and add'l.: 2611 3823 3554 3621 3531 3491

CIK No: 0001013626

Subsidiaries: AAF Controle Ambiental Ltda, Allis Mineral Systems Inc, Cable Belt Conveyors Pty Ltd, Caldebro S.L., Compusystems Oy, Construcciones Y Estudios Industriales S.A., Ebroelec S.L., Etix (UK)Ltd, Etix SA, Farros Blatter AG, Finbow Oy, Inmobiliria Los Retamos Ltda, Jamesbury de Mexico SA de CV, Jamesbury Shanghai Valve (USA)Inc, Kato Cranes (UK)Ltd 219 Subsidiaries included in the Index

Officers: Jorma Eloranta/57/CEO, Pres., Aleksanteri Lebedeff/General Counsel, Olli Vaartimo/CFO, Exec. VP, Bertel Langenskiold/58/Pres. - Metso Paper, Harri Nikunen/Sr. VP - Finance, Metso Paper, Juha Seppala/VP - Stakeholder Relations, Trade Policy, Eeva-Liisa Virkkunen/Sr. VP - Finance, Metso Minerals, Sari Aitokallio/Sr. VP - Finance, Administration, Metso Automation, Matti Kahkonen/52/Pres. - Metso Minerals, Satu Huber/50/Dir., MD - Federation, Finnish Financial Services, Risto Hautamaki/63/Pres. - Metso Paper, Pasi Laine/45/Pres. - Metso Automation, Mike Phillips/Sr. VP - Finance, Administration, Metso USA Inc, Jaana Lappalainen/Mgr. - External Communications, Anne-Mari Ylikulppi/Assist. - Investor Relations *(21 Officers included in Index)*

Directors: Jaakko Rauramo/67/Vice Chmn., Matti Kavetvuo/64/Chmn., Maija-Liisa Friman/56/Dir., Satu Huber/50/Dir., MD - Federation, Finnish Financial Services, Svante Adde/52/Dir., Yrjo Neuvo/65/Dir., Jukka Leppanen/59/Dir., Eva Liljeblom/50/Dir., Christer Gardell/48/Dir.

Owners: Bertel Langenskild, Pasi Laine, Risto Hautamaki, Matti Kahkonen, Jorma Eloranta, Olli Vaartimo

Financial Data: ***Fiscal Year End:***12/31 ***Latest Annual Data;*** 12/31/2006

Year	***Sales***	***Net Income***
2006	$6,542,087,000	$501,714,000
2005	$4,999,352,000	$280,703,000
2004	$5,424,854,000	$2,729,000

Curr. Assets:	$3,954,299,000	***Curr. Liab.:***	$3,445,983,000		
Plant, Equip.:	$811,985,000	***Total Liab.:***	$4,599,926,000	***Indic. Yr. Divd.:***	$1.720
Total Assets:	$6,458,908,000	***Net Worth:***	$1,851,061,000	***Debt/ Equity:***	NA

Mettler-Toledo International Inc

1900 Polaris Pkwy., Columbus, OH, 43240; ***PH:*** 1-614-438-4511; ***Fax:*** 1-614-438-4900;
http:// www.mt.com; ***Email:*** tech@thorntoninc.com

General - Incorporation	DE	***Stock***- Price on:12/24/2007	$94.93
Employees	9,100	Stock Exchange	NYSE
Auditor	PricewaterhouseCoopers LLP	Ticker Symbol	MTD
Stk Agt	Mellon Investor Services LLC	Outstanding Shares	37,770,000
Counsel	NA	E.P.S	$4.33
DUNS No.	48-000-3797	Shareholders	NA

Business: The groups principle activity is to provide precision instruments and services. The groups products are used for laboratory, industrial, packaging, logistics and food retailing applications. The group also manufactures metal detection and other inspection systems. The group operates from United States.

Primary SIC and add'l.: 3821 3826 7389 3823

CIK No: 0001037646

Subsidiaries: 2869-1632 Qubec Inc., Balances Experts, Inc., Branch of Rainin Instrument, LLC[Delaware], Cargoscan A/S, Exact Equipment Corporation [Pennsylvania], Gelan Detectiesystemen B.V., Gelan Holding B.V., Getmore Ges. fr Marketing& Media Service mbH, Mesoma Verwaltungs GmbH, Mettler-Toledo (Albstadt) GmbH, Mettler-Toledo (Changzhou) Measurement Technology Ltd., Mettler-Toledo (Changzhou) Precision Instruments Ltd., Mettler-Toledo (Changzhou) Scale& System Ltd., Mettler-Toledo (HK) Ltd., Mettler-Toledo (Korea) Ltd. 92 Subsidiaries included in the Index

Officers: Robert F. Spoerry/Chmn., CEO, Pres./$3,704,758.00, Beat E. Luthi/Laboratory Division/$1,327,002.00, Peter Burker/Contact - Human Resources, Jean-Lucien Gloor/55/Head - Information Systems, Olivier A. Filloi/Global Sales, Service, Marketing, Prosses Analycs Division/$1,563,412.00, Willam P. Donnelly/CFO/$1,264,592.00, Ken A. Peters/Contact - North

Amirica, Urs Widmer/Contact - Industrial Division/$970,507.00, Karl M. Long/Contact - Aisa, Pacific, Joakim Weldemanis/Contact - Product Inspection Division, Hans-Peter Von Arb/Contact - Retail Division, James T. Bellerjeau/General Counsel, Sec., Mary T. Finnegan/Treasurer, Investor Relations Officer

Directors: Robert F. Spoerry/Chmn., CEO, Pres., Francis A. Contino/Dir., John T. Dickson/Dir., Philip H. Geier/Dir., Hans Ulrich Maerki/Dir., George M. Milne/Dir., Thomas P. Salice/Dir., Wah-Hui Chu/Dir.

Owners: Olivier A. Filliol, Franklin Resources, Inc./6.00%, Insiders/3.80%, William P. Donnelly, Robert F. Spoerry/1.00%, John T. Dickson, George M. Milne, Wah-Hui Chu, Beat Luethi, Fidelity Management & Research Company/11.10%, Urs Widmer, Francis A. Contino, Hans Ulrich Maerki, Thomas P. Salice, Philip H. Geier

Financial Data: *Fiscal Year End:* 12/31 *Latest Annual Data:* 12/31/2006

Year	Sales	Net Income
2006	$1,594,912,000	$157,532,000
2005	$1,482,472,000	$108,902,000
2004	$1,404,454,000	$107,957,000

Curr. Assets:	$669,770,000	**Curr. Liab.:**	$384,379,000	**P/E Ratio:**	21.92
Plant, Equip.:	$229,138,000	**Total Liab.:**	$956,223,000	**Indic. Yr. Divd.:**	NA
Total Assets:	$1,587,085,000	**Net Worth:**	$630,862,000	**Debt/ Equity:**	0.5512

Metwood Inc

819 Naff Rd., Boones Mill, VA, 24065; *PH:* 1-540-334-4294; *Fax:* 1-540-334-4293; *http://* www.metwood.com; *Email:* information@metwood.com

General		**Stock**	
Incorporation	NV	Price on:12/24/2007	$0.7
Employees	35	Stock Exchange	OTC
Auditor	Lake & Assoc. CPA's LLC	Ticker Symbol	MTWD
Stk Agt	Colonial Stock Transfer Co Inc	Outstanding Shares	11,920,000
Counsel	NA	E.P.S.	$0.03
DUNS No.	NA	Shareholders	NA

Business: The groups principle activity is to manufacture light-gage steel construction materials, for use in residential and commercial applications. Services of the group include metal framing, square structural columns, garage and post-and-beam buildings and engineering, design and custom building services. The products of the group include girders and headers, floor joists, roof and floor trusses and rafters. The group operates through two segments namely construction and engineering services. The group operates from the United States.

Primary SIC and add'l.: 3448 2439 8711 2493 3441 3446 2499 1521 3499 3429

CIK No: 0000032567

Subsidiaries: Metwood Inc.

Officers: Robert M. Callahan/Dir., CEO, Pres., Shawn A. Callahan/Dir., Sec., Treasurer, VP, GM, CFO, Al Smith/VP - National Sales, Matt Tobey/VP - Residential Sales, Dave Beckner/Member - Residential Sales, Craig McDonald/Product Specialist, Sean C. Goldsmith/Pres., Justin Powell/Sales Technician, Travis Richardson/Commercial Sales Mgr., Landon Horne/Lead Sales Technician, Chris Pugh/Lead Structural Engineer, James C. Pugh/VP, Mark Wilson/Engineering Designer

Directors: Robert M. Callahan/Dir., CEO, Pres., Shawn A. Callahan/Dir., Sec., Treasurer, VP, GM, CFO

Owners: Ronald Shiflett/18.00%, Robert Callahan/54.50%

Financial Data: *Fiscal Year End:* 06/30 *Latest Annual Data:* 6/30/2006

Year	Sales	Net Income
2006	$4,242,000	$171,000
2005	$4,181,000	$121,000
2004	$3,110,000	$222,000

Curr. Assets:	$1,661,000	**Curr. Liab.:**	$318,000	**P/E Ratio:**	23.33
Plant, Equip.:	$462,000	**Total Liab.:**	$425,000	**Indic. Yr. Divd.:**	NA
Total Assets:	$2,376,000	**Net Worth:**	$1,951,000	**Debt/ Equity:**	NA

Mexco Energy Corp

214 W Texas Ave., Ste. 1101, Midland, TX, 79701; *PH:* 1-915-682-1119

General		**Stock**	
Incorporation	CO	Price on:12/24/2007	$5.31
Employees	2	Stock Exchange	AMEX
Auditor	Grant Thornton LLP	Ticker Symbol	NA
Stk Agt	Computershare Trust Co	Outstanding Shares	1,770,000
Counsel	NA	E.P.S.	$0.15
DUNS No.	06-421-8928	Shareholders	NA

Business: The group's principal activities are to acquire, explore and develop oil and gas properties in the United States. The group owns interests in and operates 22 producing wells and four shut-in wells. It also owns partial interests in an additional 1,704 producing wells located in the states of Texas, New Mexico, Oklahoma, Louisiana, Arkansas, Wyoming, Kansas, Colorado, Alabama, Montana and North Dakota. The majority of the operations are carried out in permian basin of west Texas. The group also acquires interests in producing and non-producing oil and gas leases from landholders and leaseholders in areas considered favorable for oil and gas exploration, development and extraction. Sid richardson energy services, co. Is one of the major customers of the group.

Primary SIC and add'l.: 1311

CIK No: 0000066418

Subsidiaries: Forman Energy Corporation

Officers: Nicholas C. Taylor/70/Dir., CEO, Pres./$4,500.00, Donna Gail Yanko/Dir., VP, Sec./$42,580.00, Tamala L. McComic/39/CFO, VP, Treasurer, Assist. Sec./$163,100.00

Directors: Nicholas C. Taylor/70/Dir., CEO, Pres., Thomas Graham/Chmn., Arden R. Grover/Dir., Donna Gail Yanko/Dir., VP, Sec., Thomas R. Craddick/Dir., Jack D. Ladd/Dir., Jeffry A. Smith/Dir.

Owners: Arden R. Grover/1.45%, Nicholas C. Taylor/50.18%, Jeffry A. Smith/0.95%, Tamala L. McComic/1.91%, Howard E. Cox/12.05%, Insiders/61.24%, Donna Gail Yanko/3.18%, Thomas R. Craddick/1.69%, Thomas Graham/7.29%, Jack D. Ladd/1.65%

Financial Data: *Fiscal Year End:* 03/31 *Latest Annual Data:* 3/31/2007

Year	Sales	Net Income
2007	$2,972,000	$608,000
2006	$3,720,000	$789,000
2005	$2,970,000	$578,000

Curr. Assets:	$558,000	**Curr. Liab.:**	$118,000	**P/E Ratio:**	16.09
Plant, Equip.:	$8,400,000	**Total Liab.:**	$2,077,000	**Indic. Yr. Divd.:**	NA
Total Assets:	$8,978,000	**Net Worth:**	$6,899,000	**Debt/ Equity:**	NA

Mexican Economic Development Inc

General Anaya No. 601 Pte, Colonia Bella Vista, Monterrey; *PH:* 52-8183286000; *http://* www.femsa.com; *Email:* investor@femsa.com.mx

General		**Stock**	
Incorporation	Mexico	Price on:12/24/2007	$40.8
Employees	97,770	Stock Exchange	NYSE
Auditor	Gabriel Gonzlez Martnez	Ticker Symbol	FMX
Stk Agt	Donald Puglisi	Outstanding Shares	357,820,000
Counsel	Cleary Gottlieb Steen & Hamilton	E.P.S.	$1.81
DUNS No.	81-205-0714	Shareholders	NA

Business: The group's principal activities are the production, distribution and marketing of beer and certain coca-cola trademark beverages in two territories in Mexico and one territory in Argentina. It also produces and distributes packaging materials to the beverage and food industries, including products such as aluminum beverage cans and tops, steel food cans, bottle caps and other closures, glass beverage bottles, labels and other flexible packaging materials, plastic cases, coolers, commercial refrigeration equipment, detergents, lubricants and adhesives. The group operates a chain of convenience stores under the trade name 'OXXO' and provides transportation, logistics and maintenance services.

Primary SIC and add'l.: 2086 5411 2082 8742 3411 7389

CIK No: 0001061736

Subsidiaries: Administracin y Asesora Integral, S.A. de C.V., Cadena Comercial Oxxo, S.A. de C.V., Cervecera Cuauhtmoc Moctezuma, S.A. de C.V., Cervezas Cuauhtmoc Moctezuma, S.A. de C.V., Coca-Cola FEMSA, Corporacin Interamericana de Bebidas, S.A. de C.V. (Panamco), FEMSA Cerveza, FEMSA Comercio, Kristine Oversease, S.A. de C.V. (holding company of Brazilian operations), Oxxo Express, S.A. de C.V., Panamco Bajo, S.A. de C.V., Panamco Mxico, S.A. de C.V., Propimex, S.A. de C.V.

Officers: Jorge Luis Ramos/CEO - Femsa Cerveza, Jose Antonio Fernandez Carbajal/Chmn., CEO - Femsa, Eduardo Padilla Silva/CEO - Femsa Comercio, Carlos Salazar Lomelin/CEO - Coca Cola Femsa, Eugenio Garza Laguera/Honorary Life Chmn. - Femsa, Alfonso Garza Garza/Exec. VP - Human Resources, Jose Gonzalez Ornelas/VP - Management, Operating Control, Hector Trevino Gutierrez/52/CFO - Coca, Cola Femsa, David Alberto Gonzalez/Alternate Sec. - Femsa, Federico Reyes Garcia/VP - Corporate Development, Femsa, Javier Astaburuaga Sanjines/CFO, VP - Strategic Development, Femsa, Carlos Aldrete Ancira/52/General Counsel, Sec. - Femsa

Directors: Jose Antonio Fernandez Carbajal/Chmn., CEO - Femsa, Alberto Bailleres/77/Dir., Barbara Garza De Braniff/50/Dir., Roberto Servitje Sendra/80/Dir., Alexis E. Rovzar De La Torre/57/Dir., Alfredo Livas. Cantu/57/Dir., Consuelo Garza De Garza/78/Dir., Helmut Paul/68/Dir., Alexis E. Rovzar De La Torre/57/Dir., Armando Garza Sada/51/Dir., Paulina Garza De Marroqui/36/Dir., Javier Fernandez Carbajal/Dir. - Femsa, Jose Calderon Rojas/54/Dir., Jose Manual Canal Hernando/68/Dir., Carlos Salguero/79/Dir. *(22 Directors included in Index)*

Owners: Consuelo Garza de Garza/0.75%, Max Michel Suberville/0.06%, Jos Caldern Rojas/0.35%, Consuelo Garza de Garza/0.30%, Eugenio Garza Lagera/0.62%, Alberto Bailleres/0.09%, Eugenio Garza Lagera/0.15%, Max Michel Suberville/0.24%, Alberto Bailleres/0.25%, Jos Caldern Rojas/0.35%, Max Michel Suberville/0.24%, Jos Caldern Rojas/0.08%, Alberto Bailleres/0.25%, Consuelo Garza de Garza/0.30%, Eugenio Garza Lagera/0.62%

Financial Data: *Fiscal Year End:* 12/31 *Latest Annual Data:* 12/31/2006

Year	Sales	Net Income
2006	$6,770,595,000	$623,616,000
2005	$5,429,526,000	$495,969,000
2004	$4,467,239,000	$590,944,000

Curr. Assets:	$1,381,606,000	**Curr. Liab.:**	$1,324,998,000	**P/E Ratio:**	12.64
Plant, Equip.:	$2,786,042,000	**Total Liab.:**	$3,646,298,000	**Indic. Yr. Divd.:**	$0.680
Total Assets:	$10,257,926,000	**Net Worth:**	$6,611,629,000	**Debt/ Equity:**	NA

Mexican Restaurants Inc

1135 Edgebrook, Houston, TX, 77034; *PH:* 1-713-943-7574; *Fax:* 1-713-943-9554; *http://* www.mexicanrestaurantsinc.com; *Email:* comments@mexicanrestaurantsinc.com

General		**Stock**	
Incorporation	TX	Price on:12/24/2007	$7.77
Employees	2,877	Stock Exchange	NDQ
Auditor	UHY LLP	Ticker Symbol	CASA
Stk Agt	Computershare Investor Services LLC	Outstanding Shares	3,460,000
Counsel	Locke Liddell & Sapp LLP	E.P.S.	-$0.25
DUNS No.	06-727-7947	Shareholders	NA

Business: The group's principal activity is to operate and franchise Mexican-theme restaurants. The restaurants feature various elements associated with the casual dining under the names: casa ole, monterey's tex-mex cafe, monterey's little Mexico, tortuga coastal cantina and la senorita. The menus of the restaurants consist of a variety of traditional Mexican and tex-mex selections, complemented by the group's original Mexican-based recipes, the menu also includes soup, salads, appetizers and desserts. From time to time the company also introduces new dishes designed to keep the menus fresh. . The group operates 64 restaurants, franchises 31 restaurants and licenses 1 restaurant in various communities across Texas, Louisiana, Oklahoma, Idaho and Michigan in 2003.

Primary SIC and add'l.: 5812 6719 6794

CIK No: 0001009244

Officers: Curt Glowacki/CEO, Pres./$1,037,467.00, Andrew J. Dennard/Exec. VP, CFO, Corp. Sec./$311,958.00, Lou Porry/COO

Directors: Larry N. Forehand/Vice Chmn., Louis P. Neeb/Chmn., Cara Denver/Dir., Lloyd Fritzmeier/Dir., Stuart J. Sargent/Dir., Thomas E. Martin/Dir., Michael D. Domec/Dir., J. J. Fitzsimmons/Dir.

Owners: David Nierenberg/34.80%, Michael D. Domec/5.90%, Loic M. Porry/1.80%, Thomas E. Martin, Curt Glowacki, J. J. Fitzsimmons, Andrew J. Dennard/2.20%, Dennis D. Vegas/1.80%, Louis P. Neeb/3.60%, Insiders/66.70%, Larry N. Forehand and Forehand Family Partnership, Ltd./19.90%

Financial Data: *Fiscal Year End:* 12/28 *Latest Annual Data:* 12/31/2006

Year	Sales	Net Income
2006	$82,264,000	$1,138,000
2005	$78,640,000	$1,761,000

Curr. Assets:	$3,572,000	**Curr. Liab.:**	$5,499,000		
Plant, Equip.:	$17,511,000	**Total Liab.:**	$12,702,000	**Indic. Yr. Divd.:**	NA
Total Assets:	$33,276,000	**Net Worth:**	$20,573,000	**Debt/ Equity:**	0.2435

Mexoro Minerals Ltd

880-609 Granville St., Vancouver, BC, V7Y 1G5; ; *http://* www.mexoro.com; *Email:* info@mexoro.com

General - Incorporation	CO	**Stock**- Price on:12/24/2007	$1.3
Employees	NA	Stock Exchange	OTC
Auditor	Pannell Kerr Forster	Ticker Symbol	MXOM
Stk Agt	Corporate Stock Transfer, Inc.	Outstanding Shares	NA
Counsel	NA	E.P.S	NA
DUNS No.	NA	Shareholders	NA

Business: The groups principal activities include exploring and developing gold exploration properties. The group operates from the United States and Mexico.

Primary SIC and add'l.: 1040

CIK No: 0001046672

Subsidiaries: Sierra Minerals and Mining, Inc.,

Officers: Robert Knight/Dir., CEO, Mario Ayub/Dir., COO, Tracy A. Moore/Dir., Sec., Francisco Quiroz/Exploration Team, Manuel J. Carrillo/Exploration Team, Filiberto Navarro/Exploration Team, Kurt Bordian/39/CFO

Directors: Robert Knight/Dir., CEO, Mario Ayub/Dir., COO, Tracy A. Moore/Dir., Sec., Robert W. Schafer/Member - Advisory Bord

Owners: Mario Ayub/7.38%, Robert Knight/2.38%, Insiders/11.31%, Tracy A. Moore/0.48%, Kurt Bordian/0.36%, Walter Stapher/5.70%, Alpine Atlantic Asset Management/6.42%

Financial Data: *Fiscal Year End:*02/28 *Latest Annual Data:* 02/28/2007

Year	Sales	Net Income
2007	NA	-$7,393,000
2006	NA	-$4,426,000
2005	NA	-$1,618,000

MFA Mortgage Investments

Formerly: America First Mortgage Investments Inc
350 Pk. Ave., 21st Fl., New York, NY, 10022; *PH:* 1-212-207-6400; *http://* www.mfa-reit.com

General - Incorporation	MD	**Stock**- Price on:12/24/2007	$7.22
Employees	15	Stock Exchange	NYSE
Auditor	Ernst& Young LLP	Ticker Symbol	NA
Stk Agt	Mellon Investor Services LLC	Outstanding Shares	81,160,000
Counsel	Clifford Chance	E.P.S	-$0.06
DUNS No.	NA	Shareholders	NA

Business: The groups principal activity is to provide investing services. The group operates from the United States. The assets of the group for the year 2006 were6 $443,967 (thousands)

Primary SIC and add'l.: 6798

CIK No: 0001055160

Officers: Stewart Zimmerman/Chmn., CEO, Pres./$1,319,683.00, William S. Gorin/CFO, Exec. VP/$906,427.00, Ronald A. Freydberg/Exec. VP, Chief Portfolio Mgr./$904,427.00, Teresa D. Covello/Sr. VP, Chief Accounting Officer, Treasurer/$389,261.00, Timothy W. Korth/General Counsel, Sr. VP - Business Development, Sec./$443,497.00

Directors: Stewart Zimmerman/Chmn., CEO, Pres., Stephen R. Blank/Dir., James Brodsky/Dir., Edison C. Buchanan/Dir., Michael L. Dahir/Dir., Alan Gosule/Dir., George H. Krauss/Dir.

Owners: Alan L. Gosule, Stewart Zimmerman, Edison C. Buchanan, James A. Brodsky, Teresa D. Covello, William S. Gorin, Michael L. Dahir, Ronald A. Freydberg, George H. Krauss, Timothy W. Korth, Stephen R. Blank, Insiders/1.80%

Financial Data: *Fiscal Year End:*12/31 *Latest Annual Data:* 12/31/2006

Year	Sales	Net Income
2006	$198,343,000	$8,758,000
2005	$243,257,000	$6,708,000
2004	$180,456,000	$78,073,000

Curr. Assets:	$80,382,000	**Curr. Liab.:**	$5,753,910,000		
Plant, Equip.:	$11,789,000	**Total Liab.:**	$5,765,409,000	**Indic. Yr. Divd.:**	$0.320
Total Assets:	$6,443,967,000	**Net Worth:**	$678,558,000	**Debt/ Equity:**	0.0205

MFB Financial Corp

4100 Edison Lakes Pkwy., Ste. 300, Mishawaka, IN, 46546; *PH:* 1-574-273-7600; *Fax:* 1-574-257-0167; *http://* www.mfbbank.com; *Email:* more-bank@mfbbank.com

General - Incorporation	IN	**Stock**- Price on:12/24/2007	$34.17
Employees	140	Stock Exchange	NDQ
Auditor	Crowe Chizek & Co. LLC	Ticker Symbol	NA
Stk Agt	Registrar & Transfer Co	Outstanding Shares	1,320,000
Counsel	Barnes & Thornburg	E.P.S	$2.37
DUNS No.	84-060-1751	Shareholders	NA

Business: The group's principal activity is to offer residential real estate, home equity and second mortgage, construction, commercial loans and loans secured by deposits. The deposit account services include now, passbook savings, certificate of deposits, consumer and commercial demand deposit, individual retirement accounts, trust services and brokerage services. These services are provided through six branch offices located in mishawaka, south bend, elkhart and goshen in Indiana. The group also offers general property, casualty and life insurance services to its customers.

Primary SIC and add'l.: 6712 6035

CIK No: 0000916396

Subsidiaries: MFB Investments I, MFB Investments II, Inc., MFB Investments, LP, Mishawaka Financial Services, Inc.

Officers: Charles J. Viater/53/Dir., Pres., CEO - MFB, MFB Financial, Gilbert M. Eberhart/74/Dir., Sec. - MFB, MFB Financial, Donald R. Kyle/61/COO, Exec. VP, James P. Coleman/62/Exec. VP, Dir. - Wealth Management, MFB Financial, Grady Gaynor/Contact - Private Banking Professional, Martha Wargo Oprea/Contact - Estate Planning Professional, Shayne Nagy/Contact - Asset, Investment Management, Terry McDevit/Contact - Asset, Investment Management, Jeffrey Remble/Business Banker, VP, Tim Goldy/VP, Sr. Business Banker, Michael Ryan/AVP - Business Banker, Kathy Sears/VP - Business Banker, Kenneth Byrd/AVP - Business Banker, Amy Karkiewicz/Contact - Private Banking Professional, Scott Taylor/42/VP, Chief Deposit Officer *(17 Officers included in Index)*

Directors: Charles J. Viater/53/Dir., Pres., CEO - MFB, MFB Financial, Reginald H. Wagle/65/Dir., Edward C. Levy/60/Dir., Michael J. Marien/60/Dir., Gilbert M. Eberhart/74/Dir., Sec. - MFB, MFB Financial, Jonathan E. Kintner/65/Dir., Robert C. Beutter/73/Dir., Christine A. Lauber/63/Dir., James P. Coleman/62/Exec. VP, Dir. - Wealth Management, MFB Financial, Jonathan W. Housand/69/Dir.

Owners: Edward C. Levy/0.60%, Insiders/27.30%, Jonathan E. Kintner/2.40%, Robert C. Beutter/1.20%, Christine A. Lauber/1.30%, Principal Trust Company/7.50%, Charles J. Viater/12.50%, Donald R. Kyle/1.20%, Michael J. Marien/3.30%, James P. Coleman, Jonathan W. Housand, Gilbert M. Eberhart/3.60%, Charles J. Viater/13.60%, Scott A. Taylor/0.10%, First Manhattan Co., General Partner/5.80% *(18 Owners included in Index)*

Financial Data: *Fiscal Year End:*09/30 *Latest Annual Data:* 9/30/2006

Year	Sales	Net Income
2006	$34,941,000	$2,166,000
2005	$33,884,000	$2,496,000
2004	$28,582,000	$1,790,000

Curr. Assets:	$16,289,000	**Curr. Liab.:**	$447,633,000	**P/E Ratio:**	12.56
Plant, Equip.:	$19,477,000	**Total Liab.:**	$457,133,000	**Indic. Yr. Divd.:**	$0.760
Total Assets:	$496,072,000	**Net Worth:**	$38,939,000	**Debt/ Equity:**	0.1223

MFIC Corp

30 Ossipee Rd., Newton, MA, 02464; *PH:* 1-617-969-5452; *Fax:* 1-617-965-1213; *http://* www.mficcorp.com; *Email:* info@mfics.com

General - Incorporation	DE	**Stock**- Price on:12/24/2007	$1.66
Employees	53	Stock Exchange	OTC
Auditor	UHY LLP	Ticker Symbol	MFIC
Stk Agt	Brown & Brown LLP	Outstanding Shares	10,180,000
Counsel	Gadsby Hannah	E.P.S	$0.08
DUNS No.	10-117-3045	Shareholders	NA

Business: The group's principal activity is to produce and market fluid materials processing systems. The systems are used for a variety of grinding, dispersing, milling and blending applications across a variety of industries and for use in numerous applications within those industries. Microfluidizer(R) a fluid processing equipment is used to formulate stable emulsions, dispersions and liposomes, used in general for deagglomeration and for cell disruption for the biotech industry. In addition, the equipment is used in biotechnology applications to harvest through cell disruption, the cultivated product contents of plant and animal cells. The group markets its products in the United States, Europe and Asia.

Primary SIC and add'l.: 3823

CIK No: 0000723889

Subsidiaries: Microfluidics Corporation, NuSil Corporation, Teva Pharmaceuticals Industries Ltd.

Officers: Thomas Hoarty/VP - Sales, Marketing, Thomai Panagiotou/VP - Research - Development, David Harney/Mgr. - Design Engineering, Jack M. Swig/VP - Corporate Development, General Counsel/$135,250.00, Robert P. Bruno/COO, Pres./$218,024.00, Dennis P. Rriordan/61/Controller/$128,990.00

Directors: James N. Little/Acting Chmn., Irwin Gruverman/Chmn. Emeritus, Leo Pierre Roy/Dir., George Uveges/Dir., Eric Walters/Dir.

Owners: George Uveges, Insiders/28.00%, Leo Pierre Roy, Jack M. Swig/1.50%, Irwin J. Gruverman/19.20%, Eric G. Walters, James N. Little, Joseph P. Daly/5.00%, Robert P. Bruno/4.40%, Dennis P. Riordan/1.70%

Financial Data: *Fiscal Year End:*12/31 *Latest Annual Data:* 12/31/2006

Year	Sales	Net Income
2006	$15,654,000	$1,277,000
2005	$11,645,000	-$989,000
2004	$12,159,000	$874,000

Curr. Assets:	$7,857,000	**Curr. Liab.:**	$2,213,000	**P/E Ratio:**	13.83
Plant, Equip.:	$303,000	**Total Liab.:**	$2,278,000	**Indic. Yr. Divd.:**	NA
Total Assets:	$8,226,000	**Net Worth:**	$5,948,000	**Debt/ Equity:**	NA

MFRI Inc

7720 N Lehigh Ave., Niles, IL, 60714; *PH:* 1-847-966-1000; *Fax:* 1-847-966-8563; *http://* www.mfri.com

General - Incorporation	DE	**Stock**- Price on:12/24/2007	$27.9
Employees	1,058	Stock Exchange	NDQ
Auditor	Grant Thornton, LLP	Ticker Symbol	MFRI
Stk Agt	Continental Stock Transfer & Trust Co	Outstanding Shares	6,550,000
Counsel	Piper, Marbury, Rudnick & Wolf	E.P.S	$0.47
DUNS No.	60-621-1977	Shareholders	NA

Business: The group's principal activities are to design, manufacture and market filter elements, specialty piping systems, leak detection and location systems and industrial process cooling equipment. The group operates through three segments: filtration products; piping systems and industrial process cooling equipment. Filtration products business sells a wide variety of filter elements for air filtration and particulate collection systems. Piping systems consists of industrial and secondary containment piping systems for transporting chemicals, waste streams and petroleum liquids, insulated and jacketed district heating and cooling piping systems. Industrial process cooling equipment business engineers, manufactures chillers, mold temperature controllers, cooling towers, plant circulating systems and coolers for industrial process applications. The group's trademarks include seamless tube(R), leak seeker(R), prekote(R), pleatkeeper(R) and pleat plus (r).

Primary SIC and add'l.: 3823 3599 3564

CIK No: 0000914122

Subsidiaries: Midwesco Filter Resources, Inc., Perma-Pipe, Inc., TDC Filter Manufacturing, Inc., Thermal Care, Inc.

Officers: David Unger/73/Chmn., CEO/$543,877.00, Dennis Kessler/Dir., Pres. - Kessler Management Consulting, Michael D. Bennett/VP, CFO, Sec., Treasurer/$315,967.00, Bradley E. Mautner/Dir., COO, Pres./$373,156.00

Directors: David Unger/73/Chmn., CEO, Henry M. Mautner/Vice Chmn., Jorgen B. Poulsen/Dir., Thomas Benson/Dir., Gene K. Ogilvie/Dir., Billy Ervin/Dir., Arnold F. Brookstone/Dir., Fati A. Elgendy/Dir., Mcleod Stephens/Dir., Bradley E. Mautner/Dir., COO, Pres., Stephen B. Schwartz/Dir., Robert A. Maffei/Dir., Don Gruenberg/Dir., Eugene Miller/Dir. - Executive, In, Residence, Adjunct Professor, Florida Atlantic University, John Carusiello/Dir. *(17 Directors included in Index)*

Owners: Arnold F. Brookstone, Insiders/23.60%, Henry M. Mautner/7.80%, Babson Capital Management/7.30%, Bradley E. Mautner/2.50%, Fati A. Elgendy, Michael D. Bennett, Edward W. Wedbush/5.60%, Stephen B. Schwartz, David Unger/9.30%, J. Carlo Cannell/9.30%, Dennis Kessler, Tontine Capital Partners, L.P./5.10%, Eugene Miller, Heartland Advisors, Inc./5.40%

Financial Data: *Fiscal Year End:*01/31 *Latest Annual Data:* 1/31/2007

Year	Sales	Net Income
2007	$213,471,000	$4,593,000
2006	$154,587,000	$531,000
2005	$145,096,000	$2,813,000

Curr. Assets:	$80,674,000	Curr. Liab.:	$49,940,000	P/E Ratio:	30.00
Plant, Equip.:	$33,441,000	Total Liab.:	$82,624,000	Indic. Yr. Divd.:	NA
Total Assets:	$121,440,000	Net Worth:	$38,816,000	Debt/ Equity:	0.3996

MGE Energy Inc

133 S Blair St., Madison, WI, 53703; *PH:* 1-608-252-7000; *Fax:* 1-608-252-7098;
http:// www.mgeenergy.com; *Email:* mge@mge.com

General - Incorporation ....WI
Employees..740
Auditor ....PricewaterhouseCoopers LLP
Stk Agt...........Mge Energy Shareholder Services
Counsel..NA
DUNS No.......................................00-794-6346

Stock- Price on:12/24/2007 ....$32.07
Stock Exchange...NDQ
Ticker Symbol...MGEE
Outstanding Shares 21,220,000
E.P.S..$2.20
Shareholders...NA

Business: The group's principal activity is to generating and distributing electricity and natural gas. The group operates in three segments: electric, gas and nonutility. The electric business generates and distributes electricity and contracts for transmission service. The gas business purchases and distributes natural gas and contracts for the transportation of natural gas. The nonutility energy business constructs and owns new electric generating capacity. At 31-Dec-2003, the group supplied electric service to nearly 132,000 customers located in the cities of fitchburg, madison, middleton, monona and adjacent areas. On 31-Dec-2003, it supplied natural gas service to more than 129,000 customers in the cities of elroy, fitchburg, lodi, madison, middleton, monona, prairie du chien, verona and viroqua; 24 villages; and all or parts of 46 townships. The group operates only in the United States.

Primary SIC and add'l.: 6719 4924 4931

CIK No: 0001161728

Subsidiaries: Central Wisconsin Development Corporation, Madison Gas and Electric Company, Magael, LLC, MGE Construct LLC, MGE Power Elm Road, LLC, MGE Power LLC, MGE Power West Campus, LLC

Officers: Gary J. Wolter/53/Chmn., CEO, Pres./$775,427.00, Jeffrey C. Newman/45/VP, Treasurer/$313,453.00, Kristine A. Euclide/55/VP, General Counsel/$342,767.00, Peter J. Waldron/50/VP - Energy Supply Operations, Joseph P. Pellitteri/59/Assist. VP - Human Resources, Lynn K. Hobbie/49/Sr. VP, James G. Bidlingmaier/61/VP - Administration, CIO, Scott A. Neitzel/47/VP - Energy Supply Policy/$345,191.00, Gregory A. Bollom/47/Assist. VP - Energy Planning, John M. Yogerst/50/Assist. VP - Gas Operations, Craig A. Fenrick/48/Assist. VP - Electric Transmission - Distribution

Directors: Gary J. Wolter/53/Chmn., CEO, Pres., John R. Nevin/64/Dir., Donna K. Sollenberger/58/Dir., Frederic E. Mohs/70/Dir., Richard E. Blaney/71/Dir., Regina M. Millner/63/Dir., Curtis F. Hastings/62/Dir., Lee H. Swanson/69/Dir.

Owners: Terry A. Hanson, Lee H. Swanson, Insiders, Jeffrey C. Newman, Kristine A. Euclide, John R. Nevin, Scott A. Neitzel, Regina M. Millner, Gary J. Wolter, Curtis F. Hastings, Richard E. Blaney, Frederic E. Mohs, Donna K. Sollenberger

Financial Data: *Fiscal Year End:*12/31   *Latest Annual Data:* 12/31/2006

Year	Sales	Net Income
2006	$507,546,000	$42,423,000
2005	$513,370,000	$32,091,000
2004	$424,881,000	$33,840,000

Curr. Assets:	$149,413,000	Curr. Liab.:	$143,861,000	P/E Ratio:	15.34
Plant, Equip.:	$769,612,000	Total Liab.:	$606,884,000	Indic. Yr. Divd.:	$1.390
Total Assets:	$982,232,000	Net Worth:	$375,348,000	Debt/ Equity:	0.6147

MGI Pharma Inc

5775 W Old Shakopee Rd., Ste. 100, Bloomington, MN, 55437; *PH:* 1-952-346-4700;
Fax: 1-952-346-4800; *http://* www.mgipharma.com; *Email:* ir@mgipharma.com

General - Incorporation .... MN
Employees..540
Auditor ....KPMG LLP
Stk Agt........... Wells Fargo Shareowner Services
Counsel.......................... Hogan & Hartson LLP
DUNS No.......................................02-157-4355

Stock - Price on:12/24/2007 ....$23.56
Stock Exchange...NDQ
Ticker Symbol...MOGN
Outstanding Shares 79,770,000
E.P.S..-$0.19
Shareholders...NA

Business: The group's principle activities include acquiring, developing and commercializing proprietary pharmaceutical products for cancer patients. The products include salagen tablets, hexalen capsules, didronel iv infusion, palonosetron, irofulven, mg98, dna methyltransferase inhibitors and other acylfulvene analogs. Currently, the products are promoted in the United States directly to radiation oncologists, select medical oncologists, hematology oncologists, rheumatologists and internal medicine physicians, and other physician specialists. International markets for the products include Europe, Japan, Australia, Canada, Colombia, egypt, Hong Kong, Israel, Korea, Singapore, Malaysia and Taiwan. The group operate from United States.

Primary SIC and add'l.: 2834 5122 6794

CIK No: 0000702131

Subsidiaries: Artery, LLC, Canvas Informatics, Inc., GPI (Canada) Inc., GPI Investments, LLC, Gpi Ip, LLC, MGI GP, Inc., Mgi Msl, LLC, MGI OM, Inc., Mgi Pharma Biologics, Inc., Mgi Pharma Canada, Co., Mgi Pharma Limited, MGI Products, Inc., ProQuest Pharmaceuticals, Inc., Zycos Services Corporation, Inc.

Officers: Leon O. Moulder/Dir., CEO, Pres./$1,200,528.00, Mary Lynne Hedley/Chief Scientific Officer, Exec. VP/$704,222.00, William F. Spengler/CFO, Exec. VP/$928,654.00, Eric P. Loukas/Exec. VP, COO, Sec./$659,849.00

Directors: Leon O. Moulder/Dir., CEO, Pres., Hugh E. Miller/Chmn., James O. Armitage/Dir., Andrew J. Ferrara/Dir., Edward W. Mehrer/Dir., Dean J. Mitchell/Dir., David B. Sharrock/Dir., Waneta C. Tuttle/Dir., Arthur L. Weaver/Dir.

Owners: David E. Shaw& Co./6.33%, Insiders/2.38%, Leon O. Moulder/1.28%, Edward W. Mehrer, Waneta Tuttle, Dean J. Mitchell, Eric P. Loukas, Andrew J. Ferrara, Mary Lynne Hedley, James O. Armitage, Wellington Management Company, LLP/10.94%, Arthur L. Weaver, Hugh E. Miller, Barclays Global Investors, N.A/6.51%, David B. Sharrock (*18 Owners included in Index*)

Financial Data: *Fiscal Year End:*12/31   *Latest Annual Data:* 12/31/2006

Year	Sales	Net Income
2006	$342,788,000	-$40,161,000
2005	$279,362,000	-$132,410,000
2004	$195,667,000	-$85,723,000

Curr. Assets:	$299,733,000	Curr. Liab.:	$94,621,000		
Plant, Equip.:	$10,119,000	Total Liab.:	$376,101,000	Indic. Yr. Divd.:	NA
Total Assets:	$482,975,000	Net Worth:	$106,874,000	Debt/ Equity:	2.1932

Mgic Investment Corp

MGIC Plz., 250 East Kilbourn Ave., Milwaukee, WI, 53202; *PH:* 1-414-347-6480;
Fax: 1-800-558-9900; *http://* www.mgic.com; *Email:* customer_service@mgic.com

General - Incorporation ....WI
Employees...1,200
Auditor ....PricewaterhouseCoopers LLP
Stk Agt .... Wells Fargo Shareowner Services
Counsel..NA
DUNS No...................................10-829-5650

Stock- Price on:12/24/2007 ....$60
Stock Exchange..NYSE
Ticker Symbol..MTL
Outstanding Shares 83,070,000
E.P.S...-$1
Shareholders...NA

Business: The group's principal activities are to provide private mortgage insurance to lenders throughout the United States. The group operates through mortgage guaranty insurance corporation and other subsidiaries. The services provided for the mortgage finance industry include contract underwriting and portfolio analysis and retention. The group covers lenders to protect against loss from defaults on low down payment residential mortgage loans. The mortgage insurance coverage is provided to home mortgage lending industry in all 50 states of the United States, the district of columbia and Puerto Rico.

Primary SIC and add'l.: 6719 6351

CIK No: 0000876437

Subsidiaries: Credit-Based Asset Servicing and Securitization LLC, eMagic.com LLC, MGIC Assurance Corporation, MGIC Credit Assurance Corporation, MGIC Indemnity Corporation, MGIC Insurance Services Corporation, MGIC Investor Services Corporation, MGIC Mortgage and Consumer Asset I LLC, MGIC Mortgage and Consumer Asset II LLC, MGIC Mortgage Insurance Corporation, MGIC Mortgage Marketing Corporation, MGIC Mortgage Reinsurance Corporation, MGIC Mortgage Securities Corporation, MGIC Reinsurance Corporation, MGIC Reinsurance Corporation of Vermont 19 Subsidiaries included in the Index

Officers: Curt S. Culver/Chmn., CEO, Patrick Sinks/COO, Pres., Lawrence J. Pierzchalski/Exec. VP - Risk Management, Jeffrey H. Lane/Sr. VP, General Counsel, Sec., Michael J. Lauer/CFO, Exec. VP, Mike Zimmerman/Investor Relations Officer, Katie Monfre/Contact - Media, James A. Karpowicz/60/Sr. VP, Chief Investment Officer, Treasurer, Michael G. Meade/58/Sr. VP - Information Services, CIO

Directors: Curt S. Culver/Chmn., CEO

Owners: JP Morgan Chase& Co./5.53%, Michael J. Lauer, Curt S. Culver, LSV Asset Management/5.27%, ClearBridge Advisors, LLC/6.36%, Putnam, LLC d/b/a Putnam Investments/9.72%, Jeffrey H. Lane, Insiders/2.60%, NWQ Investment Management Company, LLC/8.27%, Patrick Sinks, Lawrence J. Pierzchalski, Barrow, Hanley, Mewhinney& Strauss, Inc./5.67%

Financial Data: *Fiscal Year End:*12/31   *Latest Annual Data:* 12/31/2006

Year	Sales	Net Income
2006	$1,469,169,000	$564,739,000
2005	$1,526,530,000	$626,873,000
2004	$1,612,693,000	$553,186,000

Curr. Assets:	$404,846,000	Curr. Liab.:	$815,757,000	P/E Ratio:	11.81
Plant, Equip.:	$32,603,000	Total Liab.:	$2,325,794,000	Indic. Yr. Divd.:	$0.100
Total Assets:	$6,621,671,000	Net Worth:	$4,295,877,000	Debt/ Equity:	0.0130

MGM MIRAGE

3600 Las Vegas Blvd. S, Las Vegas, NV, 89109; *PH:* 1-702-693-7111; *Fax:* 1-702-693-8626;
http:// www.mgmmirage.com

General - Incorporation .... DE
Employees...56,800
Auditor ....Deloitte & Touche LLP
Stk Agt .... Mellon Investor Services LLC
Counsel..NA
DUNS No............................... 17-578-1913

Stock- Price on:12/24/2007 ....$80.81
Stock Exchange..NYSE
Ticker Symbol..MGM
Outstanding Shares 283,650,000
E.P.S...$3.02
Shareholders...NA

Business: The groups principle activity is to operate casino restaurants and resorts. The group operates from United States.

Primary SIC and add'l.: 7993 5812 7011 7999

CIK No: 0000789570

Subsidiaries: AC Holding Corp., AC Holding Corp. II, Beau Rivage Distribution Corp., Beau Rivage Resorts, Inc., dba Beau Rivage, Bella Lounge, LLC, Bellagio II, LLC, Bellagio, LLC, dba Bellagio, Boardwalk Casino, Inc., Bungalow, Inc., Circus Circus Casinos, Inc., dba Circus Circus Hotel and Casino-Las Vegas and Circus Circus Hotel and Casino-Reno, Circus Circus Mississippi, Inc., dba Gold Strike Casino Resort, Circus Circus New Jersey, Inc., Colorado Belle Corp., dba Colorado Belle Hotel and Casino, Country Star Las Vegas, LLC, Destron, Inc. 115 Subsidiaries included in the Index

Officers: Terrence J. Lanni/Chmn., CEO/$15,687,120.00, Robert C. Selwood/52/Sr. VP - Accounting, Daniel J. Darrigo/CFO, Exec. VP, Alan Feldman/49/Sr. VP - Public Affairs, Phyllis A. James/55/Sr. VP - Sr. Counsel, Bryan Wright/Sr. VP, Assist. General Counsel, Assist. Sec., James J. Murren/46/Dir., Pres., Treasurer/$10,320,520.00, Gary N. Jacobs/Dir., Exec. VP, General Counsel, Sec./$5,235,910.00, Shawn T. Sani/Sr. VP - Taxes, Aldo Manzini/Exec. VP, Chief Administrative Officer, Punam Mathur/47/Sr. VP - Corporate Diversity, Community Affairs, Bruce J. Gebhardt/59/Sr. VP - Global Security

Directors: Terrence J. Lanni/Chmn., CEO, Alexander M. Haig/Dir., John T. Redmond/49/Dir., Robert H. Baldwin/57/Dir., James J. Murren/46/Dir., Pres., Treasurer, Gary N. Jacobs/Dir., Exec. VP, General Counsel, Sec., Rose McKinney-James/Dir., Anthony Mandekic/Dir., Ronald M. Popeil/Dir., Kenny G. Guinn/Dir., Dan Taylor/Dir., Kirk Kerkorian/Dir., Willie D. Davis/Dir., Melvin B. Wolzinger/Dir., Roland Hernandez/Dir. (*16 Directors included in Index*)

Owners: Terrence J. Lanni, Gary N. Jacobs, James J. Murren, Tracinda Corporation, Insiders, Private Capital Management, Marisco Capital Management, LLC, John T. Redmond, Robert H. Baldwin

Financial Data: *Fiscal Year End:*12/31   *Latest Annual Data:* 12/31/2006

Year	Sales	Net Income
2006	$7,175,956,000	$648,264,000
2005	$6,481,967,000	$443,256,000
2004	$4,238,104,000	$412,332,000

Curr. Assets:	$1,514,751,000	Curr. Liab.:	$1,648,100,000	P/E Ratio:	26.76
Plant, Equip.:	$17,430,293,000	Total Liab.:	$18,296,689,000	Indic. Yr. Divd.:	NA
Total Assets:	$22,146,238,000	Net Worth:	$3,849,549,000	Debt/ Equity:	3.3676

MGN Technologies Inc

409 Granville St. , Ste. 1505, Vancouver, BC, V6C 1T2; *PH:* 1-604-602-9596;
http:// www.mgnmobile.com; *Email:* info@mobilegamingnow.com

General - Incorporation............................ BC	Stock- Price on:12/24/2007 ....$0.025
Employees...NA	Stock Exchange...OTC
Auditor .... BDO Dunwoody LLP	Ticker Symbol.......................................MGNLF
Stk Agt.................... Pacific Corporate Trust Co	Outstanding Shares ....NA
Counsel...NA	E.P.S..NA
DUNS No. ....NA	Shareholders..NA

Business: The groups principle activities include developing and licensing mobile media entertainment applications for online wireless gaming activities. In October 2005, the group acquired Ignition Technologies. The group operates from the United States and Canada.

Primary SIC and add'l.: 3694

CIK No: 0001258786

Subsidiaries: Ignition Technologies, Inc., MGN Technologies UK Limited

Officers: Mark Jensen/45/Dir., CEO, Pres.

Directors: Mark Jensen/45/Dir., CEO, Pres., Michael Hu/33/Dir.

Owners: Mark Jensen/16.45%, Androgas Property S.A./34.06%, Adam Morand/8.37%, Insiders/16.23%, Daniel Goldman/9.41%, Michael Hu

Financial Data: *Fiscal Year End:*12/31   *Latest Annual Data:* 12/31/2006

Year	Sales	Net Income
2006	$45,000	-$8,273,000
2005	NA	-$50,000
Curr. Assets:	$802,000	Curr. Liab.:	$606,000		
Plant, Equip.:	NA	Total Liab.:	$606,000	Indic. Yr. Divd.:	NA
Total Assets:	$802,000	Net Worth:	$196,000	Debt/ Equity:	NA

MGP Ingredients Inc

100 Commercial St., Atchison, KS, 66002; *PH:* 1-913-367-1480; *Fax:* 1-913-367-0192;
http:// www.mgpingredients.com

General - Incorporation.............................KS	Stock- Price on:12/24/2007 ....$16.16
Employees..462	Stock Exchange..NDQ
Auditor ....BKD LLP	Ticker Symbol..MGPI
Stk Agt .... UMB Bank, N.A.	Outstanding Shares 16,490,000
Counsel...NA	E.P.S...$1.38
DUNS No. 00-712-8218	Shareholders..NA

Business: The group's principal activity is to produce ingredients and distillery products through ingredients and distillery products segments. Ingredients consist of specialty ingredients, primarily of specialty wheat starches and proteins, commodity ingredients, including commodity wheat starches and vital wheat gluten, and mill feeds. Distillery products consist of food grade alcohol, including beverage alcohol and industrial alcohol, fuel alcohol, commonly known as ethanol, and distillers grain and carbon dioxide, which are by-products of the group's distillery operations. The group markets its products on normal credit terms to customers in a variety of industries.

Primary SIC and add'l.: 2869 2045 2085 2046 2041

CIK No: 0000835011

Subsidiaries: Kansas City Ingredient Technologies, Inc., MGP Ingredients of Illinois, Inc., Midwest Grain Pipeline, Inc.

Officers: Ladd M. Seaberg/Dir., CEO, Pres./$682,052.00, Randall M. Schrick/Dir., VP - Manufacturing, Engineering/$326,680.00, Selma Key/Contact - Customer Service, John Wohlgemuth/Contact - Alcohol Products, Steve Pickman/Contact - Stockholder Information, David E. Rindom/Contact - Human Resources, Timothy W. Newkirk/40/COO, Pres./$317,068.00

Directors: Ladd M. Seaberg/Dir., CEO, Pres., Cloud L. Cray/Chmn., John R. Speirs/Dir., Gary J. Gradinger/Dir., Randall M. Schrick/Dir., VP - Manufacturing, Engineering, John E. Byom/Dir., Daryl Schaller/Dir., Linda E. Miller/Dir., Michael Braude/Dir.

Owners: Daryl Schaller, Insiders, Sukh Bassi, Goldman Sachs Asset Management L.P./6.60%, MGP Ingredients Voting Trust, Cloud L. Cray/21.30%, Richard B. Cray, Richard Larson, Richard B. Cray, Tim Newkirk, Trustees of the Companys ESOPs/7.50%, Gary Gradinger, Randy M. Schrick, Michael Braude, Linda E. Miller (23 Owners included in Index)

Financial Data: *Fiscal Year End:*06/30   *Latest Annual Data:* 6/30/2006

Year	Sales	Net Income
2006	$322,477,000	$13,995,000
2005	$275,177,000	$4,004,000
2004	$270,673,000	$9,468,000
Curr. Assets:	$82,538,000	Curr. Liab.:	$38,069,000	P/E Ratio:	11.71
Plant, Equip.:	$121,835,000	Total Liab.:	$69,672,000	Indic. Yr. Divd.:	$0.200
Total Assets:	$204,584,000	Net Worth:	$134,912,000	Debt/ Equity:	0.0660

MGT Capital Investments Inc

Formerly: Medicsight Inc
46 Berkeley Sq., 66 Hammersmith, London, W1J 5AT; *PH:* 44-207-598-4070;
http:// www.medicsight.com

General - Incorporation............................. DE	Stock- Price on:12/24/2007 ....$4.85
Employees...53	Stock Exchange..AMEX
Auditor ....Amper, Politziner & Mattia P.C	Ticker Symbol..NA
Stk Agt.....................Atlas Stock Transfer Corp	Outstanding Shares 38,900,000
Counsel...NA	E.P.S...-$0.39
DUNS No. 83-632-5605	Shareholders..NA

Business: The group's principal activity is to develop software technology for medical diagnostic applications and provide medical diagnostic services. The group's stochastic perception engine technology processes and classifies unstructured data into meaningful outputs, enabling it to be viewed, interpreted or further manipulated by the user of the application. It is comprised of four principal modules: cluster analysis, statistical modeling, classification and prediction. This technology offers unsurpassed processing speed, accuracy and comprehensiveness of results when compared to existing data classification or neural network based technologies. The group operates two scanning centers in london, one located at ravenscourt hospital and the other at flagship center in westminster.

Primary SIC and add'l.: 7372

CIK No: 0001001601

Subsidiaries: HTTP Tech, Inc., Medical Vision Systems, Inc., MedicExchange, Inc, Medicsight Asset Management Limited, Medicsight Finance Limited, Medicsight International Limited, Medicsight KK, Medicsight Nominees Limited, Medicsight PLC, Medicsight USA, Inc

Officers: Christopher Morse/Sec.

Owners: General Mediterranean Holding SA/6.70%, Insiders, Peter Venton, Macniven and Cameron Equity Holdings Limited/27.40%, Tim Paterson-Brown, Christopher Paine

Financial Data: *Fiscal Year End:*12/31   *Latest Annual Data:* 12/31/2006

Year	Sales	Net Income
2006	NA	-$14,935,000
2005	NA	-$12,216,000
2004	$538,000	-$15,030,000
Curr. Assets:	$25,306,000	Curr. Liab.:	$3,378,000		
Plant, Equip.:	$683,000	Total Liab.:	$25,088,000	Indic. Yr. Divd.:	NA
Total Assets:	$38,469,000	Net Worth:	$13,381,000	Debt/ Equity:	NA

MHI Hospitality Corp

814 Capitol Landing Rd., Williamsburg, VA, 23185; *PH:* 1-757-229-5648; *Fax:* 1-757-564-8801;
http:// www.MHIHospitality.com

General - Incorporation .... MD	Stock- Price on:12/24/2007 ....$10.25
Employees..8	Stock Exchange..AMEX
Auditor ....PKF Witt Mares, PLC	Ticker Symbol..MDH
Stk Agt...... American Stock Transfer & Trust Co.	Outstanding Shares 6,850,000
Counsel...NA	E.P.S...$0.52
DUNS No. ....NA	Shareholders..NA

Business: The groups principle activity is to acquire and lease hotel properties. In the year 2005, the group acquired Crowne Plaza Jacksonville. The group operates from the United States. The group's quarterly revenue for September 2007 was 16.73 millions of USD.

Primary SIC and add'l.: 7011 6798

CIK No: 0001301236

Subsidiaries: Brownestone Partners, LLC, Capitol Hotel Associates L.P., L.L.P., Laurel Hotel Associates LLC, Louisville Hotel Associates, LLC, MHI GP LLC, MHI Hollywood LLC, MHI Hospitality TRS Holding, Inc., MHI Hospitality TRS, LLC, MHI Hospitality, L.P., MHI Jacksonville LLC, MHI Laurel West LLC, Philadelphia Hotel Associates LP, Savannah Hotel Associates LLC

Officers: Andrew M. Sims/Chmn., CEO, Pres./$244,515.00, William J. Zaiser/CFO/$191,795.00, David R. Folsom/COO/$157,799.60, Julia F. Connolly/Chief Compliance Officer/$133,850.00, Anthony E. Domalski/Chief Accounting Officer/$136,787.50, Diana D. Johnson/Dir. - Investor Relations, Administration, Scott M. Kucinski/Dir. - Construction Services, Rhonda L. Smith/Executive Assist.

Directors: Andrew M. Sims/Chmn., CEO, Pres., Anthony C. Zinni/Dir., Paul J. Carey/Dir., Edward S. Stein/Dir., Christopher L. Sims/Dir., Kim E. Sims/Dir., James P. O'Hanlon/Dir.

Owners: Anthony E. Domalski, Paul J. Carey, David R. Folsom, Anthony C. Zinni, William J. Zaiser/3.10%, Christopher L. Sims/9.30%, Insiders/29.00%, Andrew M. Sims/9.40%, Wilmington Hotel Associates Corp./5.20%, Julia Farr Connolly, Ferris, Baker Watts, Incorporated/17.50%, Edward S. Stein/4.70%, Kim E. Sims/9.40%, Elpizo Limited Partnership/9.60%

Financial Data: *Fiscal Year End:*12/31   *Latest Annual Data:* 12/31/2006

Year	Sales	Net Income
2006	$67,242,000	$3,181,000
2005	$57,856,000	$2,481,000
2004	$26,531,000	-$1,541,000
Curr. Assets:	$6,307,000	Curr. Liab.:	$7,235,000	P/E Ratio:	19.12
Plant, Equip.:	$111,416,000	Total Liab.:	$85,581,000	Indic. Yr. Divd.:	$0.680
Total Assets:	$127,603,000	Net Worth:	$42,022,000	Debt/ Equity:	NA

MI Developments Inc

455 Magna Dr., 2nd Fl., Aurora, ON, L4G 7A9; *PH:* 1-905-713-6322;
http:// www.midevelopments.com

General - Incorporation ....Canada	Stock- Price on:12/24/2007 ....$36.77
Employees...40	Stock Exchange..NYSE
Auditor ....Ernst & Young LLP	Ticker Symbol..MIM
Stk Agt..... Computershare Investor Services LLC	Outstanding Shares 48,370,000
Counsel...NA	E.P.S...$1.17
DUNS No. ....NA	Shareholders..NA

Business: The groups principle activities include managing, leasing, developing and acquiring industrial and commercial real estate properties. The group operates from Canada.

Primary SIC and add'l.: NA

CIK No: 0001252509

Subsidiaries: 1346457 Ontario Inc., Magna Entertainment Corp, MEC Maryland Racing, Inc., MI Developments (America) Inc., MI Developments Austria GmbH, MID Europa Liegenschaftsverwaltungs GmbH, The Los Angeles Turf Club, Incorporated, The Santa Anita Companies Inc.

Officers: John D. Simonetti/Dir., CEO, Richard J. Crofts/Exec. VP - Corporate Development, General Counsel, Sec., Robert S. Mintzberg/Controller, Robert Kunihiro/Exec. VP, CFO - Ontario, Canada, Douglas B. Nathanson/VP, Assoc. General Counsel, Don Cameron/COO, Richard J. Smith/CFO, Exec. VP

Directors: John D. Simonetti/Dir., CEO, Dennis J. Mills/Vice Chmn., Frank Stronach/Chmn., Judson D. Whiteside/Dir., Neil G. Davis/Dir., Philip K. Fricke/Dir., Barry B. Byrd/Dir., Manfred Jakszus/Dir., John Barnett/Dir., Frank Vasilkioti/Dir. - Ontario, Canada

Financial Data: *Fiscal Year End:*12/31   *Latest Annual Data:* 12/31/2006

Year	Sales	Net Income
2006	$866,456,000	$45,247,000
2005	$783,451,000	$7,283,000
2004	$853,875,000	-$7,465,000
Curr. Assets:	$352,681,000	Curr. Liab.:	$265,338,000		
Plant, Equip.:	$2,282,180,000	Total Liab.:	$1,145,000,000	Indic. Yr. Divd.:	$0.600
Total Assets:	$2,822,296,000	Net Worth:	$1,677,296,000	Debt/ Equity:	NA

Michael S Stores Inc

8000 Bent Br. Dr, Irving, TX, 75063; *PH:* 1-972-409-1300; *http://* www.michaels.com

General - Incorporation .... DE
Employees .... NA
Auditor .... Ernst & Young LLP
Stk Agt..... Computershare Investor Services LLC
Counsel .... Debevoise & Plimpton LLP
DUNS No. 05-440-2896

Stock- Price on:12/24/2007 .... NA
Stock Exchange .... NA
Ticker Symbol .... NA
Outstanding Shares .... NA
E.P.S .... NA
Shareholders .... NA

Business: The group's principal activities are to own and operate specialty retail stores featuring arts, crafts, framing, floral, decorative wall decor as well as seasonal merchandise. It operates michaels retail stores, which offer products for the do-it-yourself home decorator and art and craft supplies. The group's wholly-owned subsidiary operates aaron brothers stores, which offer photo frames, ready-made frames and custom framing services and art supplies. As of 24-Mar-2004, the group operated 812 michaels retail stores, 158 aaron brothers stores, 11 village crafts stores by michaels, two recollections stores and two star wholesale stores.

Primary SIC and add'l.: 5999

CIK No: 0000740670

Subsidiaries: Aaron Brothers, Inc, Michaels Finance Company, Inc., Michaels of Canada, ULC, Michaels Stores Card Services, LLC, Michaels Stores Procurement Company

Officers: Brian C. Cornell/CEO, Harvey Kanter/Exec. VP, Chief Merchant, Gregory A. Sandfort/52/COO, Pres., Jeff Boyer/CFO, Pres., David Abelman/Sr. VP - Marketing, Carolyn Sutton/Media Contact, Jennifer Munoz/Media Contact, Erin Brunemann/Media Contact, Thomas C. Decaro/53/Exec. VP - Supply Chain, Thomas M. Bazzone/41/Exec. VP - Specialty Businesses

Directors: Josh Bekenstein/49/Dir., Michael S. Chae/39/Dir., Todd Cook/36/Dir., Matthew Kabaker/31/Dir., Lewis Klessel/40/Dir., Matthew S. Levin/42/Dir., David McVeigh/40/Dir., James A. Quella/58/Dir.

Owners: Insiders, Affiliates of The Blackstone Group, L.P., Bain Capital Investors, LLC and related funds, Thomas C. DeCaro, Michaels Holdings LLC, Jeffrey N. Boyer, Gregory A. Sandfort, Highfields Capital Management, LP and related funds

Michigan Heritage Bancorp Inc

28300 Orchard Lake Rd., Ste. 200, Farmington Hills, MI, 48334; ***PH:*** 1-248-538-2525; ***Fax:*** 1-248-538-2515; ***http://*** www.miheritage.com

General - Incorporation .... MI
Employees .... NA
Auditor .... Plante & Moran, PLLC
Stk Agt............ Registrar & Transfer Co
Counsel .... NA
DUNS No. .... NA

Stock- Price on:12/24/2007 .... $11.77
Stock Exchange .... OTC
Ticker Symbol .... MHBC
Outstanding Shares 1,550,000
E.P.S .... -$0.09
Shareholders .... NA

Business: The groups principal activity is to provide banking services. The services of the group include consumer services, business service and online banking. The group operates from the United States.

Primary SIC and add'l.: 6022 6712

CIK No: 0001027623

Officers: Raymond Biggs/CEO - Michigan Heritage Bank, Catherine Ballard/AVP, Operations Mgr. - Michigan Heritage Bank, Michelle Nagy/Loan Operations Mgr. - Michigan Heritage Bank, Mark Mckay/Sr. Corporate Accountant - Michigan Heritage Bank, Janice Donahue/Credit Mgr. - Michigan Heritage Bank, Cathy Palazzolo/Human Reserace Representative, Michigan Heritage Bank, Debbie Steadman/Sr. Mgr. - Farm Hills Branch, Michigan Heritage Bank, William Vance/AVP, Commercial Loan Officer - Michigan Heritage Bank, Richard Klein/AVP, Commercial Loan Officer - Michigan Heritage Bank, Mark Boettcher/AVP, Commercial Loan Officer - Michigan Heritage Bank, Nick Delegram/Mgr. - Troy Branch, Michigan Heritage Bank, Karen Prymak/Mgr. - Novi Branch, Michigan Heritage Bank, Constance Trylong/Mgr. - Wixom Branch, Michigan Heritage Bank, Sandra Mirek/Sr. Accounting Mgr. - Michigan Heritage Bank, Natalie Conyers/Business Relations Mgr. - Michigan Heritage Bank *(41 Officers included in Index)*

Directors: Perry Driggs/Chmn. - Michigan Heritage Bank

Financial Data: ***Fiscal Year End:***12/31 ***Latest Annual Data:*** 12/31/2003

Year	Sales	Net Income
2003	$11,351,000	$1,261,000
2002	$12,592,000	$1,252,000
2001	$11,681,000	$110,000

Curr. Assets:	$5,072,000	***Curr. Liab.:***	$127,207,000		
Plant, Equip.:	$554,000	***Total Liab.:***	$130,207,000	***Indic. Yr. Divd.:***	NA
Total Assets:	$145,383,000	***Net Worth:***	$15,176,000	***Debt/ Equity:***	NA

Micrel Inc

2180 Fortune Dr., San Jose, CA, 95131; ***PH:*** 1-408-944-0800; ***Fax:*** 1-408-944-0970; ***http://*** www.micrel.com; ***Email:*** recruit2@micrel.com

General - Incorporation .... CA
Employees 932
Auditor .... PricewaterhouseCoopers LLP
Stk Agt............ Mellon Investor Services LLC
Counsel .... NA
DUNS No. 09-260-9585

Stock- Price on:12/24/2007 .... $12.74
Stock Exchange .... NDQ
Ticker Symbol .... MCRL
Outstanding Shares 77,570,000
E.P.S $0.57
Shareholders .... NA

Business: The group's principal activities are to design, develop, manufacture and market high-performance analog power integrated circuits and mixed-signal and digital integrated circuits. The group operates in two segments: standard products and custom and foundry products. Standard products include power analog circuits for the cellular telephones, battery powered computers and desktop personal computers markets, and also products for power supplies and industrial, defense, avionics, automotive and electronics industries and networking, communications and computing markets. Custom and foundry products address high bandwidth communications, consumer, automotive and military applications using analog and digital technologies. The products of the group are sold principally in North America, Asia and Europe. On 03-Mar-2004, the group acquired bluechip communications as.

Primary SIC and add'l.: 3674

CIK No: 0000932111

Subsidiaries: Micrel Semiconductor

Officers: Raymond D. Zinn/Chmn., Co - Founder, CEO, Pres./$979,040.00, Richard Crowley/VP - Finance, CFO/$554,402.00, Thomas Wong/VP - High Bandwidth Products, Bob Whelton/Exec. VP - Operations, Robert Barker/VP - Corporate Business Development, Guy Gandenberger/VP - Wafer Fab, Foundry Operations, Jc Lin/VP - Ethernet Group, Mark Lunsford/VP - Worldwide Sales, Carlos Mejia/57/VP - Human Resources, Vince Tortolano/VP, General Counsel, Sec., Scott Ward/VP - Test Division/$515,653.00, Richard Zelenka/VP - Quality Assurance, Robert Whelton/68/Exec. VP - Operations/$583,027.00, James G. Gandenberger/47/VP - Wafer Fab, Foundry Operations/$525,960.00, Jung-Chen Lin/54/VP - Ethernet Products

Directors: Raymond D. Zinn/Chmn., Co - Founder, CEO, Pres., David W. Conrath/Dir., Michael J. Callahan/Dir., Neil J. Miotto/Dir., Frank W. Schneider/66/Dir.

Owners: James G. Gandenberger, Richard D. Crowley, Scott Ward, Wasatch Advisors, Inc./12.70%, Warren H. Muller/13.80%, Kornitzer Capital Management, Inc./5.20%, Raymond D. Zinn/15.00%, David W. Conrath, Donald H. Livingstone, Robert Whelton, Michael J. Callahan, Insiders/18.40%

Financial Data: ***Fiscal Year End:***12/31 ***Latest Annual Data:*** 12/31/2006

Year	Sales	Net Income
2006	$276,307,000	$38,308,000
2005	$250,356,000	$25,358,000
2004	$257,551,000	$31,253,000

Curr. Assets:	$204,393,000	***Curr. Liab.:***	$61,778,000	***P/E Ratio:***	21.59
Plant, Equip.:	$78,665,000	***Total Liab.:***	$62,231,000	***Indic. Yr. Divd.:***	$0.120
Total Assets:	$300,273,000	***Net Worth:***	$238,042,000	***Debt/ Equity:***	0.0084

Micro Component Technology Inc

2340 W County Rd. C, St. Paul, MN, 55113; ***PH:*** 1-651-697-4000; ***Fax:*** 1-651-697-4200; ***http://*** www.mct.com; ***Email:*** sales@mct.com

General - Incorporation .... MN
Employees 91
Auditor .... Olsen, Thielen & Co. Ltd.
Stk Agt .... Wells Fargo Shareowner Services
Counsel .... Best & Flanagen LLP
DUNS No. 05-967-9902

Stock- Price on:12/24/2007 .... $0.24
Stock Exchange .... OTC
Ticker Symbol .... MCTI
Outstanding Shares 36,670,000
E.P.S .... -$0.04
Shareholders .... NA

Business: The group's principal is to supply integrated automation solutions for the global semiconductor test and assembly industry. The group offers complete and comprehensive equipment automation solutions for the test, laser mark, mark inspect singulation, sort and packaging for shipment portions of the back-end of the semiconductor manufacturing process. The process significantly improves the customers' productivity, yield and throughput. The customers of the group include leading semiconductor companies such as microchip technologies, analog devices, national semiconductor, phillips semiconductor, cypress semiconductor and st microelectronics and many of the leading back-end contract test and assembly companies including amkor and ns electronic bangkok. The group has operations in Europe and Asia.

Primary SIC and add'l.: 3825

CIK No: 0000911149

Subsidiaries: MCT Asia (Penang) Sdn. Bhd., MCT Philippines, Inc (Philippines)., Micro Component Technology Asia Pte. Ltd

Owners: Roger E. Gower, Richard L. Sidell, Donald R. VanLuvanee, David M. Sugishita, Patrick Verderico, Donald J. Kramer, Perkins Capital Management, Inc./20.60%, Insiders/2.60%, Laurus Master Fund, Ltd./9.90%

Financial Data: ***Fiscal Year End:***12/31 ***Latest Annual Data:*** 12/31/2006

Year	Sales	Net Income
2006	$12,214,000	-$3,653,000
2005	$7,069,000	-$5,103,000
2004	$14,602,000	-$2,048,000

Curr. Assets:	$5,201,000	***Curr. Liab.:***	$5,865,000		
Plant, Equip.:	$91,000	***Total Liab.:***	$11,371,000	***Indic. Yr. Divd.:***	NA
Total Assets:	$5,556,000	***Net Worth:***	-$5,815,000	***Debt/ Equity:***	NA

Micro Imaging Technology Inc

Formerly: Electropure Inc
23456 S Pointe Dr, Laguna Hills, CA, 92653; ***PH:*** 1-949-770-9347; ***http://*** www.electropure-inc.com

General - Incorporation .... CA
Employees 5
Auditor .... Jeffrey S. Gilbert, Cpa
Stk Agt ..... American Stock Transfer & Trust Co.
Counsel .... NA
DUNS No. 15-538-5602

Stock- Price on:12/24/2007 .... $0.24
Stock Exchange .... OTC
Ticker Symbol .... MMTC
Outstanding Shares 29,550,000
E.P.S .... -$0.19
Shareholders .... NA

Business: The group's principal activities are to manufacture and market electrodeionization water treatment devices for high purity water applications for both industrial and commercial users. Its operations are conducted through two wholly owned subsidiaries: electropure edi inc and micro imaging technology. The group has two product segments: water purification and fluid monitoring. The water purification segment produces water purification modules for sale to manufacturers of high purity water treatment systems. The fluid segment is developing a technology that is anticipated to enable real time identification of contamination in fluids. The group operates in the United States, Asia, Europe and other foreign countries.

Primary SIC and add'l.: 3823

CIK No: 0000808015

Subsidiaries: Micro Imaging Technology

Officers: Michael W. Brennan/64/Chmn., CEO, George R. Farquhar/66/COO, Catherine Patterson/55/CFO, Sec., Michael Snow/Contact - Pres. - Snowpure, LLC

Directors: Michael W. Brennan/64/Chmn., CEO, Ralph W. Emerson/61/Dir., Victor A. Hollander/74/Dir.

Financial Data: ***Fiscal Year End:***10/31 ***Latest Annual Data:*** 10/31/2006

Year	Sales	Net Income
2006	NA	-$3,799,000
2005	NA	$1,118,000
2004	$1,129,000	-$1,403,000

Curr. Assets:	$26,000	***Curr. Liab.:***	$660,000		
Plant, Equip.:	$111,000	***Total Liab.:***	$2,660,000	***Indic. Yr. Divd.:***	NA
Total Assets:	$137,000	***Net Worth:***	-$2,522,000	***Debt/ Equity:***	NA

Micro Laboratories Inc

29 Lakeside Dr., Johnston, RI, 02919; ***PH:*** 1-401-949-3562; ***Fax:*** 1-401-949-3405; ***http://*** www.microsprayvitamins.com; ***Email:*** contactus@microsprayvitamins.com

General

General - Incorporation	NV
Employees	NA
Auditor	James E. Scheifley & Assoc. P.C
Stk Agt	Computershare Investor Services LLC
Counsel	NA
DUNS No.	NA

Stock - Price on:12/24/2007	$0.0023
Stock Exchange	OTC
Ticker Symbol	MLAR
Outstanding Shares	NA
E.P.S.	-$0.89
Shareholders	NA

Business: The group's principle activities include producing, marketing and distributing a line of oral spray vitamins with the trade name 'micro sprayt'. This delivery system is in the form of a spray that is sprayed directly onto the mouth in the form of a fine mist. The company also produces, markets and distributes an additional line of minerals, herbs and other oral absorption products as well as gel capsules in the United States and in the international market. The company currently has six different nutritional health products: adult multiple vitamin, children's multiple vitamin, vitamin b-12, adult b-complex with c, children's b complex with c and zinc plus vitamin c. The group operates from United States.

Primary SIC and add'l.: 2834

CIK No: 0001102276

Financial Data: Fiscal Year End:03/31   Latest Annual Data: 3/31/2005

Year	Sales	Net Income
2005	$28,000	$37,000
2004	$28,000	-$44,000
2003	$13,000	-$66,000

Curr. Assets:	$0	Curr. Liab.:	$402,000		
Plant, Equip.:	NA	Total Liab.:	$402,000	Indic. Yr. Divd.:	NA
Total Assets:	$2,000	Net Worth:	-$400,000	Debt/ Equity:	NA

Microchip Technology Inc

2355 W Chandler Blvd., Chandler, AZ, 85224; *PH:* 1-480-792-7200; *Fax:* 1-480-792-7277; *http://* www.microchip.com; *Email:* events@mail.microchip.com

General - Incorporation	DE
Employees	4,336
Auditor	Ernst & Young LLP
Stk Agt	Wells Fargo Bank Minnesota N.A
Counsel	Wilson Sonsini Goodrich & Rosati
DUNS No.	18-691-7969

Stock - Price on:12/24/2007	$37.91
Stock Exchange	NDQ
Ticker Symbol	MCHP
Outstanding Shares	218,350,000
E.P.S.	$1.63
Shareholders	NA

Business: The group's principal activity is to design, develop, manufacture and market specialized semiconductor products for embedded control applications. The group's product portfolio comprises field-programmable risc-based microcontrollers that serve 8 and 16-bit embedded control applications and high-performance linear and mixed-signal, power management and thermal management devices. It also offers complementary microperipheral products such as interface devices, serial eeproms and keeloq(R) security devices. Customers of the group include distributors and original equipment manufacturers in the automotive, communications, computing, consumer and industrial control markets. These products are sold in North America, Europe and Asia.

Primary SIC and add'l.: 3674

CIK No: 0000827054

Subsidiaries: Microchip Technology (Barbados) Incorporated, Microchip Technology (Thailand) Co., Ltd.

Officers: Steve Sanghi/Chmn., CEO, Pres./$4,407,666.00, David S. Lambert/VP - Fab Operations/$756,270.00, Gary P. Marsh/VP - European Sales, Deborah L. Wussler/Investor Relations Officer, Derek P. Carlson/VP - Development Tools Group, Kathryn A. Clevenger/VP - Fab 4 Operations, Mathew B. Bunker/VP - Pacific Rim Manufacturing Operations, Joseph R. Krawczyk/VP - Asia Sales, Kenneth N. Pye/VP - Worldwide Applications Engineering, Gordon W. Parnell/CFO, VP/$743,236.00, Mitchell R. Little/VP - Worldwide Sales, Applications/$848,405.00, Ganesh Moorthy/Exec. VP/$1,032,680.00, Richard J. Simoncic/VP - Analog, Interface Products Division, Stephen V. Drehobl/VP - Security, Microcontroller, Technology Division, Eric J. Bjornholt/Sec. *(24 Officers included in Index)*

Directors: Steve Sanghi/Chmn., CEO, Pres., Wade F. Meyercord/Dir., Matthew W. Chapman/Dir., L. B. Day/Dir., Albert J. Hugo-Martinez/Dir.

Owners: Wade F. Meyercord, Mitchell R. Little, Steve Sanghi/2.70%, FMR Corp./6.22%, Insiders/3.33%, Capital Research & Management Co./10.88%, David S. Lambert, Albert J. Hugo-Martinez, Gordon W. Parnell, Ganesh Moorthy, L.B. Day, Matthew W. Chapman

Financial Data: Fiscal Year End:03/31   Latest Annual Data: 3/31/2007

Year	Sales	Net Income
2007	$1,039,671,000	$357,029,000
2006	$927,893,000	$242,369,000
2005	$846,936,000	$213,785,000

Curr. Assets:	$1,084,737,000	Curr. Liab.:	$255,920,000	P/E Ratio:	23.40
Plant, Equip.:	$605,722,000	Total Liab.:	$265,173,000	Indic. Yr. Divd.:	$1.120
Total Assets:	$2,269,541,000	Net Worth:	$2,004,368,000	Debt/ Equity:	NA

Microfield Group Inc

1631 NW Thurman, Ste 200, Portland, OR, 97209; *PH:* 1-503-419-3580; *http://* www.microfield.com; *Email:* operations@microfield.com

General - Incorporation	OR
Employees	293
Auditor	RBS Mirchandani LLP
Stk Agt	Mellon Investor Services LLC
Counsel	NA
DUNS No.	NA

Stock - Price on:12/24/2007	$0.85
Stock Exchange	OTC
Ticker Symbol	MICG
Outstanding Shares	80,660,000
E.P.S.	$0.02
Shareholders	NA

Business: The group's principal activity is installation of electrical products and services. The group's main products and services are electrical design and construction services, digital video cctv systems and infrastructure, telecommunications systems and infrastructure, enterprise security and life safety systems, wireless networking solutions and information technology (IT) network design and engineering. On 16-Sep-2003, the group two wholly-owned subsidiaries, christenson technology services inc and velagio inc. During the year the group discontinued the operations of innovative safety technologies, llc and velagio inc.

Primary SIC and add'l.: 1731

CIK No: 0000944947

Subsidiaries: Christenson Electric, Inc., Christenson Velagio, Inc., ECI Acquisition Co., Energy Connect, Inc.

Owners: Robert J. Jesenik/9.80%, Mark A. Walter, William C. McCormick/3.20%, Michael Stansell, Insiders/29.20%, Rodney M. Boucher/16.70%, Randall R. Reed, Gene Ameduri/10.90%, CEAC/7.60%, Vince Cushing/9.90%, Gary D. Conley

Microfinancial Inc

10M Commerce Way, Woburn, MA, 01801; *PH:* 1-781-994-4800; *Fax:* 1-781-994-4710; *http://* www.microfinancial.com; *Email:* info@microfinancial.com

General - Incorporation	MA
Employees	67
Auditor	Vitale, Caturano & Co. Ltd
Stk Agt	Timepayment Corp. LLC
Counsel	NA
DUNS No.	NA

Stock - Price on:12/24/2007	$6.15
Stock Exchange	AMEX
Ticker Symbol	MFI
Outstanding Shares	NA
E.P.S.	$0.38
Shareholders	NA

Business: The group's principle activities are to provide commercial finance leasing, equipment leasing and other financial services. The group leases and rents microticket equipment, advertising and display equipment, coffee machines, paging systems, water coolers and restaurant equipment. It sources the leasing transactions through a network of independent sales organizations and other dealer-based lease origination networks. The group also provides financial services, such as processing, billing and collection functions under the service contracts. The group operates in California, Florida, Texas, Massachusetts and New York. The group's quarterly revenue for September 2007 was 8.10 millions of USD.

Primary SIC and add'l.: 7359 6719 6153

CIK No: 0000827230

Subsidiaries: Leasecomm Corporation, MFI Finance Corporation I, TimePayment Corp. LLC

Officers: Richard F. Latour/Dir., CEO, Pres./$550,194.00, Steven J. Lacreta/VP - Legal, Vendor, Lessee Relations/$151,629.00, Stephen J. Constantino/VP - Human Resources/$150,255.00, James R. Jackson/CFO, VP/$283,419.00

Directors: Richard F. Latour/Dir., CEO, Pres., Peter R. Bleyleben/Chmn., Torrence C. Harder/Dir., Brian E. Boyle/Dir., Fritz Von Mering/Dir., Alan J. Zakon/Dir., John Everets/Dir.

Owners: Austin W. Marxe/5.70%, Fritz von Mering, Peter R. Bleyleben/11.30%, Insiders/42.40%, Steven J. LaCreta, James R. Jackson, Brian E. Boyle/11.00%, Wasatch Advisors, Inc./8.10%, Richard F. Latour/6.50%, Torrence C. Harder/12.80%, John W. Everets, Thomas Herlihy, Stephen Constantino, Alan J. Zakon/2.10%

Financial Data: Fiscal Year End:12/31   Latest Annual Data: 12/31/2006

Year	Sales	Net Income
2006	$32,442,000	$3,915,000
2005	$39,284,000	-$1,660,000
2004	$60,367,000	-$10,216,000

Curr. Assets:	$28,737,000	Curr. Liab.:	$2,470,000	P/E Ratio:	16.18
Plant, Equip.:	$655,000	Total Liab.:	$3,585,000	Indic. Yr. Divd.:	$0.200
Total Assets:	$59,721,000	Net Worth:	$56,136,000	Debt/ Equity:	0.0004

Microhelix Inc

19500 SW 90th Ct., Tualatin, OR, 97062; *PH:* 1-503-692-5333; *Fax:* 1-503-692-0878; *http://* www.microhelix.com; *Email:* oem-ultrasound@microhelix.com

General - Incorporation	OR
Employees	139
Auditor	Peterson Sullivan, PLLC
Stk Agt	UMB Bank, N.A.
Counsel	NA
DUNS No.	NA

Stock - Price on:12/24/2007	NA
Stock Exchange	OTC
Ticker Symbol	MHLX
Outstanding Shares	NA
E.P.S.	-$0.409
Shareholders	NA

Business: The group's principal activities are to design, manufacture and market customized electronic interconnect systems for the medical and commercial markets. The group operates in two segments: ultrasound division and wire and cable division. The ultrasound division designs and manufactures cable assemblies for original equipment manufacturer customers that are used in applications such as medical ultrasound probes, patient monitoring devices and heads-up displays. The wire and cable division manufactures and markets coated wire, including ultra-thin wall pinhole-free wire and custom cable for a number of applications. It also designs and manufactures specialty connectors and flex circuits and offers a range of laser micro-machining services. On 21-Apr-2004, the group sold its wire and cable division to advanced neuromodulation systems inc of Dallas, Texas.

Primary SIC and add'l.: 3841

CIK No: 0001142406

Subsidiaries: Alcatel NA Cable Systems, Inc, BioElectric Corporation, microHelix Acquisition Corp., Moore Electronics, Inc.

Officers: Steven G. Ashton/63/CEO, Pres., Assist. Sec.

Directors: Steven G. Ashton/63/CEO, Pres., Assist. Sec., William C. McCormick/73/Dir.

Financial Data: Fiscal Year End:12/31   Latest Annual Data: 12/31/2006

Year	Sales	Net Income
2006	$15,282,000	-$1,993,000
2005	$9,164,000	-$1,703,000
2004	$1,300,000	-$1,554,000

Curr. Assets:	$3,590,000	Curr. Liab.:	$4,776,000		
Plant, Equip.:	$904,000	Total Liab.:	$5,875,000	Indic. Yr. Divd.:	NA
Total Assets:	$5,577,000	Net Worth:	-$298,000	Debt/ Equity:	NA

Microlslet Inc

6370 Nancy Ridge Dr., Ste. 112, San Diego, CA, 92121; *PH:* 1-858-657-0287; *Fax:* 1-858-657-0288; *http://* www.microislet.com; *Email:* info@microislet

General - Incorporation	NV
Employees	25
Auditor	Deloitte & Touche LLP
Stk Agt	Integrity Stock Transfer, Inc.
Counsel	Sheppard Mullin Richter & Hampton LLP
DUNS No.	NA

Stock - Price on:12/24/2007	NA
Stock Exchange	OTC
Ticker Symbol	MIIS
Outstanding Shares	NA
E.P.S.	NA
Shareholders	NA

Business: The group's principal activity is research, development and commercialization of patented technologies in the field of transplantation therapy for patients with insulin-dependent diabetes. The group has licensed several technologies from duke university medical center developed over the last decade for the isolation, culture, storage and encapsulation (microencapsulation) of insulin-producing islet cells from porcine sources. These methods are among advances in the field of transplantation that may enable diabetic patients to become free from insulin injections.

Primary SIC and add'l.: 8731

CIK No: 0001092050

Subsidiaries: MicroIslet, Inc.

Officers: James R. Gavin/62/Dir., CEO, Pres., Kevin A. Hainley/Interim CFO, Mgr., Jonathan R.T. Lakey/Dir., Pres., Chief Scientific Officer, Mgr., Amaresh Basu/VP - Research, Development, Mgr.

Directors: James R. Gavin/62/Dir., CEO, Pres., John J. Hagenbuch/56/Chmn., Myron A. Wick/64/Dir., Barry Ritholtz/Dir., Robert W. Anderson/Dir., Steven T. Frankel/Dir., Bassam Damaj/Member - Scientific Advisory Board, Jonathan R.T. Lakey/Dir., Pres., Chief Scientific Officer, Mgr., Keith B. Hoffman/Dir., Bertram E. Walls/56/Dir., Daniel R. Salomon/Member - Scientific Advisory Board, James Shapiro/Member - Scientific Advisory Board, Nora Sarvetnick/Member - Scientific Advisory Board, Athanassios Sambanis/Member - Scientific Advisory Board

Owners: Insiders/13.70%, Robert W. Anderson, John J. Hagenbuch/9.40%, Bertram E. Walls, John F. Steel/18.10%, Kevin A. Hainley, Richard Schoninger/7.00%, James R. Gavin/1.40%, Myron A. Wick/1.90%, Steven T. Frankel

Curr. Assets:	$2,354,000	**Curr. Liab.:**	$508,000		
Plant, Equip.:	$295,000	**Total Liab.:**	$533,000	**Indic. Yr. Divd.:**	NA
Total Assets:	$2,717,000	**Net Worth:**	$2,184,000	**Debt/ Equity:**	NA

MicroMed Cardiovascular Inc

8965 Interchange Dr., Houston, TX, 77054; *PH:* 1-713-838-9210; *http://* www.micromedtech.com; *Email:* micromed@micromedtech.com

General - Incorporation	DE	**Stock**- Price on:12/24/2007	$0.88
Employees	34	Stock Exchange	OTC
Auditor	Ernst & Young LLP	Ticker Symbol	MMCV
Stk Agt	NA	Outstanding Shares	40,080,000
Counsel	NA	E.P.S	-$0.22
DUNS No.	NA	Shareholders	NA

Business: The groups principle activities include developing, manufacturing, and selling heart assist devices. The product of the group is DeBakey VAD System. The group operates from the United States.

Primary SIC and add'l.: 3841

CIK No: 0001269515

Subsidiaries: MicroMed Technology, Inc.

Officers: Robert J. Benkowski/CEO

Directors: Clifford Zur Nieden/Chmn., Norwick B.H. Goodspeed/Dir., Matt Borenzweig/Dir.

Owners: Absolute Octane Fund/11.58%, Juliet Markovich, Robert J. Benkowski, Essex Woodlands Health Ventures/5.61%, Mitsui& Co Venture Partners/5.59%, Absolute Return Europe Fund/26.71%, Alan Totah, Absolute East West Fund/8.15%, SV Life Sciences/5.19%, European Catalyst Fund/9.49%, Norwick Goodspeed, Insiders, Charterhouse Equity Partners/10.26%, Oxford Bioscience Partners/5.70%

Financial Data: ***Fiscal Year End:***12/31 ***Latest Annual Data:*** 12/31/2006

Year	Sales	Net Income
2006	$3,049,000	-$8,229,000
2005	$5,158,000	-$8,946,000
2004	NA	-$27,000

Curr. Assets:	$13,491,000	**Curr. Liab.:**	$2,067,000		
Plant, Equip.:	$385,000	**Total Liab.:**	$2,067,000	**Indic. Yr. Divd.:**	NA
Total Assets:	$13,889,000	**Net Worth:**	$11,822,000	**Debt/ Equity:**	NA

Micromem Technologies Inc

777 Bay St., Ste. 1910, Toronto, ON, M5G 2E4; *PH:* 1-416-364-6513; *http://* www.micromeminc.com; *Email:* info@micromeminc.com

General - Incorporation	Canada	**Stock**- Price on:12/24/2007	$0.44
Employees	NA	Stock Exchange	OTC
Auditor	Schwartz Levitsky Feldman LLP	Ticker Symbol	MMTIF
Stk Agt	Equity Transfer Services Inc	Outstanding Shares	NA
Counsel	Chitiz Pathak LLP	E.P.S	NA
DUNS No.	NA	Shareholders	NA

Business: The group's principle activity is to develop memory device based on ferromagnetic technology which provides digital memory which can be both read and written randomly and will not lose its information when its power is cut off. The group operates from United States.

Primary SIC and add'l.: 6719 3674

CIK No: 0001085921

Subsidiaries: Memtech International (USA) Inc., Memtech International Inc, Micromem Technologies B.V, Micromem Technologies S.p.A., Pageant International, Pageant Technologies (USA) Inc.

Officers: Joseph Fuda/Dir., CEO, Pres., Cynthia Kuper/CTO, Dan Amadori/CFO, Manoj Pundit/43/Dir., Sec., Larry Blue/Dir., Advisor, Jason Baun/Investor Relations Officer, Harry Ruda/Lead Scientist

Directors: Joseph Fuda/Dir., CEO, Pres., Salvatore Fuda/Chmn., Manoj Pundit/43/Dir., Sec., David Sharpless/Dir., Andrew Brandt/Dir., Steven Van Fleet/Dir., Oliver Nepomuceno/Dir., Larry Blue/Dir., Advisor

Owners: Dan Amadori/1.29%, Joseph Fuda/3.82%, Salvatore Fuda/8.10%, Manoj Pundit/0.14%, David Sharpless/0.57%, Oliver Nepomuceno/1.73%, Andrew Brandt/0.57%, Stephen Fleming/0.43%

Financial Data: ***Fiscal Year End:***10/31 ***Latest Annual Data:*** 10/31/2006

Year	Sales	Net Income
2006	$10,000	-$4,058,000
2005	$9,000	-$4,035,000
2004	$5,000	-$944,000

Curr. Assets:	$465,000	**Curr. Liab.:**	$914,000		
Plant, Equip.:	NA	**Total Liab.:**	$914,000	**Indic. Yr. Divd.:**	NA
Total Assets:	$465,000	**Net Worth:**	-$449,000	**Debt/ Equity:**	NA

Micron Enviro Systems Inc

789 W Pender St., Ste. 1250, Vancouver, BC, V6C 1H2; *PH:* 1-604-646-6903; *http://* www.micronenviro.com; *Email:* info@micronenviro.com

General - Incorporation	NV	**Stock**- Price on:12/24/2007	$0.034
Employees	NA	Stock Exchange	OTC
Auditor	Williams & Webster, P.S	Ticker Symbol	MENV
Stk Agt	Pacific Stock Transfer Company	Outstanding Shares	NA
Counsel	NA	E.P.S	NA
DUNS No.	NA	Shareholders	NA

Business: The group's principal activities are to acquire, explore and develop natural gas and oil mineral properties. The group is in the exploration stage and has a 5% working interest in an oil and gas well near fresno, ca. As on 15-Oct-2002 group acquired a 5% working interest in an oil and gas target located in kern county, California in the prolific san joaquin valley, which hosts 5 of the top 25 largest fields in the United States.

Primary SIC and add'l.: 1311

CIK No: 0001082285

Subsidiaries: Pinnacle Plastics Inc.

Officers: Bernard McDougall/Dir., Pres., Negar Towfigh/CFO, Sec.

Directors: Bernard McDougall/Dir., Pres., Stephen J. Amdahl/62/Dir.

Owners: Insiders/1.30%, Negar Towfigh/0.40%, Stephen Amdahl/0.50%, Bernard McDougall/0.40%

Financial Data: ***Fiscal Year End:***12/31 ***Latest Annual Data:*** 12/31/2006

Year	Sales	Net Income
2006	$18,000	-$1,881,000
2005	$25,000	-$916,000
2004	$17,000	-$992,000

Curr. Assets:	$90,000	**Curr. Liab.:**	$318,000		
Plant, Equip.:	$3,000	**Total Liab.:**	$318,000	**Indic. Yr. Divd.:**	NA
Total Assets:	$233,000	**Net Worth:**	-$85,000	**Debt/ Equity:**	NA

Micron Technology Inc

8000 S Federal Way, Boise, ID, 83707; *PH:* 1-208-368-4000; *Fax:* 1-208-368-2536; *http://* www.micron.com

General - Incorporation	DE	**Stock**- Price on:12/24/2007	$12.72
Employees	21,100	Stock Exchange	NYSE
Auditor	PricewaterhouseCoopers LLP	Ticker Symbol	MU
Stk Agt	Wells Fargo Shareowner Services	Outstanding Shares	756,360,000
Counsel	NA	E.P.S	-$0.91
DUNS No.	09-312-0871	Shareholders	NA

Business: The group operates through its subsidiaries whose activities include designing, developing, manufacturing and marketing semiconductor products. The groups semiconductor products include dynamic random access memory (DRAM), NAND Flash memory (NAND), metal-oxide semiconductor (CMOS) and image sensors. The groups products are used in mobile phones, digital still cameras, webcams and other consumer, security and automotive applications. The group operates from United States.

Primary SIC and add'l.: 5045 7375 3672 3674 3571 5065

CIK No: 0000723125

Subsidiaries: Acclaim Innovations, LLC, Lexar (Shanghai) Electronic Company Limited, Lexar Hong Kong Limited, Lexar Media (Europe) Limited, Lexar Media International Limited, Lexar Media K.K., Lexar Media Pty Ltd., Lexar Media, Inc., Lexar Singapore Pte. Ltd., Micron Customs Brokerage Services, Inc., Micron Europe Limited, Micron Japan, Ltd., Micron Semiconductor (Deutschland) GmbH, Micron Semiconductor (Shanghai) Co., Ltd., Micron Semiconductor (Xian) Co., Ltd. 35 Subsidiaries included in the Index

Officers: Steven R. Appleton/Chmn., CEO, Michael W. Sadler/VP - Worldwide Sales, Jan R. Reimer/Assist. Sec., Kipp A. Bedard/VP - Investor Relations, Jay L. Hawkins/VP - Operations, Norman L. Schlachter/Treasurer, Roderic W. Lewis/VP - Legal Affairs, General Counsel, Corp. Sec., Mark Adams/VP - Digital Media, Mark D. Durcan/COO, Pres., Frankie F. Roohparvar/VP - Nand Development, John F. Schreck/VP - Dram Development, Brian M. Shirley/VP - Memory, Ivan Donaldson/Mgr. - Investor Relations, Daniel Francisco/Dir. - Media Relations, Jason Kreizenbeck/Dir. - Government Affairs *(28 Officers included in Index)*

Directors: Steven R. Appleton/Chmn., CEO, Gordon C. Smith/Dir., Teruaki Aoki/Dir., Mercedes Johnson/Dir., Robert E. Switz/Dir., Robert L. Bailey/51/Dir., James W. Bagley/Dir., Lawrence N. Mondry/Dir.

Owners: Gordon C. Smith, Lawrence N. Mondry, James W. Bagley, William P. Weber, Robert E. Switz, Mark W. Adams, Steven R. Appleton, ClearBridge Advisors, LLC/6.64%, Brian M. Shirley, Wilbur G. Stover, Brandes Investment Partners, L.P./10.79%, Insiders/2.43%, Teruaki Aoki, Goldman Sachs Asset Management, L.P./6.62%, Mercedes Johnson *(19 Owners included in Index)*

Financial Data: ***Fiscal Year End:***09/02 ***Latest Annual Data:*** 8/30/2007

Year	Sales	Net Income
2007	$5,688,000,000	-$320,000,000
2006	$5,272,000,000	$408,000,000
2005	$4,880,200,000	$188,000,000

Curr. Assets:	$2,638,700,000	**Curr. Liab.:**	$972,100,000	**P/E Ratio:**	44.79
Plant, Equip.:	$4,712,700,000	**Total Liab.:**	$2,145,200,000	**Indic. Yr. Divd.:**	NA
Total Assets:	$7,760,000,000	**Net Worth:**	$5,614,800,000	**Debt/ Equity:**	NA

Micronetics Inc

26 Hampshire Dr., Hudson, NH, 03051; *PH:* 1-603-883-2900; *Fax:* 1-603-882-8987; *http://* www.mwireless.com

General - Incorporation	DE	**Stock**- Price on:12/24/2007	$8.51
Employees	125	Stock Exchange	NDQ
Auditor	Grant Thornton LLP	Ticker Symbol	NOIZ
Stk Agt	Computershare Investor Services LLC	Outstanding Shares	5,010,000
Counsel	Kalin & Associates	E.P.S	$0.34
DUNS No.	07-870-8690	Shareholders	NA

Business: The group's principal activity is to manufacture microwave and radio frequency components and integrated subassemblies, test equipment, sub- assemblies and components used to test the strength, durability and integrity of signals in communications equipment. The group operates in two business groups: defense electronics and commercial products. The defense electronics group develops and manufactures microwave and radio frequency components and subassemblies used in microwave

products. It consists of four operating groups: enon electronics, micro-con and microwave, video systems, inc and micronetics' receiver components division. The commercial group produces components and test equipment used in the development, test and deployment of wireless communications and automated testing systems. It consists of three operating groups: noise products, test solutions and vco product groups. Major customers include the us government , aerostat and raytheon.

Primary SIC and add'l.: 3679 3825

CIK No: 0000820097

Subsidiaries: Enon Microwave, Inc., Microwave and Video Systems, Inc., Microwave Concepts, Inc., Stealth Microwave, Inc.

Officers: David Robbins/43/Dir., CEO, Pres./$276,326.00, Diane Bourque/54/CFO/$169,662.00, Floyd Parin/Pres. - Microwave, Video Systems, Donna Hillsgrove/59/Sec., Treasurer, Peter Matthews/Sales Mgr., Patrick Robbins/Dir. - Sales, Kevin Beals/46/VP - Business Development

Directors: David Robbins/43/Dir., CEO, Pres., David Siegel/82/Dir., Gerald Y. Hattori/56/Dir., Danne Hurd/57/Dir.

Owners: FMR Corp/7.20%, Potomac Capital Management LLC/6.10%, David Siegel/3.90%, Stephen N. Barthelmes/1.20%, David Robbins/2.90%, Gerald Y. Hattori, Noelle Kalin/12.30%, Diane Bourque, Insiders/8.30%

Financial Data: *Fiscal Year End:*03/31 *Latest Annual Data:* 3/31/2006

Year	Sales		Net Income
2006	$26,909,000		$2,540,000
2005	$14,059,000		$1,275,000
2004	$13,832,000		$1,511,000
Curr. Assets:	$17,324,000	Curr. Liab.:	$5,487,000	P/E Ratio:	60.79
Plant, Equip.:	$4,017,000	Total Liab.:	$11,842,000	Indic. Yr. Divd.:	NA
Total Assets:	$29,819,000	Net Worth:	$17,977,000	Debt/ Equity:	NA

Micropac Industries Inc

905 E Walnut St., Garland, TX, 75040; *PH:* 1-972-272-3571; *Fax:* 1-972-494-2281; *http://* www.micropac.com

General - Incorporation	DE	Stock- Price on:12/24/2007	$5.92
Employees	134	Stock Exchange	OTC
Auditor	KPMG LLP	Ticker Symbol	MPAD
Stk Agt	Transfer Agent & Registrar	Outstanding Shares	2,580,000
Counsel	Glast, Phillips & Murray	E.P.S.	$0.51
DUNS No.	05-636-7113	Shareholders	NA

Business: The group's principle activities include manufacturing and distributing various types of hybrid microelectronic circuits, solid state relays, power operational amplifiers and optoelectronic components and assemblies. The company's products are used as components in a broad range of military, space and industrial systems, including aircraft instrumentation and navigation systems, power supplies, electronic controls, computers, medical devices, and high-temperature (200o c) products. The company's products are either custom designed and manufactured to meet the client's requirements or standard proprietary components such as catalog items. The company's customers include United States government department of defense and national aeronautics and space administration. The group operates from United States.

Primary SIC and add'l.: 3674 3679

CIK No: 0000065759

Officers: Mark King/53/Dir., CEO, Pres., Barbara Hall/Human Resources, Patrick Cefalu/50/CFO, VP, Gary Collins/Multi, Chip Module Business Mgr., Carla Anderson/Opto Inside Sales, Barbel Meier/Assist. European Sales Mgr., Richard Dahlberg/Opto Engineeringmgr, Dorothy Lindemann/Microcircuits Inside Sales, Cecil Miller/Mgr. - Corporate Quality, Bill King/Microcircuits New Business Unit Mgr., Dennis Granger/Regional Sales Mgr., Jim Wesberry/Microcircuits Mgr. - Operations, Manufacturing, Karen Ferris/Corporate Administrator, Bill Nail/Mgr. - Purchasing, Materials, Tracy Dotson/Mgr. - Accounting (19 Officers included in Index)

Directors: Mark King/53/Dir., CEO, Pres., Connie Wood/68/Dir., James K. Murphey/65/Dir., Nicholas Nadolsky/74/Dir., Kent H. Hearn/71/Dir., Heinz-Werner Hempel/79/Dir.

Owners: Heinz-Werner Hempel/75.70%, Insiders/76.10%, Kent H. Hearn, Connie Wood

Financial Data: *Fiscal Year End:*11/30 *Latest Annual Data:* 11/30/2006

Year	Sales		Net Income
2006	$17,156,000		$1,419,000
2005	$19,030,000		$2,176,000
2004	$15,356,000		$1,408,000
Curr. Assets:	$11,853,000	Curr. Liab.:	$1,535,000	P/E Ratio:	11.17
Plant, Equip.:	$1,215,000	Total Liab.:	$1,614,000	Indic. Yr. Divd.:	NA
Total Assets:	$13,068,000	Net Worth:	$11,454,000	Debt/ Equity:	NA

Micros Systems Inc

7031 Columbia Gateway Dr., Columbia, MD, 21046; *PH:* 1-443-285-6000; *Fax:* 1-443-285-8000; *http://* www.micros.com; *Email:* info@micros.com

General - Incorporation	MD	Stock- Price on:12/24/2007	$52.86
Employees	3,800	Stock Exchange	NDQ
Auditor	PricewaterhouseCoopers LLP	Ticker Symbol	MCRS
Stk Agt	Registrar & Transfer Co	Outstanding Shares	40,520,000
Counsel	NA	E.P.S.	NA
DUNS No.	09-240-2726	Shareholders	NA

Business: The group's principle activities are to design, manufacture, market and service enterprise information solutions for the global hospitality industry. These solutions include hotel information systems and restaurant information systems. Hotel information systems comprise software encompassing property management systems, sales and catering systems, central reservation systems and customer information under the brand micros-fidelio. Restaurant information systems include hardware and software for point-of-sale and operational applications, and a suite of back office applications including inventory, labor and finance management. The group also markets products such as spare parts, media supplies, network products and provides services such as credit card software support, network support and consulting. The group's total revenue for year 2007 was 785.73 millions of USD.

Primary SIC and add'l.: 7379 7372 3578

CIK No: 0000320345

Subsidiaries: CommercialWare, Inc., Datavantage Corporation, Fidelio Cruise GmbH, Fidelio Cruise, Inc., Fidelio India Private Ltd., Fidelio Nordic Norway A/S, Fidelio Nordic Oy, Fidelio Nordic Sverige A.B., Hospitality Technologies, S.A., Hotelbk A.B., JTECH Communications, Inc., Micros Fidelio Caribbean, Inc., Micros Fidelio Chile, S.A., Micros Fidelio Israel Ltd., Micros-Fidelio (Canada) Ltd. 32 Subsidiaries included in the Index

Officers: A. L. Giannopoulos/Chmn., CEO, Pres., Cynthia A. Russo/VP, Corporate Controller, Gary C. Kaufman/Exec. VP - Finance, Administration, CFO, Thomas L. Patz/Exec. VP - Strategic Initiatives, General Counsel, Corp. Sec., Kaweh Niroomand/Pres. - Micros, Fidelio, Eame, Europe, Africa, Middle East, Stefan Piringer/Pres. - Micros, Fidelio, Asia Pacific, Jenny M. Kurdle/Exec. VP - Leisure, Entertainment, Thomas M. Moran/VP - Restaurant Sales, Strategies, John E. Gularson/Sr. VP - Retail Systems, Jim Borkowski/VP - Business Services, Louise J. Casamento/VP - Marketing, Customer Relations, Debra McIntyre/VP - Human Resources, Peter J. Rogers/Sr. VP - Investor Relations, Business Development, James T. Walsh/VP - Customer Service, Julie Griffin/Executive Assist. - Investor Relations Coordinator (20 Officers included in Index)

Directors: A. L. Giannopoulos/Chmn., CEO, Pres., Lou Brown/Vice Chmn., Dwight S. Taylor/Dir., John G. Puente/Dir., Gary B. Dando/Dir., William S. Watson/Dir.

Owners: Thomas L. Patz, Louis M. Brown, Bernard Jammet, William S. Watson, Gary B. Dando, John G. Puente, Columbia Wanger Asset Management/5.56%, Gary C. Kaufman, Insiders/3.10%, Dwight S. Taylor, Daniel G. Interlandi, Barclays Global Investors/5.28%, A. L. Giannopoulos, Neuberger Berman LLC/6.67%

Financial Data: *Fiscal Year End:*06/30 *Latest Annual Data:* 6/30/2006

Year	Sales		Net Income
2006	$678,953,000		$63,528,000
2005	$597,264,000		$53,660,000
2004	$487,443,000		$33,279,000
Curr. Assets:	$457,152,000	Curr. Liab.:	$204,031,000		
Plant, Equip.:	$23,794,000	Total Liab.:	$227,599,000	Indic. Yr. Divd.:	NA
Total Assets:	$647,857,000	Net Worth:	$417,116,000	Debt/ Equity:	NA

Microsemi Corp

2381 Morse Ave., Irvine, CA, 92614; *PH:* 1-949-221-7100; *Fax:* 1-949-756-0308; *http://* www.microsemi.com

General - Incorporation	DE	Stock- Price on:12/24/2007	$22.72
Employees	2,049	Stock Exchange	NDQ
Auditor	PricewaterhouseCoopers LLP	Ticker Symbol	NA
Stk Agt	Mellon Investor Services LLC	Outstanding Shares	76,270,000
Counsel	NA	E.P.S.	NA
DUNS No.	05-155-0838	Shareholders	NA

Business: The group's principle activities are to design, manufacture and market analog, mixed-signal and discrete semiconductors. Products include individual components as well as complete circuit solutions that provide battery optimization, reduce size or protect circuits. These products manage and regulate power, protect against transient voltage spikes and transmit, receive and amplify signals. The group markets its products through domestic electronic component sales representatives, direct sales offices and 26 overseas sales representatives to original equipment and serves the satellite, telecommunications, computer and peripherals, military, aerospace, industrial, commercial and medical markets. The group has international operations in Thailand, the Philippines, Taiwan, Ireland, and China. Customers include boeing, compaq, dell, lockheed martin, guidant/cardiac pace makers, seagate technology, zenitron corporation, raytheon systems, bae systems, and medtronics. The group's total revenue for year 2007 was 442.25 millions of USD.

Primary SIC and add'l.: 3679 3674

CIK No: 0000310568

Subsidiaries: Micro (Bermuda), Ltd., Micro WaveSys, Inc., Microsemi Corp. Colorado, Microsemi Corp. Integrated Products, Microsemi Corp. Massachusetts, Microsemi Corp. Santa Ana, Microsemi Corp. Scottsdale, Microsemi Real Estate, Inc.

Officers: James J. Peterson/Dir., CEO, Pres., Steven Litchfield/Exec. VP, Pres. - Analog Mixed Signal, David Sonksen/CFO, Exec. VP, Sec., Ralph Brandi/Exec. VP, COO, Pres. - High Reliability, John Holtrust/Sr. VP - Human, James Gentile/VP - Worldwide Sales, Michael G. Sivetts/VP - Distribution Sales, John Costello/VP - Hi, Rel Sales, John Hohener/VP - Finance, Treasurer, Chief Accounting Officer

Directors: James J. Peterson/Dir., CEO, Pres., Dennis R. Leibel/Chmn., Paul F. Folino/Dir., William E. Bendush/Dir., Thomas R. Anderson/Dir., William L. Healey/Dir., Matthew E. Massengill/Dir.

Owners: Paul F. Folino, Franklin Resources, Inc./12.50%, Wells Fargo& Company/6.80%, AXA Financial, Inc./5.80%, Delaware Management Business Trust/5.20%, David R. Sonksen, Matthew E. Massengill, Dennis R. Leibel, William L. Healey, James J. Peterson/1.40%, William E. Bendush, Thomas R. Anderson, Stephen G. Litchfield, James H. Gentile, Insiders/4.60% (16 Owners included in Index)

Financial Data: *Fiscal Year End:*10/02 *Latest Annual Data:* 10/1/2006

Year	Sales		Net Income
2006	$370,477,000		$35,665,000
2005	$297,440,000		$29,223,000
2004	$244,805,000		$5,636,000
Curr. Assets:	$152,361,000	Curr. Liab.:	$43,904,000		
Plant, Equip.:	$59,098,000	Total Liab.:	$48,121,000	Indic. Yr. Divd.:	NA
Total Assets:	$232,998,000	Net Worth:	$184,877,000	Debt/ Equity:	NA

Microsmart Devices Inc New

3046 E Brighton Pl., Salt Lake City, UT, 84121; *PH:* 1-801-201-7635

General - Incorporation	NV	Stock- Price on:12/24/2007	NA
Employees	NA	Stock Exchange	OTC
Auditor	Mantyla, Mcreynolds & Assoc.	Ticker Symbol	MCMVE
Stk Agt	Colonial Stock Transfer Co Inc	Outstanding Shares	NA
Counsel	Mr. Meriwether	E.P.S.	NA
DUNS No.	NA	Shareholders	NA

Business: The groups principle activity is to provide recruiting services. The groups service area includes the research and development, engineering, marketing, sales, information technology and manufacturing industries. The group operates from United States.

Primary SIC and add'l.: 6770

CIK No: 0001339225

Officers: Mark L. Meriwether/49/Dir., CEO, Pres., Sec., Treasurer

Directors: Mark L. Meriwether/49/Dir., CEO, Pres., Sec., Treasurer

Owners: George Tsentas/25.90%, Insiders/86.20%, Mark L. Meriwether/60.30%

Financial Data: *Fiscal Year End:*12/31 *Latest Annual Data:* 12/31/2006

Year	Sales	Net Income
2006	NA	-$63,000

Curr. Assets:	NA	**Curr. Liab.:**	$90,000		
Plant, Equip.:	NA	**Total Liab.:**	$90,000	**Indic. Yr. Divd.:**	NA
Total Assets:	NA	**Net Worth:**	-$90,000	**Debt/ Equity:**	NA

Microsoft Corp

1 Microsoft Way, Redmond, WA, 98052; *PH:* 1-425-882-8080; *Fax:* 1-425-936-7329; *http://* www.microsoft.com

General - Incorporation .... WA
Employees 71,000
Auditor .... Deloitte & Touche LLP
Stk Agt .... Mellon Investor Services LLC
Counsel .... NA
DUNS No. 08-146-6849

Stock - Price on:12/24/2007 .... $29.96
Stock Exchange .... AMEX
Ticker Symbol .... MSI
Outstanding Shares 9,570,000,000
E.P.S. $1.52
Shareholders .... NA

Business: The group's principle activities include developing, manufacturing, licensing and supporting a wide range of software products for computing devices. The groups are divided into three business divisions namely Platform Products and Services, Business, and Entertainment and Devices. The group operates from United States.

Primary SIC and add'l.: 7375 7371 7373 7372

CIK No: 0000789019

Subsidiaries: Bagheera International Limited, Fidalgo Insurance Company, Flat Island Company Limited, GraceMac Corporation, MACS Holdings, Limited, Microsoft Asia Island Limited, Microsoft Capital Group, L.P., Microsoft Company, Limited, Microsoft Development Center Copenhagen ApS, Microsoft General Management Company, Microsoft Global Finance, Microsoft Holdings V, Inc., Microsoft Investments, Inc., Microsoft Ireland Capital, Microsoft Ireland Operations Limited 28 Subsidiaries included in the Index

Officers: Steve A. Ballmer/Dir., CEO/$1,279,821.00, Timothy Chen/CEO - Greater China Region, Corporate VP, Darren Huston/CEO, Pres. - Microsoft Co Ltd, Japan, Corporate VP, Umberto Paolucci/Sr. Chmn. - Microsoft Europe, Middle East, Africa, Corporate VP - Microsoft Corp, Bernard Vergnes/Sr. VP, Chmn. Emeritus - Microsoft Europe, Middle East, Africa, EMEA, Bill Veghte/Corporate VP - North America, Henry P. Vigil/Sr. VP - Consumer Strategy, Partnerships, Todd Warren/Corporate VP - Mobile, Embedded Devices, Allison L. Watson/Corporate VP - Worldwide Partner Group, Blair Westlake/Corporate VP - Media, Content, Partner Strategy Group, Simon Witts/Corporate VP - Enterprise, Partner Group, Ya-Qin Zhang/Corporate VP, George Zinn/Corporate VP, Treasurer, Brian Kevin Turner/COO, Klaus Holse Andersen/Corporate VP - MBS Sales, Operations *(125 Officers included in Index)*

Directors: Steve A. Ballmer/Dir., CEO, William H. Gates/52/Chmn., Reed Hastings/Dir., Korologos McLaughlin/Dir., David F. Marquardt/Dir., Dina Dublon/Dir., Helmut Panke/Dir., Raymond V. Gilmartin/Dir., Jon A. Shirley/Dir., James I. Cash/Dir., Charles H. Noski/Dir.

Owners: Insiders/13.95%, Jon A. Shirley, Helmut Panke, Kevin R. Johnson, Dina Dublon, Steven A. Ballmer/4.34%, Kevin B. Turner, David F. Marquardt, William H. Gates/9.33%, Jeffrey S. Raikes, Christopher P. Liddell, Raymond V. Gilmartin, James I. Cash, Charles H. Noski, Reed Hastings

Financial Data: *Fiscal Year End:*06/30 *Latest Annual Data:* 06/30/2007

Year	Sales	Net Income
2007	$51,122,000,000	$14,065,000,000
2006	$44,282,000,000	$12,599,000,000
2005	$39,788,000,000	$12,254,000,000

Curr. Assets:	$40,168,000,000	**Curr. Liab.:**	$23,754,000,000	**P/E Ratio:**	21.10
Plant, Equip.:	$4,350,000,000	**Total Liab.:**	$32,074,000,000	**Indic. Yr. Divd.:**	$0.400
Total Assets:	$63,171,000,000	**Net Worth:**	$31,097,000,000	**Debt/ Equity:**	NA

Microstrategy Inc

1861 International Dr., McLean, VA, 22102; *PH:* 1-703-848-8600; *Fax:* 1-703-848-8610; *http://* www.microstrategy.com; *Email:* education@microstrategy.com

General - Incorporation .... DE
Employees 1,274
Auditor .... Grant Thornton LLP
Stk Agt...... American Stock Transfer & Trust Co.
Counsel .... NA
DUNS No. 62-289-5613

Stock - Price on:12/24/2007 .... $95.31
Stock Exchange .... NYSE
Ticker Symbol .... MT
Outstanding Shares 12,400,000
E.P.S. $4.85
Shareholders .... NA

Business: The group's principal activity is to provide business intelligence software that enable companies to analyze raw data stored across their enterprise. The solutions offered by the group include microstrategy 7i, microstrategy intelligence server, microstrategy Web, microstrategy narrowcast server, microstrategy mdx adapter and microstrategy agent. The group also offers product support and other services such as technical account management, consulting, education and technical support. These solutions and services are marketed worldwide to the retail, telecommunications, financial services, pharmaceuticals, manufacturing and technology industries. Customers include bank of montreal, best buy, at&t, glaxosmithkline, honda, kimberly-clark, estee lauder and us postal service.

Primary SIC and add'l.: 7372 7376 7379 7371

CIK No: 0001050446

Subsidiaries: Alarm.com Incorporated, Lagrummet AB d/b/a MicroStrategy Sweden AB, MicroStrategy Administration Corporation, MicroStrategy Benelux B.V., MicroStrategy Brasil Ltda., MicroStrategy Canada Incorporated, MicroStrategy Deutschland GmbH, MicroStrategy France SARL, MicroStrategy Iberica, S.L.U., MicroStrategy International II Limited, MicroStrategy International Limited, MicroStrategy Italy S.r.l., MicroStrategy Korea Co., Ltd., MicroStrategy Limited, MicroStrategy Management Corporation 24 Subsidiaries included in the Index

Officers: Michael J. Saylor/Chmn., CEO, Pres./$3,189,696.00, Sanju K. Bansal/Vice Chmn., Exec. VP, COO, Sec./$719,598.00, Arthur S. Locke/VP - Finance, CFO/$866,030.00, Paul Zolfaghari/VP - Worldwide Sales, Operations/$781,929.00, Adam M. McDonald/VP - Worldwide Services, Jeffrey A. Bedell/VP - Technology, CTO, Jonathan F. Klein/VP - Law, General Counsel/$826,620.00

Directors: Michael J. Saylor/Chmn., CEO, Pres., Sanju K. Bansal/Vice Chmn., Exec. VP, COO, Sec., Matthew W. Calkins/Dir., Robert H. Epstein/Dir., David W. Larue/Dir., Jarrod M. Patten/Dir., Carl J. Rickertsen/Dir., Thomas P. Spahr/Dir.

Owners: Jonathan F. Klein/1.00%, Insiders/26.20%, Robert H. Epstein, Goldman Sachs Group Inc./18.70%, Putnam, LLC and affiliates/5.40%, Paul N. Zolfaghari, Carl J. Rickertsen, Sanju K. Bansal/3.80%, Arthur S. Locke, Michael J. Saylor/22.20%, Barclays Global Investors, NA and affiliates/8.00%, Thomas P. Spahr, Renaissance Technologies Corp./6.00%

Financial Data: *Fiscal Year End:*12/31 *Latest Annual Data:* 12/31/2006

Year	Sales	Net Income
2006	$313,823,000	$70,876,000
2005	$268,662,000	$64,743,000
2004	$231,208,000	$168,313,000

Curr. Assets:	$175,406,000	**Curr. Liab.:**	$112,828,000	**P/E Ratio:**	20.63
Plant, Equip.:	$11,102,000	**Total Liab.:**	$115,665,000	**Indic. Yr. Divd.:**	NA
Total Assets:	$248,816,000	**Net Worth:**	$133,151,000	**Debt/ Equity:**	NA

Microtek Medical Holdings Inc

13000 Deerfield Pkwy., Ste. 300, Alpharetta, GA, 30004; *PH:* 1-678-896-4400; *http://* www.microtekmed.com; *Email:* mtinfo@microtekmed.com

General - Incorporation .... GA
Employees 1,829
Auditor .... KPMG LLP
Stk Agt .... Computershare Investor Services
Counsel .... NA
DUNS No. 18-857-7050

Stock - Price on:12/24/2007 .... $4.52
Stock Exchange .... NDQ
Ticker Symbol .... MTOX
Outstanding Shares 43,450,000
E.P.S. $0.18
Shareholders .... NA

Business: The group's principle activities of the group are to develop, manufacture and market proprietary and other products and services for patient care, occupational safety and management of potentially infectious and hazardous waste primarily for the domestic healthcare market. The group markets its products to hospitals and other end users through a broad distribution system consisting of multiple channels including distributors, directly through its own sales force, original equipment manufacturers and private label customers. The group also markets certain of its products through customer procedure tray companies. The group has two operating units, microtek medical inc and orex technologies international.

Primary SIC and add'l.: 3842 2389

CIK No: 0000929299

Subsidiaries: Microtek Medical, Inc, OREX Technologies International

Officers: Dan R. Lee/Chmn., CEO, Pres./$609,384.00, Roger G. Wilson/CFO/$300,529.00, Mark J. Alvarez/COO/$327,372.00

Directors: Dan R. Lee/Chmn., CEO, Pres., Kenneth F. Davis/Dir., Michael E. Glasscock/Dir., Rosdon Hendrix/Dir., Gene R. McGrevin/Dir., Marc R. Sarni/Dir., Ronald L. Smorada/Dir.

Owners: Kenneth F. Davis, Insiders/5.04%, Rosdon Hendrix, Marc R. Sarni, Roger G. Wilson/1.28%, Mark Alvarez, Ronald L. Smorada, Dan R. Lee/2.24%, Michael E. Glasscock, Gene R. McGrevin, Rutabaga Capital Management/8.32%, Dimensional Fund Advisors Inc./8.42%

Financial Data: *Fiscal Year End:*12/31 *Latest Annual Data:* 12/31/2006

Year	Sales	Net Income
2006	NA	NA
2005	NA	NA
2004	NA	NA

Curr. Assets:	$2,294,000	**Curr. Liab.:**	NA	**P/E Ratio:**	25.11
Plant, Equip.:	NA	**Total Liab.:**	NA	**Indic. Yr. Divd.:**	NA
Total Assets:	$2,294,000	**Net Worth:**	NA	**Debt/ Equity:**	0.0141

Microtune Inc

2201 10th St., Plano, TX, 75074; *PH:* 1-972-673-1600; *Fax:* 1-972-673-1602; *http://* www.microtune.com; *Email:* info@microtune.com

General - Incorporation .... DE
Employees 204
Auditor .... Ernst & Young LLP
Stk Agt .... Computershare Investor Services LLC
Counsel .... Baker & Botts LLP
DUNS No. .... NA

Stock - Price on:12/24/2007 .... $5.13
Stock Exchange .... NDQ
Ticker Symbol .... TUNE
Outstanding Shares 53,590,000
E.P.S. .... -$0.03
Shareholders .... NA

Business: The group's principal activities are to design, manufacture and market high performance radio frequency based solutions for the global broadband communications, automotive electronics and wireless connectivity markets. The products provide digital communications at a high data transfer rate. The group's highly integrated broadband gateway radio frequency integrated circuits and modules are used in cable modems, PC/tvs, set-top boxes, cable telephony, digital TV and other consumer electronic devices. The customers of the group are daimler chrysler, ati technologies, motorola, Texas instruments and others. The group discontinued the development of wireless products in Dec 2003.

Primary SIC and add'l.: 3674 3679

CIK No: 0001108058

Subsidiaries: HMTF Acquisition (Bermuda) Ltd., HMTF Erste Beteilingungs GmbH, Microtune (Japan), Inc., Microtune (Korea), Ltd., Microtune (San Diego), Inc., Microtune (Taiwan), Ltd., Microtune (Texas), L.P., Microtune GmbH& Co. KG, Microtune RF-Technologies (Phils.), Inc., Microtune Verwaltungs GmbH, Microtune, (GP) LLC, Microtune, (LP) LLC, NSF-Technologies (Phils.), Inc., Transilica Singapore Pte Ltd

Officers: James A. Fontaine/Dir., CEO, Pres./$963,788.00, Jeffrey A. Kupp/CFO/$484,019.00, Albert H. Taddiken/COO/$574,729.00, Michael T. Schueppert/Dir. - Industry Expert, Phillip D. Peterson/General Counsel, Walter S. Ciciora/Dir., Independent Consultant, Robert S. Kirk/VP - Worldwide Sales/$532,800.00, Travis White/Dir., Independent Consultant

Directors: James A. Fontaine/Dir., CEO, Pres., James H. Clardy/Dir., Michael T. Schueppert/Dir. - Industry Expert, Bernard T. Marren/Dir., Steven Craddock/Dir., William P. Tai/Dir., Walter S. Ciciora/Dir., Independent Consultant, Travis White/Dir., Independent Consultant, Anthony J. Levecchio/Dir.

Owners: Walter S. Ciciora, Barry F. Koch, Robert S. Kirk, James H. Clardy, Institutional Venture Partners VII/5.20%, Steven Craddock, Travis A. White, Albert H. Taddiken/1.10%, William P. Tai/5.20%, Bernard T. Marren/1.00%, Simon J. Michael/7.30%, Jeffrey A. Kupp, James A. Fontaine/1.60%, Anthony J. LeVecchio, Insiders/11.00%

Financial Data: *Fiscal Year End:*12/31 *Latest Annual Data:* 12/31/2006

Year	Sales	Net Income
2006	$69,232,000	-$5,152,000
2005	$56,991,000	-$2,438,000
2004	$56,162,000	$5,529,000

Curr. Assets:	$100,484,000	**Curr. Liab.:**	$9,247,000		
Plant, Equip.:	$4,275,000	**Total Liab.:**	$9,334,000	**Indic. Yr. Divd.:**	NA
Total Assets:	$105,602,000	**Net Worth:**	$96,268,000	**Debt/ Equity:**	NA

Microvision Inc WA

6222 185th Ave. NE, Redmond, WA, 98052; **PH:** 1-425-936-6847; **Fax:** 1-425-882-6600; **http://** www.microvision.com; **Email:** ir@microvision.com

General - Incorporation	DE	**Stock** - Price on:12/24/2007	$5.45
Employees	127	Stock Exchange	NYSE
Auditor	PricewaterhouseCoopers LLP	Ticker Symbol	MVL
Stk Agt	American Stock Transfer & Trust Co.	Outstanding Shares	43,390,000
Counsel	NA	E.P.S	-$0.91
DUNS No.	83-870-7941	Shareholders	NA

Business: The group's principal activity is to design and market information display and image capture products and products utilizing its optical and related materials technology. The group operates through two segments: microvision and lumera. Microvision segment develops and commercializes scanned beam technology for information displays and image capture products. Lumera segment develops and commercialises organic non-linear optical materials that can be used to change the properties of light waves used to transmit information. The group markets the nomad(tm) augmented vision system, a see-through monochrome head-worn display product and flic(tm) laser bar code scanner, a hand-held scanner that uses proprietary scanning technology. Customers of the group include the United States government and commercial enterprises.

Primary SIC and add'l.: 3679 3827 8731 7375 7372

CIK No: 0000065770

Subsidiaries: Ethicon Endo-Surgery, Inc., Lumera Corporation

Officers: Alexander Tokman/Dir., CEO, Pres./$1,080,490.00, Todd R. McIntyre/Sr. VP - Global Strategic Marketing, Business Development/$259,936.00, Thomas M. Walker/VP, General Counsel, Sec./$295,424.00, Jeff T. Wilson/CFO/$262,607.00, Stephen R. Willey/Pres. - Sales, Marketing, Asia/$393,507.00, Ian D. Brown/VP - Sales, Marketing/$265,091.00, Sid Madhavan/VP - Research, Product Development, Julie Marshall/Contact - Investor Relations, Cale Smith/Contact - Investor Relations, Matt Nichols/Contact - Media

Directors: Alexander Tokman/Dir., CEO, Pres., Slade Gorton/Chmn., Richard A. Cowell/Dir., Marc Onetto/Dir., Brian Turner/Dir., Jeanette Horan/Dir.

Owners: Insiders/3.20%, Todd R. McIntyre, Alexander Tokman, Marc Onetto, Slade Gorton, Richard Cowell, Brian Turner, Jeanette Horan, Richard F. Rutkowski, Dorset Management Corporation/9.00%, Jeff T. Wilson, Thomas M. Walker, Stephen R. Willey/1.00%, Richard A. Raisig, Ian D. Brown

Financial Data: *Fiscal Year End:*12/31 *Latest Annual Data:* 12/31/2006

Year	Sales	Net Income
2006	$7,043,000	-$23,984,000
2005	$14,746,000	-$28,183,000
2004	$11,418,000	-$33,197,000

Curr. Assets:	$30,005,000	**Curr. Liab.:**	$10,845,000		
Plant, Equip.:	$4,011,000	**Total Liab.:**	$13,461,000	**Indic. Yr. Divd.:**	NA
Total Assets:	$35,325,000	**Net Worth:**	$21,864,000	**Debt/ Equity:**	NA

Microwave Filter Co Inc NY

6743 Kinne St., East Syracuse, NY, 13057; **PH:** 1-315-438-4700; **Fax:** 1-315-463-1467; **http://** www.microwavefilter.com; **Email:** mfcsales@microwavefilter.com

General - Incorporation	NY	**Stock** - Price on:12/24/2007	NA
Employees	56	Stock Exchange	OTC
Auditor	Rotenberg & Co. LLP	Ticker Symbol	MFCO
Stk Agt	NA	Outstanding Shares	NA
Counsel	Wiles & Wiles	E.P.S	NA
DUNS No.	04-158-9433	Shareholders	NA

Business: The group's principal activities are to design, develop, manufacture and sell electronic filters for radio and microwave frequencies. These products are used in the process of signal distribution and to prevent unwanted signals from disrupting transmit or receive operations. Niagara scientific, inc., the group's subsidiary, designs case packing machines to automatically pack products into shipping cases. The group's filter business serves cable television, television and radio broadcast, satellite broadcast, mobile radio, commercial and defense electronics and shipping cases. Other custom equipment's designed by the group are used for inspection-rejection, counting, analyzing or monitoring, reporting or controlling a continuous manufacturing or industrial process.

Primary SIC and add'l.: 3823 3565

CIK No: 0000716688

Subsidiaries: East Syracuse, Microwave Filter International, LTD., Niagara Scientific, Inc

Officers: Carl F. Fahrenkrug/Dir., CEO, Pres., Phil B. /Technical Sales Specialist, Nancy Y. /Assoc. - Sales, Joel F. /Technical Sales Specialist, Richard L. Jones/59/Dir., CFO, P. Scott/Dir. - Sales, Sherry B. /Sales Specialist, Sandy N. /Sr. Marketing, Sales Assoc

Directors: Carl F. Fahrenkrug/Dir., CEO, Pres., Robert R. Andrews/66/Chmn., Sidney K. Chong/66/Dir., Frank S. Markovich/Dir., Daniel Galbally/Dir., Richard L. Jones/59/Dir., CFO, Trudi B. Artini/Dir., Milo Peterson/Dir., Arnold Poltenson/71/Dir.

Owners: Frederick A. Dix/8.40%

Curr. Assets:	$2,572,000	**Curr. Liab.:**	$509,000		
Plant, Equip.:	$554,000	**Total Liab.:**	$509,000	**Indic. Yr. Divd.:**	NA
Total Assets:	$3,126,000	**Net Worth:**	$2,617,000	**Debt/ Equity:**	NA

Micrus Endovascular Corp

821 Fox Ln., San Jose, CA, 95131; **PH:** 1-408-433-1400; **Fax:** 1-408-433-1401; **http://** www.micruscorp.com

General - Incorporation	DE	**Stock** - Price on:12/24/2007	$25.02
Employees	287	Stock Exchange	NDQ
Auditor	PricewaterhouseCoopers LLP	Ticker Symbol	MEND
Stk Agt	American Stock Transfer & Trust Co.	Outstanding Shares	15,340,000
Counsel	Herrington & Sutcliffe LLP	E.P.S	-$0.45
DUNS No.	NA	Shareholders	NA

Business: The groups principle activities include developing, manufacturing and marketing implantable and disposable medical devices. The groups product is microcoil. The group products sold under the trade names HeliPaq(R), HeliPaq SR(R), InterPaq(R), Cerecyte(R), Pharos(TM), MicruSphere(R) and Presidio(TM). The group operates from the United States, Europe, Asia Pacific and other. The group's quarterly revenue for September 2007 was 14.36 millions of USD.

Primary SIC and add'l.: 3841

CIK No: 0001028318

Subsidiaries: Micrus Endovascular SA, Micrus Endovascular UK Ltd.

Officers: John T. Kilcoyne/49/Chmn., CEO/$482,665.00, Robert A. Stern/51/COO, Pres./$607,757.00, Robert C. Colloton/VP - US Sales, Global Marketing/$479,932.00, Edward F. Ruppel/VP - Technical Operations, William G. Rigas/VP - Sales, Asia, Latin America, David A. Watson/VP - Research, Development, Carolyn M. Bruguera/VP, General Counsel/$343,845.00, Mitchell D. Auran/VP - Micrus Design Technology/$348,617.00, Mike Crompton/VP - Regulatory, Clinical Affairs, Quality, Jim B. Robbins/VP - Finance, Richard J. Snyder/VP - Human Resources

Directors: John T. Kilcoyne/49/Chmn., CEO, Michael R. Henson/Dir., Jeff Thiel/Dir., Gregory H. Wolf/Dir., Nelson L. Hopkins/Dir., Francis Shammo/Dir., Michael L. Eagle/Dir., Fred Holubow/Dir.

Owners: HBM Bioventures (Cayman) Ltd/12.00%, Michael L. Eagle, Robert C. Colloton/1.00%, Francis J. Shanmo, Gregory H. Wolf, Jeffrey H. Thiel, Carolyn M. Bruguera, John T. Kilcoyne/2.00%, Wellington Management Group/6.00%, Nelson L. Hopkins, Fred Holubow, Jim B. Robbins, Michael R. Henson, Insiders/5.00%, Delaware Management Holdings/6.00% *(16 Owners included in Index)*

Financial Data: *Fiscal Year End:*03/31 *Latest Annual Data:* 3/31/2007

Year	Sales	Net Income
2007	$58,795,000	-$5,483,000
2006	$32,781,000	-$8,261,000
2005	$24,012,000	-$6,704,000

Curr. Assets:	$53,195,000	**Curr. Liab.:**	$14,093,000		
Plant, Equip.:	$4,648,000	**Total Liab.:**	$16,803,000	**Indic. Yr. Divd.:**	NA
Total Assets:	$73,097,000	**Net Worth:**	$56,294,000	**Debt/ Equity:**	NA

Mid Penn Bancorp Inc

349 Union St., Millersburg, PA, 17061; **PH:** 1-717-692-2133; **Fax:** 1-717-692-4861; **http://** www.midpennbank.com

General - Incorporation	PA	**Stock** - Price on:12/24/2007	$24.75
Employees	125	Stock Exchange	AMEX
Auditor	Parente Randolph LLC	Ticker Symbol	MBP
Stk Agt	Registrar & Transfer Co	Outstanding Shares	3,500,000
Counsel	NA	E.P.S	$1.38
DUNS No.	09-422-8590	Shareholders	NA

Business: The group's principal activities are to provide commercial banking, trust business and financial services through wholly owned subsidiary, mid penn bank. The services provided include personal loans, mortgage, home equity loans, secured and unsecured commercial loans and farm loans. The group also offers cash management, mobile and telephone banking, check card and ATM services. Other services include trust services, real estate planning, retirement planning and investment services. The operations are conducted through twelve offices located in dauphin, northumberland, schuylkill and cumberland counties of Pennsylvania.

Primary SIC and add'l.: 6712 6022

CIK No: 0000879635

Subsidiaries: Mid Penn Bank, Mid Penn Insurance Services, LLC, Mid Penn Investment Corp.

Officers: Alan W. Dakey/Chmn., CEO, Pres./$262,523.00, Kevin W. Laudenslager/CFO, Exec. VP/$111,055.00, Cindy L. Wetzel/VP, Corp. Sec., Michael Lehmer/VP, Sr. Trust Officer, Jean Lauver/Assist., Trust Officer, Alice Camerini/Trust Administrative Officer, Denise Lepley/Retirement Savings Specialist, Eric S. Williams/46/Exec. VP, Chief Lending Officer/$128,379.00

Directors: Alan W. Dakey/Chmn., CEO, Pres., Edwin D. Schlegel/69/Vice Chmn., Robert C. Grubic/56/Dir., Jere M. Coxon/65/Dir., Theodore W. Mowery/49/Dir., Guy J. Snyder/70/Dir., Gregory M. Kerwin/57/Dir., Donald E. Sauve/66/Dir., James A. Durica/60/Dir., William A. Specht/46/Dir.

Owners: Insiders/8.84%, James A. Durica, Cindy L. Wetzel/0.07%, Gregory M. Kerwin/0.63%, William A. Specht, Donald E. Sauve/0.07%, Robert C. Grubic/0.22%, Kevin W. Laudenslager/0.05%, Theodore W. Mowery/0.04%, Edwin D. Schlegel/2.29%, Guy J. Snyder/3.42%, Jere M. Coxon/1.56%, Alan W. Dakey/0.37%, CEDE & Co./32.93%

Financial Data: *Fiscal Year End:*12/31 *Latest Annual Data:* 12/31/2006

Year	Sales	Net Income
2006	$31,242,000	$4,888,000
2005	$26,247,000	$4,603,000
2004	$23,534,000	$4,369,000

Curr. Assets:	$59,241,000	**Curr. Liab.:**	$390,413,000	**P/E Ratio:**	18.07
Plant, Equip.:	$9,708,000	**Total Liab.:**	$452,609,000	**Indic. Yr. Divd.:**	$0.800
Total Assets:	$491,694,000	**Net Worth:**	$39,085,000	**Debt/ Equity:**	1.5309

Mid Wisconsin Financial Services Inc

132 W State St., Medford, WI, 54451; **PH:** 1-715-748-8300; **Fax:** 1-715-748-6553; **http://** www.midwisc.com; **Email:** netconnection@midwisc.com

General - Incorporation	WI	**Stock** - Price on:12/24/2007	$33
Employees	145	Stock Exchange	OTC
Auditor	Wipfli LLP	Ticker Symbol	MWFS
Stk Agt	Registrar & Transfer Co	Outstanding Shares	1,640,000
Counsel	NA	E.P.S	-$0.71
DUNS No.	78-239-3490	Shareholders	NA

Business: The group's principle activities are to provide a full range of personal banking services which includes checking, saving and time accounts, installment and other personal loans as well as mortgage loans. The group is a holding company operating through subsidiary mid-Wisconsin bank. It offers investment and brokerage services through its investment sales centers. The group serves individuals, businesses and governmental units and offers all forms of commercial and consumer lending, including line of credit, term loans, real estate financing and mortgage lending.

Primary SIC and add'l.: 6712 6022

CIK No: 0000785024

Subsidiaries: Excel Real Estate Services, Inc., Mid-Wisconsin Bank, Mid-Wisconsin Investment Corporation, Mid-Wisconsin Statutory Trust I

Officers: James F. Warsaw/Dir., CEO, Pres./$267,209.00, Laurie Peterso/Insurance Specialist, Paul H. Ewig/CFO, VP, Michelle Teeters/Investment Representative, John W. Lohre/60/VP, Scot G. Thompson/45/VP, Pierce Dopp/Investment Representative, William A. Weiland/53/Sec., Treasurer/$147,322.00, Sharon Wilsmann/Investment Representative, Laura Kuhnert/Investment Representative, Amy Schuh/Investment Representative, Marilee Kelley/Trust Experts, Joan Steliga/Trust Experts

Directors: James F. Warsaw/Dir., CEO, Pres., Kim Gowey/Chmn., Kurt Mertens/Dir., Donald Schimdt/Dir., Gene C. Knoll/Dir., Robert Schoofs/Dir., Brian Hallgren/Dir., James P. Hager/Dir., Darlene York/Dir., Frederick T. Lundin/Dir., James Melvin/Dir., Kathryn Hemer/Dir., William Ball/Dir., Craig Sigurdson/Dir., Joanne Frasier/Dir. *(16 Directors included in Index)*

Owners: Insiders/9.38%, James F. Melvin/2.64%, Brian B. Hallgren, James F. Warsaw/1.48%, Kim A. Gowey/3.31%, William A. Weiland, James P. Hager, Robert J. Schoofs, Kurt D. Mertens, Kathryn M. Hemer

Financial Data: **Fiscal Year End:**12/31 **Latest Annual Data:** 12/31/2006

Year	Sales	Net Income
2006	$33,067,000	$1,095,000
2005	$27,262,000	$4,388,000
2004	$23,259,000	$4,476,000

Curr. Assets:	$14,976,000	**Curr. Liab.:**	$416,208,000	**P/E Ratio:**	66.00
Plant, Equip.:	$9,332,000	**Total Liab.:**	$426,518,000	**Indic. Yr. Divd.:**	$0.880
Total Assets:	$460,651,000	**Net Worth:**	$34,133,000	**Debt/ Equity:**	NA

Mid-America Apartment Communities Inc

6584 Poplar Ave., Ste. 300, Memphis, TN, 38138; ***PH:*** 1-901-682-6600; ***Fax:*** 1-901-682-6667; ***http://*** www.maac.net; ***Email:*** customersvc@maac.net

General - Incorporation	TN	**Stock**- Price on:12/24/2007	$55.9
Employees	1,164	Stock Exchange	NYSE
Auditor	Ernst& Young LLP	Ticker Symbol	MAA
Stk Agt	American Stock Transfer & Trust CO.	Outstanding Shares	25,450,000
Counsel	NA	E.P.S.	$0.90
DUNS No.	NA	Shareholders	NA

Business: The groups principle activity is to invest real estate properties. The group operates from the United States.

Primary SIC and add'l.: 6798

CIK No: 0000912595

Subsidiaries: Jefferson at Sunset Valley, LP, Jefferson Village LP, JPI Coral Springs LP, MAAC of Duval LP, MAACOD, MAC II of Delaware, Inc, MAC III of Delaware, Inc, MAC of Delaware Inc, MAC of Huntington Chase LLC, Mid America Apartments LP, Mid America Apartments of Duval LP, Mid America Apartments of Savannah, Monthaven Management, Inc., Monthaven Park, LLC, Paddock Club Florence LP 16 Subsidiaries included in the Index

Officers: Eric H. Bolton/Chmn., CEO/$1,196,537.00, David Nischwitz/Sr. VP, Dir. - Property Redevelopment, Kathy Allen/VP - Coastal Region Operations, Kim Banks/VP - North Region Operations, Diane Chastain/Sr. VP - South Regions Operations, Cynthia Cloud/Sr. VP - West Regions Operations, Jackie Melnick/VP - East Region Operations, Beth Brock/Assist. VP - Central Region Operations, Leslie Wolfgang/VP, Dir. - External Reporting, Corp. Sec., Shelton Barron/VP - Management Information Systems, Melintha Ogle/VP - Marketing, Doug Clark/VP, Dir. - Risk Management, Larry Davis/Dir. - Internal Audit, Melanie Carter/VP - Human Resources, Sandy Brown/Community Outreach Dir. *(24 Officers included in Index)*

Directors: Eric H. Bolton/Chmn., CEO, George E. Cates/Dir., Philip W. Norwood/Dir., Alan B. Graf/Dir., John S. Grinalds/Dir., Ralph Horn/Dir., Mary Elizabeth McCormick/Dir., William B. Sansom/Dir., Simon R. C. Wadsworth/Dir., Exec. VP, CFO

Owners: Insiders/6.92%, George E. Cates/2.52%, Barclays/5.80%, The Vanguard Group, Inc/5.40%, Alan B. Graf, Cohen & Steers, Inc./6.33%, AMVESCAP PLC/5.64%, Eric H. Bolton, William B. Sansom, Ralph Horn, Mary Beth McCormick, AXA Financial, Inc./5.65%, John S. Grinalds, Michael S. Starnes, Simon R. C. Wadsworth *(16 Owners included in Index)*

Financial Data: **Fiscal Year End:**12/31 **Latest Annual Data:** 12/31/2006

Year	Sales	Net Income
2006	$325,999,000	$20,945,000
2005	$297,455,000	$19,744,000
2004	$267,784,000	$25,198,000

Curr. Assets:	$9,690,000	**Curr. Liab.:**	$68,362,000		
Plant, Equip.:	$1,673,289,000	**Total Liab.:**	$1,297,580,000	**Indic. Yr. Divd.:**	$2.420
Total Assets:	$1,746,646,000	**Net Worth:**	$449,066,000	**Debt/ Equity:**	NA

Mid-Southern Savings Bank IN

300 N Water St., Salem, IN, 47167; ***PH:*** 1-812-883-2639; ***http://*** www.mid-southern.com; ***Email:*** mssb@mid-southern.com

General - Incorporation		**Stock**- Price on:12/24/2007	$19.48
Employees	NA	Stock Exchange	OTC
Auditor	NA	Ticker Symbol	MSVB
Stk Agt	Registrar & Transfer Co	Outstanding Shares	1,470,000
Counsel	NA	E.P.S.	NA
DUNS No.	NA	Shareholders	NA

Business: The groups principal activity is to provide banking services. The services of the group include personal banking, business banking, loans, mortgage, safe deposit boxes, wire transfer, and fax boxes, ATM and debit card, and ACH direct deposit. The group operates from the United States.

Primary SIC and add'l.: 6035

CIK No:

Officers: Michael W. Smith/CEO, Pres., Kermit A. Lamb/Sr. VP, Orleans Mgr., Dixie Soliday/Treasurer, Controller

Directors: Paul G. Allemeier/Chmn., Joseph C. Etzler/Dir., Trent L. Fisher/Dir., Charles Lamb/Dir., Dana J. Dunbar/Dir., Benjamin F. Weathers/Dir., David E. Branaman/Dir. Emeritus

Midamerican Energy Co

PO Box 657, Des Moines, IA, 50303; ***PH:*** 1-515-242-4300; ***http://*** www.midamericanenergy.com; ***Email:*** info@midamerican.com

General - Incorporation	IA	**Stock**- Price on:12/24/2007	$86
Employees	NA	Stock Exchange	OTC
Auditor	Deloitte & Touche LLP	Ticker Symbol	MDPWK
Stk Agt	NA	Outstanding Shares	NA
Counsel	NA	E.P.S.	$1.32
DUNS No.	88-471-8768	Shareholders	NA

Business: The group's principle activities include generating, transmiting, distributing and selling electric energy; and transmits and sells natural gas. The group operates from United States.

Primary SIC and add'l.: 4931 4923

CIK No: 0000928576

Subsidiaries: CBEC Railway Inc, Cordova Energy Company, LLC, Exelon Generation Company, LLC, InterCoast Capital Company, MEC Construction Services Co, MHC Inc., MidAmerican Energy Holdings, MidAmerican Funding, MidAmerican Funding, LLC, MidAmerican Services Company, Midwest Capital Group, Inc, Northern Natural Gas Company

Officers: William J. Fehrman/CEO, Pres., Joellen Petrik/Administrative Specialist, Brian K. Hankel/45/Dir., VP, Todd M. Raba/51/Dir., Pres., Thomas B. Specketer/51/CFO, VP, Controller, Steven R. Weiss/53/Dir., VP, Keith D. Hartje/58/Sr. VP, Kathryn Kunert/VP - Community Relations, Economic Development, Marion Burns/Economic Development Consultant, Debra L. Calvert/Economic Development Consultant, Plastics, Mark Rodvold/Economic Development Consultant, Greg Theis/Economic Development Consultant, Logistics, Pharmaceuticals, Jamie Van Fossen/Economic Development Analyst, Donna Higgins/Administrative Assist., Gail Stender/Administrative Assist. *(19 Officers included in Index)*

Directors: Todd M. Raba/51/Dir., Pres., Steven R. Weiss/53/Dir., VP, Brian K. Hankel/45/Dir., VP

Financial Data: **Fiscal Year End:**12/31 **Latest Annual Data:** 12/31/2006

Year	Sales	Net Income
2006	$3,447,931,000	$266,676,000
2005	$3,160,337,000	$221,297,000
2004	$2,696,353,000	$210,455,000

Curr. Assets:	$693,804,000	**Curr. Liab.:**	$802,240,000	**P/E Ratio:**	65.15
Plant, Equip.:	$5,003,071,000	**Total Liab.:**	$4,528,485,000	**Indic. Yr. Divd.:**	NA
Total Assets:	$6,509,593,000	**Net Worth:**	$1,981,108,000	**Debt/ Equity:**	0.8895

Midamerican Energy Holdings Co

666 Grand Ave., Des Moines, IA, 50309; ***PH:*** 1-515-242-4300; ***http://*** www.midamerican.com

General - Incorporation	IA	**Stock**- Price on:12/24/2007	NA
Employees	NA	Stock Exchange	NA
Auditor	Deloitte & Touche LLP	Ticker Symbol	NA
Stk Agt	Chase Mellon Shareholder Services LLC	Outstanding Shares	NA
Counsel	NA	E.P.S.	NA
DUNS No.	07-465-5770	Shareholders	NA

Business: The group's principal activities are generating, distributing and supplying electricity to utilities, government entities, retail customers and other customers through out the world. The group is organized and managed on four separate platforms namely midamerican, northern electric, calenergy and homeservices. Midamerican energy generates, transmits, distributes and sells electric energy and distributes, sells and transports natural gas. Northern electric receives electricity from the national grid transmission system and distributes it to customers. Calenergy develops, owns and operates environmentally responsible independent power production facilities worldwide. Homeservices operates in residential real estate brokerage.

Primary SIC and add'l.: 4923 4924 6531 4911

CIK No: 0001081316

Subsidiaries: Academy of Real Estate, Inc., Allerton Capital, LTD., Allied Title Services, LLC, American Pacific Finance Company, Arizona Home Services, LLC, BE Energy Holding LLC, BE Energy LLC, Big Spring Pipeline Company, Caldwell Mill, LLP, CalEnergy Capital Trust II, CalEnergy Capital Trust III, CalEnergy Company Inc., CalEnergy Gas (Australia) Limited, CalEnergy Gas (Holdings) Limited, CalEnergy Gas (Polska) sp. z.o.o. 260 Subsidiaries included in the Index

Officers: David L. Sokol/52/Chmn., CEO, Gregory E. Abel/46/COO, Pres., Maureen E. Sammon/45/Sr. VP, Chief Administrative Officer, Patrick J. Goodman/41/Sr. VP, CFO, Jo M. Williams/VP - Business Development, Royce Ramsay/VP - Operations, Cathy S. Woollums/Sr. VP - Environmental Services, Allan Urlis/Dir. - Midamerican Energy, Des Moines/Contact - Media Relations, Midamerican Energy, Mark Reinders/Mgr. - Communications, Midamerican, Chuck Wilkinson/Project Sponsor, Douglas L. Anderson/50/Sr. VP, General Counsel, Paul Maakestad/VP - Information Technology, Thomas A. Mertz/VP - Field Operations, Kent E. Miller/VP - Pricing, Storage *(17 Officers included in Index)*

Directors: David L. Sokol/52/Chmn., CEO

Owners: Insiders, Maureen E. Sammon, Patrick J. Goodman, David L. Sokol, Insiders, Walter Scott, Insiders, Warren E. Buffett, Gregory E. Abel, Walter Scott, Douglas L. Anderson, David L. Sokol, Warren E. Buffett, Patrick J. Goodman, Berkshire Hathaway *(16 Owners included in Index)*

Midas Inc

1300 Arlington Hts. Rd., Itasca, IL, 60143; ***PH:*** 1-630-438-3000; ***Fax:*** 1-630-438-3880; ***http://*** www.midas.com

General - Incorporation	DE	**Stock**- Price on:12/24/2007	$23.3
Employees	550	Stock Exchange	NYSE
Auditor	KPMG LLP	Ticker Symbol	MDS
Stk Agt	EquiServe Trust Co N.A	Outstanding Shares	14,780,000
Counsel	NA	E.P.S.	$0.66
DUNS No.	00-812-8394	Shareholders	NA

Business: The group's principal activity is to provide retail automotive services. The group operates 2,700 auto service shops worldwide that provide auto repair and maintenance services including exhaust, brake, suspension and air conditioning. The group's retail shops, which are operated by the company, its franchisees and licensees, provide repair and maintenance services through 1,884 north American shops located in United States and Canada. The group also manufactures and distributes exhaust products under the ipc brand name and shop equipment under the huth trademark. In addition, through a subsidiary, it selects, leases, acquires and constructs sites for its shops in North America.

Primary SIC and add'l.: 7533 6531 3714 7539 6794

CIK No: 0001046131

Subsidiaries: Cosmic Holdings LLC, Dealers Wholesale, Inc., Huth, Inc., International Parts Corporation, MDS Automotive Holdings, B.V., Midas Automotive International, B.V., Midas Canada Holdings Ltd, Midas Canada Inc., Midas Illinois, Inc., Midas International Corporation, Midas Properties, Inc., Midas Realty Corporation, Midas Realty Corporation of Canada, Inc., Midas, Inc. (Registrant), Muffler Corporation of America 16 Subsidiaries included in the Index

Officers: Alan D. Feldman/55/Chmn., CEO, Pres./$2,831,961.00, William M. Guzik/48/CFO, Exec. VP/$939,109.00, James M. Haeger/42/VP, Controller, Alvin K. Marr/42/Sr. VP, Sec., General Counsel/$568,927.00, Ben Parma/43/VP - Human Resources, John A. Warzecha/59/Sr. VP - Franchise Operations/$727,396.00, Rick Dow/56/Sr. VP, Chief Marketing Officer/$710,832.00, Frederick W. Dow/57/Sr. VP, Chief Marketing Officer, John E. Brisson/VP - Finance, Planning

Directors: Alan D. Feldman/55/Chmn., CEO, Pres., Robert R. Schoeberl/71/Dir., Thomas L. Bindley/63/Dir., Archie R. Dykes/76/Dir., Jarobin Gilbert/61/Dir., Diane L. Routsen/51/Dir.

Owners: Archie R. Dykes, Frederick W. Dow, Diane L. Routson, Insiders/8.22%, Jarobin Gilbert, RGM Capital, LLC/5.34%, Keeley Asset Management Corp./5.89%, Alan D. Feldman/4.92%, Thomas L. Bindley, Alvin K. Marr, Barclays Global Investors, NA/5.48%, William M. Guzik/1.02%, Mario J. Gabelli/12.63%, Robert R. Schoeberl, Farallon Capital Management, L.L.C./5.23% *(16 Owners included in Index)*

Financial Data: **Fiscal Year End:**12/31 **Latest Annual Data:** 12/30/2006

Year	Sales	Net Income
2006	$176,700,000	$10,500,000
2005	$192,500,000	$2,200,000

Curr. Assets:	$57,300,000	**Curr. Liab.:**	$47,200,000	**P/E Ratio:**	38.20
Plant, Equip.:	$104,600,000	**Total Liab.:**	$189,700,000	**Indic. Yr. Divd.:**	NA
Total Assets:	$239,200,000	**Net Worth:**	$49,500,000	**Debt/ Equity:**	3.2825

MidCarolina Financial Corp

3101 S Church St., Burlington, NC, 27215; ***PH:*** 1-336-538-1600; ***Fax:*** 1-336-538-1603; ***http://*** www.midcarolinabank.com

General - Incorporation	NC	**Stock**- Price on:12/24/2007	$14.95
Employees	71	Stock Exchange	OTC
Auditor	Dixon Hughes PLLC	Ticker Symbol	MCFI
Stk Agt	First Citizens Bank	Outstanding Shares	4,520,000
Counsel	NA	E.P.S	$0.76
DUNS No.	NA	Shareholders	NA

Business: The group operates through its subsidiaries whose principal activity is to provide banking services. The group operates from the United States. The total assets of the group in the year 2006, was $397,514 (thousands).

Primary SIC and add'l.: 6712 6022

CIK No: 0001174872

Subsidiaries: MidCarolina Bank, MidCarolina I, MidCarolina Investments, Inc., MidCarolina Trust II

Officers: Randy Cary/Pres., CEO - Midcarolina Bank, Craig R. Patterson/46/Sr. VP, Chief Credit Officer, Charles T. Canaday/46/COO, Exec. VP, Christopher B. Redcay/55/Sr. VP, CFO

Directors: James R. Copland/Chmn., Ralph M. Holt/Vice Chmn., John K. Roberts/Dir., Robert A. Ward/Dir., Thomas H. Bobo/Dir., F. D. Hornaday/Dir., Teena Marie Koury/Dir., John H. Love/Dir., James B. Powell/Dir., Dexter R. Barbee/Dir., Thomas E. Chandler/Dir., J. Anthony Holt/Dir., James H. Smith/Dir.

Owners: James H. Smith/1.10%, Teena Marie Koury, Christopher B. Redcay, James B. Powell/2.32%, Thomas E. Chandler/1.96%, John K. Roberts/1.52%, Robert A. Ward/1.34%, R.CraigPatterson/1.76%, John H. Love, Ralph M. Holt/2.89%, Anthony J. Holt, Randolph J. Cary/2.99%, F. D. Hornaday/1.07%, James R. Copland/2.72%, Thomas H. Bobo *(18 Owners included in Index)*

Financial Data: **Fiscal Year End:**12/31 **Latest Annual Data:** 12/31/2006

Year	Sales	Net Income
2006	$29,582,000	$3,896,000
2005	$21,965,000	$2,368,000
2004	$16,315,000	$1,942,000

Curr. Assets:	$12,438,000	**Curr. Liab.:**	$365,827,000	**P/E Ratio:**	19.67
Plant, Equip.:	$6,624,000	**Total Liab.:**	$392,591,000	**Indic. Yr. Divd.:**	NA
Total Assets:	$420,850,000	**Net Worth:**	$28,259,000	**Debt/ Equity:**	0.9096

MiddleBrook Pharmaceuticals Inc

Formerly: Advancis Pharmaceutical Corp

20425 Seneca Meadows Pk.way, Germantown, MD, 20878; ***PH:*** 1-301-944-6600; ***http://*** www.advancispharm.com

General - Incorporation	MD	**Stock**- Price on:12/24/2007	$2.56
Employees	76	Stock Exchange	NDQ
Auditor	PricewaterhouseCoopers LLP	Ticker Symbol	MBRK
Stk Agt	American Stock Transfer & Trust Co.	Outstanding Shares	46,560,000
Counsel	NA	E.P.S	-$1.5
DUNS No.	NA	Shareholders	NA

Business: The group's principle activities include developing and commercializing pulsatile drug products which is used in the treatment of infectious disease. It has developed a proprietary technology called pulsys based on the biological finding that bacteria exposed to antibiotics in front-loaded, sequential bursts, or pulses, are killed more efficiently and effectively than those exposed to standard antibiotic treatment regimens. The group operates from United States.

Primary SIC and add'l.: 2384 8731 5122

CIK No: 0001161924

Subsidiaries: STADA

Officers: Edward M. Rudnic/Dir., CEO, Pres./$1,345,340.00, Sandra E. Wassink/VP - Pharmaceutical Development, Technical Operations/$460,556.00, Susan P. Clausen/VP - Clinical Research, Robert C. Low/VP - Finance/$430,728.00, Donald C. Anderson/VP, Robert Guttendorf/VP - Preclinical Research, David J. Kudla/VP - Quality Assurance, Joseph J. Rogus/Sr. VP - Tech Operations, Colin E. Rowlings/Sr. VP - Pharm Research, Devel, Kevin S. Sly/Sr. VP - Bus Dev't, Strat Marketing, Juan N. Walterspiel/VP, Beth A. Burnside/VP - Pharmaceutical Research/$443,428.00, Donald J. Treacy/VP - Analytical Sciences/$420,130.00, James Bruno/VP, Darren W. Buchwald/VP - Commercial Development, Sales, Marketing *(16 Officers included in Index)*

Directors: Edward M. Rudnic/Dir., CEO, Pres., Gordon R. Douglas/Chmn., James H. Cavanaugh/Dir., Wayne T. Hockmeyer/Dir., Harold R. Werner/Dir., Richard W. Dugan/Dir., William A. Craig/Member - Scientific Advisory Board, Joseph T. Dipiro/Member - Scientific Advisory Board, George L. Drusano/Member - Scientific Advisory Board, Jenefir D. Isbister/Member - Scientific Advisory Board, James W. McGinity/Member - Scientific Advisory Board, Robert C. Moellering/Member - Scientific Advisory Board, Czerepak Elizabeth/Dir., Douglas R. Gordon/Dir., Martin A. Vogelbaum/44/Dir.

Owners: Sandra E. Wassink, Deerfield group, Edward M. Rudnic, Robert C. Low, Martin A. Vogelbaum, Donald J. Treacy, Harold R. Werner, Richard W. Dugan, Millennium group, Wayne T. Hockmeyer, HealthCare Ventures group, Rho Ventures group, Gordon R. Douglas, Beth A. Burnside, Federated Kaufmann Fund *(18 Owners included in Index)*

Financial Data: **Fiscal Year End:**12/31 **Latest Annual Data:** 12/31/2006

Year	Sales	Net Income
2006	$4,810,000	-$41,990,000
2005	$16,848,000	-$32,989,000
2004	$11,358,000	-$34,005,000

Curr. Assets:	$19,443,000	**Curr. Liab.:**	$17,256,000		
Plant, Equip.:	$11,765,000	**Total Liab.:**	$30,134,000	**Indic. Yr. Divd.:**	NA
Total Assets:	$42,006,000	**Net Worth:**	$11,872,000	**Debt/ Equity:**	NA

Middleburg Financial Corp

Middleburg Bank, Middleburg, VA, 20118; ***PH:*** 1-703-777-6327; ***Fax:*** 1-703-737-3426; ***http://*** www.middleburgbank.com

General - Incorporation	VA	**Stock**- Price on:12/24/2007	$32.8
Employees	168	Stock Exchange	NDQ
Auditor	Yount, Hyde & Barbour, P.C	Ticker Symbol	MBRG
Stk Agt	American Stock Transfer & Trust Co.	Outstanding Shares	4,510,000
Counsel	NA	E.P.S	$1.62
DUNS No.	NA	Shareholders	NA

Business: The group's principal activity is to provide banking services to individuals and small businesses. The group operates as a holding company to middleburg bank, the tredegar trust company and gilkison patterson investment advisors, inc. It provides checking and savings deposits accounts and commercial and consumer demand and term loans. The consumer services provided by the group include ATMs, Internet banking, travelers' checks, money orders and other traditional bank services. The group also provides investment management and fiduciary services including trust and estate settlements. These services are provided in the loudoun county of Virginia, an area included in the Washington-baltimore metropolitan statistical area. The group operates solely in the domestic market.

Primary SIC and add'l.: 6712 6022

CIK No: 0000914138

Subsidiaries: ICBI Capital Trust I, MFC Capital Trust II, Middleburg Bank, Middleburg Bank Service Corporation, Middleburg Investment Advisors, Inc., Middleburg Investment Group, Inc., Middleburg Trust Company

Officers: Joseph L. Boling/Chmn., CEO/$690,654.00, James H. Patterson/63/Pres., CEO - Middleburg Investment Advisors/$375,500.00, John Mason L. Antrim/55/Pres., CEO - Middleburg Trust Company, Kathleen J. Chappell/Sr. VP, CFO/$155,164.00, Gary R. Shook/Dir., Pres., Suzanne Withers/57/Sr. VP - Human Resources, Organizational Development, Arch A. Moore/Exec. VP, Sr. Loan Officer/$249,819.00, Alice P. Frazier/42/CFO, Exec. VP/$252,777.00

Directors: Joseph L. Boling/Chmn., CEO, Lynn J. Cornwell/Dir., John C. Lee/Dir., Janet A. Neuharth/Dir., James R. Treptow/Dir., John Sherman/Dir., Childs Frick Burden/Dir., Millicent W. West/Dir., Edward T. Wright/Dir., Howard M. Armfield/Dir., Henry F. Atherton/Dir., Keith Wood Meurlin/Dir., Gary R. Shook/Dir., Pres.

Owners: Alice P. Frazier/1.14%, Keith W. Meurlin, Childs F. Burden, Lynn J. Cornwell, James H. Patterson/1.36%, Arch A. Moore, Henry F. Atherton, Joseph L. Boling/2.49%, John Mason L. Antrim, Millicent W. West/10.15%, John Sherman, Howard M. Armfield, Edward T. Wright/1.83%, Kathleen J. Chappell, Gary R. Shook *(17 Owners included in Index)*

Financial Data: **Fiscal Year End:**12/31 **Latest Annual Data:** 12/31/2006

Year	Sales	Net Income
2006	$53,818,000	$8,018,000
2005	$45,233,000	$7,174,000
2004	$35,261,000	$7,092,000

Curr. Assets:	$48,091,000	**Curr. Liab.:**	$649,252,000		
Plant, Equip.:	$18,429,000	**Total Liab.:**	$694,407,000	**Indic. Yr. Divd.:**	$0.760
Total Assets:	$772,305,000	**Net Worth:**	$77,898,000	**Debt/ Equity:**	0.5061

Middleby Corp

1400 Toastmaster Dr., Elgin, IL, 60120; ***PH:*** 1-847-741-3300; ***Fax:*** 1-847-741-0015; ***http://*** www.middleby.com; ***Email:*** board@middleby.com

General - Incorporation	DE	**Stock**- Price on:12/24/2007	$61.2
Employees	1,282	Stock Exchange	NYSE
Auditor	Deloitte & Touche LLP	Ticker Symbol	MIG
Stk Agt	Corporation Trust Center	Outstanding Shares	7,980,000
Counsel	D'ancona & Pflaum	E.P.S	$2.79
DUNS No.	08-893-2108	Shareholders	NA

Business: The group's principal activities are to design, manufacture and market a broad line of cooking and warming equipment used in all types of food service operations. The group conducts its business through two principal business divisions: the cooking systems group and the international distribution division. The product line includes heavy-duty cooking equipment, steam cooking equipment, mixers, conveyor ovens, toasters, hot food servers, food-warmers, convection ovens, charbroilers and catering equipment. The group's end-user customers are fast food or quick service restaurants, full-service restaurants, retail outlets, public and private institutions, military facilities and government agencies. Trademarks include Blodgett (R), Blodgett Combi (R), CTX (R), Magikitch'n (R), Middleby Marshall (R), Pitco Frialator (R), Southebend (R), Steammaster(R) and Toastmaster (r).

Primary SIC and add'l.: 3556 3585

CIK No: 0000769520

Subsidiaries: Alkar Holdings, Inc., Alkar-RapidPak Brasil, LLC, Alkar-RapidPak, Inc., Blodgett Holdings, Inc., Cloverleaf Properties, Inc., Fab-Asia Inc., Frialator International Limited (UK), G.S. Blodgett Corporation, G.S. Blodgett International, LTD, MagiKitchn Inc., Middleby China Corporation, Middleby Espana SL, Middleby Marshall Holdings, LLC, Middleby Marshall, Inc., Middleby Mexico SA de CV 21 Subsidiaries included in the Index

Officers: Selim A. Bassoul/51/Chmn., CEO, Pres./$9,952,364.00, Mark A. Sieron/59/Division Pres./$598,586.00, Martin M. Lindsay/43/Corporate Treasurer, Nazih Ibrahim/54/Division Pres. - Southbend/$423,478.00, Phil D. Dolori/48/Group Pres./$1,024,715.00, Timothy J. Fitzgerald/38/CFO, VP/$1,631,196.00

Directors: Selim A. Bassoul/51/Chmn., CEO, Pres., Robert L. Yohe/71/Dir., John R. Miller/67/Dir., Sabin C. Streeter/66/Dir., Philip G. Putnam/67/Dir., Robert B. Lamb/66/Dir., Ryan Levenson/32/Dir., Gordon Obrien/42/Dir.

Owners: Nazih Ibrahim, Gordon OBrien, Selim A. Bassoul/10.60%, Robert L. Yohe, Sabin C. Streeter, John R. Miller, Philip G. Putnam, Ryan Levenson, Phil Dei Dolori, Timothy J. FitzGerald/1.50%, Mark Sieron, Morgan Stanley/7.80%, Insiders/14.50%

Financial Data: **Fiscal Year End:**12/31 **Latest Annual Data:** 12/30/2006

Year	Sales	Net Income
2006	$403,131,000	$42,377,000
2005	$316,668,000	$32,178,000

Curr. Assets:	$101,635,000	**Curr. Liab.:**	$94,045,000	**P/E Ratio:**	11.25
Plant, Equip.:	$25,331,000	**Total Liab.:**	$215,418,000	**Indic. Yr. Divd.:**	NA
Total Assets:	$263,918,000	**Net Worth:**	$48,500,000	**Debt/ Equity:**	NA

Middlefield Banc Corp

15985 E High St., Middlefield, OH, 44062; ***PH:*** 1-440-632-1666; ***Fax:*** 1-440-632-1700; ***http://*** www.middlefieldbank.com

General - Incorporation .... OH
Employees 80
Auditor .... S R Snodgrass, A.C
Stk Agt...... American Stock Transfer & Trust Co.
Counsel .... NA
DUNS No. .... NA

Stock- Price on:12/24/2007 .... $38.7
Stock Exchange .... OTC
Ticker Symbol .... MBCN
Outstanding Shares 1,520,000
E.P.S $2.65
Shareholders .... NA

Business: The group's principal activity is to provide commercial banking services. The deposit products include checking, savings, and negotiable order of withdrawal (now) accounts, money market accounts and time certificates of deposit. The group originates operational and working capital loans, loans to finance capital purchases, term business loans, residential construction loans, loans for small businesses, professional loans, residential and commercial mortgage loans and consumer installment loans. The other services include safe deposit facilities and travelers' checks. The group provides online banking services to individuals and online cash management services to business customers. The services are provided primarily in geauga, portage, trumbull and ashtabula counties, Ohio.

Primary SIC and add'l.: 6022 6712

CIK No: 0000836147

Subsidiaries: The Middlefield Banking Company

Officers: Thomas G. Caldwell/CEO, Pres./$277,800.00, James R. Heslop/COO, Exec. VP/$204,903.00, Donald L. Stacy/Treasurer, CFO/$127,225.00, Sharon Jarold/VP - Middlefield Banking Company, Jay P. Giles/Sr. VP - Middlefield, OH, Middlefield Banking Company/$116,072.00, Matt Bellin/Commercial Lender, Middlefield Banking Company, Dennis Linville/Sr. VP - Area Executive, Middlefield Banking Company, R. E. West/Branch Mgr. - Middlefield Banking Company, Tom Neikirk/Branch Mgr. - Middlefield Banking Company, Kathy Vanek/Branch Supervisor - Middlefield Banking Company, Joan Sweet/Branch Supervisor - Middlefield Banking Company, Tim McCreary/Branch Mgr. - Middlefield Banking Company, Karen Graham/Branch Supervisor - Middlefield Banking Company, Jeremy Bailey/Branch Supervisor - Middlefield Banking Company

Directors: William J. Skidmore/51/Dir.

Owners: Thomas G. Caldwell/1.70%, James J. McCaskey, Other executive officers/1.50%, Frances H. Frank, Thomas C. Halstead, Richard T. Coyne, Donald L.Stacy, William J. Skidmore, Donald D. Hunter, Carolyn J. Turk, Jay P. Giles, Donald E. Villers, Insiders/8.70%, James R. Heslop/1.00%

Financial Data: ***Fiscal Year End:*** 12/31 ***Latest Annual Data:*** 12/31/2006

Year	**Sales**	**Net Income**
2006	$21,928,000	$3,884,000
2005	$19,498,000	$3,701,000
2004	$17,610,000	$3,273,000

Curr. Assets:	$14,751,000	**Curr. Liab.:**	$273,549,000		
Plant, Equip.:	$6,742,000	**Total Liab.:**	$310,388,000	**Indic. Yr. Divd.:**	NA
Total Assets:	$340,852,000	**Net Worth:**	$30,464,000	**Debt/ Equity:**	1.1854

Middlesex Water Co

1500 Ronson Rd., Iselin, NJ, 08830; ***PH:*** 1-732-634-1500; ***http://*** www.middlesexwater.com; ***Email:*** info@middlesexwater.com

General - Incorporation .... NJ
Employees 243
Auditor .... Beard Miller Co. LLP
Stk Agt........ Registrar & Transfer Co
Counsel .... NA
DUNS No. 00-697-5122

Stock- Price on:12/24/2007 .... $18.98
Stock Exchange .... NDQ
Ticker Symbol .... MSEX
Outstanding Shares 13,190,000
E.P.S $0.79
Shareholders .... NA

Business: The group's principal activities are to collect, treat, store and distribute water for domestic, commercial, industrial and fire prevention purposes. It supplies water to customers located in an area of approximately 55 square miles of New Jersey. The group's subsidiary, tidewater utilities inc, provides water to community water systems located throughout Delaware.

Primary SIC and add'l.: 9999 4941

CIK No: 0000066004

Subsidiaries: Pinelands Wastewater Company, Pinelands Water Company, Tidewater Environmental Services, Inc., Tidewater Utilities, Inc., Utility Service Affiliates (Perth Amboy) Inc., Utility Service Affiliates, Inc.

Officers: Dennis W. Doll/Dir., CEO, Pres./$352,477.00, Bruce A. O'Connor/CFO, VP/$254,296.00, Richard M. Risoldi/VP - Subsidiary Operations/$217,300.00, Ronald F. Williams/VP - Operations, COO/$254,539.00, Kenneth J. Quinn/VP, General Counsel, Sec., Treasurer/$190,602.00, Bernadette M. Sohler/VP - Corporate Affairs, James P. Garrett/VP - Human Resources

Directors: Dennis W. Doll/Dir., CEO, Pres., Richard J. Tompkins/69/Chmn., Walter G. Reinhard/62/Dir., John R. Middleton/63/Dir., Annette Catino/51/Dir., John C. Cutting/71/Dir., John P. Mulkerin/70/Dir., Jeffries Shein/68/Dir.

Owners: Richard M. Risoldi, Ronald F. Williams, Richard J. Tompkins, Dennis W. Doll, John R. Middleton, John C. Cutting, Verona Construction Company/5.31%, Insiders, Kenneth J. Quinn, Jeffries Shein, Walter G. Reinhard, Bruce A. OConnor, Annette Catino, John P. Mulkerin

Financial Data: ***Fiscal Year End:*** 12/31 ***Latest Annual Data:*** 12/31/2006

Year	**Sales**	**Net Income**
2006	$81,061,000	$10,039,000
2005	$74,613,000	$8,476,000
2004	$70,991,000	$8,446,000

Curr. Assets:	$20,912,000	**Curr. Liab.:**	$18,139,000	**P/E Ratio:**	24.03
Plant, Equip.:	$317,128,000	**Total Liab.:**	$236,964,000	**Indic. Yr. Divd.:**	$0.690
Total Assets:	$370,267,000	**Net Worth:**	$133,302,000	**Debt/ Equity:**	NA

Middleton Doll Co

1050 Walnut Ridge Dr., Hartland, WI, 53029; ***PH:*** 1-262-369-8163; ***Fax:*** 1-262-523-4193; ***http://*** www.leemiddleton.com

General - Incorporation .... WI
Employees 44
Auditor .... Virchow, Krause & Co. LLP
Stk Agt .... U.S. Bank, N.A.,
Counsel .... NA
DUNS No. .... NA

Stock- Price on:12/24/2007 .... $0.36
Stock Exchange .... OTC
Ticker Symbol .... DOLL
Outstanding Shares 3,800,000
E.P.S $0.21
Shareholders .... NA

Business: The group operates through its subsdiary whose principle activity is to provide real estate investment trust that makes loans and leases buildings to small businesses, as well as participates in loans with third-party loan originators; and manufactures and distributes vinyl play and collectible dolls, plastic clocks and other licensed consumer products. The group operates from United States.

Primary SIC and add'l.: 6512 3942 6519 6719

CIK No: 0000723209

Subsidiaries: Lee Middleton Original Dolls, Inc., License Products, Inc.

Officers: Salvatore L. Bando/Dir., CEO, Pres./$84,000.00, Craig R. Bald/VP - Finance, CFO/$123,000.00

Directors: Salvatore L. Bando/Dir., CEO, Pres., Kenneth A. Werner/Dir., Peter A. Fischer/Dir., David A. Geraldson/Dir., Jeffrey B. Rusinow/53/Dir., Douglas M. Schosser/38/Dir.

Owners: Insiders/7.00%, Thomas G. Berlin/10.40%, Insiders/7.00%, Thomas G. Berlin/10.40%, Jeffrey B. Rusinow, Richard Margolin/6.80%, Kenneth A. Werner, Salvatore L. Bando/3.60%, Salvatore L. Bando/3.60%, Richard Margolin/6.80%, Peter A. Fisher, David A. Geraldson/1.30%, David A. Geraldson/1.30%

Financial Data: ***Fiscal Year End:*** 12/31 ***Latest Annual Data:*** 9/30/2007

Year	**Sales**	**Net Income**
2007	NA	NA
2006	$15,492,000	-$1,750,000
2005	$19,661,000	-$650,000

Curr. Assets:	$9,318,000	**Curr. Liab.:**	$1,474,000		
Plant, Equip.:	$6,806,000	**Total Liab.:**	$1,474,000	**Indic. Yr. Divd.:**	NA
Total Assets:	$16,359,000	**Net Worth:**	$4,520,000	**Debt/ Equity:**	NA

MidgardXXI Inc

Formerly: Exabyte Corp
2108 - 55th St., Boulder, CO, 80301; ***PH:*** 1-303-442-4333; ***http://*** www.exabyte.com

General - Incorporation .... DE
Employees 162
Auditor .... PricewaterhouseCoopers LLP
Stk Agt .... Bank Boston EquiServe
Counsel .... Certance LLC
DUNS No. 14-428-9006

Stock- Price on:12/24/2007 .... NA
Stock Exchange .... OTC
Ticker Symbol .... MGXX
Outstanding Shares .... NA
E.P.S $0.025
Shareholders .... NA

Business: The group's principal activity is to design, manufacture and market information storage products, including tape drive products, automated tape libraries and recording media. The group's tape drive products include vxa(R) and mammothtapetm tape drives, as well as vxa(R), mammothtapetm and ltotm (ultriumtm) automated tape libraries. It also provides its own brand of recording media and provides worldwide service and support to customers and end users. The products address the need for reliable, high-performance and affordable data storage in the fastest growing segments of the computer industry such as windows nt, unix, macos and linux application and database servers, workstations and computer networks. It operates in Netherlands, Germany, Japan, Canada and Singapore.

Primary SIC and add'l.: 3577 7378 3572

CIK No: 0000855109

Subsidiaries: Ecrix Corporation, Exabyte (Europe) B.V., Exabyte (Singapore) Pte. Ltd., Nihon Exabyte Corporation

Officers: Marije Stijnen/Corporate Marketing Mgr., Meghan Turner/Dir. - Marketing, Americas, Merissa Leow/Marketing Mgr. - Apac

Owners: Leonard W. Busse, Stephanie Smeltzer McCoy, Juan A. Rodriguez, Meritage Investment Partners LLC, Carroll A. Wallace, Imation Corp., Insiders, John R. Garrett, Laurence A. Jones, Crestview Capital Master, LLC, Jackson G. Tankersley, Tom W. Ward, Thomas E. Pardun

Financial Data: ***Fiscal Year End:*** 12/31 ***Latest Annual Data:*** 12/31/2005

Year	**Sales**	**Net Income**
2005	$90,968,000	-$12,070,000
2004	$102,051,000	-$9,914,000

Curr. Assets:	$23,854,000	**Curr. Liab.:**	$24,896,000		
Plant, Equip.:	$2,720,000	**Total Liab.:**	$105,606,000	**Indic. Yr. Divd.:**	NA
Total Assets:	$34,715,000	**Net Worth:**	-$70,891,000	**Debt/ Equity:**	NA

Midland Capital Holdings Corp

8929 S Harlem Ave., Bridgeview, IL, 60455; ***PH:*** 1-708-598-9400; ***Fax:*** 1-708-598-5445; ***http://*** www.midlandfederal.com

General - Incorporation .... DE
Employees 39
Auditor .... Cobitz, Vandenberg & Fennessy
Stk Agt .... Registrar & Transfer Co
Counsel........ Luse, Gorman, Pomerenk & Schick, P.c.
DUNS No. .... NA

Stock- Price on:12/24/2007 .... $42
Stock Exchange .... OTC
Ticker Symbol .... MCPH
Outstanding Shares .... NA
E.P.S $1.79
Shareholders .... NA

Business: The group's principal activities are to accept deposits from the general public and use such deposits to originate residential mortgage, consumer, multi-family and other loans. It is a holding company of midland federal savings and loan association. The operations are conducted through its main office in bridgeview and 3 branch offices located in southwest Chicago. These offices serve a market area consisting of southwest Chicago and the southwest suburban communities of bridgeview, oak lawn, palos hills, hickory hills, burbank, Chicago ridge, homer glen, lockport, orland park and lemont.

Primary SIC and add'l.: 6035 6712

CIK No: 0001061234

Subsidiaries: Midland Capital Holdings Corporation, Midland Federal Savings and Loan Association, Midland Federal Service Corporation

Officers: Paul M. Zogas/53/Chmn., CEO, CFO, Pres./$240,058.00, Charles A. Zogas/54/Dir., Exec. VP, Sec., Richard Taylor/58/Dir., VP/$139,357.00

Directors: Paul M. Zogas/53/Chmn., CEO, CFO, Pres., Charles A. Zogas/54/Dir., Exec. VP, Sec., Michael J. Kukanza/48/Dir., Jonas Vaznelis/88/Dir., Richard Taylor/58/Dir., VP

Owners: Charles A. Zogas/23.61%, Richard Taylor/2.23%, Jeffrey S. Halis/5.37%, Paul M. Zogas/28.96%, Insiders/59.00%, Richard A. Horstman/5.37%, Algerd A. Brazis & Aldona Brazis Trust/5.37%

Financial Data: Fiscal Year End:06/30 **Latest Annual Data:** 6/30/2006

Year	Sales	Net Income
2006	$7,720,000	$1,011,000
2005	$7,650,000	$1,203,000
2004	$7,903,000	$1,043,000

Curr. Assets:	$11,746,000	Curr. Liab.:	$116,394,000	P/E Ratio:	19.18
Plant, Equip.:	$2,241,000	Total Liab.:	$117,521,000	Indic. Yr. Divd.:	$0.960
Total Assets:	$130,817,000	Net Worth:	$13,296,000	Debt/ Equity:	NA

Midland Co

7000 Midland Blvd., Amelia, OH, 45102; **PH:** 1-513-943-7100; **Fax:** 1-513-947-4022; **http://** www.midlandcompany.com; **Email:** investorinfo@amig.com

General - Incorporation	OH	Stock- Price on:12/24/2007	$47.07
Employees	1,200	Stock Exchange	NDQ
Auditor	Deloitte & Touche LLP	Ticker Symbol	NA
Stk Agt	National City Bank	Outstanding Shares	19,330,000
Counsel	Cohen, Todd, Kite & Stanford	E.P.S	$4.40
DUNS No.	04-661-6918	Shareholders	NA

Business: The group's principal activity is to provide specialty insurance products and services. The group operates in three segments: manufactured housing insurance, other insurance and transportation. Manufactured housing insurance includes physical damage insurance and related coverage for manufactured homes. Other insurance products include site-built dwelling, collateral protection, motorsport and watercraft insurance, as well as manufactured housing park and dealer insurance. Transportation segment provides charter barges and broker freight for the movement of dry bulk commodities such as petroleum coke, ores and barite primarily on the lower Mississippi river and its tributaries. The group's specialty insurance operations are conducted through American modern insurance group and transportation business through m/g transport services, inc. The group operates solely in the domestic market.

Primary SIC and add'l.: 4449 6311 6331

CIK No: 0000066025

Subsidiaries: American Family Home Insurance Company, American Modern Financial Services, Inc., American Modern Home Insurance Company, American Modern Home Service Company, American Modern Insurance Group, Inc., American Modern Life Insurance Company, American Modern Lloyds Insurance Company, American Southern Home Insurance Company, American Western Home Insurance Company, G.u.i.c. Insurance Company, Lloyds Modern Corporation, M/G Transport Services, Inc., MGT Services, Inc., Midland-Guardian Co., Modern Services Group, Inc.

Officers: John W. Hayden/CEO, Pres./$2,507,733.00, Joseph P. Hayden/55/Chmn., COO, Anthony W. Dirksing/Controller, John M. O'Mara/Dir., Corp. Dir. - Financial Consultant, Jennifer W. Colvin/Assist., Sec./$2,495,152.00, John R. Labar/Dir., Sec., John I. Von Lehman/Exec. VP, Sec./$1,139,184.00, Paul T. Brizzolara/50/Chief Legal Officer, Assist. Sec./$911,191.00, Paul F. Gelter/Exec. VP/$819,213.00, Todd W. Gray/CFO, Exec. VP/$513,172.00, Elisabeth E. Baldock/VP - Human Resources, Learning, Development, Michael L. Flowers/VP, Assist. Sec., Mark E. Burke/Dir. - Taxation, James E. Kroeger/Dir. - Internal Audit, Alisa E. Poe/VP (20 Officers included in Index)

Directors: Joseph P. Hayden/55/Chmn., COO, James E. Bushman/Dir., Rene J. Robichaud/Dir., Francis Marie Thrailkill/Dir., James H. Carey/Dir., Michael J. Conaton/Dir., Jerry A. Grundhofer/Dir., J. P. Hayden/Dir., William T. Hayden/Dir., William J. Keating/Dir., John R. Labar/Dir., Sec., Richard M. Norman/Dir., David B. O'Maley/Dir., John M. O'Mara/Dir., Corp. Dir. - Financial Consultant

Owners: Thomas R. Hayden/5.90%, Ren J. Robichaud, Francis Marie Thrailkill, Jerry A. Grundhofer, John M. OMara, John W. Hayden/6.60%, David B. OMaley, J. P. Hayden/10.90%, Michael J. Conaton, Richard M. Norman, John Von Lehman, Todd W. Gray, Paul F. Gelter, James E. Bushman, T. Rowe Price Associates, Inc./7.20% (23 Owners included in Index)

Financial Data: Fiscal Year End:12/31 **Latest Annual Data:** 12/31/2006

Year	Sales	Net Income
2006	$789,268,000	$70,695,000
2005	$733,430,000	$65,326,000
2004	$783,841,000	$54,238,000

Curr. Assets:	$281,769,000	Curr. Liab.:	$157,038,000	P/E Ratio:	12.90
Plant, Equip.:	$118,879,000	Total Liab.:	$994,782,000	Indic. Yr. Divd.:	$0.400
Total Assets:	$1,569,528,000	Net Worth:	$574,746,000	Debt/ Equity:	0.1653

MidNet Inc

1055 Hastings St. W , Ste. 300, Vancouver, BC, V6E 2E9; **PH:** 1-604-609-6188; **http://** www.midnetinc.org; **Email:** info@midnetinc.org

General - Incorporation	DE	Stock- Price on:12/24/2007	NA
Employees	NA	Stock Exchange	OTC
Auditor	Williams & Webster, P.S.	Ticker Symbol	MIDX
Stk Agt	Signature Stock Transfer, Inc.	Outstanding Shares	NA
Counsel	NA	E.P.S	NA
DUNS No.	NA	Shareholders	NA

Business: The groups principle activity is to provide data communications environment among telecommunications infrastructure companies. The group operates from the United States and Canada.

Primary SIC and add'l.: 4813

CIK No: 0001080313

Subsidiaries: MidNet Canada, Inc., MidNet USA, Inc, Tugboat Acquisition Corp

Officers: Tilo Kunz/CEO, Kent Hendrickson/Dir., Sec., Stuart Doescher/Dir., Treasurer

Directors: Del Johnson/Chmn., George Covert/Vice Chmn., Kent Hendrickson/Dir., Sec., Stuart Doescher/Dir., Treasurer, J. L. Albert/Dir., Gary Ott/Dir., Rob Otte/Dir., J. C. Ruch/Dir., Bob Zimmerman/Dir.

Financial Data: Fiscal Year End:12/31 **Latest Annual Data:** 12/31/2005

Year	Sales	Net Income
2005	$27,000	-$3,072,000
2004	$3,000	-$1,057,000
2003	$21,000	-$60,000

Curr. Assets:	$174,000	Curr. Liab.:	$499,000		
Plant, Equip.:	$45,000	Total Liab.:	$499,000	Indic. Yr. Divd.:	NA
Total Assets:	$259,000	Net Worth:	-$240,000	Debt/ Equity:	NA

Midnight Candle Company

79013 Bayside Ct, Indio, CA, 92203; **PH:** 1-760-772-1872; **http://** www.midnightcandle.com

General - Incorporation	NV	Stock- Price on:12/24/2007	NA
Employees	NA	Stock Exchange	OTC
Auditor	Bagell, Levine & Company, LLC	Ticker Symbol	MIDC
Stk Agt	Holladay Stock Transfer, Inc.	Outstanding Shares	NA
Counsel	NA	E.P.S	NA
DUNS No.	NA	Shareholders	NA

Business: The groups principle activity is to market scented candles to consumers and businesses. The products of the group include jar candles, pillar candles and tea lights. The group operates from the United States.

Primary SIC and add'l.: 5199

CIK No: 0001321573

Officers: Helen C. Cary/50/Dir., Pres., Chief Executive Fficer, Principal Financial Officer

Directors: Helen C. Cary/50/Dir., Pres., Chief Executive Fficer, Principal Financial Officer

Owners: Helen C. Cary/95.60%, Insiders/95.60%

Midsouth Bancorp Inc

102 Versailles Blvd., Lafayette, LA, 70501; **PH:** 1-337-237-8343; **Fax:** 1-337-267-4434; **http://** www.midsouthbank.com; **Email:** support@midsouthbank.com

General - Incorporation	LA	Stock- Price on:12/24/2007	$24.96
Employees	371	Stock Exchange	AMEX
Auditor	Porter Keadle Moore, LLP	Ticker Symbol	MSL
Stk Agt	Mellon Investor Services LLC	Outstanding Shares	6,270,000
Counsel	NA	E.P.S	$1.359
DUNS No.	13-122-3273	Shareholders	NA

Business: The group's principal activity is to provide banking services to commercial and retail customers through its wholly owned subsidiary, midsouth national bank. It also provides consumer loan services to individuals through its wholly owned subsidiary, the financial services of the south, inc. The group is community oriented and focuses primarily on offering commercial and consumer loan and deposit services to individuals small and middle market businesses. The group along with six other banking offices provides services in lafayette, new iberia, breaux bridge, cecilia, jeanerette, opelousas, morgan city, jennings, lake charles and sulphur Louisiana.

Primary SIC and add'l.: 6021 6712

CIK No: 0000745981

Subsidiaries: Financial Services of the South, Inc., Lamar Bank, MidSouth Bank, N.A., MidSouth Statutory Trust I, MidSouth Statutory Trust II

Officers: C. R. Cloutier/61/Dir., CEO, Pres./$435,481.00, William M. Simmons/74/Dir. - Investor, Karen L. Hail/54/Dir., COO, Sec., Sr. Exec. VP/$294,230.00, Donald R. Landry/Chief Lending Officer, Exec. VP/$233,382.00, Dwight A. Utz/Sr. VP, Retail Executive Mgr./$139,708.00, J. Eustis Corrigan/CFO/$151,677.00

Directors: C. R. Cloutier/61/Dir., CEO, Pres., Will G. Charbonnet/60/Chmn., William M. Simmons/74/Dir. - Investor, J. B. Hargroder/77/Dir., Clayton Paul Hilliard/82/Dir., Stephen C. May/59/Dir., Joseph V. Tortorice/58/Dir., James R. Davis/55/Dir., Karen L. Hail/54/Dir., COO, Sec., Sr. Exec. VP, Milton B. Kidd/59/Dir., Timothy J. Lemoine/57/Dir., Glenn R. Pumpelly/49/Dir.

Owners: William M. Simmons/3.19%, J. B. Hargroder/6.95%, Will G. Charbonnet/2.39%, Insiders/35.37%, MidSouth Bancorp, Inc/8.00%, Dwight A. Utz, C. R. Cloutier/6.16%, Timothy J. Lemoine, Glenn R. Pumpelly, Clayton Paul Hilliard/3.69%, Donald R. Landry/1.54%, Karen L. Hail/1.70%, James R. Davis/1.12%, Eustis J. Corrigan, Milton B. Kidd/3.60% (19 Owners included in Index)

Financial Data: Fiscal Year End:12/31 **Latest Annual Data:** 12/31/2006

Year	Sales	Net Income
2006	$62,580,000	$8,220,000
2005	$50,805,000	$7,274,000
2004	$36,966,000	$6,979,000

Curr. Assets:	$62,896,000	Curr. Liab.:	$727,502,000	P/E Ratio:	18.37
Plant, Equip.:	$30,609,000	Total Liab.:	$745,279,000	Indic. Yr. Divd.:	$0.280
Total Assets:	$805,022,000	Net Worth:	$59,743,000	Debt/ Equity:	0.2507

Midway Games Inc

2704 W Roscoe St., Chicago, IL, 60618; **PH:** 1-773-961-2222; **http://** www.midway.com

General - Incorporation	DE	Stock- Price on:12/24/2007	$6.1
Employees	850	Stock Exchange	AMEX
Auditor	Ernst & Young LLP	Ticker Symbol	MXC
Stk Agt	Bank of New York	Outstanding Shares	91,390,000
Counsel	Shack Siegel Katz Flaherty & Goodman	E.P.S	-$0.77
DUNS No.	95-671-9835	Shareholders	NA

Business: The group's principal activity is the development and marketing of interactive entertainment software. It develops and publishes games for all new generation home video game consoles and handheld game platforms like sony's playstation 2, microsoft's xbox and nintendo's gamecube and game boy. The titles developed include mortal kombat, spyhunter, nhl hitz 20-02, ready 2 rumble boxing, hydro thunder, san francisco rush extreme racing, nfl blitz, area 51, cruis'n usa, nba jam, centipede, asteroids and pong. In 2003, the group released 28 videogames directly or under licensing arrangements. Home video games are marketed worldwide to mass merchants, video rental retailers and entertainment software distributors. Principal customers of the group for home video games include the mass merchandisers, wal-Mart and toys r us. On 06-Apr-2004, the group acquired surreal software inc.

Primary SIC and add'l.: 7372

CIK No: 0001022080

Subsidiaries: K. K. Midway Games, Midway Amusement Games, LLC, Midway Australia Holdings Pty Ltd, Midway Games (Europe) GmbH, Midway Games Australia Pty Ltd, Midway Games Canada Corp., Midway Games GmbH, Midway Games Limited, Midway Games Sales Corporation, Midway Games SAS, Midway Games West Inc., Midway Home Entertainment Inc., Midway Home Studios Inc., Midway Interactive Inc., Midway Sales Company, LLC 24 Subsidiaries included in the Index

Officers: David F. Zucker/CEO, Pres./$3,113,610.00, James R. Boyle/VP - Finance, Controller, Assist. Treasurer, Principal Accounting Officer, Deborah K. Fulton/Sr. VP, Sec., General Counsel, Miguel Iribarren/VP - Publishing/$271,771.00, Thomas E. Powell/46/Exec. VP - Finance, Treasurer, CFO/$352,467.00, Steven M. Allison/Sr. VP - Marketing, CMO/$343,799.00, Matthew V. Booty/Sr. VP - Worldwide Studios/$433,445.00

Directors: Shari E. Redstone/Vice Chmn., Kenneth D. Cron/Chmn., William C. Bartholomay/Dir., Peter C. Brown/Dir., Joseph A. Califano/Dir., Ira S. Sheinfeld/Dir., Robert J. Steele/Dir., Robert N. Waxman/Dir.

Owners: Sumner M. Redstone, Matthew V. Booty, Robert N. Waxman, Steven M. Allison, William C. Bartholomay, Miguel Iribarren, Kenneth D. Cron, Ira S. Sheinfeld, Insiders, Peter C. Brown, National Amusements Inc., Thomas E. Powell, David F. Zucker, Sumco, Inc., Shari E. Redstone *(17 Owners included in Index)*

Financial Data: Fiscal Year End:12/31 Latest Annual Data: 12/31/2006

Year	Sales	Net Income
2006	$165,574,000	-$77,783,000
2005	$150,078,000	-$112,487,000
2004	$161,595,000	-$19,945,000

Curr. Assets:	$175,684,000	Curr. Liab.:	$45,934,000		
Plant, Equip.:	$20,407,000	Total Liab.:	$201,354,000	Indic. Yr. Divd.:	NA
Total Assets:	$254,061,000	Net Worth:	$52,707,000	Debt/ Equity:	4.3145

Midwest Air Group Inc

6744 S Howell Ave., Oak Creek, WI, 53154; **PH:** 1-414-570-4000; **Fax:** 1-414-570-9666; http:// www.midwestairlines.com

General - Incorporation	WI	Stock- Price on:12/24/2007	$14.78
Employees	2,657	Stock Exchange	AMEX
Auditor	Deloitte & Touche LLP	Ticker Symbol	MEH
Stk Agt	Firstar Trust Co	Outstanding Shares	24,470,000
Counsel	NA	E.P.S.	$0.72
DUNS No.	92-846-7091	Shareholders	NA

Business: The group's principal activity is to provide scheduled passenger services, aircraft charter and air freight services in the United States. The group is a holding company and operates principally through midwest airlines, Inc. ('midwest airlines') and skyway airlines, inc. ('midwest connect'). Midwest airlines operates a single-class passenger jet airline that caters to business travelers and serves 15 destinations from milwaukee and Kansas city. Midwest connect builds feeder traffic and provides regional scheduled passenger service. The group also provides aircraft charter services, transport air freight and mail and other airline services.

Primary SIC and add'l.: 4512 4522

CIK No: 0000948845

Subsidiaries: Midwest Airlines, Inc., Midwest Express Services Kansas City, Inc., Midwest Express Services Omaha, Inc, Skyway Airlines, Inc., YX Properties, LLC

Officers: Timothy E. Hocksema/Chmn., CEO, Pres., Christopher I. Stone/Sr. VP - Human Resources, Dennis J. O'Reilly/Treasurer, Dir. - Investor Relations, Curtis E. Sawyer/Sr. VP, CFO, Scott R. Dickson/Sr. VP, Chief Marketing Officer, David C. Reeve/Sr. VP - Operations, Carol N. Skornicka/Sr. VP - Corporate Affairs, Sec., General Counsel

Directors: Timothy E. Hocksema/Chmn., CEO, Pres., David H. Treitel/Dir., Elizabeth T. Solberg/Dir., Richard H. Sonnentag/Dir., Ulice Payne/Dir., Samuel K. Skinner/Dir., John M. Albertine/Dir., Jeffrey H. Erickson/Dir., Charles F. Kalmbach/Dir.

Owners: Litespeed Management LLC/5.80%, Samuel K. Skinner, Insiders/6.80%, Curtis E. Sawyer, Richard H. Sonnentag, Ulice Payne, Timothy E. Hocksema/3.40%, Charles F. Kalmbach, Scott R. Dickson, T. Rowe Price Associates, Inc./4.90%, David C. Reeve, Octavian Master Fund, L.P./6.00%, Jeffrey H. Erickson, Carol N. Skornicka, Fursa Alternative Strategies LLC/5.50% *(19 Owners included in Index)*

Financial Data: Fiscal Year End:12/31 Latest Annual Data: 12/31/2006

Year	Sales	Net Income
2006	$664,501,000	$5,412,000
2005	$522,989,000	-$64,886,000
2004	$415,246,000	-$43,132,000

Curr. Assets:	$187,401,000	Curr. Liab.:	$163,367,000		
Plant, Equip.:	$154,962,000	Total Liab.:	$334,629,000	Indic. Yr. Divd.:	NA
Total Assets:	$356,451,000	Net Worth:	$21,822,000	Debt/ Equity:	0.3500

Midwest Banc Holdings Inc

501 W N Ave., Melrose Park, IL, 60160; **PH:** 1-708-865-1053; **Fax:** 1-708-865-7013; http:// www.midwestbanc.com

General - Incorporation	DE	Stock - Price on:12/24/2007	$15.3
Employees	496	Stock Exchange	NDQ
Auditor	PricewaterhouseCoopers LLP	Ticker Symbol	MBHI
Stk Agt	Computershare Investor Services LLC	Outstanding Shares	24,650,000
Counsel	NA	E.P.S.	$0.69
DUNS No.	06-701-1759	Shareholders	NA

Business: The group's principal activities are to provide services such as traditional banking, personal and corporate trust, residential mortgage insurance brokerage and retail securities brokerage services. It accepts checking and now accounts, savings and money market accounts and time deposits. The lending products include commercial loans, commercial real estate loans, agricultural loans and consumer real estate loans. The operations of the group are carried out through fifteen banking centers in Chicago metropolitan area and six banking centers in western Illinois. The group has a network of 29 ATM sites. On 03-Jan-2003, the group acquired big foot financial corp.

Primary SIC and add'l.: 6022 6712

CIK No: 0001051379

Subsidiaries: MBHI Capital Trust II, MBHI Capital Trust III, MBHI Capital Trust IV, MBHI Capital Trust V, MBTC Investment Company, Midwest Bank and Trust Company, Midwest Bank Insurance Services, LLC, Midwest Financial and Investment Services, Inc.

Officers: James J. Giancola/Dir., CEO, Pres./$2,036,394.00, Daniel R. Kadolph/CFO, Exec. VP/$294,095.00, Mary C. Ceas/49/Sr. VP - Human Resources, Donald L. Weist/54/Exec. VP, Chief Investment Officer, Jan R. Thiry/Chief Accounting Officer, Sr. VP

Directors: James J. Giancola/Dir., CEO, Pres., E. V. Silveri/Chmn., Barry I. Forrester/Dir., Robert J. Genetski/Dir., Gerald F. Hartley/Dir., Joseph R. Rizza/Dir., Kenneth Velo/Dir., Angelo A. Dipaolo/Dir., J. J. Fritz/Dir., Homer J. Livingston/Dir., Thomas A. Rosenquist/Dir., Leon Wolin/Dir., Dennis M. O'Hara/Dir.

Owners: Stephen L. Markovits/1.20%, Wayne Pavlicek, Charles Bruning/4.60%, Michael R. Campbell/3.60%, John G. Eilering/6.10%, Insiders/20.00%, Linda K. Larson/2.50%, Ronald L. Spiekhout/1.10%, Peter J. Wifler, Dennis M. OHara

Financial Data: Fiscal Year End:12/31 Latest Annual Data: 12/31/2006

Year	Sales	Net Income
2006	$173,966,000	$17,746,000
2005	$123,439,000	$5,944,000
2004	$117,485,000	$2,376,000

Curr. Assets:	$100,532,000	Curr. Liab.:	$2,544,772,000	P/E Ratio:	20.96
Plant, Equip.:	$24,600,000	Total Liab.:	$2,654,804,000	Indic. Yr. Divd.:	$0.520
Total Assets:	$2,942,046,000	Net Worth:	$287,242,000	Debt/ Equity:	0.2291

Midwestone Financial Group Inc

222 1st Ave. E, Oskaloosa, IA, 52577; **PH:** 1-641-673-8448; **Fax:** 1-641-673-7836; http:// www.midwestonefinancial.com; **Email:** midwestonefg@mwofg.com

General - Incorporation	IA	Stock - Price on:12/24/2007	$17.47
Employees	225	Stock Exchange	NDQ
Auditor	KPMG LLP	Ticker Symbol	OSKY
Stk Agt	Illinois Stock Transfer Co	Outstanding Shares	3,690,000
Counsel	NA	E.P.S.	$1.501
DUNS No.	06-520-2715	Shareholders	NA

Business: The group's principal activities are to provide retail and commercial banking and related financial services through its subsidiaries. The services rendered by the group include acceptance of deposits, offering loans and trust services. The deposits accepted include demand, now accounts, savings and certificates of deposits. The loans offered include agricultural, commercial, real estate 1-4 family residences, constructions and residential property loans, installment loans and lease financing. The group also provides data processing and check processing services, brokerage services and one drive-up automated teller machine. The operations are conducted in south central Iowa and all of mahaska county, two branch offices in oskaloosa and portions of keokuk and Iowa counties. As of Dec 31, 2003, the group had approximately 54 other banks having 159 offices or branches operating within the 11 counties.

Primary SIC and add'l.: 6712 6035

CIK No: 0000741390

Subsidiaries: Central Valley Bank, Cook& Son Agency, Inc., MIC Financial, Inc., MidwestOne Bank, MidWestOne Bank& Trust, MidWestOne Investment Services, Inc., Pella State Bank

Officers: Charles S. Howard/Chmn., CEO, Pres./$359,999.00, David A. Meinert/Dir., Exec. VP, CFO/$292,324.00, Karen K. Binns/Sec.

Directors: Charles S. Howard/Chmn., CEO, Pres., Michael R. Welter/Dir., Donal D. Hill/Dir., Barbara J. Kniff-Mcculla/Dir., James G. Wake/Dir., Richard R. Donohue/Dir., David A. Meinert/Dir., Exec. VP, CFO, John P. Pothoven/Dir., Robert D. Wersen/Dir., Edward C. Whitham/Dir., Scott Zaiser/Dir.

Owners: Insiders/16.10%, Barbara J. Kniff-McCulla, MidWestOne Financial Group, Inc./12.10%, Thomas W. Campbell, Charles S. Howard/6.90%, Jerry D. Krause, Michael R. Welter, Richard R. Donohue, Robert D. Wersen, James G. Wake, David A. Meinert/3.20%, John P. Pothoven/3.00%, Donal D. Hill, Jeffrey L. Gendell/6.70%, Edward C. Whitham *(16 Owners included in Index)*

Financial Data: Fiscal Year End:12/31 Latest Annual Data: 12/31/2006

Year	Sales	Net Income
2006	$52,594,000	$6,441,000
2005	$44,508,000	$6,088,000
2004	$41,648,000	$5,829,000

Curr. Assets:	$27,313,000	Curr. Liab.:	$662,984,000	P/E Ratio:	11.97
Plant, Equip.:	$12,515,000	Total Liab.:	$682,378,000	Indic. Yr. Divd.:	$0.720
Total Assets:	$744,911,000	Net Worth:	$62,533,000	Debt/ Equity:	NA

Migami Inc

3701 Wilshire Blvd., Ste. 506, Los Angeles, CA, 90010; **PH:** 1-213-739-1700; http:// www.migami.net; **Email:** info@migami.net

General - Incorporation	NV	Stock - Price on:12/24/2007	NA
Employees	NA	Stock Exchange	OTC
Auditor	Chisholm, Bierwolf & Nilson, LLC	Ticker Symbol	MIGA
Stk Agt	Interwest Transfer Company, Inc.	Outstanding Shares	NA
Counsel	NA	E.P.S.	-$0.06
DUNS No.	NA	Shareholders	NA

Business: The groups principal activities include leveraging its expertise and understanding product formulation, product branding, and proprietary technologies to be applied to product launches. The group operates from Migami in the United States.

Primary SIC and add'l.: 4959 8711 2844 3714 8999 4959 3714 2844 8999 8711

CIK No: 0000789885

Officers: John Park/41/Dir., CEO, CFO, Pres., Tehan Oh/52/Dir., Sec.

Directors: John Park/41/Dir., CEO, CFO, Pres., Tehan Oh/52/Dir., Sec., Young Suh/46/Dir.

Owners: Langley Park Investment Trust Plc/6.32%, Tehan Oh/4.86%, Innovay, Inc./60.00%, Lionel Simons/7.08%, John Park/12.95%, Jubilee Investment Trust Plc/6.34%

Financial Data: Fiscal Year End:12/31 Latest Annual Data: 12/31/2005

Year	Sales	Net Income
2005	$50,000	-$918,000
2004	$41,000	-$1,605,000
2003	$755,000	-$2,147,000

Curr. Assets:	$365,000	Curr. Liab.:	$697,000		
Plant, Equip.:	$58,000	Total Liab.:	$697,000	Indic. Yr. Divd.:	NA
Total Assets:	$1,550,000	Net Worth:	$852,000	Debt/ Equity:	NA

MIGENIX Inc

12780 High Bluff Dr., Ste. 210, San Diego, CA, 92130; **PH:** 1-858-793-7800; **Fax:** 1-858-793-7805; http:// www.mbiotech.com; **Email:** info@migenix.com

General - Incorporation	BC	Stock - Price on:12/24/2007	$0.635
Employees	NA	Stock Exchange	OTC
Auditor	Ernst & Young LLP	Ticker Symbol	MGIFF
Stk Agt	Pacific Corporate Trust Co	Outstanding Shares	NA
Counsel	Farris, Vaughan, Wills & Murphy	E.P.S.	NA
DUNS No.	NA	Shareholders	NA

Business: The group's principle activity is to research, develop and commercialize drugs and develop therapeutic products that advance therapy, improve health and enrich lives. The group's focus is toward anti-infective drugs, with two product candidates in clinical development: mbi 226 for preventing catheter-related bloodstream infections (phase iii) and mbi 594an for treating acne (phase ii). Currently, the group has no products or license revenues. The group operates in Canada.

Primary SIC and add'l.: 2834 8731

CIK No: 0000915458

Subsidiaries: M&M Holdings Inc, MIGENIX Corp

Officers: James M. Demesa/Dir., CEO, Pres., Annkatrin Petersen-Japelli/54/VP - Clinical Development, Arthur J. Ayres/VP - Finance, CFO, William D. Milligan/Sr. VP - Corporate Development, Chief Business Officer, David K. Campagnari/VP - Operations, Jacob J. Clement/Sr. VP - Science, Technology, Chief Science Officer, Robert C. Cory/VP - Business Development, Neil A. Howell/VP - Research, San Diego

Directors: James M. Demesa/Dir., CEO, Pres., David Scott/Chmn., Walter H. Moos/Dir., Alistair Duncan/Dir., Steven Gillis/Dir., Richard W. Devries/Dir., Colin R. Mallet/Dir., Michael J. Abrams/Dir., Keith W. Schilit/Dir.

Owners: Richard DeVries/5.00%, BVF Partners, L.P./8.70%

Financial Data: *Fiscal Year End:*04/30 *Latest Annual Data:* 4/30/2006

Year	Sales	Net Income
2006	$514,000	-$9,412,000
2005	$1,948,000	-$13,354,000

Curr. Assets:	$9,038,000	**Curr. Liab.:**	$3,433,000		
Plant, Equip.:	$838,000	**Total Liab.:**	$3,433,000	**Indic. Yr. Divd.:**	NA
Total Assets:	$15,111,000	**Net Worth:**	$11,677,000	**Debt/ Equity:**	NA

Migo Software, Inc

555 Twin Dolphin Dr., Ste. 650, Redwood City, CA, 94065; *PH:* 1-650-232-2600; *Fax:* 1-650-232-2699; *http://* www.pwhtgroup.com; *Email:* info@pwhtgroup.com

General		Stock	
Incorporation	DE	Price on:12/24/2007	$0.2
Employees	36	Stock Exchange	OTC
Auditor	Hein & Assoc. LLP	Ticker Symbol	MIGO
Stk Agt	American Stock Transfer & Trust Co.	Outstanding Shares	93,730,000
Counsel	Greenberg Traurig	E.P.S	-$0.11
DUNS No.	87-951-6250	Shareholders	NA

Business: The group's principle activities are to design, develop and market removable storage devices and complementary software. The group provides software solutions, associated hardware and services enabling cross personal computer platform connectivity that enables data and device sharing and reduces computer downtime. The products include plug and play software, components for hot swap solutions, peripheral products for date back-up, instant data recovery and usb digital storage devices and applications. The products are marketed through resellers, direct telephone and Internet sales. The group has operations in the United States, Europe and the Pacific Rim. The group's quarterly revenue for September 2007 was 2.20 millions of USD.

Primary SIC and add'l.: 7372 7373 6719

CIK No: 0001006762

Subsidiaries: PowerHouse Acquisition, LLC, PowerHouse Studios, Inc.

Officers: Kent Heyman/Chmn., CEO, Jay Elliot/Chief Strategy Officer, Richard Liebman/CFO/$732,670.00, Syed Aamer Azam/Sr. VP - Research - Development, Robert Halligan/COO

Directors: Kent Heyman/Chmn., CEO, Greg Osborn/43/Dir., Alex Mashinsky/Dir., Mel S. Lavitt/Dir., Malcolm Elvey/66/Dir., Timothy Wallace/Dir., Carm Santoro/Dir.

Owners: Software Capital Partners LP/7.40%, Alex Mashinsky/10.10%, Jay Elliot/4.40%, Insiders/24.80%, Greg Osborn/1.80%, AIGH Investment Partners, LLC/5.30%, Timothy Wallace, Richard Liebman/2.50%, Software Seed Capital Partners IV, L.P/5.40%, Mel Lavitt/1.70%, Lifeboat Holdings, Inc/21.30%, Malcolm Elvey/1.10%, Lehman Brothers Holdings, Inc./8.00%, Kent Heyman/5.80%

Financial Data: *Fiscal Year End:*12/31 *Latest Annual Data:* 12/31/2006

Year	Sales	Net Income
2006	$345,000	-$11,467,000
2005	$308,000	-$10,145,000

Curr. Assets:	$586,000	**Curr. Liab.:**	$2,158,000		
Plant, Equip.:	$12,000	**Total Liab.:**	$2,158,000	**Indic. Yr. Divd.:**	NA
Total Assets:	$3,026,000	**Net Worth:**	$868,000	**Debt/ Equity:**	NA

MIIX Group Inc

2 Princess Rd. , Lawrenceville, NJ, 08648; *PH:* 1-609-896-2404; *http://* www.miix.com

General		Stock	
Incorporation	DE	Price on:12/24/2007	$0.002
Employees	94	Stock Exchange	OTC
Auditor	Ernst & Young LLP	Ticker Symbol	MIIX
Stk Agt	NA	Outstanding Shares	13,990,000
Counsel	Drinker Biddle & Reath LLP	E.P.S	-$3.47
DUNS No.	NA	Shareholders	NA

Business: The group's principal activity is to provide insurance products to the medical profession and health care institutions. The products include medical professional liability insurance for physicians and other medical professional or health care institutions. The group has insured approximately 5,000 physicians and other medical professionals and also more than 23 hospitals, extended care facilities and other health care organizations. It also offers complementary insurance products to its insured and operates other fee-based consulting and service businesses.

Primary SIC and add'l.: 6320 6324 6719

CIK No: 0001064063

Financial Data: *Fiscal Year End:*12/31 *Latest Annual Data:* 12/31/2006

Year	Sales	Net Income
2006	$779,728,000	$158,702,000
2005	$535,957,000	$111,011,000
2004	$320,707,000	$42,231,000

Curr. Assets:	$766,686,000	**Curr. Liab.:**	NA		
Plant, Equip.:	NA	**Total Liab.:**	$1,575,597,000	**Indic. Yr. Divd.:**	NA
Total Assets:	$1,616,863,000	**Net Worth:**	$41,266,000	**Debt/ Equity:**	NA

Mikohn Gaming Corp

920 Pilot Rd., Las Vegas, NV, 89119; *PH:* 1-702-896-3890; *http://* www.mikohn.com

General		Stock	
Incorporation	NV	Price on:12/24/2007	$5.4
Employees	308	Stock Exchange	NDQ
Auditor	BDO Seidman LLP	Ticker Symbol	NA
Stk Agt	U.S. Stock Transfer Corp	Outstanding Shares	34,840,000
Counsel	NA	E.P.S	-$2.6
DUNS No.	15-184-4222	Shareholders	NA

Business: The group's principle activity is to develop and market technology based products for the gaming industry. It operates through three segments: slot and table games: develops, acquires, licenses and distributes its proprietary branded and non-branded slot and table games. Product sales: designs, develops, manufactures and distributes interior signage, progressive jackpot systems, related electronic components, special order slot games and slot game glass displays. Systems: designs and develops electronic player tracking, game monitoring and accounting systems for slot and table games. The major brands include yahtzee (R), battleship (R), ripley's believe it or not ! (R), clue(R) and trivial pursuit (r). The group operates in North America, the Netherlands and Australia. The group's quarterly revenue for September 2007 was 18.32 millions of USD.

Primary SIC and add'l.: 7993 7373

CIK No: 0000912241

Subsidiaries: EndX Group, Ltd., EndX Inc., EndX Ltd., EndX Pty. Ltd., Games of Nevada, Inc., MGC, Inc., Mikohn Europe B.V., Mikohn Gaming Australasia Pty. Ltd., Mikohn Holdings, Inc., Mikohn International, Inc., Mikohn Nevada, P&S Leasing Corporation, Inc., P&S Leasing LLC, PGIC Holdings, Ltd., Progressive Games, Inc. 16 Subsidiaries included in the Index

Officers: Russel H. McMeekin/CEO, Pres./$2,203,757.00, Heather A. Rollo/VP - Finance, Chief Accounting Officer/$442,446.00, Robert J. Parente/Exec. VP - Americas/$686,333.00, Thomas M. Galanty/CTO, Exec. VP/$702,386.00, Robert B. Ziems/Exec. VP, General Counsel, Sec./$440,389.00, Neil Crossan/39/Exec. VP - International/$576,752.00

Directors: Peter G. Boynton/Chmn., Douglas M. Todoroff/Dir., Terrance W. Oliver/Dir., Rick L. Smith/Dir., Paul A. Harvey/Dir.

Owners: Thomas Galanty, Douglas M. Todoroff, Russel H. McMeekin/1.10%, Robert J. Parente, Insiders/4.70%, Delta Partners LLC/9.10%, Michael A. Sicuro, Gerald Catenacci/5.00%, Rick L. Smith, SMALLCAP World Fund, Inc./7.60%, Paul A. Harvey, Heather A. Rollo, Neil Crossan, Robert B. Ziems, Capital Research and Management/8.40% *(17 Owners included in Index)*

Financial Data: *Fiscal Year End:*12/31 *Latest Annual Data:* 12/31/2006

Year	Sales	Net Income
2006	$69,509,000	-$36,624,000
2005	$78,221,000	-$5,983,000
2004	$96,374,000	$259,000

Curr. Assets:	$47,341,000	**Curr. Liab.:**	$27,658,000		
Plant, Equip.:	$5,456,000	**Total Liab.:**	$102,259,000	**Indic. Yr. Divd.:**	NA
Total Assets:	$186,186,000	**Net Worth:**	$83,927,000	**Debt/ Equity:**	0.8228

Mikron Infrared Inc

16 Thornton Rd., Oakland, NJ, 07436; *PH:* 1-201-405-0900; *http://* www.mikroninst.com

General		Stock	
Incorporation	NJ	Price on:12/24/2007	NA
Employees	140	Stock Exchange	NDQ
Auditor	BDO Seidman LLP	Ticker Symbol	MIKR
Stk Agt	American Stock Transfer & Trust Co.	Outstanding Shares	NA
Counsel	NA	E.P.S	NA
DUNS No.	04-634-2564	Shareholders	NA

Business: The group's principal activities are to develop, manufacture, market and service equipment and instruments for non-contact temperature measurement. The products of the group are used to measure the temperature of moving objects or stationery objects and used in environment where contact temperature measurement would be difficult and it must be accurately tracked instantaneously. The group also manufactures high resolution thermal imaging products under the name pyrovision (R), calibration sources and a variety of accessories and optional equipment for infrared thermometers.

Primary SIC and add'l.: 3829 6794

CIK No: 0000787809

Subsidiaries: Mikron Europe, Mikron Europe GmbH

Officers: Gerald Posner/CEO, Paul Kohmescher/CFO, Dennis Stoneman/VP, Keikhosrow Irani/Dir., Founder, CTO

Directors: Lawrence C. Karlson/64/Chmn., Keikhosrow Irani/Dir., Founder, CTO, William J. Eckenrode/72/Dir., Henry M. Rowan/83/Dir., James L. Hamling/65/Dir.

Owners: Henry M. Rowan, James L. Hamling, Gerald D. Posner/6.80%, Dennis L. Stoneman/2.10%, Keikhosrow Irani/9.30%, Insiders/22.20%, William Eckenrode, Lawrence C. Karlson/2.30%, Glazer Capital, LLC and Paul J. Glazer/5.10%

Mikros Systems Corp

707 Alexander Rd. , Ste 208, Princeton, NJ, 08540; *PH:* 1-609-987-1513; *http://* www.mikros.us; *Email:* info@Mikros.us

General		Stock	
Incorporation	DE	Price on:12/24/2007	$0.6
Employees	5	Stock Exchange	OTC
Auditor	Beard Miller Co. LLP	Ticker Symbol	MKRS
Stk Agt	Continental Stock Transfer & Trust Co	Outstanding Shares	31,770,000
Counsel	NA	E.P.S	$0.01
DUNS No.	08-910-7643	Shareholders	NA

Business: The group's principal activities are to develop and supply radio data transmission and wireless technology products. The group has developed a business model for the AM technology. This model combines the AM data transmission technology with the operations of a nationwide or area wide network of AM radio stations equipped with the minor modifications to the radio station's transmitter. Data could be broadcast from point to multi-point based on the prototype being used in the group's experimental trials. The group operates in the United States.

Primary SIC and add'l.: 8731 3669 3812

CIK No: 0000317340

Officers: Thomas J. Meaney/Dir., CEO, CFO, Pres., Patricia A. Kapp/41/Sec., Treasurer, David C. Bryan/COO, Exec. VP, Chuck Bristow/VP - Engineering

Directors: Thomas J. Meaney/Dir., CEO, CFO, Pres., Wayne E. Meyer/Chmn., Thomas C. Lynch/Dir., Tom L. Schaffnit/Dir., Paul G. Casner/Dir.

Owners: JoAnne E. Burns/10.00%, Frederick C. Tecce/20.00%, Thomas J. Meaney/59.00%, George W. Taylor/10.00%, Princeton Valuation Consultants LLC/8.90%, Insiders/19.60%, Insiders/31.90%, Insiders/40.00%, Thomas J. Meaney/100.00%, Wayne E. Meyer/20.00%, Princeton Valuation Consultants,LLC/20.00%, Wayne E. Meyer/9.70%, Princeton Valuation Consultants LLC/79.40%, Thomas J. Meaney/16.50%, The Mercantile & General Reinsurance Company, PLC/8.30% (24 Owners included in Index)

Financial Data: Fiscal Year End:12/31　Latest Annual Data: 12/31/2006

Year	Sales		Net Income
2006	$2,275,000		$130,000
2005	$1,550,000		$135,000
2004	$1,044,000		$92,000
Curr. Assets:	$447,000	**Curr. Liab.:** $184,000	**P/E Ratio:** 60.00
Plant, Equip.:	$7,000	**Total Liab.:** $200,000	**Indic. Yr. Divd.:** NA
Total Assets:	$508,000	**Net Worth:** $227,000	**Debt/ Equity:** NA

Milacron Inc

2090 Florence Ave., Cincinnati, OH, 45206; *PH:* 1-513-487-5000; *Fax:* 1-513-487-5057; *http://* www.milacron.com; *Email:* info@milacron.com

General - Incorporation	DE	**Stock** - Price on:12/24/2007	$9.12
Employees	3,430	Stock Exchange	NYSE
Auditor	Ernst & Young LLP	Ticker Symbol	NA
Stk Agt	Mellon Investor Services LLC	Outstanding Shares	5,570,000
Counsel	NA	E.P.S.	-$6.78
DUNS No.	00-128-7812	Shareholders	NA

Business: The group's principal activities are to manufacture and distribute plastics processing equipment and supplies. It also blends and distributes industrial fluids for metalworking applications. The group operates in four segments: machinery technologies - North America; machinery technologies - Europe; mold technologies and industrial fluids. The first three segments provide plastics processors with technologically advanced products and services, machinery, tooling, parts and applications expertise required for plastic processing techniques. The fourth segment supplies industrial fluids, whose formulations meet many stringent performances, health and safety requirements of metalworking applications. The group has operations in the United States, Italy, Netherlands, Canada, Mexico, Germany, western Europe and Asia. In 2003, the group sold its round metalcutting tools business.

Primary SIC and add'l.: 3541 3229 3559 3542 3569

CIK No: 0000716823

Subsidiaries: 450500 Ontario Limited, Cimcool Europe B.V, Cimcool Industrial Products B.V, Cimcool Industrial Products Inc., Cincinnati Milacron IPK, Inc., Cincinnati Milacron Trading Co. Ltd., D-M-E Belgium CVBA, D-M-E China Ltd., D-M-E Company, D-M-E Manufacturing Inc., D-M-E Normalien GmbH, D-M-E of Canada Limited, D-M-E USA, EOC France S.A.R.L, EOC Normalien Praha s.r.o 57 Subsidiaries included in the Index

Officers: Ronald D. Brown/Chmn., CEO, Pres./$1,111,330.00, John C. Francy/VP, Treasurer, Robert C. Mckee/VP, Pres. - Global Industrial Fluids/$475,159.00, Ross A. Anderson/CFO, Sr. VP - Finance/$439,544.00, Bradley M. Baker/VP - Human Resources, Danny L. Gamez/Controller, Hugh C. O'Donnell/Sr. VP, General Counsel, Sec./$411,010.00, David E. Lawrence/VP, Pres. - Global Mold Technologies, Michael Ferlic/International Dir. - Latin America, All Lines, Machinery, Hercules Piazzo/Mgr. - Sales, SAO Paulo, Brazil, Injection Molding Machinery, Grant Jefferson/Contact - Canada, Injection Molding Machinery, Rich Smith/Mgr. - Sales, Mexico, Latin America, Canada, Blow Molding Machinery, Hans Steupert/Mgr. - Export Sales, Europe, Injection Molding Machinery, Herb Hutchison/Dir. - International Business Development, Europe, Extrusion Systems, Steve Jones/Mgr. - European Technical Sales, Marketing, Europe, Extrusion Systems (26 Officers included in Index)

Directors: Ronald D. Brown/Chmn., CEO, Pres., Sallie B. Bailey/Dir., Larry D. Yost/Dir., John P. Bolduc/Dir., John Caple/Dir., Steven N. Isaacs/Dir., Norman Cohen/Dir., Tiffany F. Kosch/Dir., Donald R. McIlnay/Dir., Lewis Schoenwetter/Dir., Eric Schneider/Dir., Mark L. Segal/Dir., Charles F.C. Turner/Dir.

Owners: Charles F. C. Turner, JPMorgan Chase Bank/PCS Shared Services/11.60%, Insiders/6.90%, Steven N. Isaacs/1.00%, Milacron Geier Foundation/6.50%, Mellon Trust of New England/18.50%, Pzena Investment Management, LLC/6.20%, Fine Capital Partners, L.P/5.00%, Donald R. McIlnay, Hugh C. ODonnell, Ore Hill Hub FundLtd./10.50%, Linden Capital L.P/7.40%, Goldman, Sachs& Co/13.70%, David J. Greene& Company, LLC/6.80%, Ross A. Anderson/1.10% (28 Owners included in Index)

Financial Data: Fiscal Year End:12/31　Latest Annual Data: 9/30/2007

Year	Sales		Net Income
2007	$203,700,000		-$4,500,000
2006	$820,100,000		-$39,700,000
2005	$808,900,000		-$14,000,000
Curr. Assets:	$365,600,000	**Curr. Liab.:** $212,500,000	
Plant, Equip.:	$114,300,000	**Total Liab.:** $671,800,000	**Indic. Yr. Divd.:** NA
Total Assets:	$650,500,000	**Net Worth:** -$21,300,000	**Debt/ Equity:** NA

Mile Marker International Inc

2121 Blount Rd., Pompano Beach, FL, 33069; *PH:* 1-954-782-0604; *Fax:* 1-954-782-0770; *http://* www.milemarker.com

General - Incorporation	FL	**Stock** - Price on:12/24/2007	NA
Employees	60	Stock Exchange	OTC
Auditor	Berenfeld Spritzer Shechter & Sheer	Ticker Symbol	MMRK
Stk Agt	Jersey Transfer & Trust Co	Outstanding Shares	NA
Counsel	NA	E.P.S.	-$0.11
DUNS No.	94-770-8285	Shareholders	NA

Business: The group's principal activities are to assemble and distribute specialized automobile parts for 4-wheel drive utility, recreational and military vehicle markets. The group distributes an innovative line of hydraulic winches used by the U.S. Military, owners of sport utility vehicles and light trucks and a line of hubs, which are components in four-wheel drive automobile transmission systems. It also assembles and markets unique hydraulic winches that use vehicle's power steering pump as the energy source as well as an electric drive full-time 4 wheel drive coupling device. The group sells full-line of locking wheel hubs conversion kits and related accessory items. The activities of the group are conducted through the wholly owned subsidiary, mile marker, inc. The group primarily operates in North America and Europe.

Primary SIC and add'l.: 6719 3714

CIK No: 0000930121

Subsidiaries: Mile Marker Automotive Electronics (ShenZhen), Ltd, Mile Marker West, Inc., Mile Marker, Inc.

Officers: Richard E. Aho/64/Chmn., CEO, Pres., Drew V. Aho/41/Dir., Exec. VP, Alvin A. Hirsch/64/CFO, Sec., Treasurer, Leslie J. Aho/51/Dir., Mgr. - Production

Directors: Richard E. Aho/64/Chmn., CEO, Pres., Drew V. Aho/41/Dir., Exec. VP, Leslie J. Aho/51/Dir., Mgr. - Production, George R. Shelley/77/Dir.

Owners: Alvin A. Hirsch, Leslie J. Aho, Drew V. Aho, Cede & Company, Richard E. Aho, George R. Shelley, Insiders

Financial Data: Fiscal Year End:12/31　Latest Annual Data: 12/31/2005

Year	Sales		Net Income
2005	$24,812,000		$3,178,000
2004	$23,336,000		$3,553,000
2003	$13,238,000		$1,316,000
Curr. Assets:	$10,047,000	**Curr. Liab.:** $6,578,000	
Plant, Equip.:	$2,153,000	**Total Liab.:** $6,687,000	**Indic. Yr. Divd.:** NA
Total Assets:	$12,378,000	**Net Worth:** $5,692,000	**Debt/ Equity:** NA

Milestone Scientific Inc

220 S Orange Ave., Livingston, NJ, 07039; *PH:* 1-973-535-2717; *Fax:* 1-973-535-2829; *http://* www.milesci.com; *Email:* info@milestonescientific.com

General - Incorporation	DE	**Stock** - Price on:12/24/2007	$1.95
Employees	15	Stock Exchange	OTC
Auditor	Eisner LLP	Ticker Symbol	MLSS
Stk Agt	Continental Stock Transfer & Trust Co	Outstanding Shares	11,700,000
Counsel	NA	E.P.S.	-$0.29
DUNS No.	00-689-1188	Shareholders	NA

Business: The group's principle activities are to develop, manufacture, market and sell Compudent(TM) computer controlled and precision metered local anesthetic injection systems and SafetyWand(TM) disposable handpieces. The group's products also include system kits, dental needles and prophy angles. The group's quarterly revenue for September 2007 was 1.16 millions of USD.

Primary SIC and add'l.: 5047 3843

CIK No: 0000855683

Officers: Leonard A. Osser/60/Chmn., CEO/$300,000.00, Eugene Casagrande/63/Dir. - Professional Relations, Mark Hochman/49/Dir. - Clinical Affairs, Malamed Hndbk/Dental Advisor, CRA, Reality, Thomas R. Ronca/61/COO, Pres./$203,814.00, David Cohn/56/CFO

Directors: Leonard A. Osser/60/Chmn., CEO, Leonard M. Schiller/66/Dir., Jeffrey Fuller/62/Dir., Leslie Bernhard/63/Dir., Pablo F. Serna C/32/Dir.

Owners: Pablo F. C. Serna, Jeffrey Fuller, Leslie Bernhard, Thomas R. Ronca, Insiders/16.14%, David Cohn, Tucker K. Andersen/13.75%, Leonard Osser/14.32%, Leonard M. Schiller

Financial Data: Fiscal Year End:12/31　Latest Annual Data: 12/31/2006

Year	Sales		Net Income
2006	$5,844,000		-$3,152,000
2005	$6,433,000		-$2,754,000
2004	$4,751,000		-$2,997,000
Curr. Assets:	$4,065,000	**Curr. Liab.:** $1,428,000	
Plant, Equip.:	$459,000	**Total Liab.:** $1,428,000	**Indic. Yr. Divd.:** NA
Total Assets:	$5,142,000	**Net Worth:** $3,713,000	**Debt/ Equity:** NA

Milk Bottle Cards Inc

2032 W 1ST Ave., Vancouver, BC, V6J 1G8; *PH:* 1-604-733-6194; *Fax:* 1-604-733-6195; *http://* www.milkbottlecards.com; *Email:* info@milkbottlecards.com

General - Incorporation	NV	**Stock** - Price on:12/24/2007	$0.26
Employees	NA	Stock Exchange	OTC
Auditor	Dale Matheson Carr-Hilton Labonte LLP	Ticker Symbol	MBTL
Stk Agt	Holladay Stock Transfer, Inc.	Outstanding Shares	NA
Counsel	NA	E.P.S.	NA
DUNS No.	NA	Shareholders	NA

Business: The groups principle activities include producing, distributing and marketing greeting cards. The group operates from the United States and Canada.

Primary SIC and add'l.: 2771

CIK No: 0001321516

Officers: Nicole Milkovich/35/Dir., CEO, Pres., Sec., Treasurer, CFO, Principal Accounting Officer, Carlos Bolbrugge/36/VP - Design

Directors: Nicole Milkovich/35/Dir., CEO, Pres., Sec., Treasurer, CFO, Principal Accounting Officer

Owners: Patrick Palmer, Jose Alonso, John A Britchford-Steel, Gina Palmer, Insiders, Palmer Trust, TWE International, LLC

Financial Data: Fiscal Year End:01/31　Latest Annual Data: 01/31/2007

Year	Sales		Net Income
2007	NA		-$12,000
2006	$0		-$13,000
Curr. Assets:	$7,000	**Curr. Liab.:** $3,000	
Plant, Equip.:	NA	**Total Liab.:** $3,000	**Indic. Yr. Divd.:** NA
Total Assets:	$7,000	**Net Worth:** $5,000	**Debt/ Equity:** NA

Millar Western Forest Products Ltd

Bag Service 2200, Edmonton, AB, T6E 5G8; *PH:* 1-780-486-8200; *http://* www.millarwestern.com; *Email:* mwfp@millarwestern.com

General - Incorporation	Canada	**Stock** - Price on:12/24/2007	NA
Employees	NA	Stock Exchange	NA
Auditor	PricewaterhouseCoopers LLP	Ticker Symbol	NA
Stk Agt	Coopers & Lybrand	Outstanding Shares	NA
Counsel	NA	E.P.S.	NA
DUNS No.	NA	Shareholders	NA

Business: The group's principle activity is to produce and market hardwood and softwood bleached chemi-thermo-mechanical pulp (bctmp) and softwood lumber. The company owns and operates three production facilities in the province of alberta. The bctmp mill and sawmill are located in whitecourt and a sawmill located in boyle. In addition, the company manages and markets all pulp produced by the

meadow lake pulp mill. The products of the company are hardwood, softwood and blended wood bctmp which are used in the production of printing and writing papers, tissue, toweling, boxboard and specialty papers. The sawmills produce lumber for residential and commercial construction industries, which are sold in Canada and the United States.

Primary SIC and add'l.: 2610 2621 5211

CIK No: 0001064408

Officers: Mackenzie H. Millar/Dir., CEO, Pres., Kevin Edgson/CFO, Joe Costantino/Sr. VP - Lumber, Craig J. Armstrong/COO, Exec. VP, Robert J. Turner/Dir., Sec., General Counsel, David Anderson/Mgr. - Lumber Sales, Steve Lord/Dir. - Pulp Sales, Marketing, Carol Cotton/Sr. VP, Ronald J. Reis/Sr. VP - Pulp, Jack Joys/Dir. - Energy, Procurement, Purchasing, Wendy Boucher/Purchasing Mgr., Mgr. - Materials Management, Dave Martell/Mill Mgr. - Whitecourt Pulp, David M. Keir/VP - Human Resources, Janet Millar/Dir. - Communications, Trevor Wakelin/Dir. - Fibre Resources, Operations *(23 Officers included in Index)*

Directors: Mackenzie H. Millar/Dir., CEO, Pres., James B. Millar/Chmn., W. K. Davidson/Dir., Doug Hall/Dir., William D. Grace/Dir., Robert J. Turner/Dir., Sec., General Counsel, Don Ching/Dir.

Millea Holdings Inc

Tokyo Kaijo Nichido Bldg Shinkan 9f, 1-2-1 Marunouchi, Chiyoda-Ku, Tokyo; ;
http:// www.millea.co.jp; *Email:* ir@millea.co.jp

General		Stock	
Incorporation	Japan	Price on:12/24/2007	$41.79
Employees	19,761	Stock Exchange	OTC
Auditor	Chuoaoyama PricewaterhouseCoopers	Ticker Symbol	MLEAY
Stk Agt	Mitsubishi UFJ Trust & Banking Corp	Outstanding Shares	823,340,000
Counsel	NA	E.P.S	$0.91
DUNS No.	NA	Shareholders	NA

Business: The group's principle activity is the provision of non-life and life insurances including fire, marine, personal accidents, voluntary automobile and compulsory automobile liability. Operations are carried out through the following divisions: non-life (non-life insurance, related investment); life (life insurance, related investment); other operations (investment management, security investment trust, derivatives, personnel supply services). At 31-Mar-2003 the group consisted of the parent company, which is a pure holding company established by its now wholly-owned subsidiaries tokio marine & fire insurance co ltd and nichido fire & marine insurance co ltd in Apr 2002, six domestic consolidated subsidiaries, nine overseas subsidiaries and a Hawaii-based associated company.

Primary SIC and add'l.: 6311 6331 6719

CIK No: 0001169486

Subsidiaries: Real Seguros S.A., The Tokio Marine and Fire Insurance Company (Hong Kong) Limited, The Tokio Marine and Fire Insurance Company (Singapore) Pte. Limited, Tokio Marine Asia Pte. Ltd., Tokio Marine Asset Management Company, Limited, Tokio Marine Brasil Seguradora S.A., Tokio Marine Europe Insurance Limited, Tokio Marine Financial Solutions Ltd., Tokio Marine Global Limited, Tokio Marine Global Re Limited, Tokio Marine& Nichido Career Service Co., Ltd., Tokio Marine& Nichido Facilities, Inc., Tokio Marine& Nichido Financial Life Co., Ltd., Tokio Marine& Nichido Fire Insurance Co., Ltd., Tokio Marine& Nichido Life Insurance Co., Ltd. 17 Subsidiaries included in the Index

Officers: Toshiro Yagi/Dir., Exec. VP, Tetsuo Kamioka/Dir., Standing Corporate Auditor, Shigemitsu Miki/Dir., Corporate Auditor, Hiroshi Fukuda/Dir., Corporate Auditor, Yuko Kawamoto/Dir., Corporate Auditor, Shuzo Sumi/Dir., Pres., Shin-Ichiro Okada/MD, Hiroshi Mitsunaga/MD, Yasuo Yaoita/Dir., Standing Corporate Auditor

Directors: Kunio Ishihara/Chmn., Toshiro Yagi/Dir., Exec. VP, Masamitsu Sakurai/Dir., Haruo Shimada/Dir., Tomochika Iwashita/Dir., Hiroshi Amemiya/Dir., Hiroshi Miyajima/Dir., Takaaki Tamai/Dir., Tetsuo Kamioka/Dir., Standing Corporate Auditor, Shigemitsu Miki/Dir., Corporate Auditor, Hiroshi Fukuda/Dir., Corporate Auditor, Yuko Kawamoto/Dir., Corporate Auditor, Shuzo Sumi/Dir., Pres., Minoru Makihara/Dir., Yasuo Yaoita/Dir., Standing Corporate Auditor

Owners: The Master Trust Bank of Japan, Ltd./6.90%, Meiji Yasuda Life Insurance Company/2.30%, The Chase Manhattan Bank N.A. London/1.50%, Japan Trustee Services Bank, Ltd./5.90%, Trust& Custody Services Bank, Ltd./1.70%, The Bank of Tokyo-Mitsubishi UFJ, Ltd./2.40%, State Street Bank and Trust Company 505103/2.00%, State Street Bank and Trust Company/3.20%, Mizuho Corporate Bank, Ltd./1.60%, Moxley& Co./5.30%

Financial Data: *Fiscal Year End:* 03/31 *Latest Annual Data:* 3/31/2006

Year	Sales	Net Income
2006	$22,403,323,000	$1,334,160,000
2005	$22,404,602,000	$855,219,000
2004	$20,838,877,000	$977,379,000

Curr. Assets:	$18,555,569,000	**Curr. Liab.:**	$31,441,934,000	**P/E Ratio:**	21.92
Plant, Equip.:	$1,596,411,000	**Total Liab.:**	$94,144,929,000	**Indic. Yr. Divd.:**	$0.230
Total Assets:	$131,886,995,000	**Net Worth:**	$37,742,066,000	**Debt/ Equity:**	NA

Millenia Hope Inc

4055 St., Catherine W, Ste. 151, Montreal, QC, H3Z 3J8; *PH:* 1-514-846-5757;
http:// www.milleniahope.com; *Email:* admin@milleniahope.com

General		Stock	
Incorporation	DE	Price on:12/24/2007	NA
Employees	NA	Stock Exchange	OTC
Auditor	Stark Winter Schenkein & Co. LLP	Ticker Symbol	MLHP
Stk Agt	I'Continental Reg & Trnsfer Agency	Outstanding Shares	NA
Counsel	NA	E.P.S	NA
DUNS No.	NA	Shareholders	NA

Business: The group's principal activity is to develop and distribute an anti-malarial drug called malarex (formerly known as aspidos). Malarex is produced in two forms, capsules and injectables. It has had successful tests in the treatment and prevention of malaria and is continuing with further ongoing tests to allow it to receive final approval for consumer usage. The group acquired the rights to another anti-material agent, strychnos mytroides. The group is also engaged in developing and marketing an interactive knowledge based application system combined with intelligent agents in order to sort, create and transact medical data.

Primary SIC and add'l.: 2834 8731 7375

CIK No: 0001060827

Subsidiaries: MHB, Millenia Hope Inc Canadian, Millenia Hope Pharmaceuticals Ltd, Sword Comp-Soft Corp

Officers: Leonard Stella/Chmn., CEO, Yehuda Kops/Dir., COO, Joseph Daniele/Dir., Chief Legal Advisor, Bahige Baroudy/Pres., Chief Scientific Officer, Member - Scientific Advisory Board, Soriba Cisse/VP - Research - Development, Member - Scientific Advisory Board, Jeffrey Brooks/VP - Operations, Manufacturing, Jacky Quan/Dir., Exec. VP, Treasurer, Hugo Valente/Dir., Sr. VP, CFO, Adboulaye Bah/Member - Scientific Advisory Board

Directors: Leonard Stella/Chmn., CEO, Yehuda Kops/Dir., COO, Jacky Quan/Dir., Exec. VP, Treasurer, Hugo Valente/Dir., Sr. VP, CFO, Joseph Daniele/Dir., Chief Legal Advisor, Bahige Baroudy/Pres., Chief Scientific Officer, Member - Scientific Advisory Board, Abel Namsemmo/Member - Scientific Advisory Board, Albert Same-Ekobo/Member - Scientific Advisory Board, Jean Pierre Willem/Member - Scientific Advisory Board, Max Koula/Member - Scientific Advisory Board, Wilfred Sylvain Nambei/Member - Scientific Advisory Board

Owners: Jacky Quan/3.12%, Yehuda Kops/3.94%, Insiders/17.61%, Hugo Valente/1.78%, Joseph Daniele/1.76%, Bahige Baroudy, Leonard Stella/6.20%

Financial Data: *Fiscal Year End:* 11/30 *Latest Annual Data:* 11/30/2006

Year	Sales	Net Income
2006	$624,000	-$8,105,000
2005	$260,000	-$7,289,000
2004	NA	-$2,774,000

Curr. Assets:	$438,000	**Curr. Liab.:**	$1,567,000		
Plant, Equip.:	$646,000	**Total Liab.:**	$3,362,000	**Indic. Yr. Divd.:**	NA
Total Assets:	$1,084,000	**Net Worth:**	-$2,278,000	**Debt/ Equity:**	NA

Millenium Holding Group Inc

12 Winding Rd. , Henderson, NV, 89052; *PH:* 1-702-492-7721; *http://* www.mnhginc.com

General		Stock	
Incorporation	NV	Price on:12/24/2007	NA
Employees	2	Stock Exchange	OTC
Auditor	Mendoza Berger & Co LLP	Ticker Symbol	MNHGE
Stk Agt	Computershare Trust Co	Outstanding Shares	NA
Counsel	NA	E.P.S	-$0.03
DUNS No.	NA	Shareholders	NA

Business: The group is development stage company providing financial services. Incorporated on Dec 22, 1969 under the name amex systems corporation for the purpose of merging other corporations together to achieve savings from consolidations.

Primary SIC and add'l.: 6159

CIK No: 0001100674

Subsidiaries: FYNRE

Officers: Richard L. Ham/Dir., CEO, CFO, Pres., Carla Aufdenkamp/45/Dir., VP, Sec.

Directors: Richard L. Ham/Dir., CEO, CFO, Pres., Carla Aufdenkamp/45/Dir., VP, Sec.

Owners: Dennis Eliassen/8.90%, Insiders/56.00%, Ham Consulting Company/9.70%, Richard L. Ham/46.30%

Financial Data: *Fiscal Year End:* 12/31 *Latest Annual Data:* 12/31/2006

Year	Sales	Net Income
2006	$140,740,000	-$9,531,000
2005	$130,493,000	-$2,182,000
2004	$113,785,000	-$30,413,000

Millennium Bankshares Corp

1601 Washington Plz., Reston, VA, 20190; *PH:* 1-703-464-0100; *Fax:* 1-703-464-0064;
http:// www.millenniumbankshares.com; *Email:* ir@millenniumbankshares.com

General		Stock	
Incorporation	VA	Price on:12/24/2007	$8.76
Employees	78	Stock Exchange	NDQ
Auditor	Crowe Chizek & Co. LLC	Ticker Symbol	MBVA
Stk Agt	EquiServe Trust Co.	Outstanding Shares	8,930,000
Counsel	NA	E.P.S	-$0.2
DUNS No.	NA	Shareholders	NA

Business: The group's principal activities are to provide commercial, retail and consumer banking services to individuals, small and medium sized businesses. The group provides variety of deposits, which includes demand, savings, time deposits and now accounts. Advances provided include mortgage loans, commercial real estate, construction and land, commercial business and consumer loans. It also provides investment services and products to bank customers and the professional community. At 31-Dec-2003, it operated through 6 offices in reston, great falls, herndon, colonial heights and richmond, Virginia

Primary SIC and add'l.: 6021 6712

CIK No: 0001158678

Subsidiaries: Millennium Bank Mortgage, LLC, Millennium Bank, National Association, Millennium Brokerage Services, Inc., Millennium Capital Trust I, Millennium Capital, Inc., Millennium Financial, Inc., Millennium Hyland Mortgage, LLC, Millennium Sunbelt Mortgage, LLC

Officers: Richard I. Linhart/64/Dir., CEO, Pres., John F. Novak/COO, Exec. VP, Barbara J. Chapman/Corp. Sec., Dale G. Phelps/52/CFO, Exec. VP/$187,177.00

Directors: Richard I. Linhart/64/Dir., CEO, Pres., Robert T. Smoot/57/Chmn., Joseph W. Paulini/53/Dir., William P. Haggerty/62/Dir., David M.W. Harvey/51/Dir., James W. Wolfe/52/Dir., Grayson P. Hanes/70/Dir., David B. Morey/60/Dir.

Owners: David M.W. Harvey/6.10%, Dale G. Phelps, Carroll C. Markley/5.20%, Anita L. Shull, Arthur J. Novick/1.00%, Robert T. Smoot/1.00%, Grayson P. Hanes, David B. Morey, Insiders/18.30%, Barbara Wortley/8.50%, Randall F. Kinoshita/6.10%, Joseph W. Paulini, William P. Haggerty

Financial Data: *Fiscal Year End:* 12/31 *Latest Annual Data:* 12/31/2006

Year	Sales	Net Income
2006	$30,636,000	-$481,000
2005	$33,671,000	$1,634,000
2004	$26,435,000	$2,009,000

Curr. Assets:	$61,878,000	**Curr. Liab.:**	$535,990,000		
Plant, Equip.:	$2,029,000	**Total Liab.:**	$543,990,000	**Indic. Yr. Divd.:**	$0.080
Total Assets:	$591,542,000	**Net Worth:**	$47,552,000	**Debt/ Equity:**	0.1651

Millennium Biotechnologies Group Inc

665 Martinsville Rd. , Ste 219, Basking Ridge, NJ, 07920; *PH:* 1-908-604-2500;
http:// www.milbiotech.com; *Email:* info@milbiotech.com

General		Stock	
Incorporation	DE	Price on:12/24/2007	$0.18
Employees	9	Stock Exchange	OTC
Auditor	Bagell, Josephs, Levine & Co. LLC	Ticker Symbol	MBTG
Stk Agt	American Stock Transfer & Trust Co.	Outstanding Shares	77,890,000
Counsel	NA	E.P.S	-$0.21
DUNS No.	07-329-9307	Shareholders	NA

Business: The group's principal activity is to provide nutritional adjunct to the medical treatment for chronic immuno-compromising debilitating diseases like acquired immune deficiency syndrome, hepatitis and cancer. The group is a research based bio-nutraceutical corporation in the field of nutritional science. The group developed two novel enteral nutritional formulas resurgex(R) and resurgex plus(tm), which plays an important role as a nutritional adjunct to the medical treatment for certain chronic immuno-compromising debilitating diseases. The resurgex(R) and resurgex plus(tm) have been formulated to address the loss of lean muscle, nutrient depletion, immune support, mitochondrial dysfunction and oxidative stress in individuals, undergoing medical treatment for chronic immuno-compromised medical conditions.

Primary SIC and add'l.: 8731 6719 2834

CIK No: 0000072170

Subsidiaries: Millennium Biotechnologies, Inc.

Officers: Jerry E. Swon/57/Chmn., CEO, Pres., Frank Guarino/32/CFO, Carl Germano/52/Exec. VP - Research, Product Development

Directors: Jerry E. Swon/57/Chmn., CEO, Pres., Michael G. Martin/55/Dir., David Sargoy/47/Dir.

Owners: Jerry E. Swon/2.70%, David Sargoy/0.70%, Insiders/8.50%, Michael G. Martin/0.70%, Carl Germano/3.00%, Jane Swon/4.80%, Frank Guarino/1.30%

Financial Data: *Fiscal Year End:*12/31 *Latest Annual Data:* 12/31/2006

Year	Sales	Net Income
2006	$823,000	-$13,687,000
2005	$798,000	-$6,949,000
2004	$1,083,000	-$5,399,000

Curr. Assets:	$445,000	**Curr. Liab.:**	$9,605,000		
Plant, Equip.:	$10,000	**Total Liab.:**	$9,620,000	**Indic. Yr. Divd.:**	NA
Total Assets:	$482,000	**Net Worth:**	-$9,139,000	**Debt/ Equity:**	NA

Millennium Cell Inc

1 Industrial Way W, Eatontown, NJ, 07724; *PH:* 1-732-542-4000; *Fax:* 1-732-542-4010; *http://* www.millenniumcell.com

General - Incorporation	DE	**Stock**- Price on:12/24/2007	$0.65
Employees	39	Stock Exchange	NDQ
Auditor	Ernst & Young LLP	Ticker Symbol	MCEL
Stk Agt	American Stock Transfer & Trust Co.	Outstanding Shares	55,010,000
Counsel	Dickstein Shapiro M & O LLP	E.P.S	-$0.21
DUNS No.	NA	Shareholders	NA

Business: The group's principal activity is to develop innovative fuel systems for the safe storage, transportation and generation of hydrogen for use as an energy source. It has developed and applied for patents for a proprietary process called Hydrogen on Demand(tm) that safely generates hydrogen from environmentally friendly raw materials. The technology developed by the group can be used to generate hydrogen for use by fuel cells in the production of electricity, generate hydrogen for use by modified internal combustion engines and provide hydrogen for other industrial purposes. The group has also designed and produced prototype direct fuel cells and batteries that utilize the sodium borohydride process to provide electricity for the portable and stationary power markets.

Primary SIC and add'l.: 3629 8732 5169 2899

CIK No: 0001114872

Subsidiaries: MCE Ventures LLC.

Officers: David H. Ramm/Dir., CEO/$263,000.00, John V. Battaglini/VP - Sales, Marketing, Product Management/$236,396.00, Adam P. Briggs/Pres./$496,719.00, Rex E. Luzader/VP - Government Relations/$309,828.00, George C. Zalepa/VP - Administration, John D. Giolli/CFO, Corp. Sec./$250,388.00

Directors: David H. Ramm/Dir., CEO, L. J. Evans/Dir., Alexander MacLachlan/Dir., Chris G. Andersen/Dir., Kenneth R. Baker/Dir., Peter A. McGuigan/Dir., Zoltan Merszei/Dir., James L. Rawlings/Dir., Hideo Ito/Dir.

Owners: Gemini Master Fund Ltd./7.40%, JGB Capital L.P./2.30%, James L. Rawlings, Portside Growth & Opportunity Fund/4.99%, L. J. Evans, Rex E. Luzader, Portside Growth & Opportunity Fund/47.40%, Zoltan Merszei, Peter A. McGuigan, David H. Ramm, John V. Battaglini, Kenneth R. Baker, The Dow Chemical Company/100.00%, John D. Giolli, Iroquois Master Fund Ltd./26.40% *(25 Owners included in Index)*

Financial Data: *Fiscal Year End:*12/31 *Latest Annual Data:* 12/31/2006

Year	Sales	Net Income
2006	$222,000	-$12,271,000
2005	$417,000	-$14,600,000
2004	$198,000	-$10,805,000

Curr. Assets:	$5,357,000	**Curr. Liab.:**	$4,418,000		
Plant, Equip.:	$307,000	**Total Liab.:**	$4,561,000	**Indic. Yr. Divd.:**	NA
Total Assets:	$9,867,000	**Net Worth:**	$2,950,000	**Debt/ Equity:**	2.8009

Millennium Pharmaceuticals Inc

40 Landsdowne St., Cambridge, MA, 02139; *PH:* 1-617-679-7000; *Fax:* 1-617-374-7788; *http://* www.mlnm.com; *Email:* info@mlnm.com

General - Incorporation	DE	**Stock**- Price on:12/24/2007	$10.36
Employees	947	Stock Exchange	NDQ
Auditor	Ernst & Young LLP	Ticker Symbol	NA
Stk Agt	EquiServe Trust Co N.A	Outstanding Shares	321,120,000
Counsel	Wilmer Cutler Pickering H & D LLP	E.P.S	-$0.06
DUNS No.	80-417-8757	Shareholders	NA

Business: The group's principal activity is the development and commercialisation of proprietary therapeutic products. The research and development activities are focused on the disease areas of cancer, cardiovascular disease and inflammatory disease. The group's commercial drugs include integrilin, for the treatment of patients with acute coronary syndromes and velcade, for treatment of patients with relapsed and refractory multiple myeloma, a form of bone marrow cancer. The trademarks include millenium (R), millennium pharmaceuticals tm, velcade tm, integrilin (r). The group has international operations in the United Kingdom and Bermuda.

Primary SIC and add'l.: 8731 2834

CIK No: 0001002637

Subsidiaries: Millennium Pharmaceuticals Research and Development, Ltd., Millennium Pharmaceuticals, Ltd.

Officers: Deborah Dunsire/CEO, Pres./$3,874,464.00, Christophe Bianchi/Exec. VP - Commercial Operations/$1,509,385.00, Robert Tepper/52/Pres. - Research, Development/$1,891,566.00, Marsha Fanucci/CFO, Sr. VP/$1,855,599.00, Stephen M. Gansler/Sr. VP - Human Resources, Laurie Bartlett Keating/Sr. VP, General Counsel/$1,286,721.00, Anna Protopapas/Sr. VP - Corporate Development, Joel Goldberg/Chief Compliance Officer, Kyle Kuvalanka/Dir. - Investor Relations, Joseph B. Bolen/Chief Scientific Officer, Nancy Simonian/Chief Medical Officer - Clinical, Medical, Regulatory Affairs, Peter F. Smith/Sr. VP - Non - Clinical Development Sciences, Michael Eging/VP - Government Relations

Directors: Kenneth E. Weg/Chmn., Norman C. Selby/Dir., Mark J. Levin/Dir., Robert F. Friel/Dir., Grant A. Heidrich/Dir., Charles J. Homcy/Dir., Raju S. Kucherlapati/Dir., Anthony Wild/Dir.

Owners: Mark J. Levin/1.50%, Deborah Dunsire, Norman C. Selby, Capital Group International, Inc./7.60%, Raju S. Kucherlapati, Robert F. Friel, ClearBridge Advisors, LLC/10.90%, Christophe Bianchi, Laurie B. Keating, Charles J. Homcy, Insiders/3.50%, Grant A. Heidrich, Kenneth E. Weg, Eric S. Lander, Robert I. Tepper *(20 Owners included in Index)*

Financial Data: *Fiscal Year End:*12/31 *Latest Annual Data:* 12/31/2006

Year	Sales	Net Income
2006	$486,830,000	-$43,953,000
2005	$558,308,000	-$198,249,000
2004	$448,206,000	-$252,297,000

Curr. Assets:	$1,015,654,000	**Curr. Liab.:**	$225,519,000		
Plant, Equip.:	$153,349,000	**Total Liab.:**	$606,635,000	**Indic. Yr. Divd.:**	NA
Total Assets:	$2,751,812,000	**Net Worth:**	$2,145,177,000	**Debt/ Equity:**	0.1508

Miller Diversified Corp

23360 Weld County Rd. , Ste. 35, La Salle, CO, 80645; *PH:* 1-970-284-5556

General - Incorporation	NV	**Stock**- Price on:12/24/2007	$0.07
Employees	NA	Stock Exchange	OTC
Auditor	Comiskey & Co. P.C	Ticker Symbol	MILR
Stk Agt	Interwest Transfer Company, Inc.	Outstanding Shares	NA
Counsel	NA	E.P.S	NA
DUNS No.	19-412-8070	Shareholders	NA

Business: The group's principal activity is cattle feeding. The group sells feed and provides services to customers who place their cattle in the group's feedlot as well as feeding cattle for its own account. The group provides complete feedlot services which include assisting customers with outside financing, purchasing feeder cattle, making trucking arrangements, selling finished cattle, and assisting with hedging transactions. The group, through its subsidiary, derives commissions and fees from buying and selling customers' cattle. The major customers of the group include charles micale dba my way land & cattle.

Primary SIC and add'l.: 0211

CIK No: 0000844856

Financial Data: *Fiscal Year End:*08/31 *Latest Annual Data:* 8/31/2002

Year	Sales	Net Income
2002	$11,421,000	-$310,000
2001	$14,639,000	-$58,000
2000	$12,009,000	-$117,000

Curr. Assets:	$4,200,000	**Curr. Liab.:**	$3,383,000		
Plant, Equip.:	$932,000	**Total Liab.:**	$4,328,000	**Indic. Yr. Divd.:**	NA
Total Assets:	$5,794,000	**Net Worth:**	$1,467,000	**Debt/ Equity:**	0.6756

Miller Industries Inc

8503 Hilltop Dr., Ooltewah, TN, 37363; *PH:* 1-423-238-4171; *Fax:* 1-423-238-5371; *http://* www.millerind.com; *Email:* sales@millerind.com

General - Incorporation	TN	**Stock**- Price on:12/24/2007	$25.33
Employees	1,000	Stock Exchange	NYSE
Auditor	Joseph Decosimo & Co. PLLC	Ticker Symbol	MLR
Stk Agt	Registrar & Transfer Co	Outstanding Shares	11,540,000
Counsel	Kilpatrick Stockton	E.P.S	$3.53
DUNS No.	00-862-3969	Shareholders	NA

Business: The group's principal activities are to manufacture a broad range of towing and recovery equipment products. The group manufactures the bodies of wreckers, car carriers and trailers which are installed on truck chassis manufactured by third parties. The brand names of the group include century, challenger, holmes, champion, eagle, jige, boniface, vulcan, and chevron. The manufacturing facilities are located in the United States, France and England. The group has a customer base consisting of 175 distributors in North America, serving 50 states in Canada and Mexico and 50 distributors serving other foreign markets. As of 31-12-2003, the group disposed of roadone terminals and three distributors.

Primary SIC and add'l.: 7549 3713

CIK No: 0000924822

Subsidiaries: 407664 British Columbia Ltd., AETEX, Inc., All American Towing Services, Inc., APACO, Inc., B&B Associated Industries, Inc., B-G Towing, Inc., BASIEX, Inc., BBSX, Inc., Bear Transportation, Inc., Boniface Engineering, Ltd., BTRCX, Inc., BTRX, Inc., Cal West Towing, Inc., CBTX, Inc., CCASX, Inc. 62 Subsidiaries included in the Index

Officers: William G. Miller/61/Chmn., Co - CEO/$180,007.00, Jeffrey I. Badgley/56/Dir., Co - CEO, Pres./$447,961.00, Vincent J. Mish/57/Exec. VP, CFO, Pres. - Financial Services Group/$262,700.00, Frank Madonia/59/Exec. VP, Sec., General Counsel/$276,025.00

Directors: William G. Miller/61/Chmn., Co - CEO, Jeffrey I. Badgley/56/Dir., Co - CEO, Pres., Russell A. Chandler/63/Dir., Richard H. Roberts/53/Dir., Paul E. Drack/79/Dir.

Owners: Wellington Management Company, LLC/6.34%, Frank Madonia, Jeffrey I. Badgley, Paul E. Drack, Ashford Capital Management, Inc./13.82%, Richard H. Roberts, Hotchkiss and Wiley Capital Management, LLC/11.14%, J. Vincent Mish, Scopia Management Inc./7.14%, William G. Miller/11.97%, A. Russell Chandler/1.02%, Insiders/13.96%

Financial Data: *Fiscal Year End:*12/31 *Latest Annual Data:* 12/31/2006

Year	Sales	Net Income
2006	$22,384,000	$45,343,000
2005	$9,552,000	$18,586,000
2004	$348,905,000	$5,475,000

Curr. Assets:	$149,778,000	**Curr. Liab.:**	$73,512,000	**P/E Ratio:**	6.67
Plant, Equip.:	$27,527,000	**Total Liab.:**	$84,049,000	**Indic. Yr. Divd.:**	NA
Total Assets:	$197,432,000	**Net Worth:**	$113,383,000	**Debt/ Equity:**	0.0929

Miller Petroleum Inc

3651 Baker Hwy., Huntsville, TN, 37756; *PH:* 1-423-663-9457; *Fax:* 1-423-663-9461; *http://* www.millerpetroleum.com

General - Incorporation	TN	Stock- Price on:12/24/2007	$0.31
Employees	15	Stock Exchange	OTC
Auditor	Rodefer Moss & Co, PLLC	Ticker Symbol	MILL
Stk Agt	Interwest Transfer Company, Inc.	Outstanding Shares	14,370,000
Counsel	NA	E.P.S.	NA
DUNS No.	NA	Shareholders	NA

Business: The groups principle activities include exploring, developing, producing and acquiring crude oil and natural gas. The group operates from the United States and Canada.

Primary SIC and add'l.: 1311

CIK No: 0000785968

Subsidiaries: MPC, Inc.

Officers: Deloy Miller/Founder, Chmn., CEO, Ernie Payne/Pres., Gary Bible/VP - Geology, Teresa Cotton/Sec., Treasurer, David Wright/Land Mgr. - Miller, Herb White/Development Engineer

Directors: Deloy Miller/Founder, Chmn., CEO

Owners: Charles M. Stivers, Wind City Oil & Gas LLC/20.18%, Prospect Energy Corporation/11.69%, Insiders/34.90%, Deloy Miller/28.50%, Ernest Payne/4.20%, Herman E. Gettelfinger/2.40%

Curr. Assets:	$371,000	Curr. Liab.:	$793,000		
Plant, Equip.:	$3,309,000	Total Liab.:	$5,470,000	Indic. Yr. Divd.:	NA
Total Assets:	$4,564,000	Net Worth:	-$906,000	Debt/ Equity:	NA

Millicom International Cellular

15 rue Leon Laval, L-3372 Leudelange, Bertrange; *PH:* 352-27759101; *Fax:* 352-27759359; *http://* www.millicom.com

General - Incorporation	Luxembourg	Stock- Price on:12/24/2007	$92
Employees	3,243	Stock Exchange	NDQ
Auditor	PricewaterhouseCoopers LLP	Ticker Symbol	MIDD
Stk Agt	Morgan ADR Service Center	Outstanding Shares	100,850,000
Counsel	NA	E.P.S.	$6.08
DUNS No.	40-061-9367	Shareholders	NA

Business: The group is a major developer and operator of cellular telephone systems. It develops and operates cellular telephone networks throughout the world, especially in developing countries where the telephone service is often inadequate, such as Latin America, Africa and Asia. It is present in more than 20 countries. There were 3,366,551 subscribers in 2001.

Primary SIC and add'l.: 4813 3663 5065

CIK No: 0000912958

Subsidiaries: Motorola, Inc, Telefonica Celullar S.A

Officers: Marc Beuls/Presidant, CEO, Mario Zanotti/Cluster GM - Central America, Mikael Grahne/COO, Iain Williams/Cluster GM - Africa, Won-Suck Song/Cluster GM - South Asia, Ricardo Maiztegui/Cluster GM - South America, Judy Tan/Cluster GM - South East Asia, David Sach/CFO

Directors: Daniel Johannesson/65/Non Exec. Chmn., Donna Cordner/Non Exec. Dir., Michel Massart/Non Exec. Dir., Cristina Stenbeck/Non Exec. Dir., Kent Atkinson/63/Dir., Mia Brunell/43/Dir.

Owners: The Stenbeck Family/2.00%, Investment AB Kinnevik/37.60%

Financial Data: *Fiscal Year End:*12/31 *Latest Annual Data:* 12/31/2006

Year		Sales			Net Income
2006		$1,576,100,000			$230,670,000
2005		$1,083,669,000			$82,329,000
2004		$1,009,777,000			$188,871,000
Curr. Assets:	$1,209,451,000	Curr. Liab.:	$988,757,000	P/E Ratio:	21.92
Plant, Equip.:	$1,819,380,000	Total Liab.:	$3,193,346,000	Indic. Yr. Divd.:	NA
Total Assets:	$3,682,590,000	Net Worth:	$489,244,000	Debt/ Equity:	NA

Millipore Corp

290 Concord Rd., Billerica, MA, 01821; *PH:* 1-978-715-4321; *Fax:* 1-800-645-5439; *http://* www.millipore.com

General - Incorporation	MA	Stock- Price on:12/24/2007	$76.63
Employees	6,100	Stock Exchange	NYSE
Auditor	PricewaterhouseCoopers LLP	Ticker Symbol	MIL
Stk Agt	American Stock Transfer & Trust CO.	Outstanding Shares	53,980,000
Counsel	NA	E.P.S.	$1.62
DUNS No.	00-105-0152	Shareholders	NA

Business: The group's principal activities are to provide technologies, tools and services for the discovery, development and production of therapeutic drugs. The group markets consumables products, hardware products and services. The consumable products include handheld laboratory sample preparation and screening devices and kits in various low and high throughput formats, specialty membranes, chromatography media and large process scale cartridges used to filter thousands of liters of fluid. The hardware products include products ranging from small benchtop laboratory water purification systems and cartridge integrity testers to large stainless steel process scale filtration and chromatography systems. The services include field services for the maintenance of laboratory water systems and validation services offered to biopharmaceutical customers. The group operates in the United States, Europe, Japan and other Asia-Pacific regions.

Primary SIC and add'l.: 3826 3845 3823 3589

CIK No: 0000066479

Subsidiaries: Amicon Ltd., Bioprocessing Corporation Limited, Bioprocessing Limited, MicroSafe B.V., Millilux S.a.r.L., Millipart S.a.r.L., Millipore (Canada) Ltd., Millipore (Shanghai) Trading Company Ltd., Millipore (U.K.) Ltd., Millipore A/S, Millipore AB, Millipore AG, Millipore AS, Millipore Asia Ltd., Millipore Australia Pty. Ltd. 50 Subsidiaries included in the Index

Officers: Martin D. Madaus/Chmn., CEO, Pres./$2,946,642.00, Gregory J. Sam/Corporate VP - Quality, Jeffrey Rudin/Corporate VP, General Counsel, Sec./$945,408.00, Jean-Paul Mangeolle/Pres. - Bioprocess Division/$1,008,525.00, Peter C. Kershaw/Corporate VP - Global Supply Chain, Dominique F. Baly/Pres. - Bioscience Division/$1,138,182.00, Kathleen B. Allen/VP/$1,152,486.00, Charles F. Wagner/CFO, Corporate VP, Bruce Bonnevier/Corporate VP - Global Human Resources, Dennis Harris/Corporate VP, Chief Scientific Officer, Geoffrey Ide/Corporate VP - International Markets

Directors: Martin D. Madaus/Chmn., CEO, Pres., Karen E. Welke/Dir., Daniel Bellus/Dir., Melvin D. Booth/Dir., Edward M. Scolnick/Dir., John F. Reno/Dir., Maureen A. Hendricks/Dir., Mark Hoffman/Dir., Robert C. Bishop/Dir., Rolf Classon/Dir.

Owners: FMR CORP./10.66%, Jean-Paul Mangeolle, Kathleen B. Allen, PRIMECAP MANAGEMENT COMPANY/11.56%, Melvin D. Booth, Karen E. Welke, Edward M. Scolnick, Insiders, AMVESCAP PLC/5.60%, CRAMER ROSENTHAL MCGLYNN LLC/5.77%, John F. Reno, Jeffrey Rudin, SELECT EQUITY GROUP INC./10.14%, Daniel Bellus, Martin D. Madaus *(21 Owners included in Index)*

Financial Data: *Fiscal Year End:*12/31 *Latest Annual Data:* 12/31/2006

Year		Sales			Net Income
2006		$1,255,371,000			$96,984,000
2005		$991,031,000			$80,168,000
2004		$883,263,000			$105,556,000
Curr. Assets:	$709,355,000	Curr. Liab.:	$401,830,000	P/E Ratio:	46.73
Plant, Equip.:	$525,903,000	Total Liab.:	$1,818,000,000	Indic. Yr. Divd.:	NA
Total Assets:	$2,771,491,000	Net Worth:	$948,411,000	Debt/ Equity:	NA

Mills Ltd Partnership

1300 Wilson Blvd., Ste. 400, Arlington, VA, 22209;

General - Incorporation	DE	Stock- Price on:12/24/2007	NA
Employees	NA	Stock Exchange	NA
Auditor	Ernst & Young LLP	Ticker Symbol	NA
Stk Agt	Mellon Investor Services LLC	Outstanding Shares	NA
Counsel	NA	E.P.S.	NA
DUNS No.	NA	Shareholders	NA

Business: The group's principle activity is to provide development, redevelopment, leasing, financing, management and marketing services to its properties. The group is a part of a fully integrated, self-managed Real Estate Investment Trust with various subsidiaries. The group operates from United States.

Primary SIC and add'l.: 6798

CIK No: 0001142028

Subsidiaries: 108 North State Street II, LLC, Arizona Mills SPE Corp., Arizona Mills SPE, LLC, Arizona Mills, LLC, Arundel Finance, LLC, Arundel Mills Holdings, L.P., Arundel Mills Limited Partnership, Arundel Mills Marketplace Finance, LLC, Arundel Mills Marketplace GP, LLC, Arundel Mills Marketplace Limited Partnership, Arundel Mills Mezzanine GP, LLC, Arundel Mills Mezzanine Limited Partnership, Arundel Mills Residual Limited Partnership, Arundel Mills Residual, LLC, Arundel Mills SPE Corp. 329 Subsidiaries included in the Index

Officers: Leslie T. Chao/CEO - Premium Outlet Centers, Chelsea, David Simon/Dir., CEO - Simons Property Group Inc, Hans C. Mautner/Advisory Dir. - Simon Property Group Inc, Pres., International Division, Simon Property Group, Inc, Chmn. - Simon Global Ltd, David Bloom/Advisory Dir. - Simon Property Group Inc, Chmn. - Chelsea Property Group, a Division, Simon, Michael E. McCarty/Pres. - Community, Lifestyle Centers, Myles H. Minton/Sr. VP - Development, Community, Lifestyle Centers, Scott J. Mumphrey/Exec. VP, Pres. - Simon Management Group, Carl Dieterle/Exec. VP - Development, Thomas J. Schneider/Exec. VP - Development, John R. Klein/Co - Pres. - Premium Outlet Centers - Chelsea, Stephen E. Sterrett/Exec. VP, CFO - Simons Property Group Inc, James M. Barkley/Sec., General Counsel - Simons Property Group Inc, Andrew Juster/Sr. VP, Treasurer - Simons Property Group Inc, John Dahl/Sr. VP, Chief Accounting Officer - Simons Property Group Inc, John Rulli/Exec. VP, COO - Operating Properties *(23 Officers included in Index)*

Directors: David Simon/Dir., CEO - Simons Property Group Inc, Hans C. Mautner/Advisory Dir. - Simon Property Group Inc, Pres., International Division, Simon Property Group, Inc, Chmn. - Simon Global Ltd, Denise M. Debartolo York/Dir. - Simons Property Group Inc, Melvin Simon/Dir. - Simons Property Group Inc, Albert J. Smith/Dir. - Simons Property Group Inc, Herbert Simon/Dir. - Simons Property Group Inc, Reuben S. Leibowitz/Dir. - Simons Property Group Inc, Fredrick W. Petri/Dir. - Simons Property Group Inc, Birch Bayh/Dir., Melvyn E. Bergstein/Dir. - Simons Property Group Inc, Linda Walker Bynoe/Dir. - Simons Property Group Inc, Karen N. Horn/Dir. - Simons Property Group Inc

Millstream II Acquisition Corp

435 Devon Pk. Dr., Bldg. 400, Wayne, PA, 19087; *PH:* 1-610-975-4909

General - Incorporation	DE	Stock- Price on:12/24/2007	NA
Employees	NA	Stock Exchange	OTC
Auditor	Goldstein Golub Kessler LLP	Ticker Symbol	MSMA
Stk Agt	Continental Stock T & T Co.	Outstanding Shares	NA
Counsel	NA	E.P.S.	$0.06
DUNS No.	NA	Shareholders	NA

Business: The groups principle activity is to provide recruiting services. The groups service area includes the research and development, engineering, marketing, sales, information technology and manufacturing industries. The group operates from United States.

Primary SIC and add'l.: 6770

CIK No: 0001304562

Officers: Arthur Spector/Chmn., CEO, Pres.

Directors: Arthur Spector/Chmn., CEO, Pres., Don K. Rice/Dir.

Owners: Andrew M. Weiss/5.90%, Arthur Spector/7.10%, Insiders/10.80%, Don K. Rice/1.20%, Heinz C. Schimmelbusch/1.20%, Robert E. Keith/1.20%, The Baupost Group, L.L.C./6.10%, Octavian Global Partners LLC/10.30%, Castlecomb Family Trust/7.10%

Financial Data: *Fiscal Year End:*12/31 *Latest Annual Data:* 12/31/2005

Year		Sales			Net Income
2005		NA			$72,000
2004		NA			-$13,000
Curr. Assets:	$25,144,000	Curr. Liab.:	$228,000	P/E Ratio:	92.00
Plant, Equip.:	NA	Total Liab.:	$5,114,000	Indic. Yr. Divd.:	NA
Total Assets:	$25,144,000	Net Worth:	$20,030,000	Debt/ Equity:	NA

Minco Gold Corp

Formerly: Minco Mining & Metals Corp
PO Box 11176, 1055 West Georgia St., Ste. 2772, Vancouver, BC, V6E3P3;

General - Incorporation	BC	Stock- Price on:12/24/2007	$1.471
Employees	NA	Stock Exchange	NYSE
Auditor	Ernst& Young LLP	Ticker Symbol	MMM
Stk Agt	Computershare Trust Co	Outstanding Shares	NA
Counsel	NA	E.P.S.	NA
DUNS No.	NA	Shareholders	NA

Business: The groups principal activities include exploring and acquiring of gold, silver and base metal properties. The group operates from China and the United States.

Primary SIC and add'l.: 1000

CIK No: 0001020825

Subsidiaries: Minco Base Metals Corporation, Minco Mining (China) Corporation, Minco Silver Corporation

Officers: Dwayne Melrose/VP - Exploration, Matthew Kavanagh/CFO

Owners: Ken Cai/14.55%, Insiders/17.40%, Pacific Canada Resources Inc./12.50%, Ken Cai/14.55%

MIND CTI Ltd

777 Ter. Ave., Hasbrouck Heights, NJ, 07604; **PH:** 1-201-288-3900; **Fax:** 1-201-288-4590; **http://** www.mindcti.com; **Email:** sales@mindcti.com

General - Incorporation	Israel	Stock- Price on:12/24/2007	$2.75
Employees	300	Stock Exchange	NDQ
Auditor	Kesselman & Kesselman	Ticker Symbol	NA
Stk Agt	NA	Outstanding Shares	21,570,000
Counsel	NA	E.P.S.	$0.12
DUNS No.	NA	Shareholders	NA

Business: The group's principle activities are the development, manufacture and marketing of real-time billing and customer care software for voice over Internet protocol service providers. It also provides a call management system used by organizations for call accounting, traffic analysis and fraud detection. The billing and customer care software is known as mind-iphoneex and it enables providers of multiple ip-based services to meet complex, mission-critical billing and customer care needs. The company also provides professional services to its customers, consisting of project management, customization, installations, customer support, training and maintenance services.

Primary SIC and add'l.: 7372

CIK No: 0001119083

Subsidiaries: Dirot Comp Srl, Mind C.t.i. Inc., MIND Software SRL, Sentori Inc.

Officers: Monica Eisinger/Founder, Chmn., CEO, Pres., Danny Engle/VP - Sales, North America, Doron Segal/CTO, Liviu Serea/GM - Romania Office, Sagee Aran/VP - Apac, Africa, Oren Bryan/CFO, Tal Shain/VP - Professional Services, Karl Wills/MD - Abacus Billing, Andrea Dray/Investor Relations Officer

Directors: Monica Eisinger/Founder, Chmn., CEO, Pres., Menahem Shalgi/58/Dir., Rimon Ben-Shaoul/63/Dir., Zamir Bar-Zion/51/Dir.

Owners: Monica Eisinger/19.00%

Financial Data: Fiscal Year End:12/31   Latest Annual Data: 12/31/2006

Year	Sales	Net Income
2006	$20,060,000	$909,000
2005	$15,601,000	$4,062,000
2004	$17,806,000	$6,877,000

Curr. Assets:	$33,376,000	Curr. Liab.:	$4,450,000	P/E Ratio:	21.92
Plant, Equip.:	$1,558,000	Total Liab.:	$5,932,000	Indic. Yr. Divd.:	$0.200
Total Assets:	$53,791,000	Net Worth:	$47,859,000	Debt/ Equity:	NA

Minden Bancorp Inc LA

415 Main St., Minden, LA, 71055; **PH:** 1-318-377-0523; **Fax:** 1-318-377-0038; **http://** www.mblminden.com; **Email:** info@mblminden.com

General - Incorporation	USA	Stock- Price on:12/24/2007	$25
Employees	21	Stock Exchange	OTC
Auditor	Heard, McElroy & Vestal, LLP	Ticker Symbol	MDNB
Stk Agt	NA	Outstanding Shares	1,380,000
Counsel	NA	E.P.S.	$0.84
DUNS No.	NA	Shareholders	NA

Business: The group operates through its subsidiary whose principle activity is to provide commercial banking services. The services of the group include providing commercial real state loans, consumer loans, commercial business loans and construction loans. The group operates from the United States.

Primary SIC and add'l.: 6712 6036

CIK No: 0001169352

Subsidiaries: Minden Services Inc.

Officers: David A. Evans/Chmn., CEO, Pres., Russell A. Adams/Dir., Sec., Kristal Adams/Teller, Michael P. Burton/Sr. VP, Sec., Becky T. Harrell/Treasurer, CFO, Gregory A. Lee/VP - Mortgage, Personal Lender, Don E. Hart/VP - Lending, Anita W. Hay/Office Mgr. - Cashier, Lee Ann Sitzes/Administrative Assist. - Lending, Ginger L. Davis/Administrative Assist. - Lending, Judy C. Holloway/Customer Service Representative, Penny James/Customer Service Representative, Robee T. Siler/Administrative Assist. - Accounting, IS, Jeffory Lee/Assist. Office Mgr. - Insurance Coordinator, Mary Johnson/Information Systems (19 Officers included in Index)

Directors: David A. Evans/Chmn., CEO, Pres., Russell A. Adams/Dir., Sec., Jack E. Byrd/61/Dir., John B. Benton/Dir., John P. Collins/Dir., Michael S. Harper/Dir., Loye A. Jones/Dir., Dare F. Lott/Dir., Michael W. Wise/Dir., R. E. Woodard/Dir.

Owners: Michael P. Burton/1.60%, Michael S. Harper, John B. Benton, Insiders/13.60%, Dare F. Lott, John P. Collins/2.10%, David A. Evans/3.30%, R. E. Woodard/2.30%, Becky T. Harrell, Michael W. Wise, Jack E. Byrd, Russell A. Adams, Minden Bancorp, Inc./3.80%, Minden Mutual Holding Company/58.10%, Loye A. Jones

Financial Data: Fiscal Year End:12/31   Latest Annual Data: 12/31/2006

Year	Sales	Net Income
2006	$8,271,000	$1,335,000
2005	$6,759,000	$1,362,000
2004	$5,931,000	$1,374,000

Curr. Assets:	$3,073,000	Curr. Liab.:	$95,003,000	P/E Ratio:	28.09
Plant, Equip.:	$6,343,000	Total Liab.:	$95,806,000	Indic. Yr. Divd.:	$0.400
Total Assets:	$115,966,000	Net Worth:	$20,160,000	Debt/ Equity:	NA

Mindray Medical International Ltd

MinDr.ay Bldg., Keji 12th Rd. S, High-tech Industrial Pk., Shenzhen, Nanshan, 518057; **PH:** 86-75526582888; **Fax:** 86-26582500; **http://** www.mindray.com; **Email:** intl-market@mindray.com

General - Incorporation	Cayman Islands	Stock- Price on:12/24/2007	$28.69
Employees	2,744	Stock Exchange	NYSE
Auditor	NA	Ticker Symbol	MR
Stk Agt	Bank of New York	Outstanding Shares	105,740,000
Counsel	NA	E.P.S.	$0.66
DUNS No.	NA	Shareholders	NA

Business: The groups principle activities include developing, manufacturing and marketing of medical devices. The group operates through three segments namely, patient monitoring devices, diagnostic laboratory instruments and ultrasound imaging systems. The group operates from the China. The groups quarterly revenue for sept 2007 was 573.24 millions of CNY.

Primary SIC and add'l.: 3841

CIK No: 0001373060

Subsidiaries: Beijing Shen Mindray Medical Electronics Technology Research Institute Company Limited, Giant Glory Investments Limited, Greatest Elite Limited, Mindray (UK) Limited, Mindray Global Limited, Mindray Medical USA Corp., Mindray Research and Development Limited, Mindray USA Corp., Shenzhen Mindray Bio-Medical Electronics Co., Ltd.

Officers: Xu Hang/Chmn., Co - CEO, Li Xiting/Dir., Pres., Co - CEO, Joyce I-Yin Hsu/Dir., CFO, Cheng Minghe/Exec. VP - Sales, Marketing, Mu Lemin/Exec. VP - Administration, Yan Baiping/Exec. VP - Research & Development, Tim Fitzpatrick/General Counsel, Justin Knapp/Investor Relations Officer

Directors: Xu Hang/Chmn., Co - CEO, Li Xiting/Dir., Pres., Co - CEO, Joyce I-Yin Hsu/Dir., CFO, Chen Qingtai/Dir., Ronald Ede/Dir., Andrew Wolff/39/Dir., Wu Qiyao/Dir., Jixun Lin/Dir.

Owners: Able Choice Investments Limited/6.60%, Cheng Minghe/2.90%, Li Xiting/17.70%, The GS Funds/5.30%, Andrew Wolff/5.30%, Xu Hang/20.40%

Financial Data: Fiscal Year End:12/31   Latest Annual Data: 12/31/2006

Year	Sales	Net Income
2006	$194,126,000	$46,358,000
2005	$134,918,000	$25,654,000
2004	$84,438,000	$21,991,000

Curr. Assets:	$254,154,000	Curr. Liab.:	$45,154,000		
Plant, Equip.:	$23,959,000	Total Liab.:	$47,950,000	Indic. Yr. Divd.:	$0.150
Total Assets:	$327,664,000	Net Worth:	$279,714,000	Debt/ Equity:	NA

Mindspeed Technologies Inc

4000 MacArthur Blvd., East Tower, Newport Beach, CA, 92660; **PH:** 1-949-579-3000; **Fax:** 1-949-579-3020; **http://** www.mindspeed.com

General - Incorporation	DE	Stock- Price on:12/24/2007	$2.29
Employees	512	Stock Exchange	NDQ
Auditor	Deloitte & Touche LLP	Ticker Symbol	MSTR
Stk Agt	Mellon Investor Services LLC	Outstanding Shares	114,790,000
Counsel	Chadbourne & Parke LLP	E.P.S.	-$0.28
DUNS No.	NA	Shareholders	NA

Business: The group's principal activity is to design, develop and market semiconductor networking solutions for communications applications in enterprise, access, metropolitan and wide-area networks. The group's three key product families include multiservice access solutions designed to support voice and data services across wireline and wireless networks, t/e carrier physical-layer and link-layer products, and ATM/mpls network processors. The products of the group are used in a wide variety of network infrastructure equipment including voice and media gateways, high-speed routers, switches, access multiplexers, cross-connect systems, add-drop multiplexers and digital loop carrier equipment. On 27-Jun-2003, the group began operations as an independent, publicly held company from wholly owned subsidiary after the distribution.

Primary SIC and add'l.: 3674

CIK No: 0001224370

Subsidiaries: Applied Telecom, Inc., Brooktree Corporation, HotRail, Inc., Maker Communications, Inc., Microcosm Communications Ltd., Mindspeed Technologies (Mauritius) Ltd., Mindspeed Technologies Asia Pacific Ltd., Mindspeed Technologies B.V., Mindspeed Technologies Cayman Islands, Ltd., Mindspeed Technologies Company, Mindspeed Technologies GmbH, Mindspeed Technologies Israel Ltd., Mindspeed Technologies K.K., Mindspeed Technologies Korea Ltd., Mindspeed Technologies Ltd. 19 Subsidiaries included in the Index

Officers: Raouf Y. Halim/Dir., CEO, Jay Cormier/Sr. VP, GM - High Performance Analog, Richard J. Burns/44/Sr. VP, GM - Wide, Area Networking, Gerald J. Hamilton/Sr. VP - Worldwide Sales, Bradley W. Yates/49/Sr. VP, Chief Administrative Officer, Thomas A. Stites/Sr. VP - Communications, Thomas J. Medrek/Sr. VP, GM - Multiservice Access, Simon Biddiscombe/Sr. VP, CFO, Treasurer, Sec., Wayne K. Nesbit/Sr. VP, GM - Operations, Ron Cates/Sr. VP, GM - WAN Communications, Tom Stites/Sr. VP - Communications

Directors: Raouf Y. Halim/Dir., CEO, Dwight W. Decker/Chmn., Donald R. Beall/69/Dir., Michael T. Hayashi/51/Dir., Ming Louie/62/Dir., Jerre L. Stead/64/Dir., Thomas A. Madden/54/Dir., Donald Gips/47/Dir.

Owners: David W. Carroll, Simon Biddiscombe, Thomas J. Medrek, Gerald J. Hamilton, Wayne K. Nesbit, Raouf Y. Halim/1.90%, Conexant Systems, Inc./21.10%, Dwight W. Decker/1.30%, Michael T. Hayashi, Donald R. Beall, CNH Partners, LLC/7.30%, Daryush Shamlou, Kopp Investment Advisors, LLC/6.10%, Ming Louie, Insiders/6.30% (19 Owners included in Index)

Financial Data: Fiscal Year End:09/30   Latest Annual Data: 9/30/2006

Year	Sales	Net Income
2006	$135,919,000	-$24,514,000
2005	$111,777,000	-$62,629,000
2004	$119,435,000	-$93,247,000

Curr. Assets:	$78,720,000	Curr. Liab.:	$27,840,000		
Plant, Equip.:	$12,961,000	Total Liab.:	$73,066,000	Indic. Yr. Divd.:	NA
Total Assets:	$96,542,000	Net Worth:	$23,476,000	Debt/ Equity:	3.8856

Mine Safety Appliances Co

121 Gamma Dr., RIDC Industrial Pk., O'Hara Township, Pittsburgh, PA, 15238; **PH:** 1-412-967-3000; **Fax:** 1-412-967-3451; **http://** www.msanet.com; **Email:** info@msanet.com

General - Incorporation	PA	Stock - Price on:12/24/2007	$42.54
Employees	4,900	Stock Exchange	NYSE
Auditor	PricewaterhouseCoopers LLP	Ticker Symbol	MSC
Stk Agt	Wells Fargo Shareowner Services	Outstanding Shares	35,920,000
Counsel	NA	E.P.S.	$1.79
DUNS No.	00-432-1865	Shareholders	NA

Business: The group's principal activities are to manufacture and market health and safety products. These products include respiratory protective equipment, instruments to monitor and analyze workplace environments and control industrial processes, thermal imaging cameras and personal protective products such as hearing protectors and fall protection equipment. Workers in the manufacturing, mining, chemicals, petroleum, construction, transportation and hazardous materials clean-up industries, fire departments and public utilities use these products. In addition, the group also manufactures and markets boron-based and other specialty chemicals. On 30-Jun-2004, the group acquired sordin ab.

Primary SIC and add'l.: 3842

CIK No: 0000066570

Subsidiaries: Aritron Instrument A.G., Compaia MSA de Argentina S.A., Microsensor Systems, Inc., MSA (Aust.) Pty. Limited, MSA (Britain) Limited, MSA Africa (Pty.) Ltd., MSA Auer, MSA Belgium NV, MSA Canada, MSA de Chile Ltda., MSA de Mexico, S.A. de C.V., MSA del Peru S.A.C., MSA do Brasil Ltda., MSA Espaola S.A., MSA Europe 29 Subsidiaries included in the Index

Officers: John T. Ryan/64/Chmn., CEO/$2,694,347.00, Kerry M. Bove/VP - Global Operational Excellence, Stephen C. Plut/CIO, VP, Joseph A. Bigler/VP, Pres. - MSA North America, Dennis L. Zeitler/Sr. VP, CFO/$975,203.00, Douglas K. McClaine/VP, Sec., General Counsel, Ronald N. Herring/VP - Global Product Leadership, Roberto Canizares/Exec. VP, Pres. - MSA International/$664,548.00, Paul R. Uhler/VP - Global Human Resources

Directors: John T. Ryan/64/Chmn., CEO, Diane M. Pearse/50/Dir., Thomas B. Hotopp/66/Dir., Thomas H. Witmer/66/Dir., John C. Unkovic/64/Dir., James A. Cederna/57/Dir., Edward L. Shaw/63/Dir., Robert A. Bruggeworth/47/Dir.

Owners: Thomas H. Witmer/0.08%, John T. Ryan/1.02%, William M. Lambert/0.82%, John C. Unkovic/0.51%, Columbia Wanger Asset Management, L.P./6.14%, Dennis L. Zeitler/0.47%, Capital Research and Management Company/8.33%, Insiders/1.53%, Calvin A. Campbell, James A. Cederna/0.04%, Rob Caizares/0.54%, Thomas B. Hotopp/0.15%, The PNC Financial Services/7.47%, Diane M. Pearse/0.01%, Private Capital Management, Inc./8.52% *(19 Owners included in Index)*

Financial Data: Fiscal Year End:12/31 Latest Annual Data: 12/31/2006

Year	Sales	Net Income
2006	$919,098,000	$63,918,000
2005	$911,970,000	$81,783,000
2004	$857,513,000	$71,047,000

Curr. Assets:	$416,859,000	Curr. Liab.:	$127,435,000	P/E Ratio:	24.31
Plant, Equip.:	$120,651,000	Total Liab.:	$460,767,000	Indic. Yr. Divd.:	NA
Total Assets:	$898,620,000	Net Worth:	$437,853,000	Debt/ Equity:	NA

Minefinders Corp Ltd

1177 W Hastings St., Ste. 2288, Vancouver, BC, V6E 2K3; **PH:** 1-604-687-6263; *http://* www.minefinders.com

General - Incorporation	Canada	Stock - Price on:12/24/2007	$11.4001
Employees	27	Stock Exchange	AMEX
Auditor	BDO Dunwoody LLP	Ticker Symbol	MFN
Stk Agt	Bdo Dunwoody LLP	Outstanding Shares	NA
Counsel	Campney & Murphy	E.P.S.	-$0.29
DUNS No.	20-635-1421	Shareholders	NA

Business: The group's principal activities are to explore and develop precious metals in Mexico and United States. The group controls over 3 million ounces of gold resource and 165 million ounces of silver resource and is actively seeking new discoveries. The group has interests in dolores property, northern sonora, reserva/ el correo in Mexico and oro blanco in United States. The group is in joint venture in el malacate gold properties. The subsidiaries of the group are minera minefinders s.a. De c.v. And compania minera dolores s.a. De c.v. In Mexico and minefinders (u.s.a.) inc.

Primary SIC and add'l.: 3295 1099

CIK No: 0000926479

Subsidiaries: Compania Minera Dolores, S.A de C.V., Minefinders (U.S.A.) Inc, Minera Minefinders, S.A. de C.V., Servicios Mineros Sierra, S.A. de C.V.

Officers: Mark H. Bailey/Dir., CEO, Pres., Tench C. Page/VP - Exploration, Paul C. MacNeill/Dir., Corp. Sec., Greg Smith/CFO

Directors: Mark H. Bailey/Dir., CEO, Pres., Robert L. Leclerc/Chmn., Paul C. MacNeill/Dir., Corp. Sec., James M. Dawson/Dir., Leo H. King/Dir., Tony Luteijn/Dir.

Financial Data: Fiscal Year End:12/31 Latest Annual Data: 12/31/2006

Year	Sales	Net Income
2006	NA	-$16,733,000
2005	NA	-$11,598,000
2004	NA	-$9,804,000

Curr. Assets:	$127,091,000	Curr. Liab.:	$7,899,000		
Plant, Equip.:	$60,405,000	Total Liab.:	$94,087,000	Indic. Yr. Divd.:	NA
Total Assets:	$191,552,000	Net Worth:	$97,465,000	Debt/ Equity:	NA

Minera Andes Inc

111 E Magnesium Rd. Ste. A, Spokane, WA, 99208; **PH:** 1-509-921-7322; *http://* www.minandes.com; **Email:** info@minandes.com

General - Incorporation	AB	Stock - Price on:12/24/2007	$2.07
Employees	NA	Stock Exchange	OTC
Auditor	BDO Dunwoody LLP	Ticker Symbol	MNEAF
Stk Agt	Computershare Trust Co	Outstanding Shares	165,920,000
Counsel	NA	E.P.S.	-$0.07
DUNS No.	NA	Shareholders	NA

Business: The group's principal activities include exploring and developing mineral properties. The group operates from the United States, Argentina and Canada.

Primary SIC and add'l.: 1481

CIK No: 0001030219

Subsidiaries: Minera Andes (Cayman 2) Inc., Minera Andes (Cayman) Inc., Minera Andes (USA) Inc., Minera Andes S.A. (Argentina), Minera Santa Cruz S.A.

Officers: Art Johnson/Contact - Investor Relations, US, Krister A. Kottmeier/Contact - Investor Relations, Canada, Allen V. Ambrose/Dir., Pres., Brian Gavin/VP - Exploration, Bonnie L. Kuhn/Dir., Sec., William V. Schara/Principal Accounting, Financial Officer, Henry John/CFO

Directors: Allen V. Ambrose/Dir., Pres., Gary A. Craig/Dir., A. D. Drummond/Dir., John Johnson Crabb/Dir., Bonnie L. Kuhn/Dir., Sec., Allan J. Marter/Dir.

Financial Data: Fiscal Year End:12/31 Latest Annual Data: 12/31/2006

Year	Sales	Net Income
2006	NA	-$14,919,000
2005	NA	-$15,536,000
2004	NA	-$6,951,000

Curr. Assets:	$2,513,000	Curr. Liab.:	$894,000		
Plant, Equip.:	$56,000	Total Liab.:	$10,787,000	Indic. Yr. Divd.:	NA
Total Assets:	$24,618,000	Net Worth:	$13,831,000	Debt/ Equity:	NA

Minerals Technologies Inc

405 Lexington Ave., New York, NY, 10174; **PH:** 1-212-878-1800; **Fax:** 1-212-878-1801; *http://* www.mineralstech.com; **Email:** investor.relations@mineralstech.com

General - Incorporation	DE	Stock - Price on:12/24/2007	$65.3
Employees	2,809	Stock Exchange	NYSE
Auditor	KPMG LLP	Ticker Symbol	MTZ
Stk Agt	Computershare Ltd.	Outstanding Shares	19,090,000
Counsel	NA	E.P.S.	-$3.64
DUNS No.	79-692-9313	Shareholders	NA

Business: The group's principal activities are to develop, manufacture and market specialty minerals, mineral-based and synthetic mineral products. The group operates in two segments: specialty minerals and refractories. The specialty minerals segment produces and sells the synthetic mineral product precipitated calcium carbonate and the processed mineral product quicklime. The group also mines, processes and sells natural mineral products, limestone and talc. The refractories segment produces and markets monolithic and shaped refractory materials and specialty products and services. These products are marketed worldwide to the paper, building materials, paints and coatings, glass, ceramic, polymers, food, pharmaceutical, steel and cement industries.

Primary SIC and add'l.: 2819

CIK No: 0000891014

Subsidiaries: APP China Specialty Minerals Pte Ltd., Barretts Minerals Inc., ComSource Trading Ltd., Ferrotron Technologies GmbH, Gold Lun Chemicals (Zhenjiang)., Gold Sheng Chemicals (Zhenjiang) Co., Ltd., Gold Zuan Chemicals (Suzhou)., Hi-Tech Specialty Minerals Company, Limited, Minerals Technologies do Brasil Comercio e Industria de Minerais Ltda., Minerals Technologies Europe N.V., Minerals Technologies Holdings Ltd., Minerals Technologies Mexico Holdings, S. de R. L. de C.V., Minerals Technologies South Africa (Pty) Ltd., Mintech Canada Inc., Mintech Japan K.K. 55 Subsidiaries included in the Index

Officers: Paul R. Saueracker/65/Chmn., CEO, Pres./$3,784,425.00, Joseph C. Muscari/Chmn., CEO, Kirk G. Forrest/VP, General Counsel, Sec./$677,360.00, Gregory P. Kelm/Treasurer, John A. Sorel/CFO, Sr. VP - Finance/$1,224,865.00, Alain F. Bouruet-Aubertot/MD, Sr. VP/$970,041.00, William A. Kromberg/VP - Taxes, Gordon S. Borteck/Corporate VP - Organization, Human Resources, Michael A. Cipolla/VP, Controller, Chief Accounting Officer

Directors: Paul R. Saueracker/65/Chmn., CEO, Pres., Joseph C. Muscari/Chmn., CEO, John T. Reid/Dir., Paula H.J. Cholmondeley/Dir., Kristina M. Johnson/Dir., William C. Stivers/Dir., Michael F. Pasquale/Dir., Steven J. Golub/Dir., Duane R. Dunham/Dir.

Owners: K. G. Forrest, W. C. Stivers, J. A. Sorel, J. T. Reid, American Century Companies, Inc./10.90%, K. L. Massimine, M. F. Pasquale, A. F. Bouruet-Aubertot, P. H. J. Cholmondeley, M&G Investment Management, Ltd./9.70%, D. R. Dunham, M & G Investment Funds/5.10%, S. J. Golub, Primecap Management Company/10.60%, Vanguard Specialized Funds/5.10% *(23 Owners included in Index)*

Financial Data: Fiscal Year End:12/31 Latest Annual Data: 12/31/2006

Year	Sales	Net Income
2006	$1,059,307,000	$49,951,000
2005	$995,838,000	$53,264,000
2004	$923,667,000	$58,563,000

Curr. Assets:	$411,762,000	Curr. Liab.:	$212,063,000	P/E Ratio:	25.41
Plant, Equip.:	$652,797,000	Total Liab.:	$440,567,000	Indic. Yr. Divd.:	$0.200
Total Assets:	$1,193,124,000	Net Worth:	$752,557,000	Debt/ Equity:	0.1551

Mines Mgmt Inc

905 W Riverside Ave., Ste. 311, Spokane, WA, 99201; **PH:** 1-509-838-6050; **Fax:** 1-509-838-0486; *http://* www.minesmanagement.com

General - Incorporation	ID	Stock - Price on:12/24/2007	$3.82
Employees	7	Stock Exchange	AMEX
Auditor	Lemaster & Daniels PLLC	Ticker Symbol	MGN
Stk Agt	Computershare Trust Co	Outstanding Shares	NA
Counsel	NA	E.P.S.	NA
DUNS No.	NA	Shareholders	NA

Business: The group's principal activity is to acquire, explore and develop mineral properties, primarily those containing silver and associated base and precious metals mainly in North America. It also has working interest in four oil wells located in Kansas.

Primary SIC and add'l.: 1044 1382

CIK No: 0000066649

Subsidiaries: Newhi, Inc.

Officers: Glenn M. Dobbs/Chmn., CEO, Pres./$293,560.00, Douglas Dobbs/41/VP - Corporate Development, Corp. Sec./$146,560.00, Eric C. Klepfer/VP - Operations/$176,560.00, James H. Moore/63/CFO, Treasurer/$374,691.00

Directors: Glenn M. Dobbs/Chmn., CEO, Pres., Jerry G. Pogue/Dir., Russell C. Babcock/Dir., Robert L. Russell/Dir., Roy G. Franklin/Dir.

Owners: Praetorian Capital Management, LLC/7.11%, Douglas D. Dobbs/1.10%, James H. Moore, Glenn M. Dobbs/7.47%, Jerry G. Pogue, Insiders/11.30%, Roy G. Franklin

Financial Data: Fiscal Year End:12/31 Latest Annual Data: 12/31/2006

Year	Sales	Net Income
2006	$13,000	-$5,984,000
2005	$11,000	-$5,210,000
2004	$9,000	-$2,516,000

Curr. Assets:	$879,000	Curr. Liab.:	$308,000		
Plant, Equip.:	$1,003,000	Total Liab.:	$308,000	Indic. Yr. Divd.:	NA
Total Assets:	$6,330,000	Net Worth:	$6,023,000	Debt/ Equity:	NA

Ministry Partners Investment Corp

955 W Imperial Hwy, Ste. 101, Brea, CA, 92821; *PH:* 1-714-671-5720;
http:// www.ministrypartners.org; *Email:* partners@eccu.org

General - Incorporation	CA	Stock - Price on:12/24/2007	NA
Employees	NA	Stock Exchange	NA
Auditor	Hutchinson & Bloodgood, LLP	Ticker Symbol	NA
Stk Agt	NA	Outstanding Shares	NA
Counsel	NA	E.P.S.	NA
DUNS No.	NA	Shareholders	NA

Business: The group's principle activity is to provide funds for real property secured loans for the benefit of evangelical churches and church organizations through funding provided by members of and persons associated with such churches and organizations. The company is a wholly owned subsidiary of evangelical christian credit union. The company's offices, mortgage loan investments and all of the business operations are currently conducted in California. The group operates from United States.

Primary SIC and add'l.: 6159

CIK No: 0000944130

Officers: Mark G. Holbrook/55/Chmn., CEO, Stephen A. Ballas/VP - Sales, Mark A. Johnson/49/Dir., CFO, Treasurer, Harold Woodall/VP - Lending, Billy M. Dodson/47/Pres. - Acting Principal Financial, Accounting Officer

Directors: Mark G. Holbrook/55/Chmn., CEO, Arthur G. Black/68/Dir., Scott T. Vandeventer/50/Dir., Van C. Elliott/69/Dir., Shirley M. Bracken/54/Dir., Mark A. Johnson/49/Dir., CFO, Treasurer, Juli A. Callis/54/Dir., Jeffrey Lauridsen/58/Dir., John Bommarito/50/Dir.

Owners: Credit Union of Southern California/8.12%, USA Federal Credit Union/8.13%, Wescom Credit Union/8.13%, Financial Partners Credit Union/8.19%, Keypoint Credit Union/5.46%, Evangelical Christian Credit Union/42.31%, Western Federal Credit Union/8.13%

Minn Dak Farmers Cooperative

7525 Red River Rd. , Wahpeton, ND, 58075; *PH:* 1-701-642-8411; *http://* www.mdfarmerscoop.com

General - Incorporation	ND	Stock - Price on:12/24/2007	NA
Employees	NA	Stock Exchange	NA
Auditor	Eide Bailly LLP	Ticker Symbol	NA
Stk Agt	NA	Outstanding Shares	NA
Counsel	NA	E.P.S.	NA
DUNS No.	06-653-2086	Shareholders	NA

Business: The group's principal activities are to produce and market fresh baker's yeast in North Dakota. The group is owned by its member-growers for the purpose of processing sugar beets and marketing sugar and by-products. The products are pooled and marketed through the services of marketing agent under contract. The marketing agents of the group are united sugars corporation, American crystal sugar company, southern Minnesota beet sugar cooperative and the United States sugar corporation. The group's beet molasses and beet pulp are also marketed through a marketing agent, midwest agri commodities company. The membership is limited to sugar beet growers located in the areas of North Dakota and Minnesota. The group holds 80% interest in minn-dak yeast company, inc. Which produces baker's yeast.

Primary SIC and add'l.: 2063

CIK No: 0000948218

Subsidiaries: Minn-Dak Yeast

Officers: Dave Roche/CEO, Pres., Richard Ames/Yeast Plant Mgr., John Wieser/Information Systems Mgr., Allen Larson/Controller, Russell Mauch/Dir., Treasurer, Charles Steiner/57/Dir., Sec., Simone Sandberg/Dir. - Legal Counsel, Steve Caspers/CFO, Exec. VP, Susan Johnson/Mgr. - Communications, John Haugen/VP - Engineering, Tom Knudsen/VP - Agriculture, John Nyquist/Purchasing Mgr., Jeff Carlson/VP - Operations, Kevin Shannon/Safety Dir., Greg Schmalz/Mgr. - Human Resources

Directors: Douglas Etten/Vice Chmn., Mike Hasbargen/Chmn., Alton Theede/Dir., Russell Mauch/Dir., Treasurer, Charles Steiner/57/Dir., Sec., Dennis Klosterman/Dir., Simone Sandberg/Dir. - Legal Counsel, Dennis Butenhoff/Dir., Dale Blume/Dir., Brent Davison/Dir.

Owners: Russell Mauch, Douglas Etten, Brent Davison/1.40%, Dale Blume, Dennis Klosterman, Dennis Butenhoff, Michael Hasbargen, Charles Steiner, Alton Theede, Insiders/5.23%

Minrad International Inc

50 Cobham Dr., Orchard, NY, 14127; *PH:* 1-716-855-1068; *Fax:* 1-716-855-1078;
http:// www.minrad.com; *Email:* customerservice@minrad.com

General - Incorporation	DE	Stock - Price on:12/24/2007	$6.01
Employees	122	Stock Exchange	AMEX
Auditor	Freed Maxick & Battaglia, CPAs, PC	Ticker Symbol	BUF
Stk Agt	Holladay Stock Transfer, Inc.	Outstanding Shares	47,090,000
Counsel	NA	E.P.S.	-$0.33
DUNS No.	NA	Shareholders	NA

Business: The groups principle activities include anesthesia and analgesia, real-time image guidance, and conscious sedation. The groups products include halothane, enflurane, isoflurane, sevoflurane and desflurane.The group marketed its products under the trade names SabreSource (TM) and Light Sabre (TM). The group operates from the United States. The group's quarterly revenue for September 2007 was 2.69 millions of USD.

Primary SIC and add'l.: 3841 2834

CIK No: 0001121225

Subsidiaries: Minrad Inc

Officers: William H. Burns/58/Chmn., CEO/$701,905.00, John McNeirney/75/CTO, Sr. VP/$221,518.00, Kirk Kamsler/57/Sr. VP - Commercial Development/$245,841.00, Jose I. Pena Castellanos/Pres., William Rolfe/62/VP, Controller, Acting CFO, Eduardo Rados/Argentina Sales Representative, Jun Li/Area Mgr. - North Pacific, Juan M. Rodriguez/Pres., Thomas Poelling/Brazil Area Mgr., Erica Ota/Sao Paulo Sales Representative, Marcelo Guerrero Alvarez-Tostado/Marketing Mgr. - Anesthetics, Yuki Yu/Executive Pres., Noelene Lee/Sales Representative - South Africa, Fawzi A. Addala/Clinic Dir. - Libya, Art Scolari/New York City, Connecticut Territory Sales Representative *(66 Officers included in Index)*

Directors: William H. Burns/58/Chmn., CEO, Theodore Stanley/Dir., Robert Lifeso/Dir., John Rousseau/Dir., Dave Digiacinto/Dir., Dave Donaldson/Dir., Don Farley/Dir., Duane B. Hopper/Dir., Brett Zbar/Dir., Enrique Herrera/Dir. - Isemed, SA de CV, Claudio M. Di Laudadio/Dir. - Unifarma SA

Owners: HealthCor Management L.P./5.10%, John McNeirney/0.40%, Theodore Stanley, David Donaldson/0.10%, Duane Hopper/0.30%, Robert Lifeso/1.60%, William H. Burns/5.00%, Richard Tamulski/0.20%, Insiders/8.70%, William Rolfe, New England Partners Capital LLC/8.50%, Aisling CapitalII L.P./5.50%, David DiGiacinto/0.10%, Kevin Kimberlin Partners L.P./15.60%, Donald F. Farley/0.60% *(19 Owners included in Index)*

Financial Data: *Fiscal Year End:*12/31   *Latest Annual Data:* 12/31/2006

Year	Sales	Net Income
2006	$16,341,000	-$6,603,000
2005	$8,345,000	-$5,084,000
2004	$460,000	-$1,380,000

Curr. Assets:	$28,309,000	Curr. Liab.:	$2,227,000		
Plant, Equip.:	$6,981,000	Total Liab.:	$2,227,000	Indic. Yr. Divd.:	NA
Total Assets:	$35,729,000	Net Worth:	$33,503,000	Debt/ Equity:	NA

Mips Technologies Inc

1225 Charleston Rd., Mountain View, CA, 94043; *PH:* 1-650-567-5000; *Fax:* 1-650-567-5150;
http:// www.mips.com; *Email:* sales@mips.com

General - Incorporation	DE	Stock - Price on:12/24/2007	$8.66
Employees	NA	Stock Exchange	NDQ
Auditor	Ernst & Young LLP	Ticker Symbol	MIPS
Stk Agt	EquiServe Trust Co N.A	Outstanding Shares	43,380,000
Counsel	NA	E.P.S.	$0.19
DUNS No.	80-884-6299	Shareholders	NA

Business: The group's principal activity is to design, develop and license intellectual property relating to embedded processors based on 32- and 64-bit risc (reduced instruction-set computing) microprocessor architectures and cores. The products developed include mips32 4k cores, mips64 5k cores, mips64 20k family, mips16e ase, mips-3D ase and smartmips ase. The technology has been incorporated into video games, set-top boxes, broadband products, handheld mobile devices, automotive products, office automation products and networking equipment. Product licensees include advanced micro devices, inc, broadcom corporation, conexant systems, inc, infineon technologies, ag, lsi logic corporation, micron technology inc, philips semiconductor, Texas instruments inc and toshiba corporation. The operations are conducted primarily in the United States, Japan and Europe.

Primary SIC and add'l.: 7372 3674 7373

CIK No: 0001059786

Subsidiaries: MIPS Technologies (UK) Limited, MIPS Technologies International AG, MIPS Technologies International Ltd.

Officers: John E. Bourgoin/Dir., CEO, Pres., Mervin S. Kato/CFO, VP, Jack Browne/VP - Marketing, Sandy Creighton/VP - Human Resources, Corporate Administration, Brad Holtzinger/VP - Worldwide Sales, Mark Tyndall/VP - Business Development, Corporate Relations, Roger Milton/VP - Sales, Americas, Jess Herrera/Dir. - Sales, US Northwest, North, East Bay Area, Tony Chang/Dir. - Sales, Karin Neubert/Contact - Europe, Gail H. Knittel/Assoc. General Counsel, Assist. Sec., Stefan Buechmann/Accounting Dir., George Nakagami/Dir. - Business Development, Country Mgr. Japan, Mauro Diamant/Accounting Dir. - Israel, Michael Uhler/CTO *(22 Officers included in Index)*

Directors: John E. Bourgoin/Dir., CEO, Pres., Anthony B. Holbrook/Chmn., Fred M. Gibbons/Dir., Kenneth L. Coleman/Dir., William M. Kelly/Dir., Jose E. Franca/Dir., Robert R. Herb/Dir.

Owners: Brad Holtzinger, Kenneth L. Coleman, Sandy Creighton/2.16%, Insiders/13.96%, FMR Corp./12.89%, Fred M. Gibbons, Anthony B. Holbrook, Trivium Capital Management, LLC/6.36%, Pacific Edge Investment Management, LLC/5.20%, William M. Kelly, John E. Bourgoin/4.90%, Schroder Investment Management Inc./6.80%, Mervin S. Kato/1.31%, Barclays Global Investors, NA/6.37%, Robert R. Herb *(19 Owners included in Index)*

Financial Data: *Fiscal Year End:*06/30   *Latest Annual Data:* 06/30/2006

Year	Sales	Net Income
2006	$64,054,000	$11,021,000
2005	$61,219,000	$14,909,000
2004	$47,885,000	-$1,531,000

Curr. Assets:	$116,868,000	Curr. Liab.:	$16,229,000	P/E Ratio:	45.58
Plant, Equip.:	$2,899,000	Total Liab.:	$19,167,000	Indic. Yr. Divd.:	NA
Total Assets:	$127,546,000	Net Worth:	$108,379,000	Debt/ Equity:	NA

Miracor Diagnostics Inc

9191 Towne Ctr. Dr., Ste. 400, San Diego, CA, 92122; *PH:* 1-858-455-7127; *Fax:* 1-858-455-7295;
http:// www.miracor.com; *Email:* info@miracor.com

General - Incorporation	UT	Stock - Price on:12/24/2007	NA
Employees	106	Stock Exchange	OTC
Auditor	Tschopp, Whitcomb & Orr P.A	Ticker Symbol	MRDG
Stk Agt	Corporate Stock Transfer, Inc.	Outstanding Shares	NA
Counsel	NA	E.P.S.	-$0.201
DUNS No.	05-639-8415	Shareholders	NA

Business: The group's principal activity is to provide medical diagnostic imaging services through magnetic resonance imaging centers. The group provides medical diagnostic imaging services through the operation of thirteen centers in five states. The group operates in the United States.

Primary SIC and add'l.: 3842

CIK No: 0000723906

Subsidiaries: computed tomography, medical diagnostic imaging services

Officers: Ross S. Seibert/45/CEO, CFO, Pres. - CPA, Robert S. Muehlberg/Dir., COO, Pres., Leslie Weber/COO, Chief Marketing Officer, Ann Wadsworth/Chief Accounting Officer

Directors: Robert S. Muehlberg/Dir., COO, Pres., Howard Salmon/Dir., Stephen A. McConnell/Dir., Don L. Arnwine/Dir., David Schack/Dir., Gregory S. Anderson/Dir.

Owners: Gregory S. Anderson, Insiders/42.41%, Ross S. Seibert/9.78%, Lee M. Hulsebus/10.51%, David J. Schack/12.18%, Howard W. Salmon, Stephen A. McConnell/1.93%, Robert S. Muehlberg/4.03%, Don L. Arnwine/2.57%, Leslie Weber, Ann Wadsworth

Financial Data: *Fiscal Year End:* 12/31   *Latest Annual Data:* 12/31/2005

Year	Sales	Net Income
2005	$19,513,000	$662,000
2004	$18,933,000	-$2,236,000
2003	$19,200,000	-$1,724,000

Curr. Assets:	$7,457,000	Curr. Liab.:	$6,864,000		
Plant, Equip.:	$5,776,000	Total Liab.:	$18,485,000	Indic. Yr. Divd.:	NA
Total Assets:	$21,426,000	Net Worth:	$2,940,000	Debt/ Equity:	NA

Mirae Bank CA

2104 Olimpic bl, Los Angeles, CA, 90006; **PH:** 1-213-427-8800; *http://* www.miraebank.com

General - Incorporation	NA	**Stock** - Price on:12/24/2007	NA
Employees	NA	Stock Exchange	NA
Auditor	NA	Ticker Symbol	NA
Stk Agt	NA	Outstanding Shares	NA
Counsel	NA	E.P.S	NA
DUNS No.	NA	Shareholders	NA

Business: The groups principal activity is to provide banking services. The services of the group include personal banking, business banking, loans, mortgage, safe deposit boxes, wire transfer, and fax boxes, ATM and debit card, and ACH direct deposit. The group operates from the United States.

Primary SIC and add'l.: 6029

CIK No:

Officers: Kwang Soon Park/Dir., CEO, Pres., Myungjoon Kim/Sr. VP, Mgr., Seattle Loan Production Officer, Wonmi Park/FVP, Note Mgr., Jennifer Lee/FVP, Mgr. - Wilshire VIP Department, Dongwon Kim/VP, Mgr., Denver Loan Production Officer, Sung Lee/FVP, IS Mgr. - Information Systems, Eunice Lee/VP, Operation Administrator, Jennifer Kong/Sr. VP, Mgr., Torrance Branch Mgr., Henry Ha/FVP, Mgr. - SBA, Timothy T. Chang/CFO, Exec. VP, Jeff Kim/Sr. VP, Chief Credit Officer - Credit Administration Department, Phillip Kim/FVP, BSA Compliance Officer - BSA Department, Bomi Kim/FVP, Mgr. - International Department, Jessica Lee/AVP, Compliance Officer - Compliance Department, Christine Chung/FVP, Marketing Mgr. - Olympic VIP Department *(20 Officers included in Index)*

Directors: Kwang Soon Park/Dir., CEO, Pres., Choon Taik Lim/Chmn., Theodore C. Yoon/Dir., Duk Hee Cho/Dir., Simon C. Chun/Dir., Henry Ungsik Kim/Dir., Jay K. Kim/Dir., Soon I. Kim/Dir., Jong Taek Lim/Dir., Chris Moonkey Nam/Dir., Chase C. Rhee/Dir.

Financial Data: *Fiscal Year End:*NA *Latest Annual Data:* 12/31/2005

Year	Sales	Net Income
2005	$106,305,000	-$21,166,000
2004	$66,881,000	-$41,155,000
2003	$79,211,000	-$20,362,000

Curr. Assets:	$109,218,000	Curr. Liab.:	$103,758,000		
Plant, Equip.:	$48,298,000	Total Liab.:	$110,379,000	Indic. Yr. Divd.:	NA
Total Assets:	$173,918,000	Net Worth:	$63,539,000	Debt/ Equity:	NA

Mirae Corp

No. 714 Baekseok-Dong, Cheonan-si, Chungcheongnam-Do; **PH:** 82-416215070; *http://* www.mirae.com

General - Incorporation	Korea	**Stock** - Price on:12/24/2007	$1.4
Employees	335	Stock Exchange	NDQ
Auditor	Deloitte Anjin LLC	Ticker Symbol	MRAE
Stk Agt	NA	Outstanding Shares	91,530,000
Counsel	NA	E.P.S	NA
DUNS No.	NA	Shareholders	NA

Business: The group's principal activity is manufacturing of other instruments and appliances for measuring, checking, testing and navigating.

Primary SIC and add'l.: 3674 3825

CIK No: 0001099196

Subsidiaries: AIO Corporation, Cyber Bank Co., Ltd, GLD Co., Ltd., Korea Internet.com Co., Ltd., Mirae (Hong Kong) Co., Ltd., Mirae America Inc., Mirae Online, Co., Ltd.

Officers: Soondo Kwon/51/Chmn., CEO, Pres., Chung Soo Kim/56/VP - Display Division, Do Young Cho/49/Dir. - Display Division, Hyochul Yun/COO, Hee Rak Beom/49/Executive Dir. - Mechatronics, Plasma Division, Hyeon Tae Kyeong/45/Executive Dir. - SMT Business Unit, Hyo Chul Yoon/51/VP, Laurent Robert/40/Dir. - SMT Software Team, Jae Myeong Song/45/Dir. - ATE Business Unit, Jeoung Han Choi/48/Dir. - Display Division, Gi-Hoon Joung/CFO

Directors: Soondo Kwon/51/Chmn., CEO, Pres., Kyung Won Chung/58/Dir., Byung Taeck Song/54/Dir. - ATE Business Unit Overseas Customer Support, Jong Ook Yoo/50/Dir. - ATE Business Unit Domestic Sales, Kwang Hyung Lee/53/Dir., Yeon Ho Lee/48/Dir.

Owners: Hyo Chul Yun, Soon Do Kwon, Moon Soul Chung/12.90%

Miramar Mining Corp

889 Harbourside Dr., Ste. 300, North Vancouver, BC, V7P 3S1; **PH:** 1-604-985-2572; **Fax:** 1-604-980-0731; *http://* www.miramarmining.com; **Email:** info@miramarmining.com

General - Incorporation	Canada	**Stock** - Price on:12/24/2007	$4.45
Employees	NA	Stock Exchange	AMEX
Auditor	KPMG LLP	Ticker Symbol	MNG
Stk Agt	Pacific Corporate Services Ltd	Outstanding Shares	217,630,000
Counsel	Owen Bird	E.P.S	-$0.04
DUNS No.	24-672-9560	Shareholders	NA

Business: The group's principal activities are to develop and explore gold mines. The group operates two mines in Canada: the con and giant gold mines in yellowknife, in the northwest territories of Canada.

Primary SIC and add'l.: 1041

CIK No: 0000940947

Subsidiaries: Miramar Con Mine Ltd., Miramar Hope Bay Ltd

Officers: Anthony Walsh/Dir., CEO, Pres., David Fennell/Executive Vice Chmn., Heather Duggan/VP - Human Resources, John Wakeford/VP - Exploration, Elaine Bennett/VP, Controller - Principal Financial, Accounting Officer, David A. Long/Corp. Sec., Alex Buchan/Mgr. - Community Relations, James A. Currie/VP - Operations

Directors: Anthony Walsh/Dir., CEO, Pres., William E. Stanley/Vice Chmn., David Fennell/Executive Vice Chmn., Anthony J. Petrina/Chmn., Christopher Pollard/Dir., Lawrence Bell/Dir., Peter B. Nixon/Dir., Catherine McLeod-Seltzer/Dir., William Myckatyn/Dir.

Financial Data: *Fiscal Year End:*12/31 *Latest Annual Data:* 12/31/2006

Year	Sales	Net Income
2006	NA	-$33,338,000
2005	$2,202,000	-$15,260,000
2004	$10,184,000	-$26,951,000

Curr. Assets:	$135,144,000	Curr. Liab.:	$11,874,000		
Plant, Equip.:	$181,436,000	Total Liab.:	$44,279,000	Indic. Yr. Divd.:	NA
Total Assets:	$338,001,000	Net Worth:	$293,722,000	Debt/ Equity:	NA

Miranda Gold Corp

15782 Marine Dr. Unit 1, White Rock, BC, V4B 1E6; **PH:** 1-604-536-2711; *http://* www.mirandagold.com; **Email:** mad@mirandagold.com

General - Incorporation	Canada	**Stock** - Price on:12/24/2007	NA
Employees	NA	Stock Exchange	OTC
Auditor	Morgan & Co	Ticker Symbol	MRDDF
Stk Agt	Pacific Corporate Trust Co	Outstanding Shares	NA
Counsel	NA	E.P.S	NA
DUNS No.	25-533-1506	Shareholders	NA

Business: The groups principle activities include mining and exploration of gold. The group also provides discovery of gold. The group operates from United States.

Primary SIC and add'l.: NA

CIK No: 0000942149

Subsidiaries: Minas Miranda S.A. de C.V., Miranda U.S.A., Inc

Officers: Kenneth D. Cunningham/Dir., CEO, Pres., Joe Hebert/VP - Exploration, Doris Meyer/CFO, Corp. Sec., Brian Cellura/Sr. Geologist, Steve Koehler/Sr. Geologist, Fiona Grant/Investor Relations, Drew Wells/Legal Counsel

Directors: Kenneth D. Cunningham/Dir., CEO, Pres., Dennis L. Higgs/Chmn., Steve Ristorcelli/Dir., James F. Cragg/Dir., Ross G. McDonald/Dir.

Owners: James G. Cragg/0.53%, Dennis L. Higgs/2.64%, Kenneth Cunningham/3.96%, Doris Meyer/0.68%, Steve Ristorcelli/1.79%, Ross G. McDonald/0.37%, Joseph Hebert/1.96%

Financial Data: *Fiscal Year End:*08/31 *Latest Annual Data:* 8/31/2006

Year	Sales	Net Income
2006	NA	-$1,551,000
2005	NA	-$1,424,000
2004	NA	-$1,328,000

Curr. Assets:	$5,906,000	Curr. Liab.:	$80,000		
Plant, Equip.:	$390,000	Total Liab.:	$80,000	Indic. Yr. Divd.:	NA
Total Assets:	$6,003,000	Net Worth:	$5,922,000	Debt/ Equity:	NA

Mirant Corp

1155 Perimeter Ctr. W, Ste. 100, Atlanta, GA, 30338; **PH:** 1-678-579-5000; **Fax:** 1-678-579-5001; *http://* www.mirant.com; **Email:** environment@mirant.com

General - Incorporation	DE	**Stock** - Price on:12/24/2007	$43.54
Employees	4,440	Stock Exchange	NYSE
Auditor	KPMG LLP	Ticker Symbol	NA
Stk Agt	Mellon Investor Services LLC	Outstanding Shares	255,880,000
Counsel	Shearman & Sterling LLP	E.P.S	$11.78
DUNS No.	NA	Shareholders	NA

Business: The group's principle activities include electricity generation and distribution, fuel procurement and marketing of energy and energy-linked commodities. The group operates from United States, North America, the Caribbean, Europe and Asia.

Primary SIC and add'l.: 4911 4923

CIK No: 0001010775

Subsidiaries: ARB Power Ventures, Inc., Avon River Power Holdings, Corp., Cayman Energy Traders, CEMIG Investments, LLC, Cheng Power Systems, Inc., Claredon Towers Holdings, Inc., Coyote Springs 2, LLC, CUC Holdings, N.V., Curacao Energy Company, Ltd., Curacao Utilities Company N.V., Curacao Utilities Operating Company N.V., Grand Bahama Power Company Limited, Hijos de F. Escao, Inc., Hudson Valley Gas Corporation, ICD Utilities Limited 186 Subsidiaries included in the Index

Officers: Edward R. Muller/Chmn., CEO, Pres./$8,646,648.00, Mary Ann Arico/Investor Relations Officer, Thomas E. Legro/56/Sr. VP, Principal Accounting Officer, Controller, Julia A. Houston/Corp. Sec., James V. Iaco/CFO, Exec. VP/$2,614,758.00, Robert M. Edgell/Exec. VP, US Region Head/$3,179,487.00, Linn S. Williams/Exec. VP, General Counsel/$2,658,148.00, Jose P. Leviste/63/Sr. VP, William P. Von Blasingame/49/Sr. VP, GM - Caribbean/$1,375,717.00

Directors: Edward R. Muller/Chmn., CEO, Pres., William L. Thacker/Dir., A. D. Correll/Dir., Thomas W. Cason/Dir., Thomas H. Johnson/Dir., John T. Miller/Dir., Robert C. Murray/Dir., John M. Quain/Dir., Terry G. Dallas/Dir.

Owners: Insiders, Robert C. Murray, Terry G. Dallas, A. D. Correll, John M. Quain, Linn S. Williams, Paulson & Co./5.78%, John T. Miller, Edward R. Muller, William L. Thacker, Thomas H. Johnson, Thomas W. Cason, William P. Von Blasingame, Robert M. Edgell, James V. Iaco

Financial Data: *Fiscal Year End:*12/31 *Latest Annual Data:* 12/31/2006

Year	Sales	Net Income
2006	$3,103,000,000	$1,864,000,000
2005	$4,184,000,000	-$1,307,000,000
2004	$4,572,000,000	-$476,000,000

Curr. Assets:	$7,985,000,000	Curr. Liab.:	$3,259,000,000	P/E Ratio:	4.72
Plant, Equip.:	$2,212,000,000	Total Liab.:	$7,093,000,000	Indic. Yr. Divd.:	NA
Total Assets:	$11,536,000,000	Net Worth:	$4,443,000,000	Debt/ Equity:	0.6601

Miravant Medical Technologies

336 Bollay Dr., Santa Barbara, CA, 93117; **PH:** 1-805-685-9880; *http://* www.miravant.com; **Email:** communications@miravant.com

General - Incorporation	DE	**Stock** - Price on:12/24/2007	$0.006
Employees	NA	Stock Exchange	OTC
Auditor	Ernst & Young LLP	Ticker Symbol	MRVT
Stk Agt	NA	Outstanding Shares	NA
Counsel	Nida & Maloney	E.P.S	NA
DUNS No.	60-694-1227	Shareholders	NA

Business: The group's principal activity is to develop light activated drugs and associated devices for a medical procedure called photodynamic therapy ('pdt'). The group has developed photopoint (TM) pdt, a proprietary technology that creates site-specific treatments for patients with serious eye and skin conditions, cancer and cardiovascular diseases. This technology includes the integration of synthetic photoselective drugs with software-controlled, portable light producing devices and fiber optic light delivery and measurement devices to achieve a photochemical effect on targeted diseased cells and blood vessels.

Primary SIC and add'l.: 8731 2835 2834

CIK No: 0000933745

Subsidiaries: Miravant Cardiovascular, Inc., Miravant Pharmaceuticals, Inc., Miravant Systems, Inc.

Financial Data: Fiscal Year End:12/31 Latest Annual Data: 12/31/2004

Year	Sales	Net Income
2004	NA	-$15,896,000
2003	NA	-$7,465,000
2002	$499,000	-$15,960,000

Curr. Assets:	$6,413,000	Curr. Liab.:	$1,858,000		
Plant, Equip.:	$125,000	Total Liab.:	$9,491,000	Indic. Yr. Divd.:	NA
Total Assets:	$7,509,000	Net Worth:	-$1,982,000	Debt/ Equity:	NA

Mirenco Inc

206 May St., Radcliffe, IA, 50230; *PH:* 1-515-899-2164; *Fax:* 1-515-899-2147; *http://* www.mirenco.com; *Email:* info@mirenco.com

General - Incorporation	IA	Stock- Price on:12/24/2007	NA
Employees	18	Stock Exchange	OTC
Auditor	Stark Winter Schenkein & Co. LLP	Ticker Symbol	MREO
Stk Agt	Signature Stock Transfer, Inc.	Outstanding Shares	NA
Counsel	NA	E.P.S.	-$0.02
DUNS No.	NA	Shareholders	NA

Business: The group's principle activities include developing and marketing technologically advanced products for throttle control of internal combustion vehicles. The products reduce environmental emissions, reduce vehicle maintenance costs and improve fuel efficiency. The company provides a product incorporating global positioning system technology into a throttle-control application using 'satellite-to-throttle' technology. The products offered include drivermax(R), drivermax(R) software, hydrofire(R) injection, hydrofire(R) fluid, hydrofire(R) lubricant and econocruise(R) and these products are derived from technology patented in the United States, Mexico and Canada. The group operates from United States.

Primary SIC and add'l.: 3714

CIK No: 0001041609

Officers: Dwayne L. Fosseen/Chmn., CEO, Paul Fournier/Engineering, Richard A. Musal/61/Dir., CFO, COO

Directors: Dwayne L. Fosseen/Chmn., CEO, Jerry Handsaker/Dir., Don Williams/Dir., Richard A. Musal/61/Dir., CFO, COO, Merlin Hanson/Dir., Timothy Neugent/57/Dir.

Owners: Insiders/45.35%, Dwayne Fosseen/38.30%, Tim Neugent/0.17%, Merlin Hanson/0.06%, Richard A. Musal/5.20%, Don Williams/1.62%

Financial Data: Fiscal Year End:12/31 Latest Annual Data: 12/31/2006

Year	Sales	Net Income
2006	$591,000	-$620,000
2005	$720,000	-$720,000
2004	$354,000	-$1,229,000

Curr. Assets:	$187,000	Curr. Liab.:	$478,000		
Plant, Equip.:	$496,000	Total Liab.:	$619,000	Indic. Yr. Divd.:	NA
Total Assets:	$691,000	Net Worth:	$58,000	Debt/ Equity:	NA

Miscor Group Ltd

821 Bev Rd. , Youngstown, OH, 44512; *PH:* 1-330-758-0941; *http://* www.magnetech.com

General - Incorporation	IN	Stock- Price on:12/24/2007	$0.41
Employees	452	Stock Exchange	OTC
Auditor	NA	Ticker Symbol	MCGL
Stk Agt	Registrar & Transfer Co	Outstanding Shares	187,410,000
Counsel	NA	E.P.S.	-$0.04
DUNS No.	NA	Shareholders	NA

Business: The group's principle activity is to provide electrical and mechanical solutions to industrial, commercial and institutional customers. The group operates through three segments namely industrial services, electrical contracting services, and diesel engine components. The group operates from the United States.

Primary SIC and add'l.: 7699

CIK No: 0001295503

Subsidiaries: HK Engine Components LLC, Magnetech Industrial Services of Alabama LLC, Magnetech Industrial Services, Inc, Magnetech Power Services LLC, Martell Electric LLC

Officers: John A. Martell/Founder, Chmn., CEO, Pres., Richard Mullin/CFO, James M. Lewis/General Counsel, Jeff Lambert/Investor Relations Contact, Patrick Kane/Investor Relations Contact

Directors: John A. Martell/Founder, Chmn., CEO, Pres., William J. Schmuhl/64/Dir., Richard A. Tamborski/59/Dir.

Owners: Richard J. Mullin, William J. Schmuhl, Anthony W. Nicholson, Insiders, James M. Lewis, Richard A. Tamborski, William Wisniewski

Financial Data: Fiscal Year End:NA Latest Annual Data: 12/31/2006

Year	Sales	Net Income
2006	$60,754,000	-$2,661,000

Curr. Assets:	$22,438,000	Curr. Liab.:	$18,350,000		
Plant, Equip.:	$6,320,000	Total Liab.:	$27,174,000	Indic. Yr. Divd.:	NA
Total Assets:	$30,867,000	Net Worth:	$3,693,000	Debt/ Equity:	0.2081

Misonix Inc

1938 New Hwy., Farmingdale, NY, 11735; *PH:* 1-631-694-9555; *Fax:* 1-631-694-9412; *http://* www.misonix.com

General - Incorporation	NY	Stock- Price on:12/24/2007	$6.23
Employees	207	Stock Exchange	NDQ
Auditor	Grant Thornton, LLP	Ticker Symbol	MSON
Stk Agt	Continental Stock Transfer & Trust Co	Outstanding Shares	7,000,000
Counsel	Hartman & Craven LLP	E.P.S.	-$0.15
DUNS No.	06-596-3449	Shareholders	NA

Business: The group's principal activities are to design, manufacture and market ultrasonic medical devices. The group also develops and markets ultrasonic equipment for use in the scientific and industrial markets, ductless fume enclosures for filtration of gaseous contaminates and environmental control products for the abatement of air pollution. The group operates through two segments: medical devices segment manufactures and sells the auto sonix ultrasonic cutting and coagulatory system, ultrasound systems and replacement transducers for the medical diagnostic ultrasound industry, ultrasonic lithotriptor, ultrasonic neuroaspirator (used for neurosurgery) and soft tissue aspirator and laboratory and scientific products segment manufactures and sells sonicator(R) ultrasonic liquid processors and cell disruptors, aura(tm) ductless fume hood products and mystaire(R) scrubbers for the abatement of air pollution.

Primary SIC and add'l.: 3822 3845 3589

CIK No: 0000880432

Subsidiaries: Acoustic Marketing Research Inc., d/b/a Sonora Medical Systems, Inc., Fibra-Sonics (NY) Inc., Hearing Innovations, Inc., Labcaire Systems, Ltd., Misonix, Ltd., UKHIFU Ltd.

Officers: Michael A. McManus/Dir., CEO, Pres., Richard Zaremba/CFO, Sr. VP, Ronald Manna/VP - Regulatory Affairs, Dan Voic/VP - Research, Development, Engineering, Frank Napoli/VP - Operations

Directors: Michael A. McManus/Dir., CEO, Pres., Thomas F. O'Neill/Dir., John W. Gildea/Dir., Charles Miner/Dir., Guy T. Minetti/Dir., Howard Alliger/Dir.

Owners: Frank Napoli, Richard Zaremba/1.30%, Ronald Manna/1.50%, Insiders/24.50%, Charles Miner, Dan Voic, Howard Alliger/6.20%, Thomas F. ONeill, Michael A. McManus/15.20%, Guy T. Minetti, Gary Gelman/6.60%, John W. Gildea

Financial Data: Fiscal Year End:06/30 Latest Annual Data: 6/30/2006

Year	Sales	Net Income
2006	$39,067,000	-$3,759,000
2005	$45,907,000	$936,000
2004	$39,059,000	$1,719,000

Curr. Assets:	$21,791,000	Curr. Liab.:	$9,688,000		
Plant, Equip.:	$6,496,000	Total Liab.:	$11,916,000	Indic. Yr. Divd.:	NA
Total Assets:	$34,513,000	Net Worth:	$22,255,000	Debt/ Equity:	0.0508

Mission Bancorp CA

1330 Truxtun Ave., Bakersfield, CA, 93301; *PH:* 1-661-859-2500; *Fax:* 1-661-321-4821; *http://* www.missionbank.com

General - Incorporation	CA	Stock- Price on:12/24/2007	$62
Employees	NA	Stock Exchange	OTC
Auditor	NA	Ticker Symbol	MSBC
Stk Agt	Computershare Investor Services LLC	Outstanding Shares	NA
Counsel	NA	E.P.S.	NA
DUNS No.	NA	Shareholders	NA

Business: The group operates through its subsidiary whose principle activity is to provide financial services. Services of the group include providing deposits including personal and business checking accounts and savings accounts, interest-bearing negotiable withdrawal accounts, money market accounts and time certificates of deposit, and lending activities including real estate mortgage, commercial and industrial, real estate construction, agricultural and consumer loans. The group operates from California in the United States.

Primary SIC and add'l.: 6022 6163 6153 6712

CIK No: 0001169483

Officers: Richard E. Fanucchi/Dir., CEO, Pres., Grady Buck/Sr. VP, Chief Credit Officer, Stan Newman/Sr. VP - Commercial Lending, Craig Swenson/Sr. VP, CFO, Cindy Talley/VP, Administrative Operations Officer, Terry Redwine/VP, Mgr. - Greenfield Branch, A. J. Antongiovanni/VP, Mgr., Rob Hallum/Sr. VP - Commercial Lending

Directors: Richard E. Fanucchi/Dir., CEO, Pres., Arnold T. Cattani/Chmn., Bruce L. Beretta/Dir., Donice Boylan/Dir., Salvador Chipres/Dir., Daniel Rodriguez/Dir., Paramjit Dosanjh/Dir., Curtis E. Floyd/Dir., Mary Jane Wilson/Dir., Kurt C. Thomas/Dir.

Financial Data: Fiscal Year End:12/31 Latest Annual Data: 12/31/2002

Year	Sales	Net Income
2002	$3,730,000	$409,000
2001	$3,572,000	$314,000
2000	$2,915,000	$486,000

Curr. Assets:	$26,426,000	Curr. Liab.:	$67,603,000		
Plant, Equip.:	$282,000	Total Liab.:	$67,603,000	Indic. Yr. Divd.:	NA
Total Assets:	$73,801,000	Net Worth:	$6,198,000	Debt/ Equity:	NA

Mission Broadcasting Inc

544 Red Rock Dr., Wadsworth, OH, 44281; *PH:* 1-330-335-8808

General - Incorporation	DE	Stock- Price on:12/24/2007	NA
Employees	NA	Stock Exchange	NA
Auditor	PricewaterhouseCoopers LLP	Ticker Symbol	NA
Stk Agt	NA	Outstanding Shares	NA
Counsel	NA	E.P.S.	NA
DUNS No.	NA	Shareholders	NA

Business: The groups principle activities include licensing and broadcasting for 15 television stations. The group operates TV stations under Nexstar Broadcasting. The group operates from United States.

Primary SIC and add'l.: NA

CIK No: 0001142412

Subsidiaries: Bastet Broadcasting, Inc., Mission Broadcasting of Joplin, Inc.

Officers: Dennis Thatcher/60/COO, Exec. VP, Nancie J. Smith/54/VP, Sec., David S. Smith/52/Dir., Pres., Treasurer, Principal Executive Officer, Principal Financial, Accounting Officer

Directors: David S. Smith/52/Dir., Pres., Treasurer, Principal Executive Officer, Principal Financial, Accounting Officer

Mission Community Bancorp

581 Higuera St., Ste. A, San Luis Obispo, CA, 93401; *PH:* 1-805-782-5000; *Fax:* 1-805-782-5034; *http://* www.missioncommunitybank.com

General - Incorporation	CA	*Stock*- Price on:12/24/2007	$19
Employees	53	Stock Exchange	OTC
Auditor	Vavrinek, Trine, Day & Co. LLP	Ticker Symbol	MISS
Stk Agt	Karla S. Cool	Outstanding Shares	NA
Counsel	NA	E.P.S	$0.94
DUNS No.	NA	Shareholders	NA

Business: The group's principle activity is to offer a wide variety of deposit, loan and other financial services to small businesses, entrepreneurs and their employees and families. The group is a bank holding company for mission community bank, which operates two branches in the central coast area of California. The group offers checking and savings accounts, money market accounts and time certificates of deposits; offers commercial, agribusiness, government guaranteed, real estate, automobile and other installment and term loans and leases; issues drafts, sells travelers' checks and provides other customary banking services.

Primary SIC and add'l.: 6021 6712

CIK No: 0001129920

Subsidiaries: Mission Community Bank, Mission Community Capital Trust I

Officers: Anita M. Robinson/Dir., CEO, Pres./$213,572.00, Ronald B. Pigeon/58/CFO, Exec. VP/$158,527.00

Directors: Anita M. Robinson/Dir., CEO, Pres., Roxanne M. Carr/Vice Chmn., William B. Coy/Chmn., Karl F. Wittstrom/Dir., Richard Korsgaard/Dir., Bruce M. Breault/Dir., Robin L. Rossi/Dir., Gary E. Stemper/Dir.

Owners: Department of the Treasury Community Development Financial Institutions Fund/12.90%, William B. Coy/2.50%, James M. Judge/0.20%, Anita M. Robinson/6.30%, Robin L. Rossi/4.00%, Patrick W. Hopper Trust/6.30%, Karl F. Wittstrom/3.80%, Bruce M. Breault/5.40%, Richard Korsgaard/0.70%, Ronald B. Pigeon/0.20%, Insiders/27.20%, Roxanne M. Carr/2.90%, Gary E. Stemper/2.80%

Financial Data: Fiscal Year End:12/31   Latest Annual Data: 12/31/2006

Year	Sales	Net Income
2006	$12,107,000	$870,000
2005	$10,240,000	$957,000
2004	$10,181,000	$1,492,000

Curr. Assets:	$12,737,000	*Curr. Liab.:*	$125,523,000	*P/E Ratio:*	20.21
Plant, Equip.:	$3,724,000	*Total Liab.:*	$146,016,000	*Indic. Yr. Divd.:*	$0.120
Total Assets:	$158,169,000	*Net Worth:*	$12,153,000	*Debt/ Equity:*	1.6217

Mission Energy Holding Co

2600 Michelson Dr., Ste. 1700, Irvine, CA, 92612; *PH:* 1-949-852-3576

General - Incorporation	DE	*Stock*- Price on:12/24/2007	NA
Employees	NA	Stock Exchange	NA
Auditor	PricewaterhouseCoopers LLP	Ticker Symbol	NA
Stk Agt	NA	Outstanding Shares	NA
Counsel	NA	E.P.S	NA
DUNS No.	NA	Shareholders	NA

Business: The groups principle activity is to generate electric power. The groups operating power plants include merchant power plants and contracted power plants. The group operates from United States.

Primary SIC and add'l.: NA

CIK No: 0001158323

Subsidiaries: Aguila Energy Company, Anacapa Energy Company, Arrowhead Energy Company, Athens Funding, LLC, Beheer-en Beleggingsmaatschappij Plogema B.V., Brookhaven Cogeneration, L.P., Camino Energy Company, Caresale Services Limited, Chester Energy Company, Chestnut Ridge Energy Company, Citizens Power Holdings One, LLC, CL Power Sales Eight, LLC, CL Power Sales One, LLC, CL Power Sales Seven, LLC, CL Power Sales Ten LLC 126 Subsidiaries included in the Index

Officers: Mark C. Clarke/VP, Controller

Directors: John E. Bryson/Chmn., Jacob A. Bouknight/Dir.

Mission Oaks Bancorp

41530 Enterprise Cir. S, Ste. 100, Temecula, CA, 92590; *PH:* 1-951-719-1200; *Fax:* 1-951-719-1201; *http://* www.missionoaksbank.com; *Email:* info@missionoaksbank.com

General - Incorporation		*Stock*- Price on:12/24/2007	$10.85
Employees	NA	Stock Exchange	OTC
Auditor	NA	Ticker Symbol	MOKB
Stk Agt	U.S. Stock Transfer Corp	Outstanding Shares	NA
Counsel	NA	E.P.S	NA
DUNS No.	NA	Shareholders	NA

Business: The groups principal activity is to provide exceptional customer banking service to residents and businesses owners. The group operates from United States.

Primary SIC and add'l.: 6021

CIK No:

Officers: Gary W. Votapka/Dir., Pres., CEO - Mission Oaks National Bank, Walter F. Combs/MD, Vice - Chmn., Keith O. Johnson/Dir., Co - Founder, Exec. VP, COO, Chief Lending Officer - Mission Oaks National Bank, Scott Butler/National Mgr. - Strategic Alliance Partners, Mission Oaks Funding, Mission Oak National Bank, James Duggan/Commercial Loan Officer, Steven Johnston/Southwest Regional Mgr. - Strategic Alliance Partners, Mission Oaks Funding, Mission Oak National Bank, Nancy Tangorra/VP, Assist. Loan Production Mgr. - Mission Oaks Funding, Mission Oak National Bank, David Manser/VP, Loan Officer - Mission Oaks Funding, Mission Oak National Bank, Paul Hanson/Assist. VP, Sr. Loan Administrator - Mission Oaks Funding, Mission Oak National Bank, Donald Coop/Dir. - Real Estate Investor, Michael D. Crews/Dir. - Residential Developer, Valley Center, Mission Oaks National Bank, Joseph J. Kuebler/Dir., Certified Public Accountant - Temecula, Darol H. Caster/Sr. VP, CFO - Mission Oak National Bank, Timothy Freese/Sr. VP, Credit Administrator, Richard Lawless/Sr. VP - Commercial Lending, Mission Oak National Bank *(50 Officers included in Index)*

Directors: Gary W. Votapka/Dir., Pres., CEO - Mission Oaks National Bank, Robert D. Knogge/Chmn., Walter F. Combs/MD, Vice - Chmn., Keith O. Johnson/Dir., Co - Founder, Exec. VP, COO, Chief Lending Officer - Mission Oaks National Bank, Irma L. Atillo/Dir., Donald Coop/Dir. - Real Estate Investor, Michael D. Crews/Dir. - Residential Developer, Valley Center, Mission Oaks National Bank, Gregory L. Gissler/Dir., Fred D. Grimes/Dir., Joseph J. Kuebler/Dir., Certified Public Accountant - Temecula, Patrick W. Utnehmer/Dir.

Mission Valley BCP CA

9116 Sunland Blvd., Sun Valley, CA, 91352; *PH:* 1-818-394-2300; *Fax:* 1-818-394-2035; *http://* www.missionvalleybank.com; *Email:* info@missionvalleybank.com

General - Incorporation		*Stock*- Price on:12/24/2007	$10.5
Employees	NA	Stock Exchange	OTC
Auditor	NA	Ticker Symbol	MVLY
Stk Agt	NA	Outstanding Shares	NA
Counsel	NA	E.P.S	NA
DUNS No.	NA	Shareholders	NA

Business: The groups principal activity is to provide banking services. The services of the group include personal banking, business banking, originating loans and online banking. The group operates from the United States.

Primary SIC and add'l.: 6029

CIK No:

Officers: Tamara Gurney/Dir., CEO, Pres., Carrie Burrell/VP, Marketing Mgr. - Administration, Cindy Brown/VP - Loan Operations - Specialized Lending Division, Amy Gibbs/VP - Operations Mgr. - Santa Clarita Valley, Frankie Powell/VP, Business Development Officer, Julian Sandoval/VP, Relationship Mgr., Jahun Smith/VP, Branch Mgr. - Sun Valley Office, Anto Touloumdjian/Assist. Operations Mgr. - Valencia Office, Marti Heinbaugh/VP - Branch Mgr. - Centre Point Office, Pat McMillian/VP - Operations Mgr. - Centre Point Office, Rhonda Pinuelas/VP - Business Banking Officer - Centre Point Office, Laura Soto/Assist. Operations Officer - Centre Point Office, Greg Spencer/VP - Business Banking Officer - Centre Point Business Banking Office, Carol Dignard/VP, Assist. Branch Mgr. - Sun Valley Office, Elizabeth Halif/VP - Operations Mgr. - SAN Fernando Valley *(26 Officers included in Index)*

Directors: Tamara Gurney/Dir., CEO, Pres., Earle S. Wasserman/Chmn., John Richardson/Dir., Darlynn C. Morgan/Dir., Jerold Neuman/Dir., Jim Bagge/Dir., Marc Foulkrod/Dir., Mark Lefever/Dir.

Mission West Properties Inc

10050 Bandley Dr., Cupertino, CA, 95014; *PH:* 1-408-725-0700; *Fax:* 1-408-725-1626; *http://* www.missionwest.com; *Email:* irmail@missionwest.com

General - Incorporation	MD	*Stock*- Price on:12/24/2007	$13.7
Employees	5	Stock Exchange	AMEX
Auditor	BDO Seidman, LLP	Ticker Symbol	MSW
Stk Agt	NA	Outstanding Shares	19,640,000
Counsel	NA	E.P.S	$1.13
DUNS No.	NA	Shareholders	NA

Business: The groups principle activities include acquiring, marketing, leasing, and manages research and development properties. The group operates from the United States. The groups quarterly revenue for September 2007 was 71.59 millions of USD.

Primary SIC and add'l.: 6798

CIK No: 0001067419

Officers: Carl E. Berg/69/Chmn., CEO/$122,500.00, Raymond V. Marino/49/Pres., Dir., COO, Sec./$374,351.00, Wayne N. Pham/38/VP - Finance, Controller, Principal Accounting Officer/$173,168.00, Ray Marino/Contact - Leasing, Acquisition Information

Directors: Carl E. Berg/69/Chmn., CEO, Raymond V. Marino/49/Pres., Dir., COO, Sec., John C. Bolger/61/Dir., William A. Hasler/66/Dir., Lawrence B. Helzel/59/Dir.

Owners: Raymond V. Marino/3.02%, Teachers Advisors, Inc./6.39%, Cohen & Steers Capital Management, Inc./14.12%, Ingalls & Snyder, LLC/15.93%, William A. Hasler, John C. Bolger, Neuberger Berman, LLC/7.89%, Lawrence B. Helzel/1.10%, Wayne N. Pham, Insiders/5.08%

Financial Data: Fiscal Year End:12/31   Latest Annual Data: 12/31/2006

Year	Sales	Net Income
2006	$123,828,000	$14,630,000
2005	$120,133,000	$10,027,000
2004	$141,383,000	$13,312,000

Curr. Assets:	$82,030,000	*Curr. Liab.:*	$32,698,000	*P/E Ratio:*	21.08
Plant, Equip.:	$898,889,000	*Total Liab.:*	$898,609,000	*Indic. Yr. Divd.:*	$0.640
Total Assets:	$1,027,487,000	*Net Worth:*	$128,878,000	*Debt/ Equity:*	2.7759

Mississippi Power Co

2992 W Beach, Gulfport, MS, 39501; *PH:* 1-228-864-1211; *http://* www.southernco.com

General - Incorporation	MS	*Stock*- Price on:12/24/2007	NA
Employees	NA	Stock Exchange	NYSE
Auditor	Deloitte & Touche LLP	Ticker Symbol	NA
Stk Agt	NA	Outstanding Shares	NA
Counsel	Balch & Bingham	E.P.S	NA
DUNS No.	00-696-4118	Shareholders	NA

Business: The group's principle activity is to provide electricity. The company generates and purchases electricity and then distributes and sells such energy within the state of Mississippi as well as in rural areas, and at wholesale to one municipality, six rural electric distribution, cooperative associations and one generating and transmitting cooperative. The group operates from United States.

Primary SIC and add'l.: 4911

CIK No: 0000066904

Subsidiaries: Alabama Power Capital Trust IV, Alabama Power Capital Trust V, Alabama Power Capital Trust VI, Alabama Power Capital Trust VII, Alabama Power Capital Trust VIII, Alabama Power Company, Alabama Property Company, Georgia Power Capital Trust IV, Georgia Power Capital Trust IX, Georgia Power Capital Trust V, Georgia Power Capital Trust VI, Georgia Power Capital Trust VII, Georgia Power Capital Trust VIII, Georgia Power Capital Trust X, Georgia Power Capital Trust XI 38 Subsidiaries included in the Index

Officers: Anthony J. Topazi/CEO, Pres./$1,346,304.00, Vicki L. Pierce/Corp. Sec., Frances V. Turnage/VP, Treasurer, CFO/$615,023.00, Kimberly D. Flowers/VP - Generation, Sr. Production Officer/$446,224.00, Johnny W. Atherton/VP - External Affairs/$408,554.00, Donald R. Horsley/VP - Customer Services, Retail Marketing, Wayne Boston/Assist. Sec.

Directors: Tommy E. Dulaney/69/Dir., Robert C. Khayat/70/Dir., Aubrey B. Patterson/65/Dir., Philip J. Terrell/54/Dir.

Owners: Aubrey B. Patterson, Donald R. Horsley, Insiders, Warren A. Hood, Anthony J. Topazi, George A. Schloegel, Kimberly D. Flowers, Robert C. Khayat, Frances V. Turnage, Phillip J. Terrell, John W. Atherton, Thomas E. Dulaney

Mitcham Industries Inc

8141 SH 75 S, Huntsville, TX, 77342; *PH:* 1-936-291-2277; *Fax:* 1-936-295-1922; *http://* www.mitchamindustries.com

General - Incorporation	TX	Stock - Price on:12/24/2007	$20
Employees	131	Stock Exchange	NDQ
Auditor	Hein & Assoc. LLP	Ticker Symbol	MIPS
Stk Agt	North American Transfer Co	Outstanding Shares	9,640,000
Counsel	Norton, Jacobs, Kuhn & McTopy	E.P.S.	$0.87
DUNS No.	02-648-5250	Shareholders	NA

Business: The group's principle activity is to lease and sell geophysical and other equipment. The group operates in two segments: equipment leasing and sales and front-end services. The equipment is used for the seismic data survey on land and transition zones. The group's leasing and sales are primarily for seismic industry worldwide, pool includes many types of equipment used in seismic data acquisition, including all components of land and transition zone seismic data acquisition systems, geophones and cables, earth vibrators, peripheral equipment, survey and other equipment. The group operates in the United States, Canada, Europe, Mexico, South America, Asia and other foreign countries. The group's total revenue for year 2007 was 48.91 millions of USD.

Primary SIC and add'l.: 5084 7359

CIK No: 0000926423

Subsidiaries: Mitcham Canada Ltd., Mitcham Seismic Eurasia LLC, Seamap (UK)Ltd., Seamap Inc., Seamap International Holdings Pte Ltd., Seamap Pte. Ltd., Seismic Asia Pacific Pty Ltd.

Officers: Billy F. Mitcham/Dir., CEO, Pres./$860,481.00, Guy Malden/VP - Marine Systems/$307,197.00, Robert P. Capps/Dir., Exec. VP - Finance, CFO/$399,921.00, Guy Rogers/VP - Business Development/$313,667.00, Cheryl Wilson/Accounting, Tim Holden/Sales, Jim Croix/Sales, Pascal Hythier/Sales, Howard White/Sales, Cyndi Miller/Accounting, Jack Lascar/Investor Relations Officer

Directors: Billy F. Mitcham/Dir., CEO, Pres., Peter H. Blum/Non Exec. Chmn., John F. Schwalbe/Dir., Robert P. Capps/Dir., Exec. VP - Finance, CFO, Randal Dean Lewis/Dir., Dean R. Lewis/65/Dir.

Owners: Robert P. Capps, Paul Guy Rogers, R. Dean Lewis, John F. Schwalbe/1.00%, Insiders/15.80%, Peter H. Blum/5.90%, Guy Malden, Billy F. Mitcham/8.00%, First Wilshire Securities Management, Inc./6.10%

Financial Data: *Fiscal Year End:*01/31 *Latest Annual Data:* 1/31/2007

Year	Sales			Net Income
2007	$48,910,000			$9,285,000
2006	$34,589,000			$10,855,000
2005	$26,368,000			$2,129,000
Curr. Assets:	$35,986,000	Curr. Liab.:	$22,296,000	P/E Ratio: 20.41
Plant, Equip.:	$35,432,000	Total Liab.:	$23,796,000	Indic. Yr. Divd.: NA
Total Assets:	$83,302,000	Net Worth:	$59,506,000	Debt/ Equity: NA

Mitchells & Butlers Plc

27 Fleet St., Birmingham, B3 1JP; *PH:* 44-8706093000; *Fax:* 44-1212332246; *http://* www.mbplc.com; *Email:* investor.relations@mbplc.com

General - Incorporation	UK	Stock - Price on:12/24/2007	NA
Employees	NA	Stock Exchange	NA
Auditor	Ernst & Young LLP	Ticker Symbol	NA
Stk Agt	Puglisi & Associates	Outstanding Shares	NA
Counsel	Sullivan & Cromwell	E.P.S.	NA
DUNS No.	NA	Shareholders	NA

Business: The group's principal activity is the operation of managed pubs, bars and restaurants. The group has two main retail operating segments: pubs & bars, focusing on drink and entertainment-led sites, and restaurants, focusing on food and accommodation-led sites. The other group activity is property development. The group's predominantly freehold estate comprises over 2,000 sites throughout the UK and over sites in Germany. On 11-Apr-2003, the group acquired six continents plc.

Primary SIC and add'l.: NA

CIK No: 0001224480

Subsidiaries: Alex Alsterpavillon Immobilien GmbH & Co KG, Alex Alsterpavillon Management GmbH, Alex Gaststatten Gesellschaft mbH & Co KG, Alex Gaststatten Management GmbH, Alex Gaststattenbetrieb Immobiliengesellschaft mbH, All Bar One Gaststatten Betriebsgesellschaft mbH, Bede Retail Investments Ltd, Browns Restaurant (Brighton) Ltd, Browns Restaurant (Bristol) Ltd, Browns Restaurant (Cambridge) Ltd, Browns Restaurant (London) Ltd, Browns Restaurant (Oxford) Ltd, Browns Restaurants Ltd, Crownhill Estates (Derriford) Ltd, East London Pubs & Restaurants Ltd 43 Subsidiaries included in the Index

Officers: Tony Hughes/59/Executive Dir., Alison Wheaton/43/Portfolio, Information Technology Dir., Mike Bramley/57/Dir., MD - Pubs, Bars, Bronagh Kennedy/43/Dir. - Human Resources, General Counsel, Adam Martin/44/Marketing Dir., Tim Clarke/50/Dir., Chief Executive, John Butterfield/42/Strategy Dir., Richard Pratt/52/Commercial Dir., Adam Fowle/48/Dir., MD - Restaurants, Karim Naffah/44/Dir., Dir. - Finance, Jeremy Townsend/43/Deputy Dir. - Finance, Victoria Penrice/Head - Secretariat, Erik Castenskiold/Head - Investor Relations

Directors: Roger Carr/61/Chmn., Karim Naffah/44/Dir., Dir. - Finance, Tony Hughes/59/Executive Dir., Drummond Hall/58/Non Exec. Dir., Mike Bramley/57/Dir., MD - Pubs, Bars, Tim Lankester/65/Non Exec. Dir., Tim Clarke/50/Dir., Chief Executive, Adam Fowle/48/Dir., MD - Restaurants, Sara Weller/46/Non Exec. Dir., George Fairweather/50/Non Exec. Dir.

Mitek Systems Inc

8911 Balboa Ave., Ste B, San Diego, CA, 92123; *PH:* 1-858-503-7810; *Fax:* 1-858-503-7820; *http://* www.miteksystems.com; *Email:* info@miteksystems.com

General - Incorporation	DE	Stock - Price on:12/24/2007	$0.65
Employees	22	Stock Exchange	OTC
Auditor	Mayer Hoffman Mccann, P.C	Ticker Symbol	MITK
Stk Agt	Mellon Investor Services LLC	Outstanding Shares	16,750,000
Counsel	NA	E.P.S.	-$0.05
DUNS No.	00-492-4841	Shareholders	NA

Business: The group's principle activities include designing, manufacturing and marketing advanced character recognition products for intelligent forms processing applications, document imaging system products and solutions systems integration services. The company's automated document recognition products include proprietary intelligent character recognition (icr), software engine quickstrokes, licensed icr software engine checkscript, checkquest and quickfx pro. The major end users include chevron, gte, citibank, nynex, fleet bank, chase manhattan and british telecom. The company primarily operates in the United States. It also markets its products in Australia, Canada, Chile, czech republic, United Kingdom, France, Germany, Hong Kong, Israel, India, Italy, jamaica, Japan, Malaysia, Mexico, Netherlands, Portugal, Spain, Sweden, Thailand and uruguay. The group operates from United States.

Primary SIC and add'l.: 7373 7372

CIK No: 0000807863

Officers: James B. Debello/Dir., CEO, Pres., Tesfaye Hailemichael/CFO, Grigori Nepomniachtchi/CTO, David Youngerman/VP - Sales, Mari Sese/Contact - Marketing

Directors: James B. Debello/Dir., CEO, Pres., John M. Thornton/Chmn., Michael W. Bealmear/Dir., Vinton Cunningham/Dir., Gerald I. Farmer/Dir., Sally B. Thornton/74/Dir., William P. Tudor/Dir.

Owners: William Tudor, James B. DeBello/6.87%, John M. Thornton/16.98%, John Harland Company/14.71%, Tesfaye Hailemichael/1.64%, Gerald I. Farmer, Michael Bealmear, Vinton Cunningham, Insiders/26.77%, White Pine Capital, LLC/5.88%

Financial Data: *Fiscal Year End:*09/30 *Latest Annual Data:* 9/30/2006

Year	Sales		Net Income
2006	$6,021,000		-$717,000
2005	$6,594,000		-$1,027,000
2004	$5,240,000		-$3,846,000
Curr. Assets:	$2,738,000	Curr. Liab.: $942,000	
Plant, Equip.:	$78,000	Total Liab.: $987,000	Indic. Yr. Divd.: NA
Total Assets:	$2,845,000	Net Worth: $1,858,000	Debt/ Equity: NA

Mitsubishi Tokyo Financial Group Inc

7-1, Marunouchi 2-chome, Chiyoda-ku, Tokyo, 100-8330; ; *http://* www.mufg.jp

General - Incorporation	Japan	Stock - Price on:12/24/2007	$11.38
Employees	80,000	Stock Exchange	NYSE
Auditor	Deloitte Touche Tohmatsu	Ticker Symbol	MTX
Stk Agt	Mitsubishi UFJ Trust & Banking Corp	Outstanding Shares	NA
Counsel	NA	E.P.S.	$0.00
DUNS No.	NA	Shareholders	NA

Business: The group's principle activity is the provision of banking and other financial services. At 31-Mar-2003 it consisted of the parent company, a pure holding company which was established as a result of the integration of the operations of the bank of Tokyo-mitsubishi ltd, the mitsubishi trust and banking corp and nippon trust bank ltd in Apr 2001and to manage and administer the businesses of its banking, trust banking and specialist securities subsidiaries as well as to provide ancillary business, 184 domestic and overseas consolidated companies and 31 associated companies. Operations are carried out through the following divisions: banking, trust business, securities, other (securities, credit cards). The group's quarterly revenue for Mar '07 was 301,381.00 millions of JPY.

Primary SIC and add'l.: 6021 6141 6211 6733 6712

CIK No: 0000067088

Subsidiaries: Banco de Tokyo-Mitsubishi UFJ Brasil S/A, Bank of Tokyo-Mitsubishi UFJ (Canada), Bank of Tokyo-Mitsubishi UFJ (Holland) N.V., Bank of Tokyo-Mitsubishi UFJ (Luxembourg) S.A., Bank of Tokyo-Mitsubishi UFJ (Malaysia) Berhad, Bank of Tokyo-Mitsubishi UFJ (Mexico) S.A., Bank of Tokyo-Mitsubishi UFJ Trust Company, BOT Lease Co., Ltd., BTMU North America International, Inc., DC Card Co., Ltd, DC Card Co., Ltd., Defined Contribution Plan Consulting of Japan Co., Ltd., Mitsubishi UFJ Asset Management Co., Ltd., Mitsubishi UFJ Factors Limited, Mitsubishi UFJ Home Loan Credit Co., Ltd. 36 Subsidiaries included in the Index

Officers: Nobuo Kuroyanagi/Dir., CEO, Pres., Representative Dir., Tsutomu Takasuka/Corporate Auditor, Outside Auditor, Toshihide Mizuno/Sr. MD, Representative Dir., Yoshihiro Watanabe/Sr. MD, Representative Dir., Yuya Saijo/53/Exec. Officer, Co - GM - Asset Management, Administration Planning Division, Integrated Trust Assets Business Group, Mikiyasu Hiroi/53/Exec. Officer - Branches, Eastern Japan, Integrated Retail Banking Business Group, Hiroshi Saito/Sr. MD, Shota Yasuda/Corporate Auditor, Haruo Matsuki/Corporate Auditor, Kunie Okamoto/Corporate Auditor, Outside Auditor, Kazuaki Kido/57/Exec. Officer, Deputy Chief Compliance Officer, Noriaki Hanamizu/61/Managing Officer, Deputy Group Head - Integrated Corporate Banking Business Group, Tetsuya Wada/54/Managing Officer, Group Head - Integrated Retail Banking Business Group, Norimichi Kanari/62/Managing Officer, Deputy Group Head - Integrated Corporate Banking Business Group, Ryusaburo Harasawa/57/Managing Officer in Charge - Operations, Systems Planning Division *(36 Officers included in Index)*

Directors: Nobuo Kuroyanagi/Dir., CEO, Pres., Representative Dir., Ryosuke Tamakoshi/Chmn., Haruya Uehara/Dep. Chmn., Yoshinari Tsutsumi/Dir., Taihei Yuki/Dir., Naotake Okubo/Member - Advisory Board, Kastunori Nagayasu/Deputy Pres., Representative Dir., Takuma Otoshi/Dir., Toshihide Mizuno/Sr. MD, Representative Dir., Shintaro Yasuda/Dir., Hirohisa Aoki/Dir., Fumiyuki Akikusa/Dir., Nobuyuki Hirano/Dir., Iwao Okijima/Dir., Akio Harada/Dir. *(19 Directors included in Index)*

Owners: The Chase Manhattan Bank, N.A. London/1.60%, State Street Bank and Trust Company 505103/1.47%, Daido Life Insurance Company/33.53%, Hero & Co./3.20%, The Norinchukin Bank/66.46%, Nippon Life Insurance Company/2.50%, Japan Trustee Services Bank, Ltd./1.53%, The Master Trust Bank of Japan, Ltd./3.78%, Nippon Life Insurance Company/20.00%, Japan Trustee Services Bank, Ltd./4.17%, UFJ Trustee Services PVT. (Bermuda) Limited/100.00%, Meiji Yasuda Life Insurance Company/1.26%, The Norinchukin Bank/100.00%, Meiji Yasuda Life Insurance Company/40.00%, State Street Bank and Trust Company/1.24% *(17 Owners included in Index)*

Financial Data: *Fiscal Year End:*03/31 *Latest Annual Data:* 3/31/2006

Year	Sales		Net Income
2006	$33,323,307,000		$3,089,844,000
2005	$23,107,831,000		$3,860,942,000
2004	$25,921,634,000		$7,811,366,000
Curr. Assets:	$292,522,154,000	Curr. Liab.: $1,307,313,873,000	P/E Ratio: 21.92
Plant, Equip.:	$9,753,844,000	Total Liab.: $1,494,041,592,000	Indic. Yr. Divd.: NA
Total Assets:	$1,582,724,744,000	Net Worth: $88,683,152,000	Debt/ Equity: NA

Mitsui & Co Ltd

200 Pk. Ave., New York, NY, 10166; *PH:* 1-212-878-4000; *Fax:* 1-212-878-4800;
http:// www.mitsui.co.jp/en

General - Incorporation	Japan	**Stock**- Price on:12/24/2007	$416.6
Employees	40,993	Stock Exchange	NDQ
Auditor	Deloitte Touche Tohmatsu	Ticker Symbol	FWHT
Stk Agt	Chuo Mitsui Trust & Banking Co Ltd	Outstanding Shares	89,230,000
Counsel	NA	E.P.S	NA
DUNS No	69-054-6403	Shareholders	NA

Business: The group's principal activity is to distribute various commodities, finance for customers and organise and coordinate industrial projects. The group is involved in the development of natural resources such as oil and gas, iron and steel raw materials. The group is also engaged in the strategic business investments in new areas such as information technology, biotechnology and nanotechnology.

Primary SIC and add'l.: 5160 5140 5090 7349 5050 5080 5130

CIK No: 0000067099

Subsidiaries: Ak & M Trading Co., Ltd., Al-abar Al-thalath Trading Co. W.l.l., Alta Moda International Limited, Aluminum Metals & Products Corp., Argo Sales Ltd., Asashi Trading Co., Ltd, Asia Investment Fund, Baf (thailand) Co., Ltd., Bangkok Coil Center Co., Ltd., Bay Maritime Limited, Beta-chem, Inc, Bioproducts Inc., Blue Sky Investment Co., Ltd., Buongiorno (hong Kong) Limited, Bussan Asset Management Co., Ltd. 376 Subsidiaries included in the Index

Officers: Shoei Utsudaq/Dir., CEO, Pres., Naoto Nakamura/Corporate Auditor, Terukazu Okahashi/Managing Officer, Osamu Takahashi/Managing Officer, Hideyo Hayakawa/Managing Officer, Hiraku Shimomaki/Managing Officer, Shunichi Miyazaki/Executive Managing Officer, Masahiko Okamura/Managing Officer, Noriaki Sakamoto/Managing Officer, Fuminobu Kawashima/Managing Officer, Katsumi Ogawa/Managing Officer, Yoshinori Setoyama/Managing Officer, Kazuya Imai/Executive Dir., Exec. VP, Yasunori Yokote/Exec. VP, Gempachiro Aihara/Exec. VP *(47 Officers included in Index)*

Directors: Shoei Utsudaq/Dir., CEO, Pres., Nobuo Ohashi/Chmn., Hiroshi Tada/Executive Dir., Exec. VP, Nobuko Matsubara/Dir., Ikujiro Nonaka/Dir., Hiroshi Hirabayashi/Dir., Hiroshi Ito/Executive Dir., Sr. Executive Managing Officer, Junichi Matsumoto/Executive Dir., Sr. Executive Managing Officer, Toshihiro Soejima/Executive Dir., Exec. VP, Motokazu Yoshida/Executive Dir., Sr. Executive Managing Officer, Akishige Okada/Dir., Kazuya Imai/Executive Dir., Exec. VP

Owners: State Street Bank and Trust Company 505103/2.05%, Japan Trustee Services Bank, Ltd./1.76%, The Master Trust Bank of Japan, Ltd./11.23%, Sumitomo Mitsui Banking Corporation/2.15%, Mizuho Corporate Bank, Ltd./1.73%, Japan Trustee Services Bank, Ltd./9.13%, The Chuo Mitsui Trust and Banking Company, Limited/1.72%, Mitsui Life Insurance Company Limited/2.56%, The Bank of Tokyo-Mitsubishi UFJ, Ltd./1.69%, Nippon Life Insurance Company/1.96%

Financial Data: *Fiscal Year End:*03/31 *Latest Annual Data:* 03/31/2007

Year		Sales		Net Income
2007		$41,363,000,000		$2,555,000,000
2006		$34,981,563,000		$1,720,477,000
2005		$32,951,000,000		$1,132,000,000
Curr. Assets:	$40,348,064,000	**Curr. Liab.:**	$29,842,999,000	**P/E Ratio:** 21.92
Plant, Equip.:	$8,200,392,000	**Total Liab.:**	$58,613,204,000	**Indic. Yr. Divd.:** NA
Total Assets:	$72,875,413,000	**Net Worth:**	$14,262,210,000	**Debt/ Equity:** NA

Mity Enterprises Inc

1301 W 400 N, Orem, UT, 84057; *PH:* 1-801-224-0589; *http://* www.mityenterprises.com

General - Incorporation	UT	**Stock**- Price on:12/24/2007	$21.4
Employees	378	Stock Exchange	NYSE
Auditor	Deloitte & Touche LLP	Ticker Symbol	MKC
Stk Agt	Computershare Trust Co	Outstanding Shares	3,330,000
Counsel	Dorsey & Whitney LLP	E.P.S	NA
DUNS No	18-107-2521	Shareholders	NA

Business: The group's principal activity is to design, manufacture and market innovative institutional furniture. It operates through two segments: multipurpose room furniture and healthcare seating. The multipurpose room furniture segment manufactures lightweight, durable, folding leg tables, stacking chairs, lecterns, portable partitions and other related products used in multipurpose rooms. These products are sold to educational, recreational, hotel and hospitality, governmental, office products, health care, church, public assembly and church markets. The healthcare seating segment designs, manufactures and markets healthcare seating and accessories used in long term healthcare facilities. The trademarks of the group include mity-lite(R), mitytuff(R), mitystack(R), mityhost(tm), swiftset(R), xpeditor(tm), xtreme edge(tm), summit(tm) lectern, mitysnap(tm), broda(tm) and versipanel(tm). On 01-Apr-2004, the group acquired versipanel, llc.

Primary SIC and add'l.: 2521 2511 2519 2531 2512 2522

CIK No: 0000921030

Subsidiaries: BOCCC, Inc, Broda Enterprises Inc, Broda Enterprises USA, Inc, DO Group Holding, Inc., Mity-Lite, Inc

Owners: Lewis C. Wilson/1.07%, Peter Najar and Constance S. Crump/3.42%, Hal B. Heaton, Insiders/31.90%, Bradley T. Nielson/3.72%, Paul R. Killpack/1.10%, Bares Capital Management, Inc./7.66%, Gregory D. Dye, Royce & Associates, LLC/9.49%, Dalton, Greiner, Hartman, Maher & Co LLC/4.97%, Gregory L. Wilson

Financial Data: *Fiscal Year End:*03/31 *Latest Annual Data:* 3/31/2006

Year		Sales		Net Income
2006		$55,701,000		$5,541,000
2005		$50,272,000		$2,469,000
2004		$44,348,000		$4,753,000
Curr. Assets:	$19,696,000	**Curr. Liab.:**	$4,416,000	
Plant, Equip.:	$12,485,000	**Total Liab.:**	$4,416,000	**Indic. Yr. Divd.:** NA
Total Assets:	$34,819,000	**Net Worth:**	$30,403,000	**Debt/ Equity:** 0.1476

MIV Therapeutics Inc

1-8765 Ash St., Vancouver, BC, V6P 6T3; *PH:* 1-604-301-9545; *http://* www.mivtherapeutics.com;
Email: contact@mivtherapeutics.com

General - Incorporation	NV	**Stock**- Price on:12/24/2007	$0.59
Employees	NA	Stock Exchange	OTC
Auditor	Ernst & Young LLP	Ticker Symbol	MIVT
Stk Agt	Interwest Transfer Company, Inc.	Outstanding Shares	NA
Counsel	NA	E.P.S	NA
DUNS No	NA	Shareholders	NA

Business: The group's principal activities are to design, develop and manufacture advanced biocompatible stent coatings and drug-delivery technologies. These medical devices are used to treat cardiovascular disorder caused by narrowing or blockage of coronary arteries. Stents are compressible tubular devices that are mounted on a balloon catheter, inserted into the circulatory system by a team of cardiologists, and directed to the location of a blocked coronary artery. The MIVI laser-cut stent is specifically designed and engineered to be used as a drug and therapeutics delivery platform to combat cardiovascular disease, including restenosis.

Primary SIC and add'l.: 3841

CIK No: 0001083011

Subsidiaries: M-I Vascular Innovations, Inc., MIVI Technologies, Inc., SagaX Inc.

Officers: Alan P. Lindsay/Chmn., CEO, Pres., Arc Rajtar/VP - Operations, Patrick A. McGowan/Dir., Exec. VP, CFO, Mark Landy/Dir., Pres., Tom Troczynski/VP - Coating Technologies

Directors: Alan P. Lindsay/Chmn., CEO, Pres., Wilbert Keon/Chmn. - Scientific Advisory Board, Arun Chockalingam/Member - Scientific Advisory Board, Daniel Savard/Dir., Member - Scientific Advisory Board, Patrick A. McGowan/Dir., Exec. VP, CFO, Mark Landy/Dir., Pres.

Owners: Millennium Partners, L.P./13.43%, Mark I. Landy/4.80%, Insiders/12.47%, Rajesh Vaishnav, Pequot Capital Management, Inc./12.53%, Tom Troczynski/1.15%, Alan P. Lindsay/4.96%, Patrick A. McGowan/1.19%, Daniel Savard

Financial Data: *Fiscal Year End:*05/31 *Latest Annual Data:* 5/31/2006

Year		Sales		Net Income
2006		NA		-$9,095,000
2005		NA		-$6,609,000
2004		NA		-$3,472,000
Curr. Assets:	$1,715,000	**Curr. Liab.:**	$194,000	
Plant, Equip.:	$339,000	**Total Liab.:**	$221,000	**Indic. Yr. Divd.:** NA
Total Assets:	$2,054,000	**Net Worth:**	$1,833,000	**Debt/ Equity:** NA

MIVA Inc

Formerly: FindWhat.com
5220 Summerlin Commons Blvd, N/a, Fort Myers, FL, 33907; *PH:* 1-239-561-7229;
http:// www.miva.com

General - Incorporation	DE	**Stock**- Price on:12/24/2007	$6.18
Employees	401	Stock Exchange	NDQ
Auditor	BDO Seidman LLP	Ticker Symbol	FWHT
Stk Agt	Interwest Transfer Company, Inc.	Outstanding Shares	33,060,000
Counsel	Porter Wright Morris & Arthur LLP	E.P.S	-$2.83
DUNS No	NA	Shareholders	NA

Business: The group's principal activities are to develop and market performance-based advertising services for the Internet. The group offers broadly two proprietary services: findwhat.com, a bid-for-position search engine which distributes its listings to third-party Web sites and befirst.com rankpro, a search engine optimization service. The services of the group are designed to connect consumers and businesses that are most likely to purchase specific goods and services to the businesses that provide those goods and services. The group's network has 22,400 managed active advertiser accounts. On 01-Jan-2004, the group acquired miva corporation and on 22-Mar-2004, it acquired comet systems, inc.

Primary SIC and add'l.: 7376 7375

CIK No: 0001094808

Subsidiaries: B&B Advertising, Inc., Espotting Media Ireland Ltd., Espotting Scandinavia, MIVA (Deutschland) GmbH, MIVA (France) S.a.r.l, MIVA (Italia) S.r.l. a socio unico, Miva (uk) Ltd., MIVA Direct, Inc., MIVA Media International, Inc., MIVA Media S.L., MIVA Small Business Solutions, Inc., Who Midco Corporation

Officers: Peter A. Corrao/Dir., CEO/$987,655.00, Seb Bishop/Dir., Pres. - CMO/$738,855.00, James David/Country Mgr. - France, Italy, Miva Ad Network, William H. Seippel/C-Level Exec./$1,072,195.00, Brian S. Mukherjee/Sr. VP, Group MD - Miva Ad Network, Lowell W. Robinson/CFO, COO/$29,581.00, Sloan Gaon/Sr. VP, GM - Consumer Entertainment, Rob Roe/GM - Miva Direct, Dave McCarthy/Sr. VP, GM - Advertising, Joanie Glance/Complaint Review Board, David Scarfpin/Complaint Review Board, Tony Garcia/CTO, Bob Protheroe/Sr. VP - Technology, Wolfhart Frohlich/Country Mgr. - Germany, Spain, Miva Ad Network, Dominique Loumaye/Country Mgr. - Spain *(17 Officers included in Index)*

Directors: Peter A. Corrao/Dir., CEO, Larry Weber/Non - Exec. Chmn., Lee Simonson/Dir., Gerald W. Hepp/Dir., Seb Bishop/Dir., Pres. - CMO, Mark W. Opzoomer/Dir., Adele Goldberg/Dir., Joseph P. Durrett/Dir.

Owners: Mark W. Opzoomer, Peter A. Corrao, Lawrence Weber, David Rae, Joseph W. Durrett, Craig Pisaris-Henderson/5.34%, John B. Pisaris, Adam Poulter, Lee S. Simonson, Andrew Lessman/5.62%, Phillip R. Thune, Gerald W. Hepp, William Seippel, Insiders/3.85%, Adele Goldberg *(21 Owners included in Index)*

Financial Data: *Fiscal Year End:*12/31 *Latest Annual Data:* 12/31/2006

Year		Sales		Net Income
2006		$172,595,000		-$87,626,000
2005		$194,616,000		-$130,167,000
2004		$169,470,000		$17,028,000
Curr. Assets:	$53,407,000	**Curr. Liab.:**	$34,998,000	
Plant, Equip.:	$15,446,000	**Total Liab.:**	$35,393,000	**Indic. Yr. Divd.:** NA
Total Assets:	$106,302,000	**Net Worth:**	$70,909,000	**Debt/ Equity:** NA

Mizuho Financial Group Inc

1-5-5, Otemachi, Chiyoda-ku, Tokyo; *PH:* 81-0352241111; *http://* www.mizuho-fg.co.jp

General - Incorporation		**Stock**- Price on:12/24/2007	$14.4
Employees	NA	Stock Exchange	NYSE
Auditor	NA	Ticker Symbol	MFG
Stk Agt	NA	Outstanding Shares	11,610,000
Counsel	NA	E.P.S	$400.97
DUNS No	NA	Shareholders	NA

Business: The groups principal activities include domestic and international financial services. The groups services include banking, securities, trust and asset management services. The group operates from the Japan and other countries.

Primary SIC and add'l.: 6282 6712 6211 6029

CIK No: 0001335730

Subsidiaries: Mizuho Bank, Ltd, Mizuho Corporate Bank, Ltd.,, Mizuho Financial Strategy Co., Ltd., Mizuho Trust & Banking Co., Ltd, Trust & Custody Services Bank, Ltd.,

Officers: Terunobu Maeda/Dir., CEO, Pres., Satoru Nishibori/Exec. Officer, CFO, Masanori Murakami/Exec. Officer, Yoshiaki Sugita/Corporate Auditor, Hidemi Hiroi/Exec. Officer, Yukio Nozaki/Corporate Auditor, Masahiro Seki/Corporate Auditor, Masahiko Kadotani/Corporate Auditor, Masayuki Saito/Managing Exec. Officer, Tsuneo Morita/Exec. Officer, Masato Ono/Dir., Deputy Pres., Hiroshi Motoyama/Dir., MD, Shigeru Yamamoto/Corporate Auditor

Directors: Terunobu Maeda/Dir., CEO, Pres., Hiroshi Saito/Dir., Seiji Sugiyama/Dir., Mitsuo Ohashi/Dir., Masato Ono/Dir., Deputy Pres., Hiroshi Motoyama/Dir., MD, Akihiko Nomiyama/Dir., Kanemitsu Anraku/Dir.

Owners: Trust & Custody Services Bank, Ltd./1.15%, Japan Trustee Services Bank, Ltd./2.52%, ITOCHU Corporation/1.02%, The Dai-ichi Mutual Life Insurance Company/2.35%, Fukoku Mutual Life Insurance Company/1.53%, Nippon Express Co., Ltd./1.02%, Sompo Japan Insurance Inc./1.94%, State Street Bank And Trust Company 505103/1.01%, Mizuho Financial Strategy/2.20%, Insiders/21.04%, The Chase Manhattan Bank, N.A. London/2.07%, The Dai-ichi Mutual Life Insurance Company/2.75%, Japan Trustee Services Bank, Ltd./5.21%, The Master Trust Bank of Japan, Ltd./4.81%, Meiji Yasuda Life Insurance Company/2.55% (27 Owners included in Index)

Financial Data: Fiscal Year End:NA　Latest Annual Data: 03/31/2007

Year	Sales	Net Income
2007	$34,616,514,000	$5,302,997,000

Curr. Assets:	$205,712,402,000	**Curr. Liab.:**	$1,001,972,895,000			
Plant, Equip.:	$7,203,946,000	**Total Liab.:**	$1,213,107,922,000	**Indic. Yr. Divd.:**	NA
Total Assets:	$1,252,740,872,000	**Net Worth:**	$39,632,950,000	**Debt/ Equity:**	NA

MKS Instruments Inc

90 Industrial Way, Wilmington, MA, 01887; **PH:** 1-978-284-4000; **Fax:** 1-978-284-4999; http:// www.mksinst.com

General - Incorporation	MA	**Stock**- Price on:12/24/2007	$27.48
Employees	2,960	Stock Exchange	NDQ
Auditor	PricewaterhouseCoopers LLP	Ticker Symbol	MKSI
Stk Agt	American Stock Transfer & Trust Co.	Outstanding Shares	57,290,000
Counsel	Hale & Dorr LLP	E.P.S.	$1.70
DUNS No.	00-105-3982	Shareholders	NA

Business: The group's principal activity is to provide instruments, components and subsystems that measure, control, power and monitor critical parameters of semiconductor and other advanced manufacturing process environments. It has three main product groups: instruments & control systems, power & reactive gas products & vacuum products. Instruments & control systems of the group includes pressure measurement & control products, materials delivery products, gas & thin-film composition analysis products and control and information management products. Power and reactive gas products include power delivery products and reactive gas generation products. Vacuum products of the group include vacuum gauging products & vacuum valves & components. The customers of the group include applied materials, asm international, celerity group, lam research, micromass UK ltd, novellus systems, phillips medical, toyko electron, ulvac & unaxis. In 2003, the group acquired wenzel instruments.

Primary SIC and add'l.: 3823

CIK No: 0001049502

Subsidiaries: Applied Science and Technology, GmbH, ASTeX GmbH, ASTeX Realty Corporation, Ion Systems, Inc., M.K.S. Tenta Products Ltd., MKS (Bermuda) Ltd., MKS Denmark APS, MKS East, Inc., MKS Germany Holding GmbH, MKS Holding, MKS Instruments (Asia) Ltd., MKS Instruments (China) Company Ltd., MKS Instruments (Hong Kong) Ltd., MKS Instruments (Shanghai) Ltd, MKS Instruments Deutschland GmbH 30 Subsidiaries included in the Index

Officers: Leo Berlinghieri/Dir., CEO, Pres., Ronald C. Weigner/CFO, VP/$787,233.00, John A. Smith/CTO, VP, Joseph M. Tocci/Treasurer, Kathleen F. Burke/General Counsel, Assist. Sec., Ron Hadar/46/VP, GM, William D. Stewart/VP, GM - Vacuum Products Group/$843,579.00, Robert L. Klimm/57/VP, GM, Gerald G. Colella/VP, Chief Business Officer/$1,196,997.00, Frank W. Schneider/VP, GM - Ion Systems, Seth H. Bagshaw/VP, Corporate Controller, Philip F. Zucchi/VP - Global Human Resources

Directors: Leo Berlinghieri/Dir., CEO, Pres., John R. Bertucci/Chmn., Louis P. Valente/Dir., Richard S. Chute/Dir., Hans-Jochen Kahl/Dir., Robert R. Anderson/70/Dir., Gregory R. Beecher/Dir., Cristina H. Amon/Dir.

Owners: FMR Corp./12.00%, Louis P. Valente, John R. Bertucci/11.40%, Leo Berlinghieri, Gerald G. Colella, Owen W. Robbins, Ronald C. Weigner, Robert R. Anderson, William D. Stewart, Insiders/14.80%, Richard S. Chute, Gregory R. Beecher, Hans-Jochen Kahl, Barclays Global Investors/6.20%, Dimensional Fund Advisors LP/6.60%

Financial Data: Fiscal Year End:12/31　Latest Annual Data: 12/31/2006

Year	Sales	Net Income
2006	$782,801,000	$94,235,000
2005	$509,294,000	$34,565,000
2004	$555,080,000	$69,839,000

Curr. Assets:	$591,438,000	**Curr. Liab.:**	$129,897,000	**P/E Ratio:**	15.02
Plant, Equip.:	$79,463,000	**Total Liab.:**	$142,501,000	**Indic. Yr. Divd.:**	NA
Total Assets:	$1,043,720,000	**Net Worth:**	$901,219,000	**Debt/ Equity:**	0.0064

ML Appleton FuturesAccess LLC

800 Scudders Mill Rd., Section 2g, Plainsboro, NJ, 08536; **PH:** 1-609-282-6091

General - Incorporation	DE	**Stock**- Price on:12/24/2007	NA
Employees	NA	Stock Exchange	NA
Auditor	Deloitte & Touche LLP	Ticker Symbol	NA
Stk Agt	NA	Outstanding Shares	NA
Counsel	NA	E.P.S.	NA
DUNS No.	NA	Shareholders	NA

Business: The group's principal activity is managing investment funds, currency trading, and US and international futures markets. Merrill Lynch Alternative Investments Llc is the manager of the fund. The company retains a single professional "commodity trading advisor" to manage the Fund speculative trading of commodity futures and forward contracts, other commodity interests and options. The Fund's offering materials were prepared in accordance with applicable CFTC rules and filed with and reviewed by NFA. The Fund's units of limited liability company interest ("Units") are privately offered.

Primary SIC and add'l.: 6221

CIK No: 0001311385

Subsidiaries: Merrill Lynch, Pierce, Fenner & Smith Incorporated

Officers: Benjamin C. Weston/54/CEO, Pres., Robert M. Alderman/48/VP, Mgr., Robert D. Ollwerther/52/COO, Mgr., Barbra E. Kocsis/CFO, Andrew B. Weisman/49/Mgr.

ML Aspect FuturesAccess LLC

800 Scudders Mill Rd., Section 2g, Plainsboro, NJ, 08536; **PH:** 1-609-282-6091

General - Incorporation	DE	**Stock**- Price on:12/24/2007	NA
Employees	NA	Stock Exchange	NA
Auditor	Deloitte & Touche LLP	Ticker Symbol	NA
Stk Agt	NA	Outstanding Shares	NA
Counsel	NA	E.P.S.	NA
DUNS No.	NA	Shareholders	NA

Business: The group's principle activity is to provide financial services. The group operates from United States.

Primary SIC and add'l.: 6221

CIK No: 0001309132

Subsidiaries: Merrill Lynch Alternative Investments LLC, Merrill Lynch Investment Managers, L.P., Merrill Lynch, Pierce, Fenner & Smith Incorporated

Officers: Benjamin C. Weston/CEO, Pres., Robert D. Ollwerther/52/COO, Mgr., Robert M. Alderman/48/VP, Mgr., Steven B. Olgin/COO, Mgr., Barbra E. Kocsis/42/CFO, Andrew B. Weisman/49/Mgr.

MI Cornerstone Futuresaccess LLC

800 Scudders Mill Rd., Section 2g, Plainsboro, NJ, 08536; **PH:** 1-609-282-6091

General - Incorporation	DE	**Stock**- Price on:12/24/2007	NA
Employees	NA	Stock Exchange	NA
Auditor	Deloitte & Touche LLP	Ticker Symbol	NA
Stk Agt	NA	Outstanding Shares	NA
Counsel	NA	E.P.S.	NA
DUNS No.	NA	Shareholders	NA

Business: The group's principal activity is that of a commodity-trading advisor. The group is a Delaware limited liability company that retains a single professional "commodity trading advisor" to manage the Fund speculative trading of commodity futures and forward contracts, other commodity interests and options on each of the foregoing.

Primary SIC and add'l.: 6221

CIK No: 0001309133

Officers: Benjamin C. Weston/54/CEO, Pres., Mgr., Robert M. Alderman/48/VP, Mgr., Robert D. Ollwerther/52/COO, Mgr., Barbra E. Kocsis/42/CFO, Andrew B. Weisman/49/Mgr.

ML Macadamia Orchards LP

26-238 Hawaii Belt Rd., Hilo, HI, 96720; **PH:** 1-808-969-8057; **Fax:** 1-808-928-8434; http:// www.mlmacadamia.com; **Email:** mlmo@mlnut.com

General - Incorporation	DE	**Stock**- Price on:12/24/2007	$5.05
Employees	215	Stock Exchange	NYSE
Auditor	PricewaterhouseCoopers LLP	Ticker Symbol	NUT
Stk Agt	Mellon Investor Services LLC	Outstanding Shares	7,500,000
Counsel	NA	E.P.S.	$0.05
DUNS No.	NA	Shareholders	NA

Business: The groups principle activities include growing and farming macadamia nuts. The group operates from the Hawaii. The groups quarterlu revenue for Sept 2007 was 2.78 millions of USD.

Primary SIC and add'l.: 0173

CIK No: 0000792161

Officers: Dennis J. Simonis/51/Dir., CEO, Pres., Randolph H. Cabral/55/Sr. VP, Orchard Mgr., Wayne W. Roumagoux/61/CFO, VP, Treasurer, Corp. Sec., James H. Case/General Counsel

Directors: Dennis J. Simonis/51/Dir., CEO, Pres., Jeffrey M. Kissel/58/Chmn., Alan E. Kennett/64/Dir., Scott C. Wallace/52/Dir., David McClain/61/Dir., John K. Kai/42/Dir., James S. Kendrick/60/Dir.

Owners: Insiders/0.06%, James S. Kendrick, Ebrahimi Family Group/9.20%, Berggruen Holdings North America, Ltd./5.10%, John K. Kai, Jeffrey M. Kissel

Financial Data: Fiscal Year End:12/31　Latest Annual Data: 12/31/2006

Year	Sales	Net Income
2006	$17,072,000	$804,000
2005	$17,378,000	$771,000
2004	$13,665,000	-$1,649,000

Curr. Assets:	$6,409,000	**Curr. Liab.:**	$2,527,000		
Plant, Equip.:	$47,232,000	**Total Liab.:**	$5,340,000	**Indic. Yr. Divd.:**	$0.200
Total Assets:	$53,963,000	**Net Worth:**	$48,623,000	**Debt/ Equity:**	NA

MI Winton Futuresaccess LLC

800 Scudders Mill Rd., Section 2g, Plainsboro, NJ, 08536; **PH:** 1-609-282-6091

General - Incorporation	DE	**Stock**- Price on:12/24/2007	NA
Employees	NA	Stock Exchange	NA
Auditor	Deloitte & Touche LLP	Ticker Symbol	NA
Stk Agt	NA	Outstanding Shares	NA
Counsel	NA	E.P.S.	NA
DUNS No.	NA	Shareholders	NA

Business: The group's principle activity is to provide diversification to a limited portion of the risk segment of the investors portfolios into an investment field that has historically often demonstrated a low degree of performance correlation with traditional stock and bond holdings. Traditional portfolios invested in stocks, bonds and cash equivalents can be diversified by allocating a portion of their assets to non-traditional investments such as managed futures. The group operates from United States.

Primary SIC and add'l.: 6221

CIK No: 0001309136

Subsidiaries: Merrill Lynch & Co., Inc. (Merrill Lynch)

Officers: Benjamin C. Weston/CEO, Pres., Robert M. Alderman/VP, Mgr., Robert D. Ollwerther/COO, Mgr., Barbra E. Kocsis/42/CFO, Andrew B. Weisman/49/Mgr.

Owners: Robert D. Ollwerther/0.04%, Insiders/0.04%

MM2 Group Inc

5 Regent St., Ste. 520, Livingston, NJ, 07039; **PH:** 1-732-290-0019; **Fax:** 1-973-758-9449; **http://** www.mm2group.net; **Email:** information@mm2group.net

General - Incorporation	NJ	**Stock** - Price on:12/24/2007	$0.03
Employees	NA	Stock Exchange	OTC
Auditor	Bagell, Josephs, Levine & Co., L.l.c.	Ticker Symbol	MMGP
Stk Agt	Fidelity Transfer Co	Outstanding Shares	155,730,000
Counsel	NA	E.P.S	NA
DUNS No.	NA	Shareholders	NA

Business: The groups principal activities include operating and retailing music and entertainment, and health care industries. Services of the group include general corporate finance, merger and acquisition advisory, consulting, facilitating asset-based lending, and arranging equipment-leasing contracts. The group operates from the United States.

Primary SIC and add'l.: 5499

CIK No: 0001141500

Officers: Mark Meller/CEO, Pres., CFO

Directors: Jerome Mahoney/Non - Exec. Chmn.

Owners: Mark Meller, Cornell Capital Partners, LP, Jerome R. Mahoney, Jerome R. Mahoney, Insiders, Mark Meller, Insiders

Curr. Assets:	$1,626,000	**Curr. Liab.:**	$8,300,000		
Plant, Equip.:	$4,000	**Total Liab.:**	$8,301,000	**Indic. Yr. Divd.:**	NA
Total Assets:	$1,649,000	**Net Worth:**	-$6,652,000	**Debt/ Equity:**	NA

MMA Media Inc

Formerly: Commerce Development Corp Ltd
9440 Little Santa Monica Blvd., Ste.400, Beverly Hills, CA, 90210; **PH:** 1-310-402-5901

General - Incorporation	MD	**Stock** - Price on:12/24/2007	NA
Employees	NA	Stock Exchange	NA
Auditor	Lawrence Scharfman CPA	Ticker Symbol	NA
Stk Agt	NA	Outstanding Shares	NA
Counsel	Raffi A. Nahabedian	E.P.S	NA
DUNS No.	NA	Shareholders	NA

Business: The groups principal activity is to provide services to modular building leases. The group operates from the United States.

Primary SIC and add'l.: 8742

CIK No: 0001208790

Subsidiaries: USM Financial Solutions, Inc

Officers: Michael Kurdziel/CEO, Richard Gammill/36/Chmn., Pres., Raffi A. Nahabedian/General Counsel, Exec. VP - Business Affairs

Directors: Richard Gammill/36/Chmn., Pres.

Owners: ARC Investment Partners/77.00%, Sam Nazarian/6.70%, David & Angelina Nazarian Family Trust/6.70%, Younes & Soraya Nazzarian Revocable Trust/6.70%

Financial Data: Fiscal Year End:12/31 **Latest Annual Data:** 12/31/2006

Year	Sales	Net Income
2006	NA	-$83,000
2005	$36,000	$0
2004	NA	-$21,000

Curr. Assets:	NA	**Curr. Liab.:**	$6,000		
Plant, Equip.:	NA	**Total Liab.:**	$6,000	**Indic. Yr. Divd.:**	NA
Total Assets:	NA	**Net Worth:**	-$6,000	**Debt/ Equity:**	NA

MMC Energy Inc

26 Broadway, Ste. 907, New York, NY, 10004; **PH:** 1-212-977-0900; **http://** www.mmcenergy.com; **Email:** contact@mmcenergy.com

General - Incorporation	DE	**Stock** - Price on:12/24/2007	NA
Employees	NA	Stock Exchange	OTC
Auditor	Russell Bedford Stefanou Mirchandani	Ticker Symbol	MMCY
Stk Agt	Continental Stock Transfer & Trust Co	Outstanding Shares	NA
Counsel	NA	E.P.S	NA
DUNS No.	NA	Shareholders	NA

Business: The groups principle activities include acquiring and managing below 250 megawatt, power generation assets. The group merged with Energy North America LLC in May 2006, and acquired Mid-Sun in November 2006. The group operates from the United States. The group's quarterly revenue for Sep'07 was 2.75 millions of USD.

Primary SIC and add'l.: 4911

CIK No: 0001312206

Subsidiaries: MMC Energy North America, LLC

Officers: Karl W. Miller/Chmn., Founder, CEO, Denis Gagnon/CFO, Harry Scarborough/Sr. VP - MMC Energy North America, LLC, Simba Dutt-Mazumdar/Controller

Directors: Karl W. Miller/Chmn., Founder, CEO, George Rountree/Dir., Richard H. Bryan/Dir., Peter W. Likins/Dir., Frederick W. Buckman/Dir., Michael Hamilton/61/Dir.

Owners: Peter Likins, George Rountree/1.00%, Denis G. Gagnon/1.30%, Michael Hamilton, Balyasny Asset Management L.P./5.10%, Stephens Investment Management, LLC/13.10%, Richard Bryan, Insiders/6.50%, Frederick W. Buckman, Karl W. Miller/4.00%

Curr. Assets:	$5,342,000	**Curr. Liab.:**	$2,489,000		
Plant, Equip.:	$7,356,000	**Total Liab.:**	$4,896,000	**Indic. Yr. Divd.:**	NA
Total Assets:	$13,522,000	**Net Worth:**	$8,626,000	**Debt/ Equity:**	NA

MNB Corp (BANGOR PA)

25 Broadway, Bangor, PA, 18013; **PH:** 1-610-588-0981; **http://** merchantsbangor2.com

General - Incorporation		**Stock** - Price on:12/24/2007	$31.15
Employees	NA	Stock Exchange	OTC
Auditor	NA	Ticker Symbol	MNBC
Stk Agt	NA	Outstanding Shares	NA
Counsel	NA	E.P.S	NA
DUNS No.	NA	Shareholders	NA

Business: The groups principal activity is to provide banking services. The services of the group include checking accounts, saving accounts, loans, investment and trust services and online banking. The group operates from the United States.

Primary SIC and add'l.: 6021

CIK No:

Officers: Anthony Biondi/Dir., CEO - Merchants National Bank, Bangor, Robert Bond/Sr. VP, CFO - Merchants National Bank, Bangor, James Sampson/Sr. VP - Lending, Merchants National Bank, Bangor, Tracey Smith/Sr. VP - Branch Administrat, Merchants National Bank, Bangor, James S. Garofalo/Pres. - Merchants National Bank, Bangor

Directors: Richard M. Hotchkiss/Chmn. - Merchants National Bank, Bangor

MNB Holdings Corp CA

3060 16th St., San Francisco, CA, 94103;

General - Incorporation		**Stock** - Price on:12/24/2007	$20.7
Employees	NA	Stock Exchange	OTC
Auditor	NA	Ticker Symbol	MNBO
Stk Agt	NA	Outstanding Shares	NA
Counsel	NA	E.P.S	NA
DUNS No.	NA	Shareholders	NA

Business: The groups principle activity is to provide recruiting services. The groups service area includes the research and development, engineering, marketing, sales, information technology and manufacturing industries. The group operates from United States.

Primary SIC and add'l.: 6712

CIK No:

MobiClear Inc

140 Broadway 46th Fl., New York, NY, 10005; **PH:** 1-212-208-1448; **Fax:** 1-212-858-7750; **http://** www.mobiclear.com; **Email:** info@mobiclear.com

General - Incorporation	PA	**Stock** - Price on:12/24/2007	$0.032
Employees	1	Stock Exchange	OTC
Auditor	Goff Backa Alfera & Company, LLC	Ticker Symbol	MBIR
Stk Agt	Continental Stock Transfer & Trust Co	Outstanding Shares	377,680,000
Counsel	NA	E.P.S	NA
DUNS No.	NA	Shareholders	NA

Business: The group's principal activity is to provide electronic personal identification verification solutions related to credit and debit card transactions. Services of the group include credit card present transaction; card not-present transactions and business-to-business purchasing transactions. The group acquired BICO, Inc. in May 2006, and MobiClear, Ltd. in July 2006. The group operates from the United States and United Kingdom.

Primary SIC and add'l.: 7374

CIK No: 0000225211

Subsidiaries: MobiClear, Ltd.

Officers: Anders Ericsson/CEO, Pres., Lim Wong/Chmn., Founder - CVO, Stephan Knowles/Engineering, Ian Simpkin/Finance

Directors: Lim Wong/Chmn., Founder - CVO, Simoun Ung/Dir.

Owners: Lim Wong/5.75%, Insiders/5.75%

Financial Data: Fiscal Year End:12/31 **Latest Annual Data:** 12/31/2006

Year	Sales	Net Income
2006	NA	-$2,898,000
2005	NA	-$800,000
2004	NA	-$195,000

Curr. Assets:	$319,000	**Curr. Liab.:**	$2,733,000		
Plant, Equip.:	NA	**Total Liab.:**	$2,733,000	**Indic. Yr. Divd.:**	NA
Total Assets:	$319,000	**Net Worth:**	-$2,414,000	**Debt/ Equity:**	NA

Mobile Area Networks Inc

2772 Depot St., Sanford, FL, 32773; **PH:** 1-407-333-2350; **Fax:** 1-407-333-9903; **http://** www.mobilan.com; **Email:** investment@mobilan.com

General - Incorporation	FL	**Stock** - Price on:12/24/2007	$0.1
Employees	9	Stock Exchange	OTC
Auditor	Randall N. Drake	Ticker Symbol	MANW
Stk Agt	Atlas Stock Transfer Corp	Outstanding Shares	46,760,000
Counsel	NA	E.P.S	-$0.01
DUNS No.	01-555-2953	Shareholders	NA

Business: The group's principle activity is to provide digital communication devices with wireless data communications service to remote home-office network services and to the Internet. The group operates from United States.

Primary SIC and add'l.: 3669 7379 7375

CIK No: 0001029454

Owners: George E. Wimbish/54.53%, Jerald R. Hoeft/0.58%, Insiders/61.83%, Jerome L. Nettuno/2.09%, Robert M. Good/4.60%, Noah V. Savant/0.03%

Financial Data: Fiscal Year End:12/31 **Latest Annual Data:** 12/31/2006

Year	Sales	Net Income
2006	$342,000	-$551,000
2005	$256,000	-$507,000
2004	$503,000	-$378,000

Curr. Assets:	$173,000	**Curr. Liab.:**	$404,000		
Plant, Equip.:	$86,000	**Total Liab.:**	$1,568,000	**Indic. Yr. Divd.:**	NA
Total Assets:	$266,000	**Net Worth:**	-$1,302,000	**Debt/ Equity:**	NA

Mobile Mini Inc

7420 S Kyrene Rd., Ste. 101, Tempe, AZ, 85283; *PH:* 1-480-894-6311; *Fax:* 1-480-894-6433; *http://* www.mobilemini.com

General - Incorporation	DE	**Stock**- Price on:12/24/2007	$31.11
Employees	1,943	Stock Exchange	NYSE
Auditor	Ernst & Young LLP	Ticker Symbol	MIR
Stk Agt	Wells Fargo Shareowner Services	Outstanding Shares	35,900,000
Counsel	Bryan Cave LLP	E.P.S.	$1.25
DUNS No.	11-806-2157	Shareholders	NA

Business: The group's principal activity is to provide portable storage solutions. The group offers fixed self-storage and portable storage solutions and includes products such as refurbished and modified storage units, manufactured storage units, steel mobile storage units, wood mobile office units, records storage units and van trailers. These products are leased or sold to retailers, construction companies, medical centers, schools, utilities, distributors, the United States military, hotels, restaurants, entertainment complexes and households. As of 31-Dec-2003, the group has a lease fleet of over 89,500 portable storage and office units. Customers include wal-Mart, motorola, frito lay, holiday inns (R), target, home depot, toys r us and walgreens. As of 31-Dec-2003, the group operated 47 branches located in 27 states and one Canadian province. In oct 2003, the group acquired the portable storage assets of mckinney vehicle services inc.

Primary SIC and add'l.: 7519 3448

CIK No: 0000911109

Subsidiaries: Mobile Mini Holdings, Inc., Mobile Mini I, Inc., Mobile Mini of Ohio LLC, Mobile Mini Texas Limited Partnership, LLP, Mobile Mini, LLC

Officers: Steven G. Bunger/Chmn., CEO, Pres./$1,247,213.00, Lawrence Trachtenberg/51/Dir., CFO, Exec. VP/$886,676.00, Deborah K. Keeley/Chief Accounting Officer, Sr. VP/$342,648.00, Russell C. Lemley/Sr. VP - Western Division, Kyle G. Blackwell/Sr. VP - Eastern Division, Martin Crayden/Sr. VP - European Division

Directors: Steven G. Bunger/Chmn., CEO, Pres., Ronald J. Marusiak/60/Dir., Lawrence Trachtenberg/51/Dir., CFO, Exec. VP, Michael L. Watts/60/Dir., Stephen A. McConnell/55/Dir., Jeffrey S. Goble/47/Dir.

Owners: Stephen A. McConnell, TimesSquare Capital Management, LLC/6.00%, Steven G. Bunger/2.90%, Munder Capital Management/6.30%, Ronald J. Marusiak, Deborah K. Keeley, Jeffrey S. Goble, Lawrence Trachtenberg/1.20%, T. Rowe Price Associates, Inc./7.50%, Insiders/5.50%, Michael L. Watts

Financial Data: *Fiscal Year End:*12/31 *Latest Annual Data:* 06/30/2007

Year	Sales	Net Income
2007	$78,250,000	$6,331,000
2006	$273,363,000	$42,776,000
2005	$207,170,000	$33,988,000

Curr. Assets:	$64,186,000	**Curr. Liab.:**	$58,474,000	**P/E Ratio:**	24.89
Plant, Equip.:	$740,511,000	**Total Liab.:**	$458,026,000	**Indic. Yr. Divd.:**	NA
Total Assets:	$900,030,000	**Net Worth:**	$442,004,000	**Debt/ Equity:**	0.6950

Mobile TeleSystems OJSC

Ul. Vorontsovskaya 5, Bldg. 2, Moscow, 109147; *PH:* 74952232025; *http://* www.mtsgsm.com; *Email:* ir@mts.ru

General - Incorporation	Russia	**Stock**- Price on:12/24/2007	$59.51
Employees	27,668	Stock Exchange	NYSE
Auditor	Zao Deloitte & Touche CIS	Ticker Symbol	MBT
Stk Agt	Ing Bank N.V.	Outstanding Shares	395,480,000
Counsel	NA	E.P.S.	$4.35
DUNS No.	NA	Shareholders	NA

Business: The group's principal activity is provision of mobile cellular communications services in the russian federation and ukraine. The group's services are based on gsm technology and include standard voice services and value-added services, such as voice mail, sms, gprs, mms and other entertainment services and data and fax transmission. At 31-12-2003, the group had licenses to operate in 76 regions of Russia and for the entire territory of ukraine, and its subscriber base reached 16.7 million.

Primary SIC and add'l.: 4812

CIK No: 0001115837

Subsidiaries: Astrakhan Mobile, BCTI, Mar Mobile GSM, MSS, MTS Belarus, MTS Finance, MTS Kostroma, MTS LLP, MTS-Capital, MTS-Komi Republic, MTS-Tver, Novitel, Primtelefon, ReCom, Sibintertelecom 20 Subsidiaries included in the Index

Officers: Leonid Melamed/41/Dir., CEO, Pres., Tatiana Evtushenkova/32/VP - Strategy - Corporate Development, Dir., Andrei Terebenin/46/VP - Corporate Communications, Pavel D. Belik/VP - Corporate Security, A. B. Nikitin/Editor in Chief, Vsevolod Rozanov/37/CFO, VP, Yury Gromakov/62/VP - Technology Development, Cynthia Gordon/VP - Chief Marketing Officer, Sergey Aslanyan/35/VP - Network, Information Technology, Ruslan Ibragimov/45/Dir. - Corporate, Legal Matters, Pavel Pavlovsky/VP, Dir. - Business Unit mts Ukraine, Raspopov Oleg/Acting VP, Dir. - Business, Unit mts, Foreign Subsidiaries, Sergey Nikonov/VP - Human Resources, Administrative Activity, Michael Hecker/Dir. - Strategy, Mikhail Shamolin/38/VP, Dir. - Business Unit, Sales, Customer Service

Directors: Leonid Melamed/41/Dir., CEO, Pres., Sergey D. Schebetov/42/Chmn., Sergei A. Drozdov/Dep. Chmn., Alexei N. Buyanov/39/Chmn., Vladimir S. Lagutin/61/Dep. Chmn., Helmut Reuschenbach/60/Dir., Tatiana Evtushenkova/32/VP - Strategy - Corporate Development, Dir., Mohanbir Gyani/Dir., Abugov V. Anton/Non - Exec. Dir., Paul J. Ostling/Dir., Peter Middleton/74/Dir., Alexander E. Gorbunov/41/Dir.

Owners: Sistema/32.20%, Sistema Holding Limited/9.80%, ING Bank (Eurasia) ZAO/40.80%, Invest-Svyaz/8.10%, Insiders/6.10%, VAST/3.00%

Financial Data: *Fiscal Year End:*12/31 *Latest Annual Data:* 12/31/2006

Year	Sales	Net Income
2006	$6,384,254,000	$1,075,738,000
2005	$5,011,018,000	$1,126,405,000
2004	$3,886,994,000	$987,878,000

Curr. Assets:	$1,629,119,000	**Curr. Liab.:**	$1,720,304,000	**P/E Ratio:**	21.92
Plant, Equip.:	$5,297,669,000	**Total Liab.:**	$4,822,164,000	**Indic. Yr. Divd.:**	NA
Total Assets:	$8,573,945,000	**Net Worth:**	$3,751,781,000	**Debt/ Equity:**	NA

Mobilepro Corp

6701 Democracy Blvd., Ste. 202, Bethesda, MD, 20817; *PH:* 1-301-315-9040; *Fax:* 1-301-315-9027; *http://* www.mobileprocorp.com; *Email:* info@mobileprocorp.com

General - Incorporation	DE	**Stock**- Price on:12/24/2007	$0.031
Employees	314	Stock Exchange	OTC
Auditor	Bagell, Josephs, Levine & Co. LLC	Ticker Symbol	MOBL
Stk Agt	Interwest Transfer Company, Inc.	Outstanding Shares	641,560,000
Counsel	NA	E.P.S.	-$0.079
DUNS No.	NA	Shareholders	NA

Business: The group's principal activity is to provide modem solutions to support third generation (3g) wireless communication systems. The company is a development stage company. The 3g technology features integrated voice and data, access to high-speed Internet and intranet applications, interactive e-mail, data exchange, global roaming and full motion video transmission. The products of the group include micro cell base station modems and handset modems. The base station solution targets smaller systems called micro and pico cell base stations. The handset modem solution also targets pda's and laptop plug-in cards. In fiscal 2004, the group acquired nationwide Internet and exp Internet services. In fiscal 2004, it also acquired Aug.net, shrevenet inc, us1, ticon.net, affinity telecom, Web one, inc and world trade network inc.

Primary SIC and add'l.: 4899

CIK No: 0000769592

Subsidiaries: Affinity Telecom, Inc., American Fiber Network, Inc., August.net Services, Inc., CloseCall America, Inc., Clover Computer Corporation, Davel Acquisition Corp., Davel Communications Group, Inc., Davel Communications, Inc., Davel de Mexico, S. de RL, Davel Financing Company, LLC, Davel Mexico, Ltd., DFW Internet Services, Inc. (d/b/a Nationwide Internet), InReach Internet, Inc., Internet Express, Inc. (d/b/a EXP Internet Services), Kite Broadband, LLC 28 Subsidiaries included in the Index

Officers: Jay Wright/Chmn., CEO/$590,468.00, Thomas Mazerski/Exec. VP - Retail, Customer Service Unit, Geoff Amend/Sr. VP, General Counsel, Jerry Sullivan/COO, Pres./$427,026.00, Hank Deily/Chief Accounting Officer, Sr. VP, Tammy Martin/Sr. VP, Chief Administrative Officer/$295,850.00, Richard H. Deily/Chief Accounting Officer, Sr. VP/$317,978.00, Douglas Bethell/Exec. VP/$309,567.00

Directors: Jay Wright/Chmn., CEO, Paul B. Silverman/Chmn. - Advisory Board, Larry D. Bouts/Member - Advisory Board, Don Gunther/Member - Advisory Board, Fred B. Tarter/Member - Advisory Board, Chris MacFarland/Dir., Michael G. Oneil/Dir., Don Sledge/Dir., Philip F. Otto/Member - Advisory Board, Paul S. Latchford/Member - Advisory Board, Bryon Wagner/Member - Advisory Board

Owners: Michael G. ONeil, Tammy L. Martin, Doug Bethell/1.38%, Richard H. Deily, Insiders/6.69%, Donald H. Sledge, Jerry M. Sullivan/1.83%, Christopher W. MacFarland

Financial Data: *Fiscal Year End:*03/31 *Latest Annual Data:* 03/31/2007

Year	Sales	Net Income
2007	$21,297,000	-$31,022,000
2006	$99,013,000	-$10,176,000
2005	$46,508,000	-$5,360,000

Curr. Assets:	$16,273,000	**Curr. Liab.:**	$41,390,000		
Plant, Equip.:	$18,783,000	**Total Liab.:**	$47,351,000	**Indic. Yr. Divd.:**	NA
Total Assets:	$69,309,000	**Net Worth:**	$21,958,000	**Debt/ Equity:**	NA

Mobility Electronics Inc

17800 N Perimeter Dr., Ste. 200, Scottsdale, AZ, 85255; *PH:* 1-480-596-0061; *Fax:* 1-480-368-2856; *http://* www.mobilityelectronics.com; *Email:* IR@mobl.com

General - Incorporation	DE	**Stock**- Price on:12/24/2007	$3.25
Employees	163	Stock Exchange	NDQ
Auditor	KPMG LLP	Ticker Symbol	NA
Stk Agt	Computershare Trust Co	Outstanding Shares	31,820,000
Counsel	Jackson Walker	E.P.S.	-$0.47
DUNS No.	NA	Shareholders	NA

Business: The group's principal activities are to manufacture and distribute ac and dc power adapters, portable computer docking stations, handheld device cradles, handheld software, monitor stands and other portable computing products and solutions. The group also designs, develops and markets connectivity and remote pci bus technology and products for the computer industry and a broad range of related embedded processor applications. The mobile computing solutions are provided to pda (personal digital assistant), smartphone, and other mobile computing device users. The products are distributed in the United States, Canada and Europe. In 2003, the group acquired certain assets, including a software license, customer relationships and consulting/employment agreements relating to the handheld hardware business of invision software inc and invision wireless, llc.

Primary SIC and add'l.: 3577

CIK No: 0001075656

Subsidiaries: iGo Direct Corporation, Mobility 2001 Limited, Mobility California, Inc., Mobility Idaho, Inc., Mobility Texas, Inc.

Officers: Charles Mollo/56/Chmn., CEO, Pres./$545,809.00, Joan Brubacher/54/CFO, Exec. VP, Treasurer/$489,283.00, Darryl S. Baker/VP, Chief Accounting Officer, Controller, Brian M. Roberts/VP, General Counsel, Sec./$238,495.00, Jonathan Downer/Sr. VP - Worldwide Sales, Distribution/$260,493.00, Randy Jones/Sr. VP, GM - Connectivity/$219,818.00

Directors: Charles Mollo/56/Chmn., CEO, Pres., Jeffrey Harris/Dir., Larry Car/Dir., Robert Shaner/Dir., William O. Hunt/Dir.

Owners: Insiders/10.10%, Jerre L. Stead, Adage Capital Partners, L.P./23.10%, Jeffrey R. Harris/4.50%, Joan W. Brubacher, Robert W. Shaner, Alydar Partners, LLC/6.40%, Charles R. Mollo/5.80%, Larry M. Carr/1.10%, William O. Hunt, Darryl S. Baker, Brian M. Roberts

Financial Data: *Fiscal Year End:*12/31 *Latest Annual Data:* 12/31/2006

Year	Sales	Net Income
2006	$92,464,000	-$16,842,000
2005	$85,501,000	$5,007,000
2004	$70,213,000	-$2,200,000

Curr. Assets:	$50,954,000	**Curr. Liab.:**	$16,459,000		
Plant, Equip.:	$2,980,000	**Total Liab.:**	$16,459,000	**Indic. Yr. Divd.:**	NA
Total Assets:	$65,864,000	**Net Worth:**	$49,405,000	**Debt/ Equity:**	NA

MobiVentures.com

Formerly: MobileMail (US) Inc
130 Shaftesbury Ave., Ste. 518, London, WID 5EU; **PH:** 44-207-031-1193;
http:// www.mailsms.co.uk

General - Incorporation	NV	**Stock** - Price on:12/24/2007	$0.42
Employees	NA	Stock Exchange	OTC
Auditor	Staley, Okada & Partners	Ticker Symbol	MBLV
Stk Agt	Pacific Stock Transfer Company	Outstanding Shares	NA
Counsel	NA	E.P.S.	NA
DUNS No.	NA	Shareholders	NA

Business: The groups principle activity is to provide platform for delivering short message service messaging traffic to wireless devices using the Internet. The group operates from the United States and Western Europe.

Primary SIC and add'l.: 7372
CIK No: 0001343460
Subsidiaries: MobileMail Limited
Officers: Gary Flint/30/Dir., CEO, Pres.
Directors: Gary Flint/30/Dir., CEO, Pres.
Owners: Tracebit Holding OY/15.30%, Simon Adahl/2.20%, Insiders/25.60%, Insiders/25.60%, Gary Flint/3.80%, Peter Ahman/15.30%, Miro Wikgren/4.40%, The Mobilemail Technology Partnership LLP/26.60%

Financial Data: Fiscal Year End:09/30 *Latest Annual Data:* 9/30/2006

Year	Sales	Net Income
2006	$11,000	-$2,817,000

Curr. Assets:	$172,000	**Curr. Liab.:**	$177,000		
Plant, Equip.:	$1,000	**Total Liab.:**	$277,000	**Indic. Yr. Divd.:**	NA
Total Assets:	$173,000	**Net Worth:**	-$105,000	**Debt/ Equity:**	NA

Mocon Inc

7500 Boone Ave. N, Minneapolis, MN, 55428; **PH:** 1-763-493-6370; **Fax:** 1-763-493-6358;
http:// www.mocon.com; **Email:** mocon@mocon.com

General - Incorporation	MN	**Stock** - Price on:12/24/2007	$11.38
Employees	118	Stock Exchange	NDQ
Auditor	KPMG LLP	Ticker Symbol	MOCO
Stk Agt	Wells Fargo Shareowner Services	Outstanding Shares	5,480,000
Counsel	NA	E.P.S.	$0.65
DUNS No.	00-644-8112	Shareholders	NA

Business: The group's principal activities are to develop, manufacture and market measurement, analytical, monitoring, sample preparation and consulting products. The products are used to detect, measure and analyze gases and chemical compounds. The group also provides consulting and analytical services to customers who require unique problem solving capabilities. The products are used by barrier packaging, food and pharmaceutical industries throughout the world. Some of the trademarks of the group are mocon (R), vericap (R), coulox(R) and hersch (r). On 01-Jan-2004, the group acquired paul lippke handels-gmbh prozess- und laborsysteme and vaculok(R) vacuum insulated panel product line from advantek inc in 2003.

Primary SIC and add'l.: 3829 3565
CIK No: 0000067279
Subsidiaries: Baseline-MOCON, Inc., Microanalytics Instrumentation Corp., Paul Lippke Handels-GmbH Prozess- und Laborsysteme
Officers: Robert L. Demorest/Chmn., CEO, Pres./$474,145.00, Darrell Lee/VP, Finance Treasurer, CFO
Directors: Robert L. Demorest/Chmn., CEO, Pres., Donald N. Demorett/49/Dir.
Owners: Douglas J. Lindemann/1.00%, Ronald A. Meyer/2.50%, Daniel W. Mayer/2.80%, FMR Corp./6.10%, Leonard J. Frame, Tom C. Thomas, Robert L. Demorest/5.50%, Dane D. Anderson, Robert F. Gallagher, Dean B. Chenoweth/1.10%, Richard A. Proulx, Insiders/13.50%, Darrell B. Lee

Financial Data: Fiscal Year End:12/31 *Latest Annual Data:* 12/31/2006

Year	Sales	Net Income
2006	$26,290,000	$3,911,000
2005	$24,582,000	$2,915,000
2004	$25,108,000	$2,429,000

Curr. Assets:	$21,023,000	**Curr. Liab.:**	$4,817,000	**P/E Ratio:**	17.51
Plant, Equip.:	$1,557,000	**Total Liab.:**	$4,917,000	**Indic. Yr. Divd.:**	$0.320
Total Assets:	$26,877,000	**Net Worth:**	$21,960,000	**Debt/ Equity:**	NA

Mod Pac Corp

1801 Elmwood Ave., Buffalo, NY, 14207; **PH:** 1-716-873-0640; **Fax:** 1-716-447-9201;
http:// www.modpac.com

General - Incorporation	NY	**Stock** - Price on:12/24/2007	$10.11
Employees	416	Stock Exchange	NDQ
Auditor	Ernst & Young LLP	Ticker Symbol	MPAC
Stk Agt	American Stock Transfer & Trust Co.	Outstanding Shares	3,450,000
Counsel	Hodgson Russ	E.P.S.	-$0.96
DUNS No.	NA	Shareholders	NA

Business: The group's principle activity is to short-run print, design and manufacture paperboard packaging. It provides its products in two different categories: folding cartons, and full color print. Folding cartons engineer, print and finish paper-board packaging for consumer goods and stock boxes primarily for the global confectionary market. Full color print operates through its single Internet-based outlet, vistaprint limited to provide select products such as business cards, direct mail pieces and marketing brochures on an as ordered basis. It also provides distinctive designs for social occasions by personalizing items such as invitations, napkins, and stationery. The group spun-off from astronics corporation on 14-Mar-2003.

Primary SIC and add'l.: 2679 2657
CIK No: 0001191857
Subsidiaries: 1803-1807 Elmwood Avenue, LLC, MOD-PAC Pilot CORP
Officers: Daniel G. Keane/Dir., CEO, Pres., Larry N. Kessler/VP - Operations, Philip C. Rechin/VP - Sales, Daniel J. Geary/Corporate Controller, David B. Lupp/CFO, Deborah K. Pawlowski/Kei Advisor, Joseph A. Burgio/Dir. - Sales, Commercial Print

Directors: Daniel G. Keane/Dir., CEO, Pres., Kevin T. Keane/Chmn., William G. Gisel/Dir., Howard Zemsky/Dir., Robert J. McKenna/Dir.
Owners: Robert J. McKenna, David B. Lupp, Daniel G. Keane/32.50%, Robert J. McKenna, Insiders/15.90%, Arbiter Partners, L.P./5.10%, Philip C. Rechin, William G. Gisel, Kevin T. Keane/11.00%, Insiders/43.50%, Philip C. Rechin, John H. Lewis/12.20%, Daniel J. Geary, Howard Zemsky/2.00%, Daniel G. Keane/7.10% *(17 Owners included in Index)*

Financial Data: Fiscal Year End:12/31 *Latest Annual Data:* 12/31/2006

Year	Sales	Net Income
2006	$46,559,000	-$3,431,000
2005	$71,193,000	$11,028,000
2004	$50,280,000	$3,722,000

Curr. Assets:	$11,817,000	**Curr. Liab.:**	$4,957,000		
Plant, Equip.:	$25,737,000	**Total Liab.:**	$9,345,000	**Indic. Yr. Divd.:**	NA
Total Assets:	$39,006,000	**Net Worth:**	$29,661,000	**Debt/ Equity:**	0.0664

Modavox Inc

2617S.46thst., Ste.300, Phoniex, AZ, 85034; **PH:** 1-480-643-5626; **http://** www.modavox.com;
Email: info@kinocom.net

General - Incorporation	DE	**Stock** - Price on:12/24/2007	$1.73
Employees	51	Stock Exchange	OTC
Auditor	Epstein Weber & Conover, PLC	Ticker Symbol	MDVX
Stk Agt	Interwest Transfer Company, Inc.	Outstanding Shares	35,880,000
Counsel	NA	E.P.S.	$0.00
DUNS No.	NA	Shareholders	NA

Business: The group's principle activity is to distribute audio video streaming products over the Internet. The group also provides online audio video streaming products for communication and advertising. The group operates from United States.

Primary SIC and add'l.: 6799
CIK No: 0001137204
Subsidiaries: Kino Acquisition Sub, Inc.
Officers: David J. Ide/Dir., CEO, Nathaniel T. Bradley/Vice Chmn., Chief Technology, Product Officer, Paul Lyons/Sales Mgr., Ivan Martinez/Dir. - Interactive Sales, Richard Keppler/Internet Radio, Ad Dir., Jeff Spenard/Dir., Pres. - Internet Radio, Sonja Darte/Host Services, Mgr., Christopher Hambright/Project Mgr., James G. Crawford/Dir., CIO
Directors: David J. Ide/Dir., CEO, Nathaniel T. Bradley/Vice Chmn., Chief Technology, Product Officer, Hubert Glover/Dir., Jay Stulberg/Dir., James G. Crawford/Dir., CIO, Jeff Spenard/Dir., Pres. - Internet Radio
Owners: Insiders/14.90%, Robert Arkin/7.20%, C&H Capital/6.20%, Nathan Bradley/5.10%, Dana LLC/8.20%, Jim Crawford/4.30%, David Ide/4.30%, Arlan Van Wyck/7.20%, Jay Stulberg/1.30%

Financial Data: Fiscal Year End:02/28 *Latest Annual Data:* 2/28/2007

Year	Sales	Net Income
2007	$2,660,000	-$554,000
2006	$1,412,000	-$2,186,000
2005	$967,000	-$2,436,000

Curr. Assets:	$1,426,000	**Curr. Liab.:**	$501,000		
Plant, Equip.:	$310,000	**Total Liab.:**	$501,000	**Indic. Yr. Divd.:**	NA
Total Assets:	$4,584,000	**Net Worth:**	$4,083,000	**Debt/ Equity:**	NA

Modern Medical Modalities Corp

439 Chestnut St., Union, NJ, 07083; **PH:** 1-908-687-8840; **http://** www.modn.com

General - Incorporation	NJ	**Stock** - Price on:12/24/2007	$0.64
Employees	44	Stock Exchange	OTC
Auditor	Liebman Goldberg & Drogin LLP	Ticker Symbol	MODM
Stk Agt	North American Transfer Co	Outstanding Shares	22,680,000
Counsel	NA	E.P.S.	-$0.11
DUNS No.	77-993-0775	Shareholders	NA

Business: The group's principal activity is to provide high technology medical equipment and management services to hospitals and physicians. The group leases magnetic resonance imaging and computerized axial tomography equipment. The services of the group include selection and acquisition of appropriate equipment, design and supervision of facility construction, provision and training of technical and support staff. The groups' services also include patient billing and collection and marketing and management services throughout New Jersey and new orleans. The group has government reimbursement programs including medicaid and medicare. The group delivers its services to its customers through either contractual arrangements with hospitals and clinics or medical technology center arrangements with hospitals or physician groups.

Primary SIC and add'l.: 8099 8741 7352 8744
CIK No: 0000902635
Subsidiaries: Amherst Medical Equipment Leasing Corp., Independence Imaging Center, LLC., Medical Marketing and Management, Inc., Metairie Medical Equipment Leasing Corp, Metairie Medical Equipment Leasing Corp., Modern Medical Imaging at Atrium, LLC, Modern Medical Imaging Centers, LLC, MRI & Imaging of Metairie, LLC, MRI Imaging Center at PBI Corporation, Ohio Medical Equipment Leasing Corp., Somerset Imaging Corporation, Union Imaging Center, LLC, West Paterson Medical Equipment Leasing Corp.
Officers: Baruh Hayut/44/Chmn., CEO, Minesh Patel/35/Dir., CFO
Directors: Baruh Hayut/44/Chmn., CEO, Minesh Patel/35/Dir., CFO, Paul W. Harrison/52/Dir.
Owners: Issak Hayut/12.41%, Paul W. Harrison/4.58%, Jacov Hayut/6.73%, Minesh Patel/0.11%, BIBY Family Partners, LLC/36.84%, Ronnie Antebi/9.28%

Financial Data: Fiscal Year End:12/31 *Latest Annual Data:* 12/31/2006

Year	Sales	Net Income
2006	$6,854,000	-$531,000
2005	$2,248,000	$195,000
2004	$7,249,000	$194,000

Curr. Assets:	$1,909,000	**Curr. Liab.:**	$3,028,000		
Plant, Equip.:	$1,667,000	**Total Liab.:**	$4,770,000	**Indic. Yr. Divd.:**	NA
Total Assets:	$3,631,000	**Net Worth:**	-$1,143,000	**Debt/ Equity:**	NA

Modern Technology Corp

14860 Montfort Dr., Ste. 210, Dallas, TX, 75240; *PH:* 1-972-386-3372; *Fax:* 1-972-386-8165; *http://* www.moderntechnologycorp.com; *Email:* ir@moderntechnologycorp.com

General - Incorporation	NV	**Stock**- Price on:12/24/2007	NA
Employees	400	Stock Exchange	OTC
Auditor	Greenberg & Co. LLC	Ticker Symbol	MODC
Stk Agt	Registrar & Transfer Co	Outstanding Shares	NA
Counsel	Jim Parsons Parsons Law Firm	E.P.S.	-$1.331
DUNS No.	10-370-3468	Shareholders	NA

Business: The group's principal activity is to aid prospective clients to obtain finance and to provide managerial services to client companies. It has concluded agreements with atlas exportaciones e importaciones s.a. ("Atlas") and esmeralda s.a., ("Esmeralda") which grants the group the exclusive rights to represent their products for sale in Israel. On 01-Apr-2003, the group signed a memorandum of understanding with centrovet, ltda. ("Centrovet"), a chilean veterinary pharmaceutical company which will result in the group being compensated for the introduction of buyers worldwide for centrovet's veterinary products or chilean human pharmaceutical products marketed by centrovet. On 15-Apr-2003, it established its subsidiary pharmavet inc. The group operates in Israel, Chile , India, Spain, ethiopia. On 31-Mar-2004, the group owns 100% of pharmavet inc.

Primary SIC and add'l.: 8741

CIK No: 0000711422

Subsidiaries: portfolio companies

Officers: Anthony Welch/Chmn., CEO, CFO, Pres.

Directors: Anthony Welch/Chmn., CEO, CFO, Pres.

Owners: Insiders/22.50%, Anthony Welch/22.50%

Financial Data: *Fiscal Year End:*06/30   *Latest Annual Data:* 6/30/2006

Year		Sales		Net Income
2006		$11,472,000		-$7,764,000
2005		$3,078,000		-$941,000
2004		$1,000		-$118,000
Curr. Assets:	$1,569,000	**Curr. Liab.:**	$5,431,000	
Plant, Equip.:	$644,000	**Total Liab.:**	$7,876,000	**Indic. Yr. Divd.:** NA
Total Assets:	$4,859,000	**Net Worth:**	-$3,016,000	**Debt/ Equity:** 0.1858

Modigene Inc

Formerly: LDG Inc
4944 Windy Hill Dr., Raleigh, NC, 27587; *PH:* 1-919-855-9200; *http://* www.modigenetech.com

General - Incorporation	NV	**Stock**- Price on:12/24/2007	NA
Employees	NA	Stock Exchange	NA
Auditor	Hansen, Barnett & Maxwell P.C.	Ticker Symbol	NA
Stk Agt	NA	Outstanding Shares	NA
Counsel	NA	E.P.S.	-$1.01
DUNS No.	NA	Shareholders	NA

Business: The groups principle activities include designing, developing and producing corporate identity packages, newspaper and magazine, ads and design for promotional materials. The group operates from the United States. The revenue of the group in the year 2006, were $96,328.

Primary SIC and add'l.: 8641

CIK No: 0001268659

Subsidiaries: Liaison Design Group, LLC

Officers: Abraham Havron/Dir., CEO, Fuad Fares/Dir., Chief Scientific Officer, Shai Novik/Dir., Pres., Eyal Fima/VP - Product Development, Peter L. Coker/65/Dir., Pres., Principal Executive Officer, Treasurer, Principal Chief - Financial Office, Sec.

Directors: Abraham Havron/Dir., CEO, Eugene Bauer/Chmn., Alastair Clemow/Dir., Fuad Fares/Dir., Chief Scientific Officer, David Hochman/Dir., Joel Kanter/Dir., Shai Novik/Dir., Pres., Adam Stern/Dir., Edward P. Amento/Member - Scientific Advisory Board, Barry M. Sherman/Member - Scientific Advisory Board, Dan Shochat/Member - Scientific Advisory Board, Judith L. Swain/Member - Scientific Advisory Board, Peter L. Coker/65/Dir., Pres., Principal Executive Officer, Treasurer, Principal Chief - Financial Office, Sec., Jane Hsiao/Dir.

Owners: Shai Novik/4.59%, Alastair Clemow/1.10%, Phillip Frost/13.21%, Adam Stern/4.33%, Abraham Havron/1.42%, Joel Kanter/1.69%, Jane H. Hsiao/3.16%, Insiders/34.40%, Eugene Bauer/1.45%, Fuad Fares/5.15%

Financial Data: *Fiscal Year End:*12/31   *Latest Annual Data:* 12/31/2006

Year		Sales		Net Income
2006		$96,000		-$49,000
Curr. Assets:	$70,000	**Curr. Liab.:**	$80,000	
Plant, Equip.:	$3,000	**Total Liab.:**	$80,000	**Indic. Yr. Divd.:** NA
Total Assets:	$72,000	**Net Worth:**	-$7,000	**Debt/ Equity:** NA

Modine Manufacturing Co

1500 DeKoven Ave., Racine, WI, 53403; *PH:* 1-262-636-1200; *Fax:* 1-262-636-1424; *http://* www.modine.com

General - Incorporation	WI	**Stock**- Price on:12/24/2007	$22.23
Employees	7,700	Stock Exchange	NYSE
Auditor	PricewaterhouseCoopers LLP	Ticker Symbol	MOD
Stk Agt	Wells Fargo Shareowner Services	Outstanding Shares	32,420,000
Counsel	NA	E.P.S.	$1.13
DUNS No.	00-609-2555	Shareholders	NA

Business: The groups principle activity is to provide thermal management technology and components. The group also designs, engineers, tests and manufactures heat transfer products for a range of applications and markets. Customers served by the group include the light, medium and heavy-duty vehicles, HVAC (heating, ventilating, air conditioning) equipment, industrial equipment, refrigeration systems, fuel cells, and electronic industries. The group operates from United States.

Primary SIC and add'l.: 3433 9999 3714 3443 3585

CIK No: 0000067347

Subsidiaries: Airedale Air Conditioning (Zhongshan) Co. Limited, Airedale Air Conditioning SA PTY Limited, Airedale Compact Systems Limited, Airedale Group Limited, Airedale Hong Kong Limited, Airedale North America, Inc., Airedale Sheet Metal Limited, Airedale, Inc., Industrial Airsystems, Inc., Modine Austria GmbH, Modine Automobiltechnik GmbH, Modine Climate Systems GmbH, Modine Climate Systems Inc., Modine Delaware, LLC, Modine Europe GmbH 44 Subsidiaries included in the Index

Officers: David B. Rayburn/60/Dir., CEO, Pres./$2,444,851.00, Robert R. Kampstra/Corporate Controller, Thomas A. Burke/51/COO, Exec. VP/$990,069.00, Dean R. Zakos/55/VP, General Counsel, Sec., Bradley C. Richardson/50/CFO, Exec. VP - Finance/$944,568.00, Klaus A. Feldmann/Regional VP - Europe/$784,273.00, Charles R. Katzfey/61/Regional VP - Americas/$815,279.00, James R. Rulsch/53/Regional VP - Asia/$819,068.00, Anthony C. De Vuono/59/CTO, VP, Gregory T. Troy/53/VP, Chief Human Resources Officer, Gary A. Fahl/53/VP - Environmental, Safety, Security, Margaret C. Kelsey/44/Corporate Treasurer, Assist. Sec.

Directors: David B. Rayburn/60/Dir., CEO, Pres., Dennis J. Kuester/66/Dir., Gary L. Neale/67/Dir., Vincent L. Martin/69/Dir., Marsha C. Williams/57/Dir., Frank P. Incropera/Dir., Michael T. Yonker/66/Dir., Richard J. Doyle/76/Dir., Frank W. Jones/68/Dir., Charles P. Cooley/Dir.

Owners: Michael T. Yonker, Charles R. Katzfey, Thomas A. Burke, Dimensional Fund Advisors LP/6.45%, Frank W. Jones, Dennis J. Kuester, Bradley C. Richardson, Gary L. Neale, Insiders/32.50%, Marsha C. Williams, David B. Rayburn/1.15%, Klaus A. Feldmann, Vincent L. Martin, Mario J. Gabelli/10.77%, Frank P. Incropera *(19 Owners included in Index)*

Financial Data: *Fiscal Year End:*03/31   *Latest Annual Data:* 3/31/2007

Year		Sales		Net Income
2007		$1,757,472,000		$42,332,000
2006		$1,628,900,000		$7,641,000
2005		$1,543,930,000		$61,662,000
Curr. Assets:	$456,857,000	**Curr. Liab.:**	$307,953,000	**P/E Ratio:** 16.97
Plant, Equip.:	$520,664,000	**Total Liab.:**	$608,306,000	**Indic. Yr. Divd.:** $0.700
Total Assets:	$1,101,573,000	**Net Worth:**	$493,267,000	**Debt/ Equity:** NA

Modtech Holdings Inc

2830 Barrett Ave., Perris, CA, 92571; *PH:* 1-951-943-4014; *Fax:* 1-951-943-9655; *http://* www.modtech.com; *Email:* pr@modtech.com

General - Incorporation	DE	**Stock**- Price on:12/24/2007	$2.73
Employees	710	Stock Exchange	NDQ
Auditor	Squar, Peterson, LLP	Ticker Symbol	MOGN
Stk Agt	Mellon Investor Services LLC	Outstanding Shares	21,420,000
Counsel	Halddan & Zepfl	E.P.S.	-$4.71
DUNS No.	NA	Shareholders	NA

Business: The group's principle activities are to design, manufacture, market and install modular relocatable classrooms and light industrial modular buildings for commercial use. The group constructs and installs both standardized and custom built units. The group also designs and manufactures modular, portable buildings to customer specifications for a wide variety of uses, including governmental, healthcare, educational, airport and correctional facilities, office and retail space, day care centers, libraries, churches, construction trailers, golf clubhouses, police station, convenience stores, fast food restaurants and sales offices. The buildings are sold primarily through a network of sales and leasing companies to a wide range of users. The group primarily caters to customers in California, Nevada, Arizona, New Mexico, Utah, Colorado, Texas and Florida. The group's quarterly revenue for September 2007 was 21.82 millions of USD.

Primary SIC and add'l.: 2452 2451

CIK No: 0001075066

Subsidiaries: Coastal Modular Buildings, Inc, Innovative Modular Structures, Inc., Trac Modular Manufacturing, Inc.

Officers: Dennis L. Shogren/Dir., CEO, Pres./$686,459.00, Karen Andreasen/Sr. VP - Administration, Dan Matsui/Investor Relations Officer - Silverman Heller Associates, Gene Heller/Investor Relations Officer - Silverman Heller Associates, Ronald C. Savona/Sr. VP - Operations/$514,009.00, Kenneth Cragun/CFO

Directors: Dennis L. Shogren/Dir., CEO, Pres., Charles C. McGettigan/63/Chmn., Daniel J. Donahoe/Dir., Myron A. Wick/Dir., Robert W. Campbell/Dir., Stanley N. Gaines/Dir., Charles R. Gwirtsman/54/Dir.

Owners: Austin W. Marxe, Charles C. McGettigan, Dennis L. Shogren, Dimensional Fund Advisors Inc., Rutabaga Capital Management LLC, Gruber & McBaine Capital Management, The TCW Group, Inc., John Hancock Advisers LLC, Heartland Advisors, Inc., Kenneth S. Cragun, Daniel J. Donahoe, Insiders, Robert W. Campbell, Ronald C. Savona, Stanley N. Gaines *(21 Owners included in Index)*

Financial Data: *Fiscal Year End:*12/31   *Latest Annual Data:* 12/31/2006

Year		Sales		Net Income
2006		$156,033,000		-$54,691,000
2005		$230,324,000		-$21,104,000
2004		$185,194,000		-$18,546,000
Curr. Assets:	$70,446,000	**Curr. Liab.:**	$44,126,000	
Plant, Equip.:	$11,118,000	**Total Liab.:**	$55,969,000	**Indic. Yr. Divd.:** NA
Total Assets:	$122,810,000	**Net Worth:**	$66,841,000	**Debt/ Equity:** 0.1413

Mohawk Industries Inc

160 S Industrial Blvd., Calhoun, GA, 30701; *PH:* 1-706-629-7721; *Fax:* 1-706-624-3825; *http://* www.mohawkind.com; *Email:* mohawkind@mohawkind.com

General - Incorporation	DE	**Stock**- Price on:12/24/2007	$99.24
Employees	37,100	Stock Exchange	NYSE
Auditor	KPMG LLP	Ticker Symbol	MHO
Stk Agt	Wachovia Bank N.A	Outstanding Shares	68,140,000
Counsel	Alston & Bird LLP	E.P.S.	$6.69
DUNS No.	61-275-7070	Shareholders	NA

Business: The groups principle activity is to produce floor-covering products for residential and commercial applications. The groups floor-covering products line include ceramic tile, laminate, rugs, carpet pad, hardwood and resilient. The group operates through three business segments namely mohawk, dal-tile and unilin. The group operates from United States.

Primary SIC and add'l.: 2273 3253

CIK No: 0000851968

Subsidiaries: Aladdin Manufacturing Corporation, Aladdin of Texas Holding, LLC, Aladdin Texas, LLC, Cevotrans BV, Dal Italia LLC, Dal-Elit, L.P, Dal-Tile Corporation, Dal-Tile Group, Inc., Dal-Tile I, LLC., Dal-Tile International, Inc, Dal-Tile Mexico S.A. de C.V., Dal-Tile of Canada Inc., Dal-Tile Puerto Rico, Inc., Dal-Tile Services, Inc., Dal-Tile SSC East, Inc. 67 Subsidiaries included in the Index

Officers: Jeffrey S. Lorberbaum/Chmn., CEO/$1,891,620.00, Frank H. Boykin/CFO/$1,114,537.00, Christopher W. Wellborn/Dir., COO/$2,281,122.00, Herbert M. Thornton/Pres. - Mohawk Flooring, Frans G. De Cock/Dir., Pres. - Unilin/$1,087,999.00, Monte H. Thornton/67/Pres. - Mohawk Flooring/$1,205,855.00, Harold G. Turk/Pres. - Dal, Tile, Barbara M. Goetz/Corp. Sec., Thomas J. Kanuk/Chief Accounting Officer, Corporate Controller, James T. Lucke/VP, General Counsel, Assist. Sec.

Directors: Jeffrey S. Lorberbaum/Chmn., CEO, Bruce C. Bruckmann/Dir., John F. Fiedler/Dir., Phyllis O. Bonanno/Dir., Christopher W. Wellborn/Dir., COO, David L. Kolb/Dir., Larry W. McCurdy/Dir., Robert N. Pokelwaldt/Dir., Frans G. De Cock/Dir., Pres. - Unilin

Owners: Frank H. Boykin, Jeffrey S. Lorberbaum/17.80%, Leo Benatar, Monte H. Thornton, Harold G. Turk, Thomas J. Kanuk, Robert N. Pokelwaldt, Bruce C. Bruckmann, Fairholme Capital Management, L.L.C./5.00%, Ruane, Cunniff & Goldfarb, Inc./19.00%, Insiders/19.20%, Larry W. McCurdy, Select Equity Group, Inc./6.30%, Phyllis O. Bonanno, David L. Kolb *(19 Owners included in Index)*

Financial Data: **Fiscal Year End:**12/31 **Latest Annual Data:** 12/31/2006

Year	Sales	Net Income
2006	$7,905,842,000	$455,833,000
2005	$6,620,099,000	$358,195,000
2004	$5,880,372,000	$368,622,000

Curr. Assets:	$2,378,911,000	**Curr. Liab.:**	$1,595,763,000	**P/E Ratio:**	14.62
Plant, Equip.:	$1,888,088,000	**Total Liab.:**	$4,463,131,000	**Indic. Yr. Divd.:**	NA
Total Assets:	$8,178,394,000	**Net Worth:**	$3,715,263,000	**Debt/ Equity:**	0.5684

Mohegan Tribal Gaming Authority

1 Mohegan Sun Blvd., Uncasville, CT, 06382; ***PH:*** 1-860-862-8150; ***Fax:*** 1-860-862-7824; ***http://*** www.mtga.com

General - Incorporation	CT	**Stock**- Price on:12/24/2007	NA
Employees	NA	Stock Exchange	NA
Auditor	PricewaterhouseCoopers LLP	Ticker Symbol	NA
Stk Agt	NA	Outstanding Shares	NA
Counsel	NA	E.P.S	NA
DUNS No.	87-282-3109	Shareholders	NA

Business: The group's principle activity is to provide various gaming facilities along with food and beverage amenities. The company is governed by a management board, which consists of nine members of the tribal council. The company also offers an arcade style recreation area and children care facility and own 30 different retail shops and a luxury hotel. The gaming and entertainment services are provided through 3,640 slot machines, 160 table games including blackjack roulette craps and baccarat and 36 poker tables. Food and beverage amenities include a 610-seat buffet, three full service themed restaurants, a 24-hour coffee shop and multiple full and floor service bars. The group operates from United States.

Primary SIC and add'l.: 7999 7011 7993

CIK No: 0001005276

Subsidiaries: Commercial Ventures PA, LLC, Mohegan Basketball Club LLC, Mohegan Commercial Ventures PA, LLC, Mohegan Ventures-NW, Penn National Gaming, Inc

Officers: Robert Soper/CEO, Mitchell Grossinger Etess/CEO, Roland J. Harris/Sr. VP - Project Management, Jeffrey E. Hartmann/COO, Roberta Harris-Payne/Corresponding Sec., William Quidgeon/Treasurer, Ralph James Gessner/Councilor, Paul Brody/VP - Corporate Development, Allison D. Johnson/Recording Sec., Leo M. Chupaska/CFO, Mark F. Brown/Councilor, Mark W. Hamilton/Councilor, Michael J. Ciaccio/General Counsel, VP - Legal Administration, Melissa McCray/Executive Assist., Peter J. Roberti/VP - Corporate Finance *(16 Officers included in Index)*

Directors: Bruce Bozsum/Chmn., Marilynn Malerba/Vice Chairwoman

Moldflow Corp

492 Old Connecticut Path, Ste. 401, Framingham, MA, 01701; ***PH:*** 1-508-358-5848; ***Fax:*** 1-508-358-5868; ***http://*** www.moldflow.com

General - Incorporation	DE	**Stock**- Price on:12/24/2007	$22.8
Employees	331	Stock Exchange	NDQ
Auditor	Grant Thornton, LLP	Ticker Symbol	MFLO
Stk Agt	EquiServe Trust Co N.A	Outstanding Shares	11,450,000
Counsel	NA	E.P.S	-$0.37
DUNS No.	NA	Shareholders	NA

Business: The group's principal activity is to provide a wide range of automation and optimization software solutions for the plastic injection molding industry. The operations are carried out under two business units: design analysis and manufacturing solutions. Design analysis solutions include the moldflow plastics advisers series for part design and high-level mold design and the moldflow plastics insight series for more in-depth part and mold design. The manufacturing solutions products allow manufacturing professionals to monitor, control and optimize their process on the shop floor and also provides hot runner control system solutions to the injection molding industry. The customers include microsoft, daimlerchrysler, apple computer, baxter international, bmw, dupont, fuji xerox, hewlett-packard, motorola, nokia and samsung. The products are sold to customers in the United States, Europe, Asia and Australia. On 23-Jan-2004, the group acquired American msi corp.

Primary SIC and add'l.: 3577 7372

CIK No: 0001103234

Subsidiaries: Advanced CAE Technology, Inc., American MSI Corporation LLC, Branden Technologies, Inc., Moldflow (Europe) Ltd., Moldflow (Guangzhou) Ltd., Moldflow B.V., Moldflow France, Moldflow Iberia S.L., Moldflow International Pty. Ltd., Moldflow Ireland, Ltd., Moldflow Italia S.r.l, Moldflow Japan KK, Moldflow Korea Ltd., Moldflow Merger Corp., Moldflow Pty. Ltd. 20 Subsidiaries included in the Index

Officers: Roland A. Thomas/Chmn., CEO, Pres./$769,575.00, Gregory W. Magoon/CFO, Exec. VP - Finance, Treasurer, Assist. Sec./$205,978.00, Lori M. Henderson/Exec. VP, General Counsel, Sec./$392,837.00, Fred Humbert/VP, GM - Manufacturing Solutions/$521,198.00, Ian M. Pendlebury/Exec. VP - Product Development, Kenneth R. Welch/Exec. VP, GM - Design Analysis Solutions/$485,346.00, Peter K. Kennedy/CTO, Exec. VP, Frank W. Haydu/Corp. Dir.

Directors: Roland A. Thomas/Chmn., CEO, Pres., Robert P. Schechter/Corp. Dir., Frank W. Haydu/Corp. Dir., Roger E. Brooks/Dir., Robert J. Lepofsky/Corp. Dir.

Owners: Robert P. Schechter, Insiders/9.38%, Fidelity Management & Research/13.62%, Gregory W. Magoon, Roland A. Thomas/4.10%, Roger E. Brooks, Christopher L. Gorgone, Fred G. Humbert, Frank W. Haydu, Robert J. Lepofsky, Kenneth R. Welch, Lori M. Henderson, Paradigm Capital Management, Inc./7.89%

Financial Data: **Fiscal Year End:**06/30 **Latest Annual Data:** 6/30/2007

Year	Sales	Net Income
2007	$55,853,000	-$3,789,000
2006	$65,558,000	$1,001,000
2005	$64,418,000	$6,757,000

Curr. Assets:	$101,500,000	**Curr. Liab.:**	$26,460,000		
Plant, Equip.:	$3,137,000	**Total Liab.:**	$28,347,000	**Indic. Yr. Divd.:**	NA
Total Assets:	$113,761,000	**Net Worth:**	$85,414,000	**Debt/ Equity:**	NA

Molecular Diagnostics Inc

414 N Orleans St., Ste. 502, Chicago, IL, 60610; ***PH:*** 1-312-222-9550; ***Fax:*** 1-312-222-9580; ***http://*** www.molecular-dx.com

General - Incorporation	DE	**Stock**- Price on:12/24/2007	NA
Employees	3	Stock Exchange	NA
Auditor	Amper, Politziner & Mattia P.c	Ticker Symbol	NA
Stk Agt	LaSalle Bank N.A	Outstanding Shares	NA
Counsel	NA	E.P.S	-$0.016
DUNS No.	05-323-8150	Shareholders	NA

Business: The group's principal activities are to design, develop and market inpath system and related image analysis systems used to detect cancer and cancer related diseases. The group has designed and manufactured accell computer aided automated microscopy instrument which collects quantitative cellular information used in support of a diagnostic process.these products may be used in a laboratory, clinic or doctor's office. On 19-Dec-2003, the group sold samba technologies assets, its wholly- owned subsidiary and treated as discontinued operation

Primary SIC and add'l.: 3841 8071 7372

CIK No: 0000075439

Subsidiaries: AccuMed International, Inc., Bell National Corporation, Inpath, LLC, Oncometrics Imaging Corp., PFI National Corporation

Officers: Floyd Taub/CEO, Richard Domanik/Pres., Robert McCullough/CFO/$550,400.00, George Gorodeski/Lead Research Scientist

Directors: Steven Waggoner/Member - Medical Advisory Board, Stephen Raab/Member - Medical Advisory Board

Owners: Monsun, AS/10.00%, David J. Weissberg/5.60%, Standard General Holdings, LLC/7.20%, Augusto Ocana, Floyd E. Taub, Insiders/6.90%, Robert F. McCullough/3.20%, John H. Abeles, Alexander M. Milley/2.80%, BSI Multihelvetia/5.30%, Edward G. Renner, Richard A. Domanik

Financial Data: **Fiscal Year End:**12/31 **Latest Annual Data:** 12/31/2006

Year	Sales	Net Income
2006	$183,000	-$973,000
2005	$3,000	-$75,000
2004	$3,000	-$330,000

Curr. Assets:	$167,000	**Curr. Liab.:**	$848,000		
Plant, Equip.:	$235,000	**Total Liab.:**	$1,054,000	**Indic. Yr. Divd.:**	NA
Total Assets:	$1,989,000	**Net Worth:**	$935,000	**Debt/ Equity:**	0.1897

Molecular Imaging Corp

9530 Towne Ctr. Dr., Ste.120, San Diego, CA, 92121; ***PH:*** 1-858-642-0032; ***Fax:*** 1-858-642-0052; ***http://*** www.molecularimagingcorp.com

General - Incorporation	DE	**Stock**- Price on:12/24/2007	$0.0055
Employees	NA	Stock Exchange	OTC
Auditor	Peterson & Co. LLP	Ticker Symbol	MLRI
Stk Agt	OTC Corporate Transfer Service Co	Outstanding Shares	NA
Counsel	NA	E.P.S	NA
DUNS No.	NA	Shareholders	NA

Business: The group's principal activity is to provide molecular imaging services to the healthcare industry. Mi is a diagnostic procedure used to diagonise, monitor and assess disease severity for many cancers, cardiovascular disease and neurological disorders. The group also provides combined imaging services through mi/ct systems which improves the time to diagnosis, staging of many cancers, cardiovascular disease and neurological disorders and is also used to observe patient response to treatment. The group provides services to hospitals, physician groups, diagnostic imaging centres and other healthcare providers in selected marketplaces in the United States.

Primary SIC and add'l.: 8071

CIK No: 0001097181

Subsidiaries: Mbpt #1 LLC, Mbpt #2 LLC, Mbpt #3 LLC, Mbpt #5 LLC, Mobile P.E.T. Systems (UK) Limited, Molecular Imaging Bellevue LLC, Molecular Imaging Cyclotron LLC, Molecular Imaging Houston LLC, Molecular Imaging MicroPET LLC, Molecular Imaging Services Corp I, Molecular Imaging Sorrento Valley LLC, Molecular Imaging St. Pete LLC, PET Billing Solutions LLC

Officers: Kenneth C. Frederick/CEO

Directors: Peter S. Conti/Chmn., Medical Member - Advisory Board, William G. Bradley/Member - Medical Advisory Board

Financial Data: **Fiscal Year End:**06/30 **Latest Annual Data:** 6/30/2004

Year	Sales	Net Income
2004	$21,207,000	-$8,801,000
2003	$20,888,000	$964,000
2002	$17,603,000	-$5,823,000

Curr. Assets:	$3,645,000	**Curr. Liab.:**	$22,440,000		
Plant, Equip.:	$14,141,000	**Total Liab.:**	$22,550,000	**Indic. Yr. Divd.:**	NA
Total Assets:	$19,022,000	**Net Worth:**	-$3,528,000	**Debt/ Equity:**	NA

Molecular Pharmacology (USA) Ltd

8721 Santa Monica Blvd., Ste. 1023, Los Angeles, CA, 90069; ***PH:*** 1-310-694-8976; ***http://*** www.mpl-usa.com

General - Incorporation	NV
Employees	NA
Auditor	James Stafford, Inc
Stk Agt	NA
Counsel	NA
DUNS No.	NA

Stock - Price on:12/24/2007	$0.135
Stock Exchange	OTC
Ticker Symbol	MLPH
Outstanding Shares	111,550,000
E.P.S.	-$0.005
Shareholders	NA

Business: The groups principal activities include developing and commercializing analgesic and anti-inflammatory molecule known as Tripeptofen. In May 2006, the group acquired Molecular Pharmacology Limited. The group operates from the United States and Australia.

Primary SIC and add'l.: 5122

CIK No: 0001191357

Officers: Jeffery Edwards/56/Dir., CEO, Pres., Maud Eijkenboom/Chief Scientist, Simon Watson/Dir., CFO, Corp. Sec., Lucio Van Rooijen/Contact - European Business Development, Ravi Riron/Contact - USA Business Development

Directors: Jeffery Edwards/56/Dir., CEO, Pres., Simon Watson/Dir., CFO, Corp. Sec.

Financial Data: Fiscal Year End:10/31 **Latest Annual Data:** 10/31/2006

Year	Sales	Net Income
2006	NA	NA
2005	NA	NA

Curr. Assets:	$32,000	Curr. Liab.:	$866,000		
Plant, Equip.:	$5,000	Total Liab.:	$866,000	Indic. Yr. Divd.:	NA
Total Assets:	$37,000	Net Worth:	-$829,000	Debt/ Equity:	NA

Molex Inc

2222 Wellington Ct., Lisle, IL, 60532; **PH:** 1-630-969-4550; **Fax:** 1-630-968-8356; **http://** www.molex.com; **Email:** amerinfo@molex.com

General - Incorporation	DE
Employees	32,400
Auditor	Ernst & Young LLP
Stk Agt	Computershare Investor Services LLC
Counsel	NA
DUNS No.	00-524-6673

Stock - Price on:12/24/2007	$31
Stock Exchange	NDQ
Ticker Symbol	MOLX
Outstanding Shares	184,460,000
E.P.S.	$1.30
Shareholders	NA

Business: The groups principle activity is to supply interconnect products. The groups products include connectors, sockets, fiber optics and cable assemblies. In the year 2007 the group acquired Polymicro Technologies, LLC. The group operates from United States.

Primary SIC and add'l.: 3679

CIK No: 0000067472

Subsidiaries: Automotive Connectors India Private Ltd., Cardell Corporation, Cardell USVI International Sales Corporation, Dongguan Molex Interconnect Co Ltd. (DG2), Dongguan Molex South-China Connector Co. Ltd. (DG 1), G. stervig-Molex A/S, Hi-P Tool & Die Pte.Ltd., KYBERNEX s.r.o., Landwin Engineering, MEC International Pte. Ltd., MI European Holdings CV, MLX Acquisition Corp, MOL Automotive Lda, Molex (Dalian) Co. Ltd., Molex (Dalien) Logistics Co., Ltd 75 Subsidiaries included in the Index

Officers: Martin P. Slark/Vice Chmn., CEO/$4,012,723.00, Fred L. Krehbiel/Dir., Pres. - Connector Products Division, Ana G. Rodriguez/VP, Co - General Counsel, Sec., Liam G. McCarthy/52/COO, Pres., James E. Fleischhacker/64/Exec. VP, Pres. - Global Transportation Products Division/$2,119,308.00, David D. Johnson/52/CFO, Exec. VP, Treasurer/$1,409,913.00, Graham C. Brock/54/Exec. VP, Katsumi Hirokawa/61/Exec. VP, Pres. - Global Micro Products Division, David B. Root/54/Exec. VP, Pres. - Global Commercial Products Division, Michael J. Nauman/46/Sr. VP, Pres. - Global Integrated Products Division, Hans A. Van Delft/53/Sr. VP, Pres. - Global Automation, Electrical Products Division, Travis K. George/Corporate Controller, Chief Accounting Officer, Principal Accounting Officer

Directors: Martin P. Slark/Vice Chmn., CEO, Frederick A. Krehbiel/Chmn., John H. Krehbiel/Chmn., Michael J. Birck/Dir., Michelle L. Collins/Dir., Edgar D. Jannotta/Dir., Kazumasa Kusaka/Dir., Robert J. Potter/Dir., Donald G. Lubin/Dir., David L. Landsittel/Dir., Fred L. Krehbiel/Dir., Pres. - Connector Products Division

Owners: Michael J. Birck, Michael J. Birck, David D. Johnson, Frederick A. Krehbiel/49.90%, Edgar D. Jannotta, Insiders/38.30%, David L. Landsittel, Martin P. Slark, Frederick A. Krehbiel/26.12%, AMVESCAP PLC, Frederick A. Krehbiel, Martin P. Slark, Insiders/7.50%, John H. Krehbiel/32.00%, Robert J. Potter *(35 Owners included in Index)*

Financial Data: Fiscal Year End:06/30 **Latest Annual Data:** 06/30/2007

Year	Sales	Net Income
2007	$3,265,874,000	$240,768,000
2006	$2,861,289,000	$236,091,000
2005	$2,548,652,000	$154,434,000

Curr. Assets:	$1,548,233,000	Curr. Liab.:	$594,812,000	P/E Ratio:	20.67
Plant, Equip.:	$1,025,852,000	Total Liab.:	$691,669,000	Indic. Yr. Divd.:	$0.300
Total Assets:	$2,974,420,000	Net Worth:	$2,281,869,000	Debt/ Equity:	0.0535

Molina Healthcare Inc

200 Oceangate, Ste. 100, Long Beach, CA, 90802; **PH:** 1-562-435-3666; **Fax:** 1-562-499-0790; **http://** www.molinahealthcare.com

General - Incorporation	DE
Employees	2,000
Auditor	Ernst & Young LLP
Stk Agt	Continental Stock Transfer & Trust Co
Counsel	NA
DUNS No.	NA

Stock - Price on:12/24/2007	$30.38
Stock Exchange	NYSE
Ticker Symbol	MOH
Outstanding Shares	28,220,000
E.P.S.	$1.66
Shareholders	NA

Business: The group's principle activity is to provide multi-state managed care that arranges for the delivery of health care services to persons eligible for medicaid and other programs for low-income families and individuals. The group generates revenue primarily from the premiums received from the contracts with state medicaid agencies and other managed care organizations with which the group operates as a subcontractor. The group has health plans in California, Washington, Michigan and Utah. The group's quarterly revenue for September 2007 was 636.03 millions of USD.

Primary SIC and add'l.: 6324

CIK No: 0001179929

Subsidiaries: Health Care Horizons, Inc., Molina Healthcare Insurance Company, Inc., Molina Healthcare of California, Molina Healthcare of California Partner Plan, Inc., Molina Healthcare of Georgia, Inc., Molina Healthcare of Indiana, Inc., Molina Healthcare of Michigan, Inc., Molina Healthcare of Nevada, Inc., Molina Healthcare of New Mexico, Inc. (indirect), Molina Healthcare of Ohio, Inc., Molina Healthcare of Texas, Inc., Molina Healthcare of Utah, Inc., Molina Healthcare of Washington, Inc.

Officers: Ann O. Wehr/CEO - New Mexico, Jesse Thomas/CEO, Pres. - Ohio, Mario J. Molina/49/Chmn., CEO, Pres., Peggy Wanta/Dir. - Contracts, Compliance, Washington, Ward B. Hurlburt/Chief Medical Officer - Leads, Washington, Amy Bingham/Compliance Mgr. - Utah, Paul Muench/Pres. - Utah, Gary Call/Chief Medical Officer - Utah, Stephen T. ODell/Pres. - California, Roberta Holtzman/COO - California, Kathie Mancini/COO - Ohio, Kevin Smith/Chief Medical Officer - Ohio, Danielle Angel/Dir. - Government Contracts, Ohio, Kimberly Blackwell/Mgr. - Compliance, Ohio, Kelly Miller/Mgr. - Human Resources, Ohio *(32 Officers included in Index)*

Directors: Mario J. Molina/49/Chmn., CEO, Pres., Charles Z. Fedak/Dir., John P. Szabo/Dir., Sally K. Richardson/Dir., John C. Molina/Dir., CFO, Ronna Romney/Dir., Steven Orlando/Dir., Frank E. Murray/Dir., Wayne B. Lowell/52/Dir.

Owners: Sally K. Richardson, Mary R. Molina Living Trust/12.80%, Wayne B. Lowell, Curtis Pedersen/29.50%, Molina Siblings Trust/11.90%, J. Mario Molina/2.50%, Ronna E. Romney, Steven J. Orlando, John C. Molina/14.90%, Mark L. Andrews, John P. Szabo, Insiders/20.80%, Frank E. Murray, William Dentino/30.80%, Charles Z. Fedak *(18 Owners included in Index)*

Financial Data: Fiscal Year End:12/31 **Latest Annual Data:** 12/31/2006

Year	Sales	Net Income
2006	$2,004,995,000	$45,727,000
2005	$1,650,058,000	$27,596,000
2004	$1,175,268,000	$55,773,000

Curr. Assets:	$613,502,000	Curr. Liab.:	$354,893,000	P/E Ratio:	18.30
Plant, Equip.:	$41,903,000	Total Liab.:	$444,309,000	Indic. Yr. Divd.:	NA
Total Assets:	$864,475,000	Net Worth:	$420,166,000	Debt/ Equity:	0.0694

Moliris Corp

4710 Kingsway, Ste. 1424, Burnaby, BC, V5H 4M2; **PH:** 1-604-628-8900

General - Incorporation	FL
Employees	NA
Auditor	Killman, Murrell & Co. P.C
Stk Agt	Signature Stock Transfer, Inc.
Counsel	NA
DUNS No.	NA

Stock - Price on:12/24/2007	$0.05
Stock Exchange	NA
Ticker Symbol	NA
Outstanding Shares	NA
E.P.S.	NA
Shareholders	NA

Business: The groups principle activity is to provide telecommunication services. The group provides personal and business telephone services. The group operates from United States.

Primary SIC and add'l.: NA

CIK No: 0001211229

Subsidiaries: Digifonica (International) Limited, Digifonica Canada Limited, Digifonica Intellectual Properties Limited, Moliris Corp., Moliris Packaging Corp., Shenzen Sino-Can Inter-Communication Technology Limited

Financial Data: Fiscal Year End:12/31 **Latest Annual Data:** 12/31/2005

Year	Sales	Net Income
2005	NA	-$2,313,000
2004	$673,000	-$4,281,000

Curr. Assets:	$158,000	Curr. Liab.:	$2,452,000		
Plant, Equip.:	$452,000	Total Liab.:	$2,452,000	Indic. Yr. Divd.:	NA
Total Assets:	$1,455,000	Net Worth:	-$997,000	Debt/ Equity:	NA

Moller International Inc

1222 Research Pk. Dr., Davis, CA, 95616; **PH:** 1-530-756-5086; **Fax:** 1-530-756-5179; **http://** www.moller.com; **Email:** info@moller.com

General - Incorporation	CA
Employees	NA
Auditor	Malone & Bailey, P.C
Stk Agt	Olde Monmouth Stk Trnsfer Co. Inc.
Counsel	NA
DUNS No.	NA

Stock - Price on:12/24/2007	NA
Stock Exchange	OTC
Ticker Symbol	MLER
Outstanding Shares	NA
E.P.S.	-$0.05
Shareholders	NA

Business: The group's principle activities are to design, develop, manufacture and market a line of vertical take-off and landing (vtol) aircraft. The activities of the group are aimed at designing and producing an aircraft that combines the speed and efficiency advantages of the fixed-wing airplane with the vertical-flight capabilities of the helicopter. The group's principal products will be the m400 skycar vtol and the aerobot remotely-operated aerial vehicles. Currently, the group derives contract revenues from design work to adapt its products to customer applications and through the leasing of a full scale skycar model for various exhibitions. The group also sells t-shirts, model cars, information packets and other items. The group's total revenue for year 2007 was 0.08 millions of USD.

Primary SIC and add'l.: 7359 3721 3714 5947 3728

CIK No: 0000871344

Officers: Paul Moller/Chmn., CEO, CFO, Bob Shebusky/Group Leader - Manufacture, Rotary Engines, Consultants, Advisors, Jennifer Moller/Office Mgr., George L. Stevens/Chief Engineer, Mike Griffith/Mgr. - Industrial Engine Project, Charles H. Guenther/Financial Consultant, Advisor, Hal Sliney/Chief Scientist - Material Section, Nasa, Peter Levin/Mgr. - Supertrapp Production, Bruce Calkins/GM, Otto Scharft/OMC Group Leader - Rotary Engine Research, Mike Shanley/Dir., Dir. - International Sales, Marketing, Stacey Horigan/Controller, Justin T. Blumetti/Project Engineer, Winstone Jordaan/International Contact - South Africa, Hendrik Ten Cate/International Contact - Netherlands

Directors: Paul Moller/Chmn., CEO, CFO, Mike Shanley/Dir., Dir. - International Sales, Marketing, Faulkner White/57/Dir., Jim Toreson/65/Dir.

Owners: Paul S. Moller/48.53%

Financial Data: Fiscal Year End:06/30 **Latest Annual Data:** 6/30/2006

Year	Sales	Net Income
2006	$74,000	-$6,902,000
2005	$639,000	-$1,433,000

Curr. Assets:	$48,000	Curr. Liab.:	$8,948,000		
Plant, Equip.:	$12,000	Total Liab.:	$9,410,000	Indic. Yr. Divd.:	NA
Total Assets:	$158,000	Net Worth:	-$9,252,000	Debt/ Equity:	NA

Molson Coors Brewing Co

1225 17th St., Denver, CO, 80202; ***PH:*** 1-303-279-6565; ***Fax:*** 1-303-277-5415;
http:// www.coors.com

General - Incorporation	DE	**Stock**- Price on:12/24/2007	$93.22
Employees	9,550	Stock Exchange	NYSE
Auditor	PricewaterhouseCoopers LLP	Ticker Symbol	TAP
Stk Agt	EquiServe Trust Co N.A	Outstanding Shares	89,340,000
Counsel	NA	E.P.S	$2.36
DUNS No.	00-705-7342	Shareholders	NA

Business: The group's principle activity is to provide beer and other malt-based beverages. The group operates from United States.

Primary SIC and add'l.: 6719 2082

CIK No: 0000024545

Subsidiaries: Carling O'Keefe Company, Cervejarias Kaiser Brasil S.A. (CKB), Coors Brewers Limited, Coors Brewing Company, Coors Brewing Company International, Inc., Coors Global Properties, Inc., Coors Global Properties,Inc., Coors Holding Ltd., Coors Intercontinental, Inc., Coors International Market Development, L.L.L.P., Coors Worldwide, Inc., Golden Acquisition Ltd., Kaiser Paricipacoes S.A. (KP), MC Finance General ULC, Molson Canada 21 Subsidiaries included in the Index

Officers: Frits D. Van Paasschen/46/CEO, Pres. - Coors Brewing Company/$2,399,966.00, Kevin Boyce/CEO, Pres. - Molson Canada/$2,037,860.00, Leo W. Kiely/61/Dir., CEO, Pres./$6,682,208.00, Peter Swinburn/CEO, Pres. - Coors Brewers Limited/$3,529,808.00, Dave Perkins/Global Chief Commercial Officer, Timothy V. Wolf/Global CFO/$2,962,991.00, Ralph Hargrow/Global Chief People Officer, Gregory L. Wade/Global Chief Supply Chain Officer, Martin L. Miller/45/VP, Global Controller, Samuel D. Walker/Chief Legal Officer, Sec., Cathy Noonan/Global Chief Synergies Officer

Directors: Leo W. Kiely/61/Dir., CEO, Pres., Peter H. Coors/Vice Chmn., Eric H. Molson/Chmn., Andrew T. Molson/Dir., Franklin W. Hobbs/Dir., Gary Matthews/Dir., Rosalind G. Brewer/Dir., Francesco Bellini/Dir., Melissa Coors Osborn/35/Dir., Pamela Patsley/Dir., Sanford H. Riley/Dir., John E. Cleghorn/66/Dir., Charles M. Herington/48/Dir., David P. O'Brien/66/Dir.

Owners: Adolph Coors Company LLC, Francesco Bellini, Peter H. Coors/13.60%, Frits D. van Paasschen, Kevin Boyce, Eric H. Molson/2.80%, Timothy V. Wolf, Pamela H. Patsley, Leo Kiely/1.30%, Charles M. Herington, Franklin W. Hobbs, Insiders, Adolph Coors,Jr. Trust/12.40%, Gary S. Matthews, Adolph Coors,Jr. Trust *(28 Owners included in Index)*

Financial Data: ***Fiscal Year End:***12/25 ***Latest Annual Data:*** 12/31/2006

Year	Sales	Net Income
2006	$5,844,985,000	$361,031,000
2005	$5,506,906,000	$134,944,000
2004	$4,305,816,000	$196,736,000

Curr. Assets:	$1,458,356,000	**Curr. Liab.:**	$1,800,116,000	**P/E Ratio:**	20.62
Plant, Equip.:	$2,421,484,000	**Total Liab.:**	$5,739,275,000	**Indic. Yr. Divd.:**	$0.640
Total Assets:	$11,603,413,000	**Net Worth:**	$5,817,356,000	**Debt/ Equity:**	0.4059

Momenta Pharmaceuticals Inc

675 W Kendall St., Cambridge, MA, 02142; ***PH:*** 1-617-491-9700; ***Fax:*** 1-617-621-0431;
http:// www.momentapharma.com; ***Email:*** info@momentapharma.com

General - Incorporation	DE	**Stock**- Price on:12/24/2007	$11.21
Employees	153	Stock Exchange	NDQ
Auditor	Ernst & Young LLP	Ticker Symbol	MNTA
Stk Agt	American Stock Transfer & Trust Co.	Outstanding Shares	36,330,000
Counsel	NA	E.P.S	-$1.72
DUNS No.	NA	Shareholders	NA

Business: The group's principle activity is to provide drugs. The company formed a collaboration with sandoz to jointly develop, manufacture and commercialize m-enoxaparin. The group operates from United States.

Primary SIC and add'l.: 8731 2834

CIK No: 0001235010

Subsidiaries: Momenta Pharmaceuticals Securities Corporation

Officers: Craig A. Wheeler/Dir., CEO, Pres., Ian Fier/VP - Development Operations, Richard P. Shea/CFO, VP, Ganesh Venkataraman/Founder, Sr. VP - Research, CSO, Barbara Rosengren/VP - Strategic Product Development, John E. Bishop/Sr. VP - Pharmaceutical Sciences, Susan K. Whoriskey/VP - Intellectual Property, Steven B. Brugger/COO - Strategic Business Operations, Lisa Carron Shmerling/VP - Legal Affairs, Gerard E. Riedel/VP - Regulatory Affairs

Directors: Craig A. Wheeler/Dir., CEO, Pres., Peter Barrett/Chmn., Paul D. Goldenheim/Dir., Peter Barton Hutt/Dir., Robert S. Langer/Dir., Ganesh Venkataraman/Founder, Sr. VP - Research, CSO, Ram Sasisekharan/Dir., Bennett M. Shapiro/Dir., Stephen T. Reeders/Dir., Alan L. Crane/Dir., John K. Clarke/Dir., Marsha H. Fanucci/Dir.

Owners: Robert S. Langer/2.80%, Steven B. Brugger, Paul G. Goldenheim, Ziff Asset Management, L.P. and related entities and individual/8.30%, Alan L. Crane/1.70%, John K. Clarke/1.70%, John E. Bishop, OrbiMed Advisors LLC,/7.50%, Atlas Venture entities/6.80%, Insiders/22.00%, Marsha H. Fanucci, Stephen T. Reeders/3.90%, FMR Corp. and affiliates/9.50%, Palo Alto Investors LLC/6.10%, Peter Barton Hutt *(24 Owners included in Index)*

Financial Data: ***Fiscal Year End:***12/31 ***Latest Annual Data:*** 12/31/2006

Year	Sales	Net Income
2006	$15,999,000	-$51,913,000
2005	$14,479,000	-$21,662,000
2004	$7,832,000	-$14,075,000

Curr. Assets:	$198,061,000	**Curr. Liab.:**	$12,762,000		
Plant, Equip.:	$13,603,000	**Total Liab.:**	$33,794,000	**Indic. Yr. Divd.:**	NA
Total Assets:	$216,385,000	**Net Worth:**	$182,591,000	**Debt/ Equity:**	0.0379

Monaco Coach Corp

91320 Coberg Industrial Way, Coburg, OR, 97408; ***PH:*** 1-541-686-8011; ***Fax:*** 1-541-681-8899;
http:// www.monaco-online.com

General - Incorporation	DE	**Stock**- Price on:12/24/2007	$15.12
Employees	5,292	Stock Exchange	NYSE
Auditor	PricewaterhouseCoopers LLP	Ticker Symbol	MNC
Stk Agt	Wells Fargo Shareowner Services	Outstanding Shares	29,940,000
Counsel	Wilson Sonsini Goodrich & Rosati	E.P.S	$0.30
DUNS No.	17-549-5985	Shareholders	NA

Business: The group' principal activity is to manufacture premium motor coaches, bus conversions, and towable recreational vehicles at manufacturing facilities in Oregon and Indiana. The product lines of the group consist of 29 models of motor coaches and 13 models of towables. Its products are sold under the brand names of "Monaco," "Holiday Rambler," "Royale Coach," "Beaver," "Safari" and "McKenzie". The products of the group are sold through an extensive network of 332 dealer lots located primarily in the United States and Canada. The group also owns two motor coach resort properties, the developed lots, of which, are sold to retail customers.

Primary SIC and add'l.: 3792 3713

CIK No: 0000910619

Subsidiaries: Bison Manufacturing LLC., Harney County Operations Inc., MCC Acquisition Corporation, Outdoor Resorts Motorcoach Country Club Inc., Outdoor Resorts of Las Vegas Inc., Outdoor Resorts of Naples Inc., R-Vision Holdings LLC, R-Vision Inc., R-Vision Motorized LLC., Roadmaster LLC, Royale Coach by Monaco Inc.

Officers: Kay Toolson/Chmn., CEO/$2,204,770.00, John Nepute/Pres./$603,218.00, Richard Bond/Sr. VP, Sec., Chief Administrative Officer/$342,110.00, Marty Daley/CFO, VP/$394,315.00, Pat Carroll/VP - Product Development, Mike Snell/VP - Sales, Marketing/$335,938.00, John Healey/VP - Corporate Purchasing, Richard Kangail/VP - Human Resources, Garth Herring/VP - Service Operations, April Lynch-Klein/VP - Customer Support Services, Marty Garriott/VP - Oregon Manufacturing, Irv Yoder/VP - Indiana Manufacturing, Craig Swisher/VP - Towable Operations, Charlie Kimball/Corporate Controller, Chief Accounting Office

Directors: Kay Toolson/Chmn., CEO, Richard A. Rouse/Dir., Dennis D. Oklak/Dir., Robert P. Hanafee/Dir., John F. Cogan/Dir., Roger A. Vandenberg/Dir., Ben L. Lytle/Dir., Daniel C. Ustian/Dir., Richard E. Colliver/Dir.

Owners: Richard A. Rouse, L. Ben Lytle, John W. Nepute, Royce& Associates, LLC/7.80%, Dennis D. Oklak, FMR Corp./12.34%, Roger A. Vandenberg/2.49%, Michael P. Snell, P. Martin Daley, Kay L. Toolson/6.31%, Franklin Resources,Inc./7.32%, Richard E. Bond, Insiders/10.89%, Daniel C. Ustian, Dimensional Fund Advisors LP/8.16% *(18 Owners included in Index)*

Financial Data: ***Fiscal Year End:***12/31 ***Latest Annual Data:*** 12/30/2006

Year	Sales	Net Income
2006	$1,297,986,000	$1,004,000
2005	$1,236,238,000	$2,648,000

Curr. Assets:	$341,516,000	**Curr. Liab.:**	$214,325,000		
Plant, Equip.:	$159,304,000	**Total Liab.:**	$270,735,000	**Indic. Yr. Divd.:**	$0.240
Total Assets:	$587,467,000	**Net Worth:**	$316,732,000	**Debt/ Equity:**	0.0869

Monadnock Bancorp Inc

Formerly: Monadnock Community Bancorp Inc
One Jaffrey Rd., Peterborough, NH, 03458; ***PH:*** 1-603-924-9654; ***http://*** www.monadnockbank.com

General - Incorporation	Federal	**Stock**- Price on:12/24/2007	$6.55
Employees	20	Stock Exchange	OTC
Auditor	Shatswell, MacLeod & Co. P.C	Ticker Symbol	MNKB
Stk Agt	Registrar & Transfer Co	Outstanding Shares	1,290,000
Counsel	NA	E.P.S	$0.07
DUNS No.	NA	Shareholders	NA

Business: The group's principle activity is to provide banking services. The groups services include certificate of deposit, savings, money market and demand deposit accounts. The group operates from United States.

Primary SIC and add'l.: NA

CIK No: 0001283899

Subsidiaries: Monadnock Community Bank

Officers: William M. Pierce/54/Dir., CEO, Pres./$122,994.00, Donald R. Blanchette/54/Sr. VP, Kenneth R. Simonetta/66/Dir., Assist. Sec., Karl F. Betz/44/Sr. VP, CFO, Treasurer, Thomas C. Lafortune/69/Dir., Sec., William C. Gilson/59/Sr. VP, Sr. Loan Officer, Wayne Gordon/Contact - Auto, Personal Loans

Directors: William M. Pierce/54/Dir., CEO, Pres., Kenneth A. Christian/63/Chmn., Samuel J. Hackler/63/Vice Chmn., Thomas C. Lafortune/69/Dir., Sec., Nancy L. Carlson/62/Dir., Kenneth R. Simonetta/66/Dir., Assist. Sec., Edward J. Shea/70/Dir.

Owners: Monadnock Community Bank/5.07%

Financial Data: ***Fiscal Year End:***12/31 ***Latest Annual Data:*** 12/31/2006

Year	Sales	Net Income
2006	$4,889,000	$75,000
2005	$3,737,000	-$30,000
2004	$2,756,000	$32,000

Curr. Assets:	$1,626,000	**Curr. Liab.:**	$86,327,000	**P/E Ratio:**	93.57
Plant, Equip.:	$787,000	**Total Liab.:**	$86,509,000	**Indic. Yr. Divd.:**	NA
Total Assets:	$96,185,000	**Net Worth:**	$9,676,000	**Debt/ Equity:**	NA

Monarch Casino & Resort Inc

3800 S Virginia St., Reno, NV, 89502; ***PH:*** 1-775-335-4600; ***Fax:*** 1-775-332-9171;
http:// www.monarchcasino.com

General - Incorporation	NV	**Stock**- Price on:12/24/2007	$27.3
Employees	1,900	Stock Exchange	NDQ
Auditor	Ernst & Young LLP	Ticker Symbol	MCRI
Stk Agt	American Stock Transfer & Trust Co.	Outstanding Shares	19,090,000
Counsel	Kummer, Kaempfer, Bonner & Renshaw	E.P.S	$1.32
DUNS No.	80-755-0280	Shareholders	NA

Business: The group's principal activity is to own and operate the tropically themed atlantis casino resort. The resort is a hotel/casino facility in reno, Nevada. The resort features approximately 51,000 square feet of casino space, a hotel and a motor lodge with 980 guest rooms, nine food outlets, a nightclub, an enclosed pool with waterfall features. It has an outdoor pool, health club, two retail outlets featuring traditional gift shop merchandise as well as clothing and other merchandise, family entertainment center and banquet, convention and meeting room space. The group caters to reno area residents, leisure travelers and conventioneers.

Primary SIC and add'l.: 7011

CIK No: 0000907242

Subsidiaries: Golden Road Motor Inn, Inc., Golden Town Inc.

Officers: John Farahi/Co - Chmn., CEO/$1,052,033.00, Bob Farahi/Co - Chmn., Pres., Sec., Debra Robinson/General Counsel, Ron Rowan/CFO/$355,277.00

Directors: John Farahi/Co - Chmn., CEO, Bob Farahi/Co - Chmn., Pres., Sec., Charles W. Scharer/Dir., Ronald R. Zideck/Dir., Craig F. Sullivan/Dir.

Owners: Akre Capital Management, LLC/8.90%, Bob Farahi/11.00%, Ronald R. Zideck, Charles W. Scharer, Ben Farahi/10.40%, Barclays Global Investors NA/6.00%, Craig F. Sullivan, Friedman, Billings, Ramsey Group, Inc./5.20%, John Farahi/15.50%, Ronald M. Rowan, Insiders/26.70%

Financial Data: *Fiscal Year End:*12/31 *Latest Annual Data:* 12/31/2006

Year	Sales	Net Income
2006	$151,969,000	$22,080,000
2005	$139,785,000	$21,035,000
2004	$129,457,000	$16,526,000

Curr. Assets:	$45,524,000	**Curr. Liab.:**	$18,486,000	**P/E Ratio:**	21.16
Plant, Equip.:	$92,626,000	**Total Liab.:**	$22,735,000	**Indic. Yr. Divd.:**	NA
Total Assets:	$138,381,000	**Net Worth:**	$115,646,000	**Debt/ Equity:**	NA

Monarch Cement Co

449 1200 St., Humboldt, KS, 66748; *PH:* 1-620-473-2222; *Fax:* 1-620-473-2447;
http:// www.monarchcement.com; *Email:* monarch@monarchcement.com

General - Incorporation	KS	**Stock**- Price on:12/24/2007	$31.35
Employees	605	Stock Exchange	OTC
Auditor	BKD LLP	Ticker Symbol	MCEM
Stk Agt	Monarch Cement Co	Outstanding Shares	4,030,000
Counsel	NA	E.P.S	$3.13
DUNS No.	00-714-4884	Shareholders	NA

Business: The group's principal activity is to manufacture and sell portland cement. The group operates in two business segments: cement manufacturing and the sale of ready-mixed concrete and sundry building materials. The products are sold to contractors, ready-mixed concrete plants, concrete product plants, building material dealers and governmental agencies. Portland cement products are sold under the monarch brand name in the state of Kansas, the state of Iowa, southeast Nebraska, western Missouri, northwest Arkansas and northern Oklahoma.

Primary SIC and add'l.: 3241 1422 3273

CIK No: 0000067517

Subsidiaries: Beaver Lake Concrete, Inc., Capitol Concrete Products Co., Inc., City Wide Construction Products Co., Concrete Enterprises, Inc., Concrete Materials, Inc., Dodge City Concrete, Inc., Joplin Concrete Company, Inc., Kansas Sand and Concrete, Inc., Monarch Cement of Iowa, Inc., Salina Concrete Products, Inc., Springfield Ready Mix Co., Tulsa Dynaspan, Inc.

Officers: Walter H. Wulf/34/Chmn., Principal Executive Officer, Pres., Byron K. Radcliff/70/Vice Chmn., Sec., Treasurer, Debra P. Roe/52/CFO, Assist. Sec., Treasurer/$154,795.00, Robert M. Kissick/71/Dir., VP, Rick E. Rush/55/VP/$153,362.00, Harvey D. Buckley/58/VP - Cement Mfg/$143,477.00

Directors: Walter H. Wulf/34/Chmn., Principal Executive Officer, Pres., Byron K. Radcliff/70/Vice Chmn., Sec., Treasurer, David L. Deffner/57/Dir., Byron J. Radcliff/51/Dir., Michael R. Wachter/47/Dir., Gayle C. McMillen/58/Dir., Richard N. Nixon/66/Dir., Jack R. Callahan/76/Dir., Robert M. Kissick/71/Dir., VP

Owners: Michael R. Wachter, Rick E. Rush, Robert M. Kissick/2.60%, Gayle C. McMillen/2.49%, David L. Deffner/1.07%, Richard N. Nixon, Richard N. Nixon, Gayle C. McMillen/4.51%, Robert M. Kissick/1.23%, Debra P. Roe, Byron K. Radcliff/13.80%, Ronald E. Callaway, Byron K. Radcliff/8.13%, Jack R. Callahan, Walter H. Wulf *(31 Owners included in Index)*

Financial Data: *Fiscal Year End:*12/31 *Latest Annual Data:* 12/31/2006

Year	Sales	Net Income
2006	$154,213,000	$13,215,000
2005	$141,320,000	$9,658,000
2004	$145,077,000	$2,569,000

Curr. Assets:	$41,478,000	**Curr. Liab.:**	$20,106,000	**P/E Ratio:**	9.83
Plant, Equip.:	$95,112,000	**Total Liab.:**	$69,524,000	**Indic. Yr. Divd.:**	$0.880
Total Assets:	$162,504,000	**Net Worth:**	$91,956,000	**Debt/ Equity:**	NA

Monarch Community Bancorp Inc

375 N Willowbrook Rd., Coldwater, MI, 49036; *PH:* 1-517-278-4566; *Fax:* 1-517-279-0221;
http:// www.monarchcommunitybank.com

General - Incorporation	MD	**Stock**- Price on:12/24/2007	$11.58
Employees	79	Stock Exchange	NDQ
Auditor	Plante & Moran, PLLC	Ticker Symbol	MCBF
Stk Agt	Registrar & Transfer Co	Outstanding Shares	2,530,000
Counsel	NA	E.P.S	$0.70
DUNS No.	NA	Shareholders	NA

Business: The group's principal activity is to provide broad range of banking services in Michigan through five full service offices. The principal business consists of attracting retail deposits from the general public and investing those funds primarily in permanent loans secured by first mortgages, one-to-four family residences and variety of consumer loans. The group also originates loans secured by commercial and multi-family real estate, commercial business loans and construction loans secured primarily by residential real estate. The deposit accounts include passbook and statement savings accounts, money market deposit accounts, now and non-interest bearing checking accounts and certificates of deposit. On 08-Jun-2004, the group acquired marshall savings bank.

Primary SIC and add'l.: 6712 6035

CIK No: 0001169769

Subsidiaries: Monarch Community Bank

Officers: Don Denney/CEO, Pres., Vicki Morris/AVP - Mortgage Lending, Monarch Community Bank, Denise Maurer/AVP, Mgr. - New Accounting, Monarch Community Bank, Bill Kurtz/COO, Sr. VP - Monarch Community Bank, Rebecca Crabill/AVP, Controller - Monarch Community Bank, Scott McQueen/VP, COO - Monarch Community Bank, Joni Manchester/AVP - Mortgage Lending, Monarch Community Bank, Christine Maxson/AVP, Human Resources Mgr. - Monarch Community Bank, Kim Emerson/AVP, Deposit Services Mgr. - Monarch Community Bank, Kim Furton/AVP - Mortgage Lending, Monarch Community Bank, Tim Muckel/AVP - Commercial Lending, Monarch Community Bank, Jerry Yoder/AVP - Commercial Lending - Monarch Community Bank, Vicki Bassage/VP - Retail, Teller Operations, Marketing Mgr. - Monarch Community Bank, Kirk Schwarz/AVP - Commercial Lending, Monarch Community Bank, Jamie Smoker/VP - Mortgage, Consumer Lending Mgr. - Monarch Community Bank *(18 Officers included in Index)*

Directors: Stephen M. Ross/64/Chmn., Lauren L. Bracy/73/Dir., Craig W. Dally/61/Dir., Richard L. Dobbins/63/Dir., James R. Vozar/72/Dir., Gordon L. Welch/61/Dir., Martin L. Mitchell/57/Dir., Harold A. Adamson/67/Dir.

Owners: Craig W. Dally, Insiders/10.70%, James R. Vozar, Jeffrey L. Gendell/9.00%, Stephen M. Ross, Lauren L. Bracy/1.60%, Monarch Community Bancorp, Inc/7.00%, Gordon L. Welch, Donald L. Denney/1.40%, Harold A. Adamson, Martin L. Mitchell, Andrew J. Van Doren/1.30%, William C. Kurtz/1.10%, Richard L. Dobbins/1.00%

Financial Data: *Fiscal Year End:*12/31 *Latest Annual Data:* 12/31/2006

Year	Sales	Net Income
2006	$20,429,000	$1,548,000
2005	$18,630,000	$1,440,000
2004	$17,303,000	-$2,511,000

Curr. Assets:	$15,297,000	**Curr. Liab.:**	$250,001,000	**P/E Ratio:**	16.54
Plant, Equip.:	$6,941,000	**Total Liab.:**	$250,001,000	**Indic. Yr. Divd.:**	$0.280
Total Assets:	$289,987,000	**Net Worth:**	$39,986,000	**Debt/ Equity:**	NA

Monarch Financial Holdings Inc

750 Volvo Pkwy., Chesapeake, VA, 23320; *PH:* 1-757-222-2100; *Fax:* 1-757-222-2101;
http:// www.monarchbank.com; *Email:* info@monarchbank.com

General - Incorporation	VA	**Stock**- Price on:12/24/2007	$15.8
Employees	121	Stock Exchange	NDQ
Auditor	Goodman & Co., LLP	Ticker Symbol	MNRTA
Stk Agt	Registrar & Transfer Co	Outstanding Shares	4,080,000
Counsel	NA	E.P.S	$0.603
DUNS No.	NA	Shareholders	NA

Business: The groups principle activity is to provide commercial and retail banking, investment and insurance sales, and mortgage origination and brokerage services. The groups services include safe deposit boxes, cash management services, check and bankcard services, direct deposit of payroll and social security checks and automatic drafts for various accounts. In June 1, 2006 the group acquired Monarch Bank. The group operates through two segments namely commercial and other banking and mortgage banking operations. The group operates from the United States.

Primary SIC and add'l.: 6712 6022

CIK No: 0001364856

Subsidiaries: Monarch Capital, LLC,, Monarch Financial Holdings, Inc., Monarch Investments, LLC,

Officers: William F. Rountree/Dir., CEO, Pres./$451,297.00, Barry A. Mathias/Pres. - Chesapeake Region, Monarch Bank/$175,447.00, Dennis R. Jones/Member - Monarch Bank - Chesapeake City, Terry L. Neal/Member - Monarch Bank - Chesapeake City, Sidney M. Oman/Member - Monarch Bank - Chesapeake City, James E. Reece/Member - Monarch Bank - Chesapeake City, Herbert L. Ansell/Member - Monarch Bank - Chesapeake City, Brian M. Clements/Member - Monarch Bank - Chesapeake City, Jeffrey J. Wermers/Member - Monarch Bank - Chesapeake City, Vernon Richard Divers/Member - Monarch Bank - Chesapeake City, Dennis M. Ellmer/Member - Monarch Bank - Chesapeake City, Jane C. Gaffney/Member - Monarch Bank - Chesapeake City, Randal K. Bregman/Member - Monarch Bank - Virginia Beach City, Kirk J. Woodruff/Member - Monarch Bank - Chesapeake City, James P. Karides/Member - Monarch Bank - Virginia Beach City *(56 Officers included in Index)*

Directors: William F. Rountree/Dir., CEO, Pres., Virginia Sancilio/Chmn. - Monarch Bank, Virginia Beach City, Lawton H. Baker/Vice Chmn. - Monarch Bank, Jeffrey F. Benson/Dir., Joe P. Covington/Dir. - Monarch Bank, Taylor B. Grissom/Dir. - Monarch Bank, Robert M. Oman/Dir. - Monarch Bank, Dwight C. Schaubach/Dir. - Monarch Bank, Lawrence L. Sutton/Dir. - Monarch Bank, Kevin L. Hubbard/Dir. - Monarch Bank, Chesapeake City

Owners: Dwight C. Schaubach/1.41%, Robert M. Oman/1.15%, Brad E. Schwartz, Cassell D. Basnight, William F. Rountree/3.12%, Lawrence L. Sutton/1.26%, Neal E. Crawford, James R. Ferber, Lawton H. Baker/1.11%, Elizabeth T. Patterson/1.48%, Taylor B. Grissom, Jeffrey F. Benson/1.20%, Barry A. Mathias/1.40%, Insiders/15.46%, Joe P. Covington

Financial Data: *Fiscal Year End:*12/31 *Latest Annual Data:* 12/31/2006

Year	Sales	Net Income
2006	$28,725,000	$3,626,000
2005	$18,688,000	$2,102,000
2004	$11,827,000	$757,000

Curr. Assets:	$18,967,000	**Curr. Liab.:**	$362,188,000		
Plant, Equip.:	$6,685,000	**Total Liab.:**	$373,706,000	**Indic. Yr. Divd.:**	NA
Total Assets:	$407,720,000	**Net Worth:**	$34,014,000	**Debt/ Equity:**	0.2821

Monarch Services Inc

112 W Main St., Durham, NC, 27701; *PH:* 1-919-490-0006; *Fax:* 1-919-490-8574;
http:// www.girlslife.com; *Email:* monarchaccounting@monarchsvc.com

General - Incorporation	MD	**Stock**- Price on:12/24/2007	$0.6
Employees	59	Stock Exchange	OTC
Auditor	Stegman & Co	Ticker Symbol	MAHI
Stk Agt	StockTrans, Inc.	Outstanding Shares	1,620,000
Counsel	Venable, Baetjer & Howard LLP	E.P.S	$0.82
DUNS No.	08-260-6666	Shareholders	NA

Business: The group's principal activity is to publish magazine through its subsidiary, girl's life, inc. The group operates in three segments namely, publishing, retail and restaurant. The group is engaged in the publication of girls' life magazine in the publishing segment, adam leaf and bean tobacco shop in the retail segment and peerce's plantation in the restaurant segment. The group publishes bi-monthly magazine for young girls between the age ten to fifteen. It also plans to establish young men's magazine and a theme restaurant that is based on girls' life magazine. The group discontinued adam leaf and bean tobacco shop from 19-Aug-2004.

Primary SIC and add'l.: 5812 5993 2721

CIK No: 0000202685

Subsidiaries: Girls' Life Plantation Mansion, LLC, Girls' Life Plantation Parcel, LLC, Girls' Life, Inc., Peerce's Plantation GL, LLC

Officers: Jackson Y. Dott/CEO, Pres., Marshall Chadwell/Controller, CFO, Katie Matarazzo-Speca/National Advertising Sales Representative, Mandy Forr/Assoc. Editor, Karen Bokram/Publisher, Founder Editor, Chun Kim/Dir. - Creative, Kelly White/Executive Editor, Lizzie Skurnick/Special Projects Editor, Katie Abbondanza/Editorial Assist., Andrea Thompson/Assoc. Web Editor, Patty O'Donnell/Sales Dir. - National Advertising, Lisa Michocki/National Advertising, Marketing Assist., Suzanne Long Tegeler/Circulation Dir.

Financial Data: *Fiscal Year End:* 04/30 *Latest Annual Data:* 4/30/2006

Year	Sales	Net Income
2006	$5,010,000	-$1,371,000
2005	$5,629,000	-$833,000
2004	$5,405,000	-$1,112,000

Curr. Assets:	$969,000	**Curr. Liab.:**	$1,713,000	**P/E Ratio:**	0.73
Plant, Equip.:	$2,970,000	**Total Liab.:**	$2,425,000	**Indic. Yr. Divd.:**	NA
Total Assets:	$4,143,000	**Net Worth:**	$1,718,000	**Debt/ Equity:**	NA

Monarch Staffing Inc

110A Baltimore Pike, Springfield, PA, 19064; *PH:* 1-610-604-0202; *Fax:* 1-610-604-0280; *http://* www.monarchstaffing.com; *Email:* resumes@monarchstaffing.com

General - Incorporation	NV	**Stock** - Price on: 12/24/2007	$0.017
Employees	24	Stock Exchange	OTC
Auditor	Chisholm, Bierwolf & Nilson, LLC	Ticker Symbol	MSTF
Stk Agt	Transfer Online, Inc.	Outstanding Shares	10,060,000
Counsel	NA	E.P.S.	-$0.135
DUNS No.		Shareholders	NA

Business: The groups principle activity is to provide healthcare staffing services to commercial and government sector. In November 2005 the group acquired Drug Consultants International, Inc. and Drug Consultants, Inc. The group operates from the United States.

Primary SIC and add'l.: 7363

CIK No: 0001177326

Officers: Joel Williams/52/CEO, David Walters/45/Chmn., CFO, Pres., Treasurer, Keith Moore/47/Dir., Sec., Pam /Branch Mgr., Kathy /Staffing Dir., Denise /Recruiting Assist., Sandy /Recruiting Assist., Laurie /Branch Mgr.

Directors: David Walters/45/Chmn., CFO, Pres., Treasurer, Keith Moore/47/Dir., Sec.

Owners: Nite Capital, L.P./9.30%, Joel Williams/3.20%, David Walters/42.00%, Insiders/86.30%, Keith Moore/42.00%

Financial Data: *Fiscal Year End:* 12/31 *Latest Annual Data:* 12/31/2006

Year	Sales	Net Income
2006	$7,728,000	-$866,000
2005	$1,851,000	$299,000
2004	$2,072,000	-$3,046,000

Curr. Assets:	$1,300,000	**Curr. Liab.:**	$1,847,000		
Plant, Equip.:	NA	**Total Liab.:**	$3,690,000	**Indic. Yr. Divd.:**	NA
Total Assets:	$2,621,000	**Net Worth:**	-$1,069,000	**Debt/ Equity:**	NA

Mondial Ventures Inc

8416 Angus Dr., Vancouver, BC, V6P 1L3; *PH:* 1-604-317-0568

General - Incorporation	NV	**Stock** - Price on: 12/24/2007	NA
Employees	NA	Stock Exchange	OTC
Auditor	Dale Matheson Carr-hilton Labonte LLP	Ticker Symbol	MNVNE
Stk Agt	Empire Stock Transfer Inc.	Outstanding Shares	NA
Counsel	NA	E.P.S.	NA
DUNS No.	NA	Shareholders	NA

Business: The group's principal activities include acquiring and exploring mineral properties. The group operates from the United States.

Primary SIC and add'l.: 1000

CIK No: 0001284452

Officers: Scott Taylor/28/Pres., CEO - Promoter, a Dir., Joe Alvaro/60/Dir., Sec., Treasurer, Principal Accounting Officer

Directors: Scott Taylor/28/Pres., CEO - Promoter, a Dir., Joe Alvaro/60/Dir., Sec., Treasurer, Principal Accounting Officer

Owners: Joe Alvaro/30.06%, Scott Taylor/30.06%, Insiders/60.12%

Money Centers Of America Inc

Formerly: iGames Entertainment Inc
700 S Henderson Rd., Ste. 325, King of Prussia, PA, 19406; *PH:* 1-610-354-8888; *Fax:* 1-610-992-0338; *http://* www.moneycenters.com

General - Incorporation	DE	**Stock** - Price on: 12/24/2007	$0.33
Employees	43	Stock Exchange	NA
Auditor	Sherb & Co. LLP	Ticker Symbol	NA
Stk Agt	Florida Atlantic Stock Transfer, Inc.	Outstanding Shares	30,770,000
Counsel	NA	E.P.S.	-$0.16
DUNS No.	NA	Shareholders	NA

Business: The group's principal activity is to develop, manufacture, market and distribute cash access services to the gaming industry. The group has four primary products like credit/debit card cash advance, creditplus credit services, automated teller machines (ATM's) and check cashing solutions. Currently it has contracts to provide some or all of the cash access services in 22 locations across the United States. On 06-Jan-2004, the group acquired available money.

Primary SIC and add'l.: 7389

CIK No: 0001165271

Subsidiaries: Available Money, Inc.

Officers: Christopher M. Wolfington/Chmn., CEO, Jeremy Stein/VP - Product Development, Earl S. Jarosh/VP - Information Technology, Thomas Scott Kruse/VP - Business Management, Ted J. Gaddis/VP - Sales, Bobby Sharp/VP - Operations, Priscilla Contreras/Dir. - Personnel Management, Darlene A. Brown/Dir. - Product Management, Cristina Ortenzi/Dir. - Guest, Client Relations

Directors: Christopher M. Wolfington/Chmn., CEO, Jeremy Stein/VP - Product Development, Dennis Gomes/64/Dir., John Ziegler/42/Dir.

Owners: Insiders/64.89%, Christopher M. Wolfington/63.12%, Dennis Gomes/1.28%, John Ziegler, Jason P. Walsh/1.70%, Jonathan Robinson, Jeremy Stein/1.32%

Financial Data: *Fiscal Year End:* 12/31 *Latest Annual Data:* 12/31/2006

Year	Sales	Net Income
2006	$11,722,000	-$4,342,000
2005	$19,409,000	-$1,666,000
2004	$16,258,000	-$11,842,000

Curr. Assets:	$4,920,000	**Curr. Liab.:**	$5,791,000		
Plant, Equip.:	$1,063,000	**Total Liab.:**	$13,492,000	**Indic. Yr. Divd.:**	NA
Total Assets:	$8,360,000	**Net Worth:**	-$5,131,000	**Debt/ Equity:**	NA

Money Tree Lending Group Inc

3400 Tamiami Trl., Ste. 203, Port Charlotte, FL, 33952; *PH:* 1-941-764-6767

General - Incorporation	DE	**Stock** - Price on: 12/24/2007	NA
Employees	NA	Stock Exchange	NA
Auditor	Gately & Assoc. LLC	Ticker Symbol	NA
Stk Agt	Corporate Stock Transfer, Inc.	Outstanding Shares	NA
Counsel	Anslow & Jaclin, LLP	E.P.S.	NA
DUNS No.	NA	Shareholders	NA

Business: The groups principle activity is to provide lend mortgage. The group also sells fixed-rate annuities which are considered insurance products. The group operates from United States.

Primary SIC and add'l.: 6199

CIK No: 0001294605

MoneyFlow Systems International Inc

7003 5th St. SE, Ste. N, Calgary, AB, T2H 2G2; *PH:* 1-403-319-0236; *http://* www.moneyflowsystems.com; *Email:* hal@moneyflowsystems.com

General - Incorporation	NV	**Stock** - Price on: 12/24/2007	$0.05
Employees	NA	Stock Exchange	OTC
Auditor	Hein & Assoc. LLP	Ticker Symbol	MFLW
Stk Agt	Transfer Online, Inc.	Outstanding Shares	NA
Counsel	Gammage & Burnham	E.P.S.	NA
DUNS No.	NA	Shareholders	NA

Business: The group's principal activities are to operate as a holding company for acquisitions of subsidiaries. The group operates in two segments: automated teller machines & point of sale terminals. The group's business is to supply, install, maintain and manage automated teller machines (ATM's) and other electronic funds transfer devices. The group also provides transaction-processing services. The automated teller machines are placed on the premises of property owners and businesses for the purpose and convenience of dispensing cash and other services to the public. The group has operations in Canada and the United States.

Primary SIC and add'l.: 3578 3643 6719

CIK No: 0001159464

Subsidiaries: Interglobe Investigation Services Inc., Interglobe Ltd., Security Bancorp Inc

Officers: Hal Schultz/Dir., CEO, Chmn., Maureen Armstrong/Accounting Administrator, Whitney Dragland/Administrative Assist., Jamie Fisher/National Technical Service Mgr.

Directors: Hal Schultz/Dir., CEO, Chmn., Richard Landerman/65/Dir.

Owners: Dale Tingley/6.89%, Insiders/39.04%, Darwyn Ross/2.10%, Richard Landerman/4.60%, Harold F. Schultz/29.90%, Douglas A. McDougall/4.20%

Financial Data: *Fiscal Year End:* 10/31 *Latest Annual Data:* 10/31/2006

Year	Sales	Net Income
2006	$753,000	-$31,000
2005	$889,000	-$1,468,000
2004	$872,000	-$136,000

Curr. Assets:	$275,000	**Curr. Liab.:**	$79,000		
Plant, Equip.:	$33,000	**Total Liab.:**	$79,000	**Indic. Yr. Divd.:**	NA
Total Assets:	$311,000	**Net Worth:**	$232,000	**Debt/ Equity:**	NA

Moneygram International Inc

1550 Utica Ave. S St., Louis Park, MN, 55416; *PH:* 1-952-591-3000; *Fax:* 1-952-591-3121; *http://* www.moneygram.com

General - Incorporation	DE	**Stock** - Price on: 12/24/2007	$28.62
Employees	2,076	Stock Exchange	NYSE
Auditor	Deloitte & Touche LLP	Ticker Symbol	MGI
Stk Agt	Wells Fargo Shareowner Services	Outstanding Shares	83,440,000
Counsel	NA	E.P.S.	$1.44
DUNS No.	NA	Shareholders	NA

Business: The group's principal activity is to provide global payment service. The group operates three segments: global fund transfer segment, payment systems segment and travel and recreation services. The fund transfer segment provides money transfer services, money orders and bill payment services. The payment systems segment provides financial institutions with payment processing services, primarily for official checks, and with money orders for sale to their consumers. The travel and recreation services segment operates tours and charters in Canadian rockies, conducts hotel operations and snowcoach tours of the columbia icefield and offers gondola rides of sulphur mountain. On 30-Jun-2004 the group spun-off from viad corp.

Primary SIC and add'l.: 7389

CIK No: 0001273931

Subsidiaries: CAG Inc., Ferrum Trust, FSMC, Inc., Hematite Trust, Long Lake Partners, LLC, Mid-America Money Order Company, MIL Overseas Limited, MLE, Inc., Monazite Trust, MoneyGram International Holdings Limited, MoneyGram International Limited, MoneyGram of New York LLC, MoneyGram Oversees, MoneyGram Payment Systems Canada, Inc., MoneyGram Payment Systems Italy S.r.l. 19 Subsidiaries included in the Index

Officers: Philip W. Milne/Chmn. - Elect, CEO, Pres./$4,809,692.00, Teresa H. Johnson/Exec. VP, General Counsel, Sec./$1,047,706.00, Anthony P. Ryan/Exec. VP, Pres. - Moneygram Global Payment Products, Services/$1,499,691.00, William J. Putney/Exec. VP, Chief Investment Officer/$1,404,407.00, Mary A. Dutra/Exec. VP - Global Payment Processing, Settlement, David J. Parrin/CFO, Exec. VP/$1,478,772.00, David A. Albright/CIO, Exec. VP, Cindy J. Stemper/Exec. VP - Human Resources, Corporate Services, Moneygram International, Inc, Thomas E. Haider/Sr. VP - Government Affairs, Chief Compliance Officer

Directors: Philip W. Milne/Chmn. - Elect, CEO, Pres., Robert C. Krueger/Dir., Albert Teplin/Dir., Jess Hay/Dir., Timothy R. Wallace/Dir., Othon Ruiz-Montemayor/Dir., Douglas L. Rock/Dir., Judith K. Hofer/Dir., Donald E. Kiernan/Dir., Monte E. Ford/Dir., Linda Johnson Rice/Dir.

Owners: Timothy R. Wallace, Insiders/1.90%, FMR Corp./13.10%, T. Rowe Price Associates, Inc./5.70%, Albert M. Teplin, Donald E. Kiernan, Judith K. Hofer, Robert C. Krueger, Jess T. Hay, Othn Ruiz Montemayor, Wellington Management Company, LLP/13.20%, Douglas L. Rock, Linda Johnson Rice, William J. Putney, Teresa H. Johnson *(19 Owners included in Index)*

Financial Data: Fiscal Year End:12/31   Latest Annual Data: 12/31/2006

Year	Sales	Net Income
2006	$595,900,000	$124,054,000
2005	$971,236,000	$112,946,000
2004	$423,057,000	$86,412,000

Curr. Assets:	$2,732,613,000	**Curr. Liab.:**	$139,848,000	**P/E Ratio:**	19.88
Plant, Equip.:	$148,849,000	**Total Liab.:**	$8,607,074,000	**Indic. Yr. Divd.:**	$0.200
Total Assets:	$9,276,137,000	**Net Worth:**	$669,063,000	**Debt/ Equity:**	12.9037

Monmouth Real Estate Investment Corp

3499 Rte. 9 N, Ste. 3-c, Ste. 3-c, Freehold, NJ, 07728; *PH:* 1-732-577-9996; *http://* www.mreic.com

General - Incorporation	MD	Stock- Price on:12/24/2007	$8.92
Employees	10	Stock Exchange	NDQ
Auditor	KPMG LLP	Ticker Symbol	MNRTA
Stk Agt	American Stock Transfer & Trust Co.	Outstanding Shares	20,210,000
Counsel	NA	E.P.S	NA
DUNS No.	NA	Shareholders	NA

Business: The groups principal activity is to operating as a real estate investment trust. The group operates from the United States.

Primary SIC and add'l.: 4225 6798

CIK No: 0000067625

Subsidiaries: MRC I LLC, MREIC Financial, Inc

Officers: Eugene W. Landy/Chmn., Pres., Cynthia J. Morgenstern/Dir., Exec. VP, Anna T. Chew/Dir., CFO, Maureen E. Vecere/Treasurer, Controller, Michael P. Landy/Dir., VP - Investments, Rosemarie Faccone/Investor Relations Contact, Susan Jordan/Investor Relations Contact

Directors: Eugene W. Landy/Chmn., Pres., Neal Herstik/Dir., Daniel D. Cronheim/Dir., Samuel A. Landy/Dir., Matthew I. Hirsch/Dir., Cynthia J. Morgenstern/Dir., Exec. VP, Scott L. Robinson/Dir., Stephen B. Wolgin/Dir., Peter J. Weidhorn/Dir., Anna T. Chew/Dir., CFO, Michael P. Landy/Dir., VP - Investments, Joshua D. Kahr/Dir., Catherine B. Elflein/Dir.

Owners: UMH Properties, Inc./7.13%, Cynthia J. Morgenstern, Palisade Concentrated Equity Partnership L.P./2.61%, Maureen E. Vecere, Samuel A. Landy/1.56%, Scott Robinson, Neal Herstik, Oakland Financial Corporation/7.66%, Anna T. Chew/1.12%, Catherine B. Elflein, Matthew I. Hirsch, Insiders/11.00%, Michael P. Landy, Eugene W. Landy/5.94%, Stephen B. Wolgin *(16 Owners included in Index)*

Financial Data: Fiscal Year End:09/30   Latest Annual Data: 9/30/2006

Year	Sales	Net Income
2006	$26,534,000	$6,166,000
2005	$24,512,000	$9,047,000
2004	$21,330,000	$7,673,000

Curr. Assets:	$4,063,000	**Curr. Liab.:**	$1,725,000		
Plant, Equip.:	$220,211,000	**Total Liab.:**	$134,340,000	**Indic. Yr. Divd.:**	$0.600
Total Assets:	$241,907,000	**Net Worth:**	$107,567,000	**Debt/ Equity:**	0.8692

Monogram Biosciences Inc

Formerly: Virologic Inc
345 Oyster Point Blvd., South Sab Francisco, CA, 94080; *PH:* 1-650-635-1100;
http:// www.monogrambio.com

General - Incorporation	DE	Stock- Price on:12/24/2007	$1.69
Employees	323	Stock Exchange	NDQ
Auditor	Pricewaterhousecoopers LLP	Ticker Symbol	NA
Stk Agt	American Stock Transfer & Trust Co.	Outstanding Shares	131,940,000
Counsel	Cooley Godward LLP	E.P.S	-$0.19
DUNS No.	NA	Shareholders	NA

Business: The group's principle activities include developing, marketing and selling innovative products to guide and improve the treatment of viral diseases. The company develops a way of directly measuring the impact of genetic mutations on drug resistance and using this information to guide therapy. The company has a proprietary technology called phenosense, for testing drug resistance in viruses that cause serious diseases such as aids, hepatitis b and hepatitis c. It collects phenosense test results and related clinical data in an interactive database that can be made available to physicians for use in therapy guidance. The group operates from United States.

Primary SIC and add'l.: 8731 2834

CIK No: 0001094961

Subsidiaries: ACLARA BioSciences, Inc.

Officers: William D. Young/Chmn., CEO/$1,582,661.00, Patricia Wray/VP - Human Resources, William J. Welch/Sr. VP, Chief Commercial Officer/$624,194.00, Kenneth N. Hitchner/VP - Pharmaceutical Collaborations, Timothy G. Henn/VP - Finance, Michael G. Vicari/VP - Sales, Michael P. Bates/VP - Clinical Research, Alfred G. Merriweather/Sr. VP, CFO/$475,235.00, Jeannette M. Whitcomb/VP - Operations, Jeremiah Hall/Media Contact, Kas Das/Media Contact, Manuel Hidalgo/Member - Scientific Advisory Board, Michael J. Dunn/Chief Business Officer, Kathy L. Hibbs/Sr. VP, General Counsel/$485,533.00, Christos J. Petropoulos/VP - Research, Development, Virology, Chief Scientific Officer/$656,554.00

Directors: William D. Young/Chmn., CEO, Cristina H. Kepner/Dir., Thomas R. Baruch/Dir., David H. Persing/Dir., Pj Utz/Member - Scientific Advisory Board, Owen N. Witte/Member - Scientific Advisory Board, John D. Mendlein/Dir., Edmon R. Jennings/Dir., William Jenkins/Dir., Carlos L. Arteaga/Member - Scientific Advisory Board, Jose Baselga/Member - Scientific Advisory Board, Stephen P. Goff/Member - Scientific Advisory Board, Roy S. Herbst/Member - Scientific Advisory Board, David D. Ho/Member - Scientific Advisory Board, Douglas D. Richman/Member - Scientific Advisory Board *(17 Directors included in Index)*

Owners: John D. Mendlein, Insiders/7.00%, Pfizer, Inc./8.70%, Kathy L. Hibbs, Alfred G. Merriweather, Federated Investors, Inc./17.70%, Cristina H. Kepner, William J. Welch, Edmon R. Jennings, William Jenkins, David H. Persing, Entities affiliated with Highbridge International LLC/8.30%, Kenneth F. Siebel/7.30%, Christos J. Petropoulos, William D. Young/2.20% *(17 Owners included in Index)*

Financial Data: Fiscal Year End:12/31   Latest Annual Data: 12/31/2006

Year	Sales	Net Income
2006	$47,958,000	-$38,703,000
2005	$48,252,000	-$37,586,000
2004	$36,801,000	-$81,430,000

Curr. Assets:	$40,552,000	**Curr. Liab.:**	$18,949,000		
Plant, Equip.:	$7,463,000	**Total Liab.:**	$46,937,000	**Indic. Yr. Divd.:**	NA
Total Assets:	$60,845,000	**Net Worth:**	$13,908,000	**Debt/ Equity:**	NA

Monolithic Power Systems Inc

6409 Guadalupe Mines Rd., San Jose, CA, 95120; *PH:* 1-408-826-0600; *Fax:* 1-408-826-0601; *http://* www.monolithicpower.com; *Email:* usinfo@monolithicpower.com

General - Incorporation	DE	Stock- Price on:12/24/2007	$16.89
Employees	393	Stock Exchange	NYSE
Auditor	Deloitte & Touche LLP	Ticker Symbol	MR
Stk Agt	Mellon Investor Services LLC	Outstanding Shares	31,370,000
Counsel	NA	E.P.S	$0.01
DUNS No.	NA	Shareholders	NA

Business: The groups principle activities include designing, developing, and marketing analog and mixed signal semiconductors. The products of the group include direct current to dc converters, liquid crystal display backlight inverters and audio amplifiers. The group products sold under the trade name BCD Plus(TM). The group operates from the United States, Taiwan, China, Korea, Japan, Europe and the United States of America. The group's quarterly revenue for September 2007 was 40.19 millions of USD.

Primary SIC and add'l.: 3674

CIK No: 0001280452

Subsidiaries: Chengdu Monolithic Power Systems Co., Ltd, MPS International Korea Co., Ltd, MPS International Ltd., MPS International Ltd. (SH), MPS Japan K.K.

Officers: Michael R. Hsing/Dir., CEO, Pres., Jim C. Moyer/Dir., Chief Design Engineer, Rick Neely/CFO, Deming Xiao/VP - Operations, Adriana Chiocchi/Chief Legal Officer, Corp. Sec., Maurice Sciammas/47/VP - Sales, Marketing

Directors: Michael R. Hsing/Dir., CEO, Pres., Jim C. Moyer/Dir., Chief Design Engineer, Herbert Chang/Dir., Alan L. Earhart/Dir., Victor Lee/Dir., Umesh Padval/Dir., Douglas M. McBurnie/Dir., Karen A. Smith Bogart/Dir.

Owners: James C. Moyer/6.00%, Maurice Sciammas/2.00%, Alan Earhart, Funds affiliated with J.& W. Seligman/12.00%, Philippe Laffont/7.00%, Herbert Chang/13.00%, Deming Xiao/1.00%, Umesh Padval, Scale Venture Management I, LLC andBAVP, L.P/7.00%, Shares associated with Artis CapitalManagement, L.P/14.00%, C. Richard Neely, Funds affiliated with Investar Capital Inc/13.00%, Insiders/27.00%, Michael R. Hsing/6.00%

Financial Data: Fiscal Year End:12/31   Latest Annual Data: 12/31/2006

Year	Sales	Net Income
2006	$105,015,000	-$2,863,000
2005	$99,131,000	$5,107,000
2004	$47,595,000	-$3,719,000

Curr. Assets:	$97,160,000	**Curr. Liab.:**	$20,122,000		
Plant, Equip.:	$11,358,000	**Total Liab.:**	$22,375,000	**Indic. Yr. Divd.:**	NA
Total Assets:	$117,327,000	**Net Worth:**	$94,952,000	**Debt/ Equity:**	NA

Monongahela Power Co

1310 Fairmont Ave., Fairmont, WV, 26554; *PH:* 1-304-366-3000; *http://* www.alleghenypower.com

General - Incorporation	OH	Stock- Price on:12/24/2007	$87
Employees	NA	Stock Exchange	NA
Auditor	PricewaterhouseCoopers LLP	Ticker Symbol	NA
Stk Agt	Mellon Investor Services LLC	Outstanding Shares	NA
Counsel	NA	E.P.S	NA
DUNS No.	00-794-4812	Shareholders	NA

Business: The group's principal activity is to operate its electric transmission and distribution system in northern west Virginia and in an adjacent portion of Ohio. The group owns generating capacity in west Virginia and Pennsylvania. The group operates in two segments namely delivery and services and generation and marketing. The delivery and services segment comprises our regulated electric and natural gas transmission and distribution operations and includes other unregulated operations. The generation and marketing segment develops, owns, operates, and manages electric generating capacity. As of 31-Dec-2003, the group served about 397,000 electric customers and 230,000 natural gas customers in a service area of about 13,000 square miles with a population of about 1,223,000.

Primary SIC and add'l.: 4911 4924

CIK No: 0000067646

Subsidiaries: Allegheny Generating Company, Allegheny Pittsburgh Coal Company

Monro Muffler Brake Inc

200 Holleder Pkwy., Rochester, NY, 14615; *PH:* 1-585-647-6400; *Fax:* 1-585-647-0945; *http://* www.monro.com

General - Incorporation	NY	Stock- Price on:12/24/2007	$36.44
Employees	3,561	Stock Exchange	NDQ
Auditor	PricewaterhouseCoopers LLP	Ticker Symbol	MNST
Stk Agt	Continental Stock Transfer & Trust Co	Outstanding Shares	14,380,000
Counsel	NA	E.P.S	$1.03
DUNS No.	01-313-5058	Shareholders	NA

Business: The group's principal activity is to provide repair services for passenger cars, light trucks and vans. The services include repair of mufflers and exhaust systems, brakes and steering, drive train, suspension and wheel alignment. It also provides other products and services including tires, scheduled maintenance, repair and replacement of parts and state inspections. The group also renders tune-up, oil change and a flush-and-fill service for heating and cooling systems. On 27-Mar-2004, the group had 595 group-operated stores and 18 dealer-operated stores in the United States. On 01-Mar-2004,the group acquired 36 tire and automotive repair locations from mr. Tire inc.

Primary SIC and add'l.: 7538 7539

CIK No: 0000876427

Subsidiaries: Monro Leasing, LLC, Monro Service Corporation

Officers: Robert G. Gross/50/Dir., CEO, Pres./$865,450.00, Catherine Damico/52/CFO, Exec. VP - Finance, Treasurer/$239,100.00, Christopher R. Hoornbeck/57/VP - Western Operations/$186,000.00, Craig L. Hoyle/54/Divisional VP - Southern Operations, Joseph Tomarchio/52/Divisional VP - Tire Stores/$378,400.00, John W. Van Heel/42/Exec. VP - Store Support, Chief Administrative Officer, Sec./$205,700.00

Directors: Robert G. Gross/50/Dir., CEO, Pres., Peter J. Solomon/69/Chmn., Lionel B. Spiro/69/Dir., Frederick M. Danziger/68/Dir., Francis R. Strawbridge/70/Dir., Richard A. Berenson/72/Dir., Donald Glickman/75/Dir., Robert E. Mellor/64/Dir.

Owners: Frederick M. Danziger, Robert G. Gross/5.20%, Catherine DAmico, John W. van Heel, Richard A. Berenson, Christopher R. Hoornbeck, Peter J. Solomon/6.50%, T. Rowe Price Associates, Inc./8.00%, TimesSquare Capital Management/5.50%, Joseph Tomarchio, Wellington Management Company, LLP/5.30%, Francis R. Strawbridge, Donald Glickman/3.40%, Lionel B. Spiro, Robert E. Mellor

Financial Data: **Fiscal Year End:**03/31 **Latest Annual Data:** 3/25/2006

Year	Sales	Net Income
2006	$368,727,000	$22,666,000
2005	$337,409,000	$19,669,000
2004	$279,457,000	$17,005,000

Curr. Assets:	$88,836,000	**Curr. Liab.:**	$60,508,000	**P/E Ratio:**	24.96
Plant, Equip.:	$184,249,000	**Total Liab.:**	$124,904,000	**Indic. Yr. Divd.:**	$0.240
Total Assets:	$340,023,000	**Net Worth:**	$215,119,000	**Debt/ Equity:**	0.2641

Monroe Bancorp

210 E Kirkwood Ave., Bloomington, IN, 47408; *PH:* 1-812-331-3444; *Fax:* 1-812-331-3460; *http://* www.monroebank.com

General - Incorporation	IN	**Stock**- Price on:12/24/2007	$16.83
Employees	236	Stock Exchange	NDQ
Auditor	BKD LLP	Ticker Symbol	MORE
Stk Agt	Registrar & Transfer Co	Outstanding Shares	6,350,000
Counsel	NA	E.P.S	$1.19
DUNS No.	NA	Shareholders	NA

Business: The group's principal activities are to provide a variety of financial services to its customers. The services include accepting deposits, providing commercial, mortgage and installment loan, originating fixed rate residential mortgage loans for sale into the secondary market. The group also provides personal and corporate trust services, investment advisory and brokerage services and fixed and variable annuities. The various types of deposits accepted by the group are now and money market deposits, savings deposits, certificates and other time deposits. As on 31-Dec-2003, it operates with its primary office located in bloomington, Indiana, conducts business from 16 locations in monroe, hendricks, jackson and lawrence counties, Indiana.

Primary SIC and add'l.: 6712 6022

CIK No: 0000745456

Subsidiaries: MB Portfolio Management, Inc., Monroe Bank

Officers: Mark D. Bradford/Dir., CEO, Pres./$280,693.00, Scott R. Walters/Sr. VP, Trust Officer/$190,281.00, Susan Johnson/Commercial Lender, Southern Indiana Region, Brownstown, Clayton Mitchell/Banking Center Mgr., Vickie Rader/Banking Center Mgr. - Brownsburg, Susie Glasgow/Banking Center Mgr. - Brownstown, Shannon Taylor/Business Development Officer, Brenda Wilson/Business Development Assist., Vicki Hensley/VP, Commercial Loan Officer, Mary Jo Huffman/Mortgage Loan Officer, Reverse Mortgage Specialist, Karan Rastall/Consumer Loan Officer, Zain MacKey/Assist. VP, Assist. Dir. - Finance, Jewell Frazier/Assist. VP, Consumer Loan Mgr., Jim Parcell/VP - Commercial Lender, South Central Indiana, Scot J. Davidson/Sr. VP - Retail Services *(84 Officers included in Index)*

Directors: Mark D. Bradford/Dir., CEO, Pres., Charles R. Royal/75/Chmn., Harry F. McNaught/53/Dir., Paul W. Mobley/67/Dir., Bradford J. Bomba/46/Dir., James G. Burkhart/Dir., Steven R. Crider/Dir., James D. Bremner/Dir., Joyce Claflin Harrell/60/Dir.

Owners: Gordon M. Dyott, Mark D. Bradford, Scott R. Walters/1.20%, Joyce Claflin Harrell, John E. Christy, Steven R. Crider, James D. Bremner, Paul W. Mobley, Insiders/12.95%, Timothy D. Ellis, Charles R. Royal/6.88%, Christopher G. Tietz, Bradford J. Bomba, Harry F. McNaught

Financial Data: **Fiscal Year End:**12/31 **Latest Annual Data:** 12/31/2006

Year	Sales	Net Income
2006	$54,135,000	$7,586,000
2005	$44,137,000	$7,223,000
2004	$37,034,000	$6,705,000

Curr. Assets:	$37,103,000	**Curr. Liab.:**	$589,328,000	**P/E Ratio:**	14.14
Plant, Equip.:	$15,078,000	**Total Liab.:**	$694,688,000	**Indic. Yr. Divd.:**	$0.480
Total Assets:	$748,193,000	**Net Worth:**	$53,505,000	**Debt/ Equity:**	1.8331

Monsanto Co

800 N Lindbergh Blvd., St. Louis, MO, 63167; *PH:* 1-314-694-1000; *Fax:* 1-314-694-8394; *http://* www.monsanto.com

General - Incorporation	DE	**Stock**- Price on:12/24/2007	$65.85
Employees	17,500	Stock Exchange	NYSE
Auditor	Deloitte & Touche LLP	Ticker Symbol	MON
Stk Agt	Mellon Investor Services LLC	Outstanding Shares	544,260,000
Counsel	NA	E.P.S	$1.79
DUNS No.	NA	Shareholders	NA

Business: The groups principle activity is to provide agricultural products. The groups products include corn, cotton and oil seeds. The groups products are sold under the brand names Asgrow(R), Dekalb and Deltapine. The group operates from United States.

Primary SIC and add'l.: 2074 2879

CIK No: 0001110783

Subsidiaries: American Seeds, Inc., Asgrow Seed Company LLC, Channel Bio Corp., Compania Agricola Colombiana Ltda. Y Cia, S.C.A., Corn States Hybrid Service LLC, DEKALB Genetics Corporation, Emergent Genetics India Private Limited, Fontanelle Hybrids, Inc., Holdens Foundation Seeds, LLC, Mahyco Monsanto Biotech (I)Pvt. Ltd., Monsanto Ag Products LLC, Monsanto Ag Technologies, LLC, Monsanto Agricoltura Italia S.p.A., Monsanto Argentina S.A.I.C., Monsanto Australia Ltd. 41 Subsidiaries included in the Index

Officers: Hugh Grant/49/Chmn., CEO, Pres., Carl M. Casale/Exec. VP - Strategy, Operations, Mark J. Leidy/Exec. VP - Manufacturing, Gerald A. Steiner/Exec. VP - Commercial Acceptance, Brett D. Begemann/Exec. VP - Global Commercial, Terrell K. Crews/CFO, Exec. VP, Matheu Escobar/Contact - Seminis, Argentina, Martin Gomez/Plant Mgr. - Argentina, Robert T. Fraley/CTO, Exec. VP, David F. Snively/54/Sr. VP, Sec., General Counsel, Steven C. Mizell/Sr. VP - Human Resources, Cheryl Morley/Sr. VP - Corporate Strategy, Richard B. Clark/VP, Controller, Janet M. Holloway/VP, Chief - Staff, Community Relations, Scarlett Lee Foster/VP - Investor Relations *(17 Officers included in Index)*

Directors: Hugh Grant/49/Chmn., CEO, Pres., Sharon R. Long/Dir., John W. Bachmann/68/Dir., Frank V. Atlee/67/Dir., Steven C. McMillan/61/Dir., William U. Parfet/60/Dir., George H. Poste/63/Dir., Gwendolyn S. King/67/Dir., Robert J. Stevens/56/Dir., Arthur H. Harper/51/Dir.

Owners: Robert J. Stevens, George H. Poste, Marsico Capital Management, LLC, John W. Bachmann, Steven C. McMillan, Robert T. Fraley, Frank V. AtLee, Carl M. Casale, Arthur H. Harper, Hugh Grant, Gwendolyn S. King, Brett D. Begemann, Insiders, FMR Corp., William U. Parfet *(16 Owners included in Index)*

Financial Data: **Fiscal Year End:**08/31 **Latest Annual Data:** 08/31/2007

Year	Sales	Net Income
2007	$8,563,000,000	$993,000,000
2006	$7,344,000,000	$689,000,000
2005	$6,294,000,000	$255,000,000

Curr. Assets:	$5,461,000,000	**Curr. Liab.:**	$2,279,000,000	**P/E Ratio:**	44.19
Plant, Equip.:	$2,418,000,000	**Total Liab.:**	$5,203,000,000	**Indic. Yr. Divd.:**	$0.500
Total Assets:	$11,728,000,000	**Net Worth:**	$6,525,000,000	**Debt/ Equity:**	0.2205

Monster Worldwide Inc

622 3rd Ave., 39th Fl., New York, NY, 10017; *PH:* 1-212-351-7000; *Fax:* 1-646-658-0541; *http://* www.monsterworldwide.com

General - Incorporation	DE	**Stock**- Price on:12/24/2007	$41.99
Employees	5,000	Stock Exchange	NDQ
Auditor	BDO Seidman LLP	Ticker Symbol	MNTA
Stk Agt	Bank of New York	Outstanding Shares	130,590,000
Counsel	Fulbright & Jaworski LLP	E.P.S	$1.065
DUNS No.	05-047-1754	Shareholders	NA

Business: The group operates under three business segments: monster, advertising and communications, and directional marketing. The monster segment provides its clients with one-stop-shopping for their recruitment needs online. The online services include providing free access to national and international job listings. The advertising and communications business designs global, national and local recruitment advertising campaigns for clients. The services provided include recruitment advertising, interactive communications, employer branding and employee communications. The directional marketing is a yellow pages advertising agency based on annual gross billings. The group provides its services in North America, Europe and the Asia/pacific region. On 31-Mar-2003, the group spinned-off its subsidiary company hudson highland group inc. The group's quarterly revenue for September 2007 was 337.14 millions of USD.

Primary SIC and add'l.: 7311 7361 7375

CIK No: 0001020416

Subsidiaries: General Yellow Pages Consultants, Inc

Officers: Sal Iannuzzi/Chmn., CEO, Douglas E. Klinger/43/Pres. - Monster Careers North AmericaPres., Monster Careers North America, Robert Jones/VP - Corporate Communications, Chris Power/44/CFO - Global Operations/$1,291,654.00, Jon Trumbull/Global Controller, Chief Accounting Officer, Charles Baker/41/Sr. VP, CFO/$2,268,431.00, Steve Pogorzelski/Exec. VP - Global Sales, Customer Development/$2,142,387.00, Timothy T. Yates/Dir., CFO, Exec. VP, Darko Dejanovic/Exec. VP - Global, CIO, Lori Erickson/Sr. VP - Human Resources, Evan Kornrich/Acting General Counsel, Steve Pemberton/Chief Diversity Officer, VP - Diversity, Inclusion, Alice Wang/Sr. VP - Corporate Development, Art O'Donnell/Exec. VP - Customer Service, Lise Poulos/Exec. VP *(17 Officers included in Index)*

Directors: Sal Iannuzzi/Chmn., CEO, Timothy T. Yates/Dir., CFO, Exec. VP, John Swann/71/Dir., Michael Kaufman/Dir., Robert J. Chrenc/Dir., Philip R. Lochner/Dir., George R. Eisele/Dir., Ronald J. Kramer/Dir., David A. Stein/Dir., John Gaulding/Dir.

Owners: Charles Baker, Michael Kaufman, Andrew J. McKelvey/100.00%, George R. Eisele, William M. Pastore, T. Rowe Price Associates, Inc., John Gaulding, David A. Stein, John Swann, Capital Research and Management Company, Bradford J. Baker, Steven Pogorzelski, Phillip R. Lochner, John Mclaughlin, Morgan Stanley *(22 Owners included in Index)*

Financial Data: **Fiscal Year End:**12/31 **Latest Annual Data:** 12/31/2006

Year	Sales	Net Income
2006	$1,116,676,000	$37,137,000
2005	$986,917,000	$98,194,000
2004	$845,519,000	$73,104,000

Curr. Assets:	$1,123,808,000	**Curr. Liab.:**	$826,244,000	**P/E Ratio:**	233.28
Plant, Equip.:	$102,402,000	**Total Liab.:**	$860,118,000	**Indic. Yr. Divd.:**	NA
Total Assets:	$1,969,803,000	**Net Worth:**	$1,109,685,000	**Debt/ Equity:**	0.0708

Montana Mining Corp

1403 E 900 S, Salt Lake City, UT, 84105; *PH:* 1-801-582-9609

General - Incorporation	NV	**Stock**- Price on:12/24/2007	$0.15
Employees	1	Stock Exchange	OTC
Auditor	Pritchett, Siler & Hardy, P.c.	Ticker Symbol	MMGC
Stk Agt	NA	Outstanding Shares	6,310,000
Counsel	NA	E.P.S	$0.00
DUNS No.	NA	Shareholders	NA

Business: The group intends to merge with or acquire a business entity. Previously, the group was engaged in the identification and exploration of precious metal properties. Montana Mining was founded in 1999. It was formerly known as Aswan Investments, Inc. and changed its name to Montana Mining Corp. in 2002. The company is based in Salt Lake City, Utah. The group operates from United States.

Primary SIC and add'l.: 6799

CIK No: 0001104672

Officers: Ruairidh Campbell/44/Dir., CEO, CFO

Directors: Ruairidh Campbell/44/Dir., CEO, CFO

Owners: Insiders/9.50%, Ruairidh Campbell/9.50%

Financial Data: **Fiscal Year End:**12/31 **Latest Annual Data:** 12/31/2006

Year	Sales	Net Income
2006	NA	-$24,000
2005	NA	-$28,000
2004	NA	-$37,000

Curr. Assets:	$5,000	Curr. Liab.:	$42,000		
Plant, Equip.:	NA	Total Liab.:	$42,000	Indic. Yr. Divd.:	NA
Total Assets:	$5,000	Net Worth:	-$36,000	Debt/ Equity:	NA

Monterey Gourmet Foods Inc

1528 Moffett St., Salinas, CA, 93905; PH: 1-831-753-6262; Fax: 1-831-753-6255;
http:// www.montereypasta.com

General - Incorporation .... DE	**Stock**- Price on:12/24/2007 ....$4.34
Employees...299	Stock Exchange...NDQ
Auditor .... BDO Seidman LLP	Ticker Symbol..PSTA
Stk Agt................. Corporate Stock Transfer, Inc.	Outstanding Shares 17,320,000
Counsel..NA	E.P.S..$0.09
DUNS No. 16-054-8608	Shareholders...NA

Business: The group's principal activities are to produce and market refrigerated gourmet pastas, soups, gnocchi, pasta sauces, stuffed pizzas and other foods. It offers over 200 varieties of contemporary gourmet food products as well as soups and gnocchi that are produced using the its proprietary recipes. The production facility and distribution centers of the group are located in monterey county and California. At 28-Dec-2003, the group had 9,000 grocery and club stores. The group markets its products throughout the United States, selected regions in Canada and part of Latin America. The group acquired 84.5% of cibo naturals llc in 2004.

Primary SIC and add'l.: 2099

CIK No: 0000913032

Subsidiaries: Borsellini, Casual Gourmet, CIBO Naturals, Homestyle Fresh Soups, Monterey Pasta Development Company, Sonoma, Sonoma Jack

Officers: Eric Eddings/CEO/$278,302.00

Owners: Dimensional Fund Advisors/8.10%, Scott S. Wheeler, Charles B. Bonner/1.00%, Gruber and McBaine Capital Management/14.60%, C. David Viviani, Martin A. Adams, AWM Investment Co., Inc./6.40%, James M. Williams, T. Rowe Price Associates, Inc./7.30%, James Wong, Michael P. Schall, Walter L. Henning, Eric C. Eddings, Van Tunstall, F. Christopher Cruger (16 Owners included in Index)

Financial Data: Fiscal Year End:12/31   Latest Annual Data: 12/31/2006

Year	Sales	Net Income
2006	$94,297,000	-$3,112,000
2005	$85,248,000	-$537,000
2004	$62,491,000	-$1,344,000

Curr. Assets:	$23,413,000	Curr. Liab.:	$11,917,000		
Plant, Equip.:	$15,303,000	Total Liab.:	$12,046,000	Indic. Yr. Divd.:	NA
Total Assets:	$62,468,000	Net Worth:	$50,263,000	Debt/ Equity:	0.0020

Montgomery Street Income Securities Inc

225 W Wacker Dr., Ste. 950, Chicago, IL, 60606; PH: 1-213-270-9991;
http:// www.montgomerystreetincome.com

General - Incorporation .... MD	**Stock**- Price on:12/24/2007 ....$17.13
Employees..NA	Stock Exchange...NDQ
Auditor ....Pricewaterhousecoopers LLP	Ticker Symbol..MTSL
Stk Agt................. Mellon Investor Services LLC	Outstanding Shares 10,380,000
Counsel.................... Howard, Rice, Nemerovski	E.P.S..$1.19
DUNS No. ....NA	Shareholders...NA

Business: The groups principal activity is to provide fund for management investment companies. The group operates from the United States.

Primary SIC and add'l.: 6199

CIK No: 0000067813

Officers: Mark D. Nerud/41/CEO, Pres., Susan S. Rhee/36/Sec., Chief Legal Officer, Charles Moon/Portfolio Mgr., Nasri A. Toutoungi/Portfolio Mgr., Toni M. Bugni/34/Chief Compliance Officer, Daniel W. Koors/CFO, Treasurer, Principal Financial Officer

Directors: Richard J. Bradshaw/59/Chmn., Victor L. Hymes/50/Dir., John T. Packard/74/Dir., Wendell G. Van Auken/63/Dir., James C. Van Horne/72/Dir.

Financial Data: Fiscal Year End:12/31   Latest Annual Data: 12/31/2006

Year	Sales	Net Income
2006	$12,848,000	$8,988,000
2005	$11,813,000	$5,329,000
2004	$15,431,000	$12,641,000

Curr. Assets:	$3,285,000	Curr. Liab.:	$341,000		
Plant, Equip.:	NA	Total Liab.:	$19,663,000	Indic. Yr. Divd.:	$1.080
Total Assets:	$214,985,000	Net Worth:	$195,322,000	Debt/ Equity:	NA

Montpelier Re Holdings Ltd

94 Pitts Bay Rd., Pembroke; PH: 441-2965550; Fax: 441-2965551; http:// www.montpelierre.bm;
Email: info@montpelierre.bm

General - Incorporation .... Bermuda	**Stock**- Price on:12/24/2007 ....$18.29
Employees...70	Stock Exchange...NDQ
Auditor ....PricewaterhouseCoopers LLP	Ticker Symbol...MRLN
Stk Agt..................... Bank of New York	Outstanding Shares 111,780,000
Counsel...NA	E.P.S..$3.42
DUNS No. ....NA	Shareholders...NA

Business: The group operates through its subsidiaries whose principle activity is to provide reinsurance services, for the global insurance market. The group operates from United States.

Primary SIC and add'l.: 6351 6719

CIK No: 0001165880

Subsidiaries: Montpelier Agency Ltd., Montpelier Holdings (Barbados) SRL, Montpelier Marketing Services (UK) Ltd., Montpelier Reinsurance Ltd.

Officers: Anthony Taylor/Chmn., CEO, Pres. - Montpelier Re Holdings, Jon Hughes/VP - Terrorism Underwritermontpelier Marketing Services Ltd, Christopher Harris/Exec. VP, Chief Underwriting, Risk Officer - Montpelier Re Holdings, Kernan Oberting/Exec. VP, CFO, Exec. VP, David Sinnott/Exec. VP, Chief Reinsurance Officer - Montpelier Re Bermuda, Paul Hopwood/Sr. VP - US Treaty Underwriting, Malcolm Graham-Taylor/Sr. VP - Direct, Facultative Underwriter, Richard

Chattock/Sr. VP - Direct, Facultative Underwriter, Tom Busher/Exec. VP, COO - Montpelier Re Holdings, Helena Bickley/Assist. VP - Risk Management, Claire Johnson/Reinsurance Analyst, Nicholas Newman-Young/Exec. VP, MD - Montpelier Marketing Services, UK Limited, William Pollett/Treasurer, Sr. VP, Neil Greenspan/Chief Accounting Officer, VP, Aline Harris/VP, Financial Controller (29 Officers included in Index)

Directors: Anthony Taylor/Chmn., CEO, Pres. - Montpelier Re Holdings, John F. Shettle/Dir., Morgan Wesley Davis/Dir., Clement S. Dwyer/Dir., Allan W. Fulkerson/Dir., Thomas K. Kemp/Dir., Wilbur L. Ross/Dir., Candace Lee Straight/Dir., Karl Thomas Kemp Thomas Kemp/Dir., John Roderick Heller/Dir., Ian M. Winchester/Dir.

Owners: Russell C. Fletcher, Thomas G.S. Busher, Clement S. Dwyer, Kernan V. Oberting, Nicholas Newman-Young, C. Russell Fletcher, John F. Shettle, Insiders/1.50%, Morgan W. Davis, White Mountains Insurance Group, Ltd./7.30%, WL Ross& Co. LLC/6.20%, White Mountains Insurance Group, Ltd./7.30%, Insiders/1.50%, Anthony Taylor/1.00%, Christopher L. Harris (20 Owners included in Index)

Financial Data: Fiscal Year End:12/31   Latest Annual Data: 12/31/2006

Year	Sales	Net Income
2006	$735,707,000	$302,860,000
2005	$967,863,000	-$752,902,000
2004	$870,834,000	$240,281,000

Curr. Assets:	$769,858,000	Curr. Liab.:	$431,764,000	P/E Ratio:	5.18
Plant, Equip.:	NA	Total Liab.:	$2,405,841,000	Indic. Yr. Divd.:	$0.300
Total Assets:	$3,898,756,000	Net Worth:	$1,492,915,000	Debt/ Equity:	0.4390

Monument Resources Inc

2050 S Oneida St., Ste. 106, Denver, CO, 80224; PH: 1-303-692-9468

General - Incorporation .... CO	**Stock**- Price on:12/24/2007 ....$0.3
Employees..3	Stock Exchange...OTC
Auditor .... Gordon Hughes & Banks LLP	Ticker Symbol..MNMN
Stk Agt .... Computershare Investor Services LLC	Outstanding Shares 5,320,000
Counsel...NA	E.P.S...-$0.05
DUNS No. 18-614-8987	Shareholders...NA

Business: The group's principal activities are to search for, acquire, evaluate, and market oil and gas and mineral properties. The products of the group include crude oil, natural gas and other petroleum products. These products are sold to various producers, including pipeline companies. The group's oil and gas properties are located in webb and knox counties, Texas, leavenworth county, Kansas and kimball county. Mineral properties of the group are located in Montana.

Primary SIC and add'l.: 1041 1311 1499 4922

CIK No: 0000818468

Subsidiaries: COG Transmission Corporation., Hecla Mining Co., King Resources, Inc.

Officers: A. G. Foust/64/Dir., CEO, Pres. - Principal Financial, Accounting Officer, Dru E. Campbell/56/Sec.

Directors: A. G. Foust/64/Dir., CEO, Pres. - Principal Financial, Accounting Officer, John J. Womack/87/Dir.

Owners: Stewart A. Jackson/8.50%, John J. Womack/3.80%, Dru E. Campbell/3.40%, A. G. Foust/25.30%, Insiders/32.50%

Financial Data: Fiscal Year End:09/30   Latest Annual Data: 9/30/2006

Year	Sales	Net Income
2006	$590,000	$143,000
2005	$515,000	$447,000
2004	$468,000	$40,000

Curr. Assets:	$1,185,000	Curr. Liab.:	$62,000		
Plant, Equip.:	$954,000	Total Liab.:	$143,000	Indic. Yr. Divd.:	NA
Total Assets:	$2,139,000	Net Worth:	$1,996,000	Debt/ Equity:	NA

Mony Life Insurance Co of America

PO Box 871642, Canton, MI, 48187; PH: 1-212-969-1000; Fax: 1-212-969-2229;
http:// www.life-insurance-companies.com

General - Incorporation .... AZ	**Stock**- Price on:12/24/2007 ....$88.5112
Employees..4,914	Stock Exchange..NA
Auditor ....PricewaterhouseCoopers LLP	Ticker Symbol..NA
Stk Agt .... The Advest Group Inc	Outstanding Shares 86,060,000
Counsel..NA	E.P.S..$4.20
DUNS No. 80-794-8294	Shareholders...NA

Business: The group's principle activity is to provide life insurance and annuity products to business owners, growing families and pre-retirees. The products of the company include term life insurance, variable life insurance, variable annuity, universal life products, group universal life products and corporate-owned and bank-owned life insurance. The insurance and financial products are marketed and distributed directly to individuals primarily through parent company's career agency sales force and complementary distribution channels. The products are sold in 49 states, the district of columbia, the U.S. Virgin islands and Puerto Rico.

Primary SIC and add'l.: 6311

CIK No: 0000835357

Subsidiaries: AXA Financial, Inc., Mloa, U.s. Financial Life Insurance Company (usfl), MONY Holdings, LLC

Financial Data: Fiscal Year End:12/31   Latest Annual Data: 12/31/2006

Year	Sales	Net Income
2006	$4,138,240,000	$1,108,601,000
2005	NA	$248,064,000
2004	NA	$195,173,000

Curr. Assets:	$6,044,893,000	Curr. Liab.:	$5,641,692,000		
Plant, Equip.:	$288,575,000	Total Liab.:	$5,976,593,000	Indic. Yr. Divd.:	$4.640
Total Assets:	$10,601,105,000	Net Worth:	$4,570,997,000	Debt/ Equity:	NA

Moody's Corp

99 Church St., New York, NY, 10007; PH: 1-212-553-0300; Fax: 1-212-553-4820;
http:// www.moodys.com

General - Incorporation DE | Employees 3,400 | Auditor PricewaterhouseCoopers LLP | Stk Agt Bank of New York | Counsel NA | DUNS No. 04-997-7473

Stock- Price on:12/24/2007 $66.08 | Stock Exchange NYSE | Ticker Symbol MCO | Outstanding Shares 273,800,000 | E.P.S $3.07 | Shareholders NA

Business: The groups principle activity is to provide credit ratings, research and risk analysis services. The group provides research data and analytic tools for assessing credit risk, and publishes market-leading credit opinions, deal research and commentary. Customers served by the group include corporate and governmental issuers of securities, including institutional investors, depositors, creditors, investment banks, commercial banks and other financial intermediaries. The group operates from United States.

Primary SIC and add'l.: 7323 2741 8748

CIK No: 0001059556

Subsidiaries: Administracin de Calificadoras, S.A. de C.V., Economy.com (Canada) Inc., Economy.com (U.K.) Ltd., Economy.com Pty. Inc., KIS Pricing, Inc., KMV Asia, Korea Investors Service, Inc., MIS Quality Management Corp., Moodys America Latina Ltda., Moodys Asia Pacific Ltd., Moodys Assurance Company, Inc., Moodys Assureco, Inc., Moodys Canada, Inc., Moodys Central Europe (BVI) Ltd., Moodys Central Europe Ltd. 51 Subsidiaries included in the Index

Officers: Raymond W. McDaniel/Chmn., CEO/$8,195,767.00, Jeanne Dering/Exec. VP - Global Regulatory Affairs, Compliance/$3,365,205.00, Linda S. Huber/CFO, Exec. VP/$2,526,923.00, Jay McCabe/Sr. VP, Corporate Controller, Andrew E. Kimball/Chief Credit Officer, Jennifer Elliott/42/VP, Chief Human Resources Officer, John J. Goggins/General Counsel, Sr. VP/$1,857,919.00, Brian M. Clarkson/COO, Pres., Mark E. Almeida/Sr. VP - Moody's Analytics, Andrew J. Kriegler/Sr. VP, Chief Human Resources Officer, Perry Rotella/CIO, Sr. VP, Philip Braverman/VP - Global Tax, Jeffrey Hare/VP - Corporate Planning, Lisa S. Westlake/VP - Investor Relations, Noel E.D. Kirnon/Exec. VP - Global Structured Finance, US Public Finance *(20 Officers included in Index)*

Directors: Raymond W. McDaniel/Chmn., CEO, Christopher T. Mahoney/Vice Chmn., Henry A. McKinnell/65/Dir., Basil L. Anderson/62/Dir., Ewald Kist/64/Dir., John K. Wulff/59/Dir., Nancy S. Newcomb/62/Dir., Robert R. Glauber/69/Dir., Connie Mack/67/Dir.

Owners: Raymond W. McDaniel, John J. Goggins, Jeanne M. Dering, John K. Wulff, Nancy S. Newcomb, Ewald Kist, Davis Selected Advisers, L.P./6.82%, Connie Mack, Linda S. Huber, Insiders/0.80%, Basil L. Anderson, Jennifer Elliott, Robert R. Glauber, Berkshire Hathaway Inc./17.23%, Henry A. McKinnell

Financial Data: *Fiscal Year End:*12/31 *Latest Annual Data:* 12/31/2006

Year	Sales	Net Income
2006	$2,037,100,000	$753,900,000
2005	$1,731,600,000	$560,800,000
2004	$1,438,300,000	$425,100,000

Curr. Assets:	$1,001,900,000	**Curr. Liab.:**	$700,000,000		
Plant, Equip.:	$62,000,000	**Total Liab.:**	$1,330,300,000	**Indic. Yr. Divd.:**	$0.400
Total Assets:	$1,497,700,000	**Net Worth:**	$167,400,000	**Debt/ Equity:**	NA

Moog Inc

Plant 4, Jamison Rd., East Aurora, NY, 14052; ***PH:*** 1-716-687-4567; ***Fax:*** 1-716-687-5969; ***http://*** www.moog.com; ***Email:*** web.admin@moog.com

General - Incorporation NY | Employees 7,273 | Auditor Ernst & Young LLP | Stk Agt Mellon Shareholder Services LLC | Counsel NA | DUNS No. 00-210-3166

Stock- Price on:12/24/2007 $42.12 | Stock Exchange NYSE | Ticker Symbol NA | Outstanding Shares 42,470,000 | E.P.S NA | Shareholders NA

Business: The group's principal activities are carried out through three segments: aircraft controls: designs and manufactures flight and engine controls for manufacturers of military and commercial aircraft. Space controls: designs and manufactures controls and systems that control the flight, positioning or thrust of tactical and strategic missiles, launch vehicles, satellites and space shuttles. Industrial controls: designs and manufactures hydraulic and electric controls used in a variety of industrial applications. These include plastic injection and blow molding machines, steam and gas turbines, fatigue testing machines, motion simulators and ammunition-loadin systems on combat vehicles. The group operates in the unites states, Germany, Japan, Italy and other areas.

Primary SIC and add'l.: 3625 3492 3812

CIK No: 0000067887

Subsidiaries: Electro-Tec Corporation, FCS Com, Inc, FCS Control Systems BV, FCS Kelsey Limited, FCS Simulator Systems BV, Focal Technologies Corporation, IDM Technologies Limited, Moog AG, Moog Australia Pty. Ltd., Moog Components Group Inc., Moog Controls (India) Private Ltd, Moog Controls Corporation, Moog Controls Hong Kong Ltd., Moog Controls Ltd., Moog de Argentina Srl 35 Subsidiaries included in the Index

Officers: Robert T. Brady/67/Chmn., CEO, Pres., Richard A. Aubrecht/64/Vice Chmn., VP - Strategy, Technology, Stephen A. Huckvale/59/VP, Warren C. Johnson/49/VP, Martin J. Berardi/52/VP, Robert R. Banta/66/Dir., CFO, Exec. VP, Assist. Sec., John B. Drenning/71/Sec., Joe C. Green/67/Dir., Exec. VP, Chief Administrative Officer, Lawrence J. Ball/54/VP, Harald E. Seiffer/49/VP, Sasidhar Eranki/54/VP, John R. Scannell/45/VP, Jay K. Hennig/48/VP, Donald R. Fishback/52/Principal Accounting Officer, Controller, Ann Marie Luhr/Contact - Shareholder Relations *(16 Officers included in Index)*

Directors: Robert T. Brady/67/Chmn., CEO, Pres., Richard A. Aubrecht/64/Vice Chmn., VP - Strategy, Technology, Robert H. Maskrey/Dir., Robert R. Banta/66/Dir., CFO, Exec. VP, Assist. Sec., Joe C. Green/67/Dir., Exec. VP, Chief Administrative Officer, Albert F. Myers/Dir., Raymond W. Boushie/Dir., James L. Gray/Dir., John D. Hendrick/Dir., Kraig H. Kayser/Dir., Brian J. Lipke/Dir.

Owners: All directors and officers as a group/2.60%, Richard A. Aubrecht/2.00%, Brian J. Lipke, Joe C. Green, Kraig H. Kayser, Robert R. Banta, Moog Inc. Employee Retirement Plan/0.40%, Fidelity Management and Research/11.00%, Earnest Partners/7.30%, Albert F. Myers, Robert T. Brady, Robert R. Banta, Insiders/5.40%, Moog Family Agreement as to Voting/0.40%, Richard A. Aubrecht *(28 Owners included in Index)*

Financial Data: *Fiscal Year End:*09/24 *Latest Annual Data:* 9/30/2006

Year	Sales	Net Income
2006	$1,306,494,000	$81,346,000
2005	$1,051,342,000	$64,792,000
2004	$938,852,000	$57,287,000

Curr. Assets:	$728,101,000	**Curr. Liab.:**	$307,606,000	**P/E Ratio:**	19.68
Plant, Equip.:	$310,011,000	**Total Liab.:**	$844,798,000	**Indic. Yr. Divd.:**	NA
Total Assets:	$1,607,654,000	**Net Worth:**	$762,856,000	**Debt/ Equity:**	0.4635

Morgain Minerals Inc

402 - 121 Richmond St. W, Toronto, ON, M5H 2K1; ***PH:*** 1-416-364-5756; ***http://*** www.morgainminerals.com

General - Incorporation Canada | Employees NA | Auditor NA | Stk Agt Computershare Trust Co. of Canada | Counsel Fraser Milner Casgrain LLP | DUNS No. NA

Stock- Price on:12/24/2007 $0.25 | Stock Exchange NA | Ticker Symbol NA | Outstanding Shares NA | E.P.S NA | Shareholders NA

Business: The group's principal activities include mining and developing a portfolio of profitable low-grade gold mines in Mexico. The group holds a number of precious-base-metal and industrial mineral properties in Mexico. The three main projects of the company include: El Castillo (formerly El Cairo Gold Project), Cuatro Hermanos (copper-molybdenum sulfide mineralization) and La Fortuna (gold-silver-copper mineralization). The company is focused on bringing their Castillo project into production. Castillo project is currently undergoing a series of mining and leaching tests designed to determine the best operating methods and machinery. The company has not yet started commercial production and expected to commence sometime during the first half of 2006.

Primary SIC and add'l.: 1081

CIK No: 0001289570

Officers: Christopher E. Babcock/CEO, Pres., Bryan Morris/Dir., CFO, Richard J. Adams/Dir., VP - Corporate Development, Darren M. Koningen/Dir., VP - Engineering, Sharon L. Fleming/Corp. Sec.

Directors: Chester F. Millar/Chmn., Bryan Morris/Dir., CFO, Richard J. Adams/Dir., VP - Corporate Development, Darren M. Koningen/Dir., VP - Engineering, Leonard Harris/Dir., Rodrigo Sanchez-Mejorada/Dir.

Morgan Creek Energy Corp

3625 N Hall St., Ste. 900, Dallas, Texas, 75219; ***PH:*** 1-214-321-0603; ***Fax:*** 1-866-414-0467; ***http://*** www.morgancreekenergy.com; ***Email:*** info@morgancreekenergy.com

General - Incorporation NV | Employees NA | Auditor Dale Matheson Carr-Hilton LaBonte LLP | Stk Agt Transfer Online, Inc. | Counsel Thomas J. Deutsch | DUNS No. NA

Stock- Price on:12/24/2007 $0.6 | Stock Exchange OTC | Ticker Symbol MCRE | Outstanding Shares 29,810,000 | E.P.S -$0.19 | Shareholders NA

Business: The groups principal activities include exploring, acquiring and developing oil and gas properties. The group operates from the United States.

Primary SIC and add'l.: 1382

CIK No: 0001323143

Officers: Marcus M. Johnson/Dir., Pres., Thomas Markham/Dir., Chief Geologist, William P. Begley/Mgr. - Operations, Bruce D. Horton/Dir., CFO, Thomas J. Deutsch/Legal Counsel

Directors: Marcus M. Johnson/Dir., Pres., Thomas Markham/Dir., Chief Geologist, Bruce D. Horton/Dir., CFO, Erik Essiger/42/Dir., Grant Atkins/Dir., Stephen Jewett/69/Dir.

Owners: Bruce D. Horton/1.30%, Insiders/17.87%, Marcus Johnson/11.79%, Erik Essiger, Steve Jewett, Thomas Markham/3.77%

Financial Data: *Fiscal Year End:*12/31 *Latest Annual Data:* 12/31/2006

Year	Sales	Net Income
2006	NA	-$3,918,000
2005	NA	-$204,000

Curr. Assets:	$20,000	**Curr. Liab.:**	$473,000	**P/E Ratio:**	14.33
Plant, Equip.:	$310,000	**Total Liab.:**	$473,000	**Indic. Yr. Divd.:**	NA
Total Assets:	$330,000	**Net Worth:**	-$144,000	**Debt/ Equity:**	NA

Morgan Stanley

1585 Broadway, New York, NY, 10036; ***PH:*** 1-212-761-4000; ***Fax:*** 1-212-762-8131; ***http://*** www.morganstanley.com; ***Email:*** genlfeedback@morganstanley.com

General - Incorporation DE | Employees 55,310 | Auditor Deloitte & Touche LLP | Stk Agt Mellon Investor Services LLC | Counsel NA | DUNS No. 10-114-7130

Stock- Price on:12/24/2007 $88.83 | Stock Exchange NYSE | Ticker Symbol MS | Outstanding Shares 1,050,000,000 | E.P.S $8.80 | Shareholders NA

Business: The group's principle activity is to provide products and services to customers including corporations, governments, financial institutions and individuals. The group's services include sales and trading, investment banking and management, prime brokerage and research. On December 21, 2006, Morgan Stanley acquired CityMortgage Bank. The group operates from United States.

Primary SIC and add'l.: 6211 6282 6221 6289

CIK No: 0000895421

Subsidiaries: AB Asesores Burstiles Cordoba, S.A., AB Asesores Ceuta, S.L., Aircraft SPC-5, Inc., Alltransair Nevada, Inc., Alsea LLC, Always Limited, Ancon Inc., Anfal Inc., Angar Nevada, Ansett Finance (Europe) B.V., Ansett Worldwide Aviation (Labuan) Inc., Ansett Worldwide Aviation Equipment, Ansett Worldwide Aviation Ireland Limited, Ansett Worldwide Aviation Limited, Ansett Worldwide Aviation Netherlands B.V. 783 Subsidiaries included in the Index

Officers: Wei Christianson/CEO - Morgan Stanley China, Hans Schuettler/CEO - Morgan Stanley Asia, John J. Mack/Chmn., CEO, Jerker Johansson/Co - Head - Institutional Sales, Trading, David H. Sidwell/54/CFO, Exec. VP, Jonathan Chenevix-Trench/COO - Institutional Securities, Gary G. Lynch/Chief Legal Officer, Owen D. Thomas/COO, Pres. - Investment Management, Philip Newcomb/Co - Head - Americas Sales, Trading, Jialin Liu/Co - Head - Asia Sales, Trading, Colm Kelleher/CFO, Exec. VP, Co - Head - Strategic Planning, Jonathan Kindred/Pres. - Morgan Stanley Japan Securities Co, Ltd, John Shapiro/Global Head - Commodities, Franck Petitgas/Head - International Investment Banking, Michael Petrick/Global Head - Corporate Credit Group And Head, Morgan Stanley Principal Investments *(39 Officers included in Index)*

Directors: John J. Mack/Chmn., CEO, Klaus Zumwinkel/Dir., Roy J. Bostock/Dir., Laura D. Tyson/Dir., Howard J. Davies/Dir., Griffith O. Sexton/Dir., Erskine B. Bowles/Dir., Robert C. Kidder/Dir., Donald T. Nicolaisen/Dir., Charles H. Noski/Dir., Hutham S. Olayan/Dir., Charles E. Phillips/Dir.

Owners: Howard J. Davies, Hutham S. Olayan, State Street Bank and Trust Company/12.01%, Robert C. Kidder, Erskine B. Bowles, Donald T. Nicolaisen, Klaus Zumwinkel, Griffith O. Sexton, Laura D. Tyson, Charles E. Phillips, John J. Mack, Zoe Cruz, Barclays Global Investors, N.A./6.05%, Roy J. Bostock, Charles H. Noski *(19 Owners included in Index)*

Financial Data: *Fiscal Year End:* 11/30   *Latest Annual Data:* 11/30/2006

Year	Sales	Net Income
2006	$76,551,000,000	$7,472,000,000
2005	$52,081,000,000	$4,939,000,000
2004	$39,549,000,000	$4,486,000,000

Curr. Assets:	$325,301,000,000	**Curr. Liab.:**	$655,408,000,000	**P/E Ratio:**	10.09
Plant, Equip.:	$4,086,000,000	**Total Liab.:**	$1,085,281,000,000	**Indic. Yr. Divd.:**	$1.080
Total Assets:	$1,120,645,000,000	**Net Worth:**	$35,364,000,000	**Debt/ Equity:**	12.0132

Morgan's Foods Inc

4829 Galaxy Pkwy., Ste. S, Cleveland, OH, 44128; *PH:* 1-216-359-9000; *Fax:* 1-216-359-2110; *http://* www.morgansfoods.com

General - Incorporation	OH	**Stock**- Price on:12/24/2007	$11.07
Employees	303	Stock Exchange	OTC
Auditor	Grant Thornton, LLP	Ticker Symbol	MRFD
Stk Agt	Computershare Investor Services LLC	Outstanding Shares	2,880,000
Counsel	Baker & Hostetler	E.P.S.	$0.76
DUNS No.	00-446-9771	Shareholders	NA

Business: The group's principal activity is to operate franchise restaurants. The group operates through wholly-owned subsidiaries kfc restaurants under franchises from kfc corporation, taco bell restaurants under franchises from taco bell corporation, pizza hut express restaurants under licenses from pizza hut corporation and an a&w restaurant under a license from a&w restaurants, inc. The group's kfc restaurants prepare and sell the distinctive kfc branded chicken products along with related food items. The group's taco bell restaurants prepare and sell a full menu of quick serve Mexican food items using appropriate taco bell containers and packages. As on 30-May-2003 the group operates 75 kfc restaurants, 7 taco bell restaurants, 16 kfc/taco bell "2n1" restaurants, 3 taco bell/pizza hut express "2n1" restaurants, 1 kfc/pizza hut express "2n1" and 1 kfc/a&w "2n1", in the states of Illinois, Missouri, Ohio, Pennsylvania, west Virginia and New York.

Primary SIC and add'l.: 7011 5812

CIK No: 0000068145

Subsidiaries: Morgans Creative Restaurant Concepts, Inc., Morgans Foods of Missouri, Inc., Morgans Restaurants of New Jersey, Inc., Morgans Restaurants of New York, Inc., Morgans Restaurants of Ohio, Inc., Morgans Restaurants of Pennsylvania, Inc., Morgans Restaurants of West Virginia, Inc., Morgans Tacos of Pennsylvania, Inc.

Owners: Kenneth L. Hignett/1.50%, Lawrence S. Dolin/3.60%, James J. Liguori/2.70%, Insiders/43.10%, Blackhorse Capital Advisors LLC/11.60%, Steven S. Kaufman, Bernard Lerner/3.50%, Bahman Guyuron/3.00%, Moab Partners LP/10.50%, Leonard R. Stein-Sapir/28.70%

Financial Data: *Fiscal Year End:* 02/26   *Latest Annual Data:* 2/25/2007

Year	Sales	Net Income
2007	$91,248,000	$3,527,000
2006	$87,457,000	$3,437,000
2005	$80,960,000	-$1,858,000

Curr. Assets:	$5,223,000	**Curr. Liab.:**	$51,271,000	**P/E Ratio:**	8.72
Plant, Equip.:	$31,607,000	**Total Liab.:**	$53,364,000	**Indic. Yr. Divd.:**	NA
Total Assets:	$48,790,000	**Net Worth:**	-$4,574,000	**Debt/ Equity:**	NA

Morgans Hotel Group Company

475 10th Ave., New York, NY, 10018; *PH:* 1-212-277-4100; *Fax:* 1-212-277-4260; *http://* www.morganshotelgroup.com

General - Incorporation	DE	**Stock**- Price on:12/24/2007	$23.53
Employees	1,950	Stock Exchange	AMEX
Auditor	BDO Seidman, LLP	Ticker Symbol	MHJ
Stk Agt	Bank of New York	Outstanding Shares	31,990,000
Counsel	NA	E.P.S.	NA
DUNS No.	NA	Shareholders	NA

Business: The groups principal activities include operating, owning, acquiring, developing and redeveloping boutique hotels. The groups services include restaurants and bars, and rooms. The group operates from New York, Miami, Los Angeles, Scottsdale, San Francisco and London.

Primary SIC and add'l.: 5813 5812 7011

CIK No: 0001342126

Subsidiaries: 1100 West Holdings, LLC, 1100 West Properties, LLC, 43rd Restaurant LLC, 495 ABC License LLC, 495 Geary LLC, 58th Street Bar Company LLC, 8440 LLC, Beach Hotel Associates LLC, Clift Holdings LLC, Collins Hotel Associates LLC, Henry Hudson Holdings LLC, Henry Hudson Senior Mezz LLC, Hudson Leaseco LLC, Hudson Managing Member LLC, Hudson Pledgor LLC 42 Subsidiaries included in the Index

Officers: Edward W. Scheetz/Dir., CEO, Marc Gordon/Chief Investment Officer, Exec. VP - Capital Markets, Richard Szymanski/CFO, David Smail/Chief Legal Officer, David Weidlich/Exec. VP - Operations, Blake T. Danner/Sr. VP - Sales, Thomas M. Buoy/Sr. VP - Distribution, Revenue Management, David Freiberger/VP - Brand Integrity, James Zito/Dir. - E - Commerce, Kim Walker/Dir. - Creative Services, Scott S. Williams/Exec. VP, Chief Marketing Officer, Kathy M. Chalmers/Exec. VP - Human Resources

Directors: Edward W. Scheetz/Dir., CEO, David T. Hamamoto/Chmn., Edwin L. Knetzger/Dir., Fred J. Kleisner/Dir., Thomas L. Harrison/Dir., Robert Friedman/Dir., Lance Armstrong/Dir.

Owners: Richard Szymanski, Morgan Stanley/17.90%, Thomas L. Harrison, David T. Hamamoto/7.00%, Lance Armstrong, FMR Corp./14.20%, Marc Gordon, Fred J. Kleisner, The Bear Stearns Companies Inc./7.40%, W. Edward Scheetz/7.30%, NorthStar Capital Investment Corp./31.80%, Citadel Limited Partnership/7.00%, Insiders/15.00%, Robert Friedman, Edwin L. Knetzger

Financial Data: *Fiscal Year End:* 12/31   *Latest Annual Data:* 12/31/2006

Year	Sales	Net Income
2006	$278,593,000	-$13,925,000
2005	$260,349,000	-$30,216,000

Curr. Assets:	$64,170,000	**Curr. Liab.:**	$35,039,000		
Plant, Equip.:	$494,537,000	**Total Liab.:**	$635,560,000	**Indic. Yr. Divd.:**	NA
Total Assets:	$758,006,000	**Net Worth:**	$122,446,000	**Debt/ Equity:**	5.6268

Morningstar Inc

225 W Wacker Dr., Chicago, IL, 60606; *PH:* 1-312-696-6000; *Fax:* 1-312-696-6001; *http://* www.morningstar.com

General - Incorporation	IL	**Stock**- Price on:12/24/2007	$47.57
Employees	1,440	Stock Exchange	NDQ
Auditor	Deloitte& Touche LLP	Ticker Symbol	MORN
Stk Agt	Computershare Investor Services LLC	Outstanding Shares	42,710,000
Counsel	NA	E.P.S.	$1.42
DUNS No.	NA	Shareholders	NA

Business: The groups principle activity is to provide investment services. The groups services include print and online publications and retirement plan. The group products sold under the trade names Morningstar(R) Licensed Data(SM), Morningstar Rating(TM) and Portfolio X-Ray(R). The groups operates through three segments namely individual, advisor, and institutional. In the year 2006, the group acquired Aspect Huntley Pty Limited and Ibbotson Associates, Inc. The group operates from the United States. The group's quarterly revenue for September 2007 was 111.86 millions of USD.

Primary SIC and add'l.: 2731 6282 2741 7375 2721 7372 7379 7389

CIK No: 0001289419

Subsidiaries: Aspect Financial Pty Limited (4), Aspect Huntley Pty Limited (3), Aspect Huntley Thailand Limited (5), Fund Information Research, G.K., Huntleys Investment Information Pty Limited (4), Ibbotson Associates Advisors, LLC (15), Ibbotson Associates Japan, K.K. (16), Ibbotson Associates, Inc., InvestorInfo Limited (4), Morningstar Asia, Ltd., Morningstar Associates Europe Limited (1), Morningstar Associates, LLC, Morningstar Canada Group, Inc., Morningstar Danmark A/S (8), Morningstar Deutschland GmbH (10) 35 Subsidiaries included in the Index

Officers: Joe Mansueto/Chmn., CEO, Richard E. Robbins/General Counsel, Corp. Sec., Patrick Reinkemeyer/Pres. - Morningstar Associates, Tao Huang/COO, Catherine Gillis Odelbo/Pres. - Individual Business, Dan Piscatelli/Dir. - Mergers, Acquisitions, Kishore Gangwani/Sr. VP - Corporate Sales, Margaret Kirch Cohen/Contact - Corporate Inquiries, Nadine Youssef/Analyst Interviews, Alexa Auerbach/Contact - Ibbotson Associates Morningstar Associates, Tory Neff/Advisor Business Inquiries, Courtney Goethals Dobrow/Contact - Analyst Interviews, Investor Products, Annette Larson/Morningstar Data Requests, Mark Komissarouk/Contact - Morningstar Data Requests, Scott Cooley/CFO

Directors: Joe Mansueto/Chmn., CEO, Don Phillips/Dir., Cheryl Francis/Dir., Steve Kaplan/Dir., Jack Noonan/Dir., Paul Sturm/Dir., Frank Ptak/Dir.

Owners: Martha Dustin Boudos, Don Phillips/3.84%, Steve Kaplan, Paul Sturm1, Catherine Gillis Odelbo, Insiders/74.51%, Patrick Reinkemeyer, Morgan Stanley/6.01%, Cheryl Francis, Jack Noonan, Joe Mansueto/68.85%, Tao Huang/3.39%

Financial Data: *Fiscal Year End:* 12/31   *Latest Annual Data:* 12/31/2006

Year	Sales	Net Income
2006	$315,175,000	$51,762,000
2005	$227,114,000	$31,117,000
2004	$179,658,000	$8,809,000

Curr. Assets:	$237,484,000	**Curr. Liab.:**	$167,463,000	**P/E Ratio:**	41.29
Plant, Equip.:	$15,869,000	**Total Liab.:**	$178,415,000	**Indic. Yr. Divd.:**	NA
Total Assets:	$447,838,000	**Net Worth:**	$269,423,000	**Debt/ Equity:**	NA

Mortgage Assistance Center Corp

1341 W Mockingbird Ln., Ste. 1200, Dallas, TX, 75247; *PH:* 1-214-670-0005

General - Incorporation	FL	**Stock**- Price on:12/24/2007	$0.4
Employees	21	Stock Exchange	OTC
Auditor	Sutton Robinson Freeman & Co. P.C	Ticker Symbol	MTGC
Stk Agt	Sutton Robinson Freeman & Co	Outstanding Shares	12,730,000
Counsel	NA	E.P.S.	-$0.18
DUNS No.	78-681-4988	Shareholders	NA

Business: The group's principle activities include developing, marketing and selling paint stripping products used to remove lead-base paints, latex, alkyd, varnish, polyurethane and epoxy resin coatings from structural metal, cement, fiberglass, wood, mica and plaster; and designs supplement existing refrigeration systems for commercial refrigeration units such as walk-in and reach-in coolers. The group operates from United States.

Primary SIC and add'l.: 2851

CIK No: 0001025856

Subsidiaries: (MAC) Mortgage Assistance Corporation

Officers: Dale J. Hensel/38/Dir., CEO, CFO, Pres., Chief Accounting Officer, Dan Barnett/49/Dir., COO, VP, Michelle Taylor/62/Exec. VP - Corporate Development, MAC, Sandra Valiquette/67/CFO - MAC

Directors: Dale J. Hensel/38/Dir., CEO, CFO, Pres., Chief Accounting Officer, Dan Barnett/49/Dir., COO, VP, William G. Payne/42/Dir., Rod Jones/42/Dir.

Owners: Michelle Taylor/9.39%, Insiders/100.00%, Dale J. Hensel/45.59%, Dan Barnett/45.01%

Financial Data: *Fiscal Year End:* 12/31   *Latest Annual Data:* 12/31/2006

Year	Sales	Net Income
2006	$2,784,000	-$2,010,000
2005	$679,000	-$1,508,000
2004	NA	-$914,000

Curr. Assets:	$8,198,000	**Curr. Liab.:**	$2,236,000		
Plant, Equip.:	$1,352,000	**Total Liab.:**	$4,765,000	**Indic. Yr. Divd.:**	NA
Total Assets:	$9,553,000	**Net Worth:**	-$678,000	**Debt/ Equity:**	NA

Mortgagebrokers.com Inc

788 Island Pk. Dr., Ottawa, ON, K1Y 0C2; *PH:* 1-613-274-0055; *https://* www.mortgagebrokers.com

General - Incorporation	DE	**Stock**- Price on:12/24/2007	$0.53
Employees	NA	Stock Exchange	OTC
Auditor	SF Partnership, LLP	Ticker Symbol	MBKR
Stk Agt	Registrar & Transfer Co	Outstanding Shares	NA
Counsel	NA	E.P.S.	NA
DUNS No.	NA	Shareholders	NA

Business: The groups principle activity is to provide consulting and technical support services to Internet Service Providers to develop e-commerce market intelligence services. The group operates from the United States and Canada. The group's quarterly revenue for Sep '07 was 3.38 millions of USD.

Primary SIC and add'l.: 6163

CIK No: 0001222218
Officers: Alex Haditaghi/Chmn., CEO, Scott MacKenzie/Regional VP - Atlantic Canada, Dong Lee/VP - Operations, Matthew Laverty/VP - Production Eastern Canada, Exec. VP - Sales - Eastern Canada, Michael Barta/Regional VP - Sales SW Ontario, Davindra Persaud/Corporate Controller, Sue Wong/Regional Sales Dir. - GTA East, Allen O'Dell/Regional VP - Sales - GTA, David Mercer/VP - Production Western Canada, Exec. VP - Sales - Western Canada, Robert Hyde/VP - Finance, Administration, Jody Janson/Contact - Investor, Investors Stock Daily
Directors: Alex Haditaghi/Chmn., CEO
Owners: Alex Haditaghi/75.83%, Insiders/75.83%
Financial Data: Fiscal Year End:12/31 Latest Annual Data: 12/31/2006

Year	Sales	Net Income
2006	$4,023,000	-$2,009,000
2005	$197,000	-$429,000
2004	NA	-$53,000

Curr. Assets:	$1,347,000	Curr. Liab.:	$2,002,000		
Plant, Equip.:	$104,000	Total Liab.:	$2,115,000	Indic. Yr. Divd.:	NA
Total Assets:	$1,451,000	Net Worth:	-$665,000	Debt/ Equity:	NA

Morton Industrial Group Inc

1021 W Birchwood St., Morton, IL, 61550; *PH:* 1-309-266-7176

General - Incorporation	GA	Stock- Price on:12/24/2007	NA
Employees	518	Stock Exchange	NA
Auditor	KPMG LLP	Ticker Symbol	NA
Stk Agt...... American Stock Transfer & Trust Co.		Outstanding Shares	NA
Counsel	Husch & Eppenberger	E.P.S.	NA
DUNS No.	00-532-0247	Shareholders	NA

Business: The group's principal activities are to manufacture engineered metal components and subassemblies for industrial, construction, agricultural and recreational vehicle original equipment manufacturers (OEM's). Metal products include cabs, engine enclosures, panels, platforms, frames and complex weldments used in backhoes, excavators, tractors, motor homes and similar industrial equipment. The customers include deere and co and caterpillar inc. The group's five manufacturing facilities are located in the midwestern and southeastern United States in close proximity to the customers. In 2003, the group discontinued the operations of mid-central plastics inc.
Primary SIC and add'l.: 3316
CIK No: 0000064247
Subsidiaries: B & W Metal Fabricators, Inc, Mid-Central Plastics, Inc, Morton Metalcraft Co

Mosaic Company (The)

3033 Campus Dr., Ste. E490, Plymouth, MN, 55441; *PH:* 1-763-577-2700; *Fax:* 1-763-559-2860; *http://* www.mosaicco.com; *Email:* newdeals@mvccapital.com

General - Incorporation	DE	Stock- Price on:12/24/2007	$38.83
Employees	7,600	Stock Exchange	NYSE
Auditor	KPMG LLP	Ticker Symbol	MOS
Stk Agt...... American Stock Transfer & Trust Co.		Outstanding Shares	440,390,000
Counsel	NA	E.P.S.	NA
DUNS No.	NA	Shareholders	NA

Business: The groups principle activity is to produce phosphate, nitrogen, animal feed and potash. The group operates from the United States, India, Canada, and Thailand. The group's quarterly revenue for Sept 2007 was 90.16 millions of USD.
Primary SIC and add'l.: 1474 2873 2874 2879
CIK No: 0001285785
Subsidiaries: 4160142 Canada Ltd, Agrico Chemical Company, Big Bend Transfer Co., LLC, Canadian Resources Limited Partnership, CASA14 LLC, CASA15 LLC, CASA16 LLC, CASA2 LLC, CASA3 LLC, CASA4 LLC, Fertifos Administracao e Participacao S.A., Fertilizantes Mosaic Servicios, S. de R.L. de C.V., Fertilizantes Mosaic, S. de R.L. de C.V., FMRP Inc., Fospar S.A. 85 Subsidiaries included in the Index
Officers: James T. Prokopanko/Dir., CEO, Pres./$2,941,987.00, Norman B. Beug/Sr. VP - Potash Operations/$1,731,070.00, Donald Fred Gill/Pres., Richard L. Mack/Sr. VP, General Counsel, Corp. Sec./$1,382,665.00, Steven L. Pinney/Sr. VP - Phosphate Operations/$1,493,335.00, Lawrence W. Stranghoener/CFO, Exec. VP/$2,420,982.00, Linda K. Thrasher/VP - Public Affairs, Linda Thrasher, Anthony T. Brausen/49/VP - Finance, Chief Accounting Officer, Richard N. McLellan/51/Sr. VP - Commercial, Cindy C. Redding/49/VP - Human Resources, Douglas Hoadley/Investor Contact, David Townsend/Media Contact - Florida, Brad Delorey/Media Contact - Canada, David Jellerson/Environment Contact
Directors: James T. Prokopanko/Dir., CEO, Pres., Robert L. Lumpkins/Chmn., Guillaume Bastiaens/Dir., Richard D. Frasch/53/Dir., Raymond F. Bentele/Dir., Phyllis E. Cochran/Dir., William R. Graber/Dir., Harold H. MacKay/Dir., David B. Mathis/Dir., Bernard M. Michel/Dir., William T. Monahan/Dir., Steven M. Seibert/Dir.
Owners: Raymond F. Bentele, Cargill Fertilizer, Inc., Norman B. Beug, Insiders, Richard L. Mack, Cargill, Incorporated, David B. Mathis, Guillaume F. Bastiaens, Robert L. Lumpkins, William T. Monahan, Lawrence W. Stranghoener, GNS I (U.S.) Corp., Fredric W. Corrigan, William R. Graber, Steven L. Pinney *(17 Owners included in Index)*
Financial Data: Fiscal Year End:05/31 Latest Annual Data: 5/31/2006

Year	Sales	Net Income
2006	$5,305,800,000	-$121,400,000
2005	$4,396,700,000	$165,600,000

Curr. Assets:	$1,580,400,000	Curr. Liab.:	$1,126,100,000		
Plant, Equip.:	$4,416,600,000	Total Liab.:	$5,169,400,000	Indic. Yr. Divd.:	NA
Total Assets:	$8,720,600,000	Net Worth:	$3,530,800,000	Debt/ Equity:	0.6673

Mosaic Nutraceuticals Corp

4100 Spring Valley Rd. , Dallas, TX, 75244; *PH:* 1-469-556-2986; *http://* www.mosaicnutracorp.com

General - Incorporation	NV	Stock- Price on:12/24/2007	$0.06
Employees	1	Stock Exchange	OTC
Auditor	Kyle L. Tingle, Cpa LLC	Ticker Symbol	MCNJ
Stk Agt......Standard Registrar & Transfer Co Inc.		Outstanding Shares	55,210,000
Counsel	NA	E.P.S.	-$0.01
DUNS No.	NA	Shareholders	NA

Business: The group's principal activity is to distribute a line of dietary supplement nutraceutical products focused on categories including osteoarthritis and associated pain, low-carbohydrate functional foods, cholesterol health, weight loss/appetite suppression, anti-aging and general wellness. The company currently has trademark rights with respect to Joint-2-Life capsules, 24/7 Instant Pain Relief topical rub, and Lipotrene chews. The group is also in the process of releasing its Premium Noni chews and its VitalHealth product line which includes Premium Calcium with vitamins D & K, Premium Vitamin C, Premium Multivitamin, Premium Creatine and LeanLicious chews. Most products of the company are available in a soft candy chew that allows the active ingredients to be absorbed through the lining of the mouth as the candy dissolves.
Primary SIC and add'l.: 5122
CIK No: 0001332832
Financial Data: Fiscal Year End:12/31 Latest Annual Data: 12/31/2005

Year	Sales	Net Income
2005	$10,000	-$1,287,000

Curr. Assets:	$355,000	Curr. Liab.:	$140,000		
Plant, Equip.:	$35,000	Total Liab.:	$140,000	Indic. Yr. Divd.:	NA
Total Assets:	$413,000	Net Worth:	$273,000	Debt/ Equity:	NA

Most Home Corp

Unit 1 - 11491 Kingston St., Maple Ridge, BC, V2X 0Y6; *PH:* 1-360-945-2490;
Fax: 1-800-347-4701; *http://* www.mosthome.com

General - Incorporation	NV	Stock- Price on:12/24/2007	$0.52
Employees	NA	Stock Exchange	OTC
Auditor	Manning Elliott LLP	Ticker Symbol	MHME
Stk Agt................Corporate Stock Transfer, Inc.		Outstanding Shares	NA
Counsel	NA	E.P.S.	NA
DUNS No.	NA	Shareholders	NA

Business: The group's principle activity is to provide real estate transaction services. The group's lead management software realtor(R) assists a homebuyer or seller to purchase or sell a property or residence in another city. These services are available through its mostreferred.com (TM) and related websites. The group has 2,600 service areas across the United States and Canada with a population base of about 100,000 people. Substantially, all of the its customers are located in the United States. The group is in development stage and derives its revenues from referral fees, earned when a customer buys or sells a house through a member realtor and though membership dues resulting from its licensed software.
Primary SIC and add'l.: 7375
CIK No: 0001047965
Subsidiaries: Amrr.com, Inc., Most Home Management Ltd., Most Home Real Estate Services Inc.
Officers: Ken Galpin/Dir., CEO, Pres., Michael Schutz/CFO, Treasurer, Jim Secord/Pres., Todd Shyiak/VP - Business Development, Brad Miller/VP - Sales, Customer Service, Lisa Gaetz/VP - Operations
Directors: Ken Galpin/Dir., CEO, Pres.
Owners: William G. Spears/12.40%, Michael Schutz/0.30%, Andrew Hoff/33.30%, David Smalley/1.10%, Khachik Toomian/11.50%, Farshad Moftakhar/8.10%, Jim Secord/0.30%, George Shahnazarian/7.40%, David Woodcock/1.40%, Kenneth Galpin/5.80%, Insiders/18.60%, Ken Landis/8.00%
Financial Data: Fiscal Year End:07/31 Latest Annual Data: 07/31/2007

Year	Sales	Net Income
2007	$1,963,000	-$3,679,000
2006	$1,792,000	-$2,948,000
2005	$1,743,000	-$1,561,000

Curr. Assets:	$357,000	Curr. Liab.:	$1,256,000		
Plant, Equip.:	$125,000	Total Liab.:	$1,256,000	Indic. Yr. Divd.:	NA
Total Assets:	$1,513,000	Net Worth:	$257,000	Debt/ Equity:	NA

MoSys Inc

Formerly: Monolithic System Technology Inc
755 N Matihilda Ave., Sunnyvale, CA, 94085; *PH:* 1-408-731-1800; *http://* www.mosysinc.com

General - Incorporation	DE	Stock- Price on:12/24/2007	$8.17
Employees	80	Stock Exchange	NDQ
Auditor	BDO Seidman, LLP	Ticker Symbol	NA
Stk Agt.............. Wells Fargo Bank Minnesota N.A		Outstanding Shares	31,920,000
Counsel...... McCutchen Doyle Brown & Enersen		E.P.S.	-$0.11
DUNS No.	NA	Shareholders	NA

Business: The group's principal activities are to design, develop and market high performance semiconductor memory products and technologies. Its patented semiconductor memory technology, 1t-sram, combines the high-density advantages of dynamic random access memory with the high performance and utility of sram. This technology is offered to semiconductor companies, electronic product manufacturers, foundries, intellectual property and design companies through product development, technology licensing and co-Marketing relationships. The major customers of the group include sony corporation, nec electronics corporation & umc. The group also sells memory chips based on its 1t-sram technology. The trademarks include mosys (R), multibank (R), mdram (R), mcache(R) and 1t-sram (r). The operations are conducted in North America, Japan, Asia and Europe.
Primary SIC and add'l.: 3674 3679
CIK No: 0000890394
Subsidiaries: ATMOS Corporation, MoSys Europe EURL, MoSys International, Inc.
Officers: Chet Silvestri/Dir., CEO, Pres./$624,056.00, Dhaval Ajmera/VP - Strategic Accounting/$475,815.00, Mehdi Bathaee/COO, Michael Maia/VP - Marketing, Wingyu Leung/53/Dir., Exec. VP - Engineering, CTO/$446,378.00, Hem Hingarh/VP - Engineering/$344,225.00, James Pekarsky/CFO/$378,621.00
Directors: Chet Silvestri/Dir., CEO, Pres., Hsu Chi-Ping/53/Dir., Chi-Ping Hsu/Dir., Tommy Eng/Dir., Wingyu Leung/53/Dir., Exec. VP - Engineering, CTO, Carl E. Berg/Dir., Chenming Calvin Hu/Dir., Jim Kupec/Dir.
Owners: Hemraj Hingarh, Chi-Ping Hsu, 1981 Kara Ann Berg Trust/7.30%, James Pekarsky, Ingalls & Snyder LLC/20.00%, Carl E. Berg, Tommy Eng, Insiders/5.70%, Wingyu Leung/1.90%, Litespeed Management LLC/8.50%, Dhaval Ajmera, Chenming Hu, James Kupec
Financial Data: Fiscal Year End:12/31 Latest Annual Data: 12/31/2006

Year	Sales	Net Income
2006	$14,909,000	-$5,338,000
2005	$12,282,000	-$2,982,000
2004	$10,821,000	-$1,907,000

Curr. Assets:	$87,489,000	**Curr. Liab.:**	$2,791,000		
Plant, Equip.:	$855,000	**Total Liab.:**	$2,845,000	**Indic. Yr. Divd.:**	NA
Total Assets:	$103,760,000	**Net Worth:**	$100,915,000	**Debt/ Equity:**	NA

Mother Lode Bank CA

172 W Stockton Rd., Sonora, CA, 95370; *PH:* 1-209-694-8400; *http://* www.motherlodebank.com; *Email:* info@motherlodebank.com

General - Incorporation		**Stock** - Price on:12/24/2007	$13
Employees	NA	Stock Exchange	OTC
Auditor	NA	Ticker Symbol	MOLB
Stk Agt	NA	Outstanding Shares	NA
Counsel	NA	E.P.S.	NA
DUNS No.	NA	Shareholders	NA

Business: The groups principle activity is to provide recruiting services. The groups service area includes the research and development, engineering, marketing, sales, information technology and manufacturing industries. The group operates from United States.

Primary SIC and add'l.: 6029

CIK No:

Officers: Charles Milazzo/CEO, Pres., Robert Dancke/Sr. VP, Chief Credit Officer, Laurie Mitchum/Sr. VP, CFO, Joanne McDonald/VP, Operations Officer, Robert Featherstone/VP, Mortgage Division Mgr., Ty Wivell/Sr. VP - Marketing, Lisa Melville/VP, Loan Officer - Sonora Branch, Tammy Hammond/AVP, Loan Officer - Sonora Branch, Terry Blakemore/VP, Sr. Credit Officer - Sonora Branch, Judy Block/VP, Loan Officer - Calaveras Loan Processing Office, Sally Mole/AVP, Loan Officer - Calaveras Loan Processing Office

Directors: Barry A. Hillman/Dir., Randolph H. Holder/Dir., Peter A. Johnson/Dir., Peter J. Kerns/Dir., Kate Powell Segerstrom/Dir., Carroll M. Sinclair/Dir., Raymond M. Suess/Dir., Samuel E. Wheeler/Dir., Gary P. Dambacher/Dir.

Mother Lode Gold Mines Consolidated

1440 Concannon Blvd., Livermore, CA, 94550; *PH:* 1-510-530-7257

General - Incorporation	CA	**Stock** - Price on:12/24/2007	$0.01
Employees	NA	Stock Exchange	OTC
Auditor	PricewaterhouseCoopers LLP	Ticker Symbol	MLGM
Stk Agt	NA	Outstanding Shares	7,330,000
Counsel	NA	E.P.S.	-$0.02
DUNS No.	03-885-0954	Shareholders	NA

Business: The group's principle activities include acquiring and developing mining properties, primarily gold producing properties. The group operates from United States.

Primary SIC and add'l.: 1041

CIK No: 0000802595

Subsidiaries: Amador United Gold Mines, Pacific FarEast Minerals, Inc.

Officers: Frank M. Orrell/74/Chmn., CEO, Byron S. James/75/Dir., Sec., CFO

Directors: Frank M. Orrell/74/Chmn., CEO, Kevin J. Keen/57/Dir., Peter S. Adams/56/Dir., Byron S. James/75/Dir., Sec., CFO, Paul Yuan/52/Dir.

Owners: Byron S. James/10.44%, Frank M. Orrell/24.20%

Financial Data: *Fiscal Year End:*12/31 *Latest Annual Data:* 12/31/2006

Year	Sales	Net Income
2006	$13,000	-$146,000
2005	$71,000	-$27,000
2004	$16,000	-$707,000

Curr. Assets:	$0	**Curr. Liab.:**	$1,000		
Plant, Equip.:	NA	**Total Liab.:**	$9,000	**Indic. Yr. Divd.:**	NA
Total Assets:	$309,000	**Net Worth:**	$300,000	**Debt/ Equity:**	NA

Mothers Work Inc

456 N 5th St., Philadelphia, PA, 19123; *PH:* 1-215-873-2200; *Fax:* 1-215-873-0869; *http://* www.motherswork.com

General - Incorporation	DE	**Stock** - Price on:12/24/2007	$32.83
Employees	2,520	Stock Exchange	NDQ
Auditor	KPMG LLP	Ticker Symbol	MWRK
Stk Agt	StockTrans, Inc.	Outstanding Shares	5,950,000
Counsel	Pepper Hamilton LLP	E.P.S.	-$0.07
DUNS No.	05-531-6459	Shareholders	NA

Business: The group's principle activity is to manufacture maternity clothing in the United States and Canada. The group offers a full range of career, casual and special occasion maternity wear. The group operates with 851 stores under Mimi Maternity, A Pea in the Pod, and Motherhood Maternity brands. In addition it operates 132 leased maternity departments in stores such as Macy's, Babies, Lazarus and Rich's. The group takes sales order by phone and Internet. The group's total revenue for year 2007 was 581.37 millions of USD.

Primary SIC and add'l.: 5621 2331

CIK No: 0000896985

Subsidiaries: Cave Springs, Inc., Confecciones Acona S.A., Maternity Factory Warehouse Centre, Inc., Mothers Work Canada, Inc.

Officers: Dan W. Matthias/Chmn., CEO, Edward M. Krell/CFO, COO, David Mangini/Exec. VP, General Merchandise Mgr., Rebecca C. Matthias/Dir., Pres.

Directors: Dan W. Matthias/Chmn., CEO, Rebecca C. Matthias/Dir., Pres., William A. Schwartz/69/Dir., Elam M. Hitchner/62/Dir., Joseph A. Goldblum/59/Dir., David Schlessinger/53/Dir., Anne T. Kavanagh/49/Dir.

Owners: Edward M. Krell/1.40%, Rebecca C. Matthias/6.70%, FMR Corp./14.80%, Stadium Capital Management, LLC/13.00%, Anne T. Kavanagh, Elam M. Hitchner, David Schlessinger, MVP Distribution Partners/6.30%, Tiger Consumer Management, LLC/6.50%, Insiders/10.80%, Wells Fargo & Company/10.80%, William A. Schwartz, Joseph A. Goldblum/2.10%, Renaissance Technologies Corp./6.50%

Financial Data: *Fiscal Year End:*09/30 *Latest Annual Data:* 9/30/2006

Year	Sales	Net Income
2006	$602,744,000	$9,102,000
2005	$561,627,000	-$175,000
2004	$518,051,000	$5,039,000

Curr. Assets:	$148,632,000	**Curr. Liab.:**	$64,860,000	**P/E Ratio:**	45.60
Plant, Equip.:	$72,130,000	**Total Liab.:**	$207,036,000	**Indic. Yr. Divd.:**	NA
Total Assets:	$287,736,000	**Net Worth:**	$80,700,000	**Debt/ Equity:**	1.0078

Motive Inc

12515 Research Blvd., Bldg. 5, Austin, TX, 78759; *PH:* 1-512-339-8335; *Fax:* 1-512-339-9040; *http://* www.motive.com; *Email:* ir@motive.com

General - Incorporation	DE	**Stock** - Price on:12/24/2007	$2.85
Employees	NA	Stock Exchange	OTC
Auditor	Ernst & Young LLP	Ticker Symbol	MOTV
Stk Agt	Mellon Investor Services LLC	Outstanding Shares	NA
Counsel	NA	E.P.S.	NA
DUNS No.	NA	Shareholders	NA

Business: The group's principal activity is to provide service management software that enables companies to build management and service directly into their customer-facing products and services. The service management software of the group helps in optimizing time and reducing waste from labor-intensive management processes. It serves the following markets: enterprise service providers, hardware manufacturers, software companies, telecommunications and cable companies and the global 2000. The major customers of the group include mercury interactive corporation, hewlett-packard development company, l.p., advanced digital information corp. And british telecommunications plc. The group operates in the United States, Europe and Asia-Pacific.

Primary SIC and add'l.: 7372

CIK No: 0001112422

Officers: Alfred Mockett/Chmn., CEO, Aramis Alvarez/VP - Worldwide Services, Richard Hanna/COO, Jack Greenberg/General Counsel, Sec., Alasdhair Campbell/Dir. - Strategic Accounting Services, Ben Geller/Dir. - Industry Marketing, Russ Keveryn/Sr. Accounting Executive, Eivind Skildheim/Program Mgr. - HDM, Lawrence J. Sternberg/Practice Mgr. - Motive, Didier Verheye/Mgr. - Industry Marketing

Directors: Alfred Mockett/Chmn., CEO, Michael J. Maples/Dir., David Sikora/Dir., Virginia Gambale/Dir., Harvey White/Dir., Tom Meredith/Dir.

Financial Data: *Fiscal Year End:*12/31 *Latest Annual Data:* 12/31/2004

Year	Sales	Net Income
2004	$97,969,000	$427,000
2003	$92,292,000	-$1,210,000
2002	$58,056,000	-$10,514,000

Curr. Assets:	$91,141,000	**Curr. Liab.:**	$25,405,000		
Plant, Equip.:	$6,850,000	**Total Liab.:**	$29,931,000	**Indic. Yr. Divd.:**	NA
Total Assets:	$173,915,000	**Net Worth:**	$143,984,000	**Debt/ Equity:**	NA

MotivNation Inc

18101 Von Karman Ave., Ste. 330, Irvine, CA, 92612; *PH:* 1-888-258-6458; *http://* www.motivnation.com; *Email:* info@MotivNation.com

General - Incorporation	NV	**Stock** - Price on:12/24/2007	$0.018
Employees	29	Stock Exchange	OTC
Auditor	Spector & Wong, LLP	Ticker Symbol	MOVT
Stk Agt	Fidelity Transfer Co	Outstanding Shares	7,240,000
Counsel	NA	E.P.S.	-$0.23
DUNS No.	NA	Shareholders	NA

Business: The groups principle activities include selling, manufacturing, converting, customizing, armor protecting, and installing custom-built motorcycles and auto parts and accessories, and repairing, and servicing motorcycles. The group operates through two segments namely custom motorcycle and custom automotive. The group operates from the United States.

Primary SIC and add'l.: 3751

CIK No: 0000001853

Subsidiaries: TrixMotive Inc.

Officers: George Lefevre/CEO, Jay Isco/CFO, Sec., Leslie Ann McPhail/COO, Richard Perez/Operations

Directors: David Psachie/Dir., Mark Absher/Dir., Richard Holt/Dir.

Owners: David McPhail/9.08%, Mark Absher, David Psachie, Richard Holt, Thomas Prewitt/10.62%, George R. Lefevre/9.69%, Insiders/39.55%, Jay Isco/4.50%, Richard Perez/10.62%, Leslie McPhail/9.08%, Scott Absher/3.52%

Financial Data: *Fiscal Year End:*12/31 *Latest Annual Data:* 12/31/2006

Year	Sales	Net Income
2006	$2,330,000	-$3,683,000
2005	$3,287,000	-$1,470,000
2004	$1,136,000	-$374,000

Curr. Assets:	$707,000	**Curr. Liab.:**	$971,000		
Plant, Equip.:	$164,000	**Total Liab.:**	$5,101,000	**Indic. Yr. Divd.:**	NA
Total Assets:	$1,197,000	**Net Worth:**	-$3,905,000	**Debt/ Equity:**	NA

Motorcar Parts of America Inc

2929 California St., Torrance, CA, 90503; *PH:* 1-310-212-7910; *Fax:* 1-310-212-6315; *http://* www.motorcarparts.com; *Email:* info@motorcarparts.com

General - Incorporation	NY	**Stock** - Price on:12/24/2007	$13
Employees	1,538	Stock Exchange	NDQ
Auditor	Grant Thornton LLP	Ticker Symbol	MPAA
Stk Agt	Continental Stock Transfer & Trust Co	Outstanding Shares	8,370,000
Counsel	NA	E.P.S.	-$0.28
DUNS No.	04-447-7123	Shareholders	NA

Business: The group's principal activity is to remanufacture replacement alternators and starters for imported and domestic cars and light trucks. It also assembles and distributes starter ignition wire sets for cars and light trucks. These products are sold to retail automotive stores, autozone, csk automotive,

and o'reilly automotive. The group services automotive retail chain store accounts servicing approximately 5,500 retail outlets. It deals with approximately 1,700 different alternators and 1,100 starters. The remanufactured alternators and starters are supplied to general motors, ford, chrysler, toyota, honda, nissan, mazda and volkswagen. It operates in the United States, Singapore, Canada and Malaysia.

Primary SIC and add'l.: 3625 3694

CIK No: 0000918251

Subsidiaries: Motorcar Parts de Mexico, S.A. de C.V., MVR Products Pte. Limited, Unijoh Sdn. Bhd.

Officers: Selwyn Joffe/Chmn., CEO, Pres., Michael Umansky/VP, General Counsel, Sec., Mervyn McCulloch/CFO, Tom Stricker/VP - Sales, Bill Laughlin/VP - Traditional Aftermarket Sales, Steve Kratz/VP - QA, Engineering, John Foster/VP - Marketing, Doug Schooner/VP - Manufacturing, Joe Terlikosky/VP - Purchasing, Regina Gov/Dir. - Information Technology, Vincent Quek/Pres. - MPA Asia Subsidiary

Directors: Selwyn Joffe/Chmn., CEO, Pres.

Owners: Irv Siegel, Mel Marks/14.50%, Midwood Capital Management LLC/6.10%, Rudolph Borneo, Mervyn McCulloch, Costa Brava Partnership III L.P./8.20%, Philip Gay, Third Point LLC/9.40%, Insiders/20.10%, Thomas Stricker, Douglas Schooner, Michael Umansky, Selwyn Joffe/5.20%

Financial Data: Fiscal Year End:03/31   Latest Annual Data: 3/31/2006

Year	Sales	Net Income
2006	$108,397,000	$2,085,000
2005	$95,785,000	$6,288,000

Curr. Assets:	$87,741,000	Curr. Liab.:	$41,311,000		
Plant, Equip.:	$12,164,000	Total Liab.:	$49,541,000	Indic. Yr. Divd.:	NA
Total Assets:	$101,136,000	Net Worth:	$51,595,000	Debt/ Equity:	0.0792

Motorola Inc

1303 E Algonquin Rd., Schaumburg, IL, 60196; *PH:* 1-847-576-5000; *Fax:* 1-847-576-5372; *http://* www.motorola.com

General - Incorporation	DE	Stock- Price on:12/24/2007	$18.13
Employees	66,000	Stock Exchange	NYSE
Auditor	KPMG LLP	Ticker Symbol	MOT
Stk Agt	Harris Trust and Savings Bank	Outstanding Shares	2,310,000,000
Counsel	NA	E.P.S.	$0.20
DUNS No.	77-992-0735	Shareholders	NA

Business: The group's principle activity is to provide wireless and broadband communication services. The group's products include cell phones and accessories, bluetooth products, two-way radio, wireless sensors and digital audio players. In August 2007, Motorola, Inc. acquired Leapstone Systems, Inc. The group operates from United States.

Primary SIC and add'l.: 3663 3661 3699 3674 3669

CIK No: 0000068505

Subsidiaries: General Instrument Corporation, Hangzhou Motorola Cellular Equipment Co. Ltd., Motorola (China) Electronics Ltd., Motorola (China) Investment Ltd., Motorola Asia Limited, Motorola Asia Treasury Pte. Ltd., Motorola Canada Limited, Motorola Credit Corporation, Motorola Electronics Pte. Limited, Motorola Electronics Sdn. Bhd., Motorola Electronics Taiwan, Limited, Motorola Finance EMEA Limited, Motorola G.m.b.h., Motorola India Private Limited, Motorola Industrial Ltda. 25 Subsidiaries included in the Index

Officers: Edward J. Zander/61/Chmn., CEO, Ruth A. Fattori/Exec. VP - Human Resources, Patricia B. Morrison/CIO, Exec. VP, Stu Reed/Exec. VP - Integrated Supply Chain, Eugene A. Delaney/Sr. VP, Peter A. Lawson/Exec. VP, General Counsel, Sec., Daniel M. Moloney/Exec. VP, Pres. - Connected Home Solutions, Richard N. Nottenburg/Chief Strategy Officer, Exec. VP, Juli Burda/Mobile Devices, Consumer Products, North America, Pattie Schiele/Dir. - Communications, Integrated Supply Chain, Daisy Fung/Asia Pacific Business, Technology, Hamid Ahmadi/Motorola Sr. Fellow, Chief Architect, Frank Bentley/Sr. Research Engineer, Dragan Boscovic/Dir. - Engineering, Technology, Ron Buskey/Fellow, Technical Staff *(102 Officers included in Index)*

Directors: Edward J. Zander/61/Chmn., CEO, David W. Dorman/Dir., Laurance H. Fuller/Dir., Judy C. Lewent/Dir., Nicholas Negroponte/Dir., Indra K. Nooyi/Dir., Samuel C. Scott/Dir., Ron Sommer/Dir., James R. Stengel/Dir., Douglas A. Warner/Dir., John A. White/Dir., Miles D. White/Dir.

Owners: Nicholas Negroponte, Douglas A. Warner, Edward J. Zander, Peter A. Lawson, Thomas J. Meredith, Miles D. White, Barclays Global Investors, NA./6.97%, Judy C. Lewent, Insiders, Indra K. Nooyi, David W. Dorman, Laurance H. Fuller, Samuel C. Scott, John A. White, Gregory Q. Brown *(18 Owners included in Index)*

Financial Data: Fiscal Year End:12/31   Latest Annual Data: 12/31/2006

Year	Sales	Net Income
2006	$42,879,000,000	$3,661,000,000
2005	$36,843,000,000	$4,578,000,000
2004	$31,323,000,000	$1,532,000,000

Curr. Assets:	$30,975,000,000	Curr. Liab.:	$15,425,000,000	P/E Ratio:	31.81
Plant, Equip.:	$2,267,000,000	Total Liab.:	$21,451,000,000	Indic. Yr. Divd.:	$0.200
Total Assets:	$38,593,000,000	Net Worth:	$17,142,000,000	Debt/ Equity:	NA

Motorsports Emporium' Inc

7525 E Williams Dr., Ste. B, Scottsdale, AZ, 85255; *PH:* 1-480-596-4002; *http://* www.motorsportsemporium.com

General - Incorporation	NV	Stock- Price on:12/24/2007	$0.0382
Employees	4	Stock Exchange	OTC
Auditor	HJ Assoc. & Consultants LLP	Ticker Symbol	INBG
Stk Agt	NA	Outstanding Shares	5,610,000
Counsel	NA	E.P.S.	-$0.425
DUNS No.	NA	Shareholders	NA

Business: The group's principle activities include designing, developing and marketing unique card games and other gaming products for the gaming industry. The two types of gaming products designed by the company consist of table game with electronics and layout games. Table game with electronics includes ten to win and shotgun 21 card games that utilizes an electronics system. The layout game is a table game utilizing a table cover or layout with no electronic system. The company also manufactures, leases and markets shufflers under the name pro shuffle. Casinos use automatic card shufflers to save time and eliminate the possibility of a dealer manipulating the cards while hand shuffling. The card games are marketed to casinos located in the states of Arizona, California, Colorado, New Mexico, Nevada, South Dakota and Wisconsin. The group operates from United States.

Primary SIC and add'l.: 7999

CIK No: 0001075993

Subsidiaries: Scottsdale Diecast, Inc

Officers: David W. Keaveney/Dir., CEO, CFO/$241,565.00, Rhonda Keaveney/41/Dir., COO, Sec./$60,000.00, Kenneth Yeung/52/Pres.

Directors: David W. Keaveney/Dir., CEO, CFO

Owners: Insiders/95.63%, Kenneth Yeung/95.63%

Financial Data: Fiscal Year End:12/31   Latest Annual Data: 12/31/2006

Year	Sales	Net Income
2006	$58,000	-$1,190,000
2005	$222,000	-$1,010,000
2004	$22,000	-$1,691,000

Curr. Assets:	$20,000	Curr. Liab.:	$754,000		
Plant, Equip.:	$18,000	Total Liab.:	$754,000	Indic. Yr. Divd.:	NA
Total Assets:	$49,000	Net Worth:	-$705,000	Debt/ Equity:	NA

Mountain 1st Bank & Trust Company NC

101 Jack St., Hendersonville, NC, 28792; *PH:* 1-828-697-3100; *http://* www.mountain1st.com

General - Incorporation		Stock- Price on:12/24/2007	$19
Employees	NA	Stock Exchange	OTC
Auditor	NA	Ticker Symbol	MOBT
Stk Agt	First-citizens Bank & Trust Co	Outstanding Shares	4,980,000
Counsel	NA	E.P.S.	NA
DUNS No.	NA	Shareholders	NA

Business: The groups principal activity is to provide banking services. The services of the group include personal banking, business banking, loans, mortgage, safe deposit boxes, wire transfer, and fax boxes, ATM and debit card, and ACH direct deposit. The group operates from the United States.

Primary SIC and add'l.: 6021

CIK No:

Officers: Greg Gibson/CEO, Vince Rees/Pres., Peggy Denny/Chief Administrative Officer, Lee Beason/COO

Mountain National Bancshares Inc

PO Box 6519, Sevierville, TN, 37864; *PH:* 1-865-428-7990; *http://* www.mountainnationalbank.com

General - Incorporation	TN	Stock- Price on:12/24/2007	$29
Employees	150	Stock Exchange	OTC
Auditor	Crowe Chizek & Co. LLC	Ticker Symbol	MNBT
Stk Agt	Illinois Stock Transfer Co	Outstanding Shares	2,070,000
Counsel	NA	E.P.S.	$1.86
DUNS No.	NA	Shareholders	NA

Business: The group's principal activities are to accept deposits and originate loans. The group seeks savings and other time deposits and demand deposits from households and businesses in its primary marketing area by offering a full range of deposit accounts. It includes savings accounts, demand deposit accounts, retirement and professional accounts, including individual retirement accounts, checking accounts and time certificates. The group solicits mortgage, commercial, and consumer loans, as well as other authorized investments. The group has opened two branches in gatlinburg, pigeon forge and in seymour, Tennessee. It also offers additional services such as 24-hour automatic teller machines and other financial services. At 30-Jun-2003, the group had forty two commercial bank branches and four savings institutions branches located in sevier county.

Primary SIC and add'l.: 6712 6021

CIK No: 0001177070

Subsidiaries: MNB Capital Trust I, MNB Holdings, Inc, MNB Investments, Inc., MNB Real Estate, Inc, Mountain National Bank

Officers: Dwight Grizzell/Dir., CEO, Pres. - Mountain National Bank, Angelene Lamy/Banking Officer, Seymour Branch Mgr., Beverly J. Brosch/Sr. VP - Administration, Devon G. McKinzie/Exec. VP, Chief Lending Officer, Michael L. Brown/COO, Exec. VP, Rick Hubbs/CFO, Sr. VP - Mountain National Bank, Ashley Singleton/Banking Officer, Kodak Branch Mgr., Janie Hodge/Loan Operations Officer, Renee Ford/Loan Operations Officer, Michael Zorio/Regional Pres. - Blount County, Michael Hearon/First VP - Blount County, Pam Davis/Banking Officer - Blount County, Rosa Clure/Banking Officer - Blount County, Richard A. Hubbs/CFO, Sr. VP, Marsha Coggins/VP, Blount County Branch Mgr. *(55 Officers included in Index)*

Directors: Jeffrey Jay Monson/Dir., James E. Bookstaff/Dir., Gary A. Helton/Dir., Charlie R. Johnson/Dir., Sam L. Large/Dir., Ruth A. Reams/Dir., John M. Parker/Dir., Michael C. Ownby/Dir., Linda N. Ogle/Dir., Jim Bookstaff/Dir.

Owners: James E. Bookstaff/6.88%, Michael C. Ownby/1.26%, Sam L. Large/2.88%, Michael L. Brown/0.75%, Ruth Reams/1.68%, Charlie R. Johnson/2.18%, John M. Parker/5.45%, Gary A. Helton/4.18%, Linda N. Ogle/4.13%, Grace D. McKinzie/1.55%, Insiders/32.80%, Jeffrey J. Monson/2.22%, Dwight B. Grizzell/3.07%

Financial Data: Fiscal Year End:12/31   Latest Annual Data: 12/31/2006

Year	Sales	Net Income
2006	$32,247,000	$3,897,000
2005	$21,900,000	$3,124,000
2004	$15,690,000	$2,133,000

Curr. Assets:	$16,034,000	Curr. Liab.:	$420,831,000	P/E Ratio:	15.59
Plant, Equip.:	$19,944,000	Total Liab.:	$435,571,000	Indic. Yr. Divd.:	NA
Total Assets:	$469,982,000	Net Worth:	$34,411,000	Debt/ Equity:	0.3728

Mountain Province Diamonds Inc

401 Bay St., Toronto, ON, M5H 2Y4; *PH:* 1-416-361-3562; *http://* www.mountainprovince.com; *Email:* mpvifsec@att.net

General - Incorporation	Canada	Stock- Price on:12/24/2007	$4.66
Employees	NA	Stock Exchange	AMEX
Auditor	KPMG LLP	Ticker Symbol	MDM
Stk Agt	Computershare Trust Co of Canada	Outstanding Shares	55,670,000
Counsel	Campney & Murphy	E.P.S.	-$0.01
DUNS No.	24-957-1225	Shareholders	NA

Business: The group's principal activity is to explore commercial-grade diamond deposit in North America primarily in Canada's northwest territories. The group holds 44.1% interest in the property of ak/cj site located in the district of mackenzie. De beers Canada is a joint venture partner of the group. The group owns a mining subsidiary in the United States.

Primary SIC and add'l.: 1099

CIK No: 0001004530

Subsidiaries: Mountain Glen Mining Inc.

Officers: Patrick Evans/Dir., CEO, Pres., Jennifer Dawson/CFO

Directors: Patrick Evans/Dir., CEO, Pres., Jonathan Comerford/Chmn., Elizabeth J. Kirkwood/Dir., Carl G. Verley/Dir., D. H.W Dobson/Dir., David Whittle/Dir.

Owners: Jonathan Comerford, Harry D. Dobson/2.00%, Patrick C. Evans, Elizabeth J. Kirkwood, Carl G. Verley, De Beers Canada Exploration Ltd./5.20%, David E. Whittle, Peeyush Varshney, Insiders/3.40%, Bottin (International) Investments Ltd./22.20%, Desmond P. Sharkey/8.70%

Financial Data: Fiscal Year End:03/31   **Latest Annual Data:** 03/31/2007

Year	Sales	Net Income
2007	NA	-$1,774,000
2006	NA	-$1,669,000
2005	NA	$1,509,000

Curr. Assets:	$848,000	Curr. Liab.:	$155,000		
Plant, Equip.:	$3,000	Total Liab.:	$155,000	Indic. Yr. Divd.:	NA
Total Assets:	$2,929,000	Net Worth:	$2,774,000	Debt/ Equity:	NA

Mountains West Exploration Inc

PO Box 57819, Chicago, IL, 60657; **PH:** 1-312-952-7100

General - Incorporation	NM	**Stock**- Price on:12/24/2007	$0.41
Employees	NA	Stock Exchange	OTC
Auditor	Jaspers & Hall, PC	Ticker Symbol	MWXI
Stk Agt	American Stock Transfer & Trust Co.	Outstanding Shares	NA
Counsel	NA	E.P.S.	-$0.61
DUNS No.	NA	Shareholders	NA

Business: The groups principle activity is to provide recruiting services. The groups service area includes the research and development, engineering, marketing, sales, information technology and manufacturing industries. The group operates from United States.

Primary SIC and add'l.: 6799

CIK No: 0000319040

Officers: Lee Wiskowski/41/Dir., Pres., Douglas Stukel/38/Dir., Treasurer, Sec.

Directors: Lee Wiskowski/41/Dir., Pres., Douglas Stukel/38/Dir., Treasurer, Sec.

Owners: Douglas Stukel, Insiders, Lee Wiskowski

Financial Data: Fiscal Year End:12/31   **Latest Annual Data:** 12/31/2006

Year	Sales	Net Income
2006	NA	-$652,000
2005	NA	-$217,000
2004	$164,000	$1,000

Curr. Assets:	$0	Curr. Liab.:	$232,000		
Plant, Equip.:	NA	Total Liab.:	$879,000	Indic. Yr. Divd.:	NA
Total Assets:	$0	Net Worth:	-$879,000	Debt/ Equity:	NA

Movado Group Inc

650 From Rd., Paramus, NJ, 07652; **PH:** 1-201-267-8000; **Fax:** 1-201-267-8070;
http:// www.movadogroupinc.com

General - Incorporation	NY	**Stock**- Price on:12/24/2007	$33.49
Employees	1,300	Stock Exchange	NYSE
Auditor	PricewaterhouseCoopers LLP	Ticker Symbol	MOV
Stk Agt	Bank of New York	Outstanding Shares	25,920,000
Counsel	Paul Weiss Rifkind Wharton & Garrison	E.P.S.	$2.03
DUNS No.	04-619-5103	Shareholders	NA

Business: The group's principal activity is to design, manufacture and distribute quality watches. The group conducts its business primarily in two operating segments: wholesale and retail. The wholesale segment includes the designing, manufacturing and distribution of quality watches. The retail segment includes the movado boutiques and outlet stores. The group operates internationally through its wholly owned subsidiaries in Switzerland, France, Hong Kong, Canada, Japan and Singapore. On 01-Mar-2004, the group acquired ebel s. A.

Primary SIC and add'l.: 5094 3873

CIK No: 0000072573

Subsidiaries: Concord Deutschland G.m.b.H., Concord Watch Company, S.A., Ebel Watches S.A., EWC Marketing Corp., MGI International, Ltd, MGI Japan Co., Ltd., MGI Luxury Group G.m.b.H., MGI Luxury Group UK Ltd., MGI Luxury Group, S.A., Movado Deutschland G.m.b.H., Movado Group Delaware Holdings Corporation, Movado Group of Canada, Inc., Movado International, Ltd., Movado LLC, Movado Retail Group, Inc. 21 Subsidiaries included in the Index

Officers: Efraim Grinberg/Dir., CEO, Pres./$2,204,936.00, Richard J. Cote/Dir., Exec. VP, COO/$1,457,490.00, Eugene J. Karpovich/Sr. VP, CFO/$509,558.00, Frank V. Kimick/VP, Treasurer, Assist. Sec., Timothy F. Michno/Sec., General Counsel/$458,297.00, Suzanne J. Rosenberg/Dir. - Corporate Communications

Directors: Efraim Grinberg/Dir., CEO, Pres., Gedalio Grinberg/Chmn., Alan H. Howard/Dir., Richard J. Cote/Dir., Exec. VP, COO, Richard D. Isserman/Dir., Margaret Hayes Adame/Dir., Nathan Leventhal/Dir., Donald Oresman/Dir., Leonard L. Silverstein/Dir.

Owners: Eugene J. Karpovich, Alan H. Howard, Dimensional Fund Advisors LP/8.00%, Barclays/5.50%, Efraim Grinberg/6.10%, AXA Mutuelle/5.90%, Miriam Phalen, Donald Oresman, Insiders/12.00%, Gedalio Grinberg, Nathan Leventhal, Timothy F. Michno, Donald Oresman, Alexander Grinberg, Margaret Hayes Adame (22 Owners included in Index)

Financial Data: Fiscal Year End:01/31   **Latest Annual Data:** 1/31/2007

Year	Sales	Net Income
2007	$532,865,000	$50,138,000
2006	$470,941,000	$26,617,000
2005	$418,966,000	$26,307,000

Curr. Assets:	$472,879,000	Curr. Liab.:	$89,457,000	P/E Ratio:	18.20
Plant, Equip.:	$56,823,000	Total Liab.:	$198,794,000	Indic. Yr. Divd.:	$0.320
Total Assets:	$577,618,000	Net Worth:	$378,381,000	Debt/ Equity:	NA

Move Inc

Formerly: Homestore Inc
30700 Russell Ranch Rd. , Westlake Village, CA, 91362; **PH:** 1-805-557-2300;
http:// www.homestore.com

General - Incorporation	DE	**Stock**- Price on:12/24/2007	$4.5
Employees	1,666	Stock Exchange	NDQ
Auditor	Ernst & Young LLP	Ticker Symbol	NA
Stk Agt	Mellon Investor Services LLC	Outstanding Shares	154,980,000
Counsel	NA	E.P.S.	$0.12
DUNS No.	NA	Shareholders	NA

Business: The group's principle activity is to provide an online service for home and real estate-related information, products and media services. The group operates in three segments namely, media services, software and print. The media services segment provides products and services that promote and connect real estate professionals to consumers through their websites such as realtor.com(R), homebuilder.com, rentnet.com and homestore.com. The software segment includes property listing management and customer relationship management applications for realtors(R), multiple listing services and home builders. The print segment provides new-mover advertising products, sales of new home plans and related magazines.

Primary SIC and add'l.: 7319 6531 8999 7371 6719 7375

CIK No: 0001085770

Subsidiaries: 3041776 Nova Scotia Company, GTKY Printing& Mailing Corp., HomeBuilder.com (Delaware), Inc., Homestore Europe Corporation, Homestore International Limited (BVI), Immoclick Online S.A., InteliQ, LLC, Move Sales, Inc., Move, Inc., Movedotcom (UK) Limited, Moving.com, Inc., National New Homes Co., Inc., RealSelect, Inc., The Enterprise of America, Ltd., Top Producer Systems Company 18 Subsidiaries included in the Index

Officers: Michael W. Long/Dir., CEO/$4,382,467.00, Lewis R. Belote/CFO/$1,483,527.00, Allan D. Dalton/Pres. - Move new Business Venture/$1,736,474.00, Jack D. Dennison/51/COO/$2,075,550.00, Lorna M. Borenstein/Pres., James S. Caulfield/Exec. VP, General Counsel, Sec., Eric G. Thorkilsen/Pres. - Move, Related Services Division, Errol Samuelson/Pres. - Realtorcom, R, Top Producer Systems, Mollie O'Brien/Primary Investor Relations Officer

Directors: Michael W. Long/Dir., CEO, Joe F. Hanauer/70/Chmn., John L. Doerr/Dir., Geraldine B. Laybourne/Dir., Roger B. McNamee/Dir., Fred D. Anderson/Dir., Kenneth K. Klein/Dir., Alan Yassky/72/Dir., Paul V. Unruh/Dir., Bruce G. Willison/Dir., William E. Kelvie/Dir.

Owners: Fred D. Anderson/13.86%, Mazama Capital Management, Inc/8.75%, FMR Corp./11.49%, National Association of REALTORS, Jack D. Dennison/2.04%, TCS Capital GP, LLC/8.83%, Paul V. Unruh, Michael W. Long/4.46%, Bruce G. Willison, Alan Yassky, Alan Yassky/2.48%, Fred D. Anderson, Insiders, Insiders, Insiders/25.90% (29 Owners included in Index)

Financial Data: Fiscal Year End:12/31   **Latest Annual Data:** 12/31/2006

Year	Sales	Net Income
2006	$290,384,000	$22,105,000
2005	$252,622,000	$545,000
2004	$216,860,000	-$7,886,000

Curr. Assets:	$210,595,000	Curr. Liab.:	$83,621,000	P/E Ratio:	50.00
Plant, Equip.:	$29,245,000	Total Liab.:	$184,497,000	Indic. Yr. Divd.:	NA
Total Assets:	$285,949,000	Net Worth:	$101,452,000	Debt/ Equity:	0.0152

Moventis Capital Inc

1959-152nd St., Ste. 304, White Rock, BC, V4A 9P3; **PH:** 1-604-535-3900; **Fax:** 1-604-357-1266;
http:// www.moventiscapital.com; **Email:** info@moventiscapital.com

General - Incorporation	DE	**Stock**- Price on:12/24/2007	$0.45
Employees	NA	Stock Exchange	OTC
Auditor	Smythe Ratcliffe LLP	Ticker Symbol	MVTS
Stk Agt	Signature Stock Transfer, Inc.	Outstanding Shares	NA
Counsel	NA	E.P.S.	NA
DUNS No.	NA	Shareholders	NA

Business: The groups principal activities include acquiring and controlling interests in businesses through asset acquisition, capital stock exchange or similar business combination. The group operates from the United States and Canada.

Primary SIC and add'l.: 6799 6726

CIK No: 0001104734

Officers: Blake Ponuick/Chmn., CEO, Tom Gill/Dir., CFO, Corp. Sec., Travis Taylor/Dir. - Corporate Development, Nicole Croizier/Dir. - Marketing, Communication, Iain Mant/Legal Counsel, David Katz/Legal Counsel, Matt Clawson/Investor Contact

Directors: Blake Ponuick/Chmn., CEO, Tom Gill/Dir., CFO, Corp. Sec., Fraser Atkinson/Dir., Marlene Schluter/Dir., Mark Reed/Member - Advisory Board, Miljenko Horvat/Member - Advisory Board, George Dorin/Member - Advisory Board

Owners: Chad Lee/5.20%, Insiders/53.50%, Walter Kloeble/1.50%, Fraser Atkinson/4.80%, Marlene Schluter/10.50%, Blake Ponuick/17.80%, Stanley Ross/15.00%

Financial Data: Fiscal Year End:06/30   **Latest Annual Data:** 6/30/2006

Year	Sales	Net Income
2006	NA	-$740,000
2005	NA	-$474,000
2004	$1,000	-$369,000

Curr. Assets:	$116,000	Curr. Liab.:	$126,000		
Plant, Equip.:	$9,000	Total Liab.:	$126,000	Indic. Yr. Divd.:	NA
Total Assets:	$125,000	Net Worth:	-$1,000	Debt/ Equity:	1.1474

Movie Gallery Inc

900 W Main St., Dothan, AL, 36301; **PH:** 1-334-677-2108; **Fax:** 1-334-794-4688;
http:// www.moviegallery.com

General - Incorporation	DE	**Stock**- Price on:12/24/2007	$2.3699
Employees	7,900	Stock Exchange	OTC
Auditor	Ernst & Young LLP	Ticker Symbol	MOVIQ
Stk Agt	American Stock Transfer & Trust Co.	Outstanding Shares	31,890,000
Counsel	NA	E.P.S.	-$11.794
DUNS No.	13-965-1384	Shareholders	NA

Business: The groups principle activity is to operate home entertainment retail stores. The group operates three store brands namely Movie Gallery, Hollywood Video and Game Crazy. In the year 2007, the group acquired MovieBeam, Inc. The group operates from United States.

Primary SIC and add'l.: 5735 7841

CIK No: 0000925178

Subsidiaries: Concord Deutschland G.m.b.H., Concord Watch Company, S.A., Ebel Watches S.A., EWC Marketing Corp., Hollywood Entertainment Corp., M.G. Digital, LLC, M.G.A Realty I, LLC, MG Automation LLC, MGI International, Ltd., MGI Japan Co., Ltd., MGI Luxury Group G.m.b.H., MGI Luxury Group UK Ltd., MGI Luxury Group, S.A., Movado Deutschland G.m.b.H., Movado Group Delaware Holdings Corporation 28 Subsidiaries included in the Index

Officers: J. T. Malugen/Chmn., CEO, Pres./$2,993,898.00, Harrison H. Parrish/Vice Chmn., Sr. VP - Concessions, Thomas D. Johnson/CFO, Exec. VP/$596,657.00, Keith A. Cousins/Exec. VP, Chief Development Officer/$738,064.00, Mark S. Loyd/Exec. VP, Chief Merchandising Officer, Jeffrey S. Stubbs/Pres. - Retail Operations/$801,364.00, Page S. Todd/Exec. VP, Sec., General Counsel, Chief Compliance Officer/$829,347.00

Directors: J. T. Malugen/Chmn., CEO, Pres., Harrison H. Parrish/Vice Chmn., Sr. VP - Concessions, William B. Snow/Dir., John J. Jump/Dir., James C. Lockwood/Dir.

Owners: John J. Jump, William B. Snow, Insiders/16.20%, LaGrange Capital Partners, L.P./6.50%, Schultze Master Fund, Ltd./12.90%, Joe T. Malugen/11.20%, Keith A. Cousins, Thomas D. Johnson, Page S. Todd, Harrison H. Parrish/3.10%, Jeffrey S. Stubbs, James C. Lockwood

Financial Data: *Fiscal Year End:*01/01 *Latest Annual Data:* 12/31/2006

Year	Sales	Net Income
2006	$2,541,933,000	-$25,720,000
2005	$791,177,000	$49,488,000

Curr. Assets:	$239,311,000	Curr. Liab.:	$268,117,000		
Plant, Equip.:	$582,916,000	Total Liab.:	$1,389,708,000	Indic. Yr. Divd.:	NA
Total Assets:	$1,153,277,000	Net Worth:	-$236,431,000	Debt/ Equity:	NA

Movie Star Inc

1115 Broadway, 11th Fl., New York, NY, 10010; *PH:* 1-212-684-3400; *Fax:* 1-212-684-3295; *http://* www.moviestarinc.com

General - Incorporation	NY	**Stock**- Price on:12/24/2007	$2.6
Employees	297	Stock Exchange	AMEX
Auditor	Mahoney Cohen & Co	Ticker Symbol	MSI
Stk Agt	American Stock Transfer & Trust Co	Outstanding Shares	16,420,000
Counsel	NA	E.P.S.	-$0.02
DUNS No.	05-154-5200	Shareholders	NA

Business: The group's principal activities are to design, manufacture, market and sell ladies' ready to wear apparels and screen-printed t-shirts. Ladies' ready to wear apparels include pajamas, nightgowns, short sets, beachwear, leisurewear, rompers and undergarments. The group markets its products through discount, specialty, national and regional chain stores, mass merchandise and department stores and direct mail catalog marketers. Registered trademarks of the group include movie star, movie star loungewear, cinema etoile, cine jour, night magic, private property and heather nicole. On 04-Aug-2004, the company acquired sidney bernstein & son lingerie, inc.

Primary SIC and add'l.: 5621 2321 2341 2331

CIK No: 0000093631

Subsidiaries: Cinejour Lingerie, Inc.

Officers: Melvyn Knigin/Chmn., CEO, Pres., Thomas Rende/CFO, Saul Pomerantz/Dir., Exec. VP, COO, Sec.

Directors: Melvyn Knigin/Chmn., CEO, Pres., Abraham David/78/Founder, Michael A. Salberg/Dir., John L. Eisel/Dir., Peter Cole/Dir., Saul Pomerantz/Dir., Exec. VP, COO, Sec., Joel M. Simon/Dir.

Owners: Michael A. Salberg, Insiders/5.90%, Joel M.Simon, John L. Eisel, Milton J. Walters, Thomas Rende/1.40%, Rose Peabody Lynch, Melvyn Knigin/1.20%, Tokarz Investments, LLC/29.40%, Linda LoRe/1.50%, Saul Pomerantz/2.80%, TTG Apparel, LLC/8.80%, Fursa Alternative Strategies LLC/29.40%, Peter Cole/1.10%

Financial Data: *Fiscal Year End:*06/30 *Latest Annual Data:* 6/30/2006

Year	Sales	Net Income
2006	$51,639,000	-$1,000,000
2005	$58,533,000	-$3,122,000
2004	$53,691,000	$128,000

Curr. Assets:	$16,944,000	Curr. Liab.:	$7,354,000		
Plant, Equip.:	$943,000	Total Liab.:	$7,733,000	Indic. Yr. Divd.:	NA
Total Assets:	$22,338,000	Net Worth:	$14,605,000	Debt/ Equity:	NA

Moving Bytes Inc

100 Wall St., 15th Fl., New York, NY, 10005; *PH:* 1-212-232-0120

General - Incorporation	Canada	**Stock**- Price on:12/24/2007	$0.105
Employees	NA	Stock Exchange	NA
Auditor	Kabani & Co.,Inc.	Ticker Symbol	NA
Stk Agt	Pacific Corporate Trust Co	Outstanding Shares	NA
Counsel	NA	E.P.S.	NA
DUNS No.	NA	Shareholders	NA

Business: The group's principle activities are to market and sell telecommunication voice and data, electronic customer relationship management, electronic document delivery and Internet marketing solutions. The group operates in two segments: telecommunication services and electronic media services. Telecommunication services consist of traditional 1+ and 800 (toll free) telecommunication services, data services and audio conferencing. Electronic media services provide email and fax electronic document delivery services to organizations of all sizes. The group sells the services through independent companies that sell, lease, install and service telephone and other telecommunication equipment to end users. These services are operational twenty-four hours a day, seven days a week. The brand names of the group are moving bytes and gooeymail.

Primary SIC and add'l.: 7375 4899

CIK No: 0001085104

Subsidiaries: California corporation, Moving Bytes Broadband Corporation, USV Telemanagement, Inc

Officers: Yang Kuidong/CEO, Yuan Qing Li/39/Chmn., Pres./$14,877.00, Ding Hong Shen/39/CFO, Chief Accounting Officer, Qing Biao Yu/40/Sec.

Directors: Yuan Qing Li/39/Chmn., Pres., Xiao Kang An/57/Dir.

Owners: Yuan Qing Li/2.40%, Insiders/23.50%, Yang Kuidong/18.50%, Zhang Liwei/5.00%

Financial Data: *Fiscal Year End:*12/31 *Latest Annual Data:* 12/31/2006

Year	Sales	Net Income
2006	$2,151,000	$94,000
2005	$1,880,000	$171,000
2004	$61,000	-$434,000

Curr. Assets:	$2,047,000	Curr. Liab.:	$301,000		
Plant, Equip.:	$312,000	Total Liab.:	$301,000	Indic. Yr. Divd.:	NA
Total Assets:	$2,359,000	Net Worth:	$2,058,000	Debt/ Equity:	NA

MPC Corp

Formerly: HyperSpace Communications Inc

906 E Karcher Rd., Nampa, ID, 83687; *PH:* 1-208-893-3434; *http://* www.ehyperspace.com

General - Incorporation	CO	**Stock**- Price on:12/24/2007	NA
Employees	680	Stock Exchange	NA
Auditor	Ehrhardt Keefe Steiner & Hottman P.C	Ticker Symbol	NA
Stk Agt	Computershare Trust Co	Outstanding Shares	NA
Counsel	NA	E.P.S.	-$4.6
DUNS No.	NA	Shareholders	NA

Business: The group's principle activity is to provide computer products and services. The group manufactures desktop, notebook, server and storage products. The group's products sold under the brand name ClientPro(R), TransPort(R), MPC Rack Optimized Servers and MPC NAS Storage Solutions. The groups markets include mid-sized businesses, government agencies and education organizations. The group operates from United States.

Primary SIC and add'l.: NA

CIK No: 0001289871

Subsidiaries: GTG PC Holdings, LLC, MPC Computers, LLC, MPC Solutions Sales, LLC, Mpc-g, LLC

Officers: John P. Yeros/Chmn., CEO, Pres., Jeff Fillmore/51/COO, Sr. VP - MPC Computers, LLC, Ross Ely/Exec. VP - Sales, Marketing, Curtis M. Akey/CFO, Doug Ellis/VP - Supply Chain Operations, MPC, Joyce M. Popp/VP - Information Technology, Web Operations, Glenda Smith/VP - Service Operations, Jody Sitts/Area VP - Human Resources

Directors: John P. Yeros/Chmn., CEO, Pres., Eric D. Murphy/47/Dir., David A. Young/63/Dir., Kent Swanson/63/Dir.

Owners: David J. Lies, Longview Fund, LP, Kent L. Swanson, Enable Growth Partners LP, Adam M. Lerner, GTG PC Investments Inc., Eric D. Murphy, John P. Yeros, Jeffrey E. Fillmore, David A. Young, Whalehaven Capital Fund Limited, Toibb Investment LLC, MIC Holding Company, LLC, Crestview Capital Master, LLC, Insiders (20 Owners included in Index)

Financial Data: *Fiscal Year End:*12/31 *Latest Annual Data:* 12/31/2006

Year	Sales	Net Income
2006	$284,971,000	-$58,716,000
2005	$187,496,000	-$16,741,000
2004	$458,000	-$3,121,000

Curr. Assets:	$80,582,000	Curr. Liab.:	$91,091,000		
Plant, Equip.:	$4,914,000	Total Liab.:	$143,560,000	Indic. Yr. Divd.:	NA
Total Assets:	$122,437,000	Net Worth:	-$21,123,000	Debt/ Equity:	NA

mPhase Technologies Inc

150 Clove Rd., Little Falls, NJ, 07424; *PH:* 1-973-256-3737; *Fax:* 1-973-256-9387; *http://* www.mphasetech.com; *Email:* info@mphasetech.com

General - Incorporation	NJ	**Stock**- Price on:12/24/2007	$0.118
Employees	23	Stock Exchange	OTC
Auditor	Rosenberg Rich Baker Berman & Co	Ticker Symbol	XDSL
Stk Agt	Jersey Transfer & Trust Co	Outstanding Shares	361,760,000
Counsel	Piper Rudnick LLP	E.P.S.	-$0.078
DUNS No.	NA	Shareholders	NA

Business: The group's principal activity is to design, develop, manufacture and market high-bandwidth telecommunications products. The group's products enable telephone companies and telecommunications service providers to provide up to 384 channels of digital television and high-speed Internet and voice simultaneously. The products include traverser digital video and data delivery system (dvdds), pots splitter shelves, intelligent pots splitter and universal bypass, mphasestretch and microfilters. The group also provides contracts, licensing agreements, marketing and legal support to service providers interested in deploying television over DSL through mphase television.net, inc.

Primary SIC and add'l.: 3669

CIK No: 0000825322

Subsidiaries: mPhaseTV.net, Inc., TLI Industries, Inc.

Officers: Ronald A. Durando/Dir., CEO, Pres., Philip Thompson/Exec. VP - Product Management, Tim Clemensen/Primary Investor Relations Officer, Mary K. Whelan/Exec. VP - Marketing, Communications, Martin S. Smiley/Dir., CFO, Exec. VP, General Counsel, Steve Simon/Exec. VP - Engineering, Research, Development, Gustave T. Dotoli/Dir., Exec. VP, COO

Directors: Ronald A. Durando/Dir., CEO, Pres., Necdet F. Ergul/Chmn., Martin S. Smiley/Dir., CFO, Exec. VP, General Counsel, Gustave T. Dotoli/Dir., Exec. VP, COO

Owners: Abraham Biderman/0.56%, Gus Doteli/4.39%, Microphase Corp/5.84%, Ron Durando/8.76%, Anthony Guerino/0.22%, Janifast LTD/4.78%, Ned Ergul/1.73%, Martin Smiley/2.74%

Financial Data: *Fiscal Year End:*06/30 *Latest Annual Data:* 6/30/2006

Year	Sales	Net Income
2006	$975,000	-$24,451,000
2005	$1,711,000	-$11,234,000
2004	$4,641,000	-$7,759,000

Curr. Assets:	$1,694,000	Curr. Liab.:	$2,788,000		
Plant, Equip.:	$350,000	Total Liab.:	$2,788,000	Indic. Yr. Divd.:	NA
Total Assets:	$2,182,000	Net Worth:	-$606,000	Debt/ Equity:	NA

MPLC Inc

42 Corp. Pk., Ste. 250, Irvine, CA, 92606; *PH:* 1-949-777-3700; *http://* www.mplc.com

General - Incorporation: DE
Employees: NA
Auditor: Carlin, Charron & Rosen LLP
Stk Agt: NA
Counsel: NA
DUNS No.: 60-718-3753

Stock - Price on:12/24/2007: NA
Stock Exchange: OTC
Ticker Symbol: MPLCF
Outstanding Shares: NA
E.P.S.: -$0.43
Shareholders: NA

Business: The group's principle activity is to provide publication of children's fiction and non-fiction books in hardcover and paperback for schools, libraries and consumer markets. The company's books have been placed on numerous recommended lists by libraries, retail bookstores, and educational organizations. The company publishes books under the millbrook, copper beech and twenty-first century imprints. The books published under the millbrook imprint includes a mix of highly graphic, consumer oriented books. Majority of copper beech books are published for both the consumer and the library markets. Twenty-first century books titles are published primarily for the educational market at a secondary school level. Roaring brook press, the company's new fiction imprint, publishes children's picture books and young peoples novels for both the school and library and trade markets. The group operates from United States.

Primary SIC and add'l.: 2731

CIK No: 0001022899

Officers: David Allen/CEO, CFO, Pres., Sec., Burton Katz/36/Dir., CEO/$170,127.00, Raymond Musci/47/Dir., Pres./$307,500.00, Issac Kier/Dir., Pres., Sec., Treasurer, Allan Legator/37/CFO, Sec./$231,888.00, Scott Walker/46/Chief Marketing Officer/$411,788.00, Shane Maidy/Sr. VP - Marketing, Licensing/$184,247.00

Directors: Burton Katz/36/Dir., CEO, Raymond Musci/47/Dir., Pres., Drew Larner/43/Dir., Robert S. Ellin/43/Dir., Barry I. Regenstein/51/Dir., Issac Kier/Dir., Pres., Sec., Treasurer, Jerome Chazen/80/Dir.

Owners: Trinad Capital Master Fund, Ltd., Drew Larner, Raymond Musci, Insiders, Brad Greenspan, Sue Swenson, Robert S. Ellin, Gil Klier, Allan Legator, Destar, LLC, Jeffrey Akres, Scott Walker, Jerome Chazen, Barry I. Regenstein, Burton Katz *(17 Owners included in Index)*

Financial Data: **Fiscal Year End:**07/31 **Latest Annual Data:** 7/31/2006

Year	Sales	Net Income
2006	NA	-$78,000
2005	NA	-$94,000

Curr. Assets:	$4,965,000	**Curr. Liab.:**	$4,271,000		
Plant, Equip.:	$146,000	**Total Liab.:**	$4,271,000	**Indic. Yr. Divd.:**	NA
Total Assets:	$5,494,000	**Net Worth:**	$1,223,000	**Debt/ Equity:**	NA

MPM Technologies Inc

199 Pomeroy Rd., Parsippany, NJ, 07054; ***PH:*** 1-973-428-5009; ***Fax:*** 1-973-428-5027; ***http://*** www.mpmtech.com

General - Incorporation: WA
Employees: 7
Auditor: Rosenberg Rich Baker Berman & Co
Stk Agt: TranSecurities International, Inc
Counsel: NA
DUNS No.: 15-651-2733

Stock - Price on:12/24/2007: $0.51
Stock Exchange: OTC
Ticker Symbol: MPML
Outstanding Shares: 6,260,000
E.P.S.: -$0.57
Shareholders: NA

Business: The group's principal activities are to design, engineer, supply and service air pollution control systems using heat, chemicals and wet and dry scrubbers. The group's operating segments are: air pollution control (heat) and air pollution control (scrubber). The group also develops waste-to-energy process system known as skygas. This process system converts solid and semi-solid wastes like municipal solid waste, municipal sewage sludge, pulp, auto fluff and medical waste into a clean burning medium btu gas. The btu gas can be used for steam production for electric power generation and building block for downstream conversion into valuable chemicals. The group operates in the United States and other foreign countries.

Primary SIC and add'l.: 3822 3564

CIK No: 0000799268

Subsidiaries: AirPol, Inc., Environmental Systems Inc., MPM Mining Inc, Nupower, Inc.

Officers: Michael J. Luciano/Chmn., CEO, Frank E. Hsu/COO, Robert D. Little/Corp. Sec.

Directors: Michael J. Luciano/Chmn., CEO

Owners: Richard Kao/1.03%, Frank E. Hsu/3.14%, Michael J. Luciano/64.89%, Robert D. Little/4.60%, Craig Cary L. Smith/4.26%, Richard E. Appleby/3.37%, Glen Hjort/1.87%, Insiders/86.43%

Financial Data: **Fiscal Year End:**12/31 **Latest Annual Data:** 12/31/2006

Year	Sales	Net Income
2006	$1,729,000	-$1,652,000
2005	$1,959,000	$1,898,000
2004	$1,850,000	-$1,905,000

Curr. Assets:	$566,000	**Curr. Liab.:**	$6,455,000		
Plant, Equip.:	$1,081,000	**Total Liab.:**	$10,286,000	**Indic. Yr. Divd.:**	NA
Total Assets:	$2,082,000	**Net Worth:**	-$8,204,000	**Debt/ Equity:**	NA

Mpower Holding Corp

175 Sully, Ste. 300, Pittsford, NY, 14534; ***PH:*** 1-585-218-6550; ***http://*** www.mpowercom.com

General - Incorporation: DE
Employees: NA
Auditor: Deloitte & Touche LLP
Stk Agt: Continental Stock Transfer & Trust Co
Counsel: NA
DUNS No.: NA

Stock - Price on:12/24/2007: NA
Stock Exchange: NA
Ticker Symbol: NA
Outstanding Shares: NA
E.P.S.: NA
Shareholders: NA

Business: The group's principle activity is to provide voice and high-speed data services using symmetrical digital subscriber line and trunk level 1 technology. The services include Internet access, local and long distance voice service, Web hosting and custom email. The services are provided to small and medium-sized business customers with a full suite of communications services and features integrated on one bill with the convenience of a single source provider. These services are marketed through direct sales offices, telemarketing and programs with agents and vendors.

Primary SIC and add'l.: 4813 4899

CIK No: 0001117042

Subsidiaries: CDM On-Line, Inc., Mpower Communications Central Corp, Mpower Communications Corp, Mpower Communications of NY, Corp., Mpower Communications of VA, Inc., Mpower Holding Corporation - Registrant, Mpower Management Corp, Primary Network Holdings, Inc., Q-Networks, Inc.

MPS Group Inc

1 Independent Dr., Ste. 2500, Jacksonville, FL, 32202; ***PH:*** 1-904-360-2000; ***Fax:*** 1-904-360-2972; ***http://*** www.mpsgroup.com; ***Email:*** investors@mpsgroup.com

General - Incorporation: FL
Employees: 2,800
Auditor: PricewaterhouseCoopers LLP
Stk Agt: SunTrust Bank
Counsel: Leboeuf, Lamb, Greene & Macrae
DUNS No.: 09-660-2008

Stock - Price on:12/24/2007: $13.18
Stock Exchange: NYSE
Ticker Symbol: MPS
Outstanding Shares: 102,530,000
E.P.S.: $0.82
Shareholders: NA

Business: The groups principle activities include staffing, consulting, and solutions for the information technology, finance and accounting, law, engineering, marketing and creative, property and healthcare industries. In the year 2007 the group acquired The Paladin Companies, Inc. The group operates from United States.

Primary SIC and add'l.: 7389 7371

CIK No: 0000924646

Subsidiaries: Accounting Principals, Inc., Alderson Reporting Company, Inc., Amicus Staffing, Inc., Badenoch and Clark Limited, Beeline International Company, Beeline Operations Corp., Beeline.com, Inc., Data Management Consultants, Inc., Entegee, Inc., First Shore, Inc., Idea Integration Corp., Idea.com, Inc., LIT, Inc., Modis Consulting Partners, Inc., Modis International Co. 31 Subsidiaries included in the Index

Officers: Timothy D. Payne/CEO, Pres./$2,696,924.00, Robert P. Crouch/39/CFO, Sr. VP, Treasurer/$1,327,928.00, Richard L. White/49/CIO, Sr. VP/$733,820.00, Gregory D. Holland/42/Sr. VP, Chief Legal Officer, Sec./$573,528.00, Tyra H. Tutor/39/Nior VP - Corporate Development/$438,894.00

Directors: Derek E. Dewan/53/Chmn., Peter J. Tanous/69/Dir., Wayne T. Davis/61/Dir., John R. Kennedy/77/Dir., Michael D. Abney/72/Dir., William M. Isaac/64/Dir., Darla D. Moore/53/Dir., Arthur B. Laffer/67/Dir.

Owners: T. Rowe Price Associates, Inc./7.16%, Tyra H. Tutor/0.11%, John R. Kennedy/0.15%, William M. Isaac/0.23%, Timothy D. Payne/1.14%, Barclay Global Investors, NA/7.20%, Arthur B. Laffer/0.14%, Richard L. White/0.22%, Goldman Sachs Asset Management, L.P./5.82%, Peter J. Tanous/0.16%, Michael D. Abney/0.10%, Darla D. Moore/0.15%, Derek E. Dewan/0.21%, T. Wayne Davis/0.57%, Dimensional Fund Advisors LP/8.16% *(18 Owners included in Index)*

Financial Data: **Fiscal Year End:**12/31 **Latest Annual Data:** 12/31/2006

Year	Sales	Net Income
2006	$1,876,622,000	$75,214,000
2005	$1,684,699,000	$59,597,000
2004	$1,426,842,000	$35,420,000

Curr. Assets:	$479,922,000	**Curr. Liab.:**	$161,043,000	**P/E Ratio:**	16.90
Plant, Equip.:	$28,472,000	**Total Liab.:**	$178,981,000	**Indic. Yr. Divd.:**	NA
Total Assets:	$1,142,279,000	**Net Worth:**	$963,298,000	**Debt/ Equity:**	NA

MR3 Systems Inc

883 Sneath Ln., Ste. 222, San Bruno, CA, 94066; ***PH:*** 1-415-947-1090; ***Fax:*** 1-415-723-7022; ***http://*** www.mr3systems.com; ***Email:*** info@mr3systems.com

General - Incorporation: DE
Employees: NA
Auditor: Pohl, McNabola, Berg & Co LLP
Stk Agt: Computershare Trust Co
Counsel: Frank J. Hariton Esq
DUNS No.: NA

Stock - Price on:12/24/2007: $0.01
Stock Exchange: OTC
Ticker Symbol: MRMR
Outstanding Shares: NA
E.P.S.: NA
Shareholders: NA

Business: The group's principal activity is to develop technology for metal extraction and recovery. It includes research in microbiology on how microbial cells efficiently acquire their essential nutrient metals such as calcium, copper, zinc, etc. The group's technology has applications like recovery of precious metals from ore and concentrates, processing of industrial wastes into purified metals and specialty chemical products and environmental remediation of hazardous metals from contaminated sites. It developed a proprietary process for the recovery, separation and purifying of a range of metals.

Primary SIC and add'l.: NA

CIK No: 0001133541

Subsidiaries: Bioponic AGS, Inc., Bioponic International, Tech Mining, LLC.

Officers: Randall S. Reis/64/Chmn., Sec., Frank J. Hariton/Corporate Counsel, Jody J. Sitkoski/45/Sr. VP, Lorraine Artinger/Contact - Corporate, Joseph S. Jaswinski/Sr. VP - Environmental Remediation

Directors: Randall S. Reis/64/Chmn., Sec.

Financial Data: **Fiscal Year End:**12/31 **Latest Annual Data:** 12/31/2004

Year	Sales	Net Income
2004	$380,000	-$2,360,000
2003	NA	-$1,649,000

Curr. Assets:	$81,000	**Curr. Liab.:**	$1,606,000		
Plant, Equip.:	$510,000	**Total Liab.:**	$2,403,000	**Indic. Yr. Divd.:**	NA
Total Assets:	$594,000	**Net Worth:**	-$1,809,000	**Debt/ Equity:**	NA

MRU Holdings Inc

1114 Ave. Of The Americas, 30th Fl., New York, NY, 10036; ***PH:*** 1-212-754-0774; ***http://*** www.mruholdings.com

General - Incorporation: DE
Employees: 70
Auditor: Bagell, Josephs, Levine & Co. LLC
Stk Agt: American Stock Transfer & Trust Co.
Counsel: NA
DUNS No.: NA

Stock - Price on:12/24/2007: $6.6
Stock Exchange: NDQ
Ticker Symbol: UNCL
Outstanding Shares: 25,400,000
E.P.S.: -$1.25
Shareholders: NA

Business: The group's principal activity is to provide students with funds for higher education. It has a unique approach of analyzing future income potential to profile and provide customized financial products to students. The group also provides consulting and student loan services to entities and individuals. The group targets students with high-income prospectus and provides them with private student loans, loan guarantees and education investments. The group operates solely in the domestic market.

Primary SIC and add'l.: 6111

CIK No: 0001145202

Subsidiaries: Iempower, Inc, MRU Funding SPV, Inc, MRU Lending Holdco, LLC, MRU Lending, Inc, MRU Originations, Inc, MRU Universal Guaranty Agency, Inc., Nomura Credit & Capital, Inc.

Officers: Edwin McGuinn/Chmn., CEO, Raza Khan/Co - Founder, Pres., Assist. Sec., Dir., Vishal Garg/Co - Founder, Dir., CFO, Sec., Denise Gillen/VP - Investor Relations, Karin Pellmann/VP - Public Relations

Directors: Edwin McGuinn/Chmn., CEO, Raza Khan/Co - Founder, Pres., Assist. Sec., Dir., Vishal Garg/Co - Founder, Dir., CFO, Sec., David C. Bushley/Dir., Richmond T. Fisher/Dir., Andrew D. Mathieson/Dir., Michael Brown/Dir., Sunil Dhaliwal/Dir.

Owners: BlackRock, Inc./10.54%, Andrew Mathieson, Y&S Nazarian Revocable Trust/5.92%, Insiders/26.52%, Perry Corp./5.25%, Raza Khan/12.71%, Richmond T. Fisher, Battery Partners VII, LL/15.61%, Vishal Garg/12.40%, Edwin J. McGuinn/2.68%, Jonathan Coblentz, C. David Bushley

Financial Data: Fiscal Year End:06/30 Latest Annual Data: 6/30/2006

Year	Sales	Net Income
2006	$1,244,000	-$24,989,000
2005	$239,000	-$4,071,000
2004	$8,000	-$1,871,000

Curr. Assets:	$60,017,000	Curr. Liab.:	$21,113,000		
Plant, Equip.:	$537,000	Total Liab.:	$41,172,000	Indic. Yr. Divd.:	NA
Total Assets:	$62,735,000	Net Worth:	$21,562,000	Debt/ Equity:	NA

MRV Communications Inc

20415 Nordhoff St., Chatsworth, CA, 91311; **PH:** 1-818-773-0900; **Fax:** 1-818-773-0906; **http://** www.mrv.com; **Email:** ir@mrv.com

General - Incorporation	DE	**Stock**- Price on:12/24/2007	$3.07
Employees	1,450	Stock Exchange	NYSE
Auditor	Ernst & Young LLP	Ticker Symbol	MRX
Stk Agt	American Stock Transfer & Trust Co.	Outstanding Shares	125,970,000
Counsel	K & L Nicholson Graham LLP	E.P.S	-$0.13
DUNS No.	19-202-1608	Shareholders	NA

Business: The group's principal activities are to design, manufacture, sell, distribute, integrate and support network infrastructure equipment and services and optical components. The group conducts business through three segments: networking group, optical components group and development stage enterprise group. The networking group provides equipment used by commercial customers, governments and telecommunications service providers. The optical components group designs, manufactures and sell optical communications components, primarily through our wholly owned subsidiary luminent, inc. The development stage enterprise group seeks to develop new optical components, subsystems and networks and other products for the infrastructure of the Internet. It has operations in Argentina, China, Denmark, France, Finland, Germany, Israel, Japan and the United Kingdom.

Primary SIC and add'l.: 3674 6719

CIK No: 0000887969

Subsidiaries: Alcadon AB, Charlottes Networks, Inc., Creative Electronic Systems SA, EDSLan SpA, Interdata, LuminentOIC, Inc., MRV Communications Boston Division, Inc., MRV Communications GmbH, MRV International, Ltd., Tecnonet SpA, TurnKey Communications AG

Officers: Noam Lotan/Dir., CEO, Pres./$416,063.00, Shlomo Margalit/Chmn., CTO, Sec./$117,096.00, Near Margalit/VP - Marketing, Business Development/$390,979.00, Kevin Rubin/33/CFO/$369,030.00, Michael Blust/32/VP - Finance/$242,650.00, Guy Avidan/Acting CFO

Directors: Noam Lotan/Dir., CEO, Pres., Shlomo Margalit/Chmn., CTO, Sec., Daniel Tsui/Dir., Igal Shidlovsky/Dir., Baruch Fischer/Dir., Guenter Jaensch/Dir., Harold W. Furchtgott-Roth/Dir.

Owners: Kevin Rubin, Igal Shidlovsky, Noam Lotan/1.30%, Harold Furchtgott-Roth, Wells Fargo& Company/5.50%, Daniel Tsui, Guenter Jaensch, Insiders/4.70%, Baruch Fischer, Sun Life Inc./6.20%, Michael Blust, Near Margalit, Deutsche Bank/7.30%, Shlomo Margalit/2.60%

Financial Data: Fiscal Year End:12/31 Latest Annual Data: 12/31/2006

Year	Sales	Net Income
2006	$356,489,000	-$5,515,000
2005	$283,698,000	-$16,299,000
2004	$271,658,000	-$10,680,000

Curr. Assets:	$289,514,000	Curr. Liab.:	$116,927,000		
Plant, Equip.:	$14,172,000	Total Liab.:	$147,222,000	Indic. Yr. Divd.:	NA
Total Assets:	$346,222,000	Net Worth:	$193,752,000	Debt/ Equity:	0.1190

MSC Industrial Direct Co Inc

75 Maxess Rd., Melville, NY, 11747; **PH:** 1-516-812-2000; **Fax:** 1-516-349-1301; **http://** www.MSCdirect.com

General - Incorporation	NY	**Stock**- Price on:12/24/2007	$52.08
Employees	3,607	Stock Exchange	NYSE
Auditor	Ernst & Young LLP	Ticker Symbol	MSM
Stk Agt	Computershare Trust Co	Outstanding Shares	65,790,000
Counsel	Katten, Muchin, Zavis & Rosenman	E.P.S	NA
DUNS No.	93-261-9265	Shareholders	NA

Business: The group's principal activity is to market a broad range of industrial products to industrial customers throughout the United States. The products of the group include cutting tools, measuring instruments, tooling components, fasteners, flat stock, raw materials, abrasives, machinery hand and power tools, safety, janitorial, plumbing, material handling, power transmission, electrical supplies and other categories. The group distributes a full line of industrial products intended to satisfy its customers' maintenance, repair and operations supplies requirements. It offers 500,000 stock-keeping units through 4,475 page master catalog, weekly, monthly and quarterly specialty and promotional catalogs, newspapers and brochures. The group serves customers from approximately 90 branch offices and 4 distribution centers. The customers of the group include a range of purchasers of industrial supply products, from one-man machine shops to fortune 1,000 companies.

Primary SIC and add'l.: 5085 5084

CIK No: 0001003078

Subsidiaries: Anderson Industrial Supply,Inc., Brooks Precision Supply,Inc., Corbin Acquisition Corporation, Corbin Corporation, Corbin Integrated Services, Cut-Rite Tool Corp., D.T.C. Tool Corp., Discount Tool and Supply Company, Dolin Supply,Inc., Drake-Atwood Tool& Supply Company,Inc., Enco Manufacturing Co.,Inc., Holloway Bros. Tools,Inc., Industrial Specialty Company Incorporated, Industrial Specialty Company,Inc. of Tupelo, J&L America,Inc. 27 Subsidiaries included in the Index

Officers: David K. Sandler/50/Dir., CEO, Pres., Thomas Cox/46/Exec. VP - Sales, Shelley Boxer/60/VP - Finance, Thomas Eccleston/59/VP - Plant, Property, Corp. Sec., Charles Boehlke/51/Dir., CFO, Exec. VP, Eileen McGuire/42/Sr. VP - Human Resources, Erik Gershwind/36/Sr. VP - Product Management, Marketing, Douglas Jones/43/Sr. VP - Logistics, Charles Bonomo/42/CIO, VP

Directors: David K. Sandler/50/Dir., CEO, Pres., Mitchell Jacobson/56/Chmn., Charles Boehlke/51/Dir., CFO, Exec. VP, Roger Fradin/54/Dir., Raymond Langton/63/Dir., Denis Kelly/58/Dir., Philip Peller/68/Dir.

Owners: David Sandler, Marjorie Gershwind/18.80%, Marjorie Gershwind/1.20%, Roger Fradin, Charles Boehlke, Capital Research and Management Company/7.10%, Thomas Cox, Insiders/2.70%, Stacey Bennett, Eileen McGuire, Trust under Trust Agreement Dated September 12, 2005/6.20%, Mitchell Jacobson, Mitchell Jacobson/61.20%, Erik Gershwind, Philip Peller (20 Owners included in Index)

Financial Data: Fiscal Year End:08/27 Latest Annual Data: 05/26/2007

Year	Sales	Net Income
2007	NA	NA
2006	$1,317,519,000	$136,389,000
2005	$1,099,915,000	$112,270,000

Curr. Assets:	$411,389,000	Curr. Liab.:	$85,013,000	P/E Ratio:	21.88
Plant, Equip.:	$103,284,000	Total Liab.:	$111,181,000	Indic. Yr. Divd.:	$0.720
Total Assets:	$729,387,000	Net Worth:	$618,206,000	Debt/ Equity:	0.2734

MSC.Software Corp

2 MacArthur Pl., Santa Ana, CA, 92707; **PH:** 1-714-540-8900; **Fax:** 1-714-784-4056; **http://** www.mscsoftware.com

General - Incorporation	DE	**Stock**- Price on:12/24/2007	$13.02
Employees	1,234	Stock Exchange	NDQ
Auditor	Deloitte & Touche LLP	Ticker Symbol	MSFG
Stk Agt	Mellon Investor Services LLC	Outstanding Shares	43,880,000
Counsel	NA	E.P.S	$0.18
DUNS No.	NA	Shareholders	NA

Business: The groups principle activities include developing, marketing and supporting enterprise simulation solutions. The groups services include enterprise simulation automation, engineering consulting, funded development, and training and onsite support. The groups operates through two segments namely software and services. The products of the group include MSC Nastran, Patran, Adams, Marc, Dytran, Easy5 and SOFY. Specific customers of the group include Boeing, Airbus, BAE, Lockheed Martin, Nissan Motor, Toyota, Northrop Grumman and Honda. The group operates from Europe, Asia Pacific and America. The group's quarterly revenue for September 2007 was 57.19 millions of USD.

Primary SIC and add'l.: 7374 7372

CIK No: 0000717238

Subsidiaries: Compumod Sdn. Bhd., MSC (Beijing) Technical Service Co., Ltd., MSC International Company, MSC.Brasil Software e EngenhariaLtda., MSC.Flyer, LLC, MSC.Software (Singapore)Pte.Ltd., MSC.Software AS, MSC.Software Asia PtyLtd., MSC.Software Australia PtyLtd., MSC.Software Benelux B.V., MSC.Software Corporation India Private Limited, MSC.Software GmbH, MSC.Software Korea Corporation, MSC.Software Limited, MSC.Software S.r.l. 22 Subsidiaries included in the Index

Officers: William Weyand/Chmn., CEO/$3,107,534.00, Glenn Wienkoop/COO, Pres./$1,510,961.00, John Mongelluzzo/Sr. VP - Business Administration, General Counsel, Corp. Sec./$853,769.00, John Laskey/58/CFO, Exec. VP/$1,029,562.00, Amir A. Mobayen/Sr. VP - EMEA Operations, Christopher St. John/Sr. VP - Asia Pacific Operations, John Howaniec/Sr. VP - Americas Sales Operations, Frank Kovacs/VP - Strategic Alliances, Sam M. Auriemma/CFO, Exec. VP, Reza Sadeghi/CTO, Douglas Peterson/Sr. VP - Product Development

Directors: William Weyand/Chmn., CEO, Donald Glickman/Dir., William F. Grun/Dir., Ashfaq Munshi/Dir., George N. Riordan/Dir., Randolph H. Brinkley/Dir.

Owners: MSD Capital L.P./7.20%, Glenn R. Wienkoop, William J. Weyand/1.83%, Silver Point Capital, L.P./9.72%, William F. Grun, Donald Glickman, ICM Asset Management, Inc./5.08%, Insiders/3.00%, John A. Mongelluzzo, George N. Riordan, Morgan Stanley/6.64%, John J. Laskey

Financial Data: Fiscal Year End:12/31 Latest Annual Data: 12/31/2006

Year	Sales	Net Income
2006	$259,686,000	$13,802,000
2005	$295,637,000	$11,818,000
2004	$277,296,000	$10,879,000

Curr. Assets:	$219,600,000	Curr. Liab.:	$121,240,000	P/E Ratio:	130.20
Plant, Equip.:	$19,055,000	Total Liab.:	$147,930,000	Indic. Yr. Divd.:	NA
Total Assets:	$458,838,000	Net Worth:	$310,908,000	Debt/ Equity:	0.0223

MSGI Security Solutions Inc

575 Madison Ave., 10th Fl., New York, NY, 10022; **PH:** 1-917-339-7150; **Fax:** 1-917-339-7166; **http://** msgisecurity.com; **Email:** info@msgisecurity.com

General - Incorporation	NV	**Stock**- Price on:12/24/2007	NA
Employees	8	Stock Exchange	OTC
Auditor	Amper, Politziner & Mattia P.C	Ticker Symbol	MSGI
Stk Agt	Continental Stock Transfer & Trust Co	Outstanding Shares	NA
Counsel	NA	E.P.S	-$0.112
DUNS No.	NA	Shareholders	NA

Business: The group's principal activity is to provide proprietary solutions to develop a global combination of innovative emerging businesses that leverage information and technology. The group provides solutions to homeland security, surveillance industry and the media sector. The group was providing telemarketing and telefundraising services. In Mar 2004, the group discontinued its telemarketing and telefunding business. On 19-Aug-2004, the group acquired majority interest in innalogic llc.

Primary SIC and add'l.: 7389

CIK No: 0000014280

Subsidiaries: Future Developments America, Inc., Innalogic LLC, MSGI Italia

Officers: Jeremy J. Barbera/Chmn., CEO, Richard J. Mitchell/Chief Accounting Officer, Joseph Peters/Dir., Pres., Robert A. Martin/Sr. Security Advisor, Carl Ottersen/Dir. - European Operations, Chris Witty/Contact Information

Directors: Jeremy J. Barbera/Chmn., CEO, David Stoller/57/Dir., John T. Gerlach/75/Dir., Seymour Jones/76/Dir., Joseph Peters/Dir., Pres.

Owners: Insiders/17.80%, Jeremy J. Barbera/10.70%, Coda Octopus Group, Inc./8.24%, Seymour Jones/1.00%, Richard Mitchell/1.50%, Anyuser, Inc./8.39%, Joseph Peters/2.90%, David Stoller, John Gerlach/1.00%

Financial Data: *Fiscal Year End:*06/30 *Latest Annual Data:* 06/30/2006

Year	Sales	Net Income
2006	$127,000	-$17,586,000
2005	$812,000	-$6,756,000
2004	NA	-$3,311,000

Curr. Assets:	$3,535,000	**Curr. Liab.:**	$3,250,000		
Plant, Equip.:	$20,000	**Total Liab.:**	$5,907,000	**Indic. Yr. Divd.:**	NA
Total Assets:	$4,879,000	**Net Worth:**	-$1,028,000	**Debt/ Equity:**	NA

MSX International Inc

1950 Concept Dr., Warren, MI, 48091; *PH:* 1-248-299-1000; *Fax:* 1-248-829-6130; *http://* www.msxi.com

General - Incorporation	DE	**Stock**- Price on:12/24/2007	NA
Employees	NA	Stock Exchange	NA
Auditor	Grant Thornton LLP	Ticker Symbol	NA
Stk Agt	JP Morgan Chase Bank, N.A.	Outstanding Shares	NA
Counsel	NA	E.P.S	NA
DUNS No.		Shareholders	NA

Business: The group's principle activity is to provide outside staffing, engineering and business services, including technical and professional staffing services, engineering, design and related technical services and other business and marketing services principally to the automotive industry. New registrant. The group operates from United States.

Primary SIC and add'l.: 7363

CIK No: 0001059274

Subsidiaries: Chelsea Computer Consultants, Inc., Intranational Computer Consultants, Management Resources International, Inc., MegaTech Engineering, Inc., Millennium Computer Systems, Inc., MSX International (Holdings), Inc., MSX International Australia Pty Limited, MSX International Business Services France, MSX International Canada Limited, MSX International DealerNet Services B.V., MSX International DealerNet Services, Inc., MSX International do Brasil Ltda., MSX International Engineering GmbH, MSX International Engineering Services, Inc., MSX International European (Holdings), LLC 31 Subsidiaries included in the Index

Officers: Peter Leger/CEO, Pres., Bruce V. Culver/49/VP, Wolfgang P. Kurth/Sr. VP - Europe, Frederick K. Minturn/CFO, Exec. VP, Craig Schmelzer/59/VP

Owners: Erwin H. Billig/0.20%, Citicorp and affiliates/76.50%, Frederick K. Minturn/1.80%, Insiders/8.90%, Charles E. Corpening, Insiders/1.10%, Michael A. Delaney/1.50%, Erwin H. Billig/5.20%, Citicorp and affiliates/88.20%, Charles E. Corpening, Frederick K. Minturn, Michael A. Delaney/0.90%, Wolfgang Kurth

Msystems Ltd

Formerly: M-Systems Flash Disk Pioneers Ltd
7 Atir Yeda St., Kfar Saba, 44425; ; *http://* www.m-sys.com

General - Incorporation	Israel	**Stock**- Price on:12/24/2007	NA
Employees	NA	Stock Exchange	NA
Auditor	Ernst & Young LLP	Ticker Symbol	NA
Stk Agt	NA	Outstanding Shares	NA
Counsel	NA	E.P.S	NA
DUNS No.	60-000-7397	Shareholders	NA

Business: The group's principle activities are the development, manufacturing and distribution of data storage cards and disks for computers known as flash disks. The disks provide the functionality of a mechanical hard drive on a solid-state silicon chip. The group's products are based on its patented true flash file system (trueffs) technology and are mainly divided into the following types: diskonchip, used in embedded systems and Internet appliances; diskonkey, used in personal computers and laptops; fast flash disk (ffd), used in network infrastructure equipment.

Primary SIC and add'l.: 3572

CIK No: 0000895361

Subsidiaries: M-Systems (Cayman) Limited., M-Systems Asia Ltd., M-Systems B.V, M-Systems Finance Inc., M-Systems Flash Disk Pioneers (Japan), Inc., M-Systems Flash Disk Pioneers (Shenzhen) Trading Ltd., M-Systems Holdings LLC, M-Systems UK Ltd., M-Systems, Inc., M. Systems Flash Disk Pioneers Espana S.L.U., Microelectronica Espanola S.A.U., MR Flash L.P., MR Flash Ltd., P.P.S. von Koppen Pensioen B.V., TwinSys Data Storage L.P. 17 Subsidiaries included in the Index

MTC Technologies Inc

4032 Linden Ave., Dayton, OH, 45432; *PH:* 1-937-252-9199; *Fax:* 1-937-258-3863; *http://* www.modtechcorp.com

General - Incorporation	DE	**Stock**- Price on:12/24/2007	NA
Employees	2,800	Stock Exchange	NDQ
Auditor	Ernst & Young LLP	Ticker Symbol	MTCT
Stk Agt	Mellon Financial Services LLC	Outstanding Shares	15,150,000
Counsel	Jones, Day, Reavis & Pogue	E.P.S	$1.10
DUNS No.	NA	Shareholders	NA

Business: The group's principal activities are to provide systems engineering, information technology, intelligence operations and program management services. It offers a broad range of systems engineering services to enhance the functionality and performance of defense systems, weapons platforms, battlefield personnel and delivery systems. It also designs, develops, upgrades and integrates complex, mission-critical information technology systems. Services to intelligence agencies include designing, developing and managing reconnaissance platforms, real-time signal processing systems, sensors and ground stations and data links. Program management support services include services provided to extend the useful life of the existing defense systems and reduce life-cycle costs. The services are provided mainly to U.S. Defense, intelligence and civilian federal government agencies. In oct 2003, the group acquired international consultants inc and vitronics inc.

Primary SIC and add'l.: 7373

CIK No: 0001172243

Subsidiaries: AMCOMP Corporation, Command Technologies, Inc., International Consultants, Inc., Manufacturing Technology, Inc., MTC Guam, LLC, MTC Technologies, Inc., OnBoard Software, Inc., Vitronics Inc.

Officers: Rajesh K. Soin/Chmn., CEO, Michael I. Gearhardt/CFO, Exec. VP/$378,744.00, John E. Longhouser/Pres./$332,037.00, James C. Clark/Exec. VP/$320,291.00, Stephen T. Catanzarita/VP, Corporate Controller, Mark N. Brown/COO, Pres., Therese C. McNea/VP, Treasurer, Kerry Gentry/Contact - Business Development, Michael L. Cauldwell/Sr. VP, Robert D. Shuey/Sr. VP, Dir. - Legacy Systems Solutions Sector, Joseph F. Thumser/VP - Contracts, Bruce A. Teeters/VP, General Counsel, Sec., Daniel Bigelow/Contact - Investor Relations, Corporate Communications, Penny Viteo/Contact - Human Resources, Clifton A. Gilmore/Sr. VP

Directors: Rajesh K. Soin/Chmn., CEO, Lester L. Lyles/Dir., Lawrence A. Skantze/Dir., William E. MacDonald/Dir., Kenneth A. Minihan/Dir., Don R. Graber/Dir.

Owners: James C. Clark, Lawrence A. Skantze, Neuberger Berman, Inc. et al./12.20%, Insiders/38.40%, William E. MacDonald, Don R. Graber, Rajesh K. Soin/37.20%, Kenneth A. Minihan, Carlson Capital, LP/5.60%, TimesSquare Capital Management, LLC/5.40%, Lester L. Lyles, Schroder Investment Management North America, Inc./6.40%, John E. Longhouser, David S. Gutridge, Michael I. Gearhardt *(16 Owners included in Index)*

Financial Data: *Fiscal Year End:*12/31 *Latest Annual Data:* 12/31/2006

Year	Sales	Net Income
2006	$415,477,000	$18,671,000
2005	$373,284,000	$21,322,000
2004	$273,027,000	$17,661,000

Curr. Assets:	$121,953,000	**Curr. Liab.:**	$69,056,000		
Plant, Equip.:	$20,559,000	**Total Liab.:**	$155,426,000	**Indic. Yr. Divd.:**	NA
Total Assets:	$334,309,000	**Net Worth:**	$178,883,000	**Debt/ Equity:**	0.4705

MTI Technology Corp

Riverview House, Weyside Pk., Catteshall Lane, GU7 1XE; *PH:* 483-520-200; *Fax:* 483-520-222; *http://* www.mti.com

General - Incorporation	DE	**Stock**- Price on:12/24/2007	NA
Employees	302	Stock Exchange	OTC
Auditor	Grant Thornton LLP	Ticker Symbol	MTIC
Stk Agt	Mellon Investor Services LLC	Outstanding Shares	NA
Counsel	Morrison & Foerster LLP	E.P.S	-$0.495
DUNS No.	03-485-1535	Shareholders	NA

Business: The group's principal activity is to provide storage solutions for the mid-range enterprise market. The group serves third party hardware and software and its professional services organization provides planning, consulting and implementation support for storage products from other vendors. It has become a reseller and service provider of emc automated networked storagetm systems and software. The group supports and serves customers that continue to use mti-branded raid controller technology and partnered independent storage technology. It sells its solutions and services to global 2000 companies for their data center computing environments. The customers of the group include governmental agencies, Fortune 500 companies and small businesses. The group has international operations in Europe.

Primary SIC and add'l.: 3577 3572 7372

CIK No: 0000901696

Subsidiaries: MTI France SA, MTI Technology BV, MTI Technology BV-Irish Branch, MTI Technology GMBH, MTI Technology Ireland Ltd., MTI Technology Limited

Officers: Thomas P. Raimondi/Chmn., CEO, Pres., Scott Poteracki/CFO, Exec. VP, Edward Taylor/Exec. VP - US Services, Edward Kirnbauer/VP, Corporate Controller, Principal Accounting Officer

Directors: Thomas P. Raimondi/Chmn., CEO, Pres., Kent D. Smith/Dir., Franz L. Cristiani/Dir., Michael Pehl/Dir., Lawrence P. Begley/Dir., William Atkins/Dir., Ronald E. Heinz/Dir.

Owners: Edward C. Ateyeh, Thomas P. Raimondi, Keith Clark, Michael Pehl, Ronald E. Heinz, EMC Corporation, The Canopy Group, Inc, Franz L. Cristiani, Lawrence P. Begley, Scott Poteracki, Kent D. Smith, William J. Kerley, Insiders, Advent International Corporation

Financial Data: *Fiscal Year End:*04/03 *Latest Annual Data:* 4/1/2006

Year	Sales	Net Income
2006	$155,043,000	-$8,102,000
2005	$132,613,000	-$15,787,000
2004	$83,165,000	-$3,866,000

Curr. Assets:	$53,290,000	**Curr. Liab.:**	$53,017,000		
Plant, Equip.:	$710,000	**Total Liab.:**	$62,877,000	**Indic. Yr. Divd.:**	NA
Total Assets:	$70,553,000	**Net Worth:**	-$14,400,000	**Debt/ Equity:**	NA

MTM Technologies Inc

1200 High Ridge Rd., Stamford, CT, 06905; *PH:* 1-203-975-3700; *Fax:* 1-203-975-3701; *http://* www.mtm.com

General - Incorporation	NY	**Stock**- Price on:12/24/2007	$1
Employees	749	Stock Exchange	NYSE
Auditor	Goldstein Golub Kessler LLP	Ticker Symbol	MTN
Stk Agt	American Stock Transfer & Trust Co.	Outstanding Shares	11,860,000
Counsel	NA	E.P.S	-$2.13
DUNS No.	NA	Shareholders	NA

Business: The group's principal activities are to provide technology solutions, including design and consulting, communication services and products, Internet/intranet development services, network and security managed services. It also markets, installs and services microcomputers, microcomputer software products, supplies, accessories and custom designed microcomputer systems. The group operates through the following three segments: micros-to-mainframes, data.com and pivot technologies. The products of the group include printers, displays, plotters, software and other peripheral products, LAN and wan products and video conferencing products. The customers consist of clients in banking and finance, insurance, pharmaceutical, utility, technology, manufacturing, distribution and education and government sectors.

Primary SIC and add'l.: 7373 7379 7371

CIK No: 0000906282

Subsidiaries: Info Systems, Inc., MTM Technologies (Massachusetts), LLC., MTM Technologies (US), Inc.

Officers: Steven Stringer/COO, Pres., Michael Muehlberg/Sr. VP - Field Operations, Dave Shimp/Sr. VP - Human Resources, John Centinaro/Sr. VP - National Services, J. W. Braukman/Sr. VP, CFO, John Carne/CIO, Jed Ayres/VP - Partner Management, Marketing

Directors: Gerald A. Poch/Chmn., Richard R. Heitzmann/Dir., William Lerner/Dir., Thomas Wasserman/Dir., Alvin E. Nashman/Dir., Arnold J. Wasserman/Dir.

Owners: Arnold Wasserman, William Lerner, Insiders, Gerald A. Poch, Insiders, Steven Stringer, Clifford Rucker, Pequot Capital Management, Inc., Steven H. Rothman, Constellation Group, Gerald A. Poch, Alvin E. Nashman, J. W. Braukman, Howard A. Pavony, Pequot Capital Management, Inc. *(16 Owners included in Index)*

Financial Data: *Fiscal Year End:*03/31 *Latest Annual Data:* 3/31/2006

Year	Sales	Net Income
2006	$236,719,000	-$8,474,000
2005	$101,194,000	-$7,681,000
2004	$52,264,000	-$8,109,000

Curr. Assets:	$75,586,000	**Curr. Liab.:**	$64,882,000		
Plant, Equip.:	$15,942,000	**Total Liab.:**	$89,535,000	**Indic. Yr. Divd.:**	NA
Total Assets:	$166,253,000	**Net Worth:**	$76,718,000	**Debt/ Equity:**	0.4185

MTR Corp Ltd

Mtr Tower Telford Plz., 33 Wai Yip St., Kowloon Bay, Hong Kong; *PH:* 852-29932111; *http://* www.mtr.com.hk

General - Incorporation	Hong Kong	**Stock** - Price on:12/24/2007	$24.25
Employees	NA	Stock Exchange	OTC
Auditor	KPMG	Ticker Symbol	MTRJY
Stk Agt	Computershare Hong Kong Inv Srvcs	Outstanding Shares	NA
Counsel	Leonard B. Turk	E.P.S.	NA
DUNS No.	NA	Shareholders	NA

Business: The group's principle activities are to construct and to operate mass transit railway system in Hong Kong. The group is comprised of the mtr lines, consisting of the kwun tong line, tsuen wan line, island line, tung chung line and tseung kwan o line and the airport express line. Other activities include development and sale of residential and commercial properties with various third-party developers and manages, and in some cases owns certain developed properties. It also leases advertising and retail space, provides other services within the group network and operates the octopus smart card system which it uses to collect the majority of the fare revenue.

Primary SIC and add'l.: 1629 4119 7319 6552 4789

CIK No: 0001159204

Subsidiaries: Candiman Limited, Chongqing Premier Property Management Co. Ltd. (Incorporated), Fasttrack Insurance Ltd., Glory Goal Limited, Hong Kong Cable Car Limited, Lantau Cable Car Limited, MTR (Beijing) Commercial Facilities Management Co. Ltd. (Incorporated), MTR (Beijing) Property Services Co. Limited (Incorporated), MTR (Estates Management) Limited, MTR (Shanghai Metro Management) Limited, MTR (Shanghai Project Management) Limited, MTR Beijing Line 4 Investment Company Limited, MTR China Consultancy Company Limited, MTR China Property Limited, MTR Consultancy (Beijing) Co. Ltd. (Incorporated) 40 Subsidiaries included in the Index

Officers: Chung-Kong Chow/57/Dir., CEO, Alan Wong Chi-Kong/53/Non Exec. Dir. - Commissioner, Transport, Leonard Bryan Turk/58/Legal Dir., Sec., William Chan Fu-Keung/59/Dir. - Human Resources, S. H. Chau/Contact - Hong Kong Island, Y. Y. Yeung/Contact - Hong Kong Island, Richard Fung/Contact - Kowloon, New Territories, Andy Yeung/Contact, Andrew McCusker/62/Operations Dir., Thomas Ho Hang-Kwong/Property Dir., Francis Ka-Kui Lung/49/China, International Business Dir., Lincoln Leong Kwok-Kuen/47/Dir. - Finance, Russell John Black/61/Project Dir.

Directors: Chung-Kong Chow/57/Dir., CEO, Raymond Kuo-Fung Ch'Ien/56/Non Exec. Chmn., Lo Chung-Hing/56/Dir., David Gordon Eldon/62/Dir., Brian T. Stevenson/63/Dir., Cheung Yau-Kai/73/Dir., Eva Cheng/48/Non Exec. Dir., K. C. Chan/51/Non Exec. Dir., Christine Fang Meng-Sang/49/Dir., Edward Sing-Tin Ho/69/Non Exec. Dir., Alan Wong Chi-Kong/53/Non Exec. Dir. - Commissioner, Transport

Financial Data: *Fiscal Year End:*12/31 *Latest Annual Data:* 12/31/2005

Year	Sales	Net Income
2005	$1,180,737,000	$731,946,000
2004	$1,073,939,000	$498,196,000

Curr. Assets:	$497,424,000	**Curr. Liab.:**	$499,746,000	**P/E Ratio:**	5.18
Plant, Equip.:	$11,948,754,000	**Total Liab.:**	$5,284,485,000	**Indic. Yr. Divd.:**	NA
Total Assets:	$12,404,511,000	**Net Worth:**	$7,120,026,000	**Debt/ Equity:**	NA

MTR Gaming Group Inc

Rte. 2 Chester, W Virginia 26034, Chester, WV, 26034; *PH:* 1-304-387-5712; *Fax:* 1-304-387-2167; *http://* www.mtrgaming.com

General - Incorporation	DE	**Stock** - Price on:12/24/2007	$15.29
Employees	3,500	Stock Exchange	NDQ
Auditor	Ernst & Young LLP	Ticker Symbol	MNTG
Stk Agt	Continental Stock Transfer & Trust Co	Outstanding Shares	27,550,000
Counsel	NA	E.P.S.	$0.02
DUNS No.	18-200-0430	Shareholders	NA

Business: The group's principal activity is to own and operate gaming and hotel properties in west Virginia and Nevada. Through subsidiaries, the group owns and operates the mountaineer racetrack & gaming resort in chester, west Virginia and the ramada inn and speedway casino in north las vegas, Nevada. The resort complex offers video lottery gaming areas, a thoroughbred horse racetrack, parimutuel wagering, 359 hotel rooms, a convention center, and the harvey e. Arneault entertainment center. The ramada inn and speedway casino property includes a 95-room hotel and a casino with approximately 400 slot machines and seven table games. On 31-Jul-2003, the group acquired scioto downs, inc.

Primary SIC and add'l.: 7997 7011 7948 7993

CIK No: 0000834162

Subsidiaries: Jackson Racing,Inc., Mountaineer Park,Inc., MTRHarness,Inc., Presque Isle Downs,Inc., Scioto Downs,Inc., Speakeasy Fremont Street Experience Operating Company, Speakeasy Gaming of Fremont,Inc., Speakeasy Gaming of Las Vegas,Inc.

Officers: Edson R. Arneault/Chmn., CEO, Pres./$3,135,670.00, Richard Knight/CEO, Pres., GM - Presque Isle Downs, Inc, Dawn Clayton/Exec. VP - Gaming Operations, Mountaineer Park, Inc, John W. Bittner/CFO/$259,224.00, Rose Mary Williams/Sec., William H. Robinson/COO, VP - Nevada Properties, Patrick J. Arneault/VP - Mountaineer, Presque Isle Downs/$254,846.00, David R. Hughes/Exec. VP - Strategic Operations/$344,071.00, Kenneth P. Zern/Chief Accounting Officer, Steven D. Overly/VP - Business, Legal Affairs

Directors: Edson R. Arneault/Chmn., CEO, Pres., Robert A. Blatt/Vice Chmn., Donald J. Duffy/Dir., Richard Delatore/Dir., James V. Stanton/Dir., L. C. Greenwood/Dir.

Owners: Patrick J. Arneault, John W. Bittner, Edson R. Arneault/7.80%, Donald J. Duffy, The Richard E. Jacobs Revocable Trust/12.98%, Insiders/12.24%, James V. Stanton, Steven D. Overly, Richard Knight, Rose Mary Williams, Robert A. Blatt/3.41%, Litespeed Management LLC/5.33%

Financial Data: *Fiscal Year End:*12/31 *Latest Annual Data:* 12/31/2006

Year	Sales	Net Income
2006	$372,834,000	$4,446,000
2005	$349,915,000	$7,769,000
2004	$310,604,000	$14,455,000

Curr. Assets:	$54,401,000	**Curr. Liab.:**	$60,381,000	**P/E Ratio:**	764.50
Plant, Equip.:	$377,926,000	**Total Liab.:**	$350,843,000	**Indic. Yr. Divd.:**	NA
Total Assets:	$479,207,000	**Net Worth:**	$122,984,000	**Debt/ Equity:**	2.8596

MTS Medication Technologies Inc

2003 Gandy Blvd. N, Ste. 800, St. Petersburg, FL, 33702; *PH:* 1-727-576-6311; *Fax:* 1-727-573-1100; *http://* www.mtsp.com; *Email:* ir@mts-mt.com

General - Incorporation	DE	**Stock** - Price on:12/24/2007	$12.25
Employees	200	Stock Exchange	AMEX
Auditor	Grant Thornton LLP	Ticker Symbol	MPP
Stk Agt	Continental Stock Transfer & Trust Co	Outstanding Shares	6,130,000
Counsel	Holland & Knight LLP	E.P.S.	NA
DUNS No.	NA	Shareholders	NA

Business: The group's principal activities are to manufacture and sell disposable medication punch cards, packaging equipment and allied ancillary products throughout the United States. The proprietary products are manufactured through a process that uses integrated machinery for manufacturing the disposable medication punch cards. The disposable medication punch cards and packaging equipment are designed to provide a cost-effective method for pharmacies to dispense medications. The medication dispensing systems and products provide innovative methods for dispensing medications in disposable packages. The customers of the group are predominantly pharmacies that supply nursing homes, assisted living and correctional facilities with prescription medications for their patients. The group is presently directing its product development efforts towards ondemand(tm) packaging machines and various products for the assisted living and home care markets.

Primary SIC and add'l.: 3565 6719

CIK No: 0000823560

Subsidiaries: BAF Printers, Ltd., MTS Packaging Systems, Inc.

Officers: Todd E. Siegel/50/Chmn., CEO, Pres./$383,318.00, Ronald M. Rosenbaum/VP - Technology, Michael D. Stevenson/VP, COO/$246,710.00, Michael P. Conroy/CFO/$242,372.00, Dennis H. Ayo/Sr. VP - Sales, Marketing/$210,619.00, Robert Ropoza/Accounting Mgr. - CA, Mark Sampson/National Sales Mgr. - TX, Richard Warner/Accounting Mgr. - OK, Perry Larson/VP - Sales, Marketing/$148,654.00, Robert Barrett/VP - Software Development, Customer Support, Teresa Dunbar/39/Controller, Stephanie Mueller/Contact - Investor Relations, Stacie Wright/Sr. Customer Care Specialist, Antonio Rubalcava/Customer Care Specialist - Oregon, Duc Luong/Customer Care Specialist - Nebraska *(22 Officers included in Index)*

Directors: Todd E. Siegel/50/Chmn., CEO, Pres., John Stanton/Vice Chmn., Allen Braswell/50/Dir., Irv I. Cohen/57/Dir., David W. Kazarian/66/Dir.

Owners: John Stanton/1.40%, Boston Partners Asset Management, L.L.C./6.10%, Dennis H. Ayo/1.30%, Michael D. Stevenson/2.60%, David W. Kazarian, Perry W. Larson, Michael P. Conroy, Todd E. Siegel/27.30%, Insiders/33.90%, Allen S. Braswell

Financial Data: *Fiscal Year End:*03/31 *Latest Annual Data:* 03/31/2007

Year	Sales	Net Income
2007	$51,095,000	$2,531,000
2006	$42,522,000	$1,652,000
2005	$40,224,000	$1,294,000

Curr. Assets:	$14,510,000	**Curr. Liab.:**	$6,595,000		
Plant, Equip.:	$5,015,000	**Total Liab.:**	$10,649,000	**Indic. Yr. Divd.:**	NA
Total Assets:	$23,082,000	**Net Worth:**	$12,433,000	**Debt/ Equity:**	0.7854

MTS Systems Corp

14000 Technology Dr., Eden Prairie, MN, 55344; *PH:* 1-952-937-4000; *Fax:* 1-952-937-4515; *http://* www.mts.com; *Email:* info@mts.com

General - Incorporation	MN	**Stock** - Price on:12/24/2007	$43.19
Employees	1,510	Stock Exchange	NDQ
Auditor	KPMG LLP	Ticker Symbol	MTSN
Stk Agt	Wells Fargo Shareowner Services	Outstanding Shares	17,740,000
Counsel	Robins, Kaplan, Miller & Ciresi LLP	E.P.S.	$2.28
DUNS No.	00-645-2312	Shareholders	NA

Business: The group's principal activities are to provide hardware, software and engineering services to researchers, designers and manufacturers. The group's operations are organized into two business segments: the mechanical testing and simulation ('mt&s') segment and the factory automation ('fa') segment. The mechanical testing segment manufactures and markets systems for vehicle and component manufacturers to aid in the acceleration of design development work and to decrease the cost of product manufacturing. The systems also aid the customers in quality control and offers highly customized systems primarily for simulation and manufacturing. The factory automation segment manufactures and markets products for high performance industrial machine applications and displacement and liquid level sensors used to monitor and automate industrial processes. The group has operations in the United States, Europe and Asia.

Primary SIC and add'l.: 8711 3829 3823

CIK No: 0000068709

Subsidiaries: MTS (Japan) Ltd., MTS Automotive Sensors GmbH, MTS Holdings France, SARL, MTS Korea, Inc., MTS Sensor Technologie GmbH and Co. KG, MTS Sensor Technologie und Verwaltungs-GmbH, MTS Sensors Technology K.K., MTS Systems (China) Inc., MTS Systems (Hong Kong) Inc., MTS Systems Beteiligungs-GmbH, MTS Systems GmbH, MTS Systems Ltd., MTS Systems Norden AB, MTS Systems SAS, MTS Systems srl 16 Subsidiaries included in the Index

Officers: Sidney W. Emery/Chmn., CEO, Joachim Hellwig/VP - Sensors Division, Kathleen M. Staby/VP - Human Resources, Susan E. Knight/CFO, VP, Laura B. Hamilton/COO, Pres., John R. Houston/Sec., Paul Runice/Treasurer, Dir. - Investor Relations

Directors: Sidney W. Emery/Chmn., CEO, Merlin E. Dewing/Dir., Barbara J. Samardzich/Dir., Jean-Lou Chameau/Dir., Brendan C. Hegarty/Dir., Lois M. Martin/Dir., Ricardo Artigas/Dir.

Owners: Brendan C. Hegarty, Kathleen M. Staby, Lois M. Martin, Sidney W. Emery/2.00%, Joachim Hellwig, Insiders/3.60%, Laura B. Hamilton, Merlin E. Dewing, Jean-Lou Chameau, Susan E. Knight, Barclays Global Investors/5.40%, Ricardo Artigas, T. Rowe Price Associates, Inc/6.50%, Barb J. Samardzich, Royce & Associates/5.80% *(16 Owners included in Index)*

Financial Data: *Fiscal Year End:*09/28 *Latest Annual Data:* 9/30/2006

Year	Sales	Net Income
2006	$396,785,000	$39,323,000
2005	$374,377,000	$37,058,000
2004	$366,969,000	$28,983,000

Curr. Assets:	$272,328,000	**Curr. Liab.:**	$130,798,000	**P/E Ratio:**	19.81
Plant, Equip.:	$43,614,000	**Total Liab.:**	$154,802,000	**Indic. Yr. Divd.:**	$0.600
Total Assets:	$324,123,000	**Net Worth:**	$169,321,000	**Debt/ Equity:**	NA

Mueller Industries Inc

8285 Tournament Dr., Ste. 150, Memphis, TN, 38125; ***PH:*** 1-901-753-3200; ***Fax:*** 1-901-753-3250; ***http://*** www.muellerindustries.com

General - Incorporation .... DE
Employees 4,700
Auditor .... Ernst & Young LLP
Stk Agt .... Continental Stock Transfer & Trust Co
Counsel .... NA
DUNS No. 62-203-1748

Stock - Price on:12/24/2007 .... $34.91
Stock Exchange .... NYSE
Ticker Symbol .... MLI
Outstanding Shares 37,040,000
E.P.S. $2.47
Shareholders .... NA

Business: The groups principle activity is to manufacture copper, brass, plastic, and aluminum products. The groups products include copper tube and fittings, brass and copper alloy rod, bar, and shapes, aluminum and brass forgings, aluminum and copper impact extrusions, plastic fittings and valves, refrigeration valves and fittings, and fabricated tubular products. The group operates through two business segments namely the plumbing and refrigeration segment and the original equipment manufacturers segment. The group operates from United States.

Primary SIC and add'l.: 3089 3354 3494 3351 3463 3432

CIK No: 0000089439

Subsidiaries: Aegis Oil & Gas Leasing Ltd., Amwest Exploration Company, Arava Exploration Company, Arava Natural Resources Company, Inc., B & K Industries, Inc., Bayard Mining Corporation, Brasscapri Limited, Brassware Sales Limited, Canco Oil & Gas Ltd., Carpentertown Coal & Coke Company, DENO Acquisition EURL, DENO Holding Company, Inc., DENO Investment Company II, Inc., DENO Investment Company, Inc., Instox Limited 85 Subsidiaries included in the Index

Officers: William D. O'Hagan/Dir., CEO, Pres./$3,595,448.00, Gary C. Wilkerson/VP, General Counsel, Sec., Kent A. McKee/CFO, Exec. VP/$1,286,224.00, Roy C. Harris/65/CIO, VP, James H. Rourke/Pres. - Industrial Products, Gregory L. Christopher/Pres. - Standard Products/$1,185,685.00, Patrick W. Donovan/Pres. - European Operations/$730,232.00, Karl J. Bambas/47/VP - Tax, Richard W. Corman/51/VP, Controller, Jeffrey A. Martin/41/VP - Operations, Standard Products Division

Directors: William D. O'Hagan/Dir., CEO, Pres., Harvey L. Karp/Chmn., Alexander P. Federbush/Dir., Gennaro J. Fulvio/Dir., Terry Hermanson/Dir., Paul J. Flaherty/Dir., Gary S. Gladstein/Dir., Robert B. Hodes/82/Dir.

Owners: Jeffrey A. Martin, Roy C. Harris, Richard W. Corman, William D. OHagan/1.72%, Alexander P. Federbush, Gary S. Gladstein, Robert B. Hodes, Insiders/3.99%, Karl J. Bambas, Gary C. Wilkerson, James H. Rourke, Harvey L. Karp, Kent A. McKee, Terry Hermanson, Gregory L. Christopher *(16 Owners included in Index)*

Financial Data: ***Fiscal Year End:***12/31 ***Latest Annual Data:*** 12/30/2006

Year	Sales	Net Income
2006	$2,510,912,000	$148,869,000
2005	$1,729,923,000	$92,542,000
2004	$1,379,056,000	$79,416,000

Curr. Assets:	$611,986,000	**Curr. Liab.:**	$251,392,000	**P/E Ratio:**	11.60
Plant, Equip.:	$307,046,000	**Total Liab.:**	$674,793,000	**Indic. Yr. Divd.:**	$0.400
Total Assets:	$1,104,638,000	**Net Worth:**	$422,908,000	**Debt/ Equity:**	0.5099

Mueller Water Products Inc

1200 Abernathy Rd., Atlanta, GA, 30328; ***PH:*** 1-770-206-4200; ***Fax:*** 1-770-206-4235; ***http://*** www.muellerwaterproducts.com

General - Incorporation .... DE
Employees 6,800
Auditor .... PricewaterhouseCoopers LLP
Stk Agt .... Bank of New York
Counsel .... NA
DUNS No. .... NA

Stock - Price on:12/24/2007 .... $16.68
Stock Exchange .... NYSE
Ticker Symbol .... MWA
Outstanding Shares 114,770,000
E.P.S. $0.44
Shareholders .... NA

Business: The groups principle activity is to manufacture water infrastructure and flow products. The group operates from the United States. The groups quarterely revenue for September 2007 was 474.90 millinons of USD.

Primary SIC and add'l.: 3498 3492 3491

CIK No: 0001291000

Subsidiaries: Anvil International, LLC, Anvil International,Inc., AnvilStar, LLC, Henry Pratt Company, Henry Pratt International Ltd., Hersey Meters Co., Hydro Gate Acquisition Corp., J.B. Smith Mfg Co., James Jones Company, Jingmen Pratt Valve Co. Ltd., Milliken Acquisition Corp., Mueller Canada Holding Corp., Mueller Canada Ltd., Mueller Co., Mueller Financial Services, LLC 24 Subsidiaries included in the Index

Officers: Gregory E. Hyland/Chmn., CEO, Pres., Marietta Edmunds Zakas/Sr. VP - Strategic Planning, Investor Relations, Dale B. Smith/COO, Ray Torok/Pres. - US Pipe Segment, Thomas E. Fish/Pres. - Anvil Segment, Doyce Gaskin/VP - Manufacturing, Robert Barker/Exec. VP, General Counsel, Corp. Sec., Jeffery W. Sprick/Chief Accounting Officer, Sr. VP, Michael T. Vollkommer/CFO, Exec. VP, Robert P. Keefe/CIO, Sr. VP

Directors: Gregory E. Hyland/Chmn., CEO, Pres., Donald N. Boyce/Dir., Howard L. Clark/Dir., Jerry W. Kolb/Dir., Joseph B. Leonard/Dir., Mark J. O'Brien/Dir., Bernard G. Rethore/Dir., Neil A. Springer/Dir., Michael T. Tokarz/Dir.

Financial Data: ***Fiscal Year End:***09/30 ***Latest Annual Data:*** 12/31/2006

Year	Sales	Net Income
2006	NA	NA

Curr. Assets:	$935,200,000	**Curr. Liab.:**	$251,600,000		
Plant, Equip.:	$337,000,000	**Total Liab.:**	$1,762,900,000	**Indic. Yr. Divd.:**	$0.070
Total Assets:	$2,989,900,000	**Net Worth:**	$1,227,000,000	**Debt/ Equity:**	NA

Multi Color Corp

50 E- Business Way, Ste. 400, Sharonville, OH, 45241; ***PH:*** 1-513-381-1480; ***Fax:*** 1-513-381-2813; ***http://*** www.multicolorcorp.com

General - Incorporation .... OH
Employees 829
Auditor .... Grant Thornton LLP
Stk Agt .... Computershare Trust Co
Counsel .... NA
DUNS No. 12-129-8590

Stock - Price on:12/24/2007 .... $39.29
Stock Exchange .... NDQ
Ticker Symbol .... LABL
Outstanding Shares 6,670,000
E.P.S. $1.62
Shareholders .... NA

Business: The group's principal activities are to supply decorative label solutions and to provide packaging services to consumer product companies, national retailers and container manufacturers. The group operates in two divisions. The decorating solutions division produces in-mold labels and manufactures high-end pressure sensitive labels and shrink sleeves. The packaging services division provides promotional packaging, assembly and fulfillment services. The customers include manufacturers of home care, personal care, lawn care, automotive and food and beverage products. The group operates in the United States, Canada, Mexico, South America and Asia. On 16-Jul-2003, the group acquired heat transfer business of international playing card and label co inc.

Primary SIC and add'l.: 2759 2796 2754 7389

CIK No: 0000819220

Subsidiaries: Laser Graphic Systems, Inc., MCC-Batavia, LLC, MCC-Dec Tech, LLC, MCC-Finance, LLC, MCC-Norway, Inc., MCC-Quick Pak, LLC, MCC-Troy, LLC, MCC-Uniflex, LLC, MCC-Wisconsin, LLC

Officers: Francis D. Gerace/55/Dir., CEO, Pres./$1,373,222.00, Dawn H. Bertsche/51/Sr. VP - Finance, CFO, Sec./$673,107.00, Donald E. Kneir/44/Pres. - Decorating Solutions Division/$719,104.00, James H. Reynolds/42/VP, Corporate Controller, Chief Accounting Officer/$317,902.00

Directors: Francis D. Gerace/55/Dir., CEO, Pres., Lorrence T. Kellar/70/Chmn., Roger A. Keller/63/Dir., Charles B. Connolly/51/Dir., Robert B. Buck/60/Dir., Thomas M. Mohr/56/Dir.

Owners: Donald E. Kneir, Wellington Management Company, LLP/10.60%, Roger A. Keller/4.00%, Charles B. Connolly, John C. Court/6.50%, Thomas M. Mohr, Insiders/12.00%, James H. Reynolds, Francis D. Gerace/2.30%, Lorrence T. Kellar/3.10%, Dawn H. Bertsche/1.60%, Robert R. Buck, T. Rowe Price Associates, Inc./8.50%, Ashford Capital Management, Inc./9.70%

Financial Data: ***Fiscal Year End:***03/31 ***Latest Annual Data:*** 3/31/2007

Year	Sales	Net Income
2007	$222,374,000	$11,026,000
2006	$205,272,000	$9,633,000
2005	$139,466,000	$7,982,000

Curr. Assets:	$47,806,000	**Curr. Liab.:**	$31,974,000	**P/E Ratio:**	23.67
Plant, Equip.:	$45,790,000	**Total Liab.:**	$42,658,000	**Indic. Yr. Divd.:**	$0.200
Total Assets:	$107,081,000	**Net Worth:**	$64,423,000	**Debt/ Equity:**	NA

Multi Fineline Electronix Inc

3140 E Coronado St., Ste. A, Anaheim, CA, 92806; ***PH:*** 1-714-996-1248; ***Fax:*** 1-714-996-3834; ***http://*** www.mflex.com; ***Email:*** info@mflex.com

General - Incorporation .... DE
Employees 10,691
Auditor .... PricewaterhouseCoopers LLP
Stk Agt .... NA
Counsel .... NA
DUNS No. .... NA

Stock - Price on:12/24/2007 .... $16.27
Stock Exchange .... NDQ
Ticker Symbol .... MFLX
Outstanding Shares 24,550,000
E.P.S. $0.12
Shareholders .... NA

Business: The group's principal activity is to design and manufacture flexible printed circuit boards along with related component assemblies. These flexible printed circuits are used in mobile phones, smart mobile devices, portable bar code scanners, personal digital assistants, power supplies, and consumable medical sensors. The group's products consists of flexible printed circuit component assemblies found in rotating scanner, keypad, camera, hinge, display transformer, computer chip connector, track wheel. The customers of the group are original equipment manufacturers, electronics manufacturing service providers and display manufacturers of the electronics industry. The major customers of the group are motorola, symbol technologies inc, emc corporation, celestica inc and others. The products are marketed in the North America, China, Hong Kong, Japan, and Europe markets. The group has operations in United States and China.

Primary SIC and add'l.: 3679 3678 3672

CIK No: 0000830916

Subsidiaries: Aurora Optical, Inc., Multi-Fineline Electronix (Suzhou No. 2) Co., Ltd., Multi-Fineline Electronix (Suzhou) Co., Ltd.

Officers: Philip A. Harding/Chmn., CEO, Craig Riedel/CFO, Charles Tapscott/CTO, VP, Thomas Lee/VP - Operations, Reza Meshgin/COO, Pres.

Directors: Philip A. Harding/Chmn., CEO, Choon Seng Tan/Dir., Richard J. Dadamo/Dir., Peter Blackmore/Dir., Sam Yau/Dir., Sanford L. Kane/Dir., Huat-Seng Lim/Dir.

Owners: Richard J. Dadamo, Insiders/5.00%, Entities affiliated with WBL Corporation Limited/60.50%, Huat Seng Lim, Sam Yau, Peter Blackmore, Craig Riedel, Reza Meshgin, Charles Tapscott, Sanford L. Kane, Philip A. Harding/2.80%, Stark Investments and its affiliated hedge funds/18.40%, Thomas Lee

Financial Data: ***Fiscal Year End:***09/30 ***Latest Annual Data:*** 9/30/2007

Year	Sales	Net Income
2007	$508,147,000	$3,038,000
2006	$504,204,000	$40,357,000
2005	$357,090,000	$37,166,000

Curr. Assets:	$234,558,000	**Curr. Liab.:**	$127,077,000	**P/E Ratio:**	23.93
Plant, Equip.:	$133,633,000	**Total Liab.:**	$127,281,000	**Indic. Yr. Divd.:**	NA
Total Assets:	$377,287,000	**Net Worth:**	$250,006,000	**Debt/ Equity:**	NA

Multi Media Tutorial Services Inc

1214 E 15th St., Brooklyn, NY, 11230; ***PH:*** 1-800-872-6284; ***Fax:*** 1-718-758-3808; ***http://*** www.mathmadeeasy.com; ***Email:*** info@mmtsusa.com

General - Incorporation .... DE
Employees 26
Auditor .... Sherb & Co. LLP
Stk Agt .... NA
Counsel .... NA
DUNS No. 15-349-4257

Stock - Price on:12/24/2007 .... $0.11
Stock Exchange .... OTC
Ticker Symbol .... MMTS
Outstanding Shares 45,480,000
E.P.S. .... -$0.03
Shareholders .... NA

Business: The group's principal activities are to produce, acquire and distribute a variety of products to educational institutions and consumers using direct marketing through television, radio, print advertising and Internet advertising. The group's product provides proprietary tutorial education programs on videotape, DVD and CD rom for use by adults and children in homes, workplaces, schools, libraries

and other locales. The products consists of an extensive line of math made easy(tm) and reading made easy(tm) videotapes and ancillary material for direct sale to consumers. The math made easy(tm) product consist a series of over 100 videotapes, DVD's, CD roms and supplemental materials on mathematics. This product line uses colorful computer graphics and real life vignettes. The reading made easy(tm) products include reading readiness, letter identification, grammar and reading comprehension, which covers topics from preschool through junior high school.

Primary SIC and add'l.: 5735 8748

CIK No: 0000935496

Subsidiaries: Math Channel, Inc, Video Tutorial Service, Inc

Officers: Barry Reichman/57/Dir., CEO, CFO

Directors: Barry Reichman/57/Dir., CEO, CFO, Anne Reichman/54/Dir.

Owners: Barry Reichman/25.05%, Josh B. Scheinfeld/9.99%, Insiders/25.05%, Mike Lee/7.48%, Anne Reichman/25.05%

Financial Data: **Fiscal Year End:** 02/28 **Latest Annual Data:** 2/28/2007

Year	Sales	Net Income
2007	$787,000	-$823,000
2006	$1,136,000	-$449,000
2005	$878,000	-$433,000

Curr. Assets:	$124,000	**Curr. Liab.:**	$6,481,000		
Plant, Equip.:	$11,000	**Total Liab.:**	$6,527,000	**Indic. Yr. Divd.:**	NA
Total Assets:	$197,000	**Net Worth:**	-$6,331,000	**Debt/ Equity:**	NA

Multiband Corp

9449 Science Ctr. Dr., New Hope, MN, 55428; *PH:* 1-763-504-3000; *Fax:* 1-763-504-3060; *http://* www.multibandusa.com; *Email:* info@multibandusa.com

General - Incorporation	MN	**Stock** - Price on:12/24/2007	$0.57
Employees	88	Stock Exchange	NDQ
Auditor	Virchow, Krause & Co. LLP	Ticker Symbol	MBND
Stk Agt	Corporate Stock Transfer, Inc.	Outstanding Shares	35,410,000
Counsel	NA	E.P.S	-$1.62
DUNS No.	03-001-6992	Shareholders	NA

Business: The group's principle activities are to provide voice, data and video communications systems and service. It also provides system integration, training and related communication sales and support activities for commercial, professional and institutional customers. The group purchases products and equipment from nec America inc, siemens enterprise networks, cisco systems inc, nortel networks corp and uses it to design telecommunications systems to fit its customers' specific needs and demands. It operates through two operating divisionssegments: ctu and multiband usa. Ctu provides integrated voice, video, data networking and computer technologies products and services. Multiband usa provides voice, data, and video services to residential multi-dwelling units. The group's quarterly revenue for September 2007 was 3.65 millions of USD.

Primary SIC and add'l.: 3661 4899

CIK No: 0000732412

Subsidiaries: Corporate Technologies, USA, Inc, MB USA, Minnesota Digital Universe, Inc, Minnesota Digital, Inc, Multiband Subscriber Services, Inc, Multiband USA, Inc, Multiband, Inc., Rainbow Satellite Group, LLC, URON, Inc

Officers: James Mandel/Dir., CEO/$283,500.00, Steve Bell/49/CFO, Pres./$208,000.00, Dave Ekman/CIO/$150,000.00, Kent Whitney/COO, Sr. VP - Sales, Operations/$110,000.00

Directors: James Mandel/Dir., CEO, Donald Miller/68/Chmn., Eugene Harris/Dir., Frank Bennett/Dir., Jonathan Dodge/Dir.

Owners: Special Situations Fund II QP, LP/30.40%, Eugene Harris, David Ekman/5.10%, Frank Bennett/1.20%, James L. Mandel/3.10%, Marathon Capital Management, LLP/6.30%, Jonathan Dodge, Insiders/17.40%, Donald Miller/4.30%, Steven Bell/2.70%

Financial Data: **Fiscal Year End:** 12/31 **Latest Annual Data:** 12/31/2006

Year	Sales	Net Income
2006	$18,052,000	-$10,184,000
2005	$16,515,000	-$7,475,000
2004	$11,068,000	-$9,784,000

Curr. Assets:	$3,571,000	**Curr. Liab.:**	$8,865,000		
Plant, Equip.:	$4,604,000	**Total Liab.:**	$12,326,000	**Indic. Yr. Divd.:**	NA
Total Assets:	$17,986,000	**Net Worth:**	$5,659,000	**Debt/ Equity:**	NA

Multicell Technologies Inc

701 George Washington Hwy., Lincoln, RI, 02865; *PH:* 1-401-333-0610; *Fax:* 1-401-333-0659; *http://* www.multicelltech.com; *Email:* info@multicelltech.com

General - Incorporation	DE	**Stock** - Price on:12/24/2007	$0.076
Employees	8	Stock Exchange	OTC
Auditor	J. H. Cohn LLP	Ticker Symbol	MCET
Stk Agt	U.S. Stock Transfer Corp	Outstanding Shares	42,490,000
Counsel	NA	E.P.S	-$0.18
DUNS No.	NA	Shareholders	NA

Business: The group's principal activities is to focus on the development of cells, medical products and associated research and development activities. The group has two subsidiaries, multicell technologies, inc and xenogenics corporation. Multicell develops, sells and licenses hepatic or liver cells, cell lines, and associated products to be used in drug development, diagnostic and therapeutic applications. Xenogenics develops sybiol(R) bio-synthetic liver device, the key product of the group, which will not be ready to be marketed before the end of the year 2006, at the earliest. On 24-Mar-2004, the group acquired exten industries inc.

Primary SIC and add'l.: NA

CIK No: 0000811779

Subsidiaries: Exten Industries, Inc, MCT Rhode Island Corp., MultiCell Immunotherapeutics, Inc, Xenogenics Corporation

Officers: Stephen M. Chang/Dir., CEO, Pres., Gerald W. Newmin/Chmn., Acting CFO, Alan Tuchman/Member - Scientific Advisory Board

Directors: Stephen M. Chang/Dir., CEO, Pres., Gerald W. Newmin/Chmn., Acting CFO, Richard Houghten/Member - Scientific Advisory Board, Markus Grompe/Member - Scientific Advisory Board, John G. Coles/Member - Scientific Advisory Board, Mattias Von Herrath/Member - Scientific Advisory Board, Paul Grint/Member - Scientific Advisory Board, Thomas A. Page/Dir., Edward Sigmond/Dir., Anthony Altig/Dir., Sangeeta Bhatia/Member - Scientific Advisory Board, Douglas Hixson/Member - Scientific Advisory Board, Edward T. Maggio/Member - Scientific Advisory Board, Richard Ulevitch/Member - Scientific Advisory Board

Owners: Affiliated Entities of Asset Managers International, Ltd., La Jolla Cove Investors, Inc., Mercator Momentum Fund, LP, Insiders, Thomas A. Page, Gerald W. Newmin, Mercator Momentum Fund III, LP, Ronald A. Faris, Pentagon Special Purposes Fund, LTD, Edward Sigmond, Monarch Pointe Fund, LTD, Stephen Chang, David Firestone, Anthony Altig, Asset Managers International, LTD

Financial Data: **Fiscal Year End:** 11/30 **Latest Annual Data:** 11/30/2006

Year	Sales	Net Income
2006	$680,000	-$5,418,000
2005	$209,000	-$5,683,000
2004	$760,000	-$1,739,000

Curr. Assets:	$138,000	**Curr. Liab.:**	$1,163,000		
Plant, Equip.:	$132,000	**Total Liab.:**	$1,215,000	**Indic. Yr. Divd.:**	NA
Total Assets:	$1,505,000	**Net Worth:**	-$1,385,000	**Debt/ Equity:**	NA

Multimedia Games Inc

206 Wild Basin Rd., Bldg. B., 4th Fl., Austin, TX, 78746; *PH:* 1-512-334-7500; *Fax:* 1-512-334-7695; *http://* www.multimediagames.com; *Email:* investor.relations@mm-games.com

General - Incorporation	TX	**Stock** - Price on:12/24/2007	$12.7
Employees	503	Stock Exchange	NDQ
Auditor	BDO Seidman, LLP	Ticker Symbol	MGAM
Stk Agt	Corporate Stock Transfer, Inc.	Outstanding Shares	27,820,000
Counsel	NA	E.P.S	-$0.03
DUNS No.	NA	Shareholders	NA

Business: The groups principle activity is to provide gaming systems. The products of the group include player terminals, stand-alone player terminals, video lottery terminals, electronic scratch ticket systems, electronic instant lottery systems, player tracking systems and casino cash management systems. The group products sold under the trade names layers Passport(R), MGAMe(R) System, Reel Time Bingo(R), MegaNanza(R), MegaBingo(R), and MegaMania(R). The group operates from the United States. The group's quarterly revenue for September 2007 was 31.24 millions of USD.

Primary SIC and add'l.: 7999

CIK No: 0000896400

Subsidiaries: Innovative Sweepstakes Systems Inc., MegaBingo Inc., Megabingo International LLC, MGAM Services LLC, MGAM Systems Inc., MGAM Systems International Inc., Multimedia Games de Mexico S. de R.L. de C.V., Servicios de Wild Basin S. de R.L. de C.V.

Officers: Clifton E. Lind/Dir., CEO, Pres., Randy S. Cieslewicz/CFO, VP - Tax, Budget, Corporate Compliance, Gary Loebig/Exec. VP - Sales, Brendan O'Connor/CTO, Exec. VP, James A. Bannerot/Legal Coordinator, Howard P. Chalmers/Sr. VP - Planning, Corporate Communications, Scott A. Zinnecker/Sr. VP - Human Resources, Central Operations, Robert F. Lannert/Exec. VP - Class II Gaming, Gordon T. Sjodin/Exec. VP, Shannon C. Brooks/VP, Controller, Joseph R. Enzminger/VP, Chief Software Architect, Ruby S. Fernandez/VP - Customer Service, Troy W. Jungmann/VP - Database Development, Jefferson C. Lind/VP - Content, Gaming Technology, Nimai C. Malle/VP - Server Software Architecture *(19 Officers included in Index)*

Directors: Clifton E. Lind/Dir., CEO, Pres., Michael J. Maples/Chmn., John M. Winkelman/Dir., Robert D. Repass/Dir., Neil E. Jenkins/Dir., Emanuel R. Pearlman/Dir.

Owners: Barclays Global Investors, NA./5.90%, Robert D. Repass, Emanuel R. Pearlman/8.30%, Prentice Capital Management, LP/9.30%, Clifton E. Lind/7.40%, Cortina Asset Management, LLC/6.40%, Royce& Associates, LLC/9.90%, Insiders/20.80%, The Baupost Group, L.L.C./5.40%, Gary L. Loebig/1.40%, Brendan M. OConnor/1.50%, Sowood Capital Management LP/8.00%, Liberation Investment Group LLC/8.30%, FMR Corp./11.30%, John M. Winkelman *(21 Owners included in Index)*

Financial Data: **Fiscal Year End:** 09/30 **Latest Annual Data:** 9/30/2006

Year	Sales	Net Income
2006	$145,112,000	$3,532,000
2005	$153,216,000	$17,643,000
2004	$153,675,000	$32,772,000

Curr. Assets:	$47,518,000	**Curr. Liab.:**	$53,353,000		
Plant, Equip.:	$117,359,000	**Total Liab.:**	$100,596,000	**Indic. Yr. Divd.:**	NA
Total Assets:	$268,541,000	**Net Worth:**	$167,945,000	**Debt/ Equity:**	0.2945

Muncy Bank FINL PA

2 N Main St., Muncy, PA , 17756; *PH:* 1-570-546-2211; *http://* www.muncybank.com

General - Incorporation		**Stock** - Price on:12/24/2007	$32.5
Employees	NA	Stock Exchange	OTC
Auditor	NA	Ticker Symbol	MYBF
Stk Agt	NA	Outstanding Shares	NA
Counsel	NA	E.P.S	NA
DUNS No.	NA	Shareholders	NA

Business: The groups principle activity is to provide recruiting services. The groups service area includes the research and development, engineering, marketing, sales, information technology and manufacturing industries. The group operates from United States.

Primary SIC and add'l.: 6712

CIK No:

Municipal Mortgage & Equity LLC

621 E Pratt St., Ste. 300, Baltimore, MD, 21202; *PH:* 1-443-263-2900; *Fax:* 1-410-727-5387; *http://* www.munimae.com; *Email:* investments@munimae.com

General - Incorporation	DE	**Stock** - Price on:12/24/2007	$25.4
Employees	450	Stock Exchange	AMEX
Auditor	PricewaterhouseCoopers LLP	Ticker Symbol	MMG
Stk Agt	Registrar & Transfer Co	Outstanding Shares	38,520,000
Counsel	NA	E.P.S	$2.09
DUNS No.	NA	Shareholders	NA

Business: The groups principle activity is to provide debt and equity financing to real estate developers. The group operates through four segments namely, debt, tax credit, structured finance and fund management. The group acquired Mony Realty Capital, Inc. in February 2005 and Glaser Financial Group, Inc. in July 2005. The groups operates from the United States.

Primary SIC and add'l.: 6159 6162 6162 6159 6500

CIK No: 0001003201

Subsidiaries: Acquisitions Investments Corp., Affordable Property Holdings, LLC, BF Institutional Tax Credits Acquisitions Limited Partner, CAPREIT Tera Venture, LLC, FM Sponsor I, LLC, Lend Lease MSR Corp., MFH Financial Trust I, Midland Realty Investment Corporation, MMA Advisory Services (formerly Midland Advisory Services, Inc.), MMA Capital Corporation, MMA Construction Finance, LLC, MMA Credit Enhancement I, LLC, MMA Equity Corporation1, MMA Financial BFG Investments, LLC, MMA Financial BFGLP, LLC 50 Subsidiaries included in the Index

Officers: Michael L. Falcone/Dir., CEO, Pres., Matt Cheney/CEO - MMA Renewable Ventures, Earl W. Cole/Exec. VP, Frank G. Creamer/Exec. VP, Stephen A. Goldberg/General Counsel, Melanie M. Lundquist/Chief Accounting Officer, Sr. VP, Gary A. Mentesana/Exec. VP, Head - MMA Financial, Loan, Acquisition Officer - Baltimore, Jenny Netzer/Exec. VP, Charles M. Pinckney/COO, Jeffrey Muller/Sr. VP - Finance, Planning, Ken Dayton/Loan, Acquisition Officer - St. Paul, Chris Diaz/Loan, Acquisition Officer - Tampa, Jerry Flannelly/Loan, Acquisition Officer - Boston, Kevin Filter/Loan, Acquisition Officer - St. Paul, Dan Flick/Loan, Acquisition Officer - Dallas *(40 Officers included in Index)*

Directors: Michael L. Falcone/Dir., CEO, Pres., Mark K. Joseph/Chmn., Robert S. Hillman/Dir., Barbara B. Lucas/Dir., Douglas A. McGregor/Dir., Eddie C. Brown/Dir., Charles C. Baum/Dir., Richard O. Berndt/Dir., Arthur S. Mehlman/Dir., Fred N. Pratt/Dir.

Financial Data: Fiscal Year End:12/31   Latest Annual Data: 12/31/2004

Year	Sales	Net Income
2004	$218,406,000	$27,037,000
2003	$171,967,000	$72,495,000
2002	$133,628,000	$28,949,000

Curr. Assets:	$111,249,000	Curr. Liab.:	$467,426,000	P/E Ratio:	12.15
Plant, Equip.:	$182,773,000	Total Liab.:	$2,469,395,000	Indic. Yr. Divd.:	NA
Total Assets:	$3,310,330,000	Net Worth:	$672,935,000	Debt/ Equity:	NA

Municipal Securities Purchase Inc

Formerly: FGIC Securities Purchase Inc
201 High Ridge Rd., Stamford, CT, 06927; *PH:* 1-203-357-4000

General - Incorporation	DE	Stock- Price on:12/24/2007	NA
Employees	NA	Stock Exchange	NA
Auditor	KPMG LLP	Ticker Symbol	NA
Stk Agt	NA	Outstanding Shares	NA
Counsel	NA	E.P.S.	NA
DUNS No.	94-423-3790	Shareholders	NA

Business: The group's principle activity is to purchase floating rate municipal securities, in the event they are tendered by the holders there of as permitted under the terms of the respective bond indentures. The group is wholly owned by fgic holdings, inc., which in turn is owned by general electric capital corporation, the ultimate parent. The group's parent, ge capital provides a standby loan to purchase these securities. The liquidity agreements are for a term of approximately five years or earlier if the bonds are no longer outstanding. During the year 2003, the group changed its name from fgic securities purchase inc to municipal securities purchase inc. The group operates from United States.

Primary SIC and add'l.: 6289
CIK No: 0000880407
Subsidiaries: GE Funding Services, Inc., Municipal Securities Purchase, Inc.
Officers: Leann Rogers/Chmn., Principal Executive Officer, Peter Graham/VP, Treasurer, Principal Financial, Accounting Officer
Directors: Leann Rogers/Chmn., Principal Executive Officer

Murphy Oil Corp

200 Peach St., El Dorado, AR, 71731; *PH:* 1-870-862-6411; *Fax:* 1-870-864-6373;
http:// www.murphyoilcorp.com; *Email:* customerservice@murphyoilcorp.com

General - Incorporation	DE	Stock- Price on:12/24/2007	$59.94
Employees	2,479	Stock Exchange	NYSE
Auditor	KPMG LLP	Ticker Symbol	NA
Stk Agt	Computershare Investor Services LLC	Outstanding Shares	188,130,000
Counsel	NA	E.P.S.	$3.37
DUNS No.	00-805-3712	Shareholders	NA

Business: The groups principle activities include exploring, producing, refining and marketing oil and gas. The group operates from United States, Canada and United Kingdom.

Primary SIC and add'l.: 5171 0811 2911 4612 1311
CIK No: 0000717423
Subsidiaries: 864 Beverage, Inc., Alnery No.166 Ltd., Arkansas Oil Company, Caledonia Land Company, Canam Offshore Limited, Eastern Canadian Coal Gas Venture Ltd., El Dorado Contractors Inc., El Dorado Engineering Inc., El Dorado Exploration, S.A., Environmental Technologies Inc., European Petroleum Distributors Ltd., H. Hartley (Doncaster) Ltd., Marine Land Company, Mentor Excess and Surplus Lines Insurance Company, Mentor Holding Corporation 60 Subsidiaries included in the Index
Officers: Claiborne P. Deming/Dir., CEO, Pres./$8,664,781.00, John W. Eckart/49/VP, Controller/$1,007,181.00, Steven A. Cosse/60/Exec. VP/$3,467,682.00, Mindy K. West/38/VP, Treasurer, Bill H. Stobaugh/56/Sr. VP/$1,450,427.00, David M. Wood/50/Exec. VP, Kevin G. Fitzgerald/52/CFO, Sr. VP, Dory Stiles/Investor Relations Officer, Katie Sandifer/Community Relations, Harvey Doerr/49/Exec. VP, Walter K. Compton/45/Sec.
Directors: William C. Nolan/68/Chmn., Madison R. Murphy/50/Dir., Frank W. Blue/66/Dir., Robert A. Hermes/68/Dir., Ivar B. Ramberg/70/Dir., Neal E. Schmale/61/Dir., David J.H. Smith/66/Dir., Caroline G. Theus/64/Dir., James V. Kelley/Dir.
Owners: C. P. Deming/2.04%, C. G. Theus/1.07%, R. M. Murphy/5.54%, Insiders/10.15%
Financial Data: Fiscal Year End:12/31   Latest Annual Data: 12/31/2006

Year	Sales	Net Income
2006	$14,307,387,000	$638,279,000
2005	$11,877,151,000	$846,452,000
2004	$8,359,839,000	$701,315,000

Curr. Assets:	$2,107,091,000	Curr. Liab.:	$1,311,105,000	P/E Ratio:	17.95
Plant, Equip.:	$5,106,282,000	Total Liab.:	$3,369,711,000	Indic. Yr. Divd.:	$0.750
Total Assets:	$7,445,727,000	Net Worth:	$4,052,676,000	Debt/ Equity:	NA

Mustang Resources Inc

1574 Gulf Rd. No.1505, Point Roberts, WA, 98281; *PH:* 1-604-261-6100

General - Incorporation	NV	Stock- Price on:12/24/2007	NA
Employees	NA	Stock Exchange	NA
Auditor	Telford Sadovnick, PLLC	Ticker Symbol	NA
Stk Agt	Valient Trust Co	Outstanding Shares	NA
Counsel	NA	E.P.S.	NA
DUNS No.	NA	Shareholders	NA

Business: The group's principle activity is to explore oil and gas properties. Mustang's shares trade on the Toronto Stock Exchange under the trading symbol "MUS.A" and "MUS.B". The company has entered into an equity financing agreement, on a bought deal basis, with a group of underwriters, co-led by GMP Securities Ltd., FirstEnergy Capital Corp., and Tristone Capital Inc. The group along with two other named Thunder Energy Inc. and Forte Resources Inc. has jointly announced shareholder support and Court approval for the proposed plan of arrangement to combine the three entities and create a new oil & gas trust, two exploration focused producers and a resource based coal bed methane company on 17-06-2005. The group operates from United States.

Primary SIC and add'l.: 1400
CIK No: 0001281842
Financial Data: Fiscal Year End:12/31   Latest Annual Data: 12/31/2006

Year	Sales	Net Income
2006	$83,350,000	$1,928,000
2005	$84,941,000	$3,424,000

Curr. Assets:	$34,309,000	Curr. Liab.:	$23,858,000		
Plant, Equip.:	$13,664,000	Total Liab.:	$25,393,000	Indic. Yr. Divd.:	NA
Total Assets:	$53,434,000	Net Worth:	$28,041,000	Debt/ Equity:	NA

Mutual Community SVG

315 E Chapel Hill St. , Durham, NC, 27701; *PH:* 1-919-688-1308; *Fax:* 1-919-682-1380;
http:// www.mcsbk.com; *Email:* MCSB@mcsbk.com

General - Incorporation	NA	Stock- Price on:12/24/2007	$10.3
Employees	32	Stock Exchange	OTC
Auditor	NA	Ticker Symbol	MTUC
Stk Agt	Registrar & Transfer Co	Outstanding Shares	NA
Counsel	NA	E.P.S.	NA
DUNS No.	NA	Shareholders	NA

Business: The groups principal activity is to provide community-banking services. The services of the group include personal banking, business banking, originating loans and online banking. The group operates from North Carolina in the United States.

Primary SIC and add'l.: 6021
CIK No:
Officers: William G. Smith/Dir., CEO, Pres., Beverly W. Jones/Dir., Corp. Sec., Donna Sylver/Sr. VP, CFO, Carmen Thompson/Branch Mgr. - Fayetteville Street, Kaye Gantt/Sr. VP, Retail Operations Officer, Lillian Johnson/Assist. VP, Credit Department Mgr., Teresa Melvin-Davis/Branch Services Mgr. - Chapel Hill Street, William J. Pickens/Greensboro Marketing Pres., Tamica Huntley/Branch Services Mgr. - Greensboro
Directors: William G. Smith/Dir., CEO, Pres., William V. Bell/Chmn., James A. Welch/Vice Chmn., Beverly W. Jones/Dir., Corp. Sec., Ruby G. Bowden/Dir., George W. Brooks/Dir., Elroy Lewis/Dir.

Mutual Federal Bancorp Inc

701 Lee Rd., Ste. 300, Chesterbrook, PA, 19087; *Fax:* 1-610-560-1501;
http:// www.mutualfederalbank.com

General - Incorporation	Federal	Stock- Price on:12/24/2007	$13.25
Employees	NA	Stock Exchange	OTC
Auditor	Crowe, Chizek and Company LLC	Ticker Symbol	MFDB
Stk Agt	Registrar & Transfer Co	Outstanding Shares	3,640,000
Counsel	NA	E.P.S.	$0.13
DUNS No.	NA	Shareholders	NA

Business: The groups principle activity is to provide banking services. Services of the group include insurance brokerage and attracting retail deposits. The group operates from the United States.

Primary SIC and add'l.: 6712
CIK No: 0001344802
Subsidiaries: Emeffs Service Corporation, Mutual Federal Savings and Loan Association of Chicago
Officers: Adriana Jaime/Personal Banking Officer, Maribel Islas/Loan Officer
Owners: Mutual Federal Bancorp, MHC/70.00%, John L. Garlanger, Stanley Balzekas, Amy P. Keane, Julie H. Oksas/1.30%, Stephen M. Oksas/1.30%, Stephanie Simonaitis, Robert P. Kazan, Insiders/3.60%, Leonard F. Kosacz
Financial Data: Fiscal Year End:12/31   Latest Annual Data: 12/31/2006

Year	Sales	Net Income
2006	$4,042,000	$530,000

Curr. Assets:	$2,607,000	Curr. Liab.:	$46,363,000	P/E Ratio:	10.28
Plant, Equip.:	$289,000	Total Liab.:	$46,830,000	Indic. Yr. Divd.:	NA
Total Assets:	$75,063,000	Net Worth:	$28,233,000	Debt/ Equity:	NA

Mutualfirst Financial Inc

110 E Charles St., Muncie, IN, 47305; *PH:* 1-765-747-2800; *Fax:* 1-765-289-1201;
http:// www.mfsbank.com

General - Incorporation	MD	Stock- Price on:12/24/2007	$19.25
Employees	253	Stock Exchange	NDQ
Auditor	BKD LLP	Ticker Symbol	MFSF
Stk Agt	Continental Stock Transfer & Trust Co	Outstanding Shares	4,350,000
Counsel	Beasley & Gilkison LLP	E.P.S.	$1.00
DUNS No.	NA	Shareholders	NA

Business: The group's principle activity is to offer a variety of financial services to customers in the United States. The group accepts retail deposits from the general public and invests them primarily in permanent loans secured by first mortgages on owner-occupied, one- to four-family residences and a variety of consumer loans. It also originates loans secured by commercial and multi-family real estate, commercial business loans and construction loans secured primarily by residential real estate. The group

offers deposit accounts, which generally include passbook and statement savings accounts, money market deposit accounts, now and non-interest bearing checking accounts and certificates of deposit. The products and services of the group are offered through seventeen retail offices primarily in Delaware, randolph, kosciusko and grant counties in Indiana.

Primary SIC and add'l.: 6712 6035

CIK No: 0001094810

Subsidiaries: First M.F.S.B. Corporation, Indiana Title Insurance Co., LLC, Mutual Federal Savings Bank

Officers: Dave Heeter/CEO, Pres., Debra Jones-Price/Branch Mgr. - West Bethel, Starr Manning/Branch Mgr. - Charles Street, Nikki Bastian/Branch Mgr. - Winchester Pearl Street, Steve Campbell/Sr. VP/$253,182.00, Steve Selby/Sr. VP/$199,150.00, Tim McArdle/Sr. VP/$221,317.00, Scott Green/VP, Kevin J. Zachary/Sr. Advisory Dir., Kevin A. Carey/VP, Jenny Yarbrough/Mgr. - Marketing, Sales, Todd Yarbrough/Mgr. - Jurisdiction, Sonya Counce/Branch Mgr. - Wabash, Chase Batt/Training Mgr., Dianne Harris/Audit Mgr. *(67 Officers included in Index)*

Directors: Wilbur R. Davis/Chmn., Jon R. Marler/Dir., Jack E. Buckles/Sr. Dir., Jerry McVicker/Dir., Donn R. Roberts/Dir., Richard G. Benson/Sr. Dir., Robert Morris/Member - Winchester Advisory Board, Clark G. Loney/Member - Winchester Advisory Board, Conan Wallace/Member - Winchester Advisory Board, Candace Wolkins/Member - Warsaw Advisory Board, John Sadler/Member - Warsaw Advisory Board, David Carey/Member - Warsaw Advisory Board, Steve Harris/Member - Warsaw Advisory Board, Philip J. Harris/Member - Warsaw Advisory Board, Edward J. Dobrow/Dir. *(19 Directors included in Index)*

Owners: Insiders/17.40%, David W. Heeter/2.10%, Jon R. Marler, Wilbur R. Davis/1.60%, Linn A. Crull/1.50%, Timothy J. McArdle/1.20%, Patrick C. Botts/1.40%, Steven R. Campbell, Mutual Federal Savings Bank Employee Stock Ownership Plan/10.10%, Donn R. Roberts/4.00%, Edward J. Dobrow/1.60%, Private Capital Management, L.P./9.90%, Stephen C. Selby, Jerry D. McVicker, Lynne D. Richardson *(18 Owners included in Index)*

Financial Data: Fiscal Year End:12/31 Latest Annual Data: 12/31/2006

Year	Sales	Net Income
2006	$63,613,000	$4,757,000
2005	$55,211,000	$6,452,000
2004	$50,626,000	$5,522,000

Curr. Assets:	$25,208,000	**Curr. Liab.:**	$860,784,000		
Plant, Equip.:	$15,431,000	**Total Liab.:**	$873,579,000	**Indic. Yr. Divd.:**	$0.600
Total Assets:	$960,842,000	**Net Worth:**	$87,264,000	**Debt/ Equity:**	0.0137

Mvb Financial Corp

301 Virginia Ave., Fairmont, WV, 26554; **PH:** 1-304-363-4800

General - Incorporation	WV	**Stock**- Price on:12/24/2007	$17
Employees	59	Stock Exchange	OTC
Auditor	Brown, Edwards & Co LLP	Ticker Symbol	MVBF
Stk Agt	NA	Outstanding Shares	1,470,000
Counsel	NA	E.P.S.	$0.72
DUNS No.	NA	Shareholders	NA

Business: The group's principal activity is to provide banking services to individual, businesses and local government customers in west Virginia. It operates through eighteen banking offices. The group's deposit account includes individual retirement accounts, money market accounts, now accounts, savings accounts and time open accounts. The lending products of the group include personal lines of credit, commercial, real estate, and instalment loans and deposit products, including checking, savings, now and money market accounts, certificates of deposit, and individual retirement accounts. The other services include trust services, non-deposit investment products, ATM services, home banking services and Internet banking services. The group operates solely in the domestic market.

Primary SIC and add'l.: 6022

CIK No: 0001277902

Subsidiaries: The Monongahela Valley Bank, Inc.

Officers: James R. Martin/60/CEO, Pres./$194,898.00

Directors: Larry F. Mazza/47/Dir., Roger J. Turner/57/Dir., Barbara L. Alexander/51/Dir., Stephen R. Brooks/59/Dir., Harvey M. Havlichek/58/Dir., Saad Mossallati/59/Dir., Kelly R. Nelson/48/Dir., Leonard W. Nossokoff/69/Dir., Nitesh S. Patel/44/Dir., Louis W. Spatafore/51/Dir., Michael F. Trent/59/Dir.

Owners: Samuel J. Warash/1.27%, Barbara Alexander, Leonard W. Nossokoff/4.11%, Michael F. Trent, Louis W. Spatafore, James R. Martin/3.97%, Stephen R. Brooks, Wayne Stanley, Saad Mossallati/5.92%, Christopher J. Pallotta/2.05%, Nitesh S. Patel/2.07%, Larry F. Mazza/5.81%, Richard L. Toothman, Eric L. Tichenor, Roger J. Turner/1.69% *(18 Owners included in Index)*

Financial Data: Fiscal Year End:12/31 Latest Annual Data: 12/31/2006

Year	Sales	Net Income
2006	$11,255,000	$973,000
2005	$7,532,000	$562,000
2004	$6,213,000	$1,058,000

Curr. Assets:	$13,366,000	**Curr. Liab.:**	$169,629,000		
Plant, Equip.:	$6,493,000	**Total Liab.:**	$169,629,000	**Indic. Yr. Divd.:**	NA
Total Assets:	$191,284,000	**Net Worth:**	$21,655,000	**Debt/ Equity:**	0.1824

MVC Capital Inc

287 Bowman Ave., Purchase, NY, 10577; **PH:** 1-914-701-0310; **Fax:** 1-914-701-0315; http:// www.mvccapital.com; **Email:** newdeals@mvccapital.com

General - Incorporation	DE	**Stock**- Price on:12/24/2007	$19.74
Employees	13	Stock Exchange	NYSE
Auditor	Ernst& Young LLP	Ticker Symbol	MVC
Stk Agt	Computershare Trust Co	Outstanding Shares	24,260,000
Counsel	NA	E.P.S.	$6.76
DUNS No.	NA	Shareholders	NA

Business: The groups principal activity is to provide fund to the business development company. The group operates from the United States.

Primary SIC and add'l.: 6726 6799

CIK No: 0001099941

Subsidiaries: MVC Financial Services, Inc.

Officers: Michael Tokarz/Chmn., Principal Exec. Officer, Bruce Shewmaker/Sr. Investment Professional, David Hadani/Investment, Portfolio Support, Operations Management Team, Ben Harris/Investment, Portfolio Support, Operations Management Team, Shivani Khurana/Investment, Portfolio Support, Operations Management Team, Forrest Mertens/Investment, Portfolio Support,

Operations Management Team, Puneet Sanan/Investment, Portfolio Support, Operations Management Team, Scott Schuenke/Investment, Portfolio Support, Operations Management Team, Peter Seidenberg/CFO, Jaclyn Shapiro-Rothchild/VP, Sec., Christopher Sullivan/Investment, Portfolio Support, Operations Management Team, Warren Holtsberg/Dir., Co - Head - Portfolio Management, Amy Francetic/Manages Investments The Firm, Mark Kaltenbacher/Investment, Portfolio Support, Operations Management Team

Directors: Michael Tokarz/Chmn., Principal Exec. Officer, Emilio Dominianni/Dir., Gerald Hellerman/Dir., Robert Knapp/Dir., William Taylor/Dir., Warren Holtsberg/Dir., Co - Head - Portfolio Management

Owners: Wynnefield Partners Small Cap Value, L.P./5.28%, Robert Knapp/6.71%, Insiders/8.72%, Scott Schuenke, Warren Holtsberg, William Taylor, Michael Tokarz/1.75%, Gerald Hellerman, Millenco, L.P./5.64%, Jaclyn Shapiro, Bruce Shewmaker, The Anegada Master FundLtd./12.83%, Peter Seidenberg, Emilio Dominianni, Western Investment, LLC/5.67% *(16 Owners included in Index)*

Financial Data: Fiscal Year End:10/31 Latest Annual Data: 10/31/2006

Year	Sales	Net Income
2006	$18,508,000	$47,336,000
2005	$12,199,000	$26,268,000
2004	$3,986,000	$11,606,000

Curr. Assets.	$67,955,000	**Curr. Liab.:**	$808,000	**P/E Ratio:**	2.37
Plant, Equip.:	NA	**Total Liab.:**	$110,053,000	**Indic. Yr. Divd.:**	$0.480
Total Assets.	$347,047,000	**Net Worth:**	$236,993,000	**Debt/ Equity:**	0.3957

MWI Veterinary Supply Inc

651 S Stratford Dr., Ste. 100, Meridian, ID, 83642; **PH:** 1-208-955-8930; **Fax:** 1-208-955-8902; http:// www.mwivet.com

General - Incorporation	DE	**Stock**- Price on:12/24/2007	$37.7
Employees	719	Stock Exchange	NDQ
Auditor	Deloitte& Touche LLP	Ticker Symbol	MWIV
Stk Agt	Wells Fargo Shareowner Services	Outstanding Shares	12,000,000
Counsel	NA	E.P.S.	NA
DUNS No.	NA	Shareholders	NA

Business: The groups principle activity is to manufacturer animal health products. The groups services include E-commerce platform, Pharmacy fulfillment, Inventory management system and Pet cremation. The group products sold under the trade names VETONE and VETRIMEC. The group acquired Northland Veterinary Supply, Ltd in the year 2006 and Vetpo Distributors, Inc in the year 2005. The group operates from the United States. The group's total revenue in the year 2007 was 710.11 millions of USD.

Primary SIC and add'l.: 2047 2833 2835 3841 5122 2899 3826 2836 5191 2834 3821

CIK No: 0001323974

Subsidiaries: Memorial Pet Care, Inc., MWI Veterinary Supply Co.

Officers: James F. Cleary/Dir., CEO, Pres., Mary Patricia B. Thompson/CFO, Sr. VP - Finance, Administration, James W. Culpepper/VP - Inventory Management, Jeffrey J. Danielson/VP - Sales, John J. Francis/VP, GM - Specialty Resources Group, James S. Hay/CIO, VP, Bryan P. Mooney/VP - Operations, John R. Ryan/VP - Marketing, Kyle Baird/Mgr. - Sales, Northwest Region, Susan Donnelly/Mgr. - Sales, California Region, Steve Fitzjames/Mgr. - Sales, Rocky Mountain Region, Eric Scott/Mgr. - Sales, Central States Region, Jeff Hicks/Mgr. - Sales, Southwest Region, Bob Weinschenk/Mgr. - Sales, Southeast Region, Terry Walsh/Mgr. - Sales, Great Lakes Region *(17 Officers included in Index)*

Directors: James F. Cleary/Dir., CEO, Pres., Keith E. Alessi/Dir., John F. McNamara/Dir., Robert N. Rebholtz/Dir., Bruce C. Bruckmann/Dir., Craig A. Olson/Dir., William J. Robison/Dir.

Owners: James S. Hay, John J. Francis, James W. Culpepper, Insiders/10.70%, FMR Corp./5.90%, John R. Ryan, James F. Cleary/1.70%, Keith E. Alessi, Robert N. Rebholtz/6.10%, John F. McNamara, Massachusetts Financial Services Company/10.10%, Bruce C. Bruckmann, Bryan P. Mooney, William J. Robison, Neuberger Berman LLC/11.80% *(19 Owners included in Index)*

Curr. Assets.	$187,791,000	**Curr. Liab.:**	$100,136,000		
Plant, Equip.:	$7,053,000	**Total Liab.:**	$100,933,000	**Indic. Yr. Divd.:**	NA
Total Assets.	$230,559,000	**Net Worth:**	$129,626,000	**Debt/ Equity:**	NA

My Quote Zone, Inc

6130 Elton Ave., Las Vegas, NV, 89107; **PH:** 1-702-874-3131

General - Incorporation	NV	**Stock**- Price on:12/24/2007	NA
Employees	NA	Stock Exchange	NA
Auditor	Ramirez International	Ticker Symbol	NA
Stk Agt	NA	Outstanding Shares	NA
Counsel	NA	E.P.S.	NA
DUNS No.	NA	Shareholders	NA

Business: The group's principle activity is to technology based marketing firm that specializes in online lead generation. The group markets its lead generation sales prospects in an auction format to business seeking new sales leads. The product would include directory products, vertical databases, online sales leads, and custom sales leads and products for sales people and small office home office markets. Sales of subscription-based products require the Company to recognize revenues over the subscription period instead of at the time of sale.

Primary SIC and add'l.: 6770

CIK No: 0001321223

Officers: Zheng Ying/41/Chmn., CEO, Yanbin Wang/38/CFO, Zhongzhi Yu/36/Sec.

Directors: Zheng Ying/41/Chmn., CEO, Ying Luo/46/Dir., Jingsong Li/40/Dir., Song Cai/36/Dir., Yufei Yu/35/Dir.

Owners: Insiders/34.27%, Max Time Enterprise Limited - Hui Ping Cheng/34.27%, Guo-Hong Zhou/7.53%, Guo-Tuan Zhou/7.53%

Myers Industries Inc

1293 S Main St., Akron, OH, 44301; **PH:** 1-330-253-5592; **Fax:** 1-330-761-6156; http:// www.myersind.com

General - Incorporation .... OH
Employees 3,689
Auditor .... KPMG LLP
Stk Agt .... National City Bank
Counsel .... Brouse McDowell
DUNS No. 00-195-0849

Stock- Price on:12/24/2007 .... $22.22
Stock Exchange .... NYSE
Ticker Symbol .... MYE
Outstanding Shares 35,140,000
E.P.S. $1.44
Shareholders .... NA

Business: The group's principal activities are to manufacture and market polymer products and distribute tools, equipment and supplies used in automotive underbody repair. Its operations are classified into two segments: manufacturing and distribution. Manufacturing segment designs, manufactures and markets polymer based plastic and rubber products for the industrial, agricultural, automotive, commercial and consumer markets worldwide. Products include plastic material handling containers, storage boxes, rubber OEM parts and tire repair materials sold under the buckhorn, dillen, listo, patch rubber and raaco brand names. Distribution segment includes tools, equipment and supplies such as computerized alignment systems, tire balancers, tire patches, repair cement and small hand tools distributed to the tire, wheel and automotive underbody service specialists. On 10-Mar-2004, the group acquired atp automotive, inc.

Primary SIC and add'l.: 5014 3585 5013 3089 3069 3052 2542

CIK No: 0000069488

Subsidiaries: AC Buckhorn LLC, AC Buckhorn LLC(50%), AkroMils (of Myers Industries, Inc.), Allibert (Anshan) Plastic Anticorrosive Equipement Co. Ltd., Allibert Buckhorn France, SAS, Allibert Buckhorn UK Limited, Allibert Contenitori SpA, Allibert ContentoresSistemas de Armazenagem, S.A., Allibert Equipement Sprl, Allibert Manutencion S.A., Allibert Transport und Lagertechnik GmbH & Co Kg, Allibert Transport und Lagertechnik GmbH & Verwaltungsgesellschaft mbH, AllibertBuckhorn Europe, SAS, AmeriKart (MI) Corp., AmeriKart Corp. 56 Subsidiaries included in the Index

Officers: John C. Orr/57/Dir., CEO, Pres./$1,360,465.00, Dave Grider/MD - Distribution Segment, Mohsen Eskandar/MD - Lawn, Garden Segment, Don Thomas/MD - North American Material Handling Segment, Dennis Roberts/MD - Automotive, Custom Segment, Donald A. Merril/42/VP, CFO, Corp. Sec./$533,487.00, Garee Daniska/Assist. Treasurer, Max Barton/Mgr. - Investor Relations

Directors: John C. Orr/57/Dir., CEO, Pres., Stephen E. Myers/64/Chmn., Richard P. Johnston/77/Dir., Keith A. Brown/56/Dir., Richard L. Osborne/70/Dir., Edward W. Kissel/66/Dir., Jon H. Outcalt/71/Dir., Karl S. Hay/78/Dir., Vincent C. Byrd/Dir.

Owners: GAMCO Investors/7.82%, Stephen E. Myers/8.48%, Rowe T. Price/5.53%, Vincent C. Byrd, John C. Orr, Richard L. Osborne, Edward W. Kissel, Mary S. Myers/10.89%, Insiders/9.40%, Keith A. Brown, Richard P. Johnston, Jon H. Outcalt, Dimensional FundAdvisors, Inc./5.57%, Karl S. Hay, Donald A. Merril

Financial Data: *Fiscal Year End:*12/31 *Latest Annual Data:* 12/31/2006

Year	Sales	Net Income
2006	$779,984,000	-$69,024,000
2005	$903,679,000	$26,556,000
2004	$803,070,000	$25,710,000

Curr. Assets:	$307,523,000	**Curr. Liab.:**	$134,727,000		
Plant, Equip.:	$151,300,000	**Total Liab.:**	$381,325,000	**Indic. Yr. Divd.:**	$0.240
Total Assets:	$661,983,000	**Net Worth:**	$280,659,000	**Debt/ Equity:**	NA

Mylan Laboratories Inc

1500 Corporate Dr., Ste. 400, Canonsburg, PA, 15317; ***PH:*** 1-724-514-1800; ***Fax:*** 1-724-514-1870; ***http://*** www.mylan.com

General - Incorporation .... PA
Employees 6,400
Auditor .... Deloitte & Touche LLP
Stk Agt .... American Stock Transfer & Trust Co.
Counsel .... NA
DUNS No. 05-929-8141

Stock- Price on:12/24/2007 .... $18.79
Stock Exchange .... NYSE
Ticker Symbol .... NA
Outstanding Shares 248,660,000
E.P.S. $0.99
Shareholders .... NA

Business: The group's principal activity is to develop and manufacture generic and brand pharmaceutical products. The group operates through two segments: generic segment and brand segment. The generic segment manufactures generic pharmaceutical products that are therapeutically equivalent to a brand name product. These products are marketed to pharmaceutical wholesalers and distributors, drug store chains, group purchasing organizations, institutions and governmental agencies. The brand segment manufactures branded pharmaceutical products that are generally patent protected products marketed directly to health care professionals by a single provider.

Primary SIC and add'l.: 6794 2834

CIK No: 0000069499

Subsidiaries: American Triumvirate Insurance Company, Milan Holding Inc., MLRE LLC, Mylan Bertek Pharmaceuticals Inc., Mylan Caribe, Inc., Mylan Inc., Mylan International Holdings, Inc., Mylan Pharmaceuticals Inc., Mylan TechnologiesInc., UDL Laboratories, Inc.

Officers: N. Prasad/Head - Global Strategies in The Office of The CEO, Robert J. Coury/Vice Chmn., CEO/$7,593,909.00, Edward J. Borkowski/CFO/$1,780,323.00, Heather Bresch/Head - North American Operations, Rajiv Malik/Head - Global Technical Operations, Daniel C. Rizzo/VP, Corporate Controller, Carolyn Myers/Pres. - Mylan Technologies Inc, VP, Harry A. Korman/Pres. - Mylan Pharmaceuticals Inc, Sr. VP/$968,483.00, John Patrick O'Donnell/Chief Scientific Officer/$1,644,656.00, Stuart A. Williams/Chief Legal Officer/$1,722,472.00

Directors: Robert J. Coury/Vice Chmn., CEO, Milan Puskar/Chmn., Co - Founder, C. B. Todd/Dir., Randall L. Vanderveen/Dir., Wendy Cameron/Dir., Neil Dimick/Dir., Douglas J. Leech/Dir., Joseph C. Maroon/Dir., Rodney L. Piatt/Dir.

Owners: Edward J. Borkowski, Douglas J. Leech, Insiders/4.10%, Barclays Global Investors NA/5.60%, Lord, Abbett& Co LLC/8.50%, Harry A. Korman, Milan Puskar/1.80%, C. B. Todd, John P. ODonnell, Rod Piatt, Louis J. DeBone, Stuart A. Williams, N. Prasad, Robert J. Coury, Wendy Cameron

Financial Data: *Fiscal Year End:*03/31 *Latest Annual Data:* 3/31/2007

Year	Sales	Net Income
2007	$1,611,819,000	$217,284,000
2006	$1,257,164,000	$184,542,000
2005	$1,253,374,000	$203,592,000

Curr. Assets:	$2,412,044,000	**Curr. Liab.:**	$700,535,000	**P/E Ratio:**	18.98
Plant, Equip.:	$686,739,000	**Total Liab.:**	$2,561,800,000	**Indic. Yr. Divd.:**	$0.240
Total Assets:	$4,253,867,000	**Net Worth:**	$1,648,860,000	**Debt/ Equity:**	NA

Mymetics Corp

14, Rue De La Colombiere, Nyon, 1260; ; ***http://*** www.mymetics.com; ***Email:*** info@mymetics.com

General - Incorporation .... DE
Employees .... NA
Auditor .... Peterson Sullivan PLLC
Stk Agt .... Continental Stock Transfer & Trust Co
Counsel .... NA
DUNS No. 87-710-1410

Stock- Price on:12/24/2007 .... $0.18
Stock Exchange .... OTC
Ticker Symbol .... MYMX
Outstanding Shares .... NA
E.P.S. $3.91
Shareholders .... NA

Business: The group's principle activity is to conducts research and development of human health products. The group's main research efforts are concentrated in the prevention and treatment of the aids virus. The group has established a network which enables it to work with education centers, research centers, pharmaceutical laboratories and biotechnology companies. The group is in its development stage and has not generated significant revenues.

Primary SIC and add'l.: 8731 2834 6719

CIK No: 0000927761

Subsidiaries: 6543 Luxembourg S.A., Mymetics S.A.

Officers: Christian J.F. Rochet/Dir., CEO, Pres., Marc Girard/Head - Vaccine Development, Chmn. - Scientific Advisory Board, Ernst Lubke/Dir., Sec., CFO, Sylvain Fleury/Dir., VP, Chief Scientific Officer, Lucia Lopalco/Strategic Academic, Govermental Partners, Additional Research Staff Partners, Dimiter Dimitrov/Strategic Academic, Govermental Partners, Additional Research Staff Partners, Nancy Miller/Strategic Academic, Govermental Partners, Additional Research Staff Partners, Pierre Coudert/Technical Academic Partners, Additional Research Staff Partners, Quin Chuan/Technical Academic Partners, Additional Research Staff Partners, Christiane Moog/Technical Academic Partners, Additional Research Staff Partners, Uriel Hazan/Technical Academic Partners, Additional Research Staff Partners

Directors: Christian J.F. Rochet/Dir., CEO, Pres., Marc Girard/Head - Vaccine Development, Chmn. - Scientific Advisory Board, Ernst Lubke/Dir., Sec., CFO, Sylvain Fleury/Dir., VP, Chief Scientific Officer, Ronald H. Gray/Member - Scientific Advisory Board, Morgane Bomsel/Member - Scientific Advisory Board

Owners: Martine Reindle/8.15%, Insiders/8.07%, Anglo Irish Bank/25.84%, Sylvain Fleury/1.35%, Ernst Luebke/4.58%, Marc Girard, Christian Rochet/1.24%

Financial Data: *Fiscal Year End:*12/31 *Latest Annual Data:* 12/31/2006

Year	Sales	Net Income
2006	NA	-$2,093,000
2005	NA	-$2,297,000
2004	NA	-$3,004,000

Curr. Assets:	$79,000	**Curr. Liab.:**	$8,711,000	**P/E Ratio:**	0.05
Plant, Equip.:	NA	**Total Liab.:**	$9,031,000	**Indic. Yr. Divd.:**	NA
Total Assets:	$475,000	**Net Worth:**	-$8,556,000	**Debt/ Equity:**	NA

Myoffiz Inc

5770 El Camino Rd., Las Vegas, NV, 89118; ***PH:*** 1-702-222-9076; ***http://*** www.PublicCompanyManagement.com

General - Incorporation .... NV
Employees 1
Auditor .... Malone & Bailey, P.C
Stk Agt .... Pacific Stock Transfer Company
Counsel .... NA
DUNS No. .... NA

Stock- Price on:12/24/2007 .... $0.07
Stock Exchange .... NA
Ticker Symbol .... NA
Outstanding Shares 24,810,000
E.P.S. .... -$0.04
Shareholders .... NA

Business: The groups principle activity is to provide a broad spectrum of services and solutions to small businesses wishing to access the U.S. Capital Markets and companies that currently trade on the OTC BB or Pink Sheets. The group operates from United States.

Primary SIC and add'l.: NA

CIK No: 0001141964

Subsidiaries: GoPublicToday.com, Nevada Fund, Pubco White Papers, Inc., Public Company Management Services, Inc

Officers: Stephen Brock/Dir., CEO, Pres., Kipley J. Lytel/COO, Sec., Trae O'neil High/CFO, Michael T. Williams/Professional, John Malone/Professional, Lawrence E. Wilson/Professional, Rick Marshall/Professional, Dan Scheff/Professional

Directors: Stephen Brock/Dir., CEO, Pres., Kipley J. Lytel/COO, Sec., Stephen A. Boyko/Dir., Steven Chaussy/Dir., Peter J. Chepucavage/Dir., Gary N. Clark/Dir., William Bradford Smith/Dir.

Owners: Kipley J. Lytel/1.90%, Stephen Brock/67.30%, Trae O'Neil/1.50%, Insiders/70.70%

Financial Data: *Fiscal Year End:*09/30 *Latest Annual Data:* 9/30/2006

Year	Sales	Net Income
2006	$1,813,000	-$528,000
2005	$1,423,000	-$2,302,000
2004	$20,000	-$45,000

Curr. Assets:	$993,000	**Curr. Liab.:**	$4,101,000		
Plant, Equip.:	$53,000	**Total Liab.:**	$4,131,000	**Indic. Yr. Divd.:**	NA
Total Assets:	$5,027,000	**Net Worth:**	$895,000	**Debt/ Equity:**	0.0244

Myriad Entertainment & Resorts Inc

10050-112 St., Ste. 1000, 10th Fl., Edmonton, AB, T5K 2J1; ***PH:*** 1-780-430086; ***http://*** www.myriadgolf.com; ***Email:*** info@myriadgolf.com

General - Incorporation .... DE
Employees 1
Auditor .... Moore Stephens Frost
Stk Agt .... Securities Transfer Corp
Counsel .... NA
DUNS No. .... NA

Stock- Price on:12/24/2007 .... $0.439
Stock Exchange .... OTC
Ticker Symbol .... MYRA
Outstanding Shares 41,300,000
E.P.S. .... -$0.17
Shareholders .... NA

Business: The group's principal activities are to provide information technology and organizational management products and services. It offers a suite of products and services for solving systems problems related to their rapidly changing technology needs. The group also provides management consulting services for project management, organizational and workforce issues related to company reorganizations, mergers and acquisitions. These services are provided primarily to financial services industry.

Primary SIC and add'l.: 7379 7372 7374 8748

CIK No: 0001042501

Subsidiaries: Infinity Technology Solutions, Inc, Statewide General Synergy S2K, Inc

Officers: John Meeske/Dir., CEO, Scott Hawrelechko/Chmn. - Myriad Botanical Resort, Robert Leahy/CFO, Exec. VP - Finance, Elizabeth Meister/47/Exec. VP - People Development, Dir.

Directors: John Meeske/Dir., CEO, Nicholas A. Lopardo/Chmn., Robert Ross/Dir., William Callnin/Dir., Dale Cheek/Dir., Tom Chema/Dir., John Daniel/Dir., Paul Ma/Dir., Beth Meister/Dir., Fiona Sutton/Dir., Jerry Wayne/Dir., Jack Vaughn/Dir., Elizabeth Meister/47/Exec. VP - People Development, Dir.

Owners: Fiona Sutton, Paul Ma, Whitmore Trust/8.89%, Jerry Anthony Wayne, Robert S. Ross, Dale Cheek, John Meeske/7.50%, Scott Hawrelechko/9.51%, John M. Daniel, William J. Callnin, Insiders/8.30%

Financial Data: Fiscal Year End:12/31 Latest Annual Data: 12/31/2006

Year	Sales	Net Income
2006	NA	-$5,569,000
2005	NA	-$640,000
2004	NA	-$629,000

Curr. Assets:	$0	Curr. Liab.:	$3,124,000		
Plant, Equip.:	$2,000	Total Liab.:	$3,124,000	Indic. Yr. Divd.:	NA
Total Assets:	$60,000	Net Worth:	-$3,064,000	Debt/ Equity:	NA

Myriad Genetics Inc

320 Wakara Way, Salt Lake City, UT, 84108; **PH:** 1-801-584-3600; **Fax:** 1-801-584-3640; **http://** www.myriad.com; **Email:** investor@myriad.com

General - Incorporation	DE	**Stock**- Price on:12/24/2007	$36.89
Employees	722	Stock Exchange	NYSE
Auditor	KPMG LLP	Ticker Symbol	MYS
Stk Agt	American Stock Transfer & Trust Co.	Outstanding Shares	43,050,000
Counsel	Mintz Levin Cohn Ferris Et Al	E.P.S.	-$0.73
DUNS No.	79-757-1668	Shareholders	NA

Business: The group's principal activity is to develop and market novel therapeutic and predictive medicine products. The group operates in two segments, research and predictive medicine. The research segment focuses on the discovery of genes and proteins related to major common diseases, the discovery of their related biological pathways and the development of therapeutic products for the treatment and prevention of major diseases. The predictive medicine segment provides testing to determine predisposition to common diseases. The group has made discoveries in the fields of cancer, viral diseases such as aids and acute thrombosis. It has alliances with 12 major multinational companies including abbott laboratories, bayer corporation, e.i. Du pont de nemours and company (dupont), eli lilly and company, hitachi ltd, hoffmann-laroche inc, novartis corporation, oracle corporation, pharmacia corporation, schering ag, schering-plough corporation and torrey mesa research institute.

Primary SIC and add'l.: 8731 2834

CIK No: 0000899923

Subsidiaries: Myriad Financial, Inc., Myriad Genetic Laboratories, Inc., Myriad Pharmaceuticals, Inc.

Officers: Peter D. Meldrum/Dir., CEO, Pres., Jay M. Moyes/CFO, Jerry Lanchbury/Exec. VP - Research, Richard Marsh/Exec. VP, General Counsel, Sec., Mark H. Skolnick/Dir., Chief Scientific Officer, William A. Hockett/Exec. VP - Corporate Communications, Patrick Burke/Sr. Dir. - Business Development

Directors: Peter D. Meldrum/Dir., CEO, Pres., John T. Henderson/Chmn., Wayne Laslie/Dir., Adrian N. Hobden/Dir., Linda S. Wilson/Dir., Dennis Langer/Dir., Mark H. Skolnick/Dir., Chief Scientific Officer, Arthur H. Hayes/Dir., Gregory C. Critchfield/Dir., Walter Gilbert/Dir., Robert S. Attiyeh/Dir., Mark C. Capone/Dir., James S. Evans/Dir.

Owners: Gregory C. Critchfield/1.10%, T. Rowe Price Associates, Inc./9.30%, Arthur H. Hayes, Linda S. Wilson, Walter Gilbert, Mark H. Skolnick/2.20%, Insiders/8.80%, FMR Corp./10.00%, Robert S. Attiyeh, John T. Henderson, Peter D. Meldrum/1.40%, Adrian N. Hobden/1.40%, Citadel Limited Partnership/5.40%, Dennis H. Langer, Jay M. Moyes

Financial Data: Fiscal Year End:06/30 Latest Annual Data: 6/30/2007

Year	Sales	Net Income
2007	$157,126,000	-$34,962,000
2006	$114,279,000	-$38,189,000
2005	$82,406,000	-$39,978,000

Curr. Assets:	$343,262,000	Curr. Liab.:	$31,704,000		
Plant, Equip.:	$24,888,000	Total Liab.:	$31,704,000	Indic. Yr. Divd.:	NA
Total Assets:	$372,067,000	Net Worth:	$340,363,000	Debt/ Equity:	NA

MyStarU.com Inc

Formerly: Telecom Communications Inc
9/f., Beijing Business World, 56 Dongxinglong Ave., Cw District, Beijing, 100062; **PH:** 86-10-6702-6968

General - Incorporation	IN	**Stock**- Price on:12/24/2007	$0.17
Employees	NA	Stock Exchange	NA
Auditor	Child, Van Wagoner & Bradshaw, PLLC	Ticker Symbol	NA
Stk Agt	Livingston, Wachtell & Co. LLP	Outstanding Shares	NA
Counsel	NA	E.P.S.	NA
DUNS No.	NA	Shareholders	NA

Business: The groups principle activity is to provide integrated information and entertainment services. The group operates through four segments namely investments in entertainment arts productions, online content and member services provider, software sales, and importing and exporting of goods. The groups online content and member services provider segment provides online content and member services for commercial use. The group operates from United States.

Primary SIC and add'l.: NA

CIK No: 0001139570

Subsidiaries: 3G Dynasty, Inc., Alpha Century Holdings Limited, IC Star MMS Limited

Officers: Tim T. Chen/42/Dir., CEO, Pres., Yan Liu/31/Dir., VP, COO, Victor Z. Li/34/Dir., CFO, Controller, Sec., Treasurer, Yaofu Su/28/Dir., VP

Directors: Tim T. Chen/42/Dir., CEO, Pres., Victor Z. Li/34/Dir., CFO, Controller, Sec., Treasurer, Yaofu Su/28/Dir., VP, Hongtao Zhang/31/Dir., Yan Liu/31/Dir., VP, COO

Owners: Guiwen Cai/4.22%, World East Corporation Limited/3.25%, China IPTV Industry Park Holdings Limited/4.39%, Auto Treasure Holdings Limited/8.03%, Yan Liu, Taikang Capital Managements Corporation/16.25%, Free Productions Limited/2.44%, Songbin Deng/1.30%, Leyi Yang/4.06%, Insiders/1.06%, Top Rider Group Limited/2.84%, Bloomen Limited/4.31%, Yaofu Su

Financial Data: Fiscal Year End:09/30 Latest Annual Data: 9/30/2006

Year	Sales	Net Income
2006	$15,546,000	$1,072,000
2005	$9,072,000	$2,048,000
2004	$1,431,000	-$8,901,000

Curr. Assets:	$8,624,000	Curr. Liab.:	$4,262,000		
Plant, Equip.:	$11,516,000	Total Liab.:	$7,524,000	Indic. Yr. Divd.:	NA
Total Assets:	$22,964,000	Net Worth:	$15,440,000	Debt/ Equity:	NA

Mystica Candle Corp

136 Bradley Rd., Salt Spring Island, BC, V8K 1J5; **PH:** 1-604-638-2283; **http://** www.mysticacandle.com; **Email:** contact@mysticacandle.com

General - Incorporation	NV	**Stock**- Price on:12/24/2007	NA
Employees	NA	Stock Exchange	OTC
Auditor	Chang G. Park, CPA	Ticker Symbol	MYTC
Stk Agt	Holladay Stock Transfer, Inc.	Outstanding Shares	NA
Counsel	NA	E.P.S.	NA
DUNS No.	NA	Shareholders	NA

Business: The groups principle activities include manufacturing, marketing, distributing and selling soy blend wax candles. The group markets its products under the brand name Mystica. The group operates from the United States.

Primary SIC and add'l.: 3999

CIK No: 0001334699

Officers: Jon Suk/43/Dir., CEO, CFO, Pres.

Directors: Jon Suk/43/Dir., CEO, CFO, Pres.

Owners: Insiders/30.00%, Candace Sikorski/30.00%, Jon Suk/30.00%

MyZipSoft Inc

Formerly: Freedom 4 Wireless Inc
1016 Clemons St., Ste. 302, Jupiter, FL, 33477; **PH:** 1-561-745-6789; **http://** www.freedom4wireless.com

General - Incorporation	FL	**Stock**- Price on:12/24/2007	NA
Employees	NA	Stock Exchange	NA
Auditor	Wieseneck, Andres & Co P.A	Ticker Symbol	NA
Stk Agt	Corporate Stock Transfer, Inc.	Outstanding Shares	NA
Counsel	NA	E.P.S.	NA
DUNS No.	NA	Shareholders	NA

Business: The group is in the business of Development and distribution of software. The group operates from United States.

Primary SIC and add'l.: 7372

CIK No: 0001290785

Subsidiaries: American Environmental, Inc

Officers: Barney A. Richmond/56/Chmn., CEO, Sec., Richard C. Turner/48/Dir., CFO, Treasurer, Harry M. Timmons/Pres., Keith J. Money/COO, Phil Dumas/VP - Research, Development, Harris Chasen/Sr. - Software Development, Software Architect

Directors: Barney A. Richmond/56/Chmn., CEO, Sec., Jonathan Pierce/56/Dir., Richard C. Turner/48/Dir., CFO, Treasurer

Owners: Jonathan Pierce/0.30%, American Capital Holdings, Inc./16.30%, Insiders/30.40%, Richard C. Turner/1.50%, Barney A. Richmond/28.60%

Curr. Assets:	$67,000	Curr. Liab.:	$155,000		
Plant, Equip.:	$0	Total Liab.:	$876,000	Indic. Yr. Divd.:	NA
Total Assets:	$67,000	Net Worth:	-$809,000	Debt/ Equity:	NA

N Viro International Corp

3450 W Central Ave, Ste 328, Toledo, OH, 43606; **PH:** 1-419-535-6374; **http://** www.nviro.com

General - Incorporation	DE	**Stock**- Price on:12/24/2007	$2.82
Employees	15	Stock Exchange	OTC
Auditor	UHY LLP	Ticker Symbol	NVIC
Stk Agt	National City Bank	Outstanding Shares	3,980,000
Counsel	NA	E.P.S.	-$0.48
DUNS No.	80-856-3332	Shareholders	NA

Business: The group's principle activity is to own and license the n-viro process. The n-viro process is a patented process for the treatment and recycling of bio-organic wastes, utilizing certain alkaline by-products produced by the cement, lime, electric utilities and other industries. The group operates through four segments: management operations, other domestic operations, foreign operations and research and development. The management operations segment provides employee and management services to operate the toledo wastewater treatment facility. The domestic and foreign operations segments license the use of n-viro technology. The research and development segment contracts with federal and state agencies to perform research and development on the company's technology. The group operates solely in the domestic market. The group's quarterly revenue for September 2007 was 0.94 millions of USD.

Primary SIC and add'l.: 6794 8731 9511

CIK No: 0000904896

Subsidiaries: American N-Viro Resources, Inc., BioCheck Laboratories, Inc., Midwest N-Viro, Inc., N-Viro Honolulu, Inc., National N-Viro Tech., Inc., Pan-American N-Viro, Inc., Tennessee-Carolina N-Viro, Inc., Viro Soil South, Inc.

Officers: Timothy R. Kasmoch/46/Dir., CEO, Pres/$488,575.00, Michael G. Nicholson/41/Chief Development Officer, James K. McHugh/49/CFO, Sec., Treasurer/$199,699.00, Howard E. Hartung/37/COO

Directors: Timothy R. Kasmoch/46/Dir., CEO, Pres., James H. Hartung/65/Chmn., Carl Richard/81/Dir., Francis R. Diprete/53/Dir., Joseph H. Scheib/51/Dir., Mark D. Hagans/41/Dir., Thomas L. Kovacik/60/Dir.

Owners: James H. Hartung/0.53%, Carl Richard/3.26%, Thomas L. Kovacik/0.03%, Howard E. Hartung/0.25%, James K. McHugh/2.77%, Patrick J. Nicholson/5.39%, Michael G. Nicholson/3.26%, Insiders/22.84%, Mark D. Hagans/0.03%, N-Viro Energy Systems, Inc./5.39%, Cooke Family Trust/21.13%, Francis R. DiPrete/3.68%, Timothy R. Kasmoch/9.60%, Joseph H. Scheib/4.10%

Financial Data: Fiscal Year End:12/31 Latest Annual Data: 12/31/2006

Year	Sales		Net Income
2006	$3,620,000		-$1,690,000
2005	$4,184,000		-$273,000
2004	$5,453,000		-$72,000

Curr. Assets:	$1,212,000	**Curr. Liab.:**	$1,562,000		
Plant, Equip.:	$932,000	**Total Liab.:**	$2,116,000	**Indic. Yr. Divd.:**	NA
Total Assets:	$2,946,000	**Net Worth:**	$830,000	**Debt/ Equity:**	0.9524

Nabi Biopharmaceuticals

5800 Pk. of Commerce Blvd. NW, Boca Raton, FL, 33487; *PH:* 1-561-989-5800; *Fax:* 1-561-989-5801; *http://* www.nabi.com; *Email:* irpr@nabi.com

General - Incorporation		**Stock**- Price on:12/24/2007	$4.94
Employees	653	Stock Exchange	NDQ
Auditor	NA	Ticker Symbol	NAFC
Stk Agt	American Stock Transfer & Trust Co.	Outstanding Shares	60,660,000
Counsel	NA	E.P.S	-$0.84
DUNS No.	NA	Shareholders	NA

Business: The groups principal activity is to develop medical prodict. The products of the group include Nabi-HB(R) and Aloprim(TM). The group operates from the United States.

Primary SIC and add'l.: 2836 2834

CIK No: 0001326676

Financial Data: *Fiscal Year End:*NA *Latest Annual Data:* 12/30/2006

Year	Sales		Net Income
2006	$89,868,000		-$58,703,000
2005	$108,055,000		-$128,449,000
2004	$179,763,000		-$50,390,000

Curr. Assets:	$155,067,000	**Curr. Liab.:**	$46,102,000		
Plant, Equip.:	$94,084,000	**Total Liab.:**	$166,570,000	**Indic. Yr. Divd.:**	NA
Total Assets:	$328,397,000	**Net Worth:**	$161,827,000	**Debt/ Equity:**	NA

NABO Inc

1221 Brickell Ave, 9th Fl., Miami, FL, 33131; *PH:* 1-305-397-2818

General - Incorporation	NV	**Stock**- Price on:12/24/2007	NA
Employees	NA	Stock Exchange	NA
Auditor	NA	Ticker Symbol	NA
Stk Agt	Empire Stock Transfer Inc.	Outstanding Shares	NA
Counsel	NA	E.P.S	NA
DUNS No.	NA	Shareholders	NA

Business: The group's principle activity is to provide community services. The group operates from United States.

Primary SIC and add'l.: 1040

CIK No: 0001364139

Officers: Enrique Abaroa Martinez/34/Dir., CEO, Pres., Treasurer, CFO, David Craven/51/Dir., Sec., Jacqueline Jordan/Dir., Sec., John Ellis/Dir., Treasurer, Janice Bispham/Public Relations Officer, Cora Rawlins/Regional Dir. - East, John Noel/Regional Dir. - West, Sheena Aimey-Petrolito/Regional Dir. - North, Wesley Lynch/Regional Dir. - South

Directors: Enrique Abaroa Martinez/34/Dir., CEO, Pres., Treasurer, CFO, Michael Cummins/Chmn., Earl Ashby/Vice Chmn., John Ellis/Dir., Treasurer, Fitzgerald Rowe/Dir., Jacqueline Jordan/Dir., Sec., David Craven/51/Dir., Sec.

Owners: Katrina MacAlpine/6.25%, Isobel Campbell/5.56%, Gerry Birmingham/5.56%, David Craven/30.56%, Rush & Co./7.24%, Insiders/30.56%, Iain MacAlpine/5.56%, Dan Easter/5.56%

Financial Data: *Fiscal Year End:*03/31 *Latest Annual Data:* 03/31/2007

Year	Sales		Net Income
2007	NA		-$56,000

Curr. Assets:	$2,000	**Curr. Liab.:**	$1,000		
Plant, Equip.:	NA	**Total Liab.:**	$1,000	**Indic. Yr. Divd.:**	NA
Total Assets:	$2,000	**Net Worth:**	$1,000	**Debt/ Equity:**	NA

Nabors Industries Ltd

Mintflower Pl., 8 Par-La-Ville Rd., Hamilton, HM08; *PH:* 441-2921510; *Fax:* 441-2921334; *http://* www.nabors.com

General - Incorporation	Bermuda	**Stock**- Price on:12/24/2007	$34.88
Employees	25,218	Stock Exchange	NDQ
Auditor	PricewaterhouseCoopers LLP	Ticker Symbol	NBTB
Stk Agt	Mellon Trust Co	Outstanding Shares	281,380,000
Counsel	NA	E.P.S	$3.57
DUNS No.	00-691-5748	Shareholders	NA

Business: The group's principal activities are to conduct oil, gas and geothermal land drilling operations in the United States, Canada, south and Central America, the Middle East and Africa. The group offers a number of ancillary well-site services, including oilfield management, engineering, transportation, construction, maintenance, well logging and other support services in selected domestic and international markets. The group owns and operates over 600 land drilling rigs, 745 domestic and 40 international land workover and well-servicing rigs, 43 offshore platform rigs, 16 jackups, three barge rigs, 30 marine transportation and support vessels and a large component of trucks and fluid hauling vehicles. The trademarks of the group are sundowner(R), mase(R) tru vu(R) and rigwatch(tm).

Primary SIC and add'l.: 1381 8711

CIK No: 0001163739

Subsidiaries: Nabors Canada LP, Nabors Drilling Canada ULC, Nabors Drilling International Ltd, Nabors Drilling Limited (Canada), Nabors Drilling USA, LP, Nabors Global Holdings Ltd, Nabors Holding Company, Nabors Hungary KFT, Nabors Industries, Inc., Nabors International Finance Inc, Nabors International Holdings Ltd, Nabors Well Services Co, Oak Leaf Investments Inc, Pool Company, Ryan Energy Technologies Inc. 17 Subsidiaries included in the Index

Officers: Eugene M. Isenberg/Chmn., CEO, Anthony G. Petrello/Dep. Chmn., COO, Pres., Bruce P. Koch/CFO, VP, Daniel McLachlin/70/VP - Administration, Sec.

Directors: Eugene M. Isenberg/Chmn., CEO, Anthony G. Petrello/Dep. Chmn., COO, Pres., Alexander M. Knaster/Dir., Hans W. Schmidt/Dir., James L. Payne/Dir., Marty J. Whitman/Dir., Mickey M. Sheinfeld/Dir., Jack Wexler/Dir. Emeritus, Myron M. Sheinfeld/Dir.

Owners: Eugene M. Isenberg/6.99%, James L. Payne, Insiders/10.84%, Bruce P. Koch, Anthony G. Petrello/3.60%, Daniel McLachlin, Alexander M. Knaster, Myron M. Sheinfeld, Martin J. Whitman, Hans W. Schmidt

Financial Data: *Fiscal Year End:*12/31 *Latest Annual Data:* 12/31/2006

Year	Sales		Net Income
2006	$4,942,714,000		$1,020,736,000
2005	$3,551,009,000		$648,695,000
2004	$2,448,152,000		$302,457,000

Curr. Assets:	$2,504,856,000	**Curr. Liab.:**	$854,360,000	**P/E Ratio:**	9.85
Plant, Equip.:	$5,410,101,000	**Total Liab.:**	$5,605,650,000	**Indic. Yr. Divd.:**	NA
Total Assets:	$9,142,303,000	**Net Worth:**	$3,536,653,000	**Debt/ Equity:**	1.0451

Nacco Industries Inc

5875 Landerbrook Dr., Ste. 300, Cleveland, OH, 44124; *PH:* 1-440-449-9600; *Fax:* 1-440-449-9607; *http://* www.nacco.com; *Email:* ir@naccoind.com

General - Incorporation	DE	**Stock**- Price on:12/24/2007	$157.68
Employees	10,700	Stock Exchange	NYSE
Auditor	Ernst & Young LLP	Ticker Symbol	NC
Stk Agt	National City Bank Corp Trust Ops	Outstanding Shares	8,270,000
Counsel	NA	E.P.S	$12.75
DUNS No.	14-720-4127	Shareholders	NA

Business: The groups principle activity is to provide lift trucks, housewares and mining services. The group operates from United States.

Primary SIC and add'l.: 1221 3537 6719 3634

CIK No: 0000789933

Subsidiaries: Bellaire Corporation, Grupo HB/PS, S.A. de C.V., Hamilton Beach/Proctor-Silex de Mexico, S.A. de C.V., Hamilton Beach/Proctor-Silex, Inc., Hyster (H.K.) Limited, Hyster-Yale Materials Handling, Inc., Mississippi Lignite Mining Company, NACCO Materials Handling Distribution (France) S.A.S., NACCO Materials Handling Distribution France S.A.R.L., NACCO Materials Handling Group Brasil Ltda., NACCO Materials Handling Group Pty, Ltd., NACCO Materials Handling Group, Inc., NACCO Materials Handling Group, Ltd., NACCO Materials Handling Limited, NACCO Materials Handling, B.V. 40 Subsidiaries included in the Index

Officers: Randolph J. Gawelek/60/CEO, Pres. - KCI, From Prior to 2002, Robert L. Benson/CEO, Pres. - North American Coal Corporation/$1,078,140.00, Michael J. Morecroft/CEO, Pres. - Hamilton Beach, Proctor, Silex/$1,778,174.00, Alfred M. Rankin/Chmn., CEO, Pres./$7,040,444.00, Michael P. Brogan/CEO, Pres. - Nacco Materials Handling Group, Inc/$1,348,675.00, Jeffrey C. Mattern/Treasurer - Nacco Materials Handling Group, Inc, J. C. Butler/VP - Corporate Development, Treasurer, Emil S. Wepprich/VP - Supply Chain - Kitchen Collection, Inc, L. J. Kennedy/Sec., Treasurer - Kitchen Collection, Inc, Constantine E. Tsipis/49/Assist. General Counsel, Assist. Sec., Charles A. Bittenbender/VP, General Counsel, Sec., Gregory J. Dawe/VP - Manufacturing, Americas, Nacco Materials Handling Group, Inc, Raymond C. Ulmer/VP - Finance, Information Systems, Americas, Nacco Materials Handling Group, Inc, Donald L. Chance/VP, Pres. - Yale Materials Handling Corporation, America, Nacco Materials Handling Group, Inc, Paul D. Laroia/VP, Pres. - Hyster Company, America, Nacco Materials Handling Group, Inc *(47 Officers included in Index)*

Directors: Alfred M. Rankin/Chmn., CEO, Pres., Michael E. Shannon/Dir., Eugene Wong/Dir., Owsley Brown/Dir., Britton T. Taplin/Dir., John F. Turben/Dir., David F. Taplin/Dir., Richard De J. O'Sborne/Dir., Ian M. Ross/Dir., Dennis W. Labarre/Dir.

Owners: Ian M. Ross, Dimensional FundAdvisors LP/5.15%, David F. Taplin, Owsley Brown, Richard de J. Osborne, Eugene Wong, Dennis W. LaBarre, Dennis W. LaBarre, Britton T. Taplin, Michael E. Shannon, John F. Turben, David F. Taplin, Thomas E. Taplin/5.84%, Thomas E. Taplin/19.26%, Alfred M. Rankin/11.91% *(20 Owners included in Index)*

Financial Data: *Fiscal Year End:*12/31 *Latest Annual Data:* 12/31/2006

Year	Sales		Net Income
2006	$3,349,000,000		$106,200,000
2005	$3,157,400,000		$62,500,000
2004	$2,782,600,000		$47,900,000

Curr. Assets:	$1,153,800,000	**Curr. Liab.:**	$751,000,000	**P/E Ratio:**	12.37
Plant, Equip.:	$371,400,000	**Total Liab.:**	$1,363,200,000	**Indic. Yr. Divd.:**	$2.000
Total Assets:	$2,156,300,000	**Net Worth:**	$793,100,000	**Debt/ Equity:**	0.4680

Nalco Holding Company

1601 W Diehl Rd., Naperville, IL, 60563; *PH:* 1-630-305-1000; *Fax:* 1-630-305-2900; *http://* www.nalco.com

General - Incorporation	DE	**Stock**- Price on:12/24/2007	NA
Employees	11,100	Stock Exchange	AMEX
Auditor	Ernst& Young LLP	Ticker Symbol	NLN
Stk Agt	Computershare Trust Co	Outstanding Shares	144,360,000
Counsel	NA	E.P.S	$0.92
DUNS No.	NA	Shareholders	NA

Business: The groups principal activity is to provide integrated water treatment and process improvement services, chemicals and equipment programs for industrial and institutional applications. The group operates through three segments namely, industrial and institutional services, energy services and paper services. The group operates from the United States.

Primary SIC and add'l.: 2865 1629 2899

CIK No: 0001298341

Subsidiaries: Adecom Quimica Ltda., Derypol SA, Katayama Nalco Inc., Nalco (Shanghai) Trading Co. Ltd., Nalco Anadolu Kimya Sanayii Ve Ticaret AS, Nalco Argentina S.R.L., Nalco Australia Pty. Ltd., Nalco Belgium NV/SA, Nalco Brasil Ltda, Nalco Canada Co., Nalco Company, Nalco de Colombia Ltda, Nalco de Mexico, S. de R.L. de C.V., Nalco Deutschland GmbH, Nalco Egypt Trading 49 Subsidiaries included in the Index

Officers: William H. Joyce/Chmn., CEO/$2,451,080.00, Richard J. O'Shanna/Division VP, Tax Officer, Mary T. Manupella/VP - Human Resources, Frederic Jung/Controller, Mark Stoll/Pres. - Pacific Support Operations, Mark Stoll, Group VP, Steve Taylor/Pres. - Energy Services Division, Group VP, Rich Bendure/Pres. - Pacific Division, Group VP/$1,281,060.00, David Johnson/Pres. - European Operations, Group VP/$1,225,731.00, Mary Kay Kaufmann/Pres. - Industrial, Institutional Services Middle Marketing, Group VP, Manian Ramesh/VP - Research, Development, Bradley J. Bell/CFO, Exec. VP, Treasurer/$946,014.00, William J. Roe/COO, Pres. - Industrial, Institutional Services Division, Exec. VP/$1,257,163.00, Daniel M. Harker/55/Sr. VP - Global Supply Chain, John P. Yimoyines/Pres. - Paper Services Division, Group VP, Louis L. Loosbrock/Pres. - Industrial, Institutional Services Heavy Industry, Group VP *(20 Officers included in Index)*

Directors: William H. Joyce/Chmn., CEO, Rodney F. Chase/Dir., Chinh E. Chu/41/Dir., Joshua J. Harris/43/Dir., Richard B. Marchese/Dir., Sanjeev K. Mehra/49/Dir., Paul H. O'Neill/Dir., Douglas A. Pertz/Dir., Daniel S. Sanders/Dir.

Owners: Mark Irwin, Insiders/3.50%, Philippe Creteur, Ziff Asset Management, L.P./5.20%, Arnhold & S. Bleichroeder Advisers Inc./7.00%, Daniel S. Sanders, Richard B. Marchese, Bradley J. Bell, Rodney F. Chase, Douglas A. Pertz, Paul H. O'Neil, Gregory Nelson, Joshua J. Harris, Glenview Capital Management LLC/5.50%, John Gigerich (*18 Owners included in Index*)

Financial Data: Fiscal Year End:12/31 Latest Annual Data: 3/31/2007

Year	Sales	Net Income
2007	$909,300,000	$19,600,000
2006	$915,400,000	$30,700,000
2005	$3,312,400,000	$47,800,000

Curr. Assets:	$1,167,400,000	Curr. Liab.:	$719,400,000	P/E Ratio:	2.37
Plant, Equip.:	$743,400,000	Total Liab.:	$4,765,600,000	Indic. Yr. Divd.:	$0.140
Total Assets:	$5,656,500,000	Net Worth:	$890,900,000	Debt/ Equity:	NA

Nam Tai Electronics Inc

Unit A & C, 17/F, Edificio Comercial Rodrigues, 559 Da Avenida Da Praia Grande, Macao; **PH:** 853-28356333; **Fax:** 853-28356262; **http://** www.namtai.com

General - Incorporation. British Virgin Islands	Stock- Price on:12/24/2007 ....$12.23
Employees 7,473	Stock Exchange..........................NYSE
Auditor ....Deloitte Touche Tohmatsu	Ticker Symbol.............................NTE
Stk Agt........................Registrar & Transfer Co	Outstanding Shares 44,800,000
Counsel.................................White & Case LLP	E.P.S.......................................$1.28
DUNS No. 66-219-0412	Shareholders...............................NA

Business: The group's principle activities are the manufacturing and trading of consumer electronic products, subassemblies, liquid crystal display panels and transformers. Other activities include the provision of management services and software development. The group is also involved in hardware and software design, plastic molding, component purchasing, assembly into finished products or electronic subassemblies, post-assembly testing, and shipping services. It is also engaged in the manufacturing, producing and selling of telecommunication products, personal digital assistants, calculators, electronic dictionaries and rechargeable lithium ion battery packs. Component subassemblies include LCD modules and lithium ion rechargeable battery packs for mobile phones, LCD panels and transformers. It operates in Hong Kong and the People's Republic of China. The group's quarterly revenue for Sep '07 was 204.49 millions of USD.

Primary SIC and add'l.: 5045 5044 8741 6719

CIK No: 0000829365

Subsidiaries: J.I.C. (Macao Commercial Offshore) Company Limited, J.I.C. Technology Company Limited, Jetup Electronic (Shenzhen) Co. Ltd, Jetup Electronic (Shenzhen) Co., Limited (Jetup), Nam Tai Electronic & Electrical Products Limited, Nam Tai Investments Consultant (Macao Commercial Offshore) Company Limited, Namtai Electronic (Shenzhen) Co., Ltd., Namtek Japan Company Limited, Namtek Software Development Company Limited, Shenzhen Namtek Co., Ltd., Zastron (Macao Commercial Offshore) Company Limited, Zastron Electronic (Shenzhen) Co. Ltd., Zastron Precision-Tech Limited (ZPTL)

Officers: Warren Lee/44/CEO, Patrick Lee/43/CEO - Zastron Group, Joseph Li/Consultant - Hong Kong, Tadao Murakami/Consultant - Tokyo, Japan, Tadashi Sasaki/Consultant, Tokyo, Japan, C. S. Chuang/Consultant - Taipei, Taiwan, Patinda Lei/41/CFO, Lorne Waldman/41/Corp. Sec., Eve Leung/Corp. Sec., John Farina/CFO

Directors: M. K. Koo/Chmn., Mark Waslen/Dir., Seitaro Furukawa/66/Dir., Peter R. Kellogg/Dir., Wing Yan Lo/Dir., Charles Chu/Dir.

Owners: M. K. Koo/12.70%, Karene Wong, Seitaro Furukawa, Lorne Waldman, Charles Chu, Ivan Chui/2.30%, Patinda Lei, Colin Yeoh, Peter R. Kellogg/13.00%, Mark Waslen, I.A.T. Reinsurance Syndicate Ltd./11.70%, Wing Yan Lo

Financial Data: Fiscal Year End:12/31 Latest Annual Data: 12/31/2006

Year	Sales	Net Income
2006	$879,432,000	$40,756,000
2005	$797,237,000	$51,306,000
2004	$533,861,000	$66,885,000

Curr. Assets:	$400,718,000	Curr. Liab.:	$162,613,000	P/E Ratio:	9.85
Plant, Equip.:	$102,721,000	Total Liab.:	$212,141,000	Indic. Yr. Divd.:	$0.840
Total Assets:	$529,235,000	Net Worth:	$317,094,000	Debt/ Equity:	NA

Nano Chemical Systems Holdings Inc

105 Pk. Ave., Seaford, DE, 19973; **PH:** 1-480-816-6140; **http://** www.nanochemical.com

General - Incorporation............................NV	Stock- Price on:12/24/2007 ....NA
Employees ....NA	Stock Exchange..........................OTC
Auditor ....Madsen & Associates, CPA's Inc.	Ticker Symbol.............................NCSH
Stk Agt..........................NA	Outstanding Shares ....NA
Counsel.................................NA	E.P.S.......................................NA
DUNS No. ....NA	Shareholders...............................NA

Business: The groups principle activity is to manufacture chemicals. The products of the group include waxes, lubricants, and polishes. The group acquired SeaSpray Aerosol, Inc. in April 2006, and GreenTree Spray Technologies, LLC in March 2005. Specific customers of the group is Pioneer Manufacturing, Inc. The group operates from the United States.

Primary SIC and add'l.: 2842

CIK No: 0001172324

Subsidiaries: Nano Chemical Systems, Inc., SeaSpray Aerosol, Inc.

Officers: Alexander H. Edwards/CEO, Pres., Treasurer

Owners: Robert Esposito/9.37%, Treya, Inc./14.14%, Marc Mathys/56.56%, GreenTree Spray Technologies, LLC/56.56%, Katrina Cleburn/7.07%

Curr. Assets:	$1,078,000	Curr. Liab.:	$2,344,000		
Plant, Equip.:	$183,000	Total Liab.:	$2,344,000	Indic. Yr. Divd.:	NA
Total Assets:	$1,330,000	Net Worth:	-$1,014,000	Debt/ Equity:	NA

Nano Proprietary Inc

3006 Longhorn Blvd., Ste. 107, Austin, TX, 78758; **PH:** 1-512-339-5020; **Fax:** 1-512-339-5021; **http://** www.nano-proprietary.com

General - Incorporation ....TX	Stock- Price on:12/24/2007 ....$1.38
Employees 35	Stock Exchange..........................OTC
Auditor ....Sprouse & Anderson LLP	Ticker Symbol.............................NNPP
Stk Agt.... Computershare Investor Services LLC	Outstanding Shares 107,120,000
Counsel.................................NA	E.P.S.......................................-$0.05
DUNS No. 60-215-9972	Shareholders...............................NA

Business: The group's principal activity is develop products and services based on novel applications of carbon nanotube technology. The group conducts research on identifying key applications of the carbon nanotube technology particularly on the display and sensor industries. The group is also conducting research on applications of this technology in the medical, X-ray, wireless communication, and other industries. The group conducts contract research and development for United States governmental agencies and large companies.

Primary SIC and add'l.: 6794

CIK No: 0000891417

Subsidiaries: Applied Nanotech, Inc., Electronic Billboard Technology, Inc., Sign Builders of America, Inc.

Officers: Thomas F. Bijou/Chmn., CEO/$687,422.00, Zvi Yaniv/Dir., Pres./$527,369.00, Douglas P. Baker/Dir., CFO, Corp. Sec./$318,684.00

Directors: Thomas F. Bijou/Chmn., CEO, Douglas P. Baker/Dir., CFO, Corp. Sec., Ronald J. Berman/Dir., Zvi Yaniv/Dir., Pres., Howard Westerman/Dir., Patrick V. Stark/Dir., Tracy K. Bramlett/Dir., Bradford S. Lamb/Dir.

Owners: Douglas P. Baker, Howard Westerman, Eddie Lee, Bradford S. Lamb, Zvi Yaniv, Insiders/3.87%, Robert Ronstadt, Marc W. Eller, Pinnacle Fund, L.P./8.74%, Thomas F. Bijou, Ronald J. Berman/1.07%

Financial Data: Fiscal Year End:12/31 Latest Annual Data: 12/31/2006

Year	Sales	Net Income
2006	$1,117,000	-$6,594,000
2005	$566,000	-$4,662,000
2004	$383,000	-$4,612,000

Curr. Assets:	$2,529,000	Curr. Liab.:	$2,051,000		
Plant, Equip.:	$155,000	Total Liab.:	$2,051,000	Indic. Yr. Divd.:	NA
Total Assets:	$2,693,000	Net Worth:	$642,000	Debt/ Equity:	NA

Nano Superlattice Technology Inc

NO. 666 JHENSING RD., Gueishan Township, Taoyuan County, 333; **PH:** 886-33498677; **Fax:** 886-33494288; **http://** www.supernano.com.tw; **Email:** service@supernano.com.tw

General - Incorporation ....DE	Stock- Price on:12/24/2007 ....$0.16
Employees ....NA	Stock Exchange..........................OTC
Auditor ....Simon & Edward, LLP	Ticker Symbol.............................NSLT
Stk Agt.....................Transfer Online, Inc.	Outstanding Shares ....NA
Counsel.................................NA	E.P.S.......................................NA
DUNS No. ....NA	Shareholders...............................NA

Business: The groups principle activities include developing and producing nano-scale coating technology that is applied to mechanical tools and metal surfaces for sale to manufacturers in the computer, mechanical and molding industries. The group operates from China and the United States.

Primary SIC and add'l.: 3470

CIK No: 0001080316

Subsidiaries: Nano Superlattice Technology Inc. (BVI)

Officers: Alice Tzu-shia Hwang/53/Chmn., CEO, Pres., Yu-Chien Cheng/57/Dir., Chief Supervisor - Technology, Chien-Fang Wang/55/Dir., VP, Principal Financial Officer, Tzu-Hsia Huang/Contact Person

Directors: Alice Tzu-shia Hwang/53/Chmn., CEO, Pres., Tzu-Sheng Su/46/Dir., Yu-Chien Cheng/57/Dir., Chief Supervisor - Technology, Chien-Fang Wang/55/Dir., VP, Principal Financial Officer, Kevin Chung-chieh Lin/47/Dir., Yun-Chun Tseng/46/Dir.

Owners: Yo-Chien Cheng/9.28%, Insiders/25.58%, Yun Chun Tseng, Alice Tzu-Shia Hwang/9.89%, Chien-Fang Wang/2.50%, Tzu-Sheng Su, Kevin Chung-Chien Lin/3.09%

Financial Data: Fiscal Year End:12/31 Latest Annual Data: 12/31/2006

Year	Sales	Net Income
2006	$9,470,000	-$193,000
2005	$9,142,000	-$864,000
2004	$2,628,000	-$1,313,000

Curr. Assets:	$3,900,000	Curr. Liab.:	$5,278,000		
Plant, Equip.:	$8,160,000	Total Liab.:	$7,383,000	Indic. Yr. Divd.:	NA
Total Assets:	$12,152,000	Net Worth:	$4,770,000	Debt/ Equity:	0.3903

Nano-Jet Corp

15321 Main St. NE, Ste. 102, Duvall, WA, 98019; **PH:** 1-425-788-9823; **http://** www.nanojetcorp.com; **Email:** info@nanojetcorp.com

General - Incorporation ....NV	Stock- Price on:12/24/2007 ....$2.5
Employees ....NA	Stock Exchange..........................OTC
Auditor ....Bateman & Co., Inc., P.C.	Ticker Symbol.............................NNJT
Stk Agt............ Pacific Stock Transfer Company	Outstanding Shares ....NA
Counsel.................................NA	E.P.S.......................................NA
DUNS No. ....NA	Shareholders...............................NA

Business: The groups principal activity is to develop fuel-efficient products and fuel additives. In September 2006 the group acquired Nano-Jet Corp. The group operates from the United States and Canada.

Primary SIC and add'l.: 3510

CIK No: 0001224006

Officers: Ken Martin/Dir., CEO, Chief Accounting Officer, Mohamed Khayr/Consultant in The Middle East, North Africa, Dan Miller/Sales Mgr. - USA, Brian J. Walsh/Sales Mgr. UK - Europe, Xiao Lin/MD, Harry Hartz/MD, William Hitsman/COO, Exec. VP

Directors: Ken Martin/Dir., CEO, Chief Accounting Officer

Owners: Arthur Brian Bage, Port Mercantile Capital Inc., Paul Walsh, Khurram Bri Chohan, Christopher Walsh, Lin Xiao, Marion Walsh, Mussarat Hanif Chohan, Harald Hartz, John Darmarin, Robert Terence Harron, Gerard Walsh, Bari Chohan, Lucy Walsh, Insiders (*17 Owners included in Index*)

Financial Data: Fiscal Year End:12/31 Latest Annual Data: 12/31/2006

Year	Sales	Net Income
2006	NA	-$70,000
2005	NA	-$42,000
2004	NA	-$82,000

Curr. Assets:	$151,000	**Curr. Liab.:**	$215,000		
Plant, Equip.:	NA	**Total Liab.:**	$465,000	**Indic. Yr. Divd.:**	NA
Total Assets:	$366,000	**Net Worth:**	-$99,000	**Debt/ Equity:**	NA

Nanobac Pharmaceuticals Inc

4730 N Habana Ave., Ste. 205, Tampa, FL, 33614; ***PH:*** 1-813-264-2241; ***Fax:*** 1-813-264-5512; ***http://*** www.nanobaclabs.com; ***Email:*** info@nanobaclabs.com

General - Incorporation	FL	**Stock**- Price on:12/24/2007	$0.07
Employees	13	Stock Exchange	OTC
Auditor	Aidman, Piser & Co. P.A	Ticker Symbol	NNBP
Stk Agt	Continental Stock Transfer & Trust Co	Outstanding Shares	247,470,000
Counsel	NA	E.P.S	-$0.029
DUNS No.	NA	Shareholders	NA

Business: The group's principal activity is to operate through its wholly owned subsidiary healthcentrics, inc. Healthcentrics, inc was formed to organize, develop and market a suite of Web-based medical accounting, billing and management information services to third party billing companies, practice management and health care provider organizations. The group intends to organize health care and related application service provider delivered software and services, and to act as a hub through which users exchange information, conduct transactions and communicate in real-time. During 2003, the group acquired infovault inc and mdi systems inc. On 28-Aug-2003, the group acquired nanobac oy.

Primary SIC and add'l.: 8071

CIK No: 0000925894

Subsidiaries: Nanobac OY, Nanobac Pharmaceuticals, Incorporated, Nanobac Sciences LLC, NanobacLabs Research Institute, LLC

Officers: John D. Stanton/Co - Chmn., CEO, CFO, Benedict S. Maniscalco/Co - Chmn., Chief Medical Officer, Head - Operations, Olavi E. Kajander/Chief Research, Scientific Dir., Neva Cifteioglu/Dir. - Science

Directors: John D. Stanton/Co - Chmn., CEO, CFO, Benedict S. Maniscalco/Co - Chmn., Chief Medical Officer, Head - Operations, Stephan Rechtschaffen/Dir., Alex H. Edwards/Dir., Olavi E. Kajander/Chief Research, Scientific Dir.

Owners: Alexander Edwards/4.92%, John D. Stanton/43.45%, Benedict Maniscalco/1.85%, Insiders/51.43%, Gary S. Mezo/9.93%, Stephan Rechtschaffen/1.21%

Financial Data: ***Fiscal Year End:***12/31 ***Latest Annual Data:*** 12/31/2006

Year	Sales	Net Income
2006	$225,000	-$4,973,000
2005	$657,000	-$3,687,000
2004	$358,000	-$8,518,000

Curr. Assets:	$127,000	**Curr. Liab.:**	$6,300,000		
Plant, Equip.:	$60,000	**Total Liab.:**	$9,137,000	**Indic. Yr. Divd.:**	NA
Total Assets:	$7,825,000	**Net Worth:**	-$1,312,000	**Debt/ Equity:**	NA

Nanogen Inc

10398 Pacific Ctr. Ct., San Diego, CA, 92121; ***PH:*** 1-877-626-6436; ***Fax:*** 1-858-410-4952; ***http://*** www.nanogen.com; ***Email:*** technicalassistance@nanogen.com

General - Incorporation	DE	**Stock**- Price on:12/24/2007	$1.37
Employees	288	Stock Exchange	NDQ
Auditor	Ernst & Young LLP	Ticker Symbol	NGEN
Stk Agt	Computershare Investor Services LLC	Outstanding Shares	72,470,000
Counsel	Wilson Sonsini Goodrich & Rosati	E.P.S	-$0.59
DUNS No.	84-061-0273	Shareholders	NA

Business: The group's principal activity is to develop products that integrate advanced microelectronics and molecular biology. These products are used in the fields of biomedical research, genomics, medical diagnostics, genetic testing, drug discovery, forensics, agriculture and environmental testing. The group's products include the nanochip(R) system consisting of nanochip(R) molecular biology workstation and the nanochip(R) cartridge which enables identification and precision analysis of biological test samples containing charged molecules. Its products are marketed primarily in the United States, Europe and Mexico. The group has collaborative alliances with hitachi, ltd, aventis and becton dickinson. On 21-Apr-2004, the group acquired synx pharma inc.

Primary SIC and add'l.: 3826

CIK No: 0001030339

Subsidiaries: Delta Point Cardiac Diagnostics, Inc., Epoch Biosciences, Inc., Nanogen Europe B.V., Nanogen Recognomics GmbH, Nanotronics, Inc., SynX Pharma, Inc.

Officers: Howard C. Birndorf/Chmn., CEO, Company Founder/$1,368,508.00, Merl F. Hoekstra/VP - Business Development, Robert Saltmarsh/CFO/$567,658.00, William L. Respess/Sr. VP, General Counsel, Sec./$768,341.00, David Ludvigson/COO, Pres./$1,153,828.00, Graham Lidgard/Sr. VP - Research, Development/$577,845.00, Robert Proulx/VP - Marketing, Sales, David Boudreau/VP - Operations, Carl T. Foster/VP - Alliance Management, Walt Mahoney/VP - Research, Development, David H. Ray/VP - Operations, Point, Care Division, Leanne M. Kiviharju/VP - Clinical, Regulatory Affairs, Quality Assurance

Directors: Howard C. Birndorf/Chmn., CEO, Company Founder, Stelios B. Papadopoulos/Dir., Robert E. Whalen/Dir., William G. Gerber/61/Dir., David Schreiber/Dir., Heiner Dreismann/Dir.

Owners: Robert Whalen, Howard C. Birndorf/2.80%, Robert Saltmarsh, William L. Respess, Fisher Scientific International, Inc./7.70%, Stelios Papadopoulos, Heiner Dreisman, Insiders/5.50%, David Schreiber, David G. Ludvigson/1.10%, Graham Lidgard

Financial Data: ***Fiscal Year End:***12/31 ***Latest Annual Data:*** 12/31/2006

Year	Sales	Net Income
2006	$26,852,000	-$49,070,000
2005	$12,544,000	-$96,494,000
2004	$5,374,000	-$38,907,000

Curr. Assets:	$46,501,000	**Curr. Liab.:**	$25,880,000		
Plant, Equip.:	$9,388,000	**Total Liab.:**	$59,040,000	**Indic. Yr. Divd.:**	NA
Total Assets:	$119,253,000	**Net Worth:**	$60,213,000	**Debt/ Equity:**	0.1965

Nanometrics Inc

1550 Buckeye Dr., Milpitas, CA, 95035; ***PH:*** 1-408-435-9600; ***Fax:*** 1-408-232-5910; ***http://*** www.nanometrics.com; ***Email:*** investors@nanometrics.com

General - Incorporation	CA	**Stock**- Price on:12/24/2007	$0.37
Employees	522	Stock Exchange	NDQ
Auditor	BDO Seidman LLP	Ticker Symbol	NANO
Stk Agt	U.S. Stock Transfer Corp	Outstanding Shares	18,150,000
Counsel	Wilson Sonsini Goodrich & Rosati	E.P.S	-$0.83
DUNS No.	07-630-3858	Shareholders	NA

Business: The group's principal activities are to design, manufacture and market metrology systems used in the manufacture of semiconductors, integrated circuits and flat panel displays. The group's metrology system measures various thin film properties, critical circuit dimensions and layer-to-layer circuit alignment and inspects for surface defects during various steps of the manufacturing process. Customers include applied materials, hynix semiconductor, samsung, powerchip, chimei, tricenti technology inc, au optronics, hannstar, semiconductor manufacturing international corp and wacker. The group operates in the United States, Japan, Korea, Taiwan, Germany and other countries.

Primary SIC and add'l.: 3829 7389 3827

CIK No: 0000704532

Subsidiaries: Nanometrics Incorporated

Officers: John D. Heaton/47/Dir., CEO, Pres./$739,026.00, Timothy Stultz/Dir., CEO, Pres., Quentin B. Wright/51/Chief Accounting Officer/$219,265.00, Gary C. Schaefer/CFO, Douglas J. McCutcheon/59/Exec. VP - Finance, Administration, CFO/$404,700.00, Bruce Crawford/COO, Rajeev Mundhe/53/Sr. VP - Global Sales

Directors: John D. Heaton/47/Dir., CEO, Pres., Timothy Stultz/Dir., CEO, Pres., Bruce C. Rhine/Chmn., Vincent J. Coates/Vice Chmn., Thomas J. Bentley/Dir., William G. Oldham/Dir., Stephen Smith/Dir., Edmond R. Ward/Dir., Joseph Dox/Dir.

Owners: Douglas J. McCutcheon, Bruce C. Rhine/5.30%, Insiders/25.20%, Royce and Associates, LLC/6.40%, Wasatch Advisors, Inc./5.80%, Dimensional Fund Advisors LP/5.90%, Roger Ingalls, Edmond R. Ward, Peter M. Joost/8.00%, Quentin B. Wright, The TCW Group/9.90%, Vincent J. Coates/18.80%

Financial Data: ***Fiscal Year End:***12/31 ***Latest Annual Data:*** 12/30/2006

Year	Sales	Net Income
2006	$96,374,000	-$22,127,000
2005	$70,543,000	$1,511,000

Curr. Assets:	$91,292,000	**Curr. Liab.:**	$14,561,000		
Plant, Equip.:	$42,928,000	**Total Liab.:**	$15,957,000	**Indic. Yr. Divd.:**	$0.340
Total Assets:	$136,300,000	**Net Worth:**	$120,343,000	**Debt/ Equity:**	NA

Nanophase Technologies Corp

1319 Marquette Dr., Romeoville, IL, 60446; ***PH:*** 1-630-771-6700; ***Fax:*** 1-630-771-0825; ***http://*** www.nanophase.com; ***Email:*** investor-relations@nanophase.com

General - Incorporation	DE	**Stock**- Price on:12/24/2007	$6.2
Employees	60	Stock Exchange	NDQ
Auditor	McGladrey & Pullen LLP	Ticker Symbol	NAPS
Stk Agt	LaSalle Bank N.A	Outstanding Shares	19,080,000
Counsel	Ehrenreich Eilenberg KZ LLP	E.P.S	-$0.21
DUNS No.	62-350-2044	Shareholders	NA

Business: The group's principal activities are to develop and market nanocrystalline materials. Nanocrystalline materials generally are made of particles that are less than 100 nanometers (billionths of a meter) in diameter. When the structural features are sized between individual molecules and bulk materials, the range of about 10 to 100 nanometers,the objects display physical attributes different from those found in bulk materials. Thus nanomaterials enable to enhance material properties and devise functions beyond those normally found in a material. The products consist of coated materials and uncoated materials. Coated material includes ingredients for sunscreens and uncoated materials includes ingredients for personal care applications, anti-fungal aids, automotive catalytic converters and abrasion-resistant flooring. E products are sold to domestic and international markets. Its largest customer is basf corporation.

Primary SIC and add'l.: 2899

CIK No: 0000883107

Officers: Joseph E. Cross/Dir., CEO, Pres./$557,945.00, Jess Jankowski/42/Controller, VP, Sec., Treasurer, CFO/$304,500.00, David W. Nelson/VP - Sales, Kevin J. Wenta/Exec. VP - Sales, Marketing, Richard W. Brotzman/Sr. Scientist, VP - Research, Development/$305,068.00, Daniel S. Bilicki/64/VP - Sales, Marketing/$319,007.00, Edward G. Ludwig/VP - Business Development, Robert Haines/VP - Operations/$425,841.00

Directors: Joseph E. Cross/Dir., CEO, Pres., Donald S. Perkins/Chmn., Janet R. Whitmore/Dir., Jerry Pearlman/Dir., Richard W. Siegel/Co - Founder, Dir., James A. McClung/Dir., James A. Henderson/Dir.

Owners: Jess Jankowski, Grace Investments, Ltd./1.57%, Richard W. Brotzman, James A. Henderson, Robert Haines, Spurgeon Corporation/17.22%, Rohm and Haas Electronic Materials CMP. Inc./4.44%, Janet R. Whitmore, James McClung, Donald S. Perkins, Bradford T. Whitmore/18.65%, Richard W. Siegel/1.20%, Jerry Pearlman, AMVESCAP PLC/6.63%, Joseph E. Cross/2.44% *(18 Owners included in Index)*

Financial Data: ***Fiscal Year End:***12/31 ***Latest Annual Data:*** 12/31/2006

Year	Sales	Net Income
2006	$8,991,000	-$5,178,000
2005	$6,802,000	-$5,384,000
2004	$5,208,000	-$6,447,000

Curr. Assets:	$11,484,000	**Curr. Liab.:**	$2,283,000		
Plant, Equip.:	$7,608,000	**Total Liab.:**	$3,919,000	**Indic. Yr. Divd.:**	NA
Total Assets:	$19,744,000	**Net Worth:**	$15,825,000	**Debt/ Equity:**	0.0992

NanoSensors Inc

1800 Wyatt Dr. Ste. 2, Santa Clara, CA, 95054; ***PH:*** 1-408-855-0051; ***Fax:*** 1-408-855-0079; ***http://*** www.nanosensorsinc.net

General - Incorporation...............................NV
Employees 2
Auditor ....Lazar, Levine & Felix, LLP
Stk Agt............ Continental Stock Transfer & Trust Co
Counsel..NA
DUNS No. ....NA

Stock- Price on:12/24/2007 ....$0.0044
Stock Exchange...OTC
Ticker Symbol...NNSR
Outstanding Shares 406,730,000
E.P.S. $0.01
Shareholders...NA

Business: The groups principle activities include developing, manufacturing and marketing sensors and instruments. In January 2007 the group acquired DKL International, Inc. The group operates from the United States.

Primary SIC and add'l.: 3829

CIK No: 0001286648

Officers: Ted Wong/Chmn., CEO, Josh Moser/VP, COO

Directors: Ted Wong/Chmn., CEO, Robert Baron/Dir.

Owners: Insiders/12.80%, Robert A. Baron/1.20%, Ted Wong/9.80%, James Batmasian/7.90%, Blue Green T, LLC/7.20%, Matthew Zuckerman/6.40%, Imtiaz Khan/5.90%, Joshua Moser/1.80%

Financial Data: Fiscal Year End:11/30 Latest Annual Data: 11/30/2006

Year	Sales	Net Income
2006	NA	-$2,110,000
2005	NA	-$334,000

Curr. Assets:	$988,000	Curr. Liab.:	$3,148,000		
Plant, Equip.:	$14,000	Total Liab.:	$3,148,000	Indic. Yr. Divd.:	NA
Total Assets:	$1,009,000	Net Worth:	-$2,139,000	Debt/ Equity:	NA

Napco Security Systems Inc

333 Bayview Ave., Amityville, NY, 11701; **PH:** 1-631-842-9400; **Fax:** 1-631-789-9292; **http://** www.napcosecurity.com; **Email:** salesinfo@napcosecurity.com

General - Incorporation...........................DE
Employees 950
Auditor ....Marcum & Kliegman LLP
Stk Agt............ Continental Stock Transfer & Trust Co
Counsel.............Forchelli, Curto, Schwartz Et Al
DUNS No. 05-497-9125

Stock- Price on:12/24/2007 ....$6.26
Stock Exchange..NDQ
Ticker Symbol..NSSC
Outstanding Shares 19,820,000
E.P.S. $0.27
Shareholders...NA

Business: The group's principal activity is to develop, manufacture and distribute security alarm products for commercial and residential uses. The products of the group include alarm systems, automatic communicators, control panels, combination control panels and digital communicators and digital keypad systems. Alarm systems consists of various detectors, a control panel, a digital keypad and signaling equipment. It also manufactures a variety of exit alarm locks and multi-zone fire alarm control panels. The group conducts its operations principally in the United States but has a foreign subsidiary, napco/alarm lock group international, s.a., located in the Dominican Republic where assemblies and subassemblies of goods are carried out. The group operates in North America, Europe and South America.

Primary SIC and add'l.: 3669 7382

CIK No: 0000069633

Subsidiaries: Alarm Lock Systems, Inc., Continental Instruments, LLC, Napco Group Europe, Limited, Napco Gulf Security Group, LLC, Napco Security Systems International, Inc., Napco/Alarm Lock Exportadora, S.A., Napco/Alarm Lock Grupo Internacional, S.A.

Officers: Richard L. Soloway/Chmn., CEO, Paul Hoey/Sales Mgr. - Eastern Regional, Frank Keel/VP - Eastern Region Sales, Mike McBride/Dir. - National Accounting, Ed Merten/Dir. - National Accounting, Anne Gaudino/Sales Mgr. - International, Yasser Shaaban/MD, Hiba F. El-Breidi/Administrative Operations Assist., Dave Sheffey/VP - Western Region Sales, Dale Clement/Sales Mgr. - Western Regional, Pat Corte/Sales Mgr. - Western Regional, Terry Fielding/GM - Europe, Middle East, Scott Cusmano/Sales Mgr. - Eastern Regional, Joe Guernica/Sales Mgr. - Western Regional, Richard Tare/Sales Mgr. - Western Regional (21 Officers included in Index)

Directors: Richard L. Soloway/Chmn., CEO

Owners: Rutabaga Capital/8.46%, Jorge Hevia/1.29%, Heartland Advisors/5.93%, Michael Carrieri, Insiders/38.48%, Donna A. Soloway, Arnold Blumenthal, Randy B. Blaustein, Kevin S. Buchel/1.77%, Richard L. Soloway/33.81%, Andrew J. Wilder, Paul Stephen Beeber

Financial Data: Fiscal Year End:06/30 Latest Annual Data: 6/30/2006

Year	Sales	Net Income
2006	$69,548,000	$6,119,000
2005	$65,229,000	$5,629,000
2004	$58,093,000	$3,335,000

Curr. Assets:	$50,890,000	Curr. Liab.:	$9,410,000	P/E Ratio:	23.19
Plant, Equip.:	$16,016,000	Total Liab.:	$23,381,000	Indic. Yr. Divd.:	NA
Total Assets:	$76,785,000	Net Worth:	$53,257,000	Debt/ Equity:	NA

Napster Inc

Formerly: Roxio Inc
9044 Melrose Ave., Los Angeles, CA, 90069; **PH:** 1-310-281-5000; **http://** www.roxio.com

General - Incorporation...........................DE
Employees 138
Auditor ....PricewaterhouseCoopers LLP
Stk Agt.................Mellon Investor Services LLC
Counsel...NA
DUNS No. ....NA

Stock- Price on:12/24/2007 ....$3.38
Stock Exchange..NDQ
Ticker Symbol..NASB
Outstanding Shares 46,400,000
E.P.S. ....-$0.63
Shareholders...NA

Business: The group's principal activity is to provide digital media software and services. The group operates in two segments. The consumer software products division develops consumer software products that allow customers to create, manage and move their rich digital media. The software products enable individuals to record digital content onto cds and dvds. The online music distribution division allow customers to access, archive, create, customize and share digital materials in formats compatible with the growing number of digital entertainment devices such as personal computers, CD and DVD players, compressed audio players and personal digital assistants. On 19-May-2003, it acquired napster llc.

Primary SIC and add'l.: 3577 7373

CIK No: 0001122787

Subsidiaries: CG1Verwaltungsgesellschaft mbH, Napster Card Company, Napster Deutschland GmbH, Napster Luxembourg, S. r. l., Napster UK Ltd., Napster, LLC, Roxio ApS

Officers: Christopher Wm. Gorog/55/Dir., CEO/$2,321,986.00, Nand Gangwani/40/CFO, VP/$531,129.00, Bradford D. Duea/39/Pres./$580,056.00, Laura B. Goldberg/40/COO/$577,333.00

Directors: Christopher Wm. Gorog/55/Dir., CEO, Richard J. Boyko/59/Dir., Robert Rodin/54/Dir., Ross Levinsohn/45/Dir., Philip J. Holthouse/49/Dir., Joseph C. Kaczorowski/52/Dir., Brian C. Mulligan/49/Dir., Vernon E. Altman/62/Dir.

Owners: Bradford D. Duea/1.05%, Richard J. Boyko, Robert Rodin, Nand Gangwani, Wm. Christopher Gorog/6.47%, Ross Levinsohn, Laura B. Goldberg, Vernon E. Altman, Joseph C. Kaczorowski, Philip J. Holthouse, Eminence Capital, LLC/7.76%, Brian C. Mulligan

Financial Data: Fiscal Year End:03/31 Latest Annual Data: 3/31/2007

Year	Sales	Net Income
2007	$111,081,000	-$36,826,000
2006	$94,691,000	-$54,945,000
2005	$46,729,000	-$29,506,000

Curr. Assets:	$74,448,000	Curr. Liab.:	$33,406,000		
Plant, Equip.:	$4,736,000	Total Liab.:	$37,023,000	Indic. Yr. Divd.:	NA
Total Assets:	$121,729,000	Net Worth:	$84,706,000	Debt/ Equity:	NA

Nara Bancorp Inc

3731 Wilshire Blvd., Ste. 1000, Los Angeles, CA, 90010; **PH:** 1-213-639-1700; **Fax:** 1-213-235-3033; **http://** www.narabank.com

General - Incorporation ....DE
Employees 408
Auditor ....Crowe Chizek & Co. LLC
Stk Agt...................U.S. Stock Transfer Corp
Counsel..NA
DUNS No. ....NA

Stock- Price on:12/24/2007 ....$16.05
Stock Exchange..NDQ
Ticker Symbol...NARA
Outstanding Shares 26,130,000
E.P.S. $1.29
Shareholders...NA

Business: The group's principal activities are to provide banking services, trade finance services and small business administration lending services. The banking services business provides lending products, including commercial and real estate loans. The trade finance services include the issuance and collection of letters of credit, international collection and import/export financing. The small business administration lending services provides customers of the group with an access to sba guaranteed lending programs. The group carries on its business through fourteen branches in los angeles, san jose, New York city, seattle, Chicago and surrounding areas. On 25-Aug-2003, the group purchased asiana bank , on 30-Oct-2003, certain loans and deposits from Korea exchange bank.

Primary SIC and add'l.: 6712 6021

CIK No: 0001128361

Subsidiaries: Nara Capital Trust I, Nara Capital Trust III, Nara Loan Center, Nara Real Estate Trust, Nara Statutory Trust II, Nara Statutory Trust IV, Nara Statutory Trust V.

Officers: Min Kim/Dir., CEO, Pres./$480,850.00, Alvin Kang/CFO, Exec. VP/$523,341.00, Kyu S. Kim/Sr. VP, Eastern Regional Mgr./$262,803.00, Bonita I. Lee/Exec. VP, Chief Credit Officer/$423,329.00, Myung Hee Hyun/COO, Sr. VP/$261,913.00, Jasna Penich/Sr. VP, Chief Risk Officer/$258,064.00

Directors: Min Kim/Dir., CEO, Pres., Ki Suh Park/Vice Chmn., Chong-Moon Lee/Chmn., Howard Gould/Dir., Jesun Paik/71/Dir., James Staes/Dir., John H. Park/Dir.

Owners: Jasna Penich, Thomas Chung/5.73%, Fidelity Management Corp./9.98%, Chong-Moon Lee/8.75%, Yong H. Kim/1.93%, John H. Park/1.31%, James P. Staes, Myung Hee Hyun, Insiders/14.36%, Alvin D. Kang, Bonita I. Lee, Min J. Kim, Jesun Paik, Ki Suh Park, Kyu S. Kim (16 Owners included in Index)

Financial Data: Fiscal Year End:12/31 Latest Annual Data: 12/31/2006

Year	Sales	Net Income
2006	$175,100,000	$33,806,000
2005	$137,416,000	$26,857,000
2004	$100,786,000	$19,782,000

Curr. Assets:	$97,339,000	Curr. Liab.:	$1,804,058,000	P/E Ratio:	12.74
Plant, Equip.:	$11,941,000	Total Liab.:	$1,860,358,000	Indic. Yr. Divd.:	$0.110
Total Assets:	$2,046,985,000	Net Worth:	$186,627,000	Debt/ Equity:	0.2016

Narrowstep Inc

116 Village Blvd. Ste. 200, Princeton, NJ, 08540; **PH:** 1-609-951-2221; **http://** www.narrowstep.com

General - Incorporation ....DE
Employees ....NA
Auditor ....Rothstein, Kass & Company, P.C.
Stk Agt..NA
Counsel..NA
DUNS No. ....NA

Stock- Price on:12/24/2007 ....$0.41
Stock Exchange..OTC
Ticker Symbol...NRWS
Outstanding Shares ....NA
E.P.S. ....NA
Shareholders...NA

Business: The groups principle activities include developing, producing, transmitting and managing, streaming video broadcasts via the Internet which are tailored for, and targeted to, specific audiences. The group operates through two segments namely Narrowcasting and production services. The group operates from Europe, Asia, the United States and Canada.

Primary SIC and add'l.: 8748

CIK No: 0001232951

Subsidiaries: High Television Ltd., Narrowstep Ltd.

Officers: David McCourt/51/Chmn., Interim CEO, Lisa Vanpatten/44/CFO, Louis Holder/37/CTO

Directors: David McCourt/51/Chmn., Interim CEO, Rajan Chopra/56/Dir., John Whyte/67/Dir.

Owners: Dennis Edmonds, Barry Sternlich/5.00%, David C. McCourt/13.20%, Roger Werner/1.40%, Austin Lewis/9.00%, Stiassni Capital Partners LP/6.70%, Iolo Jones/3.80%, Oded Aboodi/7.70%, John Whyte, Renaissance Capital/17.10%, Insiders/18.70%

Curr. Assets:	$2,203,000	Curr. Liab.:	$2,411,000		
Plant, Equip.:	$1,235,000	Total Liab.:	$2,546,000	Indic. Yr. Divd.:	NA
Total Assets:	$3,586,000	Net Worth:	$1,040,000	Debt/ Equity:	0.0366

NASB Financial Inc

12498 S Hwy. 71, Grandview, MO, 64030; **PH:** 1-816-765-2200; **Fax:** 1-816-316-4504; **http://** www.nasb.com

General - Incorporation ....MO
Employees 362
Auditor ....BKD LLP
Stk Agt...UMB Bank, N.A.
Counsel..NA
DUNS No. ....NA

Stock- Price on:12/24/2007 ....$33.87
Stock Exchange..NDQ
Ticker Symbol...NASB
Outstanding Shares ....NA
E.P.S. $1.88
Shareholders...NA

Business: The group's principal activity is to provide banking services in Missouri and Kansas. The group is a unitary thrift holding company of north American savings bank fsb, a federally chartered stock savings bank. The group accepts savings and checking deposits from the public and uses those funds to originate and purchase real estate loans and other loans. It also purchases mortgage-backed securities and other investment securities. The various kinds of deposits accepted include demand, savings, money market demand and certificates accounts. The group offers a variety of loans that include mortgage, commercial and installment loans. The operations are conducted through eight full service offices located in jackson, cass, clay, buchanan, andrew and lafayette in Missouri and johnson and wyandotte counties in Kansas. On 19-Dec-2002, the group acquired cbes bancorp inc.

Primary SIC and add'l.: 6035 6712

CIK No: 0001059131

Subsidiaries: CBES Bancorp, Inc, Nor-Am Service Corporation, North American Savings Bank, F.S.B.

Officers: David H. Hancock/Chmn., CEO, Theresa Lahiff/Assist. - Mortgage Consultant, Amy Strope/Assist. - Mortgage Consultant, Lee's Summit, Carren Miller/Assist. - Mortgage Consultant, Lee's Summit, Judy Tate/Assist. - Mortgage Consultant, Christi Bukaty/Mortgage Consultant, Springfield, Trudy Anderson/Mortgage Consultant, North Kansas City, Mark Trigg/Mortgage Consultant, Springfield, Dave Graham/Mortgage Consultant, North Kansas City, Brandon Fisher/Mortgage Consultant, Springfield, Terri Snow/Mortgage Consultant, Springfield, Mike O'Neill/Mortgage Consultant, Mortgage Consultant, Chrissy Eisennman/Assitant Consultant, Kenna Williams/Assist. Mortgage Consultant - North Kansas City, Rhonda Nyhus/CFO *(30 Officers included in Index)*

Directors: David H. Hancock/Chmn., CEO, Frederick V. Arbanas/Dir., Russell W. Welsh/Dir., Fletcher M. Lamkin/Dir., Barrett Brady/Dir., Ray A. Ceerle/Dir., Keith B. Cox/Dir., Paul L. Thomas/Dir., Linda S. Hancock/Dir.

Owners: Wade Hall, Barrett Brady, Rhonda Nyhus, Paul L. Thomas, Linda S. Hancock, Insiders, Frederick V. Arbanas, Russell W. Welsh, Brad Lee, David H. Hancock, Michael G. Dunn, Keith B. Cox, Ray A. Ceerle

Financial Data: *Fiscal Year End:*09/30 *Latest Annual Data:* 09/30/2007

Year	Sales	Net Income
2007	$125,611,000	$15,319,000
2006	$123,666,000	$20,768,000
2005	$112,285,000	$25,826,000

Curr. Assets:	$19,647,000	*Curr. Liab.:*	$1,359,314,000	*P/E Ratio:*	15.75
Plant, Equip.:	$18,225,000	*Total Liab.:*	$1,368,224,000	*Indic. Yr. Divd.:*	$0.900
Total Assets:	$1,524,796,000	*Net Worth:*	$156,572,000	*Debt/ Equity:*	0.2138

Nascent Wine Company Inc

2355 Paseo De Las Americas, San Diego, CA, 92154; *PH:* 1-619-661-0458; *Fax:* 1-619-661-9735; *http://* www.pianconegroup.com; *Email:* spiancone@pianconegroup.com

General - Incorporation	NV	**Stock**- Price on:12/24/2007	$1.29
Employees	65	Stock Exchange	OTC
Auditor	Gruber & Co., LLC	Ticker Symbol	NCTW
Stk Agt	Holladay Stock Transfer, Inc.	Outstanding Shares	52,120,000
Counsel	NA	E.P.S	-$0.13
DUNS No.	NA	Shareholders	NA

Business: The groups principle activity is to distribute food products and beer. The products of the group include meats, entrees and desserts, canned and dry goods, fresh meats, imported specialties and Miller beer. Customers served by the group include grocery stores, convenience stores, hotels, resorts, cafeterias, schools, industrial caterers and restaurants. The group operates from the United States and Mexico.

Primary SIC and add'l.: 5182

CIK No: 0001310213

Subsidiaries: Best Beer S.A. de C. V, International Food Services, Inc, Palermo Italian Foods, LLC

Officers: Sandro Piancone/CEO - Nascent Foodservice, Victor Petrone/Pres. - Nascent Foodservice, William Lindberg/CFO, Derek Scallet/COO, MD, Randy Sasaki/Investor Relations Contact, Patrick Deparini/Dir., Sec., Treasurer

Directors: Sandro Piancone/CEO - Nascent Foodservice, Victor Petrone/Pres. - Nascent Foodservice, Patrick Deparini/Dir., Sec., Treasurer

Owners: Insiders/32.00%, Sandro Piancone/27.00%, William Lindberg/1.00%, Victor Petrone/4.00%

Financial Data: *Fiscal Year End:*12/31 *Latest Annual Data:* 12/31/2006

Year	Sales	Net Income
2006	$4,680,000	-$2,037,000
2005	$1,000	-$14,000

Curr. Assets:	$3,119,000	*Curr. Liab.:*	$6,928,000		
Plant, Equip.:	$594,000	*Total Liab.:*	$7,115,000	*Indic. Yr. Divd.:*	NA
Total Assets:	$23,759,000	*Net Worth:*	$16,644,000	*Debt/ Equity:*	NA

Nasdaq Stock Market Inc (The)

1 Liberty Plz., 165 Broadway, 50th Fl., New York, NY, 10006; *PH:* 1-212-401-8700; *Fax:* 1-212-401-1024; *http://* www.nasdaq.com; *Email:* Invesotr.Relations@nasdaq.com

General - Incorporation	DE	**Stock**- Price on:12/24/2007	$30.56
Employees	898	Stock Exchange	NYSE
Auditor	Ernst& Young LLP	Ticker Symbol	NDN
Stk Agt	Mellon Investor Services LLC	Outstanding Shares	112,700,000
Counsel	NA	E.P.S	$3.38
DUNS No.	NA	Shareholders	NA

Business: The groups principle activity is to provide securities listing, trading, and information products and services. The groups services include trade execution, trade reporting and trade comparison. The groups operates through two segments namely market services and issuer services. In the year 2005, the group acquired INET ATS, Inc. The group operates from the United States. The group's quarterly revenue for September is 651.96 millions of USD.

Primary SIC and add'l.: 6200

CIK No: 0001120193

Subsidiaries: Brut, Inc., Carpenter Moore (San Francisco) LLC, Carpenter Moore Insurance Services Ltd, Carpenter Moore Insurance Services, Inc., Direct Report Corporation, Independent Research Network, LLC, INET Clearing, LLC, Inet Futures Exchange, LLC, Inet Holding Company LLC, Inet Stock Exchange, LLC, INET Technology Services, LLC, Nasdaq Canada Inc., Nasdaq Execution Services, LLC, Nasdaq Global Funds (Ireland) Limited, Nasdaq Global Funds, Inc. 30 Subsidiaries included in the Index

Officers: Robert Greifield/Chmn., CEO, Pres., Bruce E. Aust/Exec. VP - Corporate Client Group, Christopher R. Concannon/Exec. VP - Transaction Services/$1,476,433.00, Anna Ewing/CIO, Exec. VP - Operations, Technology/$1,939,828.00, Adena Friedman/Exec. VP - Corporate Strategy, Data Products/$1,481,583.00, John L. Jacobs/Chief Marketing Officer, Exec. VP, Edward S. Knight/Exec. VP, General Counsel, David P. Warren/CFO, Exec. VP/$1,712,119.00, Ronald Hassen/56/Sr. VP, Controller, Principal Accounting Officer

Directors: Robert Greifield/Chmn., CEO, Pres., Furlong H. Baldwin/Dir., Michael Casey/Dir., Daniel B. Coleman/Dir., Lon Gorman/Dir., Patrick Healy/Dir., Glenn H. Hutchins/Dir., Merit E. Janow/Dir., John D. Markese/Dir., Thomas F. O'Neill/Dir., James S. Riepe/Dir., Arvind Sodhani/54/Dir., Thomas G. Stemberg/Dir., Deborah L. Wince-Smith/Dir.

Owners: Kinetics Asset Management, Inc./8.60%, John D. Markese, David P. Warren, Perry Corp/5.70%, Ron Hassen, Thomas G. Stemberg, Lon Gorman, Bruce Aust, James S. Riepe, Deborah L. Wince-Smith, Merit E. Janow, Michael Casey, Robert Greifeld/1.90%, Christopher R. Concannon, Edward Knight *(27 Owners included in Index)*

Financial Data: *Fiscal Year End:*12/31 *Latest Annual Data:* 12/31/2006

Year	Sales	Net Income
2006	$1,657,776,000	$127,893,000
2005	$879,919,000	$61,690,000
2004	$540,441,000	$11,362,000

Curr. Assets:	$2,312,546,000	*Curr. Liab.:*	$460,535,000	*P/E Ratio:*	33.22
Plant, Equip.:	$65,269,000	*Total Liab.:*	$2,259,097,000	*Indic. Yr. Divd.:*	NA
Total Assets:	$3,716,452,000	*Net Worth:*	$1,457,355,000	*Debt/ Equity:*	1.0337

Nash Finch Co

7600 France Ave. S, Minneapolis, MN, 55440; *PH:* 1-952-832-0534; *Fax:* 1-952-844-1237; *http://* www.nashfinch.com; *Email:* investor@nashfinch.com

General - Incorporation	DE	**Stock**- Price on:12/24/2007	$50.39
Employees	4,847	Stock Exchange	NDQ
Auditor	Ernst & Young LLP	Ticker Symbol	NAFC
Stk Agt	Wells Fargo Bank Minnesota N.A	Outstanding Shares	13,410,000
Counsel	NA	E.P.S.	-$1.2
DUNS No.	00-696-2294	Shareholders	NA

Business: The group's principle activity is to distribute food products. The group also operates conventional supermarkets, military commissaries, multicultural stores, urban stores and extreme price stores. The groups services include promotion, advertising and merchandising programs, computerized ordering, receiving and scanning systems, computerized retail accounting, budgeting and payroll systems, personnel management and employee training, consumer and market research, store development services and insurance programs. The group operates from United States.

Primary SIC and add'l.: 5148 5143 5411 5147 5141

CIK No: 0000069671

Subsidiaries: Ericksons Diversified Corporation, GTL Truck Lines, Inc., Hinky Dinky Supermarkets, Inc., NFCG, LLC, Super Food Services, Inc., T.J. Morris Company, U Save Foods, Inc.

Officers: Alec C. Covington/50/Dir., CEO, Pres./$1,944,539.00, Calvin S. Sihilling/CIO, Exec. VP/$453,993.00, Jeffrey E. Poore/Exec. VP - Supply Chain Management/$699,171.00, Kathleen M. Mahoney/Sr. VP, General Counsel, Sec./$563,975.00, Libby Freer/EDI Systems Specialist - Lead, Edward L. Brunot/Sr. VP - Military, Denise M. Wilson/Sr. VP - Human Resources, Mohan Kanagala/EDI Systems Specialist, Christopher A. Brown/Exec. VP - Food Distribution, Robert B. Dimond/CFO, Exec. VP, Treasurer

Directors: Alec C. Covington/50/Dir., CEO, Pres., William R. Voss/54/Chmn., Carole F. Bitter/62/Dir., Jerry L. Ford/67/Dir., Mickey P. Foret/62/Dir., William H. Weintraub/65/Dir., Robert L. Bagby/64/Dir., Sam K. Duncan/Dir., Hawthorne L. Proctor/61/Dir., John H. Grunewald/71/Dir., Douglas A. Hacker/52/Dir.

Owners: Mickey P. Foret/0.02%, John H. Grunewald/0.28%, William R. Voss/0.29%, Robert L. Bagby/0.07%, T. Rowe Price Associates, Inc./9.64%, William H. Weintraub/0.10%, LeAnne M. Stewart/0.27%, Brandywine Global Investment Management, LLC/7.14%, Douglas A. Hacker/0.04%, Dimensional FundAdvisors LP/8.13%, Kathleen M. Mahoney/0.07%, Insiders/3.07%, Barclays Global Investors, N.A./10.83%, Wells Fargo& Company/6.09%, Olstein Capital Management, L.P./7.10% *(22 Owners included in Index)*

Financial Data: *Fiscal Year End:*12/31 *Latest Annual Data:* 12/30/2006

Year	Sales	Net Income
2006	$4,631,629,000	-$22,999,000
2005	$4,555,507,000	$41,252,000

Curr. Assets:	$512,207,000	*Curr. Liab.:*	$325,859,000		
Plant, Equip.:	$242,707,000	*Total Liab.:*	$754,846,000	*Indic. Yr. Divd.:*	$0.720
Total Assets:	$1,077,424,000	*Net Worth:*	$322,578,000	*Debt/ Equity:*	1.1151

Nashua Corp

11 Trafalgar Sq., Nashua, NH, 03063; *PH:* 1-603-880-2323; *Fax:* 1-603-880-5671; *http://* www.nashua.com

General - Incorporation	MA	**Stock**- Price on:12/24/2007	$10.55
Employees	784	Stock Exchange	NYSE
Auditor	Ernst & Young LLP	Ticker Symbol	NSM
Stk Agt	American Stock Transfer & Trust Co.	Outstanding Shares	6,260,000
Counsel	NA	E.P.S.	$1.02
DUNS No.	00-107-9433	Shareholders	NA

Business: The group's principal activities are manufacturing, converting and marketing of labels, specialty papers and imaging products. The group's products include thermal coated papers, pressure-sensitive labels and tags, bond papers, transaction receipts and toners/ developers for use in photocopiers. The group operates through label products, specialty paper products and imaging supplies segment. The label product segment consists of converts, prints and sells pressure-sensitive labels and tags to distributors and end-users. The specialty paper products segment consists of coats, converts and sells papers and films. The imaging supplies segment consists of manufacturing and selling of consumable products used in producing hard copy images. The operations of the group are conducted in the United States, Asia and Europe. On 07-Feb-2003, it acquired the label company.

Primary SIC and add'l.: 2621 5045 7384 2672

CIK No: 0000069680

Subsidiaries: Nashua FSC Limited, Nashua International, Inc., Nashua P.R., Inc., Nashua Photo Inc.

Officers: Thomas G. Brooker/Dir., CEO, Pres./$344,216.00, John L. Patenaude/VP - Finance, CFO/$263,253.00, Thomas M. Kubis/VP - Operations/$169,426.00, Todd McKeown/VP - Sales, Marketing, Suzanne L. Ansara/Sec., Margaret M. Callan/Chief Accounting Officer, Corporate Controller, Linda J. Madden/Assist., Sec., Michael D. Travis/VP - Marketing/$213,533.00, Donald A. Granholm/VP - Supply Chain Management

Directors: Thomas G. Brooker/Dir., CEO, Pres., Andrew B. Albert/Chmn., Scott L. Barnard/Dir., Avrum Gray/Dir., Michael T. Leatherman/Dir., George R. Mrkonic/Dir., Mark E. Schwarz/Dir.

Owners: Andrew B. Albert/5.40%, John L. Patenaude/1.70%, Bank of America, N.A./Columbia Management Group, LLC/8.70%, Avrum Gray/1.60%, Thomas M. Kubis, Insiders/29.90%, Franklin Resources, Inc./Charles B. Johnson/Rupert H./7.60%, Gabelli Funds, LLC/GAMCO Asset Management Inc./22.70%, Donna J. DiGiovine, Scott L. Barnard, Newcastle Partners, L.P./Newcastle Capital Group, L.L.C./17.20%, Mark E. Schwarz/17.20%, Michael T. Leatherman, Thomas G. Brooker/1.70%, George R. Mrkonic *(17 Owners included in Index)*

Financial Data: ***Fiscal Year End:***12/31 ***Latest Annual Data:*** 12/31/2006

Year	Sales	Net Income
2006	$269,043,000	$3,599,000
2005	$294,864,000	$596,000
2004	$289,217,000	$3,787,000

Curr. Assets:	$56,291,000	***Curr. Liab.:***	$25,342,000	***P/E Ratio:***	15.98
Plant, Equip.:	$26,399,000	***Total Liab.:***	$58,588,000	***Indic. Yr. Divd.:***	NA
Total Assets:	$127,615,000	***Net Worth:***	$69,027,000	***Debt/ Equity:***	NA

Nashville BK & TR TN

4525 Harding Pike, Nashville, TN, 37205; ***PH:*** 1-615-515-1700; ***Fax:*** 1-615-515-1717; ***http://*** www.nbandt.com

General - Incorporation		***Stock***- Price on:12/24/2007	$12.5
Employees	NA	Stock Exchange	OTC
Auditor	NA	Ticker Symbol	NVBT
Stk Agt	NA	Outstanding Shares	NA
Counsel	NA	E.P.S	NA
DUNS No.	NA	Shareholders	NA

Business: The groups principal activities include providing banking and financial services to the customers. Products and services of the group include relationship banking, free checking, savings account, Loans and Mortgages and financial calculations. The group operates from the United States.

Primary SIC and add'l.: 6022

CIK No:

Officers: Donald W. Thurmond/Chmn., CEO, Barbara A. Taylor/VP - Operations, Judy Adams/Sr. Personal Banker, Brooke Bowman/Private Banking, Overton J. Colton/MD - Finance, Administration, Chief Administrative Officer, Steve Davis/Sr. VP, Trust Officer - Wealth Management Services, Thomas S. Stumb/Pres., Richard A. Fleming/Assist. VP - Private Banking, Bryant Tirrill/Sr. VP - Private Banking, Seth Cole/Private Banker, Jamie Smith Nicholson/VP, Trust Officer - Wealth Management Services, Pam Gardiner/VP, Operations Officer - Wealth Management Services, Jocelynne Garrett/Business Services Analyst, Allison Griffin/Private Banking, Kate Helms/Personal Banker *(26 Officers included in Index)*

Directors: Donald W. Thurmond/Chmn., CEO, Charles W. Cook/Vice Chmn., Overton J. Colton/MD - Finance, Administration, Chief Administrative Officer

Naspers Ltd

40 Heerengracht, Cape Town, 8001; ***PH:*** 27-214062041; ***http://*** www.naspers.co.za

General - Incorporation	South Africa	***Stock***- Price on:12/24/2007	$25.55
Employees	12,067	Stock Exchange	NDQ
Auditor	PricewaterhouseCoopers Inc	Ticker Symbol	NPTE
Stk Agt	NA	Outstanding Shares	NA
Counsel	NA	E.P.S	NA
DUNS No.	NA	Shareholders	NA

Business: The group's principal activities are the operation of pay-television, Internet and instant-messaging subscriber platforms and the provision of related technologies, the publishing, distribution and printing of magazines, newspapers and books, and the provision of private education services. The group primarily operates in South Africa, sub-saharan Africa, Greece, cyprus, Thailand, China, the Netherlands and the United States of America. The group comprises mih group, operates pay television and Internet subscriber platforms; media 24, publishes prints and distributes newspapers, magazines, printing and related products; and via afrika, publishes and distributes books and conducts private education businesses. Major brands include action x, big brother Africa, m-Web, m-Web (Thailand), entriq, irdeto access, beeld, die burger, baba & kleuter, bicycling sa, finance24, food 24, paarl gravure, paarl media, tafelberg, human & rousseau van schaik bookstore and lux verbi.

Primary SIC and add'l.: 4822 2721 2752 2731 9411 2711 4833

CIK No: 0001106051

Subsidiaries: Boland Newspapers (Proprietary) Limited, Educor Holdings Limited, Entriq Inc., Irdeto Access BV, M-Web (Thailand) Limited, M-Web Holdings (Proprietary) Limited, Media24 Limited, Mih (bvi) Limited, MIH Holdings Limited, MIH Investments (Proprietary) Limited, MultiChoice Africa (Proprietary) Limited, MultiChoice Africa Limited, MultiChoice Cyprus Holdings Limited, MultiChoice Cyprus Limited, MultiChoice Hellas SA 22 Subsidiaries included in the Index

Officers: Koos Bekker/Dir., CEO - Naspers, Roberto Civita/Chmn., Editor In Chief, Giancarlo Civita/COO, VP, Carel Snyman/Investor Relations Officer, Musa Shezi/MD - Via Afrika, Mark Sorour/Chief Investment Officer, Steve Ward/CFO - MIH Holdings, Andre Coetzee/Group Counsel, MIH Group, Beverley Branford/Investor Relations Officer, G. M. Coetzee/Investor Relations Officer, Denise Vos/Investor Relations Officer

Directors: Koos Bekker/Dir., CEO - Naspers, Roberto Civita/Chmn., Editor In Chief, Francine-Ann Du Plessis/Dir., Neil Van Heerden/Dir., Lourens Jonker/Dir., Jakes Gerwel/Dir., Fred Phaswana/Dir., Rachel Jafta/Dir., Cobus Stofberg/Dir. - MIH BV, Hein Willemse/Dir., Steve Pacak/Dir., Ton Vosloo/Dir., Boetie Van Zyl/Dir., Ben Van Der Ross/Dir.

Nastech Pharmaceutical Co Inc

3830 Monte Villa Pkwy., Bothell, WA, 98021; ***PH:*** 1-425-908-3600; ***Fax:*** 1-425-908-3650; ***http://*** www.nastech.com; ***Email:*** hr@nastech.com

General - Incorporation	DE	***Stock***- Price on:12/24/2007	$11.79
Employees	197	Stock Exchange	AMEX
Auditor	KPMG LLP	Ticker Symbol	NSU
Stk Agt	American Stock Transfer & Trust Co.	Outstanding Shares	25,480,000
Counsel	Pryor Cashman Sherman & Flynn LLP	E.P.S	-$2.12
DUNS No.	11-413-1113	Shareholders	NA

Business: The group's principal activities are research, development, manufacture and commercialization of nasally administered prescription pharmaceuticals. They are into developing molecular biology-based technologies for delivering both small and large molecule drugs. The group has commercial interest in two nasal drug products, stadol(R) ns(TM) (butorphanol tartrate) and nascobal(R) (cyanocobalamin, usp). Stadol(R) ns(TM) (butorphanol tartrate) is a nasally administered opioid pain relief medication for the treatment of acute pain. Nascobal(R) (cyanocobalamin, usp) is a nasal vitamin b-12 product that provides patient benefits over the injectable therapy for chronic b-12 deficiency anaemia. At 31-Dec-2003, the group has 195 patents.

Primary SIC and add'l.: 8731 2834

CIK No: 0000737207

Subsidiaries: Atossa Acquisition Corporation, Atossa HealthCare, Inc, Delaware corporation

Officers: Steven C. Quay/Chmn., CEO, Pres./$2,917,959.00, Philip C. Ranker/CFO, Corp. Sec./$601,858.00, Gordon C. Brandt/Exec. VP - Clinical Research, Medical Affairs/$538,991.00, Paul H. Johnson/Sr. VP - Research, Development, Chief Scientific Officer/$550,336.00, David E. Wormuth/Sr. VP - Operations, Timothy M. Duffy/Exec. VP - Marketing, Business Development/$586,492.00, Matt Haines/Media Contact, Bruce R. York/CAO, Assist. Sec.

Directors: Steven C. Quay/Chmn., CEO, Pres., Devin N. Wenig/Dir., Bruce R. Thaw/Dir., Alexander D. Cross/Dir., Ian R. Ferrier/Dir., Gerald T. Stanewick/Dir., Leslie D. Michelson/Dir., John V. Pollock/Dir., Susan B. Bayh/Dir., Myron Z. Holubiak/Dir.

Owners: Bruce R. Thaw, Bruce R. York, Paul H. Johnson, Leslie D. Michelson, FMR Corp/12.30%, Philip C. Ranker, Gordon C. Brandt, Myron Z. Holubiak, Ian R. Ferrier, Insiders/11.20%, Susan B. Bayh, Carter J. Beese, Gerald T. Stanewick, David E. Wormuth, Delaware Management Holdings/7.10% *(20 Owners included in Index)*

Financial Data: ***Fiscal Year End:***12/31 ***Latest Annual Data:*** 12/31/2006

Year	Sales	Net Income
2006	$28,490,000	-$26,877,000
2005	$7,449,000	-$32,163,000
2004	$1,847,000	-$28,609,000

Curr. Assets:	$57,558,000	***Curr. Liab.:***	$14,725,000		
Plant, Equip.:	$15,444,000	***Total Liab.:***	$30,496,000	***Indic. Yr. Divd.:***	NA
Total Assets:	$73,832,000	***Net Worth:***	$43,336,000	***Debt/ Equity:***	NA

Natco Group Inc

11210 Equity Dr., Ste. 100, Houston, TX, 77041; ***PH:*** 1-713-849-7500; ***Fax:*** 1-713-849-8973; ***http://*** www.natcogroup.com

General - Incorporation	DE	***Stock***- Price on:12/24/2007	$47.05
Employees	2,304	Stock Exchange	NYSE
Auditor	KPMG LLP	Ticker Symbol	NA
Stk Agt	Mellon Investor Services LLC	Outstanding Shares	17,400,000
Counsel	NA	E.P.S	$2.26
DUNS No.	60-563-2884	Shareholders	NA

Business: The group's principle activity is to provide equipment, systems and services used in the production of crude oil and natural gas. The group operates through three business lines. The north American operations segment provides standardized components, replacement parts and used components and equipment servicing. The engineered systems segment provides customized, large scale integrated oil and gas production systems. The automation and control systems segment provides and services control panels and systems that monitor and control production of oil and gas. The group operates seven primary manufacturing facilities in the us and Canada and 36 sales and service facilities in the us and Canada. The products of the group include heaters, dehydration and desalting units, separators, gas conditioning units and oily water treatment equipment. Exxonmobil corporation, british petroleum and chevrontexaco corporation are the major customers of the group. The group's quarterly revenue for September 2007 was 145.19 millions of USD.

Primary SIC and add'l.: 3569 3559 3823 3669 3443 3533

CIK No: 0001057693

Subsidiaries: Axsia Group, Ltd., Axsia Holdings, Ltd., NATCO Canada, Ltd., National Tank Company, NTC Technical Services, Inc., TEST Automation& Controls, Inc., Total Engineering Services Team, Inc.

Officers: John U. Clarke/Chmn., CEO, Acting CFO/$1,440,757.00, Knut Eriksen/Sr. VP - Engineered Systems/$717,797.00, Joseph H. Wilson/Sr. VP - Global Marketing, Katherine P. Ellis/Sr. VP, Sec., General Counsel, Frank C. Smith/Exec. VP/$548,004.00, Patrick M. McCarthy/Dir., COO, Pres./$806,959.00, David R. Volz/Sr. VP - Automation, Controls, Pres. - Test, Robert A. Curcio/Sr. VP - Gas Technologies, Technology, Product Development/$548,710.00, James D. Graves/VP, Controller, Bradley P. Farnsworth/54/Sr. VP, CFO/$409,980.00

Directors: John U. Clarke/Chmn., CEO, Acting CFO, Thomas C. Knudson/Dir., Keith K. Allan/Dir., Thomas R. Bates/Dir., Patrick M. McCarthy/Dir., COO, Pres., Julie H. Edwards/Dir., George K. Hickox/Dir.

Owners: Robert A. Curcio, Julie H. Edwards, Patrick M. McCarthy, Herbert S. Winokur/5.30%, Insiders/10.70%, The D3 Family Funds/9.40%, Keith K. Allan, Thomas C. Knudson, Bradley P. Farnsworth, Frank C. Smith, George K. Hickox/1.40%, John U. Clarke/1.30%, FMR Corp./13.70%, Knut Eriksen, Thomas R. Bates

Financial Data: ***Fiscal Year End:***03/31 ***Latest Annual Data:*** 12/31/2006

Year	Sales	Net Income
2006	$519,041,000	$37,971,000
2005	$400,486,000	$14,185,000
2004	$321,451,000	$614,000

Curr. Assets:	$204,450,000	***Curr. Liab.:***	$126,913,000	***P/E Ratio:***	22.09
Plant, Equip.:	$34,603,000	***Total Liab.:***	$135,333,000	***Indic. Yr. Divd.:***	NA
Total Assets:	$322,541,000	***Net Worth:***	$172,649,000	***Debt/ Equity:***	NA

Natco International Inc

8559 - 132 Streeet, Surrey, BC, V3W 4N8; ***PH:*** 1-604-592-0047

General - Incorporation	DE
Employees	NA
Auditor	Moore & Assoc., Chartered
Stk Agt	Pacific Stock Transfer Company
Counsel	NA
DUNS No.	NA

Stock - Price on:12/24/2007	$2.08
Stock Exchange	OTC
Ticker Symbol	NCII
Outstanding Shares	NA
E.P.S.	NA
Shareholders	NA

Business: The groups principle activity is to manufacture jewelry sealent and tire sealent. The group operates through two segments namely jewelry cleaner and accessories, and tire sealent. The group operates from Canada, India and the United States.

Primary SIC and add'l.: 2842

CIK No: 0001172069

Officers: Raj-Mohinder S. Gurm/48/Dir., CEO, CFO, Pres., John H. Rennie/71/Dir., Sec.

Directors: Raj-Mohinder S. Gurm/48/Dir., CEO, CFO, Pres., John H. Rennie/71/Dir., Sec., Gerry Podersky-Cannon/61/Dir., Stephen Sleigh/55/Dir.

Owners: John Herman Rennie/3.88%, Insiders/60.14%, Raj-Mohinder S. Gurm/50.63%, Gerry Podersky-Cannon/5.63%

Financial Data: Fiscal Year End:03/31   Latest Annual Data: 03/31/2007

Year	Sales	Net Income
2007	NA	-$235,000
2006	$1,000	-$201,000

Curr. Assets:	$12,000	Curr. Liab.:	$1,246,000		
Plant, Equip.:	$9,000	Total Liab.:	$1,246,000	Indic. Yr. Divd.:	NA
Total Assets:	$21,000	Net Worth:	-$1,225,000	Debt/ Equity:	NA

Nathan's Famous Inc

1400 Old Country Rd., Ste. 400, Westbury, NY, 11590; **PH:** 1-516-338-8500; **Fax:** 1-516-338-7220; **http://** www.nathansfamous.com; **Email:** investor@nathansfamous.com

General - Incorporation	DE
Employees	216
Auditor	Grant Thornton LLP
Stk Agt	Grant Thornton LLP
Counsel	Blau, Kramer, Wactlar & Liebarman
DUNS No.	01-260-6737

Stock - Price on:12/24/2007	$15
Stock Exchange	NDQ
Ticker Symbol	NATL
Outstanding Shares	5,900,000
E.P.S.	$1.12
Shareholders	NA

Business: The group's principal activity is to operate and franchise fast food units. These units feature beef frankfurters, crinkle-cut French fried potatoes and a variety of other menu offerings. Nathans' hot dogs are all-beef and are free from all fillers and starches and are flavored with the original secret blend of spices. The group offers management training courses for management personnel of company-owned and franchised restaurants. The group also provides development and construction support services to miami subs franchisees. The group consists of 343 franchised units, 12 group-owned units and 2,200 nathan's branded product points of sale that feature all-beef hot dogs, located in 41 states, the district of columbia and 12 foreign countries.

Primary SIC and add'l.: 5812 6794

CIK No: 0000069733

Subsidiaries: Denek of Hicksville, Inc., MGIII, Inc., Miami Subs Corporation, Miami Subs of Delaware, Inc., Miami Subs Real Estate Corp., Miami Subs USA, Inc., Namasil Realty Corp., Nathan's Famous of 325 Fifth Avenue, Inc., Nathan's Famous of Crossgates, Inc., Nathan's Famous of Farmingdale, Inc., Nathan's Famous of H.D., Inc., Nathan's Famous of Hicksville, Inc., Nathan's Famous of Kings Plaza, Inc., Nathan's Famous of New Jersey, Inc., Nathan's Famous of Times Square, Inc. 25 Subsidiaries included in the Index

Officers: Eric Gatoff/Dir., CEO, VP, Corporate Counsel/$376,033.00, Howard M. Lorber/Exec. Chmn./$482,367.00, Donald L. Perlyn/Dir., Exec. VP/$353,465.00, Wayne Norbitz/Dir., COO, Pres./$537,957.00, Donald Schedler/VP - Development, Architecture, Construction, Randy Watts/VP - Franchise Operations, Karen C. Brown/Sr. Dir. - Human Resources, Ronald G. Devos/CFO, VP - Finance/$284,858.00, Jerry Krevans/Sr. Dir. - Branded Product Program, Nancy Murphy/Sr. Dir. - Purchasing, Carl Paley/VP - Franchise Operations

Directors: Eric Gatoff/Dir., CEO, VP, Corporate Counsel, Howard M. Lorber/Exec. Chmn., Charles Raich/Dir., Wayne Norbitz/Dir., COO, Pres., Robert J. Eide/Dir., Brian S. Genson/Dir., A. F. Petrocelli/Dir., Donald L. Perlyn/Dir., Exec. VP, Barry Leistner/Dir.

Owners: Barry Leistner, Wayne Norbitz/3.20%, Prime Logic Capital, LLC/6.00%, Donald L. Perlyn/3.60%, Howard M. Lorber/14.90%, Eric Gatoff, Brian S. Genson, A. F. Petrocelli/2.00%, Steel Partners II, L.P./16.50%, Ronald G. DeVos, Insiders/24.20%, Robert J. Eide/1.30%, Quest Equities Corp./5.80%, Charles Raich

Financial Data: Fiscal Year End:03/26   Latest Annual Data: 03/25/2007

Year	Sales	Net Income
2007	$45,730,000	$5,543,000
2006	$41,360,000	$5,677,000
2005	$34,112,000	$2,737,000

Curr. Assets:	$12,554,000	Curr. Liab.:	$6,619,000	P/E Ratio:	13.16
Plant, Equip.:	$6,263,000	Total Liab.:	$9,503,000	Indic. Yr. Divd.:	NA
Total Assets:	$25,886,000	Net Worth:	$16,383,000	Debt/ Equity:	NA

Nathaniel Energy Corp

8001 S InterPort Blvd., Ste. 260, Englewood, CO, 80112; **PH:** 1-303-690-8300; **Fax:** 1-303-539-0741; **http://** www.nathanielenergy.com; **Email:** investors@nathanielenergy.com

General - Incorporation	DE
Employees	16
Auditor	Comiskey & Company
Stk Agt	Computershare Trust Co
Counsel	NA
DUNS No.	NA

Stock - Price on:12/24/2007	$0.065
Stock Exchange	OTC
Ticker Symbol	NECX
Outstanding Shares	90,730,000
E.P.S.	-$0.02
Shareholders	NA

Business: The groups principle activity is to provide energy alternative to fossil fuels. The group operates through two segments namely fuel and renewable energy and EfW. for Sep 2005, the group acquired Nathaniel Energy Oklahoma Holdings Corporation. The group operates from the United States.

Primary SIC and add'l.: 4959 3999

CIK No: 0001096939

Subsidiaries: Cleanergy, Inc., MNS Eagle Equity Group IV, Inc., Nathaniel Energy Oklahoma Holdings Corporation

Officers: Barry Kemble/CEO, Dir., Russell Bailey/68/VP, Sec., Timothy Peach/CFO

Directors: Barry Kemble/CEO, Dir., Karen Smythe/46/Dir., Michael Burdis/55/Dir.

Owners: Karen Smythe, Brad E. Bailey, Insiders, Richard Strain/61.30%

Financial Data: Fiscal Year End:12/31   Latest Annual Data: 12/31/2006

Year	Sales	Net Income
2006	$1,149,000	$4,303,000
2005	$689,000	-$238,000
2004	$14,037,000	-$5,656,000

Curr. Assets:	$419,000	Curr. Liab.:	$1,196,000		
Plant, Equip.:	$1,069,000	Total Liab.:	$1,238,000	Indic. Yr. Divd.:	NA
Total Assets:	$1,755,000	Net Worth:	$517,000	Debt/ Equity:	0.0812

National Atlantic Holdings Corp

4 Paragon Way, Freehold, NJ, 07728; **PH:** 1-732-665-1100; **Fax:** 1-732-303-6770; **http://** www.national-atlantic.com; **Email:** investorrelations@national-atlantic.com

General - Incorporation	NJ
Employees	269
Auditor	Deloitte& Touche LLP
Stk Agt	Computershare Investor Services LLC
Counsel	NA
DUNS No.	NA

Stock - Price on:12/24/2007	$13.9
Stock Exchange	AMEX
Ticker Symbol	NAK
Outstanding Shares	11,120,000
E.P.S.	-$0.1
Shareholders	NA

Business: The groups principle activity is to provide property and casualty insurance. The products of the group include high performance policy, commercial automobile, commercial general liability, and commercial excess liability. The group operates from the United States. The group's quarterly revenue for September is 47.15 millions of USD.

Primary SIC and add'l.: 6331 6399

CIK No: 0000946492

Subsidiaries: Mayfair Reinsurance Company Limited, National Atlantic Insurance Agency, Inc., Proformance Insurance Company, Riverview Professional Services, Inc.

Officers: James V. Gorman/Chmn., CEO/$754,542.00, Bruce C. Bassman/COO, Sr. VP, Chief Actuary/$525,262.00, Cynthia L. Codella/58/Exec. VP, Sec./$587,348.00, Frank J. Prudente/Exec. VP, Chief Accounting Officer/$591,747.00, John E. Scanlan/Exec. VP, Chief Underwriting Office/$563,272.00, Douglas A. Wheeler/General Counsel, Peter A. Cappello/Dir., CFO - Proformance/$512,157.00

Directors: James V. Gorman/Chmn., CEO, Candace L. Straight/Dir., Martin Krupnick/Dir., Thomas M. Mulhare/Dir., Peter A. Cappello/Dir., CFO - Proformance, Neal Golding/Dir., Thomas J. Sharkey/Dir., Steven V. Stallone/Dir., Cornelius E. Golding/60/Dir.

Owners: Boston Partners Asset/6.73%, Loeb Partners Corp./5.05%, James V. Gorman/14.49%, Eric D. Hovde/15.56%

Financial Data: Fiscal Year End:12/31   Latest Annual Data: 12/31/2006

Year	Sales	Net Income
2006	$175,856,000	$14,382,000
2005	$187,341,000	$6,436,000
2004	$208,672,000	$17,448,000

Curr. Assets:	$103,631,000	Curr. Liab.:	$5,446,000		
Plant, Equip.:	$1,988,000	Total Liab.:	$301,942,000	Indic. Yr. Divd.:	NA
Total Assets:	$452,830,000	Net Worth:	$150,888,000	Debt/ Equity:	NA

National Australia Bank Ltd

PO Box 2333V, Melbourne, 30001; ; **http://** www.nab.com.au/About_Us/0,,175,00.html?ncID=ZBA

General - Incorporation	Victoria
Employees	NA
Auditor	Ernst & Young LLP
Stk Agt	Bank of New York
Counsel	Mallesons Stephen Jaques
DUNS No.	75-346-1714

Stock - Price on:12/24/2007	NA
Stock Exchange	OTC
Ticker Symbol	NABZY
Outstanding Shares	NA
E.P.S.	NA
Shareholders	NA

Business: The group's principal activities are the provision of banking services, credit and access card facilities, leasing, housing and general finance, international banking, investment banking, mortgage servicing, wealth management, funds management, life insurance, and custodian, trustee and nominee services.

Primary SIC and add'l.: 6021

CIK No: 0000833029

Subsidiaries: Bank of New Zealand, Clydesdale Bank PLC, MLC Limited, National Australia Financial Management Limited, National Irish Bank Limited, Northern Bank Limited, Yorkshire Bank

Financial Data: Fiscal Year End:09/30   Latest Annual Data: 09/30/2006

Year	Sales	Net Income
2006	$24,188,852,000	$3,160,458,000
2005	$16,172,341,000	$3,249,522,000
2004	$8,365,773,000	$1,969,050,000

Curr. Assets:	$81,617,026,000	Curr. Liab.:	$222,470,227,000		
Plant, Equip.:	$1,392,035,000	Total Liab.:	$341,189,769,000	Indic. Yr. Divd.:	NA
Total Assets:	$360,414,642,000	Net Worth:	$19,224,872,000	Debt/ Equity:	NA

National Bancshares Corp OH

112 W Market St., Orrville, OH, 44667; **PH:** 1-330-682-1010; **Fax:** 1-330-684-2154; **http://** www.fnborrville.com

General - Incorporation	OH
Employees	132
Auditor	Crowe Chizek & Co. LLC
Stk Agt	Registrar & Transfer Co
Counsel	NA
DUNS No.	80-443-9974

Stock - Price on:12/24/2007	$19.3
Stock Exchange	OTC
Ticker Symbol	NBOH
Outstanding Shares	2,230,000
E.P.S.	$0.49
Shareholders	NA

Business: The group's principal activity is to provide commercial banking services. The group offers services which include checking accounts, savings accounts, certificates of deposit, personal loans, loans to business and industry, installment loans, safety deposit boxes and credit cards. The group competes with insurance companies, consumer finance companies, credit unions, mortgage banking companies, and commercial finance and leasing companies. The loan portfolio includes commercial and residential mortgage loans, commercial loans and consumer installment loans. The group operates through fourteen banking offices located in orrville, dalton, kidron, smithville, mt. Eaton, apple creek, lodi, wooster, seville and massillon, Ohio.

Primary SIC and add'l.: 6022 6712
CIK No: 0000790362
Subsidiaries: First Kropf Title, LLC, National Bancshares Corporation
Officers: David C. Vernon/Pres., CEO - National Bancshares, First National Bank/$30,306.00, Heather Kiner/Mgr., Darrell Smucker/VP, Marc Valentin/40/Sr. VP, Treasurer/$108,368.00, Kathy Barnes/Mortgage Loan Officer, Harold Berkey/VP - Business Banking, Steve Riddick/VP, Sr. Credit Officer, John Shultz/VP - Business Banking, Kenneth R. Vansickle/61/Sr. VP, Sec./$127,192.00, Jim Griffith/Assist. VP - Cashier, Dean Karhan/Assist. VP, Patty Massaro/Loan Officer, Matthew Miller/Assist. VP, Mgr., Cindy Wagner/Assist. VP, Mgr., Sue Weygandt/Assist. VP, Mgr. *(23 Officers included in Index)*
Directors: Bobbi E. Douglas/49/Dir., John E. Sprunger/70/Dir., Howard J. Wenger/65/Dir., Sara Steinbrenner Balzarini/51/Dir., Steve Schmid/56/Dir., Albert W. Yeagley/60/Dir., John P. Cook/60/Dir., John W. Kropf/64/Dir.
Owners: Kenneth R. VanSickle, Marc Valentin, John P. Cook, Howard J. Wenger/2.90%, John E. Sprunger, Steve Schmid, John W. Kropf/1.80%, Sara Steinbrenner Balzarini, Insiders/6.00%, Albert W. Yeagley, David C. Vernon, Bobbi E. Douglas
Financial Data: *Fiscal Year End:*12/31 *Latest Annual Data:* 12/31/2006

Year	Sales	Net Income
2006	$18,839,000	$1,164,000
2005	$17,876,000	$2,100,000
2004	$17,207,000	$2,911,000

Curr. Assets:	$20,525,000	**Curr. Liab.:**	$273,678,000	**P/E Ratio:**	39.39
Plant, Equip.:	$5,652,000	**Total Liab.:**	$273,678,000	**Indic. Yr. Divd.:**	$0.640
Total Assets:	$308,358,000	**Net Worth:**	$34,680,000	**Debt/ Equity:**	NA

National Bank of Greece

86 Eolou St., Athens, 10232; ; *http://* www.nbg.gr

General - Incorporation	Hellenic Republic	**Stock**- Price on:12/24/2007	$11.32
Employees	24,187	Stock Exchange	NYSE
Auditor	Deloitte, Sofianos & Cambanis S.A	Ticker Symbol	NBL
Stk Agt	NA	Outstanding Shares	2,370,000,000
Counsel	NA	E.P.S	$0.87
DUNS No.	NA	Shareholders	NA

Business: The groups principle activity is to provide provision of financial services including retail and commercial banking, asset management, intermediation activities, investment banking, venture capital, insurance products, securities brokerage and real estate management. The group operates from United States.
Primary SIC and add'l.: 6035 6399 6153 6021 6099 6029 6211
CIK No: 0001096061
Subsidiaries: Banca Romaneasca, Diethniki S.A., ETEBA Advisory, ETEBA Bulgaria A.D. Sofia, ETEBA Emerging Markets Fund Ltd., ETEBA Estate Fund Ltd., ETEBA Romania S.A., ETEBA Venture Capital Management S.A., Ethniki Kefalaiou S.A., Ethniki Leasing S.A., Ethniki Mutual Fund Management S.A., EURIAL Leasing SA, Innovative Ventures S.A. (I-Ven), Interlease A.D. Sofia, National Bank of Greece Cyprus Ltd. 30 Subsidiaries included in the Index
Officers: Ioannis Pechlivanidis/Deputy CEO, Efstrations Georgios Arapoglou/57/Chmn., CEO, Michalis Kokkinos/64/Key Management, Petros Economou/71/General Counsel, omer A. Aras/54/Key Management, Marinos Stratopoulos/44/Key Management, Michael Oratis/51/GM - Risk Management, George Paschas/52/Chief Internal Auditor, Paul Mylonas/49/Chief Economist, Chief Strategist, Head - Investor Relations, Hector Zarca/48/Key Management, Stilian Vatev/51/Key Management, Gligor Bishev/50/Key Management, Agis Leopoulos/40/Chief - International, Stavros Gatopoulos/64/Head - Human Resources, Group Internal Communications, Demetrios Lefakis/47/Chief Risk Officer *(22 Officers included in Index)*
Directors: Efstrations Georgios Arapoglou/57/Chmn., CEO, Ioannis Panagopoulos/53/Non Exec. Dir., Ioannina Theoklitos/77/Non Exec. Dir., George Lanaras/87/Dir., Dimitrios A. Daskalopoulos/Dir., Constantinos D. Pilarinos/Dir., Drakoulis K. Fountoukakos-Kyriakakos/69/Non Exec. Dir., Nikolaos D. Efthymiou/62/Non Exec. Dir., Ploutarchos Sakellaris/44/Dir., Ioannis Giannidis/58/Non Exec. Dir., Konstantinos Pilarinos/74/Non Exec. Dir., John P. Panagopoulos/Dir., Achilleas Mylonopoulos/51/Non Exec. Dir., Ioannis C. Yiannidis/Dir., George Mergos/Non Exec. Dir. *(17 Directors included in Index)*
Owners: Legal Entities/51.40%, George Pashas, Ioannis Panagopoulos, Stefanos Pantzopoulos, Petros Economou, Achilleas Mylonopoulos, Pension Funds/17.90%, H.E. the Metropolitan of Ioannina Theoklitos, Petros Christodoulou, Domestic Private Investors/18.60%, Alexandros Georgitsis, Drakoulis Fountoukakos-Kyriakakos, Ioannis Yiannidis, Agis Leopoulos, Other Domestic Legal Entities/12.00% *(22 Owners included in Index)*
Financial Data: *Fiscal Year End:*12/31 *Latest Annual Data:* 12/31/2006

Year	Sales	Net Income
2006	$6,944,853,000	$1,132,902,000
2005	$4,568,421,000	$657,572,000
2004	$4,264,706,000	$254,565,000

Curr. Assets:	$23,687,535,000	**Curr. Liab.:**	$81,733,656,000	**P/E Ratio:**	9.85
Plant, Equip.:	$1,376,485,000	**Total Liab.:**	$92,520,261,000	**Indic. Yr. Divd.:**	$0.270
Total Assets:	$99,964,848,000	**Net Worth:**	$7,444,587,000	**Debt/ Equity:**	NA

National Bankshares Inc

101 Hubbard St., Blacksburg, VA, 24060; *PH:* 1-540-951-6300; *Fax:* 1-540-951-6324; *http://* www.nationalbankshares.com

General - Incorporation	VA	**Stock**- Price on:12/24/2007	$20.34
Employees	248	Stock Exchange	NDQ
Auditor	Yount, Hyde & Barbour, P.C	Ticker Symbol	NKSH
Stk Agt	National Bankshares Inc	Outstanding Shares	6,980,000
Counsel	NA	E.P.S	$1.81
DUNS No.	15-650-4698	Shareholders	NA

Business: The group's principle activities are the provision of general, retail and commercial banking services to individuals, businesses, local government units and institutional customers. The products and services include deposits in the form of checking accounts, money market deposit accounts, interest-bearing demand deposit accounts, savings accounts, certificates of deposit and time deposits. As a part of its lending activities, the group provides real estate, commercial, revolving, consumer and agricultural loans, offering letters of credit. The group also provides other consumer financial services, such as automatic funds transfer, collections, night depository, safe deposit, travelers checks, savings bond sales, utility payment services and services normally offered by commercial banks.
Primary SIC and add'l.: 6712 6021
CIK No: 0000796534
Subsidiaries: Bank of Tazewell County, National Bankshares Financial Services, Inc., The National Bank of Blacksburg
Officers: James G. Rakes/Chmn., CEO, Pres./$958,407.00, Robert J. Buchanan/Treasurer, Principal Financial Officer/$155,459.00, Marilyn B. Buhyoff/Sec., Counsel/$193,959.00, Brad F. Denardo/55/Corp. Officer/$256,139.00
Directors: James G. Rakes/Chmn., CEO, Pres., James M. Shuler/Dir., William A. Peery/Dir., Jack M. Lewis/Dir., Jeffrey R. Stewart/Dir., Mary G. Miller/Dir., Jack H. Harry/Dir., Lawrence J. Ball/Dir., Glenn P. Reynolds/Dir., Jack W. Bowling/Dir.
Owners: Jack H. Harry/1.24%, James G. Rakes/1.75%, Robert J. Buchanan, Jack M. Lewis, Jack W. Bowling, Marilyn B. Buhyoff, James M. Shuler, Lawrence J. Ball, Glenn P. Reynolds, Insiders/6.67%, William A. Peery, Mary G. Miller, Brad F. Denardo, Jeffrey R. Stewart
Financial Data: *Fiscal Year End:*12/31 *Latest Annual Data:* 12/31/2006

Year	Sales	Net Income
2006	$56,703,000	$12,632,000
2005	$52,993,000	$12,424,000
2004	$48,634,000	$12,230,000

Curr. Assets:	$40,582,000	**Curr. Liab.:**	$765,555,000	**P/E Ratio:**	11.24
Plant, Equip.:	$13,092,000	**Total Liab.:**	$771,448,000	**Indic. Yr. Divd.:**	$0.740
Total Assets:	$868,203,000	**Net Worth:**	$96,755,000	**Debt/ Equity:**	NA

National Beverage Corp

1 N University Dr., Fort Lauderdale, FL, 33324; *PH:* 1-954-581-0922; *Fax:* 1-954-473-4710; *http://* www.nbcfiz.com; *Email:* investorrelations@nationalbeverage.com

General - Incorporation	DE	**Stock**- Price on:12/24/2007	NA
Employees	1,400	Stock Exchange	NDQ
Auditor	Mcgladrey & Pullen, LLP	Ticker Symbol	FIZ
Stk Agt	Mellon Investor Services LLC	Outstanding Shares	NA
Counsel	NA	E.P.S	$0.50
DUNS No.	10-340-2343	Shareholders	NA

Business: The group's principal activities are to develop, manufacture, market and distribute branded cola and multi-flavored soft drinks. The group sells its products under brand names shasta, faygo, ritz, lacroix, everfresh, big shot, mr. Pure, home juice, clearfruit, mt. Shasta, crystal bay, ohana, st. Nick's and voodoo rain. The group's brands are produced in its fourteen manufacturing facilities, which are located in major metropolitan markets throughout the continental United States. The manufacturing facilities are situated mainly in Michigan, California, Texas, Kansas, Utah and Washington. The customers of the group include retail grocery chains, warehouse clubs, mass-merchandisers and wholesalers, retail gas station markets, hospitals, schools, military bases, airlines, hotels and food service wholesalers as well as soft drinks for other beverage companies.
Primary SIC and add'l.: 6719 2086
CIK No: 0000069891
Subsidiaries: BevCo Sales, Inc., Beverage Corporation International, Inc., Big Shot Beverages, Inc., Everfresh Beverages, Inc., Faygo Beverages, Inc., Home Juice Corp., National Beverage Vending Company, National Retail Brands, Inc., NewBevCo, Inc., PACO, Inc., Shasta Beverages International, Inc., Shasta Beverages, Inc., Shasta Midwest, Inc., Shasta Northwest, Inc., Shasta Sales, Inc. 18 Subsidiaries included in the Index
Officers: Nick A. Caporella/72/Chmn., CEO, Joseph G. Caporella/48/Dir., Pres./$671,502.00, Edward F. Knecht/74/Exec. VP - Procurement/$256,034.00, George R. Bracken/Sr. VP - Finance, Dean A. McCoy/51/Chief Accounting Officer, Sr. VP/$199,046.00
Directors: Nick A. Caporella/72/Chmn., CEO, Joseph G. Caporella/48/Dir., Pres., Samuel C. Hathorn/65/Dir., Lee S. Kling/79/Dir., Joseph P. Klock/59/Dir.
Owners: IBS Partners Ltd., Joseph P. Klock, Lee S. Kling, Edward F. Knecht, Insiders, Joseph G. Caporella, George R. Bracken, Samuel C. Hathorn, Nick A. Caporella, Dean A. McCoy
Financial Data: *Fiscal Year End:*04/29 *Latest Annual Data:* 4/29/2006

Year	Sales	Net Income
2006	$516,802,000	$22,226,000
2005	$495,572,000	$16,886,000
2004	$512,061,000	$18,691,000

Curr. Assets:	$139,846,000	**Curr. Liab.:**	$57,884,000		
Plant, Equip.:	$62,879,000	**Total Liab.:**	$81,291,000	**Indic. Yr. Divd.:**	$0.800
Total Assets:	$224,587,000	**Net Worth:**	$143,296,000	**Debt/ Equity:**	NA

National City Corp

1900 E 9th St., Cleveland, OH, 44114; *PH:* 1-216-222-2000; *Fax:* 1-216-222-9957; *http://* www.nationalcity.com

General - Incorporation	DE	**Stock**- Price on:12/24/2007	$33.81
Employees	31,270	Stock Exchange	NYSE
Auditor	Ernst & Young LLP	Ticker Symbol	NCC
Stk Agt	National City Bank	Outstanding Shares	575,760,000
Counsel	NA	E.P.S	$3.32
DUNS No.	00-790-1010	Shareholders	NA

Business: The groups principle activity is to provide financial services. The groups services include commercial and retail banking, mortgage financing and servicing, consumer finance and asset management. In the year 2007, the group acquired MAF Bancorp, Inc. The group operates from United States.
Primary SIC and add'l.: 6712 6162 6153 6021
CIK No: 0000069970
Subsidiaries: 1stChoice Mortgage, LLC, 1stFredericksburg Mortgage, LLC, 1stPremier Mortgage, LP, Access Financial Corp., AccuLend Mortgage, LP, Advent Guaranty Corporation, Affirmative Mortgage, LLC, Afleet Mortgage, LP, All American First Mortgage, LLC, Allegiant Asset Management Company, Allegiant Capital Corporation, Allegiant Capital TrustII, Allegiant Community Development Corporation, Allegiant Insurance Services Co., Alliance First Mortgage, LLC 186 Subsidiaries included in the Index
Officers: David A. Daberko/Chmn., CEO/$9,078,280.00, Todd C. Moules/CEO, Pres. - Pennsylvania, Philip L. Rice/CEO, Pres. - Ohio, Exec. VP - National City Bank, Charles P. Denny/CEO, Pres. - Kentucky, Tennessee, Joseph A. Gregoire/CEO, Pres. - Illinois, Vincent A. Elhilow/CEO, Pres. - Southeast Florida, Michael J. Brown/CEO - Florida, David P. Boyle/CEO - Michigan, Shaun R. Hayes/CEO, Pres. - Missouri, Stephen A. Stitle/CEO, Exec. VP - Indiana

Banking, Jeffrey D. Kelly/Vice Chmn., CFO/$4,994,851.00, Jane Grebenc/Sr. VP, National Sales Mgr. - Private Client Group, Peter E. Raskind/Dir., Pres./$4,340,328.00, Daniel J. Frate/Exec. VP/$3,248,535.00, Tanisha L. Hughes/Assist. VP - Community Development *(67 Officers included in Index)*

Directors: David A. Daberko/Chmn., CEO, Jeffrey D. Kelly/Vice Chmn., CFO, William E. MacDonald/Vice Chmn., Mike Dowdell/Exec. Dir., VP - Ohio, Northeast, Akron, Youngstown, Community Development, Morry Weiss/Dir., Jerry Sue Thornton/Dir., Gerald L. Shaheen/Dir., Paul A. Ormond/Dir., Bernadine P. Healy/Dir., Christopher M. Connor/Dir., Peter E. Raskind/Dir., Pres., Michael J. Taylor/Exec. Dir., Pres. - Community Development, Jon E. Barfield/Dir., Michael B. McCallister/Dir., James S. Broadhurst/Dir. *(16 Directors included in Index)*

Owners: David A. Daberko, Jon E. Barfield, Craig S. Lindner, Jeffrey D. Kelly, Christopher M. Connor, Peter E. Raskind, National City Corporation/11.50%, Morry Weiss, William E. MacDonald, James S. Broadhurst, Jerry Sue Thornton, Gerald L. Shaheen, Insiders/2.05%, Michael B. McCallister, Daniel J. Frate *(17 Owners included in Index)*

Financial Data: *Fiscal Year End:*12/31 *Latest Annual Data:* 12/31/2006

Year	Sales	Net Income
2006	$12,953,210,000	$2,299,836,000
2005	$11,036,138,000	$1,985,229,000
2004	$10,559,929,000	$2,779,934,000

Curr. Assets:	$5,072,503,000	**Curr. Liab.:**	$96,887,366,000	**P/E Ratio:**	9.74
Plant, Equip.:	$2,204,172,000	**Total Liab.:**	$125,609,839,000	**Indic. Yr. Divd.:**	$1.640
Total Assets:	$140,190,842,000	**Net Worth:**	$14,581,003,000	**Debt/ Equity:**	NA

National Coal Corp

8915 George Williams Rd., Knoxville, TN, 37923; *PH:* 1-865-690-6900; *Fax:* 1-865-691-9982; *http://* www.nationalcoal.com

General - Incorporation	FL	**Stock**- Price on:12/24/2007	$4.75
Employees	279	Stock Exchange	NYSE
Auditor	Gordon Hughes & Banks LLP	Ticker Symbol	NCR
Stk Agt	Manhattan Transfer Registrar Co	Outstanding Shares	20,280,000
Counsel	NA	E.P.S.	-$1.4
DUNS No.	NA	Shareholders	NA

Business: The groups principle activities include mining, processing and selling bituminous steam coal. The group operates two underground mines, two surface mines and two highwall mines. The group operates from United States.

Primary SIC and add'l.: 6799

CIK No: 0001089575

Subsidiaries: National Coal Corporation, NC Transportation, Inc.

Officers: Daniel A. Roling/Dir., CEO, Pres./$424,047.00, Michael T. Love/Dir., CFO, Sr. VP/$407,739.00, Charles W. Kite/Sr. VP, General Counsel/$278,691.00, William R. Snodgrass/Sr. VP - Business Development/$276,528.00, Christine Pietryla/Contact - Press, Investor Relations

Directors: Daniel A. Roling/Dir., CEO, Pres., Kenneth Scott/Chmn., Robert Heinlein/Dir., Michael T. Love/Dir., CFO, Sr. VP, Gerald Malys/Dir.

Owners: Crestview Capital Master LLC, Jon Nix, Kenneth Scott, Insiders, Scott Filstrup, Stewart & Jennifer Flink, Jenco Capital Corporation, Nancy Hoyt Revocable Trust, Robert Heinlein, Daniel A. Roling, Charles Kite, Kenneth Hodak, NorthSound Capital, The J-K Navigator Fund L.P., William R. Snodgrass *(16 Owners included in Index)*

Financial Data: *Fiscal Year End:*12/31 *Latest Annual Data:* 12/31/2006

Year	Sales	Net Income
2006	$87,517,000	-$23,421,000
2005	$65,873,000	-$6,791,000
2004	$16,999,000	-$10,429,000

Curr. Assets:	$8,983,000	**Curr. Liab.:**	$18,433,000		
Plant, Equip.:	$56,478,000	**Total Liab.:**	$87,914,000	**Indic. Yr. Divd.:**	NA
Total Assets:	$85,992,000	**Net Worth:**	-$1,923,000	**Debt/ Equity:**	9.8454

National Community Bank

570 Lausch Ln., Lancaster, PA, 17601; *PH:* 1-717-492-2222; *http://* www.uncb.com

General - Incorporation	PA	**Stock**- Price on:12/24/2007	$20.05
Employees	1,352	Stock Exchange	OTC
Auditor	Beard Miller Co. LLP	Ticker Symbol	NA
Stk Agt	UN Community Bank Wealth Mgt Grp	Outstanding Shares	30,090,000
Counsel	NA	E.P.S.	$1.28
DUNS No.	18-140-4427	Shareholders	NA

Business: The group's principal activity is to provide a wide range of banking services. The services are provided to individuals and small to medium sized businesses through its subsidiary, union national community bank. The group accepts time, demand and savings deposits and provides secured and unsecured commercial, real estate and consumer loans. The group also provides investment, custodial, estate planning and trust services. It group has a main office with an annex and six full service branch offices located in columbia, elizabethtown, hempfield, manheim, maytown and mount joy, Pennsylvania.

Primary SIC and add'l.: 6712 6021

CIK No: 0000874482

Subsidiaries: Home Team Financial, LLC, TA of Lancaster, LLC, Union National Capital Trust I, Union National Capital Trust II, Union National Community Bank, Union National Insurance Agency,Inc

Officers: Mark D. Gainer/Chmn., CEO, Pres., Charles R. Starr/61/Insider Trading Compliance Officer

Directors: Mark D. Gainer/Chmn., CEO, Pres., Darwin A. Nissley/50/Dir., James R. Godfrey/63/Dir., Donald Cargas/60/Dir., Carl R. Hallgren/70/Dir., Barry C. Huber/56/Dir., Lloyd C. Pickell/61/Dir., Kevin D. Dolan/54/Dir., Thomas J. McGrath/50/Dir., William M. Nies/60/Dir.

Owners: Mark D. Gainer/1.53%, Michael A. Frey/1.15%, William M. Nies, Clement M. Hoober, Darwin A. Nissley, Thomas J. McGrath, Kevin D. Dolan, James R. Godfrey, Donald Cargas, Charles R. Starr, Carl R. Hallgren, Insiders/5.95%, Lloyd C. Pickell, Donegal Mutual Insurance Company/7.16%, Nancy Shaub Colarik *(16 Owners included in Index)*

Financial Data: *Fiscal Year End:*12/31 *Latest Annual Data:* 12/31/2006

Year	Sales	Net Income
2006	$283,580,000	$38,377,000
2005	$280,040,000	$50,805,000
2004	$257,240,000	$50,196,000

Curr. Assets:	$258,829,000	**Curr. Liab.:**	$3,230,774,000	**P/E Ratio:**	15.66
Plant, Equip.:	$66,199,000	**Total Liab.:**	$4,036,269,000	**Indic. Yr. Divd.:**	$0.840
Total Assets:	$4,497,797,000	**Net Worth:**	$461,528,000	**Debt/ Equity:**	1.7452

National Consumer Cooperative Bank

1725 Eye St. N W, Ste 600, Washington, DC, 20006; *PH:* 1-202-336-7700; *http://* www.ncb.coop

General - Incorporation	US	**Stock**- Price on:12/24/2007	NA
Employees	NA	Stock Exchange	NA
Auditor	KPMG LLP	Ticker Symbol	NA
Stk Agt	NA	Outstanding Shares	NA
Counsel	NA	E.P.S.	NA
DUNS No.	09-777-8633	Shareholders	NA

Business: The group's principal activities are to provide financial and technical assistance to eligible cooperatives. It originates and sells real estate and commercial loans to cooperatives through its subsidiaries. The other services provided include brokering insurance, independent, fee-based financial consulting services to the nonprofit community. In addition, the group provides services to educational institutions, museums, membership groups and community-based organizations. It also builds and offers Internet technology platforms.

Primary SIC and add'l.: 6035 6712 6111

CIK No: 0000356801

Subsidiaries: Grocers Capital Company (GCC), NCB Capital Corporation (NCBCC), NCB Financial Corporation (NCBFC), United Resources, Inc. (URI)

Officers: Charles E. Snyder/CEO, Pres., Richard L. Reed/Exec. MD, CFO, Patrick N. Connealy/MD, Kathleen H. Luzik/MD, COO, Mark W. Hiltz/MD, Chief Risk Officer, Michele Fantt Harris/MD, Terry D. Simonette/Exec. MD, John Levo/Contact - Banking Specialist, Thomas Cyr/Contact - Financing Specicalist, Alyson Young/Contact - Commercial Middle Marketing, Brad Keare/Contact - Specialized Lending, Karyn Mann/Contact - Co-op Housing, Community Associations, Jeremy Morgan/Contact - Homes, Co - Operations, Condos, Richard Dines/Contact - Co-op Development, Felicia Grammas/Contact - Media Inquiries *(19 Officers included in Index)*

Directors: William F. Casey/Vice Chmn., Walden Swanson/Dir., Grady Hedgespeth/Dir., Alfred A. Plamann/65/Dir., Richard A. Parkinson/Dir., Stuart M. Saft/Dir., Rafael E. Cuellar/54/Dir., Rosemary K. Mahoney/Dir., Steven F. Cunningham/Dir., Roger B. Collins/Dir., Janis Herschkowitz/Dir., David G. Nason/Dir., Nguyen Van Hanh/Dir., Jeffrey H. Leonard/Dir.

Owners: Greenbelt Homes, Inc./12.05%, The Co-operative Central Bank/12.05%, The Co-operative Central Bank/1.87%, Group Health, Inc./6.11%, Greenbelt Homes, Inc./0.89%, Group Health, Inc./0.87%

National Datacomputer Inc

900 Middlesex Tpke., Bldg. 5, Billerica, MA, 01821; *PH:* 1-978-663-7677; *Fax:* 1-978-667-1869; *http://* www.ndcomputer.com; *Email:* investors@ndcomputer.com

General - Incorporation	DE	**Stock**- Price on:12/24/2007	$0.025
Employees	12	Stock Exchange	OTC
Auditor	Carlin, Charron & Rosen LLP	Ticker Symbol	IDCP
Stk Agt	American Stock Transfer & Trust Co.	Outstanding Shares	35,240,000
Counsel	Mintz Levin Cohn Ferris Et Al	E.P.S.	-$0.015
DUNS No.	05-889-8453	Shareholders	NA

Business: The group's principle activity is to provide solutions to workplace problems through the use of mobile information systems. The company designs, manufactures, sells and services computerized systems used to automate the collection, processing and communication of information related to product sales, distribution and inventory control. The products and services include data communication networks, application-specific software, hand-held computers and related peripherals, as well as associated training and support services. The group's hand-held Datacomputer(R) includes a microprocessor, keyboard, LCD displays, and full alphabetic and numeric character sets. The software solutions include RouteRider (R), NDI-SurveyPro (TM), smartRoute 2000(R), Wireless Inventory Network and NDI-DeJa View(TM). The group's quarterly revenue for September 2007 was 0.67 millions of USD.

Primary SIC and add'l.: 7372 3577 3571 7379

CIK No: 0000812880

Officers: William B. Berens/Dir., CEO, Pres./$140,473.00, Bruna A. Bucacci/COO, Chief Accounting Officer/$103,151.00, Stephen W. Bergmann/Dir. - Product Marketing

Directors: William B. Berens/Dir., CEO, Pres., Anthony Stafford/Chmn., William R. Smart/Dir., John P. Ward/Dir., John H. MacKinnon/Dir.

Owners: John P. Ward, William B. Berens, Insiders, Mary Lee Ingoldsby, John H. MacKinnon, Paula Stafford, Bruna A. Bucacci, Ronan Stafford, William R. Smart, Anthony Stafford, Conor Stafford, Fiona Stafford

Financial Data: *Fiscal Year End:*12/31 *Latest Annual Data:* 12/31/2006

Year	Sales	Net Income
2006	$2,045,000	-$27,000
2005	$2,672,000	-$768,000
2004	$3,248,000	-$494,000

Curr. Assets:	$296,000	**Curr. Liab.:**	$974,000		
Plant, Equip.:	$23,000	**Total Liab.:**	$999,000	**Indic. Yr. Divd.:**	NA
Total Assets:	$334,000	**Net Worth:**	-$665,000	**Debt/ Equity:**	NA

National Dentex Corp

2 Vision Dr., Natick, MA, 01760; *PH:* 1-508-358-4422; *Fax:* 1-508-358-6199; *http://* www.nationaldentex.com; *Email:* investorrelations@nationaldentex.com

General - Incorporation	MA	**Stock**- Price on:12/24/2007	$19.53
Employees	2,156	Stock Exchange	NDQ
Auditor	PricewaterhouseCoopers LLP	Ticker Symbol	NAHC
Stk Agt	Registrar & Transfer Co	Outstanding Shares	5,530,000
Counsel	Posternak, Blankstein & Lund	E.P.S.	$1.05
DUNS No.	05-531-2342	Shareholders	NA

Business: The group's principal activity is to design, fabricate, market and sell dental prosthetic appliances to dentists. The group owns and operates dental laboratories throughout the United States. The group designs and fabricates dentures, crowns, bridges and other dental prosthetic appliances. As of Dec 2003, the group owned and operated 40 dental laboratories, consisting of 38 full-service dental laboratories and 2 branch laboratories located in 29 states throughout the United States. The products are

made by trained technicians who work in dental laboratories in accordance with work orders and cases provided by the dentist. The group's products are categorized into three categories: restorative products, reconstructive products and cosmetic products. On 11-Aug-2004 the group acquired d. H. Baker dental laboratory, inc.

Primary SIC and add'l.: 3843

CIK No: 0000913616

Subsidiaries: Green Dental Laboratories, Inc.

Officers: David L. Brown/Dir., CEO, Pres./$512,166.00, Arthur B. Champagne/Sr. VP/$206,420.00, Richard F. Becker/Exec. VP, Treasurer, Assist. Sec./$239,286.00, Wayne M. Coll/CFO, VP/$173,959.00, Lynn D. Dine/VP - Research, Development, Richard G. Mariacher/VP - Technical Services, Donald E. Merz/Sr. VP/$253,886.00, Donald H. Siegel/Sec., Dean Ribeiro/VP - Client Relations, Josh Green/Exec. VP - Laboratory Operations, Doug Baker/VP - Operations, Bill Keller/VP - Operations, Tom Keller/Vice Presidens, Operations, Dick Becker/Exec. VP, Treasurer, CFO, Phillip Gold/Mgr. - Oral Arts

Directors: David L. Brown/Dir., CEO, Pres., David V. Harkins/Chmn., Jack R. Crosby/Dir., Thomas E. Callahan/Dir., Norman F. Strate/Dir., James E. Mulvihill/67/Dir.

Owners: ClearBridge Advisors, LLC/10.60%, David L. Brown/4.20%, Richard F. Becker/1.40%, Artisan Partners Limited Partnership/15.10%, Wayne M. Coll/0.30%, Royce& Associates, LLC/7.50%, Donald E. Merz/1.40%, Jack R. Crosby/0.10%, David V. Harkins/0.90%, Thomas E. Callahan, Arthur B. Champagne/0.90%, Insiders/9.10%, FMR Corp./9.60%, Norman F. Strate/0.20%

Financial Data: ***Fiscal Year End:***12/31 ***Latest Annual Data:*** 12/31/2006

Year	Sales	Net Income
2006	$150,107,000	$5,763,000
2005	$135,843,000	$7,089,000
2004	$111,753,000	$5,159,000

Curr. Assets:	$29,052,000	**Curr. Liab.:**	$22,820,000	**P/E Ratio:**	18.60
Plant, Equip.:	$27,882,000	**Total Liab.:**	$65,697,000	**Indic. Yr. Divd.:**	NA
Total Assets:	$148,490,000	**Net Worth:**	$82,794,000	**Debt/ Equity:**	0.3339

National Energy Group Inc

4925 Greenville Ave., Ste. 1400, Dallas, TX, 75206; ***PH:*** 1-214-692-9211; ***Fax:*** 1-214-692-9310; ***http://*** www.negx.com; ***Email:*** neg@negx.com

General - Incorporation	DE	***Stock***- Price on:12/24/2007	$5.03
Employees	3	Stock Exchange	OTC
Auditor	Grant Thornton LLP	Ticker Symbol	NEGI
Stk Agt	Wells Fargo Bank Minnesota N.A	Outstanding Shares	11,170,000
Counsel	Baker & Botts LLP	E.P.S	$8.056
DUNS No.	78-329-1123	Shareholders	NA

Business: The group's principal activity is to manage the exploration, development, production and operations of natural gas and oil properties. The group operates in the properties, which are primarily located in Texas, Oklahoma and Louisiana (both onshore and in the gulf of Mexico).

Primary SIC and add'l.: 1382 1311 1389 8741 1381

CIK No: 0000870756

Subsidiaries: American Casino & Entertainment Properties, NEG Oil & Gas

Officers: Bob G. Alexander/Chmn., CEO, Pres., Wayne F. Campbell/VP - Exploration, Philip D. Devlin/VP, General Counsel, Sec., Rick L. Kirby/VP - Drilling, Production, Kent R. Lueders/Dir. - Corporate Development, Lori K. Mauk/VP - Marketing, David V. Rigsby/VP - Land, Jenny V. Robins/VP - Non - Operated Properties, Mgr. - Reservoir Engineering, Grace Bricker/VP - Administration, Hillel Moerman/35/CFO

Directors: Bob G. Alexander/Chmn., CEO, Pres., Martin L. Hirsch/Dir., Jack G. Wasserman/Dir., Robert J. Mitchell/Dir., Robert H. Kite/Dir., Vincent Intrieri/Dir.

Owners: Bob G. Alexander, Robert H. Kite, AREP Oil& Gas LLC, Insiders

Financial Data: ***Fiscal Year End:***12/31 ***Latest Annual Data:*** 12/31/2006

Year	Sales	Net Income
2006	$176,760,000	$103,459,000
2005	$58,971,000	$25,274,000
2004	$46,034,000	$14,285,000

Curr. Assets:	$88,440,000	**Curr. Liab.:**	$2,895,000	**P/E Ratio:**	0.62
Plant, Equip.:	$63,000	**Total Liab.:**	$2,902,000	**Indic. Yr. Divd.:**	NA
Total Assets:	$88,503,000	**Net Worth:**	$85,601,000	**Debt/ Equity:**	NA

National Energy Services Company Inc

3153 Fire Rd. Ste. 2c, Egg Harbor Township, NJ, 08234; ***PH:*** 1-800-758-9288; ***http://*** www.nescorporation.com; ***Email:*** info@nescorporation.com

General - Incorporation	NV	***Stock***- Price on:12/24/2007	$0.3
Employees	7	Stock Exchange	OTC
Auditor	Bagell, Levine & Company, LLC	Ticker Symbol	NEGS
Stk Agt	Interwest Transfer Company, Inc.	Outstanding Shares	27,930,000
Counsel	NA	E.P.S	-$0.02
DUNS No.	NA	Shareholders	NA

Business: The group's principle activity is to provide expert service to energy service professionals.The group's services include software, training and technical support services. The group operates from United States.

Primary SIC and add'l.: 8748

CIK No: 0001165336

Owners: John A. Grillo/11.20%, John & Deborah ONeill/51.70%, Insiders/63.80%

Financial Data: ***Fiscal Year End:***10/31 ***Latest Annual Data:*** 10/31/2006

Year	Sales	Net Income
2006	$1,149,000	-$610,000

Curr. Assets:	$480,000	**Curr. Liab.:**	$1,502,000		
Plant, Equip.:	$6,000	**Total Liab.:**	$2,134,000	**Indic. Yr. Divd.:**	NA
Total Assets:	$722,000	**Net Worth:**	-$1,412,000	**Debt/ Equity:**	NA

National Financial Partners Corp

787 7th Ave., 11th Fl., New York, NY, 10019; ***PH:*** 1-212-301-4000; ***Fax:*** 1-212-301-4001; ***http://*** www.nfp.com; ***Email:*** ir@nfp.com

General - Incorporation	DE	***Stock***- Price on:12/24/2007	$46.71
Employees	2,642	Stock Exchange	NDQ
Auditor	PricewaterhouseCoopers LLP	Ticker Symbol	NFSB
Stk Agt	Mellon Investor Services LLC	Outstanding Shares	37,660,000
Counsel	NA	E.P.S	NA
DUNS No.	NA	Shareholders	NA

Business: The group's principal activity is the distribution of financial services products to high net worth individuals and small to medium-size corporations. The group deals as an insurance agency and brokerage agent. The group operates as a bridge between large financial service product manufacturers and network of independent financial service distributors. As of 31-Dec-2003, the group operated a national distribution network with over 1,400 producers in 40 states and Puerto Rico consisting of 130 owned firms. On 01-Jan-2003, the group acquired wharton equity corporation ii llc and affiliates, international risk consultants inc and occupational health underwriters inc and administrative systems inc and the balanced program inc.

Primary SIC and add'l.: 6411

CIK No: 0001183186

Subsidiaries: Administrative Systems, Inc., Advanced Settlements, Inc., Alan H. Horowitz C.L.U., Inc., Alan Kaye Insurance Agency, Inc., Alternative Benefit Solutions, Inc., American Benefits Insurance Corporation, American Financial Solutions, Inc. f/k/a Earl& Associates, Inc., Arnone, Lowth, Fanning, Wilson& Rubin, Inc., Arthur D. Shankman& Company, Inc., Asgard Incorporated, Barry Kaye Associates, Inc., Beacon Retirement Planning Services, Inc., Benefit Associates, Inc., Benefit Consultants and Administrators, Inc., Benefit Information Services, Inc. 222 Subsidiaries included in the Index

Officers: Jessica M. Bibliowicz/Chmn., CEO, Pres., Jeffrey A. Montgomery/CEO - NFP Securities, Inc, Emily Arean/Sr. VP, Dir. - Human Resources, Mark C. Biderman/CFO, Exec. VP, Robert R. Carter/Pres. - NFP Insurance Services, Inc, Elliot M. Holtz/Exec. VP - Marketing, Firm Operations, Robert S. Zuccaro/Exec. VP, Chief Accounting Officer, Douglas W. Hammond/Exec. VP, General Counsel, Stancil E. Barton/Sr. VP, Chief Compliance, Ethics Officer, Mia Dammen Mihopoulos/CTO, Sr. VP, Michael N. Goldman/Sr. VP, Head - Mergers, Acquisitions, Milton P. Henry/Sr. VP, Chief Auditor, Marc Gordon/Contact

Directors: Jessica M. Bibliowicz/Chmn., CEO, Pres., Shari Loessberg/Dir., John A. Elliott/Dir., Bruce R. Callahan/68/Dir., Kenneth C. Mlekush/Dir., Stephanie W. Abramson/Dir., Arthur S. Ainsberg/Dir., Marc E. Becker/Dir.

Owners: John A. Elliott, Arthur S. Ainsberg, Jeffrey A. Montgomery, The Atticus Group/5.50%, Bruce R. Callahan, Douglas W. Hammond, Janus Capital Management LLC/6.80%, Robert R. Carter, Kenneth C. Mlekush, Jessica M. Bibliowicz/1.80%, Insiders/3.40%, Stephanie W. Abramson, Wellington Management Company, LLP/5.80%, Mark C. Biderman, Shari Loessberg *(16 Owners included in Index)*

Financial Data: ***Fiscal Year End:***12/31 ***Latest Annual Data:*** 12/31/2006

Year	Sales	Net Income
2006	$1,077,113,000	$57,578,000
2005	$891,446,000	$56,182,000
2004	$639,472,000	$40,142,000

Curr. Assets:	$321,659,000	**Curr. Liab.:**	$332,128,000		
Plant, Equip.:	$27,749,000	**Total Liab.:**	$462,172,000	**Indic. Yr. Divd.:**	NA
Total Assets:	$1,237,044,000	**Net Worth:**	$774,872,000	**Debt/ Equity:**	0.3374

National Fuel Gas Co

6363 Main St., Williamsville, NY, 14221; ***PH:*** 1-716-857-7000; ***Fax:*** 1-716-857-7195; ***http://*** www.natfuel.com

General - Incorporation	NJ	***Stock***- Price on:12/24/2007	$44.7
Employees	1,993	Stock Exchange	NYSE
Auditor	Netherland, Sewell & Assoc., Inc.	Ticker Symbol	NFG
Stk Agt	Bank of New York	Outstanding Shares	83,480,000
Counsel	NA	E.P.S	$1.58
DUNS No.	00-697-6666	Shareholders	NA

Business: The groups principle activity is to provide energy services. The group operates through five business segments namely exploration and production, pipeline and storage, utility, energy marketing and timber. The group operates from United States.

Primary SIC and add'l.: 2421 1382 4923

CIK No: 0000070145

Subsidiaries: Horizon Energy Holdings, Inc., Seneca Energy Canada Inc.

Officers: Philip C. Ackerman/Chmn., CEO, Jay W. Lesch/VP, Donna L. Decarolis/National Fuel Resources, Inc, Pres., James D. Ramsdell/National Fuel Gas Distribution Corporation, Sr. VP, Ronald J. Tanski/Treasurer, Principal Financial Officer, Anna M. Cellino/Sec., Carl M. Carlotti/National Fuel Gas Distribution Corporation, VP, Bruce D. Heine/National Fuel Gas Distribution Corporation, VP, Matthew D. Cabell/50/Pres. - Seneca, David F. Smith/Dir., COO, Pres., Karen M. Camiolo/Principal Accounting Officer, Controller, Paula M. Ciprich/General Counsel, John R. Pustulka/56/Sr. VP - Supply Corporation

Directors: Philip C. Ackerman/Chmn., CEO, Rolland E. Kidder/67/Dir., Don R. Cash/Dir., Stephen E. Ewing/Dir., John F. Riordan/Dir., Robert T. Brady/Dir., Craig G. Matthews/Dir., George L. Mazanec/Dir., Richard G. Reiten/Dir., David F. Smith/Dir., COO, Pres.

Owners: NMV Advisers/5.80%, CalPERS/3.90%, NMVSH/3.20%, David M. DiDomenico, Vantage GP/6.40%, NMV Offshore HoldCo/2.60%, Steven B. Klinsky/9.00%, NMVC/1.10%, Fox F. Benton, NMV Offshore/2.60%, Frederic V. Salerno, NMV/1.10%, NMVT/1.00%

Financial Data: ***Fiscal Year End:***09/30 ***Latest Annual Data:*** 9/30/2006

Year	Sales	Net Income
2006	$2,311,659,000	$138,091,000
2005	$1,923,549,000	$189,488,000
2004	$2,031,393,000	$166,586,000

Curr. Assets:	$519,453,000	**Curr. Liab.:**	$290,345,000	**P/E Ratio:**	28.29
Plant, Equip.:	$2,877,726,000	**Total Liab.:**	$2,290,769,000	**Indic. Yr. Divd.:**	$1.240
Total Assets:	$3,734,331,000	**Net Worth:**	$1,443,562,000	**Debt/ Equity:**	NA

National Grid Transco Plc

1-3 Strand, London, WC2N 5EH; ; ***http://*** www.nationalgrid.com

General - Incorporation ....England and Wales
Employees ....NA
Auditor ....PricewaterhouseCoopers LLP
Stk Agt ....Bank of New York
Counsel ....NA
DUNS No. ....NA

Stock- Price on:12/24/2007 ....NA
Stock Exchange ....NYSE
Ticker Symbol ....NA
Outstanding Shares 543,800,000
E.P.S. $11.64
Shareholders ....NA

Business: The groups principal activity is to transmit electricity and gas. The group operates from the Scotland, England and Wales.

Primary SIC and add'l.: 4922

CIK No: 0001004315

Subsidiaries: 99.999 LIMITED, ADVANTICA CORPORATE VENTURES LIMITED, ADVANTICA LIMITED, ADVANTICA PTY LIMITED, ADVANTICA, INC., AERIAL GROUP LIMITED, AERIAL UK LIMITED, AGL SYSTEMS INTERNATIONAL LIMITED, AMPLE DESIGN LIMITED, ARTERION LIMITED, ASSETHALL LIMITED, BEEGAS NOMINEES LIMITED, BLACKWATER 1 LIMITED, BLACKWATER 3 LIMITED, BLACKWATER 4 LIMITED 373 Subsidiaries included in the Index

Officers: Steve Holliday/51/CEO, Steve Lucas/54/Dir. - Finance, Nick Winser/47/Executive Dir., Edward Astle/54/Executive Dir., Mark Fairbairn/49/Executive Dir., David Rees/Dir. - Investor Relations, Richard Smith/Mgr. - Investor Relations, James Waite/Mgr. - Investor Relations, Debbie Taylor/Investor Relations Advisor

Directors: John Parker/66/Chmn., Nick Winser/47/Executive Dir., Edward Astle/54/Executive Dir., Mark Fairbairn/49/Executive Dir., Ken Harvey/67/Dir., John Allan/59/Non Exec. Dir., Stephen Pettit/57/Non Exec. Dir., Maria Richter/53/Non Exec. Dir., George Rose/56/Non Exec. Dir., Linda Adamany/56/Non Exec. Dir.

Owners: Legal and General Investment Management Ltd/4.12%, Fidelity International Limited/3.06%

Financial Data: *Fiscal Year End:*03/31 *Latest Annual Data:* 3/31/2006

Year	Sales	Net Income
2006	$16,120,987,000	$2,273,919,000
2005	$16,140,610,000	$2,450,216,000
2004	$16,496,065,000	$1,822,548,000

Curr. Assets:	$6,357,229,000	**Curr. Liab.:**	$9,213,981,000	**P/E Ratio:**	2.37
Plant, Equip.:	$35,204,853,000	**Total Liab.:**	$39,215,092,000	**Indic. Yr. Divd.:**	$2.430
Total Assets:	$56,172,923,000	**Net Worth:**	$16,957,831,000	**Debt/ Equity:**	NA

National Health Investors Inc

100 Vine St., Ste. 1202, Murfreesboro, TN, 37130; ***PH:*** 1-615-890-9100; ***Fax:*** 1-615-890-0123; ***http://*** www.nhinvestors.com

General - Incorporation ....MD
Employees ....NA
Auditor ....BDO Seidman, LLP
Stk Agt ....SunTrust Bank
Counsel ....NA
DUNS No. ....NA

Stock- Price on:12/24/2007 ....$34.23
Stock Exchange ....NYSE
Ticker Symbol ....NA
Outstanding Shares 27,750,000
E.P.S. $3.26
Shareholders ....NA

Business: The groups principle activities include owning and acquiring real estate properties. The group operates from the United States. The groupsquarterely revenue for September 2007 was 39.08 millions of USD.

Primary SIC and add'l.: 6798

CIK No: 0000877860

Officers: Andrew W. Adams/Chmn., CEO, Roger R. Hopkins/Chief Accounting Officer/$106,379.00, Richard F. Laroche/61/Dir., Sec., Kenneth D. Denbesten/54/Dir., Sec./$896,780.00

Directors: Andrew W. Adams/Chmn., CEO, Richard F. Laroche/61/Dir., Sec., Robert A. McCabe/Dir., Robert T. Webb/Dir., Ted H. Welch/74/Dir., Kenneth D. Denbesten/54/Dir., Sec.

Owners: Insiders/16.20%, Roger R. Hopkins, Richard F. LaRoche/2.10%, Andrew W. Adams/9.90%, Ted H. Welch, Robert T. Webb, Charlotte A. Swafford/1.60%, The Vanguard Group, Inc./5.10%, Kenneth D. DenBesten, Robert A. McCabe, Donald K. Daniel

Financial Data: *Fiscal Year End:*12/31 *Latest Annual Data:* 12/31/2006

Year	Sales	Net Income
2006	$150,724,000	$69,228,000
2005	$157,382,000	$54,408,000
2004	$155,559,000	$56,379,000

Curr. Assets:	$183,898,000	**Curr. Liab.:**	$50,138,000	**P/E Ratio:**	2.37
Plant, Equip.:	$235,199,000	**Total Liab.:**	$163,793,000	**Indic. Yr. Divd.:**	$2.000
Total Assets:	$595,464,000	**Net Worth:**	$431,671,000	**Debt/ Equity:**	NA

National Health Realty Inc

100 Vine St., Ste. 1402, Murfreesboro, TN, 37130; ***PH:*** 1-615-890-2020; ***Fax:*** 1-615-890-0123; ***http://*** www.nationalhealthrealty.com

General - Incorporation ....MD
Employees ....NA
Auditor ....BDO Seidman, LLP
Stk Agt ....SunTrust Bank
Counsel ....NA
DUNS No. ....NA

Stock- Price on:12/24/2007 ....$23.8
Stock Exchange ....NA
Ticker Symbol ....NA
Outstanding Shares 9,960,000
E.P.S. $1.23
Shareholders ....NA

Business: The groups principle activity is to provide real estate business and financial services. The group operates from the United States.

Primary SIC and add'l.: 6798

CIK No: 0001047334

Subsidiaries: NHR/Delaware, Inc, NHR/OP, L.P.

Officers: Robert G. Adams/61/Dir., CEO, Pres., Donald K. Daniel/61/Sr. VP, Controller, Principal Accounting Officer, Charlotte A. Swafford/60/Sr. VP, Treasurer

Directors: Robert G. Adams/61/Dir., CEO, Pres., Andrew W. Adams/61/Chmn., Ernest G. Burgess/68/Dir., James R. Jobe/46/Dir., Richard F. Laroche/62/Dir.

Owners: T. Rowe Price Associates, Inc./9.60%, T. Rowe Price Small-Cap Value Fund, Inc./7.60%, National Health Corporation/12.80%, Andrew W. Adams/12.80%

Financial Data: *Fiscal Year End:*12/31 *Latest Annual Data:* 12/31/2006

Year	Sales	Net Income
2006	$20,137,000	$12,407,000
2005	$19,772,000	$11,277,000
2004	$20,191,000	$11,435,000

Curr. Assets:	$10,847,000	**Curr. Liab.:**	$5,871,000	**P/E Ratio:**	21.08
Plant, Equip.:	$109,363,000	**Total Liab.:**	$14,621,000	**Indic. Yr. Divd.:**	$1.330
Total Assets:	$140,305,000	**Net Worth:**	$112,385,000	**Debt/ Equity:**	NA

National Healthcare Corp

100 E Vine St., Murfreesboro, TN, 37130; ***PH:*** 1-615-890-2020; ***Fax:*** 1-615-890-0123; ***http://*** www.nhccare.com

General - Incorporation ....DE
Employees ....NA
Auditor ....BDO Seidman, LLP
Stk Agt ....Suntrust Bank
Counsel ....NA
DUNS No. 06-910-0097

Stock- Price on:12/24/2007 ....$52.39
Stock Exchange ....AMEX
Ticker Symbol ....NHC
Outstanding Shares 12,540,000
E.P.S. $3.38
Shareholders ....NA

Business: The group's principal activities are to operate health care centers and to provide home health care programs in United States. The health care centers provide sub-acute, skilled and intermediate nursing and rehabilitative care. The health care services include a comprehensive range of services through related or separately structured long-term health care centers, home care programs, specialized care units, pharmacy operations, rehabilitative services, assisted living centers and retirement centers. As of 31-Dec-2003, the group operated 76 long-term health care centers, 844 assisted living units at 19 centers. The group serves as a compensated investment advisor to both national health investors inc and national health realty inc. The group also provides advisory, management, accounting, financial and insurance services.

Primary SIC and add'l.: 8051

CIK No: 0001047335

Subsidiaries: National Health Investors, Inc., National Health Realty, Inc.

Officers: John K. Lines/48/Sr. VP, Sec., General Counsel

Owners: Andrew W. Adams/11.30%, Robert G. Adams/4.80%, Emil E. Hassan, Lawrence C. Tucker/6.30%, Ira Sochet/8.20%, Andrew W. Adams/11.30%, Insiders/34.30%, Donald K. Daniel/1.70%, Richard F. LaRoche/3.20%, Gerald D. Coggin/2.90%, Ernest G. Burgess/1.50%, FMR Corp./6.90%, The 1818 Fund II/6.30%, Michael Ussery, Charlotte A. Swafford/1.50% *(17 Owners included in Index)*

Financial Data: *Fiscal Year End:*12/31 *Latest Annual Data:* 12/31/2006

Year	Sales	Net Income
2006	$562,958,000	$36,740,000
2005	$542,381,000	$28,635,000
2004	$521,829,000	$23,972,000

Curr. Assets:	$290,611,000	**Curr. Liab.:**	$168,548,000	**P/E Ratio:**	17.01
Plant, Equip.:	$126,203,000	**Total Liab.:**	$222,335,000	**Indic. Yr. Divd.:**	$0.840
Total Assets:	$471,477,000	**Net Worth:**	$249,142,000	**Debt/ Equity:**	0.0393

National Holdings Corp

120 Broadway , 27th Fl., New York, NY, 10271; ***PH:*** 1-212-417-8000

General - Incorporation ....DE
Employees 89
Auditor ....Marcum & Kliegman LLP
Stk Agt ....Computershare Trust Co
Counsel ....NA
DUNS No. ....NA

Stock- Price on:12/24/2007 ....$3.2
Stock Exchange ....OTC
Ticker Symbol ....NHLD
Outstanding Shares 5,410,000
E.P.S. $0.13
Shareholders ....NA

Business: The groups principle activity is to provide commercial services. Services of the group include brokerage and investment. Customers served by the group include retail and institutional clientele, corporate finance, corporations and businesses. In March 2005, the group acquired Fiserv Securities, Inc. The group operates from the United States and Canada. The group's quarterly revenue for Sep '07 was 20.69 millions of USD.

Primary SIC and add'l.: 6289 6411 6211 6799

CIK No: 0001023844

Subsidiaries: National Insurance Corporation, National Securities Corporation, Robotic Ventures Group LLC

Owners: Insiders, Gregory C. Lowney and Maryanne K. Snyder, Brian Friedman, Bedford Oak Advisors, LLC, Robert J. Rosan, David McCoy, Robert H. Daskal, Norman J. Kurlan, Gary A. Rosenberg, Gregory P. Kusnick and Karen Jo Gustafson, Steven A. Rothstein, Marshall S. Geller, Christopher C. Dewey, Triage Partners LLC, Strategic Turnaround Equity Partners, LP *(17 Owners included in Index)*

Financial Data: *Fiscal Year End:*09/30 *Latest Annual Data:* 09/30/2007

Year	Sales	Net Income
2007	$72,819,000	$1,372,000
2006	$58,727,000	$595,000
2005	$45,730,000	-$1,183,000

Curr. Assets:	$7,225,000	**Curr. Liab.:**	$4,218,000	**P/E Ratio:**	320.00
Plant, Equip.:	$305,000	**Total Liab.:**	$6,864,000	**Indic. Yr. Divd.:**	NA
Total Assets:	$9,707,000	**Net Worth:**	$2,843,000	**Debt/ Equity:**	0.9314

National Home Health Care Corp

700 White Plains Rd., Ste. 275, Scarsdale, NY, 10583; ***PH:*** 1-914-722-9000; ***Fax:*** 1-914-722-9239; ***http://*** www.nhhc.net; ***Email:*** info@nhhc.net

General - Incorporation ....DE
Employees 3,410
Auditor ....BDO Seidman LLP
Stk Agt ..... American Stock Transfer & Trust Co.
Counsel ....Troutman Saunders LLP
DUNS No. 11-543-5935

Stock- Price on:12/24/2007 ....$12.57
Stock Exchange ....NA
Ticker Symbol ....NA
Outstanding Shares 5,660,000
E.P.S. $0.48
Shareholders ....NA

Business: The group's principle activity is to provide personal home health care services. These services include nursing, physical therapy, occupational therapy, speech therapy, medical social services, home health aid services and other specialty services. Other specialty services include mental health and wellness, primatial/high risk pregnancy and disease management. The group provides its services to four types of payor sources. These sources include federal and state funded public assistance programs

(medicare and medicaid), other third party payors (subcontracts), insurance companies and private payors. A substantial portion of the group's revenue is derived from subcontracts that the group has with medicare certified home health care agencies and long-term health care provider programs that subcontract their patients to the group.

Primary SIC and add'l.: 8741 8093 8082 6719

CIK No: 0000728389

Subsidiaries: Accredited Health Services, Inc., Connecticut Staffing Works Corp., Health Acquisition Corp., d/b/a Allen Health Care Services, Medical Resources Home Health Corp., National HMO (N.Y.) Inc., New England Home Care, Inc.

Owners: Bernard Levine, Insiders, Frederick H. Fialkow, Robert P. Heller, Robert C. Pordy, Lawndale Capital Management, LLC, Steven Fialkow, Heartland Advisors, Inc. and William J. Nasgovitz, Salvatore Alternative, AG Home Health Acquisition Corp, Ira Greifer

Financial Data: ***Fiscal Year End:***07/31 ***Latest Annual Data:*** 7/31/2006

Year	Sales	Net Income
2006	$102,365,000	$3,655,000
2005	$98,461,000	$3,567,000
2004	$94,592,000	$4,720,000

Curr. Assets:	$39,389,000	***Curr. Liab.:***	$4,356,000	***P/E Ratio:***	26.19
Plant, Equip.:	$1,865,000	***Total Liab.:***	$4,356,000	***Indic. Yr. Divd.:***	$0.300
Total Assets:	$57,219,000	***Net Worth:***	$52,863,000	***Debt/ Equity:***	NA

National Instruments Corp

11500 N MoPac Expwy., Austin, TX, 78759; ***PH:*** 1-888-280-7645; ***Fax:*** 1-512-683-8411; ***http://*** www.ni.com

General -		***Stock***-	
Incorporation	DE	Price on:12/24/2007	$33.04
Employees	4,149	Stock Exchange	NDQ
Auditor	Ernst & Young, LLP	Ticker Symbol	NA
Stk Agt	Computershare Trust Co	Outstanding Shares	79,830,000
Counsel	Wilson Sonsini Goodrich & Rosati	E.P.S	$1.02
DUNS No.	07-048-7657	Shareholders	NA

Business: The group's principle activities are to design, develop, manufacture and market instrumentation software and computer plug-in cards and accessories. These are combined with industry standard computers, networks and the Internet to create measurement and automation systems. Its application software includes labview, measurement studio, lookout, measure, virtual bench, diadem and dasylab. Hardware and related driver software products include gpib interfaces, vxi modules, daq hardware and machine vision/image acquisition hardware. The group sells its products through its direct sales force, distributors, OEMs, value added resellers, system integrators and consultants. The group serves the advanced research, automotive, commercial aerospace, computers and electronics, continuous process manufacturing, education, government, defense, medical research, pharmaceutical, power and energy, semiconductors, automated test equipment and telecommunications industries worldwide. The group's quarterly revenue for September 2007 was 184.43 millions of USD.

Primary SIC and add'l.: 3577 7372 7373

CIK No: 0000935494

Subsidiaries: Dasytec Usa Incorporated, Electronic Workbench Corporation, Enterprise International Holding B.V., Hyperception inc, Iotech inc, Measurement Computing Corporation, National Instruments (Czech Republic) s.r.o., National Instruments (Ireland) Limited, National Instruments (Korea) Corporation, National Instruments Australia Corporation, National Instruments Belgium N.V., National Instruments Brazil Ltda., National Instruments Canada Corporation, National Instruments China Corporation, National Instruments Corporation (UK) Limited 55 Subsidiaries included in the Index

Officers: James J. Truchard/Chmn., CEO, Pres./$228,960.00, John Graff/VP - Marketing, Customer Operations/$408,939.00, David Hugley/VP, General Counsel, Sec., Jeff Kodosky/Co - Founder - NI Business, Technology Fellow, Rob Porterfield/VP - Manufacturing, Ray Almgren/VP - Product Marketing, Academic Relations, Mark Finger/VP - Human Resources, Alex Davern/CFO, Sr. VP - Manufacturing, Information Technology Operations/$617,579.00, Tim Dehne/National Instruments Sr. VP - Research & Development/$531,964.00, Pete Zogas/Sr. VP - Sales, Marketing/$509,652.00, Jon Bellin/VP - Research & Development, Application and System Software, Kevin Schultz/VP - Research & Development, Data Acquisition and Distributed I, O, Arleene Porterfield/VP - Global Information Technology, Owen Golden/VP - Sales, Americas, Francis Griffiths/VP - Sales, Europe *(18 Officers included in Index)*

Directors: James J. Truchard/Chmn., CEO, Pres., Jeff Kodosky/Co - Founder - NI Business, Technology Fellow, Charles J. Roesslein/Dir., Jeffrey L. Kodosky/Dir., Donald M. Carlton/Dir., Ben G. Streetman/Dir., Gary R. Daniels/Dir., Duy Loan T. Le/Dir.

Owners: Alexander M. Davern, Insiders/29.00%, John Graff, Gary R. Daniels, Capital Research and Management Company/5.50%, Charles J. Roesslein, Peter Zogas, Donald M. Carlton, Duy-Loan T. Le, James J. Truchard/22.10%, Jeffrey L. Kodosky/5.50%, Timothy R. Dehne, Ben G. Streetman, Neuberger Berman Inc./6.10%

Financial Data: ***Fiscal Year End:***12/31 ***Latest Annual Data:*** 12/31/2006

Year	Sales	Net Income
2006	$660,407,000	$72,708,000
2005	$571,841,000	$61,517,000
2004	$514,088,000	$48,610,000

Curr. Assets:	$477,094,000	***Curr. Liab.:***	$102,582,000	***P/E Ratio:***	32.39
Plant, Equip.:	$145,425,000	***Total Liab.:***	$124,538,000	***Indic. Yr. Divd.:***	$0.400
Total Assets:	$721,220,000	***Net Worth:***	$596,682,000	***Debt/ Equity:***	NA

National Interstate Corp

3250 Interstate Dr., Richfield, OH, 44286; ***PH:*** 1-330-659-8900; ***Fax:*** 1-330-659-8901; ***http://*** www.nationalinterstate.com; ***Email:*** sales@nationalinterstate.com

General -		***Stock***-	
Incorporation	OH	Price on:12/24/2007	$24.51
Employees	309	Stock Exchange	NDQ
Auditor	Ernst& Young LLP	Ticker Symbol	NATL
Stk Agt	National City Bank	Outstanding Shares	19,210,000
Counsel	NA	E.P.S	$2.27
DUNS No.	NA	Shareholders	NA

Business: The group operates through its subsidiaries whose principle activity is to provide property and casualty insurance. The group operates from California, Hawaii, Florida, North Carolina and Texas. The group's quarterly revenue for September 2007 was 73.12 millions of USD.

Primary SIC and add'l.: 6351 6331

CIK No: 0001301106

Subsidiaries: American Highways Insurance Agency, Inc., Explorer RV Insurance Agency, Inc., Hudson Indemnity, Ltd., Hudson Management Group, Ltd., National Interstate Insurance Agency, Inc., National Interstate Insurance Company, National Interstate Insurance Company of Hawaii, Inc., Safety, Claims & Litigation Services, Inc., Safety, Claims & Litigation Services, LLC., Triumphe Casualty Company

Officers: Alan R. Spachman/Chmn., CEO, David W. Michelson/COO, Pres., Terry E. Phillips/Sr. VP, Gary N. Monda/VP, Chief Investment Officer, Julie A. McGraw/CFO, VP, Paul F. Haffner/39/VP, Sec., General Counsel

Directors: Alan R. Spachman/Chmn., CEO, Theodore H. Elliott/Dir., Gary J. Gruber/Dir., Keith A. Jensen/Dir., Joel Schiavone/Dir., Joseph E. Consolino/Dir., James C. Kennedy/Dir., Donald D. Larson/Dir.

Owners: James C. Kennedy, David W. Michelson, Julie A. McGraw, Gary N. Monda, Terry E. Phillips, Keith A. Jensen, Donald D. Larson, Gary J. Gruber, Joel Schiavone, Insiders/17.00%, The TCW Group, Inc./5.90%, Theodore H. Elliott, Joseph E. Consolino, Great American Insurance Company/47.00%, Alan R. Spachman/14.30%

Financial Data: ***Fiscal Year End:***12/31 ***Latest Annual Data:*** 12/31/2006

Year	Sales	Net Income
2006	$238,478,000	$35,700,000
2005	$209,176,000	$30,280,000
2004	$171,708,000	$22,768,000

Curr. Assets:	$233,328,000	***Curr. Liab.:***	$36,519,000	***P/E Ratio:***	12.63
Plant, Equip.:	$18,586,000	***Total Liab.:***	$632,485,000	***Indic. Yr. Divd.:***	$0.200
Total Assets:	$806,248,000	***Net Worth:***	$173,763,000	***Debt/ Equity:***	1.0343

National Investment Managers Inc

545 Metro Pl. S, Ste. 100, Dublin, OH, 43017; ***PH:*** 1-614-760-3703; ***http://*** www.nivm.com; ***Email:*** info@nationalinvestmentmanagers.com

General -		***Stock***-	
Incorporation	FL	Price on:12/24/2007	$0.76
Employees	350	Stock Exchange	OTC
Auditor	Rothstein, Kass & Company, P.C.	Ticker Symbol	NIVM
Stk Agt	Continental Stock T & T Co.	Outstanding Shares	NA
Counsel	NA	E.P.S	-$0.29
DUNS No.	NA	Shareholders	NA

Business: The groups principle activities include providing financial services and purchasing interests from small to medium-sized pension advisory, investment management and insurance organizations. In the year 2005, the group acquired Duncan Capital Financial Group, Inc., Haddon Strategic Alliance, Stephen H. Rosen & Associates, Inc., Valley Forge Enterprises, Ltd., Lamoriello & Co., Inc., Circle Pension, Inc., Southeastern Pension Services, Inc., Benefit Dynamics, Inc., National Actuarial Pension Services, Inc., Pentec, Inc., Pentec Capital Management, Inc. and The Pension Alliance, Inc. The group operates from the United States.

Primary SIC and add'l.: 8742

CIK No: 0000770461

Subsidiaries: Asset Preservation, Inc, Complete Investment Management Inc, Duncan Capital Financial Group, Inc., Haddon Strategic Alliances, Inc., Pension Administration Services, Inc, Stephen H. Rosen & Associates, Inc., Valley Forge Enterprises, Ltd.

Officers: Steven J. Ross/Dir., CEO, John M. Davis/COO, Pres., Michael Mallon/Contact - Regional Offices, Bend, Michael Porter/Investor Relations Contact, Chuck McLeod/Contact - Regional Offices, Houston, Joe McGarry/Contact - Regional Offices, North Attleboro, Steve Zito/Contact - Regional Offices, Providence, Jean Grace/Contact - Regional Offices, Southington, Michael E. Callahan/Contact - Regional Offices, Southington, Rhonda Becker/Contact - Regional Offices, White Plains, Stephen Rosen/Contact - Regional Offices, Haddonfield, Irene A. Feeley/Contact - Regional Offices, Horsham, Jack Holland/Contact - Regional Offices, Wayne, Steven Zimmerman/Contact - Regional Offices, Wayne, Jo-Ann Massanova/Contact - Regional Offices, Cherry Hill *(17 Officers included in Index)*

Directors: Steven J. Ross/Dir., CEO, Richard Berman/Chmn., Arthur D. Emil/Dir., Steven B. Ruchefsky/Dir., Jeff Cooke/Dir.

Owners: Michael Crow/8.60%, Drake Investments Limited/8.48%, John Davis, Laurus Master Fund Ltd./4.99%, Steven B. Ruchefsky/9.12%, The Lamco Group, Inc./11.21%, Richard Berman/4.99%, Stephen Eyer/7.90%, Leonard Neuhaus/3.05%, Jack C. Holland/8.10%, Insiders/21.04%, Richard Stierwalt/5.64%, Jeff Cooke, Steven J. Ross/1.94%, Arthur D. Emil/1.94% *(16 Owners included in Index)*

Financial Data: ***Fiscal Year End:***12/31 ***Latest Annual Data:*** 12/31/2006

Year	Sales	Net Income
2006	$22,892,000	-$5,204,000
2005	$4,825,000	-$2,808,000
2004	NA	-$10,000

Curr. Assets:	$9,442,000	***Curr. Liab.:***	$12,008,000	***P/E Ratio:***	17.93
Plant, Equip.:	$814,000	***Total Liab.:***	$36,547,000	***Indic. Yr. Divd.:***	NA
Total Assets:	$53,081,000	***Net Worth:***	$16,535,000	***Debt/ Equity:***	NA

National Lampoon Inc

8228 Sunset Blvd., Los Angeles, CA, 90046; ***PH:*** 1-310-474-5252; ***Fax:*** 1-310-474-1219; ***http://*** www.nationallampoon.com; ***Email:*** feedback@nationallampoon.com

General -		***Stock***-	
Incorporation	CA	Price on:12/24/2007	$2.12
Employees	25	Stock Exchange	AMEX
Auditor	Weinberg & Co., P.A	Ticker Symbol	NLN
Stk Agt	U.S. Stock Transfer Corp	Outstanding Shares	8,150,000
Counsel	NA	E.P.S	-$0.67
DUNS No.	15-751-7731	Shareholders	NA

Business: The group's principal activity is to license its trademark for use in the titles of the films. The operations of the group are carried out in three divisions: trademark, consumer products and television. The trademark division licenses and exploits the national lampoon trademark and related properties in connection with the production and distribution of feature films, television series and made-for-television movies. The activity of the television division is comprised of video distribution. The consumer products division operates through nationallampoon.com Website. The Website offers a wide array of comedy projects in motion pictures, television programming, multimedia, books, audio, video, and a wide array of merchandise.

Primary SIC and add'l.: 6794 7379 7812

CIK No: 0000798078

Subsidiaries: Stonefield Josephson, Inc.

Owners: Timothy Durham/27.75%, Insiders/61.60%, Daniel S. Laikin/49.60%, Timothy Durham/20.36%, James P. Jimirro/17.46%, Paul Skjodt/9.49%, Paul Skjodt/10.22%, Timothy Durham/31.59%, Insiders/12.15%, Insiders/12.94%, Robert Levy/5.88%, Daniel S. Laikin/49.88%, Daniel S. Laikin/40.43%, Robert Levy/4.16%

Financial Data: Fiscal Year End:07/31   Latest Annual Data: 7/31/2006

Year	Sales	Net Income
2006	$3,688,000	-$6,859,000
2005	$3,673,000	-$8,669,000
2004	$1,922,000	-$5,127,000

Curr. Assets:	$884,000	Curr. Liab.:	$4,964,000		
Plant, Equip.:	$18,000	Total Liab.:	$4,964,000	Indic. Yr. Divd.:	NA
Total Assets:	$3,458,000	Net Worth:	-$1,506,000	Debt/ Equity:	NA

National Medical Health Card Systems Inc

26 Harbor Pk. Dr., Port Washington, NY, 11050; **PH:** 1-800-251-3883; **Fax:** 1-516-605-6981; http://www.nmhc.com

General - Incorporation ....NY	Stock- Price on:12/24/2007 ....$15.91
Employees.............................436	Stock Exchange...........................NDQ
Auditor ....Ernst & Young LLP	Ticker Symbol...............................NMHC
Stk Agt..........Continental Stock Transfer & Trust Co	Outstanding Shares 5,470,000
Counsel.....................................NA	E.P.S. ....-$0.16
DUNS No. ....NA	Shareholders.................................NA

Business: The group's principal activity is to provide comprehensive pharmacy benefit management services in the United States. The pharmacy benefit management services include claims management, pharmacy network, benefit design consultation, drug review and analysis, formulary design and disease information services, data access, reporting and information analysis, physician profiling, specialty pharmacy and mail order. These services are provided to plan sponsors, which include managed care organizations, local governments, unions, corporations and third party health care plan administrators through its network of licensed pharmacies throughout the United States. During the year 2003, the group acquired portland professional pharmacy and assets of integrail.

Primary SIC and add'l.: 6324

CIK No: 0000813562

Subsidiaries: Centrus Corporation, Integrail Inc, Inteq Corp, Inteq PBM, LP, Inteq TX Corp, Interchange PMP, Inc, National Medical Health Card IPA, Inc, NMHC Funding, LLC, NMHC Group Solutions Insurance, Inc, NMHCRX Contracts, Inc, NMHCRX Mail Order, Inc, NMHCRX, Inc, PBM Technology, Inc, PCN DE Corp, Pharmaceutical Care Network 19 Subsidiaries included in the Index

Officers: Robert Kordella/Chief Clinical Officer, Mark A. Adkison/Chief Specialty Pharmacy Officer, Martin A. Magill/Chief Marketing Officer, George McGinn/General Counsel, Stuart Diamond/CFO, Patrick Moroney/CIO - Interim, Neil Carfagna/Chief Human Resources Officer

Directors: Thomas W. Erickson/57/Chmn.

Owners: Steven B. Klinsky, Millenco, L.L.C., Gerald Angowitz, Pequot Capital Management, Inc., S.A.C. Capital Advisors, LLC, T. Rowe Price Associates, Inc., Discovery Group I, LLC, Tery Baskin, Highbridge International LLC, Insiders, New Mountain Partners, L.P., New Mountain Affiliated Investors, L.P.

Financial Data: Fiscal Year End:06/30   Latest Annual Data: 6/30/2006

Year	Sales	Net Income
2006	$862,853,000	$9,657,000
2005	$800,592,000	$12,381,000
2004	$651,098,000	$7,953,000

Curr. Assets:	$155,098,000	Curr. Liab.:	$162,196,000		
Plant, Equip.:	$13,653,000	Total Liab.:	$170,809,000	Indic. Yr. Divd.:	NA
Total Assets:	$272,153,000	Net Worth:	$25,006,000	Debt/ Equity:	0.0623

National Mercantile Bancorp

1840 Century Pk. E, Ste. 800, Los Angeles, CA, 90067; **PH:** 1-310-277-2265; http://www.nationalmercbancorp.com

General - Incorporation ....CA	Stock- Price on:12/24/2007 ....NA
Employees.....................................NA	Stock Exchange...........................NA
Auditor ....Ernst & Young, LLP	Ticker Symbol...............................NA
Stk Agt..............U.S. Stock Transfer Corp	Outstanding Shares ....NA
Counsel.....................................NA	E.P.S. ....NA
DUNS No. ....NA	Shareholders.................................NA

Business: The groups principal activity is to provide banking and financial service. The products of the group include lines of credit, term loans, commercial real estate loans, construction loans and consumer and home equity loans. The group operates from South Bay, Century City and San Fernando Valley. The assets of the group for the year 2006 were $448.8 (million).

Primary SIC and add'l.: 6022

CIK No: 0000714801

Subsidiaries: Mercantile National Bank, South Bay Bank, National Association

Officers: C. G. Kum/Dir., CEO, Pres., Romolo C. Santarosa/CFO, Exec. VP, Thomas E. Anthony/Exec. VP, Head - Commercial Banking

Directors: C. G. Kum/Dir., CEO, Pres., Robert E. Gipson/Chmn., John W. Birchfield/Vice Chmn., Richard D. Aldridge/Dir., Syble R. Roberts/Dir., Thomas Tignino/Dir., Donald E. Benson/Dir., Joseph N. Cohen/Dir., Antoinette Hubenette/Dir., Douglas W. Hile/Dir.

Owners: Equity compensation plans approved by security holders/8.28%

National Oilwell Inc

10000 Richmond Ave., Houston, TX, 77042; **PH:** 1-713-346-7500; **Fax:** 1-713-435-2195; http://www.natoil.com; **Email:** customer.service@natoil.com

General - Incorporation ....DE	Stock- Price on:12/24/2007 ....$107.34
Employees.............................22,976	Stock Exchange...........................NYSE
Auditor ....Ernst & Young LLP	Ticker Symbol...............................NA
Stk Agt......American Stock Transfer & Trust Co.	Outstanding Shares 177,610,000
Counsel.....................................NA	E.P.S. $3.385
DUNS No. 16-168-1044	Shareholders.................................NA

Business: The groups principle activity is to provide equipment and components used in oil, gas drilling and production operations. The group operates through three segments namely rig technology, petroleum services and supplies, and distribution services. In the year 2006, the group acquired Soil Recovery A/S. The group operates from United States.

Primary SIC and add'l.: 5084 3533 3561

CIK No: 0001021860

Subsidiaries: Advanced Wirecloth, Inc., Amclyde UK Limited, Bowen Downhole LLC, Bowen Downhole, Inc., Brandt Energy Environmental, L.P., Brandt Interests, Inc., Brandt Oilfield Services (M)Sdn. Bhd., Brandt Servicios Petroleros S.A., Chargewood Limited, Church Oil Tools, Inc., Coil Services (North Sea) Limited, Corlac Equipment Corp, Ctes, L.p., Dreco DHT, Inc., Dreco Eastern Europe Ltd. 175 Subsidiaries included in the Index

Officers: Merrill A. Miller/Chmn., CEO, Pres./$4,932,064.00, Clay C. Williams/CFO, Sr. VP/$1,764,751.00, Mark A. Reese/Pres. - Expendable Products/$1,477,658.00, Haynes B. Smith/Pres. - Services, Dwight W. Rettig/VP, General Counsel/$1,382,660.00, Robert W. Blanchard/VP, Corporate Controller, Chief Accounting Officer, Kevin Neveu/Pres. - Rig Technology/$1,471,196.00

Directors: Merrill A. Miller/Chmn., CEO, Pres., Eric L. Mattson/Dir., Robert E. Beauchamp/Dir., Ben A. Guill/Dir., Jeffery A. Smisek/Dir., David D. Harrison/Dir., Roger L. Jarvis/Dir., Greg L. Armstrong/Dir.

Owners: Insiders, Merrill A. Miller, Ben A. Guill, Roger L. Jarvis, Robert E. Beauchamp, Mark A. Reese, Greg L. Armstrong, Dwight W. Rettig, David D. Harrison, Eric L. Mattson, Robert Blanchard, Haynes B. Smith, Kevin A. Neveu, FMR Corp./14.03%, Jeffery A. Smisek (16 Owners included in Index)

Financial Data: Fiscal Year End:12/31   Latest Annual Data: 12/31/2006

Year	Sales	Net Income
2006	$7,025,800,000	$684,000,000
2005	$4,644,500,000	$286,900,000
2004	$2,318,100,000	$115,200,000

Curr. Assets:	$4,965,600,000	Curr. Liab.:	$2,665,200,000	P/E Ratio:	18.83
Plant, Equip.:	$1,022,100,000	Total Liab.:	$3,960,300,000	Indic. Yr. Divd.:	NA
Total Assets:	$9,019,300,000	Net Worth:	$5,023,500,000	Debt/ Equity:	0.1374

National Patent Development Corp

777 Wchester Ave., White Plains, NY, 10640; **PH:** 1-914-249-9700

General - Incorporation ....DE	Stock- Price on:12/24/2007 ....$2.75
Employees.............................295	Stock Exchange...........................OTC
Auditor ....Eisner LLP	Ticker Symbol...............................NPDV
Stk Agt....Computershare Investor Services LLC	Outstanding Shares 17,880,000
Counsel.....................................NA	E.P.S. ....-$0.07
DUNS No. ....NA	Shareholders.................................NA

Business: The groups principle activity is to provide paint sundry items, interior and exterior stains, brushes, rollers, caulking compounds and hardware products. The group operates through two segments include MXL Segment and Five Star Segment. The group operates from United States, Japan, Europe, Middle East, Mexico, Canada and Australia.

Primary SIC and add'l.: NA

CIK No: 0001279715

Subsidiaries: Five Star Products, Inc., JL Distributors, MXL Industries, Inc.

Officers: Harvey P. Eisen/65/Chmn., CEO, Pres., Scott N. Greenberg/52/Dir., CFO, John C. Belknap/62/Dir., VP, Ira J. Sobotko/51/VP - Finance, Sec., Treasurer

Directors: Harvey P. Eisen/65/Chmn., CEO, Pres., Talton R. Embry/61/Dir., Scott N. Greenberg/52/Dir., CFO, John C. Belknap/62/Dir., VP, Leslie S. Flegel/71/Dir., Lawrence G. Schafran/70/Dir.

Owners: Lawrence G. Schafran, Insiders/20.02%, Harvey P. Eisen/14.59%, Carl E. Warden/5.54%, Leslie S. Flegel/1.20%, Advisory Research, Inc./10.89%, Goldman Capital Management, Inc./9.92%, John C. Belknap, Jerome I. Feldman/3.59%, Bedford Oak Advisors, LLC/14.61%, Gabelli Asset Management, Inc./10.73%, Talton R. Embry, Scott N. Greenberg, Black Horse Capital LP/6.59%

Financial Data: Fiscal Year End:12/31   Latest Annual Data: 12/31/2006

Year	Sales	Net Income
2006	$117,084,000	-$1,207,000
2005	$114,366,000	-$2,919,000
2004	$110,223,000	-$4,529,000

Curr. Assets:	$40,725,000	Curr. Liab.:	$28,543,000		
Plant, Equip.:	$2,925,000	Total Liab.:	$30,401,000	Indic. Yr. Divd.:	NA
Total Assets:	$53,234,000	Net Worth:	$21,137,000	Debt/ Equity:	0.0745

National Penn Bancshares Inc

PO Box 547, Philadelphia and Reading Ave., Boyertown, PA, 19512; **PH:** 1-610-367-6001; **Fax:** 1-610-369-6118; http://www.natpennbank.com

General - Incorporation ....PA	Stock- Price on:12/24/2007 ....$17.74
Employees.............................1,197	Stock Exchange...........................NDQ
Auditor ....Grant Thornton LLP	Ticker Symbol...............................NPLA
Stk Agt..............Mellon Investor Services LLC	Outstanding Shares 47,630,000
Counsel.....Ellsworth Carlton Mixell & Waldman	E.P.S. $1.33
DUNS No. 07-937-3247	Shareholders.................................NA

Business: The group's principal activity is to provide commercial and retail banking services. The group operates primarily through its wholly-owned banking subsidiary, national penn bank. The group provides checking and savings accounts, time deposits, personal, business, residential mortgage and educational loans, credit cards, safe deposit and night depository facilities and international banking services. The group also provides trust and investment management services, brokerage services and insurance services through its subsidiaries. The group serves the residents and businesses of southeastern Pennsylvania and northern New Jersey through 66 branch locations. In 2003, the group acquired firstservice bank and hometowne heritage bank and disposed panasia bank, na. On 10-Jun-2004 and 01-Jul-2004, the group acquired peoples first inc and pennsurance, inc.

Primary SIC and add'l.: 6021 6712

CIK No: 0000700733

Subsidiaries: d/b/a/ National Penn Mortgage Company, FTF Investmets, Inc., Link Financial Services, Inc., National Penn Bancshares, Inc., National Penn Bank, National Penn Capital Advisors, Inc., National Penn Insurance Agency, Inc., National Penn Investment Company, National Penn Investors Trust Company, National Penn Leasing Company, National Penn Life Insurance Company, National Penn Management Services, LLC, Nittany Asset Management, Inc., Nittany Bank, NPB Capital Trust II 26 Subsidiaries included in the Index

Officers: Wayne R. Weidner/Chmn., CEO/$1,379,431.00, Sandra L. Spayd/Sec. - Shareholder Services, Anderson H. Ellsworth/60/Exec. VP, Securities Law Compliance Dir., Janice S. McCracken/43/Exec. VP, Dir. - Finance, Management Accounting, Glenn E. Moyer/Dir., Pres./$8,986,637.00, Gary L. Rhoads/Chief Accounting Officer/$3,357,971.00, Michelle H. Debkowski/Contact - Investor Relations, Garry D. Koch/53/Group Exec. VP, Dir. - Risk Management, Bruce G. Kilroy/Group Exec. VP/$385,002.00, Paul W. McGloin/60/Group Exec. VP, Chief Lending Officer/$353,141.00, Sharon L. Weaver/Group Exec. VP, Michael R. Reinhard/CFO

Directors: Wayne R. Weidner/Chmn., CEO, Robert E. Rigg/55/Dir., Donald P. Worthington/Dir., Kenneth A. Longacre/Dir., Patricia L. Langiotti/61/Dir., George C. Mason/Dir., Ralph J. Borneman/69/Dir., Robert L. Byers/69/Dir., Fred D. Hafer/66/Dir., Frederick P. Krott/Dir., Thomas A. Beaver/Dir., John Ralph Borneman/Dir., Glenn E. Moyer/Dir., Pres., Robert C. Roth/Dir., Albert H. Kramer/Dir. *(17 Directors included in Index)*

Owners: Bruce G. Kilroy, Robert L. Byers, Paul W. McGloin, Thomas A. Beaver, Natalye Paquin, Kenneth A. Longacre, Wayne R. Weidner/1.25%, Albert H. Kramer, Frederick P. Krott, Insiders/6.80%, Robert C. Roth, Donald P. Worthington, Robert E. Rigg/1.14%, Ralph J. Borneman, Fred D. Hafer *(20 Owners included in Index)*

Financial Data: Fiscal Year End:12/31 Latest Annual Data: 12/31/2006

Year	Sales	Net Income
2006	$369,052,000	$64,109,000
2005	$299,602,000	$59,755,000
2004	$245,633,000	$47,914,000

Curr. Assets:	$136,828,000	Curr. Liab.:	$4,306,116,000	P/E Ratio:	13.34
Plant, Equip.:	$55,231,000	Total Liab.:	$4,909,419,000	Indic. Yr. Divd.:	$0.670
Total Assets:	$5,452,288,000	Net Worth:	$542,869,000	Debt/ Equity:	1.0742

National Presto Industries Inc

3925 N Hastings Way, Eau Claire, WI, 54703; **PH:** 1-715-839-2121; **Fax:** 1-715-839-2122; http:// www.gopresto.com

General - Incorporation	WI	Stock- Price on:12/24/2007	NA
Employees	552	Stock Exchange	NYSE
Auditor	Virchow, Krause & Co., LLP	Ticker Symbol	NPK
Stk Agt	Computershare Investor Services LLC	Outstanding Shares	6,830,000
Counsel	NA	E.P.S.	$4.09
DUNS No.	00-619-6174	Shareholders	NA

Business: The group's principal activities are to manufacture and distribute small electrical appliances and housewares. The group operates in three segments: housewares/small appliances, defense products and the absorbent products. The housewares/small appliance segment manufactures and distributes small electrical appliances and housewares, including pressure cookers, canners, pizza ovens, can openers, slicer, shredders, electric heaters, corn poppers, coffeemakers, electric grills, electric tea kettles, electric knives, electric knife sharpeners and timers. The defense products segment manufactures precision mechanical, electromechanical and electronic assembly components for the United States government and sub-contractors. The absorbent products segment manufactures and sells primarily private label diapers. In 2003, the group acquired spectra technologies llc and assets of ncn hygienic products inc.

Primary SIC and add'l.: 3634 3545 5641 3631

CIK No: 0000080172

Subsidiaries: AMTEC Corporation, Canton Sales & Storage Company, Jackson Sales and Storage Company, National Holding Investment Company, National Presto Industries, Inc, Presto Absorbent Products, Presto Absorbent Products, Inc., Presto Manufacturing Company, Spectra Technologies LLC

Owners: Royce & Associates, LLC/12.10%, Maryjo Cohen/30.20%, Dimensional Fund Advisors, Inc./6.20%, Melvin S. Cohen/5.70%, Patrick J. Quinn, Donald E. Hoeschen, Insiders/30.20%, Lawrence J. Tienor, Neil L. Brown

Financial Data: Fiscal Year End:12/31 Latest Annual Data: 12/31/2006

Year	Sales	Net Income
2006	$304,681,000	$27,960,000
2005	$184,565,000	$18,967,000
2004	$158,956,000	$15,441,000

Curr. Assets:	$273,182,000	Curr. Liab.:	$63,028,000		
Plant, Equip.:	$62,559,000	Total Liab.:	$64,634,000	Indic. Yr. Divd.:	$0.950
Total Assets:	$344,976,000	Net Worth:	$280,342,000	Debt/ Equity:	NA

National Quality Care Inc

9033 Wilshire Blvd, No.501, Beverly Hills, CA, 90211; **PH:** 1-310-550-6242

General - Incorporation	DE	Stock- Price on:12/24/2007	$0.16
Employees	31	Stock Exchange	OTC
Auditor	PMB Helin Donovan, LLP	Ticker Symbol	NQCI
Stk Agt	Colonial Stock Transfer Co Inc	Outstanding Shares	48,920,000
Counsel	Jenkens & Gilchrist LLP	E.P.S.	-$0.02
DUNS No.	96-260-4930	Shareholders	NA

Business: The group's principal activity is to provide dialysis services for patients suffering from chronic kidney failure. The group also provides inpatient dialysis services by contract to eleven hospitals in the state of California. Treatment options for chronic kidney failure include hemodialysis, peritoneal dialysis and kidney transplantation. Chronic kidney failure patients are treated predominantly in outpatient treatment facilities. Hemodialysis is the most common form of chronic kidney failure treatment. Hemodialysis is generally performed either in a freestanding facility or in a hospital-based facility. Peritoneal dialysis is generally performed by the patient at home.

Primary SIC and add'l.: 8092 6519

CIK No: 0000872544

Subsidiaries: Los Angeles community Dialysis, Inc.

Owners: Robert M. Snukal/28.80%, Insiders/45.20%, Victor Gura/31.50%, Ronald P. Lang/7.40%, Leonardo Berezovsky/8.70%, Jose Spiwak/2.60%

Financial Data: Fiscal Year End:12/31 Latest Annual Data: 12/31/2006

Year	Sales		Net Income
2006	NA		-$1,538,000
2005	$4,137,000		-$2,345,000
2004	$4,001,000		-$1,669,000

Curr. Assets:	$1,943,000	Curr. Liab.:	$1,485,000		
Plant, Equip.:	NA	Total Liab.:	$1,485,000	Indic. Yr. Divd.:	NA
Total Assets:	$2,017,000	Net Worth:	$532,000	Debt/ Equity:	NA

National Realty

One N.E. First Ave., Ste. 306, Ocala, FL, 34470; **PH:** 1-352-867-5183; http:// www.nationalrealtyfla.com

General - Incorporation	NV	Stock- Price on:12/24/2007	$0.015
Employees	NA	Stock Exchange	OTC
Auditor	Bagell, Levine & Company, LLC	Ticker Symbol	NRMG
Stk Agt	Transfer Online, Inc.	Outstanding Shares	7,140,000
Counsel	NA	E.P.S.	NA
DUNS No.	NA	Shareholders	NA

Business: The groups principal activity is to provide real estate development and mortgage lending business. The group operates from the United States.

Primary SIC and add'l.: 1520

CIK No: 0001096840

Subsidiaries: Connecticut Acquisition Corp. No. 1, DC Power Products Acquisition Corp

Officers: Bo Liu/Chmn., CEO, Acting CFO, Sandra Shaw/Professional Staff, Indialantic Office, Claire Sliptchuik/Professional Staff, Indialantic Office, Tracy Fortman/Professional Staff, Suntree Office, Liane Ivey/Professional Staff, Suntree Office, Cyndi Jones/Professional Staff, Suntree Office, Cary Kuschel/Professional Staff, Satellite Beach Office, Elsa Rebello/Professional Staff, Satellite Beach Office, Chad Wamsley/Professional Staff, Palm Bay Office, Andrew Waterman/Professional Staff, Palm Bay Office, Richard Astrom/61/Dir., Pres., Christopher Astrom/37/Dir., VP, Sec., CFO, Theresa Santee/Professional Staff, Satellite Beach Office, Todd Cowan/Professional Staff, Suntree Office, Julie Cowan/Professional Staff, Suntree Office *(90 Officers included in Index)*

Directors: Bo Liu/Chmn., CEO, Acting CFO, Richard Astrom/61/Dir., Pres., Christopher Astrom/37/Dir., VP, Sec., CFO

Owners: Insiders, Rise Elite International Limited, Liang Deli, Vision Opportunity Master Fund, Ltd./97.01%, Liu Bo, Vision Opportunity Master Fund, Ltd.

Financial Data: Fiscal Year End:09/30 Latest Annual Data: 09/30/2006

Year	Sales		Net Income
2006	NA		-$126,000
2005	$1,408,000		-$687,000
2004	$1,600,000		-$1,127,000

Curr. Assets:	$2,000	Curr. Liab.:	$40,000		
Plant, Equip.:	NA	Total Liab.:	$240,000	Indic. Yr. Divd.:	NA
Total Assets:	$2,000	Net Worth:	-$238,000	Debt/ Equity:	NA

National Research Corp

1245 Q. St., Lincoln, NE, 68508; **PH:** 1-402-475-2525; **Fax:** 1-402-475-9061; http:// www.nationalresearch.com

General - Incorporation	WI	Stock- Price on:12/24/2007	$24.79
Employees	186	Stock Exchange	NYSE
Auditor	KPMG LLP	Ticker Symbol	NRG
Stk Agt	U.S. Bank, N.A.,	Outstanding Shares	6,920,000
Counsel	Foley & Lardner LLP	E.P.S.	$0.94
DUNS No.	05-085-7788	Shareholders	NA

Business: The group's principle activity is the provision of ongoing survey-based performance measurement, analysis and tracking services to the healthcare industry. The group provides performance tracking services, custom research and renewable syndicated services. It offers market research services to hospitals and insurance companies on an unsecured credit basis. It recognizes revenue from its renewable service nrc listening system (performance tracking services). Under the performance tracking services, the group provides interim and annual performance tracking to its clients under annual client service contracts. The group's quarterly revenue for September 2007 was 13.95 millions of USD.

Primary SIC and add'l.: 8732

CIK No: 0000070487

Officers: Michael D. Hays/CEO/$263,754.00, Joseph W. Carmichael/Pres./$540,383.00, Pat Beans/CFO - Contact - Investor Relations/$294,100.00

Directors: Joann M. Martin/53/Dir., Paul C. Schorr/Dir., Gail L. Warden/69/Dir.

Owners: Paul C. Schorr, Gail L. Warden, JoAnn M. Martin, Insiders/73.00%, Joseph W. Carmichael, Jona S. Raasch, Michael D. Hays/69.80%, John N. Nunnelly, Patrick E. Beans/1.24%

Financial Data: Fiscal Year End:12/31 Latest Annual Data: 12/31/2006

Year	Sales	Net Income
2006	$43,771,000	$5,884,000
2005	$32,437,000	$5,236,000
2004	$29,683,000	$4,551,000

Curr. Assets:	$12,997,000	Curr. Liab.:	$14,479,000	P/E Ratio:	27.54
Plant, Equip.:	$11,716,000	Total Liab.:	$24,782,000	Indic. Yr. Divd.:	$0.480
Total Assets:	$61,532,000	Net Worth:	$36,751,000	Debt/ Equity:	NA

National Rural Utilities Coop Finance Corp DC

2201 Cooperative Way, Herndon, VA, 20171; **PH:** 1-703-709-6700; http:// www.nrucfc.org; **Email:** InvestorRelations@nrucfc.coop

General - Incorporation	DC	Stock- Price on:12/24/2007	$23.16
Employees	NA	Stock Exchange	NA
Auditor	Deloitte & Touche LLP	Ticker Symbol	NA
Stk Agt	NA	Outstanding Shares	NA
Counsel	NA	E.P.S.	NA
DUNS No.	07-483-3401	Shareholders	NA

Business: The group's principal activities are to provide its members with dependable source of low cost capital and state-of-the-art financial products and services. The group provides its members with low cost loans, which enable them to acquire, construct, generate and transmit electricity. The group also provides guarantees to its members for tax-exempt financing of pollution control facilities and other properties constructed or acquired by its members, debt in connection with certain leases and various other transactions. The finance is provided to supplement the loan programs of the rural utility service of the United States department of agriculture.

Primary SIC and add'l.: 6159

CIK No: 0000070502

Officers: Sheldon C. Petersen/CEO, Governor, Lawrence Zawalick/Sr. VP - Rural Telephone Finance Cooperative, RTFC, John M. Borak/Sr. VP - Credit Risk Management, John T. Evans/Sr. VP - Operations, Terryl Jacobs/49/Dir., Pres., Steven L. Lilly/CFO, Sr. VP, John J. List/Sr. VP, Richard Larochelle/Sr. VP - Corporate Relations, Roger Arthur/61/Dir., VP, Darryl Schriver/43/Dir., Sec., Treasurer - CFC

Directors: Terryl Jacobs/49/Dir., Pres., Harold Foley/74/Dir., Charles Wayne Whitaker/58/Dir., Reuben B. McBride/61/Dir., Gary Harrison/46/Dir., Ronald P. Salyer/43/Dir., Roger Arthur/61/Dir., VP, Gale Rettkowski/62/Dir., Darryl Schriver/43/Dir., Sec., Treasurer - CFC, David J. Wasson/62/Dir., William A. Kopacz/61/Dir., Jack F. Wolfe/64/Dir., F. E. Wolski/57/Dir., Wayne R. Stratton/60/Dir., Steven J. Haaven/57/Dir. *(20 Directors included in Index)*

Financial Data: Fiscal Year End:05/31 Latest Annual Data: 5/31/2007

Year	Sales	Net Income
2007	$1,151,957,000	$11,701,000
2006	$1,007,912,000	$95,746,000
2005	$1,026,126,000	$122,974,000

Curr. Assets:	$574,134,000	**Curr. Liab.:**	$5,643,215,000		
Plant, Equip.:	$127,035,000	**Total Liab.:**	$18,369,751,000	**Indic. Yr. Divd.:**	NA
Total Assets:	$19,179,621,000	**Net Worth:**	$787,976,000	**Debt/ Equity:**	NA

National RV Holdings Inc

100 W Sinclair St., Perris, CA, 92571; *PH:* 1-951-436-3000; *Fax:* 1-951-943-8498; *http://* www.nrvh.com; *Email:* ir@nrvh.com

General - Incorporation .... DE	**Stock** - Price on:12/24/2007 ....$1.76
Employees ....NA	Stock Exchange..OTC
Auditor ....Swenson Advisors, LLP	Ticker Symbol..NVRH
Stk Agt..............................Transfer & Trust Co.	Outstanding Shares 10,340,000
Counsel ....NA	E.P.S..-$2.538
DUNS No. ....NA	Shareholders...NA

Business: The groups principal activity is to provide motorized recreational vehicles. The group operates from the United States.

Primary SIC and add'l.: 3716

CIK No: 0000910655

Subsidiaries: National R.V., Inc

Officers: Bradley Albrechtsen/CEO, Pres., Tom Martini/CFO, Treasurer, Len Southwick/Pres. - National RV

Directors: Doy B. Henley/Chmn., David J. Humphreys/Dir., Gregory McCaffery/Dir., James B. Roszak/Dir.

Owners: Aegis Financial Corporation/9.00%, Dimensional Fund Advisors Inc./8.30%, Yorktown Avenue Capital, LLC/7.40%, Bradley C. Albrechtsen, Thomas J. Martini, David J. Humphreys, FMR Corp./5.30%, James B. Roszak, Doy B. Henley/1.20%, Insiders/3.20%, Bryant R. Riley/11.60%, Gregory McCaffery, Gary N. Siegler/9.00%, Jonathan C. Corn

Financial Data: Fiscal Year End:12/31 Latest Annual Data: 12/31/2006

Year	Sales	Net Income
2006	$397,118,000	-$24,333,000
2005	$463,610,000	-$19,768,000
2004	$436,813,000	-$9,454,000

Curr. Assets:	$96,398,000	**Curr. Liab.:**	$94,004,000		
Plant, Equip.:	$37,430,000	**Total Liab.:**	$99,405,000	**Indic. Yr. Divd.:**	NA
Total Assets:	$135,524,000	**Net Worth:**	$36,119,000	**Debt/ Equity:**	0.0032

National Scientific Corp

8361 E Evans Rd., Ste. 106, Scottsdale, AZ, 85260; *PH:* 1-480-948-8324; *Fax:* 1-480-483-8893; *http://* www.national-scientific.com; *Email:* info@nscus.com

General - Incorporation .... TX	**Stock** - Price on:12/24/2007 ....$0.02
Employees 2	Stock Exchange..OTC
Auditor .... Semple, Marchal & Cooper, LLP	Ticker Symbol..NSCT
Stk Agt.....Computershare Investor Services LLC	Outstanding Shares 111,130,000
Counsel ....Susan L. Regan Esq	E.P.S..-$0.004
DUNS No. ....NA	Shareholders...NA

Business: The group's principal activity is to develop and sell electronic devices for the location services market. The group is a development stage company. The products are made from several dozen or more semiconductor chips mounted on small boards and sold as complete products. These products are designed to provide the product user with information regarding the unit's current location. Some of the products report this information back to central locations and people or objects in the field can be tracked as they move from place to place. Many of the location products use global positioning systems technology commonly referred to as gps technology. Prior to 2002 the group was into research and development.

Primary SIC and add'l.: 3674

CIK No: 0001022505

Subsidiaries: Eden Systems, Inc

Officers: Michael Grollman/46/Chmn., CEO, Acting CFO, Graham Clark/Dir., Pres., Corp. Sec., Rhonda Jobe/Part, Time Marketing Mgr., El-Badawy El-Sharawy/Sr. Scientific Consultant, Susan L. Regan/Part-Time Legal Counsel, Oscar Quadros/Chartered Accountant, David Mandala/Chief Systems Architect

Directors: Michael Grollman/46/Chmn., CEO, Acting CFO, Gregory Szabo/Dir., Graham Clark/Dir., Pres., Corp. Sec.

Owners: Insiders/10.50%, Michael A. Grollman/6.30%, Graham L. Clark/3.80%, Gregory Szabo/0.40%

Financial Data: Fiscal Year End:09/30 Latest Annual Data: 9/30/2006

Year	Sales	Net Income
2006	$227,000	-$945,000
2005	$73,000	-$1,141,000
2004	$78,000	-$952,000

Curr. Assets:	$197,000	**Curr. Liab.:**	$1,494,000		
Plant, Equip.:	$1,000	**Total Liab.:**	$1,619,000	**Indic. Yr. Divd.:**	NA
Total Assets:	$220,000	**Net Worth:**	-$1,400,000	**Debt/ Equity:**	NA

National Security Group Inc

661 E Davis St., Elba, AL, 36323; *PH:* 1-334-897-2273; *http://* www.nationalsecuritygroup.com; *Email:* info@nationalsecuritygroup.com

General - Incorporation .... DE	**Stock** - Price on:12/24/2007 ....$18.78
Employees 159	Stock Exchange..NDQ
Auditor .... Barfield, Murphy, Shank & Smith P.C	Ticker Symbol..NSHA
Stk Agt .... Registrar and Transfer CO.	Outstanding Shares 2,470,000
Counsel ....NA	E.P.S..$2.26
DUNS No. 07-896-3022	Shareholders...NA

Business: The group's principal activity is to provide property, casualty and life insurance through its subsidiaries. The group, through its life insurance subsidiary, offers a basic line of life, health and accident insurance products. The group writes primarily low value dwelling fire and windstorm, homeowners and personal non-standard automobile lines of insurance. The group also writes commercial lines of insurance for small businesses. The group's subsidiaries provide life insurance service, which include a basic line of life, health and accident insurance.

Primary SIC and add'l.: 6331 6719 6321 6311

CIK No: 0000865058

Subsidiaries: Mobile Attic Franchising Company, National Security Fire & Casualty Company, National Security Insurance Company, Omega One Insurance Company, The National Security Group, Inc

Officers: William L. Brunson/Dir., CEO, Pres. The National Security Group - Incelba, Alabama/$195,107.00, Brian McLeod/CFO, Treasurer The National Security Group - Inc/$142,960.00, Mickey Murdock/Dir., COO, Sr. VP/$181,130.00, Jack E. Brunson/Dir., Pres. - National Security Fire, Casualty Co/$148,046.00

Directors: William L. Brunson/Dir., CEO, Pres. The National Security Group - Incelba, Alabama, Winfield Baird/Chmn., Carolyn E. Brunson/Dir., Frank B. O'Neil/Dir., Mickey Murdock/Dir., COO, Sr. VP, Jack E. Brunson/Dir., Pres. - National Security Fire, Casualty Co, Fleming Brooks/Dir., Paul C. Wesch/Dir., Walter P. Wilkerson/Dir., Donald S. Pittman/Dir., Fred Clark/Dir., Brunson L. White/Dir., James B. Saxon/Dir.

Owners: Edna Brunson Elba/6.31%, Brunson Properties/14.86%

Financial Data: Fiscal Year End:12/31 Latest Annual Data: 12/31/2006

Year	Sales	Net Income
2006	$69,050,000	$4,250,000
2005	$66,030,000	$1,558,000
2004	$63,246,000	$3,113,000

Curr. Assets:	$9,001,000	**Curr. Liab.:**	$12,785,000	**P/E Ratio:**	8.31
Plant, Equip.:	$11,689,000	**Total Liab.:**	$88,832,000	**Indic. Yr. Divd.:**	$0.900
Total Assets:	$134,911,000	**Net Worth:**	$45,379,000	**Debt/ Equity:**	0.2021

National Semiconductor Corp

2900 Semiconductor Dr., Santa Clara, CA, 95050; *PH:* 1-408-721-5000; *http://* www.national.com; *Email:* invest.group@nsc.com

General - Incorporation .... DE	**Stock** - Price on:12/24/2007 ....$28.5
Employees 8,500	Stock Exchange..NYSE
Auditor ....KPMG LLP	Ticker Symbol..NSM
Stk Agt .... Computershare Investor Services LLC	Outstanding Shares 310,300,000
Counsel ....NA	E.P.S..$1.12
DUNS No. 04-147-2986	Shareholders...NA

Business: The groups principle activity is to manufacture high performance analog devices and subsystems. The groups products include power management circuits, display drivers, audio and operational amplifiers, communication interface products and data conversion solutions. The group operates from United States.

Primary SIC and add'l.: 3679 3674

CIK No: 0000070530

Subsidiaries: Algorex Inc., ASIC II Limited, DigitalQuake, Inc., Electronica NSC de Mexico, S.A. de C.V., innoCOMM Wireless, Malaysia SDN. BHD., Mediamatics, Inc., National Semiconductor (Far East) Limited, National Semiconductor (I.C.) Ltd., National Semiconductor (Maine), Inc., National Semiconductor (Suzhou) Ltd., National Semiconductor (U.K.) Holdings Ltd., National Semiconductor (U.K.) Ltd., National Semiconductor (U.K.) Pension Trust Company Ltd., National Semiconductor Aktiebolog 52 Subsidiaries included in the Index

Officers: Brian L. Halla/Chmn., CEO/$12,009,180.00, Donald MacLeod/COO, Pres./$6,936,031.00, Detlev Kunz/Sr. VP - Power Management Group/$2,736,320.00, Mohan Yegnashankaran/Sr. VP - Technology Support, Michael Noonen/Sr. VP - Worldwide Marketing, Sales, John M. Clark/Sr. VP, General Counsel, Sec., Pam Baich/Government Affairs Administrator, Project Mgr., Ahmad Bahai/National Fellow, CTO - NS Labs, Dennis Monticelli/National Fellow, CTO - Analog, Lewis Chew/CFO, Sr. VP/$3,303,938.00, Suneil Parulekar/Sr. VP - Analog Signal Path Group/$2,586,022.00, Julie Lacross/Export Administration, C. S. Liu/Sr. VP - Worldwide Manufacturing, Gerry Fields/VP - Quality Assurance, Reliability, Jamie E. Samath/Corporate Controller *(19 Officers included in Index)*

Directors: Brian L. Halla/Chmn., CEO, Gary P. Arnold/Dir., Edward R. McCracken/Dir., Robert J. Frankenberg/Dir., Floyd E. Kvamme/Dir., Modesto A. Maidique/Dir., Steven R. Appleton/Dir., Richard J. Danzig/Dir., John T. Dickson/Dir.

Owners: Floyd E. Kvamme, Gary P. Arnold, Donald Macleod/1.07%, FMR Corp/15.84%, Robert J. Frankenberg, John T. Dickson, Insiders/5.18%, Lewis Chew, Detlev Kunz, Edward R. McCracken, Steven R. Appleton, Modesto A. Maidique, Brian L. Halla/2.58%, Suneil Parulekar, Relational Investors, LLC/14.80% *(16 Owners included in Index)*

Financial Data: Fiscal Year End:05/28 Latest Annual Data: 05/27/2007

Year	Sales	Net Income
2007	$1,929,900,000	$375,300,000
2006	$2,158,100,000	$449,200,000
2005	$1,913,100,000	$415,300,000

Curr. Assets:	$1,245,800,000	**Curr. Liab.:**	$461,300,000	**P/E Ratio:**	25.45
Plant, Equip.:	$699,600,000	**Total Liab.:**	$599,900,000	**Indic. Yr. Divd.:**	$0.160
Total Assets:	$2,280,400,000	**Net Worth:**	$1,680,500,000	**Debt/ Equity:**	NA

National Steel Corp

Av. Brigadeiro Faria Lima, 3.400 - 20andar, Sao Paulo, 04538-132; ***PH:*** 55-11-3049-7100

General - Incorporation	Federative Republic of Brazil	***Stock*** - Price on:12/24/2007	$0.004
Employees	8,229	Stock Exchange	OTC
Auditor	Deloitte& Touche LLP	Ticker Symbol	NSTLQ
Stk Agt	Mellon Investor Services LLC	Outstanding Shares	41,290,000
Counsel	NA	E.P.S	NA
DUNS No.	NA	Shareholders	NA

Business: The groups principle activity is to produce steel. The products of the group include carbon steel and Slabs. The group operates through four segments namely steel, mining, logistics and cement. The group operates from Asia, North America, Latin America and Europe.

Primary SIC and add'l.: 3310

CIK No: 0001049659

Subsidiaries: Cia. Metalic Nordeste, Cinnabar, Companhia Siderrgica Nacional LLC, CSN Aceros, CSN Cayman, CSN Cimentos, CSN Energia, CSN Energy, CSN Export, CSN Holding LLC, CSN I, CSN Iron, CSN Islands IX, CSN Islands VII, CSN Islands VIII 29 Subsidiaries included in the Index

Officers: Otavio De Garcia Lazcano/39/CFO, Marcos Marinho Lutz/39/Executive Officer, Juarez Saliba De Avelar/47/Executive Officer

Owners: Vicunha Siderurgia S.A/42.74%, BNDESPAR/6.28%

National Technical Systems Inc CA

24007 Ventura Blvd., Ste. 200, Calabasas, CA, 91302; ***PH:*** 1-818-591-0776; ***Fax:*** 1-818-591-0899; ***http://*** www.ntscorp.com; ***Email:*** sales@ntscorp.com

General - Incorporation	CA	***Stock*** - Price on:12/24/2007	$6.99
Employees	540	Stock Exchange	NYSE
Auditor	Ernst & Young LLP	Ticker Symbol	NTT
Stk Agt	U.S. Stock Transfer Corp	Outstanding Shares	8,800,000
Counsel	NA	E.P.S	$0.27
DUNS No.	06-381-8587	Shareholders	NA

Business: The group's principal activities are to provide technical services and solutions to a variety of industries. The group operates in two segments: engineering and evaluations and technical staffing. The engineering and evaluations segment provides technical personnel for product certification, product safety testing and product evaluations. Other services include development of product screening procedures, design and fabrication of test fixtures, failure analysis and design modification support and systems testing. The technical staffing services segment provides staffing services. The customers portfolio include aerospace, defense, commercial, automotive, electronics and nuclear industries, information technology, information systems and software companies. Nts and xxcal are the registered service marks of the group. The operations are conducted in the United States, the United Kingdom and Japan. The group acquired dynamic testing holdings llc on 23-Jan-2004.

Primary SIC and add'l.: 7363 7361 8732 8711

CIK No: 0000110536

Subsidiaries: Acton Environmental Testing Corporation, Aetl Testing, Inc., Approved Engineering Testing Laboratories, Inc., ETCR INC., National Quality Assurance, Inc., Nts Europe, Nts, Technical Systems, Phase Seven Laboratories, XXCAL, Inc.

Officers: William McGinnis/Dir., CEO, Pres./$467,800.00, Aaron Cohen/Vice Chmn., Sr. VP - Corporate Development, Raffy Lorentzian/Sr. VP CFO, Marty Dresser/VP - Contracts, Arturo Villa/Dir. - Information Technology, Richard D. Short/Pres. - Aerospace, Defense Group, Bill Schoneman/Dir. - Customer Service, Dwight Moore/COO/$256,692.00, Marvin Hoffman/CIO, Derek A. Coppinger/Dir. - Corporate Development, Andrea Korfin/Pres. - NTS Technical Resources Group, Lloyd Blonder/Sr. VP, Treasurer/$314,178.00, Douglas Briskie/Exec. VP - Development/$254,018.00, Osman Sakr/CTO, Cynthia Maher/Corp. Dir. - Human Resources, Corporate Counsel Secretary *(17 Officers included in Index)*

Directors: William McGinnis/Dir., CEO, Pres., Aaron Cohen/Vice Chmn., Sr. VP - Corporate Development, Jack Lin/Chmn., Donald J. Tringali/Vice Chmn., Norman S. Wolfe/Dir., John M. Gibbons/Dir., Ralph F. Clements/Dir., Dan C. Yates/Dir., Robert I. Lin/Dir.

Owners: Dimensional Fund Advisors Inc./7.00%, Ralph Clements, Donald Tringali, Jeffrey Gendell/5.80%, Dwight Moore, Norman Wolfe, Aaron Cohen/15.20%, Dan Yates, John Gibbons, Douglas Briskie, Jack Lin/13.10%, William McGinnis/2.70%, Lloyd Blonder/2.10%, Robert Lin/1.60%, Insiders/35.60%

Financial Data: Fiscal Year End:01/31 ***Latest Annual Data:*** 1/31/2007

Year	Sales	Net Income
2007	$115,673,000	$1,581,000
2006	$111,524,000	$2,939,000
2005	$106,997,000	$1,682,000

Curr. Assets:	NA	**Curr. Liab.:**	NA		
Plant, Equip.:	NA	**Total Liab.:**	NA	**Indic. Yr. Divd.:**	NA
Total Assets:	NA	**Net Worth:**	NA	**Debt/ Equity:**	NA

National Telephone Co of Venezuela

Avenida Libertador, Centro Nacional De Telecomunicaciones, Nuevo Edificio Administrativo, Piso 1, Apartado Postal 1226, Caracas, 1010; ***PH:*** 58-2125006800; ***http://*** www.cantv.com.ve

General - Incorporation	Venezuela	***Stock*** - Price on:12/24/2007	NA
Employees	NA	Stock Exchange	NA
Auditor	Espinerira, Sheldon y Asociados	Ticker Symbol	NA
Stk Agt	Banco Venezolano de Credito	Outstanding Shares	NA
Counsel	NA	E.P.S	NA
DUNS No.	NA	Shareholders	NA

Business: The group's principal activity is the provision of telecommunications services within venezuela and is the holder of a telecommunication network with local coverage through which it provides local fixed telephone services, national and international, as well as private telecommunications network services, data network, public telephone, rural telephone and telex services. Additionally, the group, through its subsidiaries, provides other telecommunications services such as Internet access, mobile/cellular telephone and telephone directories.

Primary SIC and add'l.: 4813 4812 1731

CIK No: 0001025862

Subsidiaries: CANTV Finance, LTD., CANTV International, LTD., Cantv.net, C.a., Compaa Annima Venezolana de GuasCAVEGUAS, Invercantv, S.a., Telecomunicaciones Movilnet, C.A.

Owners: Telefnica Venezuela Holding B.V., Ministerio del Poder Popular para la Infraestructura, GTE Venholdings B.V./24.95%, GTE Venholdings B.V./3.56%, Banco de Desarrollo Econmico y Social de Venezuela/6.59%, Banco Mercantil, C.A./0.05%, Insiders/5.72%, Brandes Investment Partners, LLC/14.66%

National Western Life Insurance Co

850 E Anderson Ln., Austin, TX, 78752; ***PH:*** 1-512-836-1010; ***Fax:*** 1-512-835-2729; ***http://*** www.nwlic.com

General - Incorporation	CO	***Stock*** - Price on:12/24/2007	$256.92
Employees	273	Stock Exchange	NDQ
Auditor	KPMG LLP	Ticker Symbol	NWLIA
Stk Agt	Continental Stock Transfer & Trust Co	Outstanding Shares	3,620,000
Counsel	Will D. Davis, Heath Davis & McCalla	E.P.S	$22.07
DUNS No.	00-787-5206	Shareholders	NA

Business: The group's principal activity is to provide whole life, universal life and term insurance plans and annuities, including single and flexible premium deferred annuities, single premium immediate annuities, and equity-indexed annuities. It operates in 48 states, the district of columbia and four U.S. Territories as well as accepts applications from and issues policies in central and South America, the Caribbean and the Pacific Rim. The group's operations also include small real estate, nursing home and other investments through its wholly owned subsidiaries. The group markets and distributes its products primarily through independent marketing organizations.

Primary SIC and add'l.: 6411 6311

CIK No: 0000070684

Subsidiaries: NWL Financial, Inc., NWL Investments, Inc., NWL Services, Inc., The Westcap Corporation

Officers: Robert L. Moody/Chmn., CEO, Brian M. Pribyl/Sr. VP, Chief Actuary, Ross R. Moody/Dir., COO, Pres., Scott E. Arendale/Sr. VP, Mark D. Gulas/VP - Actuarial Services, Carol Jackson/VP - Human Resources, Paul T. Garofoli/VP - Marketing, Kitty S. Kennedy/VP - Actuarial Services, Paul D. Facey/Sr. VP - Actuary, James P. Payne/Sr. VP, Sec., Partricia L. Scheuer/Sr. VP, Chief Investment Officer, Charles D. Milos/Dir., Sr. VP, Benjamin B. Taylor/VP - Actuarial Services, Larry D. White/VP - Policyowner Services, Carbs Gray/Medical Dir. *(21 Officers included in Index)*

Directors: Robert L. Moody/Chmn., CEO, Ross R. Moody/Dir., COO, Pres., Frances A. Moody Dahlberg/Dir., Harry L. Edwards/86/Dir., Stephen E. Glasgow/Dir., Douglas E. McLeod/Dir., Russell S. Moody/Dir., Louis E. Pauls/Dir., E. J. Pederson/Dir., Charles D. Milos/Dir., Sr. VP

Owners: FMR Corp./7.07%, Louis E. Pauls, Insiders/99.76%, Insiders/34.07%, E. J. Pederson, Charles D. Milos, Westport Asset Management, Inc./5.03%, Robert L. Moody/33.88%, Douglas E. McLeod, Third Avenue Management, LLC/5.28%, Robert L. Moody/99.04%, Harry L. Edwards

Financial Data: Fiscal Year End:12/31 ***Latest Annual Data:*** 12/31/2006

Year	Sales	Net Income
2006	$521,859,000	$76,343,000
2005	$441,043,000	$77,267,000
2004	$434,146,000	$122,169,000

Curr. Assets:	$49,901,000	**Curr. Liab.:**	$1,666,000	**P/E Ratio:**	11.60
Plant, Equip.:	NA	**Total Liab.:**	$5,760,459,000	**Indic. Yr. Divd.:**	NA
Total Assets:	$6,693,443,000	**Net Worth:**	$932,984,000	**Debt/ Equity:**	NA

National Westminster Bank Plc

135 Bishopsgate, London, E14 4QA; ***PH:*** 44-02073755000; ***http://*** www.natwest.com

General - Incorporation	UK	***Stock*** - Price on:12/24/2007	NA
Employees	NA	Stock Exchange	NA
Auditor	Deloitte & Touche LLP	Ticker Symbol	NA
Stk Agt	NA	Outstanding Shares	NA
Counsel	NA	E.P.S	NA
DUNS No.	21-021-2338	Shareholders	NA

Business: The groups principle activity is to provide banking, financial and related services. The group operates from United States.

Primary SIC and add'l.: 6021

CIK No: 0000702162

Subsidiaries: Coutts & Co, Greenwich Capital Markets, Inc, National Westminster Home Loans Limited, Ulster Bank Limited

Officers: Fred Goodwin/Group Chief Executive, Miller McLean/Sec., Guy Whittaker/Group Dir. - Finance

Directors: Tom McKillop/Chmn.

Nationshealth Inc

13630 NW 8th St., Ste. 210, Sunrise, FL, 33325; ***PH:*** 1-954-903-5000; ***Fax:*** 1-954-903-5002; ***http://*** www.nationshealth.com

General - Incorporation	DE	***Stock*** - Price on:12/24/2007	$1.59
Employees	496	Stock Exchange	NDQ
Auditor	Ernst & Young, LLP	Ticker Symbol	NHTB
Stk Agt	Continental Stock Transfer & Trust Co	Outstanding Shares	28,930,000
Counsel	NA	E.P.S	$0.038
DUNS No.	NA	Shareholders	NA

Business: The group's principle activity is to medical products and services. The group operates through two segments include Medical Products and Insurance Services. The groups other services include marketing, insurance agent training and licensing, member enrollment and service, distribution and billing, and collections. The group operates from United States.

Primary SIC and add'l.: NA

CIK No: 0001233426

Subsidiaries: NationsHealth Holdings, LLC, United States Pharmaceutical Group, LLC

Officers: Glenn Parker/Dir., CEO, Joshua Weingard/Exec. VP, Chief Legal Officer, Lewis Stone/Pres., CIO, Dir., Timothy Fairbanks/Dir., CFO, Sec., Rodney Carson/Exec. VP - Operations

Directors: Glenn Parker/Dir., CEO, Arthur Spector/Chmn., Richard R. Howard/Dir., Gary D. Small/Dir., Lewis Stone/Pres., CIO, Dir., Don K. Rice/Dir., Timothy Fairbanks/Dir., CFO, Sec., Raymond N. Steinman/Dir., Michael D. Tabris/Dir., Elliot F. Hahn/Dir., George F. Raymond/Dir., Mark H. Rachesky/Dir.

Owners: Wellington Management Company, LLP/6.10%, Gilberto E. Restrepo, Massachusetts Financial Services Company/12.30%, Philip McWeeny, Anastasia D. Kelly, Corbin A. McNeill, Janus Capital Management LLC/11.80%, Robert J. Dineen, AXA Financial Inc/15.00%, Steven R. McCracken, John J. McMackin, James W. Baehren, Gary F. Colter, State Street Bank and Trust Company/5.80%, FMR Corp./7.70%

Financial Data: **Fiscal Year End:** 12/31 **Latest Annual Data:** 12/31/2006

Year	Sales	Net Income
2006	$87,216,000	-$11,278,000
2005	$87,556,000	-$19,819,000
2004	$74,222,000	-$26,424,000

Curr. Assets:	$13,248,000	**Curr. Liab.:**	$14,595,000	**P/E Ratio:**	41.84
Plant, Equip.:	$3,557,000	**Total Liab.:**	$23,021,000	**Indic. Yr. Divd.:**	NA
Total Assets:	$30,388,000	**Net Worth:**	$7,367,000	**Debt/ Equity:**	1.0163

Nationwide Financial Services Inc

1 Nationwide Plz., Columbus, OH, 43215; ***PH:*** 1-614-249-7111; ***Fax:*** 1-614-854-5036; ***http://*** www.nationwidefinancial.com

General - Incorporation	DE	**Stock** - Price on:12/24/2007	$64.64
Employees	4,800	Stock Exchange	NYSE
Auditor	KPMG LLP	Ticker Symbol	NFX
Stk Agt	Mellon Investor Services LLC	Outstanding Shares	142,650,000
Counsel	NA	E.P.S.	$4.80
DUNS No.	00-790-2026	Shareholders	NA

Business: The group's principle activity is to provide variety of products to help the customers for building a better financial future. The group's products include mutual funds, stocks, bonds, and variable insurance policies. The group operates from United States.

Primary SIC and add'l.: 6719 6311

CIK No: 0001029786

Subsidiaries: 1717 Advisory Services, Inc., 1717 Brokerage Services, Inc., 1717 Capital Management Company, 1717 Insurance Agency of Massachusetts, Inc., 401(k) Investment Advisors, Inc., 401(k) Investment Services, Inc., Cap Pro Advisory Services, Inc., Cap Pro Brokerage Services, Inc., Cap Pro Holding, Inc. (63% owned), Cap Pro Insurance Agency Services, Inc., Capital Professional Advisors, Inc., Financial Horizons Distributors Agency of Alabama, Inc., Financial Horizons Distributors Agency of Ohio, Inc., Financial Horizons Distributors Agency of Texas, Inc., Gardiner Point Hospitality LLC 55 Subsidiaries included in the Index

Officers: Jerry Jurgensen/CEO - Nationwide, W. G. Jurgensen/Dir., CEO/$3,812,830.00, Michael C. Keller/CIO, Exec. VP - Nationwide, Stephen S. Rasmussen/COO, Pres. - Property, Casualty Insurance Operations, Peter A. Golato/54/Sr. VP, Individual Protection Business Head, Terri L. Hill/Exec. VP, Chief Administrative Officer - Nationwide, Patricia R. Hatler/Exec. VP, Chief Legal, Governance Officer - Nationwide, James Lyski/Exec. VP, Chief Marketing Officer - Nationwide, Kelly A. Hamilton/43/Sr. VP - Internal Audits, Gregory S. Lashutka/63/Sr. VP - Corporate Relations, William S. Jackson/54/Sr. VP - Nationwide Retirement Plans, Mark R. Thresher/51/COO, Pres./$3,279,388.00, Keith I. Millner/47/Sr. VP - Retail Distribution, In, Retirement Business, Brian W. Nocco/55/Sr. VP, Enterprise Chief Risk Officer, Mark Barnett/VP - Investor Relations *(22 Officers included in Index)*

Directors: W. G. Jurgensen/Dir., CEO, Arden L. Shisler/Chmn., Alex Shumate/Dir., Lydia M. Marshall/Dir., Donald L. McWhorter/Dir., Lewis J. Alphin/Dir., Irv Bell/Dir., Timothy Corcoran/Dir., Yvonne M. Curl/Dir., Joseph A. Alutto/Dir., James G. Brocksmith/Dir., Keith W. Eckel/Dir., David O. Miller/Dir., Martha Miller De Lombera/Dir., Gerald D. Prothro/Dir. *(24 Directors included in Index)*

Owners: Robert A. Rosholt, Mark R. Thresher, Alex Shumate, James G. Brocksmith, Joseph A. Alutto, Keith W. Eckel, W. G. Jurgensen, Arden L. Shisler, Nationwide Corporation/100.00%, John L. Carter, Franklin Mutual Advisers, LLC/5.10%, Insiders, Barclays Global Investors, N.A./5.75%, David O. Miller, James F. Patterson *(21 Owners included in Index)*

Financial Data: **Fiscal Year End:** 12/31 **Latest Annual Data:** 12/31/2006

Year	Sales	Net Income
2006	$4,415,500,000	$713,800,000
2005	$4,339,900,000	$598,700,000
2004	$4,180,200,000	$502,000,000

Curr. Assets:	$2,260,100,000	**Curr. Liab.:**	$85,200,000	**P/E Ratio:**	13.36
Plant, Equip.:	NA	**Total Liab.:**	$113,873,300,000	**Indic. Yr. Divd.:**	$1.040
Total Assets:	$119,411,600,000	**Net Worth:**	$5,538,300,000	**Debt/ Equity:**	0.2447

Nationwide Health Properties Inc

610 Newport Ctr. Dr., Ste. 1150, Newport Beach, CA, 92660; ***PH:*** 1-949-718-4400; ***Fax:*** 1-949-759-6876; ***http://*** www.nhp-reit.com; ***Email:*** investorrelations@nhp-reit.com

General - Incorporation	MD	**Stock** - Price on:12/24/2007	$29.63
Employees	23	Stock Exchange	NDQ
Auditor	Ernst& Young LLP	Ticker Symbol	NHRX
Stk Agt	Bank of New York	Outstanding Shares	89,250,000
Counsel	NA	E.P.S.	$2.03
DUNS No.	NA	Shareholders	NA

Business: The groups principle activity is to invest in real estate properties. The group operates from the United States. The groups quarterly revenue for September 2007 was 87.33 millions of USD.

Primary SIC and add'l.: 6798

CIK No: 0000780053

Subsidiaries: HN Texas Properties, JER/NHP Senior Housing, LLC, JER/NHP Senior Living Acquisition, LLC, MLD Delaware Trust, MLD Financial Capital Corporation, MLD Properties Limited Partnership, MLD Properties, Inc., MLD Properties, LLC, Nationwide Health Properties Finance Corporation, NH Texas Properties Limited Partnership, NHP Brownstown, LLC, NHP Carillon, LLC, NHP Properties Business Trust, NHP Senior Housing, Inc., NHP/Broe, LLC

Officers: Douglas M. Pasquale/53/Dir., CEO, Pres./$2,664,871.00, Abdo H. Khoury/Sr. VP, Chief Financial, Portfolio Officer/$1,126,339.00, Donald D. Bradley/Sr. VP, Chief Investment Officer/$1,143,476.00, David E. Snyder/VP, Controller/$472,465.00, Brent Chappell/VP - Portfolio Management, John J. Sheehan/VP, Sr. Investment Officer, David M. Boitano/VP, Sr. Investment Officer - West, Robert Noonan/VP, Sr. Investment Officer - Northeast, William Henry/VP, Sr. Investment Officer - Midwest, Stephen F. Graham/VP, Sr. Investment Officer - Southcentral

Directors: Douglas M. Pasquale/53/Dir., CEO, Pres., Charles D. Miller/80/Dir., Bruce R. Andrews/67/Dir., David R. Banks/71/Dir., William K. Doyle/61/Dir., Robert D. Paulson/62/Dir., Keith P. Russell/62/Dir., Jack D. Samuelson/83/Dir.

Owners: William K. Doyle, Jack D. Samuelson, Abdo H. Khoury, Insiders/1.30%, Donald D. Bradley, Bruce R. Andrews, Robert D. Paulson, David E. Snyder, Keith P. Russell, ING Groep N.V./10.52%, The Vanguard Group, Inc./5.43%, David R. Banks, Charles D. Miller, Douglas M. Pasquale, Cohen& Steers, Inc./10.55%

Financial Data: **Fiscal Year End:** 12/31 **Latest Annual Data:** 12/31/2006

Year	Sales	Net Income
2006	$261,676,000	$185,577,000
2005	$216,477,000	$69,941,000
2004	$186,611,000	$74,822,000

Curr. Assets:	$48,637,000	**Curr. Liab.:**	$77,829,000	**P/E Ratio:**	14.60
Plant, Equip.:	$2,486,070,000	**Total Liab.:**	$1,459,740,000	**Indic. Yr. Divd.:**	$1.640
Total Assets:	$2,704,814,000	**Net Worth:**	$1,243,809,000	**Debt/ Equity:**	1.0815

Nationwide Life Insurance Co

One Nationwide Plz., Columbus, OH, 43215; ***PH:*** 1-614-249-7111; ***https://*** www.nationwide.com

General - Incorporation	OH	**Stock** - Price on:12/24/2007	NA
Employees	NA	Stock Exchange	NA
Auditor	KPMG LLP	Ticker Symbol	NA
Stk Agt	Mellon Investor Services LLC	Outstanding Shares	NA
Counsel	NA	E.P.S.	NA
DUNS No.	00-790-2026	Shareholders	NA

Business: The group's principal activities are to provide variable annuities, fixed annuities, public and private sector pension plans and life insurance on a participating and non-participating basis. The operations are carried on through three segments individual annuity, institutional products and life insurance. The individual annuity provides customer with tax-deferred accumulation of savings and flexible payout options. The institutional products consist of private and public sectors pension plans, medium-term note program and structured product transactions. Life insurance consists of investment life products, including individual variable life and coli products, traditional life insurance products and universal life insurance. The group is a wholly owned subsidiary of nationwide financial services inc.

Primary SIC and add'l.: 6311

CIK No: 0000205695

Subsidiaries: Nationwide Financial Services, Inc., Nationwide Investment Services Corporation, Nationwide Life and Annuity Insurance Company, Nationwide Life Insurance Company

Officers: W. G. Jurgensen/Dir., CEO, Mark Barnett/VP - Investor Relations

Directors: W. G. Jurgensen/Dir., CEO, Arden L. Shisler/Chmn., Lydia M. Marshall/Dir., Gerald D. Prothro/Dir., Keith W. Eckel/Dir., Alex Shumate/Dir., James F. Patterson/Dir., Martha Miller De Lombera/Dir., David O. Miller/Dir., Joseph A. Alutto/Dir., Donald L. McWhorter/Dir., James G. Brocksmith/Dir.

Natrol Inc

21411 Prairie St., Chatsworth, CA, 91311; ***PH:*** 1-818-739-6000; ***Fax:*** 1-818-739-6001; ***http://*** www.natrol.com; ***Email:*** customer-service@natrol.com

General - Incorporation	DE	**Stock** - Price on:12/24/2007	$3.3199
Employees	251	Stock Exchange	NA
Auditor	Stonefield Josephson, Inc	Ticker Symbol	NA
Stk Agt	EquiServe Trust Co N.A	Outstanding Shares	14,150,000
Counsel	NA	E.P.S.	$0.10
DUNS No.	NA	Shareholders	NA

Business: The group's principal activities are to manufacture and market branded dietary supplement products. The dietary supplement products include vitamins, minerals, hormonal supplements, herbal products, specialty combination formulations and sports nutrition supplements. The group sells flavored herbal teas under the brand name laci le beau. The group also markets nutraceutical grade ingredients, garlic, vegetable powders, kava kava, melatonin and arabinogalactan to other manufacturers. As at 31-Dec-2003, the group discontinued the operations of annasa inc and tamson inc.

Primary SIC and add'l.: 2833

CIK No: 0001025573

Subsidiaries: Annasa, Inc., Natrol Acquisition, Inc., Natrol Direct, Inc., Natrol Products, Inc., Natrol Real Estate, Inc., Natrol Real Estate, Inc. II, Prolab Nutrition, Inc., Tamsol, Inc.

Officers: Wayne M. Bos/Dir., CEO, Pres., Elliott Balbert/Founder, Executive Chmn., Michael S. Surmeian/VP - Sales, Craig Cameron/COO, Michael T. Yatcilla/Pres. - Research, Development, Dennis R. Jolicoeur/CFO, Jenia G. Khudagulyan/VP - Manufacturing, Logistics, Steven Spitz/VP, General Counsel, Peter Gil/Dir. - International Sales, Chris Kurjanowicz/VP - Marketing, Loida C. Rubio/Sec.

Directors: Wayne M. Bos/Dir., CEO, Pres., Elliott Balbert/Founder, Executive Chmn., Dennis W. Deconcini/70/Dir., Thomas L. Doorley/Dir., James R. Peters/Dir., Ralph Simon/Dir., Joel A. Katz/Dir.

Owners: Dennis R. Jolicoeur, Joel A. Katz, Heartland Advisors, Inc., Craig D. Cameron, James R. Peters, Boston Partners Asset Management, L.L.C., Dennis W. DeConcini, Wayne M. Bos, Insiders, EOS Partners L.P., Financial & Investment Management Group, LTD, Michael S. Surmeian, Elliott Balbert, Thomas L. Doorley, Steven S. Spitz *(16 Owners included in Index)*

Financial Data: **Fiscal Year End:** 12/31 **Latest Annual Data:** 12/31/2006

Year	Sales	Net Income
2006	$65,564,000	$435,000
2005	$67,530,000	-$2,633,000
2004	$79,269,000	$1,868,000

Curr. Assets:	$23,024,000	**Curr. Liab.:**	$10,909,000		
Plant, Equip.:	$13,811,000	**Total Liab.:**	$17,210,000	**Indic. Yr. Divd.:**	NA
Total Assets:	$54,600,000	**Net Worth:**	$37,390,000	**Debt/ Equity:**	0.1632

Naturade Inc

2099 S State College Blvd., Ste. 210, Anaheim, CA, 92806; ***PH:*** 1-714-860-7600; ***Fax:*** 1-714-935-9837; ***http://*** www.naturade.com; ***Email:*** customerservice@naturade.com

General - Incorporation.............................. DE
Employees 17
Auditor .... Squar, Peterson, LLP
Stk Agt......................Registrar & Transfer Co
Counsel..NA
DUNS No. 02-842-4620

Stock- Price on:12/24/2007 ....$0.021
Stock Exchange...OTC
Ticker Symbol......................................NRDCQ
Outstanding Shares 43,450,000
E.P.S ....-$0.27
Shareholders..NA

Business: The group's principal activity is to market scientifically supported natural products formulated to improve the health and well being of consumers. The group's products include naturade total soy, a full line of nutritionally complete meal replacements available in several flavours of powders, ready-to-drink products and bars, naturade soy protein boosters, aloe vera 80 health, beauty care products and other niche dietary supplements. These products are sold to supermarkets, club stores, drug stores, health food stores, natural food supermarkets and the military. These products are generally marketed under the trademarks naturade(R), naturade total soy(TM) and aloe vera 80(r). The group markets through a network of 20 key distributors, who together service approximately 5,000 retail health food stores and natural supermarkets in the United States. In 2003, the group introduced the diet leantm, which help people to lose weight.

Primary SIC and add'l.: 2834 2844

CIK No: 0000797167

Officers: Richard L. Munro/49/Dir., CEO, Dee S. Kelly/46/CFO, Gary C. Cannon/56/Dir., Sec.

Directors: Richard L. Munro/49/Dir., CEO, Adam M. Michelin/63/Chmn., Stephen L. Scott/56/Dir., Gary C. Cannon/56/Dir., Sec.

Owners: Jay W. Brown/100.00%, Westgate Equity Partners, L.P./100.00%, Health Holdings & Botanicals, LLC, Jay W. Brown, Westgate Equity Partners, L.P., William B. Doyle, David Weil, Bill D. Stewart, Robert V. Vitale/100.00%, Lionel P. Boissiere, Insiders/100.00%, Robert V. Vitale, Lawrence Batina, Insiders

Financial Data: Fiscal Year End:12/31 Latest Annual Data: 12/31/2006

Year	Sales	Net Income
2006	$9,432,000	-$11,251,000
2005	$12,756,000	-$3,748,000
2004	$14,141,000	$368,000

Curr. Assets:	$1,234,000	Curr. Liab.:	$2,962,000		
Plant, Equip.:	$52,000	Total Liab.:	$14,322,000	Indic. Yr. Divd.:	NA
Total Assets:	$2,949,000	Net Worth:	-$16,964,000	Debt/ Equity:	NA

Natural Alternatives International Inc

1185 Linda Vista Dr., San Marcos, CA, 92078; *PH:* 1-760-744-7340; *Fax:* 1-760-744-9589; *http://* www.nai-online.com; *Email:* info@nai-onoine.com

General - Incorporation.............................. DE
Employees 211
Auditor .... Ernst & Young LLP
Stk Agt.................. Mellon Investor Services LLC
Counsel...............................Fisher Thurber
DUNS No. 05-479-3658

Stock- Price on:12/24/2007 ....$7.14
Stock Exchange.......................................NYSE
Ticker Symbol...NAL
Outstanding Shares 6,890,000
E.P.S $0.35
Shareholders..NA

Business: The group's principal activity is the formulation, manufacturing and packaging of encapsulated and compressed tablets and powder blended vitamins and related nutritional supplements including phytochemicals derived from botanicals and foods. The group provides private label contract manufacturing services to various companies engaged in the marketing and distribution of vitamins, mineral supplements, herbs and other health and nutrition consumer products. The major customers of the company include nsa international and mannatech incorporated.

Primary SIC and add'l.: 2834

CIK No: 0000787253

Subsidiaries: Custom Nutrition, LLC, Natural Alternatives International Europe S.A., Real Health Laboratories, Inc., Transformative Health Products, Inc.

Officers: Mark A. Ledoux/Chmn., CEO, Randell Weaver/Pres., Sec., John Wise/Chief Science Officer, John Reaves/CFO

Directors: Mark A. Ledoux/Chmn., CEO, Joe E. Davis/Dir., Alan G. Dunn/Dir., Alan J. Lane/Dir., Lee G. Weldon/Dir.

Owners: Dimensional Fund Advisors LP/5.45%, Trust U/W of Vincent Terranova/13.71%, Alan J. Lane/0.35%, Joe E. Davis/0.86%, Randell Weaver/4.73%, John R. Reaves/0.85%, Mark A. LeDoux/18.37%, Alan G. Dunn/0.33%, Insiders/29.35%, Alvin McCurdy/0.48%, Lee G. Weldon/1.57%, John F. Dullea/4.03%

Financial Data: Fiscal Year End:06/30 Latest Annual Data: 6/30/2006

Year	Sales	Net Income
2006	$99,131,000	$2,670,000
2005	$91,492,000	$2,199,000
2004	$78,534,000	$3,000,000

Curr. Assets:	$27,884,000	Curr. Liab.:	$11,668,000	P/E Ratio:	20.40
Plant, Equip.:	$15,059,000	Total Liab.:	$17,358,000	Indic. Yr. Divd.:	NA
Total Assets:	$47,380,000	Net Worth:	$30,022,000	Debt/ Equity:	NA

Natural Gas Services Group Inc

3204 Merrimack Ln., Flower Mound, TX, 75022; *PH:* 1-972-355-6070; *Fax:* 1-972-355-5399; *http://* www.ngsgi.com

General - Incorporation.............................. CO
Employees 266
Auditor .... Hein & Assoc. LLP
Stk Agt.........................Computershare Trust Co
Counsel................................Jones & Keller
DUNS No. ....NA

Stock- Price on:12/24/2007 ....$18.471
Stock Exchange.......................................AMEX
Ticker Symbol...NGS
Outstanding Shares 12,070,000
E.P.S $0.829
Shareholders..NA

Business: The group's principal activity is to provide equipment and services to the natural gas and oil industry. The group manufactures, fabricates, markets and leases natural gas compressors that enhance the production of oil and gas wells and provides maintenance services for those compressors. The natural gas compressors are leased to third parties. On 29-Feb-2004, the group had leased 385 natural gas compressors. The group also designs, manufactures, installs and services flare stacks and related ignition and control devices for onshore and offshore burning of gas compounds such as hydrogen sulfide, carbon dioxide, natural gas and liquefied petroleum gases. The group has produced two ignition systems for varied applications, which includes a standing jet-like pipe for minimal fuel consumption, with a patented electronic igniter and an electronic sparked ignition system.

Primary SIC and add'l.: 3533 7359

CIK No: 0001084991

Subsidiaries: Screw Compression Systems, Inc.

Officers: Stephen C. Taylor/Chmn., CEO, Pres., Earl R. Wait/VP - Accounting, Treasurer/$158,634.00, Jim Drewitz/Contact - Creative Options Communications, Investor, Public Relations, James R. Hazlett/VP - Technical Services/$153,588.00

Directors: Stephen C. Taylor/Chmn., CEO, Pres., Paul D. Hensley/Dir., Gene A. Strasheim/Dir., Charles G. Curtis/Dir., William F. Hughes/52/Dir., Alan A. Baker/Dir., Rick L. Yadon/Dir., John W. Chisholm/Dir.

Owners: Earl R. Wait, Gene A. Strasheim, Keeley Asset Management Corp./6.26%, Charles G. Curtis, Wellington Management Company, LLP/11.00%, James R. Hazlett, Mazama Capital Management, Inc./8.52%, Richard L. Yadon/2.31%, Paul D. Hensley/2.71%, Alan A. Baker, Stephen C. Taylor, Westcliff Capital Management, LLC/7.68%, John W. Chisholm, William F. Hughes/1.67%, Insiders/8.46%

Financial Data: Fiscal Year End:12/31 Latest Annual Data: 12/31/2006

Year	Sales	Net Income
2006	$62,729,000	$7,588,000
2005	$49,311,000	$4,446,000
2004	$15,958,000	$3,374,000

Curr. Assets:	$55,170,000	Curr. Liab.:	$10,637,000	P/E Ratio:	22.28
Plant, Equip.:	$66,580,000	Total Liab.:	$34,351,000	Indic. Yr. Divd.:	NA
Total Assets:	$135,552,000	Net Worth:	$101,201,000	Debt/ Equity:	0.1162

Natural Golf Corp

431 Lakeview Ct., Ste. B, Mt. Prospect, IL, 60056; *PH:* 1-888-628-4653; *Fax:* 1-847-795-0101; *http://* www.naturalgolf.com

General - Incorporation IL
Employees 23
Auditor ....Hein & Assoc. LLP
Stk Agt........................Registrar & Transfer Co
Counsel..NA
DUNS No. ....NA

Stock- Price on:12/24/2007 ....$0.0001
Stock Exchange...OTC
Ticker Symbol......................................NAXG
Outstanding Shares 5,290,000
E.P.S ....-$0.919
Shareholders..NA

Business: The group's principal activity is to manufacture and market golf equipment and operate golf school that focuses on improving golfers' abilities. It produces and markets instructional video tapes explaining their natural golf swing system. The group operates in three segments: natural golf products, natural golf field and natural golf schools. The natural golf products segment markets the products through advertising and telemarketing. The natural golf field segment markets products on the field. The natural golf schools segment conducts golf instruction. The golf instruction segment consists of approximately 25,000 pga professionals and over 335 golf schools in the United States. The products are marketed directly to the consumers that include the new golfer, the high handicapper, the good golfer wanting to improve, the occasional golfer, the woman golfer and the golfer with bad back or arthritis.

Primary SIC and add'l.: 3949 7999

CIK No: 0001039387

Subsidiaries: Natural Golf Field Sales Corporation, Natural Golf Products Corporation, Natural Golf Schools Corporation

Officers: Manny Brown/CEO, Pres., Ken Martin/Dir. - Golf Instruction, Harry J. Snyder/Pres., Andy Grzynkowicz/Dir. - Operations

Financial Data: Fiscal Year End:11/30 Latest Annual Data: 11/30/2004

Year	Sales	Net Income
2004	$8,561,000	-$7,382,000
2003	$9,744,000	-$5,303,000

Curr. Assets:	$778,000	Curr. Liab.:	$2,048,000		
Plant, Equip.:	$375,000	Total Liab.:	$2,152,000	Indic. Yr. Divd.:	NA
Total Assets:	$1,207,000	Net Worth:	-$946,000	Debt/ Equity:	NA

Natural Health Trends Corp

2050 Diplomat Dr., Dallas, TX, 75234; *PH:* 1-972-241-4080; *Fax:* 1-972-243-5428; *http://* www.naturalhealthtrendscorp.com

General - Incorporation .... DE
Employees 233
Auditor ....Lane Gorman Trubitt, L.l.p.
Stk Agt...... American Stock Transfer & Trust Co.
Counsel..NA
DUNS No. 61-301-3580

Stock- Price on:12/24/2007 ....$3.68
Stock Exchange...NDQ
Ticker Symbol...BHIP
Outstanding Shares 8,810,000
E.P.S ....-$2.02
Shareholders..NA

Business: The group's principal activity is to distribute products that promote health, wellness and vitality through a multi-level marketing channel. The group operates through its subsidiaries, lexxus international, inc, ekaire.com and lighthouse marketing corporation. Lexxus sells certain cosmetic products and products that heightening sexual arousal, health and beauty and ekaire.com distributes nutritional supplements. The group operates in the United States, Canada, Australia, New Zealand, Taiwan, Hong Kong, Singapore, Philippines, Brazil, South Korea, India and sixteen countries in eastern Europe, including Russia.

Primary SIC and add'l.: 5122

CIK No: 0000912061

Subsidiaries: Distribuidora NHTC de Mexico, S. de R.L. de C.V., eKaire.com, Inc., I Luv My Pet, Inc., Importadora NHTC de Mexico, S. de R.L. de C.V., Kaire Neutraceuticals Australia Pty. Limited, Kaire Neutraceuticals New Zealand Limited, Kaire Worldwide (Canada) Company, KGC Networks Pte. Ltd., Lexxus International (Canada) Company, Lexxus International (China) Co., Ltd., Lexxus International (NZ)Limited, Lexxus International (SW Pacific) Pty. Ltd., Lexxus International Co. Ltd., Lexxus International Co., Ltd., Lexxus International Network Marketing, Inc. 36 Subsidiaries included in the Index

Officers: John Cavanaugh/CEO - Marketvision/$309,587.00, Curtis Broome/Pres. - Worldwide, Timothy S. Davidson/37/Sr. VP, CFO, Chief Accounting Officer/$184,236.00, Chris Sharng/Exec. VP/$399,327.00, Paul Rogers/Pres. - NHT Global North America, Europe, Gary C. Wallace/General Counsel, Corp. Sec./$197,962.00

Directors: Anthony B. Martino/66/Dir., Randall A. Mason/49/Dir., Brian Wolfson/72/Dir.

Owners: Chris Sharng/1.80%, Gary C. Wallace, Brian Wolfson/1.20%, Mark D. Woodburn/6.20%, John Cavanaugh/5.30%, Randall A. Mason/1.80%, Insiders/11.80%, Anthony B. Martino, Terry A. LaCore/6.20%, Robert H. Hesse, Timothy S. Davidson

Financial Data: Fiscal Year End:12/31 Latest Annual Data: 12/31/2006

Year	Sales	Net Income
2006	$133,428,000	-$11,460,000
2005	$194,472,000	-$5,502,000
2004	$133,225,000	$1,241,000

Curr. Assets:	$22,626,000	**Curr. Liab.:**	$21,588,000		
Plant, Equip.:	$2,944,000	**Total Liab.:**	$21,588,000	**Indic. Yr. Divd.:**	NA
Total Assets:	$48,585,000	**Net Worth:**	$26,975,000	**Debt/ Equity:**	NA

Natural Nutrition

109 N Post Oak Ln., Ste. 422, Houston, TX, 77024; ***PH:*** 1-713-621-2737; ***Fax:*** 1-713-586-6678; ***http://*** corporate-strategies.net; ***Email:*** news@corporate-strategies.net

General - Incorporation	FL	**Stock**- Price on:12/24/2007	$0.02
Employees	NA	Stock Exchange	OTC
Auditor	Thomas Leger & Co. LLP	Ticker Symbol	NNTN
Stk Agt	American Stock Transfer & Trust CO.	Outstanding Shares	12,740,000
Counsel	NA	E.P.S	-$0.38
DUNS No.	NA	Shareholders	NA

Business: The groups principle activities include financing and investing services. The services of the group include equipment leasing, factoring and loan brokerage activities and selling business leases, providing short term secured lending, and investing in marketable securities. The group operates from the United States and Canada. The group's quarterly revenue for Sep '07 was 4.25 millions of USD.

Primary SIC and add'l.: 6199

CIK No: 0001070050

Officers: Timothy J. Connolly/CEO, Pres. - Turnaround Partners, Inc, Corporate Strategies, Inc, Gary Cella/Executive Dir. - Business Development, William Chris Mathers/CFO, COO

Directors: Fred Zeidman/Dir. - Turnaround Partners, Inc, Neil R. Reisman/59/Dir.

Owners: Timothy J. Connolly, Charles Bleiwise, Dobrowski, LLP, Jan Carson Connolly, Jan Carson Connolly, Susan Greenfield, Michael O. Sutton, Michael O. Sutton, iVoice, Inc., Timothy J. Connolly

Financial Data: ***Fiscal Year End:***12/31 ***Latest Annual Data:*** 12/31/2006

Year	Sales	Net Income
2006	$609,000	-$1,978,000
2005	$30,000	-$1,700,000
2004	$88,000	-$1,289,000

Curr. Assets:	$3,184,000	**Curr. Liab.:**	$271,000		
Plant, Equip.:	$5,000	**Total Liab.:**	$16,386,000	**Indic. Yr. Divd.:**	NA
Total Assets:	$12,752,000	**Net Worth:**	-$3,634,000	**Debt/ Equity:**	NA

Natural Resource Partners LP

601 Jefferson St., Ste. 3600, Houston, TX, 77002; ***PH:*** 1-713-751-7507; ***Fax:*** 1-713-650-0606; ***http://*** www.nrplp.com; ***Email:*** info@nrplp.com

General - Incorporation	DE	**Stock**- Price on:12/24/2007	$37.75
Employees	NA	Stock Exchange	NYSE
Auditor	Ernst& Young LLP	Ticker Symbol	NRT
Stk Agt	American Stock Transfer & Trust Co.	Outstanding Shares	64,890,000
Counsel	NA	E.P.S	$1.282
DUNS No.	NA	Shareholders	NA

Business: The groups principle activities include owning and managing coal properties. The group acquired Dingess-Rum, Cline in the 2007 and Quadrant, Bluestone, Red Fox, Coal Mountain, Allegany County and Indiana Reserves. The group operates from the United States. The groups quarterly revenue for Septmber 2007 was 56.37 millions of USD.

Primary SIC and add'l.: 1221 1222 1241 6519 5052

CIK No: 0001171486

Subsidiaries: ACIN LLC, Gatling Mineral, LLC, Hod LLC, Independence Land Company, LLC, Little River Transport, LLC, NRP (Operating) LLC, Shepard Boone Coal Company LLC, WBRD LLC, Williamson Transport, LLC, WPP LLC

Officers: Corbin J. Robertson/Chmn., CEO, Nick Carter/COO, Pres., Dwight L. Dunlap/CFO, Treasurer, Kevin F. Wall/VP, Chief Engineer, Kevin J. Craig/VP - Business Development, Kathy E. Hager/VP - Investor Relations, Wyatt L. Hogan/VP, General Counsel, Sec., Kenneth Hudson/Controller

Directors: Corbin J. Robertson/Chmn., CEO, Robert T. Blakely/Dir., David M. Carmichael/Dir., Matthew J. Fifield/Dir., Robert B. Karn/Dir., Reed S. Morian/Dir., W. W. Scott/Dir., Stephen P. Smith/Dir., Leo A. Vecellio/Dir.

Owners: Wyatt L. Hogan, Adena Minerals LLC/15.10%, David M. Carmichael, Great Northern Properties/3.60%, Kenneth Hudson, Reed S. Morian, Dingess-Rum Properties, Inc/9.20%, Western Pocahontas Properties/22.20%, Corbin J. Robertson/23.40%, Nick Carter, Robert B. Karn, Neuberger Berman Inc./1.70%, Kathy E. Hager, Kevin F. Wall, W. W. Scott *(17 Owners included in Index)*

Financial Data: ***Fiscal Year End:***12/31 ***Latest Annual Data:*** 12/31/2006

Year	Sales	Net Income
2006	$170,673,000	$102,090,000
2005	$159,053,000	$91,839,000
2004	$121,432,000	$58,994,000

Curr. Assets:	$90,833,000	**Curr. Liab.:**	$24,282,000	**P/E Ratio:**	14.60
Plant, Equip.:	$47,396,000	**Total Liab.:**	$503,806,000	**Indic. Yr. Divd.:**	$1.900
Total Assets:	$939,493,000	**Net Worth:**	$435,687,000	**Debt/ Equity:**	NA

Naturally Advanced Technologies Inc

Formerly: Hemptown Clothing Inc

1307 Venables St., Vancouver, BC, V5L 2G1; ***PH:*** 1-604-255-5005; ***http://*** www.hemptown.com

General - Incorporation	Canada	**Stock**- Price on:12/24/2007	$0.9
Employees	NA	Stock Exchange	NA
Auditor	Dale Matheson Carr-Hilton Labonte	Ticker Symbol	NA
Stk Agt	Pacific Stock Transfer Company	Outstanding Shares	NA
Counsel	NA	E.P.S.	NA
DUNS No.	NA	Shareholders	NA

Business: The groups principle activity is to develop proprietary technology for production of bast fibers, cellulose pulp, and their resulting by products. The group operates from Canada.

Primary SIC and add'l.: NA

CIK No: 0001210294

Subsidiaries: 0697072 B.c. Ltd, Crailar Fiber Technologies Inc, Hemptown USA, Inc

Officers: Kenneth Barker/Dir., CEO, Guy Prevost/Dir., CFO, Jason Finnis/Dir., Pres., Larisa Harrison/Dir., Chief Administration Officer, Sec., Treasurer

Directors: Kenneth Barker/Dir., CEO, Miljenko Horvat/Chmn., John Hoekman/Member - Advisory Board, Robert Edmunds/Dir., Jason Finnis/Dir., Pres., Jerry Kroll/Dir., Larisa Harrison/Dir., Chief Administration Officer, Sec., Treasurer, Guy Prevost/Dir., CFO, Lesley Hayes/Member - Advisory Board

Owners: Robert Edmunds, Jerry Kroll, Guy Carpenter, Insiders, Jason Finnis

Financial Data: ***Fiscal Year End:***12/31 ***Latest Annual Data:*** 12/31/2006

Year	Sales	Net Income
2006	$1,267,000	-$1,375,000
2005	$958,000	-$877,000
2004	$832,000	-$897,000

Curr. Assets:	$1,144,000	**Curr. Liab.:**	$896,000		
Plant, Equip.:	$7,000	**Total Liab.:**	$926,000	**Indic. Yr. Divd.:**	NA
Total Assets:	$1,204,000	**Net Worth:**	$278,000	**Debt/ Equity:**	0.0895

NaturalNano Inc

15 Schoen Pl., Pittsford, NY, 14534; ***PH:*** 1-585-214-8005; ***Fax:*** 1-585-214-4855; ***http://*** www.naturalnano.com; ***Email:*** info@naturalnano.com

General - Incorporation	NV	**Stock**- Price on:12/24/2007	NA
Employees	7	Stock Exchange	OTC
Auditor	Goldstein Golub Kessler LLP	Ticker Symbol	NNAN
Stk Agt	Interstate Transfer Company	Outstanding Shares	121,900,000
Counsel	NA	E.P.S	-$0.05
DUNS No.	NA	Shareholders	NA

Business: The groups principle activities include developing and commercializing material science technologies. The product of the group is Pleximer. The group markets its product under the brand name Pleximer(TM). for Sep 2005, the group acquired Cementitious Acquisitions, Inc. The group operates from the United States. The group's quarterly revenue for Sep '07 was 0.01millions of USD.

Primary SIC and add'l.: 8731

CIK No: 0000863895

Subsidiaries: NaturalNano Research Inc.

Officers: Kent A. Tapper/CFO, Patrick Kane/Contact - Investor Relations, Cathy A. Fleischer/Pres., CTO, Aaron Wagner/Dir. - Research, Development

Directors: Steven Katz/59/Dir., John Lanzafame/Dir., Sharell L. Mikesell/Dir., Michael L. Weiner/60/Dir., David J. Arthur/Member - Scientific Advisory Board, Robert Corkery/Member - Scientific Advisory Board, Emmanuel P. Giannelis/Member - Scientific Advisory Board, John R. Hickman/Member - Scientific Advisory Board, Harold W. Kroto/Member - Scientific Advisory Board, Raymond Kurzweil/Member - Scientific Advisory Board, Duncan T. Moore/Member - Scientific Advisory Board, Gary W. Beall/Dir., Klaus E.T. Siebert/Dir., James Wemett/Dir.

Owners: Insiders/1.80%, James Wemett, John F. Lanzafame, Technology Innovations, LLC/57.00%, Sharell L. Mikesell, Cathy A. Fleischer

Financial Data: ***Fiscal Year End:***12/31 ***Latest Annual Data:*** 12/31/2006

Year	Sales	Net Income
2006	$15,000	-$8,863,000
2005	$1,000	-$2,666,000
2004	NA	-$16,000

Curr. Assets:	$204,000	**Curr. Liab.:**	$1,144,000	**P/E Ratio:**	17.93
Plant, Equip.:	$159,000	**Total Liab.:**	$1,172,000	**Indic. Yr. Divd.:**	NA
Total Assets:	$863,000	**Net Worth:**	-$310,000	**Debt/ Equity:**	NA

Nature Vision Inc

1480 Nern Pacific Rd., Brainerd, MN, 56401; ***PH:*** 1-218-825-0733; ***Fax:*** 1-218-374-4501; ***http://*** www.naturevisioninc.com; ***Email:*** aquavu@naturevisioninc.com

General - Incorporation	MN	**Stock**- Price on:12/24/2007	$2.2
Employees	47	Stock Exchange	NDQ
Auditor	Virchow, Krause & Co. LLP	Ticker Symbol	NRVN
Stk Agt	Corporate Stock Transfer, Inc.	Outstanding Shares	2,310,000
Counsel	Gray Plant Mooty	E.P.S	-$0.49
DUNS No.	NA	Shareholders	NA

Business: The group's principal activities are to design, manufacture and market professional photographic equipment and the bookendz docking station for the apple powerbook, ibook and ipod. Photographic equipment consists of professional camerz film and digital cameras, photographic accessories, norman electronic flash equipment and lindahl photographic accessories. These products are used primarily for high volume portrait, commercial and school photography and marketed primarily under the tradenames, 'camerz', 'norman' and 'lindahl'.

Primary SIC and add'l.: 3861 3679

CIK No: 0000078311

Subsidiaries: Nature Vision Operating, Inc.

Officers: Jeffery P. Zernov/55/Chmn., CEO, Pres./$200,000.00, Michael R. Day/44/CFO/$150,000.00, Robin K. Sheeley/Pres. - Photo Control Division/$444,075.00

Directors: Jeffery P. Zernov/55/Chmn., CEO, Pres., Scott S. Meyers/54/Dir., Richard P. Kiphart/64/Dir., Curtis A. Sampson/74/Dir., Steve Shanesy/51/Dir., Phil McLaughlin/Dir.

Owners: Richard P. Kiphart/20.30%, Dean Capra/6.70%, Jeffrey P. Zernov/19.30%, Insiders/43.40%, Michael R. Day, Curtis A. Sampson, Steve Shanesy, Scott S. Meyers, Philip M. McLaughlin, Anthony Capra/6.70%

Financial Data: ***Fiscal Year End:***12/31 ***Latest Annual Data:*** 12/31/2006

Year	Sales	Net Income
2006	$8,994,000	-$1,081,000
2005	$24,254,000	$887,000
2004	$12,362,000	$139,000

Curr. Assets:	$11,775,000	**Curr. Liab.:**	$7,617,000		
Plant, Equip.:	$2,261,000	**Total Liab.:**	$8,175,000	**Indic. Yr. Divd.:**	NA
Total Assets:	$15,746,000	**Net Worth:**	$7,572,000	**Debt/ Equity:**	NA

Nature's Sunshine Products Inc

75 E 1700 S, Provo, UT, 84606; *PH:* 1-801-342-4300; *Fax:* 1-801-342-4305;
http:// www.naturessunshine.com

General		Stock	
Incorporation	UT	Price on:12/24/2007	$12.35
Employees	NA	Stock Exchange	OTC
Auditor	KPMG LLP	Ticker Symbol	NATR
Stk Agt	American Stock Transfer & Trust Co.	Outstanding Shares	NA
Counsel	NA	E.P.S	NA
DUNS No.	08-183-2388	Shareholders	NA

Business: The group's principal activity is to manufacture and market herbal products, vitamin and mineral supplements, personal care and other products. The personal care products include products for external use, such as oils and lotions, aloe vera gel, herbal shampoo, herbal skin treatment, toothpaste and skin cleanser. The group sells products through a separate division, synergy worldwide. It sells products in Japan, Taiwan, Thailand and the United States. The operations are conducted in the United States as well as in certain other countries. The subsidiaries are located in South Korea, Mexico, venezuela, Japan, Brazil, Canada, Central America, Colombia, Dominican Republic, Ecuador, Peru, the United Kingdom, Israel, Taiwan, Thailand and Singapore. The group exports products to several other countries, including Argentina, Australia, Chile, New Zealand, Norway and the russian federation. As of 31-Dec-2003, the products were distributed by 562,000 active distributors.

Primary SIC and add'l.: 2844 2834

CIK No: 0000275053

Subsidiaries: Natures Sunshine Products (Israel) Ltd., Natures Sunshine Products de Centroamrica, Natures Sunshine Products de Colombia, S.A., Natures Sunshine Products de El Salvador, S.A. de C.V., Natures Sunshine Products de Guatemala, S.A., Natures Sunshine Products de Honduras, S.A., Natures Sunshine Products de Mexico, S.A. de C.V., Natures Sunshine Products de Nicaragua, S.A., Natures Sunshine Products de Panam, S.A., Natures Sunshine Products del Ecuador, S.A., Natures Sunshine Products del Peru, S.A., Natures Sunshine Products Dominicana, S.A., Natures Sunshine Products N.S.P. de Venezuela, C.A., Natures Sunshine Products of Canada, Ltd., Natures Sunshine Produtos Naturais Ltda. 24 Subsidiaries included in the Index

Officers: Douglas Faggioli/Dir., CEO, John R. Dewyze/Exec. VP - Operations, Stephen M. Bunker/VP - Over Finance, CFO, Jamon A. Jarvis/General Counsel, Chief Compliance Officer, Kay R. Olsen/VP - Information Technology, Gregory R. Halliday/Pres., Bryant Yates/Pres. - International, Lynda Hammons/VP - QA, QC, Regulatory Affairs, William Keller/VP - Health Sciences, Educational Services

Directors: Douglas Faggioli/Dir., CEO

Financial Data: *Fiscal Year End:*12/31 *Latest Annual Data:* 12/31/2004

Year	Sales	Net Income
2004	$331,063,000	$17,078,000
2003	$258,208,000	$5,099,000
2002	$298,734,000	$7,064,000

Curr. Assets:	$92,506,000	**Curr. Liab.:**	$51,812,000		
Plant, Equip.:	$34,731,000	**Total Liab.:**	$53,857,000	**Indic. Yr. Divd.:**	NA
Total Assets:	$145,076,000	**Net Worth:**	$91,219,000	**Debt/ Equity:**	NA

NatureWell Inc

110 W "C" St., Ste. 1300, San Diego, CA, 92101; *PH:* 1-619-234-0222; *Fax:* 1-619-234-0200;
http:// www.naturewell.com; *Email:* corporate@naturewell.com

General		Stock	
Incorporation	CA	Price on:12/24/2007	$0.0013
Employees	3	Stock Exchange	OTC
Auditor	Chang G. Park, Cpa	Ticker Symbol	NAWL
Stk Agt	Computershare Trust Co	Outstanding Shares	447,390,000
Counsel	NA	E.P.S	-$0.005
DUNS No.	87-845-7431	Shareholders	NA

Business: The group's principal activities are to develop, manufacture and market health care products and provide certain laboratory services. The group has two divisions namely healthcare products division and diagnostic division. The healthcare division prepares healthcare and nutraceutical solutions which are used for eye and nose. The diagnostic division develops and markets clinical diagnostic products using immunology and molecular biologic technologies.

Primary SIC and add'l.: 8099

CIK No: 0000945617

Subsidiaries: Nasal Mist, Inc.

Officers: James R. Arabia/Chmn., CEO, Pres.

Directors: James R. Arabia/Chmn., CEO, Pres.

Owners: Milan Mandaric/3.40%, Insiders/14.90%, John W. Huemoeller/0.50%, Financial Acquisition Partners, LP/2.60%, Lowell Blankfort/4.20%, Insiders/14.90%, Robert T. Malasek/1.10%, James R. Arabia/13.00%, Timothy R. Scott, AK Trust./5.30%

Financial Data: *Fiscal Year End:*11/30 *Latest Annual Data:* 06/30/2007

Year	Sales	Net Income
2007	$285,000	-$2,300,000
2006	$51,000	-$788,000
2005	$71,000	-$364,000

Curr. Assets:	$180,000	**Curr. Liab.:**	$3,305,000		
Plant, Equip.:	$339,000	**Total Liab.:**	$4,737,000	**Indic. Yr. Divd.:**	NA
Total Assets:	$520,000	**Net Worth:**	-$4,217,000	**Debt/ Equity:**	NA

Natus Medical Inc

1501 Industrial Rd., San Carlos, CA, 94070; *PH:* 1-650-802-0400; *Fax:* 1-650-802-0401;
http:// www.natus.com; *Email:* purchasing@natus.com

General		Stock	
Incorporation	DE	Price on:12/24/2007	$15.82
Employees	360	Stock Exchange	NDQ
Auditor	Deloitte & Touche, LLP	Ticker Symbol	BABY
Stk Agt	EquiServe Trust Co N.A	Outstanding Shares	21,570,000
Counsel	Wilson Sonsini Goodrich & Rosati	E.P.S	$0.29
DUNS No.	NA	Shareholders	NA

Business: The group's principal activity is to develop, manufacture and market newborn screening products for the identification and monitoring of common medical disorders that may occur during the critical development period of infants. The group's main products include algo series, which use automated auditory brainstem response technology, or aabr, to enable simple, non-invasive and accurate screening for hearing impairment in newborns and the co-stat analyzers which accurately and non-invasively measure the rate of hemolytic through the detection of carbon monoxide in exhaled breath. The group's customers include hospitals, clinics, laboratories, physicians, nurses, audiologists and governmental agencies. On 01-Jul-2003, the group acquired neometrics inc and on 29-Sep-2004, acquired fischer-zoth gmbh.

Primary SIC and add'l.: 3845

CIK No: 0000878526

Officers: James B. Hawkins/Dir., CEO, Pres./$890,871.00, William L. Mince/VP - Operations, Christopher D. Chung/VP - Medical Affairs, Research & Development, and Engineering/$387,242.00, Kenneth M. Traverso/VP - Marketing, Sales/$431,585.00, Steven J. Murphy/VP - Finance, CFO/$371,912.00

Directors: James B. Hawkins/Dir., CEO, Pres., Robert A. Gunst/Chmn., President Ceo/Dir., Doris Engibous/Dir., Mark D. Michael/Dir., William M. Moore/Dir.

Owners: Steven J. Murphy, Mark D. Michael, Insiders/8.60%, Nierenberg Investment Management Company/17.90%, Kenneth E. Ludlum, William M. Moore/1.40%, Christopher D. Chung/1.00%, James B. Hawkins/2.00%, Kenneth M. Traverso/2.00%, Robert A. Gunst, Doris E. Engibous, William L. Mince

Financial Data: *Fiscal Year End:*12/31 *Latest Annual Data:* 12/31/2006

Year	Sales	Net Income
2006	$89,915,000	-$927,000
2005	$43,045,000	$6,152,000
2004	$36,506,000	-$2,407,000

Curr. Assets:	$51,596,000	**Curr. Liab.:**	$20,793,000	**P/E Ratio:**	54.55
Plant, Equip.:	$7,897,000	**Total Liab.:**	$23,137,000	**Indic. Yr. Divd.:**	NA
Total Assets:	$124,163,000	**Net Worth:**	$101,026,000	**Debt/ Equity:**	NA

Natuzzi SpA

130 W Commerce Ave., High Point, NC, 27260; *PH:* 1-336-887-8300; *Fax:* 1-336-887-8500;
http:// www.natuzzi.com

General		Stock	
Incorporation	Italy	Price on:12/24/2007	$8.01
Employees	7,846	Stock Exchange	NYSE
Auditor	KPMG S.P.A	Ticker Symbol	NU
Stk Agt	Bank of New York	Outstanding Shares	54,820,000
Counsel	NA	E.P.S	-$0.76
DUNS No.	43-232-3525	Shareholders	NA

Business: The group's principal activities are to design, manufacture and distribute traditional and contemporary leather and fabric upholstered furniture (sofas, armchairs, recliners). These furnitures are manufactured in Italy, romania, Brazil and China. The group improved the quality of its franchise divani & divani and created a second franchising line with novum, offering a wide range of home furnishing in the domestic market. The group operates in Europe, u.s.a., the Middle East and the Far East.

Primary SIC and add'l.: 3111 5948 2515 2295 5199

CIK No: 0000900391

Subsidiaries: Divani Due S.r.l., I.m.p.e. S.p.a., Italholding S.r.l., Italsofa Bahia Ltd, Italsofa Romania, Italsofa Shanghai Ltd, Kingdom of Leather Limited, Kingdom of Leather Trustees Limited, Koine S.r.l., La Galleria Limited, Lagene S.r.l., Minuano Nordeste S.A., Nacon S.p.A., Natco S.p.A., Natuzzi Americas Inc. 28 Subsidiaries included in the Index

Officers: Ernesto Greco/57/Dir., CEO, Dir. - Human Resources, Organization, Pasquale Natuzzi/Chmn., CEO, Fredrick Starr/CEO, Pres. - Natuzzi Americas, Annunziata Natuzzi/44/CEO - Natco SpA, Giuseppe Desantis/Vice Chmn., Worldwide Operations, GM, Nicola Coropulis/Regional Mgr. South - West Europe, Giovanni Mercadante/Accounting Dir., Gaetano D. Cataldo/Exec. VP - Natuzzi Americas, Giuseppe Firrao/House Agency Mgr., Giovanni Costantino/Product, Retail Development GM, Francesco Basile/Human Resources, Organization Corp. Dir., Ottavio Milano/Control Mgr., Giambattista Massaro/46/Purchasing Corp. Dir., Stefano Rezzin/Country Mgr. Austria - Switzerland, Filippo Simonetti/CFO *(40 Officers included in Index)*

Directors: Pasquale Natuzzi/Chmn., CEO, Ernesto Greco/57/Dir., CEO, Dir. - Human Resources, Organization, Giuseppe Desantis/Vice Chmn., Worldwide Operations, GM, Armando P. Branchini/Dir., Giuseppe R. Corvace/Dir., Maurizia Olga Iachino Leto Di Priolo/Dir., Stelio Campanale/Dir.

Owners: Pasquale Natuzzi/47.50%, Royce & Associates, LLC/10.00%, Tweedy, Browne Company, L.L.C./6.90%, Brandes Investment Partners, LP/8.60%

Financial Data: *Fiscal Year End:*12/31 *Latest Annual Data:* 12/31/2006

Year	Sales	Net Income
2006	$971,000,000	$19,130,000
2005	$793,460,000	-$8,159,000
2004	$1,027,985,000	$25,587,000

Curr. Assets:	$537,769,000	**Curr. Liab.:**	$175,587,000	**P/E Ratio:**	9.85
Plant, Equip.:	$324,444,000	**Total Liab.:**	$258,557,000	**Indic. Yr. Divd.:**	NA
Total Assets:	$877,019,000	**Net Worth:**	$618,462,000	**Debt/ Equity:**	NA

Naugatuck Valley Financial Corp

333 Church St., Naugatuck, CT, 06770; *PH:* 1-203-720-5000; *Fax:* 1-203-720-5016;
http:// www.nvsl.com

General		Stock	
Incorporation	US	Price on:12/24/2007	$11.8
Employees	111	Stock Exchange	NDQ
Auditor	Whittlesey & Hadley, P.C	Ticker Symbol	NVSL
Stk Agt	Registrar & Transfer Co	Outstanding Shares	7,410,000
Counsel	NA	E.P.S	$0.17
DUNS No.	NA	Shareholders	NA

Business: The groups principle activity is to provide traditional financial services. The group attracts deposits from the general public and uses those funds to originate one- to four-family, multi-family and commercial real estate, construction, commercial business and consumer loans. The group operates from United States.

Primary SIC and add'l.: NA

CIK No: 0001293413

Subsidiaries: Naugatuck Valley Mutual

Officers: John C. Roman/Dir., Pres., CEO - Naugatuck Valley Savings, Loan/$263,978.00, Diane L. Hanley/Assist. VP - Naugatuck Valley Savings, Loan, Bill Partington/VP - Naugatuck Valley Savings, Loan, William C. Nimons/Sr. VP - Naugatuck Valley Savings, Loan/$191,573.00, Janet L. Walsh/Assist. VP - Naugatuck Valley Savings, Loan, Joseph A. Nagrabski/VP - Naugatuck Valley Savings, Loan, Kathleen A. McPadden/VP - Naugatuck Valley Savings, Loan, Judy Guisto/Branch Mgr., Assist. Sec. - Naugatuck Valley Savings, Loan, Sonia Araujo/Branch Mgr. - Naugatuck, New

Haven Road, Assist. Sec. - Naugatuck Valley Savings, Loan, Carol Rumino/Branch Mgr. - Cheshire, Assist. Sec. - Naugatuck Valley Savings, Loan, Sandra Perrelli/Branch Mgr. - Waterbury, Assist. Sec. - Naugatuck Valley Savings, Loan, Kathy Katrenya/Branch Mgr. - Southbury, Assist. Sec. - Naugatuck Valley Savings, Loan, Sue Schmelcke/Assist. Branch Mgr. - Naugatuck Valley Savings, Loan, David Chopak/Assist. Branch Mgr. - Naugatuck, New Haven Road, Naugatuck Valley Savings, Loan, Allan Montiero/Assist. Branch Mgr. - Beacon Falls, Naugatuck Valley Savings, Loan *(40 Officers included in Index)*

Directors: John C. Roman/Dir., Pres., CEO - Naugatuck Valley Savings, Loan, Ronald D. Lengyel/Chmn. - Naugatuck Valley Savings, Loan, Lawrence J. Mambrino/Dir. Emeritus - Naugatuck Valley Savings, Loan, Frederick E. Hennick/Dir. Emeritus - Naugatuck Valley Savings, Loan, Frank Rodrigues/Dir. Emeritus - Naugatuck Valley Savings, Loan, Gerald Labriola/Dir. Emeritus - Naugatuck Valley Savings, Loan, Robert E. Ruccio/Dir. Emeritus - Naugatuck Valley Savings, Loan, Richard M. Famiglietti/Dir. - Naugatuck Valley Savings, Loan, Camilo P. Vieira/Dir. - Naugatuck Valley Savings, Loan, Carlos S. Batista/Dir. - Naugatuck Valley Savings, Loan, Michael S. Plude/Dir. - Naugatuck Valley Savings, Loan, Jane H. Walsh/Dir. - Naugatuck Valley Savings, Loan, James A. Mengacci/Dir.

Owners: Naugatuck Valley Mutual Holding Company/56.50%, Insiders/3.40%, Camilo P. Vieira, William C. Nimons, Michael S. Plude, Lee R. Schlesinger, James A. Mengacci, Richard M. Famiglietti, Dominic J. Alegi, Jane H. Walsh, John C. Roman, Carlos S. Batista, Ronald D. Lengyel

Financial Data: *Fiscal Year End:* 12/31 *Latest Annual Data:* 12/31/2006

Year	Sales	Net Income
2006	$22,698,000	$1,448,000
2005	$17,425,000	$1,905,000
2004	$13,947,000	$415,000

Curr. Assets:	$9,846,000	**Curr. Liab.:**	$357,686,000	**P/E Ratio:**	69.41
Plant, Equip.:	$11,209,000	**Total Liab.:**	$362,771,000	**Indic. Yr. Divd.:**	$0.200
Total Assets:	$413,855,000	**Net Worth:**	$51,084,000	**Debt/ Equity:**	1.2899

Nautilus Inc

16400 SE Nautilus Dr., Vancouver, WA, 98683; *PH:* 1-360-859-2900; *Fax:* 1-360-694-7755; *http://* www.nautilus.com

General - Incorporation	WA	**Stock** - Price on:12/24/2007	$12.6
Employees	1,500	Stock Exchange	NYSE
Auditor	Deloitte & Touche LLP	Ticker Symbol	NA
Stk Agt	Computershare Trust Co	Outstanding Shares	31,550,000
Counsel	Garvey Schubert Barer	E.P.S.	$0.09
DUNS No.	15-766-1877	Shareholders	NA

Business: The group's principle activities are to market, develop and manufacture health and fitness products. The group's products are sold under brand names such as Nautilus, Bowflex, Schwinn, Stairmaster, Treadclimber and Trimline. The products are distributed through diversified direct, retail and commercial sales channels. The group markets and sells Bowflex, Treadclimber and Nautilus sleep systems products through the direct-Marketing channel utilizing an effective combination of television commercials, infomercials, response mailings, the Internet and inbound/outbound call centers. It also markets and sells Nautilus, Schwinn and Stairmaster commercial fitness equipment through sales force and selected dealers to health clubs, government agencies, hotels, corporate fitness centers, colleges, universities and assisted living facilities worldwide. The group has operations in the United States, Switzerland, Italy, Germany and the United Kingdom. The group's quarterly revenue for September 2007 was 133.64 millions of USD.

Primary SIC and add'l.: 2515 3949

CIK No: 0001078207

Subsidiaries: BFI Advertising, Inc., DashAmerica, Inc., DF Hebb Industries, Inc., DFI Leaseco, LLC, DFI Properties, LLC, Nautilus Direct, Inc., Nautilus Fitness Academy UK Ltd., Nautilus Fitness Canada, Inc., Nautilus Fitness Deutschland GmbH, Nautilus Fitness Italy S.r.l., Nautilus Fitness UK Ltd., Nautilus Human Performance Systems, Inc., Nautilus International Holdings, S.A., Nautilus International, S.A., Nautilus Switzerland, S.A. 23 Subsidiaries included in the Index

Officers: Robert S. Falcone/61/Dir., CEO, Acting Pres., Gregg Hammann/45/Chmn., CEO, Pres./$1,943,700.00, Tim E. Hawkins/41/Pres. - Fitness Equipment Business/$465,887.00, Juergen Eckmann/Acting Pres. - Nautilus Apparel Business/$382,354.00, Ron D. Arp/Sr. VP - Corporate Communications, Timothy Joyce/Sr. VP - Global Sales, Darryl Thomas/Pres. - International Equipment Business/$462,110.00, Wayne Bolio/Chief Administrative Officer, William D. Meadowcroft/45/CFO, Sec., Treasurer, Danny Langton/International GSA Mgr., Steve Eichen/CIO, Deborah Marsh/Sr. VP - Human Resources, Mark A. Meussner/Sr. VP - Global Manufacturing, Operations, Brian Edwards/Eastern GSA Mgr., Bob Kettles/Western GSA Mgr.

Directors: Robert S. Falcone/61/Dir., CEO, Acting Pres., Gregg Hammann/45/Chmn., CEO, Pres., Peter A. Allen/47/Dir., Evelyn V. Follit/62/Dir., Frederick T. Hull/Dir., Donald W. Keeble/59/Dir., Paul F. Little/Dir., Diane L. Neal/51/Dir., Ronald P. Badie/65/Dir., Marvin G. Siegert/59/Dir.

Owners: Marvin G. Siegert, Robert S. Falcone, William D. Meadowcroft, Peter A. Allen, U.S. Bancorp/6.19%, SCSF Equities, LLC/9.89%, ICM Asset Management, Inc./6.57%, Diane L. Neal, Darryl K. Thomas, Insiders/1.01%, Ronald P. Badie, Juergen Eckmann, Snyder Capital Management, L.P./9.87%, Sherborne Investors LP/25.00%, Donald W. Keeble

Financial Data: *Fiscal Year End:* 12/31 *Latest Annual Data:* 12/31/2006

Year	Sales	Net Income
2006	$680,295,000	$29,100,000
2005	$631,310,000	$23,000,000
2004	$523,837,000	$29,985,000

Curr. Assets:	$250,761,000	**Curr. Liab.:**	$147,358,000	**P/E Ratio:**	15.56
Plant, Equip.:	$52,658,000	**Total Liab.:**	$168,308,000	**Indic. Yr. Divd.:**	$0.400
Total Assets:	$424,942,000	**Net Worth:**	$256,634,000	**Debt/ Equity:**	0.0158

Navarre Corp

7400 49th Ave. N, New Hope, MN, 55428; *PH:* 1-763-535-8333; *Fax:* 1-763-533-2156; *http://* www.navarre.com; *Email:* info@navarre.com

General - Incorporation	MN	**Stock** - Price on:12/24/2007	$3.91
Employees	798	Stock Exchange	NYSE
Auditor	Grant Thornton LLP	Ticker Symbol	NBD
Stk Agt	Wells Fargo Shareowner Services	Outstanding Shares	36,070,000
Counsel	Lindquist & Vennum PLLP	E.P.S.	$0.11
DUNS No.	10-227-6177	Shareholders	NA

Business: The group's principal activity is to publish and distribute home entertainment and multimedia products including PC software, audio and video titles and interactive games. The group operates through two segments. The distribution services segment distributes entertainment products including PC software, CD and DVD audio, DVD and vhs video, video games and accessories provided by publishers, independent and major music labels, and movie studios. The publishing segment licenses, packages, markets and sells proprietary PC software, CD and DVD audio, DVD and vhs video, and video game titles. The major customers of the group include best buy co., inc., sam's clubs and compusa, inc. The products are distributed in the United States and Canada. On 3-Nov-2003, the group acquired bci eclipse llc.

Primary SIC and add'l.: 7822 5099 7372

CIK No: 0000911650

Subsidiaries: BCI Eclipse Company, LLC, Encore Software, Inc., FUNimation, Mix & Burn

Officers: Gen Fukunaga/CEO, Pres. - Funimation Entertainment/$415,692.00, Cary L. Deacon/Dir., CEO, Pres./$681,416.00, Diane Lapp/VP - Finance, Marvin Gleicher/Sr. VP - DVD Content, Marketing, Reid J. Porter/CFO, Exec. VP/$400,185.00, Brian Burke/Pres. - Navarre Distribution Services/$360,738.00, Rick Vick/VP - Merchandising, David Ginsberg/VP - Operations, Joyce Fleck/VP - Sales, Marketing, Bob Freese/Pres. - BCI, Margot McManus/VP - Human Resources, Lina Shurslep/CIO, Ward Thomas/COO - Funimation Entertainment, John Turner/Sr. VP - Global Logistics/$300,143.00, Ryan Urness/General Counsel

Directors: Cary L. Deacon/Dir., CEO, Pres., Eric H. Paulson/Chmn., Founder, James G. Sippl/Dir., Michael L. Snow/Dir., Timothy R. Gentz/Dir., Gary St. Marie/Dir., Keith A. Benson/Dir., Richard Gary St. Marie/68/Dir., Tom F. Weyl/Dir., Deborah L. Hopp/Dir.

Owners: Michael L. Snow, James G. Sippl, Gen Fukunaga/2.57%, Cary L. Deacon/1.08%, Insiders/12.44%, Charles E. Cheney/1.91%, Keith A. Benson, Tom F. Weyl, Eric H. Paulson/4.65%, Deborah L. Hopp, John Turner, Timothy R. Gentz, Richard Gary St. Marie, Tracer Capital Management L.P./6.01%, Reid J. Porter *(18 Owners included in Index)*

Financial Data: *Fiscal Year End:* 03/31 *Latest Annual Data:* 3/31/2007

Year	Sales	Net Income
2007	$698,371,000	$4,059,000
2006	$686,126,000	-$3,175,000
2005	$596,615,000	$10,166,000

Curr. Assets:	$151,144,000	**Curr. Liab.:**	$152,679,000	**P/E Ratio:**	15.64
Plant, Equip.:	$14,042,000	**Total Liab.:**	$174,774,000	**Indic. Yr. Divd.:**	NA
Total Assets:	$288,225,000	**Net Worth:**	$113,451,000	**Debt/ Equity:**	0.1319

Navidec Financial Services Inc

456 Madison St., Denver, CO, 80206; *PH:* 1-303-222-1000

General - Incorporation	CO	**Stock** - Price on:12/24/2007	NA
Employees	23	Stock Exchange	NA
Auditor	Jaspers & Hall, P.C	Ticker Symbol	NA
Stk Agt	Computershare Trust Co	Outstanding Shares	NA
Counsel	NA	E.P.S.	-$0.33
DUNS No.	NA	Shareholders	NA

Business: The group's principle activity is to provide quality integrated e-business solutions and services that rapidly transform traditional Global 2000 businesses into e-businesses. The group's dedicated Financial Services Practice team provides extensive Internet solutions experience and broad financial services domain knowledge.The company's Financial Services Practice integrates targeted eFinancial Services Management (eFSM) applications that help the customers and partners to focus on their business. Utilizing its time-tested NPact process, the company defines, builds and manages custom Internet solutions that deliver meaningful and measurable progress toward an organization's business vision. The group also continue to focus on finding technology sector business opportunities that offer cash flow, strong management and an opportunity for growth. The group operates from United States.

Primary SIC and add'l.: 6199

CIK No: 0001302946

Subsidiaries: Northsight Mortgage Group, Swiftsure, Inc

Officers: John R. McKowen/58/Chmn., CEO, Robert D. Grizzle/46/CFO, COO, Pres.

Directors: John R. McKowen/58/Chmn., CEO, Howard L. Farkas/84/Dir.

Owners: Insiders/35.91%, John McKowen/19.85%, Howard Farkas/10.35%, Robert Grizzle/6.71%

Financial Data: *Fiscal Year End:* 12/31 *Latest Annual Data:* 12/31/2006

Year	Sales	Net Income
2006	NA	-$15,487,000
2005	NA	-$6,407,000
2004	NA	-$10,653,000

Curr. Assets:	$32,402,000	**Curr. Liab.:**	$10,345,000		
Plant, Equip.:	$38,727,000	**Total Liab.:**	$10,401,000	**Indic. Yr. Divd.:**	NA
Total Assets:	$74,037,000	**Net Worth:**	$63,636,000	**Debt/ Equity:**	0.0008

Navigant Consulting Inc

615 N Wabash Ave., Chicago, IL, 60611; *PH:* 1-312-573-5600; *Fax:* 1-312-573-5678; *http://* www.navigantconsulting.com

General - Incorporation	DE	**Stock** - Price on:12/24/2007	$19.52
Employees	2,475	Stock Exchange	NDQ
Auditor	KPMG LLP	Ticker Symbol	NCOC
Stk Agt	LaSalle Bank N.A	Outstanding Shares	58,100,000
Counsel	NA	E.P.S.	$0.83
DUNS No.	19-345-8635	Shareholders	NA

Business: The group's principal activity is to provide litigation, financial services, healthcare, energy and operational consultancy services to government agencies and large companies. It operates through its two segments: financial and-claims consulting and energy and water consulting. The financial and claims consulting segment provides data management, quality control, business and property valuation, research and analysis, litigation support, bankruptcy and solvency management, and claims management services. The energy and water consulting segment provides consulting and transaction support services to the energy, network based and regulatory industries. The group has international operations in the United Kingdom, Canada and Australia. On 15-Dec-2003, the group acquired front line strategic consulting inc and on 30-Jan-2004, tucker alan inc and on 07-Jun-2004, capital advisory services llc and invalesco group inc on 01-Sep-2004.

Primary SIC and add'l.: 8742

CIK No: 0001019737

Subsidiaries: Peterson Consulting, LLC

Officers: William M. Goodyear/Chmn., CEO, Ben W. Perks/Exec. VP/$952,463.00, David Tortorello/MD - International Consulting, Peter Badala/MD - Construction, Jeffrey H. Stoecklein/VP - Corporate Development, Julie M. Howard/COO, Pres., Richard X. Fischer/VP, General Counsel,

Corp. Sec., Bob Groves/MD - Construction, Greg Crider/MD - Construction, William D. Guernier/MD - Construction, William J. Keating/MD - Government Contractor Services, Glenn Beitl/Dir. - Cost Segregation Services, Amy L. Cuiffo/Assoc. Dir. - Cost Segregation Services, Don Harvey/MD - Construction, Chad Hutchison/MD - Construction *(47 Officers included in Index)*

Directors: William M. Goodyear/Chmn., CEO, Valerie B. Jarrett/Dir., Thomas A. Gildehaus/Dir., James R. Thompson/Dir., Peter B. Pond/Dir., Samuel K. Skinner/Dir.

Owners: Royce & Associates, Inc./5.50%, Richard X. Fischer, Valerie B. Jarrett, Peter B. Pond, Thomas A. Gildehaus, Samuel K. Skinner, Insiders/2.90%, T. Rowe Price Associates, Inc./5.00%, FMR Corp./13.90%, Ben W. Perks, Julie M. Howard, James R. Thompson, William M. Goodyear/1.60%

Financial Data: Fiscal Year End:12/31 **Latest Annual Data:** 06/30/2007

Year	Sales	Net Income
2007	$189,633,000	$11,350,000
2006	$681,745,000	$52,974,000
2005	$575,492,000	$49,856,000

Curr. Assets:	$200,245,000	Curr. Liab.:	$129,742,000	P/E Ratio:	22.44
Plant. Equip.:	$51,164,000	Total Liab.:	$165,782,000	Indic. Yr. Divd.:	NA
Total Assets:	$652,358,000	Net Worth:	$486,576,000	Debt/ Equity:	0.0028

Navigant International Inc

84 Inverness Cir. E, Englewood, CO, 80112; *PH:* 1-303-706-0800; *Fax:* 1-303-706-0770; *http://* www.navigant.com

General - Incorporation	DE	Stock- Price on:12/24/2007	$11.1
Employees	NA	Stock Exchange	OTC
Auditor	Deloitte & Touche LLP	Ticker Symbol	FLYR
Stk Agt	American Stock Transfer & Trust Co.	Outstanding Shares	NA
Counsel	NA	E.P.S.	NA
DUNS No.	18-808-0352	Shareholders	NA

Business: The group's principal activity is to provide corporate travel management services and other travel services. The group provides comprehensive accounting systems that track and reconcile travel expenses, processes and classifies billing information and provides management reports. It focuses on reducing the travel expenses of its clients. The group provides the services through on-site travel agencies, regional travel agency offices and satellite ticket printers. It also provides reservations and ticketing services, quality control and reduction systems, travel accounting and management reporting services. The group has operations in the United States, Canada, the United Kingdom, Germany, France, Belgium, the Netherlands, Spain, Italy, Greece, Ireland, Scotland, Norway, Iceland, turkey, kuwait, qatar, Japan, Singapore, guam, Puerto Rico, cuba and Brazil. On 17-Jun-2004, the group acquired northwestern travel service, l.p.

Primary SIC and add'l.: 4724 4729

CIK No: 0001055455

Subsidiaries: AQUA Software Products Inc., Associated Travel Services of Texas Inc., Associated Travel Services of Texas Ltd., Atlas Travel GP Inc., Atlas Travel Services Corp., Birth Investments Limited, Cornerstone Enterprises Inc., Envision Vacations Canada Inc., Incentive Connections Inc., International Travel Consultants N.V., Maple Leaf Collection Inc., Marine & Oilfield Travel Logistics LP, Navigant Australia Pty Ltd, Navigant Cruise Center Inc., Navigant International Funding Corporation 36 Subsidiaries included in the Index

Officers: Edward S. Adams/Chmn., CEO - Tq3navigant, John S. Coffman/Chief Accounting Officer - Tq3navigant, Ken Migaki/CIO - Tq3navigant, Keith Taylor/Sr. VP - Sales, Accounting Management, Tq3navigant, Gary Alexander/VP - Product Management, Tq3navigant, Regina Q. Keating/VP - Operations, Pres. - Rocky Mountain Region, Eugene A. Over/Sr. VP - Administration, General Counsel, Sec., Robert C. Griffith/CFO, COO, Treasurer, Laurie Alexander/Contact - Media Relations

Directors: Edward S. Adams/Chmn., CEO - Tq3navigant

Navigators Group Inc (The)

One Penn Plz., New York, NY, 10119; *PH:* 1-914-934-8999; *http://* www.navg.com

General - Incorporation	DE	Stock- Price on:12/24/2007	$53.3
Employees	342	Stock Exchange	NDQ
Auditor	KPMG LLP	Ticker Symbol	NAVG
Stk Agt	LaSalle Bank N.A	Outstanding Shares	16,780,000
Counsel	KMZ Rosenman Law Firm	E.P.S.	$4.91
DUNS No.	14-463-8251	Shareholders	NA

Business: The group's principal activities are to underwrite and manage property and casualty insurance. The group's segments include the insurance companies, the navigators agencies and the lloyd's operations. The insurance companies are primarily engaged in underwriting marine insurance and related lines of business, contractors' general liability insurance and professional liability insurance. The navigators agencies are underwriting management companies, which produce, manage and underwrite insurance and reinsurance for both affiliated and unaffiliated companies. The lloyd's operations underwrite marine and related lines of business at lloyd's of london.

Primary SIC and add'l.: 6351 6331

CIK No: 0000793547

Subsidiaries: Millennium Underwriting Ltd., Navigators California Insurance Services, Inc., Navigators Corporate Underwriters Ltd., Navigators Holdings (UK) Ltd., Navigators Insurance Company, Navigators Insurance Services of Texas, Inc., Navigators Insurance Services of Washington, Inc., Navigators Management (UK) Ltd., Navigators Management Company, Inc., Navigators NV, Navigators Special Risk, Inc., Navigators Underwriting Agency Ltd., Navigators Underwriting Limited, NIC Insurance Company

Officers: Stanley A. Galanski/Dir., CEO, Pres./$1,292,152.00, Doug Fischer/Contact - Marine, Energy, Alan Vernon/Inland Marine, Navigators Insurance Services, Texas, Inc, Ed Helfers/Inland Marine, Navigators Management Company, Inc, Jane E. Keller/Sr. VP, Chief Claims Officer, Bradley D. Wiley/Sr. VP, Financial Compliance Officer, Paul J. Malvasio/CFO, VP/$954,527.00, Salvatore A. Margarella/VP, Treasurer, John Grimaldi/Excess Casualty, Navigators Management Company, Inc, Robert Philhower/Excess Casualty, Navigators Management Company, Inc, Daniel Marriage/Excess Casualty, Navigators California Insurance Services, Inc, Dennis Nicholson/Primary Casualty, Navigators Insurance Services, Washington, Inc, Jan Dela Ruelle/Marine Underwriter, Navigators NV, Ivan Eggermont/Marine Claims Mgr., Chris Butcher/Regional Operations, Development Dir. *(35 Officers included in Index)*

Directors: Stanley A. Galanski/Dir., CEO, Pres., Terence N. Deeks/Chmn., Mervyn H.J. Blakeney/Dir., Peter A. Cheney/Dir., Robert W. Eager/Dir., Marc M. Tract/Dir., Robert F. Wright/Dir., Leandro S. Galban/Dir., John F. Kirby/61/Dir., Thomas W. Forrester/Dir.

Owners: Insiders/21.80%, H. J. Mervyn Blakeney, John F. Kirby, Peter A. Cheney, Noel Higgitt, Leandro S. Galban, FMR Corp./9.00%, Dimensional Fund Advisors LP/7.50%, Paul J. Malvasio, Terence N. Deeks/16.60%, Thomas W. Forrester, Christopher C. Duca, Robert W. Eager, Marc M. Tract/3.40%, Stanley A. Galanski *(17 Owners included in Index)*

Financial Data: Fiscal Year End:12/31 **Latest Annual Data:** 06/30/2007

Year	Sales	Net Income
2007	$164,020,000	$24,375,000
2006	NA	NA
2005	NA	NA

Curr. Assets:	$1,546,131,000	Curr. Liab.:	$259,132,000	P/E Ratio:	11.74
Plant. Equip.:	NA	Total Liab.:	$2,405,343,000	Indic. Yr. Divd.:	NA
Total Assets:	$2,956,686,000	Net Worth:	$551,343,000	Debt/ Equity:	0.2151

NaviSite Inc

400 Minuteman Rd., Andover, MA, 01810; *PH:* 1-978-682-8300; *Fax:* 1-978-688-8100; *http://* www.navisite.com

General - Incorporation	DE	Stock- Price on:12/24/2007	$7.45
Employees	564	Stock Exchange	NDQ
Auditor	KPMG LLP	Ticker Symbol	NBAN
Stk Agt	EquiServe Trust Co N.A	Outstanding Shares	31,370,000
Counsel	NA	E.P.S.	-$0.88
DUNS No.	NA	Shareholders	NA

Business: The group's principal activity is to provide Web hosting and application services for companies conducting mission-critical business on the Internet. The services offered include managed applications, managed servers, managed infrastructure and managed facilities. The managed applications include end-to-end management of e-business application. The managed servers include the management of the infrastructure software such as operating systems, Web servers, database servers and application servers. The managed infrastructure include services related to value added security, network and storage options. The group also provides related professional and consulting services. These services are provided over the Internet in many states in the United States and internationally. On 14-Jun-2004, the group acquired all assets of surebridge, inc.

Primary SIC and add'l.: 7379

CIK No: 0001084750

Subsidiaries: Avasta, Inc., Clear Blue Technologies/Las Vegas, Inc., ClearBlue Technologies Management, Inc., ClearBlue Technologies/Chicago-Wells, Inc., ClearBlue Technologies/Dallas, Inc., ClearBlue Technologies/Los Angeles, Inc., ClearBlue Technologies/Milwaukee, Inc., ClearBlue Technologies/New York, Inc., ClearBlue Technologies/Oak Brook, Inc., ClearBlue Technologies/San Francisco, Inc., ClearBlue Technologies/Vienna, Inc., Conxion Corporation, Intrepid Acquisition Corp., Lexington Acquisition Corp., NaviSite Europe Limited 16 Subsidiaries included in the Index

Officers: Arthur P. Becker/Dir., CEO, Nasir Cochinwala/Sr. VP - Professional Services, Denis Martin/CTO, Exec. VP, Mark Clayman/Sr. VP - Hosting Services, Sumeet Sabharwal/Sr. VP - Global Delivery, Jim Pluntze/CFO, Investor Relations Officer, Monique Cormier/40/General Counsel, Rathin Sinha/Chief Marketing Officer, Jim Fanella/Sr. VP - Strategic Business Development

Directors: Arthur P. Becker/Dir., CEO, Andrew Ruhan/Chmn., Larry Schwartz/Dir., James Dennedy/Dir., Thomas R. Evans/Dir.

Owners: Monique Cormier, Insiders/6.00%, netASPx Holdings, Inc./92.10%, SPCP Group, LLC and SPCP GroupIII LLC/5.70%, Atlantic Investors, LLC/44.70%, James W. Pluntze, Arthur P. Becker/3.90%, Larry Schwartz, Janus Capital Management LLC/10.70%, James Dennedy, Andrew Ruhan, Thomas R. Evans

Financial Data: Fiscal Year End:07/31 **Latest Annual Data:** 04/30/2007

Year	Sales	Net Income
2007	$32,748,000	-$2,359,000
2006	$109,087,000	-$13,931,000
2005	$109,863,000	-$16,084,000

Curr. Assets:	$24,496,000	Curr. Liab.:	$33,568,000		
Plant. Equip.:	$14,914,000	Total Liab.:	$104,385,000	Indic. Yr. Divd.:	NA
Total Assets:	$102,409,000	Net Worth:	-$1,976,000	Debt/ Equity:	195.2000

Navistar Financial Corp

2850 W Golf Rd. , Rolling Meadows, IL, 60008; *PH:* 1-630-753-5000; *http://* www.internationaldelivers.com

General - Incorporation	DE	Stock- Price on:12/24/2007	NA
Employees	NA	Stock Exchange	NA
Auditor	KPMG LLP	Ticker Symbol	NA
Stk Agt	Mellon Investor Services LLC	Outstanding Shares	NA
Counsel	NA	E.P.S.	NA
DUNS No.	02-516-7669	Shareholders	NA

Business: The group's principle activity is to provide wholesale, retail and lease financing in the United States for sales of new and used trucks sold by the parent corporation, International Truck and Engine Corporation and dealers. It also finances wholesale accounts and selected retail accounts receivable. The group finances sales of new products including trailers of other manufacturers.

Primary SIC and add'l.: 6159

CIK No: 0000051303

Subsidiaries: International Truck Leasing Corporation, Navistar Financial Retail Receivables Corporation, Navistar Financial Securities Corporation, Truck Engine Receivables Financing Co, Truck Retail Accounts Corporation, Truck Retail Instalment Paper Corp

Officers: Pamela Turbeville/Dir., CEO, William A. Caton/Dir., Pres., John V. Mulvaney/Dir., VP, CFO, Treasurer, David L. Derfelt/VP, Controller

Directors: Pamela Turbeville/Dir., CEO, William A. Caton/Dir., Pres., Terry M. Endsley/Dir., John V. Mulvaney/Dir., VP, CFO, Treasurer, Richard C. Tarapchak/Dir., Alice M. Peterson/Dir.

Navistar International Corp

4201 Winfield Rd., Warrenville, IL, 60555; *PH:* 1-630-753-2143; *Fax:* 1-630-753-2303; *http://* www.navistar.com; *Email:* investor.relations@nav-international.com

General - Incorporation	DE	**Stock**- Price on:12/24/2007	NA
Employees	NA	Stock Exchange	NDQ
Auditor	KPMG LLP	Ticker Symbol	NAVI
Stk Agt	Mellon Investor Services LLC	Outstanding Shares	NA
Counsel	NA	E.P.S.	NA
DUNS No.	00-521-4200	Shareholders	NA

Business: The group's principal activities are divided into three segments namely: truck, engine and financial services. The truck segment manufactures and distributes a full line of diesel-powered trucks and school buses in the common carrier, private carrier, government/service, leasing, construction and student transportation markets. The engine segment designs and manufactures diesel engines for use in the group's class 5, 6 and 7 medium trucks, school buses and selected class 8 heavy truck models. This segment also sells engines for industrial, agricultural and marine applications. The financial services segment provides retail, wholesale and lease financing of products sold by the truck segment and its dealers within the United States and Mexico. The operations are carried on in the United States, Canada, Mexico and Brazil.

Primary SIC and add'l.: 6719 6141 6159 3519 3714 6411 3713

CIK No: 0000808450

Subsidiaries: Camiones y Motores International de Mexico, S.A. de C.V., IC Corporation, International of Mexico Holding Corporation LLC, International Truck and Engine Corporation, International Truck and Engine Corporation Canada, International Truck and Engine Corporation Cayman, Islands Holding Company, Navistar Financial Corporation, Navistar Severe Service Truck Company, Truck and Engine Corporation:

Officers: Daniel C. Ustian/Chmn., CEO, Pres., William Caton/CFO, Exec. VP

Directors: Daniel C. Ustian/Chmn., CEO, Pres., Michael N. Hammes/Dir., Marc Y. Belton/Dir., Egenio Clariond/Dir., John D. Correnti/Dir., Abbie J. Griffin/Dir., James H. Keyes/Dir., Southwood J. Morcott/Dir., Dennis D. Williams/Dir., David D. Harrison/Dir.

Owners: John J. Allen, Marc Y. Belton, Pamela J. Turbeville, Tontine Overseas Associates, LLC/7.49%, Daniel C. Ustian/1.10%, Schneider Capital Management Corporation/5.69%, James H. Keyes, International Truck and Engine Corporation/10.30%, Deepak T. Kapur, Oppenheimer Funds, Inc/6.18%, William A. Caton, Michael N. Hammes, Harbinger Capital Partners Master Fund I, Ltd/14.78%, Insiders/2.80%, LSV Asset Management/5.22% *(21 Owners included in Index)*

Financial Data: *Fiscal Year End:*10/31 *Latest Annual Data:* 10/31/2004

Year	Sales	Net Income
2004	$9,724,000,000	$247,000,000
2003	$7,340,000,000	-$18,000,000
2002	$6,784,000,000	-$536,000,000

Curr. Assets:	$3,167,000,000	**Curr. Liab.:**	$3,250,000,000		
Plant, Equip.:	$1,444,000,000	**Total Liab.:**	$7,061,000,000	**Indic. Yr. Divd.:**	NA
Total Assets:	$7,592,000,000	**Net Worth:**	$531,000,000	**Debt/ Equity:**	3.9534

Navitone Technologies Inc

4850 W Flamingo Rd. No.22, Las Vegas, NV, 89103; ***PH:*** 1-714-257-0105; ***http://*** www.citycaps.com

General - Incorporation	NV	**Stock**- Price on:12/24/2007	NA
Employees	43	Stock Exchange	OTC
Auditor	Moore Stephens Wurth F & T LLP	Ticker Symbol	NVTN
Stk Agt	Pacific Stock Transfer Company	Outstanding Shares	NA
Counsel	NA	E.P.S.	-$0.096
DUNS No.	NA	Shareholders	NA

Business: The group's principle activity is to provide logistics and asset tracking for mobile assets. The company is planning a merger with chirp technologies, inc.

Primary SIC and add'l.: 7375

CIK No: 0001114302

Subsidiaries: Citycaps Information Technology Co. Ltd, Navitone China

Financial Data: *Fiscal Year End:*12/31 *Latest Annual Data:* 12/31/2005

Year	Sales	Net Income
2005	$86,000	-$1,377,000
2004	$35,000	-$597,000
2003	NA	-$166,000

Curr. Assets:	$275,000	**Curr. Liab.:**	$222,000		
Plant, Equip.:	$89,000	**Total Liab.:**	$222,000	**Indic. Yr. Divd.:**	NA
Total Assets:	$379,000	**Net Worth:**	$157,000	**Debt/ Equity:**	NA

Navstar Media Holdings Inc

26, Chaowai Rd., Ste. A2205, Chaoyang District, Beijing, 100020; ***PH:*** 86-646-688-4413; ***Fax:*** 1-646-349-3864

General - Incorporation	NV	**Stock**- Price on:12/24/2007	$0.125
Employees	NA	Stock Exchange	OTC
Auditor	Moore Stephens Wurth F & T LLP	Ticker Symbol	NVMHE
Stk Agt	Pacific Stock Transfer Company	Outstanding Shares	NA
Counsel	NA	E.P.S.	NA
DUNS No.	NA	Shareholders	NA

Business: The groups principle activity is to own majority interests in firms specializing in media content production and distribution in the peoples Republic of China. The group operates from the United States.

Primary SIC and add'l.: 7389

CIK No: 0001177274

Subsidiaries: Beijing Broadcasting and Television Media Co., Ltd., Beijing Lucky Star Century Advertisement Co. Ltd., Navistar Communications Holdings, Ltd.

Officers: Edward Meng/Dir., CFO

Directors: Edward Meng/Dir., CFO, John Chen/36/Dir., Ross Warner/43/Dir., John Wong/41/Dir.

Owners: Forum Global Opportunities Master Fund, L.P./7.10%, Ranny Liang/8.00%, Lester Schecter, Whalehaven Capital Fund/7.10%, Yang Wenquan/14.60%, Insiders/23.00%

Financial Data: *Fiscal Year End:*12/31 *Latest Annual Data:* 12/31/2006

Year	Sales	Net Income
2006	$2,300,000	-$2,414,000
2005	$3,307,000	-$255,000
2004	$197,000	$39,000

Curr. Assets:	$2,426,000	**Curr. Liab.:**	$2,527,000		
Plant, Equip.:	$1,414,000	**Total Liab.:**	$3,172,000	**Indic. Yr. Divd.:**	NA
Total Assets:	$4,482,000	**Net Worth:**	$1,310,000	**Debt/ Equity:**	NA

Navtech Inc

295 Hagey Blvd., Ste. 200, Waterloo, ON, N2L 6R5; ***PH:*** 1-519-747-1170; ***http://*** www.navtechinc.com; ***Email:*** ir@navtechinc.com

General - Incorporation	DE	**Stock**- Price on:12/24/2007	$2.35
Employees	252	Stock Exchange	NA
Auditor	Deloitte & Touche LLP	Ticker Symbol	NA
Stk Agt	Continental Stock Transfer & Trust Co	Outstanding Shares	NA
Counsel	Certilman Balin Adler & Hyman LLP	E.P.S.	NA
DUNS No.	01-790-6603	Shareholders	NA

Business: The group's principal activities are to develop, market and support flight operations and crew management systems for the commercial aviation industry. The group's systems are designed to assist commercial passenger and cargo air carriers in the dynamic environment of their daily flight operations. The group offers comprehensive software support and customer account management in the United States, Canada, Africa, Europe and the Asia-Pacific region designed to maximize the benefits and utility of the software at the customer's location. These services include training and installation support, software updates and telephone hot-line support.

Primary SIC and add'l.: 7371 7372 7375 7373

CIK No: 0000790272

Subsidiaries: European Aeronautical Group AB, European Aeronautical Group UK Limited, Navtech (Sweden) AB, Navtech (UK) Limitedq, Navtech Systems Support Inc., Navtech, LLC

Officers: David Strucke/Dir., CEO, Pres., Sec., Britt Bowra/VP Sales - Business Development, Regional VP - Americas, Mike Neudoerffer/VP - Software Development, Johan Holmqvist/VP - Operations, Graeme Wilcox/Dir. - Accounting Management, Bjorn Olsson/Contact - Europe, Africa, Middle East, George Hitchins/Contact - Sales, Asia, Andrea Murray/Contact - Marketing, Public Relations, Gordon Kilpatric/CFO

Directors: David Strucke/Dir., CEO, Pres., Sec., Thomas D. Beynon/Dir., Michael Jakobowski/Dir., John Hunt/Dir., Andrew M. Snyder/Dir., Francoise Macq/Dir.

Owners: Dorothy English, Michael Jakobowski, Britt Bowra, David Strucke, Robert N. Snyder/75.00%, Robert N. Snyder, John Hunt, Andrew M. Snyder, Alain Mallart/25.00%, Gordon Heard, Alain Mallart, Johan Holmqvist, Thomas D. Beynon, Insiders

Financial Data: *Fiscal Year End:*10/31 *Latest Annual Data:* 10/31/2006

Year	Sales	Net Income
2006	$36,823,000	$438,000
2005	$11,143,000	$673,000
2004	$7,901,000	$394,000

Curr. Assets:	$14,735,000	**Curr. Liab.:**	$13,124,000		
Plant, Equip.:	$4,410,000	**Total Liab.:**	$36,422,000	**Indic. Yr. Divd.:**	NA
Total Assets:	$42,156,000	**Net Worth:**	$5,734,000	**Debt/ Equity:**	3.5884

Navteq Corp

222 Merchandise Mart, Ste. 900, Chicago, IL, 60654; ***PH:*** 1-312-894-7000; ***Fax:*** 1-312-894-7050; ***http://*** www.navteq.com

General - Incorporation	DE	**Stock**- Price on:12/24/2007	$44.1
Employees	2,198	Stock Exchange	NYSE
Auditor	KPMG LLP	Ticker Symbol	NVT
Stk Agt	Computershare Investor Services LLC	Outstanding Shares	97,690,000
Counsel	NA	E.P.S.	$1.29
DUNS No.	NA	Shareholders	NA

Business: The group's principal activities are to provide digital map information and related software and services used in navigation, mapping and geographic-related applications. The group also provides maps, driving directions, turn-by-turn route guidance, fleet management and tracking and geographic information systems. The group's products and services are provided to end-users by customers on various platforms, which include self-contained hardware and software systems installed in vehicles, personal computing devices, server-based systems and paper media. The group's database is a digital representation of road transportation networks in the United States, Canada, western Europe and selected other countries which are constructed to provide a high level of accuracy and useful level of detail. The group's database includes extensive road, route and related travel information, including attributes collected by road segment.

Primary SIC and add'l.: 7372

CIK No: 0000834208

Subsidiaries: Austria, Belgium, Chinese, Czech, Delaware, Geoinformation NAVTEQ - Tecnologias de Navegacao, Unipessoal, Lda., Korean, Malaysian, Mexican, NAV2 Co., Ltd., Navigation Technologies CIS LLC, Navigation Technologies S.L., Navigation Technologies Sweden AB, NAVTEQ Austria GmbH, Navteq B.v. 34 Subsidiaries included in the Index

Officers: Judson C. Green/Dir., CEO, Pres./$4,339,290.00, Clifford I. Fox/Sr. VP - Navteq Map, John K. MacLeod/Exec. VP - Navteq Connected Services/$886,553.00, David B. Mullen/CFO, Exec. VP/$1,142,967.00, Christine C. Moore/VP - Human Resources, Winston V. Guillory/Sr. VP - Consumer, Business Sales, Lawrence M. Kaplan/Sr. VP, General Counsel, Corp. Sec., Richard E. Shuman/Sr. VP - Asia, Pacific Sales, Jeffrey L. Mize/Sr. VP - Vehicle Sales/$1,580,133.00, Denise M. Doyle/VP - Business Affairs, Kristen Dove/Contact - Sales, Neil T. Smith/VP, Corporate Controller, Principal Accounting Officer, Amreesh Modi/CTO, Sr. VP, Kelly A. Smith/VP - Corporate Marketing

Directors: Judson C. Green/Dir., CEO, Pres., Christopher Galvin/Non Exec. Chmn., Dirk-Jan Van Ommeren/Dir., Richard J.A. De Lange/Dir., Scott D. Miller/Dir., William Kimsey/Dir., Andrew J. Green/Dir.

Owners: T. Rowe Price Associates, Inc/8.10%, Judson C. Green/2.00%, Andrew J. Green, Jeffrey L. Mize, William L. Kimsey, Dirk-Jan van Ommeren, Insiders/2.50%, David B. Mullen, Christopher Galvin, Scott D. Miller, AXA Financial, Inc/7.00%, John K. MacLeod, Richard J. A. de Lange, Salahuddin M. Khan

Financial Data: *Fiscal Year End:*12/31 *Latest Annual Data:* 12/31/2006

Year	Sales	Net Income
2006	NA	NA
2005	NA	NA
2004	NA	NA

Curr. Assets:	$412,555,000	**Curr. Liab.:**	$140,411,000		
Plant, Equip.:	$27,462,000	**Total Liab.:**	$145,320,000	**Indic. Yr. Divd.:**	NA
Total Assets:	$794,701,000	**Net Worth:**	$649,381,000	**Debt/ Equity:**	NA

Nayna Networks Inc

4699 Old Ironsides Dr., Santa Clara, CA, 95054; *PH:* 1-408-956-8000; *Fax:* 1-408-956-8730; *http://* www.nayna.com; *Email:* sales@nayna.com

General		**Stock**	
Incorporation	NV	Price on:12/24/2007	$0.065
Employees	NA	Stock Exchange	OTC
Auditor	Nareshkumar H. Arora	Ticker Symbol	NAYN
Stk Agt	Interwest Transfer Company, Inc.	Outstanding Shares	NA
Counsel	NA	E.P.S	NA
DUNS No.	NA	Shareholders	NA

Business: The groups principal activities include designing, developing and marketing next generation broadband access solutions. Customers served by the group include carriers, cable television service providers, integrators and municipal, defense and enterprise networks. The group acquired Nayna Networks, Inc. in April 2005 and Abundance Networks (India) Pvt. Ltd. in January 2006. Specific customers of the group include InformaCorp, Crystal-Clear.TV, EthoStream, HITs, University of Evry and Revenga Ingerieros, S.A. The group operates from the North America, Europe and Asia.

Primary SIC and add'l.: 7371

CIK No: 0000769591

Subsidiaries: Nayna Networks K.K., Nayna Networks, Inc., Xpeed Inc.

Officers: Naveen S. Bisht/Dir., CEO, Pres., Gautam Chanda/Sr. VP - Business Development, Operations, Raj Jain/Co - Founder, CTO, Suresh R. Pillai/Dir., Pres., Dominique Rodriguez/VP - Product Management, Hari Hirani/VP - Engineering, Jim Connor/Dir. - Marketing, Thomas P. Richtarich/CFO, R. Muralidharan/Contact - India

Directors: Naveen S. Bisht/Dir., CEO, Pres., Tsuyoshi Taira/Chmn., William Boller/Dir., Won-Gil Choe/Dir., Raj Jain/Co - Founder, CTO, Suresh R. Pillai/Dir., Pres.

Owners: Won-Gil Choe, Raj Jain/1.62%, Eric McAfee/5.66%, Ignite Ventures/7.23%, Insiders/14.79%, Pacesetter/ MVHC, Inc/7.28%, Apex Ventures/6.56%, Gautam Chanda/1.58%, Thomas Richtarich, Berg McAfee Companies, LLC/4.56%, Hari Hirani/1.05%, Tsuyoshi Taira/3.47%, William Boller, Naveen S. Bisht/5.43%

Financial Data: *Fiscal Year End:*12/31 *Latest Annual Data:* 12/31/2006

Year	Sales	Net Income
2006	$480,000	-$19,999,000
2005	NA	-$11,065,000
2004	NA	-$138,000

Curr. Assets:	$135,000	*Curr. Liab.:*	$27,614,000		
Plant, Equip.:	$42,000	*Total Liab.:*	$27,614,000	*Indic. Yr. Divd.:*	NA
Total Assets:	$3,734,000	*Net Worth:*	-$23,880,000	*Debt/ Equity:*	NA

NB Capital Corp

65 E 55th St., 31st Fl., New York, NY, 10022; *PH:* 1-212-632-8697

General		**Stock**	
Incorporation	MD	Price on:12/24/2007	$26.06
Employees	10	Stock Exchange	NYSE
Auditor	Deloitte & Touche LLP	Ticker Symbol	NA
Stk Agt	NA	Outstanding Shares	NA
Counsel	NA	E.P.S	NA
DUNS No.	NA	Shareholders	NA

Business: The groups principle activity is to invest in residential mortgages and other real estate properties. The group operates through three segments namely, personal and commercial, wealth management and financial markets. The group operates from United States and Canada.

Primary SIC and add'l.: 6798

CIK No: 0001049551

Subsidiaries: 1261095 Ontario Limited, 3562719 Canada Inc., 4166540 Canada Inc., 4166558 Canada Inc., 4166566 Canada Inc., Altamira Investment Services Inc., Assurances gnrales Banque Nationale Inc., CABN Investments Inc., FMI Acquisition Inc., Innocap Investment Management Inc., Natbank, National Association, NatBC Holding Corporation, Natcan Acquisition Holdings Inc., Natcan Holdings International Limited, Natcan Insurance Company Limited 34 Subsidiaries included in the Index

Officers: Donna Goral/50/Chmn., Pres., Principal Executive Officer, Monique Baillergeau/49/Dir., VP, Jean Dagenais/49/CFO, Hoda Abdelmessih/53/Dir., VP, Vincent Lima/50/Dir., VP

Directors: Donna Goral/50/Chmn., Pres., Principal Executive Officer, Christian Dube/51/Dir., Andre Belzile/46/Dir., Alain Michel/58/Dir., Monique Baillergeau/49/Dir., VP, Hoda Abdelmessih/53/Dir., VP, Vincent Lima/50/Dir., VP

Financial Data: *Fiscal Year End:*12/31 *Latest Annual Data:* 12/31/2006

Year	Sales	Net Income
2006	$33,044,000	$31,194,000
2005	$35,343,000	$33,345,000
2004	$36,322,000	$34,459,000

Curr. Assets:	$285,812,000	*Curr. Liab.:*	$409,000		
Plant, Equip.:	NA	*Total Liab.:*	$409,000	*Indic. Yr. Divd.:*	NA
Total Assets:	$479,617,000	*Net Worth:*	$479,208,000	*Debt/ Equity:*	NA

NB&T Financial Group Inc

48 N S St., Wilmington, OH, 45177; *PH:* 1-937-382-1441; *Fax:* 1-937-382-4385; *http://* www.nbtdirect.com; *Email:* nbt@nbtdirect.com

General		**Stock**	
Incorporation	OH	Price on:12/24/2007	$20.75
Employees	223	Stock Exchange	NDQ
Auditor	BKD LLP	Ticker Symbol	NA
Stk Agt	Illinois Stock Transfer Co	Outstanding Shares	3,230,000
Counsel	NA	E.P.S	$1.51
DUNS No.	NA	Shareholders	NA

Business: The group's principal activities are to provide a full range of banking and financial services to individual and corporate customers. The group acts as a holding company to the national bank and trust company, chartered under the laws of the United States. The primary business consists of accepting deposits, through various consumer and commercial deposit products and using such deposits to fund consumer loans, including automobile loans, loans secured by residential and non-residential real estate, commercial and agricultural loans. The group's wholly owned subsidiary, nb&t insurance agency inc sells a full line of insurance products, including property and casualty, life, health, and annuities.

Primary SIC and add'l.: 6712 6022

CIK No: 0000908837

Subsidiaries: NB&T Insurance Agency Group, Inc., NB&T Insurance Agency, Inc., NB&T Statutory Trust I, The National Bank and Trust Company

Officers: John J. Limbert/Pres., CEO - National Bank, Trust Company/$423,826.00, Ken Blendea/AVP, Bank Security Officer - Financial Services Division, National Bank, Trust Company, Sandra F. Waits/VP - Human Resources, National Bank, Trust Company, Jill Green/AVP - Technical Staff Support, Wealth Planning, National Bank, Trust Company, Walter H. Rowsey/Sr. VP, Sr. Credit Officer - National Bank, Trust Company, Kenneth Donaldson/VP - Investment, Financial Planning, Wealth Planning, National Bank, Trust Company, Thomas J. MacDonald/Sr. VP - Wealth Planning, National Bank, Trust Company, Janet Dixon/AVP, Personal Trust Administrator - Wealth Planning, National Bank, Trust Company, Richard A. Jones/VP - Business Development, Loan Division, National Bank, Trust Company, Kelly Ward/AVP - Hillsboro, Customer Relations Division, National Bank, Trust Company, Darrell L. Baumann/VP - Milford, Customer Relations Division, National Bank, Trust Company, Tracy L. Taylor/VP, Regional Mgr. - Customer Relations Division, National Bank, Trust Company, Mary Jane West/VP - Direct Sales, Customer Relations Division, National Bank, Trust Company, Kelli Crutcher/AVP - Mt. Orab, Customer Relations Division, National Bank, Trust Company, Sharon K. Wells/AVP - Batavia, Customer Relations Division, National Bank, Trust Company *(47 Officers included in Index)*

Directors: Timothy L. Smith/57/Chmn., Charlie Dehner/Dir., Craig S. Beam/Dir., Darlene Myers/Dir., Darleen M. Myers/Dir., Charles L. Dehner/Dir., Daniel A. Dibiasio/Dir., Jeffrey Lykins/Dir., Brooke Williams James/Dir., David G. Hawley/Dir., Robert A. Raizk/Dir.

Owners: Janet M. Williams/11.58%, Darleen M. Myers/0.28%, Beth Ellingwood/6.49%, Jeffery D. Lykins, Howard T. Witherby/1.63%, Craig F. Fortin/0.61%, Craig S. Beam, John J. Limbert/0.52%, Timothy L. Smith/2.98%, Andrew J. McCreanor/1.33%, Dana L. Williams/5.68%, Daniel A. DiBiasio/0.01%, Charles L. Dehner/2.86%, Brooke W. James/5.65%, Lynn W. Cowan/5.63% *(20 Owners included in Index)*

Financial Data: *Fiscal Year End:*12/31 *Latest Annual Data:* 12/31/2006

Year	Sales	Net Income
2006	$43,290,000	$1,856,000
2005	$41,253,000	$4,105,000
2004	$41,374,000	$4,954,000

Curr. Assets:	$22,648,000	*Curr. Liab.:*	$460,211,000	*P/E Ratio:*	17.89
Plant, Equip.:	$13,424,000	*Total Liab.:*	$496,959,000	*Indic. Yr. Divd.:*	$1.120
Total Assets:	$555,182,000	*Net Worth:*	$58,223,000	*Debt/ Equity:*	0.6311

NBT Bank

52 S Broad St., Norwich, NY, 13815; *PH:* 1-607-337-2265; *Fax:* 1-607-336-6545; *http://* www.nbtbancorp.com; *Email:* info@nbtbci.com

General		**Stock**	
Incorporation	DE	Price on:12/24/2007	$22.38
Employees	1,314	Stock Exchange	NDQ
Auditor	KPMG LLP	Ticker Symbol	NA
Stk Agt	American Stock Transfer & Trust Co.	Outstanding Shares	34,010,000
Counsel	Kowalczyk, Tolles Et Al	E.P.S	$1.59
DUNS No.	36-225-0391	Shareholders	NA

Business: The group's principal activity is to provide commercial banking and financial services. It accepts deposits and invests them primarily in loans, leases and marketable securities. The group's products and services include checking, savings, money market deposit accounts, consumer and home equity loans, agricultural lending, residential mortgage, trust and investment services. The services are provided to individuals, corporations and municipalities located in its market areas. The group's market area consists of the central and upstate New York and northeastern Pennsylvania region. As of 31-Dec-2003, it operated 72 divisional offices and 148 ATMs in New York and Pennsylvania.

Primary SIC and add'l.: 6021 6712

CIK No: 0000790359

Subsidiaries: CNBF Capital Trust 1, Hathaway Agency, Inc., NBT Bank, National Association, NBT Financial Services, Inc., NBT Statutory Trust I, NBT Statutory Trust II

Officers: Martin A. Dietrich/Pres., CEO - NBT Bank/$1,262,457.00, David E. Raven/45/Pres. - Retail Banking, NBT/$765,740.00, Jeffrey M. Levy/Exec. VP, Pres. - Commercial Banking, Capital Region Pres. - NBT Bank/$309,688.00

Directors: Ronald M. Bentley/Dir., Richard Chojnowski/Dir., Joseph G. Nasser/Dir., Michael J. Chewens/Dir., Joseph A. Santangelo/Dir., Michael H. Hutcherson/Dir., Janet H. Ingraham/Dir., William L. Owens/Dir., Paul D. Horger/Dir., Daryl R. Forsythe/Dir., Patricia T. Civil/Dir., Peter B. Gregory/Dir., John C. Mitchell/Dir., Michael M. Murphy/Dir., William C. Gumble/Dir. *(16 Directors included in Index)*

Owners: David E. Raven, William L. Owens, Michael J. Chewens, Jeffrey M. Levy, William C. Gumble, Paul D. Horger, John C. Mitchell, Michael H. Hutcherson, Michael M. Murphy, Joseph G. Nasser, Daryl R. Forsythe, Robert A. Wadsworth, Janet H. Ingraham, Joseph A. Santangelo, Richard Chojnowski *(19 Owners included in Index)*

Financial Data: *Fiscal Year End:*12/31 *Latest Annual Data:* 12/31/2006

Year	Sales	Net Income
2006	$338,346,000	$55,947,000
2005	$280,152,000	$52,438,000
2004	$251,068,000	$50,047,000

Curr. Assets:	$138,793,000	*Curr. Liab.:*	$4,141,646,000	*P/E Ratio:*	14.08
Plant, Equip.:	$66,982,000	*Total Liab.:*	$4,683,755,000	*Indic. Yr. Divd.:*	$0.800
Total Assets:	$5,087,572,000	*Net Worth:*	$403,817,000	*Debt/ Equity:*	1.1487

NBTY

90 Orville Dr., Bohemia, NY, 11716; *PH:* 1-631-567-9500; *Fax:* 1-631-567-7148; *http://* www.nbty.com

General		**Stock**	
Incorporation	DE	Price on:12/24/2007	$40.67
Employees	10,900	Stock Exchange	NYSE
Auditor	Pricewaterhousecoopers LLP	Ticker Symbol	NTY
Stk Agt	American Stock Transfer & Trust Co.	Outstanding Shares	67,360,000
Counsel	Irene Fisher	E.P.S	$2.54
DUNS No.	05-279-0318	Shareholders	NA

Business: The groups principle activities include manufacturing and distributing a broad line of nutritional supplements. The groups products are sold under the brand names Natures Bounty, Vitamin World, Puritans Pride, Holland and Barrett, Rexall, Osteo-Bi-Flex and Flex-a-min. The group operates from United States.

Primary SIC and add'l.: 2844 5961 5122 2834 5912

CIK No: 0000070793

Subsidiaries: Arco Pharmaceuticals, Carb Wise (USA), D&F Industries, De Tuinen, B.V., Health & Diet Centres Limited, Health & Diet Food Company Limited, Holland & Barrett Retail Limited, Hudson Co., Knox (a fictitious name of NBTY, Inc.), Le Naturiste J.M.B. Inc., Met-Rx Nutrition, Inc., Met-Rx USA, Inc., Nature Bounty de Mexico S. de R.L. de C.V., Natures Bounty, Inc., Natures Way Limited 42 Subsidiaries included in the Index

Officers: Scott Rudolph/Chmn., CEO, James P. Flaherty/Sr. VP - Marketing, Advertising, Michael Slade/Dir., Sr. VP - Strategic Planning, Sec., Harvey Kamil/CFO, Pres., William J. Shanahan/VP - Information Technology

Directors: Scott Rudolph/Chmn., CEO, Glenn Cohen/Dir., Murray Daly/Dir., Michael Slade/Dir., Sr. VP - Strategic Planning, Sec., Arthur Rudolph/Dir., Michael Ashner/Dir., Aram G. Garabedian/Dir., Peter White/Dir., Neil Koenig/Dir.

Owners: Scott Rudolph/11.70%, ESOP/3.10%, Harvey Kamil/2.40%, Michael L. Ashner, Barclay's Global Investors/5.20%, William J. Shanahan, Arthur Rudolph, James P. Flaherty, Insiders/17.00%, Neuberger Berman, LLC/6.30%, Glenn Cohen, Peter J. White, Michael C. Slade/2.30%, Neil H. Koenig, Aram G. Garabedian

Financial Data: *Fiscal Year End:*09/30 *Latest Annual Data:* 9/30/2006

Year	Sales	Net Income
2006	$1,880,222,000	$111,785,000
2005	$1,737,187,000	$78,137,000
2004	$1,652,031,000	$111,849,000

Curr. Assets:	$602,352,000	**Curr. Liab.:**	$210,639,000	**P/E Ratio:**	16.01
Plant, Equip.:	$309,437,000	**Total Liab.:**	$464,878,000	**Indic. Yr. Divd.:**	NA
Total Assets:	$1,304,310,000	**Net Worth:**	$839,432,000	**Debt/ Equity:**	NA

NCAL Bancorp CA

145 S Fairfax Ave., Los Angeles, CA, 90036; ***PH:*** 1-323-655-6001; ***Fax:*** 1-323-931-7031; ***http://*** www.nbcal.com; ***Email:*** request@nbcal.com

General - Incorporation	NA	**Stock**- Price on:12/24/2007	$35.25
Employees	NA	Stock Exchange	OTC
Auditor	NA	Ticker Symbol	NCAL
Stk Agt	U.S. Stock Transfer Corp	Outstanding Shares	2,280,000
Counsel	NA	E.P.S.	NA
DUNS No.	NA	Shareholders	NA

Business: The group's principle activity is to provide information related services. The group operates from United States.

Primary SIC and add'l.: 6712 6021

CIK No:

Officers: Barry W. Uzel/Dir., CEO, Pres., Richard P. Ritter/CFO, Exec. VP, Scott G. Peterson/Exec. VP, Chief Credit Officer, Timothy J. Herles/Sr. VP, Mgr. - Business Banking, John J.G. Batiste/Regional VP, Adrienne Caldwell/Regional VP, Anthony D. Kourounis/Regional VP, Normand F. Leduc/Regional VP, Patty McAdams/Regional VP

Directors: Barry W. Uzel/Dir., CEO, Pres.

NCI Building Systems Inc

10943 N Sam Houston Pkwy. W, Houston, TX, 77064; ***PH:*** 1-281-897-7788; ***Fax:*** 1-281-477-9674; ***http://*** www.ncilp.com; ***Email:*** info@ncilp.com

General - Incorporation	DE	**Stock**- Price on:12/24/2007	$50.29
Employees	6,010	Stock Exchange	NYSE
Auditor	Ernst & Young LLP	Ticker Symbol	NCS
Stk Agt	Computershare Investor Services LLC	Outstanding Shares	20,020,000
Counsel	Gardere, Wynne Sewell LLP	E.P.S.	$3.07
DUNS No.	13-023-4529	Shareholders	NA

Business: The groups principle activities include manufacturing and marketing metal products. The group also provides metal coil coating services for non-residential construction applications. The group operates through three segments namely metal components, engineered building systems and metal coil coating. The group operates from United States.

Primary SIC and add'l.: 3448

CIK No: 0000883902

Subsidiaries: A&S Building Systems, L.P., Building Systems de Mexico, S.A. de C.V., Metal Building Components, L.P., Metal Coaters of California, Inc., NCI Building Systems, L.P., NCI Group, L.P., NCI Holding Corp., NCI Operating Corp., Steelbuilding.com, Inc.

Officers: Norman C. Chambers/CEO, Pres., Kenneth W. Maddox/Exec. VP - Administration, Charles W. Dickinson/Pres. - Metal Building Components Division, Frances Powell Hawes/CFO, Exec. VP, Treasurer - NCI, Mark W. Dobbins/Pres. - Engineered Building Systems Division, Marla Endler/Customer Service, Russell Ford/Customer Service, Todd R. Moore/VP, General Counsel, Sec., Eric J. Brown/CIO, VP, Kelly R. Ginn/Exec. VP - Operations, Keith E. Fischer/Pres. - all Robertson, Ceco Divisions, Bradley D. Robeson/Pres. - Metal Coil Coating Division, Mark E. Johnson/VP, Controller, Chief Accounting Officer, Mario Sanchez/Customer Service

Directors: A. R. Ginn/Chmn., John K. Sterling/Dir., William D. Breedlove/Dir., Philip J. Hawk/Dir., Bernard W. Pieper/Dir., Gary L. Forbes/Dir., Max L. Lukens/Dir., George Martinez/Dir.

Owners: Kenneth W. Maddox, Friess Associates, LLC/5.48%, Norman C. Chambers/0.82%, Barclays Global Investors; Barclays Global Fund/5.00%, William D. Breedlove, Kelly R. Ginn, Bernard W. Pieper, Gary L. Forbes, FMR Corp./15.35%, Frances Powell Hawes, Philip J. Hawk, Dimensional Fund Advisors Inc./6.13%, Max L. Lukens, Lord, Abbett & Co. LLC/9.87%, Insiders/4.70% *(19 Owners included in Index)*

Financial Data: *Fiscal Year End:*10/29 *Latest Annual Data:* 10/28/2007

Year	Sales	Net Income
2007	$1,624,273,000	$63,729,000
2006	$1,570,482,000	$73,796,000
2005	$1,130,066,000	$55,951,000

Curr. Assets:	$274,818,000	**Curr. Liab.:**	$147,581,000	**P/E Ratio:**	16.02
Plant, Equip.:	$185,687,000	**Total Liab.:**	$381,680,000	**Indic. Yr. Divd.:**	NA
Total Assets:	$782,857,000	**Net Worth:**	$401,177,000	**Debt/ Equity:**	1.0560

NCI Inc

11730 Plz. America Dr., Reston, VA, 20190; ***PH:*** 1-703-707-6900; ***Fax:*** 1-703-707-6901; ***http://*** www.nciinc.com; ***Email:*** contactus@nciinc.com

General - Incorporation	DE	**Stock**- Price on:12/24/2007	$16.56
Employees	1,400	Stock Exchange	NDQ
Auditor	Ernst& Young LLP	Ticker Symbol	NCOG
Stk Agt	American Stock Transfer & Trust Co.	Outstanding Shares	13,330,000
Counsel	NA	E.P.S.	$0.92
DUNS No.	NA	Shareholders	NA

Business: The groups principle activity is to provide information technology services and solutions. The groups services include network engineering, information assurance, systems development and integration and enterprise systems management. Specific customers of the group include United States Army, United States Air Force, United States Transportation Command, National Guard Bureau, Department of Transportation, Department of Energy, National Aeronautics and Space Administration. The group operates from the United States. The group's quarterly revenue for September 2007 was 85.21 millions of USD.

Primary SIC and add'l.: 7371 7379 7376 7389 7373

CIK No: 0001334478

Subsidiaries: NCI Information Systems, Inc, Scientific & Engineering Solutions, Inc.

Officers: Charles K. Narang/Chmn., CEO, Terry Glasgow/Dir., COO, Pres., Judith L. Bjornaas/Sr. VP, CFO, Linda Allan/Exec. VP - Corporate Strategic Program Development, Michele Cappello/General Counsel, Sec., John R. Grobmeier/Sr. VP, GM - Army Programs Group, Karl Leatham/CTO, VP, Maureen Crystal/VP - Investor Relations, Christopher M. Bishop/Sr. VP - Business Development, Capture Management, Clarence D. Johnson/Sr. VP, GM - Army Programs Group, William M. Parker/Pres. - Karta Technologies, Inc, GM - Air Force Group, Norman W. Pierce/VP - Human Resources, Administration, Frederic A. Zafran/Sr. VP, GM - Civilian Programs Group

Directors: Charles K. Narang/Chmn., CEO, Dan Young/Dir., Member - Compensation - Nominating, Governance, Terry Glasgow/Dir., COO, Pres., Steve Waechter/Dir., James P. Allen/Dir., John E. Lawler/Dir., Paul V. Lombardi/Dir., Pat McMahon/Dir.

Owners: SunTrust Banks, Inc./6.80%, Wellington Trust Company, NA/5.80%, Fidelity Management& Research Corp./7.70%, Michele R. Cappello, Insiders/100.00%, Bank of America Corporation/5.40%, Paul V. Lombardi, Charles K. Narang/100.00%, Charles K. Narang/6.80%, Judith L. Bjornaas, Oppenheimer Funds Inc./7.20%, Terry W. Glasgow, James P. Allen, Patrick J. McMahon, Neuberger Berman, Inc./6.70% *(19 Owners included in Index)*

Financial Data: *Fiscal Year End:*12/31 *Latest Annual Data:* 12/31/2006

Year	Sales	Net Income
2006	$218,340,000	$9,259,000
2005	$191,319,000	$12,315,000
2004	$171,253,000	$6,128,000

Curr. Assets:	$82,729,000	**Curr. Liab.:**	$36,409,000		
Plant, Equip.:	$4,925,000	**Total Liab.:**	$40,213,000	**Indic. Yr. Divd.:**	NA
Total Assets:	$106,799,000	**Net Worth:**	$66,586,000	**Debt/ Equity:**	NA

NCR Corp

1700 S Patterson Blvd., Dayton, OH, 45479; ***PH:*** 1-937-445-1936; ***Fax:*** 1-937-445-5541; ***http://*** www.ncr.com

General - Incorporation	MD	**Stock**- Price on:12/24/2007	$52.49
Employees	28,900	Stock Exchange	NDQ
Auditor	PricewaterhouseCoopers LLP	Ticker Symbol	NCST
Stk Agt	Mellon Investor Services LLC	Outstanding Shares	179,900,000
Counsel	NA	E.P.S.	$2.17
DUNS No.	00-131-6090	Shareholders	NA

Business: The group's principle activity is to provide innovative technology imaginatively to solve the customers business problems. The group operates through five segments namely financial self service, peyment and imaging soloution, and point of sale and kiosk solutions. The group operates from United States.

Primary SIC and add'l.: 5045 7379 7372 7373

CIK No: 0000070866

Subsidiaries: 4Front Group UK Ltd., 4Front Networks Limited, 4Front Technologies SA France, 4Soft Limited, Afrique Investments Ltd., Compris Technologies, Inc., Compu Search Sdn Bhd, Data Pathing Incorporated, Data Pathing LLC, Data Processing Printing and Supplies Limited, DecisionPoint Applications, Inc., EPNCR (Malaysia) Sdn. Bhd., Eurographic Industries Limited, First Level Technology LLC, Fluiditi Ltd. 131 Subsidiaries included in the Index

Officers: William Nuti/Chmn., CEO, Pres. - NCR Corporation, James M. Ringler/62/Chmn. - Teradata Corporation, Michael Koehler/55/Sr. VP - Teradata Division/$2,064,356.00, Christine Wallace/Sr. VP - Worldwide Customer Services/$1,285,233.00, Eric A. Berg/Sr. VP, Chief Administrative Officer, Lorena Gandolfini/Worldwide Customer Services, Italy, Lorraine Willson/Worldwide Customer Services, Canada, Winnie Sze/Worldwide Customer Services, Greater China Area, Alan Chow/CTO, Emily Riojas/Retail, Hospitality, Self, Service, Mel Walter/VP - Self, Service Business Development, Rakesh Aulaya/Worldwide Customer Services, India, Janet Brewer/VP - Corporate Communications, Nancy Berry/Worldwide Customer Services, United States, Lorraine Russell/Contact - Financial Solution *(32 Officers included in Index)*

Directors: William Nuti/Chmn., CEO, Pres. - NCR Corporation, Edward P. Boykin/Dir., Gary Daichendt/Dir., Mark P. Frissora/Dir., Linda Fayne Levinson/Dir., Victor L. Lund/60/Dir., C. K. Prahalad/Dir., William S. Stavropoulos/68/Dir.

Owners: William Stavropoulos, Christine Wallace, Victor L. Lund, Dodge& Cox/7.70%, Peter Bocian, James M. Ringler, Mark Frissora, FMR Corp/12.39%, Edward P. Boykin, C. K. Prahalad, Gary Daichendt, Malcolm Collins, Insiders, Linda Fayne Levinson, William R. Nuti *(16 Owners included in Index)*

Financial Data: *Fiscal Year End:*12/31 *Latest Annual Data:* 12/31/2006

Year	Sales	Net Income
2006	$6,142,000,000	$382,000,000
2005	$6,028,000,000	$529,000,000
2004	$5,984,000,000	$290,000,000

Curr. Assets:	$3,332,000,000	**Curr. Liab.:**	$1,770,000,000	**P/E Ratio:**	25.48
Plant, Equip.:	$378,000,000	**Total Liab.:**	$3,326,000,000	**Indic. Yr. Divd.:**	NA
Total Assets:	$5,227,000,000	**Net Worth:**	$1,881,000,000	**Debt/ Equity:**	NA

NCT Group Inc

375 Bridgeport Ave., 2nd Floor, Shelton, CT, 06484; ***PH:*** 1-203-944-9533; ***Fax:*** 1-203-944-9733; ***http://*** www.nct-active.com; ***Email:*** sales@nctclearspeech.com

General		Stock	
Incorporation	DE	Price on:12/24/2007	NA
Employees	58	Stock Exchange	OTC
Auditor	Eisner LLP	Ticker Symbol	NCTIE
Stk Agt	American Stock Transfer & Trust Co.	Outstanding Shares	NA
Counsel	NA	E.P.S	NA
DUNS No.	13-178-0892	Shareholders	NA

Business: The group's principal activities are to develop and market speech and communications applications. These applications integrate noise and echo cancellation technologies and utilize sound and signal waves to reduce noise, improve signal-to-noise ratio and enhance sound quality. The group's systems are designed for integration of products, which serves the transportation, manufacturing, commercial, consumer products and communication industries.

Primary SIC and add'l.: 3679 4841

CIK No: 0000722051

Subsidiaries: 2020 Science Limited, Advancel Logic Corporation, Artera (UK) Limited, Artera Group, Inc., Chaplin Patents Holding Company, Inc, ConnectClearly.com, Inc., Distributed Media Corporation, Distributed Media Corporation International Ltd., Distributed Media Corporation Ltd., DMC Cinema, Inc., DMC New York, Inc., Hospital Radio Network, Inc., Midcore Software Limited, Midcore Software, Inc., NCT Audio Products, Inc. 22 Subsidiaries included in the Index

Officers: Cy E. Hammond/Sr. VP, CFO, Treasurer

Curr. Assets:	$1,545,000	Curr. Liab.:	$138,352,000		
Plant, Equip.:	$849,000	Total Liab.:	$143,379,000	Indic. Yr. Divd.:	NA
Total Assets:	$4,720,000	Net Worth:	-$147,314,000	Debt/ Equity:	NA

NDS Group Plc

3500 Hyland Ave., Costa Mesa, CA, 92626; *PH:* 1-714-434-2100; *Fax:* 1-714-434-2474; *http://* www.nds.com

General		Stock	
Incorporation	UK	Price on:12/24/2007	$49.84
Employees	2,989	Stock Exchange	NYSE
Auditor	Ernst & Young LLP	Ticker Symbol	NOA
Stk Agt	Lloyds TSB Registrars	Outstanding Shares	57,570,000
Counsel	NA	E.P.S	$2.52
DUNS No.	NA	Shareholders	NA

Business: The group's principal activities are the provision of conditional access, broadcast control software and related products and services for the management, control and secure distribution of entertainment and information to televisions and personal computers. It also provides consulting, system design, integration, and maintenance support services to digital broadcasters and content providers. It also has started to provide interactive TV applications and data broadcasting solutions.

Primary SIC and add'l.: 7373 7372 7379 7371

CIK No: 0001098074

Subsidiaries: Digi-Media Vision Limited, NDS Americas, Inc., NDS Asia Pacific Limited, NDS Asia Pacific Pty Limited, NDS Beijing Information Technology Company, NDS Denmark A/S, NDS Limited, NDS Marketing Israel Limited, NDS Services Pay-TV Technology Private Limited, NDS Technologies France SAS, NDS Technologies Israel Limited, News Datacom Limited, NT Media Limited, Orbis Technology Limited, Svp La LLC

Officers: Abraham Peled/Chmn., CEO/$4,499,976.00, Alexander Gersh/Dir., CFO/$2,159,869.00, Raffi Kesten/Dir., COO/$1,224,142.00, Cedric Ros/Dir. - Human Resources - France, Linda Rudolph/Contact - Human Resources, USA, Lina Joergensen/Human Resources Advisor - United Kingdom, Yael Fainaro/Investor Relations Contact

Directors: Abraham Peled/Chmn., CEO, Lawrence A. Jacobs/Dir., Peter J. Powers/Dir., Nathan Gantcher/Dir., Arthur M. Siskind/Dir., Roger W. Einiger/Dir., Alexander Gersh/Dir., CFO, David F. Devoe/Dir., Raffi Kesten/Dir., COO

Owners: FMR Corp/6.70%, Renaissance Technologies Corp./6.00%, News Corporation/100.00%, Abe Peled, Nathan Gantcher, Raffi Kesten, Janus Capital Management LLC/10.70%, Insiders/1.40%, Peter J. Powers, AKO Capital LLP/10.00%, Alexander Gersh, Roger W. Einiger, Egerton Capital Limited Partnership/9.00%

Financial Data: *Fiscal Year End:*06/30 *Latest Annual Data:* 06/30/2007

Year	Sales	Net Income
2007	$709,492,000	$135,727,000
2006	$600,123,000	$100,950,000
2005	$556,330,000	$73,998,000

Curr. Assets:	$701,235,000	Curr. Liab.:	$161,151,000	P/E Ratio:	21.39
Plant, Equip.:	$46,239,000	Total Liab.:	$329,427,000	Indic. Yr. Divd.:	NA
Total Assets:	$897,121,000	Net Worth:	$567,694,000	Debt/ Equity:	NA

NEC Corp

6535 N State Hwy. 161, Irving, TX, 75039; *PH:* 1-214-262-2000; *Fax:* 1-214-262-2586; *http://* www.nec.com

General		Stock	
Incorporation	Japan	Price on:12/24/2007	$5.129
Employees	154,786	Stock Exchange	NDQ
Auditor	Ernst & Young Shinnihon	Ticker Symbol	NITE
Stk Agt	Sumitomo Trust & Banking Co Ltd	Outstanding Shares	2,030,000,000
Counsel	NA	E.P.S	$0.04
DUNS No.	69-054-1685	Shareholders	NA

Business: The group's principal activities are to provide systems, components, services and integrated solutions for computing and communications applications to corporations and public sectors. The group operates through three principal segments: nec it solutions develops, designs, manufactures and sells computer systems, Internet-related services, support and software to government agencies and enterprises. Nec networks provides Internet solutions systems such as w-cdma mobile communications systems to the broadband and communication service providers. Nec electron devices include develops, designs, manufactures and sells semiconductors, displays, electronic components and other electron devices such as color lcds, etc to equipment manufacturers. The group's manufacturing facilities are located in Japan, the United States of America, Europe and Asia and markets products throughout the world.

Primary SIC and add'l.: 7377 3571 3577 3679 7373 3669 3674

CIK No: 0000072127

Subsidiaries: NEC (UK)Ltd., NEC Access Technica, Ltd., NEC Business Coordination Centre (Singapore) Pte. Ltd., NEC Computers International B.V., NEC Electronics (Europe) GmbH, NEC Electronics America, Inc., NEC Electronics Corporation, NEC Fielding, Ltd., NEC Mobiling, Ltd., NEC Nexsolutions, Ltd., NEC Personal Products, Ltd., NEC Saitama, Ltd., NEC Soft, Ltd., NEC Solutions (America), Inc., NEC System Integration & Construction, Ltd. 16 Subsidiaries included in the Index

Officers: Minoru Terao/Sr. VP, Yukihiro Fujiyoshi/Assoc. Sr. VP, Takemitsu Kunio/Assoc. Sr. VP, Tazoh Ogawa/Assoc. Sr. VP, Junji Yasui/Assoc. Sr. VP, Kazuo Tsuzuki/Assoc. Sr. VP, Kunitomo Matsuoka/Sr. VP, Takao Ono/60/Dir., Sr. VP, Toshikazu Morikawa/Dir., Assoc. Sr. VP, Kiyoshi Nakanishi/Assoc. Sr. VP, Takuji Tomiyama/Assoc. Sr. VP, Masaru Murakami/Assoc. Sr. VP, Takayuki Okada/Assoc. Sr. VP, Fujio Okada/Assoc. Sr. VP, Shigeki Satake/Assoc. Sr. VP *(49 Officers included in Index)*

Directors: Hajime Sasaki/72/Chmn., Toshio Morikawa/75/Dir., Yoshinari Hara/65/Dir., Sawako Nohara/50/Dir., Takao Ono/60/Dir., Sr. VP, Toshikazu Morikawa/Dir., Assoc. Sr. VP, Kenji Miyahara/Dir., Hideaki Takahashi/Dir., Tsutomu Nakamura/60/Dir., Sr. VP, Kazumasa Fujie/64/Dir., Sr. Exec. VP, Saburo Takizawa/60/Dir., Exec. VP, Masatoshi Aizawa/62/Dir., Exec. VP, Kaoru Yano/64/Dir., Pres., Konosuke Kashima/62/Dir., Exec. VP, Toshimitsu Iwanami/59/Dir., Sr. VP - Domestic Sales Business Unit

Financial Data: *Fiscal Year End:*03/31 *Latest Annual Data:* 3/31/2004

Year	Sales	Net Income
2004	$48,120,445,000	$390,241,000
2003	$40,243,646,000	-$203,831,000
2002	$39,085,590,000	-$2,340,150,000

Curr. Assets:	$20,232,682,000	Curr. Liab.:	$16,554,577,000	P/E Ratio:	21.39
Plant, Equip.:	$7,317,033,000	Total Liab.:	$29,559,327,000	Indic. Yr. Divd.:	NA
Total Assets:	$38,421,249,000	Net Worth:	$6,758,870,000	Debt/ Equity:	NA

Neenah Paper Inc

3460 Preston Ridge Rd., Ste. 600, Alpharetta, GA, 30005; *PH:* 1-678-566-6500; *Fax:* 1-678-518-3284; *http://* www.neenah.com

General		Stock	
Incorporation	DE	Price on:12/24/2007	$42.89
Employees	1,900	Stock Exchange	NYSE
Auditor	Deloitte & Touche LLP	Ticker Symbol	NPK
Stk Agt	Computershare Trust Co	Outstanding Shares	14,810,000
Counsel	NA	E.P.S	$5.12
DUNS No.	NA	Shareholders	NA

Business: The group's principal activities are manufacturing and distribution of a wide range of premium and specialty paper grades, and bleached kraft pulp. The three primary segments of the company: fine paper, technical paper, and pulp business. The fine paper business produces premium writing, text, cover, and specialty papers used in corporate annual reports, corporate identity packages, invitations, personal stationery, and high-end packaging. The technical paper business produces durable, saturated, and coated base papers for various end users. It also produces and sells bleached pulp, primarily for use in the manufacture of tissue and writing papers. The company customers include authorized paper distributors, converters, specialty businesses, tape, label, abrasive, medical packaging, and heat transfer technical paper markets. The company produces approximately 700,000 metric tons of pulp annually, and rights to harvest wood from 5.9 million acres of Canadian timberlands. The company is based in Alpharetta, Georgia, and has manufacturing operations in Wisconsin, Michigan and in the Canadian provinces of Ontario and Nova Scotia. The company brands include Classic, Classic Crest, Environment, Neenah, Kimdura,and Munising LP. The Neenah Paper logo is a Registered Trademark of Neenah Paper Inc. In 2004, this stand-alone company was created from Kimberly-Clark's fine paper, technical paper and pulp operations. On 2/12/2004, this spin-off company was listed at the New York Stock Exchange.

Primary SIC and add'l.: 2621

CIK No: 0001296435

Subsidiaries: Neenah and Menasha Water Power Company, Neenah Paper Company of Canada, Nova Scotia, Neenah Paper Michigan, Inc., Quality Systems Inc

Officers: Sean T. Erwin/56/Chmn., CEO, Pres., James R. Piedmonte/51/Sr. VP - Operations, Steven S. Heinrichs/40/Sr. VP, General Counsel, Sec., Bonnie C. Lind/49/Sr. VP, CFO, Treasurer, Bill McCarthy/VP - Financial Analysis - Investor Relations, Dennis P. Runsten/Pres. - Technical Products, US, Walter M. Haegler/MD - Neenah Germany

Directors: Sean T. Erwin/56/Chmn., CEO, Pres., Stephen M. Wood/61/Dir., Edward D. Grzedzinski/53/Dir., Mary Ann Leeper/67/Dir., Timothy S. Lucas/61/Dir., Philip C. Moore/54/Dir., John F. McGovern/61/Dir.

Owners: Steven S. Heinrichs, Timothy S. Lucas, John F. McGovern, Bonnie C. Lind, William K. OConnor, Stephen M. Wood, Philip C. Moore, Mary Ann Leeper, James R. Piedmonte, Edward Grzedzinski, Insiders/4.10%, Sean T. Erwin/1.90%

Financial Data: *Fiscal Year End:*12/31 *Latest Annual Data:* 12/31/2006

Year	Sales	Net Income
2006	$594,300,000	$62,500,000
2005	$733,400,000	-$29,700,000
2004	$772,100,000	-$26,400,000

Curr. Assets:	$222,400,000	Curr. Liab.:	$129,500,000	P/E Ratio:	8.38
Plant, Equip.:	$355,600,000	Total Liab.:	$559,800,000	Indic. Yr. Divd.:	$0.400
Total Assets:	$744,700,000	Net Worth:	$184,900,000	Debt/ Equity:	1.7457

Neffs Bancorp Inc

5629 RtE 873, Neffs, PA, 18065; *PH:* 1-610-767-3875; *Fax:* 1-610-767-1890; *http://* www.neffsnatl.com

General		Stock	
Incorporation	PA	Price on:12/24/2007	$263
Employees	27	Stock Exchange	OTC
Auditor	Carlin, Charron & Rosen LLP	Ticker Symbol	NEFB
Stk Agt	NA	Outstanding Shares	NA
Counsel	NA	E.P.S	$13.84
DUNS No.	NA	Shareholders	NA

Business: The group's principal activity is to provide a broad range of retail banking services. The products and services of the group include free checking personal checking accounts and business checking accounts, regular savings accounts, interest checking accounts, overdraft checking protection, fixed rate certificates of deposits, individual retirement accounts, club accounts and safe deposit facilities. The group also provides full range of lending activities including commercial construction and real estate loans.

Primary SIC and add'l.: 6022 6712

CIK No: 0000797838

Officers: John J. Remaley/Dir., CEO, Pres./$1,000.00, Herman P. Snyder/Chmn., VP, Kevin A. Schmidt/Dir., Treasurer/$97,355.00, Michael J. Bailey/COO - Cashier, The Neffs National Bank, Carol L. Jones/Operations Officer, Assist. Cashier - Neffs National Bank, David C. Matulevich/Sec.

Directors: John J. Remaley/Dir., CEO, Pres., Herman P. Snyder/Chmn., VP, John F. Sharkey/Dir., Duane A. Schleicher/Dir., Mary Ann Wagner/Dir., John F. Simock/Dir., Robert B. Heintzelman/Dir., Kevin A. Schmidt/Dir., Treasurer

Owners: Carol L. Jones/0.01%, Insiders/19.58%, Michael J. Bailey/0.01%, Herman P. Snyder/6.84%, Duane A. Schleicher/1.12%, John F. Sharkey, Mary Ann Wagner/3.05%, William F. and Alma P. Deibert/5.86%, John J. Remaley/5.53%, John F. Simock/0.86%, Robert B. Heintzelman/1.10%, Kevin A. Schmidt/0.51%, CEDE & Co.3/15.13%

Financial Data: ***Fiscal Year End:*** 12/31 ***Latest Annual Data:*** 12/31/2006

Year	Sales	Net Income
2006	$11,249,000	$2,823,000
2005	$10,730,000	$3,072,000
2004	$10,315,000	$3,205,000

Curr. Assets:	$2,345,000	***Curr. Liab.:***	$173,458,000	***P/E Ratio:***	19.00
Plant, Equip.:	$2,505,000	***Total Liab.:***	$174,654,000	***Indic. Yr. Divd.:***	NA
Total Assets:	$215,876,000	***Net Worth:***	$41,222,000	***Debt/ Equity:***	NA

Nektar Therapeutics

201 Industrial Rd., San Carlos, CA, 94070; ***PH:*** 1-650-631-3100; ***Fax:*** 1-650-631-3150; ***http://*** www.nektar.com; ***Email:*** nektarsc@nektar.com

General - Incorporation DE	***Stock*** - Price on:12/24/2007 NA
Employees 793	Stock Exchange NYSE
Auditor Ernst & Young LLP	Ticker Symbol NLC
Stk Agt Mellon Investor Services LLC	Outstanding Shares 91,680,000
Counsel Cooley Godward LLP	E.P.S. -$1.21
DUNS No. 78-329-6023	Shareholders NA

Business: The group's principal activity is to provide a portfolio of technologies and expertise for pharmaceutical partners to improve drug. The technologies are designed to improve either the performance of a drug molecule or how the drug is delivered. The group operates in three technology platforms. Advanced peglation technology is designed to enhance the efficacy and performance of most drug classes including macromolecules such as peptides and proteins along with small molecules and other drugs. Pulmonary technology enables the efficient and reproducible deep lung delivery of particles and greater lung deposition in a single breath. Supercritical fluid technology uses substances such as carbon dioxide at elevated temperatures and pressures as non-solvents to control the formation of powder particles for a wide variety of chemical substances. The group has international operations in the United Kingdom and other European countries.

Primary SIC and add'l.: 8731 2834

CIK No: 0000906709

Subsidiaries: Aerogen, Inc., Inhale Therapeutic Systems Deutschland GmbH, Nektar Therapeutics (India) Pvt. Ltd, Nektar Therapeutics AL, Nektar Therapeutics UK, Ltd.

Officers: Howard W. Robin/Dir., CEO, Pres., Tim Harkness/Sr. VP - Finance, CFO, David Johnston/Sr. VP - Research, Development/$701,947.00, Truc Le/Sr. VP - Operations, Corporate Quality, Mike Simms/Sr. VP - Operations, Tim Warner/Sr. VP - Investor Relations, Corporate Affairs, Stephan Herrera/Sr. Dir. - Investor Relations, Corporate Affairs, Timothy A. Harkness/Sr. VP, CFO, Nevan Elam/Sr. VP - Corporate Operations, General Counsel, Sec./$649,598.00, John S. Patton/Dir., Co - Founder, Chief Scientific Officer/$822,397.00, Hoyoung Huh/COO, Head - Pegylation Business Unit, Christopher J. Searcy/Sr. VP - Corporate Development, Louis Drapeau/63/Sr. VP - Finance/$669,372.00, Jennifer Ruddock/Assoc Dir. - Corporate Communications, Gil M. Labrucherie/General Counsel, Sec. *(17 Officers included in Index)*

Directors: Michael A. Brown/Dir., Joseph J. Krivulka/Dir., John S. Patton/Dir., Co - Founder, Chief Scientific Officer, Christopher A. Kuebler/Dir., Robert B. Chess/Dir., Irwin Lerner/Dir., Susan Wang/Dir., Roy A. Whitfield/Dir., Lutz Lingnau/Dir.

Owners: Nevan C. Elam, Louis Drapeau, Robert B. Chess/1.24%, David Johnston, OppenheimerFunds, Inc./16.54%, Joseph J. Krivulka, TIAA-CREF Investment Management, LLC/6.30%, Wells Fargo& Company/5.86%, Roy A. Whitfield, John S. Patton, Christopher A. Kuebler, Susan Wang, Michael A. Brown, Irwin Lerner

Financial Data: ***Fiscal Year End:*** 12/31 ***Latest Annual Data:*** 12/31/2006

Year	Sales	Net Income
2006	$217,718,000	-$154,761,000
2005	$126,279,000	-$185,111,000
2004	$114,270,000	-$101,886,000

Curr. Assets:	$535,039,000	***Curr. Liab.:***	$165,314,000		
Plant, Equip.:	$133,812,000	***Total Liab.:***	$541,117,000	***Indic. Yr. Divd.:***	NA
Total Assets:	$768,177,000	***Net Worth:***	$227,060,000	***Debt/ Equity:***	1.5883

Nelnet Inc

121 S 13th St., Ste. 201, Lincoln, NE, 68508; ***PH:*** 1-402-458-2370; ***Fax:*** 1-402-458-2399; ***http://*** www.nelnet.net

General - Incorporation NE	***Stock*** - Price on:12/24/2007 $25.79
Employees 4,000	Stock Exchange NDQ
Auditor KPMG LLP	Ticker Symbol NOBH
Stk Agt Mellon Investor Services LLC	Outstanding Shares 49,600,000
Counsel NA	E.P.S. $0.00
DUNS No. 13-496-0447	Shareholders NA

Business: The groups principle activity is to provide education planning, and financing products and services to students, families and schools nationwide. The groups services include a range of pre-college, in-college, and post-college products and services to students, families, schools and financial institutions. The group operates from United States.

Primary SIC and add'l.: 6141

CIK No: 0001258602

Subsidiaries: 5280 Solutions, LLC, American Card Services, Inc., Charter Account Systems, Inc., Chela Education Funding, Inc., ClassCredit, Inc., College Bound Loans, Inc., EDULINX Canada Corporation, EFS Finance Co., EMT Corp., FACTS Management Co., FirstMark Services, LLC, Foresite Solutions, Inc., Idaho Financial Associates, Inc., infiNET Integrated Solutions, Inc., InTuition, Inc. 52 Subsidiaries included in the Index

Officers: Michael S. Dunlap/44/Chmn., CEO, David A. Bottegal/51/CEO - Nelnet's Education Services Division, David J. Byrnes/57/CEO - Nelnet Enrollment Solutions, Jeffrey R. Noordhoek/42/Pres., Evan Roth/47/Chief Learning Officer, William J. Munn/40/Chief Legal Officer, Sec., Corporate Governance Officer, General Counsel, Ben Kiser/Dir. - Corporate Communications, Investor Relations, Todd M. Eicher/38/Chief Merger, Acquisition Officer, Raymond J. Ciarvella/51/Pres. - 5280 Solutions, Cheryl E. Watson/47/Chief Communications Officer, Matthew D. Hall/48/COO - Nelnet Education Services, Terry J. Heimes/44/CFO, Edward P. Martinez/54/Exec. Dir., Corporate Counsel

Directors: Michael S. Dunlap/44/Chmn., CEO, Stephen F. Butterfield/56/Vice Chmn., Arturo Moreno/62/Dir., James P. Abel/57/Dir., Brian J. O'Connor/52/Dir., James H. Vanhorn/56/Dir., Michael Reardon/55/Dir., Don R. Bouc/61/Dir., Thomas E. Henning/55/Dir.

Owners: Brian J. OConnor, Arturo R. Moreno, Jeffery R. Noordhoek, Edward P. Martinez, Todd M. Eicher, Stephen F. Butterfield, James P. Abel, Cheryl E. Watson, Insiders, Stephen F. Butterfield, James H. Van Horn, Terry J. Heimes, Raymond J. Ciarvella, William J. Munn, David A. Bottegal *(29 Owners included in Index)*

Financial Data: ***Fiscal Year End:*** 12/31 ***Latest Annual Data:*** 12/31/2006

Year	Sales	Net Income
2006	$1,881,997,000	$68,155,000
2005	$1,233,389,000	$181,122,000
2004	$777,305,000	$149,179,000

Curr. Assets:	$2,216,586,000	***Curr. Liab.:***	$273,768,000	***P/E Ratio:***	43.71
Plant, Equip.:	$67,924,000	***Total Liab.:***	$26,125,023,000	***Indic. Yr. Divd.:***	$0.280
Total Assets:	$26,796,873,000	***Net Worth:***	$671,850,000	***Debt/ Equity:***	43.4391

Nelx Inc

300 Summers St., Ste. 970, Charleston, WV, 25301; ***PH:*** 1-304-343-8171

General - Incorporation KS	***Stock*** - Price on:12/24/2007 $0.025
Employees 7	Stock Exchange NA
Auditor Malin, Bergquist & Co., LLP	Ticker Symbol NA
Stk Agt Mountain Share Transfer	Outstanding Shares 157,000,000
Counsel NA	E.P.S. -$0.016
DUNS No. 88-347-2912	Shareholders NA

Business: The group's principle activity is to provide investment advisory and surety bond brokerage services. The company operates through two segments. Investment advisory, surety bond brokerage and corporate. Investment advisory service segment derives revenue from asset based fees. Surety brokerage service consists of placing surety bonds with insurance companies for clients engaged in regulated industries, such as the extraction of coal, oil and gas. This segment derives commission income from the placement of these bonds.

Primary SIC and add'l.: 6282 6211

CIK No: 0000857501

Subsidiaries: Crystal Mountain Water, Inc., FS Investments, Inc., Jacobs & Company, Triangle Surety Agency, Inc.

Officers: John M. Jacobs/54/Dir., CEO, Pres., Robert J. Kenney/61/VP, Robert L. Neal/52/CFO

Directors: John M. Jacobs/54/Dir., CEO, Pres., Frederick E. Ferguson/74/Dir., David C. Thomas/55/Dir.

Owners: Frederick E. Ferguson/1.01%, John M. Jacobs/15.11%, William D. Jones/6.77%, Fay S. Alexander/8.32%, Robert L. Neal, Robert J. Kenney/2.45%, Insiders/18.93%, Charles L. Stout/8.39%, Sue C. Hunt/5.43%, C. David Thomas

Financial Data: ***Fiscal Year End:*** 05/31 ***Latest Annual Data:*** 5/31/2006

Year	Sales	Net Income
2006	$407,000	-$1,494,000
2005	$260,000	-$1,120,000
2004	$316,000	-$971,000

Curr. Assets:	$1,265,000	***Curr. Liab.:***	$1,063,000		
Plant, Equip.:	$30,000	***Total Liab.:***	$1,840,000	***Indic. Yr. Divd.:***	NA
Total Assets:	$4,301,000	***Net Worth:***	-$5,355,000	***Debt/ Equity:***	NA

Neoforma Inc

3061 Zanker Rd., San Jose, CA, 95134; ***PH:*** 1-408-654-5700; ***http://*** www.neoforma.com

General - Incorporation DE	***Stock*** - Price on:12/24/2007 NA
Employees NA	Stock Exchange NA
Auditor PricewaterhouseCoopers LLP	Ticker Symbol NA
Stk Agt American Stock Transfer & Trust Co.	Outstanding Shares NA
Counsel NA	E.P.S. NA
DUNS No. NA	Shareholders NA

Business: The group's principal activity is to provide supply chain management solutions for the healthcare industry. It combines technology, information and services to provide Web-based solutions that propel efficient collaboration between hospitals and suppliers, enabling them to eliminate inefficiencies and lower costs. Its solutions enable hospitals, suppliers and group purchasing organizations to improve communications, receive accurate information, improve day-to-day operations, accelerate order, enhance strategic planning and gain organization-wide visibility into supply chain activities. Its major customers include novation, llc, vha inc. And university healthsystem consortium. Neoforma contract management solution, neoforma cms, neoforma data management solution, neoforma dms, neoforma materials management solution, neoforma mms, neoconnect, healthcare products information services, hpis, med-ecom, medcontrax and the neoforma logo are some of the group's trademarks.

Primary SIC and add'l.: 7375 7389

CIK No: 0001096219

Subsidiaries: Neolocity Corporation, Neomedacq, Inc.

Neogen Corp

620 Lesher Pl., Lansing, MI, 48912; ***PH:*** 1-517-372-9200; ***Fax:*** 1-517-372-2006; ***http://*** www.neogen.com; ***Email:*** foodsafety@neogen.com

General - Incorporation MI	***Stock*** - Price on:12/24/2007 $28
Employees 393	Stock Exchange NDQ
Auditor Ernst & Young LLP	Ticker Symbol NEON
Stk Agt American Stock Transfer & Trust Co.	Outstanding Shares 9,250,000
Counsel Foster Zack & Lowe	E.P.S. $0.68
DUNS No. 06-955-0929	Shareholders NA

Business: The group's principal activity is to develop, manufacture and market diverse line of products dedicated to food and animal safety. The group operates in two segments: food safety and animal safety. The food safety segment produces and markets diagnostic test kits and related products used by food producers and processors to detect harmful natural toxins, drug residues. They include food-borne bacteria, food allergens, genetic modifications, ruminant by-products, drug residues, pesticide residues, plant disease infections and levels of general sanitation. The animal safety segment produces and markets products dedicated to animal health. They include 250 different veterinary instruments and a complete line of consumable products marketed to veterinarians and animal health product distributors. On 21-Nov-2003, the group acquired hacco, inc and hess & clark, inc.

Primary SIC and add'l.: 3841 2835

CIK No: 0000711377

Subsidiaries: Acumedia Manufacturers, Inc., Centrus International, Inc., Hacco, Inc., Hess& Clark, Inc., Ideal Instruments, Inc., Neogen Acquisition Corporation, Neogen Europe Limited, Neogen Properties, LLC, Neogen Properties, LLCII, Neogen Properties, LLCIII, Neogen Properties, LLCIV

Owners: Insiders/11.50%, Gordon E. Guyer, Mark A. Mozola, Paul S. Satoh, James L. Herbert/6.00%, Terri A. Morrical, Richard R. Current, Joseph M. Madden, Edward L. Bradley, Jack C. Parnell, G. Bruce Papesh, Thomas H. Reed, Lon M. Bohannon/2.00%, Kenneth V. Kodilla, Anthony E. Maltese *(16 Owners included in Index)*

Financial Data: *Fiscal Year End:*05/31 *Latest Annual Data:* 5/31/2006

Year	Sales		Net Income
2006	$72,433,000		$7,941,000
2005	$62,756,000		$5,916,000
2004	$55,498,000		$5,099,000

Curr. Assets:	$51,098,000	**Curr. Liab.:**	$10,038,000	**P/E Ratio:**	27.72
Plant, Equip.:	$16,402,000	**Total Liab.:**	$13,339,000	**Indic. Yr. Divd.:**	NA
Total Assets:	$105,284,000	**Net Worth:**	$91,945,000	**Debt/ Equity:**	NA

NeoGenomics Inc

12701 Commonwealth Dr., Ste. 9, Fort Myers, FL, 33913; ***PH:*** 1-239-768-0600; ***Fax:*** 1-239-768-0711; ***http://*** www.neogenomics.org; ***Email:*** info@neogenomics.org

General - Incorporation	NV	**Stock**- Price on:12/24/2007	$1.66
Employees	48	Stock Exchange	OTC
Auditor	Kingery & Crouse P.A	Ticker Symbol	NGNM
Stk Agt	Standard Registrar & Transfer Co Inc.	Outstanding Shares	28,060,000
Counsel	NA	E.P.S	-$0.08
DUNS No.	NA	Shareholders	NA

Business: The group's principal activity is to develop clinical laboratory to offer routine cytogenetics testing and high-end molecular genetics services. The group serves human healthcare products industry. The group offers three types of genetic diagnostic services: cytogenetic testing, molecular biology testing and sponsored research services. Cytogenetic tests are routinely used to identify genetic abnormalities in pregnancy, as well as hematologic cancers. Sponsored research tests discovers underlying genetic causes of female diseases, cancers and other diseases of the ovary, uterus, cervix, and breast all have an underlying genetic basis. Molecular biology test includes dna tests used in the screening and diagnosis of single gene disorders and hematological cancers.

Primary SIC and add'l.: 8071

CIK No: 0001077183

Officers: Michael T. Dent/43/Chmn., CEO, Pres., Robert P. Gasparini/53/Dir., Pres., Chief Science Officer, Steven C. Jones/44/Dir., Acting Principal Financial Officer, Jerome J. Dvonch/39/Dir. - Finance, Principal Accounting Officer, Robert J. Feeney/40/VP - Sales, Marketing, Matthew William Moore/34/VP - Research, Development

Directors: Michael T. Dent/43/Chmn., CEO, Pres., George G. Oleary/Dir., Peter M. Peterson/Dir., Robert P. Gasparini/53/Dir., Pres., Chief Science Officer, Steven C. Jones/44/Dir., Acting Principal Financial Officer

Owners: Peter M. Peterson, Robert J. Feeney, Jerome J. Dvonch, George OLeary, Michael T. Dent, Aspen Capital Advisors, Marvin Jaffe, Aspen Select Healthcare, LP, 1837 Partners, LP, William Robison, Steven C. Jones, Insiders, Matthew W. Moore, SKL Family Limited Partnership, Robert P. Gasparini

Financial Data: *Fiscal Year End:*12/31 *Latest Annual Data:* 12/31/2006

Year	Sales		Net Income
2006	$6,476,000		-$130,000
2005	$1,885,000		-$997,000
2004	$558,000		-$819,000

Curr. Assets:	$1,896,000	**Curr. Liab.:**	$2,628,000		
Plant, Equip.:	$1,202,000	**Total Liab.:**	$3,077,000	**Indic. Yr. Divd.:**	NA
Total Assets:	$3,132,000	**Net Worth:**	$55,000	**Debt/ Equity:**	0.7721

NeoMagic

3250 Jay St., Santa Clara, CA, 95054; ***PH:*** 1-408-988-7020; ***Fax:*** 1-408-988-7036; ***http://*** www.neomagic.com; ***Email:*** ir@neomagic.com

General - Incorporation	DE	**Stock**- Price on:12/24/2007	$3.71
Employees	103	Stock Exchange	NDQ
Auditor	Stonefield Josephson, Inc	Ticker Symbol	NMGC
Stk Agt	Computershare Investor Services LLC	Outstanding Shares	12,300,000
Counsel	Wilson Sonsini Goodrich & Rosati	E.P.S	-$1.26
DUNS No.	80-895-9027	Shareholders	NA

Business: The group's principle activities are to design, develop and market high-performance semiconductor solutions for sale to original equipment manufacturers (OEMs) of handheld systems. The group designs the overall product, including the logic and analog circuitry. The group is focused on leveraging its core competencies in integrating logic, analog and memory along with graphics, video, 3D and other multimedia technologies. In addition, the group focuses on operating system software and power management. The group's new product direction is to produce integrated system-on-chip semiconductor products for the handheld Internet appliance market place. The group sells its products to key customers primarily through a direct sales and marketing organization in the United States and through manufacturer's sales representatives in regions where significant customer opportunities exist such as Japan, Taiwan, Hong Kong, Europe and United States. The group's total revenue for year 2007 was 0.57 millions of USD.

Primary SIC and add'l.: 3674

CIK No: 0001030485

Subsidiaries: NeoMagic Israel Ltd, NeoMagic Semiconductor India Private Ltd.

Officers: Doug Young/Dir., CEO, Pres./$434,068.00, Scott Sullinger/CFO, VP - Finance/$309,683.00, Sudhir Chandratreya/VP - Vlsi Design Engineering, Technology, Syed Zaidi/Dir., COO, VP, Corporate Engineering/$333,557.00, Deep Puar/VP - Operations/$374,648.00, Steven P. Berry/CFO, Michael J. Danaher/Sec.

Directors: Doug Young/Dir., CEO, Pres., Brett A. Moyer/Dir., Anil Gupta/Dir., Carl Stork/Dir., Syed Zaidi/Dir., COO, VP, Corporate Engineering, Steve Valenzuela/Dir.

Owners: Carl Stork, Syed Zaidi, Insiders/4.08%, Raffles Associates, L.P./6.68%, Deepraj Puar, Douglas Young, Scott Sullinger, Entities affiliated with Special Situations/15.98%, Steve Valenzuela, Anil Gupta

Financial Data: *Fiscal Year End:*01/29 *Latest Annual Data:* 4/29/2007

Year	Sales		Net Income
2007	NA		NA
2006	NA		NA
2005	$2,466,000		-$28,225,000

Curr. Assets:	$27,675,000	**Curr. Liab.:**	$5,607,000		
Plant, Equip.:	$2,368,000	**Total Liab.:**	$6,986,000	**Indic. Yr. Divd.:**	NA
Total Assets:	$30,494,000	**Net Worth:**	$23,508,000	**Debt/ Equity:**	NA

NeoMedia Technologies Inc

Corporate Ctr. II, Ste. 500 , Two Concourse Pkwy., Atlanta, GA, 30328; ***PH:*** 1-678-638-0460; ***Fax:*** 1-678-638-0466; ***http://*** www.neom.com

General - Incorporation	DE	**Stock**- Price on:12/24/2007	$16.65
Employees	134	Stock Exchange	OTC
Auditor	Stonefield Josephson, Inc	Ticker Symbol	NEOM
Stk Agt	American Stock Transfer & Trust Co.	Outstanding Shares	891,400,000
Counsel	Merrick & Klimek	E.P.S	-$0.127
DUNS No.	60-935-4410	Shareholders	NA

Business: The group's principal activities are to develop proprietary technologies that link physical information and objects to the Internet. It operates in two distinct business units: neomedia Internet switching services (niss) and neomedia consulting and integration services (ncis). Niss develops and supports the group's Internet core technology, which includes linking switch and application platforms. Niss also manages the group's intellectual property portfolio, which includes the identification and execution of licensing opportunities surrounding the patents. Ncis resells client-server equipment and related software. Ncis also provides consulting services targeted at software driven print applications. On 08-Oct-2003, the group acquired secure source technologies inc and on 10-Feb-2004, csi international inc. The group operates only in the United States.

Primary SIC and add'l.: 7379 7373

CIK No: 0001022701

Subsidiaries: Distribuidora Vallarta S.A., NeoMedia Technologies UK Limited, NeoMedia EDV GMBH, NeoMedia established Mobot Acquisition, Inc, NeoMedia Micro Paint Repair Inc., NeoMedia Migration de Mexico S.A. de C.V, NeoMedia Migration Inc., NeoMedia Tech Inc., NeoMedia Technologies de Mexico S.A. de C.V, NeoMedia Technologies do Brazil Ltd., NeoMedia Technologies Holding Company B.V., NeoMedia Technologies of Canada Inc., NeoMedia Telecom Services Inc.

Officers: Charles W. Fritz/51/Chmn., Interim CEO, William J. Hoffman/CEO, Frank Pezera/CFO, David A. Dodge/32/VP, Christian Steinborn/COO, Scott Womble/Controller

Directors: Charles W. Fritz/51/Chmn., Interim CEO, James J. Keil/Dir., Hayes A. Barclay/76/Dir., George Oleary/Dir.

Owners: Charles W. Fritz/4.40%, James J. Keil, Insiders/6.40%, William Fritz/8.30%, David A. Dodge/1.00%, Hayes A. Barclay

Financial Data: *Fiscal Year End:*12/31 *Latest Annual Data:* 12/31/2006

Year	Sales		Net Income
2006	$10,309,000		-$67,438,000
2005	$2,156,000		-$9,147,000
2004	$1,700,000		-$7,230,000

Curr. Assets:	$11,492,000	**Curr. Liab.:**	$92,659,000		
Plant, Equip.:	$439,000	**Total Liab.:**	$92,659,000	**Indic. Yr. Divd.:**	NA
Total Assets:	$38,125,000	**Net Worth:**	-$54,534,000	**Debt/ Equity:**	NA

NeoPharm

1850 Lakeside Dr., Waukegan, IL, 60085; ***PH:*** 1-847-887-0800; ***Fax:*** 1-847-887-9281; ***http://*** www.neophrm.com; ***Email:*** medinfo@neophrm.com

General - Incorporation	DE	**Stock**- Price on:12/24/2007	$1.33
Employees	53	Stock Exchange	AMEX
Auditor	KPMG LLP	Ticker Symbol	NEP
Stk Agt	Computershare Investor Services LLC	Outstanding Shares	28,090,000
Counsel	Burke, Warren, Mackay & Serritella	E.P.S	-$0.89
DUNS No.	92-903-3959	Shareholders	NA

Business: The group's principal activity is the research, development and commercialization of drugs for the treatment of various cancers. The group has a portfolio of six anti-cancer drugs which are in clinical trials. The group has two novel proprietary technology platforms for drug portfolio: the proprietary neolipid(TM) liposomal drug delivery platform and a tumor-targeting platform. The platforms are used for the treatment of various forms of cancer and brain tumors. The group develops liposome encapsulated doxorubicin (led), liposome encapsulated paclitaxel (lep) liposome encapsulated antisene oligonucleotides (le-aon) and liposome encapsulated mitoxantrone (lem). The group operates solely in the domestic market.

Primary SIC and add'l.: 8731 2834

CIK No: 0000942788

Subsidiaries: NeoPharm EU Limited

Officers: Laurence P. Birch/48/Dir., CEO, Acting CFO, Pres., Sec., Timothy P. Walbert/Exec. VP - Commercial Operations, Information, Jeffrey W. Sherman/Chief Medical Officer, Exec. VP/$380,224.00

Directors: Erick E. Hanson/61/Chmn., Kaveh T. Safavi/47/Dir., Frank C. Becker/72/Dir., Ronald G. Eidell/64/Dir., Paul E. Freiman/73/Dir., John N. Kapoor/64/Dir., Bernard A. Fox/54/Dir.

Owners: Insiders/22.22%, Ronald G. Eidell, John N. Kapoor 1994A Annuity Trust/6.96%, GAM Holding AG/6.08%, Ronald Pauli, Lawrence A. Kenyon, Kaveh T. Safavi, Timothy Walbert, Bernard A. Fox, Paul E. Freiman, Frank C. Becker, Nikos Hecht/8.99%, Insiders/22.22%, Erick E. Hanson, Jeffrey W. Sherman/1.29% *(16 Owners included in Index)*

Financial Data: *Fiscal Year End:*12/31 *Latest Annual Data:* 12/31/2006

Year	Sales		Net Income
2006	$11,000		-$33,208,000
2005	$543,000		-$38,725,000
2004	$157,000		-$57,609,000

Curr. Assets:	$39,214,000	**Curr. Liab.:**	$9,577,000		
Plant, Equip.:	$1,266,000	**Total Liab.:**	$11,818,000	**Indic. Yr. Divd.:**	NA
Total Assets:	$40,689,000	**Net Worth:**	$28,871,000	**Debt/ Equity:**	0.0085

Neoprobe Corp

425 Metro Pl. N, Ste. 300, Dublin, OH, 43017; *PH:* 1-614-793-7500; *Fax:* 1-614-793-7520; *http://* www.neoprobe.com; *Email:* info@neoprobe.com

General - Incorporation	DE	*Stock* - Price on:12/24/2007	$0.27
Employees	22	Stock Exchange	OTC
Auditor	BDO Seidman LLP	Ticker Symbol	NEOP
Stk Agt	Continental Stock Transfer & Trust Co	Outstanding Shares	61,260,000
Counsel	NA	E.P.S.	-$0.09
DUNS No.	13-189-1467	Shareholders	NA

Business: The group's principal activity is to develop and commercialize surgical and diagnostic products for healthcare professionals. The group manufactures two lines of medical devices: gamma radiation detection equipment, used in the application of intraoperative lymphatic mapping and blood flow monitoring devices, for a variety of diagnostic and surgical applications. The gamma detection device products are marketed throughout most of the world through a distribution arrangement with ethicon endo-surgery inc., a johnson and johnson company. The group primarily operates in the United States and Europe.

Primary SIC and add'l.: 3841

CIK No: 0000810509

Subsidiaries: Cardiosonix Ltd., Cira Biosciences, Inc.

Officers: David C. Bupp/Dir., CEO, Pres./$393,105.00, Anthony K. Blair/VP - Manufacturing Operations, Brent L. Larson/VP - Finance, CFO, Treasurer, Sec./$185,751.00, Rodger A. Brown/VP - Regulatory Affairs, Quality Assurance, Douglas L. Rash/VP - Marketing, Tim Ryan/Investor Relation Officer

Directors: David C. Bupp/Dir., CEO, Pres., Julius R. Krevans/Chmn., Reuven Avita/Dir., Frank J. Whitley/Dir., Fred B. Miller/Dir., Kirby I. Bland/Dir., Carl J. Aschinger/Dir.

Owners: Carl J. Aschinger, Reuven Avital, David C. Bupp/9.50%, Great Point Partners, L.P./29.00%, Insiders/12.90%, Brent L. Larson/1.00%, Fred B. Miller, Carl M. Bosch, Frank J. Whitley, Kirby I. Bland

Financial Data: Fiscal Year End:12/31 Latest Annual Data: 12/31/2006

Year	Sales		Net Income
2006	$6,051,000		-$4,741,000
2005	$5,919,000		-$4,929,000
2004	$5,953,000		-$3,541,000
Curr. Assets:	$5,334,000	*Curr. Liab.:*	$3,409,000
Plant, Equip.:	$356,000	*Total Liab.:*	$8,331,000	*Indic. Yr. Divd.:*	NA
Total Assets:	$8,034,000	*Net Worth:*	-$298,000	*Debt/ Equity:*	NA

Neose Technologies Inc

102 Rock Rd., Horsham, PA, 19044; *PH:* 1-215-315-9000; *Fax:* 1-215-315-9100; *http://* www.neose.com; *Email:* info@neose.com

General - Incorporation	DE	*Stock* - Price on:12/24/2007	$2.67
Employees	78	Stock Exchange	NDQ
Auditor	KPMG LLP	Ticker Symbol	NTEC
Stk Agt	American Stock Transfer & Trust Co.	Outstanding Shares	54,400,000
Counsel	Pepper Hamilton LLP	E.P.S.	-$0.85
DUNS No.	78-622-8098	Shareholders	NA

Business: The group's principal activity is to develop proprietary technologies for the synthesis and manufacture of complex carbohydrates. Through its proprietary enzymatic technology platform, the group enables the production and manipulation of complex carbohydrates either as stand-alone carbohydrate molecules or as carbohydrate structures attached to recombinant therapeutic glycoproteins and glycolipids. It uses its technology in its glycoadvance program to complete the human carbohydrate structures on therapeutic glycoprotein; glycotherapeutics program to develop carbohydrate-based therapeutics; and glycoactives program to develop carbohydrate-based food and nutritional ingredients. The group has commercial and collaborative agreements with wyeth pharmaceuticals, neuronyx, inc and progenics pharmaceuticals, inc. The group is in development stage.

Primary SIC and add'l.: 8731 2833

CIK No: 0000877902

Officers: George J. Vergis/Dir., CEO, Pres./$1,100,298.00, Shawn Defrees/VP - Research, David A. Zopf/Chief Scientific Officer, Exec. VP/$577,441.00, Brian A. Davis/Sr. VP, CFO/$601,369.00, Debra J. Poul/Sr. VP, General Counsel, Sec./$563,525.00, Barbara Krauter/Mgr. - Investor Relations, Kathryn J. Gregory/VP - Business Development, Licensing, Elliot Morales/VP - Project Management, Analytical Operations, Valerie M. Mulligan/VP - Quality, Regulatory Affairs/$315,768.00, Bruce A. Wallin/VP - Clinical Development, Chief Medical Officer

Directors: George J. Vergis/Dir., CEO, Pres., Patrick L. Gage/Chmn., Brian H. Dovey/Dir., William F. Hamilton/Dir., Douglas J. MacMaster/Dir., Stewart H. Parker/Dir., Mark H. Rachesky/Dir., Sandy Keller/Dir. - Human Resources, Administration, Henrik Clausen/Member - Scientific Advisory Board, Glycoadvance Advisory Board, Richard D. Cummings/Member - Scientific Advisory Board, Glycoadvance Advisory Board, David James/Member - Scientific Advisory Board, Glycoadvance Advisory Board, James C. Paulson/Member - Scientific Advisory Board, Glycoadvance Advisory Board

Owners: Stewart H. Parker, Boyd C. Clarke/2.10%, Insiders/21.50%, William F. Hamilton, Elizabeth Wyatt, Valerie M. Mulligan, Douglas J. MacMaster, Debra J. Poul, OrbiMed Advisors, LLC/5.20%, Kopp Investment Advisors, LLC/9.20%, Eastbourne Capital Management, L.L.C./8.40%, Patrick L. Gage, Brian H. Dovey/8.30%, Lowell E. Sears, Mark H. Rachesky/9.30% *(19 Owners included in Index)*

Financial Data: Fiscal Year End:12/31 Latest Annual Data: 12/31/2006

Year	Sales		Net Income
2006	$6,184,000		-$27,107,000
2005	$6,137,000		-$51,839,000
2004	$5,070,000		-$41,642,000
Curr. Assets:	$17,958,000	*Curr. Liab.:*	$10,265,000
Plant, Equip.:	$13,104,000	*Total Liab.:*	$15,684,000	*Indic. Yr. Divd.:*	NA
Total Assets:	$31,243,000	*Net Worth:*	$15,559,000	*Debt/ Equity:*	0.0193

NeoStem Inc

420 Lexington Ave. Rm 450, New York, NY, 10170; *PH:* 1-212-584-4180; *Fax:* 1-646-514-7787; *http://* www.neostem.com

General - Incorporation	DE	*Stock* - Price on:12/24/2007	$0.45
Employees	12	Stock Exchange	AMEX
Auditor	Holtz Rubenstein Reminick LLP	Ticker Symbol	NBS
Stk Agt	Continental Stock Transfer & Trust Co	Outstanding Shares	36,500,000
Counsel	NA	E.P.S.	-$0.38
DUNS No.	NA	Shareholders	NA

Business: The groups principle activities include operating commercial autologous adult stem cell bank and pre-disease collecting, processing and long-term storing of adult stem cells. The group operates through two segments namely collection, processing and banking of adult stem cells and warranties and service contracts via the Internet. In January 2006 the group acquired NS California, Inc. The group operates from the United States. The group's quarterly revenue for Sep '07 was 0.01 millions of USD.

Primary SIC and add'l.: 8099

CIK No: 0000320017

Subsidiaries: NeoStem Therapies, Inc.

Officers: Robin Smith/Chmn., CEO/$531,672.00, Mark Weinreb/Dir., Pres./$437,096.00, Larry A. May/CFO/$183,894.00, George Smith/Medical Dir. - Laboratory Operations, California, Catherine M. Vaczy/VP, General Counsel/$245,078.00, Julio C. Guerra/Dir. - Sales, Marketing

Directors: Robin Smith/Chmn., CEO, Wayne A. Marasco/Chmn. - Scientific Advisory Board, Denis Rodgerson/Dir. - Stem Cell Science, Mark Weinreb/Dir., Pres., Douglas W. Losordo/Member - Scientific Advisory Board, Stephen D. Nimer/Member - Scientific Advisory Board, Joseph Zuckerman/56/Dir., Richard Berman/65/Dir., Steven S. Myers/61/Dir.

Owners: Colin Poole, David Azus, Isaac Michalovsky, 305 Investments LP, Diversified Equity Funding, LP, Robert M. Cohen, Robert Edinger, Koby Huberman, Simon Lam, Fred Ophus, Sara Boyce, Beacon Trust Co., Migosa Enterprises Inc., Richard Berman, Hanka Lew *(179 Owners included in Index)*

Financial Data: Fiscal Year End:12/31 Latest Annual Data: 12/31/2006

Year	Sales		Net Income
2006	$46,000		-$6,051,000
2005	$35,000		-$1,745,000
2004	$49,000		-$1,748,000
Curr. Assets:	$528,000	*Curr. Liab.:*	$838,000
Plant, Equip.:	$96,000	*Total Liab.:*	$903,000	*Indic. Yr. Divd.:*	NA
Total Assets:	$1,195,000	*Net Worth:*	$292,000	*Debt/ Equity:*	NA

Nephros Inc

3960 Broadway, 4th Fl., New York, NY, 10032; *PH:* 1-212-781-5113; *Fax:* 1-212-781-5166; *http://* www.nephros.com; *Email:* info@nephros.com

General - Incorporation	DE	*Stock* - Price on:12/24/2007	$1.38
Employees	18	Stock Exchange	NDQ
Auditor	Deloitte & Touche LLP	Ticker Symbol	NETC
Stk Agt	Continental Stock Transfer & Trust Co	Outstanding Shares	12,320,000
Counsel	NA	E.P.S.	-$0.64
DUNS No.	NA	Shareholders	NA

Business: The groups principle activity is to develop end stage renal disease therapy technology products and services. The group provides HDF machine and associated filter technology. The group operates from United States.

Primary SIC and add'l.: NA

CIK No: 0001196298

Subsidiaries: Nephros International Limited

Officers: Norman J. Barta/Dir., CEO, Pres., Gregory Collins/Sr. Scientist, Nick Staub/Dir. - Sales, US, Dara Gannon/Nephros International, Customer Service Mgr., Mark W. Lerner/CFO

Directors: Norman J. Barta/Dir., CEO, Pres., William Fox/Chmn., Lawrence J. Centella/Dir., Eric A. Rose/Dir., John T. Daugirdas/Member - Scientific Advisory Board, Detlef Krieter/Member - Scientific Advisory Board, Leonard Stern/Member - Scientific Advisory Board, Bernard Salick/Dir., Townsend W. Ziebold/Dir., Judy S. Slotkin/Dir., Arthur H. Amron/Dir.

Owners: Ronald O. Perelman/28.70%, Howard Davis, William J. Fox/3.00%, Wasserstein Entities/15.70%, Wasserstein SBIC Ventures II, L.P./6.70%, Insiders/19.80%, Townsend W. Ziebold/7.00%, Donald G. Drapkin/5.20%, Lawrence J. Centella, WPPN, LP/7.50%, Judy Slotkin, Eric A. Rose/7.30%, Mark W. Lerner, Norman J. Barta/3.60%

Financial Data: Fiscal Year End:12/31 Latest Annual Data: 12/31/2006

Year	Sales		Net Income
2006	$793,000		-$8,013,000
2005	$2,424,000		-$5,468,000
2004	$138,000		-$7,596,000
Curr. Assets:	$4,233,000	*Curr. Liab.:*	$1,691,000
Plant, Equip.:	$911,000	*Total Liab.:*	$7,263,000	*Indic. Yr. Divd.:*	NA
Total Assets:	$5,167,000	*Net Worth:*	-$2,096,000	*Debt/ Equity:*	NA

Neptune Industries Inc

21218 St. Andrews Blvd., No. 645, Boca Raton, FL, 33433; *PH:* 1-561-482-6408; *Fax:* 1-561-483-7821; *http://* www.neptuneindustries.net; *Email:* info@neptuneindustries.net

General - Incorporation	FL	*Stock* - Price on:12/24/2007	$0.57
Employees	7	Stock Exchange	OTC
Auditor	Dohan and Company CPAs, P.A.	Ticker Symbol	NPDI
Stk Agt	Interwest Transfer Company, Inc.	Outstanding Shares	12,700,000
Counsel	NA	E.P.S.	NA
DUNS No.	NA	Shareholders	NA

Business: The groups principle activity is to supply seafood products. Services of the group include fish farms, hatchery operations and wholesale distribution. The group operates from the United States, Canada and the Caribbean.

Primary SIC and add'l.: 7373

CIK No: 0001138659

Subsidiaries: Aqua Biologics Inc.,

Officers: Ernest D. Papadoyianis/49/Chmn., CEO, Pres., Sal T. Cherch/COO, Robert Hipple/CFO, Michael Steinberg/Contact - Investor Relations

Directors: Ernest D. Papadoyianis/49/Chmn., CEO, Pres., Don C. Tewksbury/58/Dir., James M. Harvey/63/Dir., William H. Ryan/50/Dir.

Owners: James Harvey/0.06%, Insiders/61.44%, Robert Hipple, Gregry A. Lewbart/0.06%, Don C. Tewksbury/0.06%, Xavier T. Cherch/30.57%, Ernest D. Papadoyianis/30.69%

Curr. Assets:	$2,082,000	Curr. Liab.:	$1,082,000
Plant, Equip.:	$387,000	Total Liab.:	$4,219,000	Indic. Yr. Divd.:	NA
Total Assets:	$2,469,000	Net Worth:	-$1,750,000	Debt/ Equity:	NA

Neptune Society Inc

100 N First St. , Ste. 205, Sburbank, CA, 91502; **PH:** 1-818-953-9995;
http:// www.neptunesociety.com

General - Incorporation	FL	Stock- Price on:12/24/2007	NA
Employees	7	Stock Exchange	NA
Auditor	Stonefield Josephson, Inc	Ticker Symbol	NA
Stk Agt	Interwest Transfer Company, Inc.	Outstanding Shares	NA
Counsel	NA	E.P.S	NA
DUNS No.	NA	Shareholders	NA

Business: The group's principal activities are to offer cremation services and products related to cremation services. The group markets and administers pre-need and at-need cremation services in the states of California, Florida, Iowa, New York, Oregon, Colorado and Washington. Pre-need program is designed to eliminate as much of the emotional and financial burden as possible for the individuals' heirs and successors. Pre-need program allows individuals to pre-arrange simple and basic cremation services at a guaranteed fixed price by entering into a pre-need contract. At-need program provides a full range of cremation services and merchandise and care for all aspects of the deceased's cremation needs according to the decisions and plans of the decedent's heirs, including service planning, optional services for scattering remains, and delivery of ashes to family members.

Primary SIC and add'l.: 6553

CIK No: 0001098532

Subsidiaries: Heritage Alternatives, Inc., Neptune Society of America, Inc., Neptune Management Corporation, Trident Society, Inc.

Ness Technologies Inc

3 University Plz., Ste. 600, Hackensack, NJ, 07601; **PH:** 1-201-488-7222; **Fax:** 1-866-637-7380;
http:// www.ness.com; **Email:** nessna@ness-usa.com

General - Incorporation	DE	Stock- Price on:12/24/2007	$12.75
Employees	7,515	Stock Exchange	NDQ
Auditor	Kost Forer Gabbay & Kasierer	Ticker Symbol	NSTR
Stk Agt	American Stock Transfer & Trust Co.	Outstanding Shares	39,020,000
Counsel	NA	E.P.S	$0.78
DUNS No.	NA	Shareholders	NA

Business: The groups principle activity is to provide end-to-end IT services and solutions designed to help clients improve competitiveness and efficiency. The group operates from United States.

Primary SIC and add'l.: NA

CIK No: 0001089638

Subsidiaries: Aliatic Consulting GMBH, AT Ltd., Gilad Integration Computers Systems and Software (1999) Ltd., Ness AT Ltd., Ness Australia Ltd, Ness Benelux B.V., Ness BSG Ltd., Ness Canada Inc., NESS Czech s.r.o, Ness DM a.s., Ness Global Services Ltd, Ness Global Services Ltd., NESS Global Services Pte, Ness Global Services Pte. Ltd, Ness Innovative Business Services,Inc. 28 Subsidiaries included in the Index

Officers: Sachi Gerlitz/Pres., CEO - Ness Technologies, Vinod Sharma/Sr. VP - Delivery Ness IBS, Ofer Segev/CFO, Exec. VP, Bharath Kalyanram/Pres., MD - Ness India, Satyajit Bandyopadhyay/Sr. VP, Chief Delivery Officer - Ness NA, Sudhir Saran Singh/VP - Human Resources - Ness India, Puneet Chaddah/VP, Delivery Head - Bangalore Center, Shashi Bhargava/VP, Delivery Head - Mumbai Center, Gabriela Mardarasevici/VP - Operations, Vaclav Klein/Sr. VP, MD - Slovakia, Shai Onn/45/Exec. VP - Business Development, Strategy, Petr Mandelik/Dir. - Division Utilities, Karol Kubeczka/Dir. - Division Manufacturing, Outsourcing, Roman Kamart/Dir. - Division Public, Czech Republic, Damodara Baliga/VP - Ness UK (74 Officers included in Index)

Directors: Aharon Fogel/Chmn., Raviv Zoller/44/Dir., Henry Kressel/74/Dir., Morris Wolfson/48/Dir., Satyam C. Cherukuri/51/Dir., Dan S. Suesskind/64/Dir., Kenneth A. Pickar/68/Dir., Ravikumar Velagapudi/41/Dir.

Owners: Shashank Samant, Tuvia Feldman, Ivan Hrulka, Dan S. Suesskind, Henry Kressel/8.60%, Satyam C. Cherukuri, Raviv Zoller/1.10%, FMR Corporation/7.90%, Warburg Pincus/8.60%, Ytzhak Edelman, Morris Wolfson/3.90%, Aharon Fogel, Kenneth A. Pickar, Insiders/13.50%

Financial Data: Fiscal Year End:12/31   Latest Annual Data: 12/31/2006

Year	Sales	Net Income
2006	$474,318,000	$29,813,000
2005	$385,668,000	$21,689,000
2004	$304,525,000	$14,377,000

Curr. Assets:	$230,776,000	Curr. Liab.:	$158,620,000	P/E Ratio:	17.71
Plant, Equip.:	$28,279,000	Total Liab.:	$208,962,000	Indic. Yr. Divd.:	NA
Total Assets:	$541,617,000	Net Worth:	$332,655,000	Debt/ Equity:	0.0114

Nestor Inc

42 Oriental St., Providence, RI, 02908; **PH:** 1-401-274-5658; **Fax:** 1-401-274-5707;
http:// www.nestor.com; **Email:** info@nestor.com

General - Incorporation	DE	Stock- Price on:12/24/2007	$0.35
Employees	110	Stock Exchange	NDQ
Auditor	Carlin, Charron & Rosen LLP	Ticker Symbol	NEST
Stk Agt	American Stock Transfer & Trust Co.	Outstanding Shares	20,240,000
Counsel	Snow & Hahn LLP	E.P.S	-$0.17
DUNS No.	11-600-9499	Shareholders	NA

Business: The group's principal activity is to license its patented intelligent software solutions for decision and data-mining applications in real time environments. The group's products employ proprietary neural network predictive models to convert existing data and business experiences into meaningful recommendations and actions. The group through its wholly owned subsidiary nestor traffic systems inc offers products in intelligent traffic-management systems. The group's main product line is crossingguard, an automated traffic-intersection red-light enforcement and safety system.

Primary SIC and add'l.: 7372 6794

CIK No: 0000720851

Subsidiaries: CrossingGuard, Inc, Nestor Traffic, Nestor Traffic Systems, Inc.

Officers: Clarence A. Davis/66/Dir., CEO, Nigel P. Hebborn/49/Exec. VP, Treasurer, CFO, Tadas A. Eikinas/42/VP, COO, Teodor Klowan/39/VP, Corporate Controller, Chief Accounting Officer, Brian R. Haskell/45/VP, General Counsel, Sec.

Directors: Clarence A. Davis/66/Dir., CEO, George L. Ball/69/Chmn., David N. Jordan/64/Dir., Michael C. James/49/Dir., Nina R. Mitchell/49/Dir., Thodore Petroulas/53/Dir., Daryl Silzer/53/Dir., Harold E. Ford/63/Dir., Edward F. Heil/64/Dir.

Owners: Edward F. Heil/20.20%, Insiders/9.40%, Daryl Silzer, George L. Ball, William B. Danzell/35.20%, Michael C. James/3.40%, Tadas A. Eikinas, David N. Jordan/2.70%, Nigel P. Hebborn/1.70%, Teodor Klowan, Clarence A. Davis, Nina R. Mitchell, Silver Star Partners I, LLC/34.30%, Theodore Petroulas

Financial Data: Fiscal Year End:12/31   Latest Annual Data: 12/31/2006

Year	Sales	Net Income
2006	$8,087,000	-$7,491,000
2005	$7,769,000	-$6,764,000
2004	$6,035,000	-$4,473,000

Curr. Assets:	$7,500,000	Curr. Liab.:	$4,067,000
Plant, Equip.:	$789,000	Total Liab.:	$19,009,000	Indic. Yr. Divd.:	NA
Total Assets:	$24,511,000	Net Worth:	$5,502,000	Debt/ Equity:	NA

Nestor-Partners

411 W Putnam Ave., Greenwich, CT, 06830; **PH:** 1-203-625-7554; **http://** www.nestor-partners.fi;
Email: info@nestor-partners.fi

General - Incorporation	NJ	Stock- Price on:12/24/2007	NA
Employees	NA	Stock Exchange	NA
Auditor	Deloitte & Touche LLP	Ticker Symbol	NA
Stk Agt	NA	Outstanding Shares	NA
Counsel	NA	E.P.S	NA
DUNS No.	NA	Shareholders	NA

Business: The group's principal activity is to engage in speculative trading of futures, options on futures and forward contracts. The Partnerships business constitutes only one segment, a speculative commodity pool. The partnerships sole trading adviser is the General Partner. The partnership trades, pursuant to the General Partners Diversified Portfolio, in the agricultural, metals, energy, interest rate and stock index futures and futures options markets and in the currency markets, trading primarily forward contracts in the interbank market. The objective of the General Partners trading method is to participate in all major sustained price moves in the markets traded. The General Partner regards its approach as long-term in nature.

Primary SIC and add'l.: 6221

CIK No: 0000888471

Officers: Harvey Beker/54/Co - Chmn., Co - CEO, George E. Crapple/63/Co - Chmn., Co - CEO, Gregg R. Buckbinder/49/COO, Sr. VP, Steven M. Felsenthal/38/General Counsel, Chief Compliance Officer, Mark B. Fitzsimmon/60/Sr. VP, Eino Malinen/Partner, Alexander Marschan/Partner, Erkki Miettinen/Partner, Christian Van Niftrik/Partner, Barry Goodman/50/Exec. VP, Dir. - Trading, Dennis B. Newton/56/Sr. VP, Matti Oksanen/Partner, Rolf Hasselblatt/Partner, Antti Helenius/Partner, Heikki K. Helenius/Partner (60 Officers included in Index)

Directors: Harvey Beker/54/Co - Chmn., Co - CEO

Owners: Grant Smith/1.06%, Insiders/1.75%, George Crapple/0.02%, Harvey Beker/0.67%, ALFA Investors/5.13%

Net Bank Inc

1015 Windward Ridge Pkwy., Alpharetta, GA, 30005; **PH:** 1-770-343-6006; **Fax:** 1-770-343-6464;
http:// www.netbankinc.com

General - Incorporation	GA	Stock- Price on:12/24/2007	$0.29
Employees	2,589	Stock Exchange	OTC
Auditor	Ernst & Young LLP	Ticker Symbol	NTBKQ
Stk Agt	Computershare Investor Services LLC	Outstanding Shares	52,980,000
Counsel	Powell, Goldstein, Frazer & Murphy	E.P.S	-$4.359
DUNS No.	85-842-3866	Shareholders	NA

Business: The group's principal activity is to provide on-line retail banking and mortgage lending services. The group operates through its subsidiaries, netbank, fsb, market street mortgage corporation, netbank partners, llp and nb partners, inc. It operates in two segments: retail banking and mortgage lending. Retail banking includes consumer banking products such as checking, money market and certificates of deposit, as well as, online bill payment and presentment, estatements, wireless account access, account consolidation and securities brokerage services. Mortgage lending includes origination of first mortgage loans and related services. These services are provided to retail and commercial customers in the United States and 20 foreign countries. As on 08-Dec-2003, financial technologies inc and on 09-Feb-2004, select assets of electronic cash systems inc.

Primary SIC and add'l.: 6712 6035

CIK No: 0001035826

Subsidiaries: Financial Technologies, Inc., First Choice Lending Group, L.P., H&P Mortgage Financial Group, L.P., Market Street Mortgage Corporation, Meritage Mortgage Corporation, NetBank, NetBank d/b/a Beacon Credit Services, NetBank d/b/a NetBank Business Finance, NetBank d/b/a NetBank Funding Services, NetBank d/b/a Resource Mortgage Solutions, NetBank Payment Systems, Inc., NeuMark Mortgage Services, LLC, River City Mortgage Services, LLC

Officers: Dwight Galloway/Pres. - Netbank Business Finance, Steven F. Herbert/Chief Finance Executive, James P. Gross/CFO, Randall C. Johnson/Pres. - Marketing Street Mortgage Corporation, Charles E. Mapson/Chief Legal Counsel, Patricia M. Hart/Chief Human Resources - Executive, Joyce Bellows/Chief Risk Officer, Chip Register/CIO, Daniel P. Gavin/Treasurer

Directors: Thomas H. Muller/Dir., Joel A. Smith/Dir., Eula L. Adams/Dir., Stephen J. Heard/Dir., David W. Johnson/Dir.

Financial Data: Fiscal Year End:12/31   Latest Annual Data: 12/31/2005

Year	Sales	Net Income
2005	$464,673,000	-$180,000
2004	$439,514,000	$4,220,000
2003	$521,174,000	$50,514,000

Curr. Assets:	$166,954,000	Curr. Liab.:	$2,935,319,000
Plant, Equip.:	$54,420,000	Total Liab.:	$4,370,764,000	Indic. Yr. Divd.:	NA
Total Assets:	$4,771,619,000	Net Worth:	$400,179,000	Debt/ Equity:	2.4719

Net Servicos De Comunicacao

Rua Verbo Divino, 1356, So Paulo; **PH:** 55-1121112785; **http://** www.globocabo.com

General - Incorporation	Brazil	**Stock**- Price on:12/24/2007	$16.43
Employees	5,108	Stock Exchange	NDQ
Auditor	Ernst & Young LLP	Ticker Symbol	NETM
Stk Agt	Bank of New York	Outstanding Shares	29,540,000
Counsel	NA	E.P.S.	$8.29
DUNS No.	90-005-7811	Shareholders	NA

Business: The group's principal activities are the provision of cable television, pay-per-view programs and high speed Internet access. The group also offers broad band Internet services, data communication and multimedia services for corporate networks . It operates in Brazil's three largest cities:sao paulo, rio de janeiro and belo horizonte.

Primary SIC and add'l.: 4841

CIK No: 0001024446

Subsidiaries: Antenas Comunitrias Brasileiras Ltda, CMA Participaes S.A, DR-Empresa de Distribuio e Recepo de TV Ltda, Horizonte Sul Comunicaes Ltda, Jonquil Ventures Limited, Multicanal Telecomunicaes S.A, Net Anpolis Ltda, Net Arapongas Ltda, Net Bauru Ltda, Net Belo Horizonte Ltda, Net Braslia Ltda, Net Campinas Ltda, Net Campo Grande Ltda, Net Curitiba Ltda, Net Florianpolis Ltda 33 Subsidiaries included in the Index

Officers: Francisco Tosta Valim Filho/CEO, Leonardo P. Gomes Pereira/CFO, Jose Paulo De Freitas/Chief Human Resources Officer, Jose Antonio Guaraldi Felix/COO, Andre Muller Borges/Chief Legal Counsel

Directors: Roberto Irineu Marinho/Chmn., Martin Roberto Glogowsky/Chmn. - Fiscal Board, Mauro Szwarcwald/Dir., Charles Barnsley Halland/Dir., Juarez D. Campos/Dir., Sergio Lourenco Marques/Dir., Augusto Cesar Roxo De Rocha Filho/Dir., Ivan Magalhaes/Dir., Stefan Alexander/Dir., Rossana Fontenele Berto/Dir., Jose Formoso Martinez/Dir., Antonio Jose Alves/Dir., Joao Adalberto Elek/Dir., Marcos Da Cunha Carneiro/Dir., Carlos Henrique Moreira/Dir.

Owners: GB Empreendimentos e Participaes, Distel Holding S.A., Embratel Participaes S.A., Globo Comunicao e Participaes ., Empresa Brasileira de Telecomunicaes, Empresa Brasileira de Telecomunicaes, Embratel Participaes S.A.

Financial Data: *Fiscal Year End:*12/31 *Latest Annual Data:* 12/31/2006

Year	Sales	Net Income
2006	$900,903,000	$204,681,000
2005	$660,665,000	$56,414,000
2004	$574,329,000	-$95,818,000

Curr. Assets:	$401,485,000	**Curr. Liab.:**	$257,097,000	**P/E Ratio:**	17.71
Plant, Equip.:	$610,552,000	**Total Liab.:**	$971,968,000	**Indic. Yr. Divd.:**	$0.040
Total Assets:	$1,811,025,000	**Net Worth:**	$839,057,000	**Debt/ Equity:**	NA

Net1 UEPS Technologies Inc

PO Box 2424, Parklands, 2121; ***PH:*** 27-113432000; ***http://*** www.net1ueps.com; ***Email:*** net1@net-1.org

General - Incorporation	FL	**Stock**- Price on:12/24/2007	$24.44
Employees	1,763	Stock Exchange	NDQ
Auditor	Deloitte & Touche LLP	Ticker Symbol	UEPS
Stk Agt	Bank of New York	Outstanding Shares	50,880,000
Counsel	NA	E.P.S.	$1.16
DUNS No.	NA	Shareholders	NA

Business: The group's principal activity is to commercialize the smart card based universal electronic payment system. It commercializes the universal electronic payment system through the development of strategic alliances with national and international bank, card service or retail organizations. The ueps is a software application that utilizes fund transfer system. The group also licenses entities that will operate specific applications that use fts intellectual property or the combined fts/ueps payment system. The group is a development stage company. On 07-Jun-2004, the group acquired net 1 applied technology holdings limited.

Primary SIC and add'l.: 3572

CIK No: 0001041514

Subsidiaries: Cash Paymaster Service (Pty) Limited, Cash Paymaster Services (Eastern Cape) (Pty) Limited, Cash Paymaster Services (Gauteng) (Pty) Limited, Cash Paymaster Services (KwaZulu Natal) (Pty) Limited, Cash Paymaster Services (North West) (Pty) Limited, Cash Paymaster Services (Northern Cape) (Pty) Limited, Cash Paymaster Services (Northern) (Pty) Limited, Friedland 035 Investments (Pty) Limited, Moneyline Financial Services (Pty) Limited, Net 1 Applied Technologies South Africa Limited, Net1 Finance Holdings (Pty) Limited, New World Finance (Pty) Limited, NUEP Holdings S.a.r.l., Prism Holdings Limited, Sinqobile Security Services (Gauteng) (Pty) Limited 16 Subsidiaries included in the Index

Officers: Serge Christian Pierre Belamant/Chmn., CEO, Nitin Soma/Executive Mgr. - Software Development, Brenda Stewart/Sr. VP - Sales, Marketing, Herman Kotze/Dir., CFO

Directors: Serge Christian Pierre Belamant/Chmn., CEO, Herman Kotze/Dir., CFO

Owners: Investment entities affiliated with Brait S.A./17.90%, Alasdair J.K. Pein, Serge C.P Belamant/4.10%, Florian P. Wendelstadt/12.20%, Investment entities affiliated with General Atlantic LLC/12.20%, Herman G. Kotz, Antony C. Ball, Gilder, Gagnon, Howe & Co. LLC/5.10%, Insiders/17.10%, Paul Edwards, Chris S. Seabrooke, Nitin Soma, Brookside Capital Partners Fund, L.P./5.20%, Brenda L. Stewart

Financial Data: *Fiscal Year End:*06/30 *Latest Annual Data:* 06/30/2007

Year	Sales	Net Income
2007	$223,968,000	$63,679,000
2006	$196,098,000	$59,232,000
2005	$176,290,000	$44,562,000

Curr. Assets:	$240,718,000	**Curr. Liab.:**	$43,123,000	**P/E Ratio:**	22.84
Plant, Equip.:	$3,757,000	**Total Liab.:**	$60,969,000	**Indic. Yr. Divd.:**	NA
Total Assets:	$269,979,000	**Net Worth:**	$209,010,000	**Debt/ Equity:**	NA

Net2phone Inc

520 Brd. St., Newark, NJ, 07102; ***PH:*** 1-973-438-3111; ***http://*** www.net2phone.com

General - Incorporation	DE	**Stock**- Price on:12/24/2007	$11.49
Employees	3,000	Stock Exchange	NDQ
Auditor	Ernst & Young LLP	Ticker Symbol	NTOP
Stk Agt	NA	Outstanding Shares	82,310,000
Counsel	NA	E.P.S.	$0.99
DUNS No.	NA	Shareholders	NA

Business: The group's principal activity is to provide voice over Internet protocol (voip) telephony products and services. It's products and services are marketed through three units: international communications services, domestic retail services and broadband telephony solutions. It's largest customers are located in Middle East, Asia and Latin America. The international communications services unit markets international long distance solutions utilizing voip technology. The domestic retail services unit sells voip minutes via both disposable and rechargeable calling cards primarily to consumers in the United States. The broadband telephony solutions unit provides cable operators with a fully outsourced end-to-end telecommunications solution utilizing existing high speed cable data networks and access into consumers' homes provided by the cable operator via cable modems.

Primary SIC and add'l.: 3661 4813 4822 7379

CIK No: 0001086472

Subsidiaries: Dekkam Holdings, B.V, Net2Phone America do Sul Comunicacoes Ltda, Net2Phone Cable Telephony, LLC, Net2Phone do Brasil Comunicacoes Ltda, Net2Phone Global Services, LLC, Net2Phone Global Servicos de Comunicacoes, Net2Phone MEA Ltd, Net2Phone, B.V, Sprewell Consultadorio e Projectos, Lda, VoIP Technology Holdings, LLC

Officers: Liore Alroy/Dir., CEO, Jonathan Reich/CEO - Net2phone Global Services, David Lando/COO - Net2phone Global Services, David Span/VP - Product Management, Marketing, Net2phone Global Services, Jose Colagrossi/Sr. VP, GM - International Channel Sales, Sr. VP, Jeffrey Skelton/CTO - Net2phone Global Services, Michael Pastor/Pres. - Net2phone Cable Telephony, Claude Pupkin/Exec. VP - Finance, Corporate Development, Net2phone Cable Telephony, Jeff Goldberg/Chief Scientist - Net2phone Cable Telephony

Directors: Liore Alroy/Dir., CEO

Financial Data: *Fiscal Year End:*07/31 *Latest Annual Data:* 7/31/2006

Year	Sales	Net Income
2006	$2,226,422,000	-$178,654,000
2005	$2,468,522,000	-$43,814,000
2004	$2,216,905,000	-$95,711,000

Curr. Assets:	$1,243,171,000	**Curr. Liab.:**	$679,812,000	**P/E Ratio:**	11.61
Plant, Equip.:	$292,152,000	**Total Liab.:**	$916,260,000	**Indic. Yr. Divd.:**	$1.000
Total Assets:	$1,762,839,000	**Net Worth:**	$803,352,000	**Debt/ Equity:**	0.1556

NetEase.com Inc

SP Tower D,26th Floor,Tsinghua Science Pk. Building, 8,No.1 Zhongguancun East Rd., Haidian District, Beijing, 100084; ***PH:*** 86-1082558163; ***Fax:*** 86-1082618163; ***http://*** www.netease.com; ***Email:*** ir@service.netease.com

General - Incorporation	Cayman Islands	**Stock**- Price on:12/24/2007	$17.25
Employees	1,601	Stock Exchange	NDQ
Auditor	PricewaterhouseCoopers	Ticker Symbol	NTES
Stk Agt	CT Corporation System	Outstanding Shares	126,410,000
Counsel	Morrison & Foerster LLP	E.P.S.	$1.23
DUNS No.	NA	Shareholders	NA

Business: The group's principal activities are the developing and providing Internet-related services including online games, wireless value-added and other fee based premium services and advertising services in China.

Primary SIC and add'l.: 7379 7372 5734 7311 4899 7312 7319

CIK No: 0001110646

Subsidiaries: Guangzhou Boguan Telecommunication Technology Limited, Guangzhou NetEase Interactive Entertainment Ltd., NetEase Information Technology (Beijing) Co., Ltd., NetEase Interactive Entertainment Ltd.

Officers: William Ding/Dir., CEO, Michael Tong/Dir., COO, Janelle Wu/Sr. VP - Product, Zhonghui Zhan/Co - COO, Feng Zhou/Sr. VP, Onward Choi/Acting CFO

Directors: William Ding/Dir., CEO, Michael Tong/Dir., COO, Denny Lee/Dir., Donghua Ding/Dir., Lun Feng/Dir., Michael Leung/Dir., Joseph Tong/Dir., Ted Sun/Dir., Alice Cheng/47/Dir.

Owners: Shining Globe International Limited/William Ding/47.20%, Michael Tong, Insiders/47.60%, Zhonghui Zhan, Legg Mason, Inc./5.30%, Lone Pine Capital LLC/6.30%, Denny Lee

Financial Data: *Fiscal Year End:*12/31 *Latest Annual Data:* 12/31/2006

Year	Sales	Net Income
2006	$277,336,000	$159,247,000
2005	$199,792,000	$115,485,000
2004	$109,335,000	$53,412,000

Curr. Assets:	$529,105,000	**Curr. Liab.:**	$86,673,000	**P/E Ratio:**	17.71
Plant, Equip.:	$28,729,000	**Total Liab.:**	$188,111,000	**Indic. Yr. Divd.:**	NA
Total Assets:	$560,437,000	**Net Worth:**	$372,326,000	**Debt/ Equity:**	NA

Netflix Inc

100 Winchester Cir., Los Gatos, CA, 95032; ***PH:*** 1-408-540-3700; ***http://*** www.netflix.com

General - Incorporation	DE	**Stock**- Price on:12/24/2007	$19.809
Employees	1,300	Stock Exchange	NYSE
Auditor	KPMG LLP	Ticker Symbol	NFS
Stk Agt	EquiServe Trust Co N.A	Outstanding Shares	68,260,000
Counsel	Wilson Sonsini Goodrich & Rosati	E.P.S.	$0.95
DUNS No.	NA	Shareholders	NA

Business: The group's principal activity is to provide online movie rental subscription service. The group provides more than 1,487,000 subscribers access to a comprehensive library of more than 18,000 movie, television and other filmed entertainment titles. It also provides background information on DVD releases, including critic reviews, member reviews and ratings and personalized movie recommendations. The standard subscription plan allows subscribers to have three titles out at the same time with no due dates, late fees or shipping charges for $19.95 per month. The group operates throughout the United States and reaches more than 80% of its subscribers with generally next-day delivery.

Primary SIC and add'l.: 7375 7841

CIK No: 0001065280

Officers: Reed Hastings/47/Founder, Chmn., CEO, Pres./$2,303,112.00, Patty McCord/Chief Talent Officer, Bill Henderson/COO, Ted Sarandos/Chief Content Officer, Leslie Kilgore/Chief Marketing Officer/$1,653,044.00, Neil Hunt/Chief Product Officer, Barry McCarthy/CFO/$1,763,849.00

Directors: Reed Hastings/47/Founder, Chmn., CEO, Pres., Michael Schuh/Dir., Richard N. Barton/Dir., Timothy Haley/Dir., George A. Battle/Dir., Jay Hoag/Dir., Greg Stanger/Dir., Charles Giancarlo/Dir.

Owners: Reed Hastings/6.88%, Gregory S. Stanger, Timothy M. Haley, Jay C. Hoag/21.24%, Richard N. Barton, Michael N. Schuh, Insiders/30.22%, George A. Battle, Entities related to Technology Crossover Ventures/21.22%, LMM, LLC/10.91%, Barry McCarthy/1.00%, Leslie Kilgore

Financial Data: *Fiscal Year End:*12/31 *Latest Annual Data:* 06/30/2007

Year	Sales	Net Income
2007	NA	NA
2006	$996,660,000	$49,082,000
2005	$682,213,000	$42,027,000

Curr. Assets:	$428,418,000	Curr. Liab.:	$193,447,000	P/E Ratio:	25.40
Plant, Equip.:	$55,503,000	Total Liab.:	$194,568,000	Indic. Yr. Divd.:	NA
Total Assets:	$608,779,000	Net Worth:	$414,211,000	Debt/ Equity:	NA

Netfone Inc

1030 W Georgia St., Ste. 918, Vancouver, BC, V6E 2Y3; *PH:* 1-604-676-3410;
Fax: 1-604-662-7950; *http://* www.netfone.ca; *Email:* info@netfone.ca

General - Incorporation	NV	Stock - Price on:12/24/2007	$1.75
Employees	NA	Stock Exchange	OTC
Auditor	Dale Matheson Carr-Hilton LaBonte LLP	Ticker Symbol	NFON
Stk Agt	Nevada Agency & Trust Company	Outstanding Shares	NA
Counsel	NA	E.P.S.	NA
DUNS No.	NA	Shareholders	NA

Business: The groups principle activity is to develop communication technology and services for internet protocol, telephone and video applications. The group operates from Canada and the United states.

Primary SIC and add'l.: 4813

CIK No: 0001307345

Subsidiaries: Netfone Services, Inc.,

Officers: Rafeh Hulays/40/Dir., Principal Executive Officer, Principal Financial Officer, Principal Accounting Officer, Pres., Treasurer, Sec.

Directors: Rafeh Hulays/40/Dir., Principal Executive Officer, Principal Financial Officer, Principal Accounting Officer, Pres., Treasurer, Sec., Walid Salem/33/Dir.

Owners: Rafeh Hulays/62.00%, Walid Salem/1.30%, Insiders/63.60%

Financial Data: Fiscal Year End:09/30 Latest Annual Data: 09/30/2006

Year	Sales	Net Income
2006	NA	NA
2005	NA	NA

Curr. Assets:	$21,000	Curr. Liab.:	$36,000		
Plant, Equip.:	$12,000	Total Liab.:	$169,000	Indic. Yr. Divd.:	NA
Total Assets:	$47,000	Net Worth:	-$122,000	Debt/ Equity:	NA

NETGEAR

4500 Great American Pkwy., Santa Clara, CA, 95054; *PH:* 1-408-907-8000; *Fax:* 1-408-907-8097; *http://* www.netgear.com

General - Incorporation	DE	Stock - Price on:12/24/2007	$37.13
Employees	388	Stock Exchange	NDQ
Auditor	PricewaterhouseCoopers LLP	Ticker Symbol	NTGR
Stk Agt	Mellon Investor Services LLC	Outstanding Shares	34,610,000
Counsel	NA	E.P.S.	$1.32
DUNS No.	NA	Shareholders	NA

Business: The group's principal activities are to design, develop and market technologically advanced, branded networking products that address the specific needs of small business and home users. The group supplies networking products that meet the ease-of-use, quality, reliability, performance and affordability requirements of these users. The suite of approximately 100 products enables users to share Internet access, peripherals, files, digital multimedia content and applications among multiple personal computers and other Internet-enabled devices. The group's products are sold in North America, Europe and Asia-Pacific.

Primary SIC and add'l.: 4841

CIK No: 0001122904

Subsidiaries: Netgear Holdings, Ltd., Netgear International, Inc.

Officers: Patrick C. Lo/Chmn., CEO/$1,003,040.00, Mark Merrill/CTO, Deborah A. Williams/50/Sr. VP - Marketing, Chief Marketing Officer, Albert Liu/VP - Legal, Corporate Development, Company Sec., Christine M. Gorjanc/Chief Accounting Officer/$331,860.00, David Soares/Sr. VP - Worldwide Sales, Support/$612,825.00, Michael F. Falcon/Sr. VP - Operations/$550,465.00, Charles Olson/Sr. VP - Engineering/$648,121.00, Michael Werdann/VP - Americas Sales, David Pasquale/Contact - Investor, Ken Hagihara/Contact - Integrity Public Relations, Lisa Hawes/Contact - Sterling Communications, Shira Litvak/Contact - Sterling Communications

Directors: Patrick C. Lo/Chmn., CEO, Gregory J. Rossmann/Dir., Timothy A. Godwin/Dir., Linwood A. Lacy/Dir., Ralph E. Faison/Dir., Jef Graham/Dir., George G.C. Parker/Dir., Julie A. Shimer/Dir.

Owners: Charles T. Olson, Insiders/3.90%, David S. Soares, Michael F. Falcon, Christine M. Gorjanc, Jonathan R. Mather, Linwood A. Lacy, Royce& Associates, LLC/7.50%, Ralph E. Faison, FMR Corp./14.70%, Timothy A. Godwin, Barclays Global Investors/5.60%, Patrick C.S. Lo/2.00%

Financial Data: Fiscal Year End:12/31 Latest Annual Data: 12/31/2006

Year	Sales	Net Income
2006	$573,570,000	$41,132,000
2005	$449,610,000	$33,623,000
2004	$383,139,000	$23,465,000

Curr. Assets:	$424,359,000	Curr. Liab.:	$143,482,000	P/E Ratio:	28.56
Plant, Equip.:	$6,568,000	Total Liab.:	$143,482,000	Indic. Yr. Divd.:	NA
Total Assets:	$437,904,000	Net Worth:	$294,422,000	Debt/ Equity:	0.0154

NetIQ

3553 N First St., San Jose, CA, 95134; *PH:* 1-408-330-7000; *http://* www.attachmate.com

General - Incorporation	DE	Stock - Price on:12/24/2007	$25.55
Employees	NA	Stock Exchange	NA
Auditor	Deloitte & Touche LLP	Ticker Symbol	NA
Stk Agt	Richard H. Van Hoesen	Outstanding Shares	NA
Counsel	Davis Polk & Wardwell	E.P.S.	NA
DUNS No.	NA	Shareholders	NA

Business: The group's principle activities are to develop, market and support systems management, security management and Web analytics solutions. It provides enterprise systems management software solutions for managing, securing and analyzing the key components of corporate enterprise computing infrastructure. Through its subsidiary, mission critical software inc, the group provides systems administration and operations management software products for corporate and Internet-based windows nt and windows 2000 networks. The products are marketed through direct sales force, distributors, systems integrators and value-added resellers. The group has operations in Australia, Belgium, Brazil, Canada, Denmark, France, Germany, Hong Kong, Italy, Japan, Korea, Singapore, South Africa, Spain, Sweden, Switzerland and the UK.

Primary SIC and add'l.: 7372 7379

CIK No: 0001084827

Subsidiaries: Database Tools Development (Proprietary) Limited, Marshal International Limited, Marshal Software Limited, Marshal Software LLC, Mission Critical Software, Inc., NetIQ Asia Limited, NetIQ Asia Pty Ltd., NetIQ Benelux, NetIQ Canada Corporation, NetIQ Denmark Aps, NetIQ Deutschland GmbH, NetIQ do Brasil Ltda., NetIQ Europe Limited, NetIQ France Sarl, NetIQ Ireland Limited 30 Subsidiaries included in the Index

Officers: Roberto Reiner/CTO, VP - Engineering, Netiq Business Unit, Thomas W. Hull/VP - Attachmate, Netiq North America Sales, Chris Pick/VP - Products, Marketing, Netiq Business Unit, Mike Steinmetz/VP - Worldwide Services, Support, Netiq Business Unit

Netlist Inc

475 Goddard, Irvine, CA, 92618; *PH:* 1-949-435-0025; *Fax:* 1-949-435-0031; *http://* www.netlistinc.com

General - Incorporation	DE	Stock - Price on:12/24/2007	$3.35
Employees	146	Stock Exchange	NYSE
Auditor	Corbin & CO., LLP	Ticker Symbol	NLY
Stk Agt	Computershare Trust CO.	Outstanding Shares	19,640,000
Counsel	NA	E.P.S.	-$0.29
DUNS No.	NA	Shareholders	NA

Business: The groups principal activities include designing and manufacturing memory subsystems. The products of the group include DDR, DDR2 and DRAM technologies. Specific customers of the group include IBM, Dell and Lenovo. The group operates from the United States. The net sale of the group for the year 2006 was $151,448 (thousands).

Primary SIC and add'l.: 3674 3572

CIK No: 0001282631

Subsidiaries: Netlist Holdings GP, Inc., Netlist Holdings LP, Inc., Netlist International, Netlist Technology Texas, L.P

Officers: Chun K. Hong/Chmn., CEO, Pres., Christopher Lopes/VP - Sales, Jayesh Bhakta/CTO, Devon Park/VP - Sales Operations, Paik Ki Hong/VP - Procurement, Jill Bertotti/Primary Investor Relations Officer, Gail Itow/VP - Finance, Jon Siann/VP - Marketing, Rick Hazell/VP - Emerging Marketing Sales, Harrison Jin/VP - Manufacturing Technology, Operations, Nita Moritz/CFO

Directors: Chun K. Hong/Chmn., CEO, Pres., David M. Rickey/Dir., Alan H. Portnoy/Dir., Preston Romm/Dir., Nam Ki Hong/Dir., Thomas F. Lagatta/Dir.

Owners: Nam Ki Hong, Jun S. Cho/5.20%, Alan H. Portnoy, Jayesh Bhakta/4.60%, Jae Dong Lee/6.70%, Preston Romm, Lee Kim, Chun Ki Hong/28.40%, David M. Rickey, Thomas F. Lagatta, Insiders/38.30%, Christopher Lopes/4.60%

Financial Data: Fiscal Year End:12/31 Latest Annual Data: 12/30/2006

Year	Sales	Net Income
2006	$151,448,000	$5,068,000
2005	$79,856,000	-$2,347,000

Curr. Assets:	$22,504,000	Curr. Liab.:	$19,785,000	P/E Ratio:	10.15
Plant, Equip.:	$2,437,000	Total Liab.:	$22,987,000	Indic. Yr. Divd.:	NA
Total Assets:	$25,842,000	Net Worth:	$2,855,000	Debt/ Equity:	0.0197

NetLogic Microsystems

1875 Charleston Rd., Mountain View, CA, 94043; *PH:* 1-650-961-6676; *Fax:* 1-650-961-1092; *http://* www.netlogicmicro.com; *Email:* info@netlogicmicro.com

General - Incorporation	DE	Stock - Price on:12/24/2007	$29.12
Employees	170	Stock Exchange	NYSE
Auditor	PricewaterhouseCoopers LLP	Ticker Symbol	NEU
Stk Agt	Wells Fargo Shareowner Services	Outstanding Shares	20,760,000
Counsel	NA	E.P.S.	NA
DUNS No.	NA	Shareholders	NA

Business: The group's principal activities are to design, develop and market high performance knowledge-based processors for a variety of advanced Internet, corporate and other networking systems. Knowledge-based processors are integrated circuits that employ an advanced processor architecture and a large integrated circuits that employ an advanced processor architecture and a large complex decisions about individual packets of information travelling through the network. The principal customers of the group are alcatel, arris group, inc., atrica Israel, ltd., cisco systems, inc.,cloudshield technologies, inc., extreme networks, inc., fujitsu limited, hitachi, ltd., huawei technologies co., ltd., juniper networks, inc., and nortel networks corporation.

Primary SIC and add'l.: 3674

CIK No: 0001135711

Officers: Ron Jankov/Dir., CEO, Pres./$1,117,458.00, Donald Witmer/54/CFO, VP/$556,904.00, Varad Srinivasan/CTO, VP - Product Development/$577,292.00, Leslie Green/Contact, Roland B. Cortes/43/Sr. Dir. - Legal Affairs, IP Management, Sec., Michael T. Tate/CFO, VP, Mo Maghsoudnia/VP - Worldwide Manufacturing, Niall Bartlett/VP - Corporate Development, Ibrahim Korgav/Sr. VP - Manufacturing, Business Operations/$540,263.00, Dimitrios Dimitrelis/VP - Engineering, Marcia Zander/Sr. VP - Worldwide Sales/$698,948.00

Directors: Ron Jankov/Dir., CEO, Pres., Len Perham/Chmn., Steve Domenik/Dir., Doug Broyles/Dir., Alan Krock/Dir., Norman Godinho/Founder, Dir.

Owners: Citadel Investment Group, LLC/5.20%, The Godinho Family Revocable Living Trust/15.00%, Leonard Perham, Shigeyuki Hamamatsu, Franklin Advisers, Inc./6.50%, Douglas Broyles, Norman Godinho/15.00%, Marcia Zander, Insiders/23.00%, Wasatch Advisors, Inc./5.40%, Ibrahim Korgav, Steve Domenik, Alan Krock, Varadarajan Srinivasan/1.20%, Ronald Jankov/3.80% *(17 Owners included in Index)*

Curr. Assets:	$109,705,000	Curr. Liab.:	$13,719,000	P/E Ratio:	66.18
Plant, Equip.:	$5,530,000	Total Liab.:	$15,245,000	Indic. Yr. Divd.:	NA
Total Assets:	$157,769,000	Net Worth:	$142,524,000	Debt/ Equity:	NA

Netmanage Inc

20883 Stevens Creek Blvd., Cupertino, CA, 95014; *PH:* 1-408-973-7171; *Fax:* 1-408-257-6405; *http://* www.netmanage.com; *Email:* sales@netmanage.com

General - Incorporation	DE	Stock - Price on:12/24/2007	$4.85
Employees	215	Stock Exchange	NDQ
Auditor	Deloitte & Touche LLP	Ticker Symbol	NA
Stk Agt	Computershare Investor Services LLC	Outstanding Shares	9,560,000
Counsel	Kirkland & Ellis LLP	E.P.S	-$0.41
DUNS No.	62-339-7494	Shareholders	NA

Business: The group's principal activity is to develop and market software and service solutions. The group provides specific personal computer and network or application server-based software and tools. These products enable the customers to access and use their mission-critical line of business host applications and resources. The group also provides professional support, maintenance, and technical consultancy services. The group operates in two segments: host access and host integration. Host acess segment provides the technology to make the connection between personal computers and large corporate computers possible. The host integration segment provides the technology to allow customers to leverage the investment they have in existing host-based systems, applications and business processes for new Web-based presentations, applications, and solutions. Netmanage(R), onweb(R) , rumba(R), viewnow(R), onnet(R), chameleon(R), supportnow(R) are the trademarks of the group.

Primary SIC and add'l.: 7372

CIK No: 0000909793

Subsidiaries: FTP Software Worldwide, Inc. - Branch, FTP Software, Inc., N.Y. NetManage (Yerushalayim) Ltd., NetManage Canada Inc., NetManage Iberia, S.L., NetManage Italia SRL, NetManage Japan K.K., NetManage SARL, NetManage Software GmbH, NetManage UK Limited, NetManage Veenendaal HFL, NetManage, Inc., NetManage, Ltd., NetSoft Benelux BVBA, NetSoft, Inc. 19 Subsidiaries included in the Index

Officers: Zvi Alon/Chmn., CEO, Pres./$655,932.00, Ido Hardonag/Sr. VP - Worldwide Engineering/$299,759.00, Ron Rudolph/VP - Human Resources, Cheli Dudai-Karpel/VP - Operations Europe, Israel/$276,601.00, George Bennett/VP - North America Sales/$360,803.00, Omer Regev/CFO, VP - Finance

Directors: Zvi Alon/Chmn., CEO, Pres., Uzia Galil/83/Dir., Darrell Miller/61/Dir., Abraham Ostrovsky/65/Dir., Harry J. Saal/65/Dir.

Owners: Cheli Aflalo-Karpel, Darrell Miller, Ido Hardonag, Abraham Ostrovsky, Shelley Harrison/1.19%, Zvi Alon/18.73%, Riley Investment Management LLC/7.04%, Emancipation Capital Master, Ltd./7.24%, Uzia Galil, Insiders/23.16%, Spectrum Galaxy Fund Ltd./8.40%, George Bennett, John Bosch

Financial Data: *Fiscal Year End:*12/31 *Latest Annual Data:* 12/31/2006

Year	Sales	Net Income
2006	$35,561,000	-$2,536,000
2005	$43,434,000	$4,711,000
2004	$47,666,000	$1,424,000

Curr. Assets:	$39,601,000	Curr. Liab.:	$22,214,000		
Plant, Equip.:	$2,243,000	Total Liab.:	$26,176,000	Indic. Yr. Divd.:	NA
Total Assets:	$47,353,000	Net Worth:	$21,177,000	Debt/ Equity:	0.0106

Netopia Inc

6001 Shellmound St. 4th Fl., Market Place, CA, 94608; *PH:* 1-510-420-7400; *http://* www.netopia.com

General - Incorporation	DE	Stock - Price on:12/24/2007	NA
Employees	NA	Stock Exchange	NDQ
Auditor	Burr, Pilger & Mayer LLP	Ticker Symbol	NTRI
Stk Agt	Mellon Investor Services LLC	Outstanding Shares	NA
Counsel	Gunderson Dettmer Stough Et Al	E.P.S	NA
DUNS No.	17-543-2608	Shareholders	NA

Business: The group's principal activities are to develop, market and support broadband and wireless products and services to simplify and enhance the delivery of broadband services to their residential and business-class customers. The group's products are Internet equipment and Web platform. Internet equipment includes modems, routers and gateways, which enable telecommunications carriers to provide cost-effective and high-speed services over existing copper infrastructure. Web platform includes the netoctopus suite of server software products and systems management software products. Netoctopus suite includes edgemanager, ecare and desktop support, and Web ecommerce server. Systems management software includes timbuktu, which provides remote computer control, configuration, support and file transfer. The markets for the products include the United States, Canada, Europe and Asia-Pacific and other. In Oct 2003, the group acquired jadesail systems, inc.

Primary SIC and add'l.: 7379 3661 7371

CIK No: 0001012482

Subsidiaries: Business Solutions Division of the Siemens Subscriber Networks, Inc, JadeSail, Siemens AG, Westell Technologies, Inc, Wire, Inc

Officers: Philip Simmons/VP - Hardware Engineering

Owners: Howard T. Slayen, Charles Constanti, Alan B. Lefkof/3.21%, Harold S. Wills, Glazer Capital, LLC/8.60%, Insiders/11.07%, Raymond J. Smets, David A. Kadish/1.62%, Reese M. Jones/3.76%, Brooke A. Hauch/1.10%, Francois J. Crepin, Robert Lee

Netratings Inc

770 Broadway, 13th Fl., 35th Fl., New York, NY, 10003; *PH:* 1-646-654-7990; *Fax:* 1-212-703-5901; *http://* www.nielsen-netratings.com

General - Incorporation	DE	Stock - Price on:12/24/2007	$20.96
Employees	397	Stock Exchange	NDQ
Auditor	Ernst & Young LLP	Ticker Symbol	NTST
Stk Agt	Continental Stock Transfer & Trust Co	Outstanding Shares	36,080,000
Counsel	Gray, Cary, Ware & Freidenrich	E.P.S	$0.08
DUNS No.	NA	Shareholders	NA

Business: The group's principal activity is to provide Internet audience measurement and analysis. These services include measurement of audience behaviour for the world wide Web and the digital media universe, including proprietary channels, instant messaging, media players and other online applications. Primary products of the group include netview, adrelevance/lemonad, @plan, megapanel and sitecensus. Customers include advertising agencies, media companies, financial services institutions, e-commerce companies and traditional marketers requiring analysis of the online environment. The group sells its products also in Europe, Asia-Pacific, Latin America, France, Japan and Brazil. The group acquired mmxi Switzerland, netcrawling sa and majority interest in red sheriff limited in 2003.

Primary SIC and add'l.: 7379 7375 7389 8732 7371

CIK No: 0001095480

Subsidiaries: ACNielsen eRatings.com, Mediametrie NetRatings, MMXI Switzerland GmbH, Netcrawling Deutschland GmbH, Netcrawling UK Limited, NetRatings (Shanghai) Company,Ltd, NetRatings Australia Pty Ltd, NetRatings France SARL, NetRatings Italia S.r.l., NetRatings Japan, NetRatings Spain, S.L., NetRatings UK Ltd, NetValue Internet Measurement SA, NetValue USA,Inc., Nielsen-NetRatings Pty Ltd 24 Subsidiaries included in the Index

Officers: William Pulver/Dir., CEO, Pres., Manish Bhatia/42/Exec. VP - Global Operations, US Sales, Susan Hickey/42/Sr. VP, Todd Sloan/Exec. VP - Corporate Development, CFO, Sec., Forrest Didier/MD - Apla, John Kleine/54/CTO, Sr. VP - Engineering, Operations, Alan Shapiro/39/Sr. VP, General Counsel, Louise Ainsworth/41/MD - EMEA

Directors: William Pulver/Dir., CEO, Pres., John Dimling/Chmn., David Harkness/Dir., Scott Mercer/57/Dir., Jerrell W. Shelton/Dir., Thomas Mastrelli/60/Dir., James O'Hara/45/Dir., Arthur F. Kingsbury/Dir., Susan D. Whiting/51/Dir.

Owners: John A. Dimling, Forrest Didier, Scott D. Mercer, David H. Harkness, Valcon Acquisition Holding, William R. Pulver, Susan D. Whiting, John Kleine, Manish Bhatia, Arthur F. Kingsbury, James M. OHara, Jerrell W. Shelton, Insiders, Thomas A. Mastrelli, Todd Sloan *(16 Owners included in Index)*

Financial Data: *Fiscal Year End:*12/31 *Latest Annual Data:* 12/31/2006

Year	Sales	Net Income
2006	$81,769,000	$2,829,000
2005	$68,017,000	-$8,395,000
2004	$59,294,000	-$17,419,000

Curr. Assets:	$201,566,000	Curr. Liab.:	$40,977,000	P/E Ratio:	262.00
Plant, Equip.:	$9,582,000	Total Liab.:	$41,041,000	Indic. Yr. Divd.:	NA
Total Assets:	$315,473,000	Net Worth:	$272,211,000	Debt/ Equity:	NA

NetScout Systems Inc

310 Littleton Rd., Westford, MA, 01886; *PH:* 1-978-614-4000; *Fax:* 1-978-614-4004; *http://* www.netscout.com

General - Incorporation	DE	Stock - Price on:12/24/2007	$8.03
Employees	364	Stock Exchange	NDQ
Auditor	PricewaterhouseCoopers LLP	Ticker Symbol	NTCT
Stk Agt	Mellon Investor Services LLC	Outstanding Shares	32,190,000
Counsel	Sullivan & Worcester LLP	E.P.S	$0.23
DUNS No.	NA	Shareholders	NA

Business: The group's principal activities are to design, develop, manufacture and market a family of integrated products that optimize performance and cost management of complex, high-speed networks. These products are sold under the ngenius(R) brand to enterprises, large governmental agencies and service providers worldwide. The ngenius solution generates information, analyzes it and publishes it in real-time displays and customizable historical reports. These reports summarize the status of network activity, service levels, application performance, device capacity, and other critical aspects of network availability, utilization and performance, and are delivered to the end-user in an easy-to-read, Web-based newspaper format.

Primary SIC and add'l.: 6794 7373 7372

CIK No: 0001078075

Subsidiaries: NetScout Service Level Corporation, NetScout Systems (HK) Limited, NetScout Systems (UK) Limited, NetScout Systems Canada Inc., NetScout Systems France, SARL, NetScout Systems Germany GmbH, NetScout Systems India Pvt. Ltd., NetScout Systems Japan K.K., NetScout Systems Mexico, S.A. de C.V., NetScout Systems Norway AS, NetScout Systems Security Corporation, NetScout Systems Singapore Pte Ltd., NetScout Systems Switzerland GmbH

Officers: Anil K. Singhal/Chmn., CEO, Pres./$550,567.00, John Downing/Sr. VP - Worldwide Sales Operations/$328,040.00, Bruce Sweet/VP - Business Development, David P. Sommers/CFO, Sr. VP - General Operations/$290,000.00, Bruce Kelley/CTO, VP, Michael Szabados/COO/$300,064.00, Ashwani Singhal/Sr. VP - Research, Development, Jim Frey/VP - Marketing, Tracy Steele/VP - Manufacturing, Business Operations, Jeff Wakely/VP - Finance, Chief Accounting Officer/$197,308.00, Alan Fink/VP - Corporate Development, Catherine Taylor/Dir. - Investor Relations

Directors: Anil K. Singhal/Chmn., CEO, Pres., Narendra V. Popat/Founder, Joseph G. Hadzima/Dir., John R. Egan/Dir., Vincent J. Mullarkey/Dir., Victor A. Demarines/Dir., Stuart M. McGuigan/Dir., Stephen G. Pearse/Dir.

Owners: John W. Downing, Anil K. Singhal/9.00%, Brown Capital Management, Inc./9.10%, Stephen Pearse, David P. Sommers/1.00%, Joseph G. Hadzima, Vincent J. Mullarkey, John R. Egan, Narendra V. Popat/7.00%, Victor A. DeMarines, Michael Szabados, Jyoti Popat/7.50%, Stuart McGuigan, Jeffrey R. Wakely, TA Entities/10.20% *(16 Owners included in Index)*

Financial Data: *Fiscal Year End:*03/31 *Latest Annual Data:* 3/31/2007

Year	Sales	Net Income
2007	$102,472,000	$7,737,000
2006	$97,876,000	$5,797,000
2005	$85,214,000	$2,870,000

Curr. Assets:	$117,580,000	Curr. Liab.:	$38,087,000	P/E Ratio:	29.74
Plant, Equip.:	$8,262,000	Total Liab.:	$42,012,000	Indic. Yr. Divd.:	NA
Total Assets:	$180,419,000	Net Worth:	$138,407,000	Debt/ Equity:	NA

NetSol Technologies

23901 Calabasas Rd., Ste. 2072, Calabasas, CA, 91302; *PH:* 1-818-222-9195; *Fax:* 1-818-222-9197; *http://* www.netsoltek.com; *Email:* info@netsoltek.com

General - Incorporation	NV	Stock - Price on:12/24/2007	NA
Employees	708	Stock Exchange	NYSE
Auditor	Kabani & Co, Inc	Ticker Symbol	NTZ
Stk Agt	Computershare Trust Co	Outstanding Shares	19,660,000
Counsel	Patti L. W. Mcglasson	E.P.S	-$0.17
DUNS No.	NA	Shareholders	NA

Business: The group's principal activities are to design, develop, market and export proprietary software products for the automobile finance and leasing industries. The group also provides outsourcing, systems integration, customized it solutions, project/program management and i/t management consultancy services, as well as, e-business solutions. Products include epos, proposal management

system, wholesale finance system, settlement management system and contract management system. These products are sold as an integrated lease and finance package. Customers include daimlerchrysler finance, Singapore; mercedes benz leasing, Thailand; debis portfolio systems, United Kingdom; yamaha motors, Australia and citibank, pakistan. The group has international operations in Europe, the Pacific Rim, Australia and pakistan.

Primary SIC and add'l.: 7379 7372

CIK No: 0001039280

Subsidiaries: McCue Systems, Inc., NetSol Abraxas, Inc., NetSol Connect (Pvt) Limited, NetSol Omni, NetSol Technologies Ltd, NetSol Technologies Ltd., NetSol USA, Inc., NetSol-CQ Ltd., TIG-NetSol (Pvt) Limited

Officers: Najeeb Ghauri/Chmn., CEO, Andrew Lea/VP - Marketing, Corporate Communications, Todd Brinkmeier/VP - Sales North America, Gary Lowrey/Commercial Dir., Naeem Ghauri/Dir., Pres. - European Region, Tina Gilger/CFO, Fred Firth/MD - Netsol, Abraxas Pty Limited, Salim Ghauri/Dir., Pres., Patti L.W. McGlasson/Company Sec., Corporate Counsel, Sajjad Kirmani/Exec. VP - Information Technology - Operations, Netsol Technologies, Ltd, Malea Farsai/Corporate Counsel

Directors: Najeeb Ghauri/Chmn., CEO, Shahid Javed Burki/Dir., Naeem Ghauri/Dir., Pres. - European Region, Graham Tarrant/Dir., Eugen Beckert/Dir., Salim Ghauri/Dir., Pres., Mark Caton/Dir., Alexander Shakow/Dir.

Owners: Salim Ghauri/11.12%, Najeeb Ghauri/11.28%, Tina Gilger, Mark Caton, Patti McGlasson, Eugen Beckert, Shahid Javed Burki, Naeem Ghauri/10.58%, Insiders/35.42%, The Tail Wind Fund Ltd./9.90%

Financial Data: Fiscal Year End:06/30 Latest Annual Data: 06/30/2007

Year	Sales	Net Income
2007	$29,282,000	-$4,878,000
2006	$18,690,000	-$1,353,000
2005	$12,438,000	$663,000

Curr. Assets:	$22,230,000	Curr. Liab.:	$11,555,000		
Plant, Equip.:	$6,472,000	Total Liab.:	$15,243,000	Indic. Yr. Divd.:	NA
Total Assets:	$43,025,000	Net Worth:	$26,145,000	Debt/ Equity:	0.0075

Nettel Holdings Inc

1260 Commerce Ave., Longview, WA, 98632; **PH:** 1-360-369-6367; **Fax:** 1-360-326-1750; **http://** www.nettelholdings.com; **Email:** info@nettelholdings.com

General - Incorporation	FL	Stock - Price on:12/24/2007	$0.568
Employees	3	Stock Exchange	OTC
Auditor	Kabani & Company, Inc.	Ticker Symbol	NTTL
Stk Agt	Florida Atlantic Stock Transfer, Inc.	Outstanding Shares	44,230,000
Counsel	Dieterich & Associates	E.P.S.	-$0.096
DUNS No.	NA	Shareholders	NA

Business: The groups principle activities include selling telecommunication minutes and prepaid calling cards. The group operates through two segments namely equipment sales and telecommunications. The group operates from the United States. The group's quarterly revenue for Sep '07 was 5.32 millions of USD.

Primary SIC and add'l.: 4813

CIK No: 0001084883

Officers: Michael Nguyen/37/Chmn., CFO, CEO, Pres.

Directors: Michael Nguyen/37/Chmn., CFO, CEO, Pres.

Owners: Michael Nguyen/24.00%

Financial Data: Fiscal Year End:12/31 Latest Annual Data: 12/31/2006

Year	Sales	Net Income
2006	$7,833,000	-$784,000
2005	$9,617,000	-$1,780,000
2004	$2,663,000	-$2,740,000

Curr. Assets:	$489,000	Curr. Liab.:	$526,000		
Plant, Equip.:	$99,000	Total Liab.:	$526,000	Indic. Yr. Divd.:	NA
Total Assets:	$588,000	Net Worth:	$62,000	Debt/ Equity:	NA

NETtime Solutions Inc

Formerly: Time America Inc
8840 E Chaparral Rd., Ste. 100, Scottsdale, AZ, 85250; **PH:** 1-480-296-0400; **http://** www.timeamerica.com

General - Incorporation	NV	Stock - Price on:12/24/2007	NA
Employees	41	Stock Exchange	NYSE
Auditor	Semple, Marchal & Cooper, LLP	Ticker Symbol	TWX
Stk Agt	American Stock Transfer & Trust Co.	Outstanding Shares	NA
Counsel	NA	E.P.S.	NA
DUNS No.	NA	Shareholders	NA

Business: The group's principle activity is to design, develop, manufacture and market a line of time and labor management hardware and software products targeting small to mid-sized companies. The products are designed to improve productivity by automating time and attendance, workforce scheduling and management of labor resources. The products of the company are internally developed, proprietary software applications that maintain and automate the process of collecting time sheet information and provide reports to help companies track and analyze how their employees spend their time. Professional and educational services are designed to support the customers throughout the life cycle of the company's products. The group's quarterly revenue for Sep '07 was 11,676.00 millions of USD.

Primary SIC and add'l.: 7375 7372 7379

CIK No: 0000836937

Subsidiaries: NetEdge Devices, LLC, Time America, Inc.

Officers: Bahan Sadegh/35/Dir., CEO, Pres., Jon Weiss/Interim CEO, VP - Business Delopment, Thomas J. Klitzke/34/VP - Finance, Administration, Principal Accounting Officer, Controller, James Martin/VP

Directors: Bahan Sadegh/35/Dir., CEO, Pres., Todd P. Belfer/Chmn., Robert W. Zimmerman/Dir., Lise Lambert/Dir., Robert J. Novak/Dir., Timothy S. Jeffries/45/Dir.

Owners: Circle F. Ventures LLC/6.40%, Todd P. Belfer/10.90%, Lise M. Lambert/2.10%, Tim Jeffries, Robert W. Zimmerman/2.60%, Anthony Silverman/11.00%, Laurus Capital Management LLC/7.00%, Bahan Sadegh/1.80%, Thomas S. Bednarik/6.70%, Insiders/17.60%, Thomas J. Klitzke, Joseph L. Simek/26.30%

Financial Data: Fiscal Year End:06/30 Latest Annual Data: 06/30/2007

Year	Sales			Net Income
2007	$5,377,000			$140,000
2006	$6,716,000			-$1,946,000
2005	$6,082,000			-$2,020,000

Curr. Assets:	$1,274,000	Curr. Liab.:	$2,321,000		
Plant, Equip.:	$294,000	Total Liab.:	$3,438,000	Indic. Yr. Divd.:	NA
Total Assets:	$1,603,000	Net Worth:	-$1,835,000	Debt/ Equity:	NA

Netwolves Corp

4710 Eisenhower Blvd, Tampa, FL, 33634; **PH:** 1-813-286-8644; **Fax:** 1-813-286-8744; **http://** www.netwolves.com

General - Incorporation	NY	Stock - Price on:12/24/2007	NA
Employees	NA	Stock Exchange	OTC
Auditor	Marcum & Kliegman LLP	Ticker Symbol	WOLV
Stk Agt	American Stock Transfer & Trust Co.	Outstanding Shares	NA
Counsel	Beckman, Lieberman & Barandes LLP	E.P.S.	NA
DUNS No.	NA	Shareholders	NA

Business: The group's principal activity is to design, develop, manufacture and market products that provide a secure, integrated, modular Internet gateway. The group's products, netwolves security suite and gateway platforms, provide sophisticated, easy-to-use devices for securely connecting people and networks to the Internet by combining a wide range of functionalities and communications choices. These functionalities include Internet access, firewall security, Web access control, e-mail, ip routing, Web server, Web caching server, dns caching server, dhcp server, and file sharing in an easy-to-configure integrated software and hardware gateway solution. The group provides consulting, educational and training services primarily to the oil and gas and automotive industries.

Primary SIC and add'l.: 7372 8748

CIK No: 0001084103

Subsidiaries: ComputerCOP Corp., NetWolves Technologies Corporation, NNS, Inc., Norstan Network Services, Inc, TSG Global Education, Inc.

Officers: Scott Foote/Dir., CEO, Pres., Peter Castle/Dir., CFO, Ryan Kelly/VP - Sales, Leonard Luttinger/Sr. VP - Enterprise Sales

Directors: Scott Foote/Dir., CEO, Pres., Fassil Gabremariam/Dir., Peter Castle/Dir., CFO, Gerald Gagliardi/Dir., Michael Rocque/Dir.

Owners: Scott E. Foote/1.80%, Gerald A. Gagliardi/1.20%, Fassil Gabremariam/1.50%, Walter M. Groteke/5.70%, Triage Management LLC/17.00%, Walter R. Groteke/2.80%, Insiders/10.40%, Peter C. Castle/4.00%, Triage Management LLC/62.80%, Michael R.Rocque/1.30%, Ryan Kelly/1.20%, Triage Management LLC/4.60%

Curr. Assets:	$5,512,000	Curr. Liab.:	$6,394,000		
Plant, Equip.:	$149,000	Total Liab.:	$7,513,000	Indic. Yr. Divd.:	NA
Total Assets:	$10,724,000	Net Worth:	$3,212,000	Debt/ Equity:	0.0825

Network 1 Security Solutions Inc

445 Pk. Ave., Ste 1028, New York, NY, 10022; **PH:** 1-212-829-5770; **http://** www.network-1.com; **Email:** info@network-1.com

General - Incorporation	DE	Stock - Price on:12/24/2007	$1.7
Employees	1	Stock Exchange	OTC
Auditor	Radin, Glass & Co. LLP	Ticker Symbol	NSSI
Stk Agt	American Stock Transfer & Trust Co.	Outstanding Shares	23,170,000
Counsel	Olshan Grundman Frome Et Al	E.P.S.	-$0.16
DUNS No.	61-945-4143	Shareholders	NA

Business: The group's principle activities include acquiring, developing, licensing and protecting intellectual property. The products are designed to prevent unauthorized access to critical information residing on networked servers, desktops and laptops. The company's cyberwallplus family of security software combines the benefits of firewall and intrusion detection technology. It completed the sale of its cyberwallplus technology and related intellectual property in may 2003. On 18-Nov-2003, it acquired a portfolio of telecommunications and data networking patents (the 'patent portfolio'). The patent portfolio consists of six patents issued by the U.S. Patent office that relate to various telecommunications and data networking technologies. It provides the transmission of audio, video and data over computer and telephony networks and the delivery of power over ethernet network. The company is currently pursuing licensing opportunities related to its patent portfolio technologies. The group operates from United States.

Primary SIC and add'l.: 7372 7379

CIK No: 0001065078

Subsidiaries: Emigrant Bancorp, Inc, Emigrant Savings Bank, New York Private Bank & Trust Corporation

Officers: Corey M. Horowitz/Chmn., CEO, David C. Kahn/CFO, Jonathan Greene/Member - Technical Advisory Board, Marketing, Business Development Consultant

Directors: Corey M. Horowitz/Chmn., CEO, Robert Pons/Dir., Robert Graifman/Dir., Harry B. Schessel/Dir., George Conant/Member - Technical Advisory Board, Ron Keenan/Member - Technical Advisory Board, Andrew Maslow/Member - Technical Advisory Board, Jonathan Greene/Member - Technical Advisory Board, Marketing, Business Development Consultant

Owners: Hound Partners Offshore Fund, L.P./6.90%, Wheatley Partners II, L.P./5.50%, David C. Kahn, Laurent Ohana, Robert Pons, Insiders/34.60%, Emigrant Capital Corporation/5.50%, Harry B. Schessel, Hound Partners, L.P./6.80%, Barry Fingerhut/8.70%, Emigrant Savings Bank/5.50%, Eric Singer/5.30%, Irwin Lieber/8.80%, Steve Heinemann/5.00%, Robert Graifman/1.50%

Financial Data: Fiscal Year End:12/31 Latest Annual Data: 12/31/2006

Year	Sales	Net Income
2006	NA	-$1,958,000
2005	NA	-$1,332,000
2004	NA	-$1,953,000

Curr. Assets:	$1,875,000	Curr. Liab.:	$569,000		
Plant, Equip.:	NA	Total Liab.:	$569,000	Indic. Yr. Divd.:	NA
Total Assets:	$1,971,000	Net Worth:	$1,402,000	Debt/ Equity:	NA

Network Appliance Inc

495 E Java Dr., Sunnyvale, CA, 94089; **PH:** 1-408-822-6000; **Fax:** 1-408-822-4501; **http://** www.netapp.com

General - Incorporation	DE	**Stock**- Price on:12/24/2007	$31.794
Employees	4,976	Stock Exchange	NYSE
Auditor	Deloitte & Touche LLP	Ticker Symbol	NTE
Stk Agt	Computershare Investor Services LLC	Outstanding Shares	371,060,000
Counsel	Wilson Sonsini Goodrich & Rosati	E.P.S	$0.72
DUNS No.	80-205-4742	Shareholders	NA

Business: The groups principle activity is to provide data management solutions. The groups products include FC SAN, NAS, secure operating systems, Data Retention and Archive Software Products, NearStore, Virtual Tape Library, and manageability software. The groups services include SupportEdge, ConsultingEdge and NetApp University. The group operates from United States.

Primary SIC and add'l.: 3572

CIK No: 0001002047

Subsidiaries: Alacritus, Inc., Decru BV, Decru Ltd., Decru, Inc., Nagano Sub, Inc., NetApp Holding Ltd., Network Appliance, Network Appliance Argentina, Network Appliance BV, Network Appliance Canada Ltd., Network Appliance Denmark ApS, Network Appliance Federal Systems, Inc., Network Appliance Financial Solutions, Inc., Network Appliance Finland Oy, Network Appliance FSC Incorporated 36 Subsidiaries included in the Index

Officers: Daniel J. Warmenhoven/Dir., CEO/$6,429,982.00, Rich Clifton/Sr. VP, GM - Networked Storage Business Units, Jay Kidd/Chief Marketing Officer, Ed Deenihan/Exec. VP - Netapp Global Services, Rob Salmon/Exec. VP - Field Operations/$2,748,946.00, Tom Georgens/Exec. VP, Product OperationsExec. VP - Product Operations/$3,548,035.00, Thomas F. Mendoza/Pres./$3,301,107.00, James Lau/Founder, Exec. VP, Chief Strategy Officer, Suresh Vasudevan/Sr. VP, GM - Networked Storage, Manageability Group, Steve Kleiman/Sr. VP, Chief Scientist, David Hitz/Founder, Exec. VP, D. P. Linehan/Sr. VP, GM - EMEA, Mark Jon Bluth/Sr. VP - Operations, Steve Gomo/CFO, Exec. VP - Finance/$1,642,692.00, George Bennett/Sr. VP - Americas Sales *(21 Officers included in Index)*

Directors: Daniel J. Warmenhoven/Dir., CEO, Donald T. Valentine/Chmn., Robert T. Wall/Dir., Mark Leslie/Dir., Nicholas G. Moore/Dir., George T. Shaheen/Dir., Carol A. Bartz/59/Dir., Edward Kozel/52/Dir., David Hitz/Founder, Exec. VP, Jeffry R. Allen/56/Dir., James Lau/Founder, Exec. VP, Chief Strategy Officer, Alan L. Earhart/Dir.

Owners: George T. Shaheen, Alan L. Earhart, Wellington Company Management/7.40%, Carol A. Bartz, Edward Kozel, Thomas F. Mendoza, TCW Asset Management/8.40%, Steven J. Gomo, Jeffry R. Allen, Insiders/3.90%, Daniel J. Warmenhoven/2.30%, AllianceBernstein Capital Management/9.40%, Robert F. Salmon, Donald T. Valentine, Robert T. Wall *(19 Owners included in Index)*

Financial Data: *Fiscal Year End:*04/30 *Latest Annual Data:* 04/27/2007

Year	Sales	Net Income
2007	$2,804,282,000	$297,735,000
2006	$2,066,456,000	$266,452,000
2005	$1,598,131,000	$225,754,000

Curr. Assets:	$2,033,210,000	**Curr. Liab.:**	$917,163,000		
Plant, Equip.:	$513,193,000	**Total Liab.:**	$1,337,512,000	**Indic. Yr. Divd.:**	NA
Total Assets:	$3,260,965,000	**Net Worth:**	$1,923,453,000	**Debt/ Equity:**	0.0137

Network CN Inc

Formerly: TEDA Travel Group Inc

21/f., Chinachem Century Tower, 178 Gloucester Rd., Wanchai, Hong Kong; ***PH:*** 852-283-32186; ***http://*** www.tedatravelgroup.com

General - Incorporation	DE	**Stock**- Price on:12/24/2007	$2.76
Employees	NA	Stock Exchange	NA
Auditor	Webb & Co P.A	Ticker Symbol	NA
Stk Agt	Holladay Stock Transfer, Inc.	Outstanding Shares	NA
Counsel	Crone Rozynko LLP	E.P.S	NA
DUNS No.	NA	Shareholders	NA

Business: The group has no business and is now seeking a reverse merger partner. The group was initially formed to attempt to distribute an anticancer drug in Mexico. The group failed to raise enough capital to obtain the exclusive distribution rights to the drug.

Primary SIC and add'l.: 8742 7372 7311

CIK No: 0000934796

Subsidiaries: British Virgin Islands Corporation, Landmark International Hotel Development Limited, Landmark International Hotel Group Ltd., Teda (Beijing) Hotels Management Limited, Teda BV, Teda Hotels Management Company Limited, Teda Hotels Management Limited

Owners: Bloompoint Investment Limited/21.05%, Insiders/1.50%, Daley Mok, Gerd Jakob, Godfrey Hui, Benedict Fung

Financial Data: *Fiscal Year End:*12/31 *Latest Annual Data:* 12/31/2006

Year	Sales	Net Income
2006	$4,443,000	-$4,469,000
2005	$894,000	-$2,051,000
2004	$568,000	-$4,516,000

Curr. Assets:	$3,649,000	**Curr. Liab.:**	$1,012,000		
Plant, Equip.:	$87,000	**Total Liab.:**	$1,102,000	**Indic. Yr. Divd.:**	NA
Total Assets:	$10,527,000	**Net Worth:**	$9,425,000	**Debt/ Equity:**	NA

Network Engines Inc

25 Dan Rd., Canton, MA, 02021; ***PH:*** 1-781-332-1000; ***Fax:*** 1-781-770-2000; ***http://*** www.networkengines.com; ***Email:*** ir@networkengines.com

General - Incorporation	DE	**Stock**- Price on:12/24/2007	$1.82
Employees	145	Stock Exchange	NDQ
Auditor	PricewaterhouseCoopers LLP	Ticker Symbol	NENG
Stk Agt	Computershare Ltd.	Outstanding Shares	40,830,000
Counsel	Wilmer Cutler Pickering H & D LLP	E.P.S	$0.06
DUNS No.	NA	Shareholders	NA

Business: The group's principal activity is to develop, manufacture and distribute server appliance solutions. These solutions enable network equipment providers and independent software vendors to deliver data storage and security networking applications to their customers. The group operates in two segments: OEM appliance and distribution. The OEM appliance segment includes server appliance development, manufacturing and logistics services. The distribution segment includes distribution of third party products and components related to data storage area networking and server appliances. The group currently offers the products under the trademarks network engines and tidalwire. The group operates in the United States and other foreign countries. On 27-Dec-2002, it acquired tidalwire inc.

Primary SIC and add'l.: 3577 5045 7373 7379

CIK No: 0001110903

Subsidiaries: Network Engines International, Inc., Network Engines Securities Corporation, Network Engines UK, Ltd

Officers: Gregory A. Shortell/Dir., CEO, Pres., Rich Graber/VP - Engineering, Operations, Doug Bryant/CFO, Kevin Murphy/CTO, Hugh Kelly/VP - Worldwide Marketing, Bob Joyce/Financial Dynamics, Primary Investor Relations Officer, Peter Schmidt/Financial Dynamics, Primary Investor Relations Officer, Wilmer Cutler/Legal, Richard P. Graber/48/Pres. - Engineering, Operations, Paul Butler/47/VP - Worldwide Sales, Leads, Jim Herlihy/VP - Finance, Administration

Directors: Gregory A. Shortell/Dir., CEO, Pres., Robert Wadsworth/Dir., Charles Foley/Dir., John A. Blaeser/Dir., Dennis Kirshy/Dir., Gary Haroian/Dir., Fontaine Richardson/Dir., Jack Blaeser/Dir.

Owners: Dennis A. Kirshy, John A. Blaeser, Kevin J. Murphy, Robert M. Wadsworth/14.70%, HarbourVest Partners, LLC and affiliated entities/14.50%, Fontaine K. Richardson, Gary E. Haroian, Richard P. Graber, Gregory A. Shortell, Douglas G. Bryant/1.10%, Insiders/18.70%

Financial Data: *Fiscal Year End:*09/30 *Latest Annual Data:* 9/30/2006

Year	Sales	Net Income
2006	$118,696,000	-$5,447,000
2005	$98,071,000	-$15,583,000
2004	$136,755,000	-$1,619,000

Curr. Assets:	$59,948,000	**Curr. Liab.:**	$12,057,000	**P/E Ratio:**	182.00
Plant, Equip.:	$1,093,000	**Total Liab.:**	$12,658,000	**Indic. Yr. Divd.:**	NA
Total Assets:	$61,061,000	**Net Worth:**	$48,403,000	**Debt/ Equity:**	0.0009

Network Equipment Technologies Inc

6900 Paseo PaDr.e Pkwy., Fremont, CA, 94555; ***PH:*** 1-510-713-7300; ***Fax:*** 1-510-574-4000; ***http://*** www.net.com; ***Email:*** info@net.com

General - Incorporation	DE	**Stock**- Price on:12/24/2007	$9.61
Employees	238	Stock Exchange	NYSE
Auditor	Deloitte & Touche LLP	Ticker Symbol	NWK
Stk Agt	EquiServe Trust Co N.A	Outstanding Shares	26,360,000
Counsel	NA	E.P.S	-$0.648
DUNS No.	10-277-6481	Shareholders	NA

Business: The group's principle activities are to design, develop, manufacture and market multiservice wide area networking equipment. The group also provides associated services including product installation, software maintenance programs, parts repair, remote and on-site technical assistance and customer training. The group's product brands include scream service creation manager(tm) platform, promina and shoutip Internet telephony platform. The group sells its products and services through both direct and indirect sales channels worldwide. The customers of the group include financial, banking, insurance, energy, transportation, manufacturing and retail enterprises, carriers, service providers and government agencies. The group's quarterly revenue for September 2007 was 27.33 millions of USD.

Primary SIC and add'l.: 5065 7373 3663 7379

CIK No: 0000752431

Subsidiaries: N.E.T. Federal, Inc

Officers: Nicholas C. Keating/Dir., CEO, Pres./$617,422.00, David Wagenseller/VP - Finance, Terry Fore/VP - Operations, Matthew D. Krueger/VP - Business Development, Talbot Harty/VP, GM - Voice, Mobility Solutions/$304,366.00, John F. McGrath/CFO, VP/$408,179.00, Frank Slattery/VP, General Counsel/$340,079.00, Gary L. Lau/Sr. VP - Government Sales/$666,242.00, Leigh Salvo/Investor Relations Officer, John Sandschulte/VP, GM - Broadband Technology Group, Francois Le/VP - International

Directors: Nicholas C. Keating/Dir., CEO, Pres., Dixon R. Doll/Chmn., Frederick D'Alessio/Dir., David R. Laube/Dir.

Owners: Royce & Associates, Inc./9.10%, John F. McGrath/1.10%, Dixon R. Doll/1.10%, Talbot A. Harty, KCM Investment Advisors/8.30%, David R. Laube, Gary L. Lau, R. Eliot King & Associates Incorporated and John K. Nelson/6.90%, Insiders/5.60%, Frank Slattery, Kopp Investment Advisors,/5.60%, Renaissance Technologies Corp./5.10%, Nicholas C. Keating, Frederick D. DAlessio, Peter Sommerer *(16 Owners included in Index)*

Financial Data: *Fiscal Year End:*03/31 *Latest Annual Data:* 3/30/2007

Year	Sales	Net Income
2007	$84,094,000	-$16,194,000
2006	$69,768,000	-$27,235,000
2005	$114,218,000	-$6,432,000

Curr. Assets:	$111,562,000	**Curr. Liab.:**	$19,153,000		
Plant, Equip.:	$20,749,000	**Total Liab.:**	$44,532,000	**Indic. Yr. Divd.:**	NA
Total Assets:	$136,678,000	**Net Worth:**	$92,146,000	**Debt/ Equity:**	NA

Neuberger Berman Inc

605 Third Ave, New York, NY, 10158; ***PH:*** 1-212-476-9000; ***http://*** www.nb.com

General - Incorporation	DE	**Stock**- Price on:12/24/2007	$23.41
Employees	NA	Stock Exchange	NYSE
Auditor	NA	Ticker Symbol	NA
Stk Agt	American Stock Transfer & Trust Co.	Outstanding Shares	27,370,000
Counsel	Willkie Farr & Gallagher	E.P.S	$5.72
DUNS No.	NA	Shareholders	NA

Business: The groups principal activity is to provide private asset management, mutual fund and institutional and professional securities services. The group operates from the United States.

Primary SIC and add'l.: 6282

CIK No: 0001068144

Officers: Jeffrey L. Maier/Contact, Kevin Handwerker/General Counsel

Financial Data: *Fiscal Year End:*12/31 *Latest Annual Data:* 10/31/2006

Year	Sales	Net Income
2006	$217,797,000	$211,310,000
2005	$101,290,000	$95,298,000
2004	$137,774,000	$132,259,000

Curr. Assets:	$1,474,000	**Curr. Liab.:**	$1,785,000		
Plant, Equip.:	NA	**Total Liab.:**	$32,945,000	**Indic. Yr. Divd.:**	$2.440
Total Assets:	$1,011,470,000	**Net Worth:**	$978,525,000	**Debt/ Equity:**	NA

Neurobiological Technologies Inc

2000 Powell St., Ste. 800, Emeryville, CA, 94608; ***PH:*** 1-510-595-6000; ***Fax:*** 1-510-595-6006; ***http://*** www.ntii.com

General - Incorporation	DE	**Stock**- Price on:12/24/2007	$2.01
Employees	33	Stock Exchange	NDQ
Auditor	Odenberg, Muranishi & Co. LLP	Ticker Symbol	NA
Stk Agt	Mellon Investor Services LLC	Outstanding Shares	32,820,000
Counsel.	Heller Ehrman White & McAuliffe LLP	E.P.S	-$2.82
DUNS No.	62-387-7842	Shareholders	NA

Business: The group's principle activity is to develop drugs. The company is in the development stages and is conducting clinical evaluation and regulatory approval of neuroscience drugs. Its strategy is to in-license and develop early-stage and later-stage drug candidates that target major medical needs and can be commercialized. Currently, the company has two product candidates: memantime and xerecept (TM). Memantime is an orally dosed compound that helps in restoring the function of impaired neurons. Xerecept is applied for the treatment of brain swelling due to brain tumors. The company seeks partnerships with pharmaceutical and biotechnology companies to complete development and marketing of its product candidates. On 15-Jul-2004, the company acquired empire pharmaceuticals inc. The group operates from United States.

Primary SIC and add'l.: 2834 8731

CIK No: 0000918112

Subsidiaries: NTI-Empire, Inc.

Officers: Paul E. Freiman/Dir., CEO, Pres., Craig W. Carlson/CFO, VP, Karl G. Trass/VP - Regulatory Affairs, Quality Assurance, David E. Levy/VP - Clinical Development, Maureen Wesley/Mgr. - Administration, Human Resources, Warren W. Wasiewski/VP - Clinical Programs

Directors: Paul E. Freiman/Dir., CEO, Pres., Abraham E. Cohen/Chmn., John B. Stuppin/Dir., Abraham D. Sofaer/Dir., F. Van Kasper/Dir., Theodore L. Eliot/Dir., Enoch Callaway/Dir., Ronald E. Cape/Dir., William A. Fletcher/Dir.

Owners: Paul E. Freiman/2.59%, John B. Stuppin/2.76%, Theodore L. Eliot, Ronald E. Cape, Insiders/48.58%, BVF, Inc./7.76%, Abraham D. Sofaer/1.99%, Abraham E. Cohen/1.97%, Stephen J. Petti/6.19%, Van F. Kasper, Ronald E. Cape/8.10%, Abraham D. Sofaer/20.02%, Karl G. Trass, David E. Levy, John B. Stuppin/20.02% *(18 Owners included in Index)*

Financial Data: ***Fiscal Year End:***06/30 ***Latest Annual Data:*** 06/30/2007

Year	Sales	Net Income
2007	$17,673,000	-$14,128,000
2006	$12,339,000	-$27,839,000
2005	$3,100,000	-$17,322,000

Curr. Assets:	$21,664,000	***Curr. Liab.:***	$9,609,000		
Plant, Equip.:	$752,000	***Total Liab.:***	$33,901,000	***Indic. Yr. Divd.:***	NA
Total Assets:	$22,499,000	***Net Worth:***	-$11,402,000	***Debt/ Equity:***	NA

Neurochem Inc

275 Armand-Frappier Blvd., Laval, PQ, H7V 4A7; ***PH:*** 1-450-680-4500; ***http://*** www.neurochem.com; ***Email:*** webinfo@neurochem.com

General - Incorporation	Canada	**Stock**- Price on:12/24/2007	$7.15
Employees	218	Stock Exchange	NDQ
Auditor	KPMG LLP	Ticker Symbol	NA
Stk Agt	Computershare Trust Co	Outstanding Shares	38,780,000
Counsel	NA	E.P.S	-$1.94
DUNS No.	NA	Shareholders	NA

Business: The groups principle activities include discovering, developing and commercializing products to provide innovation health solutions to patients suffering from serious diseases. The group operates from Canada.

Primary SIC and add'l.: NA

CIK No: 0001259942

Subsidiaries: Neurochem (International) Limited, Neurochem Holdings Limited, Neurochem Luxco II S.A.R.L

Officers: Francesco Bellini/61/Chmn., CEO, Pres., Andreas Orfanos/Exec. VP - Strategic Planning, Scientific Affairs, Colin Bier/Dir., Consultant, David Skinner/VP, General Counsel, Corp. Sec., Denis Garceau/Sr. VP - Drug Development, Philippe Calais/Pres. - Global Business, Judith Paquin/VP - Human Resources, Mariano Rodriguez/VP - Finance, CFO, Daniel Delorme/VP - Research, Shona McDiarmid/VP - Intellectual Property, Compliance, Christine Lennon/VP - Business Development, Neil Flanzraich/Consultant, Dir., Lise Hebert/VP - Corporate Communications, Laurent Choppe/General Managerneurochem, International Limited

Directors: Francesco Bellini/61/Chmn., CEO, Pres., Francois Legault/Dir., Jean-Guy Desjardins/Dir., Peter Kruyt/Dir., Emil Skamene/Dir., John Molloy/Dir., Andre Desmarais/Dir., Neil Flanzraich/Consultant, Dir., Calin Rovinescu/Dir., Laura M. Dember/Member - Advisory Board, Philip N. Hawkins/Member - Advisory Board, Bouke P.C. Hazenberg/Member - Advisory Board, Martha Skinner/Member - Advisory Board, Paul Aisen/Member - Advisory Board, Howard Chertkow/Member - Advisory Board *(30 Directors included in Index)*

Financial Data: ***Fiscal Year End:***06/30 ***Latest Annual Data:*** 12/31/2006

Year	Sales	Net Income
2006	$2,743,000	-$65,311,000
2005	$3,810,000	-$58,148,000
2004	$110,000	-$41,597,000

Curr. Assets:	$59,219,000	***Curr. Liab.:***	$22,378,000		
Plant, Equip.:	$3,912,000	***Total Liab.:***	$81,834,000	***Indic. Yr. Divd.:***	NA
Total Assets:	$71,403,000	***Net Worth:***	-$10,431,000	***Debt/ Equity:***	NA

Neurocrine Biosciences Inc

12790 El Camino Real, San Diego, CA, 92130; ***PH:*** 1-858-617-7600; ***Fax:*** 1-858-617-7601; ***http://*** www.neurocrine.com; ***Email:*** info@neurocrine.com

General - Incorporation	DE	**Stock**- Price on:12/24/2007	$12.55
Employees	261	Stock Exchange	NDQ
Auditor	Ernst & Young LLP	Ticker Symbol	NBIX
Stk Agt	American Stock Transfer & Trust Co.	Outstanding Shares	37,990,000
Counsel	Margaret Valeur-Jensen	E.P.S	-$2.48
DUNS No.	80-098-1276	Shareholders	NA

Business: The group's principal activities are to discover and develop pharmaceutical products for neurologic and endocrine diseases and disorders. The group has developed therapeutic interventions for anxiety, depression, insomnia, stroke, malignant brain tumors, multiple sclerosis, obesity and diabetes. The product candidates in clinical development include indiplon for insomnia, gnrh antagonist for endometriosis, altered peptide ligand for multiple sclerosis and diabetes, d2 receptor agonist for sexual dysfunction, crf r1 antagonist for anxiety and depression, crf r2 peptide agonist for cardiovascular system and il-4 fusion toxin for tumors and malignant glioma. The group currently has 13 programs in various stages of research and development, including clinical development. It currently has active product development collaborations with pfizer, inc., glaxosmithkline , wyeth and taisho pharmaceutical co., ltd.

Primary SIC and add'l.: 2834 8731 2836

CIK No: 0000914475

Subsidiaries: Neurocrine Continental, Inc., Neurocrine HQ, Inc., Neurocrine International LLC, Science Park Center LLC

Officers: Gary A. Lyons/Dir., CEO, Pres./$3,490,668.00, Margaret Valeur-Jensen/Exec. VP, General Counsel, Corp. Sec./$942,186.00, Kevin C. Gorman/Dir., COO/$847,082.00, Richard Ranier/Sr. VP - Human Resources/$859,044.00, Tim Coughlin/CFO, VP/$434,783.00, Bill Wilson/VP - Information Technology, Carol Baum/VP - Marketing, Barbara Finn/VP - Regulatory Affairs - Quality Assurance, Dimitri E. Grigoriadis/VP - Research, Haig Bozigian/Sr. VP - Pharmaceutical, Preclinical Development, Christopher O'Brien/Chief Medical Officer, Elizabeth Foster/Dir. - Investor Relations

Directors: Gary A. Lyons/Dir., CEO, Pres., Joseph A. Mollica/Chmn., Richard F. Pops/Dir., Stephen A. Sherwin/Dir., Thomas W. Mitchell/Dir., Wylie W. Vale/Dir., Kevin C. Gorman/Dir., COO, Corinne Lyle/Dir.

Owners: Adrian Adams, Thomas W. Mitchell, Stephen A. Sherwin, Federated Investors Inc/12.90%, FMR Corp./13.80%, Janus Capital Management LLC/5.60%, Wendell Wierenga, Timothy P. Coughlin, Insiders/6.40%, Joseph A. Mollica, Kevin C. Gorman, Margaret Valeur-Jensen, Corinne H. Lyle, Richard Ranieri, Richard F. Pops *(18 Owners included in Index)*

Financial Data: ***Fiscal Year End:***12/31 ***Latest Annual Data:*** 12/31/2006

Year	Sales	Net Income
2006	$39,234,000	-$107,205,000
2005	$123,889,000	-$22,191,000
2004	$85,176,000	-$45,773,000

Curr. Assets:	$193,658,000	***Curr. Liab.:***	$20,116,000		
Plant, Equip.:	$91,378,000	***Total Liab.:***	$74,961,000	***Indic. Yr. Divd.:***	NA
Total Assets:	$389,677,000	***Net Worth:***	$314,716,000	***Debt/ Equity:***	0.1663

Neurogen Corp

35 NE Industrial Rd., Branford, CT, 06405; ***PH:*** 1-203-488-8201; ***Fax:*** 1-203-481-8683; ***http://*** www.neurogen.com

General - Incorporation	DE	**Stock**- Price on:12/24/2007	$8.22
Employees	166	Stock Exchange	NDQ
Auditor	PricewaterhouseCoopers LLP	Ticker Symbol	NRGN
Stk Agt	American Stock Transfer & Trust Co.	Outstanding Shares	41,860,000
Counsel	NA	E.P.S	-$1.56
DUNS No.	36-149-4743	Shareholders	NA

Business: The group's principal activities are to discover and develop new drugs for the treatment of neurological, inflammatory, pain and metabolic disorders. Through its accelerated intelligent drug discovery (TM) platform, it discovers compounds that hit new potential drug targets, evaluates the utility of those targets and optimizes useful leads into new drug candidates. The group has collaboration agreements with aventis pharmaceuticals for the discovery and research of crf1 receptor-based drugs. It also has a technology transfer agreement with pfizer inc. For the licensing and transfer of the group's proprietary technologies for the discovery of new drugs to pfizer as well as collaboration agreements for the discovery of gaba-based drugs for anxiety and cognitive disorders.

Primary SIC and add'l.: 2834 8731

CIK No: 0000849043

Subsidiaries: Neurogen Properties, LLC

Officers: William H. Koster/Dir., CEO/$837,514.00, Charles A. Ritrovato/VP - Discovery Technologies/$513,849.00, Stephen R. Davis/Dir., Pres./$560,496.00, Charles J. Manly/VP - Discovery Technologies, James E. Krause/Sr. VP - Biology/$446,369.00, Alan J. Hutchison/Exec. VP - Discovery Research/$533,384.00, Thomas A. Pitler/VP - Business Development, Bertrand L. Chenard/Sr. VP - Chemistry, Process Research/$473,002.00, Julian C. Baker/Dir., Managing Partner - Baker Brothers Investments, Elaine Dodge/Assoc. Dir. - Investor, Public Relations, Ricardo Ochoa/VP - Preclinical Safety, Arunee Changchit/VP - Drug Metabolism, Pharmacokinetics, Jeffrey Dill/VP, General Counsel, Sec., George D. Maynard/VP - Early Development

Directors: William H. Koster/Dir., CEO, Craig Saxton/Chmn., Julian C. Baker/Dir., Managing Partner - Baker Brothers Investments, Stewart Hen/Dir., Eran Broshy/Dir., Stephen R. Davis/Dir., Pres., John Simon/Dir., Felix J. Baker/Dir., Jonathan S. Leff/Dir.

Owners: James E. Krause, Daniel R. Tisch/2.30%, Stephen Uden, Stephen R. Davis, Pfizer Inc/6.80%, Jonathan S. Leff, Eran Broshy, Thomas J. Tisch/3.00%, Andrew H. Tisch/2.30%, Craig Saxton, John Simon, Alan J. Hutchison, James S. Tisch/2.30%, Julian C. Baker/12.70%, BlackRock Financial Management, Inc./5.20% *(22 Owners included in Index)*

Financial Data: ***Fiscal Year End:***12/31 ***Latest Annual Data:*** 12/31/2006

Year	Sales	Net Income
2006	$9,813,000	-$53,776,000
2005	$7,558,000	-$37,120,000
2004	$19,180,000	-$18,593,000

Curr. Assets:	$110,593,000	***Curr. Liab.:***	$17,455,000		
Plant, Equip.:	$27,085,000	***Total Liab.:***	$33,199,000	***Indic. Yr. Divd.:***	NA
Total Assets:	$137,739,000	***Net Worth:***	$104,540,000	***Debt/ Equity:***	0.0992

Neurologix Inc

One Bridge Plz., Fort Lee, NJ, 07024; ***PH:*** 1-205-926-6451; ***http://*** www.neurologix.net

General - Incorporation	DE	**Stock**- Price on:12/24/2007	$0.9
Employees	8	Stock Exchange	OTC
Auditor	BDO Seidman, LLP	Ticker Symbol	NRGX
Stk Agt	Computershare Trust Co	Outstanding Shares	26,540,000
Counsel	NA	E.P.S	-$0.28
DUNS No.	09-414-4433	Shareholders	NA

Business: The group's principal activities are to design and produce interactive media, primarily for the entertainment industry. He broad range of professional consulting services provided by the group includes e-business and technology strategy, online branding, Web architecture and design, systems integration, systems architecture and outsourcing. The group assists its clients to reinvent their traditional business model and adapt their business to the Internet and the digital economy and identify and act upon opportunities in communications technology and e-services.

Primary SIC and add'l.: 7389 7375 7373 6719 7372

CIK No: 0000356591

Subsidiaries: Neurologix Research Inc

Officers: John E. Mordock/Dir., CEO, Pres./$394,008.00, Marc L. Panoff/CFO, Treasurer/$289,158.00, Christine V. Sapan/Exec. VP, Chief Development Officer/$206,554.00, Matthew J. During/Member - Scientific Advisory Board, Company Consultants, Michael G. Kaplitt/Member - Scientific Advisory Board, Company Consultants

Directors: John E. Mordock/Dir., CEO, Pres., Paul Greengard/Chmn. - Scientific Advisory Board, Martin J. Kaplitt/Chmn., Craig J. Nickels/Dir., Jeffrey B. Reich/44/Dir., Cornelius E. Golding/60/Dir., Clark A. Johnson/Dir., Austin M. Long/Dir., Elliott H. Singer/Dir., Andres M. Lozano/Member - Scientific Advisory Board, Andrew Brooks/Member - Scientific Advisory Board, Eric J. Nestler/Member - Scientific Advisory Board, Daniel H. Lowenstein/Member - Scientific Advisory Board, Matthew J. During/Member - Scientific Advisory Board, Company Consultants, Michael G. Kaplitt/Member - Scientific Advisory Board, Company Consultants (16 Directors included in Index)

Owners: Michael Sorell/2.25%, Medtronic, Inc./6.73%, Elliott H. Singer, DaimlerChrysler Corp. Master Retirement Trust/11.73%, Clark A. Johnson/1.88%, Jeffrey B. Reich, Warwick J. Greenwood, Trustee ATEC Trust/9.90%, John E. Mordock, Trustees of General Electric Pension Trust/11.73%, Austin M. Long, Craig J. Nickels, Insiders/13.06%, Insiders/13.06%, Marc L. Panoff, Palisade Private Partnership, L.P./19.99% (18 Owners included in Index)

Financial Data: Fiscal Year End:12/31 Latest Annual Data: 12/31/2006

Year	Sales	Net Income
2006	NA	-$7,046,000
2005	NA	-$5,345,000
2004	NA	-$2,937,000

Curr. Assets:	$10,891,000	**Curr. Liab.:**	$729,000		
Plant, Equip.:	$169,000	**Total Liab.:**	$729,000	**Indic. Yr. Divd.:**	NA
Total Assets:	$11,580,000	**Net Worth:**	$10,851,000	**Debt/ Equity:**	NA

NeuroMetrix Inc

62 4th Ave., Waltham, MA, 02451; **PH:** 1-781-890-9989; **Fax:** 1-781-890-1556; **http://** www.neurometrix.com; **Email:** info@neurometrix.com

General - Incorporation	DE	**Stock** - Price on:12/24/2007	$10.75
Employees	123	Stock Exchange	NDQ
Auditor	PricewaterhouseCoopers LLP	Ticker Symbol	NURO
Stk Agt	American Stock Transfer & Trust Co.	Outstanding Shares	12,610,000
Counsel	NA	E.P.S.	-$0.41
DUNS No.	NA	Shareholders	NA

Business: The groups principle activities include designing, developing and selling medical devices. The products of the group include diagnostic device and biosensor. The group products sold under the trade names DigiScope(R), NEUROMetrix(R), NC-stat(R), ADVANCE(TM) and onCall(TM). Customers served by the group include orthopedic surgeons, endocrinologists, rheumatologists, and pain medicine physicians. The group operates from the United States. The group's quarterly revenue for September 2007 was 11.29 millions of USD.

Primary SIC and add'l.: 3845 3821 3841

CIK No: 0001289850

Officers: Shai N. Gozani/Chmn., CEO, Pres., Gary L. Gregory/COO, Bradford W. Smith/52/CFO, Sec., Guy Daniello/Sr. VP - Information Technology, Michael Williams/Sr. VP - Engineering

Directors: Shai N. Gozani/Chmn., CEO, Pres., Allen Hinkle/Dir., David E. Goodman/Dir., Charles R. Lamantia/Dir., Jonathan T. Lord/53/Dir., Mark W. Lortz/Dir.

Owners: State of Wisconsin Investment Board/9.70%, JPMorgan Chase & Co/6.60%, Wells Fargo & Company/5.40%, Allen Hinkle, Charles R. Lamantia, Michael Williams, Gary L. Gregory, Barclays Global Investors NA/6.40%, Guy Daniello, Mark W. Lortz, FMR Corp./15.00%, Jonathan T. Lord, Shai N. Gozani/5.70%, Insiders/7.40%, Bradford W. Smith (16 Owners included in Index)

Financial Data: Fiscal Year End:12/31 Latest Annual Data: 12/31/2006

Year	Sales	Net Income
2006	$55,250,000	$4,268,000
2005	$34,394,000	$938,000
2004	$17,920,000	-$4,284,000

Curr. Assets:	$52,784,000	**Curr. Liab.:**	$10,890,000		
Plant, Equip.:	$1,115,000	**Total Liab.:**	$12,298,000	**Indic. Yr. Divd.:**	$0.600
Total Assets:	$55,706,000	**Net Worth:**	$43,409,000	**Debt/ Equity:**	NA

Neustar Inc

46000 Ctr. Oak Plz., Sterling, VA, 20166; **PH:** 1-571-434-5400; **Fax:** 1-571-434-5401; **http://** www.neustar.biz

General - Incorporation	DE	**Stock** - Price on:12/24/2007	$0.095
Employees	822	Stock Exchange	NDQ
Auditor	Ernst& Young LLP	Ticker Symbol	NSSC
Stk Agt	Wachovia Bank N.A	Outstanding Shares	75,840,000
Counsel	NA	E.P.S.	$0.92
DUNS No.	NA	Shareholders	NA

Business: The groups principle activity is to provide communication services, critical technology services and addressing services. In the year 2006, the group acquired UltraDNS Corporation and Followap, Inc. The group operates from the United States. The groups quarterly revenue for September 2007 was 110.76 millions of USD.

Primary SIC and add'l.: 3661 4899 7389

CIK No: 0001265888

Subsidiaries: Followap GmbH, Followap Inc., Followap Limited, Followap R&D (2000)Ltd., NeuLevel, Inc., NeuStar Secretariat Services, LLC, UltraDNS Corporation

Officers: Jeffrey E. Ganek/Chmn., CEO, Lawrence J. Bouman/COO, Jeffrey A. Babka/Sr. VP, CFO, Mark D. Foster/CTO, Sr. VP, John Spirtos/Sr. VP - Corporate Development, Marketing, Martin Lowen/Sr. VP, General Counsel, Ray Saulino/Sr. VP - Sales, Business Development, Douglas Arnold/Sr. VP - Human Resources, Allen Scott/GM - Next Generation Messaging, Steve Johnson/Sr. VP - Marketing, Jerry Kovach/Sr. VP - External Affairs

Directors: Jeffrey E. Ganek/Chmn., CEO, James G. Cullen/Dir., Ross Ireland/Dir., Kenneth A. Pickar/Dir., Hellene Runtagh/Dir., Joel Friedman/Dir., Michael Rowny/Dir., Paul Lacouture/Dir.

Owners: Mark D. Foster/1.45%, Kenneth A. Pickar, James G. Cullen, John B. Spirtos, Michael Lach, Michael J. Rowny, Jeffrey E. Ganek/1.67%, Jeffrey A. Babka, Wellington Management Company, LLP/7.20%, Janus Capital Management LLC/7.44%, Insiders/4.02%, AXA Financial, Inc. and affiliates/6.96%, Transamerica Investment Management, LLC/5.07%

Financial Data: Fiscal Year End:12/31 Latest Annual Data: 12/31/2006

Year	Sales	Net Income
2006	$332,957,000	$73,899,000
2005	$242,469,000	$55,398,000
2004	$165,001,000	$45,376,000

Curr. Assets:	$135,675,000	**Curr. Liab.:**	$81,705,000	**P/E Ratio:**	0.10
Plant, Equip.:	$42,678,000	**Total Liab.:**	$107,113,000	**Indic. Yr. Divd.:**	NA
Total Assets:	$448,259,000	**Net Worth:**	$341,146,000	**Debt/ Equity:**	0.0084

Neutron Enterprises Inc

450 Matheson Blvd. E, Mississauga, ON, L4Z 1R5; **PH:** 1-905-238-1777; **http://** www.neutrongroup.com

General - Incorporation	NV	**Stock** - Price on:12/24/2007	$0.88
Employees	NA	Stock Exchange	OTC
Auditor	Staley, Okada & Partners	Ticker Symbol	NTRN
Stk Agt	Interwest Transfer Company, Inc.	Outstanding Shares	NA
Counsel	NA	E.P.S.	NA
DUNS No.	NA	Shareholders	NA

Business: The groups principle activity is to provide software and services to the education and corporate markets. The services of the group include advertising, marketing and brand messaging sales on innovative fixed and mobile. The group operates through two segments namely event marketing and stock market. The group operates from the United States and Canada.

Primary SIC and add'l.: 7389

CIK No: 0001135140

Subsidiaries: 4234260 Canada, Inc., Neutron Media, Inc., Stock-Trak, Inc.

Officers: Rory Olson/49/Chmn., CEO, Mitchell Rosen/48/CFO, Exec. VP, Mark Wolinsky/34/COO, Mark T. Brookshire/Pres. - Stock, Track, Inc, Ray Shapira/VP - Event, Screen Marketing

Directors: Rory Olson/49/Chmn., CEO, Andrew Gertler/46/Vice Chmn., Paul Denommee/50/Dir., Bryson F. Farrill/79/Dir., Steve Shaper/Dir.

Owners: Mark Brookshire/1.30%, Mitchell Rosen, William Friedman/19.30%, Blue Moon Holdings Ltd/6.30%, Mark Wolinsky, Jason Baybutt/6.10%, Rory Olson/3.50%, Insiders/7.50%, Ciaran Griffin, Bryson F. Farrill, Paul Denommee, Andrew Gertler/1.30%

Financial Data: Fiscal Year End:12/31 Latest Annual Data: 12/31/2006

Year	Sales	Net Income
2006	$2,099,000	-$9,161,000
2005	$1,021,000	-$4,391,000
2004	NA	-$23,480,000

Curr. Assets:	$3,459,000	**Curr. Liab.:**	$939,000		
Plant, Equip.:	$85,000	**Total Liab.:**	$939,000	**Indic. Yr. Divd.:**	NA
Total Assets:	$3,807,000	**Net Worth:**	$2,868,000	**Debt/ Equity:**	NA

Nevada Chemicals Inc

9149 S Monroe Plz. Way, Ste. B, Sandy, UT, 84070; **PH:** 1-801-984-0228; **Fax:** 1-801-984-0231; **http://** www.nevadachemicals.com

General - Incorporation	UT	**Stock** - Price on:12/24/2007	$10.3
Employees	2	Stock Exchange	NDQ
Auditor	Tanner LC	Ticker Symbol	NCIT
Stk Agt	Zions Bank Corporate Trust Services	Outstanding Shares	6,980,000
Counsel	NA	E.P.S.	$0.62
DUNS No.	09-776-5788	Shareholders	NA

Business: The group's principle activity is to market chemicals to the gold mining industry. The group's revenues consist mainly of earnings from cyanco. The group has retained fifty percent interest in cyanco company, a non-corporate joint venture. The group's quarterly revenue for September 2007 was 1.88 millions of USD.

Primary SIC and add'l.: 2899

CIK No: 0000356342

Subsidiaries: Degussa AG, Winnemucca Chemicals, Inc.

Officers: John T. Day/Dir., CEO, Pres./$280,227.00, Kevin Davis/CFO, Becky McIntyre/Office Mgr.

Directors: John T. Day/Dir., CEO, Pres., Bryan E. Bagley/Chmn., Nathan L. Wade/Dir., James E. Solomon/55/Dir., Garfield M. Cook/Dir.

Owners: Bryan E. Bagley/29.70%, Insiders/42.40%, Edward Dallin Bagley/7.60%, James Solomon/0.30%, Garfield M. Cook, Nathan L. Wade/4.60%, John T. Day/7.60%

Financial Data: Fiscal Year End:12/31 Latest Annual Data: 12/31/2006

Year	Sales	Net Income
2006	$7,002,000	$3,224,000
2005	$3,072,000	$1,779,000
2004	$3,657,000	$1,704,000

Curr. Assets:	$16,215,000	**Curr. Liab.:**	$1,572,000	**P/E Ratio:**	24.52
Plant, Equip.:	NA	**Total Liab.:**	$2,552,000	**Indic. Yr. Divd.:**	$0.360
Total Assets:	$25,662,000	**Net Worth:**	$23,110,000	**Debt/ Equity:**	NA

Nevada Geothermal Power Inc

409 Granville St., Ste. 900, Vancouver, BC, V6C 1T2; **PH:** 1-604-688-1553; **Fax:** 1-604-688-5926; **http://** www.nevadageothermal.com; **Email:** info@nevadageothermal.com

General - Incorporation	BC	**Stock**- Price on:12/24/2007	$0.82
Employees	NA	Stock Exchange	OTC
Auditor	Morgan & Company	Ticker Symbol	NGLPF
Stk Agt	Computershare Trust Co	Outstanding Shares	NA
Counsel	Miller Thomson	E.P.S	NA
DUNS No.	NA	Shareholders	NA

Business: The groups principle activity is to provide recruiting services. The groups service area includes the research and development, engineering, marketing, sales, information technology and manufacturing industries. The group operates from United States.

Primary SIC and add'l.: 1781

CIK No: 0001177440

Subsidiaries: Blue Mountain Power Company Inc., Nevada Geothermal Power Company

Officers: Brian D. Fairbank/Dir., CEO, Pres., Donald J.A. Smith/CFO, Sec., Kim Niggemann/Project Dir. - Technical Team, Frank Misseldine/Geothermal Development Mgr., Susan Petty/Independent Geothermal Reservoir Engineer, Miller Thomson/Legal Counsel, Max Walenciak/Geothermal Development Mgr.

Directors: Brian D. Fairbank/Dir., CEO, Pres., Domenic Falcone/Dir., Markus K. Christen/Dir., Richard Campbell/Dir., Gordon R. Bloomquist/Dir., James Yates/Dir., Ted Fitzpatrick/Member - Advisory Board, Alexander Korelin/Member - Advisory Board, Jack W. Milligan/Dir.

Owners: Don Smith/0.30%, Markus Christen/0.50%, Brian Fairbank/11.20%, Richard Campbell/0.40%, Gordon Bloomquist/1.40%, Jack W. Milligan/1.20%, James Yates/0.30%, Domenic Falcone/0.50%

Financial Data: ***Fiscal Year End:*** 06/30 ***Latest Annual Data:*** 06/30/2006

Year	Sales	Net Income
2006	NA	-$5,992,000
2005	NA	-$2,537,000
2004	NA	-$1,677,000

Curr. Assets:	$14,617,000	***Curr. Liab.:***	$1,785,000		
Plant, Equip.:	$27,000	***Total Liab.:***	$1,785,000	***Indic. Yr. Divd.:***	NA
Total Assets:	$14,645,000	***Net Worth:***	$12,860,000	***Debt/ Equity:***	NA

Nevada Gold & Casinos Inc

50 Briar Hollow Ln., Ste. 500w, Houston, TX, 77027; ***PH:*** 1-713-621-2245; ***Fax:*** 1-713-621-6919; ***http://*** www.nevadagold.com; ***Email:*** info@nevadagold.com

General - Incorporation	NV	**Stock**- Price on:12/24/2007	$2.12
Employees	117	Stock Exchange	AMEX
Auditor	Pannell Kerr Forster Of Texas, P.C	Ticker Symbol	UWN
Stk Agt	American Stock Transfer & Trust CO.	Outstanding Shares	12,940,000
Counsel	NA	E.P.S	-$0.26
DUNS No.	09-901-2221	Shareholders	NA

Business: The group's principal activities are to develop gaming properties and own interests in undeveloped real estate restaurant franchises and gold mining claims. The group operates in three segments: gaming, real estate and other. The gaming segment operates a casino entertainment complex in black hawk, Colorado. It consists of isle of capri- black hawk, l.l.c., dry creek casino, l.l.c. And route 66 casinos, l.l.c. The real estate segment develops planned residential and commercial property adjacent to black hawk, Colorado and another at wellesley island, New York. The restaurant franchise involves an ownership interest in pizza hut franchises in sao paulo, Brazil. The mining property segment involves leasing of property and retaining a royalty interest under the lease.

Primary SIC and add'l.: 6719 6553 9999 7999 1041

CIK No: 0000277058

Subsidiaries: Black Hawk Gold, Ltd., CGC Holdings, LLC, Colorado Grande Enterprises, Inc., Dry Creek Casino, LLC, Gold Mountain Development, LLC, Gold River, LLC, Goldfield Resources, Inc., Nevada Gold BVR, LLC, Nevada Gold NY, Inc., Nevada Gold Tulsa, Inc.

Officers: Robert B. Sturges/Dir., CEO/$411,084.00, Jim Kohn/Sr. VP, CFO/$145,619.00, Donald A. Brennan/Sr. VP - Development/$155,103.00, Jonathan A. Arnesen/COO, Pres./$418,370.00, Ernest E. East/General Counsel, Chief Compliance Officer, Sr. VP, Elgin D. McClain/VP - Development/$166,923.00, James J. Kohn/58/CFO, Sr. VP, Treasurer

Directors: Robert B. Sturges/Dir., CEO, Joseph A. Juliano/Chmn., Francis M. Ricci/Dir., Thomas H. Winn/Dir., William G. Jayroe/Dir., William J. Sherlock/Dir., Wayne H. White/Dir., John M. Gallaway/Dir.

Owners: Robert B. Sturges/1.20%, James J. Kohn, John Gallaway, Ernest E. East, William G. Jayroe/1.60%, Donald A. Brennan, Nelson Obus/9.90%, Joseph A. Juliano, Louise H. Rogers/7.30%, William J. Sherlock, John Arnesen, Francis M. Ricci, Thomas H. Winn/5.60%, Wayne H. White, Kennedy Capital Management, LLC/5.20% *(16 Owners included in Index)*

Financial Data: ***Fiscal Year End:*** 04/30 ***Latest Annual Data:*** 4/30/2006

Year	Sales	Net Income
2006	$13,149,000	$372,000
2005	$7,412,000	$4,158,000
2004	$8,544,000	$7,524,000

Curr. Assets:	$6,165,000	***Curr. Liab.:***	$5,730,000		
Plant, Equip.:	$2,580,000	***Total Liab.:***	$62,982,000	***Indic. Yr. Divd.:***	NA
Total Assets:	$88,143,000	***Net Worth:***	$24,883,000	***Debt/ Equity:***	NA

Nevada Star Resource Corp

95 Wellington St. W, Ste. 900, Fall City, WA, 98024; ***PH:*** 1-425-467-1836; ***http://*** www.nevadastar.com

General - Incorporation	YT	**Stock**- Price on:12/24/2007	$0.2
Employees	2	Stock Exchange	OTC
Auditor	Smythe Ratcliffe LLP	Ticker Symbol	NVSRF
Stk Agt	Pacific Corporate Trust Co	Outstanding Shares	NA
Counsel	Harder & Co	E.P.S	NA
DUNS No.	NA	Shareholders	NA

Business: The group's principal activities are acquiring, exploring and developing mineral properties. The group is exploring mineral properties containing nickel, platinum group elements, copper, gold, silver and associated base and precious metals. The group's properties are currently in exploration stage. The group operates through its subsidiaries namely Nevada star resource corp and m.a.n. Resources inc. The group acquired m.a.n. Resources inc on 03-Jul-2002.

Primary SIC and add'l.: 1099

CIK No: 0000877019

Subsidiaries: Nevada Star Resource Corp., Nevada Star Resource Corp. (U.S.)

Officers: Robert Angrisano/53/Dir., CEO, Pres., Jay J. Jaski/Chmn., CEO, James Richardson/CFO

Directors: Robert Angrisano/53/Dir., CEO, Pres., Jay J. Jaski/Chmn., CEO, Rodney Blakestad/59/Dir., David R. Russell/51/Dir., Donald Bosnick/56/Dir., Edward H. Waale/61/Dir., Richard W. Graeme/66/Dir., Michael W. Sharon/51/Dir.

Owners: Donald Bosnick/5.80%, Michael Sharon/0.70%, Insiders/51.00%, Robert Angrisano/17.20%, Richard W. Graeme/0.50%, Edward H. Waale/0.60%, Monty Moore/26.30%

NevStar Corp

12890 Hilltop Rd., Argyle, TX, 76226; ***PH:*** 1-972-233-0300

General - Incorporation	NV	**Stock**- Price on:12/24/2007	$0.15
Employees	NA	Stock Exchange	OTC
Auditor	Rose, Snyder & Jacobs	Ticker Symbol	NVSC
Stk Agt	Transfer Online, Inc.	Outstanding Shares	NA
Counsel	NA	E.P.S	NA
DUNS No.	NA	Shareholders	NA

Business: The groups principal activities include acquiring, developing, constructing, owning and managing hotel/casino projects. The group operates from the United States.

Primary SIC and add'l.: 7011

CIK No: 0001006384

Officers: Timothy P. Halter/42/Dir., CEO, CFO, Pres.

Directors: Timothy P. Halter/42/Dir., CEO, CFO, Pres.

Owners: Insiders/77.89%, Halter Financial Investments, L. P./77.89%, W/F Investment Corp./8.56%

Curr. Assets:	$9,000	***Curr. Liab.:***	$47,000		
Plant, Equip.:	NA	***Total Liab.:***	$47,000	***Indic. Yr. Divd.:***	NA
Total Assets:	$9,000	***Net Worth:***	-$38,000	***Debt/ Equity:***	NA

Nevsun Resources Ltd

1075 W Georgia St., Ste. 800, Vancouver, BC, V6E 3C9; ***PH:*** 1-604-623-4700; ***http://*** www.nevsun.com

General - Incorporation	BC	**Stock**- Price on:12/24/2007	$2.2
Employees	210	Stock Exchange	AMEX
Auditor	KPMG LLP	Ticker Symbol	NSU
Stk Agt	Computershare Investor Services LLC	Outstanding Shares	116,960,000
Counsel	Miller Thomson LLP	E.P.S	-$0.9
DUNS No.	NA	Shareholders	NA

Business: The group's principle activities include acquisition, exploration and development of mineral properties. The group operates from United States.

Primary SIC and add'l.: 1040

CIK No: 0000919991

Officers: John A. Clarke/Dir., CEO, Pres., Cliff T. Davis/Dir., CFO, Exec. VP, Gerry Gauthier/COO, Bill Nielsen/VP - Exploration, Judith C. Baker/Investor Relations, Maureen Carse/Corp. Sec., Pierre Matte/GM - Mali, Stan Rogers/Bisha Project GM

Directors: John A. Clarke/Dir., CEO, Pres., Stuart R. Angus/Chmn., Cliff T. Davis/Dir., CFO, Exec. VP, Robert J. Gayton/Dir., Gary E. German/Dir., Gerard E. Munera/Dir., Gerry Gauthier/COO

Financial Data: ***Fiscal Year End:*** 12/31 ***Latest Annual Data:*** 12/31/2006

Year	Sales	Net Income
2006	$23,156,000	-$109,325,000
2005	NA	-$9,852,000
2004	NA	-$12,331,000

Curr. Assets:	$35,608,000	***Curr. Liab.:***	$11,741,000	***P/E Ratio:***	8.38
Plant, Equip.:	$11,293,000	***Total Liab.:***	$15,644,000	***Indic. Yr. Divd.:***	NA
Total Assets:	$49,127,000	***Net Worth:***	$33,483,000	***Debt/ Equity:***	NA

New Brunswick Scientific Co Inc

44 Talmadge Rd. , Edison, NJ, 08818; ***PH:*** 1-732-287-1200; ***http://*** www.nbsc.com

General - Incorporation	NJ	**Stock**- Price on:12/24/2007	$7.91
Employees	437	Stock Exchange	NDQ
Auditor	KPMG LLP	Ticker Symbol	NBTF
Stk Agt	American Stock Transfer & Trust Co.	Outstanding Shares	9,220,000
Counsel	NA	E.P.S	NA
DUNS No.	00-215-7782	Shareholders	NA

Business: The group's principal activity is to design, manufacture and market a variety of equipment used in biotechnology to create, maintain, measure and control the physical and biochemical conditions required for the growth and detection of microorganisms. This equipment is used in medical, biological, chemical, and environmental research and for the commercial development of antibiotics, proteins, hormones, enzymes, monoclonal antibodies, agricultural products, fuels, vitamins, vaccines and other substances. The equipment sold by the group includes fermentation equipment, bioreactors, biological shakers, ultra-low temperature freezers, nutrient sterilizing and dispensing equipment, tissue culture apparatus and air samplers. The group sells its products in the United States, in the former soviet union, eastern Europe, Africa, other Asian countries and Latin America. On 14-Nov-2003, the group acquired rs biotech laboratory equipment limited.

Primary SIC and add'l.: 3821 8732

CIK No: 0000071241

Subsidiaries: NBS Cryo-Research Limited, NBS ULT Limited, New Brunswick Scientific (U.K.) Limited, New Brunswick Scientific B.V., New Brunswick Scientific GmbH, New Brunswick Scientific International, Inc., New Brunswick Scientific N.V., New Brunswick Scientific of Delaware, Inc., New Brunswick Scientific S.a.r.l., New Brunswick Scientific West Inc., RS Biotech Laboratory Equipment Limited

Officers: James T. Orcutt/50/Dir., CEO, Pres./$370,011.00, Lee Eppstein/VP - Technology/$228,877.00, Adele Lavender/Corp. Sec., Thomas E. Bocchino/CFO, VP - Finance, Investor Relations/$231,483.00, Matthew Dennis/Investor Relations Officer

Directors: James T. Orcutt/50/Dir., CEO, Pres., David Freedman/87/Chmn., Ernest Gross/Dir., David Pramer/Dir., Peter Schkeeper/Dir., Kenneth Freedman/Dir., Jerome Birnbaum/Dir., Daniel S. Van Riper/Dir., William J. Murphy/Dir.

Curr. Assets:	NA	***Curr. Liab.:***	NA	***P/E Ratio:***	22.60
Plant, Equip.:	NA	***Total Liab.:***	NA	***Indic. Yr. Divd.:***	NA
Total Assets:	NA	***Net Worth:***	NA	***Debt/ Equity:***	0.0167

New Century Bancorp Inc

700 W Cumberland St., Dunn, NC, 28334; *PH:* 1-910-892-7080; *Fax:* 1-910-892-9225;
http:// www.newcenturybanknc.com

General - Incorporation	NC	**Stock**- Price on:12/24/2007	$13.08
Employees	156	Stock Exchange	NYSE
Auditor	Dixon Hughes PLLC	Ticker Symbol	NCC
Stk Agt	Dixon Hughes PLLC	Outstanding Shares	6,540,000
Counsel	Gaeta & Eveson	E.P.S.	$0.20
DUNS No.	NA	Shareholders	NA

Business: The group's principal activity is to provide general commercial and retail banking services through two banking offices. The group offers a range of services including checking and savings accounts, commercial, consumer, mortgage and personal loans and other associated financial services to individuals and small to medium sized businesses. The group operates in harnett, cumberland, johnston and sampson counties, North Carolina.

Primary SIC and add'l.: 6022 6712

CIK No: 0001263762

Subsidiaries: New Century Bank, New Century Statutory Trust I

Officers: Bill Hedgepeth/Dir., CEO, Pres., Watson G. Caviness/Dir. - New Century Bank South, Bobby Bryant/Dir. - New Century Bank, Robert B. Carr/Dir. - New Century Bank, Raymond L. Mulkey/Dir. - New Century Bank, Dale E. Parker/Dir. - New Century Bank, Kevin Bunn/Exec. VP, Chief Banling Officer, John McFadyen/Sr. VP - New Century Bank South, Joan I. Patterson/COO, Exec. VP, Lisa Campbell/CFO, Exec. VP, Pete Siemion/Exec. VP, Chief Credit Officer - New Century Bank, New Century Bank South, Sidney E. Thompson/Dir. - New Century Bank South, Sharlene Riddle Williams/Dir. - New Century Bank South, Lyndo W. Tippett/Dir. - New Century Bank South, Shelton Barefoot/Dir. - New Century Bank *(30 Officers included in Index)*

Directors: Bill Hedgepeth/Dir., CEO, Pres., C. L. Tart/Chmn., Oscar N. Harris/Vice Chmn., Carlie C. McLamb/Dir., Thurman C. Godwin/Dir., John W. McCauley/Dir., Gary J. Ciccone/Dir., Tracy L. Johnson/Dir., Paul Perry/Dir., Anthony E. Rand/Dir., Irvin Warren/Dir., George D. Wise/Dir., Lester Phillips/Dir., Sharon L. Raynor/Dir., Lehmon Tart/Dir. *(17 Directors included in Index)*

Owners: Anthony Rand/1.09%, Peter J. Siemion/0.04%, John Q. Shaw/1.20%, Carlie C. McLamb/2.88%, Darrell B. Fowler, William L. Hedgepeth, John McCauley/0.54%, Gary J. Ciccone/1.37%, Insiders/15.27%, Lisa F. Campbell/0.20%, C. L. Tart/1.93%, Gerald W. Hayes/1.37%, Oscar N. Harris/3.55%, T. C. Godwin

Financial Data: *Fiscal Year End:*12/31 *Latest Annual Data:* 03/31/2007

Year	*Sales*	*Net Income*
2007	NA	NA
2006	$39,090,000	$3,970,000
2005	$27,175,000	$3,621,000

Curr. Assets:	$36,045,000	*Curr. Liab.:*	$483,154,000	*P/E Ratio:*	32.70
Plant, Equip.:	$10,019,000	*Total Liab.:*	$495,526,000	*Indic. Yr. Divd.:*	NA
Total Assets:	$552,965,000	*Net Worth:*	$57,439,000	*Debt/ Equity:*	0.2097

New Century Cos Inc

9835 Santa Fe Springs Rd. , Santa Fe Springs, CA, 90670; *PH:* 1-562-906-8455;
http:// www.newcenturyinc.com.; *Email:* info@newcenturyinc.com

General - Incorporation	DE	**Stock**- Price on:12/24/2007	$0.82
Employees	42	Stock Exchange	OTC
Auditor	Squar, Milner, Rachl & Williamson	Ticker Symbol	NCNC
Stk Agt	U.S. Stock Transfer Corp	Outstanding Shares	12,260,000
Counsel	NA	E.P.S.	-$0.06
DUNS No.	03-928-1282	Shareholders	NA

Business: The group's principal activities are to acquire, re-manufacture and sell pre-owned computer numerically controlled ('cnc') machine tools to manufacturing customers. The group provides rebuilt, retrofit and remanufacturing services for numerous brands of machine tools. The remanufacture of a machine tool consists of replacement of all components, realignment of the machine, adding updated computer numerically controlled capability and electrical and mechanical enhancements. The group manufactures original equipment, cnc large turning lathes and attachments under the trade name century turn. Cnc machines use commands from an on-board computer to control the movement of cutting tools and rotation speeds of the parts being produced. The group's machines are used in aerospace, energy, valves, fittings, oil and gas, machinery and equipment, and transportation. The products are marketed in the United States, Canada and Mexico.

Primary SIC and add'l.: 3541

CIK No: 0000318716

Subsidiaries: California corporation, New Century Remanufacturing

Officers: David Duquette/61/Chmn., CEO, CFO, Pres., Josef Czikmantori/52/Dir., VP, Sec.

Directors: David Duquette/61/Chmn., CEO, CFO, Pres., Josef Czikmantori/52/Dir., VP, Sec.

Owners: David Duquette/11.00%, Josef Czikmantori/5.00%, Insiders/15.00%

Financial Data: *Fiscal Year End:*12/31 *Latest Annual Data:* 12/31/2006

Year	*Sales*	*Net Income*
2006	$8,319,000	-$1,052,000
2005	$6,038,000	$668,000
2004	$4,606,000	-$1,423,000

Curr. Assets:	$3,140,000	*Curr. Liab.:*	$2,406,000		
Plant, Equip.:	$285,000	*Total Liab.:*	$2,679,000	*Indic. Yr. Divd.:*	NA
Total Assets:	$3,843,000	*Net Worth:*	$1,164,000	*Debt/ Equity:*	0.1407

New Century Energy Corp

5851 San Felipe, Ste 775, Houston, TX, 77057; *PH:* 1-713-266-4344;
http:// www.newcenturyenergy.com; *Email:* contact@newcenturyenergy.com

General - Incorporation	CO	**Stock**- Price on:12/24/2007	$0.09
Employees	4	Stock Exchange	OTC
Auditor	PMB Helin Donovan, LLP	Ticker Symbol	NCEY
Stk Agt	Continental Stock Transfer & Trust Co	Outstanding Shares	56,010,000
Counsel	NA	E.P.S.	-$0.2
DUNS No.	NA	Shareholders	NA

Business: The group's principle activity is to develop Internet/intranet software products and services and an Internet Website for the hazardous material and environmental industries. The company has developed a software management system known as icomply. This system helps companies to comply with their environmental regulation and related activities for common industrial applications. The company has designed a Website called hazweb.com. This Website provides e-commerce business solutions that help companies to streamline the sales process and allow hazardous materials marketers to operate more efficiently. The company's services are provided to industries and government agencies like transportation, manufacturing, engineering and research services, utility companies and other industries including mining, agriculture, construction, insurance and training. The group's quarterly revenue for September 2007 was 3.38 millions of USD.

Primary SIC and add'l.: 7372 7375 7378

CIK No: 0001079797

Officers: Edward R. Destefano/55/Dir., CEO, CFO, Pres., Sec., Treasurer/$319,750.00

Directors: Edward R. Destefano/55/Dir., CEO, CFO, Pres., Sec., Treasurer

Owners: Insiders/67.00%, Edward R. DeStefano/67.00%, Laurus Master Fund, Ltd./6.60%

Financial Data: *Fiscal Year End:*12/31 *Latest Annual Data:* 12/31/2006

Year	*Sales*	*Net Income*
2006	$14,927,000	-$6,098,000
2005	$7,017,000	-$3,399,000
2004	$2,106,000	-$3,992,000

Curr. Assets:	$15,117,000	*Curr. Liab.:*	$15,648,000		
Plant, Equip.:	$50,813,000	*Total Liab.:*	$69,721,000	*Indic. Yr. Divd.:*	NA
Total Assets:	$66,046,000	*Net Worth:*	-$3,675,000	*Debt/ Equity:*	NA

New Century Equity Holdings Corp

300 Crescent Ct., Ste. 1400, Dallas, TX, 75201; *PH:* 1-214-661-7488;
http:// www.newcenturyequity.com

General - Incorporation	DE	**Stock**- Price on:12/24/2007	$0.25
Employees	2	Stock Exchange	OTC
Auditor	Burton McCumber & Cortez LLP	Ticker Symbol	NCEH
Stk Agt	NA	Outstanding Shares	53,880,000
Counsel	Timothy N. Tuggey	E.P.S.	-$0.002
DUNS No.	17-759-0858	Shareholders	NA

Business: The group's principal activity is to own and operate technology-based companies. The group's holdings include princeton ecom corporation and sharps compliance corporation. Through its subsidiary, it designs, manufactures and markets production level automated test equipment for memory technologies. The group also offers electronic bill presentment and payment services via the Internet and telephone, as well as, credit bureau data access and retrieval to the financial, healthcare, leasing, insurance, law enforcement, educational and utilities industries. In addition, it provides cost-effective logistical and training solutions for the hospitality and healthcare industries.

Primary SIC and add'l.: 7375 3823 7379 7373 7389

CIK No: 0001013706

Subsidiaries: New Century Equity Holdings of Texas, Inc.

Officers: Steven J. Pully/48/CEO/$157,500.00, John P. Murray/39/CFO/$12,175.00

Directors: Mark E. Schwarz/Chmn., James A. Risher/65/Dir., Jonathan Bren/Dir.

Owners: Insiders, John Murray, Mark E. Schwarz, James Risher, Newcastle Partners, L.P., Steven J. Pully

Financial Data: *Fiscal Year End:*12/31 *Latest Annual Data:* 12/31/2006

Year	*Sales*	*Net Income*
2006	$69,000	-$591,000
2005	$33,000	-$543,000
2004	NA	-$1,903,000

Curr. Assets:	$12,687,000	*Curr. Liab.:*	$174,000		
Plant, Equip.:	NA	*Total Liab.:*	$174,000	*Indic. Yr. Divd.:*	NA
Total Assets:	$13,490,000	*Net Worth:*	$13,316,000	*Debt/ Equity:*	NA

New Century Financial Corp

18400 Von Karman Ave., Ste. 1000, Irvine, CA, 92612; *PH:* 1-949-440-7030; *Fax:* 1-949-440-7033;
http:// www.ncen.com

General - Incorporation	MD	**Stock**- Price on:12/24/2007	NA
Employees	NA	Stock Exchange	OTC
Auditor	KPMG LLP	Ticker Symbol	NEWCQ
Stk Agt	Mellon Investor Services LLC	Outstanding Shares	NA
Counsel	NA	E.P.S.	NA
DUNS No.	NA	Shareholders	NA

Business: The groups principle activity is to provide mortgage products and services. The group operates through three segments namely, portfolio, wholesale and retail. In the year 2005, the group acquired mortgage origination platform from the RBC Mortgage Company. The group operates from the United States.The group's quarterly revenue for september 2007 was 514.17 millions of USD.

Primary SIC and add'l.: 6798

CIK No: 0001287286

Subsidiaries: Access Investments II, L.L.C, Anyloan Financial Corporation, Capital Standard Origination Company, CSOC XI, Inc., CSOC XIV, Inc., CSOC XXIII, Inc., CSOC XXV, Inc., CSOC XXVII, Inc., CSOC XXXII, Inc., CSOC XXXVII, Inc., CSOC XXXVIII, Inc., eConduit Corporation, Home123 Corporation, Home123.com, Inc., NC Asset Holding, L.P. 43 Subsidiaries included in the Index

Officers: Brad A. Morrice/51/Dir., CEO, Pres., Holly Etlin/CEO, Pres., Chief Restructuring Officer, Anthony T. Meola/50/Exec. VP - Production, Stergios Theologides/40/Exec. VP, General Counsel, Michelle Cullinan/Dir. - Corporate Communications, Corporate Web Group, Taj S. Bindra/45/CFO, Exec. VP, Jennifer R. Jewett/VP, Corporate Counsel, Corp. Sec., Diane Denny/Customer Advocacy Supervisor, Kevin M. Cloyd/35/Exec. VP, Patti M. Dodge/47/Exec. VP - Investor Relations, Joseph F. Eckroth/48/Exec. VP, Robert J. Lambert/53/Sr. VP - Leadership, Organizational Development

Directors: Brad A. Morrice/51/Dir., CEO, Pres., Fredric J. Forster/62/Chmn., Edward F. Gotschall/53/Vice Chmn., Harold A. Black/61/Dir., Robert K. Cole/60/Dir., Donald E. Lange/61/Dir., Michael M. Sachs/65/Dir., Richard A. Zona/62/Dir.

New Dragon Asia Corp

10 Huangcheng Rd. (N), Longkou; *PH:* 86-5358528666; *Fax:* 86-5358526908;
http:// www.newdragonasia.com

General - Incorporation.............................FL
Employees 1,500
Auditor .... Grobstein, Horwath & Co. LLP
Stk Agt...... American Stock Transfer & Trust Co.
Counsel..NA
DUNS No...NA

Stock - Price on:12/24/2007 ....$1.26
Stock Exchange..AMEX
Ticker Symbol..NWD
Outstanding Shares 53,820,000
E.P.S...$0.12
Shareholders..NA

Business: The group's principal activities are to manufacture, market and distribute instant noodles and flour in the People's Republic of China. It operates in two segments: flour and instant noodles. The group produces and markets a broad range of wheat flour for use in bread, dumplings, noodles and confectionary products. The flour products are marketed under the brand name, 'long feng' and sold throughout the country at both wholesale and retail levels. Noodles are separated into two broad categories for selling and marketing purposes: packet noodles for home preparation and for snacks. The group consists of four manufacturing plants located in dalian, Beijing and yantai.

Primary SIC and add'l.: 2098 2041

CIK No: 0001089590

Subsidiaries: Hero Treasure Limited (HT), Keen General Limited (KG), Longkou City Longyuan Packing Materials Company Limited (LCLPM), Mix Creation Limited (MC), New Dragon Asia (LongKou) Food Company Limited (NDALS), New Dragon Asia Flour (Yantai) Company Limited (NDAFLY), New Dragon Asia Food (Sanhe) Company Limited (NDAFS), New Dragon Asia Food (Yantai) Company Limited (NDAFY), Penglai New Dragon Jin Qiao Food Company Limited (PNDJQ), Rich Delta Limited (RD), Shandong Xinlongya Industry and Trade Company Limited (SXDC)

Officers: Li Xia Wang/Dir., CEO/$20,000.00, Peter Mak/CFO/$5,920,000.00, Ling Wang/Dir., VP

Directors: Li Xia Wang/Dir., CEO, Heng Jing Lu/Chmn., Ling Wang/Dir., VP, Zhi Yong Jiang/41/Non Exec. Dir., De Lin Yang/53/Non Exec. Dir., Qi Xue/55/Non Exec. Dir., Feng Ju Chen/52/Non Exec. Dir.

Owners: Peter Mak, New Dragon Asia Food Ltd., Heng Jing Lu, Insiders

Financial Data: Fiscal Year End:12/25 Latest Annual Data: 12/25/2006

Year	Sales	Net Income
2006	$53,439,000	-$2,604,000
2005	$44,180,000	$1,747,000
2004	$39,221,000	$4,645,000

Curr. Assets:	$38,152,000	*Curr. Liab.:*	$20,597,000	*P/E Ratio:*	31.50
Plant, Equip.:	$24,248,000	*Total Liab.:*	$21,292,000	*Indic. Yr. Divd.:*	NA
Total Assets:	$69,508,000	*Net Worth:*	$44,012,000	*Debt/ Equity:*	NA

New England Bancshares Inc

885 Enfield St., Enfield, CT, 06082; *PH:* 1-860-253-5200; *Fax:* 1-860-253-5205; *http://* www.enfieldfederal.com

General - Incorporation.............................US
Employees 62
Auditor .... Shatswell, MacLeod & Co. P.C
Stk Agt..NA
Counsel...NA
DUNS No...NA

Stock - Price on:12/24/2007 ....$12.96
Stock Exchange..NDQ
Ticker Symbol...NEBS
Outstanding Shares 4,900,000
E.P.S...$0.14
Shareholders..NA

Business: The groups principle activity is to provide banking services. The group provides residential and commercial real estate loans, consumer, construction, commercial and small business loans. The group operates from United States.

Primary SIC and add'l.: NA

CIK No: 0001166760

Subsidiaries: Enfield Federal, Enfield Mutual Holding Company, Federally chartered mutual holding company

Financial Data: Fiscal Year End:03/31 Latest Annual Data: 03/31/2007

Year	Sales	Net Income
2007	$16,154,000	$970,000
2006	$12,789,000	$1,309,000
2005	$10,994,000	$1,188,000

Curr. Assets:	$43,856,000	*Curr. Liab.:*	$198,011,000	*P/E Ratio:*	86.40
Plant, Equip.:	$4,441,000	*Total Liab.:*	$200,978,000	*Indic. Yr. Divd.:*	$0.120
Total Assets:	$257,799,000	*Net Worth:*	$56,821,000	*Debt/ Equity:*	NA

New England Power Co

25 Research Dr., Westborough, MA, 01582; *PH:* 1-508-389-2000; *http://* www.conectiv.com

General - Incorporation.............................MA
Employees ....NA
Auditor ....PricewaterhouseCoopers LLP
Stk Agt..NA
Counsel...NA
DUNS No..00-695-2881

Stock - Price on:12/24/2007 ....$93
Stock Exchange..OTC
Ticker Symbol...NEWEN
Outstanding Shares ....NA
E.P.S...NA
Shareholders..NA

Business: The group's principal activity is to transmit electric energy in wholesale quantities to other electric utilities, principally its distribution affiliates. The group distributes electric energy to national grid usa's four new England electricity delivery companies, Massachusetts electric company (mass. Electric), the narragansett electric company (narragansett), granite state electric company (granite state) and nantucket electric company (nantucket). The group owns a system of transmission lines and substations. The group's integrated system consists of 2,848 circuit miles of transmission lines and 122 substations. The group operates in two segment electricity transmission and stranded/other.

Primary SIC and add'l.: 4911

CIK No: 0000071337

Financial Data: Fiscal Year End:03/31 Latest Annual Data: 3/31/2005

Year	Sales	Net Income
2005	$458,261,000	$76,808,000
2004	$457,811,000	$72,490,000
2003	$514,006,000	$77,427,000

Curr. Assets:	$570,071,000	*Curr. Liab.:*	$195,332,000		
Plant, Equip.:	$750,261,000	*Total Liab.:*	$1,572,831,000	*Indic. Yr. Divd.:*	NA
Total Assets:	$2,675,908,000	*Net Worth:*	$1,103,077,000	*Debt/ Equity:*	NA

New England Realty Associates LP

39 Brighton Ave., Allston, MA, 02134; *PH:* 1-617-783-0039; *Fax:* 1-617-783-0568; *http://* www.thehamiltoncompany.com

General - Incorporation ....MA
Employees 45
Auditor ....Dionne & Gass LLP
Stk Agt..NA
Counsel...NA
DUNS No...NA

Stock - Price on:12/24/2007 ....$84.5
Stock Exchange..AMEX
Ticker Symbol...NA
Outstanding Shares ....NA
E.P.S...$8.099
Shareholders..NA

Business: The groups principle activities include acquiring, developing, holding for investment, operating and selling real estate. The group operates from the United States. The groups quarterly revenue for September 2007 was 8.06 millions of USD.

Primary SIC and add'l.: 6519

CIK No: 0000746514

Officers: Ronald Brown/72/Dir., CEO, Principal Financial Officer, Principal Accounting Officer, Harold Brown/83/Dir., Treasurer

Directors: Ronald Brown/72/Dir., CEO, Principal Financial Officer, Principal Accounting Officer, Harold Brown/83/Dir., Treasurer, Guilliaem Aertsen/60/Dir., Conrad Digregorio/82/Dir., Thomas Raffoul/82/Dir., Edward Sarkisian/80/Dir.

Owners: Conrad DiGregorio, Harold Brown/75.00%, Silver Creek SAV LLC/0.80%, Ronald Brown/25.00%, Mercury Special Situations Fund, LP/1.30%, GPC LXV, LLC/1.00%, Charles Frischer/5.10%, Insiders/100.00%, Gregory Dube/0.10%, Edward Sarkisian, Ronald Brown/0.60%, Thomas Raffoul/0.50%, Robert J. Nahigian, Insiders/18.70%, Mercury Special Situations Offshore/5.80%

Financial Data: Fiscal Year End:12/31 Latest Annual Data: 12/31/2006

Year	Sales	Net Income
2006	$32,117,000	$1,403,000
2005	$31,745,000	$9,456,000
2004	$30,865,000	$1,612,000

Curr. Assets:	$10,354,000	*Curr. Liab.:*	$4,182,000	*P/E Ratio:*	10.43
Plant, Equip.:	$98,284,000	*Total Liab.:*	$118,841,000	*Indic. Yr. Divd.:*	$2.800
Total Assets:	$130,483,000	*Net Worth:*	$11,642,000	*Debt/ Equity:*	11.0287

New Frontier Energy Inc

1789 W Littleton Blvd, Littleton, CO, 80120; *PH:* 1-303-730-9994; *http://* www.nfeinc.com.; *Email:* investerinfo@NFEInc.com

General - Incorporation ....CO
Employees 5
Auditor ....Stark Winter Schenkein & Co. LLP
Stk Agt.................Corporate Stock Transfer, Inc.
Counsel...NA
DUNS No...NA

Stock - Price on:12/24/2007 ....$1.26
Stock Exchange..OTC
Ticker Symbol...NFEI
Outstanding Shares 6,140,000
E.P.S...-$1.107
Shareholders..NA

Business: The group's principal activities are the exploration and development of oil and natural gas reserves in the continental United States. The group currently have an interest in two principle properties, the slater dome/coal bank draw prospect, located in northwest Colorado and southwest Wyoming, and the nucla prospect, located in central Colorado.

Primary SIC and add'l.: NA

CIK No: 0001140586

Subsidiaries: Skyline Resources, Inc, Wyoming Oil & Minerals, Inc.

Officers: Paul G. Laird/Dir., CEO, Pres./$436,806.00, Les Bates/Dir., Sec., Treasurer - Principal Accounting, Financial Officer/$369,341.00, Jubal S. Terry/Mgr. - Exploration

Directors: Paul G. Laird/Dir., CEO, Pres., Les Bates/Dir., Sec., Treasurer - Principal Accounting, Financial Officer, Grant I. Gaeth/Dir.

Owners: John O'Shea, Paul G. Laird, Candace McKey, Wellington Management Company, LLP, Aviel Faliks, Helen DeBove, Echo's Voice LLC, John D. McKey, Les Bates, Roger May, Apollo Trust, Insiders, Grant I. Gaeth, Iris Energy Holding Corp, Vision Opportunity Master Fund, LP

Financial Data: Fiscal Year End:02/28 Latest Annual Data: 2/28/2007

Year	Sales	Net Income
2007	$361,000	-$4,574,000
2006	$159,000	-$3,012,000
2005	$28,000	-$721,000

Curr. Assets:	$13,673,000	*Curr. Liab.:*	$4,691,000		
Plant, Equip.:	$15,341,000	*Total Liab.:*	$4,831,000	*Indic. Yr. Divd.:*	NA
Total Assets:	$29,048,000	*Net Worth:*	$23,796,000	*Debt/ Equity:*	0.1892

New Frontier Media Inc

7007 Winchester Cir., Ste. 200, Boulder, CO, 80301; *PH:* 1-303-444-0900; *Fax:* 1-303-444-0734; *http://* www.noof.com

General - Incorporation ....CO
Employees 162
Auditor ....Grant Thornton LLP
Stk Agt.................Corporate Stock Transfer, Inc.
Counsel.................................Lehman & Eilen
DUNS No..93-973-0321

Stock - Price on:12/24/2007 ....$8.81
Stock Exchange..NDQ
Ticker Symbol...NOVA
Outstanding Shares 24,310,000
E.P.S...$0.42
Shareholders..NA

Business: The group's principle activity is to distribute adult entertainment programs through electronic distribution platforms. These platforms include cable, hotels television, c-band, dbs and video on demand. It offers these programming services to multi-channel providers and low-powered direct-to-home households. The group operates in two segments namely pay TV group and Internet group. Pay TV group distributes entertainment programming and video-on-demand content through electronic distribution platforms. Internet group aggregates and resells adult content via the Internet. The Internet group sells content to monthly subscribers through its broadband Web site, partners with third-party gatekeepers and wholesales pre-packaged content to various Web masters. The group offers seven adult programming networks: Pleasure, Ten, Ten Clips, Ten Blue, Ten Blox, Ten Xtsy and Ten Max. The group's total revenue for year 2007 was 63.27 millions of USD.

Primary SIC and add'l.: 4841 7812 6719 7372

CIK No: 0000847383

Subsidiaries: Colorado Satellite Broadcasting, Inc., Lifestyles Entertainment, Lightning Entertainment, Mainline Releasing, MRG Entertainment, Inc., The Erotic Networks

Officers: Michael Weiner/Chmn., CEO, Sec./$1,034,457.00, Karyn L. Miller/CFO/$443,837.00, Ken Boenish/Pres./$886,367.00, Ira Bahr/COO/$770,123.00, Matthew T. Pullam/CFO

Directors: Michael Weiner/Chmn., CEO, Sec., Walter Timenshenko/Dir., Melissa Hubbard/Dir., David Nicholas/Dir., Hiram J. Woo/Dir., Alan Isaacman/Dir.

Owners: Royce & Associates/8.00%, Alan Isaacman/1.00%, Ira Bahr, Ken Boenish/1.00%, Hiram Woo, Michael Weiner/2.00%, David Nicholas, Stephens Investment Management, LLC/5.00%, FMR Corp./14.00%, Melissa Hubbard, Loeb Partners Corporation/5.00%, Insiders/5.00%, Karyn Miller, Steel Partners II LP/12.00%

Financial Data: *Fiscal Year End:*03/31 **Latest Annual Data:** 3/31/2007

Year	Sales		Net Income
2007	$63,271,000		$12,309,000
2006	$46,851,000		$11,283,000
2005	$46,277,000		$11,122,000

Curr. Assets:	$43,376,000	**Curr. Liab.:**	$12,833,000	**P/E Ratio:**	20.98
Plant, Equip.:	$4,534,000	**Total Liab.:**	$16,517,000	**Indic. Yr. Divd.:**	$0.500
Total Assets:	$88,216,000	**Net Worth:**	$71,699,000	**Debt/ Equity:**	0.0240

New Generation Holdings Inc

245 Pk. Ave., New York, NY, 10167; *PH:* 1-212-792-4030

General - Incorporation	DE	**Stock** - Price on:12/24/2007	$0.01
Employees	5	Stock Exchange	OTC
Auditor ... Russell Bedford Stefanou Mirchandani		Ticker Symbol	NGPX
Stk Agt	Colonial Stock Transfer Co Inc	Outstanding Shares	88,750,000
Counsel	NA	E.P.S.	-$0.025
DUNS No.	NA	Shareholders	NA

Business: The groups principal activities include owning and developing patented and proprietary plastic blending technology. The group operates from the United States.

Primary SIC and add'l.: 3089

CIK No: 0001024605

Subsidiaries: Plastinum Corp

Owners: Jacques Mot/44.40%, Alfons De Maeseneir/10.40%, Lombard Odier Darier Hentsch & CIE/9.30%, Robert Scherne, Insiders/44.50%, Marcel Rokegem

Financial Data: *Fiscal Year End:*12/31 **Latest Annual Data:** 12/31/2006

Year	Sales		Net Income
2006	NA		-$8,584,000
2005	NA		-$4,744,000
2004	NA		-$621,000

Curr. Assets:	$39,000	**Curr. Liab.:**	$2,050,000		
Plant, Equip.:	NA	**Total Liab.:**	$15,052,000	**Indic. Yr. Divd.:**	NA
Total Assets:	$39,000	**Net Worth:**	-$15,013,000	**Debt/ Equity:**	NA

New Gold Inc

595 Howe St., Ste. 601, Vancouver, BC, V6C 2T5; *PH:* 1-604-687-1629; *Fax:* 1-604-687-2845; *http://* www.newgoldinc.com; *Email:* invest@newgoldinc.com

General - Incorporation	BC	**Stock** - Price on:12/24/2007	$6.87
Employees	NA	Stock Exchange	NYSE
Auditor	De Visser Gray	Ticker Symbol	NGG
Stk Agt	Computershare Trust Co	Outstanding Shares	24,170,000
Counsel	NA	E.P.S.	-$0.744
DUNS No.	NA	Shareholders	NA

Business: The groups principal activities include exploring, acquiring and developing natural resources. The group operates from the United States.

Primary SIC and add'l.: 1021 1041

CIK No: 0000800166

Officers: Chris Bradbrook/Dir., CEO, Pres., Kevin Ross/COO, Paul D. Martin/VP - Finance, CFO, Brian O'Connor/Chief Geologist, John Pitcher/Corporate Counsel

Directors: Chris Bradbrook/Dir., CEO, Pres., Clifford J. Davis/Chmn., Robert C. Edington/Dir., Gregory R. Laing/Dir., Mike Muzylowski/Dir., Paul Sweeney/Dir., John R. Mondin/Dir.

Financial Data: *Fiscal Year End:*12/31 **Latest Annual Data:** 12/31/2006

Year	Sales		Net Income
2006	$2,356,000		-$18,562,000
2005	$419,000		-$18,112,000
2004	$469,000		-$3,069,000

Curr. Assets:	$59,429,000	**Curr. Liab.:**	$3,249,000	**P/E Ratio:**	10.43
Plant, Equip.:	$1,681,000	**Total Liab.:**	$3,249,000	**Indic. Yr. Divd.:**	NA
Total Assets:	$61,110,000	**Net Worth:**	$57,862,000	**Debt/ Equity:**	NA

New Hampshire Thrift Bancshares Inc

PO Box 29, 9 Main St., Newport, NH, 03773; *PH:* 1-603-863-5772; *Fax:* 1-603-863-5025; *http://* www.lakesunbank.com

General - Incorporation	DE	**Stock** - Price on:12/24/2007	$14.8
Employees	172	Stock Exchange	NDQ
Auditor	Shatswell, MacLeod & Co. P.C	Ticker Symbol	NA
Stk Agt	Registrar & Transfer Co	Outstanding Shares	4,060,000
Counsel	Thacher Proffitt & Wood LLP	E.P.S.	$1.00
DUNS No.	60-319-8185	Shareholders	NA

Business: The group's principal activity is to provide loans to customers who are predominately small and middle-Market businesses and individuals. The group operates through its subsidiary, lake sunapee bank, a federal stock savings bank operating fourteen branches. The bank's operations are conducted from its home office located in newport, New Hampshire and its branch offices located in sunapee, newbury, new london, bradford, grantham, guild, lebanon, west lebanon, hillsboro, and andover, New Hampshire. Through its subsidiary, lake sunapee financial services corporation, the bank offers brokerage services to its customers. The group's deposits consist of business checking, money market accounts, savings, now and certificate of accounts. The loans offered by the group include residential, consumer, commercial, and municipal and home equity loans.

Primary SIC and add'l.: 6035 6712

CIK No: 0000846931

Subsidiaries: Charter Holding Corp., Charter New England Agency, Lake Sunapee Bank, NHTB Capital Trust I, NHTB Capital Trust II, NHTB Capital Trust III, Phoenix New England Trust Company

Officers: Stephen W. Ensign/Chmn., CEO, Pres., Stephen R. Theroux/Vice Chmn., CFO, COO, Exec. VP, Corp. Sec., Sheffield J. Halsey/Advisor - Lake Sunapee Bank, FSB, Jacqueline C. Cote/Advisor - Lake Sunapee Bank, FSB, Robert J. Cricenti/Advisor - Lake Sunapee Bank, FSB, John W. Flynn/Advisor - Lake Sunapee Bank, FSB, Paul J. Linehan/Advisor - Lake Sunapee Bank, FSB, Victor W. Laro/Advisor - Lake Sunapee Bank, FSB, Ernest G. Dennis/Advisor - Lake Sunapee Bank, FSB, Harry Dorman/Advisor - Lake Sunapee Bank, FSB, William J. Faccone/Advisor - Lake Sunapee Bank, FSB, John W. Wiggins/Advisor - Lake Sunapee Bank, FSB, Robert S. Burgess/Advisor - Lake Sunapee Bank, FSB, Ruth I. Clough/Advisor - Lake Sunapee Bank, FSB, John J. Marcotte/Advisor - Lake Sunapee Bank, FSB *(89 Officers included in Index)*

Directors: Stephen W. Ensign/Chmn., CEO, Pres., John J. Kiernan/Chmn. - Lake Sunapee Bank, FSB, Stephen R. Theroux/Vice Chmn., CFO, COO, Exec. VP, Corp. Sec., Jack H. Nelson/Dir., Michael T. Putziger/Dir., William C. Horn/Dir., Peter R. Lovely/Dir., Leonard R. Cashman/Dir., Peter Terwilliger/Dir., Scott A. Cooper/Dir., Dennis A. Morrow/Dir., Joseph B. Willey/Dir.

Owners: Robert Sennott/3.03%, Thomas Hayes, Lawrence Curtis/1.78%, Michael T. Putziger/14.61%, Samuel Ross, Insiders/39.27%, James H. Miller/3.52%, Roger M. Cassin, Myrna Putziger/6.24%, Kevin Meskell, James J. Ford, Mark Foley, Phillip Cabot Camp, Charles M. Petersen/4.75%, Kenneth E. Howe/3.27% *(16 Owners included in Index)*

Financial Data: *Fiscal Year End:*12/31 **Latest Annual Data:** 12/31/2006

Year	Sales		Net Income
2006	$39,548,000		$5,040,000
2005	$32,739,000		$5,524,000
2004	$29,359,000		$5,098,000

Curr. Assets:	$37,329,000	**Curr. Liab.:**	$603,002,000		
Plant, Equip.:	$16,067,000	**Total Liab.:**	$623,622,000	**Indic. Yr. Divd.:**	$0.520
Total Assets:	$672,031,000	**Net Worth:**	$48,409,000	**Debt/ Equity:**	0.4380

New Jersey Mining Company

89 Appleberg Rd., Kellogg, ID, 83837; *PH:* 1-208-783-1032; *Fax:* 1-208-783-3331; *http://* www.newjerseymining.com; *Email:* ir@newjerseymining.com

General - Incorporation	ID	**Stock** - Price on:12/24/2007	$0.66
Employees	11	Stock Exchange	OTC
Auditor	DeCoria, Maichel & Teague P.S.	Ticker Symbol	NJMC
Stk Agt	Columbia Stock Transfer Co	Outstanding Shares	30,420,000
Counsel	NA	E.P.S.	-$0.05
DUNS No.	NA	Shareholders	NA

Business: The groups principle activities include exploring and developing gold, silver and base metal ore resources. The group operates from the Pacific Northwest in the United States.

Primary SIC and add'l.: 1044 1041

CIK No: 0001030192

Officers: Fred W. Brackebusch/Chmn., Pres., Grant A. Brackebusch/Dir., VP, Tina Brackebusch/Corp. Sec.

Directors: Fred W. Brackebusch/Chmn., Pres., Grant A. Brackebusch/Dir., VP, Ivan Linscott/Dir., Kathleen M. Sims/Dir., William C. Rust/Dir.

Owners: Ivan R. Linscott, William C. Rust, Insiders/33.22%, Kathleen M. Sims, Tina C. Brackebusch, Grant A. Brackebusch/3.96%, Constance Meisel/6.62%, Terry & Marguerite Tyson/8.44%, Fred W. Brackebusch/28.56%

Financial Data: *Fiscal Year End:*12/31 **Latest Annual Data:** 12/31/2006

Year	Sales		Net Income
2006	$339,000		-$992,000
2005	$261,000		-$590,000
2004	NA		-$923,000

Curr. Assets:	$1,341,000	**Curr. Liab.:**	$192,000	**P/E Ratio:**	17.93
Plant, Equip.:	$1,872,000	**Total Liab.:**	$322,000	**Indic. Yr. Divd.:**	NA
Total Assets:	$3,216,000	**Net Worth:**	$2,893,000	**Debt/ Equity:**	NA

New Jersey Resources Corp

1415 Wyckoff Rd., Wall, NJ, 07719; *PH:* 1-732-938-1480; *Fax:* 1-732-919-8118; *http://* www.njliving.com; *Email:* investcont@njresources.com

General - Incorporation	NJ	**Stock** - Price on:12/24/2007	$52.95
Employees	766	Stock Exchange	NYSE
Auditor	Deloitte & Touche LLP	Ticker Symbol	NJR
Stk Agt .... Computershare Investor Services LLC		Outstanding Shares	27,990,000
Counsel	NA	E.P.S.	$2.33
DUNS No.	00-697-1592	Shareholders	NA

Business: The groups principle activity is to provide retail and wholesale energy services. The group operates through three business segments namely Natural Gas Distribution, Energy Services, and Retail and Other. The groups services include appliance repair, sales and installation services, natural gas and natural gas-related investments, commercial real estate development and other corporate services. The group operates from United States.

Primary SIC and add'l.: 6719 6552 4923 6531 1311 7389

CIK No: 0000356309

Subsidiaries: Commercial Realty& Resources Corp., New Jersey Natural Gas Company, NJNR Pipeline Company, NJR Capital Services Corporation , NJR Energy Corp. Subsidiaries:, NJR Energy Holdings Corporation Subsidiary:, NJR Energy Services Company Subsidiaries:, NJR Home Services Company, NJR Investment Company, NJR Natural Energy Company , NJR Plumbing Services,Inc., NJR Retail Holdings Corporation Subsidiaries:, NJR Service Corporation, NJR Storage Partners (Limited Partnership)

Officers: Laurence M. Downes/Chmn., CEO

Directors: Laurence M. Downes/Chmn., CEO, William H. Turner/Dir., Alfred C. Koeppe/Dir., Nina Aversano/Dir., Terry J. Strange/Dir., George R. Zoffinger/Dir., Jane M. Kenny/Dir., Gary W. Wolf/Dir., Duncan Thecker/Dir. Emeritus, Lawrence R. Codey/Dir., David Trice/Dir.

Owners: Alfred C. Koeppe, Terry J. Strange, Mariellen Dugan, Joseph P. Shields, George R. Zoffinger, William M. Howard, Barclays Global Investors, NA/5.40%, Jane M. Kenny, Glenn C. Lockwood, William H. Turner, Kathleen T. Ellis, Nina Aversano, Insiders, David A. Trice, Laurence M. Downes *(17 Owners included in Index)*

Financial Data: *Fiscal Year End:*09/30 **Latest Annual Data:** 9/30/2006

Year	Sales	Net Income
2006	$3,299,608,000	$78,519,000
2005	$3,148,262,000	$76,340,000
2004	$2,533,607,000	$71,574,000

Curr. Assets:	$799,866,000	Curr. Liab.:	$703,266,000	P/E Ratio: 16.05
Plant, Equip.:	$970,871,000	Total Liab.:	$1,585,948,000	Indic. Yr. Divd.: $1.520
Total Assets:	$2,230,745,000	Net Worth:	$644,797,000	Debt/ Equity: NA

New Life Scientific Inc

4400 Rte. 9 S, Ste 1000, Freehold, NJ, 07728; *PH:* 1-732-303-7341; *http://* www.newlifesci.com; *Email:* nwlf@optonline.com

General - Incorporation	NV	Stock - Price on:12/24/2007	$0.007
Employees	2	Stock Exchange	OTC
Auditor	Larry O'donnell, CPA, P.C	Ticker Symbol	NWLS
Stk Agt	NA	Outstanding Shares	NA
Counsel	NA	E.P.S.	-$0.045
DUNS No.	NA	Shareholders	NA

Business: The group's principle activity is to acquire equity positions in start-up and existing companies. The company intends to seek long-term growth potential in a business venture, rather than to seek immediate, short-term earnings. The company has adopted the policy to provide management services and acquire equity positions in companies that will provide the shareholders with potential for increases in their shareholder equity. The company will provide bridge capital, development of superior management teams, implement successful marketing programs when appropriate and then file registration statements to facilitate the public market for their securities. The group operates from United States.

Primary SIC and add'l.: 6799

CIK No: 0001134011

Subsidiaries: Contract Research Organizations, Florida corporation, Novo Life, Novo Life Scientific, PharmaTrials International

Owners: Alexander Yelsky, Michael Val, Yevsey Tseytelman, Power Network Inc., Insiders, Invapharm LLC, MBA Investors. Inc.

Financial Data: *Fiscal Year End:* 12/31   *Latest Annual Data:* 12/31/2006

Year	Sales	Net Income
2006	$368,000	-$2,004,000
2005	$116,000	-$258,000
2004	NA	-$277,000

Curr. Assets:	$527,000	Curr. Liab.:	$1,119,000	
Plant, Equip.:	$8,000	Total Liab.:	$1,119,000	Indic. Yr. Divd.: NA
Total Assets:	$610,000	Net Worth:	-$508,000	Debt/ Equity: NA

New Media Lottery Services Inc

370 Neff Ave, Ste. L, Harrisonburg, VA, 22801; *PH:* 1-540-437-1688

General - Incorporation	DE	Stock - Price on:12/24/2007	NA
Employees	NA	Stock Exchange	OTC
Auditor	Bouwhuis, Morrill & Company	Ticker Symbol	NWMDE
Stk Agt	NA	Outstanding Shares	NA
Counsel	NA	E.P.S.	NA
DUNS No.	NA	Shareholders	NA

Business: The groups principle activities include designing, building, implementing, managing, hosts and supports Internet and wireless device based lottery programs operated by governments and their licensees, such as charitable organizations, outside of the United States. The group also designs and distributes games for use on video lottery terminals and other electronic kiosks. In February 2005, the Virginia Corporation merged with and into New Media Lottery Services, Inc. The group operates from the United States.

Primary SIC and add'l.: 7999

CIK No: 0001172635

Subsidiaries: New Media Lottery Services (International), Ltd., New Media Lottery Services plc, New Media Lottery Services, Inc. (Canada)

Officers: John Carson/Dir., CEO, Pres., Randolph H. Brownell/Dir., CFO, COO, Sterling Herbst/41/Sec.

Directors: John Carson/Dir., CEO, Pres., Randolph H. Brownell/Dir., CFO, COO, Joseph Dresner/Dir., Milton Dresner/Dir., Frederick Winters/Dir.

Owners: Joseph Dresner/3.64%, Insiders/7.68%, Sterling Herbst, Paula Horan, Milton Dresner/32.65%, The Rt. Hon. Lord, Frederick Winters, Joseph Dresner/32.65%, John Carson/9.62%, Milton Dresner/3.64%, Randolph H. Brownell/6.51%

Curr. Assets:	$632,000	Curr. Liab.:	$4,324,000	
Plant, Equip.:	$299,000	Total Liab.:	$7,767,000	Indic. Yr. Divd.: NA
Total Assets:	$931,000	Net Worth:	-$6,836,000	Debt/ Equity: NA

New Medium Enterprises Inc

8721 W Sunset Blvd. Ste. P8, West Hollywood, CA, 90069; *PH:* 1-310-967-3084; *http://* www.nmeinc.com

General - Incorporation	NV	Stock - Price on:12/24/2007	$0.28
Employees	NA	Stock Exchange	OTC
Auditor	Morgenstern, Svoboda & Baer CPA's PC	Ticker Symbol	NMEN
Stk Agt	Olde Monmouth Stk Trnsfer Co. Inc.	Outstanding Shares	NA
Counsel	NA	E.P.S.	NA
DUNS No.	NA	Shareholders	NA

Business: The groups principal activity ids to develop the technology called Versatile Multilayer Disc. The group operates from the United Kingdom and the United States.

Primary SIC and add'l.: 3699

CIK No: 0001126983

Subsidiaries: New Medium Enterprises Asia Pacific, New Medium Enterprises China Ltd, New Medium Enterprises UK Ltd, New Medium Management Ltd

Officers: Mahesh Jaranayaran/Dir., CEO, Pres., Sanjay Khar/Dir., Optical Division Head, Eugene Levich/Dir., CTO, Alexander B. Hagerty/Exec. VP - Business Development, Irene Kuan/Dir., CFO, Treasurer, Sec.

Directors: Mahesh Jaranayaran/Dir., CEO, Pres., Michael Jay Solomon/Chmn., Barry Williamson/Dir., Thomas Berglund/Dir., Per Bergstrom/Dir., Rupert Stow/Dir., Eugene Levich/Dir., CTO, Irene Kuan/Dir., CFO, Treasurer, Sec., Sanjay Khar/Dir., Optical Division Head, Lawrence Lichter/Dir.

Owners: MetCash Limited/8.91%, Ann Kallgren/16.48%, New Medium Management/9.25%, Thomas Berglund, Insiders/22.67%, Mahesh Jayanarayan/4.04%, Per Bergstrom/13.70%, Rupert Stow, Eugene Levich/2.89%, Michael Solomon, Barry Williamson, Semilla Capital Ltd HK/7.42%, Sanjay Khar, Irene Kuan, May Ltd./9.09%

Financial Data: *Fiscal Year End:* 06/30   *Latest Annual Data:* 06/30/2007

Year	Sales	Net Income
2007	NA	-$35,766,000
2006	NA	-$6,441,000
2005	NA	-$2,074,000

Curr. Assets:	$3,873,000	Curr. Liab.:	$736,000	P/E Ratio: 17.93
Plant, Equip.:	$1,298,000	Total Liab.:	$3,005,000	Indic. Yr. Divd.: NA
Total Assets:	$5,228,000	Net Worth:	$2,223,000	Debt/ Equity: NA

New Mexico Software Inc

5021 Indian School Rd. NE, Ste. 100, Albuquerque, NM, 87110; *PH:* 1-505-255-1999; *Fax:* 1-505-255-7201; *http://* www.nmxs.com; *Email:* ceo@nmxs.com

General - Incorporation	NV	Stock - Price on:12/24/2007	$0.05
Employees	14	Stock Exchange	OTC
Auditor	Epstein Weber & Conover, PLC	Ticker Symbol	NMXC
Stk Agt	Beckstead & Watts LLP	Outstanding Shares	94,760,000
Counsel	Manhattan Scientifics Lawsuit	E.P.S.	-$0.019
DUNS No.	NA	Shareholders	NA

Business: The group's principal activities are to develop and market proprietary Internet technology-based software for the management of digital high resolution graphic images, video clips and audio files. The software segment performs digital asset management, high-speed transfer of high resolution graphic images, single image in multiple resolutions, media storage, digital branding for security of images, photographic quality printing and other functions. The group's software has applications for the media, advertising, publishing, medical, entertainment, e-commerce and university markets. The group's operations are classified based on its separate legal entities: nms and working knowledge inc. Nms develops and markets the software and working knowledge inc provides data maintenance services related to nms digital asset management system.

Primary SIC and add'l.: 7379 7372

CIK No: 0001101865

Subsidiaries: NMXS.com, Inc., Working Knowledge, Inc.

Officers: Richard F. Govatski/63/Chmn., CEO, Pres., Teresa B. Dickey/64/Dir., Sec., Treasurer, Principal Financial Officer, Bruce Stabile/Healthcare Division Pres., Rafael Rubio/Technology, Development VP, Toby Dickey/Exec. VP, Bruce A. Jack/DDS, Medical Dir., Ricardo Schwartz/Dir. - South America Operation

Directors: Teresa B. Dickey/64/Dir., Sec., Treasurer, Principal Financial Officer, John E. Handley/46/Dir., Frank A. Reidy/66/Dir.

Owners: Richard Govatski/17.32%, Insiders/18.81%, John Handley, Teresa B. Dickey/1.12%, Frank Reidy

Financial Data: *Fiscal Year End:* 12/31   *Latest Annual Data:* 12/31/2006

Year	Sales	Net Income
2006	$913,000	-$2,723,000
2005	$1,399,000	-$1,048,000
2004	$1,018,000	-$703,000

Curr. Assets:	$232,000	Curr. Liab.:	$362,000	
Plant, Equip.:	$103,000	Total Liab.:	$362,000	Indic. Yr. Divd.: NA
Total Assets:	$339,000	Net Worth:	-$23,000	Debt/ Equity: NA

New Millennium Bank NJ

57 Livingston Ave., New Brunswick, NJ, 08901; *PH:* 1-732-729-1100; *Fax:* 1-732-729-4399; *http://* www.nmbonline.com; *Email:* information@nmbonline.com

General - Incorporation		Stock - Price on:12/24/2007	$30.75
Employees	NA	Stock Exchange	OTC
Auditor	NA	Ticker Symbol	NMNB
Stk Agt	NA	Outstanding Shares	NA
Counsel	NA	E.P.S.	NA
DUNS No.	NA	Shareholders	NA

Business: The groups principle activity is to provide banking products and services. The group provides personal banking products, certificates of deposits, business banking products, loan products and e-banking. The group operates from United States.

Primary SIC and add'l.: 6022

CIK No:

New Millennium Development Grp Inc

723 Casino Blvd. 2nd Fl., Las Vegas, NV, 89101; *PH:* 1-877-711-3535

General - Incorporation	NV	Stock - Price on:12/24/2007	NA
Employees	NA	Stock Exchange	NA
Auditor	MacKay LLP	Ticker Symbol	NA
Stk Agt	NA	Outstanding Shares	NA
Counsel	NA	E.P.S.	NA
DUNS No.	NA	Shareholders	NA

Business: The group's principal activity is to promote events, which owns and operates 30 events, nationwide. The group books and promotes almost every type of event from live entertainment events such as music and sports, to tours such as music festivals, comedy tours, magic acts, figure skating shows, boxing, gymnastics tours, motivational speaking tours and other special events. The group books and promotes such events in a number of venue types showcased in stadiums with seating of 32,000 or more, amphitheatres or arenas with seating of 5,000 to 32,000, clubs, theatres and playhouses seating 100 to 5,000. As a producer or manager of an event, the group develops the event, hires artistic talent, schedules performances in select venues, promotes tours and sells sponsorships. The current roster of event sponsors includes wm wrigley, American express, office depot, verizon, Italian rose, cox broadcasting, clear channel communications and other.

Primary SIC and add'l.: 7372 7375

CIK No: 0001082121

New Oriental Education & Technology Group Inc

No.6 Haidian Zhongjie, Beijing, Haidian District, 100080; *PH:* 86-1062605566; *Fax:* 86-1062605511; *http://* www.neworiental.org; *Email:* info@neworiental.org

General - Incorporation	Cayman Islands	Stock- Price on:12/24/2007	$50.39
Employees	370	Stock Exchange	NYSE
Auditor	NA	Ticker Symbol	EDU
Stk Agt	NA	Outstanding Shares	36,950,000
Counsel	Latham & Watkins	E.P.S.	$1.12
DUNS No.	NA	Shareholders	NA

Business: The groups principal activity is to provide private educational services. The group provides their services under the brand New Oriental. The group operates from the United States

Primary SIC and add'l.: 8331 8244 8211 8249 8299

CIK No: 0001372920

Subsidiaries: Beijing Decision Education and Consulting Co, Ltd., Beijing Hewstone Technology Co., Ltd., Beijing Judgment Education & Consulting Co,. Ltd., Beijing New Oriental Education & Technology (Group) Co., Ltd., New Oriental Education Corporation

Officers: Michael M. Yu/Founder, Chmn., CEO, Chenggang Zhou/Dir., Exec. VP, Louis Hsieh/Dir., CFO, Xiangdong Chen/Sr. VP, Xiuwen Wang/VP, Yunlong Sha/VP, Joseph Kauffman/Assist. VP, Dir. - Business Development, Sisi Zhao/Mgr. - Investor Relations

Directors: Michael M. Yu/Founder, Chmn., CEO, Chenggang Zhou/Dir., Exec. VP, Robin Li/Dir., Denny Lee/Dir., Louis Hsieh/Dir., CFO, John Zhuang Yang/Dir.

Owners: Michael Minhong Yu/22.89%, Investment entities affiliated with Tiger Global Private Investment Partners II, L.P./4.84%, Tigerstep Developments Limited/22.89%, Insiders/24.04%

*Financial Data: Fiscal Year End:*05/31 *Latest Annual Data:* 05/31/2006

Year	Sales	Net Income
2006	$96,057,000	$6,159,000
2005	$77,836,000	$17,179,000
2004	$53,459,000	$6,339,000

Curr. Assets:	$42,395,000	Curr. Liab.:	$58,016,000	P/E Ratio:	0.10
Plant, Equip.:	$88,114,000	Total Liab.:	$70,841,000	Indic. Yr. Divd.:	NA
Total Assets:	$135,876,000	Net Worth:	$65,035,000	Debt/ Equity:	NA

New Oriental Energy & Chemical Corp

Xicheng Industrial Zone Of Luoshan, Xinyang; *PH:* 86-278-537-5701

General - Incorporation	DE	Stock- Price on:12/24/2007	NA
Employees	NA	Stock Exchange	NDQ
Auditor	Weinberg & Co., P.A	Ticker Symbol	NOEC
Stk Agt	Corporate Stock Transfer, Inc.	Outstanding Shares	NA
Counsel	NA	E.P.S.	NA
DUNS No.	NA	Shareholders	NA

Business: The groups principle activities include owning and operating fantasy sports website. The services of the group include sports headlines, news stories by sports, sports scores, links for leading online fantasy games, game lines, message forum and tickers with news & scores. The group operates from the United States.

Primary SIC and add'l.: 7389

CIK No: 0001312547

Officers: Chen Si Qiang/45/Chmn., CEO, Wang Gui Quan/40/Dir., Pres., Li Dong Lai/43/VP, Wu Peng/43/VP, Wang Xiang Fu/42/VP, Ben Wang/35/CFO

Directors: Chen Si Qiang/45/Chmn., CEO, Wang Gui Quan/40/Dir., Pres., Zhou Dian Chang/43/Dir., Mai Xiao Fu/46/Dir., Chen Ran/36/Dir., Howard S. Barth/Dir., Xiaokai Cao/Dir., Qi Lei/Dir., Yan Shi/Dir.

Owners: Auto Chance International Limited/59.34%

Curr. Assets:	$33,000	Curr. Liab.:	$1,000		
Plant, Equip.:	NA	Total Liab.:	$1,000	Indic. Yr. Divd.:	NA
Total Assets:	$33,000	Net Worth:	$32,000	Debt/ Equity:	NA

New Paradigm Productions Inc

2600 Tenth St., Ste. 611, Berkeley, CA, 94710; *PH:* 1-510-883-9814; *http://* www.paradigmproductions.org; *Email:* info@paradigmproductions.org

General - Incorporation	NV	Stock- Price on:12/24/2007	$0.8
Employees	NA	Stock Exchange	OTC
Auditor	Pritchett Siler & Hardy P.C	Ticker Symbol	NPDP
Stk Agt	Interwest Transfer Company, Inc.	Outstanding Shares	NA
Counsel	NA	E.P.S.	NA
DUNS No.	NA	Shareholders	NA

Business: The group's principle activity is to investigate potential acquisitions. The company is not presently engaged in any significant business activities and has no operations. In 2002, it discontinued its operations of producing and marketing meditation music and supplies. The company is seeking other business opportunities. The company is in its development stage. The group operates from United States.

Primary SIC and add'l.: 9999

CIK No: 0001099977

Officers: Jody St. Clair/44/Dir., CEO, CFO, Pres., Sec., Treasurer

Directors: Jody St. Clair/44/Dir., CEO, CFO, Pres., Sec., Treasurer

Owners: Pengfei Liu/50.96%, Insiders/50.96%, Tradelink Securities, LLC/9.75%

New Peoples Bankshares Inc

2 Gents Dr., Honaker, VA, 24260; *PH:* 1-276-873-7000; *http://* www.newpeoplesbank.com

General - Incorporation	VA	Stock- Price on:12/24/2007	NA
Employees	NA	Stock Exchange	NA
Auditor	Brown, Edwards & Co LLP	Ticker Symbol	NA
Stk Agt	New Peoples Bankshares Inc	Outstanding Shares	NA
Counsel	NA	E.P.S.	NA
DUNS No.	NA	Shareholders	NA

Business: The groups principle activity is to provide financial services. The group operates from United States.

Primary SIC and add'l.: NA

CIK No: 0001163389

Subsidiaries: New Peoples Bank, Inc., NPB Capital Trust I, NPB Financial Services, Inc., NPB Web Services, Inc.

Officers: Kenneth Hart/CEO, Pres., Frank Sexton/COO, Exec. VP, Todd C. Asbury/37/Sr. VP, CFO, Treasurer, John D. Maxfield/65/Dir., Sec.

Directors: Tim Ball/Dir., Joe Carter/Dir., John Cox/Dir., John D. Maxfield/65/Dir., Sec., Mickey McGlothlin/Dir., Charles Gent/Dir., Frank Kilgore/Dir., Lynn Keene/Dir., Bill Ed Sample/Dir., Virgil Sampson/Dir., Stephen H. Starnes/50/Dir., Fred Meade/Dir., Paul Vencill/Dir., Scott White/Dir., William Wampler/Dir. *(16 Directors included in Index)*

Owners: Paul R. Vencill, Joe M. Carter, Harold Lynn Keene, Tim W. Ball, Insiders/13.81%, William C. Wampler, Virgil E. Sampson, Frank A. Kilgore/1.05%, Fred W. Meade, Kenneth D. Hart/1.65%, John D. Cox, John D. Maxfield, Stephen H. Starnes, Charles H. Gent, Michael G. McGlothlin/1.31% *(19 Owners included in Index)*

New Plan Excel Realty Trust Inc

420 Lexington Ave., New York, NY, 10170; *PH:* 1-212-869-3000; *http://* www.newplan.com

General - Incorporation	MD	Stock- Price on:12/24/2007	NA
Employees	NA	Stock Exchange	NA
Auditor	PricewaterhouseCoopers LLP	Ticker Symbol	NA
Stk Agt	Computershare Trust Co	Outstanding Shares	NA
Counsel	NA	E.P.S.	NA
DUNS No.	NA	Shareholders	NA

Business: The groups principle activities include owning, managing and developing community and neighborhood shopping centers. In the year 2006, the group acquired four shopping centers. The group operates from the United States.

Primary SIC and add'l.: 6552

CIK No: 0000798288

Subsidiaries: Arapahoe Crossings, L.P., Avion Service Corp., BPR Land Partnership, LP, BPR Shopping Center, L.P., Briar Preston Ridge Partners LP, Briar Preston Ridge South, L.P., CA Harwood Holdings SPE, LLC, CA Harwood, LP, CA New Plan Acquisition Fund Delaware, LLC, CA New Plan Acquisition Fund Louisiana, LLC, CA New Plan Acquisition Fund Texas I, LP, CA New Plan Acquisition Fund Texas, LLC, CA New Plan Acquisition Fund, LLC, CA New Plan Asset Partnership IV, LP, CA New Plan Asset,Inc. 202 Subsidiaries included in the Index

Officers: Glenn J. Rufrano/CEO, John B. Roche/CFO, Exec. VP, Steven Splain/VP, Chief Accounting Officer

Directors: William Newman/Chmn., Raymond H. Bottorf/Dir., Irwin Engelman/Dir., Norman Gold/Dir., Matthew Goldstein/Dir., Nina Matis/Dir., Carl H. McCall/Dir., Melvin D. Newman/Dir., George Puskar/Dir., Gregory A. White/Dir.

Owners: Nina Matis, Irwin Engelman, George Puskar, Morgan Stanley/5.10%, Dean Bernstein, Capital Research and Management Company/7.50%, Glenn J. Rufrano/1.40%, Raymond H. Bottorf, Spectrum Asset Management, Inc./29.00%, Carl H. McCall, Matthew Goldstein, Melvin Newman, The Vanguard Group, Inc./6.30%, William Newman/1.80%, Barclays Global Investors, NA/7.20% *(20 Owners included in Index)*

New Resource Bank CA

405 Howard St. Ste. 110, San Francisco, CA, 94105; *PH:* 1-415-357-1353; *http://* www.newresourcebank.com; *Email:* info@newresourcebank.com

General - Incorporation		Stock- Price on:12/24/2007	$16.5
Employees	NA	Stock Exchange	OTC
Auditor	NA	Ticker Symbol	NWBN
Stk Agt	Mellon Investor Services LLC	Outstanding Shares	NA
Counsel	NA	E.P.S.	NA
DUNS No.	NA	Shareholders	NA

Business: The groups principle activities include providing banking by offering personalized services of a community bank along with the convenience and security. Services of the group include community banking, free checking, savings account, Loans and Mortgages and financial calculations and personal loans. The group operates from the United States.

Primary SIC and add'l.: 6021

CIK No:

Officers: Gloria Ferguson/Sr. VP - Business Banking, Joanne Marquez/Sr. VP, Operations Officer, Steve Jones/CFO, Clay Jones/Dir., Bank Pres., Geoff Butner/Exec. VP, Head - Commercial Finance

Directors: Daniel Yohannes/Chmn., Peter Liu/Initial Founder, Vice Chmn., Clay Jones/Dir., Bank Pres., Bob Epstein/Dir., Mark Finser/Dir., Rick Holmstrom/Dir., Rosemary Oda/Dir., Fran A. Streets/Dir., Michael Van Den Akker/Dir.

New River Pharmaceuticals Inc

1881 Grove Ave., Radford, VA, 24141; *PH:* 1-540-633-7900; *http://* www.nrpharma.com

General - Incorporation	VA	Stock- Price on:12/24/2007	NA
Employees	29	Stock Exchange	NDQ
Auditor	KPMG LLP	Ticker Symbol	NRVN
Stk Agt	KPMG LLP	Outstanding Shares	NA
Counsel	NA	E.P.S.	NA
DUNS No.	NA	Shareholders	NA

Business: The group's principal activity is to develop safer and improved versions of widely prescribed drugs in large and growing markets. Utilizing proprietary carrierwave technology, the group is developing novel pharmaceuticals to address the significant drawbacks and adverse side effects of currently marketed drugs. The group's carrierwave technology can be applied in various ways to improve

existing drugs. The group is in the development of three lead product candidates. The first product is nrp104, which is a prodrug of amphetamine. Nrp290, the second product candidate, is a prodrug of hydrocodone, an opioid widely used to treat acute pain. The third pipeline program is nrp369. This program is focused on developing a prodrug of oxycodone, an opioid widely used to treat chronic pain.

Primary SIC and add'l.: 8731 2834

CIK No: 0001288379

Subsidiaries: Lotus Biochemical (Bermuda) Ltd.

Officers: Randal J. Kirk/Chmn., CEO, Pres., Principal Executive Officer, Garen Z. Manvelian/44/Chief Medical Officer, VP - Clinical - Regulatory Affairs, Clifton R. Herndon/40/VP - Finance, Controller, Suma M. Krishnan/42/VP - Product Development, Krish S. Krishnan/43/Dir., CFO, COO, John K. Thottathil/55/Chief Scientific Officer, Samir D. Roy/49/VP - Product Development

Directors: Randal J. Kirk/Chmn., CEO, Pres., Principal Executive Officer, Cesar L. Alvarez/60/Dir., Krish S. Krishnan/43/Dir., CFO, COO, David S. Barlow/51/Dir., Larry D. Horner/73/Dir., Burton E. Sobel/70/Dir.

Owners: S.A.C. Capital Advisors, Larry D. Homer, David S. Barlow, Randal J. Kirk, Cesar L. Alvarez, FMR Corp., Insiders, John K. Thottathil, Suma M. Krishnan, Burton E. Sobel, Krish S. Krishnan

New Taohuayuan Culture & Tourism Company Ltd

1no. Dongfeng Rd., Xi'an Weiyang Tourism Development District, Xian; **PH:** 86-298-667-1555

General - Incorporation	NV	**Stock**- Price on:12/24/2007	$7.5
Employees	NA	Stock Exchange	OTC
Auditor	Michael Pollack Cpa	Ticker Symbol	NTYN
Stk Agt	Corporate Stock Transfer, Inc.	Outstanding Shares	NA
Counsel	NA	E.P.S.	NA
DUNS No.	NA	Shareholders	NA

Business: The groups principle activity is to own and operate the Taohuayuan Inn hotel and resort. Services of the group include heating systems, television, telephone, fully-equipped bathrooms, a gym and health club, swimming pool, fishing gardens, beauty and hair salons, restaurants, steam baths, tea services, karaoke services and mini bars . The group operates from the United States.

Primary SIC and add'l.: 7011

CIK No: 0001311185

Owners: Cai Danmei, Chen Jingmin/18.00%, Rising Star Hold ings Investment Corporation/9.10%, Insiders/18.20%

Financial Data: Fiscal Year End: 12/31 **Latest Annual Data:** 12/31/2006

Year	Sales	Net Income
2006	$5,607,000	$1,850,000
2005	$5,546,000	$1,052,000

Curr. Assets:	$1,076,000	Curr. Liab.:	$4,244,000		
Plant, Equip.:	$9,321,000	Total Liab.:	$4,244,000	Indic. Yr. Divd.:	NA
Total Assets:	$29,119,000	Net Worth:	$24,875,000	Debt/ Equity:	NA

New Ulm Telecom Inc

27 N Minnesota St., New Ulm, MN, 56073; **PH:** 1-507-354-4111; **Fax:** 1-507-354-1982; **http://** www.newulmtel.net

General - Incorporation	MN	**Stock**- Price on:12/24/2007	$13
Employees	71	Stock Exchange	OTC
Auditor	Kiesling Assoc. LLP	Ticker Symbol	NULM
Stk Agt	NA	Outstanding Shares	5,120,000
Counsel	NA	E.P.S.	$6.90
DUNS No.	00-890-4641	Shareholders	NA

Business: The group's principal activity is the operation of local exchange telephone companies. The business consists of connecting customers to the telephone network, providing switched service and dedicated private lines, connecting customers to long distance service providers and other services. The company also provides cable television services, Internet access services, long distance service and installs and maintains telephone systems to the areas surrounding its exchange service territory in southern Minnesota and northern Iowa. Nortel is the supplier of communications equipment to the group's incumbent local exchange carrier and competitive local exchange carrier central office switches. The digital loop carrier equipment is supplied by next level communications. The group acquired additional interest in midwest wireless holdings l.l.c.

Primary SIC and add'l.: 4841 5065 4812 4813

CIK No: 0000071557

Subsidiaries: New Ulm Cellular #9, Inc., New Ulm Long Distance, Inc., New Ulm Phonery, Inc., Peoples Telephone Company, Western Telephone Company

Owners: Mary Ellen Domeier, Ruth B. Wines/5.40%, Duane Lambrecht, Bill Otis/4.10%, Rosemary Dittrich, Paul Erick, Barbara Bornhoft, Nancy Blankenhagen, Patricia Matthews, Gary Nelson, James Jensen, Perry Meyer, Insiders/5.70%

Financial Data: Fiscal Year End: 12/31 **Latest Annual Data:** 12/31/2006

Year	Sales	Net Income
2006	$16,882,000	$35,111,000
2005	$17,345,000	$5,460,000
2004	$15,101,000	$3,292,000

Curr. Assets:	$32,242,000	Curr. Liab.:	$23,505,000	P/E Ratio:	1.90
Plant, Equip.:	$22,707,000	Total Liab.:	$29,307,000	Indic. Yr. Divd.:	$0.400
Total Assets:	$80,056,000	Net Worth:	$50,748,000	Debt/ Equity:	0.0014

New Valley Corp

International Pl., 100 Se, 2nd St., Miami, FL, 33131; **PH:** 1-305-579-8000; **http://** www.newvalley.com

General - Incorporation	DE	**Stock**- Price on:12/24/2007	NA
Employees	NA	Stock Exchange	NA
Auditor	PricewaterhouseCoopers LLP	Ticker Symbol	NA
Stk Agt	American Stock Transfer & Trust Co.	Outstanding Shares	NA
Counsel	NA	E.P.S.	NA
DUNS No.	00-699-2242	Shareholders	NA

Business: The group's principal activity is to manage real estate business. The group owns two commercial office buildings in princeton, New Jersey and a 50% interest in the former kona surf hotel in kailua-kona, Hawaii through its new valley realty division. It also holds a 50% interest in douglas elliman realty llc, which operates the largest residential real estate brokerage company in the New York city metropolitan area.

Primary SIC and add'l.: 6512 6531

CIK No: 0000106374

Subsidiaries: ALKI Corp., New Valley Real Estate Corporation

Officers: Bennett S. Lebow/Chmn., CEO, Richard J. Lampen/Dir., Exec. VP, General Counsel, Bryant Kirkland/CFO, VP, Treasurer, Marc Bell/VP, Sec., Assoc. General Counsel, Howard M. Lorber/Dir., COO, Pres., Carrie Bloom/Investor Inquiries

Directors: Bennett S. Lebow/Chmn., CEO, Richard J. Lampen/Dir., Exec. VP, General Counsel, Howard M. Lorber/Dir., COO, Pres., Ronald Kramer/Dir., Henry Beinstein/Dir., Victor Rivas/Dir., Arnold Burns/Dir., Barry Ridings/Dir.

New World Batteries Inc

11718-232B St., Maple Ridge, BC, V2X 7Z2; **PH:** 1-604-476-9080; **http://** www.newworldbatteries.com

General - Incorporation	Canada	**Stock**- Price on:12/24/2007	NA
Employees	NA	Stock Exchange	NA
Auditor	Cinnamon, Jang, Willoughby & Co	Ticker Symbol	NA
Stk Agt	NA	Outstanding Shares	NA
Counsel	NWB	E.P.S.	NA
DUNS No.	NA	Shareholders	NA

Business: The group's principal activity is commercializing of patents and products developed by Dr. Robert O'Brien relating to the development of electrochemical technologies that improve the capacity of rechargeable batteries, capacitance and discharge parameters of supercapacitors, and the processes of electrorefining, electroplating and electromachining.

Primary SIC and add'l.: 3690

CIK No: 0001315260

Officers: Patrick O'Brien/Dir., CEO, CFO, Pres., Treasurer, Robert N. O'Brien/Dir., Chief Science Officer

Directors: Patrick O'Brien/Dir., CEO, CFO, Pres., Treasurer, George Devlin/Dir., Robert N. O'Brien/Dir., Chief Science Officer, Daniel B. O'Brien/Dir.

Owners: Robert O'Brien/47.00%, Daniel O'Brien/23.00%, George Devlin/12.00%, Patrick O'Brien/10.00%, Insiders/92.00%

New World Brands Inc

340 W 5th Ave., Eugene, OR, 97401; **PH:** 1-541-683-2892; **Fax:** 1-541-683-4009; **http://** www.qualmax.net

General - Incorporation	DE	**Stock**- Price on:12/24/2007	$0.065
Employees	52	Stock Exchange	OTC
Auditor	Berenfeld, Spritzer, Shechter & Sheer	Ticker Symbol	NWBD
Stk Agt	Continental Stock Transfer & Trust Co	Outstanding Shares	44,300,000
Counsel	NA	E.P.S.	NA
DUNS No.	12-277-5703	Shareholders	NA

Business: The group's principal activity is to import and distribute wine and spirits in the United States. The group holds the exclusive distribution rights for the wines of vinicola l.a. Cetto in the United States. It has established arrangements for distribution of its products with major wine and spirit wholesale distributors from New York to California. The group is in the initial stages of developing its relationships with suppliers and customers.

Primary SIC and add'l.: 5182

CIK No: 0000799426

Subsidiaries: International Importers, Inc, Oak Tree Spirits, Inc.

Officers: David M. Kamrat/Chmn., CEO - IP Gear/$120,000.00, Noah Kamrat/Dir., COO, Pres./$120,000.00, Duy Tran/Dir. - Inode Division/$120,000.00, Ian Richardson/Corporate Counsel/$120,000.00, Shehryar Wahid/43/CFO, Shalom Amsalem/MD - Israel Division

Directors: Jacob M. Schorr/63/Dir.

Owners: Noah Kamrat/42.66%, B.O.S. Better Online Solutions Ltd./18.11%, David M. Kamrat/42.66%, Jacob Schorr/14.55%, P&S Spirit LLC/29.11%, Insiders/53.18%, Oregon Spirit LLC/1.91%, Qualmax, Inc./76.05%, Selvin Passen/17.65%, Duy Tran/5.41%, Selvin Passen/4.88%, Maple Leaf Distillers, Inc./1.78%

Financial Data: Fiscal Year End: 05/31 **Latest Annual Data:** 03/31/2007

Year	Sales	Net Income
2007	NA	NA
2006	$717,000	-$804,000
2005	$515,000	-$804,000

Curr. Assets:	$366,000	Curr. Liab.:	$376,000		
Plant, Equip.:	NA	Total Liab.:	$601,000	Indic. Yr. Divd.:	NA
Total Assets:	$392,000	Net Worth:	-$209,000	Debt/ Equity:	0.1345

New World Restaurant Group Inc

555 Zang St., Ste. 300, Lakewood, CO, 80228; **PH:** 1-303-568-8000; **http://** www.nwcb.com

General - Incorporation	DE	**Stock**- Price on:12/24/2007	NA
Employees	292	Stock Exchange	NA
Auditor	Grant Thornton LLP	Ticker Symbol	NA
Stk Agt	American Stock Transfer & Trust Co.	Outstanding Shares	NA
Counsel	NA	E.P.S.	NA
DUNS No.	80-382-9258	Shareholders	NA

Business: The group's principal activities are to own, operate and franchise coffee bars and integrated bagel bakeries throughout the United States and columbia. The group specializes in high-quality foods for breakfast and lunch in a cafe atmosphere with a neighborhood emphasis. The group's product offerings include fresh baked goods, made-to-order sandwiches on a variety of breads and bagels, soups, salads, desserts, premium coffees and other cafe beverages. The group also operates a dough production and a coffee roasting facility. The group's trademarks and service marks include einstein bros, noah's New York bagels, manhattan bagel, chesapeake bagel bakery and new world coffee. As of 30-Dec-2003, the group's retail system consisted of 464 company-operated, 231 franchised and 41 licensed locations.

Primary SIC and add'l.: 5499 2051 5812

CIK No: 0000949373

Subsidiaries: Chesapeake Bagel Franchise Corp., Einstein and Noah Corp., Einstein/Noah Bagel Partners, Inc., I. & J. Bagel, Inc., Manhattan Bagel Company, Inc.

Officers: Paul J.B. Murphy/Dir., CEO, Pres./$771,960.00, Dan J. Dominguez/COO/$456,186.00, Jill B.W. Sisson/General Counsel, Sec./$329,720.00, Richard Dutkiewicz/CFO/$372,830.00

Directors: Paul J.B. Murphy/Dir., CEO, Pres., Nelson E. Heumann/Chmn., Garrett S. Stonehouse/Dir., James Hood/Dir., Frank C. Meyer/Dir., Leonard Tannenbaum/Dir., Michael W. Arthur/Dir.

Owners: Paul J.B. Murphy/1.70%, James W. Hood, Frank C. Meyer, Daniel J. Dominguez, Greenlight Capital, LLC and affiliates/94.10%, Garrett S. Stonehouse, Michael W. Arthur, Richard P. Dutkiewicz, Insiders/5.10%, Leonard M. Tannenbaum, Jill B. W. Sisson

Curr. Assets:	$24,728,000	**Curr. Liab.:**	$43,390,000		
Plant, Equip.:	$41,855,000	**Total Liab.:**	$213,939,000	**Indic. Yr. Divd.:**	NA
Total Assets:	$158,456,000	**Net Worth:**	-$112,483,000	**Debt/ Equity:**	NA

New York & Company Inc

450 W 33rd St., 5th Fl., New York, NY, 10001; **PH:** 1-212-884-2000; **Fax:** 1-212-884-2396; http:// www.nyandcompany.com

General - Incorporation	DE	**Stock**- Price on:12/24/2007	$11.11
Employees	2,448	Stock Exchange	NYSE
Auditor	Ernst& Young LLP	Ticker Symbol	NA
Stk Agt	Mellon Investor Services LLC	Outstanding Shares	57,880,000
Counsel	NA	E.P.S.	$0.21
DUNS No.	NA	Shareholders	NA

Business: The groups principle activity is to retail fashion oriented womens apparel, footwear and accessories. The groups apparels marketed under the brand names New York & Company(TM). In the year 2005, the group acquired Jasmine Company, Inc. The group operates from the United States. The groups quarterly revenue in November 2007 was 286.98 millions of USD.

Primary SIC and add'l.: 2337 2389 2339 2251 2335 2844 2331

CIK No: 0001211351

Subsidiaries: Associated Lerner Shops of America,Inc., Jasmine Company,Inc., Lernco,Inc., Lerner New York GC, LLC, Lerner New York Holding,Inc., Lerner New York, Inc, Nevada Receivable Factoring,Inc.

Officers: Richard P. Crystal/Chmn., CEO, Ronald W. Ristau/Dir., CFO, Pres., Sandra Brooslin Viviano/Exec. VP - Human Resources, John E. Dewolf/Exec. VP - Real Estate, Strategic Initiatives, Sheamus G. Toal/Chief Accounting Officer, Sr. VP, Allison Malkin/Contact - Investor Relations, Kellie Baldyga/Media Contact

Directors: Richard P. Crystal/Chmn., CEO, Ronald W. Ristau/Dir., CFO, Pres., Bodil M. Arlander/Dir., Philip M. Carpenter/Dir., David H. Edwab/Dir., Pamela Grunder Sheiffer/Dir., John D. Howard/Dir., Louis Lipschitz/Dir., Edward W. Moneypenny/Dir., Richard L. Perkal/Dir., Arthur E. Reiner/Dir.

Owners: Snow Capital Management, L.P, Arthur E. Reiner, Edward W. Moneypenny, Ronald W. Ristau, Louis Lipschitz, Sheamus G. Toal, BSMB/NYCG LLC, Robert J. Luzzi, David H. Edwab, Richard P. Crystal, Insiders, Sandra Brooslin Viviano, M. Katherine Dwyer, John D. Howard, John E. DeWolf

Financial Data: Fiscal Year End:01/28 Latest Annual Data: 2/3/2007

Year	Sales			Net Income
2007	$1,193,193,000			$46,170,000
2006	$1,130,544,000			$58,488,000
2005	$1,040,028,000			$17,438,000
Curr. Assets:	$214,862,000	**Curr. Liab.:**	$144,898,000	**P/E Ratio:** 16.34
Plant, Equip.:	$210,163,000	**Total Liab.:**	$229,000,000	**Indic. Yr. Divd.:** NA
Total Assets:	$469,799,000	**Net Worth:**	$240,799,000	**Debt/ Equity:** 0.1058

New York Community Bancorp Inc

615 Merrick Ave., Westbury, NY, 11590; **PH:** 1-516-683-4100; **Fax:** 1-516-683-4424; http:// www.mynycb.com; **Email:** ir@mynycb.com

General - Incorporation	DE	**Stock**- Price on:12/24/2007	$41.71
Employees	22,961	Stock Exchange	NYSE
Auditor	KPMG LLP	Ticker Symbol	NYB
Stk Agt	Mellon Investor Services LLC	Outstanding Shares	758,520,000
Counsel	NA	E.P.S.	$0.87
DUNS No.	00-699-3018	Shareholders	NA

Business: The group's principal activities are to attract retail deposits and originate multi-family mortgage loans. It operates through six divisions, including queens county savings bank, richmond county savings bank, cfs bank, first savings bank of New Jersey, ironbound bank and south jersey bank. The group's lending portfolio comprises primarily of multi-family mortgage loans on rental and cooperative apartment buildings as well as one-to-four family, commercial real estate and construction loans. Deposits include certificates of deposit, savings accounts, now and money market accounts and demand deposits. As of 31-Dec-2003, it served its customers through 140 banking offices in New York city, long island, westchester county and New Jersey and 52 in-store branches. On 31-Oct-2003, the group acquired roslyn bancorp, inc.

Primary SIC and add'l.: 6712 6036

CIK No: 0000910073

Subsidiaries: 1400 Corp., Bellingham Corp., BlizzardRealtyCorp., Bsr 1400 Corp., CFS Investments,Inc., Columbia Preferred Capital Corp., Ironbound Investment Company, Inc., Main Omni Realty Corp., Mt. Sinai Ventures, LLC, New York Municipal Bank, NYCBCommunityDevelopmentCorp., O.B. Ventures, LLC, Pacific Urban Renewal Corp., Peter B. Cannell& Co., Inc., RCBK Mortgage Corp. 31 Subsidiaries included in the Index

Officers: Joseph R. Ficalora/Dir., CEO, Pres./$1,541,413.00, Robert Wann/COO, Sr. Exec. VP/$1,077,281.00, Thomas R. Cangemi/Sr. Exec. VP, CFO/$921,762.00, John J. Pinto/Exec. VP, Chief Accounting Officer, James J. Carpenter/Sr. Exec. VP, Chief Lending Officer/$794,233.00, Patrick R. Quinn/Exec. VP, Chief Corporate Governance Officer, Corp. Sec., Russ Dibenedetto/First Sr. VP, Dir. - Audit, Mark Ricca/Exec. VP, General Counsel, Assist., COO

Directors: Joseph R. Ficalora/Dir., CEO, Pres., Michael F. Manzulli/Chmn., Dominick Ciampa/Dir., Thomas A. Doherty/Dir., Max L. Kupferberg/Dir., Guy V. Molinari/Dir., John A. Pileski/Dir., Spiros J. Voutsinas/Dir., Donald M. Blake/Dir., Maureen E. Clancy/Dir., Robert S. Farrell/Dir., William C. Frederick/Dir., Michael J. Levine/Dir., James J. O'Donovan/Dir., John M. Tsimbinos/Dir. (16 Directors included in Index)

Owners: Max L. Kupferberg/1.53%, James J. ODonovan/0.80%, William C. Frederick, James J. Carpenter, Maureen E. Clancy, Guy V. Molinari, Thomas A. Doherty/0.03%, Robert S. Farrell/0.14%, John A. Pileski, John M. Tsimbinos/0.86%, Hanif W. Dahya, Dominick Ciampa/0.32%, Joseph R. Ficalora/1.79%, Michael J. Levine/0.11%, Insiders/7.43% (21 Owners included in Index)

Financial Data: Fiscal Year End:12/31 Latest Annual Data: 12/31/2006

Year	Sales			Net Income
2006	$1,505,933,000			$232,585,000
2005	$1,276,719,000			$292,085,000
2004	$1,282,526,000			$355,086,000
Curr. Assets:	$230,759,000	**Curr. Liab.:**	$23,709,495,000	**P/E Ratio:** 10.53
Plant, Equip.:	$196,084,000	**Total Liab.:**	$24,792,533,000	**Indic. Yr. Divd.:** $1.000
Total Assets:	$28,482,370,000	**Net Worth:**	$3,689,837,000	**Debt/ Equity:** 0.9802

New York Health Care Inc

1850 McDonald Ave., Brooklyn, NY, 11223; **PH:** 1-718-375-6700; **Fax:** 1-718-375-1555; http:// www.nyhc.com; **Email:** info@nyhc.com

General - Incorporation	NY	**Stock**- Price on:12/24/2007	$0.09
Employees	1,784	Stock Exchange	OTC
Auditor	Weiser LLP	Ticker Symbol	BBAL
Stk Agt	Continental Stock Transfer & Trust Co	Outstanding Shares	33,530,000
Counsel	NA	E.P.S.	-$0.048
DUNS No.	10-367-0485	Shareholders	NA

Business: The group operates in two industry segments, the health care and bio balance. The health care segment provide home health and personal care support services in capacities ranging from companions to live-ins, including assistance with personal hygiene, dressing and feeding, meal preparation, light housekeeping and shopping and, to a limited extent, physical therapy and standard skilled nursing services. Biobalance segment is focused on the development of novel treatments and dietary products for various gastrointestinal (gi) disorders including irritable bowel syndrome (ibs), inflammatory bowel disease and diarrhea caused by antibiotics, chemotherapy or aids. The group acquired bio balance in 2003. The group's customers include various county departments of social services, nyc hra, New Jersey medicaid, beth abraham health services in the bronx and westchester county, kingsbridge medical center, mt. Sinai medical center, etc.

Primary SIC and add'l.: 2834 8082

CIK No: 0001018354

Subsidiaries: BioBalance, NYHC Newco Paxxon, Inc.

Officers: Dennis M. O'Donnell/CEO, Joseph Segel/CEO - Health Care Division, Murray Englard/49/Dir., Acting CEO, Stewart W. Robinson/53/CFO, Shalom Yurman/Dir. - Information Services, Anthony Acquaviva/Controller

Directors: Murray Englard/49/Dir., Acting CEO, Howard Berg/53/Dir., Yoram Hacohen/37/Dir.

Owners: Howard Berg/4.09%, Insiders/5.75%, Yoram Hacohen/0.07%, Insiders/5.75%, Bernard Korolnick/5.13%, Pinchas Stefansky/6.00%, Rivvi Rose/5.78%, Murry Englard/1.71%

Financial Data: Fiscal Year End:12/31 Latest Annual Data: 12/31/2006

Year	Sales			Net Income
2006	$45,558,000			-$3,756,000
2005	$44,723,000			-$6,322,000
2004	$48,854,000			-$6,072,000
Curr. Assets:	$10,232,000	**Curr. Liab.:**	$14,682,000	
Plant, Equip.:	$121,000	**Total Liab.:**	$14,682,000	**Indic. Yr. Divd.:** NA
Total Assets:	$12,880,000	**Net Worth:**	-$1,803,000	**Debt/ Equity:** NA

New York Mortgage Trust Inc

1301 Ave. of the Americas, 7th Fl., New York, NY, 10019; **PH:** 1-212-634-9400; **Fax:** 1-212-655-6269; http:// www.nymtrust.com; **Email:** investorrelations@nymtrust.com

General - Incorporation	MD	**Stock**- Price on:12/24/2007	$1.98
Employees	616	Stock Exchange	NDQ
Auditor	Deloitte & Touche LLP	Ticker Symbol	NTRS
Stk Agt	American Stock Transfer & Trust Co.	Outstanding Shares	18,100,000
Counsel	NA	E.P.S.	-$1
DUNS No.	NA	Shareholders	NA

Business: The groups principle activities include acquiring and investing in real mortgage properties. The group operates through two segments namely, mortgage portfolio management and mortgage lending. The group operates from the United States.

Primary SIC and add'l.: 6798 6798

CIK No: 0001273685

Subsidiaries: New York Mortgage Funding, LLC, New York Mortgage Trust 2005-1, New York Mortgage Trust 2005-2, New York Mortgage Trust 2005-3, New York Mortgage Trust 2006-1, The New York Mortgage Company, LLC

Officers: David A. Akre/50/Vice Chmn., Co - CEO, Steve R. Mumma/Dir., Co - CEO, CFO, Pres., Bradley A. Howe/Sr. VP, General Counsel

Directors: David A. Akre/50/Vice Chmn., Co - CEO, Steven B. Schnall/42/Chmn., David R. Bock/Dir., Alan L. Hainey/Dir., Steven G. Norcutt/Dir., Mary Dwyer Pembroke/Dir., Jerome F. Sherman/Dir., Thomas W. White/Dir.

Owners: Steven G. Norcutt, Joseph V. Fierro/5.30%, Wellington Management Company, LLP/7.30%, Jerome F. Sherman, Huntleigh Advisors, Inc./5.60%, Insiders/18.70%, NWQ Investment Management Company, LLC/14.30%, David A. Akre, David R. Bock, Alan L. Hainey, Thomas W. White, Steven B. Schnall/12.30%, Mary Dwyer Pembroke, Steven R. Mumma

Financial Data: Fiscal Year End:12/31 Latest Annual Data: 12/31/2006

Year	Sales			Net Income
2006	$64,881,000			-$15,031,000
2005	$116,689,000			-$5,340,000
2004	$56,030,000			$4,947,000
Curr. Assets:	$8,244,000	**Curr. Liab.:**	$5,575,000	**P/E Ratio:** 16.34
Plant, Equip.:	NA	**Total Liab.:**	$1,251,336,000	**Indic. Yr. Divd.:** $0.200
Total Assets:	$1,322,908,000	**Net Worth:**	$71,572,000	**Debt/ Equity:** NA

New York Regional Rail Corp

5266 Seneca St., West Seneca, NY, 14224; **PH:** 1-716-675-6015; http:// www.nyrr.com

General - Incorporation	DE
Employees	12
Auditor	Sherb & Co. LLP
Stk Agt	Florida Atlantic Stock Transfer, Inc.
Counsel	NA
DUNS No.	NA

Stock - Price on:12/24/2007	$0.0095
Stock Exchange	OTC
Ticker Symbol	NYRR
Outstanding Shares	216,730,000
E.P.S.	NA
Shareholders	NA

Business: The group's principal activity is to operate an icc certified railroad through its majority-owned subsidiary, New York cross harbor railroad terminal corporation. The group transports and delivers rail traffic via barges across New York harbor and the east river, thus connecting the long island railroad and other lines. In addition, it receives and delivers railcars at certain industrial facilities located on partially owned and partially leased track located in brooklyn, New York and jersey city, New Jersey. The group also operates regional trucking company, which is in the business of short-haul freight transportation and landfill management.

Primary SIC and add'l.: 4213 4011

CIK No: 0001020173

Subsidiaries: JST, NYCH

Officers: James W. Cornell/Chmn., CEO

Directors: James W. Cornell/Chmn., CEO

Financial Data: Fiscal Year End:12/31   Latest Annual Data: 12/31/2004

Year	Sales	Net Income
2004	$8,361,000	-$2,025,000
2003	$5,624,000	-$839,000
2002	$5,432,000	-$52,000

Curr. Assets:	$1,304,000	Curr. Liab.:	$6,491,000		
Plant, Equip.:	$4,587,000	Total Liab.:	$8,377,000	Indic. Yr. Divd.:	NA
Total Assets:	$6,336,000	Net Worth:	-$2,040,000	Debt/ Equity:	NA

New York Times Co

620 8th Ave., New York, NY, 10018; **PH:** 1-212-556-1234; **Fax:** 1-212-556-7389; *http://* www.nytimes.com; **Email:** circulation@nytimes.com

General - Incorporation	NY
Employees	11,585
Auditor	Deloitte & Touche LLP
Stk Agt	EquiServe Trust Co N.A
Counsel	NA
DUNS No.	00-131-5613

Stock - Price on:12/24/2007	$25.77
Stock Exchange	NYSE
Ticker Symbol	NYT
Outstanding Shares	143,910,000
E.P.S.	-$3.42
Shareholders	NA

Business: The groups principle activity is to publish newspapers. The group operates Internet businesses, television and radio stations, and invests in paper mills. In May 2007, the group sold Broadcast Media Group to Oak Hill Capital Partners. The group operates from United States.

Primary SIC and add'l.: 4832 2711 2621 7375 2721 4833

CIK No: 0000071691

Subsidiaries: About, Inc., Boston Globe Electronic Publishing, LLC, Boston Globe Marketing, LLC, City & Suburban Delivery Systems, Inc, Comet-Press Newspapers Holdings, Inc., Comet-Press Newspapers, Inc., Community Newsdealers Holdings, Inc., Discovery Times Channel LLC, Donohue Malbaie Inc., Globe Newspaper Company, Inc, Globe Specialty Products, LLC, Hendersonville Newspaper Corporation, Hendersonville Newspaper Holdings, Inc., International Herald Tribune S.A.S., International Media Concepts, Inc. 53 Subsidiaries included in the Index

Officers: Janet L. Robinson/Dir., CEO, Pres./$4,402,678.00, Bill Keller/Exec. Editor, The New York Times, Scott H. Heekin-Canedy/56/Pres., GM - Times, Rhonda L. Brauer/Sec., Corporate Governance Officer, David K. Norton/Sr. VP, Martin A. Nisenholtz/Sr. VP, Stuart P. Stoller/Sr. VP, Kenneth A. Richieri/VP, General Counsel, George A. Barrios/VP, Treasurer, Catherine J. Mathis/VP - Corporate Communications, David Allan/Producer, Craig Allen/Producer, David Goodman/Producer, Julie Bloom/Producer, Simone Bridges/Producer (87 Officers included in Index)

Directors: Janet L. Robinson/Dir., CEO, Pres., Michael Golden/Vice Chmn., Arthur O. Sulzberger/Chmn., Cathy J. Sulzberger/Dir., Lynn G. Dolnick/Dir., CFO, VP, Doreen A. Toben/Dir., Raul E. Cesan/Dir., Thomas Middelhoff/Dir., David E. Liddle/Dir., Brenda C. Barnes/Dir., VP, Corporate Controller, William E. Kennard/Dir., James M. Kilts/Dir., Ellen R. Marram/Dir.

Owners: Cathy J. Sulzberger/4.70%, James M. Cohen/4.70%, Arthur Sulzberger/5.30%, Massachusetts Financial Services Company/8.30%, Eric M. A. Lax/4.50%, 1997 Trust/4.50%, Morgan Stanley/7.10%, Lynn G. Dolnick/4.70%, Michael Golden/4.90%, FMR Corp/5.80%, Susan W. Dryfoos/4.90%, T.Rowe Price Associates, Inc./15.00%, Daniel H. Cohen/4.70%, Private Capital Management, L.P./9.30%

Financial Data: Fiscal Year End:12/25   Latest Annual Data: 12/31/2006

Year	Sales	Net Income
2006	$3,289,903,000	-$543,443,000
2005	$3,372,775,000	$259,753,000
2004	$3,303,642,000	$292,557,000

Curr. Assets:	$1,185,043,000	Curr. Liab.:	$1,297,994,000		
Plant, Equip.:	$1,375,365,000	Total Liab.:	$3,030,119,000	Indic. Yr. Divd.:	$0.920
Total Assets:	$3,855,928,000	Net Worth:	$819,842,000	Debt/ Equity:	NA

Newalliance Bancshares Inc

195 Church St., New Haven, CT, 06510; **PH:** 1-203-789-2767; **Fax:** 1-203-789-2650; *http://* www.newalliancebank.com

General - Incorporation	DE
Employees	904
Auditor	PricewaterhouseCoopers LLP
Stk Agt	American Stock Transfer & Trust Co.
Counsel	NA
DUNS No.	NA

Stock - Price on:12/24/2007	$15.06
Stock Exchange	NYSE
Ticker Symbol	NAL
Outstanding Shares	113,450,000
E.P.S.	$0.47
Shareholders	NA

Business: The group's principal activity is the provision of banking services in new haven and middlesex counties. The banking services include acceptance of deposits and provision of residential and commercial real estate loans through its 36 banking offices in new haven and middlesex counties. It also offers a range of banking services to individuals and corporate customers primarily located in south central Connecticut.

Primary SIC and add'l.: 6712 6021

CIK No: 0001264755

Subsidiaries: Alliance Capital Trust I, Alliance Capital Trust II, NewAlliance Bank, NewAlliance Bank Community Development Corporation, NewAlliance Investments, Inc, NewAlliance Servicing Company, The Loan Source, Inc.

Officers: Peyton R. Patterson/Chmn., CEO, Pres./$4,031,839.00, Brian S. Arsenault/Exec. VP - Corporate Communications, Investor Relations, Merrill B. Blanksteen/Exec. VP, CFO, Treasurer/$1,947,713.00, Gail E.D. Brathwaite/COO, Exec. VP/$1,724,231.00, Donald T. Chaffee/Exec. VP, Chief Credit Officer/$977,029.00, Edward J. Diamond/Exec. VP - Wealth Management, Diane L. Wishnafski/Exec. VP - Business, Retail Services/$1,095,190.00, Koon-Ping Chan/Exec. VP, Chief Risk Officer, Poul A. McCraven/Sr. VP - Community Development Banking, Mark F. Doyle/47/Chief Accounting Officer, Sr. VP

Directors: Peyton R. Patterson/Chmn., CEO, Pres., John F. Croweak/Dir., Robert J. Lyons/Dir., Roxanne J. Coady/Dir., Sheila B. Flanagan/Dir., Eric A. Marziali/Dir., Carlton L. Highsmith/Dir., Richard J. Grossi/Dir., Joseph A. Zaccagnino/Dir., Joseph H. Rossi/Dir., Nathaniel D. Woodson/Dir., Gerald B. Rosenberg/Dir., Julia M. McNamara/Dir., Douglas K. Anderson/Dir.

Owners: NewAlliance Bancshares, Inc./6.60%, Third Avenue Management LLC/6.90%, Eric A. Marziali, Joseph H. Rossi, Gail E. D. Brathwaite, Peyton R. Patterson/1.60%, Insiders/7.00%, Cornell Scott, Douglas K. Anderson, Richard J. Grossi, Donald T. Chaffee, Nathaniel D. Woodson, Diane L. Wishnafski, Sheila B. Flanagan, Gerald B. Rosenberg (22 Owners included in Index)

Financial Data: Fiscal Year End:12/31   Latest Annual Data: 12/31/2006

Year	Sales	Net Income
2006	$382,663,000	$48,837,000
2005	$322,174,000	$52,599,000
2004	$243,740,000	$4,069,000

Curr. Assets:	$188,963,000	Curr. Liab.:	$3,900,667,000	P/E Ratio:	32.04
Plant, Equip.:	$52,479,000	Total Liab.:	$5,885,391,000	Indic. Yr. Divd.:	$0.260
Total Assets:	$7,247,696,000	Net Worth:	$1,362,305,000	Debt/ Equity:	1.4154

Newave Inc

404 E 1st St., Long Beach, CA, 90802; **PH:** 1-562-983-5331; *http://* www.nwve.com

General - Incorporation	UT
Employees	96
Auditor	Jaspers & Hall, P.C
Stk Agt	Interwest Transfer Company, Inc.
Counsel	NA
DUNS No.	NA

Stock - Price on:12/24/2007	$1.27
Stock Exchange	OTC
Ticker Symbol	CPNE
Outstanding Shares	50,860,000
E.P.S.	$0.11
Shareholders	NA

Business: The group's principal activities are to provide comprehensive line of products and services at wholesale prices. The operations of the group are conducted through wholly owned subsidiary, onlinesupplier.com. The group's integrated suite of electronic commerce products enables individuals and businesses to conduct electronic commerce over the Internet at affordable price levels. The group's products integrate transaction processing, accounting and financial systems, customer relationship management, advertising, merchant processing and a wide array of wholesale products. On 15-Jan-2004, the group acquired onlinesupplier.com.

Primary SIC and add'l.: 1455 1499

CIK No: 0001028070

Subsidiaries: Auction Liquidator, Inc., Online Supplier, Inc.

Officers: David Foucar/47/Dir., CFO, Charlie Gugliuzza/33/Dir., Pres.

Directors: David Foucar/47/Dir., CFO, Charlie Gugliuzza/33/Dir., Pres.

Owners: David Foucar, Charlie Gugliuzza, Aaron Gravitz, Douglas Leighton, Insiders, eFund Capital Parthers, LLC, Michael Hill, eFund Small-Cap Fund, Dutchess Advisors, LLC, Michael A. Novielli, Barrett Evans

Financial Data: Fiscal Year End:12/31   Latest Annual Data: 12/31/2006

Year	Sales	Net Income
2006	$27,488,000	$8,741,000
2005	$7,340,000	-$6,266,000
2004	$6,813,000	-$3,885,000

Curr. Assets:	$9,475,000	Curr. Liab.:	$3,546,000	P/E Ratio:	5.70
Plant, Equip.:	$1,306,000	Total Liab.:	$3,546,000	Indic. Yr. Divd.:	NA
Total Assets:	$10,800,000	Net Worth:	$7,254,000	Debt/ Equity:	NA

Newcastle Investment Corp

1345 Ave. of the Americas, New York, NY, 10105; **PH:** 1-212-798-6100; **Fax:** 1-212-798-6133; *http://* www.newcastleinv.com

General - Incorporation	MD
Employees	NA
Auditor	Ernst & Young LLP
Stk Agt	American Stock Transfer & Trust Co.
Counsel	NA
DUNS No.	NA

Stock - Price on:12/24/2007	$28.4
Stock Exchange	NYSE
Ticker Symbol	NCX
Outstanding Shares	52,770,000
E.P.S.	$2.71
Shareholders	NA

Business: The groups principle activity is to invest in real estate properties. The group operates through three segments namely, real estate securities and real estate related loans, residential mortgage loans, and operating real estate. In the year 2006, the group acquired 300 residential mortgage loans. The group operates from the United States. The group's quarterly revenue for Septmber 2007 was 168.87 millions of USD.

Primary SIC and add'l.: 6798

CIK No: 0001175483

Subsidiaries: 1. 2520 Ridgewood GP, LLC, 10. Fortress CBO Investments I Corp., 11. Fortress CBO Investments I, Ltd., 12. Fortress Realty Holdings, Inc., 13. Impac CMB Trust 1998-C1, 14. Impac Commercial Assets Corporation, 15. Impac Commercial Capital Corporation, 16. Impac Commercial Holdings, Inc., 17. Karl S.A., 18. LIV Holdings LLC, 19. NC Circle Holdings II LLC, 2. Commercial Asset Holdings LLC, 20. NC Circle Holdings LLC, 21. NCT Holdings II LLC, 22. NCT Holdings LLC 83 Subsidiaries included in the Index

Officers: Kenneth M. Riis/Dir., CEO, Pres., Jonathan Ashley/COO, Debra A. Hess/CFO, Randal A. Nardone/Sec., Phillip J. Evanski/Chief Investment Officer, Lilly Donohue/Dir. - Investor Relations, Nadean Finke/Assoc., Investor Relations

Directors: Kenneth M. Riis/Dir., CEO, Pres., Wesley R. Edens/Chmn., Kevin J. Finnerty/Dir., Stuart A. McFarland/Dir., David K. McKown/Dir., Peter M. Miller/Dir.

Owners: Kenneth M. Riis/1.00%, Debra A. Hess, Cohen & Steers/11.00%, Insiders/11.50%, Phillip J. Evanski, Jonathan Ashley, Stuart A. McFarland, Kevin J. Finnerty, Wesley R. Edens/4.90%, Randal A. Nardone/4.60%, David K. McKown, Peter M. Miller

Financial Data: Fiscal Year End:12/31   Latest Annual Data: 12/31/2006

Year	Sales	Net Income
2006	$552,609,000	$127,923,000
2005	$378,213,000	$116,955,000
2004	$258,146,000	$98,415,000

Curr. Assets:	$241,571,000	Curr. Liab.:	$1,984,061,000	P/E Ratio:	10.64
Plant, Equip.:	$29,626,000	Total Liab.:	$7,602,412,000	Indic. Yr. Divd.:	$2.880
Total Assets:	$8,604,392,000	Net Worth:	$1,001,980,000	Debt/ Equity:	5.3704

Newell Rubbermaid Inc

10 B Glenlake Pkwy., Ste. 300, Atlanta, GA, 30328; *PH:* 1-770-407-3800; *Fax:* 1-770-407-3970; *http://* www.newellrubbermaid.com

General - Incorporation .... DE	Stock- Price on:12/24/2007 ....$29.82
Employees 23,500	Stock Exchange................................NYSE
Auditor .... Ernst & Young LLP	Ticker Symbol.................................NWL
Stk Agt.... Computershare Investor Services LLC	Outstanding Shares 276,300,000
Counsel......................................NA	E.P.S.......................................$1.44
DUNS No. 00-523-8183	Shareholders..................................NA

Business: The groups principle activities include manufacturing and distributing brand name consumer products. The group operates through four segments namely rubbermaid, sharpie, irwin and calphalon home. The group operates from United States.

Primary SIC and add'l.: 2591 3231 3069 3556 2499 3951

CIK No: 0000814453

Subsidiaries: Amerock Hardware Systems de Mexico, Berol Corporation, Berol Limited, Berol Pen Company, Berol S. de R.L. de C.V., Calphalon Corporation, Comercial Berol S. de R.L. de C.V., Dymo Holdings SPRL, Ember Investment Corporation, Furth Corporation, Gardinia Home Dcor GmbH, Goody Products, Inc., Graco Childrens Products, Inc., Imaco, Inc., Irwin Industrial Tool Company 74 Subsidiaries included in the Index

Officers: Mark D. Ketchum/Dir., CEO, Pres./$7,577,901.00, Hartley Blaha/Pres. - Corporate Development, James J. Roberts/Group COO, Pres. - Rubbermaid, Irwin Group/$3,023,635.00, Paul G. Boitmann/Pres. - Sales Operations, Global Wal, Mart, Timothy J. Jahnke/Group Pres. - Home, Family Products Group/$2,167,105.00, Patrick J. Robinson/CFO, Exec. VP, James M. Sweet/Exec. VP - Human Resources, Corporate Communications, Steven G. Marton/Group Pres. - Office Products Group/$1,840,323.00, Magnus R. Nicolin/Pres. - Newell Rubbermaid Europe, Middle East, Africa, EMEA, Gordon Steele/CIO, Sr. VP, Ted Woehrle/Sr. VP - Marketing, Brand Management, Ricky T. Dillon/VP, Corporate Controller, Chief Accounting Officer, Raymond J. Johnson/Pres. - Global Manufacturing, Supply Chain, Dale L. Matschullat/VP, General Counsel, Corp. Sec.

Directors: Mark D. Ketchum/Dir., CEO, Pres., William D. Marohn/68/Chmn., Cynthia A. Montgomery/55/Dir., Gordon R. Sullivan/70/Dir., Allan P. Newell/Dir., Scott S. Cowen/61/Dir., Steven J. Strobel/50/Dir., Michael A. Todman/50/Dir., Michael T. Cowhig/61/Dir., Thomas E. Clarke/56/Dir., Raymond G. Viault/63/Dir., Elizabeth Cuthbert Millett/51/Dir.

Owners: James J. Roberts, Cynthia A. Montgomery, Thomas E. Clarke, Allan P. Newell, Goldman Sachs Asset Management, L.P./5.10%, Timothy J. Jahnke, Michael T. Cowhig, William D. Marohn, Elizabeth Cuthbert Millett, Steven G. Marton, T. Rowe Price Associates, Inc./7.60%, Edward C. Johnson 3d/5.02%, Steven J. Strobel, Patrick J. Robinson, Raymond G. Viault *(20 Owners included in Index)*

Financial Data: Fiscal Year End:12/31   Latest Annual Data: 12/31/2006

Year	Sales	Net Income
2006	$6,201,000,000	$385,000,000
2005	$6,342,500,000	$251,300,000
2004	$6,748,400,000	-$116,100,000

Curr. Assets:	$2,476,900,000	Curr. Liab.:	$1,896,600,000	P/E Ratio:	20.71
Plant, Equip.:	$746,900,000	Total Liab.:	$4,420,300,000	Indic. Yr. Divd.:	$0.840
Total Assets:	$6,310,500,000	Net Worth:	$1,890,200,000	Debt/ Equity:	1.2257

Newfield Exploration Co

363 N Sam Houston Pkwy. E, Ste. 2020, Houston, TX, 77060; *PH:* 1-281-847-6000; *Fax:* 1-281-405-4242; *http://* www.newfld.com; *Email:* info@newfld.com

General - Incorporation .... DE	Stock- Price on:12/24/2007 ....$49.14
Employees 871	Stock Exchange................................NDQ
Auditor ....PricewaterhouseCoopers LLP	Ticker Symbol.................................NGA
Stk Agt...... American Stock Transfer & Trust Co.	Outstanding Shares 129,980,000
Counsel......................Vinson & Elkins LLP	E.P.S.......................................$1.69
DUNS No. 19-706-7267	Shareholders..................................NA

Business: The groups principle activity is to provide crude oil and natural gas exploration and production services. The group operates from United States.

Primary SIC and add'l.: 1321 1311 1382

CIK No: 0000912750

Subsidiaries: EEX Capital, Inc., EEX E&P Company, L.P., EEX Exploration & Production Company LLC, EEX Operating L.P., EEX Operating LLC, EEX Reserves Company LLC, EEX Reserves Funding LLC, Newfield Exploration Gulf Coast Inc., Newfield Exploration Mid-Continent Inc., Newfield Production Company, Newfield Rocky Mountains Inc.

Officers: David A. Trice/Chmn., CEO/$4,585,820.00, Terry W. Rathert/CFO, Sr. VP, Sec./$2,379,962.00, Elliott Pew/Exec. VP - Exploration/$1,410,957.00, Mona Leigh Bernhardt/VP - Human Resources, William D. Schneider/VP - International, Founder Member, Penny McKnight/Investor Relations Officer, Michael D. Van Horn/Sr. VP - Exploration, David F. Schaible/Dir., Exec. VP - Operations, Acquisitions, Newfield/$2,440,233.00, Mark W. Blumenshine/VP - Land, Lee K. Boothby/VP - Mid, Continent/$1,916,029.00, Stephen C. Campbell/VP - Investor Relations, George T. Dunn/VP - Gulf Coast, James J. Metcalf/VP - Drilling, Gary D. Packer/VP - Rocky Mountains, Mark Spicer/VP - Information Technology *(16 Officers included in Index)*

Directors: David A. Trice/Chmn., CEO, David F. Schaible/Dir., Exec. VP - Operations, Acquisitions, Newfield, Dennis R. Hendrix/Dir., Michael J. Lacey/Dir., Terry J. Strange/Dir., Thomas G. Ricks/Dir., Joseph H. Netherland/Dir., Howard H. Newman/Dir., Philip J. Burguieres/Dir., Juanita F. Romans/Dir., C. E. Shultz/Dir., John R. Kemp/Dir., Pamela J. Gardner/Dir.

Owners: Terry W. Rathert, John Randolph Kemp, Michael J. Lacey, Howard H. Newman, Insiders/2.40%, Lee K. Boothby, Dennis R. Hendrix, Thomas G. Ricks, David A. Trice, Elliott Pew, Joseph H. Netherland, Capital Research and Management Company/10.80%, C. E. Shultz, Juanita F. Romans, David F. Schaible *(18 Owners included in Index)*

Financial Data: Fiscal Year End:12/31   Latest Annual Data: 12/31/2006

Year	Sales	Net Income
2006	$1,673,000,000	$591,000,000
2005	$1,762,000,000	$348,000,000
2004	$1,352,700,000	$312,100,000

Curr. Assets:	$851,000,000	Curr. Liab.:	$1,123,000,000	P/E Ratio:	15.85
Plant, Equip.:	$5,683,000,000	Total Liab.:	$3,573,000,000	Indic. Yr. Divd.:	NA
Total Assets:	$6,635,000,000	Net Worth:	$3,062,000,000	Debt/ Equity:	0.4506

Newgen Technologies Inc

6000 Fairview Rd., 12th Fl., Charlotte, NC, 28210; *PH:* 1-704-552-3590; *Fax:* 1-704-552-3705; *http://* www.refuelamerica.com

General - Incorporation .... NV	Stock- Price on:12/24/2007 ....$0.45
Employees 52	Stock Exchange................................OTC
Auditor .... Weinberg & Co. P.A	Ticker Symbol.................................NWGN
Stk Agt .... Computershare Investor Services LLC	Outstanding Shares 66,980,000
Counsel......................................NA	E.P.S......................................-$0.27
DUNS No. ....NA	Shareholders..................................NA

Business: The group's principle activity is to conceptualize and produce television programs for worldwide distribution across multiple media platforms from traditional television broadcasters, either terrestrial or cable/satellite to Internet and broadband. The group is an entertainment content provider and independent record label, whose market is the global entertainment/music consumer. The group intends to market and sell recorded material through customary industry methods including traditional music retailers, chain stores, retail mega-stores, music clubs and Internet-based retailers. The group also intends to target and acquire revenue-producing, entertainment-based assets such as existing music publishing catalogs.

Primary SIC and add'l.: 4833

CIK No: 0000833837

Subsidiaries: Cornell Capital Partners LP, NewGen International, Inc., PowerSHIFT Energy Company, Inc, Refuel America, Inc, Refuel Terminal Operations, Inc.

Officers: Bruce S. Wunner/Chmn., CEO, Blois Olson/Contact - Investor Relations Media Relations, Tadas Norvaisa/Corporate Controller, James E. Peeples/Sr. VP - Business Development - Government Relations, Ian Williamson/Pres., Dir. - Research & Development, Dir., Michael F. D'Onofrio/Dir., COO, Michael Woods/CFO

Directors: Bruce S. Wunner/Chmn., CEO, Ian Williamson/Pres., Dir. - Research & Development, Dir., Michael F. D'Onofrio/Dir., COO, Cliff Hazel/Dir., Conrad Lee/Dir.

Owners: Bruce S. Wunner, Noel M. Corcoran/20.24%, Michael F. D'Onofrio, Cliff Hazel/14.93%, Scott Deininger, Insiders/49.95%, Ian Williamson/12.83%, Michael W. Woods

Financial Data: Fiscal Year End:12/31   Latest Annual Data: 12/31/2006

Year	Sales	Net Income
2006	$916,000	-$14,560,000
2005	NA	-$4,264,000
2004	NA	-$362,000

Curr. Assets:	$1,993,000	Curr. Liab.:	$5,963,000		
Plant, Equip.:	$6,359,000	Total Liab.:	$15,499,000	Indic. Yr. Divd.:	NA
Total Assets:	$8,806,000	Net Worth:	-$6,693,000	Debt/ Equity:	NA

NewMarket China Inc

Formerly: Intercell International Corp
14860 Montfort Dr., Ste. 210, Dallas, TX, 75254; *PH:* 1-631-393-5130; *http://* www.intercellinternational.com

General - Incorporation .... NV	Stock- Price on:12/24/2007 ....NA
Employees ....NA	Stock Exchange................................NA
Auditor .... Pollard-kelley Auditing Services, Inc	Ticker Symbol.................................NA
Stk Agt ....Interwest Transfer Co., Inc.	Outstanding Shares ....NA
Counsel......................................NA	E.P.S......................................$0.009
DUNS No. 08-545-6515	Shareholders..................................NA

Business: The group has no business operations. It is attempting to arrange for financing and investigating several different business opportunities. The group owns nanopierce technologies, inc. Which designs, develops and licenses products using its intellectual property, the pi technology. The pi technology is designed to improve electrical, thermal and mechanical characteristics of electronic products. Nanopierce has designated and is commercializing its pi technology as the nanopierce connection system and markets the pi technology to companies in various industries for a wide range of applications. On 20th oct 2003, the group acquired brunetti inc.

Primary SIC and add'l.: 3674 3559

CIK No: 0000745655

Officers: John T. Verges/39/CEO, Pres., Philip J. Rauch/46/Dir., CFO

Directors: Charles E. Bauer/54/Dir., Philip J. Rauch/46/Dir., CFO, Philip Verges/43/Dir., Bruce Noller/51/Dir.

Owners: Insiders/0.92%, Cheri L. Metzinger/6.00%, NewMarket Technology, Inc./33.16%, Paul H. Metzinger/6.00%, Charles E. Bauer/0.92%

Financial Data: Fiscal Year End:09/30   Latest Annual Data: 12/31/2006

Year	Sales	Net Income
2006	$29,510,000	$245,000
2005	NA	-$284,000

Curr. Assets:	$271,000	Curr. Liab.:	$375,000		
Plant, Equip.:	NA	Total Liab.:	$375,000	Indic. Yr. Divd.:	NA
Total Assets:	$279,000	Net Worth:	-$96,000	Debt/ Equity:	NA

Newmarket Corp

330 S 4th St., Richmond, VA, 23219; *PH:* 1-804-788-5000; *Fax:* 1-804-788-5688; *http://* www.newmarket.com

General - Incorporation .... VA	Stock- Price on:12/24/2007 ....$47.76
Employees 1,185	Stock Exchange................................NDQ
Auditor .... PricewaterhouseCoopers LLP	Ticker Symbol.................................NEWP
Stk Agt .... Computershare Investor Services LLC	Outstanding Shares 17,300,000
Counsel......................................NA	E.P.S.......................................$3.45
DUNS No. ....NA	Shareholders..................................NA

Business: The group's principal activities are to develop, manufacture, blend and market fuel and lubricant additive products around the world. Its two distinct business segments include petroleum additives and tetraethyl lead. Petroleum additives are used in lubricants or fuels and have different applications. The lubricant additives are used in oils, automatic transmission fluids and greases. The fuel additives are used in applications including gasoline, diesel fuels, aviation fuels, racing fuels, power generation fuels and heating oils. Tetraethyl lead is an octane enhancer used in leaded gasoline. Few of the trademarks include ethyl(R), mmt(R), hitec(R), and greenburn(r). The group sold phenolic antioxidant business to albemarle corporation on 21-Jan-2003. It has operations in the United States, Europe, Asia, Latin America, Australia and Canada.

Primary SIC and add'l.: NA

CIK No: 0001282637

Subsidiaries: Afton Chemical Additives Corporation, Afton Chemical Asia Pacific LLC, Afton Chemical Canada Corporation, Afton Chemical Canada Holdings, Inc., Afton Chemical Corporation, Afton Chemical de Mexico S.A. de C.V., Afton Chemical de Venezuela, C.A., Afton Chemical GmbH, Afton Chemical Industria de Aditivos Ltda, Afton Chemical Intangibles LLC, Afton Chemical Japan Corporation, Afton Chemical Japan Holdings, Inc., Afton Chemical Limited, Afton Chemical S.P.R.L., Afton Cooper Limited 36 Subsidiaries included in the Index

Officers: Thomas E. Gottwald/Dir., CEO, Pres./$941,817.00, Rudolph M. West/Sec.

Directors: Thomas E. Gottwald/Dir., CEO, Pres., Bruce C. Gottwald/74/Chmn., Phyllis L. Cothran/61/Dir., James E. Rogers/62/Dir., Sidney Buford Scott/75/Dir., Charles B. Walker/69/Dir., Patrick D. Hanley/63/Dir.

Owners: Charles B. Walker, Sidney Buford Scott, Bruce C. Gottwald, Bruce C. Gottwald/9.50%, Warren C.S. Huang, Goldman Sachs Asset Management, L.P./9.60%, Steven M. Edmonds, Patrick D. Hanley, Phyllis L. Cothran, Bruce R. Hazelgrove, James E. Rogers, Renaissance Technologies Corp./5.84%, Thomas E. Gottwald/1.25%, David A. Fiorenza, Insiders/11.62%

Financial Data: Fiscal Year End:12/31 Latest Annual Data: 12/31/2006

Year	Sales	Net Income
2006	$1,263,297,000	$57,522,000
2005	$1,075,544,000	$42,381,000
2004	$894,109,000	$33,058,000

Curr. Assets:	$461,960,000	Curr. Liab.:	$160,183,000	P/E Ratio:	13.84
Plant, Equip.:	$162,114,000	Total Liab.:	$443,391,000	Indic. Yr. Divd.:	$0.500
Total Assets:	$744,793,000	Net Worth:	$301,402,000	Debt/ Equity:	0.4798

Newmarket Technology Inc

14860 Montfort Dr., Ste. 210, Dallas, TX, 75254; **PH:** 1-972-386-3372; **Fax:** 1-972-386-8165; **http://** www.newmarkettechnology.com; **Email:** info@newmarkettechnology.com

General - Incorporation	NV	**Stock**- Price on:12/24/2007	$0.301
Employees	600	Stock Exchange	OTC
Auditor	Pollard-Kelley Auditing Services, Inc	Ticker Symbol	NMKT
Stk Agt	Interwest Transfer Company, Inc.	Outstanding Shares	193,580,000
Counsel	NA	E.P.S.	$0.028
DUNS No.	NA	Shareholders	NA

Business: The group's principle activities include developing and producing proprietary software solutions for use in Internet telephony. It provides consulting and computer programming services, principally to the telecom industry. The company's multicom business management software is the business management system behind the company's trueconnect gateway product. Our target markets are located domestically in all fifty states and internationally in developing economies to include Asia-Pacific, Latin America, and eastern Europe. On 05-Apr-2004, the group acquired rkm it solutions.The group operates from United States.

Primary SIC and add'l.: 7372

CIK No: 0001092083

Subsidiaries: IPGV

Officers: Philip Verges/Chmn., CEO, John T. Verges/CEO - Newmarket China, James Jiang/Pres. - Chinese Operations, Stasi Turrell/Contact - Sales, Staffing, Larry Wu/VP - Business Development, Philip J. Rauch/Dir., CFO, Rick Lutz/Investor Contact

Directors: Philip Verges/Chmn., CEO, Philip J. Rauch/Dir., CFO, James Mandel/Dir., Hugh G. Robinson/Dir., Kenneth Blow/Dir., Bruce Noller/Dir.

Owners: Philip J. Rauch, VergeTech, Inc., Bruce Noller, Philip M. Verges, Insiders

Financial Data: Fiscal Year End:12/31 Latest Annual Data: 06/30/2007

Year	Sales	Net Income
2007	$21,892,000	$606,000
2006	$24,461,000	$3,593,000
2005	$50,138,000	$2,909,000

Curr. Assets:	$18,264,000	Curr. Liab.:	$8,245,000	P/E Ratio:	10.03
Plant, Equip.:	$1,248,000	Total Liab.:	$18,161,000	Indic. Yr. Divd.:	NA
Total Assets:	$64,576,000	Net Worth:	$45,168,000	Debt/ Equity:	NA

Newmil Bancorp Inc

19 Main St. , New Milford, CT, 06776; **PH:** 1-860-355-7600; **http://** www.newmil.com

General - Incorporation	DE	**Stock**- Price on:12/24/2007	$43.45
Employees	3,204	Stock Exchange	NA
Auditor	PricewaterhouseCoopers LLP	Ticker Symbol	NA
Stk Agt	American Stock Transfer & Trust Co.	Outstanding Shares	56,520,000
Counsel	NA	E.P.S.	$2.11
DUNS No.	61-717-1095	Shareholders	NA

Business: The group's principal activity is to accept deposits from the general public and use such deposits with other funds, to make various types of loans and investments. The group accepts both consumer and commercial deposit accounts including checking accounts, interest bearing now accounts, money market accounts, certificates of deposit, savings accounts and individual retirement accounts. The loan services provided by the group include mortgage and consumer loans to the residents including residential mortgages, home equity credit lines and loans, installment loans and collateral loans. The group operates through 19 full-service offices and one special needs offices located in fairfield, litchfield and new haven counties.

Primary SIC and add'l.: 6035 6712

CIK No: 0000807524

Subsidiaries: Asset Recovery Management Company, NewMil Asset Company, NewMil Bank, NewMil Mortgage Company, NewMil Statutory Trust I

Financial Data: Fiscal Year End:12/31 Latest Annual Data: 12/31/2006

Year	Sales			Net Income
2006	$1,239,801,000			$133,790,000
2005	$1,092,732,000			$185,855,000
2004	$951,815,000			$153,833,000

Curr. Assets:	$582,943,000	Curr. Liab.:	$14,581,820,000		
Plant, Equip.:	$195,909,000	Total Liab.:	$15,211,031,000	Indic. Yr. Divd.:	$1.200
Total Assets:	$17,097,471,000	Net Worth:	$1,876,863,000	Debt/ Equity:	0.3270

Newmont Mining Corp

1700 Lincoln St., Denver, CO, 80203; **PH:** 1-303-863-7414; **Fax:** 1-303-837-5837; **http://** www.newmont.com

General - Incorporation	DE	**Stock**- Price on:12/24/2007	$39.93
Employees	15,000	Stock Exchange	NDQ
Auditor	PricewaterhouseCoopers LLP	Ticker Symbol	NENG
Stk Agt	Mellon Investor Services LLC	Outstanding Shares	451,100,000
Counsel	NA	E.P.S.	-$3.49
DUNS No.	00-698-8414	Shareholders	NA

Business: The group's principle activities include exploring, acquiring, developing and producing gold properties. The group also produces silver, copper and zinc. The group operates mining operations in United States, Australia, Peru, Indonesia, Canada, Uzbekistan, Turkey, Bolivia, New Zealand and Mexico.

Primary SIC and add'l.: 1041

CIK No: 0001164727

Subsidiaries: ACM Gold Pty Ltd, AGR Management Services Pty Ltd, AGR Matthey (NZ) Limited, Albion Downs Pty Ltd, Australian Consolidated Minerals Pty Ltd., Australian Gold Alliance Pty Ltd, Australian Metals Corporation Pty Ltd, Autin Investments BV, Balkhash Mining and Exploration Inc., Bardini Pty Ltd, Battle Mountain (Irian Jaya) Ltd., Battle Mountain Exploration Company, Battle Mountain Gold Company, Battle Mountain Resources Inc., BGM Management Company Pty Ltd 201 Subsidiaries included in the Index

Officers: Darla Caudle/Sr. VP - Human Resources, Thomas P. Mahoney/VP, Treasurer, Jeffrey R. Huspeni/VP - Exploration Business Development, Thomas L. Enos/56/Exec. VP - Operations/$4,247,150.00, Robert J. Gallagher/VP - Asia Pacific Operations, Brant Hinze/VP - North American Operations, William M. Zisch/VP - Planning, David Harquail/Exec. VP - Exploration, Business Development/$1,420,662.00, Richard T. O'Brien/CFO, Exec. VP/$1,523,227.00, Sharon E. Thomas/VP, Sec., Russell Ball/CFO, Sr. VP, Carlos Santa Cruz/VP - South American Operations, Stephen M. Enders/Sr. VP - Worldwide Exploration, Alex G. Morrison/VP - Information Technology, Guy Lansdown/Sr. VP - Project Development, Operations Services (21 Officers included in Index)

Directors: Wayne W. Murdy/Chmn., James V. Taranik/Dir., Glen A. Barton/Dir., Seymour Schulich/Dir., John B. Prescott/Dir., Michael S. Hamson/Dir., Robert J. Miller/Dir., Vincent A. Calarco/Dir., Noreen Doyle/Dir., Veronica M. Hagen/Dir., Donald C. Roth/Dir., Joseph A. Carrabba/Dir., Robin A. Plumbridge/Dir., Pierre Lassonde/Dir.

Owners: Michael S. Hamson, Noreen Doyle, Veronica M. Hagen, David Harquail, Glen A. Barton, Bruce D. Hansen, Insiders/1.84%, Robert J. Miller, Robin A. Plumbridge, John B. Prescott, Vincent A. Calarco, Pierre Lassonde, Donald C. Roth, Thomas L. Enos, Seymour Schulich (18 Owners included in Index)

Financial Data: Fiscal Year End:12/31 Latest Annual Data: 12/31/2006

Year	Sales	Net Income
2006	$4,987,000,000	$791,000,000
2005	$4,406,000,000	$322,000,000
2004	$4,524,185,000	$443,327,000

Curr. Assets:	$2,642,000,000	Curr. Liab.:	$1,739,000,000	P/E Ratio:	27.73
Plant, Equip.:	$7,659,000,000	Total Liab.:	$5,166,000,000	Indic. Yr. Divd.:	$0.400
Total Assets:	$15,601,000,000	Net Worth:	$9,337,000,000	Debt/ Equity:	0.1878

Newnan Coweta Bancshares Inc

145 Millard Farmer Industrial Blvd., Newnan, GA, 30263; **PH:** 1-770-683-6222

General - Incorporation	GA	**Stock**- Price on:12/24/2007	$37
Employees	56	Stock Exchange	OTC
Auditor	McNair, Middlebrooks & Co. LLP	Ticker Symbol	NWCB
Stk Agt	Registrar & Transfer Co	Outstanding Shares	1,010,000
Counsel	NA	E.P.S.	$2.62
DUNS No.	NA	Shareholders	NA

Business: The group's principal activities are attracting deposits from the general public, originating real estate loans, consumer loans, business loans and residential and commercial construction loans. The deposits accepted by the group are noninterest-bearing demand deposits, interest-bearing demand and savings deposits and time deposits.

Primary SIC and add'l.: 6021 6712

CIK No: 0001157282

Subsidiaries: NCB Statutory Trust I, Neighborhood Community Bank

Officers: James B. Kimsey/55/Dir., CEO, Pres./$347,777.00, Karen P. Duffey/42/Sr. VP, Sec./$126,243.00, Allan C. Payton/50/Sr. VP/$183,771.00

Directors: James B. Kimsey/55/Dir., CEO, Pres., Donald L. Sprayberry/49/Chmn., Joe S. Crain/42/Dir., Otis F. Jones/42/Dir., Dennis H. McDowell/36/Dir., James S. Van Mottola/53/Dir., Melvin Samuels/56/Dir., Douglas T. Daviston/65/Dir., Walker J. Moody/64/Dir., David Laguardia/48/Dir., Bob Baker Mann/54/Dir., Theo D. Mann/57/Dir., Woodie T. Wood/46/Dir., Jennifer J. Thomasson/44/Dir., Robert E. Cordle/51/Dir.

Owners: Robert E. Cordle/1.63%, David LaGuardia/7.08%, Insiders/52.30%, James S. Mottola/6.05%, Donald L. Sprayberry/3.14%, Walker J. Moody/3.13%, James B. Kimsey/3.73%, Jennifer J. Thomasson/0.95%, Allan C. Payton/0.05%, Dennis H. McDowell/2.04%, Karen P. Duffey/0.10%, Douglas T. Daviston/2.81%, Melvin Samuels/0.20%, Joe S. Crain/2.90%, Dennis H. McDowell/6.95% (18 Owners included in Index)

Financial Data: Fiscal Year End:12/31 Latest Annual Data: 12/31/2006

Year	Sales	Net Income
2006	$17,995,000	$2,506,000
2005	$12,360,000	$1,709,000
2004	$8,397,000	$1,362,000

Curr. Assets:	$12,907,000	Curr. Liab.:	$201,216,000	P/E Ratio:	14.12
Plant, Equip.:	$5,846,000	Total Liab.:	$206,427,000	Indic. Yr. Divd.:	NA
Total Assets:	$224,107,000	Net Worth:	$17,681,000	Debt/ Equity:	0.1641

Newpark Resources Inc

2700 Research Forest Dr., Ste. 100, The Woodlands, TX, 77381; *PH:* 1-281-362-6800; *Fax:* 1-281-362-6801; *http://* www.newpark.com; *Email:* jbraun@newpark.com

General - Incorporation	DE	**Stock**- Price on:12/24/2007	$7.94
Employees	1,816	Stock Exchange	NDQ
Auditor	Ernst & Young LLP	Ticker Symbol	NRCI
Stk Agt	American Stock Transfer & Trust Co.	Outstanding Shares	89,900,000
Counsel	Bertram K. Massing	E.P.S	-$0.25
DUNS No.	00-697-0982	Shareholders	NA

Business: The group's principle activity is to provide drilling fluids, site access and environmental products and services to oil and gas exploration and production industry. The group operates in three segments. The exploration and production ('e&p') waste disposal segment provides disposal services for both oilfield e&p waste and e&p waste contaminated with radioactive material. The fluids sales and engineering segment provides services for technical drilling projects such as horizontal drilling, geographically deep and deep water drilling. Mat and integrated services segment provides prefabricated interlocking mat systems for constructing drilling and work sites as well as environmental services. Customers include independent oil and gas exploration and production companies in Louisiana and Texas. The group's quarterly revenue for September 2007 was 153.78 millions of USD.

Primary SIC and add'l.: 3533 4953 2421

CIK No: 0000071829

Subsidiaries: Ava Africa S.a.r.l., Ava Algerie E.u.r.l., Ava International Ltd., Ava Romania 2000 S.r.l., Ava Tunisi S.a.r.l., AVA, S.p.A., Batson-mill, L.p., Composite Mat Solutions, LLC, Crilio Due Exim S.r.l., Darcom International, L.p., Dura-base De Mexico S.a. De C.v., Dura-base Nevada, Inc., Eurocontinental Df Gmbh, Excalibar Minerals Of La. LLC, Excalibar Minerals, Inc. 43 Subsidiaries included in the Index

Officers: Paul Howes/Dir., CEO, Pres., Sammy Cooper/51/VP, Pres. - Environmental Services, Joe Gocke/Treasurer, Frank Lyon/VP - Technical Services, James E. Braun/CFO, VP, Sean Mikaelian/Sr. VP, Mark Airola/VP, General Counsel, Corp. Sec., Chief Administrative Officer, Gregg Piontek/Controller, Chief Accounting Officer, Bruce Smith/Sr. VP

Directors: Paul Howes/Dir., CEO, Pres., Jerry W. Box/Chmn., Roger C. Stull/Dir., David P. Hunt/Dir., Alan J. Kaufman/Dir., James H. Stone/81/Dir. Emeritus, Walker F. Tucei/Dir., Gary L. Warren/Dir., David C. Anderson/Dir., Stephen G. Finley/Dir., James W. McFarland/Dir.

Owners: Steinberg Asset Management, LLC/6.98%, Wells Fargo & Company/11.95%, Heartland Advisors, Inc./7.60%

Financial Data: *Fiscal Year End:*12/31 *Latest Annual Data:* 12/31/2006

Year	Sales		Net Income
2006	$668,199,000		-$32,281,000
2005	$555,018,000		$22,781,000
2004	$433,422,000		$4,956,000

Curr. Assets:	$319,718,000	**Curr. Liab.:**	$101,995,000		
Plant, Equip.:	$227,962,000	**Total Liab.:**	$304,526,000	**Indic. Yr. Divd.:**	NA
Total Assets:	$627,669,000	**Net Worth:**	$323,143,000	**Debt/ Equity:**	NA

Newport Bancorp Inc

100 Bellevue Ave., Newport, RI, 02840; *PH:* 1-401-847-5500; *http://* www.newportfederal.com; *Email:* info@newportfederal.com

General - Incorporation		**Stock**- Price on:12/24/2007	$13.6
Employees	58	Stock Exchange	NDQ
Auditor	Wolf & Co., P.c.	Ticker Symbol	NFSB
Stk Agt.	Registrar & Transfer Co	Outstanding Shares	4,880,000
Counsel	NA	E.P.S	$0.27
DUNS No.	NA	Shareholders	NA

Business: The groups principal activity is to provide traditional financial services. The products of the group include one to four family residential loans, multi family loans, commercial real estate loans, construction loans and consumer loans. The group operates from the United States. The assets of the group for the year 2006 were $290,444 (thousands).

Primary SIC and add'l.: 6035

CIK No: 0001355855

Subsidiaries: Newport Federal Savings Bank

Officers: Kevin M. McCarthy/CEO, Pres./$456,867.00, Nino Moscardi/56/Dir., COO, Exec. VP/$221,987.00, Ray D. Gilmore/60/Exec. VP, Chief Lending/$263,976.00, Bruce Walsh/CFO, Sr. VP/$183,582.00, Carol R. Silven/64/Sr. VP - Retail Banking Officer/$236,594.00, Paul Nardone/Compliance Officer

Directors: Peter W. Rector/69/Chmn., Peter T. Crowley/59/Dir., Michael J. Hayes/58/Dir., Arthur H. Lathrop/53/Dir., Kathleen A. Nealon/55/Dir., Nino Moscardi/56/Dir., COO, Exec. VP, William R. Harvey/61/Dir., Robert S. Lazar/63/Dir., Alicia S. Quirk/66/Dir., Donald N. Kaull/62/Dir., Arthur P. MacAuley/65/Dir., Michael S. Pinto/69/Dir., Barbara Saccucci Radebach/55/Dir.

Owners: Alicia S. Quirk, Robert S. Lazar, Michael J. Hayes, Michael S. Pinto, Barbara Saccucci Radebach, Bruce A. Walsh, Peter T. Crowley, Kathleen A. Nealon, Daniel S. Och/9.00%, Peter W. Rector, Nino Moscardi, Kevin M. McCarthy, Arthur P. Macauley, Ray D. Gilmore, Insiders/4.37% *(20 Owners included in Index)*

Financial Data: *Fiscal Year End:*12/31 *Latest Annual Data:* 12/31/2006

Year	Sales		Net Income
2006	$17,909,000		-$1,656,000

Curr. Assets:	$8,299,000	**Curr. Liab.:**	$198,514,000		
Plant, Equip.:	$6,099,000	**Total Liab.:**	$230,464,000	**Indic. Yr. Divd.:**	NA
Total Assets:	$290,444,000	**Net Worth:**	$59,980,000	**Debt/ Equity:**	0.5088

Newport Corp

1791 Deere Ave., Irvine, CA, 92606; *PH:* 1-949-863-3144; *Fax:* 1-949-253-1680; *http://* www.newport.com; *Email:* sales@newport.com

General - Incorporation	NV	**Stock**- Price on:12/24/2007	$15.66
Employees	1,950	Stock Exchange	NDQ
Auditor	Ernst & Young LLP	Ticker Symbol	NEXC
Stk Agt.	Wells Fargo Shareowner Services	Outstanding Shares	38,890,000
Counsel	Stradling Yocca Carlson & Rauth	E.P.S	$0.76
DUNS No.	00-914-5814	Shareholders	NA

Business: The group's principal activities are to design, manufacture and market high precision components, instruments and integrated systems. The group provides components and integrated subsystems to manufacturers of semi conductor front-end processing. The group operates in two segments. The industrial and scientific technologies segment includes motion control devices and systems, wafer handling robots, vibration isolation products, mechanical components, instruments and subassemblies. The advanced packaging and automation systems segment provides dispensing systems to the semiconductor packaging, microwave and fiber optic communication industries. The group also provides device testing, characterization systems and process automation workstations.

Primary SIC and add'l.: 5734 3829 3571 3821 5047

CIK No: 0000225263

Subsidiaries: Birch Nantucket Holding Company, LLC, Hilger Crystals Limited (indirect), Micro Controle Finance Holding 1 (indirect), Micro Controle Finance Holding 2 (indirect), Micro Controle Italia S.r.l., Micro Controle Spectra-Physics S.A., Micro Robotics Systems, Inc., MRSI (Europe), B.V. (indirect), MRSI Asia Pte. Ltd. (indirect), Newport B.V., Newport Corporation (Barbados) SRL, Newport European Distribution Company, Newport Finance Company I, LLC, Newport Finance Company II, LLC, Newport Franklin, Inc. (indirect) 28 Subsidiaries included in the Index

Officers: Robert G. Deuster/57/Chmn., CEO/$1,881,109.00, Robert J. Phillippy/48/Dir., Pres./$1,185,141.00, Charles F. Cargile/43/Sr. VP, CFO, Treasurer/$1,052,284.00, Jeffrey B. Coyne/General Counsel/$711,403.00, Gary J. Spiegel/57/VP - Worldwide Sales, Service/$751,864.00, David J. Allen/53/VP, GM - Lasers Division

Directors: Robert G. Deuster/57/Chmn., CEO, Richard E. Schmidt/76/Dir., Jack R. Aplin/77/Dir., Robert L. Guyett/71/Dir., Michael T. Oneill/67/Dir., Kumar C.N. Patel/70/Dir., Kenneth F. Potashner/50/Dir., Peter J. Simone/61/Dir., Robert J. Phillippy/48/Dir., Pres.

Owners: Jeffrey B. Coyne, SouthernSun Asset Management, Inc./5.70%, Jack R. Aplin, Private Capital Management, L.P./10.60%, Robert L. Guyett, Insiders/6.50%, Gary J. Spiegel, Michael T. O'Neil, Joseph L. Harrosh/10.10%, Dimensional Fund Advisors LP/8.40%, Robert G. Deuster/2.10%, C. N. Patel, Peter J. Simone, Richard E. Schmidt, Robert J. Phillippy *(17 Owners included in Index)*

Financial Data: *Fiscal Year End:*12/31 *Latest Annual Data:* 12/30/2006

Year	Sales		Net Income
2006	$454,724,000		$37,427,000
2005	$403,733,000		$11,632,000

Curr. Assets:	$237,539,000	**Curr. Liab.:**	$87,168,000	**P/E Ratio:**	18.21
Plant, Equip.:	$50,424,000	**Total Liab.:**	$152,823,000	**Indic. Yr. Divd.:**	NA
Total Assets:	$529,406,000	**Net Worth:**	$376,583,000	**Debt/ Equity:**	0.1196

Newport Gold Inc

220 1495 Ridgeview Dr., Reno, NV, 89509; *PH:* 1-905-542-4990; *http://* www.newportgold.info/profile.htm,www.newportgold.info/derek.htm

General - Incorporation	NV	**Stock**- Price on:12/24/2007	$0.65
Employees	NA	Stock Exchange	OTC
Auditor	Pannell Kerr Forster	Ticker Symbol	NWPG
Stk Agt	Nevada Agency & Trust Company	Outstanding Shares	15,180,000
Counsel	NA	E.P.S	-$0.03
DUNS No.	NA	Shareholders	NA

Business: The groups principal activity is presently in the pre exploration stage and there is no assurance that a commercially viable mineral deposit exists in groups property until further exploration is done and a comprehensive evaluation concludes economic and legal feasibility. The group operates from the United States.

Primary SIC and add'l.: 1041

CIK No: 0001289223

Subsidiaries: 2038052 Ontario Inc

Officers: Derek Bartlett/Pres., Joseph G. Ricci/Contact - Corporate Affairs, John Martin Arnold/Officer, Chet Idziszek/Special Advisor, Cindy Bartlett/VP - Corporate Development

Directors: Alex Johnston/Dir.

Owners: John Arnold, Insiders/46.61%, Alex Johnston/46.60%, Derek Bartlett, Donald W. Kohls

Financial Data: *Fiscal Year End:*12/31 *Latest Annual Data:* 12/31/2006

Year	Sales		Net Income
2006	NA		-$339,000

Curr. Assets:	$129,000	**Curr. Liab.:**	$329,000		
Plant, Equip.:	$289,000	**Total Liab.:**	$329,000	**Indic. Yr. Divd.:**	NA
Total Assets:	$418,000	**Net Worth:**	$89,000	**Debt/ Equity:**	NA

News Communications Inc

2 Pk. Ave. Ste. 1405, New York, NY, 10016; *PH:* 1-718-357-3380

General - Incorporation	NV	**Stock**- Price on:12/24/2007	$74
Employees	NA	Stock Exchange	OTC
Auditor	BDO Seidman LLP	Ticker Symbol	NWCM
Stk Agt	Continental Stock Transfer & Trust Co	Outstanding Shares	NA
Counsel	Piper Marbury Rudnick & Wolfe LLP	E.P.S	NA
DUNS No.	NA	Shareholders	NA

Business: The group's principal activity is to publish and distribute weekly advertiser-supported community oriented newspapers. It sells advertising space in these publications since these publications are distributed free of charge. Its publications include Dan's Papers, Montauk Pioneer and the Hill. Dan's Papers focuses on the lifestyle, culture, arts, entertainment, politics and social issues of interest to the resort areas of the south and north forks of eastern Long Island, New York. Its articles and columns include humor, news, celebrity profiles, reviews of art gallery shows, restaurants, concerts, nightclubs and movies, social satire, editorial cartoons and political issues, entertainment listings as well as special sections. The staff at Dan's Papers also publish the Montauk Pioneer. The Hill is devoted to the coverage of the United States congress. It operates solely in the domestic market.

Primary SIC and add'l.: 2711

CIK No: 0000794487

Financial Data: *Fiscal Year End:*12/31 *Latest Annual Data:* 12/31/2004

Year	Sales		Net Income
2004	$12,168,000		-$1,062,000

Curr. Assets:	$1,665,000	**Curr. Liab.:**	$3,144,000		
Plant, Equip.:	$244,000	**Total Liab.:**	$3,444,000	**Indic. Yr. Divd.:**	NA
Total Assets:	$2,824,000	**Net Worth:**	-$621,000	**Debt/ Equity:**	NA

News Corp Ltd (The)

1211 Ave. Of The Americas, New York, NY, 10036; *PH:* 1-212-852-7000;
http:// www.newscorp.com

General - Incorporation	DE	**Stock**- Price on:12/24/2007	$23.6
Employees	NA	Stock Exchange	NYSE
Auditor	Ernst& Young LLP	Ticker Symbol	NA
Stk Agt.... Computershare Investor Services LLC		Outstanding Shares	NA
Counsel	NA	E.P.S	NA
DUNS No.	NA	Shareholders	NA

Business: The groups principle activity is to provide entertaining services. The group operates through eight segments namely, Filmed Entertainment, Television, Cable Network Programming, Direct Broadcast Satellite Television, Magazines and Inserts, Newspapers, Book Publishing and Other. In the year 2006, the group acquired Turner Regional Entertainment Networks, Inc. The group operates from the United States, the United Kingdom, Europe, Australia, Asia and Pacific Basin. The group's quarterly revenue for September 2007 was 7067.00 millions of USD.

Primary SIC and add'l.: 2711

CIK No: 0001308161

Subsidiaries: 18 Street Productions, Inc, 19th Holdings Corporation, 21st Century Fox Film Corporation, 21st Century Holdings Limited, 99 Productions, Inc., A Team EOOD, A.C.N. 000 024 028 Pty. Limited, A.C.N. 075 969 265 Pty. Limited, A.C.N. 105 222 026 Pty. Limited, A.N. Investments Pty. Limited, Abudi Nur Outdoor Advertising Co, ACA2, Inc., Acetic Investments Ltd, Admacroft Limited, Advert LLC 1300 Subsidiaries included in the Index

Officers: Rupert K. Murdoch/Chmn., CEO, Peter Chernin/Dir., COO, Pres., David F. Devoe/Dir., CFO, Anthea Disney/Exec. VP - Content, Gary Ginsberg/Exec. VP - Global Marketing, Corporate Affairs, Leon Hertz/Exec. VP, John Nallen/Deputy CFO, Exec. VP, Martin Pompadur/Exec. VP, Michael Regan/Exec. VP - Government Affairs, Genie Gavenchak/Chief Compliance, Ethics Officer, Sr. VP, Deputy General Counsel, Tsalem Mueller/Invester Relations Officer, Beryl Cook/Chief Officer - Human Resources, Teri Everett/Sr. VP - Corporate Affairs, Communications, Reed Nolte/Sr. VP - Investor Relations, Craig Felenstein/VP - Investor Relations *(16 Officers included in Index)*

Directors: Rupert K. Murdoch/Chmn., CEO, Jose Maria Aznar/Dir., Peter Barnes/Dir., Chase Carey/Dir., Peter Chernin/Dir., COO, Pres., Kenneth E. Cowley/Dir., David F. Devoe/Dir., CFO, Viet Dinh/Dir., Roderick Eddington/Dir., Andrew S.B. Knight/Dir., Lachlan Murdoch/Dir., Rod Paige/Dir., Thomas J. Perkins/Dir., Arthur M. Siskind/Dir., John L. Thornton/Dir.

Owners: Murdoch Family Trust/1.60%, Andrew S.B. Knight, Stanley S. Shuman, Roger Ailes, Murdoch Family Trust/30.10%, Thomas J. Perkins, Lachlan K. Murdoch, Peter Chernin, Viet Dinh, HRH Prince Alwaleed Bin Talal Bin/5.70%, Stanley S. Shuman, Lawrence A. Jacobs, Liberty Media Corporation/15.20%, Arthur M. Siskind, Andrew S.B. Knight *(27 Owners included in Index)*

NewTech Brake Corp

779, Industriel Blvd., Blainville, QC, J7C 3V3; *PH:* 1-450-434-6432; *http://* www.newtechbrake.com

General - Incorporation	DE	**Stock**- Price on:12/24/2007	$0.15
Employees	NA	Stock Exchange	OTC
Auditor	Daszkal Bolton LLP	Ticker Symbol	NWTB
Stk Agt	Bank of Montreal Trust Co	Outstanding Shares	NA
Counsel	NA	E.P.S	NA
DUNS No.	NA	Shareholders	NA

Business: The group's principal activities are to identify, develop and exploit opportunities to provide a new generation of safer, more efficient and cost-effective contact disc brakes and related components to the north American and European heavy vehicle market. The brake system stops a vehicle by converting kinetic energy into thermal energy through friction. The group mainly operates in North America.

Primary SIC and add'l.: 3714

CIK No: 0001080008

Subsidiaries: Newtech Brake Mfg. (Suzhou) Co., Ltd

Financial Data: *Fiscal Year End:* 02/28   *Latest Annual Data:* 2/28/2005

Year		Sales		Net Income
2005		NA		-$2,388,000
2004		NA		-$859,000
2003		NA		-$130,000
Curr. Assets:	$137,000	**Curr. Liab.:**	$1,518,000	
Plant, Equip.:	$200,000	**Total Liab.:**	$1,594,000	**Indic. Yr. Divd.:** NA
Total Assets:	$336,000	**Net Worth:**	-$1,257,000	**Debt/ Equity:** NA

Newtech Resources Ltd

2610-1066 W Hastings St., Vancouver, BC, V6E 3X2; *PH:* 1-604-684-4691

General - Incorporation	NV	**Stock**- Price on:12/24/2007	$0.015
Employees	NA	Stock Exchange	OTC
Auditor	Jones Simkins P.C.	Ticker Symbol	NTHR
Stk Agt	Interwest Transfer Company, Inc.	Outstanding Shares	NA
Counsel	NA	E.P.S	NA
DUNS No.	NA	Shareholders	NA

Business: The group's principal activity is to conduct research and develop a technology known as glycosylated cystatins and non-glycosylated cystatins. Cystatins are proteins that tightly bind and inhibit the harmful effects of cysteine proteases. Cysteine proteases, also known as cysteine proteases, actively degrade proteins and detrimentally affect human health by facilitating diseases and food spoilage. Glycosylated cystatin enhances activity and stability against heating and proteolysis. Non-glycosylated cystatin only enhances activity and stability and not against heating and proteolysis. Proteolysis is the process by which to degrade protein or peptides by hydrolyzing the peptide bond. The group is a development stage company.

Primary SIC and add'l.: 8731 2834 9999

CIK No: 0001080001

Financial Data: *Fiscal Year End:* 08/31   *Latest Annual Data:* 08/31/2007

Year		Sales		Net Income
2007		NA		-$102,000
2006		NA		-$100,000
2005		NA		-$170,000
Curr. Assets:	$4,000	**Curr. Liab.:**	$150,000	
Plant, Equip.:	NA	**Total Liab.:**	$150,000	**Indic. Yr. Divd.:** NA
Total Assets:	$4,000	**Net Worth:**	-$146,000	**Debt/ Equity:** NA

Newtek Business Services Inc

1440 Broadway, 17th Fl., New York, NY, 10018; *PH:* 1-212-356-9500; *Fax:* 1-212-643-1006;
http:// www.newtekbusinessservices.com; *Email:* ir@newtekbusinessservices.com

General - Incorporation	NY	**Stock**- Price on:12/24/2007	$1.92
Employees	382	Stock Exchange	NDQ
Auditor	J.H. Cohn, LLP	Ticker Symbol	NEWT
Stk Agt	NA	Outstanding Shares	36,790,000
Counsel	NA	E.P.S	-$0.15
DUNS No.	NA	Shareholders	NA

Business: The group's principal activities are to provide investment banking and business development services. The group also provides general business consulting services, strategic planning, due diligence, merger and acquisition analysis, technology design and implementation support, joint venture negotiations and litigation support services. The services include financial and management reporting and planning, back-office data processing, software development and systems integration, merchant credit card processing, small business brokerage services, specialized directories to serve various markets through various media. The group operates as a holding company for a network of its acquisitions and investments in partner companies. The acquisitions are made in a collaborative and coordinated effort to develop successful businesses in a number of emerging and small business markets. On 02-Aug-2004, it acquired vistar insurance services.

Primary SIC and add'l.: 6799

CIK No: 0001094019

Subsidiaries: Alabama Community Financial Services, LLC, Automated Merchant Services, Inc., BJB Holdings, Inc., Business Connect, LLC, CCC Real Estate Holdings, LLC, Channel Management Partners, LLC, CrystalTech Web Hosting, Inc, Exponential Business Development Company, Inc., First BankCard Alliance, LLC, Fortress Data Management, LLC, Global Business Advisers of Wisconsin, LLC, Global Small Business Services, LLC, Group Management Technologies of Louisiana, LLC, Group Management Technologies, LLC, Harvest Strategies, LLC 61 Subsidiaries included in the Index

Officers: Barry Sloane/Chmn., CEO/$350,000.00, Peter Downs/Business Lending, Jeffrey Rubin/Dir., Pres., Chief Investment Officer/$336,668.00, Michael Holden/CFO/$310,000.00, Joseph J. Carvalho/Digital Bookkeeping, Derek Depuydt/Electronic Payment Processing, Bill Bayer/Newtek Insurance Services, Commercial, Personal, Robert P. Cichon/WEB Hosting, Data Storage, Craig Brunet/Exec. VP - Strategic Planning, Marketing/$288,000.00

Directors: Barry Sloane/Chmn., CEO, Jeffrey Rubin/Dir., Pres., Chief Investment Officer, David Beck/Dir., Sal Mulia/Dir., Christopher Payan/Dir., Jeffrey M. Schottenstein/Dir., Michael A. Schwartz/Dir.

Owners: Jeffrey M. Schottenstein, Michael J. Holden, Salvatore F. Mulia, Michael A. Schwartz, Christopher G. Payan, Barry Sloane/12.60%, Tim Uzzanti, Seth A. Cohen, Jeffrey G. Rubin/11.66%, Insiders/28.18%, Tracy A. Schmidt, David C. Beck, Craig J. Brunet

Financial Data: *Fiscal Year End:* 12/31   *Latest Annual Data:* 12/31/2006

Year		Sales		Net Income
2006		$87,905,000		-$2,120,000
2005		$96,799,000		$7,727,000
2004		$70,180,000		$10,615,000
Curr. Assets:	$28,772,000	**Curr. Liab.:**	$8,509,000	
Plant, Equip.:	$5,988,000	**Total Liab.:**	$149,072,000	**Indic. Yr. Divd.:** NA
Total Assets:	$240,737,000	**Net Worth:**	$87,069,000	**Debt/ Equity:** 0.3768

NexCen Brands Inc

Formerly: Aether Systems Inc
1330 Ave. Of The Americas, 40th Fl., New York, NY, 10019; *PH:* 1-212-277-1100;
http:// www.aethersystems.com

General - Incorporation	DE	**Stock**- Price on:12/24/2007	$11.41
Employees	36	Stock Exchange	NA
Auditor	KPMG LLP	Ticker Symbol	NA
Stk Agt..... Computershare Investor Services LLC		Outstanding Shares	50,530,000
Counsel	Kirkland & Ellis LLP	E.P.S	-$0.05
DUNS No.	NA	Shareholders	NA

Business: The group's principal activities are to design, develop, sell and support wireless data services and systems for mobile data communications and real-time transactions. The group operates through two segment namely: transportation and mobile government. The transportation segment offers mobilemax, a vehicle location and messaging solution for long-haul trucks and other products, including geologic, trailermax and 20/20v. The mobile government segment is a service provider in the area of wireless data solutions for public safety. The group's products are marketed in the United States, london, hamburg and Munich.

Primary SIC and add'l.: 7375 7372 9999 7373 7379

CIK No: 0001093434

Subsidiaries: Aether Capital, LLC, AS Monterey LLC, Cerulean Technology, Inc., NetSearch, LLC, Sinope Corporation, SunPro, Inc.

Owners: James Haran/1.01%, Marvin Traub, David S. Oros/4.18%, Truman Semans, George P. Stamas, Edward J. Mathias, David Reymann, Robert W. DLoren/6.22%, James T. Brady, Insiders/12.67%, Jack Rovner

Financial Data: *Fiscal Year End:* 12/31   *Latest Annual Data:* 12/31/2006

Year		Sales		Net Income
2006		$1,924,000		-$2,120,000
2005		$10,367,000		-$4,520,000
2004		$2,754,000		-$48,328,000
Curr. Assets:	$88,299,000	**Curr. Liab.:**	$9,237,000	
Plant, Equip.:	$389,000	**Total Liab.:**	$11,772,000	**Indic. Yr. Divd.:** NA
Total Assets:	$158,385,000	**Net Worth:**	$146,613,000	**Debt/ Equity:** 0.1544

Nexen Inc

801-7th Ave. S.W, Calgary, AB, TP2 3P7; *PH:* 1-403-699-4000; *http://* www.nexeninc.com

General - Incorporation	Canada	**Stock**- Price on:12/24/2007	$31.43
Employees	NA	Stock Exchange	NYSE
Auditor	Deloitte & Touche LLP	Ticker Symbol	NXY
Stk Agt	Mellon Trust Co	Outstanding Shares	NA
Counsel	NA	E.P.S	$0.003
DUNS No.	NA	Shareholders	NA

Business: The group's principle activities are the manufacturing and production of energy and chemicals. The group operates through three segments: oil and gas, synthetic crude oil and chemicals. The oil and gas segment explores, develops and produces crude oil, natural gas and related products. The synthetic crude oil segment develops and produces synthetic crude oil from oil sands in northern alberta, Canada. The chemical segment manufactures, markets and distributes industrial chemicals, mainly sodium chlorate, chlorine and caustic soda. The group operates in Canada, the United States, Australia, Brazil, yemen, nigeria, columbia and other foreign countries.

Primary SIC and add'l.: 2899 1311 4925 2911 1499 2813

CIK No: 0000016873

Subsidiaries: 1187433 Alberta Ltd., Canadian Nexen Petroleum East Al Hajr Ltd., Canadian Nexen Petroleum Yemen, Canadian Petroleum Vietnam Ltd., Canadian Petroleum Yemen Limited, Canadianoxy Offshore Production Co., Canexus Limited Partnership, Cnyl No. 2 Ltd., Cnyl No. 6 Ltd., Cnyl No. 7 Ltd., Ich Capital Management Hungary Limited Liability Company, Icm Assurance Ltd., Icm Capital Limited, International Capital Holdings Limited, Long Lake Finance Management Ltd. 64 Subsidiaries included in the Index

Officers: Charles Fischer/57/Dir., CEO, Pres., Una M. Power/43/Treasurer, Sean Noe/Investor Relations Analyst, Gary H. Nieuwenburg/49/VP - Synthetic Crude, Laurence Murphy/56/Sr. VP - International Oil, Gas, Douglas B. Otten/65/Sr. VP - US Oil, Gas, Michael J. Harris/VP - Investor Relations, Lavonne Zdunich/Investor Relations Analyst, Marvin F. Romanow/CFO, Exec. VP, Nancy F. Foster/48/Sr. VP - Human Resources, Corporate Services, John B. McWilliams/60/Sr. VP, General Counsel, Sec., Kevin J. Reinhart/49/VP - Corporate Planning, Business Development, Roger D. Thomas/55/Sr. VP - Canadian Oil, Gas

Directors: Charles Fischer/57/Dir., CEO, Pres., Francis M. Saville/69/Chmn., Barry Jackson/55/Dir., Victor J. Zaleschuk/Dir., Richard M. Thomson/74/Dir., Anne A. McLellan/57/Dir., John Willson/68/Dir., Thomas O'Neill/62/Dir., Kevin Jenkins/51/Dir., Dennis Flanagan/68/Dir., Eric Newell/63/Dir., David Hentschel/74/Dir.

Owners: Capital Research and Management Company/5.20%, Ontario Teachers Pension Plan Board/11.50%, Jarislowsky, Fraser Limited/11.19%

Financial Data: Fiscal Year End:12/31   Latest Annual Data: 12/31/2006

Year	Sales	Net Income
2006	$4,621,727,000	$515,718,000
2005	$4,141,566,000	$988,416,000
2004	$3,228,206,000	$654,276,000

Curr. Assets:	$3,930,956,000	Curr. Liab.:	$3,522,501,000		
Plant, Equip.:	$10,073,236,000	Total Liab.:	$10,679,055,000	Indic. Yr. Divd.:	NA
Total Assets:	$14,721,564,000	Net Worth:	$3,978,152,000	Debt/ Equity:	1.0620

Nexia Holdings Inc

59 W 100 S, 2nd Fl., Salt Lake City, UT, 84101; *PH:* 1-800-575-8073;
http:// www.nexiaholdings.com; *Email:* mail@nexiaholdings.com

General - Incorporation	NV	Stock - Price on:12/24/2007	NA
Employees	5	Stock Exchange	OTC
Auditor	De Joya Griffith & Co LLC	Ticker Symbol	NXHL
Stk Agt	Corporate Stock Transfer, Inc.	Outstanding Shares	NA
Counsel	NA	E.P.S.	-$0.004
DUNS No.	83-607-6620	Shareholders	NA

Business: The group's principal activity is to acquire, manage, lease and sell commercial and residential real estate properties. It also provides financial consulting services through its subsidiary hudson consulting group, inc. The group provides expanded scope of financial, business, and investment oriented consulting services to select start-up companies and existing public companies. The group's real estate properties are located in Utah and other parts of United States.

Primary SIC and add'l.: 8748 6531

CIK No: 0000833209

Subsidiaries: Hudson Consulting Group, Inc

Officers: Richard D. Surber/35/CEO, CFO, Pamela Kushlan/Executive Assist., Guy R. Cook/Controller, John Mortensen/Accounting, Michael Golightly/In House Counsel, Sean Pasinsky/Business Development, Jared Gold/Founder, Sr. Designer, Black Chandelier, Rachel Domingo/Assist. Designer, Production Mgr., Morgen Swenson/Dir. - Retail, Advertising, Ashley Haak/Head Patternmaker - Designer, Aja Sicks/Manufacturing, Internal Products Mgr., Matthew Stevens/Graphic Designer, Dir. - Creative, Andy Pitts/Graphic Designer, Visual Artist, Johnna Spikes/Retail Stores, Online Store Merchandiser, Matthew Landis/Founder, Sr. Stylist, Landis Lifestyle Salon *(16 Officers included in Index)*

Directors: Jared Gold/Founder, Sr. Designer, Black Chandelier, Matthew Landis/Founder, Sr. Stylist, Landis Lifestyle Salon, Gerald Einhorn/68/Dir., VP, Sec., Adrienne Bernstein/63/Dir.

Owners: Oasis International Hotel & Casino, Inc., Insiders/10.40%, Adrienne Bernstein, Richard Surber/96.67%, Richard Surber/100.00%, Gerald Einhorn, Richard Surber/10.40%, Diversified Holdings I, Inc.

Financial Data: Fiscal Year End:12/31   Latest Annual Data: 12/31/2006

Year	Sales	Net Income
2006	$1,834,000	-$1,967,000
2005	$416,000	-$131,000
2004	$634,000	-$3,004,000

Curr. Assets:	$1,023,000	Curr. Liab.:	$2,013,000		
Plant, Equip.:	$3,667,000	Total Liab.:	$4,765,000	Indic. Yr. Divd.:	NA
Total Assets:	$4,735,000	Net Worth:	-$121,000	Debt/ Equity:	NA

Nexicon

400 Gold SW, Ste 1000, Albuquerque, NM, 87102; *PH:* 1-505-248-0000; *Fax:* 1-505-244-4115;
http:// www.nexiconinc.com; *Email:* info@nexiconinc.com

General - Incorporation	NV	Stock - Price on:12/24/2007	$0.055
Employees	8	Stock Exchange	OTC
Auditor	Stark Winter Schenkein & Co. LLP	Ticker Symbol	NXCN
Stk Agt	Corporate Stock Transfer, Inc.	Outstanding Shares	212,180,000
Counsel	NA	E.P.S.	-$0.03
DUNS No.	NA	Shareholders	NA

Business: The group's principal activity is to provide computer network and management solutions via satellite communication. The group has two products: ossi comsecure(c) and ossi satsecure(c) surveillance system. The comsecure(c) controller is designed to give a global network enterprise full control of all traffic, devices and subscribers within an ip network. It breaks the network processing bottleneck and increases total performance. The satsecure(c) surveillance system can use a variety of communication channels such as isdn, ip, pstn (public switched telephone networks), inmarsat satphones (64 kbps) and gsm phones (9.6 kbps) to transfer and remotely control video, audio, alarm/sensor and data between two units at different locations. On 24-Nov-2003, the group acquired orion security services inc. During the year the group sold its tobacco operations to American Indian cigco, llc.

Primary SIC and add'l.: 5194 7375

CIK No: 0001053113

Subsidiaries: Cyco Net, Inc, Orion Security Services, Inc

Officers: Richard Urrea/CEO, Pres., Daniel Urrea/CFO, Tommy Stiansen/CTO, Founder

Directors: Tommy Stiansen/CTO, Founder

Owners: Cornell Capital Partners, LP/23.93%, Richard Urrea/4.10%, Daniel Urrea/4.24%, Insiders/8.34%, Mathew Urrea - Tres Santos Limited Partnership/4.71%, Mathew Urrea - Urrea Family Limited Partnership/3.77%

Financial Data: Fiscal Year End:12/31   Latest Annual Data: 12/31/2005

Year	Sales	Net Income
2005	$394,000	-$3,146,000
2004	$496,000	-$5,930,000
2003	$54,000	-$4,902,000

Curr. Assets:	$261,000	Curr. Liab.:	$1,260,000		
Plant, Equip.:	$45,000	Total Liab.:	$3,549,000	Indic. Yr. Divd.:	NA
Total Assets:	$456,000	Net Worth:	-$3,093,000	Debt/ Equity:	NA

Nexity Financial Corp

3500 Blue Lake Dr., Ste. 330, Birmingham, AL, 35243; *PH:* 1-205-298-6391; *Fax:* 1-205-298-6395;
http:// www.nexitybank.com

General - Incorporation	DE	Stock - Price on:12/24/2007	$10.72
Employees	94	Stock Exchange	NDQ
Auditor	Mauldin & Jenkins, LLC	Ticker Symbol	NXTY
Stk Agt	NA	Outstanding Shares	8,340,000
Counsel	NA	E.P.S.	$0.67
DUNS No.	NA	Shareholders	NA

Business: The group's principle activity is to provide various correspondent banking services to community banks located primarily in the southeastern United States and Texas. Its correspondent banking services include the purchase and sale of loan participations with community banks; fixed income investment services, including the sale of government agency securities, asset/liability management services, bond accounting, and safekeeping services; and cash management programs, including clearing programs for customer bank accounts and overnight Fed funds services to customer banks. The company offers a range of deposits, including no interest-bearing demand deposits, interest-bearing checking, money market accounts, savings accounts, brokered deposits, and time deposits. The group operates from United States.

Primary SIC and add'l.: 6199

CIK No: 0001084727

Subsidiaries: Nexity Bank, Nexity Capital Trust II

Officers: Greg L. Lee/Chmn., CEO/$831,311.00, John J. Moran/Dir., Exec. VP, CFO - Investor Relation Contact/$581,999.00, Cindy W. Russo/Exec. VP - Operations/$267,692.00, David E. Long/Dir., Pres./$592,029.00, Kenneth T. Vassey/Sr. Lending Officer, Exec. VP/$429,783.00

Directors: Greg L. Lee/Chmn., CEO, David E. Long/Dir., Pres., Bradford R. Burnette/Dir., John J. Moran/Dir., Exec. VP, CFO - Investor Relation Contact, Randy K. Dolyniuk/Dir., Tommy E. Looper/Dir., Denise N. Slupe/Dir., William L. Thornton/Dir., Mark A. Stevens/Dir.

Owners: John J. Moran/4.36%, David E. Long/4.25%, Tommy E. Looper/0.22%, Mark A. Stevens/0.03%, Bradford R. Burnette, William L. Thornton/1.31%, Randy K. Dolyniuk/3.33%, Kenneth T. Vassey/1.14%, Insiders/23.25%, Cindy W. Russo/0.48%, Denise N. Slupe/3.22%, Greg L. Lee/4.67%

Financial Data: Fiscal Year End:12/31   Latest Annual Data: 12/31/2006

Year	Sales	Net Income
2006	$59,627,000	$6,095,000
2005	$43,043,000	$4,541,000
2004	$30,317,000	$5,375,000

Curr. Assets:	$34,342,000	Curr. Liab.:	$702,400,000	P/E Ratio:	16.00
Plant, Equip.:	$5,720,000	Total Liab.:	$825,851,000	Indic. Yr. Divd.:	NA
Total Assets:	$891,022,000	Net Worth:	$65,170,000	Debt/ Equity:	1.8285

Nexmed Inc

89 Twin Rivers Dr., East Windsor, NJ, 08520; *PH:* 1-609-371-8123; *Fax:* 1-609-426-9116;
http:// www.nexmed.com

General - Incorporation	NV	Stock - Price on:12/24/2007	$1.77
Employees	18	Stock Exchange	NDQ
Auditor	PricewaterhouseCoopers LLP	Ticker Symbol	NEXM
Stk Agt	Wells Fargo Shareowner Services	Outstanding Shares	81,070,000
Counsel	Kmz Rosenman	E.P.S.	-$0.11
DUNS No.	78-994-8239	Shareholders	NA

Business: The group's principal activity is to design, develop and commercialize therapeutic products based on proprietary delivery systems. The group develops products for topical treatments including cream, gel, patch and tape products based on a penetration enhancement technology known as nexact (r). Nexact enables an active drug to be better absorbed through the skin. The products under development include alprox-td(R), femprox (TM) and viratrol (r). Alprox-td(R) and femprox(R) creams are used for the treatment of male erectile dysfunction and female sexual arousal disorder respectively. Viratrol(R) is a therapeutic medical device for the treatment of herpes simplex diseases without the use of drugs. The group has international operations in Hong Kong and Canada.

Primary SIC and add'l.: 2834 8731

CIK No: 0001017491

Subsidiaries: NexMed (U.S.A.), Inc., NexMed Holdings, Inc., NexMed International (Hong Kong) Ltd, NexMed International Limited

Officers: Vivian Lu/Dir., CEO, Pres./$520,162.00, Richard J. Berman/Chmn., CEO, Pres./$473,309.00, Mark Westgate/CFO, VP/$312,923.00, Paula Schwartz/Investor Relations Officer

Directors: Vivian Lu/Dir., CEO, Pres., Richard J. Berman/Chmn., CEO, Pres., Leonard A. Oppenheim/Chmn., Arthur D. Emil/Dir., Martin R. Wade/Dir., David S. Tierney/Dir.

Owners: FMR Corp/8.38%, David S. Tierney, Southpoint Capital/17.90%, Loeb Partners Corporation/6.25%, Vivian H. Liu/1.12%, RA Capital/11.20%, Insiders/5.03%, Richard J. Berman/2.04%, Arthur D. Emil, Mark Westgate, Leonard A. Oppenheim/1.03%, Martin R. Wade, Sami A. Hashim

Financial Data: Fiscal Year End:12/31 Latest Annual Data: 03/31/2007

Year	Sales	Net Income
2007	$287,000	-$2,039,000
2006	$1,867,000	-$8,043,000
2005	$2,399,000	-$15,442,000

Curr. Assets:	$12,446,000	Curr. Liab.:	$7,371,000		
Plant, Equip.:	$7,488,000	Total Liab.:	$8,429,000	Indic. Yr. Divd.:	NA
Total Assets:	$19,934,000	Net Worth:	$11,504,000	Debt/ Equity:	NA

Nexstar Broadcasting Group Inc

909 Lake Carolyn Pkwy., Ste. 1450, Irving, TX, 75039; *PH:* 1-972-373-8800; *Fax:* 1-972-373-8888; *http://* www.nexstar.tv

General - Incorporation	DE	**Stock**- Price on:12/24/2007	$14.29
Employees	1,900	Stock Exchange	NDQ
Auditor	PricewaterhouseCoopers LLP	Ticker Symbol	NXST
Stk Agt	American Stock Transfer & Trust Co.	Outstanding Shares	28,400,000
Counsel	NA	E.P.S	-$0.44
DUNS No.	NA	Shareholders	NA

Business: The group's principal activity is to own, operate and program television stations in the United States of America. The group operates 27 stations in the United States of America. The television stations are located in New York, Pennsylvania, Illinois, Indiana, Missouri, Texas, Louisiana, Arkansas, Alabama, Montana and Maryland. On 30-Dec-2003, the group acquired quorum broadcast holdings, llc and on 01-Aug-2003, acquired kark television station.

Primary SIC and add'l.: 4841 4833

CIK No: 0001142417

Subsidiaries: Nexstar Broadcasting, Inc., Nexstar Finance Holdings, Inc.

Officers: Perry A. Sook/Chmn., CEO, Pres./$2,159,682.00, Duane A. Lammers/Exec. VP, COO, GM - Wtwo/$616,169.00, Paul Greeley/VP - Marketing, Promotions, Shirley E. Green/VP - Finance, Gary Hood/General Sales Mgr. - Kode, Larry Young/News Dir. - KODE, Blake Russell/GM - Knwa, Richard Stolpe/VP, Dir. - Engineering, Chris Tingle/General Sales Mgr. - Kard, Randall Kamm/News Dir. - KARD, Brad Dawson/General Sales Mgr. - Kbtv, Alan Little/News Dir. - KFTA, Kirk Keller/General Sales Mgr. - Kmid, Dirk Allsbury/Local Sales Mgr. - Kqtv, Caron Keesee/Station Mgr. - Krbc *(105 Officers included in Index)*

Directors: Perry A. Sook/Chmn., CEO, Pres., Jay M. Grossman/Dir., Geoff Armstrong/Dir., Erik Brooks/Dir., Martin I. Pompadur/Dir., Michael Donovan/Dir., Brent Stone/Dir., Blake R. Battaglia/Dir., Royce Yudkoff/Dir., Lis McNabb/Dir.

Owners: Matthew E. Devine, Insiders/30.90%, ABRY, Jay M. Grossman, Duane A. Lammers, FMR Corp./12.30%, Royce Yudkoff, Act II Management, L.P./5.00%, Timothy C. Busch, Royce Yudkoff/24.40%, Banc of America Capital Investors L.P./100.00%, Insiders, ABRY/24.40%, Michael Donovan, Perry A. Sook/3.30% *(19 Owners included in Index)*

Financial Data: Fiscal Year End:12/31 Latest Annual Data: 12/31/2006

Year	Sales	Net Income
2006	$265,169,000	-$8,992,000
2005	$226,053,000	-$48,730,000
2004	$280,745,000	-$20,500,000

Curr. Assets:	$77,123,000	Curr. Liab.:	$55,098,000		
Plant, Equip.:	$110,903,000	Total Liab.:	$797,999,000	Indic. Yr. Divd.:	NA
Total Assets:	$724,709,000	Net Worth:	-$73,290,000	Debt/ Equity:	NA

Next Generation Media Corp

7644 Dynatech Ct., Springfield, VA, 22153; *PH:* 1-703-644-0200; *Fax:* 1-703-455-8519; *http://* www.unitedol.com; *Email:* info@unitedol.com

General - Incorporation	NV	**Stock**- Price on:12/24/2007	$0.075
Employees	67	Stock Exchange	OTC
Auditor	Turner, Jones & Assoc., P.l.l.c	Ticker Symbol	NGMC
Stk Agt	OTR Transfer Agency	Outstanding Shares	12,370,000
Counsel	NA	E.P.S	$0.01
DUNS No.	05-664-1343	Shareholders	NA

Business: The group's principal activity is to provide marketing in three communication mediums: direct mail, direct marketing and Internet marketing. The group offers advertising and marketing products and services through a network of franchisees in twenty states, with the largest concentration being in the northeast United States. The group provides full-service design, layout, printing, packaging and distribution of marketing products and promotional coupons sold by the franchise network. The group provides its services to local market businesses, service providers and professionals as resources to help them generate 'trial and repeat' customers.

Primary SIC and add'l.: 7331 7319 7311 6719

CIK No: 0000356292

Subsidiaries: United Marketing Solutions, Inc.

Officers: Darryl Reed/Dir., CEO, Pres., Sec., Olin Greene/CFO, Treasurer

Directors: Darryl Reed/Dir., CEO, Pres., Sec., Leon Zajdel/Chmn., Melissa Held Marsden/Dir., Fernando Mathov/Dir.

Owners: Insiders/45.80%, Leon Zajdel/3.90%, Christopher Boeman/15.60%, Melissa Marsden/1.00%, Darryl Reed/24.30%, Fernando Mathov/1.00%

Financial Data: Fiscal Year End:12/31 Latest Annual Data: 12/31/2006

Year	Sales	Net Income
2006	$7,950,000	$24,000
2005	$8,220,000	$18,000
2004	$7,822,000	$183,000

Curr. Assets:	$472,000	Curr. Liab.:	$539,000		
Plant, Equip.:	$1,067,000	Total Liab.:	$655,000	Indic. Yr. Divd.:	NA
Total Assets:	$2,532,000	Net Worth:	$1,876,000	Debt/ Equity:	NA

Next Inc

7625 Hamilton Pk. Dr., Ste. 12, Chattanooga, TN, 37421; *PH:* 1-423-296-8213; *Fax:* 1-423-510-7058; *http://* www.nextinc.net

General - Incorporation	DE	**Stock**- Price on:12/24/2007	$0.32
Employees	150	Stock Exchange	OTC
Auditor	Tauber & Balser, Joseph Decosimo & Co	Ticker Symbol	NXTI
Stk Agt	NA	Outstanding Shares	18,490,000
Counsel	NA	E.P.S	-$0.037
DUNS No.	NA	Shareholders	NA

Business: The group's principle activities are to design, develop, market and distribute branded promotional products and imprinted sportswear. The items that are imprinted include headwear, polo shirts, long-sleeve shirts, fleece wear, shorts, jackets, beach towels, souvenir blankets and t-shirts. The imprinted sportswear is sold primarily through traditional and specialty retailers ranging from the large national and regional chains to sporting goods stores, casinos, golf and tennis pro shops, souvenir shops and sports stadiums. The corporate sales market is comprised primarily of corporations that purchase imprinted sportswear bearing the corporation's logo, name, or a theme. The products are sold throughout the United States primarily under licensing agreements. The group's quarterly revenue for August 2007 was 5.86 millions of USD.

Primary SIC and add'l.: 3949

CIK No: 0001071991

Subsidiaries: Blue Sky Graphics, Inc., Choice International Inc., CMJ Ventures, Inc., Lil Fan, Inc., Next Marketing Inc., S-2-S Acquisition Corporation

Officers: Robert M. Budd/CEO, Charles Thompson/CFO, Exec. VP, David Gleason/VP - Sourcing, Program Development, Joe Ferragina/Exec. VP - Sales Marketing, Ross Litz/VP - Sales Merchandising, Rick Talbert/VP - Operations, Chuck Thompson/Contact - Corporate Office in Tennessee

Directors: Ronald Metz/49/Chmn., Salvatore Geraci/Dir., Dan F. Cooke/59/Dir.

Owners: Salvatore Geraci/0.50%, Ronald J. Metz/0.90%, Robert M. Budd/0.70%, Charles L. Thompson/7.10%, Hensley Family Limited Partnership/11.30%, Insiders/25.40%, Dan F. Cooke/17.60%

Financial Data: Fiscal Year End:11/30 Latest Annual Data: 12/1/2006

Year	Sales	Net Income
2006	$28,767,000	$47,000
2005	$26,677,000	-$681,000
2004	$21,519,000	-$281,000

Curr. Assets:	$12,073,000	Curr. Liab.:	$9,521,000		
Plant, Equip.:	$2,663,000	Total Liab.:	$13,057,000	Indic. Yr. Divd.:	NA
Total Assets:	$20,759,000	Net Worth:	$7,702,000	Debt/ Equity:	0.4917

Nextel Partners Inc

4500 Carillon Point, Kirkland, WA, 98033; *PH:* 1-425-576-3600; *http://* www.nextelpartners.com

General - Incorporation	DE	**Stock**- Price on:12/24/2007	$22.1
Employees	64,600	Stock Exchange	NA
Auditor	KPMG LLP	Ticker Symbol	NA
Stk Agt	Mellon Investor Services LLC	Outstanding Shares	2,890,000,000
Counsel	Summit Law Group	E.P.S	$0.24
DUNS No.	NA	Shareholders	NA

Business: The group's principle activity is to provide a wide range of wireless and wireline communication products and services to individuals, business and government customers. In August 2007, Sprint Nextel acquired Northern PCS Services, LLC. The group operates from United States.

Primary SIC and add'l.: 4899 4812

CIK No: 0001085707

Subsidiaries: New York, Inc., Nextel Partners Equipment LLC, Nextel Partners Operating Corp., Nextel WIP Expansion Corp., Nextel WIP Expansion Two Corp., Nextel WIP Lease Corp., Nextel WIP License Corp., NPCR, Inc., NPFC, Inc.

Financial Data: Fiscal Year End:12/31 Latest Annual Data: 12/31/2006

Year	Sales	Net Income
2006	$41,028,000,000	$1,329,000,000
2005	$34,680,000,000	$1,785,000,000
2004	$27,428,000,000	-$1,012,000,000

Curr. Assets:	$10,304,000,000	Curr. Liab.:	$9,798,000,000	P/E Ratio:	184.17
Plant, Equip.:	$25,868,000,000	Total Liab.:	$44,030,000,000	Indic. Yr. Divd.:	$0.100
Total Assets:	$97,161,000,000	Net Worth:	$53,131,000,000	Debt/ Equity:	0.4145

Nextera Enterprises Inc

6644 Valjean Ave., Van Nuys, CA, 91406; *PH:* 1-818-902-5537; *Fax:* 1-818-902-5527; *http://* www.nextera.com

General - Incorporation	DE	**Stock**- Price on:12/24/2007	$0.16
Employees	15	Stock Exchange	OTC
Auditor	Ernst & Young LLP	Ticker Symbol	NXRA
Stk Agt	Mellon Investor Services LLC	Outstanding Shares	42,340,000
Counsel	Testa, Hurwitz & Thibeault	E.P.S	-$0.205
DUNS No.	NA	Shareholders	NA

Business: The group's principal activity is to provide consulting services. The group has provided law firms, corporations and regulatory agencies with expert analysis of complex economic issues in connection with legal and government proceedings, strategic planning and other business activities. The services of the group fall into three broad areas: litigation support, public policy studies and business consulting. The customers of the group include major law firms and the corporations that they represent, government and regulatory agencies, public and private utilities and national and multinational corporations.

Primary SIC and add'l.: 7375 8742

CIK No: 0001070534

Subsidiaries: CE Acquisition Corp., ERG Acquisition Corp., Lexecon Inc., Nextera Business Performance Solutions Group, Inc., Nextera Canada Co, Nextera Economics, Inc, W Lab Acquisition Corp.

Officers: Michael P. Muldowney/44/CFO, COO/$703,539.00, Michael J. Dolan/41/Chief Accounting Officer, Corporate Controller/$332,830.00, Joseph J. Millin/Dir., Pres., Principal Executive Officer/$317,653.00, Scott J. Weiss/Dir., CFO - Woodridge Labs, Inc, Antonio Rodriquez/CFO, Robin Deyo/Corporate Controller

Directors: Richard V. Sandler/Chmn., Alan B. Levine/Dir., Ralph Finerman/Dir., Stanley E. Maron/Dir., Joseph J. Millin/Dir., Pres., Principal Executive Officer, Scott J. Weiss/Dir., CFO - Woodridge Labs, Inc, Steven B. Fink/Dir., Keith D. Grinstein/Dir.

Owners: Scott J. Weiss, Michael R. Milken, Michael R. Milken, Lawrence J. Ellison, Steven B. Fink, Insiders, Michael P. Muldowney, Insiders, Jocott Enterprises, Inc., Lowell J. Milken, Mounte LLC, Michael R. Milken, Lowell J. Milken, David Michael Schneider Trust, Lawrence J. Ellison *(29 Owners included in Index)*

Financial Data: *Fiscal Year End:*12/31   *Latest Annual Data:* 12/31/2006

Year	Sales	Net Income
2006	$7,481,000	-$7,317,000
2005	NA	-$1,901,000
2004	NA	-$2,349,000

Curr. Assets:	$3,579,000	*Curr. Liab.:*	$4,364,000		
Plant, Equip.:	$284,000	*Total Liab.:*	$17,652,000	*Indic. Yr. Divd.:*	NA
Total Assets:	$28,143,000	*Net Worth:*	$10,491,000	*Debt/ Equity:*	NA

Nextest Systems Corp

875 Embedded Way, San Jose, CA, 95138; *PH:* 1-408-960-2400; *Fax:* 1-408-960-7660; *http://* www.nextest.com; *Email:* sales@nextest.com

General - Incorporation	DE	Stock- Price on:12/24/2007	$12.87
Employees	199	Stock Exchange	NDQ
Auditor	PricewaterhouseCoopers LLP	Ticker Symbol	NEXT
Stk Agt	Computershare Trust Co	Outstanding Shares	17,750,000
Counsel	NA	E.P.S.	$0.26
DUNS No.	NA	Shareholders	NA

Business: The groups principle activities include designing, developing, manufacturing, selling and servicing automated test equipment. The products of the group include Magnum, Maverick and Maverick II. Customers served by the group include integrated device manufacturers, fabless semiconductor companies, packaging assembly and test provider and wafer fabrication foundries. Specific customers of the group include Samsung Electronics Co., Ltd., Intel Corp, SanDisk Corp., Lattice Semiconductor Corp and Amkor Technology, Inc. The group operates from the North America and United States, Asia Pacific and, Europe, Middle East and Africa. The group's quarterly revenue for September 2007 was 22.98 millions of USD.

Primary SIC and add'l.: 3825 3559

CIK No: 0001167896

Subsidiaries: Nextest Systems (Philippines) Corporation, Nextest Systems (Thailand) Ltd, Nextest Systems Europe S.R.L., Nextest Systems France S.A.R.L., Nextest Systems Japan K.K., Nextest Systems Korea Co., Ltd., Nextest Systems UK LTD

Officers: Robin Adler/Chmn., CEO, Howard Marshall/Dir., VP - Operations, James P. Moniz/CFO, VP, Treasurer, Tim F. Moriarty/Pres., Craig Z. Foster/VP - Engineering, Victor A. Hebert/Corp. Sec., Paul M. Barics/45/VP, Corporate Controller

Directors: Robin Adler/Chmn., CEO, Howard Marshall/Dir., VP - Operations, Juan Benitez/Dir., Stephen G. Newberry/Dir., Richard Dissly/Dir., Eugene R. White/Dir.

Owners: Juan A. Benitez, Needham Investment Management L.L.C./6.70%, James P. Moniz, Robin Adler/13.50%, Magnetar Investment Management, L.L.C./5.50%, Tim F. Moriarty/2.60%, Insiders/31.50%, Craig Z. Foster/1.90%, Royce& Associates, LLC/10.20%, Eugene R. White, Howard D. Marshall/11.90%, Paul M. Barics, Trivium Capital Management, LLC/6.40%, T. Rowe Price Associates, Inc./6.60%, Richard L. Dissly *(16 Owners included in Index)*

Financial Data: *Fiscal Year End:*06/24   *Latest Annual Data:* 06/30/2007

Year	Sales	Net Income
2007	$79,721,000	$7,817,000
2006	$87,669,000	$11,088,000
2005	$48,447,000	-$312,000

Curr. Assets:	$39,593,000	*Curr. Liab.:*	$11,370,000	*P/E Ratio:*	19.50
Plant, Equip.:	$3,750,000	*Total Liab.:*	$11,989,000	*Indic. Yr. Divd.:*	NA
Total Assets:	$45,815,000	*Net Worth:*	$3,042,000	*Debt/ Equity:*	NA

NextPhase Wireless Inc

300 S Harbor Blvd. Ste. 500, Anaheim, CA, 92805; *PH:* 1-714-765-0010; *Fax:* 1-714-765-0015; *http://* www.npwireless.com; *Email:* info@nptinc.net

General - Incorporation	NV	Stock- Price on:12/24/2007	$0.13
Employees	13	Stock Exchange	OTC
Auditor	Kmj	Corbin & Co. LLP	Ticker Symbol	NPHS
Stk Agt	Pacific Stock Transfer Company	Outstanding Shares	29,950,000
Counsel	NA	E.P.S.	NA
DUNS No.	NA	Shareholders	NA

Business: The groups principle activities include delivering integrated Internet, voice and data communications solutions to customers. Services of the group include connectivity solutions, including dial up access, DSL, wireless, T1, co location and web hosting. The group operates from the United States.

Primary SIC and add'l.: 4812

CIK No: 0001003933

Subsidiaries: NextPhase Technologies, Inc., Speedfactory, Inc.

Officers: Robert Ford/CEO, Thomas Hemingway/51/Chmn., COO, David Noyes/65/CFO, Principal Accounting Officer

Directors: Thomas Hemingway/51/Chmn., COO

Owners: Michael Jones/2.60%, Insiders/19.95%, Robert Ford/9.81%, Tom Hemingway/7.54%

Curr. Assets:	$255,000	*Curr. Liab.:*	$1,394,000		
Plant, Equip.:	$317,000	*Total Liab.:*	$3,713,000	*Indic. Yr. Divd.:*	NA
Total Assets:	$1,876,000	*Net Worth:*	-$1,838,000	*Debt/ Equity:*	NA

NextWave Wireless WI

12670 High Bluff Dr., San Diego, CA, 92130; *PH:* 1-858-480-3100; *Fax:* 1-858-480-3105; *http://* www.nextwave.com; *Email:* nwinfo@nextwave.com

General - Incorporation	DE	Stock- Price on:12/24/2007	NA
Employees	NA	Stock Exchange	NDQ
Auditor	Ernst & Young, LLP	Ticker Symbol	WAVE
Stk Agt	Computershare Investor Services LLC	Outstanding Shares	NA
Counsel	NA	E.P.S.	-$3.05
DUNS No.	NA	Shareholders	NA

Business: The groups principle activities include developing mobile broadband and wireless multimedia products and technologies. In December 2006, the group acquired 3.5 GHz BWA spectrums in Germany. The group operates from the United States, Japan and Europe. The group's quarterly revenue for Sep'07 was 17.75 millions of USD.

Primary SIC and add'l.: 3663

CIK No: 0001374993

Subsidiaries: AWS Wireless Inc., Cygnus Acquisition Co., Cygnus Communications Canada Co., CYGNUS Communications, Inc., Cygnus Multimedia Communications, Inc., Cygnus Multimedia Communications, Limited, Go Acquisition Corporation, GWireless, LLC, Inquam Broadband GmbH, Inquam Broadband Holding Limited, NextWave Broadband Inc., NextWave Metropolitan Inc., NextWave Wireless LLC, NextWave Wireless Sub, LLC, NW Spectrum Co. 26 Subsidiaries included in the Index

Officers: Allen Salmasi/Chmn., CEO, Pres., Oz Leave/Pres., CEO - GO Networks, Inc, Amir Adler/CTO - GO Networks, Inc, Hans Hoelsken/Sr. VP, GM - Europe, GO Networks, Inc, Markus Boemelburg/Sr. VP - Sales EMEA, GO Networks, Inc, Osama Alshaykh/CTO - Packetvideo Corporation, Mark R. Banham/VP - Engineering, Packetvideo Corporation, Cathy Pucher/Exec. VP - Worldwide Sales - Marketing, Packetvideo Corporation, Joel B. Espelien/Chief Business Officer, General Counsel, VP - Strategic Relationships, Packetvideo Corporation, Jeff Baher/VP - Corporate, Product Marketing, GO Networks, Inc, Peter Humphreys/VP - Asia Pacific, Ipwireless, Inc, Kevin Worral/VP - Global Services, Ipwireless, Inc, Michael Gury/VP - External Relations, Ed Redmond/Sr. VP - Engineering, Program Execution, Asic Development, Nextwave Broadband Inc, Barbara Emond/VP - Program Management - Packetvideo Corporation *(53 Officers included in Index)*

Directors: Allen Salmasi/Chmn., CEO, Pres., Douglas F. Manchester/Dir., Jack Rosen/Dir., Robert T. Symington/Dir., William H. Webster/Dir., William Jones/Dir., James C. Brailean/Dir.

Owners: Pitango Venture Capital Fund III (Israel Investors) L.P., Yoni Yosef, Yuval Mor, Heikki Makijarvi, Israel Seed IV, L.P., Lior Mozel, Oz Leave, Amir Adler, Ephraim Gildor, Mike Foster, Bill Jarvis, The Gideon and Bina Ben-Efraim Family Trust, Blumberg Capital I, L.P., Shlomi Atias, Pitango Venture Capital Fund III (USA) L.P. *(79 Owners included in Index)*

Financial Data: *Fiscal Year End:*12/31   *Latest Annual Data:* 12/30/2006

Year	Sales	Net Income
2006	$24,284,000	-$105,020,000

Curr. Assets:	$215,975,000	*Curr. Liab.:*	$49,725,000		
Plant, Equip.:	$17,529,000	*Total Liab.:*	$427,901,000	*Indic. Yr. Divd.:*	NA
Total Assets:	$897,079,000	*Net Worth:*	$469,178,000	*Debt/ Equity:*	NA

Nexus Telocation Systems Ltd

1 Korazin St., Givatayim, 53583; *PH:* 972-357-23111; *http://* www.nexus.telocation.com

General - Incorporation	Israel	Stock- Price on:12/24/2007	$8.02
Employees	506	Stock Exchange	NA
Auditor	Kost Forer Gabbay & Kasierer	Ticker Symbol	NA
Stk Agt	American Stock Transfer & Trust Co.	Outstanding Shares	3,220,000
Counsel	Yigal Arnon & Co	E.P.S.	-$0.2
DUNS No.	60-027-9392	Shareholders	NA

Business: The groups principle activities include development, manufacturing and marketing of two-way, wireless communication paging and acknowledgement messaging systems, and an automatic vehicle location system. The group operates from United States.

Primary SIC and add'l.: 3663 3669

CIK No: 0000920532

Subsidiaries: Pointer Localizacion Y Asistencia S.A., Pointer S.A, Shagrir Motor Vehicle Systems Ltd.

Officers: Danny Stern/CEO, Pres., Micha Kraus/CEO - Shagrir, Ruben Brailovsky/CEO - Pointer Argentina, Arturo Ortiz Rabasa/General Dir. - Pointer Mexico, Israel Ron/GM - Product, Technology Business Division, Ofer Kelman/VP - Research, Delopment, Yossi Regev/VP - Shagrir, Ilan Goldstein/VP - Shagrir, Gideon Rossman/VP - Business Development, Marketing, Zvi Fried/CFO, Antony Freedman/VP - Operations

Directors: Yossi Ben Shalom/Chmn., Barak Dotan/Dir., Gov Ben Ami/Dir., Alicia Rotbard/Dir., Ken Lalo/Dir., Yoel Rosenthal/Dir.

Owners: Fort Mason Partners, LP, DBSI Investment Ltd./21.86%, Portside Growth and Opportunity Fund/2.84%, LB I Group Inc./12.28%, Fort Mason Master, LP/10.24%

Financial Data: *Fiscal Year End:*12/31   *Latest Annual Data:* 12/31/2006

Year	Sales	Net Income
2006	$41,912,000	$1,169,000
2005	$36,964,000	-$2,727,000
2004	$10,969,000	-$3,764,000

Curr. Assets:	$16,980,000	*Curr. Liab.:*	$27,854,000		
Plant, Equip.:	$7,346,000	*Total Liab.:*	$56,969,000	*Indic. Yr. Divd.:*	NA
Total Assets:	$76,399,000	*Net Worth:*	$19,430,000	*Debt/ Equity:*	NA

Nexxus Lighting Inc

Formerly: Super Vision International Inc
9400-200 Sridge Pk. Ct., Orlando, FL, 32819; *PH:* 1-407-857-9900; *http://* www.svision.com

General - Incorporation	DE	Stock- Price on:12/24/2007	NA
Employees	58	Stock Exchange	NA
Auditor	Cross, Fernandez & Riley LLP	Ticker Symbol	NA
Stk Agt	American Stock Transfer & Trust Co.	Outstanding Shares	NA
Counsel	Beusau, Brownlee, Bowdain & Woller	E.P.S.	-$0.529
DUNS No.	61-193-2856	Shareholders	NA

Business: The group's principal activity is to design, manufacture and market fiber optics, lighting products and signs and displays. Fiber optics consists of cables marketed as an alternative to neon and other conventional lighting products and for use in accent lighting, theme lighting and other areas. Lighting products consist of light sources that are used in conjunction with the group's side-glow and end glow fiber optic cables, lighting accessories and a line of products using led technology for signs, safety/warning lamps, lighting strips, swimming pools and architectural lighting. Signs and displays consist of products used for advertising, signage and point of purchase displays. The group also markets fiber optically lit waterfalls and water features that are used in swimming pools and spas. The group has operations in Europe, Middle East and Africa, Asia-Pacific and Japan.

Primary SIC and add'l.: 3645 3357 3993 3648 3272 3646

CIK No: 0000917523

Officers: Michael A. Bauer/Dir., CEO, Pres./$340,350.00, Ralph Genova/VP - Sales, Commercial Lighting, Carina Betts/North American Sales Mgr., Brenda Eckrose/Mgr. Pool - Spa Lighting, Marolyn Merrell/Regional Sales Associate - International, Alvin Pasag/Regional Sales Associate - Northern Region, Allan Santos/Regional Sales Associate - Western Region, Canada, Dennis Bonet/Regional Sales Associate - Southern Region, John Oakley/CFO

Directors: Michael A. Bauer/Dir., CEO, Pres., Brett Kingstone/Chmn., Anthony Nicolosi/Dir., Anthony T. Castor/Dir., Brian McCaan/Dir., Edgar Protiva/Dir., Fritz Zeck/Dir.

Owners: James H. McCroy, Robert K. Green Trust, Potomac Capital Partners LP, Anthony Nicolosi, Tebo Partners II, LLC, Tebo Capital, LLC, Orion Capital Investments, LLC, Michael J. Brown, Michael Bauer, Gregory H. Ekizian Revocable Trust, Brett M. Kingstone, Anthony T. Castor, Brian McCann, J. Shawn Chalmers Revocable Trust UAD 8/13/96, Kyle Krueger, Pleiades Investment Partners - RLP *(22 Owners included in Index)*

Financial Data: *Fiscal Year End:*12/31 *Latest Annual Data:* 12/31/2006

Year	Sales	Net Income
2006	$11,001,000	-$2,235,000
2005	$11,983,000	-$488,000
2004	$11,895,000	-$332,000

Curr. Assets:	$12,481,000	Curr. Liab.:	$2,468,000		
Plant, Equip.:	$1,029,000	Total Liab.:	$2,468,000	Indic. Yr. Divd.:	NA
Total Assets:	$13,850,000	Net Worth:	$11,382,000	Debt/ Equity:	NA

NGAS Resources Inc

120 Prosperous Pl., Ste. 201, Lexington, KY, 40509; ***PH:*** 1-859-263-3948; ***Fax:*** 1-859-263-4228; ***http://*** www.ngas.com; ***Email:*** ngas@ngas.com

General		Stock	
Incorporation	BC	Price on:12/24/2007	$8.16
Employees	106	Stock Exchange	NDQ
Auditor	Hall Kistler & Co., LLP	Ticker Symbol	NGAS
Stk Agt	Cohen & March LLP	Outstanding Shares	21,780,000
Counsel	Ronald Paton, Barrister & Solicitor	E.P.S	-$0.02
DUNS No.	NA	Shareholders	NA

Business: The group's principal activities are the acquisition, exploration, development, production and sale of natural gas, oil, and related business activity. The principal products produced by the group are natural gas and oil. The group, through it's wholly owned subsidiary Daugherty Petroleum, pursues it's exploration and development activities through the identification and drilling of new productive wells and the acquisition of existing producing wells. Through Sentra, the wholly owned subsidiary of Daugherty Petroleum, the group sells natural gas to two communities in south central Kentucky. The principal markets for group's oil and gas are refineries and transmission companies.

Primary SIC and add'l.: 1311

CIK No: 0000746834

Subsidiaries: Daugherty Petroleum ND Ventures, LLC, Daugherty Petroleum, Inc., NGAS Gathering, LLC, NGAS Securities, Inc., Sentra Corporation

Officers: William S. Daugherty/54/Chmn., CEO, Pres./$947,205.00, William G. Barr/58/VP/$872,208.00, Michael P. Windisch/33/CFO/$517,873.00, Michael D. Wallen/53/VP/$869,320.00

Directors: William S. Daugherty/54/Chmn., CEO, Pres., James K. Klyman/53/Dir., Charles L. Cotterell/82/Dir., Thomas F. Miller/62/Dir.

Owners: James K. Klyman/0.12%, Cannell Capital, LLC/5.07%, Thomas F. Miller/0.10%, Michael D. Wallen/2.04%, Charles L. Cotterell/0.25%, Michael P. Windisch/1.16%, Insiders/8.73%, William G. Barr/1.24%, William S. Daugherty/4.17%

Financial Data: *Fiscal Year End:*12/31 *Latest Annual Data:* 12/31/2006

Year	Sales	Net Income
2006	$79,820,000	$1,992,000
2005	$62,228,000	$953,000
2004	$47,980,000	$1,612,000

Curr. Assets:	$24,656,000	Curr. Liab.:	$25,484,000		
Plant, Equip.:	$147,560,000	Total Liab.:	$101,863,000	Indic. Yr. Divd.:	NA
Total Assets:	$178,219,000	Net Worth:	$76,357,000	Debt/ Equity:	0.9312

Niagara Mohawk Power Corp

300 Erie Blvd. W, Syracuse, NY, 13202; ***PH:*** 1-315-474-1511; ***Fax:*** 1-315-460-7041; ***http://*** www.niagaramohawk.com

General		Stock	
Incorporation	NY	Price on:12/24/2007	$98
Employees	NA	Stock Exchange	OTC
Auditor	PricewaterhouseCoopers LLP	Ticker Symbol	NMPWM
Stk Agt	Bank of New York	Outstanding Shares	NA
Counsel	NA	E.P.S	NA
DUNS No.	00-699-4735	Shareholders	NA

Business: The group operates throug its subsdiary shoe principle activities include generating, purchasing, transmiting and selling electricity; and purchase, distribute and sell natural gas. The group operates from United States.

Primary SIC and add'l.: 6719 4923 4931

CIK No: 0000071932

Subsidiaries: Hudson Pointe, Inc., Land Management & Development, Inc., Landwest, Inc., Moreau Park, Inc., NM Properties, Inc., NM Receivables Corp. II, NM Uranium, Inc., OPropCo., Inc., Port of the Islands North, LLC, Riverview Galusha LLC, Riverview, Inc., Salmon Shores Partnership, Salmon Shores, Inc., Second Street Associates, LLC, Upper Hudson Development Inc.

Officers: William F. Edwards/51/Dir., CEO, Pres., Joseph T. Ash/59/VP - Regulatory Proceedings, NY, Lawrence J. Reilly/52/Exec. VP, Anthony C. Pini/55/Dir., Sr. VP, Steven W. Tasker/50/Sr. VP, Treasurer, Paul J. Bailey/50/Controller, Barbara A. Hassan/58/Dir., Sr. VP, Masheed H. Saidi/53/VP, Colin Buck/58/CFO, Sr. VP, Susan Crossett/47/Dir., VP

Directors: William F. Edwards/51/Dir., CEO, Pres., Anthony C. Pini/55/Dir., Sr. VP, Barbara A. Hassan/58/Dir., Sr. VP, Cheryl A. Lafleur/53/Dir., Susan Crossett/47/Dir., VP

Owners: Joseph T. Ash, Insiders, Cheryl A. LaFleur, Susan M. Crossett, Anthony C. Pini, Colin Buck, Lawrence J. Reilly, Steven W. Tasker, Masheed H. Saidi, William F. Edwards, Barbara Hassan, Paul J. Bailey

Financial Data: *Fiscal Year End:*03/31 *Latest Annual Data:* 3/31/2007

Year	Sales	Net Income
2007	$4,131,655,000	$189,577,000
2006	$4,344,023,000	$317,076,000
2005	$3,925,171,000	$263,249,000

Curr. Assets:	$1,183,572,000	Curr. Liab.:	$1,378,489,000		
Plant, Equip.:	$5,489,901,000	Total Liab.:	$8,048,206,000	Indic. Yr. Divd.:	NA
Total Assets:	$12,166,755,000	Net Worth:	$4,118,549,000	Debt/ Equity:	NA

NIC Inc

25501 W Valley Pkwy., Ste. 300, Olathe, KS, 66061; ***PH:*** 1-877-234-3468; ***Fax:*** 1-913-498-3472; ***http://*** www.nicusa.com

General		Stock	
Incorporation	CO	Price on:12/24/2007	$6.41
Employees	339	Stock Exchange	NDQ
Auditor	PricewaterhouseCoopers LLP	Ticker Symbol	EGOV
Stk Agt	Computershare Ltd.	Outstanding Shares	61,760,000
Counsel	Rothgerber Johnson & Lyons	E.P.S	$0.18
DUNS No.	NA	Shareholders	NA

Business: The group's principal activity is to provide electronic government services that enable businesses and citizens to exchange information with the government online. The group operates through two segments: portal outsourcing and software and services. Portal outsourcing designs, builds and operates Internet-based portals, which allow businesses and citizens to access government information online and complete transactions. Software and services business include corporate filings, ethics and elections, transportation and aol businesses. Aol includes government information, services and applications provided under an agreement with America online inc through aol's government guide.

Primary SIC and add'l.: 7372 7375

CIK No: 0001065332

Subsidiaries: Alabama Interactive, LLC, Arkansas Information Consortium, LLC, Bay Area Interactive, LLC, Colorado Interactive, LLC, Florida Information Consortium, Inc., Hawaii Information Consortium, LLC, Idaho Information Consortium, LLC, Indiana Interactive, LLC, Intelligent Decision Technologies, LLC, Iowa Interactive, LLC, Kansas Information Consortium, Inc., Kentucky Interactive, LLC, Michigan Local Interactive, LLC, Montana Interactive, LLC, National Information Consortium Technologies, LLC 28 Subsidiaries included in the Index

Officers: Jeffery S. Fraser/Chmn., CEO/$829,295.00, Elizabeth Proudfit/VP - Business Development, Betsy Wills/General Legal Counsel, David Oboyski/Dir. - Investor Relations, Communications, Candy Irven/Dir. - Partnerships, Alliances, Harry H. Herington/Pres./$563,081.00, Stephen M. Kovzan/CFO, William F. Bradley/COO, General Counsel/$367,088.00, Samuel R. Somerhalder/Chief Administrative Officer/$349,422.00

Directors: Jeffery S. Fraser/Chmn., CEO, Art N. Burtscher/Dir., Pete Wilson/Dir., John L. Bunce/Dir., Daniel J. Evans/Dir., Ross C. Hartley/Dir.

Owners: Insiders, Harry H. Herington, Daniel J. Evans, Art N. Burtscher, Samuel R. Somerhalder, National Information Consortium Voting Trust, Eric J. Bur, Jeffery S. Fraser, Stephen M. Kovzan, William F. Bradley, Pete Wilson, Ross C. Hartley, John L. Bunce

Financial Data: *Fiscal Year End:*12/31 *Latest Annual Data:* 12/31/2006

Year	Sales	Net Income
2006	$71,376,000	$10,739,000
2005	$59,243,000	$6,363,000
2004	$55,762,000	$7,105,000

Curr. Assets:	$113,907,000	Curr. Liab.:	$40,880,000	P/E Ratio:	40.06
Plant, Equip.:	$3,790,000	Total Liab.:	$40,880,000	Indic. Yr. Divd.:	NA
Total Assets:	$140,134,000	Net Worth:	$99,254,000	Debt/ Equity:	NA

NICE Systems Ltd

301 Rt. 17 N, 10th Fl., Rutherford, NJ, 07070; ***PH:*** 1-201-964-2600; ***Fax:*** 1-201-964-2610; ***http://*** www.nice.com

General		Stock	
Incorporation	Israel	Price on:12/24/2007	$36.04
Employees	1,779	Stock Exchange	NDQ
Auditor	Kost Forer Gabbay & Kasierer	Ticker Symbol	NICE
Stk Agt	Bank of New York	Outstanding Shares	51,390,000
Counsel	Goldfarb, Levy, Eran & Partners	E.P.S	$0.73
DUNS No.	60-018-3149	Shareholders	NA

Business: The group's principal activity is the provision of integrated multimedia digital recording and quality management solutions. These products capture, evaluate and analyze voice communications, Internet collaboration, voice over Internet protocol, call data, desktop screens, e-mail storage and video. The solutions are used in customer contact centers, financial institutions, air traffic control sites, public safety centers, closed circuit television, security installations and government agencies.

Primary SIC and add'l.: 7373

CIK No: 0001003935

Subsidiaries: Fast Video Security (UK) Ltd., Fast Video Security GmbH, Nice Apac Ltd., Nice Cti Systems Uk Ltd., Nice Interactive Solutions India Private Ltd., Nice Japan Ltd., Nice Switzerland AG, Nice Systems (Singapore) Pte. Ltd., Nice Systems Australia PTY Ltd., NICE Systems Canada Ltd., NICE Systems GmbH, Nice Systems Inc., Nice Systems Latin America, Inc., Nice Systems S.A.R.L, NiceEye BV 18 Subsidiaries included in the Index

Officers: Eran Gorev/CEO, Pres. - Nice Systems Inc, Haim Shani/CEO, Yechiam Cohen/Corporate VP, General Counsel, Penny Baker/Contact - Sales, UK, Ireland, Nice CTI Systems UK Ltd, Zvi Baum/Corporate VP, Pres. - Enterprise Interaction Solutions, Craig Pumfrey/Mgr. - Marketing Communications, EMEA, Rachel Ho/Dir. - Marketing Apac - Nice Systems, Gildo Deoliveira/Contact - Sales, Nice Systems Inc, Jacques Tchenio/Contact - Sales, France, Benelux, Italy, Iberia, Nice Systems Sarl, Carmela Avner/VP - Global Operations, CIO, Avi Menkes/Corporate VP, GM Global Services, Shuli Sharabaniishai/Corporate VP - Human Resources, Israel Livnat/Corporate VP, Pres. - Security Group, Dafna Gruber/CFO, Debbie May/Pres. - IEX Corporation *(31 Officers included in Index)*

Directors: Joseph Atsmon/59/Vice Chmn., Ron Gutler/50/Chmn., Leora Meridor/60/Dir., Yoseph Dauber/72/Dir., David Kostman/43/Dir., Rimon Ben-Shaoul/63/Dir., Dan Falk/63/Dir., John Hughes/56/Dir.

Owners: FMR Corp./14.40%, Massachusetts/8.70%

Financial Data: *Fiscal Year End:*12/31 *Latest Annual Data:* 12/31/2006

Year	Sales	Net Income
2006	$409,644,000	$22,401,000
2005	$311,110,000	$36,569,000
2004	$252,643,000	$24,555,000

Curr. Assets:	$286,162,000	Curr. Liab.:	$169,835,000		
Plant, Equip.:	$15,813,000	Total Liab.:	$214,770,000	Indic. Yr. Divd.:	NA
Total Assets:	$784,344,000	Net Worth:	$569,574,000	Debt/ Equity:	NA

Nicholas Financial Inc

2454 McMullen Booth Rd., Bldg. C, Clearwater, FL, 33759; *PH:* 1-727-726-0763;
Fax: 1-727-726-2140; *http://* www.nicholasfinancial.com

General - Incorporation	BC	Stock - Price on:12/24/2007	$10.92
Employees	236	Stock Exchange	NDQ
Auditor	Dixon Hughes PLLC	Ticker Symbol	NILE
Stk Agt..... Computershare Investor Services LLC		Outstanding Shares	10,020,000
Counsel	Foley & Lardner LLP	E.P.S.	$1.125
DUNS No.	13-177-0059	Shareholders	NA

Business: The group's principle activity is to provide and sell direct consumer loans and related products. The group also designs, develops, markets and supports computer application software. The group operates through two segments: general financing and computer application software and support. The group also acquires and services installment sales contracts for purchases of new and used automobiles and light trucks. The group operates solely in the United States of America. The group's total revenue for year 2007 was 46.71 millions of USD.

Primary SIC and add'l.: 6141 6153 7372

CIK No: 0001000045

Subsidiaries: Nicholas Data Services, Inc.

Officers: Peter L. Vosotas/Chmn., CEO, Pres./$780,321.00, Ralph T. Finkenbrink/Dir., Sr. VP, CFO, Corp. Sec./$363,567.00, Matthew J. Foget/VP - Marketing, Sotirios A. Kakalis/Dir. - Loss Recovery, Douglas W. Marohn/VP - Branch Operations, Michael J. Marika/CIO, Chad W. Steinorth/VP - Finance, Laura S. Botto/Dir. - Human Resources

Directors: Peter L. Vosotas/Chmn., CEO, Pres., Ralph T. Finkenbrink/Dir., Sr. VP, CFO, Corp. Sec., Alton R. Neal/Dir., Scott Fink/Dir., Stephen M. Bragin/Dir.

Owners: Scott Fink, Mahan Family, LLC/5.40%, Peter L. Vosotas/14.50%, Fidelity Management & Research Company/5.00%, Insiders/16.60%, Southpoint Capital Advisors LLC/6.00%, Stephen Bragin/1.20%, Midwood Capital Management LLC/5.10%, Ralph T. Finkenbrink, Alton R. Neal

Financial Data: Fiscal Year End:03/31 Latest Annual Data: 3/31/2007

Year	Sales		Net Income
2007	$46,709,000		$11,580,000
2006	$42,677,000		$10,559,000
2005	$32,832,000		$8,080,000
Curr. Assets:	$1,741,000	Curr. Liab.:	$7,234,000	P/E Ratio:	9.93
Plant, Equip.:	$1,678,000	Total Liab.:	$91,245,000	Indic. Yr. Divd.:	NA
Total Assets:	$149,495,000	Net Worth:	$58,249,000	Debt/ Equity:	1.3467

Nicor Inc

1844 Ferry Rd., Naperville, IL, 60563; *PH:* 1-630-305-9500; *Fax:* 1-630-983-9328;
http:// www.nicor.com

General - Incorporation	IL	Stock - Price on:12/24/2007	$43.89
Employees	3,900	Stock Exchange	NYSE
Auditor	Deloitte & Touche LLP	Ticker Symbol	GAS
Stk Agt..... Computershare Investor Services LLC		Outstanding Shares	45,020,000
Counsel	NA	E.P.S.	$3.06
DUNS No.	01-024-4069	Shareholders	NA

Business: The groups principle activity is to distribute natural gas. The group also provides containerized freight services. The group operates from United States. The group operates from United States.

Primary SIC and add'l.: 8999 1311 4424 4924

CIK No: 0000072020

Subsidiaries: Birdsall, Inc., Northern Illinois Gas Company

Officers: Russ M. Strobel/Chmn., CEO, Pres./$2,055,154.00, Paul C. Gracey/Sr. VP, General Counsel, Sec./$614,145.00, Claudia J. Colalillo/Sr. VP - Human Resources, Corporate Communications/$562,896.00, Karen K. Pepping/VP, Controller, Daniel R. Dodge/Sr. VP - Diversified Ventures, Corporate Planning/$585,096.00, Mark A. Knox/Dir. - Investor Relations, Gerald P. O'Connor/Sr. VP - Finance, Treasurer, Rocco J. Dalessandro/49/Exec. VP - Operations, Richard L. Hawley/CFO, Exec. VP/$940,390.00, Barbara A. Zeller/VP - Information Technology, Annette Martinez/Sr. Mgr. - Corporate Communications, Richard Caragol/Public Relations Mgr.

Directors: Russ M. Strobel/Chmn., CEO, Pres., Norman R. Bobins/Dir., Bruce P. Bickner/Dir., John Rau/Dir., John H. Birdsall/Dir., Robert M. Beavers/Dir., John F. Riordan/Dir., Georgia R. Nelson/Dir., Thomas A. Donahoe/Dir., Brenda J. Gaines/Dir., Raymond A. Jean/Dir., Dennis J. Keller/Dir., Eden R. Martin/Dir.

Owners: John Rau, Richard L. Hawley, Brenda J. Gaines, Bruce P. Bickner, R. Eden Martin, John H. Birdsall, Paul C. Gracey, Russ M. Strobel, Insiders/1.70%, Claudia J. Colalillo, Daniel R. Dodge, Barclays Global Investors, NA/11.00%, Georgia R. Nelson, George M. Behrens, Dennis J. Keller *(19 Owners included in Index)*

Financial Data: Fiscal Year End:12/31 Latest Annual Data: 12/31/2006

Year	Sales		Net Income
2006	$2,960,000,000		$128,300,000
2005	$3,357,800,000		$136,300,000
2004	$2,739,700,000		$75,100,000
Curr. Assets:	$910,700,000	Curr. Liab.:	$1,142,400,000	P/E Ratio:	14.98
Plant, Equip.:	$2,714,700,000	Total Liab.:	$3,216,900,000	Indic. Yr. Divd.:	$1.860
Total Assets:	$4,090,100,000	Net Worth:	$872,600,000	Debt/ Equity:	NA

Nidec Corp

318 Industrial Ln., Torrington, CT, 06790; *PH:* 1-860-482-4422; *Fax:* 1-860-489-7201;
http:// www.nidec.co.jp

General - Incorporation	Japan	Stock - Price on:12/24/2007	$14.31
Employees	NA	Stock Exchange	NYSE
Auditor	Misuzu Pricewaterhousecoopers	Ticker Symbol	NJ
Stk Agt......... Sumitomo Trust & Banking Co Ltd		Outstanding Shares	578,940,000
Counsel	NA	E.P.S.	$0.61
DUNS No.	NA	Shareholders	NA

Business: The group's principal activity is to manufacture small-scale spindle motors for hard disk drives. The group operates through the following divisions: small precision motors division manufactures hdd spindle motors, small brush less dc motors and fan motors. The power source devices and machinery division manufactures power supplies and fluid dynamic bearings. The medium motors division manufactures medium size brush less dc motors for automobiles, home appliances and industrial equipment and other division, which offers pivot assemblies and automobile parts.

Primary SIC and add'l.: 3613 3674 3621 3714

CIK No: 0001158967

Subsidiaries: Nidec, Nidec Read Corporation, Nidec Shibaura, Nidec Tosok Corporation, Nidec-Shimpo Corporation, Shibaura Mechatronics, Toshiba

Officers: Shigenobu Nagamori/Chmn., CEO, Pres., Representative Dir., Kenji Sawamura/Exec. VP, Juntaro Fujii/Exec. VP, Shiro Kuniya/Outside Corporate Auditor, Yoshiro Kitano/Outside Corporate Auditor, Tsutomu Katsuyama/Outside Corporate Auditor, Tadayoshi Sano/Corporate Auditor, Hideo Asahina/Outside Corporate Auditor, Seizaburo Kawaguchi/MD, Hiroshi Kobe/Dir., Exec. VP, COO, Yasunobu Toriyama/Dir., Exec. VP, Chief Financial, Accounting Officer, Yasuo Hamaguchi/Sr. MD, Tadaaki Hamada/MD

Directors: Shigenobu Nagamori/Chmn., CEO, Pres., Representative Dir., Seiichi Hattori/Dir., Takashi Iwata/Dir., Satoru Kaji/Dir., Akira Kagata/Dir., Tetsuo Inoue/Dir., Hiroshi Kobe/Dir., Exec. VP, COO, Yasunobu Toriyama/Dir., Exec. VP, Chief Financial, Accounting Officer, Kiyoyoshi Takegami/Dir., Toru Kodaki/Dir., Osamu Narumiya/57/Dir., Norimasa Goto/61/Dir.

Owners: Shigenobu Nagamori/16.10%, Fidelity Investments Japan/8.50%

Financial Data: Fiscal Year End:03/31 Latest Annual Data: 03/31/2007

Year	Sales		Net Income
2007	$5,333,901,000		$338,263,000
2006	$4,570,171,000		$348,591,000
2005	$4,524,267,000		$311,528,000
Curr. Assets:	$2,652,141,000	Curr. Liab.:	$1,584,490,000		
Plant, Equip.:	$1,500,196,000	Total Liab.:	$2,573,517,000	Indic. Yr. Divd.:	$0.100
Total Assets:	$4,817,996,000	Net Worth:	$2,244,479,000	Debt/ Equity:	NA

NightHawk Radiology Holdings Inc

250 Nwest Blvd., Ste. 202, Coeur dAlene, ID, 83814; *PH:* 1-208-676-8321; *Fax:* 1-208-664-2720;
http:// www.nighthawkrad.net; *Email:* info@nighthawkrad.net

General - Incorporation	DE	Stock - Price on:12/24/2007	$18.43
Employees	223	Stock Exchange	NDQ
Auditor	Touche LLP	Ticker Symbol	NA
Stk Agt	Mellon Investor Services LLC	Outstanding Shares	29,980,000
Counsel	NA	E.P.S.	$0.45
DUNS No.	NA	Shareholders	NA

Business: The groups principle activity is to provide radiology services. The groups services include off hours preliminary reads and final reads. Customers served by the group include radiology groups and hospitals. The group acquired Teleradiology Diagnostic Service, Inc in the year 2007 and American Teleradiology Nighthawks, Inc in the year 2005. The group operates from the United States.

Primary SIC and add'l.: 8090 7374 7374 8099 8099

CIK No: 0001292470

Subsidiaries: American Teleradiology Nighthawks, Inc., DayHawk Radiology Services, LLC, Nighthawk Radiology Services, LLC, NightHawk Services GmbH, Teleradiology Diagnostic Service, Inc

Officers: Paul E. Berger/Chmn., CEO, Jon D. Berger/Sr. VP - Strategy, Business Deveopment, Andrea M. Clegg/VP - Finance, Corporate Treasurer, Timothy M. Mayleben/Dir., COO, Pres., Michael J. Karaman/CIO

Directors: Paul E. Berger/Chmn., CEO, Timothy M. Mayleben/Dir., COO, Pres., Ernest G. Ludy/Dir., David J. Brophy/Dir., Peter Y. Chung/Dir.

Owners: Paul E. Berger/14.70%, Waddell& Reed Financial, Inc./5.50%, Jon D. Berger/6.20%, BAMCO, Inc./7.10%, FMR Corp./11.90%, Peter Y. Chung, Christopher R. Huber/8.80%, David J. Brophy, Insiders/30.00%, Timothy M. Mayleben

Financial Data: Fiscal Year End:12/31 Latest Annual Data: 12/31/2006

Year	Sales		Net Income
2006	$92,168,000		-$28,401,000
2005	$64,062,000		-$29,960,000
2004	$39,283,000		$3,325,000
Curr. Assets:	$99,460,000	Curr. Liab.:	$11,437,000	P/E Ratio:	32.33
Plant, Equip.:	$6,193,000	Total Liab.:	$13,437,000	Indic. Yr. Divd.:	NA
Total Assets:	$116,066,000	Net Worth:	$102,630,000	Debt/ Equity:	NA

Nighthawk Systems Inc

8200 E Pacific Pls, Ste 204, Denver, CO, 80231; *PH:* 1-210-341-4811;
http:// www.nighthawksystems.com; *Email:* sales@nighthawksystems.com

General - Incorporation	NV	Stock - Price on:12/24/2007	$0.1
Employees	9	Stock Exchange	OTC
Auditor	GHP Horwath, P.C	Ticker Symbol	NIHK
Stk Agt .... Interwest Transfer Company, Inc.		Outstanding Shares	100,210,000
Counsel	NA	E.P.S.	-$0.05
DUNS No.	NA	Shareholders	NA

Business: The group's principal activity is to design and manufacture intelligent remote monitoring and power control products that are easy to use, inexpensive and can remotely control virtually any device from any location. The products give the customers the flexibility to move their application from place to place, without re-engineering their network. During the year the group discontinued its paging business segment.

Primary SIC and add'l.: 4812 3669

CIK No: 0001084475

Subsidiaries: GlobalSCAPE, Inc., Peregrine Control Technologies

Officers: Douglas Saathoff/CEO, CFO, Rex Lee/45/VP, GM, Steve Wilburn/Project Mgr., Angelica Rosa/Sales Coordinator, Michael Mayer/46/VP - Utility Products Division

Directors: Raymond Romero/54/Dir.

Owners: Patrick Gorman/2.70%, Douglas H. Saathoff/1.80%, Myron Anduri, Market Pulse LLC/6.50%, Max Polinsky/2.90%, Dutchess Private Equities Fund, LP and Dutchess Private Equities Fund, II, LP/6.10%, Insiders/7.30%

Financial Data: Fiscal Year End:12/31 Latest Annual Data: 12/31/2006

Year	Sales	Net Income
2006	$899,000	-$3,675,000
2005	$529,000	-$2,693,000
2004	$610,000	-$1,377,000

Curr. Assets:	$758,000	Curr. Liab.:	$3,008,000
Plant, Equip.:	$18,000	Total Liab.:	$3,008,000	Indic. Yr. Divd.: NA
Total Assets:	$1,088,000	Net Worth:	-$1,920,000	Debt/ Equity: NA

NII Holdings Inc

10700 Pk.ridge Blvd., Ste. 600, Reston, VA, 20191; *PH*: 1-703-390-5100; *Fax*: 1-703-547-5269; http://www.nii.com

General - Incorporation............................DE
Employees...7,749
Auditor ....PricewaterhouseCoopers LLP
Stk Agt.............Relevant Prov of Our Cert of Inc
Counsel..NA
DUNS No...NA

Stock- Price on:12/24/2007 ....$80
Stock Exchange.................................NDQ
Ticker Symbol....................................NIHD
Outstanding Shares 163,600,000
E.P.S...$1.99
Shareholders.....................................NA

Business: The groups principle activity is to provide digital wireless communication services. The groups products include Nextel Direct Connect, wireless data solutions and Nextel Online, and handsets. The group operates from United States.

Primary SIC and add'l.: 4899 4812 5999

CIK No: 0001037016

Subsidiaries: Airfone Holdings, Inc., Centennial Cayman Corp., Centennial Cayman Corp. Chile Ltda., Comunicaciones Nextel de Mxico, S.A. de C.V., Conect S.A., Delta Comunicaciones Digitales, S.A. de C.V., Fonotransportes Nacionales S.A. de C.V., Fonotransportes, S.A. de C.V., Inversiones Nextel de Mxico, S.A. de C.V., McCaw International (Brazil), Ltd., Multifon S.A. de C.V., Multikom S.A., Nextel Chile S.A., Nextel Communications Argentina, S.A., Nextel del Per, S.A. 38 Subsidiaries included in the Index

Officers: Steven M. Shindler/Chmn., CEO/$5,249,102.00, Daniel E. Freiman/VP, Controller, Alan Strauss/CTO, VP, Robert J. Gilker/VP - Regulatory Affairs, Sec., Peter A. Foyo/Pres. - Nextel de Mexico/$2,502,115.00, John M. McMahon/VP - Business Operations, Greg Santoro/VP, Chief Strategy, Marketing Officer, Sergio Borges Chaia/Pres. - Nextel Brazil, Ruben Butvilofsky/Pres. - Nextel Argentina, Ivan Montalvo/Global Corporate Accounting, Claudia E. Restrepo/Contact - Media Relations, Veronica Alvarez Puente/Contact - Media Relation, Nextel Argentina, Dayna Parker/VP - Human Resources, Byron R. Siliezar/CFO, VP/$2,340,863.00, Catherine Neel/VP, Treasurer, Assist. Sec. *(20 Officers included in Index)*

Directors: Steven M. Shindler/Chmn., CEO, Carolyn Katz/46/Dir., Donald E. Morgan/39/Dir., George A. Cope/46/Dir., John Donovan/47/Dir., Steven P. Dussek/51/Dir., Neal P. Goldman/38/Dir., Charles M. Herington/48/Dir., John W. Risner/48/Dir.

Owners: Donald E. Morgan, Charles M. Herington, John W. Risner, Peter Foyo, Jose Felipe, George A. Cope, Neal P. Goldman, Insiders/1.59%, Lo van Gemert, Byron R. Siliezar, Carolyn Katz, Steven P. Dussek, John Donovan, Steven M. Shindler

Financial Data: *Fiscal Year End*:12/31 *Latest Annual Data:* 12/31/2006

Year	Sales	Net Income
2006	$2,371,340,000	$294,490,000
2005	$1,745,839,000	$174,781,000
2004	$1,279,908,000	$57,289,000

Curr. Assets:	$1,209,134,000	Curr. Liab.:	$569,101,000	P/E Ratio: 41.88
Plant, Equip.:	$1,395,120,000	Total Liab.:	$1,951,198,000	Indic. Yr. Divd.: NA
Total Assets:	$3,297,678,000	Net Worth:	$1,346,480,000	Debt/ Equity: 0.8424

Nike Inc

1 Bowerman Dr., Beaverton, OR, 97005; *PH*: 1-503-671-6453; *Fax*: 1-503-671-6300; http://www.nikebiz.com

General - Incorporation............................OR
Employees...28,000
Auditor ....PricewaterhouseCoopers LLP
Stk Agt..........Computershare Trust Co., N.A.
Counsel..NA
DUNS No. 05-095-7364

Stock- Price on:12/24/2007 ....$53.63
Stock Exchange.................................NDQ
Ticker Symbol....................................NKTR
Outstanding Shares 505,510,000
E.P.S...$3.38
Shareholders.....................................NA

Business: The group's principle activities include designing, producing, developing and marketing sports and fitness footwear, apparel, equipment and accessory products The groups products portfolio include running, training, basketball, soccer, and sport-inspired. The group operates from United States, Europe, Canada and Africa.

Primary SIC and add'l.: 3149 2339 2329 3949

CIK No: 0000320187

Subsidiaries: NIKE (Suzhou) Sports Company, Ltd., Triax Insurance, Inc.

Officers: Jack Boys/CEO, VP - Converse Inc, James Seuss/CEO, VP - Cole Haan, Roger Wyett/CEO, Pres. - Hurley International, Mark Duggan/CEO - Nike Bauer Hockey, Mark G. Parker/Dir., CEO, Pres./$6,227,968.00, Bob Hurley/CEO, Pres. - Hurley International, Heidi O'Neill/VP - Global Womens Fitness, Elliott Hill/VP - Global Retail, Gerald P. Karver/VP - Global Sourcing, Manufacturing, Sandy Bodecker/VP - Nike Global Design, David Clark/VP - USA Human Resources, John F. Coburn/Corp. Sec. - Sr. Governance Counsel, Greg Hoffman/VP - Global Brand Design, Bob Woodruff/VP, Treasurer, Charlie D. Denson/Pres. - Nike Brand/$5,519,308.00 *(72 Officers included in Index)*

Directors: Mark G. Parker/Dir., CEO, Pres., Philip H. Knight/67/Chmn., Ralph D. Denunzio/73/Dir., John G. Connors/47/Dir., Douglas G. Houser/70/Dir., Timothy D. Cook/45/Dir., John R. Thompson/64/Dir., Orin C. Smith/Dir., Jill Ker Conway/70/Dir., Alan B. Graf/51/Dir., Jeanne P. Jackson/53/Dir., Johnathan A. Rodgers/61/Dir.

Owners: Cardinal Investment Sub I, L.P./1.70%, Massachusetts Financial Services Company/5.80%, Philip H. Knight/22.30%, Insiders/23.20%, Insiders/93.50%, Douglas G. Houser, Jill K. Conway, Ralph D. DeNunzio, John G. Connors, Gary M. DeStefano/0.10%, John R. Thompson, Sojitz Corporation of America/100.00%, Alan B. Graf, Orin C. Smith, Lindsay D. Stewart *(22 Owners included in Index)*

Financial Data: *Fiscal Year End*:05/31 *Latest Annual Data:* 05/31/2007

Year	Sales	Net Income
2007	$16,325,900,000	$1,491,500,000
2006	$14,954,900,000	$1,392,000,000
2005	$13,739,700,000	$1,211,600,000

Curr. Assets:	$7,359,000,000	Curr. Liab.:	$2,623,300,000	P/E Ratio: 18.30
Plant, Equip.:	$1,657,700,000	Total Liab.:	$3,584,100,000	Indic. Yr. Divd.: $0.920
Total Assets:	$9,869,600,000	Net Worth:	$6,285,200,000	Debt/ Equity: NA

Nilam Resources Inc

42 Camden St., Ste. 503, Toronto, ON, M5V 1V1; *PH*: 1-416-823-0915

General - Incorporation............................NV
Employees...NA
Auditor ....Webb & Co., P.A.
Stk Agt................Empire Stock Transfer Inc.
Counsel..NA
DUNS No...NA

Stock- Price on:12/24/2007 ....NA
Stock Exchange.................................OTC
Ticker Symbol....................................NILR
Outstanding Shares ....NA
E.P.S...NA
Shareholders.....................................NA

Business: The groups principle activity is to provide recruiting services. The groups service area includes the research and development, engineering, marketing, sales, information technology and manufacturing industries. The group operates from United States.

Primary SIC and add'l.: 1000

CIK No: 0001368714

Officers: Sandy Sandhu/26/Chmn., CEO, Pres., Treasurer, Sec.

Directors: Sandy Sandhu/26/Chmn., CEO, Pres., Treasurer, Sec.

Owners: Karamjit Gill/26.10%, Michael Sklavenitis/26.10%, Erskine Management, Inc/5.20%, Insiders/26.10%

Curr. Assets:	$13,000	Curr. Liab.:	$3,000
Plant, Equip.:	NA	Total Liab.:	$3,000	Indic. Yr. Divd.: NA
Total Assets:	$15,000	Net Worth:	$12,000	Debt/ Equity: NA

Nile Therapeutics Inc

Formerly: SMI Prouducts Inc
2850 Telegraph Ave., Ste. 310, Berkeley, CA, 94705; *PH*: 1-510-281-7700

General - Incorporation............................NV
Employees...NA
Auditor ....Amisano Hanson
Stk Agt..NA
Counsel..NA
DUNS No...NA

Stock- Price on:12/24/2007 ....NA
Stock Exchange.................................NA
Ticker Symbol....................................NA
Outstanding Shares ....NA
E.P.S...-$0.1
Shareholders.....................................NA

Business: The group's principle activity is to provide information for the mortgage and real estate industry. Under a hosting service for mortgagecommunicator.com, the site offers both free information services, as well as "Subscribed For" member services, the free information services include; a daily mortgage commentary, a listing of the top online mortgage companies, and the daily top news headlines and stories for the mortgage and real estate industry. New registrant. The group operates from United States.

Primary SIC and add'l.: 7375 6798

CIK No: 0001133869

Officers: Peter Strumph/CEO, Geoffrey Alison/35/Pres., Treasurer, Sec., Daron Evans/CFO

Directors: Geoffrey Alison/35/Pres., Treasurer, Sec.

Owners: Joshua A. Kazam/5.11%, Insiders/19.65%, David M. Tanen/6.26%, Scott L. Navins, Pedro Granadillo, Allan Gordon/2.46%, RIT Capital Partners, Plc/7.23%, Wexford Capital LLC/10.88%, Peter M. Kash/6.19%

Financial Data: *Fiscal Year End*:12/31 *Latest Annual Data:* 12/31/2006

Year	Sales	Net Income
2006	NA	-$61,000
2005	NA	-$19,000
2004	NA	-$18,000

Curr. Assets:	NA	Curr. Liab.:	$135,000	
Plant, Equip.:	NA	Total Liab.:	$135,000	Indic. Yr. Divd.: NA
Total Assets:	NA	Net Worth:	-$135,000	Debt/ Equity: NA

Ninetowns Internet Technology Group Company Ltd

5th Fl. Union Plz., 20 Chaowai St., Chaoyang District, Beijing, 100020; *PH*: 86-1065882256; http://www.ninetowns.com; *Email*: ir@ninetowns.com

General - Incorporation............................
Employees...NA
Auditor ....Deloitte& Touche LLP
Stk Agt............Morgan ADR Service Center
Counsel..NA
DUNS No...NA

Stock- Price on:12/24/2007 ....$3.82
Stock Exchange.................................NDQ
Ticker Symbol....................................NINE
Outstanding Shares ....NA
E.P.S...-$0.057
Shareholders.....................................NA

Business: The groups principle activity is to provide software services. The products of the group include IProcess, iValue and iMonitor.CGA. The groups operates through three segments namely enterprise software, software development services and computer hardware sales. Specific customers of the group include Shanghai Xianghua Shipping Consulting Company, eGrid, Ninetowns Enke and Beijing iTowNet. The group operates from China. The group's quarterly revenue for September 2007 was 21.80 millions of USD.

Primary SIC and add'l.: 7372

CIK No: 0001285735

Subsidiaries: Asia Pacific Logistics Limited, Beijing New Take Electronic Commerce Limited, Beijing Ninetowns Digital Technology Limited, Beijing Ninetowns Network and Software Co., Ltd., Beijing Ninetowns Ports Software and Technology Co., Ltd., Beijing Ninetowns Times Electronic Commerce Limited, Beprecise Investments Limited, Better Chance International Limited, Guangdong Ninetowns Technology Co., Ltd., Ixworth Enterprises Limited, New Take Limited, Shanghai New Take Digital Technology Limited, Shielder Limited, Tsingdao Fujin Commerce and Finance Software Limited

Officers: Shuang Wang/Founder, Dir., CEO, Xiaoguang Ren/Pres., Tommy Siu Lun Fork/CFO, Bolin Wu/CTO, John Yan Wang/Sr. VP - Business Development, Min Dong/Sr. VP - Legal Affairs, Human Resources

Directors: Shuang Wang/Founder, Dir., CEO, Kin Fai Ng/Dir., Xiaomin Sun/Dir., Mark Ming Hsun Lee/Dir., Dachun Zhang/Dir., Fushan Chen/Dir.

Owners: Kin Fai Ng/1.89%, Mark Ming Hsun Lee, Value Chain International Limited/5.72%, Technology Pioneer Corp./8.77%, John Yan Wang, Fushan Chen, Xiaomin Sun, Shuang Wang/17.99%, Min Dong/17.99%, Tommy Siu Lun Fork/1.59%, Dachun Zhang, Xiaoguang Ren/1.80%, Bolin Wu/1.42%, Yong Ping Duan/13.26%, Insiders/24.32%

Financial Data: **Fiscal Year End:** 12/31 **Latest Annual Data:** 12/31/2006

Year	Sales	Net Income
2006	$19,637,000	$5,885,000
2005	$29,722,000	$18,785,000
2004	$24,351,000	$16,184,000

Curr. Assets:	$126,855,000	**Curr. Liab.:**	$7,648,000	**P/E Ratio:**	32.33
Plant, Equip.:	$5,983,000	**Total Liab.:**	$7,728,000	**Indic. Yr. Divd.:**	NA
Total Assets:	$174,945,000	**Net Worth:**	$167,217,000	**Debt/ Equity:**	NA

Nippon Telegraph and Telephone Corp

101 Pk. Ave., 41st Fl., New York, NY, 10178; **PH:** 1-212-661-0810; **Fax:** 1-212-661-1078; **http://** www.ntt.co.jp; **Email:** investors@hco.ntt.co.jp

General - Incorporation	Japan	**Stock**- Price on:12/24/2007	$22.2
Employees	199,750	Stock Exchange	NYSE
Auditor	Chuoaoyama PricewaterhouseCoopers	Ticker Symbol	NTY
Stk Agt	Chuo Mitsui Trust & Banking Co Ltd	Outstanding Shares	1,380,000,000
Counsel	NA	E.P.S.	$3.05
DUNS No.	69-062-6718	Shareholders	NA

Business: The group's principle activities are to provide fixed and mobile voice transmission, data transmission, leased circuit, telecommunication equipment sales, systems integration and other telecommunications services. The group is comprised of 422 other subsidiaries and 97 affiliated companies as of Mar 31, 2004. It operates in five divisions: regional communications; long distance and international communications; wireless services: mobile phones, car phones, phs services, pager services; data communications services: system integration, network system services and other services: engineering, real estate, finance, information dealing. The group's quarterly revenue for Sep '07 was 2,602,380.00 millions of USD.

Primary SIC and add'l.: 4813 4812 4822

CIK No: 0000769594

Subsidiaries: Airec Engineering Corporation, DoCoMo Businessnet, Inc., DoCoMo Engineering Inc., DoCoMo Mobile Inc., DoCoMo Sentsu, Inc., DoCoMo Service, Inc., DoCoMo Support Inc., DoCoMo Systems, Inc., DoCoMo Technology, Inc., HKNet Company Limited, Milletechno, Inc., Nippon Telegraph And Telephone East Corporation, Nippon Telegraph And Telephone West Corporation, Ntt Advanced Technology Corporation, Ntt Advertising, Inc. 77 Subsidiaries included in the Index

Officers: Satoshi Miura/64/Representative Dir., CEO, Pres., Yasuchika Negoro/76/Corporate Auditor, Lawyer, Masamichi Tanabe/68/Corporate Auditor, Susumu Fukuzawa/62/Full, Time Corporate Auditor, Johji Fukada/65/Full, Time Corporate Auditor, Shin Hashimoto/59/Dir., Exec. VP, Dir. - Technology Planning Department, Kiyoshi Kousaka/57/Dir., Sr. VP, Dir. - General Affairs Department, Hiroo Unoura/59/Dir., Exec. VP, Dir. - Corporate Strategy Planning Department, Shigeru Iwamoto/67/Corporate Auditor, Certified Public Accountant, Tsutomu Ebe/61/Representative Dir., Sr. Exec. VP - In Charge, Business Strategy, Dir. - Corporate Business Strategy Division, CFO, Noritaka Uji/59/Representative Dir., Sr. Exec. VP, In Charge - Technical Strategy, CTO, CIO, Dir. - Executive Counsel, Advanced Telecommunication Research Institute International, Kaoru Kanazawa/63/Representative Dir., Sr. Exec. VP - In Charge, Risk Management, International Standardization, Chief Compliance Officer, Takashi Hanazawa/57/Dir., Sr. VP, Dir. - Research, Development Planning Department, Toshio Kobayashi/57/Dir., Sr. VP, Dir. - Finance, Accounting Department

Directors: Satoshi Miura/64/Representative Dir., CEO, Pres., Norio Wada/68/Chmn., Yotaro Kobayashi/75/Dir., Shin Hashimoto/59/Dir., Exec. VP, Dir. - Technology Planning Department, Kiyoshi Kousaka/57/Dir., Sr. VP, Dir. - General Affairs Department, Tsutomu Ebe/61/Representative Dir., Sr. Exec. VP - In Charge, Business Strategy, Dir. - Corporate Business Strategy Division, CFO, Takashi Imai/79/Dir., Hiroo Unoura/59/Dir., Exec. VP, Dir. - Corporate Strategy Planning Department, Noritaka Uji/59/Representative Dir., Sr. Exec. VP, In Charge - Technical Strategy, CTO, CIO, Dir. - Executive Counsel, Advanced Telecommunication Research Institute International, Kaoru Kanazawa/63/Representative Dir., Sr. Exec. VP - In Charge, Risk Management, International Standardization, Chief Compliance Officer, Takashi Hanazawa/57/Dir., Sr. VP, Dir. - Research, Development Planning Department, Toshio Kobayashi/57/Dir., Sr. VP, Dir. - Finance, Accounting Department

Owners: Government of Japan/33.72%, Insiders

Financial Data: **Fiscal Year End:** 03/31 **Latest Annual Data:** 03/31/2007

Year	Sales	Net Income
2007	$91,191,000,000	$4,042,000,000
2006	$91,805,000,000	$4,262,000,000
2005	$100,990,000,000	$6,637,000,000

Curr. Assets:	$36,361,000,000	**Curr. Liab.:**	$33,954,000,000		
Plant, Equip.:	$89,196,000,000	**Total Liab.:**	$87,637,000,000	**Indic. Yr. Divd.:**	$0.320
Total Assets:	$161,420,000,000	**Net Worth:**	$57,944,000,000	**Debt/ Equity:**	NA

NIS Group Company Ltd

6-1, 1-chome, Nishi-Shinjuku, Shinjuku L-Tower 25F, Shinjuku-ku, Tokyo; **PH:** 81-333482424; **Fax:** 81-333485099; **http://** www.nisgroup.jp; **Email:** info-ir@nisgroup.co.jp

General - Incorporation	Japan	**Stock**- Price on:12/24/2007	$4.04
Employees	NA	Stock Exchange	NYSE
Auditor	BDO Sanyu & Co	Ticker Symbol	NIS
Stk Agt	Bank of New York	Outstanding Shares	1,420,000,000
Counsel	NA	E.P.S.	-$0.19
DUNS No.	NA	Shareholders	NA

Business: The groups principle activity is to provide financial services to the small and medium-sized enterprises and their owners. The group operates through two segments namely, integrated financial services and loan servicing. In the year 2005, the group acquired Aprek Co., Ltd. The group's quarterly revenue for Sept 2007 was 36,695.00 millions of USD.

Primary SIC and add'l.: 7359 6159 6153 6163 6141

CIK No: 0001178551

Subsidiaries: Aprek Co., Ltd., NIS Lease Co., Ltd., NIS Property Co., Ltd., NIS Real Estate Co., Ltd., NIS Securities Co., Ltd., Nissin Insurance Co., Ltd., Nissin Leasing (China) Co., Ltd., Nissin Servicer Co., Ltd., Woodnote Corporation

Officers: Kunihiko Sakioka/Chmn., Co - CEO, Shinsuke Amiya/Dir., Co - CEO, Pres., Hitoshi Higaki/Statutory Auditor, Toshioki Otani/Sr. Dir., Exec. Officer, Akihiro Nojiri/Sr. Dir., Exec. Officer, Yunwei Chen/Sr. Dir., Exec. Officer, Keishi Ishigaki/Dir., Exec. Officer, Akira Imaki/Dir., Exec. Officer, Katsutoshi Shimizu/Dir., Exec. Officer, Akio Sakioka/Statutory Auditor, Katsuhiko Asada/Statutory Auditor, Outside Auditors, Hirofumi Mihara/Exec. Officer, Hidetoshi Sawamura/Dir., Exec. Officer, Masaaki Uchino/Statutory Auditor, Outside Auditor, Shigeharu Nakashima/Exec. Officer

Directors: Kunihiko Sakioka/Chmn., Co - CEO, Shinsuke Amiya/Dir., Co - CEO, Pres., Hideo Sakioka/Dir., Akihiro Nojiri/Sr. Dir., Exec. Officer, Yunwei Chen/Sr. Dir., Exec. Officer, Keishi Ishigaki/Dir., Exec. Officer, Akira Imaki/Dir., Exec. Officer, Katsutoshi Shimizu/Dir., Exec. Officer, Hidenori Nakagawa/Dir., Hidetoshi Sawamura/Dir., Exec. Officer

Owners: Katsuhiko Asada, Yunwei Chen, Akira Imaki, Michimasa Sakioka/13.10%, Hideo Sakioka/26.00%, Kunihiko Sakioka/26.40%, Katsutoshi Shimizu, Toshioki Otani, Akio Sakioka, Shinsuke Amiya, Hitoshi Higaki, Keishi Ishigaki, Akihiro Nojiri, Midori Moriyama/13.20%

Financial Data: **Fiscal Year End:** 03/31 **Latest Annual Data:** 03/31/2007

Year	Sales	Net Income
2007	$327,209,000	-$13,638,000
2006	$374,045,000	$71,976,000
2005	$364,503,000	$67,623,000

Curr. Assets:	$337,078,000	**Curr. Liab.:**	$752,960,000	**P/E Ratio:**	10.64
Plant, Equip.:	$641,889,000	**Total Liab.:**	$3,147,090,000	**Indic. Yr. Divd.:**	NA
Total Assets:	$3,846,481,000	**Net Worth:**	$699,391,000	**Debt/ Equity:**	NA

Nisource Inc

801 E 86th Ave., Merrillville, IN, 46410; **PH:** 1-219-647-5990; **Fax:** 1-219-647-5589; **http://** www.nisource.com; **Email:** questions@nisource.com

General - Incorporation	DE	**Stock**- Price on:12/24/2007	$20.86
Employees	7,439	Stock Exchange	NDQ
Auditor	Deloitte & Touche LLP	Ticker Symbol	NICH
Stk Agt	Mellon Investor Services LLC	Outstanding Shares	274,070,000
Counsel	NA	E.P.S.	$1.15
DUNS No.	18-565-4076	Shareholders	NA

Business: The group operates through its subsidiary whose principle activity is to provide natural gas and electricity. The group operates from United States.

Primary SIC and add'l.: NA

CIK No: 0001111711

Subsidiaries: Bay State Gas Company, Columbia Gas of Kentucky, Inc., Columbia Gas of Maryland, Inc., Columbia Gas of Ohio, Inc., Columbia Gas of Pennsylvania, Inc., Columbia Gas of Virginia, Inc., Columbia Gas Transmission Corporation, Columbia Gulf Transmission Company, Crossroads Pipeline Company, Kokomo Gas and Fuel Company, NiSource Retail Services, Inc., Northern Indiana Fuel and Light Company, Inc., Northern Indiana Public Service Company, Northern Utilities, Inc.

Officers: Robert C. Skaggs/53/Dir., CEO, Pres./$1,866,595.00, Christopher A. Helms/Pipeline Group Pres./$955,487.00, Robert D. Campbell/Sr. VP - Human Resources/$533,183.00, Kathleen O'Leary/Sr. VP - Energy Distribution Regulated Revenue, Gary W. Pottorff/VP - Administration, Corp. Sec., Larry J. Francisco/VP - Audit, Jeffrey W. Grossman/VP, Controller/$607,132.00, David J. Vajda/VP, Treasurer, Michael W. O'Donnell/CFO, Exec. VP/$2,367,358.00, Glen L. Kettering/Sr. VP - Corporate Affairs, Jerry L. Godwin/Sr. VP - Electric Generation, Transmission, Harris W. Marple/Sr. VP - Distribution Operations, Violet G. Sistovaris/Sr. VP - Administrative Services, Arthur E. Smith/Sr. VP - Environmental Counsel

Directors: Robert C. Skaggs/53/Dir., CEO, Pres., Ian M. Rolland/74/Chmn., Steven R. McCracken/54/Dir., Dennis E. Foster/67/Dir., Peter McCausland/58/Dir., Lee W. Nutter/64/Dir., Deborah Coleman/Dir., Marty R. Kittrell/51/Dir., Steven C. Beering/75/Dir., Richard L. Thompson/68/Dir., Carolyn Y. Woo/53/Dir., Roger A. Young/62/Dir.

Owners: Robert J. Welsh, UBS Global Asset Management (America), Inc./6.90%, Christopher A. Helms, Steven C. Beering, Michael W. ODonnell, Roger A. Young, Dennis E. Foster, Insiders, Lord, Abbett& Co. LLC/5.60%, T. Rowe Price Associates, Inc./7.80%, Carolyn Y. Woo, Gary L. Neale, Richard L. Thompson, Peter McCausland, Ian M. Rolland *(18 Owners included in Index)*

Financial Data: **Fiscal Year End:** 12/31 **Latest Annual Data:** 12/31/2006

Year	Sales	Net Income
2006	$7,490,000,000	$282,200,000
2005	$7,899,100,000	$306,500,000
2004	$6,666,200,000	$436,300,000

Curr. Assets:	$2,782,900,000	**Curr. Liab.:**	$3,821,200,000	**P/E Ratio:**	17.24
Plant, Equip.:	$9,694,500,000	**Total Liab.:**	$13,142,900,000	**Indic. Yr. Divd.:**	$0.920
Total Assets:	$18,156,500,000	**Net Worth:**	$5,013,600,000	**Debt/ Equity:**	1.0050

Nissan Motor Company Ltd

333 Commerce St., Nashville, TN, 37201; **PH:** 1-617-725-1000; **Fax:** 1-615-725-3343; **http://** www.nissan-global.com

General - Incorporation		**Stock**- Price on:12/24/2007	NA
Employees	NA	Stock Exchange	NDQ
Auditor	NA	Ticker Symbol	NSEC
Stk Agt	JP Morgan Chase Bank	Outstanding Shares	NA
Counsel	NA	E.P.S.	NA
DUNS No.	NA	Shareholders	NA

Business: The groups principal activities include manufacturing and selling automobiles. The products of the group include passenger cars, trucks, buses and forklifts. The group operates from the United States.

Primary SIC and add'l.: 6141 3711

CIK No: 0000800937

Officers: Philippe Klein/Sr. VP, CEO, COO Office - Global Motorsports, Alliance Coordination Office, Security Office, Legal Dept, Carlos Ghosn/Co - Chmn., Pres., Itaru Koeda/Co - Chmn., Exec. VP, Tadao Takahashi/Vice Chmn. External - Government Affairs Intellectual Asset Management, Hiroto Saikawa/Dir., Exec. VP - American Operations, MC, America, MC, US, Haruo Murakami/Auditor, Toshiyuki Shiga/Representative Dir., COO, Auditors, Mitsuhiko Yamashita/Dir., Exec. VP - Research, Development, Carlos Tavares/Dir., Exec. VP - Corporate Planning, Shiro Nakamura/Sr. VP - Design, Brand Management, Kazuhiko Toida/Sr. VP - Japan Sales, Fleet Business Div, Yo Usuba/Sr. VP - Powertrain Engineering Div, Shigeo Shingyoji/Sr. VP - Purchasing, Rnpo, Common Purchasing Dept, Service Support, Yoshiaki Watanabe/Sr. VP - Manufacturing, Industrial Engineering Div, Hisayoshi Kojima/Auditor *(26 Officers included in Index)*

Directors: Carlos Ghosn/Co - Chmn., Pres., Itaru Koeda/Co - Chmn., Exec. VP, Tadao Takahashi/Vice Chmn. External - Government Affairs Intellectual Asset Management, Toshiyuki Shiga/Representative Dir., COO, Auditors, Hiroto Saikawa/Dir., Exec. VP - American Operations, MC, America, MC, US, Mitsuhiko Yamashita/Dir., Exec. VP - Research, Development, Carlos Tavares/Dir., Exec. VP - Corporate Planning, Shemaya Levy/Dir., Patrick Pelata/Dir., Hidetoshi Imazu/Dir., Exec. VP - European Operations, MC, E Manufacturing SCM

Financial Data: **Fiscal Year End:** 03/30 **Latest Annual Data:** 3/31/2006

Year	Sales	Net Income
2006	$80,583,692,000	$4,427,778,000
2004	$70,086,972,000	$4,751,575,000

Curr. Assets:	$51,472,256,000	**Curr. Liab.:**	$41,467,598,000	**P/E Ratio:**	46.72
Plant, Equip.:	$37,938,530,000	**Total Liab.:**	$69,295,299,000	**Indic. Yr. Divd.:**	NA
Total Assets:	$98,131,846,000	**Net Worth:**	$26,393,017,000	**Debt/ Equity:**	NA

Nissin Co Ltd

6-1, 1-chome, Nishi-shinjuku, Shinjuku L-tower 25f, Shinjuku-ku, Tokyo, 163-1525; ;
http:// www.nisgroup.jp

General - Incorporation	Japan	**Stock** - Price on:12/24/2007	NA
Employees	NA	Stock Exchange	NYSE
Auditor	BDO Sanyu & Co	Ticker Symbol	NA
Stk Agt	Mitsubishi UFJ Trust & Banking Corp	Outstanding Shares	NA
Counsel	NA	E.P.S	NA
DUNS No.	NA	Shareholders	NA

Business: The group's principal activity is the provision of comprehensive financing services including unsecured/secured consumer loans, commercial/industrial loans, mortgage loans, factoring and bills/notes discount. Operation are carried out through the following divisions: finance services (consumer loans, business loans); credit monitoring/recovery (credit management, monitoring and recovery services); entrepreneur support business (on-line distribution of food materials); other (comprehensive bridal services including booking of wedding ceremony halls, jewelry/accessories and costume rental and the organizing of honeymoon trips, financial strategy consulting) . At 31-Mar-2003 the group consisted of the parent company, three domestic consolidated subsidiaries and five associated companies.

Primary SIC and add'l.: 6159 6141 7299 6153

CIK No: 0001178551

Subsidiaries: Aprek Co., Ltd., NIS Lease Co., Ltd., NIS Property Co., Ltd., NIS Real Estate Co., Ltd., NIS Securities Co., Ltd., Nissin Insurance Co., Ltd., Nissin Leasing (China) Co., Ltd., Nissin Servicer Co., Ltd., Woodnote Corporation

Officers: Kunihiko Sakioka/Chmn., CEO, Pres., Shinsuke Amiya/Vice Chmn., Exec. Officer, Yunwei Chen/Sr. Exec. Dir., Akira Imaki/Dir., Exec. Officer, Katsutoshi Shimizu/Exec. Dir., Exec. Officer, Hirofumi Mihara/Dir., Exec. Officer, Hidetoshi Sawamura/Dir., Exec. Officer, Masaaki Uchino/Dir., Statutory Auditor, Shigeharu Nakashima/Dir., Exec. Officer, Akio Sakioka/Dir., Statutory Auditor, Akihiro Nojiri/Sr. Exec. Dir., Hideo Sakioka/Dir., Advisor, Keishi Ishigaki/Dir., Exec. Officer, Katsuhiko Asada/Dir., Statutory Auditor, Hitoshi Higaki/Dir., Statutory Auditor *(16 Officers included in Index)*

Directors: Kunihiko Sakioka/Chmn., CEO, Pres., Shinsuke Amiya/Vice Chmn., Exec. Officer, Yunwei Chen/Sr. Exec. Dir., Akira Imaki/Dir., Exec. Officer, Katsutoshi Shimizu/Exec. Dir., Exec. Officer, Hidenori Nakagawa/Dir., Hirofumi Mihara/Dir., Exec. Officer, Hidetoshi Sawamura/Dir., Exec. Officer, Masaaki Uchino/Dir., Statutory Auditor, Akio Sakioka/Dir., Statutory Auditor, Akihiro Nojiri/Sr. Exec. Dir., Hideo Sakioka/Dir., Advisor, Keishi Ishigaki/Dir., Exec. Officer, Katsuhiko Asada/Dir., Statutory Auditor, Hitoshi Higaki/Dir., Statutory Auditor *(17 Directors included in Index)*

Owners: Michimasa Sakioka/13.10%, Midori Moriyama/13.20%, Hideo Sakioka/26.00%, Kunihiko Sakioka/26.40%

Nitar Tech Corp

2283 Argentia Rd., Unit 8, Mississauga, ON, L5N 5Z2; ***PH:*** 1-905-824-5306; ***Fax:*** 1-866-585-1408;
http:// www.nitartech.com; ***Email:*** info@nitartech.com

General - Incorporation	DE	**Stock** - Price on:12/24/2007	NA
Employees	NA	Stock Exchange	OTC
Auditor	Rotenberg & Co., LLP	Ticker Symbol	NCHP
Stk Agt	Olde Monmouth Stk Trnsfer Co. Inc.	Outstanding Shares	NA
Counsel	Richard Lane	E.P.S	NA
DUNS No.	NA	Shareholders	NA

Business: The groups principle activity is to provide software products that help parents to ensure their children are safe while learning and playing online. The group operates through two segments namely software licensing fees and consulting. The group operates from the United States and Canada.

Primary SIC and add'l.: 7372

CIK No: 0001326853

Officers: Luiz Augusto Brasil/Chmn., CEO, Richard Lane/Legal Counsel, Richard Doyle/Dir. - Sales, North America, George Parselias/Dir., Sec., Treasurer, Principal Financial Officer, Principal Accounting Officer, Luiz O. Brasil/Dir., Pres., Jose Gustavo Brasil/Dir., VP, David Taylor/VP - Sales, Marketing

Directors: Luiz Augusto Brasil/Chmn., CEO, Luiz O. Brasil/Dir., Pres., Jose Gustavo Brasil/Dir., VP, George Parselias/Dir., Sec., Treasurer, Principal Financial Officer, Principal Accounting Officer

Financial Data: **Fiscal Year End:** 07/31 **Latest Annual Data:** 07/31/2006

Year	Sales	Net Income
2006	$235,000	-$381,000

Curr. Assets:	$9,000	**Curr. Liab.:**	$137,000		
Plant, Equip.:	$35,000	**Total Liab.:**	$137,000	**Indic. Yr. Divd.:**	NA
Total Assets:	$890,000	**Net Worth:**	$753,000	**Debt/ Equity:**	NA

Nitches Inc

10280 Camino Santa Fe, San Diego, CA, 92121; ***PH:*** 1-858-625-2633; ***Fax:*** 1-858-625-0746;
http:// www.nitches.com; ***Email:*** corp@nitches.com

General - Incorporation	CA	**Stock** - Price on:12/24/2007	$3.95
Employees	82	Stock Exchange	NDQ
Auditor	J.H. Cohn, LLP	Ticker Symbol	NICH
Stk Agt	American Stock Transfer & Trust Co.	Outstanding Shares	5,250,000
Counsel	NA	E.P.S	$0.15
DUNS No.	06-763-7504	Shareholders	NA

Business: The group's principal activities are to import and distribute finished garments for men and women. The products offered by the group include sleep wear and western wear in cotton and cotton-blend knit and woven clothing. These products are distributed under the group's brand label and private retailer labels. The major retail customers of the group include cavender's, kohl's, mervyns, sears and sheplers. The group currently owns 35 registered trademarks.

Primary SIC and add'l.: 5136 5137

CIK No: 0000772263

Subsidiaries: Nitches Far East Limited

Officers: Steven P. Wyandt/63/Chmn., CEO, CFO, Paul M. Wyandt/39/Dir., COO, Pres.

Directors: Steven P. Wyandt/63/Chmn., CEO, CFO, Jefferson T. Straub/66/Dir., Michael D. Sholtis/60/Dir., Paul M. Wyandt/39/Dir., COO, Pres., Eugene B. Price/64/Dir.

Owners: Steven P. Wyandt/22.80%, Eugene B. Price/1.30%, Paul M. Wyandt/0.30%, Haresh T. Tharani/15.80%, Insiders/24.80%, Jefferson T. Straub, Michael D. Sholtis/0.10%

Financial Data: **Fiscal Year End:** 08/31 **Latest Annual Data:** 8/31/2006

Year	Sales	Net Income
2006	$54,832,000	$468,000
2005	$26,320,000	-$1,201,000
2004	$32,179,000	$557,000

Curr. Assets:	$28,747,000	**Curr. Liab.:**	$21,548,000	**P/E Ratio:**	197.50
Plant, Equip.:	$223,000	**Total Liab.:**	$23,871,000	**Indic. Yr. Divd.:**	NA
Total Assets:	$38,101,000	**Net Worth:**	$14,230,000	**Debt/ Equity:**	NA

Nitromed Inc

45 Hayden Ave., Ste. 3000, Lexington, MA, 02421; ***PH:*** 1-781-266-4000; ***Fax:*** 1-781-274-8080;
http:// www.nitromed.com; ***Email:*** info@nitromed.com

General - Incorporation	DE	**Stock** - Price on:12/24/2007	$2.28
Employees	50	Stock Exchange	NDQ
Auditor	Ernst & Young LLP	Ticker Symbol	NTMD
Stk Agt	American Stock Transfer & Trust Co.	Outstanding Shares	38,230,000
Counsel	NA	E.P.S	-$0.88
DUNS No.	NA	Shareholders	NA

Business: The group's principle activities include discovering, developing and commercializing proprietary pharmaceuticals based on naturally occurring molecule nitric oxide. The company uses nitric oxide biology and chemistry to develop novel drugs and also the existing drugs. The operations of the company are carried out in the United States. The group operates from United States.

Primary SIC and add'l.: 2834

CIK No: 0000927829

Subsidiaries: NitroMed Securities Corp.

Officers: Kenneth M. Bate/Dir., CEO, Pres./$1,160,015.00, Gordon L. Letts/60/Sr. VP - Research, Development, Chief Scientific Officer/$1,242,915.00, Jane A. Kramer/52/VP - Corporate Affairs/$675,967.00, Welton O'Neal/VP - Medical Affairs, William B.J. Jones/44/VP - Marketing, Business Development, James G. Ham/VP, CFO, Sec., Treasurer, Manuel Worcel/Chief Medical Officer, Gerald W. Bruce/Sr. VP - Commercial Operations

Directors: Kenneth M. Bate/Dir., CEO, Pres., Argeris N. Karabelas/Chmn., Davey S. Scoon/Dir., Robert S. Cohen/Dir., John W. Littlechild/Dir., Joseph Loscalzo/Dir., Frank L. Douglas/Dir., Zola P. Horovitz/Dir., Mark Leschly/Dir., Christopher J. Sobecki/Dir.

Owners: Gordon L. Letts, Rho Ventures, Robert S. Cohen, Michael Sabolinski, Frank L. Douglas, Mark Leschly, Joseph Loscalzo, Michael D. Loberg, Funds Managed by HealthCare Ventures, L.L.C., Jane A. Kramer, Invus Public Equities, L.P., Davey S. Scoon, Kenneth M. Bate, Lawrence E. Bloch, John W. Littlechild *(19 Owners included in Index)*

Financial Data: **Fiscal Year End:** 12/31 **Latest Annual Data:** 12/31/2006

Year	Sales	Net Income
2006	$12,086,000	-$71,337,000
2005	$6,047,000	-$105,852,000
2004	$16,458,000	-$29,773,000

Curr. Assets:	$46,939,000	**Curr. Liab.:**	$15,898,000		
Plant, Equip.:	$963,000	**Total Liab.:**	$19,626,000	**Indic. Yr. Divd.:**	NA
Total Assets:	$48,705,000	**Net Worth:**	$29,079,000	**Debt/ Equity:**	0.0880

Nl Industries Inc

5430 LBJ Fwy., Ste. 1700, Dallas, TX, 75240; ***PH:*** 1-972-233-1700; ***Fax:*** 1-972-448-1445;
http:// www.nl-ind.com

General - Incorporation	NJ	**Stock** - Price on:12/24/2007	$10.46
Employees	3,587	Stock Exchange	NYSE
Auditor	PricewaterhouseCoopers LLP	Ticker Symbol	NA
Stk Agt	PricewaterhouseCoopers LLP	Outstanding Shares	48,590,000
Counsel	Bartlit Beck Herman Palenchar	E.P.S	$0.04
DUNS No.	00-131-7577	Shareholders	NA

Business: The group's principal activity is to manufacture and market titanium dioxide pigments through its wholly owned subsidiary kronos inc. The group produces over 40 grades of titanium dioxide, which it sells under the kronos trademark. The group also mines and sells ilmenite ore and manufactures and sells iron-based water treatment chemicals. The group's products are sold to domestic and international manufacturers of paint, ink, coatings, plastics, ceramics, rubber, paper and man-made fibers. The group has six manufacturing facilities located in Germany, Canada, Belgium and Norway and owns a 50% interest in a titanium dioxide manufacturing joint venture located in Louisiana, United States.

Primary SIC and add'l.: 2816 2865

CIK No: 0000072162

Officers: Harold C. Simmons/76/Chmn., CEO/$3,062,081.00, Tim C. Hafer/46/VP, Controller, Kelly D. Luttmer/44/VP, Tax Dir./$505,700.00, Gregory M. Swalwell/51/CFO, VP - Finance/$508,000.00, John A. St Wrba/51/VP, Treasurer/$348,700.00, Robert D. Graham/52/VP, General Counsel/$584,200.00

Directors: Harold C. Simmons/76/Chmn., CEO, Steven L. Watson/57/Dir., Cecil H. Moore/68/Dir., Glenn R. Simmons/80/Dir., Terry N. Worrell/63/Dir., Thomas P. Stafford/77/Dir.

Owners: Terry N. Worrell, TIMET Finance Management Company, Cecil H. Moore, Insiders/85.30%, Annette C. Simmons, Thomas P. Stafford, Valhi, Inc./83.10%, Glenn R. Simmons, Harold C. Simmons/1.10%, Steven L. Watson

Financial Data: **Fiscal Year End:** 12/31 **Latest Annual Data:** 12/31/2006

Year	Sales	Net Income
2006	$190,123,000	$26,110,000
2005	$186,350,000	$32,888,000
2004	$741,687,000	$162,813,000

Curr. Assets:	$121,065,000	Curr. Liab.:	$46,595,000	P/E Ratio:	20.12
Plant, Equip.:	$70,655,000	Total Liab.:	$235,416,000	Indic. Yr. Divd.:	$0.500
Total Assets:	$529,344,000	Net Worth:	$248,512,000	Debt/ Equity:	NA

NMHG Holding Co

650 N E Holladay St. , Ste. 1600, Portland, OR, 97232; *PH:* 1-503-721-6000

General - Incorporation	DE	*Stock*- Price on:12/24/2007	NA
Employees	NA	Stock Exchange	NA
Auditor	Ernst & Young LLP	Ticker Symbol	NA
Stk Agt	NA	Outstanding Shares	NA
Counsel	NA	E.P.S.	NA
DUNS No.	NA	Shareholders	NA

Business: The groups principle activities include designing, engineering, manufacturing and selling lift trucks and aftermarket parts. The group operates through two segments include wholesale manufacturing and retail distribution. The group's products sold under the brand name Hyster and Yale. The group operates from United States.

Primary SIC and add'l.: NA

CIK No: 0001173514

NMS Communications Corp

100 Crossing Blvd., Framingham, MA, 01702; *PH:* 1-508-271-1000; *Fax:* 1-508-271-1300; *http://* www.nmscommunications.com; *Email:* info@nmss.com

General - Incorporation	DE	*Stock*- Price on:12/24/2007	$1.87
Employees	425	Stock Exchange	NDQ
Auditor	PricewaterhouseCoopers LLP	Ticker Symbol	NMSS
Stk Agt	Computershare Investor Services LLC	Outstanding Shares	45,540,000
Counsel	Dianne Callan	E.P.S.	-$0.42
DUNS No.	10-116-4879	Shareholders	NA

Business: The group's principal activities are to design, deliver and support technology systems and system building blocks for voice, video and data services on wireless and wireline networks. Products include voice quality enhancement and echo cancellation systems, voice applications systems and system building blocks that provide connectivity to communications networks, call processing and real-time media processing. Accessgate, convergence generation (cg), e256, mercury, natural access, mycaller, nms hearsay, open access, packetmedia, sonata, studio sound and alliance generation (ag) are some of its product brands. The group operates mainly in the United States, Europe and Asia.

Primary SIC and add'l.: 7372 7373

CIK No: 0000915866

Subsidiaries: NMS Communications Europe Ltd., NMS Communications Europe S.A., NMS Communications International, Inc., NMS Communications Securities Corporation

Officers: Robert P. Schechter/59/Chmn., CEO/$603,245.00, Daniel Daly/VP, GM - Network Infrastructure/$239,795.00, Dianne L. Callan/VP, General Counsel, Herb Shumway/Sr. VP - Finance, Operations, CFO/$362,030.00, Brough R. Turner/CTO, Sr. VP, John Orlando/VP, Chief Marketing Officer, Joel Hughes/Sr. VP, GM - Mobile Applications/$611,095.00, Todd Donahue/VP, Corporate Controller, Chief Accounting Officer, Jose Freitas/VP - Human Resources, Steve Gladstone/Sr. VP, GM - Communications Platforms

Directors: Robert P. Schechter/59/Chmn., CEO, William E. Foster/63/Dir., Pamela D.A. Reeve/Dir., Ronald W. White/Dir., Frank W. King/Dir., Ofer Gneezy/Dir.

Owners: Insiders/5.20%, Austin W. Marxe/10.10%, Ofer Gneezy, Pamela D.A. Reeve, Ronald W. White, Robert P. Schechter/2.60%, Frank W. King, Daniel Daly, Joel Hughes, Gerrold Walker, Paul Deeley, Herbert Shumway, William E. Foster

Financial Data: Fiscal Year End:12/31 Latest Annual Data: 12/31/2006

Year	Sales	Net Income
2006	$99,606,000	-$15,751,000
2005	$109,474,000	$4,972,000
2004	$101,512,000	$4,102,000

Curr. Assets:	$52,277,000	Curr. Liab.:	$16,460,000		
Plant, Equip.:	$6,625,000	Total Liab.:	$18,686,000	Indic. Yr. Divd.:	NA
Total Assets:	$69,330,000	Net Worth:	$50,644,000	Debt/ Equity:	NA

NMT Medical Inc

27 Wormwood St., Boston, MA, 02210; *PH:* 1-617-737-0930; *Fax:* 1-617-737-0924; *http://* www.nmtmedical.com; *Email:* info@nmtmedical.com

General - Incorporation	DE	*Stock*- Price on:12/24/2007	$12.08
Employees	115	Stock Exchange	NDQ
Auditor	Ernst & Young LLP	Ticker Symbol	NNBR
Stk Agt	American Stock Transfer & Trust Co.	Outstanding Shares	12,960,000
Counsel	Hale & Dorr LLP	E.P.S.	-$0.76
DUNS No.	19-240-2949	Shareholders	NA

Business: The group's principal activities are to design, develop and markets proprietary implant technologies that allow interventional cardiologists to treat cardiac sources of stroke through minimally invasive, catheter-based procedures. The group's products are designed to offer alternative approaches to existing complex treatments, thereby reducing patient trauma, shortening procedure, hospitalization and recovery times and lowering overall treatment costs. These products also serve the pediatric interventional cardiologist with a broad range of cardiac septal repair implants delivered with nonsurgical catheter techniques.

Primary SIC and add'l.: 3841

CIK No: 0001017259

Subsidiaries: Nitinol Medical Technologies FSC, Inc., Nitinol Medical Technologies International B.V., NMT Heart, Inc., NMT Investments Corp., NMT Medical (UK) Limited, NMT Medical GmbH, NMT Medical SARL, NMT Neurosciences Holdings (UK) Limited

Owners: Richard E. Davis, James E. Lock, John E. Ahern, Glenhill Advisors, LLC and affiliates, Cheryl L. Clarkson, Daniel F. Hanley, Harry A. Schult, Francis J. Martin, MFC Global Investment Management (U.S.), LLC, Steven A. Cohen, Insiders

Financial Data: Fiscal Year End:12/31 Latest Annual Data: 12/31/2006

Year	Sales	Net Income
2006	$28,151,000	$5,886,000
2005	$23,916,000	-$7,792,000
2004	$21,460,000	-$1,909,000

Curr. Assets:	$50,144,000	Curr. Liab.:	$11,283,000		
Plant, Equip.:	$1,039,000	Total Liab.:	$11,283,000	Indic. Yr. Divd.:	NA
Total Assets:	$51,183,000	Net Worth:	$39,899,000	Debt/ Equity:	NA

NN Inc

2000 Waters Edge Dr., Ste. 12, Johnson City, TN, 37604; *PH:* 1-423-743-9151; *Fax:* 1-423-743-2670; *http://* www.nnbr.com

General - Incorporation	DE	*Stock*- Price on:12/24/2007	$12.33
Employees	2,249	Stock Exchange	NYSE
Auditor	PricewaterhouseCoopers LLP	Ticker Symbol	NNI
Stk Agt	Suntrust Bank	Outstanding Shares	16,850,000
Counsel	Blackwell Sanders Peper Martin LLP	E.P.S.	-$0.49
DUNS No.	03-790-5247	Shareholders	NA

Business: The group's principal activity is to manufacture and supply of precision steel balls and rollers. The group supplies precision steel balls and rollers to bearing manufacturers, automotive original equipment manufacturers, the automotive aftermarket, gas and mining industries, producers of water, gas and oil well drilling bits and stainless steel valves and pumps. The group also provides full-service design and manufacture of plastic injection molded components to the bearing, automotive, electronic, leisure and consumer markets. The group supplies its products to both domestic and international anti-friction bearing manufacturers. The primary customers include skf bearing industries, fag bearings corporation, snr roulements, and the torrington company.

Primary SIC and add'l.: 3089 3562

CIK No: 0000918541

Subsidiaries: Euroball S.p.A., Industrial Molding GP, LLC, Industrial Molding LP, Industrial Molding LP,LLC, Kugelfertigung Eltmann GmbH, NN Arte S De R.L. De D.V., NN Euroball Ireland, Ltd., NN Europe ApS, NN Holdings B.V., NN Mexico LLC, NN Netherlands B.V., NN Precision Bearing Products Company Co., Ltd, NN Slovakia, s.r.o, The Delta Rubber Company

Officers: Roderick R. Baty/Chmn., CEO/$749,372.00, Will Kelly/VP, Chief Administrative Officer, Johannes Cihak/Contact - NN Europe

Directors: Roderick R. Baty/Chmn., CEO

Owners: Frank T. Gentry, Insiders/5.80%, The TCW Group, Inc.,/5.50%, Robert M. Aiken, Wells Capital Management Incorporated/11.00%, Nicola Trombetti, James H. Dorton, Robert R. Sams, Paradigm Capital Management, Inc./6.90%, Steven T. Warshaw, Richard G. Fanelli, Michael E. Werner, Roderick R. Baty/2.30%, Dimensional Fund Advisors LP/7.80%, Ronald G. Morris (17 Owners included in Index)

Financial Data: Fiscal Year End:12/31 Latest Annual Data: 12/31/2006

Year	Sales	Net Income
2006	$330,325,000	$14,435,000
2005	$321,387,000	$15,012,000
2004	$304,089,000	$7,102,000

Curr. Assets:	$125,864,000	Curr. Liab.:	$74,869,000		
Plant, Equip.:	$156,447,000	Total Liab.:	$209,532,000	Indic. Yr. Divd.:	$0.320
Total Assets:	$342,701,000	Net Worth:	$133,169,000	Debt/ Equity:	0.7318

NNN 2002 Value Fund LLC

1551 N Tustin Ave., Ste 200, Santa Ana, CA, 92705; *PH:* 1-877-888-7348; *http://* www.1031nnn.com

General - Incorporation	VA	*Stock*- Price on:12/24/2007	NA
Employees	NA	Stock Exchange	NA
Auditor	Deloitte & Touche LLP	Ticker Symbol	NA
Stk Agt	American Stock Transfer & Trust Co.	Outstanding Shares	NA
Counsel	Hirschler Fleischer	E.P.S.	NA
DUNS No.	NA	Shareholders	NA

Business: The group's principle activities include purchasing, operating and subsequently sell all or a portion of up to three properties. The group operates from United States.

Primary SIC and add'l.: 6512

CIK No: 0001178132

Subsidiaries: NNN Netpark 25, LLC

Officers: Scott D. Peters/50/CEO, Kevin K. Hull/CEO, Pres. - NNN Capital Corp, Jeff Hanson/CEO, Pres. - Triple Net Properties Realty, Chief Investment Officer - NNN Realty Advisors, Inc Inc, Jessica Hu/Sr. Due Diligence Coordinator, Acquisitions, Elena-Joji Dia/Administrative Assist. - Finance, Doris Albay-Lacson/Portfolio Controller, Elizabeth Luciano/Administrative Assist., Julia Peterson/Transition Mgr. - Asset, Property Management, Kent Peters/Exec. VP - Real Estate, Michael Anaya/Regional Asset Mgr. - Asset, Property Management, Jean Skillman/Accounting Payable Clerk, Jenny Tran/Corporate Controller, Jessica Vega/Office Assist. - Finance, Jorge Montano/Staff Accountant - Finance, Elizabeth Monzon/Administrative Assist. - Office Administration (255 Officers included in Index)

Directors: Tony Thompson/Chmn., Founder, Talle A. Voorhies/60/Dir., COO, Sec., Mgr.

NNN 2003 Value Fund LLC

1551 N Tustin Ave., Ste 200, Santa Ana, CA, 92705; *PH:* 1-714-667-8252; *http://* www.1031nnn.com; *Email:* sylvial@1031NNN.com

General - Incorporation	DE	*Stock*- Price on:12/24/2007	NA
Employees	NA	Stock Exchange	NA
Auditor	Deloitte & Touche LLP	Ticker Symbol	NA
Stk Agt	NA	Outstanding Shares	NA
Counsel	Hirschler Fleischer	E.P.S.	NA
DUNS No.	NA	Shareholders	NA

Business: The group's principal activity is a diverse line of investment products as well as a full-range of services including asset and property management, brokerage, leasing, analysis and consultation. The groups is headquartered in Santa Ana, California and has a diverse portfolio of real estate throughout the western United States and Hawaii. The group can operate a stabilized asset for maximum profitability, identifies and acquires the sought-after, stabilized assets. The group keeps constant communication with investors, through informative, timely updates and accessible staff members.

Primary SIC and add'l.: 6512

CIK No: 0001260429
Officers: Rick Hutton/Exec. VP, Chief Investment Officer, CEO - Value Fund 2003, Alma Centeno/Portfolio Controller - Value Fund 2003, Jovita Perez/Property Accountant - Value Fund 2003, Lorraine Calvez/Accounting Payable Processor - Value Fund 2003, Melissa Campos-Amaya/Accounting Payable Processor - Value Fund 2003, Stephen Javier/CAM Accountant - Value Fund 2003, Francene La Point/43/Mgr.
Owners: Insiders

No Borders Inc

18301 Von Karman, Irvine, CA, 92612; PH: 1-949-251-0722; Fax: 1-866-329-3762;
http:// www.no-borders.com; Email: info@no-borders.com

General - Incorporation	NV	Stock - Price on:12/24/2007	$0.02
Employees	NA	Stock Exchange	OTC
Auditor	Mendoza Berger & Co., LLP	Ticker Symbol	NBDR
Stk Agt	Nevada Agency & Trust Company	Outstanding Shares	NA
Counsel	NA	E.P.S.	NA
DUNS No.	03-873-0479	Shareholders	NA

Business: The groups principle activity is to manufacture high-end toys for motorcyclists. The group operates from United States.
Primary SIC and add'l.: 7389 6211
CIK No: 0001091418
Subsidiaries: Harbour Front Holdings, Inc, Intercommunity Financing Corp.
Officers: Robert Michael Rosenfeld/Acting CEO, Raul Hinojosa/Chmn., Pres., Willie Rodriguez/VP - Sales, Jorge Hinojosa/VP - Business Development
Directors: Raul Hinojosa/Chmn., Pres.
Owners: RM ROSENFELD/4.10%, Insiders/10.90%, RAUL HINOJOSA-OJEDA/4.90%, Infospan Inc/50.20%, Guillermo Rodriguez/0.30%, Randy Gutierriz/3.00%, Jorge Hinojosa/1.30%

Financial Data: Fiscal Year End:12/31 Latest Annual Data: 12/31/2005
Year		Sales		Net Income
2005		NA		-$13,076,000
2004		$310,000		-$1,239,000
Curr. Assets:	$1,138,000	Curr. Liab.:	$765,000	
Plant, Equip.:	$663,000	Total Liab.:	$1,167,000	Indic. Yr. Divd.: NA
Total Assets:	$1,865,000	Net Worth:	$698,000	Debt/ Equity: NA

Nobel Learning Communities Inc

1615 W Chester Pike, Ste. 200, West Chester, PA, 19382; PH: 1-484-947-2000;
Fax: 1-484-947-2004; http:// www.nobellearning.com

General - Incorporation	DE	Stock - Price on:12/24/2007	$15
Employees	4,166	Stock Exchange	AMEX
Auditor	Grant Thornton, LLP	Ticker Symbol	NLP
Stk Agt	StockTrans, Inc.	Outstanding Shares	10,360,000
Counsel	NA	E.P.S.	$0.71
DUNS No.	11-261-9762	Shareholders	NA

Business: The group's principal activity is to provide private education and school management services for the pre-elementary through twelfth grade market. These schools provide summer camps and before-and-after school programs and are located in Arizona, California, Pennsylvania, New Jersey, Virginia, Florida, Maryland, North Carolina, South Carolina, Illinois, Nevada, Texas, Oregon and Washington. The schools operate under various names, including chesterbrook academy, merryhill school, evergreen academy, paladin academy and houston learning academy and saber academy. As of 33-Dec-2003 the group has 172 schools located in 14 states.
Primary SIC and add'l.: 8211
CIK No: 0000721237
Subsidiaries: Merryhill Schools Nevada, Inc., Nedi, Inc., Nobel School Management Services, Inc, Paladin Academy LLC, The Houston Learning Academy, Inc.
Officers: George H. Bernstein/CEO, Pres./$899,376.00, Lee G. Bohs/49/Sec., Sr. VP - Corporate Development/$470,068.00, Jeanne Marie Welsko/53/VP - Human Resources/$270,694.00, Osborne F. Abbey/62/Sr. VP - Education/$275,021.00, Patricia B. Miller/58/COO, Sr. VP/$433,912.00, Thomas Frank,/52/ Sr. VP, CFO/$478,760.00
Directors: Michael J. Rosenthal/64/Dir., Peter H. Havens/54/Dir., Ralph Smith/60/Dir., Richard J. Pinola/62/Dir., David L. Warnock/50/Dir., Therese Kreig Crane/58/Dir., Steven B. Fink/57/Dir., David Beale/47/Dir.
Owners: Peter H. Havens, Richard J. Pinola, Steven B. Fink/9.90%, David Beale, Camden Partners Strategic II, LLC/17.10%, Therese Kreig Crane, Insiders/30.90%, George H. Bernstein/1.40%, Midwood Capital Management LLC/5.90%, Insiders/30.90%, Lawrence J. Ellison/9.70%, Osborne F. Abbey, Patricia Miller, Jeanne Marie Welsko, David L. Warnock/17.30% (23 Owners included in Index)

Financial Data: Fiscal Year End:07/02 Latest Annual Data: 7/1/2006
Year		Sales		Net Income
2006		$168,329,000		$4,479,000
2005		$164,204,000		$2,516,000
2004		$155,158,000		-$6,081,000
Curr. Assets:	$18,598,000	Curr. Liab.:	$27,286,000	P/E Ratio: 25.42
Plant, Equip.:	$24,924,000	Total Liab.:	$51,590,000	Indic. Yr. Divd.: NA
Total Assets:	$85,865,000	Net Worth:	$34,275,000	Debt/ Equity: NA

Nobility Homes Inc

PO Box 1659, Ocala, FL, 34478; PH: 1-352-732-5157; Fax: 1-352-622-6766;
http:// www.nobilityhomes.com; Email: info@nobilityhomes.com

General - Incorporation	FL	Stock - Price on:12/24/2007	$20.56
Employees	208	Stock Exchange	NYSE
Auditor	Tedder, James, Worden & Assoc. P.A	Ticker Symbol	NOC
Stk Agt	Registrar & Transfer Co	Outstanding Shares	4,090,000
Counsel	Foley & Lardner LLP	E.P.S.	$1.00
DUNS No.	04-239-2761	Shareholders	NA

Business: The group's principle activities are to design, manufacture and sell manufactured homes. The manufactured homes are available in approximately 100 active models. The size of these homes range from 672 to 2,259 square feet and contain one to five bedrooms. The homes are primarily unfurnished dwellings ready for permanent occupancy. These manufactured homes are sold through a network of retail sales centers in Florida and on a wholesale basis to manufactured home dealers and home parks. Trade names for the homes include kingswood, richwood, springwood, tropic isle, regency manor and tropic manor. Prestige home centers, inc (prestige), a wholly owned subsidiary, of the group, operates 17 retail centers in north and central Florida. Prestige provides mortgage brokerage services, credit life, extended warranty coverage and property and casualty insurance to its customers, through its wholly owned subsidiary, mountain financial, inc. The group's total revenue for year 2007 was 40.62 millions of USD.
Primary SIC and add'l.: 2451
CIK No: 0000072205
Subsidiaries: Majestic Homes, Inc., Mountain Financial, Inc., Prestige Home Centers, Inc.
Officers: Terry E. Trexler/68/Chmn., CEO, Pres., Thomas W. Trexler/44/Dir., CFO, Exec. VP, Jean Etheredge/62/Sec., Lynn J. Cramer/62/Treasurer, Principal Accounting Officer
Directors: Terry E. Trexler/68/Chmn., CEO, Pres., Thomas W. Trexler/44/Dir., CFO, Exec. VP, Richard C. Barberie/69/Dir., Robert P. Holliday/69/Dir., Robert P. Saltsman/55/Dir.
Owners: Gabelli Group/6.87%, Robert P. Holliday, Terry E. Trexler Irrevocable Trust/53.42%, Richard C. Barberie, Thomas W. Trexler/10.04%, Robert P. Saltsman, Terry E. Trexler, Insiders/11.47%

Financial Data: Fiscal Year End:11/05 Latest Annual Data: 11/4/2006
Year		Sales		Net Income
2006		$59,958,000		$6,470,000
2005		$56,711,000		$6,172,000
2004		$50,019,000		$4,633,000
Curr. Assets:	$24,933,000	Curr. Liab.:	$8,449,000	P/E Ratio: 17.13
Plant, Equip.:	$3,265,000	Total Liab.:	$8,602,000	Indic. Yr. Divd.: $0.500
Total Assets:	$39,975,000	Net Worth:	$31,374,000	Debt/ Equity: NA

Noble Corp

13135 S Dairy Ashford, Ste. 800, Sugar Land, TX, 77478; PH: 1-281-276-6100;
Fax: 1-281-491-2092; http:// www.noblecorp.com

General - Incorporation	Cayman Islands	Stock - Price on:12/24/2007	$96.07
Employees	6,000	Stock Exchange	NYSE
Auditor	PricewaterhouseCoopers LLP	Ticker Symbol	NE
Stk Agt	Bank One Trust Company, N.A.	Outstanding Shares	134,020,000
Counsel	NA	E.P.S.	$6.99
DUNS No.	NA	Shareholders	NA

Business: The group's principal activities are to provide diversified services for the oil and gas industry. The contract drilling services are performed with a fleet of 57 offshore drilling units located in markets worldwide. The group also provides technologically advanced drilling-related products and services, labor contract drilling services, well site and project management services and engineering services. The operations are conducted in the United States, Middle East, U.S. Gulf of Mexico, Mexico, the north sea, Brazil, west Africa, India, the Mediterranean Sea and Canada.
Primary SIC and add'l.: 8711 1381
CIK No: 0001169055
Subsidiaries: 372733 Alberta Inc., Arktik Drilling Limited, Inc., Bawden Drilling Inc., Bawden Drilling International Ltd., International Directional Services Ltd., Maregem AS, Maurer Technology Incorporated, Noble (Gulf of Mexico) Inc., Noble (Middle East) Limited, Noble Asset (U.K.) Limited, Noble Asset Company Limited, Noble Asset Mexico LLC, Noble Bill Jennings LLC, Noble Brasil Investimentos e Participacoes Ltda., Noble Campeche Limited 85 Subsidiaries included in the Index
Officers: William A. Sears/Chmn., CEO, Pres., Julie J. Robertson/Exec. VP, Corp. Sec./$2,053,907.00, Robert D. Campbell/Sr. VP, General Counsel/$1,179,942.00, Thomas L. Mitchell/Sr. VP, CFO, Treasurer, Controller/$351,718.00, David W. Williams/COO, Sr. VP
Directors: William A. Sears/Chmn., CEO, Pres., James C. Day/64/Chmn., Lawrence J. Chazen/Dir., Jack E. Little/Dir., Marc E. Leland/Dir., Mark A. Jackson/Dir., Mary P. Ricciardello/Dir., Luke R. Corbett/Dir., Michael A. Cawley/Dir., Julie H. Edwards/Dir.
Owners: Mary P. Ricciardello, Bruce W. Busmire, Mark A. Jackson/0.20%, Robert D. Campbell/0.20%, Luke R. Corbett, Massachusetts Financial Services Company/5.20%, Marc E. Leland, Julie H. Edwards, FMR Corp./15.00%, Lawrence J. Chazen, Thomas L. Mitchell, Insiders/2.20%, William A. Sears/0.10%, James C. Day/1.20%, Michael A. Cawley/0.70% (17 Owners included in Index)

Financial Data: Fiscal Year End:12/31 Latest Annual Data: 12/31/2006
Year		Sales		Net Income
2006		$2,100,239,000		$731,866,000
2005		$1,382,137,000		$296,696,000
2004		$1,066,231,000		$146,086,000
Curr. Assets:	$569,980,000	Curr. Liab.:	$426,260,000	P/E Ratio: 15.67
Plant, Equip.:	$3,858,393,000	Total Liab.:	$1,364,269,000	Indic. Yr. Divd.: $0.160
Total Assets:	$4,585,914,000	Net Worth:	$3,228,993,000	Debt/ Equity: 0.2270

Noble Energy Inc

100 Glenborough Dr., Ste. 100, Houston, TX, 77067; PH: 1-281-872-3100; Fax: 1-281-872-3111;
http:// www.nobleenergyinc.com; Email: info@nobleenergyinc.com

General - Incorporation	DE	Stock - Price on:12/24/2007	$64.51
Employees	1,243	Stock Exchange	NYSE
Auditor	KPMG LLP	Ticker Symbol	NA
Stk Agt	American Stock Transfer & Trust Co.	Outstanding Shares	170,860,000
Counsel	NA	E.P.S.	$4.65
DUNS No.	05-287-7586	Shareholders	NA

Business: The groups principle activities include exploration, development, production and marketing of crude oil and natural gas. The group operates from United States.
Primary SIC and add'l.: 4924 1311
CIK No: 0000072207
Subsidiaries: Alba Associates LLC, Alba Plant LLC, AMPCO Marketing, LLC, AMPCO Services, LLC, Atlantic Methanol Associates LLC, Atlantic Methanol Capital Company, Atlantic Methanol Production Company LLC, Brabant Oil Limited, EDC (Denmark) Inc., Edc (uk) Limited, EDC Australia Ltd., EDC Ecuador Ltd., EDC Ireland, EDC Portugal Ltd., Elysium Energy, LLC 60 Subsidiaries included in the Index
Officers: Charles D. Davidson/55/Chmn., CEO, Pres./$6,718,751.00, David L. Stover/COO, Exec. VP/$2,027,745.00, Arnold J. Johnson/VP, General Counsel, Sec., Jay Smith/Sr. Mgr. - Accounting, Natural Gas Marketing, Daryl Landry/Sr. Mgr. - Accounting, Natural Gas Marketing, Elisa

Donoho/Dir. - International Marketing, Crude Oil Marketing, Buddy Brinkley/Producer Services Analyst, Producer Services, Jim Heis/Dir. - Corporate Risk Management, Joe Lacambra/Risk Analyst, Risk Management, Tammy Stevens/Assoc. Contract Analyst, Contract Administration, Archie Wright/Mgr. - Accounting, Accounting, Clara Morales/Accountant III - Accounting, Mary Mayo/Accountant II - Accounting, Dee Dang/Accountant I - Accounting, Greg Lannin/Sr. Gas Scheduler, Natural Gas Operations *(31 Officers included in Index)*

Directors: Charles D. Davidson/55/Chmn., CEO, Pres., Jeffrey L. Berenson/55/Dir., Thomas J. Edelman/55/Dir., Kirby L. Hedrick/52/Dir., Bruce A. Smith/Dir., William T. Van Kleef/Dir., Edward F. Cox/58/Dir., Michael A. Cawley/Dir.

Owners: Chris Tong/0.05%, Thomas J. Edelman/1.92%, Insiders/2.94%, William T. Van Kleef, Michael A. Cawley/0.03%, Kirby L. Hedrick/0.03%, Susan M. Cunningham/0.12%, Bruce A. Smith/0.04%, Edward F. Cox/0.02%, David L. Stover/0.07%, Charles D. Davidson/0.52%, Jeffrey L. Berenson/0.03%, Alan R. Bullington/0.08%

Financial Data: *Fiscal Year End:* 12/31 *Latest Annual Data:* 12/31/2006

Year	Sales	Net Income
2006	$2,940,082,000	$678,428,000
2005	$2,186,723,000	$645,720,000
2004	$1,351,176,000	$328,710,000

Curr. Assets:	$1,068,546,000	*Curr. Liab.:*	$1,184,262,000	*P/E Ratio:*	17.20
Plant, Equip.:	$7,170,757,000	*Total Liab.:*	$5,474,808,000	*Indic. Yr. Divd.:*	$0.480
Total Assets:	$9,588,625,000	*Net Worth:*	$4,113,817,000	*Debt/ Equity:*	NA

Noble International Ltd

840 W Long Lake Rd., Ste. 601, Troy, MI, 48098; *PH:* 1-248-519-0700; *Fax:* 1-248-519-0701; *http://* www.nobleintl.com

General - Incorporation	DE	**Stock** - Price on:12/24/2007	$20.2
Employees	2,100	Stock Exchange	NDQ
Auditor	Deloitte & Touche LLP	Ticker Symbol	NOBL
Stk Agt	American Stock Transfer & Trust Co.	Outstanding Shares	14,140,000
Counsel	Oppenheimer Wolff & Donnelly	E.P.S.	-$0.28
DUNS No.	93-339-8075	Shareholders	NA

Business: The group's principal activities are to manufacture and provide services to the automobile industry. The operations of the group are carried out in two segments: automotive and distribution. Automotive segment provides laser welding and cutting services for automotive components. Distribution segment distributes tooling components including adjustable handles, hand wheels, plastic knobs, levers, handles and hydraulic clamps to non-automotive customers. The customers of the group include general motors, daimlerchrysler ag, ford motor company, toyota motor corporation, American honda motor company inc and nissian north American inc. The operations of the group are carried out in the United States and Canada. On 21-Mar-2003, the group completed the sale of its logistics business. On 08-Aug-2003, it acquired Michigan steel processing, inc and on 21-Jan-2004 it acquired laser welding international inc.

Primary SIC and add'l.: 7389 3549 7532 5013 3714

CIK No: 0001034258

Subsidiaries: Central Transportation& Delivery, Inc., NMP Holding de Mxico, S. de R.L. de C.V., Noble Advanced Technologies, Inc., Noble Components& Systems, Inc., Noble Construction Equipment, Inc., Noble Land Holdings, Inc., Noble Logistic Services, Inc., Noble Manufacturing Group, Inc., Noble Metal Processing Australia Pty. Ltd., Noble Metal Processing Kentucky, GP, Noble Metal Processing Ohio, LLC, Noble Metal Processing Canada, Inc., Noble Metal Processing, Inc., Noble Silao de Mxico, S. de R.L. de C.V.+, Noble Summit Metal Processing de Mxico, S. de R.L. de C.V.++ 17 Subsidiaries included in the Index

Officers: Thomas L. Saeli/CEO, Greg Salchow/Dir. - Investor Relations, Michael C. Azar/VP - Administration, Sec., David J. Fallon/CFO, Andrew J. Tavi/VP, General Counsel, Scott Kehoe/Treasurer, Charlie Palms/Business Unit Dir.

Directors: Robert J. Skandalaris/Chmn.

Owners: Thomas L. Saeli, Munder Capital Management/7.00%, Mark T. Behrman, Robert J. Skandalaris/15.50%, Christopher L. Morin, David J. Fallon, Larry R. Wendling, Insiders/17.10%, Wellington Management Company, LLP/7.50%, Jay J. Hansen, Michael C. Azar, Fred L. Hubacker, St. Denis J. Villere& Company, L.L.C/20.20%, Van E. Conway, Glacier Bay Capital LLC/5.40%

Financial Data: *Fiscal Year End:* 12/31 *Latest Annual Data:* 12/31/2006

Year	Sales	Net Income
2006	$441,372,000	$7,779,000
2005	$363,820,000	$5,093,000
2004	$332,611,000	$15,361,000

Curr. Assets:	$166,114,000	*Curr. Liab.:*	$157,038,000	*P/E Ratio:*	155.39
Plant, Equip.:	$109,648,000	*Total Liab.:*	$295,242,000	*Indic. Yr. Divd.:*	$0.320
Total Assets:	$387,148,000	*Net Worth:*	$87,266,000	*Debt/ Equity:*	1.4407

Noble Roman's Inc

1 Virginia Ave., Ste. 800, Indianapolis, IN, 46204; *PH:* 1-317-634-3377; *Fax:* 1-317-636-3207; *http://* www.nobleromans.com; *Email:* franchise@nobleromans.com

General - Incorporation	IN	**Stock** - Price on:12/24/2007	$7.2
Employees	40	Stock Exchange	OTC
Auditor	Larry E. Nunn & Assoc. LLC	Ticker Symbol	NROM
Stk Agt	Computershare Investor Services LLC	Outstanding Shares	16,770,000
Counsel	NA	E.P.S.	$0.13
DUNS No.	06-281-2243	Shareholders	NA

Business: The group's principle activity is to operate casual dining Italian pizza restaurants.The group operates from United States.

Primary SIC and add'l.: 6794 5812

CIK No: 0000709005

Subsidiaries: GNR, Inc., LPS, Inc., N.R. East, Inc., N.R. Realty, Inc., Pizzaco, Inc.

Owners: Special Situations Fund III QP, L.P./7.70%, Troy Branson, Zyville E. Lewis/6.80%, Scott A. Mobley/8.30%, Robert P. Stiller/6.00%, James W. Lewis/10.20%, Mitchell Grunat, Paul W. Mobley/20.70%, Insiders/31.00%, Geovest Capital Partners, L.P./7.00%, Insiders/31.00%, Douglas H. Coape-Arnold/1.50%

Financial Data: *Fiscal Year End:* 12/31 *Latest Annual Data:* 12/31/2006

Year	Sales	Net Income
2006	$9,487,000	$1,895,000
2005	$8,431,000	$2,851,000
2004	$7,912,000	$935,000

Curr. Assets:	$5,319,000	*Curr. Liab.:*	$1,896,000	*P/E Ratio:*	72.00
Plant, Equip.:	$636,000	*Total Liab.:*	$7,521,000	*Indic. Yr. Divd.:*	NA
Total Assets:	$16,138,000	*Net Worth:*	$8,617,000	*Debt/ Equity:*	NA

NOCOPI Technologies Inc

9C Portland Rd., West Conshohocken, PA, 19428; *PH:* 1-610-834-9600; *Fax:* 1-610-834-7777; *http://* www.nocopi.com; *Email:* info@nocopi.com

General - Incorporation	MD	**Stock** - Price on:12/24/2007	$0.58
Employees	3	Stock Exchange	OTC
Auditor	Morison Cogen LLP	Ticker Symbol	NNUP
Stk Agt	American Stock Transfer & Trust Co.	Outstanding Shares	51,790,000
Counsel	NA	E.P.S.	$0.00
DUNS No.	62-745-9449	Shareholders	NA

Business: The group's principal activities are the development and distribution of document security products and the licensing of patented authentication technologies. Anti-counterfeiting and anti-diversion technologies have the ability to print invisibly on certain areas of a document. This technology is marketed under the trademark copimark(tm). The company's rub & reveal(R) system permits the invisible printing of an authenticating symbol or code that can be revealed by rubbing a fingernail over the printed area. Document security products include a line of burgundy colored papers that deter photocopying and transmission by facsimile. It offers user defined, pre-printed forms selective nocopi(tm), several inks that impede photocopying by color copiers colorbloc(r). In addition, it distributes pantograph security paper copi-alert. In 2003, the group developed removable dyes under the name rub-n-color. Products of the group are marketed in the United States and Europe.

Primary SIC and add'l.: 2672 2899

CIK No: 0000888981

Officers: Michael A. Feinstein/61/Chmn., CEO, Rudolph A. Lutterschmidt/61/CFO, VP, Chief Accounting Officer

Directors: Michael A. Feinstein/61/Chmn., CEO, Herman M. Gerwitz/54/Dir., Stanley G. Hart/47/Dir., Richard Levitt/51/Dir., Philip B. White/69/Dir.

Owners: Westvaco Brand Security, Inc./7.30%, Michael A. Feinstein/6.40%, Insiders/9.80%, Richard Levitt/1.20%, Philip B. White, Philip N. Hudson/6.90%, Stanley G. Hart, Herman Gerwitz, Ross. L Campbell/6.10%

Financial Data: *Fiscal Year End:* 12/31 *Latest Annual Data:* 12/31/2006

Year	Sales	Net Income
2006	$767,000	-$190,000
2005	$528,000	-$216,000
2004	$628,000	-$339,000

Curr. Assets:	$278,000	*Curr. Liab.:*	$811,000		
Plant, Equip.:	$24,000	*Total Liab.:*	$811,000	*Indic. Yr. Divd.:*	NA
Total Assets:	$302,000	*Net Worth:*	-$509,000	*Debt/ Equity:*	NA

NoFire Technologies Inc

21 Industrial Ave., Upper Saddle River, NJ, 07458; *PH:* 1-201-818-1616; *Fax:* 1-201-818-8775; *http://* www.nofiretechnologies.com; *Email:* nofire@nofire.net

General - Incorporation	DE	**Stock** - Price on:12/24/2007	$0.9
Employees	6	Stock Exchange	OTC
Auditor	Sherb & Co., LLP	Ticker Symbol	NFTI
Stk Agt	Continental Stock Transfer & Trust Co	Outstanding Shares	37,930,000
Counsel	NA	E.P.S.	NA
DUNS No.	NA	Shareholders	NA

Business: The groups principle activities include developing, manufacturing and marketing fire retardant products and providing related consulting services. The group operates from the United States. The group's quarterly revenue for Aug '07 was 0.45 millions of USD.

Primary SIC and add'l.: 2851

CIK No: 0000823070

Owners: Iroquois Capital Management LLC, Gerald H. Litwin, Lavin Holdings, LLC, Insiders, Bernard J. Koster, Alphonso Margino, Carole Salkind, Samuel Gottfried, John Cavanna, Sam Oolie

Curr. Assets:	$90,000	*Curr. Liab.:*	$4,785,000		
Plant, Equip.:	$1,000	*Total Liab.:*	$4,785,000	*Indic. Yr. Divd.:*	NA
Total Assets:	$128,000	*Net Worth:*	-$4,658,000	*Debt/ Equity:*	NA

Nokia Corp

6000 Connection Dr., Irving, TX, 75039; *PH:* 1-972-894-5000; *Fax:* 1-972-894-5106; *http://* www.nokia.com

General - Incorporation	Finland	**Stock** - Price on:12/24/2007	$28
Employees	68,483	Stock Exchange	NYSE
Auditor	PricewaterhouseCoopers LLP	Ticker Symbol	NOV
Stk Agt	Citibank N.A	Outstanding Shares	3,920,000,000
Counsel	NA	E.P.S.	$2.47
DUNS No.	36-840-0438	Shareholders	NA

Business: The group's principal activity is the supply of mobile phones, broadband, ip network infrastructure and related services. It also develops mobile Internet applications and solutions for operators and Internet service providers. The group operates through the following divisions: nokia mobile phones: manufacture of mobile phones; nokia network: provide Internet and multimedia mobile connection; nokia ventures organization: development of new ideas for the home environment and the corporate world. It is involved in technological research through cooperation with business groups, universities, research institutes and other corporations.

Primary SIC and add'l.: 3651 3661 3663

CIK No: 0000924613

Subsidiaries: Nokia Capitel Telecommunications Ltd, Nokia do Brazil Technologia Ltda, Nokia Finance International B.V., Nokia GmbH, Nokia Inc., Nokia India Ltd., Nokia Komrom Kft, Nokia TMC Limited, Nokia UK Limited

Officers: Olli-Pekka Kallasvuo/Dir., CEO, Pres., Simon Beresford-Wylie/50/CEO - Nokia Siemens Networks, Niklas Savander/Exec. VP - Technology Platforms, Richard A. Simonson/50/CFO, Exec. VP, Per Karlsson/53/Dir., Independent Corporate Advisor, Timo Ihamuotila/Exec. VP - Sales, Portfolio Management, Mobile Phones, Robert Andersson/48/Exec. VP - Customer, Marketing Operations, Tero Ojanpera/42/CTO, Exec. VP, Veli Sundback/62/Exec. VP -

Corporate Relations, Responsibility, Alexander Von Nandelstadh/Dir. - Investor Relations, Kenneth Lampinen/Mgr. - Investor Relations, Finland, Matt Shimao/Mgr. - Investor Relations, Anja Korhonen/Sr. VP, Corporate Controller, Kaarina Stahlberg/VP, Assist. General Counsel, Kumiko Koyama/Mgr. - Investor Relations *(20 Officers included in Index)*

Directors: Olli-Pekka Kallasvuo/Dir., CEO, Pres., Dame Marjorie Scardino/61/Vice Chmn., Jorma Ollila/58/Chmn., Paul J. Collins/72/Vice Chmn., Mary T. McDowell/44/Exec. VP, GM - Enterprise Solutions, Henning Kagermann/Dir., Daniel R. Hesse/55/Dir., Lalita D. Gupte/Dir., Keijo Suila/Dir., Vesa Vainio/66/Dir., Bengt Holmstrom/59/Dir., Georg Ehrnrooth/68/Dir., Per Karlsson/53/Dir., Independent Corporate Advisor

Financial Data: *Fiscal Year End:*12/31 *Latest Annual Data:* 12/31/2006

Year	Sales	Net Income
2006	$54,292,056,000	$5,644,283,000
2005	$40,495,820,000	$4,242,521,000
2004	$39,931,895,000	$4,561,189,000
Curr. Assets:	$24,539,096,000 **Curr. Liab.:**	$13,415,568,000
Plant, Equip.:	$1,980,450,000 **Total Liab.:**	$14,059,875,000 **Indic. Yr. Divd.:** $0.480
Total Assets:	$30,051,348,000 **Net Worth:**	$15,991,474,000 **Debt/ Equity:** NA

Nomura Holdings Inc

1-9-1, Nihonbashi, Chuo-ku, Tokyo, 8011; *PH:* 81 3-5255-1000; *http://* www.nomuraholdings.com

General - Incorporation	Japan	Stock- Price on:12/24/2007	$20.24
Employees	14,668	Stock Exchange	NYSE
Auditor	Ernst & Young Shinnihon	Ticker Symbol	NMR
Stk Agt	Nomura Bank (Luxembourg) S.A.	Outstanding Shares	1,910,000,000
Counsel	NA	E.P.S.	$0.85
DUNS No.	NA	Shareholders	NA

Business: The group's principal activity is the provision of investment and financing services with securities as the core business. The activities include securities brokerage, dealing, underwriting, distribution, assets management, advisory and consulting, financing and related services for diversified types of customers worldwide. The group has three principal business segments: domestic retail: provides investment consultation services to retail customers; global wholesale: deals with fixed income and equity trading, investment banking and merchant banking in and outside Japan; asset management: involved in development and management of investment trusts and advisory services.

Primary SIC and add'l.: 6282 6021 6211 6719

CIK No: 0001163653

Subsidiaries: Banque Nomura France, Joinvest Securities Co., Ltd., Nomura Asia Holding N.V., Nomura Asset Capital Corporation, Nomura Asset Management Co., Ltd., Nomura Australia Limited, Nomura Babcock& Brown Co., Ltd., Nomura Bank (Deutschland) GmbH, Nomura Bank (Luxembourg) S.A., Nomura Bank (Switzerland) Ltd., Nomura Bank International plc, Nomura Business Services Co., Ltd., Nomura Capital Investment Co., Ltd., Nomura Corporate Research and Asset Management Inc., Nomura Derivative Products, Inc. 41 Subsidiaries included in the Index

Officers: Nobuyuki Koga/58/Dir., CEO, Pres., Shogo Sakaguchi/Exec. MD, Kenichi Watanabe/Deputy Pres. - Retail Business Unit, Nomura Securities Co, Ltd, Tetsu Ozaki/Head - Group Corporate Strategy, Sr. MD, Hiroshi Tanaka/Dir., Exec. MD - Nomura Securities Co, Ltd, Hitoshi Tada/Exec. VP - Marketing Division, Nomura Securities Co, Ltd, Yasuo Yoshihara/Sr. MD - Human Resources, Nomura Securities Co, Ltd, Takashi Yanagiya/Investment Banking Unit, Nomura Securities Co, Ltd, Shigesuke Kashiwagi/Head - Regional Management, Americas, Yusuke Yamada/Exec. MD - Operations, Infrastructure Services, Nomura Securities Co, Ltd, Hideyuki Takahashi/Head - Internal Audit, Exec. MD, Manabu Matsumoto/Exec. VP - Nomura Securities Co, Ltd, Akihito Watanabe/Head - Group Human Resources Development, Sr. MD, Hiroshi Toda/57/Dir., COO, International Operations Officer, Yugo Ishida/Head - Regional Management, Europe *(25 Officers included in Index)*

Directors: Nobuyuki Koga/58/Dir., CEO, Pres., Junichi Ujiie/63/Chmn., Hiroshi Toda/57/Dir., COO, International Operations Officer, Kazutoshi Inano/Dir., Co - COO, Group Compliance Officer, Masaharu Shibata/71/Dir., Masanori Itatani/55/Dir., Hideaki Kubori/64/Dir., Hiroshi Tanaka/Dir., Exec. MD - Nomura Securities Co, Ltd, Fumihide Nomura/74/Dir., Yukio Suzuki/58/Dir., Shinichiro Watanabe/Dir. - Nomura Securities Co, Ltd, Kazuhiro Okada/Dir. - Nomura Securities Co, Ltd, Haruo Tsuji/76/Dir., Koji Tajika/72/Dir.

Owners: Kazutoshi Inano, Hiroshi Toda, Masafumi Nakada, Tetsu Ozaki, Yukio Suzuki, Masanori Itatani, Hideyuki Takahashi, Akihito Watanabe, Masaharu Shibata, Akihiko Nakamura, Japan Trustee Services Bank, Ltd./5.40%, Fumihide Nomura, Yugo Ishida, Junichi Ujiie, Noriaki Nagai *(21 Owners included in Index)*

Financial Data: *Fiscal Year End:*03/31 *Latest Annual Data:* 03/31/2007

Year	Sales	Net Income
2007	$17,601,000,000	$1,496,000,000
2006	$15,261,000,000	$2,590,000,000
2005	$10,504,000,000	$884,000,000
Curr. Assets:	$83,712,000,000 **Curr. Liab.:**	$159,813,000,000
Plant, Equip.:	$2,817,000,000 **Total Liab.:**	$280,582,000,000 **Indic. Yr. Divd.:** $0.260
Total Assets:	$298,145,000,000 **Net Worth:**	$17,563,000,000 **Debt/ Equity:** NA

Non-Invasive Monitoring Systems Inc

1666 Kennedy Causeway, Ste. 308, North Bay Village, FL, 33141; *PH:* 1-305-861-0075; *http://* www.nims-inc.com; *Email:* info@nims-inc.com

General - Incorporation	FL	Stock - Price on:12/24/2007	$1.14
Employees	5	Stock Exchange	OTC
Auditor	Eisner LLP	Ticker Symbol	NIMU
Stk Agt	American Stock Transfer & Trust Co.	Outstanding Shares	67,050,000
Counsel	NA	E.P.S.	-$0.02
DUNS No.	13-738-6397	Shareholders	NA

Business: The group's principal activities are to research, develop, manufacture and market non-invasive, therapeutic, periodic acceleration, cardiorespiratory device. In addition, the group has developed computer assisted, non-invasive monitoring devices and related software designed to detect abnormal respiratory, cardiac and other medical conditions from sensors placed externally on the body's surface. These devices provide diagnostic information regarding cardiorespiratory and sleep disorders in infants, children and adults. Further, alarms are sounded for adverse cardiac and respiratory events in critically ill patients.

Primary SIC and add'l.: 3845 8731

CIK No: 0000720762

Officers: Gary W. MacLeod/Dir., CEO, Morton J. Robinson/75/Dir., Sec.

Directors: Gary W. MacLeod/Dir., CEO, Marvin A. Sackner/Chmn., Founder, Taffy Gould/Vice Chmn., Morton J. Robinson/75/Dir., Sec., Gerard Kaiser/Dir., Leila Kight/Dir., John G. Clawson/Dir.

Owners: Insiders/44.50%, Marvin A. Sackner/59.40%, Taffy Gould/2.10%, Marvin A. Sackner/19.20%, Gary Macleod/2.20%, Morton J. Robinson/1.70%, Gerard Kaiser, Frost Gamma Investment Trust/17.00%, Gerard Kaiser, Frost Gamma Investment Trust/5.30%, Leila Kight/1.60%, Morton J. Robinson/1.30%, John G. Clawson, Insiders/66.50%

Financial Data: *Fiscal Year End:*07/31 *Latest Annual Data:* 7/31/2006

Year	Sales	Net Income
2006	$341,000	-$613,000
2005	$462,000	-$397,000
2004	$852,000	$26,000
Curr. Assets:	$1,635,000 **Curr. Liab.:**	$742,000
Plant, Equip.:	$20,000 **Total Liab.:**	$744,000 **Indic. Yr. Divd.:** NA
Total Assets:	$1,655,000 **Net Worth:**	$910,000 **Debt/ Equity:** NA

NorAm Capital Holdings Inc

Formerly: Harrell Hospitality Group Inc
PO Box 9250, Dallas, TX, 75209; *PH:* 1-888-886-6726; *http://* www.harrellhospitality.com

General - Incorporation	DE	Stock- Price on:12/24/2007	NA
Employees	147	Stock Exchange	NA
Auditor	Whitley Penn	Ticker Symbol	NA
Stk Agt	Computershare Investor Services	Outstanding Shares	NA
Counsel	NA	E.P.S.	-$0.09
DUNS No.	00-117-6528	Shareholders	NA

Business: The group's principal activity is to provide hotel management services and investing in hotels. The group manages nationally recognized franchises, including sheraton, holiday inn and ramada. The customers of the group include biltmore hotel and suites and rancho santa barbara marriott. The company has also been approved by hilton hotels to operate its hilton garden inn products.

Primary SIC and add'l.: 8741 8742

CIK No: 0000045694

Subsidiaries: Hotel Management Group - California, Inc

Officers: Paul L. Barham/54/Dir., CEO, Jonathan Tripp/58/Dir., VP, Controller

Directors: Paul L. Barham/54/Dir., CEO, Clive Russell/67/Dir., Jonathan Tripp/58/Dir., VP, Controller

Owners: Insiders/88.00%, Global Trek Property Holdings, L.P./44.00%, Square Rock Ltd. Pension Plan/44.00%

Financial Data: *Fiscal Year End:*09/30 *Latest Annual Data:* 09/30/2006

Year	Sales	Net Income
2006	NA	$1,964,000
2005	$5,100,000	-$23,000
2004	$5,074,000	-$747,000
Curr. Assets:	$693,000 **Curr. Liab.:**	$19,000
Plant, Equip.:	NA **Total Liab.:**	$19,000 **Indic. Yr. Divd.:** NA
Total Assets:	$1,720,000 **Net Worth:**	$1,701,000 **Debt/ Equity:** NA

Norbord Inc

1 Toronto St., Ste. 600
, Toronto, M5C 2W4 ; *PH:* 1-416-365-0705; *http://* www.norbord.com; *Email:* info@norbord.com

General - Incorporation	Canada	Stock- Price on:12/24/2007	$8.27
Employees	NA	Stock Exchange	OTC
Auditor	KPMG LLP	Ticker Symbol	NBDFF
Stk Agt	Mellon Trust Co	Outstanding Shares	NA
Counsel	NA	E.P.S.	NA
DUNS No.	NA	Shareholders	NA

Business: The group's principle activity is to manufactures panel boards, pulp, recycled paper and high quality coated and uncoated paper. The company has its operations in Canada, the United States and the United Kingdom. The group's quarterly revenue for october 2007 was 292.00 millions of USD.

Primary SIC and add'l.: 2621 2672 2421 2611 2411

CIK No: 0000877365

Subsidiaries: Norbord Alabama Inc, Norbord Georgia Inc, Norbord Industries Inc, Norbord Industries, Inc, Norbord Limited, Norbord Minnesota, Norbord Mississippi, Inc, Norbord NV, Norbord South Carolina Inc, Norbord Texas LP

Officers: Barrie J. Shineton/Dir., CEO, Pres., Karl Morris/Sr. VP - European Operations, Peter Wijnbergen/Sr. VP - Marketing, Sales, Logistics, Robert Kinnear/Sr. VP - Corporate Services, Steve Roebuck/Dir. - Environment, Health, Safety, Europe, Lynne C. Taylor/Assist. Corp. Sec., Anita Veel/Dir. - Corporate Affairs, John C. Tremayne/CFO, Exec. VP, Michael Botha/VP, Controller, Robin Lampard/VP, Treasurer, Peter Quosai/Mgr. - Environment Health, Safety, North America

Directors: Barrie J. Shineton/Dir., CEO, Pres., Robert J. Harding/Chmn., Margot Northey/Dir., Dominic Gammiero/Dir., Jack L. Cockwell/Dir., Dian Cohen/Dir., Pierre Dupuis/Dir., Gordon E. Forward/Dir., Neville W. Kirchmann/Dir.

Owners: GORDON E. FORWARD, JACK L. COCKWELL, Robert Kinnear, PIERRE DUPUIS, MARGOT NORTHEY, ROBERT J. HARDING, BARRIE J. SHINETON, DOMINIC GAMMIERO, DIAN COHEN, Peter Wijnbergen, John Tremayne

Financial Data: *Fiscal Year End:*12/31 *Latest Annual Data:* 12/31/2006

Year	Sales	Net Income
2006	$247,000,000	$97,000,000
2005	$495,000,000	$248,000,000
2004	$1,486,000,000	$331,000,000
Curr. Assets:	$284,000,000 **Curr. Liab.:**	$228,000,000
Plant, Equip.:	$1,008,000,000 **Total Liab.:**	$865,000,000 **Indic. Yr. Divd.:** NA
Total Assets:	$1,299,000,000 **Net Worth:**	$434,000,000 **Debt/ Equity:** NA

NorCal Community Bancorp CA

1701 Harbor Bay Pkwy.., Ste. 201, Alameda, CA, 94502; *PH:* 1-510-748-8450; *Fax:* 1-510-814-4988; *http://* www.bankofalameda.com; *Email:* ir@norcalcommunitybancorp.com

General		Stock	
Incorporation		Price on:12/24/2007	$16
Employees	NA	Stock Exchange	OTC
Auditor	NA	Ticker Symbol	NCLC
Stk Agt	U.S. Stock Transfer Corp	Outstanding Shares	2,980,000
Counsel	NA	E.P.S.	NA
DUNS No.	NA	Shareholders	NA

Business: The group's principle activity is to provide banking services.The group's services include personal, money market and savings accounts. The group operates from United States.

Primary SIC and add'l.: 6022

CIK No:

Officers: Stephen G. Andrews/Dir., CEO, Pres., Grant Kwok/Assist. VP, Relationship Mgr., Ana Long/Assist. VP - Consumer Loans, Cynthia Torres/VP - Cash Management Services, Ron Barrett/VP, SBA Mgr., Patricia Young/Sr. VP, Commercial Banking Team Leader, Lorna Goforth/Assist. VP, Branch Service Mgr. - Towne Centre, George Nishi/VP - Commercial Lending, Kathy Shaughnessy/Assist. VP, Personal Banking Officer, Troy P. Williams/Exec. VP, COO - Bank, Alameda, Jeanette E. Reynolds/Exec. VP, CFO, Corp. Sec., Michael K. Roberts/CIO, Exec. VP, Faye Garcia/Human Resources Mgr. - Bank, Alameda, Blake Brydon/VP - Mortgage Services, Wendell Coval/VP, Relationship Mgr. *(23 Officers included in Index)*

Directors: Stephen G. Andrews/Dir., CEO, Pres., James B. Davis/Chmn., Eric C. Cross/Dir., Robert K. Dahl/Dir., Michael G. Gorman/Dir., James L. McKenna/Dir., David S. Oliver/Dir., Joel Vuylsteke/Dir.

Nordic American Tanker Shipping Ltd

LOM Building, 27 Reid St., Hamilton; ***PH:*** 1-441-2927202; ***Fax:*** 1-441-2925962; ***http://*** www.nat.bm; ***Email:*** ir@nat.bm

General		Stock	
Incorporation	Islands Of Bermuda	Price on:12/24/2007	$39.5
Employees	1	Stock Exchange	NDQ
Auditor	Deloitte Statsautoriseret	Ticker Symbol	NATI
Stk Agt	NA	Outstanding Shares	26,910,000
Counsel	Langangen & Helset Advokatfirma	E.P.S.	$2.06
DUNS No.	NA	Shareholders	NA

Business: The groups principle activity is to provide charter of oil tankers. The group operates from United States.

Primary SIC and add'l.: 4499 7359

CIK No: 0001000177

Subsidiaries: Ugland Nordic Shipping ASA

Officers: Herbjorn Hansson/Chmn., CEO, Pres., Rolf Amundsen/Investor Relations, Advisor to The Chmn., Turid M. Sorensen/CFO, Jan Erik Langangen/Exec. VP - Business Development, Legal, Frithjof Bettum/VP - Technical Operations, Chartering, Peter Pubenzer/Company Sec., Gary Wolfe/Investor Relations Officer

Directors: Herbjorn Hansson/Chmn., CEO, Pres., Andreas Ove Ugland/Vice Chmn., George C. Lodge/80/Dir., David Gibbons/Dir., Torbjorn Gladso/Dir., Andrew W. March/Dir., Paul J. Hopkins/Dir., Richard H.K. Vietor/Dir.

Owners: Herbjorn Hansson/2.00%

Financial Data: ***Fiscal Year End:***12/31 ***Latest Annual Data:*** 12/31/2006

Year	Sales	Net Income
2006	$175,520,000	$67,393,000
2005	$117,110,000	$46,318,000
2004	$67,452,000	$40,816,000

Curr. Assets:	$44,478,000	**Curr. Liab.:**	$14,734,000		
Plant, Equip.:	$752,478,000	**Total Liab.:**	$188,234,000	**Indic. Yr. Divd.:**	$1.600
Total Assets:	$800,180,000	**Net Worth:**	$611,946,000	**Debt/ Equity:**	NA

Nordson Corp

28601 Clemens Rd., Westlake, OH, 44145; ***PH:*** 1-440-892-1580; ***Fax:*** 1-440-892-9507; ***http://*** www.nordson.com

General		Stock	
Incorporation	OH	Price on:12/24/2007	$50.08
Employees	3,800	Stock Exchange	NDQ
Auditor	Ernst & Young LLP	Ticker Symbol	NDSN
Stk Agt	National City Bank	Outstanding Shares	33,680,000
Counsel	NA	E.P.S.	$2.65
DUNS No.	00-416-6005	Shareholders	NA

Business: The group's principal activity is to design, manufacture and market precision dispensing systems that apply adhesives, sealants and coatings. The group operates in three segments: adhesive dispensing and nonwoven fiber segment (includes automated systems for adhesive dispensing, sealing, coating, laminating and producing synthetic nonwoven fabrics). Coating and finishing segment (includes automated and manual spray systems for liquid and powder paints). Advanced technology systems segment (includes dispensing equipment for printed circuit boards, drying and curing systems). These products are used in the appliance, automotive, bookbinding, container, electronics, food and beverage, medical, metal finishing, nonwovens and packaging industries. It markets its products in the United States and 30 other countries.

Primary SIC and add'l.: 2297 3563 3559 3569

CIK No: 0000072331

Subsidiaries: Asymptotic Technologies, Inc., Dosage2000, EFD, International, Inc., Electron Fusion Devices, Inc., Electrostatic Technology, Inc., H.P. Solutions, Inc., Horizon Lamps, Inc., J and M Laboratories, Inc, March Plasma Systems, Inc., Nordson (China) Co. Ltd., Nordson (Malaysia) Sdn. Bhd., Nordson (Schweiz) A.G., Nordson (U.K.) Limited, Nordson AB, Nordson Andina Limitada 45 Subsidiaries included in the Index

Officers: Edward P. Campbell/Chmn., CEO, Donald J. McLane/Sr. VP, Pres. - Pacific South Division, Raymond L. Cushing/Treasurer, Beverly J. Coen/Assist. Controller, Bradford J. Leaheey/Assist. General Counsel, Peter Lambert/VP, Gregory Thaxton/VP, Controller, William W. Colville/Dir. - Legal Consultant, David W. Ignat/Dir., Consulting Physicist, John J. Keane/Sr. VP, Shelly M. Peet/VP - Public Relations, CIO, Robert E. Veillette/VP, General Counsel, Bruce H. Fields/VP - Human Resources, John Dillon/Dir. - Supply Chain Management, Michael Groos/VP *(20 Officers included in Index)*

Directors: Edward P. Campbell/Chmn., CEO, Eric T. Nord/Chmn. Emeritus, William P. Madar/Dir., David W. Ignat/Dir., Consulting Physicist, Joseph P. Keithley/Dir., William L. Robinson/Dir., William D. Ginn/Dir., William W. Colville/Dir. - Legal Consultant, Stephen R. Hardis/Dir., Peter S. Hellman/Dir., Pres., Chief Financial, Administrative Officer, Mary G. Puma/Dir., Benedict P. Rosen/Dir.

Owners: Donald J. McLane/0.90%, William L. Robinson/0.10%, William P. Madar/0.50%, William D. Ginn/1.10%, William W. Colville/0.10%, Mary G. Puma, Columbia Wanger Asset Management LP/6.40%, Benedict P. Rosen/0.10%, Peter S. Hellman/1.00%, Eric T. Nord/6.50%, David W. Ignat/4.70%, Robert A. Dunn, Stephen R. Hardis/0.30%, Insiders/11.50%, Joseph P. Keithley *(18 Owners included in Index)*

Financial Data: ***Fiscal Year End:***10/30 ***Latest Annual Data:*** 10/31/2006

Year	Sales	Net Income
2006	$892,221,000	$90,598,000
2005	$839,162,000	$78,338,000
2004	$793,544,000	$63,334,000

Curr. Assets:	$409,924,000	**Curr. Liab.:**	$509,914,000	**P/E Ratio:**	19.19
Plant, Equip.:	$132,917,000	**Total Liab.:**	$680,723,000	**Indic. Yr. Divd.:**	$0.700
Total Assets:	$1,211,840,000	**Net Worth:**	$531,117,000	**Debt/ Equity:**	0.0990

Nordstrom Credit Inc

1617 6th Ave., Seattle, WA, 98101; ***PH:*** 1-206-628-2111; ***Fax:*** 1-206-628-1795; ***http://*** about.nordstrom.com

General		Stock	
Incorporation	CO	Price on:12/24/2007	$50.59
Employees	52,900	Stock Exchange	NA
Auditor	Deloitte & Touche LLP	Ticker Symbol	NA
Stk Agt	Mellon Investor Services LLC	Outstanding Shares	252,200,000
Counsel	NA	E.P.S.	$2.71
DUNS No.	18-707-1535	Shareholders	NA

Business: The group's principal activity is to finance customer accounts receivable generated under revolving charge accounts. The receivables are generated through the use of credit cards issued by national banking association. The accounts and visa accounts are originated through the use of credit cards issued by the bank and federal savings association. The group pays a monthly marketing fee to the bank for its marketing efforts to increase customer accounts receivable balances upon which the service income is generated. Rental income is generated from lease of a group owned building.

Primary SIC and add'l.: 6141 6519

CIK No: 0000757439

Subsidiaries: Nordstrom National Credit Bank, Nordstrom Private Label Receivables LLC

Officers: Mark S. Brashear/46/Exec. VP, Pres. - Faconnable, Paul Favaro/49/Exec. VP - Strategy Development, Linda Toschi Finn/60/Exec. VP - Marketing, Kevin T. Knight/52/Pres., James R. O'Neal/49/Exec. VP, Pres. - Nordstrom Product Group, Loretta Soffe/41/Exec. VP, General Merchandise Mgr. - Women's Apparel Division, Delena M. Sunday/47/Exec. VP - Human Resources, Diversity Affairs, David M. Witman/49/Exec. VP, General Merchandise Mgr. - Men's, Kidswear Division, Lisa G. Iglesias/42/Exec. VP, General Counsel, Corp. Sec., David Loretta/40/Treasurer, Divisional VP, James F. Nordstrom/35/Exec. VP, Pres. - Nordstrom Direct, Blake W. Nordstrom/47/Dir., Pres., Erik B. Nordstrom/44/Dir., Pres., Laurie M. Black/48/Exec. VP, General Merchandise Mgr. - Cosmetic Division, Michael G. Koppel/51/CFO, Exec. VP *(19 Officers included in Index)*

Directors: Enrique Hernandez/52/Chmn., Phyllis J. Campbell/56/Dir., Jeanne P. Jackson/56/Dir., Robert G. Miller/63/Dir., Blake W. Nordstrom/47/Dir., Pres., Erik B. Nordstrom/44/Dir., Pres., Peter E. Nordstrom/46/Dir., Philip G. Satre/58/Dir., Alison A. Winter/61/Dir.

Financial Data: ***Fiscal Year End:***01/29 ***Latest Annual Data:*** 2/3/2007

Year	Sales	Net Income
2007	$8,560,698,000	$677,999,000
2006	$1,872,103,000	$135,673,000
2005	$7,131,388,000	$393,450,000

Curr. Assets:	$2,742,193,000	**Curr. Liab.:**	$1,433,143,000	**P/E Ratio:**	18.95
Plant, Equip.:	$1,757,215,000	**Total Liab.:**	$2,653,057,000	**Indic. Yr. Divd.:**	$0.540
Total Assets:	$4,821,578,000	**Net Worth:**	$2,168,521,000	**Debt/ Equity:**	0.6358

Nordstrom Inc

1617 6th Ave., Ste. 500, Seattle, WA, 98101; ***PH:*** 1-206-628-2111; ***Fax:*** 1-206-628-1795; ***http://*** www.nordstrom.com

General		Stock	
Incorporation	WA	Price on:12/24/2007	$51.23
Employees	52,900	Stock Exchange	NYSE
Auditor	Deloitte & Touche LLP	Ticker Symbol	JWN
Stk Agt	Mellon Investor Services LLC	Outstanding Shares	252,200,000
Counsel	Lane Powell Spears Lubersky	E.P.S.	$2.87
DUNS No.	00-794-2915	Shareholders	NA

Business: The groups principle activity is to retail apparel, shoes and accessories for women, men and childrens. The group operates through three segments namely industrial packaging and services, paper, packaging and services, and timber. In the year 2006, the group acquired Delta Petroleum Company, Inc. The group operates from United States.

Primary SIC and add'l.: 5611 5621 5651 5632 5961 5661 5641

CIK No: 0000072333

Subsidiaries: N2HC, Inc., Nordstrom Credit Card Receivables, LLC, Nordstrom Credit, Inc., Nordstrom Distribution, Inc., Nordstrom European Capital Group, Nordstrom fsb, Nordstrom International Limited, Nordstrom Private Label Receivables, LLC

Officers: Delena M. Sunday/47/Exec. VP - Human Resources, Diversity Affairs, Daniel F. Little/46/Exec. VP, Chief Administrative Officer/$1,892,530.00, Peter E. Nordstrom/46/Dir., Pres. - Merchandising/$3,854,162.00, Kevin T. Knight/52/Exec. VP, James F. Nordstrom/35/Pres., Exec. VP, James R. ONeal/49/Exec. VP, Pres. - Nordstrom Product Group, Scott Meden/45/Pres., Exec. VP, Paul Favaro/49/Exec. VP - Strategy, Development, Laurie M. Black/48/Exec. VP, General Merchandise Mgr. - Cosmetic Division, Mark S. Brashear/46/Exec. VP, Pres. - Faconnable, Blake W. Nordstrom/47/Dir., Pres./$4,810,766.00, Michael G. Koppel/52/CFO, Exec. VP/$2,319,410.00, Erik B. Nordstrom/44/Dir., Pres. - Stores/$3,779,383.00, Linda Toschi Finn/60/Exec. VP - Marketing, Peter F. Collins/43/Divisional VP, Corporate Controller, Principal Accounting Officer *(24 Officers included in Index)*

Directors: Enrique Hernandez/52/Chmn., Peter E. Nordstrom/46/Dir., Pres. - Merchandising, Robert G. Miller/63/Dir., Philip G. Satre/58/Dir., Alison A. Winter/61/Dir., Erik B. Nordstrom/44/Dir., Pres. - Stores, Phyllis J. Campbell/56/Dir., Jeanne P. Jackson/56/Dir., Blake W. Nordstrom/47/Dir., Pres.

Owners: Daniel F. Little, Peter E. Nordstrom, Phyllis J. Campbell, Michael G. Koppel, Enrique Hernandez, Jeanne P. Jackson, Philip G. Satre, Erik B. Nordstrom, Robert G. Miller, Insiders/3.82%, Alison A. Winter, Bruce A. Nordstrom/8.36%, Blake W. Nordstrom/1.11%, Anne E. Gittinger/8.14%

Financial Data: ***Fiscal Year End:***01/28 ***Latest Annual Data:*** 2/3/2007

Year	Sales	Net Income
2007	$8,560,698,000	$677,999,000
2006	$7,722,860,000	$551,339,000
2005	$7,131,388,000	$393,450,000

Curr. Assets:	$2,742,193,000	Curr. Liab.:	$1,433,143,000	P/E Ratio:	19.19
Plant, Equip.:	$1,757,215,000	Total Liab.:	$2,653,057,000	Indic. Yr. Divd.:	$0.540
Total Assets:	$4,821,578,000	Net Worth:	$2,168,521,000	Debt/ Equity:	NA

Norfolk Southern Corp

3 Commercial Pl., Norfolk, VA, 23510; *PH:* 1-757-629-2600; *Fax:* 1-757-664-5069; *http://* www.nscorp.com

General - Incorporation	VA	Stock- Price on:12/24/2007	$55.24
Employees	30,541	Stock Exchange	NDQ
Auditor	KPMG LLP	Ticker Symbol	NSFC
Stk Agt	Bank of New York	Outstanding Shares	393,220,000
Counsel	NA	E.P.S.	$3.66
DUNS No.	00-692-0417	Shareholders	NA

Business: The groups principle activity is to provide rail transportation of raw materials, intermediate products and finished goods. The group operates from United States.

Primary SIC and add'l.: 4011 6719

CIK No: 0000702165

Subsidiaries: Consolidated Rail Corporation, Norfolk Southern Railway Company

Officers: Charles W. Moorman/Chmn., CEO, Pres./$12,053,140.00, Stephen C. Tobias/Vice Chmn., COO/$8,013,581.00, Henry C. Wolf/65/Vice Chmn., CFO/$8,113,350.00, Kathryn B. McQuade/51/Exec. VP - Planning, CIO, Dezora M. Martin/Corp. Sec., David T. Lawson/VP - Industrial Products, William A. Galanko/VP - Law, John P. Rathbone/Exec. VP - Administration, Gerhard A. Thelen/VP - Operations Planning, Support, Joseph C. Dimino/VP - Compliance, Tim A. Heilig/VP - Mechanical, Terry N. Evans/VP - Operations Planning, Budget, Fredric M. Ehlers/VP - Customer Service, Timothy J. Drake/VP - Engineering, Daniel M. Mazur/VP - Strategic Planning *(34 Officers included in Index)*

Directors: Charles W. Moorman/Chmn., CEO, Pres., Stephen C. Tobias/Vice Chmn., COO, Henry C. Wolf/65/Vice Chmn., CFO, Daniel A. Carp/Dir., Landon Hilliard/Dir., Gerald L. Baliles/Dir., Burton M. Joyce/Dir., Jane Margaret O'Brien/Dir., Gene R. Carter/Dir., Alston D. Correll/Dir., Steven F. Leer/Dir., Paul J. Reason/Dir.

Owners: Henry C. Wolf, Daniel A. Carp, Burton M. Joyce, Jane Margaret OBrien, Mark D. Manion, Donald W. Seale, L. I. Prillaman, Insiders, Charles W. Moorman, Stephen C. Tobias, David R. Goode, Gene R. Carter, Alston D. Correll, Paul J. Reason, Landon Hilliard *(17 Owners included in Index)*

Financial Data: Fiscal Year End:12/31 Latest Annual Data: 12/31/2006

Year	Sales	Net Income
2006	$9,407,000,000	$1,481,000,000
2005	$8,527,000,000	$1,281,000,000
2004	$7,312,000,000	$923,000,000

Curr. Assets:	$2,400,000,000	Curr. Liab.:	$2,093,000,000	P/E Ratio:	15.09
Plant, Equip.:	$21,098,000,000	Total Liab.:	$16,413,000,000	Indic. Yr. Divd.:	$1.040
Total Assets:	$26,028,000,000	Net Worth:	$9,615,000,000	Debt/ Equity:	0.6231

NorPac Technologies Inc

103 E Holly St., Ste. 410, Bellingham, WA, 98225; *PH:* 1-360-201-9591

General - Incorporation	NV	Stock- Price on:12/24/2007	NA
Employees	NA	Stock Exchange	OTC
Auditor	Peterson Sullivan PLLC	Ticker Symbol	NRPT
Stk Agt	Signature Stock Transfer, Inc.	Outstanding Shares	37,600,000
Counsel	NA	E.P.S.	NA
DUNS No.	NA	Shareholders	NA

Business: The groups principle activities include developing and marketing technology used for licensing and manufacturing of commercially viable self-chilling beverage container. The group operates from the United States.

Primary SIC and add'l.: 2080

CIK No: 0001067286

Officers: John P. Thornton/75/Dir., CEO, CFO, Pres., Sec., Treasurer

Directors: John P. Thornton/75/Dir., CEO, CFO, Pres., Sec., Treasurer

Owners: Insiders/8.00%, John P. Thornton/8.00%

Curr. Assets:	$1,000	Curr. Liab.:	$111,000		
Plant, Equip.:	NA	Total Liab.:	$111,000	Indic. Yr. Divd.:	NA
Total Assets:	$1,167,000	Net Worth:	$1,055,000	Debt/ Equity:	NA

Norsat International Inc

110-4020 Viking Way, Richmond, BC, V6V 2L4; *PH:* 1-604-821-2800; *http://* www.norsat.com

General - Incorporation	BC	Stock- Price on:12/24/2007	$0.845
Employees	NA	Stock Exchange	OTC
Auditor	Ernst & young LLP	Ticker Symbol	NSATF
Stk Agt	Computershare Trust Co	Outstanding Shares	NA
Counsel	NA	E.P.S.	NA
DUNS No.	NA	Shareholders	NA

Business: The group's principle activities are to design and market premium infrastructure products for high-speed data transmission. These services are provided to the global wireless communication industry. The company operates in two segments: microwave and open network. The microwave segment provides radio frequency and associated components, including satellite receivers, transmitters, transceivers and other ground station products. The open network segment offers digital video broadcasting (dvb) satellite networks and digital products designed for flexibility, performance and reliability. The group's quarterly revenue for September 2007 was 3.96 millions of CAD.

Primary SIC and add'l.: 4812 4841 4899

CIK No: 0000748213

Subsidiaries: Norsat (UK) Ltd, Norsat Intl

Officers: Amiee Chan/CEO, Pres., Pervez Siddiqui/Vice President, Marketing, Randy Witten/Vice President, Sales, William R. Witten/VP - Sales

Directors: Ugo Angelo Doninelli/Chmn., James Sharpe/Vice Chmn., Christopher Hoyle/Dir., Joseph Caprio/Dir.

Owners: Ugo A. Doninelli/4.20%, Joseph Caprio/0.10%, Cathy Zhai/0.02%, James Sharpe/0.10%, William R. Witten/0.25%, Amiee Chan/0.05%, Michael Schefter/0.02%, Pervez R. Siddiqui/0.02%

Financial Data: Fiscal Year End:12/31 Latest Annual Data: 12/31/2006

Year	Sales	Net Income
2006	$13,091,000	-$3,376,000
2005	$15,544,000	-$4,967,000
2004	$14,547,000	$1,346,000

Curr. Assets:	$7,287,000	Curr. Liab.:	$5,949,000		
Plant, Equip.:	$1,128,000	Total Liab.:	$5,949,000	Indic. Yr. Divd.:	NA
Total Assets:	$8,424,000	Net Worth:	$2,476,000	Debt/ Equity:	NA

Norsk Hydro ASA

1200 Smith St., Ste. 800, Houston, TX, 77002; *PH:* 1-713-759-1770; *Fax:* 1-713-759-1773; *http://* www.hydro.com; *Email:* corporate@hydro.com

General - Incorporation . Kingdom of Norway		Stock- Price on:12/24/2007	$36.91
Employees	33,605	Stock Exchange	NYSE
Auditor	NA	Ticker Symbol	NI
Stk Agt	US transfer agent	Outstanding Shares	1,230,000,000
Counsel	NA	E.P.S.	$2.42
DUNS No.	NA	Shareholders	NA

Business: The groups principal activities include acquiring, developing and operating oil and gas properties. The group operates from the Canada.

Primary SIC and add'l.: 3363 3355 3334 3354

CIK No: 0000900268

Subsidiaries: Hydro Aluminium AS, Hydro Aluminium Deutschland GmbH, Norsk Hydro Produksjon AS

Officers: Eivind Reiten/CEO, Svein Steen Thomassen/Chmn. - Corporate Assembly, Siri Teigum/Deputy Chmn. - Corporate Assembly, Westye Hoegh/Member - Corporate Assembly, Idar Kreutzer/Member - Corporate Assembly, Jan Oyri/Human Resources, Sr. VP, Jan Arve Haugan/Technology, Part Owned Smelters, Sr. VP, Oliver Bell/Rolled Products, Cologne, Pres., Tom Rotjer/Exec. VP - Projects, Merete Oiestad Jonas/Deputy Member - Corporate Assembly, Arne Kjolberg/Deputy Member - Corporate Assembly, Anne Helen Augestad Madsen/Deputy Member - Corporate Assembly, Tor Egil Skulstad/Deputy Member - Corporate Assembly, Bente Linnerud Ostlyngen/Deputy Member - Corporate Assembly, Kathrine Fog/Head - Energy Analysis, Policy *(63 Officers included in Index)*

Directors: Finn Jebsen/Dir., Heidi M. Petersen/Dir., Bente Rathe/Dir., Svein Rennemo/Dir., Jorn B. Lilleby/Dir., Grete Faremo/53/Dir., Sten Roar Martinsen/46/Dir., Billy Fredagsvik/Dir.

Owners: Goldman Sachs & Co, Euroclear Bank, SIS Segaintersettle, Investors Bank & Trust Company, Clearstream Banking, Capital EuroPacific Growth Fund, Vital Forsikring, State Street Bank and Trust, Capital World Growth and Income Fund, Goldman Sachs International, DnB NOR Norge, Capital New Perspective Fund, Hydro, JPMorgan Chase Bank, JPMorgan Chase Bank *(20 Owners included in Index)*

Financial Data: Fiscal Year End:12/31 Latest Annual Data: 12/31/2006

Year	Sales	Net Income
2006	$31,515,180,000	$2,792,995,000
2005	$25,694,648,000	$2,306,605,000
2004	$25,707,295,000	$2,077,424,000

Curr. Assets:	$13,190,239,000	Curr. Liab.:	$9,808,806,000	P/E Ratio:	10.64
Plant, Equip.:	$20,483,727,000	Total Liab.:	$21,968,635,000	Indic. Yr. Divd.:	$0.700
Total Assets:	$37,579,436,000	Net Worth:	$15,497,258,000	Debt/ Equity:	NA

Nortech Systems Inc

1120 Wayzata Blvd. E, Ste. 201, Wayzata, MN, 55391; *PH:* 1-952-345-2244; *Fax:* 1-218-765-2300; *http://* www.nortechsys.com; *Email:* sales@nortechsys.com

General - Incorporation	MN	Stock- Price on:12/24/2007	$7.7
Employees	911	Stock Exchange	NDQ
Auditor	KPMG LLP, McGladrey & Pullen LLP	Ticker Symbol	NSYS
Stk Agt	Wells Fargo Shareowner Services	Outstanding Shares	2,710,000
Counsel	NA	E.P.S.	$0.56
DUNS No.	01-042-9728	Shareholders	NA

Business: The group's principle activities are to manufacture wire harnesses, cables, electromechanical assemblies, printed circuit boards and higher level assemblies for commercial and defense industries. The majority of revenue is derived from products that are built to the customer's design specifications. The group maintains various manufacturing facilities in Minnesota locations of bemidji, fairmont, baxter, merrifield, augusta and Wisconsin. Major customers of the group are g.e. Medical systems, raytheon, spx corporation, kodak, thermo king, polaris, cubic, icon systems, allen-bradley, semitool, silicon graphics and united defense. The group sells its products to companies in the computer, medical, governmental and various other industries. The group's quarterly revenue for September 2007 was 105.15 millions of USD.

Primary SIC and add'l.: 3679

CIK No: 0000722313

Subsidiaries: Manufacturing Assembly Solutions of Monterrey, Inc

Officers: Michael J. Degen/Dir., CEO, Pres./$382,967.00, Keith A. Pieper/VP - Operations/$260,469.00, Donald E. Horne/VP - Global Supply Chain Management, Garry M. Anderly/Sr. VP - Corporate Finance, Treasurer/$209,427.00, Richard G. Wasielewski/CFO, VP/$289,341.00, Peter L. Kucera/VP - Corporate Quality, Curtis J. Steichen/VP - Sales, Marketing/$259,511.00

Directors: Michael J. Degen/Dir., CEO, Pres., Myron Kunin/Vice Chmn., Kenneth Larson/Dir., Richard W. Perkins/Dir., Trent C. Riley/Dir.

Owners: Michael J. Degen/2.70%, Insiders/62.40%, Keith A. Pieper, Richard W. Perkins/1.70%, Richard G. Wasielewski, Garry M. Anderly/1.80%, Trent C. Riley, Myron Kunin/50.40%, Curtis J. Steichen, Kenneth Larson

Financial Data: Fiscal Year End:12/31 Latest Annual Data: 12/31/2006

Year	Sales	Net Income
2006	$105,147,000	$1,312,000
2005	$84,216,000	$929,000
2004	$72,674,000	$587,000

Curr. Assets:	$32,753,000	Curr. Liab.:	$20,041,000	P/E Ratio:	15.40
Plant, Equip.:	$8,255,000	Total Liab.:	$23,576,000	Indic. Yr. Divd.:	NA
Total Assets:	$41,878,000	Net Worth:	$18,302,000	Debt/ Equity:	NA

Nortel Investments Inc

Alicia Moreau De Justo 50, Piso 11, Buenos Aires; **PH:** 54-1149683631; **http://** www.telecom.com.ar

General - Incorporation	AR	Stock- Price on:12/24/2007	$27.09
Employees	14,542	Stock Exchange	NYSE
Auditor	Price Waterhouse & Co. S.R.L.	Ticker Symbol	NA
Stk Agt	Bank of New York	Outstanding Shares	106,610,000
Counsel	NA	E.P.S.	NA
DUNS No.	NA	Shareholders	NA

Business: The group's principle activities are the provision of national and international telephone services, data transmission services, Internet services and cellular telephony. It also edits, prints and distributes telephone directories, magazines, annuals, and other types of publications.

Primary SIC and add'l.: 4899 4822 4810 2721 7389 7375 3661

CIK No: 0000877691

Subsidiaries: Cable Insignia SA, Micro Sistemas SA, Ncleo S.A., Publicom SA, Telecom Argentina USA Inc, Telecom Personal S.A

Officers: Jose G. Pozzi/GM, Sole Officer - Nortel

Directors: Ricardo Alberto Ferreiro/Vice Chmn., Oscar Carlos Cristianci/Chmn., Franco Alfredo Livini/Dir., Horacio Walter Bauer/Alternate Dir., Alejandro Borda/Alternate Dir., Bruno Iapadre/Alternate Dir., Eduardo Federico Bauer/58/Dir., Guillermo M. Irusta/Dir., Gustavo Sebastian Viramonte Olmos/Dir., Jorge Alberto Firpo/Alternate Dir., Pablo Ginnetty/Alternate Dir., Joaquin Acuna/Alternate Dir.

Owners: Galisteo Investments C.V./9.86%, JPMorgan Chase& Co./12.12%, Sofora Telecomunicaciones S.A/100.00%, Fintech Advisory Inc./11.75%, Renaissance Technologies Corp./5.47%, Fimex International Limited/32.61%, D.E. Shaw Laminar Portfolios, L.L.C./13.34%, Banco Santander Rio, Buenos Aires/61.63%

Financial Data: *Fiscal Year End:*12/31 **Latest Annual Data:** 12/31/2006

Year		Sales		Net Income	
2006		$2,427,437,000		$65,933,000	
2005		$1,884,081,000		$161,785,000	
2004		$1,512,680,000		-$174,695,000	
Curr. Assets:	$578,054,000	Curr. Liab.:	$1,101,600,000		
Plant, Equip.:	$1,880,064,000	Total Liab.:	$2,412,422,000	Indic. Yr. Divd.:	NA
Total Assets:	$2,884,070,000	Net Worth:	-$17,626,000	Debt/ Equity:	NA

Nortel Networks Corp

2221 Lakeside Blvd., Richardson, TX, 75082; **PH:** 1-972-684-1000; **Fax:** 1-888-901-7286; **http://** www.nortelnetworks.com; **Email:** investor@nortel.com

General - Incorporation	Canada	Stock- Price on:12/24/2007	$24.55
Employees	33,760	Stock Exchange	NYSE
Auditor	Deloitte & Touche LLP	Ticker Symbol	NT
Stk Agt	Computershare Trust Company of Canada	Outstanding Shares	436,580,000
Counsel	NA	E.P.S.	-$0.41
DUNS No.	20-228-6415	Shareholders	NA

Business: The group's principle activity is to design, develop, manufacture, assemble and distribute network solutions. The group provides finance, installation, license and support for network solutions. The network solutions include network equipment, software and other technologies. The group operates in three segments: metro and enterprise, wireless and optical long-haul networks. Trademarks of the group include baystack, callpilot, contivity, dms, epicon, meridian, norstar, optera, passport, periphonics, preside, shasta, succession, symposium and universal edge. The group operates in Canada, the United States, Europe, Middle East, Africa, Latin America and the pacific region. The group's quarterly revenue for September 2007 was 2,705.00 millions of USD.

Primary SIC and add'l.: 4899 3679 3612 3695 3661 3669

CIK No: 0000072911

Subsidiaries: 1328556 Ontario Inc., AC Technologies, Inc., Alteon WebSystems AB, Alteon WebSystems International Limited, Alteon WebSystems International, Inc., Alteon WebSystems, Inc., Architel Systems (U.S.) Corporation, Architel Systems (UK)Limited, Architel Systems Corporation, Brightspeed SAS, Capital Telecommunications Funding Corporation, CoreTek, Inc., CTFC Canada Inc., Guandong-Nortel Telecommunications Equipment Company Ltd., LG-Nortel Co. Ltd. 122 Subsidiaries included in the Index

Officers: Mike S. Zafirovski/Dir., CEO, Pres./$8,277,421.00, Chuck Saffell/CEO - Nortel Government Solutions, Peter MacKinnon/Chmn. - LG, Nortel JV, GM - Nortel Wimax, Wireless Mesh, Bob Bartzokas/Chief Compliance Officer, Dennis Carey/Exec. VP - Corporate Operations, Steven J. Bandrowczak/CIO, Alvio Barrios/Pres. - Caribbean, Latin America, Joel Hackney/Pres. - Enterprise Solutions/$1,686,313.00, George Riedel/Chief Strategy Officer, Peter William Currie/57/CFO, Exec. VP/$2,253,088.00, Richard Lowe/Pres. - Mobility, Converged Core Networks/$2,186,505.00, David Drinkwater/59/Chief Legal Officer, Lauren P. Flaherty/Chief Marketing Officer, John J. Roese/CTO, Darryl Edwards/Pres. - Europe, Middle East, Africa, EMEA *(22 Officers included in Index)*

Directors: Mike S. Zafirovski/Dir., CEO, Pres., Peter MacKinnon/Chmn. - LG, Nortel JV, GM - Nortel Wimax, Wireless Mesh, Harry Jonathan Pearce/Chmn., Manfred Bischoff/Dir., John P. Manley/Dir., Richard David McCormick/Dir., Kristina M. Johnson/Dir., Claude Mongeau/Dir., John D. Watson/Dir., John Alan MacNaughton/Dir., Jalynn H. Bennett/Dir., James B. Hunt/Dir.

Owners: Insiders, J. J. Hackney, D. Joannou, P. W. Currie, J. A. MacNaughton, R. S. Lowe, H. J. Pearce, R. D. McCormick, M. S. Zafirovski

Financial Data: *Fiscal Year End:*12/31 **Latest Annual Data:** 12/31/2006

Year		Sales		Net Income	
2006		$11,418,000,000		$28,000,000	
2005		$10,523,000,000		-$2,575,000,000	
2004		$9,828,000,000		-$51,000,000	
Curr. Assets:	$9,923,000,000	Curr. Liab.:	$6,726,000,000	P/E Ratio:	111.59
Plant, Equip.:	$1,530,000,000	Total Liab.:	$17,858,000,000	Indic. Yr. Divd.:	NA
Total Assets:	$18,979,000,000	Net Worth:	$1,121,000,000	Debt/ Equity:	2.0676

North American Energy Partners Inc

Zone 3, Acheson Industrial Area, Nr. 2 53016 Hwy. 60, Acheson, AB, T7X 5A7; **PH:** 1-780-960-7171; **Fax:** 1-780-960-7103; **http://** www.nacg.ca; **Email:** IR@nacg.ca

General - Incorporation	Canada	Stock- Price on:12/24/2007	$21.24
Employees	1,330	Stock Exchange	NDQ
Auditor	KPMG LLP	Ticker Symbol	NOBL
Stk Agt	Mellon Trust Co	Outstanding Shares	35,600,000
Counsel	NA	E.P.S.	-$0.05
DUNS No.	NA	Shareholders	NA

Business: The groups principle activity is to provide resource services to oil and natural gas companies. The group operates through three segments namely, mining and site preparation, piling, and pipeline. The group operates from the Canada. The group's quarterly revenue for sptember 2007 was 223.57 millions of USD.

Primary SIC and add'l.: 1382

CIK No: 0001272869

Subsidiaries: Equipment Ltd., NACG Acquisition Inc., NACG Holdings Inc., NACG Preferred Corp., Norama Ltd.

Officers: Rodney Ruston/Dir., CEO, Pres., Vincent Gallant/VP - Corporate, Christopher Hayman/VP - Supply Chain, Miles W. Safranovich/VP - Operations, Doug Wilkes/VP - Finance, CFO, Robert Harris/VP - Human Resources, Health Safety, Environment, William M. Koehn/VP - Operations, COO, Pam Winters/Dir. - Information Technology, CIO, Kevin Rowand/Mgr. - Investor Relations, Bernie Robert/VP - Business Development, Estimating

Directors: Rodney Ruston/Dir., CEO, Pres., Ronald A. McIntosh/Chmn., William Oehmig/Dir., George Brokaw/Dir., Richard Paterson/Dir., John Brussa/Dir., Peter Tomsett/Dir., Allen Sello/Dir., Rick K. Turner/Dir., John D. Hawkins/Dir.

Owners: William C. Oehmig/1.48%, John A. Brussa, Gordon Parchewsky, Gary K. Wright, Ronald A. McIntosh, Vincent Gallant, Jim G. Gardiner, William Koehn, Donald R. Getty

Financial Data: *Fiscal Year End:*03/31 **Latest Annual Data:** 03/31/2007

Year		Sales		Net Income	
2007		$544,786,000		$19,105,000	
Curr. Assets:	$198,252,000	Curr. Liab.:	$128,777,000	P/E Ratio:	10.64
Plant, Equip.:	$221,536,000	Total Liab.:	$403,719,000	Indic. Yr. Divd.:	NA
Total Assets:	$616,612,000	Net Worth:	$212,893,000	Debt/ Equity:	NA

North American Galvanizing & Coatings Inc

5314 S Yale Ave., Ste. 1000, Tulsa, OK, 74135; **PH:** 1-918-488-9420; **Fax:** 1-918-488-8172; **http://** www.nagalv.com

General - Incorporation	DE	Stock- Price on:12/24/2007	$9.38
Employees	368	Stock Exchange	NDQ
Auditor	Deloitte & Touche LLP	Ticker Symbol	NGA
Stk Agt	Mellon Investor Services LLC	Outstanding Shares	12,250,000
Counsel	King & Spalding LLP	E.P.S.	$0.637
DUNS No.	00-884-1058	Shareholders	NA

Business: The group's principal activity is to provide hot dip galvanizing and coating for metal products fabricated by its customers. The galvanizing process provides effective corrosion protection of fabricated steel which is used in numerous markets such as petrochemical, highway and transportation, energy, utilities, communications, irrigation, pulp and paper, waste water treatment, food processing, recreation and the manufacture of original equipment. The galvanizing plants are located in Oklahoma, Missouri, Texas, Colorado, Tennessee and Kentucky.

Primary SIC and add'l.: 4226 3479

CIK No: 0000055805

Subsidiaries: NAGalv-Ohio, Inc.

Officers: Judy A. Johnson/Human Resources Mgr., Beth B. Hood/CFO/$180,933.00, Rick Page/Controller

Owners: Patrick J. Lynch/1.27%, Joseph J. Morrow/21.76%, Insiders/32.14%, Beth B. Hood/0.10%, Gilbert L. Klemann/1.63%, Stephen T. Gregory, Edmund A. Schwesinger/5.57%, Ronald J. Evans/2.81%, Linwood J. Bundy/1.64%, John H. Sununu/2.47%

Financial Data: *Fiscal Year End:*12/31 **Latest Annual Data:** 12/31/2006

Year		Sales		Net Income	
2006		$74,054,000		$4,535,000	
2005		$47,870,000		$644,000	
2004		$35,822,000		$403,000	
Curr. Assets:	$23,386,000	Curr. Liab.:	$14,090,000	P/E Ratio:	18.76
Plant, Equip.:	$21,135,000	Total Liab.:	$22,645,000	Indic. Yr. Divd.:	NA
Total Assets:	$48,211,000	Net Worth:	$25,566,000	Debt/ Equity:	NA

North American Gaming & Entnt Corp

3300 Oak Lawn Ave., Dallas, TX, 75219; **PH:** 1-972-671-1133

General - Incorporation	DE	Stock- Price on:12/24/2007	$0.05
Employees	1	Stock Exchange	OTC
Auditor	Sartain Fischbein & Co	Ticker Symbol	NAGMB
Stk Agt	NA	Outstanding Shares	24,220,000
Counsel	Glast, Phillips & Murray	E.P.S.	-$0.01
DUNS No.	88-420-2029	Shareholders	NA

Business: The group's principle activity was to operate video poker machines located in truck stops in Louisiana. The company operated this business through its partial ownership of three operating companies: o.m. Operating, llc, river port truck stop, llc and ozdon investments, inc.

Primary SIC and add'l.: 7993 7999

CIK No: 0000029952

Officers: E. H. Hawes/69/Chmn., CEO, CFO, Pres., Richard P. Crane/69/Dir., Sec.

Directors: E. H. Hawes/69/Chmn., CEO, CFO, Pres., Richard P. Crane/69/Dir., Sec.

Owners: James Bowyer, Insiders, International Tours, Inc, E. H. Hawes, Hawes Partners, Richard P. Crane, Mike D. Case, Daryl N. Snadon

Financial Data: *Fiscal Year End:*12/31 **Latest Annual Data:** 12/31/2006

Year	Sales	Net Income
2006	NA	-$203,000
2005	NA	-$109,000
2004	NA	-$222,000

Curr. Assets:	$34,000	**Curr. Liab.:**	$531,000		
Plant, Equip.:	$3,000	**Total Liab.:**	$531,000	**Indic. Yr. Divd.:**	NA
Total Assets:	$170,000	**Net Worth:**	-$361,000	**Debt/ Equity:**	NA

North American Insurance Leaders Inc

885 Third Ave., 31st Fl., New York, NY, 10022; **PH:** 1-212-319-9407

General - Incorporation	DE	**Stock**- Price on:12/24/2007	$7.66
Employees	NA	Stock Exchange	AMEX
Auditor	BDO Seidman, LLP	Ticker Symbol	NAO
Stk Agt	NA	Outstanding Shares	NA
Counsel	NA	E.P.S.	NA
DUNS No.	NA	Shareholders	NA

Business: The groups principal activities include merging, capital stock exchanging, asset acquiring, and stock purchasing with one or more businesses in the insurance or insurance services industry. The group operates from North America. The groups asset in the year 2006 was $111,924,873.

Primary SIC and add'l.: 6399

CIK No: 0001336249

Officers: William R. De Jonge/51/Dir., Pres., Paula S. Butler/58/Exec. VP, Francis E. Lauricella/53/Dir., Exec. VP

Directors: Scott A. Levine/59/Chmn., William R. De Jonge/51/Dir., Pres., Francis E. Lauricella/53/Dir., Exec. VP, Robert Sroka/59/Dir., Miles E. Prentice/66/Dir.

Owners: Satellite Fund Management LLC/7.60%, The Baupost Group, L.L.C./7.20%, HBK Investments L.P./6.30%, Azimuth Opportunity, Ltd./6.20%, Context Capital Management, LLC/5.40%, Fir Tree, Inc./11.10%, Jonathan M. Glaser/9.40%

Financial Data: ***Fiscal Year End:***06/30 ***Latest Annual Data:*** 6/30/2006

Year	Sales	Net Income
2006	$1,345,000	$663,000

Curr. Assets:	$111,574,000	**Curr. Liab.:**	$546,000	**P/E Ratio:**	55.51
Plant, Equip.:	NA	**Total Liab.:**	$25,586,000	**Indic. Yr. Divd.:**	NA
Total Assets:	$111,925,000	**Net Worth:**	$86,339,000	**Debt/ Equity:**	NA

North American Natural Gas Inc

580 Hornby St., Ste. 490, Vancouver, BC, V6C 3B6; **PH:** 1-604-687-6991

General - Incorporation	WA	**Stock**- Price on:12/24/2007	$0.3
Employees	NA	Stock Exchange	OTC
Auditor	Manning Elliott LLP	Ticker Symbol	NAGA
Stk Agt	NA	Outstanding Shares	NA
Counsel	NA	E.P.S.	NA
DUNS No.	NA	Shareholders	NA

Business: The group's principle activities include marketing and distributing vitamins, minerals, nutritional supplements and other health and fitness products through a license agreement. The license agreement grants an exclusive right to distribute vitamineralherb.com products to health and fitness professionals in Minnesota via the Internet. The products are marketed to medical professionals, alternative health professionals, martial art studios and instructors, sports and fitness trainers, schools and other fund raising programs. The company is in the development stage. The group operates from United States.

Primary SIC and add'l.: 7375 5122

CIK No: 0001112425

Officers: Jim Glavas/45/Dir., CEO, CFO, Pres., Sec., Treasurer, Principal Accounting Officer

Directors: Jim Glavas/45/Dir., CEO, CFO, Pres., Sec., Treasurer, Principal Accounting Officer

Owners: Jim Glavas/62.15%

Financial Data: ***Fiscal Year End:***04/30 ***Latest Annual Data:*** 04/30/2007

Year	Sales	Net Income
2007	NA	-$29,000
2006	NA	-$22,000
2005	NA	-$30,000

Curr. Assets:	$5,000	**Curr. Liab.:**	$17,000		
Plant, Equip.:	NA	**Total Liab.:**	$17,000	**Indic. Yr. Divd.:**	NA
Total Assets:	$5,000	**Net Worth:**	-$12,000	**Debt/ Equity:**	NA

North American Palladium Ltd

130 Adelaide St. W, Ste. 2116, Toronto, ON, M5H 3P5; **PH:** 1-416-360-7590; **http://** www.napalladium.com

General - Incorporation	Canada	**Stock**- Price on:12/24/2007	$10.22
Employees	NA	Stock Exchange	AMEX
Auditor	KPMG LLP	Ticker Symbol	PAL
Stk Agt	Computershare Investor Services LLC	Outstanding Shares	53,600,000
Counsel	Cheadle Johnson Shanks & Macivor	E.P.S.	-$0.39
DUNS No.	24-540-1997	Shareholders	NA

Business: The group's principal activities are the exploration and mining of platinum group metals and certain base metals. The platinum group metals are palladium, platinum, gold, copper and nickel. Palladium is used in autocatalysts to reduce harmful engine exhaust emission from automobiles. The group's principal asset lac des iles is located in the thunder bay district in ontario. The group operates solely in Canada.

Primary SIC and add'l.: 1021 1041 1099

CIK No: 0000887701

Subsidiaries: 2750538 Canada Inc, Lacdes Iles Mines Ltd

Officers: James D. Excell/CEO, Pres., Michael C. Thompson/Mgr. - Administration, Sr. Controller, David Passfield/VP - Operations, Reno Pressacco/VP - Exploration - Development, Fraser Sinclair/VP - Finance, CFO, Trent C.A. Mell/VP, General Counsel, Corp. Sec.

Directors: Andre J. Douchane/Chmn., Steven R. Berlin/Dir., Gregory J. Van Staveren/Dir., David A.C. Comba/Dir., Robert J. Quinn/Dir., William J. Weymark/Dir.

Financial Data: ***Fiscal Year End:***12/31 ***Latest Annual Data:*** 12/31/2006

Year	Sales	Net Income
2006	$136,610,000	-$16,542,000
2005	$79,456,000	-$48,193,000
2004	$153,775,000	-$74,618,000

Curr. Assets:	$93,746,000	**Curr. Liab.:**	$50,127,000		
Plant, Equip.:	$248,000	**Total Liab.:**	$90,249,000	**Indic. Yr. Divd.:**	NA
Total Assets:	$227,531,000	**Net Worth:**	$137,282,000	**Debt/ Equity:**	NA

North American Scientific Inc

20200 Sunburst St., Chatsworth, CA, 91311; **PH:** 1-818-734-8600; **Fax:** 1-818-734-5200; **http://** www.nasmedical.com

General - Incorporation	DE	**Stock**- Price on:12/24/2007	$1.02
Employees	177	Stock Exchange	NDQ
Auditor	Singer Lewak Greenbaum & Goldstein	Ticker Symbol	NATH
Stk Agt	U.S. Stock Transfer Corp	Outstanding Shares	29,300,000
Counsel	Seyfarth Shaw	E.P.S.	-$0.787
DUNS No.	62-015-1878	Shareholders	NA

Business: The group's principal activity is manufacture and market radioisotopic products used in the treatment and diagnosis of disease. The products, including brachytherapy seeds and radiopharmaceuticals, are used in medical and environmental research and industrial applications. Other products include radiation calibration and reference source products. The group manufactures catalog and customized products for commercial laboratories serving the environmental sector. The group's commercial customers include federal and state government agencies, medical equipment manufacturers, nuclear utilities and private organizations. Brachytherapy seeds are marketed and sold under the trademark Prospera (R). The group operates mainly in the United States of America. The group acquired Radiation Therapy Products in Aug 2003. On 05-May-2004, the group acquired Nomos Corporation.

Primary SIC and add'l.: 2835 3829 8731

CIK No: 0000949876

Subsidiaries: NOMOS China USA, Inc., NOMOS Corporation, NOMOS Germany GmbH, NOMOS Netherlands B.V., North American Scientific, Inc., ROCS Acquisition, Inc., Theseus Imaging Corporation

Officers: John B. Rush/Dir., CEO, Pres., Troy Barring/COO, Sr. VP, James W. Klingler/Sr. VP, CFO, Michael L. Cutrer/Dir., CTO, Exec. VP, David N. King/Sec., Michael C. Ryan/Sr. VP

Directors: John B. Rush/Dir., CEO, Pres., Gary N. Wilner/Chmn. - North American Scientific, John A. Friede/Dir. - North American Scientific, Jonathan P. Gertler/Dir., Nancy J. Wysenski/Dir., Michael L. Cutrer/Dir., CTO, Exec. VP, Wilfred E. Jaeger/Dir. - North American Scientific, John M. Sabin/Dir., Richard A. Sandberg/Dir., Roderick A. Young/Dir.

Owners: John B. Rush, Wells Fargo & Company, Nancy J. Wysenski, John A. Friede, Roderick A. Young, Three Arch Partners, Wilfred E. Jaeger, James W. Klingler, Richard A. Sandberg, Insiders, SF Capital Partners Ltd., John M. Sabin, Michael L. Cutrer, Gary N. Wilner, CHL Medical Partners

Financial Data: ***Fiscal Year End:***10/31 ***Latest Annual Data:*** 10/31/2006

Year	Sales	Net Income
2006	$28,988,000	-$17,130,000
2005	$32,224,000	-$55,513,000
2004	$24,737,000	-$36,307,000

Curr. Assets:	$19,321,000	**Curr. Liab.:**	$10,010,000		
Plant, Equip.:	$2,400,000	**Total Liab.:**	$10,010,000	**Indic. Yr. Divd.:**	NA
Total Assets:	$27,198,000	**Net Worth:**	$17,188,000	**Debt/ Equity:**	NA

North American Technologies Group Inc

429 Memory Ln., Marshall, TX, 75672; **PH:** 1-713-462-0303; **http://** www.tietek.com

General - Incorporation	DE	**Stock**- Price on:12/24/2007	$0.183
Employees	124	Stock Exchange	OTC
Auditor	KBA Group, LLP	Ticker Symbol	NAMC
Stk Agt	Continental Stock Transfer & Trust Co	Outstanding Shares	183,440,000
Counsel	Buchanan Ingersoll P.C.	E.P.S.	-$0.221
DUNS No.	80-483-3093	Shareholders	NA

Business: The group's principal activity is to manufacture and market tietek(tm) products. The main product of the group is a composite railroad crosstie, which is used as a direct substitute for wood crossties. The tietek(tm) crosstie formula is a proprietary mixture of rubber from recycled tires, plastics, other waste materials, additives, fillers and reinforcement agents. The group's crosstie can be installed either manually or with automated equipment and can be fastened with cut spikes or other systems. The group manufactures its products through its wholly owned subsidiary, tietek inc.

Primary SIC and add'l.: 3089

CIK No: 0000808013

Subsidiaries: EET Holdings, Inc., GAIA Technologies, Inc., Natk Ipf, Inc., Natk Rii, Inc., TieTek LLC, TieTek Technologies, Inc.

Officers: Alex C. Rankin/CEO, Joe B. Dorman/62/Dir., General Counsel, Henry W. Sullivan/67/Dir., Chief Scientist - Strategist, Mahesh Shetty/48/Dir., CFO

Directors: Franklin A. Mathias/Chmn., Robert E. Chain/Dir., Henry W. Sullivan/67/Dir., Chief Scientist - Strategist, John C. Malone/49/Dir., Neal P. Kaufman/39/Dir., Mahesh Shetty/48/Dir., CFO, Joe B. Dorman/62/Dir., General Counsel, John T. Corcia/62/Dir., Scott Kaufman/35/Dir., Kenneth Z. Scott/64/Dir., Richard Guiltinan/53/Dir.

Owners: Sponsor Investments, LLC, Big Bend XI Investments, Ltd., Big Bend XI Investments, Ltd., MidSummer Investments, Ltd., MidSummer Investments, Ltd., Crestview Capital Master, LLC, Herakles Investments, Inc., Sponsor Investments, LLC, Herakles Investments, Inc., Crestview Capital Master, LLC, Islandia, L.P., Henry W. Sullivan, Kenneth Z. Scott, Opus 5949 LLC, Richard Guiltinan *(20 Owners included in Index)*

Financial Data: ***Fiscal Year End:***12/31 ***Latest Annual Data:*** 10/1/2006

Year	Sales	Net Income
2006	$10,622,000	-$15,482,000
2005	$5,171,000	-$15,686,000
2004	$3,348,000	-$11,636,000

Curr. Assets:	$3,008,000	**Curr. Liab.:**	$22,587,000		
Plant, Equip.:	$11,807,000	**Total Liab.:**	$22,587,000	**Indic. Yr. Divd.:**	NA
Total Assets:	$16,347,000	**Net Worth:**	-$6,240,000	**Debt/ Equity:**	NA

North Atlanta National Bank

10500 Old Ala Conectr Rd. , Alpharetta, GA, 30022; *PH:* 1-678-277-8400; *Fax:* 1-678-277-8440;
http:// www.nanb.com

General - Incorporation		**Stock** - Price on:12/24/2007	$18.2
Employees	22	Stock Exchange	NA
Auditor	NA	Ticker Symbol	NA
Stk Agt	NA	Outstanding Shares	NA
Counsel	NA	E.P.S.	NA
DUNS No.	NA	Shareholders	NA

Business: The group's principle activity is to provide banking services.The group's services include personal, money market and savings accounts. The group operates from United States.

Primary SIC and add'l.: 6029

CIK No:

Officers: James A. Walker/Chmn., CEO, Eugene B. Ansley/Sr. VP, Deepal Gajjar/Teller, Jeffe Herrick/VP, Hillary Coy/Sr. VP, Tony Webb/Exec. VP, Chuck Gordon/Sr. VP, Yolanda Prince/Customer Service Representative, Ryan Hammack/Commercial Loan Associate, Kristen Phillips/Operations Specialist, Brian McGuire/Business Development, Leslie W. Green/Credit Administration Specialist, Vickie Ray/Head - Teller, Kellie Pressnall/Assist. VP, Amber Hollifield/Customer Service Representative *(19 Officers included in Index)*

Directors: James A. Walker/Chmn., CEO

North Bay Bancorp

1500 Soscol Ave, Napa, CA, 94559; *PH:* 1-707-257-8500; *http://* www.northbaybancorp.com

General - Incorporation	CA	**Stock** - Price on:12/24/2007	NA
Employees	151	Stock Exchange	NYSE
Auditor	Perry-smith LLP	Ticker Symbol	NBG
Stk Agt	Registrar & Transfer Co	Outstanding Shares	NA
Counsel	Wyman G. Smith, III	E.P.S.	NA
DUNS No.	NA	Shareholders	NA

Business: The group's principal activity is to provide commercial banking services to individuals, business and agricultural communities in napa and solano counties in California. It operates five offices in napa county and four offices in solano county. Retail commercial banking operations include accepting deposits and providing consumer loans, commercial loans, construction loans and real estate loans. The group is a member of the star, visa and plus ATM networks, providing customers with access to point of sale and ATM service worldwide. It offers Internet banking services to support accounts inquiries, transfer between accounts and automatic reconciliation and bill payment services.

Primary SIC and add'l.: 6022 6712

CIK No: 0001102595

Subsidiaries: The Vintage Bank

Officers: Terry L. Robinson/Dir., CEO, Pres., Michael Wengel/CFO, Exec. VP

Directors: Terry L. Robinson/Dir., CEO, Pres., David B. Gaw/Chmn., Richard S. Long/Vice Chmn., Stephen C. Spencer/Dir., Dennis G. Schmal/Dir., Fred J. Hearn/Dir., Thomas N. Gavin/Dir., Denise C. Suihkonen/Dir., Gary C. Wallace/Dir., James E. Tidgewell/Dir., Thomas F. Malloy/Dir., Thomas H. Shelton/Dir.

North Central Bancshares Inc

825 Central Ave., Fort Dodge, IA, 50501; *PH:* 1-515-576-7531; *Fax:* 1-515-576-3398;
http:// www.firstfederaliowa.com

General - Incorporation	IA	**Stock** - Price on:12/24/2007	$40
Employees	119	Stock Exchange	NDQ
Auditor	McGladrey & Pullen LLP	Ticker Symbol	FFFD
Stk Agt	Computershare Investor Services LLC	Outstanding Shares	1,370,000
Counsel	Thacher Proffitt & Wood LLP	E.P.S.	$3.10
DUNS No.	96-677-2055	Shareholders	NA

Business: The group's principal activity is to provide real estate mortgage loans. The group operates through 9 branch units and main office located in fort dodge, Iowa. The group provides its services in Nevada, ames, perry, ankeny, burlington and mount pleasant, Iowa. The loan portfolio includes fixed-and adjustable-rate first mortgage loans secured by one-to-four family owner-occupied residential real estate and multifamily residential, commercial real estate and consumer loans. Deposit services include demand deposit, now accounts, savings accounts and money market accounts.

Primary SIC and add'l.: 6712 6035

CIK No: 0001005188

Subsidiaries: First Federal Investment Services, Inc., First Iowa Mortgage, Inc., First Iowa Title Services, Inc.

Officers: David M. Bradley/55/Chmn., CEO, Pres./$369,158.00, Paul F. Bognanno/Dir., Sr. Exec. VP, Thomas C. Chalstrom/Dir., COO, Pres./$203,977.00, Marilyn Nelson/Branch Mgr. - Nevada, Linda Moeller/Branch Mgr. - Mount Pleasant, Willis F. Fry/Pres. - Marketing, Burlington, Roosevelt, Corky Wolbert/Branch Mgr. - Burlington, Downtown, Reggie Eischeid/Mgr. - Branch, Sales, Ankeny, William Boord/VP, Branch Mgr. - West Des Moines, Jordan Creek, Jean L. Lake/65/Sec., David W. Edge/49/CFO, Treasurer/$145,020.00, Kirk A. Yung/45/Sr. VP/$145,490.00, David Tucker/Branch Mgr. - Ames, Joanna Piasecka/Branch Mgr. - Clive, Cindy Baedke/Branch Mgr. - Fort Dodge, Crossroads *(17 Officers included in Index)*

Directors: David M. Bradley/55/Chmn., CEO, Pres., Paul F. Bognanno/Dir., Sr. Exec. VP, Melvin R. Schroeder/Dir., Robert H. Singer/Dir., Randall L. Minear/Dir., Mark Thompson/Dir., Thomas C. Chalstrom/Dir., COO, Pres.

Owners: Randall L. Minear, David M. Bradley/3.80%, Kirk A. Yung, Dimensional Fund Advisors, Inc./8.90%, Employee Stock Ownership Plan of/11.90%, Insiders/18.50%, Paul F. Bognanno, Mark M. Thompson/1.50%, Melvin R. Schroeder, Thomson Horstmann & Bryant, Inc./5.70%, C. Thomas Chalstrom/1.10%, Robert H. Singer, FMR Corp./10.20%, David W. Edge

Financial Data: *Fiscal Year End:*12/31 *Latest Annual Data:* 12/31/2006

Year	Sales	Net Income
2006	$35,649,000	$4,812,000
2005	$33,500,000	$5,015,000
2004	$30,871,000	$5,399,000

Curr. Assets:	$22,284,000	**Curr. Liab.:**	$363,364,000
Plant, Equip.:	$15,685,000	**Total Liab.:**	$473,323,000	**Indic. Yr. Divd.:** $1.400
Total Assets:	$515,515,000	**Net Worth:**	$42,192,000	**Debt/ Equity:** 2.4329

North Coast Partners Inc

3495 Winton Pl., Ste. E200, Rochester, NY, 14623; *PH:* 1-516-887-8200; *Fax:* 1-585-427-7632;
http:// www.northcoastpartners.com; *Email:* info@northcoastpartners.com

General - Incorporation	DE	**Stock** - Price on:12/24/2007	NA
Employees	NA	Stock Exchange	OTC
Auditor	Malone & Bailey, PC	Ticker Symbol	NCPR
Stk Agt	National Stock Transfer	Outstanding Shares	NA
Counsel	NA	E.P.S.	$0.00
DUNS No.	NA	Shareholders	NA

Business: The groups principle activities include producing and distributing musical CD's and musical performances. The group operates from the United States and Canada.

Primary SIC and add'l.: 3652

CIK No: 0001092800

Subsidiaries: Trans Media Inc

Officers: Craig Moody/CEO, Wong Peck Ling/38/Dir., CFO, F. L. Wurzburg/Founder, Managing Partner, Doug Johnston/Principle, Mike Mills/Principle, Craig Eckert/Principle

Directors: F. L. Wurzburg/Founder, Managing Partner, Wong Peck Ling/38/Dir., CFO, Mel Venkateswaran/62/Dir.

Owners: Mel Venkateswaran/3.80%, Wong Peck Ling/12.70%, Stamford Bridge Holdings Limited/12.70%, Insiders/16.40%

Financial Data: *Fiscal Year End:*08/31 *Latest Annual Data:* 08/31/2007

Year	Sales	Net Income
2007	NA	-$35,000
2006	$2,000	-$28,000

Curr. Assets:	$1,000	**Curr. Liab.:**	$112,000
Plant, Equip.:	NA	**Total Liab.:**	$112,000	**Indic. Yr. Divd.:** NA
Total Assets:	$1,000	**Net Worth:**	-$111,000	**Debt/ Equity:** NA

North Dallas Bank & Trust Co TEX

12900 Preston Rd., Dallas, TX, 75230; *PH:* 1-972-387-1300; *Fax:* 1-972-387-2815;
http:// www.ndbt.com

General - Incorporation		**Stock** - Price on:12/24/2007	$60.9
Employees	NA	Stock Exchange	OTC
Auditor	NA	Ticker Symbol	NODB
Stk Agt	NA	Outstanding Shares	NA
Counsel	NA	E.P.S.	NA
DUNS No.	NA	Shareholders	NA

Business: The groups principle activity is to provide personal and business banking services. The groups personal banking services include checking accounts, Interest checking, Savings accounts, Money market accounts, loans, safe deposit boxes, Internet banking, merchant credit cards, Certificates of deposits, and Sweep accounts. The group operates from United States.

Primary SIC and add'l.: 6022 6029 6021

CIK No:

Financial Data: *Fiscal Year End:*NA *Latest Annual Data:* 12/31/2006

Year	Sales	Net Income
2006	$13,116,000	$3,105,000
2005	$11,002,000	$2,841,000
2004	$10,830,000	$2,694,000

North European Oil Royality Trust

43 W Front St., Ste. 19A, Red Bank, NJ, 07701; *PH:* 1-732-741-4008; *Fax:* 1-732-741-3140;
http:// www.neort.com

General - Incorporation	DE	**Stock** - Price on:12/24/2007	$38.6
Employees	NA	Stock Exchange	NDQ
Auditor	Ernst & Young LLP	Ticker Symbol	NSANY
Stk Agt	Registrar & Transfer Co	Outstanding Shares	9,190,000
Counsel	NA	E.P.S.	$2.91
DUNS No.	NA	Shareholders	NA

Business: The groups principle activities include owning, acquiring and operating oil, sulfur and gas properties. The group operated from the United States and Germany. The groups quarterly revenue for September 2007 was 6.05 millions of USD.

Primary SIC and add'l.: 6792

CIK No: 0000072633

Officers: John R. Van Kirk/MD

Financial Data: *Fiscal Year End:*10/31 *Latest Annual Data:* 10/31/2006

Year	Sales	Net Income
2006	$31,243,000	$30,259,000
2005	$21,144,000	$20,223,000
2004	$15,083,000	$14,308,000

Curr. Assets:	$7,204,000	**Curr. Liab.:**	$7,169,000	**P/E Ratio:** 10.64
Plant, Equip.:	NA	**Total Liab.:**	$7,169,000	**Indic. Yr. Divd.:** $2.560
Total Assets:	$7,204,000	**Net Worth:**	$36,000	**Debt/ Equity:** NA

North Fork BanCorp Inc

275 Brd. Hollow Rd. , Melville, NY, 11747; *PH:* 1-631-844-1004; *http://* www.northforkbank.com

General - Incorporation	DE	**Stock** - Price on:12/24/2007	$28.07
Employees	NA	Stock Exchange	NYSE
Auditor	KPMG LLP	Ticker Symbol	NFI
Stk Agt	Computershare Investor Services LLC	Outstanding Shares	NA
Counsel	NA	E.P.S.	NA
DUNS No.	10-382-9552	Shareholders	NA

Business: The group's principle activities are to provide banking and financial services. The banking services provided by the group are issuance of loans, the acceptance of customer deposits and related fee based services and products. It also offers other financial services such as asset management, securities brokerage and sales of alternative investment products. The services are provided to middle market and small business organizations, local governmental units and retail customers. The group operates through 177 branch offices located in the New York.

Primary SIC and add'l.: 6021 6712

CIK No: 0000352510

Subsidiaries: 298 15thStreet Realty Corp., 3090 Ocean Avenue Realty Corp., All Points Capital Corp., All Points Public Funding, LLC, Alpha REO Corporation, Amivest Corporation, Beta REO Corp., CBMC Inc. (d/b/a Money Centers), Clare-Elm Corp., Compass Food Service Corp., Cutchco Corp., GP Asset LLC, GPCC Mississippi, LLC, GPM Food Services, LLC, GreenPoint Agency Inc. 58 Subsidiaries included in the Index

North Penn Bancorp Inc PA

216 Adams Ave., Scranton, PA, 18503; **PH:** 1-570-344-6113

General - Incorporation	PA	Stock - Price on:12/24/2007	$13.95
Employees	30	Stock Exchange	NA
Auditor	McGrail Merkel Quinn & Associates	Ticker Symbol	NA
Stk Agt	Registrar & Transfer Co	Outstanding Shares	1,440,000
Counsel	NA	E.P.S	NA
DUNS No.	NA	Shareholders	NA

Business: The groups principle activities include owning and supervising the bank. The services of the group include real estate loans, residential mortgage loans, home equity loans and lines of credit, auto loans, demand and time deposit accounts, NOW accounts, money market accounts, individual retirement accounts and holiday accounts, direct payroll and social security, deposit services, bank-by-mail services, automated teller machine network, safe deposit boxes, night depository facilities, notary services and travelers checks, internet banking and electronic bill payment. The group operates from the United States.

Primary SIC and add'l.: 6035

CIK No: 0001309127

Subsidiaries: North Penn Bank

Officers: Frederick L. Hickman/52/Dir., CEO, Pres., Frank H. Mechler/88/Dir., Pres., Sec. - North Penn Bank, Thomas J. Dziak/52/Exec. VP, Thomas A. Byrne/46/Sr. VP, Glenn J. Clark/35/Assist. VP, Controller

Directors: Frederick L. Hickman/52/Dir., CEO, Pres., Frank H. Mechler/88/Dir., Pres., Sec. - North Penn Bank, Herbert C. Kneller/63/Dir., David Samuel/81/Dir., Kevin M. Lamont/49/Dir., Otto P. Robinson/69/Dir., Gordon S. Florey/82/Dir., James W. Reid/56/Dir., Virginia D. McGregor/45/Dir.

Financial Data: Fiscal Year End:12/31 Latest Annual Data: 12/31/2006

Year	Sales	Net Income
2006	$7,380,000	$315,000
2005	$5,671,000	-$124,000

North Pittsburgh Systems Inc

4008 Gibsonia Rd., Gibsonia, PA, 15044; **PH:** 1-724-443-9600; **Fax:** 1-724-443-9431; http:// www.northpittsburgh.com

General - Incorporation	PA	Stock - Price on:12/24/2007	$21.06
Employees	357	Stock Exchange	NDQ
Auditor	KPMG LLP	Ticker Symbol	NPSP
Stk Agt	Wells Fargo Bank Minnesota N.A	Outstanding Shares	15,010,000
Counsel	NA	E.P.S	$1.00
DUNS No.	00-791-0953	Shareholders	NA

Business: The group's principal activity is to provide wireline telecommunications services and equipment. The services offered include local network services, network access services, long distance toll service, Internet access service, directory advertising, billing and other services as well as telecommunications equipment services. The group operates through its subsidiaries, north pittsburgh telephone company, penn telecom, inc. And pinnatech, inc. These services are provided to businesses and residences throughout western Pennsylvania.

Primary SIC and add'l.: 4813 5065 7375 4899 6719

CIK No: 0000764765

Subsidiaries: Boulevard Communications, capital stock of Multi, Inc, L.L.P, North Pittsburgh Telephone Company, Penn Telecom, Inc, Pinnatech, Inc

Officers: Matthew D. Poleski/33/VP, Treasurer, Albert W. Weigand/49/VP

Owners: Frederick J. Crowley, Insiders/1.24%, Harry R. Brown, Allen P. Kimble, Charles E. Cole, Stephen G. Kraskin, Royce & Associates, LLC/7.59%, Bulldog Investors/5.36%, David E. Nelsen, William N. Barthlow, Frank A. Macefe, Charles E. Thomas

Financial Data: Fiscal Year End:12/31 Latest Annual Data: 12/31/2006

Year	Sales			Net Income
2006	$103,465,000			$31,755,000
2005	$109,804,000			$23,056,000
2004	$108,469,000			$18,960,000
Curr. Assets:	$65,259,000	**Curr. Liab.:**	$19,511,000	**P/E Ratio:** 9.93
Plant, Equip.:	$75,352,000	**Total Liab.:**	$56,137,000	**Indic. Yr. Divd.:** $0.800
Total Assets:	$157,433,000	**Net Worth:**	$101,296,000	**Debt/ Equity:** 0.1749

North Pointe Holdings Corp

28819 Franklin Rd., Southfield, MI, 48034; **PH:** 1-248-358-1171; **Fax:** 1-877-229-6743; http:// www.npic.com

General - Incorporation	MI	Stock - Price on:12/24/2007	$11.46
Employees	218	Stock Exchange	NDQ
Auditor	PricewaterhouseCoopers LLP	Ticker Symbol	NA
Stk Agt	SunTrust Bank	Outstanding Shares	9,120,000
Counsel	NA	E.P.S	$0.759
DUNS No.	NA	Shareholders	NA

Business: The group operates through its subsidiaries whose principle activity is to provide property and casualty insurance. The products of the group include coverage for liquor liability, property, general liability, commercial multi-peril and, commercial automobiles and flood insurance. The groups operates through three segments namely commercial insurance lines, personal insurance lines and administrative services. The group operates from the United States. The group's quarterly revenue for September 2007 was 40.88 millions of USD.

Primary SIC and add'l.: 6351 6331

CIK No: 0001171218

Subsidiaries: Home pointe Insurance Company, Mictfield Insurance Company, North point financial Services. Inc, North pointe Casualty Insurance Company, North pointe Insurance Company, NP capital Trust, NP premium fommce Company, South pointe financial Services. Inc

Officers: James G. Petcoff/Chmn., CEO, Pres., Matthew B. Petcoff/COO, Exec. VP, Sec., Dir., Brian J. Roney/CFO, Sr. VP - Finance, John H. Berry/Treasurer, Bradford T. Lyons/Sr. VP, Matthew L. MacLean/Sr. VP - Claims, Paul B. Deemer/VP, Natalie M. Bradley/CIO, Gregory M. Skinner/Regional VP

Directors: James G. Petcoff/Chmn., CEO, Pres., Matthew B. Petcoff/COO, Exec. VP, Sec., Dir., Richard J. Lindberg/Dir., Joon S. Moon/Dir., Jorge J. Morales/Dir., Jamison R. Williams/Dir., Julius A. Otten/Dir., Joseph D. Sarafa/Dir.

Owners: Matthew L. MacLean, Hovde Capital Advisors LLC/6.10%, Security Management Company, LLC/8.60%, Joseph D. Sarafa, Wells Fargo Capital Management Incorporated/9.70%, Becker Capital Management, Inc./6.20%, Richard J. Lindberg, Insiders/45.10%, Wellington Management Company, LLP/9.80%, James G. Petcoff/31.20%, Jorge J. Morales, Joon S. Moon/4.60%, Jamison R. Williams/1.40%, Brian J. Roney/1.90%, Wells Fargo & Company/10.70% (19 Owners included in Index)

Financial Data: Fiscal Year End:12/31 Latest Annual Data: 12/31/2006

Year	Sales			Net Income
2006	$88,421,000			$4,676,000
2005	$90,474,000			$3,850,000
2004	$86,727,000			$11,433,000
Curr. Assets:	$114,020,000	**Curr. Liab.:**	$14,136,000	**P/E Ratio:** 23.88
Plant, Equip.:	$5,946,000	**Total Liab.:**	$169,342,000	**Indic. Yr. Divd.:** NA
Total Assets:	$257,577,000	**Net Worth:**	$88,235,000	**Debt/ Equity:** 0.2571

North Shore Capital Advisors Corp

20 Marlin Ln., Port Washington, NY, 11050; **PH:** 1-516-765-6220; http:// nscapitaladvisors.com

General - Incorporation	DE	Stock - Price on:12/24/2007	NA
Employees	NA	Stock Exchange	NA
Auditor	Raich Ende Malter & Co. LLP	Ticker Symbol	NA
Stk Agt	NA	Outstanding Shares	NA
Counsel	NA	E.P.S	NA
DUNS No.	NA	Shareholders	NA

Business: The group's principal activity is providing hands-on business and financial consulting services including corporate advisory services, business development services, mergers & acquisitions, and divestitures, including business and asset valuations. The focus is on small and emerging growth public and private companies that historically have not had the access to or resources to hire the larger, more established financial services and management consulting firms.

Primary SIC and add'l.: 6211

CIK No: 0001319647

Officers: Steve Cohen/Dir., CEO, CFO, Pres.

Directors: Steve Cohen/Dir., CEO, CFO, Pres., Dov Perlysky/44/Dir.

Owners: Steven Cohen/3.50%, Alison Bell/7.10%, Rosalind Davidowitz/8.90%, Pamela Turkel/8.90%, Pamela Katz/9.95%, Insiders/3.50%, Krovim LLC/39.00%

North Shore Gas Co

24th Floor, 130 East Randolph Dr., Chicago, IL, 60601; **PH:** 1-312-240-4000; http:// www.PeoplesEnergy.com

General - Incorporation	IL	Stock - Price on:12/24/2007	NA
Employees	2,223	Stock Exchange	NA
Auditor	Deloitte & Touche LLP	Ticker Symbol	NA
Stk Agt	American Stock Transfer & Trust Co.	Outstanding Shares	NA
Counsel	NA	E.P.S	NA
DUNS No.	00-693-6306	Shareholders	NA

Business: The group's principle activities are to purchase, store, distribute and market natural gas. The company is a wholly owned subsidiary of peoples energy corporation. The company has approximately 150,000 residential, commercial and industrial retail sales and transportation customers within its service area of approximately 275 square miles, located in northeastern Illinois.

Primary SIC and add'l.: 4924

CIK No: 0000110101

Subsidiaries: North Shore Gas Company, Peoples Elwood, LLC, Peoples Energy Production Texas, L.P., Peoples Energy Production Company, Peoples Energy Production Operating Company, Peoples Energy Production Partners, L.P., Peoples Energy Resources Company, LLC, Peoples Energy Services Corporation, PEP Holdings, LLC, PERC Power, LLC, The Peoples Gas Light and Coke Company

Officers: Thomas M. Patrick/Chmn., CEO, Douglas M. Ruschau/VP, Treasurer - Peoples Energy Corporation, Theodore R. Tetzlaff/General Counsel, Linda M. Kallas/VP, Controller, Peter H. Kauffman/Assist. General Counsel, Sec., Katherine A. Donofrio/Sr. VP - Business Services, Thomas A. Nardi/CFO, Exec. VP, Desiree G. Rogers/Pres., Denise J. Cooper/VP - Human Resources, Edward A. Doerk/VP, Willard S. Evans/VP - Pglc, Gerard T. Fox/VP, Deputy General Counsel, Joseph P. Phillips/VP - Information Technology Services, Richard M. Taglienti/VP

Directors: Thomas M. Patrick/Chmn., CEO, William E. Morrow/Vice Chmn., Keith E. Bailey/Dir. - Peoples Energy Corporation, James R. Boris/Dir. - Peoples Energy Corporation, William J. Brodsky/Dir. - Peoples Energy Corporation, Pastora San Juan Cafferty/Dir. - Peoples Energy Corporation, Diana S. Ferguson/Dir. - Peoples Energy Corporation, John W. Higgins/Dir. - Peoples Energy Corporation, Dipak C. Jain/Dir. - Peoples Energy Corporation, Michael E. Lavin/Dir. - Peoples Energy Corporation, Homer J. Livingston/Dir. - Peoples Energy Corporation, Richard P. Toft/Dir. - Peoples Energy Corporation

Owners: Homer J. Livingston, Thomas M. Patrick, Richard P. Toft, William E. Morrow, Keith E. Bailey, William J. Brodsky, James R. Boris, Michael E. Lavin, Dipak C. Jain, Pastora San Juan Cafferty, Steven W. Nance, Insiders/1.51%, John W. Higgins, Diana S. Ferguson, Thomas A. Nardi (16 Owners included in Index)

North State Bank Inc

4270 Cir. at N Hills, Raleigh, NC, 27609; *PH:* 1-919-787-9696; *Fax:* 1-919-719-4481;
http:// www.northstatebank.com

General - Incorporation	NC	**Stock** - Price on:12/24/2007	$24.5
Employees	75	Stock Exchange	NA
Auditor	Dixon Hughes PLLC	Ticker Symbol	NA
Stk Agt	NA	Outstanding Shares	4,600,000
Counsel	NA	E.P.S.	$0.68
DUNS No.	NA	Shareholders	NA

Business: The group's principal activity is the provision of general commercial and retail banking services in North Carolina. A holding company of the north state bank, the group offers checking, savings and investment accounts, commercial installment, mortgage and personal loans. It also provides safe deposit boxes, savings bonds, wire transfer and other associated services. Through its subsidiary, north state bank financial services inc, the group offers brokerage services. The operations are conducted through two full-service banking offices in raleigh and garner that serve individuals, professional firms and businesses in the cities.

Primary SIC and add'l.: 6022 6712

CIK No: 0001175029

Subsidiaries: North State Bank, North State Bank Financial Services, Inc., North State Statutory Trust I, North State Statutory Trust II

Officers: Larry D. Barbour/Dir., CEO, Pres., Allyson Rayfield/Sr. Mortgage Loan Officer, David Bannister/Member - Garner Advisory Board, Sandra A. Temple/COO, Exec. VP, Virginia W. Watson/Sr. VP - Sr. Mortgage Lender, Phil Whittington/Sr. VP - Sr. Commercial Banker, Kenneth W. Goetze/Member - Wake Forest Advisory Board, James B. Pierce/Member - West Raleigh Advisory Board, Judy Stephenson/Exec. VP - Business Development, Commercial Lending, Gerry Rogers/Chief Credit Officer, Greg Asbelle/VP, Dir. - Cash Management Services, James M. Brothers/VP, Christopher R. Bruffey/Sr. VP - Garner Marketing Executive, Barbara Doolittle/VP, Accounting Relationship Mgr., Jonathan Hand/VP - Wake Forest Marketing Executive *(24 Officers included in Index)*

Directors: Larry D. Barbour/Dir., CEO, Pres., Fred J. Smith/Chmn., Nutan J. Shah/Dir., Jim Massengill/Member - Garner Advisory Board, Jason D. Moore/Member - Garner Advisory Board, George Rucker/Member - Garner Advisory Board, Gary W. Lyons/Member - Wake Forest Advisory Board, Robert P. Pace/Member - Wake Forest Advisory Board, George Pittman/Member - Wake Forest Advisory Board, David F. Boerner/Member - West Raleigh Advisory Board, Tony C. Gurley/Member - West Raleigh Advisory Boardc, Robert E. Monroe/Member - West Raleigh Advisory Board, Jack M. Stancil/Dir., Charles T. Francis/Dir., George C. Venters/Dir. *(39 Directors included in Index)*

Owners: Barry W. Partlo, Larry D. Barbour/2.72%, Kirk A. Whorf, Jeanette W. Hyde/1.52%, Burley B. Mitchell, James C. Branch/1.12%, George C. Venters/1.83%, Sandra A. Temple, Keith J. Keener/2.95%, Glenn E. Futrell/4.52%, Harold W. Perry/5.40%, Charles T. Francis/1.08%, Jack M. Stancil/1.23%, Insiders/50.69%, Nutan T. Shah/3.88% *(20 Owners included in Index)*

Financial Data: *Fiscal Year End:*12/31 *Latest Annual Data:* 12/31/2006

Year	Sales		Net Income
2006	$27,586,000		$3,272,000
2005	$20,091,000		$2,438,000
2004	$13,634,000		$1,376,000
Curr. Assets:	$59,251,000	**Curr. Liab.:** $417,684,000	**P/E Ratio:** 36.03
Plant, Equip.:	$7,810,000	**Total Liab.:** $428,880,000	**Indic. Yr. Divd.:** NA
Total Assets:	$455,477,000	**Net Worth:** $26,597,000	**Debt/ Equity:** 0.4042

North Valley Bancorp

300 Pk. Marina Cir., Redding, CA, 96001; *PH:* 1-530-226-2900; *Fax:* 1-530-226-0514;
http:// www.northvalleybank.com

General - Incorporation	CA	**Stock** - Price on:12/24/2007	$24.8
Employees	429	Stock Exchange	NDQ
Auditor	Perry-Smith LLP	Ticker Symbol	NOVB
Stk Agt	Mellon Investor Services LLC	Outstanding Shares	7,360,000
Counsel	Wells, Small, Selke & Graham	E.P.S.	$1.21
DUNS No.	06-525-0318	Shareholders	NA

Business: The group's principal activity is to conduct commercial and retail banking business in northern California. The business consists of accepting demand, savings, money market rate deposit accounts and time deposits and making commercial, real estate and consumer loans. It also offers installment note collections, issues cashier's checks and money orders, sells travelers' checks and provides safe deposit boxes and other customary banking services. The federal deposit insurance corporation insures the deposits. The group wholly owns its principal subsidiaries, north valley bank, north valley trading company, bank processing, inc and north valley capital trust i and north valley capital trust ii. The group operates fourteen banking offices in shasta and trinity counties.

Primary SIC and add'l.: 6712 6022

CIK No: 0000353191

Subsidiaries: Bank Processing, Inc., North Valley Bank, North Valley Capital Statutory Trust IV, North Valley Capital Trust I, North Valley Capital Trust II, North Valley Capital Trust III, North Valley Trading Company, NVB Business Bank

Officers: Michael J. Cushman/Dir., CEO, Pres., J. M. Wells/Chmn., Attorney at Law, John B. Johnson/VP, Business Banking Officer - North Valley Bank, Business Banking Center, Sharon L. Benson/Sr. VP, Controller - Administration, Glenn R. Huffaker/VP, Business Banking Officer - North Valley Bank, Business Banking Center, Jerald L. Ricketts/Sr. VP, Commercial Loan Officer - Woodland, Regional Headquarters, North Valley Bank, Linda U. Konietzko/VP, Branch Mgr. - Woodland, Regional Headquarters, North Valley Bank, Vicki L. Whetten/Sr. VP, Branch Administrator - Fairfield, North Valley Bank, Susan B. Vargas/VP, Regional Mgr. - Fairfield, North Valley Bank, Ann L. Alumbaugh/Assist. VP, Branch Mgr. - Willits, North Valley Bank, Peter Faye/Regional Pres. - Woodland, Regional Headquarters, North Valley Bank, Cheri Skudlarek/Assist. VP, Branch Mgr. - Cottonwood, North Valley Bank, Terri Christensen/Assist. VP, Branch Mgr. - Eureka Mall Office, North Valley Bank, Lisa Mitchell/Assist. VP, Branch Mgr. - Mckinleyville, North Valley Bank, Sandee Blalock/Assist. VP, Branch Mgr. - Palo Cedro, North Valley Bank *(51 Officers included in Index)*

Directors: Michael J. Cushman/Dir., CEO, Pres., J. M. Wells/Chmn., Attorney at Law, Royce L. Friesen/Dir., William W. Cox/Dir., Dolores M. Vellutini/Dir., Martin A. Mariani/Dir., Kevin D. Hartwick/Dir., Dan W. Ghidinelli/Dir., Roger B. Kohlmeier/Dir.

Owners: William W. Cox, Royce L. Friesen/3.07%, Roger D. Nash, Kevin D. Hartwick/3.25%, Kevin R. Watson, Roger B. Kohlmeier/2.81%, Dante W. Ghidinelli/3.67%, Michael J. Cushman/2.47%, Scott R. Louis, J. M. Wells/2.27%, Martin A. Mariani, Insiders/10.80%, Leo J. Graham, Dolores M. Vellutini/3.93%, Gary S. Litzsinger

---

Financial Data: *Fiscal Year End:*12/31 *Latest Annual Data:* 12/31/2006

Year	Sales		Net Income
2006	$69,832,000		$10,396,000
2005	$61,892,000		$9,149,000
2004	$48,393,000		$8,379,000
Curr. Assets:	$45,334,000	**Curr. Liab.:** $760,721,000	**P/E Ratio:** 17.97
Plant, Equip.:	$14,699,000	**Total Liab.:** $830,182,000	**Indic. Yr. Divd.:** $0.400
Total Assets:	$905,673,000	**Net Worth:** $75,491,000	**Debt/ Equity:** NA

Northeast Bancorp

500 Canal St., Lewiston, ME, 04240; *PH:* 1-207-786-3245; *Fax:* 1-207-782-7230;
http:// www.northeastbank.com

General - Incorporation	ME	**Stock** - Price on:12/24/2007	$16.866
Employees	188	Stock Exchange	NDQ
Auditor	Shatswell, Macleod & Co., P.c	Ticker Symbol	NA
Stk Agt	Registrar & Transfer Co	Outstanding Shares	2,450,000
Counsel	NA	E.P.S.	$0.76
DUNS No.	19-150-4950	Shareholders	NA

Business: The group's principal activities are to accept deposits and apply such funds in the origination and retention of mortgage and residential real estate loans. The group is a federally chartered unitary savings and loan holding bank. Its operations are conducted through twelve retail-banking branches located throughout the western, the central and the mid-coastal regions of the state of Maine.

Primary SIC and add'l.: 6712 6035

CIK No: 0000811831

Subsidiaries: ASI Data Services Inc, NBN Capital Trust, NBN Capital Trust II, NBN Capital Trust III, NBN Capital Trust IV, Northeast Savings Bank, F.S.B.

Officers: Jim Delamater/Dir., CEO, Pres. - Northeast Bank, Robert S. Johnson/56/CFO, Leslie Couper/VP - Northeast Bank Investment Group, Suzanne Carney/Corporate Clerk, Rob Johnson/CFO, Sr. VP - Northeast Bank, Joline Daigle/Branch Mgr. - Auburn, Northeast Bank, Liza Crenshaw/Branch Mgr. - Augusta, Northeast Bank, Deb Ricker/Branch Mgr. - Bethel, Northeast Bank, Elsa McGary/Branch Mgr. - Gateway, Northeast Bank, Lynn Hamper/Branch Mgr. - Mechanic Falls, Northeast Bank, Pender J. Lazenby/Dir., Chief Risk Officer - Northeast Bank, Jessie Wickham/Branch Mgr. - Portland, Northeast Bank, Karen Danforth/Branch Mgr. - South Paris, Northeast Bank, Philip C. Jackson/63/Dir., Sr. VP - Northeast Bank, Marcel Blais/COO, Sr. VP - Northeast Bank *(20 Officers included in Index)*

Directors: Jim Delamater/Dir., CEO, Pres. - Northeast Bank, Judith W. Kelley/Chmn. - Northeast Bank, John Rosmarin/Vice Chmn., James P. Day/48/Dir., Pender J. Lazenby/Dir., Chief Risk Officer - Northeast Bank, Stephen W. Wight/Dir., Philip C. Jackson/63/Dir., Sr. VP - Northeast Bank, John H. Schiavi/Dir., Dennis A. Wilson/Dir., John B. Bouchard/Dir., Ronald J. Goguen/Dir.

Owners: James D. Delamater/3.32%, Pender J. Lazenby, Robert S. Johnson, Sandler ONeill Asset Management LLC/5.29%, James W. Nichols d/b/a Nichols Investment Management/7.19%, Thompson Hortsmann & Bryant, Inc./8.85%, Judith W. Kelley, Phillip C. Jackson/1.04%, Tontine Financial Partners, LP/8.90%, John B. Bouchard, Marcel C. Blais, Insiders/9.21%, James P. Day, John C. Orestis

Financial Data: *Fiscal Year End:*06/30 *Latest Annual Data:* 6/30/2006

Year	Sales		Net Income
2006	$42,051,000		$4,004,000
2005	$37,825,000		$4,019,000
2004	$32,995,000		$3,512,000
Curr. Assets:	$14,783,000	**Curr. Liab.:** $500,819,000	**P/E Ratio:** 22.19
Plant, Equip.:	$7,326,000	**Total Liab.:** $523,821,000	**Indic. Yr. Divd.:** $0.360
Total Assets:	$562,918,000	**Net Worth:** $39,096,000	**Debt/ Equity:** 0.5087

Northeast Community Bancorp Inc

325 Hamilton Ave., White Plains, NY, 10601; *PH:* 1-914-684-2500; http:// www.fourthfed.com

General - Incorporation		**Stock** - Price on:12/24/2007	$12.18
Employees	71	Stock Exchange	AMEX
Auditor	Beard Miller Co. LLP	Ticker Symbol	NEN
Stk Agt	Registrar & Transfer Co	Outstanding Shares	13,230,000
Counsel	NA	E.P.S.	$0.90
DUNS No.	NA	Shareholders	NA

Business: The groups principal activity is to provide banking and financial services. The products of the group include multi-family residential, mixed-use and non-residential real estate and consumer loans. The group operates from the United States. The assets of the group for the year 2006 were $288,417 (thousands).

Primary SIC and add'l.: 6712

CIK No: 0001354772

Subsidiaries: Northeast Community Bank

Officers: Kenneth A. Martinek/55/Chmn., CEO, Pres., Salvatore Randazzo/40/Dir., CFO, Exec. VP, Treasurer, Anne Stevenson-Deblasi/Corp. Sec.

Directors: Kenneth A. Martinek/55/Chmn., CEO, Pres., Arthur M. Levine/73/Dir., Salvatore Randazzo/40/Dir., CFO, Exec. VP, Treasurer, Harry A.S. Read/71/Dir., Linda M. Swan/58/Dir., Diane B. Cavanaugh/51/Dir., Charles A. Martinek/46/Dir., Kenneth H. Thomas/60/Dir.

Owners: Diane B. Cavanaugh, Salvatore Randazzo, Charles A. Martinek, Northeast Community Bancorp, MHC, Linda M. Swan, Kenneth H. Thomas, Harry A.S. Read, Kenneth A. Martinek, John F. McKenzie, Insiders, Arthur M. Levine

Financial Data: *Fiscal Year End:*12/31 *Latest Annual Data:* 12/31/2006

Year	Sales		Net Income
2006	$15,972,000		$1,558,000
Curr. Assets:	$37,850,000	**Curr. Liab.:** $189,737,000	
Plant, Equip.:	$11,117,000	**Total Liab.:** $191,666,000	**Indic. Yr. Divd.:** $0.120
Total Assets:	$288,417,000	**Net Worth:** $96,751,000	**Debt/ Equity:** NA

Northeast Indiana Bancorp Inc New

648 N Jefferson St., Huntington, IN, 46750; *PH:* 1-260-356-3311; http:// www.firstfedhuntington.com

General - Incorporation	DE	Stock- Price on:12/24/2007	$15.6
Employees	NA	Stock Exchange	OTC
Auditor	Crowe, Chizek and Company LLC	Ticker Symbol	NIDB
Stk Agt	Registrar & Transfer Co	Outstanding Shares	1,340,000
Counsel	NA	E.P.S	$0.25
DUNS No.	NA	Shareholders	NA

Business: The groups principle activity is to provide banking services and products. The group provides deposit products, loan products, credit card products, financial services and other services. The group operates from United States.

Primary SIC and add'l.: 6035

CIK No: 0000942898

Subsidiaries: First Federal Savings Bank, Northeast Indiana Financial, Inc

Officers: Stephen E. Zahn/Chmn., CEO, Randy J. Sizemore/CFO, Sr. VP, Treasurer, Michael S. Zahn/Dir., Pres., Dee Ann Hammel/Sr. VP, Sec., COO, Vincent Haupert/Financial Advosor, Investment Specialist, Marti Evans/Investments Specialist, Shirley Dinius/Investment Specialist, Kary Monroe/Investment Specialist, Seth Kimmel/Investments Specialist

Directors: Stephen E. Zahn/Chmn., CEO, Dan L. Stephan/Dir., Michael S. Zahn/Dir., Pres., William A. Zimmer/Dir., David J. Carnes/Dir., Randall C. Rider/Dir.

Financial Data: Fiscal Year End:12/31 Latest Annual Data: 12/31/2004

Year		Sales		Net Income
2004		$13,540,000		$982,000
2003		$14,108,000		$1,930,000
2002		$15,772,000		$1,590,000
Curr. Assets:	$4,216,000	Curr. Liab.:	$202,626,000	P/E Ratio: 17.93
Plant, Equip.:	$2,176,000	Total Liab.:	$202,626,000	Indic. Yr. Divd.: $0.660
Total Assets:	$228,672,000	Net Worth:	$26,047,000	Debt/ Equity: 2.7708

Northeast Utilities

107 Selden St., Berlin, CT, 06037; *PH:* 1-800-286-5000; *Fax:* 1-860-665-5418; *http://* www.nu.com

General - Incorporation	MA	Stock- Price on:12/24/2007	$28.01
Employees	5,869	Stock Exchange	NYSE
Auditor	Deloitte & Touche LLP	Ticker Symbol	NA
Stk Agt	Bank of New York	Outstanding Shares	154,550,000
Counsel	NA	E.P.S	$3.36
DUNS No.	13-794-0847	Shareholders	NA

Business: The groups principle activity is to provide electricity. The group also provides retail natural gas services. The group operates from United States.

Primary SIC and add'l.: 4911 6719 4939

CIK No: 0000072741

Subsidiaries: CL&P Funding LLC, CL&P Receivables Corporation, E. S. Boulos Company, Holyoke Power and Electric Company, Holyoke Water Power Company, Mode 1 Communications, Inc., North Atlantic Energy Corporation, North Atlantic Energy Service Corporation, Northeast Generation Company, Northeast Generation Services Company, Northeast Nuclear Energy Company, Northeast Utilities (a Massachusetts business trust), Northeast Utilities Service Company, NU Enterprises, Inc., PSNH Funding LLC 29 Subsidiaries included in the Index

Officers: Charles W. Shivery/62/Chmn., CEO, Pres./$4,993,148.00, Patricia C. Cosgel/Assist. Treasurer - Finance, Kay O. Comendul/Assist. Sec., Michael Dipietro/Assist. Controller - Accounting Services, Leon J. Olivier/Exec. VP - Operations/$1,330,365.00, Gregory B. Butler/Sr. VP, General Counsel/$1,219,874.00, Randy A. Shoop/VP, Treasurer, Jeffrey R. Kotkin/VP - Investor Relations, Timothy J. Griffin/Assist. Controller - Corporate Accounting, Gary A. Long/COO, Pres. - Psnh, Raymond P. Necci/COO, Pres. - CL, P, Yankee Gas, Peter J. Clarke/VP - Customer Operations, CL, P, Yankee Gas, John M. MacDonald/VP - Energy Delivery, Generation, Psnh, Laurie E. Aylsworth/VP - Transmission Projects, Engineering, Maintenance, Robert A. Bersak/Assist. Sec. - CL, P, Psnh, Wmeco (37 Officers included in Index)

Directors: Charles W. Shivery/62/Chmn., CEO, Pres., Elizabeth T. Kennan/70/Trustee, Richard H. Booth/61/Trustee, Cotton Mather Cleveland/55/Trustee, Sanford Cloud/63/Trustee, James F. Cordes/67/Trustee, Gail E. De Planque/63/Trustee, John G. Graham/69/Trustee, Robert E. Patricelli/68/Trustee, John F. Swope/69/Trustee, Kenneth R. Leibler/59/Trustee

Owners: Insiders, John G. Graham, James F. Cordes, Sanford Cloud, Lord, Abbett & Co./8.37%, Lawrence E. DeSimone, Gail E. dePlanque, Cheryl W. Grise, Kenneth R. Leibler, David R. McHale, John F. Swope, Elizabeth T. Kennan, Cotton Mather Cleveland, Leon J. Olivier, Gregory B. Butler (17 Owners included in Index)

Financial Data: Fiscal Year End:12/31 Latest Annual Data: 12/31/2006

Year		Sales		Net Income
2006		$6,884,388,000		$470,578,000
2005		$7,397,390,000		-$253,488,000
2004		$6,686,699,000		$122,147,000
Curr. Assets:	$1,731,051,000	Curr. Liab.:	$1,363,835,000	P/E Ratio: 7.78
Plant, Equip.:	$6,242,186,000	Total Liab.:	$8,388,857,000	Indic. Yr. Divd.: $0.800
Total Assets:	$11,303,236,000	Net Worth:	$2,798,179,000	Debt/ Equity: NA

Northern Dynasty Minerals Ltd

800 W Pender St., Ste. 1020, Vancouver, BC, V6C 2V8; *PH:* 1-604-684-6365; *Fax:* 1-604-684-8092; *http://* www.northerndynastyminerals.com; *Email:* info@hdgold.com

General - Incorporation	BC	Stock- Price on:12/24/2007	$12.21
Employees	NA	Stock Exchange	AMEX
Auditor	De Visser Gray LLP	Ticker Symbol	NA
Stk Agt	Computershare Trust Co	Outstanding Shares	91,890,000
Counsel	NA	E.P.S	-$1.08
DUNS No.	NA	Shareholders	NA

Business: The groups principal activities include exploring, acquiring and developing minerals. The group operates from the United States.

Primary SIC and add'l.: 1040

CIK No: 0001164771

Officers: Ronald W. Thiessen/Exec. Dir., Pres. CEO, Robert Dickinson/Executive Chmn., Jeffrey Mason/CFO, Sec., Bruce Jenkins/COO, Stephen Hodgson/VP - Engineering, Bernhard Zinkhofer/Outside General Counsel

Directors: Ronald W. Thiessen/Exec. Dir., Pres. CEO, Robert Dickinson/Executive Chmn., Scott Cousens/Non Exec. Dir., David Elliott/Non Exec. Dir., Gordon Fretwell/Non Exec. Dir., David Copeland/Non Exec. Dir., Wayne Kirk/Non Exec. Dir., Walter Segsworth/Non Exec. Dir.

Financial Data: Fiscal Year End:12/31 Latest Annual Data: 12/31/2006

Year		Sales		Net Income
2006		NA		-$50,098,000
2005		NA		-$43,318,000
2004		NA		-$34,622,000
Curr. Assets:	$84,190,000	Curr. Liab.:	$6,727,000	P/E Ratio: 10.43
Plant, Equip.:	$544,000	Total Liab.:	$59,587,000	Indic. Yr. Divd.: NA
Total Assets:	$229,085,000	Net Worth:	$169,498,000	Debt/ Equity: NA

Northern Ethanol Inc

Formerly: Beaconsfield I Inc
193 King St. E, Ste. 300, Toronto, ON, M5A 1J5; *PH:* 1-416-366-5511

General - Incorporation	DE	Stock- Price on:12/24/2007	NA
Employees	NA	Stock Exchange	NA
Auditor	KPMG LLP	Ticker Symbol	NA
Stk Agt	Corporate Stock Transfer, Inc.	Outstanding Shares	NA
Counsel	NA	E.P.S	NA
DUNS No.	NA	Shareholders	NA

Business: The group's principle activity is to develop two ethanol plants to meet the growing needs of Ontario. The group operates from United States.

Primary SIC and add'l.: 2860

CIK No: 0001323923

Officers: Gordon Laschinger/60/Chmn., CEO, Pres., Andrew I. Telsey/55/Corp. Sec., Dir.

Directors: Gordon Laschinger/60/Chmn., CEO, Pres., Andrew I. Telsey/55/Corp. Sec., Dir., Robert Richards/56/Dir., Paul T. Durst/55/Dir., Frank F. Klees/56/Dir.

Owners: Andrew Gertler, 1019562 Ontario Limited/9.50%, Robert Watson/9.50%, Paul Durst, Steven Reader, Ronald Wyles/9.50%, Gordon Laschinger/1.00%, Andrew I. Telsey, Richard Smith, Robert Mark Young/9.50%, Robert Richards, Lou Pupolin/9.50%, Richard Brezzi/9.50%, Zoran Bakich/9.50%, Frank Klees (19 Owners included in Index)

Northern Illinois Gas Co

1844 Ferry Rd. , Naperville, IL, 60563; *PH:* 1-630-983-8888; *http://* www.nicor.com

General - Incorporation	IL	Stock- Price on:12/24/2007	NA
Employees	NA	Stock Exchange	NA
Auditor	Deloitte & Touche LLP	Ticker Symbol	NA
Stk Agt	Computershare Investor Services LLC	Outstanding Shares	NA
Counsel	NA	E.P.S	NA
DUNS No.	00-692-7792	Shareholders	NA

Business: The group's principal activity is to distribute natural gas. It also provides transportation service, gas storage and supply to commercial and industrial customers who purchase their own gas supplies. The group is a wholly owned subsidiary of nicor inc. The group's operations are carried on in northern Illinois.

Primary SIC and add'l.: 4923 4922

CIK No: 0000110104

Officers: Russ M. Strobel/Chmn., CEO, Pres., Richard L. Hawley/CFO, Exec. VP, Claudia J. Colalillo/Sr. VP - Human Resources, Corporate Communications, Daniel R. Dodge/Sr. VP - Diversified Ventures, Corporate Planning, Paul C. Gracey/Sr. VP, General Counsel, Sec., Gerald P. O'Connor/Sr. VP - Finance, Treasurer, Karen K. Pepping/VP, Controller, Barbara A. Zeller/VP - Information Technology, Mark A. Knox/Dir. - Investor Relations

Directors: Russ M. Strobel/Chmn., CEO, Pres., Bruce P. Bickner/Dir., Robert M. Beavers/Dir., John H. Birdsall/Dir., Thomas A. Donahoe/Dir., Eden R. Martin/Dir., John Rau/Dir., Dennis J. Keller/Dir., John F. Riordan/Dir., Brenda J. Gaines/Dir., Raymond A. Jean/Dir., Georgia R. Nelson/Dir., Norman R. Bobins/Dir.

Northern Indiana Public Service Co

801 E 86th Ave., Merrillville, IN, 46410; *PH:* 1-877-647-5990; *http://* www.nipsco.com; *Email:* nipscoquestions@nisource.com

General - Incorporation	IN	Stock- Price on:12/24/2007	NA
Employees	7,822	Stock Exchange	NA
Auditor	Deloitte & Touche LLP	Ticker Symbol	NA
Stk Agt	NA	Outstanding Shares	NA
Counsel	NA	E.P.S	NA
DUNS No.	00-693-7585	Shareholders	NA

Business: The group's principal activities are to supply natural gas and electric energy to the public. The group operates in two segments namely electric and gas operations. The electric operation segment distributes electricity in 21 counties in the northern part of Indiana. The group also engages in electric wholesale and wheeling transactions. The gas distribution segment provides natural gas service and transportation for residential, commercial and industrial customers in Indiana. The group is wholly-owned by nisource inc.

Primary SIC and add'l.: 4924 4931 4911

CIK No: 0000072843

Subsidiaries: NIPSCO Receivables Corporation

Officers: Timothy A. Dehring/Dir., GM, Mark T. Maassel/Dir., Pres., Carol M. Fox/VP - Large Customer Relations, Gas Transportation Management, Jeffrey W. Grossman/VP, Peggy Landini/VP - Support Operations, Scott C. MacDonald/VP - Retail Products, Services, Shawn L. Patterson/VP - Engineering, Gary W. Pottorff/VP - Administration, Corp. Sec., Edward A. Santry/VP - Human Resources, Charles E. Shafer/VP - Meter to Cash, David J. Vajda/VP, Treasurer, Frank Andrew Venhuizen/VP - Electric Transmission, Michael D. Watson/VP - Energy Supply Services, Jerome B. Weeden/VP - Generation, Linda E. Miller/Controller (18 Officers included in Index)

Directors: Timothy A. Dehring/Dir., GM, Mark T. Maassel/Dir., Pres.

Northern Oil & Gas Inc

Formerly: Kentex Petroleum Inc
4685 S Highland Dr., Ste. 202, Salt Lake City, UT, 84117; *PH:* 1-801-278-9424

General - Incorporation	NV	Stock - Price on:12/24/2007	NA
Employees	NA	Stock Exchange	NA
Auditor	Mantyla McReynolds, LLC	Ticker Symbol	NA
Stk Agt	NA	Outstanding Shares	NA
Counsel	NA	E.P.S.	NA
DUNS No.	NA	Shareholders	NA

Business: The group's principal activity is seeking and investigating potential assets, property or business to acquire. The Company is not currently engaged in any substantive business activity. It is a development stage Company.

Primary SIC and add'l.: 1311

CIK No: 0001104485

Officers: Michael L. Reger/CEO, Lisa Howells/45/Dir., Sec., Treasurer, Sarah E. Jenson/36/Dir., Pres., Victoria Jenson/40/Dir., VP, Ryan R. Gilbertson/CFO

Directors: Sarah E. Jenson/36/Dir., Pres., Victoria Jenson/40/Dir., VP, Lisa Howells/45/Dir., Sec., Treasurer

Owners: Ryan R. Gilberton, Joseph A. Geraci, Carter Stewart, Douglas M. Polinsky, Lisa Bromiley Meier, Michael L. Reger, Saracen Energy, LP, Millenium Partners, LP, Insiders

Financial Data: Fiscal Year End:12/31   Latest Annual Data: 12/31/2006

Year	Sales	Net Income
2006	NA	-$8,000
2005	NA	$13,000

Curr. Assets:	NA	Curr. Liab.:	$39,000		
Plant, Equip.:	NA	Total Liab.:	$39,000	Indic. Yr. Divd.:	NA
Total Assets:	NA	Net Worth:	-$39,000	Debt/ Equity:	NA

Northern Orion Resources Inc

Ste. 250 - 1075 W Georgia St., Vancouver, BC, V6E 3C9; **PH:** 1-604-689-9663;
http:// www.northernorion.com

General - Incorporation	BC	Stock - Price on:12/24/2007	$5.65
Employees	1,100	Stock Exchange	NDQ
Auditor	Deloitte & Touche LLP	Ticker Symbol	NTPA
Stk Agt	Pacific Corporate Trust Co	Outstanding Shares	153,970,000
Counsel	DuMoulin Black	E.P.S.	$0.485
DUNS No.	NA	Shareholders	NA

Business: The groups principle activity is to produce copper and gold. The group operates from Canada.

Primary SIC and add'l.: 1041

CIK No: 0001200525

Subsidiaries: Canada Pampas Ltd, Cayman Pampas Ltd., Cooper Internation LLC, Minera Alumbrera Ltd, Minera Auga Rica LLC, Minera Auga Rica Succursal, Musto Exploration (Bermuda), Northern Orion Argentina Holding S.A., Northern Orion Canada Pampas Ltd., Northern Orion Cayman Pampas Ltd, RAA Holding S.A.

Officers: David Cohen/CEO, Pres., Horng Dih Lee/VP - Finance, CFO, Pablo Marcet/Pres. - Minera Agua Rica, Operations Mgr. - Argentina, Brian Montpellier/VP - Project Development, Richard Knight/Dir. - Victoria, Australia

Directors: Robert Cross/Chmn. - Vancouver, BC, Canada, Robert Gayton/Dir. - Vancouver, BC, Canada, John K. Burns/Dir. - Philadelphia, PA, USA, Michael Beckett/Dir.

Financial Data: Fiscal Year End:12/31   Latest Annual Data: 12/31/2006

Year	Sales	Net Income
2006	NA	$73,171,000
2005	$46,755,000	$27,433,000
2004	$32,659,000	$24,303,000

Curr. Assets:	$180,560,000	Curr. Liab.:	$3,106,000		
Plant, Equip.:	$208,000	Total Liab.:	$17,087,000	Indic. Yr. Divd.:	NA
Total Assets:	$343,871,000	Net Worth:	$326,784,000	Debt/ Equity:	NA

Northern States Financial Corp

1601 N Lewis Ave., Waukegan, IL, 60085; **PH:** 1-847-244-6000; **Fax:** 1-847-244-7485;
http:// www.nsfc.net

General - Incorporation	DE	Stock - Price on:12/24/2007	$22.37
Employees	180	Stock Exchange	NDQ
Auditor	Plant & Moran, PLLC	Ticker Symbol	NSFC
Stk Agt	American Stock Transfer & Trust Co.	Outstanding Shares	4,200,000
Counsel	NA	E.P.S.	$1.00
DUNS No.	11-605-4933	Shareholders	NA

Business: The group's principal activity is to conduct banking business. The group accepts demand, savings, time deposits, securities sold under repurchase agreements and individual retirement accounts. It offers commercial loans, mortgage loans, consumer loans, installment loans, student loans, line of credit and overdraft checking. It also offers trust services, traveler's checks, money orders, cashier's checks, foreign currency and direct deposit services. The group provides these services through five branches to individuals, businesses, corporations, partnerships and local units of governmental units in the northeastern Illinois and southeastern Wisconsin. On 05-Jan-2004, the group acquired round lake bankcorp inc.

Primary SIC and add'l.: 6712 6022

CIK No: 0000744485

Subsidiaries: NorStates Bank, Northern States Community Development Corporation, Northern States Statutory Trust I

Officers: Fred Abdula/Chmn., CEO, Pres./$195,070.00, Kerry J. Biegay/VP/$164,396.00, Helen Rumsa/Dir., Sec., Thomas Nemeth/VP, Treasurer/$126,700.00, Shelly Christian/Exec. VP, Chief Lending Officer, Norstates Bank/$153,082.00

Directors: Fred Abdula/Chmn., CEO, Pres., Jack H. Blumberg/Dir., James A. Hollensteiner/Dir., Kenneth W. Balza/Dir., Helen Rumsa/Dir., Sec., Raymond Mota/Dir., Harry Gaples/Dir., Frank Furlan/Dir., Theodore Bertrand/Dir., Allan J. Jacobs/Dir.

Owners: Frank J. Furlan, Kerry J. Biegay, Helen Rumsa/1.60%, Kenneth W. Balza, Thomas M. Nemeth, Raymond M. Mota, Theodore A. Bertrand/8.10%, Fred Abdula/20.60%, Insiders/35.80%, Allan J. Jacobs, Harry S. Gaples/2.10%, Jack H. Blumberg, James A. Hollensteiner/1.20%

Financial Data: Fiscal Year End:12/31   Latest Annual Data: 12/31/2006

Year	Sales	Net Income
2006	$41,979,000	$3,092,000
2005	$39,595,000	$2,087,000
2004	$36,644,000	$4,001,000

Curr. Assets:	$34,221,000	Curr. Liab.:	$627,752,000	P/E Ratio:	23.30
Plant, Equip.:	$12,377,000	Total Liab.:	$638,546,000	Indic. Yr. Divd.:	NA
Total Assets:	$710,009,000	Net Worth:	$71,463,000	Debt/ Equity:	0.1367

Northern States Power Co

414 Nicollet Mall, Minneapolis, MN, 55401; **PH:** 1-612-330-5500; **http://** www.nspco.com

General - Incorporation	MN	Stock - Price on:12/24/2007	$25.04
Employees	2,595	Stock Exchange	NA
Auditor	Deloitte & Touche LLP	Ticker Symbol	NA
Stk Agt	Depository Trust Co	Outstanding Shares	1,000,000
Counsel	NA	E.P.S.	$255.87
DUNS No.	00-794-5868	Shareholders	NA

Business: The group's principle activities include generating and distributing electricity. The company distributes its electricity to approximately 230,000 retail customers in northwestern Wisconsin and in the western portion of the upper peninsula of Michigan. The company also distributes and sells natural gas in the same service territory to approximately 90,000 customers in Wisconsin and Michigan. The company operates as a wholly owned subsidiary of xcel energy inc. The group operates from United States.

Primary SIC and add'l.: 4923 4931

CIK No: 0001123852

Subsidiaries: Xcel Energy Inc.

Officers: Richard C. Kelly/Chmn., Principal Executive Officer, Benjamin G.S. Fowke/Dir., VP, CFO, Teresa S. Madden/VP, Controller, Principal Accounting Officer, Gary R. Johnson/Dir., VP, General Counsel, Paul J. Bonavia/Dir., VP, Patricia K. Vincent/Dir., VP, David M. Sparby/Chiefexecutive Officer, Exec. VP, Acting Pres., Principal Operating Officer

Directors: Richard C. Kelly/Chmn., Principal Executive Officer, Paul J. Bonavia/Dir., VP, Gary R. Johnson/Dir., VP, General Counsel, Benjamin G.S. Fowke/Dir., VP, CFO, Patricia K. Vincent/Dir., VP

Financial Data: Fiscal Year End:12/31   Latest Annual Data: 12/31/2006

Year	Sales	Net Income
2006	$4,027,615,000	$272,310,000
2005	$3,853,584,000	$237,744,000
2004	$3,319,562,000	$230,274,000

Curr. Assets:	$1,000,972,000	Curr. Liab.:	$902,162,000	P/E Ratio:	0.10
Plant, Equip.:	$5,988,508,000	Total Liab.:	$6,455,376,000	Indic. Yr. Divd.:	NA
Total Assets:	$9,079,048,000	Net Worth:	$2,623,672,000	Debt/ Equity:	0.9645

Northern Technologies International Corp

4201 Woodland Rd., Circle Pines, MN, 55014; **PH:** 1-763-225-6600; **Fax:** 1-763-225-6645;
http:// www.ntic.com; **Email:** sales@zerust.com

General - Incorporation	DE	Stock - Price on:12/24/2007	$9.51
Employees	44	Stock Exchange	NDQ
Auditor	Virchow, Krause & Co. LLP	Ticker Symbol	NTIQ
Stk Agt	Wells Fargo Shareowner Services	Outstanding Shares	3,680,000
Counsel	NA	E.P.S.	$0.87
DUNS No.	05-448-4001	Shareholders	NA

Business: The group's principal activity is to develop, manufacture and market corrosion inhibiting products, science based packaging materials. The dry corrosion inhibiting products is marketed under the name zerust which is utilized in protective packaging. The group's materials science based industrial packaging products and systems includes the rusting of ferrous (iron and steel) metals and the deterioration by oxidation of nonferrous (aluminum, copper, brass, etc.) metals. The group participates in various international corporate joint ventures in countries outside the United States and in similar non-contractual arrangements in various other countries. The international joint ventures provide for the manufacturing, marketing and distribution of materials science based industrial packaging products. The group discontinued its electronic sensing instruments business.

Primary SIC and add'l.: 2671

CIK No: 0000875582

Subsidiaries: Northern Technologies Holding Company, LLC, NTI Facilities, Inc., React-NTI LLC

Officers: Patrick Lynch/CEO

Directors: Barry Rosenbaum/Dir.

Owners: Sunggyu Lee, Inter Alia Holding Company/24.90%, Patrick G. Lynch/25.60%, Donald A. Kubik/3.60%, Ramani Narayan, Matthew C. Wolsfeld, Barry Rosenbaum, Mark J. Stone, Insiders/30.70%, Mark M. Mayers, Kern Capital Management, LLC/14.50%, Pierre Chenu

Financial Data: Fiscal Year End:08/31   Latest Annual Data: 8/31/2006

Year	Sales	Net Income
2006	$16,605,000	$1,719,000
2005	$14,817,000	$1,193,000
2004	$10,916,000	$1,036,000

Curr. Assets:	$6,210,000	Curr. Liab.:	$3,989,000	P/E Ratio:	15.85
Plant, Equip.:	$3,431,000	Total Liab.:	$5,230,000	Indic. Yr. Divd.:	NA
Total Assets:	$23,271,000	Net Worth:	$17,986,000	Debt/ Equity:	0.0607

Northern Trust Corp

50 S La Salle St., Chicago, IL, 60603; **PH:** 1-312-630-6000; **Fax:** 1-312-630-1512;
http:// www.northerntrust.com

General - Incorporation	DE	Stock - Price on:12/24/2007	$65.18
Employees	9,726	Stock Exchange	NDQ
Auditor	KPMG LLP	Ticker Symbol	NTSC
Stk Agt	Wells Fargo Shareowner Services	Outstanding Shares	219,410,000
Counsel	NA	E.P.S.	$3.46
DUNS No.	00-693-1968	Shareholders	NA

Business: The group's principle activity is to provide investment management, asset and fund administration, fiduciary, and banking solutions. The group provides services include personal trust, custody and investment management services. The groups servicing areas include corporate and public retirement funds, foundations, endowments, fund managers, insurance companies and Government funds. The group operates from United States.

Primary SIC and add'l.: 9999 6221 6021 6082 6712

CIK No: 0000073124

Subsidiaries: Admiral Nominees Limited, Arnold Limited, Bafsc/tnt-nl Cx Hul I, Ltd., Bafsc/tnt-nl Cx Huo, Ltd., Barfield Nominees (IOM) Limited, Barfield Nominees Limited, BBI Nominees Limited, Clenston Ltd., Control Nominees Limited, Doyle Administration Limited, Equilend Holdings LLC, Fiduciary Services Inc., Financial Service Group Limited, Fort Administration Limited, Helaba Northern Trust GmbH 99 Subsidiaries included in the Index

Officers: Alison Winter/CEO, Pres. - Personal Financial Services, Northeast Region, William A. Osborn/Chmn., CEO/$11,010,320.00, Frederick H. Waddell/Dir., COO, Pres./$3,564,155.00, Sherry S. Barrat/Pres. - Personal Financial Services/$2,948,051.00, Stephen N. Potter/Exec. VP, Head - International, Global Fund Services, Terence J. Toth/Pres. - Northern Trust Global Investments/$2,019,167.00, William L. Morrison/Pres. - Personal Financial Services/$3,091,191.00, Aileen B. Blake/Exec. VP, Controller, Chief Accounting Officer, Kelly R. Welsh/Exec. VP, General Counsel, Steven L. Fradkin/CFO, Exec. VP/$2,077,028.00, Rose A. Ellis/Corp. Sec., Joyce St. Clair/Exec. VP, Head - Corporate Risk Management, Timothy P. Moen/Exec. VP - Head - Human Resources, Administration, Jana R. Schreuder/Pres. - Worldwide Operations, Technology, Timothy J. Theriault/Pres. - Worldwide Operations, Technology/$2,348,828.00

Directors: William A. Osborn/Chmn., CEO, John W. Rowe/Dir., Robert C. McCormack/Dir., Edward J. Mooney/Dir., Harold B. Smith/Dir., Frederick H. Waddell/Dir., COO, Pres., William D. Smithburg/Dir., Charles A. Tribbett/Dir., Nicholas D. Chabraja/Dir., Enrique J. Sosa/Dir., Linda W. Bynoe/Dir., Susan Crown/Dir., Dipak C. Jain/Dir., Arthur L. Kelly/Dir.

Owners: Sherry S. Barrat, The Northern Trust Company/5.41%, Insiders/9.61%, Edward J. Mooney, Charles A. Tribbett, Timothy J. Theriault, William D. Smithburg, Enrique J. Sosa, William A. Osborn/1.02%, William L. Morrison, John W. Rowe, Frederick H. Waddell, Harold B. Smith/5.94%, Linda Walker Bynoe, Nicholas D. Chabraja (22 Owners included in Index)

Financial Data: Fiscal Year End:12/31   Latest Annual Data: 12/31/2006

Year	Sales	Net Income
2006	$4,473,000,000	$665,400,000
2005	$3,554,400,000	$584,400,000
2004	$2,829,100,000	$505,600,000

Curr. Assets:	$21,752,500,000	**Curr. Liab.:**	$48,592,300,000	**P/E Ratio:**	21.03
Plant, Equip.:	$487,200,000	**Total Liab.:**	$56,768,300,000	**Indic. Yr. Divd.:**	$1.120
Total Assets:	$60,712,200,000	**Net Worth:**	$3,943,900,000	**Debt/ Equity:**	NA

Northfield Laboratories Inc

1560 Sherman Ave., Ste. 1000, Evanston, IL, 60201; **PH:** 1-847-864-3500; **Fax:** 1-847-864-3577; **http://** www.northfieldlabs.com; **Email:** investor_relations@northfieldlabs.com

General - Incorporation	DE	**Stock** - Price on:12/24/2007	$1.52
Employees	83	Stock Exchange	NDQ
Auditor	KPMG LLP	Ticker Symbol	NFLD
Stk Agt	Computershare Investor Services LLC	Outstanding Shares	26,910,000
Counsel	NA	E.P.S.	-$0.93
DUNS No.	13-187-1139	Shareholders	NA

Business: The group's principle activities include developing and test, as well as manufacturing, marketing and distributing a hemoglobin-based blood substitute product. The company's product, polyheme(R) blood substitute, provides an alternative to transfused blood for use in the treatment of acute blood loss. It uses a proprietary process of separation, filtration and chemical modification to produce polyheme. Clinical trials of polyheme have been conducted at multiple locations in the United States. The company has entered into licensing agreements with pharmacia corporation and hemocare ltd. To develop, manufacture and distribute polyheme in certain European, Middle Eastern and african countries. The company is in development stage. The group operates from United States.

Primary SIC and add'l.: 2836

CIK No: 0000920947

Officers: Steven A. Gould/Chmn., CEO/$507,689.00, Sophia H. Twaddell/VP - Corporate Communications, Robert L. McGinnis/Sr. VP - Operations/$277,781.00, John J. Hinds/VP - Finance, George A. Hides/VP - Clinical Operations, Marc D. Doubleday/CTO, Laurel A. Omert/Chief Medical Officer/$296,606.00, Jack J. Kogut/Sr. VP - Administration/$349,247.00, Donna Oneill-Mulvihill/VP - Finance/$163,149.00

Directors: Steven A. Gould/Chmn., CEO, John F. Bierbaum/Dir., David A. Savner/Dir., Jack Olshansky/Dir., Paul M. Ness/Dir., Bruce S. Chelberg/Dir., Alan L. Heller/Dir., Edward C. Wood/Dir.

Owners: Bruce S. Chelberg, George A. Hides, Alan L. Heller, Marc D. Doubleday, Insiders/6.20%, State of Wisconsin Investment Board/5.40%, Edward C. Wood, Bank of American Corporation/7.50%, David A. Savner, Donna ONeill-Mulvihill, Steven A. Gould/3.10%, Paul M. Ness, John Bierbaum, Visium Asset Management LLC/9.60%, Robert L. McGinnis (19 Owners included in Index)

Financial Data: Fiscal Year End:05/31   Latest Annual Data: 05/31/2007

Year	Sales	Net Income
2007	NA	-$27,671,000
2006	NA	-$26,775,000
2005	NA	-$20,321,000

Curr. Assets:	$74,723,000	**Curr. Liab.:**	$6,534,000		
Plant, Equip.:	$1,079,000	**Total Liab.:**	$6,534,000	**Indic. Yr. Divd.:**	NA
Total Assets:	$75,871,000	**Net Worth:**	$69,337,000	**Debt/ Equity:**	NA

Northgate Minerals Corp

815 Hornby St., Ste. 404, Vancouver, BC, V6Z 2E6; **PH:** 1-604-681-4004; **http://** www.northgateminerals.ca; **Email:** ngx@northgateminerals.com

General - Incorporation	Canada	**Stock** - Price on:12/24/2007	$3.04
Employees	360	Stock Exchange	AMEX
Auditor	KPMG LLP	Ticker Symbol	NXG
Stk Agt	Computershare Trust Co	Outstanding Shares	254,160,000
Counsel	NA	E.P.S.	$0.11
DUNS No.	NA	Shareholders	NA

Business: The group's principle activities include exploring, developing, financing and operating gold properties in Canada and Chile. The group operates from United States.

Primary SIC and add'l.: 6719 1041

CIK No: 0000072931

Officers: Kenneth G. Stowe/Dir., CEO, Pres., Jon A. Douglas/Sr. VP, CFO, Maurice Ethier/GM - Kemess South Mine, Christopher J. Rockingham/VP - Business Development, Exploration, Peter MacPhail/VP - Operations, Bruce M. Mckay/Corp. Sec., Eugene Lee/Corporate Controller

Directors: Kenneth G. Stowe/Dir., CEO, Pres., Terry A. Lyons/Non Exec. Chmn., Keith C. Hendrick/Dir., Douglas P. Hayhurst/Dir., Conrad A. Pinette/Dir., William C. Daniel/Dir., Patrick D. Downey/Dir., Klaus V. Konigsmann/Dir.

Financial Data: Fiscal Year End:12/31   Latest Annual Data: 12/31/2006

Year	Sales	Net Income
2006	$411,313,000	$98,217,000
2005	$257,153,000	$30,965,000
2004	$192,034,000	$30,145,000

Curr. Assets:	$322,419,000	**Curr. Liab.:**	$24,462,000		
Plant, Equip.:	$167,723,000	**Total Liab.:**	$82,638,000	**Indic. Yr. Divd.:**	NA
Total Assets:	$502,192,000	**Net Worth:**	$419,554,000	**Debt/ Equity:**	NA

Northrim Bancorp Inc

PO Box 241489, Anchorage, AK, 99524; **PH:** 1-907-562-0062; **Fax:** 1-907-562-1758; **http://** www.northrim.com

General - Incorporation	AK	**Stock** - Price on:12/24/2007	$25.93
Employees	277	Stock Exchange	NDQ
Auditor	KPMG LLP	Ticker Symbol	NRIM
Stk Agt	American Stock Transfer & Trust Co.	Outstanding Shares	6,120,000
Counsel	Davis Wright Tremaine LLP	E.P.S.	$2.02
DUNS No.	62-250-5659	Shareholders	NA

Business: The group's principal activity is to provide banking services. The group is a bank holding company with three wholly owned subsidiaries: northrim bank, a state chartered full-service commercial bank, northrim investment services company and northrim capital trust 1. The deposits accepted by the group are checking accounts, savings account, money market accounts, time deposits and certificates of deposits. The loans offered include short term and medium term loans, commercial and personal loans and real estate loans. The group operates through ten branch locations, seven in anchorage and one each in fairbanks, eagle river and wasilla. The banking services are provided in south central and interior Alaska to businesses, professional and individuals.

Primary SIC and add'l.: 6022 6712

CIK No: 0001163370

Subsidiaries: Elliott Cove Capital Management LLC, Northrim Bank, Northrim Benefits Group, LLC, Northrim Capital Investments Co, Northrim Capital Trust 1, Northrim Investment Services Company, Residential Mortgage Holding Company LLC

Officers: Marc Langland/Chmn., CEO, Pres., Northrim Bank Co - Founder/$538,049.00, Blythe Campbell/VP - Marketing, Communications, Tara Tetzlaff/Sr. VP, Residential Construction Mgr., Suzanne Whittle/VP - Information Services, Rich Jerger/CTO, Sr. VP, Robert Shake/Sr. VP, Executive Loan Mgr. - Northrim Bank Charter Employee, Steve Hartung/Exec. VP, Quality Assurance Officer, Joseph Beedle/Exec. VP, Chief Lending Officer/$208,019.00, Victor Mollozzi/Sr. VP, Sr. Credit Officer Northrim Bank Charter Employee/$231,758.00, Kate Rice/Sr. VP, Human Resources Mgr., Carolyn Jennings/Sr. VP - Branch Administration, Ken Ferguson/Sr. VP, Commercial Real Estate Lending Mgr., Gary Roderick/Sr. VP, Commercial Loan Mgr. - Fairbanks Financial Center, Paul Wellman/Sr. VP - Credit Administration, Chris Knudson/Exec. VP, COO - Northrim Bank Charter Employee (19 Officers included in Index)

Directors: Marc Langland/Chmn., CEO, Pres., Northrim Bank Co - Founder, David G. Wight/67/Dir.

Owners: FMR Corp./6.60%, Dalton, Greiner, Hartman, Maher& Co., LLC/7.60%, Richard L. Lowell, Wedbush Inc./6.00%, Anthony Drabek, David G. Wight, Irene Sparks Rowan, Joseph M. Beedle, John C. Swalling, Insiders/6.60%, Frank A. Danner, Marc R. Langland/2.90%, Christopher N. Knudson/1.20%, Mark G. Copeland, Ronald A. Davis (18 Owners included in Index)

Financial Data: Fiscal Year End:12/31   Latest Annual Data: 12/31/2006

Year	Sales	Net Income
2006	$77,409,000	$12,974,000
2005	$64,038,000	$11,170,000
2004	$52,803,000	$10,700,000

Curr. Assets:	$70,381,000	**Curr. Liab.:**	$794,904,000	**P/E Ratio:**	12.59
Plant, Equip.:	$12,874,000	**Total Liab.:**	$830,173,000	**Indic. Yr. Divd.:**	$0.600
Total Assets:	$925,620,000	**Net Worth:**	$95,418,000	**Debt/ Equity:**	0.2807

Northrop Grumman Corp

1840 Century Pk. E, Los Angeles, CA, 90067; **PH:** 1-310-553-6262; **Fax:** 1-310-556-4561; **http://** www.northropgrumman.com

General - Incorporation	DE	**Stock** - Price on:12/24/2007	$77.11
Employees	122,200	Stock Exchange	NYSE
Auditor	Deloitte & Touche LLP	Ticker Symbol	NOC
Stk Agt	EquiServe Trust Co N.A	Outstanding Shares	345,110,000
Counsel	NA	E.P.S.	$4.54
DUNS No.	NA	Shareholders	NA

Business: The group's principle activity is to provide innovative systems, products, and solutions in information and services, electronics, aerospace and shipbuilding to government and commercial customers. The group's servicing areas include information and services, electronics, aerospace and ships. The group operates from United States.

Primary SIC and add'l.: 3721 4491 4581 3679 3728 3812 3825

CIK No: 0001133421

Subsidiaries: Newport News Shipbuilding Inc., Northrop Grumman Space& Mission Systems Corp., Northrop Grumman Systems Corporation

Officers: Ronald D. Sugar/Chmn., CEO/$21,655,730.00, Juli Ballesteros/Information Technology Sector, Philip A. Teel/Corporate VP, Pres. - Northrop Grumman Ship Systems, James F. Pitts/Corporate VP, Pres. - Northrop Grumman Electronic Systems, Kenneth N. Heintz/Corporate VP, Controller, Chief Accounting Officer - Northrop Grumman Corporation, Burks W. Terry/Corporate VP, General Counsel - Northrop Grumman Corporation/$4,261,250.00, Rosanne O'Brien/Corporate VP - Communications, Northrop Grumman Corporation, Scott J. Seymour/Corporate VP, Pres. - Northrop Grumman Integrated Systems/$6,069,942.00, Brooks McKinney/Mgr. - Public Relations, Space Exploration Systems, Dan McClain/Corp. Dir. - Media Relations, Tom Henson/Mgr. - Media Relations, Randy Belote/VP - Corporate, International Communications, Gus Gulmert/Corp. Dir. - Communications, Washington, Jack M. Martin/Sector Media Relations, Tom Delaney/Electronic Systems Sector Space Sensors (84 Officers included in Index)

Directors: Ronald D. Sugar/Chmn., CEO, Phillip Frost/Dir., Stephen E. Frank/Dir., Philip A. Odeen/Dir., Donald E. Felsinger/Dir., John T. Chain/73/Dir., Victor H. Fazio/Dir., Charles R. Larson/Dir., Richard B. Myers/Dir., Aulana L. Peters/Dir., Kevin W. Sharer/Dir., Lewis W. Coleman/Dir., Graham K. Thornton/Exec. Dir. - United Kingdom Northrop Grumman Corporation

Owners: Charles R. Larson, Kevin W. Sharer, Phillip Frost, Ronald D. Sugar, Stephen E. Frank, Scott J. Seymour, Victor H. Fazio, State Street Bank and Trust Company/9.60%, Capital Research and Management Company/9.40%, Philip A. Odeen, Barclays Global Investors, NA/6.40%, James R. ONeill, Aulana L. Peters, John T. Chain, Lewis W. Coleman (18 Owners included in Index)

Financial Data: Fiscal Year End:12/31 Latest Annual Data: 12/31/2006

Year	Sales	Net Income
2006	$30,148,000,000	$1,542,000,000
2005	$30,721,000,000	$1,400,000,000
2004	$29,853,000,000	$1,084,000,000

Curr. Assets:	$6,719,000,000	**Curr. Liab.:**	$6,753,000,000	**P/E Ratio:**	17.37
Plant, Equip.:	$4,531,000,000	**Total Liab.:**	$15,044,000,000	**Indic. Yr. Divd.:**	$1.480
Total Assets:	$32,009,000,000	**Net Worth:**	$16,615,000,000	**Debt/ Equity:**	0.2442

Northstar Electronics Inc

409 Granville St., Ste. 1455, Vancouver, BC, V6C 1T2; **PH:** 1-604-685-0364;
http:// www.northstarelectronics.com

General - Incorporation	DE	**Stock**- Price on:12/24/2007	$0.07
Employees	NA	Stock Exchange	OTC
Auditor	Pannell Kerr Forster	Ticker Symbol	NEIK
Stk Agt	Signature Stock Transfer, Inc.	Outstanding Shares	NA
Counsel	NA	E.P.S.	NA
DUNS No.	NA	Shareholders	NA

Business: The group's principal activities are to develop, manufacture and distribute undersea wireless communications systems and produces, under contract , defense and aerospace electronic systems.

Primary SIC and add'l.: 4899

CIK No: 0001082027

Subsidiaries: Northstar Network Ltd, Northstar Technical Inc

Officers: Wilson Russell/CEO, Pres., Principal Financial Officer, David Buttle/Technical Dir., Don Vokey/Pres. - Northstar Technical Inc, Brian Gamberg/VP - Research, Development, Northstar Technical Inc, Philomena Kavanagh/VP - Administration, Northstar Technical Inc, Howard Nash/Pres. - Northstar Network Ltd

Directors: Harry Davis/Member - Advisory Board, Keith Guelpa/Member - Advisory Board, Lauren Blair/Member - Advisory Board, Robert Blair/Dir., Terry McLeod/Member - Advisory Board

Owners: David Buttle, Insiders/15.33%, Wilson Russell/14.93%

Financial Data: Fiscal Year End:12/31 Latest Annual Data: 12/31/2006

Year	Sales	Net Income
2006	$1,344,000	-$969,000
2005	$1,630,000	-$985,000
2004	$1,462,000	-$832,000

Curr. Assets:	$467,000	**Curr. Liab.:**	$1,307,000		
Plant, Equip.:	$49,000	**Total Liab.:**	$2,482,000	**Indic. Yr. Divd.:**	NA
Total Assets:	$542,000	**Net Worth:**	-$1,940,000	**Debt/ Equity:**	NA

Northstar Neuroscience Inc

2401 4th Ave., Ste. 300, Seattle, WA, 98121; **PH:** 1-206-728-1477; **Fax:** 1-206-728-1497;
http:// www.northstarneuro.com; **Email:** info@northstarneuro.com

General - Incorporation	WA	**Stock**- Price on:12/24/2007	NA
Employees	70	Stock Exchange	NDQ
Auditor	Ernst & Young, LLP	Ticker Symbol	NSYS
Stk Agt	Registrar & Transfer Co	Outstanding Shares	25,800,000
Counsel	NA	E.P.S.	-$0.94
DUNS No.	NA	Shareholders	NA

Business: The groups principal activities include developing and commercializing neurostimulation therapies. The group products sold under the trade name Renova(TM).The group operates from the United States. The assets of the group for the year 2006 were $107,443 (thousands).

Primary SIC and add'l.: 3842 3845 3841

CIK No: 0001351509

Officers: John S. Bowers/Dir., CEO, Pres., Raymond N. Calvert/VP - Finance, CFO, Matthew J. Gani/VP - Product Development, Bradford E. Gliner/VP - Research, Scott C. Lynch/VP - Marketing, Nawzer Mehta/VP - Clinical Affairs, Amy J. Peterson/VP - Regulatory Affairs, Quality Systems, John M. Ray/VP - Product Quality, Operations, Allen R. Wyler/Medical Dir., Mark Klausner/Investor Relations Officer, Bob East/Investor Relations Officer, Helen Shik/Contact - Media, Wendy Ryan/Contact - Media

Directors: John S. Bowers/Dir., CEO, Pres., Alan J. Levy/Chmn., Susan K. Barnes/Dir., Albert J. Graf/Dir., Wende S. Hutton/Dir., Robert E. McNamara/Dir., Dale A. Spencer/Dir., Jesse I. Treu/Dir., Carol D. Winslow/Dir., Michael Ellwein/Dir.

Owners: John S. Bowers, Jesse I. Treu/3.70%, Robert E. McNamara, Nawzer Mehta, Albert J. Graf, Dale A. Spencer, Carol D. Winslow/1.30%, Lori J. Glastetter, Insiders/11.40%, Alan J. Levy/3.40%, Susan K. Barnes, Boston Scientific Corporation/12.50%, Raymond N. Calvert, Bradford E. Gliner, FMR Corp./12.90% (17 Owners included in Index)

Financial Data: Fiscal Year End:12/31 Latest Annual Data: 12/31/2006

Year	Sales	Net Income
2006	NA	-$25,083,000
2005	NA	-$14,574,000
2004	NA	-$13,411,000

Curr. Assets:	$81,785,000	**Curr. Liab.:**	$4,197,000		
Plant, Equip.:	$865,000	**Total Liab.:**	$4,705,000	**Indic. Yr. Divd.:**	NA
Total Assets:	$107,443,000	**Net Worth:**	$102,738,000	**Debt/ Equity:**	NA

Northway Bank

9 Main St., Berlin, NH, 03570; **PH:** 1-603-752-1171; http:// www.pemibank.com

General - Incorporation	NH	**Stock**- Price on:12/24/2007	$36
Employees	249	Stock Exchange	NA
Auditor	Shatswell, MacLeod & Co. P.C	Ticker Symbol	NA
Stk Agt	EquiServe Trust Co N.A	Outstanding Shares	1,490,000
Counsel	NA	E.P.S.	$2.03
DUNS No.	01-976-5619	Shareholders	NA

Business: The group's principal activity is to provide banking and related services in New Hampshire. The group is a holding company of the berlin city bank, a state chartered bank and pemigewasset national bank, a national bank. The subsidiaries attract deposits from the general public and invest those deposits in securities, commercial loans, real estate loans and consumer loans. The services are provided to individuals and small and medium sized companies. The group operates through twenty-one branch offices and one loan origination facility. The offices and facilities are located in the central and northern New Hampshire communities of berlin, conway, gorham, groveton, littleton, west ossipee, west plymouth, plymouth, campton, ashland, north woodstock, tilton, franklin, laconia, belmont, pittsfield and concord.

Primary SIC and add'l.: 6712 6022

CIK No: 0001041753

Subsidiaries: Northway Capital Trust I, Northway Capital Trust II

Officers: William J. Woodward/62/Chmn., CEO, Pres., Richard T. Brunelle/65/Sr. VP, John A. Gobel/63/Sr. VP, John H. Stratton/61/Sr. VP, Ronald P. Goudreau/54/Sr. VP

Directors: William J. Woodward/62/Chmn., CEO, Pres.

Owners: Richard P. Orsillo, Insiders/16.91%, William J. Woodward/6.16%, Richard T. Brunelle, John H. Stratton, Jeffrey L. Gendell/9.82%

Financial Data: Fiscal Year End:12/31 Latest Annual Data: 12/31/2006

Year	Sales	Net Income
2006	$41,838,000	$3,215,000
2005	$36,651,000	$2,673,000
2004	$35,374,000	$3,388,000

Curr. Assets:	$24,808,000	**Curr. Liab.:**	$521,174,000	**P/E Ratio:**	17.73
Plant, Equip.:	$13,749,000	**Total Liab.:**	$598,728,000	**Indic. Yr. Divd.:**	$0.800
Total Assets:	$650,877,000	**Net Worth:**	$52,149,000	**Debt/ Equity:**	1.6634

Northway Financial Inc

9 Main St., Berlin, NH, 03570; **PH:** 1-603-752-1171; **Fax:** 1-603-752-6291;
http:// www.northwaybank.com

General - Incorporation	NH	**Stock**- Price on:12/24/2007	$36.1
Employees	249	Stock Exchange	OTC
Auditor	Goodwin Procter LLP	Ticker Symbol	NWYF
Stk Agt	Bank Boston EquiServe	Outstanding Shares	1,490,000
Counsel	NA	E.P.S.	$1.98
DUNS No.	NA	Shareholders	NA

Business: The groups principal activity is to provide commercial banking services. The products of the group include commercial and construction loans, real estate mortgages, consumer loans, including personal secured and unsecured loans, and lines of credit. The group operates from the United States. The assets of the group for the year 2006 were $650,877 (thousands).

Primary SIC and add'l.: 6712 6022 6712 6022

CIK No: 0001041753

Subsidiaries: Northway Bank, Northway Capital Trust I, Northway Capital Trust II

Officers: William J. Woodward/62/Chmn., CEO, Pres./$557,249.00, Joseph N. Rozek/Sec., Richard T. Brunelle/65/Sr. VP - Northway Bank/$189,522.00, John A. Gobel/63/Sr. VP/$143,517.00, Ronald P. Goudreau/54/Sr. VP, Richard P. Orsillo/59/CFO, Sr. VP/$170,829.00, John H. Stratton/61/Sr. VP/$163,189.00

Directors: William J. Woodward/62/Chmn., CEO, Pres., Frederick C. Anderson/56/Dir., Brien L. Ward/56/Dir., Fletcher W. Adams/71/Dir., Arnold P. Hanson/57/Dir., John H. Noyes/61/Dir., Stephen G. Boucher/61/Dir., Barry J. Kelley/Dir., Randall G. Labnon/54/Dir.

Owners: Labnon G. Randall, John H. Stratton, Frederick C. Anderson, Stephen G. Boucher, Insiders/16.91%, William J. Woodward/6.16%, Richard T. Brunelle, Brien L. Attorney, John H. Noyes/1.65%, Arnold P. Hanson/1.29%, Fletcher W. Adams/3.68%, Barry J. Kelley/2.85%, Jeffrey L. Gendell/9.82%, Richard P. Orsillo

Financial Data: Fiscal Year End:12/31 Latest Annual Data: 12/31/2006

Year	Sales	Net Income
2006	$41,838,000	$3,215,000
2005	$36,651,000	$2,673,000
2004	$35,374,000	$3,388,000

Curr. Assets:	$24,808,000	**Curr. Liab.:**	$521,174,000	**P/E Ratio:**	18.23
Plant, Equip.:	$13,749,000	**Total Liab.:**	$598,728,000	**Indic. Yr. Divd.:**	$0.800
Total Assets:	$650,877,000	**Net Worth:**	$52,149,000	**Debt/ Equity:**	1.6634

Northwest Airlines Corp

2700 Lone Oak Pkwy., Eagan, MN, 55121; **PH:** 1-612-726-2111; **Fax:** 1-612-726-7123;
http:// www.nwa.com

General - Incorporation	DE	**Stock**- Price on:12/24/2007	NA
Employees	32,460	Stock Exchange	NYSE
Auditor	Ernst & Young LLP	Ticker Symbol	NWA
Stk Agt	Wells Fargo Shareowner Services	Outstanding Shares	NA
Counsel	NA	E.P.S.	$10.83
DUNS No.	00-696-3508	Shareholders	NA

Business: The group's principle activity is to provide airline services. The group operates from United States.

Primary SIC and add'l.: 4512 6719

CIK No: 0001058033

Subsidiaries: Aircraft Foreign Sales, Inc, Cardinal Insurance Company (Cayman) Ltd, Margoon Holding B.V, MLT Inc, Montana Enterprises, Inc, Northwest Aerospace Training Corporation, Northwest Airlines Cargo, Inc, Northwest Airlines Corporation, Northwest Airlines Holdings Corporation, Northwest Airlines, Inc., NW Red Baron LLC, NWA Aircraft Finance, Inc, NWA Fuel Services Corporation, NWA Inc, NWA Real Estate Holding Company LLC 20 Subsidiaries included in the Index

Officers: Douglas M. Steenland/Dir., CEO, Pres., Jim Cron/CEO - MLT, Sr. VP - Revenue Management, Planning, Loyalty Marketing, Ben Hirst/Sr. VP - Consumer Affairs, Administration, Laura Liu/VP - International, Julie Showers/Sr. VP - Inflight Services, Daniel B. Matthews/Sr. VP,

Treasurer, Andrea Fischer Newman/Sr. VP - Government Affairs, Timothy J. Rainey/Sr. VP - Flight Operations, System Operations Control, Kenneth J. Hylander/Sr. VP - Safety, Engineering, Chief Safety Officer, Theresa Wise/CIO, Sr. VP - Northwest Airlines - Inc, Tom Bach/Pres. - Northwest Airlines Cargo, Timothy J. Griffin/Exec. VP - Marketing, Distribution, Philip C. Haan/52/Exec. VP - International, Alliances, Information Technology, Neal Cohen/CFO, Exec. VP, Andrew C. Roberts/Exec. VP - Operations Northwest Airlines, Inc *(22 Officers included in Index)*

Directors: Douglas M. Steenland/Dir., CEO, Pres., Gary L. Wilson/66/Chmn., Roy J. Bostock/Chmn., John M. Engler/Dir., Robert L. Friedman/Dir., Ray W. Benning/62/Dir., George J. Kourpias/73/Dir., Doris Kearns Goodwin/Dir., V. A. Ravindran/59/Dir., Dennis F. Hightower/64/Dir., Frederic V. Malek/69/Dir., Leo M. Van Wijk/59/Dir., William S. Zoller/Dir., David Brandon/Dir., Mike Durham/Dir. *(20 Directors included in Index)*

Owners: Trusts for pilots/2.00%, Gary L. Wilson/1.00%, Douglas M. Steenland, Dennis F. Hightower, Trust for flight attendants/23.00%, Neal S. Cohen, Philip C. Haan, Timothy J. Griffin, Insiders/2.00%, Trusts for pilots, Andrew C. Roberts, William S. Zoller, Robert L. Friedman, Morgan Stanley/6.00%, Trust for ground employees/74.00%

Financial Data: *Fiscal Year End:*12/31 *Latest Annual Data:* 12/31/2006

Year		Sales			Net Income
2006		$12,568,000,000			-$2,835,000,000
2005		$12,286,000,000			-$2,533,000,000
2004		$11,279,000,000			-$862,000,000
Curr. Assets:	$3,566,000,000	**Curr. Liab.:**	$3,211,000,000		
Plant, Equip.:	$8,192,000,000	**Total Liab.:**	$20,929,000,000	**Indic. Yr. Divd.:**	NA
Total Assets:	$13,215,000,000	**Net Worth:**	-$7,991,000,000	**Debt/ Equity:**	NA

Northwest Bancorp Inc

421 W Riverside, Ste.113, Spokane, WA, 99201; ***PH:*** 1-509-456-8888; ***Fax:*** 1-509-742-6669; ***http://*** www.inb.com

General - Incorporation	United States	**Stock**- Price on:12/24/2007	$28.09
Employees	1,619	Stock Exchange	NDQ
Auditor	KPMG LLP	Ticker Symbol	NWSB
Stk Agt	American Stock Transfer & Trust Co.	Outstanding Shares	49,420,000
Counsel	NA	E.P.S	$0.87
DUNS No.	88-346-0958	Shareholders	NA

Business: The group's principal activity is to provide financial services through 137 banking locations in Pennsylvania, 8 banking locations in southwestern New York & 5 banking locations in eastern Ohio. The group offers loans through 45 consumer finance offices in Pennsylvania & two in New York. The lending activities include providing loans secured by first mortgages on owner-occupied, one- to four-family residences. Lending activities also include the origination of consumer loans, including home equity & second mortgage. It provides a variety of deposits consisting of checking accounts, savings accounts, money market deposit accounts, term certificate accounts and individual retirement accounts. On 31-Aug-2003, the group acquired first bell bancorp inc & bell federal savings and loan association and on 20-Oct-2003, the group acquired bell federal savings bank. On 30-Apr-2004, the group acquired skibo financial corp, first carnegie deposit & skibo bancshares m.h.c.

Primary SIC and add'l.: 6712 6035

CIK No: 0001042064

Subsidiaries: Allegheny Services, Inc., Altoona Financial Services in Altoona, Belle Vernon Financial Services in Belle Vernon, Bloomsburg Financial Services in Bloomsburg, Brookville Financial Services in Brookville, Butler Consumer Discount Company in eight locations in Southwestern PA, Clearfield Consumer Discount in Clearfield, Community Consumer Discount in Warren, Corry Consumer Discount in Corry, Dubois Financial Services in Dubois, Erie Consumer Discount in three locations in Erie, Franklin Consumer Discount in Franklin, Hazleton Financial Services in Hazleton, Huntingdon Financial Services in Huntingdon, Jeannette Financial Services in Jeannette 35 Subsidiaries included in the Index

Officers: William J. Wagner/Chmn., CEO, Pres./$814,075.00, Michael G. Smelko/Sr. VP - Retail Lending, William W. Harvey/Sr. VP - Finance, CFO/$276,254.00, Richard F. Seibel/Sr. VP - Risk Management, Andrew C. Young/Sr. VP - Technology, Gregory C. Larocca/Exec. VP - Administration, Investment Services, Corp. Sec./$342,351.00, Timothy A. Huber/Sr. VP - Commercial Lending, David E. Westerburg/Sr. VP - Operations, Robert A. Ordiway/Exec. VP - Marketing, Facilities/$399,969.00, Steven G. Fisher/Exec. VP - Banking Services/$281,825.00, Robert Bablak/Sr. VP - Community Banking, Richard L. Rausch/Sr. VP - Human Resources, James E. Vecellio/Sr. VP - Information Systems

Directors: William J. Wagner/Chmn., CEO, Pres., John M. Bauer/Dir., Joseph F. Long/Dir., Paul A. King/Dir., Robert G. Ferrier/Dir., Richard E. McDowell/Dir., Thomas K. Creal/Dir., Richard L. Carr/Dir., Philip M. Tredway/Dir.

Owners: Thomas K. Creal, Insiders, Robert G. Ferrier, Richard L. Carr, Gregory C. LaRocca, Steven G. Fisher, John M. Bauer, Paul A. King, Joseph F. Long, Richard E. McDowell, William W. Harvey, Robert A. Ordiway, William J. Wagner, Northwest Bancorp, MHC

Financial Data: *Fiscal Year End:*06/30 *Latest Annual Data:* 12/31/2006

Year		Sales			Net Income
2006		$414,599,000			$51,536,000
2005		$353,928,000			$55,804,000
Curr. Assets:	$160,275,000	**Curr. Liab.:**	$5,191,966,000	**P/E Ratio:**	30.20
Plant, Equip.:	$102,713,000	**Total Liab.:**	$5,748,292,000	**Indic. Yr. Divd.:**	$0.800
Total Assets:	$6,330,482,000	**Net Worth:**	$582,190,000	**Debt/ Equity:**	0.8318

Northwest Bancorporation Inc

421 W Riverside, Spokane, WA, 99201; ***PH:*** 1-509-456-8888; ***Fax:*** 1-509-742-6669; ***http://*** www.inb.com; ***Email:*** inb@inb.com

General - Incorporation	WA	**Stock**- Price on:12/24/2007	$16.5
Employees	105	Stock Exchange	OTC
Auditor	Moss Adams LLP	Ticker Symbol	NBCT
Stk Agt	NA	Outstanding Shares	2,350,000
Counsel	NA	E.P.S	$1.10
DUNS No.	NA	Shareholders	NA

Business: The group's principal activity is to provide commercial and retail banking services. The deposit products include non-interest bearing checking accounts, interest bearing checking and savings accounts, money market accounts and fixed and variable rate time certificates of deposit. The loan portfolio includes commercial, real estate, installment, consumer and other loans. The other services provided include cash management services, wire transfers, direct deposit of payroll and social security checks, visa debit cards for automated teller machine access and purchases, Internet banking and automatic drafts and transfers to and from various accounts. The activities are carried out through seven branch offices in Washington and two in Idaho.

Primary SIC and add'l.: 6022 6712

CIK No: 0000893467

Subsidiaries: Inland Northwest Bank

Officers: Randall L. Fewel/Pres., CEO - Inland Northwest Bank, Ronald G. Jacobson/Sr. VP, North Idaho Division Mgr., Commercial Loan Officers - Coeur D'alene, Inland Northwest Bank, Elizabeth A. Herndon/Sr. VP, Branch Administrator - Inland Northwest Bank, Christopher C. Jurey/Exec. VP, CFO - Inland Northwest Bank, Janet Dibler/Airway Heights, Indian Trail Branches Mgr. - Inland Northwest Bank, Shar Widner/Branch, Operations Mgr. - Northpointe Branch, Gerry Berube/Business Services Officer - Inland Northwest Bank, Dan Pearse/Commercial Loan Officers - Spokane, Inland Northwest Bank, Nathan Vore/Commercial Loan Officers - Coeur D'alene, Inland Northwest Bank, Fred Becker/Commercial Loan Officers - Coeur D'alene, Inland Northwest Bank, Shawn Gochenour/Branch, Operations Mgr. - Northpointe Branch, Kalee Quanz/Human Resources - Inland Northwest Bank, Stanly V. Anderson/Information Technology Management, VP, Information Tech Mgr. - Inland Northwest Bank, Roxanne Kusler/Branch, Operations Mgr. - Coeur Dalene Branch, Inland Northwest Bank, Katie Stillinger/Branch Operations Mgr. - Coeur D'alene Branch, Inland Northwest Bank *(36 Officers included in Index)*

Directors: William E. Shelby/69/Chmn., Freeman B. Duncan/61/Dir., Jennifer West/43/Dir., Katie Brodie/61/Dir., Donald A. Ellingsen/70/Dir., Bryan S. Norby/50/Dir., Richard H. Peterson/73/Dir., Jimmie T.G. Coulson/74/Dir., Dwight B. Aden/65/Dir., Harlan D. Douglass/70/Dir., Clark H. Gemmill/64/Dir., Phillip L. Sandberg/75/Dir., Frederick M. Schunter/71/Dir., James R. Walker/74/Dir.

Owners: Bryan S. Norby, Donald A. Ellingsen, Holly A. Austin, Dwight B. Aden, Clark H. Gemmill/2.22%, Christopher C. Jurey, Randall L. Fewel, Phillip L. Sandberg/1.81%, Freeman B. Duncan, William E. Shelby, Harlan D. Douglass/9.97%, Richard H. Peterson/1.59%, Jimmie T.G. Coulson/2.09%, James R. Walker/1.70%, Frederick M. Schunter/2.92%

Financial Data: *Fiscal Year End:*12/31 *Latest Annual Data:* 12/31/2006

Year		Sales			Net Income
2006		$20,091,000			$2,780,000
2005		$15,883,000			$2,160,000
2004		$13,581,000			$1,964,000
Curr. Assets:	$13,741,000	**Curr. Liab.:**	$241,112,000	**P/E Ratio:**	14.86
Plant, Equip.:	$7,252,000	**Total Liab.:**	$254,425,000	**Indic. Yr. Divd.:**	$0.170
Total Assets:	$278,947,000	**Net Worth:**	$24,521,000	**Debt/ Equity:**	0.3807

Northwest Biotherapeutics Inc

7600 Wisconsin Ave., Ste. 750, Bethesda, MD, 20814; ***PH:*** 1-425-608-3000; ***Fax:*** 1-425-608-3009; ***http://*** www.nwbio.com

General - Incorporation	DE	**Stock**- Price on:12/24/2007	$0.125
Employees	3	Stock Exchange	OTC
Auditor	Peterson Sullivan PLLC	Ticker Symbol	NWBO
Stk Agt	Mellon Investor Services LLC	Outstanding Shares	65,240,000
Counsel	Lane Powell Spears Lubersky	E.P.S	-$3.55
DUNS No.	NA	Shareholders	NA

Business: The group's principal activities are to discover, develop and commercialize immunotherapy products that safely generate and enhance immune system responses to effectively treat cancer. The group develops cancer therapies by combining its expertise in the biology of dendritic cells, monoclonal antibodies, immunology and antigen discovery. These therapies are derived from two product development programs dcvax (TM) and hurx (TM). The group is in its development stage.

Primary SIC and add'l.: 8731 2834

CIK No: 0001072379

Officers: Alton L. Boynton/64/Dir., CEO, Pres., Chief Scientific Officer, Marnix L. Bosch/49/CTO, Anthony P. Deasey/59/Dir., Sr. VP - Finance, CFO, Jim D. Johnston/CFO - Principal Financial, Accounting Officer

Directors: Linda F. Powers/52/Non Exec. Chmn., Steve R. Harris/65/Non Exec. Dir., Anthony P. Deasey/59/Dir., Sr. VP - Finance, CFO

Owners: Toucan Capital Fund II, L.P., Al Rajhi Holdings, Toucan Partners, LLC, Insiders, Alton L. Boynton, Marnix L. Bosch, IS Partners Investment Solutions AG, Linda F. Powers

Financial Data: *Fiscal Year End:*12/31 *Latest Annual Data:* 12/31/2006

Year		Sales			Net Income
2006		$80,000			-$1,395,000
2005		$124,000			-$9,937,000
2004		$390,000			-$8,508,000
Curr. Assets:	$455,000	**Curr. Liab.:**	$6,453,000	**P/E Ratio:**	13.89
Plant, Equip.:	$15,000	**Total Liab.:**	$6,453,000	**Indic. Yr. Divd.:**	NA
Total Assets:	$504,000	**Net Worth:**	-$5,949,000	**Debt/ Equity:**	NA

Northwest Indiana Bancorp

9204 Columbia Ave., Munster, IN, 46321; ***PH:*** 1-219-853-7500; ***Fax:*** 1-219-836-2396; ***http://*** www.peoplesbanksb.com

General - Incorporation	IN	**Stock**- Price on:12/24/2007	NA
Employees	139	Stock Exchange	OTC
Auditor	Crowe Chizek & Co. LLC	Ticker Symbol	NWIN
Stk Agt	Peoples Bank	Outstanding Shares	NA
Counsel	Baker & Daniels	E.P.S	$2.09
DUNS No.	87-867-3797	Shareholders	NA

Business: The group's principal activities are to accept deposits and originate loans. The deposits include demand deposits, now accounts, money market demand accounts, savings accounts and certificates of deposit. Loans are provided to real estate, construction, consumer and commercial business. Through its trust department, the group provides estate administration, estate planning, guardianships, land trusts, retirement planning, self-directed ira, keogh and investment agency accounts. The group acts as a representative of estates and trustee for revocable and irrevocable trusts. The group is a holding company of peoples bank sb. At 31-Dec-2003, it operates through 8 branch offices located in munster, east Chicago, hammond, merrillville, dyer, schererville and hobart, Indiana.

Primary SIC and add'l.: 6035 6712

CIK No: 0000919864

Subsidiaries: NWIN, LLC, Peoples Bank SB, Peoples Service Corporation

Officers: Stephan A. Ziemba/VP, Sr. Trust Officer - Investment, Trust Services Group, Randall H. Walker/VP, Trust Investment Officer - Investment, Trust Services Group, Igor Marjanovic/Assist. VP, Trust Investment Officer - Investment, Trust Services Group, Joyce Barr/Assist. VP, Assistant Trust Officer - Investment, Trust Services Group, Todd Scheub/Sr. VP, Sr. Lending Officer, Commercial

Lending Mgr. - Peoples Bank, Dan Moser/VP - Construction, Development Lending Officer - Peoples Bank, Brian Rusin/VP, Commercial Loan Officer - Peoples Bank, Ron Knestrict/VP, Commercial Loan Officer - Peoples Bank, Catherine Gonzalez/VP, Retail Lending Mgr. - Corporate Loan Center, Peoples Bank, Jeremy Gorelick/Assist. VP, Residential Lending Specialist - Peoples Bank, Alicia Quinones-McMahon/Assist. VP, Consumer Lending Specialist - Peoples Bank, Leslie J. Bernacki/Assist. VP, Residential Lending Specialist - Peoples Bank, Austin P. Logue/Assist. VP, Residential Lending Specialist - Peoples Bank, Rachel Lentz/Assist. VP, Consumer Lending Specialist - Peoples Bank, Michael Matlock/Consumer Lending Specialist - Peoples Bank *(19 Officers included in Index)*

Owners: Kenneth V. Krupinski/0.20%, Banc Fund V L.P./6.30%, Insiders/24.30%, Don Fesko/0.02%, Frank J. Bochnowski/1.08%, David A. Bochnowski/12.00%, Stanley E. Mize/1.28%, Robert T. Lowry/0.70%, Lourdes M. Dennison/1.48%, Jon E. DeGuilio/0.20%, James L. Wieser/0.40%, Anthony Puntillo, Edward J. Furticella/2.40%, Leroy F. Cataldi/2.30%, Joel Gorelick/2.40%

Financial Data: *Fiscal Year End:* 12/31 *Latest Annual Data:* 12/31/2006

Year	Sales	Net Income
2006	$39,198,000	$6,475,000
2005	$33,564,000	$6,672,000
2004	$29,926,000	$6,290,000
Curr. Assets:	$19,095,000	Curr. Liab.: $517,471,000
Plant, Equip.:	$14,926,000	Total Liab.: $568,972,000 Indic. Yr. Divd.: $1.440
Total Assets:	$618,982,000	Net Worth: $50,010,000 Debt/ Equity: NA

Northwest Natural Gas Co

220 NW 2nd Ave., Portland, OR, 97209; *PH:* 1-503-226-4211; *Fax:* 1-503-721-2506; *http://* www.nwnatural.com

General - Incorporation	OR	**Stock** - Price on: 12/24/2007	$46.76
Employees	1,211	Stock Exchange	NYSE
Auditor	PricewaterhouseCoopers LLP	Ticker Symbol	NWN
Stk Agt	American Stock Transfer & Trust Co.	Outstanding Shares	26,990,000
Counsel	Beth A. Ugoretz	E.P.S.	$2.75
DUNS No.	00-790-8916	Shareholders	NA

Business: The group's principal activities are to distribute natural gas and provide natural gas storage services. The group operates in three segments: utility, gas storage and other. The utility segment distributes natural gas. The gas storage segment provides gas storage services to interstate customers using its storage capacity not required for utility services. The other segment includes non-regulated investments in alternative energy projects in California and a Boeing 737-300 aircraft leased to Continental Airlines. It also serves the pulp, paper, electronics, electrochemicals, electrometallurgicals, farm and food products, minerals, metal fabrication and casting, machine tools, machinery and textiles industries. The group operates in the United States.

Primary SIC and add'l.: 4924 4922

CIK No: 0000073020

Subsidiaries: Financial Corporation, Gas Pipeline

Officers: Mark S. Dodson/Dir., CEO, Pres./$2,376,533.00, Elisa M. Larson/General Counsel, Assist. Sec., Chief Compliance Officer - Kbpc, Grant M. Yoshihara/VP - Utility Operations, David W. Aimone/Treasurer - Kbpc, Conrad J. Rue/Corp. Sec., Gregg S. Kantor/COO, Pres./$583,087.00, David H. Anderson/Sr. VP, CFO/$735,886.00, Stephen P. Feltz/Treasurer, Controller, Principal Accounting Officer, Lea Anne Doolittle/VP - Human Resources/$502,041.00, Margaret D. Kirkpatrick/VP, General Counsel/$416,566.00, Robert S. Hess/Dir. - Investor Relations, Charles E. Stinson/Pres. - KBPC, Keith J. White/VP - Business Development, Energy Supply, David A. Weber/CIO, David R. Williams/VP - Utility Services

Directors: Mark S. Dodson/Dir., CEO, Pres., Richard G. Reiten/Chmn., Scott C. Gibson/Dir., Timothy P. Boyle/Dir., John D. Carter/Dir., Kenneth Thrasher/Dir., Russell F. Tromley/Dir., Randall C. Pape/57/Dir., Martha L. Byorum/Dir., Jane L. Peverett/Dir., George J. Puentes/Dir., Tod R. Hamachek/Dir.

Owners: John D. Carter, Russell F. Tromley, Kenneth Thrasher, Margaret D. Kirkpatrick, Timothy P. Boyle, Gregg S. Kantor, Tod R. Hamachek, C. Scott Gibson, Richard G. Reiten, Insiders/1.30%, Randall C. Pap, David H. Anderson, Lea Anne Doolittle, Michael S. McCoy, Mark S. Dodson *(17 Owners included in Index)*

Financial Data: *Fiscal Year End:* 12/31 *Latest Annual Data:* 12/31/2006

Year	Sales	Net Income
2006	$1,013,172,000	$63,415,000
2005	$324,993,000	$58,149,000
2004	$707,604,000	$50,572,000
Curr. Assets:	$308,793,000	Curr. Liab.: $339,479,000
Plant, Equip.:	$1,425,141,000	Total Liab.: $1,357,311,000 Indic. Yr. Divd.: $1.500
Total Assets:	$1,956,856,000	Net Worth: $599,545,000 Debt/ Equity: 0.8250

Northwest Pipe Co

200 SW Market St., Ste. 1800, Portland, OR, 97201; *PH:* 1-503-946-1200; *Fax:* 1-503-240-6615; *http://* www.nwpipe.com

General - Incorporation	OR	**Stock** - Price on: 12/24/2007	$33.54
Employees	1,185	Stock Exchange	NDQ
Auditor	PricewaterhouseCoopers LLP	Ticker Symbol	NWPX
Stk Agt	Mellon Investor Services LLC	Outstanding Shares	8,930,000
Counsel	Ater Wynne LLP	E.P.S.	$2.36
DUNS No.	00-399-3060	Shareholders	NA

Business: The group's principle activity is to manufacture welded steel pipe. The group operates through two segments: water transmission and tubular products. The water transmission segment manufactures large diameter and high-pressure steel pipe products used for water transmission and also for piling, hydroelectric projects, wastewater transmission and treatment plant piping. These products are sold primarily to public water agencies. The tubular product segment manufactures and markets smaller diameter, electric resistance welded steel pipe for use in a wide range of construction, agricultural, energy and industrial applications. The group's products are marketed through direct sales personnel, installation contractor and independent distributors throughout the United States and Canada. The group's quarterly revenue for September 2007 was 91.98 millions of USD.

Primary SIC and add'l.: 3317

CIK No: 0001001385

Subsidiaries: Northwest Pipe Mexico S.A. de C.V., Thompson Tank Holdings, Inc., Thompson Tanks Mexico S.A. de C.V.

Officers: Brian W. Dunham/Dir., CEO, Pres./$628,126.00, Charles L. Koenig/Sr. VP, GM - Water Transmission/$317,900.00, Gary Stokes/Sr. VP - Sales, Marketing/$332,731.00, Robert L. Mahoney/46/VP, Chief Strategic Officer/$260,211.00, Bob Mahoney/VP - Corporate Development, Stephanie J. Welty/CFO, VP

Directors: Brian W. Dunham/Dir., CEO, Pres., William R. Tagmyer/Chmn., Wayne B. Kingsley/Dir., Richard A. Roman/Dir., Neil R. Thornton/Dir., Michael C. Franson/Dir.

Owners: Insiders/8.60%, Dimensional Fund/5.40%, William R. Tagmyer/2.60%, Richard A. Roman, Gary A. Stokes, Neil R. Thornton, Wayne B. Kingsley, John D. Murakami, Charles L. Koenig/1.30%, Brian W. Dunham/2.70%, Bank of America Corporation/6.60%, Michael C. Franson, Robert L. Mahoney, Wells Fargo& Company/10.10%

Financial Data: *Fiscal Year End:* 12/31 *Latest Annual Data:* 12/31/2006

Year	Sales	Net Income
2006	$346,591,000	$20,019,000
2005	$329,006,000	$13,386,000
2004	$291,910,000	$12,377,000
Curr. Assets:	$237,514,000	Curr. Liab.: $70,771,000 P/E Ratio: 14.09
Plant, Equip.:	$160,776,000	Total Liab.: $193,625,000 Indic. Yr. Divd.: NA
Total Assets:	$424,451,000	Net Worth: $230,826,000 Debt/ Equity: 0.3690

Northwest Pipeline Corp

295 Chipeta Way, Salt Lake, UT, 84108; *PH:* 1-801-583-8800; *http://* www.williams.com

General - Incorporation	DE	**Stock** - Price on: 12/24/2007	$34.13
Employees	1,185	Stock Exchange	NA
Auditor	Ernst & Young LLP	Ticker Symbol	NA
Stk Agt	Computershare Investor Services LLC	Outstanding Shares	8,930,000
Counsel	NA	E.P.S.	$2.38
DUNS No.	06-797-7322	Shareholders	NA

Business: The group's principal activity is to own and operate an interstate natural gas pipeline system, including facilities for mainline transmission and gas storage. This system extends from the san juan basin in northwestern New Mexico and southwestern Colorado through Colorado, Utah, Wyoming, Idaho, Oregon and Washington to a point on the Canadian border near sumas, Washington. In 2003, the group transported natural gas for a total of 175 customers. The group provides services for markets in California, New Mexico, Colorado, Utah, Nevada, Wyoming, Idaho, Oregon and Washington. The group also provides gas storage services to certain major customers. The group owns and operates a liquefied natural gas storage facility located near plymouth, Washington, which provides standby service for the group's customers during extreme peaks in demand.

Primary SIC and add'l.: 4922

CIK No: 0000110019

Subsidiaries: Llc (wgp)., Williams Gas Pipeline Company

Officers: Phillip D. Wright/Dir., Sr. VP, Principal Executive Officer, Richard D. Rodekohr/VP, Treasurer, Principal Financial Officer, Allison G. Bridges/Dir., VP, Rand R. Clark/Principal Accounting Officer, Controller

Directors: Steven J. Malcolm/Chmn., Phillip D. Wright/Dir., Sr. VP, Principal Executive Officer, Allison G. Bridges/Dir., VP

Financial Data: *Fiscal Year End:* 12/31 *Latest Annual Data:* 12/31/2006

Year	Sales	Net Income
2006	NA	NA
2005	$329,006,000	$13,386,000
2004	$291,910,000	$12,377,000
Curr. Assets:	$237,514,000	Curr. Liab.: $70,771,000 P/E Ratio: 14.34
Plant, Equip.:	$160,776,000	Total Liab.: $193,625,000 Indic. Yr. Divd.: NA
Total Assets:	$424,451,000	Net Worth: $230,826,000 Debt/ Equity: 0.3690

Northwestern Corp

3010 W 69th St., Sioux Falls, SD, 57108; *PH:* 1-605-978-2900; *Fax:* 1-605-978-2840; *http://* www.northwesternenergy.com

General - Incorporation	DE	**Stock** - Price on: 12/24/2007	$30.6
Employees	1,354	Stock Exchange	NDQ
Auditor	Deloitte & Touche LLP	Ticker Symbol	NWEC
Stk Agt	Lasalle Bank N.A	Outstanding Shares	35,910,000
Counsel	NA	E.P.S.	$1.08
DUNS No.	00-792-0291	Shareholders	NA

Business: The group's principle activity is to provide financial risk and achieve financial security through our insurance and investment products. The group's products include mutual fund and annuities.

Primary SIC and add'l.: 4923 4911

CIK No: 0000073088

Subsidiaries: Blue Dot Services, LLC, Canadian-Montana Pipe Line Corporation, Clark Fork and Blackfoot, LLC, Montana Megawatts I, LLC, Nekota Resources, Inc., Netexit, Inc., NorthWestern Corporation, NorthWestern Energy Development, LLC, NorthWestern Energy Marketing, LLC, NorthWestern Generation I, LLC, NorthWestern Investments, LLC, NorthWestern Services Corporation, Risk Partners Assurance, Ltd.

Officers: Michael J. Hanson/Dir., CEO, Pres./$896,743.00, Brian B. Bird/CFO, VP/$496,910.00, Jesse Heier/Administrative Specialist, Barry J. O'Leary/Dir. - Safety, Health, Environmental Services, Kathleen Griffith/Administrative Specialist, Elizabeth A. Stimatz/Coordinator, Safety, Environmental, Teresa S. McGrath/Safety, Coordinator, Robin G. Hess/Specialist - Administrative, Patrick R. Corcoran/VP - Government, Regulatory Affairs, Paul J. Evans/Treasurer, David G. Gates/VP - Wholesale Operations/$318,071.00, Mark I. Hallgrimson/Safety, Environmental Coordinator, William W. Thompson/Sr. Engineer, Sam Milodragovich/Biologist Wildlife, Dan Rausch/Dir. - Investor Relations *(26 Officers included in Index)*

Directors: Michael J. Hanson/Dir., CEO, Pres., Linn E. Draper/Chmn., Julia L. Johnson/Dir., Jon S. Fossel/Dir., Philip L. Maslowe/Dir., Louis D. Peoples/Dir., Stephen P. Adik/Dir.

Owners: Franklin Mutual Advisors, LLC/6.10%, Thomas J. Knapp, Michael J. Hanson, Lehman Brothers, Inc./7.10%, Angelo, Gordon & Co./5.40%, Brian B. Bird, E. Linn Draper, Julia L. Johnson, Jon S. Fossel, Philip L. Maslowe, David G. Gates, Insiders, D. Louis Peoples, Gregory G. A. Trandem, Stephen P. Adik *(16 Owners included in Index)*

Financial Data: *Fiscal Year End:* 12/31 *Latest Annual Data:* 12/31/2006

Year	Sales	Net Income
2006	$1,132,653,000	$37,900,000
2005	$1,165,750,000	$59,467,000
2004	$1,038,989,000	$544,433,000

Curr. Assets:	$268,474,000	**Curr. Liab.:**	$278,936,000	**P/E Ratio:**	32.21
Plant, Equip.:	$1,491,855,000	**Total Liab.:**	$1,653,166,000	**Indic. Yr. Divd.:**	$1.320
Total Assets:	$2,395,937,000	**Net Worth:**	$742,771,000	**Debt/ Equity:**	NA

Norwood Financial Corp

717 Main St., Honesdale, PA, 18431; *PH:* 1-570-253-1455; *Fax:* 1-570-253-3725; *http://* www.norwoodfc.com

General - Incorporation.....PA
Employees.....117
Auditor.....Beard Miller Co. LLP
Stk Agt.....Illinois Stock Transfer Co
Counsel.....NA
DUNS No......00-893-6270

Stock- Price on:12/24/2007.....$32.75
Stock Exchange.....NDQ
Ticker Symbol.....NWFL
Outstanding Shares.....2,790,000
E.P.S.....$2.26
Shareholders.....NA

Business: The group's principal activities are to provide personal, business credit services and trust and investment products to the consumers, businesses, nonprofit organizations and municipalities. The loans are offered mainly to local small and mid-sized businesses for personal and business use. Commercial lending activities include lines of credit, revolving credit, term loans, mortgages, various forms of secured lending and a limited amount of letter of credit facilities. The services are provided through six offices located in wayne county, three offices in pike county and one office in monroe county. The group also operates twelve automated teller machines with ten in branch locations and two remote service facility.

Primary SIC and add'l.: 6712 6022

CIK No: 0001013272

Subsidiaries: Norwood Investment Corp., Norwood Settlement Services, LLC, Wayne Bank, WCB Realty Corp., WTRO Properties Inc.

Officers: William W. Davis/Dir., Pres., CEO - Norwood Financial Corp's/$433,564.00, Alice Klinger/Sales Assist., Michele Bound/Sr. VP, Sandy Halas/Sr. VP, Annette Jurkowski/Trust Officer, Bill Henigan/Commercial Lender, John Carmody/Commercial Lender , Honesdale, Scott Rickard/Investment Representative, Lewis J. Critelli/Exec. VP, CFO - Norwood Financial Corp/$264,885.00, Ed Kasper/Sr. VP/$218,041.00, Bill Kerstetter/Commercial Lender, Renee Gilbert/Mgr. - Tannersville, Nancy Worobey/Mgr. - Lakewood, Marianne Glamann/Mgr. - Marshalls Creek, Maryalice Petzinger/Mgr. - Milford *(23 Officers included in Index)*

Directors: William W. Davis/Dir., Pres., CEO - Norwood Financial Corp's, Russell L. Ridd/78/Chmn., Daniel J. O'Neill/Dir. - Norwood Financial Corp's, Richard L. Snyder/Dir. - Norwood Financial Corp's, John E. Marshall/Dir. - Norwood Financial Corp's, Gary P. Rickard/Dir. - Norwood Financial Corp's, Ralph A. Matergia/Dir. - Norwood Financial Corp's, Kenneth A. Phillips/Dir. - Norwood Financial Corp's

Owners: William W. Davis/2.60%, Daniel J. O'Neil, Ralph A. Matergia, Richard L. Snyder, Wayne Bank Trust Department/6.80%, John E. Marshall, Lewis J. Critelli/1.70%, Joseph A. Kneller, Susan Gumble Cottell, Kenneth A. Phillips, Insiders/12.80%, Edward C. Kasper/1.30%, John H. Sanders, Gary P. Rickard/1.10%

Financial Data: *Fiscal Year End:*12/31 *Latest Annual Data:* 12/31/2006

Year	Sales	Net Income
2006	$29,532,000	$5,910,000
2005	$25,316,000	$5,497,000
2004	$22,552,000	$5,010,000

Curr. Assets:	$11,646,000	**Curr. Liab.:**	$383,733,000		
Plant, Equip.:	$6,020,000	**Total Liab.:**	$402,125,000	**Indic. Yr. Divd.:**	$1.000
Total Assets:	$454,356,000	**Net Worth:**	$52,231,000	**Debt/ Equity:**	0.2488

Notify Technology Corp

1054 S De Anza Blvd., Ste. 105, San Jose, CA, 95129; *PH:* 1-408-777-7920; *Fax:* 1-408-996-7405; *http://* www.notifycorp.com; *Email:* sales@notifycorp.com

General - Incorporation.....CA
Employees.....44
Auditor.....LL Bradford & Co
Stk Agt.....American Stock Transfer & Trust Co.
Counsel.....Wilson Sonsini Goodrich & Rosati
DUNS No......92-729-4561

Stock- Price on:12/24/2007.....$0.3
Stock Exchange.....OTC
Ticker Symbol.....NTFY
Outstanding Shares.....13,970,000
E.P.S......-$0.03
Shareholders.....NA

Business: The group's principal activities are to provide innovative communications application services of wireline and wireless messaging services and a supplier of innovative call and message notification products and services. The group's products include visual got mail, notifylink, call manager and centres receptionist. Visual got mail is designed to provide voice mail notification services to the customers of a long distance telephone company providing local services. Notifylink provides Internet services to mobile "Dial-Up" e-mail users and wireless e-mail notification and management. Call manager products incorporate caller-ID, call waiting caller-ID and voice mail message alert features. The centrex receptionist is a stand-alone unit, which provides the centrex customer with automatic call answer and transfer capability twenty-four hours a day. The group sells its products to bell operating companies and local exchange carriers in the United States of America.

Primary SIC and add'l.: 4822

CIK No: 0001031980

Officers: Paul F. Depond/Founder, Chmn., CEO, Pres., Chris Barker/Systems Administrator, Gerald W. Rice/CFO, Investor Relations Officer, Rhonda Chicone-Shick/VP - Engineering, Product Development, Rodney Truelove/Dir. - Information Services, Adam Sorensen/Tech Support Specialist II - Department, Transportation, Midwest US, Linda M.D. Kosek/Email Administrator - Dept, Information Technology Services, Chad Haatvedt/Dir. - Computer Services, James Eason/Information Systems, Mike Plemmons/Network Administrator, Kathy Tyler/Systems Administrator, Robert Beckwith/National Counsel Community Behavioral Healthcare, Chris J. Peterson/VP - Information Technology, CTO, Paul Kendall/Network Technologist, Brian Cline/Network Administrator *(23 Officers included in Index)*

Directors: Paul F. Depond/Founder, Chmn., CEO, Pres., Inder Tallur/Dir., David A. Brewer/Dir.

Owners: Paul F. DePond, Entities and persons affiliated, David A. Brewer, David A. Brewer, 21X Investments LLC, Insiders, Gerald W. Rice, Rhonda Chicone, Insiders, 21X Investments LLC

Financial Data: *Fiscal Year End:*09/30 *Latest Annual Data:* 9/30/2006

Year	Sales	Net Income
2006	$4,356,000	-$315,000
2005	$5,018,000	-$557,000
2004	$3,528,000	-$656,000

Curr. Assets:	$1,319,000	**Curr. Liab.:**	$2,033,000		
Plant, Equip.:	$100,000	**Total Liab.:**	$2,042,000	**Indic. Yr. Divd.:**	NA
Total Assets:	$1,419,000	**Net Worth:**	-$624,000	**Debt/ Equity:**	NA

Nova Biogenetics Inc

227 Sandy Springs Pl., D-341, Sandy Springs, GA, 30328; *PH:* 1-770-650-6508; *Fax:* 1-770-650-0411; *http://* www.novabiogenetics.com; *Email:* contact@novabiogenetics.com

General - Incorporation.....DE
Employees.....NA
Auditor.....Bouwhuis, Morrill & Co LLC
Stk Agt.....North American Transfer Co
Counsel.....NA
DUNS No......NA

Stock- Price on:12/24/2007.....NA
Stock Exchange.....OTC
Ticker Symbol.....NVBG
Outstanding Shares.....NA
E.P.S......-$0.137
Shareholders.....NA

Business: The group's principle activity is to provide non-medical services to physicians and small medical practice groups. The company's services include billing and scheduling, supply ordering, personnel staffing, marketing and providing access to patient information services. The company also distributes physician practice management system that has the capability of electronically submitting the claims. There are approximately 9,000 small practice groups in the United States. The group operates from United States.

Primary SIC and add'l.: 8062 8999

CIK No: 0001160078

Subsidiaries: Nova BioPharmaceutical, Inc

Officers: Kevin Smith/49/Chmn., CEO, Pres., William Crook/55/MD - Europe, Robert McMahon/50/Exec. VP, Shelley Moses/49/Dir., Sec., Treasurer

Directors: Kevin Smith/49/Chmn., CEO, Pres., Shelley Moses/49/Dir., Sec., Treasurer

Owners: Shelley S. Moses/2.36%, Domus Trust Fund/1.36%, M5 Trust Funds I and II/18.33%, Insiders/37.36%, International Biochemical Industries Inc/6.73%, Timothy C. Moses/3.60%, Kevin Smith/5.00%

Financial Data: *Fiscal Year End:*06/30 *Latest Annual Data:* 6/30/2006

Year	Sales	Net Income
2006	$221,000	-$1,669,000
2005	$483,000	-$1,940,000
2004	$262,000	-$704,000

Curr. Assets:	$119,000	**Curr. Liab.:**	$1,553,000		
Plant, Equip.:	$21,000	**Total Liab.:**	$1,553,000	**Indic. Yr. Divd.:**	NA
Total Assets:	$144,000	**Net Worth:**	-$1,408,000	**Debt/ Equity:**	NA

Nova Biosource Fuels Inc

363 N Sam Houston Pkwy E, Ste. 630, Houston, TX, 77060; *PH:* 1-713-869-6682; *http://* www.novaenergyholding.com; *Email:* info@novabiosource.com

General - Incorporation.....NV
Employees.....NA
Auditor.....Malone & Bailey, PC
Stk Agt.....American Stock Transfer & Trust Co.
Counsel.....NA
DUNS No......NA

Stock- Price on:12/24/2007.....NA
Stock Exchange.....AMEX
Ticker Symbol.....NA
Outstanding Shares.....NA
E.P.S......-$0.31
Shareholders.....NA

Business: The groups principle activity is to refines and markets standard biodiesel. Biodiesel is blended with petroleum diesel to create a biodiesel blend that is nearly indistinguishable from, and in some respects superior to, 100% petroleum diesel. In the year 2006, the group acquired Nova Oil and Biosource Fuels, LLC. The group operates from the United States. The group's quarterly balance for July '07 was 5.64 millions of USD.

Primary SIC and add'l.: 2911

CIK No: 0001137469

Subsidiaries: Biosource America, Nova Biofuels Oklahoma LLC, Nova Biofuels Seneca LLC, Nova Biofuels Trade Group LLC, Nova Holding Oklahoma LLC, Nova Holding Seneca LLC, Nova Holding Trade Group LLC

Officers: Kenneth T. Hern/Chmn., CEO, Mark Chadek/Sr. Mechanical Engineer - Biosource America, Jody Powers/Dir., COO, J. D. McGraw/Dir., Pres., John Mckee/Instrumentation, Controls Technician, Project Mgr. - Biosource America, Russell D. Sammons/VP - Refining Operations, Leon Van Kraayenburg/Principal Financial Officer, Controller, Treasurer, Dallas Neil/VP - Marketing, Lewis W. Powers/62/Dir., COO, Richard Talley/VP - Technology, Projects, John Jackam/Dir. - Biosource America, Jeff Jones/Sr. Chemical Process Engineer, Project Mgr. - Biosource America, Joel Pierce/Sr. Process Engineer, Project Mgr. - Biosource America

Directors: Kenneth T. Hern/Chmn., CEO, Jody Powers/Dir., COO, J. D. McGraw/Dir., Pres., Robert C. Black/Dir., Robert White/Dir., John Reiland/Dir., James L. Rainey/Dir., Charlie Vignieri/Dir., Lewis W. Powers/62/Dir., COO, David Gullickson/Dir., Fred S. Zeidman/62/Dir., John W. Sinders/55/Dir.

Owners: Credit Suisse Securities (USA) LLC, UBS OConnor LLC F/B/O: OConnor Global Convertible Arbitrage Master Limited, JBWere Global Small Companies Pooled Fund, Valens Offshore SPV I, Ltd., GLG Market Neutral Fund, UBS OConnor LLC F/B/O: OConnor Global Convertible Arbitrage II Master Limited, New Zealand Administration Services Limited - Global Equity Small Companies Pool, Telstra Superannuation Scheme, Seligman Global Smaller Companies Fund, Small/Mid Cap Diversified Alpha Fund, SEI Institutional Investments Trust - Small Cap Fund, Quattro Fund Limited, Aristeia Partners, L.P., Fonds voor Gemene Rekening Beroepsvervoer, The Central States, Southeast and Southwest Areas Pension Fund *(39 Owners included in Index)*

Financial Data: *Fiscal Year End:*10/31 *Latest Annual Data:* 10/31/2006

Year	Sales	Net Income
2006	$16,211,000	-$28,515,000
2005	$19,000	-$112,000
2004	$18,000	-$37,000

Curr. Assets:	$50,000	**Curr. Liab.:**	$0		
Plant, Equip.:	NA	**Total Liab.:**	$0	**Indic. Yr. Divd.:**	NA
Total Assets:	$50,000	**Net Worth:**	$50,000	**Debt/ Equity:**	NA

NOVA Chemicals Corp

1000 Seventh Ave., S.W., Calgary, AB, T2P 5C6; *PH:* 1-403-750-3600; *http://* www.novachem.com; *Email:* mycareer@novachem.com

General - Incorporation.....Canada
Employees.....3,330
Auditor.....Ernst & Young LLP
Stk Agt.....Mellon Trust Co
Counsel.....NA
DUNS No......24-345-5466

Stock- Price on:12/24/2007.....$33.98
Stock Exchange.....NYSE
Ticker Symbol.....NA
Outstanding Shares.....82,750,000
E.P.S......-$6.76
Shareholders.....NA

Business: The group's principle activities are to manufacture and distribute ethylene, polyethylene, styrene monomer and polystyrene resins. The company has operations in Canada, the United States, Europe and other countries. The group's revenue for September 2007 was 1,755.00 millions of USD.

Primary SIC and add'l.: 2821 2869 2899 2822

CIK No: 0000922960

Subsidiaries: NOVA Chemicals (Canada) Ltd./NOVA Chimie (Canada) Lte, NOVA Chemicals (International) S.A., NOVA Chemicals Inc., NOVA Investments (U.S.) Inc., NOVA Petrochemicals Ltd., NOVAChemicals Quimica Holdings, S.L., Novacor Chemicals Investments B.V.

Officers: Jeffrey M. Lipton/Dir., CEO, Pres., Jack S. Mustoe/Sr. VP - Legal, General Counsel, Christopher D. Pappas/Dir., COO, Sr. VP, Dale H. Spiess/Sr. VP, Pres. - Olefins, Polyolefins, John L. Wheeler/CIO, Sr. VP, Chuck Magro/VP - Investor Relations, Terence A. Poole/Exec. VP - Corporate Strategy, Development, Larry A. MacDonald/Sr. VP, CFO

Directors: Jeffrey M. Lipton/Dir., CEO, Pres., Edward J. Newall/Chmn., Jacques Bougie/Dir., Yves L. Fortier/Dir., Arnold M. Ludwick/Dir., Joanne V. Creighton/Dir., Janice G. Rennie/Dir., Joanne V. Creightonn/Dir., Peter F. Boer/Dir., Kerry L. Hawkins/Dir., Robert E. Dineen/Dir., Jerald A. Blumbergg/Dir., James M. Stanford/Dir., Christopher D. Pappas/Dir., COO, Sr. VP

Financial Data: Fiscal Year End:12/31 Latest Annual Data: 12/31/2006

Year	Sales	Net Income
2006	$6,519,000,000	-$699,000,000
2005	$5,616,000,000	-$115,000,000
2004	$5,270,000,000	$260,000,000

Curr. Assets:	$1,323,000,000	Curr. Liab.:	$1,189,000,000		
Plant, Equip.:	$2,719,000,000	Total Liab.:	$3,609,000,000	Indic. Yr. Divd.:	$0.420
Total Assets:	$4,155,000,000	Net Worth:	$546,000,000	Debt/ Equity:	NA

Nova Measuring Instruments Ltd

4701 Patrick Henry Dr., Ste. 1701, Santa Clara, CA, 95054; **PH:** 1-408-200-4344; **Fax:** 1-408-200-4349; **http://** www.nova.co.il; **Email:** info@nova.co.il

General - Incorporation	Israel	**Stock**- Price on:12/24/2007	$2.83
Employees	280	Stock Exchange	NDQ
Auditor	Brightman Almagor & Co	Ticker Symbol	NVMI
Stk Agt	Nova Measuring Inst.	Outstanding Shares	17,240,000
Counsel	Gilead Sher, Brenner & Kadari	E.P.S.	-$0.22
DUNS No.	NA	Shareholders	NA

Business: The group's principle activities are design, development and production of an integrated process control systems for use in the manufacture of semiconductors. In Oct 1995 the company began manufacturing and marketing systems for chemical mechanical polishing. The company has since expanded its product offering to include systems designed for chemical vapor deposition. The company has four wholly owned subsidiaries in the usa, Japan, Taiwan and the Netherlands. These are engaged in marketing activities and provide technical support to customers. The group's quarterly revenue for Sep '07 was 13.89 millions of USD.

Primary SIC and add'l.: 3674

CIK No: 0001109345

Subsidiaries: Nova Measuring Instruments Inc., Nova Measuring Instruments K.K., Nova Measuring Instruments Netherlands B.V., Nova Measuring Instruments Taiwan Ltd.

Officers: Gabi Seligsohn/CEO, Pres., Moshe Finarov/Dir., Co - Founder, CTO, VP - Technology, Dov Farkash/VP - Sales, Dror David/CFO, VP - Resources, Gabi Sharon/VP - Operations, Avi Kerbs/Dir., Exec. VP - Global Business Management Group, Boaz Brill/VP - Technology Development, Avron Ger/VP - Thin Film Business Unit, David Scheiner/CTO, Avi Magid/Exec. VP - Global Business Management Group, Ehud Helft/Investor Relations Officer - USA, Kenny Green/Investor Relations Officer - USA, Zvi Rabin/Investor Relations Officer - Israel, Orly Dean/Investor Relations Officer, Sec.

Directors: Michael Brunstein/Chmn., Moshe Finarov/Dir., Co - Founder, CTO, VP - Technology, Alon Dumanis/Dir., Giora Dishon/Dir., Avi Kerbs/Dir., Exec. VP - Global Business Management Group, Dan Falk/Dir., Nick Bright/Dir., Naama Zeldis/Dir.

Owners: Tamir Fishman Ventures II, L.L.C., Clal Electronics Industries Ltd., Shai Saul, Teuza - A Fairchild Technology Venture Ltd., Rima Managenent, LLC, Eldad Tamir, Danny Fishman, Tamir Fishman & Co. Ltd., Teuza Management & Development, Michael Elias, Giora Dishon, Austin W. Marxe, Richard Mashaal

Financial Data: Fiscal Year End:12/31 Latest Annual Data: 12/31/2006

Year	Sales	Net Income
2006	$48,292,000	-$1,934,000
2005	$30,142,000	-$8,414,000
2004	$36,806,000	-$1,420,000

Curr. Assets:	$31,444,000	Curr. Liab.:	$15,571,000		
Plant, Equip.:	$2,601,000	Total Liab.:	$19,844,000	Indic. Yr. Divd.:	NA
Total Assets:	$44,419,000	Net Worth:	$24,575,000	Debt/ Equity:	NA

Novacea Inc

601 Gateway Blvd., Ste. 800, South San Francisco, CA, 94080; **PH:** 1-650-228-1800; **Fax:** 1-650-228-1088; **http://** www.novacea.com; **Email:** info@novacea.com

General - Incorporation	DE	**Stock**- Price on:12/24/2007	$10.65
Employees	59	Stock Exchange	NDQ
Auditor	Ernst & Young, LLP	Ticker Symbol	NOVC
Stk Agt	American Stock Transfer & Trust Co.	Outstanding Shares	23,270,000
Counsel	NA	E.P.S.	-$1.61
DUNS No.	NA	Shareholders	NA

Business: The groups principal activities include licensing, developing and commercializing novel therapies. The group products sold under the trade name Asentar (TM). The group operates from the United States.

Primary SIC and add'l.: 2834

CIK No: 0001178711

Officers: John P. Walker/Chmn., CEO, John G. Curd/Pres., Chief Medical Officer, Amar Singh/Chief Commercialization Officer, Edward C. Albini/CFO, VP, Ivy Ang/VP - Human Resources

Directors: John P. Walker/Chmn., CEO, Eckard Weber/Dir., James Healy/Dir., Camille Samuels/Dir., Michael Raab/Dir., Lowell E. Sears/Dir., Daniel M. Bradbury/Dir.

Owners: Daniel M. Bradbury, Lowell E. Sears, Ivy Ang, Jay Moorin, Entities affiliated with ProQuest Investments, Entities affiliated with New Enterprise Associates, Michael G. Raab, Entities affiliated with Domain Associates, L.L.C., John P. Walker, Fong Wang Clow, John G. Curd, Edward C. Albini, James I. Healy, Eckard Weber, James C. Blair *(21 Owners included in Index)*

Financial Data: Fiscal Year End:12/31 Latest Annual Data: 12/31/2006

Year	Sales	Net Income
2006	$371,000	-$29,628,000
2005	$56,000	-$23,805,000
2004	$1,120,000	-$17,952,000

Curr. Assets:	$65,678,000	Curr. Liab.:	$6,240,000	P/E Ratio:	18.23
Plant, Equip.:	$150,000	Total Liab.:	$6,240,000	Indic. Yr. Divd.:	NA
Total Assets:	$66,064,000	Net Worth:	$59,824,000	Debt/ Equity:	NA

Novadel Pharma Inc

25 Minneakoning Rd., Flemington, NJ, 08822; **PH:** 1-908-782-3431; **Fax:** 1-908-782-2445; **http://** www.novadel.com

General - Incorporation	DE	**Stock**- Price on:12/24/2007	$1.21
Employees	21	Stock Exchange	AMEX
Auditor	J. H. Cohn LLP	Ticker Symbol	NVD
Stk Agt	American Stock Transfer & Trust Co.	Outstanding Shares	NA
Counsel	NA	E.P.S.	NA
DUNS No.	NA	Shareholders	NA

Business: The group's principle activity is to provide consulting services in connection with product development for various pharmaceutical companies. The company also develops novel application drug delivery systems for marketed prescription and over-the-counter therapeutics. The company's delivery systems are lingual sprays capsules which enables drug absorption through the oral mucosa and more rapid absorption into the bloodstream. The delivery of a therapeutic agent through the oral mucosa leads to a faster onset of action and avoids degradation in the gastrointestinal tract and liver. The group operates from United States.

Primary SIC and add'l.: 2834

CIK No: 0001043873

Officers: Jan H. Egberts/49/Dir., CEO, Pres./$496,912.00, Michael E. Spicer/CFO, Corp. Sec./$860,745.00, David H. Bergstrom/COO, Sr. VP/$757,076.00, Deni M. Zodda/Chief Business Officer, Sr. VP

Directors: Jan H. Egberts/49/Dir., CEO, Pres., Steven B. Ratoff/65/Chmn., Charles B. Nemeroff/Dir., Mark J. Baric/Dir., Jay J. Lobell/Dir., William F. Hamilton/Dir., Thomas Bonney/Dir.

Owners: Jan H. Egberts, Charles Nemeroff, Lindsay A. Rosenwald/14.20%, Insiders/3.40%, Jean W. Frydman, William Harris Investors, Inc./6.40%, Steven B. Ratoff, Caisse de dpt et placement du Qubec/9.60%, Jay J. Lobell, Michael E. Spicer, Barry C. Cohen, William F. Hamilton, ProQuest Investments, II, L.P./13.70%, Thomas E. Bonney, Wachovia Corporation/9.80%

Financial Data: Fiscal Year End:07/31 Latest Annual Data: 7/31/2006

Year	Sales	Net Income
2006	$1,890,000	-$10,084,000
2005	$439,000	-$9,450,000

Curr. Assets:	$11,774,000	Curr. Liab.:	$2,200,000		
Plant, Equip.:	$2,704,000	Total Liab.:	$4,777,000	Indic. Yr. Divd.:	NA
Total Assets:	$14,822,000	Net Worth:	$10,045,000	Debt/ Equity:	0.0062

Novagold Resources Inc

200 Granville St., Ste. 2300, Vancouver, BC, V6C 1S4; **PH:** 1-604-669-6227; **Fax:** 1-604-669-6272; **http://** www.novagold.net; **Email:** info@novagold.net

General - Incorporation	NS	**Stock**- Price on:12/24/2007	$14.67
Employees	NA	Stock Exchange	AMEX
Auditor	PricewaterhouseCoopers LLP	Ticker Symbol	NG
Stk Agt	Computershare Trust Co	Outstanding Shares	92,000,000
Counsel	NA	E.P.S.	-$0.3
DUNS No.	NA	Shareholders	NA

Business: The groups principle activity is to explore mineral properties. The groups mining products include copper, silver and zinc resources. The groups operating projects include Galore Creek project, and the Ambler project. The group operates from United States.

Primary SIC and add'l.: 9999

CIK No: 0001173420

Subsidiaries: Alaska Gold Company, NovaGold (Bermuda) Alaska Limited, NovaGold Canada Inc., NovaGold Resources (Bermuda) Limited, NovaGold Resources Alaska, Inc.

Officers: Rick Van Nieuwenhuyse/Dir., CEO, Pres., Greg S. Johnson/VP - Corporate Communications, Strategic Development, Joe Piekenbrock/VP - Exploration, Doug Nicholson/VP, GM - Novagold Alaska, Alaska Gold Co, Elaine Sanders/VP - Finance, Susan Mathieu/VP - Environment, Sustainability, Delaney Fisher/General Counsel, Patricia Pracher/Controller, Sacha Iley/VP - Human Resources, Peter Harris/COO, Sr. VP, Robert J. MacDonald/Sr. VP, CFO, Corp. Sec., Doug Brown/VP - Business Development, Carl Gagnier/Exec. VP - Novagold Canada

Directors: Rick Van Nieuwenhuyse/Dir., CEO, Pres., Patrick Downey/Dir., Kalidas Madhavpeddi/Dir., James Philip/Dir., George L. Brack/Dir., Michael H. Halvorson/Dir., Gerald J. McConnell/Dir., Cole McFarland/Dir., Clynton R. Nauman/Dir.

Financial Data: Fiscal Year End:11/30 Latest Annual Data: 11/30/2006

Year	Sales	Net Income
2006	$7,322,000	-$143,179,000
2005	$3,150,000	-$44,919,000
2004	$3,162,000	-$28,842,000

Curr. Assets:	$101,038,000	Curr. Liab.:	$35,259,000		
Plant, Equip.:	$142,420,000	Total Liab.:	$84,855,000	Indic. Yr. Divd.:	NA
Total Assets:	$290,559,000	Net Worth:	$205,703,000	Debt/ Equity:	NA

Novamed Inc

980 N Michigan Ave., Ste. 1620, Chicago, IL, 60611; **PH:** 1-312-664-4100; **Fax:** 1-312-664-4250; **http://** www.novamed.com; **Email:** irinfo@novamed.com

General - Incorporation	DE	**Stock**- Price on:12/24/2007	$5.52
Employees	439	Stock Exchange	NDQ
Auditor	Pricewaterhousecoopers LLP	Ticker Symbol	NOVC
Stk Agt	American Stock Transfer & Trust Co.	Outstanding Shares	24,390,000
Counsel	NA	E.P.S.	$0.24
DUNS No.	NA	Shareholders	NA

Business: The group's principle activity is to provide eye care services and operate ambulatory surgery centers. The group operates through three business segments: surgical facilities segment, product sales segment and management services segment. Currently the group owns and operates 17 ambulatory surgery centers which provide single speciality ophthalmic surgical facilities such as cataract and refractive surgery. It also owns optical products and services organization that sells corrective lenses, eyeglass frames and contact lenses. The group operates under service agreements where it supplies eyeglasses, contact lenses and other optical products and provides excimer lasers and other services to eye care professionals for their use in performing laser vision correction surgery. The group provides research services for eye care devices or pharmaceuticals being developed or tested in clinical trials. The group's quarterly revenue for September 2007 was 33.39 millions of USD.

Primary SIC and add'l.: 3851 3827 8042 8090

CIK No: 0001086939

Subsidiaries: Blue Ridge NovaMed, Inc., Blue Ridge Surgical Center, LLC, Midwest Uncuts, Inc., NMGK, Inc., NMI, Inc., NMLO, Inc., NovaMed Acquisition Company, Inc., NovaMed Alliance, Inc., NovaMed Eye Surgery and Laser Center of St. Joseph, Inc., NovaMed Eye Surgery Center (Plaza) LLC, NovaMed Eye Surgery Center of Cincinnati, LLC, NovaMed Eye Surgery Center of Maryville, LLC, NovaMed Eye Surgery Center of New Albany, LLC, NovaMed Eye Surgery Center of North County, LLC, NovaMed Eye Surgery Center of Overland Park, LLC 47 Subsidiaries included in the Index

Officers: Thomas S. Hall/Chmn., CEO, Pres./$1,400,765.00, Scott T. MacOmber/CFO, Exec. VP/$472,452.00, Michele E. Vickery/Exec. VP - Operations/$410,144.00, Jack M. Clark/Exec. VP, Chief Revenue Officer/$334,736.00, Thomas J. Chirillo/Sr. VP - Corporate Development, Robert C. Goettling/Sr. VP - Corporate Development, William J.L. Kennedy/Sr. VP - Business Development, John W. Lawrence/Sr. VP, General Counsel, Sec., John P. Hart/VP, Corporate Controller, Frank L. Soppa/VP - Optical Services Group, Robert D. Watson/VP - Marketing Services Group

Directors: Thomas S. Hall/Chmn., CEO, Pres., Robert J. Kelly/Dir., Steven V. Napolitano/Dir., Scott H. Kirk/Dir., Judd R. Jessup/Dir., Lance C.A. Piccolo/Dir.

Owners: Thomas S. Hall/1.37%, Michele E. Vickery, Scott H. Kirk/6.55%, R. Judd Jessup/1.20%, Pequot Capital Management, Inc./8.07%, Kent A. Kirk/6.28%, Scott T. Macomber/2.09%, Insiders/13.20%, C.A. Lance Piccolo, Robert J. Kelly, Jack M. Clark, Steven V. Napolitano

Financial Data: *Fiscal Year End:*12/31 *Latest Annual Data:* 12/31/2006

Year	Sales	Net Income
2006	$108,434,000	$5,737,000
2005	$81,226,000	$5,589,000
2004	$64,575,000	$4,459,000

Curr. Assets:	$24,643,000	**Curr. Liab.:**	$14,403,000	**P/E Ratio:**	24.00
Plant, Equip.:	$15,066,000	**Total Liab.:**	$78,135,000	**Indic. Yr. Divd.:**	NA
Total Assets:	$160,547,000	**Net Worth:**	$68,116,000	**Debt/ Equity:**	0.9792

Novamerican Steel Inc

6001 Irwin St., LaSalle, PQ, H8N 1A1; *PH:* 1-514-335-6682; *Fax:* 1-514-683-5285; *http://* www.novamerican.com

General - Incorporation	Canada	**Stock**- Price on:12/24/2007	$49.3
Employees	1,062	Stock Exchange	NDQ
Auditor	Raymond Chabot Grant Thornton LLP	Ticker Symbol	NA
Stk Agt	Computershare Trust Co	Outstanding Shares	10,450,000
Counsel	Stikeman Elliott	E.P.S	$0.10
DUNS No.	25-502-8169	Shareholders	NA

Business: The group's principal activity is to process and distribute stainless steel, carbon steel and aluminum products. It also operates as an intermediary between primary metal producers and manufacturers. In addition, it produces steel tubing for structural and automotive markets and manufactures steel components for heavy equipment. The group is a holding company for two main operating groups: nova, which operates in twelve locations in Canada and American steel which, operates in nine locations in the northeastern and mid-Atlantic United States.

Primary SIC and add'l.: 6719 3325 3312 3353 3914

CIK No: 0001046687

Subsidiaries: 156499 Canada Inc., American Steel& Aluminum Corporation, Argo Steel Ltd., Cresswell Industries Inc., Delta Tube and Company, Limited, Integrated Steel Industries,Inc., Nova Steel Ltd., Nova Steel Processing Centre Ltd., Nova Tube and Steel,Inc., Nova Tube Inc., Nova Tube Indiana, LLC, Nova Tube Ontario Inc., Novamerican Tube Holdings,Inc.

Officers: Roger Daigneault/VP - Corporate Purchasing, Lawrence P. Cannon/44/CFO, VP, Pina Santillo/39/Sec.

Owners: FMR Corp./12.50%, Christopher H. Pickwoad, Michael L. Richards, Alexander Adam, Robert Panet-Raymond, Scott B. Jones/13.30%, Bryan D. Jones/54.30%, Insiders/68.20%, John LeBoutillier

Financial Data: *Fiscal Year End:*11/26 *Latest Annual Data:* 11/25/2006

Year	Sales	Net Income
2006	$840,798,000	$44,298,000
2005	$834,689,000	$36,938,000
2004	$768,627,000	$72,911,000

Curr. Assets:	$312,480,000	**Curr. Liab.:**	$132,249,000		
Plant, Equip.:	$106,308,000	**Total Liab.:**	$204,172,000	**Indic. Yr. Divd.:**	NA
Total Assets:	$434,880,000	**Net Worth:**	$230,708,000	**Debt/ Equity:**	NA

Novartis AG

608 5th Ave., New York, NY, 10020; *PH:* 1-212-307-1122; *Fax:* 1-212-246-0185; *http://* www.novartis.com; *Email:* Corporate.Enquiries@novartis.com

General - Incorporation	Switzerland	**Stock**- Price on:12/24/2007	$55.71
Employees	100,735	Stock Exchange	NYSE
Auditor	PricewaterhouseCoopers LLP	Ticker Symbol	NVS
Stk Agt	Morgan ADR Service Center	Outstanding Shares	2,340,000,000
Counsel	NA	E.P.S	$5.41
DUNS No.	NA	Shareholders	NA

Business: The groups principle activity is to provide pharmaceuticals, vaccines and diagnostics products. The group operates through four segments namely, pharmaceuticals, vaccines and diagnostics, sandoz, and consumer health. The group operates from the Canada, Europe, Asia Pacific, Africa and Australia.

Primary SIC and add'l.: 2834

CIK No: 0001114448

Owners: Daniel Vasella, Paul Choffat, Wendelin Wiedeking, Rolf M. Zinkernagel, Raymund Breu, Urs Baerlocher, Ulrich Lehner, Hans-Joerg Rudloff, Pierre Landolt, Srikant Datar, Andreas Rummelt, Alexandre F. Jetzer, Peter Burckhardt, Juergen Brokatzky-Geiger, Thomas Ebeling *(19 Owners included in Index)*

Financial Data: *Fiscal Year End:*12/31 *Latest Annual Data:* 12/31/2006

Year	Sales	Net Income
2006	$36,749,000,000	$5,264,000,000
2005	$32,526,000,000	$5,190,000,000
2004	$28,247,000,000	$4,989,000,000

Curr. Assets:	$20,668,000,000	**Curr. Liab.:**	$16,234,000,000	**P/E Ratio:**	10.64
Plant, Equip.:	$10,498,000,000	**Total Liab.:**	$26,897,000,000	**Indic. Yr. Divd.:**	$0.930
Total Assets:	$68,567,000,000	**Net Worth:**	$41,670,000,000	**Debt/ Equity:**	NA

NovaStar Financial Inc

8140 Ward Pkwy., Ste. 300, Kansas City, MO, 64114; *PH:* 1-816-237-7000; *Fax:* 1-816-237-7515; *http://* www.novastarmortgage.com; *Email:* question@novastar1.com

General - Incorporation	MD	**Stock**- Price on:12/24/2007	$9.66
Employees	2,048	Stock Exchange	NDQ
Auditor	Deloitte & Touche LLP	Ticker Symbol	NFLX
Stk Agt	UMB Bank, N.A.	Outstanding Shares	37,900,000
Counsel	NA	E.P.S	$0.07
DUNS No.	NA	Shareholders	NA

Business: The groups principal activities include originating, purchasing, selling and investing in residential nonconforming loans and mortgage-backed securities. The group operates through three segments namely, mortgage portfolio management, mortgage lending and loan servicing. The group operates from the United States. Of the total assets in the year 2006, the mortgage portfolio management segment accounted for $3,234,848, mortgage lending $2,137,297 and loan servicing $41,123 (thousands).

Primary SIC and add'l.: 6798

CIK No: 0001025953

Subsidiaries: Acceleron Lending, Inc, Ampro Financial Services, Inc, Homeview Lending, Inc, HVL Repurchase Corporation, HVL Repurchase Corporation II, NFI Holding Corporation, NFI Repurchase Corporation, NMI Property Financing, Inc, NMI REO Financing, Inc, NMI Repurchase Corporation, NMI Repurchase Corporation II, NovaStar ABS CDO 1, Inc, NovaStar ABS CDO 1, Ltd, NovaStar Assets Corporation, NovaStar Capital Access Corporation 32 Subsidiaries included in the Index

Officers: Scott Hartman/Chmn., CEO/$1,597,657.00, Steve Haslam/Sr. VP - Retail Division, Lance W. Anderson/Dir., COO, Pres./$1,599,851.00, Michael L. Bamburg/CIO, Exec. VP/$927,702.00, Gregory S. Metz/Sr. VP, CFO/$469,286.00, Jeffrey D. Ayers/47/Sr. VP, General Counsel, Corp. Sec., Todd M. Phillips/VP, Controller, Treasurer

Directors: Scott Hartman/Chmn., CEO, Donald M. Berman/Dir., Lance W. Anderson/Dir., COO, Pres., Gregory T. Barmore/Dir., Art N. Burtscher/Dir., Edward W. Mehrer/Dir.

Owners: Insiders/7.96%, Dreman Value Management, LLC/5.70%, Gregory S. Metz, Scott F. Hartman/3.39%, Michael L. Bamburg/1.13%, Gregory T. Barmore, David A. Pazgan, Lance W. Anderson/2.22%, Art N. Burtscher, Donald M. Berman, Edward W. Mehrer

Financial Data: *Fiscal Year End:*12/31 *Latest Annual Data:* 12/31/2006

Year	Sales	Net Income
2006	$578,316,000	$72,938,000
2005	$453,266,000	$139,124,000
2004	$478,339,000	$115,389,000

Curr. Assets:	$229,137,000	**Curr. Liab.:**	$2,246,600,000	**P/E Ratio:**	3.91
Plant, Equip.:	$21,534,000	**Total Liab.:**	$4,513,693,000	**Indic. Yr. Divd.:**	$22.400
Total Assets:	$5,028,263,000	**Net Worth:**	$514,570,000	**Debt/ Equity:**	7.1228

Novatel Wireless Inc

9645 Scranton Rd., Ste. 205, San Diego, CA, 92121; *PH:* 1-858-812-3400; *Fax:* 1-858-812-3402; *http://* www.novatelwireless.com

General - Incorporation	DE	**Stock**- Price on:12/24/2007	$25.01
Employees	235	Stock Exchange	NDQ
Auditor	KPMG LLP	Ticker Symbol	NVTL
Stk Agt	U.S. Stock Transfer Corp	Outstanding Shares	30,420,000
Counsel	NA	E.P.S	$0.94
DUNS No.	NA	Shareholders	NA

Business: The group's principal activity is to provide wireless broadband access solutions for the worldwide mobile communications market. The products of the group include wireless data modems, software for laptop pcs, embedded wireless modules for original equipment manufacturers and ruggedized wireless data modems for public safety and telemetry applications. The group also offers software engineering and design services to customers to facilitate the use of products. Products are designed to operate across 2.5g wireless networks, including gprs and cdma 1xrtt, and 3g networks, including w-cdma/umts and cdma 1xev-do, using single or multiple radio band frequencies. The group operates in the United States and Canada.

Primary SIC and add'l.: 3669 7372

CIK No: 0001022652

Subsidiaries: Electro Rent (Tianjin) Rental Co., Ltd, Electro Rent Asia, Inc, Electro Rent Europe NV, ER International, Inc, Genstar Rental Electronics, Inc

Officers: Peter V. Leparulo/Executive Chmn./$2,683,893.00, Catherine F. Ratcliffe/Sr. VP - Business Affairs, General Counsel/$1,346,999.00, Slim S. Souissi/CTO, Sr. VP/$1,106,308.00, Brad Weinert/Pres., Rob M. Hadley/Sr. VP - Worldwide Sales, Marketing/$1,131,346.00, Chris Ross/Sr. VP - Operations, Marcy Graham/Dir. - Investor Relations

Directors: Peter V. Leparulo/Executive Chmn., David A. Werner/Dir., Horst J. Pudwill/Dir., Greg Lorenzetti/Dir., John Ross/Dir.

Owners: Catherine F. Ratcliffe, Peter V. Leparulo/3.36%, Artis Capital Management, LLC/11.48%, Robert H. Getz, Robert M. Hadley, Dan L. Halvorson/1.02%, David A. Werner, Peng K. Lim, Horst J. Pudwill/1.05%, Buckhead Capital, LLC/5.73%, George B. Weinert, Insiders/8.92%, Slim S. Souissi

Financial Data: *Fiscal Year End:*12/31 *Latest Annual Data:* 12/31/2006

Year	Sales	Net Income
2006	$217,972,000	$443,000
2005	$161,736,000	$11,116,000
2004	$103,727,000	$13,819,000

Curr. Assets:	$165,394,000	**Curr. Liab.:**	$57,409,000	**P/E Ratio:**	38.48
Plant, Equip.:	$15,501,000	**Total Liab.:**	$57,409,000	**Indic. Yr. Divd.:**	NA
Total Assets:	$191,645,000	**Net Worth:**	$134,236,000	**Debt/ Equity:**	NA

Novavax Inc

9920 Belward Campus Dr., Rockville, MD, 20850; ***PH:*** 1-240-268-2000; ***http://*** www.novavax.com; ***Email:*** ir@novavax.com

General - Incorporation .... DE | **Stock**- Price on:12/24/2007 .... $3.04
Employees .... 56 | Stock Exchange .... NDQ
Auditor .... Grant Thornton, LLP | Ticker Symbol .... NVAX
Stk Agt .... EquiServe Trust Co N.A | Outstanding Shares 61,910,000
Counsel .... White & McDermott | E.P.S .... -$0.521
DUNS No. .... 80-883-7520 | Shareholders .... NA

Business: The group's principle activities are to research, develop and commercialize proprietary products focused on drug delivery and vaccine development. The group sells, markets and distributes a line of women's health prescription pharmaceuticals throughout the United States. It also conducts research and development on preventative and therapeutic vaccines and proteins for a variety of infectious diseases, including smallpox, HIV, sars, papilloma, influenza and e-selection tolerogen for the prevention of stroke. The group markets its products through its specialty sales force calling on obstetricians and gynecologists. The products of the group include nestabs(R) , novanatal(R) and novastart(R), a line of prescription prenatal vitamins, gynodiol(R) (estradiol tablets, usp), an oral form of estrogen therapy, avc(tm) cream (sulphanilamide vaginal cream) for vaginal infections and analpram hc(R), a prescription corticosteroid and antipruritic product for hemorrhoids. The group's quarterly revenue for September 2007 was 1.31 millions of USD.

Primary SIC and add'l.: 2834 2836

CIK No: 0001000694

Subsidiaries: Fielding Pharmacuetical Company

Officers: Rahul Singhvi/Dir., CEO, Pres., Gale Smith/VP - Vaccine Development, Raymond J. Hage/Sr. VP - Commercial Operations, Robert W. Lee/VP - Pharmaceutical Development, Rick Bright/VP - Global Influenza Programs, Len F. Stigliano/CFO, VP, Treasurer, Penny M. Heaton/Chief Medical Officer, VP, James B. Robinson/VP - Technical, Quality Operations

Directors: Rahul Singhvi/Dir., CEO, Pres., John Lambert/Chmn., James B. Tananbaum/Dir., Thomas P. Monath/Dir., Michael A. McManus/Dir., Gary C. Evans/Dir., John O. Marsh/Dir.

Owners: Gale E. Smith, James B. Tananbaum/5.00%, Thomas P. Monath/4.60%, John O. Marsh, Michael A. McManus, Patricia Hall, Insiders/14.20%, OppenheimerFunds, Inc./11.40%, Denis M. ODonnell/1.00%, Stephen I. Bandak, Prospect Venture Partners III, L.P./5.00%, Dennis W. Genge, Raymond J. Hage, Rick A. Bright, Rahul Singhvi/1.20% *(17 Owners included in Index)*

Financial Data: ***Fiscal Year End:***12/31 ***Latest Annual Data:*** 12/31/2006

Year	Sales	Net Income
2006	$4,683,000	-$23,068,000
2005	$7,388,000	-$11,174,000
2004	$8,260,000	-$25,920,000

Curr. Assets:	$77,342,000	**Curr. Liab.:**	$5,339,000		
Plant, Equip.:	$9,861,000	**Total Liab.:**	$27,876,000	**Indic. Yr. Divd.:**	NA
Total Assets:	$121,877,000	**Net Worth:**	$94,001,000	**Debt/ Equity:**	0.2570

Novel Denim Holdings Ltd

Novel Industrial Bldg., Lai Chi Kok Rd., Cheung Sha Wan, Kowloon, 850-870;

General - Incorporation British Virgin Islands | **Stock**- Price on:12/24/2007 .... NA
Employees .... NA | Stock Exchange .... NA
Auditor .... PricewaterhouseCoopers LLP | Ticker Symbol .... NA
Stk Agt .... Mellon Investor Services LLC | Outstanding Shares .... NA
Counsel .... Simpson Thacher & Bartlett LLP | E.P.S .... NA
DUNS No. .... NA | Shareholders .... NA

Business: The group operates through its subsidiaries whose principle activity is to manufacture and supply high-quality denim and chino garments and fabric as well as knitted garments. The group also produces a wide variation of garments, including jeans, chinos, shirts, skirts, shorts and jackets in a variety of styles, colors and finishes, such as overdyed, stonewashed, sandblasted and stretch. The group operates from United States.

Primary SIC and add'l.: 2339 2325 6719 2211 2369

CIK No: 0001041868

Subsidiaries: Battel Ltd., Byren Trading Ltd., Good Port Finance Ltd., Income Pearl Ltd., Kotten Ltd., NDP Fabrics Ltd., NDP Holdings Ltd., NDP Investment Ltd., NDP Trading Ltd., Nomacotex Ltd., Novel Denim (HK) Ltd., Novel Dyeing and Printing Mills Ltd., Novel Dyers (S.A.) (Pty) Ltd., Novel Garments (Madagascar) S.A., Novel Garments (Mauritius) Ltd. 21 Subsidiaries included in the Index

Novelis Inc

3399 Peachtree Rd. Ne, Ste. 1500, Atlanta, GA, 30326; ***PH:*** 1-404-814-4200; ***http://*** www.novelis.com

General - Incorporation .... Canada | **Stock**- Price on:12/24/2007 .... NA
Employees .... 12,500 | Stock Exchange .... NA
Auditor .... PricewaterhouseCoopers LLP | Ticker Symbol .... NA
Stk Agt .... Mellon Shareholder Services LLC | Outstanding Shares .... NA
Counsel .... NA | E.P.S .... NA
DUNS No. .... NA | Shareholders .... NA

Business: The groups principle activity is to produce aluminum sheet and foil products. The groups markets include automotive, transportation, packaging, construction and printing industries. The group's specific customers include Anheuser-Busch, Ball, Coca-Cola, Crown Cork & Seal, Daching Holdings, Ford, General Motors, Lotte Aluminum, Kodak, Pactiv, Rexam, and Ryerson Tull. The group operates from United States.

Primary SIC and add'l.: 3350

CIK No: 0001304280

Subsidiaries: 4260848 Canada Inc., 4260856 Canada Inc., Al Dotcom Sdn Berhad, Alcom (Singapore) Pte Ltd, Alcom Aluminium Services Sdn Berhad, Alcom Nikkei Specialty Coatings Sdn Berhad, Alumnio do Brasil Indstria e Comrcio Ltda., Aluminium Company of Malaysia Berhad, Aluminium Norf GmbH, Aluminum Upstream Holdings LLC, Consorcio Candonga, Deutsche Aluminium Verpackung Recycling GmbH, Eurofoil Inc. (USA), EuroNorca Partners, France Aluminium Recyclage S.A. 44 Subsidiaries included in the Index

Officers: Edward A. Blechschmidt/55/Dir., Acting CEO, Robert Patterson/VP, Controller, Martha Finn Brooks/COO, Pres., Kevin R. Greenawalt/Pres. - North America, Antonio Tadeu Coelho Nardocci/Pres. - Novelis South America, Les Parrette/General Counsel, Chief Compliance Officer, Corp. Sec., David Godsell/52/VP - Human Resources, Environment, Health, Safety, Orville G. Lunking/52/VP, Treasurer, Brenda Pulley/VP - Corporate Affairs, Communicatio, Tom Walpole/Pres. - Novelis Asia, Eunice Lima/Mgr. - Communications, South America, John Gardner/VP - Communications, Europe, Soohyun Oh/Mgr. - Corporate Affairs, Communications, Asia, Nichole A. Robinson/37/Corp. Sec., Thomas Walpole/53/Sr. VP, Pres. - Asia *(21 Officers included in Index)*

Directors: Edward A. Blechschmidt/55/Dir., Acting CEO, William T. Monahan/Chmn., Suzanne Labarge/Dir., Roberto C. Cordaro/Dir., Helmut Eschwey/Dir., Rudolf Rupprecht/Dir., Edward V. Yang/Dir., Charles G. Cavell/Dir., Clarence Chandran/59/Dir., Kevin M. Twomey/Dir., Kumar Mangalam Birla/41/Dir., Debnarayan Bhattacharya/59/Dir., Askaran K. Agarwala/74/Dir., Donald A. Stewart/61/Dir., David J. Fitzpatrick/Dir.

Novell Inc

404 Wyman St., Ste. 500, Waltham, MA, 02451; ***PH:*** 1-781-464-8000; ***Fax:*** 1-781-464-8100; ***http://*** www.novell.com; ***Email:*** crc@novell.com

General - Incorporation .... DE | **Stock**- Price on:12/24/2007 .... $7.91
Employees .... 4,549 | Stock Exchange .... NDQ
Auditor .... PricewaterhouseCoopers LLP | Ticker Symbol .... NOVL
Stk Agt .... Mellon Investor Services LLC | Outstanding Shares 348,290,000
Counsel .... NA | E.P.S .... -$0.03
DUNS No. .... 86-950-7491 | Shareholders .... NA

Business: The group's principal activity is to provide ebusiness solutions and net service software. The group secures and simplifies networks and enables businesses and governments to accelerate their moves to a one net solution. The business solutions provided include identity management and Web services, cross-platform services, worldwide services and celerant management consulting. The group serves large-scale corporations, government entities and educational institutions both domestically and internationally. The products and services are marketed in the United States, Europe, Africa, the Middle East, Canada, South America, Australia, and Asia-Pacific. On 12-Jan-2004, the group acquired suse linux ag and on 19-Jul-2004, salmon ltd.

Primary SIC and add'l.: 7379 7372 7373

CIK No: 0000758004

Subsidiaries: Cambridge PCHL LLC, Cambridge Technology Capital Fund I, L.P., Cambridge Technology Capital Management, Inc., Cambridge Technology CGP, Inc., Cambridge Technology Colombia S.A., Cambridge Technology GPLP, L.P., Cambridge Technology Partners (Benelux) B.V., Cambridge Technology Partners (Mexico), S/A. de C.V., Cambridge Technology Partners (Puerto Rico), Inc., Cambridge Technology Partners (Switzerland) SA, Cambridge Technology Partners (UK)LTD., Cambridge Technology Partners (Venezuela) C.A., Cambridge Technology Partners CTP, Skandinavien Aktiebolag, Cambridge Technology Partners do Brasil s.c. Ltda, Cambridge Technology Partners India Private Limited 100 Subsidiaries included in the Index

Officers: Ronald W. Hovsepian/46/Dir., CEO, Pres., Joseph A. Lasala/Sr. VP, General Counsel, Sec., Dana Henriksen/Distinguished Engineer, Scott Isaacson/Distinguished Engineer, Alan Friedman/Sr. VP - People, Jeffrey Jaffe/CTO, Exec. VP, Roger Levy/Sr. VP, GM - Open Platform Solutions, Joe Wagner/Sr. VP, GM - Systems, Resource Management, John Dragoon/Sr. VP, Chief Marketing Officer, Tom Francese/Exec. VP - Worldwide Sales, Susan Heystee/GM - Global Strategic Alliances, Joe Lasala/Sr. VP, General Counsel, Sec., Dana Russell/CFO, Brady Anderson/Distinguished Engineer, Lloyd Burch/Distinguished Engineer *(34 Officers included in Index)*

Directors: Ronald W. Hovsepian/46/Dir., CEO, Pres., Thomas G. Plaskett/64/Chmn., Fred Corrado/67/Dir., Richard L. Crandall/64/Dir., Claudine B. Malone/71/Dir., Albert Aiello/64/Dir., Kathy Brittain White/58/Dir., Richard L. Nolan/67/Dir., John W. Poduska/69/Dir., James D. Robinson/72/Dir., Patrick S. Jones/63/Dir.

Owners: James D. Robinson, Ronald W. Hovsepian, Columbia Wanger Asset Management, L.P./7.00%, Richard L. Nolan, Thomas G. Plaskett, Richard L. Crandall, Thomas Francese, John W. Poduska, Joseph A. LaSala, Susan Heystee, OppenheimerFunds, Inc./6.64%, Jack L. Messman, Fred Corrado, Insiders/1.56%, Claudine B. Malone *(20 Owners included in Index)*

Financial Data: ***Fiscal Year End:***10/31 ***Latest Annual Data:*** 10/31/2006

Year	Sales	Net Income
2006	$967,277,000	$18,656,000
2005	$1,197,696,000	$376,722,000
2004	$1,165,917,000	$57,188,000

Curr. Assets:	$2,154,336,000	**Curr. Liab.:**	$822,118,000		
Plant, Equip.:	$180,537,000	**Total Liab.:**	$1,696,068,000	**Indic. Yr. Divd.:**	NA
Total Assets:	$2,854,394,000	**Net Worth:**	$1,158,326,000	**Debt/ Equity:**	0.5309

Novellus Systems Inc

4000 N 1st St., San Jose, CA, 95134; ***PH:*** 1-408-943-9700; ***Fax:*** 1-408-943-3422; ***http://*** www.novellus.com; ***Email:*** info@novellus.com

General - Incorporation .... CA | **Stock**- Price on:12/24/2007 .... $30.3
Employees .... 3,725 | Stock Exchange .... NDQ
Auditor .... Ernst & Young LLP | Ticker Symbol .... NA
Stk Agt .... Mellon Investor Services LLC | Outstanding Shares 126,360,000
Counsel .... Morrison & Foerster LLP | E.P.S $1.79
DUNS No. .... 11-330-3416 | Shareholders .... NA

Business: The groups principle activity is to supply chemical vapor, physical vapor, electrochemical, chemical mechanical planarization, ultraviolet thermal processing, and surface preparation equipment for the manufacture of semiconductors. The group operates from United States and Germany.

Primary SIC and add'l.: 3674 3559

CIK No: 0000836106

Subsidiaries: Novellus Singapore Pte LTD, Novellus Systems (H.K.) Ltd., Novellus Systems (India) Pvt. Ltd., Novellus Systems (Malaysia) Sdn. Bhd., Novellus Systems BV, Novellus Systems Export, Inc., Novellus Systems GmbH, Novellus Systems International Trading (Shanghai) Co. Ltd., Novellus Systems International, Inc., Novellus Systems Ireland Ltd., Novellus Systems Israel Ltd., Novellus Systems Italy, Novellus Systems Japan, Novellus Systems Korea Co. Ltd., Novellus Systems SARL 28 Subsidiaries included in the Index

Officers: Richard S. Hill/Chmn., CEO/$6,223,095.00, Thomas Caulfield/Exec. VP - Sales, Marketing, Customer Service/$2,009,054.00, Pushpita Prasad/Worldwide Public Relations Mgr., Patrick J. Lord/42/Sr. VP - Business Development, Strategic Planning, Gino Addiego/Exec. VP - Corporate Operations/$1,857,699.00, Fusen Chen/CTO, Exec. VP - General, William H. Kurtz/CFO, Exec. VP/$2,065,068.00, Jeffrey C. Benzing/Exec. VP, Chief Business Officer, Timothy M. Archer/Sr. VP - Dielectrics Business Group, Martin J. Collins/Sr. VP, General Counsel, Corp. Sec.

Directors: Richard S. Hill/Chmn., CEO, Neil R. Bonke/66/Dir., Yoshio Nishi/68/Dir., David J. Litster/69/Dir., William R. Spivey/61/Dir., Delbert A. Whitaker/64/Dir., Ann D. Rhoads/42/Dir., Glen G. Possley/67/Dir., Youssef A. El-Mansy/63/Dir.

Owners: Neil R. Bonke, BlackRock, Inc./7.99%, Glen G. Possley, Private Capital Management, L.P./7.40%, William H. Kurtz, Tudor Investment Corporation/5.90%, William R. Spivey, David J. Litster, Sasson Somekh, Delbert Whitaker, Yoshio Nishi, Richard S. Hill/1.52%, Ann D. Rhoads, Youssef A. El-Mansy, Thomas Caulfield *(19 Owners included in Index)*

Financial Data: Fiscal Year End:12/31   Latest Annual Data: 12/31/2006

Year	Sales	Net Income
2006	$1,658,516,000	$190,016,000
2005	$1,340,471,000	$110,107,000
2004	$1,357,288,000	$156,690,000

Curr. Assets:	$1,505,293,000	Curr. Liab.:	$361,369,000	P/E Ratio:	16.93
Plant, Equip.:	$364,599,000	Total Liab.:	$527,787,000	Indic. Yr. Divd.:	NA
Total Assets:	$2,362,492,000	Net Worth:	$1,834,705,000	Debt/ Equity:	0.0679

Novelos Therapeutics Inc

1 Gateway Ctr Ste. 504, Newton, MA, 02458; **PH:** 1-617-244-1616; **Fax:** 1-617-964-6331; http:// www.novelos.com

General - Incorporation	DE	**Stock**- Price on:12/24/2007	$1
Employees	7	Stock Exchange	OTC
Auditor	Stowe & Degon	Ticker Symbol	NVLT
Stk Agt..... American Stock Transfer & Trust CO.		Outstanding Shares	39,240,000
Counsel	NA	E.P.S.	-$0.65
DUNS No.	NA	Shareholders	NA

Business: The groups principal activities include commercializing oxidized glutathione based compounds for the treatment of cancer and hepatitis. In May and June 2005, the group completed a two-step reverse merger with Common Horizons, Inc. The group operates from the United States.

Primary SIC and add'l.: 2834

CIK No: 0001279704

Officers: Harry S. Palmin/Dir., CEO, Pres., Christopher J. Pazoles/VP - Research, Development, Taylor M. Burtis/VP - Regulatory, Quality, Compliance, Kristin C. Schuhwerk/Sr. Dir. - Operations, George R. Vaughn/CFO, Joanne M. Protano/Sr. Dir. - Finance, Controller, Simyon Palmin/Dir., Dir. - Russian Relations, Jeffrey Gelfand/Sr. Medical Advisor, Stephen Lichaw/Investor Relations, Michael Kurman/Oncology Consultant, Raymond S. Koff/Hepatology Consultant

Directors: Harry S. Palmin/Dir., CEO, Pres., Kenneth Tew/Chmn. - Scientific Advisory Board, Stephen A. Hill/Chmn., David B. McWilliams/Dir., Howard M. Schneider/Dir., Simyon Palmin/Dir., Dir. - Russian Relations, Michael J. Doyle/Dir., Sim Fass/Dir., James S. Manuso/Dir.

Owners: Insiders/11.10%, Harry S. Palmin/2.80%, David McWilliams, Taylor M. Burtis, Christopher J. Pazoles, Howard Schneider, Margie Chassman/6.40%, Simyon Palmin/6.10%, Michael J. Doyle, Sim Fass

Financial Data: Fiscal Year End:12/31   Latest Annual Data: 12/31/2006

Year	Sales	Net Income
2006	NA	-$8,286,000
2005	$13,000	-$3,053,000

Curr. Assets:	$11,889,000	Curr. Liab.:	$1,313,000		
Plant, Equip.:	$24,000	Total Liab.:	$1,313,000	Indic. Yr. Divd.:	NA
Total Assets:	$11,923,000	Net Worth:	$10,610,000	Debt/ Equity:	NA

Noven Pharmaceuticals Inc

11960 SW 144th St., Miami, FL, 33186; **PH:** 1-305-253-1916; **Fax:** 1-305-251-1887; http:// www.noven.com

General - Incorporation	DE	**Stock**- Price on:12/24/2007	$23.89
Employees	518	Stock Exchange	NDQ
Auditor	Deloitte & Touche LLP	Ticker Symbol	NPBC
Stk Agt..... American Stock Transfer & Trust Co.		Outstanding Shares	24,840,000
Counsel	SHD Strategic	E.P.S.	$0.99
DUNS No.	14-858-5441	Shareholders	NA

Business: The group's principal activity is to research, develop, manufacture and market advanced transdermal drug delivery products and technologies and prescription transdermal products. The group's products include first generation transdermal estrogen delivery system marketed as vivelle (R), menorest(R) and femiest (r); second generation transdermal estrogen delivery system marketed as vivelle-dot(R) and estradot (r); transdermal combination estrogen/progestin delivery system marketed under the brand name combipatch (r); and dentipatch (r). The group operates in United States and Ireland.

Primary SIC and add'l.: 3841

CIK No: 0000815838

Subsidiaries: Vivelle Ventures LLC

Officers: Robert C. Strauss/Chmn., CEO, Pres./$1,475,079.00, Eduardo G. Abrao/VP - Clinical Development, Chief Medical Officer, Joseph C. Jones/VP - Corporate Affairs, Diane M. Barrett/CFO, VP/$604,056.00, Jeffrey F. Eisenberg/Sr. VP - Strategic Alliances/$663,797.00, Neil W. Jones/VP - Marketing, Sales/$568,894.00, Juan A. Mantelle/VP, Chief Technical Office/$595,009.00, Carolyn Donaldson/VP - Human Resources, Richard P. Gilbert/VP - Operations, Pavan Handa/VP - Business Development, James W. Harris/VP - Quality Assurance, Quality Control, Jeff T. Mihm/VP, General Counsel

Directors: Robert C. Strauss/Chmn., CEO, Pres., Robert G. Savage/Dir., Wayne P. Yetter/Dir., Phillip M. Satow/Dir., Sidney Braginsky/Dir., John G. Clarkson/Dir., Donald A. Denkhaus/Dir., Pedro P. Granadillo/Dir.

Owners: Neil W. Jones, Pedro P. Granadillo, John G. Clarkson, Donald A. Denkhaus, Jeffrey F. Eisenberg, Sidney Braginsky, Robert C. Strauss/2.60%, Robert G. Savage, Wayne P. Yetter, Insiders/5.60%, Juan A. Mantelle, Diane M. Barrett

Financial Data: Fiscal Year End:12/31   Latest Annual Data: 12/31/2006

Year	Sales		Net Income
2006	$60,689,000		$15,988,000
2005	$52,532,000		$9,972,000
2004	$45,891,000		$11,224,000

Curr. Assets:	$210,207,000	Curr. Liab.:	$29,386,000		
Plant, Equip.:	$37,010,000	Total Liab.:	$104,690,000	Indic. Yr. Divd.:	NA
Total Assets:	$281,365,000	Net Worth:	$176,675,000	Debt/ Equity:	0.0013

Novint Technologies Inc

PO Box 66956, Albuquerque, NM, 87193; **PH:** 1-866-298-4420; http:// www.novint.com; **Email:** info@novint.com

General - Incorporation	DE	**Stock**- Price on:12/24/2007	$0.99
Employees	12	Stock Exchange	OTC
Auditor	A.J. Robbins P.C.	Ticker Symbol	NVNT
Stk Agt..........Interwest Transfer Company, Inc.		Outstanding Shares	31,360,000
Counsel	NA	E.P.S.	-$0.28
DUNS No.	NA	Shareholders	NA

Business: The groups principle activities include developing, marketing and selling products, applications and technologies that allow people to use their sense of touch to interact with computers. The group also planning to license technology to game developers and publishers, providing them with a product differentiator that can be seamlessly and cost effectively added to content, generating new creative and revenue opportunities. The group operates from the United States.

Primary SIC and add'l.: 7371

CIK No: 0001282980

Officers: Tom Anderson/Chmn., CEO, CFO, Pres., Walter Aviles/CTO, VP - Engineering, Antonia Chappell/VP - Marketing, Kevin Resnick/VP - Sales, Bill Anderson/Dir. - Game Development, Ed Zanelli/Dir. - Community Software

Directors: Tom Anderson/Chmn., CEO, CFO, Pres.; Marvin Maslow/Dir., Gerald V. Grafe/Dir.

Owners: Marvin Maslow/2.70%, Insiders/25.70%, Gerald V. Grafe, Paul Packer/7.30%, Dean R. Danielson/6.00%, Walter Aviles/5.50%, RAB Special Situations (Master) Fund Limited/6.80%, AIGH Investment Partners, LLC/8.80%, Tom Anderson/19.40%, Walter M. Zierman/9.90%, Manhattan Scientifics, Inc/5.70%

Financial Data: Fiscal Year End:12/31   Latest Annual Data: 12/31/2006

Year	Sales		Net Income
2006	$90,000		-$4,310,000
2005	$362,000		-$3,386,000

Curr. Assets:	$687,000	Curr. Liab.:	$1,206,000		
Plant, Equip.:	$288,000	Total Liab.:	$1,206,000	Indic. Yr. Divd.:	NA
Total Assets:	$1,376,000	Net Worth:	$170,000	Debt/ Equity:	NA

Novo Nordisk

100 College Rd. W, Princeton, NJ, 08540; **PH:** 1-609-987-5800; **Fax:** 1-609-921-8082; http:// www.novonordisk.com

General - Incorporation	Denmark	**Stock**- Price on:12/24/2007	$101.53
Employees	23,172	Stock Exchange	NYSE
Auditor	PricewaterhouseCoopers LLP	Ticker Symbol	NVO
Stk Agt.Danske Bank, JPMorgan Chase Bank N.A.		Outstanding Shares	317,500,000
Counsel	NA	E.P.S.	$2.87
DUNS No.	30-591-4798	Shareholders	NA

Business: The group's principal activities are manufacturing and marketing health care products. It is divided into four distinctive units; diabetes care, coagulation disorders, human growth hormone and hormone replacement therapy. The diabetes care brand names include novo-rapid, innolet, innoco and novonorm. Brand name for treating coagulation disorders is novoseven. Growth hormones include norditropin simplexx. Hormone replacement products are novofem, activelle, kliogest, trisequens, estrofem and vagifem.

Primary SIC and add'l.: 8731 2833 2834

CIK No: 0000353278

Officers: Lars Rebien Sorensen/CEO, Pres., Jesper Brandgaard/CFO, Exec. VP, Lise Kingo/Exec. VP, Chief - Staffs, Kare Schultz/COO, Exec. VP, Christian Qvist Frandsen/Dir. - Investor Relations, Mads Veggerby Lausten/Head - Investor Relations, Hans Rommer/Mgr. - Investor Relations, Celena Lund Pedersen/Investor Relations Coordinator

Directors: Sten Scheibye/Chmn., Goran A. Ando/Vice Chmn., Henrik Gurtler/Dir., Niels Jacobsen/Dir., Kurt Anker Nielsen/Dir., Anne M. Kverneland/Dir., Kurt Briner/Dir., Johnny Henriksen/Dir., Soren Thuesen Pedersen/Dir., Stig Strobk/Dir., Jorgen Wedel/Dir.

Owners: Insiders, The Capital Group Companies Inc./15.51%, Novo Nordisk A/S and affiliates/6.96%, Novo A/S/11.36%, Novo A/S/100.00%

Financial Data: Fiscal Year End:12/31   Latest Annual Data: 12/31/2006

Year	Sales	Net Income
2006	$6,857,511,000	$1,116,870,000
2005	$5,350,960,000	$776,333,000
2004	$5,324,285,000	$859,229,000

Curr. Assets:	$3,687,795,000	Curr. Liab.:	$1,797,789,000		
Plant, Equip.:	$3,626,376,000	Total Liab.:	$2,674,824,000	Indic. Yr. Divd.:	$0.610
Total Assets:	$7,849,419,000	Net Worth:	$5,174,595,000	Debt/ Equity:	NA

Novogen Ltd

1 Landmark Sq., Ste. 240, Stamford, CT, 06901; **PH:** 1-203-327-1188; **Fax:** 1-203-327-0011; http:// www.novogen.com; **Email:** usa@novogen.com

General - Incorporation	New South Wales	**Stock**- Price on:12/24/2007	$8.47
Employees	67	Stock Exchange	NDQ
Auditor	Bdo Kendalls (nsw)	Ticker Symbol	NVGN
Stk Agt.... Computershare Investor Services LLC		Outstanding Shares	19,550,000
Counsel	NA	E.P.S.	-$0.9
DUNS No.	NA	Shareholders	NA

Business: The group's principal activities are pharmaceutical research and development and manufacturing and marketing of health supplements. It operates in Australia, New Zealand, North America and Europe.

Primary SIC and add'l.: 8731 2834 2836

CIK No: 0001075880

Subsidiaries: Glycotex, Inc, Marshall Edwards, Inc., Novogen Research Pty Ltd

Officers: Christopher Naughton/MD, Alan J. Husband/Executive Dir.

Directors: Philip A. Johnston/Non Exec. Chmn., Paul J. Nestel/Non Exec. Dir., Peter B. Simpson/Non Exec. Dir., Geoffrey M. Leppinus/Non Exec. Dir., Alan J. Husband/Executive Dir.

Owners: P. B. Simpson, C. Naughton/0.60%, A. J. Husband/0.10%, B. M. Palmer, P. A. Johnston/0.10%, R. L. Erratt, D. R. Seaton, P. J. Nestel, C. D. Kearney

*Financial Data: Fiscal Year End:*06/30 *Latest Annual Data:* 06/30/2007

Year	Sales	Net Income
2007	$12,645,000	-$16,960,000
2006	$9,856,000	-$13,084,000
2005	$13,471,000	-$8,545,000

Curr. Assets:	$31,942,000	*Curr. Liab.:*	$4,513,000		
Plant, Equip.:	$5,365,000	*Total Liab.:*	$4,761,000	*Indic. Yr. Divd.:*	NA
Total Assets:	$36,458,000	*Net Worth:*	$30,987,000	*Debt/ Equity:*	NA

Novori Inc

1313 E Maple St., Ste. 425, Bellingham, WA, 98225; *PH:* 1-360-306-5309; *Fax:* 1-360-306-5835; *http://* www.novori.com; *Email:* info@novori.com

General - Incorporation .... DE	*Stock*- Price on:12/24/2007 ....$1.49
Employees..NA	Stock Exchange...OTC
Auditor .... Manning Elliott LLP	Ticker Symbol...NOVO
Stk Agt.............................. Island Stock Transfer	Outstanding Shares ....NA
Counsel...NA	E.P.S..NA
DUNS No. ....NA	Shareholders...NA

Business: The groups principle activity is to sell diamonds and diamond jewelry on the Internet. The group operates from the United States and Canada.

Primary SIC and add'l.: 5960

CIK No: 0001343257

Subsidiaries: Novori Marketing Inc

Officers: Harold Schaffrick/46/Dir., CEO, Pres., Mark Neild/41/Dir., CFO, Sec., Chief Accounting Officer, Treasurer, Nashrulla Jamani/38/Sr. VP - Investor Relations

Directors: Harold Schaffrick/46/Dir., CEO, Pres., Mark Neild/41/Dir., CFO, Sec., Chief Accounting Officer, Treasurer

Owners: Insiders/59.00%, Mark Neild/50.00%, Harold Schaffrick/29.00%, Nashrulla Jamani/1.50%, Mark Neild/29.00%, Harold Schaffrick/50.00%, Insiders/100.00%

*Financial Data: Fiscal Year End:*05/31 *Latest Annual Data:* 05/31/2007

Year	Sales	Net Income
2007	NA	NA

Curr. Assets:	$44,000	*Curr. Liab.:*	$261,000		
Plant, Equip.:	$0	*Total Liab.:*	$802,000	*Indic. Yr. Divd.:*	NA
Total Assets:	$44,000	*Net Worth:*	-$757,000	*Debt/ Equity:*	NA

Novoste Corp

4350 International Blvd., Norcross, GA, 30093; *PH:* 1-770-717-0904; *http://* www.novoste.com

General - Incorporation .... FL	*Stock*- Price on:12/24/2007 ....$2.6
Employees..18	Stock Exchange...OTC
Auditor .... Ernst & Young LLP	Ticker Symbol...NVTP
Stk Agt...... American Stock Transfer & Trust Co.	Outstanding Shares ....NA
Counsel........................... Dorsey & Whitney LLP	E.P.S...$0.80
DUNS No. 79-295-7185	Shareholders...NA

Business: The group's principle activity is to develop and market the beta-cath (TM) system, an intraluminal beta radiation catheter delivery system. This system delivers beta, or low penetration, radiation to the site of a treated blockage in a coronary artery to decrease the likelihood of restenosis. The group also develops treatments for coronary, vascular and peripheral arterial diseases. It markets its products through a direct sales force in the United States and a combination of direct sales representatives and independent distributors in western Europe, Canada, Asia and South America.

Primary SIC and add'l.: 3841

CIK No: 0001012131

Subsidiaries: Novoste BV, Novoste Europe SA/NV, Novoste France SAS, Novoste GmbH, Novoste Sales Corporation

*Financial Data: Fiscal Year End:*12/31 *Latest Annual Data:* 12/31/2005

Year	Sales	Net Income
2005	$7,887,000	-$15,329,000
2004	$23,268,000	-$26,921,000
2003	$62,901,000	-$868,000

Curr. Assets:	$14,007,000	*Curr. Liab.:*	$3,800,000	*P/E Ratio:*	2.99
Plant, Equip.:	$81,000	*Total Liab.:*	$3,800,000	*Indic. Yr. Divd.:*	NA
Total Assets:	$14,088,000	*Net Worth:*	$10,288,000	*Debt/ Equity:*	NA

NPS Pharmaceuticals Inc

Morris Corporate Ctr. 1 4th Floor, Bldg. B 300 Interpace Pkwy., Bedminster, NJ, 07921; *PH:* 1-973-394-8600; *Fax:* 1-973-316-6463; *http://* www.npsp.com

General - Incorporation .... DE	*Stock*- Price on:12/24/2007 ....$4.39
Employees..196	Stock Exchange...NDQ
Auditor ....KPMG LLP	Ticker Symbol...NA
Stk Agt....................... Computershare Trust Co	Outstanding Shares 46,340,000
Counsel...NA	E.P.S..NA
DUNS No. 18-187-1427	Shareholders...NA

Business: The group's principal activity is to discover, develop and market small molecule drugs and recombinant proteins. Its current product candidates are primarily for the treatment of bone and mineral disorders, gastrointestinal disorders and central nervous system disorders. The group's drug candidates in active clinical development and preclinical stages include preos (TM) for treating osteoporosis, alx-0600 for treating gastrointestinal disorders and amg 073 for treating hyperparathyroidism. The group has collaborative research and development agreements with amgen inc,

kirin brewery company, ltd, glaxosmithkline and astrazeneca ab. It has licensing agreements with eli lilly and company for technology related to excitatory amino acid receptor antagonists to treat pain, and with janssen. Pharmaceutica nv for technology related to glycine reuptake inhibitors to treat schizophrenia. The group operates in the United States and Canada.

Primary SIC and add'l.: 2834 8731

CIK No: 0000890465

Subsidiaries: NPS Allelix Corp., NPS Allelix Inc., NPS Holdings Company, NPS Services, L.C.

Officers: Anthony N. Coles/Dir., CEO, Pres./$2,636,607.00, Gerard J. Michel/CFO/$798,435.00, Alan L. Mueller/VP - Drug Discovery/$664,926.00, Gail Brophy/Executive Assist., Investor Relations Officer Coordinator, Val Antczak/Sr. VP - Legal Affairs, General Counsel/$438,416.00, Francois Nader/COO, Exec. VP, Gregory M. Torre/Sr. VP - Regulatory Affairs/$469,750.00

Directors: Donald E. Kuhla/Dir., James G. Groninger/Dir., Rachel R. Selisker/Dir., Joseph Klein/Dir., Calvin R. Stiller/Dir., Peter G. Tombros/Dir., Michael W. Bonney/Dir.

Owners: James G. Groninger, Donald E. Kuhla, Rachel R. Selisker, Santo J. Costa, Anthony N. Coles, OrbiMed Advisors LLC/9.62%, Gerard J. Michel, Soros Fund Management/6.26%, Peter G. Tombros, Insiders/4.11%, Thomas G. Heath, Wellington Management/10.73%, Edward F. Nemeth, Barclays Global Investors/5.31%, Eaton Vance Management/6.95% *(21 Owners included in Index)*

*Financial Data: Fiscal Year End:*12/31 *Latest Annual Data:* 12/31/2006

Year	Sales	Net Income
2006	$48,502,000	-$112,668,000
2005	$12,825,000	-$169,723,000
2004	$14,237,000	-$168,251,000

Curr. Assets:	$189,689,000	*Curr. Liab.:*	$44,467,000		
Plant, Equip.:	$19,849,000	*Total Liab.:*	$417,984,000	*Indic. Yr. Divd.:*	NA
Total Assets:	$224,740,000	*Net Worth:*	-$193,244,000	*Debt/ Equity:*	NA

NRG Energy Inc

211 Carnegie Ctr., Princeton, NJ, 08540; *PH:* 1-609-524-4500; *Fax:* 1-609-524-4501; *http://* www.nrgenergy.com

General - Incorporation .... DE	*Stock*- Price on:12/24/2007 ....$42.81
Employees...3,217	Stock Exchange..NYSE
Auditor ....KPMG LLP	Ticker Symbol...NRG
Stk Agt .... BNY Mellon Shareowner Services	Outstanding Shares 242,320,000
Counsel...NA	E.P.S...$1.53
DUNS No. ....NA	Shareholders...NA

Business: The groups principle activities include owning, developing, constructing and operating power generation facilities. In the year 2006, the group acquired Dynegy, Inc. and Texas Genco LLC. The group operates from the United States.The group's quarterly revenuie for sept 2007 was 1,786.00 millions of USD.

Primary SIC and add'l.: 6221 6289 4911 5172

CIK No: 0001013871

Subsidiaries: Arthur Kill Power LLC, Astoria Gas Turbine Power LLC, Bayou Cove Peaking Power, LLC, Berrians I Gas Turbine Power LLC, Beteiligungs GmbH, Big Cajun I Peaking Power LLC, Big Cajun II Unit 4 LLC, Cabrillo Power I LLC, Cabrillo Power II LLC, Camas Power Boiler Limited Partnership, Camas Power Boiler, Inc., Central and Eastern Europe Power Fund, Ltd., Chickahominy River Energy Corp., Commonwealth Atlantic Power LLC, Conemaugh Fuels, LLC 242 Subsidiaries included in the Index

Officers: David W. Crane/Dir., CEO, Pres./$5,528,530.00, Clint Freeland/VP, Treasurer, John B. Hill/40/Pres. - Texas Region, Exec. VP, Tanuja M. Dehne/Corp. Sec., Steve Hoffmann/Pres. - Western Region, Sr. VP, Christine A. Jacobs/55/Sr. VP - Plant Operations, Jan C. Paulin/Sr. VP - NRG, Pres. - Padoma Wind Power, Carolyn Burke/VP, Controller, Robert C. Flexon/CFO, Exec. VP/$1,830,140.00, Denise M. Wilson/48/Chief Administrative Officer, Exec. VP, John P. Brewster/Exec. VP - Development Engineering, Procurement, Construction/$932,331.00, Thad Hill/Pres. - NRG Texas Region, Exec. VP, Kevin T. Howell/Exec. VP - Commercial Operations/$3,157,890.00, Andrew J. Murphy/Exec. VP, General Counsel, John Ragan/Pres. - Northeast Region, Exec. VP *(18 Officers included in Index)*

Directors: David W. Crane/Dir., CEO, Pres., Howard E. Cosgrove/Chmn., John F. Chlebowski/Dir., Lawrence S. Coben/Dir., Stephen L. Cropper/Dir., William E. Hantke/Dir., Paul W. Hobby/Dir., Maureen J. Miskovic/Dir., Anne C. Schaumburg/Dir., Herbert H. Tate/Dir., Thomas H. Weidemeyer/Dir., Walter R. Young/Dir.

Owners: David Crane, Kevin T. Howell, Massachusetts Financial Services Company/6.00%, Janus Capital Management LLC/7.30%, Walter R. Young, Lawrence S. Coben, Steven C. Winn, John F. Chlebowski, John P. Brewster, Orbis Investment Management Limited/6.10%, Anne C. Schaumburg, Maureen Miskovic, Prudential Financial, Inc./6.90%, Thomas H. Weidemeyer, Paul W. Hobby *(21 Owners included in Index)*

*Financial Data: Fiscal Year End:*12/31 *Latest Annual Data:* 12/31/2006

Year	Sales	Net Income
2006	$5,623,000,000	$621,000,000
2005	$2,708,000,000	$84,000,000
2004	$2,361,424,000	$185,617,000

Curr. Assets:	$3,083,000,000	*Curr. Liab.:*	$2,032,000,000	*P/E Ratio:*	21.30
Plant, Equip.:	$11,600,000,000	*Total Liab.:*	$13,777,000,000	*Indic. Yr. Divd.:*	NA
Total Assets:	$19,435,000,000	*Net Worth:*	$5,658,000,000	*Debt/ Equity:*	1.9731

NS8 Corp

Two Union Sq Ctr, 601 Union St., Ste. 4200, Seattle, WA, 98101; *PH:* 1-310-242-5754; *http://* www.ns8corp.net; *Email:* contact@ns8corp.net

General - Incorporation .... DE	*Stock*- Price on:12/24/2007 ....$0.02
Employees..28	Stock Exchange...OTC
Auditor .... KMJ Corbin & Co. LLP	Ticker Symbol...NSEO
Stk Agt ....Continental Stock Transfer & Trust Co	Outstanding Shares 119,690,000
Counsel...NA	E.P.S...-$0.041
DUNS No. ....NA	Shareholders...NA

Business: The group's principle activity is to deliver envelopes by bike messenger and packages by van in the metropolitan New York city area. The group receives phone calls from customers seeking such deliveries and then dispatches its messengers via two-way radio to deliver the envelopes and packages via bike and van. The job orders are obtained through referrals from existing customers and through the group's sales force. The customers of the group consist of small and medium size businesses throughout manhattan. The current operations of the group are conducted through its wholly owned subsidiary, bmw messenger service, inc. The group's quarterly revenue for September 2007 was 0.10 millions of USD.

Primary SIC and add'l.: 4215 6719

CIK No: 0001156893
Subsidiaries: BMW Messenger Services, Inc., CGMI and CMC
Officers: Anthony Alda/Chmn., CEO, Pres., Chief Technology Architect, George O'Leary/Dir., CFO, Cam Levitt/Accounting Exec., Uriel Kusiatin/Pres., Leslie J. Ames/Sr. VP - Legal Affairs, Melanie Thomson/COO, Carl Segal/Exec. VP - Sales, Brent R. Bysouth/Dir., Chief Software Architect, Ricardo Rosado/VP - Product Management
Directors: Anthony Alda/Chmn., CEO, Pres., Chief Technology Architect, Brent R. Bysouth/Dir., Chief Software Architect, Michael W. Waage/59/Dir., George O'Leary/Dir., CFO
Owners: Insiders/29.58%, William Kunzweiler/6.10%, Leslie J. Ames/3.86%, Melanie Thomson/0.67%, Ricardo Rosado/3.65%, Carl Segal/1.26%, Michael Waage/1.84%, Anthony J. Alda/6.59%, Brent Richard Bysouth/14.40%

Financial Data: Fiscal Year End:12/31 **Latest Annual Data:** 12/31/2006

Year	Sales	Net Income
2006	$218,000	-$10,136,000
2005	NA	-$6,587,000
2004	NA	-$6,093,000

Curr. Assets:	$261,000	**Curr. Liab.:**	$8,392,000		
Plant, Equip.:	$174,000	**Total Liab.:**	$19,229,000	**Indic. Yr. Divd.:**	NA
Total Assets:	$695,000	**Net Worth:**	-$18,535,000	**Debt/ Equity:**	NA

NSTAR

PO Box 4508, Woburn, MA, 01888; **PH:** 1-617-424-2000; **Fax:** 1-781-441-8886;
http:// www.nstaronline.com

General - Incorporation	MA	**Stock**- Price on:12/24/2007	$33.06
Employees	3,100	Stock Exchange	NDQ
Auditor	PricewaterhouseCoopers LLP	Ticker Symbol	NSTK
Stk Agt	Computershare Investor Services LLC	Outstanding Shares	106,810,000
Counsel	NA	E.P.S	$2.08
DUNS No.	NA	Shareholders	NA

Business: The groups principle activity is to deliver energy. The group operates from United States.
Primary SIC and add'l.: 6719 4924 4911
CIK No: 0001035675
Subsidiaries: Advanced Energy Systems, Inc., BEC Funding II, LLC, BEC Funding LLC, Boston Edison Company, Cambridge Electric Light Company, Canal Electric Company, CEC Funding, LLC, Commonwealth Electric Company, Harbor Electric Energy Company, Hopkinton LNG Corp., Matep, LLC, NSTAR Communications, Inc., NSTAR Electric& Gas Corporation, NSTAR Gas Company
Officers: Thomas J. May/Chmn., CEO, Pres. - Trustee/$7,619,738.00, Werner Schweiger/Sr. VP - Operations/$1,470,220.00, Jim Judge/CFO, Sr. VP, Treasurer/$1,586,604.00, Joe Nolan/Sr. VP - Customer, Corporate Relations/$960,416.00, Doug Horan/Sr. VP - Strategy, Law, Policy, Sec., General Counsel/$1,708,939.00, John F. Gavin/Mgr. - Investor Relations, Paul Vaitkus/VP - Electric Operations, Geoff Lubbock/VP - Financial Strategic Planning, Policy, Larry Gelbien/VP - Engineering, Philip J. Lembo/Assist. Treasurer, Bob Weafer/VP, Controller, Chief Accounting Officer, Gene Zimon/Sr. VP - Information Technology, Tim Manning/Sr. VP - Human Resources, Rich Morrison/Assist. Sec., Don Anastasia/Assist. Treasurer (20 Officers included in Index)
Directors: Thomas J. May/Chmn., CEO, Pres. - Trustee, Daniel Dennis/Trustee, Matina S. Horner/Trustee, William C. Van Faasen/Trustee, Sherry H. Penney/Trustee, Gerald L. Wilson/Trustee, Thomas G. Dignan/Trustee, Paul A. La Camera/Trustee, Gary L. Countryman/Trustee, Charles K. Gifford/Trustee
Owners: Matina S. Horner, Gary L. Countryman, Joseph R. Nolan, Paul A. La Camera, Daniel Dennis, Thomas J. May/1.02%, Charles K. Gifford, Thomas G. Dignan, Sherry H. Penney, James J. Judge, Douglas S. Horan, Insiders/1.82%, Werner J. Schweiger, William C. Van Faasen, Gerald L. Wilson

Financial Data: Fiscal Year End:12/31 **Latest Annual Data:** 12/31/2006

Year	Sales	Net Income
2006	$3,577,702,000	$206,774,000
2005	$3,243,120,000	$198,095,000
2004	$2,954,332,000	$188,481,000

Curr. Assets:	$959,754,000	**Curr. Liab.:**	$1,239,933,000	**P/E Ratio:**	16.45
Plant, Equip.:	$4,086,127,000	**Total Liab.:**	$6,143,832,000	**Indic. Yr. Divd.:**	$1.400
Total Assets:	$7,769,395,000	**Net Worth:**	$1,625,563,000	**Debt/ Equity:**	1.3866

NT Holding Corp Inc

385 Freeport, No. 1, Sparks, NV, 89431; **PH:** 1-852-28366202; http:// www.ntholdingcorp.com;
Email: info@ntholdingcorp.com

General - Incorporation	NV	**Stock**- Price on:12/24/2007	NA
Employees	NA	Stock Exchange	OTC
Auditor	Madsen & Assoc. CPA's, Inc.	Ticker Symbol	NTHH
Stk Agt	Olde Monmouth Stk Trnsfer Co. Inc.	Outstanding Shares	NA
Counsel	NA	E.P.S	NA
DUNS No.	NA	Shareholders	NA

Business: The group's principal activity was to produce and market a line of medium to luxurious women's clothing and fashion brands. On 17-Mar-2003, the group terminated all of its business activities. The group is changing its focus and now looks to enter into the biotechnology, nutraceutical, nanotechnology and communications sectors of the economy.
Primary SIC and add'l.: 9999
CIK No: 0000797564
Subsidiaries: American - Asia Metallurgical Industry Limited, FJCC, Fujia Coking and Chemical Company Limited, Hopeful Asia Limited, PNC Labs, Inc., Tagalder C3 Holdings Inc
Officers: Chun Ka Tsun/33/Chmn., CEO, Teo Chong Nghee/60/Dir., COO, Loo Pak Hong/55/Dir., CFO
Directors: Chun Ka Tsun/33/Chmn., CEO, Woo Chi Wai/38/Dir., Teo Chong Nghee/60/Dir., COO, Loo Pak Hong/55/Dir., CFO
Owners: Chan Tsz King/74.73%

Financial Data: Fiscal Year End:12/31 **Latest Annual Data:** 12/31/2006

Year	Sales	Net Income
2006	$9,891,000	-$642,000
2005	NA	-$1,139,000
2004	NA	-$79,000

Curr. Assets:	$9,724,000	**Curr. Liab.:**	$18,197,000		
Plant, Equip.:	$11,390,000	**Total Liab.:**	$18,504,000	**Indic. Yr. Divd.:**	NA
Total Assets:	$21,114,000	**Net Worth:**	-$705,000	**Debt/ Equity:**	NA

NT Media Corp of California Inc

7800 Oceanus Dr., Los Angeles, CA, 90046; **PH:** 1-323-445-4833

General - Incorporation	DE	**Stock**- Price on:12/24/2007	$0.007
Employees	1	Stock Exchange	NA
Auditor	Aj. Robbins, P.C	Ticker Symbol	NA
Stk Agt	Pacific Stock Transfer Company	Outstanding Shares	75,710,000
Counsel	NA	E.P.S	-$0.014
DUNS No.	NA	Shareholders	NA

Business: The group's principal activities are to develop and produce feature films and television programs and provide international business development and strategy consulting services. The group is currently exploring opportunities among various types of companies including feature film and television production, commercial and broadcast design, animation, visual effects, marketing/branding firms, commercial production and interactive television design and production.
Primary SIC and add'l.: 7812
CIK No: 0000318622
Subsidiaries: Ecast Media Corporation, Inc., SU Distribution LLC
Officers: Ali Moussavi/37/Chmn., CEO, Acting CFO, Pres., Chief Accounting Officer
Directors: Ali Moussavi/37/Chmn., CEO, Acting CFO, Pres., Chief Accounting Officer, Christopher Briggs/37/Dir.
Owners: Christopher Briggs, Insiders, Chris Mehringer/4.20%, Dana O'Connor/4.20%, Delta Capital Partners, Ltd./4.70%, Britannica Associates Limited/14.70%, Astor Capital, Inc./3.00%

Financial Data: Fiscal Year End:12/31 **Latest Annual Data:** 12/31/2006

Year	Sales	Net Income
2006	NA	-$729,000
2005	$0	-$510,000
2004	$62,000	-$1,448,000

Curr. Assets:	$0	**Curr. Liab.:**	$2,948,000		
Plant, Equip.:	NA	**Total Liab.:**	$2,948,000	**Indic. Yr. Divd.:**	NA
Total Assets:	$0	**Net Worth:**	-$2,947,000	**Debt/ Equity:**	NA

Ntelos Holdings Corp

401 Spring Ln., Ste. 300, Waynesboro, VA, 22980; **PH:** 1-540-946-3500; **Fax:** 1-540-946-3595;
http:// www.ntelos.com; **Email:** customerfirst@ntelos.com

General - Incorporation	DE	**Stock**- Price on:12/24/2007	$26.5
Employees	1,305	Stock Exchange	NDQ
Auditor	KPMG LLP	Ticker Symbol	NA
Stk Agt	Computershare Trust Co	Outstanding Shares	41,980,000
Counsel	NA	E.P.S	$0.73
DUNS No.	NA	Shareholders	NA

Business: The groups principle activity is to provide wireless and wireline communications services. The groups services include voice, long distance, portable broadband access, web hosting and integrated access. The group products sold under the trade name NTELOS. In the year 2005, the group acquired NTELOS Inc. The group operates from Virginia and West Virginia. The group's quarterly revenue for September 2007 was 126.93 millions of USD.
Primary SIC and add'l.: 7375 4813 4812
CIK No: 0001328571
Subsidiaries: NA Communications Inc., NH Licenses LLC, NTELOS Cable Inc., NTELOS Cable of Virginia Inc., NTELOS Communications Inc., NTELOS Communications Services Inc., NTELOS Cornerstone Inc., NTELOS Inc., NTELOS Licenses Inc., NTELOS Media Inc., NTELOS Net LLC, NTELOS Netaccess Inc., NTELOS Network Inc., NTELOS of West Virginia Inc., NTELOS PCS Inc. 32 Subsidiaries included in the Index
Officers: James S. Quarforth/Chmn., CEO, Pres./$6,403,788.00, Carl A. Rosberg/Exec. VP, Pres. - Wireless Operations/$2,935,604.00, David R. MacCarelli/Exec. VP, Pres. - Wireline Operations/$2,230,736.00, Michael B. Moneymaker/CFO, Exec. VP/$2,479,678.00, Mary McDermott/Sr. VP - Legal, Regulatory Affairs/$1,032,147.00
Directors: James S. Quarforth/Chmn., CEO, Pres., Timothy G. Biltz/49/Dir., Christopher Bloise/32/Dir., Andrew Gesell/34/Dir., Daniel J. Heneghan/52/Dir., Eric B. Hertz/53/Dir., Michael Huber/Dir., Steven Rattner/55/Dir.
Owners: Insiders, Michael Huber, James S. Quarforth, Mary McDermott, David R. Maccarelli, Steven Rattner, Eric B. Hertz, Christopher Bloise, Andrew Gesell, Citigroup Venture Capital Equity Partners, L.P, Quadrangle Capital Partners LP, Carl A. Rosberg, Daniel J. Heneghan, Michael B. Moneymaker

Financial Data: Fiscal Year End:12/31 **Latest Annual Data:** 12/31/2006

Year	Sales	Net Income
2006	$440,076,000	-$7,185,000
2005	$264,490,000	$1,098,000

Curr. Assets:	$98,386,000	**Curr. Liab.:**	$73,412,000		
Plant, Equip.:	$376,772,000	**Total Liab.:**	$749,082,000	**Indic. Yr. Divd.:**	$0.600
Total Assets:	$900,847,000	**Net Worth:**	$151,765,000	**Debt/ Equity:**	3.7234

NTN Communications Inc

5966 La Pl. Ct, Ste. 100, Carlsbad, CA, 92008; **PH:** 1-760-438-7400; http:// www.ntn.com

General - Incorporation	DE	**Stock**- Price on:12/24/2007	$1.1
Employees	217	Stock Exchange	NDQ
Auditor	Haskell & White LLP	Ticker Symbol	NTOL
Stk Agt	American Stock Transfer & Trust Co.	Outstanding Shares	55,240,000
Counsel	O'melveny & Myers	E.P.S	-$0.08
DUNS No.	13-118-5373	Shareholders	NA

Business: The group's principal activity is to provide out-of-home hospitality services. The group's activities are carried out through its subsidiary, buzztime entertainment inc and the ntn hospitality technologies division. Ntn hospitality technologies is comprised of the ntn interactive television (itv) network, ntn wireless communications and ntn software solutions. The ntn itv network delivers entertainment and sports content games to thousands of sports bars and premier casual restaurants nationwide. Ntn wireless communications manufactures, sells and repairs paging equipment to hospitality

locations as well as hospitals, church nurseries and retail establishments. Ntn software solutions designs, develops and markets innovative software for the restaurant and hospitality industry along with customer incentive programs. Buzztime entertainment inc, develops and distributes sports and trivia games to a variety of interactive platforms.

Primary SIC and add'l.: 4841 5065

CIK No: 0000748592

Subsidiaries: Buzztime Entertainment, Inc., NTN Canada, Inc., NTN Software Solutions, Inc., NTN Wireless Communications, Inc.

Officers: Kendra Berger/Dir., CFO/$155,759.00, Dario L. Santana/Dir., Chief Exec Officer/$424,569.00, Michele Richards/CTO/$267,320.00, John A. Boozer/Sr. VP - Global Sales/$235,270.00

Directors: Neal Fondren/Dir., Kendra Berger/Dir., CFO, Michael Fleming/Dir., Gary H. Arlen/Dir., Barry Bergsman/Dir., Robert B. Clasen/Dir., Dario L. Santana/Dir., Chief Exec Officer, Mark D. Buckner/Dir.

Owners: Robert B. Clasen, Neal Fondren, John Boozer, Insiders/8.89%, Gary Arlen, Kendra Berger, Mark Buckner, Dario Santana, Michele Richards, Tyrone V. Lam/1.46%, Michael Fleming, Stanley B. Kinsey/5.77%, Media General, Inc./5.96%, Fidelity National Financial, Inc./12.10%, Barry Bergsman (16 Owners included in Index)

Financial Data: Fiscal Year End:12/31   Latest Annual Data: 12/31/2006

Year	Sales	Net Income
2006	$32,985,000	-$4,773,000
2005	$40,759,000	-$2,019,000
2004	$35,655,000	-$4,979,000
Curr. Assets:	$16,058,000	Curr. Liab.:	$7,729,000	
Plant, Equip.:	$5,919,000	Total Liab.:	$7,995,000	Indic. Yr. Divd.: NA
Total Assets:	$26,525,000	Net Worth:	$18,530,000	Debt/ Equity: 0.0006

NTS Realty Holdings LP

10172 Linn Sta. Rd., Louisville, KY, 40223; **PH:** 1-502-426-4800; **Fax:** 1-502-426-4994; **http://** www.ntsdevelopment.com

General - Incorporation	DE	Stock- Price on:12/24/2007	$7.2
Employees	NA	Stock Exchange	AMEX
Auditor	Ernst & Young, LLP	Ticker Symbol	NLP
Stk Agt.	NA	Outstanding Shares	11,380,000
Counsel	NA	E.P.S.	$0.47
DUNS No.	NA	Shareholders	NA

Business: The groups principle activity is real estate operation. The group operates through four segments namely multifamily, commercial, retail and land real estate operations. In the year 2005, the group acquired lakes apartment. The group operates from the United States. The group's quarterly revenue for September 2007 was 10.85 millions of USD.

Primary SIC and add'l.: 1541 6519 6552

CIK No: 0001278384

Owners: John Daly, Brian F. Lavin, Insiders/57.44%, J. D. Nichols/57.25%, Gregory A. Wells, Mark D. Anderson, NTS Realty Partners, LLC/6.28%, John S. Lenihan

Financial Data: Fiscal Year End:12/31   Latest Annual Data: 12/31/2006

Year	Sales	Net Income
2006	$38,180,000	$41,115,000
2005	$29,908,000	-$1,768,000
2004	NA	-$3,270,000
Curr. Assets:	$2,310,000	Curr. Liab.:	$7,794,000	P/E Ratio: 15.32
Plant, Equip.:	$303,082,000	Total Liab.:	$231,777,000	Indic. Yr. Divd.: $0.400
Total Assets:	$309,251,000	Net Worth:	$77,475,000	Debt/ Equity: NA

NTT DoCoMo Inc

Sanno Pk. Tower, 11-1 Nagata-Cho 2-Chome, Chiyoda-Ku, Tokyo; ; **http://** www.nttdocomo.com

General - Incorporation	Japan	Stock - Price on:12/24/2007	$16.12
Employees	21,591	Stock Exchange	NYSE
Auditor	KPMG Azsa & Co	Ticker Symbol	DCM
Stk Agt.	Bank of New York	Outstanding Shares	4,360,000,000
Counsel	NA	E.P.S.	$0.79
DUNS No.	NA	Shareholders	NA

Business: The group's principal activity is to provide wireless telecommunications services. The group offers cellular services, 3g wireless services, packet communications services, personal handyphone system services, paging services, satellite mobile communications services and in-flight telephone services. The group is also involved in marketing handsets, pagers and related equipment to resellers. The group's parent company is ntt and the group has thirty six consolidated subsidiaries all based in Japan.

Primary SIC and add'l.: 4813 5999 4812

CIK No: 0001166141

Subsidiaries: allucher Inc., Business Expert Inc., Business Expert Kansai, Inc., Business Expert Kyushu, Inc., Business Expert Tokai, Inc., D2 Communications Inc., DCM Investment Inc., DoCoMo Beijing Communications Laboratories Co., Ltd., DoCoMo Business Net, inc., DoCoMo Capital, Inc., DoCoMo Communications Laboratories Europe GmbH, DoCoMo Communications Laboratories USA, Inc., DoCoMo Engineering Chugoku, Inc., DoCoMo Engineering Hokkaido Inc., DoCoMo Engineering Hokuriku Inc. 61 Subsidiaries included in the Index

Officers: Masao Nakamura/Dir., CEO, Pres., Shoichi Matsuhashi/Corporate Auditor, Noriaki Ito/Dir., Sr. VP, MD - Corporate Strategy, Planning Department, Mitsunobu Komori/Sr. VP, GM - Kanagawa Branch, Haruo Imai/Corporate Auditor, Kyouichi Yoshizawa/Corporate Auditor, Takaaki Wakasugi/Corporate Auditor, Kazuhiro Yoshizawa/Sr. VP, Yuji Araki/Sr. VP, Deputy MD - Corporate Branding Division, MD - Public Relations Department, MD - Advertisement Department, Kiyoshi Tokuhiro/Sr. VP, MD - Network Planning Department, Network Division, Masatoshi Suzuki/Sr. VP, MD - Public Relations Department, Kiyoyuki Tsujimura/Dir., Exec. VP, MD - Products, Services Division, Masayuki Hirata/Dir., Sr. Exec. VP, MD - Global Business Division, CFO, Takeshi Natsuno/Sr. VP, MD - Multimedia Services Department, Products, Services Division, Takashi Tanaka/Dir., Sr. VP, MD - General Affairs Department (31 Officers included in Index)

Directors: Masao Nakamura/Dir., CEO, Pres., Noriaki Ito/Dir., Sr. VP, MD - Corporate Strategy, Planning Department, Kiyoyuki Tsujimura/Dir., Exec. VP, MD - Products, Services Division, Masayuki Hirata/Dir., Sr. Exec. VP, MD - Global Business Division, CFO, Harunari Futatsugi/Dir., Exec. VP, MD - Human Resources Management Department, Takanori Utano/Dir., Exec. VP, MD -

Research, Development Division, CTO, Bunya Kumagai/Dir., Sr. VP, MD - Marketing Division, Kazuto Tsubouchi/Dir., Sr. VP, MD - Accounting, Finance Department, Akiko Ide/Sr. VP, MD - Corporate Citizenship Department, Takashi Tanaka/Dir., Sr. VP, MD - General Affairs Department, Toshiki Nakayama/Dir.

Owners: Insiders/100.00%, Foreign corporations and individuals/16.32%, Other Japanese corporations/61.42%, Japanese securities companies, Japanese individuals, treasury shares and others/10.92%, Japanese financial institutions/10.44%

Financial Data: Fiscal Year End:03/31   Latest Annual Data: 03/31/2007

Year	Sales	Net Income
2007	$40,728,930,000	$3,889,741,000
2006	$40,567,518,000	$5,196,467,000
2005	$45,183,828,000	$6,972,244,000
Curr. Assets:	$16,400,732,000	Curr. Liab.:	$11,647,080,000	
Plant, Equip.:	$23,641,930,000	Total Liab.:	$19,690,500,000	Indic. Yr. Divd.: $0.310
Total Assets:	$54,181,622,000	Net Worth:	$34,491,122,000	Debt/ Equity: NA

Nu Horizons Electronics Corp

70 Maxess Rd., Melville, NY, 11747; **PH:** 1-631-396-5000; **Fax:** 1-631-396-5050; **http://** www.nuhorizons.com; **Email:** info@nuhorizons.com

General - Incorporation	DE	Stock- Price on:12/24/2007	$13.14
Employees	748	Stock Exchange	NDQ
Auditor	Lazar Levine & Felix LLP	Ticker Symbol	NA
Stk Agt	American Stock Transfer & Trust Co.	Outstanding Shares	18,160,000
Counsel Kramer, Coleman, Wactiar & Lieberman		E.P.S.	$0.53
DUNS No.	07-724-5942	Shareholders	NA

Business: The group's principal activities are to distribute high technology active and passive electronic components. Active components include semiconductor products such as memory chips, digital and linear circuits, microwave, rf and fiber-optic components, transistors and diodes. Passive components consist of high technology line of chip and leaded components including capacitors, resistors and related networks. The manufacturers of sophisticated electronic products including industrial instrumentation, computers and peripheral equipment utilize these components. The group distributes and exports its products throughout the United States, Asia and Europe.

Primary SIC and add'l.: 5065

CIK No: 0000718074

Subsidiaries: Components Corp. (NIC), Diplomat Electronics Corp, Nu Horizons Electronics Asia PTE LTD (NUA), Nu Horizons Electronics Hong Kong Limited (NUK), Nu Horizons Europe Limited, Nu Horizons International Corp. (International), Nu Visions Manufacturing Inc (Nu Visions), NUHC Inc. (NUC), Titan Supply Chain Services Limited (TSE)

Officers: Arthur Nadata/Chmn., CEO/$1,234,000.00, Kent Smith/Sr. VP - Sales, Americas, Burt Silverman/VP - Information Technology, Wendell Boyd/Pres. - Nu Horizons Electronics Asia Pte Ltd, Teresa Shatsoff/VP - Global Customer Business Unit, Dave Bowers/Pres. - Semiconductor Distribution Division, Rita Megling/VP - Marketing, Geoff Annesi/Regional VP - Central, Steve Mussmacher/Sr. VP - Global Operations, Dan Romanelli/VP - OEM System Sales, Elaine Givner/VP - Human Resources, Training Development, Richard S. Schuster/Pres./$1,228,000.00, Kurt Freudenberg/CFO, Exec. VP/$280,000.00, Tom Dow/VP - Sales, David Owens/Regional VP - Eastern (18 Officers included in Index)

Directors: Arthur Nadata/Chmn., CEO

Owners: Wasatch Advisors Inc./9.60%, Richard S. Schuster/6.10%, David Siegel, Keeley Asset Management Corp./6.00%, Dimensional Fund Advisors/8.40%, Insiders/14.80%, Deutsche Bank Investment Management/9.70%, Herbert M. Gardner, Kurt Freudenberg, Dominic A. Polimeni, Arthur Nadata/7.00%, Donald Smith& Co.,Inc./5.40%, Martin Novick

Financial Data: Fiscal Year End:02/28   Latest Annual Data: 2/28/2007

Year	Sales	Net Income
2007	$737,463,000	$9,913,000
2006	$561,291,000	$4,884,000
2005	$467,849,000	$3,073,000
Curr. Assets:	$248,629,000	Curr. Liab.:	$81,681,000	P/E Ratio: 24.79
Plant, Equip.:	$3,381,000	Total Liab.:	$117,784,000	Indic. Yr. Divd.: NA
Total Assets:	$267,479,000	Net Worth:	$147,747,000	Debt/ Equity: NA

Nu Skin Enterprises Inc

75 W Ctr. St., Provo, UT, 84601; **PH:** 1-801-345-1000; **Fax:** 1-801-345-2799; **http://** www.nuskinenterprises.com; **Email:** investorrelations@nuskin.com

General - Incorporation	DE	Stock- Price on:12/24/2007	$17.34
Employees	11,360	Stock Exchange	NYSE
Auditor	PricewaterhouseCoopers LLP	Ticker Symbol	NUS
Stk Agt	American Stock Transfer & Trust Co.	Outstanding Shares	64,490,000
Counsel	NA	E.P.S.	$0.81
DUNS No.	96-681-7975	Shareholders	NA

Business: The group's principal activities are to develop and distribute personal care products and nutritional supplements. The group has three product divisions: nu skin, pharmanex and big planet. Nu skin offers effective personal care products with an emphasis on skin care. Pharmanex offers high-quality nutritional supplements. Big planet offers high-technology products and services and a line of home care products. The group has operations in the United States, Japan, South Korea, Taiwan, Hong Kong, Canada, Philippines, Australia, New Zealand, Singapore, Malaysia and other countries. The group also runs a non-profit humanitarian organization, nu skin force for good foundation that provides funds and products to create a better world for children by improving human life, continuing indigenous cultures and protecting fragile environments.

Primary SIC and add'l.: 7375 5122

CIK No: 0001021561

Subsidiaries: Big Planet Inc., First Harvest International LLC, Niksun Acquisition Corporation, NSE Korea Ltd., Nu Family Benefits Insurance Brokerage Inc., Nu Skin (China) Daily-Use and Health Products Co. Ltd., Nu Skin (Malaysia) Sdn. Bhd., Nu Skin Asia Investment Inc., Nu Skin Belgium NV, Nu Skin Brazil Ltda., Nu Skin Canada Inc., Nu Skin Enterprises (Thailand) Ltd., Nu Skin Enterprises Australia Inc., Nu Skin Enterprises Hong Kong Inc., Nu Skin Enterprises New Zealand Inc. 47 Subsidiaries included in the Index

Officers: Truman Hunt/CEO, Pres./$2,306,229.00, Janet Lephart/Sr. Dir. - Nu Skin Research, Development, Frankie Kiow/Pres. - Nu Skin China, Agung Karso Sardjono/45/GM - Indonesia, Nigel Sinclair/GM - New Zealand, Sandie N. Tillotson/51/Dir., Sr. VP, Giovanni Lopez/GM - Nu Skin Central America, Win Duersch/Sr. Dir. - Global Product Regulatory Affairs, Helen E. Knaggs/VP - Nu Skin Global Research, Development, Jack Petersen/54/VP - Corporate Strategy, Development,

Robert Conlee/Pres. - North Asia Region, Pres. - Nu Skin Japan/$1,864,681.00, Andrew Fan/Country GM - Hong Kong, Michael N. Chang/Chief Scientific Advisor - Nu Skin Enterprises, Charles Ngai/Mgr. - Sales, Distributor Development, Hongkong, Kelly Cheng/Accounting Mgr. - Sales, Distributor Development, Hong Kong (63 Officers included in Index)

Directors: Truman Hunt/CEO, Pres., Steven J. Lund/54/Vice Chmn., Blake M. Roney/50/Chmn., Paul Alan Cox/Member - Scientific Advisory Board, Michael Jeffrey Balick/Member - Scientific Advisory Board, Alfred T. Lane/Member - Scientific Advisory Board, Etienne Soudant/Member - Scientific Advisory Board, Zoe Draelos/Member - Scientific Advisory Board, Bryan Fuller/Member - Scientific Advisory Board, Patricia K. Farris/Member - Scientific Advisory Board, Alexa Boer Kimball/Member - Scientific Advisory Board, Joe Ferreira/Dir., Senator E.J Garn/Dir., Senator Paula F. Hawkins/Dir., Takashi Bamba/Dir. (24 Directors included in Index)

Owners: Steven Lund/2.80%, Insiders/25.40%, Ritch Wood, Blake Roney/12.90%, Daniel Campbell, Robert Conlee, Blum Capital Partners, L.P./8.80%, Andrew Lipman, Patricia Negrn, Wellington Management Company, LLP/6.70%, Paula Hawkins, Royce and Associates, LLC/16.10%, Sandra Tillotson/5.70%, Allen Andersen, Truman Hunt/1.00% (18 Owners included in Index)

Financial Data: Fiscal Year End:12/31   Latest Annual Data: 12/31/2006

Year	Sales	Net Income
2006	$1,115,409,000	$32,817,000
2005	$1,180,930,000	$74,033,000
2004	$1,137,864,000	$77,674,000

Curr. Assets:	$276,959,000	Curr. Liab.:	$167,541,000	P/E Ratio:	21.95
Plant, Equip.:	$85,883,000	Total Liab.:	$345,869,000	Indic. Yr. Divd.:	$0.420
Total Assets:	$664,849,000	Net Worth:	$318,980,000	Debt/ Equity:	0.6361

Nuance Communications Inc

1 Wayside Rd., Burlington, MA, 01803; **PH:** 1-781-565-5000; **Fax:** 1-781-565-5001; *http://* www.nuance.com

General - Incorporation	DE	**Stock**- Price on:12/24/2007	$16.54
Employees	1,681	Stock Exchange	NYSE
Auditor	BDO Seidman LLP	Ticker Symbol	NUE
Stk Agt	U.S. Stock Transfer Corp	Outstanding Shares	176,390,000
Counsel	Wilson Sonsini Goodrich & Rosati	E.P.S.	-$0.079
DUNS No.	79-740-7517	Shareholders	NA

Business: The group's principal activity is to provide software that allows users to incorporate documents, images and speech into digital applications. The products and technologies automate manual processes and help enterprises, professionals and consumers increase productivity, reduce costs and save time. These products are built upon digital capture and speech technologies, and are sold as solutions into the financial, legal, healthcare, government, telecommunications and automotive industries. The group's digital capture technologies transform text and images into digital form. These products are designed to address the needs of a broad group of users ranging from consumers and small office to medium-sized businesses and large corporations. The group has operations in North America and other foreign countries. On 11-Aug-2003, the group acquired speechworks international inc.

Primary SIC and add'l.: 7372 7371

CIK No: 0001002517

Subsidiaries: 1448451 Ontario Inc., ART Advanced Recognition Technologies, Inc., ART Advanced Recognition Technologies, Ltd., Caere Corporation, Caere FSC Corporation, Caere Kft, Formonix, Inc., Locus Dialogue Technologies USA, Inc., McGwire LLC, Nova Acquisition LLC, Nuance Communications Australia, Nuance Communications Gmbh, Nuance Communications Hong Kong Limited, Nuance Communications International, Inc., Nuance Communications Italy SRL 52 Subsidiaries included in the Index

Officers: Paul Ricci/Chmn., CEO, William H. Janeway/Member, James Arnold/Sr. VP, CFO, Don Hunt/Sr. VP - Worldwide Sales, Scott Floeck/CIO, Sr. VP, Wes Hayden/Pres. - Nuance Enterprise Division, Richard Palmer/Sr. VP - Corporate Development, Steve Chambers/Pres. - Mobile, Consumer Services Division, Jeanne McCann/Exec. VP - Operations, Robert Wise/Pres. - Dictaphone Healthcare Division, Jo-Anne Sinclair/VP, General Counsel, John Shagoury/Pres. - Imaging Division, Dawn Fournier/VP - Human Resources, Steven E. Hebert/Chief Accounting Officer

Directors: Paul Ricci/Chmn., CEO, Robert J. Frankenberg/Dir., Mark B. Myers/Dir., Jeffrey A. Harris/Dir., Philip Quigley/Dir., Katharine A. Martin/Dir., Charles Berger/Dir., Robert G. Teresi/Dir.

Owners: John D. Shagoury, William H. Janeway/23.10%, Warburg Pincus/23.10%, Insiders/28.50%, Franklin Resources, Inc./5.30%, Mark B. Myers, Jeffrey A. Harris/23.10%, Steven G. Chambers, Katharine A. Martin, Robert J. Frankenberg, Philip J. Quigley, Robert M. Finch, Paul A. Ricci/2.30%, James R. Arnold, Robert G. Teresi (17 Owners included in Index)

Financial Data: Fiscal Year End:09/30   Latest Annual Data: 9/30/2006

Year	Sales	Net Income
2006	$388,510,000	-$22,887,000
2005	$232,388,000	-$5,417,000
2004	$130,907,000	-$9,378,000

Curr. Assets:	$263,321,000	Curr. Liab.:	$212,048,000		
Plant, Equip.:	$30,700,000	Total Liab.:	$658,478,000	Indic. Yr. Divd.:	NA
Total Assets:	$1,235,074,000	Net Worth:	$576,596,000	Debt/ Equity:	0.5667

Nuclear Solutions Inc

5505 Connecticut Ave. NW, Ste. 191, Washington, DC, 20015; **PH:** 1-202-787-1951; **Fax:** 1-202-318-2487; *http://* www.nuclearsolutions.com; **Email:** info@nuclearsolution.com

General - Incorporation	NV	**Stock**- Price on:12/24/2007	$0.51
Employees	1	Stock Exchange	OTC
Auditor	Russell Bedford Stefanou Mirchandani	Ticker Symbol	NSOL
Stk Agt	Standard Registrar & Transfer Co Inc.	Outstanding Shares	57,310,000
Counsel	NA	E.P.S.	-$0.08
DUNS No.	NA	Shareholders	NA

Business: The group's principle activities include researching, developing and commercialize innovativing nuclear technologies. The company's objective is to identify, screen and develop selected technologies to the point that they may be either licensed, joint-ventured, sold to an industrial partner, or otherwise commercialized. The company's business is focused on commercial product technologies for homeland security and defense, nanotechnology applications and nuclear remediation. The company is in the development stage. The group operates from United States.

Primary SIC and add'l.: 9511 7375

CIK No: 0001116112

Subsidiaries: Fuel Frontiers, Inc.

Officers: Patrick G. Herda/Chmn., CEO, Pres., John Dempsey/VP - Industry Relations, Jack C. Young/VP - Developement, Kenneth Faith/38/CFO, Principal Accounting Officer

Directors: Patrick G. Herda/Chmn., CEO, Pres., John Powers/73/Dir.

Owners: Insiders/0.60%, John Powers/0.50%, Ken Faith/14.00%

Financial Data: Fiscal Year End:12/31   Latest Annual Data: 12/31/2006

Year	Sales	Net Income
2006	$223,000	-$3,885,000
2005	$40,000	-$933,000

Curr. Assets:	$112,000	Curr. Liab.:	$3,524,000		
Plant, Equip.:	$16,000	Total Liab.:	$3,524,000	Indic. Yr. Divd.:	NA
Total Assets:	$131,000	Net Worth:	-$3,394,000	Debt/ Equity:	NA

Nuco2 Inc

2800 SE Market Pl., Stuart, FL, 34997; **PH:** 1-772-221-1754; **Fax:** 1-772-781-3500; *http://* www.nuco2.com; **Email:** info@nuco2.com

General - Incorporation	FL	**Stock**- Price on:12/24/2007	$26.07
Employees	700	Stock Exchange	NDQ
Auditor	Margolin, Winer & Evens LLP	Ticker Symbol	NUHC
Stk Agt	Continental Stock Transfer & Trust Co	Outstanding Shares	15,360,000
Counsel	Olshan Et Al	E.P.S.	$0.52
DUNS No.	10-768-8822	Shareholders	NA

Business: The group's principal activity is to supply carbon dioxide to retail establishments for use in the carbonation and dispensing of fountain beverages. The group installs stationary bulk carbon dioxide system on the customer's site and also provides routine filling of the system with bulk carbon dioxide. Bulk carbon dioxide involves delivery of carbon dioxide in its liquid form, which is then converted to gaseous form, the necessary ingredient for beverage carbonation. The group currently has 108 service locations and approximately 82,000 bulk and high-pressure carbon dioxide customers in 45 states, providing bulk carbon dioxide systems ranging from 300 to 600 lbs. The group markets these products under the trademark nuco2 (r). The group's customers include major national and regional restaurant and convenience store chains, movie theater operators, theme parks, resorts and sports venues.

Primary SIC and add'l.: 2813 5169

CIK No: 0000947577

Officers: Michael E. Dedomenico/Chmn., CEO, Randy Gold/Sr. VP - Sales, Customer Support, Eric M. Wechsler/General Counsel, Sec., Scott W. Wade/COO, Exec. VP, Jeffrey S. Gilheney/VP - Human Resources, Robert R. Galvin/CFO, Exec. VP

Directors: Michael E. Dedomenico/Chmn., CEO, Robert L. Frome/69/Dir., Steven J. Landwehr/60/Dir., Daniel Raynor/48/Dir., Robert J. Vipond/62/Dir., Christopher White/62/Dir.

Owners: Steven J. Landwehr, BAMCO, INC/10.20%, Federated Investors, Inc/11.70%, Christopher White, Robert R. Galvin/1.40%, Janus Capital Management LLC/6.80%, Daniel Raynor, Avenir Corporation/15.00%, Shamrock Partners Activist Value Fund, LLC/8.10%, William Scott Wade/1.60%, T. Rowe Price Associates, Inc./7.80%, Michael E. DeDomenico/3.10%, Eric M. Wechsler, TimesSquare Capital Management LLC/7.00%, Robert J. Vipond (17 Owners included in Index)

Financial Data: Fiscal Year End:06/30   Latest Annual Data: 06/30/2007

Year	Sales	Net Income
2007	$130,128,000	$7,639,000
2006	$116,196,000	$10,348,000
2005	$97,340,000	$25,591,000

Curr. Assets:	$29,507,000	Curr. Liab.:	$12,828,000		
Plant, Equip.:	$119,603,000	Total Liab.:	$52,083,000	Indic. Yr. Divd.:	NA
Total Assets:	$199,007,000	Net Worth:	$146,924,000	Debt/ Equity:	0.2488

Nucor Corp

1915 Rexford Rd., Charlotte, NC, 28211; **PH:** 1-704-366-7000; **Fax:** 1-704-362-4208; *http://* www.nucor.com; **Email:** info@nucor.com

General - Incorporation	DE	**Stock**- Price on:12/24/2007	$62.26
Employees	11,900	Stock Exchange	NYSE
Auditor	PricewaterhouseCoopers LLP	Ticker Symbol	NA
Stk Agt	American Stock Transfer & Trust Co.	Outstanding Shares	301,700,000
Counsel	NA	E.P.S.	$5.02
DUNS No.	00-344-6796	Shareholders	NA

Business: The groups principle activities include manufacturing and selling steel and steel products. The group operates through two segments namely steel mills and steel products. In the year 2007, the group acquired Magnatrax Corporation. The group operates from United States.

Primary SIC and add'l.: 3316 3312

CIK No: 0000073309

Subsidiaries: Nucor-Yamato Steel Company

Officers: Daniel R. Dimicco/Chmn., CEO, Pres./$8,555,906.00, John J. Ferriola/Exec. VP/$4,104,384.00, James M. Coblin/64/VP - Human Resources, Joseph A. Rutkowski/Exec. VP/$3,644,579.00, Hamilton Lott/Exec. VP/$4,121,055.00, Terry S. Lisenby/CFO, Treasurer, Exec. VP/$4,972,046.00, Bill Prescott/Sales Mgr. - Nucor Building Systems, South Carolina, Tom Batterbee/GM - Nucor Building Systems, Texas, Rex Query/VP, GM - Nucor Steel, Decatur, LLC, John Sacco/Sales Mgr. - Nucor Steel, Decatur, LLC, Bob McCracken/GM - Nucor Steel, Hertford, Jeff Whiteman/Sales Mgr. - Nucor Steel, Hertford, Ron Dickerson/VP, GM - Nucor Steel, Indiana, Tim Hill/Sales Mgr. - Nucor Steel, Indiana, Peter Campbell/Castrip Sales Mgr. - Nucor Steel, Indiana (96 Officers included in Index)

Directors: Daniel R. Dimicco/Chmn., CEO, Pres., Peter C. Browning/Dir., Clayton C. Daley/Dir., Victoria F. Haynes/Dir., Harvey B. Gantt/Dir., James D. Hlavacek/Dir., Raymond J. Milchovich/58/Dir., Bernard L.M. Kasriel/Dir.

Owners: Peter C. Browning, Daniel R. DiMicco, Harvey B. Gantt, State Farm Mutual Automobile Insurance Company and related entities/10.00%, Michael D. Parrish, Terry S. Lisenby, Insiders, Raymond J. Milchovich, Joseph A. Rutkowski, Clayton C. Daley, Barclays Global Investors, NA and related entities/10.41%, Victoria F. Haynes, John J. Ferriola, Hamilton Lott, James D. Hlavacek

Financial Data: Fiscal Year End:12/31   Latest Annual Data: 12/31/2006

Year	Sales	Net Income
2006	$14,751,270,000	$1,757,681,000
2005	$12,700,999,000	$1,310,284,000
2004	$11,376,828,000	$1,121,485,000

Curr. Assets:	$4,675,036,000	Curr. Liab.:	$1,450,028,000	P/E Ratio:	10.87
Plant, Equip.:	$2,856,415,000	Total Liab.:	$2,820,412,000	Indic. Yr. Divd.:	$1.200
Total Assets:	$7,884,989,000	Net Worth:	$4,825,989,000	Debt/ Equity:	NA

Nucryst Pharmaceuticals Corp

50 Audubon Rd., Ste. B, Wakefield, MA, 01880; ***PH:*** 1-781-224-1444; ***Fax:*** 1-781-246-6002; ***http://*** www.nucryst.com; ***Email:*** info@nucryst.com

General - Incorporation	AL	***Stock***- Price on:12/24/2007	$2.17
Employees	158	Stock Exchange	NDQ
Auditor	Deloitte & Touche LLP	Ticker Symbol	NCST
Stk Agt	Computershare Trust Co of Canada	Outstanding Shares	18,310,000
Counsel	NA	E.P.S	-$0.52
DUNS No.	NA	Shareholders	NA

Business: The groups principle activities include developing, manufacturing and commercializing medical products. The group products sold under the trade names SILCRYST(TM) and Acticoat(TM). Specific customer of the group is Smith and Nephew. The group operates from the United States and Canada. The group's quarterly revenue for September 2007 was 7.53 millions of USD.

Primary SIC and add'l.: 2834 3841 8731

CIK No: 0001344674

Subsidiaries: Nucryst Pharmaceuticals Inc.

Officers: Scott H. Gillis/55/Dir., CEO, Pres., Paul J. Schechter/68/VP - Drug Development, Regulatory Affairs, Chief Medical Officer, Eliot M. Lurier/49/CFO, VP - Finance, Administration, David C. McDowell/VP - Manufacturing Operations, Catherine Cloft/Contact - Investor Relations, Media Relations, Carol Amelio/VP, General Counsel, Corp. Sec., Ed Gaj/VP - Corporate Development, Katherine J. Turner/VP - Research, Development

Directors: Scott H. Gillis/55/Dir., CEO, Pres., Barry M. Heck/Chmn., Neil Carragher/Dir., Roger G.H. Downer/Dir., David Poorvin/Dir., Richard W. Zahn/Dir., Allen J. Bard/Member - Scientific Advisory Board, Robert H. Demling/Member - Scientific Advisory Board, Byron D. McLees/Member - Scientific Advisory Board, Robert S. Stern/Member - Scientific Advisory Board, Michael Weintraub/Member - Scientific Advisory Board

Owners: Eliot M. Lurier, Paul J. Schechter, Roger G.H. Downer, Richard W. Zahn, David Poorvin, The Westaim Corporation/74.70%, Neil Carragher, Royce & Associates LLC/7.77%, Scott H. Gillis/1.47%, David C. McDowell, AMVESCAP PLC/5.40%, Insiders/2.08%

Financial Data: ***Fiscal Year End:***12/31 ***Latest Annual Data:*** 12/31/2006

Year	Sales	Net Income
2006	$24,369,000	-$10,499,000
2005	$23,636,000	-$2,641,000
2004	$24,682,000	$1,348,000

Curr. Assets:	$33,591,000	**Curr. Liab.:**	$2,306,000		
Plant, Equip.:	$11,350,000	**Total Liab.:**	$2,306,000	**Indic. Yr. Divd.:**	NA
Total Assets:	$45,892,000	**Net Worth:**	$43,586,000	**Debt/ Equity:**	NA

Nugget Resources Inc

778 Ft. St. St., Victoria, BC, V8W 1H2; ***PH:*** 1-250-385-8444

General - Incorporation	NV	***Stock***- Price on:12/24/2007	NA
Employees	NA	Stock Exchange	OTC
Auditor	James Stafford	Ticker Symbol	NUGR
Stk Agt	EquiServe Trust Co N.A	Outstanding Shares	NA
Counsel	NA	E.P.S	NA
DUNS No.	NA	Shareholders	NA

Business: The groups principal activity is to engage in the acquisition and exploration of mineral properties. The group operates from the United States.

Primary SIC and add'l.: 1000

CIK No: 0001356371

Officers: Peter Sorel/55/Dir., CEO, Pres., David Matzele/51/Dir., Sec., Treasurer, Principal Accounting Officer

Directors: Peter Sorel/55/Dir., CEO, Pres., David Matzele/51/Dir., Sec., Treasurer, Principal Accounting Officer

Owners: Insiders/47.60%, David Matzele/47.60%

Numerex Corp

1600 Pk.wood Cir., Ste. 500, Atlanta, GA, 30339; ***PH:*** 1-770-693-5950; ***Fax:*** 1-770-693-5951; ***http://*** www.nmrx.com; ***Email:*** public_relations@nmrx.com

General - Incorporation	PA	***Stock***- Price on:12/24/2007	$11.58
Employees	110	Stock Exchange	NDQ
Auditor	Grant Thornton LLP	Ticker Symbol	NMTI
Stk Agt	American Stock Transfer & Trust Co.	Outstanding Shares	14,540,000
Counsel	Salisbury & Ryan LLP	E.P.S	$0.13
DUNS No.	82-675-1232	Shareholders	NA

Business: The group's principal activities are to design, manufacture and market communication and information products and services in wireless communications and multimedia networking. The group offers products and services in wireless data communications through cellemetry(R) and data1 source tm, and digital multimedia through powerplay tm. Cellemetry llc provides two-way wireless data transport and digital multimedia business provides integration services, installation, and operator training for interactive voice, video, and data via fiber optic transport. Through uplink security inc, the group offers wireline alarm security products and services. In addition, the group provides telecommunications network operational support systems and services through its subsidiary digilog inc to operating telephone companies.

Primary SIC and add'l.: 4899 7382 3669

CIK No: 0000870753

Subsidiaries: BNI Solutions LLC, Broadband Networks, Inc., Cellemetry LLC, CellemetryXG Customer Services, LLC, DCX Systems (Australia) Pty Limited, DCX Systems, Inc., Digilog, Inc., MobileGuardian LLC, Numerex Investment Corp., Numerex Solutions LLC, Uplink Security, Inc.

Officers: Stratton Nicolaides/Chmn., CEO/$697,780.00, Louis Fienberg/Sr. VP - Corporate Development, Michael A. Marett/COO/$630,933.00, Alan Catherall/CFO, Exec. VP/$480,777.00, Chuck Horne/Sr. VP - Marketing, Michael W. Lang/Sr. VP - Sales

Directors: Stratton Nicolaides/Chmn., CEO, Matthew J. Flanigan/Dir., Nicholas A. Davidge/Dir., George Benson/Dir., Andrew J. Ryan/Dir., Brian C. Beazer/Dir., John G. Raos/Dir., Allan H. Liu/Dir.

Owners: Laurus Master Fund, Ltd., George Benson, Potomac Capital Management LLC, Kenneth F. Manser, Gwynedd Resources, Ltd., Maria E. Nicolaides, Matthew J. Flanigan, Nicholas A. Davidge, Allan H. Liu, Insiders, Douglas Holsclaw, Elizabeth Baxavanis, Trustee, Stratton J. Nicolaides, John G. Raos, Andrew J. Ryan *(18 Owners included in Index)*

Financial Data: ***Fiscal Year End:***12/31 ***Latest Annual Data:*** 12/31/2006

Year	Sales	Net Income
2006	$52,788,000	$4,103,000
2005	$29,946,000	$593,000
2004	$22,993,000	-$2,079,000

Curr. Assets:	$37,773,000	**Curr. Liab.:**	$11,871,000	**P/E Ratio:**	55.14
Plant, Equip.:	$1,287,000	**Total Liab.:**	$24,973,000	**Indic. Yr. Divd.:**	NA
Total Assets:	$66,393,000	**Net Worth:**	$41,420,000	**Debt/ Equity:**	0.2954

NUR Macroprinters Ltd

12 Abba Hillel Silver St., Lod, 71111; ***PH:*** 972-89145555; ***Fax:*** 972-89211220; ***http://*** www.nur.com

General - Incorporation	Israel	***Stock***- Price on:12/24/2007	$0.5
Employees	NA	Stock Exchange	OTC
Auditor	Kost Forer Gabbay & Kasierer	Ticker Symbol	NURMF
Stk Agt	Continental Stock Transfer & Trust Co	Outstanding Shares	NA
Counsel	Katten Muchin Rosenman LLP	E.P.S	NA
DUNS No.	60-006-8480	Shareholders	NA

Business: The group's principle activities are the development, manufacture, marketing and service of wide format and super wide format digital color printing systems worldwide. These to be used for the printing of large images such as billboards, posters and banners, point of purchase displays, exhibition and trade show displays as well as decorations and backdrops for construction scaffolding covers, showrooms, television and film studios, museums and exhibits. The company also supplies inks and solvents for use with printers, and print substrates for use with all brands of wide and super wide format digital printers.

Primary SIC and add'l.: 2893 3577

CIK No: 0000946394

Subsidiaries: NUR America, Inc, NUR Asia Pacific Ltd., NUR DO Brazil Ltda., NUR Europe S.A., NUR Japan Ltd.

Officers: David Reis/CEO, Pres., Yossy Zylberberg/CFO, COO, Andrew Middleton/45/MD - NUR Europe SA, Marco Baio/45/MD - NUR Europe SA, Assaf Eyal/Exec. VP, Shuki Garibi/VP - Research, Development, Itzik Arbesfeld/VP - Human Resources, Eran Cohen/VP - Operations, Roni Zomber/52/VP - Operations, Menashe Ben Chaim/VP - Consumables - Bus, Operations, David Bartram/Public Relations Contact, Thibault Dejaiffe/Public Relations Contact, Winnie Chu/Public Relations Contact, Yael Hazan/Public Relations Contact, Jude Liemburg/Public Relations Contact *(22 Officers included in Index)*

Directors: Yuval Cohen/45/Chmn., Lauri A. Hanover/External Dir., Shmoulik Barashi/Dir., Marc Lesnick/41/Dir., Eli Blatt/Dir., Menachem Raphael/Dir., Hemi Raphael/56/Dir., Alon Lumbroso/51/Dir., Koby Shtaierman/External Dir., Oded Akselrod/Dir.

Owners: Dan and Edna Purjes/12.51%, Kanir Joint Investments (2005) Limited Partnership/19.05%, Old LaneLuxemburg Master Fund S.a.r.l/6.56%, Bank Hapoalim B.M/6.44%, Meitav Entities/6.34%, Fortissimo Entities/49.12%

Financial Data: ***Fiscal Year End:***12/31 ***Latest Annual Data:*** 12/31/2006

Year	Sales	Net Income
2006	$77,968,000	-$1,921,000
2005	$71,378,000	-$14,706,000
2004	$76,723,000	-$21,967,000

Curr. Assets:	$33,995,000	**Curr. Liab.:**	$33,639,000		
Plant, Equip.:	$5,758,000	**Total Liab.:**	$62,206,000	**Indic. Yr. Divd.:**	NA
Total Assets:	$41,203,000	**Net Worth:**	-$21,003,000	**Debt/ Equity:**	NA

NuStar GP Holdings LLC

Formerly: Valero GP Holdings LLC

1 Valero Way, San Antonio, TX, 78249; ***PH:*** 1-210-918-2000 ; ***Fax:*** 1-210-918-5055; ***http://*** www.nustargpholdings.com; ***Email:*** investorrelations@nustargp.com

General - Incorporation	DE	***Stock***- Price on:12/24/2007	NA
Employees	NA	Stock Exchange	NYSE
Auditor	KPMG LLP	Ticker Symbol	NA
Stk Agt	Computershare Trust Co	Outstanding Shares	NA
Counsel	NA	E.P.S	$1.05
DUNS No.	NA	Shareholders	NA

Business: The groups principle activities include owning, acquiring and developing natural gas and liquefied petroleum pipeline. The group operates through four segments namely, refined product terminals, refined products pipelines, crude oil pipelines and crude oil storage tanks. In the year 2006, the group acquired Kaneb Pipe Line Operating Partnership, L.P. The group operates from the United States.

Primary SIC and add'l.: 4610

CIK No: 0001223786

Subsidiaries: Bicen Development Corporation N.V., Diamond K Limited, Kaneb Investment, LLC, Kaneb LLC, Kaneb Management Company LLC, Kaneb Management, LLC, Kaneb Pipe Line Company LLC, Kaneb Pipe Line Holding Company, LLC, Kaneb Pipe Line Operating Partnership, L.P., Kaneb Pipe Line Partners, L.P., Kaneb Services LLC, Kaneb Terminals (Eastham) Limited, Kaneb Terminals B.V., Kaneb Terminals Limited, Kaneb, Inc. 23 Subsidiaries included in the Index

Officers: Curtis V. Anastasio/Dir., CEO, Pres., Frank Padilla/Mgr. - Sparks, Robert Condon/Mgr. - Los Angeles, Ed Vega/Mgr. - Pittsburg, CA, David Tidmore/Mgr. - Moundville, AL, Jamie Smith/Area Mgr. - Savannah, GA, Terry Ennis/Terminal Mgr. - Savannah, GA, Ian Vaughan/Mgr. - Texas City, Larry Pomeroy/Mgr. - Winona, WI, Jim Siciliano/Dir. - Gulf Coast Region, TX, LA, Dave Keefer/Dir. - West Region, Dilio Baptista/National Accounting Mgr. - Southeast, Joe Clinch/Mgr. - Brunswick, Sandra Lloyd/Mgr. - Jacksonville, FL, Eddie Nobles/Mgr. - Macon, GA *(55 Officers included in Index)*

Directors: Curtis V. Anastasio/Dir., CEO, Pres., William E. Greehey/Chmn., Dan J. Bates/Dir., Dan J. Hill/Dir., Rodman D. Patton/Dir., William B. Burnett/Dir., Fully Clingman/Dir., Stan L. McLelland/Dir.

Owners: William E. Greehey/12.13%, Lehman Brothers Holdings Inc./7.70%

Financial Data: ***Fiscal Year End:***12/31 ***Latest Annual Data:*** 12/31/2006

Year	Sales	Net Income
2006	$42,983,000	$30,718,000
2005	$37,646,000	$20,293,000
2004	$35,314,000	$18,447,000

Curr. Assets:	$5,032,000	**Curr. Liab.:**	$4,516,000		
Plant, Equip.:	NA	**Total Liab.:**	$14,850,000	**Indic. Yr. Divd.:**	$1.440
Total Assets:	$570,493,000	**Net Worth:**	$555,643,000	**Debt/ Equity:**	NA

Nutech Digital Inc

3841 Hayvenhurst Dr., Encino, CA, 91436; *PH:* 1-818-994-3841; *Fax:* 1-818-994-1575;
http:// www.nutechdvd.com; *Email:* info@nutechdvd.com

General - Incorporation	CA	Stock- Price on:12/24/2007	$0.021
Employees	1	Stock Exchange	OTC
Auditor	Weaver & Martin LLC	Ticker Symbol	NTDL
Stk Agt	Registrar & Transfer Co	Outstanding Shares	34,170,000
Counsel	NA	E.P.S	NA
DUNS No.	NA	Shareholders	NA

Business: The group's principal activities are to license and distribute general entertainment products for children and adults. The products of the group are made available through digital versatile disc. The products include children's animated films and video games, karaoke software, Japanese anime and late night programming.the group's products are sold in two formats DVD and CD + g. The products are sold through retail stores, the Internet and wholesale distributors.

Primary SIC and add'l.: 7841

CIK No: 0001144347

Officers: Lee Kasper/Dir., CEO, CFO, Pres., Joe Giarmo/VP, Dir., Yegia Eli Aramyan/Dir., Accountant

Directors: Lee Kasper/Dir., CEO, CFO, Pres., Joe Giarmo/VP, Dir., Yegia Eli Aramyan/Dir., Accountant, Jay S. Hergott/Dir.

Owners: Insiders/96.40%, Lee Kasper/41.80%, Insiders, Frederick A. Greenberg

Financial Data: Fiscal Year End:12/31   *Latest Annual Data:* 12/31/2006

Year	Sales	Net Income
2006	$1,027,000	-$3,531,000
2005	$2,784,000	-$3,948,000
2004	$4,181,000	-$1,235,000

Curr. Assets:	$43,000	Curr. Liab.:	$3,286,000		
Plant, Equip.:	$51,000	Total Liab.:	$3,286,000	Indic. Yr. Divd.:	NA
Total Assets:	$101,000	Net Worth:	-$3,185,000	Debt/ Equity:	NA

Nutra Pharma Corp

791 Pk. of Commerce Blvd., Ste. 300, Boca Raton, FL, 33487; *PH:* 1-954-509-0911;
Fax: 1-877-895-5647; *http://* www.nutrapharma.com; *Email:* info@nutrapharma.com

General - Incorporation	CA	Stock- Price on:12/24/2007	$0.065
Employees	3	Stock Exchange	OTC
Auditor	Stark Winter Schenkein & Co. LLP	Ticker Symbol	NPHC
Stk Agt	Atlas Stock Transfer Corp	Outstanding Shares	73,280,000
Counsel	NA	E.P.S	-$0.006
DUNS No.	NA	Shareholders	NA

Business: The group's principal activity is to develop drugs for HIV and multiple sclerosis. The group is a biotechnology holding company that owns non-exclusive license rights to patents and intellectual property related to the development of drugs. These technologies are being developed by receptopharm, inc. The group's subsidiary infectech, inc is engaged in the research and development of diagnostic test kits designed to be used for the rapid identification of infectious human diseases such as tuberculosis (tb) and mycobacterium avium-intracellulare (mai). On 19-Sep-2003, the group acquired infectech inc.

Primary SIC and add'l.: 8731 2834

CIK No: 0001119643

Subsidiaries: Designer Diagnostics, Inc., Receptopharm, Inc

Officers: Rik J. Deitsch/Chmn., CEO, Neil Roth/Pres. - Designer Diagnostics, Inc

Directors: Rik J. Deitsch/Chmn., CEO, Stewart Lonky/Dir., Stanley J. Cherelstein/Dir.

Owners: Insiders/4.10%, Rik J. Deitsch/2.00%, Stewart Lonky, Tanvir Khandaker, Opus International/16.00%, Stanley J. Cherelstein/0.70%

Financial Data: Fiscal Year End:12/31   *Latest Annual Data:* 12/31/2006

Year	Sales	Net Income
2006	$20,000	-$2,431,000
2005	NA	-$5,152,000
2004	NA	-$7,987,000

Curr. Assets:	$30,000	Curr. Liab.:	$1,969,000		
Plant, Equip.:	$38,000	Total Liab.:	$1,969,000	Indic. Yr. Divd.:	NA
Total Assets:	$106,000	Net Worth:	-$1,863,000	Debt/ Equity:	NA

Nutracea

5090 N 40th St., Ste. 400, Phoenix, AZ, 85018; *PH:* 1-602-522-3000; *Fax:* 1-602-522-3001;
http:// www.nutracea.com; *Email:* info@nutracea.com

General - Incorporation	CA	Stock- Price on:12/24/2007	$3.87
Employees	51	Stock Exchange	OTC
Auditor	Malone & Bailey, P.C	Ticker Symbol	NTRZ
Stk Agt	Fidelity Transfer Co	Outstanding Shares	135,630,000
Counsel	NA	E.P.S	-$0.02
DUNS No.	NA	Shareholders	NA

Business: The group's principal activities are to develop and distribute various products based upon the use of stabilized rice bran and proprietary rice bran formulations. These products include various health food supplements and cosmetic and beauty aids. The group also develops and markets rice bran food supplements for animals. The activities of the group are carried out through four divisions: therafoods, nutracea1, nutraglo, and nutrabeauticals. The therafoods division consists of the sale of consumer products such as risolubles(R), ricemucil(R), nutraflex(tm), and stabran(r). The nutracea division consists of distribution of medical foods like synbiotics(tm)1, synbiotics(tm)2 and nutrabetics. The nutraglo division distributes animal products, which prevents and rehabilitates debilitating joint degeneration in horses. The nutrabeauticals(R) division is focused on providing natural products to improve skin health.

Primary SIC and add'l.: 2834

CIK No: 0001063537

Subsidiaries: NutraStar Incorporated, Nutrients, Inc., RiceX Nutrients, Inc., The RiceX Company

Officers: Bradley D. Edson/Dir., CEO, Pres./$183,030.00, Michael Lindsey/Western Dir. - Sales, Equine, Animal Nutrition Division, Leo G. Gingras/COO, Kurt Kreuter/VP - Sales, Food Ingredient Division, Jerry Eggenberger/Central Dir. - Sales, Food Ingredient Division, Bruce Sloan/Western VP - Sales, Food Ingredient Division, Ed Newton/Contact - New Business Development, Food Ingredient

Division, Darin Barney/Dir. - Marketing, Marilyn Meek/Financial Relations Board, Investor Relations, Julie Tu/Financial Relations Board, Investor Relations, Todd C. Crow/CFO/$172,489.00, Margie Adelman/Sr. VP/$170,828.00, Kody Newland/Sr. VP - Sales/$386,526.00, Matthew Butler/VP - Sales, US, International, Equine, Animal Nutrition Division, Ed Dingledine/Eastern Dir. - Sales, Equine, Animal Nutrition Division

Directors: Bradley D. Edson/Dir., CEO, Pres., David Bensol/52/Chmn., Wesley K. Clark/Dir., Jim C. Lintzenich/Dir., Edward L. McMillan/Dir., Steven W. Saunders/Dir., Kenneth L. Shropshire/Dir.

Owners: Kenneth L. Shropshire, Bradley D. Edson/4.36%, Wesley K. Clark, Kody K. Newland, Margie D. Adelman, David S. Bensol, Ike E. Lynch/1.22%, Todd C. Crow/1.10%, Patricia McPeak/9.97%, Insiders/18.30%, Steven W. Saunders, Edward L. McMillan, James C. Lintzenich/2.13%

Financial Data: Fiscal Year End:12/31   *Latest Annual Data:* 12/31/2006

Year	Sales	Net Income
2006	$18,090,000	$1,585,000
2005	$5,564,000	-$3,872,000
2004	$1,224,000	-$23,574,000

Curr. Assets:	$26,201,000	Curr. Liab.:	$2,881,000	P/E Ratio:	193.50
Plant, Equip.:	$8,961,000	Total Liab.:	$2,881,000	Indic. Yr. Divd.:	NA
Total Assets:	$73,255,000	Net Worth:	$64,884,000	Debt/ Equity:	NA

Nutraceutical International Corp

1400 Kearns Blvd., 2nd Fl., Park City, UT, 84060; *PH:* 1-800-669-8877; *Fax:* 1-800-767-8514;
http:// www.nutraceutical.com; *Email:* info@nutraceutical.com

General - Incorporation	DE	Stock- Price on:12/24/2007	$16.46
Employees	660	Stock Exchange	NDQ
Auditor	PricewaterhouseCoopers LLP	Ticker Symbol	NUTR
Stk Agt	American Stock Transfer & Trust Co.	Outstanding Shares	11,020,000
Counsel	Kirkland & Ellis LLP	E.P.S	$1.15
DUNS No.	00-512-7654	Shareholders	NA

Business: The group's principal activities are to manufacture and market nutritional supplements to health and natural food stores. The group also publishes, prints and markets a line of natural health and lifestyle books and booklets, national retail bookstores and health and natural food stores under the name woodland publishing tm. In addition, the group manufactures bulk materials for use in its own pdts and for sale to other manufacturers in the nutritional supplement industry. The products include vitamins and minerals, herbs, specialty formulas and natural foods. The group sells products under the brand names solaray(R), kal(R), nature's life(R), naturalmax(R), veglife(R), premier one(R), sunny green(R), natural sport(R), actipet(R), action labs(R), thompson(R) and funfresh foodstm. On 30-Jun-2003 the group acquired the assets of Arizona health foods inc & m k health food distributors inc, on 14-May-2004, natural balance(R) & on 08-Jun-2004, Montana big skytm

Primary SIC and add'l.: 2834 2833 2741

CIK No: 0001050007

Subsidiaries: A Delaware corporation (fka Makers of KAL,Inc, American Nutritional Casualty,Inc, Au Naturel (Canada),Inc, Au Naturel (Japan),Inc, Au Naturel (Netherlands),Inc, Au Naturel (UK),Inc, Au Naturel,Inc, Fresh Organics,Inc, Fresh To You,Inc, Fresh Vitamins,Inc, FunFresh Foods,Inc, Great Basin Botanicals,Inc, Healthway Corporation, a Delaware corporation, KAL Nutritionals,Inc, M. K Health Food Distributors,Inc 30 Subsidiaries included in the Index

Officers: Frank W. Gay/62/Chmn., CEO, Gary M. Hume/59/Exec. VP, Jeffrey A. Hinrichs/51/Dir., COO, Exec. VP, Sec., Stanley E. Soper/45/VP - Legal Affairs, Cory J. McQueen/39/CFO, VP, Bruce R. Hough/54/Pres., Christopher B. Neuberger/42/VP - Marketing, Sales, Andrew Seelos/41/Assist. VP, Controller

Directors: Frank W. Gay/62/Chmn., CEO, Jeffrey A. Hinrichs/51/Dir., COO, Exec. VP, Sec., Kimo J. Esplin/Dir., Michael D. Burke/Dir., James D. Stice/Dir., Gregory M. Benson/Dir.

Owners: Cory J. McQueen, Burgundy Asset Management Ltd./8.80%, Leslie M. Brown, Gregory M. Benson, Jeffrey A. Hinrichs/2.70%, Dalton, Greiner, Hartman, Maher & Co LLC/8.60%, Insiders/13.50%, Frank W. Gay/8.20%, James D. Stice, Royce & Associates, LLC/12.90%, Michael D. Burke, Kiluva, S.A./5.00%, Kimo J. Esplin, FMR Corp./12.40%, Stanley E. Soper *(16 Owners included in Index)*

Financial Data: Fiscal Year End:09/30   *Latest Annual Data:* 09/30/2007

Year	Sales	Net Income
2007	$156,548,000	$12,972,000
2006	$150,405,000	$14,940,000
2005	$148,187,000	$12,520,000

Curr. Assets:	$44,437,000	Curr. Liab.:	$14,494,000	P/E Ratio:	13.83
Plant, Equip.:	$32,669,000	Total Liab.:	$17,178,000	Indic. Yr. Divd.:	NA
Total Assets:	$107,960,000	Net Worth:	$90,782,000	Debt/ Equity:	0.1727

Nutradyne Inc

Formerly: Digital Learning Mgmt Corp
927 Canada Ct., City Of Industry, CA, 91748; *PH:* 1-626-581-9098

General - Incorporation	DE	Stock- Price on:12/24/2007	$0.055
Employees	2	Stock Exchange	NA
Auditor	Kabani & Co, Inc	Ticker Symbol	NA
Stk Agt	Pacific Stock Transfer Company	Outstanding Shares	65,860,000
Counsel	NA	E.P.S	-$0.02
DUNS No.	NA	Shareholders	NA

Business: The group's principal activity is to provide post secondary education and training in the niche markets such as, information technology and business. Planning to even begin specialized nurses training in future.

Primary SIC and add'l.: 7375

CIK No: 0001087848

Owners: Yongmei Wang/4.00%, Full Spring Group Ltd. BVI/6.00%, Master Power Holdings Coup Ltd./14.00%, Al Jinnah/92.00%, Accord Success Ltd./18.00%, Gregory Frazer/1.00%, Umesh Patel/5.23%, Insiders, Yongkui Liu/18.00%, Grand Opus Co. Ltd., BVI/8.00%, Umesh Patel/5.23%, Craig Nagasugi/46.00%, Brad Stewart/2.12%, Yongxin Liu/2.00%, Faisel H. Khan/1.35%

Financial Data: Fiscal Year End:12/31   *Latest Annual Data:* 12/31/2006

Year	Sales	Net Income
2006	$94,000	-$1,267,000
2005	$164,000	-$3,122,000
2004	$3,711,000	-$6,336,000

Curr. Assets:	$4,000	**Curr. Liab.:**	$6,894,000		
Plant, Equip.:	$11,000	**Total Liab.:**	$6,894,000	**Indic. Yr. Divd.:**	NA
Total Assets:	$17,000	**Net Worth:**	-$6,876,000	**Debt/ Equity:**	NA

NutriSystem Inc

300 Welsh Rd., Bldg. 1, Ste. 100, Horsham, PA, 19044; ***PH:*** 1-215-706-5300; ***Fax:*** 1-215-706-5388; ***http://*** www.nutrisystem.com; ***Email:*** info@nutrisystem.com

General - Incorporation	DE	**Stock**- Price on:12/24/2007	$67.44
Employees	680	Stock Exchange	NDQ
Auditor	KPMG LLP	Ticker Symbol	NA
Stk Agt	StockTrans, Inc.	Outstanding Shares	34,350,000
Counsel	Morgan, Lewis & Bockius LLP	E.P.S	$3.17
DUNS No.	NA	Shareholders	NA

Business: The group's principal activity is to provide a comprehensive weight management program, consisting of support for dieters and a pre-packaged food program. Online support for dieters include individualized diet and exercise plans, online counselling, support groups, bulletin boards and chat rooms. The group also provides relevant information on diet, nutrition, exercise and well being, provided on the Web site and in a weekly newsletter. The group's program allows members to participate conveniently and privately from their own homes or offices. The group currently offers menu customization from over 100 food selections, which have been developed under the guidance of its team of registered nutritionists. The group's pre-packaged foods are now sold to weight loss program participants through the Internet, qvc, independent distributors and the remaining franchised weight loss centers.

Primary SIC and add'l.: 7991 7299

CIK No: 0001096376

Subsidiaries: Nutri/System IPHC, INC., NutriSystem Direct, LLC, NutriSystem Media, LLC, Slim and Tone, LLC

Officers: Michael J. Hagan/Chmn., CEO, Pres./$497,772.00, Bruce Blair/CIO/$768,111.00, James D. Brown/Exec. VP, CFO, Treasurer, Sec./$632,486.00, Thomas Connerty/Exec. VP - Program Development, Chief Marketing Officer/$1,092,661.00, Joseph M. Redling/COO, Pres., Sanjay M. Hurry/Investor Relations Counsel

Directors: Michael J. Hagan/Chmn., CEO, Pres., Ian Berg/Dir., Brian P. Tierney/Dir., Warren V. Musser/Dir., Stephen T. Zarrilli/Dir., Robert Bernstock/Dir., Michael A. Dipiano/Dir., Michael F. Devine/Dir.

Owners: Thomas F. Connerty, Michael J. Hagan/5.30%, Robert F. Bernstock, James D. Brown, Insiders/8.40%, Michael A. DiPiano/1.50%, Warren V. Musser, Brian P. Tierney, Bridger Management, LLC/5.00%, Trafelet& Company, LLC/5.10%, Turner Investments Partners, Inc./6.50%, Ian J. Berg, Stephen T. Zarrilli, Bruce Blair

Financial Data: ***Fiscal Year End:***12/31 ***Latest Annual Data:*** 12/31/2006

Year	Sales	Net Income
2006	$568,209,000	$85,130,000
2005	$212,506,000	$21,015,000
2004	$37,996,000	$1,019,000

Curr. Assets:	$185,783,000	**Curr. Liab.:**	$51,734,000	**P/E Ratio:**	24.70
Plant, Equip.:	$9,374,000	**Total Liab.:**	$52,565,000	**Indic. Yr. Divd.:**	NA
Total Assets:	$197,867,000	**Net Worth:**	$145,302,000	**Debt/ Equity:**	NA

Nutrition 21 Inc

4 Manhattanville Rd., Purchase, NY, 10577; ***PH:*** 1-914-701-4500; ***Fax:*** 1-914-696-0860; ***http://*** www.nutrition21.com; ***Email:*** contactn21@nutrition21.com

General - Incorporation	NY	**Stock**- Price on:12/24/2007	$1.71
Employees	30	Stock Exchange	NDQ
Auditor	J. H. Cohn LLP	Ticker Symbol	NXXI
Stk Agt	American Stock Transfer & Trust Co.	Outstanding Shares	60,370,000
Counsel	NA	E.P.S	-$0.27
DUNS No.	15-061-2844	Shareholders	NA

Business: The group's principal activities are to develop and market clinically substantiated proprietary nutritional products. It operates in two segments, nutritional products and pharmaceutical products while the products are categorized as ingredients and consumer products. Ingredients are proprietary essential trace elements, sold to vitamin and nutritional supplement manufacturers, wholesalers and consumers. They include the chromax (TM) chromium picolinate, a form of the trace mineral chromium. The group is also developing forms of other minerals such as calcium taurate, arginine silicate, magnesium taurate and others. Consumer products consist of applications for the proprietary ingredients. Lite bites(R) is the primary brand of the line and is sold on the qvc television network.

Primary SIC and add'l.: 8731 2834

CIK No: 0000744962

Officers: Paul S. Intlekofer/Dir., CEO, Pres., James Komorowski/VP - Technical Services, Scientific Affairs, Benjamin T. Sporn/General Counsel, Sec., Alan J. Kirschbaum/63/CFO, VP - Finance, Treasury, Dean Dimaria/VP - Sales, Marketing, Mark H. Stenberg/Sr. VP

Directors: Paul S. Intlekofer/Dir., CEO, Pres., John H. Gutfreund/Chmn., Marvin Moser/Dir., Audrey T. Cross/Dir., George P. Benson/Dir., John L. Cassis/Dir., Warren D. Cooper/Dir., Robert Golden/Member - Scientific Advisory Board, Francine R. Kaufman/Member - Scientific Advisory Board, Ronald M. Krauss/Member - Scientific Advisory Board, Louis Ignarro/Member - Scientific Advisory Board, Peter C. Mann/66/Dir.

Owners: George P. Benson, Warren D. Cooper, Audrey T. Cross, Wyeth/5.56%, Peter C. Mann, John L. Cassis/4.99%, Marvin Moser, John H. Gutfreund, Arnold Blair/6.92%, Alan Kirschbaum, Paul Intlekofer/1.95%, Insiders/14.99%, Mark Stenberg/6.92%, Dean DiMaria

Financial Data: ***Fiscal Year End:***06/30 ***Latest Annual Data:*** 6/30/2006

Year	Sales	Net Income
2006	$10,664,000	-$10,317,000
2005	$10,711,000	-$7,044,000
2004	$10,232,000	-$5,901,000

Curr. Assets:	$10,993,000	**Curr. Liab.:**	$11,425,000		
Plant, Equip.:	$64,000	**Total Liab.:**	$18,757,000	**Indic. Yr. Divd.:**	NA
Total Assets:	$34,694,000	**Net Worth:**	$15,937,000	**Debt/ Equity:**	NA

Nutrition Management Services Company

725 Kimberton Rd., Kimberton, PA, 19442; ***PH:*** 1-610-935-2050; ***Fax:*** 1-610-935-8287; ***http://*** www.nmsc.com; ***Email:*** company@nmsc.com

General - Incorporation	PA	**Stock**- Price on:12/24/2007	$0.44
Employees	250	Stock Exchange	OTC
Auditor	Moore Stephens, P.C	Ticker Symbol	NMSCA
Stk Agt	Continental Stock Transfer & Trust Co	Outstanding Shares	2,850,000
Counsel	NA	E.P.S	-$0.31
DUNS No.	09-816-3611	Shareholders	NA

Business: The group's principal activities are to provide professional management expertise and food services to continuing care and health care facilities in the United States. The services include complete management and supervision of the dietary operations in its customers' facilities through the use of on-site management staff, quality and cost-control programs, and training and education of dietary staff. The market for the group's services consists of a large number of facilities involved in various aspects of the continuing care and health care fields, including nursing homes, retirement communities, hospitals and rehabilitation centers.

Primary SIC and add'l.: 8748 8322 8299 5812

CIK No: 0000879303

Subsidiaries: Apple Management Company, Conference and Training Center, Inc

Officers: Joseph V. Roberts/Dir., Chmn., CEO, Kathleen A. Hill/Dir., Pres., Linda J. Haines/Principal Financial Mgr.

Directors: Joseph V. Roberts/Dir., Chmn., CEO, Kathleen A. Hill/Dir., Pres., Michael M. Gosman/Dir., Samuel R. Shipley/Dir., Michelle Roberts-O'Donnell/Dir., Jane Scaccetti/Dir., Richard Kresky/Dir.

Owners: Samuel R. Shipley, Michelle Roberts-ODonnell, Insiders/75.40%, Michael Gosman, Jane Scaccetti, Joseph V. Roberts/74.20%, Kathleen A. Hill/3.70%, Richard Kresky

Financial Data: ***Fiscal Year End:***06/30 ***Latest Annual Data:*** 06/30/2007

Year	Sales	Net Income
2007	$20,912,000	-$771,000
2006	$23,366,000	-$820,000
2005	$26,602,000	$776,000

Curr. Assets:	$4,355,000	**Curr. Liab.:**	$3,668,000		
Plant, Equip.:	$6,637,000	**Total Liab.:**	$9,383,000	**Indic. Yr. Divd.:**	NA
Total Assets:	$13,967,000	**Net Worth:**	$4,585,000	**Debt/ Equity:**	0.5134

Nutritional Sourcing Corp

1300 NW 22nd St., Pompano Beach, FL, 33069; ***PH:*** 1-954-977-2500; ***Fax:*** 1-954-979-5770; ***http://*** www.puebloxtra.com

General - Incorporation	DE	**Stock**- Price on:12/24/2007	NA
Employees	NA	Stock Exchange	NA
Auditor	Deloitte & Touche LLP	Ticker Symbol	NA
Stk Agt	NA	Outstanding Shares	NA
Counsel	NA	E.P.S	NA
DUNS No.	NA	Shareholders	NA

Business: The group's principal activity is to operate supermarkets and video rental stores. As of 01-Nov-2003, the group operated 41 supermarkets in Puerto Rico and 5 supermarkets in the U.S. Virgin islands. In Puerto Rico, the group operates its supermarkets under the names pueblo and puebloxtra. As of 1-Nov-2003, the group also operated 40 in-home movie and game entertainment stores Puerto Rico and 2 in the U.S. Virgin islands. The group operates video rental outlets its franchise rights with blockbuster, inc. The video rental outlets of the group offer a range of recorded and blank video tapes, music compact discs, video game cartridges, self-activated cellular phones, prepaid phone cards, accessories and snack food products.

Primary SIC and add'l.: 5411 7841

CIK No: 0000906307

Nuvasive Inc

4545 Towne Ctr. Ct., San Diego, CA, 92121; ***PH:*** 1-800-455-1476; ***Fax:*** 1-858-909-2000; ***http://*** www.nuvasive.com; ***Email:*** info@nuvasive.com

General - Incorporation	DE	**Stock**- Price on:12/24/2007	$25.81
Employees	233	Stock Exchange	NDQ
Auditor	Ernst & Young LLP	Ticker Symbol	NUVA
Stk Agt	U.S. Stock Transfer Corp	Outstanding Shares	34,520,000
Counsel	NA	E.P.S	-$0.37
DUNS No.	05-395-0783	Shareholders	NA

Business: The group's principal activity is to design, develop and market products for the surgical treatment of spine disorders. The group's principal product offering includes a minimally invasive surgical platform called maximum access surgery (mas), as well as classic fusion products. Mas combines three of its current product offerings-neurovision, a proprietary software-driven nerve avoidance system, maxcess, a split blade-design minimally invasive surgical system and specialized implants-that collectively minimize soft tissue disruption during spine surgery. It provides a surgeon with enhanced visibility and access to the spine for fusion. The group's also offers a portfolio of classic fusion products, including spine allografts and spine implants such as rods, plates and screws that are necessary for a variety of spine surgery procedures. The group became publicly held on 12-May-2004.

Primary SIC and add'l.: 3841

CIK No: 0001142596

Subsidiaries: NuVasive Europe, GmbH, Nuvasive UK Limited

Officers: Alexis V. Lukianov/Chmn., CEO/$2,545,870.00, Keith Valentine/COO, Pres./$1,376,850.00, Kevin C. O'Bolyle/CFO, Exec. VP/$1,035,737.00, Patrick Miles/Sr. VP - Marketing, Development/$933,381.00, Jeffrey Rydin/Sr. VP - US Sales/$1,196,155.00, Jason M. Hannon/Sr. VP, General Counsel, Jonathan D. Spangler/VP, Chief Patent Counsel, Bryan G. Cornawall/VP - Research, Clinical Resources, Lisa Brockman/VP - Accounting

Directors: Alexis V. Lukianov/Chmn., CEO, Robert J. Hunt/Dir., Hansen A. Yuan/Dir., Eileen More/Dir., James C. Blair/Dir., Jack Blair/Dir., Peter C. Farrell/Dir., Lesley H. Howe/Dir.

Owners: Hansen A. Yuan, Delaware Management Holdings/7.58%, Patrick Miles, FMR Corp./14.73%, Insiders/5.53%, Kevin C. OBoyle, Capital Research and Management Company/9.31%, Keith C. Valentine, Jeffrey P. Rydin, Jack R. Blair, James C. Blair, Robert J. Hunt, Alexis V. Lukianov/2.41%, Peter C. Farrell, Lesley H. Howe

Financial Data: Fiscal Year End:12/31 Latest Annual Data: 12/31/2006

Year	Sales	Net Income
2006	$98,091,000	-$47,910,000
2005	$61,789,000	-$30,339,000
2004	$38,403,000	-$14,210,000

Curr. Assets:	$154,718,000	Curr. Liab.:	$18,482,000		
Plant, Equip.:	$30,573,000	Total Liab.:	$19,881,000	Indic. Yr. Divd.:	NA
Total Assets:	$196,184,000	Net Worth:	$176,303,000	Debt/ Equity:	NA

Nuveen Investments Inc

333 W Wacker Dr., Chicago, IL, 60606; **PH:** 1-312-917-7700; **Fax:** 1-312-917-8049;
http:// www.nuveen.com

General - Incorporation	DE	**Stock**- Price on:12/24/2007	$63.16
Employees	828	Stock Exchange	NA
Auditor	KPMG LLP	Ticker Symbol	NA
Stk Agt	Bank of New York	Outstanding Shares	79,440,000
Counsel	NA	E.P.S	$2.36
DUNS No.	04-252-9396	Shareholders	NA

Business: The group's principal activities are asset management and related research and development, marketing and distribution of investment products and services through financial advisors who serve the affluent and high-net-worth market segments. The investment products of the group include mutual funds and exchange-traded funds. These are distributed through registered representatives associated with unaffiliated broker-dealers, commercial banks, affiliates of insurance providers, financial planners, accountants, consultants and investment advisers.

Primary SIC and add'l.: 6282

CIK No: 0000885708

Subsidiaries: Nuveen Asia Investments, Inc., Nuveen Asset Management, Nuveen Commodities Asset Management, LLC, Nuveen Investments Advisers Inc., Nuveen Investments Canada Co., Nuveen Investments Holdings, Inc., Nuveen Investments Institutional Services Group LLC, Nuveen Investments, LLC, NWQ Holdings, LLC, NWQ Investment Management Company, LLC, Rittenhouse Asset Management, Inc., Santa Barbara Asset Management, LLC, Symphony Asset Management LLC, Tradewinds NWQ Global Investors, LLC

Officers: John P. Amboian/Dir., CEO/$10,249,130.00, George P. Webb/MD - Institutional Services Group, Cheryl Wilks/Assist. - Denver, CO, Marcia Nilles/Assist. - Minneapolis, MN, George M. Tharakan/Dir. - Research, Portfolio Mgr., James R. Boothe/Portfolio Mgr., Michael G. Mayfield/Pres., Chief Investment Officer, Brian A. Anderson/Portfolio Mgr., Nancy M. Crouse/MD, Portfolio Mgr., Christopher Leonard/VP - Research Analyst, Mark T. Hackett/VP - Research Analyst, Bridgot S. Basile/Assist. VP - Quantitative Analyst, Robert A. Norton/VP, Portfolio Mgr., Mark E. Devaul/VP - Research Analyst, Daniel C. Roarty/MD, Portfolio Mgr. *(138 Officers included in Index)*

Directors: John P. Amboian/Dir., CEO, Timothy R. Schwertfeger/59/Chmn., Duane R. Kullberg/Dir., Roderick A. Palmore/Dir., Willard L. Boyd/Dir., Connie K. Duckworth/Dir., Pierre E. Leroy/59/Dir.

Owners: Connie K. Duckworth, Glenn R. Richter, Wellington Management Company, LLP/6.20%, William Adams, Timothy R. Schwertfeger/3.60%, Roderick A. Palmore, Alan G. Berkshire, Insiders/7.30%, Willard L. Boyd, Duane R. Kullberg, Alan A. Brown, John P. Amboian/2.40%

Financial Data: Fiscal Year End:12/31 Latest Annual Data: 12/31/2006

Year	Sales	Net Income
2006	$709,828,000	$187,680,000
2005	$589,129,000	$171,156,000
2004	$505,637,000	$156,408,000

Curr. Assets:	$337,895,000	Curr. Liab.:	$259,278,000	P/E Ratio:	26.76
Plant, Equip.:	$33,454,000	Total Liab.:	$892,084,000	Indic. Yr. Divd.:	$0.960
Total Assets:	$1,227,772,000	Net Worth:	$290,719,000	Debt/ Equity:	1.6901

Nuvelo Inc

201 Industrial Rd., Ste. 310, San Carlos, CA, 94070; **PH:** 1-650-517-8000; **Fax:** 1-650-517-8001;
http:// www.nuvelo.com; **Email:** ir@nuvelo.com

General - Incorporation	DE	**Stock** - Price on:12/24/2007	$3.41
Employees	146	Stock Exchange	NDQ
Auditor	KPMG LLP	Ticker Symbol	NUVO
Stk Agt	U.S. Stock Transfer Corp	Outstanding Shares	53,300,000
Counsel	NA	E.P.S	-$1.24
DUNS No.	84-931-7615	Shareholders	NA

Business: The group's principal activity is to undertake the research and development of novel biopharmaceutical protein-based products for the treatment of human disease from its collection of proprietary genes discovered using its high-throughput signature-by-hybridization platform and from genes licensed-in from partners. It is researching several product candidates to treat various serious diseases and medical conditions. These product candidates target several markets, including cardiovascular disease and oncology. The group intends to develop and commercialize these product candidates on its own or in collaboration with other biotechnology or pharmaceutical companies. The group has two segments: nuvelo, which develops and plans to market therapeutic drugs for the treatment of human diseases; and callida, which develops and plans to commercialize the group's sequencing-by-hybridization (sbh) technology. On 31-Jan-2003, the group acquired variagenics, inc.

Primary SIC and add'l.: 2835 8731 3826

CIK No: 0000907654

Subsidiaries: Hyseq Diagnostics, Inc

Officers: Ted W. Love/Chmn., CEO/$3,844,442.00, Michael Levy/Exec. VP - Research, Development/$1,490,688.00, Jill Pergande/VP - Human Resources, Lee Bendekgey/Sr. VP, CFO, General Counsel/$1,166,315.00, Ralph J. Zitnik/VP - Development, Brian S. Kersten/VP - Regulatory Affairs, Quality Assurance, Analytical Sciences, Ward H. Wolff/Sr. VP - Finance/$396,748.00, Shelly D. Guyer/VP - Business Development, Investor Relations

Directors: Ted W. Love/Chmn., CEO, Barry L. Zubrow/Vice Chmn., George B. Rathmann/Chmn. Emeritus, Mary K. Pendergast/Dir., James R. Gavin/Dir., Burton E. Sobel/Dir., Kimberly Popovits/Dir., Mark L. Perry/Dir.

Owners: Ward H. Wolff/17.03%, Lee Bendekgey/16.74%, Insiders/16.81%, Gary S. Titus/16.74%, Michael D. Levy/16.74%, Ted W. Love/16.74%

Financial Data: Fiscal Year End:12/31 Latest Annual Data: 06/30/2007

Year	Sales	Net Income
2007	NA	NA
2006	$3,888,000	-$130,553,000
2005	$545,000	-$71,611,000

Curr. Assets:	$166,335,000	Curr. Liab.:	$43,839,000		
Plant, Equip.:	$11,978,000	Total Liab.:	$114,562,000	Indic. Yr. Divd.:	NA
Total Assets:	$184,405,000	Net Worth:	$69,843,000	Debt/ Equity:	NA

NuVim Inc

12 Rt E 17 N, Ste. 210, Paramus, NJ, 07652; **PH:** 1-201-556-1010; **Fax:** 1-201-556-1012;
http:// www.nuvim.com

General - Incorporation	DE	**Stock**- Price on:12/24/2007	$0.3
Employees	5	Stock Exchange	OTC
Auditor	WithumSmith+Brown, P.C.	Ticker Symbol	NUVM
Stk Agt	American Stock Transfer & Trust Co.	Outstanding Shares	14,410,000
Counsel	NA	E.P.S	-$0.14
DUNS No.	NA	Shareholders	NA

Business: The groups principle activities include producing, marketing and distributing NuVim(R) dietary supplement beverages. The group operates from the United States. The group's quarterly revenue for Sep'07 was 0.18 millions of USD.

Primary SIC and add'l.: 2023 2086 2099

CIK No: 0001170652

Subsidiaries: NuVim, Inc

Officers: Richard P. Kundrat/64/Chmn., CEO, Peter B. Hutt/Special Advisor, Paul Young/Special Advisor, Michael H. Maizes/Special Advisor

Directors: Richard P. Kundrat/64/Chmn., CEO, Calvin Hodock/70/Dir., Stanley H. Moger/69/Dir., Douglas Scott/39/Dir., Peter V. Decrescenzo/56/Dir.

Owners: Insiders/19.29%, Stanley Moger/3.19%, Richard P. Kundrat/11.98%, Cede & Co./11.23%, Calvin L. Hodock, Dick Clark/5.27%, Doug Scott/1.54%, Peter V. DeCrescenzo

Financial Data: Fiscal Year End:12/31 Latest Annual Data: 12/31/2006

Year	Sales	Net Income
2006	$944,000	-$1,779,000
2005	$721,000	-$2,397,000

Curr. Assets:	$469,000	Curr. Liab.:	$976,000		
Plant, Equip.:	$1,000	Total Liab.:	$2,160,000	Indic. Yr. Divd.:	NA
Total Assets:	$625,000	Net Worth:	-$1,534,000	Debt/ Equity:	NA

NVE Corp

11409 Valley View Rd., Eden Prairie, MN, 55344; **PH:** 1-952-829-9217; **Fax:** 1-952-829-9189;
http:// www.nve.com

General - Incorporation	MN	**Stock**- Price on:12/24/2007	$30.51
Employees	48	Stock Exchange	NDQ
Auditor	Ernst & Young LLP	Ticker Symbol	NVEC
Stk Agt	Corporate Stock Transfer, Inc.	Outstanding Shares	4,630,000
Counsel	Moss & Barnett P.A	E.P.S	$1.00
DUNS No.	13-321-9550	Shareholders	NA

Business: The group's principal activity is to develop, produce and distribute components that combine giant magnetoresistance(gmr) materials with integrated circuits. The products of the group include sensors, isolators and magnetoresistive computer memory technology ('mram'). Sensors are combined with integrated circuits deposited in layers to form magnetic field. Isolators eliminate ground noise in communication and are commonly used in communication networks. Magnetoresistive computer memory technology is a nonvolatile memory where the data is stored in the magnetism of thin films of iron, nickel and cobalt and then recovered through the magnetoresistive properties.

Primary SIC and add'l.: 3672 6794 8731 3676 3674

CIK No: 0000724910

Officers: Daniel A. Baker/Dir., CEO, Pres./$201,409.00, Curt A. Reynders/CFO/$112,686.00

Directors: Daniel A. Baker/Dir., CEO, Pres., Terrence W. Glarner/Chmn., Patricia M. Hollister/Dir., Robert H. Irish/Dir., James D. Hartman/Dir.

Owners: Patricia M. Hollister, Daniel A. Baker/4.30%, James D. Hartman, Robert H. Irish, Terrence W. Glarner, Insiders/5.70%, Curt A. Reynders, Citadel Limited Partnership/8.30%

Financial Data: Fiscal Year End:03/31 Latest Annual Data: 3/31/2007

Year	Sales	Net Income
2007	$16,461,000	$4,781,000
2006	$12,171,000	$1,798,000
2005	$11,616,000	$1,758,000

Curr. Assets:	$7,063,000	Curr. Liab.:	$1,122,000	P/E Ratio:	30.51
Plant, Equip.:	$1,038,000	Total Liab.:	$1,122,000	Indic. Yr. Divd.:	NA
Total Assets:	$25,010,000	Net Worth:	$23,888,000	Debt/ Equity:	NA

Nvidia Corp

2701 San Tomas Expwy., Santa Clara, CA, 95050; **PH:** 1-408-486-2000; **Fax:** 1-408-486-2200;
http:// www.nvidia.com

General - Incorporation	DE	**Stock**- Price on:12/24/2007	$42.69
Employees	4,083	Stock Exchange	NDQ
Auditor	PricewaterhouseCoopers LLP	Ticker Symbol	NVDA
Stk Agt	Mellon Investor Services LLC	Outstanding Shares	362,910,000
Counsel	NA	E.P.S	$1.24
DUNS No.	NA	Shareholders	NA

Business: The groups principle activity is to provide visual computing technologies. The groups products include desktops, downloadable games and servers. The group's solutions include ESA, MXM and PCI Express. The group operates from United States.

Primary SIC and add'l.: 7372 3679

CIK No: 0001045810

Subsidiaries: Blue Ash Holdings Limited, Nvidia Bvi Holdings Limited, NVIDIA Development, Inc, NVIDIA GmbH, NVIDIA Graphics Holding Company, NVIDIA Graphics Private Limited, NVIDIA Hong Kong Development Limited, NVIDIA Hong Kong Holdings Limited, NVIDIA Hong Kong Limited, NVIDIA International Holdings, Inc., NVIDIA International, Inc., NVIDIA KK, NVIDIA Ltd., NVIDIA Pty Limited, NVIDIA Semiconductor Holding Company 21 Subsidiaries included in the Index

Officers: Jen-Hsun Huang/Chmn., CEO, Co - Founder/$4,632,002.00, Jonah M. Alben/VP - GPU Engineering, Marvin D. Burkett/CFO/$2,322,151.00, Dwight Diercks/VP - Software Engineering, Joseph D. Greco/VP - Vlsi Engineering, Tommy Lee/VP - Systems, Application Engineering, Philip J. Carmack/Sr. VP - Wireless Media Processor Business Unit, Brian M. Kelleher/Sr. VP - GPU Engineering, Gopal Solanki/Sr. VP - Platform Business Unit, David B. Kirk/Chief Scientist, Frank Fox/VP - Digital Media Processor Engineering, Chris A. Malachowsky/Co - Founder - Nvidia Fellow, Sr. VP - Engineering, Operations, David M. Shannon/Sr. VP, General Counsel, Sec./$1,486,772.00, Jeff D. Fisher/Sr. VP - GPU Business Unit, Michael W. Hara/VP - Investor Relations, Communications *(21 Officers included in Index)*

Directors: Jen-Hsun Huang/Chmn., CEO, Co - Founder, William J. Miller/Dir., Mark L. Perry/Dir., Brooke A. Seawell/Dir., Chris A. Malachowsky/Co - Founder - Nvidia Fellow, Sr. VP - Engineering, Operations, Steven Chu/Dir., Tench Coxe/Dir., James C. Gaither/Dir., Harvey C. Jones/Dir.

Owners: Marvin D. Burkett, William J. Miller, Ajay K. Puri, Jen-Hsun Huang/5.70%, AXA and affiliates/6.80%, Insiders/7.50%, Barclays Global Investors, NA. and Affiliates/10.50%, Tench Coxe, David M. Shannon, Harvey C. Jones, James C. Gaither, Brooke A. Seawell

Financial Data: Fiscal Year End:01/29   Latest Annual Data: 1/28/2007

Year	Sales	Net Income
2007	$3,068,771,000	$448,834,000
2006	$2,375,687,000	$301,176,000
2005	$2,010,033,000	$100,356,000

Curr. Assets:	$1,304,926,000	**Curr. Liab.:**	$421,156,000		
Plant, Equip.:	$178,955,000	**Total Liab.:**	$450,268,000	**Indic. Yr. Divd.:**	NA
Total Assets:	$1,628,536,000	**Net Worth:**	$1,178,268,000	**Debt/ Equity:**	NA

NVR

Plz. America Tower 1, 11700 Plz. America Dr., Ste. 500, Reston, VA, 20190; *PH:* 1-703-956-4000; *Fax:* 1-703-956-4750; *http://* www.nvrinc.com; *Email:* info@nvrinc.com

General - Incorporation	VA	**Stock**- Price on:12/24/2007	$679.99
Employees	4,548	Stock Exchange	AMEX
Auditor	KPMG LLP	Ticker Symbol	NVR
Stk Agt	EquiServe Trust Co N.A	Outstanding Shares	5,610,000
Counsel	Sack & Harris	E.P.S.	$63.18
DUNS No.	80-839-4621	Shareholders	NA

Business: The group's principle activities are carried out through two segments: homebuilding and mortgage banking. The group's homebuilding segment constructs and sells single-family detached homes, townhomes and condominium buildings. Ryan homes, nvhomes and fox ridge homes are the trade names used by the group. The ryan homes and fox ridge homes products are moderately priced and marketed primarily to first-time homeowners and first-time move-up buyers. The nvhomes product is marketed primarily to move-up and upscale buyers. The group's mortgage banking business are conducted through its wholly owned subsidiary, nvr mortgage finance inc. Nvr's mortgage banking business generates revenues primarily from origination fees, gains on sales of loans, title fees, and sales of servicing rights. The group's quarterly revenue for September 2007 was 1,297.69 millions of USD.

Primary SIC and add'l.: 1531 6162 6513

CIK No: 0000906163

Subsidiaries: NVR Funding II, Inc., NVR Funding III, Inc., NVR Mortgage Finance, Inc., NVR Services, Inc., NVR Settlement Services, Inc., RVN, Inc.

Officers: Brian Moyer/Sr. VP - Pittsburgh, PA, Nashville, TN, Cleveland, Dayton, Cincinnati OH, William J. Inman/Pres. - NVR Mortgage Finance, Inc/$1,783,836.00, Paul C. Saville/Principal Executive Officer/$4,157,617.00, Dennis M. Seremet/Principal Financial Officer/$1,750,876.00, Michael Abrams/VP - North Carolina, Robert W. Henley/VP, Controller/$451,732.00, Matt Beck/Regional VP - Virginia, John Duffy/Regional VP - Maryland, John Harper/Regional VP - Philadelphia, PA, Delaware, New Jersey, Jim Brekovsky/Marketing Land Mgr. - Buffalo, Rochester, Syracuse NY, James M. Sack/Sec., General Counsel

Directors: Dwight C. Schar/66/Chmn., Scott C. Bartlett/75/Dir., Robert C. Butler/77/Dir., Timothy M. Donahue/59/Dir., Manuel H. Johnson/59/Dir., William A. Moran/61/Dir., David A. Preiser/51/Dir., George E. Slye/77/Dir., John M. Toups/82/Dir., Paul W. Whetsell/Dir.

Owners: Insiders/19.00%, Manuel H. Johnson, Timothy M. Donahue, George E. Slye, Putnam, LLC/6.70%, Dwight C. Schar/9.40%, Robert C. Butler, Janus Capital Management LLC/5.30%, Scott C. Bartlett, John M. Toups, Paul C. Saville/5.10%, Barclays Global Investors, N.A./12.70%, William J. Inman/2.10%, Dennis M. Seremet/1.20%, David A. Preiser *(17 Owners included in Index)*

Financial Data: Fiscal Year End:12/31   Latest Annual Data: 12/31/2006

Year	Sales	Net Income
2006	$6,156,771,000	$587,412,000
2005	$5,275,097,000	$697,559,000
2004	$4,327,701,000	$523,204,000

Curr. Assets:	$1,301,948,000	**Curr. Liab.:**	$680,252,000	**P/E Ratio:**	10.06
Plant, Equip.:	$41,598,000	**Total Liab.:**	$1,321,734,000	**Indic. Yr. Divd.:**	NA
Total Assets:	$2,473,808,000	**Net Worth:**	$1,152,074,000	**Debt/ Equity:**	0.2396

NWH Inc

156 W 56th St., Ste. 2001, New York, NY, 10019; *PH:* 1-212-582-1212; *http://* www.nwhinc.com

General - Incorporation	DE	**Stock**- Price on:12/24/2007	NA
Employees	NA	Stock Exchange	NA
Auditor	PricewaterhouseCoopers LLP	Ticker Symbol	NA
Stk Agt	Continental Stock Transfer & Trust Co	Outstanding Shares	NA
Counsel	Hahn & Hessen LLP	E.P.S.	NA
DUNS No.	87-904-6480	Shareholders	NA

Business: The group's principal activity is to operate telecommunications, e-commerce and other strategically linked businesses. The group provides links between healthcare providers and payers through its subsidiary electronic network systems, a business-to-business healthcare e-commerce company. It provides a full-cycle suite of payer-driven services and products known as health-e-network that establishes a transaction processing environment for payers, physicians and other healthcare providers,

including hospitals and laboratories. The group's principal customers consist of healthcare providers, such as physicians, hospitals, clinics and billing services and third-party payers, such as indemnity insurers, managed care organizations, preferred provider organizations, claims submitters and state governmental agencies.

Primary SIC and add'l.: 7372 4899

CIK No: 0000915016

Subsidiaries: Anagram International Communications Ltd., Electronic Network Systems, Inc., National Wireless Holdings Inc., NW Media, LLC

Officers: Terrence S. Cassidy/Dir., CEO, Pres., Carl Nicola/Dir. - Investor Relations

Directors: Terrence S. Cassidy/Dir., CEO, Pres., Thomas R. Dibenedetto/Dir., Paul J. Tobin/Dir., Michael A. McManus/Dir.

NWT Uranium Corp

Formerly: Northwestern Mineral Ventures Inc
36 Toronto St., Ste. 1000, Toronto, ON, M5C 2C5; *PH:* 1-866-437-9551;
http:// www.northwestmineral.com

General - Incorporation	ON	**Stock**- Price on:12/24/2007	$1.06
Employees	NA	Stock Exchange	NA
Auditor	McGovern, Hurley, Cunningham LLP	Ticker Symbol	NA
Stk Agt	Equity Transfer & Trust Company	Outstanding Shares	NA
Counsel	NA	E.P.S.	NA
DUNS No.	NA	Shareholders	NA

Business: The groups principle activities include acquiring, developing and exploring uranium, silver and gold properties. The group operates from Western Africa and Niger.

Primary SIC and add'l.: 1000

CIK No: 0001290982

Subsidiaries: Northwestern Mineral Ventures (USA) Inc

Officers: Marek Kreczmer/Dir., CEO, Pres., Bill Thomas/CFO

Directors: Marek Kreczmer/Dir., CEO, Pres., Anton Esterhuizen/Dir., Simon J. Lawrence/Dir., David Subotic/Dir., John P. Lynch/Dir.

Financial Data: Fiscal Year End:12/31   Latest Annual Data: 12/31/2005

Year	Sales	Net Income
2005	NA	-$1,862,000
2004	NA	-$1,538,000

Curr. Assets:	$1,522,000	**Curr. Liab.:**	$147,000	**P/E Ratio:**	16.00
Plant, Equip.:	$6,000	**Total Liab.:**	$147,000	**Indic. Yr. Divd.:**	NA
Total Assets:	$1,528,000	**Net Worth:**	$1,382,000	**Debt/ Equity:**	NA

NxStage Medical Inc

439 S Union St., 5th Fl., Lawrence, MA, 01843; *PH:* 1-978-687-4700; *Fax:* 1-978-687-4809;
http:// www.nxstage.com

General - Incorporation	DE	**Stock**- Price on:12/24/2007	$12.6
Employees	208	Stock Exchange	NDQ
Auditor	Ernst & Young LLP	Ticker Symbol	NXTM
Stk Agt	Computershare Shareholder Ser Inc	Outstanding Shares	29,920,000
Counsel	NA	E.P.S.	NA
DUNS No.	NA	Shareholders	NA

Business: The groups principle activities include developing, manufacturing and marketing medical systems. The group products sold under the trade name NxStage System One(TM). The groups services include Medicare and Medicaid. The group operates from the United States. The group's quarterly revenue for September 2007 was 11.62 millions of USD.

Primary SIC and add'l.: 3841 3845 3842

CIK No: 0001333170

Subsidiaries: EIR Medical, Inc, NxStage GmbH & Co. KG, NxStage Verwaltungs GmbH

Officers: Jeffrey H. Burbank/Dir., CEO, Pres., Robert S. Brown/CFO, Alan R. Hull/Member - Chronic Therapy Scientific Advisory Board, Philip R. Licari/COO, Sr. VP, Michael A. Kraus/Member - Chronic Therapy Scientific Advisory Board, Allan Collins/Member - Chronic Therapy Scientific Advisory Board, Frederic Finkelstein/Member - Chronic Therapy Scientific Advisory Board, Joel Glickman/Member - Chronic Therapy Scientific Advisory Board, Bertrand L. Jaber/Member - Chronic Therapy Scientific Advisory Board, Winifred L. Swan/Sr. VP, General Counsel, James McCarthy/Member - Chronic Therapy Scientific Advisory Board, Brent Miller/Member - Chronic Therapy Scientific Advisory Board, Agustin M. Azel/Sr. VP - Manufacturing, Joseph E. Turk/Sr. VP - Commercial Operations, Michael J. Webb/Sr. VP - Quality, Regulatory, Clinical Affairs

Directors: Jeffrey H. Burbank/Dir., CEO, Pres., Philippe Chambon/Chmn., David S. Utterberg/Dir., Peter Phildius/Dir., Daniel A. Giannini/Dir., Craig Moore/Dir., Reid S. Perper/Dir.

Owners: T. Rowe Price Associates, Inc./6.10%, Peter P. Phildius, Insiders/47.60%, Federated Investors, Inc./6.90%, David S. Utterberg/23.40%, Philippe O. Chambon/16.30%, Joseph E. Turk, Credit Suisse/17.00%, Craig W. Moore, Philip R. Licari, Daniel A. Giannini, Reid S. Perper/3.60%, Jeffrey H. Burbank/2.30%, Atlas Venture entities/7.10%, Winifred L. Swan

Financial Data: Fiscal Year End:12/31   Latest Annual Data: 3/31/2007

Year	Sales	Net Income
2007	NA	NA
2006	NA	NA
2005	$5,994,000	-$24,480,000

Curr. Assets:	$77,677,000	**Curr. Liab.:**	$13,310,000		
Plant, Equip.:	$23,642,000	**Total Liab.:**	$18,316,000	**Indic. Yr. Divd.:**	NA
Total Assets:	$101,725,000	**Net Worth:**	$83,408,000	**Debt/ Equity:**	NA

Nyer Medical Group Inc

1292 Hammond St., Bangor, ME, 04401; *PH:* 1-207-942-5273; *Fax:* 1-207-941-9392;
http:// www.nyermedicalgroup.com; *Email:* info@nyermedicalgroup.com

General - Incorporation	FL	**Stock**- Price on:12/24/2007	$2.01
Employees	128	Stock Exchange	NDQ
Auditor	Sweeney, Gates & Co	Ticker Symbol	NYER
Stk Agt	Continental Stock Transfer & Trust Co	Outstanding Shares	3,980,000
Counsel	NA	E.P.S.	$0.01
DUNS No.	79-362-6029	Shareholders	NA

Business: The group's principal activity is to provide medical products and services, distributes equipment and supplies novelty items to emergency medical service companies, fire and police departments. The group operates through three segments namely: diabetic, medical and surgical supplies, emt, fire, police equipment and supplies and pharmacy chain. The group's interactive Website, medicalmailorder.com aids consumers in fulfilling their medical needs. The products offered by the group include fire, police and rescue equipment, blood glucose meters, test strips, lancets and penlets, control solutions and other products to individual diabetics directly at their homes, surgical and diagnostic equipment.

Primary SIC and add'l.: 5912 5047 3841

CIK No: 0000884647

Subsidiaries: ADCO South Medical Supplies, Inc., ADCO Surgical Supply, Inc., Anton Investments, Inc., Conway Associates Inc, D.A.W., Inc.

Officers: Karen L. Wright/46/Dir., CEO, Pres.

Directors: Karen L. Wright/46/Dir., CEO, Pres., Robert Landis/49/Dir., Donald C. Lewis/70/Dir., Kenneth L. Nyer/50/Dir., James Schweiger/73/Dir., Gerald Weston/66/Dir.

Owners: Insiders/6.50%, Samuel Nyer/100.00%, Samuel Nyer/38.30%, Mark Dumouchel/100.00%, Gerald Weston, James J. Schweiger/1.00%, Donald C. Lewis/1.50%, Mark Dumouchel/38.30%, Karen L. Wright/1.70%, Around the Clock Partners, LP/10.60%, Samuel Nyer/100.00%, Mark Dumouchel/100.00%, Kenneth L. Nyer/1.90%, Donato Mazzola, Robert J. Landis *(16 Owners included in Index)*

Financial Data: Fiscal Year End: 06/30   **Latest Annual Data:** 06/30/2007

Year	Sales		Net Income
2007	$69,908,000		$86,000
2006	$63,597,000		$858,000
2005	$61,184,000		$224,000
Curr. Assets:	$12,750,000	**Curr. Liab.:**	$5,181,000	**P/E Ratio:** 14.36
Plant, Equip.:	$1,491,000	**Total Liab.:**	$5,473,000	**Indic. Yr. Divd.:** NA
Total Assets:	$15,450,000	**Net Worth:**	$8,329,000	**Debt/ Equity:** 0.0180

Nyfix Inc

100 Wall St., 26th Fl., New York, NY, 10005; **PH:** 1-646-525-3000; **Fax:** 1-212-809-1013; **http://** www.nyfix.com; **Email:** info@nyfix.com

General - Incorporation	DE	Stock- Price on:12/24/2007	$6.5
Employees	NA	Stock Exchange	OTC
Auditor	Friedman LLP	Ticker Symbol	NYFX
Stk Agt	Mellon Investor Services LLC	Outstanding Shares	NA
Counsel	Olshan Grundman Frome Et Al	E.P.S.	-$1.37
DUNS No.	78-288-1908	Shareholders	NA

Business: The group's principal activity is to provide electronic trading technology infrastructure and execution services to the professional trading segment of the brokerage industry. The group operates in two segments: technology services and transaction services. Technology services segment provides desktop solutions, wireless exchange floor systems, electronic automation systems and straight through processing to the professional trading segment of the brokerage community. Transaction services segment provides an electronic order routing and matching environment, anonymous order matching and executing services for existing technology customers and Web-based desktop users, and execution and smart order routing solutions. It operates in stamford, New York, Chicago, london and san francisco. On 01-Jul-2003, the group acquired renaissance trading technologies inc and on 29-Mar-2004, it acquired eurolink network inc.

Primary SIC and add'l.: 7389 6719 7373

CIK No: 0000099047

Subsidiaries: EuroLink Network, Inc, Javelin Technologies, Inc., NYFIX Clearing Corporation., NYFIX International, Ltd., NYFIX Millennium LLC, NYFIX Overseas, Inc., NYFIX Partners, Inc., NYFIX Transaction Services, Inc., Nyfix Usa, LLC., Renaissance Trading Technologies, LLC

Officers: Howard P. Edelstein/Dir., CEO/$509,923.00, Brian Bellardo/General Counsel/$404,055.00, Steven R. Vigliotti/CFO/$599,292.00, Don Duffy/Integrated Corporate Relations, Scott A. Bloom/42/Exec. VP - Corporate Development, Chief Administrative Officer, Sec., Brian Prenoveau/Integrated Corporate Relations, Donald P. Henderson/44/CTO, Brennan W. Carley/47/Exec. VP, Head - Business Operations, Chief Strategy Officer, David A. Merrill/47/Exec. VP, Chief - Client Operations

Directors: Howard P. Edelstein/Dir., CEO, Lon Gorman/Chmn., Mitchel A. Lenson/54/Dir., William J. Lynch/Dir., Richard Y. Roberts/Dir., William C. Jennings/Dir., George O. Deehan/Dir., Thomas C. Wajnert/Dir., Cary J. Davis/Dir., William H. Janeway/Dir., Michael J. Passarella/67/Dir.

Owners: Lars Kragh, William Lynch, Insiders, Insiders, Howard P. Edelstein, William Janeway, Cary Davis, Thomas Wajnert, Warburg Pincus Private Equity IX, LP, Wellington Management Company, LLP, George Deehan, Frank E. Lawatsch, Brian Bellardo, Robert Gasser, William Jennings *(18 Owners included in Index)*

Financial Data: Fiscal Year End: 12/31   **Latest Annual Data:** 12/31/2006

Year	Sales		Net Income
2006	$98,353,000		-$12,904,000
2005	$97,617,000		-$6,417,000
2004	$75,135,000		-$32,702,000
Curr. Assets:	$546,947,000	**Curr. Liab.:**	$454,420,000	
Plant, Equip.:	$14,808,000	**Total Liab.:**	$465,955,000	**Indic. Yr. Divd.:** NA
Total Assets:	$629,328,000	**Net Worth:**	$163,373,000	**Debt/ Equity:** 0.1219

Nymagic Inc

919 3rd Ave., 10th Fl., New York, NY, 10022; **PH:** 1-212-551-0600; **Fax:** 1-212-986-1310; **http://** www.nymagic.com

General - Incorporation	NY	Stock- Price on:12/24/2007	$42.12
Employees	146	Stock Exchange	NYSE
Auditor	KPMG LLP	Ticker Symbol	NYM
Stk Agt	Mellon Investor Services LLC	Outstanding Shares	8,880,000
Counsel	Lane & Mittendorf	E.P.S.	$3.661
DUNS No.	61-030-8074	Shareholders	NA

Business: The group's principal activities are to underwrite insurance. The group underwrites ocean marine, inland marine, aircraft and other liability insurance through insurance pools managed by mutual marine office inc, pacific mutual marine office inc and mutual marine office of the midwest inc. The group accepts, on behalf of the pools, insurance risks brought to the pools by brokers and others. All

premiums, losses and expenses are prorated among the pool members in accordance with their percentage participation in the pools. The group also participates in the risks underwritten for the pools through New York marine and general insurance company and gotham insurance company. The operations are carried on in the United States, Europe, Asia and Latin America.

Primary SIC and add'l.: 6331 6719

CIK No: 0000847431

Subsidiaries: Gotham Insurance Company, MMO EU, Ltd., Mutual Marine Office of the Midwest, Inc., Mutual Marine Office, Inc., New York Marine And General Insurance Company, Pacific Mutual Marine Office, Inc.

Officers: Mark Blackman/56/Chief Underwriting Officer - Insurance Inquiries, Mutual Marine Office, Midwest, Surety/$867,690.00, Tom Iacopelli/CFO - Pacific Mutual Marine Office/$489,655.00, Diane Votinelli/VP - Human Resources, Mutual Marine Office, Midwest, Molly Singh/Insurance Inquiries - Ocean Marine, Hull, Liability, Nick Chen/Insurance Inquiries - Professional Liability, Mutual Marine Office, Midwest, Dianne Competiello/Insurance Inquiries - Ocean Marine, Cargo, Pacific Mutual Marine Office, Matt Rubin/Insurance Inquiries - Property, Inland Marine, Mutual Marine Office, Midwest, Timothy Crowe/Insurance Inquiries - Casualty, Pacific Mutual Marine Office, Ozzie Rodriguez/Insurance Inquiries - Energy, Mutual Marine Office, Midwest

Owners: Mark W. Blackman/10.83%, William D. Shaw, Robert G. Simses/10.33%, David E. Hoffman, George R. Trumbull/4.59%, Dimensional Fund Advisors, Inc./7.37%, Paul J. Hart, Royce & Associates, Inc./10.73%, Louise B. Tollefson/10.93%, Lionshead Investments, LLC/5.35%, Mark W. Blackman/11.72%, Mariner Partners, Inc., et al./15.50%, Louise B. Tollefson/9.93%, John R. Anderson, David W. Young *(24 Owners included in Index)*

Financial Data: Fiscal Year End: 12/31   **Latest Annual Data:** 12/31/2006

Year	Sales		Net Income
2006	$200,467,000		$29,850,000
2005	$171,344,000		$9,701,000
2004	$142,941,000		$14,631,000
Curr. Assets:	$566,417,000	**Curr. Liab.:**	$45,582,000	**P/E Ratio:** 11.51
Plant, Equip.:	$9,950,000	**Total Liab.:**	$848,597,000	**Indic. Yr. Divd.:** $0.320
Total Assets:	$1,119,296,000	**Net Worth:**	$270,700,000	**Debt/ Equity:** 0.3694

Nymex Holdings Inc

1 N End Ave., World Financial Ctr., New York, NY, 10282; **PH:** 1-212-299-2000; **Fax:** 1-212-301-4623; **http://** www.nymex.com

General - Incorporation	DE	Stock- Price on:12/24/2007	$136.49
Employees	500	Stock Exchange	NYSE
Auditor	KPMG LLP	Ticker Symbol	NMX
Stk Agt	American Stock Transfer & Trust Co.	Outstanding Shares	92,080,000
Counsel	NA	E.P.S.	$2.24
DUNS No.	NA	Shareholders	NA

Business: The groups principle activity is to explore energy and precious metals. The group operates through two divisions include NYMEX and COMEX. The group operates from United States.

Primary SIC and add'l.: NA

CIK No: 0001105018

Subsidiaries: Commodity Exchange, Inc, Commodity Exchange, Inc., New York Mercantile Exchange, Inc, New York Mercantile Exchange, Inc., NYMEX Europe Exchange Holdings Limited

Officers: James Newsome/Dir., CEO, Pres./$2,984,625.00, Ellen Steuerer/VP - Contract Administration, Financial Services, Sean Keating/Sr. VP - Clearing Services, Samuel Gaer/CIO/$1,165,747.00, Christopher Bowen/General Counsel, Chief Administrative Officer/$1,078,208.00, Thomas F. Lasala/Chief Regulatory Officer, Robert Levin/Sr. VP - Research, Joseph Raia/Sr. VP - Marketing, Donna Talamo/VP, Assist. Corp. Sec., Ian Wall/Sr. VP - Technology, Daniel Brusstar/VP - Research, Anthony Di Benedetto/VP - Clearing, Keil Decker/VP - Corporate Communications, Investor Relations, Deana Dow/VP - Counsel, Legislative, Regulatory Affairs, Mark Francetic/VP - Software Development *(38 Officers included in Index)*

Directors: James Newsome/Dir., CEO, Pres., Richard Schaeffer/Chmn., Robert Halper/Vice Chmn., William Ford/Dir., William Maxwell/Dir., Melvyn J. Falis/Public Dir., Harvey Gralla/Dir., Stephen Ardizzone/Dir., Frank Siciliano/Dir., Daniel Rappaport/Dir., Neil Citrone/Dir., Thomas Gordon/Dir., Dennis Suskind/Public Dir., Robert Steele/Public Dir., George A. Gero/Dir.

Owners: Mitchell Steinhause, Kenneth Shifrin, George A. Gero/7.88%, Investment entities affiliated with General Atlantic LLC/7.88%, Frank Siciliano, David Greenberg, Thomas Gordon, Richard Schaeffer, William Maxwell, Stephen Ardizzone, Robert Halper, Daniel Rappaport, Harvey Gralla, William Ford, Samuel Gaer *(16 Owners included in Index)*

Financial Data: Fiscal Year End: 12/31   **Latest Annual Data:** 12/31/2006

Year	Sales		Net Income
2006	$497,249,000		$154,801,000
2005	$346,561,000		$71,128,000
2004	$241,325,000		$27,367,000
Curr. Assets:	$3,118,676,000	**Curr. Liab.:**	$2,632,909,000	**P/E Ratio:** 77.55
Plant, Equip.:	$183,193,000	**Total Liab.:**	$2,849,009,000	**Indic. Yr. Divd.:** $0.400
Total Assets:	$3,623,931,000	**Net Worth:**	$774,922,000	**Debt/ Equity:** NA

Nymox Pharmaceutical Corp

Nymox Corporation, 230 W Passaic St., Maywood, NJ, 07607; **Fax:** 1-514-332-2227; **http://** www.nymox.com; **Email:** info@nymox.com

General - Incorporation	Canada	Stock- Price on:12/24/2007	$5.95
Employees	16	Stock Exchange	NDQ
Auditor	KPMG LLP	Ticker Symbol	NYMX
Stk Agt	CT Corporation System	Outstanding Shares	28,720,000
Counsel	NA	E.P.S.	-$0.18
DUNS No.	25-330-7326	Shareholders	NA

Business: The group's principle activities include researching and developing neurological diagnostics and pharmaceuticals for the aging population with emphasis on alzheimer's disease. The group operates from United States.

Primary SIC and add'l.: 2834

CIK No: 0001018735

Subsidiaries: Nymox Corporation, Serex Inc

Officers: Paul Averback/Chmn., CEO, Pres., Celine Dupuis/49/Chief Clinical Officer, Jack Gemmell/Dir., General Counsel, CIO, Brian Doyle/53/Sr. Mgr. Global Sales - Marketing, Roy M. Wolvin/Sec., Treasurer, CFO

Directors: Paul Averback/Chmn., CEO, Pres., Jack Gemmell/Dir., General Counsel, CIO, Randall Lanham/Dir., Paul F. McDonald/Dir., David Morse/Dir., Roger Guy/Dir.

Owners: Roy Wolvin, Brian Doyle, David Morse, Celine Dupuis/3.00%, Insiders/48.90%, Paul Averback/45.70%, Jack Gemmell, Roger Guy

Financial Data: Fiscal Year End:12/31 Latest Annual Data: 12/31/2006

Year	Sales	Net Income
2006	$443,000	-$4,894,000
2005	$426,000	-$3,609,000
2004	$322,000	-$3,771,000

Curr. Assets:	$379,000	Curr. Liab.:	$2,115,000		
Plant, Equip.:	$8,000	Total Liab.:	$4,369,000	Indic. Yr. Divd.:	NA
Total Assets:	$5,386,000	Net Worth:	$1,016,000	Debt/ Equity:	NA

NYSE Group Inc

11 Wall St., New York, NY, 10005; *PH:* 1-212-656-3000; *http://* www.nyse.com

General - Incorporation	DE	Stock- Price on:12/24/2007	$78.93
Employees	2,578	Stock Exchange	NA
Auditor	PricewaterhouseCoopers LLP	Ticker Symbol	NA
Stk Agt	Wells Fargo Shareowner Services	Outstanding Shares	263,900,000
Counsel	NA	E.P.S	NA
DUNS No.	NA	Shareholders	NA

Business: The groups principle activity is to provide securities listing, trading and related information products and services. The group operates through two segments namely, market and regulation. The group operates from the United States.

Primary SIC and add'l.: 6200

CIK No: 0001326579

Subsidiaries: ARCA GNC Acquisition, L.L.C., Archipelago Direct, L.L.C., Archipelago Europe, Ltd, Archipelago Holdings, Inc., Archipelago Market Data Services, L.L.C., Archipelago Securities, L.L.C., Archipelago Trading Services, Inc., Jefferson Merger Sub, Inc., NASD/NYSE Trade Reporting Facility LLC, New York Stock Exchange, New York Stock Exchange LLC, New York Stock Exchange, Inc., Newex Corporation, Newin Corporation, NYSE Arca Equities, Inc. 30 Subsidiaries included in the Index

Officers: John A. Thain/53/Dir., CEO, Jan-Michiel Hessels/65/Chmn. - Nyse Euronext, Margaret D. Tutwiler/57/Exec. VP - Communications, Gov Relations, Rachel F. Robbins/General Counsel, Corp. Sec., Dale B. Bernstein/53/Exec. VP - Human Resources, Catherine R. Kinney/Co - COO, Pres., Gerald D. Putnam/49/Co - COO, Pres., Nelson Chai/CFO, Exec. VP, Lawrence Leibowitz/48/Co - COO, Exec. VP

Directors: John A. Thain/53/Dir., CEO, Marshall N. Carter/67/Chmn., Ellyn L. Brown/Dir., William E. Ford/Dir., Shirley Ann Jackson/Dir., James S. McDonald/Dir., Duncan M. McFarland/Dir., James J. McNulty/Dir., Alice M. Rivlin/77/Dir., Robert B. Shapiro/Dir., Karl M. Von Der Heyden/Dir.

Owners: Alice M. Rivlin, Shirley Ann Jackson, Marshall N. Carter, Ellyn L. Brown, Robert B. Shapiro, Nelson Chai, Insiders, Gerald D. Putnam, James S. McDonald, John A. Thain, Atticus Capital LP/6.40%, William E. Ford, James J. McNulty, Investment entities affiliated with General Atlantic LLC/5.20%, Karl M. von der Heyden *(17 Owners included in Index)*

Financial Data: Fiscal Year End:12/31 Latest Annual Data: 12/31/2006

Year	Sales	Net Income
2006	$2,375,950,000	$204,977,000

Curr. Assets:	$1,443,068,000	Curr. Liab.:	$832,193,000		
Plant, Equip.:	$378,128,000	Total Liab.:	$1,796,523,000	Indic. Yr. Divd.:	$0.250
Total Assets:	$3,465,542,000	Net Worth:	$1,669,019,000	Debt/ Equity:	NA

O Reilly Automotive Inc

233 S Patterson, Springfield, MO, 65802; *PH:* 1-417-862-6708; *Fax:* 1-417-874-7163; *http://* www.oreillyauto.com

General - Incorporation	MO	Stock- Price on:12/24/2007	$36.84
Employees	17,153	Stock Exchange	NDQ
Auditor	Ernst & Young LLP	Ticker Symbol	ORLY
Stk Agt	UMB Bank, N.A.	Outstanding Shares	114,130,000
Counsel	Gallop, Johnson & Neuman LC	E.P.S	$1.67
DUNS No.	03-114-1534	Shareholders	NA

Business: The groups principle activity is to operate auto parts retail stores. The groups product line includes new and remanufactured automotive hard parts, accessories, and a line of auto body paint and related materials, automotive tools and professional service equipment. The groups services include battery testing, drum/rotor resurfacing and fluid recycling services. The group operates from United States.

Primary SIC and add'l.: 5531

CIK No: 0000898173

Subsidiaries: Greene County Realty Co., Hi-LO Investment Company, Hi-LO Management Company, OReilly II Aviation, Inc., Ozark Automotive Distributors, Inc., Ozark Services, Inc.

Officers: Greg Henslee/Co - CEO, Pres./$1,036,776.00, Tricia Headley/VP, Corp. Sec., Ted Wise/Co - COO, Pres./$1,207,789.00, Tom McFall/CFO, Exec. VP - Finance/$341,474.00, Brett Heintz/VP - Retail Systems, James R. Batten/Treasurer/$335,861.00, Kenny Martin/VP - Northern Division, Brad Beckham/VP - Eastern Division, Barry Sabor/VP - Loss Prevention, Jeff Shaw/VP - Store Sales, Operations/$219,342.00, Randy Johnson/VP - Store Inventories, Charlie Downs/VP - Real Estate, Wayne Price/VP - Risk Management, Greg Johnson/VP - Distribution Operations, Gregory A. Beck/VP - Purchasing *(27 Officers included in Index)*

Directors: David OReilly/58/Chmn., Lawrence P. OReilly/61/Vice Chmn., Charles H. OReilly/68/Vice Chmn., Rosalie OReilly-Wooten/66/Dir., John Murphy/57/Dir., Paul R. Lederer/69/Dir., Joe C. Greene/71/Dir., Jay D. Burchfield/61/Dir., Ronald Rashkow/67/Dir.

Owners: Wasatch Advisors, Inc./6.50%, Joe C. Greene, Paul R. Lederer, Ted F. Wise, Thomas G. McFall, John Murphy, Rosalie O'Reilly-Wooten/1.40%, David E. O'Reilly/2.70%, Jeff Shaw, Greg Henslee, Insiders/7.40%, Jay D. Burchfield, Ronald Rashkow, Lawrence P. O'Reilly, T. Rowe Price Associates, Inc./8.60% *(18 Owners included in Index)*

Financial Data: Fiscal Year End:12/31 Latest Annual Data: 12/31/2006

Year	Sales	Net Income
2006	$2,283,222,000	$178,085,000
2005	$2,045,318,000	$164,266,000
2004	$1,721,241,000	$139,566,000

Curr. Assets:	$1,000,676,000	Curr. Liab.:	$433,784,000	P/E Ratio:	22.60
Plant, Equip.:	$883,095,000	Total Liab.:	$613,400,000	Indic. Yr. Divd.:	NA
Total Assets:	$1,977,496,000	Net Worth:	$1,364,096,000	Debt/ Equity:	0.0706

O'Charley's Inc

3038 Sidco Dr., Nashville, TN, 37204; *PH:* 1-615-256-8500; *http://* www.ocharleys.com

General - Incorporation	TN	Stock- Price on:12/24/2007	$19.99
Employees	25,000	Stock Exchange	NDQ
Auditor	KPMG LLP	Ticker Symbol	CHUX
Stk Agt	Wachovia Bank N.A	Outstanding Shares	23,900,000
Counsel	NA	E.P.S	$0.49
DUNS No.	10-176-5436	Shareholders	NA

Business: The group's principle activities are to own and operate full-service restaurant facilities. It operates in two segments: restaurant sales and commissary sales. Its restaurants are casual dining restaurants that cater to mainstream casual dining customers as well as upscale casual dining and value-oriented customers. As of 28-Dec-2003, the group operates 293 restaurants and six stoney river legendary steaks in various parts of United States. The group also operates a commissary, which services its restaurants and sells food products and supplies to retail grocery chains, mass merchandisers and wholesales clubs. The groups' quarterly revenue for September 2007 was 220.90 millions of USD.

Primary SIC and add'l.: 5411 6794 5812

CIK No: 0000864233

Subsidiaries: 99 Commissary, LLC, a Delaware, 99 Restaurants of Boston, LLC, Delaware, 99 Restaurants of Massachusetts, Massachusetts, 99 Restaurants of Vermont, LLC, Vermont, 99 Restaurants, LLC, Delaware, 99 West, Inc., Massachusetts, Air Travel Services, Inc., DFI, Inc., JFC Enterprises, LLC, Delaware, O'Charley's Finance Company, Inc., Tennessee, O'Charley's Restaurant Properties, LLC, Delaware, O'Charley's Service Company, Inc., Tennessee, O'Charley's Sports Bar, Inc., Alabama, OCI, Inc., Delaware, OPI, Inc., Colorado 25 Subsidiaries included in the Index

Officers: Gregory L. Burns/Chmn., CEO/$1,420,214.00, John R. Grady/Ninety Nine Concept Pres./$686,104.00, Stephen W. McMillen/VP - Human Resources Development, Lawrence E. Hyatt/CFO, Sec., Treasurer/$783,821.00, Colin M. Daly/Sr. Corporate Counsel, Anthony J. Halligan/Stoney River Concept Pres., Jeff D. Warne/O'charley's Concept Pres./$917,964.00, Jeffrey R. Williams/Chief Accounting Officer, Corporate Controller, Principal Accounting Officer, Lawrence D. Taylor/Chief Supply Chain Officer

Directors: Gregory L. Burns/Chmn., CEO, Dale Polley/Dir., Shirley A. Zeitlin/Dir., Robert J. Walker/Dir., John E. Stokely/Dir., William F. Andrews/Dir., Richard Reiss/Dir., Nicholas G. Spiva/Dir., Steve H. Tidwell/Dir.

Owners: John R. Grady, Robert J. Walker, Gregory L. Burns/2.70%, Dimensional Fund Advisors Inc./8.10%, John E. Stokely, Dale W. Polley, Steve H. Tidwell, Bank of America Corporation/6.30%, Lawrence E. Hyatt, Randall C. Harris, Nicholas G. Spiva, Jeffrey D. Warne, William F. Andrews, Shirley A. Zeitlin, Insiders/6.00% *(16 Owners included in Index)*

Financial Data: Fiscal Year End:12/25 Latest Annual Data: 12/31/2006

Year	Sales	Net Income
2006	$989,524,000	$18,890,000
2005	$930,188,000	$11,878,000
2004	$871,386,000	$23,319,000

Curr. Assets:	$80,749,000	Curr. Liab.:	$110,343,000	P/E Ratio:	33.88
Plant, Equip.:	$464,107,000	Total Liab.:	$305,686,000	Indic. Yr. Divd.:	$0.240
Total Assets:	$686,512,000	Net Worth:	$380,826,000	Debt/ Equity:	0.3624

O2 Secure Wireless Inc

4898 S Old Peachtree Rd. , Norcross, GA, 30071; *PH:* 1-678-942-0684; *http://* www.o2securewireless.com; *Email:* investors@o2securewireless.net

General - Incorporation	GA	Stock- Price on:12/24/2007	$0.1
Employees	8	Stock Exchange	OTC
Auditor	Braverman International, P.C.	Ticker Symbol	OTOW
Stk Agt	Stalt, Inc.	Outstanding Shares	26,180,000
Counsel	NA	E.P.S	-$0.03
DUNS No.	NA	Shareholders	NA

Business: The groups principle activity is to provide Wi Fi Internet Service Provider. The group provides wireless Internet service to five multi dwelling units in Atlanta, Georgia, three in Charlotte, North Carolina, and one in Tampa, Florida. In July 2005, the group acquired Epiphony Voice Solutions, LLC. The group operates from the Southeastern United States.

Primary SIC and add'l.: 4813

CIK No: 0001326852

Subsidiaries: Epiphony Voice Solutions, LLC

Officers: Craig C. Sellars/Dir., CEO/$80,000.00, India C. Creery/Interim CFO, Juan Ferreira/Investor Relations Contact

Directors: Craig C. Sellars/Dir., CEO, Kendrick Armistead/Member - Advisory Board, Scott T. Conley/Dir., Keith A. Greaves/Dir., Marjorie Singley-Hall/Member - Advisory Board, Terri Theisen/Member - Advisory Board, Lance Wetherby/Member - Advisory Board

Owners: Scott T. Conley/20.80%, Insiders/20.10%, Keith A. Greaves/17.30%, Craig C. Sellars/2.80%

Financial Data: Fiscal Year End:09/30 Latest Annual Data: 9/30/2006

Year	Sales	Net Income
2006	$212,000	-$847,000

Curr. Assets:	$526,000	Curr. Liab.:	$108,000		
Plant, Equip.:	$491,000	Total Liab.:	$108,000	Indic. Yr. Divd.:	NA
Total Assets:	$1,022,000	Net Worth:	$913,000	Debt/ Equity:	NA

O2Diesel Inc

100 Commerce Dr., Newark, DE, 19713; *PH:* 1-302-266-6000; *Fax:* 1-302-266-7076; *http://* www.o2diesel.net; *Email:* info@o2diesel.net

General - Incorporation	DE	Stock- Price on:12/24/2007	$0.5298
Employees	17	Stock Exchange	AMEX
Auditor	Ernst & Young LLP	Ticker Symbol	OTD
Stk Agt	Interwest Transfer Company, Inc.	Outstanding Shares	76,430,000
Counsel	NA	E.P.S	-$0.11
DUNS No.	NA	Shareholders	NA

General - Incorporation	DE
Employees	17
Auditor	Ernst & Young LLP
Stk Agt	Interwest Transfer Company, Inc.
Counsel	NA
DUNS No.	NA

Stock - Price on:12/24/2007	$0.5298
Stock Exchange	AMEX
Ticker Symbol	OTD
Outstanding Shares	76,430,000
E.P.S.	-$0.11
Shareholders	NA

Business: The groups principle activities include developing, producing and marketing new diesel fuel. The groups markets include Urban truck fleets, Agriculture and construction equipment, Mobile or stationary power generators, Shipping fleets and railroads, Municipal transit vehicles, and Government fleets. The group operates from United States.

Primary SIC and add'l.: NA

CIK No: 0001117458

Subsidiaries: 02Diesel Qumicos, Ltda, 02Diesel R&D SPA, S.L., 02Diesel, Inc.

Officers: Alan Rae/Sec., CEO/$298,141.00, Peter Gross/GM - Brazil, David H. Shipman/CFO/$242,017.00

Directors: Arthur E. Meyer/80/Chmn., Hendrik Rethwilm/43/Dir., David L. Koontz/65/Dir., Jeffrey L. Cornish/56/Dir., Gerson Santos-Leon/48/Dir., Karim Jobanputra/44/Dir.

Owners: Holt E. Williams, Insiders/6.40%, Hendrik Rethwilm, Standard Bank Plc/6.00%, Jeffrey L. Cornish, UBS AG/9.50%, David H. Shipman, Arthur E. Meyer, Abengoa Bioenergy R&D Inc./11.10%, Alan R. Rae/3.20%, Karim Jobanputra, David L. Koontz

Financial Data: Fiscal Year End:12/31   Latest Annual Data: 12/31/2006

Year	Sales	Net Income
2006	$251,000	-$7,608,000
2005	$196,000	-$6,852,000
2004	$127,000	-$6,728,000

Curr. Assets:	$7,966,000	Curr. Liab.:	$1,329,000		
Plant, Equip.:	$230,000	Total Liab.:	$1,329,000	Indic. Yr. Divd.:	NA
Total Assets:	$8,197,000	Net Worth:	$6,868,000	Debt/ Equity:	NA

O2micro International Ltd

3118 Patrick Henry Dr., Santa Clara, CA, 95054; **PH:** 1-408-987-5920; **Fax:** 1-408-987-5929; **http://** www.o2micro.com; **Email:** ir@o2micro.com

General - Incorporation	Cayman Islands
Employees	644
Auditor	Deloitte & Touche LLP
Stk Agt	Computershare Ltd.
Counsel	NA
DUNS No.	NA

Stock - Price on:12/24/2007	$10.45
Stock Exchange	NDQ
Ticker Symbol	OIIM
Outstanding Shares	38,100,000
E.P.S.	$0.49
Shareholders	NA

Business: The groups principle activities include designing and development of products used in notebook computers, cellular phone, Internet appliance and others. The group operates from United States.

Primary SIC and add'l.: 3674

CIK No: 0001095348

Subsidiaries: Aotu Micro (Wuhan) Co., Ltd, Micro (Beijing) Co., Ltd, Micro (Chengdu) Co., Ltd, Micro (China) Co., Ltd, Micro Electronics, Inc, Micro International Japan Limited, Micro PTE Limited-Singapore, Micro, Inc.

Officers: Sterling Du/Chmn., CEO, Marc Cram/Contact - Sales, United States, Chuan Chiung Kuo/Dir., CFO, Sec., James Keim/Head - Marketing, Sales, Dir., Tania Hall/Contact - Sales, United States

Directors: Sterling Du/Chmn., CEO, Geok Ling Goh/Dir., Michael Austin/Dir., Xiaolang Yan/Dir., Lawrence Lin/Dir., Chuan Chiung Kuo/Dir., CFO, Sec., James Keim/Head - Marketing, Sales, Dir., Keisuke Yawata/Dir., Ji Liu/Dir.

Owners: Insiders/12.97%, Wasatch Advisors, Inc./18.73%, Capital Research & Management Co./8.02%, Wellington Management Co. LLP/9.85%, RS Investment Management Co/6.11%

Financial Data: Fiscal Year End:12/31   Latest Annual Data: 12/31/2006

Year	Sales	Net Income
2006	$124,915,000	$743,000
2005	$105,552,000	$8,147,000
2004	$92,196,000	$14,084,000

Curr. Assets:	$113,919,000	Curr. Liab.:	$23,054,000		
Plant, Equip.:	$41,427,000	Total Liab.:	$23,509,000	Indic. Yr. Divd.:	NA
Total Assets:	$197,020,000	Net Worth:	$173,511,000	Debt/ Equity:	NA

OAK Financial Corp

2445 84th St. SW, Byron Center, MI, 49315; **PH:** 1-616-588-3801; **Fax:** 1-616-878-4418; **http://** www.snl.com

General - Incorporation	MI
Employees	158
Auditor	Plante & Moran, PLLC
Stk Agt	Registrar & Transfer Co
Counsel	NA
DUNS No.	78-201-5663

Stock - Price on:12/24/2007	$36.15
Stock Exchange	OTC
Ticker Symbol	OKFC
Outstanding Shares	2,700,000
E.P.S.	$2.64
Shareholders	NA

Business: The group's principal activities are to offer commercial and personal banking services. The consumer services of the group include checking accounts, savings accounts, certificate of deposit, commercial loans, real estate loan, installment loans, collections, traveler's checks, night depository, safe deposit boxes and U.S. Savings bonds. The bank also provides loans to other financial institutions. The bank conducts its operations through 12 branch offices located in kent, ottawa and allegan counties. The bank's subsidiary, o.a.k. Financial services, offers mutual fund products, securities brokerage services, retirement planning services, investment management and advisory services.

Primary SIC and add'l.: 6712 6022

CIK No: 0001038459

Subsidiaries: Byron Bank, Byron Insurance Agency, Inc, Byron Investment Services, Inc, OAK Title Insurance Agency, Inc

Officers: Patrick K. Gill/Dir., CEO, Pres./$421,750.00, James A. Luyk/Exec. VP, CFO, COO/$234,107.00, Joel Rahn/CLO/$196,724.00

Directors: Patrick K. Gill/Dir., CEO, Pres., Stephanie Leonardos/Dir., Grace O. Shearer/Dir., Robert F. Dentzman/Dir., James B. Meyer/Dir., David G. Van Solkema/Dir., Norman J. Fifelski/Dir.

Owners: Robert F. Dentzman, Charles Andringa/5.27%, Patrick K. Gill, Norman J. Fifelski, David G. Van Solkema, Grace O. Shearer, Willard J. Van Singel/12.71%, The Banc Funds Company, L.L.C/5.34%, James B. Meyer

Financial Data: Fiscal Year End:12/31   Latest Annual Data: 12/31/2006

Year	Sales	Net Income
2006	$47,578,000	$7,022,000
2005	$37,535,000	$6,058,000
2004	$30,470,000	$4,504,000

Curr. Assets:	$18,016,000	Curr. Liab.:	$594,294,000	P/E Ratio:	13.49
Plant, Equip.:	$16,001,000	Total Liab.:	$603,551,000	Indic. Yr. Divd.:	$0.880
Total Assets:	$669,372,000	Net Worth:	$65,821,000	Debt/ Equity:	0.0439

Oak Hill Financial Inc

14621 State Rte 93, Jackson, OH, 45640; **PH:** 1-740-286-3283; **http://** www.oakf.com

General - Incorporation	OH
Employees	421
Auditor	Grant Thornton LLP
Stk Agt	Registrar & Transfer Co
Counsel	NA
DUNS No.	83-260-8541

Stock - Price on:12/24/2007	$22.95
Stock Exchange	NA
Ticker Symbol	NA
Outstanding Shares	5,340,000
E.P.S.	$0.34
Shareholders	NA

Business: The group's principle activity is to provide commercial banking services and other related services. It operates through wholly owned subsidiaries: oak hill banks, action finance company, mcnelly, patrick & associates and oak hill financial insurance agency, llc. The services rendered by the group include commercial lending, real estate lending, consumer credit, credit card, other personal loan financing, group health insurance and other employee benefits.

Primary SIC and add'l.: 6022 6712

CIK No: 0000949953

Subsidiaries: Oak Hill Banks, Oak Hill Banks Community Development Corp., Oak Hill Capital Trust 1, Oak Hill Capital Trust 2, Oak Hill Capital Trust 3, Oak Hill Capital Trust 4, Oak Hill Financial Insurance Agency, Inc., Oak Hill Financial Services Company, Oak Hill Title Agency, LLC

Officers: David G. Ratz/Exec. VP/$157,643.00

Owners: Dale B. Shafer, Barry M. Dorsey, Neil S. Strawser/1.34%, John D. Kidd/4.26%, Evan E. Davis/11.43%, R. E. Coffman/3.71%, Candice R. DeClark-Peace, Grant H. Stephenson, Donald P. Wood, Ron J. Copher, Scott J. Hinsch, Insiders/20.24%, Miles R. Armentrout, David G. Ratz, William S. Siders/1.64% (17 Owners included in Index)

Financial Data: Fiscal Year End:12/31   Latest Annual Data: 12/31/2006

Year	Sales	Net Income
2006	$92,914,000	$9,582,000
2005	$81,358,000	$11,379,000
2004	$69,829,000	$10,662,000

Curr. Assets:	$29,035,000	Curr. Liab.:	$1,161,878,000	P/E Ratio:	12.82
Plant, Equip.:	$33,023,000	Total Liab.:	$1,184,878,000	Indic. Yr. Divd.:	$0.840
Total Assets:	$1,275,635,000	Net Worth:	$90,757,000	Debt/ Equity:	0.2475

Oak Ridge Micro Energy Inc

275 Midway Ln., Oak Ridge, TN, 37830; **PH:** 1-865-220-8886; **Fax:** 1-865-220-8895; **http://** www.oakridgemicro.com

General - Incorporation	CO
Employees	3
Auditor	Mantyla Mcreynolds, LLC
Stk Agt	Colonial Stock Transfer Co Inc
Counsel	NA
DUNS No.	11-806-9892

Stock - Price on:12/24/2007	$0.13
Stock Exchange	OTC
Ticker Symbol	OKME
Outstanding Shares	74,380,000
E.P.S.	-$0.01
Shareholders	NA

Business: The group's principal activities are to develop thin-film lithium battery technology for commercial, consumer, industrial, security and military use. The battery is lithium-based and is manufactured to be thinner than common plastic wrap, like the larger, traditional lithium batteries that power laptops and cell phones, this lithium battery is also rechargeable. The group operates solely in the United States.

Primary SIC and add'l.: NA

CIK No: 0000830483

Subsidiaries: Oak Ridge Nevada

Officers: Mark Meriwether/Dir., CEO, Pres., Sec., Treas, John B. Bates/Dir., CTO

Directors: Mark Meriwether/Dir., CEO, Pres., Sec., Treas, John B. Bates/Dir., CTO

Owners: Mark L. Meriwether/20.50%, John B. Bates/24.30%

Financial Data: Fiscal Year End:12/31   Latest Annual Data: 12/31/2006

Year	Sales	Net Income
2006	$1,000	-$1,887,000
2005	NA	-$2,619,000
2004	$1,000	-$3,217,000

Curr. Assets:	$843,000	Curr. Liab.:	$73,000		
Plant, Equip.:	$673,000	Total Liab.:	$73,000	Indic. Yr. Divd.:	NA
Total Assets:	$1,532,000	Net Worth:	$1,459,000	Debt/ Equity:	NA

Oak Valley Community Bank CA

125 N 3rd Ave., Oakdale, CA, 95361; **PH:** 1-209-848-2265; **Fax:** 1-866-844-7500; **http://** www.ovcb.com; **Email:** CustomerService@ovcb.com

General - Incorporation	
Employees	NA
Auditor	NA
Stk Agt	U.S. Stock Transfer Corp
Counsel	NA
DUNS No.	NA

Stock - Price on:12/24/2007	NA
Stock Exchange	OTC
Ticker Symbol	OVYB
Outstanding Shares	NA
E.P.S.	NA
Shareholders	NA

Business: The groups principal activities include providing community banking offers a full range of products and financial services for today's varied businesses. Services of the group include check writing, use ATM/Debit card, no minimum balance required, overdraft privilege available, free check safe keeping, saving account, loans and business online banking. The group operates from the United States.

Primary SIC and add'l.: 6022

CIK No:

Officers: Ronald C. Martin/Dir., CEO, Christopher M. Courtney/Dir., Pres., Richard A. McCarty/CFO, Exec. VP, Elisa Luna/Customer Service Mgr. - Oakdale, Julie Dehart/Branch Mgr. - Escalon, June Lopez/Customer Service Mgr. - Escalon, Ron Davenport/Branch Mgr. - Modesto, Laura Weaver/Customer Service Mgr. - Modesto, Jennifer Jackson/Mortgage Loan Officer - Central Valley, Florencia Baldwin/New Accounting Representative Mortgage Loan Specialist Sonora, Alan Wilbur/VP - Investment Representative Central Valley, Petra Welsh/AVP - Investment Representative Central Valley, Jeff Buss/Commercial Loan Officerbishop, Caleb Gervase/Commercial Loan Officer Oakdale - Stockton, Ripon, Frank Middleton/VP - Commercial Loan Officer Agriculture - Central Valley *(34 Officers included in Index)*

Directors: Ronald C. Martin/Dir., CEO, Michael Q. Jones/Vice Chmn., Thomas A. Haidlen/Chmn., James L. Gilbert/Dir., Arne J. Knudsen/Dir., Corp. Sec., Danny L. Titus/Dir., Richard J. Vaughan/Dir., Roger M. Schrimp/Dir., Don Barton/Dir., Christopher M. Courtney/Dir., Pres.

Curr. Assets:	$244,898,000	**Curr. Liab.:**	$4,601,000		
Plant, Equip.:	$6,975,000	**Total Liab.:**	$6,606,000	**Indic. Yr. Divd.:**	NA
Total Assets:	$254,817,000	**Net Worth:**	$248,211,000	**Debt/ Equity:**	NA

Oakley Inc

One Icon, Foothill Ranch, CA, 92610; ***PH:*** 1-949-951-0991; ***http://*** www.oakley.com

General - Incorporation	WA	**Stock**- Price on:12/24/2007	$25.94
Employees	3,400	Stock Exchange	NA
Auditor	Deloitte & Touche LLP	Ticker Symbol	NA
Stk Agt	American Stock Transfer & Trust Co.	Outstanding Shares	69,260,000
Counsel	Skadden, Meagher & Flom LLP	E.P.S	$0.75
DUNS No.	08-538-6522	Shareholders	NA

Business: The group's principal activities are to design, manufacture and distribute consumer products. These products include performance and prescription eyewear, athletic equipment, apparel, footwear and watches. Its products are sold through four o store(R) retail stores, two outlet stores, as well as 15,600 locations in the United States comprised of optical stores, sunglass retailers, specialty sports stores for bikes, surfs, skis and golf, athletic footwear and sporting goods stores. Internationally, products are sold in 70 countries with direct operations in Europe, Australia, New Zealand, South Africa, Mexico, Japan and Canada. Customers include sunglass hut international. The group has 800 trademarks that include square wire (R), straight jacket (R), kevlar (R), big smoke (TM), crush (TM), bullet (TM), icon(R) small and time bomb (r).

Primary SIC and add'l.: 2389 3870 3851 5139

CIK No: 0000946356

Subsidiaries: Bazooka, Inc.

Officers: Scott Olivet/Dir., CEO/$2,380,365.00, Link Newcomb/Sr. Advisor, CEO/$1,095,843.00, Richard Shields/CFO/$560,992.00, Kent Lane/Sr. VP - Manufacturing, Sourcing/$567,277.00, Scott Bowers/VP - Marketing Worldwide, Donna Gordon/VP - Finance, Sec., Colin Baden/Pres./$738,162.00, Cos Lykos/VP - Business Development, Jon Krause/Sr. VP - Operations/$587,684.00, Carlos Reyes/VP - Research, Development, Cliff Neill/VP - US Sales, Giuseppe Servidori/VP, Head - European Strategy, Lance Allega/Dir. - Investor Relations, Corporate Communications

Directors: Scott Olivet/Dir., CEO, Jim Jannard/Chmn., Colombe Nicholas/63/Dir., Mary George/Dir., Tom Davin/50/Dir., Frits Van Paasschen/Dir., Greg Trojan/Dir., Michael J. Puntoriero/Dir., Jeff Moorad/Dir.

Owners: Frits van Paasschen, Jim Jannard/63.80%, Jon Krause, Scott D. Olivet, Michael Puntoriero, Jeffrey Moorad, Richard Shields, Insiders/64.90%, Mary George, Kent Lane, Colin Baden, Link Newcomb, Greg Trojan, Tom Davin

Financial Data: ***Fiscal Year End:***12/31 ***Latest Annual Data:*** 06/30/2007

Year	Sales	Net Income
2007	$263,162,000	$21,452,000
2006	$196,364,000	$7,668,000
2005	$648,131,000	$59,660,000

Curr. Assets:	$334,113,000	**Curr. Liab.:**	$154,367,000	**P/E Ratio:**	37.06
Plant, Equip.:	$177,400,000	**Total Liab.:**	$174,943,000	**Indic. Yr. Divd.:**	$0.160
Total Assets:	$633,834,000	**Net Worth:**	$458,891,000	**Debt/ Equity:**	NA

Oakridge Energy Inc

4613 Jacksboro Hwy., Wichita Falls, TX, 76302; ***PH:*** 1-940-322-4772; ***Fax:*** 1-940-322-9452; ***http://*** oakridgeenergy.com

General - Incorporation	UT	**Stock**- Price on:12/24/2007	$6.9
Employees	4	Stock Exchange	OTC
Auditor	Whitley Penn	Ticker Symbol	OAKR
Stk Agt	Stock Transfer Co of America Inc	Outstanding Shares	4,260,000
Counsel	Sherrill, Crosnoe & Goff	E.P.S	-$0.04
DUNS No.	06-836-5691	Shareholders	NA

Business: The group's principal activity is to explore, develop, produce and sell oil and gas, primarily in Texas. It also receives lease and royalty income from gravel deposits and holds real estate properties in colarado for future development. The oil and gas operations are primarily conducted in madison, freestone, red river, panola, gregg and smith counties of east Texas and in various areas of north Texas. The group's gravel property is located on approximately 43 acres of its 1,965 acres land in la plata county, Colorado.

Primary SIC and add'l.: 1222 1442 1311

CIK No: 0000216748

Officers: Sandra Pautsky/66/Chmn., CEO, Pres., Sec., Treasurer, Danny Croker/58/Dir., VP, Assist. Sec., Treasurer, Carol J. Cooper/61/Principal Financial Officer, Accounting Officer

Directors: Sandra Pautsky/66/Chmn., CEO, Pres., Sec., Treasurer, Danny Croker/58/Dir., VP, Assist. Sec., Treasurer, Randy Camp/55/Dir.

Owners: Robert S. Allen, Insiders, Randy Camp, Sandra Pautsky, Flem Noel Pautsky, Jr. Trust, Noel Pautsky Trust

Financial Data: ***Fiscal Year End:***02/28 ***Latest Annual Data:*** 02/28/2007

Year	Sales	Net Income
2007	$1,357,000	-$175,000
2006	$1,561,000	$324,000
2005	$1,278,000	-$250,000

Curr. Assets:	$3,461,000	**Curr. Liab.:**	$203,000		
Plant, Equip.:	$4,340,000	**Total Liab.:**	$809,000	**Indic. Yr. Divd.:**	NA
Total Assets:	$8,724,000	**Net Worth:**	$7,914,000	**Debt/ Equity:**	NA

Oakridge Holdings Inc

400 W Ontario St. No.1003, Chicago, IL, 60610; ***PH:*** 1-312-823-8772

General - Incorporation	MN	**Stock**- Price on:12/24/2007	$0.51
Employees	65	Stock Exchange	OTC
Auditor	Wipfli LLP	Ticker Symbol	OKRG
Stk Agt	Mellon Investor Services LLC	Outstanding Shares	1,430,000
Counsel	NA	E.P.S	$0.02
DUNS No.	04-901-3543	Shareholders	NA

Business: The group's principal activities are to operate cemeteries and manufacture and market aviation ground support equipment. The cemetery services are provided through two wholly owned subsidiaries, oakridge cemetery (hillside) inc and glen oak cemetery inc. In addition the group provides internment services, burial plots and crypts and sells cremation services. The aviation ground support equipment business is operated through stinar corporation, a subsidiary of the group. The principal products of stinar corporation are: truck-mounted stairways and push stairs for loading aircraft, lavatory trucks and carts, water trucks, bobtails and carts and catering trucks for servicing aircraft; cabin cleaning trucks and maintenance hi-lifts. These products are sold to airports, airlines and government and military customers in the United States.

Primary SIC and add'l.: 6719 6553 3537

CIK No: 0000073605

Subsidiaries: Glen Oak Cemetery Company, Lain and Son, Inc., Oakridge Cemetery (Hillside), Inc., Stinar Corporation

Officers: Robert C. Harvey/57/Chmn., CEO, CFO, Robert B. Gregor/57/Dir., VP - Sales, Marketing

Directors: Robert C. Harvey/57/Chmn., CEO, CFO, Robert Lindman/65/Dir., Hugh McDaniel/69/Dir., Pamela Whitney/56/Dir., Robert B. Gregor/57/Dir., VP - Sales, Marketing

Owners: Jerry Kenline/9.00%, Insiders/41.30%, Robert C. Harvey/28.00%, Robert B. Gregor/13.00%, Hugh McDaniel/0.30%

Financial Data: ***Fiscal Year End:***06/30 ***Latest Annual Data:*** 6/30/2006

Year	Sales	Net Income
2006	$15,697,000	$82,000
2005	$16,836,000	-$26,000
2004	$14,539,000	-$18,000

Curr. Assets:	$7,834,000	**Curr. Liab.:**	$7,653,000	**P/E Ratio:**	25.50
Plant, Equip.:	$2,358,000	**Total Liab.:**	$9,243,000	**Indic. Yr. Divd.:**	NA
Total Assets:	$17,549,000	**Net Worth:**	$1,496,000	**Debt/ Equity:**	NA

OAO Rostelecom

14, 1st Tverskaya-Yamskaya St., Moscow, 125047; ***PH:*** 7-4957872849; ***Fax:*** 7-4999728222; ***http://*** www.rt.ru; ***Email:*** info@rostelecom.ru

General - Incorporation	Russia	**Stock**- Price on:12/24/2007	$56.37
Employees	22,519	Stock Exchange	NYSE
Auditor	Ernst & Young LLC	Ticker Symbol	ROS
Stk Agt	CT Corporation System	Outstanding Shares	NA
Counsel	NA	E.P.S	NA
DUNS No.	64-463-1392	Shareholders	NA

Business: The group's principal activity is the provision of telecommunication services on international and inter city connections. Additionally, the group provides communication services such as television, broadcasting, audio text, Internet information, data transmission for telex, fax, electronic mail and video teleconferences, switched and non-switched transit, leasing of circuits and network trunks and other related services. The group's services are based on ATM technology. The group operates in the following geographical markets: Russia, cis, usa, western and eastern Europe and other countries.

Primary SIC and add'l.: 4822 4899 3669 4813

CIK No: 0001054487

Subsidiaries: GlobalTel, MTs NTT, Westelcom

Officers: Vladimir Mironov/Deputy General Dir., Galina Rysakova/Dir. - Department, Organizational Development, Human Resources, Rostelecom, Vladimir Terekhov/First Deputy General Dir., Nikolai Mylnikov/Dir. - Legal Department, CIT Finance Investment Bank, Yevgeny Gerasimov/Deputy General Dir., Dir. - Rostelecom's North, Western Branch, Roman Frolov/Chief Accountant, Andrei Baklykov/Dir. - Information Technology Department, Rostelecom, Andrei Gaiduk/First Deputy General Dir., Financial Dir. - Rostelecom, Rodion Levochka/Dir. - Products, Marketing Department, Olga Rumyantseva/Dir. - Sales, Customer Service Department, Rostelecom, Dmitry Gurevich/Dir. - Project Management Department, Sergei Akopov/Dir. - Administrative Department, Dmitry Sigalov/Dir. - Legal Affairs Department, Rostelecom

Directors: Mikhail Alexeev/Dir., Maxim Tsyganov/Dir., Yekaterina Vasilyeva/Dir., Yevgeny Logovinsky/Dir., Anatoly Gavrilenko/Dir., Elena Selvich/Dir., Yevgeny Chechelnitsky/Dir., Sergei Kuznetsov/Dir., Alexander Kiselev/Dir., Valery Degtyarev/Dir.

Owners: Depository Clearing Company, a closed joint stock company, as a nominee holder/6.26%, ING Bank (Eurasia) /ING DEPOSITARY ING Barings, as a nominee holder/7.48%, Insiders/1.81%, Svyazinvest/50.67%, National Depositary Center, a non-commercial partnership, as a nominee holder/33.79%

Financial Data: ***Fiscal Year End:***12/31 ***Latest Annual Data:*** 12/31/2006

Year	Sales	Net Income
2006	$2,339,242,000	$10,298,000
2005	$1,425,234,000	$120,130,000
2004	$1,343,448,000	$132,444,000

Curr. Assets:	$774,744,000	**Curr. Liab.:**	$482,448,000		
Plant, Equip.:	$1,649,276,000	**Total Liab.:**	$667,014,000	**Indic. Yr. Divd.:**	NA
Total Assets:	$2,730,642,000	**Net Worth:**	$2,063,628,000	**Debt/ Equity:**	NA

OAO Tatneft

75 Lenin St., Almetyevsk, Tatarstan, 423400; ***PH:*** 8553-371-111; ***Fax:*** 8553-376-151; ***http://*** www.tatneft.ru/eng; ***Email:*** tnr@tatneft.ru

General - Incorporation	Russia	**Stock**- Price on:12/24/2007	NA
Employees	NA	Stock Exchange	NA
Auditor	Ernst & Young LLC	Ticker Symbol	NA
Stk Agt	Aktsionerny Kapital	Outstanding Shares	NA
Counsel	NA	E.P.S	NA
DUNS No.	NA	Shareholders	NA

Business: The group's principle activities are the exploration of crude oil and production of petroleum products. The company is also involved in refining and marketing of crude oil and oil related products. The group's export markets include both the commonwealth independent states and non-commonwealth independent states, such as Germany, France and Poland. The company's oil reserves are estimated to 838,403 thousand tons.

Primary SIC and add'l.: 4613 1311 4612 1381 1389 1321

CIK No: 0001058255

Subsidiaries: OAO Nizhnekamskshina, Tatneft Europe AG

Officers: Nail Gabdulbarievich Ibraghimov/Dir., First Deputy General Dir. on Production, Chief Engineer, Vladimir Pavlovich Lavushchenko/Deputy General Dir., Nail Ulfatovich Maganov/First Deputy General Dir., Head - Crude Oil, Oil Product Sales Dept, Shafagat Fakhrazovich Takhautdinov/General Dir., Rais Salikhovich Khisamov/Deputy General Dir., Chief Geologist

Directors: Rustam Nurgaliyevich Minnikhanov/Chmn., Nail Ulfatovich Maganov/First Deputy General Dir., Head - Crude Oil, Oil Product Sales Dept, Sushovan Ghosh/Dir., Radik Raufovich Gaizatullin/Dir., Maria Leonidovna Voskresenskaya/Dir., David William Waygood/Dir., Veleriy Yuryevich Sorokin/Dir., Valery Pavlovich Vasilyev/Dir., Rishat Fazlutdinovich Abubakirov/Dir., Nail Gabdulbarievich Ibraghimov/Dir., First Deputy General Dir. on Production, Chief Engineer, Renat Khaliullovich Muslimov/Dir., Mirgaziyan Zakiyevich Taziyev/Dir., Rais Salikhovich Khisamov/Deputy General Dir., Chief Geologist

Oasys Mobile Inc

Formerly: Summus Inc

5400 Trinity Rd., Ste. 208, Raleigh, NC, 27601; **PH:** 1-919-807-5600;
http:// www.oasysmobileinc.com

General - Incorporation	DE	Stock- Price on:12/24/2007	$0.2
Employees	38	Stock Exchange	OTC
Auditor	Ernst & Young LLP	Ticker Symbol	OYSME
Stk Agt	Interwest Transfer Company, Inc.	Outstanding Shares	13,780,000
Counsel	NA	E.P.S.	-$1.003
DUNS No.	NA	Shareholders	NA

Business: The group's principal activity is to develop information solutions for the mobile and wireless markets. It also licenses its photo ID compression and decompression technology. The group has developed proprietary software, technology and applications to enable information processing and resource management. Products of the group are bluefuel platform and picture this!tm .'the bluefuel platform the foundation for a majority of its applications is constructed from a set of modules, application programmers interfaces (apis) and services that connect various elements of the value chain from content provider to mobile devices through the wireless carrier's channel. The picture this!tm l which loads all pictures to view and share from the mobile phone. Group's technology platform enables mobile, high-speed access to a wide range of telecommunications services supported by fixed telecommunications networks and other services to mobile users.

Primary SIC and add'l.: 7389 7372

CIK No: 0001104332

Officers: Doug Dyer/CEO, Tracy T. Jackson/CFO, Donald T. Locke/VP - Corporate Development

Directors: Stephen M. Finn/58/Dir., Winder J. Hughes/49/Dir., Richard B. Ruben/52/Dir., Bernard Stolar/61/Dir., James A. Taylor/62/Dir.

Owners: Stephen M. Finn, Donald T. Locke/2.64%, Andrew L. Fox/2.54%, Donald D. Hammett/6.98%, Tracy T. Jackson, Gary E. Ban/3.68%, JDS Capital Management, LLC/15.55%, Empire Capital LP/19.03%, Scott W. Hamilton, RHP Master Fund, Ltd./9.90%, Andrew L. Fox/2.54%, Gary E. Ban/3.68%, James A. Taylor, Douglas B. Dyer, LAP Summus Holdings, LLC/9.90% (18 Owners included in Index)

Financial Data: Fiscal Year End:12/31   Latest Annual Data: 12/31/2006

Year	Sales	Net Income
2006	$8,688,000	-$14,570,000
2005	$7,795,000	-$5,921,000
2004	$5,171,000	-$3,873,000

Curr. Assets:	$3,953,000	Curr. Liab.:	$9,219,000		
Plant, Equip.:	$153,000	Total Liab.:	$9,238,000	Indic. Yr. Divd.:	NA
Total Assets:	$4,106,000	Net Worth:	-$5,132,000	Debt/ Equity:	NA

OBN Holdings Inc

8275 S Eern Ave., Ste 200, Las Vegas, NV, 89123; **PH:** 1-702-435-0544;
http:// www.obnholdings.com

General - Incorporation	NV	Stock- Price on:12/24/2007	NA
Employees	5	Stock Exchange	OTC
Auditor	Corbin & Co LLP	Ticker Symbol	OBNI
Stk Agt	Atlas Stock Transfer Corp	Outstanding Shares	NA
Counsel	NA	E.P.S.	NA
DUNS No.	NA	Shareholders	NA

Business: The group's principal activities are television broadcasting, feature film and television production, music production, distribution and merchandising. The group produces motion pictures for theatrical release. Film production includes identifying scripts, developing budgets and creating film packages. The group broadcast television network designed to deliver quality programming to viewers nationwide and also provides production services and facilitating merchandising activities for all of the entities under the obn holdings.

Primary SIC and add'l.: 6719 4833

CIK No: 0001261204

Subsidiaries: Omni Broadcasting Network

Officers: Roger Neal Smith/Chmn., CEO, Pres., Larry Taylor/Dir., VP, Treasurer, CFO, Christine Ohama/Dir., Sr. VP - Marketing, Enviro Board, Donald K. Wilson/Corp. Sec.

Directors: Roger Neal Smith/Chmn., CEO, Pres., Larry Taylor/Dir., VP, Treasurer, CFO, Dennis Johnson/Dir., Dennis Severson/Dir., Christine Ohama/Dir., Sr. VP - Marketing, Enviro Board, Barry Allen/Dir., Anita L. Defrantz/Dir.

Owners: Roger N. Smith/29.63%, Insiders/49.85%, Anita L. DeFrantz, Larry Taylor/10.10%, Commerce Street Venture Group/9.22%, Donald Wilson/2.95%, L. G. Hancher/5.16%, Dennis Johnson/4.94%, Dennis Severson/2.06%

Financial Data: Fiscal Year End:06/30   Latest Annual Data: 06/30/2006

Year	Sales	Net Income
2006	$247,000	-$1,007,000
2005	$35,000	-$1,296,000
2004	NA	-$1,461,000

Curr. Assets:	$2,000	Curr. Liab.:	$3,153,000		
Plant, Equip.:	$41,000	Total Liab.:	$3,153,000	Indic. Yr. Divd.:	NA
Total Assets:	$523,000	Net Worth:	-$2,630,000	Debt/ Equity:	NA

OC Financial Inc OH

6033 Perimeter Dr., Dublin, OH, 43017; **PH:** 1-800-687-6228

General - Incorporation	MD	Stock- Price on:12/24/2007	$10.85
Employees	14	Stock Exchange	OTC
Auditor	NA	Ticker Symbol	OCFL
Stk Agt	NA	Outstanding Shares	NA
Counsel	NA	E.P.S.	-$1.46
DUNS No.	NA	Shareholders	NA

Business: The groups principal activity is the stock holding company for Ohio Central Savings. The services of the group include general and local economic conditions, changes in interest rates, deposit flows, demand for mortgage, and other loans, real estate values, competition, changes in accounting principles, policies, or guidelines, changes in legislation or regulation, and other economic, competitive, governmental, regulatory, and technological factors. The group operates from the United States.

Primary SIC and add'l.: 6035

CIK No: 0001310273

Subsidiaries: AutoARMtm, Ohio Central Savings

Officers: Robert W. Hughes/49/Chmn., CEO, Pres., Diane M. Gregg/40/Dir., VP, COO, Danny E. Hosler/43/CFO, VP

Directors: Robert W. Hughes/49/Chmn., CEO, Pres., Thomas H. Lagos/57/Dir., Christophjer L. Lardiere/52/Dir., Diane M. Gregg/40/Dir., VP, COO, Thomas J. Parliment/61/Dir., Nils C. Muladore/50/Dir., Michael B. Bowman/53/Dir.

Owners: Robert W. Hughes/5.44%, OC Financial Employee Stock Ownership Plan/8.00%, Lance S. Gad/9.28%, Thomas H. Lagos/9.43%, Insiders/27.41%

Financial Data: Fiscal Year End:09/30   Latest Annual Data: 9/30/2006

Year	Sales	Net Income
2006	$3,690,000	-$615,000
2005	$3,504,000	-$64,000

Curr. Assets:	$6,959,000	Curr. Liab.:	$58,576,000		
Plant, Equip.:	$680,000	Total Liab.:	$60,130,000	Indic. Yr. Divd.:	NA
Total Assets:	$66,945,000	Net Worth:	$6,815,000	Debt/ Equity:	0.1927

Occam Networks

6868 Cortona Dr., Santa Barbara, CA, 93117; **PH:** 1-805-692-2900; **Fax:** 1-805-692-2999;
http:// www.occamnetworks.com; **Email:** sales@occamnetworks.com

General - Incorporation	DE	Stock- Price on:12/24/2007	$9.9672
Employees	101	Stock Exchange	NDQ
Auditor	Singer Lewak Greenbaum & Goldstein	Ticker Symbol	OCNW
Stk Agt	U.S. Stock Transfer Corp	Outstanding Shares	19,710,000
Counsel	NA	E.P.S.	-$0.22
DUNS No.	NA	Shareholders	NA

Business: The group's principal activities are to develop, manufacture and market telecommunication products that enable the bundling of voice and data services over a single broadband access network. These products are designed to allow the group's customers to efficiently and cost-effectively deliver and manage multiple voice and data services using various broadband access technologies including digital subscriber line, copper-line technologies such as t1 and nxt1 and higher bandwidth technologies such as ds3.

Primary SIC and add'l.: 3661

CIK No: 0001108185

Subsidiaries: Occam Networks (California), Inc

Officers: Robert L. Howard-Anderson/52/Dir., CEO, Pres., Chris Farrell/CFO, Nathan Harrell/VP - Sales, Scott Remillard/VP - Sales, Western Region, Mark Johnson/VP - Sales, Eastern Region, Clive Hallatt/VP - Business Development, Drusie Davis/Member - Advisory Board, Consultant, Mark Rumer/Founder, CTO, Dave Mason/VP - Engineering, Greg Dion/VP - Operations, Russ Sharer/VP - Sales, Marketing

Directors: Robert L. Howard-Anderson/52/Dir., CEO, Pres., Steven M. Krausz/Chmn., Mark Rumer/Founder, CTO, Robert B. Abbott/Dir., Juha Heinanen/Member - Advisory Board, Albert J. Moyer/65/Dir., Drusie Davis/Member - Advisory Board, Consultant, Frederick J. Baker/Member - Advisory Board, Jeff Pulver/Member - Advisory Board, Asher Waldfogel/Member - Advisory Board, Robert E. Bylin/Dir., Brian H. Strom/Dir., Wilson /Member - Advisory Board, Corporate Counsel, Sonsini /Member - Advisory Board, Corporate Counsel, Goodrich /Member - Advisory Board, Corporate Counsel (22 Directors included in Index)

Owners: Robert B. Abbott/10.30%, Insiders/31.20%, Christopher B. Farrell, Russell J. Sharer, Norwest Venture Partners/10.10%, David C. Mason, Kenneth R. Cole, Robert L. Howard-Anderson/0.90%, Albert J. Moyer, U.S. Venture Partners/17.60%, Thomas E. Pardun, Conus Partners, Inc./5.50%, Brian H. Strom, Robert E. Bylin, Steven M. Krausz/17.70% (16 Owners included in Index)

Financial Data: Fiscal Year End:12/31   Latest Annual Data: 12/31/2006

Year	Sales	Net Income
2006	$68,203,000	$1,235,000
2005	$39,238,000	-$7,438,000
2004	$17,329,000	-$14,989,000

Curr. Assets:	$85,701,000	Curr. Liab.:	$19,615,000		
Plant, Equip.:	$1,766,000	Total Liab.:	$19,615,000	Indic. Yr. Divd.:	NA
Total Assets:	$87,758,000	Net Worth:	$68,143,000	Debt/ Equity:	NA

Occidental Petroleum Corp

10889 Wilshire Blvd., Los Angeles, CA, 90024; **PH:** 1-310-208-8800; **Fax:** 1-310-443-6690;
http:// www.oxy.com

General - Incorporation	DE	Stock- Price on:12/24/2007	$59.02
Employees	8,886	Stock Exchange	NYSE
Auditor	KPMG LLP	Ticker Symbol	OXY
Stk Agt	Mellon Investor Services LLC	Outstanding Shares	833,810,000
Counsel	NA	E.P.S.	$5.77
DUNS No.	00-690-8354	Shareholders	NA

Business: The groups principle activites include exploring and producing oil and natural gas. The group operates from United States, Qatar, Yemen, Colombia, Oman, Pakistan, and Canada.

Primary SIC and add'l.: 1311 4922 2812

CIK No: 0000797468

Subsidiaries: Basic Chemicals Company, LLC, Centurion Pipeline GP, Inc., Centurion Pipeline L.P., Centurion Pipeline LP, Inc., D. S. Ventures, Inc., Glenn Springs Holdings, Inc., INDSPEC Chemical Corporation, INDSPEC Holding Corporation, INDSPEC Technologies, Ltd., La Porte Chemicals Corp., Laguna Petroleum Corporation, NGL Ventures LLC, Occidental Andina, LLC, Occidental Chemical Chile Limitada, Occidental Chemical Corporation 80 Subsidiaries included in the Index

Officers: Ray R. Irani/Chmn., CEO, Pres./$55,626,230.00, Stephen I. Chazen/CFO, Sr. Exec. VP/$19,822,390.00, Donald P. De Brier/Exec. VP, General Counsel, Sec./$8,531,301.00, John W. Morgan/Exec. VP, Pres. - Oil, Gas, Western Hemisphere/$7,976,666.00, Casey R. Olson/Exec. VP, Jim A. Leonard/58/VP, Controller, Richard W. Hallock/63/Exec. VP - Human Resources/$5,920,802.00, James R. Havert/66/VP, Treasurer, Chuck B. Anderson/48/Pres. - Occidental Chemical Corporation, Christopher G. Stavros/VP - Investor Relations, James L. Siccardi/Dir. - Investor Relations

Directors: Ray R. Irani/Chmn., CEO, Pres., Irvin W. Maloney/Dir., Chad R. Dreier/Dir., John E. Feick/Dir., Spencer Abraham/Dir., Ronald W. Burkle/Dir., John S. Chalsty/Dir., Edward P. Djerejian/Dir., Rodolfo Segovia/Dir., Aziz D. Syriani/Dir., Rosemary Tomich/Dir., Walter L. Weisman/Dir.

Owners: Rodolfo Segovia, Donald P. De Brier, Richard W. Hallock, Edward P. Djerejian, Stephen I. Chazen, Irvin W. Maloney, Aziz D. Syriani, John S. Chalsty, Barclays Global Investors, N.A., Rosemary Tomich, John E. Feick, Walter L. Weisman, Spencer Abraham, John W. Morgan, Ray R. Irani *(18 Owners included in Index)*

Financial Data: **Fiscal Year End:**12/31 **Latest Annual Data:** 12/31/2006

Year	Sales	Net Income
2006	$18,160,000,000	$4,182,000,000
2005	$16,259,000,000	$5,281,000,000
2004	$11,513,000,000	$2,568,000,000

Curr. Assets:	$6,006,000,000	**Curr. Liab.:**	$4,724,000,000	**P/E Ratio:**	12.14
Plant, Equip.:	$24,316,000,000	**Total Liab.:**	$12,830,000,000	**Indic. Yr. Divd.:**	$1.000
Total Assets:	$32,355,000,000	**Net Worth:**	$19,184,000,000	**Debt/ Equity:**	NA

OccuLogix Inc

2600 Skymark Ave., Unit 9, Ste. 201, Mississauga, ON, L4W 5B2; ***PH:*** 1-905-602-0887; ***http://*** www.occulogix.com

General - Incorporation	DE	**Stock**- Price on:12/24/2007	$1.09
Employees	34	Stock Exchange	NDQ
Auditor	Ernst & Young LLP	Ticker Symbol	OCCX
Stk Agt	Mellon Investor Services LLC	Outstanding Shares	57,300,000
Counsel	NA	E.P.S	-$1.68
DUNS No.	NA	Shareholders	NA

Business: The groups principle activity is to provide ophthalmic therapeutic services. The group products sold under the trade names RHEO(TM) and SOLX Glaucoma. The groups operates through two segments namely retina and glaucoma. In the year 2006, the group acquired OcuSense, Inc and SOLX.Specific customer of the group is RHEO Clinic Inc. The group operates from the United States, Canada, Europe and Israel. The group's quarterly revenue for September 2007 was 0.01 millions of USD.

Primary SIC and add'l.: 3845 3841

CIK No: 0001299139

Subsidiaries: OccuLogix ExchangeCo ULC, OccuLogix Holding, Inc., OccuLogix LLC, OccuLogix Management Inc., OccuLogix, L.P.

Officers: Elias Vamvakas/Chmn., CEO, Thomas P. Reeves/COO, Pres., Steve Westing/VP - Medical, Scientific Development, Stephen B. Parks/VP, Irving J. Siegel/VP - Clinical Affairs, Doug Adams/Pres., Founder - Solx Division, Nozhat Choudry/VP - Clinical Research, John Cornish/VP - Operations, William G. Dumencu/Interim CFO, Treasurer, David Eldridge/VP - Science, Technology, Julie A. Fotheringham/VP - Marketing, Stephen J. Kilmer/VP - Investor, Public Affairs, Steve Parks/VP - Sales

Directors: Elias Vamvakas/Chmn., CEO, Thomas N. Davidson/Dir., Adrienne L. Graves/Dir., Jay T. Holmes/Dir., Richard L. Lindstrom/Dir., Georges Noel/Dir., Gilbert S. Omenn/Dir.

Owners: Stephen J. Kilmer, Gilbert S. Omenn, Thomas N. Davidson, Diamed Medizintechnik GmbH/7.60%, John Cornish, William G. Dumencu, Thomas P. Reeves, Georges Nol, Nozait Chaudry-Rao, David C. Eldridge, Julie A. Fotheringham, Adrienne L. Graves, Insiders/6.30%, Sowood Capital Management LP/6.40%, Jay T. Holmes *(20 Owners included in Index)*

Financial Data: **Fiscal Year End:**12/31 **Latest Annual Data:** 12/31/2006

Year	Sales	Net Income
2006	$206,000	-$82,172,000
2005	$1,840,000	-$162,972,000
2004	$969,000	-$21,819,000

Curr. Assets:	$19,178,000	**Curr. Liab.:**	$5,639,000		
Plant, Equip.:	$861,000	**Total Liab.:**	$29,184,000	**Indic. Yr. Divd.:**	NA
Total Assets:	$90,404,000	**Net Worth:**	$61,220,000	**Debt/ Equity:**	NA

Oce

5450 N Cumberland Ave., Chicago, IL, 60656; ***PH:*** 1-773-714-8500; ***Fax:*** 1-773-714-4056; ***http://*** www.oce.com; ***Email:*** info@oce.com

General - Incorporation	Netherlands	**Stock**- Price on:12/24/2007	$19.23
Employees	23,784	Stock Exchange	OTC
Auditor	PricewaterhouseCoopers LLP	Ticker Symbol	OCENY
Stk Agt	NA	Outstanding Shares	84,010,000
Counsel	NA	E.P.S	$0.83
DUNS No.	40-404-6377	Shareholders	NA

Business: The group's principal activity is to provide products and services including complete solutions used in print and document management. The group also offers its customers innovative services in the areas of consultancy, outsourcing and services. The operations are carried through two segments: wide format printing systems and digital document system. The wide format printing systems offers wide format production printers, wide format scanners and financial services. The digital document system provides document output solutions through three divisions: corporate printing, commercial printing and software and professional services. The corporate printing division provides integral solutions for document output management. The commercial printing division provides commercial services to the printing industry. The software and professional services provides software products and project services for the implementation and use of digital services.

Primary SIC and add'l.: 5044 5045 7359 3861 6159

CIK No: 0000753058

Subsidiaries: BEC Digital Limited, BEC Holdings Limited, Imagistics Canada Inc., Imagistics International Limited, Imagistics International, Inc., Lakeside Office Systems Ltd., Lakeside Office Systems Ltd. and Imagistics Canada Inc., Oc Imagistics (UK) Limited, Oc Printing Systems (Asia) Pte.Ltd., Oc Rental (Shanghai) Company Ltd., Oc-Deutschland Facility Services G.m.b.H., Oc-Display Graphics Belgium N.V., Oc-Facility Services Est EURL, Oc-Reprographics Limited, Oc-Slovensko Spol. S.R.O. 18 Subsidiaries included in the Index

Officers: Rokus Van Iperen/Pres., CEO - Oce, USA Holding, Inc, Joe Marciano/Pres., CEO - Oce Business Services, Inc, Joseph D. Skrzypczak/Pres., CEO - Oce North America, Inc, Jan Hol/Sr. VP - Communications, F.W. T. Koole/Sr. VP, Corp. Sec., Chief Legal Officer, M. Reeuwijk Arentsen/69/Supervisory Dir., Mal Baboyian/Pres. - Commercial Printing Division, Pres. - Commercial Printing Division, Patrick Chapuis/Pres. - Wide Format Printing Division, Oce North America, Inc, T. Egelund/Exec. VP - WFPS, N. J. Koole/Sr. VP - Manufacturing, Logistics, Jan Van Den Belt/Executive Dir., Dan Hart/Sr. VP, General Counsel, Sec. - Oce North America, Inc, Dan Krzesinski/Sr. VP - Service, Oce North America, Inc, James A. Magrone/VP - Corporate Communications, William Midgley/Sr. VP - Administration, Logistics *(32 Officers included in Index)*

Directors: P. A.f.w. Elverding/60/Chmn., A.H. Schaaf/54/Dir., J. L. Brentjens/68/Dir., Jan Van Den Belt/Executive Dir., J. F. Dix/Exec. Dir.

Owners: Insiders, ING Groep N.V./10.00%, Fortis Utrecht N.V./1.80%, Ducatus N.V./53.60%, Fortis Utrecht N.V./36.40%, Pictet & Cie/6.70%, Foundation Fort Ginkel/100.00%, Orbis Investment Management Ltd./10.00%, ING Groep N.V./8.60%, Stichting Administratiekantoor Preferente Aandelen Oc/100.00%

Financial Data: **Fiscal Year End:**11/30 **Latest Annual Data:** 11/30/2006

Year	Sales	Net Income
2006	$4,098,473,000	$7,821,000
2005	$3,138,302,000	$9,593,000
2004	$3,516,888,000	$78,630,000

Curr. Assets:	$1,590,241,000	**Curr. Liab.:**	$1,061,471,000		
Plant, Equip.:	$711,612,000	**Total Liab.:**	$2,531,505,000	**Indic. Yr. Divd.:**	$1.120
Total Assets:	$3,797,675,000	**Net Worth:**	$1,266,170,000	**Debt/ Equity:**	NA

Ocean Bio Chem Inc

4041 SW 47th Ave., Fort Lauderdale, FL, 33314; ***PH:*** 1-954-587-6280; ***Fax:*** 1-954-587-2813; ***http://*** www.oceanbiochem.com

General - Incorporation	FL	**Stock**- Price on:12/24/2007	$1.7201
Employees	90	Stock Exchange	NDQ
Auditor	Berenfeld, Spritzer, Shechter & Sheer	Ticker Symbol	OBCI
Stk Agt	Registrar & Transfer Co	Outstanding Shares	7,610,000
Counsel	Berger Singerman P.A	E.P.S	$0.01
DUNS No.	09-346-1796	Shareholders	NA

Business: The group's principal activities are to manufacture, market and distribute appearance and maintenance products for boats, recreational vehicles, automotive and aircraft. The appearance and maintenance products include polishes, cleaners, protectors, detergents, fabric cleaners, protectors, silicone sealants, waterproofers, gasket materials, degreasers, vinyl cleaners, anti-freeze coolants and waxes of various formulations. The group's products are sold through national chains such as wal-Mart, k mart and through specialized marine retailers. The group operates in the United States and Canada.

Primary SIC and add'l.: 2842

CIK No: 0000350737

Subsidiaries: Alabama corporation, Kinpak Inc, Schlumberger B.V., Schlumberger Canada Limited, Schlumberger SA, Services Petroliers Schlumberger, WesternGeco A.S., WesternGeco B.V.

Officers: Peter G. Dornau/68/Chmn., CEO, Pres., William W. Dudman/43/Sec., VP - Operations, Gregor M. Dornau/39/VP - Sales, James Nikas/Contact - Geomarketing, Financial Relations, George W. Lindsey/50/VP - Advertising, Marketing, Jeffrey S. Baracos/60/Dir., VP - Finance, Chief Financial

Directors: Peter G. Dornau/68/Chmn., CEO, Pres., John B. Turner/60/Dir., Laz L. Schneider/68/Dir., James Kolisch/56/Dir., Sonia B. Beard/37/Dir., Jeffrey S. Baracos/60/Dir., VP - Finance, Chief Financial

Owners: Peter G. Dornau/60.40%, Jeffrey J. Tieger/4.50%, Edward Anchel/3.50%, Gregor M. Dornau/3.30%, Sonia B. Beard/0.40%, James M. Kolisch/0.60%, Insiders/74.10%, William W. Dudman/0.60%, John B. Turner/0.80%, Laz L. Schneider/0.40%

Financial Data: **Fiscal Year End:**12/31 **Latest Annual Data:** 12/31/2006

Year	Sales	Net Income
2006	$20,427,000	$392,000
2005	$17,652,000	-$1,813,000
2004	$21,657,000	$135,000

Curr. Assets:	$7,964,000	**Curr. Liab.:**	$4,044,000	**P/E Ratio:**	172.01
Plant, Equip.:	$6,800,000	**Total Liab.:**	$8,594,000	**Indic. Yr. Divd.:**	NA
Total Assets:	$15,529,000	**Net Worth:**	$6,936,000	**Debt/ Equity:**	NA

Ocean Rig

Vestre Svanholmen 6, N-4313, Sandnes, Forus; ***PH:*** 47-51969000; ***http://*** www.ocean-rig.com; ***Email:*** oras@ocean-rig.com

General - Incorporation	Kingdom Of Norway	**Stock**- Price on:12/24/2007	NA
Employees	NA	Stock Exchange	NA
Auditor	PricewaterhouseCoopers LLP	Ticker Symbol	NA
Stk Agt	NA	Outstanding Shares	NA
Counsel	NA	E.P.S	NA
DUNS No.	NA	Shareholders	NA

Business: The groups principle activities include assembling, testing and commissioning of semi-submersible deep water rigs used for oil and gas drilling operations. The group operates from United States.

Primary SIC and add'l.: 3533

CIK No: 0001065952

Subsidiaries: Ocean Rig 1 AS, Ocean Rig 2 AS, Ocean Rig AS, Ocean Rig ASA, Ocean Rig Norway AS, Ocean Rig UK Ltd.

Officers: Trygve Arnesen/CEO, Frank Tollefsen/Sr. VP - Operations, Ole Petter Landa/VP - HES - Q, Jan Rune Steinsland/CFO, John Rune Hellevik/Sr. VP - Marketing - Contracts, Rolf Brathen/Sr. VP - Accounting

Directors: Jon R. Aisbitt/Dep. Chmn., Geir Aune/Chmn., Tage Bundgaard/Dir., James Frithjof Skouveroe/Dir., George Stephen Finley/Dir., Peter Goode/Dir.

Ocean Shore Holding Company

1001 Asbury Ave., Ocean City, NJ, 08226; **PH:** 1-609-399-0012; **Fax:** 1-609-399-3614; **http://** www.ochome.com; **Email:** service@ochome.com

General - Incorporation	USA	**Stock**- Price on:12/24/2007	$12.93
Employees	102	Stock Exchange	NDQ
Auditor	Deloitte& Touche LLP	Ticker Symbol	OSHC
Stk Agt	Registrar & Transfer Co	Outstanding Shares	8,550,000
Counsel	NA	E.P.S.	$0.35
DUNS No.	NA	Shareholders	NA

Business: The groups principal activity is to provide financial services. The products of the group include one to four family residential mortgage loans, consumer loan and construction loan. The group operates from the United States. The assets of the group for the year 2006 were $562,260 (thousands).

Primary SIC and add'l.: 6035 6712

CIK No: 0001298716

Subsidiaries: Ocean City Home Bank, Seashore Financial Services, LLC

Officers: Steven E. Brady/CEO, Pres., Dir. - Ocean City Home Bank's, Kim M. Davidson/Exec. VP - Business Development, Corp. Sec. - Ocean City Home Bank's, Donald F. Morgenweck/Sr. VP, CFO - Ocean City Home Bank's, Anthony J. Rizzotte/Exec. VP, Chief Lending Officer - Ocean City Home Bank's, Janet M. Bossi/Sr. VP - Loan Administration, Ocean City Home Bank's, Paul J. Esposito/Sr. VP - Marketing, Ocean City Home Bank's

Directors: Steven E. Brady/CEO, Pres., Dir. - Ocean City Home Bank's, Robert A. Previti/Chmn. - Ocean City Home Bank's, Christopher J. Ford/Dir. - Ocean City Home Bank's, Samuel R. Young/Dir. - Ocean City Home Bank's, Sylva A. Bertini/Dir. - Ocean City Home Bank's, Frederick G. Dalzell/Dir. - Ocean City Home Bank's, John L. Van Duyne/Dir. - Ocean City Home Bank's

Owners: Hovde Capital Advisors LLC/9.60%, Kim M. Davidson, Christopher J. Ford, Robert A. Previti, Paul J. Esposito, Steven E. Brady, Insiders/4.40%, Sylva A. Bertini, Anthony J. Rizzotte, John L. Van Duyne, Frederick G. Dalzell, OC Financial MHC/54.30%, Samuel R. Young, Donald F. Morgenweck

Financial Data: Fiscal Year End:12/31 Latest Annual Data: 12/31/2006

Year	Sales	Net Income
2006	$32,170,000	$3,149,000
2005	$28,588,000	$3,076,000
2004	$25,111,000	$1,306,000

Curr. Assets:	$35,622,000	Curr. Liab.:	$479,018,000		
Plant, Equip.:	$10,181,000	Total Liab.:	$499,710,000	Indic. Yr. Divd.:	NA
Total Assets:	$562,260,000	Net Worth:	$62,551,000	Debt/ Equity:	NA

Ocean West Holding Corp

15991 Redhill Ave., Tustin, CA, 92780; **PH:** 1-949-861-2590

General - Incorporation	DE	**Stock**- Price on:12/24/2007	NA
Employees	161	Stock Exchange	OTC
Auditor	Webb & Co P.A	Ticker Symbol	AKMN
Stk Agt	Registrar & Transfer Co	Outstanding Shares	NA
Counsel	Ogden Newell & Welch	E.P.S.	$0.15
DUNS No.	NA	Shareholders	NA

Business: The groups' principal activity is to originate, package, fund and sell government-insured and non-conforming residential mortgage loans secured by one-to-four family residences. The group also originates, purchases and sells mortgage-servicing rights. The customers of the group include real estate agents, homeowners and builders. The group solely operates in the United States.

Primary SIC and add'l.: 6719 6159

CIK No: 0001104538

Subsidiaries: InfoByPhone, Inc.

Owners: Yvon Cormier/6.30%, Alan Smith/1.70%, Darryl Cohen/11.30%, Yvon Cormier/6.30%, Dolphin Offshore Partners, L.P./5.70%, Baruch Halpern Revocable Trust/6.50%, Insiders/14.00%, Noble Consultants Ltd./6.50%, Sandro Sordi/1.60%, Baruch Halpern Revocable Trust/6.50%, Insiders/14.00%, Arjent Ltd./9.90%, Sandro Sordi/1.60%, Noble Consultants Ltd./6.50%, Alan Smith/1.70% (20 Owners included in Index)

Financial Data: Fiscal Year End:12/31 Latest Annual Data: 12/31/2006

Year	Sales	Net Income
2006	$28,000	-$12,574,000
2005	$11,000	-$8,820,000
2004	$6,874,000	-$2,873,000

Curr. Assets:	$7,909,000	Curr. Liab.:	$8,734,000		
Plant, Equip.:	$252,000	Total Liab.:	$9,304,000	Indic. Yr. Divd.:	NA
Total Assets:	$8,265,000	Net Worth:	-$1,039,000	Debt/ Equity:	NA

Oceaneering International Inc

11911 FM 529, Houston, TX, 77041; **PH:** 1-713-329-4500; **Fax:** 1-713-329-4951; **http://** www.oceaneering.com

General - Incorporation	DE	**Stock**- Price on:12/24/2007	$53.07
Employees	6,500	Stock Exchange	NYSE
Auditor	Ernst & Young LLP	Ticker Symbol	OII
Stk Agt	Computershare Investor Services LLC	Outstanding Shares	54,530,000
Counsel	Baker & Botts LLP	E.P.S.	$2.40
DUNS No.	05-514-7490	Shareholders	NA

Business: The group's principal activities are to provide integrated technical services and hardware for underwater and space operations. It operates in five segments, classified into offshore oil and gas and advanced technologies. Offshore oil and gas includes remotely operated vehicles, subsea products, mobile offshore production systems and related services. The advanced technologies segment provides

underwater intervention, engineering services and related manufacturing for ship and submarine husbandry, subsea cable field support and civil works projects. Customers include oil and gas companies governments and telecommunications, aerospace, marine engineering and construction firms. On 16-Jan-2003, the group acquired ois international inspection plc and 02-Sep-2003, rotator as.

Primary SIC and add'l.: 7389 1389

CIK No: 0000073756

Subsidiaries: Consolidated Launcher Technology, Inc., Grayloc Products Ltd., Grayloc Products, LLC, Marine Production Systems do Brasil Ltda., Marine Production Systems Ltd., Marine Technologies Ltd., Nauticos Corporation, Oceaneering AS, Oceaneering Australia Pty. Limited, Oceaneering Canada, Ltd., Oceaneering FSC, Inc., Oceaneering International (Sharjah) Limited, Oceaneering International AG, Oceaneering International Dubai LLC, Oceaneering International Pte Ltd 24 Subsidiaries included in the Index

Officers: Jay T. Collins/CEO, Pres./$4,081,631.00, George R. Haubenreich/Sr. VP - General Counsel, Sec./$1,920,379.00, Kevin M. McEvoy/Exec. VP/$2,104,633.00, Marvin J. Migura/Sr. VP, CFO/$1,946,097.00, Philip D. Gardner/Sr. VP - Subsea Products/$802,778.00, Cardon W. Gerner/VP, Chief Accounting Officer

Directors: John R. Huff/62/Chmn., Harris J. Pappas/Dir., Jerold J. Desroche/71/Dir., Michael D. Hughes/69/Dir., David S. Hooker/Dir.

Owners: Insiders, EARNEST Partners, LLC/10.20%, Jerold J. DesRoche, Marvin J. Migura, Neuberger Berman, Inc./5.90%, George R. Haubenreich, Jay T. Collins, Harris J. Pappas, Philip D. Gardner, John R. Huff, FMR Corp./5.30%, Kevin M. McEvoy, David S. Hooker, Michael D. Hughes

Financial Data: Fiscal Year End:03/31 Latest Annual Data: 12/31/2006

Year	Sales	Net Income
2006	$1,280,198,000	$124,494,000
2005	$998,543,000	$62,680,000
2004	$780,181,000	$40,300,000

Curr. Assets:	$523,645,000	Curr. Liab.:	$279,706,000	P/E Ratio:	22.11
Plant, Equip.:	$523,707,000	Total Liab.:	$538,743,000	Indic. Yr. Divd.:	NA
Total Assets:	$1,242,022,000	Net Worth:	$696,764,000	Debt/ Equity:	0.3234

Oceanfirst Financial Corp

975 Hooper Ave., Toms River, NJ, 08753; **PH:** 1-732-240-4500; **Fax:** 1-732-349-5070; **http://** www.oceanfirstonline.com

General - Incorporation	DE	**Stock**- Price on:12/24/2007	$18.16
Employees	445	Stock Exchange	NDQ
Auditor	KPMG LLP	Ticker Symbol	OCFC
Stk Agt	American Stock Transfer & Trust Co.	Outstanding Shares	12,320,000
Counsel	Muldoon, Murphy & Faucette	E.P.S.	-$0.3
DUNS No.	07-514-3131	Shareholders	NA

Business: The group's principal activity is to accept retail deposits from the general public and invest these deposits in single-family, owner-occupied residential mortgage loans. The group offers commercial real estate loans, multi-family loans, construction loans, consumer and commercial loans and provides trust and asset management services. It also sells alternative investment products such as mutual funds, annuities and life insurance. In addition, the group's subsidiary, columbia equities ltd originates, sells and provides a full product line of residential mortgage loans. The group conducts its operations through its 17 branch offices located in ocean county, monmouth county and middlesex county, New Jersey.

Primary SIC and add'l.: 6035 6712

CIK No: 0001004702

Subsidiaries: Columbia Home Loans, LLC, OceanFirst REIT Holdings, Inc., OceanFirst Services, LLC

Officers: John R. Garbarino/58/Chmn., CEO, Pres./$941,756.00, John K. Kelly/Corp. Sec./$254,331.00, Michael J. Fitzpatrick/52/CFO, Exec. VP/$344,742.00, Vito R. Nardelli/58/Exec. VP/$361,431.00, Catherine Farley/VP, Trust Officer

Directors: John R. Garbarino/58/Chmn., CEO, Pres., Joseph J. Burke/60/Dir., John W. Chadwick/66/Dir., Carl Feltz/69/Dir., Donald E. McLaughlin/60/Dir., Diane F. Rhine/58/Dir. - Human Resources, John E. Walsh/54/Dir., Angelo Catania/58/Dir., Robert M. Pardes/48/Dir.

Owners: Carl Feltz, OceanFirst Bank,/18.31%, OceanFirst Foundation/12.01%, John K. Kelly/1.09%, John W. Chadwick/0.24%, James T. Snyder/0.58%, Diane F. Rhine/0.54%, Angelo Catania/0.02%, Private Capital Management/6.28%, Donald E. McLaughlin/0.70%, Vito R. Nardelli/0.34%, John R. Garbarino/6.05%, Michael J. Fitzpatrick/2.01%, John E. Walsh/0.62%, Robert M. Pardes/1.20% (17 Owners included in Index)

Financial Data: Fiscal Year End:12/31 Latest Annual Data: 12/31/2006

Year	Sales	Net Income
2006	$130,170,000	$12,633,000
2005	$126,889,000	$19,497,000
2004	$111,692,000	$17,945,000

Curr. Assets:	$40,287,000	Curr. Liab.:	$1,887,810,000		
Plant, Equip.:	$18,484,000	Total Liab.:	$1,944,682,000	Indic. Yr. Divd.:	$0.800
Total Assets:	$2,077,002,000	Net Worth:	$132,320,000	Debt/ Equity:	0.1396

Oceanic Exploration Co

7800 E Dorado Pl., Ste. 250, Greenwood, CO, 80111; **PH:** 1-303-220-8330

General - Incorporation	DE	**Stock**- Price on:12/24/2007	$0.17
Employees	9	Stock Exchange	OTC
Auditor	Grant Thornton LLP	Ticker Symbol	OCEX
Stk Agt	Mellon Investor Services LLC	Outstanding Shares	NA
Counsel	NA	E.P.S.	-$0.04
DUNS No.	04-813-2153	Shareholders	NA

Business: The group's principal activity is to acquire and develop oil and gas sites. The group conducts exploration activities, including seismic and other geophysical evaluation and exploratory drilling where appropriate. It provides full-service employment solutions to clients through strategic partnerships through its alliance employment solutions division. It offers employment services in executive search, professional and technical placement, human resources consulting, site management and contract staffing. The group's property interests are located in the north aegean sea, offshore Greece, in the east China sea and in the timor gap, a strait that lies between east timor and Australia.

Primary SIC and add'l.: 1381 8741 1382 8330

CIK No: 0000073759

Subsidiaries: Oceanic International Properties Corporation, Petrotimor Companhia de Petrleos, S.A. (Petrotimor)

Owners: Sidney H. Stires, Gene E. Burke, Cordillera Corporation, Insiders, NWO Resources, Inc./89.20%

Financial Data: Fiscal Year End: 12/31 **Latest Annual Data:** 12/31/2006

Year	Sales	Net Income
2006	$1,063,000	-$2,490,000
2005	$948,000	-$2,198,000
2004	$833,000	-$2,740,000

Curr. Assets:	$3,009,000	Curr. Liab.:	$1,210,000		
Plant, Equip.:	$20,000	Total Liab.:	$2,017,000	Indic. Yr. Divd.:	NA
Total Assets:	$3,029,000	Net Worth:	$1,012,000	Debt/ Equity:	NA

Octus Inc

Marbella, Avenida Aquilino De La Guardia Y Calle 47, Edificio Ocean Plaza, Piso 16;
PH: 507-265-1555

General - Incorporation	CA	**Stock** - Price on:12/24/2007	$0.1
Employees	NA	Stock Exchange	OTC
Auditor	Stark Winter Schenkein & Co. LLP	Ticker Symbol	OCTI
Stk Agt	Stalt, Inc.	Outstanding Shares	13,440,000
Counsel	NA	E.P.S.	$0.00
DUNS No.	10-916-7379	Shareholders	NA

Business: The group's principle activity is to design and develop computer software and associated software products that are focused on the integration of personal computer and the telephone. The group licensed its software under the trade name octus pta (personal telephone assistant). Currently, the group is seeking alternative business opportunities, which may include the acquisition of other software products or acquisition of some other technology.

Primary SIC and add'l.: 7372

CIK No: 0000891462

Officers: Josie Ben Rubi/38/Dir., CEO, CFO, Pres.

Directors: Josie Ben Rubi/38/Dir., CEO, CFO, Pres.

Owners: Grupo Dynastia S.A./6.00%

Financial Data: Fiscal Year End: 12/31 **Latest Annual Data:** 12/31/2006

Year	Sales	Net Income
2006	NA	-$46,000
2005	NA	-$70,000
2004	NA	-$59,000

Curr. Assets:	NA	Curr. Liab.:	$397,000		
Plant, Equip.:	NA	Total Liab.:	$397,000	Indic. Yr. Divd.:	NA
Total Assets:	NA	Net Worth:	-$397,000	Debt/ Equity:	NA

Ocwen Financial Corp

1661 Worthington Rd., Ste. 100, West Palm Beach, FL, 33409; **PH:** 1-561-682-8000;
Fax: 1-561-682-8177; **http://** www.ocwen.com; **Email:** international@ocwen.com

General - Incorporation	FL	**Stock** - Price on:12/24/2007	$13.55
Employees	3,303	Stock Exchange	NYSE
Auditor	PricewaterhouseCoopers LLP	Ticker Symbol	OCN
Stk Agt	American Stock Transfer & Trust Co.	Outstanding Shares	62,310,000
Counsel	NA	E.P.S.	$1.01
DUNS No.	18-695-7114	Shareholders	NA

Business: The group's principal activity is to service and resolve subperforming and nonperforming residential and commercial mortgage loans. It also provides related development of loan servicing technology and business-to-business e-commerce technology solutions for the mortgage and real estate industries. The group is a holding company operating through subsidiaries, including ocwen federal bank fsb, investors mortgage insurance holding company, ocwen technology xchange inc and ocwen asset investment corp. International operations are conducted in Tokyo, Japan and Taipei, Taiwan.

Primary SIC and add'l.: 6712 6035

CIK No: 0000873860

Subsidiaries: Global Servicing Solutions, LLC, Investors Mortgage Insurance Holding Company, Ocwen Asia Holdings Ltd., Ocwen Asset Investment - UK, LLC, Ocwen Asset Investment Corp., Ocwen Capital Trust I, Ocwen Financial Solutions Private Limited, Ocwen General, Inc., Ocwen Loan Servicing, LLC, Ocwen Luxembourg, Sarl, Ocwen Mortgage Asset Investment Company, LLC, Ocwen Mortgage Asset Trust, Ocwen Mortgage Company, LLC, Ocwen Partnership, L.P., RMSI, Inc

Officers: William C. Erbey/Chmn., CEO/$1,215,692.00, Ronald M. Faris/Dir., Pres./$1,062,431.00, William B. Shepro/39/Sr. VP/$572,159.00, David J. Gunter/49/Sr. VP, CFO/$284,149.00, Kevin J. Wilcox/Sec.

Directors: William C. Erbey/Chmn., CEO, Ronald M. Faris/Dir., Pres., Michael W. Linn/59/Dir., Barry N. Wish/66/Dir., Martha Clark Goss/58/Dir., William H. Lacy/63/Dir., W. C. Martin/59/Dir., Ronald J. Korn/67/Dir.

Owners: Ronald J. Korn, William C. Erbey/30.46%, Perry Corp./5.74%, Dimensional Fund Advisors LP/5.72%, William H. Lacy, William B. Shepro, Ronald M. Faris/1.37%, Insiders/42.97%, Barry N. Wish/11.16%, David J. Gunter, W. C. Martin, Martha C. Goss, Michael W. Linn, Altus Capital, LLC/5.19%

Financial Data: Fiscal Year End: 12/31 **Latest Annual Data:** 12/31/2006

Year	Sales	Net Income
2006	$431,719,000	$206,510,000
2005	$375,376,000	$15,065,000
2004	$246,703,000	$57,724,000

Curr. Assets:	$523,238,000	Curr. Liab.:	$2,421,000	P/E Ratio:	13.42
Plant, Equip.:	$44,033,000	Total Liab.:	$1,449,974,000	Indic. Yr. Divd.:	NA
Total Assets:	$2,009,743,000	Net Worth:	$557,979,000	Debt/ Equity:	0.9584

Odyne Corp

89 Cabot Ct., Ste. L, Hauppauge, NY, 11788; **PH:** 1-631-750-1010; **Fax:** 1-631-750-1011;
http:// www.odyne.com; **Email:** info@odyne.com

General - Incorporation	DE	**Stock** - Price on:12/24/2007	$0.38
Employees	17	Stock Exchange	OTC
Auditor	Most & Company, LLP	Ticker Symbol	ODYC
Stk Agt	Action Stock Transfer Corp	Outstanding Shares	19,240,000
Counsel	Greenberg Traurig, LLP	E.P.S.	-$0.38
DUNS No.	NA	Shareholders	NA

Business: The groups principle activities include providing and marketing, communications and computer networking and integration advice to small and medium sized businesses in the financial services industry. The group operates from the United States.

Primary SIC and add'l.: 3714

CIK No: 0001346377

Officers: Konstantinos Sfakianos/CEO, Alan Tannebaum/Chmn., CEO, Andrew Lavin/Contact - Investor Relations, Joseph M. Ambrosio/Exec. VP - Engineering, CTO, Joshua A. Hauser/Dir., COO, Pres., Daniel Bartley/CFO

Directors: Alan Tannebaum/Chmn., CEO, Bruce E. Humenik/Dir., Roger M. Slotkin/55/Dir., Joshua A. Hauser/Dir., COO, Pres., Charles S. Tabak/Dir., Stanley W. Struble/Dir.

Owners: Stanley W. Struble, Alan Tannenbaum/5.80%, Joshua A. Hauser/8.50%, Konstantinos Sfakianos/15.50%, Insiders/44.90%, Bruce E. Humenik, Joseph M. Ambrosio/14.80%, Charles S. Tabak, Roger M. Slotkin/16.10%

Financial Data: Fiscal Year End: 06/30 **Latest Annual Data:** 12/31/2006

Year	Sales	Net Income
2006	$243,000	-$2,010,000

Curr. Assets:	$3,580,000	Curr. Liab.:	$610,000		
Plant, Equip.:	$99,000	Total Liab.:	$856,000	Indic. Yr. Divd.:	NA
Total Assets:	$3,703,000	Net Worth:	$2,847,000	Debt/ Equity:	NA

Odyssey Healthcare Inc

717 N Harwood, Ste. 1500, Dallas, TX, 75201; **PH:** 1-214-922-9711; **Fax:** 1-214-922-9752;
http:// www.odyssey-healthcare.com; **Email:** info@odsyhealth.com

General - Incorporation	DE	**Stock** - Price on:12/24/2007	$12.04
Employees	4,309	Stock Exchange	NDQ
Auditor	Ernst & Young LLP	Ticker Symbol	ODSY
Stk Agt	U.S. Stock Transfer Corp	Outstanding Shares	33,770,000
Counsel	Vinson & Elkins LLP	E.P.S.	$0.38
DUNS No.	NA	Shareholders	NA

Business: The group's principal activity is to provide hospice services in the United States. As a hospice care provider, the group supports to improve the quality of life of terminally ill patients and their families. Hospice services focuses on palliative care for patients with life-limiting illnesses, which is care directed at managing pain and other discomforting symptoms and addressing the psychosocial and spiritual needs of patients and their families. The group operates through 68 hospice locations situated in 29 states. Hospice care is a covered benefit under the medicare program. In 2003, the group acquired good shepherd hospice, palliative care center llc, mahogany hospice care inc, homecare hospice inc, omega hospice ltd, first state hospice llc, Utah's heritage hospice llc, grace inc and palliative care inc. On 15-Jan-2004, it acquired crown of Texas hospice southeast, ltd.

Primary SIC and add'l.: 8059

CIK No: 0001129623

Subsidiaries: At Home Hospice, Inc., Hospice of the Palm Coast, Inc., Odyssey HealthCare GP, LLC, Odyssey HealthCare Holding Company, Odyssey HealthCare LP, LLC, Odyssey HealthCare Management, LP, Odyssey HealthCare Operating B, LP, Odyssey HelthCare Operating A, LP

Officers: Robert A. Lefton/CEO, Pres./$1,250,333.00, Woodrin Grossman/Sr. VP - Strategy, Development/$728,462.00, Deborah A. Hoffpauir/46/COO, Sr. VP/$671,178.00, Brenda A. Belger/Sr. VP - Human Resources, Bradley W. Bickham/VP, General Counsel/$456,472.00, Dirk R. Allison/Sr. VP, CFO/$59,023.00

Directors: Richard R. Burnham/Chmn., Kathleen A. Ventre/Dir. - Clinical Affairs, Shawn S. Schabel/43/Dir., Paul J. Feldstein/74/Dir., John K. Carlyle/53/Dir., David W. Cross/61/Dir., David L. Steffy/64/Dir.

Owners: FMR Corp./8.50%, Insiders/8.00%, Bradley W. Bickham, David W. Cross, Woodrin Grossman, Paul J. Feldstein, Shapiro Capital Management LLC/14.50%, John K. Carlyle, Robert A. Lefton, Deborah A. Hoffpauir, Richard R. Burnham/2.60%, Barclays Global Investors, NA/5.40%, Wellington Management Company, LLP/8.50%, Baron Capital Group, Inc./5.50%, David L. Steffy/2.30% *(16 Owners included in Index)*

Financial Data: Fiscal Year End: 12/31 **Latest Annual Data:** 12/31/2006

Year	Sales	Net Income
2006	$409,831,000	$19,729,000
2005	$381,649,000	$18,556,000
2004	$350,276,000	$34,996,000

Curr. Assets:	$145,929,000	Curr. Liab.:	$76,131,000	P/E Ratio:	23.61
Plant, Equip.:	$20,881,000	Total Liab.:	$90,390,000	Indic. Yr. Divd.:	NA
Total Assets:	$269,986,000	Net Worth:	$179,596,000	Debt/ Equity:	NA

Odyssey Marine Exploration Inc

5215 W Laurel St., Tampa, FL, 33607; **PH:** 1-813-876-1776; **Fax:** 1-813-876-1777;
http:// shipwreck.net

General - Incorporation	NV	**Stock** - Price on:12/24/2007	$6.35
Employees	57	Stock Exchange	NDQ
Auditor	Ferlita, Walsh & Gonzalez P.A	Ticker Symbol	OMEX
Stk Agt	Computershare Trust Co	Outstanding Shares	46,970,000
Counsel	NA	E.P.S.	-$0.42
DUNS No.	NA	Shareholders	NA

Business: The group's principal activity is to explore and recover the archaelogically sensitive deep-water shipwrecks throughout the world. The group employs advanced state-of-the-art technology including side scan sonar, remotely operated vehicles, or rovs, and other advanced technology, which enables the group to locate and recover shipwrecks at depths that were previously unreachable in an economically feasible manner. The group's projects are conducted in two phases. The search phase is usually conducted from a smaller vessel outfitted with survey equipment and an inspection rov. The recovery phase requires a vessel equipped with a work class rov, both long baseline and usbl acoustic positioning systems and certain odyssey technology and proprietary software, which allows the group to record the recovery in an archaeology sound fashion.

Primary SIC and add'l.: 7389

CIK No: 0000798528

Subsidiaries: Odyssey Marine Entertainment, Inc., Odyssey Marine Services, Inc., Odyssey Marine, Inc., Odyssey Retriever, Inc., OVH, Inc.

Officers: John C. Morris/Co - Founder, Chmn., CEO/$332,125.00, Davis D. Howe/49/COO/$224,334.00, George J. Becker/73/Pres./$175,066.00, David Morris/Sec., Treasurer/$175,066.00, Michael J. Holmes/CFO/$224,334.00, Jay A. Nudi/Chief Accounting Officer, Controller, Mark D. Gordon/47/Dir. - Business Development

Directors: John C. Morris/Co - Founder, Chmn., CEO, Greg Stemm/Co - Founder, Chmn., David Bederman/Dir., George Knutsson/Dir., George E. Lackman/Dir., David J. Saul/Dir.

Owners: Jay A. Nudi, George J. Becker, George E. Lackman, David A. Morris/1.10%, George Knutsson, Gregory P. Stemm/4.40%, Insiders/12.20%, David J. Saul/1.20%, Drawbridge Global Macro Master Fund Ltd./9.90%, Michael J. Holmes, David J. Bederman, Mark D. Gordon, GLG Partners LP/9.90%, GLG North American Opportunity Fund/7.70%, John C. Morris/3.70% *(17 Owners included in Index)*

Financial Data: Fiscal Year End:12/31   Latest Annual Data: 12/31/2006

Year	Sales	Net Income
2006	$5,064,000	-$19,088,000
2005	$10,037,000	-$14,920,000
2004	$17,622,000	$5,229,000

Curr. Assets:	$5,482,000	Curr. Liab.:	$5,901,000		
Plant, Equip.:	$19,288,000	Total Liab.:	$9,842,000	Indic. Yr. Divd.:	NA
Total Assets:	$27,208,000	Net Worth:	$17,366,000	Debt/ Equity:	0.1422

Odyssey Oil & Gas Inc

5005 Riverway, Ste. 440, Houston, TX, 77056; *PH:* 1-713-623-2219

General - Incorporation	FL	**Stock**- Price on:12/24/2007	$0.5
Employees	1	Stock Exchange	OTC
Auditor	Webb & Company, P. A.	Ticker Symbol	OOGI
Stk Agt.	NA	Outstanding Shares	31,100,000
Counsel	NA	E.P.S.	-$0.01
DUNS No.	NA	Shareholders	NA

Business: The groups principle activities include developing and marketing premium quality, premium priced, branded fitness and exercise equipment to the home fitness equipment market. In the year April 2006, CardioBioMedical Corporation merged with Odyssey Oil & Gas, Inc. The group operates from the United States.

Primary SIC and add'l.: 1382

CIK No: 0001160798

Subsidiaries: Advanced Sports Technologies, Inc., CardioBioMedical Corporation

Officers: James F. Mongiardo/Dir., was Elected CEO, Pres., Arthur Johnson/CFO, Pres., Principal Executive,Accounting Officer, Sole Dir.

Directors: James F. Mongiardo/Dir., was Elected CEO, Pres., Arthur Johnson/CFO, Pres., Principal Executive,Accounting Officer, Sole Dir.

Owners: Curtis Olschansky/17.00%, Centurion Gold Holdings, Inc/64.30%

Financial Data: Fiscal Year End:03/31   Latest Annual Data: 12/31/2006

Year	Sales	Net Income
2006	$19,000	-$141,000
2005	NA	-$1,697,000
2004	NA	-$196,000

Curr. Assets:	$5,000	Curr. Liab.:	$211,000		
Plant, Equip.:	NA	Total Liab.:	$211,000	Indic. Yr. Divd.:	NA
Total Assets:	$5,000	Net Worth:	-$205,000	Debt/ Equity:	NA

Odyssey Re Holdings Corp

300 First Stamford Pl., Stamford, CT, 06902; *PH:* 1-203-977-8000; *Fax:* 1-203-356-0196; *http://* www.odysseyre.com

General - Incorporation	DE	**Stock**- Price on:12/24/2007	$43.75
Employees	610	Stock Exchange	NYSE
Auditor	PricewaterhouseCoopers LLP	Ticker Symbol	ORH
Stk Agt.	Bank of New York	Outstanding Shares	72,260,000
Counsel	NA	E.P.S.	$5.19
DUNS No.	NA	Shareholders	NA

Business: The group's principal activity is to provide reinsurance services to property and casualty insurers and reinsurers. The group is a holding company for reinsurance-related subsidiaries of fairfax financial holdings limited. It approaches and conducts its business through three divisions: Americas, london market and euroasia. The Americas division writes treaty property, general casualty, specialty casualty and facultative casualty reinsurance in the United States, Canada and Latin America. The london market division primarily writes property, marine and aerospace reinsurance business as well as casualty and financial lines primary insurance. The euroasia division writes primarily treaty and facultative reinsurance property business and is comprised of offices in Paris, stockholm, Singapore and Tokyo. On 28-Oct-2003, the group acquired surplus lines shell.

Primary SIC and add'l.: 6361 6321 6719

CIK No: 0001137048

Subsidiaries: Clearwater Insurance Company, Clearwater Select Insurance Company, Hudson Insurance Company, Hudson Specialty Insurance Company, Newline Corporate Name Limited, Newline Holdings UK Limited, Newline Insurance Company Limited, Newline Underwriting Limited, O.R.E. Holdings Limited, Odyssey America Reinsurance Corporation, Odyssey Holdings Latin America, Inc., Odyssey Latin America Inc., Odyssey UK Holdings Corp.

Officers: Andrew A. Barnard/Dir., CEO, Pres./$5,582,305.00, Lucien Pietropoli/CEO - Euroasia Division, Michael G. Wacek/CEO - Americas Division/$1,369,479.00, Brian D. Young/CEO - London Marketing Division, James E. Migliorini/CEO - US Insurance Division, Mark W. Hinkley/Exec. VP - Marketing, Communications, Claude Oger/General Sec. - Communications, Euroasia Division, Herve Leduc/CFO - Reinsurance, Euroasia, Stephen L. Gordon/Active Underwriter, Newline Syndicate, Chief Underwriting Officer - Nicl, Reinsurance, London Marketing, Martin Campbell/Sr. Underwriter, Financial Instituions, Crime, Reinsurance, London Marketing, Richard Smart/Sr. Underwriter, Professional Indemnity, Reinsurance, London Marketing, Adam Harper/Sr. Underwriter, Dir., Officers Liability - Reinsurance, London Marketing, Donald L. Smith/Sr. VP, General Counsel, Corp. Sec./$726,865.00, Brian D. Quinn/Exec. VP - US Casualty Treaty, Arturo E. Falcon/Sr. VP - Latin America *(41 Officers included in Index)*

Directors: Andrew A. Barnard/Dir., CEO, Pres., James F. Dowd/Dir., Anthony F. Griffiths/Independent Business Consultant, Corp. Dir., Samuel A. Mitchell/Dir., Brandon W. Sweitzer/Dir., Prem V. Watsa/Dir., Patrick W. Kenny/Dir., Bradley P. Martin/Dir., Peter M. Bennett/Dir., Paul M. Wolff/Dir.

Owners: Anthony F. Griffiths, Scott R. Donovan, TIG Insurance Group, Inc./42.07%, James F. Dowd, Brandon W. Sweitzer, Fairfax Financial Holdings Limited/0.25%, Marshfield Associates/5.79%, ORH Holdings Inc/8.67%, TIG Insurance Company/5.50%, Anthony J. Narciso, Samuel A. Mitchell, Donald L. Smith, Insiders/1.22%, Michael G. Wacek, Fairfax Inc./1.95% *(20 Owners included in Index)*

Financial Data: Fiscal Year End:12/31   Latest Annual Data: 06/30/2007

Year	Sales	Net Income
2007	$720,339,000	$147,636,000
2006	$654,623,000	$85,867,000
2005	$2,556,778,000	-$115,722,000

Curr. Assets:	$4,142,451,000	Curr. Liab.:	$102,711,000	P/E Ratio:	7.23
Plant, Equip.:	NA	Total Liab.:	$6,870,133,000	Indic. Yr. Divd.:	$0.250
Total Assets:	$8,953,712,000	Net Worth:	$2,083,579,000	Debt/ Equity:	0.2925

Office Depot Inc

2200 Old Germantown Rd., Delray Beach, FL, 33445; *PH:* 1-561-438-4800; *Fax:* 1-561-438-4001; *http://* www.officedepot.com; *Email:* investor.relations@officedepot.com

General - Incorporation	DE	**Stock**- Price on:12/24/2007	$33.54
Employees	26,000	Stock Exchange	NYSE
Auditor	Deloitte & Touche LLP	Ticker Symbol	ODP
Stk Agt	Mellon Investor Services LLC	Outstanding Shares	274,800,000
Counsel	Kirkland & Ellis LLP	E.P.S.	$1.90
DUNS No.	15-353-1108	Shareholders	NA

Business: The group's principle activity is to provide office products and services. The groups products include general office supplies, technology products and office furniture. The group operates through three segments namely North American Retail, North American Business Solutions n and International Division. In the year 2006, the group acquired Papirius s.r.o. The group operates from United States, Canada and France.

Primary SIC and add'l.: 5712 5112 5943 5734 5045 5999 5044

CIK No: 0000800240

Subsidiaries: Eastman Office Supplies, Inc., OD International, Inc., Office Depot International BV (2), Office Depot of Texas, L.P., The Office Club, Inc., Viking Office Products, Inc.

Officers: Steve Odland/Chmn., CEO/$11,749,080.00, Carl Rubin/48/Pres. - North American Retail, Daisy Vanderlinde/Exec. VP - Human Resources/$1,882,548.00, Renny Johnson/Dir. - Real Estate, WA, OR, MT, ID, Nocal, Ken Hrabar/Dir. - Real Estate, S IL, KY, MD - DC, VA, WV, NJ, NY, Excluding Upstate, E PA, DE, Jennifer Moline/50/Sr. VP, Controller, Ana Rimkus/Sr. Dir. - Real Estate, CO, UT, WY, NM, AZ, AK, HI, NV, Scott Whitney/Dir. - Real Estate, Southern CA, Steven M. Schmidt/Pres. - North American Business Solutions Division, Elisa D. Garcia/Exec. VP, General Counsel, Corp. Sec., Rosalie Ferran/Sr. Dir. - Real Estate, Northern TX, Charles E. Brown/Pres. - International/$2,546,110.00, Patricia A. McKay/CFO, Exec. VP/$2,210,013.00, Monica Luechtefeld/Exec. VP - Business Development, Supply Chain, Information Technology, Cynthia Campbell/Exec. VP - Business Solutions Division *(27 Officers included in Index)*

Directors: Steve Odland/Chmn., CEO, Myra M. Hart/Dir., Brenda J. Gaines/Dir., David W. Bernauer/Dir., Kathleen Mason/Dir., Marsha Johnson Evans/Dir., Lee A. Ault/Dir., Abelardo E. Bru/Dir., Neil R. Austrian/Dir., David I. Fuente/Dir., Scott W. Hedrick/Dir., Michael J. Myers/Dir., Wendy K. Baumann/Member - Office Depot Women's Advisory Board, Carolyn Elman/Member - Office Depot Women's Advisory Board, Edie Fraser/Member - Office Depot Women's Advisory Board *(21 Directors included in Index)*

Owners: Insiders/1.80%, David W. Bernauer, Abelardo E. Bru, David I. Fuente, Carl Rubin, Brenda Gaines, Myra M. Hart, 45 Fremont Street, San Francisco, CA 94105 USA/9.97%, Daisy L. Vanderlinde, Lee A. Ault, Charles Brown, Kathleen Mason, Neil R. Austrian, 32 Old Slip, New York, 10005 USA/5.80%, Patricia A. McKay *(20 Owners included in Index)*

Financial Data: Fiscal Year End:12/31   Latest Annual Data: 12/30/2006

Year	Sales	Net Income
2006	$15,010,781,000	$516,135,000
2005	$14,278,944,000	$273,792,000
2004	$13,564,699,000	$335,504,000

Curr. Assets:	$3,530,062,000	Curr. Liab.:	$2,468,751,000	P/E Ratio:	17.65
Plant, Equip.:	$1,311,737,000	Total Liab.:	$3,359,304,000	Indic. Yr. Divd.:	NA
Total Assets:	$6,098,525,000	Net Worth:	$2,739,221,000	Debt/ Equity:	0.2087

Officemax Inc

263 Shuman Blvd., Naperville, IL, 60563; *PH:* 1-630-438-7800; *Fax:* 1-630-864-4422; *http://* www.officemax.com

General - Incorporation	DE	**Stock**- Price on:12/24/2007	$40.78
Employees	25,000	Stock Exchange	NYSE
Auditor	KPMG LLP	Ticker Symbol	OMX
Stk Agt	EquiServe Trust Co N.A	Outstanding Shares	75,340,000
Counsel	Baker & Hostetler	E.P.S.	$2.28
DUNS No.	18-512-2629	Shareholders	NA

Business: The group's principle activity is to operate high-volume, deep-discount office products superstores. Products offered at its retail stores include office products, business-machines and related items and copymax and furnituremax in-store modules devoted exclusively to print-for-pay services and office furniture. These products are marketed primarily to small- and medium-sized businesses, home office customers and individual consumers. The group offers its products through two business segments, namely, domestic and international. Domestic segment includes its retail store operations in the United States, ecommerce operations, catalog business and outside sales groups. International segment includes the operations of its joint venture in Mexico, officemax de Mexico. The group's quarterly revenue for September 2007 was 2,315.22 millions of USD.

Primary SIC and add'l.: 5044

CIK No: 0000012978

Subsidiaries: Clearfield Insurance Limited, Grand & Toy Limited, Loving Creek Funding Corporation, National Office Products Ltd., OfficeMax Contract, Inc., OfficeMax de Mexico, OfficeMax Nevada Company, OfficeMax New Zealand Limited, OfficeMax North America, Inc., OfficeMax Southern Company, OMX Timber Finance Holdings I, LLC, OMX Timber Finance Holdings II, LLC, Picabo Holdings, Inc.

Officers: Sam K. Duncan/Chmn., CEO/$5,572,341.00, Phillip P. Depaul/37/Sr. VP, Controller, Chief Accounting Officer/$1,029,914.00, Michael D. Rowsey/Pres. - Contract Division/$2,437,030.00, Ryan T. Vero/Exec. VP, Chief Merchandising Officer/$2,431,342.00, Don Civgin/CFO, Exec. VP - Officemax/$2,092,181.00, Harold Mulet/Exec. VP - Retail Stores, Randy Burdick/CIO, Exec. VP, Matthew Broad/Exec. VP, General Counsel, Reuben E. Slone/Exec. VP - Supply Chain, Carolynn Brooks/VP - Diversity, Inclusion, Perry Zukowski/Exec. VP - Human Resources, William Bonner/Sr. Dir. - External Relations, Officemax, Harry Dochelli/Exec. VP - US Operations, John S. Jennings/Sr. VP, Treasurer - Investor Relations

Directors: Sam K. Duncan/Chmn., CEO, Rakesh Gangwal/54/Dir., William J. Montgoris/Dir., William A. Reynolds/Dir., David M. Szymanski/51/Dir., Gary G. Michael/67/Dir., Dorrit J. Bern/Dir., Joseph M. Depinto/Dir., Brian C. Cornell/49/Dir., Warren F. Bryant/62/Dir., Francesca Ruiz De Luzuriaga/54/Dir.

Owners: State Street Bank and Trust Company,, David M. Szymanski, Edward C. Johnson, Don Civgin, Phillip P. DePaul, Barclays Global Investors, NA, Lord, Abbett&Co.LLC, Brian C. Cornell, Monte R. Haymon, Gary G. Michael, Michael D. Rowsey, Warren F. Bryant, Francesca Ruiz de Luzuriaga, Dorrit J. Bern, William A. Reynolds *(23 Owners included in Index)*

Financial Data: *Fiscal Year End:*12/31 *Latest Annual Data:* 12/30/2006

Year	Sales	Net Income
2006	$8,965,707,000	$91,721,000
2005	$9,157,660,000	-$73,762,000
2004	$13,270,196,000	$173,058,000

Curr. Assets:	$1,942,049,000	**Curr. Liab.:**	$1,588,326,000	**P/E Ratio:**	17.81
Plant, Equip.:	$535,445,000	**Total Liab.:**	$4,509,008,000	**Indic. Yr. Divd.:**	$0.600
Total Assets:	$6,272,142,000	**Net Worth:**	$1,735,679,000	**Debt/ Equity:**	NA

OGE Energy Corp

515 Central Pk. Dr., Ste. 408, Oklahoma City, OK, 73105; ***PH:*** 1-405-553-6400; ***Fax:*** 1-405-553-6498; ***http://*** www.oge.com

General - Incorporation	OK	**Stock**- Price on:12/24/2007	$34.11
Employees	3,123	Stock Exchange	NYSE
Auditor	Ernst & Young LLP	Ticker Symbol	OGE
Stk Agt	Mellon Investor Services LLC	Outstanding Shares	91,740,000
Counsel	NA	E.P.S	$2.48
DUNS No.	96-386-0044	Shareholders	NA

Business: The group's principle activity is to provide energy services in electricity, crude oil and natural gas liquids. The group provides services include asset management, transportation, storage, risk management and transmission. The group operates from United States.

Primary SIC and add'l.: 4931 4922 4911 6719 4923 4939

CIK No: 0001021635

Subsidiaries: Enogex Gas Gathering, LLC, Enogex Inc., Enogex Products Corporation, OGE Energy Resources, Inc, Oklahoma Gas and Electric

Officers: Steven E. Moore/62/Chmn., CEO/$4,772,610.00, James R. Hatfield/CFO, Sr. VP/$1,398,248.00, Steven R. Gerdes/VP - Utility Operations, OG, E Electric Services/$581,013.00, Jesse B. Langston/VP - Utility Commercial Operations OG, E Electric Services, Scott H. Forbes/Controller, Chief Accounting Officer, Cary Martin/VP - Human Resources, Peter B. Delaney/54/Dir., COO, Pres./$3,029,357.00, Deborah S. Fleming/Treasurer, Carla D. Brockman/VP - Administration, Corp. Sec., Jerry A. Peace/Chief Risk, Compliance Officer, Gary D. Huneryager/VP - Internal Audits, Melvin H. Perkins/VP - Power Delivery, OG, E Electric Services, Danny P. Harris/COO, Sr. VP/$797,352.00, Paul L. Renfrow/VP - Public Affairs, Reid V. Nuttall/VP - Enterprise Information, Performance

Directors: Steven E. Moore/62/Chmn., CEO, Peter B. Delaney/54/Dir., COO, Pres., Linda Petree Lambert/68/Dir., Ronald H. White/71/Dir., J. D. Williams/70/Dir., Robert O. Lorenz/61/Dir., Herbert H. Champlin/70/Dir., Robert Kelley/62/Dir., Luke R. Corbett/61/Dir., John D. Groendyke/63/Dir.

Owners: S.E. Moore, Linda Petree Lambert, J.R. Hatfield, Insiders, D.P. Harris, Herbert H. Champlin, Ronald H. White, Luke R. Corbett, Robert Kelley, Robert O. Lorenz, J.D. Williams, S.R. Gerdes, John D. Groendyke, William E. Durrett, P. B. Delaney

Financial Data: *Fiscal Year End:*12/31 *Latest Annual Data:* 12/31/2006

Year	Sales	Net Income
2006	$4,005,600,000	$262,100,000
2005	$5,948,200,000	$211,000,000
2004	$4,926,600,000	$153,500,000

Curr. Assets:	$664,100,000	**Curr. Liab.:**	$673,000,000		
Plant, Equip.:	$3,902,700,000	**Total Liab.:**	$3,298,200,000	**Indic. Yr. Divd.:**	$1.360
Total Assets:	$4,902,000,000	**Net Worth:**	$1,603,800,000	**Debt/ Equity:**	0.8462

Oglethorpe Power Corp

2100 E Exchange Pl., Tucker, GA, 30084; ***PH:*** 1-770-270-7600; ***Fax:*** 1-770-270-7872; ***http://*** www.opc.com

General - Incorporation	GA	**Stock**- Price on:12/24/2007	NA
Employees	NA	Stock Exchange	NA
Auditor	PricewaterhouseCoopers LLP	Ticker Symbol	NA
Stk Agt	NA	Outstanding Shares	NA
Counsel	NA	E.P.S	NA
DUNS No.	07-346-0305	Shareholders	NA

Business: The group's principle activity is to provide wholesale electric service to 39 of Georgia's 42 retail electric distribution cooperative members. These members are local consumer-owned distribution cooperatives providing retail electric service on a not-for-profit basis. The members distribute energy to approximately 3.7 million people across two-thirds of the state. The company has undivided interests in eighteen generating units which provide a total of 3,660 megawatts of nameplate capacity. The company provides this service pursuant to long-term, take-or-pay wholesale power contracts. The company's 39 members include altamaha emc, amicalola emc, canoochee emc, carroll emc, central Georgia emc, coastal emc, cobb emc, colquitt emc, flint emc, excelsior emc, habersham emc and irwin emc. The group operates from United States.

Primary SIC and add'l.: 4911

CIK No: 0000788816

Subsidiaries: American National Power, Inc., Georgia Power Company, MDU Resources Inc., National Power, PLC, Rocky Mountain Leasing Corporation, The Southern Company

Officers: Thomas A. Smith/CEO, Pres., Elizabeth B. Higgins/CFO, Hill C. Bentley/Dir., Mgr., Robert E. Rentfrow/Dir., Mgr., Jeffrey W. Murphy/Dir., Mgr., Gary W. Wyatt/Dir., Mgr., Michael W. Price/COO, Jami G. Reusch/VP - Human Resources, Clay W. Robbins/Sr. VP, Chief Administrative Officer, Gary A. Miller/Dir., Mgr., William F. Ussery/Sr. VP

Directors: Benny W. Denham/Chmn., Sam Rabun/Vice Chmn., Larry N. Chadwick/Dir., John S. Ranson/Dir., H. B. Wiley/Dir., Gary A. Miller/Dir., Mgr., Marshall S. Millwood/Dir., Hill C. Bentley/Dir., Mgr., Robert E. Rentfrow/Dir., Mgr., Jeffrey W. Murphy/Dir., Mgr., Anthony M. Ham/Dir., Gary W. Wyatt/Dir., Mgr., Ronald Duffey/Dir.

Ohana Pacific BK HI

1357 Kapiolani Blvd, Honolulu, HI, 96814; ***PH:*** 1-808-237-6551; ***Fax:*** 1-808-237-6555; ***http://*** www.ohanapacificbank.com

General - Incorporation		**Stock**- Price on:12/24/2007	$12.3
Employees	NA	Stock Exchange	OTC
Auditor	NA	Ticker Symbol	OHPB
Stk Agt	NA	Outstanding Shares	NA
Counsel	NA	E.P.S	NA
DUNS No.	NA	Shareholders	NA

Business: The groups principal activities include providing independent community banking services, which include traditional banking products, and services to the general public with a special emphasis on residents and business owners. Services of the group include money market savings accounts, certificate of deposit accounts, loans, real estates, travelers check, ATM and residential mortgage loans. The group operates from Korea.

Primary SIC and add'l.: 6021

CIK No:

Officers: Woon S. Hyun/Dir., CEO, Pres., Robert Kamemoto/Exec. VP, Chief Credit Officer, Ira Peek/Operations Utility Assist., Helen Kwok/CFO, Exec. VP, Tina Nakahara/Operations Mgr., Sue Chun/Banking Services Specialist, Yoon Kyoung No/Banking Services Specialist, Lawrence P.C. Pai/Sr. VP, Sr. Lending Officer, Paul K. Lemcke/VP, Administrative Systems Mgr., Byron T. Okino/AVP, Loan Officer, Jeena Chong Kobayashi/Documentation, Note Supervisor, Jenny K.H. Li/VP, Branch Mgr., Marie Choi Kurosu/Banking Services Specialist, Eun Ha Kim/Banking Services Specialist, Jamie Hyun Jung Han/Operations Supervisor

Directors: Woon S. Hyun/Dir., CEO, Pres., Wayne T. Miyao/Chmn., Hyung K. Cha/Dir., Nicole I. Choi/Dir., Soung Ho Yoon/Dir., Woon I. Chung/Dir., Marcy E. Fleming/Dir., David H. Jung/Dir., Donald B.S. Kang/Dir., Rex K.C. Kim/Dir., Roy Y. Morihara/Dir., Ghon S. Rhee/Dir.

Ohio Casualty Corp

9450 Seward Rd., Fairfield, OH, 45014; ***PH:*** 1-513-603-2400; ***http://*** www.ocas.com

General - Incorporation	OH	**Stock**- Price on:12/24/2007	$43.31
Employees	2,114	Stock Exchange	NA
Auditor	Ernst & Young LLP	Ticker Symbol	NA
Stk Agt	Computershare Trust Co	Outstanding Shares	60,000,000
Counsel	Vorys, Sater, Seymour & Pease	E.P.S	$4.05
DUNS No.	00-790-3040	Shareholders	NA

Business: The groups principle activity is to provide insurance services. The groups products include business and personal insurance. The group operates from United States.

Primary SIC and add'l.: 6331 6411

CIK No: 0000073952

Subsidiaries: American Fire and Casualty Company, Avomark Insurance Agency, LLC, Avomark Insurance Company, Ocasco Budget, Inc., Ocasco Securities Corporation, OCI Printing, Inc., Ohio Casualty of New Jersey, Inc., Ohio Life Brokerage Services, Inc., Ohio Security Insurance Company, The Ohio Casualty Insurance Company, West American Insurance Company

Officers: Dan R. Carmichael/Dir., CEO/$4,374,127.00, Michael A. Winner/Exec. VP, Chief Financial, Accounting Officer/$767,633.00

Directors: Dan R. Carmichael/Dir., CEO, Jack E. Brown/Dir., Stanley N. Pontius/Dir., Terrence J. Baehr/Dir., Catherine E. Dolan/Dir., Philip G. Heasley/Dir., Robert A. Oakley/Dir., Jan H. Suwinski/Dir., Ronald W. Tysoe/Dir., Michael L. Wright/Dir.

Owners: Stanley N. Pontius, Philip G. Heasley, Insiders/3.99%, Ralph S. Michael, Dan R. Carmichael/3.10%, Michael A. Winner, DIMENSIONAL FUND ADVISORS, INC./8.02%, Robert A. Oakley, Jan H. Suwinski, Paul J. Gerard, Jack E. Brown, T. Rowe Price Associates, Inc./8.35%, Catherine E. Dolan, Debra K. Crane, Michael L. Wright *(17 Owners included in Index)*

Financial Data: *Fiscal Year End:*12/31 *Latest Annual Data:* 12/31/2006

Year	Sales	Net Income
2006	$1,676,300,000	$218,300,000
2005	$1,702,400,000	$212,700,000
2004	$1,671,000,000	$128,400,000

Curr. Assets:	$1,046,600,000	**Curr. Liab.:**	NA	**P/E Ratio:**	11.80
Plant, Equip.:	$80,500,000	**Total Liab.:**	$4,142,900,000	**Indic. Yr. Divd.:**	$0.520
Total Assets:	$5,698,600,000	**Net Worth:**	$1,555,700,000	**Debt/ Equity:**	0.1249

Ohio Edison Co

76 S Main St., Akron, OH, 44308; ***PH:*** 1-216-384-5100; ***http://*** www.firstenergycorp.com

General - Incorporation	OH	**Stock**- Price on:12/24/2007	$64.49
Employees	13,739	Stock Exchange	NA
Auditor	PricewaterhouseCoopers LLP	Ticker Symbol	NA
Stk Agt	NA	Outstanding Shares	NA
Counsel	Mr. Van Ness	E.P.S	$4.24
DUNS No.	00-699-8371	Shareholders	NA

Business: The group's principle activities include generating and selling electric energy. The group also provides transmission services and electric energy for resale to third parties; and sells, purchases and interchanges electric energy with other electric companies. The group operates from United States.

Primary SIC and add'l.: 4911

CIK No: 0000073960

Subsidiaries: American Transmission Systems, Inc, Centerior Service Company, FE Acquisition Corp, FELHC, Inc, FirstEnergy Facilities Services Group, LLC, FirstEnergy Foundation, FirstEnergy Nuclear Generation Corp, FirstEnergy Nuclear Operating Company, FirstEnergy Properties Company, FirstEnergy Securities Transfer Company, FirstEnergy Service Company, FirstEnergy Solutions Corp, FirstEnergy Telecom Services, Inc, FirstEnergy Ventures Corp, GPU Capital, Inc 26 Subsidiaries included in the Index

Officers: C. D. Lasky/45/VP - Fossil Operations, FES, D. C. Luff/60/Sr. VP - Governmental Affairs, D. R. Schneider/46/VP - Energy Delivery, C. B. Snyder/62/Sr. VP, T. M. Welsh/58/Sr. VP - External Affairs, Stephen E. Morgan/Dir., Pres., G. L. Pipitone/57/Pres. - FES, Steven E. Strah/Regional Pres. - Ohio Edison Company, L. M. Cavalier/56/Sr. VP - Human Resources, M. T. Clark/57/Sr. VP - Strategic Planning, Operations, K. W. Dindo/58/VP, Chief Risk Officer, D. S. Elliott/53/Pres. - Pennsylvania Operations, A. Jamshidi/53/VP - Commodity Operations, FES

Directors: Mark A. Julian/Dir., Stanley C. Van Ness/Dir., Bradley S. Ewing/Dir., Stephen E. Morgan/Dir., Pres.

Financial Data: Fiscal Year End:12/31 **Latest Annual Data:** 12/31/2006

Year	Sales	Net Income
2006	$11,501,000,000	$1,254,000,000
2005	$11,989,000,000	$861,000,000
2004	$12,453,046,000	$878,175,000

Curr. Assets:	$2,083,000,000	**Curr. Liab.:**	$5,255,000,000		
Plant, Equip.:	$14,667,000,000	**Total Liab.:**	$22,161,000,000	**Indic. Yr. Divd.:**	$2.000
Total Assets:	$31,196,000,000	**Net Worth:**	$9,035,000,000	**Debt/ Equity:**	1.0297

Ohio Legacy Corp

305 W Liberty St., Wooster, OH, 44691; **PH:** 1-330-263-1955; **Fax:** 1-330-263-0063; *http://* www.ohiolegacycorp.com

General - Incorporation	OH	Stock- Price on:12/24/2007	$8.45
Employees	71	Stock Exchange	NDQ
Auditor	Crowe Chizek & Co. LLC	Ticker Symbol	OLCB
Stk Agt.	Illinois Stock Transfer Co	Outstanding Shares	2,210,000
Counsel	NA	E.P.S.	-$0.05
DUNS No.	NA	Shareholders	NA

Business: The group's principal activity is to provide retail and commercial banking services. The services include checking and savings accounts, time deposits, individual retirement accounts, safe deposit facilities, personal loans, commercial loans, real estate mortgage loans, installment loans and night depository facilities to customers. It also provides financial services through its full service offices in wooster, millersburg and canton, Ohio. The operations of the group are carried out through it three offices to its customers, who are located primarily in holmes, stark and wayne counties in north east-central Ohio. The group operates through its subsidiary Ohio legacy bank.

Primary SIC and add'l.: 6712 6021

CIK No: 0001096654

Subsidiaries: Ohio Legacy Bank, N.A., Wooster

Officers: David Michael Kramer/48/Dir., Pres., CEO - Contact - Investor Relations, Dwight L. Douce/57/CEO, Pres./$105,164.00, Steven G. Pettit/47/Sr. Loan Officer, Pres. - Stark County Region/$155,008.00, Robert E. Boss/49/Pres. - Holmes County Region/$118,267.00, Derek Williams/49/Sr. VP, Chief Deposit Officer/$104,217.00

Directors: David Michael Kramer/48/Dir., Pres., CEO - Contact - Investor Relations, Daniel H. Plumly/53/Chmn., Robert F. Belden/58/Dir., William D. Allen/54/Dir., Edward J. Diamond/Dir., Scott J. Fitzpatrick/52/Dir., Gregory A. Long/56/Dir., Melvin J. Yoder/60/Dir.

Owners: Robert F. Belden/5.40%, Bay Pond Partners, L.P./6.90%, Hot Creek Capital, LLC/5.40%, Gregory A. Long/2.70%, Wellington Management Company, LLP/8.80%, William D. Allen/1.20%, Steven G. Pettit/1.60%, Michael Meenan, Daniel H. Plumly/3.40%, Tontine Financial Partners, L.P./7.60%, Scott J. Fitzpatrick/4.10%, Scott E. Dodds, Robert F. Belden/4.80%, Insiders/42.60%, Robert E. Boss/1.70% (22 Owners included in Index)

Financial Data: Fiscal Year End:12/31 **Latest Annual Data:** 12/31/2006

Year	Sales	Net Income
2006	$14,726,000	$87,000
2005	$11,945,000	$362,000
2004	$9,919,000	$1,273,000

Curr. Assets:	$15,095,000	**Curr. Liab.:**	$207,800,000		
Plant, Equip.:	$6,185,000	**Total Liab.:**	$212,065,000	**Indic. Yr. Divd.:**	NA
Total Assets:	$230,484,000	**Net Worth:**	$18,419,000	**Debt/ Equity:**	NA

Ohio Power Co

301 Cleveland Ave. S W, Columbus, OH, 44702; **PH:** 1-614-223-1000; *http://* www.aep.com

General - Incorporation	OH	Stock - Price on:12/24/2007	$77
Employees	NA	Stock Exchange	OTC
Auditor	Deloitte & Touche LLP	Ticker Symbol	OHIPP
Stk Agt.	Computershare Investor Services LLC	Outstanding Shares	NA
Counsel	NA	E.P.S.	NA
DUNS No.	00-289-9953	Shareholders	NA

Business: The group's principal activities are to generate, purchase, market, transmit and distribute electric power. The group also supplies electric power at wholesale to other electric utility companies and municipalities. The industries served by the group include primary metals, rubber, plastic products, stone, clay, glass products, concrete products, petroleum refining and chemicals. The group has 704,000 retail customers in the northwestern, east central, eastern and southern sections of Ohio. It is a wholly owned subsidiary of American electric power company inc.

Primary SIC and add'l.: 4911

CIK No: 0000073986

Subsidiaries: AEGCo, APCo, CSPCo, I&M, Kingsport Power Company, KPCo, OPCo, PSO, SWEPCo, TCC, TNC, WPCo

Officers: Michael G. Morris/61/Chmn., CEO/$14,222,010.00, Robert P. Powers/54/Vice Chmn., VP/$2,938,804.00, Nicholas K. Akins/47/Dir., VP, Carl L. English/61/Dir., VP/$2,789,102.00, Dennis E. Welch/56/Dir., VP, Susan Tomasky/54/Dir., VP/$3,480,398.00, Stephen P. Smith/47/Dir., VP, Treasurer, Holly K. Koeppel/49/Dir., VP/$2,569,754.00, Heather L. Geiger/Sec., John B. Keane/61/Dir., VP/$1,743,708.00

Directors: Michael G. Morris/61/Chmn., CEO, Robert P. Powers/54/Vice Chmn., VP, Stephen P. Smith/47/Dir., VP, Treasurer, Susan Tomasky/54/Dir., VP, John B. Keane/61/Dir., VP, Dennis E. Welch/56/Dir., VP, Donald M. Carlton/Dir., Nicholas K. Akins/47/Dir., VP, Holly K. Koeppel/49/Dir., VP, Carl L. English/61/Dir., VP

Owners: J. B. Keane, H. K. Koeppel, M. G. Morris, S. Tomasky, R. P. Powers, S. P. Smith, Insiders, C. L. English, K. E. Walker, D. E. Welch, N. K. Akins

Ohio Valley Banc Corp

420 3rd Ave., Gallipolis, OH, 45631; **PH:** 1-740-446-6000; **Fax:** 1-740-446-7688; *http://* www.ovbc.com

General - Incorporation	OH	Stock- Price on:12/24/2007	$25.25
Employees	254	Stock Exchange	NDQ
Auditor	Crowe Chizek & Co. LLC	Ticker Symbol	OVBC
Stk Agt	NA	Outstanding Shares	4,160,000
Counsel	NA	E.P.S.	$1.26
DUNS No.	00-892-9697	Shareholders	NA

Business: The group's principal activities are to provide commercial, retail and agricultural banking services. The operations of the group are carried on through twenty-two branch offices located in central and southeastern Ohio and west Virginia. The group offers checking, savings and time deposits. It also provides safe deposit boxes, issuance of travelers' checks and administration of trusts. The group invests in United States government and agency obligations, interest-bearing deposits in other financial institutions and other investments permitted by applicable law.

Primary SIC and add'l.: 6021 6712

CIK No: 0000894671

Subsidiaries: Loan Central, Inc., Ohio Valley Financial Services Agency, LLC, Ohio Valley Statutory Trust I, Ohio Valley Statutory Trust II, ProAlliance Corp., The Ohio Valley Bank Company

Officers: Jeffrey E. Smith/58/Dir., CEO, Pres./$319,177.00, Richard E. Mahan/Sr. VP, Sec./$117,971.00, Scott W. Shockey/CFO, VP/$87,205.00, David L. Shaffer/Sr. VP - Main Office, Larry E. Miller/Sr. VP, Treasurer/$118,147.00, Katrinka V. Hart/Sr. VP, Risk Management Officer/$117,417.00, Ryan L. Young/Commercial Loan Officer - Main Office, Phil E. Miller/Assist. VP - Columbus Office, Ty J. Thomas/Assist. Cashier - Columbus Office, Richard D. Scott/VP - Trust Department Team, Melissa P. Mason/Assist. VP, Trust Officer - Trust Department Team

Directors: Jeffrey E. Smith/58/Dir., CEO, Pres., Robert E. Daniel/67/Dir., Lowell W. Call/71/Dir., Harold A. Howe/57/Dir., Brent A. Saunders/50/Dir., Anna P. Barnitz/45/Dir., Roger D. Williams/57/Dir., Lannes C. Williamson/63/Dir., Thomas E. Wiseman/49/Dir., Steven B. Chapman/61/Dir., Robert H. Eastman/67/Dir.

Owners: Lannes C. Williamson/0.11%, Lowell W. Call, Larry E. Miller, Anna P. Barnitz/0.03%, Thomas E. Wiseman/0.37%, Jeffrey E. Smith/0.47%, Brent A. Saunders/0.14%, Katrinka V. Hart/0.25%, Richard E. Mahan, Scott W. Shockey/0.06%, Robert H. Eastman/1.67%, Morris and Dorothy Haskins Foundation, Inc./7.90%, Roger D. Williams/0.01%, Robert E. Daniel/0.01%, Steven B. Chapman/0.04% (17 Owners included in Index)

Financial Data: Fiscal Year End:12/31 **Latest Annual Data:** 12/31/2006

Year	Sales	Net Income
2006	$58,251,000	$5,398,000
2005	$51,593,000	$7,017,000
2004	$51,482,000	$8,381,000

Curr. Assets:	$21,273,000	**Curr. Liab.:**	$627,033,000	**P/E Ratio:**	19.57
Plant, Equip.:	$9,812,000	**Total Liab.:**	$704,079,000	**Indic. Yr. Divd.:**	$0.720
Total Assets:	$764,361,000	**Net Worth:**	$60,282,000	**Debt/ Equity:**	NA

OI Corp

151 Graham Rd., College Station, TX, 77845; **PH:** 1-979-690-1711; **Fax:** 1-979-690-0440; *http://* www.oico.com; **Email:** oimail@oico.com

General - Incorporation	OK	Stock- Price on:12/24/2007	$13.51
Employees	155	Stock Exchange	NDQ
Auditor	Grant Thornton LLP	Ticker Symbol	OICO
Stk Agt	American Stock Transfer & Trust Co.	Outstanding Shares	2,890,000
Counsel	Andrews & Kurch LLP	E.P.S.	$0.52
DUNS No.	04-890-4361	Shareholders	NA

Business: The group's principle activities are to design, manufacture, market and service sample preparation, detection, measurement and monitoring instruments used to analyze chemical compounds. The products of the group include gas chromatography instruments and systems, total organic carbon analyzer systems, ion analysis systems, sample preparation products and systems and filtometers. The instruments are used for specialized applications in the analytical instrument markets. The group sells its products domestically to end users through a direct sales channel, manufacturers' representatives, distributors and resellers. The products are sold internationally through independent manufacturers' representatives and distributors. The group's quarterly revenue for September 2007 was 6.46 millions of USD.

Primary SIC and add'l.: 3823

CIK No: 0000073773

Subsidiaries: CMS Research Corp.

Officers: Bruce J. Lancaster/CEO, CFO, Donald P. Segers/COO, Pres./$180,023.00, Laura Samuelson/Corp. Sec.

Directors: Raymond E. Cabillot/Chmn., Richard W.K. Chapman/Dir., Kenneth M. Dodd/Dir., Robert L. Moore/Dir., Leo B. Womack/Dir.

Owners: Leo B. Womack/0.10%, Robert L. Moore/0.10%, Dimensional Fund Advisors, Inc./6.00%, Farnam Street Partners, L.P./8.60%, Advisory Research, Inc./7.00%, Heartland Advisors, Inc./8.30%, Insiders/10.80%, William W. Botts/10.30%, Donald P. Segers/1.10%

Financial Data: Fiscal Year End:12/31 **Latest Annual Data:** 12/31/2006

Year	Sales	Net Income
2006	$30,264,000	$2,409,000
2005	$29,853,000	$2,486,000
2004	$28,480,000	$1,762,000

Curr. Assets:	$26,117,000	**Curr. Liab.:**	$5,899,000	**P/E Ratio:**	28.15
Plant, Equip.:	$3,279,000	**Total Liab.:**	$5,899,000	**Indic. Yr. Divd.:**	$0.200
Total Assets:	$30,512,000	**Net Worth:**	$24,613,000	**Debt/ Equity:**	NA

Oil States International Inc

3 Allen Ctr., 333 Clay St., Ste. 4620, Houston, TX, 77002; **PH:** 1-713-652-0582; **Fax:** 1-713-652-0499; *http://* www.oilstatesintl.com

General - Incorporation	DE	Stock- Price on:12/24/2007	$40.16
Employees	5,124	Stock Exchange	NYSE
Auditor	Ernst & Young LLP	Ticker Symbol	OIS
Stk Agt	Mellon Investor Services LLC	Outstanding Shares	49,240,000
Counsel	Vinson & Elkins LLP	E.P.S.	$4.03
DUNS No.	NA	Shareholders	NA

Business: The groups principle activity is to manufacture products for deepwater production facilities and subsea pipelines. The group also provides land drilling, completion and production-related rental tools, logistics, and oil country tubular goods distribution services. The groups services include inventory management, remediation and threading services. The group operates from United States.

Primary SIC and add'l.: 3533

CIK No: 0001121484

Subsidiaries: A-Z Terminal Corporation, Capstar Drilling, L.P., Crown Camp Services Ltd, General Marine Leasing, LLC, HWC Energy Services, Inc., HWC Limited, HWCES International, Hydraulic Well Control, LLC, Oil States Industries (Asia) Pte Ltd, Oil States Industries (UK)Limited, Oil States Industries, Inc., Oil States Skagit SMATCO LLC, PTI Group, Inc., PTI Premium Camp Services Ltd., PTI Travco Modular Structures Ltd. 20 Subsidiaries included in the Index

Officers: Cindy B. Taylor/Dir., CEO, Pres./$1,344,984.00, Christopher E. Cragg/Sr. VP - Operations, Robert W. Hampton/Sr. VP - Accounting, Corp. Sec., Bradley J. Dodson/CFO, VP, Treasurer/$515,976.00, Ron R. Green/Pres. - PTI Group, Inc/$592,971.00, Howard Hughes/Pres. - Oil States Industries/$774,193.00

Directors: Cindy B. Taylor/Dir., CEO, Pres., Stephen A. Wells/Chmn., James S. Nelson/Dir., Mark G. Papa/Dir., William T. Van Kleef/Dir., Martin A. Lambert/Dir., Douglas E. Swanson/Dir., Gary L. Rosenthal/Dir.

Owners: Ron R. Green, Cindy B. Taylor, FMR Corp./15.21%, S. James Nelson, Douglas E. Swanson, Mark G. Papa, Gary L. Rosenthal, Mellon Financial Corporation/6.04%, Bradley J. Dodson, William T. Van Kleef, Stephen A. Wells, Howard Hughes, Insiders/1.91%, Martin Lambert

Financial Data: *Fiscal Year End:*12/31 *Latest Annual Data:* 06/30/2007

Year	Sales	Net Income
2007	$499,308,000	$52,233,000
2006	$1,923,357,000	$197,634,000
2005	$1,531,636,000	$121,813,000

Curr. Assets:	$783,989,000	**Curr. Liab.:**	$280,416,000	**P/E Ratio:**	10.30
Plant, Equip.:	$358,716,000	**Total Liab.:**	$731,258,000	**Indic. Yr. Divd.:**	NA
Total Assets:	$1,571,094,000	**Net Worth:**	$839,836,000	**Debt/ Equity:**	0.4289

Oil-Dri Corp of America

410 N Michigan Ave., Ste. 400, Chicago, IL, 60611; *PH:* 1-312-321-1515; *Fax:* 1-312-321-1271; *http://* www.oildri.com; *Email:* info@oildri.com

General - Incorporation	DE	**Stock**- Price on:12/24/2007	$17.3
Employees	765	Stock Exchange	NYSE
Auditor	PricewaterhouseCoopers LLP	Ticker Symbol	ODC
Stk Agt	Computershare Investor Services LLC	Outstanding Shares	6,870,000
Counsel	NA	E.P.S	$1.20
DUNS No.	00-521-3954	Shareholders	NA

Business: The group's principal activities are to develop, manufacture and market sorbent products and related services. The products and services are for the consumer, industrial, crop production and horticultural, specialty and automotive markets. Consumer products consist primarily of cat litter and dog treats. Specialty products consist primarily of bleaching, filtration and clarification clays. Crop production and horticultural products include carriers for crop protection chemicals and fertilizers, drying agents, soil conditioners, sports field products, pellet binders for animal feeds and flowability aids. Industrial and automotive products consist primarily of oil, grease and clay and non-clay water sorbents. In fiscal 2004, the group disposed of its wholly owned subsidiary, phoebe products co.

Primary SIC and add'l.: 5199 5191 2842 2843

CIK No: 0000074046

Subsidiaries: Blue Mountain Production Company, Favorite Products Company, Ltd., Mounds Management, Inc., Mounds Production Company, LLC, ODC Acquisition Corp., Oil-Dri (U.K.) Limited, Oil-Dri Corporation of Georgia, Oil-Dri Corporation of Nevada, Oil-Dri Production Company, Oil-Dri, S.A., Taft Production Company

Officers: Daniel S. Jaffee/Dir., CEO, Pres., Thomas Cofsky/VP - Manufacturing, Logistics, Charles Brissman/VP, General Counsel, Sec., Andrew N. Peterson/CFO, VP, Jeffrey Libert/VP - Finance, Treasurer, Daniel T. Smith/VP, Controller, Brian K. Bancroft/VP, Chief Procurement Officer

Directors: Daniel S. Jaffee/Dir., CEO, Pres., Richard M. Jaffee/Chmn., Joseph C. Miller/Vice Chmn., Arnold W. Donald/Dir., Steven J. Cole/Dir., Allan H. Selig/Dir., Paul Suckow/Dir., Michael Nemeroff/Dir.

Owners: Charles P. Brissman, Advisory Research Inc./6.80%, Heartland Advisors, Inc./15.08%, Jaffee Investment Partnership, L.P, Michael A. Nemeroff, Steven J. Cole, Paul E. Suckow, Insiders, Joseph C. Miller, Dimensional Fund Advisors, Inc./6.25%, Allan H. Selig, Arnold W. Donald, Karen Jaffee Cofsky, Daniel S. Jaffee, GAMCO Asset Management Inc./12.04% *(20 Owners included in Index)*

Financial Data: *Fiscal Year End:*07/31 *Latest Annual Data:* 7/31/2006

Year	Sales	Net Income
2006	$205,210,000	$5,259,000
2005	$187,868,000	$6,540,000
2004	$185,511,000	$5,033,000

Curr. Assets:	$78,300,000	**Curr. Liab.:**	$27,405,000	**P/E Ratio:**	18.02
Plant, Equip.:	$51,445,000	**Total Liab.:**	$61,845,000	**Indic. Yr. Divd.:**	$0.520
Total Assets:	$142,087,000	**Net Worth:**	$80,242,000	**Debt/ Equity:**	NA

Oilgear Co

2300 S 51st St. , Milwaukee, WI, 53219; *PH:* 1-414-327-1700; *http://* www.oilgear.com

General - Incorporation	WI	**Stock**- Price on:12/24/2007	NA
Employees	748	Stock Exchange	NA
Auditor	KPMG LLP	Ticker Symbol	NA
Stk Agt	Wells Fargo Shareowner Services	Outstanding Shares	NA
Counsel	Quarles & Brady LLP	E.P.S	NA
DUNS No.	00-609-5038	Shareholders	NA

Business: The group's principal activities are to manufacture and distribute engineered fluid power components and electronic controls for a broad range of industrial machinery and industrial processes. The group's products primarily involve the flow, pressure and condition control and measurement of liquids, which referred to as fluid power. It provides advanced technology in the design and production of fluid power components, systems and electronic controls. Its product line includes hydraulic pumps, high-pressure intensifier pumps, valves, controls, cylinders, motors and fluid meters. The group manufactures both radial and axial piston type hydraulic pumps. The products are sold in the United States, Canada, Europe, Asia, Latin America, Australia and Africa.

Primary SIC and add'l.: 3492 3594 3593

CIK No: 0000074058

Subsidiaries: Oilgear Canada Inc., Oilgear do Brazil Hydraulica Ltd., Oilgear Ltd., Oilgear Mexicana S.A. de C.V., Oilgear Towler Australia Pty., Oilgear Towler GmbH, Oilgear Towler Japan Co., Oilgear Towler Korea Ltd., Oilgear Towler Ltd., Oilgear Towler Polyhydron Pvt. Ltd., Oilgear Towler S.A., Oilgear Towler S.r.l., Oilgear Towler Taiwan Co. Ltd., Towler Enterprise Pvt. Ltd.

Oilsands Quest Inc

707 - 7 Ave. SW, Ste. 205, Calgary, AB, T2P 3H6; *PH:* 1-403-263-1623; *Fax:* 1-403-263-9812; *http://* www.oilsandsquest.com

General - Incorporation	CO	**Stock**- Price on:12/24/2007	$2.64
Employees	NA	Stock Exchange	AMEX
Auditor	Deloitte & Touche, LLP	Ticker Symbol	BQI
Stk Agt	Computershare Trust Co	Outstanding Shares	158,580,000
Counsel	TingleMerrett LLP	E.P.S	-$0.666
DUNS No.	NA	Shareholders	NA

Business: The group operates through its subsidiaries whose principal activity is oil and gas exploration. In the year 2005, the group acquired by Can West. In the year 2006, the group merged with private Alberta Company. The group operates from the United States and Canada.

Primary SIC and add'l.: 1090

CIK No: 0001096791

Subsidiaries: Oilsands Quest, Inc, Township Petroleum Corporation, Western Petrochemicals Corporation

Officers: Christopher H. Hopkins/Dir., CEO, Pres./$6,037,515.00, Karim Hirji/CFO/$3,330,540.00, Erdal Yildirim/Exec. VP, Errin Kimball/VP - Exploration/$3,196,892.00

Directors: Christopher H. Hopkins/Dir., CEO, Pres., Murray T. Wilson/Chmn., Thomas Milne/Dir., Ronald Phillips/Dir., Gordon Tallman/Dir., William Scott Thompson/Dir., J. K. Read/Dir.

Owners: Gordon Tallman, Insiders/18.00%, Karim Hirji/3.20%, William Scott Thompson/1.40%, Pamela Wallin, Murray T. Wilson/1.80%, Thomas Milne/1.40%, Christopher H. Hopkins/10.00%, Ronald Phillips, Errin Kimball/1.60%

Financial Data: *Fiscal Year End:*04/30 *Latest Annual Data:* 4/30/2006

Year	Sales	Net Income
2006	NA	-$52,641,000
2005	NA	-$5,109,000
2004	NA	-$1,581,000

Curr. Assets:	$23,816,000	**Curr. Liab.:**	$19,978,000		
Plant, Equip.:	$17,831,000	**Total Liab.:**	$21,059,000	**Indic. Yr. Divd.:**	NA
Total Assets:	$41,958,000	**Net Worth:**	$16,164,000	**Debt/ Equity:**	NA

Ojai Community Bk CA

402 W Ojai Ave., Ojai, CA, 93023; *PH:* 1-805-646-2445; *Fax:* 1-805-646-9919; *http://* www.ojaicommunitybank.com

General - Incorporation		**Stock**- Price on:12/24/2007	$14.5
Employees	NA	Stock Exchange	OTC
Auditor	NA	Ticker Symbol	OJCB
Stk Agt	U.S. Stock Transfer Corp	Outstanding Shares	NA
Counsel	NA	E.P.S	NA
DUNS No.	NA	Shareholders	NA

Business: The groups principal activities include providing prompt and professional services to customers. The group provides personal service to the people and businesses of the Ojai Valley, meets the credit needs of market through local decision makers. The group operates from the United States.

Primary SIC and add'l.: 6022

CIK No:

Officers: Sharon Skinner/Dir., CEO, Pres., Michelle Henson/Chief Credit Officer, Suzanne Lagos/CFO, Troy K. Norlander/Investor Relation Officer, Jodi Woolwine/Contact, Roberta Becker/Contact, Susan Lagos/Contact, Diana Trent/Contact, Joey Warmenhoven/Investor Relation Officer, Laurie Johnson/Contact, Mary Thomas/Contact, Wendy Giroux/Contact, Mary Floyd/Contact, Shari Skinner/Contact, Esther Lovio/Contact *(24 Officers included in Index)*

Directors: Sharon Skinner/Dir., CEO, Pres., John W. Russell/Chmn., Donald G. Scanlin/Vice Chmn., Robin Rossi/Dir., Dietrich Schmidt/Dir., William B. Sechrest/Dir., Lawrence E. Wilde/Dir.

Oklahoma Gas & Electric Co

PO Box 321, Oklahoma City, OK, 73101; *PH:* 1-405-553-3000; *http://* www.oge.com

General - Incorporation	OK	**Stock**- Price on:12/24/2007	NA
Employees	NA	Stock Exchange	NA
Auditor	Ernst & Young LLP	Ticker Symbol	NA
Stk Agt	Mellon Investor Services LLC	Outstanding Shares	NA
Counsel	NA	E.P.S	NA
DUNS No.	00-790-6662	Shareholders	NA

Business: The group's principle activity is to provide energy services. The group offers physical delivery and management of both electricity and natural gas in south central United States. The group operates through two business segments: the energy supply and the electric utility. The energy supply segment produces, gathers, processes, transports, markets and stores natural gas and produces, transports and markets natural gas liquids in Oklahoma, Arkansas and west Texas. This segment is also into commodity sales, services related to natural gas and electric power and provides energy-related services. The electric utility segment generates, transmits, distributes and sells electric energy in Oklahoma and western Arkansas.

Primary SIC and add'l.: 4922 4911 4931 6719 4939

CIK No: 0000074145

Officers: Steven E. Moore/60/Chmn., CEO, Steven R. Gerdes/51/VP - Utility Operations, Scott Forbes/50/Controller, Chief Accounting Officer, Jerry A. Peace/45/Chief Risk, Compliance Officer, Melvin H. Perkins/59/VP - Transmission, Gary D. Huneryager/VP - Internal Audits, James R. Hatfield/50/Sr. VP, CFO, Peter B. Delaney/54/Dir., COO, Pres., Cary W. Martin/55/VP - Human Resources, Howard W. Motley/59/VP - Regulatory Affairs, Carla D. Brockman/48/VP - Administration, Corp. Sec., Deborah S. Fleming/52/VP, Treasurer, Paul L. Renfrow/51/VP - Public Affairs, Reid Nuttall/50/VP - Enterprise Information, Performance, Jesse B. Langston/45/VP - Utility Commercial Operations

Directors: Steven E. Moore/60/Chmn., CEO, Herbert H. Champlin/Dir., J. D. Williams/Dir., Linda P. Lambert/Dir., Peter B. Delaney/54/Dir., COO, Pres., Ronald H. White/Dir., Luke R. Corbett/Dir., Robert Kelley/Dir., John D. Groendyke/Dir., Robert Lorenz/Dir.

Old Dominion Electric Cooperative

Innsbrook Corporate Ctr., Glen Allen, VA, 23058; ***PH:*** 1-804-747-0592; ***http://*** www.odec.com

General - Incorporation	VA	***Stock***- Price on:12/24/2007	NA
Employees	NA	Stock Exchange	NA
Auditor	Ernst & Young LLP	Ticker Symbol	NA
Stk Agt	NA	Outstanding Shares	NA
Counsel	NA	E.P.S.	NA
DUNS No.	07-043-1218	Shareholders	NA

Business: The group's principal activity is to provide wholesale power supply on a non-profit basis to its twelve consumer-owned electric distribution cooperatives and to tec trading inc. The twelve consumer-owned distribution co-operatives are termed as class a members and tec trading, inc. Is a class b member. The class a members sell electric service to consumers in 70 counties throughout Virginia, Delaware, Maryland and parts of west Virginia. Tec trading inc sells power in the market, manages the member distribution cooperatives exposure to changes in fuel prices and makes use of other power-related trading opportunities, which may become available in the market. During 2003, the group served more than 479,000 retail electric consumers representing a total population of approximately 1.2 million people.

Primary SIC and add'l.: 4911

CIK No: 0000885568

Officers: Jack Reasor/55/CEO, Pres., Greg White/Sr. VP - Engineering, Operations, Daryl Jaschen/Staff, Information Systems, Dan Walker/Sr. VP - Accounting, Finance, Daniel M. Walker/Dir. - RHI, Jon Reed/Staff, Facilities Management, Fred Hubbard/Dir. - RHI, Robert L. Kees/CFO, VP, Controller, Larry M. Longshore/Dir. - RHI, Bill May/Staff, Power Supply, Operations, Jeffrey Platzke/Staff, Power Supply, Operations, Kevin Miller/Staff, Asset Development, Production, Arlene Hines/Staff, Finance, Lynn Maloney/Staff, Finance, Manley J. Garber/Dir. - RHI *(82 Officers included in Index)*

Directors: Paul E. Owen/57/Dir., Vernon N. Brinkley/61/Dir., Hunter Greenlaw/Dir. - RHI, Philip B. Tankard/79/Dir., David J. Jones/59/Dir., William C. Frazier/77/Dir., Dale M. Bradshaw/54/Dir., John William Andrew/54/Dir., Wade C. House/55/Dir., Calvin P. Carter/83/Dir., Bruce A. Henry/62/Dir., Carl R. Widdowson/69/Dir., Johnson M. Bowman/62/Dir., Kent D. Farmer/50/Dir., William M. Leech/80/Dir. *(20 Directors included in Index)*

Old Dominion Freight Line Inc

500 Old Dominion Way, Thomasville, NC, 27360; ***PH:*** 1-336-889-5000; ***Fax:*** 1-336-822-5229; ***http://*** www.odfl.com; ***Email:*** information.services@odfl.com

General - Incorporation	VA	***Stock***- Price on:12/24/2007	$29.61
Employees	10,762	Stock Exchange	NDQ
Auditor	Ernst & Young LLP	Ticker Symbol	ODFL
Stk Agt	National Assoc.	Outstanding Shares	37,280,000
Counsel	Womble Carlyle Sandridge & Rice	E.P.S.	NA
DUNS No.	00-687-0877	Shareholders	NA

Business: The group's principal activity is to provide motor carrier services in the United States. The group operates through four segments: od-domestic, od-global, od-expedited and od-technology. It operates within the southeast, south central, northeast midwest and west regions of the country through fleet of 11,443 trailers. The group also offers container delivery service and nine port facilities as well as assembly and distribution services. It operates ltl shipments for full truckload transport by a truckload carrier or break down full truckload shipments from a truckload carrier into ltl shipment delivery. The group serves in Georgia, California, Illinois, Indiana, North Carolina, Pennsylvania, Tennessee and Texas.

Primary SIC and add'l.: 4213

CIK No: 0000878927

Officers: Earl E. Congdon/Chmn., CEO/$2,892,806.00, John R. Congdon/75/Vice Chmn., Sr. VP/$878,465.00, Wes J. Frye/60/CFO, Sr. VP - Finance, Treasurer, Assist. Sec./$644,890.00, Joel B. McCarty/70/Sr. VP, Sec., General Counsel, David S. Congdon/COO, Pres./$1,776,956.00, John B. Yowell/56/Exec. VP/$905,837.00

Directors: Earl E. Congdon/Chmn., CEO, John R. Congdon/75/Vice Chmn., Sr. VP, John A. Ebeling/70/Dir., Paul J. Breitbach/70/Dir., Franz F. Holscher/86/Dir., Robert G. Culp/61/Dir., Chester W. Evans/58/Dir.

Owners: David S. Congdon/7.40%, Franz F. Holscher, Robert G. Culp, John A. Ebeling, Jeffrey W. Congdon/5.50%, Earl E. Congdon/6.00%, Fidelity Management & Research Company/9.90%, Joel B. McCarty, Paul J. Breitbach, Wes J. Frye, Insiders/24.50%, John R. Congdon/5.70%, Munder Capital Management/7.60%, John B. Yowell/4.30%, John R. Congdon/4.90%

Financial Data: ***Fiscal Year End:***12/31 ***Latest Annual Data:*** 12/31/2006

Year	Sales	Net Income
2006	NA	NA
2005	NA	NA
2004	NA	NA

Curr. Assets:	$256,367,000	***Curr. Liab.:***	$121,546,000		
Plant, Equip.:	$607,588,000	***Total Liab.:***	$474,573,000	***Indic. Yr. Divd.:***	NA
Total Assets:	$892,193,000	***Net Worth:***	$417,620,000	***Debt/ Equity:***	0.5918

Old Florida Bankshares Inc

6321 Daniels Pk.way, Fort Myers, FL, 33912; ***PH:*** 1-239-561-6222; ***http://*** www.oldfloridabank.com

General - Incorporation		***Stock***- Price on:12/24/2007	NA
Employees	NA	Stock Exchange	NA
Auditor	NA	Ticker Symbol	NA
Stk Agt	American Stock Transfer & Trust Co.	Outstanding Shares	NA
Counsel	NA	E.P.S.	NA
DUNS No.	NA	Shareholders	NA

Business: The group operates through its subsidiaries whose principal activity is to provide a range of consumer and commercial banking services to individuals, businesses and industries. Services of the group include money market deposit accounts, time deposits, safe deposit services, credit cards, cash management, direct deposits, notary services, money orders, night depository, travelers checks, cashiers checks, domestic collections, savings bonds, bank drafts and automated teller services. The group operates from the United States.

Primary SIC and add'l.: 6712 6022

CIK No: 0001212565

Old Harbor BK FL

32700 Us Hwy. 19 N, Palm Harbor, FL, 34684; ***PH:*** 1-727-451-0561; ***http://*** www.oldharborbank.com; ***Email:*** customerservice@oldharborbank.com

General - Incorporation		***Stock***- Price on:12/24/2007	$15.75
Employees	NA	Stock Exchange	OTC
Auditor	NA	Ticker Symbol	OHBK
Stk Agt	Registrar & Transfer Co	Outstanding Shares	NA
Counsel	NA	E.P.S.	NA
DUNS No.	NA	Shareholders	NA

Business: The groups principal activities include providing community bank serving the businesses and residents of North Pinellas and South Pasco Counties, Florida. The group provides the personalized service and attention to the customers. The group operates from the United States. In the year 2006, the groups total assets were $171 (millions).

Primary SIC and add'l.: 6099

CIK No:

Officers: Barry K. Miller/Chmn., CEO, Michael J. Dean/Dir., CPA, Consultant, Gregory A. Mohr/Dir., Exec. VP - FT Processing, Brian M. Jones/Dir. - Management Consultant, William W. Short/Dir., COO, Pres.

Directors: Barry K. Miller/Chmn., CEO, Carl H. Keltner/Dir., Brian M. Jones/Dir. - Management Consultant, William W. Short/Dir., COO, Pres., Michael J. Dean/Dir., CPA, Consultant, Gregory A. Mohr/Dir., Exec. VP - FT Processing, James C. Hill/Dir., Gary F. Queen/Dir., Robert P. Symanski/Dir.

Old Line Bancshares Inc

1525 Pointer Ridge Pl., Bowie, MD, 20716; ***PH:*** 1-301-430-8720; ***Fax:*** 1-301-430-8723; ***http://*** www.oldlinebank.com

General - Incorporation	MD	***Stock***- Price on:12/24/2007	$9.9
Employees	52	Stock Exchange	NDQ
Auditor	Rowles & Co. LLP	Ticker Symbol	OLBK
Stk Agt	American Stock Transfer & Trust Co.	Outstanding Shares	4,250,000
Counsel	NA	E.P.S.	$0.36
DUNS No.	NA	Shareholders	NA

Business: The group's principal activity is to operate as a full service commercial bank. The group offers deposit services and loans to individuals, small businesses, associations and government entities. The services of the group include direct deposit of payroll and social security checks, automatic drafts from accounts, automated teller machine services, cash management services, safe deposit boxes, money orders and travelers cheques. The group also offers credit card services.

Primary SIC and add'l.: 6712 6022

CIK No: 0001253317

Subsidiaries: Old Line Bank

Officers: James W. Cornelsen/Dir., CEO, Pres., Erin G. Lyddane/Accounting, Old Line Bank, Denise Miller/Loan Dept, Old Line Bank Main Office, Elise Hubbard/Accounting, Old Line Bank Main Office, Brenda Martin/Bookkeeping, Old Line Bank Main Office, Cecilia McPherson/Bookkeeping, Old Line Bank Main Office, Barbara Sellner/Mgr. - Route 5, Old Line Centre Office, Charlene White/New Accounting, Old Line Bank Main Office, Debbie Hardesty/Mgr. - Clinton Office Old Line Centre Office, Joy Hinton/Mgr. - New Accounting, Accokeek Office Old Line Bank Main Office, Adelaide Copeland/New Accounting, Accokeek Office Old Line Bank Main Office, Rita King/Mgr. - 301 Office Old Line Bank Main Office, Joan McNeill/New Accounting, Route 5, Old Line Centre Office, Seble Habtemariam/New Accounting, Clinton Office Old Line Centre Office, Sandi Burnett/Mgr. - Collegepark Loan Office Old Line Centre Office *(21 Officers included in Index)*

Directors: James W. Cornelsen/Dir., CEO, Pres., Frank Lucente/65/Vice Chmn., Craig E. Clark/Chmn., Charles A. Bongar/Dir., John D. Mitchell/Dir., John M. Suit/Dir., Gail D. Manuel/Dir., Gregory Stephen Proctor/Dir., Suhas R. Shah/Dir., Daniel W. Deming/Dir., James F. Dent/Dir., Nancy L. Gasparovic/Dir.

Owners: Joseph E. Burnett/0.81%, Gregory S. Proctor/0.32%, John M. Suit/0.07%, Wellington Management Company LLP/6.34%, James W. Cornelsen/2.44%, Christine M. Rush/0.37%, Gail D. Manuel/0.37%, James F. Dent/1.25%, Craig E. Clark/2.07%, Nancy L. Gasparovic/0.39%, Jeffrey A. Miller/8.69%, Suhas R. Shah/0.05%, Frank Lucente/3.53%, Charles A. Bongar/0.70%, John D. Mitchell/0.48% *(17 Owners included in Index)*

Financial Data: ***Fiscal Year End:***12/31 ***Latest Annual Data:*** 12/31/2006

Year	Sales	Net Income
2006	$12,052,000	$1,574,000
2005	$7,624,000	$1,139,000
2004	$5,444,000	$817,000

Curr. Assets:	$40,449,000	***Curr. Liab.:***	$179,829,000	***P/E Ratio:***	27.50
Plant, Equip.:	$4,049,000	***Total Liab.:***	$183,314,000	***Indic. Yr. Divd.:***	$0.120
Total Assets:	$218,131,000	***Net Worth:***	$34,816,000	***Debt/ Equity:***	0.0853

Old National Bancorp

1 Main St., Evansville, IN, 47708; ***PH:*** 1-812-464-1294; ***Fax:*** 1-812-464-1567; ***http://*** www.oldnational.com; ***Email:*** bancorp@oldnational.com

General - Incorporation	IN	***Stock***- Price on:12/24/2007	$17.66
Employees	2,568	Stock Exchange	NYSE
Auditor	PricewaterhouseCoopers LLP	Ticker Symbol	ONB
Stk Agt	Old National Bancorp	Outstanding Shares	66,420,000
Counsel	Jeffrey L. Knight	E.P.S.	$1.05
DUNS No.	00-693-6959	Shareholders	NA

Business: The group's principal activities are to provide commercial and consumer banking services. The operating segments of the group are community banking, non-bank services and treasury. The community banking segment provides commercial, real estate and consumer loans, lease financing, checking, savings and time deposits, safe deposit facilities, debit cards and Internet banking. The non-bank services provide fiduciary and trust services, investment and brokerage services and asset management services. Treasury segment manages investments, wholesale funding, interest rate risk, liquidity, and leverage for the group. During the year 2003, it acquired insurance and risk management, graham and peat insurance agency and james l. Will insurance agency.

Primary SIC and add'l.: 6712 6021

CIK No: 0000707179

Subsidiaries: American National Trust & Investment Management Corp, Old National Bank, Old National Realty Company, Inc., ONB Finance Inc., ONB Insurance Group, Inc.

Officers: Robert G. Jones/Dir., CEO, Pres./$994,802.00, John W. Rosenthal/Region CEO, Donald A. Schroeder/Region CEO, Thomas A. Flynn/CEO - ONB Insurance Group, James A. Sandgren/Region CEO, Dennis P. Heishman/Region CEO, Richard W. Dube/Exec. VP, Chief Auditing Exec., Candice J. Rickard/44/Exec. VP, Chief Risk Officer, Candice J. Jenkins/Exec. VP, Chief Risk Officer, Allen R. Mounts/Exec. VP, Chief Administrative Officer, Daryl D. Moore/Exec. VP, Chief Credit Officer/$459,435.00, Barbara A. Murphy/57/Exec. VP, Chief Risk Officer/$378,152.00, Jeffrey L. Knight/Exec. VP, Chief Legal Counsel, Annette W. Hudgions/Exec. VP, Chief Client Services Officer/$412,205.00, Christopher A. Wolking/CFO, Sr. Exec. VP/$424,447.00 (16 Officers included in Index)

Directors: Robert G. Jones/Dir., CEO, Pres., Larry E. Dunigan/65/Chmn., Joseph D. Barnette/Dir., Arthur H. McElwee/Dir., Charles D. Storms/Dir., Phelps L. Lambert/Dir., Marjorie Z. Soyugenc/Dir., Niel C. Ellerbrook/Dir., Kelly N. Stanley/Dir., Alan W. Braun/Dir., Andrew E. Goebel/Dir.

Owners: Marjorie Z. Soyugenc, Charles D. Storms, Kelly N. Stanley, Alan W. Braun, Christopher A. Wolking, Annette W. Hudgions, Niel C. Ellerbrook, Barbara A. Murphy, David E. Eckerle, Insiders/3.48%, Phelps L. Lambert, Andrew E. Goebel, Daryl D. Moore, Robert G. Jones, Larry E. Dunigan (16 Owners included in Index)

Financial Data: Fiscal Year End:12/31   Latest Annual Data: 12/31/2006

Year	Sales	Net Income
2006	$605,633,000	$79,373,000
2005	$588,573,000	$63,764,000
2004	$599,361,000	$67,571,000

Curr. Assets:	$551,249,000	Curr. Liab.:	$6,759,601,000	P/E Ratio:	16.82
Plant, Equip.:	$122,865,000	Total Liab.:	$7,507,146,000	Indic. Yr. Divd.:	$0.880
Total Assets:	$8,149,515,000	Net Worth:	$642,369,000	Debt/ Equity:	NA

Old Point Financial Corp

1 W Mellen St., Hampton, VA, 23663; *PH:* 1-757-728-1200; *Fax:* 1-757-728-1279; http:// www.oldpoint.com

General - Incorporation	VA	Stock - Price on:12/24/2007	$25.94
Employees	285	Stock Exchange	NDQ
Auditor	Yount, Hyde & Barbour, P.C	Ticker Symbol	OPOF
Stk Agt	Computershare Investor Services LLC	Outstanding Shares	4,000,000
Counsel	NA	E.P.S.	$1.85
DUNS No.	15-019-8901	Shareholders	NA

Business: The group's principal activity is to provide full range of banking, financial and depository services. The group accepts checking accounts, savings accounts, money market deposit accounts and certificates of deposit. It lends commercial loans, industrial loans, and residential real estate and consumer loans. The other services include safekeeping services and trust services which includes retirement planning, estate planning, financial planning, trust accounts, tax services and investment management services. The products and services are provided to both individuals and commercial customers. The group's operations are conducted through twenty offices located in hampton, newport news, chesapeake, james city and york county of Indiana, North Carolina, Pennsylvania, Tennessee and Texas.

Primary SIC and add'l.: 6021 6712

CIK No: 0000740971

Subsidiaries: Old Point Trust and Financial Services N.A., The Old Point National Bank of Phoebus

Officers: Robert F. Shuford/Chmn., CEO/$282,644.00, Cary B. Epes/Sr. VP - Business Development, Lending/$173,933.00, Margaret P. Causby/Sr. VP - Risk Management/$165,523.00, Eugene M. Jordan/Exec. VP - Trust, Lani Chisman Davis/Contact - Investor Relations, Robert F. Shuford/Sr. VP - Operations, Laurie D. Grabow/Sr. VP - Finance/$147,890.00, Melissa L. Burroughs/Sr. VP - Business Development, Lending

Directors: Robert F. Shuford/Chmn., CEO, John B. Morgan/Dir., Robert L. Riddle/Dir., Ellen Clark Thacker/Dir., Arthur D. Greene/Dir., Stephen D. Harris/Dir., Eugene M. Jordan/Dir., Russell Smith Evans/Dir., James Reade Chisman/Dir., Robert H. Schappert/Dir., Melvin R. Zimm/Dir., Richard F. Clark/Dir., John Cabot Ishon/Dir., Louis G. Morris/Dir.

Owners: John B. Morgan, John Cabot Ishon, Margaret P. Causby, Richard F. Clark, Ellen Clark Thacker, VuBay Foundation, Cary B. Epes, Melvin R. Zimm, Robert F. Shuford, James Reade Chisman, Louis G. Morris, Robert H. Schappert, Arthur D. Greene, Stephen D. Harris, Laurie D. Grabow (22 Owners included in Index)

Financial Data: Fiscal Year End:12/31   Latest Annual Data: 12/31/2006

Year	Sales	Net Income
2006	$56,291,000	$7,024,000
2005	$46,852,000	$7,268,000
2004	$43,059,000	$8,580,000

Curr. Assets:	$36,784,000	Curr. Liab.:	$772,856,000	P/E Ratio:	13.51
Plant, Equip.:	$26,410,000	Total Liab.:	$772,856,000	Indic. Yr. Divd.:	$0.720
Total Assets:	$847,521,000	Net Worth:	$74,665,000	Debt/ Equity:	NA

Old Republic International Corp

307 N Michigan Ave., Chicago, IL, 60601; *PH:* 1-312-346-8100; *Fax:* 1-312-726-0309; http:// www.oldrepublic.com

General - Incorporation	DE	Stock - Price on:12/24/2007	$21.39
Employees	6,370	Stock Exchange	NYSE
Auditor	PricewaterhouseCoopers LLP	Ticker Symbol	ORI
Stk Agt	Computershare Trust Co	Outstanding Shares	231,400,000
Counsel	NA	E.P.S.	$1.90
DUNS No.	00-693-2024	Shareholders	NA

Business: The groups principle activity is to provide insurance security and related services to businesses, individuals and public institutions. The groups businesses include general insurance, mortgage guaranty, title, and life and health insurance. The group operates from United States.

Primary SIC and add'l.: 6331 6719 6311 6351 6361

CIK No: 0000074260

Officers: Aldo C. Zucaro/68/Chmn., CEO/$3,299,882.00, James A. Kellogg/COO, Pres./$1,083,200.00, Charles S. Boone/Sr. VP - Investments, Treasurer, Spencer Leroy/Sr. VP, General Counsel, Sec./$1,237,285.00, Karl W. Mueller/CFO, Sr. VP/$702,446.00, Christopher S. Nard/Sr. VP - Mortgage Guaranty/$1,416,588.00, Rande K. Yeager/Sr. VP - Title Insurance/$951,070.00, Scott R. Rager/Sr. VP - General Insurance/$987,955.00

Directors: Aldo C. Zucaro/68/Chmn., CEO, Harrington Bischof/73/Dir., William A. Simpson/66/Dir., Arnold L. Steiner/70/Dir., Peter Lardner/76/Dir., Charles F. Titterton/66/Dir., Steven R. Walker/62/Dir., Jimmy A. Dew/67/Dir., John M. Dixon/68/Dir., John W. Popp/85/Dir., Fredricka Taubitz/64/Dir., Dennis P. Van Mieghem/67/Dir., Leo E. Knight/62/Dir.

Owners: AXA Financial, Inc./5.80%, Spencer LeRoy, Jimmy A. Dew/0.60%, Leo E. Knight, Dennis Van Mieghem, Fredricka Taubitz, Charles F. Titterton, James A. Kellogg/0.20%, Steven R. Walker, Aldo C. Zucaro/1.00%, Franklin Resources, Inc./5.40%, William A. Simpson/0.50%, Franklin Mutual Advisors, LLC./7.10%, Rande K. Yeager, Insiders/3.10% (25 Owners included in Index)

Financial Data: Fiscal Year End:12/31   Latest Annual Data: 12/31/2006

Year	Sales	Net Income
2006	$3,794,200,000	$464,800,000
2005	$3,806,000,000	$551,400,000
2004	$3,491,500,000	$435,000,000

Curr. Assets:	$4,316,700,000	Curr. Liab.:	$557,900,000	P/E Ratio:	10.97
Plant, Equip.:	NA	Total Liab.:	$8,243,000,000	Indic. Yr. Divd.:	$0.640
Total Assets:	$12,612,200,000	Net Worth:	$4,369,200,000	Debt/ Equity:	NA

Old Second Bancorp Inc

37 S River St., Aurora, IL, 60506; *PH:* 1-630-892-0202; *Fax:* 1-630-892-9630; http:// www.o2bancorp.com; *Email:* supportcenter@o2bancorp.com

General - Incorporation	DE	Stock - Price on:12/24/2007	$30.06
Employees	582	Stock Exchange	NDQ
Auditor	Grant Thornton, LLP	Ticker Symbol	OSBC
Stk Agt	NA	Outstanding Shares	13,110,000
Counsel	NA	E.P.S.	$1.72
DUNS No.	00-692-7818	Shareholders	NA

Business: The group's principal activity is to provide consumer and commercial banking services. The group accepts deposits in the different forms such as demand, savings, time deposit, individual retirement and keogh deposit accounts. It provides various kinds of loans including commercial, industrial, consumer, real estate and installment loans, student loans, farm loans, line of credit and overdraft checking. The group's services also include safe deposit operations, trust services, the acquisition of treasury notes and bonds, sale of traveler's checks, money orders, cashier's checks and foreign currency, direct deposit, discount brokerage, debit and credit card services. The group's offices are located in kane, kendall, dupage, dekalb, lake, lasalle and winnebago counties of Illinois.

Primary SIC and add'l.: 6021 6712

CIK No: 0000357173

Subsidiaries: Old Second Affordable Housing Fund, LLC, Old Second Bank - Kane County, Old Second Bank - Yorkville, Old Second Capital Trust I, Old Second Financial,Inc., Old Second Mortgage,Inc., Old Second National Bank of Aurora

Officers: William B. Skoglund/57/Chmn., CEO, Pres./$530,459.00, James Eccher/Dir., COO, Exec. VP/$244,983.00, Douglas J. Cheatham/51/Dir., CFO, Sr. VP/$248,034.00, James Carl Schmitz/Dir., Tax Consultant

Directors: William B. Skoglund/57/Chmn., CEO, Pres., William Kane/Dir., Walter Alexander/Sr. Dir., Mary Krasner/55/Dir., James Eccher/Dir., COO, Exec. VP, Edward Bonifas/48/Dir., Kenneth Lindgren/Dir., Marvin Fagel/Dir., William Meyer/60/Dir., Jesse Maberry/Dir., James Carl Schmitz/Dir., Tax Consultant, Gerald Palmer/62/Dir., Barry Finn/48/Dir., Douglas J. Cheatham/51/Dir., CFO, Sr. VP, Chet D. Mckee/Dir.

Owners: Old Second Bancorp, Inc./5.50%, Jesse Maberry, Kenneth Lindgren, The Banc Funds Company, L.L.C./5.80%, Walter Alexander, Mary Krasner, Chet D. McKee, Rod Sloan, Insiders/9.20%, Barry Finn, Gerald Palmer, Marvin Fagel, William Kane, Edward Bonifas, William Meyer (19 Owners included in Index)

Financial Data: Fiscal Year End:12/31   Latest Annual Data: 12/31/2006

Year	Sales	Net Income
2006	$170,736,000	$23,656,000
2005	$148,386,000	$27,683,000
2004	$123,312,000	$26,287,000

Curr. Assets:	$118,335,000	Curr. Liab.:	$2,252,535,000	P/E Ratio:	17.28
Plant, Equip.:	$48,452,000	Total Liab.:	$2,300,585,000	Indic. Yr. Divd.:	$0.600
Total Assets:	$2,459,140,000	Net Worth:	$158,555,000	Debt/ Equity:	NA

Olin Corp

190 Carondelet Plz., Ste. 1530, Clayton, MO, 63105; *PH:* 1-314-480-1400; *Fax:* 1-314-862-7406; http:// www.olin.com

General - Incorporation	VA	Stock - Price on:12/24/2007	$20.22
Employees	6,000	Stock Exchange	NYSE
Auditor	KPMG LLP	Ticker Symbol	OLN
Stk Agt	Mellon Investor Services LLC	Outstanding Shares	73,740,000
Counsel	NA	E.P.S.	$0.03
DUNS No.	18-176-4192	Shareholders	NA

Business: The groups principle activities include manufacturing and selling chlorine and caustic soda, sodium hydrosulfite, hydrochloric acid, canister powder, reloading components, and small caliber military ammunition and components. The group operates through two business segments namely Chlor Alkali Products and Winchester. The group operates from United States.

Primary SIC and add'l.: 3341 2899 2812

CIK No: 0000074303

Subsidiaries: A.J. Oster Caribe, Inc., A.J. Oster Foils, Inc., A.J. Oster West, Inc., Bridgeport Brass Corporation, Bryan Metals, Inc., Chase Brass& Copper Company, Inc., Chase Industries Inc., Hunt Trading Co., LTC Reserve Corp., Monarch Brass& Copper Corp., Monarch Brass& Copper of New England Corp., New Haven Copper Company, Nutmeg Insurance Limited, Olin (UK) Limited, Olin Asia Pacific Pte. Ltd. 34 Subsidiaries included in the Index

Officers: Joseph D. Rupp/Chmn., CEO, Pres./$4,594,279.00, John L. McIntosh/53/VP, Pres. - Chlor Alkali Products Division/$1,204,801.00, George H. Pain/57/VP, General Counsel, Sec./$1,365,549.00, John E. Fischer/52/CFO, VP/$1,121,451.00, Dennis R. McGough/59/VP - Human Resources, Jeffrey J. Haferkamp/53/VP, Pres. - Olin Brass/$820,040.00, Stephen C. Curley/56/VP, Treasurer, Bruce G. Greer/47/VP - Strategic Planning, Richard M. Hammett/61/VP, Pres. - Winchester Division, Todd A. Slater/44/VP, Controller

Directors: Joseph D. Rupp/Chmn., CEO, Pres., Randall W. Larrimore/Dir., Anthony W. Ruggiero/Dir., Robert C. Bunch/Dir., Virginia A. Kamsky/Dir., Richard M. Rompala/Dir., Philip J. Schulz/Dir., Donald W. Bogus/Dir., Donald W. Griffin/Dir., John M.B. O'Connor/Dir.

Owners: Barclays Global Investors, NA/5.20%, State Street Bank and Trust Company/10.40%

Financial Data: Fiscal Year End:12/31 **Latest Annual Data:** 12/31/2006

Year	Sales	Net Income
2006	$3,151,800,000	$149,700,000
2005	$2,357,700,000	$133,300,000
2004	$1,997,000,000	$55,000,000

Curr. Assets:	$919,200,000	**Curr. Liab.:**	$407,800,000	**P/E Ratio:**	10.64
Plant, Equip.:	$486,900,000	**Total Liab.:**	$1,093,200,000	**Indic. Yr. Divd.:**	$0.800
Total Assets:	$1,636,500,000	**Net Worth:**	$543,300,000	**Debt/ Equity:**	NA

Oliver Creek Resources Inc

250 - 5135 Camino Al Norte, North Las Vegas, NV, 89031; *PH:* 1-702-441-0447

General - Incorporation		**Stock**- Price on:12/24/2007	NA
Employees	NA	Stock Exchange	OTC
Auditor	Chang G. Park, Cpa	Ticker Symbol	OVCR
Stk Agt	Holladay Stock Transfer, Inc.	Outstanding Shares	NA
Counsel	NA	E.P.S	NA
DUNS No.	NA	Shareholders	NA

Business: The groups principal activity is in the exploration. The groups activities to date have been limited to capital formation, organization and development of its business plan. The group operates from the United States.

Primary SIC and add'l.: 1000

CIK No: 0001353406

Officers: Bruce Thomson/60/Dir., CEO, CFO, Pres., Samantha Thomson/29/Dir., Sec.

Directors: Bruce Thomson/60/Dir., CEO, CFO, Pres., Samantha Thomson/29/Dir., Sec.

Owners: Bruce Thomson/50.00%, Insiders/50.00%

Olympic Cascade Financial Corp

1001 Fourth Ave., Ste. 2200, Seattle, WA, 98154; *PH:* 1-312-751-8833

General - Incorporation	DE	**Stock**- Price on:12/24/2007	$4.16
Employees	2,123	Stock Exchange	NA
Auditor	Marcum & Kliegman LLP	Ticker Symbol	NA
Stk Agt	Computershare Trust Co	Outstanding Shares	59,600,000
Counsel	NA	E.P.S	-$8.76
DUNS No.	04-620-7635	Shareholders	NA

Business: The group's principal activity is to provide financial services through its wholly-owned subsidiary national securities corporation. The group's business includes securities brokerage for individual and institutional clients, market-making trading activities, asset management and corporate finance services.

Primary SIC and add'l.: 6719 6211 6282

CIK No: 0001023844

Subsidiaries: National Securities Corporation, Robotic Ventures Group LLC

Officers: Mark Goldwasser/49/Chmn., CEO, Pres., Robert H. Daskal/66/CFO, Sec., David McCoy/45/COO, Brian Friedman/36/Exec. VP

Directors: Mark Goldwasser/49/Chmn., CEO, Pres., Gary A. Rosenberg/67/Dir., Marshall S. Geller/68/Dir., Robert J. Rosan/76/Dir., Norman J. Kurlan/55/Dir., Peter Rettman/Dir., Christopher C. Dewey/63/Dir.

Owners: Bedford Oak Advisors, LLC, Mark Goldwasser, Steven A. Rothstein, Gregory P. Kusnick, Robert H. Daskal, Gregory C. Lowney, Triage Partners LLC, Insiders, Robert J. Rosan, Brian Friedman, Christopher C. Dewey, David McCoy, Norman J. Kurlan, Gary A. Rosenberg, Strategic Turnaround Equity Partners, LP *(17 Owners included in Index)*

Financial Data: Fiscal Year End:09/26 **Latest Annual Data:** 12/31/2006

Year	Sales	Net Income
2006	$2,637,300,000	-$201,200,000
2005	$2,509,000,000	$218,300,000
2004	$2,135,300,000	$119,600,000

Curr. Assets:	$2,283,400,000	**Curr. Liab.:**	$632,700,000		
Plant, Equip.:	$30,000,000	**Total Liab.:**	$2,067,300,000	**Indic. Yr. Divd.:**	$0.060
Total Assets:	$2,842,200,000	**Net Worth:**	$774,900,000	**Debt/ Equity:**	1.6102

Olympic Steel Inc

5096 Richmond Rd., Bedford Heights, OH, 44146; *PH:* 1-216-292-3800; *Fax:* 1-216-292-3974; *http://* www.olysteel.com; *Email:* olysteel@bellsouth.net

General - Incorporation	OH	**Stock**- Price on:12/24/2007	$32.44
Employees	1,120	Stock Exchange	NDQ
Auditor	PricewaterhouseCoopers LLP	Ticker Symbol	ZEUS
Stk Agt	LaSalle Bank N.A	Outstanding Shares	10,580,000
Counsel	Kahn, Kleinman, Yonowitz & Arnson Co.	E.P.S	$2.28
DUNS No.	00-886-1627	Shareholders	NA

Business: The group's principle activities include processing and distribution of flat-rolled carbon, stainless and tubular steel products. The group operates as an intermediary between steel producers and manufacturers that require processed steel for their operations. The group purchases flat rolled steel from steel producers and processes as per customer specifications, provides critical inventory and just-in-time delivery services. The services of the group include traditional services and higher value-added. The traditional services include process of cutting-to-length, slitting, shearing and roll forming .the higher value-added processes include blanking, tempering, plate burning, laser welding, and precision machining of steel parts. The group's international sales office is located in miami, Florida and it services customers primarily in Mexico and Puerto Rico. The group's quarterly revenue for September 2007 was 256.09 millions of USD.

Primary SIC and add'l.: 3317 3316

CIK No: 0000917470

Subsidiaries: G.s.p., LLC, OLP LLC, Oly Steel Welding, Inc., Olympic Steel Iowa, Inc., Olympic Steel Lafayette, Inc., Olympic Steel Minneapolis, Inc., Olympic Steel Receivables LLC, Olympic Steel Receivables, Inc., Olympic Steel Trading, Inc.

Officers: Michael D. Siegal/55/Chmn., CEO, Michael Cedoz/GM - Detroit Subsidiary, Tom Ehlers/Minneapolis Subsidiary, Inside Sales Mgr. Coil, Larry Freedman/Minneapolis Subsidiary, Inside Sales Mgr. - Plate, Dave Thielman/Minneapolis Subsidiary, GM Plate, Mary Murphy/Minneapolis Subsidiary, Regional Sales Mgr. - Northern Tier, Central Region, Joe Roberts/Minneapolis Subsidiary, Operations Mgr. - Coil, Dana Henjum/Minneapolis Subsidiary, Operations Mgr. - Plate, Richard T. Marabito/CFO/$1,087,330.00, Steve Mallory/Chicago Division, VP - Central Region, Rudi Tanck/Chicago Division, GM, Ray Walker/Cleveland Division, VP - Eastern Region, John Mooney/Cleveland Division, GM, Dan Springer/Southern Division, Operations Mgr., Tina Feraci/Southern Division, Regional Sales Mgr. Southern Tier *(40 Officers included in Index)*

Directors: Michael D. Siegal/55/Chmn., CEO, Howard L. Goldstein/55/Dir., David A. Wolfort/55/Dir., COO, Pres., James B. Meathe/50/Dir., Thomas M. Forman/61/Dir., Martin H. Elrad/68/Dir., Ralph M. Della Ratta/54/Dir.

Owners: Royce & Associates, LLC/12.40%, Dimensional Fund Advisors Inc./8.50%, Michael D. Siegal/13.50%, Howard L. Goldstein, Goldman Sachs Asset Management, L.P./7.10%, Insiders/20.80%, Martin H. Elrad, Richard T. Marabito, Thomas M. Forman, Richard A. Manson, Heber MacWilliams, David A. Wolfort/6.40%, James B. Meathe, Ralph M. Della Ratta

Financial Data: Fiscal Year End:12/31 **Latest Annual Data:** 12/31/2006

Year	Sales	Net Income
2006	$981,004,000	$31,048,000
2005	$939,210,000	$22,092,000
2004	$894,157,000	$60,078,000

Curr. Assets:	$308,215,000	**Curr. Liab.:**	$92,340,000	**P/E Ratio:**	12.20
Plant, Equip.:	$87,359,000	**Total Liab.:**	$171,083,000	**Indic. Yr. Divd.:**	$0.160
Total Assets:	$405,320,000	**Net Worth:**	$234,237,000	**Debt/ Equity:**	0.2098

OM Group Inc

127 Public Sq., 1500 Key Tower, Cleveland, OH, 44114; *PH:* 1-216-781-0083; *Fax:* 1-216-781-1502; *http://* www.omgi.com; *Email:* investinfo@na.omgi.com

General - Incorporation	DE	**Stock**- Price on:12/24/2007	$59.62
Employees	1,248	Stock Exchange	NYSE
Auditor	Ernst & Young LLP	Ticker Symbol	OMG
Stk Agt	National City Bank	Outstanding Shares	29,810,000
Counsel	Squire, Sanders & Dempsey LLP	E.P.S	$10.532
DUNS No.	55-686-9238	Shareholders	NA

Business: The group's principal activity is to produce and market value-added, metal-based specialty chemicals and related materials. The group leverages its unique vertical integration in cobalt and nickel with its metal separation technologies to offer product formulations to its customers. It produces specialty chemicals and materials from barium, calcium, iron, manganese, potassium, rare earths, stainless steel, zinc and zirconium. The group supplies more than 1,700 customers in 50 countries with more than 625 different product offerings and serves more than 30 major industries. These industries include aerospace, hard metal tools, appliance, rubber, automotive, ceramics, paints & ink, catalysts, electronics, petrochemicals, stainless steel, magnetic media, rechargeable battery chemicals and other manufacturers who use specialty chemicals. The group operates manufacturing facilities in the Americas, Europe, Asia, Africa and Australia.

Primary SIC and add'l.: 2869 2819

CIK No: 0000899723

Subsidiaries: Fidelity Chemical Products Malaysia SDN.BHD, Groupement Pour Le Traitement Du teril De Lubumbashi, Harko CV, OM Holdings, Inc, OMG Americas, Inc, OMG Asia-Pacific Co., Ltd., OMG Belleville, Limited, OMG Cawse Pty Ltd., OMG Chemicals Pte, Ltd., OMG Europe GmbH, OMG Fidelity, Inc., OMG Finland Oy, OMG Harjavalta Chemicals Holding BV, OMG Harjavalta Nickel Oy, OMG Japan, Inc. 23 Subsidiaries included in the Index

Officers: Joseph M. Scaminace/54/Chmn., CEO, Pres./$5,567,130.00, Stephen D. Dunmead/45/VP, GM - Specialties Group/$1,197,142.00, Greg Griffith/Dir. - Investor Relation, VP - Corporate Affairs, Pat Deluca/Business Dir. - Inorganics, Steve Flinchbaugh/Business Dir. - Advanced Organics, Jeff Blazek/Global Business Mgr. - Powder Metallurgy, Mike Lacis/Global Business Mgr. - Ceramics, Chemicals, Hiroki Oda/Global Marketing Mgr. - Battery Products, Peter Ting/Sales, Marketing, Asia Pacific, Yutaka Tonomura/Sales, Marketing, Japan, Valerie Gentile Sachs/53/VP, General Counsel, Corp. Sec./$1,045,356.00, Kenneth Haber/57/CFO, Gregory J. Griffith/53/VP - Strategic Planning, Development, Investor Relations

Directors: Joseph M. Scaminace/54/Chmn., CEO, Pres., Katharine L. Plourde/Dir., William J. Reidy/67/Dir., Richard W. Blackburn/65/Dir., Steven J. Demetriou/49/Dir., David L. Pugh/59/Dir., Gordon A. Ulsh/62/Dir.

Owners: Stephen D. Dunmead, Katharine L. Plourde, Marcus P. Bak, Kenneth Haber, Barclays Global Investors, NA/5.43%, FMR Corporation/9.14%, Insiders, William J. Reidy, Valerie Gentile Sachs, Richard W. Blackburn, Joseph M. Scaminace, Goldman Sachs Asset Management, L.P./10.40%

Financial Data: Fiscal Year End:12/31 **Latest Annual Data:** 12/31/2006

Year	Sales	Net Income
2006	$660,104,000	$216,073,000
2005	$1,249,609,000	$38,891,000
2004	$1,347,338,000	$128,644,000

Curr. Assets:	$1,210,041,000	**Curr. Liab.:**	$749,289,000		
Plant, Equip.:	$210,953,000	**Total Liab.:**	$792,859,000	**Indic. Yr. Divd.:**	NA
Total Assets:	$1,618,224,000	**Net Worth:**	$782,079,000	**Debt/ Equity:**	0.0013

Omagine Inc

Formerly: Alfa International Holdings Corp

350 Fifth Ave., Ste. 1103, New York, NY, 10118; *PH:* 1-212-563-4141; *http://* www.alfacorp.net

General - Incorporation	NJ	**Stock**- Price on:12/24/2007	$1.55
Employees	NA	Stock Exchange	OTC
Auditor	Michael T. Studer CPA P.C	Ticker Symbol	OMAG
Stk Agt	International Holdings Corp	Outstanding Shares	39,670,000
Counsel	NA	E.P.S	-$0.01
DUNS No.	00-139-4709	Shareholders	NA

Business: The group's principal activities are to manufacture and market apparel products. The group is a holding company, which conducts substantially all of its operations through its two wholly owned subsidiaries, contact sports, inc. And ty-breakers corp. The products are marketed through industry trade shows, advertising, street teams, tie-ins with rap artists, fashion shows, direct mail, print advertising, promotional events and parties which it sponsors, as well as video presentations for major customers. Ty-breakers corp manufactures and markets apparel products, mostly jackets, and accessories made from tyvek and kensel and markets the products into the premium and incentive marketplace. 'contact sports', 'tyvek' and 'kensel' are the trademarks of the group.

Primary SIC and add'l.: 6719 2389

CIK No: 0000820600

Subsidiaries: Contact Sports, Inc, Journey of Light, Inc, Ty-Breakers Corp

Officers: Frank J. Drohan/63/Chmn., CEO, CFO, Pres., Charles P. Kuczynski/54/Dir., VP, Sec.

Directors: Frank J. Drohan/63/Chmn., CEO, CFO, Pres., Charles P. Kuczynski/54/Dir., VP, Sec., Louis J. Lombardo/63/Dir., Salvatore J. Bucchere/64/Dir., Kevin O'c Green/60/Dir.

Owners: Charles P. Kuczynski/1.90%, Salvatore S. Bucchere/0.20%, Frank J. Drohan/18.80%, Louis J. Lombardo/0.90%, Mahmoud Gebril El-Warfally/6.00%, Mohammed K. Al-Sada/9.70%, Muftah Benomran/14.50%, Robert F. Peacock/6.20%, Insiders/22.00%, Kevin O. Green/0.20%

Financial Data: ***Fiscal Year End:***12/31 ***Latest Annual Data:*** 12/31/2006

Year	Sales	Net Income
2006	$1,182,000	-$768,000
2005	$271,000	-$5,901,000
2004	$71,000	-$1,021,000

Curr. Assets:	$68,000	***Curr. Liab.:***	$988,000		
Plant, Equip.:	$16,000	***Total Liab.:***	$1,108,000	***Indic. Yr. Divd.:***	NA
Total Assets:	$97,000	***Net Worth:***	-$1,010,000	***Debt/ Equity:***	NA

Omega Financial Corp

366 Walker Dr., State College, PA, 16804; ***PH:*** 1-814-231-7680; ***Fax:*** 1-814-231-5797; ***http://*** www.omegafinancial.com

General - Incorporation	PA	***Stock***- Price on:12/24/2007	$27.68
Employees	607	Stock Exchange	NDQ
Auditor	Ernst & Young LLP	Ticker Symbol	OMEF
Stk Agt	Registrar & Transfer Co	Outstanding Shares	12,650,000
Counsel	NA	E.P.S	$1.61
DUNS No.	10-167-0925	Shareholders	NA

Business: The group's principal activity is to provide consumer and commercial banking services. Consumer services include Internet and telephone banking, automated teller machine, personal checking and savings accounts, insured money market accounts, debit cards and investment certificates. Commercial banking services include small and high-volume business checking accounts, on-line account management services, ach origination, payroll direct deposit, commercial lending, commercial cash management services and repurchase agreements. Other products and services include club accounts, installment loans, construction and mortgage loans, safe deposit facilities, credit lines with overdraft checking protection and student loans. The group also provides trust and asset management services. The group operates through 44 offices in centre, clinton, mifflin, juniata, blair, huntingdon and bedford counties.

Primary SIC and add'l.: 6712 6022

CIK No: 0000705671

Subsidiaries: Omega Financial Capital Trust I, SUBI Services Inc.

Officers: Donita R. Koval/Dir., CEO, Pres./$461,295.00, Bruce R. Erb/Pres. - Wealth Management, Omega Bank, Byron M. Mertz/Sr. VP, Daniel L. Warfel/CFO, Exec. VP/$355,641.00, John R. Franks/Exec. VP - Branch Administration, Omega Bank, David S. Runk/Exec. VP, Thomas Bixler/Sr. VP - Commercial Lending, Teresa M. Ciambotti/Sr. VP, Corporate Controller, Dir. - Investor Relations, David N. Wells/Sr. VP, Customer Relationship Mgr., Walter Kay/CIO, Sr. VP, Rodney L. Fletcher/Dir. - Omega Bank

Directors: Donita R. Koval/Dir., CEO, Pres., David B. Lee/Chmn., Maureen M. Bufalino/Dir., Allen E. Gibboney/Dir., Carl H. Baxter/Dir., Jodi L. Green/Dir., Dennis Van Benthuysen/Dir., Stephen D. Martz/Dir., Robert A. Szeyller/Dir., Philip E. Gingerich/Dir., Stanton R. Sheetz/Dir., Stephen M. Krentzman/Dir., Robert A. Hormell/Dir., Frederick J. Kissinger/Dir.

Owners: Philip E. Gingerich, Robert A. Szeyller, Stanton R. Sheetz, Daniel L. Warfel, Maureen M. Bufalino, David N. Thiel, David B. Lee/1.90%, Stephen M. Krentzman, Insiders/5.70%, Dennis J. Van Benthuysen, Donita R. Koval, Dimensional Fund Advisors, LP/7.20%, Robert A. Hormell, D. Stephen Martz, Jodi L. Green *(16 Owners included in Index)*

Financial Data: ***Fiscal Year End:***12/31 ***Latest Annual Data:*** 12/31/2006

Year	Sales	Net Income
2006	$123,673,000	$20,431,000
2005	$121,419,000	$22,875,000
2004	$82,879,000	$17,021,000

Curr. Assets:	$68,346,000	***Curr. Liab.:***	$1,391,475,000	***P/E Ratio:***	16.88
Plant, Equip.:	$31,373,000	***Total Liab.:***	$1,490,607,000	***Indic. Yr. Divd.:***	$1.240
Total Assets:	$1,815,818,000	***Net Worth:***	$325,211,000	***Debt/ Equity:***	NA

Omega Flex Inc

451 Creamery Way, Exton, PA, 19341; ***PH:*** 1-610-524-7272; ***Fax:*** 1-610-524-7282; ***http://*** www.omegaflex.com; ***Email:*** info@omegaflex.com

General - Incorporation	PA	***Stock***- Price on:12/24/2007	$19.19
Employees	115	Stock Exchange	NDQ
Auditor	Vitale, Caturano & Co. Ltd	Ticker Symbol	OFLX
Stk Agt	NA	Outstanding Shares	10,150,000
Counsel	NA	E.P.S	$0.47
DUNS No.	NA	Shareholders	NA

Business: The group's principle activities are manufacture and sale of flexible metal hose and accessories primarily in North America and the United Kingdom. Its product lines include corrugated metal hoses in various sizes and alloys, including three grades of stainless steel, bronze, Inconel, and Hastelloy. The company offers stainless annular hose, stainless high pressure hose, stainless helical hose, bronze annular hose, and monel annular hose; and hose assemblies, which include chlorine transfer hose, cargo transfer hose, formex hose, jacketed hose, oxygen lance hose, versa connector hose, and vibration absorbers. Its products are used in various applications to carry gases and liquids, including carrying liquefied gases in processing applications; fuel gases within residential and commercial buildings; vibration absorbers in high vibration applications; and other types of gases and fluids in industrial applications. The company's products are used in various industries, including construction, manufacturing, transportation, petrochemical, and pharmaceutical industries. In addition, Omega manufactures pressure reinforcing braids for its hoses in both metallic and synthetic constructions. Its products include stainless tubular and braided braid, stainless abrasion resistant braid, stainless tubular braid, bronze tubular braid, and monel tubular braid. These products are used primarily by the processing industries, transportation and construction industries, medical and semiconductor markets, and for instrumentation. Omega sells its products principally through independent outside sales organizations, including independent sales representatives, distributors, fabricating distributors, wholesalers, and equipment manufacturers. The group's quarterly revenue for Sep '07 was 18.27 millions of USD.

Primary SIC and add'l.: 3430

CIK No: 0001317945

Subsidiaries: Exton Ranch, Inc., Omega Flex Limited

Officers: Duane E. Shooltz/53/Sr. VP, GM - our Tracpipe Business

Owners: Kevin R. Hoben/10.01%, Steven A. Treichel, David W. Hunter, John E. Reed/32.61%, Stewart B. Reed/21.62%, David K. Evans, Edward J. Trainor, Bruce C. Klink, Lawrence J. Cianciolo, Mark F. Albino/4.00%

Financial Data: ***Fiscal Year End:***12/31 ***Latest Annual Data:*** 12/31/2006

Year	Sales	Net Income
2006	$73,574,000	$5,164,000
2005	$65,638,000	$7,477,000

Curr. Assets:	$38,694,000	***Curr. Liab.:***	$22,458,000	***P/E Ratio:***	40.83
Plant, Equip.:	$6,705,000	***Total Liab.:***	$24,977,000	***Indic. Yr. Divd.:***	NA
Total Assets:	$52,623,000	***Net Worth:***	$27,646,000	***Debt/ Equity:***	NA

Omega Healthcare Investors Inc

9690 Deereco Rd., Ste. 100, Timonium, MD, 21093; ***PH:*** 1-410-427-1700; ***Fax:*** 1-410-427-8800; ***http://*** www.omegahealthcare.com

General - Incorporation	MD	***Stock***- Price on:12/24/2007	$16.68
Employees	18	Stock Exchange	NYSE
Auditor	Ernst& Young LLP	Ticker Symbol	OHI
Stk Agt	First Chicago Trust Co of New York	Outstanding Shares	67,240,000
Counsel	NA	E.P.S	$0.89
DUNS No.	NA	Shareholders	NA

Business: The groups principle activity is to provide finance to the real estate properties. The group operates from the United State. The groups quarteerly revenue for September 2007 was 39.22 millions of USD.

Primary SIC and add'l.: 6798 6798

CIK No: 0000888491

Subsidiaries: Arizona Lessor - Infinia, Inc., Baldwin Health Center, Inc., Bayside Street II, Inc., Bayside Street, Inc., Canton Health Care Land, Inc., Colonial Gardens, LLC, Colorado Lessor - Conifer, Inc., Copley Health Center, Inc., Delta Investors II, LLC, Delta Investors, I, LLC, Dixon Health Care Center, Inc., Florida Lessor - Emerald, Inc., Florida Lessor - Meadowview, Inc., Georgia Lessor - Bonterra/Parkview, Inc., Hanover House, Inc. 62 Subsidiaries included in the Index

Officers: Taylor C. Pickett/46/Dir., CEO/$2,639,211.00, Robert O. Stephenson/44/CFO/$1,170,322.00, Lee R. Crabill/54/Sr. VP - Operations/$1,136,491.00, Daniel J. Booth/44/COO/$1,474,566.00

Directors: Taylor C. Pickett/46/Dir., CEO, Bernard J. Korman/76/Chmn., Thomas F. Franke/77/Dir., Harold J. Kloosterman/65/Dir., Edward Lowenthal/63/Dir., Stephen D. Plavin/48/Dir.

Owners: Insiders/2.30%, ING Groep N.V./14.40%, Taylor C. Pickett, Robert O. Stephenson, Daniel J. Booth, Thomas F. Franke, Stephen D. Plavin, ING Clarion Real Estate Securities, L.P./13.20%, Edward Lowenthal, Nomura Asset Management Co., LTD./5.90%, Bernard J. Korman, Lee R. Crabill, The Vanguard Group, Inc./5.10%, Harold J. Kloosterman

Financial Data: ***Fiscal Year End:***12/31 ***Latest Annual Data:*** 12/31/2006

Year	Sales	Net Income
2006	$135,693,000	$55,697,000
2005	$110,278,000	$38,753,000
2004	$90,451,000	$16,738,000

Curr. Assets:	$56,040,000	***Curr. Liab.:***	$33,683,000	***P/E Ratio:***	18.74
Plant, Equip.:	$1,052,545,000	***Total Liab.:***	$709,916,000	***Indic. Yr. Divd.:***	$1.080
Total Assets:	$1,175,370,000	***Net Worth:***	$465,454,000	***Debt/ Equity:***	1.4405

Omega Navigation Enterprises Inc

24 Kaningos St., Piraeus; ***PH:*** 30-2104132305; ***http://*** www.omeganavigation.com

General - Incorporation		***Stock***- Price on:12/24/2007	$22.51
Employees	172	Stock Exchange	NDQ
Auditor	NA	Ticker Symbol	ONAV
Stk Agt	Computershare Trust Co	Outstanding Shares	15,150,000
Counsel	NA	E.P.S	$0.91
DUNS No.	NA	Shareholders	NA

Business: The groups principal activity is to provide global marine transportation services. The group operates from the United States.

Primary SIC and add'l.: 4449 4412

CIK No: 0001324915

Subsidiaries: Abilene Navigation Inc., Beaumont Navigation Inc., Carrolton Navigation Inc., Decatur Navigation Inc., Elgin Navigation Inc., Fulton Navigation Inc., Galveston Navigation Inc., Hamilton Navigation Inc., Omega Management Inc.

Officers: George Kassiotis/37/Dir., CEO, Pres., Charilaos Loukopoulos/38/Dir., Exec. VP, COO, General Counsel, Gregory A. McGrath/57/CFO, Harris Loukopoulos/39/Dir., Exec. VP, COO, General Counsel, Nicolas Bornozis/Investor Relations Officer

Directors: George Kassiotis/37/Dir., CEO, Pres., Robert J. Flynn/55/Chmn., Charilaos Loukopoulos/38/Dir., Exec. VP, COO, General Counsel, Nicolas Borkmann/45/Dir., Chiang Hai Ding/69/Dir., Kevin Harding/48/Dir., Shariq Azhar/53/Dir., Matthew W. McCleery/37/Dir., Harris Loukopoulos/39/Dir., Exec. VP, COO, General Counsel

Owners: US Trust Company NA /US Trust Corporation/13.00%, MHR Fund management LLC/10.00%, George Kassiotis/100.00%, Transamerica Investment Management LLC/7.00%

Financial Data: ***Fiscal Year End:***NA ***Latest Annual Data:*** 12/31/2006

Year	Sales	Net Income
2006	$26,867,000	$14,128,000

Curr. Assets:	$87,428,000	***Curr. Liab.:***	$54,790,000		
Plant, Equip.:	$350,631,000	***Total Liab.:***	$243,734,000	***Indic. Yr. Divd.:***	$2.000
Total Assets:	$443,831,000	***Net Worth:***	$200,097,000	***Debt/ Equity:***	NA

Omega Protein Corp

2101 City W Blvd., Bldg. 3, Ste. 500, Houston, TX, 77042; ***PH:*** 1-713-623-0060; ***Fax:*** 1-713-940-6166; ***http://*** www.omegaproteininc.com; ***Email:*** hq@omegahouston.com

General - Incorporation	NV	***Stock***- Price on:12/24/2007	$8.52
Employees	567	Stock Exchange	NYSE
Auditor	PricewaterhouseCoopers LLP	Ticker Symbol	OME
Stk Agt	American Stock Transfer & Trust Co.	Outstanding Shares	16,440,000
Counsel	NA	E.P.S	$0.08
DUNS No.	00-926-8124	Shareholders	NA

Business: The group's principle activity is to produce and sell variety of protein and oil products derived from menhaden. Menhaden is a species of wild herring-like fish found along the gulf of Mexico and Atlantic coasts. The products type includes, fish meal, fish oil and fish solubles. Fish meal products are primarily used as a protein ingredient in animal feed for swine, cattle, aquaculture and household pets. Fish oil is utilized for animal and aquaculture feeds, industrial applications, and additives to human food products. Fish solubles are sold primarily to livestock feed manufacturers, aquaculture feed manufacturers and for use as an organic fertilizer. The group sells its products directly as well as through sales agents. Products of the group are primarily sold in the United States, European and Asian market. The group's quarterly revenue for September 2007 was 44.59 millions of USD.

Primary SIC and add'l.: 2077

CIK No: 0001053650

Subsidiaries: Omega International Distribution Company, Omega International Marketing Company, Omega Protein Mexico S. de R. L. de C.V., Omega Protein, Inc., Omega Shipyard, Inc., Protein Finance Company

Officers: Joseph L. Von Rosenberg/Chmn., CEO, Pres./$992,424.00, Thomas R. Wittmann/VP - Operations/$249,686.00, Richard W. Weis/59/VP - Business Development, Michael E. Wilson/VP - Marine Operations, John D. Held/Sr. VP, General Counsel, Sec., Exec. VP/$637,975.00, Scott J. Herbert/Sr. VP - Sales, Marketing/$242,466.00, Albert A. Riley/VP - Refined Oils, Robert W. Stockton/CFO, Exec. VP, Chief Accounting Officer, Treasurer - Analyst, Financial Media Relations/$668,420.00, Toby Gascon/Contact - Media Relations

Directors: Joseph L. Von Rosenberg/Chmn., CEO, Pres., Gary L. Allee/Dir., Paul M. Kearns/Dir., William E.M. Lands/Dir., Harry O. Nicodemus/Dir., Gary R. Goodwin/Dir.

Owners: Robert W. Stockton/6.60%, Kennedy Capital Management, Inc./7.60%, Scott J. Herbert, Franklin Advisory Services LLC/6.20%, Paul M. Kearns, Gary R. Goodwin, John D. Held/1.80%, Richard Weis, Gary L. Allee, Insiders/18.10%, MHR Advisors LLC,/5.40%, Harry O. Nicodemus, Albert A. Riley, William E. M. Lands, Dimensional Fund Advisors, Inc./13.20% *(21 Owners included in Index)*

Financial Data: *Fiscal Year End:*12/31 *Latest Annual Data:* 12/31/2006

Year	Sales	Net Income
2006	$139,834,000	$4,572,000
2005	$109,896,000	-$7,186,000
2004	$119,645,000	$3,202,000

Curr. Assets:	$89,759,000	*Curr. Liab.:*	$18,683,000	*P/E Ratio:*	106.50
Plant, Equip.:	$100,776,000	*Total Liab.:*	$99,628,000	*Indic. Yr. Divd.:*	NA
Total Assets:	$200,718,000	*Net Worth:*	$101,090,000	*Debt/ Equity:*	0.6633

Omega Ventures Inc

9000 Sheridan St., Ste. 7, Pembroke, FL, 33024; ***PH:*** 1-800-230-2249

General		**Stock**	
Incorporation	NV	Price on:12/24/2007	$0.04
Employees	1	Stock Exchange	OTC
Auditor	Salberg & Co P.A	Ticker Symbol	OMGV
Stk Agt	Fidelity Transfer Co	Outstanding Shares	78,490,000
Counsel	NA	E.P.S.	$0.00
DUNS No.	NA	Shareholders	NA

Business: The group operates through three subsidiaries whose principle activities include purchasing and managing land assets. The group operates under Arizona Land Corporation, Western Gas Corporation, and Vogue Environment Solutions Inc. The group operates from United States.

Primary SIC and add'l.: NA

CIK No: 0001133153

Subsidiaries: Worldwide Management. SA

Financial Data: *Fiscal Year End:*12/31 *Latest Annual Data:* 12/31/2006

Year	Sales	Net Income
2006	NA	-$141,000
2005	$1,000	-$62,000
2004	$0	-$121,000

Curr. Assets:	$29,000	*Curr. Liab.:*	$69,000		
Plant, Equip.:	$3,000	*Total Liab.:*	$69,000	*Indic. Yr. Divd.:*	NA
Total Assets:	$32,000	*Net Worth:*	-$37,000	*Debt/ Equity:*	NA

Omi Corp Marshall Islands

One Sta. Pl., Stamford, CT, 60902; ***PH:*** 1-203-602-6700; ***http://*** www.omicorp.com

General		**Stock**	
Incorporation	MH	Price on:12/24/2007	NA
Employees	68	Stock Exchange	NA
Auditor	Deloitte & Touche LLP	Ticker Symbol	NA
Stk Agt	American Stock Transfer & Trust Co.	Outstanding Shares	NA
Counsel	NA	E.P.S.	NA
DUNS No.	04-470-9004	Shareholders	NA

Business: The group's principal activity is to provide seaborne transportation services of crude oil and petroleum products. The group operates through two major segments: product carrier fleet and crude oil fleet. The product carrier fleet segment provides transportation of refined petroleum products such as gasoline, naphtha and kerosene. This fleet includes two sizes of vessels; handymax and handysize vessels. The crude oil fleet provides transportation of crude oil. This fleet includes vessels of four sizes: suezmax, ultra large crude carriers, panamax and handysize. The group's vessels are available for charter on a voyage, time or bareboat basis. The customers of the group include major independent and state-owned oil companies, major oil traders, government entities and other entities. The group's fleet of vessels comprises of 38 vessels including two product carriers.

Primary SIC and add'l.: 4424 4412

CIK No: 0001061571

Subsidiaries: Adair Shipping LLC, Alliance Chartering LLC, Alma Shipping LLC, Amazon Shipping LLC, Angelica Shipping LLC, Arlene Shipping LLC, Ashley Shipping LLC, Bandar Ayu Shipping LLC, Brazos Shipping LLC, Charente Shipping LLC, Colorado Shipping LLC, Columbia Shipping LLC, Dakota Shipping LLC, Danube Shipping LLC, Deanne Shipping LLC 81 Subsidiaries included in the Index

Officers: Craig H. Stevenson/54/Chmn., CEO/$5,222,408.00, Robert Bugbee/47/Dir., COO, Pres./$3,983,192.00, Fredric S. London/Sec./$1,653,698.00, Kathleen C. Haines/CFO, Sr. VP/$1,769,452.00

Directors: Craig H. Stevenson/54/Chmn., CEO, Philip J. Shapiro/55/Dir., James N. Hood/Dir., Donald C. Trauscht/74/Dir., Robert Bugbee/47/Dir., COO, Pres., Michael Klebanoff/87/Dir., James D. Woods/76/Dir.

Owners: James Hood, Kathleen C. Haines, Donald C. Trauscht, Freiss Associates LLC/5.39%, Insiders/5.46%, Robert L. Bugbee/1.11%, Craig H. Stevenson/1.76%, FMR Corp./15.61%, James D. Woods, Cameron K. Mackey, Michael Klebanoff, Fredric S. London, Philip J. Shapiro

Omni Energy Services Corp

4500 NE Evangeline Thruway, Carencro, LA, 70520; ***PH:*** 1-337-896-6664; ***Fax:*** 1-337-896-6655; ***http://*** www.omnienergy.com

General		**Stock**	
Incorporation	LA	Price on:12/24/2007	$12.21
Employees	600	Stock Exchange	NDQ
Auditor	Pannell Kerr Forster Of Texas, P.C	Ticker Symbol	OMNI
Stk Agt	American Stock Transfer & Trust Co.	Outstanding Shares	17,650,000
Counsel	Locke, Liddell & Sapp	E.P.S.	$0.71
DUNS No.	18-179-4538	Shareholders	NA

Business: The group's principal activity is to provide an integrated range of onshore seismic drilling, permitting, helicopter support and survey services. The group's services are offered to geophysical companies operating in logistically difficult and environmentally sensitive terrain in the United States. The group's primary market is in the marsh, swamp shallow water and contiguous dry land areas along the United States gulf coast. The group owns and operates an extensive fleet of specialized seismic drilling and transportation equipment used in the transition zone. The group also maintains a fleet of helicopters, including an inventory of aviation parts, turbine engines and other miscellaneous flight equipment. On 20-Nov-2003, the group acquired American helicopters inc.

Primary SIC and add'l.: 1380 1382

CIK No: 0001046212

Subsidiaries: American Aviation LLC, American Helicopters Inc., Gulf Coast Resources, Inc, Hamilton Drill Tech, Inc., OMNI Energia Mexicana, OMNI Energy Seismic Services Corp., OMNI Energy Services Corp., OMNI Energy Services, OMNI International Energy Services, OMNI Labor Corporation, OMNI Offshore Aviation Corp., OMNI Properties Corp., Trussco Properties, LLC, Trussco, Inc.

Officers: James C. Eckert/Chmn., CEO, Pres./$649,726.00, Darcy G. Klug/Exec. VP/$312,557.00, John A. Harris/VP - Seismic Drilling Services/$242,521.00, Gregory B. Milton/Chief Accounting Officer/$117,927.00, Robert H. Rhyne/VP - Sales, Marketing, Nolan C. Vice/VP - Trussco Operations/$285,963.00, Craig P. Rothwell/Advisory Dir., Andy J. Dufrene/GM - Preheat

Directors: James C. Eckert/Chmn., CEO, Pres., Edward E. Colson/Dir., Barry E. Kaufman/Dir., Dennis R. Sciotto/Dir., Richard C. White/Dir.

Owners: James C. Eckert/2.30%, John A. Harris, Edward Colson, III Trust/4.80%, Barry E. Kaufman, Darcy G. Klug/4.30%, Insiders/40.60%, Dennis R. Sciotto Family Trust/31.80%, Nolan C. Vice, Edward E. Colson/4.80%, Dennis Sciotto/31.80%, Richard C. White, Gregory B. Milton

Financial Data: *Fiscal Year End:*12/31 *Latest Annual Data:* 12/31/2006

Year	Sales	Net Income
2006	$98,998,000	$21,815,000
2005	$43,350,000	-$4,273,000
2004	$51,634,000	-$14,255,000

Curr. Assets:	$51,111,000	*Curr. Liab.:*	$34,499,000	*P/E Ratio:*	15.07
Plant, Equip.:	$44,827,000	*Total Liab.:*	$81,114,000	*Indic. Yr. Divd.:*	NA
Total Assets:	$120,540,000	*Net Worth:*	$39,426,000	*Debt/ Equity:*	0.8902

Omni Medical Holdings Inc

1107 Mt Rushmore Rd. , Ste 2, Rapid City, SD, 57701; ***PH:*** 1-303-703-4576; ***http://*** www.omnimedicalholdings.com; ***Email:*** ceo@omnimedical.com

General		**Stock**	
Incorporation	UT	Price on:12/24/2007	$0.011
Employees	75	Stock Exchange	OTC
Auditor	Mantyla McReynolds	Ticker Symbol	OMHI
Stk Agt	NA	Outstanding Shares	12,910,000
Counsel	NA	E.P.S.	-$0.214
DUNS No.	NA	Shareholders	NA

Business: The groups principle activity is to provide back-office suite of products and services to healthcare practitioners and healthcare facilities. The group provides back-office suite of products and services to healthcare practitioners and healthcare facilities. The groups products include GE Centricity and Misys practice management and electronic medical records solutions, and a Web-based decision support reporting tools. The group operates from United States.

Primary SIC and add'l.: 6799

CIK No: 0001085402

Subsidiaries: Omni Medical Services, Inc, Omni Medical Services, Inc.

Officers: Douglas P. Davis/Chmn., CEO, Pres., Treasurer, Careen Wilson/Dir. - Billing Operations

Directors: Douglas P. Davis/Chmn., CEO, Pres., Treasurer

Owners: Lance Weaver/0.40%, Arthur D. Lyons/8.50%, Charles D. Arbeiter/5.90%, Insiders/9.00%, Peter Pollachek/13.60%, John Globoker/0.20%, LHM Trading/10.80%, Elisa Norrick/3.40%, Interstate Advisors/1.00%, Al Rieman/8.50%

Financial Data: *Fiscal Year End:*12/31 *Latest Annual Data:* 3/31/2005

Year	Sales	Net Income
2005	$1,756,000	-$1,141,000
2004	$1,181,000	-$555,000
2002	NA	-$4,000

Curr. Assets:	$647,000	*Curr. Liab.:*	$5,096,000		
Plant, Equip.:	$1,694,000	*Total Liab.:*	$5,976,000	*Indic. Yr. Divd.:*	NA
Total Assets:	$7,714,000	*Net Worth:*	$1,888,000	*Debt/ Equity:*	NA

Omni USA Inc

2236 Rutherford Rd., Ste. 107, Carlsbad, CA, 92008; ***PH:*** 1-760-929-7500

General		**Stock**	
Incorporation	NV	Price on:12/24/2007	$0.37
Employees	12	Stock Exchange	NA
Auditor	Farber Hass Hurley & Mcewen, LLP	Ticker Symbol	NA
Stk Agt	American Stock Transfer & Trust Co.	Outstanding Shares	23,710,000
Counsel	NA	E.P.S.	-$0.07
DUNS No.	08-934-2083	Shareholders	NA

Business: The group's principal activities are to design, develop, manufacture and distribute power transmission components and trailer and implement components. Power transmission components (also known as gearboxes or enclosed geardrives) are used in agricultural, industrial, off-highway and

construction equipment. Trailer and implement components include heavy-duty implement jacks, spring return jacks, stabilizing jacks and wheel chocks for semi-trailers, a series of high density polyethylene lubricating plates and a complete line of bumper-pull and gooseneck couplers for trailers. The group's products are distributed to original equipment manufacturers and distributors in North America and in several foreign countries including Argentina, Australia, Brazil, Canada, France, Mexico, New Zealand, South Africa, Thailand and venezuela.

Primary SIC and add'l.: 3566 3523

CIK No: 0000846732

Subsidiaries: Brendan Technologies, Inc.

Officers: Paula Caroppoli/Transfer Agent, Brendan Technologies Inc

Owners: Potawatomi Business Development Corp., Steven Eisold/3.00%, Massoud Kharrazian/6.30%, Lowell W. Giffhorn/2.70%, John R. Dunn/21.00%, Theo Vermaelen/3.60%, Jason Booth, Insiders/37.30%, Robert Tabor/20.00%, George Dunn/9.40%

Financial Data: *Fiscal Year End:*06/30 *Latest Annual Data:* 6/30/2006

Year	Sales	Net Income
2006	$681,000	-$845,000
2005	$21,007,000	-$639,000
2004	$19,152,000	$282,000

Curr. Assets:	$206,000	**Curr. Liab.:**	$1,766,000		
Plant, Equip.:	$73,000	**Total Liab.:**	$1,884,000	**Indic. Yr. Divd.:**	NA
Total Assets:	$287,000	**Net Worth:**	-$1,597,000	**Debt/ Equity:**	NA

Omnicare Inc

1600 RiverCtr. II, 100 East RiverCtr. Blvd., Covington, KY, 41011; *PH:* 1-859-392-3300; *Fax:* 1-859-392-3333; *http://* www.omnicare.com

General - Incorporation	DE	**Stock** - Price on:12/24/2007	$36.01
Employees	14,950	Stock Exchange	NYSE
Auditor	PricewaterhouseCoopers LLP	Ticker Symbol	OCR
Stk Agt	Computershare Trust Co	Outstanding Shares	121,540,000
Counsel	NA	E.P.S	$1.76
DUNS No.	05-643-3907	Shareholders	NA

Business: The groups principle activity is to provide pharmaceuticals and related pharmacy services to long-term care institutions. The group operates through two segments namely pharmacy and contract research organization services. The group operates from United States.

Primary SIC and add'l.: 5912 9999 8099

CIK No: 0000353230

Subsidiaries: 3096479 Nova Scotia Company, 3096480 Nova Scotia Company, 3103-3798 Quebec, Inc., 42986 Ontario Limited, AAHS Acquisition Corp., Accu-Med Services of Washington LLC, Accu-Med Services, LLC, Accumed, Inc., Alacritas Biopharma, Inc., Ambler Acquisition Company LLC, AMC - New York, Inc., AMC - Tennessee, Inc., Anderson Medical Services, Inc., APS Acquisition LLC, APS Summit Care Pharmacy, LLC 275 Subsidiaries included in the Index

Officers: Dale B. Evans/CEO, VP - Omnicare Clinical Research, Joel F. Gemunder/Dir., CEO, Pres./$29,025,690.00, William A. Fitzpatrick/Corporate Compliance Officer, Patrick E. Keefe/COO, Exec. VP/$4,620,286.00, Gary W. Erwin/Sr. VP - Professional Services, Pres. - Omnicare Sr. Health Outcomes, Tracy Finn/Sr. VP - Strategic Planning, Development, Bradley S. Abbott/VP, Controller - Group Exec., Corporate Financial Services Group, Donald E. Amorosi/VP - Trade Relations, Paul W. Baldwin/VP - Public Affairs, Beth A. Kinerk/VP - Customer Development, Mark G. Kobasuk/VP, General Counsel, Michael D. Laney/VP - Management Information Systems, Kirk M. Pompeo/51/Sr. VP - Sales, Marketing, David W. Froesel/CFO, Sr. VP/$2,307,195.00, Cheryl D. Hodges/Sr. VP, Sec./$3,224,220.00 *(24 Officers included in Index)*

Directors: Joel F. Gemunder/Dir., CEO, Pres., Edward L. Hutton/Chmn., Charles H. Erhart/Dir., Sandra E. Laney/Dir., John T. Crotty/Dir., Andrea R. Lindell/Dir., John H. Timoney/Dir., Amy Wallman/Dir.

Owners: T. E. Bien, A. Wallman, C. H. Erhart, D. W. Froesel, E.L. Hutton Foundation, J. F. Gemunder/4.50%, S. E. Laney, J. H. Timoney, FMR Corp/11.90%, P. E. Keefe, Insiders/7.20%, C. D. Hodges, G. C. Laschober, Joel F. Gemunder Foundation, E. L. Hutton *(18 Owners included in Index)*

Financial Data: *Fiscal Year End:*12/31 *Latest Annual Data:* 12/31/2006

Year	Sales	Net Income
2006	$6,492,993,000	$183,572,000
2005	$5,292,782,000	$226,491,000
2004	$4,119,891,000	$236,011,000

Curr. Assets:	$2,424,828,000	**Curr. Liab.:**	$552,401,000	**P/E Ratio:**	25.36
Plant, Equip.:	$200,425,000	**Total Liab.:**	$4,235,020,000	**Indic. Yr. Divd.:**	$0.090
Total Assets:	$7,398,471,000	**Net Worth:**	$3,163,451,000	**Debt/ Equity:**	NA

Omnicell Inc

1201 Charleston Rd., Mountain View, CA, 94043; *PH:* 1-650-251-6100; *Fax:* 1-650-251-6266; *http://* www.omnicell.com; *Email:* info@omnicell.com

General - Incorporation	DE	**Stock** - Price on:12/24/2007	$21.04
Employees	626	Stock Exchange	NDQ
Auditor	Ernst & Young LLP	Ticker Symbol	OMCL
Stk Agt	Ernst & Young LLP	Outstanding Shares	29,170,000
Counsel	Calfee, Halter & Griswold	E.P.S	$0.95
DUNS No.	NA	Shareholders	NA

Business: The group's principal activity is to provide patient safety solutions for the healthcare industry. The end-to end solutions include medication and supply dispensing systems, central pharmacy storage, retrieval and packaging solution, a bedside automation solution, a physician order management solution, a decision support application and a Web-based procurement application. These solutions reduce medication errors, improve workflow and increase operational efficiency. The products services are marketed to healthcare facilities such as hospitals, integrated delivery networks and specialty care facilities that includes nursing homes, ambulatory surgery centers, catheterization labs and outpatient clinics. On 15-Aug-2003, the group acquired bcx technology inc and on 11-Mar-2004, ariel distributing inc.

Primary SIC and add'l.: 5047 7375

CIK No: 0000926326

Subsidiaries: APRS, Inc., BCX Technology, Inc., Omnicell Corporation (India) Private Limited, Omnicell HealthCare Canada, Inc.

Officers: Randall A. Lipps/Chmn., CEO, Pres./$1,500,786.00, Dan S. Johnston/VP, General Counsel/$648,169.00, Christopher J. Drew/Sr. VP - Operations/$1,098,069.00, John Choma/VP - OD, Learning, Performance, Renee Luhr/VP - Sales/$587,444.00, Michelle Smith/Executive Assist., Linda Capcara/Contact - Media, Rob Seim/VP - Finance, CFO/$540,416.00, Gary Robinson/VP - Corporate Sales, International, Deborah Reinert/Sr. Dir. - Marketing, Corporate Communications

Directors: Randall A. Lipps/Chmn., CEO, Pres., Mary E. Foley/Dir., Sara J. White/Dir., Randy Lindholm/Dir., Kevin L. Roberg/Dir., William H. Younger/Dir., Donald C. Wegmiller/Dir., Joseph E. Whitters/Dir., James T. Judson/Dir., Gary S. Petersmeyer/Dir.

Owners: James T. Judson, Mary E. Foley, Randy D. Lindholm, Brock D. Nelson, Donald C. Wegmiller, J. Christopher Drew/1.04%, Kevin L. Roberg, Janus Venture Fund/7.76%, William H. Younger/2.62%, Gary S. Petersmeyer, Dan S. Johnston, Veredus Asset Management LLC/6.34%, Sara J. White, Renee M. Luhr, Joseph E. Whitters *(18 Owners included in Index)*

Financial Data: *Fiscal Year End:*12/31 *Latest Annual Data:* 12/31/2006

Year	Sales	Net Income
2006	$154,710,000	$10,365,000
2005	$121,518,000	-$2,074,000
2004	$123,939,000	$10,602,000

Curr. Assets:	$129,846,000	**Curr. Liab.:**	$53,556,000	**P/E Ratio:**	22.15
Plant, Equip.:	$5,226,000	**Total Liab.:**	$64,634,000	**Indic. Yr. Divd.:**	NA
Total Assets:	$154,630,000	**Net Worth:**	$89,996,000	**Debt/ Equity:**	NA

Omnicom Group Inc

437 Madison Ave., New York, NY, 10022; *PH:* 1-212-415-3600; *Fax:* 1-212-415-3530; *http://* www.omnicomgroup.com; *Email:* ir@omnicomgroup.com

General - Incorporation	NY	**Stock** - Price on:12/24/2007	$102.95
Employees	66,000	Stock Exchange	NYSE
Auditor	KPMG LLP	Ticker Symbol	OMC
Stk Agt	Mellon Investor Services LLC	Outstanding Shares	165,400,000
Counsel	Michael J. O'Brien Esq.	E.P.S	$2.81
DUNS No.	14-785-7429	Shareholders	NA

Business: The groups principle activity is to provide professional services. The groups services include advertising, marketing and corporate communication services. The group operates from United States.

Primary SIC and add'l.: 7311 6719

CIK No: 0000029989

Subsidiaries: BBDO Worldwide Inc., Bernard Hodes Group, Inc., Cline, Davis & Mann, Inc., DAS Holdings Inc., DDB Worldwide Communications Group, Inc., Fleishman-Hillard Inc, InterOne Marketing Group, Inc., Ketchum Inc., Omnicom Capital Inc., Omnicom Europe Limited., Omnicom Finance Inc., Omnicom Holdings Inc., Omnicom Media Group Holdings Inc., Rapp Partnership Holdings Inc., TBWA Worldwide Inc. 16 Subsidiaries included in the Index

Officers: Daryl D. Simm/46/Chmn., CEO - Omnicom Media Group, John D. Wren/56/Dir., CEO, Pres./$13,241,030.00, Charles E. Brymer/48/CEO, Pres. - DDB Worldwide, Bruce Redditt/Exec. VP, Philip J. Angelastro/Sr. VP - Finance, Controller, Philip J. George/Tax Counsel, Dennis E. Hewitt/Treasurer, Michael J. O'Brien/Sr. VP, General Counsel, Sec., Randall J. Weisenburger/CFO, Exec. VP/$7,991,209.00, Asit Mehra/Exec. VP, Janet Riccio/Exec. VP, Serge Dumont/Sr. VP

Directors: Daryl D. Simm/46/Chmn., CEO - Omnicom Media Group, John D. Wren/56/Dir., CEO, Pres., William Timothy Love/Vice Chmn., Bruce Nelson/Vice Chmn., Peter Mead/Vice Chmn., Michael Birkin/Vice Chmn., Bruce Crawford/79/Chmn., John R. Purcell/76/Dir., Susan S. Denison/62/Dir., Robert Charles Clark/64/Dir., John R. Murphy/74/Dir., Leonard S. Coleman/59/Dir., Errol M. Cook/69/Dir., Michael A. Henning/68/Dir., Linda Johnson Rice/50/Dir. *(16 Directors included in Index)*

Owners: Linda Johnson Rice, Michael Henning, John Murphy, UBS Global Asset Mgt. Inc./7.50%, Susan Denison, Bruce Crawford, Andrew Robertson, Randall Weisenburger, Thomas Harrison, Robert Charles Clark, Insiders/4.10%, Gary Roubos, Leonard Coleman, Jean-Marie Dru, Errol Cook *(17 Owners included in Index)*

Financial Data: *Fiscal Year End:*12/31 *Latest Annual Data:* 12/31/2006

Year	Sales	Net Income
2006	$11,376,900,000	$864,000,000
2005	$10,481,100,000	$790,700,000
2004	$9,747,200,000	$723,500,000

Curr. Assets:	$9,646,800,000	**Curr. Liab.:**	$10,296,100,000	**P/E Ratio:**	19.91
Plant, Equip.:	$639,800,000	**Total Liab.:**	$14,094,300,000	**Indic. Yr. Divd.:**	$0.600
Total Assets:	$18,164,400,000	**Net Worth:**	$3,871,300,000	**Debt/ Equity:**	NA

Omnicorder Technologies Inc

12-8 Technology Dr., Setanket, NY, 11733; *PH:* 1-631-689-3781; *http://* www.advancedbp.com

General - Incorporation	DE	**Stock** - Price on:12/24/2007	$0.004
Employees	6	Stock Exchange	NA
Auditor	Marcum & Kliegman LLP	Ticker Symbol	NA
Stk Agt	Corporate Stock Transfer, Inc.	Outstanding Shares	946,560,000
Counsel	NA	E.P.S	-$0.13
DUNS No.	04-208-1047	Shareholders	NA

Business: The group's principle activity is to provide promotional products to other business companies. The group also provides brand marketing services. The group operates from United States.

Primary SIC and add'l.: 7311

CIK No: 0001096182

Officers: Denis A. O'Connor/Dir., CEO, Pres., Robert P. Ellis/Sr. VP - Business Development, Celia Schiffner/Controller, Principal Financial Officer, Marek Pawlowski/VP - Product Development, Kevin J. Healy/General Counsel, Erika Moran/Investor Relations Group, Loring D. Andersen/VP - Marketing Development

Directors: Denis A. O'Connor/Dir., CEO, Pres., Michael A. Davis/Chmn., James Wavle/Dir., William J. Wagner/Dir., Jed Schutz/Dir., Mark A. Fauci/Dir., Joseph T. Casey/Dir.

Owners: Jed Schutz/7.60%, Michael A. Davis/1.10%, Marek Pawlowski, Anthony A. Lombardo/1.30%, Columbia Ventures Corp./17.80%, Denis O'Connor/7.00%, Insiders/6.10%, Joseph T. Casey/3.70%, Michael A. Davis, Robert Ellis, Columbia Ventures Corp./1.50%, Joseph T. Casey/8.90%, James Wavle, Joseph T. Casey/2.60%, George Benedict/1.70% *(27 Owners included in Index)*

Financial Data: *Fiscal Year End:*12/31 *Latest Annual Data:* 12/31/2006

Year	Sales	Net Income
2006	NA	-$4,084,000
2005	NA	-$5,781,000
2004	$70,000	-$4,635,000

Curr. Assets:	$1,094,000	Curr. Liab.:	$2,399,000		
Plant, Equip.:	$179,000	Total Liab.:	$9,391,000	Indic. Yr. Divd.:	NA
Total Assets:	$2,211,000	Net Worth:	-$7,180,000	Debt/ Equity:	NA

Omniture Inc

550 E Timpanogos Cir., Orem, UT, 84097; *PH:* 1-801-722-7000; *Fax:* 1-801-722-7001;
http:// www.omniture.com

General - Incorporation	DE	**Stock**- Price on:12/24/2007	$20.71
Employees	353	Stock Exchange	NDQ
Auditor	Ernst & Young, LLP	Ticker Symbol	OMTR
Stk Agt	American Stock Transfer & Trust Co.	Outstanding Shares	49,150,000
Counsel	NA	E.P.S.	-$0.17
DUNS No.	NA	Shareholders	NA

Business: The groups principle activity is to provide online business optimization services. Specific customers of the group include America Online, Comcast Corporation, eBay, Inc., Expedia, Inc., Ford Motor Company, Gannett, Inc. and Hewlett-Packard. In the year 2007, the group acquired Instadia A/S and Touch Clarity Limited. The group operates from the United States. The group's quarterly revenue for September 2007 was 37.38 millions of USD.

Primary SIC and add'l.: 8732 7372

CIK No: 0001357525

Subsidiaries: Instadia GmbH, Instadia Limited, Omniture A/S, Omniture HK Limited, Omniture KK, Omniture Limited, Touch Clarity Limited, Touch Clarity, Inc.

Officers: Joshua G. James/Co - Founder, Dir., CEO, Mike Herring/CFO, Exec. VP, Brett Error/CTO, Exec. VP - Products, Chris Harrington/Pres. - Worldwide Sales, Client Services, Michael J. Dodd/Sr. VP - Corporate Development, Gail Ennis/Sr. VP - Worldwide Marketing, Shawn Lindquist/Chief Legal Officer, Sr. VP, Sec., John Mellor/Sr. VP - Business Development, Neil Weston/GM - EMEA, Sr. VP, Michael S. Herring/CFO, Exec. VP

Directors: Joshua G. James/Co - Founder, Dir., CEO, John R. Pestana/Chmn., Fraser D. Bullock/Dir., Gregory S. Butterfield/Dir., Dana L. Evan/Dir., Mark P. Gorenberg/Dir., Rory T. O'Driscoll/Dir.

Owners: FMR Corp/15.00%, Cocolalla, LLC/6.10%, Christopher C. Harrington, Michael S. Herring, Scale Venture Partners II, L.P./7.80%, Hummer Winblad Venture Partners V, L.P./14.80%, Mark P. Gorenberg/14.90%, Brett M. Error/3.00%, Rory T. ODriscoll/7.80%, Gregory S. Butterfield, Dana L. Evan, Joshua G. James/9.00%, TPP Capital Advisors Ltd./5.20%, Insiders/44.90%, Fraser D. Bullock/3.10% *(16 Owners included in Index)*

Financial Data: *Fiscal Year End:*12/31 *Latest Annual Data:* 12/31/2006

Year	Sales	Net Income
2006	$79,749,000	-$7,725,000
2005	$42,804,000	-$17,441,000
2004	$20,566,000	-$1,318,000

Curr. Assets:	$93,984,000	Curr. Liab.:	$41,956,000		
Plant, Equip.:	$31,128,000	Total Liab.:	$48,785,000	Indic. Yr. Divd.:	NA
Total Assets:	$135,210,000	Net Worth:	$86,425,000	Debt/ Equity:	0.0479

Omnivision Technologies Inc

1341 Orleans Dr., Sunnyvale, CA, 94089; *PH:* 1-408-542-3000; *Fax:* 1-408-542-3001;
http:// www.ovt.com; *Email:* invest@ovt.com

General - Incorporation	DE	**Stock**- Price on:12/24/2007	$16.5
Employees	1,644	Stock Exchange	NDQ
Auditor	PricewaterhouseCoopers LLP	Ticker Symbol	OVTI
Stk Agt	EquiServe Trust Co N.A	Outstanding Shares	54,940,000
Counsel	Y. Vicky Chou	E.P.S.	NA
DUNS No.	NA	Shareholders	NA

Business: The group's principal activity is to design, develop and market semiconductor image sensor devices. These devices are used for computing, communications, industrial, automotive and consumer electronics applications. The group's main product is an image sensing device called camerachip. This is used in a number of consumer applications such as personal computer cameras, digital still cameras, security and surveillance cameras, personal digital assistant cameras and mobile phone cameras and cameras for automobiles and toys for both still picture and live video applications. The group's customers include original equipment manufacturers, which include camera device manufacturers and contract manufacturers, value added resellers and indirectly through distributors. The group sells its products in the United States and the Asia-Pacific region.

Primary SIC and add'l.: 3674

CIK No: 0001106851

Subsidiaries: CDM Optics, Inc., HuaWei Semiconductor (Shanghai) Co., Ltd. (formerly OmniView Electronic (Shanghai) Co., Ltd.), HuaWei Technology International, Ltd.(formerly OmniView Technology International, Ltd.), OmniVision International Holding Ltd., OmniVision Technologies (Hong Kong) Company Limited, OmniVision Trading (Hong Kong) Company Limited, Shanghai OmniVision IC Design Co., Ltd.

Officers: Shaw Hong/Chmn., CEO, Pres./$1,680,565.00, James He/COO, Dir., Peter V. Leigh/CFO/$1,137,719.00, John T. Yue/VP - Quality, Reliability/$1,361,717.00, Vicky Y. Chou/VP - Legal, General Counsel/$854,827.00, Jeanette Ishibashi/Slaes, China, Tan Chen/Slaes, China, Jerry Lu/Sales, Taiwan, Isaac Hwang/Sales, Korea, Alex Wong/Sales, Hong Kong, Howard E. Rhodes/VP - Process Engineering, Tajima Tsuyoshi/Sales, Japan, Michael Chan/Sales, South Asia, Ian Montandon/Sales, Western Europe, Mario Heid/Sales, Europe *(22 Officers included in Index)*

Directors: Shaw Hong/Chmn., CEO, Pres., Dwight Steffensen/Dir., Joseph Jeng/Dir., Andrew Wang/Dir.

Owners: Insiders/4.90%, Andrew Wang, Galleon Management, L.P./5.12%, Shaw Hong/2.11%, FMR Corporation/13.75%, Vicky Y. Chou, Joseph Jeng, Xinping He/1.27%, Peter V. Leigh, Mac-Per-Wolf Company/6.43%, Dwight Steffensen, John Yue

Financial Data: *Fiscal Year End:*04/30 *Latest Annual Data:* 4/30/2007

Year	Sales	Net Income
2007	$528,143,000	$23,973,000
2006	$491,926,000	$89,148,000
2005	$388,062,000	$76,387,000

Curr. Assets:	$515,712,000	Curr. Liab.:	$158,685,000	P/E Ratio:	38.37
Plant, Equip.:	$64,363,000	Total Liab.:	$193,259,000	Indic. Yr. Divd.:	NA
Total Assets:	$688,059,000	Net Worth:	$490,456,000	Debt/ Equity:	NA

Omnova Solutions Inc

175 Ghent Rd., Fairlawn, OH, 44333; *PH:* 1-330-869-4200; *Fax:* 1-330-869-4288;
http:// www.omnova.com

General - Incorporation	OH	**Stock**- Price on:12/24/2007	$5.99
Employees	1,700	Stock Exchange	NYSE
Auditor	Ernst & Young LLP	Ticker Symbol	OMN
Stk Agt	Bank of New York	Outstanding Shares	42,200,000
Counsel	NA	E.P.S.	$0.14
DUNS No.	NA	Shareholders	NA

Business: The group's principal activities are to develop, manufacture and market decorative and functional surfaces, emulsion polymers and specialty chemicals. The group operates in two segments namely decorative and building products and performance chemicals. The decorative and building product segment manufactures and sells functional surfacing products such as wallcoverings, coated and performance fabrics, industrial films, transfer printed products and commercial roofing systems. The products are used in building remodeling, new construction, furniture, cabinets, flooring and home furnishings. The performance chemicals segment produces a range of emulsion polymers and specialty chemicals. These are used in paper, carpet, textiles, construction, floor care, tires and other chemical applications.

Primary SIC and add'l.: 2821

CIK No: 0001090061

Subsidiaries: CGOMNOVA Decorative Products (Shanghai) Co., Ltd, CPPCDecorative Products Company Limited, Muraspec N.A. LLC, OMNOVA Performance Chemicals (UK) Ltd., OMNOVA Wallcovering (UK), Limited, OMNOVA Wallcovering (USA), Inc.

Officers: Kevin M. McMullen/Chmn., CEO, Pres., Michael E. Hicks/Sr. VP, CFO, James C. Lemay/Sr. VP - Business Development, General Counsel, Robert H. Coleman/Pres. - Decorative Products, Douglas E. Wenger/CIO, Sr. VP, James J. Hohman/Corporate VP, Pres. Performance Chemicals, Sandra Klaasse/VP - Lean Sixsigma, Kristine C. Syrvalin/Corp. Sec., Assist. General Counsel

Directors: Kevin M. McMullen/Chmn., CEO, Pres., William R. Seelbach/Dir., Byron R. Pipes/Dir., Diane E. McGarry/Dir., Steven W. Percy/Dir., Edward P. Campbell/Dir., David A. Daberko/Dir., David J. D'Antoni/Dir., Robert A. Stefanko/Dir.

Owners: William R. Seelbach, Putnam, LLC/6.60%, James C. LeMay, Insiders/5.30%, Kevin M. McMullen/2.90%, Robert A. Stefanko, David J. DAntoni, Steven W. Percy, GAMCO Investors, Inc./10.80%, Michael E. Hicks, David A. Daberko, Byron R. Pipes, Diane E. McGarry, James J. Hohman, Edward P. Campbell *(18 Owners included in Index)*

Financial Data: *Fiscal Year End:*11/30 *Latest Annual Data:* 11/30/2006

Year	Sales	Net Income
2006	$699,100,000	$21,300,000
2005	$810,100,000	-$1,800,000
2004	$745,700,000	-$24,400,000

Curr. Assets:	$157,800,000	Curr. Liab.:	$93,500,000	P/E Ratio:	46.08
Plant, Equip.:	$138,500,000	Total Liab.:	$290,400,000	Indic. Yr. Divd.:	NA
Total Assets:	$338,900,000	Net Worth:	$48,500,000	Debt/ Equity:	3.7008

Omrix Biopharmaceuticals Inc

630 5th Ave., 22nd Fl., New York, NY, 10111; *PH:* 1-212-887-6500; *Fax:* 1-212-887-6550;
http:// www.omrix.com; *Email:* info@omrix.com

General - Incorporation	DE	**Stock**- Price on:12/24/2007	$32.16
Employees	180	Stock Exchange	NDQ
Auditor	Ernst & Young, LLP	Ticker Symbol	OMRI
Stk Agt	American Stock Transfer & Trust Co.	Outstanding Shares	NA
Counsel	NA	E.P.S.	$0.89
DUNS No.	NA	Shareholders	NA

Business: The groups principle activities include developing and marketing biological products. The products of the group include Adhexil, Evicel, Quixil and Fibrin Patch. The group operates from Israel, the United States, Europe, and Central and Latin America. The group's quarterly revenue for September 2007 was 15.83 millions of USD.

Primary SIC and add'l.: 3841 2836 2834

CIK No: 0001349426

Subsidiaries: Biopex Ltd., Omrix Biopharmaceuticals Ltd., Omrix Biopharmaceuticals, S.A.

Officers: Robert Taub/Dir., CEO, Pres., Nissim Mashiach/COO, Exec. VP, Nanci Prado/VP, General Counsel, Ana I. Stancic/CFO, Exec. VP, Matthew Haines/Dir. - Corporate Communications

Directors: Robert Taub/Dir., CEO, Pres., Fredric D. Price/Chmn., Larry Ellberger/Dir., Bernard Horowitz/Dir., Kevin Rakin/Dir., Philippe Romagnoli/Dir., Steven St. Peter/Dir.

Owners: Orbimed Advisors LLC/5.00%, FMR Corp./11.20%, Nissim Mashiach, Fredric D. Price, Harold Safferstein, Bernard Horowitz, Philippe Romagnoli, Oberweis Asset Management, Inc./5.40%, Insiders/18.70%, Robert Taub/16.20%, Michael Burshtine

Financial Data: *Fiscal Year End:*12/31 *Latest Annual Data:* 12/31/2006

Year	Sales	Net Income
2006	$63,765,000	$23,058,000
2005	$27,499,000	-$27,712,000
2004	$19,948,000	-$6,604,000

Curr. Assets:	$110,705,000	Curr. Liab.:	$15,780,000		
Plant, Equip.:	$7,692,000	Total Liab.:	$25,561,000	Indic. Yr. Divd.:	NA
Total Assets:	$121,645,000	Net Worth:	$96,084,000	Debt/ Equity:	0.0041

Omtool Ltd

6 Riverside Dr., Andover, MA, 01810; *PH:* 1-800-886-7845; *Fax:* 1-978-659-1300;
http:// www.omtool.com

General - Incorporation	DE	Stock- Price on:12/24/2007	$1.86
Employees	118	Stock Exchange	OTC
Auditor	Vitale, Caturano & Co., Ltd.	Ticker Symbol	OMTL
Stk Agt	American Stock Transfer & Trust Co.	Outstanding Shares	4,540,000
Counsel	Testa, Hurwitz & Thibeault	E.P.S	-$1.41
DUNS No.	79-442-5942	Shareholders	NA

Business: The group's principal activity is to provide e-mail and fax-based messaging software that enables secure confirmed document exchange between businesses. The products include genidocs, genifax, accuroute, fax sr. And legalfax. These products provide the users with an extensive, flexible feature set for transmitting and receiving electronic documents that enables users to improve management of their messaging activities. The group also resells hardware products including intelligent fax boards and fax modems. The group provides support services including telephone support, software support comprised of maintenance releases, minor feature enhancement releases, technical bulletins and replacement of damaged media. The products and services are marketed to large and mid-sized corporations, business and healthcare organizations, law firms and government entities.

Primary SIC and add'l.: 7379 3577

CIK No: 0001020579

Subsidiaries: Omtool Europe Limited

Officers: Robert L. Voelk/Chmn., CEO, Pres./$533,465.00, Karen Cummings/Exec. VP - Marketing, Business Development, EMEA/$279,662.00, Eamonn Doyle/VP - Information Technologies, Thaddeus Bouchard/CTO, Ann Taylor/Mgr. - Human Resources, Christopher Degnan/VP - Legal Sales, Jason Doris/VP - Channel Sales, Dan Coccoluto/CFO, Treasurer, Sec., Claudia Skilton/VP - Customer Services, William J. Rynkowski/Dir., Sr. VP

Directors: Robert L. Voelk/Chmn., CEO, Pres., Richard D. Cramer/Dir., William Drummey/Dir., Martin A. Schultz/Dir., Arnold E. Ditri/Dir., James P. Ohalloran/Dir., William J. Rynkowski/Dir., Sr. VP

Owners: Insiders/33.57%, William J. Rynkowski/8.30%, James P. OHalloran, Arnold E. Ditri/1.42%, Michael Rapoport/14.89%, Richard D. Cramer/1.13%, Robert L. Voelk/11.19%, William J. Drummey, Karen Cummings/1.11%, Martin A. Schultz/9.15%, Daniel A. Coccoluto/1.29%, Manchester Management Company, LLC/5.57%

Financial Data: ***Fiscal Year End:***12/31 ***Latest Annual Data:*** 12/31/2006

Year	Sales	Net Income
2006	$13,775,000	-$5,264,000
2005	$14,296,000	-$310,000
2004	$14,790,000	$1,600,000

Curr. Assets:	$8,850,000	**Curr. Liab.:**	$9,090,000		
Plant, Equip.:	$1,525,000	**Total Liab.:**	$11,240,000	**Indic. Yr. Divd.:**	NA
Total Assets:	$14,427,000	**Net Worth:**	$3,187,000	**Debt/ Equity:**	0.8120

On Assignment Inc

26651 W Agoura Rd., Calabasas, CA, 91302; ***PH:*** 1-818-878-7900; ***Fax:*** 1-818-878-7930; ***http://*** www.onassignment.com; ***Email:*** info@onassignment.com

General - Incorporation	DE	Stock- Price on:12/24/2007	$11.03
Employees	460	Stock Exchange	NDQ
Auditor	Deloitte & Touche LLP	Ticker Symbol	ASGN
Stk Agt	U.S. Stock Transfer Corp	Outstanding Shares	35,140,000
Counsel	Hogan & Hartson LLP	E.P.S	$0.39
DUNS No.	15-767-4896	Shareholders	NA

Business: The group's principal activity is to provide skilled temporary professionals to clients in the healthcare and science industries. It provides clients in these markets with short-term or long-term assignments of temporary professionals and permanents through two segments: the healthcare staffing segment includes nurse travel, allied travel and local healthcare staffing (offering healthcare financial, clinical lab and diagnostic imaging staffing services) lines of business. Lab support segment includes domestic and international operations offering scientific staffing services. It provides locally based temporary and temporary-to-permanent placement of scientists and other professipermanentd and beverage, personal care, chemical and environmental industries. The group has approximately 55 branches in 30 states and 3 foreign countries.

Primary SIC and add'l.: 7363 7361 8742

CIK No: 0000890564

Subsidiaries: Assignment Ready, Inc., EnviroStaff, Inc, On Assignment Clinical Research, On Assignment Engineering, On Assignment Health Information Management, On Assignment Healthcare Staffing, On Assignment Lab Support, On Assignment Nurse Travel, On Assignment Staffing Services, Inc

Officers: Peter T. Dameris/Dir., CEO, Pres./$2,373,384.00, Angela Kolarek/VP - Human Resources, Karen Keppel/VP - Support Services, Carol McNamara/VP - Recruiting, Kristi Wolff/VP - Finance, Corporate Controller/$232,603.00, Shawn Mohr/Pres. - On Assignment Healthcare Staffing, Chief Sales Officer/$894,951.00, Emmett McGrath/Pres. - Lab Support, Clinical Research, Engineering/$727,705.00, Larry Hemley/VP - Marketing, Michael C. Payne/Sr. VP - Shared Services, CIO/$415,152.00, Debbie Tiberi/Contact - Investor Relation, Michael McGowan/Pres. - Oxford Global Resources, James L. Brill/Sr. VP - Finance, CFO, Samanthe Beck/VP, General Counsel, Christina Gibson/VP - Finance, Corporate Controller, Mark S. Brouse/Pres. - Vista Staffing Solutions

Directors: Peter T. Dameris/Dir., CEO, Pres., Elliott Ettenberg/Dir., Jeremy Jones/Dir., Jonathan Holman/Dir., Senator William E. Brock/Dir., Teresa Hopp/Dir.

Owners: Teresa A. Hopp, Elliott Ettenberg, Jeremy M. Jones, Wells Fargo& Company/5.20%, Times Square Asset Management, LLC/5.50%, Barclays Global Investors Japan Limited/6.20%, Emmett McGrath, Peter T. Dameris/2.20%, Jonathan S. Holman, Insiders/4.90%, Shawn Mohr, Michael C. Payne, Michael J. Holtzman, William E. Brock, State of Wisconsin Investment Board/5.80%

Financial Data: ***Fiscal Year End:***12/31 ***Latest Annual Data:*** 12/31/2006

Year	Sales	Net Income
2006	$287,566,000	$11,044,000
2005	$237,856,000	-$96,000
2004	$193,574,000	-$42,393,000

Curr. Assets:	$155,925,000	**Curr. Liab.:**	$20,424,000	**P/E Ratio:**	28.28
Plant, Equip.:	$9,116,000	**Total Liab.:**	$21,051,000	**Indic. Yr. Divd.:**	NA
Total Assets:	$186,995,000	**Net Worth:**	$165,944,000	**Debt/ Equity:**	0.8007

On Semiconductor Corp

5005 E McDowell Rd., Phoenix, AZ, 85008; ***PH:*** 1-602-244-6600; ***Fax:*** 1-602-244-6071; ***http://*** www.onsemi.com

General - Incorporation	DE	Stock- Price on:12/24/2007	$10.87
Employees	11,691	Stock Exchange	NDQ
Auditor	PricewaterhouseCoopers LLP	Ticker Symbol	ONNN
Stk Agt	Computershare Investor Services LLC	Outstanding Shares	292,440,000
Counsel	NA	E.P.S	$0.86
DUNS No.	NA	Shareholders	NA

Business: The group's principal activity is to design, develop, manufacture and market semiconductor components. The products include power management and standard analog, metal oxide semiconductor power devices, high frequency clock and data management and standard components. Products include linear regulators, multi function integrated circuits, small signal transistors and diodes, zeners, rectifiers and thyristors. These products address applications such as portable electronics, industrial automation controls, routers, switches, computers, servers, storage-area networks, automated test equipment and automotive control systems. Customers include OEMs, electronic manufacturing service providers and global distributors such as alcatel, daimlerchrysler, delphi, intel, motorola, nokia, siemens, sony, solectron, arrow, avnet and future electronics. International operations are primarily in the United States, Japan, Malaysia, the Philippines, slovakia and the czech republic.

Primary SIC and add'l.: 3674

CIK No: 0001097864

Subsidiaries: Leshan-Phoenix Semiconductor Company Limited, ON Semiconductor (Shenzhen) Limited, ON Semiconductor Canada Trading Corporation, ON Semiconductor Czech Republic, s.r.o., legal successor, ON Semiconductor Design (Shanghai) Limited, ON Semiconductor France SAS, ON Semiconductor Germany GmbH, ON Semiconductor Hong Kong Design Limited, ON Semiconductor Italy S.r.l., ON Semiconductor Japan Ltd., ON Semiconductor Limited, ON Semiconductor Philippines, Inc., ON Semiconductor Slovakia a.s., ON Semiconductor Technology Japan Ltd., ON Semiconductor Technology Malaysia Sdn. Bhd. 32 Subsidiaries included in the Index

Officers: Keith Jackson/Dir., CEO, Pres./$2,548,821.00, Sherry Stanley/Investor Relations Coordinator, Donald Colvin/Exec. VP, CFO, Treasurer/$1,252,430.00, Sonny Cave/Sr. VP, General Counsel, Chief Compliance, Ethics Officer, Sec., William George/Exec. VP/$787,387.00, Robert Charles/Exec. VP - Sales, Marketing/$841,218.00, John Nelson/COO, Exec. VP, Bill Hall/Sr. VP, GM - Standard Products Group, Bill Schromm/Sr. VP, GM - Computing Products Group, Andy Williams/Sr. VP, GM - Automotive, Power Regulation Group, Bob Mahoney/Exec. VP - Sales - Marketing, Ken Rizvi/Dir. - Investor Relations

Directors: Keith Jackson/Dir., CEO, Pres., Daniel J. McCranie/Chmn., Emmanuel T. Hernandez/Dir., John W. Marren/Dir., Curtis J. Crawford/Dir., Robert H. Smith/Dir., Phil D. Hester/Dir.

Owners: Emmanuel T. Hernandez, Robert Charles Mahoney, Alonim Investments, Inc./6.80%, Richard W. Boyce, Curtis J. Crawford, Jerome N. Gregoire, Peter Green, Robert H. Smith, George H. Cave, TPG Advisors II Inc./17.30%, John W. Marren, Justin T. Chang, FMR Corp./16.20%, Daniel J. McCranie, Insiders/1.10% *(16 Owners included in Index)*

Financial Data: ***Fiscal Year End:***12/31 ***Latest Annual Data:*** 12/31/2006

Year	Sales	Net Income
2006	$1,531,800,000	$272,100,000
2005	$1,260,600,000	$100,600,000
2004	$1,266,900,000	-$123,700,000

Curr. Assets:	$700,800,000	**Curr. Liab.:**	$433,000,000	**P/E Ratio:**	12.35
Plant, Equip.:	$578,100,000	**Total Liab.:**	$1,621,100,000	**Indic. Yr. Divd.:**	NA
Total Assets:	$1,416,500,000	**Net Worth:**	-$225,400,000	**Debt/ Equity:**	NA

On the Go Healthcare Inc

85 Corstate Ave., Unit 1, Concord, ON, L4K 4Y2; ***PH:*** 1-905-760-2987; ***http://*** www.onthegohealthcare.com; ***Email:*** info@oghc.com

General - Incorporation	DE	Stock- Price on:12/24/2007	$0.0145
Employees	NA	Stock Exchange	OTC
Auditor	Danziger & Hochman	Ticker Symbol	ONGO
Stk Agt	Int Registrar and Transfer Agency	Outstanding Shares	NA
Counsel	NA	E.P.S	NA
DUNS No.	NA	Shareholders	NA

Business: The group's principal activity is to manufacture healthcare products for home healthcare, medical, rehabilitation and long-term care markets. It also manufactures markets and distributes portable reusable heating pads, molded cases for pills, condoms and tampons and a child padded training seat throughout Canada and the United States. The products are marketed to hospitals, nursing homes, physicians, home healthcare and rehabilitation re-distributors as well as both wholesalers and retailers of healthcare products. It includes drug stores, catalog companies, pharmacies, home-shopping related businesses and certain governmental agencies. The products are sold under the brand name healing heat sensation. On 18-May-2004 the group acquired vital baby innovations.

Primary SIC and add'l.: 3069 3089

CIK No: 0001126302

Subsidiaries: Go Technologies Inc

Owners: Insiders/30.26%, Evan Schwartzberg, Stuart Turk/30.26%, Ralph Magid, The Cellular Connection, Ltd./29.19%

Financial Data: ***Fiscal Year End:***07/31 ***Latest Annual Data:*** 7/31/2006

Year	Sales	Net Income
2006	$30,012,000	-$6,343,000
2005	$5,571,000	-$1,033,000
2004	$3,013,000	-$1,534,000

Curr. Assets:	$7,026,000	**Curr. Liab.:**	$5,117,000		
Plant, Equip.:	$646,000	**Total Liab.:**	$8,090,000	**Indic. Yr. Divd.:**	NA
Total Assets:	$12,346,000	**Net Worth:**	$4,256,000	**Debt/ Equity:**	0.8041

On Track Innovations Ltd

2 Executive Dr., Ste. 740, Fort Lee, NJ, 07024; ***PH:*** 1-201-944-5200; ***Fax:*** 1-201-944-3233; ***http://*** www.oti.co.il; ***Email:*** info@otiamerica.com

General - Incorporation	Israel	Stock- Price on:12/24/2007	$6.26
Employees	625	Stock Exchange	NDQ
Auditor	Somekh Chaikin	Ticker Symbol	OTIV
Stk Agt	Continental Stock Transfer & Trust Co	Outstanding Shares	18,900,000
Counsel	NA	E.P.S	-$0.861
DUNS No.	NA	Shareholders	NA

Business: The group's principle activities are the design, development, sale and support of contactless microprocessor-based smart cards. The company supplies technologies and components and develops smart card applications and solutions for projects such as: electronic purses which incorporate

multiple functions in a single smart card; contactless smart cards for use by passengers in mass transportation systems; national identification documentation; gasoline management systems; electronic parking systems and employee hygiene control. The company's research and development activities are based in Israel. Its manufacturing, assembly and testing and packaging facilities are located in Israel and Germany. The global sales & marketing strategy is directed from the usa. Its shares are traded on the neuer market stock exchange.

Primary SIC and add'l.: 7372 5045

CIK No: 0001021604

Subsidiaries: ASEC Spolka Akcyjna, e-Pilot Group, Easy Park Israel Ltd., Easy Park Ltd, InSeal SAS, InterCard Systemelectronic GmbH, Millennium Cards Technology Limited, Oriental Power Technology LTD, OTI Africa, Inc., OTI America, Inc., Pioneer Oriental International Ltd., Soft Chip Technologies (3000) Ltd.

Officers: Oded Bashan/Chmn., CEO, Pres., Ronnie Gilboa/Dir., VP - Projects, Nehemya Itay/VP - Hardware Engineering, David Azoulay/COO, Ohad Bashan/Dir., Chief Marketing Officer, Guy Shafran/CFO, Aharon Binur/VP - Research, Development, Moshe Aduk/VP - Petroleum Management Solutions

Directors: Oded Bashan/Chmn., CEO, Pres., Ronnie Gilboa/Dir., VP - Projects, Ohad Bashan/Dir., Chief Marketing Officer, Eli Akavia/Dir., Liora Katzenstein/Dir., Eliezer Manor/Dir., Shlomo Toussia-Cohen/Dir., Ora Setter/57/Dir.

Owners: Ronnie Gilboa, Guy Shafran, Insiders/32.70%, Ohad Bashan/1.06%, Nehemya Itay, Shlomo Toussia-Cohen, Moshe Aduk, Eliezer Manor, Oded Bashan/27.50%, Eli Akavia

Financial Data: **Fiscal Year End:** 12/31 **Latest Annual Data:** 12/31/2006

Year	Sales	Net Income
2006	$40,553,000	-$6,604,000
2005	$35,664,000	-$9,113,000
2004	$23,152,000	-$9,275,000

Curr. Assets:	$70,889,000	**Curr. Liab.:**	$10,698,000		
Plant, Equip.:	$13,318,000	**Total Liab.:**	$18,020,000	**Indic. Yr. Divd.:**	NA
Total Assets:	$117,174,000	**Net Worth:**	$99,154,000	**Debt/ Equity:**	0.3711

On2 Technologies Inc

580 White Plains Rd., Ste. 100, Tarrytown, NY, 10591; ***PH:*** 1-518-348-0099; ***Fax:*** 1-518-348-2098; ***http://*** www.on2.com

General - Incorporation	DE	**Stock**- Price on:12/24/2007	$3.08
Employees	37	Stock Exchange	AMEX
Auditor	Eisner LLP	Ticker Symbol	ONT
Stk Agt	Corporate Stock Transfer, Inc.	Outstanding Shares	112,860,000
Counsel	NA	E.P.S.	-$0.06
DUNS No.	NA	Shareholders	NA

Business: The group's principal activity is to provide video compression/decompression software and related services. The group's proprietary technology platform and video compression/decompression software delivers video at low data rates to closed area networks such as set-top boxes, the Internet and wireless devices. Products include truemotion vp3 series of codecs, open source vp3.2, vp4 codec, truemotion 2x, vp4 encoder, audio for video coding technology and truecast(R) server software. The group also provides custom engineering and consulting services. Customers include digital communication and media companies, entertainment companies, telecommunication companies and other global corporations that operate within the digital media industry. Internationally, the group operates in the United Kingdom.

Primary SIC and add'l.: 7372 7812 7375

CIK No: 0001045280

Officers: Bill Joll/CEO, Pres., Jim Bankoski/CTO, Sr. VP, Matt Frost/Exec. VP, General Counsel, Eero Kaikkonen/Exec. VP, CSO, Paul Wilkins/CTO, Sr. VP, Anthony Principe/Sr. VP, CFO

Directors: Allen J. Kosowsky/Chmn., Thomas Weigman/Dir., William A. Newman/Dir., Afsaneh Naimollah/Dir., Mike Alfant/Dir., Mike Kopetski/Dir., James Meyer/Dir.

Owners: William A. Newman, Michael J. Alfant, Thomas Weigman, Allen J. Kosowsky, Insiders/4.90%, Eric Ameres, Matthew Frost, Afsaneh Naimollah, Anthony Principe, Bill Joll, Michael Kopetski, James Meyer

Financial Data: **Fiscal Year End:** 12/31 **Latest Annual Data:** 12/31/2006

Year	Sales	Net Income
2006	$6,572,000	-$4,846,000
2005	$2,208,000	-$4,605,000
2004	$3,028,000	-$3,445,000

Curr. Assets:	$6,681,000	**Curr. Liab.:**	$1,413,000		
Plant, Equip.:	$157,000	**Total Liab.:**	$3,771,000	**Indic. Yr. Divd.:**	NA
Total Assets:	$7,887,000	**Net Worth:**	$1,033,000	**Debt/ Equity:**	1.7202

Oncolytics Biotech Inc

1167 Kensington Crescent NW, Ste. 210, Calgary, AB, T2N 1X7; ***PH:*** 1-403-670-7377; ***http://*** www.oncolyticsbiotech.com; ***Email:*** info@oncolyticsbiotech.com

General - Incorporation	Canada	**Stock**- Price on:12/24/2007	$2
Employees	NA	Stock Exchange	NDQ
Auditor	Ernst & Young LLP	Ticker Symbol	ONCY
Stk Agt	Computershare Trust Co of Canada	Outstanding Shares	NA
Counsel	NA	E.P.S.	NA
DUNS No.	NA	Shareholders	NA

Business: The group's principle activities include discovering and developing pharmaceutical products for the treatment of a wide variety of human cancers. The company's products are developed utilizing the reovirus for treatment of cancers in humans. The reovirus has been demonstrated to replicate specifically in tumor cells bearing an activated ras pathway. Activating mutations of ras and mutations along the("Activated") ras pathway occur in approximately 65% of all tumors. The company's technologies are based on discoveries made in the department of microbiology and infectious diseases at the university of calgary. The group operates from United States.

Primary SIC and add'l.: 2834

CIK No: 0001129928

Officers: Bradley G. Thompson/Chmn., CEO, Pres., Matthew Coffey/Chief Scientific Officer, George Gill/Sr. VP - Clinical, Regulatory Affairs, Karl Mettinger/Chief Medical Officer, Douglas A. Ball/Dir., CFO, Cathy Ward/Dir. - Communications, Alan Tuchman/Consultant, Member - Scientific Advisory Board, Daniel Von Hoff/Consultant, Mary Ann Dillahunty/VP - Intellectual Property, Nick Hurst/Additional Investor Relations Contact - Canada, Erika Moran/Investor Relation Officer - US

Directors: Bradley G. Thompson/Chmn., CEO, Pres., Douglas A. Ball/Dir., CFO, William A. Cochrane/Dir., Ger J. Van Amersfoort/Dir., Jim Dinning/Dir., Mark J. Lievonen/Dir., Ed Levy/Dir., Robert B. Schultz/Dir., Fred A. Stewart/Dir., Ramon Alemany/Member - Scientific Advisory Board, Richard Gorlick/Member - Scientific Advisory Board, Frank Tufaro/Member - Scientific Advisory Board

Financial Data: **Fiscal Year End:** 12/31 **Latest Annual Data:** 12/31/2006

Year	Sales	Net Income
2006	NA	-$11,959,000
2005	$672,000	-$10,657,000
2004	$581,000	-$10,457,000

Curr. Assets:	$24,315,000	**Curr. Liab.:**	$2,245,000		
Plant, Equip.:	$128,000	**Total Liab.:**	$2,374,000	**Indic. Yr. Divd.:**	NA
Total Assets:	$28,803,000	**Net Worth:**	$26,429,000	**Debt/ Equity:**	0.0048

One IP Voice Inc

Formerly: Farmstead Telephone Group Inc
22 Prestige Pk. Cir., East Hartford, CT, 06108; ***PH:*** 1-860-610-6000; ***http://*** www.farmstead.com

General - Incorporation	DE	**Stock**- Price on:12/24/2007	NA
Employees	72	Stock Exchange	NA
Auditor	Carlin, Charron & Rosen LLP	Ticker Symbol	NA
Stk Agt	Computershare Trust Co	Outstanding Shares	NA
Counsel	Pepe & Hazard LLP	E.P.S.	-$0.893
DUNS No.	13-176-2767	Shareholders	NA

Business: The group's principle activity is to resell new and refurbished business communication products. The group is the authorized remarketing supplier of classic avaya (TM) and new business communication products manufactured by avaya inc. These products are primarily customer premises-based private switching systems and peripheral telecommunications products. The group also provides telecommunications equipment repair and refurbishing, rental, inventory management, and related value-added services. It sells its products and services primarily to both large and small end-user businesses, government agencies, and other secondary market dealers. Telecommunications parts and value added services are marketed nationally through the group's direct sales staff, which includes salespersons located throughout the eastern seaboard, Illinois, Ohio, Texas and California.

Primary SIC and add'l.: 5065 7359 7629

CIK No: 0000804331

Officers: George J. Taylor/Chmn., Pres., Frederick E. Robertson/COO, Mel M. Lipes/VP - Administration

Directors: George J. Taylor/Chmn., Pres.

Financial Data: **Fiscal Year End:** 12/31 **Latest Annual Data:** 12/31/2005

Year	Sales	Net Income
2005	$15,203,000	-$3,314,000
2004	$12,344,000	-$1,424,000
2003	$14,680,000	-$709,000

Curr. Assets:	$4,351,000	**Curr. Liab.:**	$4,919,000		
Plant, Equip.:	$615,000	**Total Liab.:**	$6,101,000	**Indic. Yr. Divd.:**	NA
Total Assets:	$5,604,000	**Net Worth:**	-$497,000	**Debt/ Equity:**	NA

One Liberty Properties Inc

60 Cutter Mill Rd., Ste. 303, Great Neck, NY, 11021; ***PH:*** 1-516-466-3100; ***Fax:*** 1-516-466-3132; ***http://*** www.1liberty.com

General - Incorporation	MD	**Stock**- Price on:12/24/2007	$23.73
Employees	NA	Stock Exchange	NYSE
Auditor	Ernst& Young LLP	Ticker Symbol	OLP
Stk Agt	American Stock Transfer & Trust Co.	Outstanding Shares	10,060,000
Counsel	NA	E.P.S.	$3.26
DUNS No.	NA	Shareholders	NA

Business: The groups principle activities include owning, acquiring and managing retail, industrial, office, health, and fitness properties. In the year 2006, the group acquired eleven retail furniture stores. The group operates from the United States.

Primary SIC and add'l.: 6798

CIK No: 0000712770

Subsidiaries: OLP 6609 Grand LLC, OLP Athens LLC, OLP Baltimore LLC, OLP Baltimore, MD, Inc., OLP Batavia, Inc., OLP CC Antioch LLC, OLP CC Fairview Heights LLC, OLP CC Ferguson LLC, OLP CC Florence LLC, OLP CC St. Louis LLC, OLP Champaign, Inc., OLP Chula Vista Corp., OLP Columbus, Inc., OLP Dixie Drive Houston, Inc., OLP El Paso 1, L.P. 61 Subsidiaries included in the Index

Officers: Fredric H. Gould/Chmn., CEO/$743,926.00, Patrick J. Callan/Dir., Pres./$613,969.00, David W. Kalish/Sr. VP, CFO/$435,173.00, Simeon Brinberg/Sr. VP, Israel Rosenzweig/Sr. VP, Lawrence G. Ricketts/Exec. VP/$346,780.00, Karen Dunleavy/VP - Financial, Mark H. Lundy/Sr. VP, Sec./$560,290.00, Richard Figueroa/VP, Assist. Sec., Alysa Block/Assist. Treasurer, Jeffrey A. Gould/Dir., Sr. VP

Directors: Fredric H. Gould/Chmn., CEO, Patrick J. Callan/Dir., Pres., Marshall Rose/71/Dir., Joseph A. Amato/Dir., Charles L. Biederman/Dir., James J. Burns/Dir., Eugene Zuriff/Dir., Robert J. Lovejoy/Dir., Joseph A. Deluca/Dir., Matthew J. Gould/Dir., Jeffrey A. Gould/Dir., Sr. VP

Owners: Joseph A. Amato, Insiders/21.50%, Third Avenue Management LLC/9.30%, Eugene I. Zuriff, Robert J. Lovejoy, Marshall Rose/1.50%, Davidson Kempner Partners/6.20%, Gould Investors L.P./8.50%, David W. Kalish/2.20%, Patrick J. Callan, Charles Biederman, Fredric H. Gould/13.00%, Matthew J. Gould/10.50%, Joseph A. DeLuca, Mark H. Lundy *(18 Owners included in Index)*

Financial Data: **Fiscal Year End:** 12/31 **Latest Annual Data:** 12/31/2006

Year	Sales	Net Income
2006	NA	NA
2005	NA	NA
2004	NA	NA

Curr. Assets:	$49,640,000	**Curr. Liab.:**	$7,978,000	**P/E Ratio:**	18.74
Plant, Equip.:	$351,841,000	**Total Liab.:**	$241,912,000	**Indic. Yr. Divd.:**	$1.440
Total Assets:	$422,037,000	**Net Worth:**	$180,125,000	**Debt/ Equity:**	NA

One Voice Technologies Inc

4250 Executive Sq., Ste. 770, La Jolla, CA, 92037; ***PH:*** 1-858-552-4466; ***Fax:*** 1-858-552-4474; ***http://*** www.onevoicetech.com; ***Email:*** info@onev.com

General		Stock	
Incorporation	NV	Price on:12/24/2007	$0.028
Employees	7	Stock Exchange	OTC
Auditor	PMB Helin Donovan, LLP	Ticker Symbol	ONEV
Stk Agt	Corporate Stock Transfer, Inc.	Outstanding Shares	619,340,000
Counsel	NA	E.P.S	-$0.01
DUNS No.	NA	Shareholders	NA

Business: The group's principal activities are to develop and market computer software using intelligent voice interactive technology to Website owners. The group develops scalable, platform-independent human voice interface technologies for the telecom, telematics, and itv/Internet appliance markets. The product, 'ivan' (TM) (intelligent voice activated network) allows people to use everyday speech to conduct an open-ended, free-format interactive dialogue to quickly obtain information, execute transactions and issue orders over the Web at any time.

Primary SIC and add'l.: 7372

CIK No: 0001096088

Officers: Dean Weber/Chmn., CEO, Company Founder, Pres., Laszlo Betyar/VP - Engineering, Jack Johnson/VP - Telephony, North America, Aaron Bennett/VP - Telephony Business Development, North America, Steve Zielke/VP - Business Development, Bob Duerr/VP - Business Development

Directors: Dean Weber/Chmn., CEO, Company Founder, Pres.

Owners: RAHOUL SHARAN/0.40%, Insiders/3.80%, ALPHA CAPITAL AKTEINGESELLSCHAFT/22.30%, DEAN WEBER/3.10%, Bradley J. Ammon/0.30%, WHALEHAVEN CAPITAL FUND LIMITED/14.60%, ELLIS INTERNATIONAL/6.90%, STONESTREET LIMITED PARTNERSHIP/5.10%, BRISTOL INVESTMENTS FUND LIMITED/5.50%

Financial Data: *Fiscal Year End:*12/31 *Latest Annual Data:* 12/31/2006

Year	Sales	Net Income
2006	$691,000	-$4,419,000
2005	$142,000	-$1,060,000
2004	$2,000	-$8,752,000

Curr. Assets:	$167,000	Curr. Liab.:	$5,268,000		
Plant, Equip.:	$164,000	Total Liab.:	$6,363,000	Indic. Yr. Divd.:	NA
Total Assets:	$788,000	Net Worth:	-$5,576,000	Debt/ Equity:	NA

OneBeacon Insurance Group Ltd

1 Beacon Ln., Canton, MA, 02021; *PH:* 1-781-332-7000; *Fax:* 1-888-656-1213; *http://* www.onebeacon.com

General		Stock	
Incorporation	Bermuda	Price on:12/24/2007	$24.53
Employees	NA	Stock Exchange	NYSE
Auditor	PricewaterhouseCoopers LLP	Ticker Symbol	OB
Stk Agt	Wells Fargo Bank, N.A.	Outstanding Shares	100,010,000
Counsel	NA	E.P.S	$2.58
DUNS No.	NA	Shareholders	NA

Business: The groups principle activity is to provide insurance products. The group operates through three segments namely, primary insurance operation, affiliate quota shares and other operations. The group operates from the United States. The groups quarterly revenue for September 2007 was 566.60 millions of USD.

Primary SIC and add'l.: 6331

CIK No: 0001369817

Subsidiaries: A.W.G. Dewar, Inc., Adirondack AIF, LLC, Adirondack Insurance Exchange, American Central Insurance Company, American Employers Insurance Company, Atlantic Specialty Insurance Company, AutoOne Insurance Agency, Inc., AutoOne Insurance Company, AutoOne Management Company, Inc., AutoOne Select Insurance Company, Farmers and Merchants Insurance Company, Fund American Companies, Inc., Fund American Enterprises Holdings, Inc., Fund American Financial Services, Inc., Homeland Insurance Company of New York 48 Subsidiaries included in the Index

Officers: Michael T. Miller/Dir., CEO, Pres., Frederick J. Turcotte/VP - Investor Relations, Tax Dir., Eileen Stansbury/Contact - New England Region, Phil Spencer/Contact - New England Region, Toni Mitchell/Contact - Western Region, Mark McGregor/Contact - Western Region, Sandra Larkin/Contact - New York Region, David Devinney/Contact - New York Region, Kevin S. Pendergast/Contact - New York Region, Rick Hernandez/Contact - New York Region, Michael Preston/Contact - Atlantic Region, Joe Armeni/Contact - Atlantic Region, Scott Betlesky/Contact - Atlantic Region, Bob Bell/Contact - Western Region, Steve Schaeberle/Contact - Western Region *(30 Officers included in Index)*

Directors: Michael T. Miller/Dir., CEO, Pres., Lowndes A. Smith/Chmn., Allan L. Waters/49/Dir., Raymond Barrette/Dir., Ira H. Malis/Dir., Reid T. Campbell/Dir., Morgan W. Davis/Dir., David T. Foy/Dir., Lois W. Grady/Dir., Richard P. Howard/Dir., Robert R. Lusardi/Dir., Kent D. Urness/Dir.

Owners: Advisory Research,Inc, Lazard Asset Management LLC, RS Investment Management Company LLC, Oppenheimer Capital LLC, Lone Tree Holdings Ltd

Financial Data: *Fiscal Year End:*12/31 *Latest Annual Data:* 12/31/2006

Year	Sales	Net Income
2006	$2,470,100,000	$246,700,000
2005	$2,396,800,000	$232,600,000
2004	$2,485,000,000	$136,000,000

Curr. Assets:	$3,831,300,000	Curr. Liab.:	$83,400,000	P/E Ratio:	9.89
Plant, Equip.:	NA	Total Liab.:	$7,829,900,000	Indic. Yr. Divd.:	$0.840
Total Assets:	$9,869,400,000	Net Worth:	$1,777,200,000	Debt/ Equity:	NA

Oneida Financial Corp

182 Main St., Oneida, NY, 13421; *PH:* 1-315-363-2000; *Fax:* 1-315-366-3709; *http://* www.oneidabank.com; *Email:* service@oneidabank.com

General		Stock	
Incorporation	Federal	Price on:12/24/2007	$11.99
Employees	267	Stock Exchange	NDQ
Auditor	Crowe Chizek & Co. LLC	Ticker Symbol	ONFC
Stk Agt	Registrar & Transfer Co	Outstanding Shares	7,680,000
Counsel	Luse Gorman Pomerenk & Schick	E.P.S	$0.50
DUNS No.	NA	Shareholders	NA

Business: The group's principal activity is to provide financial services. The group is a savings and loan holding company that accepts deposits from public and provides various types of loans. The loans include one-to-four family residential, commercial real estate loans, commercial business loans and consumer loans. The group also provides trust and brokerage services. The group also conducts investing activities of residential and commercial real estate mortgages. On 01-Oct-2003, it acquired macdonald/yando agency inc.

Primary SIC and add'l.: 6712 6035

CIK No: 0001070190

Subsidiaries: Bailey & Haskell Associates, Inc., MacDonald/Yando Agency Inc., Oneida Preferred Funding Corp., The Oneida Savings Bank, The State Bank of Chittenango

Officers: Michael R. Kallet/Dir., CEO, Pres./$633,065.00, Eric E. Stickels/Exec. VP, Sec., CFO/$335,042.00, Thomas H. Dixon/Exec. VP, CCO/$332,743.00, Jim Lacy/Sr. VP - Business Banking - Oneida Savings, Cathleen Mumford/AVP, Office Mgr. - Convenience Office, Oneida Savings, Angel Rose/AVP, Office Mgr. - Canastota Office, Oneida Savings, Andrea Narrow/AVP, Office Mgr. - Cazenovia Office, Oneida Savings, Janet Briggs/Office Supervisor, Hamilton Office, Oneida Savings, George Sawner/VP - Regional Lender, Camden Office, Oneida Savings, Amanda Relyea/Consumer Banking Mgr. - Oneida Savings Bank, Paula Demo/VP - Operations, Deanne Suits/AVP, Office Mgr. - Camden Office, Oneida Savings, Roberta Button/AVP, Office Mgr. - Chittenango Office, Oneida Savings, Kathy Donegan/VP - Branch Administration - Oneida Savings, Erika Mumford/Auditor *(24 Officers included in Index)*

Directors: Michael R. Kallet/Dir., CEO, Pres., Richard B. Myers/Chmn., Patricia D. Caprio/Dir., Frank O. White/Dir., Gerald N. Volk/Dir., Rodney D. Kent/Dir., John E. Haskell/Dir., Edward J. Clarke/Dir., Marlene Constanzo Denney/Dir., Michael A. Miravalle/Dir.

Owners: Michael A. Miravalle/0.04%, Edward J. Clarke/0.33%, Frank O. White, Eric E. Stickels/1.22%, Michael R. Kallet/2.46%, Marlene C. Denny/0.19%, Oneida Financial, MHC/55.09%, William D. Matthews/0.43%, Gerald N. Volk/0.30%, Insiders/10.16%, Thomas H. Dixon/1.20%, Rodney D. Kent/0.89%, Patricia D. Caprio/0.46%, John E. Haskell/1.52%, Richard B. Myers/0.66%

Financial Data: *Fiscal Year End:*12/31 *Latest Annual Data:* 12/31/2006

Year	Sales	Net Income
2006	$39,239,000	$4,198,000
2005	$32,904,000	$3,858,000
2004	$19,664,000	$3,292,000

Curr. Assets:	$20,798,000	Curr. Liab.:	$317,270,000	P/E Ratio:	25.51
Plant, Equip.:	$17,428,000	Total Liab.:	$384,537,000	Indic. Yr. Divd.:	$0.480
Total Assets:	$442,937,000	Net Worth:	$58,400,000	Debt/ Equity:	1.0698

Oneida Ltd

163-181 Kenwood Ave., Oneida, NY, 13421; *PH:* 1-315-361-3000; *Fax:* 1-315-361-3700; *http://* www.oneida.com; *Email:* investor@oneida.com

General		Stock	
Incorporation	NY	Price on:12/24/2007	NA
Employees	NA	Stock Exchange	NA
Auditor	BDO Seidman LLP	Ticker Symbol	NA
Stk Agt	American Stock Transfer & Trust Co.	Outstanding Shares	NA
Counsel	Shearman & Sterling LLP	E.P.S	NA
DUNS No.	00-222-9128	Shareholders	NA

Business: The group's principal activity is to manufacture and market tableware products. These products are classified into metalware, dinnerware, glassware products and other tabletop accessories. Metalware products include silverplated and sterling silver flatware and holloware, cutlery and cookware. Dinnerware products include domestic and imported China, porcelain and stoneware plates, bowls, cups and mugs. Glassware products include glass and crystal stemware, barware, serveware, giftware and decorative pieces. Other tabletop products include ceramic and plastic serveware, kitchen and table linens, picture frames and decorative pieces. Customers include department store chains, mass merchandisers, discount chains and specialty shops, restaurants, resorts, airlines and cruise lines. The group's tableware operations serve 3 markets: consumer, foodservice and international. The operations are in Canada, Mexico, Italy, Australia, the United Kingdom, China and Hong Kong.

Primary SIC and add'l.: 3914 3262

CIK No: 0000074585

Subsidiaries: Buffalo China, Inc., Delco International, Ltd., Encore Promotions, Inc., Kenwood Silver Company, Inc., Oneida Australia Pty Ltd., Oneida Canada, Limited, Oneida International, Inc., Oneida Ltd., Oneida Mexicana, S.A. de C.V., Oneida Silversmiths, Inc., Oneida U.K. Limited, Oneida, S.A. de C.V., Sakura, Inc., THC Systems, Inc.

Officers: James E. Joseph/CEO, Pres., Catherine H. Suttmeier/Sr. VP, Sec., General Counsel, Andrew G. Church/Sr. VP, CFO, David Sank/Chief Marketing Officer, Sr. VP - Strategic Planning, Foster Sullivan/Pres. - Oneida's Foodservice Division, Dominick J. Trapasso/Sr. VP - Supply Chain, Rob Hack/Sr. VP - Information Technology, CIO, Tim W. Runyan/Exec. VP, Chief Global Supply Chain Officer, Bill Grannis/Sr. VP - Global Procurement, Paul E. Gebhardt/Sr. VP - Design, Advertising, Timothy J. Shine/Pres. - Oneidas Consumer Division

Directors: Diane Price Baker/Dir., Andrew Herenstein/Dir., Norman S. Matthews/Dir., Edward W. Rabin/Dir., Thomas J. Russo/Dir., Eric S. Salus/Dir., Hugh R. Rovit/47/Dir.

OneLink Corp

1 Market Plz, San Francisco, CA, 94105; *PH:* 1-415-293-8277; *http://* www.onelinkcorp.com; *Email:* sales@onelinkcorp.com

General		Stock	
Incorporation	DE	Price on:12/24/2007	NA
Employees	NA	Stock Exchange	OTC
Auditor	Mahoney Cohen & Company, CPA, P.C.	Ticker Symbol	OLNK
Stk Agt	NA	Outstanding Shares	NA
Counsel	NA	E.P.S	-$0.35
DUNS No.	NA	Shareholders	NA

Business: The groups principle activities include providing distribution and automated financial settlement services for non air products to the leisure and business travel industries. In the year April 2005, the group acquired The Call Center LLC, In May 2005, Reservation Center, Inc. The group operates from the United States.

Primary SIC and add'l.: 4724

CIK No: 0001166161

Subsidiaries: Onelink4travel Limited

Officers: Bill Guerin/Chmn., CEO, Steve Simon/Contact - Investor Relations

Directors: Bill Guerin/Chmn., CEO, Peter Boatright/Dir., Edward Nichols/Dir., Peter Short/Member - Industry Advisory Board, Peter Crouch/Member - Industry Advisory Board

Financial Data: *Fiscal Year End:*12/31 *Latest Annual Data:* 12/31/2005

Year	Sales	Net Income
2005	$4,222,000	-$8,140,000
2004	NA	-$6,093,000
2003	NA	-$7,178,000

Curr. Assets:	$1,081,000	Curr. Liab.:	$6,598,000		
Plant, Equip.:	$1,027,000	Total Liab.:	$14,482,000	Indic. Yr. Divd.:	NA
Total Assets:	$11,907,000	Net Worth:	-$2,575,000	Debt/ Equity:	NA

Oneok Inc

100 W 5th St., Tulsa, OK, 74103; *PH:* 1-918-588-7000; *Fax:* 1-918-588-7960; *http://* www.oneok.com

General - Incorporation	OK	Stock- Price on:12/24/2007	$50.92
Employees	4,536	Stock Exchange	NYSE
Auditor	KPMG LLP	Ticker Symbol	OKE
Stk Agt	UMB Bank, N.A.	Outstanding Shares	111,040,000
Counsel	NA	E.P.S.	$2.49
DUNS No.	00-790-7827	Shareholders	NA

Business: The groups principle activities include purchasing transporting, storing, and distribute natural gas. The group operates through six segments namely marketing and trading, gathering and processing, transportation and storage, distribution and production segment. The group operates from United States.

Primary SIC and add'l.: 4923 4924 4922 6519

CIK No: 0001039684

Subsidiaries: Chisholm Pipeline Company, Chisholm Pipeline Holdings, Inc., Fox Plant, LLC, Kansas Gas Marketing Company, Mercado Gas Services Inc., Mid Continent Market Center, Inc., NBP Services, LLC, Northern Border Pipeline Corporation, Northern Plains Natural Gas Company, LLC, Oasis Acquisition Corporation, Oklahoma Natural Energy Services Company, OkTex Pipeline Company, ONEOK Bushton Processing, Inc., ONEOK Energy Marketing Company, ONEOK Energy Services Canada, Ltd. 51 Subsidiaries included in the Index

Officers: John W. Gibson/Dir., CEO/$2,713,856.00, David Roth/Sr. VP - Administrative Services, Curtis L. Dinan/CFO, Sr. VP, Treasurer, Caron A. Lawhorn/Chief Accounting Officer, Sr. VP, William S. Maxwell/47/Pres. - Oneok Energy Services/$1,177,395.00, Samuel Combs/Pres. - Oneok Distribution Companies/$1,661,954.00, James C. Kneale/COO, Pres./$3,326,710.00, Dan Harrison/VP - Communications, Investor Relations, Eric Grimshaw/Corp. Sec., Assoc. General Counsel, Phyllis S. Worley/Pres. - Oklahoma Natural Gas, Bradley O. Dixon/Pres. - Kansas Gas Service, Roger N. Mitchell/Pres. - Texas Gas Service, David Arnold/VP - Customer Service, Daniel Walker/VP - Operations, Engineering, Steve Guy/Sr. VP - Technical, Corporate Services *(21 Officers included in Index)*

Directors: John W. Gibson/Dir., CEO, David L. Kyle/Chmn., Eduardo A. Rodriguez/Dir., Mollie B. Williford/Dir., Pattye L. Moore/Dir., Gary D. Parker/Dir., William L. Ford/Dir., James C. Day/Dir., William M. Bell/Dir., David J. Tippeconnic/Dir., Julie H. Edwards/Dir., Jim W. Mogg/Dir., Bert H. MacKie/Dir.

Owners: Bert H. Mackie, James C. Day, James C. Kneale, William L. Ford, Pattye L. Moore, William S. Maxwell, Insiders, Gary D. Parker, William M. Bell, Mollie B. Williford, Bank of Oklahoma, N.A./5.60%, David L. Kyle, David L. Kyle, Insiders/1.26%, John W. Gibson *(19 Owners included in Index)*

*Financial Data: Fiscal Year End:*12/31   *Latest Annual Data:* 12/31/2006

Year	Sales	Net Income
2006	$11,896,104,000	$306,312,000
2005	$12,676,230,000	$546,545,000
2004	$5,988,080,000	$242,178,000

Curr. Assets:	$3,238,600,000	Curr. Liab.:	$2,064,177,000	P/E Ratio:	20.13
Plant, Equip.:	$4,844,921,000	Total Liab.:	$7,488,118,000	Indic. Yr. Divd.:	$1.440
Total Assets:	$10,504,721,000	Net Worth:	$2,215,958,000	Debt/ Equity:	1.6406

ONEOK Partners LP

Formerly: Northern Border Partners LP
100 W Fifth St., Tulsa, OK, 74103; *PH:* 1-918-588-7000; *http://* www.oneok.com

General - Incorporation	DE	Stock- Price on:12/24/2007	$68.82
Employees	NA	Stock Exchange	NYSE
Auditor	KPMG LLP	Ticker Symbol	NA
Stk Agt	UMB Bank, N.A.	Outstanding Shares	82,890,000
Counsel	NA	E.P.S.	$3.77
DUNS No.	NA	Shareholders	NA

Business: The groups principle activities include owning, gathering, processing and managing natural gas storage centers. The group operates through four segments namely, gathering and processing, natural gas liquids, pipelines and storage, and interstates natural gas pipelines. The group operates from the United States.

Primary SIC and add'l.: 4922

CIK No: 0000909281

Subsidiaries: Bear Paw Energy, LLC., Bear Paw Investments, LLC., Bear Paw Processing Company (Canada), Ltd., Bighorn Gas Gathering, L.L.C., Black Mesa Holdings, Inc., Black Mesa Pipeline Operations, L.L.C., Black Mesa Pipeline, Inc., Black Mesa Technologies Services, LLC, Black Mesa Technologies, Inc., Border Midstream Services, Ltd., Border Midwestern Company, Border Minnesota Pipeline, LLC., Border Viking Company, Brown Bear Enterprises, LLC., China Pipeline Holdings Ltd. 60 Subsidiaries included in the Index

Officers: John W. Gibson/Dir., CEO/$2,035,391.00, Patrick McDonie/Sr. VP - Trading, Daniel Walker/VP - Operations, Engineering, Lamar D. Miller/Sr. VP - Marketing, Phyllis S. Worley/Pres. - Oklahoma Natural Gas, Bradley O. Dixon/Pres. - Kansas Gas Service, Roger N. Mitchell/Pres. - Texas Gas Service, David Arnold/VP - Customer Service, Samuel Combs/Pres., William S. Maxwell/Pres., John R. Barker/Sr. VP, General Counsel, Curtis L. Dinan/Sr. VP, CFO, Treasurer, Caron A. Lawhorn/Sr. VP, Chief Accounting Office, David Roth/Sr. VP - Administrative Services, Dan Harrison/VP - Communications, Investor Relations *(18 Officers included in Index)*

Directors: John W. Gibson/Dir., CEO, David L. Kyle/Chmn., William M. Bell/Vice Chmn., James C. Day/Dir., Julie H. Edwards/Dir., Jim W. Mogg/Dir., Bert H. MacKie/Dir., William L. Ford/Dir., Pattye Moore/Dir., Gary Parker/Dir., Eduardo A. Rodriguez/Dir., David J. Tippeconnic/Dir., Mollie B. Williford/Dir.

Owners: ONEOK Inc. and Affilates/1.08%, David L. Kyle, Pierce H. Norton, Insiders, Gary N. Petersen, William R. Cordes, Jerry L. Peters, ONEOK Inc. and Affilates/100.00%

*Financial Data: Fiscal Year End:*12/31   *Latest Annual Data:* 12/31/2006

Year	Sales	Net Income
2006	$4,714,026,000	$445,186,000
2005	$678,560,000	$147,013,000
2004	$590,383,000	$144,720,000

Curr. Assets:	$806,877,000	Curr. Liab.:	$784,672,000	P/E Ratio:	10.64
Plant, Equip.:	$2,763,648,000	Total Liab.:	$2,846,694,000	Indic. Yr. Divd.:	$4.040
Total Assets:	$5,035,356,000	Net Worth:	$2,188,662,000	Debt/ Equity:	NA

Onesource Technologies Inc

15730 N 83rd Way, Ste. 104, Scottsdale, AZ, 85260; *PH:* 1-480-889-1177; *Fax:* 1-480-889-1166; *http://* www.1sourcetech.com

General - Incorporation	DE	Stock- Price on:12/24/2007	$0.001
Employees	NA	Stock Exchange	OTC
Auditor	Epstein Weber & Conover, PLC	Ticker Symbol	OSRC
Stk Agt	Interwest Transfer Company, Inc.	Outstanding Shares	NA
Counsel	NA	E.P.S.	NA
DUNS No.	NA	Shareholders	NA

Business: The group's principle activity is to provide technology infrastructure maintenance and installation services. These services are used in business, government, banking, financial and retail industries. The group provides products and services under three areas: equipment maintenance services, equipment installation services and value added equipment supply sales. The group's customers are located in Arizona, California, Colorado, Nevada, and New Mexico.

Primary SIC and add'l.: 7389

CIK No: 0001118421

*Financial Data: Fiscal Year End:*12/31   *Latest Annual Data:* 12/31/2004

Year	Sales	Net Income
2004	$4,519,000	-$345,000
2003	$3,075,000	-$434,000
2002	$2,959,000	$16,000

Curr. Assets:	$8,708,000	Curr. Liab.:	$7,448,000		
Plant, Equip.:	$410,000	Total Liab.:	$10,408,000	Indic. Yr. Divd.:	NA
Total Assets:	$10,920,000	Net Worth:	$512,000	Debt/ Equity:	NA

Online Holdings Inc

1667 K St., Nw, Ste. 1230, Washington, DC, 20006; *PH:* 1-202-955-9490

General - Incorporation	NV	Stock- Price on:12/24/2007	NA
Employees	NA	Stock Exchange	OTC
Auditor	Moore & Assoc., Chartered	Ticker Symbol	STDRE
Stk Agt	NA	Outstanding Shares	NA
Counsel	Cletha A. Walstrand	E.P.S.	NA
DUNS No.	NA	Shareholders	NA

Business: The group's principal activity is to develop and market easily maintained Website systems. The group designs and develops corporate websites, which the end user can easily modify without the need of technical experience. The Website systems are designed to allow its clients to streamline and enhance corporate communications. In addition the group provides managed Website hosting, search engine placement, email marketing and graphic design. The group is in development stage.

Primary SIC and add'l.: 7379 7375

CIK No: 0001158694

Subsidiaries: E-Site Technologies, Inc.

Officers: Prentis B. Tomlinson/Chmn., CEO, Interim CFO, Edward L. Moses/69/Dir., COO, Pres.

Directors: Prentis B. Tomlinson/Chmn., CEO, Interim CFO, Edward L. Moses/69/Dir., COO, Pres., Richard W. Anderson/51/Dir.

*Financial Data: Fiscal Year End:*12/31   *Latest Annual Data:* 12/31/2006

Year	Sales	Net Income
2006	$473,000	-$3,624,000
2005	NA	-$22,000

Curr. Assets:	$1,048,000	Curr. Liab.:	$8,498,000		
Plant, Equip.:	$11,757,000	Total Liab.:	$8,498,000	Indic. Yr. Divd.:	NA
Total Assets:	$21,853,000	Net Worth:	$13,355,000	Debt/ Equity:	NA

Online Resources Corp

4795 Meadow Wood Ln., Ste. 300, Chantilly, VA, 20151; *PH:* 1-703-653-3100; *Fax:* 1-703-653-3105; *http://* www.orcc.com; *Email:* info@orcc.com

General - Incorporation	DE	Stock- Price on:12/24/2007	$11.14
Employees	600	Stock Exchange	NDQ
Auditor	Ernst & Young LLP	Ticker Symbol	ORCC
Stk Agt	American Stock Transfer & Trust Co.	Outstanding Shares	26,150,000
Counsel	Mintz Levin Cohn Ferris Et Al	E.P.S.	-$0.46
DUNS No.	NA	Shareholders	NA

Business: The group's principal activities are to provide Internet banking, electronic bill payment and marketing infrastructure that enable the clients to provide their customers with end-to-end Internet channel functionality and a high quality user experience. The customers of the group are primarily regional and community-based depository financial institutions. In 2003, the groups provided services to approximately 841,000 customers of 633 client financial institutions. The group's clients choose one of two primary product lines: full service, which includes a suite of Internet banking, bill payment, call center and other support services, or stand-alone bill payment and presentment services. The group provides a single source, fully integrated solution through quotiensm e-financial suite of services, which enables depository financial institutions to offer the breadth of financial services needed to remain competitive and earn profit from their Internet channel.

Primary SIC and add'l.: 7389 7372 7375

CIK No: 0000888953

Subsidiaries: Incurrent Acquisition LLC

Officers: Matthew P. Lawlor/Chmn., CEO, Co - Founder/$584,780.00, Raymond T. Crosier/COO, Pres./$430,522.00, Ronald J. Bergamesca/Exec. VP, GM - Integrated Banking Services, Paul A. Franko/Sr. VP - Banking Technology Services, CTO, William T. Kinnelly/Sr. VP - Card, Credit

Services, Daniel M. Thomas/Sr. VP - Strategic Development, Catherine A. Graham/CFO, Exec. VP/$380,783.00, Stephanie S. Chaufournier/Exec. VP, GM - Banking CSP Payments, Robert R. Craig/Exec. VP, GM - eCommerce Services, Beth Halloran/Investor Relations Officer, Michae C. Bisignano/VP, General Counsel, Sec.

Directors: Matthew P. Lawlor/Chmn., CEO, Co - Founder, Stephen S. Cole/Dir., Michael H. Heath/Dir., Barry D. Wessler/Dir., Ervin R. Shames/Dir., Joseph J. Spalluto/Dir., William H. Washecka/Dir., Michael E. Leitner/Dir., Debra A. Janssen/Dir.

Owners: Stephen S. Cole, Insiders/8.70%, Edward E. Furash, Raymond T. Crosier/1.60%, Ervin R. Shames, Federated Investors, Inc./11.40%, William H. Washecka, Tennenbaum Capital Partners, LLC/15.10%, Barry D. Wessler, Matthew P. Lawlor/5.80%, Michael H. Heath, Joseph J. Spalluto, Wellington Management Company, LLP/7.50%, Catherine A. Graham

Financial Data: *Fiscal Year End:*12/31 *Latest Annual Data:* 12/31/2006

Year	Sales	Net Income
2006	$91,736,000	$321,000
2005	$60,501,000	$22,663,000
2004	$42,285,000	$3,947,000

Curr. Assets:	$58,066,000	Curr. Liab.:	$16,583,000		
Plant, Equip.:	$19,110,000	Total Liab.:	$111,148,000	Indic. Yr. Divd.:	NA
Total Assets:	$286,591,000	Net Worth:	$103,335,000	Debt/ Equity:	0.8873

Online Vacation Center Holdings Corp

Formerly: Alec Bradley Cigar Corp
1801 Nw 66th Ave, Ste. 102, Plantation, FL, 33313; *PH:* 1-954-377-6400;
http:// www.alecbradley.com

General - Incorporation	FL	Stock - Price on:12/24/2007	$2.15
Employees	50	Stock Exchange	NA
Auditor	Jewett, Schwartz, & Assoc.	Ticker Symbol	NA
Stk Agt	NA	Outstanding Shares	18,490,000
Counsel	NA	E.P.S.	$0.00
DUNS No.	NA	Shareholders	NA

Business: The group's principle activity is to import and distribute cigars. It distributes cigars under the name bogey's stogies. Customers of the company include distributors, including wine and liquor wholesalers, retailers, which includes tobacco shops, convenience stores, bars, restaurants and country clubs. It purchases and imports the majority of its cigars from cigar manufacturing plants in Honduras and the Dominican Republic. The company supplies cigars through mail orders, direct sales and personalized and customized cigar band program. The company imports and distributes cigars in the United States and Canada with offices located in plantation, Florida. The group's quarterly revenue for September 2007 was 2.01 millions of USD.

Primary SIC and add'l.: 5194
CIK No: 0001058786
Subsidiaries: Online Vacation Center Holdings, Inc.
Officers: Edward B. Rudner/57/Dir., CEO, CFO, Pres./$343,076.00
Directors: Edward B. Rudner/57/Dir., CEO, CFO, Pres., Richard A. McKinnon/67/Chmn., Frank Bracken/67/Dir., Brian P. Froelich/61/Dir.
Owners: Simon Todd/7.90%, Reginald Flosse/16.50%, Edward B. Rudner/55.50%, Richard A. McKinnon, Frank Bracken, Brian P. Froelich, Insiders/64.50%, William A. Cataldo/6.50%

Financial Data: *Fiscal Year End:*12/31 *Latest Annual Data:* 12/31/2006

Year	Sales	Net Income
2006	$7,785,000	$238,000
2005	$2,587,000	$19,000
2004	$2,393,000	$74,000

Curr. Assets:	$4,321,000	Curr. Liab.:	$3,740,000		
Plant, Equip.:	$92,000	Total Liab.:	$4,115,000	Indic. Yr. Divd.:	NA
Total Assets:	$7,858,000	Net Worth:	$3,743,000	Debt/ Equity:	0.1217

Only Natures Best International Inc

Formerly: 51146 Inc
800 W Rainbow Blvd., Ste. 308, Las Vegas, NV, 89107;

General - Incorporation	DE	Stock - Price on:12/24/2007	NA
Employees	NA	Stock Exchange	NA
Auditor	Gately & Assoc. LLC CPAs	Ticker Symbol	NA
Stk Agt	Interwest Transfer Co.	Outstanding Shares	NA
Counsel	NA	E.P.S.	NA
DUNS No.	NA	Shareholders	NA

Business: The groups principle activity is to provide the process of setting up a method for foreign or domestic private companies to become a reporting public company. The group operates from United States.

Primary SIC and add'l.: 6770
CIK No: 0001317837

Onscreen Technologies Inc

600 NW 14th Ave., Ste. 100, Portland, OR, 97209; *PH:* 1-503-417-1700; *Fax:* 1-503-417-1717;
http:// www.onscreentech.com; *Email:* info@onscreentech.com

General - Incorporation	CO	Stock - Price on:12/24/2007	$0.43
Employees	9	Stock Exchange	OTC
Auditor	Salberg & Co P.A	Ticker Symbol	ONSC
Stk Agt	Computershare Trust Co	Outstanding Shares	149,720,000
Counsel	NA	E.P.S.	-$0.05
DUNS No.	NA	Shareholders	NA

Business: The group's principle activity is to provide innovative technology to the world of visual communications. It concentrates on motion display advertising solutions and seeks to develop innovative approaches to motion advertising products and delivery systems. The company's technology division is focused on the design, development, licensing and sale of led video displays based on the onscreen (TM) architecture. The group operates from United States.

Primary SIC and add'l.: 7311
CIK No: 0001108967

Officers: William J. Clough/Dir., CEO, Pres., Michael Schuette/Chief Technical Engineer, Walter B. Poff/Member - Scientific Advisory Board, Clifford Melby/COO, Stan Robinson/Exec. VP - Engineering, Research & Development, Larry Rightmyer/Dir. - Administrative Services, Cynthia M. Wilson/Interim CFO

Directors: William J. Clough/Dir., CEO, Pres., David Pelka/Chmn. - Scientific Advisory Board, Robert V. Steele/Member - Scientific Advisory Board, Richard Reis/Member - Scientific Advisory Board, Joseph D. Tajnai/Member - Scientific Advisory Board, Bradley J. Hallock/Dir., Steven S. Hallock/Dir., John P. Rouse/Dir., Corey Lambrecht/Dir.

Owners: Steven S. Hallock/5.09%, Russell L. Wall/1.03%, Walter and Whitney Miles/6.51%, Mark R. Chandler/6.18%, Insiders/27.18%, John P. Rouse/4.06%, Kjell H. Qvale/4.95%, William J. Clough/3.25%, Bradley J. Hallock/5.72%, Jerry Ostrin/59.57%, Charles R. Baker/1.37%, Clifford Melby/1.82%, Joel Fedder/33.09%

Financial Data: *Fiscal Year End:*12/31 *Latest Annual Data:* 12/31/2006

Year	Sales	Net Income
2006	$257,000	-$14,481,000
2005	$134,000	-$8,482,000
2004	$146,000	-$7,904,000

Curr. Assets:	$2,849,000	Curr. Liab.:	$1,682,000		
Plant, Equip.:	$102,000	Total Liab.:	$2,079,000	Indic. Yr. Divd.:	NA
Total Assets:	$8,181,000	Net Worth:	$6,103,000	Debt/ Equity:	0.0950

Onspan Networking Inc

4500 Cameron Valley Pk.way, Ste. 270, Charlotte, NC, 28211; *PH:* 1-704-366-5122

General - Incorporation	NV	Stock - Price on:12/24/2007	NA
Employees	3	Stock Exchange	NA
Auditor	Daszkal Bolton LLP	Ticker Symbol	NA
Stk Agt	American Stock Transfer & Trust Co.	Outstanding Shares	NA
Counsel	NA	E.P.S.	-$0.03
DUNS No.	94-518-4174	Shareholders	NA

Business: The group's principle activity is to develop residential real estate and provide building construction services. Until 2002, the group's business was primarily concentrated on sales of computer hardware and software. In Apr 2003, the group changed its focus to investing in and revitalizing single family homes in established residential neighbourhoods in suburban areas.

Primary SIC and add'l.: 1531
CIK No: 0000842722
Subsidiaries: Coventry 1, Inc., InterLAN Communications, Inc., Onspan SmartHouse, Inc.
Officers: Michael D. Pruitt/Chmn., CEO, Pres., M. E. Durschlag/CEO, CFO
Directors: Michael D. Pruitt/Chmn., CEO, Pres.
Owners: Insiders/4.99%, Adam Adler/19.96%, Mike Fine/5.99%, M.E. Hank Durschlag/4.99%

Financial Data: *Fiscal Year End:*09/30 *Latest Annual Data:* 09/30/2006

Year	Sales	Net Income
2006	NA	-$407,000
2005	NA	-$433,000
2004	NA	-$658,000

Curr. Assets:	NA	Curr. Liab.:	$7,000		
Plant, Equip.:	NA	Total Liab.:	$38,000	Indic. Yr. Divd.:	NA
Total Assets:	NA	Net Worth:	-$38,000	Debt/ Equity:	NA

Onstream Media Corp

1291 SW 29th Ave., Pompano Beach, FL, 33069; *PH:* 1-954-917-6655; *Fax:* 1-954-917-6660;
http:// www.onstreammedia.com

General - Incorporation	FL	Stock - Price on:12/24/2007	$2.37
Employees	64	Stock Exchange	NDQ
Auditor	Goldstein Lewin & Co	Ticker Symbol	ONSM
Stk Agt	Interwest Transfer Company, Inc.	Outstanding Shares	39,880,000
Counsel	Arnstein & Lehr LLP	E.P.S.	-$0.48
DUNS No.	80-904-7038	Shareholders	NA

Business: The group's principal activity is to service broadband media that specializes in webcasting, networking solutions for the entertainment and advertising industries and marketing solutions for the travel industry. The group operates through three segments: visual data webcasting group provides an array of corporate-oriented, Web-based media services to the corporate market including audio and video webcasting and information distribution for any business or government. Visual data networking solutions group, provides connectivity within the entertainment and advertising industries through its private network, which encompasses production companies, producers and directors. Visual data travel group produces Internet-based multi-media streaming videos such as hotel, resort, golf facility and travel destination. In Feb 2004, the group acquired certain assets from virage, inc.

Primary SIC and add'l.: 7812 7375
CIK No: 0000919130
Subsidiaries: America Online, Inc, CCBN
Officers: Randy S. Selman/Chmn., CEO, Pres., Clifford Friedland/Vice Chmn., Sr. VP - Business Development, Bradford A. Tyler/Corporate CTO, Alan M. Saperstein/Dir., COO, Treasurer, David Glassman/Sr. VP, Chief Marketing Officer, Robert Tomlinson/CFO
Directors: Randy S. Selman/Chmn., CEO, Pres., Clifford Friedland/Vice Chmn., Sr. VP - Business Development, Charles C. Johnston/Dir., Carl L. Silva/Dir., Benjamin Swirsky/Dir., Alan M. Saperstein/Dir., COO, Treasurer, Robert J. Wussler/71/Dir.
Owners: Alan M. Saperstein/3.30%, Robert Wussler/0.60%, Insiders/13.80%, Charles C. Johnston/1.70%, Carl L. Silva/0.20%, David Glassman/2.20%, Robert E. Tomlinson/0.80%, Cliff Friedland/2.20%, Fred DeLuca/9.60%, Benjamin Swirsky/0.60%

Financial Data: *Fiscal Year End:*09/30 *Latest Annual Data:* 09/30/2007

Year	Sales	Net Income
2007	$12,115,000	-$14,758,000
2006	$8,419,000	-$6,466,000
2005	$8,156,000	-$9,638,000

Curr. Assets:	$2,276,000	Curr. Liab.:	$6,039,000		
Plant, Equip.:	$4,899,000	Total Liab.:	$8,780,000	Indic. Yr. Divd.:	NA
Total Assets:	$17,166,000	Net Worth:	$8,386,000	Debt/ Equity:	0.0018

Ontv Inc

1615 Walnut St., 3rd Fl., Philadelphia, PA, 19103; *PH:* 1-215-972-1601

General - Incorporation	DE	**Stock**- Price on:12/24/2007	NA
Employees	NA	Stock Exchange	NA
Auditor	Rotenberg & Co. LLP	Ticker Symbol	NA
Stk Agt	NA	Outstanding Shares	NA
Counsel	NA	E.P.S	-$0.019
DUNS No.	NA	Shareholders	NA

Business: The group's principal activity is to market general merchandise and consumer goods through Web sites. The consumer products include health, beauty, weight loss, kitchen, sporting goods, and household appliances, etc. The products are marketed through its wholly owned subsidiary seen on TV, inc. The group operates websites 'seenontv.com' and 'asseenontv.com'. These destination websites offers as seen on TV products direct to the consumer via the Internet.

Primary SIC and add'l.: 7375

CIK No: 0001011550

Officers: Richard A. Bendis/Pres., Sec., Dir., Sergio Luz/Pres., Principal Financial Officer

Directors: James MacKay/51/Chmn., Richard A. Bendis/Pres., Sec., Dir., Li Ning/48/Dir., Michael J. Antonopolos/56/Dir.

Owners: Li Ning/2.20%, Sichuan Valencia Trading Limited/22.20%, Michael Antonopolos/0.20%, Insiders/17.30%, Richard A. Bendis/6.80%, James MacKay/14.90%

Financial Data: *Fiscal Year End:*06/30 *Latest Annual Data:* 6/30/2006

Year	Sales	Net Income
2006	NA	-$1,165,000
2005	$5,111,000	$159,000
2004	$3,935,000	-$500,000

Curr. Assets:	$78,000	**Curr. Liab.:**	$1,572,000		
Plant, Equip.:	$136,000	**Total Liab.:**	$3,902,000	**Indic. Yr. Divd.:**	NA
Total Assets:	$18,667,000	**Net Worth:**	$14,890,000	**Debt/ Equity:**	NA

Onvia Inc

1260 Mercer St., Seattle, WA, 98109; *PH:* 1-206-282-5170; *Fax:* 1-206-373-8960; *http://* www.onvia.com; *Email:* investorrelations@onvia.com

General - Incorporation	DE	**Stock**- Price on:12/24/2007	$8.47
Employees	174	Stock Exchange	NDQ
Auditor	Deloitte & Touche LLP	Ticker Symbol	ONVI
Stk Agt	U.S. Stock Transfer Corp	Outstanding Shares	8,030,000
Counsel	NA	E.P.S	-$0.41
DUNS No.	96-717-6637	Shareholders	NA

Business: The group's principal activity is to provide business-to-government information services for government agency buyers and business suppliers. Its network enables business suppliers to secure government contracts and government agencies to find suppliers online. The group also manages the distribution and reporting of requests for proposals and quotes from approximately 400 government agencies nationwide. Products include the onvia guide for suppliers and demandstar, bidwire and quotewire for buyers. It serves the architectural, engineering and environmental services, information technology, telecom, consulting services, construction services and building supplies markets.

Primary SIC and add'l.: 7375 7389 7379

CIK No: 0001100917

Officers: Mike Pickett/Chmn., CEO, Pres./$690,678.00, Irvine Alpert/Exec. VP, Founder - Onviaguides/$463,896.00, Eric Gillespie/CIO, Jill Boyle/VP - Human Resources, Michael Balsam/VP - Products, Services, Cameron Way/Chief Accounting Officer/$166,898.00, Matthew S. Rowley/44/CIO/$231,388.00, Peter Noble/44/Exec. VP - Sales/$420,204.00, Soyoung Kwon/General Counsel

Directors: Mike Pickett/Chmn., CEO, Pres., Jeffrey C. Ballowe/Dir., Roger L. Feldman/Dir., D. Van Skilling/Dir., Robert G. Brown/Dir., Steven D. Smith/Dir., James L. Brill/Dir.

Owners: James L. Brill, Insiders/21.50%, Diker GP, LLC/8.10%, Cameron S. Way, Peter W. Noble, Michael D. Pickett/8.10%, Robert G. Brown, Federated Investors, Inc/8.70%, Matthew S. Rowley, Roger L. Feldman/7.70%, Steven D. Smith, Asamara, LLC/17.70%, Irvine N. Alpert/1.30%, D. Van Skilling, Harvey Hanerfeld/7.50% *(16 Owners included in Index)*

Financial Data: *Fiscal Year End:*12/31 *Latest Annual Data:* 12/31/2006

Year	Sales	Net Income
2006	$16,739,000	-$5,544,000
2005	$14,714,000	-$6,920,000
2004	$13,076,000	-$3,900,000

Curr. Assets:	$16,031,000	**Curr. Liab.:**	$11,143,000		
Plant, Equip.:	$2,145,000	**Total Liab.:**	$14,397,000	**Indic. Yr. Divd.:**	NA
Total Assets:	$23,991,000	**Net Worth:**	$9,595,000	**Debt/ Equity:**	NA

Onyx Pharmaceuticals Inc

2100 Powell St., Emeryville, CA, 94608; *PH:* 1-510-597-6500; *Fax:* 1-510-597-6600; *http://* www.onyx-pharm.com

General - Incorporation	DE	**Stock**- Price on:12/24/2007	$27.56
Employees	125	Stock Exchange	NDQ
Auditor	Ernst & Young LLP	Ticker Symbol	ONXX
Stk Agt	Wells Fargo Bank Minnesota N.A	Outstanding Shares	47,870,000
Counsel	Cooley Godward LLP	E.P.S	-$1.42
DUNS No.	78-959-1724	Shareholders	NA

Business: The group's principle activity is to develop products for the treatment of cancer. The company is developing novel, small molecule therapies that target the molecular mechanisms that cause cancer. It's lead product candidate is bay 43-9006, an orally active small molecule in phase iii clinical development with bayer pharmaceuticals corporation. The company also has a small molecule cell cycle inhibitor from a collaboration with pfizer advancing towards clinical development. By exploiting the genetic differences between cancer cells and normal cells, the company is focused on changing the way cancer is treatedtm by creating anticancer therapies aimed at avoiding damage to healthy tissue while destroying malignant cells. The group operates from United States.

Primary SIC and add'l.: 8731 2834

CIK No: 0001012140

Officers: Hollings C. Renton/Chmn., CEO, Pres./$2,257,899.00, Laura A. Brege/Exec. VP, Chief Business Officer, Edward F. Kenney/Exec. VP, Chief Commercial Officer/$2,249,812.00, Gregory J. Giotta/VP, Chief Legal Counsel/$640,497.00, Julianna Wood/VP - Corporate Communications, Investor Relations, Julie Wood/Investor Relations Contact, Alexandra Santos/Investor Relations Contact, Randy A. Kelley/VP - Sales/$1,347,125.00, Henry J. Fuchs/Chief Medical Officer, Exec. VP/$2,323,497.00, Gregory W. Schafer/CFO, VP/$399,294.00, Todd J. Yancey/VP - Medical Affairs, Patricia A. Oto/VP - Regulatory Affairs, Kathleen Stafford/VP - Human Resources, Douglas Burcz/VP - Marketing, Paul K. Ross/VP, Chief Compliance Officer

Directors: Hollings C. Renton/Chmn., CEO, Pres., Magnus Lundberg/Dir., Wendell Wierenga/Dir., Antonio J. Grillo-Lopez/Dir., Paul Goddard/Dir., Corinne H. Lyle/Dir., Thomas G. Wiggans/Dir.

Owners: Orbimed Advisors LLC/5.46%, Edward F. Kenney, Meditor Capital Management./6.29%, Gregory W. Schafer, Hollings C. Renton/1.08%, Wellington Management Company, LLP/9.36%, Henry J. Fuchs, Randy A. Kelley, Insiders/2.71%, D.E. Shaw & Co. L.P/8.06%, Sectoral Asset Management Inc./7.17%

Financial Data: *Fiscal Year End:*12/31 *Latest Annual Data:* 06/30/2007

Year	Sales	Net Income
2007	NA	NA
2006	$250,000	-$92,681,000
2005	$1,000,000	-$95,174,000

Curr. Assets:	$279,898,000	**Curr. Liab.:**	$23,466,000		
Plant, Equip.:	$1,478,000	**Total Liab.:**	$63,466,000	**Indic. Yr. Divd.:**	NA
Total Assets:	$286,246,000	**Net Worth:**	$222,780,000	**Debt/ Equity:**	NA

Onyx Software Corp

1100 112th Ave. Ne, Ste. 100, Bellevue, WA, 98004; *PH:* 1-425-451-8060; *http://* www.onyx.com

General - Incorporation	WA	**Stock**- Price on:12/24/2007	NA
Employees	NA	Stock Exchange	NA
Auditor	KPMG LLP	Ticker Symbol	NA
Stk Agt	Mellon Investor Services LLC	Outstanding Shares	NA
Counsel	Orrick, Herrington & Sutcliffe LLP	E.P.S	NA
DUNS No.	NA	Shareholders	NA

Business: The group's principle activity is to provide enterprise-wide customer relationship management solutions. The product solution consists of a core e-business engine and three audience-specific portals: the onyx employee portal, the onyx partner portal and the onyx customer portal. Using the Internet in combination with traditional forms of interaction, including phone, mail, fax and e-mail, the group's solution enables enterprises to manage their customer relationships through one integrated, enterprise-wide technology platform. The products are marketed in the United States, Australia, Canada, France, Germany, Hong Kong, Japan, Singapore and other countries in Asia, Europe and Latin America. The customers include credit suisse financial services, agile software, Wisconsin public service, telstra, trizettogroup and australian business limited.

Primary SIC and add'l.: 7372 7378 7379

CIK No: 0001014383

Subsidiaries: Onyx CSN Computer Holding GmbH, Onyx Software Asia Pte. Ltd., Onyx Software Australia PTY, Ltd, Onyx Software Canada Corporation, Onyx Software Co., Ltd, Onyx Software GmbH, Onyx Software Hong Kong Ltd, Onyx Software Professional Services GmbH, Onyx Software UK Limited

Officers: Jeff Tognoni/CEO

OP-TECH Environmental Services Inc

6392 Deere Rd., Syracuse, NY, 13206; *PH:* 1-315-463-1643; *http://* www.op-techenvironmental.com

General - Incorporation	DE	**Stock**- Price on:12/24/2007	$0.55
Employees	180	Stock Exchange	OTC
Auditor	Dannible & Mckee LLP	Ticker Symbol	OTES
Stk Agt	Computershare Trust Co	Outstanding Shares	11,810,000
Counsel..	Rubin Bailinortoli Mayer & Baker LLP	E.P.S	$0.01
DUNS No.	78-675-1750	Shareholders	NA

Business: The group's principal activity is to provide environmental services in upstate New York, Massachusetts, northern Pennsylvania, and New Jersey. It performs industrial cleaning of hazardous and non- hazardous materials and provides varying services relating to plant facility closure, including interior and exterior demolition and asbestos removal. The group also provides remediation services for sites contaminated by hazardous and non-hazardous materials and provides 24-hour emergency spill response services. The services of the group include assessing the regulatory, technical, and construction aspects of the environmental issue and performing the necessary remediation activities. The group also provides liquid tank truck transports equipped with vacuum pumps.

Primary SIC and add'l.: 4959 1795

CIK No: 0000858748

Subsidiaries: Op-tech Avix, Inc., OP-TECH Environmental Services, Ltd.

Officers: Charles B. Morgan/CEO - Syracuse, Christopher J. Polimino/42/Pres., Dawn Glynn/Administrative Assist. - Buffalo, Kevin Cannon/Project Mgr. - Buffalo, Douglas R. Lee/37/CFO, Treasurer, Shannan Hoerger/Environmental, Transportation Compliance Officer - Syracuse, Joe Farrell/Health, Safety Dir. - Syracuse, Plattsburgh, David Roth/VP - Operations, Syracuse, Keith Kemp/Information Technology Mgr. - Syracuse, Colleen Price/Sr. Accounting Mgr. - Syracuse, Deborah Kasarda/Accounting Payable Supervisor, Syracuse, Michael Wright/Branch Mgr. - Albany, Tom Madison/Sr. Sales Mgr. - Albany, Matt Rose/Branch Mgr. - Massena, Shanda Lafave/Administrative Assist. - Massena *(51 Officers included in Index)*

Directors: Robert J. Berger/61/Chmn., Richard Messina/45/Co - Chmn., George W. Lee/59/Dir., Richard Jacobson/44/Dir., Richard L. Elander/66/Dir., Cornelius B. Murphy/63/Dir., Steven A. Sanders/62/Dir.

Owners: Richard Messina/32.00%, Kevin Eldred/6.00%, Robert Berger/9.00%, Jurg Walker/8.00%

Financial Data: *Fiscal Year End:*12/31 *Latest Annual Data:* 12/31/2006

Year	Sales	Net Income
2006	$35,070,000	$355,000
2005	$21,784,000	-$146,000
2004	$18,170,000	$200,000

Curr. Assets:	$14,110,000	**Curr. Liab.:**	$7,206,000	**P/E Ratio:**	55.00
Plant, Equip.:	$3,217,000	**Total Liab.:**	$15,066,000	**Indic. Yr. Divd.:**	NA
Total Assets:	$18,376,000	**Net Worth:**	$3,311,000	**Debt/ Equity:**	2.6160

Open Solutions Inc

455 Winding Brook Dr., Glastonbury, CT, 06033; *PH:* 1-860-652-3155; *http://* www.opensolutions.com

General		**Stock**- Price on:12/24/2007	
Incorporation	DE		NA
Employees	1,100	Stock Exchange	NA
Auditor	PricewaterhouseCoopers LLP	Ticker Symbol	NA
Stk Agt	Computershare Trust Co	Outstanding Shares	NA
Counsel	NA	E.P.S	NA
DUNS No.	NA	Shareholders	NA

Business: The group's principal activity is to provide software and services to financial institutions. The group develops, markets, licenses and supports an enterprise-wide suite of software and services that performs a financial institution's data processing and information management functions, including account transaction, lending operations, back office, client information and reporting. The group's core software and its complementary products access and update real-time data stored in a single relational database, which is designed to deliver strategic benefits to financial institutions. The software can be operated either by the financial institution internally or on an outsourced basis. The group operates primarily in the United States of America. The group acquired maxxar corporation on 24-Feb-2004 and on 23-Jul -2004, omega systems corporation llc.

Primary SIC and add'l.: 7372

CIK No: 0000873538

Subsidiaries: 6259936 Canada, Inc., BIS LP, Inc., BISYS Document Solutions, LLC, BISYS Information Solutions Holdings I, Inc., BISYS Information Solutions Holdings II, Inc., BISYS Information Solutions L.P., Maxxar Corporation, Open Solutions BIS, Inc., Open Solutions Canada (partnership), Open Solutions Canada, Inc., Open Solutions Datawest, Inc., Open Solutions DTS, Inc., Open Solutions RDS Technologies, Inc., Open Solutions Software Services Private Limited, re:Member Data Services, Inc. 17 Subsidiaries included in the Index

Officers: Louis Hernandez/Chmn., CEO, Michael D. Nicastro/Sr. VP, Chief Marketing Officer, Andrew S. Bennett/Exec. VP - International, Dave Krystowiak/Group Exec. VP, Kenneth Saunders/CFO, Exec. VP, Roswell M. Curtis/Group Exec. VP, Rashid Desai/CTO, Sr. VP

Directors: Louis Hernandez/Chmn., CEO, Douglas K. Anderson/Dir., Dennis F. Lynch/Dir., Carlos P. Naudon/Dir., Richard P. Yanak/Dir.

Owners: Massachusetts Financial Services Company/6.90%, Samuel F. McKay, Michael D. Nicastro, Dennis F. Lynch, Roswell M. Curtis, Louis Hernandez/3.40%, Artisan Partners Limited Partnership/8.40%, Howard L. Carver, Insiders/6.70%, Andrew S. Bennett/1.00%, David G. Krystowiak, Kenneth J. Saunders, Douglas K. Anderson, Anchor Capital Advisors, Inc./10.40%, T. Rowe Price Associates, Inc./7.00% *(17 Owners included in Index)*

Open Text Corp

100 Tri-State International Pkwy., 3rd Fl., Lincolnshire, IL, 60069; ***PH:*** 1-847-267-9330; ***Fax:*** 1-847-267-9332; ***http://*** www.opentext.com; ***Email:*** sales@opentext.com

General		**Stock**- Price on:12/24/2007	
Incorporation	Canada		$21.96
Employees	1,894	Stock Exchange	NDQ
Auditor	KPMG LLP	Ticker Symbol	OTEX
Stk Agt	Computershare Trust Co	Outstanding Shares	49,880,000
Counsel	Gardiner Roberts LLP	E.P.S	$0.43
DUNS No.	24-850-3187	Shareholders	NA

Business: The group's principle activities are to develop, market, license and supports collaboration and knowledge management software. These services are used on intranets, extranets and the Internet, to electronically store information and collaborative processes. The services of the group are offered to both as end-user stand-alone products and as fully integrated modules. The group also maintains a business partner support program that provides training and support for original equipment manufacturers and value-added resellers. The group operates in three segments: license and networking, customer support and service. The group's quarterly revenue for September 2007 was 163.97 millions of USD.

Primary SIC and add'l.: 7379 7372

CIK No: 0001002638

Subsidiaries: 2015603 Ontario Ltd., 2016090 Ontario Inc., 2016091 Ontario Inc., 2030928 Ontario Ltd., 6575064 Canada Inc., Artesia Technologies, Inc., Artesia Technologies, UK Limited, Brokercom Inc., Centrinity Ltd., Centrinity UK Ltd., Corechange BV, Corechange Ltd., Corechange Svenska AB, Gauss Interprise AB, Gauss Interprise AG 49 Subsidiaries included in the Index

Officers: John Shackleton/Dir., Pres., CEO - Open Text Corporation, Thomas P. Jenkins/Executive Chmn., Chief Strategy Officer - Open Text Corporation, Paul McFeeters/CFO, Randy Fowlie/Dir., Consultant, Bill Forquer/Exec. VP - ECM Business Development, Kirk Roberts/Exec. VP - Product Solutions, Marketing, John Wilkerson/Exec. VP - Global Sales, Services, Greg Secord/Dir. - Investor Relations, Sonya Mehan/Investor Relations Specialist

Directors: John Shackleton/Dir., Pres., CEO - Open Text Corporation, Thomas P. Jenkins/Executive Chmn., Chief Strategy Officer - Open Text Corporation, Stephen J. Sadler/Dir., Brian J. Jackman/Dir., Gail Hamilton/Dir., Randy Fowlie/Dir., Consultant, Michael Slaunwhite/47/Dir., Ken Olisa/Dir.

Owners: Thomas P. Jenkins/3.00%, Franklin Resources/7.30%, TAL Global Asset Management Inc/5.80%, Randy Fowlie, Beutel, Goodman& Company/12.67%, Ken Olisa, AMVESCAP PLC/9.61%, John Wilkerson, UBS AG/5.10%, FMR Corp./18.00%, Insiders/7.26%, Michael Slaunwhite, Paul McFeeters, Brian Jackman, Phillips, Hager& North Investment Management Ltd./7.10% *(21 Owners included in Index)*

Financial Data: ***Fiscal Year End:***06/30 ***Latest Annual Data:*** 06/30/2007

Year	*Sales*	*Net Income*
2007	$595,664,000	$21,660,000
2006	$409,562,000	$4,978,000
2005	$414,828,000	$20,359,000

Curr. Assets:	$231,538,000	***Curr. Liab.:***	$149,810,000	***P/E Ratio:***	53.56
Plant, Equip.:	$41,262,000	***Total Liab.:***	$206,918,000	***Indic. Yr. Divd.:***	NA
Total Assets:	$671,093,000	***Net Worth:***	$458,371,000	***Debt/ Equity:***	0.7925

Opentv Corp

275 Sacramento St., San Francisco, CA, 94111; ***PH:*** 1-415-962-5000; ***Fax:*** 1-415-962-5300; ***http://*** www.opentv.com

General		**Stock**- Price on:12/24/2007	
Incorporation	British Virgin Islands		$2.2
Employees	492	Stock Exchange	NDQ
Auditor	KPMG LLP	Ticker Symbol	OPTV
Stk Agt	Mellon Investor Services LLC	Outstanding Shares	138,580,000
Counsel	NA	E.P.S	-$0.1
DUNS No.	NA	Shareholders	NA

Business: The group's principal activity is to provide software, content and applications and professional services for interactive and enhanced television. It provides the core software and related technologies that permit cable, satellite and terrestrial operators, television programmers and advertisers to offer viewers interactive and enhanced television experiences. It develops and manages branded interactive television channels and offers a suite of managed services and applications to simplify the business of interactive television and market research for network operators, programmers and advertisers. The group's team of skilled and experienced managers and software engineers help network operators and set-top box manufacturers build, integrate and deploy interactive and enhanced television services.

Primary SIC and add'l.: 7372 6719

CIK No: 0001096958

Subsidiaries: 4G Media Ltd., ACTV Entertainment, Inc., ACTV, Inc., Advision LLC, BettingCorp. UK Ltd., Digital Adco, Inc., HyperTV Networks, Inc., Intellocity USA, Inc., Media Online Services, Inc., OpenGaming Ltd., OpenPlay (BVI)Ltd., OpenTV (Cayman) Digital Solutions, OpenTV AG, OpenTV Australia Pty Ltd, OpenTV Europe S.A.S. 31 Subsidiaries included in the Index

Officers: Ben Bennett/COO, Acting CEO/$852,845.00, Michael Ivanchenko/Sr. VP - Sales, Joel Zdepski/Sr. VP - Technology, Architecture, Shum Mukherjee/57/CFO, Exec. VP/$591,219.00, Mark Beariault/General Counsel, Sid Gregory/Sr. VP - Engineering, Tracy Geist/Sr. VP - Marketing Development, Tony Webster/Sr. VP - Human Resources, Nigel W. Bennett/Sr. VP, GM - Europe, Middle East, Africa

Directors: James A. Chiddix/Vice Chmn., Alan A. Guggenheim/58/Dir., Jerry MacHovina/Dir., David J. Wargo/54/Dir., Andre Kudelski/Dir., Joseph Deiss/Dir., Lucien Gani/Dir., Mercer Reynolds/Dir., Pierre Roy/Dir., Mauro Saladini/Dir., Claude Smadja/Dir., Eric Tveter/Dir.

Owners: Scott Wornow, Kudelski SA, Sun Microsystems, Inc./7.00%, Tim Evard, Joseph Deiss, Insiders, Alan A. Guggenheim, Kudelski SA/6.10%, David J. Wargo, Insiders/7.30%, Andr Kudelski, Andr Kudelski/6.10%, Nigel W. Bennett, Shum Mukherjee, Jerry Machovina *(16 Owners included in Index)*

Financial Data: ***Fiscal Year End:***12/31 ***Latest Annual Data:*** 12/31/2006

Year	*Sales*	*Net Income*
2006	$101,908,000	-$10,818,000
2005	$87,380,000	-$8,473,000
2004	$77,169,000	-$21,962,000

Curr. Assets:	$83,656,000	***Curr. Liab.:***	$38,259,000		
Plant, Equip.:	$7,231,000	***Total Liab.:***	$52,447,000	***Indic. Yr. Divd.:***	NA
Total Assets:	$220,764,000	***Net Worth:***	$167,831,000	***Debt/ Equity:***	NA

Openwave Systems Inc

2100 Seaport Blvd., Redwood City, CA, 94063; ***PH:*** 1-650-480-8000; ***Fax:*** 1-650-480-8100; ***http://*** www.openwave.com

General		**Stock**- Price on:12/24/2007	
Incorporation	DE		$6.731
Employees	1,452	Stock Exchange	NDQ
Auditor	KPMG LLP	Ticker Symbol	OPWV
Stk Agt	U.S. Stock Transfer Corp	Outstanding Shares	82,750,000
Counsel	NA	E.P.S	-$2.12
DUNS No.	NA	Shareholders	NA

Business: The group's principal activity is to provide software applications and services that enable the convergence of the Internet and wireless communications. The software products consist of client software for browsing and multi-media messaging, infrastructure software such as wireless application protocol, or wap, gateways and wireless and wireline applications, such as email and multimedia messaging and related services. The applications are used by network operators to provide Internet services to the wireless subscribers and wireless telephone manufacturers. The group provides call management, billing history information, pricing plan subscription and voice message management services. It also provides subscribers with a unified mailbox for e-mail, voicemail, and facsimile. The customers of the group include sprint, kddi and mm02. On 02-Aug-2004, the group acquired magic4.

Primary SIC and add'l.: 7379 7371 7373 7372

CIK No: 0001082506

Subsidiaries: Magic4 SARL, Magic4, Inc., Mobile Position AB, Nihon Openwave Systems KK, Openwave Aries Inc., Openwave ScriptEase Inc., Openwave Systems (Canada) Ltd., Openwave Systems (Denmark) ApS, Openwave Systems (Espana) S.L., Openwave Systems (Europe) Ltd., Openwave Systems (France) SAS, Openwave Systems (H.K.) Ltd., Openwave Systems (Holdings) Ltd., Openwave Systems (Ireland) Ltd., Openwave Systems (Italia) SRL 37 Subsidiaries included in the Index

Officers: Robert Vrij/Dir., CEO, Pres., Jean-Yves Dexmier/CFO, Hari Haran/Sr. VP - Worldwide Field Operations, Michael Luna/CTO, Caroline Farrar/Contact - Stock Sales, Jonathan Spinney/Sr. Marketing Mgr., Martin Dunsby/Sr. VP, GM - Global Service, Alison Simmons/Contact - Bite Communications, Europe, John Boden/Sr. VP - Product Management, Vikki Herrera/Sr. Mgr. - Public Relations, Dan Nguyen/Dir. - Product Management, Jeffrey K. Li/Corp. Sec., Jan Lowdon/Mgr. - Marketing Communications, EMEA, Europe, Mariko Kato/Contact - Japan

Directors: Robert Vrij/Dir., CEO, Pres., Kenneth D. Denman/50/Dir., Bo Hedfors/Dir., Gerald Held/Dir., William T. Morrow/Dir., Patrick Jones/Dir., Charles E. Levine/55/Dir.

Owners: Richard Lee Schwartz, David C. Peterschmidt, Harold L. Covert, Bo C. Hedfors, Entities affiliated with S Squared Technology, LLC/6.60%, Patrick Jones, Robert Vrij, William Morrow, Masood Jabbar, Entities affiliated with Galleon Management, L.P./6.10%, Charles E. Levine, Gerald Held, Bernard C. Puckett, Allen E. Snyder, Entities affiliated with FMR Corp./16.20% *(17 Owners included in Index)*

Financial Data: ***Fiscal Year End:***06/30 ***Latest Annual Data:*** 6/30/2006

Year	*Sales*	*Net Income*
2006	$412,010,000	$5,236,000
2005	$383,635,000	-$62,129,000
2004	$290,791,000	-$29,851,000

Curr. Assets:	$602,962,000	***Curr. Liab.:***	$151,534,000		
Plant, Equip.:	$20,784,000	***Total Liab.:***	$380,236,000	***Indic. Yr. Divd.:***	NA
Total Assets:	$919,831,000	***Net Worth:***	$539,595,000	***Debt/ Equity:***	0.3830

Ophthalmic Imaging Systems

221 Lathrop Way, Ste. I, Sacramento, CA, 95815; ***PH:*** 1-916-646-2020; ***Fax:*** 1-916-646-0207; ***http://*** www.oisi.com; ***Email:*** info@oisi.com

General		**Stock**- Price on:12/24/2007	
Incorporation	CA		$2
Employees	59	Stock Exchange	OTC
Auditor	Perry-Smith LLP	Ticker Symbol	OISI
Stk Agt	American Securities T & T Inc.	Outstanding Shares	16,510,000
Counsel	NA	E.P.S	$0.13
DUNS No.	16-191-9410	Shareholders	NA

Business: The group's principal activity is to design, develop, manufacture and market digital imaging system, image enhancement and analysis software and related products and services used by the practitioners in the ocular healthcare field. The group's product, targets the needs of the ophthalmic fluorescein angiography market and the indocyanine green market. The current flagship product in the group's angiography line is its digital imaging systems. The group's product includes winstation systems, digital fundus imager, digital slit lamp imager and slit lamps. Retina specialists and general ophthalmologists use the winstation systems. The digital fundus imagers are used by a majority of eye care practitioners. Eye care practitioners use the digital slit lamp imagers with an emphasis on imaging the front of the eye. Slit lamps are imaging devices used in virtually ophthalmic and optometric practices.

Primary SIC and add'l.: 7372 3845

CIK No: 0000885317

Officers: Gil Allon/CEO, Donna Turner/Midwest Regional Sales Mgr., Chris Fotos/Southeast Regional Sales Mgr., Chad A. Steward/Southwest Regional Sales Mgr., Ariel Shenhar/CFO, Tony Migon/National Sales Mgr. - Central Region, Glenn Erickson/Eastern Regional Sales Mgr., John Walton-Cale/Mid, Atlantic Regional Sales Mgr.

Directors: Yigal Berman/Chmn.

Owners: Wasatch Advisors/6.00%, Healthinvest Partners/7.60%, Ariel Shenhar/1.60%, Gil Allon/2.70%, MediVision Medical Imaging Ltd./56.00%, Insiders/4.40%

Financial Data: *Fiscal Year End:*12/31 *Latest Annual Data:* 12/31/2006

Year	Sales	Net Income
2006	$15,797,000	$2,251,000
2005	$13,651,000	$1,755,000
2004	$10,818,000	$1,705,000

Curr. Assets:	$11,594,000	Curr. Liab.:	$4,357,000	P/E Ratio:	15.38
Plant, Equip.:	$391,000	Total Liab.:	$4,511,000	Indic. Yr. Divd.:	NA
Total Assets:	$12,667,000	Net Worth:	$8,156,000	Debt/ Equity:	0.0174

Opinion Research Corp

600 College Rd. E, Ste. 4100, Princeton, NJ, 08540; *PH:* 1-609-452-5272; *http://* www.opinionresearch.com

General - Incorporation	DE	Stock- Price on:12/24/2007	NA
Employees	NA	Stock Exchange	NA
Auditor	Grant Thornton, Ernst & Young	Ticker Symbol	NA
Stk Agt	NA	Outstanding Shares	NA
Counsel	Wolf Block Schorr & Solis-Cohen LLP	E.P.S	NA
DUNS No.	00-254-3239	Shareholders	NA

Business: The group's principle activity is to conduct research on the public opinion polling. The group assists its clients to evaluate, monitor and optimize the effectiveness of their marketing and sales strategies. The group provides market research, social research, business information services, marketing services and telemarketing services. The services and products address issues like customer loyalty, market demand and forecasting, corporate image, competitive positioning and model-based telemarketing. The group collects customer market information through computer assisted telephone interviews, personal interviews, mail questionnaires and other techniques such as business panels. The group offers services to clients in north American, Europe, Asian and latin American markets.

Primary SIC and add'l.: 8732 8742

CIK No: 0000911673

Subsidiaries: European Information Centre Limited, Macro International Inc., O.R.C. International Ltd., Opinion Research Corporation, S.A. de C.V., ORC Holdings, Ltd., ORC International Holdings, Inc., ORC Korea, Ltd., ORC Telecommunications Ltd., ORC TeleService Corp., Rating Research LLC, Social& Health Services, Ltd.

Officers: Jeffrey T. Resnick/Exec. VP, Global MD, Linda G. Shea/Sr. VP, Global MD - Customer Strategies, Howard L. Lax/VP - Customer Strategies, John S. Watts/Sr. VP, Global MD - Value Based Marketing, Decision Science

Opko Health Inc

Formerly: Exegenics Inc
4400 Biscayne Blvd., Ste. 900, Miami, FL, 33137; *PH:* 1-305-575-6015

General - Incorporation	DE	Stock- Price on:12/24/2007	NA
Employees	NA	Stock Exchange	AMEX
Auditor	Rotenberg & Co. LLP	Ticker Symbol	OPK
Stk Agt	Meyers Associates LP	Outstanding Shares	NA
Counsel	Mintz Levin Cohn Ferris Et Al	E.P.S	NA
DUNS No.	78-398-0345	Shareholders	NA

Business: The group's principle activity is to exploit new enabling technologies to advance and shorten the new drug development cycle. As the group was unsuccessful at advancing research programs, it decided to focus on developing and marketing products to physicians practicing in specialist areas and entered into an agreement and plan of merger and reorganization with innovative drug delivery systems. This proposed merger had significant shareholder opposition and hence, both the companies reached a mutual decision to terminate the merger effort and completed it. During 2003, it discontinued its drug discovery operations and terminated all research activities in which it was involved before and began identifying potential business opportunities. The group operates from United States.

Primary SIC and add'l.: 2834 8731

CIK No: 0000944809

Officers: John A. Paganelli/73/Chmn., Interim CEO/$100,810.00, David F. Hostelley/68/CFO, Adam Logal/Exec. Dir. - Finance, Chief Accounting Officer, Treasurer

Directors: John A. Paganelli/73/Chmn., Interim CEO, Robert A. Baron/Dir., Adam Logal/Exec. Dir. - Finance, Chief Accounting Officer, Treasurer, Jane Hsiao/Dir., Subbarao V. Uppaluri/Dir.

Owners: Steven D. Rubin, David Eichler, Phillip Frost, Johnson & Johnson Development Corporation, Insiders, Psilos Group Partners II-S, Rao Uppaluri, The Frost Group, Michael Reich, Robert Baron, Frost Gamma Investments Trust, Richard A. Lerner, Jane H. Hsiao, John A. Paganelli, Adam Logal

Curr. Assets:	$8,752,000	Curr. Liab.:	$674,000		
Plant, Equip.:	NA	Total Liab.:	$674,000	Indic. Yr. Divd.:	NA
Total Assets:	$8,752,000	Net Worth:	$8,078,000	Debt/ Equity:	NA

Oplink Communications Inc

46335 Landing Pkwy., Fremont, CA, 94538; *PH:* 1-510-933-7200; *Fax:* 1-510-933-7300; *http://* www.oplink.com; *Email:* info@oplink.com

General - Incorporation	DE	Stock- Price on:12/24/2007	$15.42
Employees	2,067	Stock Exchange	NDQ
Auditor	Burr, Pilger & Mayer LLP	Ticker Symbol	OPLK
Stk Agt	Bank of New York	Outstanding Shares	22,280,000
Counsel	Cooley Godward LLP	E.P.S	$0.52
DUNS No.	NA	Shareholders	NA

Business: The group's principal activities are to design, manufacture and market fiber optic components and integrated optical modules that increase the performance of optical networks. The group produces fiber optic subsystems, integrated modules and components for next-generation, all-optical dense wavelength division multiplexing (dwdm), optical amplification, routing, monitoring and conditioning applications. The products are categorized into two groups: bandwidth creation products which includes wavelength expansion and optical amplification products. The bandwidth management products includes wavelength performance monitoring, protection and optical switching products. The group has manufacturing operations in san jose, California, zhuhai and fuzhou in China. On 3-Nov-2003 the group acquired redclover networks, inc and on 09-Mar-2004, the group acquired accumux technologies, inc.

Primary SIC and add'l.: 3357 3679

CIK No: 0001022225

Subsidiaries: Accumux Technologies, Inc., Cayman Oplink Communications, Inc., Commonwealth Trust Limited, F3 Inc., George Town, Grand Cayman, Cayman Islands, King Galaxy International Limited, Limited, Oplink Macau Commercial Services Company, P.O. Box 3321, Road Town, Tortola, British Virgin Islands., Shanghai Oplink Communications, Inc., Taiwan Oplink Communications, Inc., Ugland House, South Church Street, Zhuhai FTZ Oplink Communications, Inc., Zhuhai FTZ Oplink Optical Communications, Inc.

Officers: Joseph Y. Liu/Dir., CEO, Pres., Janey Lin/Contact - Investor Relations, Shirley Yin/CFO, Thomas P. Keegan/54/VP - Business Development, General Counsel, Sec., Charles Ingebretsen/Chief Quality Officer, Yanfeng Yang/Corporate VP - Operations, James Cheng/GM - China, Macau, River Gong/VP - Sales

Directors: Joseph Y. Liu/Dir., CEO, Pres., Leonard J. Leblanc/Chmn., Jesse W. Jack/Dir., Chieh Chang/Dir., Hua Lee/Dir.

Owners: Chi-Min Cheng, River Gong, FMR Corp./10.00%, Hua Lee, Chieh Chang/2.30%, Insiders/7.70%, AXA Financial, Inc,/5.20%, LeRoy C. Kopp and Kopp Investment Advisors, Inc./5.10%, Joseph Y. Liu/4.20%, Shirley Yin, Yangfeng Yang, Leonard J. LeBlanc, Jesse W. Jack, Robert Shih, Bruce D. Horn

Financial Data: *Fiscal Year End:*07/30 *Latest Annual Data:* 6/30/2006

Year	Sales	Net Income
2006	$54,846,000	$1,938,000
2005	$34,355,000	-$2,647,000
2004	$34,328,000	-$6,441,000

Curr. Assets:	$149,008,000	Curr. Liab.:	$10,732,000	P/E Ratio:	29.77
Plant, Equip.:	$23,443,000	Total Liab.:	$10,815,000	Indic. Yr. Divd.:	NA
Total Assets:	$237,955,000	Net Worth:	$227,140,000	Debt/ Equity:	NA

Opnet Technologies Inc

7255 Woodmont Ave., Bethesda, MD, 20814; *PH:* 1-240-497-3000; *Fax:* 1-240-497-3001; *http://* www.opnet.com; *Email:* info@opnet.com

General - Incorporation	DE	Stock- Price on:12/24/2007	$11.36
Employees	490	Stock Exchange	NDQ
Auditor	Deloitte & Touche LLP	Ticker Symbol	OPNT
Stk Agt	American Stock Transfer & Trust Co.	Outstanding Shares	20,610,000
Counsel	Hale & Dorr LLP	E.P.S	$0.31
DUNS No.	NA	Shareholders	NA

Business: The group's principal activity is to provide management software for network and applications. These software solutions address application performance troubleshooting; network configuration auditing; network capacity and resiliency planning; application deployment planning and network technology research and development. The products include it guru(R), netbiz(R), netdoctor(R), opnet(R), opnet modeler(R), sp guru(R), wdm guru(R), opnet technologies, inc.(R), opnetwork(R), and vne servertmare trademarks. The group's customers are large and medium-sized enterprises, service providers including telecommunications carriers and Internet service providers, network equipment manufacturers & government agencies. The group has operations in France, United Kingdom, Belgium and Australia. The products are distributed in Australia, Brazil, China,France, Germany, Greece, Italy, Israel, Japan, Latin America, the Middle East, Poland, scandinavia, Singapore, South Africa.

Primary SIC and add'l.: 7379 7372 8243 6794

CIK No: 0001108924

Subsidiaries: OPNET Technologies Limited, OPNET Technologies Pty Limited, OPNET Technologies Societe par Actions Simplifiee, OPNET Technologies, GmbH

Officers: Marc A. Cohen/Chmn., CEO/$330,144.00, Pradeep K. Singh/Sr. VP - Model Research, Development, Alain J. Cohen/Pres., CTO/$326,990.00, Melvin F. Wesley/CFO, VP/$227,714.00, Yevgeny Gurevich/Sr. VP - Core Technologies, Joseph J. Lenz/Sr. VP - International Sales, Dennis R. McCoy/VP, General Counsel, Alberto Morales/Sr. VP - Information Systems, CIO, Eric S. Nudelman/Sr. VP - Applications Engineering, Training, Edward A. Sykes/Sr. VP, Chief Scientist

Directors: Marc A. Cohen/Chmn., CEO, Steven G. Finn/Dir., Ronald W. Kaiser/Dir., William F. Stasior/Dir.

Owners: Insiders/37.30%, Marc A. Cohen/13.80%, Ronald W. Kaiser, Alain J. Cohen/22.80%, William F. Stasior, Mel F. Wesley, Steven G. Finn

Financial Data: *Fiscal Year End:*03/31 *Latest Annual Data:* 3/31/2007

Year	Sales	Net Income
2007	$95,130,000	$7,965,000
2006	$76,115,000	$2,137,000
2005	$64,243,000	$2,052,000

Curr. Assets:	$121,047,000	Curr. Liab.:	$31,679,000	P/E Ratio:	29.89
Plant, Equip.:	$8,745,000	Total Liab.:	$34,787,000	Indic. Yr. Divd.:	NA
Total Assets:	$147,658,000	Net Worth:	$112,871,000	Debt/ Equity:	NA

Oppenheimer Holdings Inc

Oppenheimer & Co. Inc, 125 Broad St., New York, NY, 10004; *PH:* 1-212-668-8000; *Fax:* 1-800-221-5588; *http://* www.opco.com; *Email:* info@opco.com

General - Incorporation	ON	**Stock** - Price on:12/24/2007	$48.79
Employees	2,993	Stock Exchange	NYSE
Auditor	PricewaterhouseCoopers LLP	Ticker Symbol	OPY
Stk Agt	Mellon Trust Co	Outstanding Shares	13,220,000
Counsel	NA	E.P.S	$3.673
DUNS No.	NA	Shareholders	NA

Business: The group is a diversified financial services holding company with subsidiaries that offer a variety of investment and financial services, including securities brokerage, investment banking, and asset management. The group's principal subsidiaries are: fahnestock & co., inc. Operating 92 branch offices in 20 states and 3 foreign countries, fahnestock asset management which provides investment advisory services and freedom investments, inc. The group also provides investment advisory services and operates discount brokerage business based in omaha and Nebraska. The group's quarterly revenue for September 2007 was 215.17 millions of USD.

Primary SIC and add'l.: 6719 6282 6211

CIK No: 0000791963

Subsidiaries: Evanston Financial, Inc., Freedom Investments, Inc., Josephthal & Co. Inc., Oppenheimer & Co. Inc., Oppenheimer Asset Management Inc, Prime Charter, Ltd.

Officers: Albert G. Lowenthal/62/Chmn., CEO/$5,156,156.00, A. W. Oughtred/65/Dir., Sec., Elaine K. Roberts/56/Dir., CFO, Pres., Treasurer/$826,610.00

Directors: Albert G. Lowenthal/62/Chmn., CEO, R. Crystal/67/Dir., A. W. Oughtred/65/Dir., Sec., J. L. Bitove/80/Dir., K. W. McArthur/72/Dir., Elaine K. Roberts/56/Dir., CFO, Pres., Treasurer, B. Winberg/83/Dir.

Owners: J. L. Bitove/3.30%, Insiders/25.10%, E. K. Roberts/1.50%, R. Crystal, Howson Tattersall Investment Counsel Ltd./9.70%, E. K. Roberts, R. Okin, A. W. Oughtred, Private Capital Management, L.P/19.70%, Insiders, Olga Roberts/2.50%, K. W. McArthur, J. L. Bitove, Albert G. Lowenthal/21.90%, Albert G. Lowenthal *(19 Owners included in Index)*

Financial Data: ***Fiscal Year End:***12/31 ***Latest Annual Data:*** 12/31/2006

Year	Sales	Net Income
2006	$800,823,000	$44,577,000
2005	$679,746,000	$22,916,000
2004	$655,140,000	$21,077,000

Curr. Assets:	$1,703,196,000	**Curr. Liab.:**	$1,577,663,000	**P/E Ratio:**	13.28
Plant, Equip.:	$16,478,000	**Total Liab.:**	$1,801,049,000	**Indic. Yr. Divd.:**	$0.440
Total Assets:	$2,160,090,000	**Net Worth:**	$359,041,000	**Debt/ Equity:**	0.3847

Opsware Inc

599 N Mathilda Ave., Sunnyvale, CA, 94086; ; ***http://*** www.opswareinc.com

General - Incorporation	DE	**Stock** - Price on:12/24/2007	$9.65
Employees	452	Stock Exchange	NA
Auditor	Ernst & Young LLP	Ticker Symbol	NA
Stk Agt	American Stock Transfer & Trust Co.	Outstanding Shares	NA
Counsel	NA	E.P.S	NA
DUNS No.	NA	Shareholders	NA

Business: The group's principal activity is to provide information technology automation software. The services provided by the using its proprietary opsware system, is comprised of two primary layers, the automation platform and automation applications. Automation platform controls and automates operations in single locations and across geographically disparate application environments. Automation applications are the modules that automate particular it processes performed by users in the operational environment. The group provides managed Internet services that address the challenges associated with deploying, maintaining and growing Internet operations for critical business functions. Currently, the customers of the group are agencies of United States government, comcast, gateway computers, new breed and metlife. The group operates in the united sates and Europe. The group acquired tangram enterprise solutions inc on Feb 20, 2004.

Primary SIC and add'l.: 7379

CIK No: 0001100813

Subsidiaries: EURL Opsware France, Opsware B.V., Opsware Germany GmbH, Opsware Singapore Pte Ltd., Opsware UK Ltd.

Officers: Benjamin Horowitz/Dir., CEO, Pres./$2,045,354.00, Scott Kupor/Sr. VP - Customer Solutions, Kevin McGuirk/Sr. VP - Corporate Communications, Jason Rosenthal/Sr. VP - Server Automation Products, Karli Overmier/Contact - Product Public Relations, Alex Burreson/Contact - Sales Inquiries, Central Region, Deirdre Boyle/Customer Contact, Victor Espino/Sales Mgr. - All Regions, Jordan Breslow/General Counsel, David Conte/CFO/$601,786.00, John Ofarrell/Exec. VP - Business Development/$783,442.00, Tim Howes/CTO, Mark Cranney/Exec. VP - Worldwide Field Operations/$1,817,352.00, Sharmila Shahani/Exec. VP - Marketing, Jim Adkins/Exec. VP - Products *(27 Officers included in Index)*

Directors: Benjamin Horowitz/Dir., CEO, Pres., Marc Andreessen/Chmn., Co - Founder, William Campbell/Dir., Michelangelo Volpi/Dir., Simon Lorne/Dir., Michael Ovitz/Dir.

Owners: David F. Conte, William V. Campbell, Mark D. Cranney, Michael S. Ovitz/1.10%, Mike J. Homer, John L. OFarrell/1.00%, Michelangelo A. Volpi, Delaware Management Holdings/5.20%, FMR Corp./14.40%, James E. Adkins, Sharlene P. Abrams, Benjamin A. Horowitz/5.50%, Insiders/24.30%, Marc L. Andreessen/9.10%, Simon M. Lorne

Financial Data: ***Fiscal Year End:***01/31 ***Latest Annual Data:*** 1/31/2007

Year	Sales	Net Income
2007	$101,726,000	-$16,069,000
2006	$61,077,000	-$14,751,000
2005	$37,792,000	-$7,246,000

Curr. Assets:	$129,119,000	**Curr. Liab.:**	$49,074,000		
Plant, Equip.:	$5,898,000	**Total Liab.:**	$51,269,000	**Indic. Yr. Divd.:**	NA
Total Assets:	$182,045,000	**Net Worth:**	$130,776,000	**Debt/ Equity:**	0.0003

Opt-Sciences Corp

1912 Bannard St., Cinnaminson, NJ, 08077; ***PH:*** 1-856-829-2800; ***Fax:*** 1-856-829-0482; ***http://*** www.optsciences.com; ***Email:*** sales@optsciences.com

General - Incorporation	NJ	**Stock** - Price on:12/24/2007	$9.5744
Employees	40	Stock Exchange	OTC
Auditor	Goff Backa, Alfera & Co. LLC	Ticker Symbol	OPST
Stk Agt	StockTrans, Inc.	Outstanding Shares	NA
Counsel	Kania, Linder, Lasak & Feeney	E.P.S	$0.64
DUNS No.	00-233-8838	Shareholders	NA

Business: The group's principal activities are to provide optical coatings, filters, faceplates and lighting wedges, which improve display readability for electronic instruments used primarily in aircraft. This includes application of different types of anti-reflection coatings, transparent conductive coatings and other optical coatings. The group's products are designed to enable pilots to read aircraft instruments in direct sunlight or at night or in covert situations using appropriate night vision filters. It also provides full glass cutting, grinding and painting operations which augment its optical coating capabilities. The group conducts its business through its wholly owned subsidiary, o & s research, inc.

Primary SIC and add'l.: 3827

CIK No: 0000074688

Subsidiaries: O & S Research, Inc, OPT-Sciences, Raytheon Corporation

Officers: Anderson L. McCabe/CEO, CFO, Pres., Arthur J. Kania/Sec., Lorraine Domask/Chief Accountant, Arthur J. Kania/75/Dir., Sec.

Owners: Anderson L. McCabe, Rose Sayen/66.00%, Insiders/3.00%, Arthur J. Kania/3.00%

Financial Data: ***Fiscal Year End:***10/29 ***Latest Annual Data:*** 10/28/2006

Year	Sales	Net Income
2006	$4,265,000	$404,000
2005	$4,323,000	$349,000
2004	$4,068,000	$199,000

Curr. Assets:	$6,966,000	**Curr. Liab.:**	$405,000	**P/E Ratio:**	21.00
Plant, Equip.:	$974,000	**Total Liab.:**	$405,000	**Indic. Yr. Divd.:**	NA
Total Assets:	$7,943,000	**Net Worth:**	$7,537,000	**Debt/ Equity:**	NA

Optelecom Inc

12920 Cloverleaf Ctr. Dr., Germantown, MD, 20874; ***PH:*** 1-301-444-2200; ***http://*** www.optelecom.com

General - Incorporation	DE	**Stock** - Price on:12/24/2007	$7.73
Employees	177	Stock Exchange	NDQ
Auditor	Grant Thornton LLP	Ticker Symbol	OPTC
Stk Agt	American Stock Transfer & Trust Co.	Outstanding Shares	3,420,000
Counsel	NA	E.P.S	$0.20
DUNS No.	07-265-8529	Shareholders	NA

Business: The group's principal activities are the designing and manufacturing of communication products and laser systems. The group operates in two segments: communication product division and electro-optics division: the communication product division develops, manufactures and sells optical fiber-based data communication equipment to both commercial and government clients. The electro-optics division focuses on interferometric fiber optic gyro coils, which are components in rotation-sensing instruments. These instruments replace mechanical and laser gyros in aircraft, missiles, and other vehicles. The group operates in the United States and the United Kingdom.

Primary SIC and add'l.: 3699 3357

CIK No: 0000275858

Subsidiaries: Optelecom UK Limited, Optelecom-NKF Limited, Optelecom-NKF S.A.S., Optelecom-NKF S.L, Optelecom-NKF, B.V., Optelecom-NKF, Inc.

Officers: Edmund Ludwig/Chmn., CEO, Pres./$612,447.00, James Armstrong/Dir., Exec. VP - US Federal Systems, Business Development, CFO/$260,153.00, Thomas W.M. Overwijn/45/Dir., COO, Exec. VP - European Union Unit/$350,773.00, Steven Tamburo/CFO/$143,817.00, Roland Hooghiemstra/VP - Sales, Marketing/$251,694.00, Greg Hall/VP - Manufacturing, Michiel Wensing/Sales Dir. - North Europe, Middle East Michiel Wensing, Ron Rogers/Regional Sales Mgr. - US Mid, Atlantic, Midwestern, Sales Office Maryland, Natividad Dominguez/Inside Sales, Customer Service - Spain, Richard De Nijs/Inside Sales Customer Service, Betsy Lanning/Integrator, Representative Support Coordinator, USA, Mgr. - Marketing Communications, USA, Yin Kiat Chan/Sales Dir. - Far East, Anthony Tan/Area Mgr. - Singapore, David Tan/Technical Support Engineer - Singapore, Fabien Haubert/Sales Dir. - South Europe, Africa *(43 Officers included in Index)*

Directors: Edmund Ludwig/Chmn., CEO, Pres., James Armstrong/Dir., Exec. VP - US Federal Systems, Business Development, CFO, Thomas W.M. Overwijn/45/Dir., COO, Exec. VP - European Union Unit, Walter Fatzinger/Dir., David Lipinski/Dir., Carl Rubbo/Dir., Robert Urso/Dir.

Owners: Insiders/11.40%, Thomas Overwijn/1.10%, Walrus Partners LLC/8.00%, Carl J. Rubbo/1.00%, Steven Tamburo, Walter R. Fatzinger, Robert F. Urso, Edmund D. Ludwig/4.10%, Roland Hooghiemstra, James Armstrong/1.30%, David R. Lipinski

Financial Data: ***Fiscal Year End:***12/31 ***Latest Annual Data:*** 12/31/2006

Year	Sales	Net Income
2006	$39,484,000	$1,554,000
2005	$33,865,000	$2,682,000
2004	$19,395,000	$1,595,000

Curr. Assets:	$20,503,000	**Curr. Liab.:**	$10,498,000	**P/E Ratio:**	38.65
Plant, Equip.:	$2,488,000	**Total Liab.:**	$28,331,000	**Indic. Yr. Divd.:**	NA
Total Assets:	$46,274,000	**Net Worth:**	$17,943,000	**Debt/ Equity:**	0.7958

Opti Inc

3430 W Bayshore Rd. , Ste. 103, Palo Alto, CA, 94303; ***PH:*** 1-650-213-8550; ***Fax:*** 1-650-213-8551; ***http://*** www.opti.com

General - Incorporation	CA	**Stock** - Price on:12/24/2007	$5.05
Employees	1	Stock Exchange	OTC
Auditor	Ernst & Young LLP	Ticker Symbol	OPTI
Stk Agt	Computershare Investor Services LLC	Outstanding Shares	11,630,000
Counsel	NA	E.P.S	-$0.26
DUNS No.	60-619-7705	Shareholders	NA

Business: The group's principal activity is licensing of its intellectual property for use principally by personal computer manufacturers and semiconductor device manufacturers.

Primary SIC and add'l.: 3577

CIK No: 0000899297

Subsidiaries: Media Chips, OPTi Acquisition, OPTi International Inc.

Officers: Bernard T. Marren/72/Chmn., CEO, Pres., Michael F. Mazzoni/45/CFO, Sec.

Directors: Bernard T. Marren/72/Chmn., CEO, Pres., Stephen F. Diamond/52/Dir., Kapil K. Nanda/62/Dir., William H. Welling/74/Dir.

Owners: Bernard T. Marren, Dimensional Fund Advisors LP/5.40%, William Welling, Kapil Nanda, Whitaker Group/8.60%, Raffles Associates, L.P./6.80%, MG Capital Management, LLC/13.80%, Insiders/1.30%, S. Muoio& Co. LLC/9.90%

Financial Data: ***Fiscal Year End:***03/31 ***Latest Annual Data:*** 03/31/2007

Year	Sales	Net Income
2007	$11,000,000	$7,008,000
2006	NA	-$1,968,000
2005	$52,000	-$1,173,000

Curr. Assets:	$12,939,000	Curr. Liab.:	$628,000	P/E Ratio:	8.42
Plant, Equip.:	$8,000	Total Liab.:	$628,000	Indic. Yr. Divd.:	NA
Total Assets:	$12,961,000	Net Worth:	$12,333,000	Debt/ Equity:	NA

Optibase Ltd

880 Maude Ave., Mountain View, CA, 94043; **PH:** 1-650-230-2400; **Fax:** 1-650-691-9998;
http:// www.optibase.com

General - Incorporation	Israel	Stock - Price on:12/24/2007	$4.48
Employees	122	Stock Exchange	NDQ
Auditor	Kost Forer Gabbay & Kasierer	Ticker Symbol	OBAS
Stk Agt	Ernest & Young LLP	Outstanding Shares	13,500,000
Counsel	NA	E.P.S.	-$0.25
DUNS No.	NA	Shareholders	NA

Business: The groups principle activity is to provide high-quality, cost-effective solutions that enable the preparation and delivery of digital video over ATM and ip-based networks. The group operates from United States.

Primary SIC and add'l.: 7372

CIK No: 0001077618

Subsidiaries: Californian corporation, Optibase B.V

Officers: Tom Wyler/Chmn., CEO, David Sackstein/CTO, VP - Research & Development, Udi Shani/Exec. VP - International Sales, Technical Support, Orna Gil-Bar/VP - Human Resources, Danny Lustiger/Contact, Yaron Comarov/VP - Operations, Adam Schadle/VP - North America Sales, Yossi Aloni/VP - Marketing, Amir Philips/CFO, Meir Sudry/VP - Professional Services, Yael Lapid/Contact, Tally Netzer/Dir. - Corporate Communications

Directors: Tom Wyler/Chmn., CEO, Alex Hilman/Dir., Gil Weiser/Dir., Dana Tamir/Dir., Haim Labenski/Dir., Chaim Labenski/60/Dir.

Owners: Tom Wyler/19.25%, Arthur Mayer - Sommer/8.87%, Kern Capital Management LLC/14.52%, Insiders/22.60%

Financial Data: Fiscal Year End:12/31 **Latest Annual Data:** 12/31/2006

Year	Sales	Net Income
2006	$17,977,000	-$3,120,000
2005	$22,388,000	-$3,445,000
2004	$20,848,000	-$3,680,000

Curr. Assets:	$54,451,000	Curr. Liab.:	$14,109,000		
Plant, Equip.:	$1,700,000	Total Liab.:	$16,480,000	Indic. Yr. Divd.:	NA
Total Assets:	$60,974,000	Net Worth:	$44,494,000	Debt/ Equity:	NA

Optical Cable Corp

5290 Concourse Dr., Roanoke, VA, 24019; **PH:** 1-540-265-0690; **Fax:** 1-540-265-0724;
http:// www.occfiber.com; **Email:** marketinginfo@occfiber.com

General - Incorporation	VA	Stock - Price on:12/24/2007	$5.15
Employees	216	Stock Exchange	NDQ
Auditor	KPMG LLP	Ticker Symbol	OCCF
Stk Agt	American Stock Transfer & Trust Co.	Outstanding Shares	6,200,000
Counsel	Woods Rogers PLC, McGuire Woods LLP	E.P.S.	$0.20
DUNS No.	10-627-8575	Shareholders	NA

Business: The group's principal activities are to manufacture and market tight-buffer fiber optic cables for high bandwidth transmission of data, video and audio communications. These cables are sold to the local area network and premises markets. They are used for both indoor and outdoor requirements and utilize a tight-buffered coating process. The group's products can also be used to connect electro-optical hardware components. The products are derived from technology originally developed for military application requiring very rugged flexible and compact fiber optic cables. The customers of the group include distributors, original equipment manufacturers, system integrators, electrical contractors, value added resellers and end-users. The end-users of the product are educational institutions, financial institutions, government agencies, industrial and manufacturing facilities, original equipment manufacturers and the military.

Primary SIC and add'l.: 3357

CIK No: 0001000230

Officers: Neil D. Wilkin/Chmn., CEO, Pres., Tracy G. Smith/CFO, VP, Luke J. Huybrechts/Dir., Sr. VP - Operations, Cherry Richardson/Contact - US Military, Government Sales, Richard Hutchinson/Contact - International Sales, Andrew Siegel/Dir., Primary Investor Relations Officer, Joele Frank/Primary Investor Relations Officer

Directors: Neil D. Wilkin/Chmn., CEO, Pres., Randall H. Frazier/Dir., John M. Holland/Dir., Luke J. Huybrechts/Dir., Sr. VP - Operations, Craig H. Weber/Dir., John B. Williamson/Dir.

Owners: Dimensional Fund Advisors LP/5.69%, FMR Corp./10.03%, John M. Holland, Tracy G. Smith/1.04%, Luke J. Huybrechts/1.60%, Craig H. Weber, Royce & Associates, LLC/5.91%, Randall H. Frazier, Insiders/7.90%, Neil D. Wilkin/4.14%, John B. Williamson

Financial Data: Fiscal Year End:10/31 **Latest Annual Data:** 10/31/2006

Year	Sales	Net Income
2006	$45,330,000	$351,000
2005	$45,899,000	$1,172,000
2004	$43,218,000	$750,000

Curr. Assets:	$18,747,000	Curr. Liab.:	$4,306,000	P/E Ratio:	39.62
Plant, Equip.:	$13,650,000	Total Liab.:	$4,356,000	Indic. Yr. Divd.:	NA
Total Assets:	$34,791,000	Net Worth:	$30,435,000	Debt/ Equity:	NA

Optical Communication Products Inc

6101 Variel Ave., Woodland Hills, CA, 91367; **PH:** 1-818-251-7100; **Fax:** 1-818-251-7111;
http:// www.ocp-inc.com; **Email:** info@ocp-inc.com

General - Incorporation	DE	Stock - Price on:12/24/2007	$1.6
Employees	591	Stock Exchange	NA
Auditor	Deloitte & Touche LLP	Ticker Symbol	NA
Stk Agt	American Stock Transfer & Trust Co.	Outstanding Shares	113,860,000
Counsel	Paul Hastings	E.P.S.	-$0.2
DUNS No.	NA	Shareholders	NA

Business: The group's principal activity is to design, manufacture and market fiber optic subsystems and modules. These are integrated into systems, which address the bandwidth limitations in metropolitan area networks, local area networks and storage area networks. The products include optical transmitters, receivers, transceivers and transponders that convert electronic signals into optical signals and back to electronic signals. The group's products enable high-speed communication of voice and data traffic over public and private fiber optic networks. Its customers include acterna corporation, alcatel, canoga perkins, ciena, cisco systems, eci telecom, huawei technologies, lucent technologies, marconi communications, and nortel networks.

Primary SIC and add'l.: 3663 3674

CIK No: 0001122668

Subsidiaries: The Furukawa Electric Co., Ltd.

Officers: David Warnes/Dir., Pres., CEO - Best Direct Networks, Philip F. Otto/Dir., CEO, Pres., Joe Liu/Chmn. - OCP, Pres., CEO - Oplink Communications, Robert Shih/VP - Business Development, Oplink Communications, Paul Hastings/Legal Counsel, Frederic T. Boyer/Sr. VP, CFO, Liew Chuang Chiu/VP - Manufacturing

Directors: David Warnes/Dir., Pres., CEO - Best Direct Networks, Philip F. Otto/Dir., CEO, Pres., Joe Liu/Chmn. - OCP, Pres., CEO - Oplink Communications, Len Leblanc/Dir., Chieh Chang/Dir., Jesse Jack/Dir., Stewart D. Personick/Dir., Hobart Birmingham/Dir.

Owners: Mohammad Ghorbanali, David Warnes, Arinobu Sato, Hobart Birmingham, Muoi Van Tran, Frederic T. Boyer, Haruki Ogoshi, Yukimasa Shiga, Insiders, Susie L. Nemeti, Stewart D. Personick, The Furukawa Electric Co., Ltd.,, Liew-Chuang Chiu

Financial Data: Fiscal Year End:09/30 **Latest Annual Data:** 9/30/2006

Year	Sales	Net Income
2006	$70,138,000	$1,395,000
2005	$55,978,000	$941,000
2004	$57,143,000	-$1,307,000

Curr. Assets:	$166,783,000	Curr. Liab.:	$15,443,000		
Plant, Equip.:	$29,313,000	Total Liab.:	$15,602,000	Indic. Yr. Divd.:	NA
Total Assets:	$207,318,000	Net Worth:	$191,716,000	Debt/ Equity:	NA

Opticare Health Systems Inc

87 Grandview Ave., Waterbury, CT, 06708; **PH:** 1-203-596-2236; http:// www.opticare.com

General - Incorporation	DE	Stock - Price on:12/24/2007	NA
Employees	NA	Stock Exchange	NA
Auditor	Deloitte & Touche LLP	Ticker Symbol	NA
Stk Agt	Mellon Investor Services LLC	Outstanding Shares	NA
Counsel	Stephen P. Fisher	E.P.S.	NA
DUNS No.	62-225-3508	Shareholders	NA

Business: The group principal activity is to provide integrated eye care services. The group operates in three segments: distribution and technology, managed vision and consumer vision. The distribution and technology segment provides products and services to eye care professionals. The consumer vision sells retail optical products to consumers and operates integrated eye health centers and surgical facilities where comprehensive eye care services are provided to patients. The managed vision contracts with insurers, managed care plans and other third party payors to manage claims payment administration of eye health benefits for those contracting parties. On 07-Feb-2003, the group purchased all of the assets and certain liabilities of the contact lens distribution business of wise optical vision group, inc.

Primary SIC and add'l.: 8042 8099 5995

CIK No: 0000311046

Subsidiaries: Accountable Eye Care Associates, Inc., AECC Total Vision Health Plan of Texas, Inc., Georgia Eye Care, Inc., Ocucare Systems, Inc., OptiCare Acquisition Corp., OptiCare Eye Health Centers, Inc., OptiCare Eye Health Network LLC, OptiCare IPA of New York, Inc., OptiCare Systems LLC, OptiCare Vision Insurance Company, Inc.

Optigenex Inc

750 Lexington Ave., 6th Fl., New York, NY, 10022; **PH:** 1-866-678-4469;
http:// www.optigenex.com; **Email:** info@optigenex.com

General - Incorporation	DE	Stock - Price on:12/24/2007	$0.016
Employees	3	Stock Exchange	OTC
Auditor	Goldstein Golub Kessler LLP	Ticker Symbol	OPGX
Stk Agt	NA	Outstanding Shares	11,270,000
Counsel	NA	E.P.S.	-$0.611
DUNS No.	NA	Shareholders	NA

Business: The group's principle activity is to distribute health and nutritional products through its Internet websites. The websites are www.vibranthealthonline.com and www.yahoovibranthealth.com. The group enters into a contract with the manufacturers or the suppliers of health and nutritional products, whereby it focuses on marketing and generating sales through Internet. As of 31-Dec-2002, the group markets celadrin(R), which is available in the form of cream and oral capsules. Celadrin(R) is a scientifically tested and formulated product developed to provide support for healthy joint function and mobility. The group is in the development stage.

Primary SIC and add'l.: 5912

CIK No: 0001168776

Subsidiaries: Merger Inc, Optigenex Acquisition Corp, Vibrant Health Inc

Officers: Daniel Zwiren/52/CEO, Pres., CFO, David Westra/Compliance Officer

Owners: Insiders/13.30%, William Walters/12.20%, Claudia Walters/5.90%, Michael Mullarkey/1.10%, Richard Serbin/8.80%, Vincent Giampapa/8.60%

Financial Data: Fiscal Year End:12/31 **Latest Annual Data:** 12/31/2006

Year	Sales	Net Income
2006	$301,000	-$7,357,000
2005	$278,000	-$6,996,000
2004	$339,000	-$5,793,000

Curr. Assets:	$1,161,000	Curr. Liab.:	$521,000		
Plant, Equip.:	$70,000	Total Liab.:	$7,675,000	Indic. Yr. Divd.:	NA
Total Assets:	$2,825,000	Net Worth:	-$4,850,000	Debt/ Equity:	NA

Optimal Group Inc

2 Pl. Alexis-Nihon, 3400 de Maisonneuve Blvd., W 12th Fl., Montreal, PQ, H3Z 3C1;
PH: 1-514-738-8885; http:// www.optimalgrp.com; **Email:** info@optimalgrp.com

General - Incorporation......................Canada	Stock- Price on:12/24/2007 ....$7.65
Employees...171	Stock Exchange...NDQ
Auditor ....KPMG LLP	Ticker Symbol..OPMR
Stk Agt........................Computershare Trust Co	Outstanding Shares 23,850,000
Counsel...NA	E.P.S...$0.11
DUNS No...NA	Shareholders..NA

Business: The group's principle activity is to provide self-checkout systems to retailers in the United States. The principal product of the group is u-scan(R) automated self-checkout system. The product enables shoppers to scan, bag and pay for their purchases with a little or no assistance from store personnel. The u-scan system can be operated quickly and easily by shoppers and makes the checkout process more convenient. The group has sold 1,937 u-scan systems, consisting of 7,706 checkout stations, across 42 states. It markets u-scan systems directly to customers through sales personnel. The group's quarterly revenue for September 2007 was 27.62 milions of USD.

Primary SIC and add'l.: 3578

CIK No: 0001015923

Subsidiaries: 3507637 Canada Inc., 4287258 Canada Inc., 4295382 Canada Inc. , FireOne Group plc., FirePay Ltd., FPA Processing Services Inc., LFPD California Corp., a corporation, Micro Tempus Corporation., Micro Tempus GmbH., OG Processing Services Holdings., Online Processing Limited., Optimal Payments Corp., Optimal Payments Holdings Limited., Optimal Payments Inc., Optimal Payments Limited. 17 Subsidiaries included in the Index

Officers: Neil S. Wechsler/Co - Chmn., CEO/$2,005,053.00, Leon P. Garfinkle/Sr. VP, General Counsel, Sec., Gary S. Wechsler/CFO, Treasurer/$1,033,539.00, Bradley O. McKenna/VP - Administration, Human Resources

Directors: Neil S. Wechsler/Co - Chmn., CEO, Holden L. Ostrin/Co - Chmn., Tommy Boman/Dir., Henry M. Karp/Dir., James S. Gertler/Dir., Jonathan J. Ginns/Dir., Thomas Murphy/Dir., Steve Shaper/Dir., Sydney Sweibel/Dir.

Owners: Magnetar Capital Partners LP/6.46%, James S. Gertler, Benjamin A. Dalfen, Neil S. Wechsler/4.25%, Gary S. Wechsler/2.40%, Stephen J. Shaper, Sydney Sweibel, Jonathan J. Ginns, Holden L. Ostrin/4.24%, Henry M. Karp/4.24%, Douglas P. Lewin, Insiders/1.96%, William Blair & Company/10.39%, Thomas D. Murphy, Tommy Boman

Financial Data: Fiscal Year End:12/31 Latest Annual Data: 12/31/2006

Year	Sales	Net Income
2006	$191,893,000	$12,779,000
2005	$181,351,000	$577,000
2004	$99,397,000	-$9,253,000

Curr. Assets:	$216,116,000	Curr. Liab.:	$99,795,000	P/E Ratio:	69.55
Plant, Equip.:	$2,121,000	Total Liab.:	$121,155,000	Indic. Yr. Divd.:	NA
Total Assets:	$340,537,000	Net Worth:	$219,382,000	Debt/ Equity:	0.0117

Optimum Interactive (USA) Ltd

30 W 61st St. Apt 25e, New York, NY, 10023; **PH:** 1-646-226-2212; **http://** www.optimuminteractive.com; **Email:** info@optimuminteractive.com

General - Incorporation.............................DE	Stock- Price on:12/24/2007 ....$0.75
Employees...NA	Stock Exchange..OTC
Auditor ....Glo Cpas, LLP	Ticker Symbol..OTMI
Stk Agt...............................Island Stock Transfer	Outstanding Shares ....NA
Counsel..NA	E.P.S...NA
DUNS No...NA	Shareholders..NA

Business: The groups principal activity is to develop educational software for the computer market. The group also develops and market educational products and related proprietary content dedicated to making learning effective and engaging. The group operates from the United States.

Primary SIC and add'l.: 7372

CIK No: 0001341997

Officers: Robert M. Rubin/68/Dir., CEO, CFO, Pres., Daniel Wainstein/28/Dir., Sec.

Directors: Robert M. Rubin/68/Dir., CEO, CFO, Pres., Daniel Wainstein/28/Dir., Sec., Barry Pomerantz/65/Dir.

Owners: Insiders/84.90%, Robert M. Rubin/84.90%, 25 Highland Partners, LLC/84.90%

Financial Data: Fiscal Year End:12/31 Latest Annual Data: 12/31/2006

Year	Sales	Net Income
2006	NA	-$26,000

Curr. Assets:	$0	Curr. Liab.:	$46,000		
Plant, Equip.:	NA	Total Liab.:	$46,000	Indic. Yr. Divd.:	NA
Total Assets:	$0	Net Worth:	-$45,000	Debt/ Equity:	NA

Optimumbank Holdings Inc

2477 E Commercial Blvd., Fort Lauderdale, FL, 33308; **PH:** 1-954-776-2332; **Fax:** 1-954-776-2281; **http://** www.optimumbank.com

General - Incorporation.............................FL	Stock- Price on:12/24/2007 ....$9.787
Employees...20	Stock Exchange...NDQ
Auditor .... Hacker, Johnson & Smith P.A, P.C	Ticker Symbol..OPHC
Stk Agt...NA	Outstanding Shares 2,960,000
Counsel..NA	E.P.S...$0.562
DUNS No...NA	Shareholders..NA

Business: The group's principal activities are to provide personal, consumer and commercial banking services and products to individuals and businesses in broward, dade and palm beach counties. The group operates through its wholly owned subsidiary optimumbank. The lending activities of the group include consumer loans and real estate loans to individuals, small businesses and to other organization. The group also offers a variety of deposits consisting of money market deposits accounts, now accounts, checking accounts and time deposits. Other services include credit cards, cash management, direct deposits, notary services, money orders, night depository, travelers checks, cashiers check, domestic collections, savings bonds, bank drafts, ATM's, drive-in tellers and banking by mail.

Primary SIC and add'l.: 6022 6712

CIK No: 0001288855

Subsidiaries: Optimumbank, Optimumbank Holdings Capital Trust I

Officers: Albert J. Finch/Chmn., CEO/$287,200.00, Richard L. Browdy/COO, Pres./$246,394.00

Directors: Albert J. Finch/Chmn., CEO

Owners: Michael Bedzow/4.29%, Thomas A. Procelli/1.43%, Wendy Mitchler/0.88%, Richard L. Browdy/3.44%, Sam Borek/6.23%, Larry Willis/3.25%, David H. Krinsky/9.80%, Albert J. Finch/6.00%, Gordon Deckelbaum/6.49%, Insiders/39.77%, Irving P. Cohen/2.23%

Financial Data: Fiscal Year End:12/31 Latest Annual Data: 12/31/2006

Year	Sales	Net Income
2006	$14,819,000	$1,834,000
2005	$11,969,000	$1,601,000
2004	$9,505,000	$1,570,000

Curr. Assets:	$2,858,000	Curr. Liab.:	$188,515,000	P/E Ratio:	17.41
Plant, Equip.:	$3,990,000	Total Liab.:	$205,280,000	Indic. Yr. Divd.:	NA
Total Assets:	$225,703,000	Net Worth:	$20,423,000	Debt/ Equity:	1.2766

Optio Software Inc

3015 Windward Plz., Windward Fairways II, Atlanta, GA, 30005; **PH:** 1-770-576-3500; **Fax:** 1-770-576-3699; **http://** www.optiosoftware.com; **Email:** info@optiosoftware.com

General - Incorporation ....GA	Stock- Price on:12/24/2007 ....$1.25
Employees...182	Stock Exchange..OTC
Auditor ....BDO Seidman LLP	Ticker Symbol..OPTO
Stk Agt......................................SunTrust Bank	Outstanding Shares 22,370,000
Counsel.................... Morris, Manning & Martin	E.P.S..-$0.04
DUNS No..NA	Shareholders..NA

Business: The group's principle activity is to provides infrastructure software and services that enhance the form, content, distribution and availability of business info. It also develops, sells and supports document customization software to companies. The group provides two suites of software products: optio enterprise suite and the optio healthcare suite. The optio enterprise suite is designed to meet the needs of the general market place. The optio healthcare suite is targeted to meet the specialized requirements of healthcare enterprises. The software products of the group enhances the performance and reliability of its customer's e-business, enterprise, legacy and custom applications and also provides a comprehensive, cost-effective solutions for organizations. The group derives revenues from software licenses, services and maintenance. Software services and maintenance include fee for consulting, implementation, training and technical support. The group's total revenue for year 2007 was 28.68 millions of USD.

Primary SIC and add'l.: 7372 7374 7378

CIK No: 0001096689

Subsidiaries: Optio Software Deutschland GmbH, Optio Software Europe, S.A, Optio Software UK, Pvt. Limited, VertiSoft Limited

Officers: Wayne C. Cape/Chmn., CEO, Pres./$297,389.00, Mike McGuire/Sr. VP, GM - Healthcare Sales/$215,969.00, David Moody/MD - EMEA Operations, Daryl G. Hatton/CTO, Donald H. French/Sr. VP - Research - Development/$318,738.00, Caroline Bembry/CFO, Sec./$202,613.00, Steven E. Kaye/Sr. VP - Sales - Services, Marketing/$239,803.00

Directors: Wayne C. Cape/Chmn., CEO, Pres., Barron Hughes/Dir., Ronald Diener/Dir., David T. Leach/Dir., Jeff Anderson/Dir., Jay A. Wolf/35/Dir., Jay Toole/63/Dir.

Owners: Jay A. Wolf/14.10%, David T. Leach, Donald H. French/6.90%, Jay Toole, Yorktown Avenue Capital, LLC/12.40%, Wayne C. Cape/34.40%, Ronald G. Diener/2.80%, Steven E. Kaye, Baron F. Hughes/1.70%, Chris Beecroft, Diane Cape/7.90%, Jeffrey J. Anderson, Michael McGuire, Trinad Capital Master Fund, Ltd./14.00%, Caroline Bembry (17 Owners included in Index)

Financial Data: Fiscal Year End:01/31 Latest Annual Data: 1/31/2007

Year	Sales	Net Income
2007	$28,677,000	$282,000
2006	$29,621,000	$898,000
2005	$28,367,000	$1,653,000

Curr. Assets:	$16,579,000	Curr. Liab.:	$10,482,000		
Plant, Equip.:	$2,714,000	Total Liab.:	$12,217,000	Indic. Yr. Divd.:	NA
Total Assets:	$22,937,000	Net Worth:	$10,720,000	Debt/ Equity:	0.0313

Option Care Inc

485 E Half Day Rd., Ste. 300, Buffalo, IL, 60089; **PH:** 1-847-465-2100; **http://** www.optioncare.com

General - Incorporation ....DE	Stock- Price on:12/24/2007 ....$15.23
Employees...1,954	Stock Exchange...NA
Auditor ....Ernst & Young LLP	Ticker Symbol...NA
Stk Agt............................U.S. Stock Transfer Corp	Outstanding Shares 34,510,000
Counsel..NA	E.P.S...NA
DUNS No..10-284-3331	Shareholders..NA

Business: The group's principal activities are to provide specialty pharmacy services, infusion therapy and other ancillary healthcare services. The services include the distribution of infused and injected medications, patient care coordination, compliance management and reimbursement support. These services are offered to patients at home or at other alternate sites such as infusion suites and physician's offices. The group provides these services on behalf of managed care organizations, government healthcare programs and biopharmaceutical manufacturers through a network of 124 owned and franchised pharmacies. The group through its subsidiary, management by information inc., supplies data management products and support services to the infusion and home medical equipment industry.

Primary SIC and add'l.: 6794 8082

CIK No: 0000884064

Subsidiaries: At Home Solutions, Inc., Chartwell Care Givers, Inc., Chartwell Southern New England, LLC, Cypress Home Medical, Inc., Excel Healthcare, LLC, Full Road Holdings, Ltd., Healthcare Options of Minnesota, Inc., Home Health of Option Care, Inc., Home I.V., Inc., Hunterdon Infusion Services, LLP, Infusion Specialties, Inc, Management by Information, Inc., North County Home I.V., Inc., Option Care Enterprises, Inc, Option Care Enterprises, Inc. 27 Subsidiaries included in the Index

Officers: Rajat Rai/Dir., CEO, Pres./$769,286.00, Joseph Bonaccorsi/Sr. VP, General Counsel/$455,385.00, Paul Mastrapa/Sr. VP, CFO/$501,249.00

Directors: Rajat Rai/Dir., CEO, Pres., John N. Kapoor/Chmn., Edward A. Blechschmidt/Dir., Kenneth Abramowitz/Dir., Leo Henikoff/Dir., Jerome F. Sheldon/Dir.

Owners: Joseph P. Bonaccorsi, Insiders/13.70%, FMR Corporation/9.50%, John N. Kapoor/9.20%, Rajat Rai/2.70%, Mellon Financial Corporation/7.10%, Wellington Management Company LLP/8.80%, Fiduciary Management Inc./6.50%, Kenneth S. Abramowitz, Paul Mastrapa, Rao Akella/11.90%, Lord Abbett& Co. LLC/8.00%, Jerome F. Sheldon, Leo Henikoff, Edward A. Blechschmidt

Financial Data: Fiscal Year End:12/31 Latest Annual Data: 12/31/2006

Year	Sales	Net Income
2006	$659,412,000	$21,685,000
2005	$506,364,000	$22,728,000
2004	$414,430,000	$18,931,000

Curr. Assets:	$176,328,000	Curr. Liab.:	$59,233,000	P/E Ratio:	23.08
Plant, Equip.:	$24,398,000	Total Liab.:	$156,196,000	Indic. Yr. Divd.:	$0.080
Total Assets:	$376,385,000	Net Worth:	$219,363,000	Debt/ Equity:	0.3776

Optionable Inc

465 Columbus Ave., Valhalla, NY, 10595; **PH:** 1-914-773-1100; **Fax:** 1-914-773-1500; **http://** www.optionable.com; **Email:** contactus@optionable.com

General - Incorporation	DE	**Stock**- Price on:12/24/2007	$0.29
Employees	18	Stock Exchange	OTC
Auditor	Sherb & Co., LLP	Ticker Symbol	OPBL
Stk Agt	Continental Stock Transfer & Trust Co	Outstanding Shares	52,260,000
Counsel	NA	E.P.S.	NA
DUNS No.	NA	Shareholders	NA

Business: The groups principle activity is to provide commodity derivative brokerage service provider to brokerage firms, financial institutions, energy traders, and hedge funds. The group operates from the United States. The group's quarterly revenue for Sep'07 was 0.06 millions of USD.

Primary SIC and add'l.: 6221

CIK No: 0001303433

Subsidiaries: Hydra Commodity Services, Inc, OPEX International, Inc.

Officers: Kevin P. Cassidy/48/Vice Chmn., CEO, Edward Oconnor/Dir., Pres., Marc-Andre Boisseau/CFO, Abe Zucker/Exec. VP, Co - Founder, Charles Wilson/CTO, Rudy Barrio/Contact - Investors

Directors: Kevin P. Cassidy/48/Vice Chmn., CEO, Mark Nordlicht/38/Founder, Chmn., Edward Oconnor/Dir., Pres., Albert Helmig/56/Dir., Abe Zucker/Exec. VP, Co - Founder

Owners: Mark Nordlicht/27.80%, Albert Helmig/0.50%, Insiders/44.10%, Edward J. O'Connor/10.40%, Kevin P. Cassidy/5.90%

Financial Data: Fiscal Year End:12/31   Latest Annual Data: 12/31/2006

Year	Sales	Net Income
2006	$16,070,000	$6,206,000
2005	$5,805,000	$1,260,000

Curr. Assets:	$12,057,000	Curr. Liab.:	$3,539,000		
Plant, Equip.:	$58,000	Total Liab.:	$5,394,000	Indic. Yr. Divd.:	NA
Total Assets:	$12,284,000	Net Worth:	$6,890,000	Debt/ Equity:	NA

optionsXpress Holdings Inc

39 S LaSalle St., Ste. 220, Chicago, IL, 60603; **PH:** 1-312-630-3300; **Fax:** 1-312-629-5256; **http://** www.optionsxpress.com; **Email:** investorrelations@optionsxpress.com

General - Incorporation	DE	**Stock**- Price on:12/24/2007	$26.34
Employees	206	Stock Exchange	NDQ
Auditor	Ernst & Young, LLP	Ticker Symbol	OXPS
Stk Agt	Continental Stock Transfer & Trust Co	Outstanding Shares	62,940,000
Counsel	NA	E.P.S.	$1.20
DUNS No.	NA	Shareholders	NA

Business: The groups principle activity is to provide brokerage services. The group products sold under the trade names Strategy Scan(R), Xspreads(R) and Xecute(SM). In January 2007, the group acquired XpressTrade, LLC. The group operates from the United States. The group's quarterly revenue for September 2007 was 64.09 millions of USD.

Primary SIC and add'l.: 6221 6289 6799 6221 6289 6799

CIK No: 0001299688

Subsidiaries: brokersXpress Illinois, Inc., brokersXpress, LLC, optionsXpress Australia Pty Limited, optionsXpress Canada Corp., optionsXpress Europe, B.V., optionsXpress Europe, LLC, optionsXpress International, Inc., optionsXpress Singapore Pte Ltd., optionsXpress Singapore, LLC, optionsXpress, Inc., OX Australia, LLC, OX Singapore, LLC, Xpresstrade, L.L.C.

Officers: David A. Fisher/Dir., CEO, Ned W. Bennett/Executive Vice Chmn., Thomas E. Stern/Chief Administrative Officer, Benjamin Morof/Chief Compliance Officer, Adam Dewitt/CFO

Directors: David A. Fisher/Dir., CEO, James A. Gray/Chmn., Ned W. Bennett/Executive Vice Chmn., Bruce Evans/Dir., Steven L. Fradkin/Dir., Howard Draft/Dir., David S. Kalt/40/Dir., Scott Wald/Dir.

Owners: Thomas E. Stern, Ned W. Bennett/3.50%, Adam J. DeWitt, David A. Fisher, Benjamin Morof, Franklin Resources Inc./5.20%, G-Bar Limited Partnership/18.30%, Insiders/30.60%, Janus Capital Management LLC/5.30%, David S. Kalt/4.20%, Steven Fradkin, Bruce R. Evans, James A. Gray/22.20%, Scott S. Wald

Financial Data: Fiscal Year End:12/31   Latest Annual Data: 12/31/2006

Year	Sales	Net Income
2006	$188,372,000	$71,729,000
2005	$128,983,000	$48,741,000
2004	$93,069,000	$31,210,000

Curr. Assets:	$675,610,000	Curr. Liab.:	$503,060,000	P/E Ratio:	20.74
Plant, Equip.:	$6,619,000	Total Liab.:	$506,696,000	Indic. Yr. Divd.:	$0.250
Total Assets:	$687,524,000	Net Worth:	$180,828,000	Debt/ Equity:	NA

Optium Corp

500 Horizon Dr., Ste. 505, Chalfont, PA, 18914; **PH:** 1-215-712-6200; **Fax:** 1-215-712-0031; **http://** www.optiumcorp.com; **Email:** customerservice@optium.com

General - Incorporation	DE	**Stock**- Price on:12/24/2007	$11.56
Employees	NA	Stock Exchange	NDQ
Auditor	Goodwin Procter LLP	Ticker Symbol	OPTM
Stk Agt	Computershare Trust Co	Outstanding Shares	25,380,000
Counsel	NA	E.P.S.	$0.24
DUNS No.	NA	Shareholders	NA

Business: The groups principal activities include designing, manufacturing and selling optical subsystems. The products of the group include transponders and ROADM. In March 5, 2006, the group acquired Engana Pty Limited. The group operates from the United States.

Primary SIC and add'l.: 3674 3661 3679

CIK No: 0001219169

Subsidiaries: Optium Australia Pty Limited

Officers: Eitan Gertel/Chmn., CEO, Pres., David Renner/CFO, VP - Finance, Mark Colyar/Sr. VP - Engineering, GM - Optium US, Anthony Musto/VP - Sales, Marketing, Christopher Brown/General Counsel, VP - Corporate Development, Steven Frisken/VP - Wavelength Products, Simon Poole/VP - Business Development, GM - Optium Australia, Veronica Rosa/Investor Relations Officer, Raymond Nering/VP - Optical Subsystems, Sagie Tsadka/VP, GM - Optium Israel

Directors: Eitan Gertel/Chmn., CEO, Pres., James Barbookles/Dir., Christopher Crespi/Dir., Kerry Dehority/Dir., Steven Foster/Dir., Russell Johnson/Dir., Morgan Jones/Dir., Joseph Chinnici/Dir.

Owners: Steven Foster, Christopher Crespi, Insiders, Christopher Brown, Russell Johnson, Mark Colyar, James Barbookles, Battery Ventures, Eitan Gertel, Anthony Musto, KPLJ Ventures, T. Rowe Price Associates, Inc., Morgan Jones, David Renner, Kerry DeHority (16 Owners included in Index)

Financial Data: Fiscal Year End:NA   Latest Annual Data: 07/28/2007

Year	Sales	Net Income
2007	$125,478,000	$11,254,000
2006	$69,477,000	-$8,123,000
2005	$37,076,000	-$1,451,000

Curr. Assets:	$17,051,000	Curr. Liab.:	$3,985,000		
Plant, Equip.:	$5,222,000	Total Liab.:	$4,078,000	Indic. Yr. Divd.:	NA
Total Assets:	$22,411,000	Net Worth:	-$47,464,000	Debt/ Equity:	NA

Oracle Corp

500 Oracle Pkwy., Redwood City, CA, 94065; **PH:** 1-650-506-7000; **http://** www.oracle.com

General - Incorporation	DE	**Stock**- Price on:12/24/2007	$19.56
Employees	56,133	Stock Exchange	NDQ
Auditor	Ernst & Young LLP	Ticker Symbol	ORCL
Stk Agt	Computershare Trust Co	Outstanding Shares	5,140,000,000
Counsel	NA	E.P.S.	NA
DUNS No.	14-470-9193	Shareholders	NA

Business: The groups principle activity is to provide software products and services. The group also provides advance product services. The group operates through two segments namely software and services. In the year 2007, the group acquired Moniforce. The group operates from United States.

Primary SIC and add'l.: 8243 7379 7372

CIK No: 0000777676

Subsidiaries: Beijing Oracle Software Systems Company Limited, Business OnLine, Inc., Centro de Capacitacion Oracles Ltda., Delphi Asset Management Corporation, Graphical Information, Inc., Healthcare Acquisition I Corporation, HighTouch Technologies, Inc., Istante Software, J.D. Edwards & Company Foreign Sales, Inc., J.D. Edwards Europe Ltd., Jade Acquisition Corp., Miracle Linux Corporation, OIC Acquisition I Corporation, OIC Acquisition II Corporation, OIC Acquisition III Corporation 155 Subsidiaries included in the Index

Officers: Lawrence J. Ellison/Dir., CEO, Masaaki Shintaku/CEO, Pres. - Oracle Japan, Derek H. Williams/Chmn., Exec. VP - Oracle Corporation Asia Pacific, Japan, Sergio Giacoletto/Exec. VP - Oracle EMEA, Charles Rozwat/Exec. VP - Oracle Server Technologies, Lenley Hensarling/VP, GM Oracle's JD Edwards Enterpriseone Product Line, Bindi Bhullar/Analyst Relations, Europe, Middle East, Africa, Dave Chappell/VP, Chief Technologist SOA, Terry Olkin/Chief Architect, VP - Collaborative Technologies Division, Mike Olson/VP - Embedded Technologies, Juergen Rottler/Exec. VP - Oracle Customer Services, Charles E. Phillips/Dir., Pres., Safra A. Catz/Dir., CFO, Pres., Roger Sullivan/VP - Business Development Oracle's Identity Management Solutions, Terrance Wampler/VP - Finanicals Applications Product Strategy (41 Officers included in Index)

Directors: Lawrence J. Ellison/Dir., CEO, Jeffrey O. Henley/Chmn., Derek H. Williams/Chmn., Exec. VP - Oracle Corporation Asia Pacific, Japan, Donald L. Lucas/Dir., Charles E. Phillips/Dir., Pres., Safra A. Catz/Dir., CFO, Pres., Michael J. Boskin/Dir., Jeffrey S. Berg/Dir., Jack F. Kemp/Dir., Hector Garcia-Molina/Dir., Raymond H. Bingham/Dir., Naomi O. Seligman/Dir.

Financial Data: Fiscal Year End:05/31   Latest Annual Data: 05/31/2007

Year	Sales	Net Income
2007	$17,996,000,000	$4,274,000,000
2006	$14,380,000,000	$3,381,000,000
2005	$11,799,000,000	$2,886,000,000

Curr. Assets:	$8,479,000,000	Curr. Liab.:	$8,063,000,000		
Plant, Equip.:	$1,442,000,000	Total Liab.:	$9,850,000,000	Indic. Yr. Divd.:	NA
Total Assets:	$20,687,000,000	Net Worth:	$10,837,000,000	Debt/ Equity:	0.3632

Oracle Health ACQ

200 Greenwich Ave., Greenwich, CT, 06830; **PH:** 1-203-862-7900

General - Incorporation		**Stock**- Price on:12/24/2007	$7.7
Employees	NA	Stock Exchange	OTC
Auditor	Rothstein, Kass & Co., P.C	Ticker Symbol	OHAQ
Stk Agt	Continental Stock T. & T Co.	Outstanding Shares	NA
Counsel	NA	E.P.S.	$0.64
DUNS No.	NA	Shareholders	NA

Business: The groups principal activity is acquiring, through a merger, capital stock exchange, asset acquisition, stock purchase or other similar business combination, an operating business in the healthcare industry. The group operates through seven segments namely healthcare services, medical devices and products, healthcare information technology, pharmaceuticals, diagnostics, biotechnology therapeutics and life sciences. The group operates from the United States.

Primary SIC and add'l.: 2834

CIK No: 0001338648

Officers: Joel D. Liffmann/47/Dir., COO, Pres., Principal Executive Officer, Mark A. Radzik/43/CFO, Sec.

Directors: Larry N. Feinberg/53/Chmn., Joel D. Liffmann/47/Dir., COO, Pres., Principal Executive Officer, George W. Bickerstaff/52/Dir., Kevin C. Johnson/53/Dir., Per G. H. Lofberg/60/Dir.

Owners: D.B. Zwirn& Co., L.P./5.30%, George W. Bickerstaff, Larry N. Feinberg/12.70%, Joel D. Liffmann/5.00%, Granite Creek Partners, L.L.C./2.00%, Andrew M. Weiss/6.60%, HBK Investments L.P./7.20%, Daniel B. Zwirn/5.30%, Oracle Healthcare Holding LLC/7.70%, Insiders/20.00%, Adage Capital Partners GP, L.L.C./5.30%, LNF OHAC LLC/5.00%, JDL OHAC LLC/5.00%, Jonathan Glaser/7.80%, Mark A. Radzik/2.00% (16 Owners included in Index)

Financial Data: Fiscal Year End:NA   Latest Annual Data: 12/31/2006

Year	Sales	Net Income
2006	$4,793,000	$6,917,000

Curr. Assets:	$553,000	Curr. Liab.:	$17,437,000	P/E Ratio:	12.62
Plant, Equip.:	NA	Total Liab.:	$40,778,000	Indic. Yr. Divd.:	NA
Total Assets:	$117,182,000	Net Worth:	$76,405,000	Debt/ Equity:	NA

Oragenics Inc

13700 Progress Blvd., Alachua, FL, 32615; PH: 1-386-418-4018; Fax: 1-386-418-1660; http://www.oragenics.com; Email: info@oragenics.com

General - Incorporation	FL	Stock- Price on:12/24/2007	$0.52
Employees	9	Stock Exchange	AMEX
Auditor .... Kirkland , Russ, Murphy & Tapp P.A.		Ticker Symbol	ONI
Stk Agt	Continental Stock Transfer & Trust Co	Outstanding Shares	23,190,000
Counsel	Shumaker Loop & Kendrick LLP	E.P.S	-$0.124
DUNS No.	NA	Shareholders	NA

Business: The group's principal activities are to develop engineered streptococcus mutans for oral and other therapeutic applications. The group has developed two healthcare products. The first technology product is a genetically altered strain of a species of bacteria called s mutans which occurs naturally on teeth in human beings. The second technology is an antibiotic known as mutacin 1140 effective against all tested gram-positive bacteria. Gram-positive bacteria cause many human ailments, such as pneumonia, pharyngitis and others. The group is a development stage company.

Primary SIC and add'l.: 8731 2834

CIK No: 0001174940

Officers: Robert T. Zahradnik/Dir., CEO, Pres., Sec., Treasurer, Interim Financial Officer, Jeffrey Hillman/Dir., Chief Scientific Officer, Eli Schwarz/Member - International Scientific Advisory Board, Howard K. Kuramitsu/Scientific Consultants, Per-Erik J. Saris/Scientific Consultants

Directors: Robert T. Zahradnik/Dir., CEO, Pres., Sec., Treasurer, Interim Financial Officer, David J. Gury/Chmn., Raman Bedi/Chmn. - International Scientific Advisory Board, Ayyaz Ali Khan/Member - International Scientific Advisory Board, Brian Mouatt/Member - International Scientific Advisory Board, Hari Parkash/Member - International Scientific Advisory Board, Jeffrey Hillman/Dir., Chief Scientific Officer, George T. Hawes/61/Dir.

Owners: Robert Zahradnik/3.81%, Jeffrey D. Hillman/17.80%, Insiders/39.50%, George Hawes/17.65%, David J. Gury/1.00%

Financial Data: Fiscal Year End:12/31   Latest Annual Data: 12/31/2006

Year	Sales	Net Income
2006	$66,000	-$2,936,000
2005	NA	-$3,251,000
2004	$196,000	-$3,078,000

Curr. Assets:	$781,000	Curr. Liab.:	$328,000		
Plant, Equip.:	$825,000	Total Liab.:	$328,000	Indic. Yr. Divd.:	NA
Total Assets:	$1,606,000	Net Worth:	$1,278,000	Debt/ Equity:	NA

Oralabs Holding Corp

18685 E Plz. Dr., Parker, CO, 80134; PH: 1-303-783-9499; http://www.oralabs.com

General - Incorporation	CO	Stock- Price on:12/24/2007	NA
Employees	153	Stock Exchange	NDQ
Auditor ..... Murrell, Hall, Mcintosh & Co., PLLP		Ticker Symbol	OLAB
Stk Agt	Corporate Stock Transfer, Inc.	Outstanding Shares	NA
Counsel	NA	E.P.S	NA
DUNS No.	05-377-3503	Shareholders	NA

Business: The group's principal activity is to produce and sell consumer products relating to oral care, lip care and to distribute nutritional supplements. The principal products of the group can be categorized into three groups: breath fresheners, lip balm products nutritional supplement and related products. Breath fresheners include ice drops(R), sour zone(tm) brand sour drops and sour sprays. Lip balm products are sold under the names ice drops(R), lip rageous(R), chap ice(R), lip naturals(tm), lip rageous glitters(tm) and essential lip moisturizer(tm). Nutritional supplement and related products consist of msm, 5-htp, glucosamine + msm, breast plus(tm) and cheat & lean(tm). In 2003, the group acquired certain assets of symbiosis, inc.

Primary SIC and add'l.: 2833 2834

CIK No: 0001044577

Subsidiaries: OraLabs, Inc., PSHL

Officers: Wo Hing Li/62/Chmn., CEO, Pres., Hai Sheng Chen/45/Dir., VP, Tammy Pierce/Contact - Contract Packaging Sales, Service, Daniel Casini/Contact - International, Leada Tak Tai/28/CFO

Directors: Wo Hing Li/62/Chmn., CEO, Pres., Hai Sheng Chen/45/Dir., VP, Tung Kuen Tsui/63/Dir., David Peter Wong/52/Dir., Che Kin Lui/46/Dir.

Owners: Wo Hing Li/59.20%, Leada Tak Tai Li/3.40%, Hung Wan/11.20%, Belmont Capital Group Limited/7.30%, Insiders/62.60%

Oramed Pharmaceuticals Inc

2 Elza St., Jerusalem, 93706; PH: 972-547909058; Fax: 972-26792336; http://www.oramedpharma.com; Email: info@oramedpharma.com

General - Incorporation	NV	Stock- Price on:12/24/2007	$0.57
Employees	NA	Stock Exchange	OTC
Auditor	Malone & Bailey, PC	Ticker Symbol	ORMP
Stk Agt	NA	Outstanding Shares	NA
Counsel	NA	E.P.S	-$0.001
DUNS No.	NA	Shareholders	NA

Business: The groups principal activity is to engage in the research and development of a method to administer insulin orally. The group operates from the United States.

Primary SIC and add'l.: 2834

CIK No: 0001176309

Subsidiaries: Iguana Explorations Inc.

Officers: Nadav Kidron/34/Dir., CEO, Pres., George Drazenovic/37/Dir., Sec., Vinisha Agnihotri/Contact - Primary Investor Relations, Alex Werber/52/CFO, Treasurer, Tara Horn/Office Mgr., Erika Moran/Contact - Investor Relations

Directors: Nadav Kidron/34/Dir., CEO, Pres., George Drazenovic/37/Dir., Sec., Derek Leroith/Member - Scientific Board, Itamar Raz/Member - Scientific Board, Brazilai /Member - Scientific Board, Ele Ferrannini/Member - Scientific Board, Harold Jacob/Member - Advisory Board, Leonard Sank/43/Dir.

Owners: George Drazenovic/1.09%, Miriam Kidron/1.85%, Leonard Sank/7.06%, Nadav Kidron/24.38%, Insiders/34.38%, CEDE & CO./36.66%, Zeev Bronfeld/13.38%, Hadassit Medical Research/8.00%

Financial Data: Fiscal Year End:08/01   Latest Annual Data: 08/31/2006

Year	Sales	Net Income
2006	NA	-$415,000
2005	NA	-$46,000
2004	NA	-$282,000

Oranco Inc

1981 E 4800 S Ste. 100, Salt Lake City, UT, 84117; PH: 1-201-777-3951; http://www.investors.ch/weboranco.htm; Email: oranco@investors.ch

General - Incorporation	NV	Stock- Price on:12/24/2007	$0.57
Employees	NA	Stock Exchange	OTC
Auditor	Madsen & Associates, CPA's Inc.	Ticker Symbol	ORNC
Stk Agt	Interwest Transfer Company, Inc.	Outstanding Shares	NA
Counsel	NA	E.P.S	NA
DUNS No.	NA	Shareholders	NA

Business: The groups principle activity may be deemed to be a vehicle to acquire or merge with a business or company. The group operates from the United States.

Primary SIC and add'l.: 7389

CIK No: 0001098996

Officers: Claudio P. Gianascio/CEO, CFO, Pres., Sec. - Treasurer, Dir.

Directors: Claudio P. Gianascio/CEO, CFO, Pres., Sec. - Treasurer, Dir., Alfredo M. Villa/Dir.

Owners: Capital One International SA/8.19%, Prestige Underwriters NV/8.19%, Progressive Emerging Ventures Ltd./9.36%, Claudio Gianascio/19.32%, Alfredo M. Villa/2.93%, Insiders/22.25%, OTC Opportunities Limited/8.19%, Comprehensive Ventures Inc. Ltd./9.36%

Orange 21 Inc

2070 Las Palmas Dr., Carlsbad, CA, 92009; PH: 1-760-804-8420; Fax: 1-760-804-8421; http://www.orangetwentyone.com

General - Incorporation	DE	Stock- Price on:12/24/2007	$6.46
Employees	88	Stock Exchange	NDQ
Auditor	Deloitte & Touche, LLP	Ticker Symbol	ORNG
Stk Agt	EquiServe Trust Co N.A	Outstanding Shares	8,100,000
Counsel	NA	E.P.S	-$0.89
DUNS No.	NA	Shareholders	NA

Business: The groups principal activities include designing, developing and marketing eyewear products. The products of the group include sunglasses and goggles. The group products sold under the trade name Spy Optic(TM). The groups operates through two segments namely the United States and foreign. The group operates from the United States and Canada. Of the net sale in the year 2006, the United States accounted for $22,904 and foreign $4,500 (thousands).

Primary SIC and add'l.: 2389 3851 2329 2325 5048 2331 5136 2321 2353 5137

CIK No: 0000932372

Subsidiaries: LEM S.r.l., Spy Optic, Inc., Spy Optic, S.r.l.

Officers: Mark Simo/Co - Founder, Co - Chmn., CEO/$15,521.00, Jerry Collazo/CFO/$107,436.00, Jerry Kohlscheen/COO/$180,283.00, John Gothard/VP - North American Sales/$167,152.00, Fran Richards/VP - Marketing

Directors: Mark Simo/Co - Founder, Co - Chmn., CEO, John Pound/Co - Chmn., Harry Casari/Dir., David Mitchell/Dir., Ted Roth/Dir., Greg Theiss/Dir., Jeff Theodosakis/Dir.

Owners: Insiders, Jerry Collazo, John Gothard, Mark Simo, John Pound, Costa Brava Partnership III L.P., Greg Theiss, Harry Casari, Barry Buchholtz, Stephens Investment Management, LLC, Michael Brower, Jerry Kohlscheen, CCM Master Qualified Fund, Ltd., David R. Mitchell, Signia Capital Management, L.L.C. (20 Owners included in Index)

Financial Data: Fiscal Year End:12/31   Latest Annual Data: 12/31/2006

Year	Sales	Net Income
2006	$42,406,000	-$7,252,000
2005	$38,568,000	-$1,708,000
2004	$33,563,000	$807,000

Curr. Assets:	$26,763,000	Curr. Liab.:	$15,478,000		
Plant, Equip.:	$8,042,000	Total Liab.:	$17,018,000	Indic. Yr. Divd.:	NA
Total Assets:	$45,706,000	Net Worth:	$28,688,000	Debt/ Equity:	0.0638

Orange Cmnty Bank CA

1045 W Katella Ave., Ste. 100, Orange, CA, 92867; PH: 1-714-532-0700; Fax: 1-714-532-0701; http://www.orangecommunitybank.net

General - Incorporation		Stock- Price on:12/24/2007	NA
Employees	NA	Stock Exchange	OTC
Auditor	NA	Ticker Symbol	OCBN
Stk Agt	U.S. Stock Transfer Corp	Outstanding Shares	NA
Counsel	NA	E.P.S	NA
DUNS No.	NA	Shareholders	NA

Business: The groups principle activity is to provide recruiting services. The groups service area includes the research and development, engineering, marketing, sales, information technology and manufacturing industries. The group operates from United States.

Primary SIC and add'l.: 6022

CIK No:

Orange County Business Bank

4675 MacArthur Ct., Ste. 100, Newport Beach, CA, 92660; PH: 1-949-221-0001; http://www.ocbusinessbank.com; Email: info@ocbusinessbank.com

General - Incorporation ....
Employees .... NA
Auditor .... NA
Stk Agt .... U.S. Stock Transfer Corp
Counsel .... NA
DUNS No. .... NA

Stock - Price on:12/24/2007 .... $16
Stock Exchange .... OTC
Ticker Symbol .... OCBB
Outstanding Shares 4,710,000
E.P.S .... NA
Shareholders .... NA

Business: The groups principal activities include service commercial bank specifically serving the needs of businesses and professionals throughout Orange County. Services of the group include operating checking accounts for sole proprietors, partnerships, and corporations, money market savings accounts, certificate of deposit accounts, courier deposit pick up services, cash management services and wire transfer facilities. The group operates from the United States.

Primary SIC and add'l.: 6022

CIK No:

Officers: J. P. Gough/Chmn., CEO, Pres., Diana Johnson/Client Services Mgr., Allan T. Gibson/COO, Exec. VP, Victor E. Guerrero/CFO, Exec. VP, Elaine P. Crouch/Sr. VP, Corp. Sec., Dir. - Human Resources, Gregory M. Savino/Exec. VP, Chief Credit Officer

Directors: J. P. Gough/Chmn., CEO, Pres., James J. Florance/Founder, Dir., Robert Delanza/Founder, Dir., Raymond J. Deriggi/Founder, Dir., Steven H. Anderson/Founder, Dir., Roger D. Billingsley/Founder, Dir., Brad L. Champlin/Founder, Dir., Viola C. Chisholm/Founder, Dir., Ralph H. Haberfeld/Founder, Dir., Larry O. Hintz/Founder, Dir., Charles I. Kosmont/Founder, Dir., William T. Morris/Founder, Dir., Christian A. Schmidt/Founder, Dir., Allan R. Uyesugi/Founder, Dir., Gregory J. Vigoren/Dir. *(17 Directors included in Index)*

Orasure Technologies Inc

220 E 1st St., Bethlehem, PA, 18015; ***PH:*** 1-610-882-1820; ***Fax:*** 1-610-882-1830; ***http://*** www.orasure.com

General - Incorporation .... DE
Employees 250
Auditor .... KPMG LLP
Stk Agt .... Mellon Investor Services LLC
Counsel .... Pepper Hamilton LLP
DUNS No. .... NA

Stock - Price on:12/24/2007 .... $8.09
Stock Exchange .... NDQ
Ticker Symbol .... OSUR
Outstanding Shares 46,180,000
E.P.S $0.08
Shareholders .... NA

Business: The group's principal activity is to develop, manufacture and market oral fluid specimen collection devices and diagnostic products. The group designs tests for alcohol abuse. The group's products include: the orasure(R) and intercept(R) oral fluid collection devices; the oraquick(R) rapid diagnostic test device; histofreezer(R) portable cryosurgical systems; immunoassay tests and reagents; western blot confirmatory tests for HIV and other products. The products are sold in the United States and certain foreign countries to government agencies, clinical laboratories, physician's offices, hospitals, commercial and industrial entities, and various distributors.

Primary SIC and add'l.: 8731 2835

CIK No: 0001116463

Officers: Douglas A. Michels/Dir., CEO, Pres./$1,723,834.00, Mark L. Kuna/44/Sr. VP - Finance, Controller, Ronald H. Spair/CFO, COO/$972,275.00, Stephen R. Lee/Exec. VP, Chief Science Officer/$718,974.00, Joseph E. Zack/Exec. VP - Marketing, Sales/$676,063.00, Michael P. Formica/Exec. VP - Operations/$775,462.00, Jack E. Jerrett/Sr. VP - General Counsel, Sec.

Directors: Douglas A. Michels/Dir., CEO, Pres., Douglas G. Watson/Chmn., Jack Goldstein/Dir., Frank G. Hausmann/Dir., Ronny B. Lancaster/Dir., Charles W. Patrick/Dir., Roger L. Pringle/Dir., Michael Celano/49/Dir.

Owners: Michael P. Formica, Ronny B. Lancaster, Roger L. Pringle, Jack Goldstein, Stephen R. Lee, Joseph E. Zack, Wells Fargo& Company/12.02%, Frank G. Hausmann, Ronald H. Spair/1.30%, Douglas A. Michels/1.75%, First Manhattan Co./7.13%, BlackRock, Inc./11.51%, Douglas G. Watson, Charles W. Patrick, Insiders/7.19% *(16 Owners included in Index)*

Financial Data: **Fiscal Year End:**12/31 **Latest Annual Data:** 12/31/2006

Year	Sales	Net Income
2006	$68,155,000	$5,268,000
2005	$69,366,000	$27,448,000
2004	$54,008,000	-$560,000

Curr. Assets:	$112,559,000	**Curr. Liab.:**	$16,580,000	**P/E Ratio:**	62.23
Plant, Equip.:	$17,375,000	**Total Liab.:**	$27,062,000	**Indic. Yr. Divd.:**	NA
Total Assets:	$156,565,000	**Net Worth:**	$129,504,000	**Debt/ Equity:**	0.0757

Orbcomm Inc

2115 Linwood Ave., Ste. 100, Fort Lee, NJ, 07024; ***PH:*** 1-703-433-6300; ***Fax:*** 1-703-433-6400; ***http://*** www.orbcomm.com; ***Email:*** investorrelations@orbcomm.com

General - Incorporation .... DE
Employees 99
Auditor .... J.H. Cohn, LLP
Stk Agt .... Mellon Investor Services LLC
Counsel .... NA
DUNS No. .... NA

Stock - Price on:12/24/2007 .... $15.96
Stock Exchange .... NDQ
Ticker Symbol .... ORBC
Outstanding Shares 40,170,000
E.P.S .... NA
Shareholders .... NA

Business: The groups principle activity is to provide commercial wireless messaging system. The groups service is satellite communications. Specific customers of the group include Caterpillar Inc., Komatsu Ltd., Hitachi Construction Machinery Co., Ltd. and Volvo Group. The group operates from the United States, Central Asia and other. The group's quarterly revenue for September 2007 was 6.91 millions of USD.

Primary SIC and add'l.: 4789 4899 7389 7382

CIK No: 0001361983

Subsidiaries: European Datacomm Holding NV, Leosatellite Services de Ecuador S.A., MITE Global Communications S.A. de C.V., Orbcomm Australia Gateway Company Pty. Limited, Orbcomm Canada Inc., Orbcomm Central America Holdings LLC, Orbcomm Curacao Gateway N.V., Orbcomm Europe LLC, Orbcomm International Holdings LLC, Orbcomm License Corp., Orbcomm LLC, ORBCOMM Maghreb, Orbcomm New Zealand Limited, Orbcomm Panama Incorporated Inc., Satcom International Group PLC 16 Subsidiaries included in the Index

Officers: Jerome B. Eisenberg/Chmn., CEO, Pres., Marc J. Eisenberg/COO, Robert G. Costantini/CFO, Exec. VP, John J. Stolte/Exec. VP - Technology, Operations

Directors: Jerome B. Eisenberg/Chmn., CEO, Pres., Marco Fuchs/Dir., Hans E.W. Hoffmann/Dir., Gary H. Ritondaro/Dir.

Owners: General Electric Capital Corporation/5.48%, Ronald Gerwig/6.69%, Jerome B. Eisenberg/3.84%, Timothy Kelleher/14.09%, John J. Stolte, Emmett Hume, Ridgewood Satellite LLC/9.33%, Estate and Family of Don Franco/5.44%, MH Investors Satellite LLC/6.69%, Marco Fuchs/7.66%, John P. Brady, Robert G. Costantini, Marc Eisenberg/1.13%, Insiders/34.67%, Hans E. W. Hoffmann *(18 Owners included in Index)*

Financial Data: **Fiscal Year End:**12/31 **Latest Annual Data:** 12/31/2006

Year	Sales	Net Income
2006	$24,520,000	-$11,215,000
2005	$15,527,000	-$9,098,000
2004	$10,866,000	-$12,389,000

Curr. Assets:	$111,233,000	**Curr. Liab.:**	$10,436,000		
Plant, Equip.:	$29,131,000	**Total Liab.:**	$19,381,000	**Indic. Yr. Divd.:**	NA
Total Assets:	$148,093,000	**Net Worth:**	$128,712,000	**Debt/ Equity:**	0.0068

Orbit E-Commerce Inc

14845 Yonge St., Aurora, ON, L4G 6H8; ***PH:*** 1-905-751-1499; ***http://*** www.orbitecommerce.com; ***Email:*** info@orbitecommerce.com

General - Incorporation .... NV
Employees .... NA
Auditor .... Mccarney Greenwood LLP
Stk Agt .... Capital Transfer Agency Inc
Counsel .... NA
DUNS No. 10-852-2988

Stock - Price on:12/24/2007 .... $0.12
Stock Exchange .... OTC
Ticker Symbol .... OECI
Outstanding Shares .... NA
E.P.S .... NA
Shareholders .... NA

Business: The group's principal activity is to provide Internet services that include Internet access and phone-to-phone voip (voice over Internet protocol) long distance. The services provided are based on advanced voip gateway technology, utilizing the public Internet. Operating in Canada, the group provides its services on a retail basis in twelve major centers across Canada from vancouver to montreal. On 12-Oct-2002, the group signed agreements with gan and associates inc to form and operate an American based company called phoenix telnet llc to offer voip and other data and long distance services in the United States and Canada.

Primary SIC and add'l.: 4813 4822 7375

CIK No: 0000071391

Subsidiaries: Orbit Canada inc

Officers: Douglas C. Lloyd/Dir., Founder, Pres., CEO - Principal Accounting, Financial Officer, Michael Somerville/Information Technology Engineer, John Neufeld/VP - Sales, Marketing, Tony Kemp/Techincal Consultant

Directors: Douglas C. Lloyd/Dir., Founder, Pres., CEO - Principal Accounting, Financial Officer

Owners: Insiders/39.70%, Orbit Reorganization Facilitator Inc/8.30%, PureNet.TV Canada Inc./38.90%, Douglas C. Lloyd/39.70%

Financial Data: **Fiscal Year End:**07/31 **Latest Annual Data:** 7/31/2006

Year	Sales	Net Income
2006	NA	-$130,000
2005	NA	-$763,000
2004	NA	-$402,000

Curr. Assets:	$0	**Curr. Liab.:**	$362,000		
Plant, Equip.:	NA	**Total Liab.:**	$362,000	**Indic. Yr. Divd.:**	NA
Total Assets:	$0	**Net Worth:**	-$362,000	**Debt/ Equity:**	NA

Orbit International Corp

80 Cabot Ct., Hauppauge, NY, 11788; ***PH:*** 1-631-435-8300; ***Fax:*** 1-631-435-8458; ***http://*** www.orbitintl.com; ***Email:*** sales@orbitintl.com

General - Incorporation .... DE
Employees 126
Auditor .... Goldstein Golub Kessler LLP
Stk Agt ..... American Stock Transfer & Trust Co.
Counsel .... Snow Becker Krauss P.C.
DUNS No. 00-204-6530

Stock - Price on:12/24/2007 .... $8.8
Stock Exchange .... NDQ
Ticker Symbol .... ORBT
Outstanding Shares 4,600,000
E.P.S $0.47
Shareholders .... NA

Business: The group's principal activity is to design, manufacture and market customized electronic components and subsystems, distortion free commercial power units, power conversion devices and electronic devices for measurement and display. It operates through orbit instrument division and behlman electronics inc, which takes care of electronic subsystems and power units respectively. The group's products include intercommunication panels, displays, keyboards and pointing devices, ac power sources, frequency converters and uninterruptible power supplies products. The major customers of the group are various agencies of the United States government, lockheed martin corp, raytheon company.

Primary SIC and add'l.: 3669 3577 3629 3679

CIK No: 0000074818

Subsidiaries: Behlman Electronics, Inc., Orbit Instrument of California, Inc., TDL Manufacturing, Inc., Tulip Development Laboratory, Inc

Officers: Dennis Sunshine/CEO/$624,500.00, Bruce Reissman/58/Exec. VP, COO, Dir./$598,144.00, Mark Tublisky/70/Dir., Sec., Pres. - Behlman Electronics, Inc/$209,879.00, David Goldman/38/Dir., Treasurer, Controller, Michael Brunone/52/Dir., CFO, Exec. VP, Mitchell Binder/Dir., CFO, Exec. VP/$433,191.00, Linda Latman/Investor Relations Counsel, Lena Cati/Investor Relations Counsel

Directors: Michael Brunone/52/Dir., CFO, Exec. VP, Mitchell Binder/Dir., CFO, Exec. VP, Bruce Reissman/58/Exec. VP, COO, Dir., Richard A. Hetherington/53/Dir., Mark Tublisky/70/Dir., Sec., Pres. - Behlman Electronics, Inc, David Goldman/38/Dir., Treasurer, Controller, Arthur Rhein/62/Dir., Bernard Karcinell/69/Dir., Lee Feinberg/61/Dir., William H. Coogan/54/Dir.

Owners: William H. Coogan, Elkhorn Partners Limited Partnership/9.40%, Dennis Sunshine/7.80%, Mitchell Binde/7.30%, Mark Tublisky, Arthur Rhein, Lee Feinberg, Bruce Reissman/10.30%, Insiders/26.50%, Oppenheimer Funds, Inc./8.70%, Richard Hetherington/2.70%, Al Frank Asset Management/13.90%, Bernard Karcinell

Financial Data: **Fiscal Year End:**12/31 **Latest Annual Data:** 12/31/2006

Year	Sales	Net Income
2006	$25,015,000	$2,419,000
2005	$24,254,000	$2,684,000
2004	$18,012,000	$1,937,000

Curr. Assets:	$21,563,000	**Curr. Liab.:**	$4,387,000	**P/E Ratio:**	17.96
Plant, Equip.:	$414,000	**Total Liab.:**	$8,919,000	**Indic. Yr. Divd.:**	NA
Total Assets:	$31,215,000	**Net Worth:**	$22,296,000	**Debt/ Equity:**	0.1649

ORBIT/FR Inc

506 Prudential Rd., Horsham, PA, 19044; *PH:* 1-215-674-5100; *Fax:* 1-215-674-1102; *http://* www.orbitfr.com; *Email:* sales@orbitfr.com

General		**Stock**	
Incorporation	DE	Price on:12/24/2007	$1.84
Employees	115	Stock Exchange	OTC
Auditor	Hoberman, Lesser, CPA's, PC	Ticker Symbol	ORFR
Stk Agt	American Stock Transfer & Trust Co.	Outstanding Shares	6,000,000
Counsel	NA	E.P.S	$0.19
DUNS No.	96-553-0397	Shareholders	NA

Business: The group's principal activity is to develop, market and support automated microwave test and measurement systems. The group also manufactures anechoic foam, a microwave absorbing material that is an external component of microwave test and measurement systems. The products are sold in the United States and throughout the world. Customers of the group include manufacturers of wireless systems and products, such as motorola, nokia and ericsson; aerospace/defense systems integrators and product manufacturers, such as lockheed martin, raytheon, northrop grumman, bae, and boeing; telecommunications service providers, such as at&t, ntt and british telecom; and automobile and automotive subassembly manufacturers. The group also sells its products to the United States government and several foreign governments.

Primary SIC and add'l.: 3679 3663 3825

CIK No: 0001037115

Subsidiaries: Advanced ElectroMagnetics, Inc., Flam & Russell,Inc., Orbit FR Engineering, Ltd, Orbit FR Europe, GmbH

Officers: Israel Adan/CEO, Pres., William Campbell/VP - Engineering, Program Management US, John F. Aubin/CTO VP - Business Development, David Lubbe/CFO, Marcel Boumans/MD - Orbit, FR Europe Gmbh, Moshe Pinkasy/MD - Orbit, FR Engineering Ltd, Gabriel A. Sanchez/Pres. - Advanced Electromagnetics, Inc, Aemi, Mark Bates/VP - Software Development US, Connie Dougherty/Investor Relations Officer

Directors: Zeev Stein/55/Chmn., Dan Goffer/56/Dir., Doron Ginat/39/Dir., Uri Jenach/54/Dir.

Owners: Wellington Trust Company, NA/5.39%, Uri Jenach, William Campbell, Dan Goffer, Dave Lubbe, Zeev Stein/61.80%, Mark Bates, John Aubin, Israel Adan, Insiders/66.20%, Doron Ginat

Financial Data: *Fiscal Year End:*12/31 *Latest Annual Data:* 12/31/2006

Year	Sales	Net Income
2006	$29,441,000	$1,161,000
2005	$22,905,000	$618,000
2004	$21,185,000	$952,000

Curr. Assets:	$15,514,000	**Curr. Liab.:**	$9,648,000	**P/E Ratio:**	10.82
Plant, Equip.:	$1,169,000	**Total Liab.:**	$9,648,000	**Indic. Yr. Divd.:**	NA
Total Assets:	$17,527,000	**Net Worth:**	$7,879,000	**Debt/ Equity:**	NA

Orbital Corp Ltd

389 W Hunters Creek Rd., Lapeer, MI, 48446; *PH:* 1-810-245-0621; *Fax:* 1-810-277-2183; *http://* www.orbeng.com.au; *Email:* info@orbeng.com

General		**Stock**	
Incorporation	Australia	Price on:12/24/2007	$10.91
Employees	NA	Stock Exchange	OTC
Auditor	KPMG LLP	Ticker Symbol	OBTLY
Stk Agt	Bank of New York	Outstanding Shares	NA
Counsel	Sullivan & Cromwell	E.P.S	NA
DUNS No.	75-768-6001	Shareholders	NA

Business: The group's principle activities are the provision of engineering services, the development of engine and related technologies, the provision of research, design and development services to producers of powertrains and engine management systems for application in marine and recreational vehicles, automobiles and trucks.marine & recreation accounted for 75% of fiscal 2003 revenues; motorcycles, 9%; automotive,89% and engineering, 7%

Primary SIC and add'l.: 3519 8711

CIK No: 0000880419

Subsidiaries: Orbital Australia Pty Limited

Officers: Rodney Houston/Dir., MD, CEO, Geoff Paul Cathcart/Dir. - Engineering, Operations, Keith Halliwell/CFO, Tony Fitzgerald/Dir. - Sales, Marketing, Brian Anthony Fitzgerald/Dir. - Sales, Marketing

Directors: Rodney Houston/Dir., MD, CEO, William Peter Day/Chmn., John Richard Marshall/Dir., John Grahame Young/64/Non - Exec. Dir.

Financial Data: *Fiscal Year End:*06/30 *Latest Annual Data:* 06/30/2007

Year	Sales	Net Income
2007	$12,569,000	$961,000
2006	$8,661,000	-$659,000
2005	$8,837,000	-$1,689,000

Curr. Assets:	$5,092,000	**Curr. Liab.:**	$3,227,000		
Plant, Equip.:	$4,696,000	**Total Liab.:**	$17,975,000	**Indic. Yr. Divd.:**	NA
Total Assets:	$17,904,000	**Net Worth:**	-$71,000	**Debt/ Equity:**	NA

Orbital Sciences Corp

21839 Atlantic Blvd., Dulles, VA, 20166; *PH:* 1-703-406-5000; *Fax:* 1-703-406-3502; *http://* www.orbital.com; *Email:* investor.relations@orbital.com

General		**Stock**	
Incorporation	DE	Price on:12/24/2007	$20.81
Employees	2,800	Stock Exchange	NYSE
Auditor	PricewaterhouseCoopers LLP	Ticker Symbol	ORB
Stk Agt	Computershare Investor Services LLC	Outstanding Shares	59,340,000
Counsel	NA	E.P.S	$0.60
DUNS No.	10-191-6062	Shareholders	NA

Business: The group's principal activity is to design, develop, manufacture and operate small space and rocket systems for the U.S. Department of defense and other U.S. Government agencies and for global commercial and scientific customers. The group operates in three segments. The launch vehicles and advanced programs segment includes ground and air launched rockets that deliver satellites into orbit and suborbital launch vehicles and missile defense boosters that are used as interceptor and target vehicles for missile defense systems. The spacecraft and related space systems segment includes low-orbit, geosynchronous-orbit and planetary spacecraft for communications, remote sensing and scientific missions and space-related technical services. The transportation management systems segment consists of satellite-based transportation management systems for public transit agencies and private vehicle fleet operators.

Primary SIC and add'l.: 9661 3812 3761 3663

CIK No: 0000820736

Officers: David W. Thompson/Chmn., CEO, Orbital Co - Founder/$1,438,439.00, Garrett E. Pierce/Vice Chmn., CFO/$1,173,415.00, James R. Thompson/Vice Chmn., COO, Pres./$1,221,995.00, Richard Kramer/Contact - Technical Services, Bob Ritter/Contact - Technical Services, Susan C. Sarner/Contact - Technical Services, Carl A. Marchetto/Exec. VP, GM - Space Systems Group/$588,441.00, Susan Herlick/Sr. VP, General Counsel, Sec., Ray Bietry/Contact - Technical Services, Paul N. Brost/Sr. VP - Finance, Business Operations, Gregory A. Jones/VP - Corporate Strategy, Business Development, Lou Amorosi/VP - Orbital - Suborbital Program, Leslie Seeman/Sec., Ronald J. Grabe/Exec. VP, GM - Launch Systems Group/$982,074.00, Mike Honaker/Program Dir. *(27 Officers included in Index)*

Directors: David W. Thompson/Chmn., CEO, Orbital Co - Founder, James R. Thompson/Vice Chmn., COO, Pres., Robert M. Hanisee/Dir., Edward F. Crawley/Dir., Daniel J. Fink/Dir., Lennard A. Fisk/Dir., Janice I. Obuchowski/Dir., Robert J. Hermann/Dir., Harrison H. Schmitt/Dir., James G. Roche/Dir., Scott L. Webster/Dir., Ronald T. Kadish/Dir., Frank L. Salizzoni/Dir.

Owners: FMR Corp./13.20%, TimesSquare Capital Management, LLC/5.90%, Edward F. Crawley, Robert M. Hanisee, Daniel J. Fink, Insiders/4.70%, David W. Thompson/1.00%, Ronald J. Grabe, Garrett E. Pierce, James R. Thompson/1.00%, Scott L. Webster, Janice I. Obuchowski, James G. Roche, Robert J. Hermann, ClearBridge Advisors, LLC/5.50% *(20 Owners included in Index)*

Financial Data: *Fiscal Year End:*12/31 *Latest Annual Data:* 12/31/2006

Year	Sales	Net Income
2006	$802,761,000	$34,884,000
2005	$703,450,000	$27,849,000
2004	$675,935,000	$200,000,000

Curr. Assets:	$450,233,000	**Curr. Liab.:**	$206,425,000	**P/E Ratio:**	34.68
Plant, Equip.:	$92,878,000	**Total Liab.:**	$350,175,000	**Indic. Yr. Divd.:**	NA
Total Assets:	$744,494,000	**Net Worth:**	$394,319,000	**Debt/ Equity:**	NA

Orbotech Ltd

44 Manning Rd., Billerica, MA, 01821; *PH:* 1-978-667-6037; *Fax:* 1-978-667-9969; *http://* www.orbotech.com; *Email:* infoisl@orbotech.com

General		**Stock**	
Incorporation	Israel	Price on:12/24/2007	$23.01
Employees	1,596	Stock Exchange	NDQ
Auditor	Kesselman & Kesselman	Ticker Symbol	ORBK
Stk Agt	American Stock Transfer & Trust Co.	Outstanding Shares	33,480,000
Counsel	Doron & David Cohen	E.P.S	$0.36
DUNS No.	60-002-2446	Shareholders	NA

Business: The group's principle activities are design, development, manufacture and marketing of automated optical inspection (aoi) systems for use in the manufacture of printed circuit boards and for use in the production of liquid crystal flat panel displays. The company also manufactures computer aided manufacturing systems and laser plotters for pcb production and provides customer support and training through its wholly-owned subsidiaries in the United States, Europe, Pacific Rim and Japan. The company maintains its main research, development and manufacturing facilities in Israel and more than 50 offices worldwide. Its shares are traded on the Nasdaq national market under the symbol 'orbk'. The group's quarterly revenue for Sep '07 was 82.32 millions of USD.

Primary SIC and add'l.: 3672 3577 7378

CIK No: 0000749037

Subsidiaries: Orbograph Ltd., Orbotech Asia Ltd., Orbotech Medical Solutions Ltd., Orbotech Pacific Ltd., Orbotech S.A., Orbotech, Inc

Officers: Raanan Cohen/CEO, Arie Weisberg/COO, Pres., Amichai Steinberg/CFO, Exec. VP, Michael Havin/Corp. Sec., Adrian Auman/Corporate VP - Finance, Investor Relations, Michelle Harnish/Mgr. - Marketing Communications, North America, Corporate Projects, Avi Gross/CTO, Exec. VP, Asher Levy/Exec. VP - Business, Strategy, Dan Falk/Dir. - Consultant, Abraham Gross/57/CTO, Exec. VP, Eliezer Tokman/Dir., Consultant

Directors: Shlomo Barak/Chmn., Yochai Richter/Active Chmn., Jacob Richter/Dir., Yehudit Bronicki/Dir., Shimon Ullman/Dir., Dan Falk/Dir. - Consultant, Aaron Ferber/Dir., Uzia Galil/Dir., Rafi Yizhar/Dir., Eliezer Tokman/Dir., Consultant

Owners: Harris Associates L.P./7.85%, Artisan Partners Limited Partnership/10.17%, T. Rowe Price Associates, Inc./6.26%, Insiders/10.06%, FMR Corp./9.14%, J. & W. Seligman & Co. Incorporated/7.31%

Financial Data: *Fiscal Year End:*12/31 *Latest Annual Data:* 12/31/2006

Year	Sales	Net Income
2006	$416,469,000	$54,970,000
2005	$379,923,000	$43,257,000
2004	$315,168,000	$29,486,000

Curr. Assets:	$474,294,000	**Curr. Liab.:**	$102,835,000		
Plant, Equip.:	$20,124,000	**Total Liab.:**	$133,511,000	**Indic. Yr. Divd.:**	NA
Total Assets:	$575,013,000	**Net Worth:**	$441,502,000	**Debt/ Equity:**	NA

Orchestra Therapeutics Inc

Formerly: Immune Response Corp (The)
5931 Darwin Ct., Carlsbad, CA, 92008; *PH:* 1-760-431-7080; *http://* www.imnr.com

General		**Stock**	
Incorporation	DE	Price on:12/24/2007	NA
Employees	38	Stock Exchange	NA
Auditor	Levitz, Zacks & Ciceric	Ticker Symbol	NA
Stk Agt	Computershare Trust Co., Inc.	Outstanding Shares	NA
Counsel	Heller Ehrman LLP	E.P.S	NA
DUNS No.	17-509-8136	Shareholders	NA

Business: The group's principle activity is to develop immune-based therapies. The group develops these therapies to induce specific immune responses for the treatment of HIV, autoimmune diseases and cancer. In addition the group is developing a targeted non-viral delivery technology for gene therapy, which is designed to enable the delivery of genes directly to the liver via intravenous injection. The group has developed an immune-based therapy to induce specific immune responses for the treatment of HIV. The group is developing complementary technology combining two platform technologies cytokines and tumor cell lines to develop cancer vaccines to treat colon, brain, prostate and melanoma cancers. The group operates from United States.

Primary SIC and add'l.: 2836 8731 2834

CIK No: 0000817785

Officers: Joseph F. Oneill/55/CEO, Pres./$914,892.00, Peter Lowry/46/VP - Manufacturing/$241,445.00, Michael K. Green/52/CFO, COO/$573,364.00, Georgia Theofan/51/VP - Clinical Development/$272,564.00

Directors: Robert E. Knowling/52/Chmn., Martyn Greenacre/66/Dir., David Hochman/33/Dir., Kevin Reilly/65/Dir., Kevin B. Kimberlin/55/Co - Founder, Jim Foght/72/Dir.

Owners: James L. Foght, Insiders/40.70%, Peter Lowry, Kevin B. Kimberlin/36.60%, James B. Glavin, Georgia Theofan, Kevin L. Reilly, Joseph F. ONeill, Michael K. Green, Martyn Greenacre, David Hochman/5.60%

Financial Data: **Fiscal Year End:**12/31 **Latest Annual Data:** 12/31/2006

Year	Sales	Net Income
2006	$932,000	$195,290,000
2005	$44,000	-$17,313,000
2004	$323,000	-$29,959,000

Curr. Assets:	$4,710,000	**Curr. Liab.:**	$10,750,000		
Plant, Equip.:	$2,785,000	**Total Liab.:**	$18,990,000	**Indic. Yr. Divd.:**	NA
Total Assets:	$8,106,000	**Net Worth:**	-$10,884,000	**Debt/ Equity:**	NA

Orchid Cellmark Inc

4390 US Rte. 1, Princeton, NJ, 08540; *PH:* 1-609-750-2200; *Fax:* 1-609-750-6400; *http://* www.orchid.com; *Email:* mail@orchid.com

General - Incorporation	DE	**Stock**- Price on:12/24/2007	$4.69
Employees	403	Stock Exchange	NDQ
Auditor	KPMG LLP	Ticker Symbol	ORCH
Stk Agt	American Stock Transfer & Trust Co.	Outstanding Shares	29,350,000
Counsel	Mintz Levin et al	E.P.S	-$0.11
DUNS No.	NA	Shareholders	NA

Business: The group's principal activity is to develop genetic diversity technologies, products and services for genetic biochemistry applications. The products include scoring single nucleotide polymorphism and microfluidics technologies. They are used in drug discovery, principally in the field of pharmacogenetics and dna synthesis. Genetic diversity information is used by the pharmaceutical and medical communities to facilitate the development of highly specific and efficacious drugs, to improve the effectiveness of existing drugs and to increase the likelihood of success of tissue transplants. The group's proprietary technologies are also used in other commercial applications outside the healthcare field including forensics, paternity testing, improved crop development and livestock breeding programs.

Primary SIC and add'l.: 5047 8734 8731

CIK No: 0001107216

Subsidiaries: GeneScreen, Inc., GeneShield, Inc., Lifecodes Corporation, Orchid BioSciences Europe Limited.

Officers: Thomas A. Bologna/Dir., CEO, Pres./$1,185,167.00, Mary Bashore/Investor Relations Officer, Bruce F. Basarab/VP - North American Sales, Marketing, James F. Smith/CFO, VP

Directors: Thomas A. Bologna/Dir., CEO, Pres., George Poste/Chmn., Nicole S. Williams/Dir., James Beery/Dir., Sidney M. Hecht/Dir., Kenneth D. Noonan/Dir.

Owners: Kenneth D. Noonan, Millenco/7.20%, Royce & Associates/9.90%, Accipiter Capital Management LLC/14.80%, James Beery, Ziff Asset Management/7.90%, Insiders/1.80%, Sidney M. Hecht, Thomas A. Bologna, Nicole S. Williams, George H. Poste, John C. Deighan

Financial Data: **Fiscal Year End:**12/31 **Latest Annual Data:** 12/31/2006

Year	Sales	Net Income
2006	$56,854,000	-$11,271,000
2005	$61,609,000	-$9,439,000
2004	$62,499,000	-$8,812,000

Curr. Assets:	$38,804,000	**Curr. Liab.:**	$8,831,000		
Plant, Equip.:	$8,469,000	**Total Liab.:**	$9,944,000	**Indic. Yr. Divd.:**	NA
Total Assets:	$60,850,000	**Net Worth:**	$50,906,000	**Debt/ Equity:**	NA

Orchids Paper Products Company

4826 Hunt St., Pryor, OK, 74361; *PH:* 1-918-825-0616; *Fax:* 1-918-825-0060; *http://* www.orchidspaper.com

General - Incorporation	DE	**Stock**- Price on:12/24/2007	$5.163
Employees	310	Stock Exchange	AMEX
Auditor	Tullius Taylor Sartain & Sartain LLP	Ticker Symbol	TIS
Stk Agt	American Stock Transfer & Trust Co.	Outstanding Shares	6,230,000
Counsel	NA	E.P.S	$0.409
DUNS No.	NA	Shareholders	NA

Business: The groups principle activity is manufacturing of tissue paper. The group products include paper towels, bathroom tissue and paper napkins. The group marketed its products under the trade names VELVET(R), COLORTEX (R), ULTRA VALU(R), DRI-MOP (R) and BIG MOPPER (R). Specific customers of the group include Freds, Variety Wholesale, Wal-Mart, Dollar Tree and Big Lots. The group operates from Pryor and Oklahoma. The group's quarterly revenue for September 2007 was 19.22 millions of USD.

Primary SIC and add'l.: 2621 2676

CIK No: 0001324189

Officers: Robert A. Snyder/CEO, Pres., Michael P. Sage/61/Dir., Pres., Keith R. Schroeder/CFO

Directors: Jay Shuster/Chmn., John C. Guttilla/Dir., Jeffery Schoen/Dir., Michael P. Sage/61/Dir., Pres., Douglas E. Hailey/Dir., Gary P. Arnold/Dir., Steven R. Berlin/Dir.

Owners: Michael P. Sage/3.00%, Michael N. Taglich/7.20%, Jay Shuster, Insiders/9.60%, Keith R. Schroeder/1.50%, Robert F. Taglich/6.80%, Gary P. Arnold/2.80%, John C. Guttilla, Jeffrey S. Schoen, Steven R. Berlin, Douglas E. Hailey/2.20%

Financial Data: **Fiscal Year End:**12/31 **Latest Annual Data:** 12/31/2006

Year	Sales	Net Income
2006	$60,190,000	$732,000
2005	$57,700,000	$1,392,000

Curr. Assets:	$12,865,000	**Curr. Liab.:**	$7,840,000		
Plant, Equip.:	$58,039,000	**Total Liab.:**	$46,324,000	**Indic. Yr. Divd.:**	NA
Total Assets:	$71,028,000	**Net Worth:**	$24,704,000	**Debt/ Equity:**	NA

Orckit Communications Ltd

126 Yigal Allon St., Tel Aviv, 67443; *PH:* 972-36962121; *Fax:* 972-36965678; *http://* www.orckit.com; *Email:* info@orckit.com

General - Incorporation	Israel	**Stock**- Price on:12/24/2007	$9.15
Employees	219	Stock Exchange	NDQ
Auditor	Kesselman & Kesselman	Ticker Symbol	ORCT
Stk Agt	Kesselman & Kesselman	Outstanding Shares	15,760,000
Counsel	NA	E.P.S	-$1.293
DUNS No.	60-020-5371	Shareholders	NA

Business: The groups principle activities include designing, development, manufacturing and selling of data access systems mainly to telephone companies and private network operators. The group also provides designing of telecom equipment targeting metro areas based on emerging resilient packet ring technology. The groups products include digital subscriber line multiplexor system (DSLAM) based on asymmetric technology (ADSL). The group operates from United States.

Primary SIC and add'l.: 3661

CIK No: 0001021620

Subsidiaries: Corrigent Systems Inc., Corrigent Systems KK., Corrigent Systems Ltd.

Officers: Eric Paneth/Chmn., CEO, Leon Bruckman/CTO, Zvika Menahemi/COO, Izhak Tamir/Dir., Pres., Aviv Boim/CFO, Eli Aloni/Exec. VP - Technology - Marketing, Oren Maymon/VP - Operations, Lee Roth/IR Contact

Directors: Eric Paneth/Chmn., CEO, Miri Gelbman/Dir., Moshe Nir/Dir., Moti Motil/Dir., Izhak Tamir/Dir., Pres., Jed Arkin/Dir.

Owners: David J. Greene and Company, LLC/7.60%, Insiders/15.90%, Eric Paneth/7.50%, Izhak Tamir/7.50%, FMR Corp./6.90%

Financial Data: **Fiscal Year End:**12/31 **Latest Annual Data:** 12/31/2006

Year	Sales	Net Income
2006	$63,648,000	$5,204,000
2005	$101,247,000	$22,226,000
2004	$11,276,000	-$20,132,000

Curr. Assets:	$53,133,000	**Curr. Liab.:**	$18,237,000		
Plant, Equip.:	$2,490,000	**Total Liab.:**	$22,494,000	**Indic. Yr. Divd.:**	NA
Total Assets:	$99,357,000	**Net Worth:**	$76,863,000	**Debt/ Equity:**	NA

Oregon Pacific Bancorp

1355 Hwy. 101, Florence, OR, 97439; *PH:* 1-541-997-7121; *Fax:* 1-541-997-2774; *http://* www.opbc.com

General - Incorporation	OR	**Stock**- Price on:12/24/2007	$11.5
Employees	95	Stock Exchange	OTC
Auditor	Moss Adams LLP	Ticker Symbol	OPBP
Stk Agt	Registrar & Transfer Co	Outstanding Shares	2,200,000
Counsel	NA	E.P.S	$0.89
DUNS No.	NA	Shareholders	NA

Business: The group's principal activity is to provide banking services in Oregon. The group provides depository and lending services to commercial enterprises, governmental entities and individuals. Its consumer deposit products include checking, savings and money market accounts and certificates of deposit. Lending products include residential real estate financing, commercial loans, installment and overdrafts, home equity and personal lines of credit, and motor vehicle loans. The group also provides trust, asset management services and investment and brokerage services. Other services consist of safe deposit boxes, letters of credit, travelers' checks, direct deposit of payroll, social security and dividend payments and automatic payment of insurance premiums and mortgage loans. The group operates through four branches in florence, roseburg, coos bay and sutherlin.

Primary SIC and add'l.: 6022 6712

CIK No: 0001216128

Subsidiaries: Oregon Pacific Banking Co., Oregon Pacific Statutory Trust I.

Officers: Jim Clark/Pres., CEO - Oregon Pacific Bank/$129,697.00, Deena Gisholt/VP, South Coast Loan Mgr., Branch Mgr. - Coos Bay, Oregon Pacific Bank, Kim Kentta/VP, Regional Mgr. - Mortgage Loans, Florence, Coos Bay, Roseburg, Oregon Pacific Bank, Ronald Green/Exec. VP, Chief Credit Officer - Financial Services Center, Oregon Pacific Bank, Judy Matheny/Trust Officer - Oregon Pacific Bank, Pat Riley/Sr. VP, Mgr. - Trust Services, Oregon Pacific Bank, Lisa Tine/Trust Officer - Oregon Pacific Bank, Carol Au Court/Trust Operations Assist, Oregon Pacific Bank, Tina Meyers/Trust Operations Specialist - Oregon Pacific Bank, Joanne A. Forsberg/CFO, Exec. VP/$117,657.00, Debbie Stinger/Supervisor, Safeway Branch, Florence, Oregon Pacific Bank, Cindy Kent/Commercial Loan Officer - Roseburg Branch, Oregon Pacific Bank

Owners: Thomas K. Grove/5.10%, Lydia G. Brackney/0.20%, Jon Thompson/0.20%, Joanne Forsberg/0.40%, Richard L. Yecny/0.20%, Insiders/19.60%, Doug Feldkamp/0.40%, James P. Clark, A.J. Brauer/6.10%, Don Mabry/0.30%, Marteen L. Wick/0.20%, Patricia Benetti/0.20%, Robert R. King/6.20%

Financial Data: **Fiscal Year End:**12/31 **Latest Annual Data:** 12/31/2006

Year	Sales	Net Income
2006	$14,474,000	$1,986,000
2005	$12,769,000	$1,865,000
2004	$10,401,000	$1,067,000

Curr. Assets:	$11,402,000	**Curr. Liab.:**	$132,986,000	**P/E Ratio:**	12.92
Plant, Equip.:	$6,986,000	**Total Liab.:**	$139,405,000	**Indic. Yr. Divd.:**	$0.280
Total Assets:	$151,305,000	**Net Worth:**	$11,901,000	**Debt/ Equity:**	0.3465

Oregon Steel Mills Inc

1000 Sw Brd.way, Ste 2200, Portland, OR, 97205; *PH:* 1-503-240-5788; *http://* www.osm.com

General - Incorporation	DE	**Stock**- Price on:12/24/2007	NA
Employees	1,680	Stock Exchange	NA
Auditor	KPMG LLP	Ticker Symbol	NA
Stk Agt	Mellon Investor Services LLC	Outstanding Shares	NA
Counsel	Parker Chapin Flattau & Klimpl	E.P.S	NA
DUNS No.	00-910-6055	Shareholders	NA

Business: The group's principal activity is to manufacture and markets specialty and commodity steel products. The group operates two steel minimills and seven finishing facilities in the western United States and Canada. The Oregon steel division's steel pipe mill in napa, California is a large diameter steel pipe mill and fabrication facility. Napa pipe mill produces pipe of a quality suitable for use in high-pressure oil and gas transmission pipelines. The rocky mountain steel mills, located in Colorado, supplies steel for the company's rail, rod and bar and seamless tubular finishing mills the principal markets for the group's products are steel service centers, steel fabricators, railroads, oil and gas producers and distributors and other industrial concerns. The group's products are primarily marketed in the United States, west of the Mississippi river and western Canada.

Primary SIC and add'l.: 3312 3317

CIK No: 0000830260

Subsidiaries: Camrose Pipe Corporation, Canadian National Steel Corporation, CF&I Steel, L.P., Colorado & Wyoming Railway Company, LSI Plate, New CF&I, Inc., Oregon Feralloy Partners, Oregon Steel de Guayana, Inc., Oregon Steel Mills Processing, Inc, OSM Distribution, Inc., OSM GlassificationTM, Inc.

Officers: James E. Declusin/Dir., CEO, Pres., Robin A. Gantt/CFO, Treasurer, Jennifer R. Murray/VP - Administration, Corp. Sec., Larry R. Lawrence/VP - Sales, OSM Tubular, Scott J. Montross/VP GM, VP - Sales, Marketing, Plate, Coil, Robert A. Simon/VP, GM - Rocky Mountain Steel Mills, Bill Groom/Contact - Octg Seamless Sales

Directors: James E. Declusin/Dir., CEO, Pres.

Oretech Inc

309 State Docks Rd. , Phenix City, AL, 36869; **PH:** 1-334-297-0663; **http://** www.oretech.net

General - Incorporation	NV	Stock - Price on:12/24/2007	NA
Employees	NA	Stock Exchange	NA
Auditor	Rotenberg & Co. LLP	Ticker Symbol	NA
Stk Agt	American Stock Transfer & Trust Co.	Outstanding Shares	NA
Counsel	NA	E.P.S.	NA
DUNS No.	NA	Shareholders	NA

Business: The group's principal activity is to acquire mineral properties and the extraction of gold, silver, platinum and other precious metals.the group is planning to operate in the extraction of precious and strategic metals from various ore tailings, dump piles and other industrial feedstock sources. The management services business, and Internet related services business were discontinued. On 03-Apr-2003, the group acquired oretech corporation.

Primary SIC and add'l.: 1044 1081 1041

CIK No: 0001090052

Orezone Resources Inc

290 Picton St., Ste. 201, Ottawa, ON, K1K 8P8; **PH:** 1-613-241-3699; **http://** www.orezone.com; **Email:** info@orezone.com

General - Incorporation	Canada	Stock - Price on:12/24/2007	$1.6
Employees	72	Stock Exchange	AMEX
Auditor	PricewaterhouseCoopers LLP	Ticker Symbol	OZN
Stk Agt	Computershare Trust Co of Canada	Outstanding Shares	133,030,000
Counsel	NA	E.P.S.	-$0.01
DUNS No.	NA	Shareholders	NA

Business: The groups principle activities include exploring, developing and operating resource properties including precious metal properties. The group operates from Canada.

Primary SIC and add'l.: 9999

CIK No: 0001215546

Subsidiaries: Channel Mining (Barbados) Ltd., Orezone Inc.

Officers: Ronald Little/Dir., CEO, Pres., Pascal Marquis/VP - Exploration, M. S. King/VP - Technical Services, Bryan Tokarsky/CFO, VP, Niel Marotta/VP - Corporate Development

Directors: Ronald Little/Dir., CEO, Pres., David Netherway/Dir., Greg Bowes/Dir., Michael Halvorson/Dir., Peter Allen/Dir., Paul Carmel/Dir.

Owners: Ronald Little, David Netherway, Paul Carmel, Gregory B. Bowes, Michael Halvorson, Niel Marotta

Financial Data: **Fiscal Year End:** 12/31   **Latest Annual Data:** 12/31/2006

Year	Sales	Net Income
2006	NA	-$9,742,000
2005	NA	-$7,703,000
2004	NA	-$7,103,000

Curr. Assets:	$23,064,000	Curr. Liab.:	$1,680,000		
Plant, Equip.:	$4,127,000	Total Liab.:	$1,680,000	Indic. Yr. Divd.:	NA
Total Assets:	$29,344,000	Net Worth:	$27,664,000	Debt/ Equity:	NA

Organetix Inc

Organix Inc, 240 Salem St., Woburn, MA, 01801; **PH:** 1-781-932-4142; **Fax:** 1-781-933-6695; **http://** organixinc.com; **Email:** organix@organixinc.com

General - Incorporation	DE	Stock - Price on:12/24/2007	$0.065
Employees	NA	Stock Exchange	OTC
Auditor	Meyler & Company, LLC	Ticker Symbol	OGTX
Stk Agt	NA	Outstanding Shares	72,520,000
Counsel	NA	E.P.S.	-$0.02
DUNS No.	NA	Shareholders	NA

Business: The groups principal activity is to produce proprietary medical discovery relating to the liver. The group operates from the United States.

Primary SIC and add'l.: 2834

CIK No: 0001106213

Officers: Raj Razdan/CEO, David F. Hostelley/68/Chmn., CEO, Pres., Sec., Anu Mahadevan/VP, Peter Meltzer/Pres., Howard Sard/VP, Paul Blundell/VP

Directors: David F. Hostelley/68/Chmn., CEO, Pres., Sec.

Financial Data: **Fiscal Year End:** 12/31   **Latest Annual Data:** 12/31/2006

Year	Sales	Net Income
2006	NA	-$1,114,000
2005	NA	-$1,269,000
2004	NA	-$1,240,000

Curr. Assets:	NA	Curr. Liab.:	NA		
Plant, Equip.:	NA	Total Liab.:	NA	Indic. Yr. Divd.:	NA
Total Assets:	NA	Net Worth:	NA	Debt/ Equity:	NA

Organic Soils Com Inc

7315 E Peakview Ave., Centennial, CO, 80111; **PH:** 1-303-796-8940

General - Incorporation	NV	Stock - Price on:12/24/2007	$0.38
Employees	NA	Stock Exchange	NA
Auditor	Cordovano & Honeck LLP	Ticker Symbol	NA
Stk Agt	First American Stock Transfer, Inc.	Outstanding Shares	14,900,000
Counsel	NA	E.P.S.	-$0.06
DUNS No.	NA	Shareholders	NA

Business: The group's principle activities include marketing and distributing services in the soil industry. The services provided by the company include assistance with package design, package design with in-store trials, as well as an introduction to various packaged soil distributors. It also provides consulting services in the area of market analysis, including determining potential profitability, potential volume, and ease of entry into specified markets. The group operates from United States.

Primary SIC and add'l.: 0711

CIK No: 0001108046

Subsidiaries: Inhibetex Therapeutics, Inc

Officers: Henry Fong/72/Dir., Pres., Principal Executive Officer, Principal Financial Officer, Principal Accounting Officer, Thomas B. Olson/42/Sec.

Directors: Henry Fong/72/Dir., Pres., Principal Executive Officer, Principal Financial Officer, Principal Accounting Officer

Owners: Gulfstream Financial Partners, LLC/20.70%, Insiders/22.60%, Henry Fong/20.70%, Thomas B. Olson/1.80%, Perkins Capital Management, Inc./18.60%, Wayne Mills/11.30%

Financial Data: **Fiscal Year End:** 01/31   **Latest Annual Data:** 1/31/2007

Year	Sales	Net Income
2007	NA	-$527,000
2006	NA	-$127,000
2004	NA	-$16,000

Curr. Assets:	$1,000	Curr. Liab.:	$45,000		
Plant, Equip.:	NA	Total Liab.:	$45,000	Indic. Yr. Divd.:	NA
Total Assets:	$1,000	Net Worth:	-$43,000	Debt/ Equity:	NA

Organic To Go Food Corp

Formerly: SP Holding Corp

3317 Third Ave. S, Seattle, WA, 98134; **PH:** 1-206-838-4670; **http://** www.organictogo.com

General - Incorporation	DE	Stock - Price on:12/24/2007	NA
Employees	NA	Stock Exchange	OTC
Auditor	Rose, Snyder & Jacobs	Ticker Symbol	OTGO
Stk Agt	American Stock Transfer & Trust Co.	Outstanding Shares	NA
Counsel	NA	E.P.S.	-$0.81
DUNS No.	NA	Shareholders	NA

Business: The groups principle activities include providing healthy alternative to typical fast food options, lunch box deliveries and casual catering. The group serves a range of organic, natural and wholesale meals, which include everything from cheese sandwiches to deli-style roast beef sandwiches and veggie packed salads. In October 2006, the group acquired Vinaigrettes LLC, In February 2007, the group acquired Organic Holding Company, Inc. and In March 2007 Jackrabbit a Seattle based catering company. The group operates from the United States.

Primary SIC and add'l.: 5812

CIK No: 0001014343

Subsidiaries: Organic To Go, Inc

Officers: Jason Brown/Chmn., CEO, Jonathan Wernick/40/CFO, Tom Rogers/Corporate Sales Mgr.

Directors: Jason Brown/Chmn., CEO, Peter Meehan/51/Dir., Roy Bingham/45/Dir., Douglas Lioon/51/Dir., S. M. Hassan/59/Dir.

Owners: Insiders/17.00%, Vicis Capital Master Fund/6.50%, Douglas Lioon/2.70%, Dave Smith, Wendy Tenenberg/1.20%, Jason Brown/10.90%, Roy Bingham, Michael Johnson, Trinad Capital Master Fund Ltd./6.40%, Peter Meehan, S. M. Hassan

Financial Data: **Fiscal Year End:** 12/31   **Latest Annual Data:** 12/31/2006

Year	Sales	Net Income
2006	$9,663,000	-$7,966,000
2005	NA	-$443,000
2004	NA	-$3,743,000

Curr. Assets:	$1,655,000	Curr. Liab.:	$8,549,000		
Plant, Equip.:	$2,148,000	Total Liab.:	$9,278,000	Indic. Yr. Divd.:	NA
Total Assets:	$5,277,000	Net Worth:	-$4,001,000	Debt/ Equity:	NA

Orgral Technologies Corp

113 Argonne Cres., Toronto, ON, M2K 2K2; **PH:** 1-416-557-9684

General - Incorporation	DE	Stock - Price on:12/24/2007	NA
Employees	NA	Stock Exchange	NA
Auditor	Gately & Assoc. LLC	Ticker Symbol	NA
Stk Agt	NA	Outstanding Shares	NA
Counsel	NA	E.P.S.	NA
DUNS No.	NA	Shareholders	NA

Business: The groups principle activity is to provide lawful corporate undertaking, including selected mergers and acquisitions. The group operates from United States.

Primary SIC and add'l.: 9995

CIK No: 0001294612

Officers: Helen Heit/Dir., CEO, CFO, Pres.

Orient Express Hotels Ltd

1114 Ave. of the Americas, 38th Fl., New York, NY, 10036; **PH:** 1-212-302-5055; **Fax:** 1-212-302-5203; **http://** www.orient-expressinvestorinfo.com

General - Incorporation	Bermuda	Stock - Price on:12/24/2007	$52.81
Employees	7,100	Stock Exchange	NYSE
Auditor	Deloitte & Touche LLP	Ticker Symbol	OEH
Stk Agt	EquiServe Trust Co N.A	Outstanding Shares	42,390,000
Counsel	Carter, Ledyard & Milburn	E.P.S.	$1.02
DUNS No.	NA	Shareholders	NA

Business: The group's principal activity is to manage and operate hotels, restaurants, tourist trains and cruises. The group owns and manages 39 properties, which consists of 30 deluxe hotels, 3 restaurants, five tourist trains and a river cruiseship. The hotels are located in the United States, Caribbean, Mexico, Europe, southern Africa, South America, Australia and south pacific. The restaurants are located in london, New York and buenos aires. The tourist trains operate in Europe, southeast Asia and Peru and the river cruiseship operates in burma. On 25-Apr-2003, the group acquired hotel ritz.

Primary SIC and add'l.: 7011 4011

CIK No: 0001115836

Subsidiaries: 21 Club Inc., 21 Club Properties Inc., 80 Westcliff (Pty) Ltd., Blanc Restaurants Ltd., Bora Bora Lagoon Resort S.A., Byblos S.r.l., Charleston Place Holdings Inc., Collection Venice Simplon-Orient-Express Ltd., Compania Hoteis Palace, Crosieres Orex S.A., CSN (San Miguel) Holdings Ltd., Cupecoy Village Development NV, Cupecoy Village Real Estate NV, El Encanto Inc., European Cruises Ltd. 80 Subsidiaries included in the Index

Officers: Paul White/CEO, Pres., Pippa Isbell/VP - Corporate Communications, Dean P. Andrews/VP - Real Estate Development, Adrian D. Constant/47/VP - Hotels Europe, Nicholas R. Varian/Chief Development Officer, Roger V. Collins/VP - Design, Technical Services, Natale Rusconi/VP, David C. Williams/VP - Sales, Marketing, Edwin S. Hetherington/VP, General Counsel, Sec., Filip Boyen/VP - Operations, Maurizio Saccani/VP - Italy

Directors: James B. Hurlock/Non Exec. Chmn., Prudence M. Leith/Dir., Georg R. Rafael/Dir., Robert J. Lovejoy/Dir., James B. Sherwood/Founder, Dir., John D. Campbell/Dir.

Owners: Orient-Express Holdings 1 Ltd./29.90%, Insiders, Insiders, Orient-Express Holdings 1 Ltd., Pippa Isbell, James B. Sherwood, John D. Campbell, Edwin S. Hetherington, Paul M. White, Dean P. Andrews, James B. Hurlock, Robert J. Lovejoy, Simon M.C. Sherwood, Nicholas R. Varian, Natale Rusconi

Financial Data: Fiscal Year End:12/31   Latest Annual Data: 12/31/2006

Year	Sales		Net Income
2006	$492,804,000		$39,767,000
2005	$433,147,000		$40,733,000
2004	$357,284,000		$28,222,000
Curr. Assets:	$254,679,000	Curr. Liab.: $238,880,000	P/E Ratio: 50.78
Plant, Equip.:	$1,183,400,000	Total Liab.: $944,667,000	Indic. Yr. Divd.: $0.100
Total Assets:	$1,751,663,000	Net Worth: $806,996,000	Debt/ Equity: 0.7548

Oriental Financial Group Inc

997 San Roberto St., Oriental Ctr. 10th Fl., San Juan, PR, 00926; **PH:** 1-787-771-6800; **Fax:** 1-787-993-4670; **http://** www.orientalfg.com

General - Incorporation	Puerto Rico	Stock- Price on:12/24/2007	$11.05
Employees	535	Stock Exchange	NYSE
Auditor	Deloitte & Touche LLP	Ticker Symbol	OFG
Stk Agt	American Stock Transfer & Trust Co.	Outstanding Shares	24,500,000
Counsel	NA	E.P.S.	$0.12
DUNS No.	80-917-1101	Shareholders	NA

Business: The group's principle activity is to provide banking services. The group operates in three segments: treasury, retail banking and financial services. These segments provide mortgage, commercial and consumer lending, saving and time deposit products, financial planning, insurance sales, money management and investment brokerage services. The subsidiaries of the group include oriental bank and trust, oriental financial services corporation, fisa insurance agency, inc. And oriental financial group, inc. The group operates with a network of 23 branch offices in san juan, Puerto Rico The group's quarterly revenue for Sep '07 was 8.45 millions of USD.

Primary SIC and add'l.: 6022 6712

CIK No: 0001030469

Subsidiaries: Caribbean Pension Consultants, Inc, Oriental Bank And Trust, Oriental Financial (pr) Statutory Trust I, Oriental Financial (pr) Statutory Trust Ii, Oriental Financial Services Corp., Oriental Insurance, Inc., Oriental International Bank Inc.

Officers: Jose Rafael Fernandez/Dir., CEO, Pres./$504,709.00, Ganesh Kumar/COO, Exec. VP/$385,351.00, Norberto Gonzalez/CFO, Exec. VP/$323,436.00, Steven Anreder/Investor Relations Officer, Jose E. Fernandez-Richards/Exec. VP - Banking Services, Carlos Velez/Pres. - Oriental Mortgage, Carlos O. Souffront/Sec., Carlos J. Nieves/Sr. Exec. VP - Financial Services/$352,725.00, Gary Fishman/Investor Relations Officer, Julio R. Micheo/Sr. Exec. VP, Chief Investment Officer, Treasurer, Lidio V. Soriano/Exec. VP - Retail Banking, Mortgage Divisions

Directors: Jose Rafael Fernandez/Dir., CEO, Pres., Jose J. Gil De Lamadrid/Chmn., Francisco Arrivi/Dir., Jose Enrique Fernandez/Dir., Pablo I. Altieri/Dir., Maricarmen Aponte/Dir., Julian S. Inclan/Dir., Efrain E. Archilla/Dir., Miguel Vazquez-Deynes/Dir., Juan Carlos Aguayo/Dir., Nelson Garcia/Dir., Pedro Morazzani Ferrer/Dir.

Owners: Maricarmen Aponte, Jose Enrique Fernandez/7.34%, Miguel Vzquez-Deynes, Juan C. Aguayo, Francisco Arrivi, Rutabaga Capital Management, LLC/8.97%, Jose J. De Lamadrid, Earnest Partners LLC/7.98%, Nelson Garcia, Jose Rafael Fernandez/1.14%, Pedro Morazzani, Pablo I. Altieri, Fidelity Management & Research Corp./9.48%

Financial Data: Fiscal Year End:06/30   Latest Annual Data: 12/31/2006

Year	Sales		Net Income
2006	$268,101,000		-$5,106,000
2005	$227,023,000		$56,612,000
Curr. Assets:	$82,273,000	Curr. Liab.: $3,822,319,000	
Plant, Equip.:	$19,455,000	Total Liab.: $3,909,485,000	Indic. Yr. Divd.: $0.560
Total Assets:	$4,250,652,000	Net Worth: $341,167,000	Debt/ Equity: 0.1518

Origen Financial Inc

27777 Franklin Rd., Ste. 1700, Southfield, MI, 48034; **PH:** 1-248-746-7000; **Fax:** 1-248-746-7091; **http://** www.origenfinancial.com

General - Incorporation	DE	Stock- Price on:12/24/2007	$7.05
Employees	278	Stock Exchange	NDQ
Auditor	Grant Thornton LLP	Ticker Symbol	ORGN
Stk Agt	American Stock Transfer & Trust Co.	Outstanding Shares	25,860,000
Counsel	NA	E.P.S.	$0.37
DUNS No.	NA	Shareholders	NA

Business: The groups principal activity is to provide manufactured housing loans services. The group operates from the United States. The assets of the group for the year 2006 were $1,073,067 (thousands).

Primary SIC and add'l.: 6798 6162

CIK No: 0001268039

Subsidiaries: OF Insurance Agency, Inc., Origen Asset-Backed Note Trust, Origen CMO Residential Holding Company, L.L.C., Origen Credit L.L.C., Origen Financial L.L.C., Origen Financial of Puerto Rico, L.L.C, Origen Financial of South Dakota, L.L.C., Origen Insurance Agency, L.L.C., Origen Manufactured Home Financial, L.L.C., Origen Manufactured Housing Contract Trust 2004-A, Origen Manufactured Housing Contract Trust 2004-B, Origen Manufactured Housing Contract Trust 2005-A, Origen Manufactured Housing Contract Trust 2005-B, Origen Manufactured Housing Contract Trust 2006-A, Origen MH Contract Company, L.L.C. 21 Subsidiaries included in the Index

Officers: Ronald Klein/50/Dir., CEO, Peter J. Scherer/Pres., Head - Operations, Anderson W. Geater/CFO, Mark Landschulz/Exec. VP - Portfolio Management, Douglas O. Burdett/58/Exec. VP, Mgr. - Loan Servicing, Paul Galaspie/CIO, Sr. VP, David M. Rand/46/Sr. VP - Marketing, Strategic Development, Jim Bramlage/Sr. VP - Strategic Development, Benton E. Sergi/Sr. VP - Operations, Laura Campbell/Sr. VP - Human Resources, Jennifer Schotte/Dir. - Training, Development, Brett Thomas/Sr. VP - Servicing, Matt Allen/VP - Marketing, Jeff Mouat/VP - Sales

Directors: Ronald Klein/50/Dir., CEO, Paul A. Halpern/55/Chmn., Richard H. Rogel/59/Dir., Gary A. Shiffman/53/Dir., Michael J. Wechsler/68/Dir., Robert S. Sher/69/Dir.

Owners: Anderson W. Geater, Insiders/30.70%, Sun OFI, LLC/19.30%, Robert E. Robotti/8.70%, Michael J. Wechsler, Ronald A. Klein/2.20%, Mark W. Landschulz, Benton E. Sergi, Richard H. Rogel, Peter J. Scherer, Ronald R. Redfield/7.40%, Third Avenue Management LLC/8.80%, Gary A. Shiffman/19.40%, Paul A. Halpern/6.90%, Woodward Holding, LLC/6.80%

Financial Data: Fiscal Year End:12/31   Latest Annual Data: 12/31/2006

Year	Sales		Net Income
2006	$92,082,000		$6,971,000
2005	$74,042,000		-$2,659,000
2004	$53,663,000		-$2,966,000
Curr. Assets:	$17,978,000	Curr. Liab.: $23,582,000	
Plant, Equip.:	$6,559,000	Total Liab.: $868,603,000	Indic. Yr. Divd.: $0.360
Total Assets:	$1,073,067,000	Net Worth: $204,464,000	Debt/ Equity: 4.2607

Origin Agritech Ltd

625 Broadway, Ste. 1111, San Diego, CA, 92101; **PH:** 1-619-795-4627; **Fax:** 1-619-795-9639; **http://** www.originagritech.com

General - Incorporation British Virgin Islands		Stock- Price on:12/24/2007	$8.25
Employees	743	Stock Exchange	NDQ
Auditor	Deloitte Touche Tohmatsu CPA Ltd.	Ticker Symbol	SEED
Stk Agt	Continental Stock Transfer & Trust Co	Outstanding Shares	NA
Counsel	NA	E.P.S.	NA
DUNS No.	NA	Shareholders	NA

Business: The groups principle activities include researching and developing, producing and selling and marketing crop seeds. The products of the group include corn, cotton, rice and canola. The group operates from China. The group's quarterly revenue for September 2007 was 447.73 millions of USD.

Primary SIC and add'l.: 5191 0131 0112 0115

CIK No: 0001321851

Subsidiaries: Beijing Origin Seed Limited, Beijing Origin State Harvest Biotechnology Limited, Changchun Origin Seed Technology Development Limited, Denong Zhengcheng Seed Limited, Henan Origin Cotton Technology Development Limited, Jilin Changji Seed Limited, Jilin Changrong High-tech Seed Limited, Shenzhen BiocenturyTransgene (China)Limited, Shijiazhuang Liyu Technology Development Limited, State Harvest Holding Limtied

Officers: Gengchen Han/52/Chmn., CEO, Liang Yuan/50/Dir., Executive Vice Chmn., Youqiang Wang/44/CFO, Yasheng Yang/44/Dir., Pres., Treasurer, COO, Irving Kau/VP - Finance

Directors: Gengchen Han/52/Chmn., CEO, Liang Yuan/50/Dir., Executive Vice Chmn., Yasheng Yang/44/Dir., Pres., Treasurer, COO, Bailiang Zhang/66/Dir., Dafang Huang/65/Dir., Kerry S. Propper/32/Dir., Steven Urbach/31/Dir., Michael W. Trimble/50/Dir., Remo Richli/44/Dir.

Owners: JLF Asset Management LLC/5.32%, Gengchen Han/14.20%, Steven Urbach/0.34%, Liang Yuan/14.20%, Kerry S. Propper/1.01%, Michael W. Trimble/0.04%, Jeff Feinberg/7.69%, Yasheng Yang/8.30%

Financial Data: Fiscal Year End:12/31   Latest Annual Data: 9/30/2006

Year	Sales		Net Income
2006	$66,169,000		$9,658,000
2005	$25,687,000		$2,034,000
Curr. Assets:	$90,895,000	Curr. Liab.: $64,474,000	
Plant, Equip.:	$15,869,000	Total Liab.: $66,490,000	Indic. Yr. Divd.: NA
Total Assets:	$124,508,000	Net Worth: $58,018,000	Debt/ Equity: NA

Original Sixteen to One Mine Inc

PO Box 1621, Allegheny, CA, 95910; **PH:** 1-916-287-3223; **http://** www.origsix.com; **Email:** corp@origsix.com

General - Incorporation	CA	Stock- Price on:12/24/2007	NA
Employees	NA	Stock Exchange	NA
Auditor	NA	Ticker Symbol	NA
Stk Agt	Norman Lamb Securities	Outstanding Shares	NA
Counsel	NA	E.P.S.	NA
DUNS No.	08-885-3601	Shareholders	NA

Business: The group's principle activity is to operate gold mines in and around the town of alleghany in the California. The company markets rare high-grade gold and quartz specimens at a premium to museums, collectors and jewelry manufacturers. The main operating site is the sixteen to one mines. Many modern mining technologies are deployed in these mines to ensure effective extraction of gold. The mines are made available to third parties for research and development, which allows the company to benefit from the same without incurring the usual cost associated with research. The company also manufactures its own jewelry and sells its own proprietary mine bars. The group operates from United States.

Primary SIC and add'l.: 0811 1041 3911

CIK No: 0000074925

Officers: Michael M. Miller/Dir., CEO, Pres., Rae Bell Arbogast/42/Sec.

Directors: Michael M. Miller/Dir., CEO, Pres., Scott K. Robertson/Dir., Hugh Daniel O'Neill/Dir.

Owners: Kathy N. Hull/12.00%, Scott K. Robertson/1.10%, Blair M. Hull/15.20%, Insiders/42.60%, Michael M. Miller/8.00%, Charles I. Brown/6.50%, Rae Bell Arbogast/0.10%, Hugh Daniel O'Neill/0.10%

Originally New York Inc

PO Box 19149, Natchez, MS, 39120; *PH:* 1-603-686-5340; *http://* www.unitedethanolgroup.com; *Email:* ethanol@unitedethanolgroup.com

General - Incorporation	NV	Stock - Price on:12/24/2007	NA
Employees	NA	Stock Exchange	NA
Auditor	Beckstead & Watts, LLP	Ticker Symbol	NA
Stk Agt	Pacific Stock Transfer Company	Outstanding Shares	NA
Counsel	NA	E.P.S.	$0.00
DUNS No.	NA	Shareholders	NA

Business: The groups principal activities include marketing a proprietary line of sports and athletic garments bearing groups logos. The group established a website to serve as the principal method of marketing, selling and distributing proprietary products.

Primary SIC and add'l.: 2300

CIK No: 0001192907

Owners: Insiders, Vineyard Creek Investments, LLC, James Monroe Capital Corp., EE Forester, LLC

*Financial Data: Fiscal Year End:*12/31   *Latest Annual Data:* 12/31/2005

Year	Sales	Net Income
2005	NA	-$22,000
2004	$0	-$41,000
2003	$0	-$40,000

Curr. Assets:	$10,000	Curr. Liab.:	$27,000		
Plant, Equip.:	NA	Total Liab.:	$27,000	Indic. Yr. Divd.:	NA
Total Assets:	$10,000	Net Worth:	-$16,000	Debt/ Equity:	NA

Oriole Inc

Cosmo Palmieri, Naples, FL, 34108;

General - Incorporation	NV	Stock - Price on:12/24/2007	$0.0001
Employees	NA	Stock Exchange	OTC
Auditor	Child, Sullivan & Co	Ticker Symbol	ORLSF
Stk Agt	Nevada Agency & Trust Company	Outstanding Shares	NA
Counsel	NA	E.P.S.	NA
DUNS No.	NA	Shareholders	NA

Business: The group has not identified any business opportunity that it plans to pursue. The group operates from United States.

Primary SIC and add'l.: 9995

CIK No: 0001098080

Subsidiaries: Mellow Anti-Counterfeit Net System (Shenzhen, Mid-Am Connelly Investments Limited, Sheffield, Shutterport Inc.

Officers: Cosmo Palmieri/35/Treasurer, James J. Charles/62/Dir., Pres.

Directors: Joseph Pioppi/78/Dir., James J. Charles/62/Dir., Pres.

Orion Diversified Technologies Inc

11 Front St. , Ste. 200, Hempstead, NY, 11550; *PH:* 1-516-220-1229

General - Incorporation	NJ	Stock - Price on:12/24/2007	$0.4
Employees	NA	Stock Exchange	OTC
Auditor	Tabriztchi & Co., CPA, P.C	Ticker Symbol	ORDTE
Stk Agt	Continental Stock Transfer & Trust Co	Outstanding Shares	9,980,000
Counsel	NA	E.P.S.	-$0.01
DUNS No.	NA	Shareholders	NA

Business: The groups principal activity is seeking to consummate a business combination with a profitable privately owned company. The group operates from the United States.

Primary SIC and add'l.: 5651

CIK No: 0000032284

Officers: Irwin Pearl/Dir., CFO, Pres., Thomas F. Regan/Dir., Pres.

Directors: Irwin Pearl/Dir., CFO, Pres., Thomas F. Regan/Dir., Pres.

Owners: Insiders/37.10%, Parthian Securities SA/2.50%, Vladimir Fabert/19.50%, Synergy Asset Management Ltd./5.00%, Alexandra Fabert/4.50%, Gilles Neveu/17.60%, Thomas F. Regan, Pasquale Catizone/0.40%, Grove Partners/3.20%, Richard Von Tscharner/5.20%, Gable International Investments, LTD/3.20%

*Financial Data: Fiscal Year End:*04/30   *Latest Annual Data:* 4/30/2006

Year	Sales	Net Income
2006	NA	-$12,000
2005	NA	-$6,000
2004	NA	-$27,000

Curr. Assets:	$798,000	Curr. Liab.:	$51,000		
Plant, Equip.:	NA	Total Liab.:	$51,000	Indic. Yr. Divd.:	NA
Total Assets:	$1,747,000	Net Worth:	$1,696,000	Debt/ Equity:	NA

Orion Ethanol Inc

307 S Main St., Pratt, KS, 67124; *PH:* 1-620-672-2814; *http://* www.orionethanol.net

General - Incorporation	UT	Stock - Price on:12/24/2007	$20
Employees	NA	Stock Exchange	OTC
Auditor	Mantyla McReynolds, LLC	Ticker Symbol	OEHL
Stk Agt	NA	Outstanding Shares	32,660,000
Counsel	NA	E.P.S.	-$0.72
DUNS No.	NA	Shareholders	NA

Business: The groups principal activity is in the business of building bio refineries to produce ethanol and animal feed products. The group operates from the United States.

Primary SIC and add'l.: 2869

CIK No: 0000812355

Subsidiaries: Gateway Ethanol, LLC, Gateway Holdco, LLC, Orion Ethanol, LLC

Officers: Joshua N. Barker/Co - CEO, Timothy C. Barker/Exec. VP - Development, Jerry Nash/Exec. VP - Distribution, Douglas Donaghue/Chief Accounting Officer

Directors: Patrick Barker/Chmn., Gary C. Evans/51/Dir., J. L. Meibergen/51/Dir., Porter Loomis/44/Dir., Wallace Stanberry/86/Dir.

Owners: Jerry Nash/24.40%, Greengroup, LLC/34.20%, Porter J. Loomis/3.20%, Insiders/69.60%, Joshua N. Barker/3.00%, J. L. Meibergen, Wallace A. Stanberry, Timothy C. Barker/3.00%, Frank H. Moore, Gary C. Evans/6.00%, Patrick N. Barker/37.80%

Financial Data: Fiscal Year End:12/31   *Latest Annual Data:* 12/31/2006

Year	Sales	Net Income
2006	$46,000	-$9,411,000
2005	NA	-$13,000

Curr. Assets:	$9,594,000	Curr. Liab.:	$7,112,000		
Plant, Equip.:	$50,400,000	Total Liab.:	$44,872,000	Indic. Yr. Divd.:	NA
Total Assets:	$64,304,000	Net Worth:	$19,432,000	Debt/ Equity:	2.6565

Orion HealthCorp Inc

1805 Old Alabama Rd., Ste. 350, Roswell, GA, 30076; *PH:* 1-678-832-1800; *Fax:* 1-678-832-1888; *http://* www.orionhealthcorp.com; *Email:* info@orionhealthcorp.com

General - Incorporation	DE	Stock - Price on:12/24/2007	$0.11
Employees	367	Stock Exchange	NA
Auditor	UHY LLP	Ticker Symbol	NA
Stk Agt	NA	Outstanding Shares	130,160,000
Counsel	NA	E.P.S.	-$0.08
DUNS No.	04-813-2674	Shareholders	NA

Business: The group's principal activity is to develop, acquire and operate freestanding ambulatory surgery centers, which are used by physicians, physician partners and their patients. The group provides management services to ambulatory surgery center services that are both wholly or partially owned by the group as well as independently owned centers. Services provided by the group include management and reporting of financial accounts, design and oversight of compliance programs, management of insurance and risk management programs, insurance of quality control and negotiation of services.

Primary SIC and add'l.: 8011

CIK No: 0000755113

Subsidiaries: Baytown SurgiCare, Inc., Bellaire ASC, LP, Bellaire SurgiCare, Inc., Dennis Cain Management, LLC, Dennis Cain Physician Solutions, Ltd., Integrated Physician Solutions, Inc., Medical Billing Services, Inc., San Jacinto Surgery Center, Ltd., SurgiCare Memorial Village, LP, Town & Country SurgiCare, Inc.

Officers: Terrence L. Bauer/Dir., CEO, Pres./$0.30, Dennis M. Cain/CEO - Medical Billing Services, Inc, MBS/$0.70, Tommy M. Smith/COO, Pres. - Medical Billing Services, Inc, MBS/$0.10, Stephen H. Murdock/CFO, Corp. Sec./$0.50, Marvin Retsky/Pres. - Rand Medical Billing, Inc/$0.13, William Suffich/Pres. - On Line Alternatives, Inc, On Line Payroll Services, Inc

Directors: Terrence L. Bauer/Dir., CEO, Pres., Paul H. Cascio/Non - Exec. Chmn., Michael J. Finn/Dir., Joseph M. Valley/Dir., David Crane/Dir., Robert P. Pinkas/Dir.

Owners: Brantley Venture Management IV, L.P., Brantley Venture Management III, L.P., Brantley Partners IV, L.P., Dennis M. Cain, David Crane, Brantley Venture Management IV, L.P., Brantley Partners IV, L.P., Brantley Venture Partners III, L.P., Insiders, D/V Cain Family, L.P., Phoenix Life Insurance Company, Pinkas Family Partners, L.P, Tommy M. Smith, Insiders, Pinkas Family Partners, L.P. *(28 Owners included in Index)*

*Financial Data: Fiscal Year End:*12/31   *Latest Annual Data:* 12/31/2006

Year	Sales	Net Income
2006	$23,401,000	-$4,128,000
2005	$29,565,000	-$20,440,000
2004	$21,711,000	-$6,175,000

Curr. Assets:	$5,406,000	Curr. Liab.:	$9,269,000		
Plant, Equip.:	$711,000	Total Liab.:	$20,799,000	Indic. Yr. Divd.:	NA
Total Assets:	$30,183,000	Net Worth:	$9,384,000	Debt/ Equity:	1.2787

Orix Corp Ads

3-22-8 Shiba, Minato-ku, Tokyo; *PH:* 81-354195102; *Fax:* 81-354195901; *http://* www.orix.co.jp; *Email:* orixir@orix.co.jp

General - Incorporation	Japan	Stock - Price on:12/24/2007	$125.8
Employees	NA	Stock Exchange	NYSE
Auditor	KPMG LLP	Ticker Symbol	IX
Stk Agt	Mitsubishi UFJ Trust & Banking Corp	Outstanding Shares	182,470,000
Counsel	NA	E.P.S.	$9.62
DUNS No.	NA	Shareholders	NA

Business: The groups principle activity is to invest in real estate properties. The group operates through seven segments in Japan and two segments overseas. In the year 2005, the group acquired Kitakanto Lease Company Limited and Houlihan Lokey Bank. The group operates from the Japan and other international countries.

Primary SIC and add'l.: 6159

CIK No: 0001070304

Subsidiaries: Alternative Investment& Development Headquarters, Asia, Oceania and Europe, BlueWave Corporation, BTA ORIX Leasing JSC, District Sales Headquarters, Hokugin Lease Co Ltd., Hyakugo Leasing Company Limited, IL&FS Education& Technology Services Limited, INFRASTRUCTURE LEASING& FINANCIAL SERVICES LIMITED, International Headquarters, Investment Banking Headquarters, Kagawagin Leasing CoLtd., Kinki (Osaka) Sales Headquarters, Kuribayashi Leasing Co Ltd., Lanka ORIX Leasing Company Limited 101 Subsidiaries included in the Index

Officers: Yoshihiko Miyauchi/Chmn., Representative Executive Officer, CEO, Yuichi Kawamura/Executive Officer - District Sales Headquarters, Chmn. - Orix Kitakanto Corporation, Yasuhiko Fujiki/Dir., Representative Executive Officer, COO, Pres., Hiroaki Nishina/Dir., Deputy Pres. - Real Estate Business Headquarters, Pres. - Orix Real Estate Corporation, Hiroshi Nakajima/Corporate Exec. VP - Risk Management Headquarters, Receivables Administration Office, Mitsuo Nishiumi/Group Executive, Pres. - Orix Asset Management, Loan Services Corporation, Tamio Umaki/Group Sr. VP, Pres. - Orix Rentec Corporation, Izumi Mizumori/Group Executive, Pres. - Orix Life Insurance Corporation, Akira Hirose/Group Executive Pres. - Orix Capital Corporation, Kenji Kajiwara/Dir., Deputy Pres. - Osaka Group Representative, Domestic Sales Headquarters, Osaka Head Office, Shintaro Agata/Corporate Sr. VP - Treasury Department, Masayuki Okamoto/Executive Officer - Investment Banking Headquarters, Yoshiyuki Yamaya/Executive Officer - OQL Headquarters, Asset Administration Department, Pres. - Orix Credit Corporation, Makoto Inoue/Corporate Sr. VP - Alternative Investment, Development Headquarters, Information Technology Planning Office Pres., Eiji Mitani/Group Sr. VP, Pres. - Orix Auto Corporation *(26 Officers included in Index)*

Directors: Yoshihiko Miyauchi/Chmn., Representative Executive Officer, CEO, Haruyuki Urata/Dir., Kenji Kajiwara/Dir., Deputy Pres. - Osaka Group Representative, Domestic Sales Headquarters, Osaka Head Office, Yoshinori Yokoyama/Dir., Hirotaka Takeuchi/Dir., Teruo Ozaki/Dir., Yasuhiko Fujiki/Dir., Representative Executive Officer, COO, Pres., Hiroaki Nishina/Dir., Deputy Pres. - Real Estate Business Headquarters, Pres. - Orix Real Estate Corporation, Yukio Yanase/Dir., Paul Sheard/Dir., Takeshi Sasaki/Dir.

Owners: The Chase Manhattan Bank, N.A. London/2.94%, Japan Trustee Services Bank, Ltd./8.47%, The Master Trust Bank of Japan, Ltd/6.04%, The Chase Manhattan Bank, N.A. London SL Omnibus Account/2.24%, The Chase Manhattan Bank/2.30%, State Street Bank and Trust Company/3.20%, JPMCB USA Residents Pension/1.78%, State Street Bank and Trust Company/8.03%, Mellon Bank NA/2.07%, Nats Cumco/1.71%

Financial Data: Fiscal Year End:03/31   Latest Annual Data: 03/31/2007

Year	Sales	Net Income
2007	$9,679,000,000	$1,665,000,000
2006	$8,069,000,000	$1,416,000,000
2005	$8,539,000,000	$852,000,000

Curr. Assets:	$4,659,000,000	**Curr. Liab.:**	$18,635,000,000	**P/E Ratio:**	9.89
Plant, Equip.:	$2,599,000,000	**Total Liab.:**	$59,407,000,000	**Indic. Yr. Divd.:**	NA
Total Assets:	$69,523,000,000	**Net Worth:**	$10,116,000,000	**Debt/ Equity:**	NA

Orleans Homebuilders Inc

1 Greenwood Sq., 3333 St. Rd., Ste. 101, Bensalem, PA, 19020; **PH:** 1-215-245-7500; **Fax:** 1-215-633-2352; **http://** www.orleanshomes.com; **Email:** info@orleanshomes.com

General - Incorporation	DE	**Stock**- Price on:12/24/2007	$8.5
Employees	988	Stock Exchange	AMEX
Auditor	PricewaterhouseCoopers LLP	Ticker Symbol	OHB
Stk Agt.	Registrar & Transfer Co	Outstanding Shares	18,500,000
Counsel..	Wolf Block Schorr & Solis-Cohen LLP	E.P.S.	-$3.937
DUNS No.	04-860-2817	Shareholders	NA

Business: The group's principal activity is to develop, build and market condominiums, townhouses and single-family homes. The group acts as a general contractor and employs subcontractors at specified prices for the installation of site improvements and construction of its residential units. The group's operations are primarily in the philadelphia metropolitan area, bucks, chester and Delaware counties in Pennsylvania and in burlington and camden and gloucestor counties in New Jersey. On 29-Jul-2004, the group acquired realen homes lp.

Primary SIC and add'l.: 6552 1531

CIK No: 0000038570

Subsidiaries: A. P. Orleans Real Estate Co., A. P. Orleans, Incorporated, Alambry Funding, Inc., Brookshire Estates, L.P., Byers Commercial LP, Byers Commercial, LLC, Byers Group II LLC, Byers Group III LLC, Byers Group LLC, Community Management Services Group, Inc., Greenwood Financial Inc., Greenwood Trade, Inc., JPO Air, LLC, Lucy Financial, Inc., Masterpiece Homes & Properties, Inc. 102 Subsidiaries included in the Index

Officers: Jeffrey P. Orleans/Chmn., CEO, Michael T. Vesey/Dir., COO, Pres., Andrew N. Heine/Dir. - Attorney, Private Investor, Garry P. Herdler/CFO, Exec. VP, Dean C. Amann/45/Exec. VP, Thomas Gancsos/56/Pres., Jeffrey Guernier/49/Pres. - Greensboro, Randy Harris/58/Pres. - Midwest Division, Russell J. Parker,/64/Pres. - Parker, Lancaster Corporation

Directors: Jeffrey P. Orleans/Chmn., CEO, Benjamin D. Goldman/Vice Chmn., Michael T. Vesey/Dir., COO, Pres., Robert N. Goodman/Dir., Jerome S. Goodman/Dir., John Temple/Dir., David Kaplan/Dir., Andrew N. Heine/Dir. - Attorney, Private Investor, Lewis Katz/Dir., Robert Segal/Dir.

Owners: Dean C. Amann, T. Rowe Price Associates, Inc., Robert M. Segal, Jerome S. Goodman, David Kaplan, Robert N. Goodman, Andrew N. Heine, John W. Temple, Jeffrey P. Orleans, Insiders, Michael T. Vesey, Lewis Katz, Benjamin D. Goldman

Financial Data: Fiscal Year End:06/30   Latest Annual Data: 6/30/2006

Year	Sales	Net Income
2006	$987,193,000	$63,041,000
2005	$919,230,000	$55,584,000
2004	$547,258,000	$38,079,000

Curr. Assets:	$80,395,000	**Curr. Liab.:**	$72,586,000		
Plant, Equip.:	$802,889,000	**Total Liab.:**	$686,410,000	**Indic. Yr. Divd.:**	$0.080
Total Assets:	$910,944,000	**Net Worth:**	$224,534,000	**Debt/ Equity:**	NA

Ormat Technologies Inc

6225 Neil Rd., Ste. 300, Reno, NV, 89511; **PH:** 1-775-356-9029; **Fax:** 1-775-356-9039; **http://** www.ormat.com; **Email:** info@ormat.com

General - Incorporation	DE	**Stock**- Price on:12/24/2007	$36.91
Employees	NA	Stock Exchange	NYSE
Auditor	PricewaterhouseCoopers LLP	Ticker Symbol	ORA
Stk Agt	American Stock Transfer & Trust Co.	Outstanding Shares	38,120,000
Counsel	NA	E.P.S.	$0.57
DUNS No.	NA	Shareholders	NA

Business: The groups principle activities include designing, developing, building, owning and operating power plants and its equipments. The group operates through two segments namely, electricity and products. In the year 2006, the group acquired Orzunil I De Electricidad, Limitada. The group operates from the United States, Canada, North America, Italy, Russia, Thailand, Germany and Spain.The group's quarterly revenue for Sept 2007 was 79.47millions of USD.

Primary SIC and add'l.: 4931 4911 5063

CIK No: 0001296445

Subsidiaries: Brady Power Partners, Heber Field Company, Heber Geothermal Company, Mammoth Pacific L.P., OrCal Geothermal, Inc., Oreg 1 Inc., OrHeber 1, Inc., Orleyte Company, OrMammoth Inc., Ormat Funding Corp., Ormat Holding Corp., Ormat International, Inc., Ormat Momotombo Power Company, Ormat Nevada, Inc., Ormat Pacific Inc. 22 Subsidiaries included in the Index

Officers: Yehudit Bronicki/Dir., CEO, Pres., Lucien Y. Bronicki/Chmn., CTO, Yoram Bronicki/Dir., COO - North America, Joseph Tenne/CFO, Hezy Ram/Exec. VP - Business Development, Nadav Amir/Exec. VP - Engineering, Joseph Shiloah/Exec. VP - Marketing, Sales, Zvi Reiss/Exec. VP - Project Management, Etty Rosner/VP, Contract Administrator, Smadar Lavi/Investor Relations Officer, Connie Stechman/52/VP

Directors: Yehudit Bronicki/Dir., CEO, Pres., Lucien Y. Bronicki/Chmn., CTO, Yoram Bronicki/Dir., COO - North America, Dan Falk/Dir., Jacob J. Worenklein/Dir., Roger W. Gale/Dir., Robert F. Clarke/Dir.

Owners: Dan Falk, Zvi Reiss, Joseph Tenne, Robert F. Clarke, Nadav Amir, Insiders, Jacob Worenklein, Roger W. Gale, Ormat Industries Ltd./59.63%

Financial Data: Fiscal Year End:12/31   Latest Annual Data: 12/31/2006

Year	Sales	Net Income
2006	$268,937,000	$34,447,000
2005	$237,992,000	$15,177,000
2004	$219,230,000	$17,791,000

Curr. Assets:	$242,592,000	**Curr. Liab.:**	$208,163,000	**P/E Ratio:**	64.75
Plant, Equip.:	$793,164,000	**Total Liab.:**	$719,308,000	**Indic. Yr. Divd.:**	$0.200
Total Assets:	$1,160,102,000	**Net Worth:**	$440,794,000	**Debt/ Equity:**	0.8574

Oromin Explorations Ltd

1055 W Hastings St., Ste. 2000, Vancouver, BC, V6E 2E9; **PH:** 1-604-331-8772; **Fax:** 1-604-331-8773; **http://** www.oromin.com

General - Incorporation	BC	**Stock**- Price on:12/24/2007	$2.12
Employees	NA	Stock Exchange	OTC
Auditor	Davidson & Company LLP	Ticker Symbol	NA
Stk Agt ...	Computershare Investor Services LLC	Outstanding Shares	NA
Counsel	NA	E.P.S.	NA
DUNS No.	NA	Shareholders	NA

Business: The groups principal activity is engaged in the business of acquiring interests in resource properties in the hope of locating reserves. The groups property interests are in the exploration stage only. In February 2006, the group had incurred net acquisition and exploration with respect to its Sabodala Property in Senegal. The group operates from Argentina, Brazil, Senegal and Canada.

Primary SIC and add'l.: 1481

CIK No: 0001109141

Subsidiaries: Carneirinho Property, Cynthia Holdings Limited, Exploraciones Oromin, S.A, Irie Isle Limited, Sabodala Property, Santa Rosa Property

Officers: Chet Idziszek/Dir., Pres., James G. Stewart/Dir., Sec., Corporate Counsel, Norman Haimila/Dir., VP - Exploration, Petroleum, David Mallo/VP - Exploration - Minerals, David J. Scott/Marketing, Investor Relations Officer, Ian Brown/CFO

Directors: Chet Idziszek/Dir., Pres., James G. Stewart/Dir., Sec., Corporate Counsel, Norman Haimila/Dir., VP - Exploration, Petroleum, Douglas S. Turnbull/Dir., Derek Bartlett/Dir., Nell M. Dragovan/Dir., Robert Sibthorpe/Dir., Robert H. Brennan/Dir., Phil E. Pearce/Member - Advisory Board

Owners: Abdullah Basodan/6.40%, Chet Idziszek/15.20%

Financial Data: Fiscal Year End:02/28   Latest Annual Data: 2/28/2006

Year	Sales	Net Income
2006	NA	-$2,864,000
2005	NA	-$1,303,000

Curr. Assets:	$6,279,000	**Curr. Liab.:**	$625,000	**P/E Ratio:**	12.62
Plant, Equip.:	$650,000	**Total Liab.:**	$625,000	**Indic. Yr. Divd.:**	NA
Total Assets:	$9,575,000	**Net Worth:**	$8,950,000	**Debt/ Equity:**	NA

Orrstown Financial Services Inc

77 E King St., Shippensburg, PA, 17257; **PH:** 1-717-532-6114; **Fax:** 1-717-532-9342; **http://** www.orrstown.com; **Email:** info@rtco.com

General - Incorporation	PA	**Stock**- Price on:12/24/2007	$33.17
Employees	220	Stock Exchange	OTC
Auditor	Smith Elliott Kearns & Co. LLC	Ticker Symbol	ORRF
Stk Agt	Registrar & Transfer Co	Outstanding Shares	6,440,000
Counsel	NA	E.P.S.	$1.79
DUNS No.	19-657-9080	Shareholders	NA

Business: The group's principal activity is to provide commercial banking, trust and insurance services in Pennsylvania. It accepts demand deposit, time deposit and savings deposits. The group offers commercial loans, financial loans, agricultural loans, real estate construction loans, mortgage loans and consumer loans. The insurance services include reinsurance of credit, life and disability insurance. The trust department acts as trustee, executor, administrator, guardian, managing agent, custodian and investment advisor and other fiduciary activities. The operations are conducted through 12 branch offices located in shippensburg, carlisle, spring run, orrstown, chambersburg, greencastle and mechanicsburg, Pennsylvania.

Primary SIC and add'l.: 6712 6022

CIK No: 0000826154

Subsidiaries: Orrstown Bank, Pennbanks Insurance Company

Officers: Kenneth R. Shoemaker/Dir., CEO, Pres./$545,756.00, Bradley S. Everly/CFO, Sr. VP/$299,083.00, Benjamin S. Stoops/CTO, Sr. VP, Robert J. Gentry/VP, Dir. - Marketing, Stephen C. Oldt/COO, Exec. VP/$261,461.00, Barbara E. Brobst/Sr. VP, Sr. Trust Officer - Financial Advisor, Greater Shippensburg Area, Paul Baynum/Business Development Officer - Carlisle Area, Chad Rosenberry/Business Development Officer - Chambersburg Area, Steve Szady/Business Development Officer - Chambersburg Area, Terry Reiber/Business Development Officer - Greencastle Area, Gary Holder/Business Development Officer - Mechanicsburg Area, Matt Jones/Business Development Officer - Shippensburg, Orrstown Area, Mindy Jones/Commercial Marketing Mgr. - Carlisle Area, Cody Carbaugh/Commercial Marketing Mgr. - Chambersburg Area, Jorie Shope/Merchant Service Sales Officer - Shippensburg, Orrstown Area (25 Officers included in Index)

Directors: Kenneth R. Shoemaker/Dir., CEO, Pres., Joel R. Zullinger/Chmn., Jeffrey W. Coy/Vice Chmn., Glenn W. Snoke/Dir., Peter C. Zimmerman/Dir., Gregory A. Rosenberry/Dir., John S. Ward/Dir., Anthony F. Ceddia/Dir., Andrea Pugh/Dir., Denver L. Tuckey/Dir.

Owners: Jeffrey W. Embly, John S. Ward, Kenneth R. Shoemaker, Peter C. Zimmerman, Jeffrey W. Coy, Anthony F. Ceddia, Bradley S. Everly, Philip E. Fague, Glenn W. Snoke, Denver L. Tuckey, Insiders, Stephen C. Oldt, Gregory Rosenberry, Orrstown Bank/13.64%, Joel R. Zullinger (16 Owners included in Index)

Financial Data: Fiscal Year End:12/31   Latest Annual Data: 12/31/2006

Year	Sales	Net Income
2006	$55,871,000	$11,632,000
2005	$41,534,000	$9,987,000
2004	$32,861,000	$7,770,000

Curr. Assets:	$43,308,000	**Curr. Liab.:**	$687,203,000	**P/E Ratio:**	18.53
Plant, Equip.:	$19,852,000	**Total Liab.:**	$719,643,000	**Indic. Yr. Divd.:**	$0.840
Total Assets:	$809,031,000	**Net Worth:**	$89,388,000	**Debt/ Equity:**	0.3629

Orsus Xelent Technologies Inc

6B Building 5, Yi Jing Yuan, Chao Yang, Peking, 100020; *PH:* 86-1085613362;
Fax: 86-1085626566; *http://* www.orsus-xelent.com

General - Incorporation	DE	Stock - Price on:12/24/2007	NA
Employees	NA	Stock Exchange	OTC
Auditor	Moores Rowland Mazars	Ticker Symbol	ORXT
Stk Agt	Corporate Stock Transfer, Inc.	Outstanding Shares	NA
Counsel	NA	E.P.S.	$0.229
DUNS No.	NA	Shareholders	NA

Business: The groups principle activity is engaged in the business of designing for retail and wholesale distribution cellular phones. The group operates from the United States, Singapore and Hong Kong. The group's quarterly revenue for Sep '07 was 22.05 millions of USD.

Primary SIC and add'l.: 7389

CIK No: 0001297024

Subsidiaries: Beijing Orsus Xelent Technology & Trading Company Limited, Orsus Xelent Holdings (BVI) Limited, Orsus Xelent Trading (HK) Company Limited, United First International Limited

Officers: Wang Xin/39/Dir., CEO, Zhao Hongwei/Dir., CFO, Xavier Xin Wang/Dir., Pres., Wang Xiaolong/Dir., Deputy GM, Yang Shulin/Dir., Deputy GM

Directors: Wang Xin/39/Dir., CEO, Liu Yu/42/Chmn., Zhao Hongwei/Dir., CFO, Xavier Xin Wang/Dir., Pres., Yang Shulin/Dir., Deputy GM, Naizhong Che/65/Dir., Peng Wang/36/Dir., Zhixiang Zhang/40/Dir., Nathaniel K. Hsieh/43/Dir., Howard S. Barth/56/Dir.

Owners: Insiders/30.25%, Wang Zhibin/20.16%, Wang Xin/10.09%, Liu Yu/20.16%

*Financial Data: Fiscal Year End:*12/31 *Latest Annual Data:* 12/31/2006

Year	Sales	Net Income
2006	$68,108,000	$6,718,000
2005	$28,705,000	$3,492,000
2004	$0	-$62,000

Curr. Assets:	$45,567,000	Curr. Liab.:	$23,604,000		
Plant, Equip.:	$320,000	Total Liab.:	$23,604,000	Indic. Yr. Divd.:	NA
Total Assets:	$45,887,000	Net Worth:	$22,283,000	Debt/ Equity:	NA

Ortec International Inc

3960 Broadway, New York, NY, 10032; *PH:* 1-212-740-6999; *Fax:* 1-212-740-6963;
http:// www.ortecinternational.com; *Email:* ir@ortecinternational.com

General - Incorporation	DE	Stock - Price on:12/24/2007	NA
Employees	36	Stock Exchange	OTC
Auditor	BDO Seidman LLP, Grant Thornton LLP	Ticker Symbol	OTCI
Stk Agt	Registrar & Transfer Co	Outstanding Shares	NA
Counsel	Feder, Kaszovitz, Isaacson Et Al	E.P.S.	$0.28
DUNS No.	78-089-7864	Shareholders	NA

Business: The group's principle activities include research and development of tissue engineered skin regeneration product, for use in the treatment of chronic and acute wounds. The group has developed a proprietary and patented technology known as orcel, which is used to stimulate the repair and regeneration of human skin. Orcel is a two layered tissue engineered dressing that consists of human derived skin cells, both dermal and epidermal, supported within a porous collagen matrix. The composite matrix is seeded with keratinocytes for epidermal growth and fibroblasts for dermal growth. The company also conducts a pivotal clinical trial for the use of orcel in its cryopreserved form for the treatment of venous leg stasis and diabetic foot ulcers. The group operates from United States.

Primary SIC and add'l.: 2834

CIK No: 0000889992

Subsidiaries: Orcel LLC

Officers: Ron Lipstein/Vice Chmn., CEO, Costantin Papastephanou/CEO, Pres., Daniel Marshak/Chmn. - Stem Cell, Regenerative Medicine, Member - Scientific Advisory Board, Consultant, Steven Peltier/Consultant - Clinical, Regulatory, Dan Lesnoy/Dir. - Biomaterials, Michel Hermans/Dir. - Medical, Chief Safety Officer, Consultant, Melvin Silberklang/Chief Scientific Officer, VP - Research, Development, Alan Schoenbart/CFO, Mel Silberklang/Chief Scientific Officer, VP - Research, Development

Directors: Ron Lipstein/Vice Chmn., CEO, Daniel Marshak/Chmn. - Stem Cell, Regenerative Medicine, Member - Scientific Advisory Board, Consultant, John R. Leone/Dir., Raphael Hofstein/Dir., Andreas Vogler/Dir., Mark Eisenberg/Dir., Steven Lilien/Dir., Allen I. Schiff/Dir., Shepard M. Goldberg/Dir., Mark Bagnall/Dir.

Owners: Ron Lipstein, Yehuda Dachs, BIP Ventures Partners SICAR SA, John Leone, Steven Putzi, Cipher 06 LLC, Platinum-Montaur Life Sciences, LLC, Vicis Capital Master Fund, SDS Capital Group SPC, Ltd., Shepard Goldberg, Thomas J. Franco, Insiders Trend Fund LP, Andreas Vogler, Melvin Silberklang, Alan W. Schoenbart *(28 Owners included in Index)*

*Financial Data: Fiscal Year End:*12/31 *Latest Annual Data:* 12/31/2006

Year	Sales	Net Income
2006	NA	-$18,000,000
2005	NA	-$30,374,000
2004	NA	-$15,378,000

Curr. Assets:	$650,000	Curr. Liab.:	$44,157,000		
Plant, Equip.:	$183,000	Total Liab.:	$44,166,000	Indic. Yr. Divd.:	NA
Total Assets:	$1,561,000	Net Worth:	-$42,605,000	Debt/ Equity:	NA

Orthodontix Inc

1428 Brickell Ave., Ste. 105, Miami, FL, 33131; *PH:* 1-305-371-4112

General - Incorporation	FL	Stock - Price on:12/24/2007	NA
Employees	1	Stock Exchange	NA
Auditor	Kesselman & Kesselman	Ticker Symbol	NA
Stk Agt	American Stock Transfer & Trust Co.	Outstanding Shares	NA
Counsel	NA	E.P.S.	NA
DUNS No.	94-131-2720	Shareholders	NA

Business: The group currently has no operations. The group was providing management services to affiliated orthodontic practices, including billing, collections, cash management, payroll processing, in exchange for a management fee. It intends to effect a merger, acquisition or other business combination with an operating company utilizing any combination of its common stock, cash on hand or other funding sources.

Primary SIC and add'l.: 8021 8999

CIK No: 0001006281

Subsidiaries: Embassy Acquisition Corp.

Officers: David Aviezer/43/Dir., CEO, Pres., Yoseph Shaaltiel/Dir., Exec. VP - Research, Development, Einat Brill Almon/48/VP - Product Development, Yossi Maimon/38/CFO, Treasurer, Sec., Iftah Katz/43/VP - Operations

Directors: David Aviezer/43/Dir., CEO, Pres., Eli Hurvitz/75/Chmn., Yoseph Shaaltiel/Dir., Exec. VP - Research, Development, Zeev Bronfeld/56/Dir., Amos Bar-Shalev/54/Dir., Sharon Toussia-Cohen/48/Dir., Eyal Sheratzki/39/Dir., Pinhas Barel Buchris/57/Dir., Phillip Frost/71/Dir., Jane H. Hsiao/60/Dir.

Owners: Insiders, Jane H. Hsiao, Zeev Bronfeld, Eli Hurvitz, Biocell Ltd., Phillip Frost, Amos Bar-Shalev, Techno-Rov Holdings (1993) Ltd., Pontifax G.P. Ltd., David Aviezer, Sharon Toussia-Cohen, Frost Gamma Investment Trust, Eyal Sheratzky, Yoseph Shaaltiel, Marathon Investments Ltd. *(16 Owners included in Index)*

*Financial Data: Fiscal Year End:*12/31 *Latest Annual Data:* 12/31/2006

Year	Sales	Net Income
2006	NA	-$9,390,000
2005	NA	-$75,000
2004	NA	-$160,000

Curr. Assets:	$24,291,000	Curr. Liab.:	$2,268,000		
Plant, Equip.:	$2,404,000	Total Liab.:	$2,704,000	Indic. Yr. Divd.:	NA
Total Assets:	$26,988,000	Net Worth:	$24,284,000	Debt/ Equity:	NA

Orthofix International

1720 Bray Central Dr., McKinney, TX, 75069; *PH:* 1-469-742-2500; *http://* www.orthofix.com

General - Incorporation	Netherlands	Stock - Price on:12/24/2007	$45.37
Employees	1,324	Stock Exchange	NDQ
Auditor	Ernst & Young LLP	Ticker Symbol	OFIX
Stk Agt	Bank of New York	Outstanding Shares	16,540,000
Counsel	Shearman & Sterling LLP	E.P.S.	$1.72
DUNS No.	85-633-6466	Shareholders	NA

Business: The group's principle activity of the group is the development & manufacturing of a diverse line of orthopedic, medical products. The company is based in the Netherlands Antilles and has its main operations in USA, United Kingdom, Italy and Seychelles. The group's quarterly revenue for Sep '07 was 121.12 millions of USD.

Primary SIC and add'l.: 3842

CIK No: 0000884624

Subsidiaries: Breg, Inc., Colgate Medical Limited, Implantes Y Sistemas Medicos, Inc., Intavent Orthofix Limited, Inter Medical Supplies Limited, Novamedix Distribution Limited, Novamedix Services Limited, Orthofix AG, Orthofix do Brasil, Orthofix GmbH, Orthofix Holdings, Inc., Orthofix II B.V., Orthofix Inc., Orthofix International B.V., Orthofix Limited 23 Subsidiaries included in the Index

Officers: Alan W. Milinazzo/Dir., Group CEO, Pres./$1,565,462.00, Oliver Burckhardt/Pres. - Orthofix Spine, Thomas Hein/CFO/$709,959.00, Raymond C. Kolls/Sr. VP, General Counsel, Corp. Sec./$590,736.00, Bradley R. Mason/VP/$912,513.00, Eric Brown/Sr. VP - Spine Sales, Scott Dodson/Pres. - Orthopedic Division, Michael Simpson/Sr. VP - Global Operations, General Mgr. - Orthofix Inc, Luigi Ferrari/VP - Europe, Keith Jansen/Sr. VP - Spine Marketing, Michael Finegan/VP - Corporate Development/$521,722.00, Dan Yarbrough/VP - Investor Relations

Directors: Alan W. Milinazzo/Dir., Group CEO, Pres., James F. Gero/Chmn., Jerry C. Benjamin/Dir., Guy Jordan/Dir., Kenneth R. Weisshaar/Dir., Walter P. Von Wartburg/Dir., Thomas J. Kester/Dir., Peter J. Hewett/Dir., Charles W. Federico/Dir.

Owners: Stefan Widensohler, Robert Gaines-Cooper/9.80%, Thomas J. Kester, Peter J. Hewett, James F. Gero, Paradigm Capital Management, Inc/8.60%, Michael M. Finegan, Bradley R. Mason/1.20%, Jerry C. Benjamin, Thomas Hein, Columbia Wanger Asset Management, L.P./7.40%, FMR Corp/14.90%, Charles W. Federico, Walter P. von Wartburg, Guy J. Jordan *(19 Owners included in Index)*

*Financial Data: Fiscal Year End:*12/31 *Latest Annual Data:* 12/31/2006

Year	Sales	Net Income
2006	$365,359,000	-$7,042,000
2005	$313,304,000	$73,402,000
2004	$286,638,000	$34,149,000

Curr. Assets:	$233,968,000	Curr. Liab.:	$61,040,000		
Plant, Equip.:	$25,311,000	Total Liab.:	$469,650,000	Indic. Yr. Divd.:	NA
Total Assets:	$862,285,000	Net Worth:	$392,635,000	Debt/ Equity:	0.7601

Orthologic Corp

1275 W Washington St., Tempe, AZ, 85281; *PH:* 1-602-286-5520; *http://* www.orthologic.com;
Email: investorinquiries@olgc.com

General - Incorporation	DE	Stock - Price on:12/24/2007	$1.44
Employees	30	Stock Exchange	NDQ
Auditor	Ernst & Young, LLP	Ticker Symbol	OLGC
Stk Agt	Bank of New York	Outstanding Shares	41,590,000
Counsel	Quarles & Brady LLP	E.P.S.	-$0.34
DUNS No.	19-439-6438	Shareholders	NA

Business: The group's principle activities are to develop, manufacture and market proprietary orthopedic products. These products are designed to promote the healing of musculoskeletal tissue, with particular emphasis on fracture healing and spinal repair. The products are designed to enhance the healing of diseased, damaged, degenerated or recently repaired musculoskeletal tissue. The products improve the clinical outcomes and cost-effectiveness of orthopedic procedures that are characterized by compromised healing, high-cost, potential for complication and long recuperation time. The product line includes bone growth stimulation and fracture fixation devices. These products are sold primarily through the company's direct sales force supplemented by regional distributors. It is in the process of developing and testing our chrysalin(R) product platform.

Primary SIC and add'l.: 2836 3842 8731 2834

CIK No: 0000887151

Officers: John M. Holliman/54/Exec. Chmn., Principal Executive Officer, Randolph C. Steer/58/Pres., Dana Shinbaum/VP - Business Development/$547,000.00, Les M. Taeger/57/CFO, Sr. VP/$635,000.00

Directors: John M. Holliman/54/Exec. Chmn., Principal Executive Officer, Michael E. Mendelsohn/Chmn. - Scientific Advisory Board, Charles A. Dinarello/Member - Scientific Advisory Board, William W. Wardell/Dir., Elwood D. Howse/68/Dir., Augustus A. White/71/Dir., Fredric J. Feldman/67/Dir., Michael D. Casey/62/Dir.

Owners: Insiders/5.30%, James T. Ryaby, Sherry A. Sturman, Augustus A. White, Randolph C. Steer, Dana B. Shinbaum, Elwood D. Howse, Fredric J. Feldman, Les M. Taeger, John M. Holliman, Michael D. Casey, William M. Wardell, James M. Pusey

Financial Data: Fiscal Year End:12/31   Latest Annual Data: 12/31/2006

Year	Sales	Net Income
2006	NA	-$31,913,000
2005	NA	-$27,202,000
2004	NA	-$41,761,000

Curr. Assets:	$55,974,000	Curr. Liab.:	$3,441,000		
Plant, Equip.:	$409,000	Total Liab.:	$3,441,000	Indic. Yr. Divd.:	NA
Total Assets:	$72,589,000	Net Worth:	$69,148,000	Debt/ Equity:	NA

Orthometrix Inc

106 Corporate Pk. Dr., Ste. 102, White Plains, NY, 10604; **PH:** 1-914-694-2285; **Fax:** 1-914-694-2286; **http://** www.orthometrix.net; **Email:** info@orthometrix.net

General - Incorporation	DE	**Stock** - Price on:12/24/2007	NA
Employees	10	Stock Exchange	OTC
Auditor	Radin, Glass & Co. LLP	Ticker Symbol	OMRX
Stk Agt	American Stock Transfer & Trust Co.	Outstanding Shares	NA
Counsel	NA	E.P.S.	-$0.041
DUNS No.	94-423-3543	Shareholders	NA

Business: The group's principal activity is to market, sell and provide services through several musculoskeletal product lines used in pharmaceutical research, diagnostis and monitoring of bone and muscle disorders, sports medicine, rehabilitative medicine, physical therapy and pain management. Distributors and third parties are the principal customers of the group. The group also sells its products directly to end-users in those markets where the group does not have third party dealers or distributors.

Primary SIC and add'l.: 3844 3845 2834

CIK No: 0000946428

Subsidiaries: CooperSurgical Acquisition Corp.

Officers: Reynald G. Bonmati/Chmn., CEO, Juri Schule/Customer Service Engineer, Pat Cunniff/Customer Service Engineer, Neil H. Koenig/Dir., CFO, Bruce M. Harvey/Sales Mgr. - Rehabilitation, Fitness, Ralph G. Theodore/VP - Operations, Christopher Gordon/Applications Mgr. - Pqct, Galileo, Chrystele B. Zawislack/Marketing Mgr.

Directors: Reynald G. Bonmati/Chmn., CEO, William Orr/Dir., Michael W. Huber/Dir., Andre-Jacques Neusy/Dir., Neil H. Koenig/Dir., CFO, Albert S. Waxman/Dir.

Owners: William Orr, Neil H. Koenig, Michael W. Huber, Reynald G. Bonmati, Andr-Jacques Neusy, Rock Creek Investment Partners, L.P., Insiders, Psilos Group Partners II SBIC, L.P., Albert S. Waxman

Financial Data: Fiscal Year End:12/31   Latest Annual Data: 12/31/2006

Year	Sales	Net Income
2006	$2,362,000	-$1,980,000
2005	$1,515,000	-$2,388,000
2004	$1,180,000	-$1,944,000

Curr. Assets:	$1,081,000	Curr. Liab.:	$2,828,000		
Plant, Equip.:	$81,000	Total Liab.:	$3,459,000	Indic. Yr. Divd.:	NA
Total Assets:	$1,174,000	Net Worth:	-$2,286,000	Debt/ Equity:	NA

Orthovita Inc

45 Great Valley Pkwy., Malvern, PA, 19355; **PH:** 1-610-640-1775; **Fax:** 1-610-640-2603; **http://** www.orthovita.com

General - Incorporation	PA	**Stock** - Price on:12/24/2007	$2.91
Employees	198	Stock Exchange	NDQ
Auditor	KPMG LLP	Ticker Symbol	VITA
Stk Agt.	StockTrans, Inc.	Outstanding Shares	61,430,000
Counsel	Morgan, Lewis & Bockius LLP	E.P.S.	-$0.3
DUNS No.	NA	Shareholders	NA

Business: The group's principal activity is to develop, manufacture and market synthetic bone substitutes for orthopaedic applications that are useful in spine and joint replacements. The products are based on two platforms: synthetic cortical bone and synthetic cancellous bone substitute. The synthetic cortical bone is a non restorable, load bearing and resin composite and the synthetic cancellous bone substitute consists of small particle restorable calcium phosphate. The products include vitoss(R) scaffold synthetic cancellous bone void filler, imbibe(tm) bone marrow aspirate syringe used with vitoss, cortoss(R) synthetic cortical bone void filler and aliquot(tm) microdelivery system used with cortoss.

Primary SIC and add'l.: 3842 3843

CIK No: 0000913756

Subsidiaries: Partisyn Corporation, Vita Licensing, Inc, Vita Special Purpose Corporation

Officers: Antony Koblish/Dir., CEO, Pres./$810,971.00, Maarten Persenaire/Chief Medical Officer, Christopher H. Smith/Sr. VP - Sales/$411,568.00, Douglas Low/Sr. VP - European Operations, David J. McLlhenny/Sr. VP - Operations, Albert J. Pavucek/CFO/$78,343.00, David McIlhenny/Sr. VP - Operations/$359,240.00

Directors: Antony Koblish/Dir., CEO, Pres., David Fitzgerald/Chmn., Mary E. Paetzold/Dir., Morris Cheston/Dir., Scott R. Barry/Dir., Paul G. Thomas/Dir., William E. Tidmore/Dir., Paul T. Touhey/Dir.

Owners: Crestview Capital Offshore Fund, Inc., Crestview Capital Fund II, LP, Crestview Capital Fund, LP, Crestview Capital Master, LLC

Financial Data: Fiscal Year End:12/31   Latest Annual Data: 12/31/2006

Year	Sales	Net Income
2006	$46,828,000	-$17,464,000
2005	$34,679,000	-$13,363,000
2004	$24,661,000	-$13,198,000

Curr. Assets:	$47,465,000	Curr. Liab.:	$8,164,000		
Plant, Equip.:	$5,295,000	Total Liab.:	$18,953,000	Indic. Yr. Divd.:	NA
Total Assets:	$62,215,000	Net Worth:	$43,262,000	Debt/ Equity:	0.0360

Osage Federal Financial Inc

239 E Main St., Pawhuska, OK, 74056; **PH:** 1-918-287-2919

General - Incorporation	US	**Stock** - Price on:12/24/2007	NA
Employees	28	Stock Exchange	NA
Auditor	BKD LLP	Ticker Symbol	NA
Stk Agt	Registrar & Transfer Co	Outstanding Shares	NA
Counsel	NA	E.P.S.	NA
DUNS No.	NA	Shareholders	NA

Business: The groups principle activity is to provide banking services and products. The group provides online banking, telephone banking, personal banking, business banking, loan products and other services. The groups personal banking services include free checking account, regular checking account, gold checking account and now checking account. The group operates from United States.

Primary SIC and add'l.: NA

CIK No: 0001272771

Subsidiaries: Osage Federal Bank

Oscient Pharmaceuticals Corp

1000 Winter St., Ste. 2200, Waltham, MA, 02451; **PH:** 1-781-398-2300; **Fax:** 1-781-893-9535; **http://** www.oscient.com; **Email:** investors@oscient.com

General - Incorporation	MA	**Stock** - Price on:12/24/2007	$4.6
Employees	336	Stock Exchange	NDQ
Auditor	Ernst & Young LLP	Ticker Symbol	OSCI
Stk Agt	Computershare Investor Services LLC	Outstanding Shares	13,760,000
Counsel	NA	E.P.S.	-$2.32
DUNS No.	04-591-4041	Shareholders	NA

Business: The group's principal activities are to develop pharmaceutical and diagnostic products. The group concentrates the product discovery and development efforts in two principal areas, infectious diseases caused by bacterial and fungal pathogens and human diseases believed to have a significant genetic component. The group has ten ongoing product development programs. Its product candidate, ramoplanin, is in phase iii clinical trials for the prevention of bloodstream infections caused by vancomycin-resistant enterococci. It also has six product discovery and development alliances with pharmaceutical companies astrazeneca, biomerieux, schering-plough and wyeth. The group also provides drug discovery services to genomevisiontm services, providing drug discovery services to pharmaceutical, biotechnology companies and national human genome research institute. The group operates solely in the domestic market. On 06-Feb-2004, the group acquired genesoft pharmaceuticals inc.

Primary SIC and add'l.: 2836 8731

CIK No: 0000356830

Subsidiaries: Pfizer Inc, Vicuron Pharmaceuticals, Inc

Officers: Steven M. Rauscher/Dir., CEO, Pres./$1,126,964.00, Patrick Obrien/Clerk, Joseph A. Pane/VP - Human Resources, Christopher J.M. Taylor/VP - Corporate Communications, Investor Relations, Nick Colangelo/Exec. VP - Corporate Development, Operations, Philippe M. Maitre/Sr. VP, CFO/$300,819.00, Inder Kaul/VP - Clinical Development, Medical, Regulatory Affairs, Diane McGuire/VP - Operations, Dominick Colangelo/44/Exec. VP - Corporate Development, Operations/$708,298.00, Aaron D. Berg/VP - Marketing, Mark A. Glickman/VP - Sales, Anthony Watkins/VP - Corporate Development

Directors: Steven M. Rauscher/Dir., CEO, Pres., David K. Stone/Chmn., Walter Flamenbaum/Dir., Robert J. Hennessey/Dir., Gary Patou/Dir., John E. Voris/Dir., Gregory B. Brown/Dir., William R. Mattson/Dir., William S. Reardon/Dir., Norbert G. Riedel/Dir.

Owners: Steven M. Rauscher/1.90%, Philippe M. Maitre, Robert J. Hennessey, David K. Stone, Gregory B. Brown, Insiders/14.80%, Walter Flamenbaum/11.90%, John E. Voris, Norbert G. Riedel, Abingworth Management Limited/5.40%, Dominick Colangelo, William R. Mattson, Paul Royalty Fund Holdings II/11.90%, William S. Reardon, Ashford Capital Management, Inc./10.90% *(16 Owners included in Index)*

Financial Data: Fiscal Year End:12/31   Latest Annual Data: 12/31/2006

Year	Sales	Net Income
2006	$46,152,000	-$78,477,000
2005	$23,609,000	-$88,593,000
2004	$6,613,000	-$93,271,000

Curr. Assets:	$70,234,000	Curr. Liab.:	$30,426,000		
Plant, Equip.:	$1,497,000	Total Liab.:	$281,403,000	Indic. Yr. Divd.:	NA
Total Assets:	$279,407,000	Net Worth:	-$1,996,000	Debt/ Equity:	NA

Ose USA Inc

2221 Old Oakland Rd. , San Jose, CA, 95131; **PH:** 1-408-383-0818

General - Incorporation	DE	**Stock** - Price on:12/24/2007	NA
Employees	NA	Stock Exchange	NA
Auditor	Grant Thornton LLP	Ticker Symbol	NA
Stk Agt	NA	Outstanding Shares	NA
Counsel	NA	E.P.S.	NA
DUNS No.	80-374-3921	Shareholders	NA

Business: The group's principle activity is to operate semiconductor-packaging foundry. The group receives wafers from its customers and assembles each integrated circuit in a protective plastic package. The group operates in two segments: manufacturing and distribution. Manufacturing comprises the semiconductor packaging services of packages designed for assembly using surface mount technology in which, leads on integrated circuits are soldered to the surface of the printed circuit board. Distribution comprises the north American sales, marketing and technical support organization for ose inc. The customers of the group are manufacturers of high-tech products such as video components, chip sets, graphics chips and logic components.

Primary SIC and add'l.: 3674

CIK No: 0000924101

Subsidiaries: OSE, Inc.

Oshkosh Truck Corp

2307 Oregon St., Oshkosh, WI, 54902; **PH:** 1-920-235-9150; **Fax:** 1-920-233-9268; **http://** www.oshkoshtruckcorporation.com

General - Incorporation.............................WI
Employees...9,387
Auditor ....Deloitte & Touche LLP
Stk Agt.............................First Union Nat'l Bank
Counsel...NA
DUNS No. 00-607-0445

Stock- Price on:12/24/2007 ....$64.13
Stock Exchange.....................................NYSE
Ticker Symbol...OSK
Outstanding Shares 74,060,000
E.P.S..$3.58
Shareholders...NA

Business: The groups principle activities include designing, manufacturing and marketing a range of specialty vehicles and vehicle bodies. The group operates through four segments namely access equipment, defense, fire and emergency, and commercial. The group operates from United States.

Primary SIC and add'l.: 5012 3713 3715 3531 3711

CIK No: 0000775158

Subsidiaries: 3841189 Canada, Inc., Bayside Underwriters Insurance Agency, Inc., Commercial Resource Services Company, Drive Insurance Holdings, Inc., Drive New Jersey Insurance Company, Drive Resource Services Company, Garden Sun Insurance Services, Inc., Greenberg Financial Insurance Services, Inc., Insurance Confirmation Services, Inc., Lakeside Insurance Agency, Inc., Midland Financial Group, Inc., Midland Risk Services, Inc., Mountain Laurel Assurance Company, National Continental Insurance Company, Pacific Motor Club 48 Subsidiaries included in the Index

Officers: John W. Randjelovic/CEO, Exec. VP - Fire, Emergency Group, Robert G. Bohn/Chmn., CEO, Michael J. Wuest/Exec. VP, Pres. - Mcneilus Companies, Inc, David M. Sagehorn/CFO, Exec. VP, Treasurer, Tom Cihowiak/New Product Information, Airport, Municipal, Arff, Michael S. Guzowski/VP - Information Technology, Matthew J. Zolnowski/Exec. VP, Chief Administration Officer, Charles L. Szews/COO, Pres., Thomas J. Polnaszek/Sr. VP - Finance, Donald H. Verhoff/Exec. VP - Technology, Thomas D. Fenner/Exec. VP, Pres. - Fire, Emergency Group, Michael K. Rohrkaste/VP - Human Resources, Joseph H. Kimmitt/Exec. VP - Government Operations, Industry Relations, John W. Stoddart/Exec. VP, Pres. - Defense Business, Scott L. Ney/Pres. - Oshkosh Capital (16 Officers included in Index)

Directors: Robert G. Bohn/Chmn., CEO, Robert A. Cornog/Dir., Richard G. Sim/Dir., William J. Andersen/Dir., Harvey Medvin/Dir., Frederick M. Franks/Dir., Kathleen J. Hempel/Dir., Richard M. Donnelly/Dir., Donald V. Fites/Dir., Peter J. Mosling/Dir., Timothy J. Roemer/Dir., Michael W. Grebe/Dir.

Owners: Kathleen J. Hempel, Bryan J. Blankfield, Charles L. Szews, Joseph H. Kimmitt, Insiders/3.98%, Robert A. Cornog, Richard M. Donnelly, T. Rowe Price Associates, Inc./9.64%, Harvey N. Medvin, Donald V. Fites, Frederick M. Franks, Matthew J. Zolnowski, Robert G. Bohn/1.35%, William J. Andersen, Richard G. Sim (18 Owners included in Index)

Financial Data: Fiscal Year End:09/30   Latest Annual Data: 9/30/2006

Year	Sales	Net Income
2006	$3,427,388,000	$205,529,000
2005	$2,959,900,000	$160,205,000
2004	$2,262,305,000	$112,806,000

Curr. Assets:	$2,194,900,000	Curr. Liab.:	$1,548,000,000	P/E Ratio: 24.57
Plant, Equip.:	$429,600,000	Total Liab.:	$5,002,400,000	Indic. Yr. Divd.: $0.400
Total Assets:	$6,399,800,000	Net Worth:	$1,393,600,000	Debt/ Equity: NA

OSI Pharmaceuticals

41 Pinelawn Rd., Melville, NY, 11747; **PH:** 1-631-962-2000; **Fax:** 1-631-752-3880; *http://* www.osip.com; **Email:** investor_info@osip.com

General - Incorporation.............................DE
Employees...611
Auditor ....KPMG LLP
Stk Agt.............................Bank of New York
Counsel...............................Saul Ewing LLP
DUNS No. 10-901-4720

Stock- Price on:12/24/2007 ....$36.99
Stock Exchange.......................................NDQ
Ticker Symbol...OSIP
Outstanding Shares 57,660,000
E.P.S..-$3.79
Shareholders...NA

Business: The group's principal activities are to discover, develop and market oncology products. The group's advanced drug tarceva(tm); an anti-cancer agent is undergoing phase iii clinical trials for non-small lung cancer and pancreatic cancer. Tarceva(tm) is being developed in a global alliance with genentech inc and roche holdings inc. In addition, it has five other drug candidates in early stages of clinical development, out of which three are next generation cytotoxic chemotherapy agents and three are gene-targeted therapies currently being developed by pfizer inc. The products of the group include novantrone(R) and gelclair(r). On, 12-Jun-2003, the group acquired cell pathways inc.

Primary SIC and add'l.: 8731 2834

CIK No: 0000729922

Subsidiaries: OSI Eyetech, Inc., OSI Pharmaceuticals (UK) Limited, Prosidion Limited

Officers: Colin Goddard/Dir., CEO/$1,905,478.00, Robert Simon/Exec. VP - Pharmaceutical Development, Manufacturing, Gabriel Leung/Pres. - OSI Oncology/$1,528,831.00, Anker Lundemose/Exec. VP, Pres. - OSI Prosidion/$1,301,307.00, Barbara A. Wood/VP, General Counsel, Sec., Michael G. Atieh/CFO, Exec. VP/$2,066,244.00, Paul G. Chaney/Exec. VP, Pres. - OSI Eyetech/$1,636,464.00, Neil Gibson/VP, Chief Scientific Officer, Linda E. Amper/VP - Business Administration, Human Resources

Directors: Colin Goddard/Dir., CEO, Robert A. Ingram/Chmn., Herbert Michael Pinedo/Dir., Daryl K. Granner/Dir., Viren Mehta/Dir., John P. White/Dir., Walter M. Lovenberg/Dir., Katharine B. Stevenson/Dir., Morgan G. Browne/Dir., Santo J. Costa/62/Dir., Joseph Klein/Dir., David W. Niemiec/Dir., Kenneth B. Lee/Dir.

Owners: Santo J. Costa, Colin Goddard, Insiders/3.20%, John P. White, OrbiMed Advisors LLC/5.70%, Daryl K. Granner, Paul G. Chaney, Gabriel Leung, T. Rowe Price Associates Inc./6.60%, Katharine B. Stevenson, Morgan G. Browne, Robert A. Ingram, Westfield Capital Management Co./8.00%, Viren Mehta, Walter M. Lovenberg (23 Owners included in Index)

Financial Data: Fiscal Year End:12/31   Latest Annual Data: 12/31/2006

Year	Sales	Net Income
2006	$375,696,000	-$582,184,000
2005	$174,194,000	-$157,123,000
2004	$42,800,000	-$260,371,000

Curr. Assets:	$275,445,000	Curr. Liab.:	$47,222,000	
Plant, Equip.:	$35,356,000	Total Liab.:	$233,796,000	Indic. Yr. Divd.: NA
Total Assets:	$388,029,000	Net Worth:	$154,233,000	Debt/ Equity: NA

OSI Restaurant Partners Inc

Formerly: Outback Steakhouse Inc
2202 N W Shore Blvd., Ste. 500, Tampa, FL, 33607; **PH:** 1-813-282-1225; *http://* www.outback.com

General - Incorporation............................DE
Employees...95,000
Auditor ....PricewaterhouseCoopers LLP
Stk Agt.............................Bank of New York
Counsel...............................Baker & Hostetler
DUNS No. 18-583-8968

Stock- Price on:12/24/2007 ....NA
Stock Exchange...NA
Ticker Symbol..NA
Outstanding Shares ....NA
E.P.S...NA
Shareholders...NA

Business: The group's principal activity is to develop and operate casual dining restaurants. It offers consumers of different demographic backgrounds an array of dining alternatives suited for differing needs. The restaurants serve dinner only and feature a limited menu of seasoned steaks, prime rib, chops, barbecued ribs, chicken, fish and pasta. The group has seven restaurant concepts, over 1000 system-wide restaurants. The operations are conducted through company-owned stores in 50 states and in 21 countries internationally. Outback steakhouse, carrabba's Italian grill, fleming's prime steakhouse and wine bar, roy's, cheeseburger in paradise, bonefish grill, lee roy selmon's and paul lee's Chinese kitchen service marks and 'bloomin' onion' are the trademarks under which the group markets its restaurants. On 01-Jul-2003, the group acquired 14 outback steakhouse restaurants operating in Alabama and Florida.

Primary SIC and add'l.: 6794 5812

CIK No: 0000874691

Subsidiaries: Bonefish Grill, Inc., Boomerang Air, Inc., Carrabba's Italian Grill, Inc., OS Asset, Inc., OS Capital, Inc., OS Cathay, Inc., OS Investments, Inc., OS Management, Inc., OS Marketing Services, Inc., OS Mortgage Holdings, Inc., OS Pacific, Inc., OS Prime, Inc., OS Realty, Inc., OS Restaurant Services, Inc., f.k.a. Outback Employee Services, Inc., OS Southern, Inc. 25 Subsidiaries included in the Index

Officers: William A. Allen/48/Dir., CEO, Dirk A. Montgomery/44/CFO, Joseph J. Kadow/51/Chief Officer - Legal, Corporate Affairs, Exec. VP, Paul E. Avery/48/COO

Directors: William A. Allen/48/Dir., CEO, Chris T. Sullivan/60/Chmn., Co - Founder, Robert D. Basham/60/Co - Founder, Vice Chmn., Debbi Fields/51/Dir., Toby S. Wilt/63/Dir., Thomas A. James/65/Dir., John A. Brabson/67/Dir., Tommy Franks/62/Dir., Lee Roy Selmon/53/Dir., William R. Carey/60/Dir.

Owners: Debbi Fields, Paul E. Avery, Capital Research and Management Company/9.10%, Toby S. Wilt, Dirk A. Montgomery, Joseph J. Kadow, OSI Investors as a group/11.90%, John A. Brabson, Steven T. Shlemon, William A. Allen, Thomas A. James, Chris T. Sullivan/3.20%, Insiders/11.40%, FMR Corp./8.10%, Tommy Franks (20 Owners included in Index)

OSI Systems Inc

12525 ChaDr.on Ave., Hawthorne, CA, 90250; **PH:** 1-310-978-0516; **Fax:** 1-310-644-7213; *http://* www.osi-systems.com

General - Incorporation ....CA
Employees..2,580
Auditor ....Deloitte & Touche LLP
Stk Agt.......................U.S. Stock Transfer Corp
Counsel...............................Richman Et Al
DUNS No. 94-837-1356

Stock- Price on:12/24/2007 ....$27.92
Stock Exchange.......................................NDQ
Ticker Symbol...OSIS
Outstanding Shares 16,980,000
E.P.S..-$0.88
Shareholders...NA

Business: The group's principal activity is to manufacture and sell optoelectronic devices and subsystems and medical imaging systems. The group designs and manufactures optoelectronic devices and value-added subsystems for original equipment manufacturers. The group utilizes the optoelectronic technology and designs to manufacture security and inspection products, sold under the brand names: rapiscan, secure and metor. In the medical field, the group manufactures and sells bone densitometers and saturation of arterial hemoglobin, under the trade names digital dolphin(tm) and dolphin 2000(TM). The group markets its products across North America, Europe and Asia. During 2004 ,the group acquired all assets of schwartz electro-optics, inc & advanced research and applications corporation. On 19-Mar-2004, the group acquired space labs medical.

Primary SIC and add'l.: 3826 3674 3841 3827 7382

CIK No: 0001039065

Subsidiaries: Advanced Micro Electronics AS, Blease Medical Equipment Limited, Blease Medical Holdings Limited, Blease Medical Services Limited, Corrigan Canada, Ltd., CXR Limited, Del Mar Reynolds GmbH, Del Mar Reynolds Medical Limited, Del Mar Reynolds Medical, Inc., Dolphin Medical Pte Ltd., Dolphin Medical, Inc., Ferson Technologies, Inc., Hertford Cardiology Limited, Hertford Medical International Limited, Metorex Security Products, Inc. 50 Subsidiaries included in the Index

Officers: Deepak Chopra/Chmn., CEO, Pres., Ajay Mehra/Dir., Exec. VP, Anuj Wadhawan/CFO, Treasurer, Alan Edrick/CFO, Exec. VP, Victor Sze/Exec. VP, Company Sec., General Counsel, Jeremy Norton/Dir. - Investor Relations, Manoocher Mansouri/Pres.

Directors: Deepak Chopra/Chmn., CEO, Pres., Steve Good/Dir., Meyer Luskin/Dir., Chand R. Viswanathan/Dir., Leslie E. Bider/58/Dir.

Owners: Steven C. Good/0.30%, Manoocher Mansouri/0.20%, Alan Edrick/0.10%, Insiders/10.60%, Wells Fargo& Company/13.00%, Leslie E. Bider, Deepak Chopra/7.80%, Chand R. Viswanathan/0.10%, Ajay Mehra/1.20%, Victor S. Sze/0.20%, Dimensional Fund Advisors,Inc./8.30%, Anuj Wadhawan/0.40%, Wellington Management Company, LLP/7.70%, Turner Investment Partners, Inc./5.20%, Meyer Luskin/0.30%

Financial Data: Fiscal Year End:06/30   Latest Annual Data: 06/30/2007

Year	Sales	Net Income
2007	$532,284,000	-$18,758,000
2006	$452,686,000	-$2,358,000
2005	$385,041,000	-$2,395,000

Curr. Assets:	$283,724,000	Curr. Liab.:	$121,568,000	
Plant, Equip.:	$42,521,000	Total Liab.:	$144,820,000	Indic. Yr. Divd.: NA
Total Assets:	$403,498,000	Net Worth:	$248,947,000	Debt/ Equity: 0.1130

Osiris Therapeutics Inc

7015 Albert Einstein Dr., Columbia, MD, 21046; **PH:** 1-443-545-1800; **Fax:** 1-443-545-1701; *http://* www.osiristx.com; **Email:** osiris@osiris.com

General - Incorporation ....DE
Employees..73
Auditor ....KPMG LLP
Stk Agt.......................Stock Transfer & Trust Co
Counsel...NA
DUNS No. ....NA

Stock- Price on:12/24/2007 ....$12.96
Stock Exchange.......................................NDQ
Ticker Symbol...OSIR
Outstanding Shares 27,470,000
E.P.S..-$2.42
Shareholders...NA

Business: The groups principal activities include developing and marketing medical services. The products of the group include Osteocel, Prochymal, Chondrogen and Provacel. The group operates from the United States.

Primary SIC and add'l.: 2836 8731

CIK No: 0001360886

Officers: Randal C. Mills/Dir., CEO, Pres., Harry E. Carmitchel/COO, Cary J. Claiborne/CFO, Lode Debrabandere/VP, GM - Inflammatory Diseases, Earl Fender/VP, GM - Orthopedics, Rodney L. Monroy/Sr. Dir. - Prochymal, Michelle Leroux Williams/VP - Development

Directors: Randal C. Mills/Dir., CEO, Pres., Peter Friedli/Co - Founder, Chmn., Felix Gutzwiller/Dir., Jay M. Moyes/Dir., Gregory H. Barnhill/Dir.

Owners: Insiders, Cary J. Claiborne, Thomas Schmidheiny/6.60%, C. Randal Mills/1.30%, Venturetec,Inc./12.80%, Gregory H. Barnhill, Felix Gutzwiller, Harry E. Carmitchel, Peter Friedli/47.20%, Jay M. Moyes

Financial Data: Fiscal Year End:12/31 Latest Annual Data: 12/31/2006

Year	Sales	Net Income
2006	$9,472,000	-$44,959,000
2005	$957,000	-$19,995,000
2004	NA	-$10,528,000

Curr. Assets:	$43,635,000	Curr. Liab.:	$10,469,000		
Plant, Equip.:	$3,942,000	Total Liab.:	$37,881,000	Indic. Yr. Divd.:	NA
Total Assets:	$49,168,000	Net Worth:	$11,287,000	Debt/ Equity:	69.3631

Osteologix Inc

425 Market St., Ste. 2230, San Francisco, CA, 94105; *PH:* 1-310-396-1691; *Fax:* 1-415-955-2727; *http://* www.osteologix.com; *Email:* ccasamento@osteologix.com

General		Stock	
Incorporation	DE	Price on:12/24/2007	$1.17
Employees	4	Stock Exchange	OTC
Auditor	Weinberg & Co., P.A	Ticker Symbol	OLGX
Stk Agt	Continental Stock Transfer & Trust Co	Outstanding Shares	21,080,000
Counsel	NA	E.P.S	-$0.38
DUNS No.	NA	Shareholders	NA

Business: The groups principal activity is developing pharmaceuticals for the treatment and prevention of diseases of bone and joint tissues. Product of the group includes NB S101, which is approved by the United States FDA. The group operates from the United States.

Primary SIC and add'l.: 2834

CIK No: 0001278129

Subsidiaries: Osteologix Aps

Officers: Philip J. Young/Dir., CEO, Baxter Phillips/Sr. Dir. - Corporate Development, Susan Greenspan/Clinical Advisor, Jens E.T. Andersen/Clinical Advisor, Matthew M. Loar/CFO, Malene Weis/Dir. - Clinical Development, Leslie Z. Benet/Clinical Advisor, Goran Samsioe/Clinical Advisor

Directors: Philip J. Young/Dir., CEO, Klaus Eldrup Jorgensen/Chmn., Christopher B. Wood/Dir., Christian Hansen/Dir., Florian Schonharting/Dir., Malene Weis/Dir. - Clinical Development, Bobby W. Sandage/Dir., Jeremy Curnock Cook/Dir., Baxter Phillips/Sr. Dir. - Corporate Development

Owners: Bobby W. Sandage, Nordic Biotech K/S, Stephan Christgau, Florian Schonharting, Visium Asset Management LLC, Christopher B. Wood, Charles J. Casamento, Klaus Eldrup Jorgensen, Matthew M. Loar, BML Healthcare I, LP, Insiders, Christian Hansen, Jeremy Curnock Cook

Financial Data: Fiscal Year End:12/31 Latest Annual Data: 12/31/2006

Year	Sales	Net Income
2006	NA	-$4,858,000
2005	NA	-$106,000
2004	$0	-$45,000

Curr. Assets:	$6,533,000	Curr. Liab.:	$745,000	P/E Ratio:	12.62
Plant, Equip.:	$9,000	Total Liab.:	$745,000	Indic. Yr. Divd.:	NA
Total Assets:	$6,542,000	Net Worth:	$5,797,000	Debt/ Equity:	NA

Osteotech Inc

51 James Way, Eatontown, NJ, 07724; *PH:* 1-732-542-2800; *Fax:* 1-732-542-9312; *http://* www.osteotech.com

General		Stock	
Incorporation	DE	Price on:12/24/2007	$7.46
Employees	354	Stock Exchange	NDQ
Auditor	BDO Seidman LLP	Ticker Symbol	OSTE
Stk Agt	Registrar & Transfer Co	Outstanding Shares	17,430,000
Counsel	Carella, Byrne, Bain, Gilfillan	E.P.S	$0.03
DUNS No.	15-738-4306	Shareholders	NA

Business: The group's principal activity is to provide the services and products used in the repair and healing of the musculoskeletal system. The group has two operating segments: demineralized bone matrix segment and base tissue segment. The demineralized bone matrix segment is engaged in the processing and marketing of grafton(R) and private label demineralized bone matrix. Demineralized bone matrix is processed using the group's advanced proprietary demineralization process. The base tissue segment primarily is engaged in the processing of mineralized weight-bearing allograft bone tissue. The group's other business units are engaged in marketing and distributing metal spinal implant products and processing, marketing and distributing bovine tissue products. These products and services are marketed primarily to the orthopedic, spinal, neurological, oral/maxillofacial, dental and general surgery customers in the United States and Europe.

Primary SIC and add'l.: 8731 8099 3842

CIK No: 0000874734

Subsidiaries: HC Implants, B.V., Medical Technical Laboratory OsteoCentre Bulgaria EAD, OST Developpement, OST Developpement Australia PTY Limited, Osteotech, Osteotech B.V., Osteotech Implants, B.V., Osteotech/CAM Services B.V.

Officers: Sam Owusu-Akyaw/Dir., CEO, Pres./$728,746.00, Donna A. Haag/VP - Supply Chain, Information Management, Roman Hitchev/VP - International, MD, Pres. Ocbg, Chuck Lanza/VP - Sales, Mark H. Burroughs/CFO, Exec. VP/$299,487.00, Robert W. Honneffer/Sr. VP - Operations/$225,752.00, Richard Russo/Pres. - International/$382,529.00, Robert M. Wynalek/Pres. - Domestic/$312,109.00, Kai H. Lo/VP, Controller Domestic Operations, Martin Rexroad/VP - Human Resources, Greg Cannedy/VP - Quality Assurance, Regulatory Affairs, Good Tissue Practices

Directors: Sam Owusu-Akyaw/Dir., CEO, Pres., Kenneth P. Fallon/Chmn., Robert J. Palmisano/Dir., Stephen S. Galliker/Dir., Robert W. Gunn/Dir., James M. Shannon/Dir.

Owners: Sam Owusu-Akyaw/1.30%, Robert W. Honneffer, Richard Russo/1.10%, Insiders/5.20%, Group comprised of Heartland Advisors, Inc./11.30%, Mark H. Burroughs, John F. White/9.60%, Kenneth P. Fallon, Stephen J. Sogin, Robert J. Palmisano, Stephen S. Galliker, Robert M. Wynalek, Dimensional Fund Advisors LP/6.50%

Financial Data: Fiscal Year End:12/31 Latest Annual Data: 12/31/2006

Year	Sales	Net Income
2006	$99,241,000	$1,907,000
2005	$93,307,000	-$21,117,000
2004	$88,577,000	-$5,283,000

Curr. Assets:	$69,320,000	Curr. Liab.:	$16,588,000	P/E Ratio:	248.67
Plant, Equip.:	$36,340,000	Total Liab.:	$39,180,000	Indic. Yr. Divd.:	NA
Total Assets:	$113,033,000	Net Worth:	$73,853,000	Debt/ Equity:	0.1998

Otelco Inc

505 3rd Ave. E, Oneonta, AL, 35121; *PH:* 1-205-625-3574; *Fax:* 1-205-625-3523; *http://* www.otelco.net; *Email:* info@otelco.net

General		Stock	
Incorporation	DE	Price on:12/24/2007	$20.8799
Employees	220	Stock Exchange	AMEX
Auditor	BDO Seidman, LLP	Ticker Symbol	OTT
Stk Agt	Wells Fargo Shareowner Services	Outstanding Shares	10,220,000
Counsel	Dorsey & Whitney, LLP	E.P.S	$0.067
DUNS No.	NA	Shareholders	NA

Business: The groups principle activity is operates and acquire rural local exchange carriers. The groups services include local services, network access, cable television, Internet and transport services. In the year 2006, the group acquired Mid-marine communications Inc. The group operates from the United States.

Primary SIC and add'l.: 4822 4899 4813 4841

CIK No: 0001288359

Subsidiaries: Blountsville Telephone Company Inc., Brindlee Holdings LLC, Brindlee Mountain Telephone Company, Hopper Holding Company, Inc., Hopper Telecommunications Company, Inc., Imagination, Inc., Mid-Maine Communications, Inc., Mid-Maine Telecom, Inc., Mid-Maine TelPlus, Mid-Missouri Telephone Corp., Otelco Holdings LLC, Otelco Telecommunications LLC, Otelco Telephone LLC, Page & Kiser Communications, Inc.

Officers: Michael D. Weaver/Chmn., CEO, Pres., Curtis L. Garner/CFO, Dennis Andrews/Sr. VP, GM - Brindlee Mountain, Blountsville Divisions, Gary B. Romig/VP, GM - Mid, Missouri Division, Jerry C. Boles/VP, Controller, Nicholas A. Winchester/Sr. VP, GM - Mid, Maine Division

Directors: Michael D. Weaver/Chmn., CEO, Pres., Stephen P. McCall/Dir., Andrew Meyers/Dir., Howard Haug/Dir., John P. Kunz/Dir., William F. Reddersen/Dir., William Bak/Dir.

Owners: Michael D. Weaver, Insiders/0.80%, CEA Capital, Gary B. Romig, Mid-Missouri Parent LLC, Insiders, Dennis K. Andrews, Stephen P. McCall, Seaport Capital, Michael D. Weaver/0.80%, BancBoston Ventures, Inc.

Financial Data: Fiscal Year End:12/31 Latest Annual Data: 12/31/2006

Year	Sales	Net Income
2006	$57,589,000	$1,161,000
2005	$46,972,000	$1,792,000
2004	$37,266,000	$6,114,000

Curr. Assets:	$25,304,000	Curr. Liab.:	$11,557,000	P/E Ratio:	311.64
Plant, Equip.:	$60,494,000	Total Liab.:	$243,725,000	Indic. Yr. Divd.:	NA
Total Assets:	$243,852,000	Net Worth:	$127,000	Debt/ Equity:	NA

Ottawa Savings Bancorp Inc IL

925 Lasalle St., Ottawa, IL, 61350; *PH:* 1-815-433-2525; *Fax:* 1-815-433-2573; *http://* www.ottawasavings.com; *Email:* customerservice@ottawasavings.com

General		Stock	
Incorporation	USA	Price on:12/24/2007	$13
Employees	22	Stock Exchange	OTC
Auditor	McGladrey & Pullen LLP	Ticker Symbol	OTTW
Stk Agt	NA	Outstanding Shares	2,220,000
Counsel	NA	E.P.S	$0.68
DUNS No.	NA	Shareholders	NA

Business: The groups principal activities include providing banking and financial services. The groups services includes to attract deposits from the general public and use those funds to originate and purchase one to four family, multi family and commercial real estate, construction and consumer loans. The group operates from the United States. In the year 2006, the groups total assets were $19,421,322(thousands).

Primary SIC and add'l.: 6021

CIK No: 0001321070

Subsidiaries: Illinois Valley Service Corporation, Ottawa Savings Bank

Officers: Gary Ocepek/CEO, Pres., Jon Kranov/Sr. VP, CFO, Phil Devermann/VP, Construction Loan Officer, Juleann Leamy/Assist. VP, Sec., Carol Collins/Assist. VP, Cathy Koch/Treasurer, Laurie Duffell/Assist. VP, Assistant Sec., Jessica Oldman/Assist. VP

Directors: Gary Ocepek/CEO, Pres., Arthur C. Mueller/54/Dir., Daniel J. Reynolds/61/Dir., Keith Johnson/54/Dir., James A. Ferrero/58/Dir.

Owners: Ottawa Savings Bancorp MHC/55.00%, Tyndall Capital Partners, LP/5.81%

Financial Data: Fiscal Year End:12/31 Latest Annual Data: 12/31/2006

Year	Sales	Net Income
2006	$10,617,000	$944,000
2005	$9,110,000	$868,000

Curr. Assets:	$11,761,000	Curr. Liab.:	$182,996,000		
Plant, Equip.:	$7,866,000	Total Liab.:	$185,316,000	Indic. Yr. Divd.:	$0.200
Total Assets:	$204,865,000	Net Worth:	$19,421,000	Debt/ Equity:	NA

Otter Tail Corp

215 S Cascade St., Fergus Falls, MN, 56538; *PH:* 1-218-739-8479; *Fax:* 1-218-998-3165; *http://* www.ottertail.com; *Email:* sharesvc@ottertail.com

General		Stock	
Incorporation	MN	Price on:12/24/2007	$78.85
Employees	NA	Stock Exchange	OTC
Auditor	Deloitte & Touche LLP	Ticker Symbol	OTTRO
Stk Agt	Otter Tail Corp	Outstanding Shares	NA
Counsel	NA	E.P.S	$1.69
DUNS No.	00-696-1353	Shareholders	NA

Business: The group's principal activities are carried out through five segments: electric, plastics, manufacturing, health services and other business operations. Electric segment includes the production, transmission, distribution and sale of electric energy. Plastics: consist of the production of polyvinyl

chloride pipe. Manufacturing consists of businesses involved in the production of waterfront equipment, wind towers, frame-straightening equipment, accessories for the auto repair industry, custom plastic pallets, handling trays and horticultural containers; fabrication of steel products; contract machining and metal parts stamping and fabrication. Health services consist of the sale of diagnostic medical equipment, supplies and accessories. Other business operations includes electrical and telephone construction contracting, transportation, telecommunications, entertainment and energy services and natural gas marketing. On 01-Nov-2003, the group acquired foley company.

Primary SIC and add'l.: 3088 4832 7352 4911 3844 8099 1623

CIK No: 0000075129

Subsidiaries: AC Equipment, Inc., Aerial Contractors, Inc., AgraWest Investments Limited, AWI Acquisition Company Limited, BTD Manufacturing, Inc., Chassis Liner Corporation, DMI Canada, Inc., DMI Industries, Inc., DMS Health Technologies, Inc., DMS Imaging Partners, LLC, DMS Imaging, Inc., DMS Leasing Corporation, E. W. Wylie Corporation, Foley Company, Galva Foam Marine Industries, Inc. 32 Subsidiaries included in the Index

Officers: Paul Wilson/CEO - DMS Health Group, VP - Health Services, John D. Erickson/Dir., CEO, Pres./$1,627,337.00, Kevin G. Moug/CFO, Treasurer/$936,702.00, Lauris N. Molbert/COO, Exec. VP/$1,568,842.00, Shane Waslaski/VP - Infrastructure Products, Services Platform, Lori Talafous/VP - Human Resources, Strategy, George A. Koeck/General Counsel, Corp. Sec./$571,850.00, Chuck Hoge/VP - Manufacturing Platform, Charles S. MacFarlane/43/Pres. - Otter Tail Power Company/$534,375.00

Directors: John D. Erickson/Dir., CEO, Pres., John MacFarlane/Chmn., Arvid R. Liebe/Dir., Kenneth L. Nelson/Dir., Karen M. Bohn/Dir., Gary J. Spies/Dir., Dennis R. Emmen/Dir., Nathan I. Partain/Dir., Edward J. McIntyre/Dir., Joyce Nelson Schuette/Dir.

Owners: Otter Tail Corporation/0.06%, Jeffrey L. Gendell/0.06%, Cascade Investment L.L.C./0.09%

Financial Data: Fiscal Year End:12/31 **Latest Annual Data:** 12/31/2006

Year	Sales	Net Income
2006	$1,104,954,000	$51,112,000
2005	$1,046,408,000	$62,551,000
2004	$882,324,000	$42,195,000

Curr. Assets:	$335,353,000	Curr. Liab.:	$215,457,000		
Plant, Equip.:	$718,609,000	Total Liab.:	$766,625,000	Indic. Yr. Divd.:	$1.170
Total Assets:	$1,258,650,000	Net Worth:	$490,770,000	Debt/ Equity:	NA

Our Glass Inc

PO Box 110310, Naples, FL, 34108; **PH:** 1-239-598-2300

General - Incorporation	NV	Stock- Price on:12/24/2007	NA
Employees	NA	Stock Exchange	NA
Auditor	Child, Sullivan & Co	Ticker Symbol	NA
Stk Agt	NA	Outstanding Shares	NA
Counsel	NA	E.P.S	NA
DUNS No.	NA	Shareholders	NA

Business: The group's principle activity is to provice glass processing service. The group's products include fused glass,glass bowl and glass tray. The group operates from United States.

Primary SIC and add'l.: 9995

CIK No: 0001302365

Officers: Cosmo Palmieri/35/Pres., Treasurer, Jose Acevedo/50/Sec.

Directors: Joseph Pioppi/78/Dir.

Curr. Assets:	$236,000	Curr. Liab.:	$167,000		
Plant, Equip.:	$3,000	Total Liab.:	$167,000	Indic. Yr. Divd.:	NA
Total Assets:	$343,000	Net Worth:	$175,000	Debt/ Equity:	NA

Ourpets Co

1300 E St., Fairport Harbor, OH, 44077; **PH:** 1-440-354-6500; **Fax:** 1-440-354-9129; http:// www.our-pets.com; **Email:** info@ourpets.com

General - Incorporation	CO	Stock - Price on:12/24/2007	$1.49
Employees	21	Stock Exchange	OTC
Auditor	S R Snodgrass, A.C	Ticker Symbol	OPCO
Stk Agt	Transfer Online, Inc.	Outstanding Shares	15,100,000
Counsel	NA	E.P.S	$0.03
DUNS No.	NA	Shareholders	NA

Business: The group's principal activities are to develop, manufacture and market various proprietary products for the retail pet business.the group develops, designs, produces and markets a broad line of innovative, high-quality accessory and consumable pet products for improving the health, safety, comfort and enjoyment of pets.the group markets products such as dog and cat feeders, dog and cat toys, cat litter, and natural and nutritional pet supplements and treats.the group has been granted fifteen United States patents for dog and cat feeders and has twenty five United States patents pending for cat and dog toys, dog feeders and wild bird feeders.

Primary SIC and add'l.: 3085

CIK No: 0001094139

Subsidiaries: Akon Plastic Enterprises, Sanar Manufacturing Company

Officers: Steven Tsengas/70/Chmn., CEO, Pres./$133,646.00, John G. Murchie/70/Principal Financial Officer, VP, Treasurer, Konstantine A. Tsengas/43/VP - Operations, Sec.

Directors: Steven Tsengas/70/Chmn., CEO, Pres., Joseph T. Aveni/76/Dir., James D. Ireland/58/Dir., John Spirk/59/Dir.

Owners: James D. Ireland, John Spirk, Evangelia S. Tsengas, Nicholas S. Tsengas, Scott T. Fitzhugh, Joseph T. Aveni, Insiders, Steven Tsengas, John G. Murchie, James W. McCourt, Pet Zone Products Ltd.

Financial Data: Fiscal Year End:12/31 **Latest Annual Data:** 12/31/2006

Year	Sales	Net Income
2006	$9,442,000	$561,000
2005	$6,566,000	$254,000
2004	$5,445,000	$13,000

Curr. Assets:	$4,088,000	Curr. Liab.:	$2,735,000	P/E Ratio:	37.25
Plant, Equip.:	$2,058,000	Total Liab.:	$2,946,000	Indic. Yr. Divd.:	NA
Total Assets:	$6,476,000	Net Worth:	$3,531,000	Debt/ Equity:	0.0461

Outdoor Channel Holdings Inc

43445 Business Pk. Dr., Ste. 113, Temecula, CA, 92590; **PH:** 1-951-699-4749; **Fax:** 1-951-699-1849; http:// www.outdoorchannel.com; **Email:** investor@pondel.com

General - Incorporation	DE	Stock - Price on:12/24/2007	$10.34
Employees	134	Stock Exchange	NDQ
Auditor	J. H. Cohn LLP	Ticker Symbol	OUTD
Stk Agt	Computershare Trust Co	Outstanding Shares	25,830,000
Counsel	NA	E.P.S.	-$0.29
DUNS No.	NA	Shareholders	NA

Business: The group's principal activities are to provide outdoor amusement and recreation services, such as hunting, fishing, shooting sports, rodeo, recreational gold prospecting and related life style programming. It also owns and operates related businesses, which serves the interest of viewers of the outdoor channel and other outdoor enthusiasts. These related businesses include: ldma-au, inc. (lost dutchman's), gold prospectors' association of America, inc. (gpaa) and the trips division. On 08-Sep-2004, the group acquired the outdoor channel.

Primary SIC and add'l.: 7999

CIK No: 0000760326

Subsidiaries: 43455 Bpd, LLC, Gold Prospectors Association of America, Inc, Gold Prospectors Association of America, LLC, Ldma-au, Inc., The Outdoor Channel, Inc.

Officers: Perry T. Massie/Chmn., CEO, Pres., Thomas H. Massie/Vice Chmn., Exec. VP, Sec., William A. Owen/Exec. VP, CFO, Treasurer, Assist. Sec., Mary Seifert/Administrative Assist. - Affiliate Relations Team, Jesi Steward/Dir. - Business Development, Brenda Pearson/Executive Assist. - California, Erik Redmond/Event Mgr. - Motor Moose Team, Cindy Collins-Berndt/Mgr. - Affiliate Relations, Reporting, Thomas E. Hornish/Exec. VP, COO, General Counsel, Sec., Alice Kim/Client Services Mgr. - California, Mark Romano/Regional VP - Northeast Region, Eugene A. Brookhart/Sr. VP - Operations, Stacy Sjogren/Affiliate Relations Coordinator, Northeast Region, Teresa Chiniaeff/National Accounting Mgr. - Central Region, Scott E. Fink/National Accounting Mgr. - Western Region (40 Officers included in Index)

Directors: Perry T. Massie/Chmn., CEO, Pres., Thomas H. Massie/Vice Chmn., Exec. VP, Sec., David C. Merritt/Dir., Bahnson T. Stanley/Dir., Thomas Bahnson Stanley/Dir., Roger L. Werner/Dir., Ajit M. Dalvi/Dir., David D. Kinley/Dir., Michael L. Pandzik/Dir.

Owners: Insiders, Bahnson T. Stanley, Andrew J. Dale, David C. Merritt, Richard K. Dickson, BlackRock, Inc, Musk Ox Investments, LP, Jerry R. Berglund, Thomas E. Hornish, Mazama Capital Management, Inc., Roger L. Werner, Thomas H. Massie, Perry T. Massie, Ray V. Miller, Elizabeth J. Sanderson (17 Owners included in Index)

Financial Data: Fiscal Year End:12/31 **Latest Annual Data:** 12/31/2006

Year	Sales	Net Income
2006	$48,522,000	-$7,325,000
2005	$42,908,000	$2,193,000
2004	$39,954,000	-$24,160,000

Curr. Assets:	$70,969,000	Curr. Liab.:	$3,623,000		
Plant, Equip.:	$15,797,000	Total Liab.:	$5,983,000	Indic. Yr. Divd.:	NA
Total Assets:	$147,957,000	Net Worth:	$141,974,000	Debt/ Equity:	NA

Outlook Group Corp

1180 American Dr, Neenah, WI, 54956; **PH:** 1-920-722-2333; http:// www.outlookgroup.com

General - Incorporation	WI	Stock - Price on:12/24/2007	NA
Employees	NA	Stock Exchange	NA
Auditor	Virchow, Krause & Co. LLP	Ticker Symbol	NA
Stk Agt	American Stock Transfer & Trust Co.	Outstanding Shares	NA
Counsel	Charles & Brady	E.P.S	NA
DUNS No.	08-330-2034	Shareholders	NA

Business: The group's principal activity is to provide a broad array of packaging, specialty printing and direct marketing services. The services offered include contract packaging, collateral information management and distribution, direct marketing components and services, packaging and label materials and specialty print and related services. The group operates through two business segments: outlook graphics and outlook Web. The outlook graphic segment produces custom printed products on a wide range of media including newsprint, coated paper and heavy board including paperboard packaging. This segment also provides finishing services for printed items such as precision trimming, folding and gluing, binding, shrink-wrapping, collating and packaging products for mailing and distribution. Outlook Web provides flexographic printing, rotary letterpress printing, laminating and slitting services.

Primary SIC and add'l.: 2759 2752

CIK No: 0000867490

Subsidiaries: Outlook Foods, Inc., Outlook Label Systems, Inc, Showcase Postcards, Inc

Officers: Lorie Gillis/Member - OG Team, Gene Bortolameolli/Member - OG Team, Diane Novak/Member - OG Team, Patricia Schuh/Member - OG Team, Melissa Krokstrom/Member - OG Team, Chris Kissinger/Member - OG Team, John Johnson/Member - OG Team, Brenda Kussow/Member - OG Team, Rebecca Oberg/Member - OG Team, Deb Spencer/Member - OG Team, Jane Vandinter/Member - OG Team, Dan Fraleigh/Member - OG Team, Stacey Steffens/Member - OG Team, Patricia Heckman/Member - OG Team, Amy Bravick/Member - OG Team (19 Officers included in Index)

Ovation Products Corp

395 E Dunstable Rd., Nashua, NH, 03062; **PH:** 1-603-891-3224; http:// www.ovationproducts.com

General - Incorporation	DE	Stock- Price on:12/24/2007	NA
Employees	NA	Stock Exchange	NA
Auditor	Wolf & Co. P.C	Ticker Symbol	NA
Stk Agt	NA	Outstanding Shares	NA
Counsel	NA	E.P.S	NA
DUNS No.	NA	Shareholders	NA

Business: The group's principle activity is to provide produced prototypes of its Clean Water Appliance for testing. The group operates from United States.

Primary SIC and add'l.: 3580

CIK No: 0001189528

Subsidiaries: Lancy Water Technologies Limited, Norman Hay Plc

Officers: William H. Zebuhr/64/CTO, Christine Cox/CFO, Treasurer, William E. Lockwood/64/Dir., COO, VP - Business Development

Directors: William E. Lockwood/64/Dir., COO, VP - Business Development

Overhill Farms Inc

2727 E Vernon Ave., Vernon, CA, 90058; ***PH:*** 1-323-582-9977; ***Fax:*** 1-323-582-6122;
http:// www.overhillfarms.com

General - Incorporation	NV	**Stock**- Price on:12/24/2007	$5.64
Employees	860	Stock Exchange	AMEX
Auditor	Ernst & Young LLP	Ticker Symbol	OFI
Stk Agt	American Stock Transfer & Trust Co.	Outstanding Shares	15,370,000
Counsel	NA	E.P.S.	$0.29
DUNS No.	NA	Shareholders	NA

Business: The group's principle activity is to manufacture frozen food products. The products of the group includes entrees, plated meals, meal components, soups, sauces, poultry, meat and fish specialties. The group manufactures products in the retail and food service areas with branded and private label entrees and components. Major customers include panda restaurant group, jenny craig products, albertson's, and American airlines. The group markets its products through an internal sales force and outside food brokers. The group's patents are overhill farms, Chicago brothers and florence pasta and cheese. The group's total revenue for September 2007 was 192.64 millions of USD.

Primary SIC and add'l.: 2048 2015 2092 2038 2035 5147

CIK No: 0001101020

Officers: James Rudis/57/Chmn., CEO, Pres., Richard A. Horvath/62/Sr. VP, Sec., Silvia Ventura/Mgr. - Human Resources, John Steinbrun/44/Dir., Sr. VP, CFO, COO, Robert Olivarez/Contact - Investor Relations

Directors: James Rudis/57/Chmn., CEO, Pres., Alexander Rodetis/65/Dir., Harold Estes/68/Dir., Geoffrey A. Gerard/63/Dir., Alexander Auerbach/64/Dir., Louis J. Giraudo/62/Dir.

Owners: Coliseum Capital Management, LLC/6.00%, Harold Estes/7.20%, Alexander Rodetis, William Blair & Company, L.L.C./10.80%, James Rudis/3.80%, Louis J. Giraudo, Insiders/11.80%, Geoffrey A. Gerard, Richard A. Horvath, Alexander Auerbach

Financial Data: **Fiscal Year End:**10/02 **Latest Annual Data:** 10/1/2006

Year	Sales	Net Income
2006	$168,310,000	$5,102,000
2005	$162,566,000	$3,696,000
2004	$133,957,000	-$2,142,000

Curr. Assets:	$27,776,000	**Curr. Liab.:**	$14,255,000	**P/E Ratio:**	15.67
Plant, Equip.:	$12,618,000	**Total Liab.:**	$62,030,000	**Indic. Yr. Divd.:**	NA
Total Assets:	$59,550,000	**Net Worth:**	-$2,481,000	**Debt/ Equity:**	NA

Overland Storage Inc

4820 Overland Ave., San Diego, CA, 92123; ***PH:*** 1-858-571-5555; ***Fax:*** 1-858-571-0982;
http:// www.overlandstorage.com

General - Incorporation	CA	**Stock**- Price on:12/24/2007	$2.78
Employees	360	Stock Exchange	NDQ
Auditor	PricewaterhouseCoopers LLP	Ticker Symbol	OVRL
Stk Agt	Wells Fargo Shareowner Services	Outstanding Shares	12,750,000
Counsel	Procopio Cory H & S LLP	E.P.S.	-$3.47
DUNS No.	03-221-0858	Shareholders	NA

Business: The group's principal activities are to design, develop, manufacture, market and support magnetic tape data storage systems for backup, archival and data interchange functions. The products of the group are installed on specific computer platforms with the appropriate backup, data interchange or storage management software. The group markets all its products on an indirect basis, primarily through three channels or types of customers: original equipment manufacturers (OEMs), commercial distributors and volume. Volume consists of systems integrators, technical distributors and value added resellers (vars).

Primary SIC and add'l.: 3572

CIK No: 0000889930

Subsidiaries: Okapi Acquisition Co., Inc., Overland Storage (Europe) Ltd., Overland Storage Export Limited, Overland Storage GmbH, Overland Storage SARL, Zetta Systems, Inc.

Officers: Robert Scroop/VP - Engineering, Michael W. Gawarecki/VP - Operations, Vernon Loforti/Dir., VP, CFO, Sec., Robert C. Farkaly/VP - Worldwide Sales, Kurt L. Kalbfleisch/Interim CFO, VP - Finance

Directors: Scott McClendon/Chmn., Robert A. Degan/Dir., William J. Miller/Dir., Michael Norkus/Dir., Vernon Loforti/Dir., VP, CFO, Sec., Nora M. Denzel/Dir., Eric L. Kelley/Dir.

Owners: Kingdon Capital Management, LLC/7.80%, Insiders/8.20%, FMR Corp./7.90%, Michael W. Gawarecki, Dimensional Fund Advisors Inc./7.40%, Wellington Management Company, LLP/7.20%, William J. Miller, Michael Norkus, Vernon A. LoForti/1.10%, Robert A. Degan/1.00%, Renaissance Technologies, Corp./5.00%, Scott McClendon/4.10%, Galleon Management, LP/6.20%

Financial Data: **Fiscal Year End:**07/03 **Latest Annual Data:** 6/30/2006

Year	Sales	Net Income
2006	$209,038,000	-$19,486,000
2005	$235,687,000	$4,578,000
2004	$238,139,000	$10,625,000

Curr. Assets:	$148,895,000	**Curr. Liab.:**	$38,532,000		
Plant, Equip.:	$8,758,000	**Total Liab.:**	$43,060,000	**Indic. Yr. Divd.:**	NA
Total Assets:	$164,554,000	**Net Worth:**	$121,494,000	**Debt/ Equity:**	NA

Overseas Shipholding Group Inc

666 3rd Ave., New York, NY, 10017; ***PH:*** 1-212-953-4100; ***Fax:*** 1-212-578-1832;
http:// www.osg.com

General - Incorporation	DE	**Stock**- Price on:12/24/2007	$81.71
Employees	3,980	Stock Exchange	NYSE
Auditor	Ernst & Young LLP	Ticker Symbol	OSG
Stk Agt	Mellon Investor Services LLC	Outstanding Shares	33,220,000
Counsel	Proskauer Rose LLP	E.P.S.	$9.62
DUNS No.	05-049-6140	Shareholders	NA

Business: The group's principal activity is the ocean transportation of crude oil and petroleum products. The group operates under four segments: foreign flag very large crude carriers (vlccs), aframaxes, product carriers, U.S. Flag crude tankers. The activity also includes transportation of crude oil, petroleum products, dry bulk cargoes, primarily grain, coal and iron ore. Of the 52 vessels owned by the group, 47 are tankers engaged in the oil transportation business, of which 41 are foreign flag tankers that operate in the international market and six are U.S. Flag tankers that operate in the us, alaskan and coastwise trades.

Primary SIC and add'l.: 4412 4424

CIK No: 0000075208

Subsidiaries: 1320 Tanker Corporation, 1321 Tanker Corporation, 1372 Tanker Corporation, 1395 Tanker Corporation, 398 Equity Corporation, 399 Equity Corporation, 400 Equity Corporation, 401 Equity Corporation, Africa Tanker Corporation, Alcesmar Limited, Alcmar Limited, Allenmar Limited, Almar Limited, Ambermar Limited, Ambermar Tanker Corporation 197 Subsidiaries included in the Index

Officers: Morten Arntzen/Dir., CEO, Pres./$3,881,399.00, Myles Itkin/Exec. VP, CFO, Treasurer/$1,919,164.00, Eric F. Smith/Head - US Flag Strategic Business Unit, Mats Berglund/Sr. VP, Head - Crude Transportation Strategic Business Unit/$1,639,964.00, Angus Campbell/Head - OSG Gas Strategic Business Unit, James I. Edelson/General Counsel, Sec., Robert R. Mozdean/Head - Worldwide Human Resources, Lois K. Zabrocky/Head - International Product Carrier Strategic Business Unit, Jennifer Schlueter/VP - Corporate Communications, Robert Johnston/Sr. VP, Head - Shipping Operations/$1,944,623.00, Ian T. Blackley/MD, COO - OSG Ship Management, UK Ltd, George Dienis/MD, COO - OSG Ship Management, GR Ltd/$893,720.00, John L. Grenier/Operational Compliance Officer, Marc Lamonte/Crude, Commercial Chartering, Jean-Paul Vettier/63/Dir. - Sr. Advisor, Investment Funds *(19 Officers included in Index)*

Directors: Morten Arntzen/Dir., CEO, Pres., Michael J. Zimmerman/Chmn., Stanley Komaroff/Dir., Charles A. Fribourg/Dir., Thomas Coleman/Dir., Solomon Merkin/Dir., Jean-Paul Vettier/63/Dir. - Sr. Advisor, Investment Funds, Allen G. Andreas/Dir., Joel I. Picket/Dir., Oudi Recanati/Dir., Alan R. Batkin/Dir., Ariel Recanati/Dir., Thomas Robards/Dir.

Owners: Myles R. Itkin, FMR Corp, Robert E. Johnston, Jean-Paul Vettier, Alan R. Batkin, Oudi Recanati, Michael Recanati, Mats Berglund, Ariel Recanati, Archer-Daniels-Midland Company, Joel I. Picket, Charles A. Fribourg, The Michael Recanati Trust, George Dienis, Goldman Sachs Asset Management, L.P *(28 Owners included in Index)*

Financial Data: **Fiscal Year End:**12/31 **Latest Annual Data:** 12/31/2006

Year	Sales	Net Income
2006	$1,047,403,000	$392,660,000
2005	$1,000,303,000	$464,829,000
2004	$810,835,000	$401,236,000

Curr. Assets:	$845,521,000	**Curr. Liab.:**	$227,576,000	**P/E Ratio:**	9.24
Plant, Equip.:	$2,532,596,000	**Total Liab.:**	$2,023,358,000	**Indic. Yr. Divd.:**	$1.250
Total Assets:	$4,230,669,000	**Net Worth:**	$2,207,311,000	**Debt/ Equity:**	NA

Overstock Com Inc

6350 S 3000 E, Salt Lake City, UT, 84121; ***PH:*** 1-801-947-3100; ***Fax:*** 1-801-944-4629;
http:// www.overstock.com

General - Incorporation	DE	**Stock**- Price on:12/24/2007	$18.95
Employees	864	Stock Exchange	NDQ
Auditor	PricewaterhouseCoopers LLP	Ticker Symbol	OSTK
Stk Agt	Computershare Investor Services LLC	Outstanding Shares	23,680,000
Counsel	Wilson Sonsini Goodrich & Rosati	E.P.S.	-$3.68
DUNS No.	NA	Shareholders	NA

Business: The group's principle activity is to provide online retailing activities. The group offers closeout, brand-name merchandise for sale over the Internet. Closeout merchandise is typically available in inconsistent quantities and prices and often is only available to consumers after it has been purchased and resold by disparate liquidation wholesalers. The group's warehouses purchase large bulks of inventory from these liquidation sales of residual products and make direct and indirect sales. The group's merchandise offering includes bed-and-bath goods, kitchenware, watches, jewelry, electronics, sporting goods and designer accessories. The group's quarterly revenue for September 2007 was 161.93 millions of USD.

Primary SIC and add'l.: 7375 5999

CIK No: 0001130713

Subsidiaries: OTravel.com, Inc., Overstock Mexico, S. de R.L. de C.V.

Officers: Patrick M. Byrne/Chmn., CEO/$137,568.00, Stormy D. Simon/Sr. VP - Branding, Customer Care/$468,770.00, David Chidester/Sr. VP - Finance, Principal Financial Officer/$367,653.00, Jonathan E. Johnson/Sr. VP - Corporate Affairs, Sam Peterson/Sr. VP - Technology, Jason Lindsey/Dir., COO, Pres./$602,717.00, Jacob Hawkins/VP - Online Marketing, Kevin Moon/Contact - Investor Relations, Stephen Tryon/Sr. VP - Logistics/$442,573.00

Directors: Patrick M. Byrne/Chmn., CEO, Allison H. Abraham/Dir., Jason Lindsey/Dir., COO, Pres., Ray Groves/72/Dir., Barclay F. Corbus/41/Dir.

Owners: David K. Chidester, Fairfax Financial Holdings Limited/16.50%, Stormy D. Simon, Insiders/30.80%, Ray J. Groves, Stephen P. Tryon, Patrick M. Byrne/29.10%, Jonathan E. Johnson, Allison H. Abraham, Jason C. Lindsey, High Plains Investments LLC/23.90%, AXA Financial, Inc. and affiliates/8.40%, Chou Associates Management Inc./9.90%

Financial Data: **Fiscal Year End:**12/31 **Latest Annual Data:** 12/31/2006

Year	Sales	Net Income
2006	$788,150,000	-$101,766,000
2005	$803,822,000	-$24,918,000
2004	$494,635,000	-$4,540,000

Curr. Assets:	$180,011,000	**Curr. Liab.:**	$114,939,000		
Plant, Equip.:	$72,792,000	**Total Liab.:**	$194,201,000	**Indic. Yr. Divd.:**	NA
Total Assets:	$256,165,000	**Net Worth:**	$61,964,000	**Debt/ Equity:**	1.7365

Owens & Minor Inc

9120 Lockwood Blvd., Mechanicsville, VA, 23116; ***PH:*** 1-804-723-7000; ***Fax:*** 1-804-723-7100;
http:// www.owens-minor.com

General - Incorporation	VA	**Stock**- Price on:12/24/2007	$34.11
Employees	4,600	Stock Exchange	NYSE
Auditor	KPMG LLP	Ticker Symbol	OMI
Stk Agt	Bank of New York	Outstanding Shares	40,510,000
Counsel	Hunton & Williams LLP	E.P.S.	$1.25
DUNS No.	00-422-9381	Shareholders	NA

Business: The group's principle activities include manufacturing and distributing medical and surgical products. The groups products lines include disposable gloves, dressings, endoscopic products, intravenous products, needles, syringes, sterile procedure trays, surgical products, urological products and wound closure products. The group also provides value-added services in supply chain management, logistics and information technology. The groups customer areas include acute-care hospitals, integrated healthcare networks, clinics, home healthcare organizations, nursing homes, physicians' offices, rehabilitation facilities and surgery centers. The group operates from United States.

Primary SIC and add'l.: 5122 5047

CIK No: 0000075252

Subsidiaries: Access Diabetic Supply, LLC, Access Respiratory Supply, Inc., O&M Canada, Inc., O&M Funding Corp., OM Solutions International, Inc., OMI International, Ltd., Owens& Minor Distribution, Inc., Owens& Minor Medical, Inc.

Officers: Craig R. Smith/Dir., CEO, Pres./$2,034,401.00, Mark A. Van Sumeren/Sr. VP - Business Development, Charles C. Colpo/Sr. VP - Operations/$542,206.00, Richard W. Mears/CIO, Sr. VP, James L. Bierman/Chielf Financial Officer, Joe Zaluzney/Area VP - Capital, John Curtis/GM - Baltimore, Washington, Tim Williams/GM - Richmond, Bill Volker/GM - Waunakee, Mike Reiss/Area VP - Mountain States Area, Mike Littlefield/GM - Denver, Darrin Lambert/GM - Salt Lake City, Bud Taber/GM - Des Moines, ISC, Vince Jerome/Area VP - Heartland Area, Steve Boyer/GM - Kansas City *(72 Officers included in Index)*

Directors: Craig R. Smith/Dir., CEO, Pres., Gilmer G. Minor/Chmn., Anne Marie Whittemore/Dir., Richard E. Fogg/Dir., James B. Farinholt/Dir., Eddie N. Moore/Dir., Peter S. Redding/Dir., Alfred J. Broaddus/Dir., Marshall A. Acuff/Dir., James E. Ukrop/Dir., John T. Crotty/Dir., James E. Rogers/Dir.

Owners: Charles C. Colpo, Craig R. Smith/1.31%, James B. Farinholt, Mark Van Sumeren, Jeffrey Kaczka, Grace R. den Hartog, Marshall A. Acuff, James E. Rogers, Vanguard Specialized FundsVanguard Health Care Fund/5.45%, Anne Marie Whittemore, Barclays Global Investors, NA,/8.74%, John T. Crotty, Insiders/4.61%, Richard E. Fogg, Gilmer G. Minor/1.06% *(21 Owners included in Index)*

Financial Data: **Fiscal Year End:**12/31 **Latest Annual Data:** 12/31/2006

Year	Sales	Net Income
2006	$5,533,736,000	$48,752,000
2005	$4,822,414,000	$64,420,000
2004	$4,525,105,000	$60,500,000

Curr. Assets:	$1,266,770,000	**Curr. Liab.:**	$670,503,000	**P/E Ratio:**	32.18
Plant, Equip.:	$70,853,000	**Total Liab.:**	$1,138,296,000	**Indic. Yr. Divd.:**	$0.680
Total Assets:	$1,685,750,000	**Net Worth:**	$547,454,000	**Debt/ Equity:**	NA

Owens Corning

1 Owens Corning Pkwy., Toledo, OH, 43659; *PH:* 1-419-248-8000; *http://* www.owenscorning.com

General - Incorporation	DE	**Stock**- Price on:12/24/2007	$33.89
Employees	19,000	Stock Exchange	NYSE
Auditor	PricewaterhouseCoopers LLP	Ticker Symbol	OC
Stk Agt	American Stock Transfer & Trust Co.	Outstanding Shares	NA
Counsel	NA	E.P.S	$72.90
DUNS No.	00-131-7452	Shareholders	NA

Business: The group's principle activity is to provide building materials systems and composites solutions for consumers and industrial customers. The group operates in two segments building materials systems and composite solutions. The group operates from United States.

Primary SIC and add'l.: 5039 9999 3084 2951 2821 2952 3296

CIK No: 0000075234

Subsidiaries: CDC Corporation, Comercializadora Owens Corning, S.A. de C.V., Crown Manufacturing Inc., Engineered Pipe Systems, Inc., Engineered Yarns America, Inc., EPS Holding AS, Eric Company, European Owens-Corning Fiberglas, S.A., Exterior Systems, Inc., Falcon Foam Corporation, Fibreboard Corporation, Flowtite Offshore Services Ltd., Goodman Ventures, Inc., HOMExperts LLC, Integrex 96 Subsidiaries included in the Index

Officers: Michael H. Thaman/43/Chmn., CEO - Elect, David T. Brown/58/Dir., CEO, Pres., Scott Deitz/Investor Relations Officer, Roy D. Dean/Pres. - Insulating Systems, Stephen K. Krull/Sr. VP, General Counsel, Sec., Chuck Dana/Pres. - Composite Solutions, Sheree Bargabos/Pres. - Roofing, Asphalt, Chuck Stein/Pres. - Masonry Products, Duncan Palmer/CFO, Ron Ranallo/VP, Corporate Controller, Jason Saragian/Public Relations, Kerry Desberg/Product Media Relations, Bill Lebaron/Pres. - Construction Services, David Johns/CIO, Sr. VP, Chief Supply Chain Officer, Joseph C. High/Sr. VP - Human Resources *(16 Officers included in Index)*

Directors: Michael H. Thaman/43/Chmn., CEO - Elect, David T. Brown/58/Dir., CEO, Pres., Robert B. Smith/69/Dir., William W. Colville/72/Dir., Daniel K.K. Tseung/Dir., Marc Sole/Dir., Joseph F. Neely/Dir., Howard W. Morris/Dir., James J. McMonagle/Dir., Philip F. Handy/Dir., Ralph F. Hake/Dir., Gaston Caperton/67/Dir., Norman P. Blake/65/Dir., Ann Iverson/62/Dir., Landon Hilliard/67/Dir. *(16 Directors included in Index)*

Financial Data: **Fiscal Year End:**12/31 **Latest Annual Data:** 12/31/2006

Year	Sales	Net Income
2006	$6,461,000,000	$8,075,000,000
2005	$6,323,000,000	-$4,099,000,000
2004	$5,675,000,000	$204,000,000

Curr. Assets:	$2,552,000,000	**Curr. Liab.:**	$2,560,000,000	**P/E Ratio:**	0.38
Plant, Equip.:	$2,521,000,000	**Total Liab.:**	$4,740,000,000	**Indic. Yr. Divd.:**	NA
Total Assets:	$8,470,000,000	**Net Worth:**	$3,686,000,000	**Debt/ Equity:**	NA

Owens Illinois Inc

1 Michael Owens Way, Perrysburg, OH, 43551; *PH:* 1-567-336-5000; *Fax:* 1-419-247-7107; *http://* www.o-i.com

General - Incorporation	DE	**Stock**- Price on:12/24/2007	$34.03
Employees	28,000	Stock Exchange	NYSE
Auditor	Ernst & Young LLP	Ticker Symbol	OI
Stk Agt	EquiServe Trust Co N.A	Outstanding Shares	154,770,000
Counsel	NA	E.P.S	$0.56
DUNS No.	00-503-4566	Shareholders	NA

Business: The groups principle activity is to manufacture packaging products and glass containers. The group operates through two segments namely glass container and plastics packaging products. The group operates from United States.

Primary SIC and add'l.: 3229 3089 3221 3466

CIK No: 0000812074

Subsidiaries: A/S Jarvakandi Klaas, ACI America Holdings Inc., ACI Beijing Ltd., ACI Finance Pty. Ltd., ACI Glass Packaging Penrith Pty. Ltd., ACI Guangdong Glass Company Ltd., ACI Guangdong Ltd., ACI India LLC, ACI International Pty. Ltd., ACI Operations NZ Ltd., ACI Operations Pty. Ltd., ACI Packaging Services Pty . Ltd., ACI Plastics Packaging (Thailand) Ltd., ACI Shanghai Glass Company Ltd., ACI Shanghai Ltd. 174 Subsidiaries included in the Index

Officers: Albert P.L. Stroucken/Chmn., CEO, Pres./$4,322,772.00, Stephen P. Bramlage/VP, Treasurer, Michael Paparone/VP, Pres. - Closure, Specialty Products, Richard L. Crawford/VP, Pres. - Global Glass, Edward C. White/CFO, Sr. VP/$1,302,022.00, Greg W. Ridder/VP, Pres. - O, I Asia Pacific, James W. Baehren/Sr. VP, Chief Administrative Officer, General Counsel/$963,573.00, Philip McWeeny/VP, General Counsel - Corporate/$920,595.00, Stephen P. Malia/Sr. VP, Chief Human Resources Officer, Raymond C. Schlaff/VP, Chief Procurement Officer, Gerard D. Doyle/CIO, VP, John Bachey/VP - Global Accounting Management, Robert E. Lachmiller/VP - Glass Container Research, Development, Joseph V. Conda/VP, Pres. - Healthcare Packaging

Directors: Albert P.L. Stroucken/Chmn., CEO, Pres., Corbin A. McNeill/Dir., Thomas L. Young/Dir., Robert J. Dineen/Dir., Gary F. Colter/Dir., John J. McMackin/Dir., Dennis K. Williams/Dir., Anastasia D. Kelly/Dir., Peter S. Hellman/Dir., Helge H. Wehmeier/Dir.

Owners: FMR Corp./7.70%, AXA Financial Inc/15.00%, John J. McMackin, Wellington Management Company, LLP/6.10%, Robert J. Dineen, Gary F. Colter, Corbin A. McNeill, Gilberto E. Restrepo, Anastasia D. Kelly, Philip McWeeny, Steven R. McCracken, Janus Capital Management LLC/11.80%, State Street Bank and Trust Company/5.80%, Massachusetts Financial Services Company/12.30%, James W. Baehren

Financial Data: **Fiscal Year End:**12/31 **Latest Annual Data:** 12/31/2006

Year	Sales	Net Income
2006	$7,523,500,000	-$27,500,000
2005	$7,189,700,000	-$558,600,000
2004	$6,263,400,000	$235,500,000

Curr. Assets:	$2,432,700,000	**Curr. Liab.:**	$2,365,700,000	**P/E Ratio:**	60.77
Plant, Equip.:	$3,336,700,000	**Total Liab.:**	$8,757,200,000	**Indic. Yr. Divd.:**	$1.190
Total Assets:	$9,320,700,000	**Net Worth:**	$356,700,000	**Debt/ Equity:**	10.4278

Oxford Bank Corp

60 S Washington St., Oxford, MI, 48371; *PH:* 1-248-628-2533; *Fax:* 1-248-969-7230; *http://* www.oxfordbank.com

General - Incorporation		**Stock**- Price on:12/24/2007	$47.75
Employees	NA	Stock Exchange	OTC
Auditor	NA	Ticker Symbol	OXBC
Stk Agt	Nicholas W. Hevron	Outstanding Shares	1,280,000
Counsel	NA	E.P.S	NA
DUNS No.	NA	Shareholders	NA

Business: The groups principal activities include providing traditional banking technology, products, and services. Services of the group include savings account, loans and mortgage, credit card facilities, Debit cards, ATM, Investment accounts and Internet banking. The group operates from the United States.

Primary SIC and add'l.: 6022 6712

CIK No:

Oxford Industries Inc

222 Piedmont Ave., NE., Atlanta, GA, 30308; *PH:* 1-404-659-2424; *Fax:* 1-404-653-1545; *http://* www.oxfordinc.com; *Email:* info@oxfordinc.com

General - Incorporation	GA	**Stock**- Price on:12/24/2007	$45.29
Employees	4,800	Stock Exchange	NYSE
Auditor	Ernst & Young LLP	Ticker Symbol	OXM
Stk Agt	Computershare Investor Services LLC	Outstanding Shares	17,830,000
Counsel	NA	E.P.S	$2.92
DUNS No.	00-326-4041	Shareholders	NA

Business: The group's principal activity is to design, manufacture and sell consumer apparel products. It operates through the following divisions: menswear group, womenswear group and tommy bahoma group. Menswear produces branded and private label dress shirts, sport shirts, dress slacks, casual slacks, suits, sportscoat etc . Womenwear produces private label women's sportswear, outwear, dresses and swimwear. Tommy bahoma group produces lifestyle branded casual attire, operates retail stores and restaurants and licenses its brands for accessories, footwear, furniture and other products. The customers include chain stores, mail order, catalog firms, department and specialty stores. Company-owned manufacturing facilities are located in Mexico, the Caribbean, Central America and Asia. On 30-Jul-2004, the group acquired ben sherman ltd.

Primary SIC and add'l.: 2321 2325 2311 2335

CIK No: 0000075288

Subsidiaries: Ben Sherman (Australia) Pty. Ltd., Ben Sherman (Lurgan) Limited, Ben Sherman (Manufacturing) Limited, Ben Sherman Clothing, Inc., Ben Sherman Group Limited, Ben Sherman Holdings Limited, Ben Sherman Limited, Camisas Bahia Kino S.A. de C.V., Confecciones Monzini SA, Dunkeld Fashions Limited, Industrias Lanier De Honduras S. de R.L., Industrias Oxford de Merida, S.A. de CV, Lionshead Clothing Company, Inc., Manufacturera de Sonora, S.A. de CV, Neal & Cooper Limited 41 Subsidiaries included in the Index

Officers: Miles Gray/62/CEO - Ben Sherman Group, Hicks J. Lanier/Chmn., CEO/$1,709,444.00, Anthony S. Margolis/CEO, Group VP - Tommy Bahama Group/$1,814,828.00, Thomas E. Campbell/VP - Law, General Counsel, Anne M. Shoemaker/VP - Capital Markets, Treasurer, Christine B. Cole/VP - Human Resources/$372,068.00, John A. Baumgartner/CIO, Sr. VP/$377,593.00, Thomas C. Chubb/Exec. VP/$691,618.00, Scott K. Grassmyer/Sr. VP, Controller, Chief Accounting Officer, James F. Tuman/60/Pres. - Lanier Clothes

Directors: Hicks J. Lanier/Chmn., CEO, Reese J. Lanier/Dir., Jenner E. Wood/Dir., Cecil D. Conlee/Dir., Clarence H. Smith/Dir., James A. Rubright/Dir., Jack Guynn/Dir., George C. Guynn/65/Dir., Robert E. Shaw/Dir., Helen Ballard Weeks/Dir.

Owners: Clarence H. Smith, Insiders/13.35%, John A. Baumgartner, Cecil D. Conlee, Kornitzer Capital Management, Inc./5.23%, Michael J. Setola, Anthony S. Margolis, Hicks J. Lanier/8.98%, Reese J. Lanier/3.09%, James A. Rubright, George C. Guynn, Christine B. Cole, Robert E. Shaw, Thomas C. Chubb, Jenner E. Wood *(17 Owners included in Index)*

Financial Data: **Fiscal Year End:**06/03 **Latest Annual Data:** 06/01/2007

Year	Sales	Net Income
2007	$1,128,907,000	$52,137,000
2006	$1,109,116,000	$70,471,000
2005	$1,313,609,000	$49,827,000

Curr. Assets:	$393,395,000	**Curr. Liab.:**	$212,449,000	**P/E Ratio:**	12.69
Plant, Equip.:	$65,051,000	**Total Liab.:**	$602,376,000	**Indic. Yr. Divd.:**	$0.720
Total Assets:	$905,877,000	**Net Worth:**	$303,501,000	**Debt/ Equity:**	NA

Oxigene Inc

230 3rd Ave., Waltham, MA, 02451; *PH:* 1-781-547-5900; *Fax:* 1-781-547-6800;
http:// www.oxigene.com

General - Incorporation	DE	**Stock**- Price on:12/24/2007	$4.25
Employees	22	Stock Exchange	NDQ
Auditor	Ernst & Young LLP	Ticker Symbol	OXGN
Stk Agt	American Stock Transfer & Trust Co.	Outstanding Shares	28,420,000
Counsel	NA	E.P.S.	-$0.65
DUNS No.	79-883-2226	Shareholders	NA

Business: The group's principal activity is to conduct research and develop biopharmaceutical products for treatment of cancer treatment agents (vtas), ocular diseases. These agents attack a tumor's network of existing and emerging blood vessels, which are its main life support system. The group is also investigating products for other applications in the field of ophthalmology in particular age-related macular degeneration and myopic macular degeneration. The group provides clinical and pre-clinical development, multiple therapeutic product candidates that were derived from its principal vascular targeting platform. The group has collaborative agreements with a number of academic and research institutions and organizations in the United States and abroad.

Primary SIC and add'l.: 2834 8731

CIK No: 0000908259

Officers: Richard Chin/CEO, Pres./$620,055.00, James B. Murphy/CFO, VP/$397,405.00, Dai Chaplin/Executive Vice Chariman, Head - Research, Development, Chief Scientific Officer/$653,036.00, Peter Harris/64/Chief Medical Officer/$308,097.00, John A. Kollins/Sr. VP, Chief Business Officer, Patricia A. Walicke/Chief Medical Officer, VP

Directors: David Chaplin/52/Vice Chmn., Joel Citron/Chmn., Richard J. Zecher/Dir., Robert S. Kerbel/Member - Scientific Advisory Board, Dietmar W. Siemann/Member - Scientific Advisory Board, Adrian L. Harris/Member - Scientific Advisory Board, Hakan Mellstedt/Member - Clinical Trial Advisory Board, Jan B. Vermorken/Member - Clinical Trial Advisory Board, Lee S. Rosen/Member - Clinical Trial Advisory Board, Gordon J.S. Rustin/Member - Advisory Board, William N. Shiebler/Dir., Dai Chaplin/Executive Vice Chariman, Head - Research, Development, Chief Scientific Officer, Arthur B. Laffer/Dir., Per-Olof Soderberg/Dir., Jeffrey S. Heier/Member - Advisory Board *(19 Directors included in Index)*

Owners: Joel-Tomas Citron/2.40%, Richard J. Zecher, Insiders/9.80%, William Shiebler, Jim Murphy, Per Olof Sderberg/2.80%, Richard Chin, David Chaplin/1.40%, Arthur Laffer/1.40%

Financial Data: *Fiscal Year End:*12/31 *Latest Annual Data:* 12/31/2006

Year	Sales	Net Income
2006	NA	-$15,457,000
2005	$1,000	-$11,909,000
2004	$7,000	-$10,024,000

Curr. Assets:	$45,989,000	**Curr. Liab.:**	$4,222,000		
Plant, Equip.:	$241,000	**Total Liab.:**	$4,222,000	**Indic. Yr. Divd.:**	NA
Total Assets:	$47,642,000	**Net Worth:**	$43,420,000	**Debt/ Equity:**	NA

Oxis International Inc

323 Vintage Pk. Dr., Ste. B, Foster City, CA, 92202; *PH:* 1-650-212-2568; *Fax:* 1-650-212-2569;
http:// www.oxis.com

General - Incorporation	DE	**Stock**- Price on:12/24/2007	$0.2
Employees	30	Stock Exchange	OTC
Auditor	Williams & Webster, P.S	Ticker Symbol	OXIS
Stk Agt	Computershare Investor Services LLC	Outstanding Shares	44,530,000
Counsel	Morrison & Foerster LLP	E.P.S.	-$0.12
DUNS No.	05-051-8505	Shareholders	NA

Business: The group's principle activities are to develop, manufacture and market selected therapeutic and diagnostic products. The group's operating segments are divided into health products and therapeutic development. As of 31-Dec-2002, the group derived revenues from the health products segment. Under the health products segment, the group markets research and commercial diagnostic assays and fine chemicals to research and clinical laboratories and other customers. The therapeutic products segment is focused on the development of new drugs to treat diseases associated with tissue damage from free radicals and reactive oxygen species. The group markets its products in the United States, the United Kingdom, France, Germany, Japan, Spain, Korea, China and other countries. The group's quarterly revenue for September 2007 was 1.52 millions of USD.

Primary SIC and add'l.: 2835 3841 2834 8731

CIK No: 0000109657

Subsidiaries: BioCheck, Inc., OXIS Acquisition Corporation, OXIS Health Products, Inc., OXIS Instruments, Inc., OXIS International S.A., OXIS Isle of Man Limited, OXIS Therapeutics, Inc.

Officers: Marvin Hausman/Chmn., CEO, Pres./$425,930.00, Colin S. Neill/Dir., Sec., Ted Michelini/Contact - Technical Service, Gary M. Post/Dir., Acting COO

Directors: Marvin Hausman/Chmn., CEO, Pres., Colin S. Neill/Dir., Sec., John Repine/Dir., Matthew Spolar/Dir., Gary M. Post/Dir., Acting COO

Owners: Gary M. Post/2.27%, John E. Repine, Bristol Investment Fund, Ltd./22.42%, Matthew Spolar, Megapolis BV/20.00%, TorreyPines Therapeutics, Inc./30.00%, Insiders/13.17%, Colin S. Neill, American Health Care Fund, L.P./80.00%, Whalehaven Capital Fund Limited/8.45%, Cranshire Capital, LP/8.18%, Alpha Capital Anstalt/10.96%, Marvin S. Hausman/9.74%

Financial Data: *Fiscal Year End:*12/31 *Latest Annual Data:* 12/31/2006

Year	Sales	Net Income
2006	$5,776,000	-$4,940,000
2005	$2,497,000	-$3,109,000
2004	$2,364,000	-$2,698,000

Curr. Assets:	$5,701,000	**Curr. Liab.:**	$7,653,000		
Plant, Equip.:	$244,000	**Total Liab.:**	$7,802,000	**Indic. Yr. Divd.:**	NA
Total Assets:	$7,997,000	**Net Worth:**	-$575,000	**Debt/ Equity:**	NA

Oyo Geospace Corp

7007 Pinemont Dr., Houston, TX, 77040; *PH:* 1-713-986-4444; *Fax:* 1-713-986-4445;
http:// www.oyogeospace.com

General - Incorporation	DE	**Stock**- Price on:12/24/2007	$76.75
Employees	975	Stock Exchange	NDQ
Auditor	UHY LLP	Ticker Symbol	OYOG
Stk Agt.	NA	Outstanding Shares	5,810,000
Counsel	NA	E.P.S.	$2.98
DUNS No.	03-924-7630	Shareholders	NA

Business: The group's principal activities are to design and manufacture instruments and equipment used in the acquisition and processing of seismic data. The group also designs and manufactures thermal imaging equipment and distributes dry thermal film products to the commercial graphics industry. It operates in Asia, Canada, Europe, Japan, the Middle East and the United States. The customers for seismic products include contractors and major independent and government-owned oil and gas companies that either operate their own seismic crews or operate through contractors. The customers for commercial graphic products include specialized resellers that focus on the newsprint, silkscreen and corrugated box printing industries.

Primary SIC and add'l.: 3829 3826

CIK No: 0001001115

Subsidiaries: Concord Technologies, LP, Geospace Engineering Resources International, LP, Geospace Technologies Corporation, Geospace Technologies, LP, OYO Geo Space Canada, Inc., OYO Geospace China, OYO Geospace J.V., LP, OYO Instruments Europe Limited, OYO Instruments, LP, OYO-GEO Impulse International, LLC, OYOG Limited Partner, LLC, OYOG Operations, LP, OYOG, LLC

Officers: Gary D. Owens/Chmn., CEO, Pres., Michael J. Sheen/Dir., CTO, Sr. VP, Thomas T. McEntire/CFO, Katsuhiko Kobayashi/Dir., Sr. Executive Officer - OYO Corporation

Directors: Gary D. Owens/Chmn., CEO, Pres., Charles H. Still/Dir., William H. Moody/Dir., Ryuzo Okuto/Dir., Katsuhiko Kobayashi/Dir., Sr. Executive Officer - OYO Corporation, Michael J. Sheen/Dir., CTO, Sr. VP, Thomas L. Davis/Dir.

Owners: Dimensional Fund Advisors Inc./6.00%, Gary D. Owens/6.10%, Eagle Asset Management, Inc./8.50%, Thomas T. McEntire/1.80%, Thomas L. Davis, OYO Corporation U.S.A./20.00%, William H. Moody, OYO Corporation/20.00%, FMR Corp./5.20%, Charles H. Still, Ryuzo Okuto, Insiders/11.60%, Michael J. Sheen/2.60%

Financial Data: *Fiscal Year End:*09/30 *Latest Annual Data:* 9/30/2006

Year	Sales	Net Income
2006	$103,700,000	$9,770,000
2005	$72,823,000	$2,507,000
2004	$63,538,000	$5,953,000

Curr. Assets:	$76,584,000	**Curr. Liab.:**	$25,969,000		
Plant, Equip.:	$25,093,000	**Total Liab.:**	$33,409,000	**Indic. Yr. Divd.:**	NA
Total Assets:	$109,176,000	**Net Worth:**	$75,767,000	**Debt/ Equity:**	0.0980

P & F Industries Inc

445 Broadhollow Rd., Melville, NY, 11747; *PH:* 1-631-694-9800; *Fax:* 1-631-694-9804;
http:// www.pfina.com; *Email:* info@pfina.com

General - Incorporation	DE	**Stock**- Price on:12/24/2007	$11.45
Employees	192	Stock Exchange	NDQ
Auditor	Grant Thornton, LLP	Ticker Symbol	PFIN
Stk Agt	American Stock Transfer & Trust Co.	Outstanding Shares	3,590,000
Counsel	Willkie Farr & Gallagher LLP	E.P.S.	$1.34
DUNS No.	00-206-0572	Shareholders	NA

Business: The group's operates through its subsidiaries, Florida pneumatic manufacturing corporation, green manufacturing, inc. And embassy industries, inc. Florida pneumatic imports, manufactures and sells pneumatic hand tools and compressor air filters for the industrial and retail markets. Green manufacturing, inc. Manufactures, develops and sells heavy-duty welded custom designed hydraulic cylinders, line of access equipment for the petro-chemical industry and line of post hole digging equipment for the agricultural industry. Embassy industries inc. Manufactures and sells baseboard heating products, radiant heating systems and a line of door and window hardware items. The major customers of the group include distributors, retailers and private label customers.

Primary SIC and add'l.: 3429 6719 3546 5072

CIK No: 0000075340

Subsidiaries: Countrywide Hardware, Inc, Embassy Industries, Inc, Florida Pneumatic Manufacturing Corporation, Green Manufacturing, Inc., Nationwide Industries, Inc, Pacific Stair Products, Inc., WILP Holdings, Inc.

Officers: Richard A. Horowitz/Chmn., CEO, Pres./$1,691,532.00, Joseph A. Molino/CFO, COO, Sec., Pres./$556,543.00, Robert Weiden/Controller, Jennifer Beach/Exec. Assist., Christopher Klieforth/Pres. - Countrywide Hardware Inc, Bart Swank/Pres. - Countrywide Hardware Inc, Larry Franklin/Pres. - Florida Pneumatic Manufacturing Corp, Sam Sherstad/Pres. - Woodmark International LP, Richard B. Goodman/General Counsel, Robert Ober/COO, Pres. - Hy, Tech Machine Inc

Directors: Richard A. Horowitz/Chmn., CEO, Pres., Sidney Horowitz/87/Chmn. Emeritus, Kenneth M. Scheriff/Dir., Dennis Kalick/Dir., Alan Goldberg/Dir., Mitchell A. Solomona/48/Dir., Jeffrey D. Franklin/Dir., Robert L. Dubofsky/Dir., Robert M. Steinberg/Dir., Marc A. Utay/Dir.

Owners: Robert L. Dubofsky, Marc A. Utay/2.00%, Steel Partners II L.P./9.80%, Jeffrey D. Franklin, Lawndale Capital Management, LLC/11.90%, Insiders/45.60%, Robert M. Steinberg, FMR Corp./10.00%, Mitchell A. Solomon, Joseph A. Molino/1.90%, Sidney Horowitz/7.30%, Richard A. Horowitz/35.60%, Dennis Kalick, Kenneth M. Scheriff, Alan I. Goldberg

Financial Data: *Fiscal Year End:*12/31 *Latest Annual Data:* 12/31/2006

Year	Sales	Net Income
2006	$111,733,000	$3,881,000
2005	$107,978,000	$6,571,000
2004	$103,632,000	$4,039,000

Curr. Assets:	$46,457,000	**Curr. Liab.:**	$25,602,000	**P/E Ratio:**	13.80
Plant, Equip.:	$7,729,000	**Total Liab.:**	$38,796,000	**Indic. Yr. Divd.:**	NA
Total Assets:	$90,317,000	**Net Worth:**	$51,521,000	**Debt/ Equity:**	0.5662

P-Com Inc

6080 Ctr. Dr., Ste. 600, Los Angeles, CA, 90045; *PH:* 1-310-242-5698; *http://* www.p-com.com

General - Incorporation	DE	**Stock**- Price on:12/24/2007	$0.0014
Employees	NA	Stock Exchange	NA
Auditor	Aidman, Piser & Co. P.A	Ticker Symbol	NA
Stk Agt	NA	Outstanding Shares	NA
Counsel	Brobeck, Phleger & Harrison	E.P.S.	$1.391
DUNS No.	78-870-3643	Shareholders	NA

Business: The group's principal activities are to develop, manufacture and market point-to-point, spread spectrum and point-to-multipoint, wireless access systems to the worldwide telecommunications market. P-com broadband wireless access systems are designed to satisfy the high-speed, integrated network requirements of Internet access associated with business to business and e-commerce business processes. The customers include cellular and personal communications service providers and network and Internet service providers. The group has operations in the United States, the United Kingdom, Italy, Europe and Asia. The group discontinued its network services segment in 2003. On 10-Dec-2003, the group acquired wave wireless networking division of speedcom wireless corporation.

Primary SIC and add'l.: 7372 3663

CIK No: 0000935493

Subsidiaries: P-Com Italia S.p.A, P-Com United Kingdom,Inc.

Owners: Smithfield Fiduciary LLC/10.00%, CGA Resources LLC/10.00%, SDS Capital Group SPC, Ltd./80.00%

Financial Data: Fiscal Year End:12/31 Latest Annual Data: 12/31/2005

Year	Sales	Net Income
2005	$11,807,000	-$12,582,000
2004	$24,175,000	-$3,320,000
2003	$20,841,000	-$12,886,000

Curr. Assets:	$2,176,000	Curr. Liab.:	$9,286,000		
Plant, Equip.:	$622,000	Total Liab.:	$10,830,000	Indic. Yr. Divd.:	NA
Total Assets:	$15,038,000	Net Worth:	$4,208,000	Debt/ Equity:	NA

P. H. Glatfelter Co

96 S George St., Ste. 500, York, PA, 17401; *PH:* 1-717-225-4711; *Fax:* 1-717-225-6834; *http://* www.glatfelter.com; *Email:* info@schoellerhoesch.de

General		Stock	
Incorporation	PA	Price on:12/24/2007	$13.59
Employees	3,704	Stock Exchange	NYSE
Auditor	Deloitte & Touche LLP	Ticker Symbol	GLT
Stk Agt	American Stock Transfer & Trust Co.	Outstanding Shares	45,030,000
Counsel	NA	E.P.S	$0.57
DUNS No.	00-300-3407	Shareholders	NA

Business: The group's principal activity is to manufacture specialized printing papers. The products are classified into four segments: engineered products consist of engineered paper products designed for pressure sensitive postage stamps, disposable medical garments, playing cards and digital inkjet applications. Long-fiber and overlay papers include a paper for tea bags and decorative laminates used for furniture, flooring and other commercial applications. Printing and converting paper products include papers for the production of high-quality hardbound books. The manufacturing facilities are located in spring grove, Pennsylvania and neenah, Wisconsin. The group operates in Germany, France and the Philippines. The group discontinued wisches, France subsidiary in 2003.

Primary SIC and add'l.: 2611 2672 2679 4911 2679 2621

CIK No: 0000041719

Subsidiaries: Balo-I Industrial, Inc., Glatfelter Holdings II, LLC, Glatfelter Holdings, LLC, Glatfelter-UK, Ltd., Glenn-Wolfe, Inc., GLT International Finance LLC, GPW Springing Member, Inc., GPW Timberlands, LLC, GW Partners, LLC, Mollanvick, Inc., Newtech Pulp Inc., Papcel-Kiew, Papcel-Papier und Cellulose, Technologie und Handels-GmbH, Papierfabrik Schoeller & Hoesch Auslandsbeteiligungen GmbH, Papierfabrik Schoeller & Hoesch GmbH & Co. KG 24 Subsidiaries included in the Index

Officers: George H. Glatfelter/Chmn., CEO/$1,659,504.00, Jeffrey J. Norton/VP, General Counsel, Sec., Mark A. Sullivan/VP - Global Supply Chain, John P. Jacunski/Sr. VP, CFO/$498,277.00, William T. Yanavitch/VP - Human Resources, Administration/$460,913.00, Dante C. Parrini/COO, Exec. VP/$938,349.00, David C. Elder/Corporate Controller, Timothy R. Hess/VP, GM - Specialty Papers Business Unit, Martin Rapp/VP, GM - Composite Fibers Business Unit

Directors: George H. Glatfelter/Chmn., CEO, Robert J. Hall/Dir., Kathleen Dahlberg/Dir., Nicholas Debenedictis/Dir., Ronald J. Naples/Dir., Richard L. Smoot/Dir., Lee C. Stewart/Dir., Richard C. Ill/Dir.

Owners: Richard C., Barclays Global Investors,NA/6.53%, Dante C. Parrini, Richard L. Smoot, Nicholas DeBenedictis, Insiders/1.32%, Dimensional Fund AdvisorsLP/8.51%, Ronald J. Naples, Kathleen A. Dahlberg, Oz Management L.L.C./6.11%, John P. Jacunski, George H. Glatfelter/1.06%, Lee C. Stewart, William T. Yanavitch, John C. vanRoden *(16 Owners included in Index)*

Financial Data: Fiscal Year End:12/31 Latest Annual Data: 12/31/2006

Year	Sales	Net Income
2006	$997,137,000	-$12,236,000
2005	$589,199,000	$38,609,000
2004	$553,477,000	$56,102,000

Curr. Assets:	$375,038,000	Curr. Liab.:	$193,290,000	P/E Ratio:	226.50
Plant, Equip.:	$528,867,000	Total Liab.:	$837,275,000	Indic. Yr. Divd.:	$0.360
Total Assets:	$1,225,643,000	Net Worth:	$388,368,000	Debt/ Equity:	NA

P.A.M. Transportation Services Inc

297 W Henri DeTonti Blvd., Tontitown, AR, 72770; *PH:* 1-479-361-9111; *Fax:* 1-479-361-5335; *http://* www.pamt.com; *Email:* hr@pamt.com

General		Stock	
Incorporation	DE	Price on:12/24/2007	$19.45
Employees	3,062	Stock Exchange	NDQ
Auditor	Grant Thornton, LLP	Ticker Symbol	PTSI
Stk Agt	Securities Transfer Corp	Outstanding Shares	10,310,000
Counsel	Smith Gambrell & Russell	E.P.S	$1.07
DUNS No.	09-857-1433	Shareholders	NA

Business: The group operates as a truckload dry van carrier transporting general commodities. The group also provides transportation services in Mexico under agreements with Mexican carriers. The freight consists primarily of automotive parts, consumer goods, such as general retail store merchandise and manufactured goods, such as heating and air conditioning units. The group operates throughout the continental United States, the Canadian provinces of ontario and quebec and in Mexico under agreements with Mexican carriers. On 31-Jan-2003, the group acquired east coast transport and logistics inc and on 03-Apr-2003, mcneill trucking inc.

Primary SIC and add'l.: 4213

CIK No: 0000798287

Subsidiaries: Allen Freight Services, Inc., Choctaw Brokerage, Inc., Choctaw Express, Inc., Decker Transport Co., Inc., East Coast Transport and Logistics, Inc., McNeill Express, Inc., P.A.M. Canada, Inc., P.A.M. Dedicated Services, Inc., P.A.M. International, Inc., P.A.M. Logistics Services, Inc., P.A.M. Transport, Inc., S & L Logistics, Inc., T.T.X., Inc., Transcend Logistics, Inc.

Officers: Robert W. Weaver/58/Co - Founder, Dir., CEO, Pres./$900,861.00, Clif W. Lawson/COO, Exec. VP/$560,167.00, Larry J. Goddard/VP - Finance, CFO, Sec., Treasurer/$459,721.00

Directors: Robert W. Weaver/58/Co - Founder, Dir., CEO, Pres., Matthew T. Moroun/35/Dir., Manuel J. Moroun/80/Dir., Christopher L. Ellis/63/Dir., Frederick P. Calderone/57/Dir., Daniel C. Sullivan/67/Dir., Charles F. Wilkins/69/Dir., Frank L. Conner/58/Dir.

Owners: Daniel C. Sullivan, FMR Corp./6.00%, Matthew T. Moroun/44.50%, Charles F. Wilkins, Robert W. Weaver/3.00%, Frank L. Conner, Insiders/48.70%, Thomas H. Cooke, Larry J. Goddard, Manuel J. Moroun, Christopher L. Ellis, Frederick P. Calderone, Clif W. Lawson

Financial Data: Fiscal Year End:12/31 Latest Annual Data: 12/31/2006

Year	Sales	Net Income
2006	$400,269,000	$17,964,000
2005	$360,880,000	$13,139,000
2004	$325,066,000	$10,588,000

Curr. Assets:	$94,552,000	Curr. Liab.:	$56,077,000	P/E Ratio:	18.18
Plant, Equip.:	$203,314,000	Total Liab.:	$129,218,000	Indic. Yr. Divd.:	NA
Total Assets:	$314,246,000	Net Worth:	$185,028,000	Debt/ Equity:	0.2134

P.F. Chang's China Bistro Inc

7676 E Pinnacle Peak Rd., Scottsdale, AZ, 85255; *PH:* 1-480-888-3000; *Fax:* 1-480-888-3001; *http://* www.pfchangs.com; *Email:* pfcomments@pfchangs.com

General		Stock	
Incorporation	DE	Price on:12/24/2007	$34.94
Employees	24,000	Stock Exchange	NDQ
Auditor	KPMG LLP	Ticker Symbol	PFCB
Stk Agt	First Chicago Trust Co of New York	Outstanding Shares	25,790,000
Counsel	Gray, Cary, Ware & Freidenrich	E.P.S	$1.30
DUNS No.	87-788-6416	Shareholders	NA

Business: The group's principal activity is to operate restaurants in the United States under the names, p. F. Chang's China bistro and pei wei Asian diner. These restaurants serve food and beverages that feature traditional Chinese cuisine and American hospitality in a contemporary bistro setting. The menu includes flavors and styles of the five major culinary regions of China namely: canton, hunan, mongolia, shanghai and szechwan. The menu consists of dishes such as chang's spicy chicken, orange peel beef, peking dumplings, chicken in soothing lettuce wrap, szechwan-style long beans and dan dan noodles. The restaurants also have a full service bar offering wines, specialty drinks, Asian beers, cappuccino and espresso. As of 27-Jun-2004, the group operates through 105 full service restaurants and 44 limited service restaurants.

Primary SIC and add'l.: 5812 7011

CIK No: 0001039889

Subsidiaries: Fleming/PFC III Corp., P.F. Changs China Bistro, Inc., P.F. Changs II, Inc., P.F. Changs III, LLC, P.F. Changs VI, Inc., P.f.c.c.b. Club Frankford, Inc., P.f.c.c.b. Texas, Inc., Pei Wei Asian Diner Eleven (Minnesota) LLC, Pei Wei Asian Diner Five (Denver) LLC, Pei Wei Asian Diner Four (Houston) LLP, Pei Wei Asian Diner One LLC, Pei Wei Asian Diner Seven (Central Texas) LLP, Pei Wei Asian Diner Six (Nevada) LLC, Pei Wei Asian Diner Ten (Florida) LLP, Pei Wei Asian Diner Three (SoCal) LLC 53 Subsidiaries included in the Index

Officers: Richard L. Federico/Chmn., CEO/$1,358,641.00, Robert T. Vivian/Pres./$1,071,152.00, Stephen K. Marr/Chief Development Officer, Russell G. Owens/Exec. VP - PF Changs China Bistro, Pres. - Pei Wei Asian Diner/$605,351.00, Michael R. Welborn/Dir., Chief Administrative Officer/$832,688.00, Mark D. Mumford/CFO/$410,214.00, John A. Johnson/CIO, Tracy M. Durchslag/Chief Legal Officer, Corp. Sec., Kc Moylan/COO - Pei Wei

Directors: Richard L. Federico/Chmn., CEO, Kenneth J. Wessels/Dir., Ann M. Rhoades/Dir., Lesley H. Howe/Dir., James G. Shennan/Dir., Lane F. Cardwell/Dir., Michael R. Welborn/Dir., Chief Administrative Officer

Owners: TransAmerica Investment Management LLC/5.20%, Insiders/6.30%, Kenneth J. Wessels, T. Rowe Price Associates, Inc./14.10%, Westfield Capital Management Co. LLC/5.30%, Michael R. Welborn, Richard L. Federico/1.90%, James G. Shennan, Kornitzer Capital Management LLC/6.30%, Lane F. Cardwell, Ann M. Rhoades, Robert T. Vivian/1.00%, Mark D. Mumford, Russell G. Owens, Lesley H. Howe *(17 Owners included in Index)*

Financial Data: Fiscal Year End:01/01 Latest Annual Data: 12/31/2006

Year	Sales	Net Income
2006	$937,606,000	$33,253,000
2005	$706,941,000	$26,054,000

Curr. Assets:	$64,816,000	Curr. Liab.:	$103,891,000	P/E Ratio:	26.07
Plant, Equip.:	$421,770,000	Total Liab.:	$191,205,000	Indic. Yr. Divd.:	NA
Total Assets:	$514,045,000	Net Worth:	$289,525,000	Debt/ Equity:	0.2846

P.T. Telekomunikasi Indonesia Tbk.

Jl. Japati No. 1, Bandung, Jawa Barat, 40133; *PH:* 62-0222500000; *Fax:* 62-0222500000; *http://* www.telkom.co.id; *Email:* investor@telkom.co.id

General		Stock	
Incorporation		Price on:12/24/2007	$43.74
Employees	NA	Stock Exchange	NYSE
Auditor	NA	Ticker Symbol	TLK
Stk Agt	Bank of New York	Outstanding Shares	499,200,000
Counsel	NA	E.P.S	$2.48
DUNS No.	NA	Shareholders	NA

Business: The groups principle activity is to provide telecommunication services. The group also provides cellular operators. The group operates through four segments namely, fixed wireline, fixed wireless, cellular, and other. The group operates from the Indonesia.

Primary SIC and add'l.: 4813

CIK No: 0001001807

Subsidiaries: PTAriaWest International, PTDayamitra Telekomunikasi, PTGraha Sarana Duta, PTIndonusa Telemedia, PTInfomedia Nusantara, PTMultimedia Nusantara, PTNapsindo Primatel Internasional, PTPramindo Ikat Nusantara, PTTelekomunikasi Selular

Officers: Rinaldi Firmansyah/48/Dir., CEO, Sudiro Asno/51/Dir., Dir. - Finance, Ermady Dahlan/55/Dir., Consumer Dir., Arief Yahya/47/Dir., Dir. - Enterprise, Wholesale, Indra Utoyo/46/Dir., Chief Information Technology, Tanri Abeng/66/Board Of Commissioners, Pres., P. Sartono/64/Independent Commissioner, Arif Arryman/52/Independent Commissioner, Rochiman Sukarno/Head - Corporate Communication, Harsya Denny Suryo/VP - Investor Relations, Corp. Sec., Arwin Rasyid/50/Dir., Pres., Garuda Sugardo/57/Dir., COO, VP, Abdul Haris/52/Dir. - Network, Solution, John Welly/53/Dir. - Human Resources, Guntur Siregar/56/Dir. - Consumer *(16 Officers included in Index)*

Directors: Rinaldi Firmansyah/48/Dir., CEO, Anggito Abimanyu/45/Chmn., Gatot Trihargo/Vice Chmn., Arwin Rasyid/50/Dir., Pres., Garuda Sugardo/57/Dir., COO, VP, Sudiro Asno/51/Dir., Dir. - Finance, Faisal Syam/52/Dir. - Human Capital, General Affair Dir., Nyoman Gede Wiryanata/49/Dir., Dir. - Network, Solution, Ermady Dahlan/55/Dir., Consumer Dir., Arief Yahya/47/Dir., Dir. - Enterprise, Wholesale, Indra Utoyo/46/Dir., Chief Information Technology, Tanri Abeng/66/Board Of Commissioners, Pres.

Owners: Government, The Bank of New York, Insiders, Government, JPMCB US Resident

Financial Data: *Fiscal Year End:*NA *Latest Annual Data:* 12/31/2006

Year	Sales	Net Income
2006	$5,129,401,000	$1,211,145,000
2005	$4,180,718,000	$784,009,000
2004	$3,394,777,000	$646,857,000

Curr. Assets:	$1,392,079,000	**Curr. Liab.:**	$2,053,569,000	**P/E Ratio:**	64.75
Plant, Equip.:	$5,560,465,000	**Total Liab.:**	$4,919,714,000	**Indic. Yr. Divd.:**	$1.320
Total Assets:	$7,550,571,000	**Net Worth:**	$2,630,857,000	**Debt/ Equity:**	NA

PAB Bankshares Inc

3250 N Valdosta Rd., Valdosta, GA, 31604; ***PH:*** 1-229-241-2775; ***Fax:*** 1-229-241-2774; ***http://*** www.pabbankshares.com

General - Incorporation	GA	**Stock**- Price on:12/24/2007	$20.43
Employees	311	Stock Exchange	NDQ
Auditor	Mauldin & Jenkins LLC	Ticker Symbol	PABK
Stk Agt	Registrar & Transfer Co	Outstanding Shares	9,520,000
Counsel	Coleman, Talley, Newbern, Kurrie	E.P.S	$1.35
DUNS No.	06-696-3067	Shareholders	NA

Business: The group's principal activities are to provide general, commercial and mortgage banking services through its subsidiaries in valdosta and Georgia. The operations are conducted through 18 banking offices. The product line of the group include loans to small- and medium-sized businesses, residential mortgage loans, home equity loans, construction and development loans, commercial real estate loans, consumer loans and a variety of commercial and consumer deposit products. The group also offers Internet banking, cash management, electronic bill payment services, safe deposit box rentals, telephone banking, credit and debit card services and the availability of a network of automatic teller machines.

Primary SIC and add'l.: 6712 6022

CIK No: 0000705200

Subsidiaries: PAB Bankshares Capital Trust I2, The Park Avenue Bank

Officers: Burke M. Welsh/61/Dir., CEO, Pres./$514,472.00, David H. Gould/60/Exec. VP - South Georgia, Florida Regional Pres./$288,697.00, Donald Jay Torbert/35/Exec. VP, CFO, Treasurer/$277,603.00, Wesley R. Fuller/47/Exec. VP, Dir. - Operations/$278,079.00, William L. Kane/57/Exec. VP, North Georgia Regional Pres./$297,646.00, George D. Henderson/56/Exec. VP, Chief Credit Officer

Directors: Burke M. Welsh/61/Dir., CEO, Pres., Douglas W. McNeill/65/Vice Chmn., James L. Dewar/65/Chmn., Joe P. Singletary/70/Dir., Michael H. Godwin/49/Dir., James B. Lanier/61/Dir., Walter W. Carroll/59/Dir., Paul E. Parker/59/Dir., John E. Mansfield/52/Dir., Kennith D. McLeod/61/Dir., Bradford R. Burnette/68/Dir., Ferrell F. Scruggs/69/Dir., David K. Williams/47/Dir.

Owners: The Estate of James L. Dewar,/11.26%, William L. Kane, Douglas W. McNeill, Walter W. Carroll/1.01%, Wesley R. Fuller, Kennith D. McLeod, Bill J. Jones/1.35%, Bradford R. Burnette/1.21%, Ferrell F. Scruggs, John E. Mansfield/1.00%, David H. Gould, Dewar Family, L.P./11.24%, Insiders/25.66%, Burke M. Welsh, James L. Dewar/14.96% *(21 Owners included in Index)*

Financial Data: *Fiscal Year End:*12/31 *Latest Annual Data:* 12/31/2006

Year	Sales	Net Income
2006	$83,488,000	$13,735,000
2005	$65,195,000	$12,453,000
2004	$46,941,000	$8,518,000

Curr. Assets:	$68,876,000	**Curr. Liab.:**	$1,006,322,000	**P/E Ratio:**	14.70
Plant, Equip.:	$20,780,000	**Total Liab.:**	$1,025,488,000	**Indic. Yr. Divd.:**	$0.580
Total Assets:	$1,120,804,000	**Net Worth:**	$95,316,000	**Debt/ Equity:**	NA

Pac-West Telecomm Inc

4210 Coronado Ave., Stockton, CA, 95204; ***PH:*** 1-209-926-3490; ***Fax:*** 1-209-926-4140; ***http://*** www.pacwest.com; ***Email:*** website@pacwest.com

General - Incorporation	CA	**Stock**- Price on:12/24/2007	$0.027
Employees	296	Stock Exchange	NA
Auditor	Macias Gini & Co LLP	Ticker Symbol	NA
Stk Agt	American Stock Transfer & Trust Co.	Outstanding Shares	37,670,000
Counsel	Latham & Watkins	E.P.S	-$0.244
DUNS No.	NA	Shareholders	NA

Business: The group's principal activity is to provide integrated business communications solutions. The services are provided to communications-intensive users including Internet service providers, enhanced communications service providers and small and medium sized enterprises businesses. Its network enables Internet service providers to provide their business and residential customers with access to Internet, paging and other data and voice services from almost any point in the state through a local call. The facilities-based network also enables to provide its customer with Internet access and high-speed data transport, giving them the ability to send and receive e-mail, exchange data between branch offices, and quickly download information from the Internet.

Primary SIC and add'l.: 4813

CIK No: 0001071598

Subsidiaries: INET, Mexico, Installnet, Inc., Pac-West Telecomm of Virginia, Inc., PWT of New York, Inc., PWT Services, Inc., U.S. Net Solutions, Inc.

Officers: Hank Carabelli/Dir., CEO, Pres., Eric Jacobs/VP, GM - Service Provider Sales, Ravi H. Brar/COO, Michael L. Sarina/CFO, VP - Finance, Michael B. Hawn/VP - Customer Network Services, Todd M. Putnam/CIO, Robert C. Morrison/VP, General Counsel, John F. Sumpter/VP - Regulatory, Reid Cox/VP - Business Development, Investor Relations, Sarita Fernandes/VP - Marketing

Directors: Hank Carabelli/Dir., CEO, Pres., Wallace W. Griffin/Chmn., Samuel A. Plum/Dir., Timothy A. Samples/Dir., Stanley P. Hanks/Dir., James F. Hensel/Dir., Kenneth D. Peterson/Dir., Richard A. Roman/Dir., Joseph J. Bonocore/Dir.

Financial Data: *Fiscal Year End:*12/31 *Latest Annual Data:* 12/31/2005

Year	Sales	Net Income
2005	$90,933,000	$8,588,000
2004	$124,006,000	-$75,033,000
2003	$134,640,000	-$15,250,000

Curr. Assets:	$38,786,000	**Curr. Liab.:**	$22,494,000		
Plant, Equip.:	$39,458,000	**Total Liab.:**	$66,086,000	**Indic. Yr. Divd.:**	NA
Total Assets:	$79,323,000	**Net Worth:**	$13,237,000	**Debt/ Equity:**	4.3506

Paccar Financial Corp

777 106th Ave. NE, Bellevue, WA, 98004; ***PH:*** 1-425-468-7400; ***Fax:*** 1-425-468-8216; ***http://*** www.paccar.com; ***Email:*** internetproducer@paccar.com

General - Incorporation	WA	**Stock**- Price on:12/24/2007	$90.01
Employees	21,000	Stock Exchange	NDQ
Auditor	Ernst & Young LLP	Ticker Symbol	NA
Stk Agt	Computershare Investor Services LLC	Outstanding Shares	248,410,000
Counsel	NA	E.P.S	$5.79
DUNS No.	00-794-2469	Shareholders	NA

Business: The group's principle activity is to provide finance and leases trucks and related equipment primarily manufactured by paccar inc. The company is a wholly owned subsidiary of paccar inc. The company operates primarily in one industry segment, truck and related equipment financing in the United States. The company provides financing to customers and dealers for new kenworth and peterbilt trucks, used trucks, truck trailers and allied equipment such as mixer and dump bodies attached to trucks. The company also finances dealer inventories of transportation equipment and franchises paccar inc dealerships to engage in full-service and finance leasing. The products include retail receivables, direct loans, master note, wholesale contracts, dealer loans, direct financing lease, operating leases, full-servicing leases and insurance services. The group operates from United States.

Primary SIC and add'l.: 7359 6411 6159

CIK No: 0000731288

Subsidiaries: PACCAR Financial Services Corporation, PACCAR Inc

Officers: Michael A. Tembreull/Vice Chmn., Principal Financial Officer, Mark C. Pigott/Chmn., Principal Executive Officer, Timothy M. Henebry/Dir., Pres., Cathy A. MacLeod/Controller

Directors: Michael A. Tembreull/Vice Chmn., Principal Financial Officer, Mark C. Pigott/Chmn., Principal Executive Officer, Timothy M. Henebry/Dir., Pres., Kenneth R. Gangl/Dir., Thomas E. Plimpton/Dir.

Financial Data: *Fiscal Year End:*12/31 *Latest Annual Data:* 12/31/2006

Year	Sales	Net Income
2006	$16,454,100,000	$1,496,000,000
2005	$14,057,400,000	$1,133,200,000
2004	$11,456,200,000	$906,800,000

Curr. Assets:	$4,245,700,000	**Curr. Liab.:**	$2,980,700,000	**P/E Ratio:**	14.83
Plant, Equip.:	$2,798,500,000	**Total Liab.:**	$11,651,200,000	**Indic. Yr. Divd.:**	$1.000
Total Assets:	$16,107,400,000	**Net Worth:**	$4,456,200,000	**Debt/ Equity:**	1.5662

Paccar Inc

777 106th Ave. NE, Bellevue, WA, 98004; ***PH:*** 1-425-468-7400; ***Fax:*** 1-425-468-8216; ***http://*** www.paccar.com; ***Email:*** internetproducer@paccar.com

General - Incorporation	DE	**Stock**- Price on:12/24/2007	$89.43
Employees	21,000	Stock Exchange	NDQ
Auditor	Ernst & Young LLP	Ticker Symbol	PCAR
Stk Agt	Wells Fargo Bank Minnesota N.A	Outstanding Shares	248,410,000
Counsel	NA	E.P.S	$5.79
DUNS No.	04-834-1267	Shareholders	NA

Business: The groups principle activity is to manufacture premium commercial vehicles. The groups services include PAC lease trucks and kenworth trucks. The group products are sold under the brand names kenworth and DAF. The group operates from United States.

Primary SIC and add'l.: 6159 5013 3711

CIK No: 0000075362

Subsidiaries: DAF Trucks Deutschland GmbH, DAF Trucks France, S.A.R.L, DAF Trucks Ltd, DAF Trucks Vlaanderen N.V., DAF Trucks, N.V., DAF Vehiculos Industriales S.A, DAF Veicoli Industriali S.p.A., Leyland Trucks Limited, PACCAR Australia Pty. Ltd., PACCAR Financial Belux BVBA, PACCAR Financial Corp, PACCAR Financial Deutschland GmbH, PACCAR Financial Espana S.r.l., PACCAR Financial Europe B.V, PACCAR Financial France S.A.S. 30 Subsidiaries included in the Index

Officers: Mark C. Pigott/54/Chmn., CEO/$7,381,514.00, Ronald E. Armstrong/52/VP, Controller, Janice B. Skredsvig/47/CIO, VP, David C. Anderson/54/VP, General Counsel, John J. Waggoner/Contact Person, Thomas E. Plimpton/Pres./$3,425,682.00, James G. Cardillo/59/Exec. VP/$1,779,507.00, Kenneth R. /62/Sr. VP/$1,437,350.00, J. M. Damato/Dir., Sec., Cathy MacLeod/Treasurer, Investor Relations Officer, Daniel D. Sobic/54/Sr. VP, Michael T. Barkley/52/VP, Controller, Operations Controller

Directors: Mark C. Pigott/54/Chmn., CEO, Michael A. Tembreull/61/Vice Chmn., William G. Reed/69/Dir., James C. Pigott/72/Dir., Stephen F. Page/68/Dir., John M. Fluke/65/Dir., Alison J. Carnwath/55/Dir., Robert T. Parry/69/Dir., Harold A. Wagner/72/Dir., Charles R. Williamson/59/Dir.

Owners: Robert T. Parry, Kenneth R. Gangl, James C. Pigott/4.90%, John M. Fluke, Mark C. Pigott/1.60%, Thomas E. Plimpton, James G. Cardillo, Charles R. Williamson, Alison J. Carnwath, Harold A. Wagner, Stephen F. Page, Merrill Lynch, Pierce, Fenner & Smith, Incorporation/6.00%, William G. Reed, Michael A. Tembreull, Insiders/7.00%

Financial Data: *Fiscal Year End:*12/31 *Latest Annual Data:* 12/31/2006

Year	Sales	Net Income
2006	$16,454,100,000	$1,496,000,000
2005	$14,057,400,000	$1,133,200,000
2004	$11,456,200,000	$906,800,000

Curr. Assets:	$4,245,700,000	**Curr. Liab.:**	$2,980,700,000	**P/E Ratio:**	15.45
Plant, Equip.:	$2,798,500,000	**Total Liab.:**	$11,651,200,000	**Indic. Yr. Divd.:**	$1.000
Total Assets:	$16,107,400,000	**Net Worth:**	$4,456,200,000	**Debt/ Equity:**	NA

Pace Medical Inc

391 Totten Pond Rd., Waltham, MA, 02451; ***PH:*** 1-781-890-5656; ***http://*** www.pacemedicalinc.com; ***Email:*** customerservice@pacemedicalinc.com

General - Incorporation	MA	**Stock**- Price on:12/24/2007	$0.25
Employees	NA	Stock Exchange	OTC
Auditor	Vitale, Caturano & Co. Ltd	Ticker Symbol	PMDL
Stk Agt	American Stock Transfer & Trust Co.	Outstanding Shares	3,350,000
Counsel	Lynch Brewer Hoffman & Sands LLP	E.P.S.	-$0.05
DUNS No.	15-779-4561	Shareholders	NA

Business: The group's principal activity is to design, manufacture and market temporary cardiac pacemakers, pacing analyzer, extension cables and heart wires used in pacemakers for surgical purposes. The group manufactures single and dual-chamber temporary cardiac pacemakers, percutaneous lead introducers and other accessories. The temporary pacemakers are used for correcting the cardiac rhythm disorders and external short time electrical conduction. The temporary pacemakers are sold to hospitals, both domestic as well as foreign. The operations are carried on in the United States, the United Kingdom and Canada.

Primary SIC and add'l.: 3841 3845

CIK No: 0000814057

Subsidiaries: APC Medical Ltd

Officers: Steven E. Hanson/53/CEO, Pres., Ralph E. Hanson/Chmn., Treasurer, Drusilla F. Hays/VP, Clerk

Directors: Ralph E. Hanson/Chmn., Treasurer, Derrick Ebden/Dir., George F. Harrington/Dir.

Financial Data: ***Fiscal Year End:***12/31 ***Latest Annual Data:*** 12/31/2004

Year	Sales	Net Income
2004	$1,217,000	-$310,000
2003	$1,320,000	-$377,000
2002	$1,205,000	-$197,000

Curr. Assets:	$1,628,000	***Curr. Liab.:***	$360,000		
Plant, Equip.:	$19,000	***Total Liab.:***	$360,000	***Indic. Yr. Divd.:***	NA
Total Assets:	$1,896,000	***Net Worth:***	$1,536,000	***Debt/ Equity:***	NA

Pacel Corp

7621 Little Ave., Ste. 101, Charlotte, NC, 28226; ***PH:*** 1-704-643-0676; ***Fax:*** 1-704-552-7946; ***http://*** www.asmarahr.com

General - Incorporation	NV	**Stock**- Price on:12/24/2007	NA
Employees	13	Stock Exchange	OTC
Auditor	Peter C. Cosmas Co., Cpas	Ticker Symbol	PCLO
Stk Agt	Olde Monmouth Stk Trnsfer Co. Inc.	Outstanding Shares	NA
Counsel	NA	E.P.S.	-$0.001
DUNS No.	NA	Shareholders	NA

Business: The group's principal activity is to develop and market computer software programs. It also provides a full line of Internet services and information technology consulting services. The products include visual writer system, win sentry, zoomer and childwatch. In Sept 2002, the group announced its intention to enter the professional employer organization (peo) industry. In addition, it plans to provide administrative service organization (aso) services. The group will provide human capital management solutions to small business clients within the United States. Subsequent to 31-Dec-2002, it acquired two peo organizations and one aso organization. Through the peo/aso business unit, the group will provide a broad range of products and services that provide an outsourced solution for the clients' human resources needs. In Apr 2003, it acquired benecorp business services inc, asmara, inc and nsc llc.

Primary SIC and add'l.: 7375 7372

CIK No: 0001044490

Subsidiaries: Asmara Benefits, Inc., Asmara Services II, Inc., Benecorp Business Services, Inc., Piedmont HR, Inc., The Resourcing Solutions Group, Inc., United Personnel Services, Inc., World Wide Personnel Services of Maine, Inc.

Officers: Gary A. Musselman/CEO, Pres.

Financial Data: ***Fiscal Year End:***12/31 ***Latest Annual Data:*** 12/31/2005

Year	Sales	Net Income
2005	$2,241,000	-$4,410,000
2004	$3,998,000	-$5,099,000
2003	$3,841,000	-$6,863,000

Curr. Assets:	$712,000	***Curr. Liab.:***	$5,914,000		
Plant, Equip.:	$125,000	***Total Liab.:***	$6,468,000	***Indic. Yr. Divd.:***	NA
Total Assets:	$1,444,000	***Net Worth:***	-$5,024,000	***Debt/ Equity:***	NA

Pacer Health Corp

7759 NW 146 St., Miami Lakes, FL, 33016; ***PH:*** 1-305-828-7660; ***http://*** www.pacerhealth.com; ***Email:*** tvidal@pacerhealth.com

General - Incorporation	FL	**Stock**- Price on:12/24/2007	$0.013
Employees	500	Stock Exchange	OTC
Auditor	Salberg & Co P.A	Ticker Symbol	PHLH
Stk Agt	Computershare Investor Services LLC	Outstanding Shares	580,700,000
Counsel	NA	E.P.S.	-$0.005
DUNS No.	NA	Shareholders	NA

Business: The group's principal activity is to provide primary healthcare services and operate medical treatment center. The group provides skilled nursing facilities and assisted living facilities. Skilled nursing facilities services include 24-hour skilled nursing services services to seniors who require such care. The facilities also provide housing, dietary and medical services to these seniors. Assisted living facilities include seniors who do not require skilled nursing services with housing that provides supportive care and services that include assistance with activities of daily living and other services. During the year 2003, the group acquired infe inc & aaa medical center inc. Aaa medical center inc provides rehabilitative therapy to patients of various ages. The rehabilitative therapy is designed to assist the patient to overcome various sustained injuries. On Mar 2004 the group acquired certain assets of camelot specialty hospital of cameron llc.

Primary SIC and add'l.: 7389

CIK No: 0000922913

Subsidiaries: Pacer Health Holdings of Lafayette, Inc., Pacer Health Management Corporation, Pacer Health Management Corporation of Georgia, Pacer Health Management of Florida LLC, Pacer Health Services, Inc, Pacer Holdings of Arkansas, Inc., Pacer Holdings of Georgia, Inc, Pacer Holdings of Lafayette, Inc, Pacer Holdings of Louisiana, Inc.

Officers: Rainier Gonzalez/Chmn., CEO, Tina M. Vidal/VP - Business Development, Integration, Contact - Investor, Antony J. Chi/34/CFO, John Chi/CFO, John Vincent/COO, Manuel Llano/VP - Finance, Paula Durham/Dir. - Patient Financial Services

Directors: Rainier Gonzalez/Chmn., CEO, Eugene Marini/Dir., Alfredo R. Jurado/Dir., Eric O. Pantaleon/Dir., Marcelo Llorente/Dir.

Owners: John Vincent, Alfredo Jurado, Eric Pantaleon, Marcelo Llorente, Eugene M. Marini, Antony J. Chi, Rainier Gonzalez/73.04%, Insiders/75.70%

Financial Data: ***Fiscal Year End:***12/31 ***Latest Annual Data:*** 12/31/2006

Year	Sales	Net Income
2006	$14,835,000	-$7,637,000
2005	$11,515,000	-$899,000
2004	$7,582,000	$391,000

Curr. Assets:	$8,044,000	***Curr. Liab.:***	$9,013,000		
Plant, Equip.:	$5,700,000	***Total Liab.:***	$13,816,000	***Indic. Yr. Divd.:***	NA
Total Assets:	$15,068,000	***Net Worth:***	-$7,361,000	***Debt/ Equity:***	NA

Pacer International Inc

2300 Clayton Rd., Ste. 1200, Concord, CA, 94520; ***PH:*** 1-925-887-1400; ***Fax:*** 1-925-887-1503; ***http://*** www.pacer-international.com; ***Email:*** info@pacerintl.com

General - Incorporation	TN	**Stock**- Price on:12/24/2007	$25.43
Employees	1,574	Stock Exchange	NDQ
Auditor	PricewaterhouseCoopers LLP	Ticker Symbol	PACR
Stk Agt	Firstar Trust Co	Outstanding Shares	36,830,000
Counsel	NA	E.P.S.	$1.61
DUNS No.	NA	Shareholders	NA

Business: The groups principle activity is to provide logistics and intermodal freight transportation services. Specific clients of the group include General Electric, Union Pacific, Toyota and Whirlpool. The group operates from United States.

Primary SIC and add'l.: 4212 4111 4731 4013

CIK No: 0001091735

Subsidiaries: Intermodal Container Service, Inc. d/b/a Harbor Rail Transport, Manufacturers Consolidation Service of Canada, Inc., Ocean World Lines, Inc., Pacer Cartage, Inc., Pacer Distribution Services, Inc., Pacer Global Logistics, Inc., Pacer Stacktrain S. de R.L. de C.V., Pacific Motor Transport Company d/b/a Pacer Transport, PDS Trucking, Inc., RF International, Ltd., S&H Leasing, Inc., S&H Transport, Inc.

Officers: Michael E. Uremovich/Chmn., CEO/$422,390.00, Michael F. Killea/Exec. VP, General Counsel/$366,952.00, Alex M. Munn/59/COO, Exec. VP - Logistics Segment/$375,364.00, Jeffrey Brashares/COO, Exec. VP - Logistics Segment, Lawrence C. Yarberry/CFO, Exec. VP/$381,754.00, Thomas C. Shurstad/Pres./$456,165.00, Dan Beers/Chief Commercial Officer - Intermodal Segment, Russ D. Oldson/Pres. - Pacer Transport, Pacer Stacktrain/Contact - Sales, Business Development, Pacer Cartage/Contact - Sales, Business Development, William Smith/Exec. VP - Human Resources Management, Brian Kane/COO, Exec. VP - Intermodal Segment, Joseph Doherty/VP, Treasurer, Lisa O. Taylor/VP, Assist. General Counsel, Sec., Val T. Noel/Pres. - Pacer Cartage *(17 Officers included in Index)*

Directors: Michael E. Uremovich/Chmn., CEO, Andrew C. Clarke/35/Dir., Michael P. Giftos/Dir., Bruce H. Spector/65/Dir., Robert S. Rennard/Dir., Donald Orris/Dir., Robert F. Starzel/Dir.

Owners: Michael P. Giftos, Robert S. Rennard, Robert F. Starzel, Michael E. Uremovich, Alex M. Munn, Bruce H. Spector, Thomas C. Shurstad, Andrew C. Clarke, Kayne Anderson Rudnick InvestmentManagement, LLC/6.60%, Michael F. Killea, Cardinal Capital Management, LLC/5.10%, Donald C. Orris, Barclays Global Investors, NA/6.60%, New Amsterdam Partners, LLC/5.50%, Lawrence C. Yarberry *(16 Owners included in Index)*

Financial Data: ***Fiscal Year End:***12/30 ***Latest Annual Data:*** 12/29/2006

Year	Sales	Net Income
2006	$1,887,800,000	$68,300,000
2005	$1,860,100,000	$50,900,000
2004	$1,808,100,000	$47,200,000

Curr. Assets:	$246,400,000	***Curr. Liab.:***	$184,700,000	***P/E Ratio:***	15.41
Plant, Equip.:	$49,100,000	***Total Liab.:***	$341,000,000	***Indic. Yr. Divd.:***	$0.600
Total Assets:	$605,500,000	***Net Worth:***	$264,500,000	***Debt/ Equity:***	NA

Pachinko World Inc

Formerly: Exam USA Inc
5912 Bolsa Ave., Ste. 108, Huntington Beach, CA, 92649; ***PH:*** 1-714-895-7772; ***http://*** www.exam-usa.com

General - Incorporation	NV	**Stock**- Price on:12/24/2007	$0.22
Employees	NA	Stock Exchange	OTC
Auditor	McKennon, Wilson & Morgan LLP	Ticker Symbol	EXMAE
Stk Agt	Interwest Transfer Company, Inc.	Outstanding Shares	NA
Counsel	NA	E.P.S.	NA
DUNS No.	NA	Shareholders	NA

Business: The group's principle activities include acquiring, licensing and distributing nonviolent, educational, informational and special interest television programs for children. The group was doing business as the 'children's cable network', which is comprised of individuals or entities, known as broadcast affiliates, who license the group's programs to air in the various cable markets throughout the United States.

Primary SIC and add'l.: 9999

CIK No: 0000934646

Subsidiaries: Exam Co., Ltd

Pacific Biometrics Inc

220 W Harrison St., Seattle, WA, 98119; ***PH:*** 1-206-298-0068; ***Fax:*** 1-206-298-9838; ***http://*** www.pacbio.com; ***Email:*** contact@pacbio.com

General - Incorporation	DE	**Stock**- Price on:12/24/2007	$0.54
Employees	53	Stock Exchange	OTC
Auditor	Williams & Webster, P.S	Ticker Symbol	PBME
Stk Agt	Grant Thornton LLP	Outstanding Shares	18,990,000
Counsel	NA	E.P.S.	-$0.06
DUNS No.	94-917-0765	Shareholders	NA

Business: The group's principal activity is to provide reference laboratory services to the pharmaceutical and diagnostics industries. The group had developed non-invasive technologies for use in diagnostics to improve the detection and management of chronic diseases. The group developed two new patented platform technologies developed to permit the use of sweat and saliva as diagnostic fluids. Salivasac(R) collects a non-invasive saliva sample that is used to replace blood and urine testing in various applications.

Primary SIC and add'l.: 8731 3821 2835 3845

CIK No: 0001020475

Subsidiaries: Pacific Biometrics, Inc.

Officers: Ronald Helm/Chmn., CEO, Michael Murphy/Sr. VP - Operations, Rick Gordon/VP - Business Development, Sales, Marketing, Kari Charbonnel/Investor Relation Officer, Elizabeth Teng Leary/Co - Founder, Chief Scientific Officer, Janice E. O'Connor/Sr. Dir. - Clinial Biomarkers, Tonya Aggoune/Dir. - Project Services, Kenneth Waters/Dir. - Strategic Planning, Timothy Carlson/Laboratory Dir., Kristin Walsh/Operations Mgr., John P. Jensen/VP - Finance, Controller, Mario R. Ehlers/Chief Medical Officer

Directors: Ronald Helm/Chmn., CEO, Elizabeth Teng Leary/Co - Founder, Chief Scientific Officer

Owners: EFG Bank SA/8.00%, Ronald R. Helm/4.90%, Saigene Corporation/12.00%, Terry M. Giles, Mario Ehlers, Paul G. Kanan/1.50%, Curtis J. Scheel, Anthony Silverman/6.00%, Elizabeth T. Leary/1.30%, Insiders/9.80%, Richard W. Palfreyman

Financial Data: *Fiscal Year End:*06/30 *Latest Annual Data:* 06/30/2007

Year	Sales	Net Income
2007	$8,480,000	-$1,213,000
2006	$10,750,000	$179,000
2005	$3,230,000	-$2,993,000

Curr. Assets:	$8,205,000	**Curr. Liab.:**	$3,829,000		
Plant, Equip.:	$693,000	**Total Liab.:**	$6,668,000	**Indic. Yr. Divd.:**	NA
Total Assets:	$9,024,000	**Net Worth:**	$2,355,000	**Debt/ Equity:**	0.6873

Pacific Booker Minerals Inc

1702 - 1166 Alberni St., Vancouver, BC, V6E 3Z3; *PH:* 1-604-681-8556; *Fax:* 1-604-687-5995; *http://* www.pacificbooker.com; *Email:* info@pacificbooker.bc.ca

General - Incorporation	BC	**Stock**- Price on:12/24/2007	NA
Employees	NA	Stock Exchange	AMEX
Auditor	Davidson & Co. LLP	Ticker Symbol	PBM
Stk Agt	Computershare Investor Services	Outstanding Shares	NA
Counsel	William Schmidt	E.P.S	NA
DUNS No.	NA	Shareholders	NA

Business: The group's principle activity is to operate in the mineral exploration sector. The group is in the advanced stage of development of its Morrison Copper/Gold property. The Morrison deposit is within 20 km (12 mi.) of two former producing mines, Bell and Granisle. The groups only active project is the Morrison/Hearne Hill project in British ColumbiaThe Company currently operates in the mineral exploration sector. All of the groups properties are located in British Columbia, Canada and are at the exploration stage. The group operates from United States.

Primary SIC and add'l.: 1000

CIK No: 0001319150

Officers: Gregory R. Anderson/Dir., CEO, Pres., Rod Smith/Consultant, John Plourde/Exec. Dir., Mark Gulbrandson/Exec. Dir., Erik A. Tornquist/Exec. Dir., COO, Exec. VP, Ruth Swan/CFO, Michael Farnsworth/Consultant, William F. Webster/Exec. Dir., Kevin A. Morin/Consultant

Directors: Gregory R. Anderson/Dir., CEO, Pres., William Deeks/Chmn., William F. Webster/Exec. Dir., John Plourde/Exec. Dir., Mark Gulbrandson/Exec. Dir., Erik A. Tornquist/Exec. Dir., COO, Exec. VP, Dennis C. Simmons/Dir.

Owners: Dennis Simmons/6.54%, Mark Gulbrandson/4.48%, Erik Tornquist/1.77%, Ruth Swan/0.73%, William Deeks/1.81%, William Webster/2.84%, Gregory Anderson/3.35%, Insiders/23.67%, John Plourde/4.69%

Pacific Capital Bancorp

1021 Anacapa St., Santa Barbara, CA, 93101; *PH:* 1-805-564-6405; *Fax:* 1-805-882-3888; *http://* www.pcbancorp.com

General - Incorporation	CA	**Stock**- Price on:12/24/2007	$25.06
Employees	1,622	Stock Exchange	NDQ
Auditor	Ernst & Young LLP	Ticker Symbol	PCBC
Stk Agt	Mellon Investor Services LLC	Outstanding Shares	47,020,000
Counsel	NA	E.P.S	$2.13
DUNS No.	00-691-3883	Shareholders	NA

Business: The group's principal activities are providing commercial banking services to households, professionals and small to medium sized businesses. The banking services include making commercial, leasing, consumer, commercial and residential real estate loans and small business administration guaranteed loans. Deposits are accepted for checking, interest-bearing checking, money-Market, savings, and time accounts. It also offers safe deposit boxes, travelers checks, money orders, foreign exchange services, and cashiers checks. The group through the trust and investment services division offers wealth management services. The services are offered through 41 banking offices under the brand names santa barbara bank and trust, first national bank of central California, south valley national bank and san benito bank.

Primary SIC and add'l.: 6712 6022

CIK No: 0000357264

Subsidiaries: Pacific Capital Bank, N.A., PCB Service Corporation, SBB&T Automobile Loan Securitization Corporation, Sbb&t Ral Funding Corporation

Officers: George Leis/Dir., CEO, Pres./$495,185.00, Gerald T. McCullough/Dir. - General Contractor & Developer, Frederick W. Clough/Exec. VP, General Counsel/$411,493.00

Directors: George Leis/Dir., CEO, Pres., Vernon D. Horton/Vice Chmn., Clayton C. Larson/Vice Chmn. - Retail Banking, Commercial Banking, Marketing, Richard S. Hambleton/Dir., Kathy J. Odell/Dir., Edward E. Birch/Dir., Robert W. Kummer/Dir., Gerald T. McCullough/Dir. - General Contractor & Developer, Roger C. Knopf/Dir., Lee E. Mikles/Dir., John R. MacKall/Dir., Richard A. Nightingale/Dir.

Financial Data: *Fiscal Year End:*12/31 *Latest Annual Data:* 12/31/2006

Year	Sales	Net Income
2006	$726,544,000	$94,540,000
2005	$538,810,000	$99,285,000
2004	$403,834,000	$87,944,000

Curr. Assets:	$186,476,000	**Curr. Liab.:**	$5,476,282,000	**P/E Ratio:**	11.77
Plant, Equip.:	$95,400,000	**Total Liab.:**	$6,877,454,000	**Indic. Yr. Divd.:**	$0.880
Total Assets:	$7,494,830,000	**Net Worth:**	$617,376,000	**Debt/ Equity:**	NA

Pacific City Bank CA

18160 Colima Rd. , City Of Industry, CA, 91748; *PH:* 1-626-363-6730; *http://* paccitybank.com

General - Incorporation		**Stock**- Price on:12/24/2007	$13.75
Employees	NA	Stock Exchange	OTC
Auditor	NA	Ticker Symbol	PFCY
Stk Agt	U.S. Stock Transfer Corp	Outstanding Shares	NA
Counsel	NA	E.P.S	NA
DUNS No.	NA	Shareholders	NA

Business: The groups principal activities include providing banking and financial services to small and medium sized businesses. Services of the group include savings accounts, loans and mortgage, housing loans, business checking and money market. The group operates from the United States.

Primary SIC and add'l.: 6099

CIK No:

Officers: Jung C. Chang/Dir., CEO, Pres., Haeyoung Cho/COO, Exec. VP, Henry Kim/Sr. VP, Chief Credit Officer, Andrew Chung/Sr. VP, CFO, Annie Jo/Sr. VP, Downtown Fashion District Branch Mgr., Justin Chon/Sr. VP, Consumer Loan Dept Mgr., Mike Kim/Sr. VP, SBA Loan Dept Mgr., Yeon Ho Lee/Sr. VP, Wilshire Branch Mgr., Karen Yi/FVP, Controller, Mimi Lee/FVP, Operations Administrator, BSA Officer, Steven Lee/FVP, Private Banking Mgr., Hyun Hee Kim/VP, Rowland Heights Branch Mgr., Linda Park/VP, Note Mgr., Sang Ui Hong/VP, Business Banking Center Mgr., Intl Dept Mgr., Scott Yi/VP, MIS Mgr.

Directors: Jung C. Chang/Dir., CEO, Pres., Kwang Jin Chung/Chmn., Cheonil Kim/Dir., Injoa Kim/Dir., Jin Woo Lee/Dir., Kijun Ahn/Dir., Marlseon Ro/Dir., Sang Young Lee/Dir., Suk Won Youn/Dir., Young Gi Joo/Dir.

Pacific Cma Inc

153-04 Rockaway Blvd., Jamaica, NY, 11434; *PH:* 1-718-949-9700; *Fax:* 1-718-949-9740; *http://* www.pacificcma.com

General - Incorporation	DE	**Stock**- Price on:12/24/2007	$0.34
Employees	277	Stock Exchange	OTC
Auditor	Virchow, Krause & Co., LLP	Ticker Symbol	PACC
Stk Agt	Corporate Stock Transfer, Inc.	Outstanding Shares	28,580,000
Counsel	NA	E.P.S	-$0.28
DUNS No.	NA	Shareholders	NA

Business: The group's principle activity is to provide financial services. The group operates from United States.

Primary SIC and add'l.: 6799

CIK No: 0001071775

Subsidiaries: AGI China Limited, AGI Freight Singapore Pte Limited, AGI Logistics (HK) Ltd, AIO Global Logistics Limited, Seabridge International Pte Limited, Shenzhen Careship International Transportation Ltd, WCL Global Logistics Limited

Officers: Alfred Lam/Chmn., CEO, Scott Turner/Dir., Pres., Kaze Chan/Dir., Exec. VP, John Mazarella/Sr. VP, Rango Lam/Sec., Ling Kwok/36/Exec. VP, Anita Chan/CFO

Directors: Alfred Lam/Chmn., CEO, Scott Turner/Dir., Pres., Kaze Chan/Dir., Exec. VP, Liu Kwong Sang/Non - Exec. Dir., Kenneth Chik/Dir., Cheung Leung Yu/Dir., Louisa Chan/47/Dir.

Owners: Scott Turner, Kaze Chan, Insiders, Alfred Lam, Rango Lam

Financial Data: *Fiscal Year End:*12/31 *Latest Annual Data:* 12/31/2006

Year	Sales	Net Income
2006	$153,986,000	-$2,497,000
2005	$125,009,000	$478,000
2004	$99,600,000	$328,000

Curr. Assets:	$32,913,000	**Curr. Liab.:**	$25,762,000		
Plant, Equip.:	$1,759,000	**Total Liab.:**	$30,989,000	**Indic. Yr. Divd.:**	NA
Total Assets:	$41,355,000	**Net Worth:**	$10,190,000	**Debt/ Equity:**	0.2677

Pacific Continental Corp

111 W 7th Ave., Eugene, OR, 97440; *PH:* 1-541-686-8685; *http://* www.therightbank.com; *Email:* info@rtco.com

General - Incorporation	OR	**Stock**- Price on:12/24/2007	$16.06
Employees	257	Stock Exchange	NDQ
Auditor	Moss Adams LLP	Ticker Symbol	PCBK
Stk Agt	Registrar & Transfer Co	Outstanding Shares	11,800,000
Counsel	NA	E.P.S	$1.07
DUNS No.	NA	Shareholders	NA

Business: The group's principal activities are to provide commercial banking and other financial services. The services of the group include secured and unsecured commercial loans to professional and community based businesses, checking accounts, savings accounts, money market accounts and time deposits. The group also provides safe deposit services, debit and automatic teller machine cards, savings bonds, cashier's checks, travelers' checks, notary services and other services. At 31-Dec 2003, the group operated ten banking offices and two consumer finance lending office serving western Oregon and clark county in southwest Washington state. In 2003 the group acquired coos bay consumer finance office of citifinancial.

Primary SIC and add'l.: 6712 6021

CIK No: 0001084717

Subsidiaries: Pacific Continental Bank

Officers: Hal M. Brown/Dir., CEO/$435,470.00, Roger S. Busse/COO, Pres./$313,932.00, Michael A. Reynolds/CFO, Exec. VP/$203,432.00, Casey Hogan/Exec. VP, Chief Credit Officer, Carol Batchelor/Sr. VP, Dir. - Human Resources - Sphr, Pat Haxby/CIO, Exec. VP, Daniel J. Hempy/Exec. VP, Dir. - Greater Portland Operations/$275,681.00, Mitchell J. Hagstrom/Exec. VP, Dir. - Lane County Operations, Basant Singh/Exec. VP, Dir. - Greater Seattle Operations/$242,078.00, Charlotte Boxer/Exec. VP, Dir. - Commercial Real Estate Markets

Directors: Hal M. Brown/Dir., CEO, Donald G. Montgomery/Vice Chmn., Robert A. Ballin/Chmn., Michael S. Holcomb/Dir., Larry G. Campbell/Dir., Donald L. Krahmer/Dir., Michael D. Holzgang/Dir., John H. Rickman/Dir., Cathi Hatch/Dir., Michael E. Heijer/Dir., Jay R. Tejera/Dir.

Owners: Larry G. Campbell, Basant Singh/1.22%, Michael D. Holzgang, Roger Busse, Michael E. Heijer, Robert A. Ballin/3.99%, Michael Reynolds, John H. Rickman, Daniel J. Hempy, Hal M. Brown/2.16%, Insiders/11.79%, Donald L. Krahmer, Donald G. Montgomery, Michael S. Holcomb/1.34%, Jay R. Tejera

Financial Data: Fiscal Year End:12/31   **Latest Annual Data:** 12/31/2006

Year	Sales	Net Income
2006	$66,373,000	$12,655,000
2005	$43,687,000	$9,578,000
2004	$33,900,000	$7,949,000

Curr. Assets:	$36,776,000	**Curr. Liab.:**	$781,368,000	**P/E Ratio:**	15.01
Plant, Equip.:	$18,591,000	**Total Liab.:**	$789,616,000	**Indic. Yr. Divd.:**	$0.360
Total Assets:	$885,351,000	**Net Worth:**	$95,735,000	**Debt/ Equity:**	1.3693

Pacific Enterprises

555 W 5th St., Los Angeles, CA, 90013; *PH:* 1-213-244-1200; *http://* www.voltviewtech.com

General - Incorporation	CA	**Stock**- Price on:12/24/2007	NA
Employees	NA	Stock Exchange	AMEX
Auditor	Deloitte & Touche LLP	Ticker Symbol	NA
Stk Agt	NA	Outstanding Shares	NA
Counsel	NA	E.P.S.	NA
DUNS No.	61-107-6928	Shareholders	NA

Business: The group's principle activity is to provide energy services. The company also markets a wide range of unregulated energy products and services, including natural gas, and has interests in international utility operations in Argentina and Mexico, interstate and offshore natural gas pipelines and centralised heating and cooling for large building complexes.principal subsidiaries: southern California gas co; pacific enterprises international; pacific interstate co; pacific interstate offshore co; pacific interstate transmission co; pacific offshore pipeline co; pacific energy. The group operates from United States.

Primary SIC and add'l.: 4932 4923

CIK No: 0000075527

Subsidiaries: Ecotrans OEM Corporation, Southern California Gas Company, Southern California Gas Tower

Officers: Debra L. Reed/51/CEO, Pres./$2,210,909.00, Anne S. Smith/54/Sr. VP - Customer Service/$1,043,330.00, Robert M. Schlax/52/VP, Controller, Chief Accounting Officer, Lee Schavrien/53/Sr. VP - Regulatory Affairs/$837,379.00, Lee M. Stewart/62/Sr. VP - Gas Operations/$1,754,969.00, Michael R. Niggli/58/COO/$2,930,639.00, Dennis V. Arriola/47/Sr. VP, CFO/$1,090,900.00

Directors: Edwin A. Guiles/Chmn., Mark A. Snell/Dir.

Owners: Debra L. Reed, Mark A. Snell, Anne S. Smith, Insiders, Dennis V. Arriola, Lee Schavrien, James P. Avery, Michael R. Niggli, Lee M. Stewart

Pacific Ethanol Inc

400 Capitol Mall, Ste. 2060, Sacramento, CA, 95814; *PH:* 1-916-403-2123; *Fax:* 1-916-446-3937; *http://* www.pacificethanol.net

General - Incorporation	DE	**Stock**- Price on:12/24/2007	$12.29
Employees	78	Stock Exchange	NDQ
Auditor	Hein & Assoc. LLP	Ticker Symbol	PEIX
Stk Agt	Continental Stock Transfer & Trust Co	Outstanding Shares	40,560,000
Counsel	NA	E.P.S.	$0.04
DUNS No.	13-088-4695	Shareholders	NA

Business: The group's principal activities are to provide collision repair management services for the insurance industry nationwide through a Website on the Internet. The group through its wholly owned subsidiary conducts the company's collision administration services for insurance carriers and provides the various auto-affinity programs for all types of businesses. The Website enables insurance carriers to utilize the group's Website to directly enter the initial vehicle claim information, find and select the most accessible automobile collision repair shop.

Primary SIC and add'l.: 7538 7549

CIK No: 0000778164

Officers: Neil M. Koehler/Dir., CEO, Pres./$849,917.00, John T. Miller/COO/$350,786.00, Christopher W. Wright/VP, General Counsel/$364,781.00, Tom Koehler/VP - Government Affairs, Communications, Jeff Manternach/VP - Finance, Terrance Kulesa/VP - Operations, Construction, Paul Koehler/VP - Business Development, Doug Dickson/VP - Ag Products, Greg Dibiase/VP - Ethanol Supply, Marketing, Mike Barwig/VP - Ethanol Sales

Directors: Neil M. Koehler/Dir., CEO, Pres., William L. Jones/58/Chmn., Douglas L. Kieta/Dir., John L. Prince/65/Dir., Terry L. Stone/Dir., Robert P. Thomas/30/Dir., Jack Prince/Dir.

Owners: Daniel A. Sanders, Robert P. Thomas, John T. Miller, Cascade Investment, L.L.C./20.60%, Douglas L. Kieta, Terry L. Stone, Neil M. Koehler/7.91%, William L. Jones/4.40%, Christopher W. Wright, Insiders/12.50%, John L. Prince

Financial Data: Fiscal Year End:12/31   **Latest Annual Data:** 12/31/2006

Year	Sales	Net Income
2006	$226,356,000	-$142,000
2005	$87,597,000	-$9,923,000
2003	$658,000	-$1,626,000

Curr. Assets:	$127,045,000	**Curr. Liab.:**	$30,594,000	**P/E Ratio:**	307.25
Plant, Equip.:	$196,156,000	**Total Liab.:**	$61,012,000	**Indic. Yr. Divd.:**	NA
Total Assets:	$453,820,000	**Net Worth:**	$298,445,000	**Debt/ Equity:**	0.3435

Pacific Financial Corp

PO Box 1826, Aberdeen, WA, 98520; *PH:* 1-360-533-8870; *Fax:* 1-360-533-0489; *http://* www.thebankofpacific.com

General - Incorporation	WA	**Stock**- Price on:12/24/2007	$15.55
Employees	203	Stock Exchange	OTC
Auditor	Deloitte & Touche, LLP	Ticker Symbol	PFLC
Stk Agt.	Mellon Investor Services LLC	Outstanding Shares	6,570,000
Counsel	NA	E.P.S.	NA
DUNS No.	NA	Shareholders	NA

Business: The group's principal activities are to accept deposit and lend loans to small medium-sized local businesses and professionals. The deposits include demand accounts, negotiable order of withdrawal accounts, money market investment accounts, savings accounts and time deposits. The loan portfolio includes commercial loans, installment loans, real estate loans, residential mortgage loans and personal and business deposit products. The group operates through ten branches located in grays harbor, pacific and wahkiakum counties in southwest Washington. On 02-Feb-2004, the group acquired bnw bancorp inc.

Primary SIC and add'l.: 6712 6021 6726

CIK No: 0001093728

Subsidiaries: Bank NorthWest, PFC Statutory Trust, The Bank of the Pacific

Officers: Dennis A. Long/Dir., CEO, Pres./$362,494.00

Directors: Dennis A. Long/Dir., CEO, Pres., Gary C. Forcum/Chmn., Douglas M. Schermer/Dir., Susan C. Freese/Dir., Robert J. Worrell/Dir., Dennis G. Archer/Dir., Stewart L. Thomas/Dir., Randy J. Rust/Dir., Joseph A. Malik/Dir., Duane E. Hagstrom/Dir., Randy W. Rognlin/Dir., John Ferlin/Dir., Edwin W. Ketel/Dir.

Owners: Douglas M. Schermer, Insiders/17.00%, Duane E. Hagstrom/1.90%, Joseph A. Malik, Denise Portmann, Robert J. Worrell/2.00%, Philippe Swaab, Bruce D. MacNaughton, Susan C. Freese, Dennis G. Archer, John R. Ferlin, Gary C. Forcum/1.20%, Stewart L. Thomas, Randy Rust, John Van Dijk/1.10% *(18 Owners included in Index)*

Financial Data: Fiscal Year End:12/31   **Latest Annual Data:** 12/31/2006

Year	Sales	Net Income
2006	$40,620,000	$6,551,000
2005	$33,712,000	$6,046,000
2004	$27,300,000	$5,707,000

Curr. Assets:	$43,794,000	**Curr. Liab.:**	$468,256,000	**P/E Ratio:**	15.87
Plant, Equip.:	$11,537,000	**Total Liab.:**	$513,400,000	**Indic. Yr. Divd.:**	NA
Total Assets:	$562,384,000	**Net Worth:**	$48,984,000	**Debt/ Equity:**	NA

Pacific Fuel Cell Corp

131 N Tustin Ave., Ste.100, Tustin, CA, 92780; *PH:* 1-714-564-1693; *Fax:* 1-714-558-9301; *http://* www.pfce.net; *Email:* investor@pfce.net

General - Incorporation	NV	**Stock**- Price on:12/24/2007	$0.31
Employees	10	Stock Exchange	OTC
Auditor	Stark Winter Schenkein & Co. LLP	Ticker Symbol	PFCE
Stk Agt	Computershare Trust Co	Outstanding Shares	73,170,000
Counsel	NA	E.P.S.	-$0.01
DUNS No.	NA	Shareholders	NA

Business: The group's principle activities include developing and producing low cost fuel cells for personal electronics or other applications. The company uses platinum, a precious metal, as the catalyst for hydrogen to separate into a proton and electron. The group operates from United States.

Primary SIC and add'l.: 4911

CIK No: 0001098578

Subsidiaries: Cellfoods Corporation, Nevada corporation

Officers: George Suzuki/65/Dir., CEO, CFO, Pres., Xin Wang/Researcher, Yushan Yan/Dir., Chief Scientific Advisor, Wenzhen Li/Researcher

Directors: George Suzuki/65/Dir., CEO, CFO, Pres., Yushan Yan/Dir., Chief Scientific Advisor

Owners: Insiders/41.70%, Fullerene USA, Inc./41.70%, Stephen G. Godwin/8.60%

Financial Data: Fiscal Year End:12/31   **Latest Annual Data:** 12/31/2006

Year	Sales	Net Income
2006	NA	-$492,000
2005	$52,000	-$521,000
2004	$114,000	-$142,000

Curr. Assets:	$117,000	**Curr. Liab.:**	$28,000		
Plant, Equip.:	$33,000	**Total Liab.:**	$28,000	**Indic. Yr. Divd.:**	NA
Total Assets:	$323,000	**Net Worth:**	$295,000	**Debt/ Equity:**	NA

Pacific Gas & Electric Co

PO Box 770000, San Francisco, CA, 94177; *PH:* 1-415-973-7000; *http://* www.pgecorp.com; *Email:* invrel@pge-corp.com

General - Incorporation	CA	**Stock**- Price on:12/24/2007	NA
Employees	19,800	Stock Exchange	AMEX
Auditor	Deloitte & Touche LLP	Ticker Symbol	NA
Stk Agt	Bank of New York	Outstanding Shares	NA
Counsel	NA	E.P.S.	NA
DUNS No.	00-691-2877	Shareholders	NA

Business: The group is an energy-based holding group. The group's northern and central California energy utility subsidiary, pacific gas and electric company, delivers electric service to approximately 4.6 million customers and natural gas service to approximately 3.8 million customers. On Sept 20, 2001, the pacific gas and electric company and the group jointly filed with the bankruptcy court a proposed plan of reorganization of the pacific gas and electric company under chapter 11 of the bankruptcy code. After the reorganization, pacific gas and electric company would operate as a stand-alone electric and gas distribution business.

Primary SIC and add'l.: 4922 4923 4911

CIK No: 0000075488

Subsidiaries: Pacific Gas and Electric Company, PG&E Energy Recovery Funding LLC

Officers: Thomas B. King/46/CEO/$4,228,109.00, Nancy E. McFadden/Sr. VP - Public Affairs, William T. Morrow/COO, Pres., Helen A. Burt/Sr. VP, Chief Customer Officer, Russell M. Jackson/50/Sr. VP - Human Resources, Donna Jacobs/VP - Nuclear Services, Roy M. Kuga/VP - Energy Supply, Patricia M. Lawicki/CIO, VP, Brian Cherry/VP - Regulatory Relations, Deann Hapner/VP - Ferc, ISO Relations, Randal S. Livingston/VP - Power Generation, John T. Conway/Site VP - Diablo Canyon Power Plant, Des Bell/VP, Chief - Staff, John R. Simon/Sr. VP - Human Resources, Edward A. Salas/Sr. VP - Engineering, Operations *(32 Officers included in Index)*

Directors: Barry Lawson Williams/Dir., Mary S. Metz/Dir., Barbara L. Rambo/Dir.

Owners: Pacific Gas and Electric/96.44%

Pacific Gold Corp

157 Adelaide St. W, Ste. 600, Toronto, ON, M5H 4E7; *PH:* 1-416-214-1483;
http:// www.pacificgoldcorp.com; *Email:* info@pacificgoldcorp.com

General - Incorporation	NV	*Stock*- Price on:12/24/2007	$0.345
Employees	NA	Stock Exchange	OTC
Auditor	Vavrinek, Trine, Day & Co.,LLP	Ticker Symbol	PCFG
Stk Agt.	Olde Monmouth Stk Trnsfer Co. Inc.	Outstanding Shares	NA
Counsel	NA	E.P.S.	-$0.096
DUNS No.	NA	Shareholders	NA

Business: The groups principal activity is to exploration and development of a mining prospect is subject to regulation by a number of federal and state government authorities. The group operates from the United States.

Primary SIC and add'l.: 1040

CIK No: 0001137855

Subsidiaries: Fernley Gold, Inc., Nevada Rae Gold, Inc., Oregon Gold, Inc., Pacific Metals Corp., Pilot Mountain Resources Inc.

Officers: Rob Landau/Chmn., CEO/$383,831.00, Mitchell Geisler/Dir., COO/$369,235.00, Jackie Glazer/CFO/$110,019.00, Cindy Roach/Dir. - Human Resources, John A. Rae/Pgeo

Directors: Rob Landau/Chmn., CEO, Mitchell Geisler/Dir., COO

Owners: Gable International Investments, Ltd./5.00%, Vladimir Fabert/19.00%, Parthian Securities/12.00%, Grove Partners/5.00%

Financial Data: Fiscal Year End:12/31   *Latest Annual Data:* 12/31/2006

Year	Sales	Net Income
2006	$86,000	-$8,836,000
2005	NA	-$5,016,000
2004	$62,000	-$994,000

Curr. Assets:	$253,000	*Curr. Liab.:*	$2,733,000		
Plant, Equip.:	$4,386,000	*Total Liab.:*	$4,944,000	*Indic. Yr. Divd.:*	NA
Total Assets:	$4,911,000	*Net Worth:*	-$34,000	*Debt/ Equity:*	0.5260

Pacific Harbour Capital Ltd

543 Granville St., Ste. 1502, Vancouver, BC, V6C 1X8; *PH:* 1-604-697-0687

General - Incorporation	Canada	*Stock*- Price on:12/24/2007	$0.19
Employees	NA	Stock Exchange	OTC
Auditor	Amisano Hanson	Ticker Symbol	PCFHF
Stk Agt.	Computershare Trust Co. of Canada	Outstanding Shares	NA
Counsel	NA	E.P.S.	NA
DUNS No.	25-536-4317	Shareholders	NA

Business: The group's principle activities of the group are operating convenience stores through joint venture and provide vehicle-leasing services. Operations of the group are carried out in Canada and the United States of America.

Primary SIC and add'l.: 5511 7549 5411

CIK No: 0000936801

Subsidiaries: incorporated in British Columbia, Venpac Nevada I, Inc., Venture Pacific Development Corporation (USA), VenPac Nevada I, Inc.

Officers: Thomas Pressello/39/Dir., CEO, Pres., Michael Reynolds/44/Dir., Interim Financial Officer, David Raffa/51/Dir., Sec.

Directors: Thomas Pressello/39/Dir., CEO, Pres., Michael Reynolds/44/Dir., Interim Financial Officer, David Raffa/51/Dir., Sec.

Owners: Michael Reynolds/14.63%, Thomas Pressello/7.62%, Michael Reynolds/9.77%, Hartford Estate Holdings Ltd./21.83%

Financial Data: Fiscal Year End:03/31   *Latest Annual Data:* 03/31/2007

Year	Sales	Net Income
2007	$446,000	$192,000
2006	$190,000	-$177,000
2005	$14,000	-$182,000

Curr. Assets:	$785,000	*Curr. Liab.:*	$149,000		
Plant, Equip.:	$2,000	*Total Liab.:*	$149,000	*Indic. Yr. Divd.:*	NA
Total Assets:	$907,000	*Net Worth:*	$759,000	*Debt/ Equity:*	NA

Pacific International Bancorp Inc WA

1155 N 130th St. , Ste. 100, Seattle, WA, 98133; *PH:* 1-206-306-7900

General - Incorporation		*Stock*- Price on:12/24/2007	NA
Employees	NA	Stock Exchange	OTC
Auditor	NA	Ticker Symbol	PIBW
Stk Agt.	NA	Outstanding Shares	NA
Counsel	NA	E.P.S.	NA
DUNS No.	NA	Shareholders	NA

Business: The groups principle activity is to provide recruiting services. The groups service area includes the research and development, engineering, marketing, sales, information technology and manufacturing industries. The group operates from United States.

Primary SIC and add'l.: 6021

CIK No: 0001374376

Pacific Land & Coffee Corp

1650 Ala Moana, Ste. 507, Honolulu, HI, 96815; *PH:* 1-808-371-4266

General - Incorporation	DE	*Stock*- Price on:12/24/2007	$0.3
Employees	NA	Stock Exchange	OTC
Auditor	Mantyla McReynolds, LLC	Ticker Symbol	PLCF
Stk Agt.	NA	Outstanding Shares	10,000,000
Counsel	NA	E.P.S.	$0.00
DUNS No.	NA	Shareholders	NA

Business: The groups principal activity is to markets its coffee and coffee related products. The group operates from the United States.

Primary SIC and add'l.: 5149

CIK No: 0001092791

Subsidiaries: Pacific Land & Coffee Corporation

Officers: Dale G. Nielsen/59/Dir., CEO, Alfred Coscina/69/Dir., CFO, Sec.

Directors: Dale G. Nielsen/59/Dir., CEO, Alfred Coscina/69/Dir., CFO, Sec.

Owners: Dennis Nielsen/31.90%, Al Coscina/21.30%, Insiders/42.60%, Dale G. Nielsen/21.30%

Financial Data: Fiscal Year End:03/31   *Latest Annual Data:* 3/31/2006

Year	Sales	Net Income
2006	$32,000	-$8,000
2005	$19,000	-$7,000

Curr. Assets:	$2,000	*Curr. Liab.:*	$14,000		
Plant, Equip.:	NA	*Total Liab.:*	$14,000	*Indic. Yr. Divd.:*	NA
Total Assets:	$2,000	*Net Worth:*	-$13,000	*Debt/ Equity:*	NA

Pacific Mercantile Bancorp

949 S Coast Dr., Third Fl., Costa Mesa, CA, 92626; *PH:* 1-714-438-2500; *Fax:* 1-714-438-1059;
http:// www.pmbank.com; *Email:* info@pmbank.com

General - Incorporation	CA	*Stock*- Price on:12/24/2007	$14.27
Employees	139	Stock Exchange	NDQ
Auditor	Grant Thornton LLP	Ticker Symbol	PMBC
Stk Agt.	U.S. Stock Transfer Corp	Outstanding Shares	10,360,000
Counsel	Stradling Yocca Carlson & Rauth	E.P.S.	$0.58
DUNS No.	NA	Shareholders	NA

Business: The group's principal activity is to provide traditional and Internet banking products services through its subsidiary, pacific mercantile bank. The activities are carried out through two segments: commercial banking and mortgage banking. The commercial banking segment provides a diversified range of products and services to small and medium-size businesses, professional firms and individuals. The products and services include various types of deposit accounts, various types of commercial and consumer loans, cash management services and Internet banking services. The mortgage banking segment originates and purchases residential mortgages and resells within 30 days to long-term investors in the secondary residential mortgage market. These products and services are offered through six banking offices located in California.

Primary SIC and add'l.: 6712 6022

CIK No: 0001109546

Subsidiaries: Pacific Mercantile Bank, Pacific Mercantile Capital Trust I, PMB Capital Trust II, PMB Capital Trust III, PMB Securities Corp., PMB Statutory Trust I

Officers: Raymond E. Dellerba/Dir., CEO, Pres./$1,216,767.00, Nancy A. Gray/CFO, Exec. VP/$277,500.00, Barbara Palermo/Investor Relations Officer, Bradford C. Hoover/51/Dir., Chief Credit Officer - Bank/$285,227.00

Directors: Raymond E. Dellerba/Dir., CEO, Pres., George H. Wells/Chmn., Ronald W. Chrislip/49/Dir., John Thomas/52/Dir., Gary M. Williams/Dir., Robert E. Williams/59/Dir., Warren T. Finley/70/Dir., Julia Mary Digiovanni/83/Dir.

Owners: Warren T. Finley/1.20%, Raymond E. Dellerba/6.10%, Brad Hoover, Ronald W. Chrislip/1.10%, Robert E. Williams/1.40%, Nancy A. Gray, John Thomas/1.40%, Julia M. DiGiovanni/1.10%, First Manhattan Co./9.50%, George H. Wells/1.50%, Insiders/13.40%

Financial Data: Fiscal Year End:12/31   *Latest Annual Data:* 06/30/2007

Year	Sales	Net Income
2007	NA	NA
2006	$65,694,000	$6,932,000
2005	$47,686,000	$5,724,000

Curr. Assets:	$31,379,000	*Curr. Liab.:*	$720,723,000	*P/E Ratio:*	22.65
Plant, Equip.:	$2,152,000	*Total Liab.:*	$954,603,000	*Indic. Yr. Divd.:*	NA
Total Assets:	$1,042,529,000	*Net Worth:*	$87,926,000	*Debt/ Equity:*	2.9575

Pacific North West Capital Corp

2303 W 41st Ave., Vancouver, BC, V6M 2A3; *PH:* 1-604-685-1870; *Fax:* 1-604-685-8045;
http:// www.pfncapital.com; *Email:* jlondry@pfncapital.com

General - Incorporation	BC	*Stock*- Price on:12/24/2007	$0.696
Employees	NA	Stock Exchange	OTC
Auditor	Staley, Okada & Partners	Ticker Symbol	NA
Stk Agt.	Computershare Investor Services LLC	Outstanding Shares	NA
Counsel	Devlin Jensen	E.P.S.	NA
DUNS No.	NA	Shareholders	NA

Business: The groups principal activity is to explores for platinum group metals and Nickel in North America. The group operates from the United States.

Primary SIC and add'l.: 1099

CIK No: 0001073238

Officers: Harry Barr/CEO, Pres., Peter Dasler/VP - Business Development, John W. Londry/VP - Exploration, John Royall/Business Consultant, Taryn Downing/Corp. Sec., Gord Steblin/CFO, Devlin Jensen/Legal Counsel

Directors: Bernard Barlin/Dir., Steve Oakley/Dir., Alex Walcott/Dir., Linda Holmes/Dir., Jordan Point/Dir., Denny Hop/Dir.

Owners: Stillwater Mining Company/10.36%, CDS & Company/68.09%

Financial Data: Fiscal Year End:04/30   *Latest Annual Data:* 4/30/2006

Year	Sales	Net Income
2006	NA	-$1,864,000
2005	NA	-$2,143,000
2004	NA	-$1,080,000

Curr. Assets:	$3,044,000	*Curr. Liab.:*	$58,000		
Plant, Equip.:	$63,000	*Total Liab.:*	$58,000	*Indic. Yr. Divd.:*	NA
Total Assets:	$3,490,000	*Net Worth:*	$3,432,000	*Debt/ Equity:*	NA

Pacific Premier Bancorp Inc

1600 Sunflower Ave., 2nd Fl., Costa Mesa, CA, 92626; *PH:* 1-714-431-4000; *Fax:* 1-714-433-3000;
http:// www.ppbi.net; *Email:* centralbranchsupport@ppbi.net

General - Incorporation: DE
Employees: 104
Auditor: Vavrinek, Trine, Day & Co. LLP
Stk Agt: American Stock Transfer & Trust Co.
Counsel: NA
DUNS No.: 92-995-4006

Stock - Price on:12/24/2007: $10.5
Stock Exchange: NDQ
Ticker Symbol: PPBI
Outstanding Shares: 5,160,000
E.P.S.: $0.74
Shareholders: NA

Business: The group's principal activity is to originate, purchase, sell and service non-conventional mortgage loans secured by first and second mortgage on one-to-four family residences. The group's consumer and other loans generally consists of overdraft line of credit, commercial loans and unsecured personal loans. The principal business of the bank is attracting retail deposits from the general public and investing those deposits, together with funds generated from operations and borrowings, primarily in one-to four-family residential mortgage and residential construction loans. The group provides the services through its subsidiaries, pacific premier bank, life financial insurance services inc and life investment holdings inc.

Primary SIC and add'l.: 6035 6712

CIK No: 0001028918

Subsidiaries: Pacific Premier Bank, Pacific Premier Investment Services, Inc.

Officers: John Shindler/CFO, Exec. VP/$286,928.00

Directors: Jeff C. Jones/53/Dir., David L. Hardin/54/Dir.

Owners: Eddie Wilcox, Kenneth A. Boudreau, Michael L. McKennon, Steven R. Gardner, Insiders, John D. Goddard, Ronald G. Skipper, Kent G. Snyder, Jeff Jones, John Shindler

Financial Data: Fiscal Year End:12/31 Latest Annual Data: 12/31/2006

Year	Sales	Net Income
2006	$50,643,000	$7,428,000
2005	$37,837,000	$7,221,000
2004	$27,469,000	$6,741,000

Curr. Assets:	$20,934,000	Curr. Liab.:	$346,035,000	P/E Ratio:	14.19
Plant, Equip.:	$8,760,000	Total Liab.:	$672,836,000	Indic. Yr. Divd.:	NA
Total Assets:	$730,874,000	Net Worth:	$58,038,000	Debt/ Equity:	5.4427

Pacific Rim Mining Corp

625 Howe St., Ste. 410, Vancouver, BC, V6C 2T6; *PH:* 1-604-689-1976; *Fax:* 1-604-689-1978; *http://* www.pacrim-mining.com; *Email:* info@pacrim-mining.com

General - Incorporation: Canada
Employees: NA
Auditor: Pricewaterhousecoopers LLP
Stk Agt: Computershare Trust Co
Counsel: Gowling, Lafleur, Henderson LLP
DUNS No.: 25-453-1494

Stock - Price on:12/24/2007: $0.9528
Stock Exchange: AMEX
Ticker Symbol: PMU
Outstanding Shares: 107,040,000
E.P.S.: -$0.08
Shareholders: NA

Business: The group's principle activities include acquiring, exploring and developing mineral resource properties, primarily gold and silver properties in Latin America. The group operates from United States.

Primary SIC and add'l.: 1044 1041

CIK No: 0001056512

Subsidiaries: Dayton Mining (U.S.) Inc

Officers: Thomas C. Shrake/Dir., CEO, Pres., Peter Neilans/COO, Barbara Henderson/VP - Investor Relations, William Gehlen/VP - Exploration, Ronda Fullerton/Corp. Sec., David Ernst/Sr. Technical, Chief Geologist, April Hashimoto/CFO

Directors: Thomas C. Shrake/Dir., CEO, Pres., Catherine McLeod-Seltzer/Chmn., William Myckatyn/Dir., Paul Sweeney/Dir., Anthony Petrina/Dir., David Fagin/Dir.

Financial Data: Fiscal Year End:04/30 Latest Annual Data: 04/30/2007

Year	Sales	Net Income
2007	$8,337,000	-$9,417,000
2006	$8,024,000	-$618,000
2005	$11,868,000	-$4,634,000

Curr. Assets:	$17,354,000	Curr. Liab.:	$1,025,000	P/E Ratio:	15.88
Plant, Equip.:	$4,307,000	Total Liab.:	$2,874,000	Indic. Yr. Divd.:	NA
Total Assets:	$24,909,000	Net Worth:	$22,035,000	Debt/ Equity:	NA

Pacific Sands Inc

1509 Rapids Dr., Racine, WI, 53404; *PH:* 1-262-619-3261; *Fax:* 1-262-619-1999; *http://* www.pacificsands.biz/index.html; *Email:* sales@pacificsandsinc.com

General - Incorporation: NV
Employees: 6
Auditor: Frank L. Sassetti & Co
Stk Agt: Corporate Stock Transfer, Inc.
Counsel: NA
DUNS No.: NA

Stock - Price on:12/24/2007: $0.09
Stock Exchange: OTC
Ticker Symbol: PFSD
Outstanding Shares: 34,320,000
E.P.S.: -$0.009
Shareholders: NA

Business: The group's principle activity is to manufacture nontoxic compound, which eliminates itching, rashes and scum lines in spas and cleaning products. It does business as natural water technologies. The target markets for the company's products include retail and industrial uses. Currently, the company markets the retail spa products and is testing equipment for industrial use. The group operates from United States.

Primary SIC and add'l.: 2842 2899

CIK No: 0001069799

Officers: Michael L. Wynhoff/CEO, Pres., Mark R. Rauscher/Dir., Sec., Jack Hagarty/Dir., Lead Research Chemist, Robert Krug/Marketing Dir., Jill Wegener/Distributor, Manufacturers Rep, Trade, Show Coordinator, Todd Taylor/Ecoone Product Support Mgr., Michael D. Michie/CFO, VP - Sale, Marketing, John Homan/Contact - Ecoone Sales, Donald Michie/Dir. - Corporate Communications, Angela Wuerker/Coordinator, Manufacturing, Shipping, Receiving, Jt Ploch/Contact - Investor Relations

Directors: Mark R. Rauscher/Dir., Sec., Jack Hagarty/Dir., Lead Research Chemist, John D. Hagarty/68/Dir.

Owners: Mark Rauscher/5.10%, John D. Hagarty, Michael D. Michie/5.50%, Michael L. Wynhoff/16.80%

Financial Data: Fiscal Year End:06/30 Latest Annual Data: 06/30/2007

Year	Sales	Net Income
2007	$597,000	-$551,000
2006	$434,000	-$310,000
2005	$220,000	-$300,000

Curr. Assets:	$202,000	Curr. Liab.:	$458,000		
Plant, Equip.:	$39,000	Total Liab.:	$481,000	Indic. Yr. Divd.:	NA
Total Assets:	$241,000	Net Worth:	-$240,000	Debt/ Equity:	NA

Pacific State Bancorp

PO Box 1649, Stockton, CA, 95201; *PH:* 1-209-870-3200; *Fax:* 1-209-870-3250; *http://* www.pacificstatebank.com

General - Incorporation: CA
Employees: 84
Auditor: Perry-Smith LLP
Stk Agt: Mellon Investor Services LLC
Counsel: Shapiro Buchman Provine Patton LLP
DUNS No.: NA

Stock - Price on:12/24/2007: $17.75
Stock Exchange: NDQ
Ticker Symbol: PSBC
Outstanding Shares: 3,680,000
E.P.S.: $1.47
Shareholders: NA

Business: The group's principal activity is to provide commercial banking services to residents and employers including professional firms and small to medium sized retail and wholesale businesses and manufacturers. These services include offering loans and acceptance of deposits. The categories of loans include commercial, agricultural, real estate and installment loans. The various deposits accepted by the group include savings, time deposits, money market and negotiable orders of withdrawal. Other services offered by the group include domestic and foreign drafts, banking by appointment, automatic transfer of funds, business courier services, domestic letters of credit and individual retirement accounts. The group operates through seven branches in stockton, modesto, groveland, arnold, angels camp and tracy.

Primary SIC and add'l.: 6712 6022

CIK No: 0001169424

Subsidiaries: Pacific State Bank, Pacific State Statutory Trust I, Pacific State Statutory Trust II

Officers: Steven A. Rosso/54/Dir., CEO, Pres., Joanne C. Roberts/CFO, Sr. VP

Directors: Steven A. Rosso/54/Dir., CEO, Pres., Harold Hand/70/Dir., Yoshikazu Mataga/65/Dir., Kathleen M. Verner/65/Dir., Michael L. Dalton/61/Dir., Patricia A. Hatton/58/Dir., Maxwell M. Freeman/70/Dir., Steven J. Kikuchi/50/Dir., Gary A. Stewart/58/Dir., Russel Munson/61/Dir.

Owners: Harold Hand/8.04%, Maxwell M. Freeman/9.25%, Steven A. Rosso/7.37%

Financial Data: Fiscal Year End:12/31 Latest Annual Data: 12/31/2006

Year	Sales	Net Income
2006	$29,078,000	$5,543,000
2005	$21,263,000	$4,286,000
2004	$16,034,000	$3,169,000

Curr. Assets:	$58,291,000	Curr. Liab.:	$344,029,000	P/E Ratio:	12.41
Plant, Equip.:	$11,957,000	Total Liab.:	$357,693,000	Indic. Yr. Divd.:	NA
Total Assets:	$386,752,000	Net Worth:	$29,059,000	Debt/ Equity:	0.4484

Pacific Sunwear of California Inc

3450 E Miraloma Ave., Anaheim, CA, 92806; *PH:* 1-714-414-4000; *Fax:* 1-714-414-4251; *http://* www.pacsun.com; *Email:* info@pacsun.com

General - Incorporation: CA
Employees: 4,700
Auditor: Deloitte & Touche LLP
Stk Agt: U.S. Stock Transfer Corp
Counsel: O'melveny & Myers
DUNS No.: 05-056-0002

Stock - Price on:12/24/2007: $22.09
Stock Exchange: NDQ
Ticker Symbol: PSUN
Outstanding Shares: 70,410,000
E.P.S.: $0.56
Shareholders: NA

Business: The group's principal activity are to operate in specialty retailer of everyday casual apparel, footwear and accessories for teenagers and young adults. The group operates through three nationwide, primarily mall-based chains of retail stores under the names pacific sunwear (pacsun), pacific sunwear outlet and d.e.m.o. Pacsun outlets stores specialize in board-sport inspired casual apparel, footwear and related accessories and d.e.m.o specializes in hip-hop inspired casual apparel and related accessories catering to teenagers and young adults. The group operates 888 stores in 50 states and in the United States of America and in Puerto Rico. The group also operates a Web site through a subsidiary that sells merchandise online, provides content and community for customers and also provides information about the group.

Primary SIC and add'l.: 5621 2389 5611 5632

CIK No: 0000874841

Subsidiaries: Miraloma Corp, Pacific Sunwear Stores Corp

Officers: Sally Frame Kasaks/63/Dir., Interim CEO/$365,091.00, Wendy E. Burden/54/COO/$972,402.00, Steven Sare/VP - GMM, Demo, Whitney Walker/VP - Business Strategy, David Schenk/CIO, Sr. VP, Lou Ann Bett/Divison Pres. - Demo/$773,010.00, Reenie Benziger/Exec. VP - Merchandising, Pacsun, Teresa Nersesyan/VP - Global Logistics, Trade Compliance, Gerald M. Chaney/Sr. VP, CFO/$983,899.00, Thomas Kennedy/Division Pres. - Pacsun/$1,280,994.00, Charlie Mescher/VP, General Merchandise Mgr. Pacsun Young Men's, Caroline Kenyon/VP - Human Resources, Mark Kibler/VP - Distribution, Linda Eddy/VP - Real Estate, Larry J. Fesler/VP - Stores *(27 Officers included in Index)*

Directors: Sally Frame Kasaks/63/Dir., Interim CEO, Reb Jensen/Dir., Pete Cummin/Dir., Tom Murnane/Dir., Michael Goldstein/Dir., Peter Starrett/Dir., Michael Weiss/66/Dir., Julius Jensen/74/Dir., Pearson C. Cummin/65/Dir.

Owners: FMR Corp. and related parties/14.50%, Gerald M. Chaney, Insiders/1.80%, Julius Jensen, Peter Starrett, Michael Weiss, Lazard Asset Management LLC/6.10%, Steven A. Cohen/5.50%, Wendy E. Burden, Thomas M. Kennedy, Thomas M. Murnane, Michael Goldstein, Pearson C. Cummin, Adage Capital Partners, LP and related parties/6.00%, Lou Ann Bett *(16 Owners included in Index)*

Financial Data: Fiscal Year End:01/28 Latest Annual Data: 2/3/2007

Year	Sales	Net Income
2007	$1,447,204,000	$39,621,000
2006	$1,391,473,000	$126,212,000
2005	$1,229,762,000	$106,904,000

Curr. Assets:	$335,235,000	Curr. Liab.:	$140,533,000	P/E Ratio:	69.03
Plant, Equip.:	$420,886,000	Total Liab.:	$269,890,000	Indic. Yr. Divd.:	NA
Total Assets:	$773,243,000	Net Worth:	$503,353,000	Debt/ Equity:	NA

Pacific Valley Bank CA

3 Rossi Cir., Ste. A, Near the Intersection Davis Rd., Rossi St., Salinas, CA, 93912; *PH:* 1-831-422-5300; *Fax:* 1-831-422-4059; *http://* www.pacificvalleybank.com

General - Incorporation................................... | **Stock**- Price on:12/24/2007 ....$16.2
Employees ....19 | Stock Exchange...OTC
Auditor ....NA | Ticker Symbol...PVBK
Stk Agt.......................Computershare Trust CO. | Outstanding Shares ....NA
Counsel...NA | E.P.S...NA
DUNS No. ....NA | Shareholders...NA

Business: The groups principal activities include providing community banking. The group offers a complete array of checking and savings accounts, along with money management products that will satisfy any individual or business banking customers needs. The group operates from the United States.

Primary SIC and add'l.: 6021

CIK No:

Officers: Ben A. Tinkey/COO, Pres., Susan M. Carlson/Sr. VP, Chief Administrative Officer, Frank H. Lippman/Sr. VP, CFO, Bruce E. Lyman/Chief Lending Officer, Sr. VP, Jon R. Moore/Dir., Corp. Sec., Tom Ragusa/Sr. VP, Chief Risk Officer, Charles A. Willis/Financial Consultant

Directors: Rodney Braga/Chmn., Louis H. Huntington/Vice Chmn., Louis P. Cosentino/Dir., Tina Lopez/Dir., Jon R. Moore/Dir., Corp. Sec., Michael D. Cling/Dir., Andrew P. Ausonio/Dir., Steven D. Bassi/Dir., Guillermo Nieto/Dir., Michael P. Shah/Dir.

Pacific WebWorks Inc

180 S 300 W, Ste. 400, Salt Lake City, UT, 84101; **PH:** 1-801-578-9020; **Fax:** 1-801-578-9019; **http://** www.pacificwebworks.com; **Email:** info@pacificwebworks.com

General - Incorporation............................NV | **Stock**- Price on:12/24/2007 ....$0.041
Employees ....19 | Stock Exchange...OTC
Auditor ....Chisholm, Bierwolf & Nilson, LLC | Ticker Symbol...PWEB
Stk Agt.............Standard Registrar & Transfer Co Inc. | Outstanding Shares 35,780,000
Counsel...NA | E.P.S...-$0.02
DUNS No. ....NA | Shareholders...NA

Business: The groups principle activity is an application service provider and software development firm that develops business software technologies and services for business merchants and organizations using Internet and other technologies. The group markets its products under the tradenames include ExpertLink(TM), LinkSmart(TM), Smart Terminal(TM), Secure Account Management System (SAMS) and IntelliPay Desktop Terminal (IDT). The group operates from the United States. The group's revenue for Sep '07 was 3.19 millions of USD.

Primary SIC and add'l.: 7372

CIK No: 0001086303

Subsidiaries: FundWorks, Inc.,, Intellipay, Inc.,, TradeWorks Marketing, Inc.,, World Commerce Network, LLC.

Owners: Insiders/11.70%, Kenneth W. Bell/4.90%, Brett R. Bell/1.80%, Christian R. Larsen/5.70%

Financial Data: Fiscal Year End:12/31 **Latest Annual Data:** 12/31/2006

Year		Sales	Net Income
2006		$5,043,000	-$1,026,000
2005		$5,914,000	-$296,000
2004		$3,617,000	-$489,000
Curr. Assets:	$584,000	**Curr. Liab.:** $579,000	
Plant, Equip.:	$91,000	**Total Liab.:** $579,000	**Indic. Yr. Divd.:** NA
Total Assets:	$2,746,000	**Net Worth:** $2,167,000	**Debt/ Equity:** NA

Pacific West Bank OR

1800 Blankenship Rd., Ste. 150, West Linn, OR, 97068; **PH:** 1-503-905-2222; **Fax:** 1-503-905-2223; **http://** www.bankpacificwest.com

General - Incorporation................................... | **Stock**- Price on:12/24/2007 ....$10.05
Employees ....NA | Stock Exchange...OTC
Auditor ....NA | Ticker Symbol...PWBO
Stk Agt...NA | Outstanding Shares ....NA
Counsel...NA | E.P.S...NA
DUNS No. ....NA | Shareholders...NA

Business: The groups principle activity is to provide personal and business banking services. The groups personal banking services include checking accounts, Interest checking, Savings accounts, Money market accounts, Certificates of deposits, and Sweep accounts. The group operates from United States.

Primary SIC and add'l.: 6022

CIK No:

Officers: Douglas H. Leeding/Dir., CEO, Pres., Lara Dewey/Business Development Officer, Donald V. Burgard/COO, Alan R. Ludlow/Chief Lending Officer, Jeff Tainer/VP, Jennifer Harry/Business Lending Officer, Scott Gaerisch/Business Development Officer, Terisa Lundy/Operations Supervisor

Directors: Douglas H. Leeding/Dir., CEO, Pres., Susan Nozaki Lamont/Dir., Patrick McCloskey/Dir., Steven F. Miller/Dir., Steven W. Gray/Dir., Timothy L. Hysell/Dir., Edwin J. Kawasaki/Dir., Michael L. Kelley/Dir., Daniel M. Taylor/Dir., Craig S. Ostbo/Dir.

Pacifica Bancorp Inc

Skyline Tower 10900 Ne 4th St., Ste. 200, Bellevue, WA, 98004; **PH:** 1-425-637-1188

General - Incorporation............................WA | **Stock**- Price on:12/24/2007 ....$18.46
Employees ....1,318 | Stock Exchange...NA
Auditor ....Moss Adams LLP | Ticker Symbol..NA
Stk Agt...NA | Outstanding Shares 99,900,000
Counsel...NA | E.P.S...$1.09
DUNS No. ....NA | Shareholders...NA

Business: The group's principal activity is to provide a full range of commercial and mortgage lending services as well as banking services to individuals and small-to-medium sized businesses through its wholly-owned subsidiary, pacifica bank. It is also subject to the regulations of certain federal and state of Washington agencies and undergoes periodic examinations by those regulatory authorities. The primary market area from which we attract the majority of our customers is king county, Washington. The group operates in a highly competitive environment, competing for deposits, loans and other financial services with both banking institutions and non-financial institutions. Effective 31-Mar-2003, the operations of its wholly owned subsidiary pacifica mortgage company were ceased.

Primary SIC and add'l.: 6022 6712

CIK No: 0001133862

Subsidiaries: Federal Deposit Insurance Corporation, Pacifica Bank, Pacifica Mortgage Company

Financial Data: Fiscal Year End:12/31 **Latest Annual Data:** 12/31/2006

Year		Sales	Net Income
2006		$583,262,000	$100,877,000
2005		$432,537,000	$97,826,000
2004		$333,151,000	$85,603,000
Curr. Assets:	$580,222,000	**Curr. Liab.:** $8,280,099,000	**P/E Ratio:** 17.58
Plant, Equip.:	$115,610,000	**Total Liab.:** $9,560,343,000	**Indic. Yr. Divd.:** $0.120
Total Assets:	$10,346,414,000	**Net Worth:** $786,071,000	**Debt/ Equity:** 1.6071

Pacificap Entertainment Holdings Inc

9100 Wilshire Blvd, Ste. 242, Beverly Hills, CA, 90212; **PH:** 1-310-550-5800; **http://** www.pacificapentertainment.com

General - Incorporation ....NV | **Stock**- Price on:12/24/2007 ....NA
Employees ....2 | Stock Exchange...OTC
Auditor ... Russell Bedford Stefanou Mirchandani | Ticker Symbol...PFEH
Stk Agt....... Olde Monmouth Stk Trnsfer Co. Inc. | Outstanding Shares ....NA
Counsel...NA | E.P.S...NA
DUNS No. ....NA | Shareholders...NA

Business: The group's principal activity is to broadcast nostalgic sports film and ethnic broadcasting. The nostalgic sports division offers a programming format that features both college and professional sports, as well as various international sports competitions. These competitions emphasize on the more popular sports such as baseball, football, basketball, hockey and boxing. The new ethnic broadcasting division has been in development. As of 31-Dec-2003, the group owned approximately 5,000 hours of vintage sports film with negotiations in process to acquire in excess of an additional 2,500 hours of footage. On 19-Sep-2003 the group acquired pacificap entertainment inc. It is a development stage company.

Primary SIC and add'l.: 4841 7812 4833

CIK No: 0001129284

Officers: Mark Schaftlein/Dir, Pres., Principal Executive, Financial, Accounting Officer

Pacificare Health Systems Inc

5995 Plz. Dr., Cypress, CA, 90630; **PH:** 1-714-952-1121; **http://** www.phs.com

General - Incorporation ....DE | **Stock**- Price on:12/24/2007 ....$51.94
Employees ....58,000 | Stock Exchange...NA
Auditor .... Ernst & Young LLP | Ticker Symbol..NA
Stk Agt........... Wells Fargo Shareowner Services | Outstanding Shares 1,340,000,000
Counsel............................Cooley Godward LLP | E.P.S...$3.19
DUNS No. ....09-171-2414 | Shareholders...NA

Business: The group's principle activity is to offer managed care and other health insurance products to employer groups and medicare beneficiaries. The group's commercial and senior plans are designed to deliver quality health care and customer service to members cost-effectively. The programs offered by the group include health maintenance organizations, preferred provider organizations and medicare supplement products. The group also offers specialty managed care products and services that employees can purchase as a supplement to the basic commercial plans or as stand-alone products. These products include pharmacy benefit management, behavioral health services, group life and health insurance and dental and vision benefit plans. The group markets its products under the trademarks pacificare (R), securehorizons (R), prescription solutions(R) and quality index (r).

Primary SIC and add'l.: 6324

CIK No: 0001027974

Subsidiaries: American Medical Security Group, Inc., American Medical Security Life Insurance Co., Continental Plan Services, Inc., Covantage, LLC, FHP Reinsurance Limited, Nurse Healthline, Inc., PacifiCare Advantage, Inc., PacifiCare Asia Pacific Insurance Brokers, Inc., PacifiCare Behavioral Health NY IPA, Inc., PacifiCare Behavioral Health of California, Inc., PacifiCare Behavioral Health of New Jersey, Inc., PacifiCare Behavioral Health, Inc., PacifiCare Dental, PacifiCare Dental of Colorado, Inc., PacifiCare eHoldings, Inc. 36 Subsidiaries included in the Index

Officers: Howard Phanstiel/Chmn., CEO, Brad A. Bowlus/Pres., CEO - Health Plan Division, Jerome V. Vaccaro/CEO, Pres., Carol Black/Sr. VP - Human Resources, Jacqueline Kosecoff/Exec. VP - Specialty Companies, Gregory W. Scott/CFO, Exec. VP, Joseph Konowiecki/General Counsel, Exec. VP - Corporate Affairs, Kathy F. Feeny/Exec. VP - Secure Horizons, Sam Ho/Chief Medical Officer, Exec. VP, James Frey/Exec. VP - Major Accounting

Directors: Howard Phanstiel/Chmn., CEO

Financial Data: Fiscal Year End:12/31 **Latest Annual Data:** 12/31/2006

Year		Sales	Net Income
2006		$71,542,000,000	$4,159,000,000
2005		$45,365,000,000	$3,300,000,000
2004		$37,218,000,000	$2,587,000,000
Curr. Assets:	$16,044,000,000	**Curr. Liab.:** $18,497,000,000	**P/E Ratio:** 16.28
Plant, Equip.:	$1,894,000,000	**Total Liab.:** $27,510,000,000	**Indic. Yr. Divd.:** $0.030
Total Assets:	$48,320,000,000	**Net Worth:** $20,810,000,000	**Debt/ Equity:** 0.2597

Pacifichealth Laboratories Inc

100 Matawan Rd., Ste. 420, Matawan, NJ, 07747; **PH:** 1-732-739-2900; **Fax:** 1-732-739-4360; **http://** www.pacifichealthlabs.com; **Email:** information@pacifichealthlabs.com

General - Incorporation ....DE | **Stock**- Price on:12/24/2007 ....$2.1
Employees ....10 | Stock Exchange...OTC
Auditor .... Weiser LLP | Ticker Symbol...PHLI
Stk Agt.................................... StockTrans, Inc. | Outstanding Shares 13,300,000
Counsel....Eckert Seamans Cherin & Mellott LLC | E.P.S...-$0.09
DUNS No. ....93-750-2573 | Shareholders...NA

Business: The group's principle activities include developing and marketing products from natural ingredients for improving the health and other well being. The company has entered into an agreement with the institute of nutrition and food hygiene of the Chinese academy of preventive medicine for utilizing natural constituents exported from China. The main product endurox (R), is a dietary supplement which is capable of shifting the fuel source from carbohydrates to fat during workouts. Endurox excel, a

developed one of endurox, is targeted at athletes and other sports persons. Endurox(R) r4 (TM) is another product and it enhances performance and extend endurance. Prosol plus(tm) is another unique product developed by the company for treating mild to moderate depression. On 22-Dec-2003, the company acquired strong research corp. The group operates from United States.

Primary SIC and add'l.: 2833

CIK No: 0001000278

Officers: Robert Portman/Chmn., CEO, Pres., Chief Scientific Officer/$378,282.00, Stephen P. Kuchen/Dir., CFO, Treasurer, Sec., COO, Treasurer, Sec./$171,951.00, Jeffrey Goldberger/Contact - Investor Relations

Directors: Robert Portman/Chmn., CEO, Pres., Chief Scientific Officer, Adam Mizel/Dir., Marc Particelli/Dir., Stephen P. Kuchen/Dir., CFO, Treasurer, Sec., COO, Treasurer, Sec., Michael Cahr/Dir., David I. Portman/Dir.

Owners: Michael Cahr/1.80%, Adam Mizel/2.80%, Insiders/31.20%, Robert Portman/22.40%, Diker Management, LLC/6.80%, Stephen P. Kuchen/1.30%, Matthew Smith/7.90%, David I. Portman/3.90%, Marc Particelli

Financial Data: Fiscal Year End: 12/31   **Latest Annual Data:** 12/31/2006

Year	Sales		Net Income
2006	$6,210,000		$2,269,000
2005	$5,445,000		-$634,000
2004	$6,807,000		-$2,521,000
Curr. Assets:	$5,124,000	Curr. Liab.:	$1,249,000	
Plant, Equip.:	$74,000	Total Liab.:	$1,249,000	Indic. Yr. Divd.: NA
Total Assets:	$5,209,000	Net Worth:	$3,959,000	Debt/ Equity: NA

PacificNet Inc

655 N Central Ave., 17th Fl., Glendale, CA, 91203; **PH:** 1-888-250-6478; **Fax:** 1-646-349-1096; **http://** www.pacificnet.com; **Email:** investor@pacificnet.com

General - Incorporation	DE	Stock- Price on:12/24/2007	$5.14
Employees	1,501	Stock Exchange	NDQ
Auditor	Clancy & Co. PLLC	Ticker Symbol	PACT
Stk Agt	American Stock Transfer & Trust Co.	Outstanding Shares	11,810,000
Counsel	Mr. Mike Fei	E.P.S.	-$1.79
DUNS No.	66-222-6851	Shareholders	NA

Business: The group's principal activities are to provide system integration, network communications, customer relationship management and information technology solutions and telecommunications in Asia. The group develops a suite of proprietary e-commerce software applications. The group also provides telecommunication, perform voice and data network communications and value-added telecommunication products and services. Consulting services establishes online e-business environments to its customers. These services include the identification of specific content nature, user-friendly interface, overall Web theme and design, target user groups, Web advertising and integrated online solutions. The customers for the group's products and services are located in Hong Kong, mainland China and other regions of Asia. The group's major customers included sony, swire travel ltd.

Primary SIC and add'l.: 4899 7379 7372 7375

CIK No: 0000815017

Subsidiaries: Bank of China Group Life ssurance Company Ltd, Pacific Solutions Technology (Shenzhen) Co. Ltd., PacificNet Strategic Investment Holdings Limited

Officers: Desmond Ng Tai Wing/CEO - Pacificnet Solutions Limited, Tony Tong/Co - Founder, Chmn., CEO/$121,552.00, Victor Tong/Dir., Pres./$93,552.00, Star Mu/39/GM - Northern China, Carol Men-yee Chang/COO - Pacificnet Epro's, Joyce Mei-wei Poon/42/GM - Pacificnet Epro, Fei Sun/42/VP - Southern China, Jack Ou/41/Vice GM - Southern China, Mike Fei/40/Chief Legal Counsel - China Operations, Andrew Tong/Dir. - Business Development, William Yeung/Project Mgr., Wong Ka Cheong/CTO - Pacificnet Solutions Lim, Telly Wai-hon Wong/46/MD, a Co - Founder - Pacificnet Epro, Becky Zhao/Contact - Investor Relations, Daniel Lui/44/CFO *(19 Officers included in Index)*

Directors: Tony Tong/Co - Founder, Chmn., CEO, Michael Chun Ha/Dir., Ho-Man Poon/Dir., Jeremy Goodwin/Dir., Victor Tong/Dir., Pres., Peter Wang/52/Dir., Shaojian Wang/Dir., Telly Wai-hon Wong/46/MD, a Co - Founder - Pacificnet Epro, Tao Jin/Dir.

Owners: Victor Tong, Tony Tong/2.06%, Kin Shing Li/8.00%, Insiders/2.91%, ShaoJian Wang, Tao Jin, Sino Mart Management Ltd./12.88%

Financial Data: Fiscal Year End: 12/31   **Latest Annual Data:** 12/31/2006

Year	Sales		Net Income
2006	$42,738,000		-$20,093,000
2005	$44,341,000		$2,489,000
2004	$29,709,000		$774,000
Curr. Assets:	$17,041,000	Curr. Liab.:	$17,376,000	
Plant, Equip.:	$4,711,000	Total Liab.:	$22,949,000	Indic. Yr. Divd.: NA
Total Assets:	$36,926,000	Net Worth:	$13,977,000	Debt/ Equity: 0.3345

Pacificorp

825 NE Multnomah St., Portland, OR, 97232; **PH:** 1-503-813-5000; **http://** www.pacificorp.com

General - Incorporation	OR	Stock- Price on:12/24/2007	NA
Employees	9,793	Stock Exchange	AMEX
Auditor	Deloitte & Touche, LLP	Ticker Symbol	NA
Stk Agt	Mellon Investor Services LLC	Outstanding Shares	NA
Counsel	Holme Roberts & Owen LLP	E.P.S.	NA
DUNS No.	00-790-9013	Shareholders	NA

Business: The group's principle activity is to provide electricity generation which conducts a retail electric utility business through pacific tower and Utah tower. The group operates from United States.

Primary SIC and add'l.: 7389 4911

CIK No: 0000075594

Subsidiaries: Berkshire Hathaway Inc, Bridger Coal Company, Intermountain Geothermal Company, MidAmerican Energy Holdings Company, PacifiCorp Holdings, Inc, PPW Holdings LLC, Scottish Power plc

Officers: David J. Mendez/40/Sr. VP, CFO

Directors: Patrick R. Reiten/46/Dir.

Owners: Insiders, Insiders/1.01%, Gregory E. Abel/1.01%, Douglas L. Anderson, Patrick J. Goodman, Mark C. Moench

Packaging Corp of America

1900 W Field Ct., Lake Forest, IL, 60045; **PH:** 1-847-482-3000; **Fax:** 1-847-482-2122; **http://** www.packagingcorp.com

General - Incorporation	DE	Stock- Price on:12/24/2007	$25.76
Employees	8,300	Stock Exchange	NYSE
Auditor	Ernst & Young LLP	Ticker Symbol	PKG
Stk Agt	Computershare Trust Co	Outstanding Shares	105,240,000
Counsel	Cahill Gordon & Reindel LLP	E.P.S.	$1.52
DUNS No.	00-521-1768	Shareholders	NA

Business: The group's principle actiivty is to produce containerboard and corrugated products. The group operates from United States.

Primary SIC and add'l.: 2653 2631 2679

CIK No: 0000075677

Subsidiaries: Dixie Container Corporation, Packaging Corporation of Illinois, Packaging Credit Company, LLC, Packaging Receivables Company, LLC, PCA Hydro, Inc., PCA International Services, LLC, PCA International, Inc., PCAI de Mexico S. de R.L. de C.V.

Officers: Paul T. Stecko/Chmn., CEO/$4,661,358.00, Mark W. Kowlzan/Sr. VP - Containerboard/$1,255,740.00, Stephen T. Calhoun/VP - Human Resources, William J. Sweeney/Exec. VP - Corrugated Products/$1,605,544.00, Richard B. West/CFO, Sr. VP, Corp. Sec./$1,274,889.00, Thomas A. Hassfurther/Sr. VP - Sales, Marketing, Corrugated Products/$1,043,520.00

Directors: Paul T. Stecko/Chmn., CEO, Henry F. Frigon/73/Dir., Louis A. Holland/66/Dir., Samuel M. Mencoff/51/Dir., Roger B. Porter/61/Dir., Thomas S. Souleles/39/Dir., Rayford K. Williamson/82/Dir.

Owners: Stephen T. Calhoun, Henry F. Frigon, Goldman Sachs Asset Management, L.P./7.30%, Thomas S. Souleles/11.20%, Paul T. Stecko, Thomas A. Hassfurther, Mark W. Kowlzan, Rayford K. Williamson, Roger B. Porter, Insiders/12.80%, Richard B. West, PCA Holdings LLC/11.20%, Samuel M. Mencoff/11.40%, Capital Research and Management Company/11.90%, Louis A. Holland *(16 Owners included in Index)*

Financial Data: Fiscal Year End: 12/31   **Latest Annual Data:** 12/31/2006

Year	Sales		Net Income
2006	NA		NA
2005	NA		NA
2004	NA		NA
Curr. Assets:	$646,718,000	Curr. Liab.:	$388,338,000	P/E Ratio: 18.53
Plant, Equip.:	$1,252,291,000	Total Liab.:	$1,295,205,000	Indic. Yr. Divd.: $1.000
Total Assets:	$1,986,976,000	Net Worth:	$691,771,000	Debt/ Equity: NA

Packaging Dynamics Corp

3900 W 43rd St. , Chicago, IL, 60632; **PH:** 1-773-843-8000; **http://** www.pkdy

General - Incorporation	DE	Stock- Price on:12/24/2007	NA
Employees	NA	Stock Exchange	NA
Auditor	PricewaterhouseCoopers LLP	Ticker Symbol	NA
Stk Agt	EquiServe Trust Co N.A	Outstanding Shares	NA
Counsel	NA	E.P.S.	NA
DUNS No.	NA	Shareholders	NA

Business: The group's principal activity is to laminate and convert paper, film and foil into various flexible-packaging products. The end products include printed bags, fast food foil and paper sandwich wrap sheets, bag stock, can liner, label stock and insulation facing. These are marketed to the food service, food processing, bakery, supermarket and certain industrial markets. The operations of the group are carried on in the United States. In Oct 2003, the group announced the closing down of detroit paper mill and exited the specialty paper operation. In Dec 2003, the group acquired the net assets of the iuka lamination division of ormet corporation. On 14-Sep-2004, the group acquired papercon inc.

Primary SIC and add'l.: 2671 3497

CIK No: 0001171159

Subsidiaries: Bagcraft Packaging, LLC, GMG International, Inc., International Converter, Inc., IPMC Acquisition, LLC, Iuka, Incorporated, Packaging Dynamics Operating Company, Papercon Canada Holding Corp., Papercon U.S. Holding, Inc., Papercon, Inc., Wolf Packaging Inc.

Officers: Rick Cote/VP - Finance

Packeteer Inc

10201 N De Anza Blvd., Cupertino, CA, 95014; **PH:** 1-408-873-4400; **Fax:** 1-408-873-4410; **http://** www.packeteer.com

General - Incorporation	DE	Stock- Price on:12/24/2007	$9.53
Employees	421	Stock Exchange	NDQ
Auditor	KPMG LLP	Ticker Symbol	PKTR
Stk Agt	Computershare Investor Services LLC	Outstanding Shares	35,980,000
Counsel	Gray, Cary, Ware & Freidenrich	E.P.S.	-$0.36
DUNS No.	NA	Shareholders	NA

Business: The group's principal activity is to provide application traffic management systems. These systems enable the enterprises and service providers to measure, control, accelerate and validate the performance of networked applications and managed application services. Packetseeker system, packetshaper system, packetshaper xpress system, appcelera system, policycentertm software and reportcentertm software are few of the products offered by the group. These products are distributed through a worldwide network of resellers, distributors and systems integrators. The group has branch offices in Australia, caymans, Canada, Denmark, France, Germany, Hong Kong, Japan, Singapore, Spain, South Korea, the Netherlands and the United Kingdom.

Primary SIC and add'l.: 7373 7372

CIK No: 0001011344

Subsidiaries: Packeteer (Thailand) Ltd., Packeteer Aps, Packeteer Asia Pacific Limited, Packeteer Australia Pty Limited, Packeteer Beijing, Packeteer Caymans, Packeteer Europe B.V., Packeteer GmbH, Packeteer Holdings, Inc., Packeteer Iberica, Packeteer India, Packeteer International Inc., Packeteer Italy s.r.l., Packeteer Korea, Packeteer Malaysia 21 Subsidiaries included in the Index

Officers: Dave Cote/Dir., CEO, Pres./$1,611,257.00, Nelu Mihai/VP - Engineering/$770,757.00, Manuel R. Freitas/VP - Operations, Customer Support/$739,421.00, David C. Yntema/CFO, Sec./$787,493.00, Greg Pappas/VP - Human Resources, Raymond Smets/VP - Worldwide Sales, Marketing, Alan Menezes/48/VP - Marketing

Directors: Dave Cote/Dir., CEO, Pres., Steven J. Campbell/Chmn., Craig W. Elliott/Dir., Joseph A. Graziano/Dir., Bernard F. Mathaisel/Dir., William L. Krause/Dir., Gregory E. Myers/Dir., Peter Van Camp/Dir.

Owners: FMR Corp./9.70%, Royce& Associates, LLC/7.20%, Arturo Czares, Bernard F. Mathaisel, Steven J. Campbell/1.20%, T. Rowe Price Associates, Inc/6.50%, Manuel R. Freitas, Barclays Global Investors, NA/5.90%, Dave Ct/1.70%, Craig W. Elliott/1.40%, Nelu Mihai, David C. Yntema, Gregory E. Myers, William L. Krause, Joseph A. Graziano (17 Owners included in Index)

Financial Data: Fiscal Year End:12/31   **Latest Annual Data:** 12/31/2006

Year	Sales	Net Income
2006	$145,123,000	$4,904,000
2005	$112,941,000	$19,158,000
2004	$92,437,000	$14,534,000

Curr. Assets:	$104,486,000	Curr. Liab.:	$52,107,000		
Plant, Equip.:	$3,968,000	Total Liab.:	$57,459,000	Indic. Yr. Divd.:	NA
Total Assets:	$216,968,000	Net Worth:	$159,509,000	Debt/ Equity:	NA

Packetport Com Inc

587 Connecticut Ave., Norwalk, CT, 06854; *PH:* 1-203-831-2214; *http://* www.packetport.com

General - Incorporation	NV	Stock - Price on:12/24/2007	NA
Employees	3	Stock Exchange	OTC
Auditor	Demetrius & Co LLC	Ticker Symbol	PKPT
Stk Agt	American Stock Transfer & Trust Co.	Outstanding Shares	NA
Counsel	NA	E.P.S	-$0.024
DUNS No.	12-082-4768	Shareholders	NA

Business: The group's principal activities are to manufacture and market computer peripheral hardware and software products for ip telephony solutions and services that are used for telephony applications for the Internet, telecommunications and other data networking industries. The group provides commercialized global hosted telephony solutions using the retained platform licenses for the voicepak soft central office (s.c.o.), media gateway control protocol (mgcp), service access point (sap) and service access transfer point (satp). The products of the group are voicepak gateway, voicepak database, voicepak call agent, voicepak integrated access device (iad), and the voicepak usb phone.

Primary SIC and add'l.: 7378 7372 3661 3577

CIK No: 0000833203

Owners: Insiders/34.30%, Gustave T. Dotoli/5.30%, Ronald A. Durando/27.90%, Edward J. Suozzo/1.10%

Financial Data: Fiscal Year End:01/31   **Latest Annual Data:** 01/31/2007

Year	Sales	Net Income
2007	NA	-$505,000
2006	NA	-$581,000
2005	$27,000	-$786,000

Curr. Assets:	$0	Curr. Liab.:	$5,065,000		
Plant, Equip.:	NA	Total Liab.:	$5,065,000	Indic. Yr. Divd.:	NA
Total Assets:	$0	Net Worth:	-$5,064,000	Debt/ Equity:	NA

Pactiv Corp

1900 W Field Ct., Lake Forest, IL, 60045; *PH:* 1-847-482-2000; *Fax:* 1-770-232-9864; *http://* www.pactiv.com

General - Incorporation	DE	Stock - Price on:12/24/2007	$32.71
Employees	11,000	Stock Exchange	NYSE
Auditor	Ernst & Young LLP	Ticker Symbol	PTV
Stk Agt	National City Bank	Outstanding Shares	130,380,000
Counsel	NA	E.P.S	NA
DUNS No.	NA	Shareholders	NA

Business: The groups principle activity is to produce consumer and food packaging products. The groups products include disposable plastic, foam, molded-fiber, pressed-paperboard and aluminum-packaging products. Customers served by the group include foodservice distributors, restaurants, food processors and grocery chains. In the year 2007, Pactiv acquired Prairie Packaging, Inc. The group operates from United States.

Primary SIC and add'l.: 2671 3089 2652 3086 2657

CIK No: 0001089976

Subsidiaries: 798795 Ontario Limited, Alpha Products (Bristol) Limited, Baldwin Packaging Limited, Brucefield Plastics Limited, Central de Bolsas, Coast-Packaging Company, Coastal Packaging Ltd., Counce Finance Corporation, E-Z Por Corporation , EKCO Products, Inc., Ha'Lakoach Ha'Neeman H' Sheeshim Ou'Shenayim Ltd, J & W Baldwin (Holdings) Ltd., J&W Baldwin (Manchester) Limited, Jiffy Rugated Products Limited, Montana Industries, Inc. 70 Subsidiaries included in the Index

Officers: Richard L. Wambold/Chmn., CEO/$7,910,548.00, Peter J. Lazaredes/Exec. VP, GM/$3,237,115.00, James V. Faulkner/VP, General Counsel/$2,570,828.00, Mary R. Henderson/Dir. - Food Industry Consultant, Andrew A. Campbell/CFO, Sr. VP/$2,869,491.00, John N. Schwab/Sr. VP, GM/$2,510,530.00, Joseph E. Doyle/VP, General Counsel, Sec., Henry M. Wells/63/VP, Chief Human Resources Officer

Directors: Richard L. Wambold/Chmn., CEO, Dane K. Brooksher/Dir., Norman H. Wesley/Dir., Roger B. Porter/Dir., Robert J. Darnall/Dir., Larry D. Brady/Dir., Thomas N. Linebarger/Dir.

Owners: Roger B. Porter, Andrew A. Campbell, Mary R. Henderson, Richard L. Wambold/1.51%, Insiders/2.95%, James V. Faulkner, Larry D. Brady, Dane K. Brooksher, Robert J. Darnall, Peter J. Lazaredes, Norman H. Wesley, John N. Schwab, Thomas N. Linebarger

Financial Data: Fiscal Year End:12/31   **Latest Annual Data:** 12/31/2006

Year	Sales	Net Income
2006	$2,917,000,000	$274,000,000
2005	$2,756,000,000	$54,000,000
2004	$3,382,000,000	$155,000,000

Curr. Assets:	NA	Curr. Liab.:	NA	P/E Ratio:	16.03
Plant, Equip.:	NA	Total Liab.:	NA	Indic. Yr. Divd.:	NA
Total Assets:	NA	Net Worth:	NA	Debt/ Equity:	0.9266

Paid Inc

236 Huntington Ave., 5th Fl., Boston, MA, 02115; *PH:* 1-617-861-6050; *Fax:* 1-508-797-5398; *http://* www.paid,com

General - Incorporation	DE	Stock - Price on:12/24/2007	$0.435
Employees	16	Stock Exchange	OTC
Auditor	Carlin, Charron & Rosen LLP	Ticker Symbol	PAYD
Stk Agt	Olde Monmouth Stk Trnsfer Co. Inc.	Outstanding Shares	225,660,000
Counsel	Bowditch & Dewey LLP	E.P.S	-$0.01
DUNS No.	NA	Shareholders	NA

Business: The group's principal activities are to provide services related to the auction industry, including management, Website hosting, consignment and merchandising services. It provides management tools for online retailers. This system provides the fundamentals structure for our celebrity Web hosting and development services, and for individuals seeking a professional and interactive presence on the Internet. The collectible industry includes items that have either economic or sentimental value, such as antiques, sports and entertainment memorabilia, stamps, coins, figurines, dolls, collector plates, plush and die cast toys, cottage and village reproductions and other decorative or limited edition items that are intended for collecting and other memorabilia. The group operates an online auction site that provides a full range of services to sellers and buyers. It also designs, hosts and maintains client websites primarily in the sports and collectibles industry.

Primary SIC and add'l.: 7372 7375

CIK No: 0001017655

Subsidiaries: Rotman Collectibles, Inc.

Officers: Gregory Rotman/Dir., CEO, Pres., Richard Rotman/Dir., CFO, VP, Treasurer, Sec., Julie Shepherd/Contact - Investor Relations, Media, Kristen Kuliga/New Business Development, Kerri Kennedy/Client Relations, Keith Garde/Pres., Andy Martel/Client Mgr.

Directors: Andrew Pilaro/38/Dir.

Owners: Andrew Pilaro, Gregory Rotman/7.21%, Richard Rotman/7.94%, Insiders/15.99%, Augustine Fund, L.P./10.06%

Financial Data: Fiscal Year End:12/31   **Latest Annual Data:** 12/31/2006

Year	Sales	Net Income
2006	$8,049,000	-$1,704,000
2005	$4,920,000	-$3,101,000
2004	$1,853,000	-$4,080,000

Curr. Assets:	$1,477,000	Curr. Liab.:	$1,409,000		
Plant, Equip.:	$192,000	Total Liab.:	$1,409,000	Indic. Yr. Divd.:	NA
Total Assets:	$1,681,000	Net Worth:	$271,000	Debt/ Equity:	NA

Pain Therapeutics Inc

2211 Bridgepointe Pkwy., Ste. 500, San Mateo, CA, 94404; *PH:* 1-650-624-8200; *Fax:* 1-650-624-8222; *http://* www.paintrials.com

General - Incorporation	DE	Stock - Price on:12/24/2007	$8.32
Employees	41	Stock Exchange	NDQ
Auditor	Ernst & Young LLP	Ticker Symbol	PTIE
Stk Agt	Mellon Investor Services LLC	Outstanding Shares	44,150,000
Counsel	Wilson Sonsini Goodrich & Rosati	E.P.S	$0.30
DUNS No.	NA	Shareholders	NA

Business: The group's principle activity is to develop novel drugs. The drugs provide pain relief and reduced tolerance and physical dependence or addiction potential compared to existing opioid painkillers. The drugs combine very low doses of opioid antagonists with standard opioid painkillers. The company has three proprietary drug candidates in clinical development: oxytrextm, remoxytm and pti-901. Oxytrex and pti-901 are in phase iii clinical trials and remoxy is in phase i clinical trials in the United Kingdom. These drugs are awaiting approval from the food and drug administration. The company is the development stage. The group operates from United States.

Primary SIC and add'l.: 2834 8731

CIK No: 0001069530

Officers: Remi Barbier/Chmn., CEO, Pres./$1,125,884.00, Peter S. Roddy/CFO/$485,216.00, Peter Butera/VP - Clinical Operations, Grant L. Schoenhard/Chief Scientific Officer/$458,514.00, Michael Zamloot/VP - Technical Operations, Nadav Friedmann/Dir., Chief Medical, Operating Officer/$894,524.00, Michael Marsman/VP - Regulatory Affairs, Roger Fu/VP - Pharmaceutical Development

Directors: Remi Barbier/Chmn., CEO, Pres., Sanford Robertson/Dir., Robert Gussin/Dir., Nadav Friedmann/Dir., Chief Medical, Operating Officer, Vernon R. Loucks/Dir., Michael O'Donnell/Dir., Leslie Z. Benet/Member - Scientific Medical Advisory Board, Sidney L. Goldfischer/Member - Scientific Medical Advisory Board, Margareta Hammarlund-Udenaes/Member - Scientific Medical Advisory Board, Mary Jeanne Kreek/Member - Scientific Medical Advisory Board, Fredrick L. Minn/Member - Scientific Medical Advisory Board, Robert B. Raffa/Member - Scientific Medical Advisory Board, Ke-Fei Shen/Member - Scientific Medical Advisory Board, Eric J. Simon/Member - Scientific Medical Advisory Board, Patrick Scannon/Member - Scientific Medical Advisory Board (20 Directors included in Index)

Owners: Vernon R. Loucks, Insiders/24.30%, Robert Z. Gussin, Remi Barbier/19.10%, Nadav Friedmann, Eastbourne Capital/18.50%, Sanford R. Robertson, Peter S. Roddy, Michael J. ODonnell, Grant L. Schoenhard

Financial Data: Fiscal Year End:12/31   **Latest Annual Data:** 12/31/2006

Year	Sales	Net Income
2006	$53,918,000	$6,188,000
2005	$5,080,000	-$30,670,000
2004	NA	-$37,776,000

Curr. Assets:	$207,114,000	Curr. Liab.:	$36,654,000		
Plant, Equip.:	$1,267,000	Total Liab.:	$130,541,000	Indic. Yr. Divd.:	NA
Total Assets:	$208,456,000	Net Worth:	$77,915,000	Debt/ Equity:	NA

Paincare Holdings Inc

1030 N Orange Ave., Ste. 105, Orlando, FL, 32801; *PH:* 1-407-367-0944; *Fax:* 1-407-367-0950; *http://* www.paincareholdings.com

General - Incorporation	FL	Stock - Price on:12/24/2007	$0.36
Employees	481	Stock Exchange	AMEX
Auditor	Beemer, Kuehnhackl & Heidbrink PA	Ticker Symbol	PRZ
Stk Agt	American Stock Transfer & Trust Co.	Outstanding Shares	67,470,000
Counsel	NA	E.P.S	-$1.837
DUNS No.	14-854-4992	Shareholders	NA

Business: The group's principal activity is to provide healthcare services for patients seeking pain relief. The services include: pain management: includes treatment such as medication, exercise, physiotherapy, chiropractic manipulation and surgery. Minimally invasive spine surgery: a specialized surgical technique that allows physicians to provide advanced treatment of back and neck pain in an

outpatient environment. Orthopedic rehabilitation: a program that advances functional restoration of the musculoskeletal system utilizing state of the art computerized medxtmmedical exercise machines. In 2003, the group acquired medical rehabilitation specialists ii p a, associated physician's group, spine & pain center PC, health care center of tampa inc., bone & joint surgical clinic and non-medical assets of dr. Kenneth m. Alo. In 2004, it group acquired the care clinics pa and the non-medical assets of denver pain management PC and Georgia pain physicians PC.

Primary SIC and add'l.: 8099 8999

CIK No: 0001003472

Subsidiaries: Advanced Orthopaedics of South Florida II, Inc., Benjamin Zolper, M.D., Inc., Caperian, Inc., Georgia Surgical Centers, Inc., Health Care Center of Tampa, Inc., Medical Rehabilitation Specialists II, Inc., Pain and Rehabilitation Network, Inc., PainCare Acquisition Company IX, Inc., PainCare Acquisition Company V, Inc., PainCare Acquisition Company VI, Inc., PainCare Acquisition Company VIII, Inc. d/b/a Bone and Joint Surgical Clinic, PainCare Acquisition Company X, Inc., PainCare Acquisition Company XI, Inc., PainCare Acquisition Company XII, Inc., PainCare Acquisition Company XIII, Inc. 45 Subsidiaries included in the Index

Officers: Randy Lubinsky/Dir., CEO, Ronald L. Riewold/Dir., Pres., Mark Szporka/Dir., CFO

Directors: Randy Lubinsky/Dir., CEO, Merrill Reuter/Chmn., Jay L. Rosen/Dir., Ronald L. Riewold/Dir., Pres., Mark Szporka/Dir., CFO, Aldo F. Berti/Dir., Robert Fusco/Dir., Arthur Hudson/Dir., Thomas J. Crane/Dir.

Owners: Ronald Riewold/3.40%, Merrill Reuter/2.80%, Arthur J. Hudson, Insiders/16.30%, Randy Lubinsky/4.80%, Jay Rosen, Mark Szporka/4.70%, Thomas J. Crane, Aldo F. Berti, Robert Fusco

Financial Data: *Fiscal Year End:*12/31 *Latest Annual Data:* 12/31/2006

Year		Sales		Net Income	
2006		$63,729,000		-$26,483,000	
2005		$68,664,000		-$5,339,000	
2004		$37,962,000		$5,730,000	
Curr. Assets:	$31,119,000	**Curr. Liab.:**	$59,598,000		
Plant, Equip.:	$10,041,000	**Total Liab.:**	$63,835,000	**Indic. Yr. Divd.:**	NA
Total Assets:	$163,378,000	**Net Worth:**	$97,351,000	**Debt/ Equity:**	0.2859

Paivis Corp

Formerly: APO Health

3475 Lenox Rd., Ste. 400, Atlanta, GA, 30326; ***PH:*** 1-404-601-2885; ***http://*** www.apohealth.com

General - Incorporation	NV	**Stock**- Price on:12/24/2007	$0.34
Employees	9	Stock Exchange	NA
Auditor	Linder & Linder	Ticker Symbol	NA
Stk Agt	Executive Registrar & Transfer, Inc.	Outstanding Shares	30,660,000
Counsel	NA	E.P.S.	-$0.12
DUNS No.	NA	Shareholders	NA

Business: The group's principle activities are to distribute and supply disposable medical products to dental, medical and veterinary professionals. It distributes approximately 5,000 different products. Its main products include protective garments like the isolation gowns, facemasks and gauze, disposable items like latex gloves, needles, syringes, health and beauty aids and pharmaceuticals. The group's products are sold directly by its employees through mail order and by independent sales representatives.

Primary SIC and add'l.: 3843 5047 3841

CIK No: 0001076607

Subsidiaries: APO Health, Inc., Universal Medical Distributors, Inc.

Officers: Edwin Kwong/Interim Pres., Interim CEO, Gregory L. Bauer/CEO, Acting Principal Accounting Officer

Directors: Guriqbal Randhawa/34/Dir.

Owners: Guriqbal Randhawa/16.37%, Insiders/19.64%, Gregory L. Bauer/3.27%

Financial Data: *Fiscal Year End:*09/30 *Latest Annual Data:* 9/30/2006

Year		Sales		Net Income	
2006		$6,905,000		-$4,085,000	
2005		$15,014,000		-$664,000	
2004		$35,919,000		-$1,049,000	
Curr. Assets:	$531,000	**Curr. Liab.:**	$7,615,000		
Plant, Equip.:	$101,000	**Total Liab.:**	$7,615,000	**Indic. Yr. Divd.:**	NA
Total Assets:	$6,875,000	**Net Worth:**	-$740,000	**Debt/ Equity:**	NA

Palatin Technologies Inc

4-C Cedar Brook Dr., Cedar Brook Corporate Ctr., Cranbury, NJ, 08512; ***PH:*** 1-609-495-2200; ***Fax:*** 1-609-495-2201; ***http://*** www.palatin.com; ***Email:*** info@palatin.com

General - Incorporation	DE	**Stock**- Price on:12/24/2007	$1.93
Employees	85	Stock Exchange	AMEX
Auditor	KPMG LLP	Ticker Symbol	PTN
Stk Agt	American Stock Transfer & Trust Co.	Outstanding Shares	84,930,000
Counsel	NA	E.P.S.	-$0.25
DUNS No.	82-743-4705	Shareholders	NA

Business: The group's principal activity is to develop and commercialize products and technologies for diagnostic imaging and ethical drug development. The group uses peptide, monoclonal antibody and radiopharmaceutical technologies for imaging, diagnosing and treating infections. The main products of the group are metal ion-induced distinctive array of structures (midas), pt-141 and leutech. Midas is useful for developing drugs to treat diseases or for diagnostic imaging. Pt-141 is a peptide hormone product for the treatment of sexual dysfunction. Leutech, a diagnostic imaging product is used to image and locate the site of infection or inflammation within the body. The group operates solely in the domestic market.

Primary SIC and add'l.: 8071 3841

CIK No: 0000911216

Subsidiaries: RhoMed Incorporated

Officers: Carl Spana/Dir., CEO, Pres., Trevor Hallam/Exec. VP - Research, Development, Shubh Sharma/VP, Chief Scientific Officer, Stephen T. Wills/CFO, Exec. VP - Operations, Sec., Treasurer

Directors: Carl Spana/Dir., CEO, Pres., John K.A. Prendergast/Chmn., Zola P. Horovitz/Dir., Stanley J. Hull/Dir., Robert K. Deveer/Dir., Perry Molinoff/Dir., Errol Desouza/Dir., Robert Taber/Dir., Robert A. Kloner/Member - Scientific Advisory Board, Harin Padma-Nathan/Member - Scientific Advisory Board, Michael A. Perelman/Member - Scientific Advisory Board, Christopher Steidle/Member - Scientific Advisory Board, Jay M. Young/Member - Scientific Advisory Board

Owners: Jonathan E. Rothschild/10.00%, Laura Gold Galleries Ltd. Profit Sharing Trust/5.00%, Steven N. Ostrovsky/10.00%, Perry B. Molinoff, Stanley J. Hull, Thomas P. and Mary E. Heiser, JTWROS/5.00%, King Pharmaceuticals, Inc./7.40%, Arthur J. Nagle/5.00%, Insiders/4.10%, Shubh D. Sharma, Zola P. Horovitz, Michael J. Wrubel/5.00%, 103336 Canada Inc./6.00%, Myron M. Teitelbaum/5.00%, Stephen T. Wills *(25 Owners included in Index)*

Financial Data: *Fiscal Year End:*06/30 *Latest Annual Data:* 6/30/2006

Year		Sales		Net Income	
2006		$19,749,000		-$28,959,000	
2005		$17,957,000		-$14,358,000	
2004		$2,315,000		-$26,318,000	
Curr. Assets:	$32,187,000	**Curr. Liab.:**	$12,445,000		
Plant, Equip.:	$6,348,000	**Total Liab.:**	$21,747,000	**Indic. Yr. Divd.:**	NA
Total Assets:	$40,047,000	**Net Worth:**	$18,300,000	**Debt/ Equity:**	0.0139

Paligent Inc

424 W 33rd St., Ste. 650, New York, NY, 10001; ***PH:*** 1-212-356-4000

General - Incorporation	DE	**Stock**- Price on:12/24/2007	$1
Employees	28	Stock Exchange	OTC
Auditor	Rothstein, Kass & Co, P.C	Ticker Symbol	IFLI
Stk Agt	American Stock Transfer & Trust Co.	Outstanding Shares	53,500,000
Counsel	NA	E.P.S.	-$0.55
DUNS No.	18-472-6115	Shareholders	NA

Business: The group currently has no business and evaluates various strategic alternatives, including acquisitions of new operating businesses and technologies as well as potential merger opportunities. The principal activity is to develop and commercialize novel drugs based on biotechnological research.

Primary SIC and add'l.: 2834 9999

CIK No: 0000885475

Subsidiaries: Pacific Pharmaceuticals, Inc, Procept, Inc

Officers: Gareb Shamus/Chmn., CEO/$60,000.00, Salvatore A. Bucci/53/Dir., CFO, Exec. VP, Treasurer/$188,301.00, Ron Kruck/IFL Ring Reporter, Play By Play, Greg Smith/Sr. Staff Tour Accountant - IFL Corp, Charlene Tanwing/Executive Assist. - IFL Corp, Lisa Faircloth/Dir. - Events, IFL Corp, Drew Archer/Operations, Operations, Las Vegas, IFL Corp, Jan Hubbard/Event Coordinator, Operations, Las Vegas, IFL Corp, Vickie Hayes/Travel Coordinator, Operations, Las Vegas, IFL Corp, Jay Zdon/Production Coordinator, Operations, Las Vegas, IFL Corp, Mike Martin/Dir. - Production Operations, Operations, New York, IFL Corp, Joe Favorito/Sr. VP - Communications, Marketing, Public Relations, New York, IFL Corp, Marie Camaya/Dir. - Marketing, Marketing, Public Relations, New York, IFL Corp, Stan Gloss/Controller - IFL Corp, Michael Keefe/Pres. - Legal, Business Affairs, IFL Corp *(35 Officers included in Index)*

Directors: Gareb Shamus/Chmn., CEO, Kevin Waldman/37/Dir., Salvatore A. Bucci/53/Dir., CFO, Exec. VP, Treasurer, Jeffrey M. Jagid/39/Dir., Kurt Otto/Founder - IFL Corp

Owners: Richard J. Kurtz/7.00%, Kurt Otto/11.70%, Paul Tudor Jones,II, James J. Pallotta and related entities/6.10%, Atlas Master Fund, Ltd./8.70%, Gareb Shamus/10.00%, Ronald Heller and related entities/5.60%, Midsummer Investment Ltd./7.40%, Michael C. Keefe, Nadir Tavakoli and related entities/10.50%, SOF Investments, L.P./7.20%, Insiders/21.90%, Enable Capital Management and related entities/6.50%

Financial Data: *Fiscal Year End:*12/31 *Latest Annual Data:* 12/31/2006

Year		Sales		Net Income	
2006		$2,365,000		-$9,603,000	
2005		NA		$40,000	
Curr. Assets:	$166,000	**Curr. Liab.:**	$353,000		
Plant, Equip.:	$0	**Total Liab.:**	$353,000	**Indic. Yr. Divd.:**	NA
Total Assets:	$166,000	**Net Worth:**	-$187,000	**Debt/ Equity:**	NA

Pall Corp

2200 Nern Blvd., East Hills, NY, 11548; ***PH:*** 1-516-484-5400; ***Fax:*** 1-516-484-5228; ***http://*** www.pall.com

General - Incorporation	NY	**Stock**- Price on:12/24/2007	$46.69
Employees	10,828	Stock Exchange	NYSE
Auditor	KPMG LLP	Ticker Symbol	PLL
Stk Agt	Computershare Trust Co	Outstanding Shares	122,600,000
Counsel	NA	E.P.S.	$1.68
DUNS No.	00-205-4419	Shareholders	NA

Business: The groups principle activity is to provide integrated filtration, separation and purification technologies for a variety of liquids and gases. The group operates through two business groups namely life sciences and industrial. The group operates from United States.

Primary SIC and add'l.: 3842 3569 3599 3841 3714

CIK No: 0000075829

Subsidiaries: Argentaurum A.G., Gelman Ireland Ltd., Gelman Sciences, Inc., Medsep Corporation, Nihon Pall Ltd., Pall (Canada) Limited, Pall (Schweiz) A.G., Pall - PASS US, Inc., Pall Acquisition LLC, Pall Aeropower Corporation, Pall Asia International Ltd., Pall Austria Filter GmbH, Pall Biomedical, Inc., Pall Corporation Filtration and Separations (Thailand) Ltd., Pall Deutschland Beteiligungs GmbH 35 Subsidiaries included in the Index

Officers: Eric Krasnoff/Chmn., CEO, Leonard Bensch/VP, Roberto Perez/Pres. - Life Sciences, Kenneth Frank/Pres. - Pall Biopharmaceuticals Global, Mary Ann Bartlett/Sr. VP, General Counsel, Corp. Sec., Patricia Iannucci/VP - Investor Relations, Communications, Lisa McDermott/CFO, Treasurer, Marcia Katz/Dir. - Public Relations, Donald Stevens/COO, Pres. - Industrial

Directors: Eric Krasnoff/Chmn., CEO, James D. Watson/Dir., Daniel J. Carroll/Dir., John H. Haskell/76/Dir., Edward Travaglianti/Dir., Edward L. Snyder/Dir., Heywood Shelley/Dir., Katharine L. Plourde/Dir., Ulric S. Haynes/Dir., Dennis N. Longstreet/Dir., Edwin W. Martin/Dir., Cheryl W. Grise/Dir.

Owners: Donald Stevens, CAM North America, LLC/10.20%, Heywood Shelley, Katharine L. Plourde, Andrew Denver, Marcus Wilson, Daniel J. Carroll, James D. Watson, Eric Krasnoff/0.40%, Insiders/0.80%, Roberto Perez, Ulric S. Haynes, Edwin W. Martin, PRIMECAP Management Company/7.90%, Edward Travaglianti *(19 Owners included in Index)*

Financial Data: *Fiscal Year End:*07/31 *Latest Annual Data:* 04/30/2007

Year	Sales	Net Income
2007	$559,347,000	$67,074,000
2006	$2,016,830,000	$145,493,000
2005	$1,902,284,000	$140,816,000

Curr. Assets:	$1,376,981,000	**Curr. Liab.:**	$530,816,000	**P/E Ratio:**	27.79
Plant, Equip.:	$620,979,000	**Total Liab.:**	$1,374,162,000	**Indic. Yr. Divd.:**	$0.480
Total Assets:	$2,552,858,000	**Net Worth:**	$1,178,696,000	**Debt/ Equity:**	NA

Palm Harbor Homes Inc

15303 Dallas Pkwy., Ste. 800, Addison, TX, 75001; ***PH:*** 1-972-991-2422; ***Fax:*** 1-972-991-5949; ***http://*** www.palmharbor.com; ***Email:*** email@palmharbor.com

General - Incorporation.....FL
Employees.....3,800
Auditor.....Ernst & Young LLP
Stk Agt.....American Stock Transfer & Trust Co.
Counsel.....Locke Liddell & Sapp LLP
DUNS No.....08-761-4780

Stock- Price on:12/24/2007.....$14.72
Stock Exchange.....NDQ
Ticker Symbol.....PHHM
Outstanding Shares.....22,850,000
E.P.S.....-$0.05
Shareholders.....NA

Business: The group's principal activity is to manufacture and market multi-section homes. The operations are vertically integrated and include manufacturing, housing, modular housing, financing and insurance. The group manufactures single and multi-section homes under various brand names including palm harbor, masterpiece, keystone, countryplace, river bend and windsor homes(tm). At 26-Mar-2004, the group 19 manufacturing facilities in nine states that sell homes in 29 states through 149 of our company-owned retail superstores and builder locations and approximately 275 independent retail dealers, builders and developers. The group through its subsidiary, countryplace mortgage, ltd, offers installment financing to purchasers of manufactured homes sold by company-owned retail superstores. Property and casualty insurance are also provided by the group for owners of manufactured homes through its subsidiary, standard casualty company.

Primary SIC and add'l.: 6513 1521 1522 6162

CIK No: 0000923473

Subsidiaries: Better Homes Systems, Inc., CountryPlace Acceptance Corporation, CountryPlace Acceptance GP, LLC, CountryPlace Acceptance LP, LLC, CountryPlace Funding, Inc., CountryPlace Mortgage, Ltd., Magic Living, Inc., Nationwide Homes, Incorporated, Palm Harbor Albemarle, LLC, Palm Harbor G.P., Inc., Palm Harbor GenPar, LLC, Palm Harbor Holding, Inc., Palm Harbor Homes I, L.P., Palm Harbor Insurance Agency of Texas, Inc., Palm Harbor Manufacturing, L.P. 19 Subsidiaries included in the Index

Officers: Larry Keener/Chmn., CEO, Pres./$512,482.00, Kelly Tacke/CFO, Exec. VP, Sec./$349,169.00

Directors: Larry Keener/Chmn., CEO, Pres., Lee Posey/Chmn. Emeritus, Walter Rosenberg/Dir., Frederick Meyer/Dir., Jerry D. Mallonee/Dir., John Wilson/Dir., William Thomas/Dir., Gary A. Shilling/Dir., Elysia Holt Ragusa/Dir., Christopher W. Wellborn/Dir., William M. Ashbaugh/53/Dir.

Owners: Frederick R. Meyer, Walter D. Rosenberg, Royce& Associates, LLC/6.61%, Larry H. Keener/1.90%, John H. Wilson, Lee Posey/17.50%, William R. Thomas/1.00%, Capital Southwest Corporation and Capital Southwest Venture Corporation/34.40%, Insiders/22.37%, Jerry D. Mallonee, Gary A. Shilling, Christopher W. Wellborn, Kelly Tacke

Financial Data: *Fiscal Year End:*03/31 *Latest Annual Data:* 3/30/2007

Year	Sales	Net Income
2007	$661,247,000	-$11,565,000
2006	$710,635,000	$11,114,000
2005	$610,538,000	-$3,823,000

Curr. Assets:	$296,083,000	**Curr. Liab.:**	$391,027,000		
Plant, Equip.:	$65,512,000	**Total Liab.:**	$391,027,000	**Indic. Yr. Divd.:**	NA
Total Assets:	$654,051,000	**Net Worth:**	$263,024,000	**Debt/ Equity:**	1.1252

Palm Inc

950 W Maude Ave., Sunnyvale, CA, 94085; ***PH:*** 1-408-617-7000; ***Fax:*** 1-408-617-0100; ***http://*** www.palm.com

General - Incorporation.....DE
Employees.....1,103
Auditor.....Deloitte & Touche LLP
Stk Agt.....EquiServe Trust Co N.A
Counsel.....Wilson Sonsini Goodrich & Rosati
DUNS No.....NA

Stock- Price on:12/24/2007.....$16.77
Stock Exchange.....NDQ
Ticker Symbol.....PALM
Outstanding Shares.....103,450,000
E.P.S.....$0.16
Shareholders.....NA

Business: The groups principle activity is to manufacture mobile products. The groups products include smartphones, handhelds and accessories. The group operates from United States.

Primary SIC and add'l.: 3571 3577 7372

CIK No: 0001100389

Subsidiaries: Handspring Corporation, Handspring Facility Company LLC, Handspring International Ltd., Palm Asia Pacific Limited, Palm Australasia Pty Limited, Palm Benelux B.V., Palm Canada Inc., Palm Chile Limitada, Palm Colombia Limitada, Palm Comrcio de Aparelhos Eletrnicos Ltda., Palm Computing Mexico S.A. de C.V., Palm Europe Limited, Palm France, Palm Geneva SARL, Palm Germany GmbH 23 Subsidiaries included in the Index

Officers: Ed Colligan/CEO, Pres., Andrew J. Brown/48/CFO, Mark Bercow/Sr. VP - Business Development, Mary E. Doyle/Sr. VP, General Counsel, Rena Lane/Sr. VP - Human Resources, John Hartnett/Sr. VP - Global Markets, Michael R. Farese/Sr. VP - Engineering, Ron Rhodes/Sr. VP - Global Operations, Brodie Keast/Sr. VP - Marketing

Directors: Eric A. Benhamou/Chmn., Robert C. Hagerty/Dir., Bruce W. Dunlevie/Dir., William T. Coleman/Dir., Jeff Hawkins/Founder, Scott D. Mercer/57/Dir., Gordon A. Campbell/Dir., Donna L. Dubinsky/Dir.

Owners: Galleon Management, L.L.C./6.10%, Donna L. Dubinsky/1.70%, Scott D. Mercer, Ronald R. Rhodes, Mark Nelson& Dana Johnson/5.90%, Eric A. Benhamou, Insiders/6.00%, John C. Hartnett, Barclays Global Investor, NA/5.30%, Gordon A. Campbell, William T. Coleman, FMR Corp./14.90%, Robert C. Hagerty, Michael R. Farese, Andrew J. Brown *(18 Owners included in Index)*

Financial Data: *Fiscal Year End:*06/02 *Latest Annual Data:* 05/31/2007

Year	Sales	Net Income
2007	$1,560,507,000	$56,383,000
2006	$1,578,509,000	$336,170,000
2005	$1,270,410,000	$66,387,000

Curr. Assets:	$937,647,000	**Curr. Liab.:**	$481,023,000	**P/E Ratio:**	25.80
Plant, Equip.:	$96,634,000	**Total Liab.:**	$485,591,000	**Indic. Yr. Divd.:**	NA
Total Assets:	$1,548,002,000	**Net Worth:**	$1,062,411,000	**Debt/ Equity:**	NA

Palmetto Bancshares Inc

PO Box 49, Laurens, SC, 29360; ***PH:*** 1-864-984-4551; ***http://*** www.palmettobank.com

General - Incorporation.....SC
Employees.....NA
Auditor.....Elliot Davis LLC
Stk Agt.....NA
Counsel.....NA
DUNS No.....14-484-4909

Stock- Price on:12/24/2007.....NA
Stock Exchange.....NA
Ticker Symbol.....NA
Outstanding Shares.....NA
E.P.S.....NA
Shareholders.....NA

Business: The group's principal activities are to accept deposits, provide loans and offer electronic fund transfers, trust services, mortgage loans and brokerage services. The group, through its wholly owned subsidiary palmetto bank, provides general banking business in the upstate South Carolina market of laurens, greenville, spartanburg, greenwood, anderson, cherokee and abbeville counties. The services offered include checking, savings, money market and other time deposits of various types of consumer and commercial depositors; loans for business, real estate and personal uses; safe deposit box rental and various electronic funds transfer services. The mortgage operation originates, sells, and services mortgage loans. The group's brokerage subsidiary offers customers stocks, treasury and municipal bonds, mutual funds and insurance annuities.

Primary SIC and add'l.: 6712 6022

CIK No: 0000706874

Subsidiaries: Palmetto Capital Inc, The Palmetto Bank

Officers: Leon L. Patterson/66/Chmn., CEO/$686,775.00, Ralph M. Burns/57/Treasurer/$317,645.00, Teresa M. Crabtree/Corp. Sec.

Directors: Leon L. Patterson/66/Chmn., CEO, Sam B. Phillips/66/Dir., Ann B. Smith/46/Dir., Edward K. Snead/48/Dir., David J. Wasson/62/Dir., Michael D. Glenn/67/Dir., Fred W. Davis/64/Dir., David P. George/66/Dir., John T. Gramling/66/Dir., John D. Hopkins/56/Dir., Paul W. Stringer/64/Dir., Jane S. Sosebee/51/Dir., Stewart L. Spinks/61/Dir., Albert V. Smith/61/Dir.

Owners: Sam B. Phillips, Albert V. Smith, Fred W. Davis, Teresa W. Knight, George A. Douglas, David J. Wasson, Keith E. Snead, John D. Hopkins, Stewart L. Spinks, Ann B. Smith, David P. George, Michael W. Ellison, Ralph M. Burns, John T. Gramling, Insiders/15.40% *(19 Owners included in Index)*

Palomar Enterprises Inc

1802 N Carson St., Ste. No. 212-7105, Carson City, NV, 89701; ***PH:*** 1-775-887-0670; ***http://*** www.palomarenterprises.com; ***Email:*** contact@palomarenterprises.com

General - Incorporation.....NV
Employees.....4
Auditor.....Gruber & Co., LLC
Stk Agt.....Signature Stock Transfer, Inc.
Counsel.....NA
DUNS No.....NA

Stock- Price on:12/24/2007.....$5.94
Stock Exchange.....OTC
Ticker Symbol.....PLMA
Outstanding Shares.....557,240,000
E.P.S.....-$0.036
Shareholders.....NA

Business: The group's principle activity is to operate high-Margin businesses that are strategically located on prime real estate. The company incubates businesses internally, as well as through acquisitions of existing, profitable ventures. The company plans to increase profits in each venture, while providing long-term value through the appreciation of the underlying properties. The company is in the development stage. The group operates from United States.

Primary SIC and add'l.: 9999

CIK No: 0001082822

Subsidiaries: The Blackhawk Fund, Zan well

Officers: Steve Bonenberger/Dir., CEO, Pres., Brent Fouch/38/Dir., CFO, COO, Sec.

Directors: Steve Bonenberger/Dir., CEO, Pres., Brent Fouch/38/Dir., CFO, COO, Sec.

Owners: Insiders/0.04%, Steve Bonenberger/0.02%, Brent Fouch/0.02%, Steve Bonenberger/50.00%, Insiders/100.00%, Brent Fouch/50.00%

Financial Data: *Fiscal Year End:*12/31 *Latest Annual Data:* 12/31/2006

Year	Sales	Net Income
2006	$683,000	-$2,440,000
2005	$531,000	-$2,102,000
2004	$737,000	-$4,666,000

Curr. Assets:	$56,000	**Curr. Liab.:**	$2,289,000		
Plant, Equip.:	$3,147,000	**Total Liab.:**	$4,380,000	**Indic. Yr. Divd.:**	NA
Total Assets:	$3,650,000	**Net Worth:**	-$733,000	**Debt/ Equity:**	NA

Palomar Medical Technologies Inc

82 Cambridge St., Burlington, MA, 01803; ***PH:*** 1-781-993-2300; ***Fax:*** 1-781-993-2330; ***http://*** www.palmed.com; ***Email:*** info@palomarmedical.com

General - Incorporation.....DE
Employees.....225
Auditor.....Ernst & Young LLP
Stk Agt.....American Stock Transfer & Trust Co.
Counsel.....NA
DUNS No.....17-819-3447

Stock- Price on:12/24/2007.....$35.03
Stock Exchange.....NDQ
Ticker Symbol.....PMTI
Outstanding Shares.....18,330,000
E.P.S.....$2.06
Shareholders.....NA

Business: The group's principle activity is to research and develop light-based systems for hair removal and other cosmetic procedures. The group researches, develops and tests new innovations for the hair removal market and other cosmetic applications including fat reduction, acne treatment and skin rejuvenation. The group offers a comprehensive range of products based on proprietary technologies including hair removal, non-invasive treatment of facial, leg veins and other benign vascular lesions, removal of benign pigmented lesions such as age and sun spots, tattoo removal, acne treatment, pseudofolliculitis barbae and other skin treatments. The group sells its products in the United States primarily through its direct sales force to dermatologists, cosmetic surgeons and other licensed practitioners. The group markets its products in Europe, Japan, Australia, south and Central America, the Far East and the Middle East through a global network of strategic distributors. The group's quarterly revenue for September 2007 was 31.28 millions of USD.

Primary SIC and add'l.: 3845 7299

CIK No: 0000881695

Subsidiaries: Esthetica Partners, Inc., Palomar Medical Products, Inc., Palomar Medical Technologies, Inc.

Officers: Joseph P. Caruso/Dir., CEO, Pres./$1,110,745.00, Paul S. Weiner/Sr. VP, CFO, Treasurer/$771,001.00, Michael H. Smotrich/CTO, Steven Armstrong/Sr. VP - Operations, Patricia A. Davis/Sr. VP, General Counsel, Sec., Douglas Baraw/VP, Chief Accounting Officer, Paul F. Wiener/Sr. VP - Sales, Marketing, Gregory Altshuler/Sr. VP - Research, Jeffrey Knight/VP - North American Sales

Directors: Joseph P. Caruso/Dir., CEO, Pres., Louis P. Valente/Chmn., Jeanne Cohane/Dir., Nicholas P. Economou/Dir., James G. Martin/Dir., Neil A. Pappalardo/Dir.

Owners: Barclays Global Investors, NA./0.70%, Louis P. Valente/0.50%, Insiders/0.50%, Westfield Capital Management Company, LLC/0.20%, Paul S. Weiner/0.50%, Jeanne Cohane, Craig Drill Capital, LLC/0.60%, Joseph P. Caruso/0.90%, James G. Martin, Neil A. Pappalardo, Nicholas P. Economou

Financial Data: Fiscal Year End:12/31   Latest Annual Data: 12/31/2006

Year	Sales	Net Income
2006	$126,544,000	$52,977,000
2005	$76,154,000	$17,453,000
2004	$54,432,000	$10,633,000

Curr. Assets:	$139,921,000	Curr. Liab.:	$24,031,000	P/E Ratio:	17.00
Plant, Equip.:	$1,130,000	Total Liab.:	$24,031,000	Indic. Yr. Divd.:	NA
Total Assets:	$141,162,000	Net Worth:	$117,132,000	Debt/ Equity:	NA

Palomine Mining Inc

595 Howe St., Ste. 507, Vancouver, BC, V6C 2T5; **PH:** 1-604-681-6466

General - Incorporation	NV	Stock - Price on:12/24/2007	NA
Employees	NA	Stock Exchange	OTC
Auditor	NA	Ticker Symbol	POMM
Stk Agt	Island Stock Transfer	Outstanding Shares	NA
Counsel	NA	E.P.S.	NA
DUNS No.	NA	Shareholders	NA

Business: The groups principal activity is in the exploration program on the Gab property. The group operates from the United States.

Primary SIC and add'l.: 1000

CIK No: 0001320729

Officers: Eugene N. Larabie/71/Dir., CEO, Pres., Sec., Treasurer, Principal Accounting Officer, Principal Financial Officer

Directors: Eugene N. Larabie/71/Dir., CEO, Pres., Sec., Treasurer, Principal Accounting Officer, Principal Financial Officer, Barry Brown/54/Dir.

Owners: Insiders/46.50%, Eugene N. Larabie/23.26%, Barry Brown/23.26%

Pamrapo Bancorp Inc

611 Ave. C, Bayonne, NJ, 07002; **PH:** 1-201-339-4600; **Fax:** 1-201-339-7375;
http:// www.pamrapo.com

General - Incorporation	NJ	Stock - Price on:12/24/2007	$20.15
Employees	92	Stock Exchange	NDQ
Auditor	Beard Miller Co. LLP	Ticker Symbol	PBCI
Stk Agt	Registrar & Transfer Co	Outstanding Shares	4,970,000
Counsel	Patton Boggs LLP	E.P.S.	$1.12
DUNS No.	04-073-6860	Shareholders	NA

Business: The group's principal activities are to accept retail deposits from the general public and provide mortgage-banking services. The services are provided through its subsidiary, pamrapo savings bank sla. It offers fixed rate one to four family residential mortgage loans, multi family residential mortgage loans, commercial real estate loans, home equity and second mortgage loans, consumer loans and mortgage backed securities. As on 31-Dec-2003, the group operated through nine retail banking offices located in bayonne, hoboken, fort lee and monroe counties of New Jersey.

Primary SIC and add'l.: 6035 6712

CIK No: 0000854071

Subsidiaries: Pamrapo Service Corporation

Officers: William J. Campbell/Dir., CEO, Pres./$514,191.00, Kenneth D. Walter/CFO, VP, Treasurer/$179,170.00, Robert A. Hughes/Investor Relations Contact, Margaret Russo/VP - Mortgage Department, Marianne Harrigan/Contact - Savings Accounting, IRA Retirement Accounting, Fast Banking by Telephone, Linda Lojewski/Contact - Checking Accounting, Teresa Caposello/Contact - Direct Deposit, Brian Campbell/Contact - Investment Accounting, Tax, Deferred Accounting, Margaret Marlow/Contact - Star ATM

Directors: William J. Campbell/Dir., CEO, Pres., John A. Morecraft/Vice Chmn., Daniel J. Massarelli/Chmn., Herman L. Brockman/Dir., Jaime Portela/Dir., Patrick D. Conaghan/Dir., Kenneth R. Poesl/Dir., Robert G. Doria/Dir., Francis J. O'Donnell/Dir.

Owners: Herman L. Brockman, Patrick D. Conaghan/1.00%, Pamrapo Savings Bank, S.L.A./5.46%, William J. Campbell/12.03%, Kenneth R. Poesl, Daniel J. Massarelli/4.01%, Robert G. Doria, Kenneth D. Walter/1.13%, Insiders/23.47%, Francis J. ODonnell, John A. Morecraft/3.15%

Financial Data: Fiscal Year End:12/31   Latest Annual Data: 12/31/2006

Year	Sales	Net Income
2006	$40,335,000	$6,542,000
2005	$39,058,000	$7,964,000
2004	$38,582,000	$7,944,000

Curr. Assets:	$16,241,000	Curr. Liab.:	$570,941,000	P/E Ratio:	17.99
Plant, Equip.:	$3,731,000	Total Liab.:	$577,992,000	Indic. Yr. Divd.:	$0.920
Total Assets:	$636,560,000	Net Worth:	$58,568,000	Debt/ Equity:	NA

Pan American Silver Corp

625 Howe St., Ste. 1500, Vancouver, BC, V6C 2T6; **PH:** 1-604-684-1175;
http:// www.panamericansilver.com; **Email:** info@panamericansilver.com

General - Incorporation	BC	Stock - Price on:12/24/2007	$27.06
Employees	6,060	Stock Exchange	NDQ
Auditor	Deloitte & Touche LLP	Ticker Symbol	PAAS
Stk Agt	Computershare Trust Co of Canada	Outstanding Shares	76,350,000
Counsel	Borden Ladner Gervais LLP	E.P.S.	$1.09
DUNS No.	24-371-2064	Shareholders	NA

Business: The group's principal activities are mining, development and exploration of silver, zinc, lead and copper. The group operates in three mines: the quiruvilca mine in northern Peru, the huaron mine in central Peru and the la colorada mine in central Mexico.

Primary SIC and add'l.: 1044

CIK No: 0000771992

Subsidiaries: Compania Minera Alto Valle S.A., Compania Minera Argentum (Argentum), Corner Bay Silver Inc., Minera Corner Bay S.A. de C.V., Minera Triton Argentina S.A., Pan American Minerals, Inc., Pan American Silver (Barbados) Corp., Pan American Silver (Bolivia) S.A., Pan American Silver Peru S.A.C., Pan American Silver S.A.C. Mina Quiruvilca, Plata Panamericana S.A. de C.V.

Officers: Geoffrey A. Burns/Dir., CEO, Pres., Joe Phillips/Pres. - Pan American Silver, Mexico, Luqman Shaheen/Dir. - Environmental Affairs, Nadia Carotenuto/Dir. - Human Resources, Andrew Pooler/Sr. VP - Mining Operations, Michael Steinmann/Sr. VP - Geology, Exploration, Martin Wafforn/VP - Engineering, Robert G. Doyle/CFO, Steven Busby/Sr. VP - Project Development, Technical Services, Stuart A. Moller/VP - Exploration, David Drips/Country Mgr. - Argentina, Ignacio Couturier/Treasury Mgr., David Travis/Pres. - Pan American Silver, Andres Dasso/Executive Dir., GM, Wayne Vincent/Controller, Assist. Sec. (17 Officers included in Index)

Directors: Geoffrey A. Burns/Dir., CEO, Pres., Ross J. Beaty/Chmn., Robert Pirooz/Dir., General Counsel, Corp. Sec., John Willson/Dir., John H. Wright/Dir., Paul B. Sweeney/Dir., Michael Larson/Dir., William A. Fleckenstein/Dir., Michael J.J. Maloney/Dir., Andres Dasso/Executive Dir., GM

Financial Data: Fiscal Year End:12/31   Latest Annual Data: 12/31/2006

Year	Sales	Net Income
2006	$255,447,000	$56,215,000
2005	$122,401,000	-$30,310,000
2004	$94,825,000	-$2,013,000

Curr. Assets:	$270,097,000	Curr. Liab.:	$65,481,000	P/E Ratio:	24.83
Plant, Equip.:	$398,379,000	Total Liab.:	$167,969,000	Indic. Yr. Divd.:	NA
Total Assets:	$671,406,000	Net Worth:	$503,437,000	Debt/ Equity:	NA

Pan Pacific Bank CA

47065 Warm Springs Blvd, Fremont, CA, 94539; **PH:** 1-510-809-8888; **Fax:** 1-510-809-8889;
http:// www.panpacificbank.com

General - Incorporation		Stock - Price on:12/24/2007	$7.1
Employees	NA	Stock Exchange	OTC
Auditor	NA	Ticker Symbol	PPFC
Stk Agt	American Stock Transfer & Trust Co.	Outstanding Shares	NA
Counsel	NA	E.P.S.	NA
DUNS No.	NA	Shareholders	NA

Business: The groups principal activities include providing community banking services to its customers. The group offers a full range of bank products and services that reflect the growing sophistication and complex financial needs of business and individual clients. The group operates from the United States.

Primary SIC and add'l.: 6021

CIK No:

Officers: Joe Ching/CEO, Pres., Nancy Lee/Founder, Exec. VP, Chief Marketing Officer, Byron Lee/Exec. VP, Chief Credit Officer, Founder

Directors: Marcel Liang/Vice Chmn., Wayne Doiguchi/Chmn., Robert Demarta/Dir., Mckenzie Moss/Dir., Joan Fong/Dir., Nancy Lee/Founder, Exec. VP, Chief Marketing Officer, Anselm Leung/Dir., Linda Leung/Dir., Karen Miyahara/Dir., C. T. Wong/Dir., Byron Lee/Exec. VP, Chief Credit Officer, Founder, Joseph Ching/Dir.

Panacos Pharmaceuticals Inc

134 Coolidge Ave., Watertown, MA, 02472; **PH:** 1-617-926-1551; **Fax:** 1-617-923-2245;
http:// www.panacos.com; **Email:** info@panacos.com

General - Incorporation	DE	Stock - Price on:12/24/2007	$3.75
Employees	43	Stock Exchange	NDQ
Auditor	KPMG LLP	Ticker Symbol	PANC
Stk Agt	American Stock Transfer & Trust Co.	Outstanding Shares	53,150,000
Counsel	Mintz, Levin, Glovsky & Popeo PC	E.P.S.	-$0.81
DUNS No.	87-918-4489	Shareholders	NA

Business: The group's principal activity is to develop innovative biotechnology products designed to improve the safety of the blood supply. The group has designed the proprietary inactine(tm) system to inactivate a wide range of viruses, bacteria, parasites and lymphocytes from red blood cells. The inactine(tm) system has also demonstrated the ability to remove prion proteins that may cause mad cow disease in cows and the human form of the disease, variant creutzfeldt-jakob disease (vcjd). The technology works by binding to the rna or dna of the pathogen. Once bound, the compound forms an irreversible bond to the pathogenic nucleic acid, preventing replication and thereby killing the pathogens.

Primary SIC and add'l.: 2836

CIK No: 0001040017

Subsidiaries: V.I. Technologies Ltd

Officers: Alan W. Dunton/CEO, Dir., Pres., Tom Lategan/VP - Regulatory Affairs, Philip C. Smith/Scientific Advisor, Robert B. Pelletier/55/VP - Finance/$100,661.00, Scott McCallister/Chief Medical Officer, Dana Conti/Media Inquiries, Graham P. Allaway/COO/$801,612.00, Peyton J. Marshall/53/CFO, Exec. VP/$1,580,608.00, David E. Martin/Sr. VP - Drug Development, John D. Richards/VP - Manufacturing Operations, Frederick Schmid/Sr. VP - Commercial Operations, Business Development/$603,752.00, Jeffrey Jacobson/Scientific Advisor, Charles Grudzinskas/Scientific Advisor, K. H. Lee/Scientific Advisor

Directors: Jeremy Hayward-Surry/65/Chmn., Irwin Lerner/Dir., John R. Fletcher/Dir., Joseph M. Limber/Dir., Laurent Fischer/Dir., Robert G. Savage/54/Dir.

Owners: Alan W. Dunton, Insiders/7.10%, Herbert H. Hooper, Robert B. Pelletier, John R. Fletcher, Frederick Schmid, OZ Management LLC/5.30%, Peyton J. Marshall, Jeremy Hayward-Surry, Samuel K. Ackerman/2.60%, Eric W. Linsley/3.50%, Joseph M. Limber, Robert G. Savage, Irwin Lerner, OrbiMed Advisors LLC/6.60% (16 Owners included in Index)

Financial Data: Fiscal Year End:12/31   Latest Annual Data: 12/31/2006

Year	Sales	Net Income
2006	$284,000	-$38,110,000
2005	$1,049,000	-$59,078,000
2004	$1,682,000	-$18,162,000

Curr. Assets:	$62,977,000	**Curr. Liab.:**	$6,510,000		
Plant, Equip.:	$2,122,000	**Total Liab.:**	$6,969,000	**Indic. Yr. Divd.:**	NA
Total Assets:	$65,653,000	**Net Worth:**	$58,684,000	**Debt/ Equity:**	NA

Panamerican Bancorp

1200 N Federal Hwy., Ste. 111a, Boca Raton, FL, 33432; ***PH:*** 1-561-826-0464; ***http://*** www.panamericanbank.com

General - Incorporation	DE	**Stock** - Price on:12/24/2007	NA
Employees	74	Stock Exchange	AMEX
Auditor	Crowe Chizek & Co. LLC	Ticker Symbol	PNB
Stk Agt	Olde Monmouth Stk Trnsfer Co. Inc.	Outstanding Shares	NA
Counsel	NA	E.P.S	NA
DUNS No.	NA	Shareholders	NA

Business: The group's principle activity is to provide a full range of commercial banking and consumer banking services to businesses and individuals. The company is a Florida state chartered bank providing services through its three full-service community-banking offices. The company considers its primary market and service area to be broward, dade and palm beach counties. Retail services offered by the company include installment loans, credit cards, checking accounts, savings accounts, now accounts and various types of time-deposit instruments. The company also provides commercial and industrial loans, commercial and residential mortgage loans and consumer and installment loans. At 31-Dec-2002, the company operated through 3 full-service banking offices. The group operates from United States.

Primary SIC and add'l.: 6022 6712

CIK No: 0001042521

Subsidiaries: Federal Reserve Bank, Sun American Bank

Officers: Michael E. Golden/Chmn., CEO, Pres./$1,179,746.00, Robert Nichols/CFO/$331,500.00, Robert Garrett/Exec. VP - Retail Sales, Services/$197,100.00, Alfredo Barriero/COO, Exec. VP, William T. Ross/Exec. VP - Retail Sales, Services, Sun American Bank/$209,200.00, Will Bermudez/Sr. VP - Finance, Eduardo Granda/Sr. VP, Chief Compliance Officer - Sun American Bank, Felipe Lozano/Sr. VP, Credit Risk Mgr. - Sun American Bank, David W. House/Sr. VP - Welth Management, Sun American Bank

Directors: Michael E. Golden/Chmn., CEO, Pres., Nelson Famadas/Vice Chmn., Stephen L. Perrone/Vice Chmn., James Partridge/Chmn., Alberto Valle/Dir., Leonard Marinello/Dir. - Sun American Bank, Michael Rosinus/Dir. - Sun American Bank

Owners: Beach Bank Liquidating Trust, Leonard F. Marinello, York Investment Limited, QVT Fund LP, Michael F. Rosinus, QVT Financial GP LLC, Robert K. Garrett, QVT Financial LLC, Pequot Capital Management, Inc., Robert L. Nichols, Insiders, QVT Associates GP LLC, JGD Management Corp., York Global Value Partners, L.P., Second Curve Capital, LLC *(27 Owners included in Index)*

Panavision Inc

6219 De Soto Ave, Woodland Hills, CA, 91367; ***PH:*** 1-818-316-1000; ***http://*** www.panavision.com

General - Incorporation	DE	**Stock** - Price on:12/24/2007	NA
Employees	NA	Stock Exchange	NA
Auditor	Ernst & Young LLP	Ticker Symbol	NA
Stk Agt	NA	Outstanding Shares	NA
Counsel	Skadden, Meagher & Flom LLP	E.P.S	NA
DUNS No.	78-523-1119	Shareholders	NA

Business: The group's principal activities are to design, manufacture and supply high precision camera systems. The group's products include cameras, lenses and accessories for the motion picture and television industries. The group also rents lighting, lighting grip, transportation equipment, distribution equipment and mobile generators. The group develops and designs all the critical components for its camera systems, including the camera movement and lens. The group provides camera systems to the television commercial market in North America, Europe and the Asia-Pacific. The group is a majority-owned subsidiary of m&f worldwide corp., which is a majority-owned indirect subsidiary of mafco holdings inc.

Primary SIC and add'l.: 3861 7359 6719

CIK No: 0001022911

Subsidiaries: Camera Bellows Limited, Camera Rentals Ireland Limited, Cinecam Sarl, Film Facilities Ltd., John Barry Group Pty. Limited, Lee Filters Limited, Lee Lighting Limited, LPPI, LLC, Panavision (1998) Limited, Panavision (Canada) Corporation, Panavision Alga Techno Eurl, Panavision Asia Pacific Pty. Limited, Panavision Asia Pte. Limited, Panavision Australia Pty. Limited, Panavision Canada Holdings Inc. 32 Subsidiaries included in the Index

Officers: Tal Kendra/Marketing Department Staff, LEE Filters USA, Sales, Jesse Friend/Marketing Department Staff, LEE Filters USA, Sales, Leo Ferrini/Marketing Department Staff, Panavision Hollywood, Lisa Harp/Marketing Department Staff, Panavision Hollywood, Sami Scott/Marketing Department Staff, LEE Filters USA, Sales, Kerstin Vitali/Marketing Department Staff, LEE Filters USA, Sales, Alec Colley/Marketing Department Staff, Panavision Florida, Scott Fleischer/Marketing Department Staff, Panavision NEW York, Sal Giarratano/Marketing Department Staff, Panavision NEW York, Paul Jackson/Marketing Department Staff, Panavision Sydney, Martin Cayzer/Marketing Department Staff, Panavision Sydney, Adam Osten/Marketing Department Staff, Panavision Vancouver, Kelli Bingham/Marketing Department Staff, Panavision NEW Orleans, Nigel Gorham/Marketing Department Staff, Panavision Melbourne, Andrea Leonard/Marketing Department Staff, Panavision NEW York *(85 Officers included in Index)*

Panda Ethanol Inc

4100 Spring Valley, Dallas, TX, 75244; ***PH:*** 1-972-361-1200; ***Fax:*** 1-972-361-1200; ***http://*** www.pandaenergy.com

General - Incorporation	NV	**Stock** - Price on:12/24/2007	$5.75
Employees	52	Stock Exchange	OTC
Auditor	Deloitte & Touche, LLP	Ticker Symbol	PDAE
Stk Agt	Pacific Stock Transfer Company	Outstanding Shares	31,070,000
Counsel	NA	E.P.S	-$0.63
DUNS No.	NA	Shareholders	NA

Business: The groups principal activities include developing, owning and operating a multi site portfolio of innovative manure fueled and gas fueled ethanol plants and to service the growing demand for and increased usage of renewable fuels. In November 2006, the group merged with and into Cirracor, a Nevada corporation. The group operates from the United States.

Primary SIC and add'l.: 2869

CIK No: 0001167880

Subsidiaries: Panda Ethanol Acquisitions, LLC, Panda Ethanol Holdings, LLC, Panda Ethanol Management, LLC, Panda Ethanol Pool, LLC, Panda Global Services Haskell, LLC, Panda Global Services Hereford, LLC, Panda Global Services Iroquois, LLC, Panda Global Services Lincoln, LLC, Panda Global Services Muleshoe, LLC, Panda Global Services Quincy, LLC, Panda Global Services Sherman, LLC, Panda Global Services Yuma, LLC, Panda Grain, LLC, Panda Haskell Ethanol, L.P., Panda Haskell Grain, LLC 47 Subsidiaries included in the Index

Officers: Darol Lindloff/CEO, Reed Fisher/Pres., Sec. - Cirracor, Franklin Byrd/CFO, Treasurer, Richard Cuccia/Assoc. General Counsel, Corp. Sec., John Zamlen/VP - Construction, Development, Asset Management, Donald J. Thorpe/VP - Operations, Wes Durham/Consultant - Grain Management, Kurt M. Landis/Dir. - Feed, Nutrition, Bill Pentak/Dir. - Corporate Communications, Investor Relations

Directors: Robert W. Carter/Chmn., Todd W. Carter/Dir., Michael G. Boswell/Dir., Donald Brown/Dir., Philip D. English/Dir.

Owners: Panda Energy International, Inc./45.80%, FrontPoint Energy Horizons Fund GP, LLC/5.90%, Seneca Capital LP/7.20%, GLG Partners LP/16.20%

Financial Data: ***Fiscal Year End:***09/30 ***Latest Annual Data:*** 12/31/2006

Year	**Sales**	**Net Income**
2006	NA	-$11,586,000

Curr. Assets:	$164,481,000	**Curr. Liab.:**	$7,853,000		
Plant, Equip.:	$68,245,000	**Total Liab.:**	$156,184,000	**Indic. Yr. Divd.:**	NA
Total Assets:	$241,629,000	**Net Worth:**	$85,445,000	**Debt/ Equity:**	NA

Panera Bread Co

6710 Clayton Rd., Richmond Heights, MO, 63117; ***PH:*** 1-314-633-7100; ***Fax:*** 1-314-633-7200; ***http://*** www.panera.com

General - Incorporation	DE	**Stock** - Price on:12/24/2007	$47.04
Employees	7,200	Stock Exchange	NDQ
Auditor	PricewaterhouseCoopers LLP	Ticker Symbol	PNRA
Stk Agt	EquiServe Trust Co N.A	Outstanding Shares	31,900,000
Counsel	NA	E.P.S	$1.79
DUNS No.	09-384-4462	Shareholders	NA

Business: The group's principal activity is to provide food for breakfast and lunch. The food items include fresh baked goods, made-to-order sandwiches, soups, salads, custom roasted coffees and other cafe beverages. The group operates in three reportable business segments: company store operations, franchise operations and commissary operations. As of 27-Dec- 2003, the group's retail operations consist of 173 company-owned bakery-cafes and 429 franchise-operated bakery-cafes. The franchise operations segment comprises the activities of the franchise business unit which licenses qualified operators to conduct business under the panera bread group name and also monitors the operations of these stores. The commissary operations segment supplies fresh dough items to both group-owned and franchise operated bakery cafes.

Primary SIC and add'l.: 5461 6794

CIK No: 0000724606

Subsidiaries: Artisan Bread, LLC, Asiago Bread, LLC, Atlanta JV, LLC, Cap City Bread, LLC, Panera Enterprises, Inc., Panera, LLC, Pumpernickel Associates, LLC, Pumpernickel, Inc.

Officers: Ronald Shaich/Co - Founder, Chmn., CEO/$875,227.00, Mark Borland/Sr. VP, Chief Supply Chain Officer/$575,930.00, Michael Nolan/Chief Development Officer, Sr. VP, Michael Kupstas/Sr. VP, Chief Franchise Officer, Rebecca Fine/Sr. VP, Chief People Officer, Thomas Kish/CIO, Sr. VP, John Maguire/Exec. VP/$555,438.00, Scott Davis/Sr. VP, Chief Concept Officer, Neal Yanofsky/Pres./$1,413,640.00, Patricia Gray/Sr. VP, Chief Legal Officer, Jeffrey Kip/Sr. VP, CFO/$457,300.00, Michael Markowitz/Sr. VP, Chief Brand Officer, William H. Simpson/45/Sr. VP

Directors: Ronald Shaich/Co - Founder, Chmn., CEO, George E. Kane/Dir., Larry Franklin/Dir., Domenic Colasacco/Dir., Fred Foulkes/Dir.

Owners: Domenic Colasacco, Ronald M. Shaich/5.60%, Neal J. Yanofsky, Ronald M. Shaich/93.80%, Fred K. Foulkes, Insiders/8.20%, Jeffrey W. Kip, Insiders/93.80%, Larry J. Franklin, John M. Maguire, Mark A. Borland

Financial Data: ***Fiscal Year End:***12/27 ***Latest Annual Data:*** 12/26/2006

Year	**Sales**	**Net Income**
2006	$828,971,000	$58,849,000
2005	$640,275,000	$52,183,000
2004	$479,139,000	$38,580,000

Curr. Assets:	$102,774,000	**Curr. Liab.:**	$86,865,000	**P/E Ratio:**	25.57
Plant, Equip.:	$268,809,000	**Total Liab.:**	$120,689,000	**Indic. Yr. Divd.:**	NA
Total Assets:	$437,667,000	**Net Worth:**	$316,978,000	**Debt/ Equity:**	NA

Pangea Petroleum Corp

9801 Westheimer, Ste. 302, Houston, TX, 77042; ***PH:*** 1-713-706-6350; ***Fax:*** 1-713-706-6351; ***http://*** www.pangeapetroleum.com; ***Email:*** info@pangeapetroleum.com

General - Incorporation	CO	**Stock** - Price on:12/24/2007	$0.0061
Employees	2	Stock Exchange	OTC
Auditor	Malone & Bailey, P.C	Ticker Symbol	PAPO
Stk Agt	Olde Monmouth Stk Trnsfer Co. Inc.	Outstanding Shares	NA
Counsel	Axelrod Smith & KRA Council	E.P.S	NA
DUNS No.	NA	Shareholders	NA

Business: The group's principal activity is to explore and develop oil and natural gas reserves in the onshore United States, primarily on the gulf coast.

Primary SIC and add'l.: 1311

CIK No: 0001077319

Officers: Charles B. Pollock/Chmn., CEO, Robert Axelrod/Legal Counsel, Scott Duncan/CFO, Mark F. Weller/Dir., Pres.

Directors: Charles B. Pollock/Chmn., CEO, Mark F. Weller/Dir., Pres., Edward R. Skaggs/42/Dir.

Owners: Charles B. Pollock/28.60%, Mark F. Weller/20.30%, Edward Skaggs, Scott Duncan, Insiders/49.90%

Financial Data: ***Fiscal Year End:***12/31 ***Latest Annual Data:*** 12/31/2006

Year	**Sales**	**Net Income**
2006	$38,000	-$1,011,000
2005	$57,000	-$543,000
2004	$82,000	$928,000

Curr. Assets:	$61,000	**Curr. Liab.:**	$601,000		
Plant, Equip.:	$210,000	**Total Liab.:**	$609,000	**Indic. Yr. Divd.:**	NA
Total Assets:	$271,000	**Net Worth:**	-$338,000	**Debt/ Equity:**	NA

Panhandle Eastern Pipe Line Co

5444 Wheimer Rd., Houston, TX, 77056; *PH:* 1-713-989-7000; *http://* www.panhandleenergy.com

General - Incorporation	DE	Stock - Price on:12/24/2007	$32.88
Employees	2,312	Stock Exchange	NA
Auditor	PricewaterhouseCoopers LLP	Ticker Symbol	NA
Stk Agt	NA	Outstanding Shares	119,840,000
Counsel	NA	E.P.S.	$0.54
DUNS No.	04-525-6641	Shareholders	NA

Business: The group's principal activity is transmission and storage of natural gas. The group is a indirect wholly owned subsidiary of southern union company. The group operates a large natural gas pipeline network, which provides customers in the midwest and southwest with a comprehensive array of transportation services. The major customers of the group include 25 utilities located primarily in the United States midwest market area, which encompasses large portions of Illinois, Indiana, Michigan, Missouri, Ohio and Tennessee. On 11-Jun-2003 southern union acquired the group.

Primary SIC and add'l.: 4922

CIK No: 0000076063

Subsidiaries: Pan Gas Storage, LLC, Panhandle Energy, Sea Robin Pipeline Company, LLC, Southern Union Company, Trunkline Gas Company, LLC, Trunkline LNG Company, LLC, Trunkline LNG Holdings, LLC

Officers: Gary W. Lefelar/Chief Accounting Officer, Sr. VP, John P. Barnett/Dir. - Public Information, Robert O. Bond/COO, Pres., Richard N. Marshall/CFO, Sr. VP

Financial Data: Fiscal Year End:12/31 Latest Annual Data: 12/31/2006

Year	Sales	Net Income
2006	$2,340,144,000	$64,131,000
2005	$2,019,430,000	$20,683,000
2004	$1,799,774,000	$114,025,000

Curr. Assets:	$690,859,000	Curr. Liab.:	$1,200,824,000	P/E Ratio:	142.96
Plant, Equip.:	$4,584,427,000	Total Liab.:	$4,732,382,000	Indic. Yr. Divd.:	$0.400
Total Assets:	$6,782,790,000	Net Worth:	$2,050,408,000	Debt/ Equity:	1.4385

Panhandle Royalty Co

Grand Ctr., 5400 Nw Grand Blvd., Ste. 300, Oklahoma City, OK, 73112; *PH:* 1-405-948-1560; *http://* www.panra.com

General - Incorporation	OK	Stock - Price on:12/24/2007	$27.31
Employees	16	Stock Exchange	AMEX
Auditor	Ernst & Young LLP	Ticker Symbol	NA
Stk Agt	UMB Bank, N.A.	Outstanding Shares	8,420,000
Counsel	Lon Foster III	E.P.S.	$0.746
DUNS No.	09-350-2821	Shareholders	NA

Business: The group's principal activities are to explore and develop oil and gas properties. The products of the group include crude oil and natural gas. These products are sold to various purchasers, including pipeline and marketing companies that are generally located in and service the areas where the group's producing wells are located. The mineral properties and other oil and gas interests are located in Oklahoma, Texas and New Mexico and nineteen other states. Oneok is one of the largest customers of the group.

Primary SIC and add'l.: 6792 1311

CIK No: 0000315131

Subsidiaries: Wood Oil Company

Officers: Ben D. Hare/62/Dir., CEO, Co - Pres., Ben Spriestersbach/VP - Land, Michael C. Coffman/Dir., CFO, Pres., Lonnie J. Lowry/VP, Controller, Chief Accounting Officer, Sec.

Directors: Chris E. Kauffman/67/Chmn., Robert A. Reece/Dir., Ben D. Hare/62/Dir., COO, Co - Pres., Michael C. Coffman/Dir., CFO, Pres., Robert E. Robotti/Dir., Bruce M. Bell/Dir., Robert O. Lorenz/Dir., Grant H. Swartzwelder/Dir., Duke R. Ligon/Dir.

Owners: Robert A. Reece, Ben Spriestersbach, Robert E. Robotti/6.90%, Lonnie J. Lowry, Insiders/9.50%, Chris E. Kauffman, Michael C. Coffman/1.30%, Grant H. Swartzwelder, Robert O. Lorenz, Ben D. Hare, Bruce M. Bell

Financial Data: Fiscal Year End:09/30 Latest Annual Data: 9/30/2006

Year	Sales	Net Income
2006	$37,486,000	$10,574,000
2005	$33,307,000	$10,485,000
2004	$24,607,000	$6,730,000

Curr. Assets:	$8,796,000	Curr. Liab.:	$27,000	P/E Ratio:	41.38
Plant, Equip.:	$61,310,000	Total Liab.:	-$196,029,000	Indic. Yr. Divd.:	$0.280
Total Assets:	$70,949,000	Net Worth:	$49,066,000	Debt/ Equity:	NA

Pantry Inc

1801 Douglas Dr., Sanford, NC, 27330; *PH:* 1-919-774-6700; *Fax:* 1-919-774-3329; *http://* www.thepantry.com; *Email:* postmaster@thepantry.com

General - Incorporation	DE	Stock - Price on:12/24/2007	$48.3
Employees	10,356	Stock Exchange	NDQ
Auditor	Deloitte & Touche LLP	Ticker Symbol	PTRY
Stk Agt	Wachovia Bank N.A	Outstanding Shares	22,890,000
Counsel	NA	E.P.S.	$2.09
DUNS No.	18-145-8357	Shareholders	NA

Business: The group's principle activity is to operate stores. The stores provide merchandise, gasoline and ancillary services. The group operates quick service restaurants or full-service fast food locations. The group also offers proprietary food service programs featuring cold beverages, snacks, fast food, tobacco products, gasoline, and other merchandise and services. The group operates from United States.

Primary SIC and add'l.: 5451 5441 5541 5993 5461 5411

CIK No: 0000915862

Subsidiaries: D&D Oil Co., Inc., Kangaroo, Inc., R & H Maxxon, Inc.

Officers: Peter J. Sodini/Chmn., CEO, Pres., Steven J. Ferreira/Sr. VP - Administration, Daniel J. Kelly/CFO, VP - Finance, Sec., David M. Zaborski/Sr. VP - Operations, Melissa H. Anderson/Sr. VP - Human Resources, Keith S. Bell/Sr. VP - Fuels

Directors: Peter J. Sodini/Chmn., CEO, Pres., Thomas M. Murnane/Dir., Robert F. Bernstock/Dir., Bryan E. Monkhouse/Dir., Paul L. Brunswick/Dir., Edwin J. Holman/Dir., Terry L. McElroy/Dir., Mark D. Miles/Dir., Wilfred A. Finnegan/50/Dir., Maria C. Richter/52/Dir.

Financial Data: Fiscal Year End:09/29 Latest Annual Data: 9/28/2006

Year	Sales	Net Income
2006	$5,961,702,000	$89,198,000
2005	$4,429,239,000	$57,810,000
2004	$3,493,085,000	$15,726,000

Curr. Assets:	$273,832,000	Curr. Liab.:	$212,535,000	P/E Ratio:	23.11
Plant, Equip.:	$582,242,000	Total Liab.:	$1,083,954,000	Indic. Yr. Divd.:	NA
Total Assets:	$1,232,881,000	Net Worth:	$148,927,000	Debt/ Equity:	2.4539

Papa Johns International Inc

2002 Papa Johns Blvd., Louisville, KY, 40299; *PH:* 1-502-261-7272; *http://* www.papajohns.com

General - Incorporation	DE	Stock - Price on:12/24/2007	$28.94
Employees	13,194	Stock Exchange	NDQ
Auditor	Ernst & Young LLP	Ticker Symbol	PZZA
Stk Agt	National City Bank	Outstanding Shares	29,920,000
Counsel	Greenebaum Doll & McDonald	E.P.S.	$1.42
DUNS No.	14-779-4812	Shareholders	NA

Business: The group's principal activity is to operate and franchise pizza delivery and carry-out restaurants under the trademarks 'papa john's' and 'perfect pizza'. The restaurants offer a menu of high-quality pizza along with limited side items, including breadsticks, cheesesticks, chicken strips and canned or bottled soft drinks. The pizzas are made from a proprietary blend of wheat flour, cheese made from 100% real mozzarella, fresh-packed pizza sauce made from vine-ripened tomatoes and a proprietary mix of savory spices, and a choice of high-quality meat and vegetable toppings. The domestic quality control centers of the group comprises of 11 regional production and distribution centers. These centers supply pizza dough, food products, paper products, smallwares and cleaning supplies twice weekly to each restaurant. The group operates and franchises in 49 states, the district of columbia, and 15 international markets.

Primary SIC and add'l.: 6794 5812

CIK No: 0000901491

Subsidiaries: Capital Delivery, Ltd., Colonels Limited, LLC., Papa Johns (U.K.) Ltd., Papa Johns Support Services, Inc., Papa Johns USA, Inc., Perfect Pizza Holdings, Ltd., Perfect Pizza Ltd, PJ Food Service, Inc., Risk Services Corp, RSC Insurance Services Ltd., Star Papa, LP

Officers: Nigel Travis/CEO, Pres./$3,272,175.00, John H. Schnatter/Founder, Executive Chmn./$1,198,953.00, Julie Larner/Pres. - PJ Food Service, Sr. VP, Bill Van Epps/Pres. - USA, Christopher J. Sternberg/Sr. VP - Corporate Communications, Charles W. Schnatter/Chief Development Officer, Sr. VP, David Flanery/Sr. VP, CFO, Treasurer/$674,603.00, Richard J. Emmett/Sr. VP, General Counsel, Sec., William M. Van Epps/Pres. - USA/$921,270.00, Lou H. Jones/Sr. VP, General Counsel, Peter McCue/Sr. VP - Human Resources, William M. Mitchell/Sr. VP - Domestic Operations, Glenn West/Sr. VP - Information Services, eCommerce

Directors: John H. Schnatter/Founder, Executive Chmn., William F. Barnett/Dir., Cole P. Norborne/66/Dir., Philip Guarascio/Dir., Olivia F. Kirtley/Dir., Wade S. Oney/Dir., William M. Street/Dir., John Hatab/Dir., Norborne P. Cole/Dir., Alex Smith/Dir.

Owners: Philip Guarascio, Olivia F. Kirtley, William M. VanEpps, FMR Corp./8.30%, William M. Street, Wade S. Oney, John H. Schnatter/27.50%, AXA Financial, Inc./5.10%, Norborne P. Cole, William F. Barnett, Insiders/31.40%, Goldman Sachs Asset Management, L.P./6.80%, David J. Flanery, Nigel Travis/2.40%, Michael R. Cortino (16 Owners included in Index)

Financial Data: Fiscal Year End:12/25 Latest Annual Data: 12/31/2006

Year	Sales	Net Income
2006	$1,001,557,000	$63,375,000
2005	$968,788,000	$46,056,000
2004	$942,426,000	$23,221,000

Curr. Assets:	$84,543,000	Curr. Liab.:	$102,096,000	P/E Ratio:	17.43
Plant, Equip.:	$197,722,000	Total Liab.:	$233,471,000	Indic. Yr. Divd.:	NA
Total Assets:	$379,639,000	Net Worth:	$146,168,000	Debt/ Equity:	0.7170

PaperFree Medical Solutions Inc

1817 Dogwood Dr, Kokomo, IN, 46902; *PH:* 1-765-456-1089

General - Incorporation	NV	Stock - Price on:12/24/2007	$0.0019
Employees	20	Stock Exchange	OTC
Auditor	Malone & Bailey, P.C	Ticker Symbol	PFMS
Stk Agt	Nevada Agency & Trust Company	Outstanding Shares	82,560,000
Counsel	NA	E.P.S.	-$0.042
DUNS No.	NA	Shareholders	NA

Business: The group's principal activity is to publish and distribute industry and profession specific wall planners. The activities are carried through its subsidiary, business publishing limited. The group sells advertising space located around the perimeter of the wall planner to businesses and professionals that wish to market their products or services to the specific industry for which the wall planner is made. The group ceased the operations of business publishing limited. It is considered a development stage company as it no longer has any business operations.

Primary SIC and add'l.: 7372

CIK No: 0001171546

Subsidiaries: KMS Computer Services, Inc

Officers: Stephen Hawksworth/53/Dir., CEO, Pres., Craig S. Barrow/56/CFO

Directors: Stephen Hawksworth/53/Dir., CEO, Pres., Richard J. Paver/47/Dir., William L. Sklar/60/Dir., David L. Bailey/67/Dir., Marshall T. Wilde/44/Dir.

Owners: William L. Skla/2.40%, William L. Sklar/33.00%, Insiders/100.00%, David L. Bailey/33.00%, Marshall T. Wilde, Richard J. Paver/33.00%, Insiders/2.40%

Financial Data: Fiscal Year End:02/28 Latest Annual Data: 2/28/2007

Year	Sales	Net Income
2007	$867,000	-$2,761,000
2006	$979,000	-$3,242,000
2005	NA	-$57,435,000

Curr. Assets:	$394,000	Curr. Liab.:	$720,000		
Plant, Equip.:	$150,000	Total Liab.:	$2,257,000	Indic. Yr. Divd.:	NA
Total Assets:	$630,000	Net Worth:	-$1,627,000	Debt/ Equity:	NA

Par Pharmaceutical Cos Inc

300 Tice Blvd., Woodcliff Lake, NJ, 07677; *PH:* 1-201-802-4000; *Fax:* 1-201-802-4600; *http://* www.parpharm.com

General - Incorporation DE
Employees 766
Auditor Deloitte & Touche LLP
Stk Agt American Stock Transfer & Trust Co.
Counsel NA
DUNS No. 09-273-3690

Stock - Price on:12/24/2007 $28.41
Stock Exchange NYSE
Ticker Symbol PRX
Outstanding Shares 35,050,000
E.P.S $1.45
Shareholders NA

Business: The group's principal activities are to develop, manufacture and distribute generic drugs and complex synthetic active pharmaceutical ingredients in the United States. The products are in the form of tablet, capsules, and semi-solid and two-piece hard shell capsule. Generic drug consists of 170 products representing various dosage strengths for 71 separate drugs. The group markets its products to wholesalers, retail drug store chains, managed health care providers, clinics, governmental agencies, health care organizations and drug distributors.

Primary SIC and add'l.: 2834

CIK No: 0000878088

Subsidiaries: Israel Pharmaceutical Resources LP, Kali Laboratories, Inc., Nutriceutical Resources, Inc., Par Pharma Group, Ltd., Par Pharmaceutical, Inc., Par SVC, LLC., ParCare Ltd., PRI-Research, Inc., PRX Pharmaceuticals, Inc.

Officers: Patrick G. Lepore/Dir., Chmn., CEO, Pres., Gerard A. Martino/COO, Exec. VP/$841,782.00, Thomas J. Haughey/Exec. VP, General Counsel, Corp. Sec., John A. MacPhee/Exec. VP, Pres. - Branded Products Division, Paul V. Campanelli/Exec. VP, Pres. - Generics Division, Veronica A. Lubatkin/CFO, Exec. VP

Directors: Patrick G. Lepore/Dir., Chmn., CEO, Pres., William L. Seidman/Dir., Melvin Sharoky/Dir., Joseph E. Smith/Dir., John D. Abernathy/Dir., Ronald M. Nordmann/Dir., Peter S. Knight/Dir.

Owners: Thomas J. Haughey, Ronald M. Nordmann, Shankar Hariharan, Peter S. Knight, Nicholas DiMaio, John A. MacPhee, John D. Abernathy, Dennis J. OConnor, Mark Auerbach, Insiders/2.40%, L. William Seidman, Joseph E. Smith, Steven A. Cohen/9.90%, Patrick G. LePore, Scott L. Tarriff/1.90% *(17 Owners included in Index)*

Financial Data: *Fiscal Year End:*12/31 *Latest Annual Data:* 12/31/2006

Year	Sales	Net Income
2006	$725,168,000	$6,741,000
2005	$432,256,000	-$15,309,000
2004	$690,016,000	$29,246,000

Curr. Assets:	$514,577,000	**Curr. Liab.:**	$389,409,000		
Plant, Equip.:	$89,155,000	**Total Liab.:**	$389,409,000	**Indic. Yr. Divd.:**	NA
Total Assets:	$810,418,000	**Net Worth:**	$421,009,000	**Debt/ Equity:**	0.4425

Par Technology Corp

PAR Technology Pk., 8383 Seneca TpkEast, New Hartford, NY, 13413; *PH:* 1-315-738-0600; *Fax:* 1-315-738-0411; *http://* www.partech.com; *Email:* askpar@partech.com

General - Incorporation DE
Employees 1,700
Auditor KPMG LLP
Stk Agt Registrar & Transfer Co
Counsel NA
DUNS No. 05-527-1183

Stock - Price on:12/24/2007 $8.69
Stock Exchange NYSE
Ticker Symbol PTC
Outstanding Shares 14,360,000
E.P.S -$0.067
Shareholders NA

Business: The group's principal activities are to provide hardware platforms, software applications and professional services to businesses in retail, hospitality and quick-services-restaurant industries. The software applications assist in the operation of hospitality and quick-service-restaurant businesses by managing data from end-to-end and improving profitability through more efficient operations. The group develops advanced prototype and operational systems for the department of defense and other government agencies. In addition, it also provides information technology and communications support services to the U.S. Navy and the U.S. Airforce. It also provides integrated solutions to the quick-service-restaurant industry.

Primary SIC and add'l.: 3571 7373 7371

CIK No: 0000708821

Subsidiaries: Ausable Solutions, Inc., PAR Government Systems Corporation, PAR Springer-Miller Systems, Inc., PAR Vision Systems Corporation, ParTech, Inc., PixelPoint ULC., Rome Research Corporation

Officers: John W. Sammon/69/Chmn., CEO, Pres./$508,567.00, Gregory T. Cortese/58/CEO, General Counsel, Sec., Pres. - Partech, Inc/$304,237.00, Ronald J. Casciano/54/CFO, VP, Treasurer/$248,487.00, Albert Lane/66/Pres./$481,004.00, Lawrence Blain/Contact - Canada, Charles A. Constantino/68/Dir., Exec. VP/$319,694.00, Christopher R. Byrnes/Dir. - Investor Relations, Deanna M. Cook/Legal, Administrative Assist., Nick Hamilton/Contact - Europe, Africa, Ahmad H.A. Abdallah/Contact - Middle East, Bob Evans/MD Asia - Pacific, Steven Leo/GM - Australasia, Glen Carroll/Contact - Latin American, Caribbean

Directors: John W. Sammon/69/Chmn., CEO, Pres., Charles A. Constantino/68/Dir., Exec. VP, James A. Simms/48/Dir., Kevin R. Jost/53/Dir., Sangwoo Ahn/69/Dir., Paul D. Nielsen/57/Dir.

Owners: Sangwoo Ahn, Insiders/44.30%, James A. Simms, Ronald J. Casciano, Paul D. Nielsen, Gregory T. Cortese/2.14%, Albert Lane, Kevin R. Jost, Charles A. Constantino/1.92%, John W. Sammon/39.80%

Financial Data: *Fiscal Year End:*12/31 *Latest Annual Data:* 12/31/2006

Year	Sales	Net Income
2006	$208,667,000	$5,721,000
2005	$205,639,000	$9,432,000
2004	$174,884,000	$5,635,000

Curr. Assets:	$95,991,000	**Curr. Liab.:**	$46,473,000		
Plant, Equip.:	$7,535,000	**Total Liab.:**	$56,713,000	**Indic. Yr. Divd.:**	NA
Total Assets:	$142,796,000	**Net Worth:**	$86,083,000	**Debt/ Equity:**	0.0886

Paradigm Holdings Inc WY

402 21st St. E , Ste. 400, Saskatoon, SK, S7K 0C3; *PH:* 1-306-931-1700; *Fax:* 1-306-934-3134; *http://* www.paradigmsolutionscorp.com

General - Incorporation WY
Employees 288
Auditor BDO Seidman, LLP
Stk Agt Corporate Stock Transfer, Inc.
Counsel Kirkpatrick & Lockhart
DUNS No. NA

Stock - Price on:12/24/2007 $0.85
Stock Exchange OTC
Ticker Symbol PDHO
Outstanding Shares 19,020,000
E.P.S -$0.09
Shareholders NA

Business: The groups principal activities include providing information technology and business continuity solutions to government and commercial customers. In October 2005, the group acquired Blair Technology. The group operates from the United States.

Primary SIC and add'l.: 6712

CIK No: 0000313353

Subsidiaries: BLAIR MANAGEMENT SERVICES, PARADIGM SOLUTIONS CORPORATION, PARADIGM SOLUTIONS INTERNATIONAL

Officers: Peter B. Lamontagne/Dir., CEO, Pres./$358,689.00, Richard P. Sawchak/Sr. VP, CFO/$218,971.00, Harry Kaneshiro/Exec. VP - Federal Operations/$348,651.00, Thomas J. Kristofco/Sr. VP - Paradigm Solutions/$601,954.00, Russell E. Blackwell/VP - Product, Professional Services, Paradigm Solutions International, Stephen Murray/Sr. VP - Federal Operations, Robert Valli/VP - Business Development, Anthony Verna/Sr. VP - Business Development - Marketing, Strategy, Robert Boakai/VP - Enterprise Solutions, Christian Kleszewski/VP - Trinity, IMS, Samuel Caldwell/VP - CTS, Diane C. Moberg/VP - Human Resources, Compliance

Directors: Peter B. Lamontagne/Dir., CEO, Pres., Raymond A. Huger/Chmn., Francis X. Ryan/Dir., John A. Moore/Dir., Edwin A. Avery/Dir.

Owners: Harry Kaneshiro/15.35%, Insiders/77.63%, Frank Jakovac/4.04%, Francis Ryan/0.21%, Peter LaMontagne/0.87%, John Moore/0.21%, Edwin Avery/0.21%, Raymond Huger/55.70%, Richard Sawchak/1.04%

Financial Data: *Fiscal Year End:*12/31 *Latest Annual Data:* 12/31/2006

Year	Sales	Net Income
2006	$59,828,000	-$3,638,000
2005	$63,515,000	$823,000
2004	$61,756,000	-$3,767,000

Curr. Assets:	$18,720,000	**Curr. Liab.:**	$17,646,000		
Plant, Equip.:	$593,000	**Total Liab.:**	$17,891,000	**Indic. Yr. Divd.:**	NA
Total Assets:	$19,547,000	**Net Worth:**	$1,655,000	**Debt/ Equity:**	NA

Paradigm Medical Industries Inc

2355 S 1070 W, Salt Lake City, UT, 84119; *PH:* 1-801-977-8970; *Fax:* 1-801-977-8973; *http://* www.paradigm-medical.com

General - Incorporation DE
Employees 21
Auditor Hynen &Ievach LLP
Stk Agt Continental Stock Transfer & Trust Co
Counsel NA
DUNS No. 78-908-1155

Stock - Price on:12/24/2007 $0.0081
Stock Exchange OTC
Ticker Symbol PMED
Outstanding Shares 205,990,000
E.P.S -$0.007
Shareholders NA

Business: The group's principal activity is to develop, manufactures, sources, markets and sells ophthalmic surgical and diagnostic instrumentation and related accessories, including disposable products. The Company's surgical equipment is designed forminimally invasive cataract treatment. The group's cataract removal system, the Photon(TM) laser system, is a laser cataract surgery system designed to be marketed as the next generation of cataract removal. In October 2004, the group entered into a Manufacturing and Distribution Agreement with E-Technologies, Inc., a Iowa based developer of software and related technology for technical applications. In September 2002, the group acquired International Bio-Immune Systems, Inc.

Primary SIC and add'l.: 3841 3851 3845

CIK No: 0000916444

Officers: Raymond Cannefax/CEO, Pres., Luis Mostacero/VP - Finance

Owners: Insiders/4.60%, David M. Silver, John C. Pingree, Raymond P.L. Cannefax/3.60%, Randall A. Mackey, Keith D. Ignotz

Financial Data: *Fiscal Year End:*12/31 *Latest Annual Data:* 12/31/2006

Year	Sales	Net Income
2006	$2,195,000	-$1,816,000
2005	$2,201,000	-$5,389,000
2004	$3,062,000	$64,000

Curr. Assets:	$1,572,000	**Curr. Liab.:**	$1,202,000		
Plant, Equip.:	$21,000	**Total Liab.:**	$3,857,000	**Indic. Yr. Divd.:**	NA
Total Assets:	$1,932,000	**Net Worth:**	-$1,925,000	**Debt/ Equity:**	NA

Paradise Inc

1200 Dr. Martin Luther King Jr. Blvd., Plant City, FL, 33563; *PH:* 1-813-752-1155; *Fax:* 1-813-754-3168; *http://* www.paradisefruitco.com

General - Incorporation FL
Employees 140
Auditor Bella, Hermida, Hancock & Mueller
Stk Agt Continental Stock Transfer & Trust Co
Counsel NA
DUNS No. 00-192-7102

Stock - Price on:12/24/2007 $18.5
Stock Exchange OTC
Ticker Symbol PARF
Outstanding Shares NA
E.P.S $0.78
Shareholders NA

Business: The group's principle activity is to operate through two segments: candied fruit and molded plastics. Candied fruit is a basic fruitcake ingredient sold to manufacturing bakers, institutional users and retailers for use in home baking. Candied fruit production also includes the processing of frozen strawberry products for sale to commercial and institutional users such as preservers, dairies and drink manufacturers. Molded plastics production involves the production of plastic containers for the company's products and other molded plastics for sale to unaffiliated customers. The principal raw materials used by the group are fruits, fruit peels, corn syrups and plastic resins. The trademarks of the group were paradise, dixie, mor-fruit and sun-ripe. Sales to retail outlets are usually generated through registered food brokers operating in exclusively franchised territories. The group's quarterly revenue for September 2007 was 10.36 millions of USD.

Primary SIC and add'l.: 3089 2051 5145 2064

CIK No: 0000076149

Subsidiaries: Paradise Plastics, Inc.

Officers: Melvin S. Gordon/74/Dir., Chmn., CEO/$418,226.00, Jack M. Laskowitz/51/CFO, Treasurer/$125,604.00, Randy S. Gordon/52/Dir., Pres./$263,103.00, Eugene L. Weiner/76/Dir., VP, Tracy W. Schulis/50/Dir., Sr. VP, Sec./$261,677.00, Mark H. Gordon/45/Dir., Exec. VP/$262,221.00

Directors: Melvin S. Gordon/74/Dir., Chmn., CEO, Randy S. Gordon/52/Dir., Pres., Eugene L. Weiner/76/Dir., VP, Tracy W. Schulis/50/Dir., Sr. VP, Sec., Mark H. Gordon/45/Dir., Exec. VP

Owners: Melvin S. Gordon/37.10%, Randy S. Gordon/1.40%, Eugene L. Weiner, Mark H. Gordon/1.70%, Insiders/41.90%, Tracy W. Schulis/1.70%

Financial Data: *Fiscal Year End:* 12/31 *Latest Annual Data:* 12/31/2006

Year	Sales		Net Income
2006	$26,072,000		$380,000
2005	$24,952,000		$557,000
2004	$22,764,000		$74,000
Curr. Assets:	$13,235,000	*Curr. Liab.:* $3,955,000	*P/E Ratio:* 23.72
Plant, Equip.:	$5,963,000	*Total Liab.:* $5,247,000	*Indic. Yr. Divd.:* $0.100
Total Assets:	$21,219,000	*Net Worth:* $15,973,000	*Debt/ Equity:* NA

ParaFin Corp

27127 Calle Arroyo, Ste. 1923, San Juan Capistrano, CA, 92675; *PH:* 1-877-613-3131; *Fax:* 1-866-613-3131; *http://* www.parafincorp.com; *Email:* ceo@parafincorp.com

General - Incorporation	NV	*Stock* - Price on:12/24/2007	NA
Employees	NA	Stock Exchange	OTC
Auditor	George Brenner, CPA	Ticker Symbol	PFNO
Stk Agt	Computershare Investor Services LLC	Outstanding Shares	NA
Counsel	NA	E.P.S.	-$0.398
DUNS No.	80-747-8110	Shareholders	NA

Business: The group's principal activity is to raise fund for charitable organizations using the proprietary 1 900 'pay-per-call' telephone numbers 1 900 'democrat', 1 900 'republican', 1 900 'stop abuse', 1 900 'HIV aids', 1 900 'HIV kids', 1 900 'get madd' and others. The group has agreements to raise funds for charitable organizations including broadway cares inc, action for peace foundation and national coalition against domestic violence.

Primary SIC and add'l.: 6733

CIK No: 0000311842

Subsidiaries: Encryption Technology Canada, Inc.

Officers: Sidney B. Fowlds/68/Chmn., Pres., John Johnston/Dir., VP, Anthony V. Feimann/Sec., Treasurer, Charles M. Gail/Drilling, Well Completion Petroleum Consultant, Frank Hariton/Corporate Legal Counsel, George Brenner/Auditor

Directors: Sidney B. Fowlds/68/Chmn., Pres., Robert M. Miller/Dir., John Johnston/Dir., VP

Financial Data: *Fiscal Year End:* 09/30 *Latest Annual Data:* 9/30/2006

Year	Sales		Net Income
2006	NA		-$9,349,000
2005	NA		-$1,022,000
2004	NA		-$730,000
Curr. Assets:	$88,332,000	*Curr. Liab.:* $70,457,000	
Plant, Equip.:	$59,643,000	*Total Liab.:* $157,687,000	*Indic. Yr. Divd.:* NA
Total Assets:	$188,547,000	*Net Worth:* $30,860,000	*Debt/ Equity:* NA

Paragon Financial Corp

2207 Sawgrass Village Dr., Ponte Vedra Beach, FL, 32082; *PH:* 1-904-285-0000; *http://* www.paragonfinancialcorp.com; *Email:* info@paragonfinancial.net

General - Incorporation	DE	*Stock* - Price on:12/24/2007	NA
Employees	33	Stock Exchange	NA
Auditor	Stevens, Powell & Co. P.A	Ticker Symbol	NA
Stk Agt	EquiServe Shareholder Services	Outstanding Shares	NA
Counsel	NA	E.P.S.	NA
DUNS No.	NA	Shareholders	NA

Business: The group's principal activity is to provide specialty financial services. The group provides mortgage products in the one-to-four family residential mortgage market. The mortgage products are offered to borrowers who generally do not satisfy the credit, documentation or other underwriting standards prescribed by conventional mortgage lenders or loan buyers. The group originates loans through wholesale and retail division. The wholesale division originates loans through a network of independent mortgage brokers and the retail division originates loans directly to the consumer through loan officers located at retail branch offices.

Primary SIC and add'l.: 6153 6159

CIK No: 0001089979

Subsidiaries: Paragon Homefunding, Inc

Officers: Aubrey Brown/CEO, Philip Rauch/CFO, Sec.

Financial Data: *Fiscal Year End:* 12/31 *Latest Annual Data:* 12/31/2005

Year	Sales		Net Income
2005	$1,502,000		-$100,000
2004	$2,034,000		-$4,661,000
2003	$13,905,000		-$1,397,000
Curr. Assets:	$118,000	*Curr. Liab.:* $1,668,000	
Plant, Equip.:	$53,000	*Total Liab.:* $1,830,000	*Indic. Yr. Divd.:* NA
Total Assets:	$1,399,000	*Net Worth:* -$431,000	*Debt/ Equity:* NA

Paragon National Bank TN

6300 Poplar Ave. Ste. 117, Memphis, TN, 38119; *PH:* 1-901-370-4968; *http://* www.bankparagon.com; *Email:* info@bankparagon.com

General - Incorporation		*Stock* - Price on:12/24/2007	$12
Employees	43	Stock Exchange	OTC
Auditor	Crowe, Chizek and Company LLC	Ticker Symbol	PGNN
Stk Agt	Michael S. Erhardt	Outstanding Shares	3,320,000
Counsel	NA	E.P.S.	NA
DUNS No.	NA	Shareholders	NA

Business: The groups principal activities include providing banking and financial services to its customers. Services of the group include checking accounts, personal banking, private banking, Debit cards, Credit Cards, ATM and online customer help. The group operates from the United States.

Primary SIC and add'l.: 6021

CIK No:

Officers: Robert S. Shaw/Dir., CEO, Pres., Michael S. Erhardt/CFO, Exec. VP, Andrew H. Taylor/Exec. VP, Sr. Credit Officer, Carol K. McConkey/Sr. VP, Sr. Consumer Banking Officer, Robert E. Word/Sr. VP, Mgr., Elizabeth W. Perry/Sr. VP - Private Banking, Gordin B. McMurtry/Sr. VP - Commercial Lending, Kimberly D. Hall/VP - Treasury Management, Harry A. Word/VP - Operations, Information Technology

Directors: Robert S. Shaw/Dir., CEO, Pres., Napoleon L. Cassibry/Chmn., Thomas E. Boggs/Dir., Glenn W. Cofield/Dir., James F. Freeman/Dir., Edith Kelly-Green/Dir., Robert J. Hussey/Dir., John T. Novarese/Dir., Deborah N. Pittman/Dir., Edwin S. Roberson/Dir., Christian J. Saenger/Dir., Dee Anna Smith/Dir., Craig L. Weiss/Dir.

Paragon Real Estate

180 Redwood St., San Francisco, CA, 94102; *PH:* 1-415-565-0500; *Fax:* 1-415-552-8367; *http://* www.paragon-re.com

General - Incorporation		*Stock* - Price on:12/24/2007	$0.42
Employees	NA	Stock Exchange	OTC
Auditor	Boulay, Heutmaker, Zibell & Co.	Ticker Symbol	PRLE
Stk Agt	American Stock Transfer & Trust Co.	Outstanding Shares	NA
Counsel	NA	E.P.S.	-$0.89
DUNS No.	NA	Shareholders	NA

Business: The groups principle activity is in the real estate dealing. The group also active acquisition of properties with many entities, including, among others, publicly traded REITs, life insurance companies, pension funds, partnerships and individual investors. The group operates from the United States.

Primary SIC and add'l.: 6798

CIK No: 0000928953

Officers: Bob Dadurka/CEO, Pres., Patrick Carlisle/Dir. - Business Development, Randy Zinn/VP - Marketing, Gil Mora/Sr. Loan Officer - Residential Pacific Mortgage, Sally Stull/COO, George McNabb/Exec. VP, Anita Head/Pres. - Paragon San Francisco, John J. Dee/56/Sr. VP, CFO - Trustee

Directors: John J. Dee/56/Sr. VP, CFO - Trustee, Daryl J. Carter/52/Trustee, Paul T. Lambert/55/Trustee, Michael T. Oliver/64/Trustee

Owners: Insiders/100.00%, James C. Mastandrea, James C. Mastandrea, James C. Mastandrea/23.30%, John J. Dee/5.10%, Insiders, Daryl J. Carter, Daniel G. DeVos/25.60%, Loeb Partners Corp., Michael T. Oliver/5.10%, Michael T. Oliver, Paragon Real Estate, Paragon Real Estate, John J. Dee, Paul T. Lambert *(18 Owners included in Index)*

Financial Data: *Fiscal Year End:* 12/31 *Latest Annual Data:* 12/31/2006

Year	Sales		Net Income
2006	$5,000		-$446,000
2005	$646,000		-$1,374,000
2004	$660,000		-$816,000
Curr. Assets:	$214,000	*Curr. Liab.:* $28,000	
Plant, Equip.:	$3,000	*Total Liab.:* $28,000	*Indic. Yr. Divd.:* NA
Total Assets:	$232,000	*Net Worth:* $204,000	*Debt/ Equity:* NA

Paragon Technologies Inc

600 Kuebler Rd., Easton, PA, 18040; *PH:* 1-610-252-3205; *Fax:* 1-610-252-3102; *http://* www.ptgamex.com; *Email:* info@ptgamex.com

General - Incorporation	DE	*Stock* - Price on:12/24/2007	$6.25
Employees	54	Stock Exchange	AMEX
Auditor	KPMG LLP	Ticker Symbol	PTG
Stk Agt	American Stock Transfer & Trust Co.	Outstanding Shares	2,770,000
Counsel	Pepper Hamilton LLP	E.P.S.	$0.01
DUNS No.	00-238-8528	Shareholders	NA

Business: The group's principal activity is to provide a variety of materials handling solutions, including systems, technologies, products and services for material flow applications. The group's capabilities include horizontal transportation, rapid dispensing, order fulfillment and integrating conveyors and conveyor systems. The products of the group include lo-tow(R), cartrac(R) and dispen-si-matic(tm). The group markets its products under the si systems, ermanco and paragon brands. The systems are designed, sold, manufactured, installed and serviced by the group's own staff or agents.

Primary SIC and add'l.: 3569 3535

CIK No: 0000090045

Subsidiaries: E Incorporated

Officers: Leonard S. Yurkovic/Dir., Acting CEO, Ronald J. Semanick/VP - Finance, CFO, Treasurer, Sec./$150,516.00, William J. Casey/COO, Pres./$187,368.00, John F. Lehr/VP/$171,168.00

Directors: Leonard S. Yurkovic/Dir., Acting CEO, Theodore W. Myers/Chmn., Anthony W. Schweiger/Dir., Robert Blyskal/Dir., Samuel L. Torrence/Dir.

Owners: Jack L. Bradt/8.00%, John F. Lehr, Anthony W. Schweiger, William J. Casey, Theodore W. Myers, Ronald J. Semanick, Emerald Advisers, Inc./11.90%, Insiders/11.20%, Leonard S. Yurkovic/1.00%

Financial Data: *Fiscal Year End:* 12/31 *Latest Annual Data:* 12/31/2006

Year	Sales		Net Income
2006	$17,788,000		$468,000
2005	$16,676,000		$1,198,000
2004	$42,255,000		$1,473,000
Curr. Assets:	$16,370,000	*Curr. Liab.:* $4,296,000	*P/E Ratio:* 625.00
Plant, Equip.:	$276,000	*Total Liab.:* $4,324,000	*Indic. Yr. Divd.:* NA
Total Assets:	$16,752,000	*Net Worth:* $12,428,000	*Debt/ Equity:* NA

Parallel Petroleum Corp

1004 N Big Spring, Ste. 400, Midland, TX, 79701; *PH:* 1-432-684-3727; *Fax:* 1-432-684-8057; *http://* www.parallel-petro.com

General - Incorporation	DE	*Stock* - Price on:12/24/2007	$22.8
Employees	41	Stock Exchange	NDQ
Auditor	BDO Seidman LLP	Ticker Symbol	PLLL
Stk Agt	Computershare Trust Co	Outstanding Shares	37,700,000
Counsel	Lynch, Chappell & Alsup	E.P.S.	$0.66
DUNS No.	02-193-7438	Shareholders	NA

Business: The group's principal activity is to explore, develop, produce and acquire oil and gas producing properties. The business activities are carried out primarily in Texas through three core areas: the onshore gulf coast area of south Texas, the permian basin of west Texas, and east Texas. The group uses 3-D seismic, avo and other technologies for successful drilling.

Primary SIC and add'l.: 1311 1381

CIK No: 0000750561

Subsidiaries: Parallel, L.P., Parallel, LLC

Officers: Larry C. Oldham/Founder, CEO, Pres./$552,773.00, Donald E. Tiffin/COO/$440,747.00, Steven D. Foster/CFO/$280,547.00, John S. Rutherford/VP - Land, Administration/$258,174.00, Eric A. Bayley/VP - Corporate Engineering/$259,321.00, Thomas W. Ortloff/Corp. Sec.

Directors: Larry C. Oldham/Founder, CEO, Pres., Thomas R. Cambridge/Chmn., Martin B. Oring/Dir., Ray M. Poage/Dir., Jeffery G. Shrader/Dir.

Owners: John S. Rutherford, Eric A. Bayley, Jeffrey G. Shrader, Donald E. Tiffin, Martin B. Oring, Thomas R. Cambridge/2.71%, Steven D. Foster, Ray M. Poage, Insiders/7.49%, Larry C. Oldham/2.39%

Financial Data: *Fiscal Year End:*12/31 *Latest Annual Data:* 12/31/2006

Year	Sales	Net Income
2006	$97,025,000	$26,155,000
2005	$66,150,000	-$1,589,000
2004	$35,837,000	$5,585,000

Curr. Assets:	$42,265,000	**Curr. Liab.:**	$50,981,000		
Plant, Equip.:	$388,506,000	**Total Liab.:**	$259,036,000	**Indic. Yr. Divd.:**	NA
Total Assets:	$442,818,000	**Net Worth:**	$183,782,000	**Debt/ Equity:**	1.1768

Parametric Technology Corp

140 Kendrick St., Needham, MA, 02494; *PH:* 1-781-370-5000; *Fax:* 1-781-370-6000; *http://* www.ptc.com

General - Incorporation	MA	**Stock**- Price on:12/24/2007	$20.3299
Employees	4,309	Stock Exchange	NDQ
Auditor	PricewaterhouseCoopers LLP	Ticker Symbol	PMTC
Stk Agt	American Stock Transfer & Trust Co.	Outstanding Shares	114,860,000
Counsel	Palmer & Dodge LLP	E.P.S	$1.22
DUNS No.	17-574-9431	Shareholders	NA

Business: The group's principal activities are to develop, market and support product lifestyle management software solutions and related services that help manufacturers improve the competitiveness of their products and product development processes. It has aligned its two business units, windchill and mcad under a common product strategy to meet the changing needs of manufacturers. The group's design solutions encompass a broad spectrum of engineering disciplines essential to the development of manufactured products. The collaboration and control solutions of the group offer a set of business software technologies for collaboration and control throughout the product lifecycle. The software solutions of the group focus on training, consulting, ancillary product offerings, implementation and support customers worldwide.

Primary SIC and add'l.: 7371 7372 7373

CIK No: 0000857005

Subsidiaries: 3rd Angle Limited, Advent 3B2 Inc., Aptavis Technologies Corporation, Arbortext Canada Inc., Arbortext France SARL, Arbortext GmbH, Arbortext Holdings B.V., Arbortext International, Inc., Arbortext Pte. Ltd., Arbortext Software GmbH, Arbortext Software Limited, Arbortext The Netherlands B.V., Arbortext United Kingdom Limited, Arbortext, Inc., Computervision (Canada) Inc. 76 Subsidiaries included in the Index

Officers: Richard C. Harrison/Dir., CEO, Pres., Barry Cohen/Exec. VP - Strategic Services, Partners, Paul J. Cunningham/Exec. VP - Worldwide Sales, Distribution, Steve Horan/Corporate VP, CIO, Aaron Von Staats/Sr. VP, General Counsel, Anthony Dibona/Exec. VP - Global Maintenance Support, Neil Moses/CFO, Exec. VP, James E. Heppelmann/Exec. VP - Software Solutions, Chief Product Officer, Cornelius F. Moses/50/CFO, Exec. VP

Directors: Richard C. Harrison/Dir., CEO, Pres., Noel G. Posternak/Chmn., Robert N. Goldman/Dir., Joseph M. O'Donnell/Dir., Donald K. Grierson/Dir., Oscar B. Marx/Dir., Michael E. Porter/Dir.

Owners: Noel G. Posternak/0.26%, Barclays Global Investors, NA/9.63%, Oscar B. Marx, Donald K. Grierson/0.11%, Cornelius F. Moses/0.40%, Robert N. Goldman/0.14%, Paul J. Cunningham/0.85%, Joseph M. ODonnell/0.03%, Richard C. Harrison/2.21%, Michael E. Porter/0.27%, James E. Heppelmann/0.90%, Insiders/5.81%, Barry F. Cohen/0.72%

Financial Data: *Fiscal Year End:*09/30 *Latest Annual Data:* 09/30/2007

Year	Sales	Net Income
2007	$941,279,000	$143,656,000
2006	$854,918,000	$60,866,000
2005	$720,719,000	$83,592,000

Curr. Assets:	$438,116,000	**Curr. Liab.:**	$346,704,000	**P/E Ratio:**	31.28
Plant, Equip.:	$51,603,000	**Total Liab.:**	$457,345,000	**Indic. Yr. Divd.:**	NA
Total Assets:	$895,444,000	**Net Worth:**	$438,099,000	**Debt/ Equity:**	NA

Paramount Gold & Silver Corp

Formerly: Paramount Gold Mining Corp

346 Waverley St., Ottawa, On, K2P 0W5; *PH:* 1-613-226-9881; *http://* www.paramountgold.com

General - Incorporation	DE	**Stock**- Price on:12/24/2007	$2.25
Employees	NA	Stock Exchange	OTC
Auditor	Cinnamon Jang Willoughby & Company	Ticker Symbol	PGDP
Stk Agt	Olde Monmouth Stk Trnsfer Co. Inc.	Outstanding Shares	NA
Counsel	NA	E.P.S	NA
DUNS No.	NA	Shareholders	NA

Business: The groups principal activity is an exploration stage, which has as its core business, precious metals exploration. The group operates from the United States, Canada, Mexico and Peru.

Primary SIC and add'l.: 1000

CIK No: 0001342854

Subsidiaries: Compania Minera Paramount SAC, Paramount Gold de Mexico S.A. de C.V.

Officers: Christopher Crupi/39/Dir., CEO, Pres., Treasurer, Charles W. Reed/Dir., Mgr. - Exploration, Mexico, Jean Depatie/Sr. Advisor to Board, John Simons/Sr. Advisor to Board, Lawrence Segerstrom/COO, Marc Slauenwhite/Sr. Project Geologist, South America, Lucie Letellier/47/CFO

Directors: Christopher Crupi/39/Dir., CEO, Pres., Treasurer, John Carden/Dir., Daniel Hachey/Dir., Charles W. Reed/Dir., Mgr. - Exploration, Mexico, Michel Yvan Stinglhamber/Dir., Ian Talbot/Dir.

Owners: Michael Clancy, Insiders/13.96%, Ian Talbot, Daniel Hachey/1.22%, Michel Yvan Stinglhamber, Charles Reed/2.55%, Christopher Crupi/8.59%, John Carden, Lucie Letellier, Sprott Asset Management Inc./9.40%, Libra Advisors Inc./9.22%

Parexel International Corp

200 W St., Waltham, MA, 02451; *PH:* 1-781-487-9900; *Fax:* 1-781-768-5512; *http://* www.parexel.com

General - Incorporation	MA	**Stock**- Price on:12/24/2007	$40.37
Employees	5,600	Stock Exchange	NDQ
Auditor	Ernst & Young LLP	Ticker Symbol	PRXL
Stk Agt	Computershare Investor Services LLC	Outstanding Shares	27,830,000
Counsel	Hale & Dorr LLP	E.P.S	$1.33
DUNS No.	04-021-0627	Shareholders	NA

Business: The group's principal activity is to provide biopharmaceutical services. It provides services in clinical research, medical marketing, consulting and informatics and advanced technology products and services to pharmaceutical, biotechnology and medical device industries. The group has four business segments. The clinical research services unit provides clinical trials management and biostatistical and data management services. The consulting group unit offers consulting and advisory services in support of product development, regulatory and marketing processes. Medical marketing services assists clients in achieving market penetration for their products by providing customized, integrated and expert product pre-launch and launch services. Perceptive provides technology products and services designed to improve clients' product development and commercialization processes. The group acquired on 31-Jan-2003 fwps group limited and on 22-Apr-2004 3clinicalresearch ag.

Primary SIC and add'l.: 8742 8071 8731 5122

CIK No: 0000799729

Subsidiaries: Bio/pharm Accelerator Management Company LLC, Broomco (2149) Ltd, Farmovs Parexel Ltd, Fraser Williams (Midlands) Ltd, FW Pharma Systems, FWPS Group Ltd, MMSQI, Inc, Parexel (imc), Inc., PAREXEL Baltics, PAREXEL Belgium B.V.B.A., Parexel Ett, S.l, PAREXEL Finland OY, PAREXEL Government Services, Inc, PAREXEL Hungary Limited, PAREXEL International 51 Subsidiaries included in the Index

Officers: Josef H. Von Rickenbach/Chmn., CEO, James F. Winschel/Sr. VP, CFO, Mark A. Goldberg/Pres. - Clinical Research Services, Perceptive Informatics, Kurt A. Brykman/Pres. - Parexel Consulting, Medical Communication Services, Ulf Schneider/Sr. VP, Chief Administrative Officer, Douglas A. Batt/Sr. VP, General Counsel, Corp. Sec., Jill L. Baker/VP - Investor Relations

Directors: Josef H. Von Rickenbach/Chmn., CEO, Dana A. Callow/55/Dir., Patrick J. Fortune/60/Dir., Richard L. Love/65/Dir., Ellen M. Zane/57/Dir., Christopher J. Lindop/50/Dir.

Owners: Wellington Management Company, LLP/8.99%, Douglas A. Batt/0.10%, Christopher J. Lindop, Richard L. Love/0.20%, Fidelity Management and Research/6.63%, Insiders/4.50%, Patrick J. Fortune, Dana A. Callow, Kurt A. Brykman/0.30%, Snyder Capital Management, L.P./5.14%, James F. Winschel, Ellen M. Zane, Mark A. Goldberg, Vanguard Specialized Funds Vanguard Health Care Fund/5.77%, Josef H. von Rickenbach/1.80% *(16 Owners included in Index)*

Financial Data: *Fiscal Year End:*06/30 *Latest Annual Data:* 6/30/2006

Year	Sales	Net Income
2006	$759,954,000	$23,544,000
2005	$671,537,000	-$35,177,000
2004	$658,603,000	$13,791,000

Curr. Assets:	$453,140,000	**Curr. Liab.:**	$334,394,000		
Plant, Equip.:	$97,233,000	**Total Liab.:**	$361,071,000	**Indic. Yr. Divd.:**	NA
Total Assets:	$680,013,000	**Net Worth:**	$316,616,000	**Debt/ Equity:**	NA

Park Bancorp Inc

5400 S Pulaski Rd., Chicago, IL, 60632; *PH:* 1-773-582-8200; *Fax:* 1-773-582-8201; *http://* www.parkfed.com

General - Incorporation	DE	**Stock**- Price on:12/24/2007	$29.92
Employees	58	Stock Exchange	NDQ
Auditor	Crowe Chizek & Co. LLC	Ticker Symbol	PFED
Stk Agt	LaSalle Bank N.A	Outstanding Shares	1,240,000
Counsel	Vedder, Price, Kaufman	E.P.S	$0.21
DUNS No.	06-748-1408	Shareholders	NA

Business: The group's principal activities are to provide banking and real estate development services. The group provides these services through its subsidiaries, park federal savings bank and pbi development corporation. The group mainly provides retail banking with operations conducted through the main office and two branches located in Chicago and westmont, Illinois. The group attracts deposits and provides fixed rate one-to-four-family residential mortgage loans, commercial real estate, construction, land and other consumer loans.

Primary SIC and add'l.: 6712 6021 6552 6035

CIK No: 0001013554

Subsidiaries: GPS Development Corp., Park Federal Savings Bank, PBI Development Corporation

Officers: David A. Remijas/Chmn., CEO, Pres./$311,375.00, Paul J. Lopez/Chief Lending Officer, Sr. VP/$156,753.00, Richard J. Remijas/COO, Exec. VP/$289,098.00, Steven J. Pokrak/Treasurer, CFO/$217,430.00, Maureen Schiesser/VP - Information Services, Savings Administration, Nancy Perchatsch/VP - Loan Administration, Curt Henry/VP, Branch Mgr. - Westmont Office, Eva Ayento/VP, Security Officer

Directors: David A. Remijas/Chmn., CEO, Pres., Robert W. Krug/Dir., Victor H. Reyes/Dir., Paul Shukis/Dir., John J. Murphy/Dir.

Owners: John J. Murphy/1.35%, Robert W. Krug/1.78%, David A. Remijas/11.02%, Insiders/33.31%, Paul J. Lopez/1.47%, Victor H. Reyes, Richard J. Remijas/8.53%, Park Federal Savings Bank/15.56%, Steven J. Pokrak/6.07%, Jeffrey L. Gendell/5.79%, Paul Shukis/2.64%

Financial Data: *Fiscal Year End:*12/31 *Latest Annual Data:* 06/30/2007

Year	Sales	Net Income
2007	NA	NA
2006	$12,959,000	NA
2005	$14,059,000	$630,000

Curr. Assets:	$16,280,000	**Curr. Liab.:**	$193,816,000		
Plant, Equip.:	$7,146,000	**Total Liab.:**	$198,069,000	**Indic. Yr. Divd.:**	$0.720
Total Assets:	$227,189,000	**Net Worth:**	$29,120,000	**Debt/ Equity:**	NA

Park City Group Inc

3160 Pinebrook Rd., Park City, UT, 84098; *PH:* 1-435-645-2000; *Fax:* 1-435-645-2010;
http:// www.parkcitygroup.com

General - Incorporation	NA	**Stock**- Price on:12/24/2007	$2.75
Employees	31	Stock Exchange	OTC
Auditor	HJ & Assoc., LLC	Ticker Symbol	PCYG
Stk Agt	Liberty Transfer Co	Outstanding Shares	8,950,000
Counsel	NA	E.P.S.	-$0.26
DUNS No.	NA	Shareholders	NA

Business: The group's principle activities are to design, develop, market and support proprietary software products. This software aims to help retail customers to boost sales while controlling their inventory and labor costs. The group offers actionmanager and fresh market manager applications as a superior set of software solutions to retailers in the store operations management and perishable product management areas. The group's customers include the home depot, foot locker, inc., the limited, albertson's, schnuck markets, pacific sunwear of California, wawa, busch entertainment and tesco lotus. The principal markets for the group's products are retail companies that have operations in North America and, to a lesser extent, in Europe and Asia. The group's total revenue for year 2007 was 2.59 millions of USD.

Primary SIC and add'l.: 7372 7379

CIK No: 0000050471

Subsidiaries: Fresh Market Manager, LLC, Riverview Financial Corp

Officers: Randall K. Fields/Chmn., CEO, Pres., William Dunlavy/53/CFO, Bob Hermanns/Dir., Sr. VP, Shaun Broadhead/Dir. - Research, Development, Carolyn Doll/VP - Marketing, Education, Russ Ruby/VP, Steve Lewis/Dir. - Business Metrics Group, Robert Hermanns/64/Dir., Sr. VP - Sales, John R. Merrill/38/CFO, Treasurer, Edward L. Clissold/52/Sec.

Directors: Randall K. Fields/Chmn., CEO, Pres., Edward C. Dmytryk/62/Dir., Bob Hermanns/Dir., Sr. VP, Robert Hermanns/64/Dir., Sr. VP - Sales, Thomas W. Wilson/76/Dir.

Owners: John R. Merrill, Robert Hermanns, Thomas W. Wilson, William Dunlavy, Randall K. Fields, Riverview Financial, Corp, Meadowbrook Opportunity Fund LLC/6.85%, London Family Trust/5.14%, Hillson Partners LP/8.56%, Edward C. Dmytryk

Financial Data: *Fiscal Year End:*06/30 *Latest Annual Data:* 6/30/2006

Year	Sales	Net Income
2006	$7,085,000	$1,394,000
2005	$3,632,000	-$3,408,000
2004	$6,030,000	-$675,000

Curr. Assets:	$6,351,000	**Curr. Liab.:**	$3,177,000		
Plant, Equip.:	$482,000	**Total Liab.:**	$3,402,000	**Indic. Yr. Divd.:**	NA
Total Assets:	$7,775,000	**Net Worth:**	$4,372,000	**Debt/ Equity:**	NA

Park Electrochemical Corp

48 S Service Rd., Melville, NY, 11747; *PH:* 1-631-465-3600; *Fax:* 1-631-465-3100;
http:// www.parkelectro.com; *Email:* pkny@parkelectro.com

General - Incorporation	NY	**Stock**- Price on:12/24/2007	$31.33
Employees	950	Stock Exchange	NYSE
Auditor	Grant Thornton, LLP	Ticker Symbol	PKE
Stk Agt	Registrar & Transfer Co	Outstanding Shares	20,200,000
Counsel	Skadden, Meagher & Flom LLP	E.P.S.	$1.68
DUNS No.	04-447-6224	Shareholders	NA

Business: The group's principal activities are to design, produce and market advanced electronic materials used to fabricate complex multilayer printed circuit boards and other electronic interconnection systems. The multilayer printed circuit board materials include copper-clad laminates and prepregs. The group specializes in advanced materials for high layer count circuit boards and high-speed digital broadband telecommunication, Internet and networking applications. It also designs, produces and manufactures specialty adhesive tapes and advanced composite materials for the electronics, aerospace and industrial markets. The group principally operates in North America, Singapore, China, Germany and France. On 27-Jun-2002, the group sold its dielectric polymers inc subsidiary.

Primary SIC and add'l.: 2891 3679

CIK No: 0000076267

Subsidiaries: Nelco Products Pte. Ltd., Nelco Products Sdn. Bhd., Nelco Products, Inc., Nelco STS, Inc., Nelco Technology (Zhuhai FTZ) Ltd., Nelco Technology, Inc., Nelcote, Inc., Neltec Europe SAS, Neltec SA, Neltec, Inc., Neluk, Inc., New England Laminates (U.K.) Ltd., New England Laminates Co., Inc., Park Advanced Product Development Corp., ParkNelco SNC 16 Subsidiaries included in the Index

Officers: Brian E. Shore/56/Chmn., CEO, Pres./$559,962.00, Stephen E. Gilhuley/63/Exec. VP, Sec., General Counsel/$265,594.00, James W. Kelly/51/VP - Taxes, Planning/$218,874.00, Anthony W. Digaudio/38/VP - Marketing, Sales/$176,018.00, Louis J. Stans/61/VP - Engineering, Quality/$167,415.00, James L. Zerby/65/CFO, VP/$103,271.00

Directors: Brian E. Shore/56/Chmn., CEO, Pres., Dale Blanchfield/70/Dir., Anthony Chiesa/87/Dir., Steven Warshaw/59/Dir., Lloyd Frank/82/Dir.

Owners: Jerry Shore/7.90%, Lloyd Frank, Louis J. Stans, Steven T. Warshaw, Insiders/4.00%, Anthony W. DiGaudio, Royce & Associates, LLC/5.20%, Wentworth, Hauser & Violich, Inc./5.40%, Anthony Chiesa, Dale Blanchfield, James W. Kelly, Stephen E. Gilhuley, Brian E. Shore/2.60%, Barclays Global Investors, NA/6.60%

Financial Data: *Fiscal Year End:*02/26 *Latest Annual Data:* 2/25/2007

Year	Sales	Net Income
2007	$257,377,000	$39,791,000
2006	$222,251,000	$26,875,000
2005	$211,187,000	$21,605,000

Curr. Assets:	$243,662,000	**Curr. Liab.:**	$42,161,000		
Plant, Equip.:	$63,251,000	**Total Liab.:**	$64,454,000	**Indic. Yr. Divd.:**	NA
Total Assets:	$307,311,000	**Net Worth:**	$242,857,000	**Debt/ Equity:**	NA

Park National Corp

50 N 3rd St., Newark, OH, 43058; *PH:* 1-740-349-8451; *Fax:* 1-740-349-3765;
http:// www.parknationalcorp.com

General - Incorporation	OH	**Stock**- Price on:12/24/2007	$87.06
Employees	1,892	Stock Exchange	AMEX
Auditor	Ernst & Young, LLP	Ticker Symbol	PRK
Stk Agt	First-Knox National Bank	Outstanding Shares	14,590,000
Counsel	NA	E.P.S.	$6.24
DUNS No.	NA	Shareholders	NA

Business: The group operates through its subsidiaries whose principal activity is banking operations. The group financial products include acceptance of savings, demand and term deposits, trust services, cash management and electronic fund transfer, on line internet banking, commercial loans. The group operates from the United States.

Primary SIC and add'l.: 6021 6022 6712

CIK No: 0000805676

Subsidiaries: Century National Bank, The First-Knox National Bank of Mount Vernon, The Park National Bank, The Richland Trust Company

Officers: Daniel C. Delawder/Chmn., CEO/$1,076,262.00, John W. Kozak/CFO/$449,336.00, David L. Trautman/Dir., Pres., Sec./$649,432.00

Directors: Daniel C. Delawder/Chmn., CEO, Harry O. Egger/Vice Chmn., David L. Trautman/Dir., Pres., Sec., William T. McConnell/Dir., Nicholas L. Berning/Dir., James J. Cullers/Dir., William A. Phillips/Dir., Rick R. Taylor/Dir., Leon Zazworsky/Dir., Maureen Buchwald/Dir., William F. Englefield/Dir., John J. O'Neill/Dir., Gilbert J. Reese/Dir.

Owners: Trust departments of bank/17.00%, Maureen Buchwald, James J. Cullers, William A. Phillips, John J. ONeill/1.30%, Leon Zazworsky, Harry O. Egger, Daniel C. DeLawder, Gilbert J. Reese/3.30%, David L. Trautman, William F. Englefield, John W. Kozak, Insiders/7.90%, William T. McConnell/1.40%, Rick R. Taylor

Financial Data: *Fiscal Year End:*12/31 *Latest Annual Data:* 12/31/2006

Year	Sales	Net Income
2006	$399,321,000	$94,091,000
2005	$374,164,000	$95,238,000
2004	$323,634,000	$91,507,000

Curr. Assets:	$212,379,000	**Curr. Liab.:**	$4,214,383,000		
Plant, Equip.:	$47,554,000	**Total Liab.:**	$4,900,437,000	**Indic. Yr. Divd.:**	$3.760
Total Assets:	$5,470,876,000	**Net Worth:**	$570,439,000	**Debt/ Equity:**	NA

Park Ohio Holdings Corp

23000 Euclid Ave., Cleveland, OH, 44117; *PH:* 1-216-692-7200; *Fax:* 1-216-692-6877;
http:// www.pkoh.com

General - Incorporation	OH	**Stock**- Price on:12/24/2007	$25.19
Employees	3,900	Stock Exchange	NDQ
Auditor	Ernst & Young LLP	Ticker Symbol	PKOH
Stk Agt	National City Bank	Outstanding Shares	11,370,000
Counsel	NA	E.P.S.	$2.22
DUNS No.	04-106-7752	Shareholders	NA

Business: The group's principal activities are to manufacture highly engineered products and to provide logistic services. It operates through three segments: integrated logistics solutions, aluminum products and manufactured products. Integrated logistics solutions supplies chain logistics provider of production components to large, multinational manufacturing companies, other manufacturers and distributors. Aluminum products manufactures cast aluminum components for automotive, agricultural equipment, heavy-duty truck and construction equipment. It also provides value-added services such as design and engineering, machining and assembly. Manufactured products operates a diverse group of niche manufacturing businesses that design and manufacture a broad range of high quality products engineered for specific customer applications. On 01-Apr-2004 the group acquired the remaining 66% of the common stock of Japan ajax magnethermic company.

Primary SIC and add'l.: 3567 3714 3089 3462 5072 3061 3463

CIK No: 0000076282

Subsidiaries: Ajax Tocco International Limited, Ajax Tocco Magnethermic (Shanghai) Co. Ltd., Ajax Tocco Magnethermic Canada Limited, Ajax Tocco Magnethermic Corporation, Ajax Tocco Magnethermic GmbH, Ajax Tocco Magnethermic Poland, Chambersburg Acquisition Corp., Control Transformer, Inc., FECO, Inc., General Aluminum Mfg. Company, ILS Technology, LLC, Integrated Holding Company, Integrated Logistics Company of Canada (1), Integrated Logistics Holding Company, Integrated Logistics Solutions de Mexico S.A. de C.V. 39 Subsidiaries included in the Index

Officers: Edward F. Crawford/68/Chmn., CEO/$2,114,111.00, Matthew V. Crawford/38/Dir., COO, Pres./$776,428.00, Richard P. Elliott/51/CFO, VP/$446,682.00, Robert D. Vilsack/Sec., General Counsel/$413,247.00, Patrick W. Fogarty/46/Dir. - Corporate Development/$355,410.00

Directors: Edward F. Crawford/68/Chmn., CEO, Matthew V. Crawford/38/Dir., COO, Pres., Patrick V. Auletta/57/Dir., Dan T. Moore/68/Dir., James W. Wert/61/Dir., Kevin R. Greene/49/Dir., Ronna Romney/64/Dir.

Owners: Matthew V. Crawford/12.30%, Dan T. Moore, GAMCO Investors, Inc./12.20%, Private Management Group, Inc./6.40%, Paulette R. Baum Revocable Living Trust u/a/d 7/21/98/5.40%, Robert D. Vilsack, Richard P. Elliott, Insiders/33.50%, Patrick W. Fogarty, James W. Wert/1.30%, Ronna Romney, Edward F. Crawford/20.80%, Kevin R. Greene, FMR Corp./9.00%, Patrick V. Auletta

Financial Data: *Fiscal Year End:*12/31 *Latest Annual Data:* 12/31/2006

Year	Sales	Net Income
2006	$1,056,246,000	$24,179,000
2005	$932,900,000	$30,808,000
2004	$808,718,000	$14,199,000

Curr. Assets:	$485,826,000	**Curr. Liab.:**	$217,392,000	**P/E Ratio:**	11.77
Plant, Equip.:	$113,045,000	**Total Liab.:**	$645,405,000	**Indic. Yr. Divd.:**	NA
Total Assets:	$784,142,000	**Net Worth:**	$138,737,000	**Debt/ Equity:**	NA

Parke Bancorp Inc

601 Delsea Dr., Sewell, NJ, 08080; *PH:* 1-856-256-2500; *Fax:* 1-856-256-2590;
http:// www.parkebank.com; *Email:* info@parkebank.com

General - Incorporation	NJ	**Stock**- Price on:12/24/2007	$17.67
Employees	35	Stock Exchange	NDQ
Auditor	McGladrey & Pullen, LLP	Ticker Symbol	PKBK
Stk Agt	LaSalle Bank N.A	Outstanding Shares	3,170,000
Counsel	NA	E.P.S.	$1.53
DUNS No.	NA	Shareholders	NA

Business: The groups principal activity is to provide banking and financial services.The products of the group include residential and commercial, real estate, construction loans, working capital loans and lines of credit and demand. The group operates from the United States. The assets of the group for the year 2006 were $60.0 (million).

Primary SIC and add'l.: 6099 6712 6022

CIK No: 0001315399

Subsidiaries: Farm Folly LLC, Parke Bank, Parke Capital Markets, Parke Capital Trust I, Parke Capital Trust II

Officers: Vito S. Pantilione/Dir., CEO, Pres./$598,944.00, Robert A. Kuehl/CFO, Sr. VP/$29,111.00, Elizabeth Milavsky/Sr. VP - Branch Administration, Systems, Parke Bank/$146,730.00, David O. Middlebrook/Sr. VP, Sr. Loan Officer - Parke Bank/$232,258.00, Paul Palmieri/Sr. VP - Philadelphia Region, Parke Bank/$139,317.00, Dolores Calvello/Assist. VP, Loan Officer, John Campbell/Dir. - Business Development, Parkebank

Directors: Vito S. Pantilione/Dir., CEO, Pres., Thomas E. Hedenberg/Vice Chmn. - Parke Bank, Celestino R. Pennoni/Chmn., Ray Tresch/Dir., Edward Infantolino/Dir., Jeff Kripitz/Dir., Jack Sheppard/Dir., Richard Phalines/Dir., Arret F. Dobson/Dir., Daniel J. Dalton/Dir., Fred G. Choate/Dir., Anthony J. Jannetti/Dir.

Owners: Arret F. Dobson/3.58%, Jeffrey H. Kripitz/6.78%, Celestino R. Pennoni/5.80%, Paul E. Palmieri, Elizabeth A. Milavsky, Jack C. Sheppard/4.27%, Daniel J. Dalton/2.81%, Fred G. Choate, Richard Phalines/3.84%, Thomas Hedenberg/2.43%, Ray H. Tresch/3.30%, David O. Middlebrook/1.12%, Banc Fund V L.P. and Banc/8.43%, Robert A. Kuehl, Vito S. Pantilione/6.31% (18 Owners included in Index)

Financial Data: Fiscal Year End:12/31 **Latest Annual Data:** 12/31/2006

Year	Sales	Net Income
2006	$26,332,000	$4,624,000
2005	$18,242,000	$3,494,000
2004	$12,627,000	$2,722,000

Curr. Assets:	$20,240,000	**Curr. Liab.:**	$318,877,000			
Plant, Equip.:	$3,432,000	**Total Liab.:**	$329,288,000	**Indic. Yr. Divd.:**	NA	
Total Assets:	$359,997,000	**Net Worth:**	$30,709,000	**Debt/ Equity:**	0.3389	

Parker Drilling Co

1401 EnclAve. Pkwy., Ste. 600, Houston, TX, 77077; **PH:** 1-281-406-2000; **Fax:** 1-281-406-2001; **http://** www.parkerdrilling.com

General - Incorporation	DE	**Stock**- Price on:12/24/2007	$11.5
Employees	2,628	Stock Exchange	NYSE
Auditor	PricewaterhouseCoopers LLP	Ticker Symbol	PKD
Stk Agt	Wells Fargo Bank, N.A.	Outstanding Shares	111,630,000
Counsel	NA	E.P.S.	$0.94
DUNS No.	00-790-7850	Shareholders	NA

Business: The group's principal activities are to provide land and offshore contract drilling services and rental tools on a worldwide basis to major, independent and foreign-owned oil and gas companies. The group specializes in the drilling of deep and difficult wells, drilling in remote and harsh environments, drilling in transition zones and offshore waters and in providing specialized rental tools. The group also provides a range of services that are ancillary to its principal drilling services, including engineering and logistics, as well as various types of project management. The group has seven shallow water jackup rigs in the gulf of Mexico. The group's drilling customer base consists of major, independent and foreign-owned oil and gas companies. Major customers of the group include royal dutch shell, tengizchevroil, and chevrontexaco corporation. In 2003, the group discontinued Latin America operations and the U.S. Jackup and platform drilling operations.

Primary SIC and add'l.: 2911 1381 7359

CIK No: 0000076321

Subsidiaries: Parker Drilling (Kazakstan), Ltd., Parker Drilling Company International Limited, Parker Drilling Company International, Inc, Parker Drilling Company Limited, Parker Drilling Company of New Guinea, Inc., Parker Drilling Company of Oklahoma, Incorporated, Parker Drilling Company(Bolivia) S.A., Parker North America Operations, Inc., Parker Technology, Inc., Parker-VSE, Inc., Universal Rig Service Corp.

Officers: Robert L. Parker/Chmn., CEO, Pres./$2,653,040.00, Robert N. White/VP - Business Development, James Hutchinson/Victoria Mgr., Ben Lacy/Odessa Mgr., Greg Sentell/Sr. Business Development Mgr., John Lechner/Sr. Business Development Mgr., Bruce Black/Sr. Business Development Mgr., Tony Petticrew/Mgr. - Contracts, Marketing, Toby Begnaud/US Sales Mgr., Kent Gerdsen/US Sales Mgr., John Prejean/US Sales Mgr., Glenn Jones/Instructor, John Stanway/Instructor, Jeremy Eubanks/Instructor, Sean Mills/Instructor (35 Officers included in Index)

Directors: Robert L. Parker/Chmn., CEO, Pres., James W. Whalen/65/Vice Chmn., John W. Gibson/Dir., Robert E. Mckee/Dir., Roger B. Plank/Dir., Rudolph R. Reinfrank/Dir., Robert W. Goldman/Dir., George J. Donnelly/Dir.

Owners: Robert L. Parker/1.42%, Kirk W. Brassfield, Denis Graham, Insiders/2.92%, R. Rudolph Reinfrank, John W. Gibson, Robert L. Parker, David C. Mannon, Ronald C. Potter, Roger B. Plank

Financial Data: Fiscal Year End:12/31 **Latest Annual Data:** 12/31/2006

Year	Sales	Net Income
2006	$586,435,000	$81,026,000
2005	$531,662,000	$98,883,000
2004	$376,525,000	-$47,083,000

Curr. Assets:	$317,574,000	**Curr. Liab.:**	$101,903,000	**P/E Ratio:**	12.64
Plant, Equip.:	$440,301,000	**Total Liab.:**	$442,202,000	**Indic. Yr. Divd.:**	NA
Total Assets:	$901,301,000	**Net Worth:**	$459,099,000	**Debt/ Equity:**	NA

Parker-Hannifin Corp

6035 Pk.land Blvd., Cleveland, OH, 44124; **PH:** 1-216-896-3000; **Fax:** 1-216-896-4000; **http://** www.parker.com; **Email:** c-parker@parker.com

General - Incorporation	OH	**Stock**- Price on:12/24/2007	$100.2
Employees	57,073	Stock Exchange	NYSE
Auditor	PricewaterhouseCoopers LLP	Ticker Symbol	PH
Stk Agt	National City Bank	Outstanding Shares	115,830,000
Counsel	NA	E.P.S.	$4.83
DUNS No.	00-417-5550	Shareholders	NA

Business: The groups principle activity is to manufacture motion control products. The group also provide fluid purification, fluid and fuel control, process instrumentation, air conditioning, refrigeration, and electromagnetic shielding. In the year 2007, the group acquired Kay Pneumatics Ltd and Scan Subsea ASA. The group operates from United States.

Primary SIC and add'l.: 3593 3594 3492 3546

CIK No: 0000076334

Subsidiaries: 265 Warwick LLC, 506655nb Inc., Acadia International Insurance Limited, Acofab SAS, Adecem SARL, Advanced Products NV, Advanced Products UK Ltd., AFL Limited, Alenco (Holdings) Ltd., Alkid Corporation, Annapurna Kenmore Tube Products Private Limited, Denison Financial Holdings Ltd., Denison Hydraulics Pty. Ltd., Denison Hydraulics UK Ltd., Denison International Ltd. 181 Subsidiaries included in the Index

Officers: Donald E. Washkewicz/Chmn., CEO, Pres./$17,065,010.00, William G. Eline/CIO, VP, Craig Maxwell/VP - Technology, Innovation, Thomas L. Williams/Sr. VP, Operating Officer, Thomas A. Piraino/VP, General Counsel, Sec., Dana A. Dennis/VP, Controller, Roger S. Sherrard/VP, Pres. - Automation Group, Timothy K. Pistell/Exec. VP - Finance, Administration, CFO/$5,965,560.00, Pamela J. Huggins/VP, Treasurer, Marwan M. Kashkoush/Corporate VP - Worldwide Sales, Marketing, Joseph J. Vicic/VP, Pres. - Asia Pacific Group, Jeffery A. Cullman/VP, Pres. - Hydraulics Group, John R. Greco/VP, Pres. - Instrumentation Group, William R. Hoelting/VP - Tax, Robert P. Barker/58/Sr. VP, Operating Officer, Pres. - Aerospace Group (24 Officers included in Index)

Directors: Donald E. Washkewicz/Chmn., CEO, Pres., Candy M. Obourn/Dir., Wolfgang R. Schmitt/Dir., Robert J. Kohlhepp/Dir., Klaus-Peter Mueller/Dir., Joseph M. Scaminace/Dir., Markos I. Tambakeras/Dir., Linda S. Harty/Dir., Giulio Mazzalupi/Dir., William E. Kassling/Dir.

Owners: L. C. Banks, J. M. Scaminace, Wellington Management Company, LLP/5.88%, W. R. Schmitt, R. J. Kohlhepp, J. D. Myslenski, D. E. Collins, Capital Research and Management Company/5.96%, P. W. Likins, N. W. Vande Steeg, R. P. Barker, D. E. Washkewicz, W. E. Kassling, C. M. Obourn, M. I. Tambakeras (20 Owners included in Index)

Financial Data: Fiscal Year End:06/30 **Latest Annual Data:** 6/30/2006

Year	Sales	Net Income
2006	$9,385,888,000	$673,167,000
2005	$8,215,095,000	$604,692,000
2004	$7,106,907,000	$345,783,000

Curr. Assets:	$3,138,978,000	**Curr. Liab.:**	$1,681,105,000	**P/E Ratio:**	14.82
Plant, Equip.:	$1,693,794,000	**Total Liab.:**	$3,932,229,000	**Indic. Yr. Divd.:**	$1.040
Total Assets:	$8,173,432,000	**Net Worth:**	$4,241,203,000	**Debt/ Equity:**	0.2468

Parkervision Inc

7915 Baymeadows Way, Ste. 400, Jacksonville, FL, 32256; **PH:** 1-800-532-8034; **Fax:** 1-904-731-0958; **http://** www.parkervision.com

General - Incorporation	FL	**Stock**- Price on:12/24/2007	$11.92
Employees	51	Stock Exchange	NDQ
Auditor	PricewaterhouseCoopers LLP	Ticker Symbol	PRKR
Stk Agt	American Stock Transfer & Trust Co.	Outstanding Shares	24,490,000
Counsel	NA	E.P.S.	-$0.7
DUNS No.	60-818-1384	Shareholders	NA

Business: The group's principal activities are to design, develop and market video systems; automated production systems and the development of wireless direct conversion radio frequency technology. The operations are categorized into two segments namely video division and wireless division. The video division is engaged in the design, development and marketing of automated live television production systems, marketed under the tradename pvtv(tm), and automated video camera control systems, marketed under the tradename cameraman(r). The group also provides training, support and other services related to these products. The wireless division is engaged in the development and initial marketing of integrated circuits based on its direct2data(tm) technology. In 2002, the group discontinued the manufacture and sale of its single-chip systems.

Primary SIC and add'l.: 3663 3861

CIK No: 0000914139

Subsidiaries: D2D, LLC, Direct2Data Technologies, Inc.

Officers: Jeffrey L. Parker/Chmn., CEO/$472,662.00, Paul G. Henning/Investor Relations Officer, David F. Sorrells/Dir., CTO/$538,827.00, Todd Parker/Dir., VP/$201,916.00, Carolyn B. Wrenn/Dir. - Investor Relations

Directors: Jeffrey L. Parker/Chmn., CEO, William A. Hightower/Dir., Papken S. Der Torossian/Dir., Nam P. Suh/Dir., John Metcalf/Dir., David F. Sorrells/Dir., CTO, Todd Parker/Dir., VP, William L. Sammons/Dir., Robert G. Sterne/Dir.

Owners: Insiders/21.63%, David F. Sorrells/2.57%, Heartland Value Fund/7.84%, Jeffrey L. Parker/12.24%, Cynthia Poehlman/0.73%, Robert G. Sterne/0.71%, William A. Hightower/0.87%, Todd Parker/4.17%, William L. Sammons/0.66%, John Metcalf/0.28%, Papken S. der Torossian/0.58%, Nam P. Suh/0.52%, Wellington Management Company, LLP/14.04%

Financial Data: Fiscal Year End:12/31 **Latest Annual Data:** 12/31/2006

Year	Sales	Net Income
2006	NA	-$15,816,000
2005	$996,000	-$23,099,000
2004	$441,000	-$14,815,000

Curr. Assets:	$14,373,000	**Curr. Liab.:**	$1,059,000		
Plant, Equip.:	$2,094,000	**Total Liab.:**	$1,492,000	**Indic. Yr. Divd.:**	NA
Total Assets:	$26,675,000	**Net Worth:**	$25,183,000	**Debt/ Equity:**	NA

Parkvale Financial Corp

4220 William Penn Hwy., Monroeville, PA, 15146; **PH:** 1-412-373-7200; **Fax:** 1-412-856-3943; **http://** www.parkvale.com

General - Incorporation	PA	**Stock**- Price on:12/24/2007	$29.7
Employees	380	Stock Exchange	NDQ
Auditor	Parente Randolph LLC	Ticker Symbol	PVSA
Stk Agt	Registrar & Transfer Co	Outstanding Shares	5,650,000
Counsel	NA	E.P.S.	$2.34
DUNS No.	19-454-0555	Shareholders	NA

Business: The group's principal activity is to provide banking services. It accepts deposits from the general public and invests such deposits together with other funds in residential real estate loans, consumer loans, commercial loans and investment securities. It provides consumer and commercial services to individuals, partnerships and corporations in pittsburgh. The group also provides different services such as various types of deposit, commercial checking accounts and automated teller machines. At 31-Mar-2004, the group operates through 39 full-service offices in allegheny, beaver, butler, fayette, Washington and westmoreland counties.

Primary SIC and add'l.: 6712 6035

CIK No: 0000820907

Subsidiaries: Parkvale, Parkvale Mortgage Corporation

Officers: Robert J. McCarthy/65/Dir., CEO, Pres./$714,596.00, Janice Bradstreet/Parkvale Insurance Mgr., Jason W. Ross/34/Audit Compliance Dir., Joseph C. Defazio/47/Assist. Treasurer, Timothy G. Rubritz/54/VP, Treasurer/$234,159.00, Gail B. Anwyll/56/Dir. - Human Resources, Marketing, Assist. Corp. Sec./$140,600.00

Directors: Robert J. McCarthy/65/Dir., CEO, Pres., Robert D. Pfischner/86/Chmn., Fred P. Burger/81/Dir., Andrea F. Fitting/54/Dir., Stephen M. Gagliardi/60/Dir., Patrick J. Minnock/51/Dir., Harry D. Reagan/75/Dir.

Owners: Tontine Partners/5.08%, Robert J. McCarthy, Insiders/18.54%, Gail B. Anwyll, Gilbert A. Riazzi, Timothy G. Rubritz/2.26%, Harry D. Reagan, Parkvale Financial Corporation/10.43%, Patrick J. Minnock, Robert D. Pfischner/2.13%, Stephen M. Gagliardi, Fred P. Burger/3.10%, Thomas R. Ondek, Andrea F. Fitting

Financial Data: Fiscal Year End:06/30 **Latest Annual Data:** 6/30/2006

Year	Sales	Net Income
2006	$98,990,000	$13,312,000
2005	$85,698,000	$11,667,000
2004	$78,111,000	$10,016,000

Curr. Assets:	$146,943,000	**Curr. Liab.:**	$1,678,371,000	**P/E Ratio:**	12.86
Plant, Equip.:	$18,567,000	**Total Liab.:**	$1,736,011,000	**Indic. Yr. Divd.:**	$0.800
Total Assets:	$1,858,715,000	**Net Worth:**	$122,704,000	**Debt/ Equity:**	0.1714

Parkway Bank

4800 N Harlem Ave., Harwood Heights, IL, 60706; **PH:** 1-708-867-6600; **Fax:** 1-708-867-1119; **http://** www.parkwaybank.com

General - Incorporation		**Stock**- Price on:12/24/2007	$12
Employees	NA	Stock Exchange	OTC
Auditor	NA	Ticker Symbol	PKWY
Stk Agt	Registrar & Transfer Co	Outstanding Shares	NA
Counsel	NA	E.P.S.	NA
DUNS No.	NA	Shareholders	NA

Business: The groups principal activities include providing banking and financial services. Services of the group include cash management, small business loans, real estate loans, International banking, ATM, Debit Cards and Credit cards. The group operates from the United States.

Primary SIC and add'l.: 6029

CIK No: 0001306708

Officers: Milos Sekulic/Branch Mgr. - Chicago, Elston, Chicago, Six Corners, Michael Swinford/Branch Mgr. - Chicago, Jefferson Park, Christine Celik/Branch Mgr. - Deerfield, Robert Makanoeich/Branch Mgr. - Elk Grove, Karen Franciere/Branch Mgr. - Glendale Heights, Walter Davidson/Branch Mgr. - Mount Prospect North, Park Ridge North, Steven Alexander/Branch Mgr. - Niles, Sandy Severin-Svizzero/Branch Mgr. - Park Ridge South, Beata Santarsieri/Branch Mgr. - Schaumburg, Diana Wrona/Branch Mgr. - Wood Dale, Erica Bosco/Mortgage Loan Consultant, Walter Latocha/Home Mortgage Consultant, Shannon Ryan/Branch Mgr. - Harwood Heights, Main, Norridge, Andrea Pilipuf/Branch Mgr. - Antioch, Grace Popovich/Branch Mgr. - Arlington Heights, Mount Prospect South *(17 Officers included in Index)*

Parkway Properties Inc

1 Jackson Pl., 188 East Capitol St., Ste. 1000, Jackson, MS, 39201; **PH:** 1-601-948-4091; **Fax:** 1-601-949-4077; **http://** www.pky.com

General - Incorporation	MD	**Stock**- Price on:12/24/2007	$49.68
Employees	282	Stock Exchange	NYSE
Auditor	Ernst & Young LLP	Ticker Symbol	PKY
Stk Agt	Computershare Investor Services LLC	Outstanding Shares	15,890,000
Counsel	NA	E.P.S.	$1.32
DUNS No.	NA	Shareholders	NA

Business: The groups principle activities include operating, leasing, acquiring and owning office properties. In the year 2006, the group acquired BellSouth Building and Centurion Centre. The group operates from the United States.

Primary SIC and add'l.: 6798

CIK No: 0000729237

Subsidiaries: 111 Capitol Building LP, 111 East Wacker LLC, Chicago OfficeInvest LLC, Golf Properties, Inc., Moore Building Associates LP, Moore Garage LLC, Parkway 233 North Michigan LLC, Parkway 233 North Michigan Manager, Inc., Parkway Capitol Center LLC, Parkway Chicago LLC, Parkway Jackson LLC, Parkway JHLIC LP, Parkway Lamar LLC, Parkway Mississippi LLC, Parkway Moore LLC 33 Subsidiaries included in the Index

Officers: Steven G. Rogers/Dir., CEO, Pres./$691,819.00, William R. Flatt/CFO, Exec. VP, Sec./$256,070.00, James M. Ingram/Exec. VP, Chief Investment Officer/$360,940.00, Thomes C. Maloney/COO, Exec. VP/$372,953.00, Barbara A. Griffin/VP - Risk Management, Carol Matheny/VP - Property Management Systems, Lee Nations/VP, John Gifford/VP, Asset Mgr., Darryl Waltman/VP, Assist. Controller, Ron Coffey/VP - Technical Services, Mandy M. Pope/Sr. VP, Controller/$193,254.00, Mitch G. Mattingly/Exec. VP, Sr. Asset Mgr./$303,733.00, John J. Buckley/Sr. VP, Asset Mgr., Roy H. Butts/Sr. VP, Treasurer, Sarah P. Clark/Sr. VP - Strategic Planning, Investor Relations *(24 Officers included in Index)*

Directors: Steven G. Rogers/Dir., CEO, Pres., Leland R. Speed/Chmn., Roger P. Friou/Dir., Daniel P. Friedman/Dir., Martin Garcia/Dir., Michael J. Lipsey/Dir., Joe F. Lynch/Dir., Matthew W. Kaplan/Dir., Lenore M. Sullivan/Dir., Troy A. Stovall/43/Dir.

Owners: Martin L. Garcia, Cohen & Steers, Inc./13.10%, Thomas C. Maloney, Daniel P. Friedman, Barclays Global Investors, NA/7.50%, The Vanguard Group, Inc./5.90%, Lenore M. Sullivan, Deutsche Bank AG/9.70%, Insiders/3.50%, Matthew W. Kaplan, Roger P. Friou, Leland R. Speed, Goldman Sachs Asset Management, L.P./6.00%, William R. Flatt, Mitch G. Mattingly *(20 Owners included in Index)*

Financial Data: Fiscal Year End:12/31 **Latest Annual Data:** 12/31/2006

Year	Sales	Net Income
2006	$215,336,000	$25,682,000
2005	$195,897,000	$20,807,000
2004	$164,375,000	$29,515,000

Curr. Assets:	$30,353,000	**Curr. Liab.:**	$67,258,000	**P/E Ratio:**	40.06
Plant, Equip.:	$1,307,748,000	**Total Liab.:**	$1,022,040,000	**Indic. Yr. Divd.:**	$2.600
Total Assets:	$1,512,346,000	**Net Worth:**	$490,306,000	**Debt/ Equity:**	NA

Parlex Corp

One Parlex Pl., Methuen, MA, 01844; **PH:** 1-978-685-4341; **http://** www.parlex.com

General - Incorporation	MA	**Stock**- Price on:12/24/2007	$5.6
Employees	NA	Stock Exchange	NA
Auditor	Deloitte & Touche LLP	Ticker Symbol	NA
Stk Agt	EquiServe Trust Co N.A	Outstanding Shares	NA
Counsel	Kuitchin & Ruffo	E.P.S.	NA
DUNS No.	05-177-8934	Shareholders	NA

Business: The group's principal activity is to design and manufacture flexible interconnect solutions. Flexible interconnects provide electrical connection between components in electronic systems and are used as a platform to support the attachment of electronic devices. The products offered include flexible circuits, laminated cable, flexible interconnect hybrid circuits, and flexible interconnect assemblies. These products are sold to automotive, telecommunications and networking, diversified electronics, military, home appliance, electronic identification and computer markets. The customers of the group include dell computer, lexmark, motorola, nortel networks, hewlett-packard, honeywell, kulicke and soffa industries, lexmark, pitney bowes, siemens, symbol technologies and visteon. The products are sold in the United States, China, Mexico and the United Kingdom.

Primary SIC and add'l.: 8711 3678

CIK No: 0000724988

Subsidiaries: Pacific Advanced Interconnect Products Ltd., Parlex (China) Investment Limited, Parlex (Europe) Limited, Parlex (Shanghai) Circuit Co., Ltd., Parlex (Shanghai) Interconnect Products, Co, Parlex (Shanghai) Interconnect Technologies, Ltd., Parlex Asia Pacific Ltd., Parlex Corporation Limited, Parlex Dynaflex Corporation, Parlex International Corporation, Poly-Flex Circuits Limited, Poly-Flex Circuits, Inc.

Parlux Fragrances Inc

3725 SW 30th Ave., Fort Lauderdale, FL, 33312; **PH:** 1-954-316-9008; **Fax:** 1-954-316-9152; **http://** www.parlux.com; **Email:** info@parlux.com

General - Incorporation	DE	**Stock**- Price on:12/24/2007	$4.67
Employees	144	Stock Exchange	NDQ
Auditor	Deloitte & Touche LLP	Ticker Symbol	PARL
Stk Agt	American Stock Transfer & Trust Co.	Outstanding Shares	18,070,000
Counsel	NA	E.P.S.	NA
DUNS No.	07-764-6362	Shareholders	NA

Business: The group's principal activity is to manufacture and distribute fragrances and beauty related products. The group's products are marketed primarily through specialty stores, national department stores and perfumeries on a worldwide basis. The brand names under which the products are marketed are perry ellis, fred hayman beverly hills, ocean pacific, jockey, and baryshnikov. The beauty and grooming products include soaps, shower gels, deodorants, body lotions, creams and dusting powders which are sold under exclusive license agreements. The group's distributors are located in Canada, Europe, the Middle East, the Far East, Latin America, the Caribbean and Russia.

Primary SIC and add'l.: 2844

CIK No: 0000802356

Subsidiaries: E Com Ventures, Inc., Parlux S.A, Parlux, Ltd., Perfumania Inc.

Officers: Neil J. Katz/63/Chmn., CEO/$62,116.00, Raymond J. Balsys/CFO, VP - Principal Financial, Principal Accounting Officer

Directors: Glenn Gopman/52/Dir., Esther Egozi Choukroun/46/Dir., David Stone/58/Dir., Anthony Dagostino/51/Dir., Robert Mitzman/53/Dir.

Owners: LaGrange Capital Administration, LLC/9.40%, Glenn Nussdorf/11.70%, Lotsoff Capital Management/6.00%, River Road Asset Management, LLC/5.80%, Neil J. Katz, Anthony DAgostino, David Stone, Dimensional Fund Advisors, Inc./6.50%, Raymond J. Balsys, Ilia Lekach/6.40%, Glenn Gopman, Frank A. Buttacavoli/4.40%, Jaya Kader Zebede, Insiders/5.00%

Financial Data: Fiscal Year End:03/31 **Latest Annual Data:** 03/31/2007

Year	Sales	Net Income
2007	$134,365,000	$2,882,000
2006	$182,237,000	$22,736,000
2005	$100,361,000	$10,824,000

Curr. Assets:	$73,762,000	**Curr. Liab.:**	$13,192,000		
Plant, Equip.:	$927,000	**Total Liab.:**	$14,895,000	**Indic. Yr. Divd.:**	NA
Total Assets:	$88,276,000	**Net Worth:**	$73,381,000	**Debt/ Equity:**	0.0151

Particle Drilling Technologies Inc

1 City Ctr., 1021 Main St., Ste. 2650, Houston, TX, 77041; **PH:** 1-713-223-3031; **Fax:** 1-713-224-6361; **http://** www.particledrilling.com; **Email:** info@particledrilling.com

General - Incorporation	NV	**Stock**- Price on:12/24/2007	$2.3201
Employees	18	Stock Exchange	NDQ
Auditor	UHY Mann Frankfort Stein & Lipp CPAs	Ticker Symbol	PDRT
Stk Agt	Computershare Trust Co	Outstanding Shares	30,620,000
Counsel	Vinson & Elkins LLP	E.P.S.	-$0.43
DUNS No.	NA	Shareholders	NA

Business: The group operates through its subsidiaries whose principle activity is to develop Particle Impact Drilling System. The group operates from the United States.

Primary SIC and add'l.: 1382 3533

CIK No: 0000759153

Subsidiaries: Particle Drilling Technologies, Inc

Officers: Jim B. Terry/Dir., CEO, Pres., Chris J. Boswell/Sr. VP, CFO, Thomas E. Hardisty/Sr. VP - Corporate Development, Gordon Tibbitts/VP - Technology, Greg Galloway/VP - Engineering, Operations

Directors: Jim B. Terry/Dir., CEO, Pres., Ken R. Lesuer/Chmn., Steve A. Weyel/Dir., Hugh Menown/Dir., Michael S. Mathews/Dir., John D. Schiller/Dir.

Owners: Insiders/19.00%, Ken R. LeSuer, Jim B. Terry/2.60%, Chris J. Boswell/5.60%, John D. Schiller/5.60%, Greywolf Capital Management LP/6.40%, LC Capital Master Fund, Ltd./5.50%, Gordon Tibbitts/1.10%, Byron Dunn, Thomas E. Hardisty/4.60%, Michael S. Mathews, Hugh A. Menown

Financial Data: Fiscal Year End:09/30 **Latest Annual Data:** 9/30/2006

Year	Sales	Net Income
2006	NA	-$10,190,000
2005	NA	-$5,724,000
2004	NA	-$19,000

Curr. Assets:	$2,912,000	**Curr. Liab.:**	$1,500,000		
Plant, Equip.:	$1,327,000	**Total Liab.:**	$1,516,000	**Indic. Yr. Divd.:**	NA
Total Assets:	$5,483,000	**Net Worth:**	$3,968,000	**Debt/ Equity:**	0.0010

Partner Communications Co Ltd

8 Amal St., Afeq Industrial Pk., Rosh Ha'ayin, 48103; ***PH:*** 972-547814888; ***http://*** www.orange.co.il/investor_site/about/597.html

General - Incorporation	Israel	**Stock**- Price on:12/24/2007	$15.91
Employees	3,403	Stock Exchange	NDQ
Auditor	Kesselman & Kesselman	Ticker Symbol	PTNR
Stk Agt	U.S. Stock Transfer Corp	Outstanding Shares	156,190,000
Counsel	Roly Klinger	E.P.S	$1.30
DUNS No.	NA	Shareholders	NA

Business: The group's principal activity is the operation of a mobile telecommunications network based upon the global system of mobile communications (GSM) standard in Israel. The group offers an additional services including international dialling and roaming, voice mail, short message services, personal numbering, data and fax transmission and other services. It also offers 24-hour customer service, as well as handset replacement services.the group's shares are traded on the Tel Aviv Stock Exchange, on the London Stock Exchange and on the Nasdaq National Market.

Primary SIC and add'l.: 4822 4813

CIK No: 0001096691

Subsidiaries: Partner Future Communications 2000 Ltd., Partner Land-Line Communications Solutions LLP

Officers: David Avner/CEO, Michal Dana/VP - Human Resources, Deborah Margalit/Mgr., Eli Glickman/VP - Customers Division, Iris Beck/VP - Marketing, Content, Adi Biran/VP - Regulation, New Business Development, Edith Shih/Joint Company Co - Sec., Alon Berman/VP - Technologies, Roly Klinger/General Counsel, Joint Company Co - Sec., Gil Rosenfeld/VP - Business Division, Chaim Beker/VP - Operations, Dan Eldar/VP - Carrier, International, Investor Relations, Emanuel Avner/CFO

Directors: Canning Fok/Chmn., Dennis Lui/Dir., Uzia Galil/Dir., Michael J. Anghel/Dir., Frank Sixt/Dir., Moshe Vidman/Dir., Susan Chow/Dir., Amikam Shorer/Dir., Erez Gissin/Dir., Ting Yu Chan/Dir., Pesach Shachar/Dir.

Owners: Hutchison Whampoa Limited, Hutchison Telecommunications, Cheung Kong (Holdings) Limited

Financial Data: ***Fiscal Year End:***12/31 ***Latest Annual Data:*** 12/31/2006

Year	Sales	Net Income
2006	$1,327,032,000	$161,488,000
2005	$1,112,957,000	$77,028,000
2004	$1,193,300,000	$109,460,000

Curr. Assets:	$301,621,000	**Curr. Liab.:**	$243,276,000	**P/E Ratio:**	13.96
Plant, Equip.:	$413,600,000	**Total Liab.:**	$815,634,000	**Indic. Yr. Divd.:**	$0.960
Total Assets:	$1,112,549,000	**Net Worth:**	$296,915,000	**Debt/ Equity:**	NA

PartnerRe Ltd

Partner Reinsurance Company of the US, One Greenwich Plz., Greenwich, CT, 06830; ***PH:*** 1-203-485-4200; ***Fax:*** 1-203-485-4300; ***http://*** www.partnerre.com

General - Incorporation	Bermuda	**Stock**- Price on:12/24/2007	$77.94
Employees	935	Stock Exchange	NYSE
Auditor	Deloitte & Touche LLP	Ticker Symbol	PRE
Stk Agt	EquiServe Trust Co N.A	Outstanding Shares	56,810,000
Counsel	Christine Patton	E.P.S	$12.37
DUNS No.	NA	Shareholders	NA

Business: The group's principal activity is to provide multi-line reinsurance to insurance companies on a worldwide basis through its wholly owned subsidiaries. The group provides risks reinsurance including property, catastrophe, agriculture, casualty, marine, aviation and space, credit and surety, technical and miscellaneous lines and life/annuity and health. The subsidiaries of the group are Partner Reinsurance Company Ltd, Safr Partnerre, Partnerre U.S. and Partnerre Life. The operations of the group are carried on throughout the United States, Europe, Asia, Australia, New Zealand, Latin America, Caribbean Islands and Africa.

Primary SIC and add'l.: 6331 6321 6311

CIK No: 0000911421

Subsidiaries: Coresa, PARC GmbH& Co KG, PARC Service GmbH, Partner Reinsurance Company Ltd., Partner Reinsurance Company of the U.S., Partner Reinsurance Ireland Limited, PartnerRe (Curacao) N.V., PartnerRe Asset Management Corporation, PartnerRe Capital Trust I, PartnerRe Capital Trust II, PartnerRe Capital Trust III, PartnerRe Finance I Inc., PartnerRe Finance II Inc., PartnerRe Holdings B.V., PartnerRe Holdings Ireland Limited 29 Subsidiaries included in the Index

Officers: Patrick Thiele/Dir., CEO, Pres./$7,961,288.00, Bruno Meyenhofer/CEO - Partnerre Global/$4,867,470.00, Scott D. Moore/Pres., CEO - Partnerre US/$2,730,166.00, Albert Benchimol/CFO, Exec. VP/$2,758,139.00, Christine Patton/Sec., Corporate Counsel, Costas Miranthis/44/Chief Actuarial Officer/$1,728,341.00, Robin Sidders/Mgr. - Investor Relations

Directors: Patrick Thiele/Dir., CEO, Pres., John A. Rollwagen/67/Chmn., Vito H. Baumgartner/67/Vice Chmn., Judith Hanratty/64/Dir., Jurgen Zech/68/Dir., Jan H. Holsboer/61/Dir., Jean-Paul Montupet/60/Dir., Remy Sautter/62/Dir., Lucio Stanca/Dir., Robert M. Baylis/69/Dir., Kevin M. Twomey/61/Dir.

Owners: FMR Corp/9.30%, AXA Financial Inc/11.00%, Jean-Paul L. Montupet, Jan H. Holsboer, Capital Group International, Inc/8.30%, Kevin M. Twomey, Rmy Sautter, Lucio Stanca, Insiders/2.57%, Jrgen Zech

Financial Data: ***Fiscal Year End:***12/31 ***Latest Annual Data:*** 12/31/2006

Year	Sales	Net Income
2006	$4,187,384,000	$749,332,000
2005	$4,205,491,000	-$51,064,000
2004	$4,172,699,000	$492,353,000

Curr. Assets:	$3,171,157,000	**Curr. Liab.:**	$746,416,000	**P/E Ratio:**	6.30
Plant, Equip.:	NA	**Total Liab.:**	$11,162,378,000	**Indic. Yr. Divd.:**	$1.720
Total Assets:	$14,948,225,000	**Net Worth:**	$3,785,847,000	**Debt/ Equity:**	0.2246

Partners Trust Financial Group Inc

233 Genesee St., Utica, NY, 13501; ***PH:*** 1-315-768-3000; ***Fax:*** 1-315-738-4978; ***http://*** www.partnerstrust.com

General - Incorporation	DE	**Stock**- Price on:12/24/2007	$10.47
Employees	649	Stock Exchange	NA
Auditor	KPMG LLP	Ticker Symbol	NA
Stk Agt	Registrar & Transfer Co	Outstanding Shares	43,590,000
Counsel	NA	E.P.S	$0.52
DUNS No.	NA	Shareholders	NA

Business: The group's principal activity is to provide retail and commercial banking services to individuals and business customers. The group offers its services through sixteen central New York locations in oneida, onondaga and herkimer counties. The services offered include origination of commercial real estate loans, including multi-family residential real estate loans, commercial business loans, consumer loans and home equity loans. The depository services offered include passbook and statement savings accounts, interest-bearing demand accounts, non-interest-bearing demand accounts, money market accounts and time deposits. The group also provides trust services, annuity and mutual fund products and customers' banking needs through a network of ATMs and automated telephone banking.

Primary SIC and add'l.: 6035 6712

CIK No: 0001163345

Subsidiaries: BSB Capital Trust I, LLC, BSB Capital Trust II, LLC, BSB Capital Trust III, LLC, Partners Trust Bank

Officers: John A. Zawadzki/59/Dir., CEO, Pres./$1,774,661.00, Daniel J. O'Toole/44/Exec. VP, Chief Credit, Risk Management Officer/$648,185.00, Howard W. Sharp/Exec. VP/$151,698.00, Stephen P. Mahler/Investor Relations Officer, Steven A. Covert/45/COO, Sr. Exec. VP/$990,792.00, Daniel J. Mohr/CFO, Sr. VP, Corp. Sec./$54,342.00, Amie Estrella/37/CFO, Sr. VP, Corp. Sec./$154,412.00, Richard F. Callahan/55/Exec. VP, Chief Retail Banking Officer/$480,838.00

Directors: John A. Zawadzki/59/Dir., CEO, Pres., William C. Craine/59/Chmn., Elizabeth B. Dugan/68/Dir., Robert H. Linn/58/Dir., Gordon M. Hayes/59/Dir., Marybeth K. McCall/55/Dir., John R. Zapisek/69/Dir.

Owners: Marybeth K. McCall, Dimensional Fund Advisors LP/8.40%, Insiders/7.25%, Daniel J. O'Toole, Steven A. Covert/1.17%, Nicholas O. Matt, Richard F. Callahan, Private Capital Management/9.30%, Elizabeth B. Dugan, Gordon M. Hayes, Robert H. Linn, Howard W. Sharp, Robert W. Allen, Amie Estrella, John A. Zawadzki/1.40% *(20 Owners included in Index)*

Financial Data: ***Fiscal Year End:***12/31 ***Latest Annual Data:*** 12/31/2006

Year	Sales	Net Income
2006	$207,017,000	$23,524,000
2005	$192,591,000	$32,807,000
2004	$124,607,000	$12,140,000

Curr. Assets:	$88,414,000	**Curr. Liab.:**	$3,161,255,000	**P/E Ratio:**	20.94
Plant, Equip.:	$23,748,000	**Total Liab.:**	$3,252,010,000	**Indic. Yr. Divd.:**	$0.280
Total Assets:	$3,746,843,000	**Net Worth:**	$494,833,000	**Debt/ Equity:**	0.0882

Patapsco Bancorp Inc

1301 Merritt Blvd., Dundalk, MD, 21222; ***PH:*** 1-410-285-1010; ***Fax:*** 1-410-285-6790; ***http://*** www.patapscobank.com

General - Incorporation	MD	**Stock**- Price on:12/24/2007	$22.75
Employees	72	Stock Exchange	OTC
Auditor	Beard Miller Co. LLP	Ticker Symbol	PATD
Stk Agt	Registrar & Transfer Co	Outstanding Shares	1,880,000
Counsel	Nolan Plumhoff & Williams	E.P.S	$0.52
DUNS No.	93-858-6237	Shareholders	NA

Business: The group's principal activities are to accept deposits from individual and corporate customers and lend a wide range of loans. The deposits offered by the group include checking accounts, christmas club accounts, money market accounts, statement and passbook savings accounts, individual retirement accounts and certificates of deposit. The loan portfolio of the group contains small business loans, construction loans, commercial real estate loans, home equity and other consumer loans and equipment leases. The group also invests in mortgage-backed securities and other securities issued or guaranteed by the us government. The group operates through three full service offices located in dundalk, parkville and carney Maryland and serving eastern baltimore county. On 01-Apr-2004, the group acquired parkville federal savings bank.

Primary SIC and add'l.: 6712 6022

CIK No: 0001003961

Subsidiaries: Patapsco Financial Services, Inc, PFSL Holding Corp., The Patapsco Bank

Officers: Michael J. Dee/48/CEO, CFO, Pres., William Peters/VP - Commercial Lending, The Patapsco Bank, Lisa Ross/Commercial Lending Assist. - Patapsco Bank, John Freese/Leasing Sales, Commercial Leasing - The Patapsco Bank, Mike McGee/Leasing Sales, Commercial Leasing - The Patapsco Bank, Joann Shorb/Assist. Branch Mgr. - Waltham Woods, The Patapsco Bank, Leslie Miller/Branch Mgr. - Hampden, The Patapsco Bank, Alan Herbst/VP - Consumer Lending, The Patapsco Bank, Francis Broccolino/VP - Real Estate Lending, The Patapsco Bank, Louis Hubberman/VP - Real Estate Lending, The Patapsco Bank, Jonna Wurster/Commercial Real Estate Officer - Patapsco Bank, Kim West/Mortgage, Equity Loan Processor, Mortgage, Real Estate Lending, The Patapsco Bank, Marie McClelland/Real Estate Lending Clerk - Mortgage, Real Estate Lending, The Patapsco Bank, John W. McClean/Sr. VP - Loan Portfolio Administration, The Patapsco Bank, Cheryl Strom/Loan Portfolio Administrator - Loan Portfolio Administration, The Patapsco Bank *(56 Officers included in Index)*

Directors: Thomas P. Oneill/55/Chmn., Douglas H. Ludwig/70/Dir., Nicole N. Glaeser/50/Dir., William R. Waters/65/Dir., Gary R. Bozel/50/Dir., Thomas J. Hoffman/60/Dir.

Owners: Thomas J. Hoffman/1.38%, William R. Waters, Insiders/14.83%, Jeffrey L. Gendell/6.98%, Gary R. Bozel/2.69%, Nicole N. Glaeser/1.19%, Laurence S. Mitchell, Frank J. Duchacek/2.30%, Douglas H. Ludwig/1.02%, Michael J. Dee/2.20%, Thomas P. O'Neil/2.52%

Financial Data: ***Fiscal Year End:***06/30 ***Latest Annual Data:*** 06/30/2007

Year	Sales	Net Income
2007	$17,301,000	$1,185,000
2006	NA	NA
2005	$12,495,000	$1,346,000

Curr. Assets:	$12,264,000	**Curr. Liab.:**	$169,732,000		
Plant, Equip.:	$2,175,000	**Total Liab.:**	$210,903,000	**Indic. Yr. Divd.:**	$0.280
Total Assets:	$228,070,000	**Net Worth:**	$17,167,000	**Debt/ Equity:**	NA

Patch International Inc

5th Ave.SW, Ste. 300, 441, Calgary, AB, T2P 2V1; *PH:* 1-403-441-4390; *Fax:* 1-403-411-4395; *http://* www.patchenergy.com

General - Incorporation	NV	**Stock**- Price on:12/24/2007	$2.02
Employees	NA	Stock Exchange	OTC
Auditor	KPMG LLP	Ticker Symbol	PTCH
Stk Agt	American Registrar & Transfer Co	Outstanding Shares	NA
Counsel	Ukrainian Legal Counsel	E.P.S.	NA
DUNS No.	NA	Shareholders	NA

Business: The group's principal activities are to develop and commercialize non-prescription therapeutics and nutraceutical drugs designed to prevent inflammation and their sequelae and also to develop cosmetics for skin conditions. The group is a development stage company that plans to develop new drugs internally. The drugs are intended to be used in the control of conditions such as skin wrinkles and surgical adhesions. The technology also has applicability in the cosmetic and nutraceutical markets and agents for wrinkles and other conditions are being developed for these markets. The group from the past several months has decided to pursue other business opportunities.

Primary SIC and add'l.: 2834

CIK No: 0001064481

Subsidiaries: Energy, Patch Oilsands Ltd., Praxis Pharmaceuticals Australia, Rothschild Bioscience Managers Limited

Officers: Jason G. Dagenais/Principal Executive Officer, COO, Terry Buchanan/VP - Exploration, Geoscience, Reservoir, Thomas K. Rouse/CFO, Donald B. Edwards/47/Corp. Sec.

Directors: Michael S. Vandale/Chmn., Greg Belzberg/Dir., Mark Bentsen/Dir., Roderick D. Maxwell/45/Dir.

Owners: Citadel Equity Fund Ltd/8.30%, Jason G. Dagenais/0.10%, Investors Group Trust Co./9.40%, Mark L. Bentsen/1.80%, Insiders/9.80%, Michael S. Vandale/4.90%, Roderick D. Maxwell/0.90%, Terry Buchanan/0.40%, Bounty Developments Ltd./10.90%, Greg Belzberg/1.30%, Donald B. Edwards/0.40%

Financial Data: Fiscal Year End:05/31 **Latest Annual Data:** 05/31/2007

Year	Sales	Net Income
2007	$16,000	-$18,622,000
2006	$179,000	$2,687,000
2005	$108,000	-$1,022,000

Curr. Assets:	$4,573,000	**Curr. Liab.:**	$2,484,000		
Plant, Equip.:	$1,000	**Total Liab.:**	$2,518,000	**Indic. Yr. Divd.:**	NA
Total Assets:	$14,780,000	**Net Worth:**	$11,691,000	**Debt/ Equity:**	NA

Path 1 Network Technologies Inc

6650 Lusk Blvd, Ste. B 100, San Diego, CA, 92121; *PH:* 1-858-450-4220; *Fax:* 1-858-450-4203; *http://* www.path1.com; *Email:* investors@path1.com

General - Incorporation	DE	**Stock**- Price on:12/24/2007	NA
Employees	26	Stock Exchange	OTC
Auditor	Swenson Advisors LLP	Ticker Symbol	PNOT
Stk Agt	Registrar & Transfer Co	Outstanding Shares	NA
Counsel	NA	E.P.S.	-$0.978
DUNS No.	NA	Shareholders	NA

Business: The group's principal activity is to develop products that enable the transportation and distribution of real-time, high-quality video over Internet protocol (ip) networks. Cable companies use the product to supply video-on-demand services. These products are also used by communication service providers to transmit high-quality, real-time video to one or more locations. The customers include cable, broadcast and satellite companies, movie studios, carriers and government and educational institutions.

Primary SIC and add'l.: 3669

CIK No: 0001059404

Officers: Tom Tullie/Dir., CEO, Jeremy L. Ferrell/Interim CFO, Sec., Robin Allbritton/Contact - Sales, Eastern US Region, Nat Collins/Contact - Sales, Western, Central US Region, Anthony Tay/Contact - Sales, Asia Region, Bart Schade/Contact - Sales, International Region, Partners

Directors: Tom Tullie/Dir., CEO, Robert B. Clasen/Chmn., Mark Buckner/Dir., Robert L. Packer/Dir., James A. Bixby/Dir.

Financial Data: Fiscal Year End:12/31 **Latest Annual Data:** 12/31/2005

Year	Sales	Net Income
2005	$2,931,000	-$9,388,000
2004	$3,193,000	-$7,134,000
2003	$2,721,000	-$7,446,000

Curr. Assets:	$2,765,000	**Curr. Liab.:**	$2,387,000		
Plant, Equip.:	$244,000	**Total Liab.:**	$3,260,000	**Indic. Yr. Divd.:**	NA
Total Assets:	$3,883,000	**Net Worth:**	-$657,000	**Debt/ Equity:**	NA

Pathfinder Bancorp Inc

214 W 1st St., Oswego, NY, 13126; *PH:* 1-315-343-0057; *Fax:* 1-315-342-9403; *http://* www.pathfinderbancorpinc.com; *Email:* contactus@pathfinderbank.com

General - Incorporation	DE	**Stock**- Price on:12/24/2007	$12.25
Employees	NA	Stock Exchange	NDQ
Auditor	Beard Miller Co. LLP	Ticker Symbol	PBHC
Stk Agt	Registrar & Transfer Co	Outstanding Shares	2,480,000
Counsel	Luse, Lehman, Gorman Et Al	E.P.S.	$0.38
DUNS No.	17-200-4038	Shareholders	NA

Business: The group's principal activities are accepting deposits from the general public and investing such deposits together with other sources of funds, in loans secured by one-to -four family residential real estate. The group has five full service offices located in oswego county. The group offers wide range of deposits including noninterest-bearing demand accounts, now accounts, passbook and club accounts, money management deposits accounts, term certificate accounts and individual retirement accounts. The group also provides commercial and consumer loans and invests a portion of its assets in securities issued by the United States government, state and municipal obligations, corporate debt securities, mutual funds and equity securities.

Primary SIC and add'l.: 6035 6712

CIK No: 0001046188

Subsidiaries: Pathfinder Bank, Pathfinder Statutory Trust

Officers: Thomas W. Schneider/CEO, Pres./$277,658.00, James A. Dowd/CFO, VP/$110,486.00, Beard Miller/Independent Auditor - Pathfinder Bank, Ronald Tascarella/49/CCO, Sr. VP/$57,115.00, Michael Quenville/VP, Business Development Officer - Pathfinder Bank, Will O'Brien/Business Relationship Mgr. - Pathfinder Bank, Robert A. Rolfe/Investment Executive, Pathfinder Investment Services, Susan M. Cahill/Branch Mgr. - Pathfinder Bank, Oswego, Barbara Cowles/Branch Mgr. - Central Square, Pathfinder Bank, Edward Mervine/VP, General Counsel, Corp. Sec. - Pathfinder Bank/$137,985.00, Denise Lyga/Branch Mgr. - Lacona, Pathfinder Bank, Cynthia Claflin/Branch Mgr. - Mexico, Pathfinder Bank, Deana Michaels/Branch Mgr. - Fulton, Pathfinder Bank, Craig Nessel/Branch Mgr. - Eastside Office, Oswego, Pathfinder Bank, Melissa A. Miller/50/COO, VP/$124,835.00 *(17 Officers included in Index)*

Directors: Janette Resnick/65/Chmn., Chris R. Burritt/54/Dir., Bruce E. Manwaring/66/Dir., George P. Joyce/57/Dir., William L. Nelson/64/Dir., Lloyd Stemple/47/Dir.

Owners: Janette Resnick, Lloyd"Buddy" Stemple, Pathfinder Bancorp, M.H.C., Melissa A. Miller, Edward A. Mervine, Chris R. Burritt, Ronald Tascarella, Pathfinder Bancorp, M.H.C., James A. Dowd, Corte J. Spencer, Bruce E. Manwaring, Steven W. Thomas, George P. Joyce, Thomas W. Schneider, William L. Nelson *(16 Owners included in Index)*

Financial Data: Fiscal Year End:12/31 **Latest Annual Data:** 12/31/2006

Year	Sales	Net Income
2006	$18,584,000	$1,028,000
2005	$17,431,000	$462,000
2004	$17,525,000	$1,405,000

Curr. Assets:	$15,417,000	**Curr. Liab.:**	$245,585,000	**P/E Ratio:**	37.12
Plant, Equip.:	$8,068,000	**Total Liab.:**	$280,532,000	**Indic. Yr. Divd.:**	$0.410
Total Assets:	$301,382,000	**Net Worth:**	$20,850,000	**Debt/ Equity:**	1.5440

Pathmark Stores Inc

200 Milik St., Carteret, NJ, 07008; *PH:* 1-732-499-3000; *Fax:* 1-732-499-3072; *http://* www.pathmark.com

General - Incorporation	DE	**Stock**- Price on:12/24/2007	$12.99
Employees	7,400	Stock Exchange	NA
Auditor	Deloitte & Touche LLP	Ticker Symbol	NA
Stk Agt	NA	Outstanding Shares	52,430,000
Counsel	NA	E.P.S.	-$0.41
DUNS No.	00-697-4950	Shareholders	NA

Business: The group's principle activity is to provide food and general merchandise through its supermarkets. The group's stores also provide customer service centers, pharmacies, expanded produced health and beauty care departments, and seafood and delicatessen departments. The group operates from United States.

Primary SIC and add'l.: 5399 5411

CIK No: 0000095585

Subsidiaries: AAL Realty Corp, Adbrett Corp, Bergen Street Pathmark, Inc, Bridge Stuart, Inc, East Brunswick Stuart LLC, Lancaster Pike Stuart LLC, MacDade Boulevard Stuart, LLC, Plainbridge LLC, PTMK LLC, Supermarkets Oil Co, Upper Darby Stuart LLC

Officers: John T. Standley/45/Dir., CEO/$6,393,989.00, Mark C. Kramer/58/Exec. VP - Store Operations/$526,074.00, John T. Derderian/49/Exec. VP - Business Strategy, Marketing, Marc A. Strassler/59/Sr. VP, Sec., General Counsel, Frank G. Vitrano/52/CFO, Pres.,Treasurer/$2,337,649.00, Robert J. Joyce/62/Exec. VP - Human Resources/$529,506.00, Kenneth A. Martindale/48/Pres., Chief Marketing, Merchandising Officer/$2,584,851.00, Kevin R. Darrington/40/Sr. VP, Corporate Controller

Directors: John T. Standley/45/Dir., CEO, David R. Jessick/54/Chmn., Bruce Hartman/54/Dir., Michael R. Duckworth/47/Dir., Daniel H. Fitzgerald/55/Dir., Sarah E. Nash/54/Dir., Larry R. Katzen/62/Dir., Gregory Mays/61/Dir., Ira Tochner/46/Dir., John J. Zillmer/52/Dir.

Owners: Bruce Hartman, Daniel Fitzgerald, David Jessick, Frank Vitrano/2.00%, John Zillmer, Gregory Mays, John Standley/1.70%, Insiders/5.80%, Sarah Nash, Kenneth Martindale, Larry Katzen, Mark Kramer, Robert Joyce

Financial Data: Fiscal Year End:01/28 **Latest Annual Data:** 1/28/2006

Year	Sales	Net Income
2006	$3,977,000,000	-$40,100,000
2005	$3,978,500,000	-$308,600,000
2004	$3,991,300,000	$16,500,000

Curr. Assets:	$330,600,000	**Curr. Liab.:**	$260,100,000		
Plant, Equip.:	$584,500,000	**Total Liab.:**	$1,145,900,000	**Indic. Yr. Divd.:**	NA
Total Assets:	$1,520,900,000	**Net Worth:**	$375,000,000	**Debt/ Equity:**	3.6855

Patient Infosystems Inc

4401 Nw 124th Ave, Coral Springs, FL, 33065; *PH:* 1-954-796-3714; *http://* www.ptisys.com

General - Incorporation	DE	**Stock**- Price on:12/24/2007	$5.45
Employees	NA	Stock Exchange	OTC
Auditor	McGladrey & Pullen LLP	Ticker Symbol	PATYE
Stk Agt	Continental Stock Transfer & Trust Co	Outstanding Shares	NA
Counsel	Gibbons Del Deo Dolan Et Al	E.P.S.	NA
DUNS No.	92-778-2995	Shareholders	NA

Business: The group's principal activities include the design and development of health care information systems and services to manage, collect and analyze patient-related information and to improve patient compliance with prescribed treatment protocols. The group has three product lines such as population management, disease management and demand management. Population management system collects, analyzes and reports data about an overall target patient population. Disease management is designed to improve patient compliance with prescribed treatment protocols and improve the process of patient management. Demand management includes services to facilitate the appropriate deployment of costly health care resources. The customers of the group include pharmaceutical and medical equipment and device manufacturers, pharmacy benefit managers and health care payors. On 31-Dec-2003, the group acquired American caresource. On 24-Sep-2004, the group acquired cbca care management.

Primary SIC and add'l.: 8099

CIK No: 0001017813

Subsidiaries: American Care Source, Inc, CBCA Care Management, Inc, CCS Consolidated, Inc, PATY Acquisition Corp

Officers: Chris E. Paterson/CEO/$237,258.00, Glen A. Spence/53/CFO, Exec. VP/$176,949.00, Rex M. Dendinger/CIO, Sr. VP, Thomas L. Tran/CFO, Pres., Julie A. Meek/COO, Exec. VP, John R. Pegues/Exec. VP, Chief Marketing Officer

Directors: John Pappajohn/Vice Chmn., Albert S. Waxman/67/Chmn., Daniel C. Lubin/Dir., Derace L. Schaffer/60/Dir., Marc L. Pacala/52/Dir., William C. Stapleton/Dir., Michael J. Barber/Dir.

Owners: Christine St. Andre, Derace L. Schaffer, Radius Venture Partners I, L.P., Daniel C. Lubin, Ashford Capital Management, Inc., John Pappajohn, Insiders, Hickory Venture Capital Corporation, Roger L. Chaufournier, Entities affiliated with Psilos Group Partners, Principal Life Insurance Company, Entities affiliated with Essex Woodlands Health Ventures, Albert S. Waxman, Chris E. Paterson, Glen A. Spence *(16 Owners included in Index)*

Patient Portal Technologies Inc

Formerly: Suncoast Naturals Inc
7108 Fairway Dr., Ste. 215, Palm Beach Gardens, FL, 33418; *PH:* 1-561-630-7688

General - Incorporation	DE	Stock - Price on:12/24/2007	$1.06
Employees	NA	Stock Exchange	OTC
Auditor	Walden Certified Public Accountant	Ticker Symbol	PPRG
Stk Agt	Liberty Transfer Co	Outstanding Shares	24,140,000
Counsel	NA	E.P.S.	-$0.05
DUNS No.	NA	Shareholders	NA

Business: The groups principle activity is to provide revenue enhancement and cost improvement services for the healthcare industry. The groups products and services utilize a proprietary software platform that optimizes patient flow, reduces administrative costs, and maximizes insurance reimbursement. The group also provides process improvement solutions. The group operates from United States.

Primary SIC and add'l.: NA
CIK No: 0001240093
Subsidiaries: Caribbean Pacific Natural Products, Inc., OptiLiving, Inc.
Officers: Kevin Kelly/48/Chmn., CEO, Pres., Thomas Hagan/67/Dir., Sec., Acting CFO, Daniel Coholan/51/Dir., VP, David Wolf/47/COO
Directors: Kevin Kelly/48/Chmn., CEO, Pres., Thomas Hagan/67/Dir., Sec., Acting CFO, Daniel Coholan/51/Dir., VP
Owners: Kevin Kelly, Thomas Hagan, William J. Reilly, David Wolf, Insiders, William Kelly, Brian Kelly, Vicki Ramundo, Daniel Coholan

Financial Data: *Fiscal Year End:*12/31 *Latest Annual Data:* 12/31/2006

Year	Sales	Net Income
2006	$14,000	-$401,000
2005	NA	-$131,000
2004	$89,000	-$1,494,000

Curr. Assets:	$30,000	Curr. Liab.:	$385,000		
Plant, Equip.:	$822,000	Total Liab.:	$385,000	Indic. Yr. Divd.:	NA
Total Assets:	$1,103,000	Net Worth:	$718,000	Debt/ Equity:	NA

Patni Computer Systems Ltd

1 Broadway, Cambridge, MA, 02142; *PH:* 1-617-914-8000; *Fax:* 1-617-914-8200;
http:// www.patni.com; *Email:* patni-mumbai@patni.com

General - Incorporation	Republic of India	Stock - Price on:12/24/2007	$25.9
Employees	NA	Stock Exchange	NYSE
Auditor	NA	Ticker Symbol	PTI
Stk Agt	Karvy Computershare Private Limited	Outstanding Shares	69,170,000
Counsel	NA	E.P.S.	$1.93
DUNS No.	NA	Shareholders	NA

Business: The groups principle activity is to provide information technology services. The groups services include application development, software implementation, infrastructure management services, engineering services, business process outsourcing and quality assurance services. The group operates from the India, the United States, Japan and others. The groups quarterly revenue for Sept 2007 was 169.45 millions of USD.

Primary SIC and add'l.: 7376 7371 7375 7373 7374 7379
CIK No: 0001324503
Subsidiaries: Cymbal Information Services (Thailand) Limited, Patni Computer Systems (UK) Limited, Patni Computer Systems GmbH, Patni Computer Systems,Inc., Patni Telecom Solutions (UK) Limited, Patni Telecom Solutions Inc., Patni Telecom Solutions Private Limited, The Reference Inc.
Officers: Narendra K. Patni/Chmn., CEO, Mrinal Sattawala/COO, Russell Boekenkroeger/Exec. VP, Neeraj Gupta/Exec. VP, Satish M. Joshi/CTO, Exec. VP, Vic Dalfonso/Sr. VP - Sales - Financial Services, Sanjay Bhatnagar/Sr. Mgr. - Software, Siddharth Shah/Software Engineer, Prashant Kharche/Sr. Consultant, Ranjana Chitale/Sr. Mgr. - Software, Valerian Harris/Sr. Mgr. - Software, Vijay P. Khare/Exec. VP, CAO, CDO, Surjeet Singh/CFO, Rajesh Padmanabhan/Exec. VP, Brian Stones/Exec. VP *(21 Officers included in Index)*
Directors: Narendra K. Patni/Chmn., CEO, Gajendra K. Patni/Non Exec. Dir., Ashok K. Patni/Non Exec. Dir., William O. Grabe/Dir., Louis Theodoor Van Den Boog/Dir., Michael A. Cusumano/Dir., Arun Duggal/Dir., Arun Maira/Dir., Pradip Shah/Dir., Ramesh Venkataraman/Dir., Abhay Havaldar/Alternate Dir.
Owners: Satish M. Joshi, Mrinal R. Sattawala, William O. Grabe/16.52%, Louis T. van den Boog, Narendra K. Patni/14.69%, Insiders/44.05%, Ashok K. Patni/14.87%, Gajendra K. Patni/14.42%, HSBC/7.75%, General Atlantic Mauritius Limited/16.52%

Financial Data: *Fiscal Year End:*12/31 *Latest Annual Data:* 12/31/2006

Year	Sales	Net Income
2006	$578,851,000	$59,251,000
2005	$450,332,000	$60,867,000
2004	$326,582,000	$56,653,000

Curr. Assets:	$450,188,000	Curr. Liab.:	$119,488,000	P/E Ratio:	40.06
Plant, Equip.:	$125,758,000	Total Liab.:	$131,747,000	Indic. Yr. Divd.:	$0.130
Total Assets:	$640,341,000	Net Worth:	$508,593,000	Debt/ Equity:	NA

Patrick Industries Inc

107 W Franklin St., Elkhart, IN, 46515; *PH:* 1-574-294-7511; *Fax:* 1-574-522-5213;
http:// www.patrickind.com; *Email:* info@patrickind.com

General - Incorporation	IN	Stock - Price on:12/24/2007	$15.47
Employees	961	Stock Exchange	NDQ
Auditor	McGladrey & Pullen LLP	Ticker Symbol	PATK
Stk Agt	NBD Bank	Outstanding Shares	4,910,000
Counsel	NA	E.P.S.	-$0.3
DUNS No.	01-627-2908	Shareholders	NA

Business: The group's principal activities are to manufacture and supply building products and materials to the manufactured housing and recreational vehicle industries. The group also supplies to certain other industrial markets, such as, furniture manufacturing, marine, architectural and the automotive aftermarket. The group manufactures decorative vinyl and paper panels, cabinet doors, countertops, aluminum extrusions, drawer sides, pleated shades, wood adhesives and laminating machines. The group is also an independent wholesale distributor of pre-finished wall and ceiling panels, particleboard, hardboard siding, passage doors, roofing products, high pressure laminates, building hardware, insulation and other related products. As of 31-Dec-2003, the group operated twelve warehouse and distribution centers and seventeen manufacturing plants.

Primary SIC and add'l.: 2434 7549 2431 3089 5031
CIK No: 0000076605
Subsidiaries: Harlan Machinery Company, Inc, Patrick Mouldings, LLC
Officers: Paul E. Hassler/60/CEO, Pres./$582,168.00, Andy L. Nemeth/39/Dir., CFO, Exec. VP - Finance, Sec., Treasurer/$315,328.00, Bill Benford/MH, RV, Industrial Sales Representative - Decatur, AL, Van Pierce/MH, RV, Industrial Sales Representative - Decatur, AL, Perry D'Amour/GM - Phoenix, AZ, Jason Stout/MH, RV, Industrial Sales Representative - Phoenix, AZ, Vince Fergen/GM - Fontana, CA, Jeff Justice/Industrial Sales Representative - Fontana, CA, Steve Mount/Industrial Sales Representative - Fontana, CA, Steve Reid/RV, M, H Sales Representative - Fontana, CA, Syd Reitz/Industrial Sales Coordinator, Fontana, CA, Stan Yoder/National Accounting Mgr. - Fontana, CA, Pat Mullen/Outside Sales, Elkhart, IN, Metals, Ron Simpson/Outside Sales, Elkhart, IN, Metals, James Winters/Outside Sales, Elkhart, IN, Metals *(51 Officers included in Index)*
Directors: Andy L. Nemeth/39/Dir., CFO, Exec. VP - Finance, Sec., Treasurer, Robert C. Timmins/Dir., Keith V. Kankel/Dir., Harold E. Wyland/Dir., John H. McDermott/Dir., Terrence D. Brennan/Dir., Walter E. Wells/Dir., Larry D. Renbarger/Dir.
Owners: Andy L. Nemeth, Gregory J. Scharnott, Keith V. Kankel, Jeffrey L. Gendell/38.20%, Clearbridge Advisors, LLC/9.70%, Robert C. Timmins/1.10%, John H. McDermott, Walter E. Wells, Harold E. Wyland, Terrence D. Brennan, Dimensional Fund Advisors, Inc./5.90%, Larry D. Renbarger, Heartland Advisors, Inc./6.50%, Insiders/5.50%, Wilen Management Company, Inc./5.00% *(16 Owners included in Index)*

Financial Data: *Fiscal Year End:*12/31 *Latest Annual Data:* 12/31/2006

Year	Sales	Net Income
2006	$347,629,000	$2,629,000
2005	$323,400,000	$1,424,000
2004	$301,554,000	$601,000

Curr. Assets:	$63,122,000	Curr. Liab.:	$26,017,000	P/E Ratio:	59.50
Plant, Equip.:	$42,927,000	Total Liab.:	$43,073,000	Indic. Yr. Divd.:	NA
Total Assets:	$109,149,000	Net Worth:	$66,076,000	Debt/ Equity:	NA

Patriot Capital Funding Inc

274 Riverside Ave., Westport, CT, 06880; *PH:* 1-203-429-2700; *Fax:* 1-203-227-5257;
http:// www.patcapfunding.com

General - Incorporation	DE	Stock - Price on:12/24/2007	$14.97
Employees	11	Stock Exchange	NDQ
Auditor	Angell Palmer & Dodge LLP	Ticker Symbol	PCAP
Stk Agt	American Stock Transfer & Trust Co.	Outstanding Shares	18,250,000
Counsel	NA	E.P.S.	$1.11
DUNS No.	NA	Shareholders	NA

Business: The groups principal activity is to provide financing solutions. The group operates from the United States. The assets of the group for the year 2006 were $257,248,376.

Primary SIC and add'l.: 6282 6726
CIK No: 0001321560
Subsidiaries: Patriot Capital Funding LLC I
Officers: Richard P. Buckanavage/Dir., CEO, Pres., Timothy W. Hassler/38/Dir., COO, Chief Compliance Officer, Clifford L. Wells/Exec. VP, Chief Investment Officer, Matthew R. Colucci/35/MD, William E. Alvarez/53/CFO, Exec. VP, Sec., Basem W. Pharaon/Sr. VP, Andrew M. Brown/VP, Ryan T. Magee/VP, Seth Tutlis/Assist. VP, Liam Pisano/Assoc., Warren Hsiung/Assoc., Melissa P. Granata/Loan Administrator, Lauren Taylor/Administrative Assist.
Directors: Richard P. Buckanavage/Dir., CEO, Pres., Mel P. Melsheimer/67/Chmn., Steven Drogin/63/Dir., Timothy W. Hassler/38/Dir., COO, Chief Compliance Officer, Richard A. Sebastiao/59/Dir., Dennis C. O'Dowd/57/Dir.
Owners: William E. Alvarez, Mel P. Melsheimer, Richard P. Buckanavage/1.70%, Compass Group Investments, Inc./5.70%, Insiders/4.60%, Matthew R. Colucci, Dennis C. ODowd, Clifford L. Wells, Timothy W. Hassler/1.70%, American Century Companies, Inc./6.70%, Richard A. Sebastiao, Steven Drogin

Financial Data: *Fiscal Year End:*12/31 *Latest Annual Data:* 3/31/2007

Year	Sales	Net Income
2007	$8,977,000	$5,373,000
2006	$10,316,000	$3,527,000
2005	$13,449,000	-$1,237,000

Curr. Assets:	$11,546,000	Curr. Liab.:	$8,034,000		
Plant, Equip.:	NA	Total Liab.:	$106,414,000	Indic. Yr. Divd.:	$1.280
Total Assets:	$270,523,000	Net Worth:	$164,109,000	Debt/ Equity:	0.4101

Patriot Gold Corp

1775 Bellevue Ave., Vancouver, BC, V7V 1A9; *PH:* 1-604-613-1334;
http:// www.patriotgoldcorp.com; *Email:* info@patriotgoldcorp.com

General - Incorporation	NV	Stock - Price on:12/24/2007	$0.12
Employees	NA	Stock Exchange	OTC
Auditor	Robison, Hill & Co.	Ticker Symbol	PGOL
Stk Agt	Holladay Stock Transfer, Inc.	Outstanding Shares	NA
Counsel	David Lubin and Associates	E.P.S.	NA
DUNS No.	NA	Shareholders	NA

Business: The groups principal activity is engaged in natural resource exploration and anticipates acquiring, exploring, and if warranted and feasible, developing natural resource properties. Currently the group is in the exploration stage and is undertaking exploration programs in Arizona and Nevada. The group operates from the United States.

Primary SIC and add'l.: 1081

CIK No: 0001080448

Officers: Robert Coale/Chmn., CEO, COO, Pres., Sec.

Directors: Robert Coale/Chmn., CEO, COO, Pres., Sec., Robert Sibthorpe/Dir., Duncan Budge/Dir.

Owners: Almir Ramic/6.30%, Robert D. Coale/12.40%, Colin Bruce Worth/5.80%, Robert A. Sibthorpe/12.80%, Insiders/25.20%, Duncan Budge

Financial Data: Fiscal Year End:05/31   Latest Annual Data: 05/31/2007

Year	Sales		Net Income
2007	NA		-$295,000
Curr. Assets:	$3,031,000	Curr. Liab.:	$2,000	
Plant, Equip.:	$2,000	Total Liab.:	$2,000	Indic. Yr. Divd.: NA
Total Assets:	$3,033,000	Net Worth:	$3,030,000	Debt/ Equity: NA

Patriot Investment Corp

6269 Jamestown Ct., Salt Lake City, UT, 84121; **PH:** 1-801-566-6627

General - Incorporation	NV	Stock - Price on:12/24/2007	$0.22
Employees	NA	Stock Exchange	OTC
Auditor	Hansen, Barnett & Maxwell P.C.	Ticker Symbol	PTRT
Stk Agt	OTC Stock Transfer, Inc.	Outstanding Shares	NA
Counsel	NA	E.P.S.	NA
DUNS No.	NA	Shareholders	NA

Business: The groups principal activity is to acquire a business opportunity in any stage of development, which includes opportunities involving start up or new companies. The group operates from the United States.

Primary SIC and add'l.: 6282

CIK No: 0000805729

Officers: Bradley S. Shepherd/47/Dir., CEO, CFO, Pres., Sec., Treasurer

Directors: Bradley S. Shepherd/47/Dir., CEO, CFO, Pres., Sec., Treasurer, Todd Gee/48/Dir.

Owners: Tse Wan Yi/5.60%, Insiders/37.00%, Degong Han/18.00%, Everwin Development Ltd/19.00%

Financial Data: Fiscal Year End:12/31   Latest Annual Data: 12/31/2006

Year	Sales		Net Income
2006	NA		-$8,000
2005	NA		-$8,000
2004	NA		-$8,000
Curr. Assets:	$0	Curr. Liab.:	$24,000	
Plant, Equip.:	NA	Total Liab.:	$24,000	Indic. Yr. Divd.: NA
Total Assets:	$0	Net Worth:	-$24,000	Debt/ Equity: NA

Patriot National Bancorp Inc

900 Bedford St., Stamford, CT, 06901; **PH:** 1-203-324-7500; **Fax:** 1-203-324-8877; http:// www.pnbdirect.com

General - Incorporation	CT	Stock - Price on:12/24/2007	$21.93
Employees	107	Stock Exchange	NDQ
Auditor	McGladrey & Pullen LLP	Ticker Symbol	PNBK
Stk Agt	Registrar & Transfer Co	Outstanding Shares	4,740,000
Counsel	NA	E.P.S.	$0.55
DUNS No.	80-857-0576	Shareholders	NA

Business: The group's principal activities are to provide a broad range of consumer and commercial banking services to individuals, small and medium-sized businesses and professionals. The group offers checking accounts, interest-bearing now accounts, insured money market accounts, time certificates of deposit, savings accounts and individual retirement accounts. The group also offers real estate loans, commercial loans and consumer loans. The other services provided by the group include money orders, traveler's checks, ATM's (automated teller machine) and Internet banking. The group also conducts mortgage brokerage operations in Connecticut, New York and New Jersey through its mortgage brokerage division, pinnacle financial. The group operates through its main office in stamford and two branch offices in greenwich, old greenwich and two branch office in norwalk and one in wilton located in Connecticut

Primary SIC and add'l.: 6712 6021

CIK No: 0001098146

Owners: Barry C. Lewis/6.50%, Donald Opatrny/8.00%, Marcus Zavattaro/1.60%, Morris L. Glucksman/1.40%, Insiders/22.70%, John J. Ferguson, Martin Noble, Charles F. Howell/1.20%, Philip W. Wolford, Harvey Sandler Revocable Trust/8.00%, Brian A. Fitzgerald, Michael F. Intrieri/1.20%, Angelo DeCaro/15.90%, Robert F. OConnell, John A. Geoghegan

Financial Data: Fiscal Year End:12/31   Latest Annual Data: 12/31/2006

Year	Sales		Net Income
2006	$40,369,000		$2,415,000
2005	$28,378,000		$1,407,000
2004	$21,380,000		$926,000
Curr. Assets:	$59,017,000	Curr. Liab.:	$573,452,000	
Plant, Equip.:	$3,691,000	Total Liab.:	$581,700,000	Indic. Yr. Divd.: $0.180
Total Assets:	$645,983,000	Net Worth:	$64,283,000	Debt/ Equity: NA

Patriot Scientific Corp

6183 Paseo Del Norte, Ste. 180, Carlsbad, CA, 92011; **PH:** 1-760-547-2700; **Fax:** 1-760-547-2705; http:// www.ptsc.com; **Email:** ir@ptsc.com

General - Incorporation	DE	Stock - Price on:12/24/2007	$0.52
Employees	5	Stock Exchange	OTC
Auditor	KMJ Corbin & Co. LLP	Ticker Symbol	PTSC
Stk Agt	Interwest Transfer Company, Inc.	Outstanding Shares	390,090,000
Counsel	Beatie & Osborn LLP	E.P.S.	$0.03
DUNS No.	61-734-1862	Shareholders	NA

Business: The group's principle activities are to develop, market and sell microprocessor technology and high-performance high-speed data communication products. These products enable computers and other data processing devices to communicate and can be used to connect to the Internet or other telecommunication networks. Technologies include ignite microprocessor technology, juicetechnology, high-speed data communications technology and radar technology. These are used in wireless devices, smart cards, home appliances, gateways, set top boxes, entertainment technologies, automotive telematics, biomedical devices and industrial controllers. The group's products and technology licenses are marketed in North America, Europe and Asia through a combination of direct sales and distributors. The group's total revenue for year 2007 was 0.64 millions of USD.

Primary SIC and add'l.: 3669 3674

CIK No: 0000836564

Subsidiaries: Metacomp Inc, Plasma Scientific Corp.

Officers: Jim L. Turley/Dir., CEO, Julie Marshall/Investor Relations Officer, Thomas J. Sweeney/CFO, Frank Hawkins/Investor Relations Officer, Cliff Flowers/CFO

Directors: Jim L. Turley/Dir., CEO, David H. Pohl/71/Chmn., Harry L. Tredennick/Dir., Nick Tredennick/Dir., Carlton M. Johnson/48/Dir., Gloria H. Felcyn/Dir., Helmut Falk/Dir.

Owners: Carlton M. Johnson, Helmut Falk, Insiders/2.74%, David H. Pohl, Lincoln Ventures, LLC/7.61%, James L. Turley, Harry L. Tredennick, Thomas J. Sweeney, Swartz Private Equity, LLC/1.48%, Gloria H. Felcyn, CPA

Financial Data: Fiscal Year End:05/31   Latest Annual Data: 5/31/2006

Year	Sales		Net Income
2006	$10,310,000		$28,673,000
2005	$2,983,000		-$10,519,000
2004	$76,000		-$5,761,000
Curr. Assets:	$8,015,000	Curr. Liab.:	$1,244,000	P/E Ratio: 17.33
Plant, Equip.:	$64,000	Total Liab.:	$1,244,000	Indic. Yr. Divd.: $0.020
Total Assets:	$12,072,000	Net Worth:	$10,828,000	Debt/ Equity: NA

Patriot Transportation Holding Inc

1801 Art Museum Dr., Jacksonville, FL, 32207; **PH:** 1-877-704-1776; **Fax:** 1-904-396-2715; http:// www.patriottrans.com

General - Incorporation	FL	Stock - Price on:12/24/2007	$89.11
Employees	981	Stock Exchange	NDQ
Auditor	Hancock Askew & Co., LLP	Ticker Symbol	PATR
Stk Agt	Wachovia Bank N.A	Outstanding Shares	3,040,000
Counsel	Lewis S. Lee, Esquire McGuirewoods	E.P.S.	$2.97
DUNS No.	19-961-5469	Shareholders	NA

Business: The group's principal activities are to provide transportation services and real estate operations. The transportation business is conducted through two wholly owned subsidiaries. One of the transportation companies concentrates in the hauling by motor carrier of liquid and dry bulk commodities. Another subsidiary serves the flatbed portion of the trucking industry in the southeast, midwest and mid-Atlantic states, hauling primarily the construction materials. Under the real estate segment, the group leases land under mining royalty agreements. The group also holds certain other real estate for investment. The real estate group acquires, constructs, leases, operates and manages land and buildings.

Primary SIC and add'l.: 6531 4213

CIK No: 0000844059

Subsidiaries: 1502 Quarry, LLC, 34 Loveton Center LLC, Florida Rock & Tank Lines, Inc., Florida Rock Properties, Inc., FRP Development Corp., FRP Maryland, Inc., Oz LLC, SunBelt Transport, Inc.

Officers: John E. Anderson/63/CEO, Pres., David H. Devilliers/57/VP, Robert E. Sandlin/Pres. - Florida Rock, Tank Lines, INc, Ray M. Vanlandingham/65/CFO, VP, Treasurer, Sec., Terry S. Phipps/44/Pres. - Sunbelt Transportation, John D. Klopfenstein/45/Controller, Chief Accounting Officer

Directors: Edward L. Baker/73/Chmn., John D. Baker/Dir., Luke E. Fichthorn/Dir., H. W. Shad/Dir., Charles E. Commander/Dir., Robert H. Paul/Dir., Thompson S. Baker/Dir., Martin E. Stein/Dir., James H. Winston/Dir.

Owners: Robert E. Sandlin, John D. Klopfenstein, Thompson S. Baker, David H. deVilliers, Edward L. Baker, John D. Baker, Ray M. Van Landingham, Martin E. Stein, H. W. Shad, Insiders, Terry S. Phipps, James H. Winston, Robert H. Paul, Baker Holdings, L.P., Luke E. Fichthorn (18 Owners included in Index)

Financial Data: Fiscal Year End:09/30   Latest Annual Data: 9/30/2006

Year	Sales		Net Income
2006	$147,374,000		$8,078,000
2005	$131,036,000		$7,609,000
2004	$115,789,000		$20,740,000
Curr. Assets:	$17,412,000	Curr. Liab.:	$18,192,000	
Plant, Equip.:	$192,073,000	Total Liab.:	$101,163,000	Indic. Yr. Divd.: NA
Total Assets:	$219,215,000	Net Worth:	$118,052,000	Debt/ Equity: 0.5002

Patron Systems Inc

5775 Flatiron Pkwy No. 230, Boulder, CO, 80301; **PH:** 1-303-541-1005; **Fax:** 1-888-335-8300; http:// www.patronsystems.net; **Email:** pr@patronsystems.com

General - Incorporation	DE	Stock - Price on:12/24/2007	$0.7
Employees	25	Stock Exchange	OTC
Auditor	Marcum & Kliegman LLP	Ticker Symbol	PTRNE
Stk Agt	American Stock Transfer & Trust Co.	Outstanding Shares	14,510,000
Counsel	NA	E.P.S.	-$1.23
DUNS No.	NA	Shareholders	NA

Business: The groups principle activity is to solve a set of enterprise level customer problems associated with electronic message management, whether in the form of e mail, eforms or instant messaging. Services of the group include e mail policy management, e mail retention policies, archiving and eDiscovery, proactive e mail supervision, and the protection of messages and their attachments. The group operates from the United States.

Primary SIC and add'l.: 7374

CIK No: 0001075043

Subsidiaries: Complete Security Solutions, Inc., Entelagent Software Corp., LucidLine, Inc., PILEC Disbursement Company

Officers: Braden Waverley/41/CEO, Dir., Martin T. Johnson/56/CFO, Mark Gergen/VP - Engineering, Heidi Newton/VP - Finance, Brett Newbold/55/Pres., CTO

Directors: Braden Waverley/41/CEO, Dir., George M. Middlemas/61/Dir.

Owners: Apex Investment Fund V, L.P., Peter Nordin, Apex Investment Fund V, L.P., Robert W. Cross/1.60%, Insiders/8.60%, George M. Middlemas, Arthur Wirth, Martin T. Johnson/1.40%, Apex Investment Fund V, L.P/49.30%, Arco Van Nieuwland/12.80%, Per Gustafsson/6.80%, Heidi B. Newton, Braden Waverley/3.80%, Logan Hurst/5.90%, Graham Smith *(20 Owners included in Index)*

Financial Data: ***Fiscal Year End:***12/31 ***Latest Annual Data:*** 12/31/2006

Year	Sales	Net Income
2006	$1,188,000	-$6,485,000
2005	$642,000	-$44,446,000
2004	NA	-$4,665,000

Curr. Assets:	$1,504,000	***Curr. Liab.:***	$4,300,000	***P/E Ratio:***	34.60
Plant, Equip.:	$386,000	***Total Liab.:***	$4,300,000	***Indic. Yr. Divd.:***	NA
Total Assets:	$11,732,000	***Net Worth:***	$7,432,000	***Debt/ Equity:***	NA

Patterson Cos Inc

1031 Mendota Hts. Rd., St. Paul, MN, 55120; ***PH:*** 1-651-686-1600; ***Fax:*** 1-651-686-9331; ***http://*** www.pattersondental.com

General - Incorporation	MN	***Stock***- Price on:12/24/2007	$37.55
Employees	6,440	Stock Exchange	NDQ
Auditor	Ernst & Young LLP	Ticker Symbol	PDCO
Stk Agt	Wells Fargo Bank Minnesota N.A	Outstanding Shares	135,700,000
Counsel	Briggs & Morgan	E.P.S	$1.61
DUNS No.	00-696-2500	Shareholders	NA

Business: The groups principle activity is to provide dental products, services and technology. The groups products include anesthetic and needles, cameras and accessories, and denture material. The group operates from United States.

Primary SIC and add'l.: 5047 5044 7359 7699 7372 5045

CIK No: 0000891024

Subsidiaries: AbilityOne Homecraft Limited, AbilityOne Kinetec S.A., AbilityOne Limited, Accu-Bite Dental Products Limited Liability Company, Accu-Bite, Inc., AO Liquidation, Inc., AOC Vertriebs GmbH, Direct Dental Supply Co., Intra Corp., Medco Supply Company, Inc., Midland Manufacturing Company, Inc., Patterson Dental Canada Inc., Patterson Dental Supply, Inc., Patterson Logistics Services, Inc., Patterson Medical Holdings, Inc. 25 Subsidiaries included in the Index

Officers: James W. Wiltz/Dir., CEO, Pres./$1,033,046.00, Stephen R. Armstrong/CFO, Exec. VP, Treasurer/$817,784.00, Lynn E. Askew/VP - Management Information Systems, Gary D. Johnson/VP - Operations/$569,394.00, Scott P. Anderson/Pres. - Patterson Dental Supply, Inc/$517,758.00, Matthew L. Levitt/Sec., General Counsel, David P. Sproat/Pres. - Patterson Medical Supply, Inc/$537,307.00, George L. Henriques/Corporate Officers, Pres. - Operating Units, Richard G. Cinquina/Contact - Additional Information

Directors: James W. Wiltz/Dir., CEO, Pres., Peter L. Frechette/Chmn., Ronald E. Ezerski/Dir., Andre B. Lacy/Dir., Charles Reich/Dir., Ellen A. Rudnick/Dir., Harold C. Slavkin/Dir., John D. Buck/Dir.

Owners: Charles Reich, U.S. Bancorp/8.30%, David P. Sproat, Sands Capital Management, LLC/5.10%, Ellen A. Rudnick, John D. Buck, Insiders/7.20%, Harold C. Slavkin, Gary D. Johnson, Andre B. Lacy, Stephen R. Armstrong, Peter L. Frechette/4.10%, Ronald E. Ezerski/1.90%, Scott P. Anderson, James W. Wiltz

Financial Data: ***Fiscal Year End:***04/29 ***Latest Annual Data:*** 04/28/2007

Year	Sales	Net Income
2007	$2,798,398,000	$208,336,000
2006	$2,615,123,000	$198,425,000
2005	$2,421,457,000	$183,698,000

Curr. Assets:	$800,037,000	***Curr. Liab.:***	$322,288,000	***P/E Ratio:***	24.87
Plant, Equip.:	$97,178,000	***Total Liab.:***	$670,229,000	***Indic. Yr. Divd.:***	NA
Total Assets:	$1,685,301,000	***Net Worth:***	$1,015,072,000	***Debt/ Equity:***	NA

Patterson Uti Energy Inc

4510 Lamesa Hwy., Snyder, TX, 79549; ***PH:*** 1-325-574-6300; ***Fax:*** 1-325-574-6390; ***http://*** www.patenergy.com; ***Email:*** investrelations@patenergy.com

General - Incorporation	DE	***Stock***- Price on:12/24/2007	$27
Employees	9,000	Stock Exchange	NDQ
Auditor	PricewaterhouseCoopers LLP	Ticker Symbol	PTEN
Stk Agt	Continental Stock Transfer & Trust Co	Outstanding Shares	156,710,000
Counsel	Fulbright & Jaworski LLP	E.P.S	$3.23
DUNS No.	08-888-9498	Shareholders	NA

Business: The groups principle activity is to provide onshore contract drilling services to exploration and production companies. The groups services include development, exploration, acquisition and production of oil and natural gas. The group operates from United States.

Primary SIC and add'l.: 1382 1311 1381

CIK No: 0000889900

Subsidiaries: Ambar Drilling Fluids LP, LLLP, Eastern Reservoir Services Company, International Petroleum Services Company, Lone Star Mud LP, LLLP, Norton Drilling Company Mexico, Inc., Norton Drilling Services, Inc., Norton Drilling, L.P., Norton GP, LLC, Patterson (GP)LLC, Patterson (GP2) LLC, Patterson (LP)LLC, Patterson Petroleum LP, LLLP, Patterson Petroleum Trading Company LP, LLLP, Patterson-UTI Aviation Services, LLC, Patterson-UTI Drilling Company LP, LLLP 25 Subsidiaries included in the Index

Officers: Douglas J. Wall/CEO, Pres., William L. Moll/General Counsel, Sec., John E. Vollmer/Sr. VP - Corporate Development, CFO, Treasurer/$2,714,941.00, Kenneth N. Berns/Dir., Sr. VP/$2,588,402.00

Directors: Mark S. Siegel/Chmn., Curtis W. Huff/Dir., Cloyce A. Talbott/Dir., Kenneth R. Peak/Dir., Terry H. Hunt/Dir., Robert C. Gist/67/Dir., Kenneth N. Berns/Dir., Sr. VP, Nadine C. Smith/50/Dir., Charles O. Buckner/Dir.

Owners: First Pacific Advisors, LLC/5.70%, Kenneth N. Berns, Cloyce A. Talbott, John E. Vollmer, Curtis W. Huff, Mark S. Siegel/1.70%, Insiders/4.50%, Robert C. Gist, Charles O. Buckner, Glenn A. Patterson, Barclays Global Investors, NA/12.30%, Kenneth R. Peak, Terry H. Hunt, Nadine C. Smith

Financial Data: ***Fiscal Year End:***12/31 ***Latest Annual Data:*** 12/31/2006

Year	Sales	Net Income
2006	$2,546,586,000	$673,254,000
2005	$1,740,455,000	$372,740,000
2004	$1,000,769,000	$94,346,000

Curr. Assets:	$652,670,000	***Curr. Liab.:***	$317,618,000	***P/E Ratio:***	7.22
Plant, Equip.:	$1,435,804,000	***Total Liab.:***	$630,037,000	***Indic. Yr. Divd.:***	$0.480
Total Assets:	$2,192,503,000	***Net Worth:***	$1,562,466,000	***Debt/ Equity:***	NA

Paula Financial

87 E Green St., Ste. 206, Pasadena, CA, 91105; ***PH:*** 1-626-844-7100; ***Fax:*** 1-626-844-7144; ***http://*** www.paula.com; ***Email:*** stockholder@paula.com

General - Incorporation	DE	***Stock***- Price on:12/24/2007	NA
Employees	86	Stock Exchange	OTC
Auditor	Ernst & Young LLP	Ticker Symbol	PFCO
Stk Agt	Mellon Investor Services LLC	Outstanding Shares	NA
Counsel	Morgan, Lewis & Bockius LLP	E.P.S	$0.19
DUNS No.	08-110-6239	Shareholders	NA

Business: The group's principal activity is to distribute commercial insurance products and services. Products and services of the group include health, property and casualty, emphasizing workers' compensation, and some life and disability insurance products. In 2003, the group acquired book of business of roudebush & avina insurance agency inc.

Primary SIC and add'l.: 6411

CIK No: 0000929031

Subsidiaries: Pan American Underwriters Insurance Agents and Brokers, Inc, Pan American Underwriters, Inc, Pan Pacific Benefit Administrators, Inc, PAULA Trading Company Insurance Agents and Brokers, Inc, Stock Incentive Plan

Officers: Jeffrey A. Snider/Chmn., CEO, Debbie Maddocks/VP, Bob Underwood/Pres., Bitsy Ming/Exec. VP, Steve Martin/Sr. VP, Robert Alderete/Accounting Executive, John Montano/VP, Fred Besana/Sr. VP, Eric Duell/Accounting Executive, Joe O'Brien/Sr. VP, Hyacinth Perera/VP - Sbdu, J. J. Stone/Accounting Executive, Harry Goodall/Business Develpoment, Florida

Directors: Jeffrey A. Snider/Chmn., CEO

Financial Data: ***Fiscal Year End:***12/31 ***Latest Annual Data:*** 12/31/2005

Year	Sales	Net Income
2005	$18,085,000	$1,213,000
2004	$18,676,000	$950,000
2003	$19,396,000	$1,428,000

Curr. Assets:	$12,164,000	***Curr. Liab.:***	$9,217,000		
Plant, Equip.:	$536,000	***Total Liab.:***	$9,822,000	***Indic. Yr. Divd.:***	NA
Total Assets:	$20,886,000	***Net Worth:***	$11,064,000	***Debt/ Equity:***	NA

Paulson Capital Corp

811 SW Naito Pkwy., Ste. 200, Portland, OR, 97204; ***PH:*** 1-503-243-6000; ***Fax:*** 1-503-243-6018; ***http://*** www.paulsoninvestment.com

General - Incorporation	OR	***Stock***- Price on:12/24/2007	$5.21
Employees	80	Stock Exchange	NDQ
Auditor	Mcgladrey & Pullen, LLP	Ticker Symbol	PLCC
Stk Agt	PIC	Outstanding Shares	6,150,000
Counsel	NA	E.P.S	$0.91
DUNS No.	10-381-2236	Shareholders	NA

Business: The group's principal activity is to provide security brokerage services through its wholly owned subsidiary paulson investment company, inc. The group is involved in the purchase and sale of investment securities. The services provided by the group include retail brokerage, corporate finance, investment banking, trading and market making. The subsidiary renders broker dealer services in securities on agency and on principal basis to its customers. As on 31-Dec-2003 the group had 30 branch offices throughout the United States.

Primary SIC and add'l.: 6211 6719

CIK No: 0000704159

Subsidiaries: Paulson Investment Company, Inc

Officers: Charles Paulson/72/Chmn., CEO, Pres., Karen Johannes/48/CFO/$105,190.00, Jacqueline M. Paulson/69/Dir., Sec., Treasurer

Directors: Charles Paulson/72/Chmn., CEO, Pres., Jacqueline M. Paulson/69/Dir., Sec., Treasurer, Steve Kleemann/67/Dir., Shannon P. Pratt/74/Dir., Paul Shoen/51/Dir.

Owners: Shannon P. Pratt, Lorraine Maxfield, Insiders/62.70%, Amy Paulson/7.80%, Jacqueline M. Paulson/49.00%, Steve Kleemann/12.10%, Harry Striplin, Trent Davis, Paul Shoen

Financial Data: ***Fiscal Year End:***12/31 ***Latest Annual Data:*** 12/31/2006

Year	Sales	Net Income
2006	$13,464,000	-$4,862,000
2005	$39,736,000	$8,492,000
2004	$32,915,000	$3,490,000

Curr. Assets:	$10,637,000	***Curr. Liab.:***	$588,000	***P/E Ratio:***	22.65
Plant, Equip.:	$272,000	***Total Liab.:***	$3,688,000	***Indic. Yr. Divd.:***	NA
Total Assets:	$38,464,000	***Net Worth:***	$34,776,000	***Debt/ Equity:***	NA

Pavilion Bancorp Inc

135 E Maumee St., Adrian, MI, 49221; ***PH:*** 1-517-265-5144; ***Fax:*** 1-517-265-3926; ***http://*** www.pavilionbancorp.com

General - Incorporation	MI	***Stock***- Price on:12/24/2007	$47
Employees	NA	Stock Exchange	OTC
Auditor	Plante & Moran, PLLC	Ticker Symbol	PVLN
Stk Agt	American Stock Transfer & Trust Co.	Outstanding Shares	NA
Counsel	NA	E.P.S	$3.38
DUNS No.	NA	Shareholders	NA

Business: The group operates through its subsdiary whose principle activity is to provide banking operations and other related financial activities. The group operates from United States.

Primary SIC and add'l.: 6712

CIK No: 0001112477

Subsidiaries: Bank of Lenawee, Pavilion Financial Services, Inc., Pavilion Mortgage Company

Officers: Richard J. Devries/Dir., CEO, Pres./$236,737.00, Mark D. Wolfe/CFO/$126,500.00

Directors: Richard J. Devries/Dir., CEO, Pres., Douglas L. Kapnick/Chmn., Daniel R. Hupp/Dir., Margaret M.S. Noe/Dir., Terence R. Sheehan/Dir., Edward J. Engle/Dir., David J. Stutzman/Dir., Fred R. Duncan/Dir., Marinus Vanooyen/Dir., Barbara A. Mitzel/Dir., Emory M. Schmidt/Dir.

Directors: Richard J. Devries/Dir., CEO, Pres., Douglas L. Kapnick/Chmn., Daniel R. Hupp/Dir., Margaret M.S. Noe/Dir., Terence R. Sheehan/Dir., Edward J. Engle/Dir., David J. Stutzman/Dir., Fred R. Duncan/Dir., Marinus Vanooyen/Dir., Barbara A. Mitzel/Dir., Emory M. Schmidt/Dir.

Owners: Richard J. DeVries/0.20%, Douglas L. Kapnick/11.97%, Emory M. Schmidt, Ryan C. Luttenton/0.03%, Fred R. Duncan/3.50%, Mark D. Wolfe/0.06%, Marinus VanOoyen, Edward J. Engle, Terence R. Sheehan, Dan R. Hupp, Pamela S. Fisher/0.66%, David J. Stutzman, Barbara A. Mitzel, Insiders/20.33%, Margaret M. S. Noe *(16 Owners included in Index)*

Financial Data: *Fiscal Year End:*12/31 *Latest Annual Data:* 12/31/2006

Year	Sales	Net Income
2006	$21,943,000	$2,401,000
2005	$19,407,000	$1,938,000
2004	$18,451,000	$7,132,000
Curr. Assets: $19,140,000	**Curr. Liab.:** $261,981,000	**P/E Ratio:** 13.91
Plant, Equip.: $8,175,000	**Total Liab.:** $267,087,000	**Indic. Yr. Divd.:** $1.040
Total Assets: $295,023,000	**Net Worth:** $27,936,000	**Debt/ Equity:** 0.0894

Pawfect Foods Inc

1325 S Congress Ave, Boynton Beach, FL, 33426; *PH:* 1-954-801-3950

General - Incorporation	FL	**Stock**- Price on:12/24/2007	NA
Employees	NA	Stock Exchange	OTC
Auditor	Baum & Co., P.A.	Ticker Symbol	PWFF
Stk Agt	NA	Outstanding Shares	NA
Counsel	NA	E.P.S.	NA
DUNS No.	NA	Shareholders	NA

Business: The groups principal activity is selling pet food via the Internet utilizing website that can be viewed at Pawfectfoods.com. The group also have targeted products that are offered on website for immediate purchase and with recent addition of credit card processing through Authorize.net. The group operates from the United States.

Primary SIC and add'l.: 5990

CIK No: 0001347613

Officers: Charles Monahan/61/Pres., Sec., Treasurer

Owners: Charles Monahan/91.70%

Paxar Corp

105 Corporate Pk. Dr., White Plains, NY, 10604; *PH:* 1-914-697-6800; *http://* www.paxarcorp.com

General - Incorporation	NY	**Stock**- Price on:12/24/2007	NA
Employees	10,800	Stock Exchange	NA
Auditor	Ernst & Young LLP	Ticker Symbol	NA
Stk Agt	Mellon Investor Services LLC	Outstanding Shares	NA
Counsel	Snow Becker Krauss P.C.	E.P.S.	NA
DUNS No.	00-128-1450	Shareholders	NA

Business: The group's principal activities are to provide innovative merchandising systems to retailers and apparel manufacturers. It develops, manufactures and markets bar code systems, apparel systems, fabric labels, graphic tags, and identification and pricing solutions products. The group also manufactures printers, paper and fabric substrates, inks for tag and label printing systems and develops operating software. Electronic bar code systems and hand-held mechanical labelers are manufactured for use in retail stores, distribution centers and for remote tracking applications. The group designs integrated systems that combine its electronic printer, scanners and specialized software for warehouse applications. In addition, the group provides service for its printers at customer locations and services mechanical labelers in its facilities. The group operates in North America, Europe and Asia-Pacific. On 04-Sep-2003, the group acquired alkahn labels, inc.

Primary SIC and add'l.: 3565 3999

CIK No: 0000075681

Subsidiaries: Bonny Nice Industries Ltd, Collitex S.r.l, Ferguson Asia Ltd, Mandhana Bornemann Industries Ltd, Paxa Italia S.r.l, Paxar Americas, Inc., Paxar B.V, Paxar Canada, Inc, Paxar Capital Corporation, Paxar Central Europe, GmbH, Paxar Corporativo Mexico S.A. de C.V, Paxar de Colombia S.A, Paxar Far East Ltd, Paxar France S.A, Paxar Honduras S.A 20 Subsidiaries included in the Index

Officers: Robert Van Der Merwe/55/Chmn., CEO, Pres., Anthony S. Colatrella/52/CFO, VP, James Wrigley/54/Group Pres. - Global Apparel Solutions, Robert S. Stone/70/VP, General Counsel, Sec., James L. Martin/61/Pres. - Global Supply Chain Solutions, Susan P. Guerin/46/Pres. - Americas Apparel Group, Timothy M. Winston/43/VP, Treasurer, Paul Chu/56/Pres. - Asia Pacific, Richard A. Maue/37/VP, Controller

Directors: Robert Van Der Merwe/55/Chmn., CEO, Pres., James R. Painter/Dir., Jack Becker/Dir., David E. McKinney/Dir., Arthur Hershaft/Dir., Joyce F. Brown/Dir., Thomas R. Loemker/Dir., James C. McGroddy/Dir., Leo Benatar/Dir., Victor Hershaft/Dir., David L. Kolb/Dir., Roger M. Widmann/Dir.

Owners: Jack Becker, Arthur Hershaft/5.61%, David E. McKinney, Anthony S. Colatrella, David L. Kolb, James R. Painter, James C. McGroddy, Paul Chu, Leo Benatar, Roger M. Widmann, Robert van der Merwe, Insiders/9.95%, Dimensional Fund Advisors, LP/7.47%, Victor Hershaft, Joyce F. Brown *(18 Owners included in Index)*

Pay88 Inc

1053 N Barnstead Rd. , Barnstead, NH, 03225; *PH:* 1-603-776-6044; *http://* www.pay88.com; *Email:* info@pay88.us

General - Incorporation	NV	**Stock**- Price on:12/24/2007	$2.6
Employees	NA	Stock Exchange	OTC
Auditor	Wolinetz, Lafazan & Company, P.C.	Ticker Symbol	PAYI
Stk Agt	Island Stock Transfer	Outstanding Shares	NA
Counsel	NA	E.P.S.	NA
DUNS No.	NA	Shareholders	NA

Business: The groups principal activity is involved in the business of facilitating money transfers from the United States to China. In September 2006, the group acquired Qianbao. The group operates from the United States.

Primary SIC and add'l.: 6099

CIK No: 0001338360

Subsidiaries: Chongqing Qianbao Technology Ltd.

Officers: Guo Fan/30/Chmn., CEO, CFO, Gordon Preston/Dir., Sec., Tao Fan/COO - China, Dir.

Directors: Guo Fan/30/Chmn., CEO, CFO, Gordon Preston/Dir., Sec., Lin Xu/Dir., Shi Qing Fu/Dir., Tao Fan/COO - China, Dir.

Owners: Whalehaven Capital Fund Limited/3.91%, Guo Fan/24.70%, Insiders/29.20%, Alpha Capital Anstalt/3.91%, Tao Fan/4.50%, Osher Capital Partners LLC/1.23%, Shiqing Fu

Financial Data: *Fiscal Year End:*12/31 *Latest Annual Data:* 12/31/2006

Year	Sales	Net Income
2006	$1,200,000	-$298,000
2005	NA	-$170,000
Curr. Assets: $241,000	**Curr. Liab.:** $381,000	
Plant, Equip.: $487,000	**Total Liab.:** $462,000	**Indic. Yr. Divd.:** NA
Total Assets: $728,000	**Net Worth:** $267,000	**Debt/ Equity:** 0.5882

Paychex Inc

911 Panorama Trl. S, Rochester, NY, 14625; *PH:* 1-585-385-6666; *Fax:* 1-585-383-3428; *http://* www.paychex.com

General - Incorporation	DE	**Stock**- Price on:12/24/2007	$39.87
Employees	10,900	Stock Exchange	NDQ
Auditor	Ernst & Young LLP	Ticker Symbol	PAYX
Stk Agt	American Stock Transfer & Trust Co.	Outstanding Shares	381,930,000
Counsel	NA	E.P.S.	$1.44
DUNS No.	09-439-9359	Shareholders	NA

Business: The group's principle activity is to provide payroll, human resource and employee benefit outsourcing solutions for small to medium-sized businesses. The services include payroll processing, tax filing and payments, retirement services administration, employee benefits administration, regulatory compliance, workers' compensation insurance and comprehensive bundled human resource administrative services. Through the Paychex Online, the group provides core payroll services such as online payroll, Internet time sheet, Internet report service and general ledger reporting service. Outsourcing of the payroll and human resource functions allows small businesses to minimize the compliance risks associated with changing administrative requirements and statutory tax regulations. The trademarks include Paychex, Taxpay, Paylink, Preview, Readychex, Pay-As-You-Go and Rapid Payroll. The group's total revenue for year 2007 was 1.886.96 millions of USD.

Primary SIC and add'l.: 7374 7375 8742 8721 7379 7291

CIK No: 0000723531

Subsidiaries: Advantage Payroll Services, Inc., Business Benefits Administrators, Inc., Paychex Agency, Inc., Paychex Business Solutions, Inc., Paychex Deutschland GmbH, Paychex Insurance Concepts, Inc., Paychex Investment Partnership LP, Paychex Management Corp., Paychex North America Inc., Paychex of New York LLC, Paychex Securities Corporation, Paychex Time & Attendance Inc., Prime Real Estate LLC, Prime Real Estate LLCDelaware, PXC Inc. 18 Subsidiaries included in the Index

Officers: Jonathan J. Judge/Dir., CEO, Pres./$4,655,740.00, John M. Morphy/CFO, Sr. VP, Sec./$1,036,330.00, Michael A. McCarthy/VP - Eastern US Sales, Melinda A. Janik/VP - Finance, Clifford Gibson/VP - Western US Sales, Brad R. Flipse/VP - Major Marketing Services Sales, Suzanne E. Vickery/VP - Central US Sales, William G. Kuchta/VP - Organizational Development, Martin Stowe/VP - Human Resources Services, Terri Allen/Investor Relations Officer, Daniel A. Canzano/VP - Information Technology/$599,059.00, Martin Mucci/Sr. VP - Operations/$1,038,196.00, Anthony Tortorella/VP - Human Resources Services Sales, Leonard E. Redon/VP - Western Operations, Lynn J. Miley/VP - Eastern Operations *(17 Officers included in Index)*

Directors: Jonathan J. Judge/Dir., CEO, Pres., Thomas B. Golisano/Chmn., Pamela A. Joseph/Dir., Joseph M. Tucci/Dir., Grant M. Inman/Dir., David J.S. Flaschen/Dir., Joseph M. Velli/Dir., Phillip Horsley/Dir.

Owners: Thomas B. Golisano/9.90%, Daniel A. Canzano, Martin Mucci, Jonathan J. Judge, Walter Turek, Pamela A. Joseph, Joseph M. Velli, Phillip Horsley, Insiders/10.40%, John M. Morphy, David J. S. Flaschen, Joseph M. Tucci, Grant M. Inman

Financial Data: *Fiscal Year End:*05/31 *Latest Annual Data:* 05/31/2007

Year	Sales	Net Income
2007	$1,886,964,000	$515,447,000
2006	$1,674,596,000	$464,914,000
2005	$1,445,143,000	$368,849,000
Curr. Assets: $4,861,319,000	**Curr. Liab.:** $4,237,470,000	**P/E Ratio:** 29.53
Plant, Equip.: $256,087,000	**Total Liab.:** $4,294,271,000	**Indic. Yr. Divd.:** $0.840
Total Assets: $6,246,519,000	**Net Worth:** $1,952,248,000	**Debt/ Equity:** NA

Payless Shoesource Inc

3231 S E Sixth St., Topeka, KS, 66607; *PH:* 1-785-233-5171; *http://* www.payless.com

General - Incorporation	DE	**Stock**- Price on:12/24/2007	$31.22
Employees	13,200	Stock Exchange	NYSE
Auditor	Deloitte & Touche LLP	Ticker Symbol	NA
Stk Agt	Securities Transfer Corp	Outstanding Shares	65,000,000
Counsel	NA	E.P.S.	$1.73
DUNS No.	NA	Shareholders	NA

Business: The groups principle activity is to operate shoe retail stores. The groups products include dress, athletic and casual shoes, slippers, boots and sandals for men, women and kids. The group operates from United States.

Primary SIC and add'l.: 5661

CIK No: 0001060232

Subsidiaries: Dyelights, Inc., Dynamic Assets Limited, Payless Ca Management Ltd., Payless Shoesource (bvi) Holdings, Ltd., Payless Shoesource Andean Holdings, Payless Shoesource Asia Pte. Ltd., Payless Shoesource Canada Gp Inc., Payless Shoesource Canada Inc., Payless Shoesource Canada Lp, Payless Shoesource Distribution, Inc., Payless Shoesource Finance, Inc., Payless Shoesource Gold Value, Inc., Payless Shoesource International Limited, Payless Shoesource Japan Co. Ltd., Payless Shoesource Merchandising, Inc. 26 Subsidiaries included in the Index

Officers: Matthew E. Rubel/Dir., CEO, Pres., Michael J. Massey/Sr. VP, Sec., General Counsel, Darrel J. Pavelka/Exec. VP - Global Supply Chain, Ullrich E. Porzig/CFO, Sr. VP, Treasurer, James Grant/Investor Relations Officer, Nikki Sloup/Investor Relations Officer, Jay A. Lentz/Sr. VP - Human Resources, Douglas Treff/Exec. VP, Chief Administrative Officer, Paul Fenaroli/Division Sr. VP - Corporate Strategy, Michael Jeppesen/Division Sr. VP - Global Sourcing, Product Development, John D. Smith/Division Sr. VP - Store Development

Directors: Matthew E. Rubel/Dir., CEO, Pres., Howard R. Fricke/Chmn., David Scott Olivet/Dir., Michael A. Weiss/Dir., Judith K. Hofer/Dir., Daniel Boggan/Dir., Mylle H. Mangum/Dir., John F. McGovern/Dir., Michael E. Murphy/Dir., Robert C. Wheeler/Dir., Scott D. Olivet/Dir., Robert F. Moran/Dir.

Owners: Barclays Global Investors, NA/5.70%, Judith K. Hofer, Scott D. Olivet, Mylle H. Mangum, Howard R. Fricke, Matthew E. Rubel, Michael J. Massey, Robert F. Moran, Jay A. Lentz, Insiders/1.60%, Daniel Boggan, Ullrich E. Porzig, Robert C. Wheeler, State Street Bank and Trust Company/7.30%, John F. McGovern *(19 Owners included in Index)*

Financial Data: *Fiscal Year End:*01/28   *Latest Annual Data:* 2/3/2007

Year	Sales	Net Income
2007	$2,796,700,000	$122,000,000
2006	$2,667,300,000	$66,400,000
2005	$2,656,500,000	-$2,000,000

Curr. Assets:	$906,600,000	**Curr. Liab.:**	$380,300,000	**P/E Ratio:**	16.61
Plant, Equip.:	$421,200,000	**Total Liab.:**	$714,600,000	**Indic. Yr. Divd.:**	NA
Total Assets:	$1,427,400,000	**Net Worth:**	$700,100,000	**Debt/ Equity:**	0.2881

Payment Data Systems Inc

12500 San PeDr.o, Ste. 120, San Antonio, TX, 78216; *PH:* 1-210-249-4100; *Fax:* 1-210-249-4130; *http://* www.paymentdata.com; *Email:* info@paymentdata.com

General - Incorporation	NV	**Stock**- Price on:12/24/2007	$0.092
Employees	8	Stock Exchange	OTC
Auditor	Akin, Doherty, Klein & Feuge, P.c.	Ticker Symbol	PYDS
Stk Agt	American Stock Transfer & Trust Co.	Outstanding Shares	70,350,000
Counsel	NA	E.P.S.	-$0.028
DUNS No.	NA	Shareholders	NA

Business: The group's principal activity is to provide integrated electronic payment processing services to merchants and businesses. The services include all types of automated clearinghouse processing and credit and debit card-based processing services. The group provides its services for consumers under the domain name www.bills.com. On 25-Jul-2003, the group sold all its assets to saro inc, a wholly owned subsidiary of cyberstarts inc.

Primary SIC and add'l.: 7374 7389

CIK No: 0001088034

Subsidiaries: bills.com, Inc., billserv.com-canada, Inc.

Officers: Michael R. Long/Co - Founder, Chmn., CEO, CFO/$427,172.00, Louis A. Hoch/Co - Founder, Vice Chmn., COO, Pres./$545,020.00, Larry Morrison/VP - Business Development/$191,008.00, Connie Allen/Mgr. - PDS Sales

Directors: Michael R. Long/Co - Founder, Chmn., CEO, CFO, Louis A. Hoch/Co - Founder, Vice Chmn., COO, Pres., Peter G. Kirby/Dir., Tom Debrooke/Member - Advisory Board, Jason Moore/Member - Advisory Board

Owners: Larry Morrison/2.00%, Robert Evans/14.80%, Peter G. Kirby/1.80%, Michael R. Long/13.50%, Insiders/32.50%, Louis A. Hoch/16.40%

Financial Data: *Fiscal Year End:*12/31   *Latest Annual Data:* 12/31/2006

Year	Sales	Net Income
2006	$2,523,000	-$1,396,000
2005	$1,181,000	-$1,196,000
2004	$358,000	-$1,515,000

Curr. Assets:	$417,000	**Curr. Liab.:**	$1,167,000		
Plant, Equip.:	$158,000	**Total Liab.:**	$1,167,000	**Indic. Yr. Divd.:**	NA
Total Assets:	$602,000	**Net Worth:**	-$565,000	**Debt/ Equity:**	NA

Payphone Wind Down Corp

Formerly: ETS Payphones Inc
1490 Westfork Dr., Ste. G, Lithia Springs, GA, 30122; *PH:* 1-770-819-1600; *http://* www.etspayphones.com

General - Incorporation	DE	**Stock** - Price on:12/24/2007	NA
Employees	NA	Stock Exchange	NA
Auditor	Tauber & Balser, P.C	Ticker Symbol	NA
Stk Agt	American Stock Transfer & Trust Co.	Outstanding Shares	NA
Counsel	NA	E.P.S.	NA
DUNS No.	NA	Shareholders	NA

Business: The groups principle activity is to operate pay telephones. The group also provides telecommunications products to certain clients. The group operates from United States.

Primary SIC and add'l.: 3661

CIK No: 0001287065

Owners: Insiders

PBS Holding Inc

433 Kitty Hawk Dr., Ste 226, Universal City, TX, 78148; *PH:* 1-210-658-4675; *http://* www.pbs-sa.com; *Email:* investorrelations@pbs-sa.com

General - Incorporation	NV	**Stock**- Price on:12/24/2007	$0.05
Employees	25	Stock Exchange	OTC
Auditor	Madsen & Assoc. CPAs, Inc	Ticker Symbol	PBHG
Stk Agt	Registrar & Transfer Co	Outstanding Shares	11,770,000
Counsel	NA	E.P.S.	-$0.03
DUNS No.	NA	Shareholders	NA

Business: The group's principle activity is to offer a range of product and services that provide a complete solution for the clients' human resources (hr) outsourcing needs. The group's products and services include benefits administration, payroll administration, governmental compliance, risk management, unemployment administration, health, welfare and retirement benefits. These products are offered to clients which are typically small to medium-sized business with between five and one hundred employees. The group acquired ahjr inc through the purchase of its outstanding shares.

Primary SIC and add'l.: 8742

CIK No: 0001077150

Subsidiaries: AHJR, Inc., Primary HR Services, LLC

Officers: Patrick Matthews/Chmn., CEO, CFO, Pres., Principal Accounting Officer, Amanda Sinclair/Dir., Sr. Exec. VP

Directors: Patrick Matthews/Chmn., CEO, CFO, Pres., Principal Accounting Officer, Michael Ellis/Dir., Amanda Sinclair/Dir., Sr. Exec. VP

Owners: Insiders/84.01%, Amanda Sinclair/6.82%, Patrick D. Matthews/72.64%, Connie Matthews/4.55%

Financial Data: *Fiscal Year End:*12/31   *Latest Annual Data:* 12/31/2006

Year	Sales	Net Income
2006	$5,638,000	-$446,000
2005	$4,919,000	-$205,000
2004	$3,339,000	-$69,000

Curr. Assets:	$575,000	**Curr. Liab.:**	$1,273,000		
Plant, Equip.:	$101,000	**Total Liab.:**	$1,328,000	**Indic. Yr. Divd.:**	NA
Total Assets:	$681,000	**Net Worth:**	-$646,000	**Debt/ Equity:**	NA

Pbsj Corp

2001 NW 107th Ave., Miami, FL, 33172; *PH:* 1-305-592-7275; *http://* www.pbsj.com

General - Incorporation	FL	**Stock**- Price on:12/24/2007	NA
Employees	NA	Stock Exchange	NA
Auditor	Deloitte & Touche LLP	Ticker Symbol	NA
Stk Agt	NA	Outstanding Shares	NA
Counsel	NA	E.P.S.	NA
DUNS No.	NA	Shareholders	NA

Business: The group's principle activities include planning, designing and construction services to the transportation, environmental, civil engineering and construction industries. The group operates from United States.

Primary SIC and add'l.: 8711

CIK No: 0001117414

Subsidiaries: Florida Construction Services, Inc., Post Buckley, Schuh & Jernigan, Inc, Post, Buckley International, Inc.

Officers: John B. Zumwalt/57/Chmn., CEO/$588,130.00, Robert J. Paulsen/Vice Chmn., Exec. VP, Sec./$454,210.00, Todd J. Kenner/46/Dir., Pres./$674,528.00, Kathe Riley Jackson/Mgr. - Corporate Communications, John S. Shearer/Dir., Sr. VP/$411,022.00, Donald J. Vrana/CFO, Sr. VP, Treasurer/$539,296.00, Cecilia R. Green/Sr. VP, National Service Dir. - Environmental Sciences, Dean L. Fox/Sr. VP, National Business Sector Mgr. - Federal Strategic Programs, Max D. Crumit/Exec./VP, National Service Dir. - Transportation, Clarence E. Anthony/Chief Marketing Officer, Becky S. Schaffer/63/Corporate Counsel, VP, Assist. Sec.

Directors: John B. Zumwalt/57/Chmn., CEO, Robert J. Paulsen/Vice Chmn., Exec. VP, Sec., John S. Shearer/Dir., Sr. VP, Todd J. Kenner/46/Dir., Pres., William D. Pruitt/67/Dir., Phillip E. Searcy/74/Dir., Frank A. Stasiowski/74/Dir.

Owners: Donald J. Vrana, John B. Zumwalt/2.85%, Max D. Crumit, The PBSJ Employee Profit Sharing and Stock Ownership Plan and Trust/50.84%, Insiders/9.15%, Todd J. Kenner/1.73%, Robert J. Paulsen/2.14%, William D. Pruitt, Phillip E. Searcy, Wayne J. Overman, Frank A. Stasiowski

PC Connection Inc

Rte. 101A, 730 Milford Rd., Merrimack, NH, 03054; *PH:* 1-603-683-2000; *Fax:* 1-603-423-5748; *http://* www.pcconnection.com; *Email:* ir@pcconnection.com

General - Incorporation	DE	**Stock**- Price on:12/24/2007	$12.75
Employees	1,635	Stock Exchange	NDQ
Auditor	Deloitte & Touche LLP	Ticker Symbol	PCCC
Stk Agt	American Stock Transfer & Trust Co.	Outstanding Shares	26,800,000
Counsel	NA	E.P.S.	$0.80
DUNS No.	94-979-0299	Shareholders	NA

Business: The groups principle activity is to market a variety of information technology (IT) products and services. The groups products include computer systems, software and peripheral equipment, networking communications and other products and accessories. The group operates from United States.

Primary SIC and add'l.: 5961

CIK No: 0001050377

Subsidiaries: GovConnection, Inc, MD Professional Services, Inc, Merrimack Services Corporation, MoreDirect, Inc, PC Connection Sales Corporation, PC Connection, Inc., PCSC, Inc.

Officers: Patricia Gallup/Chmn., CEO, Co - Founder/$1,230,031.00, Bradley Mousseau/Sr. VP - Human Resources/$433,773.00, Jack Ferguson/CFO, Sr. VP, Treasurer/$484,405.00, David Beffa-Negrini/Dir., Sr. VP - Corporate Marketing, Creative Services, Steve Baldridge/VP - Finance, Corporate Controller, Timothy McGrath/Exec. VP - Enterprise Group

Directors: Patricia Gallup/Chmn., CEO, Co - Founder, David Beffa-Negrini/Dir., Sr. VP - Corporate Marketing, Creative Services, Joseph A. Baute/Dir., Bruce Barone/Dir., David Hall/Dir., Donald Weatherson/Dir.

Owners: Patricia Gallup/32.70%, Donald Weatherson, Bruce Barone, Insiders/65.50%, Dimensional Fund Advisors, Inc./8.10%, Bear Stearns Asset Management Inc./8.80%, Jack Ferguson, David Beffa Negrini/1.10%, Robert Wilkins, Joseph Baute, Bradley Mousseau, David Hall/31.60%

Financial Data: *Fiscal Year End:*12/31   *Latest Annual Data:* 12/31/2006

Year	Sales	Net Income
2006	$1,635,651,000	$13,776,000
2005	$1,444,297,000	$4,447,000
2004	$1,353,834,000	$8,304,000

Curr. Assets:	$265,557,000	**Curr. Liab.:**	$138,592,000	**P/E Ratio:**	18.75
Plant, Equip.:	$19,542,000	**Total Liab.:**	$149,780,000	**Indic. Yr. Divd.:**	NA
Total Assets:	$346,684,000	**Net Worth:**	$196,904,000	**Debt/ Equity:**	0.0231

PC Mall Inc

2555 W 190th St., Ste. 201, Torrance, CA, 90504; *PH:* 1-310-354-5600; *Fax:* 1-310-225-4030; *http://* www.pcmall.com

General - Incorporation	DE	**Stock**- Price on:12/24/2007	$12.52
Employees	1,449	Stock Exchange	NDQ
Auditor	Morrison & Foerster LLP	Ticker Symbol	MALL
Stk Agt	U.S. Stock Transfer Corp	Outstanding Shares	12,420,000
Counsel	NA	E.P.S.	$0.71
DUNS No.	NA	Shareholders	NA

Business: The groups principal activity is to marketing computer hardware, software, peripherals, electronics, and other consumer products and services. The products of the group include notebooks, desktops and servers, displays, home electronics and printers. The groups operates through two segments namely Core business and online OnSale.com. The group operates from the United States. Of the net sale in the year 2006, Core business accounted for $993,860and online OnSale.com $11,960 (thousands).

Primary SIC and add'l.: 5961 5731 5734

CIK No: 0000937941

Subsidiaries: AF Services, LLC, Onsale, Inc., OSRP, LLC, PC Mall Canada, Inc., PC Mall Gov, Inc., PC Mall Sales, Inc., Wareforce Corp.

Officers: Frank F. Khulusi/Co - Founder, Chmn., CEO, Pres./$1,039,500.00, Theodore R. Sanders/CFO, Treasurer/$482,796.00, Daniel J. Devries/Exec. VP - Marketing/$412,673.00, Kristin M. Rogers/Exec. VP - Enterprise Sales - Business Solutions/$493,846.00, Robert I. Newton/General Counsel/$504,935.00, Rory K. Zaks/Pres. - PC Mall Sales, Inc.

Directors: Frank F. Khulusi/Co - Founder, Chmn., CEO, Pres., Thomas A. Maloof/Dir., Ronald B. Reck/Dir., Paul C. Heeschen/Dir.

Owners: Boston Avenue Capital, LLC/8.50%, Insiders/21.00%, Thomas A. Maloof, Robert I. Newton, Amre A. Youness/5.00%, Paul C. Heeschen, Wells Fargo and Company/5.20%, Citadel Limited Partnership/5.20%, Kristin M. Rogers/1.30%, Frank F. Khulusi/17.30%, Theodore R. Sanders/1.40%, Dimensional Fund Advisors LP/5.70%, Daniel J. DeVries/1.10%, Ronald B. Reck, Jonathan L. Kimerling/9.40%

Financial Data: Fiscal Year End:12/31 Latest Annual Data: 12/31/2006

Year	Sales	Net Income
2006	$1,005,820,000	$3,956,000
2005	$997,232,000	-$3,713,000
2004	$1,157,253,000	$1,013,000

Curr. Assets:	$184,379,000	Curr. Liab.:	$140,993,000	P/E Ratio: 28.45
Plant, Equip.:	$8,055,000	Total Liab.:	$142,743,000	Indic. Yr. Divd.: NA
Total Assets:	$203,567,000	Net Worth:	$60,824,000	Debt/ Equity: 0.0256

PCCW Ltd

39th Floor, PCCW Tower, Taikoo Pl., 979 Kings Rd., Quarry Bay; **PH:** 852-28882888; **Fax:** 852-28778877; **http://** www.pccw.com; **Email:** business_inquiry@pccw.com

General - Incorporation	Hong Kong	Stock - Price on:12/24/2007	NA
Employees	14,108	Stock Exchange	OTC
Auditor	PricewaterhouseCoopers LLP	Ticker Symbol	PCCWY
Stk Agt	Citigroup Global Markets Asia Ltd	Outstanding Shares	NA
Counsel	NA	E.P.S.	NA
DUNS No.	NA	Shareholders	NA

Business: The group's principal activities are the provision of international, local and mobile telecommunications services, Internet and interactive multimedia services, sale and rental of telecommunications equipment, computer, engineering and other technical services. Other activities include management services, e-commerce, broadband services, sale of advertising in the business white pages, yellow pages for businesses and yellow pages for customers, publication of directories, data center services, investment in and development of technology-related based businesses and investment in and development of infrastructure and properties in Hong Kong and elsewhere in mainland China and investment holding. Operations are carried out in Hong Kong, the cayman islands, the United States of America, the People's Republic of China, the british virgin islands, Japan, Taiwan and the United Kingdom.

Primary SIC and add'l.: 5065 4899 6519 6531 7375 6719 4812

CIK No: 0000842519

Subsidiaries: Beyond The Network Limited, BtN Access (HK) Limited, Cascade Limited, ChinaBiG Limited, Corporate Access Limited, Cyber-Port Limited, Jaleco Ltd, Omnilink Technology Limited, Pacific Century Premium Developments Limited, Pacific Century Systems Limited, PCCW (Beijing) Limited, PCCW Business eSolutions Limited, PCCW Directories Limited, Pccw Ims Limited, PCCW Powerbase Data Center Services (HK) Limited 30 Subsidiaries included in the Index

Officers: Peter Anthony Allen/52/Executive Dir., Mico Cho Yee Chung/47/Executive Dir., Alexander Anthony Arena/57/Group MD, Robert Chi Hong Lee/56/Executive Dir., Fan Xingcha/42/Executive Dir.

Directors: Richard Tzar Kai Li/41/Chmn., Zhang Chunjiang/Non Exec. Dir., Fan Xingcha/42/Executive Dir., Aman Mehta/Dir., Peter Anthony Allen/52/Executive Dir., Mico Cho Yee Chung/47/Executive Dir., Robert Chi Hong Lee/56/Executive Dir., Roger Lobo/Dir., David Ford/Non Exec. Dir., Chang Hsin-Kang/Dir., Li Kwok Po David/Dir., Raymond George Hardenbergh Seitz/Dir., Zuo Xunsheng/Dir., Li Fushen/Non Exec. Dir.

PCL Employees Holdings Ltd

5410 99 St., Edmonton, AB, T6E 3P4; **PH:** 1-780-435-9711; **http://** www.pcl.ca

General - Incorporation	AB	Stock - Price on:12/24/2007	NA
Employees	NA	Stock Exchange	NA
Auditor	KPMG LLP	Ticker Symbol	NA
Stk Agt	Computershare Investor Services LLC	Outstanding Shares	NA
Counsel	NA	E.P.S.	NA
DUNS No.	NA	Shareholders	NA

Business: The groups principle activity is to provide contracting and construction services. The groups markets include buildings, infrastructure and heavy industries. The group operates from United States, Canada and the Bahamas.

Primary SIC and add'l.: 1600

CIK No: 0001326107

Subsidiaries: 4102410 Canada Inc., GHI Holdings, Inc., Grand Sierra Construction Inc., Grand Sierra Equipment Ltd., Melloy Industrial Services Inc., Monad Industrial Constructors Inc., PCL Civil Constructors, Inc., PCL Construction Enterprises, Inc., PCL Construction Group Inc., PCL Construction Holdings Ltd., PCL Construction Management Inc., PCL Construction New Mexico, Inc., PCL Construction Resources (U.S.A.) Inc., PCL Construction Resources Inc., PCL Construction Services, Inc. 28 Subsidiaries included in the Index

Owners: Peter A. Stalenhoef, Al E. Troppmann/16.00%, Alan L. Bodie, Fred Auch/7.00%, R. Brad Nelson/8.00%, Peter E. Beaupre, Ross A. Grieve/17.00%, Alan L. Bodie/8.00%, Fred Auch/1.00%, Peter E. Beaupr/4.00%, Gordon D. Maron/7.00%, Paul G. Douglas, Al E. Troppmann/1.00%, R. Brad Nelson, Peter E. Beaupr (24 Owners included in Index)

PCS Edventures Inc

345 Bobwhite Ct., Ste. 200, Boise, ID, 83706; **PH:** 1-208-343-3110; **Fax:** 1-208-343-1321; **http://** www.pcsedu.com; **Email:** sales@pcsedu.com

General - Incorporation	ID	Stock - Price on:12/24/2007	$1.18
Employees	17	Stock Exchange	OTC
Auditor	HJ & Assoc. LLC	Ticker Symbol	PCSV
Stk Agt	Interwest Transfer Company, Inc.	Outstanding Shares	31,430,000
Counsel	Hall Farley Oberrecht & Blanton PA	E.P.S.	-$0.04
DUNS No.	NA	Shareholders	NA

Business: The group's principal activity is to develop and market educational related technologies and programs directed to the kindergarten through 12th grade after-school market. The group's products and technologies are targeted to both the classroom and home markets. Products and technologies of the group are delivered to the classroom through Internet access with group's subscription based Website. Currently, the group has developed seven innovative technology based educational programs namely academy of engineering, academy of robotics, edventures! lab, discover! lab, edventures brick lab!, young learner building box for classrooms and learning programs and edventures! online program is delivered to the home user over the Internet on a monthly subscription basis. The group has operations in the United States. Pcs (TM), academy of learning, business, edventures and pcs brick lab (TM) are some of trade names of the group.

Primary SIC and add'l.: 7379 8732 7373

CIK No: 0001122020

Subsidiaries: Northway Capital Trust I

Officers: Anthony A. Maher/Chmn., CEO, Pres./$120,000.00, Robert O. Grover/CTO, Exec. VP/$110,000.00, Christina M. Vaughn/39/VP, Chief Compliance Officer, Shannon M. Wilson/CFO, VP, Tamara Kauhaahaa/Graphic Design, Desktop Publishing, Product, Systems Development, Krystal M. Wright/Assist. to CFO, Joseph A. Khoury/COO, Pres. - PCS Labmentors, Ltd, Mark D. Veinot/Technical Dir. - Systems Administration, PCS Labmentors, Ltd, Richard Chen/Application Developer, PCS Labmentors, Ltd, Zoltan Cserna/Warehouse Mgr. - Administrative, Support, William F. Albert/National Sales Mgr. - Sales, Marketing, Suzanne C. Haislip/Regional Sales Mgr. - Sales, Marketing, Joe D. Egusquiza/International Sales Mgr. - Sales, Marketing, Mary Moiso/Procurement Specialist, Mike Law/Windows Domain Specialist, Network Administrator (21 Officers included in Index)

Directors: Anthony A. Maher/Chmn., CEO, Pres., Cecil D. Andrus/Dir., Dehryl A. Dennis/Dir., Michael K. McMurray/62/Dir., Donald J. Farley/Dir.

Owners: Shannon M. Wilson, Robert O. Grover/2.92%, Anthony A. Maher/6.74%, Insiders/19.50%, Michael K. McMurray, Donald J. Farley/4.54%, Dehryl A. Dennis, Christina M. Vaughn, Cecil D. Andrus/3.13%

Financial Data: Fiscal Year End:03/31 Latest Annual Data: 03/31/2007

Year	Sales	Net Income
2007	$1,999,000	-$1,924,000
2006	$2,602,000	-$1,205,000
2005	$1,469,000	-$939,000

Curr. Assets:	$1,098,000	Curr. Liab.:	$1,253,000	
Plant, Equip.:	$18,000	Total Liab.:	$1,253,000	Indic. Yr. Divd.: NA
Total Assets:	$1,756,000	Net Worth:	$503,000	Debt/ Equity: NA

PCTEL Inc

8725 W Higgins Rd., Ste. 400, Chicago, IL, 60631; **PH:** 1-773-243-3000; **Fax:** 1-773-243-3049; **http://** www.pctel.com; **Email:** investorrelations@pctel.com

General - Incorporation	DE	Stock - Price on:12/24/2007	$9.1
Employees	352	Stock Exchange	NDQ
Auditor	PricewaterhouseCoopers LLP	Ticker Symbol	PCTI
Stk Agt	Wells Fargo Bank Minnesota N.A	Outstanding Shares	22,440,000
Counsel	NA	E.P.S.	$0.16
DUNS No.	NA	Shareholders	NA

Business: The group's principal activity is to provide wireless connectivity products and test tool to cellular carriers, wireless Internet providers, PC OEM's and wireless equipment manufacturers. The group licenses patented and proprietary access technology related to analog modems to modem solution providers. The products offered include segue(tm), seegull(tm), clarify(tm) and wireless communication antennas. The group has intellectual property portfolio consisting of over 130 U.S. Patents and applications primarily in analog modem technology. The group's customers include distributors of wireless products. In Mar 2003, the group acquired dynamic telecommunications inc. On 02-Jan-2004, the group acquired maxrad inc.

Primary SIC and add'l.: 5065 6794 7370 3674 3661

CIK No: 0001057083

Subsidiaries: Dynamic Telecommunications, Inc., PCTEL Antenna Products Group, PCTEL Maryland, Sigma

Officers: Martin H. Singer/Chmn., CEO/$639,176.00, Varda Goldman/VP, General Counsel, Steven L. Deppe/59/Exec. VP - Strategy, Business Development/$313,621.00, Biju Nair/VP, GM - Mobility Solutions Group/$387,389.00, John Schoen/CFO/$355,774.00, Jeff Miller/VP, GM - Broadband Technology Group/$328,229.00, Luis Rugeles/GM - RF Solutions

Directors: Martin H. Singer/Chmn., CEO, Richard C. Alberding/Dir., Brian Jackman/Dir., John Sheehan/Dir., Carl Thomsen/Dir., Steven Levy/Dir., Giacomo Marini/Dir.

Owners: Richard C. Alberding, Martin H. Singer/4.21%, John R. Sheehan, Steven D. Levy, Biju Nair/1.53%, Entities affiliated with Dimensional FundAdvisors Inc./8.21%, Jeffrey A. Miller/1.50%, Royce& Associates LLC/7.86%, Entities and persons affiliated with Gruber& McBaineCapital Management, LLC/5.12%, Carl A. Thomsen, Whitman Capital, LLC/6.41%, Austin W. Marxe/7.90%, Insiders/10.58%, Steven L. Deppe, Giacomo Marini (17 Owners included in Index)

Financial Data: Fiscal Year End:12/31 Latest Annual Data: 12/31/2006

Year	Sales	Net Income
2006	$86,562,000	-$10,019,000
2005	$77,746,000	-$3,713,000
2004	$51,429,000	-$2,738,000

Curr. Assets:	$94,122,000	Curr. Liab.:	$9,743,000	
Plant, Equip.:	$12,357,000	Total Liab.:	$12,027,000	Indic. Yr. Divd.: NA
Total Assets:	$132,720,000	Net Worth:	$120,693,000	Debt/ Equity: NA

PDF Solutions

333 W San Carlos St., Ste. 700, San Jose, CA, 95110; *PH*: 1-408-280-7900; *Fax*: 1-408-280-7915; *http://* www.pdf.com; *Email*: info@pdf.com

General - Incorporation.............................. DE
Employees..369
Auditor ....Deloitte & Touche LLP
Stk Agt.............. Boston EquiServe Shareholder Services
Counsel..NA
DUNS No...NA

Stock- Price on:12/24/2007 ....$12.17
Stock Exchange...NDQ
Ticker Symbol...PDFS
Outstanding Shares 28,040,000
E.P.S..-$0.16
Shareholders..NA

Business: The group's principal activity is the provision of comprehensive technologies and services that enable semiconductor companies to improve yield and performance of manufactured integrated circuits (ic). The ic's are critical components used in applications such as computer systems, Internet, communications infrastructure equipment and consumer products. The group accomplishes this by providing infrastructure to integrate the design and manufacturing processes. The services are provided to integrated device manufacturers such as toshiba corporation, matsushita electric industrial co and sony corporation. The other services offered include proprietary manufacturing process simulation, ic yield and performance modeling software, comprehensive test chips, proven yield and performance enhancement methodologies and professional services.

Primary SIC and add'l.: 7372 7389

CIK No: 0001120914

Subsidiaries: PDF Solutions GmbH, PDF Solutions International Services, Inc., PDF Solutions KK

Officers: John K. Kibarian/Dir. - Founder, CEO Pres./$271,314.00, Zia Malik/56/VP - Sales/$380,121.00, Andrzej Strojwas/Chief Technologist, Kimon Michaels/Dir. - Founder, VP/$390,158.00, Andre Hawit/VP, GM, Keith Jones/CFO, VP - Finance, Administration/$548,021.00, Steven P. Melman/VP - Investor Relations, Strategic Initiatives, David Joseph/Chief Strategy Officer, Jim Jensen/VP - Client Services, Applications, Cees Hartgring/VP, GM Manufacturing Process Solutions, Steve Morstad/VP - Business Operations, Richard Mousties/VP, GM - Process Control Solutions, James Jensen/55/VP - Engineering Services Manufacturing Process Solutions, Becky Baybrook/VP - Human Resources, Rebecca M. Baybrook/56/VP - Human Resources/$368,491.00

Directors: John K. Kibarian/Dir. - Founder, CEO Pres., Lucio L. Lanza/Chmn., Albert Y.C. Yu/Dir., Stephen R. Heinrichs/Dir., Duane S. Boning/Dir., Member - Advisory Board, Sue Billat/Dir., Kimon Michaels/Dir. - Founder, VP, Tom Caulfield/Dir., Marco Iansiti/Dir., Member - Advisory Board, Costas J. Spanos/Dir., Member - Advisory Board

Owners: TimesSquare Capital Management, LLC/5.56%, Kimon Michaels/5.87%, John K. Kibarian/9.48%, Zia Malik, Keith Jones, Lucio L. Lanza, FMR Corp./12.77%, Insiders/23.83%, Stephen R. Heinrichs, T. Rowe Price Associates, Inc./10.76%, Albert Y. C. Yu, William Blair& Company, L.L.C./13.93%, Susan H. Billat, Rebecca Baybrook

Financial Data: Fiscal Year End:12/31 Latest Annual Data: 06/30/2007

Year	Sales	Net Income
2007	NA	NA
2006	$76,184,000	-$439,000
2005	$73,928,000	$6,524,000

Curr. Assets:	$85,805,000	Curr. Liab.:	$19,219,000		
Plant, Equip.:	$3,916,000	Total Liab.:	$20,638,000	Indic. Yr. Divd.:	NA
Total Assets:	$168,857,000	Net Worth:	$148,219,000	Debt/ Equity:	0.0080

PDG Environmental Inc

1386 Beulah Rd., Bldg. 801 Churchill, Pittsburgh, PA, 15235; *PH*: 1-412-243-3200; *Fax*: 1-412-243-4900; *http://* www.pdge.com

General - Incorporation.............................. DE
Employees..123
Auditor ....Malin, Bergquist & Co LLP
Stk Agt.........................Parente Randolph LLC
Counsel................................... Cohen & Girgsby
DUNS No..................................... 15-377-5804

Stock - Price on:12/24/2007 ....$1.03
Stock Exchange...OTC
Ticker Symbol...PDGE
Outstanding Shares 20,500,000
E.P.S..-$0.23
Shareholders..NA

Business: The group's principal activity is to provide environmental and specialty contracting services including asbestos and lead abatement, insulation, microbial remediation, demolition and related services through its subsidiaries. The group provides thermal insulation for piping, tanks, boilers and other systems in industrial, commercial and institutional facilities. The microbial remediation services provided by the group include decontamination, application of biocides and sealant, removal of building systems, duct cleaning and disposal of building furnishings. The group operates in New York, Pennsylvania, Florida, Texas, California, Arizona, Missouri, Oregon, Washington and South Carolina. The group operates solely in the domestic market.

Primary SIC and add'l.: 6719 4959 1795 1742

CIK No: 0000771485

Subsidiaries: Enviro-Tech Abatement Services Co, PDG, Inc, Project Development Group, Inc, Servestec, Inc.

Officers: John C. Regan/64/Chmn., CEO, CFO, Pres./$286,550.00, James D. Chiafullo/50/Dir., Sec., Dulcia Maire/Investor Relations, PDGE, Chris W. Witty/Assist. VP - Lippert, Heilshorn, Assoc, Inc, Shawn P. Regan/Dir. - Business Development

Directors: John C. Regan/64/Chmn., CEO, CFO, Pres., James D. Chiafullo/50/Dir., Sec., Richard A. Bendis/61/Dir., Edgar Berkey/67/Dir., Edwin J. Kilpela/62/Dir.

Owners: Insiders/15.80%, Costa Brava Partnership III LP/9.70%, Todd B. Fortier, Richard A. Bendis, Barron Partners, LP/8.80%, Edgar Berkey, John C. Regan/11.20%, James D. Chiafullo, Edwin J. Kilpela

Financial Data: Fiscal Year End:01/31 Latest Annual Data: 01/31/2007

Year	Sales	Net Income
2007	$74,977,000	-$7,177,000
2006	$78,181,000	$508,000
2005	$60,362,000	$2,186,000

Curr. Assets:	$29,295,000	Curr. Liab.:	$15,153,000		
Plant, Equip.:	$2,557,000	Total Liab.:	$27,314,000	Indic. Yr. Divd.:	NA
Total Assets:	$43,254,000	Net Worth:	$13,390,000	Debt/ Equity:	0.9313

PDI-Inc

Saddle River Executive Ctr., 1 Rte. 17 S., Saddle River, NJ, 07458; *PH*: 1-201-258-8450; *Fax*: 1-201-258-8400; *http://* www.pdi-inc.com

General - Incorporation .... DE
Employees...700
Auditor .... Ernst & Young, LLP
Stk Agt.... American Stock Transfer & Trust Co.
Counsel..NA
DUNS No..................................... 60-624-3442

Stock- Price on:12/24/2007 ....$10.07
Stock Exchange...NDQ
Ticker Symbol...PDII
Outstanding Shares 14,170,000
E.P.S..-$0.26
Shareholders..NA

Business: The group's principle activities are to design and execute customized sales and marketing campaigns for pharmaceutical, biotech and medical devices and diagnostics industries. The group operates in three segments namely: sales and marketing services, pharmaceutical products and medical devices and diagnostics. Sales and marketing services segment designs and implements product promotion programs for pharmaceutical companies. The pharmaceutical product segment sources pharmaceutical products through licensing, copromotion and acquisition arrangements. The medical devices and diagnostics segment offers sales and marketing activities to the pharmaceutical industry. The customers of the group include astrazeneca, novartis, glaxosmithkline, aventis, pfizer and pharmacia. The group's quarterly revenue for September 2007 was 23.97 millions of USD.

Primary SIC and add'l.: 2834 7389 8099

CIK No: 0001054102

Subsidiaries: LifeCycle Ventures, Inc., PDI Investment Company, Inc., ProtoCall, Inc., TVG, Inc.

Officers: Michael J. Marquard/CEO/$619,408.00, John P. Dugan/Founder, Chmn., Dir. - Strategic Planning, Kevin Connolly/Exec. VP, GM - Diversified Marketing Services/$531,624.00, Nancy McCarthy/Exec. VP - Human Resources, Stacey Morse/Executive Administrative Assist., Kerry Skolkin/VP, Assoc. General Counsel, Jeffrey Smith/Exec. VP, CFO, Treasurer/$372,769.00, Jo Ann Saitta/Sr. VP - Information Technology, David Stievater/Sr. VP - Emerging Pharma

Directors: John P. Dugan/Founder, Chmn., Dir. - Strategic Planning, Stephen Sullivan/Dir., Joseph T. Curti/Dir., Jack Stover/Dir., Frank Ryan/Dir., John Federspiel/Dir., Jan Martens Vecsi/Dir., John M. Pietruski/Dir.

Owners: Stephen P. Cotugno, DeLisle Callender, Heartland Advisors, Inc./13.90%, Steven K. Budd/1.40%, Kevin Connolly, John P. Dugan/34.40%, Michael J. Marquard, Dimensional Fund Advisors LP/8.80%, John C. Federspiel, Joseph T. Curti, Jan Martens Vecsi, Frank J. Ryan, Jack Stover, Portfolio Logic, LLC./6.60%, Larry Ellberger *(19 Owners included in Index)*

Financial Data: Fiscal Year End:12/31 Latest Annual Data: 12/31/2006

Year	Sales	Net Income
2006	$239,242,000	$11,809,000
2005	$319,415,000	-$19,454,000
2004	$364,444,000	$21,132,000

Curr. Assets:	$156,740,000	Curr. Liab.:	$44,554,000	P/E Ratio:	167.83
Plant, Equip.:	$12,809,000	Total Liab.:	$52,439,000	Indic. Yr. Divd.:	NA
Total Assets:	$201,636,000	Net Worth:	$149,197,000	Debt/ Equity:	NA

PDL Biopharma Inc

Formerly: Protein Design Labs Inc
34801 Campus Dr., Fremont, CA, 94555; *PH*: 1-510-574-1400; *http://* www.pdl.com

General - Incorporation .... DE
Employees...1,100
Auditor .... Ernst & Young LLP
Stk Agt................ Mellon Investor Services LLC
Counsel................Gray, Cary, Ware & Freidenrich
DUNS No..................................... 15-508-4460

Stock- Price on:12/24/2007 ....$23.86
Stock Exchange...NDQ
Ticker Symbol...NA
Outstanding Shares 116,600,000
E.P.S..-$0.82
Shareholders..NA

Business: The group's principal activity is the development of humanized monoclonal antibodies for the treatment of diseases. The key areas of disease focus include oncology and inflammatory and autoimmune diseases. It has several humanized antibodies in clinical development for inflammatory bowel disease, psoriasis and asthma. The group has licensed certain rights to first humanized antibody product, zenpax to hoffmann-la roche inc and its affiliates, which markets it for the prevention of kidney transplant rejection.the groups registered trademarks are protein design labs, nuvion and humanizing science. The group operates mainly in the domestic market. On 04-Apr-2003, the group acquired eos biotechnology inc.

Primary SIC and add'l.: 8731 2836

CIK No: 0000882104

Subsidiaries: Fremont Holding LLC, Specialty Pharmaceutical Services

Officers: Mark McDade/Dir., CEO/$1,758,067.00, Cynthia Shumate/VP - Legal Affairs, Corp. Sec., Chief Compliance Officer, Andrew Guggenhime/Sr. VP, CFO/$519,732.00, Richard Murray/Chief Scientific Officer, Exec. VP/$794,399.00, Peter Calcott/VP - Quality/$698,125.00, Steven E. Benner/Sr. VP, Chief Medical Officer, David Iwanicki/VP - Sales, Sales Operations/$741,251.00, Barbara K. Finck/VP - Clinical Development, Graeme Currie/VP - Clinical Operations, Eric A. Emery/VP - Manufacturing, Julie Badilo/VP - Biopharmaceutical Program Management, Debbie Law/VP - Research, Jeanmarie Guenot/VP - Corporate, Business Development, Maninder Hora/VP - Process Development, Mark McCamish/Sr. VP, Chief Medical Officer *(21 Officers included in Index)*

Directors: Mark McDade/Dir., CEO, Bradford S. Goodwin/Dir., Karen A. Dawes/Dir., Patrick L. Gage/Dir., Jon S. Saxe/Dir., Joseph Klein/Dir., Laurence J. Korn/Dir., Samuel Broder/Dir.

Owners: Mark McDade, Karen A. Dawes, Mellon Financial Corporation/5.10%, Peter Calcott, Patrick L. Gage, Samuel Broder, Laurence Jay Korn/1.30%, Jon S. Saxe, Rich Murray, Brad Goodwin, David Iwanicki, Insiders/3.10%, FMR Corp./6.70%, Third Point LLC/9.60%, Andrew Guggenhime

Financial Data: Fiscal Year End:12/31 Latest Annual Data: 12/31/2006

Year	Sales	Net Income
2006	$414,770,000	-$130,020,000
2005	$279,654,000	-$166,577,000
2004	$96,024,000	-$53,241,000

Curr. Assets:	$379,496,000	Curr. Liab.:	$105,459,000		
Plant, Equip.:	$296,529,000	Total Liab.:	$674,352,000	Indic. Yr. Divd.:	NA
Total Assets:	$1,141,893,000	Net Worth:	$467,541,000	Debt/ Equity:	1.0713

PDVSA Finance Ltd

Caledonian House, George Town, Grand Cayman; *PH*: 1-905-882-7044

General - Incorporation .... Cayman Islands
Employees .... NA
Auditor .... Alcaraz Cabrera Vazquez
Stk Agt. .... NA
Counsel .... NA
DUNS No. .... NA

Stock- Price on:12/24/2007 .... NA
Stock Exchange .... NA
Ticker Symbol .... NA
Outstanding Shares .... NA
E.P.S. .... NA
Shareholders .... NA

Business: The groups principle activity is to issue securities and lends proceeds to Petroleos De Venezuela, SA. The group operates from United States.

Primary SIC and add'l.: 6159

CIK No: 0001074512

Subsidiaries: PDV America, Inc, PDV Holding, Inc., Petrleos de Venezuela

Peabody Energy Corp

701 Market St., St. Louis, MO, 63101; **PH:** 1-314-342-3400; **Fax:** 1-314-342-7799; *http://* www.peabodyenergy.com; **Email:** pr@peabodyenergy.com

General - Incorporation .... DE
Employees 9,200
Auditor .... Ernst & Young LLP
Stk Agt. ..... American Stock Transfer & Trust Co.
Counsel .... NA
DUNS No. .... NA

Stock- Price on:12/24/2007 .... $50.65
Stock Exchange .... NYSE
Ticker Symbol .... BTU
Outstanding Shares 264,970,000
E.P.S. $1.50
Shareholders .... NA

Business: The group's principle activity is to operate coal-mining properties. The groups other services include coal trading, coal bed methane production, transportation related services, third-party coal contract restructuring and participation in the development of coal based generating plants. The group operates from United States.

Primary SIC and add'l.: 1241

CIK No: 0001064728

Subsidiaries: Affinity Mining Company, American Land Development, LLC, American Land Holdings of Illinois, LLC, American Land Holdings of Indiana, LLC, American Land Holdings of Kentucky, LLC, Appalachia Mine Services, LLC, Arclar Company, LLC, Arid Operations Inc., Baralaba Coal Pty Ltd, Beaver Dam Coal Company, Big Ridge, Inc., Big Sky Coal Company, Black Beauty Coal Company, Black Beauty Equipment Company, Black Beauty Holding Company, LLC 196 Subsidiaries included in the Index

Officers: Gregory H. Boyce/53/Dir., CEO, Pres./$6,042,712.00, Richard A. Navarre/CFO, Exec. VP - Corporate Development/$4,345,179.00, Sharon D. Fiehler/Exec. VP - Human Resources, Administration/$2,387,552.00, Roger B. Walcott/Exec. VP - Strategy, Business Services/$2,228,450.00, Richard M. Whiting/Exec. VP, Chief Marketing Officer/$3,497,661.00, Rick Bowen/Pres. - Generation, Btu Conversion, Fredrick D. Palmer/Sr. VP - Government Relations, Eric Ford/COO, Exec. VP, Alexander C. Schoch/Exec. VP, Chief Legal Officer, Jeffery L. Klinger/VP, General Counsel, Corp. Sec.

Directors: Gregory H. Boyce/53/Dir., CEO, Pres., Irl F. Engelhardt/61/Chmn., B. R. Brown/75/Dir., William A. Coley/64/Dir., Henry Givens/74/Dir., James R. Schlesinger/79/Dir., John F. Turner/65/Dir., Sandra A. Van Trease/47/Dir., William E. James/62/Dir., Henry E. Lentz/62/Dir., William C. Rusnack/63/Dir., Robert B. Karn/66/Dir., Blanche M. Touhill/76/Dir., Alan H. Washkowitz/67/Dir.

Owners: Sharon D. Fiehler, Insiders/0.90%, Sandra Van Trease, Gregory H. Boyce, FMR Corp./14.50%, Henry E. Lentz, Irl F. Engelhardt, Roger B. Walcott, John F. Turner, Richard M. Whiting, Richard A. Navarre, Henry Givens, B. R. Brown, William A. Coley, Robert B. Karn (20 Owners included in Index)

Financial Data: Fiscal Year End:12/31 Latest Annual Data: 12/31/2006

Year	Sales	Net Income
2006	$5,256,315,000	$600,697,000
2005	$4,644,453,000	$422,653,000
2004	$3,631,582,000	$175,387,000

Curr. Assets:	$1,274,340,000	**Curr. Liab.:**	$1,367,531,000	**P/E Ratio:**	26.52
Plant, Equip.:	$7,551,517,000	**Total Liab.:**	$7,142,193,000	**Indic. Yr. Divd.:**	$0.240
Total Assets:	$9,514,056,000	**Net Worth:**	$2,338,526,000	**Debt/ Equity:**	1.2947

Peace Arch Entertainment Group Inc

1867 Yonge St., Ste. 650, Toronto, ON, M4S 1Y5; **PH:** 1-416-783-8383; *http://* www.peacearch.net

General - Incorporation .... Canada
Employees .... NA
Auditor .... PricewaterhouseCoopers LLP
Stk Agt. .... PricewaterhouseCoopers LLP
Counsel .... NA
DUNS No. .... NA

Stock- Price on:12/24/2007 .... $2.22
Stock Exchange .... AMEX
Ticker Symbol .... PAE
Outstanding Shares 32,680,000
E.P.S. .... NA
Shareholders .... NA

Business: The group's principle activities include developing, financing, producing and distributing high-quality, proprietary television programming for markets worldwide, as well as provide production services for third parties on a contract basis. The group operates from United States.

Primary SIC and add'l.: 7812

CIK No: 0001038367

Subsidiaries: Peace Arch Films Limited (PAF), Peace Arch Motion Pictures Inc, Peace Arch Project Development Corp

Officers: Gary Howsam/Dir., CEO, Jeff Sagansky/Chmn., Interim CEO, Mara Di Pasquale/Dir., CFO, Dave Berenbaum/VP - Eyes, Mary Herne/Exec. VP - International Television, Home Entertainment, Comfort Alemoru/Contact - Accounting, Mark Balsam/Pres. - US Distribution, Julie Sultan/Exec. VP - International Theatrical Film Sales, John Flock/Dir., COO, Pres., Lewin Webb/Pres. - Peace Arch Motion Pictures, Michael Taylor/Pres. - Peace Arch Television, Blair Reekie/Pres. - Eyes Project Development Corp, Berry Meyerowitz/Pres. - Peace Arch Home Entertainment Inc, Paul Davis-Miller/Sr. VP - Domestic Sales, Co - Productions, Suzanne Barron/Sr. VP - International Television, Home Entertainment (18 Officers included in Index)

Directors: Jeff Sagansky/Chmn., Interim CEO, Gary Howsam/Dir., CEO, Drew Craig/Chmn., Robert Essery/Dir., Juliet Jones/Dir., Mara Di Pasquale/Dir., CFO, Ian Fodie/Dir., Nelson S. Thall/Dir., Richard Watson/Dir., John Flock/Dir., COO, Pres.

Owners: Fremantle Media/8.90%, CPC Communications Inc./20.80%, Kerry McCluggage/27.50%, Kerry McCluggage/11.90%, Jeff Sagansky/27.50%, Jeff Sagansky/29.70%, Pension Financial Services (Canada) Inc/58.40%, Todd Wagner/9.10%, Pension Financial Services (Canada) Inc/42.50%

Peak Entertainment Holdings Inc

Bagshaw Hall, Bagshaw Hill, Bakewell, DE45 1DL;

General - Incorporation .... NV
Employees .... NA
Auditor .... Garbutt & Elliott Ltd
Stk Agt .... American Stock Transfer & Trust Co.
Counsel .... NA
DUNS No. 19-658-4718

Stock- Price on:12/24/2007 .... $0.007
Stock Exchange .... OTC
Ticker Symbol .... ENCS
Outstanding Shares .... NA
E.P.S. .... NA
Shareholders .... NA

Business: The group's principal activities are the production of television entertainment, character licensing and consumer products development, including toy and gift manufacturing and distribution. It has three lines of business: entertainment, licensing and consumer products. The entertainment division is currently working on three product lines that are in the pre-production or production stages. Licensing division licenses and sublicenses intellectual properties to and from third parties. Consumer products division manufactures and sells countin' sheep products, mini flora products and pretty pony club products. The group's major customer is silly goose company. Geographically the group operates in the United States and the United Kingdom. On 22-Apr-2003, the group acquired peak entertainment ltd.

Primary SIC and add'l.: 7929 4899 4813

CIK No: 0000824851

Subsidiaries: Cameo Collectables Limited, Jusco Toys Limited, Jusco Toys Ltd, Jusco UK Limited, Jusco UK Ltd, Peak Entertainment Holdings, LLC, Peak Entertainment Limited, Wembley Sportsmaster Limited

Financial Data: Fiscal Year End:12/31 Latest Annual Data: 12/31/2005

Year	Sales	Net Income
2005	$1,545,000	-$4,498,000
2004	$1,166,000	-$1,994,000
2003	$1,015,000	-$2,967,000

Curr. Assets:	$4,537,000	**Curr. Liab.:**	$4,775,000		
Plant, Equip.:	$202,000	**Total Liab.:**	$8,176,000	**Indic. Yr. Divd.:**	NA
Total Assets:	$6,707,000	**Net Worth:**	-$1,470,000	**Debt/ Equity:**	NA

Peak International Ltd

38507 Cherry St., Unit G, Newark, CA, 94560; **PH:** 1-852-85231936000; *http://* www.peakf.com

General - Incorporation .... Bermuda
Employees .... NA
Auditor .... BDO McCabe Lo & Co
Stk Agt .... Mellon Investor Services LLC
Counsel .... NA
DUNS No. 66-228-7986

Stock- Price on:12/24/2007 .... $2.83
Stock Exchange .... NDQ
Ticker Symbol .... PEAK
Outstanding Shares 12,420,000
E.P.S. .... -$0.79
Shareholders .... NA

Business: The group's principal activities are to provide packaging products for the storage, transportation and automated handling of semiconductor devices and other electronic components. The products are designed to interface with automated handling equipment used in the production and testing of semiconductor and electronic products. Products include matrix and disk drive trays, carrier tapes, and reels, shipping tubes, lead frame boxes and interleaves used in the storage and transportation of lead frames. In addition, it collects and sells recycled matrix trays using the name 'semicycle'. Customers include semiconductor companies such as Texas instruments, st microelectronics, philips and motorola, disk drive manufacturers such as seagate, subcontract assembly and test companies such as asat, stats and ase. The group has operations in the United States, Hong Kong, Taiwan, Singapore, Malaysia, the peoples' republic of China, Philippines, Italy, Japan and South Korea.

Primary SIC and add'l.: 6719 3089

CIK No: 0001036081

Subsidiaries: Best Luck 9 Ltd., Diamond Crest Holdings Ltd., Luckygold 168J Ltd., Peak China Property Ltd, Peak Gold 3 Ltd, Peak International (Asia) Ltd., Peak International Inc., Peak Plastic& Metal Products (International) Ltd., Peak Plastics, Inc., Peak Resources Singapore Pte Ltd., Peak Semiconductor Packaging Products (Shenzhen) Co. Ltd., Peak Semiconductor Packaging SDN BHD, PIL (Mauritius) Ltd., Semicycle Hong Kong Ltd., Semicycle Resources (S)Pte Ltd. 17 Subsidiaries included in the Index

Officers: Dean Personne/Dir., CEO, Pres./$611,447.00, John Supan/CFO/$271,538.00, Splendid Zuo/VP, GM - Operations/$181,309.00, Mary Chow/VP - Supply Chain Management/$156,371.00, Chris Buckley/VP - Sales/$152,507.00, Wayne Moore/VP - Sales, Jim Steger/VP - Sales, Disk Drive Products

Directors: Dean Personne/Dir., CEO, Pres., Douglas Broyles/Dir., Christine Russell/Dir., Russ Silvestri/Dir.

Owners: Splendid Zuo, Russell Silvestri/19.90%, Aegis Financial Corporation/6.40%, Douglas Broyles/1.10%, Christine Russell, FMR Corp./9.60%, Mary Chow, Quaker Capital Management Corporation/8.30%, John Supan, SKIRITAI Capital LLC/19.90%, Luckygold 18A Limited/7.00%, Chris Buckley, Costa Brava Partnership III L.P./6.20%, Insiders/24.50%, Chadwick Capital Management LLC/5.60% (16 Owners included in Index)

Financial Data: Fiscal Year End:03/31 Latest Annual Data: 03/31/2007

Year	Sales	Net Income
2007	$60,159,000	-$3,907,000
2006	$66,119,000	-$4,575,000
2005	$67,909,000	-$9,209,000

Curr. Assets:	$42,584,000	**Curr. Liab.:**	$7,017,000		
Plant, Equip.:	$19,278,000	**Total Liab.:**	$7,017,000	**Indic. Yr. Divd.:**	NA
Total Assets:	$62,926,000	**Net Worth:**	$55,909,000	**Debt/ Equity:**	NA

Peaksoft Multinet Corp

3930 Meridian St., Ste. C117, Bellingham, WA, 98226; ; *http://* www.peak.com

General - Incorporation .... Canada
Employees .... NA
Auditor .... Gordon K.w. Gee
Stk Agt .... Computershare Trust Co of Canada
Counsel .... NA
DUNS No. .... NA

Stock- Price on:12/24/2007 .... $0.0001
Stock Exchange .... OTC
Ticker Symbol .... PEAMF
Outstanding Shares .... NA
E.P.S. .... NA
Shareholders .... NA

Business: The group's principle activity is to provide Internet software to corporate and individual users. The company also provides an Internet portal facility. It develops and publishes multi-media CD-ROM and research computer software. The group operates from United States.

Primary SIC and add'l.: 5045 7372

CIK No: 0001058429

Subsidiaries: BREEZ Business Management Systems Inc, Chameleon Bridge Technologies Corp, Peak Media, Inc

Owners: Insiders/1.84%, T. W. Metz/1.00%, Colin Morse

Financial Data: *Fiscal Year End:*09/30 *Latest Annual Data:* 9/30/2006

Year	Sales	Net Income
2006	NA	-$710,000
2005	NA	-$564,000
2004	NA	-$600,000

Curr. Assets:	$0	**Curr. Liab.:**	$411,000		
Plant, Equip.:	NA	**Total Liab.:**	$9,438,000	**Indic. Yr. Divd.:**	NA
Total Assets:	$0	**Net Worth:**	-$9,437,000	**Debt/ Equity:**	NA

Peapack Gladstone Financial Corp

158 RtE 206 N, Gladstone, NJ, 07934; *PH:* 1-908-234-0700; *Fax:* 1-908-234-0795; *http://* www.pgbank.com

General - Incorporation	NJ	**Stock**- Price on:12/24/2007	$27.4
Employees	232	Stock Exchange	AMEX
Auditor	KPMG LLP	Ticker Symbol	PGC
Stk Agt	Registrar & Transfer Co	Outstanding Shares	8,290,000
Counsel	NA	E.P.S	$1.319
DUNS No.	00-891-2263	Shareholders	NA

Business: The group's principal activity is that of a bank holding company. Its principal subsidiary, peapack-gladstone bank, is a state-chartered commercial bank of New Jersey. The group provides personalized financial, trust and investment services to individuals and small businesses. It offers them working capital lines of credit; term loans for fixed asset acquisitions, commercial mortgages and other forms of asset-based financing. Depository activities consist of savings, money market and interest bearing checking accounts and certificates of deposits. Consumer banking includes the provision of residential and construction mortgages, home equity lines of credit and other second mortgage loans. In addition, the group provides travelers' checks, money orders, cashier's checks, wire transfers and automated teller machines. The operations are conducted through sixteen full-service banking offices and one mini-branch in somerset, hunterdon and morris counties.

Primary SIC and add'l.: 6022 6712

CIK No: 0001050743

Subsidiaries: Peapack-Gladstone Investment, Peapack-Gladstone Mortgage Group, Inc.

Officers: Frank A. Kissel/57/Chmn., CEO/$426,761.00, Bridget J. Walsh/Sr. VP, Dir. - Human Resources, Mary Anne Maloney/Maloney, Chatham Main Street, Donna Gisone/Mgr. - Chatham Shunpike, Ronald Field/Mgr. - Warren, Joan Wychules/Mgr. - Chester, Carolyn Sepkowski/Mgr. - Clinton, Rohinton Madon/Mgr. - Far Hills, Janet Battaglia/Mgr. - Fellowship Village, Annette Malanga/Mgr. - Ladstone, Main Office, Teresa Lawler/Mgr. - Hillsborough, Amy Glaser/Mgr. - Long Valley, Linda Ziropoulos/Mgr. - Mendham, Arthur F. Birmingham/CFO, Exec. VP/$254,524.00, Robert M. Rogers/49/Dir., COO, Pres./$279,240.00 *(29 Officers included in Index)*

Directors: Frank A. Kissel/57/Chmn., CEO, Anthony J. Consi/62/Dir., Robert M. Rogers/49/Dir., COO, Pres., Philip W. Smith/52/Dir., Edward A. Merton/67/Dir., John R. Mulcahy/69/Dir., John D. Kissel/55/Dir., Pamela Hill/70/Dir., Craig C. Spengeman/52/Dir., Pres., James R. Lamb/65/Dir., Duffield F. Meyercord/61/Dir.

Owners: Insiders/9.49%, John R. Mulcahy, Frank A. Kissel/1.72%, Anthony J. Consi, Duffield F. Meyercord, John D. Kissel, James R. Lamb, Pamela Hill/1.44%, Arthur F. Birmingham, James M. Weichert/9.69%, Philip W. Smith, Craig C. Spengeman, Robert M. Rogers, Edward A. Merton, Garrett P. Bromley

Financial Data: *Fiscal Year End:*12/31 *Latest Annual Data:* 12/31/2006

Year	Sales	Net Income
2006	$79,315,000	$10,226,000
2005	$66,909,000	$13,130,000
2004	$54,844,000	$13,109,000

Curr. Assets:	$35,439,000	**Curr. Liab.:**	$1,160,649,000	**P/E Ratio:**	23.42
Plant, Equip.:	$24,059,000	**Total Liab.:**	$1,184,613,000	**Indic. Yr. Divd.:**	$0.640
Total Assets:	$1,288,376,000	**Net Worth:**	$103,763,000	**Debt/ Equity:**	0.2227

Pearson Plc

1330 Ave. of the Americas, New York, NY, 10019; *PH:* 1-212-641-2400; *Fax:* 1-212-641-2500; *http://* www.pearson.com

General - Incorporation	UK	**Stock**- Price on:12/24/2007	$16.6
Employees	29,283	Stock Exchange	NYSE
Auditor	PricewaterhouseCoopers LLP	Ticker Symbol	PSO
Stk Agt	Bank of New York	Outstanding Shares	797,350,000
Counsel	NA	E.P.S	$0.83
DUNS No.	NA	Shareholders	NA

Business: The group's principal activities are education, consumer publishing and business information. The group is divided into three divisions namely pearson education, the penguin group and ft group. Pearson education publishes textbooks and electronic learning tools for students of all ages from pre-school to college and on into their professional lives. The penguin group publishes books for adults and children, in fiction and non-fiction, from timeless classics to the hottest bestsellers. Ft group covers a network of newspapers and online services. The group's publishing brands include penguin, financial times, prentice hall, dorling kindersley, scott foresman and longman.

Primary SIC and add'l.: 2731 4833 2711

CIK No: 0000938323

Subsidiaries: Blue Wharf Ltd, Data Broadcasting Corporation, Dorling Kindersley Holdings Ltd, Financial Times Business Ltd, Interactive Data Corporation, Les Echos SA, NCS Pearson Inc., Pearson Capital Company LLC, Pearson DBC Holdings Inc., Pearson Dollar Finance plc, Pearson Education Holdings Inc., Pearson Education Inc., Pearson Education Ltd, Pearson Finance Partnership (Bermuda), Pearson Holdings Inc. 31 Subsidiaries included in the Index

Officers: Marjorie Scardino/61/Dir., CEO, Robin Freestone/49/Dir., CFO, Jennifer Barker/Contact - Pearson Education, UK, Helena Peacock/Community Contact - Penguin UK, Alison Boehm/Penguin Group, USA, Community Contact, Simon Mays-Smith/Investor Contact - UK, Luke Swanson/Investor Contact - UK, Jeff Taylor/Investor Contact - US, Charles Goldsmith/Contact - Media, John Coffey/Contact - General Interactive Data Media, Sue Mitchell/Contact - General Interactive Data Media, Joanna Prior/Contact - Penguin UK, Marilyn Duckworth/Contact - Penguin US, Stevie Pattison-Dick/Media Contact - Edexcel, UK, Thomasina Coombe/Community Contact *(18 Officers included in Index)*

Directors: Marjorie Scardino/61/Dir., CEO, Glen Moreno/64/Chmn., Robin Freestone/49/Dir., CFO, Rona Fairhead/46/Dir., Susan Fuhrman/64/Non Exec. Dir., Patrick Cescau/59/Non Exec. Dir., Ken Hydon/63/Non Exec. Dir., David Bell/61/Dir., John Makinson/53/Dir., David Arculus/61/Non Exec. Dir., Terry Burns/64/Non Exec. Dir.

Owners: Marjorie Scardino, Patrick Cescau, Ken Hydon, David Bell, Susan Fuhrman, Rana Talwar, Reuben Mark, Glen Moreno, David Arculus, Vernon Sankey, Terry Burns, Robin Freestone, Rona Fairhead, John Makinson

Financial Data: *Fiscal Year End:*12/31 *Latest Annual Data:* 12/31/2006

Year	Sales	Net Income
2006	$8,104,797,000	$668,053,000
2005	$7,048,397,000	$707,249,000
2004	$7,995,390,000	$350,641,000

Curr. Assets:	$4,654,822,000	**Curr. Liab.:**	$3,310,879,000		
Plant, Equip.:	$1,257,742,000	**Total Liab.:**	$7,372,093,000	**Indic. Yr. Divd.:**	$0.590
Total Assets:	$14,387,630,000	**Net Worth:**	$7,015,537,000	**Debt/ Equity:**	NA

Peco Energy Co

2301 Market St., Philadelphia, PA, 19101; *PH:* 1-215-840-4000; *http://* www.peco.com

General - Incorporation	PA	**Stock**- Price on:12/24/2007	$73.49
Employees	NA	Stock Exchange	NYSE
Auditor	PricewaterhouseCoopers LLP	Ticker Symbol	PE-PA
Stk Agt	Computershare Investor Services LLC	Outstanding Shares	NA
Counsel	NA	E.P.S	NA
DUNS No.	00-791-4468	Shareholders	NA

Business: The group's principle activities are purchase, transmission, distribution and sale of electricity to a diverse base of residential, commercial, industrial and wholesale customers in northern Illinois. The group operates in three business segments: energy delivery, generation and enterprises. The energy delivery segment consists of the retail electricity distribution and transmission businesses in northern Illinois and in southern Pennsylvania. This segment also operates natural gas distribution business in the Pennsylvania counties surrounding the city of philadelphia. The generation segment includes the operation of electric generating facility and power marketing operations. The activities of enterprises segment consist of competitive retail energy sales, energy and infrastructure services, communications and related investments.

Primary SIC and add'l.: 4922 4911 4939

CIK No: 0000078100

Officers: Denis P. O'Brien/48/CEO, Pres., John W. Rowe/62/Chmn., CEO, Pres. - Exelon, John F. Young/51/CFO, Exec. VP - Finance, Markets, CFO - Exelon, John L. Skolds/57/Exec. VP - Exelon, Pres. - Exelon Energy Delivery, Dir., Lisa Crutchfield/44/Sr. VP - Regulatory, External Affairs, Matthew R. Galvanoni/35/VP, Controller

Directors: John W. Rowe/62/Chmn., CEO, Pres. - Exelon, John L. Skolds/57/Exec. VP - Exelon, Pres. - Exelon Energy Delivery, Dir.

Owners: John W. Rogers, Sue L. Gin, Thomas J. Ridge, Ian P. McLean, Richard L. Thomas, Barry J. Mitchell, John L. Skolds, Insiders, Denis OBrien, Frank M. Clark, John W. Rogers, Edgar D. Jannotta, James W. Compton, Matthew F. Hilzinger, Christopher M. Crane *(25 Owners included in Index)*

Financial Data: *Fiscal Year End:*12/31 *Latest Annual Data:* 06/30/2007

Year	Sales	Net Income
2007	$1,269,000,000	$96,000,000
2006	$1,235,000,000	$121,000,000
2005	$4,910,000,000	$517,000,000

Curr. Assets:	$762,000,000	**Curr. Liab.:**	$978,000,000		
Plant, Equip.:	$4,651,000,000	**Total Liab.:**	$7,964,000,000	**Indic. Yr. Divd.:**	NA
Total Assets:	$9,773,000,000	**Net Worth:**	$1,809,000,000	**Debt/ Equity:**	1.9591

Peco II Inc

1376 State Rte. 598, Galion, OH, 44833; *PH:* 1-419-468-7600; *Fax:* 1-419-468-1587; *http://* www.peco2.com; *Email:* irelations@peco2.com

General - Incorporation	OH	**Stock**- Price on:12/24/2007	$0.7404
Employees	279	Stock Exchange	NDQ
Auditor	Battelle & Battelle LLP	Ticker Symbol	PIII
Stk Agt	National City Bank	Outstanding Shares	27,170,000
Counsel	Porter Wright Morris & Arthur LLP	E.P.S	-$0.33
DUNS No.	NA	Shareholders	NA

Business: The group's principal activities are to provide engineering and installation on-site services and to design and manufacture communications power systems and equipment. The group operates in two segments: product and service. The product segment consists of manufacturing operations and the production of power plants, rectifiers and power distribution equipment. The service segment consists of telecommunications contract, engineering, and installation services. The group also offers systems integration products to the communications industry. The products include power systems, power distribution equipment and systems integration products and related services. The e&i on-site services include engineering and installation management, power monitoring systems, applications software and customized products to meet customer needs.

Primary SIC and add'l.: 3669 7379 3612 4899 3661

CIK No: 0000845072

Subsidiaries: b+w II, Inc., PECO II Global Services, Inc.

Officers: John G. Heindel/Chmn., CEO, Pres./$561,804.00, Sandra A. Frankhouse/CFO, Treasurer, Sec./$161,760.00, Tony McIntosh/VP - Operations, Kevin Borders/VP - Marketing, Product Development/$217,486.00

Directors: John G. Heindel/Chmn., CEO, Pres., James L. Green/Dir., Richard E. Hottenroth/Dir., Gerard B. Moersdorf/Dir., Louis R. Schneeberger/Dir., Matthew P. Smith/Dir., Tom Thomson/Dir., Richard W. Orchard/54/Dir., Albert Chang/47/Dir.

Owners: Austin W. Marxe, Thomas R. Thomsen, Louis R. Schneeberger, George J. Dallas, Mary Janet Green, Miles A. McIntosh, Dennis J. Baughman, Linda H. Smith, Sandra A. Frankhouse, Costa Brava Partnership III L.P., James L. Green, Matthew P. Smith, John G. Heindel, Insiders, Trygve A. Ivesdal *(18 Owners included in Index)*

Financial Data: *Fiscal Year End:*12/31 *Latest Annual Data:* 12/31/2006

Year	Sales	Net Income
2006	$47,701,000	-$8,040,000
2005	$42,447,000	-$6,823,000
2004	$31,564,000	-$12,270,000

Curr. Assets:	$28,832,000	**Curr. Liab.:**	$10,038,000		
Plant, Equip.:	$5,293,000	**Total Liab.:**	$10,038,000	**Indic. Yr. Divd.:**	NA
Total Assets:	$45,041,000	**Net Worth:**	$35,003,000	**Debt/ Equity:**	NA

Pediatric Services of America Inc

310 Technology Pkwy, Norcross, GA, 30092; ***PH:*** 1-770-441-1580; ***http://*** www.psakids.com

General - Incorporation .... DE
Employees .... NA
Auditor .... Ernst & Young LLP
Stk Agt............ Mellon Investor Services LLC
Counsel............ Long Aldridge & Norman
DUNS No. 12-094-1042

Stock- Price on:12/24/2007 .... $15.99
Stock Exchange............ NA
Ticker Symbol............ NA
Outstanding Shares 7,580,000
E.P.S............ -$0.01
Shareholders............ NA

Business: The group's principal activities are to provide children's health care and related services. The group operates in two segments: pediatric home health care and adult home health care. Pediatric health care provides nursing, respiratory therapy, rental and sale of durable medical equipment, pharmaceutical services and infusion therapy services. The group provides pediatric rehabilitation services, day treatment centers for medically fragile children, pediatric well care services and special needs educational services for pediatric patients. It provides case management services to assist the family and patient by coordinating the provision of services between the insurer, physician, hospital and other health care providers. It also provides respiratory and infusion therapy and related services for adults. On 10-Jan-2003 the group acquired assets of health med one.

Primary SIC and add'l.: 8082

CIK No: 0000893430

Subsidiaries: Pediatric Home Nursing Services, Inc, Pediatric Services of America, Inc, PSA Capital Corporation, PSA Licensing Corporation, PSA Properties Corporation

Officers: Daniel J. Kohl/51/CEO, Pres., Lori J. Reel/CFO, Elizabeth A. Rubio/VP - Operations, Mark A. Kulik/VP - Business Development, Wesley E. Debnam/VP - Human Resources, Thomas D. Zeimet/VP - Information Systems, Jeffrey K. Nickell/VP - Reimbursement, John R. Hamilton/General Counsel, Chief Risk Officer, Dale Valentine/VP - Compliance

Directors: Michael E. Axelrod/50/Non Exec. Chmn., David Crane/51/Dir., Michael J. Finn/58/Dir., Robert P. Pinkas/54/Dir., Phyllis Yale/50/Dir., Joel Kimbrough/Dir.

Owners: Myca Partners Inc./5.60%, The D3 Family Funds/19.20%, Insiders/7.60%, Dimensional Fund Advisors Inc./8.40%, Ashford Capital Management, Inc./6.00%, Michael E. Axelrod, James M. McNeill/1.30%, David Crane, Robert P. Pinkas/2.70%, Portfolio Logic LLC/14.40%, Daniel J. Kohl/2.00%, Michael J. Finn, Phyllis Yale

Financial Data: ***Fiscal Year End:***09/30 ***Latest Annual Data:*** 9/30/2006

Year	Sales	Net Income
2006	$119,360,000	$21,305,000
2005	$172,183,000	$5,666,000
2004	$239,774,000	$4,012,000

Curr. Assets:	$101,271,000	**Curr. Liab.:**	$21,372,000		
Plant, Equip.:	$2,874,000	**Total Liab.:**	$34,886,000	**Indic. Yr. Divd.:**	NA
Total Assets:	$133,498,000	**Net Worth:**	$98,611,000	**Debt/ Equity:**	NA

Pediatrix Medical Group Inc

1301 Concord Ter., Sunrise, FL, 33323; ***PH:*** 1-954-384-0175; ***Fax:*** 1-954-838-9961; ***http://*** www.pediatrix.com

General - Incorporation .... FL
Employees 1,658
Auditor .... PricewaterhouseCoopers LLP
Stk Agt............ EquiServe Trust Co N.A
Counsel............ Greenberg Traurig LLP
DUNS No. 79-149-7431

Stock- Price on:12/24/2007 .... $55.2
Stock Exchange............ NYSE
Ticker Symbol............ PDX
Outstanding Shares 48,500,000
E.P.S............ $2.68
Shareholders............ NA

Business: The group's principal activity is to provide neonatal and perinatal physician services. These services are provided at hospital-based neonatal intensive care units (nicus) and pediatric intensive care units (picus). Nicus are staffed by neonatologists, who are pediatricians with additional training to care for newborn infants with low birth weight and other medical complications. Perinatal physician services are provided by perinatologists, who are obstetricians with additional training to care for women with high risk and complicated pregnancies and their fetuses. The group provided services in certain states and in Puerto Rico. These services are provided by 622 practicing physicians. The group also provides staff and manages nicus and picus in hospitals; provides physicians and professional and administrative support, including physician billing and reimbursement services.

Primary SIC and add'l.: 8069

CIK No: 0000893949

Subsidiaries: captive insurance

Officers: Roger J. Medel/Dir., CEO/$2,997,725.00, Joseph M. Calabro/COO, Pres./$2,458,003.00, Carlos A. Perez/Regional Pres. - Caribbean Region, John F. Rizzo/Sr. VP - Business Development, Thomas W. Hawkins/Sr. VP, General Counsel, Sec./$1,505,333.00, Karl B. Wagner/42/CFO/$1,889,620.00, Robert J. Balcom/Regional Pres. - Central Region, Robert C. Bryant/CIO, Sr. VP, David A. Clark/Sr. VP - Operations, Alan R. Spitzer/Sr. VP, Dir. - Center Research, Education, William C. Hawk/Sr. VP - Operations, Anesthesia Services, Michael D. Stanley/Regional Pres. - South Central Region, Eric H. Kurzweil/Regional Pres. - Mountain Region, Frederick V. Miller/Regional Pres. - Atlantic Region

Directors: Roger J. Medel/Dir., CEO, Enrique J. Sosa/Dir., Manuel Kadre/Dir., Cesar L. Alvarez/Dir., Waldemar A. Carlo/Dir., Michael B. Fernandez/Dir., Roger K. Freeman/Dir., Paul G. Gabos/Dir., Pascal J. Goldschmidt/Dir.

Owners: Cesar L. Alvarez, Enrique J. Sosa, Paul G. Gabos, Michael B. Fernandez, Karl B. Wagner, Thomas W. Hawkins, Roger J. Medel/1.70%, Insiders/2.90%, Joseph M. Calabro, Roger K. Freeman, Waldemar A. Carlo, Pascal J. Goldschmidt

Financial Data: ***Fiscal Year End:***12/31 ***Latest Annual Data:*** 12/31/2006

Year	Sales	Net Income
2006	$818,554,000	$124,465,000
2005	$693,700,000	$89,037,000
2004	$619,629,000	$98,279,000

Curr. Assets:	$301,599,000	**Curr. Liab.:**	$221,315,000	**P/E Ratio:**	21.23
Plant, Equip.:	$29,939,000	**Total Liab.:**	$269,369,000	**Indic. Yr. Divd.:**	NA
Total Assets:	$1,135,170,000	**Net Worth:**	$865,801,000	**Debt/ Equity:**	0.0550

Peerless Mfg Co

14651 N Dallas Pkwy., Ste. 500, Dallas, TX, 75254; ***PH:*** 1-214-357-6181; ***Fax:*** 1-214-351-0194; ***http://*** www.peerlessmfg.com

General - Incorporation .... TX
Employees 169
Auditor .... Grant Thornton LLP
Stk Agt .... Mellon Investor Services LLC
Counsel............ Hughes & Luce LLP
DUNS No. 00-734-4906

Stock- Price on:12/24/2007 .... $21
Stock Exchange............ NDQ
Ticker Symbol............ PMFG
Outstanding Shares 6,420,000
E.P.S............ $0.45
Shareholders............ NA

Business: The group's principle activities include designing, engineering, manufacturing and selling specialized separators and filters used in cleaning gases and liquids as they move through a piping system; and designs, manufactures and sells pulsation dampeners which reduce noise levels, improve efficiency and prolong the life of piping systems.The group operates from United States.

Primary SIC and add'l.: 3496

CIK No: 0000076954

Subsidiaries: Peerless Europe Ltd., PMC Acquisition, Inc.

Officers: David Taylor/VP - Separation Systems, Henry Schopfer/VP - Administration, CFO, Sean P. McMenamin/VP - Environmental Systems, Barry Nesbit/MD - Peerless Europe Limited, Kevin McGrath/Primary Investor Relations Officer, Jon Segelhorst/VP - Pressure Products, Charles G. Mogged/VP - Manufacturing - Supply Chain Management

Directors: Sherrill Stone/Chmn., Clayton R. Mulford/Dir., Kenneth R. Hanks/Dir., Howard G. Westerman/Dir., Robert McCashin/Dir.

Owners: Jon Segelhorst, Sean McMenamin, Clayton R. Mulford, Clayton R. Mulford, Brown Advisory Holdings Incorporated/27.60%, David Taylor, Peter J. Burlage, Dana P. Cohen/5.00%, Sherrill Stone, Kenneth R. Hanks, Insiders/2.30%, Dana P. Cohen/5.00%, Henry G. Schopfer, Insiders/2.30%, Howard G. Westerman *(16 Owners included in Index)*

Financial Data: ***Fiscal Year End:***06/30 ***Latest Annual Data:*** 6/30/2006

Year	Sales	Net Income
2006	$63,411,000	$426,000
2005	$51,063,000	-$592,000
2004	$59,761,000	$2,038,000

Curr. Assets:	$45,172,000	**Curr. Liab.:**	$22,242,000	**P/E Ratio:**	46.67
Plant, Equip.:	$2,140,000	**Total Liab.:**	$22,242,000	**Indic. Yr. Divd.:**	NA
Total Assets:	$48,159,000	**Net Worth:**	$25,917,000	**Debt/ Equity:**	NA

Peerless Systems Corp

2381 Rosecrans Ave., El Segundo, CA, 90245; ***PH:*** 1-310-536-0908; ***Fax:*** 1-310-536-0058; ***http://*** www.peerless.com; ***Email:*** info@peerless.com

General - Incorporation .... DE
Employees 99
Auditor .... Ernst & Young LLP
Stk Agt .... Wells Fargo Shareowner Services
Counsel............ NA
DUNS No. 11-311-0829

Stock- Price on:12/24/2007 .... $2.3701
Stock Exchange............ NDQ
Ticker Symbol............ PRLS
Outstanding Shares 17,250,000
E.P.S............ $0.18
Shareholders............ NA

Business: The group's principal activity is the development and licensing of software-based digital imaging and networking systems. The group provides custom engineering services to original equipment manufacturers. Digital document products include printers, copiers, fax machines, scanners and color products, as well as multifunction products that perform a combination of these imaging functions. Peerless(R), Peerlesspowered(R), Winexpress(R), Peerlessprint(R), Redips(R), Acceleprint(R), Synthesys(R), Quickprint(R) and Perfectone(R) are registered trademarks of the group. The digital document products are located primarily in the United States and Japan. The group markets its solutions directly to OEM customers including Canon, Konicaminolta, Kyocera/ Mita, Lenovo, Oki Data, Panasonic, Ricoh, and Seiko Epson.

Primary SIC and add'l.: 7373 7372

CIK No: 0000897893

Subsidiaries: Peerless Systems Imaging Products, Inc., Peerless Systems K.K

Officers: Richard L. Roll/Dir., CEO, Pres., Geoff High/Contact - High Investor Relations, Jan Bowler/Sr. Dir. - Human Resources, Eric Random/VP - Engineering, Howard J. Nellor/Pres., Chief Executives Officer, Alan D. Curtis/VP - Corporate Development, Ed Gaughan/VP - Sales, Marketing, Cary A. Kimmel/VP - Business Development, John V. Rigali/VP - Finance, CFO, Joe Szikszoy/GM - Peerless Systems Imaging Products, Robert T. Westervelt/CTO, VP - Engineering

Directors: Richard L. Roll/Dir., CEO, Pres., William B. Patton/Chmn., John C. Reece/Dir., John Thomas Zender/Dir., Timothy E. Brog/Dir., Robert G. Barrett/63/Dir., Louis C. Cole/64/Dir.

Owners: Robert T. Westervelt, Cary A. Kimmel, Marathon Capital Management LLC/6.30%, Diker Management, LLC/5.30%, Eric Random/1.00%, William R. Neil/1.90%, State of Wisconsin Investment Board/9.10%, Insiders/5.10%, Robert G. Barrett, Peerless Full Value Committee/8.40%, Alan D. Curtis/1.40%, Kaizen Capital LLC/5.00%, Howard J. Nellor/3.40%, Timothy E. Brog/8.00%

Financial Data: ***Fiscal Year End:***01/31 ***Latest Annual Data:*** 1/31/2007

Year	Sales	Net Income
2007	$33,383,000	$3,286,000
2006	$36,157,000	$4,314,000
2005	$23,078,000	-$5,805,000

Curr. Assets:	$22,884,000	**Curr. Liab.:**	$6,959,000	**P/E Ratio:**	118.51
Plant, Equip.:	$558,000	**Total Liab.:**	$7,418,000	**Indic. Yr. Divd.:**	NA
Total Assets:	$23,601,000	**Net Worth:**	$16,183,000	**Debt/ Equity:**	NA

Peet's Coffee & Tea Inc

1400 Pk. Ave., Emeryville, CA, 94608; ***PH:*** 1-510-594-2100; ***Fax:*** 1-510-594-2180; ***http://*** www.peets.com

General - Incorporation .... WA
Employees 621
Auditor .... Deloitte & Touche LLP
Stk Agt .... Continental Stock Transfer & Trust Co
Counsel............ Cooley Godward LLP
DUNS No. .... NA

Stock- Price on:12/24/2007 .... $25.35
Stock Exchange............ NDQ
Ticker Symbol............ PEET
Outstanding Shares 13,660,000
E.P.S............ $0.52
Shareholders............ NA

Business: The group's principle activity is to sell fresh roasted coffee, hand selected tea and related items. These products are sold through distribution channels, including specialty grocery and gourmet food stores, online and mail order, office and restaurant accounts and company-operated retail stores in the United States. The group operates in two reportable segments. Retail store operations consist of sale

of whole bean coffee, beverages, tea and related products. Specialty sales consist of whole bean coffee sales through online, mail order and grocery, wholesale and office coffee accounts. The group operates 76 retail stores in seven states. The patent and trademarks of the group includes peet's(R), peet's coffee and tea(R), peet's.corn(R), blend 101(R), garuda blend(R), jr reserve blend(R), maduro blend(R), major dickason's blend(R), pride of the port(R), pumphrey's blend(R), sierra dorada blend(R), summer house(R), top blend(R) and vine street blend(r). The group's quarterly revenue for September 2007 was 60.86 millions of USD.

Primary SIC and add'l.: 5499 2095
CIK No: 0000917968

Officers: Jim Reynolds/Roastmaster Emeritus, Doug Welsh/VP - Coffee, Shirin Moayyad/Dir. - Coffee Purchasing, Eliot Jordan/Dir. - Tea, John Weaver/Sr. Master Roaster, Steve Ableski/Coffee Roaster, Paul Gallegos/Coffee Roaster, John Nicolini/Coffee Roaster, Alan Kao/Coffee Roaster

Directors: Jerry Baldwin/Dir., David Deno/Dir.

Owners: Morgan Stanley/10.20%, Michael Linton, Thomas P. Cawley/1.60%, Palo Alto Investors, LLC/10.30%, Gerald Baldwin/1.80%, Baron Capital Group, Inc./7.60%, Barclays Global Investors Japan Limited/5.60%, Patrick J. Odea/5.60%, William H. Jesse, Gordon A. Bowker, David Deno, Next Century Growth Investors, LLC/6.00%, Hilary Billings, Jean-Michel Valette, James E. Grimes *(16 Owners included in Index)*

Financial Data: Fiscal Year End:01/01 **Latest Annual Data:** 12/31/2006

Year	Sales	Net Income
2006	$210,493,000	$7,816,000
2005	$145,683,000	$8,785,000

Curr. Assets:	$59,314,000	Curr. Liab.:	$22,060,000	P/E Ratio:	51.73
Plant, Equip.:	$82,447,000	Total Liab.:	$25,566,000	Indic. Yr. Divd.:	NA
Total Assets:	$153,005,000	Net Worth:	$127,439,000	Debt/ Equity:	NA

Pegasus Communications Corp

225 City Line Ave., Ste. 200, Bala Cynwyd, PA, 19004; **PH:** 1-610-934-7000; **Fax:** 1-610-934-7054; http:// www.pgtv.com

General - Incorporation	DE	Stock - Price on:12/24/2007	$2.02
Employees	72	Stock Exchange	NYSE
Auditor	Marcum & Kliegman LLP	Ticker Symbol	XAN
Stk Agt	Wachovia Bank N.A	Outstanding Shares	NA
Counsel	NA	E.P.S.	NA
DUNS No.	NA	Shareholders	NA

Business: The group's principal activity is to provide satellite television and digital services to the rural and under-served areas of the United States. The group operates in two areas: direct broadcast services and broadcast and other businesses. The direct broadcast services of the group provides multi-channel satellite audio and video programming of directv service in rural areas of the United States on a subscription basis. Under broadcast and other businesses, the group provides two way satellite accesses to the Internet through its pegasus express service. The group also owns or operates nine TV stations affiliated with the fox broadcasting company, united paramount network and the wb television network.

Primary SIC and add'l.: 4841 4833 6719
CIK No: 0001135338

Subsidiaries: Broadband Communications LLC), Pegasus Communications Management Company, Pegasus Development 107 Corporation, Pegasus Development 107 License Corporation, Pegasus Development Corporation, Pegasus Guardband, LLC, Pegasus Real Estate Company, Pegasus Rural Broadband LLC, Pegasus Satellite Communications Holdings, Inc., Pegasus Satellite Development Corporation, Pegasus Travel, Inc., PMC Satellite Development, LLC, WFXU Corporation, WFXU License Corporation

Pegasus Wireless Corp.

277 Royal Poinciana Way, Ste. 153, Palm Beach, FL, 33480; **PH:** 1-510-490-8288; **Fax:** 1-510-440-7046; http:// www.pegasuswirelesscorp.com; **Email:** sales@pegasuswirelesscorp.com

General - Incorporation	NV	Stock - Price on:12/24/2007	$0.18
Employees	500	Stock Exchange	OTC
Auditor	Pollard-Kelley Auditing Services, Inc	Ticker Symbol	PGSW
Stk Agt	Olde Monmouth Stk Trnsfer Co. Inc.	Outstanding Shares	34,610,000
Counsel	NA	E.P.S.	$0.019
DUNS No.	NA	Shareholders	NA

Business: The group's principal activity is to develop, manufacture and sell small-throughput water treatment systems and associated consumable products that provide reliable supplies of safe drinking water. The group's products give end-users a cost-effective means of filtering, treating, disinfecting and conserving water without the use of chlorine and other chemicals. The products of the company are used for residential, industrial, municipal and agricultural purposes. The group also provides technical consulting services to its customers, and sells the components and consumables that are required for the operation and maintenance of water treatment systems.

Primary SIC and add'l.: 7375 3589 7372
CIK No: 0001126752

Officers: Jasper Knabb/41/Dir., CEO, Stephen Durland/Dir., CFO

Directors: Jasper Knabb/41/Dir., CEO, Stephen Durland/Dir., CFO, Billy Horn/44/Dir.

Owners: Vision 2000 Ventures, Ltd/8.40%, Insiders/4.70%, Stephen Durland/1.10%, Jasper Knabb/3.50%, Billy Horn, Alex Tsao/8.60%

Financial Data: Fiscal Year End:12/31 **Latest Annual Data:** 03/31/2007

Year	Sales	Net Income
2007	NA	$4,046,000
2006	$103,974,000	$613,000
2005	$3,172,000	-$673,000

Curr. Assets:	$1,637,000	Curr. Liab.:	$556,000	P/E Ratio:	9.47
Plant, Equip.:	$125,000	Total Liab.:	$556,000	Indic. Yr. Divd.:	NA
Total Assets:	$1,779,000	Net Worth:	$1,222,000	Debt/ Equity:	0.0195

Pegasystems Inc

101 Main St., Cambridge, MA, 02142; **PH:** 1-617-374-9600; **Fax:** 1-617-374-9620; http:// www.pega.com

General - Incorporation	MA	Stock - Price on:12/24/2007	$10.56
Employees	547	Stock Exchange	NDQ
Auditor	Deloitte & Touche LLP	Ticker Symbol	PEGA
Stk Agt	Computershare Trust Co	Outstanding Shares	35,380,000
Counsel	Choate, Hall & Stewart LLP	E.P.S.	$0.22
DUNS No.	11-422-3183	Shareholders	NA

Business: The group's principal activity is to develop, market, license and support customer relationship management software that enables transaction intensive-organizations to manage a broad array of customer interactions and that integrates rules and business process management. It also offers consultation, training, and maintenance and support services to facilitate the installation and use of its solutions. The customers of the group represent a range of industries including banking and financial services, insurance, healthcare and telecommunications. The software of the group enables organizations to deliver high-quality consistent service across multiple channel interactions, from the traditional call centers environment to Internet self-service.

Primary SIC and add'l.: 7371 7379 7372
CIK No: 0001013857

Subsidiaries: GDOO AB, Pegasystems Company, Pegasystems Investment Inc, Pegasystems Limited, Pegasystems Private Ltd, Pegasystems Pty Ltd, Pegasystems Worldwide Inc

Officers: Alan Trefler/51/Chmn., CEO/$467,770.00, Jo Hoppe/CIO, VP, Douglas Kra/VP - Global Services/$387,920.00, Shawn Hoyt/VP, General Counsel/$308,854.00, Craig A. Dynes/CFO, Sr. VP/$198,316.00, Mike Pyle/Sr. VP - Engineering, Edward Hughes/Sr. VP - Global Sales/$615,550.00, Max Mayer/VP - Corporate Development, Carmelina Procaccini/VP, Human Resources Officer, Jay Sherry/VP - Marketing, Solution Frameworks, Michael R. Pyle/53/Sr. VP - Product Development/$377,831.00, Denise Stephenson/Exec. Assist. to CFO, James T. Reilly/53/VP - Finance, Treasurer, Chief Accounting Officer

Directors: Alan Trefler/51/Chmn., CEO, Alexander V. Darbeloff/80/Dir., Richard H. Jones/56/Dir., Steven F. Kaplan/51/Dir., James P. OHalloran/75/Dir., William W. Wyman/70/Dir.

Owners: Insiders/66.30%, Michael Pyle, Alan Trefler/58.30%, Shawn Hoyt, Edward Hughes, Richard H. Jones/3.70%, Steven F. Kaplan, Perry Corp./8.20%, James P. OHalloran, Dimensional Fund Advisors LP/6.30%, William W. Wyman, Alexander V. dArbeloff/1.80%, Craig Dynes, Douglas Kra

Financial Data: Fiscal Year End:12/31 **Latest Annual Data:** 12/31/2006

Year	Sales	Net Income
2006	$126,023,000	$1,842,000
2005	$100,209,000	$5,192,000
2004	$96,461,000	$7,554,000

Curr. Assets:	$190,598,000	Curr. Liab.:	$43,369,000	P/E Ratio:	86.56
Plant, Equip.:	$2,453,000	Total Liab.:	$47,850,000	Indic. Yr. Divd.:	$0.120
Total Assets:	$214,008,000	Net Worth:	$166,158,000	Debt/ Equity:	NA

Pekin Life Insurance Company

2505 Ct. St., Pekin, IL, 61558; **PH:** 1-309-346-1161; **Fax:** 1-309-346-8512; http:// www.pekininsurance.com

General - Incorporation	IL	Stock - Price on:12/24/2007	$15.75
Employees	NA	Stock Exchange	OTC
Auditor	NA	Ticker Symbol	PKIN
Stk Agt	NA	Outstanding Shares	17,070,000
Counsel	NA	E.P.S.	$0.80
DUNS No.	NA	Shareholders	NA

Business: The groups principal activities include providing Insurance services. Services of the group include local hometown professional agent, comprehensive product profile, competitive premiums, round the clock claim service, convenient premium payment plans and visa mastercard. The group operates from the United States.

Primary SIC and add'l.: 6311
CIK No: 0000784863

Financial Data: Fiscal Year End:12/31 **Latest Annual Data:** 12/31/2002

Year	Sales	Net Income
2002	$226,752,000	-$9,832,000
2001	$210,976,000	$11,982,000
2000	$213,098,000	$3,635,000

Curr. Assets:	$29,089,000	Curr. Liab.:	$12,761,000		
Plant, Equip.:	$1,698,000	Total Liab.:	$514,250,000	Indic. Yr. Divd.:	$0.220
Total Assets:	$595,243,000	Net Worth:	$80,994,000	Debt/ Equity:	NA

Pelican Financial Inc

3767 Ranchero Dr., Ann Arbor, MI, 48108; **PH:** 1-800-242-6698

General - Incorporation	DE	Stock - Price on:12/24/2007	$27.08
Employees	NA	Stock Exchange	NA
Auditor	Crowe Chizek & Co. LLC	Ticker Symbol	NA
Stk Agt	NA	Outstanding Shares	NA
Counsel	NA	E.P.S.	NA
DUNS No.	NA	Shareholders	NA

Business: The group's principal activity is to provide mortgage banking and retail banking services. The group operates in two segments: mortgage banking and retail banking. The mortgage banking segment involves the origination and purchase of single-family residential mortgage loans in approximately 40 states; the sale of such loans in the secondary market, generally on a pooled and securitized basis; and the servicing of mortgage loans for investors. Mortgage banking operations are conducted through offices located in ann arbor, Michigan and pleasant hill, California. The retail banking segment involves attracting deposits from the general public and using such funds to originate consumer, commercial, commercial real estate, residential construction, and single-family residential mortgage loans, from its offices in naples and fort myers, Florida.

Primary SIC and add'l.: 6712 6021 6162
CIK No: 0001037652

Subsidiaries: Pelican National, Stark Bank Group, Ltd, of Fort Dodge

Pemco Aviation Group Inc

1943 N 50th St., Birmingham, AL, 35212; **PH:** 1-205-592-0011; **Fax:** 1-205-592-6306; http:// www.pemcoaviationgroup.com

rmingham, AL, 35212; *PH:* 1-205-592-0011; *Fax:* 1-205-592-6306;
http:// www.pemcoaviationgroup.com

General - Incorporation	DE	*Stock* - Price on:12/24/2007	$9.5
Employees	1,506	Stock Exchange	NDQ
Auditor	Grant Thornton LLP	Ticker Symbol	NA
Stk Agt	Computershare Trust Co	Outstanding Shares	4,130,000
Counsel	NA	E.P.S.	$0.37
DUNS No.	18-310-1419	Shareholders	NA

Business: The group's principal activity is to provide aircraft maintenance and modification services, including complete airframe inspection, repair and custom airframe design. It operates through three segments. The government services group provides aircraft maintenance and modification services for the government and military customers. The commercial services group provides commercial aircraft maintenance and modification services to the owners and operators of large commercial aircraft. The manufacturing and components group designs and manufactures a wide array of proprietary aerospace products including various space systems such as guidance control systems and launching vehicles and precision parts and components for aircraft. The group has operations in the United States.

Primary SIC and add'l.: 3728 4581

CIK No: 0000771729

Subsidiaries: McDonnell Douglas Corporation, Pemco Aeroplex, Inc., Pemco Engineers, Inc.

Officers: Ronald A. Aramini/Dir., CEO, Pres./$1,225,764.00, Eric Wildhagen/VP - Engineering, Product Support/$167,806.00, Philip M. Panzera/Pres. - Space Vector Corp, Kevin Casey/VP - Commercial Business Development, Glenn Hess/Pres. - Pemco Aeroplex, Inc, Doris K. Sewell/VP - Legal, Corporate Affairs/$295,340.00, Randy Shealy/VP - Accounting/$335,083.00, Gil McSheehy/VP - Military Programs

Directors: Ronald A. Aramini/Dir., CEO, Pres.

Owners: Randall C. Shealy, Thomas C. Richards, Clarium LP, Hugh Steven Wilson, SVIM/MSM, LLC, Eric L. Wildhagen, Ronald W. Yates, Massachusetts Mutual Life Insurance Company, Rustic Canyon Ventures, L.P., FMR Corp., Ronald A. Aramini, Harold T. Bowling, Tennenbaum Capital Partners, LLC, Doris K. Sewell, Insiders (20 Owners included in Index)

Financial Data: Fiscal Year End:12/31 Latest Annual Data: 12/31/2006

Year	Sales		Net Income
2006	$160,709,000		$519,000
2005	$150,312,000		-$5,814,000
2004	$201,165,000		-$2,988,000
Curr. Assets:	$48,271,000	*Curr. Liab.:* $57,260,000	*P/E Ratio:* 25.68
Plant, Equip.:	$22,590,000	*Total Liab.:* $81,206,000	*Indic. Yr. Divd.:* NA
Total Assets:	$88,586,000	*Net Worth:* $7,380,000	*Debt/ Equity:* NA

Penford Corp

1001 First St. S.W., Cedar Rapids, IA, 52404; *PH:* 1-800-582-8728; *Fax:* 1-319-398-3797;
http:// www.penx.com; *Email:* ir@penx.com

General - Incorporation	WA	*Stock* - Price on:12/24/2007	$19.1
Employees	571	Stock Exchange	NDQ
Auditor	Ernst & Young LLP	Ticker Symbol	PENX
Stk Agt	Mellon Investor Services LLC	Outstanding Shares	8,980,000
Counsel	Preston Gates & Ellis	E.P.S.	NA
DUNS No.	11-302-2586	Shareholders	NA

Business: The group's principal activities are to develop, manufacture and market carbohydrate-based specialty ingredient systems for industrial and food applications. The business is carried on through two segments namely industrial and food ingredients. The principal products include ethylated starches and cationic starches. Ethylated starches are used in coatings and as binders in the manufacture of magazine, fine white and catalog paper. Cationic starches are generally used in the paper-forming process in paper production, providing strong bonding of paper fibers and other ingredients. Specialty starches produced for food applications are used in coatings to provide crispness, improved taste and texture and increased product life for products such as french fries. The group has international operations in Australia and New Zealand.

Primary SIC and add'l.: 2046 2087

CIK No: 0000739608

Subsidiaries: Penford Australia Limited, Penford Corporation, Penford Export Corporation, Penford Holdings Pty. Limited, Penford New Zealand Ltd., Penford Products Co.

Officers: Thomas D. Malkoski/Dir., CEO, Pres., Margaret Von Der Schmidt/Corporate Controller, Assist. Sec., Christopher L. Lawlor/VP - Human Resources, General Counsel, Sec., Wallace H. Kunerth/VP, Chief Science Officer, John R. Randall/VP, Steven O. Cordier/Sr. VP, CFO, Assist. Sec., Timothy M. Kortemeyer/VP

Directors: Thomas D. Malkoski/Dir., CEO, Pres., Paul H. Hatfield/Chmn., John C. Hunter/Dir., William E. Buchholz/Dir., James E. Warjone/Dir., Jeffrey T. Cook/Dir., Randolph R. Devening/Dir., Sally G. Narodick/Dir.

Owners: James E. Warjone, William E. Buchholz, Insiders/9.23%, Jeffrey T. Cook/2.16%, Sally G. Narodick, Dimensional Fund Advisors, Inc./5.58%, Steven O. Cordier/1.52%, John R. Randall, Randolph R. Devening, Bear Stearns Asset Management, Inc./5.93%, Thomas D. Malkoski/3.01%, T. Rowe Price Associates, Inc./9.27%, Timothy M. Kortemeyer, Paul H. Hatfield, John C. Hunter (16 Owners included in Index)

Financial Data: Fiscal Year End:08/31 Latest Annual Data: 8/31/2006

Year	Sales		Net Income
2006	$318,419,000		$4,228,000
2005	$296,763,000		$2,574,000
2004	$279,386,000		$3,702,000
Curr. Assets:	$105,279,000	*Curr. Liab.:* $66,246,000	*P/E Ratio:* 19.69
Plant, Equip.:	$146,663,000	*Total Liab.:* $162,712,000	*Indic. Yr. Divd.:* NA
Total Assets:	$288,388,000	*Net Worth:* $125,676,000	*Debt/ Equity:* NA

Pengrowth Energy Trust

240 - 4th Ave. SW, Ste. 2900, Calgary, AB, T2P 4H4; *PH:* 1-403-233-0224; *Fax:* 1-403-265-6251;
http:// www.pengrowth.com; *Email:* pcngrowth@pengrowth.com

General - Incorporation	AB	*Stock* - Price on:12/24/2007	$19.04
Employees	461	Stock Exchange	NYSE
Auditor	KPMG LLP	Ticker Symbol	PGH
Stk Agt	Computershare Trust Co	Outstanding Shares	244,750,000
Counsel	NA	E.P.S.	$1.54
DUNS No.	NA	Shareholders	NA

Business: The groups principle activities include owning, acquiring and producing light crude oil, natural gas, natural gas liquids, heavy oil and sulfur. The group operates from the Canada.

Primary SIC and add'l.: 1381 6792 1382

CIK No: 0001088166

Officers: James S. Kinnear/Chmn., CEO, Pres., Chris Webster/CFO, Gordon M. Anderson/VP - Finance, James Causgrove/VP - Production, Operations, William Christensen/VP - Strategic Planning, Reservoir Exploitation, Larry B. Strong/VP - Geosciences, Charles V. Selby/VP, Corp. Sec., Douglas C. Bowles/VP, Controller, Peter Cheung/Treasurer, Michael G. /VP, Chief - Staff, Wendy M. Noonan/Dir. - Human Resources, Administration, Shawn Howard/Dir. - Public, Government Affairs, Lisa Ciulka/Mgr. - Investor Relations, Wassem Khalil/Investor Relations Analyst, Kirsten Kulyk/Investor Relations Representative (17 Officers included in Index)

Directors: James S. Kinnear/Chmn., CEO, Pres., James MacDonald/Dir. - East Coast Operations, Thomas A. Cumming/Dir., Micheal S. Parrett/Dir., Stanley H. Wong/Dir., John B. Zaozirny/Dir., Terence A. Poole/Dir., Kirby L. Hedrick/Dir., Wayne K. Foo/Dir., Michael G. D. Stewart/Dir.

Financial Data: Fiscal Year End:12/31 Latest Annual Data: 12/31/2006

Year	Sales		Net Income
2006	$850,692,000		$147,863,000
2005	$819,677,000		$299,090,000
2004	$676,993,000		$149,491,000
Curr. Assets:	$164,112,000	*Curr. Liab.:* $291,435,000	*P/E Ratio:* 40.06
Plant, Equip.:	$2,968,312,000	*Total Liab.:* $1,390,537,000	*Indic. Yr. Divd.:* $2.830
Total Assets:	$3,765,154,000	*Net Worth:* $2,374,617,000	*Debt/ Equity:* NA

Penn Laurel Financial Corp

426-434 State St., Curwensville, PA, 16833; *PH:* 1-800-494-3453; *http://* www.csb-bank.com;
Email: csb@csb-bank.com

General - Incorporation	PA	*Stock* - Price on:12/24/2007	$30.63
Employees	NA	Stock Exchange	NA
Auditor	NA	Ticker Symbol	NA
Stk Agt	NA	Outstanding Shares	NA
Counsel	NA	E.P.S.	NA
DUNS No.	NA	Shareholders	NA

Business: The groups principal activity is to provide banking and financial services to the customers. The group operates from the United States.

Primary SIC and add'l.: 6022

CIK No: 0000797096

Financial Data: Fiscal Year End:12/31 Latest Annual Data: 12/31/2002

Year	Sales		Net Income
2002	$13,727,000		$1,721,000
2001	$13,160,000		$1,213,000
2000	$1,612,000		$1,151,000
Curr. Assets:	$5,162,000	*Curr. Liab.:* $162,671,000	
Plant, Equip.:	$2,318,000	*Total Liab.:* $164,624,000	*Indic. Yr. Divd.:* NA
Total Assets:	$180,943,000	*Net Worth:* $16,319,000	*Debt/ Equity:* 0.3798

Penn National Gaming Inc

825 Berkshire Blvd., Ste. 200, Wyomissing, PA, 19610; *PH:* 1-610-373-2400; *Fax:* 1-610-373-4966;
http:// www.pngaming.com; *Email:* corporate@pngaming.com

General - Incorporation	PA	*Stock* - Price on:12/24/2007	$63.3
Employees	14,874	Stock Exchange	NDQ
Auditor	Ernst & Young, LLP	Ticker Symbol	PENN
Stk Agt	Continental Stock Transfer & Trust Co	Outstanding Shares	85,560,000
Counsel	Schnader, Harrison, Segal & Lewis	E.P.S.	$2.45
DUNS No.	14-731-8356	Shareholders	NA

Business: The group's principle actiivty is to operate gaming properties including horse racetracks and associated off-track wagering facilities. The group operates from United States.

Primary SIC and add'l.: 7993 7948

CIK No: 0000921738

Subsidiaries: Alton Gaming Company, Argosy Gaming Company, Argosy of Iowa,Inc., Bangor Acquisition Corp., Bangor Historic Track,Inc., Belle of Sioux City, L.P., BSL,Inc., BTN,Inc., Casino Rama Services,Inc., CHC (Ontario) Supplies Limited, CHC Casinos Canada Limited, CHC Casinos Corp., Crazy Horses,Inc., CRC Holdings,Inc., Empress Casino Joliet Corporation 37 Subsidiaries included in the Index

Officers: Peter M. Carlino/Chmn., CEO/$7,671,978.00, Robert S. Ippolito/VP, Sec., Treasurer/$1,315,467.00, William J. Clifford/CFO/$3,054,001.00, Gene Clark/Sr. VP - Human Resources, John Finamore/Sr. VP - Regional Operations, Steven T. Snyder/Sr. VP - Corporate Development, Jordan B. Savitch/Sr. VP, General Counsel/$1,610,198.00, Leonard M. Deangelo/Exec. VP - Operations/$3,201,267.00, James Baum/Sr. VP - Project Development, Joseph N. Jaffoni/Contact - Financial, Investor Inquiries

Directors: Peter M. Carlino/Dir., CEO, David A. Handler/Dir., John M. Jacquemin/61/Dir., Robert P. Levy/Dir., Harold Cramer/Dir., Barbara Z. Shattuck/Dir.

Owners: Peter M. Carlino/13.57%, Akre Capital Management, LLC/8.50%, David A. Handler, Richard J. Carlino/11.03%, Peter D. Carlino/11.59%, Robert S. Ippolito, Barbara Z. Shattuck, David E. Carlino/11.05%, John M. Jacquemin, Kevin DeSanctis, Harold Cramer/11.74%, Jordan B. Savitch, Leonard M. DeAngelo, Robert P. Levy, William J. Clifford (17 Owners included in Index)

Financial Data: Fiscal Year End:12/31 Latest Annual Data: 12/31/2006

Year	Sales		Net Income
2006	$2,244,547,000		$327,088,000
2005	$1,412,466,000		$120,930,000
2004	$1,140,689,000		$71,484,000
Curr. Assets:	$401,963,000	*Curr. Liab.:* $415,671,000	*P/E Ratio:* 17.06
Plant, Equip.:	$1,365,871,000	*Total Liab.:* $3,592,919,000	*Indic. Yr. Divd.:* NA
Total Assets:	$4,514,082,000	*Net Worth:* $921,163,000	*Debt/ Equity:* 3.0281

Penn Octane Corp

77-530 Enfield Ln., Bldg. D, Palm Desert, CA, 92211; *PH:* 1-760-772-9080; *Fax:* 1-760-772-8588;
http:// www.pennoctane.com

General - Incorporation............................ DE
Employees..30
Auditor .... Burton McCumber & Cortez LLP
Stk Agt......................... Computershare Trust Co
Counsel..Kevin Finck
DUNS No. 80-971-2276

Stock- Price on:12/24/2007 ....NA
Stock Exchange...OTC
Ticker Symbol..POCC
Outstanding Shares ....NA
E.P.S .... -$0.08
Shareholders ....NA

Business: The group's principal activities are to purchase, transport and market liquefied petroleum gas (lpg) in the United States. It owns and operates a terminal facility in brownsville, Texas and owns a lpg terminal facility in matamoros, tamaulipas, Mexico and pipelines that connect the brownsville terminal facility to the matamoros terminal facility. The primary market for the group's lpg is the northeastern region of Mexico which includes the states of coahuila, nuevo leon and tamaulipas.

Primary SIC and add'l.: 4925

CIK No: 0000893813

Subsidiaries: Camiones Ecologicos, S.A. de C.V., Estacion Ambiental II, S.A. de C.V., Estacion Ambiental, S.A. de C.V., Foreign Consolidated Affiliate, Foreign Subsidiaries, Grupo Ecologico Industrial, S.A. de C.V., Penn CNG Holdings, Inc., Penn Octane de Mexico, S. de R.L. de C.V., Penn Octane International, LLC, Penn Wilson CNG, Inc., PennWill, S.A. de C.V., Rio Vista Energy Partners L.P., Rio Vista GP LLC, Rio Vista Operating GP LLC, Rio Vista Operating Partnership L.P. 18 Subsidiaries included in the Index

Officers: Ian T. Bothwell/48/VP, Treasurer, Assist Sec., CFO, Acting CEO, Acting Pres., VP, Charles Handly/Pres., Jerry Lockett/VP, Sec.

Directors: Richard R. Canney/53/Chmn., Emmett M. Murphy/Dir., Bruce I. Raben/54/Dir., Eugene A. Viele/53/Dir., Harvey L. Benenson/Dir., Jerome Richter/Dir., Richard Shore/Dir., Stewart J. Paperin/Dir.

Owners: Jerome B. Richter/25.54%, Jerry L. Lockett, Insiders/4.54%, Richard R. Canney, Eugene A. Viele, Swank Group, LLC, Swank Energy Income/8.04%, The Apogee Fund, Paradigm Capital/8.37%, Ian T. Bothwell, Charles C. Handly, Strategic Turnaround Equity Partners, LP/9.53%, Bruce I. Raben/1.82%

Financial Data: *Fiscal Year End:*12/31 *Latest Annual Data:* 12/31/2006

Year	Sales	Net Income
2006	$144,337,000	$4,655,000
2005	$260,314,000	-$2,033,000
2004	$177,664,000	$1,798,000

Curr. Assets:	$16,694,000	**Curr. Liab.:**	$7,295,000		
Plant, Equip.:	$10,911,000	**Total Liab.:**	$7,295,000	**Indic. Yr. Divd.:**	NA
Total Assets:	$27,620,000	**Net Worth:**	$5,379,000	**Debt/ Equity:**	NA

Penn Treaty American Corp

3440 Lehigh St., Allentown, PA, 18103; ***PH:*** 1-610-965-2222; ***Fax:*** 1-877-582-3299; ***http://*** www.penntreaty.com; ***Email:*** info@penntreaty.com

General - Incorporation..............................PA
Employees..291
Auditor .... BDO Seidman, LLP
Stk Agt.............................. Wachovia Bank N.A
Counsel.......... Ballard Spahr Andrews & Ingersoll LLP
DUNS No. 07-916-9900

Stock- Price on:12/24/2007 ....$6.03
Stock Exchange...NYSE
Ticker Symbol...PTA
Outstanding Shares 23,290,000
E.P.S ....NA
Shareholders ....NA

Business: The group's principal activity is to provide long term nursing home and home health care insurance products. It operates through independent insurance agents and underwrites its policies through its subsidiaries. The group also markets and sells life, disability, medicare supplement and other hospital care insurance products. The principal products are individual, defined benefit accident and health insurance policies covering long-term skilled, intermediate and custodial nursing home care and home health care.

Primary SIC and add'l.: 6321 6311 6719

CIK No: 0000814181

Subsidiaries: American Independent Network Insurance Company, American Network Insurance Company, Network Insurance Senior Health Division, Penn Treaty Network America Insurance Company, Senior Financial Consultants Company, United Insurance Group Agency, Inc

Officers: William W. Hunt/Dir., CEO, Pres., Bruce A. Stahl/49/Sr. VP, Chief Actuary, Jane Menin Bagley/VP, Corporate Counsel, Corp. Sec., Cameron B. Waite/Exec. VP - Strategic Operations, Mark D. Cloutier/CFO, Exec. VP, Patrick D. Patterson/55/Exec. VP, Chief Marketing Officer, Stephen R. Lapierre/Sr. VP - Claims Management, Policyholder Services, Penn Treaty Insurance Company Subsidiaries, Derrick E. Brickhouse/VP - Sales, Marketing

Directors: William W. Hunt/Dir., CEO, Pres., Gary E. Hindes/57/Chmn., Francis R. Grebe/76/Dir., Patrick E. Falconio/66/Dir., Domenic P. Stangherlin/81/Dir., Peter M. Ross/68/Dir., Alexander M. Clark/74/Dir., Matthew W. Kaplan/49/Dir., Eugene J. Woznicki/65/Dir.

Owners: Whitebox Advisors LLC/8.90%, Stephen R. La Pierre, William W. Hunt, Atlas Capital Management, L.P./5.20%, Cameron B. Waite, Elkhorn Partners, LP/9.90%, Mark D. Cloutier, Insiders/1.80%, Bruce A. Stahl, Peter M. Ross, Francis R. Grebe, Dimensional Fund Advisors LP/6.30%, Matthew W. Kaplan, Eugene J. Woznicki, Patrick E. Falconio *(19 Owners included in Index)*

Financial Data: *Fiscal Year End:*12/31 *Latest Annual Data:* 12/31/2005

Year	Sales	Net Income
2005	NA	NA
2004	$414,741,000	$20,536,000
2003	$364,063,000	-$13,353,000

Curr. Assets:	$50,918,000	**Curr. Liab.:**	$38,401,000		
Plant, Equip.:	$17,477,000	**Total Liab.:**	$1,037,550,000	**Indic. Yr. Divd.:**	NA
Total Assets:	$1,292,480,000	**Net Worth:**	$254,930,000	**Debt/ Equity:**	NA

Penn Virginia Corp

3 Radnor Corporate Ctr., Ste. 300, 100 Matsonford Rd., Radnor, PA, 19087; ***PH:*** 1-610-687-8900; ***Fax:*** 1-610-687-3688; ***http://*** www.pennvirginia.com

General - Incorporation..............................VA
Employees..282
Auditor ....KPMG LLP
Stk Agt..... American Stock Transfer & Trust Co.
Counsel..NA
DUNS No. 00-791-5093

Stock- Price on:12/24/2007 ....$41.44
Stock Exchange...NYSE
Ticker Symbol...PVA
Outstanding Shares 37,590,000
E.P.S $1.64
Shareholders ....NA

Business: The group's principal activity is to explore, develop and produce crude oil and natural gas. The group operates in two segments: oil and gas and coal royalty and land management. The oil and gas segment explores, develops and produces crude oil, condensate and natural gas primarily in the eastern and gulf coast onshore areas of the United States. The coal royalty and land management segment includes the operations of penn Virginia resource partners lp.

Primary SIC and add'l.: 1411 1222 1382 6519 1311

CIK No: 0000077159

Subsidiaries: Cantera Gas Company, Penn Virginia Resource GP, LLC, Virginia Resource GP, LLC

Officers: James A. Dearlove/Dir., CEO, Pres./$1,298,177.00, Keith D. Horton/Dir., Exec. VP/$769,383.00, Baird H. Whitehead/Exec. VP/$815,111.00, Frank A. Pici/CFO, Exec. VP/$811,874.00, Nancy M. Snyder/Sr. VP, General Counsel, Corp. Sec./$727,226.00, Ronald K. Page/VP - Corporate Development, Forrest W. McNair/VP, Controller, Dana G. Wright/VP - Planning, Steven A. Hartman/VP, Treasurer, James W. Dean/Dir. - Investor Relations

Directors: James A. Dearlove/Dir., CEO, Pres., Philippe Van Marcke De Lummen/Dir., Gary K. Wright/Dir., Marsha R. Perelman/Dir., Edward B. Cloues/Dir., Keith D. Horton/Dir., Exec. VP, Steve W. Krablin/Dir., Robert Garrett/Dir.

Owners: Robert Garrett, Marsha R. Perelman, Joe N. Averett, Steven W. Krablin, Nancy M. Snyder, T. Rowe Price Associates, Inc./9.20%, Gary K. Wright, Insiders/2.80%, Barclays Global Investors, N.A./6.00%, Frank A. Pici, Keith D. Horton, Philippe van Marcke de Lummen, Baird H. Whitehead, BlackRock, Inc./8.50%, James A. Dearlove *(16 Owners included in Index)*

Financial Data: *Fiscal Year End:*12/31 *Latest Annual Data:* 12/31/2006

Year	Sales	Net Income
2006	$753,929,000	$75,909,000
2005	$673,864,000	$62,088,000
2004	$228,425,000	$33,355,000

Curr. Assets:	$192,383,000	**Curr. Liab.:**	$172,690,000	**P/E Ratio:**	28.00
Plant, Equip.:	$1,358,383,000	**Total Liab.:**	$812,352,000	**Indic. Yr. Divd.:**	$0.230
Total Assets:	$1,633,149,000	**Net Worth:**	$382,425,000	**Debt/ Equity:**	1.2866

Penn Virginia Resource Partners LP

3 Radnor Corporate Ctr., Ste. 300, 100 Matsonford Rd., Radnor, PA, 19087; ***PH:*** 1-610-687-8900; ***Fax:*** 1-610-687-3688; ***http://*** www.pvresource.com

General - Incorporation .... DE
Employees..NA
Auditor ....KPMG LLP
Stk Agt...... American Stock Transfer & Trust Co.
Counsel...........................Vinson & Elkins L.L.P.
DUNS No. ....NA

Stock- Price on:12/24/2007 ....$30.71
Stock Exchange...NYSE
Ticker Symbol...PVR
Outstanding Shares 46,110,000
E.P.S..$1.66
Shareholders ....NA

Business: The groups principle activities include acquiring and managing coal properties and gathering and processing of natural gas. The group operates through two segments namely, coal and natural gas midstream. In the year 2006, the group acquired LG&E, Huff Creek, Green River and Wayland properties. The group's quarterly revenue for Sept 2007 was 260.53 millions of USD.The group operates from the United States.

Primary SIC and add'l.: 6519 4922 0831

CIK No: 0001144945

Subsidiaries: Connect Energy Services, LLC, Fieldcrest Resources LLC, K Rail LLC, Loadout LLC, Penn Virginia Operating Co., LLC, PVR Gas Resources, LLC, PVR Midstream LLC, Suncrest Resources LLC, Toney Fork LLC, Wise LLC

Officers: James A. Dearlove/Chmn., CEO, Frank A. Pici/Dir., VP, CFO, Nancy M. Snyder/Dir., VP, General Counsel, Keith D. Horton/Dir., COO, Pres., Forrest W. McNair/VP, Controller, Ronald K. Page/VP - Corporate Development, Jim Dean/Dir. - Investor Relations

Directors: James A. Dearlove/Chmn., CEO, Edward B. Cloues/Dir., John P. Desbarres/Dir., James L. Gardner/Dir., James R. Montague/Dir., Marsha R. Perelman/Dir., Frank A. Pici/Dir., VP, CFO, Nancy M. Snyder/Dir., VP, General Counsel, Keith D. Horton/Dir., COO, Pres.

Owners: A. James Dearlove, Keith D. Horton, Marsha R. Perelman, Ronald K. Page, Penn Virginia GP Holdings, L.P/37.00%, Penn Virginia Resource GP Corp, James L. Gardner, Frank A. Pici, Insiders, John P. DesBarres, Edward B. Cloues, Penn Virgina GP Holdings, L.P/100.00%, Nancy M. Snyder, James R. Montague

Financial Data: *Fiscal Year End:*12/31 *Latest Annual Data:* 12/31/2006

Year	Sales	Net Income
2006	$517,891,000	$73,928,000
2005	$446,348,000	$51,161,000
2004	$75,630,000	$34,315,000

Curr. Assets:	$81,463,000	**Curr. Liab.:**	$88,080,000	**P/E Ratio:**	18.50
Plant, Equip.:	$556,513,000	**Total Liab.:**	$311,843,000	**Indic. Yr. Divd.:**	$1.640
Total Assets:	$714,023,000	**Net Worth:**	$402,180,000	**Debt/ Equity:**	0.5458

Penn West Energy Trust

425 First St., S.w., Calgary, AB, T2P3L8; ; ***http://*** www.pennwest.com

General - Incorporation ....AO
Employees..700
Auditor ....KPMG LLP
Stk Agt..................................Mellon Trust Co
Counsel................. Burnet, Duckworth & Palmer
DUNS No. ....NA

Stock- Price on:12/24/2007 ....$33.51
Stock Exchange...NYSE
Ticker Symbol..PWE
Outstanding Shares ....NA
E.P.S..$0.84
Shareholders ....NA

Business: The groups principal activity is to provide natural gas and oil properties. The group operates from the Canada.

Primary SIC and add'l.: 6792 1311 1321

CIK No: 0001334388

Officers: William E. Andrew/Dir., Pres. - Zceo, David W. Middleton/COO, Exec. VP, Thane A.E. Jensen/Sr. VP - Exploration, Development, Todd Takeyasu/Sr. VP, CFO, William Tang Kong/Sr. VP - Corporate Development, Kristian Tange/VP - Business Development, Anne Thomson/VP - Exploration South, Gregg Gegunde/VP - Development North, Eric Obreiter/VP - Production, Lucas Law/VP - Asset Management, Keith Luft/VP - Land, Legal, Brett Frostad/VP - Exploration North, Don Wood/VP - Development South

Directors: William E. Andrew/Dir., Pres. - Zceo, John A. Brussa/Chmn., Thomas E. Phillips/Dir., James C. Smith/Dir., Murray R. Nunns/Dir., George H. Brookman/Dir., James E. Allard/Dir., Frank Potter/Dir., Shirley A. McClellan(/Dir.

Financial Data: *Fiscal Year End:*12/31 *Latest Annual Data:* 12/31/2006

Year	Sales	Net Income
2006	$1,519,180,000	$547,897,000

Curr. Assets:	$324,962,000	Curr. Liab.:	$398,759,000	P/E Ratio:	18.50
Plant, Equip.:	$6,040,166,000	Total Liab.:	$8,980,446,000	Indic. Yr. Divd.:	$3.850
Total Assets:	$6,924,610,000	Net Worth:	-$2,055,836,000	Debt/ Equity:	NA

Pennichuck Corp

25 Manchester St., Merrimack, NH, 03054; **PH:** 1-603-882-5191; **Fax:** 1-603-882-4125; *http://* www.pennichuck.com

General - Incorporation	NH	**Stock**- Price on:12/24/2007	$24.94
Employees	101	Stock Exchange	NDQ
Auditor	PricewaterhouseCoopers LLP	Ticker Symbol	PNNW
Stk Agt	American Stock Transfer & Trust Co.	Outstanding Shares	4,220,000
Counsel	NA	E.P.S.	$0.62
DUNS No.	00-697-1436	Shareholders	NA

Business: The group's principal activities are to collect, store, treat, distribute and sell potable water throughout southern and central New Hampshire. The operations are conducted through three segments. The water utility segment is involved in collecting, treating and distribution of water for domestic, industrial, commercial and fire protection services. Real estate segment is involved in the ownership, development, management and sale of property. Contract operations and other segment is involved in the contracts and laboratory testing activities. It serves approximately 29,400 residential, industrial and commercial customers. The group also conducts non-regulated, water related management services and contract operations. It operates through its wholly owned subsidiaries, pennichuck water works inc, pennichuck east utility inc and pittsfield aqueduct company inc.

Primary SIC and add'l.: 6552 4941

CIK No: 0000788885

Subsidiaries: Pennichuck Water Service Corporation, Southwood Corporation

Officers: Duane C. Montopoli/CEO, Pres./$244,381.00, Michael C.J. Fallon/61/Executive Officer/$195,464.00, Bonalyn J. Hartley/63/VP - Administration, Donald L. Ware/51/Pres., Sr. VP - Operations, Chief Engineer/$182,276.00, William D. Patterson/53/Sr. VP, VP, CFO/$213,903.00, Stephen J. Densberger/57/Exec. VP/$178,741.00

Directors: Steven F. Bolander/63/Dir., Joseph A. Bellavance/68/Dir., Michelle L. Chicoine/Dir., Martha E. O'Neill/Dir., Robert P. Keller/70/Dir., John R. Kreick/63/Dir., Hannah M. McCarthy/61/Dir., James M. Murphy/60/Dir.

Owners: Stephen J. Densberger/1.20%, Steven F. Bolander, Robert P. Keller, Michelle L. Chicoine, John R. Kreick, William D. Patterson, Martha E. O'Neill, Michael C.J. Fallon, Pictet (London) Limited/9.90%, Duane C. Montopoli, Joseph A. Bellavance, Insiders/5.30%, James M. Murphy, Donald L. Ware, Hannah M. McCarthy

Financial Data: Fiscal Year End:12/31 **Latest Annual Data:** 12/31/2006

Year	Sales	Net Income
2006	$24,481,000	$570,000
2005	$23,772,000	$477,000
2004	$23,025,000	$1,820,000

Curr. Assets:	$8,805,000	Curr. Liab.:	$5,567,000	P/E Ratio:	40.23
Plant, Equip.:	$123,482,000	Total Liab.:	$100,355,000	Indic. Yr. Divd.:	$0.660
Total Assets:	$144,905,000	Net Worth:	$44,550,000	Debt/ Equity:	1.0853

Penns Woods Bancorp Inc

115 S Main St., Jersey Shore, PA, 17740; **PH:** 1-570-322-1111; **Fax:** 1-570-322-9947; *http://* www.jssb.com

General - Incorporation	PA	**Stock**- Price on:12/24/2007	$34.65
Employees	187	Stock Exchange	NDQ
Auditor	S R Snodgrass, A.C	Ticker Symbol	PWOD
Stk Agt	Registrar & Transfer CO.	Outstanding Shares	3,890,000
Counsel	NA	E.P.S.	$2.40
DUNS No.	11-976-7226	Shareholders	NA

Business: The group's principal activities are providing commercial and retail banking services to customers through eleven branch offices and a mortgage loan center in northcentral Pennsylvania. The operating subsidiaries of the group include, the jersey shore state bank, woods real estate development company, woods investment company inc and the m group inc. The services provided by the group include accepting time, regular, savings and demand deposits, providing commercial, consumer and mortgage loans, safe deposit services and cash management services. The financial services are provided to individuals, partnerships, non-profit organizations and corporations.

Primary SIC and add'l.: 6712 6022

CIK No: 0000716605

Subsidiaries: Jersey Shore State Bank, The M Group,Inc., Woods Investment Company,Inc., Woods Real Estate Development Company,Inc.

Officers: Ronald A. Walko/Dir., CEO, Pres./$422,815.00, William H. Rockey/Dir., Sr. VP/$170,865.00, Paul R. Mamolen/COO, Sr. VP - Comprehensive Financial Group, David G. Gundy/Sr. VP - Customer Sales, Service Mgr., Thomas A. Donofrio/Exec. VP, Chief Administrative Officer/$187,522.00, Ann M. Riles/Sr. VP, Chief Credit Officer, Stephen M. Tasselli/Sr. VP, Commercial Loan Mgr., Janine E. Packer/Contact - Investor Relations, Brian L. Knepp/33/Principal Financial Officer/$88,088.00

Directors: Ronald A. Walko/Dir., CEO, Pres., William H. Rockey/Dir., Sr. VP, Michael J. Casale/Dir., James M. Furey/Dir., Lynn S. Bowes/Dir., Henry Thomas Davis/Dir., Leroy H. Keiler/Dir., Edward R. Nestlerode/Dir., Jay H. McCormick/Dir., James E. Plummer/Dir., Hubert A. Valencik/Dir., Michael D. Hawbaker/Dir.

Owners: Brian L. Knepp, Lynn S. Bowes/1.95%, Insiders/7.03%, William H. Rockey/0.82%, Leroy H. Keiler, Ronald A. Walko/0.47%, James E. Plummer/0.94%, Michael J. Casale, Jay H. McCormick/0.78%, James M. Furey, Thomas A. Donofrio/0.01%, Hubert A. Valencik/0.39%, Thomas H. Davis, Edward R. Nestlerode

Financial Data: Fiscal Year End:12/31 **Latest Annual Data:** 12/31/2006

Year	Sales	Net Income
2006	$42,782,000	$9,647,000
2005	$40,334,000	$10,901,000
2004	$38,896,000	$11,083,000

Curr. Assets:	$18,312,000	Curr. Liab.:	$431,420,000	P/E Ratio:	14.44
Plant, Equip.:	$6,737,000	Total Liab.:	$517,691,000	Indic. Yr. Divd.:	$1.760
Total Assets:	$592,285,000	Net Worth:	$74,594,000	Debt/ Equity:	1.0970

Pennsylvania Commerce Bancorp Inc

3801 Paxton St., Harrisburg, PA, 17111; **PH:** 1-717-412-6301; **Fax:** 1-717-412-6171; *http://* www.commercepc.com

General - Incorporation	PA	**Stock**- Price on:12/24/2007	$26.55
Employees	696	Stock Exchange	NDQ
Auditor	Beard Miller Co. LLP	Ticker Symbol	COBH
Stk Agt	Registrar & Transfer Co	Outstanding Shares	6,200,000
Counsel	NA	E.P.S.	$0.98
DUNS No.	NA	Shareholders	NA

Business: The group's principal activity is to provide retail and commercial banking services to consumers, small and mid-sized companies. The group is a bank holding company operating through its wholly-owned subsidiary, Commerce Bank/Harrisburg, NA. Banking products and services offered by the group include checking accounts, savings and money market accounts, certificates of deposits, individual retirement accounts, home equity loans, mortgage products, personal and education loans, business and small business loans and cash management services. The group also offers special services such as online banking, electronic banking, automated teller facilities, Visa(R) business card and merchant credit card services and others. As of 31-Dec-2003, the group had twenty-three banking offices located in Cumberland, Dauphin, Lebanon and York counties, Pennsylvania

Primary SIC and add'l.: 6719 6021

CIK No: 0001085706

Subsidiaries: Commerce Bank / Harrisburg, N.A., Commerce Harrisburg Capital Trust I, Commerce Harrisburg Capital Trust II

Officers: Gary L. Nalbandian/Chmn., CEO, Pres./$452,341.00, Peter J. Ressler/Sec., Counsel to The Board, Rory G. Ritrievi/Marketing Pres./$243,844.00, Mark A. Zody/CFO/$217,815.00, Scott D. Huggins/Chief Risk Officer/$134,714.00, Victoria G. Chieppa/Sr. VP - Operations

Directors: Gary L. Nalbandian/Chmn., CEO, Pres., Alan R. Hassman/Dir., Michael A. Serluco/Dir., Samir J. Srouji/Dir., James R. Adair/Dir., Douglas S. Gelder/Dir., John J. Cardello/Dir., Howell C. Mette/Dir., Jay W. Cleveland/Dir.

Owners: Commerce Bancorp, Inc./10.75%, Rory G. Ritrievi, Insiders/23.97%, Howell C. Mette/2.25%, Alan R. Hassman/2.57%, Scott D.Huggins, Wellington Management Company, LLP/9.30%, David B. Skerpon, Michael A. Serluco/2.85%, Samir J. Srouji/2.58%, John J. Cardello, Douglas S. Gelder/2.33%, Gary L. Nalbandian/8.52%, Mark A. Zody/1.65%, James R. Adair

Financial Data: Fiscal Year End:12/31 **Latest Annual Data:** 12/31/2006

Year	Sales	Net Income
2006	$123,303,000	$7,254,000
2005	$93,768,000	$8,817,000
2004	$72,278,000	$8,591,000

Curr. Assets:	$52,500,000	Curr. Liab.:	$1,729,577,000	P/E Ratio:	29.50
Plant, Equip.:	$83,679,000	Total Liab.:	$1,765,375,000	Indic. Yr. Divd.:	NA
Total Assets:	$1,866,483,000	Net Worth:	$101,108,000	Debt/ Equity:	0.2801

Pennsylvania Electric Co

76 S Main St., Akron, OH, 44308; **PH:** 1-800-736-3402; *http://* www.firstenergycorp.com

General - Incorporation	PA	**Stock**- Price on:12/24/2007	$64.49
Employees	13,739	Stock Exchange	NA
Auditor	PricewaterhouseCoopers LLP	Ticker Symbol	NA
Stk Agt	FirstEnergy Securities Transfer Co	Outstanding Shares	304,830,000
Counsel	NA	E.P.S.	$4.24
DUNS No.	00-896-7614	Shareholders	NA

Business: The group's principle activity is to distribute electricity on retail as well as wholesale basis. The company became a wholly owned subsidiary of firstenergy corp following its merger with gpu, inc in 2001. The company distributes and sells electric energy in an area of approximately 17,600 square miles in western Pennsylvania to a population of approximately 1.6 million. As a lessee of the property of its subsidiary, the waverly electric light & power, the company also serves a population of about 13,400 in waverly, New York and vicinity. It also purchases, sells and interchanges electrical energy with other electric companies. The group operates from United States.

Primary SIC and add'l.: 4911

CIK No: 0000077227

Subsidiaries: American Transmission Systems, Inc., Centerior Service Company, FE Acquisition Corp., FELHC, Inc., FirstEnergy Facilities Services Group, FirstEnergy Foundation, FirstEnergy Nuclear Generation Corp., FirstEnergy Nuclear Operating Company, FirstEnergy Properties Company, FirstEnergy Securities Transfer Company, FirstEnergy Service Company, FirstEnergy Solutions Corp., FirstEnergy Telecom Services, FirstEnergy Ventures Corp., GPU Capital, Inc. 26 Subsidiaries included in the Index

Officers: A. J. Alexander/56/Dir., CEO, Pres., Leila L. Vespoli/48/Sr. VP, General Counsel, D. S. Elliott/53/Pres. - Pennsylvania Operations, Harney L. Wagner/55/VP, Controller, Chief Accounting Officer, J. F. Pearson/53/VP, Treasurer, Charles E. Jones/Sr. VP - Energy Delivery, Customer Service, Richard H. Marsh/57/Dir., Sr. VP, CFO, Richard R. Grigg/59/Dir., Exec. VP, COO, K. W. Dindo/58/VP, Chief Risk Officer

Directors: A. J. Alexander/56/Dir., CEO, Pres., Richard H. Marsh/57/Dir., Sr. VP, CFO, Richard R. Grigg/59/Dir., Exec. VP, COO

Financial Data: Fiscal Year End:12/31 **Latest Annual Data:** 12/31/2006

Year	Sales	Net Income
2006	$11,501,000,000	$1,254,000,000
2005	$11,989,000,000	$861,000,000
2004	$12,453,046,000	$878,175,000

Curr. Assets:	$2,083,000,000	Curr. Liab.:	$5,255,000,000	P/E Ratio:	15.88
Plant, Equip.:	$14,667,000,000	Total Liab.:	$22,161,000,000	Indic. Yr. Divd.:	$2.000
Total Assets:	$31,196,000,000	Net Worth:	$9,035,000,000	Debt/ Equity:	1.0297

Pennsylvania Power Co

1 E Washington St., New Castle, PA, 16103; **PH:** 1-800-736-3402; *http://* www.pennpower.com

General - Incorporation	PA	**Stock**- Price on:12/24/2007	NA
Employees	NA	Stock Exchange	NA
Auditor	PricewaterhouseCoopers LLP	Ticker Symbol	NA
Stk Agt	StockTrans, Inc.	Outstanding Shares	NA
Counsel	NA	E.P.S.	NA
DUNS No.	00-791-2736	Shareholders	NA

Business: The group's principle activity is to provide electric services to customers. The company primarily provides electric service to residential, commercial and industrial customers in western Pennsylvania. The retail customers of the company are metered on a cycle basis. The group operates from United States.

Primary SIC and add'l.: 4911

CIK No: 0000077278

Subsidiaries: Met-Ed Funding LLC, York Haven Power Company

Pennsylvania Real Estate Investment Trust

The Bellevue, 200 S. Broad St., Philadelphia, PA, 19102; *PH:* 1-215-875-0700; *Fax:* 1-215-546-7311; *http://* www.preit.com

General - Incorporation	PA	Stock - Price on:12/24/2007	$43.25
Employees	887	Stock Exchange	NYSE
Auditor	KPMG LLP	Ticker Symbol	PEI
Stk Agt	Wells Fargo Bank, N.A.	Outstanding Shares	37,110,000
Counsel	NA	E.P.S.	$0.59
DUNS No.	NA	Shareholders	NA

Business: The groups principle activities include acquiring and investing in retail properties. In the year 2006, the group acquired three Strawbridges department stores. The group operates from the United States.

Primary SIC and add'l.: 6798

CIK No: 0000077281

Subsidiaries: 1150 Plymouth Associates, Inc., ALRO Associates, L.P., CD Development LLC, Cherry Hill Beverage II, LLC, Cherry Hill Beverage, Inc., Cherry Hill Center, LLC, Cumberland Mall Associates, Cumberland Mall Retail Condominium Association, LLC, Echelon Beverage LLC, Echelon Residential Unit Owner LLC, Echelon Title, LLC, Exton License II, LLC, Exton License, Inc., Exton Square 1, LLC, Exton Square 10, LLC 201 Subsidiaries included in the Index

Officers: Ronald Rubin/76/Trustee, Chmn., CEO/$1,828,924.00, Timothy M. Tremel/VP - Construction, Design Services, Andrew H. Bottaro/VP - Development, Daniel M. Scott/VP - Anchor, Outparcel Leasing, Harvey Diamond/Exec. VP - Site Acquisitions, Ernie Brennsteiner/VP - Mall Leasing, Daniel Donley/VP - Asset Management, Cheryl K. Dougherty/VP - Marketing, Michael Fenchak/VP - Asset Management, Richard Zeigler/VP - Development, Sean C. Byrne/VP - Mall Leasing/$4,116,884.00, Beth Desista/VP - Specialty Leasing, Tim Havener/VP - Mall Leasing, Andrew M. Ioannou/VP - Capital Markets, Treasurer, Debra Lambert/VP - Legal *(32 Officers included in Index)*

Directors: Ronald Rubin/76/Trustee, Chmn., CEO, George F. Rubin/65/Trustee, Vice Chmn., John J. Roberts/63/Trustee, Walter D'Alessio/73/Trustee, Stephen B. Cohen/62/Trustee, Joseph F. Coradino/56/Trustee, Donald F. Mazziotti/62/Trustee, Mark E. Pasquerilla/48/Trustee, Edward Glickman/50/Trustee, COO, Pres., Rosemarie B. Greco/62/Trustee, Lee H. Javitch/77/Trustee, Leonard I. Korman/72/Trustee, Ira M. Lubert/58/Trustee

Owners: Barclays Global Investors, NA/9.80%, ING Group N.V./7.00%, The Vanguard Group, Inc./5.60%

Financial Data: *Fiscal Year End:* 12/31 *Latest Annual Data:* 12/31/2006

Year		Sales		Net Income
2006		$464,570,000		$28,021,000
2005		$429,659,000		$57,629,000
2004		$406,249,000		$53,788,000
Curr. Assets:	$61,873,000	Curr. Liab.:	$105,754,000	P/E Ratio: 72.08
Plant, Equip.:	$2,826,878,000	Total Liab.:	$2,216,309,000	Indic. Yr. Divd.: $2.280
Total Assets:	$3,145,609,000	Net Worth:	$929,300,000	Debt/ Equity: 2.1278

Penseco Financial Services Corp

150 N Washington Ave., Scranton, PA, 18503; *PH:* 1-570-346-7741; *Fax:* 1-570-969-2743; *http://* www.pennsecurity.com

General - Incorporation	PA	Stock - Price on:12/24/2007	$39.79
Employees	171	Stock Exchange	OTC
Auditor	McGrail Merkel Quinn & Assoc.	Ticker Symbol	PFNS
Stk Agt	Penn Security Bank & Trust Co	Outstanding Shares	2,150,000
Counsel	NA	E.P.S.	$3.05
DUNS No.	NA	Shareholders	NA

Business: The group's principal activity is to provide banking services to individual and corporate customers in northeastern Pennsylvania. It operates through nine banking offices. The group's deposit account includes individual retirement accounts, money market accounts, now accounts, savings accounts and time open accounts. The lending products of the group include appliance loans, automobile loans, business loans, collateral loans, commercial equipment leasing, construction loans, cosmic card like debit card and check card, educational loans, home loans, installment loans, mastercard and visa, residential and commercial mortgage loans and consumer loans. The other services include ATM services, data processing services, home banking services, Internet banking services, investor services, lockbox services and trust department services. The group operates solely in the domestic market.

Primary SIC and add'l.: 6712 6022

CIK No: 0001054508

Subsidiaries: Penseco Realty

Officers: Pam Edwards/Mgr. - North Pocono Office, Penn Security Bank, Trust Company, Frank Gardner/Mgr. - East Scranton Office, Penn Security Bank, Trust Company, Robin Jenkins/Mgr. - Gouldsboro Office, Penn Security Bank, Trust Company, Elisa Rosario/Mgr. - East Stroudsburg Office, Kristin McGoff/Mgr. - South Side Office, Penn Security Bank, Trust Company, Carl Baruffaldi/Mgr. - Central City Office, Penn Security Bank, Trust Company, Susan Holweg/Mgr. - Abington Office, Penn Security Bank, Trust Company, Dominic Gianuzzi/Mgr. - Green Ridge Office, Penn Security Bank, Trust Company, Susan Kopp/Mgr. - Mount Pocono Office, Penn Security Bank, Trust Company

Owners: Steven L. Weinberger, Sandra C. Phillips/3.50%, William D. Hume, Otto P. Robinson/3.50%, Andrew A. Kettel, Emily S. Perry, Robert W. Naismith/1.40%, Edwin J. Butler/1.00%, Craig W. Best, Richard E. Grimm, Russell C. Hazelton, Patrick Scanlon, Insiders/13.70%, Peter F. Moylan, James B. Nicholas *(17 Owners included in Index)*

Financial Data: *Fiscal Year End:* 12/31 *Latest Annual Data:* 12/31/2006

Year		Sales		Net Income
2006		$40,127,000		$6,008,000
2005		$37,057,000		$5,869,000
2004		$34,979,000		$5,601,000
Curr. Assets:	$18,410,000	Curr. Liab.:	$434,199,000	P/E Ratio: 13.67
Plant, Equip.:	$9,471,000	Total Liab.:	$503,250,000	Indic. Yr. Divd.: $1.480
Total Assets:	$569,821,000	Net Worth:	$66,571,000	Debt/ Equity: 0.9399

Penson Worldwide Inc

1700 Pacific Ave., Ste. 1400, Dallas, TX, 75201; *PH:* 1-214-765-1100; *Fax:* 1-214-217-4978; *http://* www.penson.com

General - Incorporation	DE	Stock - Price on:12/24/2007	$25.87
Employees	763	Stock Exchange	NDQ
Auditor	BDO Seidman, LLP	Ticker Symbol	PNSN
Stk Agt	Continental Stock Transfer & Trust Co	Outstanding Shares	26,630,000
Counsel	NA	E.P.S.	$0.92
DUNS No.	NA	Shareholders	NA

Business: The groups principle activity is to provide critical securities and futures processing infrastructure products and services. Customers served by the group include online, direct access and traditional retail brokers. The group operates from the United States, Canada and other.

Primary SIC and add'l.: 6221 6211 6289 6211 6289 6221

CIK No: 0001123541

Subsidiaries: GHP1, Inc., GHP2, LLC, Market Essentials Group, Inc., Nexa Technologies, Inc., Penson Asia Limited, Penson Financial Futures, Inc., Penson Financial Services Canada Inc., Penson Financial Services Limited, Penson Financial Services, Inc., Penson GHCO, Penson Holdings, Inc., Penson Ventures, Inc., SAH, Inc., SAI Holdings, Inc., Turnpike Trading Systems, Inc. 16 Subsidiaries included in the Index

Officers: Philip A. Pendergraft/Dir., CEO, Daniel P. Son/Dir., Pres./$1,763,246.00, Kevin W. McAleer/Sr. VP, CFO/$623,997.00, Andrew B. Koslow/Sr. VP, General Counsel/$1,113,656.00, Andy Koslow/Sr. VP - Strategic Investments

Directors: Philip A. Pendergraft/Dir., CEO, Roger J. Engemoen/Chmn., Daniel P. Son/Dir., Pres., John L. Drew/Dir., James S. Dyer/Dir., Kelly J. Gray/Dir., William D. Gross/Dir., David Johnson/Dir., Thomas R. Johnson/Dir., David M. Kelly/Dir., David A. Reed/Dir., Roanld G. Steinhart/Dir.

Owners: John L. Drew/15.30%, Thomas R. Johnson/4.60%, William D. Gross/3.20%, Entities affiliated with TCV V, L.P./15.30%, David M. Kelly, Kelly J. Gray/6.20%, Kevin W. McAleer, Ronald G. Steinhart, Insiders/47.70%, Andrew Koslow, T. Rowe Price Associates, Inc./7.10%, David A. Reed, David R. Henkel, James S. Dyer, David Johnson

Financial Data: *Fiscal Year End:* 12/31 *Latest Annual Data:* 12/31/2006

Year		Sales		Net Income
2006		$287,618,000		$24,522,000
2005		$174,568,000		$2,904,000
2004		$116,064,000		$7,753,000
Curr. Assets:	$2,375,775,000	Curr. Liab.:	$2,833,211,000	
Plant, Equip.:	$18,698,000	Total Liab.:	$4,432,606,000	Indic. Yr. Divd.: NA
Total Assets:	$4,644,390,000	Net Worth:	$211,784,000	Debt/ Equity: 6.6781

Pentair Inc

5500 Wayzata Blvd., Ste. 800, Golden Valley, MN, 55416; *PH:* 1-763-545-1730; *Fax:* 1-763-656-5400; *http://* www.pentair.com

General - Incorporation	MN	Stock - Price on:12/24/2007	$38.02
Employees	14,800	Stock Exchange	NYSE
Auditor	Deloitte & Touche LLP	Ticker Symbol	PNR
Stk Agt	Wells Fargo Bank Minnesota	Outstanding Shares	99,790,000
Counsel	NA	E.P.S.	$2.01
DUNS No.	NA	Shareholders	NA

Business: The groups principal activity is to manufacture water and technical products. The group also provides products and systems in the movement, storage, treatment, storage and enjoyment of water. The group operates through two segments namely, water and technical products. The group acquired McLean Thermal Management, Aspen Motion Technologies and APW, Ltd in the year 2005 and Jung Pumpen GmbH, Geyers Manufacturing & Design Inc and FTA Filtration, Inc. in the year 2006. The group operates from the United States. Of the total net sales in the year 2006, the United States and Canada region accounted for $2,567,744, Europe $405,751 and Asia $180,974 (thousands).

Primary SIC and add'l.: 3494 3561 3629 3491 3621 3593 3679

CIK No: 0000077360

Subsidiaries: Alberta Electronic Company Limited, Aplex Industries, Inc., Apno S.A. de C.V., Aspen Motion Technologies, Inc., Axholme Resources Limited, Beijing Pentair Water Jieming Co., Ltd., Century Mfg. Co., Chansuba Pumps Private Ltd., Compool Inc., Davies Pumps & Co. Limited, Dongguan Jieming Tianyuan Water Purifying Equipment Co., Ltd., Epps Limited, EuroPentair GmbH, Everpure (Europe) B.V.B.A, Everpure (UK)Limited 128 Subsidiaries included in the Index

Officers: Randall J. Hogan/Chmn., CEO/$6,795,837.00, Michael V. Schrock/COO, Pres./$2,925,206.00, John Stauch/CFO, Exec. VP, Michael G. Meyer/VP - Treasury, Tax, Louis L. Ainsworth/Sr. VP, General Counsel, Sec./$1,949,309.00, Jack J. Dempsey/Sr. VP - Operations, Technology, Frederick S. Koury/Sr. VP - Human Resources

Directors: Randall J. Hogan/Chmn., CEO, Richard J. Cathcart/Vice Chmn., Barbara B. Grogan/Dir., Charles A. Haggerty/Dir., David A. Jones/Dir., Augusto Meozzi/Dir., Ronald L. Merriman/Dir., William T. Monahan/Dir., Karen E. Welke/Dir., Michael T. Glenn/Dir., David H.Y. Ho/Dir., Glynis A. Bryan/Dir.

Owners: Louis L. Ainsworth, Augusto Meozzi, Charles A. Haggerty, Ronald L. Merriman, Insiders/4.50%, Michael V. Schrock, Glynis A. Bryan, Barbara B. Grogan, Karen E. Welke, David A. Jones, David D. Harrison, William T. Monahan, Randall J. Hogan/2.00%, Richard J. Cathcart

Financial Data: *Fiscal Year End:* 12/31 *Latest Annual Data:* 12/31/2006

Year		Sales		Net Income
2006		$3,154,469,000		$183,731,000
2005		$2,946,579,000		$185,049,000
2004		$2,278,129,000		$171,225,000
Curr. Assets:	$957,628,000	Curr. Liab.:	$521,282,000	P/E Ratio: 72.08
Plant, Equip.:	$330,372,000	Total Liab.:	$1,694,980,000	Indic. Yr. Divd.: $0.600
Total Assets:	$3,364,979,000	Net Worth:	$1,669,999,000	Debt/ Equity: NA

Penton Media Inc

1300 E Ninth St., Cleveland, OH, 44114; *PH:* 1-216-696-7000; *http://* www.penton.com

General - Incorporation	DE	Stock- Price on:12/24/2007	NA
Employees	703	Stock Exchange	NA
Auditor	PricewaterhouseCoopers LLP	Ticker Symbol	NA
Stk Agt	NC Bank Shareholder Srvcs Ops	Outstanding Shares	NA
Counsel	Jones Day	E.P.S.	NA
DUNS No.	08-015-3844	Shareholders	NA

Business: The group's principal activity is to produce market-focused magazines, websites, trade shows and conferences. The integrated media portfolios of the group are divided into four segments comprising of the market sectors, industry media; technology media; lifestyle media and retail media. Industry media caters to the engineering, government compliance, manufacturing, mechanical systems construction, supply chain and aviation industries. The technology media serves in the electronics, information technology and Internet broadband industry sectors. The lifestyle media segment serves customers in the natural products industry sector whereas; the retail media segment serves customers in the retail food and leisure hospitality industry sectors.

Primary SIC and add'l.: 7319 2721

CIK No: 0001062441

Subsidiaries: Duke Communications International, Inc., Duke Investments, Inc, DVGM & Associates, Internet World Media, Inc., Penton Media Asia Limited, Penton Media Australia Pty. Limited

Officers: John French/CEO, Lisa Parks/VP - Production, Jerry Okabe/VP - Audience Marketing, Circulation, Darrell C. Denny/Exec. VP - Lifestyle Media Group, Bob Moraczewski/Sr. VP - Agricultural, Transportation, Public Services Group, Robert Feinberg/VP, General Counsel, Corp. Sec., Blair Johnson/VP - Business Development, Kurt Nelson/VP - Human Resources, Steve Martin/Corporate Controller, Margaret Pederson/Pres. - Penton Exhibitions Group, Eric Lundberg/CFO, Exec. VP, Warren Bimblick/Sr. VP - Financial Services, Marketing Media Group, David Blansfield/Sr. VP - Design Engineering Group, Shawn Etheridge/Sr. VP - Information Products Group, Eric Jacobson/Sr. VP - Administration *(18 Officers included in Index)*

Penwest Pharmaceuticals Co

39 Old Ridgebury Rd., Ste. 11, Danbury, CT, 06810; *PH:* 1-203-796-3700; *Fax:* 1-203-794-1393; *http://* www.penw.com; *Email:* investor@penwest.com

General - Incorporation	WA	Stock- Price on:12/24/2007	$13.33
Employees	75	Stock Exchange	NDQ
Auditor	Ernst & Young LLP	Ticker Symbol	PPCO
Stk Agt	Mellon Investor Services LLC	Outstanding Shares	23,290,000
Counsel	Wilmer Cutler Pickering H & D LLP	E.P.S.	-$1.47
DUNS No.	00-253-6456	Shareholders	NA

Business: The group's principal activity is to develop pharmaceutical products based on innovative proprietary oral drug delivery technologies. The group's technology platform is based on timerx, an extended release delivery system that is adaptable to soluble and insoluble drugs, and that is flexible for a variety of controlled released profiles. It has also developed two additional oral drug delivery systems, geminex and syncrodose. Geminex is a drug delivery system that is designed to provide independent release of different active ingredients contained in a drug. Syncrodose is a drug delivery system that is designed to release the active ingredient of a drug at the desired site and time in the digestive tract. On 27-Feb-2003 the group sold its excipient business to subsidiaries and affiliates of josef rettenmaier holding gmbh & co kg.

Primary SIC and add'l.: 2834

CIK No: 0001047188

Officers: Jennifer L. Good/Dir., CEO, Pres./$1,229,634.00, Mehrdad Abedin/VP - Information Technology, CIO, Anand R. Baichwal/Sr. VP - Licensing, Chief Scientific Officer/$502,130.00, Thomas R. Sciascia/Sr. VP, Chief Medical Officer/$670,525.00, Paul Hayes/VP - Strategic Marketing, Benjamin Palleiko/Sr. VP - Corporate Development, CFO/$713,295.00, Amale Hawi/Sr. VP - Pharmaceutical Development

Directors: Jennifer L. Good/Dir., CEO, Pres., Paul E. Freiman/Chmn., Robert Hennessey/Dir., John N. Staniforth/Dir., Peter F. Drake/Dir., Anne M. Vanlent/Dir., Christophe Bianchi/Dir., James W. Oshea/Dir., David P. Meeker/Dir.

Owners: Thomas R. Sciascia, Galleon Management, L.P./11.30%, Rolf H. Henel, Alan F. Joslyn, Next Century Growth Investors, LLC/7.20%, Visium Asset Management, LLC/9.00%, David P. Meeker, Benjamin L. Palleiko, Insiders/5.50%, Franklin Resources, Inc./5.30%, Wells Fargo & Company/5.30%, Jennifer L. Good/1.60%, Peter F. Drake, Ph.D., D.E. Shaw & Co., L.P./9.40%, Anand R. Baichwal *(19 Owners included in Index)*

Financial Data: *Fiscal Year End:*12/31 *Latest Annual Data:* 12/31/2006

Year	Sales	Net Income
2006	$3,499,000	-$31,312,000
2005	$6,213,000	-$22,898,000
2004	$5,108,000	-$23,785,000

Curr. Assets:	$43,069,000	Curr. Liab.:	$4,815,000		
Plant, Equip.:	$3,787,000	Total Liab.:	$7,621,000	Indic. Yr. Divd.:	NA
Total Assets:	$52,742,000	Net Worth:	$45,121,000	Debt/Equity:	0.2911

People's Liberation Inc

150 W Jefferson Blvd, Los Angeles, CA, 90007; *PH:* 1-213-745-2123; *Fax:* 1-213-745-2032; *http://* www.peoplesliberation.com; *Email:* info@peopleslib.com

General - Incorporation	DE	Stock- Price on:12/24/2007	$0.41
Employees	56	Stock Exchange	OTC
Auditor	Grobstein, Horwath & Company LLP	Ticker Symbol	PPLB
Stk Agt	Stalt, Inc.	Outstanding Shares	34,940,000
Counsel	NA	E.P.S.	-$0.05
DUNS No.	NA	Shareholders	NA

Business: The groups principle activities include designing, marketing and selling casual apparels. The group markets its products under the tradenames "People's Liberation" and "William Rast." In the year 2005, the group acquired Bella Rose and Versatile Entertainment, Inc. The group operates from the United States, Japan, Canada, Mexico, Germany and the United Kingdom. The group's quarterly revenue for Sep '07 was 6.24 millions of USD.

Primary SIC and add'l.: 2211

CIK No: 0000791770

Subsidiaries: Bella Rose, LLC, Rast Sourcing, LLC, Versatile Entertainment, Inc., William Rast Licensing, LLC

Officers: Colin Dyne/45/Co - Chmn., CEO, Daniel Guez/31/Co - Chmn., Dir. - Creative, Sec., Darryn Barber/CFO, Tom Nields/COO, Jennifer Wojinksi/Design Dir., Mark Kanights/Sales Dir., Edward Houston/40/Pres.

Directors: Colin Dyne/45/Co - Chmn., CEO, Daniel Guez/31/Co - Chmn., Dir. - Creative, Sec., Dean Oakey/Dir., Kevin R. Keating/67/Dir., Susan White/Dir., Troy Carter/Dir., Kenneth Wengrod/Dir.

Owners: MicroCapital Fund Ltd/7.70%, William Rast Enterprises/1.60%, Insiders/24.60%, Troy Carter, Dean Oakey/1.20%, Daniel Guez/31.10%, Thomas Nields, Kenneth Wengrod, Colin Dyne/21.50%, Darryn Barber/1.60%, Susan White

Financial Data: *Fiscal Year End:*12/31 *Latest Annual Data:* 12/31/2006

Year	Sales	Net Income
2006	$15,960,000	-$865,000
2005	$5,803,000	-$570,000

Curr. Assets:	$6,908,000	Curr. Liab.:	$2,301,000		
Plant, Equip.:	$577,000	Total Liab.:	$2,362,000	Indic. Yr. Divd.:	NA
Total Assets:	$8,207,000	Net Worth:	$5,845,000	Debt/ Equity:	NA

Peoples Bancorp

212 W 7th St., Auburn, IN, 46706; *PH:* 1-260-925-2500; *Fax:* 1-260-925-1733; *http://* www.peoplesbancorp.us

General - Incorporation	IN	Stock- Price on:12/24/2007	NA
Employees	531	Stock Exchange	NDQ
Auditor	BKD LLP	Ticker Symbol	PFDC
Stk Agt	Computershare Investor Services LLC	Outstanding Shares	NA
Counsel	Manatt, Phelps & Phillips LLP	E.P.S.	NA
DUNS No.	03-906-9448	Shareholders	NA

Business: The group's principal activity is to provide a wide range of consumer and commercial financial services. The services offered include consumer demand deposit accounts; now accounts; regular and term savings accounts; savings certificates; residential and commercial real estate loans and secured and unsecured consumer loans. The group also provides credit card services as well as enhancements to its loan and deposit products to add convenience to customers. The operations of the group are carried through 14 full service offices in north central and northeastern Indiana and south central Michigan. The group is the holding company for peoples federal savings bank and first savings bank.

Primary SIC and add'l.: 6712 6035

CIK No: 0000869004

Subsidiaries: financial institution , holding, WHEREAS

Officers: Cheryl L. Taylor/58/Sec., Maurice F. Winkler/52/Dir., Pres. - Peoples Bancorp, Peoples Federal, Steven H. Caryer/45/CFO, VP, Jeffrey L. Grate/45/VP - Retail Lending, Jeffrey H. Gatton/45/COO, Sr. VP

Directors: Richard G. Gatton/66/Chmn., Stephen R. Olson/65/Dir., Bruce S. Holwerda/51/Dir., Maurice F. Winkler/52/Dir., Pres. - Peoples Bancorp, Peoples Federal, John C. Thrapp/Dir., Douglas D. Marsh/Dir., Erica D. Dekko/39/Dir.

Owners: Erica D. Dekko, Jeffrey L. Grate, Douglas D. Marsh, Jeffery H. Gatton, Stephen R. Olson, Maurice F. Winkler/1.47%, Insiders/4.54%, Bruce S. Holwerda, John C. Thrapp, Richard G. Gatton

Peoples Bancorp Inc

1818 E Main St., Easley, SC, 29640; *PH:* 1-864-859-2265; *Fax:* 1-864-850-1538; *http://* www.peoplesbc.com

General - Incorporation	OH	Stock- Price on:12/24/2007	$18.66
Employees	NA	Stock Exchange	NDQ
Auditor	Ernst & Young LLP	Ticker Symbol	PEBO
Stk Agt	Shareowner Services	Outstanding Shares	3,150,000
Counsel	Vorys, Sater, Seymour & Pease	E.P.S.	$1.97
DUNS No.	00-450-4627	Shareholders	NA

Business: The group's principal activity is to provide a wide range of financial products and services through 49 financial service locations and 32 ATMs in Ohio, west Virginia and Kentucky. It accepts various deposits interest-bearing and non-interest bearing, savings, money market accounts and certificates of deposit. The loans provided include commercial, financial and agricultural loans, real estate mortgage and construction loans, consumer loans and credit card loans. The group also provides credit and debit cards, lease financing, corporate and personal trust services and safe deposit rental facilities and sells travelers checks, money orders and cashier's checks. It offers a full range of life, property and casualty insurance products through peoples insurance agency inc. On 09-May-2003, the group acquired Kentucky bancshares incorporated.

Primary SIC and add'l.: 6712 6021

CIK No: 0000318300

Subsidiaries: Pbna, LLC, PEBO Capital Trust I, PEBO Capital Trust II, Peoples Bank, National Association (Peoples Bank), Peoples Capital Corporation, Peoples Insurance Agency, Inc. (Peoples Insurance), Peoples Investment Company, Peoples Loan Services, Inc. (PLS)

Officers: Mark F. Bradley/38/Dir., CEO, Pres./$334,528.00, Carol A. Schneeberger/51/Exec. VP - Operations/$234,134.00, Joseph S. Yazombek/54/Exec. VP, Chief Lending Officer/$309,457.00, Larry E. Holdren/60/Exec. VP/$263,952.00, David T. Wesel/46/Exec. VP, Donald J. Landers/49/CFO, Treasurer/$193,345.00, Rhonda L. Mears/Corp. Sec.

Directors: Mark F. Bradley/38/Dir., CEO, Pres., Paul T. Theisen/77/Vice Chmn., Joseph H. Wesel/78/Chmn., Thomas J. Wolf/61/Dir., David L. Mead/52/Dir., Frank L. Christy/60/Dir., Robert W. Price/44/Dir., Theodore P. Sauber/74/Dir., Carl L. Baker/45/Dir., George W. Broughton/50/Dir., Wilford D. Dimit/73/Dir., Richard Ferguson/61/Dir.

Owners: Peoples Bank - Trustee/9.70%, Thomas J. Wolf, Dimensional Fund Advisors LP/6.85%, Joseph S. Yazombek, Donald J. Landers, Paul T. Theisen, David L. Mead, John W. Conlon, Frank L. Christy, Larry E. Holdren, Carl L. Baker, Joseph H. Wesel, Carol A. Schneeberger, Insiders/8.49%, George W. Broughton/1.74% *(21 Owners included in Index)*

Financial Data: *Fiscal Year End:*12/31 *Latest Annual Data:* 9/30/2006

Year	Sales	Net Income
2006	$30,713,000	$3,252,000
2004	$28,980,000	$4,734,000
2003	$32,462,000	$5,749,000

Curr. Assets: $15,805,000 **Curr. Liab.:** $435,522,000 **P/E Ratio:** 21.95
Plant, Equip.: $5,704,000 **Total Liab.:** $438,579,000 **Indic. Yr. Divd.:** $0.880
Total Assets: $501,354,000 **Net Worth:** $62,775,000 **Debt/ Equity:** NA

Peoples Bancorp Inc/MD

PO Box 210, Chestertown, MD, 21620; *PH:* 1-410-778-3500; *http://* www.pbkc.com; *Email:* main@pbkc.com

General - Incorporation MD
Employees 547
Auditor Rowles & Co LLP
Stk Agt Peoples Bank of Kent County, Maryland
Counsel NA
DUNS No. NA

Stock- Price on:12/24/2007 $27.89
Stock Exchange OTC
Ticker Symbol PEBC
Outstanding Shares 10,520,000
E.P.S. $1.97
Shareholders NA

Business: The group's principal activities are to provide deposit services and loans to individuals, small businesses, associations and government entities through five branches in kent and queen anne's countries. It offers a full range of deposit services including checking accounts, now accounts, savings and other time deposits. The group provides short to medium term commercial and personal loans, including loans for working capital, purchase of machinery and equipment, loans for financing automobiles, home improvements, education and personal investments. It also originates mortgage loans, real estate construction and acquisition loans. The other services include cash management services, safe deposit boxes, Internet banking, credit card services, direct deposit of payroll and social security checks, automated teller machine services and travelers checks.

Primary SIC and add'l.: 6712 6022

CIK No: 0001060244

Subsidiaries: Peoples Bancorp, Inc.

Officers: Benge H. Simmons/Pres., Bates L. Russell/VP, Irving W. Walker/Sec., Parks A. Rasin/Cashier

Owners: Elizabeth A. Strong, Patricia Joan Ozman Horsey/7.77%, Alexander P. Rasin/7.31%, Insiders/5.95%, Residuary Trust/5.95%, LaMonte E. Cooke, Jean E. Anthony, William G. Wheatley, Thomas G. Stevenson/1.28%, Nylon Capital Shopping Center, Inc./7.49%, Stefan R. Skipp/4.19%, Robert W. Clark, Herman E. Hill/1.36%, Gary B. Fellows, Patrick P. McClary

Financial Data: *Fiscal Year End:*12/31 *Latest Annual Data:* 12/31/2006

Year	Sales	Net Income
2006	$139,919,000	$21,558,000
2005	$124,942,000	$20,499,000
2004	$112,278,000	$18,275,000

Curr. Assets: $39,806,000 **Curr. Liab.:** $1,447,881,000 **P/E Ratio:** 14.16
Plant, Equip.: $23,455,000 **Total Liab.:** $1,678,086,000 **Indic. Yr. Divd.:** $0.880
Total Assets: $1,875,255,000 **Net Worth:** $197,169,000 **Debt/ Equity:** 1.1675

Peoples Bancorp of North Carolina Inc

518 W C St., Newton, NC, 28658; *PH:* 1-828-464-5620; *Fax:* 1-828-466-1747; *http://* www.peoplesbanknc.com

General - Incorporation NC
Employees 239
Auditor Porter Keadle Moore LLP
Stk Agt Registrar & Transfer Co
Counsel NA
DUNS No. NA

Stock- Price on:12/24/2007 $19.4062
Stock Exchange NDQ
Ticker Symbol PEBK
Outstanding Shares 5,760,000
E.P.S. $1.662
Shareholders NA

Business: The group's principal activities are to provide a full range of commercial and consumer banking services in North Carolina. It has a diversified loan portfolio including agricultural loans, real estate loans and commercial loans. The majority of the group's deposit and loan customers are individuals and small to medium-sized businesses. The group also provides investment counseling and non-deposit investment products such as stocks, bonds, mutual funds, tax deferred annuities and related brokerage services and real estate appraisal and real estate brokerage services. The group operates through 15 offices located in lincolnton, newton, denver, catawba, conover, maiden, claremont, hiddenite, and hickory, North Carolina.

Primary SIC and add'l.: 6712 6022

CIK No: 0001093672

Subsidiaries: Delaware statutory trust, PEBK Capital Trust I, Peoples Investment Services, Inc, Real Estate Advisory Services, Inc

Officers: Tony W. Wolfe/CEO, Pres./$453,980.00, William D. Cable/Exec. VP, Assist. Corporate Treasurer/$198,626.00, Benjamin I. Zachary/Dir. - Peoples Bank, John W. Lineberger/Dir. - Peoples Bank, Joseph F. Beaman/Exec. VP, Corp. Sec./$193,000.00, Lance A. Sellers/Exec. VP, Assist. Corp. Sec./$248,018.00, Joseph A. Lampron/Exec. VP, CFO, Corporate Treasurer/$204,918.00

Directors: Robert C. Abernethy/Chmn., James S. Abernethy/Dir. - Peoples Bank, Billy L. Price/Dir. - Peoples Bank, Greg W. Terry/Dir. - Peoples Bank, Dan Ray Timmerman/Dir. - Peoples Bank, Douglas S. Howard/Dir. - Peoples Bank, Larry E. Robinson/Dir. - Peoples Bank, Gary E. Matthews/Dir. - Peoples Bank

Owners: Gary E. Matthews, Douglas S. Howard, Joseph A. Lampron, William D. Cable, Tontine Partners, LP/9.03%, Billy L. Price, Christine S. Abernethy/11.15%, Larry E. Robinson, James S. Abernethy/2.97%, Insiders/11.86%, Banc Funds Company, LLC/6.14%, Lance A. Sellers, John W. Lineberger, Robert C. Abernethy/3.51%, Joseph F. Beaman *(19 Owners included in Index)*

Financial Data: *Fiscal Year End:*12/31 *Latest Annual Data:* 12/31/2006

Year	Sales	Net Income
2006	$63,647,000	$9,171,000
2005	$50,835,000	$6,331,000
2004	$42,556,000	$4,431,000

Curr. Assets: $31,644,000 **Curr. Liab.:** $733,893,000 **P/E Ratio:** 11.83
Plant, Equip.: $12,816,000 **Total Liab.:** $756,112,000 **Indic. Yr. Divd.:** $0.240
Total Assets: $818,948,000 **Net Worth:** $62,835,000 **Debt/ Equity:** 0.3289

Peoples Bancorporation Inc

1818 E Main St., Easley, SC, 29640; *PH:* 1-864-859-2265; *Fax:* 1-864-850-1538; *http://* www.peoplesbc.com

General - Incorporation SC
Employees 128
Auditor Elliot Davis LLC
Stk Agt Registrar & Transfer Co
Counsel NA
DUNS No. 15-187-7222

Stock- Price on:12/24/2007 $11.99
Stock Exchange OTC
Ticker Symbol PBCE
Outstanding Shares 6,720,000
E.P.S. $0.64
Shareholders NA

Business: The group's principal activities are to provide a variety of banking services. The services of the group include offering checking accounts, now accounts, savings and other time deposits of various types, daily repurchase agreements, and alternative investment products such as annuities, mutual funds, stocks and bonds. The group's lending products include, loans for business, agriculture, real estate, personal uses, home improvement and automobiles, credit cards, letters of credit, home equity lines of credit, accounts receivable financing program and wholesale mortgage lending program. In addition, it provides safe deposit boxes, bank money orders, write transfer services and use of automatic teller machine facilities. The group conducts its business from seven banking offices located in South Carolina.

Primary SIC and add'l.: 6712 6021

CIK No: 0000885542

Subsidiaries: Bank of Anderson, National Association, Seneca National Bank, The Peoples National Bank

Officers: Riggie R. Ridgeway/Dir., CEO, Pres./$409,622.00, Andrew L. Westbrook/45/Pres., CEO - Peoples National Bank, Bank, Anderson/$296,261.00, Patricia A. Jensen/Sr. VP, Robert E. Dye/Dir., CFO, Sr. VP/$159,298.00, William B. West/Dir., Sr. VP, CFO, Exec. VP, Treasurer/$220,173.00

Directors: Riggie R. Ridgeway/Dir., CEO, Pres., Smyth E. McKissick/Vice Chmn., George B. Nalley/Chmn., Garnet A. Barnes/Dir., A. J. Thompson/Dir., Robert E. Dye/Dir., CFO, Sr. VP, Nell W. Smith/Dir., Larry D. Reeves/Dir., James A. Black/Dir., William A. Carr/Dir., William B. West/Dir., Sr. VP, CFO, Exec. VP, Treasurer, Charles E. Dalton/Dir., Andrew M. McFall/Dir., Rutledge W. Galloway/Dir., Eugene W. Merritt/Dir. *(22 Directors included in Index)*

Owners: Insiders/22.54%, Riggie R. Ridgeway/1.64%, Gray D. Suggs, William R. Rowan, Smyth E. McKissick/2.40%, Nell W. Smith/0.52%, William B. West/0.51%, Andrew M. McFall, Charles E. Dalton/0.55%, Eugene W. Merritt/0.86%, Timothy J. Reed/0.01%, A. J. Thompson/2.63%, Rutledge W. Galloway/2.34%, George Weston Nalley/0.40%, Alexander C. Dye/6.44% *(21 Owners included in Index)*

Financial Data: *Fiscal Year End:*12/31 *Latest Annual Data:* 12/31/2006

Year	Sales	Net Income
2006	$35,688,000	$4,486,000
2005	$29,899,000	$4,128,000
2004	$26,059,000	$3,528,000

Curr. Assets: $26,484,000 **Curr. Liab.:** $456,339,000 **P/E Ratio:** 17.38
Plant, Equip.: $11,117,000 **Total Liab.:** $457,750,000 **Indic. Yr. Divd.:** $0.190
Total Assets: $503,814,000 **Net Worth:** $46,064,000 **Debt/ Equity:** 0.2961

Peoples BancTrust Co Inc

310 Brd. St. , Selma, AL, 36701; *PH:* 1-334-875-1000; *http://* www.peoplesbt.com

General - Incorporation AL
Employees 275
Auditor Mauldin & Jenkins, LLC
Stk Agt Registrar & Transfer Co
Counsel NA
DUNS No. 15-650-6982

Stock- Price on:12/24/2007 $24.69
Stock Exchange NA
Ticker Symbol NA
Outstanding Shares 5,930,000
E.P.S. NA
Shareholders NA

Business: The group's principal activities are providing commercial and retail banking services. It is a holding company operating through the peoples bank and trust company. In addition to accepting deposits and lending loans, the group also offers sale of traveler's checks, rental of safe deposit facilities, collection of domestic and foreign items, issuance of cashier's checks and money orders, automated teller machine services, bank by mail and night depository and other customary banking services. Some of the other services offered are trust and financial management services and financial services through brokerage department and insurance agency. The services are provided to individuals and corporations in Dallas, autauga, butler, bibb, shelby, tallapossa, elmore, lee and tuscaloosa counties and surrounding areas of Alabama.

Primary SIC and add'l.: 6022 6712

CIK No: 0000762128

Subsidiaries: Consolidated Balance Sheets, Consolidated Financial Statements, Consolidated Statements of Cash Flows, Consolidated Statements of Changes in Stockholders Equity, Consolidated Statements of Comprehensive Income, Consolidated Statements of Income, Notes to Consolidated Financial Statements

Officers: Don J. Giardina/Dir., CEO, Pres., Gary Pierson/Trust Officer - People Bank, Trust Company, Clyde B. Rivers/Trust Officer - People Bank, Trust Company, Victoria Newman/Contact - Helena Branch, People Bank, Trust Company, Denise Johnson/Contact - Eclectic Branch, People Bank, Trust Company, Stephanie Stephens/Contact - Tuscaloosa County, People Bank, Trust Company, Kim Coats/Contact - Tuscaloosa Skyland Branch, People Bank, Trust Company, Thomas P. Wilbourne/39/Sr. VP, CFO, Shirley Holmes/Contact - Selma Mall Branch, People Bank, Trust Company, Charles Moss/Contact - Selma Satterfield Plaza Branch, People Bank, Trust Company, Andi Ott/Contact - Valley Grande, People Bank, Trust Company, Martha Smith/Contact - Opelika Branch, People Bank, Trust Company, Melissa Bagley/Contact - Auburn Branch, People Bank, Trust Company, Kerry Edgeworth/Contact - Prattville East Branch, People Bank, Trust Company, Norma Cassidy/Contact - Millbrook Branch, People Bank, Trust Company *(27 Officers included in Index)*

Directors: Don J. Giardina/Dir., CEO, Pres.

Owners: Johnny Crear, Julius E. Talton, Don J. Giardina, Lynn D. Swindal, The Peoples Bank and Trust Company/15.30%, Harry W. Gamble, Daniel P. Wilbanks, Thomas E. Newton, David Y. Pearce, Endurance Capital Investors, L.P./9.60%, Thomas P. Wilbourne, Andrew C. Bearden, Gerald F. Holley, Insiders/11.40%, M. Scott Patterson/3.70% *(21 Owners included in Index)*

Financial Data: *Fiscal Year End:*12/31 *Latest Annual Data:* 12/31/2006

Year	Sales	Net Income
2006	$62,878,000	$8,080,000
2005	$51,062,000	$6,537,000
2004	$45,802,000	$6,042,000

Curr. Assets: $32,402,000 **Curr. Liab.:** $772,178,000
Plant, Equip.: $26,421,000 **Total Liab.:** $823,911,000 **Indic. Yr. Divd.:** $0.520
Total Assets: $910,705,000 **Net Worth:** $86,794,000 **Debt/ Equity:** 0.5424

Peoples Bank OF COM OR

234 E First Ave., Cambridge, MI, 55008; *PH:* 1-763-689-1212; *http://* www.e-peoplesbank.com

General - Incorporation

Employees ... NA
Auditor ... NA
Stk Agt ... Mellon Investor Services LLC
Counsel ... NA
DUNS No. ... NA

Stock - Price on:12/24/2007 ... $19
Stock Exchange ... OTC
Ticker Symbol ... PBCO
Outstanding Shares ... NA
E.P.S ... NA
Shareholders ... NA

Business: The groups principle activity is to provide recruiting services. The groups service area includes the research and development, engineering, marketing, sales, information technology and manufacturing industries. The group operates from United States.

Primary SIC and add'l.: 6022

CIK No:

Officers: Andrea Ferkingstad/VP - Marketing, Corporate Communications

Peoples Community Bancorp Inc

6100 W Chester Rd., West Chester, OH, 45071; *PH:* 1-513-870-3530; *Fax:* 1-513-881-5933; *http://* www.pcbionline.com; *Email:* info@pcbionline.com

General - Incorporation ... MD
Employees ... 217
Auditor ... BKD LLP
Stk Agt ... Registrar & Transfer Co
Counsel ... NA
DUNS No. ... NA

Stock - Price on:12/24/2007 ... $16.05
Stock Exchange ... NDQ
Ticker Symbol ... PCBI
Outstanding Shares ... 4,830,000
E.P.S ... -$0.88
Shareholders ... NA

Business: The group's principal activity is to accept deposits from the general public and using those funds to originate loans and invest in securities. The group, conducts its business through its wholly owned subsidiary peoples community bank, through thirteen offices in hamilton, warren and butler counties in Ohio. The various types of loans consists of single-family mortgage loans, construction and land development loans, multi-family residential real estate loans, commercial real estate loans, home equity loans and other loans.

Primary SIC and add'l.: 6712 6035

CIK No: 0001100983

Subsidiaries: Federal Reserve

Officers: Jerry D. Williams/Dir., CEO, Pres./$259,010.00, John E. Rathkamp/Dir., Sec., Stephen P. Wood/Chief Lending Officer, Sr. VP/$151,698.00, Fred L. Darlington/51/Corp. Sec., Sr. VP, General Counsel - Peoples Community Bancorp, Rick W. Wade/COO, Sr. VP, Teresa O'Quinn/CFO, Exec. VP/$191,533.00, Thomas J. Noe/Dir., Exec. VP/$226,052.00, Lori Henn/Sr. VP, Compliance Officer/$160,654.00, Joan Woodward/Sr. VP, Dir. - Human Resources, Jerry Gore/Sr. VP, Dir. - Retail Banking

Directors: Jerry D. Williams/Dir., CEO, Pres., Paul E. Hasselbring/Chmn., John L. Buchanan/Dir., Nicholas N. Nelson/Dir., James R. Van Degrift/Dir., Donald L. Hawke/Dir., Thomas J. Noe/Dir., Exec. VP, John E. Rathkamp/Dir., Sec., Joan Woodward/Sr. VP, Dir. - Human Resources

Owners: James R. Van DeGrift, John L. Buchanan, Thomas J. Noe/9.46%, Donald L. Hawke, Insiders/18.23%, Stephen P. Wood, Paul E. Hasselbring, Lori M. Henn, Teresa A. OQuinn, Nicholas N. Nelson, John E. Rathkamp, Financial Stocks Capital Partners III L.P./8.95%, Jerry D. Williams/2.29%

Financial Data: *Fiscal Year End:*09/30 *Latest Annual Data:* 12/31/2006

Year	Sales	Net Income
2006	$68,747,000	-$4,061,000
2005	$49,920,000	$2,856,000
2004	$41,352,000	$2,869,000

Curr. Assets:	$726,549,000	**Curr. Liab.:**	$886,613,000		
Plant, Equip.:	$24,174,000	**Total Liab.:**	$919,954,000	**Indic. Yr. Divd.:**	$0.600
Total Assets:	$1,006,654,000	**Net Worth:**	$86,700,000	**Debt/ Equity:**	NA

Peoples Educational Holdings Inc

299 Market St., Saddle Brook, NJ, 07663; *PH:* 1-201-712-0090; *Fax:* 1-201-712-0045; *http://* peoplespublishing.com

General - Incorporation ... DE
Employees ... NA
Auditor ... McGladrey & Pullen LLP
Stk Agt ... Wells Fargo Shareowner Services
Counsel ... NA
DUNS No. ... NA

Stock - Price on:12/24/2007 ... $3.25
Stock Exchange ... NDQ
Ticker Symbol ... PEDH
Outstanding Shares ... 4,420,000
E.P.S ... -$0.03
Shareholders ... NA

Business: The groups principle activities include publishing and marketing supplementary educational textbooks and materials for elementary and secondary school. The group provides Test Preparation, Assessment and Instruction, and College Preparation books. The group operates from United States.

Primary SIC and add'l.: 8299 8748

CIK No: 0000729156

Subsidiaries: Peoples Publishing Group, Inc

Officers: Brian T. Beckwith/52/Dir., CEO, Pres., Diane M. Miller/56/Co - Founder, Dir., Exec. VP, Chief Creative Officer, Michael L. Demarco/44/CFO, Exec. VP

Directors: Brian T. Beckwith/52/Dir., CEO, Pres., James J. Peoples/71/Co - Founder, Chmn., Sr. Advisor, Diane M. Miller/56/Co - Founder, Dir., Exec. VP, Chief Creative Officer, Anton J. Christianson/Dir., James P. Dolan/Dir., Richard J. Casabonne/Dir., John C. Bergstrom/Dir., Thomas G. Ahern/Dir.

Owners: Diane M. Miller/7.30%, Thomas G. Ahern, Brian T. Beckwith/5.60%, NAP & CO c/o Delaware State Pension Fund/13.60%, Dolphin Offshore Partners, Inc./8.10%, James P. Dolan/1.10%, Insiders/66.30%, Richard Casabonne, John C. Bergstrom/1.30%, Michael L. DeMarco/1.50%, James J. Peoples/12.90%, Anton J. Christianson/42.60%

Financial Data: *Fiscal Year End:*12/31 *Latest Annual Data:* 12/31/2005

Year	Sales	Net Income
2005	$35,454,000	-$3,156,000
2004	$32,487,000	$1,410,000
2003	$27,815,000	$1,218,000

Curr. Assets:	$11,172,000	**Curr. Liab.:**	$8,154,000		
Plant, Equip.:	$697,000	**Total Liab.:**	$24,559,000	**Indic. Yr. Divd.:**	NA
Total Assets:	$31,751,000	**Net Worth:**	$7,192,000	**Debt/ Equity:**	NA

Peoples Financial Corp

152 Lameuse St., Biloxi, MS, 39530; *PH:* 1-228-435-5511; *Fax:* 1-228-435-8418; *http://* www.thepeoples.com

General - Incorporation ... MS
Employees ... 211
Auditor ... Piltz, Williams, LaRosa & Co
Stk Agt ... NA
Counsel ... NA
DUNS No. ... 78-216-4925

Stock - Price on:12/24/2007 ... $25.2001
Stock Exchange ... NDQ
Ticker Symbol ... PFBX
Outstanding Shares ... 5,550,000
E.P.S ... $2.23
Shareholders ... NA

Business: The group's principal activities are to provide a full range of banking, financial and trust services to individuals and small and commercial businesses. It has 15 branches and operates through locations in harrison, hancock and west jackson counties. The group is a one-bank holding company for the peoples bank. The group's deposit services include interest bearing and non-interest bearing checking accounts, savings, certificates of deposits and individual retirement accounts. The loan services include business, real estate, construction, personal and installment loans. Other services offered include asset management, trust services, safe deposit box, cash management and Internet banking.

Primary SIC and add'l.: 6022 6712

CIK No: 0000770460

Subsidiaries: Peoples Financial Corporation

Officers: Chevis C. Swetman/Chmn., CEO, Pres./$422,870.00, Thomas J. Sliman/Sr. VP, CIO - Peoples Bank/$186,258.00, Robert M. Tucei/Sr. VP, Chief Credit Officer - Peoples Bank/$201,316.00, Lauri A. Wood/CFO, Sr. VP/$160,987.00, Liz Corso Joachim/Dir. - Peoples Bank, Jeannette E. Romero/Sr. VP, Retail Banking Officer - Peoples Bank, Rex E. Kelly/Dir. - Peoples Bank, Jeffrey O'Keefe/Dir. - Peoples Bank, Wes A. Fulmer/Exec. VP, Chief Lending Officer - Peoples Bank/$189,769.00, Ann F. Guice/Sr. VP, Trust Officer - Peoples Bank

Directors: Chevis C. Swetman/Chmn., CEO, Pres., Dan Magruder/Vice Chmn., Tyrone J. Gollott/Vice Chmn. - Peoples Bank, Lyle M. Page/Dir., Drew Allen/Dir.

Owners: Robert M. Tucei, Ella Mae Barq/8.74%, Chevis C. Swetman/15.16%, Andrew Tanner Swetman/6.01%, Insiders/18.76%, Wes A. Fulmer, Jeannette E. Romero, Peoples Financial Corporation Employee/8.32%, Ann F. Guice, Lyle M. Page/2.00%, Drew Allen, Lauri A. Wood, Thomas J. Sliman, Dan Magruder, Rex E. Kelly

Financial Data: *Fiscal Year End:*12/31 *Latest Annual Data:* 12/31/2006

Year	Sales	Net Income
2006	$61,203,000	$12,768,000
2005	$40,007,000	$5,882,000
2004	$34,388,000	$5,794,000

Curr. Assets:	$52,335,000	**Curr. Liab.:**	$846,470,000	**P/E Ratio:**	11.30
Plant, Equip.:	$19,703,000	**Total Liab.:**	$865,791,000	**Indic. Yr. Divd.:**	$0.500
Total Assets:	$964,023,000	**Net Worth:**	$98,233,000	**Debt/ Equity:**	0.0714

Peoples Financial Services Corp

PO Box A, Hallstead, PA, 18822; *PH:* 1-570-879-2175; *Fax:* 1-570-879-4372; *http://* www.peoplesnatbank.com

General - Incorporation ... PA
Employees ... 106
Auditor ... Beard Miller Co. LLP
Stk Agt ... NA
Counsel ... NA
DUNS No. ... NA

Stock - Price on:12/24/2007 ... $28.16
Stock Exchange ... OTC
Ticker Symbol ... PFIS
Outstanding Shares ... 3,130,000
E.P.S ... $1.40
Shareholders ... NA

Business: The group's principal activities are to provide commercial and retail banking services to individuals, small businesses and municipalities. The operations are conducted through offices located in hallstead, hop bottom, susquehanna, montrose, nicholson, meshoppen and tunkhannock. It offers consumer loans including residential real estate loans, automobile loans, manufactured housing loans, personal installment loans, student loans and home equity loans. The other banking services include demand deposits, interest bearing transaction accounts, money market accounts, savings deposits and certificates of deposit. The group has on-site automated teller machines and operates one super market branch located in the price chopper in norwich, chenango county, New York. The other services offered include safe deposit boxes, night depository services, traveler's checks, merchant credit cards, direct deposit of payroll, us savings bonds, official bank checks and money orders.

Primary SIC and add'l.: 6712 6022

CIK No: 0001056943

Subsidiaries: Peoples Advisors, LLC, Peoples National Bank

Officers: Richard S. Lochen/Dir., CEO, Pres. - Peoples National Bank, John W. Ord/Chmn. - Peoples National Bank/$359,164.00, Debra Dissinger/Exec. VP, COO - Peoples National Bank/$113,953.00, Donald Adams/VP - Peoples National Bank, Thomas Bush/VP, Mgr. - Montrose, Peoples National Bank, Joseph Ferretti/VP - Peoples National Bank, Stephen Lawrenson/VP - Peoples National Bank, Russell Sears/VP - Peoples National Bank, Darlene Slocum/VP, Mgr. - Susquehanna, Peoples National Bank, Steven Stranburg/VP, Mgr. - Nicholson, Peoples National Bank, Eric Upright/VP, Mgr. - Hallstead, Peoples National Bank, Howard Updyke/VP - Peoples National Bank, Marjorie Eberly/Assist. VP - Peoples National Bank, Frederick Malloy/Assist. VP - Peoples National Bank, Amy Walsh/Assist. VP, Mgr. - Tunkhannock, Peoples National Bank *(27 Officers included in Index)*

Directors: Richard S. Lochen/Dir., CEO, Pres. - Peoples National Bank

Owners: Richard S. Lochen, Thomas F. Chamberlain, Insiders/6.54%, Debra E. Dissinger, Joseph M. Ferretti, William E. Aubrey, John W. Ord/2.33%, George H. Stover/2.48%, Stephen N. Lawrenson, Russell D. Shurtleff

Financial Data: *Fiscal Year End:*12/31 *Latest Annual Data:* 12/31/2006

Year	Sales	Net Income
2006	$25,488,000	$4,129,000
2005	$23,713,000	$4,476,000
2004	$22,835,000	$4,453,000

Curr. Assets:	$14,235,000	**Curr. Liab.:**	$336,890,000	**P/E Ratio:**	19.69
Plant, Equip.:	$11,245,000	**Total Liab.:**	$375,028,000	**Indic. Yr. Divd.:**	$0.760
Total Assets:	$416,268,000	**Net Worth:**	$41,240,000	**Debt/ Equity:**	0.7676

Peoples Gas Light & Coke Co

130 E Randolph Dr., Chicago, IL, 60601; *PH:* 1-312-240-4000; *http://* www.pecorp.com

General - Incorporation	IL	**Stock**- Price on:12/24/2007	NA
Employees	2,223	Stock Exchange	NA
Auditor	Deloitte & Touche LLP	Ticker Symbol	NA
Stk Agt	American Stock Transfer & Trust Co.	Outstanding Shares	NA
Counsel	NA	E.P.S	NA
DUNS No.	00-693-2115	Shareholders	NA

Business: The group's principle activities are to purchase, store, distribute and transport natural gas to approximately one million customers through a 6,000-mile distribution system serving the city of Chicago, Illinois (Chicago) and 54 communities in northeastern Illinois. The company has approximately 825,000 residential, commercial and industrial retail sales and transportation customers in Chicago.

Primary SIC and add'l.: 4924

CIK No: 0000077388

Subsidiaries: North Shore Gas Company, Peoples Elwood, LLC, Peoples Energy Production Texas, L.P., Peoples Energy Production Company, Peoples Energy Production Operating Company, Peoples Energy Production Partners, L.P., Peoples Energy Resources Company, LLC, Peoples Energy Services Corporation, PEP Holdings, LLC, PERC Power, LLC, The Peoples Gas Light and Coke Company

Officers: Robert Anderson/Major Accounting Executives, John Moran/Major Accounting Executives, David R. Zielke/Contact, Tom Nash/Major Accounting Executives, Erica L. Jenni/Contact, John Cadogan/Mgr., Jerry Weber/Supervisor, Ronald S. Beugger/Contact, Timothy J. Kois/Contact, Rick Seymour/Contact, Richard C. Clotfelter/Contact, Lolethia Hardy/Contact, James McLoughlin/Major Accounting Executives, Jim Ostrander/Major Accounting Executives

Owners: John W. Higgins, Michael E. Lavin, Thomas A. Nardi, Homer J. Livingston, Pastora San Juan Cafferty, Keith E. Bailey, Diana S. Ferguson, James R. Boris, Insiders/1.51%, William E. Morrow, Desiree G. Rogers, Thomas M. Patrick, William J. Brodsky, Richard P. Toft, Dipak C. Jain *(16 Owners included in Index)*

Peoples-Sidney Financial Corp

101 E Ct. St. , Sidney, OH, 45365; ***PH:*** 1-937-492-6129

General - Incorporation	DE	**Stock**- Price on:12/24/2007	$12.6
Employees	32	Stock Exchange	OTC
Auditor	Crowe Chizek & Co. LLC	Ticker Symbol	PSFC
Stk Agt	Registrar & Transfer Co	Outstanding Shares	1,360,000
Counsel	Katten, Muchin, Zavis & Rosenman	E.P.S	$0.82
DUNS No.	03-909-3190	Shareholders	NA

Business: The group's principal activity is to attract saving deposits from the general public and invest such funds in permanent mortgage loans secured by one- to four-family residential real estate. The deposit services of the group include checking, saving and term certificate accounts. The group originates loans for the construction of one- to four-family real estate, loans secured by multi-family real estate and non-residential real estate, consumer and commercial loans. The services are provided through the main office in sidney, Ohio and branch offices in sidney, anna and jackson centre, Ohio.

Primary SIC and add'l.: 6712 6035

CIK No: 0001031340

Subsidiaries: Peoples Federal Savings & Loan Association of Sidney

Officers: Douglas Stewart/59/DDir., CEO, Pres./$233,255.00, David R. Fogt/57/VP - Operations, Debra A. Geuy/50/CFO, Treasurer, Gary N. Fullenkamp/52/VP - Mortgage Loans, Corp. Sec.

Directors: Douglas Stewart/59/DDir., CEO, Pres., Richard T. Martin/68/Chmn., James W. Kerber/66/Dir., Harry N. Faulkner/67/Dir., Jeffery S. Sargeant/40/Dir.

Owners: Insiders/25.10%, Peoples-Sidney Financial Corporation/11.50%, Jeffery S. Sargeant/0.20%, Richard T. Martin/3.60%, Harry N. Faulkner/2.00%, Douglas Stewart/8.40%, James W. Kerber/3.40%

Financial Data: ***Fiscal Year End:***06/30 ***Latest Annual Data:*** 6/30/2006

Year	Sales	Net Income
2006	$8,550,000	$1,039,000
2005	$7,933,000	$978,000
2004	$8,046,000	$975,000

Curr. Assets:	$5,543,000	**Curr. Liab.:**	$83,280,000	**P/E Ratio:**	15.37
Plant, Equip.:	$2,075,000	**Total Liab.:**	$123,548,000	**Indic. Yr. Divd.:**	$0.640
Total Assets:	$139,047,000	**Net Worth:**	$15,500,000	**Debt/ Equity:**	2.4917

PeopleSupport Inc

1100 Glendon Ave., Ste. 1250, Los Angeles, CA, 90024; ***PH:*** 1-310-824-6200; ***Fax:*** 1-310-824-6299; ***http://*** www.peoplesupport.com; ***Email:*** investor@peoplesupport.com

General - Incorporation	DE	**Stock**- Price on:12/24/2007	$11.9
Employees	8,100	Stock Exchange	NDQ
Auditor	BDO Seidman LLP	Ticker Symbol	PSPT
Stk Agt	U.S. Stock Transfer Corp	Outstanding Shares	23,560,000
Counsel	NA	E.P.S	$0.72
DUNS No.	NA	Shareholders	NA

Business: The groups principle activity is to provide value-added customer management services. The groups markets include travel and hospitality, financial services, technology, telecommunications and consumer products industries. The groups transcription and captioning business includes transcribing voice recordings and captioning television, film and educational content. The group operates from United States.

Primary SIC and add'l.: NA

CIK No: 0001289001

Subsidiaries: PeopleSupport (Costa Rica), S.R.L, PeopleSupport (Philippines), Inc., PeopleSupport Rapidtext, Inc, ProArm Management, Inc, STC Solutions, Inc, The Transcription Company

Officers: Lance Rosenzweig/Founder, Chmn., CEO, George Hines/35/CIO, Caroline Rook/CFO, Rainerio Borja/46/Pres. - Peoplesupport, Philippines, Inc, VP - Global Operations, Tim Miller/VP - Service Delivery, Jennifer Sherry/VP - Global Human Resources, Joseph S. Duryea/VP - Sales, Bong Borja/Pres. - Peoplesupport, Philippines, Inc, VP - Global Strategic Programs, Richard Bledsoe/COO

Directors: Lance Rosenzweig/Founder, Chmn., CEO, Michael Edell/Dir., Adam Berger/Dir., Joe A. Rose/Dir., Larry C. Bradford/Dir., George H. Ellis/Dir., Frank Perna/Dir.

Owners: Frank Perna, Lance Rosenzweig/3.28%, George Hines, Joe Rose, Richard Bledsoe, George Ellis, Jennifer Sherry, Michael Edell, Joseph Duryea, Insiders/5.66%, Kingdon Capital Management/5.49%, Adam Berger, Larry C. Bradford, Rainerio Borja, Caroline Rook *(16 Owners included in Index)*

Financial Data: ***Fiscal Year End:***12/31 ***Latest Annual Data:*** 12/31/2006

Year	Sales	Net Income
2006	$110,119,000	$14,152,000
2005	$62,124,000	$22,829,000
2004	$44,511,000	$8,324,000

Curr. Assets:	$146,160,000	**Curr. Liab.:**	$21,973,000	**P/E Ratio:**	16.53
Plant, Equip.:	$22,080,000	**Total Liab.:**	$25,132,000	**Indic. Yr. Divd.:**	NA
Total Assets:	$217,591,000	**Net Worth:**	$192,430,000	**Debt/ Equity:**	NA

Pep Boys

3111 W Allegheny Ave., Philadelphia, PA, 19132; ***PH:*** 1-215-430-9000; ***Fax:*** 1-215-227-7513; ***http://*** www.pepboys.com

General - Incorporation	PA	**Stock**- Price on:12/24/2007	$21.9
Employees	14,358	Stock Exchange	NYSE
Auditor	Deloitte & Touche LLP	Ticker Symbol	PBY
Stk Agt	American Stock Transfer & Trust Co.	Outstanding Shares	51,400,000
Counsel	NA	E.P.S	-$0.25
DUNS No.	00-690-8560	Shareholders	NA

Business: The groups principle activity is to operate automotive retail stores. The groups products include tire and accessories, and brakes. The groups services include tire installation, oil change packages, repair and maintenance, preventative maintenance packages and tune-ups services. The group operates from United States.

Primary SIC and add'l.: 7538 5531

CIK No: 0000077449

Subsidiaries: Carrus Supply Corporation, Colchester Insurance Company, PBY Corporation, Pep Boys - Manny, Moe & Jack of Delaware, Inc., Pep Boys - Manny, Moe & Jack of Puerto Rico, Inc., The Pep Boys Manny Moe & Jack of California

Officers: Jeffrey C. Rachor/Dir., CEO, Pres., Mark L. Page/Sr. VP - Parts, Tires/$637,871.00, Marie Gehret/Mgr. - Communications, Mark S. Bacon/Exec. VP - Operations/$948,581.00, Bernard K. McElroy/Chief Accounting Officer, Treasurer, Harry Yanowitz/CFO/$1,432,415.00, Hal Smith/Exec. VP - Merchandising, Marketing/$1,303,975.00

Directors: Jeffrey C. Rachor/Dir., CEO, Pres., William Leonard/60/Chmn., Jane Scaccetti/54/Dir., John T. Sweetwood/60/Dir., Peter A. Bassi/58/Dir., Shan M. Atkins/51/Dir., Robert H. Hotz/63/Dir., Max L. Lukens/60/Dir., James A. Mitarotonda/53/Dir., Thomas R. Hudson/42/Dir., Nick White/63/Dir., James A. Williams/65/Dir.

Owners: James A. Mitarotonda/8.20%, Max L. Lukens, Advisory Research, Inc./9.50%, Lawrence N. Stevenson, Jeffrey C. Rachor/1.40%, Pirate Capital LLC/12.50%, William Leonard, Mark S. Bacon, Insiders/23.90%, Peter A. Bassi, Shn M. Atkins, Dimensional Fund Advisors LP/8.50%, Hal Smith, Nick White, Mark L. Page *(22 Owners included in Index)*

Financial Data: ***Fiscal Year End:***01/28 ***Latest Annual Data:*** 2/3/2007

Year	Sales	Net Income
2007	$2,272,161,000	-$2,549,000
2006	$2,235,226,000	-$37,528,000
2005	$2,272,896,000	$23,579,000

Curr. Assets:	$768,140,000	**Curr. Liab.:**	$604,180,000	**P/E Ratio:**	730.00
Plant, Equip.:	$906,247,000	**Total Liab.:**	$1,199,444,000	**Indic. Yr. Divd.:**	$0.270
Total Assets:	$1,767,199,000	**Net Worth:**	$567,755,000	**Debt/ Equity:**	NA

Pepsi Bottling Group Inc

1 Pepsi Way, Somers, NY, 10589; ***PH:*** 1-914-767-6000; ***Fax:*** 1-914-767-7761; ***http://*** www.pbg.com; ***Email:*** pbgpresscenter@pepsi.com

General - Incorporation	DE	**Stock**- Price on:12/24/2007	$34.06
Employees	70,400	Stock Exchange	NYSE
Auditor	KPMG LLP	Ticker Symbol	PBG
Stk Agt	Bank of New York	Outstanding Shares	226,830,000
Counsel	David Polk & Wardwell	E.P.S	$2.48
DUNS No.	NA	Shareholders	NA

Business: The group's principle activities include manufacturing, selling and distributing carbonated and non-carbonated pepsi-cola beverages. The group's products include pepsi-cola, diet pepsi, mountain dew, aquafina, sierra mist, lipton brisk, diet mountain dew, sobe, dole and pepsi vanilla. The group operates from United States, Mexico, Canada, Spain, Greece, and Russia.

Primary SIC and add'l.: 2086

CIK No: 0001076405

Subsidiaries: Abechuko Inversiones, S.L., Alikate Inversiones, S.L., Aquafina Inversiones, S.L., Aspetuck Ireland Limited, Avalon Lake, Sarl, Bebidas Purificadas Del Noreste, S.R.L., Bedidas Purificadas Del Sureste S.R.L., Beimiguel Inversiones, S.L., Bermuda Holdings, LLC, Bienes Raices Metropolitanos, S.R.L., Bottling Group Espana, S.L., Bottling Group Holdings, Inc., Bottling Group Servicios Centrales SL, Bottling Group, LLC, C & I Leasing, Inc. 130 Subsidiaries included in the Index

Officers: Eric J. Foss/Dir., CEO, Pres./$5,496,058.00, Andrea Forster/VP, Controller, John L. Berisford/Sr. VP - Human Resources, Yiannis Petrides/Pres. - PBG Europe/$3,025,444.00, Robert C. King/Pres. - PBG North America/$1,452,460.00, Neal A. Bronzo/CIO, Sr. VP, Thomas M. Lardieri/VP, Controller, Steven M. Rapp/Sr. VP, General Counsel, Sec., Brent J. Franks/Sr. VP, Chief Customer Officer, Pablo Lagos/Pres., GM - PBG Mexico/$1,858,943.00, Victor L. Crawford/Sr. VP - Worldwide Operations, Mary Winn Settino/VP - Investor Relations, Lori Jean Rooney/Shareholder Relations Coordinator, Alfred H. Drewes/CFO, Sr. VP/$2,169,971.00, Kathleen M. Dwyer/VP - Strategy

Directors: Eric J. Foss/Dir., CEO, Pres., Barry H. Beracha/Non - Exec. Chmn., Blythe J. McGarvie/Dir., Ira D. Hall/Dir., Hugh F. Johnston/Dir., John A. Quelch/Dir., Javier G. Teruel/Dir., Clay G. Small/Dir., Margaret D. Moore/Dir., Susan D. Kronick/Dir., Linda G. Alvarado/Dir.

Owners: Robert C. King, Yiannis Petrides, Insiders/1.50%, Thomas H. Kean, Susan D. Kronick, John T. Cahill, Clay G. Small, John A. Quelch, PepsiCo, Inc./37.80%, Barclays Global Investors/14.30%, Barry H. Beracha, Linda G. Alvarado, Pablo Lagos, Alfred H. Drewes, Margaret D. Moore *(19 Owners included in Index)*

Financial Data: ***Fiscal Year End:***12/31 ***Latest Annual Data:*** 12/30/2006

Year	Sales	Net Income
2006	$12,730,000,000	$522,000,000
2005	$11,885,000,000	$466,000,000
2004	$10,906,000,000	$457,000,000

Curr. Assets:	$2,412,000,000	**Curr. Liab.:**	$2,598,000,000	**P/E Ratio:**	15.21
Plant, Equip.:	$3,649,000,000	**Total Liab.:**	$8,985,000,000	**Indic. Yr. Divd.:**	$0.560
Total Assets:	$11,524,000,000	**Net Worth:**	$2,043,000,000	**Debt/ Equity:**	2.4220

Pepsiamericas Inc

4000 Dain Rauscher Plz., 60 S. 6th St., Minneapolis, MN, 55402; ***PH:*** 1-612-661-4000; ***Fax:*** 1-612-661-3737; ***http://*** www.pepsiamericas.com; ***Email:*** info@pepsiamericas.com

General - Incorporation .... DE
Employees 17,100
Auditor .... KPMG LLP
Stk Agt........ Wells Fargo Bank Minnesota N.A
Counsel .... Briggs & Morgan
DUNS No. .... NA

Stock - Price on:12/24/2007 .... $24.5
Stock Exchange .... NYSE
Ticker Symbol .... PAS
Outstanding Shares 128,240,000
E.P.S $1.28
Shareholders .... NA

Business: The groups principle activities include manufacturing, packing, selling and distributing carbonated pepsi cola beverages and other beverages. The group operates in United States, Poland, hungary, the czech republic, republic of slovakia, Puerto Rico, jamaica, Barbados.

Primary SIC and add'l.: 2086

CIK No: 0001084230

Subsidiaries: Beverage Plastics, LLC, Caribbean Flavors, Ltd., fka PepsiAmericas Caribbean, Inc., Caribbean Juices Limited, Central K, Inc, Cove Development Corp., DakBev, LLC, Delta Beverage Group, Inc., DiLoreto & Sons, Inc, Dove Vending, Inc., Environ of Inverrary, Inc., Favarosi Asvanyviz es Uditoipari Reszvenytarsasag, GB Czech LLC, GB International, Inc., GB Slovak, LLC, Genadco Advertising Agency, Inc. 61 Subsidiaries included in the Index

Officers: Robert C. Pohlad/52/Chmn., CEO/$3,161,941.00, Jay S. Hulbert/Sr. VP - Supply Chain, Kenneth L. Johnsen/CIO, Sr. VP, Alexander H. Ware/CFO, Exec. VP/$1,258,898.00, James R. Rogers/Exec. VP - International/$1,031,483.00, Anne D. Sample/Sr. VP - Human Resources, Kenneth E. Keiser/COO, Pres./$2,690,795.00, Michael G. Durkin/Exec. VP - PAS US Operations/$1,847,273.00, Matthew E. Carter/Sr. VP - Corporate Development, Brian D. Wenger/Corp. Sec., Timothy W. Gorman/47/VP, Controller, Andrew R. Stark/44/VP, Treasurer, Sara Zawoyski/VP - Investor Relations

Directors: Robert C. Pohlad/52/Chmn., CEO, Jarobin Gilbert/61/Dir., James R. Kackley/64/Dir., Matthew M. McKenna/61/Dir., Richard G. Cline/72/Dir., Archie R. Dykes/77/Dir., Pierre S. Du Pont/72/Dir., Herbert M. Baum/70/Dir., Deborah E. Powell/Dir., Michael J. Corliss/47/Dir.

Owners: Alexander H. Ware, Robert C. Pohlad/9.50%, Kenneth E. Keiser, Michael G. Durkin, Michael J. Corliss, Pierre S. du Pont, Herbert M. Baum, Archie R. Dykes, James R. Rogers, Richard G. Cline, Deborah E. Powell, Matthew M. McKenna/44.50%, Insiders/54.50%, James R. Kackley, Jarobin Gilbert

Financial Data: ***Fiscal Year End:*** 12/31 ***Latest Annual Data:*** 12/30/2006

Year	Sales	Net Income
2006	$3,972,400,000	$158,300,000
2005	$3,726,000,000	$194,700,000

Curr. Assets:	$598,200,000	**Curr. Liab.:**	$722,000,000	**P/E Ratio:**	17.63
Plant, Equip.:	$1,114,100,000	**Total Liab.:**	$2,484,500,000	**Indic. Yr. Divd.:**	$0.520
Total Assets:	$4,053,800,000	**Net Worth:**	$1,569,300,000	**Debt/ Equity:**	0.9441

PepsiCo Inc

700 Anderson Hill Rd., Purchase, NY, 10577; ***PH:*** 1-914-253-2000; ***Fax:*** 1-914-253-2070; ***http://*** www.pepsico.com

General - Incorporation .... NC
Employees 168,000
Auditor .... KPMG LLP
Stk Agt........ Bank of New York
Counsel .... NA
DUNS No. 00-128-7762

Stock - Price on:12/24/2007 .... $65.88
Stock Exchange .... NYSE
Ticker Symbol .... PEP
Outstanding Shares 1,630,000,000
E.P.S .... NA
Shareholders .... NA

Business: The group's principle activities include manufacturing, marketing and selling a wide range of salty, sweet and grain-based snacks, carbonated and non-carbonated beverages and foods. The group's products include chips, popcorns, pretzels and snack mix, multigrain and puffed wheat snacks, candy coated popcorns and fried corn sticks. The group products are sold under the brand names Frito-Lay, Pepsi-Cola, Gatorade, Tropicana, Quaker, Walkers and Copella. The group operates from United States.

Primary SIC and add'l.: 2096 2099 2043 2086

CIK No: 0000077476

Subsidiaries: A.R. Scott Ltd., Ahmedabad Advertising and Marketing Consultants Ltd., Alcasa S.A., Alegro Internacional, S. de R.L. de C.V., Alimentos del Istmo S.A., Alimentos Quaker Oats y Compania Limitada, Alliance Canners, Alpac Corporation, Anderson Hill Insurance Limited, Aradhana Beverages& Foods Company Pvt Limited, Aradhana Carbonated Beverages Private Ltd., Aradhana Convenience Foods Private Limited, Aradhana Drinks and Beverages Private Limited, Aradhana Foods and Juices Private Limited, Aradhana Snack Food Company 503 Subsidiaries included in the Index

Officers: Indra K. Nooyi/52/Chmn., CEO/$9,377,119.00, John C. Compton/CEO - Pepsico North America/$4,956,577.00, Dawn Hudson/CEO, Pres. - Pepsi, Cola North America/$4,941,070.00, Wahid Hamid/Sr. VP - Corporate Strategy, Development, Richard Goodman/CFO/$2,595,151.00, Mitch Adamek/Sr. VP, Chief Procurement Officer, Tod J. MacKenzie/Sr. VP - Corporate Communications, Clay G. Small/Sr. VP - Managing Attorney, Sarah McGill/Sr. VP - Tax, Lionel L. Nowell/Sr. VP, Treasurer, Cynthia M. Trudell/54/Sr. VP, Chief Personnel Officer, Larry D. Thompson/Sr. VP - Government Affairs, General Counsel, Sec., Peter A. Bridgman/Sr. VP, Controller, Antonio Lucio/Chief Health, Wellness Innovation Officer, Ronald C. Parker/Sr. VP - Human Resources, Pepsico North America, Sr. VP Global Diversity - Pepsico *(16 Officers included in Index)*

Directors: Indra K. Nooyi/52/Chmn., CEO, Michael D. White/Vice Chmn., Daniel Vasella/54/Dir., Ray L. Hunt/64/Dir., Arthur C. Martinez/68/Dir., Sharon Percy Rockefeller/63/Dir., James J. Schiro/62/Dir., Dina Dublon/54/Dir., Victor J. Dzau/62/Dir., Donald M. Kendall/Co - Founder - Pepsico, Alberto Ibarguen/64/Dir.

Owners: Daniel Vasella, Richard Goodman, Dawn E. Hudson, John C. Compton, Michael D. White, Ray L. Hunt, Insiders, John F. Akers, Robert E. Allen, James J. Schiro, Victor J. Dzau, Dina Dublon, Indra K. Nooyi, Franklin A. Thomas, Sharon Percy Rockefeller *(18 Owners included in Index)*

Financial Data: ***Fiscal Year End:*** 12/31 ***Latest Annual Data:*** 12/30/2006

Year	Sales	Net Income
2006	$35,137,000,000	$5,642,000,000
2005	$32,562,000,000	$4,078,000,000
2004	$29,261,000,000	$4,212,000,000

Curr. Assets:	$10,454,000,000	**Curr. Liab.:**	$9,406,000,000	**P/E Ratio:**	19.15
Plant, Equip.:	$8,681,000,000	**Total Liab.:**	$17,407,000,000	**Indic. Yr. Divd.:**	$1.500
Total Assets:	$31,727,000,000	**Net Worth:**	$14,320,000,000	**Debt/ Equity:**	0.1171

Per Se Technologies Inc

1145 Sanctuary Pk.way, Ste. 200, Alpharetta, GA, 30004; ***PH:*** 1-770-237-4300

General - Incorporation .... DE
Employees 5,100
Auditor .... Ernst & Young LLP
Stk Agt ..... American Stock Transfer & Trust Co.
Counsel .... NA
DUNS No. 15-290-5089

Stock - Price on:12/24/2007 .... NA
Stock Exchange .... NDQ
Ticker Symbol .... NA
Outstanding Shares .... NA
E.P.S .... -$3.72
Shareholders .... NA

Business: The group's principle activities are divided into two operating segments: physician services and hospital services segment. The physician services division provides connective healthcare services and solutions that manage the revenue cycle for physician groups. The hospital services division provides connective healthcare solutions that increase revenue and decrease expenses for hospitals with a focus on revenue cycle management and resource management.

Primary SIC and add'l.: 7372 8741

CIK No: 0000878556

Subsidiaries: Knowledgeable Healthcare Solutions, Inc, NDC Health Pharmacy Systems and Services, Inc., NDC of Canada, Inc., NDCHealth Corporation, Patient Account Management Services, Inc., Per-Se Transaction Services, Inc., PhyServ Solutions, Inc, PST Products, LLC, PST Services, Inc.

Financial Data: ***Fiscal Year End:*** 12/31 ***Latest Annual Data:*** 06/30/2007

Year	Sales	Net Income
2007	NA	-$8,429,000
2006	NA	-$2,440,000
2005	NA	-$2,098,000

Curr. Assets:	$6,053,000	**Curr. Liab.:**	$733,000		
Plant, Equip.:	$468,000	**Total Liab.:**	$830,000	**Indic. Yr. Divd.:**	NA
Total Assets:	$6,727,000	**Net Worth:**	$5,897,000	**Debt/ Equity:**	NA

Per-Se Technologies

One Post St., San Francisco, California, 94104; ***PH:*** 1-415-983-8300; ***Fax:*** 1-800-826-9360; ***http://*** www.mckesson.com; ***Email:*** corp.communications@mckesson.com

General - Incorporation .... DE
Employees 5,100
Auditor .... Ernst & Young LLP
Stk Agt ..... American Stock Transfer & Trust Co.
Counsel .... NA
DUNS No. 04-297-8528

Stock - Price on:12/24/2007 .... NA
Stock Exchange .... NDQ
Ticker Symbol .... PSTI
Outstanding Shares .... NA
E.P.S .... NA
Shareholders .... NA

Business: The group's principal activity is to provide electronic healthcare information solutions. The group operates in three segments: the network services and systems segment provides electronic connectivity to the group's intelligent network and system solutions throughout the healthcare industry. The information management segment provides management information, research and consulting services to pharmaceutical manufacturers, pharmacy chains and hospitals. The pharmacy benefit services segment provides tools, resources and data for prescription benefit management services. Its services are provided primarily to pharmacies, hospitals, physicians, payers and pharmaceutical manufacturers. The company has operations in the United States of America and Canada. On 08-Apr-2004, the group acquired mckesson corporation.

Primary SIC and add'l.: 7374 7375

CIK No: 0000878556

Perceptron Inc

47827 Halyard Dr., Plymouth, MI, 48170; ***PH:*** 1-734-414-6100; ***Fax:*** 1-734-414-4700; ***http://*** www.perceptron.com; ***Email:*** inquiry@perceptron.com

General - Incorporation .... MI
Employees 241
Auditor .... Grant Thornton LLP
Stk Agt ..... American Stock Transfer & Trust Co.
Counsel .... Dykema Gossett
DUNS No. 02-840-0331

Stock - Price on:12/24/2007 .... $9.63
Stock Exchange .... NDQ
Ticker Symbol .... PRCP
Outstanding Shares 8,000,000
E.P.S $0.29
Shareholders .... NA

Business: The group's principal activities are to design, develop, manufacture and market information-based measurement and inspection solutions for process improvement. The products are designed to improve quality, increase productivity and decrease costs in manufacturing and product development. The solutions offered by the group include laser-based gauging systems that provide 100% in-line measurement for reduction of process variation; systems that guide robots in a variety of automated assembly applications; systems that inspect the quality of painted surfaces and technology components and software. The group has international operations in Germany, the Netherlands, France, Brazil, Japan, & Spain.

Primary SIC and add'l.: 7372

CIK No: 0000887226

Subsidiaries: Perceptron (Europe) GmbH, Perceptron Europe B.V.

Officers: Alfred A. Pease/Chmn., CEO, Pres., Harry T. Rittenour/62/Sr. VP - Product Production, Quality, David W. Geiss/Sec., Sylvia M. Smith/Controller, John H. Lowry/61/VP - Finance, CFO, Paul J. Eckhoff/46/Sr. VP - Commercial Products

Directors: Alfred A. Pease/Chmn., CEO, Pres., James A. Ratigan/60/Dir., Terryll R. Smith/58/Dir., Richard W. Marz/65/Dir., David J. Beattie/Dir., Kenneth R. Dabrowski/65/Dir., Philip J. Decocco/70/Dir., Robert S. Oswald/67/Dir.

Owners: Nicusa Capital Partners, L.P./6.17%, Dimensional Fund Advisors Inc./8.94%, Harry T. Rittenour/1.41%, Kenneth R. Dabrowski/1.02%, Wilfred J. Corriveau/1.15%, Sylvia M. Smith, Rutabaga Capital Management LLC/10.47%, Alfred A. Pease/6.76%, Insiders/12.33%, Philip J. DeCocco, Royce & Associates, Inc./9.21%, James A. Ratigan, Richard W. Marz, Paul J. Eckhoff, David J. Beattie *(18 Owners included in Index)*

Financial Data: ***Fiscal Year End:*** 06/30 ***Latest Annual Data:*** 06/30/2007

Year	Sales	Net Income
2007	$62,252,000	$1,459,000
2006	$57,875,000	$3,239,000
2005	$54,892,000	$3,282,000

Curr. Assets:	$50,817,000	**Curr. Liab.:**	$8,165,000		
Plant, Equip.:	$7,408,000	**Total Liab.:**	$8,165,000	**Indic. Yr. Divd.:**	NA
Total Assets:	$62,395,000	**Net Worth:**	$54,230,000	**Debt/ Equity:**	NA

Perdigao S.A.

760 Av Escola Politecnica, Jaguare, Sao Paulo; ***PH:*** 55-1137185300; ***http://*** www.perdigao.com.br

General - Incorporation	Federative Republic of Brazil	**Stock** - Price on:12/24/2007	$35.87
Employees	39,048	Stock Exchange	NYSE
Auditor	Ernst & Young LLP	Ticker Symbol	PDA
Stk Agt	Bank of New York	Outstanding Shares	82,760,000
Counsel	NA	E.P.S	$1.98
DUNS No.	NA	Shareholders	NA

Business: The groups principle activities include producing and exporting poultry. In the year 2005, the group acquired Mary Loize Indstria de Alimentos Ltda and Mary Loize Indstria e Comrcio de Raes Ltda. The group operates from the Brazil. The group's quarterely revenue for Sept 2007 was 1658.12 millions of USD.

Primary SIC and add'l.: 5191 2037 2022 2011 2038 5159 2013 5147 2015 5144 2048 2099 2079 5142 0251 0213 2051

CIK No: 0001122491

Subsidiaries: Crossban Holdings GMBH, Perdigo Agroindustrial S.A., Perdigo International Ltd., Perdix International Foods Comrcio Internacional Lda.

Officers: Antonio Augusto De Toni/45/General Officer - Perdix Business, Nilvo Mittanck/47/Dir., Supply Chain Officer, Ricardo Robert Athayde Menezes/Dir., Institutional Relations Officer, Agenor Azevedo Dos Santos/52/Member - Fiscal Counsel, Alternate, Ivan Mendes Do Carmo/45/Member - Fiscal Counsel, Decio Magno A. Stochiero/44/Member - Fiscal Counsel, Alternate, Giberto Antonio Orsatto/Dir., Human Relations Officer, Jose Antonio Do Prado Fay/54/Dir., General Officer - Perdigao Business

Directors: Giberto Antonio Orsatto/Dir., Human Relations Officer, Jose Antonio Do Prado Fay/54/Dir., General Officer - Perdigao Business, Nilvo Mittanck/47/Dir., Supply Chain Officer, Ricardo Robert Athayde Menezes/Dir., Institutional Relations Officer

Owners: Weg Participaes e Servios S.A./5.12%, Fundo Inv. em Tit. e V. M. Librium/2.24%, VALIA Fundao Vale do Rio Doce/4.14%, PREVI Caixa de Previdncia dos Funcionrios do Banco do Brasil/15.68%, Fundao Telebrs de Seguridade Social SISTEL/5.12%, Fundao de Assistncia e Previdncia Social do BNDES FAPES/3.69%, Real Grandeza Fundao de Assistncia e Previdncia Social/2.86%, PREVI BANERJ - Caixa de Previdncia dos Funcionrios do Banerj/1.20%, Insiders/0.08%, PETROS Fundao Petrobras de Seguridade Social/11.93%

Financial Data: ***Fiscal Year End:***12/31 ***Latest Annual Data:*** 12/31/2006

Year	Sales	Net Income
2006	$2,442,875,000	$66,490,000
2005	$2,210,378,000	$153,152,000
2004	$1,838,057,000	$109,989,000

Curr. Assets:	$1,334,021,000	**Curr. Liab.:**	$585,375,000	**P/E Ratio:**	72.08
Plant, Equip.:	$777,436,000	**Total Liab.:**	$1,273,439,000	**Indic. Yr. Divd.:**	$0.020
Total Assets:	$2,242,561,000	**Net Worth:**	$969,123,000	**Debt/ Equity:**	NA

Peregrine Industries Inc

90 John St., Ste. 626, Florida, FL, 10038; ***PH:*** 1-646-202-9679

General - Incorporation	FL	**Stock** - Price on:12/24/2007	$0.035
Employees	NA	Stock Exchange	OTC
Auditor	Michael F. Cronin, CPA	Ticker Symbol	HVAC
Stk Agt	Florida Atlantic Stock Transfer, Inc.	Outstanding Shares	50,420,000
Counsel	NA	E.P.S	-$0.001
DUNS No.	NA	Shareholders	NA

Business: The groups principal activities include designing and manufacturing heat pump pool heaters, residential air conditioners and parallel flow coils for the heating, ventilation and air conditioning industry. The group operates from the United States.

Primary SIC and add'l.: 3089

CIK No: 0001061164

Subsidiaries: Alcool, Inc., Thermopompe Peregrine Heat Pump

Owners: Park Avenue Group, Inc./6.35%, Richard Rubin/21.82%, Merrill Yarbrough/17.31%, Thomas J. Craft/21.82%, Ivo Heiden/20.63%, Insiders/21.13%

Financial Data: ***Fiscal Year End:***06/30 ***Latest Annual Data:*** 06/30/2007

Year	Sales	Net Income
2007	NA	-$51,000
2006	NA	-$137,000
2005	NA	-$2,000

Curr. Assets:	NA	**Curr. Liab.:**	$61,000		
Plant, Equip.:	NA	**Total Liab.:**	$61,000	**Indic. Yr. Divd.:**	NA
Total Assets:	NA	**Net Worth:**	-$61,000	**Debt/ Equity:**	NA

Peregrine Pharmaceuticals Inc

14282 Franklin Ave., Tustin, CA, 92780; ***PH:*** 1-714-508-6067; ***Fax:*** 1-714-838-5817; ***http://*** www.peregrineinc.com

General - Incorporation	DE	**Stock** - Price on:12/24/2007	$0.95
Employees	102	Stock Exchange	NDQ
Auditor	Ernst & Young LLP	Ticker Symbol	PPHM
Stk Agt	Integrity Stock Transfer	Outstanding Shares	196,110,000
Counsel	NA	E.P.S	-$0.103
DUNS No.	04-253-5740	Shareholders	NA

Business: The group's principal activities are the research, development, manufacture and commercialization of cancer therapeutics and cancer diagnostics and licensing. This is done through a series of proprietary platform technologies using monoclonal antibodies. The group operates in two segments namely, contract manufacturing and licensing. The group is focussing on the development of its collateral targeting antibody based technologies, 'collateral targeting agents'. The services include contract manufacturing of antibodies and proteins, cell culture development, process development, and testing of biologics for biopharmaceutical and biotechnology companies.

Primary SIC and add'l.: 2834 8731 6794

CIK No: 0000704562

Subsidiaries: Avid Bioservices, Inc, Vascular Targeting Technologies, Inc

Officers: Steven W. King/CEO, Pres./$436,719.00, David F. King/VP - Business Development, Joseph Shan/Executive Dir. - Clinical, Regulatory Affairs, Shelley P. Fussey/VP - Intellectual Property, Paul J. Lytle/CFO/$346,767.00, Richard Richieri/Sr. VP - Bioprocess Development - Manufacturing, John L. Quick/Head - Quality Systems, Linda Donaldson/Contact - Media Inquiries

Directors: Thomas A. Waltz/Chmn., David H. Pohl/71/Dir., Stephen M. Smith/Member - Scientific Resource Board - Anti Viral, HIV, Peter Barry/Member - Scientific Resource Board - Anti Viral , CMV, Eric S. Swartz/Dir., Carlton M. Johnson/48/Dir., Philip E. Thorpe/Member - Scientific Resource Board - Core Technologies, Alan J. Schroit/Member - Scientific Resource Board, Core Technologies, Rolf A. Brekken/Member - Scientific Resource Board, Oncology, Harold F. Dvorak/Member - Scientific Resource Board, Oncology, Michael S. Gordon/Member - Scientific Resource Board, Oncology, Donald R. Senger/Member - Scientific Resource Board, Oncology, Xianming Huang/Member - Scientific Resource Board, Oncology, John G. McHutchison/Member - Scientific Resource Board - Anti Viral, Hepatitis C, Arnold S. Monto/Member - Scientific Resource Board - Anti Viral, Influenza *(16 Directors included in Index)*

Owners: Steven W. King, Carlton M. Johnson, F. David King, Eric S. Swartz/1.44%, Insiders/3.04%, Thomas A. Waltz, David H. Pohl, Paul J. Lytle

Financial Data: ***Fiscal Year End:***04/30 ***Latest Annual Data:*** 04/30/2007

Year	Sales	Net Income
2007	$3,708,000	-$20,796,000
2006	$3,193,000	-$17,061,000
2005	$4,959,000	-$15,452,000

Curr. Assets:	$19,898,000	**Curr. Liab.:**	$5,855,000		
Plant, Equip.:	$1,840,000	**Total Liab.:**	$6,008,000	**Indic. Yr. Divd.:**	NA
Total Assets:	$22,997,000	**Net Worth:**	$16,989,000	**Debt/ Equity:**	NA

Perfectenergy International Ltd

Formerly: Crestview Development Corp

No. 479 You Dong Rd., Xinzhuang Town, Shanghai, 201100; ***PH:*** 8621-54888436

General - Incorporation	NV	**Stock** - Price on:12/24/2007	NA
Employees	NA	Stock Exchange	NA
Auditor	Jewett, Schwartz, Wolfe & Associates	Ticker Symbol	NA
Stk Agt	NA	Outstanding Shares	NA
Counsel	NA	E.P.S	NA
DUNS No.	NA	Shareholders	NA

Business: The groups principal activity is to explore minerals and natural gas. The group operates from Canada.

Primary SIC and add'l.: 3674

CIK No: 0001345432

Officers: Philip McDonald/39/Dir., CEO, CFO, Pres., Treasurer, Sec.

Directors: Philip McDonald/39/Dir., CEO, CFO, Pres., Treasurer, Sec.

Owners: Olivier Couriol/9.07%, Wennan Li/20.98%, Yunxia Yang/13.68%, Min Fan/13.68%, Insiders/48.35%

Financial Data: ***Fiscal Year End:***10/31 ***Latest Annual Data:*** 10/31/2006

Year	Sales	Net Income
2006	NA	-$93,000

Curr. Assets:	$2,000	**Curr. Liab.:**	$10,000		
Plant, Equip.:	NA	**Total Liab.:**	$10,000	**Indic. Yr. Divd.:**	NA
Total Assets:	$2,000	**Net Worth:**	-$8,000	**Debt/ Equity:**	NA

Perficient Inc

1120 S Capital of Texas Hwy., Bldg. III, Ste. 220, Austin, TX, 78731; ***PH:*** 1-512-531-6000; ***Fax:*** 1-512-531-6011; ***http://*** www.perficient.com

General - Incorporation	DE	**Stock** - Price on:12/24/2007	$20.82
Employees	774	Stock Exchange	NDQ
Auditor	BDO Seidman LLP	Ticker Symbol	PRFT
Stk Agt	Continental Stock Transfer & Trust Co	Outstanding Shares	29,300,000
Counsel	Gibbons Del Deo Dolan Griffinger	E.P.S	$0.388
DUNS No.	NA	Shareholders	NA

Business: The group's principle activity is to provide end-to-end business and technology solutions with a focus on serving the financial services, healthcare, technology and energy industries. The group markets its ebusiness solutions directly to large and major midsize companies, principally in the midwestern United States through a seven person direct sales force. The group's quarterly revenue for September 2007 was 53.08 millions of USD.

Primary SIC and add'l.: 7371 7375 7372

CIK No: 0001085869

Subsidiaries: Core Objective, Inc., Perficient Canada Corp, Perficient Genisys, Inc., Perficient International Limited, Perficient iPath, Inc., Perficient Meritage, Inc., Perficient Vivare, Inc., Perficient Zettaworks, Inc., Perficient, Inc.

Officers: John T. McDonald/Chmn., CEO/$1,859,192.00, Kathy Henely/VP - Corporate Operations, Chris Gianattasio/VP - Field Operations, Paul E. Martin/CFO, Treasurer, Sec./$216,217.00, Paul Elisii/GM - Philadelphia, Scott Nesbitt/GM - Denver CRM, Don Kasica/GM - Denver, Richard T. Kalbfleish/VP - Finance, Administration/$266,945.00, Jeffrey S. Davis/COO, Pres./$1,419,722.00, Jackie Thorn/GM - Minneapolis, Mike Minkler/GM - St. Louis, Tim Robinson/GM - San Francisco CRM, Hari Madamalla/GM - IBM EAI, Thomas Pash/VP - Field Operations, Tim Thompson/VP - Client Development/$542,000.00 *(18 Officers included in Index)*

Directors: John T. McDonald/Chmn., CEO, David S. Lundeen/Dir., Kenneth R. Johnsen/Dir., Ralph C. Derrickson/Dir., Max D. Hopper/Dir.

Owners: Ralph C. Derrickson, Paul E. Martin/0.30%, David S. Lundeen/1.20%, John T. McDonald/4.30%, Kenneth R. Johnsen, Robert H. Drysdale/6.10%, Max D. Hopper, Timothy J. Thompson/0.80%, Richard T. Kalbfleish/0.10%, Insiders/8.30%, Michael D. Hill/0.10%, Jeffrey S. Davis/1.10%

Financial Data: ***Fiscal Year End:***12/31 ***Latest Annual Data:*** 12/31/2006

Year	Sales	Net Income
2006	$160,926,000	$9,567,000
2005	$96,997,000	$7,177,000
2004	$58,848,000	$3,913,000

Curr. Assets:	$47,119,000	**Curr. Liab.:**	$22,260,000	**P/E Ratio:**	47.32
Plant, Equip.:	$1,806,000	**Total Liab.:**	$23,648,000	**Indic. Yr. Divd.:**	NA
Total Assets:	$131,000,000	**Net Worth:**	$107,352,000	**Debt/ Equity:**	0.0157

Perfisans Holdings Inc

10900 Wilshire Blvd., Ste. 500, Los Angeles, CA, 90024; *PH:* 1-905-943-9996;
Fax: 1-905-943-7560; *http://* www.perfisans.com; *Email:* info@perfisans.com

General - Incorporation	MD	*Stock*- Price on:12/24/2007	$0.035
Employees	NA	Stock Exchange	OTC
Auditor	Schwartz Levitsky Feldman LLP	Ticker Symbol	PFNH
Stk Agt	Select Fidelity Transfer Services	Outstanding Shares	NA
Counsel	NA	E.P.S.	NA
DUNS No.	NA	Shareholders	NA

Business: The groups principal activity is to provide technology focused on the development of cost effective, high performance network processing and storage chips. The group operates through three segments namely consumer, small office home office and enterprise. The group operates from the United States.

Primary SIC and add'l.: 3674
CIK No: 0001049861
Subsidiaries: Perfisans Networks Corporation
Officers: Bok Wong/Chmn., CEO, Pres., Principle Accounting Officer, To-Hon Lam/Co - Founder, Chief Technical Advisor
Directors: Bok Wong/Chmn., CEO, Pres., Principle Accounting Officer, To-Hon Lam/Co - Founder, Chief Technical Advisor, Eric Wang/42/Dir.
Owners: Alfred Morgan Capital/6.67%, To Hon Lam/4.40%, Insiders/8.80%, General Resources Co./7.60%, Bok Wong/4.40%

*Financial Data: Fiscal Year End:*12/31   *Latest Annual Data:* 12/31/2006

Year	Sales	Net Income
2006	$23,000	-$2,959,000
2005	$17,000	-$3,823,000
2004	$1,096,000	-$4,530,000

Curr. Assets:	$22,000	*Curr. Liab.:*	$4,358,000		
Plant, Equip.:	$9,000	*Total Liab.:*	$4,358,000	*Indic. Yr. Divd.:*	NA
Total Assets:	$30,000	*Net Worth:*	-$4,328,000	*Debt/ Equity:*	NA

Performance Food Group Co

12500 W Creek Pkwy., Richmond, VA, 23238; *PH:* 1-804-484-7700; *Fax:* 1-804-484-7701;
http:// www.pfgc.com

General - Incorporation	TN	*Stock*- Price on:12/24/2007	$35.12
Employees	7,000	Stock Exchange	NDQ
Auditor	KPMG LLP	Ticker Symbol	PFGC
Stk Agt	American Stock Transfer & Trust Co.	Outstanding Shares	35,330,000
Counsel	Bass, Berry & Sims PLC	E.P.S.	$1.39
DUNS No.	15-448-3457	Shareholders	NA

Business: The group's principle activities include marketing and distributing food products. The groups products include baked and sea food. The group operates from United States.

Primary SIC and add'l.: 5141 5143 5142
CIK No: 0000908254
Subsidiaries: AFFLINK Corporation, AFFLINK Holding Corporation, AFFLINK Incorporated, AFI Foodservice, LLC, All Kitchens, Inc., Caro Foods, Inc., Carroll County Foods, Inc, Empire Imports, Inc, Empire Seafood Holding Corp., Empire Seafood, LLC, Foodservice Purchasing Group, LLC, Gerken Food Company, Incorporated, Hale Brothers Summit, Inc., Kenneth O. Lester Company, Inc., Middendorf Meat Company 35 Subsidiaries included in the Index
Officers: Thomas Hoffman/CEO - Customized Division/$828,271.00, Steven L. Spinner/Dir., CEO, Pres./$929,888.00, Keith J. Middleton/Sr. VP, Controller, Charlotte Perkins/Sr. VP, Chief Human Resources Officer/$454,829.00, Joseph J. Paterak/Sr. VP - Broadline Operations, Joseph J. Traficanti/Chief Compliance Officer, Sr. VP, General Counsel, Corp. Sec., Jeffery W. Fender/VP, Treasurer, John D. Austin/CFO, Sr. VP/$686,994.00, Peter Giuffrida/CIO
Directors: Steven L. Spinner/Dir., CEO, Pres., Robert C. Sledd/Chmn., Charles E. Adair/Dir., Timothy M. Graven/Dir., Mary C. Doswell/Dir., Fred C. Goad/Dir., John E. Stokely/Dir.
Owners: Steven L. Spinner, John D. Austin, Charlotte L. Perkins, Prudential Financial, Inc./8.50%, Mary C. Doswell, Barclays Global Investors, NA/9.60%, Axa Financial, Inc./5.90%, Insiders/4.20%, Timothy M. Graven, John E. Stokely, Robert C. Sledd/2.20%, Fred C. Goad, Charles E. Adair, Joseph J. Paterak, Thomas Hoffman *(16 Owners included in Index)*

*Financial Data: Fiscal Year End:*12/31   *Latest Annual Data:* 12/30/2006

Year	Sales	Net Income
2006	$5,826,732,000	$42,786,000
2005	$5,721,372,000	$247,138,000

Curr. Assets:	$632,318,000	*Curr. Liab.:*	$489,124,000		
Plant, Equip.:	$255,816,000	*Total Liab.:*	$535,773,000	*Indic. Yr. Divd.:*	NA
Total Assets:	$1,312,290,000	*Net Worth:*	$776,517,000	*Debt/ Equity:*	0.0118

Performance Technologies Inc

205 Indigo Creek Dr., Rochester, NY, 14626; *PH:* 1-585-256-0200; *Fax:* 1-585-256-0791;
http:// www.pt.com; *Email:* info@pt.com

General - Incorporation	DE	*Stock*- Price on:12/24/2007	$4.44
Employees	211	Stock Exchange	NDQ
Auditor	PricewaterhouseCoopers LLP	Ticker Symbol	PTIX
Stk Agt	American Stock Transfer & Trust Co.	Outstanding Shares	12,890,000
Counsel	Harter, Secrest & Emery	E.P.S.	$0.14
DUNS No.	05-986-4868	Shareholders	NA

Business: The group's principal activities are to design, develop, manufacture and market communications and networking products that enable the convergence of wireline, wireless and next generation Internet protocol networks. The group is a supplier of platforms, components and software solutions for the embedded systems marketplace that can be used in a broad range of applications and end markets. The customers of the group include telecommunications equipment manufacturers, telecommunications service providers, operators, server manufacturers, international wireless carriers and platform manufacturers. The company markets its products under a variety of brand names including ipnexus, advanced managed platforms, intelligent shelf manager, nexusware and segway products. Ipnexus, nexusware, flexnat, ziatech and segway are trademarks of performancetechnologies, inc. On 23-Jan-2004, the group acquired mapletree networks.

Primary SIC and add'l.: 3577

CIK No: 0001003950
Subsidiaries: 3688283 Canada, Inc., Performance Technologies, Inc., PerfTech (PTI), PTI Massachusetts Corporation
Officers: John M. Slusser/Founder, Chmn., CEO, Pres./$58,962.00, William E. Mahuson/Sr. Corporate VP, John J. Grana/Sr. VP - Systems Engineering/$215,544.00, Dorrance W. Lamb/Sr. VP, CFO/$237,614.00, Doug Steward/Strategic Accounting Mgr. - Latin America, Carlos Fortiche/Sales Support, Latin America, Edward J. Bizari/VP - Marketing, Worldwide Sales, John J. Peters/CTO, Sr. VP - Platform Engineering, Dan Grey/Regional Sales Mgr. - United States, Patricia Beach/Sales Support, United States, Reeves Mollman/Sales Engineer, Patrick J. Rice/VP, GM - Signaling Systems Group, Jiping Cao/Sales Representative, Field Applications Engineer - Asia Pacific, Todd Haschmann/Sales Support, Asia Pacific, Rober Potter/Strategic Accounting Mgr. - Israel *(18 Officers included in Index)*
Directors: John M. Slusser/Founder, Chmn., CEO, Pres., Stuart B. Meisenzahl/Dir., Dennis C. Connors/Dir., Mark Rajkowski/Dir., Robert Tillman/Dir., Bernard Kozel/86/Dir.
Owners: Bernard Kozel/1.80%, Charles E. Maginness/5.10%, Robert L. Tillman, John J. Grana, Dimensional Fund Advisors LP/5.90%, Dorrance W. Lamb/1.10%, Stuart B. Meisenzahl, John M. Slusser/2.00%, Mark E. Rajkowski, Bank of America Corporation/12.40%, John J. Peters, Insiders/13.60%, Royce & Associates, LLC/12.80%, Michael F. Tortorello

*Financial Data: Fiscal Year End:*12/31   *Latest Annual Data:* 12/31/2006

Year	Sales	Net Income
2006	$48,405,000	$1,483,000
2005	$49,633,000	$3,045,000
2004	$53,489,000	$2,780,000

Curr. Assets:	$53,694,000	*Curr. Liab.:*	$5,994,000		
Plant, Equip.:	$2,213,000	*Total Liab.:*	$5,994,000	*Indic. Yr. Divd.:*	NA
Total Assets:	$64,261,000	*Net Worth:*	$58,267,000	*Debt/ Equity:*	NA

Pericom Semiconductor Corp

3545 N 1st St., San Jose, CA, 95134; *PH:* 1-408-435-0800; *Fax:* 1-408-435-1100;
http:// www.pericom.com

General - Incorporation	CA	*Stock*- Price on:12/24/2007	$11.14
Employees	544	Stock Exchange	NDQ
Auditor	Burr, Pilger & Mayer, LLP	Ticker Symbol	PSEM
Stk Agt	EquiServe Trust Co N.A	Outstanding Shares	26,020,000
Counsel	Morrison & Foerster LLP	E.P.S.	$0.41
DUNS No.	62-607-8794	Shareholders	NA

Business: The group's principal activity is to design, develop and market integrated circuits and frequency control products used in advanced electronic systems. The products of the group are marketed under the brand names of SiliconSwitch(TM) SiliconInterface(TM), SiliconClock(TM), SiliconConnect(TM), and SaRonix(TM). The customers of the group include original equipment manufacturers, contract manufacturers and distributors. The subcontractor plants of the group are ISO 9000 certified. In September 2005 the group acquired eCERA Comtek Corporation.

Primary SIC and add'l.: 5065 3674
CIK No: 0001001426
Subsidiaries: eCERA Comtek Corporation, Pericom Semiconductor (HK) Limited, Pericom Taiwan Limited, SaRonix, Incorporated
Officers: Alex Chi-Ming Hui/Chmn., CEO, Pres., Co - Founder, Angela Chen/VP - Finance, CFO, H. L. Hong/VP - Product, Application Engineering, Gerry Liu/Sr. VP - Marketing, Tat C. Choi/VP - Design Engineering, Michael Chen/VP - Asic Engineering, Wilfred Ling/VP - Sales, Asia, John Chi-Hung Hui/Dir., Co - Founder, VP - Technology, Sec., George Kao/VP - Operations
Directors: Alex Chi-Ming Hui/Chmn., CEO, Pres., Co - Founder, John Chi-Hung Hui/Dir., Co - Founder, VP - Technology, Sec., Millard Phelps/Dir., Hau L. Lee/Dir., Simon Wong/Dir.
Owners: Hau L. Lee, Millard Phelps, Siu-Weng Simon Wong, Dimensional Fund Advisors/8.60%, Alex Chiming Hui/7.20%, Insiders, Barclays Global Investors Japan Limited/5.90%, Wasatch Advisors, Inc./9.70%, Angela Chen, Chi-Hung Hui/4.80%

*Financial Data: Fiscal Year End:*07/02   *Latest Annual Data:* 06/30/2007

Year	Sales	Net Income
2007	$123,370,000	$8,627,000
2006	$105,878,000	$5,979,000
2005	$79,557,000	$927,000

Curr. Assets:	$171,857,000	*Curr. Liab.:*	$12,369,000	*P/E Ratio:*	34.81
Plant, Equip.:	$6,477,000	*Total Liab.:*	$12,576,000	*Indic. Yr. Divd.:*	NA
Total Assets:	$193,995,000	*Net Worth:*	$181,162,000	*Debt/ Equity:*	0.0069

Perini Corp

73 Mt. Wayte Ave., Framingham, MA, 01701; *PH:* 1-508-628-2000; *Fax:* 1-508-628-2357;
http:// www.perini.com; *Email:* dtannar@perini.com

General - Incorporation	MA	*Stock*- Price on:12/24/2007	$61.11
Employees	4,300	Stock Exchange	NYSE
Auditor	Deloitte & Touche LLP	Ticker Symbol	PCR
Stk Agt	Computershare Investor Services LLC	Outstanding Shares	26,690,000
Counsel	NA	E.P.S.	$3.43
DUNS No.	00-191-0611	Shareholders	NA

Business: The groups principle activity is to provide construction services. The groups services include diversified general contracting, construction management and design-build services. Customers served by the group include the hospitality and gaming, sports and entertainment, educational, transportation, healthcare, biotech, pharmaceutical and high-tech industries. The group operates from United States.

Primary SIC and add'l.: 1522 1540 1629 1622
CIK No: 0000077543
Subsidiaries: American International Group, Inc., Perini Environmental Services, Inc
Officers: Ronald N. Tutor/Chmn., CEO - Perini Corporation/$16,755,700.00, Richard J. Rizzo/Chmn. - Perini Building Company, Craig D. Shaw/Pres. - Perini Building Company, Robert Band/COO, Pres. - Perini Corporation/$4,428,300.00, Zohrab B. Marashlian/Pres. - Perini Civil, Michael E. Ciskey/57/CFO, VP/$1,553,300.00, Crocker Coulson/Pres. - CCG Investor Relations
Directors: Ronald N. Tutor/Chmn., CEO - Perini Corporation, Willard W. Brittain/Dir., Michael R. Klein/Dir., Robert A. Kennedy/Dir., Raymond R. Oneglia/Dir., Robert L. Miller/Dir., Peter Arkley/Dir., James A. Cummings/Dir.

Owners: Insiders/9.70%, Robert L. Miller, Tontine Capital Partners, L.P./5.89%, Jeffery L. Gendell/8.46%, AXA Courtage Assurances Mutuelle/5.00%, Craig W. Shaw, AXA/5.00%, Raymond R. Oneglia, Tontine Capital Management, L.L.C./5.89%, AXA Assurances Vie Mutuelle/5.00%, Robert A. Kennedy, AXA Assurances I.A.R.D. Mutuelle/5.00%, Ronald N. Tutor/8.76%, Michael R. Klein, Peter Arkley *(17 Owners included in Index)*

Financial Data: *Fiscal Year End:*12/31 *Latest Annual Data:* 12/31/2006

Year	Sales	Net Income
2006	$3,042,839,000	$41,536,000
2005	$1,733,477,000	$4,049,000
2004	$1,842,315,000	$36,007,000

Curr. Assets:	$1,078,253,000	**Curr. Liab.:**	$884,301,000	**P/E Ratio:**	29.38
Plant, Equip.:	$84,785,000	**Total Liab.:**	$952,133,000	**Indic. Yr. Divd.:**	NA
Total Assets:	$1,195,992,000	**Net Worth:**	$243,859,000	**Debt/ Equity:**	NA

Perkinelmer Inc

940 Winter St., Waltham, MA, 02451; *PH:* 1-781-663-6900; *Fax:* 1-203-944-4904; *http://* www.perkinelmer.com

General - Incorporation	MA	**Stock** - Price on:12/24/2007	$26.44
Employees	8,500	Stock Exchange	NYSE
Auditor	Deloitte & Touche LLP	Ticker Symbol	PKI
Stk Agt	Mellon Investor Services LLC	Outstanding Shares	119,760,000
Counsel	NA	E.P.S	$0.89
DUNS No.	00-105-3610	Shareholders	NA

Business: The group's principal activities are to design, manufacture, market and support products, systems and service offerings within the life and analytical sciences, optoelectronics and fluid sciences segments. The life and analytical sciences segment provides drug discovery, genetic screening and chemical analysis tools and instrumentation. The optoelectronics segment provides digital imaging, sensor and specialty lighting components for biomedical, consumer products and other markets. The fluid sciences segment provides critical fluid control and containment systems for highly demanding environments such as turbine engines and semiconductor fabrication facilities. The group's operations are carried out in the United States, Canada, Singapore, Germany, Finland, Philippines and other countries and serves customers in over 125 countries.

Primary SIC and add'l.: 3841 3679 3812 3825 3829

CIK No: 0000031791

Subsidiaries: Carl Consumable Products, LLC, EG&G Omni, Inc., Fluid Sciences Singapore Pte Ltd, Lumac LSC B.V., Lumen Technologies, Inc., Packard BioScience Holding, B.V., Perkin Elmer de Mexico, S.A., Perkin Elmer Italia SpA, Perkin Elmer Polska Sp zo.o., Perkin Elmer Sdn. Bhd., Perkin Elmer Yuhan Hoesa, Perkin-Elmer Argentina S.R.L., Perkin-Elmer Hungaria Kft, PerkinElmer (Hong Kong) Limited, PerkinElmer (India) Private Limited 69 Subsidiaries included in the Index

Officers: Gregory L. Summe/Chmn., CEO/$7,198,882.00, Jeffrey D. Capello/Sr. VP, CFO/$1,533,122.00, Katherine A. O'Hara/Sr. VP, General Counsel, Sec., John A. Roush/Sr. VP, Pres. - Optoelectronics/$1,570,727.00, Richard F. Walsh/Sr. VP, Chief Administrative Officer/$1,758,396.00, Robert F. Friel/Dir., COO, Pres./$3,240,299.00, Michael L. Battles/VP, Chief Accounting Officer

Directors: Gregory L. Summe/Chmn., CEO, Robert F. Friel/Dir., COO, Pres., Alexis P. Michas/Dir., James C. Mullen/Dir., Vicki L. Sato/Dir., Gabriel Schmergel/Dir., Nicholas A. Lopardo/Dir., Robert G. Tod/Dir., Kenton J. Sicchitano/Dir.

Owners: Jeffrey D. Capello, Gabriel Schmergel, Robert F. Friel/1.20%, John A. Roush, Manning & Napier Advisors, Inc./5.10%, Vicki L. Sato, Tamara J. Erickson, Gregory L. Summe/4.00%, Robert G. Tod, Insiders/7.10%, Alexis P. Michas, James C. Mullen, Kenton J. Sicchitano, Nicholas A. Lopardo, Richard F. Walsh/1.00%

Financial Data: *Fiscal Year End:*01/03 *Latest Annual Data:* 12/31/2006

Year	Sales	Net Income
2006	$1,546,358,000	$119,583,000
2005	$1,687,231,000	$96,043,000

Curr. Assets:	$744,766,000	**Curr. Liab.:**	$476,533,000	**P/E Ratio:**	29.71
Plant, Equip.:	$182,196,000	**Total Liab.:**	$932,592,000	**Indic. Yr. Divd.:**	$0.280
Total Assets:	$2,510,322,000	**Net Worth:**	$1,577,730,000	**Debt/ Equity:**	0.1155

Perma Fix Environmental Services Inc

8302 Dunwoody Pl., Ste. 250, Atlanta, GA, 30350; *PH:* 1-770-587-9898; *Fax:* 1-770-587-9937; *http://* www.perma-fix.com; *Email:* corporate@perma-fix.com

General - Incorporation	DE	**Stock** - Price on:12/24/2007	$3.03
Employees	459	Stock Exchange	NDQ
Auditor	BDO Seidman LLP	Ticker Symbol	PESI
Stk Agt	Capital Bank Stock Transfer Agent	Outstanding Shares	NA
Counsel	NA	E.P.S	$0.00
DUNS No.	79-211-7681	Shareholders	NA

Business: The group's principal activities are to offer industrial waste management, nuclear waste management and consulting engineering services. Industrial waste management services include treatment, storage, processing and disposal of hazardous and non-hazardous waste. Nuclear waste management services include treatment, storage, processing and disposal of mixed waste, which is both low-level radioactive and hazardous waste. Consulting engineering services include broad-scope environmental issues including environmental management programs, regulatory permitting, compliance and auditing, landfill design, field testing and characterization. The group provides these services to research, biotechnical development, transportation, chemicals, metal processing, electronic, automotive, petrochemical and refining industries and to governmental agencies. On 29-Mar-2004, the group acquired us liquids of Pennsylvania, inc d/b/a emax.

Primary SIC and add'l.: 8711 4952

CIK No: 0000891532

Subsidiaries: Diversified Scientific Services Inc., East Tennessee Materials and Energy, Industrial Waste Management Inc., Perma-Fix of Dayton Inc., Perma-Fix of Florida Inc., Perma-Fix of Fort Lauderdale Inc., Perma-Fix of Maryland Inc., Perma-Fix of Memphis Inc., Perma-Fix of Michigan Inc., Perma-Fix of Orlando Inc., Perma-Fix of Pittsburgh Inc., Perma-Fix of South Georgia Inc., Perma-Fix Treatment Services Inc., Schreiber Yonley & Associates

Officers: Lou Centofanti/Chmn., CEO, Pres./$475,990.00, Larry McNamara/COO/$545,804.00, Steve Baughman/CFO, VP/$283,482.00, Robert J. Schreiber/Pres. - Schreiber, Yonley, Associates/$200,409.00, Pam Ittah/Human Resources Mgr., David Waldman/Pres.

Directors: Lou Centofanti/Chmn., CEO, Pres., Charles E. Young/Dir., Larry M. Shelton/Dir., Mark Zwecker/Dir., Jon Colin/Dir., Jack Lahav/Dir., Joe R. Reeder/57/Dir.

Owners: Jeffrey L. Gendell/7.17%, Sandler Capital Management/5.48%, Pictet Asset Management, LTD/9.35%, Capital Bank- GRAWE Gruppe/9.32%, Rutabaga Capital Management/10.16%, Heartland Advisors, Inc./8.39%

Financial Data: *Fiscal Year End:*12/31 *Latest Annual Data:* 12/31/2006

Year	Sales	Net Income
2006	$87,929,000	$4,711,000
2005	$90,866,000	$3,739,000
2004	$83,373,000	-$19,361,000

Curr. Assets:	$35,575,000	**Curr. Liab.:**	$22,765,000	**P/E Ratio:**	60.60
Plant, Equip.:	$45,920,000	**Total Liab.:**	$40,259,000	**Indic. Yr. Divd.:**	NA
Total Assets:	$105,997,000	**Net Worth:**	$64,453,000	**Debt/ Equity:**	0.0936

Permian Basin Royalty Trust

901 Main St., Ste. 1700, Dallas, TX, 75202; *PH:* 1-214-209-2400; *Fax:* 1-214-209-2431; *http://* www.pbt-permianbasintrust.com; *Email:* trustee@pbt-permianbasintrust.com

General - Incorporation	TX	**Stock** - Price on:12/24/2007	$13.3
Employees	NA	Stock Exchange	NYSE
Auditor	Deloitte & Touche LLP	Ticker Symbol	PBT
Stk Agt	Mellon Investor Services LLC	Outstanding Shares	46,610,000
Counsel	Thompson & Knight L.L.P.	E.P.S	$1.41
DUNS No.	NA	Shareholders	NA

Business: The groups principle activity is to invest in any businesses. The group operates from the United States. The groups quarterly revenue for Sept 2007 was 18.03 millions of USD.

Primary SIC and add'l.: 6792

CIK No: 0000319654

Officers: Ron E. Hooper/Sr. VP

Owners: Burlington Resources Oil & Gas Company LP

Financial Data: *Fiscal Year End:*12/31 *Latest Annual Data:* 12/31/2006

Year	Sales	Net Income
2006	$66,541,000	$65,715,000
2005	$63,031,000	$62,268,000
2004	$45,037,000	$44,547,000

Curr. Assets:	$5,135,000	**Curr. Liab.:**	$5,135,000	**P/E Ratio:**	9.43
Plant, Equip.:	NA	**Total Liab.:**	$5,135,000	**Indic. Yr. Divd.:**	$1.160
Total Assets:	$6,574,000	**Net Worth:**	$1,439,000	**Debt/ Equity:**	NA

Perot Systems Corp

2300 W Plano Pkwy., Plano, TX, 75075; *PH:* 1-972-577-0000; *http://* www.perotsystems.com; *Email:* americas@ps.net

General - Incorporation	DE	**Stock** - Price on:12/24/2007	$16.82
Employees	21,200	Stock Exchange	NYSE
Auditor	PricewaterhouseCoopers LLP	Ticker Symbol	PER
Stk Agt	Mellon Investor Services LLC	Outstanding Shares	122,270,000
Counsel	NA	E.P.S	$0.83
DUNS No.	19-169-2813	Shareholders	NA

Business: The groups principle activity is to provide information technology services and business solutions. The groups services include consulting, business process, applications and infrastructure solutions. Customers served by the group include the healthcare, commercial, government and insurance industries. The group operates from United States.

Primary SIC and add'l.: 7373 7371 8742

CIK No: 0000894253

Subsidiaries: Advanced Receivables Strategy, Inc., Delphi Consulting Group LLC, Eagle Delaware Corp., Health Systems Design Corp., Hospital Revenue Associates LLC, HPS Solutions Private Limited, Kay Software, Inc., Perot Systems (Canada) Corporation, Perot Systems (Japan) Ltd., Perot Systems A.G., Perot Systems Asia Pacific Pte Ltd., Perot Systems B.V., Perot Systems BPS, LLC, Perot Systems Business Process Solutions India Private Limited, Perot Systems Business Process Solutions, Inc. 65 Subsidiaries included in the Index

Officers: Peter Altabef/Dir., CEO, Pres./$2,339,281.00, James Champy/Chmn. - Consulting/$1,181,967.00, Russell Freeman/COO/$1,377,920.00, Padma Ravichander/48/VP, Jeff Renzi/Exec. VP - Sales, Marketing, Mike McClaskey/CIO, Chuck Lyles/VP - Leads The Healthcare Group, Del Williams/VP, General Counsel, Sec., Darcy Anderson/Chief People Officer, VP - Corporate Support, John Lyon/Dir. - Investor Relations, Joe McNamara/Dir. - Corporate Communications, Robert J. Kelly/Controller, John Harper/CFO, Raj Asava/VP - Enterprise Planning, CAS Global Sales, Marketing, Scott Barnes/VP - Infrastructure Solutions *(20 Officers included in Index)*

Directors: Peter Altabef/Dir., CEO, Pres., Ross Perot/Chmn., Ross Perot/Chmn. Emeritus, John S.T. Gallagher/Dir., Jack Gallagher/Dir., Cecil H. Moore/Dir., Desoto Jordan/Dir., John King/Founder, VP, Anthony J. Principi/Dir., Tom Meurer/Dir., Carl Hahn/Dir., Steven Blasnik/Dir., Anuroop Singh/Dir.

Owners: Peter A. Altabef, Ross Perot/24.60%, James Champy, Jordan DeSoto, Insiders/29.50%, C. H. Moore, Russell Freeman, Carl Hahn, Thomas Meurer, Anuroop Singh, Ross Perot/25.20%, Steven Blasnik, John S.T. Gallagher, Charles A. Lyles, Anthony J. Principi *(17 Owners included in Index)*

Financial Data: *Fiscal Year End:*12/31 *Latest Annual Data:* 12/31/2006

Year	Sales	Net Income
2006	$2,298,000,000	$81,000,000
2005	$1,998,286,000	$111,120,000
2004	$1,773,452,000	$94,347,000

Curr. Assets:	$783,000,000	**Curr. Liab.:**	$301,000,000	**P/E Ratio:**	25.48
Plant, Equip.:	$220,000,000	**Total Liab.:**	$476,000,000	**Indic. Yr. Divd.:**	NA
Total Assets:	$1,581,000,000	**Net Worth:**	$1,105,000,000	**Debt/ Equity:**	0.1373

Perrigo Co

515 Eern Ave., Allegan, MI, 49010; *PH:* 1-269-673-8451; *Fax:* 1-269-673-9128; *http://* www.perrigo.com

General - Incorporation .... MI
Employees 5,969
Auditor .... BDO Seidman LLP
Stk Agt .... National City Bank
Counsel .... Gardner, Carton & Douglas
DUNS No. 00-601-3346

Stock- Price on:12/24/2007 .... $19.4
Stock Exchange .... NDQ
Ticker Symbol .... PRGO
Outstanding Shares 92,710,000
E.P.S .... NA
Shareholders .... NA

Business: The group's principal activity is to manufacture store brand over-the-counter pharmaceutical products and store brand nutritional products. These products include pharmaceuticals such as analgesics, antacids, cough and cold remedies, feminine hygiene, laxatives, smoking cessation and suppositories and nutritional products such as herbals, natural and synthetic vitamins and nutritional drinks. The group's segments are consumer healthcare, includes the U.S. Operations supporting the sale of otc pharmaceutical and nutritional products: pharmaceuticals include the development and eventual sale of prescription drug products: UK operations support the sale of otc pharmaceutical and nutritional products and Mexico operations support the sale of otc and prescription drug products to retail, wholesale and governmental customers. On 12-Dec-2003, the group acquired peter black pharmaceuticals ltd.

Primary SIC and add'l.: 2834

CIK No: 0000820096

Subsidiaries: Agis Commercial Agencies (1989) Ltd., Agis Distribution & Marketing (1989) Ltd., Agis Investments (2000) Ltd., Arginet Investments and Property (2003) Ltd., Barum Limited, Careline (Pharmagis) Ltd., ChemAgis B.V., ChemAgis Germany GmbH, Chemagis Ltd., ChemAgis USA Inc., Clay Park Distributors Inc., Clay Park Industries Inc., Dovechem Ltd., Elite Soap Manufacturers (1986) Ltd., L. Perrigo Company 45 Subsidiaries included in the Index

Officers: Joseph C. Papa/52/Dir., CEO, Pres./$2,417,948.00, Moshe Arkin/55/Vice Chmn., GM - Perrigo Global Generics, API/$939,009.00, Judy L. Brown/CFO, Exec. VP/$676,538.00, John T. Hendrickson/Exec. VP - Global Operations, Supply Chain/$1,021,818.00, Refael Lebel/Exec. VP, GM - Perrigo Israel/$897,982.00, Todd W. Kingma/Exec. VP, General Counsel, Sec., Thomas M. Farrington/51/CIO, Sr. VP, Sharon Kochan/40/Exec. VP - US Generics, Jeffrey R. Needham/52/Sr. VP - Commercial Business Development, Michael R. Stewart/56/Sr. VP - Global Human Resources, James C. Tomshack/57/Sr. VP - Consumer Healthcare Sales, Louis W. Yu/58/Sr. VP - Global Quality, Compliance

Directors: Joseph C. Papa/52/Dir., CEO, Pres., Moshe Arkin/55/Vice Chmn., GM - Perrigo Global Generics, API, Gary M. Cohen/49/Dir., Larry D. Fredricks/70/Dir., Laurie Brlas/51/Dir., Herman Morris/57/Dir., Michael J. Jandernoa/58/Dir., David T. Gibbons/65/Dir., Ran Gottfried/64/Dir., Gary K. Kunkle/61/Dir., Ben-Zion Zilberfarb/58/Dir.

Owners: Judy L. Brown, BenZion Zilberfarb, Ran Gottfried, Moshe Arkin/10.70%, Insiders/17.90%, Gary K. Kunkle, Gary M. Cohen, John T. Hendrickson, Refael Lebel, Joseph C. Papa, Michael J.Jandernoa/5.30%, Laurie Brlas, Larry D. Fredricks, Herman Morris, David T. Gibbons/1.00%

Financial Data: *Fiscal Year End*:06/25 *Latest Annual Data:* 7/1/2006

Year	Sales	Net Income
2006	$1,366,821,000	$71,400,000
2005	$1,024,098,000	-$352,983,000
2004	$898,204,000	$80,567,000

Curr. Assets:	$657,178,000	**Curr. Liab.:**	$371,431,000		
Plant, Equip.:	$319,358,000	**Total Liab.:**	$1,109,880,000	**Indic. Yr. Divd.:**	$0.180
Total Assets:	$1,750,624,000	**Net Worth:**	$640,744,000	**Debt/ Equity:**	1.0057

Perry Ellis International Inc

3000 NW 107th Ave., Miami, FL, 33172; *PH:* 1-305-592-2830; *Fax:* 1-305-594-2307; *http://* www.pery.com; *Email:* info@pery.com

General - Incorporation .... FL
Employees 1,930
Auditor .... Deloitte & Touche LLP
Stk Agt .... Continental Stock Transfer & Trust Co
Counsel .... NA
DUNS No. 04-402-9452

Stock- Price on:12/24/2007 .... $31.92
Stock Exchange .... NDQ
Ticker Symbol .... PERY
Outstanding Shares 14,700,000
E.P.S $1.83
Shareholders .... NA

Business: The group's principal activity is to design, market and license a broad line of high quality men's sportswear, including casual and dress casual shirts, golf sportswear, sweaters, dress casual pants and shorts, jeans wear, active wear and swimwear to all levels of retail distribution. The group's distribution channels include regional, national and international department stores, national and regional chain stores, mass merchants, green grass, specialty stores and corporate wear distributors throughout the United States, Puerto Rico and Canada. The customers of the group include wal-Mart stores, j.c. Penney company, inc., kohl's corporation, sears roebuck and co., mervyn's, and k-Mart corporation. The group operates through perry ellis, jantzen, natural issue, munsingwear, grand slam, john henry, manhattan, and cubavera. On 19-Jun-2003, it acquired salant corporation.

Primary SIC and add'l.: 5136 6794

CIK No: 0000900349

Subsidiaries: Grand Team Holdings Limited, a private company incorporated under the laws of Hong Kong, Jantzen Apparel, LLC, a Delaware limited liability company, Jantzen, LLC, a Delaware limited liability, PEI Licensing, Inc, Perry Ellis Europe Limited, a private limited company incorporated in England and Wales, Perry Ellis International Europe Limited, a private company incorporated under the laws of Ireland, Perry Ellis International Europe SARL, a private company incorporated under the laws of France, Perry Ellis International Group Holdings Limited, a private company incorporated under the laws of Ireland Perry Ellis International Group Holdings Limited, a private company incorporated under the laws of Ireland, Perry Ellis International HK Limited, a private company incorporated under the laws of Hong Kong, Perry Ellis Menswear, LLC, a Delaware limited liability, Perry Ellis Real Estate, LLC, a Delaware limited liability company formerly known as Perry Ellis Real Estate Corporation, Perry Ellis Shared Services Corporation, a Delaware corporation, Salant Holding, LLC, a Delaware limited liability, Supreme International Canada Co. Limited, a Canada corporation, Supreme International, LLC, a Delaware limited liability 22 Subsidiaries included in the Index

Officers: George Feldenkreis/73/Chmn., CEO/$1,972,868.00, Fanny Hanono/Elected Sec., Treasurer, George Pita/46/CFO/$465,911.00, Oscar Feldenkreis/Dir., COO, Pres./$1,854,812.00, Stephen Harriman/Pres./$675,112.00, Paul Rosengard/Pres./$721,057.00, Perry Ellis Brand/Contact - Licensing Inquiries, Maggie Marquetti/Contact - Savane, Farah, Customer Service, Joe Roisman/Contact - All Other Brands, Customer Service, Karen Rosenfeld/Contact - Human Resources, Britta Delaney/Contact - Human Resources, Lori Medici/Contact - Brand Marketing, Public Relations, Pablo De Echevarria/Contact - Brand Marketing, Public Relations, Jeffrey Knapp/Contact - Corporate, ASI Business Inquiries, Annette Ramos/Investor Relations Officer *(17 Officers included in Index)*

Directors: George Feldenkreis/73/Chmn., CEO, Joseph P. Lacher/Dir., Salomon Hanono/Dir., Gary Dix/Dir., Oscar Feldenkreis/Dir., COO, Pres., Joe Arriola Arriola/Dir., Linda Platzner/Dir., Ronald L. Buch/Dir., Leonard Miller/Dir.

Owners: Oscar Feldenkreis/12.00%, Paul Rosengard, Leonard Miller, Barclays Global Investors, N.A./5.30%, Dimensional Fund Advisors LP/5.60%, Ronald L. Buch, Insiders/30.40%, Stephen Harriman, Gary Dix, Salomon Hanono/3.20%, George Feldenkreis/15.30%, Joe Arriola, Joseph P. Lacher, George Pita

Financial Data: *Fiscal Year End*:01/31 *Latest Annual Data:* 1/31/2007

Year	Sales	Net Income
2007	$829,842,000	$22,409,000
2006	$849,414,000	$22,682,000
2005	$656,581,000	$20,962,000

Curr. Assets:	$314,596,000	**Curr. Liab.:**	$84,914,000	**P/E Ratio:**	19.23
Plant, Equip.:	$71,989,000	**Total Liab.:**	$344,210,000	**Indic. Yr. Divd.:**	NA
Total Assets:	$593,206,000	**Net Worth:**	$246,634,000	**Debt/ Equity:**	0.9476

Peru Copper Inc

1050 625 Howe St., Vancouver, BC, V6C2T6; *PH:* 1-604-689-0234; *Fax:* 1-604-688-0094; *http://* www.perucopper.com; *Email:* info@perucopper.com

General - Incorporation .... Canada
Employees 58
Auditor .... PricewaterhouseCoopers LLP
Stk Agt .... Computershare Trust Co
Counsel .... Brock & Blackwell LLP
DUNS No. .... NA

Stock- Price on:12/24/2007 .... $6.04
Stock Exchange .... NA
Ticker Symbol .... NA
Outstanding Shares 119,340,000
E.P.S .... -$0.04
Shareholders .... NA

Business: The groups principal activity is exploration of minerals. The group operates from Canada and the United States.

Primary SIC and add'l.: 1021

CIK No: 0001307111

Subsidiaries: Minera Peru Copper S.A., Peru Copper Syndicate Ltd.

Officers: Gerald Wolfe/CEO, Pres., David J. Lowell/Founder, Executive Chmn., David E. De Witt/Founder, Dir., VP - Corporate Development, Eric H. Peitz/CFO, Angel Alvarez/Exploration Mgr., Patrick De Witt/Dir. - Investor Relations, Armando Arrieta/Dir. - Peruvian Legal Affairs

Directors: David J. Lowell/Founder, Executive Chmn., Catherine E. McLeod Seltzer/Founder, Dir., David E. De Witt/Founder, Dir., VP - Corporate Development, Geoffrey Loudon/Founder, Luis J. Baertl/Founder, Zhengang Zhao/Dir., Wenfu Wang/Dir., Richard Miner/Dir.

Financial Data: *Fiscal Year End*:12/31 *Latest Annual Data:* 12/31/2006

Year	Sales	Net Income
2006	$1,781,000	-$36,333,000
2005	$844,000	-$20,655,000
2004	$261,000	-$11,827,000

Curr. Assets:	$36,448,000	**Curr. Liab.:**	$13,914,000		
Plant, Equip.:	$955,000	**Total Liab.:**	$13,914,000	**Indic. Yr. Divd.:**	NA
Total Assets:	$52,352,000	**Net Worth:**	$38,439,000	**Debt/ Equity:**	NA

Perusahaan Perseroan Persero Pt Telekomunikasi Indonesia TBK

Formerly: Telecommunications Indonesia
Jalan Japati, 1, Bandung, 40133; *PH:* 62-22-452-1510; *http://* www.telkom.co.id

General - Incorporation .... Indonesia
Employees .... NA
Auditor .... Lucas Kurniawan Kantor
Stk Agt .... NA
Counsel .... NA
DUNS No. 72-866-0689

Stock- Price on:12/24/2007 .... NA
Stock Exchange .... NYSE
Ticker Symbol .... NA
Outstanding Shares .... NA
E.P.S .... NA
Shareholders .... NA

Business: The group's principal activities are carried out in two segments: fixed line and cellular. Fixed line provides local and domestic telephone and other telecommunication services. Cellular segment provides telecommunication services for mobile phones. Other activities include provision for telecommunication development and services, cabled-television subscription, real estate development and services, multimedia, information and networking services. Operations of the group are carried out in Indonesia, the Netherlands and mauritius.

Primary SIC and add'l.: 3669 4899 4813 4812 4822

CIK No: 0001001807

Subsidiaries: Bridge Mobile Pte. Ltd., PTAriaWest International (AriaWest), PTBatam Bintan Telekomunikasi (BBT), PTCitra Sari Makmur (CSM), PTDayamitra Telekomunikasi (Dayamitra), PTGraha Sarana Duta (GSD), PTIndonusa Telemedia (Indonusa), PTInfomedia Nusantara (Infomedia), PTMandara Selular Indonesia (MSI), PTMultimedia Nusantara (Metra), PTNapsindo Primatel Internasional (Napsindo), PTPasifik Satelit Nusantara (PSN), PTPatra Telekomunikasi Indonesia (Patrakom), PTPembangunan Telekomunikasi Indonesia (Bangtelindo), PTPramindo Ikat Nusantara (Pramindo) 16 Subsidiaries included in the Index

Officers: Rinaldi Firmansyah/48/Dir., CEO, Dir. - Finance, Arif Arryman/52/Independent Commissioner, Tanri Abeng/66/Pres. - Commissioner, Guntur Siregar/56/Dir. - Consumer, Garuda Sugardo/57/Dir., COO, VP, Gatot Trihargo/48/Commissioner, Arief Yahya/47/Dir., Dir. - Enterprise, Wholesale, John Welly/53/Dir. - Human Resources, Arwin Rasyid/50/Dir., Pres., P. Sartono/64/Independent Commissioner, Abdul Haris/52/Dir. - Network, Solution, Anggito Abimanyu/45/Commissioner, Didik B. Santoso/Corporate Communications, Rochiman Sukarno/Head - Corporate Communication, Harsya Denny Suryo/VP - Investor Relations, Corp. Sec. *(22 Officers included in Index)*

Directors: Rinaldi Firmansyah/48/Dir., CEO, Dir. - Finance, Arwin Rasyid/50/Dir., Pres., Arief Yahya/47/Dir., Dir. - Enterprise, Wholesale, Garuda Sugardo/57/Dir., COO, VP, Sudiro Asno/51/Dir., CFO, Dir. - Finance, Faisal Syam/52/Dir. - Human Capital, Dir. - General Affair, Nyoman G. Wiryanata/49/Dir., Dir. - Network, Solution, Ermady Dahlan/55/Dir., Dir. - Consumer, Indra Utoyo/46/Dir., Chief Information Technology

Owners: JPMCB US Resident/8.71%, Government/51.19%, Insiders, The Bank of New York/7.38%, Government/100.00%

Pervasive Software Inc

12365-B Riata Trace Pkwy., Austin, TX, 78727; *PH:* 1-512-231-6000; *Fax:* 1-512-231-6010; *http://* www.pervasive.com; *Email:* info@pervasive.com

General - Incorporation	DE	**Stock**- Price on:12/24/2007	$4.58
Employees	165	Stock Exchange	NDQ
Auditor	Grant Thornton, LLP	Ticker Symbol	PVSW
Stk Agt	Computershare Trust Co	Outstanding Shares	21,380,000
Counsel	Gunderson Dettmer Stough Et Al	E.P.S	$0.26
DUNS No.	84-729-1572	Shareholders	NA

Business: The group's principal activities are to design, develop and market embedded database and information management software. The software enables cost effective development, deployment and support of low maintenance packaged server applications. The group provides data management solutions and services to simplify the development, deployment and management of business applications for small and medium enterprises. The group also offers software developer kits including tools, documentation and licenses that help the programmers to develop, test and deploy applications. The international operations are conducted in offices located in frankfurt, Paris, brussel, dublin, london, Hong Kong and Tokyo. On 08-Dec-2003, the group acquired data junction corporation.

Primary SIC and add'l.: 7372

CIK No: 0001042821

Subsidiaries: Ontario Acquisition Corp., Pervasive Software Co., Ltd., Pervasive Software Company, Pervasive Software GmbH, Pervasive Software International Inc., Pervasive Software Limited, Pervasive Software N.V., Pervasive Software S.A.R.L., PVSW Software Technologies India Private Limited, Ramal Acquisition Corp.

Officers: John Farr/Dir., CEO, Pres., Michael Hoskins/Dir., CTO, Gilbert Van Cutsem/GM - Database Products, Randy Jonkers/CFO, Steve Padgett/VP - Information Technology

Directors: John Farr/Dir., CEO, Pres., Shelby H. Carter/Chmn., Nancy Woodward/Dir., Jeff Hawn/Dir., David A. Boucher/Dir., Michael Hoskins/Dir., CTO, David R. Bradford/Dir.

Owners: Dimensional Fund Advisors, Inc./8.40%, Insiders/17.40%, Shelby H. Carter, Stephen M. Padgett, Randall G. Jonkers, John E. Farr/3.20%, David R. Bradford, FMR Corp./11.00%, David A. Boucher, Chip G. Harmon, Michele B. Thompson, Michael E. Hoskins/9.20%, Jeffrey S. Hawn, Nancy R. Woodward/3.30%, Royce & Associates/12.70%

Financial Data: ***Fiscal Year End:***06/30 ***Latest Annual Data:*** 6/30/2006

Year	Sales	Net Income
2006	$45,580,000	$4,776,000
2005	$48,352,000	$4,009,000
2004	$49,608,000	$7,314,000

Curr. Assets:	$54,598,000	***Curr. Liab.:***	$11,477,000	***P/E Ratio:***	24.11
Plant, Equip.:	$1,724,000	***Total Liab.:***	$11,477,000	***Indic. Yr. Divd.:***	NA
Total Assets:	$100,638,000	***Net Worth:***	$89,161,000	***Debt/ Equity:***	NA

Petaquilla Minerals Ltd

Formerly: Adrian Resources Ltd

475 W Georgia St., Ste. 410, Vancouver, BC, V6B 4M9; ; ***http://*** www.petaquilla.com

General - Incorporation	BC	**Stock**- Price on:12/24/2007	NA
Employees	NA	Stock Exchange	NA
Auditor	Davidson & Co LLP	Ticker Symbol	NA
Stk Agt	ComputerShare Trust Co.	Outstanding Shares	NA
Counsel	NA	E.P.S	NA
DUNS No.	24-868-3104	Shareholders	NA

Business: The group's principal activities are acquisition, exploration, exploration management, development and sale of mineral properties. The group has not yet determined whether its properties contain ore reserves that are economically recoverable. The subsidiaries include adrian resources sa, adrian resources Peru sa, adrian resources bvi inc, adrian resources Colorado inc and geo recursos international sa.The Company has one operating segment being the exploration of resource properties.

Primary SIC and add'l.: 1382 5082

CIK No: 0000947121

Subsidiaries: Adrian Resources,S.A., Georecursos Internacional, S.A, Georecursos Internacional, S.A., Panamanian corporation, Petaquilla Copper Ltd., Petaquilla Minerals, S.A.

Officers: Richard Fifer/Dir., CEO, Pres., Aurora Catibog/Accounting Mgr. - Canada, Graham Scott/Corp. Sec., Lydia De Carrizo/Controller - Panama Operations, Ricardo Tejeira/VP - Construction - Development Engineering, Octavio Choy/VP - Commercial Operations, Tom Byrne/Corporate Mgr. - Communications, Michele Merchan/VP - Corporate Affairs - Panama, Janet Francis/VP - Corporate Affairs - Canada, John Kapetas/VP - Exploration - Resources Development, Tony Ricci/Interim CFO

Directors: Richard Fifer/Dir., CEO, Pres., John Cook/Chmn., Ralph Ansley/Dir., Bob Baxter/Dir., Marco Tejeira/Dir., Micheal Levy/Dir., Kenneth W. Morgan/Dir.

Owners: Richard Fifer/1.21%, Ralph Ansley/0.02%, Graham Scott/0.03%, Michael Levy/0.69%, Robert Baxter/0.07%, Tony M. Ricci/0.03%, Marco Tejeira/0.03%, Kenneth W. Morgan/0.00%

Petcare Television Network Inc

8406 Benjamin Rd., Ste. C, Tampa, FL, 33634; ***PH:*** 1-813-888-7330; ***http://*** www.petcaretv.com

General - Incorporation	FL	**Stock**- Price on:12/24/2007	$0.015
Employees	7	Stock Exchange	NA
Auditor	Baumann, Raymondo & Co. P.A	Ticker Symbol	NA
Stk Agt	H.C. Wainwright & Co. Inc	Outstanding Shares	56,800,000
Counsel	NA	E.P.S	-$0.162
DUNS No.	NA	Shareholders	NA

Business: The groups principle activity is to provide new pet owner educational programming to animal shelters. The group operates from United States.

Primary SIC and add'l.: NA

CIK No: 0001235899

Subsidiaries: African American Medical Network, Inc., KidCARE Medical Television Network, Inc., Medical Media Television, Inc.

Officers: Philip M. Cohen/59/Chmn., CEO, Pres., Bernard J. Kouma/Pres., Donald R. Mastropietro/59/Sr. VP - Finance, CFO, Treasurer, Assist. Sec., Dir., Charles V. Richardson/63/Dir., Sr. VP - Marketing, Chief Marketing Officer, Teresa J. Bray/51/VP - Administration, Compliance, Sec., Steven Kessler/VP - Advertising Sales

Directors: Philip M. Cohen/59/Chmn., CEO, Pres., Ronald E. Whitford/Member - Advisory Board, Donald R. Mastropietro/59/Sr. VP - Finance, CFO, Treasurer, Assist. Sec., Dir., Charles V. Richardson/63/Dir., Sr. VP - Marketing, Chief Marketing Officer, W. G. Coombs/Member - Advisory Board, Gary Landsberg/Member - Advisory Board, Steven Melman/Member - Advisory Board, Gerald M. Snyder/Member - Advisory Board, Jeff Werber/50/Dir., Member - Advisory Board, Bernandine Cruz/Member - Advisory Board, Jan F. Bellows/Member - Advisory Board, Chris R. Blair/Member - Advisory Board, Nan L. Boss/Member - Advisory Board, Colin Burrows/Member - Advisory Board, Randy P. Carsch/Member - Advisory Board *(18 Directors included in Index)*

Owners: Philip M. Cohen, Donald R. Mastropietro, Teresa J. Bray, Vicis Capital Master Fund/65.96%, Holt J. Smith, Michael Marcovsky, Bernard J. Kouma, Sondra Topper, Charles V. Richardson, Jeffrey I. Werber, Insiders

Financial Data: ***Fiscal Year End:***12/31 ***Latest Annual Data:*** 12/31/2006

Year	Sales	Net Income
2006	$372,000	-$3,968,000
2005	$125,000	-$1,965,000
2004	$64,000	-$2,188,000

Curr. Assets:	$68,000	***Curr. Liab.:***	$3,615,000		
Plant, Equip.:	$7,000	***Total Liab.:***	$5,256,000	***Indic. Yr. Divd.:***	NA
Total Assets:	$303,000	***Net Worth:***	-$4,953,000	***Debt/ Equity:***	NA

Petco Animal Supplies Inc

9125 Rehco Rd., San Diego, CA, 92121; ***PH:*** 1-858-453-7845; ***Fax:*** 1-858-677-3489; ***http://*** www.petco.com

General - Incorporation	DE	**Stock**- Price on:12/24/2007	NA
Employees	NA	Stock Exchange	NA
Auditor	KPMG LLP	Ticker Symbol	NA
Stk Agt	American Stock Transfer & Trust Co.	Outstanding Shares	NA
Counsel	Latham & Watkins	E.P.S	NA
DUNS No.	02-836-4727	Shareholders	NA

Business: The group's principle activity is the retail of pet food and supplies. It operates six hundred specialty stores in forty-three states and the district of columbia that sell pet food brands like nutro, science diet and eukanuba. Supplies include grooming products, toys, novelty items, vitamins and veterinary supplies. In addition, the stores sell small pets such as fish, birds and other animals. Retail sales are also made on the Internet through the site, petco.com. The group operates three central distribution centers in mira loma, California; dayton, New Jersey; and joliet, Illinois in addition to five regional distribution centers. The major suppliers of merchandise to the group are the iams company, hill's pet products inc and nutro inc.

Primary SIC and add'l.: 5999

CIK No: 0000888455

Subsidiaries: 17187 Yukon Inc., E-Pet Services, E-Pet Services, LLC, International Pet Supplies and Distribution, Inc., Pet Concepts International, PETCO Animal Supplies Stores, Inc., PETCO Southwest, Inc., PETCO Southwest, L.P., PM Management Incorporated

Officers: James M. Myers/Dir., CEO, Bruce C. Hall/COO, Pres., Rodney Carter/Sr. VP, CFO, Frederick W. Major/Sr. VP - Information Systems, David Bolen/Exec. VP, Chief Merchandising Officer, Janet D. Mitchell/Sr. VP - Human Resources, Administration, Razia Richter/Sr. VP - Supply Chain, William M. Woodard/Sr. VP - Business Development

Directors: James M. Myers/Dir., CEO, Brian K. Devine/Chmn., David B. Appel/Dir., Sandra N. Bane/Dir., David T. Ching/53/Dir., Julian C. Day/Dir., John G. Danhakl/Dir., Charles W. Duddles/Dir., Peter Maslen/Dir.

Petmed Express Inc

1441 SW 29th Ave., Pompano Beach, FL, 33069; ***PH:*** 1-954-979-5995; ***Fax:*** 1-954-971-0544; ***http://*** www.1800petmeds.com

General - Incorporation	FL	**Stock**- Price on:12/24/2007	$12.97
Employees	216	Stock Exchange	NDQ
Auditor	Goldstein Golub Kessler LLP	Ticker Symbol	PETS
Stk Agt	Florida Atlantic Stock Transfer, Inc.	Outstanding Shares	24,340,000
Counsel	NA	E.P.S	$0.70
DUNS No.	NA	Shareholders	NA

Business: The group's principal activity is to market prescription and non- prescription pet medications, health and nutritional supplements and accessories at discounted prices through the pet med express catalog, customer service representatives and on the Internet. The group offers broad variety of products for dogs and cats. The products are prescription medications, non-prescription medications, health and nutritional supplements and accessories. Prescription medications include heartworm treatments, thyroid and arthritis medications, antibiotics, and other specialty medications, as well as generic substitutes, non-prescription medications include flea and tick control products, bone and joint care products, vitamins and supplements, and hygiene products. Group sells these products directly to retail customers.

Primary SIC and add'l.: 5912

CIK No: 0001040130

Subsidiaries: First Image Marketing, Inc., Southeastern Veterinary Exports, Inc.

Officers: Menderes Akdag/47/Dir., CEO, Pres./$669,970.00, Bruce S. Rosenbloom/CFO/$235,239.00

Directors: Menderes Akdag/47/Dir., CEO, Pres., Robert C. Schweitzer/62/Chmn., Frank J. Formica/64/Dir., Gian M. Fulgoni/60/Dir., Ronald J. Korn/68/Dir.

Owners: Bruce S. Rosenbloom, Insiders/4.30%, Menderes Akdag/3.10%, Morgan Stanley/5.80%, Barclays Global Investors, NA/6.00%, Gian M. Fulgoni, Frank J. Formica, Munder Capital Management/5.70%, Robert C. Schweitzer, Ronald J. Korn

Financial Data: ***Fiscal Year End:***03/31 ***Latest Annual Data:*** 3/31/2007

Year	Sales	Net Income
2007	$162,246,000	$14,444,000
2006	$137,583,000	$12,064,000
2005	$108,358,000	$8,010,000

Curr. Assets:	$57,968,000	***Curr. Liab.:***	$7,355,000	***P/E Ratio:***	19.95
Plant, Equip.:	$1,991,000	***Total Liab.:***	$7,355,000	***Indic. Yr. Divd.:***	NA
Total Assets:	$61,218,000	***Net Worth:***	$53,864,000	***Debt/ Equity:***	NA

Petro Resources Corp

777 Post Oak Blvd, Ste.910, Houston, TX, 77056; ***PH:*** 1-832-369-6986; ***Fax:*** 1-832-369-6992; ***http://*** www.petroresourcescorp.com; ***Email:*** investorrelations@petroresourcescorp.com

General - Incorporation
Employees 4
Auditor NA
Stk Agt Nevada Agency & Trust Company
Counsel NA
DUNS No. NA

Stock- Price on:12/24/2007 $2.4501
Stock Exchange AMEX
Ticker Symbol PRC
Outstanding Shares 21,250,000
E.P.S. -$0.2
Shareholders NA

Business: The groups principle activities include acquiring, drilling and producing oil and natural gas properties. The group operates from the United States. The group's quarterly revenue for September 2007 was 1.97 millions of USD.

Primary SIC and add'l.: 1311

CIK No: 0001335190

Subsidiaries: PRC Williston, LLC

Officers: Wayne P. Hall/Chmn., CEO, Pres., Don Kirkendall/Dir., Pres., Allen R. McGee/Dir., CFO, Harry Stout/Exec. VP, General Counsel

Directors: Wayne P. Hall/Chmn., CEO, Pres., Gary L. Hall/Dir., Raleigh J. Bailes/Dir., Brad Bynum/Dir., Don Kirkendall/Dir., Pres., Joe L. McClaugherty/Dir., Allen R. McGee/Dir., CFO, Steven Pfeifer/Dir.

Owners: Eagle Operating, Inc/14.80%, Brad Bynum, Suzanne Kerr Bryant/5.30%, Steven A. Pfeifer, Donald L. Kirkendall, Gary L. Hall/1.40%, Wayne P. Hall/9.60%, Touradji Capital Management, LP/100.00%, Harry Lee Stout, Joe L. McClaugherty, Raleigh J. Bailes, Gary E. Bryant/7.90%, Insiders/17.50%, Bonanza Master Fund, Ltd/17.00%, Allen R. McGee/3.70%

Financial Data: *Fiscal Year End:*NA *Latest Annual Data:* 12/31/2006

Year	Sales	Net Income
2006	$1,546,000	-$3,899,000

Curr. Assets:	$4,388,000	**Curr. Liab.:**	$218,000		
Plant, Equip.:	$4,256,000	**Total Liab.:**	$249,000	**Indic. Yr. Divd.:**	NA
Total Assets:	$10,948,000	**Net Worth:**	$10,699,000	**Debt/ Equity:**	0.0028

Petro-Canada

150 6th Ave. SW, Calgary, AB, T2P 3E3; ***PH:*** 1-403-296-8000; ***http://*** www.petro-canada.ca

General - Incorporation Canada
Employees 5,156
Auditor Deloitte & Touche LLP
Stk Agt. Mellon Trust Co
Counsel NA
DUNS No. 20-522-0536

Stock- Price on:12/24/2007 $52.64
Stock Exchange NYSE
Ticker Symbol PCZ
Outstanding Shares 495,830,000
E.P.S. $4.67
Shareholders NA

Business: The group's principle activities are to explore, develop and retail crude oil and natural gas. The group's business is divided into two sectors: upstream sector which develops, produces and markets crude oil, natural gas, natural gas liquids, sulphur and oil sands; downstream sector which refines crude oil and other feedstocks and markets and distributes petroleum products and related goods and services. The group's quarterly revenue for September 2007 was 5,497.00 millions of CAD.

Primary SIC and add'l.: 1321 2911 1382 1311 5541

CIK No: 0000795615

Subsidiaries: 3908968 Canada Inc., Petro-Canada U.K. Holdings Ltd., Petro-Canada U.K. Limited

Officers: Ron A. Brenneman/61/Dir., CEO, Pres., Harry Roberts/CFO, Exec. VP, Philip Churton/VP - Marketing, M. A. Raymond/VP - Environment, Health, Safety, Security, Helen Wesley/VP - Finance, Wayne R. Pennington/Treasurer, Gordon Carrick/Sr. VP - Operations, Technology, John D. Miller/VP - Natural Gas Marketing, Michael Danyluk/CIO, Hugh L. Hooker/Chief Compliance Officer, Corp. Sec., Assoc. General Counsel, Graham Lyon/VP - Business Development International, Peter S. Kallos/Exec. VP - International, Boris Jackman/Exec. VP - Downstream, Michael Barkwell/Controller, Pamela Tisdale/Sr. Advisor, Investor Relations *(32 Officers included in Index)*

Directors: Ron A. Brenneman/61/Dir., CEO, Pres., Brian F. MacNeill/68/Chmn., Daniel Valot/63/Dir., Richard J. Currie/70/Dir., Thomas E. Kierans/67/Dir., Paul Haseldonckx/59/Dir., Paul D. Melnuk/59/Dir., Maureen McCaw/53/Dir., James W. Simpson/63/Dir., Guylaine Saucier/61/Dir., Claude Fontaine/66/Dir., Gail Cook-Bennett/67/Dir.

Owners: GUYLAINE SAUCIER, THOMAS E. KIERANS, CLAUDE FONTAINE, RICHARD J. CURRIE, PAUL D. MELNUK, RON A. BRENNEMAN, MAUREEN McCAW, PAUL HASELDONCKX, Angus A. Bruneau, JAMES W. SIMPSON, GAIL COOK-BENNETT, BRIAN F. MacNEILL

Financial Data: *Fiscal Year End:*12/31 *Latest Annual Data:* 12/31/2006

Year	Sales	Net Income
2006	$16,019,869,000	$1,493,094,000
2005	$15,087,930,000	$1,664,520,000
2004	$11,937,223,000	$1,451,364,000

Curr. Assets:	$2,424,991,000	**Curr. Liab.:**	$2,872,919,000		
Plant, Equip.:	$15,940,924,000	**Total Liab.:**	$10,473,111,000	**Indic. Yr. Divd.:**	$0.480
Total Assets:	$19,432,533,000	**Net Worth:**	$8,959,422,000	**Debt/ Equity:**	NA

Petrobras Energa Participaciones

Maipu 1, 122nd Fl., Buenos Aires; ***PH:*** 54-1143446000; ***http://*** www.petrobrasenergia.com

General - Incorporation AR
Employees 5,036
Auditor Henry Martin Y Asociados SRL
Stk Agt. Citibank N.A
Counsel NA
DUNS No. NA

Stock- Price on:12/24/2007 $11.15
Stock Exchange NYSE
Ticker Symbol PZE
Outstanding Shares 213,200,000
E.P.S. $1.02
Shareholders NA

Business: The group's principal activities are the exploration and production of oil and gas; petrochemical; refining; distribution and transportation of hydrocarbon and electricity; and investment holding.

Primary SIC and add'l.: 4911 6282 4925 2911 1382

CIK No: 0001099205

Subsidiaries: Petrobras Energa Per S.A. (Per), Petrobras Energa S.A., Petrobras Energa Venezuela S.A. (Venezuela), World Fund Financial Services (Cayman)

Officers: Carlos Alberto De Meira Fontes/58/Dir., CEO, Alberto Da Fonseca Guimaraes/Dir. - Petrobras Energia SA, Pablo Maria Puiggari/Executive Mgr. - Communications, Petrobras Energia SA, Daniel Hector Casal/Dir. - Legal Affairs, Petrobras Energia SA, Michael Ditchfield/Executive Mgr. - Planning, Management Control, Petrobras Energia SA, Roberto Fortunati/Dir. - Petrobras Energia SA, Luis Miguel Sas/45/Dir., CFO

Directors: Carlos Alberto De Meira Fontes/58/Dir., CEO, Decio Fabrcio Oddone Da Costa/47/Chmn., Daniel Lima De Oliveira/56/Vice Chmn., Luis Miguel Sas/45/Dir., CFO, Hector Daniel Casal/52/Dir., Carlos Tadeuda Costa Fraga/50/Dir., Solange Da Silva Guedes/47/Dir., Venina Velosa Da Fonseca/45/Dir., Sidney Granja Affonso/56/Dir., Carlos Alberto Pereira De Oliveira/50/Dir., Joao Bezerra/50/Dir., Vison Reichemback Da Silva/57/Dir., Claudio Fontes Nunes/53/Dir., Rui Antonio Alves Da Fonseca/51/Dir., Andre Garcez Ghirardi/57/Dir. *(21 Directors included in Index)*

Owners: Petrobras Participaciones S.L./58.60%

Financial Data: *Fiscal Year End:*12/31 *Latest Annual Data:* 12/31/2006

Year	Sales	Net Income
2006	$3,618,144,000	$317,261,000
2005	$3,337,506,000	-$25,372,000
2004	$2,347,448,000	$255,816,000

Curr. Assets:	$1,648,973,000	**Curr. Liab.:**	$1,678,675,000		
Plant, Equip.:	$3,692,563,000	**Total Liab.:**	$4,705,056,000	**Indic. Yr. Divd.:**	$0.170
Total Assets:	$6,727,104,000	**Net Worth:**	$2,022,048,000	**Debt/ Equity:**	NA

PetroChina Co Ltd

16 Andelu, Beijing, Dongcheng District, 100011; ***PH:*** 86-1062094114; ***http://*** www.petrochina.com.cn

General - Incorporation China
Employees 446,290
Auditor PricewaterhouseCoopers LLP
Stk Agt Bank of New York
Counsel NA
DUNS No. NA

Stock- Price on:12/24/2007 $141.53
Stock Exchange NYSE
Ticker Symbol PTR
Outstanding Shares 1,790,000,000
E.P.S. $11.00
Shareholders NA

Business: The group's principal activities are the exploration, production, trading and sale of refined and chemical products. Other activities include the design and construction of pipelines and provision of consulting services. The group's major customers are sinopec and cnpc.

Primary SIC and add'l.: 4932 4924 1389 2999 1321 1311 2911

CIK No: 0001108329

Subsidiaries: Daqing Oilfield Company Limited, Daqing Yu Shu Lin Oilfield Company Limited, Jilin Chemical Industrial Company Limited, Jinzhou Petrochemical Limited Company, Liaohe Jinma Oilfield Company Limited, PetroChina International Indonesia Limited, PetroChina International Limited, Zhong You Kan Tan Kai Fa Company Limited

Officers: Duan Wende/56/Exec. Dir., Sr. VP, Chmn. - Health, Wen Qingshan/49/Company Supervisor, Zhang Anping/Contact - Public Relations, Duan Yarui/Contact - Foreign Affairs Office, Jia Chengzao/59/VP, Wang Guoliang/55/CFO, Wu Zhipan/51/Independent Supervisor, Sun Xianfeng/55/Supervisor, Xu Fengli/60/Supervisor, GM - Audit Department, Su Shulin/45/Dir., Sr. VP, Li Huaiqi/58/Sec., Qin Gang/54/Supervisor, Liao Yongyuan/45/VP, Hu Wenrui/58/VP, Mao Zefeng/Investor Relations Officer *(22 Officers included in Index)*

Directors: Chen Geng/61/Chmn., Duan Wende/56/Exec. Dir., Sr. VP, Chmn. - Health, Chee-Chen Tung/65/Dir., Wang Yilin/51/Non - Exec. Dir., Zeng Yukang/57/Non - Exec. Dir., Zhou Jiping/55/Non - Exec. Dir., Franco Bernab/59/Dir., Liu Hongru/77/Dir., Jiang Fan/44/Non - Exec. Dir., Zheng Hu/61/Non - Exec. Dir., Su Shulin/45/Dir., Sr. VP

Financial Data: *Fiscal Year End:*12/31 *Latest Annual Data:* 12/31/2006

Year	Sales	Net Income
2006	$88,326,980,000	$18,728,353,000
2005	$68,476,396,000	$17,095,260,000
2004	$46,956,000,000	$13,065,000,000

Curr. Assets:	$20,796,860,000	**Curr. Liab.:**	$23,060,488,000		
Plant, Equip.:	$79,800,141,000	**Total Liab.:**	$36,143,554,000	**Indic. Yr. Divd.:**	$5.400
Total Assets:	$109,790,608,000	**Net Worth:**	$73,647,054,000	**Debt/ Equity:**	0.0620

Petrogen Corp

10777 Wheimer, Ste 1100, Houston, TX, 77042; ***PH:*** 1-281-383-9403; ***http://*** www.petrogencorp.com

General - Incorporation NV
Employees 2
Auditor Dale Matheson Carr-Hilton Labonte
Stk Agt Transfer Online, Inc.
Counsel NA
DUNS No. NA

Stock- Price on:12/24/2007 $0.37
Stock Exchange OTC
Ticker Symbol PEYG
Outstanding Shares NA
E.P.S. -$0.36
Shareholders NA

Business: The group's principal activities are to acquire, explore and develop oil and natural gas properties. The group is primarily engaged in the business of acquiring oil and natural gas properties for exploration and production within the United States and internationally. The group's operations also include processing of natural gas into various natural gas liquids.

Primary SIC and add'l.: 1311 1382

CIK No: 0001057226

Subsidiaries: Petrogen, Petrogen, Inc.

Officers: Sacha H. Spindler/Chmn., CEO, Sam S. Sen/COO, Pres., Brian Fiddler/CFO, Louis J. Fruchier/Sr. VP - Corporate Development, Jose Bereskyj/Sr. VP - Exploration, Development, Eduardo Davila/Advisor to The Dir.

Directors: Sacha H. Spindler/Chmn., CEO, Justin D. Perryman/Dir.

Owners: Brian Fiddler/1.52%, Insiders/40.74%, Soumitra Sen/9.21%, Timothy G. Russell/1.49%, Justin Perryman/3.77%, Sacha H. Spindler/24.75%

Financial Data: *Fiscal Year End:*12/31 *Latest Annual Data:* 12/31/2006

Year	Sales	Net Income
2006	NA	-$5,708,000
2005	$199,000	-$3,065,000
2004	$107,000	-$4,004,000

Curr. Assets:	$225,000	**Curr. Liab.:**	$2,017,000		
Plant, Equip.:	$1,418,000	**Total Liab.:**	$2,017,000	**Indic. Yr. Divd.:**	NA
Total Assets:	$1,702,000	**Net Worth:**	-$315,000	**Debt/ Equity:**	NA

Petrohawk Energy Corp

1000 Louisiana, Ste. 5600, Houston, TX, 77002; ***PH:*** 1-832-204-2700; ***Fax:*** 1-832-204-2800; ***http://*** www.petrohawk.com; ***Email:*** investors@petrohawk.com

General - Incorporation	DE
Employees	154
Auditor	Deloitte & Touche LLP
Stk Agt	American Stock Transfer & Trust Co.
Counsel	NA
DUNS No.	NA

Stock- Price on:12/24/2007	NA
Stock Exchange	NYSE
Ticker Symbol	HK
Outstanding Shares	NA
E.P.S.	$0.62
Shareholders	NA

Business: The group's principal activity is to acquire, explore, develop and produce natural gas and crude oil. The exploration and development of oil and gas producing trends are conducted in Texas, Louisiana, Oklahoma and Kansas. In addition, the group has international operations in west queensland, Australia on the ethabuka structure. On 31-Dec-2003, it owned interests in 218 wells in the mid continent, Texas and Louisiana regions and drilled and completed 28 gross wells. These interests had a net proven reserve of 18.3 billion cubic feet of gas equivalent consisting of 14.7 billion cubic feet of natural gas and 608.6 million barrels of oil. The group's major clients include duke energy, allegro investments and ip petroleum (pure).

Primary SIC and add'l.: 1381 1311

CIK No: 0001059324

Subsidiaries: P-H Energy, LLC, Petrohawk Holdings, LLC, Petrohawk Operating Company, Petrohawk Properties, LP, Red River Field Services, LLC

Officers: Floyd C. Wilson/Chmn., CEO, Pres./$1,887,939.00, Shane M. Bayless/41/Exec. VP, Treasurer/$901,828.00, William N. Hahne/56/COO, Exec. VP/$750,933.00, Weldon H. Holcombe/Exec. VP - Mid Continent Region, Richard K. Stoneburner/COO, Exec. VP/$840,590.00, Larry L. Helm/Exec. VP - Finance, Administration/$965,420.00, Mark J. Mize/CFO, Exec. VP, Treasurer, Stephen W. Herod/Exec. VP - Corporate Development/$935,590.00, Tina Obut/VP - Corporate Reserves, Joan Dunlap/VP - Investor Relations, David Elkouri/Exec. VP, General Counsel - Secretory

Directors: Floyd C. Wilson/Chmn., CEO, Pres., Robert C. Stone/Dir., James L. Irish/Dir., Tucker S. Bridwell/Dir., James W. Christmas/Dir., Robert G. Raynolds/Dir., Christopher A. Viggiano/Dir., Thomas R. Fuller/60/Dir., Gary A. Merriman/Dir.

Owners: Edward C. Johnson/9.40%, James J. Pallota/5.10%, FMR Corp./10.00%, Fidelity Management& Research Company/9.40%, Paul Tudor Jones/5.10%

Financial Data: Fiscal Year End:12/31 **Latest Annual Data:** 12/31/2006

Year	Sales	Net Income
2006	$587,762,000	$116,563,000
2005	$258,039,000	-$16,634,000
2004	$33,577,000	$8,117,000

Curr. Assets:	$246,712,000	Curr. Liab.:	$332,019,000		
Plant, Equip.:	$3,066,043,000	Total Liab.:	$2,351,312,000	Indic. Yr. Divd.:	NA
Total Assets:	$4,279,656,000	Net Worth:	$1,928,344,000	Debt/ Equity:	0.7559

PetroHunter Energy Corp

1875 Lawrence St., 14th Fl., Denver, CO, 80202; **PH:** 1-303-572-8900; **Fax:** 1-303-572-8927; **http://** www.petrohunter.com

General - Incorporation	MD
Employees	16
Auditor	Hein & Associates LLP
Stk Agt	NA
Counsel	NA
DUNS No.	NA

Stock- Price on:12/24/2007	$0.58
Stock Exchange	OTC
Ticker Symbol	PHUN
Outstanding Shares	222,930,000
E.P.S.	NA
Shareholders	NA

Business: The groups principle activity is in oil and gas exploration and production. The group operates from the United States and Australia.

Primary SIC and add'l.: 1311

CIK No: 0001298824

Subsidiaries: PaleoTechnology Australia Pty Ltd., PaleoTechnology Inc., PetroHunter Energy NT Ltd., PetroHunter Heavy Oil Ltd., PetroHunter Operating Company, Sweetpea Petroleum Pty Ltd.

Officers: Kelly H. Nelson/51/Chmn., CEO, Charles B. Crowell/Chmn., CEO, Thomas Ahlbrandt/59/VP - Exploration, Chief Geologist, Garry Lavold/62/COO, Pres., Carmen J. Lotito/63/Dir., CFO, Treasurer, Sec., Lyle R. Nelson/VP - Operations

Directors: Kelly H. Nelson/51/Chmn., CEO, Charles B. Crowell/Chmn., CEO, Carmen J. Lotito/63/Dir., CFO, Treasurer, Sec., Anthony Keith Yeats/Dir., Martin B. Oring/Dir., Matthew R. Silverman/Dir.

Owners: Carmen J. Lotito, Marc A. Bruner/33.40%, Kelly H. Nelson, Anthony K. Yeats, Insiders/1.40%, Garry Lavold

Petrol Industries Inc

Ste. 1.1, 1st Fl., Kompleks Antarabangsa, Jalan Sultan Ismail, Kuala Lumpur, 50250; **PH:** 1-603-2142-1611; **Fax:** 1-603-2142-1826; **http://** www.umland.com.my; **Email:** pr@umland.com.my

General - Incorporation	NV
Employees	NA
Auditor	Heard Mcelroy & Vestal LLP
Stk Agt	Mellon Investor Services LLC
Counsel	NA
DUNS No.	06-704-3943

Stock- Price on:12/24/2007	$0.065
Stock Exchange	OTC
Ticker Symbol	PTLD
Outstanding Shares	NA
E.P.S.	NA
Shareholders	NA

Business: The group's principal activities are drilling and producing oil and gas and marketing to major oil companies and other purchasers. The group is a wholly owned subsidiary of sovereign industries, inc. The group drills and produces oil and gas on leased property located in the caddo pine island field and the shreveport field located in caddo parish, Louisiana. It contains 8 completed gas wells, 18 completed wells producing oil and gas, and 157 completed oil wells, principally in the annona chalk zone.

Primary SIC and add'l.: 1381 1311

CIK No: 0000077864

Subsidiaries: Sovereign Industries, Inc

Financial Data: Fiscal Year End:12/31 **Latest Annual Data:** 3/31/2004

Year	Sales	Net Income
2004	$222,000	-$8,000
2003	$764,000	-$20,000

Curr. Assets:	$150,000	Curr. Liab.:	$1,773,000		
Plant, Equip.:	$95,000	Total Liab.:	$1,773,000	Indic. Yr. Divd.:	NA
Total Assets:	$246,000	Net Worth:	-$1,526,000	Debt/ Equity:	NA

Petrol Oil & Gas Inc

Corporate Woods Bldg.51 9393W 110th St., Ste.500, OverlandPark, KS, 66210; **PH:** 1-913-323-4925; **Fax:** 1-913-323-4926; **http://** www.petroloilandgas.com

General - Incorporation	NV
Employees	8
Auditor	Weaver & Martin, LLC
Stk Agt	Madison Stock Transfer, Inc.
Counsel	NA
DUNS No.	NA

Stock- Price on:12/24/2007	$0.3
Stock Exchange	OTC
Ticker Symbol	POIG
Outstanding Shares	29,090,000
E.P.S.	-$0.27
Shareholders	NA

Business: The groups principle activity is to produce oil and gas. The group creates value through the acquisition, development and production of economic quantities of natural gas from buried coal seams, denoted as coal-bed methane and other gas bearing formations, as well as the production of oil. In the year 2006, the group acquired Savage Resources, LLC and Savage Pipeline, LLC. The group operates from the United States.

Primary SIC and add'l.: 5541

CIK No: 0001109348

Subsidiaries: Coal Creek Pipeline, Inc., Neodesha Pipeline, Inc., Petrol Oil, II LLC, Petrol Paola, LLC

Officers: Loren Moll/CEO, Pres., Paul T. Branagan/64/Dir., CEO, Pres., Sec., Treasurer, Jerry Falkner/Contact - Investor Relations

Directors: Paul T. Branagan/64/Dir., CEO, Pres., Sec., Treasurer, Suzanne Herring/43/Dir., Robert H. Kite/53/Dir., Duane D. Fadness/59/Dir.

Owners: Loren Moll/11.00%, Insiders/19.00%, Paul Branagan/8.00%, Robert Kite

Financial Data: Fiscal Year End:12/31 **Latest Annual Data:** 12/31/2006

Year	Sales	Net Income
2006	$7,489,000	-$7,795,000
2005	$6,041,000	-$5,964,000
2004	$867,000	-$4,524,000

Curr. Assets:	$6,581,000	Curr. Liab.:	$15,086,000		
Plant, Equip.:	$28,267,000	Total Liab.:	$29,222,000	Indic. Yr. Divd.:	NA
Total Assets:	$36,487,000	Net Worth:	$7,265,000	Debt/ Equity:	2.8693

Petroleo Brasileiro SA Petrobras

750 Lexington Ave., 43rd Fl., New York, NY, 10022; **PH:** 1-212-829-1517; **Fax:** 1-212-832-5300; **http://** www2.petrobras.com.br

General - Incorporation	
Employees	62,266
Auditor	Ernst & Young, LLP
Stk Agt	Registrar and Depositary Bank
Counsel	NA
DUNS No.	NA

Stock- Price on:12/24/2007	$123.19
Stock Exchange	NYSE
Ticker Symbol	PBR
Outstanding Shares	1,100,000,000
E.P.S.	$3.46
Shareholders	NA

Business: The groups principle activities include exploring and producing gas and energy. The group operates from the Angola, Argentina, Bolivia, Colombia, Nigeria and the United States.

Primary SIC and add'l.: 5171 1311 1389 1381 5984 2911 4922 2992 2999 4923 4613 4612 1382 5172 5399 5499 5983 1321 4925 3533 5541

CIK No: 0001119639

Subsidiaries: 5283 Participaes Ltda., Albacora Japan Petroleum Limited Company, Baixada Santista Energia Ltda., Barracuda e Caratinga Holding Company B.V., BEAR Insurance Company Limited, Blade Securities Limited, Braspetro Oil Company , Braspetro Oil Services Company , Cayman Cabiunas Investments Co. Ltda., Charter Development - CDC, Cia. De Desenvolvimento e Modernizao de Plantas Industriais CDMPI, Codajs Coari Participaes Ltda., Companhia de Recuperao Secundria, Companhia Locadora de Equipamentos Petrolferos S.A. CLEP, Companhia Petrolfera Marlim 43 Subsidiaries included in the Index

Officers: Armando Ramos Tripodi/Head - Ceo's Office , Gapre, Daniel Lima De Oliveira/57/Chmn., CEO, Jose Sergio Gabrielli De Azevedo/Dir., Pres., CEO - Representative, Controller, Dilma Vana Rousseff/Chmn. - Representative, Controller, Guido Mantega/Dir. - Representative, Controlling Shareholder, Silas Rondeau Cavalcante Silva/Dir. - Representative, Controller, Guilherme Pontes Galvao Franca/49/Commercial Mgr., Francisco Roberto De Albuquerque/71/Dir. - Controlling Shareholder Representative, Maria Das Gracas Silva Foster/Dir. - Gas Energy, Fabio Colletti Barbosa/Dir. - Representative, Minority Common Shareholders, Servio Tulio Da Rosa Tinoco/53/Financial Mgr., Helio Shiguenobu Fujikawa/Sec. - General , Segepe, Jorge Gerdau Johannpeter/Dir. - Representative, Preferred Shareholders, Arthur Antonio Sendas/Dir. - Representative, Controller, Almir Guilherme Barbassa/CFO, Investor Relations Officer (23 Officers included in Index)

Directors: Daniel Lima De Oliveira/57/Chmn., CEO, Jose Sergio Gabrielli De Azevedo/Dir., Pres., CEO - Representative, Controller, Dilma Vana Rousseff/Chmn. - Representative, Controller, Guido Mantega/Dir. - Representative, Controlling Shareholder, Marcos Antonio Silva Menezes/56/Dir., Silas Rondeau Cavalcante Silva/Dir. - Representative, Controller, Nilo Carvalho Vieira Filho/54/Dir., Francisco Roberto De Albuquerque/71/Dir. - Controlling Shareholder Representative, Roger Agnelli/49/Dir.

Owners: Insiders, BNDES Participaes S.A.-BNDESPAR/1.90%, Brazilian government/55.70%, Other Brazilian public sector entities/0.04%, Insiders, BNDES Participaes S.A.-BNDESPAR/15.50%, Other Brazilian public sector entities/0.10%

Financial Data: Fiscal Year End:12/31 **Latest Annual Data:** 12/31/2005

Year	Sales	Net Income
2005	$56,324,000,000	$10,344,000,000
2004	$37,452,000,000	$6,190,000,000
2003	$42,690,000,000	$6,559,000,000

Curr. Assets:	$25,778,000,000	Curr. Liab.:	$18,155,000,000	P/E Ratio:	9.43
Plant, Equip.:	$45,920,000,000	Total Liab.:	$44,634,000,000	Indic. Yr. Divd.:	$1.620
Total Assets:	$78,625,000,000	Net Worth:	$32,917,000,000	Debt/ Equity:	NA

Petroleum Development Corp

120 Genesis Blvd., Bridgeport, WV, 26330; **PH:** 1-304-842-3597; **Fax:** 1-304-842-0913; **http://** www.petd.com; **Email:** petd@petd.com

General - Incorporation ... NV
Employees ... 189
Auditor ... KPMG LLP
Stk Agt ... Transfer Online, Inc.
Counsel ... Duane, Morris & Hecksher
DUNS No. ... 05-570-0389

Stock- Price on:12/24/2007 ... $48.44
Stock Exchange ... NDQ
Ticker Symbol ... PETD
Outstanding Shares ... 14,890,000
E.P.S ... $2.22
Shareholders ... NA

Business: The group's principle activity is to develop, produce and market natural gas and oil. The activities also include drilling and development activities, acquisition of natural gas and oil producing wells and the expansion of natural gas marketing activities. The group operates under three segments namely natural gas sales, drilling and development and well operations. It drills natural gas wells for company sponsored drilling partnerships and retains an interest in each well. The group also engages in oil and gas sales to commercial and industrial end-users. The group's quarterly revenue for September 2007 was 76.28 millions of USD.

Primary SIC and add'l.: 4924 1381

CIK No: 0000077877

Subsidiaries: PDC Securities Incorporated, Riley Natural Gas

Officers: Steven R. Williams/Chmn., CEO/$1,206,285.00, Thomas E. Riley/Dir., Pres./$727,738.00, Darwin L. Stump/Chief Accounting Officer/$565,862.00, Celesta M. Miracle/VP - Investor Relations, Communications, Ersel E. Morgan/VP - Special Projects, Dewey W. Gerdom/VP - Exploration, Bart Brookman/VP - Production, Tina R. Smith/VP - Natural Gas, Oil Marketing, Eric R. Stearns/Exec. VP - Exploration, Productioin/$772,627.00, Chuck Holm/Dir. - Accounting Operations, Cindy Dalton/Dir. - Financial Reporting, Tom W. Carpenter/Dir. - Geo, Sciences, Steven W. Trippett/Dir. - Drilling, Completions, Susan A. Foster/Dir. - Reserve Engineering, Jim Wason/Dir. - Land *(23 Officers included in Index)*

Directors: Steven R. Williams/Chmn., CEO, Thomas E. Riley/Dir., Pres., Kimberly Luff Wakim/Dir., Vincent F. D'Annunzio/Dir., David C. Parke/Dir., Jeffrey C. Swoveland/Dir., Anthony Crisafio/Dir., Donald B. Nestor/Dir.

Owners: David C. Parke, Vincent F. D'Annunzio, Eric R. Stearns, Kimberly Luff Wakim, Darwin L. Stump, Barclays Global Investors, NA/6.90%, FMR Corp./16.30%, Steven R. Williams/2.10%, Kayne Anderson Rudnick/7.20%, Thomas E. Riley, Insiders/3.60%, Anthony J. Crisafio, Steinberg Asset Management, LLC/14.00%, Jeffrey C. Swoveland

Financial Data: *Fiscal Year End:*12/31 *Latest Annual Data:* 12/31/2006

Year	Sales	Net Income
2006	$286,503,000	$237,772,000
2005	$343,133,000	$41,452,000
2004	$293,660,000	$33,228,000

Curr. Assets:	$271,014,000	Curr. Liab.:	$241,834,000	P/E Ratio:	3.05
Plant, Equip.:	$394,217,000	Total Liab.:	$524,143,000	Indic. Yr. Divd.:	NA
Total Assets:	$884,287,000	Net Worth:	$360,144,000	Debt/ Equity:	NA

Petroleum Geo-Services

Strandveien 4, N-1366, Lysaker; *PH:* 47-67526400; *Fax:* 47-90855672; *http://* www.pgs.com; *Email:* ir@pgs.com

General - Incorporation ... Norway
Employees ... 5,130
Auditor ... Ernst & Young AS
Stk Agt ... Mellon Investor Services LLC
Counsel ... Baker & Botts LLP
DUNS No. ... 51-504-1853

Stock- Price on:12/24/2007 ... $25.76
Stock Exchange ... OTC
Ticker Symbol ... PGSVY
Outstanding Shares ... 177,880,000
E.P.S ... $2.41
Shareholders ... NA

Business: The group's principal activity is to provide geophysical services for the marine oil field industry. The group operates through four segments: marine geophysical, onshore, production and petra. The marine geophysical segment acquires, processes and markets 3D, 4d and multi-component marine and onshore seismic data and provides 4d and multi-component reservoir interpretation, characterization and monitoring services. Onshore segment includes all seismic operations on land and in shallow water. The production services segment owns and operates floating production storage and offloading facilities, other offshore production facilities and provides production management services. Pertra is a small oil and gas company operating for the norwegian continental shelf. The customers of the group include oil and gas companies and seismic marketing companies. The group filed for chapter 11 proceedings on 29-Jul-2003 and emerged from proceedings on 05-Nov-2003.

Primary SIC and add'l.: 1382

CIK No: 0000902053

Subsidiaries: FMR Corp, Landmark Graphics Corporation, natural gas, Norwegian Reservoir Services, Oil and Natural Gas, Petrofac Limited, Petrojarl ASA, Petroleum Geo-Services ASA, PGS Geophysical AS, PGS Tigress (UK) Ltd, Walter Herwig AS

Officers: Svein Rennemo/61/CEO, Pres., Gottfred Langseth/42/Sr. VP, CFO, Rune Eng/47/Group Pres. - Marine, Eric Wersich/45/Group Pres. - Onshore, Rune Olav Pedersen/General Counsel, Ola Bosterud/VP - Group Communications, Terje Bjolseth/VP - Global - Human Resources, Sverre Strandenes/52/Group Pres. Data Processing - Technology, Bard Stenberg/Mgr. - Investor Relations, Katrina Parrott/Contact - US Investor Services

Directors: Jens Ulltveit-Moe/Chmn., Francis Gugen/Dir., Harald Norvik/Dir., Holly Van Deursen/Dir., Wenche Kjolas/Dir., Siri Beate Hatlen/Dir., Daniel J. Piette/Dir.

Financial Data: *Fiscal Year End:*12/31 *Latest Annual Data:* 12/31/2005

Year	Sales	Net Income
2005	$1,196,326,000	$112,578,000
2004	$1,129,468,000	-$134,730,000
2001	$1,052,628,000	$4,453,000

Curr. Assets:	$498,323,000	Curr. Liab.:	$310,886,000		
Plant, Equip.:	$972,657,000	Total Liab.:	$1,387,512,000	Indic. Yr. Divd.:	NA
Total Assets:	$1,717,572,000	Net Worth:	$329,275,000	Debt/ Equity:	NA

Petroleum Helicopters Inc

PO Box 90808, Lafayette, LA, 70509; *PH:* 1-337-235-2452; *Fax:* 1-337-232-6537; *http://* www.phihelico.com

General - Incorporation ... LA
Employees ... 2,126
Auditor ... Deloitte & Touche LLP
Stk Agt ... American Stock Transfer & Trust Co.
Counsel ... NA
DUNS No. ... 00-694-7873

Stock- Price on:12/24/2007 ... $32.16
Stock Exchange ... NDQ
Ticker Symbol ... NA
Outstanding Shares ... 15,280,000
E.P.S ... $0.73
Shareholders ... NA

Business: The group's principal activities are to provide helicopter transportation services in the gulf of Mexico. It transports personnel and parts and equipment for the customers engaged in the oil and gas exploration, development and production industry. The group operates through the following segments: domestic oil and gas, air medical, international and technical services. The domestic and gas segment operates approximately 164 owed, leased and customer-owned aircraft related to its domestic oil and gas operations from several bases or helicopters. Air medical segment provides air medical transportation services for hospitals and medical programs. International segment provides helicopter services in angola, antarctica and the democratic republic of congo. The technical services segment performs maintenance and repair services of the lafayette facility pursuant to an faa repair station license, primarily for the existing customers.

Primary SIC and add'l.: 4522

CIK No: 0000350403

Subsidiaries: Air Evac Services, Inc., Energy Risk LTD, Evangeline Airmotive, Inc., Helex, LLC, Helicopter Leasing, LLC, Helicopter Management, LLC, International Helicopter Transport, Inc., Petroleum Helicopters Angola Limitada, Petroleum Helicopters International, Inc., PHI Air Medical Services, Inc., PHI Angola, PHI International, LTD, Sky Leasing

Officers: Al A. Gonsoulin/Chmn., CEO/$519,829.00, Joey White/Marketing Representative, Richard A. Rovinelli/Chief Administrative Office, Dir. - Human Resources/$266,038.00, Aren Chaisson/Mgr. - Compensation, Benefits, Jerry Loviglio/Dir. - Training, Mike Baker/Environmental Mgr., Terry Kaufman/Flight Safety Mgr., Jim Palmer/Sr. Human Resources Representative, Ed Gatza/Mgr. - Field Human Resources, John Sage/Sr. Human Resources Representative, David Motzkin/Regional Dir. - PHI Air Medical Group, Dale Johnson/Mgr. - International, Chad Broussard/Industrial Safety Mgr., Lenny Leblanc/Quality Systems Compliance Mgr., Kathy Lejeune/Administrative Assist. *(32 Officers included in Index)*

Directors: Al A. Gonsoulin/Chmn., CEO, Russell C. Luigs/Dir., Lance F. Bospflug/Dir., Arthur J. Breault/Dir., Thomas H. Murphy/Dir., Richard H. Matzke/Dir.

Owners: Arthur J. Breault, Thomas H. Murphy, Michael J. McCann, Al A. Gonsoulin, St. Dennis J. Villere & Company, L.L.C./10.59%, FMR Corp/7.61%, Wells Capital Management Incorporated/7.44%, Thomas H. Murphy, Al A. Gonsoulin/52.60%, Baron Capital/12.03%, Wells Fargo & Company/7.54%, Woodbourne Partners, L.P./8.20%, Russell C. Luigs, Al A. Gonsoulin/52.60%, Wells Fargo Funds Management, LLC/5.80% *(20 Owners included in Index)*

Financial Data: *Fiscal Year End:*12/31 *Latest Annual Data:* 12/31/2006

Year	Sales	Net Income
2006	$423,064,000	-$667,000
2005	$366,840,000	$14,154,000
2004	$294,269,000	$3,972,000

Curr. Assets:	$307,689,000	Curr. Liab.:	$53,590,000	P/E Ratio:	64.32
Plant, Equip.:	$369,465,000	Total Liab.:	$300,845,000	Indic. Yr. Divd.:	NA
Total Assets:	$700,970,000	Net Worth:	$400,125,000	Debt/ Equity:	NA

Petroquest Energy Inc

400 E Kaliste Saloom Rd., Ste. 6000, Lafayette, LA, 70508; *PH:* 1-337-232-7028; *Fax:* 1-337-232-0044; *http://* www.petroquest.com

General - Incorporation ... DE
Employees ... 70
Auditor ... Ernst & Young LLP
Stk Agt ... American Stock Transfer & Trust Co.
Counsel ... Onebane, Befnard, Torian, Diaz
DUNS No. ... 24-881-8247

Stock- Price on:12/24/2007 ... $15.17
Stock Exchange ... NYSE
Ticker Symbol ... PQ
Outstanding Shares ... 47,790,000
E.P.S ... $0.58
Shareholders ... NA

Business: The group's principal activities are to generate, explore, develop, acquire and operate oil and gas properties. It operates oil and gas properties both onshore and offshore in the gulf coast region. At 31-Dec-2003, the group has estimated proved reserves of 4,245 mbbl of oil and 57,793 mmcf of natural gas.

Primary SIC and add'l.: 1311

CIK No: 0000872248

Subsidiaries: CSP Pipeline, LLC, PetroQuest Energy, LLC, PetroQuest Oil and Gas, LLC, Pittrans, Inc., Salvador Energy Company, LLC, Sea Harvester Energy Development Company, LLC, TDC Energy LLC, TDC Energy Systems, LLC

Officers: Charles T. Goodson/Chmn., CEO, Pres./$1,412,887.00, Todd W. Zehnder/VP - Corporate Development, Stephen H. Green/Sr. VP - Exploration/$1,760,698.00, Michael O. Aldridge/Exec. VP, CFO, Treasurer/$1,084,144.00, James S. Blair/VP - Business Development, Dalton F. Smith/Sr. VP - Business Development, Land, Daniel G. Fournerat/Exec. VP, General Counsel, Chief Administrative Officer, Sec./$1,289,976.00, Mark K. Stover/Sr. VP - Business Development, Art M. Mixon/Exec. VP - Exploration, Production/$1,312,321.00, Bond J. Clement/VP, Controller

Directors: Charles T. Goodson/Chmn., CEO, Pres., Charles F. Mitchell/Dir., Michael L. Finch/Dir., William W. Rucks/Dir., Wayne E. Nordberg/Dir., W. J. Gordon/Dir.

Owners: Michael O. Aldridge, Insiders/15.70%, Arthur M. Mixon, Daniel G. Fournerat/1.10%, W. J. Gordon, William W. Rucks/2.20%, Charles F. Mitchell, Stephen H. Green, Charles T. Goodson/7.70%, E. Wayne Nordberg/1.70%, Ralph J. Daigle/5.90%, Michael L. Finch, Independence Investments LLC/6.30%

Financial Data: *Fiscal Year End:*12/31 *Latest Annual Data:* 12/31/2006

Year	Sales	Net Income
2006	$200,544,000	$23,986,000
2005	$123,348,000	$21,417,000
2004	$84,868,000	$16,348,000

Curr. Assets:	$64,190,000	Curr. Liab.:	$72,081,000	P/E Ratio:	27.58
Plant, Equip.:	$447,324,000	Total Liab.:	$328,579,000	Indic. Yr. Divd.:	NA
Total Assets:	$518,290,000	Net Worth:	$189,711,000	Debt/ Equity:	0.9552

Petrosearch Energy Corp

675 Bering Dr., Ste. 200, Houston, TX, 77057; *PH:* 1-713-961-9337; *Fax:* 1-713-961-9338; *http://* petrosearch.com; *Email:* info@piedmontir.com

General - Incorporation ... NV
Employees ... 9
Auditor ... Ham, Langston & Brezina, LLP
Stk Agt ... Corporate Stock Transfer, Inc.
Counsel ... NA
DUNS No. ... NA

Stock- Price on:12/24/2007 ... $1.39
Stock Exchange ... OTC
Ticker Symbol ... PTSG
Outstanding Shares ... 38,860,000
E.P.S ... NA
Shareholders ... NA

Business: The groups principle activity is in the production of crude oil and natural gas exploration. In the year November 2005, the group acquired 1,755 acres in the Quinduno Field in Roberts County, Texas. The group operates from the United States.

Primary SIC and add'l.: 1311

CIK No: 0001288382

Subsidiaries: Anadarko Petrosearch, L.L.C., Barnett Petrosearch LLC, Beacon Petrosearch, L.L.C., Big Sky Petrosearch, L.L.C., Black Ramn Petrosearch, L.L.C., Buena Vista Petrosearch, L.L.C., Exploration Holdings Co, LLC, Garwood Petrosearch, Inc., Great Buffalo Petrosearch, L.L.C., Guidance Petrosearch, L.L.C., Magnolia Petrosearch, L.L.C., Petrosearch Operating Company, L.L.C., Pursuit Petrosearch, L.L.C., Rancon Petrsearch, L.L.C., Rocky Mountain Petrosearch, L.L.C. 17 Subsidiaries included in the Index

Officers: Richard D. Dole/Chmn., CEO, Pres., Wayne Beninger/COO, David Collins/CFO, VP, David Arndt/Mgr. - Drilling, Operations, Petrosearch Operations Group

Directors: Richard D. Dole/Chmn., CEO, Pres., Gerald N. Agranoff/Dir., Richard Majeres/Dir.

Owners: Commonwealth Bank of Australia/18.67%, Richard Majeres/0.52%, Insiders/12.40%, Richard D. Dole/7.76%, Wellington Trust Company, NA/5.23%, Gerald Agranoff/0.31%, Wayne Beninger/1.61%, David J. Collins/2.20%

Financial Data: Fiscal Year End:12/31   Latest Annual Data: 12/31/2006

Year	Sales	Net Income
2006	$1,233,000	-$2,322,000
2005	$1,701,000	-$2,901,000

Curr. Assets:	$5,127,000	Curr. Liab.:	$5,485,000		
Plant, Equip.:	$27,564,000	Total Liab.:	$15,422,000	Indic. Yr. Divd.:	NA
Total Assets:	$33,363,000	Net Worth:	$17,941,000	Debt/ Equity:	NA

PetroSouth Energy Corp

Formerly: Mobridge Exploration Inc
20333 State Hwy. 249, Ste. 200 11, Houston, TX, 77070; *PH:* 1-281-378-1563

General - Incorporation	NV	Stock- Price on:12/24/2007	NA
Employees	NA	Stock Exchange	OTC
Auditor	Madsen & Associates, CPA's Inc.	Ticker Symbol	MBDX
Stk Agt.	Empire Stock Transfer Inc.	Outstanding Shares	NA
Counsel	NA	E.P.S	NA
DUNS No.	NA	Shareholders	NA

Business: The groups principal activities include acquiring and exploring mineral properties. The group operates from the United States.

Primary SIC and add'l.: 1000

CIK No: 0001343601

Officers: Fred B. Zaziski/55/Chmn., CEO, Pres., Felipe Pimienta Barrios/37/CFO, Treasurer, Dir.

Directors: Fred B. Zaziski/55/Chmn., CEO, Pres., Felipe Pimienta Barrios/37/CFO, Treasurer, Dir.

Owners: Insiders/4.93%, Gurminder Manhas/28.16%, Victor Rafuse/15.09%, Fred B. Zaziski/4.23%, Fred B. Zaziski/0.70%

Petsec Energy Ltd

3861 Ambassador Caffery Pkwy., Ste. 500, Lafayette, LA, 70503; *PH:* 1-337-989-1942; *Fax:* 1-337-989-7271; *http://* www.petsec.com

General - Incorporation	Australia	Stock- Price on:12/24/2007	$1.22
Employees	NA	Stock Exchange	OTC
Auditor	KPMG LLP	Ticker Symbol	PSJEF
Stk Agt	NA	Outstanding Shares	NA
Counsel	NA	E.P.S	NA
DUNS No.	75-109-0754	Shareholders	NA

Business: The group's principal activities are the exploration for, production and development of oil and gas. It holds interests in eight exploration wells in the United States of America and China. The group operates in Australia, the United States of America, and China.

Primary SIC and add'l.: 1321 1382 1311

CIK No: 0001017910

Subsidiaries: Ginida Pty. Limited, Laurel Bay Petroleum Limited, Najedo Pty. Limited, Osglen Pty. Limited, Petroleum Securities Pty. Limited, Petroleum Securities Share Plan Pty. Limited, Petsec (U.S.A.) Inc., Petsec America Pty. Limited, Petsec Energy Inc., Petsec Investments Pty. Limited, Petsec Petroleum Inc., Western Medical Products Pty. Limited

Officers: Terry N. Fern/Chmn., MD, Craig H. Jones/Company Sec. - Australian Management, GM - Corporate, Fiona A. Robertson/CFO - Australian Management, Ross Keogh/Pres. - USA Management

Directors: Terry N. Fern/Chmn., MD, David A. Mortimer/Non Exec. Dir., Peter E. Power/Non Exec. Dir.

Owners: Terrence N. Fern/19.60%, P. E. Power, Den Duyts Corporation Pty Limited/13.39%, D. A. Mortimer, F. A. Robertson, ANZ Nominees Limited/6.96%, C. H. Jones, Terrence N. Fern/19.62%, Den Duyts Corporation Pty Limited/13.40%, P. Kallenberger, National Nominees Ltd/8.78%, Insiders/22.50%, R. A. Keogh, N. Fakier, Citicorp Nominees Pty Limited/5.30%

Financial Data: Fiscal Year End:12/31   Latest Annual Data: 12/31/2005

Year	Sales	Net Income
2005	$45,462,000	$7,987,000
2004	$32,798,000	$17,734,000

Curr. Assets:	$35,184,000	Curr. Liab.:	$31,465,000		
Plant, Equip.:	$48,990,000	Total Liab.:	$33,031,000	Indic. Yr. Divd.:	NA
Total Assets:	$87,294,000	Net Worth:	$54,263,000	Debt/ Equity:	NA

Petsmart Inc

19601 N 27th Ave., Phoenix, AZ, 85027; *PH:* 1-623-580-6100; *Fax:* 1-623-580-6183; *http://* www.petsmart.com

General - Incorporation	DE	Stock- Price on:12/24/2007	$31.9228
Employees	18,500	Stock Exchange	NDQ
Auditor	Deloitte & Touche LLP	Ticker Symbol	PETM
Stk Agt.	Wells Fargo Bank, N.A.	Outstanding Shares	136,030,000
Counsel	Cooley Godward LLP	E.P.S	$1.93
DUNS No.	17-380-8684	Shareholders	NA

Business: The group's principle activity is to provide products, services and solutions for the lifetime needs of pets. The group's products include pet food, treats, litter, pet supplies, live fish, birds and small pets. The group also provides veterinary, grooming and obedience training services. The group operates from United States.

Primary SIC and add'l.: 7375 0752 5963 5999

CIK No: 0000863157

Officers: Philip L. Francis/61/Chmn., CEO/$4,054,032.00, Kenneth T. Hall/39/Sr. VP - Merchandising, Mary L. Miller/47/Sr. VP, Chief Marketing Officer, Scott A. Crozier/Sr. VP, General Counsel, Sec., Chief Compliance Officer With Lightning - Ruby, Barbara A. Munder/62/Exec. Dir., Barbara Fitzgerald/56/Sr. VP - Store Operations With Gracie, Boone/$1,517,199.00, David K. Lenhardt/Sr. VP/$1,361,214.00, Donald E. Beaver/49/CIO, Sr. VP, Francesca Spinelli/Sr. VP - People With Winston, Joseph D. O'Leary/49/Sr. VP - Supply Chain, Raymond L. Storck/47/VP - Finance, Chief Accounting Officer, Robert F. Moran/COO, Pres./$2,671,989.00

Directors: Philip L. Francis/61/Chmn., CEO, Rita V. Foley/55/Dir., Barbara A. Munder/62/Exec. Dir., Lawrence A. Del Santo/74/Dir., Rakesh Gangwal/54/Dir., Joseph S. Hardin/62/Dir., Gregory P. Josefowicz/55/Dir., Amin I. Khalifa/54/Dir., Ronald Kirk/53/Dir., Richard K. Lochridge/64/Dir., Thomas G. Stemberg/59/Dir.

Owners: Amin I. Khalifa, Jeffery W. Yabuki, Barbara A. Munder, Robert F. Moran/1.34%, Insiders/3.91%, Ronald Kirk, Gregory P. Josefowicz, Thomas G. Stemberg, Rakesh Gangwal, Philip L. Francis, Richard K. Lochridge, Rita V. Foley, Barbara A. Fitzgerald, Timothy E. Kullman, Joseph S. Hardin (18 Owners included in Index)

Financial Data: Fiscal Year End:01/31   Latest Annual Data: 1/28/2007

Year	Sales	Net Income
2007	$4,233,857,000	$185,069,000
2006	$3,760,499,000	$182,490,000
2005	$3,363,452,000	$171,228,000

Curr. Assets:	$822,808,000	Curr. Liab.:	$350,921,000	P/E Ratio:	17.68
Plant, Equip.:	$699,262,000	Total Liab.:	$704,460,000	Indic. Yr. Divd.:	$0.120
Total Assets:	$1,655,454,000	Net Worth:	$950,994,000	Debt/ Equity:	0.3992

Pfeiffer Vacuum Technology

Berliner Strasse 43, Asslar, New South Wales, 35614; *PH:* 49-64418020; *http://* www.pfeiffer-vacuum.de; *Email:* info@pfeiffer-vacuum.de

General - Incorporation	Germany	Stock- Price on:12/24/2007	$95.4
Employees	684	Stock Exchange	NA
Auditor	Ernst & Young AG	Ticker Symbol	NA
Stk Agt.	Bank of New York	Outstanding Shares	8,840,000
Counsel	NA	E.P.S	$5.26
DUNS No.	31-555-8007	Shareholders	NA

Business: The group's principal activities are the design, manufacture and sale of turbomolecular pump, rotary vane, root vacuum pumps, backing pumps and consumer specified vacuum systems for DVD production. The group supplies products to varying market segments that include analytical industry, research and development, industrial, optical and glass coating, storage media, chemical and process technology and semiconductor industry. The group's operations are carried out through five divisions: turbo pumps, measurement and analysis equipment, components, service, backing pumps and systems.

Primary SIC and add'l.: 5084 3826 3563 1796

CIK No: 0001010613

Subsidiaries: Pfeiffer Vacuum (Schweiz) AG, Pfeiffer Vacuum Austria GmbH, Pfeiffer Vacuum Belgium N.V., Pfeiffer Vacuum France SAS, Pfeiffer Vacuum GmbH, Pfeiffer Vacuum Holding B.V., Pfeiffer Vacuum Inc., Pfeiffer Vacuum India Ltd., Pfeiffer Vacuum Italia S.p.A., Pfeiffer Vacuum Korea Ltd., Pfeiffer Vacuum Ltd., Pfeiffer Vacuum Nederland B.V., Pfeiffer Vacuum Scandinavia AB, Pfeiffer Vacuum Systems GmbH i.L.

Officers: Wolfgang Dondorf/64/Chmn., CEO, Manfred Bender/43/CFO, Mark Nowotny/Sales Engineer, Klaus Reimann/Sales Engineer, Dirk Schwendel/Sales Engineer, Gerd Riemenschneider/Sales Engineer, Uwe Schmidt/Sales Engineer, Bertram Weil/Human Resources, Jurgen Schafer/Dir. - Human Resources, Gudrun Geissler/Mgr. - Investor Relations, Daniel Neth/Human Resources, Claus Gerlach/Contact - Marketing Communications, Roland Hellmer/Exec. VP - Pfeiffer Vacuum, Inc, Steven Kirsch/VP - Pfeiffer Vacuum, Inc, Michael Morin/Corporate Controller - Pfeiffer Vacuum, Inc (39 Officers included in Index)

Directors: Wolfgang Dondorf/64/Chmn., CEO, Klaus-Jurgen Kugler/57/Vice Chmn. - Supervisory Board, Michael Oltmanns/51/Chmn. - Supervisory Board, Edgar Keller/52/Member - Supervisory Board, Gunter Schneider/64/Member - Supervisory Board, Michael J. Anderson/50/Member - Supervisory Board, Gotz Timmerbeil/40/Member - Supervisory Board, Matthias Wiemer/50/Member - Executive Board, Wilfried Glaum/Member - Supervisory Board, Helmut Bernhardt/Member - Supervisory Board, Manfred Gath/Member - Supervisory Board

Owners: Arnhold and S. Bleichroeder Advisors, LLC,/10.34%, Artisan Partners Ltd., Milwaukee/U.S.A./9.99%

Financial Data: Fiscal Year End:12/31   Latest Annual Data: 12/31/2006

Year	Sales	Net Income
2006	$236,973,000	$38,870,000
2005	$188,932,000	$26,943,000
2004	$213,149,000	$15,863,000

Curr. Assets:	$156,489,000	Curr. Liab.:	$33,709,000		
Plant, Equip.:	$32,663,000	Total Liab.:	$39,211,000	Indic. Yr. Divd.:	$2.670
Total Assets:	$222,142,000	Net Worth:	$182,093,000	Debt/ Equity:	NA

PFF Bancorp Inc

9337 Milliken Ave., Rancho Cucamonga, CA, 91730; *PH:* 1-909-941-5400; *Fax:* 1-909-623-2926; *http://* www.pffbank.com; *Email:* investor.relations@pffb.com

General - Incorporation	DE	Stock- Price on:12/24/2007	$28.63
Employees	652	Stock Exchange	NYSE
Auditor	KPMG LLP	Ticker Symbol	PFB
Stk Agt.	Mellon Investor Services LLC	Outstanding Shares	24,020,000
Counsel	Patton Boggs LLP	E.P.S	$0.81
DUNS No.	94-325-7840	Shareholders	NA

Business: The group's principal activity is to provide financial services to individuals and companies located primarily in southern California through its twenty-six branches. These services include demand, time, and savings deposits; real estate, business and consumer lending; cash management; trust services and investment advisory services and diversified financial services to homebuilders. The group offers certain annuity and mutual fund non-deposit investment products and investment and asset management services through its subsidiaries. The trust services are offered through its trust department. The group also purchases one-to-four family residential mortgages to supplement internal origination activities. In addition, the group invests in mortgage-backed securities, collateralized mortgage obligations and other investment securities. In may 2004, the group opened its 27th full services branch in yucaipa California.

Primary SIC and add'l.: 6712 6035

CIK No: 0001004969

Subsidiaries: Diversified Builder Services, Inc, Diversified Services, Inc, Glencrest Insurance Services, Inc, Glencrest Investment Advisors, Inc., PFF Bancorp Capital Trust I, PFF Bancorp Capital Trust II, PFF Bank & Trust, PFF Financial Services, Inc, Pomona Financial Services, Inc

Officers: Kevin McCarthy/Dir., CEO, Pres./$985,691.00, Gregory C. Talbott/Sr. Exec. VP, Chief Operating Office, CFO/$827,214.00

Directors: Kevin McCarthy/Dir., CEO, Pres., Curtis W. Morris/Vice Chmn., Stephen C. Morgan/Dir., Richard P. Crean/Dir., Jil H. Stark/Dir., Robert W. Burwell/Dir., Larry M. Rinehart/Dir., Royce A. Stutzman/Dir.

Owners: Larry M. Rinehart, PFF Bank & Trust Employee Stock/9.30%, Robert W. Burwell, Gregory C. Talbott/1.20%, Curtis W. Morris, Lynda Scullin, Royce A. Stutzman, Kevin McCarthy/1.30%, Jerald W. Groene, Richard P. Crean, Stephen C. Morgan, Robert L. Golish, Insiders/6.70%, Goldman Sachs Asset Management, L.P./7.10%, Wellington Management Company, LLP/5.10% *(16 Owners included in Index)*

Financial Data: Fiscal Year End:03/31 Latest Annual Data: 3/31/2007

Year	Sales	Net Income
2007	$361,621,000	$55,909,000
2006	$283,275,000	$52,080,000
2005	$237,409,000	$45,773,000

Curr. Assets:	$85,291,000	Curr. Liab.:	$4,099,712,000		
Plant, Equip.:	$56,564,000	Total Liab.:	$4,156,414,000	Indic. Yr. Divd.:	$0.760
Total Assets:	$4,553,527,000	Net Worth:	$397,113,000	Debt/ Equity:	0.1427

Pfizer Inc

235 E 42nd St., New York, NY, 10017; *PH:* 1-212-733-2323; *http://* www.pfizer.com

General - Incorporation	DE	Stock- Price on:12/24/2007	$25.92
Employees	98,000	Stock Exchange	NYSE
Auditor	KPMG LLP	Ticker Symbol	PFE
Stk Agt	Computershare Investor Services LLC	Outstanding Shares	7,020,000,000
Counsel	NA	E.P.S.	$2.11
DUNS No.	00-132-5919	Shareholders	NA

Business: The group's principle activities include discovering, developing, manufacturing and marketing prescription medicines. The group's servicing areas include oncology, cardiovascular disease and diabetes. The group operates from United States.

Primary SIC and add'l.: 2048 3842 3845 3841 2844 2834

CIK No: 0000078003

Subsidiaries: 412357 Ontario Inc, A S Ruffel (Mozambique) Limitada, A.S. Ruffel (Private) Limited, A/O Pfizer, ACO AB, Adenylchemie GmbH, Agouron Pharmaceuticals, Inc., Alginate Industries (Ireland) Ltd., American Food Industries, Inc., Amicore, Inc, Andean Services S.A, Angiosyn, Inc, Backsvalan 6 Handelsbolag, Balverda S.R.L, Bharti Healthcare Limited 465 Subsidiaries included in the Index

Officers: Jeffrey B. Kindler/Chmn., CEO/$9,799,234.00, Alan G. Levin/46/CFO, Sr. VP/$4,766,299.00, Loretta V. Cangialosi/VP, Controller, Principal Accounting Officer, Ian Read/Pres. - Worldwide Pharmaceutical Operations/$4,779,299.00, Joe Feczko/Chief Medical Officer, Mary McLeod/Human Resources, Frank D'Amelio/CFO, Corey Goodman/Pres. - Biotherapeutics, Bioinnovation Center, Allen Waxman/General Counsel, Rich Bagger/Worldwide Public Affairs, Policy, Martin MacKay/Pres. - Pfizer Global Research, Development, John L. Lamattina/57/VP, Pres. - Pfizer Global Research, Development/$7,019,667.00, Natale S. Ricciardi/Pres., Team Leader - Pfizer Global Manufacturing

Directors: Jeffrey B. Kindler/Chmn., CEO, David L. Shedlarz/Vice Chmn., William C. Steere/71/Dir., James M. Kilts/Dir., William R. Howell/66/Dir., Dana G. Mead/72/Dir., William H. Gray/66/Dir., Michael S. Brown/67/Dir., Don W. Cornwell/60/Dir., Dennis A. Ausiello/62/Dir., Suzanne Nora Johnson/51/Dir., George A. Lorch/66/Dir., Robert N. Burt/70/Dir., Constance J. Horner/66/Dir., Anthony M. Burns/65/Dir.

Owners: William C. Steere, John L. LaMattina, William H. Gray, William R. Howell, Michael S. Brown, Ruth J. Simmons, M. Anthony Burns, Robert N. Burt, Jeffrey B. Kindler, George A. Lorch, Alan G. Levin, Stanley O. Ikenberry, David L. Shedlarz, Ian C. Read, Dennis A. Ausiello *(22 Owners included in Index)*

Financial Data: Fiscal Year End:12/31 Latest Annual Data: 12/31/2006

Year	Sales	Net Income
2006	$48,371,000,000	$19,337,000,000
2005	$51,298,000,000	$8,085,000,000
2004	$52,516,000,000	$11,361,000,000

Curr. Assets:	$46,949,000,000	Curr. Liab.:	$21,389,000,000	P/E Ratio:	10.05
Plant, Equip.:	$16,632,000,000	Total Liab.:	$43,479,000,000	Indic. Yr. Divd.:	$1.160
Total Assets:	$114,837,000,000	Net Worth:	$71,358,000,000	Debt/ Equity:	0.1288

PFSweb Inc

500 N Central Expwy., Ste. 500, Plano, TX, 75074; *PH:* 1-972-881-2900; *Fax:* 1-972-633-2615; *http://* www.pfsweb.com; *Email:* pfsinfo@pfsweb.com

General - Incorporation	DE	Stock- Price on:12/24/2007	$0.95
Employees	1,200	Stock Exchange	NDQ
Auditor	KPMG LLP	Ticker Symbol	PFSW
Stk Agt	Mellon Investor Services LLC	Outstanding Shares	46,560,000
Counsel	NA	E.P.S.	-$0.34
DUNS No.	NA	Shareholders	NA

Business: The group's principal activity is to provide integrated business process outsourcing services. These services rendered by the group include professional consulting, technology collaboration, managed hosting and creative Web development, order management, Web-enabled customer contact centers and customer relationship management. The group also offers financial services including billing and collection services, information management, and option kitting and assembly services, on-line credit card processing, fraud protection and invoicing. The services of the group enable the brand name companies maximize their supply chain efficiencies and to extend their traditional e-commerce initiatives. The group operates in the United States, Canada and Europe.

Primary SIC and add'l.: 7389 7379

CIK No: 0001095315

Subsidiaries: Business Supplies Distributors Europe B.V. (in liquidation), Business Supplies Distributors Holdings, LLC, eCOST.com, Inc., PFSweb BV SPRL , Priority Fulfillment Services of Canada, Inc., Priority Fulfillment Services, Inc., Supplies Distributors of Canada, Inc., Supplies Distributors S.A., Supplies Distributors, Inc.

Officers: Mark C. Layton/Chmn. - Sr. Partner, CEO/$608,825.00, Lawrence Lubrano/Partner, VP - Client Services, Jonathan Walters/Dir. - Client Services, Joe Farrell/Dir. - Client Services, Elizabeth Johnson/Group Mgr. - Client Services, Ralph Blakley/Dir. - Client Solutions, Jeff Murray/Dir. - eCommerce Services, Tracey Mewborn/Logistics Mgr., Scott R. Talley/Partner, VP - Worldwide Distribution, Harvey H. Achatz/Sr. Partner, Chief Administrative Officer, Sec./$156,129.00, Dave Reese/Partner, VP - Client Solutions - Implementation, Bruce E. McClung/Partner, VP - Sales, Steven S. Graham/Sr. Partner, CTO/$287,892.00, Michael Willoughby/Sr. Partner, Pres. - Priority Fulfillment Services/$318,443.00, Cindy Almond/Partner, VP - Client Services *(16 Officers included in Index)*

Directors: Mark C. Layton/Chmn. - Sr. Partner, CEO

Owners: James F. Reilly, Harvey H. Achatz, David I. Beatson, Steven S. Graham/1.80%, Timothy M. Murray, Austin W. Marxe/15.00%, Thomas J. Madden/1.40%, Mark C. Layton/2.90%, Insiders/7.70%, Michael C. Willoughby, Neil W. Jacobs

Financial Data: Fiscal Year End:12/31 Latest Annual Data: 12/31/2006

Year	Sales	Net Income
2006	$423,253,000	-$14,530,000
2005	$331,657,000	-$747,000
2004	$321,665,000	$226,000

Curr. Assets:	$128,411,000	Curr. Liab.:	$107,708,000		
Plant, Equip.:	$12,884,000	Total Liab.:	$115,312,000	Indic. Yr. Divd.:	NA
Total Assets:	$164,152,000	Net Worth:	$48,840,000	Debt/ Equity:	0.1265

PG&E Corp

1 Market Spear Tower, Ste. 2400, San Francisco, CA, 94105; *PH:* 1-415-267-7070; *Fax:* 1-415-267-7268; *http://* www.pge.com; *Email:* invrel@pge-corp.com

General - Incorporation	CA	Stock- Price on:12/24/2007	$46.35
Employees	20,400	Stock Exchange	NYSE
Auditor	Deloitte & Touche LLP	Ticker Symbol	PCG
Stk Agt	Mellon Investor Services LLC	Outstanding Shares	351,500,000
Counsel	NA	E.P.S.	$2.65
DUNS No.	96-489-9132	Shareholders	NA

Business: The group's principle activity is to provide electric and natural gas services. In the year 2006, the group acquired Mirant Delta's. The group operates from United States.

Primary SIC and add'l.: 4923 6719 4911 4922

CIK No: 0001004980

Subsidiaries: Pacific Gas and Electric Company, PG&E Energy Recovery Funding LLC

Officers: Peter A. Darbee/55/Chmn., CEO, Pres./$7,990,058.00, William T. Morrow/49/Dir. - PG, E Corp, CEO, Pres. - Pacific Gas, Electric Company, Sanford L. Hartman/VP, MD - Law, Pacific Gas, Electric Company, Kent M. Harvey/50/Sr. VP, Chief Risk, Audit Officer/$1,529,620.00, Thomas E. Bottorff/Sr. VP - Regulatory Relations, Pacific Gas, Electric Company/$1,439,849.00, Helen A. Burt/Sr. VP, Chief Customer Officer - Pacific Gas, Electric Company, Jeffrey D. Butler/Sr. VP - Energy Delivery, Pacific Gas, Electric Company, John S. Keenan/Sr. VP - Generation, Chief Nuclear Officer - Pacific Gas, Electric Company, Ophelia B. Basgal/VP - Civic Partnership, Community Initiatives, Pacific Gas, Electric Company, James R. Becker/VP - Plant Operations, Station Dir. - Pacific Gas, Electric Company, Brian Cherry/VP - Regulatory Relations, Pacific Gas, Electric Company, Thomas B. King/46/Dir., Sr. VP/$4,228,109.00, William H. Harper/VP - Strategic Sourcing, Operations Support, Pacific Gas, Electric Company, Leslie H. Everett/Sr. VP - Communications, Public Affairs/$1,740,468.00, Dinyar B. Mistry/VP - State Regulation, Pacific Gas, Electric Company *(43 Officers included in Index)*

Directors: Peter A. Darbee/55/Chmn., CEO, Pres., William T. Morrow/49/Dir. - PG, E Corp, CEO, Pres. - Pacific Gas, Electric Company, Barry Lawson Williams/64/Dir., Maryellen C. Herringer/64/Dir., Mary S. Metz/71/Dir., Barbara L. Rambo/56/Dir., Leslie S. Biller/60/Dir., Lee C. Cox/67/Dir., Thomas B. King/46/Dir., Sr. VP, Richard A. Meserve/63/Dir., David R. Andrews/66/Dir., David A. Coulter/61/Dir.

Owners: Thomas E. Bottorff, Thomas B. King, Barry Lawson Williams, Peter A. Darbee, Christopher P. Johns, Leslie H. Everett, Lee C. Cox, Kent M. Harvey, David R. Andrews, Leslie S. Biller, Richard A. Meserve, Insiders, David A. Coulter, Barbara L. Rambo, Mary S. Metz *(16 Owners included in Index)*

Financial Data: Fiscal Year End:12/31 Latest Annual Data: 12/31/2006

Year	Sales	Net Income
2006	$12,539,000,000	$991,000,000
2005	$11,703,000,000	$917,000,000
2004	$11,080,000,000	$4,504,000,000

Curr. Assets:	$5,867,000,000	Curr. Liab.:	$8,250,000,000	P/E Ratio:	15.66
Plant, Equip.:	$21,785,000,000	Total Liab.:	$26,740,000,000	Indic. Yr. Divd.:	$1.440
Total Assets:	$34,803,000,000	Net Worth:	$7,811,000,000	Debt/ Equity:	1.1875

PGI Inc

212 S Central, Ste. 100, St. Louis, MO, 63105; *PH:* 1-314-512-8650

General - Incorporation	FL	Stock- Price on:12/24/2007	$12.94
Employees	2,350	Stock Exchange	OTC
Auditor	BKD LLP	Ticker Symbol	PGAI
Stk Agt	Computershare Investor Services LLC	Outstanding Shares	70,780,000
Counsel	NA	E.P.S.	$0.39
DUNS No.	03-268-6255	Shareholders	NA

Business: The group's principle activity is to sell and market undeveloped, platted and residential real estate. The properties of the group include 366 acres of land located in hernando county, Florida. The group also owns about 100 acres in various sites which are scattered in charlotte county, Florida, but most of these are subject to easements which markedly reduce the value and consist of wetlands of indeterminate value. As of 30-Jun-2004, the group owns 3 single family lots, located in citrus county, Florida. The group has been actively pursuing collection on delinquent contract receivables from home site sales. The group's quarterly revenue for September 2007 was 139.84 millions of USD.

Primary SIC and add'l.: 6552
CIK No: 0000081157
Subsidiaries: Burnt Store Marina, Inc., Burnt Store Utilities, Inc, Gulf Coast Credit Corporation, Punta Gorda Isles Sales, Inc, Sugarmill Woods, Inc.
Officers: Laurence A. Schiffer/68/Dir., CEO, CFO, Pres.
Directors: Laurence A. Schiffer/68/Dir., CEO, CFO, Pres., Andrew S. Love/64/Chmn.
Owners: Insiders, Insiders, Alfred M. Johns, Laurence A. Schiffer, Love-PGI Partners, L.P., Love-PGI Partners, L.P., Andrew S. CLove, Laurence A. Schiffer, Estate of Harold Vernon, Andrew S. Love, Alfred M. Johns

Financial Data: Fiscal Year End:12/31 **Latest Annual Data:** 12/31/2006

Year	Sales	Net Income
2006	$496,472,000	$25,509,000
2005	$497,473,000	$47,417,000
2004	$449,371,000	$41,880,000

Curr. Assets:	$934,000	**Curr. Liab.:**	$109,000	**P/E Ratio:**	33.18
Plant, Equip.:	$641,000	**Total Liab.:**	$42,668,000	**Indic. Yr. Divd.:**	NA
Total Assets:	$1,774,000	**Net Worth:**	-$40,894,000	**Debt/ Equity:**	0.3880

PGMI Inc

5912 Bolsa Ave., Ste. 108, Huntington Beach, CA, 92649; **PH:** 1-714-895-7772; **http://** pgmi-inc.com

General - Incorporation	UT	**Stock**- Price on:12/24/2007	NA
Employees		Stock Exchange	OTC
Auditor	McKennon, Wilson & Morgan LLP	Ticker Symbol	PGMI
Stk Agt	Stalt, Inc.	Outstanding Shares	NA
Counsel	NA	E.P.S.	NA
DUNS No.	NA	Shareholders	NA

Business: The groups principle activity is to operate thirteen stores, which offer Pachinko Japanese pinball gaming entertainment. During the year ended June 2006, the group acquired several parcels of land in the construction of one new store. The group operates from the United States.
Primary SIC and add'l.: 7900
CIK No: 0001127005
Subsidiaries: Marugin International, Inc.
Officers: Shinichi Gakushin Kanemoto/Dir., CEO, Pres. - Marugin, Gakushin Kanemoto/Founder, Chmn., CFO - Marugin, Eiichi Kanemoto/Executive Dir.
Directors: Shinichi Gakushin Kanemoto/Dir., CEO, Pres. - Marugin, Gakushin Kanemoto/Founder, Chmn., CFO - Marugin, Eiichi Kanemoto/Executive Dir., Mark Buck/Dir., Brian Weiss/36/Dir., Akira Oyake/53/Dir.
Owners: Mark Buck/1.80%, Taiki Kanemoto/8.50%, Insiders/1.80%, Spice Island Products, Inc./12.30%, Shinichi Kanemoto/40.00%, Insiders/81.50%, Gakushin Kanemoto/1.50%, Phase One, LLC/31.60%, Antaeus Capital Partners, LLC/37.50%, Kousei Kanemoto/8.50%, Eiichi Kanemoto/40.00%, Spice Island Products, Inc./12.70%, CCC Interests Limited/12.50%, Phase One, LLC/28.20%, Antaeus Capital Partners, LLC/24.00%

Curr. Assets:	$2,000	**Curr. Liab.:**	$586,000		
Plant, Equip.:	NA	**Total Liab.:**	$586,000	**Indic. Yr. Divd.:**	NA
Total Assets:	$3,000	**Net Worth:**	-$583,000	**Debt/ Equity:**	9.7842

PGT Inc

1070 Technology Dr., North Venice, FL, 34275; **PH:** 1-941-480-1600; **Fax:** 1-941-486-8634; **http://** www.pgtindustries.com

General - Incorporation	DE	**Stock**- Price on:12/24/2007	$11.27
Employees	2,400	Stock Exchange	NDQ
Auditor	Meagher & Flom LLP.	Ticker Symbol	PGTI
Stk Agt	LaSalle Bank N.A	Outstanding Shares	27,070,000
Counsel	NA	E.P.S.	$0.10
DUNS No.	NA	Shareholders	NA

Business: The groups principal activities include manufacturing and supplying residential product. The products of the group include aluminum and vinyl windows and doors. The group products sold under the trade names WinGuard and Eze-Breeze. Customers served by the group include window distributors, building supply distributors, window replacement dealers and enclosure contractors. The group operates from the United States, Caribbean, Mexico, South America and Australia. The net sale of the group for the year 2006 was $371,598 (thousands).
Primary SIC and add'l.: 3442 3499
CIK No: 0001354327
Subsidiaries: PGT Industries, Inc.
Officers: Rodney Hershberger/Dir., CEO, Pres., Herman Moore/Exec. VP, Jeffrey T. Jackson/CFO, Treasurer, Mario Ferrucci/VP, Corporate Counsel, Sec., Linda Gavit/VP - Human Resources, Ken Hilliard/VP - Field Services, Debbie L. Lapinska/VP - Sales, Marketing, David McCutcheon/VP - Engineering, Mary J. Kotler/VP - Supply Chain, Wayne B. Varnadore/VP - Information Technology, Douglas C. Cross/VP
Directors: Rodney Hershberger/Dir., CEO, Pres., Paul S. Levy/Chmn., Alexander R. Castaldi/Dir., Richard D. Feintuch/Dir., Ramsey A. Frank/Dir., Joseph M. McHugh/Dir., Brett N. Milgrim/Dir., Floyd F. Sherman/Dir., Randy L. White/Dir., Daniel Agroskin/Dir., William J. Morgan/Dir.
Owners: Insiders, David McCutcheon, Wellington Management Company, LLP, Linda Gavit, Richard D. Feintuch, JLL Partners Fund IV, L.P., Wayne B. Varnadore, Floyd F. Sherman, Jeffrey T. Jackson, Joseph M. McHugh, Rodney Hershberger, Paul S. Levy, Randy L. White

Financial Data: Fiscal Year End:12/31 **Latest Annual Data:** 12/30/2006

Year	Sales	Net Income
2006	$371,598,000	-$969,000
2005	$332,813,000	$7,863,000

Curr. Assets:	$76,937,000	**Curr. Liab.:**	$31,137,000		
Plant, Equip.:	$65,508,000	**Total Liab.:**	$268,982,000	**Indic. Yr. Divd.:**	NA
Total Assets:	$425,553,000	**Net Worth:**	$156,571,000	**Debt/ Equity:**	0.8044

Phantom Entertainment Inc

Formerly: Infinium Labs Inc
800 Fifth Ave., Ste. 4100, Seattle, WA, 98104; **PH:** 1-941-917-0788; **http://** www.infiniumlabs.com

General - Incorporation	DE	**Stock**- Price on:12/24/2007	NA
Employees	5	Stock Exchange	NA
Auditor	Kempisty & Co.	Ticker Symbol	NA
Stk Agt	Corporate Stock Transfer, Inc.	Outstanding Shares	NA
Counsel	NA	E.P.S.	-$0.007
DUNS No.	NA	Shareholders	NA

Business: The group's principal activity is to provide management consulting services to small and medium sized entities. The group designs, develops and implements systems to increase profitability, enhance efficiencies and advance the development of its client companies. The group provides original and authoritative advice for clients in many high-stakes matters such as acquisitions, new product introductions and general corporate strategies.
Primary SIC and add'l.: 8742
CIK No: 0001145019
Subsidiaries: Infinium Labs Operating Corporation
Owners: Greg Koler/4.40%, Insiders/6.23%, Linley Management S.A./1.41%, Golden Gate Investors, Inc./9.99%, Richard Angelotti/1.83%

Financial Data: Fiscal Year End:12/31 **Latest Annual Data:** 12/31/2006

Year	Sales	Net Income
2006	NA	-$9,525,000
2005	NA	$9,646,000
2004	NA	-$70,726,000

Curr. Assets:	$58,000	**Curr. Liab.:**	$18,402,000		
Plant, Equip.:	$2,000	**Total Liab.:**	$18,687,000	**Indic. Yr. Divd.:**	NA
Total Assets:	$60,000	**Net Worth:**	-$18,627,000	**Debt/ Equity:**	NA

Phantom Fiber Corp

405 Lexington Ave., 26th Fl., New York, NY, 10174; **PH:** 1-212-907-6544; **Fax:** 1-212-368-8005; **http://** www.phantomfiber.com

General - Incorporation	DE	**Stock**- Price on:12/24/2007	$0.36
Employees	NA	Stock Exchange	OTC
Auditor	Mintz & Partners LLP	Ticker Symbol	PHFB
Stk Agt	PacWest Transfer LLC	Outstanding Shares	NA
Counsel	NA	E.P.S.	NA
DUNS No.	NA	Shareholders	NA

Business: The group's principle activity is to distribute batteries and other products in North America. During 2003, the company discontinued its battery operations. Currently, the company does not have any business and is seeking new business opportunities. The company acquired phantom fiber corp on 07-Jul-2004. The group operates from United States.
Primary SIC and add'l.: 3692 7372
CIK No: 0000049397
Subsidiaries: Phantom Fiber, Inc
Officers: Jeffrey Halloran/Chmn., CEO, Pres., Herb Sears/CTO, Shane Lourensse/VP - Business Development, Steve Henkel/VP - Finance, Administration
Directors: Jeffrey Halloran/Chmn., CEO, Pres., Chris Carmichael/Dir., Stephen Gesner/51/Dir., Konstantine Lucas/59/Dir., Shimon Constante/34/Dir.
Owners: Lorraine Halloran/4.90%, Gordon S. Fowler/1.00%, Herbert C. Sears, Stephen Gesner/1.50%, Jeffrey T. Halloran/32.40%, Insiders/46.50%, Konstantine Lucas/13.40%

Financial Data: Fiscal Year End:12/31 **Latest Annual Data:** 12/31/2006

Year	Sales	Net Income
2006	$309,000	-$2,905,000
2005	$225,000	-$2,725,000
2004	$92,000	-$1,524,000

Curr. Assets:	$493,000	**Curr. Liab.:**	$819,000		
Plant, Equip.:	$55,000	**Total Liab.:**	$3,265,000	**Indic. Yr. Divd.:**	NA
Total Assets:	$790,000	**Net Worth:**	-$2,475,000	**Debt/ Equity:**	NA

Pharma-Bio Serv Inc

Formerly: Lawrence Consulting Group Inc
373 Mendez Vigo, Ste. 110, Dorado; **PH:** 787-278-2709

General - Incorporation	DE	**Stock**- Price on:12/24/2007	$0.55
Employees	152	Stock Exchange	NA
Auditor	Horwath Vlez & Co, Psc	Ticker Symbol	NA
Stk Agt	American Stock Transfer & Trust Co.	Outstanding Shares	19,610,000
Counsel	NA	E.P.S.	$0.08
DUNS No.	NA	Shareholders	NA

Business: The group's principle activity is consulting services to companies including business solutions, sales, marketing, customer, manufacturing, finance, and information technology services and develop business and information technology strategies, technology solutions and integrated marketing programs. The group had consulting agreements with three customers as on 31 Aug 2005. The group's quarterly revenue for Sep '07 was 70.64 millions of USD.
Primary SIC and add'l.: 8742
CIK No: 0001304161
Officers: Elizabeth Plaza/44/Chmn., CEO, Pres./$207,801.00, Nelida Plaza/39/VP, Sec./$147,214.00, Manuel O. Morera/51/CFO, VP - Finance, Administration
Directors: Elizabeth Plaza/44/Chmn., CEO, Pres., Dov Perlysky/44/Dir., Kirk Michel/51/Dir., Howard Spindel/62/Dir., Irving Wiesen/53/Dir.
Owners: Barron Partners LP, Elizabeth Plaza, Dov Perlysky, Venturetek LP, Irving Wiesen, Insiders, Pentland USA, Inc., Kirk Michel, San Juan Holdings, Inc., Howard Spindel, LDP Family Partnership, LP, Fame Associates

Financial Data: Fiscal Year End:06/30 **Latest Annual Data:** 10/31/2006

Year	Sales	Net Income
2006	$14,230,000	$2,335,000

Curr. Assets:	$8,542,000	**Curr. Liab.:**	$3,952,000	**P/E Ratio:**	6.88
Plant, Equip.:	$395,000	**Total Liab.:**	$8,993,000	**Indic. Yr. Divd.:**	NA
Total Assets:	$9,140,000	**Net Worth:**	$147,000	**Debt/ Equity:**	NA

Pharmaceutical Formulations Inc

460 Plainfield Ave, Edison, NJ, 08818; *PH:* 1-732-985-7100

General - Incorporation	DE	Stock- Price on:12/24/2007	NA
Employees	13	Stock Exchange	NA
Auditor	Grant Thornton LLP	Ticker Symbol	NA
Stk Agt	Continental Stock Transfer & Trust Co	Outstanding Shares	NA
Counsel	Stroock & Stroock & Lavan	E.P.S.	NA
DUNS No.	04-550-3000	Shareholders	NA

Business: The group's principal activities are to manufacture and distribute nonprescription solid dosage pharmaceutical products. The nonprescription drugs are commonly referred to as over-the-counter products. These products are manufactured in caplet, capsule and tablet form. Bulk products are distributed to secondary distributors, repackers and also small competitors, who do not have research and development department. The group also conducts contract manufacturing for major pharmaceutical companies. The group provides testing and research and development of new drug and health care products. Presently, the group markets more than 95 different types of generic otc products. The products include cough-cold preparations, analgesics, sinus and allergy products and gastrointestinal relief products. The customers include retailers, wholesalers, distributors and brand-name pharmaceutical companies. On 15-May-2003, the group acquired konsyl pharmaceuticals inc.

Primary SIC and add'l.: 2834
CIK No: 0000353827
Subsidiaries: Konsyl Pharmaceuticals, Inc.

Pharmaceutical Product Development Inc

929 N Front St., Wilmington, NC, 28401; *PH:* 1-910-251-0081; *Fax:* 1-910-762-5820;
http:// www.ppdi.com

General - Incorporation	NC	Stock- Price on:12/24/2007	$37.6
Employees	9,150	Stock Exchange	NDQ
Auditor	Deloitte & Touche LLP	Ticker Symbol	PPDI
Stk Agt	American Stock Transfer & Trust Co.	Outstanding Shares	118,160,000
Counsel	NA	E.P.S.	$1.38
DUNS No.	36-257-4527	Shareholders	NA

Business: The group's principal activity is to provide drug discovery and development services. The development sciences segment provides preclinical programs. The activities of the discovery sciences include functional genomics, which is the study of gene functions to identify drug targets within the body. This segment also provides biological chemistry research and preclinical biology services. It offers post-Market support services for drugs receiving approval for market use. These services include product launch services, patient compliance programs and medical communications programs for consumer and healthcare providers on product use and adverse events. In 2002, the group acquired medical research laboratories international inc, medical research laboratories international bvba, piedmont research center ii inc, complete software solutions inc and propharma pte ltd. In jul 2003, the group acquired eminent research systems inc and clinsights inc.

Primary SIC and add'l.: 8731
CIK No: 0001003124
Subsidiaries: APBI Finance Corporation, APBI Holdings, LLC, Applied Bioscience International, LLC, ATP, LLC, Cambridge Applied Nutrition Toxicology & Biosciences LTD, Chelmsford Clinical Trials Unit, LTD, Clinical Science Research International, LTD, Clinical Technology Centre International LTD, CSS Informatics, Inc., Data Analysis & Research (DAR) LTD, Development Partners, LLC, Gabbay, LTD, Genupro, Inc., Leicester Clinical Research Centre, LTD, Pharmaceutical Product Development South Africa (PTY) LTD 56 Subsidiaries included in the Index
Officers: Fred Eshelman/Dir., CEO/$3,287,047.00, Stephen Smith/VP - Finance, Louise Caudle/Dir. - Corporate Communications, Fred B. Davenport/Pres., Assist. Sec./$1,867,357.00, Paul S. Covington/Exec. VP - Development/$976,132.00, Linda Baddour/CFO, Treasurer, Assist. Sec./$1,535,680.00, Colin Shannon/48/Exec. VP - Global Clinical Operations/$1,456,461.00, William Sharbaugh/COO, Peter Wilkinson/Chief Accounting Officer, Judd Hartman/General Counsel, Sec., William Richardson/Sr. VP - Global Business Development
Directors: Fred Eshelman/Dir., CEO, Ernest Mario/Chmn., David L. Grange/Dir., Marye Anne Fox/Dir., Frederick Frank/Dir., John A. McNeill/Dir., Catherine M. Klema/Dir., Terry Magnuson/Dir., Stuart Bondurant/Dir.
Owners: Insiders/12.40%, John A. McNeill/2.80%, Colin Shannon, Frederick Frank, Marye Anne Fox, Linda Baddour, Earnest Partners, LLC/9.60%, David L. Grange, Terry Magnuson, Catherine M. Klema, Paul S. Covington, Fred B. Davenport, Stuart Bondurant, FMR Corp./12.70%, Neuberger Berman Inc./5.80% *(17 Owners included in Index)*

*Financial Data: Fiscal Year End:*12/31 *Latest Annual Data:* 12/31/2006

Year	Sales	Net Income
2006	$1,247,682,000	$156,652,000
2005	$1,037,090,000	$131,483,000
2004	$841,256,000	$98,888,000

Curr. Assets:	$908,202,000	Curr. Liab.:	$495,491,000	P/E Ratio:	27.45
Plant, Equip.:	$323,539,000	Total Liab.:	$528,665,000	Indic. Yr. Divd.:	$0.400
Total Assets:	$1,481,565,000	Net Worth:	$952,900,000	Debt/ Equity:	NA

Pharmacopeia Drug Discovery Inc

3000 EPk. Blvd, Cranbury, NJ, 08512; *PH:* 1-609-452-3600; *Fax:* 1-609-452-3672;
http:// www.pharmacopeia.com; *Email:* hrreq@pharmacopeia.com

General - Incorporation	DE	Stock- Price on:12/24/2007	$5.84
Employees	150	Stock Exchange	NDQ
Auditor	Ernst & Young LLP	Ticker Symbol	NA
Stk Agt	American Stock Transfer & Trust Co.	Outstanding Shares	29,510,000
Counsel	NA	E.P.S.	-$1.7
DUNS No.	NA	Shareholders	NA

Business: The group's principal activity is to design, develop, market and support science and technology-based products and services intended to improve and accelerate the processes of drug discovery and chemical development. The group provides drug discovery services to pharmaceutical and biotechnology companies. The services are based on proprietary combinatorial chemistry and high-throughput screening technologies. Using proprietary technologies and processes, scientists identify and optimize novel drug candidates through research collaborations. The group's collaborative drug discovery is focused on the creation of new small molecule therapeutics.

Primary SIC and add'l.: 8731
CIK No: 0001273013
Officers: Leslie J. Browne/Dir., CEO, Pres./$819,181.00, Simon M. Tomlinson/Sr. VP - Business Development/$359,127.00, Rene Belder/VP - Clinical, Regulatory Affairs, Brian M. Posner/Exec. VP, CFO, Treasurer/$402,070.00, Maria L. Webb/VP - Preclinical Research, Biological, Pharmacological Sciences, Stephen C. Costalas/Exec. VP, General Counsel, Sec./$457,193.00, David M. Floyd/Chief Scientific Officer, Exec. VP/$563,700.00
Directors: Leslie J. Browne/Dir., CEO, Pres., Joseph A. Mollica/Chmn., Carol A. Ammon/Dir., Frank Baldino/Dir., Dan R. Littman/Member - Scientific Advisory Board, Paul A. Bartlett/Dir., Member - Scientific Advisory Board, John C. Chabala/Member - Scientific Advisory Board, Israel Charo/Member - Scientific Advisory Board, John B. Kostis/Member - Advisory Board, Marc A. Pfeffer/Member - Advisory Board, Neville F. Ford/Member - Scientific Advisory Board, Bruce A. Peacock/Dir., Steven J. Burakoff/Dir., Dennis H. Langer/Dir., Martin H. Soeters/Dir. *(20 Directors included in Index)*
Owners: Frank Baldino, James J. Marino, Gary E. Costley, Federated Investors,Inc./5.22%, David M. Floyd, OrbiMed Advisors L.L.C./8.87%, BVF Inc./9.44%, OZ Management, L.L.C/6.22%, Steven J. Burakoff, Brian M. Posner, Insiders/7.00%, Leslie J. Browne/1.07%, Bruce A. Peacock, Stephen C. Costalas, Paul A. Bartlett *(19 Owners included in Index)*

*Financial Data: Fiscal Year End:*12/31 *Latest Annual Data:* 12/31/2006

Year	Sales	Net Income
2006	$16,936,000	-$27,764,000
2005	$20,403,000	-$17,138,000
2004	$24,359,000	-$17,420,000

Curr. Assets:	$52,644,000	Curr. Liab.:	$18,750,000		
Plant, Equip.:	$11,287,000	Total Liab.:	$35,696,000	Indic. Yr. Divd.:	NA
Total Assets:	$66,127,000	Net Worth:	$30,431,000	Debt/ Equity:	NA

Pharmacyclics Inc

995 E Arques Ave., Sunnyvale, CA, 94085; *PH:* 1-408-774-0330; *Fax:* 1-408-774-0340;
http:// www.pharmacyclics.com; *Email:* info@pcyc.com

General - Incorporation	DE	Stock- Price on:12/24/2007	$2.88
Employees	112	Stock Exchange	NDQ
Auditor	PricewaterhouseCoopers LLP	Ticker Symbol	PCYC
Stk Agt	EquiServe Trust Co N.A	Outstanding Shares	25,970,000
Counsel	NA	E.P.S.	-$1.04
DUNS No.	79-117-9526	Shareholders	NA

Business: The group's principle activities include developing and marketing pharmaceutical products for the treatment of cancer and atherosclerosis. The products of the company include xcytrin(R) and antrin (r). These products represent a new class of drugs called texaphyrins, rationally designed, porphyrin-like molecules, that are capable of upsetting the intracellular oxidation-reduction balance and disrupting the bioenergetic processes in diseased tissue. The company is conducting a multicenter international phase iii clinical trial of xcytrin(R) (motexafin gadolinium) injection, to improve the efficacy of radiation therapy of tumors that have spread to the brain resulting from a variety of cancers, including those of the lung and breast. The company is in the development stage. The group operates from United States.

Primary SIC and add'l.: 8731 2834 5122
CIK No: 0000949699
Officers: Richard A. Miller/Dir., CEO, Pres., David Loury/VP, Markus F. Renschler/Sr. VP - Clinical Development, Leiv Lea/VP - Finance, Administration, CFO, Sec., Gregory Hemmi/VP - Chemical Operations, Michael Inouye/Sr. VP - Corporate, Commercial Development, Joseph J. Buggy/41/VP - Research
Directors: Richard A. Miller/Dir., CEO, Pres., James L. Knighton/Dir., Miles R. Gilburne/Dir., Richard M. Levy/Dir., William R. Rohn/Dir., Christine A. White/Dir., Robert W. Duggan/64/Dir.
Owners: Primecap Management Company/7.60%, See-Chun Phan, Miles R. Gilburne, Markus F. Renschler/1.20%, Robert W. Duggan/14.70%, Richard M. Levy, Leiv Lea/1.60%, Richard A. Miller/4.60%, Insiders/21.20%

*Financial Data: Fiscal Year End:*06/30 *Latest Annual Data:* 06/30/2007

Year	Sales	Net Income
2007	$126,000	-$26,217,000
2006	$181,000	-$42,158,000
2005	NA	-$31,048,000

Curr. Assets:	$41,438,000	Curr. Liab.:	$3,339,000		
Plant, Equip.:	$764,000	Total Liab.:	$3,409,000	Indic. Yr. Divd.:	NA
Total Assets:	$42,729,000	Net Worth:	$39,320,000	Debt/ Equity:	NA

Pharmafrontiers Corp

2635 N Cres. Ridge Dr., The Woodlands, TX, 77381; *PH:* 1-281-272-9331;
http:// www.pharmafrontiers.net

General - Incorporation	TX	Stock- Price on:12/24/2007	$5.4
Employees	32	Stock Exchange	NA
Auditor	Malone & Bailey, P.C	Ticker Symbol	NA
Stk Agt	Continental Stock Transfer & Trust Co	Outstanding Shares	6,700,000
Counsel	NA	E.P.S.	-$1.91
DUNS No.	NA	Shareholders	NA

Business: The group's principal activity is to distribute sports novelties and memorabilia primarily to retail outlets in the United States. The group ceased operating in early 2002. On 04-Jun-2004, the group acquired pharmafrontiers corporation.

Primary SIC and add'l.: 5091 5099
CIK No: 0001069308
Subsidiaries: Opexa Pharmaceuticals, Inc.
Officers: David B. McWilliams/Dir., CEO/$761,874.00, Donna R. Rill/VP - Operations, Jim C. Williams/COO, Lynne Hohlfeld/CFO/$172,089.00
Directors: David B. McWilliams/Dir., CEO, Eliezer Huberman/Chmn. - Scientific Advisory Board, Scott B. Seaman/Dir., Jingwu Zang/Member - Scientific Advisory Board, Norman Barton/Member - Scientific Advisory Board, Daniel R. Marshak/Member - Scientific Advisory Board, Shelly Heimfeld/Member - Scientific Advisory Board, Irun Cohen/Member - Scientific Advisory Board, Gregory H. Bailey/Dir., David Hung/Dir., Michael S. Richman/Dir., Charles F. Brunicardi/Member - Advisory Board, Diabetes, John A. Goss/Member - Advisory Board, Diabetes, Dale J. Hamilton/Member - Advisory Board, Diabetes, Saundra Hendricks/Member - Advisory Board, Diabetes *(23 Directors included in Index)*

Owners: Jimmy C. Williams/0.65%, Lorin Randall, David B. McWilliams/1.41%, Insiders/11.11%, Austin W. Marxe/20.95%, Albert and Margaret Alkek Foundation/9.99%, Donna Rill/0.30%, Michael Richman, DLD Family Investments, LLC/5.29%, Scott B. Seaman/6.82%, Lynne Hohlfeld, SF Capital Partners Ltd./14.78%, Alkek & Williams Ventures Ltd./5.95%, David Hung, Gregory H. Bailey/1.26% *(16 Owners included in Index)*

Financial Data: ***Fiscal Year End:***12/31 ***Latest Annual Data:*** 12/31/2006

Year	Sales	Net Income
2006	NA	-$12,649,000
2005	NA	-$15,517,000
2004	NA	-$4,621,000

Curr. Assets:	$15,445,000	**Curr. Liab.:**	$9,287,000		
Plant, Equip.:	$1,361,000	**Total Liab.:**	$9,383,000	**Indic. Yr. Divd.:**	NA
Total Assets:	$16,806,000	**Net Worth:**	$7,423,000	**Debt/ Equity:**	0.0036

PharmaNet Development Group Inc

Formerly: SFBC International Inc
504 Carnegie Ctr., Princeton, NJ, 08540; ***PH:*** 1-609-951-6800; ***http://*** www.sfbci.com

General - Incorporation ... DE
Employees ... 2,089
Auditor ... Grant Thornton LLP
Stk Agt...... American Stock Transfer & Trust Co.
Counsel ... Michael Harris
DUNS No. ... NA

Stock- Price on:12/24/2007 ... $31.33
Stock Exchange ... NA
Ticker Symbol ... NA
Outstanding Shares ... 18,660,000
E.P.S ... -$1.37
Shareholders ... NA

Business: The group's principal activity is to provide outsource drug development research services for pharmaceutical and biotechnology industries. It also manages clinical trials at multiple sites involving ophthalmology, dermatology and generic drug testing. The group conducts clinical trials and provides related services to pharmaceutical, biotechnology and contract research organizations. Clinical research involves the testing of new drugs and other products on humans according to guidelines set by clients and approved by the fda. The group has operations in the United States, Canada, Spain, North America, Europe and Asia. The group acquired clinical pharmacology of Florida inc on 04-Aug-2003, synfine research inc on 26-Mar-2003 and remaining 51% interest in danapharm clinical research inc on 07-Jul-2003. The group acquired taylor technology inc on 26-Jul-2004.

Primary SIC and add'l.: 8731 6719

CIK No: 0001089542

Subsidiaries: 11190 Biscayne, LLC, Anapharm Inc., Clinical Pharmacology International, Inc., CRO-PharmaNet Services GmbH, Limited Liability Company PharmaNet, Pharma Holdings, Inc., PharmaNet (C.A.), Inc., PharmaNet (Hong Kong) Limited, PharmaNet (P.A.), Inc., PharmaNet AG, PharmaNet Argentina S.R.L., PharmaNet Asia AG, PharmaNet B.V., PharmaNet B.V.B.A., PharmaNet Clinical Services Private Limited 40 Subsidiaries included in the Index

Officers: Jeffrey P. McMullen/Dir., CEO, Pres./$2,203,338.00, David Natan/Exec. VP/$801,654.00, Mark Di Ianni/Exec. VP - Strategic Initiatives/$515,959.00, John P. Hamill/CFO, Sr. VP/$760,201.00, Johane Boucher-Champagne/Exec. VP/$550,468.00, Thomas J. Newman/COO, Exec. VP/$898,046.00, Stuart Portnoy/Exec. Dir.

Directors: Jeffrey P. McMullen/Dir., CEO, Pres., Jack Levine/Chmn., Arnold Golieb/Dir., David Lucking/Dir., Lewis R. Elias/Dir., Peter G. Tombros/Dir., Rolf A. Classon/Dir., David M. Olivier/Dir., Per Wold-Olsen/Dir., Stuart Portnoy/Exec. Dir.

Owners: Jack Levine, Insiders/3.60%, Brandywine Global Investment Management, LLC/7.80%, Royce & Associates, LLC/6.00%, Per Wold-Olsen, John P. Hamill, Wellington Management Company, LLP/7.00%, David Lucking, Thomas J. Newman, David Natan, David M. Olivier, Peter G. Tombros, Johane Boucher-Champagne, Mark Di Ianni, Lewis Elias *(19 Owners included in Index)*

Financial Data: ***Fiscal Year End:***12/31 ***Latest Annual Data:*** 12/31/2006

Year	Sales	Net Income
2006	$406,955,000	-$36,025,000
2005	$429,593,000	$4,779,000
2004	$159,585,000	$19,659,000

Curr. Assets:	$199,225,000	**Curr. Liab.:**	$135,407,000		
Plant, Equip.:	$52,235,000	**Total Liab.:**	$296,361,000	**Indic. Yr. Divd.:**	NA
Total Assets:	$556,001,000	**Net Worth:**	$258,079,000	**Debt/ Equity:**	0.6145

Pharmaxis Ltd

Unit 2, 10 Rodborough Rd., Frenchs Forest, NSW, 2086; ; ***http://*** www.pharmaxis.com.au; ***Email:*** info@pharmaxis.com.au

General - Incorporation ... Australia
Employees ... 49
Auditor ... PricewaterhouseCoopers LLP
Stk Agt ... Bank of New York
Counsel ... PFM Legal Pty Ltd
DUNS No. ... NA

Stock- Price on:12/24/2007 ... $42.48
Stock Exchange ... NDQ
Ticker Symbol ... PXSL
Outstanding Shares ... 11,820,000
E.P.S ... -$1.88
Shareholders ... NA

Business: The group's principle activities include integrated development of pharmaceutical products for human use. The group's three main business segments: basis research, preclinical development, manufacture and release of its products; design, management and control of clinical trials; and sales and marketing. Main productline includes human healthcare products to treat chronic respiratory and autoimmune diseases. Products includes medicines for the management of asthma, cystic fibrosis and chronic obstructive pulmonary disease (COPD); treatment of multiple sclerosis; and rheumatoid arthritis. Aridol & Bronchitol are patented, dry powder formulation of mannitol delivered to the lungs through an inhaler.

Primary SIC and add'l.: 2834

CIK No: 0001301357

Officers: Alan D. Robertson/Dir., CEO, David McGarvey/Dir., Company Sec., CFO, Brett Charlton/Medical Dir., John F. Crapper/COO, Gary J. Phillips/Head - Commercial Development, Ian A. McDonald/CTO, Jane Sugden/Investor Relations, Communications, John W. Villiger/Non Exec. Dir.

Directors: Alan D. Robertson/Dir., CEO, Denis M. Hanley/Chmn., Peter Farrell/Non Exec. Dir., Charles P.H. Kiefel/Dir., Malcolm J. McComas/Non Exec. Dir., David McGarvey/Dir., Company Sec., CFO, Sandra Anderson/Member - Scientific Advisory Board, Norbert Berend/Member - Scientific Advisory Board, Malcolm Fisher/Member - Scientific Advisory Board, Richard Ji Morgan/Member - Scientific Advisory Board

Owners: Platypus Asset Management Pty Limited/5.10%, Malcolm J. McComas, John F. Crapper, Peter C. Farrell, David M. McGarvey, ABN AMRO Bank N.V./8.20%, Acorn Capital Limited/5.40%, Gary J. Phillips, Alan D. Robertson/1.20%, Ian A. McDonald, Brett Charlton, John Villiger, Insiders/4.30%, ABN AMRO Bank N.V./8.20%, Charles P.H. Kiefel *(17 Owners included in Index)*

Financial Data: ***Fiscal Year End:***06/30 ***Latest Annual Data:*** 6/30/2006

Year	Sales	Net Income
2006	$6,000	-$12,947,000
2005	NA	-$7,959,000

Curr. Assets:	$72,507,000	**Curr. Liab.:**	$3,888,000		
Plant, Equip.:	$2,401,000	**Total Liab.:**	$3,888,000	**Indic. Yr. Divd.:**	NA
Total Assets:	$76,086,000	**Net Worth:**	$72,198,000	**Debt/ Equity:**	NA

Pharmion Corp

2525 28th St., Ste. 200, Boulder, CO, 80301; ***PH:*** 1-720-564-9100; ***Fax:*** 1-720-564-9191; ***http://*** www.pharmion.com; ***Email:*** ir@pharmion.com

General - Incorporation ... DE
Employees ... 417
Auditor ... Ernst & Young LLP
Stk Agt...... American Stock Transfer & Trust Co.
Counsel ... Willkie Farr & Gallagher LLP
DUNS No. ... NA

Stock- Price on:12/24/2007 ... $29.55
Stock Exchange ... NDQ
Ticker Symbol ... PHRM
Outstanding Shares ... 32,190,000
E.P.S ... -$2.53
Shareholders ... NA

Business: The group's principle activity is to acquire, develop and commercialize innovative products for the treatment of hematology and oncology patients. The group has established their own regulatory, development and sales and marketing organizations covering the U.S., Europe and Australia. It also has established third party distributor network to serve the hematology and oncology markets in 20 additional countries throughout the Middle East and Asia. The products of the group are innohep(R), refludan(R), thalidomide pharmion 50mgtm and vidazatm. The products are sold to wholesale distributors and directly to hospitals, clinics, and retail pharmacies. The group's quarterly revenue for September 2007 was 67.31 millions of USD.

Primary SIC and add'l.: 8731 2834

CIK No: 0001203866

Officers: Patrick J. Mahaffy/Dir., CEO, Pres., Andrew R. Allen/Chief Medical Officer, Exec. VP, Michael Cosgrave/Chief Commercial Officer, Erle T. Mast/CFO, Exec. VP, Gillian C. Ivers-Read/Exec. VP - Development Operations, Jay T. Backstrom/VP - Global Medical, Safety, Joe Como/VP - Global Manufacturing, Jeffrey P. Davis/VP - Information Technology, Steven Dupont/VP, General Counsel, Pam Herriott/VP - Human Resources, Breanna Burkart/Dir. - Investor Relations, Corporate Communications, Anna Sussman/Dir. - Investor Relations, Corporate Communications, Andrea Bacigalupo/Scientific Advisor, John Byrd/Scientific Advisor, Norbert Schmitz/Member - Scientific Advisors *(16 Officers included in Index)*

Directors: Patrick J. Mahaffy/Dir., CEO, Pres., Grant Prentice/Chmn. - Scientific Advisor, John Reed/Dir., Thorlef Spickschen/Dir., Anna Sussman/Dir. - Investor Relations, Corporate Communications, Edward J. McKinley/Dir., Breanna Burkart/Dir. - Investor Relations, Corporate Communications, Brian G. Atwood/Dir., Cam L. Garner/Dir., James M. Barrett/Dir., James Blair/Dir.

Owners: Celgene Corporation/6.00%, Erle T. Mast, Sectoral Asset Management, Inc./6.20%, Gillian C. Ivers-Read, Entities affiliated with New Enterprise Associates/9.00%, Entities affiliated with Domain Associates/7.20%, Insiders/21.50%, Steven N. Dupont, Entities affiliated with S.A.C. Capital Advisors/5.10%, Pictet Funds Biotech/5.00%, Thorlef Spickschen, Entities affiliated with OSS Capital Management/5.60%, Patrick J. Mahaffy/1.80%, James M. Barrett/9.10%, Brian G. Atwood *(21 Owners included in Index)*

Financial Data: ***Fiscal Year End:***12/31 ***Latest Annual Data:*** 12/31/2006

Year	Sales	Net Income
2006	$238,646,000	-$91,012,000
2005	$221,244,000	$2,269,000
2004	$130,171,000	-$17,537,000

Curr. Assets:	$202,968,000	**Curr. Liab.:**	$49,971,000		
Plant, Equip.:	$7,121,000	**Total Liab.:**	$53,650,000	**Indic. Yr. Divd.:**	NA
Total Assets:	$326,732,000	**Net Worth:**	$273,082,000	**Debt/ Equity:**	NA

Pharmos Corp

99 Wood Ave. S, Ste. 311, Iselin, NJ, 08830; ***PH:*** 1-732-452-9556; ***Fax:*** 1-732-452-9557; ***http://*** www.pharmoscorp.com; ***Email:*** info@pharmos-us.com

General - Incorporation ... NV
Employees ... 51
Auditor ... PricewaterhouseCoopers LLP
Stk Agt...... American Stock Transfer & Trust Co.
Counsel...... Ehrenreich Eilenberg & Krause LLP
DUNS No. ... 55-661-3024

Stock- Price on:12/24/2007 ... $1.41
Stock Exchange ... NDQ
Ticker Symbol ... PARS
Outstanding Shares ... 25,600,000
E.P.S ... -$1.46
Shareholders ... NA

Business: The group's principal activities are to discover and develop new drugs to treat a range of inflammatory and neurological disorders. The products of the group are used to treat a range of neurological disorders such as traumatic brain injury, stroke, neuropathic pain. Lotemax is a steroid used to treat steroid responsive inflammatory eye conditions and also used for cataract surgery. Alrex is used in the treatment of ophthalmic allergies. The group's products include loteprednol etabonate and dexanabinol, which are used for traumatic brain injury and tamoxifen analogs. The group's operations are conducted in the United States and Israel. The Israel, operations are conducted through its subsidiary, pharmos ltd.

Primary SIC and add'l.: 6794 2834

CIK No: 0000713275

Subsidiaries: Pharmos Ltd

Officers: Elkan R. Gamzu/Dir., CEO, Alan L. Rubino/COO, Pres./$636,254.00, Iris Alroy/Sr. VP - Discovery, Alon Michal/GM, VP - Finance, Colin S. Neill/Sr. VP, CFO, Sec., Treasurer/$144,687.00

Directors: Elkan R. Gamzu/Dir., CEO, Haim Aviv/Chmn., Abraham Sartani/Dir., David Schlachet/62/Dir., Mony Ben Dor/Dir., Srinivas Akkaraju/Dir., Anthony B. Evnin/Dir., Lloyd I. Miller/Dir., Charles W. Newhall/Dir.

Owners: Alan L. Rubino, Srinivas Akkaraju/11.10%, New Enterprise Associates 10/7.40%, James A. Meer, Anthony B. Evnin/5.00%, JP Morgan Partners BHCA LLP/11.10%, Mony Ben Dor, David Schlachet, Haim Aviv/3.70%, Venrock Associates/5.00%, Abraham Sartani, Lloyd I. Miller/7.70%, Colin S. Neill, Insiders/33.50%, Charles W. Newhall/7.40% *(16 Owners included in Index)*

Financial Data: ***Fiscal Year End:***12/31 ***Latest Annual Data:*** 12/31/2006

Year	Sales	Net Income
2006	NA	-$35,137,000
2005	NA	-$2,930,000
2004	NA	-$21,968,000

Curr. Assets:	$26,735,000	Curr. Liab.:	$2,567,000		
Plant, Equip.:	$593,000	Total Liab.:	$3,965,000	Indic. Yr. Divd.:	NA
Total Assets:	$28,393,000	Net Worth:	$24,428,000	Debt/ Equity:	NA

Pharsight Corp

321 E Evelyn Ave., 3rd Fl., Mountain View, CA, 94041; *PH:* 1-650-314-3800; *Fax:* 1-650-314-3810; *http://* www.pharsight.com; *Email:* info@pharsight.com

General - Incorporation	DE	Stock - Price on:12/24/2007	$1.86
Employees	85	Stock Exchange	OTC
Auditor	Grant Thornton, LLP	Ticker Symbol	PHST
Stk Agt... ComputerShare Investor Services LLC		Outstanding Shares	19,730,000
Counsel	NA	E.P.S.	-$0.3
DUNS No.	NA	Shareholders	NA

Business: The group's principle activities include developing and marketing integrated products and services that help pharmaceutical and biotechnology companies improve their drug development process. It's solution combines proprietary computer-based simulation, statistical and data analysis tools with strategic decision making and the sciences of pharmacology, drug and disease modeling, human genetics and biostatistics. The company operates mainly in the United States and Europe. The products include pharsight(R) knowledgebase server(TM) (pks). The group operates from United States.

Primary SIC and add'l.: 7371 7372 7379

CIK No: 0001040853

Subsidiaries: Pharsight International Co., Pharsight International France SAS, Pharsight International UK Ltd.

Officers: Shawn M. O'Connor/Chmn., CEO, Pres./$624,625.00, Will Frederick/Sr. VP, CFO/$661,290.00, Daniel L. Weiner/CTO/$468,236.00, James Hayden/Sr. VP - Global Sales/$399,743.00, Mark Hovde/Sr. VP - Marketing/$446,231.00, Greg Lee/VP - Research, Development Projects, Rene Bruno/MD - Strategic Consulting Services, Europe, Nancy Risch/VP - Global Sales

Directors: Shawn M. O'Connor/Chmn., CEO, Pres., Philippe O. Chambon/Dir., John J. Schickling/68/Dir., Howard B. Rosen/Dir., Dean O. Morton/Dir., Douglas E. Kelly/Dir., Arthur Reidel/Dir.

Owners: Philippe O. Chambon, McKesson Corporation, Alloy Entities, William Frederick, Weiss, Peck & Greer Entities, Daniel Weiner, Howard B. Rosen, Dean O. Morton, Insiders, Sprout Entities, Douglas E. Kelly, Insiders, Sprout Entities, Douglas E. Kelly, Mark Hovde *(20 Owners included in Index)*

Financial Data: Fiscal Year End:03/31 Latest Annual Data: 03/31/2007

Year	Sales	Net Income
2007	$25,092,000	$1,871,000
2006	$22,742,000	$530,000
2005	$22,593,000	$2,733,000

Curr. Assets:	$15,715,000	Curr. Liab.:	$13,105,000		
Plant, Equip.:	$2,025,000	Total Liab.:	$13,804,000	Indic. Yr. Divd.:	NA
Total Assets:	$17,786,000	Net Worth:	-$2,659,000	Debt/ Equity:	NA

Phase Forward Inc

880 Winter St., Waltham, MA, 02451; *PH:* 1-781-890-7878; *Fax:* 1-781-890-4848; *http://* www.phaseforward.com; *Email:* info@phaseforward.com

General - Incorporation	DE	Stock - Price on:12/24/2007	$16.02
Employees	450	Stock Exchange	NDQ
Auditor	Ernst & Young LLP	Ticker Symbol	PFWD
Stk Agt..... American Stock Transfer & Trust Co.		Outstanding Shares	35,640,000
Counsel	NA	E.P.S.	$0.44
DUNS No.	NA	Shareholders	NA

Business: The group's principal activity is to provide integrated enterprise-level software products, services and hosted solutions for use in the clinical trial component of the customers' global research and development initiatives. The product-line consists of three software solutions namely, inform, clintrial and clintrace. Inform is an Internet-based electronic data capture solution for collection and transmission of patient information in clinical trials. Clintrial is a clinical data management solution. Clintrace is a solution for monitoring drug safety and reporting adverse events that occur during the clinical trial process. The customers of the group include pharmaceutical, biotechnology and medical device companies, as well as academic institutions, clinical research organizations and other entities engaged in clinical trials.

Primary SIC and add'l.: 7389

CIK No: 0001050180

Subsidiaries: Avalon Lake, Sarl, Bermuda Holdings, LLC, Bottling Group Holdings, Inc., Bottling Group, LLC, C & I Leasing, Inc., Gray Bern Holdings, Inc., Grayhawk Leasing, LLC, Hillwood Bottling, LLC, International Bottlers Management Co. LLC, Luxembourg SCS Holdings, LLC, New Bern Transport Corporation, PBG Canada Finance II, LLC, PBG Canada Finance, LLC

Officers: Robert K. Weiler/Dir., CEO, Pres./$1,196,826.00, Rodger Weismann/Sr. VP, CFO/$849,299.00, Tim Rochford/CTO, Jason Reynolds/VP - North American Sales, Victor Becker/VP - Human Resources, Compliance Officer, Pam Randhawa/VP - Marketing, Martin Young/VP - Corporate Development, Michael Owings/VP - Quality, Regulatory Compliance, Ari D. Buchler/VP, General Counsel, Sec., Steve Powell/VP - Worldwide Sales/$969,176.00, Steve Rosenberg/Sr. VP/$509,673.00, Chan Russell/Pres. - Lincoln Technologies

Directors: Robert K. Weiler/Dir., CEO, Pres., Paul A. Bleicher/Chmn., Founder, James Cash/Dir., Richard D'Amore/Dir., Axel Bichara/Dir., Gary Haroian/Dir., Dennis Shaughnessy/Dir.

Owners: Insiders/11.32%, Gary E. Haroian, Kopp Investment Advisors, LLC/5.91%, Gary E. Haroian, Robert K. Weiler/3.93%, Dennis R. Shaughnessy, Steven J. Rosenberg, Axel Bichara/3.00%, Axel Bichara/3.00%, Paul A. Bleicher/2.40%, Richard A. DAmore, Arbor Capital Management, LLC/5.38%, Eve E. Slater, Stephen J. Powell, Robert K. Weiler/3.93% *(32 Owners included in Index)*

Financial Data: Fiscal Year End:12/31 Latest Annual Data: 12/31/2006

Year	Sales	Net Income
2006	$106,613,000	$12,349,000
2005	$87,081,000	$3,341,000
2004	$73,730,000	$1,869,000

Curr. Assets:	$112,636,000	Curr. Liab.:	$68,056,000	P/E Ratio:	36.41
Plant, Equip.:	$8,561,000	Total Liab.:	$72,630,000	Indic. Yr. Divd.:	NA
Total Assets:	$160,651,000	Net Worth:	$88,021,000	Debt/ Equity:	NA

Phazar Corp

101 SE 25th Ave., Mineral Wells, TX, 76067; *PH:* 1-940-325-3301; *Fax:* 1-940-325-0716; *http://* www.phazar.com

General - Incorporation	DE	Stock - Price on:12/24/2007	$5.9
Employees	59	Stock Exchange	NDQ
Auditor	Weaver & Tidwell LLP	Ticker Symbol	ANTP
Stk Agt .... Computershare Investor Services LLC		Outstanding Shares	2,300,000
Counsel	NA	E.P.S.	-$0.02
DUNS No.	80-563-5430	Shareholders	NA

Business: The group's principal activities are to design, manufacture and market antenna systems, towers and communications accessories worldwide. The antenna products include ground to air collinear antennas, instrument landing antennas and towers, tactical quick erect antennas and masts, shipboard antenna tilting devices and surveillance antennas. The group's commercial products include panel, sector, omnidirectional and closed loop telecommunications antennas, automatic meter reading (amr), instrument scientific medical (ism), cellular, guyed towers, self supported towers and monopoles. These products are principally marketed to the United States government, military and civil agencies, prime contractors and commercial clients. The subsidiaries include antenna products corporation, phazar antenna corp, phazar aerocorp inc and thirco inc.

Primary SIC and add'l.: 6719 3679 3663 3471 7532

CIK No: 0000724267

Subsidiaries: Phazar Antenna Corp., Thirco, Inc., Tumche Corp.

Officers: James Miles/65/Dir., CEO, Pres., Clark D. Wraight/64/Dir., VP, Sec., Treasurer

Directors: James Miles/65/Dir., CEO, Pres., Allen R. Wahl/80/Dir., Gary W. Havener/68/Dir., Clark D. Wraight/64/Dir., VP, Sec., Treasurer, James Kenney/67/Dir., Dennis M. Maunder/57/Dir., Vernon Bryant/66/Dir.

Owners: James Miles/0.20%, James Kenney/0.19%, Vernon Bryant, Insiders/8.94%, Gary W. Havener/4.46%, Allen R. Wahl, Antenna Products Corporation/3.91%, Dennis Maunder/0.06%

Financial Data: Fiscal Year End:05/31 Latest Annual Data: 5/31/2006

Year	Sales	Net Income
2006	$9,489,000	$1,103,000
2005	$11,615,000	$1,737,000
2004	$11,714,000	$1,422,000

Curr. Assets:	$6,499,000	Curr. Liab.:	$434,000		
Plant, Equip.:	$1,053,000	Total Liab.:	$434,000	Indic. Yr. Divd.:	NA
Total Assets:	$7,589,000	Net Worth:	$7,155,000	Debt/ Equity:	NA

Phelps Dodge Corp

One N Central Ave, Phoenix, AZ, 85004; *PH:* 1-602-366-8100; *http://* www.phelpsdodge.com

General - Incorporation	NY	Stock - Price on:12/24/2007	NA
Employees	15,000	Stock Exchange	NA
Auditor	PricewaterhouseCoopers LLP	Ticker Symbol	NA
Stk Agt	Mellon Investor Services LLC	Outstanding Shares	NA
Counsel	NA	E.P.S.	NA
DUNS No.	00-121-3149	Shareholders	NA

Business: The groups principle activity is to exploring and trading minerals. The group operates from North America, Africa and Asia.

Primary SIC and add'l.: 2895 3331 1061 1044 3351 1021 1041

CIK No: 0000078066

Subsidiaries: Ajo Improvement Company, Alambres y Cables de Panama, S.A., Alambres y Cables Venezolanos, C.A., Amax Arizona, Inc., Amax de Chile, Inc., Amax Energy Inc., Amax Exploration (Ireland), Inc., Amax Exploration, Inc., Amax Metals Recovery, Inc., Amax Nickel Overseas Ventures, Inc., Amax Realty Development, Inc., Amax Research & Development, Inc., Amax Specialty Coppers Corporation, Amax Specialty Metals (Driver), Inc., Amax Zinc (Newfoundland) Limited 151 Subsidiaries included in the Index

Officers: Timothy R. Snider/COO, Pres.

Directors: Charles C. Krulak/Dir., Jon C. Madonna/Dir., Dustan E. McCoy/Dir.

Owners: Marie L. Knowles, Archie W. Dunham, Jon C. Madonna, Insiders, Charles C. Krulak, Robert D. Johnson, William J. Post, Steven J. Whisler, Martin H. Richenhagen, Atticus Capital, L.L.C./9.97%, Ramiro G. Peru, S.A.C. Capital Advisors, LLC/5.10%, William A. Franke, Dustan E. McCoy, David S. Colton *(19 Owners included in Index)*

PHH Corp

3000 Leadenhall Rd., Mt. Laurel, NJ, 08054; *PH:* 1-800-449-8767; *Fax:* 1-856-917-4326; *http://* www.phh.com

General - Incorporation	MD	Stock - Price on:12/24/2007	$31.11
Employees	NA	Stock Exchange	NYSE
Auditor	Deloitte & Touche LLP	Ticker Symbol	PHH
Stk Agt	Mellon Investor Services LLC	Outstanding Shares	NA
Counsel	Skadden, Meagher & Flom LLP	E.P.S.	-$0.43
DUNS No.	00-695-0349	Shareholders	NA

Business: The group operates through its business in three business segments namelyvehicle management services, real estate services and mortgage banking services.principle subsidiaries: phh vehicle management services; phh relocation; phh asset management; phh fantus; phh network services; phh us mortgage services. The group operates from United States.

Primary SIC and add'l.: 7389 6531 6162

CIK No: 0000077776

Subsidiaries: Atrium Insurance Corporation, Axiom Financial, Inc., Canadian Lease Management Limited, Cendant Home Funding, LLC(joint venture), Cendant Preferred Mortgage, LLC (joint venture), Century 21 Mortgage Corporation, Chesapeake Funding LLC, Coldwell Banker Mortgage Corporation, D.L. Peterson Trust, Dealers Holding, Inc., drivershield.com FS Corp., Edenton Motors, Inc., ERA Mortgage Corporation, FAH Company, Inc., First Fleet Corporation 62 Subsidiaries included in the Index

Officers: Terence W. Edwards/Dir., CEO, Pres., George J. Kilroy/Dir., CEO, Pres. - PHH Arval, Joseph E. Suter/CEO, Pres. - PHH Mortgage, Clair M. Raubenstine/CFO, Exec. VP, Mark E. Johnson/48/VP, Treasurer, Karen McCallson/VP - Public Relations, PHH Mortgage Services, Mark R. Danahy/CFO, Sr. VP - PHH Mortgage, William F. Brown/Sr. VP, General Counsel, Corp. Sec., Nancy Kyle/VP - Investor Relations, Michael D. Orner/40/VP, Controller

Directors: Terence W. Edwards/Dir., CEO, Pres., George J. Kilroy/Dir., CEO, Pres. - PHH Arval, A. B. Krongard/Non - Exec. Chmn., Ann D. Logan/Dir., Francis J. Van Kirk/Dir., James W. Brinkley/Dir., Jonathan D. Mariner/Dir.

Owners: Appaloosa Management L.P./5.58%, James W. Brinkley, Ann D. Logan, Francis J. Van Kirk, Dimensional FundAdvisors Inc./6.99%, Neil J. Cashen, A. B. Krongard, Jonathan D. Mariner, George J. Kilroy, Luxor Capital Partners, LP/5.01%, Pennant Capital Management, LLC/8.67%, Hotchkis and Wiley Capital Management, LLC/8.93%, William F. Brown, Mark R. Danahy, Terence W. Edwards *(16 Owners included in Index)*

Financial Data: *Fiscal Year End:*12/31 *Latest Annual Data:* 12/31/2006

Year	Sales	Net Income
2006	$2,558,000,000	-$16,000,000
2005	$2,680,000,000	$72,000,000
2004	$2,973,000,000	$182,000,000

Curr. Assets:	$1,144,000,000	**Curr. Liab.:**	$494,000,000		
Plant, Equip.:	$64,000,000	**Total Liab.:**	$9,214,000,000	**Indic. Yr. Divd.:**	NA
Total Assets:	$10,760,000,000	**Net Worth:**	$1,515,000,000	**Debt/ Equity:**	4.7980

Philadelphia Consolidated Holding Corp

1 Bala Plz., Ste. 100, Bala Cynwyd, PA, 19004; *PH:* 1-610-617-7900; *Fax:* 1-610-617-7940; *http://* www.phlyins.com; *Email:* phlysales@phlyins.com

General		**Stock**	
Incorporation	PA	Price on:12/24/2007	$41.86
Employees	1,237	Stock Exchange	NDQ
Auditor	PricewaterhouseCoopers LLP	Ticker Symbol	PHLY
Stk Agt	American Stock Transfer & Trust Co.	Outstanding Shares	71,360,000
Counsel	Wolf Block Schorr & Solis-Cohen LLP	E.P.S	$4.45
DUNS No.	17-551-0916	Shareholders	NA

Business: The group's principal activities are to design, market and underwrite specialty commercial and personal property and casualty insurance products. The group's target market includes, among others, rent-a-car industry, automobile leasing industry, non-profit organizations, the health, fitness and wellness industry and select classes of professional liability. The products of the group are marketed through 204 underwriting professionals and 36 regional offices located in the United States.

Primary SIC and add'l.: 6331 6719

CIK No: 0000909109

Subsidiaries: Liberty American Insurance Company, Liberty American Insurance Group, Liberty American Insurance Services, Inc., Liberty American Premium Finance Company, Maguire Insurance Agency, Inc, Mobile USA Insurance Company, PCHC Investment Corp, Philadelphia Indemnity Insurance Company, Philadelphia Insurance Company

Officers: James J. Maguire/Dir., CEO, Pres./$2,110,959.00, Bruce T. Meyer/CEO, Pres. - Liberty American Insurance Group, Inc, Sean S. Sweeney/Dir., Exec. VP, Chief Marketing Officer/$1,466,924.00, Christopher J. Maguire/Exec. VP, Chief Underwriting Officer/$1,617,214.00, Craig P. Keller/CFO, Exec. VP, Sec.,Treasurer/$1,326,941.00, Joseph Barnholt/Assist. VP - Fin, Tax Reporting, Investor Relations

Directors: James J. Maguire/Dir., CEO, Pres., James J. Maguire/Chmn., Michael J. Cascio/Dir., Aminta Hawkins Breaux/Dir., Michael J. Morris/Dir., Elizabeth H. Gemmill/Dir., Sean S. Sweeney/Dir., Exec. VP, Chief Marketing Officer, Donald A. Pizer/Dir., Shaun F. O'Malley/Dir., Ronald R. Rock/Dir.

Owners: Bruce T. Meyer, Frances M. Maguire/12.30%, Aminta Hawkins Breaux, Michael J. Cascio, EARNEST Partners, LLC/10.00%, James J. Maguire/2.60%, Michael J. Morris, FMR Corp./8.20%, Craig P. Keller, Christopher J. Maguire/1.70%, Shaun F. OMalley, James J. Maguire/15.30%, Ronald R. Rock, Sean S. Sweeney, Elizabeth H. Gemmill *(17 Owners included in Index)*

Financial Data: *Fiscal Year End:*12/31 *Latest Annual Data:* 12/31/2006

Year	Sales	Net Income
2006	$1,253,770,000	$288,849,000
2005	$1,051,429,000	$156,688,000
2004	$818,856,000	$83,683,000

Curr. Assets:	$728,305,000	**Curr. Liab.:**	$66,827,000	**P/E Ratio:**	9.60
Plant, Equip.:	$26,999,000	**Total Liab.:**	$2,271,270,000	**Indic. Yr. Divd.:**	NA
Total Assets:	$3,438,537,000	**Net Worth:**	$1,167,267,000	**Debt/ Equity:**	NA

Philippine Long Distance Telephone Co

4/F MGO Bldg., Makati Ave., Makati City, 721; *PH:* 632-8168915; *Fax:* 632-8451596; *http://* www.pldt.com.ph; *Email:* info@epldt.com

General		**Stock**	
Incorporation	Philippines	Price on:12/24/2007	$58.07
Employees	28,219	Stock Exchange	NYSE
Auditor	SyCip Gorres Velayo & Co	Ticker Symbol	PHI
Stk Agt	Hongkong & Shanghai Banking Corp	Outstanding Shares	188,570,000
Counsel	NA	E.P.S	$4.54
DUNS No.	71-865-7752	Shareholders	NA

Business: The group's principle activity is the provision of diversified telecommunications that are organized into three main segments: fixed line: primarily provided through pldt and its affiliate piltel, and subsidiaries clark telecom inc, subic telecom and maratel, which together account for less than 1% of total fixed lines in service. Wireless: it is provided through cellular service providers and satellite operators (mabuhay satellite, aces Philippines, and telesat). Information and communications technology: information and communications infrastructure and services for Internet applications, Internet protocol-based solutions and multimedia content delivery provided by epldt, Internet access services provided by epldt's subsidiary infocom and e-commerce, call centers and it-related services provided through other subsidiaries and affiliates of epldt.

Primary SIC and add'l.: 4899 4813 4812

CIK No: 0000078150

Subsidiaries: ACeS Philippines Cellular Satellite Corporation, Airborne Access Corporation, BCC, Bonifacio Communications Corporation, Clark Telecom, Infocom Technologies, Inc, Mabuhay Satellite, Mabuhay Satellite Corporation, netGames, Inc, PLDT Clark Telecom, Inc, PLDT Global and subsidiaries, PLDT-Maratel, Smart and subsidiaries, Smart-NTT Multimedia, Inc, Subic Telecom 16 Subsidiaries included in the Index

Officers: Napoleon L. Nazareno/Dir., CEO, Pres., Arnel S. Crisostomo/VP, Celso T. Dimarucut/VP, Anna Isabel V. Bengzon/VP, Emeraldo L. Hernandez/VP, Miguela F. Villanueva/First VP, Ramon Alger P. Obias/First VP, Ramon B. Rivera/First VP, Ernesto R. Alberto/Sr. VP, Enrique S. Pascual/VP, Alfredo S. Panlilio/Sr. VP, Jose Lauro G Pelayo/VP, Nerissa S. Ramos/First VP, Victorico P. Vargas/Sr. VP, Rebecca Jeanine R. De Guzman/VP *(52 Officers included in Index)*

Directors: Napoleon L. Nazareno/Dir., CEO, Pres., Manuel V. Pangilinan/Chmn., Bienvenido F. Nebres/Dir., Lourdes C. Rausa-Chan/Dir., Sr. VP, Ray C. Espinosa/Dir., Oscar S. Reyes/Dir., Corazon S. De La Paz/Dir., Albert F. Del Rosario/Dir., Pedro E. Roxas/Dir., Helen Y. Dee/Dir., Tatsu Kono/Dir., Tsuyoshi Kawashima/Dir., Alfred V. Ty/Dir.

Owners: NTT Communications Corporation/6.70%, Alfred V. Ty, Ma. Lourdes C. Rausa-Chan, J.P. Morgan Asset Holdings/18.50%, Ma. Lourdes C. Rausa-Chan, Rene G. Baez, Napoleon L. Nazareno, Metro Pacific Resources, Inc./9.07%, Oscar S. Reyes, PCD Nominee Corporation/46.19%, Bienvenido F. Nebres, Social Security System/5.91%, George N. Lim, Helen Y. Dee, Alfredo S. Panlilio *(40 Owners included in Index)*

Financial Data: *Fiscal Year End:*12/31 *Latest Annual Data:* 12/31/2006

Year	Sales	Net Income
2006	$2,614,488,000	$688,759,000
2005	$2,331,032,000	$767,397,000
2004	$2,157,734,000	$500,198,000

Curr. Assets:	$1,073,175,000	**Curr. Liab.:**	$1,161,407,000		
Plant, Equip.:	$3,406,998,000	**Total Liab.:**	$3,211,284,000	**Indic. Yr. Divd.:**	$2.870
Total Assets:	$5,415,998,000	**Net Worth:**	$2,176,547,000	**Debt/ Equity:**	NA

Phillips Van Heusen Corp

200 Madison Ave., New York, NY, 10016; *PH:* 1-212-381-3500; *Fax:* 1-212-381-3950; *http://* www.pvh.com

General		**Stock**	
Incorporation	DE	Price on:12/24/2007	$58.92
Employees	5,600	Stock Exchange	NYSE
Auditor	Ernst & Young LLP	Ticker Symbol	PVH
Stk Agt	Bank of New York	Outstanding Shares	56,180,000
Counsel	NA	E.P.S	$2.63
DUNS No.	00-136-1005	Shareholders	NA

Business: The groups principle activity is to operate apparel stores. The groups products include branded label dress shirts, sportswear and footwear. The groups products are sold under the brand names including Heusen, IZOD, Arrow, G.H. Bass and Co., Bass and Eagle. In the year 2007 the group acquired Superba, Inc. The group operates from United States.

Primary SIC and add'l.: 2326 3149 2339

CIK No: 0000078239

Subsidiaries: BassNet, Inc., C.A.T. Industrial, S.A. de C.V., Calvin Klein (Europe II) Corp., Calvin Klein (Europe), Inc., Calvin Klein, Inc., Camisas Modernas, S.A., Caribe M&I Ltd., CD Group Inc., CK Service Corp., Cluett Peabody Resources Corporation, Cluett, Peabody & Co., Inc., Confecciones Imperio, S.A., G. H. Bass Franchises Inc., G.H. Bass Caribbean LLC, GHB (Far East) Limited 32 Subsidiaries included in the Index

Officers: Emanuel Chirico/Chmn., CEO/$6,678,796.00, Michael Zaccaro/Vice Chmn. - Retail/$2,501,016.00, Francis K. Duane/Vice Chmn. - Wholesale/$3,015,169.00, Steven B. Shiffman/Pres. - Van Heusen Retail, Michael A. Shaffer/CFO, Exec. VP - Finance/$1,350,550.00, Arthur R. Heffner/Group Exec. VP - Logistics Services, Donna Patrick/Pres. - Izod Retail, David F. Kozel/VP - Human Resources, Margaret P. Lachance/Pres. - Geoffrey Beene Retail, Allen E. Sirkin/COO, Pres./$3,965,169.00, Theodore Sattler/Group Exec. VP - Foreign Operations, Molly Yearick/Pres. - PVH Sportswear Group, Paul Thomas Murry/COO, Pres. - Calvin Klein/$2,815,801.00, Ellen Constantinides/COO, Pres. - PVH Dress Shirt Group, Cheryl Dapolito/Pres. - Izod Womens Sportswear *(31 Officers included in Index)*

Directors: Emanuel Chirico/Chmn., CEO, Joseph B. Fuller/Dir., Edward H. Cohen/Dir., Bruce Maggin/Dir., Henry Nasella/Dir., Rita M. Rodriguez/Dir., Mary Baglivo/Dir., James V. Marino/Dir., Margaret L. Jenkins/Dir., Craig Rydin/Dir.

Owners: Bruce Maggin, Marc Grosman, Francis K. Duane, Michael A. Shaffer, Mark Weber, Joel H. Goldberg, Henry Nasella, Allen E. Sirkin, Paul Thomas Murry, Rita M. Rodriguez, Earnest Partners, LLC/9.99%, Joseph B. Fuller, Barclays Global Investors, NA/5.34%, Bruce J. Klatsky, FMR Corp./5.09% *(19 Owners included in Index)*

Financial Data: *Fiscal Year End:*01/29 *Latest Annual Data:* 2/4/2007

Year	Sales	Net Income
2007	$2,090,648,000	$155,229,000
2006	$1,908,848,000	$111,688,000
2005	$1,641,428,000	$58,615,000

Curr. Assets:	$785,003,000	**Curr. Liab.:**	$283,166,000	**P/E Ratio:**	22.40
Plant, Equip.:	$172,040,000	**Total Liab.:**	$1,056,328,000	**Indic. Yr. Divd.:**	$0.150
Total Assets:	$1,998,485,000	**Net Worth:**	$942,157,000	**Debt/ Equity:**	0.4240

Phoenix Cos Inc

1 American Row, Hartford, CT, 06102; *PH:* 1-860-403-5000; *Fax:* 1-860-403-5534; *http://* www.phoenixwm.com

General		**Stock**	
Incorporation	DE	Price on:12/24/2007	$15.16
Employees	1,500	Stock Exchange	NYSE
Auditor	PricewaterhouseCoopers LLP	Ticker Symbol	PNX
Stk Agt	Bank of New York	Outstanding Shares	114,100,000
Counsel	NA	E.P.S	$1.41
DUNS No.	NA	Shareholders	NA

Business: The groups principle activity is to provide life insurance, annuities and investment products. The group provides money management services to individuals and institutions. The group operates from United States.

Primary SIC and add'l.: 6311

CIK No: 0001129633

Subsidiaries: KAR, Phoenix Global Solutions (India) Pvt. Ltd, PXP, stock life insurance company

Officers: Dona D. Young/Chmn., CEO, Pres./$4,492,541.00, Tracy L. Rich/Exec. VP, General Counsel, Sec./$599,350.00, George R. Aylward/COO, Sr. VP - Asset Management, Lisa-Lynn Bassi/Sr. VP - Distributor Service Organization, Edward W. Cassidy/Sr. VP - Life Distribution, Katherine P. Cody/Sr. VP, Chief Accounting Officer - Corporate Finance, Michele U. Farley/Sr. VP - Corporate, Marketing Communications, Stephen D. Gresham/Sr. VP - Retail Distribution - Asset

Management, Peter A. Hofmann/Exec. VP, Joseph E. Kelleher/COO, Sr. VP - Life, Annuity, John V. Lagrasse/CIO, Sr. VP, Robert G. Lautensack/Sr. VP, Chief Risk Officer, Gina Collopy O'Connell/Sr. VP - Life - Annuity Manufacturing, Zafar Rashid/Sr. VP - Life - Annuity Finance, Christopher M. Wilkos/Sr. VP - Corporate Portfolio Management *(24 Officers included in Index)*

Directors: Dona D. Young/Chmn., CEO, Pres., Thomas S. Johnson/Dir., Ann Maynard Gray/Dir., John E. Haire/Dir., Sal H. Alfiero/Dir., Peter C. Browning/Dir., John H. Forsgren/Dir., Jerry J. Jasinowski/Dir., Sanford Cloud/Dir., Jean S. Blackwell/Dir., Gordon J. Davis/Dir., Arthur P. Byrne/62/Dir., Martin N. Baily/Dir.

Owners: Dona D. Young, Daniel T. Geraci, Jean S. Blackwell, Peter C. Browning, Jerry J. Jasinowski, Sanford Cloud, James D. Wehr, Michael E. Haylon, John H. Forsgren, Sal H. Alfiero, Ann Maynard Gray, Arthur P. Byrne, Martin N. Baily, Philip K. Polkinghorn, Tracy L. Rich *(21 Owners included in Index)*

Financial Data: Fiscal Year End:12/31   Latest Annual Data: 12/31/2006

Year	Sales	Net Income
2006	$2,578,000,000	$99,900,000
2005	$2,608,900,000	$108,400,000
2004	$2,744,000,000	$86,400,000

Curr. Assets:	$602,000,000	**Curr. Liab.:**	NA	**P/E Ratio:** 11.75
Plant, Equip.:	NA	**Total Liab.:**	$26,732,600,000	**Indic. Yr. Divd.:** $0.160
Total Assets:	$28,973,200,000	**Net Worth:**	$2,236,100,000	**Debt/ Equity:** 0.4603

Phoenix Footwear Group Inc

5840 El Camino Real, Ste. 106, Carlsbad, CA, 92008; *PH:* 1-760-602-9688; *Fax:* 1-760-602-9684; *http://* www.phoenixfootwear.com; *Email:* info@phxg.com

General - Incorporation	DE	**Stock**- Price on:12/24/2007	$3.2
Employees	543	Stock Exchange	AMEX
Auditor	Grant Thornton, LLP	Ticker Symbol	PXG
Stk Agt	Computershare Investor Services LLC	Outstanding Shares	8,050,000
Counsel	NA	E.P.S.	-$1.61
DUNS No.	00-222-8849	Shareholders	NA

Business: The group's principal activities are to design, develop and market dress and casual footwear and apparel with an emphasis on traditional style, quality and fit. Women's dress and casual footwear are sold under the trotters and softwalk brand names. Men's dress and casual footwear are sold under the strol, h.s. Trask and ducks unlimited brand names. Outdoor sportswear and travel apparel for both men and women are sold under the royal robbins brand name. The group markets over 80 different styles of footwear and over 250 different styles of apparel products. The sale of footwear and apparel products is made principally to retailers in the United States. On 19-Jul-2004, the group acquired altama delta corporation.

Primary SIC and add'l.: 3142 5139

CIK No: 0000026820

Subsidiaries: Altama Delta (Puerto Rico) Corporation, Altama Delta Corporation, Chambers Belt Company, H.S. Trask & Co., Penobscot Shoe Company, Phoenix Delaware Acquisition, Inc., PXG Canada, Inc., Royal Robbins, Inc.

Officers: Cathy Taylor/Dir., CEO, Pres., Kenneth Wolf/CFO, Treasurer, Sec./$232,383.00

Directors: Cathy Taylor/Dir., CEO, Pres., James R. Riedman/Chmn., John C. Kratzer/Dir., John M. Robbins/Dir., Frederick R. Port/Dir., Steven M. Deperrior/Dir., Wilhelm Pfander/Dir., Gregory M. Harden/Dir., Robert Gunst/Dir.

Owners: Sivaprasad Reddy, Retirement Committee of the Phoenix Footwear Group, Inc./5.60%, Robert A. Gunst, John M. Robbins, Gregory M. Harden, John C. Kratzer, Riedman Corporation/7.60%, Frederick R. Port, Wedbush, Inc. and Wedbush Morgan Securities/5.80%, Insiders/33.70%, Kenneth E. Wolf/1.70%, Steven M. DePerrior/6.30%, James R. Riedman/32.20%, Wilhelm Pfander, Dimensional FundAdvisors, Inc./7.00% *(16 Owners included in Index)*

Financial Data: Fiscal Year End:12/31   Latest Annual Data: 12/30/2006

Year	Sales	Net Income
2006	$140,589,000	-$20,378,000
2005	$109,189,000	$1,191,000

Curr. Assets:	$61,989,000	**Curr. Liab.:**	$27,937,000	
Plant, Equip.:	$4,538,000	**Total Liab.:**	$84,867,000	**Indic. Yr. Divd.:** $0.180
Total Assets:	$138,891,000	**Net Worth:**	$54,024,000	**Debt/ Equity:** NA

Phoenix India Acquisition Corp

590 Madison Ave., 6th Fl., New York, NY, 10022; *PH:* 1-212-734-4600

General - Incorporation	DE	**Stock**- Price on:12/24/2007	$7.65
Employees	NA	Stock Exchange	OTC
Auditor	NA	Ticker Symbol	PXIA
Stk Agt	American Stock Transfer & Trust Co.	Outstanding Shares	NA
Counsel	NA	E.P.S.	$0.10
DUNS No.	NA	Shareholders	NA

Business: The groups principal activity is to serve as a vehicle for the acquisition of an operating business through a merger, capital stock exchange, asset acquisition or other similar business combination. The group intends to focus efforts on identifying within the information technology, information technology enabled service and information technology enabled products industries, a prospective target business.

Primary SIC and add'l.: 7389

CIK No: 0001336775

Officers: Ramesh Akella/42/Dir., Pres., Chief Strategy Officer, CFO, Principal Executive Officer, Shekhar Wadekar/49/Dir., Exec. VP, Sec., Treasurer, Rohit Phansalkar/63/Dir., Exec. VP

Directors: Raju Panjwani/52/Chmn., Ramesh Akella/42/Dir., Pres., Chief Strategy Officer, CFO, Principal Executive Officer, Shekhar Wadekar/49/Dir., Exec. VP, Sec., Treasurer, Rohit Phansalkar/63/Dir., Exec. VP

Owners: Raju Panjwani/3.67%, Rohit Phansalkar/3.44%, Phoenix India Management Company LLC/5.35%, Shekhar Wadekar/3.85%, Insiders/20.94%, Ramesh Akella/4.62%

Financial Data: Fiscal Year End:NA   Latest Annual Data: 12/31/2006

Year	Sales	Net Income
2006	$2,111,000	$678,000

Curr. Assets:	$56,430,000	**Curr. Liab.:**	$757,000	**P/E Ratio:** 95.63
Plant, Equip.:	NA	**Total Liab.:**	$3,023,000	**Indic. Yr. Divd.:** NA
Total Assets:	$56,429,000	**Net Worth:**	$42,580,000	**Debt/ Equity:** NA

Phoenix Interests Inc

1 Riverpoint Plz., Ste. 706, Jeffersonville, IN, 47130; *PH:* 1-502-584-4434; *http://* www.phoenixinterests.com; *Email:* info@phoenixinterests.com

General - Incorporation	NV	**Stock**- Price on:12/24/2007	$0.0004
Employees	NA	Stock Exchange	OTC
Auditor	Gruber & Co., LLC	Ticker Symbol	PXIT
Stk Agt	Olde Monmouth Stk Trnsfer Co. Inc.	Outstanding Shares	1,010,000,000
Counsel	NA	E.P.S.	-$0.001
DUNS No.	NA	Shareholders	NA

Business: The group's principle activity is to engage in pinhooking and racing of thoroughbred horses. Pinhooking involves the purchase of a yearling, that is, a horse, which is between one and two years old, with a view towards training and then reselling that horse as two years old. Pinhooking also involves the purchase of a weanling, that is, a horse which is less than one year old and reselling as a yearling. The thoroughbreds are purchased from non-affiliated breeders of thoroughbred yearlings through non-affiliated industry auction houses, such as Fasig-Tipton, Keeneland and Ocala Breeders Sales Company.

Primary SIC and add'l.: 0272

CIK No: 0001092448

Subsidiaries: Legend Mobile, Inc., Online Enterprises, Inc, Phoenix Interests, Inc

Owners: Peter Klamka/2.20%, Insiders/0.00%, Peter Klamka, James D. Tilton, Insiders/97.80%, James D. Tilton/95.60%

Financial Data: Fiscal Year End:12/31   Latest Annual Data: 12/31/2006

Year	Sales	Net Income
2006	$26,000	-$147,000
2005	$26,000	-$592,000
2004	NA	-$1,160,000

Curr. Assets:	$1,000	**Curr. Liab.:**	$3,806,000	
Plant, Equip.:	$12,000	**Total Liab.:**	$3,808,000	**Indic. Yr. Divd.:** NA
Total Assets:	$13,000	**Net Worth:**	-$3,796,000	**Debt/ Equity:** NA

Phoenix Technologies Ltd

915 Murphy Ranch Rd., Milpitas, CA, 95035; *PH:* 1-408-570-1000; *Fax:* 1-408-570-1001; *http://* www.phoenix.com

General - Incorporation	DE	**Stock**- Price on:12/24/2007	$8.09
Employees	356	Stock Exchange	NDQ
Auditor	Ernst & Young LLP	Ticker Symbol	PTEC
Stk Agt	Computershare Ltd.	Outstanding Shares	25,840,000
Counsel	Orrick, Herrington & Sutcliffe LLP	E.P.S.	NA
DUNS No.	10-885-8044	Shareholders	NA

Business: The group's principal activity is to provide core system software to activate, secure, connect, and recover personal computers, information appliances and other digital devices connected to the Internet. The products are provided to platform and peripheral manufactures that include PC and information appliance manufacturers, system integrators, system builders, integrated service vendors and value-added resellers. The group also provides training, consulting, maintenance and engineering services to its customers. Its products are firstbios, firstware, firstauthority and information appliance software products families. Some of the customers of the group include dell computer corporation, IBM corporation, samsung electronics co. Ltd., toshiba, inc., sony corporation, motorola, inc., fujitsu limited and nec corporation. The group operates in North America, Japan, Taiwan, Europe and other Asian countries.

Primary SIC and add'l.: 7372 7379

CIK No: 0000832767

Subsidiaries: Award Software Far East Ltd. Hong Kong, Phoenix Acquisition Corporation, Phoenix Computer Products Corporation, Phoenix Technologies (Hungary) Ltd., Phoenix Technologies (India) Ltd., Phoenix Technologies (Korea) Ltd., Phoenix Technologies (Nanjing) Co. Ltd., Phoenix Technologies (Netherland) B.V., Phoenix Technologies (Taiwan) Ltd., Phoenix Technologies Asia Pacific Ltd., Phoenix Technologies GmbH, Phoenix Technologies Kabushiki Kaisha, Phoenix Technologies UK Ltd.

Officers: Woodson Hobbs/CEO, Pres., Shauli Chaudhuri/VP - Marketing, David Gibbs/Sr. VP, GM - Worldwide Field Operations, Tim Chu/VP, General Counsel, Sec., John Correia/VP - Worldwide Customer Engineering, Robin Eller/VP - Administration, Erica Mannion/Investor Relations Contact, Richard Arnold/CFO, COO, Gaurav Banga/Sr. VP - Engineering, CTO, Surendra Arora/VP - Business Development

Directors: Dale Fuller/Chmn., Douglas E. Barnett/Dir., Michael Clair/Dir., John Mutch/Dir., Richard Noling/Dir.

Owners: David Gibbs/1.75%, Scott Taylor, Gaurav Banga, John Mutch, Richard Arnold/2.22%, Woodson Hobbs/4.24%, Michael Clair, Dale Fuller, Insiders/9.86%, Husic Capital Management/5.89%, Douglas Barnett, Ramius Capital Group LLC/12.56%, Richard Noling, Austin W. Marxe/9.36%

Financial Data: Fiscal Year End:09/30   Latest Annual Data: 9/30/2006

Year	Sales	Net Income
2006	$60,495,000	-$43,969,000
2005	$99,536,000	$277,000
2004	$86,750,000	$449,000

Curr. Assets:	$72,928,000	**Curr. Liab.:**	$30,433,000	
Plant, Equip.:	$4,247,000	**Total Liab.:**	$34,984,000	**Indic. Yr. Divd.:** NA
Total Assets:	$95,160,000	**Net Worth:**	$60,176,000	**Debt/ Equity:** NA

PhotoChannel Networks Inc

425 Carrall St., Ste. 506, Vancouver, BC, V6B 6E3; *PH:* 1-604-893-8955; *http://* www.photochannel.com; *Email:* sales@pnidigitalmedia.com

General - Incorporation	Canada	**Stock**- Price on:12/24/2007	$15.23
Employees	NA	Stock Exchange	NYSE
Auditor	PricewaterhouseCoopers LLP	Ticker Symbol	NA
Stk Agt	Computershare Trust Co	Outstanding Shares	10,540,000
Counsel	NA	E.P.S.	$0.95
DUNS No.	NA	Shareholders	NA

Business: The group's principle activities include developing, distributing and marketing digital imaging software products for use by consumers and businesses wishing to catalog, present and display images captured using digital cameras, photo scanners, images downloaded from the Internet as well as images developed as pictures on CD and floppy disks. The group operates from United States.

Primary SIC and add'l.: 7372

CIK No: 0001036642

Subsidiaries: PhotoChannel, Inc

Officers: Peter Fitzgerald/Chmn., CEO, Pres., Kyle Hall/Exec. VP - Sales, Marketing, Business Development, Robert Chisholm/CFO, Aaron Rallo/CTO, VP - Product Development

Directors: Peter Fitzgerald/Chmn., CEO, Pres., Peter C. Scarth/Dir., Thomas Nielsen/Dir., Cory Kent/Dir., Doug Rowan/Dir.

Owners: Peter Scarth/3.66%, Thomas Nielsen, Doug Rowan, Robert Chisholm, Aaron Rallo, Kyle Hall, Peter Fitzgerald/5.79%, Patricia Spice, Cory Kent

Financial Data: Fiscal Year End:09/30   Latest Annual Data: 5/31/2006

Year	Sales		Net Income
2006	$15,223,000		$12,331,000
2005	$28,371,000		$22,774,000
2004	$13,953,000		$1,001,000
Curr. Assets:	$5,920,000	Curr. Liab.:	$1,555,000
Plant, Equip.:	NA	Total Liab.:	$42,583,000	Indic. Yr. Divd.:	$0.800
Total Assets:	$286,672,000	Net Worth:	$244,088,000	Debt/ Equity:	NA

Photomedex Inc

147 Keystone Dr., Montgomeryville, PA, 18936; **PH:** 1-215-619-3600; **Fax:** 1-215-619-3208; *http://* www.photomedex.com; **Email:** info@photomedex.com

General - Incorporation	DE	Stock- Price on:12/24/2007	$1.3
Employees	192	Stock Exchange	NDQ
Auditor	Amper, Politziner & Mattia P.C	Ticker Symbol	PHMD
Stk Agt.	StockTrans, Inc	Outstanding Shares	62,800,000
Counsel	NA	E.P.S.	-$0.12
DUNS No.	05-450-3875	Shareholders	NA

Business: The group's principal activity is to develop, manufacture and market excimer laser and fiber optic systems and techniques. These products are designed for the treatment of psoriasis, vitiligo, atopic dermatitis and leukoderma. The activities are carried out through four segments: domestic xtrac, international xtrac, surgical services and surgical products and other. The group also develops, manufactures and markets proprietary lasers and delivery systems for both contact and non-contact surgery and provides surgical services utilizing these and other manufacturers' products. The customers include doctors, hospitals and surgery centers.

Primary SIC and add'l.: 3699 3841 3674 3845

CIK No: 0000711665

Subsidiaries: ProCyte Corporation, SLT Technology, Inc, Surgical Innovations & Services, Inc, Surgical Laser Technologies, Inc.

Officers: Jeffrey F. O'Donnell/Dir., CEO, Pres./$1,888,113.00, Jeffrey L. Levatter/CTO, Michael R. Stewart/COO/$533,566.00, Dennis McGrath/CFO, VP - Finance, Administration/$1,381,486.00

Directors: Jeffrey F. O'Donnell/Dir., CEO, Pres., Rox R. Anderson/Chmn. - Scientific Advisory Board, Richard Depiano/Chmn., Warwick Alex Charlton/Dir., Alan R. Novak/Dir., Anthony J. Dimun/Dir., Kenneth Arndt/Member - Scientific Advisory Board, Steven R. Feldman/Member - Scientific Advisory Board, Richard E. Fitzpatrick/Member - Scientific Advisory Board, Roy G. Geronemus/Member - Scientific Advisory Board, Lajos Kemeny/Member - Scientific Advisory Board, John Y.M. Koo/Member - Scientific Advisory Board, Warrick L. Morison/Member - Scientific Advisory Board, Daniel Siegel/Member - Scientific Advisory Board, James Spencer/Member - Scientific Advisory Board *(19 Directors included in Index)*

Owners: Corsair Reporting Persons/7.03%, Alan R. Novak, Prides Capital Partners, L.L.C./5.71%, Wayne M. Withrow, Richard J. DePiano, Jeffrey F. O'Donnell/1.41%, LB I Group, Inc/8.31%, David W. Anderson, Warwick Alex Charlton, Insiders/4.95%, Anthony J. Dimun, Dennis M. McGrath/1.03%, Wellington Management Co., L.P/13.57%, Michael R. Stewart

Financial Data: Fiscal Year End:12/31   Latest Annual Data: 12/31/2006

Year	Sales		Net Income
2006	$33,190,000		-$7,492,000
2005	$28,385,000		-$3,936,000
2004	$17,745,000		-$4,984,000
Curr. Assets:	$25,721,000	Curr. Liab.:	$9,651,000
Plant, Equip.:	$9,054,000	Total Liab.:	$13,378,000	Indic. Yr. Divd.:	NA
Total Assets:	$57,482,000	Net Worth:	$44,103,000	Debt/ Equity:	NA

Photon Dynamics Inc

5970 Optical Ct., San Jose, CA, 95138; **PH:** 1-408-226-9900; **Fax:** 1-408-226-9910; *http://* www.photondynamics.com

General - Incorporation	CA	Stock- Price on:12/24/2007	$11.39
Employees	423	Stock Exchange	NDQ
Auditor	Ernst & Young LLP	Ticker Symbol	PHTN
Stk Agt.	Computershare Trust Co	Outstanding Shares	16,650,000
Counsel	Cooley Godward LLP	E.P.S.	-$1.46
DUNS No.	15-510-6180	Shareholders	NA

Business: The group's principal activity is to provide yield management solutions to the flat panel display industry. Its solution are designed to collect data, analyze product quality and identify and repair product defects at critical steps in the flat panel display manufacturing process. It also offers yield management solutions for the printed circuit board assembly, advanced semiconductor packaging industry and the cathode ray tube display and high quality glass industries. The optical and X-ray inspection systems are used to detect and identify defects on printed circuit board assemblies with advanced semiconductor packages mounted on the surfaces of these assemblies. The optical inspection systems use high-resolution cameras and proprietary software to locate and characterize defects in cathode ray tube displays and automotive glass panels. On 21-Jul-2004, the group acquired assets from quantum composers.

Primary SIC and add'l.: 3674 3825 3672

CIK No: 0001002663

Subsidiaries: Akcron Corporation, Ltd., Intelligent Reasoning Systems Intl KK, Intelligent Reasoning Systems, Inc., Kabushiki Kaisha Photon Dynamics, Photon Dynamics Canada, Inc., formerly known as Image Processing Systems, Inc., Photon Dynamics International Trading (Shanghai) Co., Ltd., Photon Dynamics Korea, Inc., Photon Dynamics Nova Scotia Company, Photon Dynamics Technology (Beijing) Co., Ltd.

Officers: Jeffrey A. Hawthorne/Dir., Pres., CEO - Photon Dynamics, Steve Song/VP - Sales, Mark Merrill/VP - Marketing, Michael W. Schradle/CFO, Wendell T. Blonigan/VP, COO

Directors: Jeffrey A. Hawthorne/Dir., Pres., CEO - Photon Dynamics, Malcolm J. Thompson/Chmn., Michael J. Kim/Dir., Nicholas Brathwaite/Dir., Terry Carlitz/Dir., Edward Rogas/Dir., Curt Wozniak/Dir.

Owners: Jeffrey A. Hawthorne/0.27%, Nicholas E. Brathwaite/0.24%, Jeffrey A. Hawthorne/1.51%, Clearbridge Advisors, LLC/6.55%, Curtis S. Wozniak/0.09%, FMR Corporation/9.08%, Barclays Global Investors N.A./5.27%, Terry H. Carlitz/0.09%, Maureen L. Lamb/0.16%, Steve Song/0.48%, Malcolm J. Thompson/0.43%, Insiders/3.66%, Mark Merrill/0.54%

Financial Data: Fiscal Year End:09/30   Latest Annual Data: 9/30/2006

Year	Sales		Net Income
2006	$172,872,000		$4,080,000
2005	$125,813,000		-$19,311,000
2004	$141,870,000		$9,694,000
Curr. Assets:	$154,524,000	Curr. Liab.:	$33,113,000
Plant, Equip.:	$15,891,000	Total Liab.:	$33,232,000	Indic. Yr. Divd.:	NA
Total Assets:	$177,613,000	Net Worth:	$144,381,000	Debt/ Equity:	NA

Photonic Products Group Inc

181 Legrand Ave., Northvale, NJ, 07647; **PH:** 1-201-767-1910; **Fax:** 1-201-767-9644; *http://* www.inrad.com; **Email:** corp@ppgrpinc.com

General - Incorporation	NJ	Stock- Price on:12/24/2007	$2.1
Employees	89	Stock Exchange	OTC
Auditor	Holtz Rubenstein & Co. LLP	Ticker Symbol	PHPG
Stk Agt.	First City Transfer Co	Outstanding Shares	8,970,000
Counsel	NA	E.P.S.	$0.14
DUNS No.	07-666-8458	Shareholders	NA

Business: The group's principal activities are designing, developing, manufacturing and marketing crystals, crystal devices, electro-optic and optical components and sophisticated laser subsystems and instruments. The crystals are used primarily for controlling and measuring laser radiation. The principal customers of the group include commercial instrumentation companies and OEM laser manufacturers, research laboratories, government agencies and defense contractors. The group markets its products in the United States, Canada, Europe, the near east and Japan. During 2003, it acquired the assets and liabilities of laser optics, inc.

Primary SIC and add'l.: 3827 3679 8731

CIK No: 0000719494

Subsidiaries: Laser Optics Holdings, Inc., MRC Precision Metal Optics, Inc.

Officers: Daniel Lehrfeld/Dir., CEO, Pres./$226,950.00, Devaunshi Sampat/55/VP - Northvale Sales, Ppgi Marketing Communication/$152,648.00, William J. Foote/57/VP, CFO, Chief Accounting Officer, Corp. Sec./$87,117.00

Directors: Daniel Lehrfeld/Dir., CEO, Pres., John C. Rich/70/Chmn., Luke P. Lavalle/65/Dir., Thomas H. Lenagh/82/Dir., Jan M. Winston/71/Dir.

Owners: John C. Rich, Clarex, Ltd. & Welland Ltd., Luke P. LaValle, William Nicklin, Jan M. Winston, Devaunshi Sampat, Thomas H. Lenagh, Brown Advisory Holdings, Inc., Insiders, Daniel Lehrfeld

Financial Data: Fiscal Year End:12/31   Latest Annual Data: 12/31/2006

Year	Sales		Net Income
2006	$13,921,000		$772,000
2005	$13,785,000		-$11,000
2004	$9,222,000		-$673,000
Curr. Assets:	$7,987,000	Curr. Liab.:	$3,780,000	P/E Ratio:	26.25
Plant, Equip.:	$4,426,000	Total Liab.:	$10,080,000	Indic. Yr. Divd.:	NA
Total Assets:	$15,316,000	Net Worth:	$5,237,000	Debt/ Equity:	NA

Photonics Corp

520 S Fourth Ave., Ste. 400, Louisville, KY, 40202; **PH:** 1-502-515-1515

General - Incorporation	CA	Stock- Price on:12/24/2007	NA
Employees	2	Stock Exchange	OTC
Auditor	Turner, Stone & Co. LLP	Ticker Symbol	SMCA
Stk Agt.	Securities Transfer Corp	Outstanding Shares	NA
Counsel	NA	E.P.S.	-$0.931
DUNS No.	82-640-4816	Shareholders	NA

Business: The group's principal activity is to provide Internet vertical service to the commercial real estate industry. New management is in the process of seeking additional merger candidates for shareholder growth.

Primary SIC and add'l.: 3577 3669

CIK No: 0000912844

Subsidiaries: REPipeline.com, Inc., The Sarasota Group, Inc.

Officers: Bryce Knight/24/Dir., CEO, CFO, Pres., Walter M. Fiederowicz/Dir. - Private Investor, Consultant

Directors: Bryce Knight/24/Dir., CEO, CFO, Pres., Constantine S. MacRicostas/Chmn., Willem D. Maris/Dir., George C. MacRicostas/Dir., Walter M. Fiederowicz/Dir. - Private Investor, Consultant, Paul Johnson/59/Dir., Joseph A. Fiorita/Dir., Mitchell G. Tyson/Dir., Joel Holt/77/Dir.

Owners: OTC Support, Inc./6.95%, Shocker 100 Index LP/14.53%

Financial Data: Fiscal Year End:12/31   Latest Annual Data: 12/31/2006

Year	Sales		Net Income
2006	$751,000		$499,000
2005	NA		$81,000
2004	NA		-$73,000
Curr. Assets:	$0	Curr. Liab.:	$89,000
Plant, Equip.:	NA	Total Liab.:	$89,000	Indic. Yr. Divd.:	NA
Total Assets:	$505,000	Net Worth:	$416,000	Debt/ Equity:	NA

Photoworks Inc

71 Columbia St., Ste. 200, Seattle, WA, 98104; **PH:** 1-206-281-1390; **Fax:** 1-206-284-5357; *http://* www.photoworks.com; **Email:** ir@photoworks.com

General - Incorporation .... WA
Employees 48
Auditor .... Williams & Webster, P.S
Stk Agt.............. Mellon Investor Services LLC
Counsel. Heller Ehrman White & McAuliffe LLP
DUNS No. 02-024-9348

Stock - Price on:12/24/2007 .... $0.27
Stock Exchange.. OTC
Ticker Symbol.. PHTW
Outstanding Shares 39,440,000
E.P.S. .... -$0.19
Shareholders.. NA

Business: The group's principal activities are to provide online, direct mail and retail photo services. The group offers prints, slides, digital images and online archiving. The group can process 35mm film, advanced photo systems (24mm) film or 35mm reloadable or single-use camera. The photoworks service provides film and image processing and online image storage and management services to both traditional and digital camera users, providing customers with various ways to store and organize photos online and photo related products. The group provides an array of complementary services and products primarily under the brand names photoworks (r).

Primary SIC and add'l.: 7812 7384

CIK No: 0000791050

Subsidiaries: OptiColor, Inc., PhotoWorks Digital Imaging, Inc, Seattle FilmWorks Manufacturing Company

Officers: Andy L. Wood/CEO, Pres., Thomas J. Kelley/39/VP, Chief Marketing Officer, Dan Zimmerman/VP - Engineering, David Kaill/VP - Business Development, Bruce Fischer/CFO

Directors: Paul B. Goodrich/61/Dir., Edward C. Holl/48/Dir., Mark L. Kalow/52/Dir., Joseph Waechter/54/Dir.

Owners: Paul B. Goodrich, Mark Kalow, Joseph Waechter, Dan Zimmerman, Alexandra Global Master Fund Ltd., Insiders, Carlo J. Cannell, Matinicus LP, The Tahoma Fund, L.L.C., Edward Holl, California Pacific Capital L.L.C.

Financial Data: Fiscal Year End:09/24   Latest Annual Data: 9/30/2006

Year	Sales	Net Income
2006	$11,669,000	-$3,831,000
2005	$13,723,000	-$7,370,000
2004	$20,160,000	-$1,672,000

Curr. Assets:	$1,252,000	Curr. Liab.:	$2,110,000		
Plant, Equip.:	$383,000	Total Liab.:	$3,749,000	Indic. Yr. Divd.:	NA
Total Assets:	$1,754,000	Net Worth:	-$1,995,000	Debt/ Equity:	NA

Photronics Inc

15 Secor Rd., Brookfield, CT, 06804; **PH:** 1-203-740-5664; **Fax:** 1-203-740-5618;
http:// www.photronics.com; **Email:** marketing@brk.photronics.com

General - Incorporation .... CT
Employees 1,500
Auditor .... Deloitte & Touche LLP
Stk Agt.......................... Registrar & Transfer Co
Counsel .... NA
DUNS No. 08-479-7745

Stock - Price on:12/24/2007 .... $14.97
Stock Exchange... NDQ
Ticker Symbol.. PLAB
Outstanding Shares 41,810,000
E.P.S. $0.75
Shareholders.. NA

Business: The group's principal activity is to manufacture photomasks. Photomasks are precision photographic quartz plates containing microscopic images of electronic circuits, used in the manufacture of semiconductors. The photomasks are used as masters to transfer circuit patterns onto semiconductor wafers during the fabrication of integrated circuits. The group also provides services and conducts research and development related to cleaning and etching process and provides mask-related technology consulting and data processing services. The group sells its products to semiconductor manufacturers such as agere systems inc, asm lithography, motorola inc, samsung and Texas instruments incorporated. The group has manufacturing locations in the United States, Europe, Singapore, Taiwan and Korea.

Primary SIC and add'l.: 3674

CIK No: 0000810136

Subsidiaries: Align-Rite Corporation, Align-Rite International, Inc., Align-Rite International, Ltd., Align-Rite, Inc., Beta Squared I, LLC, Beta Squared I, LP, Beta Squared, Inc., Photronics (Heilbronn) GmbH (in liquidation), Photronics (Wales) Limited, Photronics Arizona, Inc., Photronics California, Inc., Photronics Connecticut, Inc., Photronics France SAS, Photronics Hellas, S.A., Photronics Imaging Technologies (Shanghai) Co., Ltd. 34 Subsidiaries included in the Index

Officers: Michael J. Luttati/Dir., CEO, Sean T. Smith/Sr. VP, CFO, Cp Ling/Sales, Singapore, David Wang/Operations, Taiwan, Rob Lloyd/Operations, Wales, Mh Choi/Operations, Korea, Bk Chung/Sales, Korea, C. S. Song/Operations, Singapore, Zafar Ahmad/VP - Europe, North America, S. H. Jeong/Pres. - Asia, COO, Christopher J. Progler/CTO, Nicholas N. Colonese/VP, Corporate Controller, Scott Gish/VP - Global Sales, Business Development, Joseph E. Roche/VP - Supply Chain Management, P. J. Shurick/VP - Human Resources *(36 Officers included in Index)*

Directors: Michael J. Luttati/Dir., CEO, Constantine S. MacRicostas/Chmn., Willem D. Maris/Dir., George C. MacRicostas/Dir., Mitchell G. Tyson/Dir., Walter M. Fiederowicz/Dir. - Private Investor, Consultant, Joseph A. Fiorita/Dir.

Owners: Citadel Limited Partnership/6.60%, Mitchell G. Tyson, Willem D. Maris, Macricostas Partners, L.P./5.46%, Michael J. Luttati, Walter M. Fiederowicz, Insiders/9.67%, George Macricostas, Dimensional Fund Advisors LP/6.81%, Soo Hong Jeong, Christopher J. Progler, Letko, Brosseau & Ass. Inc./7.60%, Barclays Global Investors Japan Limited/8.09%, Sean T. Smith, Joseph A. Fiorita *(16 Owners included in Index)*

Financial Data: Fiscal Year End:10/31   Latest Annual Data: 10/29/2006

Year	Sales	Net Income
2006	$454,875,000	$29,332,000
2005	$440,770,000	$38,653,000
2004	$395,539,000	$24,466,000

Curr. Assets:	$345,726,000	Curr. Liab.:	$90,664,000	P/E Ratio:	19.96
Plant, Equip.:	$396,461,000	Total Liab.:	$458,674,000	Indic. Yr. Divd.:	NA
Total Assets:	$872,871,000	Net Worth:	$349,473,000	Debt/ Equity:	0.2318

Physical Spa & Fitness Inc

12/f - 15/f Lee Theatre Plz., 99 Percival St Causeway Bay, North Point; **PH:** 852-291-70000

General - Incorporation .... DE
Employees .... NA
Auditor .... Moores Rowland Mazars
Stk Agt... NA
Counsel .... NA
DUNS No. .... NA

Stock - Price on:12/24/2007 .... NA
Stock Exchange.. OTC
Ticker Symbol.. PPYH
Outstanding Shares .... NA
E.P.S. .... NA
Shareholders.. NA

Business: The group operates through its subsidiaries whose principle activity is to operate fitness and spa centers, primarily for women, and sell a variety of exercise clothing and beauty products and cosmetics. The group operates from United States.

Primary SIC and add'l.: 7997 7991 6719

CIK No: 0001048055

Subsidiaries: Dalian Physical Ladies' Club Co. Ltd., Ever Growth Ltd., Global Fitness Management Limited, Jade Regal Holdings Ltd., Physical Beauty & Fitness Holdings Limited, Physical Beauty Centre (Central) Limited, Physical Health Centre (Dalian) Ltd., Physical Health Centre (E House) Limited, Physical Health Centre (Kornhill) Limited, Physical Health Centre (Macau) Limited, Physical Health Centre (Shanghai) Ltd., Physical Health Centre (Shatin) Limited, Physical Health Centre (Shenzhen) Ltd., Physical Health Centre (TST) Limited, Physical Health Centre (Tsuen Wan) Limited 25 Subsidiaries included in the Index

Owners: NGAI KEUNG LUK, YUK WAH HO, Insiders

Financial Data: Fiscal Year End:12/31   Latest Annual Data: 12/31/2006

Year	Sales	Net Income
2006	$56,343,000	-$4,934,000
2005	$56,976,000	-$7,173,000
2004	$64,336,000	$179,000

Curr. Assets:	$9,776,000	Curr. Liab.:	$24,918,000		
Plant, Equip.:	$15,525,000	Total Liab.:	$35,632,000	Indic. Yr. Divd.:	NA
Total Assets:	$28,866,000	Net Worth:	-$6,766,000	Debt/ Equity:	NA

Physicians Formula Holdings Inc

1055 W 8th St., Azusa, CA, 91702; **PH:** 1-626-334-3395; **Fax:** 1-626-812-9462;
http:// www.physiciansformula.com; **Email:** inquiry@physiciansformula.com

General - Incorporation .... DE
Employees 153
Auditor .... Deloitte & Touche LLP
Stk Agt .... Computershare Trust Co
Counsel .... NA
DUNS No. .... NA

Stock - Price on:12/24/2007 .... $15.89
Stock Exchange... NDQ
Ticker Symbol.. FACE
Outstanding Shares 13,930,000
E.P.S. $0.02
Shareholders.. NA

Business: The groups principal activities include developing and marketing cosmetics products. The products of the group include face powders, bronzers, concealers, blushes, foundations, eye shadows, eyeliners, brow makeup and mascaras. The group products sold under the trade name Concealer Twins(R), Baked Collections(R) and Magic Mosaic(R). Specific customers of the group include Wal-Mart, Target, CVS, Walgreens and Albertsons. The group operates from the United States. The net sale of the group for the year 2006 was $95,405 (thousands).

Primary SIC and add'l.: 2844 5961

CIK No: 0001269871

Subsidiaries: Physicians Formula Cosmetics, Inc., Physicians Formula DRTV, LLC, Physicians Formula, Inc.

Officers: Ingrid Jackel/CEO, Dir., Jeff Rogers/Pres., Joseph J. Jaeger/CFO, John Mills/Integrated Corporate Relations, Anne Rakunas/Integrated Corporate Relations

Directors: Ingrid Jackel/CEO, Dir., Zvi Eiref/Chmn., Jeff Berry/Dir., Walter G. Kortschak/48/Dir., James A. Lawrence/55/Dir., Sonya T. Brown/Dir., Craig D. Frances/Dir., Claude Gros/Dir.

Owners: James A. Lawrence, Joseph Jaeger, Jeff Rogers/2.00%, Ingrid Jackel/1.90%, Insiders/4.40%

Financial Data: Fiscal Year End:12/31   Latest Annual Data: 12/31/2006

Year	Sales	Net Income
2006	$95,405,000	$606,000
2005	$78,706,000	$7,823,000
2004	$62,323,000	$4,201,000

Curr. Assets:	$57,066,000	Curr. Liab.:	$37,467,000	P/E Ratio:	529.67
Plant, Equip.:	$2,506,000	Total Liab.:	$72,742,000	Indic. Yr. Divd.:	NA
Total Assets:	$134,314,000	Net Worth:	$61,572,000	Debt/ Equity:	0.1865

PhytoMedical Technologies Inc

100 Overlook Dr., 2nd Fl., Princeton, NJ, 08540; **PH:** 1-800-611-3388; **Fax:** 1-604-659-5029;
http:// phytomedical.com; **Email:** investors@phytomedical.com

General - Incorporation .... NV
Employees 5
Auditor .... Peterson Sullivan PLLC
Stk Agt .... Holladay Stock Transfer, Inc.
Counsel .... NA
DUNS No. .... NA

Stock - Price on:12/24/2007 .... $0.355
Stock Exchange.. OTC
Ticker Symbol.. PYTO
Outstanding Shares 189,710,000
E.P.S. .... -$0.02
Shareholders.. NA

Business: The group's principal activities are developing non-surgical, non-drug, non-invasive and cost-effective treatment program for urinary incontinence, pelvic pain, chronic constipation, fecal incontinence and disorder defecation based on behavioral techniques. The technique includes biofeedback using electromyography, pelvic floor muscle exercise, bladder and bowel retraining. The physicians refer patients to undergo medical treatment program given by the group.

Primary SIC and add'l.: 8093

CIK No: 0001002422

Subsidiaries: Phytomedical Technologies Corporation

Officers: Greg Wujek/46/Dir., CEO, Pres., Harmel S. Rayat/Dir., Sec., Treasurer, CFO, Bruce David Cherksey/Scientific Founder

Directors: Greg Wujek/46/Dir., CEO, Pres., Harmel S. Rayat/Dir., Sec., Treasurer, CFO, Gary Branning/Dir., Rick Henson/58/Dir.

Owners: Greg Wujek, Insiders/62.00%, Harmel S. Rayat/62.00%

Financial Data: Fiscal Year End:12/31   Latest Annual Data: 12/31/2006

Year	Sales	Net Income
2006	NA	-$3,853,000
2005	NA	-$4,257,000
2004	NA	-$686,000

Curr. Assets:	$391,000	Curr. Liab.:	$1,602,000		
Plant, Equip.:	$10,000	Total Liab.:	$1,602,000	Indic. Yr. Divd.:	NA
Total Assets:	$421,000	Net Worth:	-$1,181,000	Debt/ Equity:	NA

Pick Ups Plus Inc

4360 Ferguson Dr., Ste. 120, Cincinnati, OH, 45245; **PH:** 1-513-943-4100; **Fax:** 1-513-398-4271;
http:// www.pickupsplus.com; **Email:** investor-relations@pickupsplus.com

General		Stock	
Incorporation	DE	Price on:12/24/2007	NA
Employees	26	Stock Exchange	OTC
Auditor	Lazar Levine & Felix LLP	Ticker Symbol	PUPS
Stk Agt	Florida Atlantic Stock Transfer, Inc.	Outstanding Shares	NA
Counsel	NA	E.P.S	NA
DUNS No.	NA	Shareholders	NA

Business: The group's principal activity is to operate and franchise retail automotive parts and accessories stores (pick-up plus stores) catering to the truck and sports utility vehicle accessories. The stores offer a variety of merchandise to accessorize trucks and sports utility vehicles. The popular product categories include: grille accessories, running boards, chrome light bars, fiberglass fender flares, ladder racks, bug guards, heavy-duty floor mats, oversized visors, headlight covers, tool boxes, bed liners, caps and step bars. The stores provide installation services of various products including running boards, bug shields and tonnue tops. As of 31-Dec-2003, there were two company-owned stores and five franchised locations in the United States. On 5-May-2004, the group acquires auto preservation division of automotive international, inc.

Primary SIC and add'l.: 5531 6794

CIK No: 0001074961

Subsidiaries: Auto Preservation, Inc

Officers: Merritt Jesson/CEO, Pres., Robert White/61/Dir., CFO

Curr. Assets:	$212,000	**Curr. Liab.:**	$3,875,000		
Plant, Equip.:	$134,000	**Total Liab.:**	$3,945,000	**Indic. Yr. Divd.:**	NA
Total Assets:	$667,000	**Net Worth:**	-$3,278,000	**Debt/ Equity:**	NA

Pico Holdings Inc

875 Prospect St., Ste. 301, La Jolla, CA, 92037; **PH:** 1-858-456-6022; **Fax:** 1-858-456-6480; **http://** www.picoholdings.com; **Email:** inbox@picoholdings.com

General		Stock	
Incorporation	CA	Price on:12/24/2007	$44.96
Employees	42	Stock Exchange	NDQ
Auditor	Deloitte & Touche LLP	Ticker Symbol	PICO
Stk Agt	Computershare Investor Services LLC	Outstanding Shares	18,700,000
Counsel	Gray, Cary, Ware & Freidenrich	E.P.S	$1.10
DUNS No.	14-464-4200	Shareholders	NA

Business: The group's principal activities are to own and develop land and water rights. It is a diversified company, the operations of which include owning and developing water rights and water storage operations; owning and developing land and the related mineral rights; the acquisition and financing of businesses and 'running off' the loss reserves of companies. The group purchases and stores water for resale in dry years. It also acquires businesses that are undervalued and have the potential to provide a superior rate of return over time. The group has operations and investments both in the United States of America and in other foreign countries.

Primary SIC and add'l.: 6719 4941 6552 6411

CIK No: 0000830122

Subsidiaries: Avalon Lake, Sarl, Bermuda Holdings, LLC, Bottling Group Holdings, Inc., Bottling Group, LLC, C & I Leasing, Inc., Gray Bern Holdings, Inc., Grayhawk Leasing, LLC, Hillwood Bottling, LLC, International Bottlers Management Co. LLC

Officers: John Hart/48/Dir., CEO, Pres./$3,219,635.00, Ron Langley/63/Executive Chmn./$3,219,635.00, Raymond Webb/VP - Investments/$619,970.00, Carlene Wilbur/GM - Investor Relations, Richard H. Sharpe/COO/$953,556.00, Maxim C.W. Webb/46/CFO, Treasurer/$785,848.00, James F. Mosier/60/General Counsel, Sec., John T. Perri/38/VP, Controller

Directors: John Hart/48/Dir., CEO, Pres., Ron Langley/63/Executive Chmn., Walter S. Foulkrod/66/Dir., Richard D. Ruppert/77/Dir., John D. Weil/67/Dir., Carlos C. Campbell/70/Dir., Kenneth J. Slepicka/52/Dir.

Owners: Dimensional Fund Advisors Inc/7.07%, John D. Weil/13.60%, Walter S. Foulkrod, Artisan Partners Limited Partnership,/6.03%, Insiders/13.93%, Carlos C. Campbell, Ronald Langley/8.94%, Richard D. Ruppert, FMR Corp./12.64%, John R. Hart/8.95%, Richard H. Sharpe, PICO Equity Investors, L.P./8.84%, Maxim C. W. Webb, Raymond W.Webb

Financial Data: *Fiscal Year End:* 12/31 *Latest Annual Data:* 12/31/2006

Year	Sales	Net Income
2006	$82,723,000	$29,243,000
2005	$146,383,000	$16,202,000
2004	$28,127,000	-$10,559,000

Curr. Assets:	$153,912,000	**Curr. Liab.:**	$317,000	**P/E Ratio:**	40.87
Plant, Equip.:	$103,057,000	**Total Liab.:**	$143,816,000	**Indic. Yr. Divd.:**	NA
Total Assets:	$549,043,000	**Net Worth:**	$405,227,000	**Debt/ Equity:**	0.0248

Piedmont Community Bank Group Inc

110 Bill Conn Pk.way, Gray, GA, 31032; **PH:** 1-478-986-5900

General		Stock	
Incorporation	GA	Price on:12/24/2007	NA
Employees	NA	Stock Exchange	OTC
Auditor	NA	Ticker Symbol	PCBN
Stk Agt	NA	Outstanding Shares	NA
Counsel	NA	E.P.S	$1.29
DUNS No.	NA	Shareholders	NA

Business: The groups principal activity is to provide banking and financial services to the customers. The group is a community oriented, service commercial bank whose primary service area is the Georgia counties of Jones, Baldwin, Bibb, Monroe, Houston, Greene and Putnam. Services of the group include checking, money market, savings, individual retirement and time deposit accounts, issues debit cards and travelers checks. The group operates from the United States.

Primary SIC and add'l.: 6712

CIK No: 0001388337

Officers: Robert D. Hulsey,/Dir., CEO, Julie Simmons/CFO, Accounting Officer, Christine A. Daniels/Dir., Sec., Mickey Parker/Dir., Pres.

Directors: Robert D. Hulsey,/Dir., CEO, John A. Hudson/Chmn., Terrell L. Fulford/Vice Chmn., Zelma A. Redding/Dir., Robert C. McMahan/Dir., Joseph S. Dumas/Dir., Angela M. Tribble/Dir., Arthur Goolsby/Dir., Mickey Parker/Dir., Pres., Franklin J. Davis/Dir., Christine A. Daniels/Dir., Sec., James R. Hawkins/Dir.

Owners: Angela Tribble/4.34%, Mickey C. Parker/5.47%, Dory Wiley/9.90%, Drew R. Hulsey/4.20%, Insiders/34.09%, John A. Hudson/2.43%, Christine A. Daniels/1.27%, James R. Hawkins/0.85%, Zelma A. Redding/2.79%, Terrell L. Fulford/1.10%, Cole M. Davis/1.10%, Franklin J. Davis/2.33%, Robert C. McMahan/2.36%, Joseph S. Dumas/3.47%, Arthur Goolsby/5.41%

Financial Data: *Fiscal Year End:* 12/31 *Latest Annual Data:* 12/31/2006

Year	Sales	Net Income
2006	$8,790,000	$732,000

Curr. Assets:	$8,382,000	**Curr. Liab.:**	$124,104,000		
Plant, Equip.:	$6,832,000	**Total Liab.:**	$124,893,000	**Indic. Yr. Divd.:**	NA
Total Assets:	$141,044,000	**Net Worth:**	$16,151,000	**Debt/ Equity:**	NA

Piedmont Natural Gas Co Inc

4720 Piedmont Row Dr., Charlotte, NC, 28210; **PH:** 1-704-364-3120; **Fax:** 1-704-365-8515; **http://** www.piedmontng.com; **Email:** investorrelations@piedmontng.com

General		Stock	
Incorporation	NC	Price on:12/24/2007	$25.14
Employees	2,051	Stock Exchange	NYSE
Auditor	Deloitte & Touche LLP	Ticker Symbol	PNY
Stk Agt	American Stock Transfer & Trust Co.	Outstanding Shares	73,910,000
Counsel	Jerry W. Amos Esq	E.P.S	$1.40
DUNS No.	00-699-6219	Shareholders	NA

Business: The groups principle activity is to distribute natural gas to residential, commercial and industrial customers. The group operates in two business segments namely regulated utility and non-utility activities. The group operates from United States.

Primary SIC and add'l.: 4925 4924

CIK No: 0000078460

Subsidiaries: Piedmont Energy Company, Piedmont Energy Partners, Inc., Piedmont Hardy Storage Company, Inc., Piedmont Interstate Pipeline Company, Piedmont Intrastate Pipeline Company, Piedmont Propane Company

Officers: Thomas E. Skains/Chmn., CEO, Pres., June B. Moore/VP - Customer Service, Leslie Ennis/VP - Information Services, David L. Trusty/VP - Corporate Communications, David J. Dzuricky/CFO, Sr. VP, Minh Tran/Regional Exec., South Carolina, Anderson, Gaffney, Greenville, Spartanburg, Tim Greenhouse/Regional Exec., Tennessee, Nashville, Kevin Shaw/Major Accounting Services Representative, Michael H. Yount/Sr. VP - Utility Operations, Jane R. Lewis-Raymond/Chief Compliance Officer, VP, General Counsel, Corp. Sec., Jose M. Simon/VP, Controller, Jeff Hedrick/Regional Exec., North Carolina, Teresa Voncannon/Regional Exec., North Carolina, Hickory, Mayland, Salisbury, Winston, Salem, Rodney Myers/Regional Exec., North Carolina, Elizabeth City, Fayetteville, Goldsboro, New Bern, Rockingham, Tarboro, Wilmington, Mike Keever/Regional Exec., North Carolina, Charlotte, Indian Trail *(31 Officers included in Index)*

Directors: Thomas E. Skains/Chmn., CEO, Pres., David E. Shi/Dir., John W. Harris/Dir., Malcolm E. Everett/Dir., Frankie T. Jones/Dir., Muriel Sheubrooks/Dir., Aubrey B. Harwell/Dir., Minor Mickel Shaw/Dir., Frank B. Holding/Dir., Jerry W. Amos/Dir., James E. Burton/Dir., Hayes D. Clement/Dir., Vicki McElreath/Dir.

Owners: Frank B. Holding, Cincinnati Financial Corporation/7.56%, Insiders, Franklin H. Yoho, Jerry W. Amos, Aubrey B. Harwell, David E. Shi, Hayes D. Clement, David J. Dzuricky, Muriel W. Sheubrooks, June B. Moore, Malcolm E. Everett, Vicki McElreath, Thomas E. Skains, Kevin M. O'Hara *(18 Owners included in Index)*

Financial Data: *Fiscal Year End:* 10/31 *Latest Annual Data:* 10/31/2006

Year	Sales	Net Income
2006	$1,924,628,000	$97,189,000
2005	$1,761,091,000	$101,270,000
2004	$1,529,739,000	$95,188,000

Curr. Assets:	$475,964,000	**Curr. Liab.:**	$400,389,000	**P/E Ratio:**	18.35
Plant, Equip.:	$2,076,464,000	**Total Liab.:**	$1,851,014,000	**Indic. Yr. Divd.:**	$1.000
Total Assets:	$2,733,939,000	**Net Worth:**	$882,925,000	**Debt/ Equity:**	NA

Pier 1 Imports Inc

100 Pier 1 Pl., Fort Worth, TX, 76102; **PH:** 1-817-252-8000; **Fax:** 1-817-252-8174; **http://** www.pier1.com

General		Stock	
Incorporation	DE	Price on:12/24/2007	$8.84
Employees	8,800	Stock Exchange	NYSE
Auditor	Ernst & Young LLP	Ticker Symbol	PIR
Stk Agt	Mellon Investor Services LLC	Outstanding Shares	88,300,000
Counsel	Testa, Hurwitz & Thibeault	E.P.S	-$1.92
DUNS No.	09-584-9360	Shareholders	NA

Business: The groups principle activity is to distribute decorative home furnishings, gifts and related items. The groups products include furniture collections, decorative accessories, bed and bath products, housewares and other seasonal assortments in its stores. The group operates from United States.

Primary SIC and add'l.: 5712 5719 5947

CIK No: 0000278130

Subsidiaries: Pier 1 Assets, Inc., Pier 1 Funding, LLC, Pier 1 Holdings, Inc., Pier 1 Imports (U.S.), Inc., Pier 1 Kids, Inc., Pier 1 Licensing, Inc., Pier 1 National Bank, a national banking association, Pier 1 Services Company, Pier 1 Value Services, LLC, Pier Alliance Ltd., Pier Direct Limited, Pier Group, Inc., Pier International Limited, Pier Lease, Inc., Pier-SNG, Inc. 19 Subsidiaries included in the Index

Officers: Alex W. Smith/Dir., CEO, Pres., Sharon M. Leite/Exec. VP - Store Operations, Jay R. Jacobs/Exec. VP - Merchandising/$622,459.00, Michael A. Carter/Sr. VP, General Counsel, Sec., Charles H. Turner/CFO, Exec. VP/$697,102.00, David A. Walker/Exec. VP - Planning, Allocations/$710,659.00, Phil E. Schneider/56/Exec. VP - Marketing/$652,846.00, Greg Humenesky/Exec. VP - Human Resources, Susan E. Barley/Principal Accounting Officer

Directors: Alex W. Smith/Dir., CEO, Pres., Tom M. Thomas/Chmn., James M. Hoak/Dir., Terry E. London/Dir., Michael R. Ferrari/Dir., Cece Smith/Dir., John H. Burgoyne/Dir., Karen W. Katz/Dir., Robert B. Holland/Dir.

Owners: David A. Walker, Insiders/7.38%, Karen W. Katz, John H. Burgoyne, Tom M. Thomas, SCSF Equities, LLC/5.10%, Charles H. Turner, Phil E. Schneider, Jakup A. Dul Jacobsen/9.80%, Terry E. London, FMR Corp./5.50%, Elliott Associates, L.P./5.50%, Jay R. Jacobs, Marvin J. Girouard/3.69%, Mitchell E. Weatherly *(20 Owners included in Index)*

Financial Data: *Fiscal Year End:* 02/25 *Latest Annual Data:* 03/03/2007

Year	Sales	Net Income
2007	$1,623,216,000	-$227,645,000
2006	$1,776,701,000	-$39,804,000
2005	$1,897,853,000	$60,457,000

Curr. Assets:	$633,968,000	**Curr. Liab.:**	$284,585,000		
Plant, Equip.:	$239,548,000	**Total Liab.:**	$555,353,000	**Indic. Yr. Divd.:**	NA
Total Assets:	$916,470,000	**Net Worth:**	$361,117,000	**Debt/ Equity:**	NA

Pierre Foods Inc

9990 Princeton Rd., Cincinnati, OH, 45246; *PH:* 1-513-874-8741; *Fax:* 1-513-874-8395;
http:// www.pierrefoods.com

General - Incorporation	NC	Stock- Price on:12/24/2007	NA
Employees	NA	Stock Exchange	NA
Auditor	Deloitte & Touche LLP	Ticker Symbol	NA
Stk Agt	First Citizens Bank & Trust Co	Outstanding Shares	NA
Counsel	NA	E.P.S.	NA
DUNS No.	55-540-8582	Shareholders	NA

Business: The group's principal activity is to produce and market fully-cooked branded and private label protein, bakery products and microwaveable sandwiches for the domestic food service market. The group produces fully-cooked beef, chicken and pork products, hand-held convenience sandwiches and value-added bakery products. It also offers proprietary product development, special ingredients and recipes, as well as custom packaging and marketing programs to its customers. The primary markets and distribution channels include national restaurant chains, primary and secondary schools, vending, convenience stores, warehouse clubs and other niche food service and packaged foods markets.

Primary SIC and add'l.: 2051 5812
CIK No: 0000067494
Subsidiaries: Fresh Foods Properties, LLC
Officers: Norbert E. Woodhams/62/Chmn., CEO, Pres., Joseph W. Meyers/41/CFO, Robert C. Naylor/56/Sr. VP - Sales, Marketing
Directors: Norbert E. Woodhams/62/Chmn., CEO, Pres., Scott W. Meader/46/Dir., George A. Peinado/38/Dir., Robin P. Selati/42/Dir., Nicholas W. Alexos/44/Dir.
Owners: Robert C. Naylor, Insiders, Joseph W. Meyers, Norbert E. Woodhams, Madison Dearborn Capital Partners IV, L.P., Nicholas W. Alexos, Robin P. Selati, Scott W. Meader

Pike Electric Corp

100 Pike Way, Mt. Airy, NC, 27030; *PH:* 1-336-789-2171; *Fax:* 1-336-719-4566;
http:// www.pike.com; *Email:* hr@pike.com

General - Incorporation	DE	Stock- Price on:12/24/2007	$23.4
Employees	6,900	Stock Exchange	NYSE
Auditor	Ernst & Young LLP	Ticker Symbol	PEC
Stk Agt	National City Bank	Outstanding Shares	32,900,000
Counsel	NA	E.P.S.	NA
DUNS No.	NA	Shareholders	NA

Business: The groups principle activities include distributing and transmitting electric services. The group operates through two segments namely, powerline and storm restoration. The group operates from the United States. The groups specific customers include Cobb EMC, Duke Energy, Entergy Corporation, Dominion Virginia PowerCo and TXU Corp. The groups quarterly revenue for September 2007 was 139.74 millions of USD.

Primary SIC and add'l.: 1623 1731 1623 1731
CIK No: 0001317577
Subsidiaries: Pike Electric, Inc, Pike Equipment and Supply Company, Red Simpson, LLC
Officers: Eric J. Pike/Chmn., CEO, Pres., Anthony Slater/CFO, James R. Fox/VP, General Counsel, Sec., Audie G. Simmons/52/Sr. VP - Operations
Directors: Eric J. Pike/Chmn., CEO, Pres., Charles E. Bayless/Dir., James R. Helvey/Dir., Robert D. Lindsay/Dir., Louis F. Terhar/Dir., Adam P. Godfrey/46/Dir., Daniel J. Sullivan/62/Dir.
Owners: Audie G. Simmons/1.20%, Robert D. Lindsay/39.90%, Tontine Capital/5.80%, Eric J. Pike/7.90%, James R. Fox, James R. Helvey, Lindsay Goldberg & Bessemer/39.90%, Insiders/49.40%, Louis F. Terhar, Anthony K. Slater, Charles E. Bayless

Curr. Assets:	$133,984,000	Curr. Liab.:	$69,906,000	P/E Ratio:	9.43
Plant, Equip.:	$267,740,000	Total Liab.:	$349,436,000	Indic. Yr. Divd.:	NA
Total Assets:	$545,497,000	Net Worth:	$196,061,000	Debt/ Equity:	NA

Pilgrims Pride Corp

4845 US Hwy. 271 N, Pittsburg, TX, 75686; *PH:* 1-903-855-1000; *Fax:* 1-903-856-7505;
http:// www.pilgrimspride.com

General - Incorporation	DE	Stock- Price on:12/24/2007	$37.24
Employees	39,900	Stock Exchange	NYSE
Auditor	Ernst & Young LLP	Ticker Symbol	PPC
Stk Agt	Computershare Investor Services LLC	Outstanding Shares	66,560,000
Counsel	NA	E.P.S.	NA
DUNS No.	00-733-4170	Shareholders	NA

Business: The group's principle activities include producing and distributing prepared and fresh chicken products. The group's products include prepared and fresh chicken. The group also prepares chicken products including portion-controlled breast fillets, tenderloins and strips, delicatessen products, frankfurters, salads, formed nuggets and patties and bone-in chicken parts. The groups specific customers include Wendy's, Stouffers and Walmart. The group operates from United States, Canada, Mexico, Eastern Europe and the Far East.

Primary SIC and add'l.: 2048 0253 2015 0254
CIK No: 0000802481
Subsidiaries: Avicola Pilgrim's Pride de Mexico, S. DE R.L. DE C. V., Comercializadora De Carnes De Mexico S. De R.I. De C. V., Gallina Pesada S.a. De C.v., Grupo Pilgrims Pride Funding Holdings S. De R.l. De C.v., Grupo Pilgrims Pride Funding S. De R.l. De C.v., Incubadora Hidalgo S. De R.I. De C. V., Inmobiliaria Avicola Pilgrims Pride, S. De R.l., Mayflower Insurance, Pfs Distribution Company, Pilgrim's Pride Affordable Housing Corporation, Pilgrim's Pride Funding Corporation, PILGRIMS PRIDE CORPORATION OF WEST VIRGINIA, INC., PILGRIMS PRIDE LUXEMBOURG FUNDING S.A.R. L., PILGRIMS PRIDE MKTG, LTD., PILGRIMS PRIDE OF NEVADA, INC. 29 Subsidiaries included in the Index
Officers: O. B. Goolsby/Dir., CEO, Pres., Clinton J. Rivers/COO, Robert A. Wright/Exec. VP - Sales, Marketing, Richard A. Cogdill/Dir., CFO, Exec. VP, Sec., Treasurer, Gary Rhodes/VP - Corporate Communications, Kathy Costner/VP - Investor Relations, Ray Atkinson/Dir. - Corporate Communications
Directors: Lonnie Ken Pilgrim/Chmn., Clifford E. Butler/Vice Chmn., Lonnie Pilgrim/Sr. Chmn., James G. Vetter/Dir., Linda Chavez/Dir., Vance C. Miller/Dir., Blake D. Lovette/Dir., Richard A. Cogdill/Dir., CFO, Exec. VP, Sec., Treasurer, Keith W. Hughes/Dir., Key S. Coker/Dir., Charles L. Black/Dir., Donald L. Wass/Dir.

Owners: Vance C. Miller, Clinton J. Rivers, Keith W. Hughes, Pilgrim Interests, Ltd, M & G Investment Management Ltd., Donald L. Wass, O. B. Goolsby, Lonnie Pilgrim, Lonnie Ken Pilgrim, James G. Vetter, Charles L. Black, Richard A. Cogdill, Insiders, Clifford E. Butler

Financial Data: Fiscal Year End:10/01   Latest Annual Data: 9/30/2006

Year	Sales	Net Income
2006	$5,235,565,000	-$34,232,000
2005	$5,666,235,000	$264,979,000
2004	$5,363,723,000	$128,340,000

Curr. Assets:	$1,105,674,000	Curr. Liab.:	$576,837,000		
Plant, Equip.:	$1,154,994,000	Total Liab.:	$1,307,582,000	Indic. Yr. Divd.:	$0.090
Total Assets:	$2,426,868,000	Net Worth:	$1,117,328,000	Debt/ Equity:	NA

Pine Valley Mining Corp

501 535 Thurlow St., Vancouver, BC, V6E 3L2; *PH:* 1-604-682-4678;
http:// www.pinevalleycoal.com; *Email:* pinevalley@pinevalleycoal.com

General - Incorporation	Canada	Stock- Price on:12/24/2007	$0.05
Employees	NA	Stock Exchange	OTC
Auditor	Deloitte & Touche LLP	Ticker Symbol	PVMCF
Stk Agt	Computershare Trust Co of Canada	Outstanding Shares	NA
Counsel	NA	E.P.S.	NA
DUNS No.	24-957-1522	Shareholders	NA

Business: The group's principal activities are the exploration, acquisition and development of coal mining properties near chetwynd, british columbia and a gold property in the northwest territories, Canada.

Primary SIC and add'l.: 1041 5052
CIK No: 0000749750
Subsidiaries: Falls Mountain Coal Inc., Globaltex Gold Mining Corporation
Officers: Mark T. Smith/CEO, CFO

Financial Data: Fiscal Year End:03/31   Latest Annual Data: 3/31/2005

Year	Sales	Net Income
2005	$16,173,000	$3,837,000
2004	$6,000	-$835,000
2003	$1,000	-$578,000

Curr. Assets:	$14,207,000	Curr. Liab.:	$22,345,000		
Plant, Equip.:	$24,470,000	Total Liab.:	$23,579,000	Indic. Yr. Divd.:	NA
Total Assets:	$42,547,000	Net Worth:	$18,968,000	Debt/ Equity:	NA

Pinnacel Resources Inc

9600 E Arapahoe Rd., Ste. 260, Englewood, CO, 80112; *PH:* 1-303-705-8600; *Fax:* 1-309-799-0912;
http:// www.pnrr.net; *Email:* info@pnrr.net

General - Incorporation	WY	Stock- Price on:12/24/2007	$0.15
Employees	NA	Stock Exchange	OTC
Auditor	Cordovano & Honeck LLP	Ticker Symbol	PNRR
Stk Agt	Corporate Stock Transfer, Inc.	Outstanding Shares	NA
Counsel	NA	E.P.S.	-$0.04
DUNS No.	NA	Shareholders	NA

Business: The group's principal activity is to provide financial services, making small commercial loans and equity investments. The loans are provided to emerging growth companies that are unable to obtain financing from traditional sources. The group is a development stage company. The group seeks and evaluates suitable candidates for financing both in the United States and on companies operating in selected stable, developing countries, principally in Africa and South America.

Primary SIC and add'l.: 6163
CIK No: 0001043825
Subsidiaries: Development Pty Ltd., Diamonaire Exploration, Magnetite Exploration 1, Plateau Resources, Vanadium
Officers: Glen R. Gamble/Chmn., CEO, Pres., Robert A. Hildebrand/Sec., Treasurer, CFO, Jan Becker/Technical Consultant
Directors: Glen R. Gamble/Chmn., CEO, Pres.
Owners: Insiders/25.79%, Robert A. Hildebrand/0.29%, Re-Group, Inc./1.54%, Beverly Jo Gamble/1.16%, Victory Minerals Corp./11.59%, Glen R. Gamble/12.75%

Financial Data: Fiscal Year End:06/30   Latest Annual Data: 06/30/2005

Year	Sales	Net Income
2005	NA	-$781,000
2004	NA	-$416,000
2003	NA	$2,519,000

Curr. Assets:	$112,000	Curr. Liab.:	$172,000		
Plant, Equip.:	$586,000	Total Liab.:	$278,000	Indic. Yr. Divd.:	NA
Total Assets:	$798,000	Net Worth:	$486,000	Debt/ Equity:	NA

Pinnacle Airlines Corp

1689 Nonconnah Blvd., Ste. 111, Memphis, TN, 38132; *PH:* 1-901-348-4100; *Fax:* 1-901-348-4130;
http:// www.pncl.com; *Email:* investorrelations@nwairlink.com

General - Incorporation	DE	Stock- Price on:12/24/2007	$18.79
Employees	3,860	Stock Exchange	NDQ
Auditor	Ernst & Young LLP	Ticker Symbol	PNCL
Stk Agt	Computershare Trust Co	Outstanding Shares	22,160,000
Counsel	Shearman & Sterling LLP	E.P.S.	$3.00
DUNS No.	NA	Shareholders	NA

Business: The group's principal activity is to operate an all-regional jet fleet providing regional airline services in United States. The group including its wholly owned subsidiary, pinnacle airlines inc. Operate as nortwest airlink. It provides the regional airline services to northwest corporation under an airline services agreement.

Primary SIC and add'l.: 4512
CIK No: 0001166291
Subsidiaries: Northwest Airlines Corporation, Pinnacle Airlines Corp., Pinnacle Airlines, Inc
Officers: Philip H. Trenary/Dir., CEO, Pres., Clive A. Seal/VP - Flight Operations, Douglas W. Shockey/VP, COO, Russ Elander/VP - Customer Service, Barry G. Baker/VP - Maintenance, Engineering, Peter D. Hunt/VP, CFO, Investor Relations Officer, Edgar C. Fell/VP - Safety,

Regulatory Compliance, Nikki M. Tinker/VP - Labor Relations, Lorraine Grubbs-West/VP - People Services, Jeffrey M. Dato/VP - Risk Management, Information Technology, Lawrence Grant/VP - Purchasing, Contract Management, David A. Hinton/VP, Corporate Controller, Ronald T. Kay/VP - Finance, Treasurer

Directors: Philip H. Trenary/Dir., CEO, Pres., Stephen E. Gorman/Chmn., Thomas S. Schreier/Dir., Ian Massey/Dir., Philip R. Shannon/Dir., James E. McGehee/Dir., Nicholas R. Tomassetti/Dir., Donald J. Breeding/Dir.

Owners: Douglas W. Shockey, Monish Pabrai/9.45%, Insiders/4.40%, Barry G. Baker, Donald J. Breeding, Northwest Airlines Corporation/11.40%, Thomas S. Schreier, James E. McGehee, Clive A. Seal, Ian Massey, Philip H. Trenary/1.80%, Peter D. Hunt, Philip R. Shannon, Stephen E. Gorman, Nicholas R. Tomassetti

Financial Data: **Fiscal Year End:** 12/31 **Latest Annual Data:** 12/31/2006

Year	Sales	Net Income
2006	$824,623,000	$77,799,000
2005	$841,605,000	$25,698,000
2004	$635,448,000	$40,725,000

Curr. Assets:	$197,394,000	**Curr. Liab.:**	$73,844,000	**P/E Ratio:**	5.76
Plant, Equip.:	$40,985,000	**Total Liab.:**	$204,252,000	**Indic. Yr. Divd.:**	NA
Total Assets:	$301,273,000	**Net Worth:**	$97,021,000	**Debt/ Equity:**	0.1505

Pinnacle Bancshares Inc

1811 2nd Ave., Jasper, AL, 35502; ***PH:*** 1-205-221-4111; ***Fax:*** 1-205-221-8860; ***http://*** www.pinnaclebancshares.com

General - Incorporation	DE	**Stock**- Price on:12/24/2007	$14.45
Employees	82	Stock Exchange	AMEX
Auditor	KPMG LLP	Ticker Symbol	PLE
Stk Agt	Registrar & Transfer Co	Outstanding Shares	1,460,000
Counsel	Maddox Maclaurin Nicholson & Thornley	E.P.S	$0.88
DUNS No.	09-775-4659	Shareholders	NA

Business: The group's principle activities are to accept savings deposits and invest in mortgage loans on single-family residential real estate. The principal sources of funds for the group's lending activities are savings deposits, federal home loan bank of atlanta advances and principal repayments of loans and sales of loans. The group's principal sources of income are interest on loans, servicing and commitment fees and interest and dividends on securities. The group operates in six offices in the central and northwest portion of Alabama.

Primary SIC and add'l.: 6712 6022

CIK No: 0001022243

Subsidiaries: First General Service(s) Corporation, First General Ventures Corporation, Pinnacle Bank

Officers: Robert B. Nolen/50/Dir., CEO, CFO, Pres./$152,222.00, Mary Jo Gunter/54/Dir., Sr. VP - Banking Services, Bankenior, Marie Guthrie/Treasurer, Principal Accounting Officer

Directors: Robert B. Nolen/50/Dir., CEO, CFO, Pres., James W. Cannon/Chmn., Max W. Perdue/Dir., Greg Batchelor/Dir., James T. Waggoner/70/Dir., O. H. Brown/Dir., Sam W. Murphy/Dir., Albert H. Simmons/Dir., Mary Jo Gunter/54/Dir., Sr. VP - Banking Services, Bankenior

Owners: Sam W. Murphy/1.70%, Robert B. Nolen/2.10%, James W. Cannon, Insiders/14.40%, Max W. Perdue/1.20%, Greg Batchelor/3.00%, Al H. Simmons/4.70%, O. H. Brown, Jeffrey L. Gendell/8.90%, James T. Waggoner

Financial Data: **Fiscal Year End:** 12/31 **Latest Annual Data:** 12/31/2006

Year	Sales	Net Income
2006	$15,155,000	$1,351,000
2005	$13,726,000	$1,517,000
2004	$12,773,000	$1,732,000

Curr. Assets:	$14,341,000	**Curr. Liab.:**	$208,839,000	**P/E Ratio:**	16.42
Plant, Equip.:	$7,285,000	**Total Liab.:**	$212,829,000	**Indic. Yr. Divd.:**	$0.440
Total Assets:	$232,234,000	**Net Worth:**	$19,406,000	**Debt/ Equity:**	0.1568

Pinnacle Bank Of OR

8880 S.W. Nimbus Ave., Ste. D, Beaverton, OR, 97008; ***PH:*** 1-503-644-3000; ***Fax:*** 1-503-643-2759; ***http://*** www.pinnaclebankoregon.com; ***Email:*** WeCare@PinnacleBankOregon.com

General - Incorporation		**Stock**- Price on:12/24/2007	$11.2
Employees	NA	Stock Exchange	OTC
Auditor	NA	Ticker Symbol	PNNB
Stk Agt	Computershare Trust CO.	Outstanding Shares	NA
Counsel	NA	E.P.S	NA
DUNS No.	NA	Shareholders	NA

Business: The groups principal activities include providing banking and financial services to its customers. Services of the group include checking accounts, personal banking, private banking, Debit cards, Credit Cards, ATM and online customer help. The group operates from the United States.

Primary SIC and add'l.: 6022

CIK No:

Officers: Ronald A. May/CEO, Pres., Karen Levear/CFO, Exec. VP, Mike Rutherford/Electronic Banking Specialist - Operations Dept, Holly J. Peterson/Operations, Human Resources Assist. - Operations Dept, Jason Haines/Project Mgr. - Operations, Operations Dept, Greg Froman/Exec. VP, Chief Credit Officer - Administration Dept, Carol Williams/Exec. VP - Human Resources, Administration, Anne Fosen/Compliance Officer, Carol E. Warneke/VP - Business Development, Marketing, Dianne Foster/Customer Service Mgr. - Customer Service, Sales Dept, Chris Lee/Personal Banking Officer - Customer Service, Sales, Sue Donovan/Personal Banking Officer - Customer Service, Sales Dept, Karen Hatch/Personal Banking Officer - Customer Service, Sales Dept, Annie Spencer/Accounting Mgr. - Financial Services, Dean L. Williams/VP, Commercial Loan Officer - Loans Dept *(18 Officers included in Index)*

Directors: Jeffrey F. Dulcich/Chmn., Kurt B. Johnson/Vice Chmn., Matthew Essieh/Dir., Kip Croskrey/Dir., William O. Carter/Dir.

Pinnacle Bankshares Corp

622 Broad St., Altavista, VA, 24517; ***PH:*** 1-434-369-3000; ***Fax:*** 1-434-369-7190; ***http://*** www.1stnatbk.com

General - Incorporation	VA	**Stock**- Price on:12/24/2007	$25.9
Employees	99	Stock Exchange	OTC
Auditor	Cherry, Bekaert & Holland LLP	Ticker Symbol	PPBN
Stk Agt	U.S. Stock Transfer Corp	Outstanding Shares	1,480,000
Counsel	NA	E.P.S	$1.76
DUNS No.	NA	Shareholders	NA

Business: The group's principal activity is to provide services to commercial and agricultural businesses and individuals in the altavista area. It conducts its operations through offices of its wholly-owned subsidiary bank, the first national bank of altavista. With an emphasis on personal service, the group offers a broad range of commercial and retail banking products and services including checking, savings and time deposits, individual retirement accounts, merchant bankcard processing, residential and commercial mortgages, home equity loans, consumer installment loans, agricultural loans, investment loans, small business loans, commercial lines of credit and letters of credit. The group serves in campbell county, northern pittsylvania county, southeastern bedford county, and the city of lynchburg from facilities located in the town of altavista and the city of lynchburg, Virginia.

Primary SIC and add'l.: 6712 6021

CIK No: 0001031233

Subsidiaries: First Properties, Inc., FNB Property Corp, The First National Bank of Altavista

Officers: Robert H. Gilliam/62/Dir., CEO, Pres./$200,112.00, Bryan M. Lemley/VP, CFO, Sec./$102,184.00, Carroll E. Shelton/57/Dir., Sr. VP, Chief Lending Officer/$114,427.00

Directors: Robert H. Gilliam/62/Dir., CEO, Pres., Michael E. Watson/53/Dir., Carroll E. Shelton/57/Dir., Sr. VP, Chief Lending Officer, James E. Burton/51/Dir., R. B. Hancock/57/Dir., John L. Waller/64/Dir., Willard A. Arthur/62/Dir., John P. Erb/64/Dir., James P. Kent/66/Dir., William F. Overacre/66/Dir.

Owners: Willard A. Arthur, James E. Burton/1.22%, William F. Overacre, Robert H. Gilliam/1.61%, Bryan M. Lemley, James P. Kent/1.34%, R. B. Hancock, John P. Erb, Insiders/6.64%, John L. Waller, Michael E. Watson, Carroll E. Shelton/1.06%

Financial Data: **Fiscal Year End:** 12/31 **Latest Annual Data:** 12/31/2006

Year	Sales	Net Income
2006	$18,117,000	$2,412,000
2005	$15,066,000	$2,107,000
2004	$13,157,000	$1,819,000

Curr. Assets:	$15,836,000	**Curr. Liab.:**	$231,681,000	**P/E Ratio:**	15.70
Plant, Equip.:	$5,264,000	**Total Liab.:**	$231,929,000	**Indic. Yr. Divd.:**	$0.600
Total Assets:	$256,421,000	**Net Worth:**	$24,492,000	**Debt/ Equity:**	NA

Pinnacle Data Systems Inc

6600 Port Rd., Groveport, OH, 43125; ***PH:*** 1-614-748-1150; ***Fax:*** 1-614-409-1269; ***http://*** www.pinnacle.com; ***Email:*** info.sales@pinnacle.com

General - Incorporation	OH	**Stock**- Price on:12/24/2007	$2.1
Employees	180	Stock Exchange	AMEX
Auditor	Hausser & Taylor, LLC	Ticker Symbol	PNS
Stk Agt	Computershare Investor Services LLC	Outstanding Shares	6,370,000
Counsel	Schottenstein Zox & Dunn Co	E.P.S	$0.05
DUNS No.	NA	Shareholders	NA

Business: The group's principal activities are to design, assemble and sell computer products and provide repair and related services. The products include complete systems, specially designed products, including boards and attach cards, and software. Complete systems include fully integrated hardware and software from multiple sources. The group resells some hardware and software manufactured by other original equipment manufacturers. It also offers complete after-the-sale service and support including repair, logistics and product end-of-life management services. The products and services are provided primarily to original equipment manufacturers in the telecommunication, medical system, process control and computer industries.

Primary SIC and add'l.: 7379 3577

CIK No: 0001004608

Officers: Michael R. Sayre/Dir., CEO, Pres./$250,966.00, John D. Bair/Chmn., Co - Founder, Chief Technology, Innovation Officer/$238,965.00, George A. Troutman/Dir., Treasurer, Corp. Sec., CFO/$161,819.00, Susan E. Rothberg/47/VP - Operations, Supply Chain

Directors: Michael R. Sayre/Dir., CEO, Pres., John D. Bair/Chmn., Co - Founder, Chief Technology, Innovation Officer, George A. Troutman/Dir., Treasurer, Corp. Sec., CFO, Hugh C. Cathey/Dir., Carl J. Aschinger/Dir., Benjamin Brussell/Dir., Thomas M. O'Leary/Dir.

Owners: Michael R. Sayre/5.10%, Thomas G. Berlin/9.10%, Robert B. Harris/1.80%, Insiders/26.00%, Carl J. Aschinger, John D. Bair/20.10%, Thomas M. OLeary/1.80%, Hugh C. Cathey

Financial Data: **Fiscal Year End:** 12/31 **Latest Annual Data:** 12/31/2006

Year	Sales	Net Income
2006	$75,920,000	-$1,862,000
2005	$44,606,000	$937,000
2004	$34,397,000	$884,000

Curr. Assets:	$31,879,000	**Curr. Liab.:**	$27,164,000		
Plant, Equip.:	$1,244,000	**Total Liab.:**	$27,839,000	**Indic. Yr. Divd.:**	NA
Total Assets:	$33,858,000	**Net Worth:**	$6,019,000	**Debt/ Equity:**	NA

Pinnacle Entertainment Inc

3800 Howard Hughes Pkwy., Las Vegas, NV, 89109; ***PH:*** 1-702-784-7777; ***Fax:*** 1-702-784-7778; ***http://*** www.pnkinc.com

General - Incorporation	DE	**Stock**- Price on:12/24/2007	$29.31
Employees	7,186	Stock Exchange	NYSE
Auditor	Deloitte & Touche LLP	Ticker Symbol	PNK
Stk Agt	American Stock Transfer & Trust Co.	Outstanding Shares	59,690,000
Counsel	Irell & Manella	E.P.S	$0.22
DUNS No.	10-815-9641	Shareholders	NA

Business: The group's principal activity is to own and operate gaming entertainment facilities. The group operates in southeastern Indiana, Reno, Nevada, Bossier City, New Orleans, Louisiana, Biloxi and Mississippi. The group also operates two casinos in Argentina and receives lease income from two card clubs in southern California. The group is also developing a hotel and casino resort in Lake Charles, Louisiana. The group's casinos are operated under the names; Belterra Casino Resort, Boomtown Reno, Boomtown New Orleans, Casino Magic Biloxi, Casino Magic Bossier City, Casino Magic Argentina.

Primary SIC and add'l.: 7948 7033 7011

CIK No: 0000356213

Subsidiaries: Belterra Resort Indiana, LLC, Biloxi Casino Corp., Boomtown, LLC, Casino Magic (Europe) B.V., Casino Magic Antofagasta, SA, Casino Magic Buenos Aires, SA, Casino Magic Calama, SA, Casino Magic Chile, SA, Casino Magic Corp., Casino Magic Hellas Management Services, SA, Casino Magic Neuquen, SA, Casino Magic Rancagua, SA, Casino Magic Talca, SA, Casino One Corporation, Casino Parking, Inc. (50%) 53 Subsidiaries included in the Index

Officers: Daniel R. Lee/Chmn., CEO/$2,764,455.00, Alain Uboldi/COO/$765,630.00, Kimberly C. Townsend/Exec. VP - Atlantic City, Sarah Lee Tucker/VP - Operations, Stephen H. Capp/CFO, Exec. VP/$1,146,628.00, Wade W. Hundley/Pres./$1,080,756.00, Carol Pride/CIO, James W. Barich/Sr. VP - Public Relations, Government, Christopher K. Plant/VP - Investor Relations, Treasurer, Clifford D. Kortman/Pres. - Pinnacle Design, Construction, Alice Mui/VP - Corporate Taxes, Larry Buck/Pres. - Atlantic City, Arthur I. Goldberg/Sr. VP - Risk Management, Benefits, Humberto Trueba/Sr. VP - Human Resources, John A. Godfrey/Exec. VP, General Counsel, Sec./$834,588.00 *(23 Officers included in Index)*

Directors: Daniel R. Lee/Chmn., CEO, John V. Giovenco/Dir., Lynn P. Reitnouer/Dir., Michael Ornest/Dir., Richard J. Goeglein/Dir., James L. Martineau/Dir., Stephen C. Comer/Dir., Ellis Landau/Dir., Bruce A. Leslie/Dir.

Owners: Daniel R. Lee/1.83%, Insiders/4.38%, John A. Godfrey, James L. Martineau, Michael Ornest, Alain Uboldi, Lynn P. Reitnouer, Wade W. Hundley, Stephen H. Capp, Richard J. Goeglein, Columbia Wanger Asset Management, L.P./5.80%, Ellis Landau, John V. Giovenco, Bruce A. Leslie

Financial Data: *Fiscal Year End:* 12/31 *Latest Annual Data:* 12/31/2006

Year	Sales	Net Income
2006	$912,357,000	$76,886,000
2005	$725,900,000	$6,125,000
2004	$553,311,000	$9,161,000

Curr. Assets:	$288,566,000	**Curr. Liab.:**	$190,740,000	**P/E Ratio:**	23.08
Plant, Equip.:	$1,260,371,000	**Total Liab.:**	$1,043,247,000	**Indic. Yr. Divd.:**	NA
Total Assets:	$1,737,830,000	**Net Worth:**	$694,583,000	**Debt/ Equity:**	NA

Pinnacle Financial Partners Inc

211 Commerce St., Ste. 300, Nashville, TN, 37201; *PH:* 1-615-744-3700; *http://* www.mypinnacle.com

General - Incorporation	TN	**Stock**- Price on:12/24/2007	$29.78
Employees	397	Stock Exchange	NDQ
Auditor	KPMG LLP	Ticker Symbol	PNFP
Stk Agt	Registrar & Transfer Co	Outstanding Shares	15,530,000
Counsel	NA	E.P.S.	$1.35
DUNS No.	NA	Shareholders	NA

Business: The group's principal activity is to provide commercial banking services. The group's services include commercial, real estate and consumer loans to individuals and small-to medium-sized businesses and professional entities. The group is a bank holding company operating through its subsidiary: pinnacle national bank. The group has branches located in the downtown, green hills and rivergate areas of nashville, cool springs area of williamson county and in brentwood, tenn.

Primary SIC and add'l.: 6021 6712

CIK No: 0001115055

Subsidiaries: PFP Title Company, Pinnacle Advisory Services, Inc., Pinnacle Community Development Corporation, Pinnacle Credit Enhancement Services, Inc., Pinnacle National Bank, PNFP Holdings, Inc., PNFP Properties, Inc., PNFP Statutory Trust I, PNFP Statutory Trust II

Officers: Terry M. Turner/Dir., CEO, Pres./$844,802.00, Robert A. McCabe/Chmn. - Pinnacle Financial Partners/$802,827.00, Jerry Hampton/Financial Advisor, Hugh M. Queener/Exec. VP, Chief Administrative Officer/$472,906.00, Harold R. Carpenter/CFO/$318,250.00, James O. Sweeney/Sr. Product Mgr., Charles McMahan/Exec. VP, Sr. Credit Officer/$286,886.00, Edward J. White/Sr. Lending Officer, Exec. VP, Joanne B. Jackson/Exec. VP, Mgr. - Client Services, Ron Carter/Rutherford, Bedford Client Services Mgr., Mike Distefano/Exec. VP - Pinnacle Knoxville, Nathan Hunter/Pres. - Pinnacle Knoxville, Kim Jenny/Sr. VP, Sr. Program Mgr., Bill Jones/Pinnacle Rutherford County Area Executive, Glenn M. Layne/Sr. VP, Credit Officer *(18 Officers included in Index)*

Directors: Terry M. Turner/Dir., CEO, Pres., Robert A. McCabe/Chmn. - Pinnacle Financial Partners, Dale W. Polley/Dir., Sue G. Atkinson/Dir., Gregory L. Burns/Dir., Colleen Conway-Welch/Dir., Hal N. Pennington/Dir., James C. Cope/58/Dir., William H. Huddleston/44/Dir., Ed C. Loughry/65/Dir., James L. Shaub/Dir., Reese L. Smith/Dir., Clay T. Jackson/Dir., Robert E. McNeilly/Dir. Emeritus

Owners: Sue G. Atkinson/0.27%, Dale W. Polley/0.51%, Ed C. Loughry/1.67%, T. Rowe Price Associates, Inc./5.71%, Hugh M. Queener/1.77%, Charles B. McMahan/0.14%, Harold R. Carpenter/0.40%, Robert A. McCabe/3.67%, Hal N. Pennington/0.02%, M. Terry Turner/2.79%, James C. Cope/0.51%, James L. Shaub/0.45%, Colleen Conway-Welch/0.20%, Reese L. Smith/0.52%, Gregory L. Burns/0.04% *(18 Owners included in Index)*

Financial Data: *Fiscal Year End:* 12/31 *Latest Annual Data:* 12/31/2006

Year	Sales	Net Income
2006	$125,483,000	$17,927,000
2005	$51,701,000	$8,055,000
2004	$33,152,000	$5,319,000

Curr. Assets:	$103,538,000	**Curr. Liab.:**	$1,822,105,000	**P/E Ratio:**	23.63
Plant, Equip.:	$36,286,000	**Total Liab.:**	$1,886,170,000	**Indic. Yr. Divd.:**	NA
Total Assets:	$2,142,187,000	**Net Worth:**	$256,017,000	**Debt/ Equity:**	0.1960

Pinnacle West Capital Corp

400 N 5th St., Phoenix, AZ, 85072; *PH:* 1-602-250-1000; *Fax:* 1-602-250-2430; *http://* www.pinnaclewest.com

General - Incorporation	AZ	**Stock**- Price on:12/24/2007	$42.26
Employees	7,400	Stock Exchange	NYSE
Auditor	Deloitte & Touche LLP	Ticker Symbol	PNW
Stk Agt	Bank of New York	Outstanding Shares	100,240,000
Counsel	NA	E.P.S.	$2.96
DUNS No.	13-115-5400	Shareholders	NA

Business: The groups principle activity is to provide energy and energy-related products to people and businesses. The group operates through two business segments namely electricity segment and real estate segment. The group operates from United States.

Primary SIC and add'l.: 4911 6552 6799

CIK No: 0000764622

Subsidiaries: Apex Power LLC, APS Energy L.P., APS Energy Services Company, Inc., APS Foundation, Inc., APSES Holdings, Inc., Arizona Public Service Company, Avimor, LLC(formerly SunCor Idaho, LLC), AXIOM Power Solutions, Inc., Bixco, Inc., BV at Hayden Ferry Lakeside, LLC, Centrepoint Associates, LLC, Club West Golf Course LLC, Crest Power, LLC, Edgewater at Hayden Ferry Lakeside, LLC, Golden Heritage Construction Nevada, LLC 44 Subsidiaries included in the Index

Officers: William J. Post/Chmn., CEO/$7,518,342.00, Jack E. Davis/Dir., COO, Pres./$6,571,496.00, Jan Bennett/Sr. VP - Energy Delivery, Arizona Public Service Company, Ajit P. Bhatti/VP - Resource Planning, Arizona Public Service Company, Donald G. Robinson/Sr. VP - Planning, Administration, Arizona Public Service Company, Nancy Loftin/Sr. VP, General Counsel, Sec., Barbara M. Gomez/VP, Treasurer, Armando Flores/Exec. VP - Corporate Business Services, Arizona Public Service Company/$2,281,441.00, Donald E. Brandt/CFO, Exec. VP/$1,583,644.00, Chris N. Froggatt/VP, Controller - Arizona Public Service Company, Martin L. Shultz/VP - Government Affairs, Robert S. Aiken/VP - Federal Affairs, Jacque Patterson/Contact - Shareholder Services, Rebecca L. Hickman/Dir. - Investor Relations, Lisa Malagon/Mgr. - Investor Relations *(29 Officers included in Index)*

Directors: William J. Post/Chmn., CEO, Jack E. Davis/Dir., COO, Pres., Bruce J. Nordstrom/Dir., William L. Stewart/Dir., Edward N. Basha/Dir., Michael L. Gallagher/Dir., Pamela Grant/Dir., Roy A. Herberger/Dir., Martha O. Hesse/Dir., William S. Jamieson/Dir., Humberto S. Lopez/Dir., Kathryn L. Munro/Dir.

Owners: Insiders/1.10%, Bruce J. Nordstrom, William L. Stewart, William J. Post, Armando B. Flores, Edward N. Basha, Pamela Grant, James M. Levine, Barclays Global Investors, NA./7.80%, State Street Bank and Trust Company/6.40%, Donald E. Brandt, Roy A. Herberger, T. Rowe Price Associates, Inc./5.90%, Michael L. Gallagher, Franklin Resources, Inc./6.70% *(20 Owners included in Index)*

Financial Data: *Fiscal Year End:* 12/31 *Latest Annual Data:* 12/31/2006

Year	Sales	Net Income
2006	$3,401,748,000	$327,255,000
2005	$2,987,955,000	$176,267,000
2004	$2,899,725,000	$243,195,000

Curr. Assets:	$1,474,662,000	**Curr. Liab.:**	$1,458,560,000	**P/E Ratio:**	14.28
Plant, Equip.:	$8,311,836,000	**Total Liab.:**	$8,009,827,000	**Indic. Yr. Divd.:**	$2.100
Total Assets:	$11,455,943,000	**Net Worth:**	$3,446,116,000	**Debt/ Equity:**	0.9240

Pioneer Bank

263 E Main St., Stanley, VA, 22851; *PH:* 1-540-778-2294; *Fax:* 1-540-778-5140; *http://* www.pioneerbks.com

General - Incorporation	VA	**Stock**- Price on:12/24/2007	$23.9
Employees	59	Stock Exchange	OTC
Auditor	Yount, Hyde & Barbour, P.C	Ticker Symbol	PNBI
Stk Agt	Registrar & Transfer Co	Outstanding Shares	1,010,000
Counsel	NA	E.P.S.	$1.66
DUNS No.	NA	Shareholders	NA

Business: The group's principal activity is that of a holding company for pioneer bank, inc. The bank provides general commercial banking business, primarily serving page, rockingham and greene counties in the commonwealth of Virginia. The bank accepts deposits, makes consumer and commercial loans, issues drafts and provides other services. Other services include business and personal checking, savings accounts, walk-up tellers, drive-in windows and 24-hour automated teller machines. The bank offers a full range of short-to-medium term commercial and personal loans. Commercial loans include both secured and unsecured loans for working capital, business expansion and purchase of equipment and machinery. Consumer loans include secured and unsecured loans for financing automobiles, home improvements, education and personal investments.

Primary SIC and add'l.: 6022 6712

CIK No: 0001113026

Subsidiaries: Pioneer Financial Services, LLC., Pioneer Special Assets, LLC

Officers: Betty Purdham/Contact - Commercial Loans, Beth Painter/VP, Dir. - Human Resources, Gene Colligan/VP, Branch Mgr. - Charlottesville, Contact - Commercial Loan, Bill Groseclose/Contact - Commercial Loans, Brad Archart/Contact - Commercial Loans, Donna Pendergast/AVP, Branch Mgr. - Main Office, Patsy Miller/Branch Mgr. - Shenandoah, Amy Atkins/Branch Mgr. - Luray, Leena Smith/Branch Mgr. - Harrisonburg, Donna Morrissey/Branch Mgr. - Stanardsville, Linda Harris/Branch Mgr. - Valley Finance Service

Owners: Powell E. Markowitz, David N. Slye, Kyle L. Miller/1.26%, Thomas R. Rosazza/1.64%, Harry F. Louderback/1.88%, Mark N. Reed, Robert E. Long/1.77%, Patricia G. Baker/1.75%, Insiders/12.29%, Louis L. Bosley/2.35%

Financial Data: *Fiscal Year End:* 12/31 *Latest Annual Data:* 12/31/2006

Year	Sales	Net Income
2006	$11,021,000	$1,662,000
2005	$9,573,000	$1,465,000
2004	$8,986,000	$1,562,000

Curr. Assets:	$11,985,000	**Curr. Liab.:**	$125,713,000	**P/E Ratio:**	13.74
Plant, Equip.:	$4,478,000	**Total Liab.:**	$136,413,000	**Indic. Yr. Divd.:**	$0.560
Total Assets:	$151,631,000	**Net Worth:**	$15,218,000	**Debt/ Equity:**	0.6062

Pioneer Behavioral Health

200 Lake St., Ste 102, Peabody, MA, 01960; *PH:* 1-978-536-2777; *http://* www.phc-inc.com; *Email:* info@phc-inc.com

General - Incorporation	MA	**Stock**- Price on:12/24/2007	NA
Employees	389	Stock Exchange	NA
Auditor	BDO Seidman LLP	Ticker Symbol	NA
Stk Agt	American Stock Transfer & Trust Co.	Outstanding Shares	NA
Counsel	NA	E.P.S.	$0.11
DUNS No.	08-852-1091	Shareholders	NA

Business: The group's principal activity is to provide psychiatric services primarily to individuals who have alcohol and drug dependency. The group is a national health care company specializing in the treatment of substance provision of psychiatric services and also provides management, administrative and online behavioral health services. The group operates substance abuse treatment facilities in Utah and Virginia, four outpatient psychiatric facilities in Michigan, two outpatient psychiatric facilities in Nevada, one outpatient psychiatric facility in Kansas and an inpatient psychiatric facility in Michigan. The group also operates a Website, wellplace.com, which provides education, training and materials to behavioral health professional's in addition to providing Internet support to all of our other subsidiaries.

Primary SIC and add'l.: 8069 8051 8063 7375

CIK No: 0000915127

Subsidiaries: North Point-Pioneer, Inc, Pivotal Research Centers, Inc

Officers: Bruce A. Shear/Chmn., CEO, Pres., Paula C. Wurts/CFO, Janet Esterkes/Investor Relations Contact, Robert A. Boswell/Sr. VP, Alexander N. Luvall/Exec. VP, Scott Kitcher/Investor Relations Contact

Directors: Bruce A. Shear/Chmn., CEO, Pres., Donald E. Robar/Dir., Howard W. Phillips/Dir., William F. Greico/54/Dir., David E. Dangerfield/Dir.

Owners: Howard W. Phillips/1.00%, Insiders/8.50%, Robert H. Boswell/1.30%, Bruce A. Shear/3.70%, William F. Grieco, Paula C. Wurts/1.00%, Bruce A. Shear/93.00%, Insiders/93.00%, Donald E. Robar, David E. Dangerfield, Boston Partners Asset Management, LLC/7.80%, Marathon Capital Mgmt, LLC/7.80%, Camden Partners Capital Management LLC/8.60%

Financial Data: *Fiscal Year End:*06/30 *Latest Annual Data:* 6/30/2006

Year	Sales	Net Income
2006	$38,013,000	$4,045,000
2005	$34,063,000	$3,156,000
2004	$26,649,000	-$257,000

Curr. Assets:	$15,434,000	**Curr. Liab.:**	$7,889,000		
Plant, Equip.:	$3,841,000	**Total Liab.:**	$9,040,000	**Indic. Yr. Divd.:**	NA
Total Assets:	$27,290,000	**Net Worth:**	$18,250,000	**Debt/ Equity:**	NA

Pioneer Corp

4-1 Meguro 1 Chome, Meguro Ku, Tokyo; *PH:* 81-334941111; *Fax:* 81-334954428; *http://* www.pioneer.co.jp

General - Incorporation	Japan	**Stock**- Price on:12/24/2007	$14.25
Employees	NA	Stock Exchange	OTC
Auditor	Deloitte Touche Tohmatsu	Ticker Symbol	PNCOF
Stk Agt	Mitsubishi UFJ Trust & Banking Corp	Outstanding Shares	NA
Counsel	NA	E.P.S	NA
DUNS No.	69-054-3715	Shareholders	NA

Business: The group's principal activity is to develop, manufacture and sell electronic products. The group's product includes audio, video and car electronics and audio/video software. The group operates in four segments, namely, car electronics, home electronics, patent licensing and other. Car electronics, manufactures and sells car audio products and car navigation systems. Home electronics, manufactures and sells audio/video equipment for home use. Patent licensing includes the licensing of patents related to optical disc technology and other includes manufacture and sale of computer peripheral equipment, factory automation system, av software, devices and parts. The principal markets for the group is Japan, the United States of America, European countries and southeast Asia. The group's products are sold under its own brand name pioneer.

Primary SIC and add'l.: 3695 6794 3651 3652 3661

CIK No: 0000078706

Subsidiaries: Discovision Associates, Pioneer China Holding Co., Ltd., Pioneer Display Products Corporation, Pioneer Electronics (USA)Inc., Pioneer Electronics Asiacentre, Pte. Ltd., Pioneer Electronics Capital Inc., Pioneer Europe NV, Pioneer North America, Inc., Pioneer Plasma Display Corporation, Tohoku Pioneer Corporation

Officers: Yoichi Sato/Sr. Executive Officers, Hajime Ishizuka/Exec. VP, Representative Dir., Yoshio Taniyama/Sr. Executive Officer, Keiichi Nishikido/Corporate Auditors, Tsutomu Haga/Executive Officer, Keiichi Yamauchi/Executive Officer, Tatsuo Takeuchi/Executive Officer, Masanori Kurosaki/Executive Officer, Buntarou Nishikawa/Sr. Executive Officers, Masao Kawabata/Sr. Executive Officer, Sumitaka Matsumura/Executive Officer, Michiyoshi Ogawa/Corporate Auditor, Hiroyuki Mineta/Executive Officer, Takashige Nakano/Executive Officer, Shinichi Yamada/Corporate Auditors *(26 Officers included in Index)*

Directors: Hajime Ishizuka/Exec. VP, Representative Dir., Shunichi Sato/Dir., Tamihiko Sudo/Dir., Pres. - Representative, Koichi Ueda/Dir.

Pioneer Drilling Co

1250 NE Loop 410, Ste. 1000, San Antonio, TX, 78209; *PH:* 1-210-828-7689; *Fax:* 1-210-828-8228; *http://* www.pioneerdrlg.com; *Email:* dglacombe@pioneerdrlg.com

General - Incorporation	TX	**Stock**- Price on:12/24/2007	$15.16
Employees	1,700	Stock Exchange	AMEX
Auditor	KPMG LLP	Ticker Symbol	PDC
Stk Agt	Registrar & Transfer Co	Outstanding Shares	49,630,000
Counsel	NA	E.P.S	$1.32
DUNS No.	04-477-3091	Shareholders	NA

Business: The group's principal activity is to provide contract land drilling services to independent and major oil and gas exploration and production companies. In addition to drilling rigs, the group provides the drilling crews, most of the ancillary equipment needed to operate the drilling rigs. The group focuses operations in the natural gas production regions of south Texas and east Texas. At 16-May-2003, the group's rig fleet consists of 25 drilling rigs, 15 of which are operating in south Texas and 10 of which are operating in east Texas.

Primary SIC and add'l.: 1381

CIK No: 0000320575

Subsidiaries: PDC Investment Corp., South Texas Drilling Company

Officers: Stacy Wm. Locke/Dir., CEO, Pres./$1,333,675.00, F. C. West/COO, Exec. VP/$1,082,264.00, Donald G. Lacombe/Sr. VP - Marketing/$505,860.00, William D. Hibbetts/59/CFO, Sr. VP, Sec./$561,238.00, David J. Blaine/VP - Operations/$375,115.00, Willie Walker/VP - Operations/$391,250.00, Kurt M. Forkheim/VP, Chief Accounting Officer, Principal Accounting Officer, Joyce M. Schuldt/CFO, Exec. VP, Sec., Investor Relations Officer

Directors: Stacy Wm. Locke/Dir., CEO, Pres., Robert C. Bunch/Chmn., Dean A. Burkhardt/Dir., James M. Tidwell/Dir., Michael F. Harness/Dir., John C. Thompson/Dir.

Owners: Insiders/2.28%, James M. Tidwell, Barclays Global Investors NA/5.28%, Robert C. Bunch, Franklin C. West, William D. Hibbetts, Stacy Locke, Michael F. Harness, Dean A. Burkhardt, John C. Thompson, The Vanguard Group, Inc./5.37%, Donald G. Lacombe

Financial Data: *Fiscal Year End:*03/31 *Latest Annual Data:* 3/31/2006

Year	Sales	Net Income
2006	$284,148,000	$50,567,000
2005	$185,246,000	$10,812,000
2004	$107,876,000	-$1,790,000

Curr. Assets:	$139,536,000	**Curr. Liab.:**	$32,632,000	**P/E Ratio:**	9.78
Plant, Equip.:	$260,783,000	**Total Liab.:**	$60,003,000	**Indic. Yr. Divd.:**	NA
Total Assets:	$400,678,000	**Net Worth:**	$340,676,000	**Debt/ Equity:**	NA

Pioneer Natural Resources Co

5205 N O'Connor Blvd., Ste. 200, Irving, TX, 75039; *PH:* 1-972-444-9001; *Fax:* 1-972-969-3576; *http://* www.pioneernrc.com; *Email:* ir@pxd.com

General - Incorporation	DE	**Stock**- Price on:12/24/2007	$53.62
Employees	1,624	Stock Exchange	NYSE
Auditor	Ernst & Young LLP	Ticker Symbol	PXD
Stk Agt	Continental Stock Transfer & Trust Co	Outstanding Shares	123,440,000
Counsel	NA	E.P.S	$1.43
DUNS No.	16-003-2199	Shareholders	NA

Business: The groups principle activity is to provide oil and gas exploration services. The group explores, develops and produces oil, natural gas liquid and gas reserves. The group operates from United States.

Primary SIC and add'l.: 1311 1381 1321

CIK No: 0001038357

Subsidiaries: DMLP CO., Long Canyon Gas Company, LLC, Lorencito Gas Gathering, LLC, Mesa Environmental Ventures Co., Mesa Offshore Royalty Partnership, Midkiff Development Drilling Program, Ltd., Parker & Parsley 87-A Conv., Ltd., Parker & Parsley 90 Spraberry Private Development, L.P., Parker & Parsley Argentina, Inc., Parker & Parsley Private Investment 88 L.P., Parker & Parsley Private Investment 89, L.P., Petroleum South Cape (Pty) Ltd., Pioneer Canada ULC, Pioneer Energy Canada Ltd., Pioneer International Resources Company 45 Subsidiaries included in the Index

Officers: Scott D. Sheffield/Chmn., CEO/$4,152,675.00, Timothy L. Dove/COO, Pres./$1,931,486.00, Richard P. Dealy/CFO, Exec. VP/$1,191,389.00, Mark S. Berg/Exec. VP, General Counsel, A. R. Alameddine/Exec. VP - Worldwide Negotiations, Chris J. Cheatwood/Exec. VP - Worldwide Exploration/$1,259,906.00, William F. Hannes/Exec. VP - Worldwide Business Development, Danny L. Kellum/Exec. VP - Domestic Operations/$1,242,990.00, Jay P. Still/Exec. VP - Western Division, Thomas C. Halbouty/CIO, VP, Darin G. Holderness/VP, Chief Accounting Officer, Frank E. Hopkins/VP - Investor Relations, Mark H. Kleinman/Corp. Sec., Chief Compliance Officer, David McManus/VP - International Operations, Larry N. Paulsen/VP - Administration, Risk Management *(17 Officers included in Index)*

Directors: Scott D. Sheffield/Chmn., CEO, Jim A. Watson/Dir., Mark S. Sexton/Dir., Robert A. Solberg/Dir., Charles E. Ramsey/Dir., James R. Baroffio/Dir., Edison C. Buchanan/Dir., Hartwell R. Gardner/Dir., Linda K. Lawson/Dir., Andrew D. Lundquist/Dir., Frank A. Risch/Dir.

Owners: Frank A. Risch, Southeastern Asset Management, Inc./19.00%, Chris J. Cheatwood, Andrew D. Lundquist, Insiders/1.50%, Robert A. Solberg, Timothy L. Dove, Edison C. Buchanan, Danny L. Kellum, Jim A. Watson, James R. Baroffio, Richard P. Dealy, Hartwell R. Gardner, Scott D. Sheffield, Charles E. Ramsey *(18 Owners included in Index)*

Financial Data: *Fiscal Year End:*12/31 *Latest Annual Data:* 12/31/2006

Year	Sales	Net Income
2006	$1,632,881,000	$739,731,000
2005	$2,373,223,000	$534,568,000
2004	$1,846,776,000	$312,854,000

Curr. Assets:	$536,558,000	**Curr. Liab.:**	$886,979,000	**P/E Ratio:**	37.50
Plant, Equip.:	$6,414,484,000	**Total Liab.:**	$4,370,728,000	**Indic. Yr. Divd.:**	$0.260
Total Assets:	$7,355,399,000	**Net Worth:**	$2,984,671,000	**Debt/ Equity:**	0.6544

Pioneer Railcorp

1318 S Johanson Rd., Peoria, IL, 61607; *PH:* 1-309-697-1400; *Fax:* 1-309-697-5387; *http://* www.pioneer-railcorp.com

General - Incorporation	IA	**Stock**- Price on:12/24/2007	$4.8
Employees	NA	Stock Exchange	OTC
Auditor	McGladrey & Pullen LLP	Ticker Symbol	PRRR
Stk Agt	Mr. Brenkman	Outstanding Shares	NA
Counsel	Daniel A Lakemper	E.P.S	NA
DUNS No.	15-650-6743	Shareholders	NA

Business: The group's principal activities are to provide railroad operations and railroad equipment leasing. The railroad operations provides shipping links for customers along its routes and interchanges with five major railroads, burlington northern santa fe railroad (bnsf), csx transportation (csx), Canadian national railway company (cn), norfolk southern railway (ns) and union pacific railroad (up). Railroad equipment leasing provides locomotives, railcars and other railroad related vehicles and equipment to the group's operating railroad subsidiaries. The group also leases railcars and locomotives to unaffiliated third parties. The group operates in Alabama, Arkansas, Kansas, Illinois, Indiana, Iowa, Michigan, Mississippi, Pennsylvania and Tennessee.

Primary SIC and add'l.: 4013 6517 6719

CIK No: 0000796374

Subsidiaries: Alabama & Florida Railway Co., Inc., Alabama Railroad Co., Decatur Junction Railway Co., Elkhart & Western Railroad Co., Fort Smith Railroad Co., Gettysburg & Northern Railroad Co., Indiana Southwestern Railway Co., Kendallville Terminal Railway Co., Keokuk Junction Railway Co., Michigan Southern Railroad Company, Mississippi Central Railroad Co., Pioneer Air, Inc., Pioneer Industrial Railway Co., Pioneer Railroad Equipment Co., Ltd., Pioneer Railroad Services, Inc. 20 Subsidiaries included in the Index

Officers: Michael J. Carr/Dir., CEO, CFO, Pres., Treasurer, Dennis Johnson/AAR Billing Mgr. - Pioneer Railroad Equipment Co, LTD, Shane D. Cullen/Superintendent, Transportation, Tom S. Black/VP - Safety, Compliance, Joseph Evans/Dir. - Operations Center, Pioneer Railroad Equipment Co, LTD, Tammy Bridson/Chief Agent, Catherine Busch/Dir. - Marketing, Frank C. May/Real Estate Agent, Pioneer Resources, Inc, Kenneth Pilgrim/Revenue Accounting Mgr. - Pioneer Railroad Equipment Co, LTD, Leora Day/Staff Accountant - Pioneer Railroad Equipment Co, LTD, Joyce Hilyard/Staff Accountant - Pioneer Railroad Equipment Co, LTD, Scott Isonhart/Staff Accountant - Pioneer Railroad Equipment Co, LTD, Prel, Nathan Johns/Marketing Mgr., Kathy Bouris/Customer Service Center Agent, Ryan Bridson/Customer Service Center Agent *(16 Officers included in Index)*

Directors: Guy L. Brenkman/Chmn.

Financial Data: *Fiscal Year End:*12/31 *Latest Annual Data:* 12/31/2004

Year	Sales	Net Income
2004	$16,775,000	$1,440,000
2003	$15,995,000	$1,425,000
2002	$14,970,000	$1,246,000

Curr. Assets:	$5,600,000	**Curr. Liab.:**	$5,108,000		
Plant, Equip.:	$25,309,000	**Total Liab.:**	$21,286,000	**Indic. Yr. Divd.:**	NA
Total Assets:	$32,211,000	**Net Worth:**	$10,190,000	**Debt/ Equity:**	0.9310

Pipeline Data Inc

1515 Hancock St., Ste. 301, Hancock, MA, 02169; *PH:* 1-671-405-2600; *Fax:* 1-678-867-6050; *http://* www.pipelinedata.com

General - Incorporation ... DE
Employees ... 92
Auditor ... Drakeford & Drakeford, LLC
Stk Agt ... American Stock Transfer & Trust Co.
Counsel ... NA
DUNS No. ... NA

Stock - Price on:12/24/2007 ... $0.95
Stock Exchange ... OTC
Ticker Symbol ... PPDA
Outstanding Shares ... 48,150,000
E.P.S ... -$0.07
Shareholders ... NA

Business: The groups principle activities include provider of merchant payment processing services and other related software products. Services of the group include credit and debit card based payment processing solutions and services to small to medium sized merchants who operate either in a physical brick and mortar business environment or over the Internet. In July 2006, the group acquired Paynet Systems, Inc. and Valadata, Inc. The group operates from the United States. The group's quarterly revenue for Sep '07 was 12.75 millions of USD.

Primary SIC and add'l.: 6099 7389 7374 4822 7379

CIK No: 0001086533

Subsidiaries: Aircharge, Inc, CardAccept, Inc.,, Charge.com, Inc.,, Northern Merchant Services, Inc, Paynet Systems, Inc, Pipeline Data Portfolio Acquisitions, Inc, Pipeline Data Processing, Inc, SecurePay.com, Inc.,, Valadata, Inc.,

Officers: Macallister Smith/Dir., CEO/$264,287.00, Kevin Smith/COO/$299,851.00, Thomas Tesmer/CTO/$321,889.00, Philip Chait/Investor Relation Officer

Directors: Macallister Smith/Dir., CEO, Jack Rubinstein/Chmn., Kevin J. Weller/Dir.

Owners: Kevin Smith, Jack Rubinstein, Kevin J. Weller/6.30%, James Plappert, MacAllister Smith/12.80%, John Reeder, Insiders/45.00%, Centrecourt Asset Management LLC/8.00%, David Danzig/9.80%, Harold Denton, Michael M. Greenburg, Gregory Danzig/9.80%, Nancy Smith Weller/7.10%, Chasm Holdings, Inc/10.70%

Financial Data: *Fiscal Year End:*12/31 *Latest Annual Data:* 12/31/2006

Year	Sales	Net Income
2006	$41,814,000	-$2,286,000
2005	$24,098,000	$369,000
2004	$15,565,000	-$700,000

Curr. Assets:	$6,445,000	**Curr. Liab.:**	$2,513,000		
Plant, Equip.:	$1,117,000	**Total Liab.:**	$34,427,000	**Indic. Yr. Divd.:**	NA
Total Assets:	$65,024,000	**Net Worth:**	$30,597,000	**Debt/ Equity:**	NA

Piper Jaffray & Co

800 Nicollet Mall, Ste. 800, Minneapolis, MN, 55402; *PH:* 1-612-303-6000; *Fax:* 1-612-303-8199; *http://* www.piperjaffray.com

General - Incorporation ... DE
Employees ... 1,104
Auditor ... Ernst & Young LLP
Stk Agt ... Mellon Investor Services LLC
Counsel ... Faegre & Benson LLP
DUNS No. ... NA

Stock - Price on:12/24/2007 ... $60.45
Stock Exchange ... NYSE
Ticker Symbol ... PJC
Outstanding Shares ... 18,880,000
E.P.S ... $12.60
Shareholders ... NA

Business: The group's principle activity is to provide security brokerage, investment banking and related financial services to individuals, institutions, corporations and municipalities in the United States of America. It operates through three segments: capital markets, private client services and corporate support and other. Capital market provides equity and fixed income institutional sales and trading. It also provides investment banking, underwriting, merger and acquisition services and public finance activities. Private client services provides financial advice and investment products and services to individual investors. Corporate support and other provide administrative support functions such as finance, legal and human resources. It also provides venture capital business and company's investment in limited partnership that invests in venture capital funds. The products and services are marketed under the single brand piper jaffray. The group's quarterly revenue for September 2007 was 98.54 millions of USD.

Primary SIC and add'l.: 6211

CIK No: 0001230245

Subsidiaries: Piper Jaffray & Co., Piper Jaffray Financial Products II Inc., Piper Jaffray Financial Products Inc., Piper Jaffray Funding LLC, Piper Jaffray Lending LLC, Piper Jaffray Ltd., Piper Jaffray Private Capital Inc., Piper Jaffray Ventures Inc., Piper Ventures Capital Inc., PJC Nominees Ltd., PJH Idaho, Inc., PJH Montana, Inc., PJH South Dakota, Inc., PJH Utah, Inc., PJH Wyoming, Inc. 16 Subsidiaries included in the Index

Officers: Andrew S. Duff/Chmn., CEO/$3,111,496.00, Thomas P. Schnettler/51/Vice Chmn., CFO/$2,875,871.00, James L. Chosy/General Counsel, Sec., Robert W. Peterson/Head - Equities/$1,793,921.00, Frank Fairman/Head - Public Finance Services/$1,009,169.00, Todd R. Firebaugh/Chief Administrative Officer, Jon W. Salveson/Head - Investment Banking/$2,823,133.00, Benjamin T. May/Head - High, Yield, Structured Products, Jennifer A. Olson-Goude/Dir. - Investor Relations

Directors: Andrew S. Duff/Chmn., CEO, Thomas P. Schnettler/51/Vice Chmn., CFO, Addison L. Piper/Dir., Michael R. Francis/Dir., Kristine B. Johnson/Dir., Samuel L. Kaplan/Dir., Frank L. Sims/Dir., Jean M. Taylor/Dir., Lisa K. Polsky/Dir.

Owners: Francis E. Fairman, Thomas P. Schnettler, Barclays Global Investors, N.A/5.71%, Insiders, Robert W. Peterson, Samuel L. Kaplan, Jean M. Taylor, Addison L. Piper, Kristine B. Johnson, Jon W. Salveson, BlackRock, Inc./10.34%, T. Rowe Price Associates, Inc./6.30%, Andrew S. Duff, Frank L. Sims, Dimensional Fund Advisors LP/5.49% *(16 Owners included in Index)*

Financial Data: *Fiscal Year End:*12/31 *Latest Annual Data:* 12/31/2006

Year	Sales	Net Income
2006	$535,237,000	$235,253,000
2005	$814,789,000	$40,083,000
2004	$815,624,000	$50,348,000

Curr. Assets:	$1,505,241,000	**Curr. Liab.:**	$781,905,000	**P/E Ratio:**	5.02
Plant, Equip.:	$25,289,000	**Total Liab.:**	$927,408,000	**Indic. Yr. Divd.:**	NA
Total Assets:	$1,851,847,000	**Net Worth:**	$924,439,000	**Debt/ Equity:**	NA

Pismo Coast Village Inc

165 S Dolliver St., Pismo Beach, CA, 93449; *PH:* 1-805-773-8111; *Fax:* 1-805-773-1507; *http://* www.pismocoastvillage.com; *Email:* rv@pismocoastvillage.com

General - Incorporation ... CA
Employees ... NA
Auditor ... McCown Starbuck & Keeter
Stk Agt ... NA
Counsel ... NA
DUNS No. ... 08-433-5819

Stock - Price on:12/24/2007 ... NA
Stock Exchange ... NA
Ticker Symbol ... NA
Outstanding Shares ... NA
E.P.S ... NA
Shareholders ... NA

Business: The group's principal activity is to own and operate a recreational vehicle resort in pismo beach, California. The group's vehicle resort operations include site rentals, rv storage business, video arcade and laundromat. Other activities of the group include owning and operating retail stores, which consists of a general store, rv parts store, rv repair shop and a recreation department, which provides youth program and recreational equipment rentals.

Primary SIC and add'l.: 7033 7538 5399

CIK No: 0000216877

Officers: Ronald Nunlist/70/Dir., VP - Policy, Chmn., Jerald Pettibone/82/Dir., Chmn., Jack Williams/58/Dir., CFO, VP - Finance, Jay Jamison/GM, Charles Amian/Operations Mgr., Kurt Brittain/78/Dir., VP, Sec., Glenn Hickman/75/Dir., Exec. VP

Directors: Elaine R. Harris/70/Dir., Chmn. Environmental - Health, Ronald Nunlist/70/Dir., VP - Policy, Chmn., Jerald Pettibone/82/Dir., Chmn., Gary Willems/54/Dir., Jack Williams/58/Dir., CFO, VP - Finance, Dennis Hearne/69/Dir., George Pappi/46/Dir., Glenn Hickman/75/Dir., Exec. VP, Terris Hughes/59/Dir., William Fischer/75/Dir., Eudaly Douglas/76/Dir., Ed Figueroa/65/Dir., Harry Buchaklian/76/Dir., Norman Gould/89/Dir., Nancy Brady/66/Dir. *(16 Directors included in Index)*

Owners: Rodney Enns, Insiders, Gary Willems, Ronald Nunlist, William Fischer, Nancy Brady, Douglas Eudaly, Louis Benedict, Glenn Hickman, Jerald Pettibone, George Pappi, Elaine R. Harris, Kurt Brittain, Harry Buchaklian, Norman Gould *(19 Owners included in Index)*

Pitney Bowes Inc

1 Elmcroft Rd., Stamford, CT, 06926; *PH:* 1-203-356-5000; *Fax:* 1-203-351-7336; *http://* www.pb.com

General - Incorporation ... DE
Employees ... 34,454
Auditor ... PricewaterhouseCoopers LLP
Stk Agt ... EquiServe Trust Co N.A
Counsel ... NA
DUNS No. ... 00-116-1793

Stock - Price on:12/24/2007 ... $46.6
Stock Exchange ... NYSE
Ticker Symbol ... PBI
Outstanding Shares ... 219,640,000
E.P.S ... $2.71
Shareholders ... NA

Business: The group's principle activity is to provide mail processing equipment and integrated mail solutions.The group's services include custom postage,multi-vendor and optimization services. In the year 2007, the group was acquire by Pitney Bowes Inc. The group operates from United States.

Primary SIC and add'l.: 7389 3579 7359 6159

CIK No: 0000078814

Subsidiaries: 1136 Corporation, Addressing Systems International Holdings Limited, Adrema Leasing Corporation, Adrema Maschinen und Auto Leasing GmbH, Adrema Maschinenbau Inc., Andeen Enterprises, Inc., Archiver Limited f/k/a Micromedia Limited, Artec International Corporation, B. Williams Funding Corp., B. Williams Holding Corp., Bell & Howell France Holding SAS, Burmas voorheen Buroservice NV, Canadian Office Services (Toronto) Limited, Cascade Microfilm Systems, Inc., CPLC Inc. 209 Subsidiaries included in the Index

Officers: Michael J. Critelli/59/Chmn., CEO/$9,368,038.00, Helen Shan/VP, Treasurer, Luis A. Jimenez/63/Sr. VP, Chief Strategy Officer, Murray D. Martin/60/Dir., COO, Pres./$4,787,900.00, Bruce P. Nolop/CFO, Exec. VP/$2,793,548.00, Leslie R. Abi-Karam/Exec. VP, Pres. - Document Messaging Technologies, Amy C. Corn/VP, Sec., Chief Governance Officer, Elise R. Debois/Exec. VP, Pres. - Global Financial Services, Vincent R. De Palma/Exec. VP, Pres. - Pitney Bowes Management Services, Steven J. Green/VP - Finance, Chief Accounting Officer, Joseph E. Wall/CTO, Sr. VP, Michele Coleman Mayes/Sr. VP, General Counsel/$1,575,567.00, Johnna G. Torsone/Sr. VP, Chief Human Resources Officer, Patrick J. Keddy/Exec. VP, Pres. - Mailstream International/$1,548,994.00, Neil Metviner/Exec. VP, Pres. - Global Small Business, Supplies *(19 Officers included in Index)*

Directors: Michael J. Critelli/59/Chmn., CEO, Anne Sutherland Fuchs/60/Dir., Ernie Green/69/Dir., James H. Keyes/67/Dir., Murray D. Martin/60/Dir., COO, Pres., John S. McFarland/59/Dir., David B. Snow/53/Dir., David L. Shedlarz/59/Dir., Eduardo R. Menasce/62/Dir., Robert E. Weissman/67/Dir., Michael I. Roth/62/Dir., Linda G. Alvarado/56/Dir.

Owners: David L. Shedlarz, James H. Keyes, Linda G. Alvarado, Murray D. Martin, Bruce P. Nolop, Michael J. Critelli, John S. McFarlane, Ernie Green, Robert E. Weissman, Wellington Management Company, LLP/5.46%, NWQ Investment Management Company, LLC/6.00%, Michael I. Roth, Michele Coleman Mayes, Patrick J. Keddy, Anne Sutherland Fuchs *(19 Owners included in Index)*

Financial Data: *Fiscal Year End:*12/31 *Latest Annual Data:* 12/31/2006

Year	Sales	Net Income
2006	$5,730,018,000	$105,347,000
2005	$5,492,183,000	$526,578,000
2004	$4,957,440,000	$480,526,000

Curr. Assets:	$2,918,670,000	**Curr. Liab.:**	$2,746,833,000	**P/E Ratio:**	108.37
Plant, Equip.:	$1,331,922,000	**Total Liab.:**	$7,397,066,000	**Indic. Yr. Divd.:**	$1.320
Total Assets:	$8,480,420,000	**Net Worth:**	$699,189,000	**Debt/ Equity:**	NA

Pittsburgh & West Virginia Railroad

2 Port Amherst Dr, Charleston, WV, 25306; *PH:* 1-304-926-1124

General - Incorporation ... PA
Employees ... NA
Auditor ... Gibbons & Kawash
Stk Agt ... NA
Counsel ... nn
DUNS No. ... NA

Stock - Price on:12/24/2007 ... $9
Stock Exchange ... AMEX
Ticker Symbol ... PW
Outstanding Shares ... 1,510,000
E.P.S ... $0.52
Shareholders ... NA

Business: The groups principle activity is to acquire business and property of a small leased railroad. The group operates from the United States. The groups quarterly revenue for September 2007 was 0.23 millions of USD.

Primary SIC and add'l.: 6798

CIK No: 0000078838

Officers: Robert A. Hamstead/VP, Sec., Treasurer, Herbert E. Jones/59/Trustee, Pres.

Directors: Herbert E. Jones/87/Chmn., Trustee, Herbert E. Jones/59/Trustee, Pres., Virgil E. Wenger/77/Trustee, Larry R. Parsons/66/Trustee, Howard C. Capito/60/Trustee

Owners: Howard C. Capito/0.07%, Virgil E. Wenger/0.01%, Larry R. Parsons/0.83%, Insiders/1.17%, Herbert E. Jones

Financial Data: Fiscal Year End: 12/31   **Latest Annual Data:** 12/31/2006

Year	Sales	Net Income
2006	$915,000	$789,000
2005	$915,000	$780,000
2004	$915,000	$805,000

Curr. Assets:	$49,000	**Curr. Liab.:**	NA	
Plant, Equip.:	NA	**Total Liab.:**	NA	**Indic. Yr. Divd:** $0.520
Total Assets:	$9,199,000	**Net Worth:**	$9,199,000	**Debt/ Equity:** NA

Pixar

1200 Pk. Ave., Emeryville, CA, 94608; **PH:** 1-510-752-3000; **http://** www.pixar.com

General - Incorporation	CA	Stock - Price on: 12/24/2007	NA
Employees	133,000	Stock Exchange	NA
Auditor	KPMG LLP	Ticker Symbol	NA
Stk Agt..... Computershare Investor Services LLC		Outstanding Shares	NA
Counsel.......... Wilson Sonsini Goodrich & Rosati		E.P.S.	NA
DUNS No.	15-151-6259	Shareholders	NA

Business: The group's principal activity is to create, develop and produce computer-animated feature films with a new three-dimensional appearance, heartwarming stories and memorable characters that appeal to audiences of all ages. The group has produced animated films and related products such as video products, toys, interactive games and other merchandise. The group has created and produced four full-length animated feature films: toy story, a bug's life, toy story 2, monsters, inc and finding nemo. The group operates solely in the domestic market.

Primary SIC and add'l.: 7372 7812

CIK No: 0001002114

Subsidiaries: Blue Sky, Walt Disney Pictures

Officers: John Lasseter/Chief Creative Officer, Ed Catmull/Pres.

Financial Data: Fiscal Year End: 12/31   **Latest Annual Data:** 9/30/2006

Year	Sales	Net Income
2006	$34,285,000,000	$3,374,000,000
2005	$31,944,000,000	$2,533,000,000
2004	$30,752,000,000	$2,345,000,000

Curr. Assets:	$9,562,000,000	**Curr. Liab.:**	$10,210,000,000	
Plant, Equip.:	$17,167,000,000	**Total Liab.:**	$26,835,000,000	**Indic. Yr. Divd.:** NA
Total Assets:	$59,998,000,000	**Net Worth:**	$31,820,000,000	**Debt/ Equity:** 0.3241

Pixelplus Company Ltd

3003 N 1st St., Ste. 330, San Jose, CA, 95134; **PH:** 1-408-519-5790; **Fax:** 1-408-519-5746; **http://** www.pixelplus.com; **Email:** info@pixelplus.com

General - Incorporation..... Republic of Korea		Stock - Price on: 12/24/2007	$0.79
Employees	NA	Stock Exchange	NDQ
Auditor .... Samil PricewaterhouseCoopers		Ticker Symbol	PXPL
Stk Agt.	Hana Bank	Outstanding Shares	12,850,000
Counsel	NA	E.P.S.	-$0.78
DUNS No.	NA	Shareholders	NA

Business: The groups principal activities include designing, developing and marketing semiconductor image sensor devices. Specific customers of the group include BYD Co., Ltd., China TechFaith, Ningbo Bird Co., Ltd., Ltd., Seiko Precision Inc. and Sharp. The group operates from United States.

Primary SIC and add'l.: 3674

CIK No: 0001331588

Subsidiaries: Pixelplus Asia Co., Limited, Pixelplus Semiconductor, Inc, Pixelplus Shanghai Ltd, Pixelplus Technology INC.

Officers: Seo-Kyu Lee/Chmn., CEO, Pres., Sang-Soo Lee/Dir., CTO, Exec. VP, Euy-Hyeon Baek/VP, Ou-Seb Lee/VP, Sung-Soo Lee/Technical Dir., Hoang Taig Choi/57/Dir., CFO, Sr. VP, Hae-su Hwang/43/COO, Chang-soo Park/52/VP

Directors: Seo-Kyu Lee/Chmn., CEO, Pres., Sang-Soo Lee/Dir., CTO, Exec. VP, Choong-Ki Kim/Dir., Taek-Jin Nam/Dir., Ha-Jin Jhun/Dir., Dong-Woo Chun/Dir., Hoang Taig Choi/57/Dir., CFO, Sr. VP

Owners: Insiders/21.66%, Sang Soo Lee, MIC 2001-4TG Venture/5.30%, Sung Su Lee/2.23%, Seo Kyu Lee/16.37%, Euy Hyeon Baek/2.63%, Ou Seb Lee

Financial Data: Fiscal Year End: 12/31   **Latest Annual Data:** 12/31/2006

Year	Sales	Net Income
2006	$34,404,000	-$18,676,000
2005	$41,173,000	$969,000

Curr. Assets:	$27,299,000	**Curr. Liab.:**	$14,212,000	**P/E Ratio:** 529.67
Plant, Equip.:	$2,311,000	**Total Liab.:**	$14,894,000	**Indic. Yr. Divd:** NA
Total Assets:	$33,966,000	**Net Worth:**	$19,072,000	**Debt/ Equity:** NA

Pixelworks Inc

8100 SW Nyberg Rd., Tualatin, OR, 97062; **PH:** 1-503-454-1750; **Fax:** 1-503-612-0848; **http://** www.pixelworks.com; **Email:** info@pixelworks.com

General - Incorporation	OR	Stock - Price on: 12/24/2007	$1.45
Employees	449	Stock Exchange	NDQ
Auditor	KPMG LLP	Ticker Symbol	PXLW
Stk Agt........... Chase Mellon Shareholder Services LLC		Outstanding Shares	48,850,000
Counsel	Ater Wynne LLP	E.P.S.	-$0.94
DUNS No.	NA	Shareholders	NA

Business: The group's principal activities are to design, develop and sell semi-conductors and software for the advanced display industry, including advanced televisions, multimedia projectors and flat panel monitors. The group's system-on-chip semiconductors process and optimize video, computer graphics and Web information for display on a wide variety of devices. The products address every major segment of the advanced display market including flat panel monitors, digital televisions and multimedia projectors. The group has international operations in Japan, Taiwan, China and Europe.

Primary SIC and add'l.: 7372

CIK No: 0001040161

Subsidiaries: Equator Technologies, Inc, Jaldi Semiconductor, nDSP Delaware, Inc, Panstera, Inc, Pixelworks Ltd, Pixelworks Semiconductor Singapore Pte. Ltd., Pixelworks Semiconductor Technology (Shanghai) Co. Ltd., Pixelworks Semiconductor Technology (Taiwan) Inc.

Officers: Hans Olsen/CEO, Pres./$1,078,637.00, Hongmin Zhang/VP - Technololgy, CTO/$714,018.00, John Y. Lau/VP - China Liaison, Foundry Management, Gang Cui/VP - Strategy, Marketing Development/$644,967.00, Michael D. Yonker/50/CFO, VP, Treasurer, Sec./$466,171.00, Jodie F.T. Brady/VP - Business Operations, Steven Moore/CFO, VP - Finance, Anthony R. Simon/VP - Marketing, Damon M. Hess/VP - Sales

Directors: Allen Alley/Chmn., James R. Fiebiger/Dir., Daniel J. Heneghan/Dir., Scott C. Gibson/Dir., Bruce Walicek/Dir., Frank Gill/Dir., Mark Christensen/Dir.

Owners: Deutsche Bank AG/8.50%, James R. Fiebiger, Mazama Capital Management, Inc./18.90%, Hans H. Olsen/1.20%, Michael D. Yonker, Mark A. Christensen, Daniel J. Heneghan, Scott C. Gibson, Hongmin Zhang, Insiders/7.60%, Gang Cui, Allen H. Alley/4.50%, Bruce A. Walicek, Frank C. Gill, Jeff B. Bouchard

Financial Data: Fiscal Year End: 12/31   **Latest Annual Data:** 12/31/2006

Year	Sales	Net Income
2006	$133,607,000	-$204,178,000
2005	$171,704,000	-$42,610,000
2004	$176,211,000	$21,781,000

Curr. Assets:	$146,578,000	**Curr. Liab.:**	$38,409,000	
Plant, Equip.:	$21,931,000	**Total Liab.:**	$185,823,000	**Indic. Yr. Divd.:** NA
Total Assets:	$207,771,000	**Net Worth:**	$21,948,000	**Debt/ Equity:** 11.6433

Pizza Inn Inc

3551 Plano Pkwy., The Colony, TX, 75056; **PH:** 1-469-384-5000; **Fax:** 1-469-384-5059; **http://** www.pizzainn.com

General - Incorporation	MO	Stock - Price on: 12/24/2007	$3.2
Employees	159	Stock Exchange	NDQ
Auditor	BDO Seidman LLP	Ticker Symbol	PZZI
Stk Agt...... American Stock Transfer & Trust Co.		Outstanding Shares	10,170,000
Counsel	NA	E.P.S.	$0.16
DUNS No.	02-628-5296	Shareholders	NA

Business: The group's principal activity is to franchise and distribute food to a system of restaurants operating under the trade name "Pizza Inn". Pizza inn system consists of 427 units, including three company operated units and 411 franchised units. These units are currently located in 20 states and 10 foreign countries. These restaurants offer pizzas with variety of toppings, pasta, salads, sandwiches, desserts and beverages including beer and wine in certain locations. Full service restaurants offer dine-in and carry-out services and also offers delivery services in most cases.

Primary SIC and add'l.: 5812 6794

CIK No: 0000718332

Subsidiaries: PIBCO, Ltd

Officers: Charles R. Morrison/Interim CEO, CFO, Mischa Chandler/Investor Relation Officer, Ward T. Olgreen/Sr. VP - Franchise Operations, Concept Development, Danny K. Meisenheimer/VP - Brand Marketing, Michael L. Iglesias/VP - Franchise Development, Darrell G. Smith/VP - Development

Directors: Mark E. Schwarz/Chmn., Steven J. Pully/Dir., Robert B. Page/Dir., Ramon D. Phillips/Dir., Clinton J. Coleman/Dir., James K. Zielke/Dir., Steven M. Johnson/Dir.

Owners: Insiders/48.70%, Jim Zeilke, Steve Johnson, Mark E. Schwarz/47.40%, Darrell G. Smith, Hoak Public Equities, L.P./5.20%, Newcastle Partners, L.P./47.00%, Steven J. Pully, Charles R. Morrison, Ramon D. Phillips, Ward T. Olgreen, Danny K. Meisenheimer

Financial Data: Fiscal Year End: 06/26   **Latest Annual Data:** 6/25/2006

Year	Sales	Net Income
2006	$50,608,000	-$5,989,000
2005	$55,269,000	$204,000
2004	$60,212,000	$2,243,000

Curr. Assets:	$7,057,000	**Curr. Liab.:**	$3,771,000	
Plant, Equip.:	$13,640,000	**Total Liab.:**	$12,189,000	**Indic. Yr. Divd:** NA
Total Assets:	$20,906,000	**Net Worth:**	$8,717,000	**Debt/ Equity:** NA

Placer Dome Inc

1055 Dunsmuir St., Ste. 1600, Vancouver, BC, V7X 1P1; **PH:** 1-604-682-7082; **http://** www.barrick.com

General - Incorporation	Canada	Stock - Price on: 12/24/2007	NA
Employees	NA	Stock Exchange	NA
Auditor	Ernst & Young LLP	Ticker Symbol	NA
Stk Agt	Mellon Trust Co	Outstanding Shares	NA
Counsel	NA	E.P.S.	NA
DUNS No.	20-163-6818	Shareholders	NA

Business: The group's principle activity is to operates in gold mining and related activities including copper, silver and other minerals exploration, extraction, processing, refining and reclamation. Major mining operations are located in Canada, the United States, Australia, papua new guinea, South Africa and Chile. The company operates 15 mines in 6 countries on 5 continents.

Primary SIC and add'l.: 1041 1021 1044

CIK No: 0000819996

Subsidiaries: Campbell Red Lake Mines Limited, Canada Business Corporations, Dome Mines Limited, Mount Isa Mines Limited, Placer Development Limited

Plains All American Pipeline LP

333 Clay St., Ste. 1600, Houston, TX, 77002; **PH:** 1-713-646-4100; **Fax:** 1-713-646-4572; **http://** www.plainsallamerican.com

General - Incorporation	DE	Stock - Price on: 12/24/2007	$62.86
Employees	2,900	Stock Exchange	NYSE
Auditor	PricewaterhouseCoopers LLP	Ticker Symbol	PAA
Stk Agt...... American Stock Transfer & Trust Co.		Outstanding Shares	109,410,000
Counsel	NA	E.P.S.	$2.57
DUNS No.	NA	Shareholders	NA

Business: The groups principle activities include transporting, storing, terminalling and marketing of crude oil, refined products and liquefied petroleum gas and other natural gas related petroleum products. The group operates through two segments namely, transportation and marketing. In the year 2006, the group acquired Pacific Atlantic Terminals LLC. The group operates from the United States. The groups quarterly revenue for September 2007 was 5,799.00 millions of USD.

Primary SIC and add'l.: 4613 4612

CIK No: 0001070423

Subsidiaries: Andrews Partners, LLC, Atchafalaya Pipeline, L.L.C., Aurora Pipeline Company, Ltd., Basin Holdings GP LLC, Basin Pipeline Holdings, L.P., Lone Star Trucking, LLC, PAA Finance Corp., Pacific Atlantic Terminals LLC, Pacific Energy Finance Corporation, Pacific Energy GP, LP, Pacific Energy Group LLC, Pacific Energy Management LLC, Pacific LA Marine Terminal LLC, Pacific Marketing and Transportation LLC, Pacific Pipeline System LLC 37 Subsidiaries included in the Index

Officers: Greg L. Armstrong/Chmn., CEO, Harry N. Pefanis/COO, Pres., Phil D. Kramer/CFO, Exec. VP, George R. Coiner/57/Sr. Group VP, Alfred A. Lindseth/Sr. VP - Technology, Process, Risk Management, Tina L. Val/VP - Accounting, Chief Accounting Officer, Troy E. Valenzuela/VP - Environmental, Health, Safety, Ralph R. Cross/VP - Business Development PMC, Nova Scotia Company, M. D. Hallahan/VP - Crude Oil PMC, Nova Scotia Company, Ron F. Wunder/VP - LPG PMC, Nova Scotia Company, Stephen L. Bart/VP - Operations PMC, Nova Scotia Company, Richard H. Henson/VP - Corporate Services, PMC, Nova Scotia Company, Canadian Management Team, John Von Berg/VP - Trading, Patrick A. Diamond/VP, Mark D. Alenius/VP *(31 Officers included in Index)*

Directors: Greg L. Armstrong/Chmn., CEO, Gary R. Petersen/Dir., Robert V. Sinnott/Dir., Arthur L. Smith/Dir., Taft J. Symonds/Dir., David N. Capobianco/Dir., Everardo Goyanes/Dir.

Owners: Arthur L. Smith, Everardo Goyanes, Phillip D. Kramer, Richard Kayne/Kayne Anderson Capital Advisors, L.P./8.40%, Robert V. Sinnott, Vulcan Energy Corporation/11.30%, Gary R. Petersen, Harry N. Pefanis, Paul G. Allen/13.10%, Taft J. Symonds, Insiders, George R. Coiner, Greg L. Armstrong

Financial Data: *Fiscal Year End:*12/31 *Latest Annual Data:* 12/31/2006

Year	Sales	Net Income
2006	$22,444,400,000	$285,100,000
2005	$31,177,300,000	$217,800,000
2004	$20,975,470,000	$130,006,000

Curr. Assets:	$3,157,600,000	**Curr. Liab.:**	$3,024,700,000	**P/E Ratio:**	22.78
Plant, Equip.:	$4,183,200,000	**Total Liab.:**	$5,738,100,000	**Indic. Yr. Divd.:**	$3.360
Total Assets:	$8,714,900,000	**Net Worth:**	$2,976,800,000	**Debt/ Equity:**	0.8921

Plains Exploration & Production Co

700 Milam St., Ste. 3100, Houston, TX, 77002; ***PH:*** 1-713-579-6000; ***Fax:*** 1-713-579-6500; ***http://*** www.plainsxp.com; ***Email:*** investor@plainsxp.com

General - Incorporation	DE	**Stock**- Price on:12/24/2007	$50.83
Employees	610	Stock Exchange	NYSE
Auditor	PricewaterhouseCoopers LLP	Ticker Symbol	PXP
Stk Agt	American Stock Transfer & Trust Co.	Outstanding Shares	71,700,000
Counsel	NA	E.P.S	$6.23
DUNS No.	NA	Shareholders	NA

Business: The group's principle activity is to acquire, exploit, develop and produce oil and gas in the United States. On 18-Dec-2002, the group spun off from plains resources inc. The group's core areas of operation are onshore California, primarily in the los angeles basin; offshore California in the point arguello unit; and the Illinois basin in southern Illinois and Indiana. The revenues of the group are derived from the sale of oil, gas and natural gas liquids. The group's quarterly revenue for September 2007 was 298.97 millions of USD.

Primary SIC and add'l.: 1311 1321

CIK No: 0000891456

Subsidiaries: Arguello Inc., Arroyo Grande Land Company LLC, Brown PXP Properties, LLC, Cane River Development Company LLC, Lompoc Land Company LLC, Montebello Land Company LLC, Nuevo Ghana Inc., Nuevo International Inc., Nuevo Offshore Company, Nuevo Resources Inc., Pacific Interstate Offshore Company, Plains Louisiana Inc., Plains Resources International Inc., PXP Gulf Coast Inc., PXP Louisiana LLC 18 Subsidiaries included in the Index

Officers: James C. Flores/Chmn., CEO, Pres./$27,292,880.00, John F. Wombwell/Exec. VP, General Counsel, Corp. Sec./$5,444,238.00, Doss R. Bourgeois/Exec. VP - Exploration, Production/$2,330,373.00, Winston M. Talbert/CFO, Exec. VP/$2,012,483.00, Steven P. Rusch/VP - Environmental - Health, Safety, Government Affairs, Scott Winters/VP - Investor Relations, Joanna Pankey/Investor Relations Analyst

Directors: James C. Flores/Chmn., CEO, Pres., Robert L. Gerry/Dir., Isaac Arnold/Dir., John H. Lollar/Dir., Tom H. Delimitros/Dir., Alan R. Buckwalter/Dir., Jerry L. Dees/Dir.

Owners: Insiders/3.10%, FMR Corp./16.10%, Stephen A. Thorington, Winston M. Talbert, Isaac Arnold, Alan R. Buckwalter, Doss R. Bourgeois, Tom H. Delimitros, Cynthia A. Feeback, Thomas M. Gladney, Robert L. Gerry, Jerry L. Dees, James C. Flores/2.20%, John F. Wombwell, John H. Lollar *(17 Owners included in Index)*

Financial Data: *Fiscal Year End:*12/31 *Latest Annual Data:* 12/31/2006

Year	Sales	Net Income
2006	$1,018,503,000	$597,528,000
2005	$1,086,566,000	-$214,012,000
2004	$671,706,000	$8,840,000

Curr. Assets:	$184,796,000	**Curr. Liab.:**	$460,192,000	**P/E Ratio:**	5.48
Plant, Equip.:	$2,107,524,000	**Total Liab.:**	$1,332,545,000	**Indic. Yr. Divd.:**	NA
Total Assets:	$2,463,228,000	**Net Worth:**	$1,130,683,000	**Debt/ Equity:**	0.4598

Plaintree Systems Inc

90 Decosta St., Arnprior, ON, K7S 0B5; ***PH:*** 1-613-623-3434; ***Fax:*** 1-613-623-4647; ***http://*** www.plaintree.com; ***Email:*** marketing@plaintree.com

General - Incorporation	Canada	**Stock**- Price on:12/24/2007	$0.005
Employees	NA	Stock Exchange	OTC
Auditor	Deloitte & Touche LLP	Ticker Symbol	LANPF
Stk Agt	Computershare Investor Services LLC	Outstanding Shares	NA
Counsel	Blake, Cassels & Graydon LLP	E.P.S	NA
DUNS No.	24-946-6186	Shareholders	NA

Business: The group's principal activity is to design, develop, manufacture, market and support optical wireless links, network switches and telecommunication products. The products of the group allow customers to improve the performance and increase the manageability of the existing local area networks. The group's wavebridge product uses led (light-emitting diode) technology to provide a local and wide area networking alternative to wire line, fiber, leased circuits and radio wave (rf) data solutions. The wavebride system can also be used to transport data, voice and video information among computer workstations, file servers and printers either in the same office or between office buildings.

Primary SIC and add'l.: 3661 8741

CIK No: 0000943946

Subsidiaries: 4178611 Canada Inc, Plaintree Systems Corporation

Officers: William David Watson/Dir., CEO, Pres., Girvan L. Patterson/Dir., Corp. Sec., Jason Lee/VP - Business Development, Lynn Saunders/VP - Operations

Directors: William David Watson/Dir., CEO, Pres., Robert E. Shea/Dir., John M. Buchanan/Dir., Girvan L. Patterson/Dir., Corp. Sec., Jerry S. Vickers/Dir.

Owners: Targa Group Inc/28.00%, Robert G. Shea, Girvan L. Patterson, Insiders/2.00%, William David Watson

Financial Data: *Fiscal Year End:*03/31 *Latest Annual Data:* 03/31/2007

Year	Sales	Net Income
2007	$1,872,000	$882,000
2005	$284,000	-$1,559,000
2004	$198,000	-$543,000

Curr. Assets:	$334,000	**Curr. Liab.:**	$11,098,000		
Plant, Equip.:	$146,000	**Total Liab.:**	$11,098,000	**Indic. Yr. Divd.:**	NA
Total Assets:	$9,341,000	**Net Worth:**	-$1,757,000	**Debt/ Equity:**	NA

Planar Systems Inc

1195 NW Compton Dr., Beaverton, OR, 97006; ***PH:*** 1-503-748-1100; ***Fax:*** 1-503-748-1244; ***http://*** www.planar.com

General - Incorporation	OR	**Stock**- Price on:12/24/2007	$7.16
Employees	590	Stock Exchange	NDQ
Auditor	KPMG LLP	Ticker Symbol	PLNR
Stk Agt	Mellon Investor Services LLC	Outstanding Shares	17,450,000
Counsel	Ater Wynne LLP	E.P.S	-$1.33
DUNS No.	10-301-7166	Shareholders	NA

Business: The group's principal activities are to develop, manufacture and market high-performance electronic display systems. It offers a wide variety of displays and display systems in a range of resolutions, formats, viewing areas and technologies. The products offered include proprietary electroluminescent flat-panel displays, active matrix liquid crystal displays and passive matrix liquid crystal display. The products are used in a wide variety of medical, industrial, transportation, communication and other applications. The major customers of the group include philips, marconi, datex ohmeda, ge medical, datascope, tokheim, sun microsystems, kodak, allen bradley and dell computer systems. The group acquired dome imaging systems inc in fiscal 2002.

Primary SIC and add'l.: 3679 3575

CIK No: 0000722392

Subsidiaries: DOME imaging systems, inc., Planar China LLC, Planar International Oy, Planar Taiwan LLC

Officers: Gerald K. Perkel/Dir., CEO, Pres., Scott Hildebrandt/CFO, VP, Brad Gleeson/VP - Business Development, Scott P. Hix/VP, GM - Home Theater Business Unit, Douglas K. Barnes/VP, GM - Industrial Business Unit, Mark A. Ceciliani/VP, GM - Commercial Business Unit, Patrick Herguth/35/VP, GM - Medical Business Unit, Jack Ehren/VP - Global Operations, Kristina Gorriaran/VP, GM - Control Room, Signage Business Unit, Paul Gulick/CTO, VP, John J. Ehren/47/VP - Global Operations, Jeffrey T. Siegal/44/Corporate Controller, Treasurer

Directors: Gerald K. Perkel/Dir., CEO, Pres., Gregory H. Turnbull/Chmn., Heinrich Stenger/Dir., Steven E. Wynne/Dir., Kay E. Stepp/Dir., William D. Walker/Dir., Carl W. Neun/Dir., Walter W. Noce/62/Dir., Michael J. Gullard/Dir.

Owners: Scott Hildebrandt, Walter W. Noce, Insiders/8.80%, Heinrich Stenger, John J. Ehren, Carl W. Neun, Patrick Herguth, Gregory H. Turnbull, Gerald K. Perkel/1.10%, Douglas K. Barnes, William D. Walker, Dimensional Fund Advisors Inc./6.10%, Royce& Associates, LLC/5.30%, Kay E. Stepp, Steven E. Wynne

Financial Data: *Fiscal Year End:*09/30 *Latest Annual Data:* 9/29/2006

Year	Sales	Net Income
2006	$212,726,000	$6,280,000
2005	$231,832,000	-$34,880,000
2004	$256,196,000	$9,278,000

Curr. Assets:	$134,708,000	**Curr. Liab.:**	$35,912,000		
Plant, Equip.:	$15,011,000	**Total Liab.:**	$40,846,000	**Indic. Yr. Divd.:**	NA
Total Assets:	$172,084,000	**Net Worth:**	$131,238,000	**Debt/ Equity:**	NA

Planet Polymer Technologies Inc

96 Danbury Rd., Ridgefield, CT, 06877; ***PH:*** 1-800-255-3749

General - Incorporation	CA	**Stock**- Price on:12/24/2007	$2.1
Employees	25	Stock Exchange	NA
Auditor	J. H. Cohn LLP	Ticker Symbol	NA
Stk Agt	OTR Inc/Oxford Transfer & Registrar	Outstanding Shares	3,990,000
Counsel	Blanchard, Krasner & French	E.P.S	-$0.27
DUNS No.	78-840-7310	Shareholders	NA

Business: The group's principle activities include designing, developing, manufacturing and marketing degradable and recycled polymer materials. The company's materials are marketed under the trademarks enviroplastic crt, aquadro and enviroplastic z. Enviroplastic crt are used in agriculture and produce products. Enviroplastic and aquadro are used to produce films, coatings and injection molded parts that serve as an alternative to conventional plastics. The group operates from United States.

Primary SIC and add'l.: 8731 2821

CIK No: 0000896861

Subsidiaries: Allergy Control Products, Kidder Peabody and Co, Inc., MCA Financial, Inc., Planet Technologies, Inc.

Officers: Edward Steube/64/Dir., CEO, Pres., Scott L. Glenn/58/Chmn. - Business Executive, Eric B. Freedus/58/Dir. - Attorney, Michael Trinkle/55/Dir. - Business Executive, Michael Walsh/Dir. - Business Executive, Francesca Dinota/45/CFO, Chief Accounting Officer

Directors: Edward Steube/64/Dir., CEO, Pres., Scott L. Glenn/58/Chmn. - Business Executive, Eric B. Freedus/58/Dir. - Attorney, H. M. Busby/69/Dir., Michael Trinkle/55/Dir. - Business Executive, Ellen M. Preston/53/Dir., Michael Walsh/Dir. - Business Executive

Owners: Michael A. Trinkle, H.M. Busby, Scott L. Glenn, Insiders, John Dawson, Fog City Fund, LLC, Francesca DiNota, Eric B. Freedus, William and Lisa Barkett, Michael Walsh, Windamere III, LLC, Brett Megargel, Ellen Preston, Edward J. Steube

Financial Data: *Fiscal Year End:* 12/31 *Latest Annual Data:* 12/31/2006

Year	Sales	Net Income
2006	$8,036,000	-$1,202,000
2005	$3,923,000	-$1,508,000
2004	$1,180,000	-$774,000

Curr. Assets:	$932,000	*Curr. Liab.:*	$1,798,000		
Plant, Equip.:	$27,000	*Total Liab.:*	$1,798,000	*Indic. Yr. Divd.:*	NA
Total Assets:	$3,499,000	*Net Worth:*	$1,702,000	*Debt/ Equity:*	NA

Planet411.com Inc

8720-a Rue Du Frost, St Leonard, QC, H1P 2Z5; *PH:* 1-514-325-4567

General - Incorporation	DE	**Stock** - Price on:12/24/2007	NA
Employees	NA	Stock Exchange	NA
Auditor	De Joya Griffith & Company LLC	Ticker Symbol	NA
Stk Agt	Nevada Agency & Trust Company	Outstanding Shares	NA
Counsel	NA	E.P.S.	-$0.03
DUNS No.	NA	Shareholders	NA

Business: The groups principal activity is an identifying additional business and/or technology for acquisition. The group operates from the United States.

Primary SIC and add'l.: 4899

CIK No: 0001096555

Officers: Derek Ivany/25/Dir., CEO, CFO, Victor Cantore/43/Dir., Pres., Sec.

Directors: Derek Ivany/25/Dir., CEO, CFO, Victor Cantore/43/Dir., Pres., Sec., Shing Lo/39/Dir.

Owners: Anna Giglio/14.82%, Victor Cantore/35.10%, Derek Ivany/49.39%, Insiders/84.49%

Financial Data: *Fiscal Year End:* 06/30 *Latest Annual Data:* 6/30/2006

Year	Sales	Net Income
2006	NA	-$35,000
2005	NA	-$34,000
2004	NA	-$4,000

Curr. Assets:	$5,000	*Curr. Liab.:*	$153,000		
Plant, Equip.:	NA	*Total Liab.:*	$153,000	*Indic. Yr. Divd.:*	NA
Total Assets:	$5,000	*Net Worth:*	-$148,000	*Debt/ Equity:*	NA

PlanetLink Communications Inc

1415 Bookhout Dr., Cumming, GA, 30341; *PH:* 1-678-455-7075; *Fax:* 1-404-781-0802; *http://* www.planettraks.com

General - Incorporation	GA	**Stock** - Price on:12/24/2007	$0.0003
Employees	1	Stock Exchange	OTC
Auditor	Chisholm, Bierwolf & Nilson, LLC	Ticker Symbol	PLKC
Stk Agt	Florida Atlantic Stock Transfer, Inc.	Outstanding Shares	1,090,000,000
Counsel	NA	E.P.S.	-$0.001
DUNS No.	NA	Shareholders	NA

Business: The groups principle activities include satellite based position location technologies with the widespread availability and use of wireless data communications. Services of the group include mobile locator units, development of the TransTRAK fleet monitoring software, map data and wireless data services. The group operates from the United States.

Primary SIC and add'l.: 4899 3812 4789 7215

CIK No: 0001123845

Subsidiaries: PlanetTRAKS, Inc.

Officers: Dewey M. Bain/Dir.,CEO, Interim CFO, Pres., Principal Accounting Officer Treasurer

Directors: Dewey M. Bain/Dir.,CEO, Interim CFO, Pres., Principal Accounting Officer Treasurer, Amy M. Trombly/40/Dir., James T. Crane/31/Dir.

Owners: Insiders/1.60%, Dewey M. Bain/1.60%

Financial Data: *Fiscal Year End:* 12/31 *Latest Annual Data:* 12/31/2006

Year	Sales	Net Income
2006	$281,000	-$2,436,000
2005	$178,000	-$3,184,000
2004	$3,000	-$2,382,000

Curr. Assets:	$54,000	*Curr. Liab.:*	$705,000		
Plant, Equip.:	$609,000	*Total Liab.:*	$708,000	*Indic. Yr. Divd.:*	NA
Total Assets:	$722,000	*Net Worth:*	$14,000	*Debt/ Equity:*	NA

PlanetOut Inc

1355 Sansome St., San Francisco, CA, 94111; *PH:* 1-415-834-6500; *Fax:* 1-415-834-6502; *http://* www.planetoutinc.com

General - Incorporation	DE	**Stock** - Price on:12/24/2007	$1.4074
Employees	273	Stock Exchange	NDQ
Auditor	Pricewaterhousecoopers LLP	Ticker Symbol	LGBT
Stk Agt	Wells Fargo Bank, N.A.	Outstanding Shares	17,690,000
Counsel	NA	E.P.S.	-$19.72
DUNS No.	NA	Shareholders	NA

Business: The groups principle activity is to provide media and entertainment services. The groups services include online and print media properties, and travel marketing business. The group operates from the United States and Canada. The group's quarterly revenue for September 2007 was 13.73 millions of USD.

Primary SIC and add'l.: 4724 2721 7375 4899 7319 2741 7379 7999

CIK No: 0001287258

Subsidiaries: LPI Media Inc., PlanetOut USA Inc., RSVP Productions, Inc., SpecPub, Inc.

Officers: Karen Magee/Dir., CEO/$413,266.00, Dan Miller/Sr. VP, CFO, Anne Moellering/VP - Brand, Product Marketing, Rob McGuire/VP - Advertising Sales, Todd Huge/VP - Business, Legal Affairs, Eric Wilson/VP - Product Planning, Strategy, Phillip S. Kleweno/Dir., Consultant, Bill Bain/CTO, Tom Cignarella/VP - Technology Operations, Kevyn Aiken/VP - Marketing, Media Sales, Jay Adams/VP - Group Publisher, East

Directors: Karen Magee/Dir., CEO, William H. Jesse/Chmn., Jerry Colonna/Dir., Robert W. King/Dir., Phillip S. Kleweno/Dir., Consultant

Owners: Jerry Colonna, William H. Jesse, Cascade Investment L.L.C./12.80%, Jeffrey T. Soukup, Lowell R. Selvin/1.90%, PAR Investment Partners, L.P./5.80%, Phillip Kleweno, Daniel J. Miller, Karen Magee, Insiders/5.00%, SF Capital Partners, Ltd./13.60%, Herbert A. Allen/5.30%, T. Rowe Price Associates, Inc./12.50%, Robert W. King, Mark D. Elderkin

Financial Data: *Fiscal Year End:* 12/31 *Latest Annual Data:* 12/31/2006

Year	Sales	Net Income
2006	$68,644,000	-$3,710,000
2005	$35,591,000	$2,740,000
2004	$24,962,000	-$537,000

Curr. Assets:	$36,941,000	*Curr. Liab.:*	$29,797,000		
Plant, Equip.:	$10,923,000	*Total Liab.:*	$42,444,000	*Indic. Yr. Divd.:*	NA
Total Assets:	$93,589,000	*Net Worth:*	$51,145,000	*Debt/ Equity:*	0.1417

Plangraphics Inc Colorado

112 E Main St., Frankfort, KY, 40601; *PH:* 1-502-223-1501; *Fax:* 1-502-223-1235; *http://* www.plangraphics.com; *Email:* info@plangraphics.com

General - Incorporation	CO	**Stock** - Price on:12/24/2007	$0.0042
Employees	NA	Stock Exchange	OTC
Auditor	Sherb & Co., LLP	Ticker Symbol	PGRA
Stk Agt	Computershare Investor Services LLC	Outstanding Shares	NA
Counsel	Davis Graham & Stubbs LLP	E.P.S.	NA
DUNS No.	05-528-5399	Shareholders	NA

Business: The group's principal activity is to provide business solutions to government and commercial entities. The group also provides Web-enabled solutions based on the advanced technologies of geographic information systems (gis), data warehouses and repositories, electronic document management systems (edms) and internal and external communication networks. The group has operations in the People's Republic of China. Its customers include federal, state and local governments, utilities, and commercial enterprises in United States and foreign markets requiring locational information. On 02-May-2002, the group changed its name from integrated spatial information solutions, inc to plangraphics, inc. The group acquired xmarc ltd on 30-Apr-2004.

Primary SIC and add'l.: 7373 6719

CIK No: 0000783284

Subsidiaries: PlanGraphics, Inc., RDT2M, Xmarc Limited

Officers: John C. Antenucci/Vice Chmn., CEO, Pres., Frederick G. Beisser/Sr. VP, Finance Sec., Treasurer Administrative Office, Gary W. Murphy/CFO, Joyce M. Rector/Sr. VP - Human Resources, John Chen/GM - International Operations

Directors: John C. Antenucci/Vice Chmn., CEO, Pres., Gary S. Murray/Chmn., William S. Strang/Dir., Raymund E. O'Mara/Dir.

Owners: Insiders/13.00%, John C. Antenucci/11.50%, Frederick G. Beisser/1.50%

Financial Data: *Fiscal Year End:* 09/30 *Latest Annual Data:* 9/30/2005

Year	Sales	Net Income
2005	$6,840,000	-$376,000
2004	$7,828,000	-$990,000
2003	$7,906,000	-$2,834,000

Curr. Assets:	$2,751,000	*Curr. Liab.:*	$4,296,000		
Plant, Equip.:	$80,000	*Total Liab.:*	$4,431,000	*Indic. Yr. Divd.:*	NA
Total Assets:	$4,922,000	*Net Worth:*	$491,000	*Debt/ Equity:*	NA

Planktos Corp

Formerly: Diatom Corp
1151-c Triton Dr., Foster City, CA, 94404; *PH:* 1-650-638-1975

General - Incorporation	NV	**Stock** - Price on:12/24/2007	NA
Employees	5	Stock Exchange	NA
Auditor	Williams & Webster, P.S	Ticker Symbol	NA
Stk Agt	Madison Stock Transfer, Inc.	Outstanding Shares	NA
Counsel	NA	E.P.S.	NA
DUNS No.	NA	Shareholders	NA

Business: The group's principle activity is to provide Internet-based online travel services for business. The group has not yet secured operations and is in the development stage. The group operates from United States.

Primary SIC and add'l.: 7375

CIK No: 0001076505

Officers: Russ George/Dir., CEO, CFO, Bill Coleman/COO, Jean Replicon/Coordinator - Education, Outreach, Julia Clark/Environmental Economist, Sarah Kelly/Environmental Policy Analyst, David Reitz/Marine Biologist, Michael Bailey/Program Mgr., Melodie Grubbs/Climatologist, Jenna Morris/Marine Biologist, Stephanie Fraker/Biologist, Adam White/Deckhand, Technician, Eric Ramirez/Information Technology Specialist, Ash Shepley/Chief Engineer

Directors: Russ George/Dir., CEO, CFO, Robert Fisher/58/Dir., Joel Dumaresq/43/Dir.

Owners: Robert Fisher, Gabriela Sameniego/41.60%, Investment Track Group/6.60%, Insiders

Curr. Assets:	$73,000	*Curr. Liab.:*	$175,000
Plant, Equip.:	NA	*Total Liab.:*	$175,000	*Indic. Yr. Divd.:*	NA
Total Assets:	$73,000	*Net Worth:*	-$102,000	*Debt/ Equity:*	NA

Plantronics Inc

345 Encinal St., Santa Cruz, CA, 95060; *PH:* 1-831-426-5858; *Fax:* 1-831-426-6098; *http://* www.plantronics.com

General - Incorporation	DE	**Stock** - Price on:12/24/2007	$23.66
Employees	7,300	Stock Exchange	NYSE
Auditor	PricewaterhouseCoopers LLP	Ticker Symbol	PLT
Stk Agt	EquiServe Trust Co N.A	Outstanding Shares	48,070,000
Counsel	Wilson Sonsini Goodrich & Rosati	E.P.S.	$1.17
DUNS No.	00-918-0902	Shareholders	NA

Business: The group's principal activities are to design, manufacture, market and sell telecommunication equipment. The products include lightweight telecommunication headsets, telephone headset systems, headset accessories and related services. The group also manufactures and markets specialty telephone products, such as telephone for hearing-impaired and other related products for people

with special communication needs. The group distributes its products through specialized headset distributors, large electronics wholesalers, original equipment manufacturers (OEMs) and retail channels, such as office supply stores, consumer electronics stores, mail order catalogs, warehouse clubs and office supplies distributors. The principal customers are distributors, retailers, telephony service providers and OEM partners. The group has operations in Europe, Middle East, Africa, Asia-Pacific, Latin America, Canada and other countries.

Primary SIC and add'l.: 3661 4813

CIK No: 0000914025

Subsidiaries: Altec Lansing Electronics (Dongguan) Limited, Altec Lansing Europe Sarl, Altec Lansing Far East Limited, Altec Lansing Hong Kong, Altec Lansing International, Inc., Altec Lansing Manufacturing Limited, Altec Lansing Technologies, Inc., Frederick Electronics Corporation, Plamex, S.A. de C.V., Plantronics Acoustics Italia, S.r.l., Plantronics APS, Plantronics B.V., Plantronics Canada Limited, Plantronics Communications Technology (Suzhou) Co. Ltd, Plantronics Europe Ltd. 26 Subsidiaries included in the Index

Officers: Gary Savadove/CEO, Pres. - Plantronics Audio Entertainment Business Group, Ken Kannappan/Dir., CEO, Pres./$887,514.00, Barbara Scherer/Sr. VP - Finance, Administration, CFO/$446,701.00, Greg Klaben/VP - Investor Relations, Barry Margerum/VP - Strategy, Business Development, Philip Vanhoutte/MD - Europe, Middle East, Africa/$489,988.00, Chuck Yort/VP, GM - B2B Solutions, Carsten Trads/Pres. - Clarity Division, Owen Brown/CTO, VP, Donald Houston/Sr. VP - Sales/$419,682.00, Greg Tyrrell/Dir. - Finance, EMEA, European Investor Relations, Joyce Shimizu/VP, GM - Home, Home Office/$414,114.00, Clay Hausmann/VP - Corporate Marketing, Renee Niemi/VP, GM - Mobile, Entertainment, Jim Sotelo/VP - Product Development, Technology *(16 Officers included in Index)*

Directors: Ken Kannappan/Dir., CEO, Pres., Marv Tseu/Chmn., Roger Wery/Dir., Trude Taylor/Dir., Greggory Hammann/Dir., John Hart/Dir., Marshall Mohr/Dir.

Owners: Philip Vanhoutte, FMR Corp./12.20%, John Hart, Trude Taylor, Barbara Scherer, Don Houston, Ken Kannappan/2.40%, Marv Tseu, Insiders/5.50%, PRIMECAP Management Company/12.20%, First Pacific Advisors, LLC/5.20%, Roger Wery, Marshall Mohr, Invesco PLC/14.70%, Joyce Shimizu *(17 Owners included in Index)*

Financial Data: Fiscal Year End:04/01   Latest Annual Data: 03/31/2007

Year	Sales	Net Income
2007	$800,154,000	$50,143,000
2006	$750,394,000	$81,150,000
2005	$559,995,000	$97,520,000

Curr. Assets:	$406,694,000	**Curr. Liab.:**	$71,171,000	**P/E Ratio:**	21.51
Plant, Equip.:	$59,745,000	**Total Liab.:**	$82,210,000	**Indic. Yr. Divd.:**	$0.200
Total Assets:	$487,929,000	**Net Worth:**	$405,719,000	**Debt/ Equity:**	NA

Platina Energy Group Inc

Formerly: Federal Security Protection Services Inc
1807 Capitol Ave., Ste. 101 - I, Cheyenne, WY, 82001; *PH:* 1-307-637-3900

General - Incorporation	DE	**Stock**- Price on:12/24/2007	$0.4999
Employees	1	Stock Exchange	OTC
Auditor	Jonathon P. Reuben CPA	Ticker Symbol	PLTG
Stk Agt	Corporate Stock Transfer, Inc.	Outstanding Shares	22,130,000
Counsel	NA	E.P.S.	-$0.272
DUNS No.	NA	Shareholders	NA

Business: The group's principle activity was to provide a commercial Internet site for boating, sports enthusiasts and the boating industry to advertise sales and services related to the professional and recreational boating industry. It markets Internet protocol based products and services with emphasis on Internet and data security. The Website of the group currently delivers an easy to use classified advertisement database advertising boats for sale and provides links to other boating and water sports related websites and services.

Primary SIC and add'l.: 7389 7375

CIK No: 0001098278

Subsidiaries: Permian Energy International, Permian Energy International, Inc

Officers: Blair J. Merriam/50/Dir., CEO, CFO, Pres., Daniel W. Thornton/47/Dir., Sec.

Directors: Blair J. Merriam/50/Dir., CEO, CFO, Pres., Daniel W. Thornton/47/Dir., Sec.

Owners: Blair J. Merriam/8.50%, Daniel W. Thornton/2.60%, Joseph F. Langston, Insiders/11.80%

Financial Data: Fiscal Year End:03/31   Latest Annual Data: 03/31/2007

Year	Sales	Net Income
2007	$18,000	-$1,151,000
2006	$5,000	-$601,000
2005	NA	-$342,000

Curr. Assets:	$189,000	**Curr. Liab.:**	$1,150,000		
Plant, Equip.:	$562,000	**Total Liab.:**	$1,150,000	**Indic. Yr. Divd.:**	NA
Total Assets:	$999,000	**Net Worth:**	-$151,000	**Debt/ Equity:**	NA

Platinum Energy Resources Inc

25 Philips Pkwy., Montvale, NJ, 07645; *PH:* 1-212-581-2401; *http://* www.platenergy.com

General - Incorporation	DE	**Stock**- Price on:12/24/2007	$7.5
Employees	10	Stock Exchange	OTC
Auditor	Marcum & Kliegman LLP	Ticker Symbol	PGRI
Stk Agt	American Stock Transfer & Trust Co.	Outstanding Shares	18,000,000
Counsel	NA	E.P.S.	NA
DUNS No.	NA	Shareholders	NA

Business: The groups principal activity is independent oil and gas E&P company headquartered in Midland Texas and a wholly owned subsidiary of Tandem Energy Holdings, Inc., operates oil fields in Texas and New Mexico. The group operates from the United States.

Primary SIC and add'l.: 1311

CIK No: 0001329605

Subsidiaries: PER Acquisition Corp.

Officers: Barry Kostiner/Dir., CEO, Sec., William C. Glass/Dir., Pres., Richard Geyser/VP, James H. Dorman/Exec. VP, Jim L. Troxel/Exec. VP, Tom Rozycki/Investor Relations Contact

Directors: Barry Kostiner/Dir., CEO, Sec., Mark Nordlicht/Chmn., William C. Glass/Dir., Pres., James E. Bashaw/Dir., Albert Helmig/Dir.

Owners: James H. Dorman, Mark Nordlicht/12.00%, David J. Rogers/7.00%, Andrew M. Weiss/6.10%, Barry Kostiner/5.20%, D. B. Zwirn Special Opportunities Fund, L.P./9.00%, Israel A. Englander/10.80%, Richard Geyser, William C. Glass/1.50%, Azimuth Opportunity,Ltd./8.60%, QVT Financial LP/7.70%, Jim L. Troxel, Insiders/19.80%

Financial Data: Fiscal Year End:12/31   Latest Annual Data: 12/31/2006

Year	Sales	Net Income
2006	NA	$1,660,000
2005	NA	$276,000

Curr. Assets:	$109,293,000	**Curr. Liab.:**	$1,763,000		
Plant, Equip.:	NA	**Total Liab.:**	$23,594,000	**Indic. Yr. Divd.:**	NA
Total Assets:	$110,956,000	**Net Worth:**	$87,361,000	**Debt/ Equity:**	NA

Platinum Research Organization Inc

1917 W 4th Ave., Ste. 421, Vancouver, BC, V6J 1M7; *PH:* 1-604-689-4088;
http:// www.platinumresearch.com

General - Incorporation	NV	**Stock**- Price on:12/24/2007	$0.675
Employees	NA	Stock Exchange	OTC
Auditor	James Stafford	Ticker Symbol	PLRO
Stk Agt	Signature Stock Transfer, Inc.	Outstanding Shares	75,000,000
Counsel	NA	E.P.S.	$0.00
DUNS No.	NA	Shareholders	NA

Business: The groups principal activities include developing, expanding and marketing two web based database programs namely one for small business and the second for community sports teams or groups. In October 2006, the group merged with Platinum Subsidiary. The group operates from the United States.

Primary SIC and add'l.: 3470

CIK No: 0001330340

Officers: John T. Jaeger/Dir., CEO, Pres., Matt Hawkins/Chief Marketing Officer, Peter R. Jones/Technical, Marketing Consultant, Stephen C. Kidwell/Marketing Consultant, Pranesh Aswath/Co - Investigator - Scientific Team, Ronald Elsenbaumer/Co - Investigator - Scientific Team, Harold Shaub/Technical Consultant, Scientific Team, Cecelia Pineda/62/Pres., Treasurer, Principal Accounting Officer, Sec., Dir., Mike Newman/Sr. VP, CFO, David Owen/VP, Chief Technical, Supply Officer

Directors: John T. Jaeger/Dir., CEO, Pres., Thomas G. Plaskett/Chmn., Theodore J. Brombach/Dir., Arnold I. Burns/Dir., Ben Dupont/Dir., Allan T. McArtor/Dir., Michael McMillan/Dir., Cecelia Pineda/62/Pres., Treasurer, Principal Accounting Officer, Sec., Dir.

Owners: Hypo Alpe-Adria-Bank (Liechtenstein) AG, Bank Sal Oppenheim Jr. & CIE, Bank Sal Oppenheim Jr. & CIE/11.10%, John T. Jaeger, Ben DuPont, Epsom Investment Services, NV, Lubrication Partners, Joint Venture, Arnold Burns, Insiders, JTE Finance Ltd, Felix Holdings Limited/11.10%, Felix Holdings Limited, Cecelia Pineda, Allan McArtor, Michael L. McMillan *(22 Owners included in Index)*

Financial Data: Fiscal Year End:12/31   Latest Annual Data: 12/31/2006

Year	Sales	Net Income
2006	NA	-$100,000

Curr. Assets:	$1,045,000	**Curr. Liab.:**	$1,031,000		
Plant, Equip.:	NA	**Total Liab.:**	$1,031,000	**Indic. Yr. Divd.:**	NA
Total Assets:	$1,045,000	**Net Worth:**	$14,000	**Debt/ Equity:**	NA

Platinum Underwriters Holdings Ltd

Platinum Underwriters Re, 2 World Financial Ctr., 225 Liberty St., Ste. 2300, New York, NY, 10281;
PH: 1-212-238-9600; *Fax:* 1-212-619-4092; *http://* www.platinumre.com;
Email: louterbridge@platinumre.com

General - Incorporation	Bermuda	**Stock**- Price on:12/24/2007	$34.5
Employees	160	Stock Exchange	NYSE
Auditor	KPMG LLP	Ticker Symbol	PTP
Stk Agt	Mellon Investor Services LLC	Outstanding Shares	59,850,000
Counsel	Dewey Ballantine	E.P.S.	$4.98
DUNS No.	NA	Shareholders	NA

Business: The group operates through its subsidiaries whose principle activity is to provide property, casualty and other reinsurance to insurers and reinsurers on a worldwide basis. The group operates from United States.

Primary SIC and add'l.: 6331 6719

CIK No: 0001171500

Subsidiaries: Platinum Administrative Services, Inc, Platinum Re (UK) Limited, Platinum Regency Holdings, Platinum Underwriters Bermuda, Ltd, Platinum Underwriters Finance, Inc, Platinum Underwriters Reinsurance, Inc

Officers: Michael D. Price/Dir., CEO, Pres./$3,893,840.00, Joseph F. Fisher/52/Exec. VP/$2,219,816.00, Neal J. Schmidt/Exec. VP, Chief Actuary - Platinum Administrative Services, Inc, Michael E. Lombardozzi/Exec. VP, General Counsel, Chief Administrative Officer, Sec./$2,883,637.00, Kenneth A. Kurtzman/Exec. VP, Chief Risk Officer - Platinum Administrative Services, Inc, Elizabeth H. Mitchell/Pres. - Platinum Underwriters Reinsurance, Inc/$1,897,655.00, Robert S. Porter/Pres. - Platinum Underwriters Reinsurance, Inc/$2,437,956.00, James A. Krantz/CFO, Exec. VP, Lily Outerbridge/VP, Dir. - Investor Relations

Directors: Michael D. Price/Dir., CEO, Pres., Steve H. Newman/Chmn., Furlong H. Baldwin/Dir., John A. Hass/Dir., Dan R. Carmichael/Dir., Robert V. Deutsch/Dir., Peter T. Pruitt/Dir., Jonathan F. Bank/Dir., Edmund R. Megna/Dir.

Owners: FMR Corp./10.00%, Robert S. Porter, James A. Krantz, Jonathan F. Bank, Wellington Management Company, LLP/9.50%, Insiders/3.80%, Peter T. Pruitt, Michael E. Lombardozzi, Neal J. Schmidt, Elizabeth H. Mitchell, Kenneth A. Kurtzman, Dan R. Carmichael, Michael D. Price, Joseph F. Fisher, Steven H. Newman/1.80% *(18 Owners included in Index)*

Financial Data: Fiscal Year End:12/31   Latest Annual Data: 06/30/2007

Year	Sales	Net Income
2007	$346,757,000	$90,650,000
2006	$1,522,906,000	$329,657,000
2005	$1,840,536,000	-$137,487,000

Curr. Assets:	$1,575,239,000	**Curr. Liab.:**	$158,432,000	**P/E Ratio:**	7.07
Plant, Equip.:	NA	**Total Liab.:**	$3,235,506,000	**Indic. Yr. Divd.:**	$0.320
Total Assets:	$5,093,567,000	**Net Worth:**	$1,858,061,000	**Debt/ Equity:**	0.1511

Plato Learning Inc

10801 Nesbitt Ave. S, Bloomington, MN, 55437; **PH:** 1-952-832-1000; **Fax:** 1-952-832-1200; **http://** www.plato.com; **Email:** info@plato.com

General - Incorporation	DE	**Stock** - Price on:12/24/2007	$4.57
Employees	540	Stock Exchange	NDQ
Auditor	PricewaterhouseCoopers LLP	Ticker Symbol	TUTR
Stk Agt	Wells Fargo Shareowner Services	Outstanding Shares	23,800,000
Counsel	NA	E.P.S	-$0.63
DUNS No.	61-319-6567	Shareholders	NA

Business: The group's principal activity is to provide computer and Web based instruction, curriculum planning and management, assessment and related professional development and support services to k-12 schools. The products and services provided by the group include the plato courseware and software, plato learning system, Web learning networks, Internet and distance learning, e-commerce and professional services. The products and services are provided to two-and four-year colleges, job training programs, correctional institutions, military education programs, corporations and individuals. The products of the group are marketed in the United States, Canada and the United Kingdom under the trademark, 'plato'. The group acquired new media (holdings) limited and lightspan inc in fiscal 2004.

Primary SIC and add'l.: 7372 7379

CIK No: 0000893965

Subsidiaries: Academic Systems Corporation, CyberEd, Inc., Edutest, Inc., Lightspan, Inc., NetSchools Corporation, New Media (Holdings) Limited, PLATO Learning (Canada), Inc., PLATO Learning (UK)Limited, PLATO, Inc., TeachMaster Technologies, Inc.

Officers: Michael A. Morache/Dir., CEO, Pres., Robert J. Rueckl/CFO, VP, David H. Lepage/Sr. VP - Operations, James T. Lynn/CTO, VP, Terri Lynn Reden/VP - Marketing Communications

Directors: Michael A. Morache/Dir., CEO, Pres., David W. Smith/Chmn., Debra Janssen/Dir., Ted J. Sanders/Dir., Lee M. Pelton/Dir., Joseph E. Duffy/Dir., Susan E. Knight/Dir., Ruth L. Greenstein/Dir., Warren Simmons/Dir., Robert S. Peterkin/Dir.

Owners: Security Management Company, LLC/5.30%, Heartland Advisors, Inc./6.30%, Wasatch Advisors, Inc./5.20%, John T. Sanders, Lee M. Pelton, James T. Lynn, Joseph E. Duffy, Debra A. Janssen, David W. Smith, Thomas G. Hudson, Dimension Fund Advisors Inc./5.90%, Reed Conner & Birdwell LLC/9.30%, Rutabaga Capital Management/7.40%, Richard M. Ferrentino, Susan E. Knight *(23 Owners included in Index)*

Financial Data: Fiscal Year End:10/31   Latest Annual Data: 10/31/2006

Year	Sales	Net Income
2006	$90,719,000	-$22,480,000
2005	$121,804,000	-$27,687,000
2004	$141,801,000	-$1,828,000

Curr. Assets:	$59,801,000	Curr. Liab.:	$51,033,000		
Plant, Equip.:	$6,308,000	Total Liab.:	$61,780,000	Indic. Yr. Divd.:	NA
Total Assets:	$176,230,000	Net Worth:	$114,450,000	Debt/ Equity:	NA

Playboy Enterprises Inc

680 N Lake Shore Dr., Chicago, IL, 60611; **PH:** 1-312-751-8000; **Fax:** 1-312-751-2818; **http://** www.playboyenterprises.com

General - Incorporation	DE	**Stock** - Price on:12/24/2007	$11.07
Employees	789	Stock Exchange	NYSE
Auditor	Ernst & Young LLP	Ticker Symbol	PLA
Stk Agt	LaSalle Bank N.A	Outstanding Shares	33,240,000
Counsel	NA	E.P.S	$0.25
DUNS No.	NA	Shareholders	NA

Business: The group operates in entertainment businesses that are related to the content and style of playboy magazine and licensing the trademarks for use on various consumer products and services. The group operates in four segments. The entertainment group develops, produces and distributes a wide range of adult television programming through domestic, international and worldwide home video markets. Publishing group includes the publication of playboy magazine and other domestic publishing businesses. Playboy online group provides a wide range of Web-based entertainment experiences under the playboy and spice brand names and is dedicated to the lifestyle and entertainment interests of the youth. The licensing businesses combine certain brand-related businesses such as the licensing of consumer products as well as playboy branded casino gaming opportunities. Playboy, the rabbit head design, playmate, spice and sarah coventry are the trademarks of the group.

Primary SIC and add'l.: 2741 2721 4841 7812

CIK No: 0001072341

Subsidiaries: 1945/1947 Cedar River C.v., Adultvision Communications, Inc., Alta Loma Distribution, Inc., Alta Loma Entertainment, Inc., Andrita Studios, Inc., Candlelight Management LLC, Chelsea Court Holdings, LLC, Cji Holdings, Inc., Claridge Organization LLC, Cpv Productions, Inc., Cyberspice, Inc., Ics Entertainment, Inc., Impulse Productions, Inc., Indigo Entertainment, Inc., Itasca Holdings, Inc. 70 Subsidiaries included in the Index

Officers: Christie Hefner/55/Chmn., CEO/$1,381,137.00, Hugh M. Hefner/Editor-In-Chief, Chief Creative Officer/$1,008,933.00, Martha O. Lindeman/Sr. VP - Corporate Communications, Investor Relations, Alex L. Vaickus/Exec. VP, Pres. - Global Licensing/$890,084.00, Linda G. Havard/CFO, Exec. VP - Finance, Operations/$758,800.00, Robert D. Campbell/Sr. VP, Treasurer, Strategic Planning Assist. Sec., Amy Williamson/Assist. Treasurer, Howard Shapiro/Exec. VP - Law, Administration, General Counsel, Sec., Louis R. Mohn/VP - Publisher, Playboy Publishing Group, Robert F. O'Donnell/Exec. VP - International Publishing, Robert Meyers/52/Exec. VP, Pres. - Media/$635,710.00, Bob Meyers/Exec. VP, Pres. - Media, Tom Hagopian/Exec. VP, GM - Digital Media, Richard S. Rosenzweig/73/Dir., Exec. VP, Jeffrey M. Jenest/Exec. VP *(21 Officers included in Index)*

Directors: Christie Hefner/55/Chmn., CEO, Richard S. Rosenzweig/73/Dir., Exec. VP, Sol Rosenthal/Dir., David I. Chemerow/Dir., Donald G. Drapkin/60/Dir., Russell I. Pillar/40/Dir., Jerome H. Kern/Dir., Dennis S. Bookshester/67/Dir., Charles Hirschhorn/Dir., Carol A. Devine/Dir., Cleo F. Wilson/Exec. Dir.

Owners: Sol Rosenthal, Dennis S. Bookshester, Insiders/34.94%, Hugh M. Hefner/27.97%, Insiders, Jerome H. Kern, Donald G. Drapkin, Hugh M. Hefner, Trustee, Christie Hefner, Sol Rosenthal, Alex Vaickus, Pequot Capital Management, Inc., David I. Chemerow, Linda G. Havard/1.03%, Hugh M. Hefner *(20 Owners included in Index)*

Financial Data: Fiscal Year End:12/31   Latest Annual Data: 12/31/2006

Year	Sales	Net Income
2006	$331,142,000	$2,285,000
2005	$338,153,000	-$735,000
2004	$329,376,000	$9,989,000

Curr. Assets:	$117,223,000	Curr. Liab.:	$105,489,000	P/E Ratio:	44.28
Plant, Equip.:	$17,407,000	Total Liab.:	$272,155,000	Indic. Yr. Divd.:	NA
Total Assets:	$435,783,000	Net Worth:	$163,628,000	Debt/ Equity:	0.6977

Players Networks Inc

4620 Polaris Ave., Las Vegas, NV, 89103; **PH:** 1-702-895-8884; **Fax:** 1-702-895-8833; **http://** www.playersnetwork.com; **Email:** info@playersnetwork.com

General - Incorporation	NV	**Stock** - Price on:12/24/2007	$0.21
Employees	6	Stock Exchange	OTC
Auditor	Weaver & Martin, LLC	Ticker Symbol	PNTV
Stk Agt	Florida Atlantic Stock Transfer, Inc.	Outstanding Shares	24,830,000
Counsel	NA	E.P.S	-$0.11
DUNS No.	NA	Shareholders	NA

Business: The groups principle activity is producing television programming to serve the gaming industry. The groups programming includes shows about gaming instruction, gaming news, wagering on sports and racing, gaming entertainment, tournaments, events and travel. The group operates from the United States.

Primary SIC and add'l.: 7812 7379 7375 4841

CIK No: 0001037131

Officers: Mark Bradley/Chmn., CEO/$288,817.00, Michael Berk/Pres. - Programming, Dir./$259,900.00, Douglas R. Miller/Financial Advisor, Dir., Roger P. Gros/Pres. - Casino Connection International

Directors: Mark Bradley/Chmn., CEO, Michael Berk/Pres. - Programming, Dir., Douglas R. Miller/Financial Advisor, Dir.

Owners: Insiders/38.49%, Douglas Miller/1.28%, Morden Lazarus/1.29%, Mark Bradley/22.93%, Joost Van Adelberg/5.55%, Michael Berk/9.22%

Financial Data: Fiscal Year End:12/31   Latest Annual Data: 12/31/2006

Year	Sales	Net Income
2006	$231,000	-$2,154,000
2005	$463,000	-$3,470,000
2004	$570,000	-$676,000

Curr. Assets:	$23,000	Curr. Liab.:	$663,000		
Plant, Equip.:	$66,000	Total Liab.:	$1,118,000	Indic. Yr. Divd.:	NA
Total Assets:	$89,000	Net Worth:	-$1,029,000	Debt/ Equity:	NA

Playtex Products Inc

300 Nyala Farms Rd., Westport, CT, 06880; **PH:** 1-203-341-4000; **http://** www.playtexproductsinc.com

General - Incorporation	DE	**Stock** - Price on:12/24/2007	$15.14
Employees	1,250	Stock Exchange	NA
Auditor	KPMG LLP	Ticker Symbol	NA
Stk Agt	Mellon Investor Services LLC	Outstanding Shares	63,460,000
Counsel	NA	E.P.S	$0.61
DUNS No.	19-855-4354	Shareholders	NA

Business: The group's principal activities are to manufacture and market a diversified portfolio of consumer and personal products. The group mainly operates in two segments: personal products and consumer products. Personal products include infant care and feminine care products such as diaper disposal system, mealtime products, reusable hard bottles, pacifiers, infant toiletries, plastic and cardboard applicator tampons. Consumer products include sun care, household products and personal grooming products such as gloves, cleaning products, oral care products and skin care products. The corporate division of the group sells these products to specialty classes of trade in the United States including warehouse clubs, military, convenience stores, subsidiaries, and specialty stores and the international division to Puerto Rico, Canada and Australia.

Primary SIC and add'l.: 3069 3999 2676 3089 3991 2844

CIK No: 0000842699

Subsidiaries: Carewell Industries, Inc., Personal Care Group, Inc., Personal Care Holdings, Inc., Playtex Enterprise Risk Management Ltd., Playtex International Corp., Playtex Investment Corp., Playtex Limited, Playtex Manufacturing, Inc., Playtex Marketing Corp., Playtex Products (Australia) Pty Ltd., Playtex Products, Inc., Playtex Sales & Services, Inc., Smile-Tote, Inc., Sun Pharmaceuticals Corp., TH Marketing Corp.

Officers: Neil P. Defeo/61/Chmn., CEO, Pres./$5,268,157.00, John J. McColgan/VP, Corporate Controller, Treasurer, Kris J. Kelley/CFO, Exec. VP/$1,466,324.00, Thomas M. Schultz/Sr. VP - Research, Development/$763,368.00, Paul E. Yestrumskas/VP, General Counsel, Sec., James S. Cook/Sr. VP - Operations/$898,091.00, Gretchen R. Crist/VP - Human Resources, Perry R. Beadon/Sr. VP - Global Sales/$843,942.00, Gary Cohen/Sr. VP - Marketing, Blair P. Hawley/VP - Supply Chain

Directors: Neil P. Defeo/61/Chmn., CEO, Pres., Michael R. Eisenson/52/Dir., Jeffrey R. Harris/53/Dir., Ann C. Merrifield/56/Dir., Herbert M. Baum/71/Dir., Douglas D. Wheat/57/Dir., Nick White/62/Dir., Ronald B. Gordon/64/Dir., Susan R. Nowakowski/43/Dir., Maureen Tart-Bezer/52/Dir.

Owners: Herbert M. Baum, Insiders/11.20%, Susan R. Nowakowski, C. Ann Merrifield, R. Jeffrey Harris, Kris J. Kelley, Harbinger Capital Partners Master Fund I, Ltd./19.70%, Michael R. Eisenson/7.40%, Nick White, Ronald B. Gordon, Douglas D. Wheat, Thomas M. Schultz, FMR Corp/12.60%, Perry R. Beadon, James S. Cook *(16 Owners included in Index)*

Financial Data: Fiscal Year End:12/26   Latest Annual Data: 12/30/2006

Year	Sales	Net Income
2006	$636,148,000	$30,204,000
2005	$643,806,000	$12,528,000
2004	$666,896,000	$55,507,000

Curr. Assets:	$270,602,000	Curr. Liab.:	$119,603,000	P/E Ratio:	24.82
Plant, Equip.:	$110,314,000	Total Liab.:	$890,421,000	Indic. Yr. Divd.:	NA
Total Assets:	$1,004,538,000	Net Worth:	$114,117,000	Debt/ Equity:	3.7468

Plaza Bank CA

19900 MacArthur Blvd, Ste. 110, Irvine, CA, 92612; **PH:** 1-949-502-4300; **http://** www.plazabank.net; **Email:** info@plazabank.net

General - Incorporation	NA	Stock - Price on:12/24/2007	$6.55
Employees	NA	Stock Exchange	OTC
Auditor	NA	Ticker Symbol	PLZB
Stk Agt	NA	Outstanding Shares	NA
Counsel	NA	E.P.S.	NA
DUNS No.	NA	Shareholders	NA

Business: The groups principal activity is to provide banking and serving small to medium sized businesses and professionals. The group is able to provide a wide range of products and services for the entrepreneur, including lines of credit, commercial loans for working capital or equipment financing, and small business administration loans for purchase or construction of a building for the business. The group operates from the United States.

Primary SIC and add'l.: 6022

CIK No:

Officers: Donald L. Solsby/Dir., CEO, Pres., Lawrence L. Luckey/Dir., Exec. VP, COO, Bruce J. McDonald/Sr. VP, CFO, Lissette Duran/Sr. VP, Dir. - Operations, Human Resources, Michael C. Miller/Exec. VP, Chief Credit Officer, David Simkin/Sr. VP, Sr. Relationship Mgr., Jon A. Bennett/VP - Construction Lending, Jacquin M. Davidson/VP, Commercial Banking Officer, Stephen E. Huelsman/VP, Commercial Banking Officer, Renee R. Leibowitz/VP, Note Department Mgr., Theresa R. Sanchez/Assist. VP - Operations, Reid Mendenhall/VP - Financial Analyst, Kristiina K. Beary/Assist. VP - Financial Analyst, Laura Ann Scott/New Accounting Office Administrator, Mirette Wassef/Financial Services Representative

Directors: Donald L. Solsby/Dir., CEO, Pres., Lawrence L. Luckey/Dir., Exec. VP, COO, Horacio Bellofiore/Dir., Lynne Pierson Doti/Dir., Robert J. Feldhake/Dir., Barry D. Foust/Dir., Bruce E. Sandler/Dir., Thomas J. Taylor/Dir., Leslee A. Temple/Dir.

Plaza Bank WA

1420 Fifth Ave., Ste. 3700, Seattle, WA, 98101; **PH:** 1-206-436-7600; **Fax:** 1-206-381-8895; *http://* www.plazabankwa.com

General - Incorporation		Stock - Price on:12/24/2007	$10.55
Employees	NA	Stock Exchange	OTC
Auditor	NA	Ticker Symbol	PZBW
Stk Agt	NA	Outstanding Shares	NA
Counsel	NA	E.P.S.	NA
DUNS No.	NA	Shareholders	NA

Business: The groups principal activities include providing banking and financial services to the customers. Services of the group include checking accounts, savings accounts, loans, checking accounts and treasury management. The group operates from the United States.

Primary SIC and add'l.: 6022

CIK No:

Officers: Carlos Guangorena/Dir., CEO, Pres., Agustin R. Ayala/CFO, Exec. VP, Carol J. Simpson/Exec. VP, Chief Administrative Officer, Frank M. Buty/Exec. VP, Chief Lending Officer

Directors: Carlos Guangorena/Dir., CEO, Pres., Michael E. Sotelo/Dir., Cristobal Guillen/Dir., Pedro Celis/Dir., Steve Johnson/Dir., Gene Juarez/Dir., Robert Flowers/Dir., George Armendariz/Dir., Priscilla J. Bell/Dir.

PLC Systems Inc

10 Forge Pk., Franklin, MA, 02038; **PH:** 1-508-541-8800; **Fax:** 1-508-541-7944; *http://* www.plcmed.com; **Email:** info@plcmed.com

General - Incorporation	Canada	Stock - Price on:12/24/2007	$0.67
Employees	30	Stock Exchange	AMEX
Auditor	Vitale, Caturano & Co. Ltd	Ticker Symbol	PLC
Stk Agt	U.S. Stock Transfer Corp	Outstanding Shares	30,310,000
Counsel	Mintz Levin Cohn Ferris Et Al	E.P.S.	-$0.05
DUNS No.	01-188-5845	Shareholders	NA

Business: The group's principal activity is to manufacture medical lasers and related products for use in the treatment of severe coronary artery diseases in a surgical laser procedure. The group's primary product is heart laser system, which is used for transmyocardial revascularization. One of the major customers of the group is edwards. The group's products are sold in the United States, Canada, Germany, Japan and Europe. During the year the group launched European clinical study with an objective of showing an improvement in angina relief, quality relief and other treatment procedure.

Primary SIC and add'l.: 3845

CIK No: 0000879682

Subsidiaries: PLC Medical Systems, Inc., PLC Sistemas Medicos Internacionais (Deutschland) GmbH

Officers: Mark R. Tauscher/Dir., CEO, Pres./$308,160.00, James Thomasch/CFO/$201,400.00

Directors: Mark R. Tauscher/Dir., CEO, Pres., Edward H. Pendergast/Chmn., Kevin J. Dunn/55/Dir., Benjamin L. Holmes/73/Dir., Alan H. Magazine/63/Dir., Brent Norton/47/Dir., Robert I. Rudko/65/Dir.

Owners: Brent Norton, Kevin J. Dunn, Benjamin L. Holmes, Kenneth J. Luppi/1.10%, Mark R. Tauscher/3.50%, Edward H. Pendergast/1.20%, Alan H. Magazine, Fred Kayne/10.10%, Vincent C. Puglisi, Robert I. Rudko/4.50%, Insiders/13.30%, James G. Thomasch/2.10%, Edwards Lifesciences Corporation/17.60%

Financial Data: Fiscal Year End: 12/31 **Latest Annual Data:** 12/31/2006

Year	Sales	Net Income
2006	$7,146,000	$1,319,000
2005	$7,636,000	-$1,268,000
2004	$7,573,000	-$833,000

Curr. Assets:	$12,802,000	Curr. Liab.:	$2,953,000		
Plant, Equip.:	$166,000	Total Liab.:	$6,047,000	Indic. Yr. Divd.:	NA
Total Assets:	$13,176,000	Net Worth:	$7,129,000	Debt/ Equity:	NA

Plexus Corp

55 Jewelers Pk. Dr., Neenah, WI, 54957; **PH:** 1-920-722-3451; **Fax:** 1-920-751-5395; *http://* www.plexus.com

General - Incorporation	WI	Stock - Price on:12/24/2007	$23.04
Employees	7,800	Stock Exchange	NDQ
Auditor	PricewaterhouseCoopers LLP	Ticker Symbol	PLXS
Stk Agt	M&I Marshall & Ilsley Bank	Outstanding Shares	46,330,000
Counsel	Quarles & Brady LLP	E.P.S.	$1.79
DUNS No.	09-854-4398	Shareholders	NA

Business: The group's principal activity is to provide product realization services to original equipment manufacturers (OEMs) in the networking, medical, industrial, computer and transportation industries. It also offers advanced electronics design, manufacturing and testing services to its customers with a focus on complex, high-end products. It enables the customers the ability to outsource all stages of product realization like development and design, materials procurement and management, testing, manufacturing configuration, logistics and test repair. It operates through 19 manufacturing and engineering facilities located in North America, Europe and Asia.

Primary SIC and add'l.: 3825 3674 3672

CIK No: 0000785786

Subsidiaries: Plexus (Xiamen) Co., Ltd, Plexus Asia, Ltd, Plexus Corp. (UK) Limited, Plexus Corp. Limited, Plexus Electronica S.de R.L., Plexus International Services, Inc, Plexus Intl. Sales & Logistics, Plexus Management Services Corporation, Plexus Manufacturing Sdn. Bhd, Plexus QS, LLC, Plexus Services Corp, PTL Information Technology Services Corp

Officers: Dean Foate/CEO, Pres., Mark Wolfgram/Sales, New Business Development, North America, Dianne Boydstun/Investor Relations Officer, George Setton/Corporate Treasurer, Chief Treasury Officer, Tom J. Czajkowski/CIO, VP, Dave Clark/VP - Materials, Supply Chain, Mike Verstegen/Sr. VP - Global Marketing Development, Kirsty Brown/New Business Development Contact - Europe, Mandy Lin/Sales, New Business Development Contact - Asia, Ginger Jones/CFO, VP, Angelo Ninivaggi/VP, General Counsel, Sec., Todd Kelsey/Sr. VP - Global Customer Services, Mike Buseman/Sr. VP - Global Manufacturing Operations, Yong Jin Lim/Regional Pres. - Plexus Asia Pacific, Steve Frisch/Sr. VP - Global Engineering Services *(16 Officers included in Index)*

Directors: John L. Nussbaum/Chmn., Rolf R. Boer/Dir., Michael V. Schrock/Dir., Charles M. Strother/Dir., Stephen P. Cortinovis/Dir., David J. Drury/Dir., Peter Kelly/Dir.

Owners: Lord, Abbett & Co. LLC/7.30%, David J. Drury, Stephen P. Cortinovis, Peter Kelly, Michael T. Verstegen, John L. Nussbaum, Dean A. Foate/1.30%, Yong Jin Lim, Barrow, Hanley, Mewhinney & Strauss, Inc./6.90%, Insiders/3.00%, Gordon F. Bitter, Robert J. Kronser, Barclays Global Investors, NA./8.20%, Ginger M. Jones, Ralf R. Boer *(18 Owners included in Index)*

Financial Data: Fiscal Year End: 10/01 **Latest Annual Data:** 9/30/2006

Year	Sales	Net Income
2006	$1,460,557,000	$100,025,000
2005	$1,228,882,000	-$12,417,000
2004	$1,040,858,000	-$31,580,000

Curr. Assets:	$645,449,000	Curr. Liab.:	$286,381,000	P/E Ratio:	12.87
Plant, Equip.:	$134,437,000	Total Liab.:	$319,895,000	Indic. Yr. Divd.:	NA
Total Assets:	$801,462,000	Net Worth:	$481,567,000	Debt/ Equity:	NA

Plug Power Inc

968 Albany-Shaker Rd., Latham, NY, 12110; **PH:** 1-518-782-7700; **Fax:** 1-518-782-9060; *http://* www.plugpower.com; **Email:** investors@plugpower.com

General - Incorporation	DE	Stock - Price on:12/24/2007	$3.11
Employees	316	Stock Exchange	NDQ
Auditor	KPMG LLP	Ticker Symbol	PLUG
Stk Agt	American Stock Transfer & Trust Co.	Outstanding Shares	86,900,000
Counsel	NA	E.P.S.	-$0.65
DUNS No.	NA	Shareholders	NA

Business: The group's principal activities are to design, develop and manufacture on-site electricity generation systems utilizing proton exchange membrane fuel cells for stationary applications. A fuel cell is an electrochemical device that combines hydrogen and oxygen from the air to produce electric power without combustion. The initial product of the company is a fully integrated, grid parallel 5-kilowatt fuel cell system that operates on natural gas. This initial product is being marketed to a select number of customers, including utilities, government entities and the group's distribution partners, ge fuel cell systems llc and dte energy technologies inc.

Primary SIC and add'l.: 3620

CIK No: 0001093691

Subsidiaries: H Power

Officers: Roger B. Saillant/Dir., CEO, Pres./$751,467.00, Gregory A. Silvestri/COO/$521,759.00, Allan S. Greenberg/VP - Sales, David P. Waldek/Interim CFO, Gerard A. Anderson/CFO, Sergey Polikarpov/Dir., Dir. - Outside Affiliated, John F. Elter/CTO/$414,069.00, Paul J. Burton/VP, Country Mgr. - South Africa, Allen K. Bucknam/VP - Strategy, Business Development, William D. Ernst/VP, Chief Scientist, Debra Scheiman/Sr. Manufacturing Engineer, Dustan Skidmore/Sr. Systems Controls, Dan Connelly/Systems Support Technician, Jill Wager/Assist. Controller, Sheila Mattice/Materials Coordinator *(22 Officers included in Index)*

Directors: Roger B. Saillant/Dir., CEO, Pres., Maureen O. Helmer/Dir., Larry G. Garberding/Dir., George C. McNamee/Dir., Douglas Grant/Dir., Peter Woicke/Dir., Lisa Rosenblum/Dir., Sergey Polikarpov/Dir., Dir. - Outside Affiliated, Joel E. Gross/Dir., Sergey L. Batekhin/42/Dir., Joel D. Gross/53/Dir., Gary K. Willis/Dir.

Owners: Mark Sperry, David A. Neumann, Sergey S. Polikarpov, Gary K. Willis, Larry G. Garberding, George C. McNamee, Roger B. Saillant, Smart Hydrogen Inc./34.20%, Gregory A. Silvestri, DTE Energy Company/7.10%, Lisa Rosenblum, Sergey L. Batekhin, John F. Elter, Joel D. Gross, Insiders/43.50% *(19 Owners included in Index)*

Financial Data: Fiscal Year End: 12/31 **Latest Annual Data:** 12/31/2006

Year	Sales	Net Income
2006	$7,836,000	-$50,310,000
2005	$13,486,000	-$51,743,000
2004	$16,141,000	-$46,739,000

Curr. Assets:	$279,281,000	Curr. Liab.:	$12,279,000		
Plant, Equip.:	$18,048,000	Total Liab.:	$13,391,000	Indic. Yr. Divd.:	NA
Total Assets:	$307,920,000	Net Worth:	$294,528,000	Debt/ Equity:	NA

Plum Creek Timber Company Inc

999 Third Ave., Ste. 4300, Seattle, WA, 98104; **PH:** 1-206-467-3600; **Fax:** 1-206-467-3795; *http://* www.plumcreek.com; **Email:** info@plumcreek.com

General - Incorporation DE
Employees 2,000
Auditor Ernst & Young LLP
Stk Agt Computershare Investor Services LLC
Counsel NA
DUNS No. NA

Stock - Price on:12/24/2007 $42.84
Stock Exchange NYSE
Ticker Symbol PCL
Outstanding Shares 176,760,000
E.P.S $1.32
Shareholders NA

Business: The groups principle activity is to provide raw material for the paper and forest products industry. The group operates through two segments namely, Southern resources and Northern resources. The group acquired 98,000 acres of timberlands in the year 2006 and 754,000 acres of timberlands in the year 2005. The group operates from the United States. The group's quarterly revenue for sept 2007 was 407.00 millions of USD.

Primary SIC and add'l.: 2421 6552 0811 2431 2436 6798 2411 2435

CIK No: 0000849213

Subsidiaries: B & C Water Resources, Inc., B & C Water Resources, L.L.C., Cypress Creek Ranch, L.L.C., Escanaba Timberlands Holding IV, L.L.C., Highland Resources Inc., PC Timberland Investment Company, Plum Creek Investment Company, Plum Creek Land Company, Plum Creek Maine Marketing, Inc., Plum Creek Maine Timberlands, L.L.C., Plum Creek Manufacturing Holding Company, Inc., Plum Creek Manufacturing, L.P., Plum Creek Marketing, Inc., Plum Creek MDF, Inc., Plum Creek Northwest Lumber, Inc. 24 Subsidiaries included in the Index

Officers: Rick R. Holley/Dir., CEO, Pres./$4,629,999.00, John Hobbs/Dir. - Investor Relations, Bob Jirsa/Dir. - Corporate Affairs, Thomas M. Lindquist/COO, Exec. VP/$1,596,649.00, James A. Kilberg/Sr. VP - Real Estate, Land Management/$969,280.00, James A. Kraft/Sr. VP, General Counsel, Sec., David W. Lambert/CFO, Sr. VP/$789,993.00, Robin Keegan/Sr. Mgr. - Communications, Larry D. Neilson/Sr. VP - Planning, Business Development, David A. Brown/VP, Chief Accounting Officer, Barbara L. Crowe/VP - Human Resources, Joan K. Fitzmaurice/VP - Audit, Financial Services, Russell Hagen/VP - Real Estate, Robert J. Olszewski/VP - Environmental Affairs, Thomas M. Reed/VP, GM - Southern Resources *(17 Officers included in Index)*

Directors: Rick R. Holley/Dir., CEO, Pres., Ian B. Davidson/Chmn., Robin Josephs/Dir., John G. McDonald/Dir., Robert B. McLeod/Dir., John F. Morgan/Dir., John H. Scully/Dir., Stephen C. Tobias/Dir., Carl B. Webb/58/Dir., Martin A. White/Dir.

Owners: Carl B. Webb, Robin Josephs, Insiders, John F. Morgan, Thomas M. Lindquist, Barclays Global Investors, NA/5.39%, Stephen C. Tobias, James A. Kilberg, Ian B. Davidson, Robert B. McLeod, Rick R. Holley, John H. Scully, John G. McDonald, Martin A. White, David W. Lambert

Financial Data: *Fiscal Year End:*12/31 *Latest Annual Data:* 12/31/2006

Year	Sales	Net Income
2006	$1,627,000,000	$317,000,000
2005	$1,576,000,000	$354,000,000
2004	$1,528,000,000	$362,000,000

Curr. Assets:	$513,000,000	**Curr. Liab.:**	$281,000,000		
Plant, Equip.:	$4,103,000,000	**Total Liab.:**	$2,572,000,000	**Indic. Yr. Divd.:**	$1.680
Total Assets:	$4,661,000,000	**Net Worth:**	$2,089,000,000	**Debt/ Equity:**	NA

Plumas Bancorp

35 S Lindan Ave., Quincy, CA, 95971; *PH:* 1-530-283-7305; *Fax:* 1-530-283-3557; *http://* www.plumasbank.com

General - Incorporation CA
Employees 181
Auditor Perry-Smith LLP
Stk Agt U.S. Stock Transfer Corp
Counsel NA
DUNS No. NA

Stock - Price on:12/24/2007 $12.9
Stock Exchange NDQ
Ticker Symbol PLBC
Outstanding Shares 4,990,000
E.P.S $0.93
Shareholders NA

Business: The group's principal activity is to provide a wide range of commercial and consumer banking services. The services include checking and savings accounts, ira accounts, certificates of deposit and direct deposit of social security, pension and payroll checks and Internet banking. The group also provides commercial, construction, inventory, automobile, home improvement, real estate, commercial real estate, single family mortgage, agricultural, small business administration, office equipment, leasehold improvement, installment and credit card loans. The other special services and products include both personal and business checking products, business cash management products and mortgage products and services. The group also provides investment and insurance services. The group operates twelve branch offices in California.

Primary SIC and add'l.: 6022

CIK No: 0001168455

Subsidiaries: Plumas Bank

Officers: Douglas N. Biddle/Dir., CEO, Pres./$381,350.00, Robert T. Herr/59/Exec. VP, Loan Administrator - Plumas Bank/$275,489.00, Andrew J. Ryback/Exec. VP, CFO - Plumas Bancorp, Plumas Bank/$188,759.00, Dennis C. Irvine/Exec. VP - Cito, Plumas Bank/$246,570.00, Monetta R. Dembosz/Sr. VP, Operations Mgr./$151,814.00

Directors: Douglas N. Biddle/Dir., CEO, Pres., Daniel E. West/Chmn., Terrance J. Reeson/Vice Chmn., William E. Elliott/Dir., Gerald W. Fletcher/Dir., Christine McArthur/Dir., Arthur C. Grohs/Dir., Alvin G. Blickenstaff/Dir., John Flournoy/Dir., Jerry V. Kehr/Dir., Thomas Watson/Dir.

Owners: Andrew J. Ryback, Robert T. Herr, Insiders/15.20%, Arthur Grohs, Daniel E. West/1.10%, Jerry V. Kehr/4.30%, Dennis C. Irvine, John Flournoy, William E. Elliott/3.70%, Alvin G. Blickenstaff/1.60%, Christine McArthur, Tom Watson, Douglas N. Biddle/1.30%, Cortopassi/9.70%, Monetta R. Dembosz *(18 Owners included in Index)*

Financial Data: *Fiscal Year End:*12/31 *Latest Annual Data:* 12/31/2006

Year	Sales	Net Income
2006	$34,642,000	$5,202,000
2005	$30,158,000	$4,528,000
2004	$24,894,000	$3,646,000

Curr. Assets:	$20,491,000	**Curr. Liab.:**	$427,077,000	**P/E Ratio:**	13.16
Plant, Equip.:	$15,190,000	**Total Liab.:**	$437,387,000	**Indic. Yr. Divd.:**	$0.300
Total Assets:	$473,239,000	**Net Worth:**	$35,852,000	**Debt/ Equity:**	0.2822

Pluristem Life Systems Inc

MATAM Advanced Technology Pk., No. 20, Haifa, 31905; *PH:* 972-48501080; *Fax:* 972-48501085; *http://* www.pluristem.com; *Email:* info@pluristem.com

General - Incorporation NV
Employees NA
Auditor Kost, Forer, Gabbay & Kassierer
Stk Agt Nevada Agency & Trust Company
Counsel NA
DUNS No. NA

Stock - Price on:12/24/2007 $0.114
Stock Exchange OTC
Ticker Symbol PLRS
Outstanding Shares NA
E.P.S NA
Shareholders NA

Business: The groups principal activities include developing the stem cell production technology and the commercializing of cell therapy products. The product of the group includes PLX-I. PLX-I. The group operates from the United States.

Primary SIC and add'l.: 2836

CIK No: 0001158780

Subsidiaries: Pluristem, Ltd

Officers: Zami Aberman/Acting Chmn., CEO, Pres., Yaky Yanay/VP - Finance, CFO, William R. Prather/Sr. VP - Corporate Development, Shai Meretzki/Founder, CTO, Ora Burger/VP - Development, Daya Lettvin/Dir. - Quality Assurance

Directors: Zami Aberman/Acting Chmn., CEO, Pres., Jacob M. Rowe/Chmn. - Scientific Advisory Board, Mark Germain/Co - Chmn., Abraham Treves/Member - Scientific Advisory Board, Arnon Nagler/Member - Scientific Advisory Board, Avinoam Kadouri/Member - Scientific Advisory Board, Edwin M. Horwitz/Member - Scientific Advisory Board, Israel Ben-Yoram/Dir., Have Klemperer Meretzki/Dir., Shai Meretzki/Founder, CTO, Doron Shorrer/Dir., Isaac Braun/Dir.

Owners: Mark Germain/1.50%, Zami Aberman/2.10%, Doron Shorrer, Insiders/10.00%, Ronald I. Heller/5.00%, Barry C. Honig/7.50%, Wood River Trust/15.00%, Israel Ben-Yoram, Shai Meretzki/4.50%, Jonathan Honig/6.00%, Hava Meretzki, Ora Burger, Isaac Braun, Yaky Yanay/1.00%

PLX Technology Inc

870 Maude Ave., Sunnyvale, CA, 94085; *PH:* 1-408-774-9060; *Fax:* 1-408-774-2169; *http://* www.plxtech.com

General - Incorporation DE
Employees 150
Auditor BDO Seidman LLP
Stk Agt Computershare Ltd.
Counsel NA
DUNS No. NA

Stock - Price on:12/24/2007 $11.04
Stock Exchange NDQ
Ticker Symbol PLXT
Outstanding Shares 28,670,000
E.P.S $0.03
Shareholders NA

Business: The group's principle activity is to develop and supply semiconductor devices that accelerate and manage the transfer of data in networking and telecommunications, enterprise storage, servers, personal computers, imaging and industrial equipment. The group's products include semiconductor devices, software development kits and hardware design kits. The group's semiconductor devices simplify the development of data transfer circuits in high-performance embedded systems and computers and are compatible with microprocessors such as motorola's powerpc, intel's i960 and strongarm, broadcom's mips, pmc-sierra's mips and dsps from companies such as Texas instruments. The group maintains United States direct sales offices in California, Connecticut, Massachusetts, North Carolina and Texas. The group markets its products in Asia, Europe, Taiwan, Singapore, France and North America. The group's quarterly revenue for September 2007 was 21.22 millions of USD.

Primary SIC and add'l.: 3674 7373

CIK No: 0000850579

Subsidiaries: PLX Technology (Europe) Ltd., PLX Technology China, PLX Technology Japan K.K.

Officers: Michael J. Salameh/Dir., CEO, Pres./$783,164.00, David K. Raun/VP - Marketing, Business Development, Lawrence Chisvin/COO/$783,429.00, Hector Berardi/VP - Operations, Jack Regula/CTO, VP, George Apostol/VP - Engineering/$613,768.00, Matt Ready/VP - Worldwide Sales/$689,210.00, Jerry Steach/Contact - Editorial, Art Whipple/CFO, Ken Murray/VP - Human Resources

Directors: Michael J. Salameh/Dir., CEO, Pres., James D. Guzy/Chmn., Pat Verderico/Dir., Tom Riordan/Dir., John H. Hart/Dir., Robert H. Smith/Dir.

Owners: Patrick Verderico, Mazama Capital Management, Inc./7.00%, Kopp Investment Advisors, LLC/7.90%, Robert H. Smith, James D. Guzy/7.70%, Wasatch Investors, Inc./13.00%, Matthew Ready, Neil Gagnon/5.50%, John H. Hart, Thomas Riordan, Lawrence Chisvin, George Apostol, Insiders/9.30%, Michael J. Salameh/1.60%, Stephen Loh

Financial Data: *Fiscal Year End:*12/31 *Latest Annual Data:* 12/31/2006

Year	Sales	Net Income
2006	$81,425,000	$3,006,000
2005	$54,615,000	-$1,748,000
2004	$54,449,000	-$642,000

Curr. Assets:	$56,043,000	**Curr. Liab.:**	$7,012,000	**P/E Ratio:**	276.00
Plant, Equip.:	$28,744,000	**Total Liab.:**	$7,012,000	**Indic. Yr. Divd.:**	NA
Total Assets:	$127,948,000	**Net Worth:**	$120,936,000	**Debt/ Equity:**	NA

PMA Capital Corp

380 Sentry Pkwy., Blue Bell, PA, 19422; *PH:* 1-610-397-5298; *Fax:* 1-610-397-5422; *http://* www.pmacapital.com; *Email:* investorrelations@pmacapital.com

General - Incorporation PA
Employees 1,010
Auditor Beard Miller Co. LLP
Stk Agt American Stock Transfer & Trust Co.
Counsel NA
DUNS No. 11-846-4031

Stock - Price on:12/24/2007 $10.72
Stock Exchange NDQ
Ticker Symbol PMACA
Outstanding Shares 32,630,000
E.P.S NA
Shareholders NA

Business: The group's principal activity is to provide property and casualty insurance. The group's property and casualty insurance segment, the pma insurance group writes workers' compensation, integrated disability and other commercial property and casualty lines of insurance primarily in the eastern part of the United States. The group also provides a range of other commercial insurance products, including commercial automobile and multi-peril coverages, general liability and related services. On Nov 6, 2003, the group withdrew from the reinsurance business operations, pma re.

Primary SIC and add'l.: 6331 6719

CIK No: 0001041665

Subsidiaries: High Mountain Reinsurance, Ltd., Manufacturers Alliance Insurance Company, Mid-Atlantic States Investment Company, Pennsylvania Manufacturers Association Insurance Company, Pennsylvania Manufacturers Indemnity Company, Pennsylvania Manufacturers International Insurance Ltd., PMA Capital Insurance Company, PMA Holdings Ltd., PMA Insurance SPC, Cayman, PMA Management Corp., PMA Re Management Company

Officers: Vincent T. Donnelly/Dir., CEO, Pres./$1,621,977.00, William E. Hitselberger/CFO, Exec. VP/$856,639.00, Robert L. Pratter/Sr. VP, General Counsel, Sec./$791,835.00

Directors: Vincent T. Donnelly/Dir., CEO, Pres., Neal C. Schneider/63/Chmn., Patricia A. Drago/Dir., John D. Rollins/Dir., L. J. Rowell/Dir., James C. Hellauer/Dir., Richard Lutenski/Dir., Charles T. Freeman/Dir., James F. Malone/Dir., Peter S. Burgess/Dir., Roderic H. Ross/Dir., Gregory J. Driscoll/Dir.

Owners: Edward H. Owlett/2.00%, Roderic H. Ross, William E. Hitselberger, Peter S. Burgess, Owl Creek Asset Management, L.P./9.80%, L. J. Rowell, Joseph H. Foster, James F. Malone, Dimensional Fund Advisors LP/8.32%, Gregory J. Driscoll, John Santulli, NWQ Investment Management Company, LLC/8.70%, Richard DeCoux, James C. Hellauer, Insiders/7.30% *(22 Owners included in Index)*

PMC Commercial Trust

17950 Preston Rd., Ste. 600, Dallas, TX, 75252; *PH:* 1-972-349-3200; *Fax:* 1-972-349-3265; *http://* www.pmctrust.com; *Email:* pmctinfo@pmctrust.com

General - Incorporation	TX	**Stock** - Price on:12/24/2007	$13.88
Employees	45	Stock Exchange	AMEX
Auditor	PricewaterhouseCoopers LLP	Ticker Symbol	PCC
Stk Agt	NA	Outstanding Shares	10,750,000
Counsel	NA	E.P.S.	$1.25
DUNS No.	NA	Shareholders	NA

Business: The group operates through its subsidiaries whose principle activity is to provide loans. The group operates from the United States. The groups quarterly revenue for September 2007 was 7.49 millions of USD.

Primary SIC and add'l.: 6798

CIK No: 0000908311

Subsidiaries: First Western SBLC, Inc., PMC Asset Holding, LLC, PMC Capital Corp. 1998-1, PMC Capital Corp. 1999-1, PMC Capital, L.P. 1998-1, PMC Capital, L.P. 1999-1, PMC Commercial Trust, Ltd. 1998-1, PMC Conduit, L.P., PMC Conduit, LLC, PMC Funding Corp., PMC Investment Corporation, PMC Joint Venture LLC 2000, PMC Joint Venture LLC 2001, PMC Joint Venture LLC 2002-1, PMC Joint Venture LLC 2003-1 28 Subsidiaries included in the Index

Officers: Lance B. Rosemore/CEO, Sec./$502,367.00, Barry N. Berlin/47/CFO/$355,414.00, Andrew S. Rosemore/61/COO, Exec. VP, Treasurer/$464,806.00, Jan F. Salit/57/Exec. VP, Chief Investment Officer, Assist. Sec./$354,838.00, Ron H. Dekelbaum/38/General Counsel/$179,828.00, Martha R. Greenberg/56/Trust Mgr.

Directors: Andrew S. Rosemore/61/COO, Exec. VP, Treasurer, Jan F. Salit/57/Exec. VP, Chief Investment Officer, Assist. Sec., Nathan G. Cohen/62/Dir., Roy H. Greenberg/50/Dir., Irving Munn/59/Dir., Ira Silver/62/Dir.

Owners: Martha R. Greenberg/3.50%, Ron H. Dekelbaum, Barry N. Berlin, Jan F. Salit, Roy H. Greenberg, Lance B. Rosemore/2.00%, Nathan G. Cohen, Barry A. Imber, Irving Munn, Andrew S. Rosemore/5.10%, Ira Silver, Insiders/11.80%

Financial Data: Fiscal Year End:12/31 **Latest Annual Data:** 12/31/2006

Year	Sales	Net Income
2006	$30,677,000	$15,684,000
2005	$25,584,000	$11,297,000
2004	$25,359,000	$24,781,000

Curr. Assets:	$5,322,000	**Curr. Liab.:**	$7,626,000		
Plant, Equip.:	$4,414,000	**Total Liab.:**	$83,113,000	**Indic. Yr. Divd.:**	$1.200
Total Assets:	$240,404,000	**Net Worth:**	$157,291,000	**Debt/ Equity:**	0.4122

PMC Sierra Inc

3975 Freedom Cir., Santa Clara, CA, 95054; *PH:* 1-408-239-8000; *Fax:* 1-408-492-1157; *http://* www.pmc-sierra.com; *Email:* investor_relations@pmc-sierra.com

General - Incorporation	DE	**Stock** - Price on:12/24/2007	$8
Employees	1,183	Stock Exchange	NDQ
Auditor	Deloitte & Touche LLP	Ticker Symbol	PMCS
Stk Agt	American Stock Transfer & Trust Co.	Outstanding Shares	213,660,000
Counsel	Wilson Sonsini Goodrich & Rosati	E.P.S.	-$0.43
DUNS No.	10-276-5476	Shareholders	NA

Business: The group's principle activity is to design, develop, market and support high-speed broadband communications and storage semiconductors and mips-based processors for service provider, enterprise, storage, and wireless networking equipment. The group has two operating segments: the networking segment consists of internetworking semiconductor devices and related technical service and support to equipment manufacturers for use in their communications and networking equipment. The non-networking segment consists of a single medical device. The group offers worldwide technical and sales support through a network of offices in North America, Europe and Asia. The group's quarterly revenue for September 2007 was 117.45 millions of USD.

Primary SIC and add'l.: 3674

CIK No: 0000767920

Subsidiaries: PMC-Sierra Europe Ltd., PMC-Sierra International Inc, PMC-Sierra Ireland Limited, PMC-Sierra Ltd, PMC-Sierra US, Inc

Officers: Robert L. Bailey/Chmn., CEO, Pres./$1,251,730.00, Alan F. Krock/47/VP - Corporate Affairs/$677,516.00, Victor Vaisleib/VP, GM, Colin C. Harris/COO, VP/$610,191.00, Tom Sun/VP - Asia Pacific Operations, Alinka Flaminia/VP, General Counsel, Corp. Sec., Robert Yung/CTO, VP, Ben Naskar/53/VP, GM, Mark C. Stibitz/VP, GM - Enterprise, Storage Division/$560,265.00, Robert M. Liszt/VP - Worldwide Sales/$578,247.00, Arun Bellary/VP - India Operations, MD - PMC, Sierra India Pvt Ltd, Steve Cadigan/VP - Worldwide Human Resources, Brian Gerson/VP - Fellow, Research, Development, Michael W. Zellner/CFO, VP, Ra'ed O. Elmurib/VP, GM - Microprocessor Products Division

Directors: Robert L. Bailey/Chmn., CEO, Pres., William H. Kurtz/Dir., Frank J. Marshall/Dir., Richard E. Belluzzo/Dir., Jonathan J. Judge/Dir., James V. Diller/Founder, Michael R. Farese/Dir.

Owners: Robert L. Bailey/1.92%, Capital Research and Management Company/6.57%, Richard E. Belluzzo, Colin C. Harris, FMR Corp./14.94%, Jonathan J. Judge, T. Rowe Price Associates, Inc/11.58%, Insiders/5.35% Adage Capital Partners, L.P./6.71%, William H. Kurtz, Mark C. Stibitz, Alan F. Krock, Frank J. Marshall, Michael R. Farese, James V. Diller/1.15%

Financial Data: Fiscal Year End:12/31 **Latest Annual Data:** 12/31/2006

Year	Sales	Net Income
2006	$424,992,000	-$99,892,000
2005	$291,411,000	$27,986,000
2004	$297,383,000	$51,681,000

Curr. Assets:	$347,886,000	**Curr. Liab.:**	$155,740,000		
Plant, Equip.:	$18,904,000	**Total Liab.:**	$436,129,000	**Indic. Yr. Divd.:**	NA
Total Assets:	$1,006,557,000	**Net Worth:**	$570,428,000	**Debt/ Equity:**	0.3900

PMI Group Inc (The)

3003 Oak Rd. , Walnut Creek, CA, 94597; *PH:* 1-925-658-7878; *http://* www.pmigroup.com

General - Incorporation	DE	**Stock** - Price on:12/24/2007	$47.24
Employees	1,000	Stock Exchange	NYSE
Auditor	Ernst & Young LLP	Ticker Symbol	PMI
Stk Agt	American Stock Transfer & Trust Co.	Outstanding Shares	86,890,000
Counsel	NA	E.P.S.	$2.33
DUNS No.	83-553-4066	Shareholders	NA

Business: The group's principle activity is to provide credit enhancement & other products that promote homeownership and facilitate mortgage transactions in the capital markets. It operates its business in four segments, us mortgage insurance operations: offers mortgage insurance products in the us. International operations: offers mortgage insurance and other credit enhancement products in Europe, Australia, New Zealand and Hong Kong. Financial guaranty: the group's subsidiary fgic corp provides financial guaranty insurance. Other: consists of holding company and contract underwriting revenue and expenses, equity in earnings primarily from unconsolidated strategic investment fairbanks. In oct 2003, the group reached a definitive agreement to sell its subsidiary American pioneer title insurance company. The group's quarterly revenue for September 2007 was 286.97 millions of USD.

Primary SIC and add'l.: 6351

CIK No: 0000935724

Subsidiaries: CMG Mortgage Assurance Company, CMG Mortgage Insurance Company, CMG Mortgage Reinsurance Company, FGIC Corporation, PMI Capital Corporation, PMI Indemnity Limited, PMI Insurance Services Limited, PMI Mortgage Guaranty Co., PMI Mortgage Insurance Australia (Holdings) Pty Limited, PMI Mortgage Insurance Co., PMI Mortgage Insurance Company Limited, PMI Mortgage Insurance Ltd, PMI Plaza LLC, RAM Holdings II Ltd, RAM Holdings Ltd 20 Subsidiaries included in the Index

Officers: Stephen L. Smith/58/Chmn., CEO/$4,475,927.00, Ian Graham/Group CEO, Sr. VP - PMI Mortgage Insurance Ltd, PMI Australia, Janet Martin/CEO, Pres. - PMI Mortgage Insurance Company Canada, Ray D. Chang/Sr. VP, Corporate Treasurer, Lloyd A. Porter/Exec. VP, MD - International MI, PMI Capital Corporation, Andrew D. Cameron/Sr. VP, Deputy General Counsel, Stanley M. Pachura/Sr. VP - Corporate Systems, PMI Mortgage Insurance Co, Charles J. Starkovich/Sr. VP - Systems Development, Enterprise Architecture, PMI Mortgage Insurance Co, Jan Walker/Sr. VP - Structured Transactions, Structured Product Development, PMI Mortgage Insurance Co, PMI US, Pete Pannes/Sr. VP - Field Sales, National Accounting, PMI Mortgage Insurance Co, Kosta Karmaniolas/Sr. Financial Analyst, Bill Horning/VP - Investor Relations, Victor J. Bacigalupi/Exec. VP, Chief Administrative Officer, General Counsel, Sec./$2,051,706.00, Glen S. Corso/Group Sr. VP - Public Policy, Bradley M. Shuster/Pres. - International, Strategic Investments/$2,214,346.00 *(27 Officers included in Index)*

Directors: Stephen L. Smith/58/Chmn., CEO, James C. Castle/71/Dir., John D. Roach/64/Dir., Kenneth T. Rosen/59/Dir., Ronald H. Zech/Dir., Louis G. Lower/62/Dir., Steven L. Scheid/54/Dir., Jose H. Villarreal/55/Dir., Raymond L. Ocampo/55/Dir., Carmine Guerro/66/Dir., Mariann Byerwalter/47/Dir., Mary Lee Widener/69/Dir., Wayne E. Hedien/74/Dir.

Owners: Insiders/3.92%, Ronald H. Zech, FMR CORP./10.50%, Victor J. Bacigalupi, Bradley M. Shuster, James C. Castle, ClearBridge Advisors, LLC./10.10%, Mary Lee Widener, Kenneth T. Rosen, Mariann Byerwalter, David H. Katkov, Raymond L. Ocampo, Louis G. Lower, Carmine Guerro, Wayne E. Hedien *(21 Owners included in Index)*

Financial Data: Fiscal Year End:12/31 **Latest Annual Data:** 12/31/2006

Year	Sales	Net Income
2006	$1,206,037,000	$419,651,000
2005	$1,117,783,000	$409,169,000
2004	$1,038,236,000	$399,333,000

Curr. Assets:	$602,816,000	**Curr. Liab.:**	$44,262,000	**P/E Ratio:**	10.59
Plant, Equip.:	$174,128,000	**Total Liab.:**	$1,751,556,000	**Indic. Yr. Divd.:**	$0.210
Total Assets:	$5,320,146,000	**Net Worth:**	$3,568,590,000	**Debt/ Equity:**	0.1354

PNC Financial Services Group Inc

1 PNC Plz., 249 5th Ave., Pittsburgh, PA, 15222; *PH:* 1-412-762-2000; *Fax:* 1-412-762-7829; *http://* www.pncbank.com

General - Incorporation	PA	**Stock** - Price on:12/24/2007	$74.92
Employees	21,455	Stock Exchange	NYSE
Auditor	Deloitte & Touche LLP	Ticker Symbol	PNC
Stk Agt	Computershare Investor Services LLC	Outstanding Shares	344,920,000
Counsel	NA	E.P.S.	$5.12
DUNS No.	05-798-0500	Shareholders	NA

Business: The groups principle activity is to provide diversified financial services. The groups services include on line banking, cards, insurance and loans. The group operates through three segments namely espanol, students banking and work place banking. The group operates from United States.

Primary SIC and add'l.: 6712 6162 6021

CIK No: 0000713676

Subsidiaries: PNC Bank Capital Securities, LLC, PNC Capital Leasing, LLC, PNC Funding Corp, Pnc Reit Corp., PNC Venture Corp

Officers: James E. Rohr/Chmn., CEO/$18,070,530.00, Richard J. Johnson/CFO, Sr. VP/$1,900,272.00, Michael J. Hannon/Sr. VP, Chief Credit Policy Officer, Helen P. Pudlin/Sr. VP, General Counsel, John J. Wixted/Sr. VP, Chief Compliance, Regulatory Officer, William E. Rosner/Chief Human Resources Officer, Samuel R. Patterson/49/Sr. VP, Controller, Timothy G. Shack/CIO, Exec. VP/$5,942,093.00, Thomas K. Whitford/Exec. VP, Chief Risk Officer, Joseph C. Guyaux/Pres./$7,915,677.00, William H. Callihan/Sr. VP, Dir. - Investor Relations

Directors: James E. Rohr/Chmn., CEO, William S. Demchak/Vice Chmn., William C. Mutterperl/Vice Chmn., Paul W. Chellgren/Dir., Robert N. Clay/Dir., George A. Davidson/Dir., Richard O. Berndt/Dir., Charles E. Bunch/Dir., Donald J. Shepard/Dir., Jane G. Pepper/Dir., Lorene K. Steffes/Dir., Dennis F. Strigl/Dir., Stephen G. Thieke/Dir., Thomas J. Usher/Dir., George H. Walls/Dir. *(20 Directors included in Index)*

Owners: William S. Demchak, George A. Davidson, Robert N. Clay, Anthony A. Massaro, Bruce C. Lindsay, Kay C. James, Timothy G. Shack, Thomas J. Usher, Lorene K. Steffes, Helge H. Wehmeier, Jane G. Pepper, George H. Walls, Stephen G. Thieke, Insiders, Paul W. Chellgren *(22 Owners included in Index)*

Financial Data: Fiscal Year End:12/31 **Latest Annual Data:** 12/31/2006

Year	Sales	Net Income
2006	$11,146,000,000	$2,595,000,000
2005	$7,937,000,000	$1,325,000,000
2004	$6,315,000,000	$1,197,000,000

Curr. Assets:	$8,416,000,000	Curr. Liab.:	$75,033,000,000	P/E Ratio:	8.35
Plant, Equip.:	NA	Total Liab.:	$90,147,000,000	Indic. Yr. Divd.:	$2.520
Total Assets:	$101,820,000,000	Net Worth:	$10,788,000,000	Debt/ Equity:	NA

PNG Venture Inc

2038 Corte Del Nogal, Ste. 110, Carlsbad, CA, 92011; *PH:* 1-760-804-8844

General - Incorporation	NV	**Stock** - Price on:12/24/2007	$0.55
Employees	1	Stock Exchange	OTC
Auditor	Chisholm, Bierwolf & Nilson, LLC	Ticker Symbol	PNGX
Stk Agt	Madison Stock Transfer, Inc.	Outstanding Shares	NA
Counsel	NA	E.P.S.	-$2.55
DUNS No.	NA	Shareholders	NA

Business: The groups principal activity is engaged in the business of edgarizing. Edgarizing is the process of electronically converting typically Microsoft Word documents into HTML. The group operates from the United States.

Primary SIC and add'l.: 6770

CIK No: 0001016900

Officers: Mark L. Baum/35/Chmn., CEO, CFO, Pres., Sec.

Directors: Mark L. Baum/35/Chmn., CEO, CFO, Pres., Sec.

Owners: Mark L. Baum/29.90%, Insiders/57.50%, Firle Trading, S.A./28.60%

Financial Data: Fiscal Year End:12/31   Latest Annual Data: 12/31/2006

Year	Sales	Net Income
2006	NA	-$460,000
2005	NA	-$319,000
2004	NA	-$151,000

Curr. Assets:	NA	Curr. Liab.:	$250,000		
Plant, Equip.:	NA	Total Liab.:	$430,000	Indic. Yr. Divd.:	NA
Total Assets:	NA	Net Worth:	-$430,000	Debt/ Equity:	NA

PNM Resources Inc

Alvarado Sq., Albuquerque, NM, 87158; *PH:* 1-505-241-2700; *Fax:* 1-505-241-2367; *http://* www.pnmresources.com

General - Incorporation	NM	**Stock** - Price on:12/24/2007	$27.43
Employees	3,294	Stock Exchange	NYSE
Auditor	Deloitte & Touche LLP	Ticker Symbol	PNM
Stk Agt	Mellon Investor Services LLC	Outstanding Shares	76,690,000
Counsel	NA	E.P.S.	$1.22
DUNS No.	NA	Shareholders	NA

Business: The groups principle activity is to deliver energy. The group operates from United States.

Primary SIC and add'l.: 4911 4932

CIK No: 0001108426

Subsidiaries: FCP Enterprises Inc, First Choice Power Special Purpose, LP, First Choice Power, LP, Public Service Company of New Mexico, Texas-New Mexico Power Company, TNP Enterprises, Inc.

Officers: Jeff Sterba/Chmn., CEO/$3,599,729.00, Ernie C'De Baca/VP - Governmental Affairs, Tom Sategna/VP, Corporate Controller, Hugh Smith/50/Sr. VP - Energy Resources, Charles Eldred/CFO, Sr. VP/$771,343.00, William J. Real/Sr. VP - Public Policy, Tom Olesen/VP - Supply Chain, Patrick Ortiz/Sr. VP, General Counsel/$857,652.00, Alice A. Cobb/Sr. VP, Chief Administrative Officer/$898,496.00, Cindy McGill/Sr. VP - Public Policy, Strategy, Joanne Reuter/VP, Deputy General Counsel, Corp. Sec., Jim Ferland/Sr. VP - Energy Resources, Terry Horn/VP - Customer Service, Pat Vincent/Utilities Pres., Frederick Bermudez/Analyst *(23 Officers included in Index)*

Directors: Jeff Sterba/Chmn., CEO, Robert R. Nordhaus/Dir., Adelmo E. Archuleta/Dir., Julie A. Dobson/Dir., Woody L. Hunt/Dir., Charles E. McMahen/Dir., Manuel T. Pacheco/Dir., Robert M. Price/Dir., Bonnie S. Reitz/Dir., Joan B. Woodard/Dir.

Owners: Bonnie S. Reitz, Julie A. Dobson, Charles N. Eldred, Insiders/1.40%, Charles E. McMahen, Joan B. Woodard, Terry R. Horn, Woody L. Hunt, Robert M. Price, Jeffry E. Sterba, Patrick T. Ortiz, Adelmo E. Archuleta, Manuel T. Pacheco, Alice A. Cobb, William J. Real

Financial Data: Fiscal Year End:12/31   Latest Annual Data: 12/31/2005

Year	Sales	Net Income
2005	$2,076,810,000	$67,227,000
2004	$1,604,792,000	$87,686,000
2003	$1,455,714,000	$95,173,000

Curr. Assets:	$596,297,000	Curr. Liab.:	$723,496,000	P/E Ratio:	15.86
Plant, Equip.:	$2,988,306,000	Total Liab.:	$3,826,721,000	Indic. Yr. Divd.:	$0.920
Total Assets:	$5,124,709,000	Net Worth:	$1,297,988,000	Debt/ Equity:	NA

Pogo Producing Co

5 Greenway Plz., Houston, TX, 77252; *PH:* 1-713-297-5000; *http://* www.pogoproducing.com

General - Incorporation	DE	**Stock** - Price on:12/24/2007	$54.06
Employees	566	Stock Exchange	NA
Auditor	PricewaterhouseCoopers LLP	Ticker Symbol	NA
Stk Agt	Computershare Investor Services LLC	Outstanding Shares	58,490,000
Counsel	NA	E.P.S.	-$0.85
DUNS No.	05-361-8104	Shareholders	NA

Business: The group's principle activities include exploring and producing oil and natural gas. The group operates from United States.

Primary SIC and add'l.: 1321 1311 4922

CIK No: 0000230463

Subsidiaries: Bennett Energy Partnership, Northrock Energy,Inc., Northrock Resources Partnership, Northrock Resources, Ltd., Pogo Alberta, ULC, Pogo Denmark ApS, Pogo Energy,Inc., Pogo Finance, ULC, Pogo New Zealand, Pogo North Sea Limited, Pogo Offshore Pipeline Co., Pogo Overseas Production B.V., Pogo Panhandle 2004, L.P., Pogo Partners,Inc., Pogo Producing 18 Subsidiaries included in the Index

Officers: Paul G. Van Wagenen/Chmn., CEO, Pres./$9,151,116.00, Bruce E. Archinal/Sr. VP, Regional Mgr. - Gulf Coast, John O. McCoy/Exec. VP, Chief Administrative Officer/$1,886,585.00, Phillip R. Laney/Sr. VP, Mgr. - Worldwide New Ventures, Michael J. Killelea/Sr. VP, General Counsel, Corp. Sec., Clay P. Jeansonne/VP - Investor Relations, J. D. McGregor/Sr. VP - Sales, Gerald A. Morton/Sr. VP, Regional Mgr. - Asia Pacific, Robert C. Marlowe/VP - Accounting, Stephen R. Brunner/Exec. VP - Operations/$1,562,894.00, Jerry A. Cooper/Exec. VP, Regional Mgr. - Western United States/$2,270,069.00, James P. Ulm/CFO, Sr. VP/$1,141,572.00, Frank Davis/VP - Land, David R. Beathard/Sr. VP - Engineering, Leah D. Smith/VP - Acquisitions *(16 Officers included in Index)*

Directors: Paul G. Van Wagenen/Chmn., CEO, Pres., Jerry M. Armstrong/Dir., Carroll W. Suggs/Dir., Thomas A. Fry/Dir., Charles G. Goat/Dir., Stephen A. Wells/Dir., Daniel S. Loeb/Dir., Bradley L. Radoff/Dir., Gerrit W. Gong/Dir., Robert H. Campbell/Dir.

Owners: Jerry M. Armstrong, TRT Holdings, Inc./9.20%, James P. Ulm, Klingenstein, Fields & Co., L.L.C./5.30%, John O. McCoy, Robert H. Campbell, Charles G. Groat, Paul G. Van Wagenen/1.30%, State Farm Mutual Automobile Insurance Company/9.50%, Third Point LLC/7.90%, Carroll W. Suggs, Stephen R. Brunner, Insiders/10.50%, Daniel S. Loeb/7.90%, PRIMECAP Management Company/10.60% *(20 Owners included in Index)*

Financial Data: Fiscal Year End:12/31   Latest Annual Data: 12/31/2006

Year	Sales	Net Income
2006	$1,745,000,000	$446,200,000
2005	$1,225,699,000	$750,703,000
2004	$1,322,979,000	$261,754,000

Curr. Assets:	$368,200,000	Curr. Liab.:	$401,800,000		
Plant, Equip.:	$6,557,100,000	Total Liab.:	$4,403,700,000	Indic. Yr. Divd.:	$0.300
Total Assets:	$6,971,100,000	Net Worth:	$2,567,400,000	Debt/ Equity:	0.9024

Point 360

2777 N Ontario St., Burbank, CA, 91504; *PH:* 1-818-565-1440; *http://* www.point360.com

General - Incorporation	CA	**Stock** - Price on:12/24/2007	$5.9
Employees	440	Stock Exchange	NDQ
Auditor	Holthouse Carlin & Van Trigt, LLP	Ticker Symbol	PTSX
Stk Agt	American Stock Transfer & Trust Co.	Outstanding Shares	9,980,000
Counsel	NA	E.P.S.	$0.02
DUNS No.	61-595-5333	Shareholders	NA

Business: The group's principal activities are to provide video and film asset management services to owners, producers and distributors of entertainment and advertising content. The group provides the services necessary to edit, master, reformat, archive and distribute its clients' audio and video content, including television programming, feature films, spot advertising and movie trailers. The group provides electronic distribution, using fiber optics, satellites and the Internet. The group markets its services to motion picture and television production companies, advertising agencies, television program suppliers, national television networks, infomercial providers, local television stations, television program syndicators, corporations and educational institutions. The group markets its services through industry referrals, formal advertising, trade shows, special client events and its Internet Website.

Primary SIC and add'l.: 7822 7812 7829

CIK No: 0001014733

Subsidiaries: Alliance Atlantis Communications, Inc.

Officers: Haig S. Bagerdjian/Chmn., CEO, Pres., Alan R. Steel/Exec. VP - Finance, Administration, Mary Kay Berg/Dir. - Human Resources

Directors: Haig S. Bagerdjian/Chmn., CEO, Pres., Robert A. Baker/Dir., Greggory J. Hutchins/Dir., Sam P. Bell/Dir., Samuel G. Oki/Dir.

Owners: Greggory J. Hutchins, Sam P. Bell, Haig S. Bagerdjian, DG FastChannel, Inc., Julia Stefanko, Insiders, Robert A. Baker, Samuel G. Oki, Alan R. Steel

Financial Data: Fiscal Year End:12/31   Latest Annual Data: 12/31/2006

Year	Sales	Net Income
2006	$64,218,000	$76,000
2005	$66,199,000	$14,000
2004	$63,344,000	$1,247,000

Curr. Assets:	$16,789,000	Curr. Liab.:	$13,068,000	P/E Ratio:	295.00
Plant, Equip.:	$14,138,000	Total Liab.:	$22,935,000	Indic. Yr. Divd.:	NA
Total Assets:	$62,956,000	Net Worth:	$40,021,000	Debt/ Equity:	0.1251

Point Blank Solutions Inc

Formerly: DHB Industries Inc

2102 S.w. 2nd St., Pompano Beach, FL, 33069; *PH:* 1-954-630-0900; *http://* www.dhbt.com

General - Incorporation	DE	**Stock** - Price on:12/24/2007	$5.22
Employees	950	Stock Exchange	NA
Auditor	Rachlin Cohen & Holtz, LLP	Ticker Symbol	NA
Stk Agt	American Stock Transfer & Trust Co.	Outstanding Shares	45,340,000
Counsel	NA	E.P.S.	-$0.4
DUNS No.	80-131-6613	Shareholders	NA

Business: The group's principal activities are to develop, manufacture and distribute bullet projectile resistant garment and protective athletic apparel and equipment. The group is a holding company of dhb armor group and dhb sports group. Dhb armor group along with four subsidiaries develops, manufactures and distributes bullet and projectile resistant garments, bullet resistant and fragmentation vests, bomb projectile blankets and related ballistic accessories. Dhb sports group manufactures and distributes protective athletic apparel and equipment, such as elbow, breast, hip, groin, knee, shin and ankle supports and braces, as well as, a line of therapy products through its two subsidiaries.

Primary SIC and add'l.: 2389 6719 3842

CIK No: 0000899166

Subsidiaries: DHB Armor Group, Inc., DHB Sports Group Inc., NDL Products Inc., Point Blank Body Armor Inc., Point Blank International S.A., Protective Apparel Corporation of America

Officers: Larry R. Ellis/62/Dir., CEO, Pres., John C. Siemer/58/COO, Chief - Staff, James F. Anderson/55/Chief Accounting Officer, Sr. VP, Sam White/49/Head - Global Sales

Directors: Larry R. Ellis/62/Dir., CEO, Pres., Senator William Campbell/Chmn., David Bell/65/Dir., Martin R. Berndt/60/Dir., Maurice Hannigan/67/Dir., Jack A. Henry/64/Dir., Suzanne Hopgood/59/Dir.

Owners: Terry S. Brooks/6.00%, Insiders/1.80%, Harbinger Capital Partners Master Fund I, Ltd./14.80%, Maurice Hannigan, Dawn Schlegel, Thomas Canfield, David H. Brooks/23.00%, Sam White, Larry Ellis, James F. Anderson, Martin R. Berndt, Jack A. Henry, Suzanne Hopgood, David Bell, William Campbell *(16 Owners included in Index)*

Financial Data: Fiscal Year End:12/31   Latest Annual Data: 12/31/2004

Year	Sales	Net Income
2004	$340,075,000	$30,435,000
2003	$230,011,000	$15,172,000
2002	$130,347,000	$15,980,000

Curr. Assets:	$142,266,000	Curr. Liab.:	$35,180,000		
Plant, Equip.:	$2,632,000	Total Liab.:	$68,400,000	Indic. Yr. Divd.:	NA
Total Assets:	$145,857,000	Net Worth:	$77,026,000	Debt/ Equity:	0.1179

Point Therapeutics Inc

70 Walnut St., Wellesley Hills, MA, 02481; **PH:** 1-781-239-7502; **Fax:** 1-781-239-8005; *http://* www.pther.com; **Email:** inquiries@pther.com

General - Incorporation	DE	Stock - Price on:12/24/2007	$0.13
Employees	40	Stock Exchange	NDQ
Auditor	Ernst & Young LLP	Ticker Symbol	POTP
Stk Agt	American Stock Transfer & Trust Co.	Outstanding Shares	39,310,000
Counsel	Ropes & Gray LLP	E.P.S.	-$0.468
DUNS No.	82-940-0415	Shareholders	NA

Business: The group's principle activity is to develops small molecule drugs for the treatment of certain hematopoietic disorders and for the treatment of cancer, pt-100, the company's lead product candidate, has the potential to treat a number of different hematopoietic disorders, such as neutropenia (an abnormally low level of a type of white blood cell called neutrophil) and anemia (an abnormally low level of red blood cells). The group operates from United States.

Primary SIC and add'l.: 2835 2836

CIK No: 0000919745

Subsidiaries: HemaPharmInc., Hemasure A/S, Point Therapeutics Massachusetts,Inc.

Officers: Donald R. Kiepert/Founder, Chmn., CEO, Pres., Barry Jones/Chief Scientific Officer, Sr. VP, Michael P. Duffy/Sr. VP, General Counsel, Sec., Richard N. Small/Sr. VP, CFO, Treasurer, David G. Shand/Chief Medical Officer

Directors: Donald R. Kiepert/Founder, Chmn., CEO, Pres., Alfred Goldberg/Member - Scientific Advisory Board, Antonio J. Grillo-Lopez/Member - Advisory Board, Charles A. Dinarello/Member - Scientific Advisory Board, Daniel T. Roble/Dir., Richard Benjamin/Dir., Robert T. Schooley/Member - Scientific Advisory Board, John Nemunaitis/Member - Advisory Board, Paul Allen/Member - Scientific Advisory Board, Michael Gordon/Member - Advisory Board, Ravi Salgia/Member - Advisory Board, Larry G. Pickering/Dir., Thomas Gajewski/Member - Advisory Board, George Demetri/Member - Advisory Board, Timothy J. Barberich/Dir. *(20 Directors included in Index)*

Owners: Timothy J. Barberich, Larry G. Pickering, Donald R. Kiepert/2.94%, Richard J. Benjamin, Daniel T. Roble, Thomas M. Claflin, Barry Jones, Insiders/7.30%, Richard N. Small/1.35%, Michael P. Duffy

Financial Data: Fiscal Year End:12/31   Latest Annual Data: 12/31/2006

Year	Sales	Net Income
2006	$439,000	-$29,365,000
2005	$161,000	-$22,674,000
2004	NA	-$15,158,000

Curr. Assets:	$12,329,000	Curr. Liab.:	$4,580,000		
Plant, Equip.:	$238,000	Total Liab.:	$4,617,000	Indic. Yr. Divd.:	NA
Total Assets:	$12,568,000	Net Worth:	$7,951,000	Debt/ Equity:	NA

Points International Ltd

179 John St., 8th Fl., Toronto, ON, M5T 1X4; **PH:** 1-416-595-0000; **Fax:** 1-416-595-6444; *http://* www.points.com

General - Incorporation	Canada	Stock - Price on:12/24/2007	$1.53
Employees	NA	Stock Exchange	OTC
Auditor	Mintz & Partners LLP	Ticker Symbol	PTSEF
Stk Agt	American Registrar & Transfer Co	Outstanding Shares	NA
Counsel	NA	E.P.S.	NA
DUNS No.	NA	Shareholders	NA

Business: The group's principal activity is to offer a portfolio of solutions, referred to as the Points Solutions, to the loyalty program industry.

Primary SIC and add'l.: 7319

CIK No: 0001204413

Officers: Rob MacLean/CEO, Christopher Barnard/Pres., Peter Lockhard/Sr. VP - Partners, Brian Miller/CIO, Anthony Lam/CFO, Marianne Borenstein/VP - Product, Marketing, Erika Boyd/VP - Human Resources

Directors: Stephen K. Bannon/Chmn., Brian Ladin/Dir., Michael Kestenbaum/Dir., John W. Thompson/Dir., Marc B. Lavine/Dir., Douglas A. Carty/Dir., Jason Rapp/Dir.

Financial Data: Fiscal Year End:12/31   Latest Annual Data: 12/31/2006

Year	Sales	Net Income
2006	$10,509,000	-$6,700,000
2005	$8,604,000	-$8,452,000
2004	$6,469,000	-$7,531,000

Curr. Assets:	$24,991,000	Curr. Liab.:	$21,054,000		
Plant, Equip.:	$2,518,000	Total Liab.:	$37,797,000	Indic. Yr. Divd.:	NA
Total Assets:	$34,736,000	Net Worth:	-$3,061,000	Debt/ Equity:	NA

PokerTek Inc

1020 Crews Rd., Ste. J, Matthews, NC, 28106; **PH:** 1-704-849-0860; *http://* pokertek.com; **Email:** info@pokertek.com

General - Incorporation	NC	Stock - Price on:12/24/2007	$12.54
Employees	69	Stock Exchange	NDQ
Auditor	McGladrey & Pullen, LLP	Ticker Symbol	PTEK
Stk Agt	American Stock Transfer & Trust Co.	Outstanding Shares	10,920,000
Counsel	NA	E.P.S.	-$1.08
DUNS No.	NA	Shareholders	NA

Business: The groups principle activities include developing and marketing the PokerPro system. The groups product is 10-seated table. The group products sold under the trade names PokerPro(R) Heads-Up(TM). Customers served by the group include casinos, commercial casinos, cruise ships and card clubs. Specific customers of the group include Seminole Tribe of Florida and Carnival Corporation and plc. The group operates from the United States.

Primary SIC and add'l.: 7372 7372 3990

CIK No: 0001302177

Officers: Chris Halligan/CEO, Mark Roberson/CFO, James Crawford/Dir., Pres., Hal Shinn/CTO, John Howard/Marketing Research Analyst, Public Relations Writer, Danny Byrd/Mechanical Engineer, Jon Lester/Sr. Software Developer

Directors: Lyle Berman/Chmn., Gehrig White/Vice Chmn., Arthur Lee Lomax/51/Dir., James Crawford/Dir., Pres., Lee Lomax/Dir., Joe Lahti/Dir.

Owners: Arthur Lee Lomax, Aristocrat International Pty. Limited, Lyle Berman, Hal Shinn, Gehrig H. White, Insiders, Joseph J. Lahti, James T. Crawford, Christopher Daniels

Financial Data: Fiscal Year End:12/31   Latest Annual Data: 12/31/2006

Year	Sales	Net Income
2006	$1,980,000	-$9,146,000
2005	$314,000	-$3,701,000
2004	NA	-$926,000

Curr. Assets:	$11,731,000	Curr. Liab.:	$1,003,000		
Plant, Equip.:	$3,046,000	Total Liab.:	$1,003,000	Indic. Yr. Divd.:	NA
Total Assets:	$15,123,000	Net Worth:	$14,120,000	Debt/ Equity:	NA

Polaris Industries Inc

2100 Hwy. 55, Medina, MN, 55340; **PH:** 1-763-542-0500; **Fax:** 1-763-542-0599; *http://* www.polarisindustries.com

General - Incorporation	MN	Stock - Price on:12/24/2007	$54.75
Employees	3,400	Stock Exchange	NYSE
Auditor	Ernst & Young LLP	Ticker Symbol	PII
Stk Agt	Wells Fargo Bank Minnesota N.A	Outstanding Shares	35,760,000
Counsel	Lindquist & Vennum PLLP	E.P.S.	$2.86
DUNS No.	05-169-1673	Shareholders	NA

Business: The groups principle activity is to manufacture all-terrain vehicles, snowmobiles and motorcycles. The group operates from United States.

Primary SIC and add'l.: 2380 3751 3714 3069 3799

CIK No: 0000931015

Subsidiaries: Polaris Acceptance Inc., Polaris Austria GmbH, Polaris Britain Limited, Polaris Direct Inc., Polaris France S.A., Polaris Industries Inc., Polaris Industries Ltd., Polaris Industries Manufacturing LLC, Polaris Insurance Services LLC, Polaris Norway AS, Polaris Sales Australia Pty Ltd., Polaris Sales Inc., Polaris Scandinavia AB

Officers: Thomas C. Tiller/46/Dir., CEO/$2,353,445.00, Bennett J. Morgan/COO, Pres./$855,691.00, Mark E. Blackwell/VP - Victory Motorcycles, International, Mary P. McConnell/VP, General Counsel, John B. Corness/VP - Human Resources/$411,827.00, Michael W. Malone/CFO, VP - Finance, Sec./$280,895.00, Jeffrey A. Bjorkman/VP - Operations/$465,534.00

Directors: Thomas C. Tiller/46/Dir., CEO, Gregory R. Palen/52/Chmn., Robert L. Caulk/56/Dir., Richard A. Zona/63/Dir., John R. Menard/68/Dir., Andris A. Baltins/62/Dir., Annette K. Clayton/44/Dir., William G. Van Dyke/63/Dir., R. M. Schreck/Dir., John P. Wiehoff/46/Dir.

Owners: John R. Menard, Gregory R. Palen, William Grant Van Dyke, R. M. Schreck, Thomas C. Tiller/5.90%, AMVESCAP PLC/14.90%, Annette K. Clayton, Robert L. Caulk, Andris A. Baltins, Richard A. Zona, John B. Corness, Bennett J. Morgan, Barclays Global Investors, N.A./5.20%, Michael W. Malone, Jeffrey A. Bjorkman *(16 Owners included in Index)*

Financial Data: Fiscal Year End:12/31   Latest Annual Data: 12/31/2006

Year	Sales	Net Income
2006	$1,656,518,000	$106,985,000
2005	$1,908,459,000	$143,278,000
2004	$1,773,206,000	$104,504,000

Curr. Assets:	$392,961,000	Curr. Liab.:	$361,420,000	P/E Ratio:	19.08
Plant, Equip.:	$204,001,000	Total Liab.:	$611,420,000	Indic. Yr. Divd.:	$1.360
Total Assets:	$778,791,000	Net Worth:	$167,371,000	Debt/ Equity:	1.4003

Polo Ralph Lauren Corp

650 Madison Ave., New York, NY, 10022; **PH:** 1-212-318-7000; **Fax:** 1-212-888-5780; *http://* www.polo.com

General - Incorporation	DE	Stock - Price on:12/24/2007	$100.56
Employees	14,000	Stock Exchange	NYSE
Auditor	Deloitte & Touche LLP	Ticker Symbol	RL
Stk Agt	Bank of New York	Outstanding Shares	103,960,000
Counsel	NA	E.P.S.	NA
DUNS No.	04-616-9595	Shareholders	NA

Business: The group's principle activities are to design, market, distribute and license men's and women's apparel, accessories, fragrances, skin care products and home furnishings. The group operates through three business segments: wholesale, retail and licensing. The wholesale segment consists of two operating units: polo brands and collection brands. Each unit designs, sources, markets and distributes discrete brands. The retail segment operates two types of stores: outlet and full price stores. The stores sell the products purchased from the wholesale segment. The licensing segment consists of product, international and home generated revenues from royalties through its licensing alliances. The licensing agreement grants the licensee rights to use the various trademarks. The group markets its product in the United States, Europe and other foreign countries. The group's total revenue for year 2007 was 4,295.40 millions of USD.

Primary SIC and add'l.: 5136 5137 5641 5632 5651 6794 5611

CIK No: 0001037038

Subsidiaries: 379 West Broadway Retail, LLC., 41 Jobs Lane, LLC., Acqui Polo CV (Netherlands)., Acqui Polo Espana (Spain)., Acqui Polo GP, LLC, Acqui Polo Limited, LLC, Acqui Polo SAS (France)., Club Monaco (Hong Kong) Limited., Club Monaco Corp. (Nova Scotia)., Club Monaco S.A.M. (Monagescue)., Club Monaco U.S., LLC, Consolidated Polo Retailers, Inc., Fashion Development Corp., Fashions Outlet of America, Inc., Fashions Outlet of Florida, LLC. 116 Subsidiaries included in the Index

Officers: Ralph Lauren/Chmn., CEO/$25,859,760.00, Roger N. Farah/Dir., COO, Pres./$12,546,360.00, Jackwyn L. Nemerov/Dir., Exec. VP/$5,486,213.00, Mitchell A. Kosh/Sr. VP - Human Resources/$1,813,703.00, Tracey T. Travis/CFO, Sr. VP/$2,133,439.00, Jonathan D. Drucker/Sr. VP, General Counsel, Sec.

Directors: Ralph Lauren/Chmn., CEO, Joyce F. Brown/Dir., Judith A. McHale/Dir., Roger N. Farah/Dir., COO, Pres., Terry S. Semel/Dir., Arnold H. Aronson/Dir., Frank A. Bennack/Dir., Joel L. Fleishman/Dir., Steven P. Murphy/Dir., Jackwyn L. Nemerov/Dir., Exec. VP, John R. Alchin/Dir., Robert C. Wright/Dir.

Owners: Frank A. Bennack, Tracey T. Travis, John R. Alchin, Ralph Lauren/2.70%, Joel L. Fleishman, D.E. Shaw & Co., L.P./5.10%, Arnold H. Aronson, Roger N. Farah/1.10%, OppenheimerFunds, Inc./5.40%, Joyce F. Brown, Judith A. McHale, Steven P. Murphy, Insiders/4.40%, Jackwyn L. Nemerov, FMR Corp./8.90% *(19 Owners included in Index)*

Financial Data: *Fiscal Year End:*04/01 *Latest Annual Data:* 3/31/2007

Year	Sales	Net Income
2007	$4,295,400,000	$400,900,000
2006	$3,746,300,000	$308,000,000
2005	$3,305,415,000	$190,425,000

Curr. Assets:	$1,413,763,000	**Curr. Liab.:**	$622,410,000	**P/E Ratio:**	26.39
Plant, Equip.:	$487,894,000	**Total Liab.:**	$1,050,961,000	**Indic. Yr. Divd.:**	NA
Total Assets:	$2,726,669,000	**Net Worth:**	$1,675,708,000	**Debt/ Equity:**	0.1909

Poly-Pacific International Inc

4755 Zinfandel Ct., Unit A, Ontario, CA, 91761; *PH:* 1-909-390-7799; *http://* www.poly-pacific.com; *Email:* poly@poly-pacific.com

General - Incorporation	Canada	**Stock** - Price on:12/24/2007	NA
Employees	NA	Stock Exchange	NA
Auditor	Collins Barrow Edmonton LLP	Ticker Symbol	NA
Stk Agt	Olympia Trust Co	Outstanding Shares	NA
Counsel	David Tam	E.P.S	NA
DUNS No.	NA	Shareholders	NA

Business: The group's activity is to manufacture plastic blasting media. The group serves commercial and industrial customers for applications including paint stripping from aluminum fiberglass and dense hardwood hulls and carbon fiber and graphite composite structure, removing light flash from cast component without affecting critical surface dimensions, coating removal and restoration, mold cleaning, removing carbon deposits and paint from aluminum parts, surface preparation and conditioning applications. The group operates in California.

Primary SIC and add'l.: 2851

CIK No: 0001319149

Subsidiaries: Everwood Agricultural Products International Inc, Poly-Pacific Technologies

Officers: Randy Hayward/Chmn., Pres., David Tam/Dir., Sec., Rick Gliege/COO, Stephen Koltai/VP - International Business Development, Michael Nayyar/Controller, Angus Ross/Dir. - Engineering

Directors: Randy Hayward/Chmn., Pres., Edward J. Chambers/Dir., David Tam/Dir., Sec., Mike Duff/Dir., Richard Oravec/Dir., Greg Pendura/Dir.

Owners: Mike Duff

Polyair Inter Pack Inc

330 Humberline Dr., Toronto, ON, 44502; *PH:* 1-416-679-6600; *http://* www.polyair.com; *Email:* marketing@polyair.com

General - Incorporation	Canada	**Stock** - Price on:12/24/2007	NA
Employees	1,200	Stock Exchange	OTC
Auditor	KPMG LLP	Ticker Symbol	PPKZ
Stk Agt	KPMG LLP	Outstanding Shares	NA
Counsel	NA	E.P.S	NA
DUNS No.	25-353-1099	Shareholders	NA

Business: The group's principle activity is to manufacture protective packaging and swimming pool accessory products. The products are marketed through a select network of 2,500 distributors across North America. The group manufactures a complete line of protective packaging products. The five major categories include durabubble, mailers, starfoam, systems and insulation. Durabubble is used for cushioning, void-filling and surface protection. Mailers combine cushioning with a variety of rugged exteriors. Starfoam is resistant to punctures and tears and helps in surface protection and cushioning. Systems consisting of the airspace inflatable pillow packaging system provides on demand air pillows for cushions and void filling. Insulation are products designed for the residential and commercial construction industry. The group's quarterly revenue for july 2007 was 30.87 millions of USD.

Primary SIC and add'l.: 3089

CIK No: 0001049984

Subsidiaries: C/P International Corporation, Inc., Cantar Pool Products Corporation, Cantar Pool Products Limited, Cantar/Polyair Canada Limited, Cantar/Polyair Corporation, Cantar/Polyair Inc., Faircove Investments Inc, Mabex Universal Corporation, Performa Corporation, PSC Moulding Corporation, PXL Cross linked Foam Corporation

Officers: Stysia Reay/Shareholder Administrator

Financial Data: *Fiscal Year End:*10/31 *Latest Annual Data:* 10/31/2005

Year	Sales	Net Income
2005	$196,174,000	-$15,669,000
2004	$191,656,000	$977,000
2003	$142,776,000	$4,664,000

Curr. Assets:	$57,846,000	**Curr. Liab.:**	$73,055,000		
Plant, Equip.:	$38,749,000	**Total Liab.:**	$77,651,000	**Indic. Yr. Divd.:**	NA
Total Assets:	$101,364,000	**Net Worth:**	$23,713,000	**Debt/ Equity:**	NA

Polycom Inc

4750 Willow Rd., Pleasanton, CA, 94588; *PH:* 1-925-924-6000; *Fax:* 1-925-924-6100; *http://* www.polycom.com

General - Incorporation	DE	**Stock** - Price on:12/24/2007	$34.1
Employees	1,727	Stock Exchange	NDQ
Auditor	PricewaterhouseCoopers LLP	Ticker Symbol	PLCM
Stk Agt	Computershare Ltd.	Outstanding Shares	91,690,000
Counsel	Wilson Sonsini Goodrich & Rosati	E.P.S	$0.70
DUNS No.	62-344-8073	Shareholders	NA

Business: The group's principle activities are to develop, manufacture, market and service video, voice, data and Web conferencing collaboration solutions. The group operates in two segments: communications and network systems. Communication segment includes videoconferencing collaboration products that facilitates video communications; desktop, conference, analog, digital and ip voice communications products. Network systems segment provides network infrastructure to facilitate video, voice and data conferencing and collaboration capabilities. The customer base of the group includes government, businesses, telecommunications service providers, and educational institutions. These sales are made through network of channel partners, which includes communications service providers, value-added resellers, distributors and retailers. In 2003, the group discontinued and sold the network access segment. The group's quarterly revenue for September 2007 was 240.05 millions of USD.

Primary SIC and add'l.: 4813 3661 4810

CIK No: 0001010552

Subsidiaries: 1414c Inc., A.S.P.I Digital, Inc., Accord Networks (UK) Ltd., Accord Networks Management, Inc., Accord Networks, Inc., Beijing Bing Fei Communications Technology Co., Ltd., Beijing Polycom Communications Products Maintenance Co., Ltd., DSTMedia Technology Co., Ltd, Octave Communications Pte Ltd., Octave Communications, Inc., PictureTel Argentina, PictureTel Audio Holdings Inc., PictureTel Australia Pty. Ltd., PictureTel Company Ltd., PictureTel Corporation 53 Subsidiaries included in the Index

Officers: Robert C. Hagerty/Chmn., CEO, Pres./$2,786,771.00, Philip B. Keenan/Sr. VP, Chief Evangelist/$1,086,307.00, Sunil K. Bhalla/Sr. VP, GM - Voice Division/$1,262,634.00, Sayed M. Darwish/VP, General Counsel, Corp. Sec., Michael R. Kourey/Dir., Sr. VP - Finance, Administration, CFO/$1,515,231.00, Donald J. Floyd/VP - Corporate Governance, Internal Audit, Robert B. Steele/VP - Manufacturing, Hans H. Schwarz/Sr. VP - Technology, CTO, Laura J. Durr/VP, Worldwide Controller, Principal Accounting Officer, Garth B. Hobden/VP, Corporate Treasurer, Gary M. Zieses/Sr. VP - Human Resources, Heidi Melin/Sr. VP, Chief Marketing Officer, James E. Ellett/Sr. VP - Strategic Initiatives/$1,185,273.00, David R. Phillips/Sr. VP - Worldwide Sales, Joseph A. Sigrist/Sr. VP, GM - Video Solutions Division/$917,354.00 *(16 Officers included in Index)*

Directors: Robert C. Hagerty/Chmn., CEO, Pres., John A. Kelley/Dir., Durk I. Jager/Dir., Michael R. Kourey/Dir., Sr. VP - Finance, Administration, CFO, Kevin T. Parker/Dir., Betsy S. Atkins/Dir., John Seely Brown/Dir., David G. Dewalt/Dir., William A. Owens/Dir.

Owners: James E. Ellett, Michael R. Kourey, Robert C. Hagerty/1.40%, Insiders/3.10%, John A. Kelley, Joseph A. Sigrist, Betsy S. Atkins, Mazama Capital Management/7.90%, David G. DeWalt, Stanley J. Meresman, Goldman Sachs Asset Management/10.10%, Barclays Global Investors/7.60%, Kevin T. Parker, John Seely Brown, Durk I. Jager *(19 Owners included in Index)*

Financial Data: *Fiscal Year End:*12/31 *Latest Annual Data:* 12/31/2006

Year	Sales	Net Income
2006	$682,385,000	$71,924,000
2005	$580,659,000	$62,745,000
2004	$540,252,000	$35,349,000

Curr. Assets:	$639,977,000	**Curr. Liab.:**	$213,883,000		
Plant, Equip.:	$39,426,000	**Total Liab.:**	$243,295,000	**Indic. Yr. Divd.:**	NA
Total Assets:	$1,190,015,000	**Net Worth:**	$946,720,000	**Debt/ Equity:**	0.0358

Polydex Pharmaceuticals Ltd

421 Comstock Rd., Toronto, ON, M1L 2H5; *PH:* 1-416-755-2231; *http://* www.polydex.com; *Email:* gu-dextran@rogers.com

General - Incorporation	Bahamas	**Stock** - Price on:12/24/2007	NA
Employees	26	Stock Exchange	NDQ
Auditor	Ernst & Young LLP	Ticker Symbol	POLXF
Stk Agt	Equity Transfer Services Inc	Outstanding Shares	3,070,000
Counsel	Katten, Muchin, Zavis & Rosenman	E.P.S	-$0.24
DUNS No.	24-719-1786	Shareholders	NA

Business: The group's principle activities include manufacturing and selling dextran and several of its derivatives including iron dextran, dextran sulphate and fetal bovine serum; and manufacture tablets and injectable products used for treatment of farm animals. The group operates from United States.

Primary SIC and add'l.: 2822 6719 2834

CIK No: 0000317158

Subsidiaries: Dextran Products Limited

Officers: George Usher/Chmn., CEO, Pres./CAD314,760.00, Linda Hughes/Contact - Investor Relations, Sharon Wardlaw/55/COO, Sec., Treasurer /CAD114,380.00, John A. Luce/61/CFO/CAD64,345.00

Directors: George Usher/Chmn., CEO, Pres., John L.E. Seidler/Dir., Derek Lederer/Dir., Joseph Buchman/Dir.

Owners: George G. Usher/6.00%, Thomas C. Usher/10.60%, Insiders/11.80%, George G. Usher/100.00%, Derek John Michael Lederer/1.20%, John L.E. Seidler, Joseph Buchman/4.30%, Sharon L. Wardlaw

Financial Data: *Fiscal Year End:*01/31 *Latest Annual Data:* 1/31/2007

Year	Sales	Net Income
2007	$6,499,000	-$261,000
2006	$5,265,000	-$1,489,000
2005	$6,372,000	$1,140,000

Curr. Assets:	$3,964,000	**Curr. Liab.:**	$1,588,000		
Plant, Equip.:	$4,308,000	**Total Liab.:**	$2,769,000	**Indic. Yr. Divd.:**	NA
Total Assets:	$10,127,000	**Net Worth:**	$7,358,000	**Debt/ Equity:**	0.0522

PolyMedica Corp

701 Edgewater Dr., Ste. 360, Wakefield, MA, 01880; *PH:* 1-781-486-8111; *Fax:* 1-781-295-0181; *http://* www.polymedica.com

General - Incorporation	MA	**Stock** - Price on:12/24/2007	$40.7
Employees	2,441	Stock Exchange	NA
Auditor	PricewaterhouseCoopers LLP	Ticker Symbol	NA
Stk Agt	EquiServe Trust Co N.A	Outstanding Shares	22,740,000
Counsel	Hale & Dorr LLP	E.P.S	$1.44
DUNS No.	61-168-8235	Shareholders	NA

Business: The group's principal activity is to provide consumer medical products and services. The group operates in three segments: liberty diabetes provides direct-to-consumer diabetes testing supplies and related products primarily to medicare-eligible customers suffering from diabetes and related chronic diseases. Liberty respiratory provides direct-to-consumer respiratory medications and supplies primarily to medicare-eligible customers suffering from chronic obstructive pulmonary disease. Pharmaceuticals provide prescription oral medications not covered by medicare directly to consumers and sell to distributors prescription urology and suppository products, over-the-counter female urinary discomfort products and home medical diagnostic kits. Polymedica, urised and azo standard are the trademarks of the group. The group provides a mail order for delivery of supplies directly to the customers at their homes and also provide 24-hour telephone support to customers.

Primary SIC and add'l.: 8731 2835 2834

CIK No: 0000878748

Subsidiaries: IntelliCare, Inc., Liberty Commercial Health Services, Inc., Liberty Direct Services Corporation, Liberty Healthcare Group, Inc., Liberty Home Pharmacy Corporation, Liberty Lane Condominium Association, Liberty Lane Development Company, Inc, Liberty Medical Supply Pharmacy, Inc., Liberty Medical Supply, Inc., Liberty Pharmacy, Inc, National Diabetic Pharmacies, LLC, PolyMedica Holdings, Inc., PolyMedica Securities, Inc

Owners: Westfield Capital Management Co., LLC/5.20%, Keith W. Jones/1.20%, Edward A. Burkhardt, William C. VanFaasen, Marcia J. Hooper, Frank W. LoGerfo, Devin J. Anderson, Patrick T. Ryan/2.40%, Samuel L. Shanaman/1.30%, James J. Mahoney, Stephen C. Farrell/1.30%, Krishna G. Palepu, Jonathan A. Starr, Bank of America Corporation/5.40%, Insiders/8.20% *(18 Owners included in Index)*

Financial Data: *Fiscal Year End:*03/31 *Latest Annual Data:* 3/31/2007

Year	Sales	Net Income
2007	$675,487,000	$33,672,000
2006	$491,515,000	$60,398,000
2005	$451,467,000	$32,434,000

Curr. Assets:	$180,087,000	**Curr. Liab.:**	$62,227,000	**P/E Ratio:**	24.23
Plant, Equip.:	$61,098,000	**Total Liab.:**	$315,530,000	**Indic. Yr. Divd.:**	$0.600
Total Assets:	$477,446,000	**Net Worth:**	$161,916,000	**Debt/ Equity:**	1.4881

PolyMedix Inc

3701 Market St. Ste. 442, Philadelphia, PA, 19104; *PH:* 1-215-966-6119; *http://* www.polymedix.com; *Email:* deringis@polymedix.com

General		Stock	
Incorporation	DE	Price on:12/24/2007	$2.25
Employees	16	Stock Exchange	OTC
Auditor	NA	Ticker Symbol	PYMX
Stk Agt	American Stock Transfer & Trust Co.	Outstanding Shares	19,440,000
Counsel	NA	E.P.S.	-$0.72
DUNS No.	NA	Shareholders	NA

Business: The groups principle activity is developed novel small molecule antibiotics that mimic the activity of host defense proteins. The group is seeking to commercialize these antibiotics in a variety of forms to combat drug resistant bacterial infections. The group operates from the United States. The group's revenue for Sep '07 was 0.60 millions of USD.

Primary SIC and add'l.: 8011

CIK No: 0001341843

Subsidiaries: PolyMedix Pharmaceuticals, Inc

Officers: Nicholas Landekic/Dir., CEO, Pres., Edward Smith/VP - Finance, CFO, Erika Moran/Investor Relations Contact, Janet Vasquez/Investor Relations Officer, Richard Scott/VP - Biology Research, Dawn Eringis/VP - Business Development, Eric McAllister/VP - Clinical Development

Directors: Nicholas Landekic/Dir., CEO, Pres., Frank Slattery/Chmn., Frank M. Delape/Dir., William N. Kelle/Dir., Michael E. Lewis/Dir., Shaun F. OMalley/Dir.

Owners: Insiders/30.90%, Michael E. Lewis/3.20%, Frank M. DeLape/5.10%, William Baquet/15.20%, Richard W. Scott/4.00%, Edward F. Smith, Frank P. Slattery/5.70%, Wistar I. Morris/7.10%, Nicholas Landekic/11.80%, William N. Kelley, Shaun F. OMalley

Financial Data: *Fiscal Year End:*NA *Latest Annual Data:* 12/31/2006

Year	Sales	Net Income
2006	$821,000	-$5,966,000

Curr. Assets:	$14,589,000	**Curr. Liab.:**	$1,002,000	**P/E Ratio:**	95.63
Plant, Equip.:	$553,000	**Total Liab.:**	$1,396,000	**Indic. Yr. Divd.:**	NA
Total Assets:	$15,142,000	**Net Worth:**	$13,746,000	**Debt/ Equity:**	NA

Polymer Group Inc

9335 Harris Corners Pkwy., Ste. 300, Charlotte, NC, 28269; *PH:* 1-704-697-5100; *Fax:* 1-919-207-3140; *http://* www.polymergroupinc.com

General		Stock	
Incorporation	DE	Price on:12/24/2007	$29.51
Employees	3,471	Stock Exchange	OTC
Auditor	Grant Thornton, LLP	Ticker Symbol	POLGA
Stk Agt	American Stock Transfer & Trust Co.	Outstanding Shares	19,390,000
Counsel	NA	E.P.S.	-$1.98
DUNS No.	79-705-0598	Shareholders	NA

Business: The group's principal activities are to develop, manufacture and market nonwoven and oriented polyolefin products. The group operates through two business segments: consumer and industrial and specialty. The consumer segment includes a variety of nonwoven materials. These materials are used in diapers, training pants, feminine sanitary protection, adult incontinence, baby wet wipes and consumer wiping products. The industrial and specialty segment includes products such as cable wrap, house wrap, furniture and bedding applications, landscape and agricultural products, protective apparel, automotive, filtration, flexible packaging and industrial wiping products. The customers of the group include the procter & gamble company and johnson and johnson. The group operates mainly in the United States, Europe, Latin America, Canada and Asia.

Primary SIC and add'l.: 2299 2297

CIK No: 0000927417

Subsidiaries: Albuma S.A.S., Bonlam (S.C.), Inc., Bonlam Andina Ltd., Bonlam Holdings BV, Bonlam S.A. de C.V., Chicopee Holdings B.V., Chicopee Holdings CV, Chicopee, Inc., DIFCO Performance Fabrics, Inc., Dominion Nonwovens Sudamerica, S.A., Dominion Textile (USA) Inc., Dominion Textile Mauritius Inc., DT Acquisition Inc., FabPro Oriented Polymers, Inc., Fabrene Corp. 40 Subsidiaries included in the Index

Officers: Veronica Hagen/Dir., CEO, Dale Tyson/VP, Corporate Controller, Daniel Rikard/VP, General Counsel, Sec., Bruce Rockenfield/VP - Human Resources, Fernando Espinosa/VP, GM - Latin America/$977,016.00, Jay Cheng/VP, GM - China, Willis Moore/CFO, VP/$1,096,243.00, Thomas Dort/VP, GM - Fabpro, Mike Hale/VP, GM - US Nonwovens/$714,387.00, William Spencer/VP, GM - Canada, Richard Ferencz/VP - Engineering, Development, Dennis Norman/VP - Strategic Planning, Communication

Directors: Veronica Hagen/Dir., CEO, William Hewitt/Chmn., James Ovenden/Dir., Ramon Betolaza/Dir., Eugene Linden/Dir., Lap W. Chan/Dir., Pedro Arias/Dir., Charles Volpe/Dir., Mark Patterson/Dir.

Owners: Willis C. Moore, Fernando Espinosa, Mark Patterson, Lap Wai Chan, Michael W. Hale, Charles E. Volpe, Insiders, MatlinPatterson Global Opportunities Partners, L.P., Ramon Betolaza, Pedro A. Arias, William B. Hewitt, Eugene Linden, James A. Ovenden

Financial Data: *Fiscal Year End:*12/31 *Latest Annual Data:* 12/30/2006

Year	Sales	Net Income
2006	$1,021,608,000	-$34,532,000
2005	$948,848,000	$6,997,000

Curr. Assets:	$298,752,000	**Curr. Liab.:**	$125,305,000		
Plant, Equip.:	$421,997,000	**Total Liab.:**	$616,908,000	**Indic. Yr. Divd.:**	NA
Total Assets:	$765,001,000	**Net Worth:**	$131,482,000	**Debt/ Equity:**	3.3126

PolyMet Mining Corp

1177 W Hastings St., Ste. 2350, Vancouver, BC, V6E 2K3; *PH:* 1-604-669-4701; *http://* www.polymetmining.com

General		Stock	
Incorporation	Canada	Price on:12/24/2007	$3.56
Employees	NA	Stock Exchange	AMEX
Auditor	Staley, Okada & Partners	Ticker Symbol	PLM
Stk Agt	Pacific Corporate Trust Co	Outstanding Shares	136,530,000
Counsel	NA	E.P.S.	-$0.03
DUNS No.	24-578-3923	Shareholders	NA

Business: The group's principle activities include exploring and developing natural resource properties. The group operates from United States.

Primary SIC and add'l.: 1021 1099

CIK No: 0000866028

Subsidiaries: Fleck Minerals Inc., Poly Met Mining, Inc.

Officers: William Murray/Dir., CEO, Pres., Don Hunter/Project Mgr., Douglas J. Newby/Dir., CFO, Jim Scott/Mgr. - Environmental, Phillip Brodie-Hall/VP - Project Development, Andrew Clark/Project Mgr. - Process Plant, Joe Scipioni/Dir., COO, Niall Moore/Dir., Corp. Sec., Group Controller, Richard Patelke/Northmet Project Geologist, Gaston Reymenants/VP - Marketing

Directors: William Murray/Dir., CEO, Pres., Ian L.W. Forrest/Chmn., James Swearingen/Dir., David Dreisinger/Dir., George Molyviatis/Dir., Douglas J. Newby/Dir., CFO, William Corneliuson/Dir., Joe Scipioni/Dir., COO, Niall Moore/Dir., Corp. Sec., Group Controller

Owners: Niall Moore, James Swearingen, Cleveland-Cliffs, Inc./6.70%, Ian L.W. Forrest/2.20%, Joseph Scipioni, George Molyviatis/6.20%, Insiders/14.10%, David Dreisinger, William D. Corneliuson, William Murray/1.90%, Douglas J. Newby

Financial Data: *Fiscal Year End:*01/31 *Latest Annual Data:* 01/31/2007

Year	Sales	Net Income
2007	NA	-$18,048,000
2006	NA	-$15,930,000
2005	NA	-$3,776,000

Curr. Assets:	$11,788,000	**Curr. Liab.:**	$2,717,000		
Plant, Equip.:	$14,247,000	**Total Liab.:**	$6,649,000	**Indic. Yr. Divd.:**	NA
Total Assets:	$26,035,000	**Net Worth:**	$19,387,000	**Debt/ Equity:**	NA

Polyone Corp

33587 Walker Rd., Avon Lake, OH, 44012; *PH:* 1-440-930-1000; *Fax:* 1-440-930-1750; *http://* www.polyone.com

General		Stock	
Incorporation	OH	Price on:12/24/2007	$7.11
Employees	4,600	Stock Exchange	NYSE
Auditor	Ernst & Young LLP	Ticker Symbol	POL
Stk Agt	Computershare Trust Co	Outstanding Shares	92,990,000
Counsel	NA	E.P.S.	NA
DUNS No.	NA	Shareholders	NA

Business: The groups principle activity is to provide polymer materials, services and solutions. The group operates through four business segments namely vinyl business, international color and engineered materials, polyone distribution, and resin and intermediates. The group operates from United States.

Primary SIC and add'l.: 3087 2821

CIK No: 0001122976

Subsidiaries: Altona Properties Pty Ltd., Auseon Limited, BayOne Urethane Systems, Chloralkali Venture, Inc., Compounding Technology, Euro S.A, Conexus, Inc., DH Compounding Company, General Compounding Partnership, Inc., Geon Development, Inc., Geon Polimeros Andios S.A., Hanna Deutschland, GmbH, Hanna France SARL, Hanna PAR Corporation, Hollinger Development Company, L. E. Carpenter & Company 62 Subsidiaries included in the Index

Officers: Stephen D. Newlin/Chmn., CEO, Pres./$3,317,350.00, David W. Wilson/CFO, VP/$962,761.00, Wendy C. Shiba/57/Sr. VP, Chief Legal Officer, Sec./$842,126.00, Michael L. Rademacher/57/VP, GM - Distribution, Kenneth M. Smith/53/Sr. VP, Chief Human Resources, CIO/$802,479.00, Robert M. Rosenau/53/VP, GM - Vinyl Business, Bernard P. Baert/58/Sr. VP, GM - Colors, Engineered Materials, Europe, Asia, Michael E. Kahler/50/Sr. VP - Commercial Development

Directors: Stephen D. Newlin/Chmn., CEO, Pres., Richard H. Fearon/Dir., Gordon D. Harnett/Dir., Farah M. Walters/Dir., Douglas J. Campbell/Dir., Robert A. Garda/Dir., Carol A. Cartwright/Dir., Gale Duff-Bloom/Dir., Edward J. Mooney/Dir.

Owners: Barrow, Hanley, Mewhinney& Strauss, Inc/6.50%, Wayne R. Embry, FMR Corp./5.90%, Douglas J. Campbell, Farah M. Walters, Stephen D. Newlin, Dimensional FundAdvisors LP/6.20%, David W. Wilson, Robert A. Garda, Insiders, Gordon D. Harnett, New York Life Trust Company, Trustee/6.00%, Edward J. Mooney, Richard H. Fearon, Barclays Global Investors, NA/7.20% *(21 Owners included in Index)*

Financial Data: *Fiscal Year End:*12/31 *Latest Annual Data:* 12/31/2006

Year	Sales	Net Income
2006	$2,622,400,000	$123,200,000
2005	$2,450,600,000	$46,900,000
2004	$2,161,500,000	$23,500,000

Curr. Assets:	$669,300,000	**Curr. Liab.:**	$341,800,000	**P/E Ratio:**	7.90
Plant, Equip.:	$442,400,000	**Total Liab.:**	$1,193,600,000	**Indic. Yr. Divd.:**	NA
Total Assets:	$1,773,600,000	**Net Worth:**	$574,500,000	**Debt/ Equity:**	0.9568

Pomeroy IT Solutions

1020 Petersburg Rd., Hebron, KY, 41048; *PH:* 1-859-586-0600; *Fax:* 1-859-586-4414; *http://* www.pomeroy.com

General - Incorporation	DE	**Stock**- Price on:12/24/2007	$9.86
Employees	2,212	Stock Exchange	NDQ
Auditor	BDO Seidman, LLP	Ticker Symbol	PMRY
Stk Agt	American Stock Transfer & Trust Co.	Outstanding Shares	12,320,000
Counsel	NA	E.P.S	-$7.22
DUNS No.	04-315-2388	Shareholders	NA

Business: The group's principal activities are to sell, install, service and lease microcomputers and microcomputer equipments. The group operates through three segments: products, services and leasing. The product segment sells a range of desktop computer equipment, including servers, infrastructure and peripherals. The services segment provides the services segment provides enterprise consulting, infrastructure solutions and lifecycle services. The leasing segment provides in-house leasing services to the group's products and service customers. These products and services are provided primarily to government and education, financial services, health care and other sectors throughout the United States, southeast and midwest regions. The group's target markets include Fortune 1000 and small and medium businesses. In 2003, the group acquired micrologic business systems of k.c inc and eserv solutions group, llc.

Primary SIC and add'l.: 7373 7377 7378 7379 7371

CIK No: 0000883979

Subsidiaries: information technology (IT), Technology Integration Financial Services (TIFS).

Officers: Keith R. Coogan/CEO, Pres., Keith M. Blachowiak/Sr. VP - Information Technology, CIO, Kristi Nelson/Legal Department, John E. McKenzie/Sr. VP - Sales, Marketing, Kevin G. Gregory/CFO, Sr. VP, Hope Griffith/Sr. VP - Services

Directors: David B. Pomeroy/Chmn., Stephen E. Pomeroy/Dir., James H. Smith/Dir., William H. Lomicka/Dir., Vincent D. Rinaldi/Dir., Debra E. Tibey/Dir., Kenneth R. Waters/Dir., David G. Boucher/Dir., Ronald E. Krieg/Dir.

Owners: Keith Blachowiak, James H. Smith, Insiders/23.38%, Kevin G. Gregory, Kenneth R. Waters, David G. Boucher, P. Hope Griffith, William H. Lomicka, FMR Corp./10.45%, Debra E. Tibey, Vincent D. Rinaldi, Wells Capital Management Inc./12.98%, Byram Capital Management LLC/7.19%, David B. Pomeroy/17.24%, John E. McKenzie *(20 Owners included in Index)*

Financial Data: **Fiscal Year End:**01/05 **Latest Annual Data:** 1/5/2007

Year	Sales	Net Income
2007	$631,632,000	$1,143,000
2006	$714,749,000	-$10,662,000
2005	$742,290,000	$10,933,000

Curr. Assets:	$188,035,000	**Curr. Liab.:**	$97,497,000	**P/E Ratio:**	82.17
Plant, Equip.:	$12,593,000	**Total Liab.:**	$99,810,000	**Indic. Yr. Divd.:**	NA
Total Assets:	$305,021,000	**Net Worth:**	$205,211,000	**Debt/ Equity:**	NA

Poniard Pharmaceuticals Inc

Formerly: NeoRx
7000 Shoreline Ct., Ste. 270, South San Francisco, CA, 94080; *PH:* 1-206-281-7001; *http://* www.poniard.com

General - Incorporation	WA	**Stock**- Price on:12/24/2007	$7.08
Employees	29	Stock Exchange	NA
Auditor	KPMG LLP	Ticker Symbol	NA
Stk Agt	Mellon Investor Services LLC	Outstanding Shares	34,660,000
Counsel	Perkins Coie LLP	E.P.S	-$1.12
DUNS No.	12-117-2209	Shareholders	NA

Business: The group's principal activity is to develop products for targeted delivery of anti-cancer agents, including radiopharmaceuticals, to tumor sites. The group's product strtm (skeletal targeted radiotherapy) is developed to treat multiple myeloma, a cancer of the body's antibody-producing cells originating in the bone marrow. This reduces exposure of healthy tissues other than bone to the potentially toxic effects of the radiation. The group's str product consists of a bone-seeking molecule called dotmp, which deposits the radioactive substance, holmium-166, in the skeleton. The operations are carried on in the United States.

Primary SIC and add'l.: 8731 2834

CIK No: 0000755806

Subsidiaries: NeoRx Manufacturing Group

Officers: Jerry McMahon/Chmn., CEO, David A. Karlin/Sr. VP - Clinical Development, Regulatory Affairs/$417,065.00, Anna Lewak Wight/VP - Legal/$392,371.00, Caroline M. Loewy/CFO/$271,840.00, Cheni Kwok/VP - Business Development, Ronald A. Martell/COO, Pres.

Directors: Jerry McMahon/Chmn., CEO, Robert M. Littauer/Dir., David R. Stevens/Dir., Alan B. Glassberg/Member - Advisory Board, Carl S. Goldfischer/Dir., Frederick B. Craves/Dir., Rolland E. Dickson/Dir., Nicholas J. Simon/Dir., Robert S. Basso/Dir., Paul A. Bunn/Member - Clinical Advisory Board, Richard M. Goldberg/Member - Clinical Advisory Board, Eric J. Small/Member - Clinical Advisory Board

Owners: Gerald McMahon, Caroline M. Loewy, Anna L. Wight, Abingworth Management Limited, Nicholas J. Simon, David A. Karlin, Carl S. Goldfischer, Alan B. Glassberg, Robert M. Littauer, David R. Stevens, Ronald A. Martell, Bay City Capital Fund IV, L.P., MPM BioVentures III, L.P, OrbiMed Advisors LLC, OrbiMed Capital LLC and Samuel D. Isaly, Rolland E. Dickson *(19 Owners included in Index)*

Financial Data: **Fiscal Year End:**12/31 **Latest Annual Data:** 12/31/2006

Year	Sales	Net Income
2006	NA	-$23,294,000
2005	$15,000	-$20,997,000
2004	$1,015,000	-$19,371,000

Curr. Assets:	$54,500,000	**Curr. Liab.:**	$12,201,000		
Plant, Equip.:	$3,149,000	**Total Liab.:**	$22,176,000	**Indic. Yr. Divd.:**	NA
Total Assets:	$69,067,000	**Net Worth:**	$46,891,000	**Debt/ Equity:**	0.2313

Pool Corp

Formerly: SCP Pool Corp
109 N Pk. Blvd., 4th Fl., Covington, LA, 70433; *PH:* 1-985-892-5521; *http://* www.scppool.com

General - Incorporation	DE	**Stock**- Price on:12/24/2007	$41.39
Employees	3,600	Stock Exchange	NDQ
Auditor	Ernst & Young LLP	Ticker Symbol	NA
Stk Agt	Computershare Investor Services LLC	Outstanding Shares	49,230,000
Counsel	Jones, Walker, Waechter Et Al	E.P.S	$1.47
DUNS No.	87-296-5363	Shareholders	NA

Business: The groups principle activity is to distribute swimming pool supplies, equipment and related leisure products. The groups products include filter accessories, santizers, heaters and pool-fiberglass. Customers served by the group include swimming pool remodelers and builders, retail swimming pool stores, swimming pool repair and service businesses. The group operates from United States.

Primary SIC and add'l.: 5091

CIK No: 0000945841

Subsidiaries: AllianceTrading,Inc., B&B s.r.l., BoninConsultoresEServicos,LDA, Cascade Swimming, Cypress Hong Kong Limited, Cypress, Inc., Garden Leisure Products, Ltd, Horizon Distributors, Inc., Les Industries R.P. Inc., Norcal Pool Supplies Ltd, Pool Development LLC, SCP (Shanghai) Purchasing Co Ltd, SCP Europe, SAS, SCP FranceSAS, SCP Mexico S.A. de C.V 34 Subsidiaries included in the Index

Officers: Manuel J. Perez De La Mesa/51/Dir., CEO, Pres./$1,406,655.00, Kenneth G. St. Romain/46/Group VP, Melanie Housey/35/Corporate Controller, Stephen C. Nelson/62/VP/$466,035.00, Richard P. Polizzotto/67/VP, David A. Cook/53/Group VP/$607,961.00, Christopher W. Wilson/53/Group VP, John M. Murphy/47/VP/$597,294.00, Craig K. Hubbard/56/Treasurer, Assist. Sec., Jennifer M. Neil/34/General Counsel, Sec., Mark W. Joslin/49/CFO, VP/$568,000.00

Directors: Manuel J. Perez De La Mesa/51/Dir., CEO, Pres., Wilson B. Sexton/71/Chmn., John E. Stokely/55/Dir., George T. Haymaker/70/Dir., Robert C. Sledd/55/Dir., James J. Gaffney/68/Dir., Andrew W. Code/50/Dir., Harlan F. Seymour/58/Dir.

Owners: John E. Stokely, T. Rowe Price Associates, Inc/5.20%, Baron Capital Group, Inc./5.50%, Stephen C. Nelson, TimesSquare Capital Management, LLC/11.60%, Mark W. Joslin, Wasatch Advisors, Inc./6.70%, James J. Gaffney, Wilson B. Sexton/2.20%, Andrew W. Code, Baillie Gifford & Co./9.10%, Robert C. Sledd, Columbia Wanger Asset Management, L.P./5.60%, Manuel J. Perez de la Mesa/2.50%, George T. Haymaker *(19 Owners included in Index)*

Financial Data: **Fiscal Year End:**12/31 **Latest Annual Data:** 12/31/2006

Year	Sales	Net Income
2006	$1,909,762,000	$95,024,000
2005	$1,552,659,000	$83,621,000
2004	$1,310,853,000	$66,941,000

Curr. Assets:	$519,421,000	**Curr. Liab.:**	$291,790,000	**P/E Ratio:**	25.55
Plant, Equip.:	$33,633,000	**Total Liab.:**	$496,878,000	**Indic. Yr. Divd.:**	$0.480
Total Assets:	$774,562,000	**Net Worth:**	$277,684,000	**Debt/ Equity:**	1.1600

Pop N Go Inc

12429 E Putnam St., Whittier, CA, 90602; *PH:* 1-562-945-9351; *http://* www.popngo.com

General - Incorporation	DE	**Stock**- Price on:12/24/2007	$0.015
Employees	5	Stock Exchange	OTC
Auditor	Kabani & Co, Inc	Ticker Symbol	POPN
Stk Agt	Liberty Transfer Co	Outstanding Shares	289,300,000
Counsel	NA	E.P.S	-$0.01
DUNS No.	NA	Shareholders	NA

Business: The group's principle activities are to develop, manufacture, market and distribute food vending machine equipment and related food products. The group is also engaged in providing specialty food service. The product of the company is a hot air based popcorn vending machine, called pop n go that delivers a fresh cup of popcorn on demand, with butter flavoring. Pop n go popcorn machines are currently located in airports, shopping centers, schools, convenience stores, supermarkets, bowling alleys, car washes, military bases and a wide range of other retail, industrial and office locations. The company has international sales in Mexico, Canada, China, cyprus, Korea, Australia and Israel. The group's quarterly revenue for June 2007 was 0.23 millions of USD.

Primary SIC and add'l.: 3581

CIK No: 0001071819

Officers: Melvin Wyman/70/Sole Dir., CEO, Sec., Ruth Williams/Dir. - Operations

Directors: Melvin Wyman/70/Sole Dir., CEO, Sec.

Owners: Insiders/5.72%, Melvin Wyman/5.72%, Haruyo DElia/22.60%

Financial Data: **Fiscal Year End:**09/30 **Latest Annual Data:** 03/31/2007

Year	Sales	Net Income
2007	NA	NA
2006	$97,000	-$9,051,000
2005	$45,000	-$2,533,000

Curr. Assets:	$893,000	**Curr. Liab.:**	$15,003,000		
Plant, Equip.:	$36,000	**Total Liab.:**	$15,246,000	**Indic. Yr. Divd.:**	NA
Total Assets:	$1,037,000	**Net Worth:**	-$14,209,000	**Debt/ Equity:**	NA

Pop Starz Inc

1801 Clint Moore Rd. , Boca Raton, FL, 33487; *PH:* 1-561-994-8414; *http://* www.popstarzinc.com; *Email:* info@popstarzinc.com

General - Incorporation	FL	**Stock**- Price on:12/24/2007	$0.07
Employees	2	Stock Exchange	OTC
Auditor	NA	Ticker Symbol	PSRZ
Stk Agt	Florida Atlantic Stock Transfer, Inc.	Outstanding Shares	37,700,000
Counsel	NA	E.P.S	NA
DUNS No.	NA	Shareholders	NA

Business: The group's principle activity is to operate dance training centers, currently concentrating on the musical genre popularly referred to as "Hip Hop" and "Pop". Pop Starz' ultimate goal is the development and operation of dance and talent development programs throughout Florida and nationally, combining the functions of traditional dance and exercise facilities with training in modeling, drama and voice development, and providing participants of all ages with an opportunity to participate in professional entertainment opportunities. The group operates from United States.

Primary SIC and add'l.: 7922

CIK No: 0001309223

Officers: Michelle Tucker/Pres., Brice Vick/Artistic Dir., Amanda Tac/Dir. - Creative

Pop3 Media Corp

2451 W Birchwood Ave., Ste. 105, Mesa, AZ, 85202; ***PH:*** 1-480-393-0423;
http:// www.viastarcorp.com

General - Incorporation	NV	**Stock**- Price on:12/24/2007	$0.0015
Employees	NA	Stock Exchange	OTC
Auditor	Shelley International CPA	Ticker Symbol	POPT
Stk Agt	Pacific Stock Transfer Company	Outstanding Shares	NA
Counsel	NA	E.P.S	NA
DUNS No.	NA	Shareholders	NA

Business: The group's principal activity is to develop and maintain portfolio companies in the field of media and entertainment. The group's portfolio includes picture perfect releasing inc, viastar partners inc, and all4entertainment inc. The group also designs and develops Web sites, establishes membership programs emphasizing the characters and themes of its productions and develop corporate partnerships, all with an emphasis on the interests and needs of children and their families. On 31-Mar-2004, the group acquired masterdisk corporation.

Primary SIC and add'l.: 7812 7822

CIK No: 0001098226

Subsidiaries: Viastar Distribution Group, Inc.

Financial Data: ***Fiscal Year End:***06/30 ***Latest Annual Data:*** 6/30/2005

Year	Sales	Net Income
2005	$452,000	-$13,452,000
2004	$3,027,000	-$3,987,000
2003	NA	-$190,000

Curr. Assets:	$960,000	***Curr. Liab.:***	$1,747,000		
Plant, Equip.:	$920,000	***Total Liab.:***	$1,747,000	***Indic. Yr. Divd.:***	NA
Total Assets:	$3,141,000	***Net Worth:***	$1,395,000	***Debt/ Equity:***	NA

Pope & Talbot Inc

1500 SW 1st Ave., Ste. 200, Portland, OR, 97201; ***PH:*** 1-503-228-9161; ***Fax:*** 1-503-220-2722;
http:// www.poptal.com; ***Email:*** info@poptal.com

General - Incorporation	DE	**Stock**- Price on:12/24/2007	$4.08
Employees	2,373	Stock Exchange	OTC
Auditor	KPMG LLP	Ticker Symbol	PTBT
Stk Agt	Mellon Investor Services LLC	Outstanding Shares	16,430,000
Counsel	NA	E.P.S	NA
DUNS No.	00-922-7372	Shareholders	NA

Business: The group's principle activity is to manufacture wood and pulp products. The group operates in two segments namely pulp products and wood products. The group's pulp product business manufactures and sells bleached softwood kraft pulp for newsprint, tissue and high-grade coated and uncoated paper and construction material. Wood products business manufactures and sells standardized and specialty lumber, residual wood chips and other by-products. The group operates three pulp mills located in halsey, Oregon and nanaimo and mackenzie in british columbia. The pulp products are marketed globally through sales offices in portland, Oregon, Brussels, Belgium and through agency sales offices around the world. The wood products are marketed from its portland, Oregon office. The group's quarterly revenue for June 2007 was 236.52 millions of USD.

Primary SIC and add'l.: 2611 2436 2411

CIK No: 0000311871

Subsidiaries: Halsey C102 Limited Partnership, Mackenzie Pulp Land Ltd., P&T Factoring Partnership, P&T Finance One Limited Partnership, P&T Finance Two Limited Partnership, P&T Funding Ltd., P&T LFP Investment Ltd. Partnership, P&T Power Company, Penn Timber, Inc., Pope& Talbot Ltd., Pope& Talbot Lumber Sales, Inc., Pope& Talbot Pulp Sales Europe SPRL, Pope& Talbot Pulp Sales U.S., Inc., Pope& Talbot Relocation Services, Inc., Pope& Talbot Spearfish Ltd. Partnership

Officers: Michael Flannery/64/Chmn., CEO, Pres./$1,690,994.00, Harold Stanton/Dir., CEO, Pres., Angel M. Diez/VP, GM - Pulp Division/$527,057.00, Maria M. Pope/VP, GM - Wood Products Division/$610,562.00, Neil R. Stuart/CFO, VP/$34,613.00

Directors: Michael Flannery/64/Chmn., CEO, Pres., Harold Stanton/Dir., CEO, Pres., Lionel G. Dodd/Chmn., David J. Barram/Dir., Peter T. Pope/Dir., Robert G. Funari/Dir., Gordon P. Andrews/Dir., Kenneth G. Hanna/Dir., Keith J. Matheney/Dir.

Owners: Michael Flannery/2.60%, Lionel G. Dodd, Gordon P. Andrews/1.50%, Angel M. Diez, Insiders/8.90%, Kenneth G. Hanna, Robert G. Funari, Maria M. Pope/1.30%, David J. Barram, Richard K. Atkinson, Harold N. Stanton, Peter T. Pope/2.50%, Neil R. Stuart

Financial Data: ***Fiscal Year End:***12/31 ***Latest Annual Data:*** 12/31/2006

Year	Sales	Net Income
2006	$841,140,000	$45,319,000
2005	$848,845,000	-$50,009,000
2004	$762,665,000	$11,127,000

Curr. Assets:	$258,336,000	***Curr. Liab.:***	$102,504,000		
Plant, Equip.:	$371,806,000	***Total Liab.:***	$541,594,000	***Indic. Yr. Divd.:***	NA
Total Assets:	$662,019,000	***Net Worth:***	$120,425,000	***Debt/ Equity:***	3.3474

Pope Resources

19245 Tenth Ave. NE, Poulsbo, WA, 98370; ***PH:*** 1-360-697-6626; ***Fax:*** 1-360-697-1156;
http:// www.poperesources.com; ***Email:*** investor@orminc.com

General - Incorporation	DE	**Stock**- Price on:12/24/2007	$47.08
Employees	51	Stock Exchange	NDQ
Auditor	KPMG LLP	Ticker Symbol	POPEZ
Stk Agt	Mellon Investor Services LLC	Outstanding Shares	4,680,000
Counsel	NA	E.P.S	$3.56
DUNS No.	NA	Shareholders	NA

Business: The groups principle activities include growing and harvesting timber from tree farms. The groups operates through three segments namely fee timber, timberland management and consulting and real estate. Customer served by the group is Lumber mills. The group operates from the United States. The group's quarterly revenue for September 2007 was 12.17 millions of USD.

Primary SIC and add'l.: 2411

CIK No: 0000784011

Subsidiaries: ORM, Inc

Officers: David L. Nunes/Dir., CEO, Pres., Thomas M. Ringo/CFO, VP, Sec., Jonathan P. Rose/Dir. - Real Estate, John T. Shea/Dir. - Business Development, Thomas Kametz/Dir. - Timberland Operations

Directors: David L. Nunes/Dir., CEO, Pres., John E. Conlin/Dir., Douglas E. Norberg/Dir., Peter T. Pope/Dir., Thurston J. Roach/Dir.

Owners: Pope EGP, Inc./1.10%, Thurston J. Roach, Douglas E. Norberg/1.40%, Insiders/11.10%, Emily T. Andrews/11.20%, Thomas M. Ringo, John E. Conlin, Peter T. Pope/6.90%, Pope MGP, Inc., Private Capital Management, Inc./24.20%, David L. Nunes/1.90%

Financial Data: ***Fiscal Year End:***12/31 ***Latest Annual Data:*** 12/31/2006

Year	Sales	Net Income
2006	$66,250,000	$24,910,000
2005	$57,006,000	$13,684,000
2004	$39,648,000	$10,176,000

Curr. Assets:	$41,127,000	***Curr. Liab.:***	$14,775,000	***P/E Ratio:***	10.37
Plant, Equip.:	$137,136,000	***Total Liab.:***	$92,677,000	***Indic. Yr. Divd.:***	$1.600
Total Assets:	$180,282,000	***Net Worth:***	$87,605,000	***Debt/ Equity:***	0.3362

Popular Inc

209 Muoz Rivera Ave., Hato Rey, PR, 00918; ***PH:*** 1-787-765-9800; ***http://*** www.popularinc.com;
Email: investor-relations@bppr.com

General - Incorporation	Puerto Rico	**Stock**- Price on:12/24/2007	$16.99
Employees	12,508	Stock Exchange	NDQ
Auditor	PricewaterhouseCoopers LLP	Ticker Symbol	BPOP
Stk Agt	Banco Popular De Puerto Rico	Outstanding Shares	279,360,000
Counsel	Brunilda Santos De lvarez	E.P.S	$1.16
DUNS No.	14-865-8529	Shareholders	NA

Business: The groups principle activity is to provide financial services. The group provides services include auto and lease financing, mortgage and consumer lending and investment services. The group operates from Puerto Rico, United States, the Caribbean, and Latin America.

Primary SIC and add'l.: 6712 6021

CIK No: 0000763901

Subsidiaries: ATH Costa Rica, S.A, Banco Popular de Puerto Rico, Banco Popular North America, Banco Popular, National Association, BanPonce Trust I, BPNA Real Estate, Inc., Crest, S.a., E-Loan Auto Fund Two, LLC, E-Loan, Inc., Equity One Consumer Loan Company, Equity One Funding Company, Equity One Holding Company, Equity One Mortgage Servicing, Inc., Equity One of West Virginia, Equity One, Inc. 48 Subsidiaries included in the Index

Officers: Richard L. Carrion/Chmn., CEO, Pres./$3,294,206.00, Ileana Gonzalez/Sr. VP, Brunilda Santos De alvarez/Exec. VP, Chief Legal Officer/$771,461.00, C. E. Williams/Exec. VP, Tere Loubriel/Exec. VP - People, Communications, Planning/$1,400,568.00, Samuel T. Cespedes/Sec., Jorge A. Junquera/CFO, Sr. Exec. VP/$1,239,298.00, Felix M. Villamil/Exec. VP/$820,408.00, Roberto R. Herencia/Exec. VP/$1,445,449.00, David H. Chafey/Sr. Exec. VP/$3,171,665.00, Amilcar Jordan/Executvie VP - Risk Management

Directors: Richard L. Carrion/Chmn., CEO, Pres., Jose B. Carrion/Dir., Maria Luisa Ferre/Dir., Manuel Morales/Dir., Francisco M. Rexach/Dir., Frederic V. Salerno/Dir., William J. Teuber/Dir., Jose R. Vizcarrondo/Dir., Michael Masin/Dir., Juan J. Bermudez/Dir.

Owners: Insiders/6.06%, Amlcar L. Jordn/0.04%, William J. Teuber/0.00%, Jos B. Carrin/0.75%, Jos R. Vizcarrondo/0.13%, David H. Chafey/0.18%, Juan J. Bermudez/0.50%, Roberto R. Herencia/0.08%, Mara Luisa Ferr/2.33%, Michael Masin/0.00%, Richard L. Carrin/1.15%, Jorge A. Junquera/0.21%, Tere Loubriel/0.07%, State Farm Mutual Automobile Insurance/6.54%, Brunilda Santos De Alvarez/0.04% *(19 Owners included in Index)*

Financial Data: ***Fiscal Year End:***12/31 ***Latest Annual Data:*** 12/31/2006

Year	Sales	Net Income
2006	$3,873,926,000	$357,676,000
2005	$3,451,134,000	$540,702,000
2004	$2,825,195,000	$489,908,000

Curr. Assets:	$1,500,106,000	***Curr. Liab.:***	$34,234,901,000	***P/E Ratio:***	14.65
Plant, Equip.:	$679,956,000	***Total Liab.:***	$43,783,571,000	***Indic. Yr. Divd.:***	$0.640
Total Assets:	$47,403,987,000	***Net Worth:***	$3,620,306,000	***Debt/ Equity:***	2.2398

Porta Systems Corp

6851 Jericho TpkE, Ste. 170, Syosset, NY, 11791; ***PH:*** 1-516-364-9300; ***Fax:*** 1-516-682-4636;
http:// www.portasystems.com

General - Incorporation	DE	**Stock**- Price on:12/24/2007	$0.14
Employees	355	Stock Exchange	OTC
Auditor	BDO Seidman LLP	Ticker Symbol	PYTM
Stk Agt	American Stock Transfer & Trust Co.	Outstanding Shares	10,070,000
Counsel	Katsky Korins LLP	E.P.S	$0.17
DUNS No.	04-920-0397	Shareholders	NA

Business: The group's principal activity is to design, develop, manufacture and market a broad range of telecommunications equipment and integrated software applications. The group operates in three segments: line connection and protection equipment, operating support systems and signal processing equipment. The line connection and protection equipment is used to connect copper-wired telecommunications networks and protect equipment from voltage surges. The operating support systems primarily focus on trouble management, line testing, network provisioning and other service delivery initiatives. The signal processing equipment is primarily used in defense and aerospace applications. The group's products are sold in Asia, south and Central America and Europe.

Primary SIC and add'l.: 7372 3669 3661

CIK No: 0000079564

Officers: Ed Kornfeld/CEO, CFO, Ralph Depascale/VP - Operations - Sales, Marketing, Protection, Security Products, Richard Schwarz/GM - Signal Processing Division, Al Squillante/Dir. - Engineering, Protection, Security Products, David Graney/Sales, Marketing Mgr. - US, South, Canada, Eric Sadler/Sales, Marketing Mgr. - US, West, Caribbean, Central America, Kurt Weber/Sales, Marketing Mgr. - US, North, Monica Gonzales/Sales, Marketing Mgr. - Mexico, South America

Owners: Marco M. Elser/3.40%, Warren H. Esanu/1.40%, Edward B. Kornfeld, Insiders/8.50%, Michael A. Tancredi, William V. Carney/2.10%, Herbert H. Feldman/1.10%

Financial Data: ***Fiscal Year End:***12/31 ***Latest Annual Data:*** 12/31/2006

Year	Sales	Net Income
2006	$32,818,000	$2,182,000
2005	$28,604,000	$810,000
2004	$29,168,000	$2,675,000

Curr. Assets:	$13,190,000	Curr. Liab.:	$44,836,000	P/E Ratio:	0.82
Plant, Equip.:	$1,571,000	Total Liab.:	$45,607,000	Indic. Yr. Divd.:	NA
Total Assets:	$17,784,000	Net Worth:	-$27,823,000	Debt/ Equity:	NA

Portal Resources Ltd

750-625 Howe St., Vancouver, BC, V6C 2T5; **PH:** 1-604-629-1929; **http://** www.portalresources.net; **Email:** info@portalresources.net

General - Incorporation	BC	**Stock**- Price on:12/24/2007	$0.75
Employees	NA	Stock Exchange	OTC
Auditor	De Visser Gray	Ticker Symbol	PLORF
Stk Agt	Pacific Corporate Trust Co	Outstanding Shares	NA
Counsel	DuMoulin Black	E.P.S.	NA
DUNS No.	NA	Shareholders	NA

Business: The group's principal activity is to discover natural resources focused primarily on the exploration and development of high potential gold-silver and copper-gold projects in Argentina and Chile. The company's dual objectives are to identify relatively early stage mineral properties that have large discovered potential, and to acquire one or more advanced projects that with further development have good production potential.

Primary SIC and add'l.: 1400

CIK No: 0001326910

Subsidiaries: El Portal de Oro, S.A., Portal de Oro (B.V.I.) Ltd.

Officers: Bruce Winfield/Dir., CEO, Pres., Gary Nordin/Dir., VP - Exploration, Christine West/CGA, CFO

Directors: Bruce Winfield/Dir., CEO, Pres., David Hottman/Chmn., Gary Nordin/Dir., VP - Exploration, Mark T. Brown/Dir., Frank Wheatley/Dir.

Owners: Bruce Winfield/6.11%, Christine West/0.21%, Frank Wheatley/0.70%, David Hottman/5.41%, Gary Nordin/3.22%, Mark T. Brown/1.21%

PortalPlayer Inc

70 W Plumeria Dr., San Jose, CA, 95134; **PH:** 1-408-521-7000; **http://** portalplayer.com

General - Incorporation	DE	**Stock**- Price on:12/24/2007	NA
Employees	NA	Stock Exchange	NA
Auditor	Deloitte & Touche LLP	Ticker Symbol	NA
Stk Agt	Bank of New York	Outstanding Shares	NA
Counsel	NA	E.P.S.	NA
DUNS No.	NA	Shareholders	NA

Business: The groups principle activities include designing , developing and marketing comprehensive platform solutions. The group products include system on chip, firmware and software. The group operates from Taiwan, China, Japan, Malaysia, Korea, the United States, Singapore and Denmark.

Primary SIC and add'l.: 3674

CIK No: 0001297633

Subsidiaries: Pinexe Systems Private, Ltd, PortalPlayer (India) Private Limited, PortalPlayer USA, Inc.

Portec Rail Products Inc

900 Old Freeport Rd., Pittsburgh, PA, 15238; **PH:** 1-412-782-6000; **Fax:** 1-412-782-1037; **http://** www.portecrail.com; **Email:** corporate@portecrail.com

General - Incorporation	WV	**Stock**- Price on:12/24/2007	$12.19
Employees	285	Stock Exchange	NDQ
Auditor	BKD LLP	Ticker Symbol	PRPX
Stk Agt	NA	Outstanding Shares	9,600,000
Counsel	NA	E.P.S.	$0.50
DUNS No.	02-920-1493	Shareholders	NA

Business: The group's principal activities are to manufacture, supply and distribute a broad range of railroad products, including rail joints, rail anchors, rail spikes and railway friction management products. It also manufactures material handling equipment. The group operates through four business units. The railway maintenance products division provides track components and friction management products and services to railroads, transit systems and railroad contractors. The shipping systems division, designs and sells load securement systems to the railroad industry. The Canadian operation produces rail anchors and spikes primarily for the Canadian railroads with some products exported to the United States and other international customers. The United Kingdom operation produces railway lubrication products at wrexam, wales's location. The group acquired salient systems, inc on Jul 20, 2004.

Primary SIC and add'l.: 3743 4011

CIK No: 0001263074

Subsidiaries: Conveyors International Ltd., JAM Enterprises, Inc., Kelsan Holdings, Inc., Kelsan Technologies (Europe) Limited, Kelsan Technologies (USA), LLC, Kelsan Technologies Corp., Portec Rail Nova Scotia Company, Portec Rail Products (UK)Ltd., Portec, Rail Products Ltd., Salient Systems, Inc., Torvale Fisher 2000 Ltd., Torvale Fisher Ltd., Whitehough Engineering Ltd.

Officers: Richard J. Jarosinski/CEO, Pres., John N. Pesarsick/CFO, Konstantinos Papazoglou/COO, Exec. VP, Michael D. Bornak/Chief Accounting Officer, Kirby J. Taylor/Dir., Sec.

Directors: John S. Cooper/Vice Chmn., Marshall T. Reynolds/Chmn., Philip Shell/Dir., Kirby J. Taylor/Dir., Sec., Michael A. Perry/Dir., Thomas W. Wright/Dir., Carl M. Callaway/Dir., Douglas V. Reynolds/Dir., Neal W. Scaggs/Dir., Daniel P. Harrington/Dir., Philip E. Cline/Dir.

Owners: Richard J. Jarosinski/0.20%, Heartland Advisors, Inc./5.60%, Kirby J. Taylor/0.20%, Daniel P. Harrington/7.80%, Jeffrey Gendell/5.20%, Phillip Todd Shell/0.10%, John S. Cooper/1.00%, Neal W. Scaggs/2.50%, Thomas W. Wright/2.20%, Konstantinos Papazoglou/0.50%, Insiders/31.30%, Douglas V. Reynolds/4.50%, Philip E. Cline/1.50%, Harold D. Harrison/5.90%, Marshall T. Reynolds/10.80%

Financial Data: Fiscal Year End:12/31   Latest Annual Data: 12/31/2006

Year	Sales	Net Income
2006	$99,225,000	$4,620,000
2005	$90,793,000	$5,827,000
2004	$69,437,000	$4,073,000

Curr. Assets:	$45,793,000	Curr. Liab.:	$21,022,000	P/E Ratio:	24.38
Plant, Equip.:	$10,403,000	Total Liab.:	$48,586,000	Indic. Yr. Divd.:	$0.240
Total Assets:	$101,682,000	Net Worth:	$53,096,000	Debt/ Equity:	0.2073

Porter Bancorp Inc

2500 Epoint Pkwy., Louisville, KY, 40223; **PH:** 1-502-499-4800; **Fax:** 1-502-499-4811; **http://** www.pbibank.com

General - Incorporation	KY	**Stock**- Price on:12/24/2007	$23.15
Employees	203	Stock Exchange	NDQ
Auditor	NA	Ticker Symbol	PBIB
Stk Agt	NA	Outstanding Shares	7,630,000
Counsel	NA	E.P.S.	$1.88
DUNS No.	NA	Shareholders	NA

Business: The group operates through its subsidiaries whose principle activity is to provide banking and financial services. The groups services include Internet banking, electronic funds transfers through ACH services, domestic and foreign wire transfers, cash management, vault services. The products of the group include automatic teller machines, night depository, personalized checks, credit cards, debit cards, travelers checks, loan and deposit sweep accounts and lock box. In January 31, 2005 the group acquired Citizens Financial Bank. The group operates from the United States. The assets of the group for the year 2006 were $1,051,006 (thousands).

Primary SIC and add'l.: 6712 6022

CIK No: 0001358356

Subsidiaries: Asencia Statutory Trust I, Durham-Mudd Insurance Agency, Inc, PBI Bank, PBI Title Services, LLC, Porter Statutory Trust II, Porter Statutory Trust III, Porter Statutory Trust IV

Officers: Maria L. Bouvette/CEO, Pres., Chester J. Porter/Chmn., General Counsel, David B. Pierce/Chief Strategy Officer, Fred Catlett/Pres. - Northern Region, Avery K. Matney/Pres. - Southern Region, James L. Grubbs/Sr. VP - Commercial Lending, Phil W. Barnhouse/CFO, Eric J. Satterly/CTO, Todd E. Young/COO, Charles R. Darst/Chief Business Development Officer

Directors: Chester J. Porter/Chmn., General Counsel, David L. Hawkins/53/Dir., Glenn Hogan/46/Dir., Michael E. Miller/56/Dir., Sidney L. Monroe/67/Dir., Stephen A. Williams/57/Dir.

Owners: Sidney L. Monroe, Glenn W. Hogan, Maria L. Bouvette/32.10%, Stephen A. Williams, David B. Pierce/1.20%, Chester J. Porter/36.40%, David L. Hawkins, Michael E. Miller, Bradford C. Harris

Financial Data: Fiscal Year End:12/31   Latest Annual Data: 12/31/2006

Year	Sales	Net Income
2006	$78,059,000	$14,339,000
2005	$67,487,000	$12,257,000
2004	$54,500,000	$8,859,000

Curr. Assets:	$87,726,000	Curr. Liab.:	$917,660,000	P/E Ratio:	11.40
Plant, Equip.:	$13,774,000	Total Liab.:	$942,660,000	Indic. Yr. Divd.:	$0.840
Total Assets:	$1,051,006,000	Net Worth:	$108,346,000	Debt/ Equity:	0.2261

Portfolio Recovery Assoc Inc

120 Corporate Blvd., Norfolk, VA, 23502; **PH:** 1-757-519-9300; **Fax:** 1-757-518-0901; **http://** www.portfoliorecovery.com

General - Incorporation	DE	**Stock**- Price on:12/24/2007	$59.24
Employees	1,291	Stock Exchange	NDQ
Auditor	PricewaterhouseCoopers LLP	Ticker Symbol	PRAA
Stk Agt	Continental Stock Transfer & Trust Co	Outstanding Shares	16,000,000
Counsel	Sidley, Austin, Brown & Wood	E.P.S.	$3.01
DUNS No.	NA	Shareholders	NA

Business: The group's principal activity is to provide outsourced receivables management services. The group purchases, collects and manages portfolios of defaulted consumer receivables. Defaulted consumer receivables are the unpaid obligations of individuals to credit originators, including banks, credit unions, consumer and auto finance companies, retail merchants and other providers of goods and services. The defaulted consumer receivables collected are either purchased from the credit originator or are collected on behalf of clients on a commission fee basis.

Primary SIC and add'l.: 6159 6153

CIK No: 0001185348

Subsidiaries: Brad Ragan, Inc, Household Recovery Services, PRA Holding I, LLC, PRA Inc, PRA Location Services, LLC, RDS, Thomas West Associates, LLC

Officers: Steven Fredrickson/Chmn., CEO, Pres., Craig Grube/Exec. VP - Acquisitions, Kevin Stevenson/Chief Administrative Officer, Exec. VP, CFO, Treasurer, Assist. Sec., Judith Scott/Exec. VP, General Counsel, Sec.

Directors: Steven Fredrickson/Chmn., CEO, Pres., William Brophey/Dir., Penelope Kyle/Dir., James Voss/Dir., Scott Tabakin/Dir., David Roberts/Dir.

Owners: Craig Grube/0.30%, Judith Scott/0.10%, Michael J. Petit/0.20%, James Voss/0.10%, Scott Tabakin, Steve Fredrickson/1.60%, William F. ODaire/0.10%, TimesSquare Capital Management, LLC/5.69%, Second Curve Capital, LLC/5.64%, David Roberts/0.60%, William Brophey, Chris Graves, Penelope Kyle, Insiders/3.60%, Kevin Stevenson/0.50% *(16 Owners included in Index)*

Financial Data: Fiscal Year End:12/31   Latest Annual Data: 12/31/2006

Year	Sales	Net Income
2006	$188,322,000	$44,490,000
2005	$148,525,000	$36,772,000
2004	$113,396,000	$27,451,000

Curr. Assets:	$26,614,000	Curr. Liab.:	$11,715,000	P/E Ratio:	20.43
Plant, Equip.:	$11,193,000	Total Liab.:	$46,100,000	Indic. Yr. Divd.:	NA
Total Assets:	$293,378,000	Net Worth:	$247,278,000	Debt/ Equity:	0.0029

Portland General Electric Company

121 SW Salmon St., Portland, OR, 97204; **PH:** 1-503-464-8000; **Fax:** 1-503-464-2676; **http://** www.portlandgeneral.com

General - Incorporation	OR	**Stock**- Price on:12/24/2007	$27.27
Employees	2,635	Stock Exchange	NYSE
Auditor	Deloitte & Touche LLP	Ticker Symbol	POR
Stk Agt	American Stock Transfer & Trust Co.	Outstanding Shares	62,510,000
Counsel	NA	E.P.S	$2.58
DUNS No.	NA	Shareholders	NA

Business: The groups principle activities include generating, purchasing, transmitting, distributing and retailing electricity. In the year 2006, the group acquired 76 wind turbines. The group operates from the United States. The group's quarterly revenue for Septmber 2007 was 435.00 millions of USD.

Primary SIC and add'l.: 4911

CIK No: 0000784977

Officers: Peggy Y. Fowler/Dir., CEO, Pres./$2,535,378.00, Jim Piro/CFO, Exec. VP - Finance, Treasurer/$669,605.00, Douglas R. Nichols/VP, General Counsel, Corp. Sec./$568,245.00, Arleen Barnett/VP - Administration/$472,457.00, Carol Dillin/VP - Public Policy, Stephen Hawke/Sr. VP - Customer Service, Delivery/$465,850.00, Cam Henderson/VP - Information Technology, Ronald W. Johnson/57/VP - Customers, Economic Development, Pamela Lesh/VP - Regulatory Affairs, Strategic Planning, James Lobdell/VP - Power Operations, Resource Planning, Joe McArthur/VP - Customer Service, Distribution Support, Stephen Quennoz/VP - Power Supply, Generation, Jay Dudley/VP, General Counsel, Corporate Compliance Officer, Bill Nicholson/VP - Customers, Economic Development, William Valach/Dir. - Investor Relations *(16 Officers included in Index)*

Directors: Peggy Y. Fowler/Dir., CEO, Pres., Corbin A. McNeill/Chmn., John W. Ballantine/Dir., Rodney L. Brown/Dir., David A. Dietzler/Dir., Mark B. Ganz/Dir., Neil J. Nelson/Dir., Lee M. Pelton/Dir., Maria M. Pope/Dir., Robert T.F. Reid/Dir.

Owners: Harbinger Capital Partners Master Fundl, Ltd. Cayman Islands/7.40%, Mark B. Ganz, Insiders, Enron Disputed Claims Reserve/51.20%, Maria M. Pope, David A. Dietzler, Neil J. Nelson, Lee M. Pelton, John W. Ballantine, Rodney L. Brown, Corbin A. McNeill, Robert T.F. Reid

Financial Data: ***Fiscal Year End:***12/31 ***Latest Annual Data:*** 12/31/2006

Year		Sales		Net Income	
2006		$1,520,000,000		$71,000,000	
2005		$1,446,000,000		$64,000,000	
2004		$1,454,000,000		$92,000,000	
Curr. Assets:	$527,000,000	**Curr. Liab.:**	$562,000,000	**P/E Ratio:**	12.92
Plant, Equip.:	$2,718,000,000	**Total Liab.:**	$2,543,000,000	**Indic. Yr. Divd.:**	$0.940
Total Assets:	$3,767,000,000	**Net Worth:**	$1,224,000,000	**Debt/ Equity:**	NA

Portola Packaging Inc

951 Douglas Rd. , Batavia, IL, 60510; ***PH:*** 1-630-406-8440; ***Fax:*** 1-630-406-8441; ***http://*** www.portpack.com; ***Email:*** info@portpack.com

General - Incorporation	DE	**Stock**- Price on:12/24/2007	NA
Employees	NA	Stock Exchange	NA
Auditor	BDO Seidman, LLP	Ticker Symbol	NA
Stk Agt		Outstanding Shares	NA
Counsel	Tomlinson Zisko LLP	E.P.S	NA
DUNS No.	04-501-6490	Shareholders	NA

Business: The group's principal activity is to design, manufacture and market tamper evident plastic closures and related equipment used for packaging applications in beverages and related food products. The group's product line is grouped into five categories: small closures five-gallon closures, wide mouth closures, fitments and push-pull dispensing closures. It designs, manufactures and supplies high speed capping equipment and turnkey water bottling systems. The products are manufactured through injection molding processes at eleven manufacturing facilities located in the United States, Canada, Mexico, China and the United Kingdom. Its major brand names are cap snap, snap cap, cap snap seal, non-spill, twist & spout, cap profile logo, cap seal, plasto-lok, product integrity, nepco and portola packaging. On 19-Sep-2003, it acquired tech industries inc.

Primary SIC and add'l.: 3085 3089

CIK No: 0000788983

Subsidiaries: Northern Engineering and Plastics Corporation, Portola (Asia Pacific) Holding Limited, Portola Allied Tool, Inc, Portola GmbH, Portola Ltd. (U.K.), Portola Packaging (ANZ) Limited, Portola Packaging Canada Ltd, Portola Packaging Limited, Portola s.r.o, Shanghai Portola Packaging Company Limited, Tech Industries UK Ltd, Tech Industries, Inc

Officers: Brian J. Bauerbach/43/Dir., CEO, Pres., Jim Funera/Technical Service Engineers - Water and Dairy Equipment, Dan Depaolo/Dir. - Technical Service, United States, Matt Mateer/Production Mgr. - Water and Dairy Equipment, Jeff Dunham/Sales, Service Representative, Northpoint Packaging Systems, Inc, Mike Bryce/Contact - Southeast Asia, Africa Australia, South Pacific Islands, Oceania, International Sales, Piet Gruwez/Contact - Continental Europe, International Sales, Kim Wehrenberg/56/VP, General Counsel, Sec., Michael T. Morefield/52/Sr. VP, CFO, Kim Rieser/Administrator - Northpoint Packaging Systems, Inc, Ralph Crompton/Sales Representative - Crompton Sales Inc, Phil Gillis/Sales, Crompton Sales Inc, Allen Witmer/Sales, Crompton Sales Inc, Lauren Fritchy/Customer Service - Crompton Sales Inc, Bob Barber/Sales, Crompton Sales Inc *(54 Officers included in Index)*

Directors: Brian J. Bauerbach/43/Dir., CEO, Pres., Martin Imbler/60/Chmn., Robert Egan/44/Dir., Jack L. Watts/60/Dir., Larry C. Williams/59/Dir., Richard Cross/60/Dir., Debra Leipman-Yale/52/Dir.

Owners: Jack L. Watts/34.00%, Jeff Swoyer, Richard Lohrman/2.00%, Robert Egan/24.50%, Suez Equity Investors, L.P., Debra Leipman-Yale, Gary L. Barry/6.20%, Brian J. Bauerbach/3.90%, Larry C. Williams/1.40%, Martin Imbler, J.P. Morgan Partners 23A/24.00%, Kim Wehrenberg/1.30%, Michael T. Morefield/1.70%, SEI Associates, Insiders/71.70%

Portrush Petroleum Corp

1687 W Broadway, Ste. 200, Vancouver, BC, V6J 1X2; ***PH:*** 1-604-696-2555; ***Fax:*** 1-604-738-8116; ***http://*** www.portrushpetroleum.com; ***Email:*** info@portrushpetroleum.com

General - Incorporation	BC	**Stock**- Price on:12/24/2007	$0.099
Employees	NA	Stock Exchange	OTC
Auditor	Davidson & Company LLP	Ticker Symbol	PRRPF
Stk Agt	Computershare Trust Co	Outstanding Shares	NA
Counsel	NA	E.P.S	NA
DUNS No.	NA	Shareholders	NA

Business: The groups principle activities include acquiring, exploring, and developing oil and gas properties. The group operates from the United States and Canada.

Primary SIC and add'l.: 1382

CIK No: 0001008112

Officers: Martin P. Cotter/56/Dir., CEO, Pres., Neal Iverson/Dir., Sec., Wes Franklin/Dir. - Consulting Geologist

Directors: Martin P. Cotter/56/Dir., CEO, Pres., Neal Iverson/Dir., Sec., Wes Franklin/Dir. - Consulting Geologist

Owners: Martin P. Cotter/15.80%, Insiders/19.20%, Wes Franklin/3.00%, Neal Iverson/0.40%

Financial Data: ***Fiscal Year End:***12/31 ***Latest Annual Data:*** 12/31/2005

Year		Sales		Net Income	
2005		$509,000		-$137,000	
2004		$367,000		-$636,000	
2003		$321,000		-$577,000	
Curr. Assets:	$226,000	**Curr. Liab.:**	$91,000		
Plant, Equip.:	$1,348,000	**Total Liab.:**	$100,000	**Indic. Yr. Divd.:**	NA
Total Assets:	$1,574,000	**Net Worth:**	$1,474,000	**Debt/ Equity:**	NA

Portsmouth Square Inc

820 Moraga Dr., Los Angeles, CA, 90049; ***PH:*** 1-310-889-2500

General - Incorporation	CA	**Stock**- Price on:12/24/2007	$35.05
Employees	3	Stock Exchange	OTC
Auditor	Pricewaterhousecoopers LLP	Ticker Symbol	PRSI
Stk Agt	U.S. Stock Transfer Corp	Outstanding Shares	NA
Counsel	NA	E.P.S	-$0.74
DUNS No.	10-852-3184	Shareholders	NA

Business: The group conducts business through the general and limited partnership interest in justice investors. The primary source of revenue for the company is from its 49.8% interest in justice investors. Justice investors owns the land, improvements and leaseholds at 750 kearny street in san francisco, California and derives income mainly from lease between the partnership and felcor lodging trust, inc.

Primary SIC and add'l.: 6512 6799

CIK No: 0000079661

Owners: Santa Fe Financial Corporation/79.70%, Insiders/86.30%, Jerold R. Babin/6.60%

Financial Data: ***Fiscal Year End:***06/30 ***Latest Annual Data:*** 6/30/2006

Year		Sales		Net Income	
2006		$271,000		-$1,603,000	
2005		NA		-$2,523,000	
2004		$3,428,000		$3,227,000	
Curr. Assets:	$3,340,000	**Curr. Liab.:**	$13,218,000		
Plant, Equip.:	$41,620,000	**Total Liab.:**	$61,386,000	**Indic. Yr. Divd.:**	NA
Total Assets:	$65,418,000	**Net Worth:**	$4,032,000	**Debt/ Equity:**	NA

Portugal Telecom

Av Fontes Pereira De Melo 40, Codex, Lisboa; ; ***http://*** www.telecom.pt; ***Email:*** geral@telecom.pt

General - Incorporation	The Portuguese Republic	**Stock**- Price on:12/24/2007	$13.99
Employees	32,058	Stock Exchange	NYSE
Auditor	Deloitte & Assoc., SROC, S.A	Ticker Symbol	PT
Stk Agt	Bank of New York	Outstanding Shares	NA
Counsel	NA	E.P.S	NA
DUNS No.	45-401-0729	Shareholders	NA

Business: The group's principal activities are the operation of public exchange telephone line networks, domestic and international transmission facilities, mobile telephone services, paging, data communication, telex, leased lines, cable television broadcasting and other related activities. The group operates through four main divisions: wire line business, mobile business, multimedia business and international business. It works mainly in Portugal and Brazil.

Primary SIC and add'l.: 3663 4812 4899 4841 4822 4813

CIK No: 0000944747

Subsidiaries: Brasilcel, N.V., Cabo Verde Telecom, S.A., CRT Celular Participaes S.A., CST Companhia Santomensa de Telecomunicaes, S.A.R.L., CTM Companhia de Telecomunicaes de Macau, S.A.R.L., Global Telecom, S.A., Lusomundo Audiovisuais, S.A., Lusomundo Cinemas, S.A., Mobitel, S.A. Unitel, Portugal Telecom Inovao, S.A., Portugal Telecom International Finance B.V., Portugal Telecom, Brasil, S.A., PT Compras Servios de Consultoria e Negociao, S.A., PT Comunicaes, S.A., PT Contact Telemarketing e Servios de Informao, S.A. 29 Subsidiaries included in the Index

Officers: Henrique Granadeiro/65/Chmn., CEO, Nuno Miguel Da Silva Anjos Machado/33/Mgr. - Planning, Control Department, Zeinal Bava/43/Dir., VP, Luis Pacheco De Melo/Dir., CFO

Directors: Henrique Granadeiro/65/Chmn., CEO, Zeinal Bava/43/Dir., VP, Luis Pacheco De Melo/Dir., CFO, Joao Pedro Baptista/Dir., Paulo Jorge Da Costa Goncalves Fernandes/42/Dir., Francisco Teixeira Pereira Soares/58/Dir., Jose Guilherme Xavier De Bastos/69/Dir., Rafael Luis Mora Funes/42/Dir., Antonio Caria/56/Dir., Rui Pedro Soares/Dir.

Owners: Brandes Investments Partners L.P./4.20%, Joao Manuel de Mello Franco/0.00%, Telefnica/9.96%, Nuno Rocha dos Santos de Almeida e Vasconcellos/5.35%, Fidelity Group/2.09%, Franquelim Fernando Garcia Alves/0.60%, Merrill Lynch International/2.20%, Antnio Aleixo Claudino Caria, Visabeira Group/2.01%, Telefnos de Mexico, S.A. de C.V./3.41%, Zeinal Abedin Mahomed Bava, Paulson & Co. Inc./2.34%, Grupo Barclays/2.06%, Amlcar Carlos Ferreria de Morais Pires/7.77%, Capital Group Companies/2.04% *(27 Owners included in Index)*

Financial Data: ***Fiscal Year End:***12/31 ***Latest Annual Data:*** 12/31/2006

Year		Sales		Net Income	
2006		$5,738,434,000		$1,033,902,000	
2005		$7,562,889,000		$362,375,000	
2004		$8,217,582,000		$662,694,000	
Curr. Assets:	$5,279,445,000	**Curr. Liab.:**	$5,133,827,000		
Plant, Equip.:	$5,018,563,000	**Total Liab.:**	$15,737,422,000	**Indic. Yr. Divd.:**	$0.510
Total Assets:	$18,216,396,000	**Net Worth:**	$2,478,974,000	**Debt/ Equity:**	NA

POSCO

2 Executive Dr., Ste. 805, Fort Lee, NJ, 07024; ***PH:*** 1-201-585-3060; ***Fax:*** 1-201-585-6001; ***http://*** www.posco.co.kr

General - Incorporation	Korea	**Stock**- Price on:12/24/2007	$127.4891
Employees	28,853	Stock Exchange	NYSE
Auditor	Samil PricewaterhouseCoopers	Ticker Symbol	PKX
Stk Agt	Kookmin Bank	Outstanding Shares	NA
Counsel	NA	E.P.S	NA
DUNS No.	68-774-1991	Shareholders	NA

Business: The group's principal activity is the production and distribution of hot and cold rolled coil steel sheets which are used in automobiles, steel structure, steel pipe, home appliances, and food containers; steel plates which are used in marine structures, pressure vessels, machinery pipes and storage tanks; wire rods which are used to make screws, nail, barbed wires, wire mesh, wire ropes, springs, welding electrodes, and underwater cables; electrical steel sheets which are used for power generators and transformers; and stainless steel products which are used in home appliances, medical equipment, machinery, automobile exhaust system, train interior and exterior panels.

Primary SIC and add'l.: 3316 3312

CIK No: 0000889132

Subsidiaries: Changwon Specialty Steel Co., Ltd., Dalian Posco-cfm Coated Steel Co., Ltd., Dongwoosa Service Inc., Guangdong Pohang Coated Steel Co., Ltd., IBC Corporation, Myanmar-POSCO Co., Ltd., Pohang Coated Steel Co., Ltd., POS-AC Co., Ltd., POS-CD Pty. Ltd., POS-GC Pty. Ltd., POS-IPC, POS-ORE Pty. Ltd., POS-Qingdao Coil Center Co., Ltd., Pos-thai Steel Service Center Co., Ltd., POS-Tianjin Coil Center Co., Ltd. 47 Subsidiaries included in the Index

Officers: Lee Ku-Taek/Dir., CEO, Cho Bong-Rae/Sr. VP - Departy General Super Intendent - Iron, Steel Making, Pohang Works, Finex Research, Development Project Dept, Cho Soung-Sik/Dir., Sr. Exec. VP, Ha Sang-Wook/Sr. VP, Kee-Yeoung Park/Sr. VP, Yun Tai-Han/Sr. VP - Marketing Strategy Dept - Sales, Production Planning Dept, Marketing Division, Kim Moon-Seok/Sr. VP - GM - Seoul Office, Chang In-Hwan/53/Sr. VP - Cold, Rolled Steel Sales Dept, Automotive Flat Products Sales Dept, Automotive Flat Products Exports Dept, Coated Steel Sales Dept, Electrical Steel Sheets Sales Dept, Marketing Division, Kwon Oh-Joon/Exec. VP - General Superintendent - Technical Research Laboratory, Operating, Technology Division, Jong-Ta Choi/Sr. Exec. VP, Won Jong-Hai/Sr. VP - Operating - Technology Division, Materials Purchasing, Supply Management Dept, Kim Tae-Man/Sr. VP - Deputy General Superintendent - Pohang Works, General Administration, Labor, Management Cooperation Group, Operating, Technology Division, Lee Sang-Young/Sr. VP - Corporate Communication Dept, Choo Wung-Yong/Sr. VP - GM - EU Office, Kim Joon-Sik/Sr. VP - Operating - Technology Division, Technology Development Department Mgr. - Magnesium Project Dept *(42 Officers included in Index)*

Directors: Lee Ku-Taek/Dir., CEO, Kim E. Han/Dir., Chmn., Jun Kwang-Woo/Dir., Park Won-Soon/Dir., Suh Yoon-Suk/Dir., Sung K. Huh/60/Dir., Lee Youn/60/Dir., Pres., Yoon Seok-Man/Dir., Pres. Chief Marketing Officer - Corporate Communication Dept, Energy Business Dept, Park Young-Ju/Dir., Ahn Charles/Dir., Sun Wook/Dir., Lee Dong-Hee/Dir., Sr. Exec. VP, Kwang-Woo Jun/Dir., Jeffrey D. Jones/Dir., Cho Soung-Sik/Dir., Sr. Exec. VP *(16 Directors included in Index)*

Owners: National Pension Corporation/2.86%, POSCO/2.95%, POSCO/8.06%, Insiders/100.00%, Pohang University of Science and Technology/2.67%, SK Telecom/2.85%, Public/80.61%, Directors and executive officers as a group

Financial Data: Fiscal Year End: 12/31   **Latest Annual Data:** 12/31/2006

Year	Sales	Net Income
2006	$28,426,559,000	$3,748,575,000
2005	$26,041,374,000	$3,971,828,000
2004	$23,973,053,000	$3,460,214,000

Curr. Assets:	$13,460,648,000	**Curr. Liab.:**	$5,590,525,000			
Plant, Equip.:	$16,214,596,000	**Total Liab.:**	$10,160,192,000	**Indic. Yr. Divd.:**	NA	
Total Assets:	$34,329,559,000	**Net Worth:**	$24,169,367,000	**Debt/ Equity:**	NA	

Poseidis Inc

222 Lake Ave., Pmb 160, West Palm Beach, FL, 33401; **PH:** 1-305-428-3758; **http://** www.poseidis.com; **Email:** info@poseidis.com

General - Incorporation	FL	**Stock**- Price on:12/24/2007	$0.049
Employees	NA	Stock Exchange	OTC
Auditor	Moore Stephens, P. C.	Ticker Symbol	PSED
Stk Agt	Interwest Transfer Company, Inc.	Outstanding Shares	70,160,000
Counsel	NA	E.P.S.	-$0.026
DUNS No.	NA	Shareholders	NA

Business: The group's principal activity is the commercial and industrial exploitation of a natural mineral water spring. The group provides water potabilization solutions that fit individual needs. Through a combination of approved methods and technology's latest breakthroughs, our equipment allows to protect against recontamination of the water supply without the use of chemicals. The group's operations have been to secure a 'source' of natural mineral water in France and negotiating with several entities to build a bottling facility. The group is also involved in two other water production areas: production and bottling of natural mineral spring waters and marketing and brand development for natural mineral spring waters.

Primary SIC and add'l.: 4941

CIK No: 0001088399

Subsidiaries: Montespan SAS

Officers: Louis Pardo/39/Chmn., CEO, Pres., Diane Boisvert/49/Dir., Sec., John J. McGovern/51/CFO, Exec. VP, Treasurer

Directors: Louis Pardo/39/Chmn., CEO, Pres., Diane Boisvert/49/Dir., Sec., Robert Prunetti/Dir., Shyam Iyer/Dir.

Owners: Diane Boisvert, Insiders/21.36%, John J. McGovern/1.58%, Louis Pardo/20.05%, Christophe Giovannetti/20.51%

Financial Data: Fiscal Year End: 02/28   **Latest Annual Data:** 2/28/2006

Year	Sales	Net Income
2006	NA	-$1,569,000
2005	NA	-$3,294,000
2004	NA	-$794,000

Curr. Assets:	$135,000	**Curr. Liab.:**	$529,000		
Plant, Equip.:	$54,000	**Total Liab.:**	$529,000	**Indic. Yr. Divd.:**	NA
Total Assets:	$232,000	**Net Worth:**	-$297,000	**Debt/ Equity:**	NA

Positron Corp

1304 Langham Creek Dr., Ste. 300, Houston, TX, 77084; **PH:** 1-281-492-7100; **Fax:** 1-281-492-2961; **http://** www.positron.com; **Email:** ir@positron.com

General - Incorporation	TX	**Stock**- Price on:12/24/2007	$0.1
Employees	10	Stock Exchange	OTC
Auditor	Frank L. Sassetti & Co.	Ticker Symbol	POSC
Stk Agt	Bank of Boston	Outstanding Shares	87,210,000
Counsel	NA	E.P.S.	-$0.08
DUNS No.	11-849-0259	Shareholders	NA

Business: The group's principle activities include designing, manufacturing, marketing and servicing advanced medical imaging devices using positron emission tomography technology. The company markets its product under the trademark posicam (TM) . Posicam(tm) systems incorporate patented and proprietary technology and enable physicians to diagnose and treat patients in the areas of cardiology, neurology and oncology. The products of the company are sold to medical institutions. Company operates solely operates in the United States. The group operates from United States.

Primary SIC and add'l.: 3845

CIK No: 0000844985

Subsidiaries: IMAGIN

Officers: Joseph G. Oliverio/38/Dir., Pres., Corey N. Conn/46/CFO, Timothy M. Gabel/38/VP - Operations

Directors: Patrick G. Rooney/45/Chmn., Sachio Okamura/56/Dir., Anthony C. Nicholls/59/Dir., Joseph G. Oliverio/38/Dir., Pres.

Owners: IMAGIN Diagnostic Centres, Inc., Jamscor, Inc./10.80%, Fleet Securities/11.00%, Positron Acquisition Corp., Corey N. Conn, John H. Wilson/7.20%, Anthony C. Nicholls, Sachio Okamura, Patrick G. Rooney, Joseph G. Oliverio, Imaging Pet Technologies, Inc., Timothy M. Gabel, Imagin Diagnostic Centres, Inc./76.10%, Insiders, Morgan Instruments, Inc./9.00% *(17 Owners included in Index)*

Financial Data: Fiscal Year End: 12/31   **Latest Annual Data:** 12/31/2006

Year	Sales	Net Income
2006	$2,213,000	-$6,586,000
2005	$762,000	-$3,806,000
2004	$2,780,000	-$1,658,000

Curr. Assets:	$4,932,000	**Curr. Liab.:**	$3,521,000		
Plant, Equip.:	$81,000	**Total Liab.:**	$6,571,000	**Indic. Yr. Divd.:**	NA
Total Assets:	$5,271,000	**Net Worth:**	-$1,132,000	**Debt/ Equity:**	NA

Possis Medical Inc

9055 Evergreen Blvd. NW, Minneapolis, MN, 55433; **PH:** 1-763-780-4555; **Fax:** 1-763-783-8463; **http://** www.possis.com

General - Incorporation	MN	**Stock**- Price on:12/24/2007	$10.87
Employees	269	Stock Exchange	NDQ
Auditor	Deloitte & Touche LLP	Ticker Symbol	POSS
Stk Agt	Norwest Bank Minnesota N.A	Outstanding Shares	17,110,000
Counsel	Dorsey & Whitney LLP	E.P.S.	$0.03
DUNS No.	00-624-7555	Shareholders	NA

Business: The group's principal activity is to develop and manufacture cardiovascular and vascular medical devices. The main product of the group is angiojet rheolytic thrombectomy system. The angiojet system is a non-surgical, minimally invasive catheter system designed to rapidly remove blood clots with minimal vascular trauma. The group markets its product to interventional cardiologists, interventional radiologists, vascular surgeons and physician specialty groups, such as nephrologists and osteopaths. The group has operations in the United States and the Netherlands.

Primary SIC and add'l.: 3841

CIK No: 0000079677

Subsidiaries: Possis Medical Europe B.v.

Officers: Robert G. Dutcher/Chmn., CEO, Pres., Jules Fisher/CFO, VP - Finance, Irving R. Colacci/VP - Legal, Human Resources, General Counsel, Sec., Chief Governance Officer, James D. Gustafson/Sr. VP - Research, Development, Engineering, Clinical Evaluation, Chief Quality Officer, Shawn McCarrey/Exec. VP - Worldwide Sales, Marketing, Robert J. Scott/VP - Manufacturing Operations, Information Technology, Chief Security Officer, Alan Kaeding/Contact - Media

Directors: Robert G. Dutcher/Chmn., CEO, Pres., Mary K. Brainerd/55/Dir., Seymour J. Mansfield/63/Dir., William C. Mattison/60/Dir., Donald C. Wegmiller/70/Dir., Rodney A. Young/53/Dir., Whitney A. McFarlin/68/Dir.

Owners: Mary K. Brainerd, Irving R. Colacci, Whitney A. McFarlin, Royce and Associates, LLC/10.90%, Black River Asset Management, LLC/6.70%, Robert G. Dutcher/3.10%, Seymour J. Mansfield/1.10%, Donald C. Wegmiller, Rodney A. Young, Shawn F. McCarrey, Jules L. Fisher, James D. Gustafson/1.10%, Insiders/10.90%, William C. Mattison

Financial Data: Fiscal Year End: 07/31   **Latest Annual Data:** 7/31/2006

Year	Sales	Net Income
2006	$61,879,000	$809,000
2005	$65,053,000	$6,155,000
2004	$72,420,000	$11,729,000

Curr. Assets:	$65,383,000	**Curr. Liab.:**	$8,225,000	**P/E Ratio:**	362.33
Plant, Equip.:	$5,090,000	**Total Liab.:**	$9,049,000	**Indic. Yr. Divd.:**	NA
Total Assets:	$81,952,000	**Net Worth:**	$72,904,000	**Debt/ Equity:**	NA

Post Properties Inc

4401 Nside Pkwy., Ste. 800, Atlanta, GA, 30327; **PH:** 1-404-846-5000; **Fax:** 1-404-846-6282; **http://** www.postproperties.com; **Email:** info@postproperties.com

General - Incorporation	GA	**Stock**- Price on:12/24/2007	$50.34
Employees	790	Stock Exchange	NYSE
Auditor	Deloitte & Touche LLP	Ticker Symbol	PPS
Stk Agt	Computershare Trust Co	Outstanding Shares	43,640,000
Counsel	NA	E.P.S.	NA
DUNS No.	NA	Shareholders	NA

Business: The groups principle activities include developing, owning and managing multifamily apartment communities. In the year 2006, the group acquired two apartments. The group operates from the United States. The group's quarterly revenue for September 2007 was 78.01 millions of USD.

Primary SIC and add'l.: 6798

CIK No: 0000903127

Subsidiaries: 1499 Massachusetts Avenue, Inc., 1499 Massachusetts Holding, LLC, 3630 Condo Holdings, LLC, 3630 North Tower Residential, LLC, 3630 Peachtree Road Holdings Limited Partnership, 3630 Residential GP, LLC, 3630 South Tower Residential, LLC, 98 San Jac Condo Investment, LLC, 98 San Jac Condo Limited Partnership, 98 San Jac Condo Management, LLC, 98 San Jac Holdings Limited Partnership, 98 San Jac Holdings Management, LLC, 98 San Jac Rental Limited Partnership, 98 San Jac Rental Management, LLC, Addison Circle Access, Inc. 91 Subsidiaries included in the Index

Officers: David P. Stockert/Dir., CEO, Pres./$1,287,774.00, Charles A. Konas/Sr. VP - Construction - Development, Jeffrey W. Harris/Exec. VP, Regional Investment Dir. Southeast Region - Post Investment Group, Holly Mudd/PCA GM, Orlala Icenberger/PCA GM, Debbie Thomas/PCA

GM, Leslie Drohan/PCA GM, Wallace Hitt/Group Relocation Assistance, Lori Hoogland/Group Relocation Assistance, Western Division, Catherine M. Howell/VP - Commercial - Post Apartment Management, Martin J. Howle/Exec. VP, Regional Investment Dir. Mid - Atlantic, New York Region, Post Investment Group, David C. Ward/Exec. VP - Regional Investment Directo Rsouthwest Region, Post Investment Group, Curtis W. Walker/Exec. VP, Regional Investment Dir. Southeast Region - Post Investment Group, Kathleen M. Mason/VP - Taxation - Post Corporate Services, Cheryl Bruce/Contact *(33 Officers included in Index)*

Directors: David P. Stockert/Dir., CEO, Pres., Robert C. Goddard/Chmn., Herschel M. Bloom/Dir., Douglas Crocker/Dir., Walter M. Deriso/Dir., Russell R. French/Dir., Nicholas B. Paumgarten/Dir., Charles E. Rice/Dir., Stella F. Thayer/Dir., Ronald De Waal/Dir.

Owners: Herschel M. Bloom, Charles E. Rice, The Vanguard Group, Inc/6.10%, Ronald de Waal, Insiders/4.30%, Walter M. Deriso, ING Groep N.V./6.20%, Stella F. Thayer, JPMorgan Chase & Co./7.30%, David P. Stockert/1.20%, Sherry W. Cohen, Nicholas B. Paumgarten, David OConnor/5.40%, Thomas D. Senkbeil, Robert C. Goddard *(23 Owners included in Index)*

Financial Data: **Fiscal Year End:**12/31 **Latest Annual Data:** 06/30/2007

Year	Sales	Net Income
2007	$78,309,000	$63,937,000
2006	$300,096,000	$101,469,000
2005	$296,803,000	$141,948,000

Curr. Assets:	$8,866,000	**Curr. Liab.:**	$110,089,000	**P/E Ratio:**	19.51
Plant, Equip.:	$2,028,580,000	**Total Liab.:**	$1,143,868,000	**Indic. Yr. Divd.:**	$1.800
Total Assets:	$2,116,647,000	**Net Worth:**	$956,454,000	**Debt/ Equity:**	1.0761

Potash Corp of Saskatchewan Inc

500-122 1st Ave. S, Saskatoon, SK, S7K 7G3; ***PH:*** 1-306-933-8500; ***Fax:*** 1-306-933-8844; ***http://*** www.potashcorp.com

General - Incorporation	Canada	**Stock**- Price on:12/24/2007	$76.7
Employees	4,871	Stock Exchange	NYSE
Auditor	Deloitte & Touche LLP	Ticker Symbol	POT
Stk Agt	Mellon Trust Co	Outstanding Shares	315,400,000
Counsel	Robertson Stromberg	E.P.S	$2.83
DUNS No.	24-819-0209	Shareholders	NA

Business: The group's principle activities of the group are the mining, production and sale of potash, phosphate ore, phosphoric acid and nitrogen fertilizers and nitrogen chemicals. The group manufactures and distributes solid and liquid fertilizers and other agricultural supplies. The group has three reportable business segments: potash, phosphate and nitrogen. The group's quarterly revenue for September 2007 was 1,295.00 millions of USD.

Primary SIC and add'l.: 2873 1474 1475

CIK No: 0000855931

Subsidiaries: 101070338 Saskatchewan Ltd., 175360 Canada Inc., 609430 Saskatchewan Ltd., 628550 Saskatchewan Ltd., AA Sulfuric Corporation, Augusta Service Company, Inc., Canpotex Bulk Terminals Limited, Chilkap Resources Ltd., El Boldo Limitada, El Roble Limitada, Inversiones PCS Chile Limitada, Inversiones RAC Chile Limitada, Minera Saskatchewan Limitada, PCS (Barbados) Holdings SRL, PCS (Barbados) Investment Company Ltd. 57 Subsidiaries included in the Index

Officers: William J. Doyle/CEO, Pres., Bill Johnson/Dir. - Public Affairs, Thomas J. Regan/Pres. - PCS Phosphate, PCS Nitrogen, Karen G. Chasez/VP - Procurement, Robert A. Jaspar/Sr. VP - Information Technology, Daphne J. Arnason/VP - Internal Audit, John R. Hunt/VP - Safety, Health and Environment, Wayne R. Brownlee/CFO, Exec. VP, Denis A. Sirois/VP, Corporate Controller, Barbara Jane Irwin/Sr. VP - Administration, Rhonda Speiss/Mgr. - Public Relations, Joseph A. Podwika/Sr. VP, General Counsel, Sec., James F. Dietz/COO, Exec. VP, David G. Delaney/Pres. - PCS Sales, Garth W. Moore/Pres. - PCS Potash *(16 Officers included in Index)*

Directors: Dallas J. Howe/Chmn., Wade Fetzer/Dir., Alice D. Laberge/Dir., Jeffrey J. McCaig/Dir., Elena Viyella De Paliza/Dir., Mary Mogford/Dir., Paul J. Schoenhals/Dir., Robert E. Stromberg/Dir., Jack G. Vicq/Dir., Keith G. Martell/Dir., Frederick J. Blesi/Dir., John W. Estey/Dir.

Financial Data: **Fiscal Year End:**12/31 **Latest Annual Data:** 12/31/2006

Year	Sales	Net Income
2006	$3,766,700,000	$625,800,000
2005	$3,847,200,000	$532,700,000
2004	$3,244,400,000	$290,500,000

Curr. Assets:	$1,354,700,000	**Curr. Liab.:**	$1,131,800,000	**P/E Ratio:**	30.20
Plant, Equip.:	$3,409,800,000	**Total Liab.:**	$3,636,000,000	**Indic. Yr. Divd.:**	$0.400
Total Assets:	$7,038,900,000	**Net Worth:**	$3,402,900,000	**Debt/ Equity:**	0.3411

Potlatch Corp

601 W 1st Ave.., Ste. 1600, Spokane, WA, 99201; ***PH:*** 1-509-835-1500; ***Fax:*** 1-509-835-1559; ***http://*** www.potlatchcorp.com; ***Email:*** info@potlatchcorp.com

General - Incorporation	DE	**Stock**- Price on:12/24/2007	$42.86
Employees	3,800	Stock Exchange	NYSE
Auditor	KPMG LLP	Ticker Symbol	PCH
Stk Agt	Computershare Investor Services LLC	Outstanding Shares	39,020,000
Counsel	Pillsbury Winthrop LLP	E.P.S	$1.92
DUNS No.	00-944-8200	Shareholders	NA

Business: The groups principle activity is to operate timberlands. The groups products include logs and fiber, paperboard and NBSK pulp. The group operates through five segments namely resource, land sales and development, wood products, pulp and paperboard, and consumer products. The group operates from United States.

Primary SIC and add'l.: 2621 2435 2493 2611

CIK No: 0000079716

Subsidiaries: NaturNorth Technologies, LLC, Prescott & Northwestern Railroad Co., St. Maries River Railroad Co., Warren & Saline River Railroad Co.

Officers: Michael J. Covey/Chmn., CEO, Pres., Pamela A. Mull/VP, General Counsel, Eric J. Cremers/CFO, VP, Matt Vanvleet/Dir. - Corporate Communications, Robert P. Devleming/VP - Consumer Product Division, Harry D. Seamans/VP - Pulp, Paperboard Division, Richard K. Kelly/VP - Wood Products Division, Brent L. Stinnett/VP - Resource Management Division, Mark J. Benson/VP - Public Affairs, Jane Crane/VP - Human Resources, William R. Dereu/VP - Real Estate Division

Directors: Michael J. Covey/Chmn., CEO, Pres., Ruth Ann M. Gillis/Dir., William T. Weyerhaeuser/Dir., Michael T. Riordan/Dir., John S. Moody/Dir., Jerome C. Knoll/Dir., Gregory L. Quesnel/Dir., Boh A. Dickey/Dir., Judith M. Runstad/Dir., Lawrence S. Peiros/Dir., William L. Driscoll/Dir.

Financial Data: **Fiscal Year End:**12/31 **Latest Annual Data:** 12/31/2006

Year	Sales	Net Income
2006	$1,607,827,000	$139,110,000
2004	$1,351,472,000	$271,249,000
2003	$1,506,634,000	$50,727,000

Curr. Assets:	$356,519,000	**Curr. Liab.:**	$196,264,000	**P/E Ratio:**	38.27
Plant, Equip.:	$962,518,000	**Total Liab.:**	$879,748,000	**Indic. Yr. Divd.:**	$1.960
Total Assets:	$1,457,607,000	**Net Worth:**	$577,859,000	**Debt/ Equity:**	NA

Potomac Bancshares Inc

111 E Washington St., Charles Town, WV, 25414; ***PH:*** 1-304-725-8431; ***Fax:*** 1-304-725-0059; ***http://*** www.bankatbct.com

General - Incorporation	WV	**Stock**- Price on:12/24/2007	$15.55
Employees	88	Stock Exchange	OTC
Auditor	Yount, Hyde & Barbour, P.C	Ticker Symbol	PTBS
Stk Agt	American Stock Transfer & Trust Co.	Outstanding Shares	3,430,000
Counsel	NA	E.P.S	$1.14
DUNS No.	00-342-5923	Shareholders	NA

Business: The group's principal activity is to provide banking services to consumers, businesses and governments in berkeley and jefferson county, west Virginia. The lending activities of the group include commercial, financial, agricultural, residential and consumer loans. The deposits services of the group include demand, now, savings, certificates of deposits and individual retirement accounts. The group operates through its wholly owned subsidiary, bank of charles town. The group operates only in the domestic market.

Primary SIC and add'l.: 6022 6712

CIK No: 0000925173

Subsidiaries: Bank of Charles Town

Officers: Robert F. Baronner/CEO, Pres./$243,701.00, David Irvin/Commercial Loan Officer/$177,429.00, Gayle Marshall Johnson/58/SrVP, CFO/$132,915.00, Tammy Miller/Consumer Loan Officer - Martinsburg, Brian Davis/Consumer Loan Officer - Martinsburg, Tammy Hefner/Consumer Loan Officer - Hedgesville, Linda Sager/Mortgage Loan Officer - Charles Town, Bev Mitchell/Mortgage Loan Officer - Charles Town, Alan Henderson/Mortgage Loan Officer - Winchester, Donald S. Smith/79/VP, Assist. Sec., Karen Hensell/Commercial Loan Officer, Matt Perks/Commercial Loan Officer, Donna Burns/Consumer Loan Officer - Charles Town, Susan Clark/Consumer Loan Officer - Harpers Ferry, Nancy Baker/Consumer Loan Officer - Harpers Ferry *(18 Officers included in Index)*

Directors: Scott J. Boyd/Dir., John P. Burns/Dir., Guy Gareth Chicchirichi/Dir., Margaret Cogswell/Dir., Thomas C.G. Coyle/Dir., William R. Harner/Dir., William E. Johnson/Dir., Barbara H. Pichot/60/Dir., John C. Skinner/Dir., Larry C. Togans/Dir.

Owners: Margaret Cogswell/0.16%, David W. Irvin, Gayle Marshall Johnson, Thomas C.G. Coyle/0.82%, Robert F. Baronner, William R. Harner/0.40%, Scott J. Boyd, Donald S. Smith, John P. Burns, William E. Johnson, Barbara H. Pichot/0.21%, John C. Skinner, Barbara H. Pichot, Larry C. Togans, Guy Gareth Chicchirichi/0.75% *(17 Owners included in Index)*

Financial Data: **Fiscal Year End:**12/31 **Latest Annual Data:** 12/31/2006

Year	Sales	Net Income
2006	$22,865,000	$4,035,000
2005	$18,978,000	$3,664,000
2004	$15,192,000	$3,090,000

Curr. Assets:	$8,357,000	**Curr. Liab.:**	$263,596,000	**P/E Ratio:**	13.64
Plant, Equip.:	$6,421,000	**Total Liab.:**	$266,032,000	**Indic. Yr. Divd.:**	$0.430
Total Assets:	$292,749,000	**Net Worth:**	$26,717,000	**Debt/ Equity:**	NA

Potomac Edison Co (The)

800 Cabin Hill Dr., Greensburg, PA, 15601; ***PH:*** 1-724-837-3000

General - Incorporation	MD	**Stock**- Price on:12/24/2007	$50.77
Employees	4,362	Stock Exchange	NA
Auditor	PricewaterhouseCoopers LLP	Ticker Symbol	NA
Stk Agt	Mellon Investor Services LLC	Outstanding Shares	165,710,000
Counsel	NA	E.P.S	$2.14
DUNS No.	04-338-1565	Shareholders	NA

Business: The group's principal activities are the generation, transmission and distribution of electric power. The group is a wholly owned utility subsidiary of allegheny energy, inc and is a part of the allegheny energy integrated electric utility system. It operates an electric transmission and distribution system in portions of Maryland, Virginia and west Virginia under the trade name allegheny power. The group serves approximately 436,000 customers in Maryland and Virginia.

Primary SIC and add'l.: 4911

CIK No: 0000079731

Financial Data: **Fiscal Year End:**12/31 **Latest Annual Data:** 12/31/2006

Year	Sales	Net Income
2006	$3,121,489,000	$319,321,000
2005	$3,037,887,000	$63,065,000
2004	$2,756,121,000	-$310,598,000

Curr. Assets:	$909,422,000	**Curr. Liab.:**	$820,779,000	**P/E Ratio:**	27.15
Plant, Equip.:	$6,512,893,000	**Total Liab.:**	$6,437,338,000	**Indic. Yr. Divd.:**	NA
Total Assets:	$8,552,446,000	**Net Worth:**	$2,080,395,000	**Debt/ Equity:**	1.5574

Potomac Electric Power Co

701 Ninth St. NW, Washington, DC, 20068; ***PH:*** 1-202-872-2000; ***http://*** www.pepco.com

General - Incorporation	VA	**Stock**- Price on:12/24/2007	$28.26
Employees	5,156	Stock Exchange	NYSE
Auditor	PricewaterhouseCoopers LLP	Ticker Symbol	NA
Stk Agt	Mellon Investor Services LLC	Outstanding Shares	193,080,000
Counsel	NA	E.P.S	$1.29
DUNS No.	00-692-0284	Shareholders	NA

Business: The group's principle activity is to transmit and distribute electric energy throughout Washington D.C. Metropolitan area. The group also offers telecommunication services, which includes local and long distance telephone, high-speed Internet and cable television and also provides energy products and services. The products and services of the group are provided through its subsidiaries: pepco holdings, inc., potomac electric power company trust i and edison capital reserves corporation.

Primary SIC and add'l.: 6159 4911

CIK No: 0000079732

Subsidiaries: Atlantic City Electric Company (ACE), Delmarva Power & Light Company (DPL), PHI

Officers: Dennis R. Wraase/63/Chmn., CEO, Pres., William T. Torgerson/63/Vice Chmn., General Counsel, Thomas S. Shaw/60/COO, Exec. VP, Ronald K. Clark/52/VP, Controller, John U. Huffman/48/Pres., Clay Anderson/Sr. Media Representative, Robert Dobkin/Principal Media Representative, Joseph M. Rigby/51/Sr. VP, CFO, David M. Velazquez/48/Pres.

Directors: Dennis R. Wraase/63/Chmn., CEO, Pres., William T. Torgerson/63/Vice Chmn., General Counsel

Financial Data: *Fiscal Year End:*12/31 *Latest Annual Data:* 12/31/2006

Year	Sales	Net Income
2006	$8,362,900,000	$248,300,000
2005	$8,065,500,000	$371,200,000
2004	$7,221,800,000	$258,700,000

Curr. Assets:	$1,981,400,000	**Curr. Liab.:**	$2,526,900,000	**P/E Ratio:** 21.74
Plant, Equip.:	$7,576,600,000	**Total Liab.:**	$10,606,900,000	**Indic. Yr. Divd.:** $1.040
Total Assets:	$14,243,500,000	**Net Worth:**	$3,612,200,000	**Debt/ Equity:** 1.2073

Powder River Basin Gas Corp

104, 3208 8th Ave. NE, Calgary, AB, T2A 7V8; *PH:* 1-403-263-4145;
http:// www.powderrivergascorp.com; *Email:* info@powderrivergascorp.com

General - Incorporation	CO	**Stock**- Price on:12/24/2007	$0.26
Employees	NA	Stock Exchange	OTC
Auditor	Chisholm Bierwolf & Nilson LLC	Ticker Symbol	PRVB
Stk Agt	Corporate Stock Transfer, Inc.	Outstanding Shares	NA
Counsel	NA	E.P.S.	NA
DUNS No.	NA	Shareholders	NA

Business: The group's principal activities are to explore and develop oil and gas properties. The group evaluates and develops coalbed methane reserves as well as shallow oil reserves within the state of Wyoming. As of 31-Dec-2003, the group owns 11,878 acres in thirteen different leases within converse, crook, johnson and sheridan counties. On 01-Jun-2004, the group acquired s & s drilling.

Primary SIC and add'l.: 1382

CIK No: 0001125557

Subsidiaries: PRBG

Officers: Brian Fox/62/Chmn., CEO, Pres., Jeffery Q. Johnson/32/CFO, Steve Weiss/Investor Relations Contact

Directors: Brian Fox/62/Chmn., CEO, Pres., Jonathan N. Havelock/52/Dir., Mark Chang/50/Dir.

Owners: Mark Chang/3.70%, Brian Fox/39.50%, Insiders/42.70%

Financial Data: *Fiscal Year End:*12/31 *Latest Annual Data:* 12/31/2006

Year	Sales	Net Income
2006	$13,174,000	$5,725,000
2005	$4,644,000	$699,000
2004	$2,185,000	$1,008,000

Curr. Assets:	$7,876,000	**Curr. Liab.:**	$11,210,000	
Plant, Equip.:	$16,637,000	**Total Liab.:**	$11,210,000	**Indic. Yr. Divd.:** NA
Total Assets:	$24,895,000	**Net Worth:**	$13,685,000	**Debt/ Equity:** NA

Powell Industries Inc

8550 Mosley Dr., Houston, TX, 77075; *PH:* 1-713-944-6900; *Fax:* 1-713-947-4435;
http:// www.powellind.com

General - Incorporation	DE	**Stock** - Price on:12/24/2007	$30.24
Employees	1,800	Stock Exchange	NDQ
Auditor	PricewaterhouseCoopers LLP	Ticker Symbol	POWL
Stk Agt	American Stock Transfer & Trust Co.	Outstanding Shares	NA
Counsel	Winstead Sechrest & Minick	E.P.S.	NA
DUNS No.	08-835-6563	Shareholders	NA

Business: The group's principal activities are to design, develop, manufacture and service systems and equipment used in the distribution, control, generation and management of electrical energy. The business of the group is managed through operating subsidiaries, which are combined into two reportable business segments: electrical power products and process control systems. The principal products are switchgear and related equipment, bus duct and process control systems. The products and services are provided to oil and gas producers, refineries, petrochemical plants, pulp and paper producers, mining operations, commuter railways and vehicular transportation facilities, as well as public and private utilities.

Primary SIC and add'l.: 3613 3823

CIK No: 0000080420

Subsidiaries: Powell Electrical Systems, Inc., Powell Industries Asia, Inc., Powell Industries International, Inc., Powell Industries, Inc., Powell International Europe B.V., Switchgear & Instrumentation Ltd, Switchgear & Instrumentation Properties Ltd, Transdyn, Inc.

Officers: Thomas W. Powell/Chmn., CEO, Don R. Madison/Chief Administrative Officer, CFO, Milburn Honeycutt/VP, Corporate Controller, Mark W. Reid/Exec. VP, Patrick L. McDonald/COO, Pres.

Directors: Thomas W. Powell/Chmn., CEO, Eugene L. Butler/Dir., Ronald J. Wolny/Dir., James F. Clark/Dir., Joseph L. Becherer/Dir., Stephen W. Seale/Dir., Robert C. Tranchon/Dir.

Owners: Nationwide Trust Company, FSB/5.20%, Stephen W. Seale, Royce& Associates, L.L.C./11.80%, Mark W. Reid, Wellington Management Company, L.L.P./5.50%, Bonnie L. Powell/7.50%, Insiders/28.90%, Thomas W. Powell/27.70%, Ronald J. Wolny, James F. Clark, Jeffrey L. Gendell/5.70%, Joseph L. Becherer, Insiders/28.90%, Robert C. Tranchon, Milburn E. Honeycutt *(17 Owners included in Index)*

Financial Data: *Fiscal Year End:*10/31 *Latest Annual Data:* 9/30/2006

Year	Sales	Net Income
2006	$374,547,000	$9,820,000
2005	$256,645,000	$2,251,000
2004	$206,142,000	$1,669,000

Curr. Assets:	$192,946,000	**Curr. Liab.:**	$96,227,000	
Plant, Equip.:	$60,336,000	**Total Liab.:**	$133,084,000	**Indic. Yr. Divd.:** NA
Total Assets:	$292,124,000	**Net Worth:**	$158,762,000	**Debt/ Equity:** NA

Power 3 Medical Products Inc

3400 Research Forest Dr., Ste. B2-3, Woodlands, TX, 77381; *PH:* 1-281-466-1600;
Fax: 1-281-466-1481; *http://* www.power3medical.com

General - Incorporation	NY	**Stock**- Price on:12/24/2007	$0.2
Employees	14	Stock Exchange	OTC
Auditor	Malone & Bailey, P.C	Ticker Symbol	PWRM
Stk Agt	Integrity Stock Transfer, Inc.	Outstanding Shares	76,970,000
Counsel	Sichenzia Ross Friedman Ference LLP	E.P.S.	-$0.08
DUNS No.	NA	Shareholders	NA

Business: The group's principal activity is to conduct research, development, production and distribution of products and services for health care. It also develops additional products and services to provide a safer and more efficient environment for healthcare workers, manufacturers and patients. The group operates through its product namely the suturemate(R) surgical safety device. This device prevent accidental needle sticks and assist in finishing surgical sutures. On 18-May-2004, the group acquired advanced bio/chem inc.

Primary SIC and add'l.: 3841 7375

CIK No: 0001063530

Subsidiaries: TenthGate, Inc.

Officers: Steven B. Rash/Chmn., CEO, John P. Burton/62/CFO, Ira L. Goldknopf/Dir., Chief Scientific Officer, Member - Scientific Advisory Board

Directors: Steven B. Rash/Chmn., CEO, Ira L. Goldknopf/Dir., Chief Scientific Officer, Member - Scientific Advisory Board, Stanley H. Appel/Member - Scientific Advisory Board, Zouhair M. Atassi/Member - Scientific Advisory Board, Thomas E. Watts/Member - Scientific Advisory Board, Alan Hollingsworth/Member - Scientific Advisory Board

Owners: Trinity Financing Investments/6.09%, Industrial Enterprises of America, Inc./18.54%, John P. Burton, Insiders/8.22%, Steven B. Rash/7.00%, Ira L. Goldknopf/1.01%

Financial Data: *Fiscal Year End:*12/31 *Latest Annual Data:* 12/31/2006

Year	Sales	Net Income
2006	$300,000	-$6,416,000
2005	NA	-$13,513,000
2004	$15,000	-$19,081,000

Curr. Assets:	$41,000	**Curr. Liab.:**	$6,265,000	
Plant, Equip.:	$16,000	**Total Liab.:**	$6,265,000	**Indic. Yr. Divd.:** NA
Total Assets:	$496,000	**Net Worth:**	-$5,769,000	**Debt/ Equity:** NA

Power Air Corp

4777 Bennett Dr., Livermore, CA, 94551; *PH:* 1-925-960-8777; *http://* www.poweraircorp.com;
Email: investors@poweraircorp.com

General - Incorporation	NV	**Stock**- Price on:12/24/2007	$0.33
Employees	12	Stock Exchange	OTC
Auditor	Dale Matheson Carr-Hilton LaBonte LLP	Ticker Symbol	PWAC
Stk Agt	Republic Stock Transfer, Inc	Outstanding Shares	45,610,000
Counsel	NA	E.P.S.	NA
DUNS No.	NA	Shareholders	NA

Business: The groups principal activities include developing, manufacturing and marketing of fuel cell based commercial products. In September 2005, the group acquired all of the issued and outstanding shares of Power Air Tech, Inc. The group operates from the United States.

Primary SIC and add'l.: 5172

CIK No: 0001310261

Subsidiaries: Power Air (Canada) Corp., Power Air Tech, Inc.

Officers: Remy Kozak/CEO, Pres., Dean H. Haley/Chmn., COO, Andrew Turnbull/Dir. - Engineering, Don Prest/CFO, Donald Ceci/VP - Sales, Marketing

Directors: Dean H. Haley/Chmn., COO, Paul Brock/Dir., Stephen Harrison/Dir., William J. Potter/Dir., Al Sylwester/Dir.

Owners: Stephen Harrison, HDH Group, LLC/16.20%, Aurora Global Energy Limited/32.20%, William J. Potter, Donald M. Prest/1.60%, Paul D. Brock/1.30%, Insiders/22.30%, Remy Kozak/1.50%, Dean H. Haley/16.50%, Don Ceci

Power Efficiency Corp

3960 Howard Hughes Pkwy, Ste. 460, Las Vegas, NV, 89169; *PH:* 1-702-697-0377;
http:// www.powerefficiencycorp.com; *Email:* info@powerefficiencycorp.com

General - Incorporation	DE	**Stock**- Price on:12/24/2007	$5.08
Employees	8	Stock Exchange	OTC
Auditor	Sobel & Co. LLC	Ticker Symbol	PEFF
Stk Agt	Continental Stock Transfer & Trust Co	Outstanding Shares	38,520,000
Counsel	NA	E.P.S.	-$0.11
DUNS No.	NA	Shareholders	NA

Business: The group's principle activities include designing, developing, marketing and selling proprietary solid state electrical devices which are designed to effectively reduce energy consumption in alternating current induction motors. The company has two principal and proprietary products: the three phase power commander(R) and the single phase power commander(r). The three phase power commander(R) is used in industrial and commercial applications. The single phase power commander(R) is used in consumer applications such as home applications. The company sells its products under the brand names performance controller(tm), power commander(R), energy master, current control and ecostart. The major customers of the company include otis elevator company, kone, inc., millar elevator service co. And the defense logistics agency of the federal government of the United States of America. The group operates from United States.

Primary SIC and add'l.: 5063

CIK No: 0001024075

Officers: Steven Strasser/Chmn., CEO, John Lackland/Dir., CFO, COO - Investor Relations, George Boyadjieff/Dir. - Sr. Technical Advisor, John Hurst/Dir. - Engineering, Christine Toledo/Mgr. - Marketing Communications, Kenneth Munson/VP - Sales, Marketing, Brian Taylor/VP - Product Management, B. J. Lackland/CFO, Investor Relations Officer

Directors: Steven Strasser/Chmn., CEO, Gary Rado/Dir., George Boyadjieff/Dir. - Sr. Technical Advisor, John Lackland/Dir., CFO, COO - Investor Relations, Raymond J. Skiptunis/Dir., Douglas Dunn/Dir., Richard Morgan/Dir.

Owners: John Lackland/2.33%, Richard Morgan, Summit Energy Ventures/12.77%, Insiders/29.06%, Douglas Dunn, Sarkowski Family L.P./7.88%, Steven Strasser/22.78%, Gary Rado, Raymond J. Skiptunis, Ron Boyer/6.33%, Commerce Energy Group/5.57%, George Boyadjieff/2.97%

Financial Data: Fiscal Year End:12/31 Latest Annual Data: 12/31/2006

Year	Sales	Net Income
2006	$189,000	-$5,021,000
2005	$276,000	-$2,571,000
2004	$284,000	-$2,466,000

Curr. Assets:	$1,914,000	Curr. Liab.:	$595,000		
Plant, Equip.:	$115,000	Total Liab.:	$1,993,000	Indic. Yr. Divd.:	NA
Total Assets:	$4,038,000	Net Worth:	$2,045,000	Debt/ Equity:	0.6342

Power Integrations Inc

5245 Hellyer Ave., San Jose, CA, 95138; **PH:** 1-408-414-9200; **Fax:** 1-408-414-9201; **http://** www.powerint.com

General - Incorporation .... DE	Stock- Price on:12/24/2007 .... $22.29
Employees .... NA	Stock Exchange .... NDQ
Auditor .... Deloitte & Touche, LLP	Ticker Symbol .... POWI
Stk Agt.... Computershare Investor Services LLC	Outstanding Shares 29,460,000
Counsel .... Gray, Cary, Ware & Freidenrich	E.P.S. $0.62
DUNS No. 18-891-9468	Shareholders .... NA

Business: The group's principal activity is to design, develop, manufacture and market proprietary, high-voltage, analog integrated circuits. These circuits are primarily used in converting alternating current to direct current power conversion. The products are marketed to high-volume power suppliers including communications, consumer, computer and industrial electronics markets. The group also provides application-engineering support to its customers. The products of the group are sold in the United States, China, England, Germany, India, Japan, Korea, Singapore and Taiwan.

Primary SIC and add'l.: 6794 3674

CIK No: 0000833640

Subsidiaries: Power Integrations (Europe) Limited, Power Integrations GmbH, Power Integrations International Limited, Power Integrations Italy S.r.l, Power Integrations KK, Power Integrations Limited, Power Integrations Netherlands B.V., Power Integrations Singapore Pte. Limited

Officers: Balu Balakrishnan/Inside Dir., CEO, Pres., Bruce Renouard/VP - Worldwide Sales, John Tomlin/VP - Operations, Derek Bell/VP - Engineering, Technology, Clifford Walker/VP - Corporate Development, Douglas Bailey/VP - Marketing, Rafael Torres/VP - Finance, Administration, CFO, Joe Shiffler/Dir. - Investor Relations, Corporate Communications, Nancy Renzullo/Mgr. - Marketing Communications

Directors: Balu Balakrishnan/Inside Dir., CEO, Pres., Nicholas E. Brathwaite/Dir., Jim Fiebiger/Dir., Balakrishnan S. Iyer/Dir., Floyd E. Kvamme/Dir., Scott R. Brown/Dir., Steven J. Sharp/Dir., Alan D. Bickell/Dir.

Owners: FMR Corp./8.25%, John Tomlin/1.13%, Balu Balakrishnan/6.13%, John Tomlin, Nicholas E. Brathwaite, Balakrishnan S. Iyer, Lord, Abbett & Co. LLC/6.17%, Franklin Resources, Inc. and affiliates/8.82%, Rafael Torres, Bruce Renouard/1.00%, Floyd E. Kvamme, Scott R. Brown, Alan D. Bickell, Wasatch Advisors, Inc./11.29%, Insiders/13.98% (18 Owners included in Index)

Financial Data: Fiscal Year End:12/31 Latest Annual Data: 12/31/2005

Year	Sales	Net Income
2005	$143,071,000	$15,698,000
2004	$136,636,000	$20,367,000
2003	$125,706,000	$18,085,000

Curr. Assets:	$160,375,000	Curr. Liab.:	$27,562,000		
Plant, Equip.:	$48,890,000	Total Liab.:	$27,562,000	Indic. Yr. Divd.:	NA
Total Assets:	$236,921,000	Net Worth:	$209,359,000	Debt/ Equity:	NA

Power One Inc

740 Calle Plano, Camarillo, CA, 93012; **PH:** 1-805-987-8741; **Fax:** 1-805-388-0476; **http://** www.power-one.com; **Email:** price.delivery@power-one.com

General - Incorporation .... DE	Stock- Price on:12/24/2007 .... $4.07
Employees 4,167	Stock Exchange .... NDQ
Auditor .... Deloitte & Touche LLP	Ticker Symbol .... PWER
Stk Agt...... American Stock Transfer & Trust Co.	Outstanding Shares 86,890,000
Counsel .... Randy Holliday	E.P.S. .... -$0.42
DUNS No. 06-458-5565	Shareholders .... NA

Business: The group's principle activity is to design and manufacture power conversion products for the communications infrastructure market. The group's products are used to convert and process electrical energy to the high levels of quality, reliability and precise levels of dc voltage required by the digital economy. The group's products include ac/dc power supplies, dc/dc converters, dc power systems, dc/dc point-of-load converters and digital power management architecture. The major customers of the group include Cisco Systems, Nokia, Nortel, Lucent, Alcatel, Hutchison 3g, Extreme Networks, Motorola, Agilent, Siemens and Teradyne. The group has operations in Dominican Republic, Norway, Switzerland, China and Ireland. The group markets its products through a global sales force with direct sales offices in Europe, North America, Asia and Australia. The group's quarterly revenue for September 2007 was 131.48 millions of USD.

Primary SIC and add'l.: 3629

CIK No: 0001042825

Subsidiaries: di/dt,Inc, HC Power,Inc, Melcher Holding,Inc, Melcher,Inc, P-O Delaware Corp, P-O Nevada Corp, Power-One AG, Power-One AS, Power-One BV, Power-One BVBA, Power-One Co Ltd, Power-One Denmark ApS, Power-One Energy Solutions Pty Ltd, Power-One Energy Solutions SDN BHD, Power-One GmbH 28 Subsidiaries included in the Index

Officers: William T. Yeates/Dir., CEO/$659,566.00, Brad W. Godfrey/COO, Pres./$535,136.00, Randall H. Holliday/Sec., General Counsel/$342,784.00, Jeffrey Kyle/VP - Finance, Treasurer, CFO, Alexander Levran/CTO

Directors: William T. Yeates/Dir., CEO, Jay Walters/Chmn., Mark Melliar-Smith/Dir., Kendall R. Bishop/Dir., Jon E.M. Jacoby/Dir., Steven J. Goldman/Dir., Gayla J. Delly/Dir., William Franciscovich/Dir., Richard J. Thompson/Dir.

Owners: Steven J. Goldman/3.80%, Wells Fargo& Company/5.20%, Kendall R. Bishop/0.20%, Jon E.M. Jacoby/2.10%, Voting Trust/11.40%, William T. Yeates/1.50%, Insiders/10.00%, Veronica Tarrant/0.10%, Security Management Company, LLC/7.80%, SF Holding Corp./7.80%, Gayla J. Delly/0.10%, Paul Ross/0.10%, Brad W. Godfrey/1.40%, Mark Melliar-Smith/0.10%, Jay Walters/0.20% (17 Owners included in Index)

Financial Data: Fiscal Year End:12/31 Latest Annual Data: 12/31/2006

Year	Sales		Net Income
2006	$338,048,000		-$14,625,000
2005	$261,557,000		-$38,282,000
2004	$280,279,000		-$21,190,000

Curr. Assets:	$300,392,000	Curr. Liab.:	$156,237,000		
Plant, Equip.:	$66,831,000	Total Liab.:	$226,043,000	Indic. Yr. Divd.:	NA
Total Assets:	$449,271,000	Net Worth:	$223,228,000	Debt/ Equity:	0.2458

Power Technology Inc

16302 Alexander Rd., Alexander, AR, 72002; **PH:** 1-501-407-0712; **Fax:** 1-501-407-0036; **http://** www.powertechnology.com; **Email:** info@pwtcbattery.com

General - Incorporation .... NV	Stock- Price on:12/24/2007 .... $0.012
Employees 2	Stock Exchange .... OTC
Auditor .... Malone & Bailey, P.C	Ticker Symbol .... PWTC
Stk Agt .... Pacific Stock Transfer Company	Outstanding Shares 161,900,000
Counsel .... NA	E.P.S. .... -$0.013
DUNS No. .... NA	Shareholders .... NA

Business: The group's principal activity is to develop improved technology for batteries to be used in the automotive and electric car industry and other uses. The research and development activities include development of batteries for the automotive and electric power industries, electronic sensors, pipeline connection technology and grain drying equipment.

Primary SIC and add'l.: 3691 8731 3824

CIK No: 0001066978

Subsidiaries: Sentry Power Technology, Inc.

Officers: Daren Ford/Sales Engineers, Kelly Crampton/East Coast Sales Engineers, Gary Wadsworth/Inside Sales Engineer, Glenn Sullivan/Inside Sales Engineer, James Jackson/Inside Sales Engineer

Owners: Bernard J. Walter/7.50%, Insiders/10.85%, Lee A. Balak/14.30%, Bryson F. Farrill, Thomas J. Hopwood/0.29%, Cornell Capital Partners, L.P./52.34%, Joey Jung/0.15%

Financial Data: Fiscal Year End:01/31 Latest Annual Data: 1/31/2007

Year	Sales	Net Income
2007	$23,000	-$1,909,000
2006	NA	-$3,246,000
2005	NA	-$2,422,000

Curr. Assets:	$246,000	Curr. Liab.:	$2,264,000	P/E Ratio:	3.00
Plant, Equip.:	$142,000	Total Liab.:	$3,172,000	Indic. Yr. Divd.:	NA
Total Assets:	$450,000	Net Worth:	-$2,723,000	Debt/ Equity:	NA

Power-Save Energy Co

Formerly: Safari Assoc Inc
3940-7 Brd. St., Ste. 200, San Luis Obispo, CA, 93401; **PH:** 1-866-297-7192

General - Incorporation .... UT	Stock- Price on:12/24/2007 .... $0.89
Employees 1	Stock Exchange .... NA
Auditor .... Gruber & Co., LLC	Ticker Symbol .... NA
Stk Agt .... American Registrar & Transfer Co	Outstanding Shares 31,230,000
Counsel .... NA	E.P.S. $0.00
DUNS No. 84-791-0817	Shareholders .... NA

Business: The groups principle activities include manufacturing, marketing and selling electricity saving devices. The group's products sold under the brand name Power-Save. The group operates from United States.

Primary SIC and add'l.: NA

CIK No: 0000922011

Subsidiaries: Safari Group Safety Products, Inc

Owners: Michael Forster/74.00%, Insiders/74.00%, Zirk Engelbrecht/7.40%

Financial Data: Fiscal Year End:12/31 Latest Annual Data: 12/31/2006

Year	Sales	Net Income
2006	$651,000	-$141,000
2005	NA	-$213,000
2004	NA	-$196,000

Curr. Assets:	$160,000	Curr. Liab.:	$48,000		
Plant, Equip.:	$2,000	Total Liab.:	$48,000	Indic. Yr. Divd.:	NA
Total Assets:	$174,000	Net Worth:	$126,000	Debt/ Equity:	NA

Powercerv Corp

400 N Ashley Dr., Ste 2700, Tampa, FL, 33602; **PH:** 1-813-979-9222; **http://** www.powercerv.com

General - Incorporation .... FL	Stock- Price on:12/24/2007 .... $0.11
Employees .... NA	Stock Exchange .... NA
Auditor .... Aidman, Piser & Co. P.A	Ticker Symbol .... NA
Stk Agt .... Continental Stock Transfer & Trust Co	Outstanding Shares .... NA
Counsel .... NA	E.P.S. .... NA
DUNS No. 80-525-6518	Shareholders .... NA

Business: The group's principal activity is to develop, market, license, implement and support enterprise application software solutions for mid-sized companies. On 26-Nov-2002, the group sold substantially all of its operating assets to pcv acquisition inc., a subsidiary of asa international, ltd. As on 31-Dec-2002, the group had no operations. It plans to continue as a separate public entity and seeks to merge with another operating business.

Primary SIC and add'l.: 7372 7371

CIK No: 0001005758

Subsidiaries: PowerCerv Technologies Corporation

Officers: Scott Galloway/Pres., Alan Goniwich/VP - Sales, Marketing, Bill Walker/VP - Operations, Rick Fox/VP - Research, Development, Scott Cranford/Dir. - Sales, Michelle Spayde/Mgr. - Accounting

Financial Data: Fiscal Year End:12/31 Latest Annual Data: 12/31/2004

Year	Sales	Net Income
2004	NA	$47,000
2001	$6,107,000	-$4,140,000
2000	$11,632,000	-$8,408,000

Curr. Assets:	$176,000	Curr. Liab.:	$449,000		
Plant, Equip.:	NA	Total Liab.:	$449,000	Indic. Yr. Divd.:	NA
Total Assets:	$176,000	Net Worth:	-$273,000	Debt/ Equity:	NA

Powerchannel Inc

16 N Main St. Ste. 395, New City, NY, 10956; **PH:** 1-845-634-7979; **Fax:** 1-845-783-5989; http:// www.powerchannel.com

General - Incorporation	DE	**Stock**- Price on:12/24/2007	$0.003
Employees	NA	Stock Exchange	OTC
Auditor	Anslow & Jacklin LLP	Ticker Symbol	PWRC
Stk Agt.	Olde Monmouth Stk Trnsfer Co. Inc.	Outstanding Shares	NA
Counsel	NA	E.P.S.	NA
DUNS No.	NA	Shareholders	NA

Business: The group's principal activity is to provide Internet access through television. They offer subscription based on-line services that enable the customers to access Internet through their television. The group provides service through a set top terminal which is attached to a television and telephone line through which customer can access Internet. The group provide physical hardware that is used to deliver the Internet through the use of the consumer's existing television. On 21-Jul-2003, the group merged with sealant solutions inc.

Primary SIC and add'l.: 7375

CIK No: 0000894049

Subsidiaries: PowerChannel Holdings, Inc.

Financial Data: Fiscal Year End:12/31 Latest Annual Data: 12/31/2004

Year	Sales	Net Income
2004	$195,000	-$6,917,000
2003	$95,000	-$4,394,000
2002	$4,000	-$425,000

Curr. Assets:	$166,000	Curr. Liab.:	$1,747,000		
Plant, Equip.:	$22,000	Total Liab.:	$1,747,000	Indic. Yr. Divd.:	NA
Total Assets:	$188,000	Net Worth:	-$2,192,000	Debt/ Equity:	NA

PowerCold Corp

PO Box 1239, La Vernia, TX, 78121; **PH:** 1-830-779-5223; http:// www.powercold.com; **Email:** pwcl@powercold.com

General - Incorporation	NV	**Stock**- Price on:12/24/2007	$0.35
Employees	14	Stock Exchange	OTC
Auditor	Williams & Webster, P.S	Ticker Symbol	PWCL
Stk Agt.	Computershare Investor Services LLC	Outstanding Shares	25,500,000
Counsel	NA	E.P.S.	-$0.22
DUNS No.	62-271-2552	Shareholders	NA

Business: The group's principle activity is to provide solutions of energy efficient products for the refrigeration, air conditioning and power industries. The group operates across many sectors from large industrial food processors to small commercial air conditioning systems. The group develops, manufactures and markets proprietary equipment to achieve electric power cost savings for commercial and industrial firms. The group's revenue is derived from three product lines. The first is a line of evaporative heat exchange systems for the hvac and refrigeration industry. The second line is the design and production of unique products for the refrigeration industry. The third is consulting engineering services, including process safety management compliance and ammonia refrigeration and carbon dioxide system design.

Primary SIC and add'l.: 3694 8711 3585

CIK No: 0000827055

Subsidiaries: PowerCold ComfortAir Solutions, Inc., PowerCold International, Ltd., PowerCold Products, Inc, PowerCold Technology, LLC

Officers: Frank L. Simola/Chmn., CEO, Pres., George H. More/Advisor to The Dir., Dean S. Calton/Dir., VP - Development, CTO, Grayling Hofer/VP - Operations, Dir., Joseph C. Cahill/Advisor to The Dir., John Papastavrou/Dir. - Product Management, Edward N. Schinner/Advisor to The Dir., Thomas M. Obrien/Special Consultant to The Dir.

Directors: Frank L. Simola/Chmn., CEO, Pres., Dean S. Calton/Dir., VP - Development, CTO, John Papastavrou/Dir. - Product Management, Michael J. Willms/Dir., Randy Rutledge/Dir.

Financial Data: Fiscal Year End:12/31 Latest Annual Data: 12/31/2005

Year	Sales	Net Income
2005	$667,000	-$6,688,000
2004	$9,091,000	-$4,337,000
2003	$4,070,000	-$2,657,000

Curr. Assets:	$967,000	Curr. Liab.:	$4,676,000		
Plant, Equip.:	$215,000	Total Liab.:	$6,095,000	Indic. Yr. Divd.:	NA
Total Assets:	$1,560,000	Net Worth:	-$4,535,000	Debt/ Equity:	NA

Powerlinx Inc

10901 A Roosevelt Blvd. N, Ste. 200, St. Petersburg, FL, 33716; **PH:** 1-727-866-7440; **Fax:** 1-727-866-7480; http:// www.power-linx.com; **Email:** general@power-linx.com

General - Incorporation	NV	**Stock**- Price on:12/24/2007	$1.1
Employees	17	Stock Exchange	OTC
Auditor	Aidman, Piser & Co. P.A	Ticker Symbol	PWNX
Stk Agt.	Island Stock Transfer	Outstanding Shares	5,760,000
Counsel	NA	E.P.S.	-$0.06
DUNS No.	NA	Shareholders	NA

Business: The group's principal activity is to develop, manufacture and market products and applications developed to transmit voice, video, audio and data over power lines, twisted pair wires and coax in ac and dc power environments on any power grids. It operates through three segments: security products segment develops, manufactures, markets and sells proprietary video security network devices and consumer electronic products. The dc transportation products segment develops, manufactures, markets, and sells powerline rear and side vision systems for all classes and types of vehicles in the transportation industry. The marine products segment develops, manufactures, markets and sells underwater video cameras, lighting and accessories principally to dealers and distributors in recreational/professional marine and fishing markets.

Primary SIC and add'l.: 3651 3714

CIK No: 0000894536

Subsidiaries: Linx Comm, LLC

Officers: Michael Tomlinson/Dir., CEO, Pres., Douglas Bauer/Exec. VP - Finance, Adminstration, CFO, Sec., Treasurer, James Markus/VP, GM - Transportation Sales Division

Directors: Michael Tomlinson/Dir., CEO, Pres., James A. Williams/Chmn., Myles J. Gould/Dir., Bradford M. Gould/Dir., Martin A. Traber/Dir., William B. Edwards/Dir., Francisco Sanchez/Dir., Ted Shalek/Dir.

Owners: Ted Shalek, Insiders/6.54%, Vatas SA/26.06%, Myles J. Gould/1.51%, William B. Edwards, Sofaer Capital Global Fund/40.67%, Francisco Sanchez, Douglas Bauer/1.79%, Mike Tomlinson, Bradford M. Gould, Martin A. Traber, RIT Capital Partners/6.75%

Financial Data: Fiscal Year End:12/31 Latest Annual Data: 12/31/2006

Year	Sales	Net Income
2006	$1,727,000	-$3,011,000
2005	$1,271,000	-$5,849,000
2004	$1,391,000	-$5,124,000

Curr. Assets:	$1,057,000	Curr. Liab.:	$4,673,000		
Plant, Equip.:	$138,000	Total Liab.:	$4,673,000	Indic. Yr. Divd.:	NA
Total Assets:	$1,591,000	Net Worth:	-$3,082,000	Debt/ Equity:	NA

PowerNova Technologies Corp

680 - 1285 W Broadway, Vancouver, BC, V6H 3X8; **PH:** 1-604-734-7488; http:// www.powernova.com; **Email:** inquiries@powernova.com

General - Incorporation	Canada	**Stock**- Price on:12/24/2007	NA
Employees	NA	Stock Exchange	NA
Auditor	Amisano Hanson	Ticker Symbol	NA
Stk Agt.	Computershare Trust Co of Canada	Outstanding Shares	NA
Counsel	Salley Bowes Harwardt LLP	E.P.S.	NA
DUNS No.	NA	Shareholders	NA

Business: The group's principle activity is to develop a hydrogen production technology to supply a new world energy economy based on hydrogen. The technology is a catalyst to produce hydrogen from hydrocarbons such a gasoline with zero emissions of greenhouse gases. The group has a patent pending on the technology. The group is a Vancouver, Canada based company founded in June 2000 to research and develop hydrogen production technology. Hydrogen is classified as a secondary source of energy, or an energy carrier that can be used to store, move and deliver energy in a practical way. It has many applications and can be used for transportation, heating and power generation, making it a versatile form of energy carrier. Moreover, it has the highest energy content per unit of weight (52,000 British Thermal Units per pound) of any known fuel, which makes it an extremely efficient source of energy. The group operates from United States and Russia.

Primary SIC and add'l.: 2810

CIK No: 0001281216

Officers: Stuart Lew/Co - Chmn., CEO, Robert Oralbekov/Co - Chmn., Pres., Phillip Webber/CFO, Avtandil Koridze/CTO, VP, Lila Chan/Financial, Office Administrator

Directors: Stuart Lew/Co - Chmn., CEO, Robert Oralbekov/Co - Chmn., Pres., William C. Kaska/Dir.

Owners: Insiders/26.28%, Stuart Lew/10.68%, Avtandil Koridze/20.43%, Bakytzhan Oralbekov/20.63%, Phillip Webber

Powersecure International Inc

Formerly: Metretek Technologies Inc

303 E 17th Ave., Ste. 660, Enver, CO, 80203; **PH:** 1-303-592-5555; http:// www.metretek.com

General - Incorporation	DE	**Stock**- Price on:12/24/2007	$14.81
Employees	335	Stock Exchange	NA
Auditor	Hein & Assoc. LLP	Ticker Symbol	NA
Stk Agt.	Computershare Trust Co	Outstanding Shares	15,920,000
Counsel	Kegler, Brown, Hill & Ritter	E.P.S.	$0.785
DUNS No.	78-108-2938	Shareholders	NA

Business: The group's principal activity is to provide energy technology measurement products, services and data management systems to industrial and commercial users. It operates under four segments: powersecure, southern flow, metretek Florida and other. Southern flow's services include on-site field services, chart processing and analysis, laboratory analysis and data management and reporting. These services are provided principally to customers involved in natural gas production, gathering, transportation and processing. Powersecure distributes generated products and services that include designing, engineering, marketing, constructing and operating turn-key systems. Metretek Florida provides automated energy data management designs that includes electronic devices and systems, recording systems and electronic gas flow computers. The group markets its products in the United Kingdom, Netherlands, pakistan, Australia, Argentina, columbia, Taiwan, Korea, Brazil and Canada.

Primary SIC and add'l.: 3825 3824 3586 3823

CIK No: 0000882154

Subsidiaries: Conquest Acquisition Company, LLC, EnergyLite, Inc., Industrial Automation, Inc., Marcum Capital Resources, Inc., Marcum Gas Transmission, Inc., Marcum Midstream 1995-2 Business Trust, Mercator Energy Incorporated, Metretek Contract Manufacturing Company, Inc., Metretek, Incorporated, PowerSecure, Inc., PowerServices, Inc., PowerSpring, Inc., Southern Flow Companies, Inc, UtilityEngineering, Inc.

Officers: John D. Bernard/CEO - Southernflow/$234,976.00, Daniel J. Packard/Pres., CEO - MGT/$223,381.00, Gary J. Zuiderveen/CFO

Directors: Anthony D. Pell/Dir., Sidney Hinton/44/Dir., Basil M. Briggs/Dir., Kevin P. Collins/Dir.

Owners: Bradley A. Gabbard/2.40%, Sidney Hinton/2.40%, Kevin P. Collins/0.60%, Anthony D. Pell/1.00%, John Bernard/0.60%, Phillip W. Marcum/4.10%, DDJ Capital Management, LLC/6.10%, Daniel J. Packard/0.30%, Independence Investments LLC/6.50%, Gruber & McBaine Capital Management, LLC/7.40%, Austin W. Marxe/6.30%, Basil M. Briggs/0.70%, Insiders/12.10%, Winslow Management Company, LLC/5.20%

Financial Data: Fiscal Year End:12/31 Latest Annual Data: 12/31/2006

Year	Sales	Net Income
2006	$120,447,000	$11,705,000
2005	$47,253,000	$2,334,000
2004	$35,177,000	-$3,244,000

Curr. Assets:	$70,536,000	Curr. Liab.:	$31,692,000		
Plant, Equip.:	$4,444,000	Total Liab.:	$31,699,000	Indic. Yr. Divd.:	NA
Total Assets:	$89,699,000	Net Worth:	$58,000,000	Debt/ Equity:	NA

Powerwave Technologies Inc

1801 E St. Andrew Pl., Santa Ana, CA, 92705; ***PH:*** 1-714-466-1000; ***Fax:*** 1-714-466-5800; ***http://*** www.powerwave.com; ***Email:*** invest@pwav.com

General - Incorporation	DE	**Stock**- Price on:12/24/2007	$6.85
Employees	4,223	Stock Exchange	NDQ
Auditor	Deloitte & Touche LLP	Ticker Symbol	PWAV
Stk Agt	U.S. Stock Transfer Corp	Outstanding Shares	130,290,000
Counsel	NA	E.P.S	-$2.11
DUNS No.	13-959-5268	Shareholders	NA

Business: The group's principal activity is to design, manufacture and market ultra-linear radio frequency power amplifiers for use in the wireless communications market. The group offers both single and multi-carrier radio frequency power amplifiers for use in cellular networks, including ultra-linear multi-carrier radio frequency power amplifiers for cdma, cdma2000, tdma and gsm digital cellular systems as well as analog systems utilizing amps and tacs protocols. The amplifiers are also used in pcs networks that operate in the international dcs-1800 frequency and the United States pcs band at 1900 mhz and multi-carrier radio frequency power amplifiers for 3g umts networks operating at 2100 mhz. The products are sold to customers worldwide, such as ericsson, lgic, motorola and lucent. The group has foreign operations in China, Finland, France, Singapore and the United Kingdom. On Jul 10, 2003, the group purchased selected assets of ericsson amplifier technologies, inc.

Primary SIC and add'l.: 3663

CIK No: 0001023362

Subsidiaries: Allgon Innovation AB, Allgon International AB, Allgon Systems AB, Allgon Systems Ltd., Allgon Telecom K.K., Allgon Telecom Ltda, Arkivator Falkoping AB, KB IR Falevi, LGP Allgon Holding AB, LGP Allgon OY, LGP Telecom Ltda., LGP Telecom Shanghai Ltd., MG Instruments AB, Microwave Ventures, Inc., Milcom International Ltd. 52 Subsidiaries included in the Index

Officers: Ronald J. Buschur/44/Dir., CEO, Pres., Bruce C. Edwards/54/Exec. Chmn., Kevin T. Michaels/48/CFO, Sec.

Directors: Ronald J. Buschur/44/Dir., CEO, Pres., Bruce C. Edwards/54/Exec. Chmn., David L. George/53/Dir., Daniel A. Artusi/52/Dir., Andrew J. Sukawaty/52/Dir., Eugene L. Goda/70/Dir., John L. Clendenin/72/Dir., Carl W. Neun/64/Dir.

Owners: David L. George, Carl W. Neun, Wellington Management Company, LLP/7.30%, Ronald J. Buschur, Delaware Management Holdings/6.20%, Marc C. Cohodes/6.00%, John L. Clendenin, Andrew J. Sukawaty, Bruce C. Edwards, Khurram P. Sheikh, Kevin T. Michaels, Eugene L. Goda, Daniel A. Artusi, FMR Corp./13.10%, Insiders/2.20%

Financial Data: ***Fiscal Year End:***01/01 ***Latest Annual Data:*** 12/31/2006

Year	Sales	Net Income
2006	$716,886,000	-$158,903,000
2005	$473,914,000	-$72,122,000

Curr. Assets:	$482,698,000	**Curr. Liab.:**	$233,234,000		
Plant, Equip.:	$144,596,000	**Total Liab.:**	$564,134,000	**Indic. Yr. Divd.:**	NA
Total Assets:	$1,215,732,000	**Net Worth:**	$651,598,000	**Debt/ Equity:**	0.5497

Pozen Inc

1414 Raleigh Rd., Ste. 400, Chapel Hill, NC, 27517; ***PH:*** 1-919-913-1030; ***Fax:*** 1-919-913-1039; ***http://*** www.pozen.com; ***Email:*** investors@pozen.com

General - Incorporation	DE	**Stock**- Price on:12/24/2007	$17.68
Employees	35	Stock Exchange	NDQ
Auditor	Ernst & Young LLP	Ticker Symbol	POZN
Stk Agt	StockTrans, Inc.	Outstanding Shares	29,490,000
Counsel	Ballard Spahr Andrews & Ingersoll LLP	E.P.S	$0.28
DUNS No.	NA	Shareholders	NA

Business: The group's principal activity is to build a portfolio of products with commercial potential in targeted therapeutic areas. The initial area of focus is migraine, where the group has built a portfolio of three product candidates through a combination of innovation and in licensing. Mt 100 is being developed by the group as an oral first-line therapy for the treatment of migraine. The group is developing mt 300 to provide safe, convenient and pain relief for patients needing an injectable therapy for severe migraine attacks. Other migraine therapeutic product candidates include mt 400, being developed as a co-active migraine therapy.

Primary SIC and add'l.: 8731 2834

CIK No: 0001059790

Subsidiaries: Jurisdiction of incorporation

Officers: John R. Plachetka/Chmn., CEO, Pres./$2,664,277.00, William L. Hodges/Sr. VP - Finance - Administration, CFO/$729,300.00, Marshall E. Reese/Exec. VP - Product Development/$810,114.00, John E. Barnhardt/VP - Finance, Administration, Principal Accounting Officer/$623,095.00, Gilda M. Thomas/Sr. VP, General Counsel

Directors: John R. Plachetka/Chmn., CEO, Pres., Peter J. Wise/73/Co - Founder, Vice Chmn., Paul J. Rizzo/Dir., Arthur S. Kirsch/Dir., Bruce A. Tomason/Dir., Kenneth B. Lee/Dir., James J. Mauzey/Dir., Jacques Rejeange/Dir.

Owners: Barclays Global Investors, N.A./5.30%, James J. Mauzey, Jacques F. Rejeange, Arthur S. Kirsch, John R. Plachetka/14.20%, Kristina M. Adomonis, Insiders/18.10%, Paul J. Rizzo, Peter J. Wise/1.50%, Vector Later-Stage Equity Fund II, L.P./8.90%, Marshall E. Reese, Kenneth B. Lee, John E. Barnhardt, William L. Hodges, Bruce A. Tomason

Financial Data: ***Fiscal Year End:***12/31 ***Latest Annual Data:*** 12/31/2006

Year	Sales	Net Income
2006	$13,517,000	-$19,310,000
2005	$28,647,000	$1,959,000
2004	$23,088,000	-$5,260,000

Curr. Assets:	$66,958,000	**Curr. Liab.:**	$19,027,000		
Plant, Equip.:	$183,000	**Total Liab.:**	$43,027,000	**Indic. Yr. Divd.:**	NA
Total Assets:	$67,141,000	**Net Worth:**	$24,114,000	**Debt/ Equity:**	NA

PPG Industries

1 PPG Pl., Pittsburgh, PA, 15272; ***PH:*** 1-412-434-3131; ***Fax:*** 1-412-434-2011; ***http://*** www.ppg.com; ***Email:*** corporateinfo@ppg.com

General - Incorporation	PA	**Stock**- Price on:12/24/2007	$74.61
Employees	32,200	Stock Exchange	NYSE
Auditor	Deloitte & Touche LLP	Ticker Symbol	PPG
Stk Agt	Mellon Investor Services LLC	Outstanding Shares	164,170,000
Counsel	NA	E.P.S	$4.15
DUNS No.	00-134-4803	Shareholders	NA

Business: The groups principle activity is to provide trust solutions. The groups services include term care and medicare supplement insurance, and related financial and wellness advisory services. The group operates through three segments namely long-term care insurance, payment protection insurance, and group life and health insurance business units. The group operates from United States.

Primary SIC and add'l.: 2812 2821 2851 3211

CIK No: 0000079879

Subsidiaries: Bellaria S.p.A., EPIC Insurance Co. Ltd., HOBA Lacke und Farben GmbH, LYNX Services, LLC, Pinetree Stockholding Corporation, Ppg Alesco Automotive Finishes Mexico, S. De R.I. De C.v., PPG Architectural Finishes, Inc., PPG Auto Glass, LLC, PPG Canada Inc., PPG Capital LLC, PPG Coatings (Hong Kong) Co., Limited, PPG Coatings (Malaysia) Sdn. Bhd., PPG Coatings (Thailand) Co., Ltd, PPG Coatings (Tianjin) Co., Ltd., PPG Coatings B.V. 62 Subsidiaries included in the Index

Officers: Charles E. Bunch/Chmn., CEO/$8,885,890.00, James C. Diggs/Sr. VP, General Counsel, Sec./$2,323,823.00, William H. Hernandez/Dir., CFO, Sr. VP - Finance, Treasurer/$3,230,728.00, Rich J. Alexander/Sr. VP - Coatings/$1,520,165.00, Dennis A. Kovalsky/VP - Automotive OEM Coatings, Lynne D. Schmidt/VP - Government, Community Affairs, Vince Morales/VP - Investor Relations, Barry N. Gillespie/VP - Aerospace Products, Charles F. Kahle/VP - Research, Development Coatings, Kathleen A. McGuire/VP - Purchasing, Distribution, Kevin F. Sullivan/Sr. VP - Chemicals/$1,888,715.00, Richard C. Elias/VP - Optical Products, David P. Morris/VP - Aerospace Coatings, Sealants, Marc P. Talman/VP - Packaging Coatings, Aziz S. Giga/VP - Strategic Planning *(37 Officers included in Index)*

Directors: Charles E. Bunch/Chmn., CEO, Victoria F. Haynes/60/Dir., James G. Berges/60/Dir., Thomas J. Usher/65/Dir., Robert Ripp/66/Dir., Robert Mehrabian/66/Dir., Erroll B. Davis/63/Dir., David R. Whitwam/66/Dir., William H. Hernandez/Dir., CFO, Sr. VP - Finance, Treasurer, Charles W. Wise/Dir., VP - Human Resources, Hugh Grant/49/Dir., Sue Sloan/Exec. Dir., Michele J. Hooper/56/Dir.

Owners: Thomas J. Usher, Capital Research and Management Company and certain of its affiliates/8.50%, Robert Mehrabian, Victoria F. Haynes, Hugh Grant, James C. Diggs, Charles E. Bunch, William H. Hernandez, Erroll B. Davis, Insiders, Michele J. Hooper, Kevin F. Sullivan, James G. Berges, Rich J. Alexander, David R. Whitwam *(16 Owners included in Index)*

Financial Data: ***Fiscal Year End:***12/31 ***Latest Annual Data:*** 12/31/2006

Year	Sales	Net Income
2006	$11,037,000,000	$711,000,000
2005	$10,201,000,000	$596,000,000
2004	$9,513,000,000	$683,000,000

Curr. Assets:	$4,592,000,000	**Curr. Liab.:**	$2,787,000,000	**P/E Ratio:**	17.23
Plant, Equip.:	$2,496,000,000	**Total Liab.:**	$6,639,000,000	**Indic. Yr. Divd.:**	$2.000
Total Assets:	$10,021,000,000	**Net Worth:**	$3,234,000,000	**Debt/ Equity:**	NA

PPL Corp

2 N 9th St., Allentown, PA, 18101; ***PH:*** 1-610-774-5151; ***Fax:*** 1-610-774-4198; ***http://*** www.pplweb.com

General - Incorporation	PA	**Stock**- Price on:12/24/2007	$46.19
Employees	12,620	Stock Exchange	NYSE
Auditor	PricewaterhouseCoopers LLP	Ticker Symbol	PPL
Stk Agt	Wells Fargo Shareowner Services	Outstanding Shares	385,950,000
Counsel	NA	E.P.S	$2.45
DUNS No.	83-543-3830	Shareholders	NA

Business: The groups principle activities include generating and marketing electricity. The group operates through three segments namely supply, delivery and international. The group operates from United States.

Primary SIC and add'l.: 4911 4925 6719

CIK No: 0000922224

Subsidiaries: PMDC International Holdings, Inc., PPL Electric Utilities Corporation, PPL Energy Funding Corporation, PPL Energy Supply, LLC, PPL EnergyPlus, LLC, PPL Generation, LLC, PPL Global, LLC, PPL Investment Corporation, PPL Montana Holdings, LLC, PPL Montana, LLC, PPL Receivables Corporation, PPL Susquehanna, LLC, PPL Transition Bond Company, LLC, WPD Investment Holdings Ltd.

Officers: James H. Miller/59/Chmn., CEO, Pres./$5,586,410.00, Bryce L. Shriver/Pres. - PPL Generation/$1,773,428.00, John R. Biggar/63/CFO, Exec. VP/$2,658,711.00, David G. Decampli/Pres. - PPL Electric Utilities, Paul T. Champagne/Pres. - PPL Energy Services Group/$1,520,781.00, Paul A. Farr/CFO, Exec. VP, Robert J. Grey/Sr. VP, General Counsel, Sec./$1,666,839.00, James E. Abel/VP - Finance, Treasurer, Timothy J. Paukovits/Dir. - Investor Relations, Clarence J. Hopf/Pres. - PPL Energyplus, William H. Spence/COO, Exec. VP, Britt T. McKinney/Sr. VP, Chief Nuclear Officer, Matt Simmons/VP, Controller, Vijay Singh/VP - Risk Management, Joanne H. Raphael/VP - External Affairs *(17 Officers included in Index)*

Directors: James H. Miller/59/Chmn., CEO, Pres., Frederick M. Bernthal/65/Dir., Susan M. Stalnecker/55/Dir., Keith H. Williamson/55/Dir., John W. Conway/62/Dir., Allen E. Deaver/72/Dir., Louise K. Goeser/54/Dir., Stuart Heydt/68/Dir., Craig A. Rogerson/51/Dir., Keith W. Smith/73/Dir.

Owners: S. M. Stalnecker, J. W. Conway, B. L. Shriver, J. R. Biggar, W. K. Smith, L. K. Goeser, W. F. Hecht, R. J. Grey, J. H. Miller, S. Heydt, P. T. Champagne, K. H. Williamson, F. M. Bernthal, E. A. Deaver, C. A. Rogerson *(16 Owners included in Index)*

Financial Data: ***Fiscal Year End:***12/31 ***Latest Annual Data:*** 12/31/2006

Year	Sales	Net Income
2006	$6,899,000,000	$865,000,000
2005	$6,219,000,000	$678,000,000
2004	$5,812,000,000	$698,000,000

Curr. Assets:	$3,630,000,000	**Curr. Liab.:**	$3,348,000,000	**P/E Ratio:**	22.75
Plant, Equip.:	$12,069,000,000	**Total Liab.:**	$14,264,000,000	**Indic. Yr. Divd.:**	$1.220
Total Assets:	$19,747,000,000	**Net Worth:**	$5,122,000,000	**Debt/ Equity:**	1.3148

PPL Energy Supply LLC

2 N 9th St., Allentown, PA, 18101; ***PH:*** 1-610-774-5151; ***http://*** www.pplweb.com; ***Email:*** invrel@pplweb.com

General - Incorporation............................ DE
Employees...8,744
Auditor ....Ernst & Young LLP
Stk Agt.......... Wells Fargo Shareowner Services
Counsel..NA
DUNS No. ....NA

Stock - Price on:12/24/2007 ....$25.93
Stock Exchange.......................................NYSE
Ticker Symbol..PLS
Outstanding Shares ....NA
E.P.S...NA
Shareholders...NA

Business: The groups principle activity is to supply coal and synthetic fuel. The group operates from the United States.

Primary SIC and add'l.: 4911

CIK No: 0001161976

Subsidiaries: PMDC International Holdings, Inc., PPL Electric Utilities Corporation, PPL Energy Funding Corporation, PPL Energy Supply, LLC, PPL EnergyPlus, LLC, PPL Generation, LLC, PPL Global, LLC, PPL Investment Corporation, PPL Montana Holdings, LLC, PPL Montana, LLC, PPL Susquehanna, LLC, PPL Transition Bond Company, LLC, WPD Holdings Ltd.

Officers: James H. Miller/59/Chmn., CEO, Pres., John R. Biggar/63/Dir., CFO, Exec. VP, William H. Spence/50/COO, Exec. VP, Robert J. Grey/57/Sr. VP, General Counsel, Sec., Paul A. Farr/40/Sr. VP, James E. Abel/56/VP - Finance, Treasurer, Matt Simmons/42/VP, Controller, Paul T. Champagne/49/Pres. - PPL Energy Services Group, LLC, Rick L. Klingensmith/47/Pres. - PPL Global, Bryce L. Shriver/60/Pres. - PPL Generation, Clarence J. Hopf/51/Pres. - PPL Energyplus, John F. Sipics/59/Pres. - PPL Electric, David G. Decampli/50/Pres. - PPL Electric Utilities, Joanne H. Raphael/VP - External Affairs, Vijay Singh/VP - Risk Management *(16 Officers included in Index)*

Directors: James H. Miller/59/Chmn., CEO, Pres., Keith H. Williamson/56/Dir., John R. Biggar/63/Dir., CFO, Exec. VP, Frederick M. Bernthal/65/Dir., John W. Conway/63/Dir., Allen E. Deaver/72/Dir., Louise K. Goeser/54/Dir., Stuart Heydt/68/Dir., Craig A. Rogerson/51/Dir., Keith W. Smith/73/Dir., Susan M. Stalnecker/55/Dir.

Financial Data: Fiscal Year End:12/31　**Latest Annual Data:** 12/31/2006

Year	Sales	Net Income
2006	$5,272,000,000	$698,000,000

Curr. Assets:	$3,192,000,000	**Curr. Liab.:**	$2,053,000,000		
Plant, Equip.:	$8,925,000,000	**Total Liab.:**	$10,121,000,000	**Indic. Yr. Divd.:**	NA
Total Assets:	$14,655,000,000	**Net Worth:**	$4,534,000,000	**Debt/ Equity:**	NA

Ppol Inc

1 City Blvd. W, Ste. 820, Orange, CA, 92868; **PH:** 1-714-937-3211; **http://** www.ppolusa.com; **Email:** ir@ppolusa.com

General - Incorporation............................CA
Employees..18
Auditor ....Windes & Mcclaughry
Stk Agt......................U.S. Stock Transfer Corp
Counsel........................Gelfend & Stein LLP
DUNS No. ....NA

Stock - Price on:12/24/2007 ....NA
Stock Exchange...OTC
Ticker Symbol...PPLI
Outstanding Shares ....NA
E.P.S..-$11.86
Shareholders...NA

Business: The groups principle activity is to provide communication and networking services. The group provides LCD screen and includes the functions of a telephone and fax. The group connects to Pan Pacific Online, the online service exclusive for MOJICO users. The group operates from United States.

Primary SIC and add'l.: NA

CIK No: 0001202507

Subsidiaries: AJOL Co., Ltd., Getefor, Inc., K.K. U Service

Officers: Masao Yamamoto/CEO, Yoshihiro Aota/Supreme Advisor, Ajol, Richard Izumi/CFO

Owners: Richard H. Izumi/0.12%, Leo Global Fund/15.28%, Foster Strategic Investment Partnership/51.34%

Financial Data: Fiscal Year End:03/31　**Latest Annual Data:** 03/31/2006

Year	Sales	Net Income
2006	$106,624,000	-$2,387,000
2005	$130,058,000	-$2,741,000
2004	$136,824,000	$7,722,000

Curr. Assets:	$55,813,000	**Curr. Liab.:**	$58,409,000		
Plant, Equip.:	$448,000	**Total Liab.:**	$110,626,000	**Indic. Yr. Divd.:**	NA
Total Assets:	$113,104,000	**Net Worth:**	$2,478,000	**Debt/ Equity:**	NA

PPT VISION Inc

12988 Valley View Rd., Eden Prairie, MN, 55344; **PH:** 1-952-996-9500; **Fax:** 1-952-996-9501; **http://** www.pptvision.com; **Email:** info@pptvision.com

General - Incorporation............................ MN
Employees..38
Auditor ....Virchow, Krause & Co. LLP
Stk Agt.......... Wells Fargo Shareowner Services
Counsel..NA
DUNS No. 04-741-9403

Stock - Price on:12/24/2007 ....$0.37
Stock Exchange...OTC
Ticker Symbol..PPTV
Outstanding Shares 7,400,000
E.P.S..-$0.32
Shareholders...NA

Business: The group's principle activities include designing, manufacturing, and marketing and integrate 2d and 3D machine vision-based automated inspection systems for manufacturing applications. The company's products enable manufacturers to realize significant economic paybacks by increasing the quality of manufactured parts and improving the productivity of manufacturing processes. The company's 2d machine vision product line is sold on a global basis to end-users, system integrators and original equipment manufacturers primarily in the electronic and semiconductor component, automotive, medical device, and packaged goods industries. The speedscan 3D(TM) sensor is sold to original equipment manufacturers for specific applications. The group operates from United States.

Primary SIC and add'l.: 3829

CIK No: 0000704460

Officers: Joseph C. Christenson/Dir., CEO, CFO, Pres., David L. Friske/63/VP - Manufacturing, Michael Hanrahan/Mgr. - Business Development, Brian Robertson/Application Engineer, Richard Thai/Application Engineer - US Southeast

Directors: Joseph C. Christenson/Dir., CEO, CFO, Pres., Robert W. Heller/Dir., Peter R. Peterson/Dir.

Owners: Fred Brenner/6.20%, David L. Friske, Robert W. Heller, Joseph C. Christenson/1.80%, Insiders/62.00%, P. R. Peterson/60.50%

Financial Data: Fiscal Year End:10/31　**Latest Annual Data:** 12/31/2006

Year	Sales	Net Income
2006	$812,138,000	$105,888,000
2005	$756,905,000	$99,034,000
2004	$660,368,000	$89,445,000

Curr. Assets:	$2,261,000	**Curr. Liab.:**	$627,000		
Plant, Equip.:	$308,000	**Total Liab.:**	$627,000	**Indic. Yr. Divd.:**	NA
Total Assets:	$2,591,000	**Net Worth:**	$1,964,000	**Debt/ Equity:**	NA

PRA International

12120 Sunset Hills Rd., Ste. 600, Reston, VA, 20190; **PH:** 1-703-464-6300; **Fax:** 1-703-464-6301; **http://** www.prainternational.com

General - Incorporation .... DE
Employees...NA
Auditor ....PricewaterhouseCoopers LLP
Stk Agt...... American Stock Transfer & Trust Co.
Counsel..NA
DUNS No. ....NA

Stock - Price on:12/24/2007 ....$23.93
Stock Exchange...NA
Ticker Symbol...NA
Outstanding Shares 24,420,000
E.P.S..$0.63
Shareholders...NA

Business: The groups principle activity is to provide clinical drug development services. The group products sold under the trade names PRA(R), PRA International(R), PRA e-TMF(R) and Project Assurance(R). The group operates from the United States, Canada, Europe and other.

Primary SIC and add'l.: 8731 8731 8734 8734

CIK No: 0001293243

Subsidiaries: Call Co 3065613, GMG BioBusiness Ltd., International Medical Technical Consultants, Inc., MFH, Inc., Parmaceutical Research Associates, Hungary Research and Development Ltd., Pharm Research Associates Russia Ltd., Pharm Research Associates UK Ltd., Pharma Bio-Research USA, Inc., Pharmaceutical Research Associates AG, Pharmaceutical Research Associates Belgium, BVBA, Pharmaceutical Research Associates Benelux, BVBA, Pharmaceutical Research Associates Espana, SA, Pharmaceutical Research Associates GmbH, Pharmaceutical Research Associates Group B.V., Pharmaceutical Research Associates HK Ltd. 40 Subsidiaries included in the Index

Officers: Terrance Bieker/Dir., CEO, Matthew J. Bond/47/CFO, Exec. VP, David W. Dockhorn/Exec. VP - Product Registration, Monika M. Pietrek/Exec. VP - Global Scientific, Medical Affairs, Bruce A. Teplitzky/Exec. VP - Business Development, William M. Walsh/Exec. VP - Corporate Development, Linda Baddour/CFO, Exec. VP, Colin Shannon/COO, Pres., Susan C. Stansfield/Exec. VP - Product Registration, Europe, Africa, Asia, Pacific, Willem Jan Drijfhout/Sr. VP - Early Development Services

Directors: Terrance Bieker/Dir., CEO, Melvin D. Booth/63/Chmn., Armin Kessler/70/Dir., Jean-Pierre L. Conte/44/Dir., Robert E. Conway/54/Dir., Judith A. Hemberger/60/Dir., Robert J. Weltman/43/Dir.

Owners: Morgan Stanley Investment Management/5.50%, FMR Corporation/14.70%, Monika Pietrek, David W. Dockhorn/1.00%, Patrick K. Donnelly, Terrance J. Bieker, Melvin D. Booth, Baron Capital Group, Inc./6.20%, Jean-Pierre L. Conte/12.60%, Insiders/16.10%, Robert E. Conway, Judith A. Hemberger, Genstar Capital III, L.P./12.60%, ValueAct Capital Master Fund, L.P./18.50%, Bruce A. Teplitzky *(16 Owners included in Index)*

Financial Data: Fiscal Year End:12/31　**Latest Annual Data:** 12/31/2006

Year	Sales	Net Income
2006	$338,166,000	$26,845,000
2005	$326,244,000	$32,223,000
2004	$307,644,000	$20,749,000

Curr. Assets:	$172,029,000	**Curr. Liab.:**	$164,132,000	**P/E Ratio:**	11.40
Plant, Equip.:	$33,663,000	**Total Liab.:**	$202,887,000	**Indic. Yr. Divd.:**	NA
Total Assets:	$454,255,000	**Net Worth:**	$251,368,000	**Debt/ Equity:**	NA

Practicexpert Inc

23975 Pk. Sorrento Dr., Ste. 110, Calabasas, CA, 91302; **PH:** 1-818-591-0081; **Fax:** 1-818-223-8816; **http://** www.pxpert.com; **Email:** info@pxpert.com

General - Incorporation .... NV
Employees...NA
Auditor ....Kabani & Co, Inc
Stk Agt............ First Global Stock Transfer LLC
Counsel..NA
DUNS No. ....NA

Stock - Price on:12/24/2007 ....NA
Stock Exchange...OTC
Ticker Symbol...PXPT
Outstanding Shares ....NA
E.P.S..-$0.095
Shareholders...NA

Business: The group's principal activity is to provide administrative services, developing and deploying systems, technologies and services designed to improve operational efficiencies, reduce billing errors and enhance cash flow for, medical practitioners. The services include medical billing and accounts receivable management, practice management, transcription, and consulting. The pxpert system provides for data capture in the physician's office, utilizing a hand-held pocket PC, or other remote data capture device. The data undergoes an electronic data review at point of entry, allowing for the immediate correction of input errors on medical claims data. On 10-Nov-2003, the group acquired national healthcare management services inc, on 01-Mar-2004, singer medscript and on 29-Apr-2004, cancer care network, inc. During 2003, the group disposed its subsidiary, castpro.com, llc.

Primary SIC and add'l.: 7389 6719 4899

CIK No: 0001113679

Subsidiaries: Practice Xpert Services Corp.

Financial Data: Fiscal Year End:12/31　**Latest Annual Data:** 12/31/2005

Year	Sales	Net Income
2005	$17,725,000	-$12,206,000
2004	$11,097,000	-$4,199,000
2003	$3,379,000	$945,000

Curr. Assets:	$2,413,000	**Curr. Liab.:**	$11,436,000		
Plant, Equip.:	$462,000	**Total Liab.:**	$11,536,000	**Indic. Yr. Divd.:**	NA
Total Assets:	$6,414,000	**Net Worth:**	-$5,122,000	**Debt/ Equity:**	NA

Prana Biotechnology Ltd

369 Royal Parade, Level 2, Parkville, Victoria, 3052; **PH:** 61-393494906; **Fax:** 61-393480377; **http://** www.pranabio.com; **Email:** info@pranabio.com

General - Incorporation .... Australia
Employees...14
Auditor ....Deloitte Touche Tohmatsu
Stk Agt..... Computershare Investor Services LLC
Counsel..NA
DUNS No. ....NA

Stock - Price on:12/24/2007 ....$2.9
Stock Exchange...NDQ
Ticker Symbol...PRAN
Outstanding Shares 15,030,000
E.P.S..-$0.69
Shareholders...NA

Business: The groups principle activity is to provide provision of therapies for age-related disease, initially focussing on the treatment of alzheimer's disease. The group operates from United States.

Primary SIC and add'l.: 2834

CIK No: 0001131343

Subsidiaries: Prana Biotechnology Inc, Prana Biotechnology UK plc

Officers: Geoffrey Paul Kempler/Chmn., CEO, Richard Revelins/Company Sec., Dianne Angus/47/COO, Steve Targum/Chief Medical Advisor, Axel Unterbeck/Chief Strategic Advisor

Directors: Geoffrey Paul Kempler/Chmn., CEO, Jeffrey L. Cummings/Chmn. - Research, Development Advisory Board, Ashley I. Bush/Member - Research, Development Advisory Board, Craig Ritchie/Member - Research, Development Advisory Board, Jean-Marc Orgogozo/Member - Research, Development Advisory Board, Colin Louis Masters/Member - Research, Development Advisory Board, Peter Marks/Non - Exec. Dir., Brian Derek Meltzer/Non - Exec. Dir., George William Mihaly/Non - Exec. Dir., Peter Colman/Member - Scientific Advisory Board, Konrad Beyreuther/Member - Scientific Advisory Board, Rudolph Tanzi/Member - Research, Development Advisory Board

Owners: AMP Ltd./7.00%, Geoffrey P. Kempler/13.00%, Jagen Nominees Pty Ltd/10.00%

Financial Data: Fiscal Year End:06/30 Latest Annual Data: 6/30/2006

Year	Sales	Net Income
2006	$767,000	-$8,556,000
2005	$2,022,000	-$13,468,000
2004	$1,602,000	-$6,356,000

Curr. Assets:	$7,534,000	Curr. Liab.:	$1,179,000			
Plant, Equip.:	$75,000	Total Liab.:	$1,235,000	Indic. Yr. Divd.:	NA
Total Assets:	$7,608,000	Net Worth:	$6,373,000	Debt/ Equity:	NA

Praxair Inc

39 Old Ridgebury Rd., Danbury, CT, 06810; **PH:** 1-203-837-2000; **Fax:** 1-716-879-2040; **http://** www.praxair.com; **Email:** info@praxair.com

General - Incorporation	DE	Stock - Price on:12/24/2007	$72.67
Employees	27,042	Stock Exchange	NYSE
Auditor	PricewaterhouseCoopers LLP	Ticker Symbol	PX
Stk Agt	Registrar & Transfer Co	Outstanding Shares	318,700,000
Counsel	NA	E.P.S.	$3.46
DUNS No.	19-715-4586	Shareholders	NA

Business: The groups principle activities include manufacturing and selling atmospheric, process and specialty gases and high performance surface coatings. The groups products include atmospheric and process gases. Customers served by the group include chemicals and refining, primary metals, food and beverage, healthcare, semiconductor materials. The group operates from United States.

Primary SIC and add'l.: 3479 3471 2813 5085

CIK No: 0000884905

Subsidiaries: 3R Associati S.p.A., 640733 British Columbia Ltd., A. I. C. E. Reti S.c.a.r.l., A.S.P. S.r.l., Accent Cay Holdings Inc., Agas Servizi S.r.l., American Home Oxygen and Hospital Equipment, Inc., AMKO Service Company, Andaluza de Gases S.A., Antwerpse Chemische Bedrijven (LCB) N. V., Argim Ltd., Arroweld Italia S.p.A., Asian Surface Technologies, Pte., Ltd., Asistencia Tecnologica Medioambiental, S.A., Asistir Ltda. 340 Subsidiaries included in the Index

Officers: Dennis H. Reilley/55/Chmn., CEO/$15,501,250.00, Nigel D. Muir/VP - Communications, Public Relations, George P. Ristevski/Pres., Sally A. Savoia/VP - Human Resources, Stephen F. Angel/52/Dir., COO, Pres./$4,587,922.00, Ricardo S. Malfitano/Exec. VP/$2,556,092.00, James S. Sawyer/CFO, Sr. VP/$2,983,911.00, James J. Fuchs/Sr. VP/$2,329,435.00, Wayne J. Yakich/50/Pres. - Praxair Distribution, Inc, Randy S. Kramer/Sr. VP - Global Sales, Patrick M. Clark/VP, Controller, James T. Breedlove/Sr. VP, General Counsel, Corp. Sec., Richard P. Kenny/VP - Global Operations Excellence, Steven L. Lerner/CTO, Sr. VP, Sunil Mattoo/VP - Strategic Planning, Marketing (39 Officers included in Index)

Directors: Dennis H. Reilley/55/Chmn., CEO, Wayne T. Smith/62/Dir., Mitchell H. Watson/70/Dir., Robert L. Wood/53/Dir., Edward G. Galante/57/Dir., Jose Paulo De Oliveira Alves/Dir., Stephen F. Angel/52/Dir., COO, Pres., Claire W. Gargalli/65/Dir., Ira D. Hall/63/Dir., Ronald L. Kuehn/72/Dir., Raymond W. Leboeuf/61/Dir., Jackson G. Ratcliffe/71/Dir.

Owners: James S. Sawyer, Dennis H. Reilley, Ira D. Hall, Wayne T. Smith, Ricardo S. Malfitano, H. Mitchell Watson, Ronald L. Kuehn, Raymond W. LeBoeuf, G. Jackson Ratcliffe, FMR Corp./6.60%, James J. Fuchs, Jose P. Alves, Insiders, Robert L. Wood, Stephen F. Angel (16 Owners included in Index)

Financial Data: Fiscal Year End:12/31 Latest Annual Data: 12/31/2006

Year	Sales	Net Income
2006	$8,324,000,000	$988,000,000
2005	$7,656,000,000	$726,000,000
2004	$6,594,000,000	$697,000,000

Curr. Assets:	$2,059,000,000	Curr. Liab.:	$1,758,000,000	P/E Ratio:	22.22
Plant, Equip.:	$6,694,000,000	Total Liab.:	$6,326,000,000	Indic. Yr. Divd.:	$1.200
Total Assets:	$11,102,000,000	Net Worth:	$4,554,000,000	Debt/ Equity:	0.7609

Precis Inc

4929 W Royal Ln., Ste. 200, Irving, TX, 75063; **PH:** 1-866-578-1665; **http://** www.precis-pcis.com

General - Incorporation	OK	Stock - Price on:12/24/2007	NA
Employees	180	Stock Exchange	NA
Auditor	BDO Seidman, Hein & Assoc. LLP	Ticker Symbol	NA
Stk Agt	UMB Bank, N.A.	Outstanding Shares	NA
Counsel	NA	E.P.S.	-$1.21
DUNS No.	NA	Shareholders	NA

Business: The group's principal activity is to provide innovative membership service programs. It offers savings on healthcare services to persons who are under-insured. These savings are offered by accessing the same preferred provider organizations that are utilized by many insurance companies. These programs are sold primarily through a network marketing strategy under the name care entree. The group also addresses the needs of organizations seeking to leverage the expertise of an outside provider in offering membership service programs. Membership service programs offer selected products and services from a variety of vendors intended to enhance the existing relationships between businesses and consumers. The group operates solely in the United States. On 18-Jun-2004, the group acquired access healthsource inc.

Primary SIC and add'l.: 7372

CIK No: 0001017440

Subsidiaries: Access HealthSource, Inc

Officers: Frank B. Apodaca/45/CEO, Pres. - Access Healthsource, Inc/$411,773.00, Peter W. Nauert/64/Chmn., CEO, Pres., Nancy L. Zalud/VP - Communications, Investor Relations Officer, Eliseo Ruiz/Exec. VP, General Counsel, Sec./$335,765.00, Robert L. Bintliff/CFO, Exec. VP/$386,478.00, David M. Wysong/VP - Business Development/$242,744.00, Ian R. Stuart/COO, Michael K. Owens/Chief Marketing Officer, Michael R. Puestow/Pres. - Foresight TPA, Carl H. Fischer/Pres., Chief Marketing Officer

Directors: Peter W. Nauert/64/Chmn., CEO, Pres., French J. Hill/Dir., Andrew A. Boemi/Dir., Kent H. Webb/Dir., Russell Cleveland/69/Dir., Nicholas J. Zaffiris/Dir., Kenneth S. George/Dir.

Owners: Nicholas J. Zaffiris, Kent H. Webb, Lewis Opportunity Fund, LP, Rodney D. Baber, Renaissance US Growth Investment Trust PLC, Carl H. Fisher, Insiders, RENN Capital Group, Inc., Peter W. Nauert, Renaissance Capital Growth & Income Fund III, Inc., Premier RENN US Emerging Growth Fund Limited, Ready One Industries, US Special Opportunities Trust PLC, Ian R. Stuart, Andrew A. Boemi (24 Owners included in Index)

Financial Data: Fiscal Year End:12/31 Latest Annual Data: 12/31/2006

Year	Sales	Net Income
2006	$21,974,000	-$7,724,000
2005	$30,143,000	-$13,371,000
2004	$38,319,000	-$1,956,000

Curr. Assets:	$6,876,000	Curr. Liab.:	$2,880,000			
Plant, Equip.:	$924,000	Total Liab.:	$2,928,000	Indic. Yr. Divd.:	NA
Total Assets:	$16,320,000	Net Worth:	$13,392,000	Debt/ Equity:	NA

Precision Auto Care Inc

748 Miller Dr. SE, Ste. G-1, Leesburg, VA, 20175; **PH:** 1-703-777-9095; **Fax:** 1-703-779-0136; **http://** www.precisionac.com; **Email:** invest@precisionac.com

General - Incorporation	VA	Stock - Price on:12/24/2007	$0.426
Employees	25	Stock Exchange	OTC
Auditor	Yount, Hyde & Barbour, P.C	Ticker Symbol	PACI
Stk Agt	First Union Nat'l Bank	Outstanding Shares	28,990,000
Counsel	NA	E.P.S.	$0.118
DUNS No.	79-994-6595	Shareholders	NA

Business: The group's principal activity is to provide franchised automotive maintenance services in the United States and in certain foreign countries. It services include diagnosis, maintenance and repair of ignition systems, fuel systems, computerized engine control systems, cooling systems, starting and charging systems, emissions control systems, engine drive train systems, electrical systems, air conditioning systems, oil and other fluid systems, and brake systems. The group operates in one segment, automotive care franchising which is comprised of precision tune auto care and precision lube express services.

Primary SIC and add'l.: 7542 7549 6794 7538 5013

CIK No: 0001038541

Subsidiaries: Acc-u-tune, Colorado Tune,Inc., Miracle Industries,Inc., Miracle Partners,Inc., National 60 Minute Tune,Inc., PAC Mexican Delaware Holding Company,Inc., Praxis Afinaciones Puerto Rico,Inc., Praxis Afinaciones, S.A. de C.V., Praxis Auto Partes, S.A. de C.V., Precision Auto Care Mexico I, S. de R.L., Precision Auto Care Mexico II, S. de R.L., Precision Building Solutions,Inc., Precision Franchising LLC, Precision Printing,Inc., Precision Tune Auto Care,Inc. 23 Subsidiaries included in the Index

Officers: Robert R. Falconi/52/CEO, Pres., Joel Burrows/51/VP - Training, Research, Development, Mark P. Francis/40/CFO, Kevin Bates/45/Sr. VP - Marketing, Glyn D. Massingill/60/VP - Franchise Services, Frederick F. Simmons/45/Sr. VP, General Counsel, Corp. Sec., John T. Wiegand/45/Sr. VP - Operational Programs, Development

Directors: Louis M. Brown/63/Chmn.

Owners: Woodley A. Allen/0.48%, John D. Sanders, Bassam N. Ibrahim/0.42%, Insiders/20.87%, Louis M. Brown/13.43%, Frederick F. Simmons/0.92%, Robert R. Falconi/3.70%, Arthur C. Kellar Charitable Lead Annuity Trust/37.84%, Peter C. Keefe/0.31%, Avenir Corporation/9.47%, Falcon Solutions Limited/21.36%

Financial Data: Fiscal Year End:06/30 Latest Annual Data: 06/30/2007

Year	Sales	Net Income
2007	$12,072,000	$3,409,000
2006	$11,719,000	$724,000
2005	$12,803,000	$4,655,000

Curr. Assets:	$5,900,000	Curr. Liab.:	$2,005,000	P/E Ratio:	35.50
Plant, Equip.:	$122,000	Total Liab.:	$2,040,000	Indic. Yr. Divd.:	NA
Total Assets:	$17,565,000	Net Worth:	$15,408,000	Debt/ Equity:	0.0018

Precision Castparts Corp

4650 SW Macadam Ave., Ste. 440, Portland, OR, 97239; **PH:** 1-503-417-4800; **Fax:** 1-503-417-4817; **http://** www.precast.com; **Email:** info@precastcorp.com

General - Incorporation	OR	Stock - Price on:12/24/2007	$119.6
Employees	19,900	Stock Exchange	NYSE
Auditor	Deloitte & Touche, LLP	Ticker Symbol	PCP
Stk Agt	Bank of New York	Outstanding Shares	137,590,000
Counsel	Stoel Rives LLP	E.P.S.	$4.59
DUNS No.	00-902-7970	Shareholders	NA

Business: The groups principle activity is to manufacture complex metal components and products, investment castings, forgings and fasteners/fastener systems for aerospace and industrial gas turbine applications. The group also provides investment castings and forgings, specialty alloys, waxes and metal processing solutions. The group operates through three segments namely investment cast products, forged products and fastener products. In April 1, 2007 PCC acquired Cherry Aerospace LLC, GSC Foundries, Inc., and Special Metals Corporation. The group operates from United States.

Primary SIC and add'l.: 3369 3546 3541 3462 3594 3463 3492

CIK No: 0000079958

Subsidiaries: 300 N West Street LLC, AAA Aircraft Supply LLC, Advanced Forming Technology, Inc., AETC Limited, AFT Europa-Advanced Forming Technology Limited, Alexander Socket Screws Limited, ATAAS LLC, Avibank Mfg., Inc, Avibank Services LLC, BI, Inc., Cameron Forged Products, Limited, Cannon-Muskegon Corporation, Carmet Company, Carmet Investors, Inc., Chevron Aerospace Group, Limited 138 Subsidiaries included in the Index

Officers: Mark Donegan/Chmn., CEO/$8,328,499.00, Christopher L. Ayers/Sr. VP, Kenneth D. Buck/Sr. VP, Roger A. Cooke/VP - Regulatory - Legal Affairs/$1,954,401.00, Byron J. Gaddis/CIO, VP, Steve Hackett/Exec. VP - Presient, Fastener Products Business, Shawn R. Hagel/42/VP, Corporate Controller, Assist. Sec., Geoffrey A. Hawkes/49/VP, Treasurer, Assist. Sec., Dennis L. Konkol/49/Sr. VP, Pres. - Industrial Products, William D. Larsson/CFO, Sr. VP/$2,987,317.00, Ross

M. Lienhart/Sr. VP, Kirk G. Pulley/VP - Stratagic Planning, Corporate Development, Mark R. Roskopf/46/VP - Corporate Taxes, Assist. Sec., Joseph I. Snowden/Sr. VP, Pres. - Special Metals Corporation/$1,754,068.00, John W. Ericksen/46/Sr. VP, Pres. - Small Structurals Casting Operations *(16 Officers included in Index)*

Directors: Mark Donegan/Chmn., CEO, Dean T. Ducray/Dir., Vernon E. Oechsle/Dir., Byron O. Pond/Dir., Don R. Graber/Dir., Peter R. Bridenbaugh/Dir., Ulrich Schmidt/Dir., Rick Schmidt/58/Dir., Steven G. Rothmeier/Dir., Frank J. Travis/Dir., Daniel J. Murphy/Dir.

Owners: Peter R. Bridenbaugh, Roger A. Cooke, Vernon E. Oechsle, Dean T. DuCray, Joseph I. Snowden, Byron O. Pond, William D. Larsson, Frank J. Travis, Steven G. Rothmeier, Steven G. Hackett, Mark Donegan, Insiders, Don R. Graber

Financial Data: *Fiscal Year End:*04/02 **Latest Annual Data:** 4/1/2007

Year	Sales		Net Income
2007	$5,361,200,000		$633,100,000
2006	$3,546,400,000		$350,600,000
2005	$2,919,000,000		-$1,700,000

Curr. Assets:	$1,213,100,000	**Curr. Liab.:**	$779,700,000	**P/E Ratio:**	26.06
Plant, Equip.:	$692,500,000	**Total Liab.:**	$1,844,600,000	**Indic. Yr. Divd.:**	$0.120
Total Assets:	$3,625,000,000	**Net Worth:**	$1,780,400,000	**Debt/ Equity:**	NA

Precision Drilling Trust

Formerly: Precision Drilling Corp
4200-150 6th Ave., SW, Calgary, AB, T2P 3Y7; *PH:* 1-403-716-4500;
http:// www.precisiondrilling.com

General - Incorporation	Canada	**Stock**- Price on:12/24/2007	$25.29
Employees	6,500	Stock Exchange	NYSE
Auditor	KPMG LLP	Ticker Symbol	PDS
Stk Agt	Computershare Trust Co	Outstanding Shares	125,760,000
Counsel	Borden Ladner Gervais LLP	E.P.S	$3.08
DUNS No.	20-077-5641	Shareholders	NA

Business: The group's principle activities are to provide access to a growing fleet of drilling and service rigs, drilling and completion services, controlled pressure drilling, sophisticated downhole completion tools and logging- while-drilling systems. The group also provides directional drilling services, drill bit and tool manufacturing, gas compression packaging, drilling and industrial maintenance services. The group has operations in Canada, the United States, Latin America. Europe/Africa, Middle East and Asia/pacific.

Primary SIC and add'l.: 1381

CIK No: 0001013605

Subsidiaries: 1194312 Alberta Ltd., Columbia Oilfield Supply Ltd., LRG Catering Ltd., PDLP, Precision Diversified Services Ltd., Precision Drilling Corporation, Precision Drilling Ltd., Precision Limited Partnership, Precision Rentals Ltd., Rostel Industries Ltd., Trust sold Energy Industries Inc.

Officers: Kevin Neveu/CEO, Hank B. Swartout/Exec. Chmn., Doug J. Strong/CFO, Gene C. Stahl/Dir., COO, Pres., Darren J. Ruhr/VP - Corporate Services, Corp. Sec.

Directors: Hank B. Swartout/Exec. Chmn., Robert L. Phillips/Dir., Garth H. Wiggins/Dir., Trustee, W. C. Dunn/Dir., Frederick W. Pheasey/Dir., Brian A. Felesky/Dir., Robert J.S. Gibson/Dir., Trustee, Patrick M. Murray/Dir., Trustee, Allen R. Hagerman/Dir., Stephen J.J. Letwin/Dir.

Financial Data: *Fiscal Year End:*12/31 **Latest Annual Data:** 12/31/2006

Year	Sales		Net Income
2006	$1,233,591,000		$497,345,000
2005	$1,088,956,000		$1,399,023,000
2004	$1,930,627,000		$216,908,000

Curr. Assets:	$319,595,000	**Curr. Liab.:**	$176,735,000		
Plant, Equip.:	$950,446,000	**Total Liab.:**	$3,173,001,000	**Indic. Yr. Divd.:**	$1.590
Total Assets:	$1,565,359,000	**Net Worth:**	-$1,607,642,000	**Debt/ Equity:**	NA

Precision Optics Corp Inc

22 E Broadway, Gardner, MA, 01440; *PH:* 1-978-630-1800; *Fax:* 1-978-630-1487;
http:// www.poci.com; *Email:* info@poci.com

General - Incorporation	MA	**Stock**- Price on:12/24/2007	$0.35
Employees	30	Stock Exchange	OTC
Auditor	Vitale, Caturano & Co., Ltd.	Ticker Symbol	POCI
Stk Agt	EquiServe Trust Co N.A	Outstanding Shares	25,460,000
Counsel	NA	E.P.S	-$0.12
DUNS No.	11-824-4987	Shareholders	NA

Business: The group's principal activities are to design, develop, manufacture and market optical systems and components and optical thin film coatings. The products of the group include arthroscopes, laparoscopes, laryngoscopes, stereo endoscopes, adapters, imagecouplers and beamsplitters. The services provided by the group include advanced lens and optical system design, image analysis, optics testing and structural design and analysis. The products are used in telecommunications and other applications, test instrumentation and advanced optical system design and development services. The customers include endoscope and video camera manufacturers and suppliers and original equipment manufacturers.

Primary SIC and add'l.: 3845 3851

CIK No: 0000867840

Officers: Chuck Gerlowski/Dir. - Business Development

Owners: Richard E. Forkey, Joel R. Pitlor, Donald A. Major, Insiders, Arnold Schumsky, AIGH Investment Partners, LLC, Austin W. Marxe, Richard Miles, Michael T. Pieniazek, Joseph N. Forkey

Financial Data: *Fiscal Year End:*06/30 **Latest Annual Data:** 06/30/2007

Year	Sales		Net Income
2007	$2,477,000		-$2,890,000
2006	$2,285,000		-$2,272,000
2005	$1,350,000		-$3,688,000

Curr. Assets:	$2,903,000	**Curr. Liab.:**	$589,000		
Plant, Equip.:	$76,000	**Total Liab.:**	$589,000	**Indic. Yr. Divd.:**	NA
Total Assets:	$3,229,000	**Net Worth:**	$2,640,000	**Debt/ Equity:**	NA

Preferred Bank

601 S Figueroa St., 24th Fl., Los Angeles, CA, 90017; *PH:* 1-213-891-1188;
http:// www.preferredbank.com

General - Incorporation		**Stock**- Price on:12/24/2007	$40.1
Employees	132	Stock Exchange	NDQ
Auditor	KPMG LLP	Ticker Symbol	PFBC
Stk Agt	U.S. Stock Transfer Corp	Outstanding Shares	10,420,000
Counsel	NA	E.P.S.	NA
DUNS No.	NA	Shareholders	NA

Business: The groups principal activity is to provide banking and financial services.The products of the group include real estate and construction loan, commercial loan, trade finance loan, electronic banking and personal banking. The group operates from the United States.

Primary SIC and add'l.: 6022

CIK No: 0001165763

Officers: Li Yu/Chmn., CEO, Pres., Edward J. Czajka/Sr. VP, CFO, Lasse Glassen/Investor Relation Officer

Directors: Li Yu/Chmn., CEO, Pres., William C.Y. Cheng/Dir., Frank T. Lin/Dir., Chih-Wei Wu/Dir., Jason C. Yuan/Dir., Richard J. Belliston/Dir., Clark Hsu/Dir., Gary S. Nunnelly/Dir., Albert Yu/Dir.

Preferred Voice Inc New

6500 Greenville Ave., Ste. 570, Dallas, TX, 75206; *PH:* 1-214-265-9580; *Fax:* 1-214-265-9663;
http:// www.preferredvoice.com; *Email:* sales@preferredvoice.com

General - Incorporation	DE	**Stock**- Price on:12/24/2007	$1.25
Employees	10	Stock Exchange	OTC
Auditor	Philip Vogel & Co. PC	Ticker Symbol	PRFV
Stk Agt	Computershare Investor Services LLC	Outstanding Shares	6,130,000
Counsel	NA	E.P.S.	NA
DUNS No.	NA	Shareholders	NA

Business: The groups principle activity is to integrate and market enhanced services to phone companies, to complement their overall package of voice services. The group markets its products under the tradenames include Rockin Ringback(TM) and Push 2 Connect(TM). The group operates from the United States.

Primary SIC and add'l.: 3663 4899 4812

CIK No: 0000946822

Officers: Mary G. Merritt/Chmn., CEO, Sec., Treasurer, Bernard Bareis/VP - Engineering

Directors: Mary G. Merritt/Chmn., CEO, Sec., Treasurer, Scott V. Ogilvie/54/Dir., Todd Parker/44/Dir.

Owners: Steven J. Emerson, JMG Capital Partners, L.P., Todd Parker, Scott Ogilvie, Mary G. Merritt, Bristol Investment Fund, Ltd., Tyler G. Runnels, JMG Triton Offshore Fund Ltd., Insiders

Preformed Line Products Co

660 Beta Dr., Mayfield Village, OH, 44143; *PH:* 1-440-461-5200; *Fax:* 1-440-442-8816;
http:// www.preformed.com; *Email:* inquiries@preformed.com

General - Incorporation	OH	**Stock**- Price on:12/24/2007	$54
Employees	1,528	Stock Exchange	NDQ
Auditor	Deloitte & Touche LLP	Ticker Symbol	PLPC
Stk Agt	National City Bank	Outstanding Shares	5,370,000
Counsel	NA	E.P.S.	$2.47
DUNS No.	NA	Shareholders	NA

Business: The group's principle activities include designing and manufacturing products and systems employed in the construction and maintenance of overhead and underground networks for the energy, communications, cable provider, information and other similar industries. The principal products offered include formed wire and related hardware products, protective closures and data communication interconnection devices. The company also manufactures a line of products serving the voice and data transmission markets. These products are used to support, protect, connect, terminate and secure cables and wires. The company's customers include public and private energy utilities and communication companies, cable operators, financial institutions, subcontractors, distributors and value-added re-sellers. The operations are conducted mainly in Australia, Brazil, Canada, great Britain, Mexico, South Africa, Spain, Japan and China. The group operates from United States.

Primary SIC and add'l.: 3357

CIK No: 0000080035

Subsidiaries: APRESA PLP Spain, S. A., Beijing PLP Conductor Line Products Co., Ltd., PLP-Produtos Para Linhas Preformados Ltd., Preformados de Mexico S.A. de C.V., Preformed Line Products (Asia) Ltd., Preformed Line Products (Australia) Ltd., Preformed Line Products (Canada) Ltd., Preformed Line Products (Great Britain) Ltd., Preformed Line Products (South Africa) Pty. Ltd., Rack Technologies Pty. Ltd., Superior Modular Products Incorporated

Officers: Dem Kambouris/MD - South Africa, Francisco Marin/Power Area, Contact - Spain, Juan Fernandez-Trueba/Telecom Area, Contact - Spain, D. L. Humphrey/Sr. Business Mgr. - Great Britain, S. W. Carley/MD - Great Britain, M. J. Spayes/Sr. Business Mgr. - Export, Great Britain, Sergio Scavone/MD - Brazil, Jesus Villota/MD - Spain, Joanne R. Cash/Supervisor, International Sales Service, Wade Cutting/Product Mgr. - Canada, Ralph S. Crane/MD - Canada, Miguel Angel Guerrero/Energy Sales Mgr. - Mexico, Wu Yu/GM - China, Li Yue/Marketing Mgr. - China, Tuck Chew/Sales Support Mgr. - Australia *(19 Officers included in Index)*

Owners: Barbara P. Ruhlman/31.20%, KeyCorp/7.60%, Frank B. Carr, J. Cecil Curlee, Eric R. Graef, Dennis F. McKenna, Robert G. Ruhlman/7.70%, Insiders/53.80%, John D. Drinko/10.40%, William H. Haag, Randall M. Ruhlman/4.80%, Thomas F. Peterson/8.70%

Financial Data: *Fiscal Year End:*12/31 **Latest Annual Data:** 12/31/2006

Year	Sales		Net Income
2006	$216,937,000		$12,060,000
2005	$205,804,000		$11,986,000
2004	$183,112,000		$13,037,000

Curr. Assets:	$105,536,000	**Curr. Liab.:**	$33,405,000	**P/E Ratio:**	22.59
Plant, Equip.:	$52,810,000	**Total Liab.:**	$40,030,000	**Indic. Yr. Divd.:**	$0.800
Total Assets:	$170,963,000	**Net Worth:**	$130,933,000	**Debt/ Equity:**	NA

Premier Commercial Bancorp CA

2400 E Katella Ave. No. 125, Anaheim, CA, 92806; *PH:* 1-714-978-2400; *Fax:* 1-714-978-6100;
http:// www.pcboc.com

General - Incorporation	CA
Employees	57
Auditor	NA
Stk Agt	U.S. Stock Transfer Corp
Counsel	NA
DUNS No.	NA

Stock- Price on:12/24/2007	$14.4
Stock Exchange	OTC
Ticker Symbol	PCBP
Outstanding Shares	3,290,000
E.P.S.	$0.17
Shareholders	NA

Business: The group is a holding bank operating through its subsidiaries, whose principal activities include providing banking and financial services to the customers. Services of the group include personal and business checking accounts and various types of interest bearing deposit accounts, including interest bearing checking, money market, savings and time certificates of deposits. The group operates from the United States. In the year 2006, the groups total assets were $341,612 (thousands).

Primary SIC and add'l.: 6022

CIK No: 0001358462

Subsidiaries: Premier Commercial Bank Arizona, N.A., Premier Commercial Bank, N.A., Premier Commercial Statutory Trust I, Premier Commercial Statutory Trust II, Premier Commercial Statutory Trust III

Officers: Kenneth J. Cosgrove/Chmn., CEO, Ash Patel/Dir., COO, Pres., Chitra Sridhar/Assist. VP - Sr. Loan Processor, Danni Remington Gilchrist/Sr. VP, Regional Mgr. - General Banking, Molly D. Millican/VP, Relationship Mgr. - General Banking, Carolyn Nix/VP, Relationship Mgr. - General Banking, Ladawn Crawford/VP, Dir. - Operations, General Banking, Stephen W. Pihl/Exec. VP, Chief Credit Officer, Viktor R. Uehlinger/CFO, Exec. VP, Jules Jomsky/First VP, Business Development Officer, Andy Weaver/Sr. VP, SBA Loan Officer, Fred Grohmann/Sr. VP, Commercial Loan Officer - Commercial Lending, Brent Walters/VP, Commercial Loan Officer, Vernon Camara/VP, Commercial Loan Officer, Carlo De Lucia/Business Development Officer *(21 Officers included in Index)*

Directors: Kenneth J. Cosgrove/Chmn., CEO, Gene Hatz/Vice Chmn., Richard T. Letwak/Dir., Ash Patel/Dir., COO, Pres., Robert Matranga/Dir., Steven Perryman/Dir., Mel Smith/Dir., Ronald P. Thon/Dir., Anthony M. Vitti/Dir.

Owners: Anthony M. Vitti/1.25%, Ashokkumar R. Patel/4.51%, Ronald P. Thon/3.87%, Eugene E. Hatz/3.04%, Insiders/34.03%, Steven Perryman/3.09%, Richard T. Letwak/1.97%, Melvin W. Smith/6.48%, Robert C. Matranga/4.90%, Kenneth J. Cosgrove/7.01%

Financial Data: Fiscal Year End:12/31   Latest Annual Data: 12/31/2006

Year	Sales	Net Income
2006	NA	-$3,853,000
2005	NA	-$4,257,000
2004	NA	-$686,000

Curr. Assets:	$36,453,000	Curr. Liab.:	$291,401,000		
Plant, Equip.:	$2,733,000	Total Liab.:	$310,155,000	Indic. Yr. Divd.:	NA
Total Assets:	$341,612,000	Net Worth:	$31,457,000	Debt/ Equity:	NA

Premier Community Bankshares Inc

4095 Valley Pike, Winchester, VA, 22602; *PH:* 1-540-869-6600;
http:// www.premiercommunitybankshares.com

General - Incorporation	VA
Employees	266
Auditor	Yount, Hyde & Barbour, P.C
Stk Agt	Registrar & Transfer Co
Counsel	Williams, Mullen, Clark & Dobbins
DUNS No.	62-422-7120

Stock- Price on:12/24/2007	$32
Stock Exchange	NA
Ticker Symbol	NA
Outstanding Shares	5,740,000
E.P.S.	$1.40
Shareholders	NA

Business: The group's principal activities are to provide a wide range of banking services to the general public. The operations of the group are conducted through its subsidiaries the marathon bank and rockingham heritage bank. The services provided by the group include checking accounts, savings and time deposits, commercial, personal, home improvement, automobile and other installment and term loans. The group lends real estate loans, commercial and industrial loans and loans to individuals for household, family and other consumer expenditures. The other services provided by the group include traveler's checks, safe deposit, collection, notary public, discount brokerage service and other customary bank services (other than trust services) to its customers.

Primary SIC and add'l.: 6712 6022

CIK No: 0000854399

Subsidiaries: Premier Bank, Inc., Premier Statutory Trust I, Premier Statutory Trust II, Premier Statutory Trust III, RHB Services, Inc., Rockingham Heritage Bank, The Marathon Bank

Officers: John A. Willingham/CFO

Owners: Frank D. Hill, Mensel D. Dean/0.09%, John K. Stephens/1.70%, Meryl G. Kiser/0.07%, Thomas M. Boyd/0.16%, Joseph W. Hollis/1.30%, Walter H. Aikens/0.53%, Donald L. Unger/0.79%, Paul R. Yoder/1.66%, Clifton L. Good/1.37%, Stephen T. Heitz/0.37%, John A. Willingham/0.09%, Frederick A. Board/0.03%, Insiders/11.50%, Wayne B. Ruck/2.80% *(17 Owners included in Index)*

Financial Data: Fiscal Year End:12/31   Latest Annual Data: 12/31/2006

Year	Sales	Net Income
2006	$60,922,000	$7,845,000
2005	$44,746,000	$7,141,000
2004	$35,891,000	$6,343,000

Curr. Assets:	$55,868,000	Curr. Liab.:	$789,573,000	P/E Ratio:	22.86
Plant, Equip.:	$25,780,000	Total Liab.:	$828,998,000	Indic. Yr. Divd.:	$0.260
Total Assets:	$900,711,000	Net Worth:	$71,713,000	Debt/ Equity:	0.5326

Premier Concepts Inc

5215 N O'connor, Ste. 200, Irving, TX, 76039; *PH:* 1-310-201-9900

General - Incorporation	CO
Employees	74
Auditor	Creason & Assoc. PLLC
Stk Agt	Corporate Stock Transfer, Inc.
Counsel	NA
DUNS No.	82-650-1215

Stock- Price on:12/24/2007	NA
Stock Exchange	NA
Ticker Symbol	NA
Outstanding Shares	NA
E.P.S.	-$0.729
Shareholders	NA

Business: The group's principle activities include marketing and retailing of high-end reproduction jewelry. The product line includes 14-karat gold jewelry with cubic zirconia and other synthetic stones and sterling silver jewelry with semi-precious and synthetic stones. As at 26-Jan-2003, the company operated 25 retail locations in southern California, northern California, the states of Arizona, Colorado, Florida, Louisiana, Maryland, Nevada, New Jersey, Pennsylvania, and in the Washington, d.c. Area. The company's registered trademarks are impostors, impostors copy jewels, elegant pretenders, joli-joli and the latest in faux. The group operates from United States.

Primary SIC and add'l.: 5094 5944 6794

CIK No: 0000879206

Subsidiaries: USN TV

Financial Data: Fiscal Year End:03/31   Latest Annual Data: 03/31/2006

Year	Sales	Net Income
2006	$27,334,000	-$14,628,000
2003	$9,883,000	-$1,997,000
2002	$10,261,000	-$1,480,000

Curr. Assets:	$2,342,000	Curr. Liab.:	$18,118,000		
Plant, Equip.:	$281,000	Total Liab.:	$18,118,000	Indic. Yr. Divd.:	NA
Total Assets:	$3,326,000	Net Worth:	-$14,792,000	Debt/ Equity:	NA

Premier Development & Investment Inc New

8910 N Dale Mabry Hwy, Ste. 37, Tampa, FL, 33614; *PH:* 1-813-932-6822

General - Incorporation	NV
Employees	NA
Auditor	Baumann, Raymondo & Company P.A.
Stk Agt	Transfer Online, Inc.
Counsel	Drinker, Biddle and Reath, LLP
DUNS No.	NA

Stock- Price on:12/24/2007	NA
Stock Exchange	OTC
Ticker Symbol	PDIV
Outstanding Shares	NA
E.P.S.	-$0.56
Shareholders	NA

Business: The groups principle activity is to generate from the sale of alcoholic beverages. The group operates from the United States.

Primary SIC and add'l.: 5812

CIK No: 0001140003

Subsidiaries: Players Grille, Inc.

Financial Data: Fiscal Year End:12/31   Latest Annual Data: 12/31/2005

Year	Sales	Net Income
2005	$1,251,000	-$2,461,000
2004	$543,000	$116,000
2003	$14,000	-$43,000

Curr. Assets:	$60,000	Curr. Liab.:	$760,000		
Plant, Equip.:	$351,000	Total Liab.:	$760,000	Indic. Yr. Divd.:	NA
Total Assets:	$859,000	Net Worth:	$100,000	Debt/ Equity:	NA

Premier Exhibitions Inc

3340 Peachtree Rd. NE, Ste. 2250, Atlanta, GA, 30326; *PH:* 1-404-842-2600; *Fax:* 1-404-842-2626; *http://* www.rmstitanic.net

General - Incorporation	FL
Employees	56
Auditor	Kempisty & Co
Stk Agt	American Stock Transfer & Trust Co.
Counsel	Brian Wainger
DUNS No.	80-792-0061

Stock- Price on:12/24/2007	$16.78
Stock Exchange	NDQ
Ticker Symbol	PRXI
Outstanding Shares	29,240,000
E.P.S.	$0.30
Shareholders	NA

Business: The group's principal activities are to conduct touring exhibitions, television programs and market still photographs, coal and titanic-related products. The group obtains oceanic material and scientific data, which includes still and moving photography and artifacts from the wreck site of the titanic for historical verification, scientific education and public awareness. The group operates solely in the domestic market. The group is in a unique position to present exhibitions of titanic artifacts for viewing by the public. The group has presented exhibitions in association with third parties throughout the world and nearly fifteen million people have attended these exhibits.the company is now presenting its own titanic exhibitions in omaha, Nebraska and salt lake city, Utah. The pending openings during the summer of 2004 include manchester, England; philadelphia, Pennsylvania and shanghai, China.

Primary SIC and add'l.: 7999

CIK No: 0000796764

Subsidiaries: Exhibitions International, LLC., Premier Acquisitions, Inc., Premier Exhibitions (UK)Ltd., Premier Exhibitions 2005A-SP, Inc., Premier Exhibitions 2005B-ATL, Inc., Premier Exhibitions No.5, Inc., Premier Exhibitions NYC, Inc., RMS Titanic (United Kingdom) Ltd., RMS Titanic, Inc., Seatron Limited

Officers: Arnie Geller/67/Chmn., CEO, Pres./$586,111.00, Paul Giguere/Dir. - Sales, Stephen Couture/38/Dir., CFO, VP/$701,528.00, Thomas Zaller/36/VP - Exhibitions/$460,026.00, Brian Wainger/39/VP, Chief Legal Counsel, Corp. Sec./$460,131.00

Directors: Arnie Geller/67/Chmn., CEO, Pres., Douglas Banker/56/Dir., Stephen Couture/38/Dir., CFO, VP, Nick N. Cretan/72/Dir., Alan Reed/51/Dir.

Owners: Arnie Geller/10.20%, Joseph B. Marsh/5.10%, Judith Geller/5.10%, Insiders/13.90%, Janice S. Gasparrini/7.70%

Financial Data: Fiscal Year End:02/28   Latest Annual Data: 2/28/2007

Year	Sales	Net Income
2007	$30,087,000	$7,421,000
2006	$13,041,000	$5,283,000
2005	$6,857,000	-$1,475,000

Curr. Assets:	$24,670,000	Curr. Liab.:	$1,986,000	P/E Ratio:	69.92
Plant, Equip.:	$3,620,000	Total Liab.:	$1,986,000	Indic. Yr. Divd.:	NA
Total Assets:	$34,886,000	Net Worth:	$32,900,000	Debt/ Equity:	NA

Premier Financial Bancorp Inc

2883 Fifth Ave., Huntington, WV, 25702; *PH:* 1-304-525-1600

General - Incorporation	KY
Employees	225
Auditor	Crowe Chizek & Co. LLC
Stk Agt	Registrar & Transfer Co
Counsel	NA
DUNS No.	92-866-1644

Stock- Price on:12/24/2007	$16.32
Stock Exchange	NDQ
Ticker Symbol	PFBI
Outstanding Shares	5,240,000
E.P.S.	$1.34
Shareholders	NA

Business: The group's principal activity is to provide traditional banking services and trust services to customers located in the counties and adjoining counties in Kentucky, Ohio and west Virginia. The group operates fourteen banking offices in Kentucky, three banking offices in Ohio and six banking offices in west Virginia. The services include commercial, real estate, agricultural and consumer lending,

depository and funds transfer services, collections, safe deposit boxes, cash management services and other services. The group's range of deposit services includes checking accounts, now accounts, savings accounts, money market accounts, club accounts, individual retirement accounts, certificates of deposit and overdraft protection.

Primary SIC and add'l.: 6712 6022

CIK No: 0000887919

Subsidiaries: Boone County Bank, Inc., Citizens Deposit Bank and Trust Company, Farmers Deposit Bank, First Central Bank, Inc., Mt. Vernon Financial Holdings, Inc., Ohio River Bank, Premier Data Services, Inc.

Officers: Robert W. Walker/61/Dir., CEO, Pres./$249,777.00, Brien M. Chase/43/CFO, VP/$116,219.00, Dennis Klingensmith/54/VP - Premier/$147,912.00

Directors: Robert W. Walker/61/Dir., CEO, Pres., Marshall T. Reynolds/71/Chmn., Neal W. Scaggs/72/Dir., E. V. Holder/75/Dir., Keith F. Molihan/65/Dir., Edsel R. Burns/57/Dir., Toney K. Adkins/58/Dir., Hosmer A. Brown/87/Dir., Thomas W. Wright/55/Dir.

Owners: Tontine Financial Partners, L.P./9.90%, Douglas V. Reynolds/5.30%, Marla Braun/8.60%, Marshall T. Reynolds/10.70%

Financial Data: Fiscal Year End:12/31 Latest Annual Data: 12/31/2006

Year	Sales	Net Income
2006	$36,565,000	$6,501,000
2005	$33,319,000	$4,434,000
2004	$31,727,000	$6,697,000
Curr. Assets:	$47,378,000	Curr. Liab.: $460,827,000	P/E Ratio: 12.85
Plant, Equip.:	$7,028,000	Total Liab.: $474,450,000	Indic. Yr. Divd.: $0.400
Total Assets:	$535,452,000	Net Worth: $61,002,000	Debt/ Equity: 0.1824

Premier Svc Bank CA

3637 Arlington Ave., Ste. B, Riverside, CA, 92506; **PH:** 1-951-274-2400; **Fax:** 1-951-274-2410; **http://** www.premierservicebank.com

General - Incorporation	NA	Stock - Price on:12/24/2007	$18.35
Employees	NA	Stock Exchange	OTC
Auditor	NA	Ticker Symbol	PSBK
Stk Agt	NA	Outstanding Shares	NA
Counsel	NA	E.P.S.	NA
DUNS No.	NA	Shareholders	NA

Business: The groups principal activities include providing banking and financial services to its customers. Services of the group include checking accounts, personal banking, private banking, Debit cards, Credit Cards, ATM and online customer help. The group operates from the United States.

Primary SIC and add'l.: 6712 6036

CIK No:

Officers: Kerry L. Pendergast/Dir., CEO, Pres. Premier Service Bank, Angela Swanson/Exec. VP, Chief Credit Officer, Jessica Lee/CFO, Exec. VP

Directors: Kerry L. Pendergast/Dir., CEO, Pres. Premier Service Bank, Kenneth B. Stream/Chmn., Robert D. Aust/Dir., Donald J. Bosic/Dir., Iheanacho Emeruwa/Dir., Carol Ann Flambures/Dir., Carole A. Gudde/Dir., Robert Jaspan/Dir., Gerald R. Luppino/Dir., Robert J. Norton/Dir., V. C. Smith/Dir., John Weiss/Dir., Jack Wyatt/Dir.

Premier Valley Bank CA

8355 N Fresno St., Ste 180, Fresno, CA, 93720; **PH:** 1-559-438-2002; **http://** www.premiervalleybank.com

General - Incorporation		Stock - Price on:12/24/2007	$8.6
Employees	NA	Stock Exchange	OTC
Auditor	NA	Ticker Symbol	PVLY
Stk Agt	Registrar & Transfer Co	Outstanding Shares	12,200,000
Counsel	NA	E.P.S.	NA
DUNS No.	NA	Shareholders	NA

Business: The groups principal activities include providing second to none customer service in every facet of business. The groups services provide a wide range of products for the entrepreneur, including lines of credit, commercial loans for working capital or equipment financing, and small business administration loans for purchase or construction of a building for the business.

Primary SIC and add'l.: 6029

CIK No:

Officers: Mike J. McGowan/Dir., Pres., CEO - Organizers, Elayne Mendoza/VP, Bank Operations Administrator, Kathy Seiler/VP - Human Resources, Thomas A. Weil/Investor Relations Officer, Jerry E. Cook/Dir., Organizer, Mateo F. De Soto/Dir., Organizer, Richard H. Lehman/Dir., Organizer, Michael S. Mathiesen/Dir., Organizer, Dave Bonaccorso/Investor Relations Officer, Troy K. Norlander/Investor Relations Officer, Lisa Gallo/Investor Relations Officer, Mike Hedrei/Investor Relations Officer, Thomas G. Richards/Dir. - Organizers, Joe Williams/Dir. - Organizers, Tony Coelho/Organizers (26 Officers included in Index)

Directors: Mike J. McGowan/Dir., Pres., CEO - Organizers, Jerry E. Cook/Dir., Organizer, Mateo F. De Soto/Dir., Organizer, Surinder P. Dhillon/Dir., Linda F. East/Dir., Richard H. Lehman/Dir., Organizer, Michael S. Mathiesen/Dir., Organizer, Thomas G. Richards/Dir. - Organizers, Joe Williams/Dir. - Organizers

Premier Wealth Management Inc

Formerly: Tally-Ho Ventures Inc
518 Oak St. 2, Glendale, CA, 91204; **PH:** 1-818-550-7886; **http://** tallyhoventures.com

General - Incorporation	DE	Stock - Price on:12/24/2007	$0.9
Employees	NA	Stock Exchange	NA
Auditor	Malone & Bailey, P.C	Ticker Symbol	NA
Stk Agt	Signature Stock Transfer, Inc.	Outstanding Shares	NA
Counsel	NA	E.P.S.	NA
DUNS No.	NA	Shareholders	NA

Business: The groups principle activity is a wealth management organization focused on serving the needs of families and high net worth individual throughout the world. The group operates from the United States.

Primary SIC and add'l.: 6282

CIK No: 0001226944

Officers: Tal L. Kapelner/CEO - Producer, Nigel Gregg/36/Chmn., CEO, Pres./$175,000.00, Emmanuel Wolf/CEO - Master Finance Holdings SA, Jose M. Meleth/Dir., Sec., CFO/$175,000.00

Directors: Nigel Gregg/36/Chmn., CEO, Pres., Jose M. Meleth/Dir., Sec., CFO

Owners: Jose Meleth/1.10%, Insiders/4.00%, Financial & Investment Management Group, Ltd/18.73%, Peter Ellery/8.59%, Nigel Gregg/2.90%, Peter Smith/8.59%, Protrust Financial Services Group, SA/6.86%

Financial Data: Fiscal Year End:12/31 Latest Annual Data: 12/31/2006

Year	Sales	Net Income
2006	$12,289,000	-$1,281,000
2005	$3,829,000	$528,000
2004	NA	-$34,000
Curr. Assets:	$10,320,000	Curr. Liab.: $17,183,000	
Plant, Equip.:	$133,000	Total Liab.: $18,541,000	Indic. Yr. Divd.: NA
Total Assets:	$25,835,000	Net Worth: $6,664,000	Debt/ Equity: 0.0911

Premiere Global Services Inc

3280 Peachtree Rd. NW, The Terminus Bldg., Ste. 1000, Atlanta, GA, 30305; **PH:** 1-404-262-8400; **Fax:** 1-404-262-8525; **http://** www.ptek.com

General - Incorporation	GA	Stock - Price on:12/24/2007	$12.63
Employees	2,350	Stock Exchange	NYSE
Auditor	Deloitte & Touche LLP	Ticker Symbol	PGI
Stk Agt	SunTrust Bank	Outstanding Shares	70,780,000
Counsel	Alston & Bird LLP	E.P.S.	$0.44
DUNS No.	79-282-7669	Shareholders	NA

Business: The group's principal activity is to provide communications and data services through two business units: premiere conferencing and xpedite. Premiere conferencing offers a full range of enhanced, automated and Web conferencing services for group communications activities such as investor relation calls, press conferences and training seminars. Xpedite offers a comprehensive suite of value-added multimedia messaging services that manage and facilitate the electronic distribution of information to all types of electronic addresses including fax, e-mail, voice and wireless. The group operates in North America, Europe and Asia-Pacific. The company acquired adval communications, inc. And its affiliates in feb, 2004 and resource communications, inc. On 01 apr, 2004.

Primary SIC and add'l.: 6719 4812 4813 4822

CIK No: 0000880804

Subsidiaries: Accucast, Inc., American Teleconferencing Services, Ltd., CCS ConferenceCallService GmbH, Clarinet, Inc., Communications Network Enhancement Inc., Comwave UK, Ltd., Fastwell Technology Limited, iMeet, Inc., Intellivoice Communications, LLC, Netspoke, Inc., PCI Network Services, Inc., Premiere Communications, Inc., Premiere Conferencing (Canada) Limited, Premiere Conferencing (Hong Kong) Limited, Premiere Conferencing (Ireland) Limited 56 Subsidiaries included in the Index

Officers: Boland T. Jones/Chmn., CEO/$3,159,841.00, Michael E. Havener/CFO/$479,162.00, Theodore P. Schrafft/Pres./$1,431,492.00, Randolph W. Salisbury/Chief Communications Officer, David M. Guthrie/CTO, Lee T. Provow/Pres. - Global Operations/$1,299,480.00, Scott L. Askins/Sec., Erik Petrik/Chief People Officer, Mark Alexander/Exec. VP - Sales, Marketing North America, Dennis Choo/MD - Asia Pacific, John Stone/MD - Europe

Directors: Boland T. Jones/Chmn., CEO, Jeffery T. Arnold/Dir., Raymond H. Pirtle/Dir., Wilkie S. Colyer/Dir., Walker J. Smith/Dir., John R. Harris/Dir., Steve W. Jones/Dir.

Owners: Jeffrey A. Allred/1.20%, T. Rowe Price Associates, Inc./7.30%, Boland T. Jones/5.90%, John R. Harris, Michael E. Havener, Theodore P. Schrafft, Walker J. Smith, Barclays Global Investors, NA et. al./5.00%, Insiders/9.30%, Wilkie S. Colyer, Jeffrey T. Arnold, Lee T. Provow, Raymond H. Pirtle

Financial Data: Fiscal Year End:12/31 Latest Annual Data: 12/31/2006

Year	Sales	Net Income
2006	$496,472,000	$25,509,000
2005	$497,473,000	$47,417,000
2004	$449,371,000	$41,880,000
Curr. Assets:	$121,566,000	Curr. Liab.: $91,397,000	P/E Ratio: 32.38
Plant, Equip.:	$88,062,000	Total Liab.: $233,024,000	Indic. Yr. Divd.: NA
Total Assets:	$549,315,000	Net Worth: $316,291,000	Debt/ Equity: 0.3880

Premiere Publishing Group Inc

386 Pk. Ave. S, 16th Fl., New York, NY, 10016; **PH:** 1-212-481-1005

General - Incorporation	NY	Stock - Price on:12/24/2007	$0.08
Employees	NA	Stock Exchange	OTC
Auditor	Gruber & Co., LLC	Ticker Symbol	PPBLE
Stk Agt	Corporate Stock Transfer, Inc.	Outstanding Shares	NA
Counsel	NA	E.P.S.	-$0.097
DUNS No.	NA	Shareholders	NA

Business: The groups principle activity is to publish the national quarterly magazine namely Trump Magazine. In March 2005, the group acquired Sobe Life, LLC. The group operates from the United States.

Primary SIC and add'l.: 2721

CIK No: 0001338929

Subsidiaries: Poker Life Magazine LLC., Sobe Life, LLC.

Officers: Michael Jacobson/Chmn., CEO, Pres.

Directors: Michael Jacobson/Chmn., CEO, Pres.

Owners: Lakefield Trading LTD/6.80%, Legend Merchant Group, Inc/4.60%, Gilman Securities LTD/6.80%, Lion Advisors LLC/5.10%, Donald J. Trump/14.60%, Michael Jacobson/14.60%, Lars Volkenberg/5.00%, Insiders/14.60%, Brenston Enterprises S.A./6.80%

Financial Data: Fiscal Year End:12/31 Latest Annual Data: 3/31/2007

Year	Sales	Net Income
2007	NA	NA
2006	NA	NA
Curr. Assets:	$1,213,000	Curr. Liab.: $2,236,000	
Plant, Equip.:	$86,000	Total Liab.: $2,496,000	Indic. Yr. Divd.: NA
Total Assets:	$1,451,000	Net Worth: -$1,045,000	Debt/ Equity: NA

Premierwest Bancorp

503 Airport Rd., Medford, OR, 97504; **PH:** 1-541-618-6003; **Fax:** 1-541-618-6001;
http:// www.premierwestbank.com; **Email:** info@premierwestbank.com

General - Incorporation .... OR	**Stock**- Price on:12/24/2007 ....$14.25
Employees.................................435	Stock Exchange.............................NDQ
Auditor ....Moss Adams LLP	Ticker Symbol...............................PRWT
Stk Agt............U.S. Stock Transfer Corp	Outstanding Shares 17,030,000
Counsel...NA	E.P.S..$0.82
DUNS No..NA	Shareholders.................................NA

Business: The group's principal activity is to provide a wide range of financial products and services principally to small and medium-sized businesses, professional and retail customers. The group provides deposit products such as checking and savings accounts, money market accounts and certificates of deposit. In addition, it also provides travelers checks, money orders and automated teller machines services at its facilities. The group originates various commercial, consumer and real estate loans. The group provides other services including insurance and related financial products, mutual funds, annuities and other investment products through a third-party registered broker-dealer. It operates primarily in jackson, josephine, douglas and klamath counties of southern Oregon and siskiyou and shasta counties of northern California. On 23-Jan-2004, the group acquired mid valley bank.

Primary SIC and add'l.: 6022 6712

CIK No: 0001102287

Subsidiaries: Blue Star Properties, Inc., Premier Finance Company, PremierWest Bank, PremierWest Investment Services, Inc., PremierWest Statutory Trust I, PremierWest Statutory Trust II, Timberline Community Bank

Officers: John L. Anhorn/Dir., CEO/$773,170.00, Richard R. Hieb/Dir., COO, Exec. VP, Sec./$470,928.00, Owen Atkinson/Sr. VP, Dir. - Information Services, Bob Dumilieu/Exec. VP - Branch Administration, James M. Ford/Dir., Pres./$317,468.00, James Earley/Exec. VP, Credit Administrator, Cher Everhart-Earl/Sr. VP - Compliance, Kathy Trautman/Sr. VP, Regional Administrator, James Servoss/Sr. VP - Loan Production, Tom Anderson/CFO, Exec. VP/$278,409.00, Mack Lai/Sr. VP, Dir. - Operations, Jim Fortner/Sr. VP, Controller, Richard Russell/VP, Regional Administrator

Directors: John L. Anhorn/Dir., CEO, John A. Duke/Chmn., Patrick G. Huycke/Vice Chmn., James L. Patterson/Dir., John B. Dickerson/Dir., Dennis N. Hoffbuhr/Dir., Rickar D. Watkins/Dir., Richard R. Hieb/Dir., COO, Exec. VP, Sec., Brian Pargeter/Dir., James M. Ford/Dir., Pres., Thomas R. Becker/Dir.

Owners: James Patterson, Jim Earley, Patrick G. Huycke/1.16%, James Ford, Thomas Becker, Tom Anderson, Richard Hieb, Insiders/15.62%, John A. Duke/7.29%, PremierWest 401K Plan/1.82%, John A. & Marilyn R. Duke Charitable Lead Annuity Trust/5.63%, Rickar Watkins, John Anhorn/1.07%, Dennis Hoffbuhr, Brian Pargeter (16 Owners included in Index)

Financial Data: Fiscal Year End:12/31   Latest Annual Data: 12/31/2006

Year	Sales	Net Income
2006	$80,953,000	$14,648,000
2005	$64,878,000	$13,189,000
2004	$49,437,000	$9,108,000

Curr. Assets:	$58,961,000	**Curr. Liab.:**	$902,788,000	**P/E Ratio:**	18.04
Plant, Equip.:	$34,102,000	**Total Liab.:**	$918,252,000	**Indic. Yr. Divd.:**	$0.240
Total Assets:	$1,034,511,000	**Net Worth:**	$116,259,000	**Debt/ Equity:**	NA

Premium Standard Farms Inc

805 Pennsylvania Ave., Ste. 200, Kansas City, MO, 64105; **PH:** 1-816-472-7675;
http:// www.psfarms.com

General - Incorporation .... DE	**Stock**- Price on:12/24/2007 .... NA
Employees.......................................NA	Stock Exchange..............................NA
Auditor ....Deloitte & Touche, LLP	Ticker Symbol.................................NA
Stk Agt...........................UMB Bank, N.A.	Outstanding Shares ....NA
Counsel..................Shook Hardy & Bacon, LLP	E.P.S...NA
DUNS No...NA	Shareholders....................................NA

Business: The groups principle activity is to provide pork products. The products of the group include tenderloins, hams, picnics, butts, ribs, marinated, case-ready, bacon, smoked hams and sausage. The group products sold under the trade names Premium Farms, Natural Excellence and Tomahawk Farms. The groups operates through two segments namely pork processing and hog production. The group operates from the United States.

Primary SIC and add'l.: 2013

CIK No: 0001143967

Subsidiaries: Crystal Peak Technologies, LLC, L&H Farms, LLC,, L&S Farms, LPC Transport, Inc., Lundy International, Inc., Oldhams, LLC,

Prepaid Legal Services Inc

1 Pre-Paid Way, Ada, OK, 74820; **PH:** 1-580-436-1234; **Fax:** 1-580-421-6305;
http:// www.pplsi.com; **Email:** customerservice@pplsi.com

General - Incorporation ....OK	**Stock**- Price on:12/24/2007 ....$63.86
Employees.....................................840	Stock Exchange.............................NYSE
Auditor ....Grant Thornton LLP	Ticker Symbol................................PPD
Stk Agt...................Computershare Trust CO.	Outstanding Shares 13,340,000
Counsel....................Crowe & Dunlvy	E.P.S..$3.94
DUNS No............................08-248-5350	Shareholders...................................NA

Business: The group's principal activities are to design, underwrite and market legal expense plans. It's legal expense plans (referred to as memberships) provide for a variety of legal services in a manner similar to medical plans. The plans offered by the group include family legal plan, preventive legal services, automobile legal protection plan, trial defense, irs audit protection services, Canadian family plan, specialty legal service plans and business owners' legal solutions plan. The memberships sold by the group allow members to access legal services through a network of independent law firms under contract with the group. At 31-Dec-2002, the group had 1,418,997 memberships in force with members in all 50 states, the district of columbia and the Canadian provinces of ontario, british columbia, alberta and manitoba.

Primary SIC and add'l.: 6311 8111 7322

CIK No: 0000311657

Subsidiaries: Ada Travel Service, Inc., American Legal Services, Inc., Legal Service Plans of Virginia, Inc., National Pre-Paid Legal Services of Mississippi, Inc., PPL Legal Care of Canada Corporation, Pre-Paid Canadian Holdings, LLC, Pre-Paid Legal Access, Inc., Pre-Paid Legal Casualty, Inc., Pre-Paid Legal Services of Tennessee, Inc., Pre-Paid Legal Services, Inc. of

Officers: Harland C. Stonecipher/Chmn., CEO, Pres./$2,123,431.00, Andrew P. Miller/Advisory Counsel Member, Randy Harp/COO/$299,427.00, Steve Williamson/CFO/$174,754.00, Duke R. Ligon/Dir., Advisory Counsel Member, Jamie Anderson/Mgr. - Membership Administration, Linda Brown/Mgr. - Customer Care, Sheila Burris/Mgr. - Marketing Services, Keith Davis/Mgr. - Group Marketing, Leslie Fisher/VP - Attorney Resources, Melanie Lawson/Retention Analyst, John Long/VP - Corporate Development, Vicky Mapp/VP - Information Technology, Kathy Pinson/VP - Regulatory Compliance, Keri Prince/General Counsel (20 Officers included in Index)

Directors: Harland C. Stonecipher/Chmn., CEO, Pres., Tom W. Smith/Dir., Orland G. Aldridge/Dir., Martin H. Belsky/Dir., Peter K. Grunebaum/Dir., John W. Hail/Dir., Duke R. Ligon/Dir., Advisory Counsel Member

Owners: Scott Vassalluzzo/16.30%, Idoya Partners./7.80%, Prescott Associates/7.60%, Thomas W. Smith/24.40%

Financial Data: Fiscal Year End:12/31   Latest Annual Data: 12/31/2006

Year	Sales	Net Income
2006	$57,952,000	$40,062,000
2005	$41,739,000	$29,846,000
2004	$41,562,000	$15,506,000

Curr. Assets:	$88,332,000	**Curr. Liab.:**	$70,457,000	**P/E Ratio:**	16.21
Plant, Equip.:	$59,643,000	**Total Liab.:**	$157,687,000	**Indic. Yr. Divd.:**	NA
Total Assets:	$188,547,000	**Net Worth:**	$30,860,000	**Debt/ Equity:**	2.1194

Prescient Applied Intelligence Inc

1247 Ward Ave., Ste. 200, West Chester, PA, 19380; **PH:** 1-610-719-1600; **Fax:** 1-610-719-8575;
http:// www.prescient.com; **Email:** info@prescient.com

General - Incorporation .... DE	**Stock**- Price on:12/24/2007 ....$0.125
Employees.......................................47	Stock Exchange.............................OTC
Auditor ....Amper, Politziner & Mattia P.c	Ticker Symbol................................PPID
Stk Agt......................UMB Bank, N.A.	Outstanding Shares 33,330,000
Counsel...NA	E.P.S..-$0.098
DUNS No......................14-803-3863	Shareholders...................................NA

Business: The group's principal activity is to provide subscription-based, business-to-business electronic commerce services. The group's services enable food industry participants to efficiently manage their complex supply chain of information. The services of group allow manufacturers, wholesalers, distributors and retailers to communicate and synchronize item, price and promotion information in a more cost-effective and accessible way. The group's clients and customers range from small, rapidly growing companies to large corporations in the consumer packaged goods and retail industries and are geographically dispersed throughout the United States. At 31-Dec-2003, the group had more than 1000 customers.

Primary SIC and add'l.: 7378 7373 7374 7379

CIK No: 0001017137

Subsidiaries: Prescient Systems Limited, Prescient Systems, Inc., viaLink Operations, Inc.

Officers: Jane F. Hoffer/Dir., CEO, Pres./$364,983.00, Betsy Hargus/Dir. - Marketing, Kent Rice/Dir. - Advanced Commerce Development, Bill Woerner/Dir. - Professional Services, Elliot Zimmerman/VP - Strategic Accounting, Services, Jim Eckels/Dir. - Development

Directors: Jane F. Hoffer/Dir., CEO, Pres., Daniel W. Rumsey/Chmn., Mary Lou Fox/Dir., Michael A. Dipiano/Dir., Warren D. Jones/Dir., Patrick L. Kiernan/Dir.

Owners: Patrick Kiernan/1.25%, Daniel W. Rumsey/1.18%, Insiders/22.27%, New Spring Ventures/12.16%, Mary Lou Fox/1.28%, Jane F. Hoffer/5.94%, CGA Resources, LLC/9.99%, Warren D. Jones/1.30%, SDS Capital Group SPC LTD/17.20%, Michael A. DiPiano/13.34%, Hudson Ventures/9.99%

Financial Data: Fiscal Year End:12/31   Latest Annual Data: 12/31/2006

Year	Sales	Net Income
2006	$9,244,000	-$2,493,000
2005	$9,390,000	-$2,334,000
2004	$5,174,000	-$7,473,000

Curr. Assets:	$2,562,000	**Curr. Liab.:**	$2,476,000		
Plant, Equip.:	$183,000	**Total Liab.:**	$4,900,000	**Indic. Yr. Divd.:**	NA
Total Assets:	$21,754,000	**Net Worth:**	$16,853,000	**Debt/ Equity:**	0.1420

President Casinos Inc

1000 N Leonor K. Sullivan Blvd., St. Louis, MO, 63102; **PH:** 1-314-622-3000;
Fax: 1-314-622-3049; **http://** www.presidentcasino.com; **Email:** investor@presidentcasino.com

General - Incorporation .... DE	**Stock**- Price on:12/24/2007 ....$0.37
Employees...5	Stock Exchange.............................OTC
Auditor ....Deloitte & Touche LLP	Ticker Symbol................................PREZQ
Stk Agt ....Mellon Investor Services LLC	Outstanding Shares 5,030,000
Counsel...NA	E.P.S..$1.58
DUNS No...................79-820-4640	Shareholders...................................NA

Business: The group's principal activities are to develop, own and operate riverboat and dockside gaming casinos and related operations. The operations of the group include riverboat gaming, dockside gaming casinos, non gaming dinner cruise, excursion and sightseeing vessels. The group also owns and manages hotel and ancillary facilities related to its casino operations in biloxi, mississippi. The group operates two main boats: the president casino-broadwater; the admiral. In may 2003, the group discontinued its leasing segment.

Primary SIC and add'l.: 5812 7993 7011 6519

CIK No: 0000888507

Subsidiaries: Broadwater Hotel, Inc., PRC Holdings Corporation, PRC Louisiana, Inc., PRC Management, Inc., President Broadwater Hotel, LLC, President Casino New Yorker, Inc., President Riverboat Casino-Iowa, Inc., President Riverboat Casino-Missouri, Inc., President Riverboat Casino-New York, Inc., President Riverboat Casino-Philadelphia, Inc., TCG/Blackhawk, Inc., The Connelly Group, L.P., The President Riverboat Casino-Mississippi, Inc., Vegas Vegas, Inc.

Officers: John S. Aylsworth/57/Dir., CEO, Pres., COO, Ralph J. Vaclavik/53/Sr. VP, CFO

Directors: John S. Aylsworth/57/Dir., CEO, Pres., COO, Karl G. Andren/61/Dir., Royal P. Walker/48/Dir.

Owners: Insiders/12.30%, John E. Connelly/12.20%, Terrence L. Wirginis/24.30%, Royal J. Walker, Karl G. Andren/1.30%, Ralph J. Vaclavik, John S. Aylsworth/9.10%

Financial Data: *Fiscal Year End:*02/28 *Latest Annual Data:* 2/28/2007

Year	Sales	Net Income
2007	NA	$10,104,000
2006	NA	$34,341,000
2005	NA	$10,192,000

Curr. Assets:	$30,453,000	**Curr. Liab.:**	$14,097,000	**P/E Ratio:**	0.18
Plant, Equip.:	$85,965,000	**Total Liab.:**	$151,514,000	**Indic. Yr. Divd.:**	NA
Total Assets:	$116,818,000	**Net Worth:**	-$52,349,000	**Debt/ Equity:**	NA

Presidential Life Corp

69 Lydecker St., Nyack, NY, 10960; *PH:* 1-845-358-2300; *Fax:* 1-845-353-0273;
http:// www.presidentiallife.com

General - Incorporation	DE	**Stock**- Price on:12/24/2007	$19.97
Employees	NA	Stock Exchange	NDQ
Auditor	BDO Seidman, LLP	Ticker Symbol	PLFE
Stk Agt	Bankers Trust Company	Outstanding Shares	29,510,000
Counsel	NA	E.P.S	$2.28
DUNS No.	10-679-5875	Shareholders	NA

Business: The group's principal activity is the sale of various annual and single premium life insurance products and single premium and flexible premium annuity products. The group operates principally in a single business segment with two primary lines of business-individual annuities and individual life insurance. Each of these products is designed to meet the needs of increasingly sophisticated consumers for supplemental retirement income, estate planning and protection from unexpected death.

Primary SIC and add'l.: 6321 6719 6311

CIK No: 0000080124

Subsidiaries: CNL, Household International, Inc, P.L. Assigned Services Corporation, Presidential Life Insurance Company, Presidential Securities Corporation

Officers: Herbert Kurz/88/Chmn., CEO, Pres./$721,185.00, Donald L. Barnes/64/Vice Chmn., COO, Pres./$509,540.00, Jerrold Scher/66/Dir., Sr. VP, Chief Actuary/$384,455.00, Charles J. Snyder/50/Dir., CFO/$371,906.00, Mark Abrams/59/Dir., Exec. VP, Chief Investment Officer/$386,761.00, Kathleen Dash/Sec.

Directors: Herbert Kurz/88/Chmn., CEO, Pres., Donald L. Barnes/64/Vice Chmn., COO, Pres., Lawrence Read/63/Dir., Jerrold Scher/66/Dir., Sr. VP, Chief Actuary, Jeffrey Keil/64/Dir., Lawrence Rivkin/86/Dir., Charles J. Snyder/50/Dir., CFO, Mark Abrams/59/Dir., Exec. VP, Chief Investment Officer, Richard A. Giesser/76/Dir., Paul Frederick Pape/75/Dir.

Owners: Herbert Kurz/26.10%, Jerrold Scher/6.00%, Dimensional Fund Advisors, Inc., Mark Abrams/6.00%, Paul Frederick Pape/6.00%, Donald Barnes/6.00%, Lawrence Read/6.00%, Jeffrey Keil/6.00%, Richard A. Giesser/6.00%, Charles Snyder/6.00%, Lawrence Rivkin/6.00%, Insiders

Financial Data: *Fiscal Year End:*12/31 *Latest Annual Data:* 12/31/2006

Year	Sales	Net Income
2006	$358,826,000	$49,713,000
2005	$458,581,000	$91,589,000
2004	$396,259,000	$65,965,000

Curr. Assets:	$884,341,000	**Curr. Liab.:**	$60,604,000	**P/E Ratio:**	11.75
Plant, Equip.:	$446,000	**Total Liab.:**	$3,979,785,000	**Indic. Yr. Divd.:**	$0.500
Total Assets:	$4,619,372,000	**Net Worth:**	$639,587,000	**Debt/ Equity:**	NA

Presidio Bank

1 Montgomery St. Ste. 2300, San Francisco, CA, 94108; *PH:* 1-415-229-8400; *Fax:* 1-415-398-3111;
http:// www.presidiobank.com

General - Incorporation		**Stock**- Price on:12/24/2007	$9.85
Employees	NA	Stock Exchange	OTC
Auditor	NA	Ticker Symbol	PDOB
Stk Agt	Computershare Trust Co., NA	Outstanding Shares	NA
Counsel	NA	E.P.S	NA
DUNS No.	NA	Shareholders	NA

Business: The groups principal activities include providing banking and financial services to small and medium sized businesses and their owners, professional service firms and their partners, non profit organizations, and real estate investors and developers. The group operates from the United States.

Primary SIC and add'l.: 6029

CIK No:

Officers: Stephen A. Fleming/Founder, Dir., CEO, Pres., James R. Woolwine/Chmn., Founding Organizer, Mary Leonard - Wilson/Exec. VP, Chief Credit Officer, Vernon Padgett/Exec. VP, East Bay Marketing Pres., Founder Organizers, Donatella Levintow/Sr. VP, North Bay Marketing Mgr., Sherry Price/COO, Exec. VP, John Cavender/Marketing Makers, Denise Gilseth/Marketing Makers, Lisa Gallo/Marketing Makers, Edward Murphy/CFO, Exec. VP, Paula R. Collins/Dir., Founder Organizers, Joey J. Warmenhoven/Marketing Maker, Investor Relations, Craig F. Andersen/Dir., Founder Organizers, Michael A. Covarrubias/Dir., Founder Organizers, Robert Leet/Dir., Founding Organizer *(28 Officers included in Index)*

Directors: Stephen A. Fleming/Founder, Dir., CEO, Pres., James R. Woolwine/Chmn., Founding Organizer, Alison Davis/Dir., Paula R. Collins/Dir., Founder Organizers, Craig F. Andersen/Dir., Founder Organizers, Michael A. Covarrubias/Dir., Founder Organizers, Robert Leet/Dir., Founding Organizer, Stephen D. Mayer/Dir., Founding Organizer

Presstek Inc

55 Executive Dr., Hudson, NH, 03051; *PH:* 1-603-595-7000; *Fax:* 1-603-595-2602;
http:// www.presstek.com

General - Incorporation	DE	**Stock**- Price on:12/24/2007	$7.84
Employees	891	Stock Exchange	NDQ
Auditor	KPMG LLP	Ticker Symbol	PRST
Stk Agt	Continental Stock Transfer & Trust Co	Outstanding Shares	35,700,000
Counsel	Testa, Hurwitz & Thibeault	E.P.S	-$0.043
DUNS No.	18-361-5426	Shareholders	NA

Business: The group's principal activities are to manufacture, develop and market digital laser imaging and chemistry-free plate technologies for the printing and graphic arts industries. The group operates in two segments, the digital imaging products segment and the lasertel segment. The digital imaging products segment develops, manufactures and markets proprietary digital imaging systems and printing plate technologies for ctp and direct-to-press applications. The lasertel segment manufactures and develops the group's high-powered laser diodes. The group operates in the United States, Germany and Japan. On 30-Jul-2004, the group acquired precision lithograining corp.

Primary SIC and add'l.: 7373 7389 3555

CIK No: 0000846876

Subsidiaries: A.B. Dick of UK Limited, ABD Canada Holdings, Inc., ABD International Company of Canada, ABD International, Inc., HIC, Inc., Lasertel, Inc., Precision Acquisition Corporation, Precision Lithograining Corporation, R/H Acquisition Corporation, SDK Realty Corporation

Officers: Edward J. Marino/Dir., CEO, Pres., Peter A. Bouchard/VP - International Business Development, Cathleen V. Cavanna/VP - Corporate Human Resources, Emile Tabassi/VP - North American Sales, Ronald T. Cardone/CIO, Hakan Elmali/VP - Engineering, Research, Geoff Loftus/VP - North American Service, Gerald N. Herman/VP, Corporate Controller, Principal Accounting Officer, James Van Horn/VP, General Counsel, Todd H. Chambers/Chief Marketing Officer, James W. Larue/VP - Worldwide Manufacturing, Supply Chain

Directors: Edward J. Marino/Dir., CEO, Pres., John W. Dreyer/Chmn., Daniel S. Ebenstein/Dir., Michael D. Moffitt/Dir., Lawrence Howard/Founder, Dir., Donald C. Waite/Dir., Brian F. Mullaney/Dir., Steven N. Rappaport/Dir.

Owners: Lawrence Howard/3.70%, Insiders/7.40%, Moosa E. Moosa, Peter A. Bouchard, Daniel S. Ebenstein, Brian F. Mullaney, Emile A. Tabassi, Quentin C. Baum, Michael D. Moffitt, Steven N. Rappaport, Edward J. Marino/1.90%, Donald C. Waite, John W. Dreyer

Financial Data: *Fiscal Year End:*12/31 *Latest Annual Data:* 12/30/2006

Year	Sales	Net Income
2006	$265,694,000	$9,744,000
2005	$274,140,000	$6,086,000

Curr. Assets:	$100,961,000	**Curr. Liab.:**	$59,569,000		
Plant, Equip.:	$45,250,000	**Total Liab.:**	$82,854,000	**Indic. Yr. Divd.:**	NA
Total Assets:	$181,487,000	**Net Worth:**	$98,633,000	**Debt/ Equity:**	0.1246

Pressure Biosciences Inc

321 Manley St., West Bridgewater, MA, 02379; *PH:* 1-508-580-1818; *Fax:* 1-508-580-1822;
http:// www.pressurebiosciences.com; *Email:* info@pressurebiosciences.com

General - Incorporation	MA	**Stock**- Price on:12/24/2007	$4.74
Employees	18	Stock Exchange	NDQ
Auditor	UHY LLP	Ticker Symbol	PBIO
Stk Agt	Computershare Trust Co	Outstanding Shares	2,070,000
Counsel	NA	E.P.S	-$1.19
DUNS No.	NA	Shareholders	NA

Business: The group's principal activity is to provide products and services for the detection and treatment of infectious diseases such as aids and viral hepatitis. The group operates in four segments: diagnostics, biotech research laboratories, source scientific and pressure cycling technology. Diagnostics segment manufactures quality control and other diagnostic products for the accuracy of vitro diagnostic tests. Biotech research laboratories undertakes research contracts and provides repository services for agencies of the United States government. Source scientific develops and manufactures laboratory and medical instruments. Pressure cycling technology introduces new solutions for a number of healthcare issues. The products of the group are made from human plasma and serum. The group also provides clinical trials. On 31-Mar-2004, the group disposed the clinical laboratory business.

Primary SIC and add'l.: 8734 8071 2835 3826

CIK No: 0000830656

Subsidiaries: BBI Biotech Research Laboratories, Inc., BBI Clinical Laboratories, Inc., PBI Source Scientific, Inc.

Officers: Richard T. Schumacher/Founder, Dir., CEO, Pres./$406,596.00, Edmund Y. Ting/Sr. VP - Engineering/$175,497.00, Nathan P. Lawrence/VP - Marketing, Business Development/$184,765.00, Alexander Lazarev/VP - Research, Development/$149,593.00, Edward H. Myles/CFO, VP - Finance/$228,329.00

Directors: Richard T. Schumacher/Founder, Dir., CEO, Pres., Wayne R. Fritzsche/Chmn., Calvin A. Saravis/Chmn. - Scientific Advisory Board, Donald J. Payne/Dir., Thomas P. Vogel/Dir.

Owners: P. Thomas Vogel/2.80%, Lloyd I. Miller/6.10%, Insiders/30.70%, Edmund Y. Ting/1.10%, Calvin A. Saravis/4.60%, Alexander V. Lazarev/0.80%, J. Donald Payne/2.90%, Richard T. Schumacher/19.00%, Nathan P. Lawrence/1.30%, Edward H. Myles/1.00%, R. Wayne Fritzsche/3.00%

Financial Data: *Fiscal Year End:*12/31 *Latest Annual Data:* 12/31/2006

Year	Sales	Net Income
2006	$210,000	-$2,413,000
2005	$106,000	$1,604,000
2004	$413,000	$12,713,000

Curr. Assets:	$8,449,000	**Curr. Liab.:**	$1,287,000		
Plant, Equip.:	$208,000	**Total Liab.:**	$2,338,000	**Indic. Yr. Divd.:**	NA
Total Assets:	$10,454,000	**Net Worth:**	$8,115,000	**Debt/ Equity:**	NA

Prestige Brand Holdings Inc

90 N Broadway, Irvington, NY, 10533; *PH:* 1-914-524-6810; *Fax:* 1-914-524-6815;
http:// www.prestigebrands.com

General - Incorporation	DE	**Stock**- Price on:12/24/2007	$23.78
Employees	92	Stock Exchange	NYSE
Auditor	PricewaterhouseCoopers LLP	Ticker Symbol	PBH
Stk Agt	Computershare Trust Co	Outstanding Shares	50,010,000
Counsel	NA	E.P.S	$0.72
DUNS No.	NA	Shareholders	NA

Business: The groups principle activities include manufacturing and selling drug, household cleaning and personal care products. The groups products marketed under the brand names Chloraseptic(R), Clear eyes(R), Compound W(R), Murine(R), Little Remedies(R) and Dermpoplast(R). The group operates through three segments namely, over the counter drug, household cleaning and personal care. In the year 2006, the group acquired Dental Concepts, LLC. The group operates from the United States. The group's quarterly revenue for September 2007 was 87.34 millions of USD.

Primary SIC and add'l.: 2834

CIK No: 0001295947

Subsidiaries: Bonita Bay Holdings, Inc., Medtech Holdings, Inc., Medtech Products, Inc., Pecos Pharmaceutical, Inc., Prestige Acquisition Holdings, LLC, Prestige Brands (UK) Limited, Prestige Brands Financial Corporation, Prestige Brands Holdings, Inc., Prestige Brands International, Inc., Prestige Brands International, LLC, Prestige Brands, Inc., Prestige Household Brands, Inc., Prestige Household Holdings, Inc., Prestige International Holdings, LLC, Prestige Personal Care Holdings, Inc. 22 Subsidiaries included in the Index

Officers: Mark Pettie/Chmn., CEO, Peter J. Anderson/CFO, Charles M. Schrank/Sr. VP - Marketing, Household, Eric M. Millar/64/Sr. VP - Operations, Charles N. Jolly/General Counsel, Sec., John F. Parkinson/Sr. VP - International, Jean A. Boyko/Sr. VP - Quality, Regulatory Affairs, David B. Talbert/Sr. VP - Sales, Lieven Nuyttens/Sr. VP - Operations

Directors: Mark Pettie/Chmn., CEO, Dick L. Buell/Dir., John E. Byom/Dir., Gary E. Costley/Dir., David A. Donnini/Dir., Ronald Gordon/Dir., Vincent J. Hemmer/Dir., Patrick Lonergan/Dir., Peter C. Mann/Dir., Raymond P. Silcock/Dir.

Owners: John E. Byom, Mark Pettie, Charles N. Jolly, Frank Palantoni, Patrick Lonergan, Insiders/32.40%, Vincent J. Hemmer/29.90%, John Parkinson, David A. Donnini/29.90%, Peter J. Anderson, GTCR Funds/29.90%, Dick L. Buell, FMR Corp./8.30%, Eric M. Millar, Gerard F. Butler (19 Owners included in Index)

Financial Data: Fiscal Year End:03/31   Latest Annual Data: 3/31/2007

Year	Sales	Net Income
2007	$318,634,000	$36,078,000
2006	$296,668,000	$26,277,000
2005	$303,318,000	$13,459,000

Curr. Assets:	$83,768,000	Curr. Liab.:	$40,910,000	P/E Ratio:	33.03
Plant, Equip.:	$1,449,000	Total Liab.:	$618,082,000	Indic. Yr. Divd.:	NA
Total Assets:	$1,063,416,000	Net Worth:	$445,334,000	Debt/ Equity:	1.0324

Prevention Insurance.com

2770 S Maryland Pk.way, Ste. 416, Las Vegas, NV, 89109; **PH**: 1-702-732-2758

General - Incorporation	NV	Stock- Price on:12/24/2007	$0.065
Employees	NA	Stock Exchange	OTC
Auditor .Beadle, McBride, Evans & Reeves, LLP		Ticker Symbol	PVNC
Stk Agt	NA	Outstanding Shares	21,520,000
Counsel	NA	E.P.S.	-$0.002
DUNS No.	NA	Shareholders	NA

Business: The groups principal activities include attempting to organize select independent insurance agencies to create a nationwide cooperative group of health, life and casualty insurance companies with the ability to negotiate fees with national insurance companies. The group operates from the United States.

Primary SIC and add'l.: 6411

CIK No: 0001134982

Officers: Scott Goldsmith/57/Chmn., CEO, Pres., Principle Financial Officer

Directors: Scott Goldsmith/57/Chmn., CEO, Pres., Principle Financial Officer, George T. Nasser/60/Dir., Richard Peterson/57/Dir.

Owners: Scott C. Goldsmith/13.82%, George Nasser, Aleene Goldsmith

Financial Data: Fiscal Year End:04/30   Latest Annual Data: 4/30/2006

Year	Sales	Net Income
2006	$159,000	-$69,000
2005	$166,000	-$104,000
2004	$124,000	-$37,000

Curr. Assets:	NA	Curr. Liab.:	$12,000		
Plant, Equip.:	NA	Total Liab.:	$12,000	Indic. Yr. Divd.:	NA
Total Assets:	NA	Net Worth:	-$12,000	Debt/ Equity:	NA

PRG-Schultz International Inc

600 Galleria Pkwy., Ste. 100, Atlanta, GA, 30339; **PH**: 1-770-779-3900; **Fax**: 1-770-779-3133; http:// www.prgx.com; **Email**: personnel@prgx.com

General - Incorporation	GA	Stock- Price on:12/24/2007	$15.5501
Employees	1,935	Stock Exchange	NDQ
Auditor	BDO Seidman, LLP	Ticker Symbol	PRGX
Stk Agt American Stock Transfer & Trust Co.		Outstanding Shares	8,770,000
Counsel	Victor A. Allums	E.P.S.	$1.64
DUNS No.	78-376-5860	Shareholders	NA

Business: The group's principal activity is to provide recovery audit services by using sophisticated proprietary technology and advanced techniques and methodologies. Trained and experienced auditors of the group examine merchandise procurement records on a post-payment basis to identify overpayments resulting from duplicate payments, missed discounts, allowances, rebates and other forms of pricing concessions offered by vendors. The group also provides specialty service offerings in the areas of direct-to-store-delivery audits, media audits, real estate audits, freight-related vendor compliance audits, and document imaging and management technology. The services are rendered to large and mid-sized businesses having numerous payment transactions. The group operates in over 40 different countries.

Primary SIC and add'l.: 8744 8721

CIK No: 0001007330

Subsidiaries: Howard Schultz & Associates (Asia) Limited, Howard Schultz de Mexico, S.A. de C.V., HS&A Acquisition - UK Inc., HS&A International PTE LTD, JA Ewing, Inc., Meridian Corporation Limited, Meridian Sverige AB, Meridian VAT Processing (International) Limited, Meridian VAT Processing (Japan) Limited, Meridian VAT Processing (N. America) Limited, Meridian VAT Reclaim (Australia) Pty. Limited, Meridian VAT Reclaim (India) Private Limited, Meridian VAT Reclaim (Schwiez) AG, Meridian VAT Reclaim (UK) Limited, Meridian VAT Reclaim Canada, Inc. 75 Subsidiaries included in the Index

Officers: James B. McCurry/59/Chmn., CEO, Pres./$52,566,900.00, Steve Riordan/Sr. VP - Managing Principle, Management Consulting Practice, John Terranova/Mgr. - Operations, Australia, Dave Schroeder/CIO, Sr. VP, Adam Simon/MD - Benelux, Antonio Augusto Orcesi Da Costa/MD - Brazil, Alan Yin/Country Mgr. - Canada, Ian Kinman/MD - Germany, Central Europe, Albert Peynsaert/MD - Hong Kong, Lee White/Exec. VP - US Operations/$778,683.00, Larry Robinson/Pres. - Canada, Latin America, Asia Pacific/$990,145.00, Bradley Roos/Exec. VP - Europe/$1,179,510.00, Peter Limeri/CFO/$796,599.00, Victor A. Allums/Sr. VP, General Counsel, Jennifer Moore/Sr. VP - Human Resources (20 Officers included in Index)

Directors: James B. McCurry/59/Chmn., CEO, Pres., Steven Rosenberg/Dir., David A. Cole/Dir., Philip J. Mazzilli/Dir., Eugene I. Davis/Dir., Patrick G. Dills/Dir., Colin N. Lind/Dir.

Owners: Morgan Stanley & Co., Blum Capital Partners, L.P., Larry Robinson, Patrick G. Dills, Peter Limeri, Sandelman Partners, LP, Wellington Capital Management, Phillip J. Mazzilli, Weintraub Capital Management, L.P., Eugene I. Davis, JANA Partners, LLC, Insiders, Steven P. Rosenberg, Bradley T. Roos, Zazove Associates LLC (19 Owners included in Index)

Financial Data: Fiscal Year End:12/31   Latest Annual Data: 12/31/2006

Year	Sales	Net Income
2006	$266,095,000	-$21,099,000
2005	$292,152,000	-$207,740,000
2004	$356,873,000	-$71,483,000

Curr. Assets:	$127,016,000	Curr. Liab.:	$121,798,000	P/E Ratio:	9.42
Plant, Equip.:	$10,403,000	Total Liab.:	$271,951,000	Indic. Yr. Divd.:	NA
Total Assets:	$178,667,000	Net Worth:	-$104,483,000	Debt/ Equity:	NA

Priceline.com Inc

800 Connecticut Ave., Norwalk, CT, 06854; **PH**: 1-203-299-8000; **Fax**: 1-203-299-8948; http:// www.priceline.com

General - Incorporation	DE	Stock- Price on:12/24/2007	$2.61
Employees	696	Stock Exchange	NDQ
Auditor	Deloitte & Touche LLP	Ticker Symbol	PCLN
Stk Agt	Mellon Financial Services LLC	Outstanding Shares	37,890,000
Counsel	NA	E.P.S.	$3.17
DUNS No.	NA	Shareholders	NA

Business: The group's principal activity is to provide e-commerce based Internet services that enable consumers to use the Internet for the transaction of a wide range of products. The group also provides e-commerce pricing system that enables consumers to use the Internet to save money on products and services. The online products include traveling, airline tickets, hotel rooms, car rentals, vacation packages and cruises. During the year 2003, the group acquired rentalcars.com and breezenet.com Internet domains. On 21-Sep-2004, the group acquired active hotels ltd.

Primary SIC and add'l.: 7375

CIK No: 0001075531

Subsidiaries: Active Hotels Ltd., Bookings B.V., Lowestfare.com Incorporated, Priceline.com Europe Holdco, Inc., priceline.com Europe Holdings N.V., priceline.com europe Ltd., Priceline.com Holdco U.K. Limited, priceline.com International Ltd., Travelweb LLC

Officers: Jeffery H. Boyd/Dir., CEO, Pres./$3,730,659.00, Stef Norden/CEO - Priceline Europe/$1,517,470.00, Patricia D'Angelo/Sr. VP - Rental Cars, Brett Keller/Chief Marketing Officer, Christopher L. Soder/Pres. - North American Travel/$1,292,054.00, Paul J. Hennessy/Chief Distribution Officer, Daniel J. Finnegan/Sr. VP, Chief Accounting Officer, Controller, Peter J. Millones/Exec. VP, General Counsel/$999,578.00, Glenn D. Fogel/MD - Corporate Development, International, Robert J. Mylod/CFO, Ronald V. Rose/CIO, Mark Koehler/Sr. VP - Air, Lisa Gillingham/Sr. VP - Customer Service, Operations, Tim Gordon/Sr. VP - Hotels

Directors: Jeffery H. Boyd/Dir., CEO, Pres., Ralph M. Bahna/Chmn., Jeffrey E. Epstein/Dir., Nancy B. Peretsman/Dir., Craig W. Rydin/Dir., Howard W. Barker/Dir., James M. Guyette/Dir.

Owners: Craig W. Rydin, Alwaleed Bin Talal Abdulaziz Al Saud/5.26%, Stef Norden, Barclays Global Investors, NA/5.16%, Wellington Management Company, LLP/8.04%, Insiders/5.11%, James M. Guyette, FMR Corp./14.47%, Nancy B. Peretsman, PAR Investment Partners, L.P./10.56%, Tudor Investment Corporation/5.67%, Jeffrey E. Epstein, Ralph M. Bahna, Howard W. Barker, Jeffery H. Boyd/1.71% (18 Owners included in Index)

Financial Data: Fiscal Year End:12/31   Latest Annual Data: 12/31/2006

Year	Sales	Net Income
2006	$1,123,103,000	$74,466,000
2005	$962,660,000	$192,729,000
2004	$914,372,000	$31,509,000

Curr. Assets:	$503,089,000	Curr. Liab.:	$100,672,000	P/E Ratio:	1.43
Plant, Equip.:	$21,691,000	Total Liab.:	$721,136,000	Indic. Yr. Divd.:	NA
Total Assets:	$1,105,648,000	Net Worth:	$348,556,000	Debt/ Equity:	NA

Pricesmart Inc

9740 Scranton Rd., San Diego, CA, 92121; **PH**: 1-858-404-8800; **Fax**: 1-858-404-8848; http:// www.pricesmart.com

General - Incorporation	DE	Stock- Price on:12/24/2007	$23.3
Employees	2,937	Stock Exchange	NDQ
Auditor	Ernst & Young LLP	Ticker Symbol	PSMT
Stk Agt	Mellon Investor Services LLC	Outstanding Shares	29,550,000
Counsel	NA	E.P.S.	$0.44
DUNS No.	17-676-6905	Shareholders	NA

Business: The group's principal activities are to own and operate international merchandising businesses consisting of membership shopping stores similar to, but smaller in size than, warehouse clubs in the United States. The group has 29 warehouse stores in operation. The group's trademarks include pricesmart in most markets and pricecostco in panama, El Salvador, north mariana island and gaum.

Primary SIC and add'l.: 5331 6794

CIK No: 0001041803

Subsidiaries: Consultant and Development Services, S.A., Gestiones Mercantiles, S.A, Importadora y Exportadora PriceSmart Mexico S.A. de C.V, Inmobiliaria PriceSmart El Salvador, S.A. deC.V, Inmobiliaria PriceSmart Mexico S.A. de C.V, Inmobiliaria PriceSmart, S.A, Inmobiliaria PSMT Nicaragua S.A, Island Foods and Distributors, N.V, PriceSmart (Guatemala), S.A, PriceSmart (Jamaica) Limited, PriceSmart (Trinidad) Limited, PriceSmart Dominicana, S.A, PriceSmart El Salvador, S.A. deC.V, PriceSmart Exempt SRL, PriceSmart Holdings, Inc 39 Subsidiaries included in the Index

Officers: Robert Price/Chmn., CEO, Glenn Harmon/VP - Food Service, Prepared Foods, Bakery, Jonathan Darcangelo/Buyer - Food Service, Prepared Foods, Bakery, Johann Pantin/Regional Buyer, Foods, HBA, Guy Zavodny/Buyer - Foods, Jose Lopez/Sr. VP - Buying - Fresh, Phillipe Jacquemin/Buyer - Produce, Edward A. Oats/Exec. VP - Information Technology - Logistics, Kelly Orme/Buyer - Major Appliances, Electronics, Business Machines, Photo, Tom Sliney/Buyer - Automotive, Hardware, Sporting Goods, Jesel G. Teigeiro/Buyer - Office Supplies, Lawn, Garden, Seasonal, Imports, Lori Adami/Buyer, Toys, Domestics, Fashion Apparel, Basic Apparel, Linda Bolton/Buyer, Housewares, Small Appliances, Luggage, Home Furnishings, Phil Wilson/Sr. VP - Buying - Non - Foods, Chris Hoehn/Buyer - Frozen (40 Officers included in Index)

Directors: Robert Price/Chmn., CEO, Murray L. Galinson/Dir., Katherine L. Hensley/Dir., Leon C. Janks/Dir., Lawrence B. Krause/Dir., Edgar A. Zurcher/Dir., Keene Wolcott/Dir.

Owners: Keene Wolcott, Leon C. Janks, The Price group, John Heffner, Edgar A. Zurcher, Grupo Gigante, S.A. de C.V., Jack McGrory, Robert E. Price, Katherine L. Hensley, William J. Naylon, Insiders, Jose Luis Laparte, Lawrence B. Krause, Murray L. Galinson, Robert M. Gans

Financial Data: *Fiscal Year End:*08/31 *Latest Annual Data:* 08/31/2007

Year	Sales	Net Income
2007	$888,801,000	$12,926,000
2006	$734,673,000	$11,858,000
2005	$618,825,000	-$42,337,000

Curr. Assets:	$139,256,000	*Curr. Liab.:*	$102,443,000	*P/E Ratio:*	35.30
Plant, Equip.:	$162,029,000	*Total Liab.:*	$121,752,000	*Indic. Yr. Divd.:*	$0.160
Total Assets:	$359,043,000	*Net Worth:*	$234,619,000	*Debt/ Equity:*	0.0002

Pricester.com Inc

5555 Hollywood Blvd, Ste.303, Hollywood, FL, 33021; *PH:* 1-954-272-1200; *http://* pricester.com; *Email:* sales@pricester.com

General - Incorporation	NV	**Stock** - Price on:12/24/2007	NA
Employees	11	Stock Exchange	OTC
Auditor	Baum & Company, P.A.	Ticker Symbol	PRCC
Stk Agt	Florida Atlantic Stock Transfer, Inc.	Outstanding Shares	25,230,000
Counsel	Howard Neu	E.P.S.	-$0.05
DUNS No.		Shareholders	NA

Business: The groups principle activity is Internet marketplace, which allows vendors to host their website with product and service listings and promote them through network. In February 2005, Pricester.Com merged into Pricester.com, Inc. The group operates from the United States. In the year 2005, the groups total revenue was $23,302.

Primary SIC and add'l.: 7371
CIK No: 0001302913
Officers: Edward C. Dillon/CEO - Contact - Investor Relations Officer, Lee Taylor/Contact - Sales Inquirie, Nelson Stark/CFO - Contact - Public Relations, Joe Puentes/Founder, Pres.
Directors: Howard M. Neu/Chmn., Joe Puentes/Founder, Pres., Ivan Jimenez/Dir., Steve Kontos/Dir., Edward J. Dillon/Dir.
Owners: Joe Puentes/15.89%, Bernard Gutman/6.59%, Insiders/41.84%, Edward J. Dillon, Edward C. Dillon/19.11%, Barbara Gutman/3.82%, Steve Kontos/1.25%, Nelson Stark/1.17%, Howard M. Neu/2.82%, Ivan Jimenez/2.09%

Financial Data: *Fiscal Year End:*12/31 *Latest Annual Data:* 12/31/2006

Year	Sales	Net Income
2006	$139,000	-$470,000

Curr. Assets:	$31,000	*Curr. Liab.:*	$191,000		
Plant, Equip.:	$7,000	*Total Liab.:*	$191,000	*Indic. Yr. Divd.:*	NA
Total Assets:	$39,000	*Net Worth:*	-$151,000	*Debt/ Equity:*	NA

Pride Business Development Holdings Inc

1230 Calle Suerte, Camarillo, CA, 93012; *PH:* 1-866-868-0461; *Fax:* 1-805-322-6515; *http://* www.pridegroup.org; *Email:* Info@pridegroup.org

General - Incorporation	NV	**Stock** - Price on:12/24/2007	NA
Employees	NA	Stock Exchange	OTC
Auditor	Malone & Bailey, PC	Ticker Symbol	PDVG
Stk Agt	Olde Monmouth Stk Trnsfer Co. Inc.	Outstanding Shares	NA
Counsel	NA	E.P.S.	-$0.61
DUNS No.	NA	Shareholders	NA

Business: The groups principal activity is to provide certain personal protective and safety products to the homeland security and safety marketplace. The group markets its products under the tradenames include "Smith & Wesson(R)" and PRIDE(TM). Customers of the group include federal, state, municipalities, foreign, military, law enforcement and other governmental agencies. The group operates from the United States.

Primary SIC and add'l.: 3842
CIK No: 0001137667
Subsidiaries: Bodyguard, Inc.

Financial Data: *Fiscal Year End:*12/31 *Latest Annual Data:* 12/31/2005

Year	Sales	Net Income
2005	$282,000	-$3,694,000
2004	$11,000	-$1,041,000

Curr. Assets:	$438,000	*Curr. Liab.:*	$2,190,000		
Plant, Equip.:	$249,000	*Total Liab.:*	$2,744,000	*Indic. Yr. Divd.:*	NA
Total Assets:	$783,000	*Net Worth:*	-$1,962,000	*Debt/ Equity:*	NA

Pride Inc

2525 Fifteenth St., Ste 3H, Denver, CO, 80211; *PH:* 1-303-480-5037; *http://* www.prideinc.org

General - Incorporation	CO	**Stock** - Price on:12/24/2007	NA
Employees	12,200	Stock Exchange	NA
Auditor	Miller & McCollom	Ticker Symbol	NA
Stk Agt	NA	Outstanding Shares	NA
Counsel	NA	E.P.S.	NA
DUNS No.	NA	Shareholders	NA

Business: The group's principal activity is to invest in real estate, real estate mortgage loans and foreclosure certificates of purchase.

Primary SIC and add'l.: 6532
CIK No: 0001302548
Subsidiaries: Pride Holdings, Inc
Officers: Charles Bisnett/CEO, Michael L. Schumacher/58/Chmn., CFO, Pres., Treasurer, Michelle Keller/Assist. Crews Supervisor - Pride Production Center, Employment Services, George A. Powell/81/Dir., VP, Sec., Kevin Marchus/Controller, Sheree Wanner/Residential Supervisor, Dave Werner/Residential Supervisor, Suzy Jans/Day Programming Supervisor, Brandi Beechie/Heritage Recovery Coordinator, Wendi Holz/Program Coordinator, Susan Owens/Licensed Practical Nurse, Mary Pierson/Program Coordinator, Corey Stewart/Behavior Analyst, Marnie Stone/Program Coordinator, Dawn Thuen/Program Coordinator *(37 Officers included in Index)*

Directors: Michael L. Schumacher/58/Chmn., CFO, Pres., Treasurer, George A. Powell/81/Dir., VP, Sec.
Owners: Insiders/53.90%, Michael Schumacher/53.80%, George A. Powell/0.10%, Harold L. Morris/28.30%

Pride International Inc

5847 San Felipe, Ste. 3300, Houston, TX, 77057; *PH:* 1-713-789-1400; *Fax:* 1-713-789-1430; *http://* www.prde.com

General - Incorporation	DE	**Stock** - Price on:12/24/2007	$37.32
Employees	14,300	Stock Exchange	NYSE
Auditor	KPMG LLP	Ticker Symbol	PDE
Stk Agt	American Stock Transfer & Trust Co.	Outstanding Shares	165,850,000
Counsel	NA	E.P.S.	$2.33
DUNS No.	04-891-0947	Shareholders	NA

Business: The group's principle activity is to provide contract drilling and related services to oil & gas exploration and production companies through the use of mobile offshore and land-based drilling rigs in both U.S. offshore and international land and offshore markets. The group operates a global fleet of 278 rigs, including two ultra-deepwater drillships, 12 semi-submersible rigs, 28 jackup rigs, 18 tender-assisted, barge and platform rigs and 218 land-based drilling and workover rigs. The group functions through five principal reporting segments including eastern hemisphere, western hemisphere, U.S. Gulf of Mexico, Latin America Land, and E&P services. The group's operations are conducted in many of the most active oil and natural gas basins of the world, including South America, the Gulf of Mexico, the Mediterranean Sea, West Africa, the Middle East, Asia Pacific and the Caspian Sea. The group's quarterly revenue for September 2007 was 540.40 millions of USD.

Primary SIC and add'l.: 1381 1389
CIK No: 0000833081
Subsidiaries: Amethyst Financial Company Ltd., Andre Maritime Ltd., C.A. Foravep, Caland Boren B.V., Compagnie Monegasque de Services Comoser S.A.M., Criwey Corporation S.A., Dayana Finance S.A., Drilling Labor Services PTE Ltd., Dundee Corporation, Dupont Maritime Ltd., Durand Maritime SNC, Forafels Inc., Foral S.N.C., Forasol S.N.C., Forasub B.V. 101 Subsidiaries included in the Index
Officers: George K. Wasaff/54/CEO - Latin America Land, E, P Services, Louis A. Raspino/Dir., CEO, Pres./$4,892,875.00, Lonnie D. Bane/Sr. VP - Human Resources/$1,559,265.00, Steven D. Oldham/VP, Treasurer, Carlos Etcheverry/VP - E, P Services, Douglas G. Smith/VP, Controller, Chief Accounting Officer, Gregory W. Looser/Sr. VP, General Counsel, Sec./$1,628,972.00, Robert E. Warren/VP - Industry, Governmental Affairs, Mario Kricorian/VP - Latin American Operations, Gary W. Casswell/VP - Eastern Hemisphere Operations, Bobby E. Benton/VP - Western Hemisphere Operations, Bruce E. Kain/VP - Qhse, Imran Toufeeq/VP - Engineering, Technical Support, David E. Bruce/VP - Western Hemisphere Operations, Jeffrey L. Chastain/VP - Investor Relations *(21 Officers included in Index)*
Directors: Louis A. Raspino/Dir., CEO, Pres., David A.B. Brown/Chmn., Frank S. Kalman/Dir., Ralph D. McBride/Dir., Archie W. Dunham/Dir., Kenneth M. Burke/Dir., David B. Robson/Dir., J. C. Burton/Dir.
Owners: Ralph D. McBride, Wellington Management Company, LLP/5.60%, Kenneth M. Burke, J. C. Burton, Lonnie D. Bane, Brian C. Voegele, Insiders, John R. Blocker, Archie W. Dunham, FMR Corp/14.40%, Rodney W. Eads, Gregory W. Looser, Louis A. Raspino, Francis S. Kalman, David B. Robson *(17 Owners included in Index)*

Financial Data: *Fiscal Year End:*12/31 *Latest Annual Data:* 12/31/2006

Year	Sales	Net Income
2006	$2,495,400,000	$296,500,000
2005	$2,033,300,000	$128,600,000
2004	$1,712,200,000	$9,839,000

Curr. Assets:	$963,200,000	*Curr. Liab.:*	$670,100,000	*P/E Ratio:*	16.02
Plant, Equip.:	$4,000,100,000	*Total Liab.:*	$2,435,300,000	*Indic. Yr. Divd.:*	NA
Total Assets:	$5,097,500,000	*Net Worth:*	$2,633,900,000	*Debt/ Equity:*	0.4427

Prima East West Model Mgmt Inc

8618 W 3Rd St., Los Angeles, CA, 90048; *PH:* 1-310-205-6922; *http://* www.qmodels.com

General - Incorporation	CA	**Stock** - Price on:12/24/2007	NA
Employees	NA	Stock Exchange	NA
Auditor	Paritz & Co P.A	Ticker Symbol	NA
Stk Agt	NA	Outstanding Shares	NA
Counsel	NA	E.P.S.	NA
DUNS No.	NA	Shareholders	NA

Business: The group's principal activities include the business of representing talent including professional fashion, models, commercial actors and theatrical actors. The company is affiliated with Q Management, Inc., a larger agency located in New York, NY. The company's principal shareholder is also the principal shareholder of Q. Both companies are under the common control of Peter Zachariou.

Primary SIC and add'l.: 7900
CIK No: 0001318387
Subsidiaries: Diva Entertainment, Inc., J.R. Consulting, Inc., Quasar Projects Company
Officers: Jeffrey Kolsrud/Dir. - Q Management

Primal Solutions Inc

19732 MacArthur Blvd, Ste. 100, Irvine, CA, 92612; *PH:* 1-949-260-1500; *Fax:* 1-949-260-1515; *http://* www.primal.com; *Email:* ir@primal.com

General - Incorporation	DE	**Stock** - Price on:12/24/2007	$0.085
Employees	25	Stock Exchange	OTC
Auditor	Haskell & White LLP	Ticker Symbol	PSOL
Stk Agt	Liberty Transfer Co	Outstanding Shares	38,370,000
Counsel	Bryan Cave LLP	E.P.S.	-$0.013
DUNS No.	NA	Shareholders	NA

Business: The group's principal activity is to deliver operations support systems for wired and wireless communications service providers. The group develops, market and support convergent network mediation and convergent integrated billing software for providers of voice and data transmission services using the Internet and wireless networks. The group operates through systems operating segment and services segment. Systems operating segment develops and markets the integrated suite of client server

and browser-based software solutions. Services segment provides after-sale support for software products, programming, maintenance, customization and consulting services in different software languages and platforms. The group was spun-off as a separate public company by avery communications, inc in Feb 2001.

Primary SIC and add'l.: 7372 7379

CIK No: 0001124217

Subsidiaries: Wireless Billing Systems

Officers: Joseph R. Simrell/Chmn., CEO, Pres., William C. Bousema/Sr. VP, CFO, Corp. Sec., Tim Hoolihan/VP - Strategy, Corporate Development, Sam Gilson/Sr. VP - Sales, John S. Vanderpool/VP - Business Development, Bob Richardson/COO, Exec. VP, Steffanie Early/Contact, William Homan-Muise/VP - Engineering, Services, Mark Dicamillo/VP - Marketing, Product Management, Robert Richardson/4l/COO

Directors: Joseph R. Simrell/Chmn., CEO, Pres., Louis Delmonico/Dir., David Haynes/Dir.

Owners: Louis A. Delmonico/1.20%, Sam Gilson, Austin W. Marxe/58.30%, John E. Rehfeld/4.70%, Insiders/16.40%, John Faltys/3.20%, Robert Richardson, Joseph R. Simrell/3.70%, David Haynes/2.60%

Financial Data: Fiscal Year End: 12/31   **Latest Annual Data:** 03/31/2007

Year	Sales	Net Income
2007	$1,605,000	-$129,000
2006	$5,648,000	-$3,162,000
2005	$8,567,000	-$1,402,000

Curr. Assets:	$995,000	Curr. Liab.:	$3,373,000		
Plant, Equip.:	$360,000	Total Liab.:	$4,620,000	Indic. Yr. Divd.:	NA
Total Assets:	$2,007,000	Net Worth:	-$2,613,000	Debt/ Equity:	NA

Prime Bank CT

7 Old TAve.rn Rd., Orange, CT, 06477; **PH:** 1-203-799-1299; **Fax:** 1-203-799-1297; **http://** www.primebankct.com

General - Incorporation		Stock - Price on:12/24/2007	$13
Employees	NA	Stock Exchange	OTC
Auditor	NA	Ticker Symbol	PMHV
Stk Agt	Registrar & Transfer Co	Outstanding Shares	NA
Counsel	NA	E.P.S.	NA
DUNS No.	NA	Shareholders	NA

Business: The groups principal activity is to provide banking and financial services to the customers. Services of the group include for the entrepreneur, credit, commercial loans, online banking, debit cards, ATM and money markets. The group operates from the United States.

Primary SIC and add'l.: 6022

CIK No:

Officers: Jasper J. Jaser/Chmn., CEO, Pres., William J. Bozelko/Dir., Pres., Marion M. Violano/Sec. to The Board, Assist. Treasurer, Edward J. Maloney/Sr. VP, CFO, Lynne A. Wozniak/Assist. VP, Assistant Sec., Michael J. Grande/VP, Sr. Lending Officer

Directors: Jasper J. Jaser/Chmn., CEO, Pres., William J. Bozelko/Dir., Robert A. Lanzi/Dir., Frank Perrotti/Dir., Thomas Santa Barbara/Dir.

Prime Companies Inc

409 Ctr. St., Yuba City, CA, 95991; **PH:** 1-530-755-3580; **http://** www.primecompanies.com; **Email:** sales@primecompanies.com

General - Incorporation	DE	Stock - Price on:12/24/2007	$0.009
Employees	NA	Stock Exchange	OTC
Auditor	Stonefield Josephson, Inc	Ticker Symbol	PRMC
Stk Agt	Mountain Share Transfer	Outstanding Shares	NA
Counsel	NA	E.P.S.	NA
DUNS No.	NA	Shareholders	NA

Business: The group's principle activity is to provide prepaid telecommunication services, interconnect services, and paging and voicemail services. The company currently provides interconnect, voicemail, and paging services to over 1,000 customers, primarily in Northern California. The company offers it prepaid customers the ability to make long distance telephone calls through the use of an 800 number. The Company also offers prepaid long distance wireline calling cards to its Distributors as a complementary product. The company's Nacc-Tel subsidiary sells and services pagers and voicemail services to its commercial and consumer customers. The company is the provider of voicemail services through the utilization of the equipment it has at its Yuba City facility. The group operates from United States.

Primary SIC and add'l.: 5045

CIK No: 0001041581

Officers: Norbert J. Lima/CEO, Pres.

Financial Data: Fiscal Year End: 12/31   **Latest Annual Data:** 12/31/2003

Year	Sales	Net Income
2003	$352,000	-$1,825,000
2002	$285,000	-$773,000
2001	$455,000	-$1,629,000

Curr. Assets:	$116,000	Curr. Liab.:	$2,904,000		
Plant, Equip.:	$392,000	Total Liab.:	$3,113,000	Indic. Yr. Divd.:	NA
Total Assets:	$801,000	Net Worth:	-$2,312,000	Debt/ Equity:	NA

Prime Pacific FNL WA

1001 Dove St. No. 100, Newport Beach, CA, 92660; **PH:** 1-949-252-8898; **Fax:** 1-949-252-8999; **http://** www.primepacific.com; **Email:** gretchen@primepacific.com

General - Incorporation		Stock - Price on:12/24/2007	$15.1
Employees	NA	Stock Exchange	OTC
Auditor	NA	Ticker Symbol	PPFS
Stk Agt	NA	Outstanding Shares	NA
Counsel	NA	E.P.S.	NA
DUNS No.	NA	Shareholders	NA

Business: The groups principal activities include processing, packaging and customer relationship concept. The group offers a full range residential mortgage loans. Services of the group include residential loans, commercial loans, and mortgages. The group operates from the United States.

Primary SIC and add'l.: 6021

CIK No: 0001268096

Officers: Steven R. Haymond/Staff, Yvonne Mckay/Staff, Don Kutz/Staff, Jean Wortley/Staff, Karen Knoche/Staff, Kathi Ruoff/Staff

Prime Resource Inc

1245 E Brickyard Rd., Ste. 590, Salt Lake City, UT, 84106; **PH:** 1-801-433-2000

General - Incorporation	UT	Stock - Price on:12/24/2007	NA
Employees	18	Stock Exchange	NA
Auditor Child, Van Wagoner & Bradshaw, PLLC		Ticker Symbol	NA
Stk Agt	NA	Outstanding Shares	NA
Counsel	NA	E.P.S.	NA
DUNS No.	NA	Shareholders	NA

Business: The group's principle activities are to provide asset management services and insurance brokerage services to individuals and employee groups. The group operates through its subsidiaries: belsen getty, llc, (belsen getty), and fringe benefits analysts, llc, (fba), with offices in salt lake city and layton, Utah. Belsen getty is a fee-only financial management firm, providing investment advice to high-wealth individuals and employee groups in connection with company retirement plans. Fringe benefits analysts, llc sells group and employee benefit products, primarily health insurance to employers and individuals. The group has operations only in the United States.

Primary SIC and add'l.: 6411

CIK No: 0001173281

Officers: Terry M. Deru/53/Chmn., CEO, Pres., Scott Deru/47/Dir., VP - Operations, Andrew W. Limpert/38/Dir., CFO, Treasurer, Sec.

Directors: Terry M. Deru/53/Chmn., CEO, Pres., Scott Deru/47/Dir., VP - Operations, Andrew W. Limpert/38/Dir., CFO, Treasurer, Sec.

Owners: Andrew Limpert/22.00%, Terry Deru/30.00%, Insiders/83.00%, Scott Deru/31.00%

Curr. Assets:	$15,000	Curr. Liab.:	$396,000		
Plant, Equip.:	NA	Total Liab.:	$396,000	Indic. Yr. Divd.:	NA
Total Assets:	$387,000	Net Worth:	-$8,000	Debt/ Equity:	NA

Primedex Health Systems Inc

1510 Cotner Ave., Los Angeles, CA, 90025; **PH:** 1-310-478-7808; **http://** www.radnetonline.com

General - Incorporation	NY	Stock - Price on:12/24/2007	NA
Employees	903	Stock Exchange	NA
Auditor	Moss Adams LLP	Ticker Symbol	NA
Stk Agt	American Stock Transfer & Trust Co.	Outstanding Shares	NA
Counsel	NA	E.P.S.	-$0.52
DUNS No.	61-228-0271	Shareholders	NA

Business: The group's principal activity is the provision of diagnostic imaging services through its ownership and operation of 58 outpatient diagnostic imaging centres. The group utilizes sophisticated technology and technical expertise to perform a broad range of imaging procedures, such as magnetic resonance imaging (or mri), computed tomography (or ct), position emission tomography (or pet), nuclear medicine, ultrasound, mammography, general radiography (or X-ray) and fluoroscopy. It contracts with radiology practices to provide professional services, including the supervision and interpretation of diagnostic imaging procedures performed in its diagnostic imaging centres. The group operates in the state of California.

Primary SIC and add'l.: 8099 8071

CIK No: 0000790526

Subsidiaries: Diagnostic Imaging Services, Inc., Primedex Corporation, RadNet Managed Imaging Services, Inc., Radnet Management I, Inc., Radnet Management II, Inc., RadNet Management, Inc., Radnet Sub, Inc., SoCal MR Site Management, Inc.

Officers: Howard Berger/CEO, Pres., Norman Hames/Dir., COO - Radnet inc, Eli J. Bendavid/Medical Staff, Radiology Groups, Matthew D. Benedict/Medical Staff, Radiology Groups, Ludmila Bojman/Medical Staff, Radiology Groups, Jerry Einzinger/Medical Staff - Radiology Groups, Radnet inc, June W. Chen/Medical Staff - Radiology Groups, Radnet inc, Shaya Ghazinoor/Medical Staff - Radiology Groups, Radnet inc, Fahim Gheybi/Medical Staff - Radiology Groups, Radnet inc, Ilyssa Golding/Medical Staff - Radiology Groups, Radnet inc, Gary Gray/Medical Staff - Radiology Groups, Radnet inc, Richard Gritz/Medical Staff - Radiology Groups, Radnet inc, Philip Hahn/Medical Staff - Radiology Groups, Radnet inc, Curtis Handler/Medical Staff - Radiology Groups, Radnet inc, Steve Henderson/Medical Staff - Radiology Groups, Radnet inc *(265 Officers included in Index)*

Directors: Norman Hames/Dir., COO - Radnet inc, John Crues/Dir. - Radnet inc, David Swartz/Dir. - Radnet inc, Larry Levitt/Dir. - Radnet inc, Marvin Cadwell/Dir. - Radnet inc, Michael L. Sherman/Dir. - Radnet inc

Owners: Contrarian Capital Management, LLC/5.20%, Howard G. Berger/17.00%, John V. Crues/1.90%, Insiders/21.70%, Lawrence L. Levitt, Jeffrey L. Linden/1.50%, Mark D. Stolper, David L. Swartz

Financial Data: Fiscal Year End: 10/31   **Latest Annual Data:** 12/31/2006

Year	Sales	Net Income
2006	$57,374,000	-$10,983,000
2005	$145,573,000	-$3,135,000

Curr. Assets:	$88,274,000	Curr. Liab.:	$58,194,000		
Plant, Equip.:	$158,542,000	Total Liab.:	$440,097,000	Indic. Yr. Divd.:	NA
Total Assets:	$394,355,000	Net Worth:	-$46,996,000	Debt/ Equity:	NA

PRIMEDIA Inc

3585 Engineering Dr., Ste. 100, Norcross, GA, 30092; **PH:** 1-678-421-3000; **Fax:** 1-800-216-1423; **http://** www.primedia.com; **Email:** information@primedia.com

General - Incorporation	DE	Stock - Price on:12/24/2007	$2.86
Employees	2,800	Stock Exchange	NYSE
Auditor	Deloitte & Touche LLP	Ticker Symbol	PRM
Stk Agt	Bank of New York	Outstanding Shares	264,530,000
Counsel	NA	E.P.S.	$11.12
DUNS No.	78-935-7894	Shareholders	NA

Business: The group's principal activities are the provision of specialized information to targeted markets, which is classified into three business segments: consumer magazines, business-to-business magazines and non-core businesses. The consumer magazines segment, which is concentrated primarily on specialty consumer magazines. Business-to-business magazines is the information segment, which produces consumer and business information products in a variety of formats for decision makers in

business, professional and special interest consumer markets. The information is compiled and sold through guides, newsletters, CD-roms, directories and via the Internet. Non-core businesses segment, which specializes in providing educational materials to the classroom learning and workplace learning markets.

Primary SIC and add'l.: 2721 2731 2741

CIK No: 0000884382

Subsidiaries: 1RoofRealty.com,Inc., AgriClick LLC, Automotive.com,Inc., Canoe& Kayak,Inc., Channel One Communications Corporation, Channel One Interactive,Inc., ConsumerClick Corp., Coterie,Inc., Cover Concepts Marketing Services, LLC, CSK Publishing Company,Inc., Distributech LLC, Enthusiast Media Subscription Company,Inc., Films For The Humanities& Sciences,Inc., Go Lo Entertainment,Inc., Guias do Brazil Ltda. 60 Subsidiaries included in the Index

Officers: Dean B. Nelson/Chmn., CEO, Pres./$1,581,523.00, Eric M. Leeds/Sr. VP - Investor Relations, Jeff Paro/Sr. VP, Steve Parr/Sr. VP/$1,022,280.00, Scott Wagner/Sr. VP, Maureen O'Mara/Assist. - Investor Relation, Kevin J. Neary/44/CFO, Sr. VP/$614,905.00, Kim Payne/CFO, Jason S. Thaler/Sr. VP, General Counsel, Sec., Bruce Abrahams/43/Sr. VP - Tax, Accounting, Robert J. Sforzo/Chief Accounting Officer, Sr. VP, Michaelanne Discepolo/Exec. VP - Human Resources, Robert C. Metz/Exec. VP/$1,346,587.00, Carl F. Salas/Sr. VP, Treasurer, Steve Aster/Sr. VP *(17 Officers included in Index)*

Directors: Dean B. Nelson/Chmn., CEO, Pres., Meyer Feldberg/Dir., David A. Bell/Dir., Perry Golkin/Dir., John H. Greeniaus/Dir., Daniel T. Ciporin/Dir., Kevin J. Smith/Dir., Beverly C. Chell/Dir., Thomas Uger/Dir.

Owners: Glenview Capital Management, LLC/6.97%, Meyer Feldberg, Insiders/2.85%, KKR 1996 GP LLC/20.92%, Marathon Asset Management Limited/8.14%, Robert C. Metz, Perry Golkin, KKR Associates, L.P./40.34%, Beverly C. Chell, Dean B. Nelson/1.14%, Steven Parr, John H. Greeniaus, David A. Bell, Amber Master Fund (Cayman) SPC/5.40%, Kevin J. Neary

Financial Data: ***Fiscal Year End:***12/31 ***Latest Annual Data:*** 12/31/2006

Year	Sales	Net Income
2006	$849,309,000	$38,252,000
2005	$990,571,000	$564,618,000
2004	$1,307,079,000	$35,470,000

Curr. Assets:	$323,104,000	**Curr. Liab.:**	$295,267,000	**P/E Ratio:**	0.84
Plant, Equip.:	$46,390,000	**Total Liab.:**	$1,777,559,000	**Indic. Yr. Divd.:**	NA
Total Assets:	$1,254,329,000	**Net Worth:**	-$523,230,000	**Debt/ Equity:**	NA

Primeenergy Corp

1 Landmark Sq., Stamford, CT, 06901; ***PH:*** 1-203-358-5700; ***Fax:*** 1-203-358-5786; ***http://*** www.selectmedicalcorp.com

General - Incorporation	DE	**Stock**- Price on:12/24/2007	$57.39
Employees	229	Stock Exchange	NDQ
Auditor	Pustorino, Puglisi & Co. LLP	Ticker Symbol	PNRG
Stk Agt	Computershare Investor Services LLC	Outstanding Shares	3,180,000
Counsel	James F. Gilbert	E.P.S	$2.31
DUNS No.	06-971-0481	Shareholders	NA

Business: The group's principal activities are to develop, explore and produce crude oil and natural gas. It participates in various joint ventures for the purpose of acquiring and developing oil and gas properties. The group operates solely in the domestic market. The pemc provides administration, accounting and tax preparation services for limited partnerships and trusts. The socc and eowsc perform oil and gas field servicing. The poc is an operator for producing oil and gas properties of the group and its affiliates. The major customers of the group include texon distributing lp, unimark llc and plains all America inc.

Primary SIC and add'l.: 1382 1311

CIK No: 0000056868

Subsidiaries: E O W S Midland Company, Eastern Oil Well Service Company, Prime Offshore LLC, Prime Operating Company, PrimeEnergy Management Corporation, Southwest Oilfield Construction Company

Officers: Charles E. Drimal/60/Dir., CEO, Pres., James F. Gilbert/75/Sec., Beverly A. Cummings/55/Dir., CFO, Exec. VP, Treasurer

Directors: Charles E. Drimal/60/Dir., CEO, Pres., Gifford H. Fong/63/Dir., Matthias Eckenstein/78/Dir., Thomas S.T. Gimbel/53/Dir., Clint Hurt/72/Dir., Jan K. Smeets/60/Dir., Beverly A. Cummings/55/Dir., CFO, Exec. VP, Treasurer

Owners: Insiders/55.37%, Clint Hurt/6.30%, Beverly A. Cummings/2.60%, H. Gifford Fong/4.30%, Charles E. Drimal/33.38%, Jan K. Smeets/6.20%, Thomas S. T. Gimbel/1.60%, Matthias Eckenstein/7.00%

Financial Data: ***Fiscal Year End:***12/31 ***Latest Annual Data:*** 12/31/2006

Year	Sales	Net Income
2006	$92,419,000	$18,300,000
2005	$75,946,000	$25,955,000
2004	$62,428,000	$7,275,000

Curr. Assets:	$71,681,000	**Curr. Liab.:**	$67,440,000	**P/E Ratio:**	12.75
Plant, Equip.:	$219,182,000	**Total Liab.:**	$235,581,000	**Indic. Yr. Divd.:**	NA
Total Assets:	$291,592,000	**Net Worth:**	$54,698,000	**Debt/ Equity:**	NA

PrimeGen Energy Corp

3625 N Hall St. Ste. 900, Dallas, TX, 75219; ***PH:*** 1-214-459-1217; ***http://*** www.primegenenergy.com; ***Email:*** info@primegenenergy.com

General - Incorporation	NV	**Stock**- Price on:12/24/2007	$0.015
Employees	NA	Stock Exchange	OTC
Auditor	De Leon & Company, P.A.	Ticker Symbol	PGNE
Stk Agt	Pacific Stock Transfer Company	Outstanding Shares	37,590,000
Counsel	NA	E.P.S	NA
DUNS No.	NA	Shareholders	NA

Business: The groups principal activity is engaged in no significant operations other than organizational activities, acquiring and staking properties and planning Phase 1 of the exploration work on SSM project. In June 2005, the group acquired one mineral property containing six mining claims in British Columbia, Canada. The group operates from the United States and Canada.

Primary SIC and add'l.: 7389

CIK No: 0001329015

PrimeWest Energy Trust

150 - 6th Ave. SW, Ste. 5100, Calgary, AB, T2P 3Y7; ***PH:*** 1-403-234-6600; ***Fax:*** 1-403-266-2825; ***http://*** www.primewestenergy.com; ***Email:*** investor@primewestenergy.com

General - Incorporation	Canada	**Stock**- Price on:12/24/2007	$21.9169
Employees	NA	Stock Exchange	NYSE
Auditor	PricewaterhouseCoopers LLP	Ticker Symbol	PWI
Stk Agt.	Computershare Trust Co	Outstanding Shares	91,140,000
Counsel	NA	E.P.S	NA
DUNS No.	NA	Shareholders	NA

Business: The groups principal activities include acquiring and holding oil and natural gas properties. The group also produced oil, natural gas and natural gas liquids. The group operates from the Canada.

Primary SIC and add'l.: 6726 6792

CIK No: 0001136201

Officers: Donald A. Garner/CEO, Pres., Dennis G. Feuchuk/VP - Finance, CFO, Timothy S. Granger/COO, Ronald J. Ambrozy/VP - Business Development, Gordon D. Haun/VP - Legal, General Counsel, Douglas Fraser/VP - Finance, CFO, Gregory Moore/VP - Operations, Lance J. Petersen/VP - Land, Bruce R. Thornhill/VP - Geosciences, George Kesteven/Mgr. - Investor Relations, Debbie Carver/Investor Relations Advisor

Directors: Harold P. Milavsky/Chmn., Barry E. Emes/Dir., Harold N. Kvisle/Dir., Kent J. MacIntyre/Dir., Michael W. O'Brien/Dir., James W. Patek/Dir., Glen W. Russell/Dir., Peter Valentine/Dir., Dave Fitzpatrick/Dir., Robert B. Hodgins/Dir., Warren D. Steckley/Dir.

Financial Data: ***Fiscal Year End:***12/31 ***Latest Annual Data:*** 12/31/2006

Year	Sales	Net Income
2006	$535,454,000	$142,187,000
2005	$518,575,000	$123,552,000
2004	$433,915,000	$102,044,000

Curr. Assets:	$147,765,000	**Curr. Liab.:**	$305,913,000	**P/E Ratio:**	33.03
Plant, Equip.:	$1,773,607,000	**Total Liab.:**	$2,474,589,000	**Indic. Yr. Divd.:**	NA
Total Assets:	$1,992,937,000	**Net Worth:**	-$481,652,000	**Debt/ Equity:**	NA

Primus Guaranty Ltd

360 Madison Ave., 23rd Fl., New York, NY, 10017; ***PH:*** 1-212-697-2227; ***Fax:*** 1-212-697-3731; ***http://*** www.primusfinancial.com; ***Email:*** investorrelations@primusguaranty.com

General - Incorporation	Bermuda	**Stock**- Price on:12/24/2007	$11.05
Employees	52	Stock Exchange	NYSE
Auditor	Ernst & Young LLP	Ticker Symbol	PRS
Stk Agt	Mellon Shareholder Services LLC	Outstanding Shares	45,020,000
Counsel	Morgan, Lewis & Bockius LLP	E.P.S	$0.40
DUNS No.	NA	Shareholders	NA

Business: The groups principle activity is to sell credit swaps through Primus Financial. The groups products include credit default swaps, leveraged loans, and investment grade and speculative grade securities. The group operates from United States.

Primary SIC and add'l.: NA

CIK No: 0001170593

Subsidiaries: Primus (Bermuda), Ltd., Primus Asset Management, Inc., Primus Financial Products, LLC, Primus Group Holdings, LLC, Primus Guaranty (UK), Ltd., Primus Re, Ltd., PRS Trading Strategies, LLC

Officers: Thomas W. Jasper/Dir., CEO/$2,748,244.00, Malcolm P. Basing/Chmn. - Primus UK, Charles Truett/Head - Portfolio Management/$1,502,884.00, Richard Claiden/CFO/$1,125,804.00, Charles McLendon/Pres. - Primus Asset Management/$1,103,905.00, Christopher N. Gerosa/Primary Investor Relations Officer, Scott H. Davis/Sec., Howard S. Yaruss/General Counsel

Directors: Thomas W. Jasper/Dir., CEO, Michael P. Esposito/Chmn., Frank P. Filipps/Dir., Duncan Goldie-Morrison/Dir., Paul S. Giordano/Dir., Thomas J. Hartlage/Dir., James K. Hunt/Dir., Robert R. Lusardi/Dir., John A. Ward/Dir., Fiona E. Luck/Dir.

Owners: Thomas W. Jasper/1.60%, Second Curve Capital, LLC/5.60%, UBS AG/5.00%, Century Capital Management, LLC/5.80%, Frank P. Filipps, Charles McLendon, TimesSquare Capital Management, LLC/6.40%, James K. Hunt, Insiders/2.50%, Robert R. Lusardi, Duncan E. Goldie-Morrison, John A. Ward, Michael P. Esposito, Transamerica Life Insurance Company/12.40%, XL Capital Ltd/33.20% *(19 Owners included in Index)*

Financial Data: ***Fiscal Year End:***12/31 ***Latest Annual Data:*** 12/31/2006

Year	Sales	Net Income
2006	$147,864,000	$94,891,000
2005	$38,202,000	$4,083,000
2004	$53,755,000	$23,685,000

Curr. Assets:	$229,361,000	**Curr. Liab.:**	$12,330,000	**P/E Ratio:**	9.78
Plant, Equip.:	$5,510,000	**Total Liab.:**	$341,856,000	**Indic. Yr. Divd.:**	NA
Total Assets:	$902,468,000	**Net Worth:**	$462,091,000	**Debt/ Equity:**	0.8580

Primus Telecommunications Group Inc

7901 Jones Branch Rd., Ste. 900, McLean, VA, 22102; ***PH:*** 1-703-902-2800; ***Fax:*** 1-703-902-2814; ***http://*** www.primustel.com; ***Email:*** primussalesusa@primustel.com

General - Incorporation	DE	**Stock**- Price on:12/24/2007	$0.41
Employees	NA	Stock Exchange	OTC
Auditor	Deloitte & Touche LLP	Ticker Symbol	PRTL
Stk Agt	StockTrans, Inc.	Outstanding Shares	NA
Counsel	NA	E.P.S	NA
DUNS No.	80-987-3136	Shareholders	NA

Business: The group's principal activity is to provide telecommunication services to business and residential customers. The group offers its telecommunication services to international and domestic voice Internet, data and voice services. These services include international and domestic long distance services and private networks; prepaid and calling cards; toll-free services and re-origination services; local services; ATM+ip broadband services. The group also provides dial-up, dedicated and high-speed Internet access; managed and shared Web hosting services and applications; voice over ip services; e-commerce applications and services and co-location services. The group has international operations in Canada, Brazil, the United Kingdom, continental Europe, Australia, India and Japan. The services of the group are provided to 3.1 million customers. On 15-Apr-2004, the group acquired magma communications ltd. On Jun 2004, the group acquired onramp network services inc.

Primary SIC and add'l.: 4812 4813

CIK No: 0001006837

Subsidiaries: 0014 Pty, Ltd., 3082833 Nova Scotia Company, 3620212 Canada, Inc., Binoche Holdings Pte, Communicacoes di Brazil Ltda, CS Communications GmbH, CS Network GmbH, Delta One America do Sul, Direct Internet Limited, Discount Calls Limited, DSLCom Pty, Ltd., European Mobile Products and Solutions Limited, Global Access Pty Ltd., Global Sales Pty, Global Telephone Holdings Inc. 82 Subsidiaries included in the Index

Officers: Paul K. Singh/Founder, CEO, Pres./$1,154,230.00, John F. Depodesta/Dir., Co - Founder, Exec. VP, Chief Legal Officer, Chief Corporate Development Officer, Sec./$815,798.00, Ravi Bhatia/MD - Primus Australia, Dg Gulati/Pres. - Primus US, Tracy B. Lawson/VP, Corporate Controller/$191,707.00, Edmund Chislett/Pres. - Primus Canada, Mark Guirgis/VP - Corporate Planning, Analysis, Assist. Sec./$245,820.00, Thomas R. Kloster/CFO/$596,423.00

Directors: Paul K. Singh/Founder, CEO, Pres., John G. Puente/Dir., John F. Depodesta/Dir., Co - Founder, Exec. VP, Chief Legal Officer, Chief Corporate Development Officer, Sec., Paul G. Pizzani/Dir., David E. Hershberg/Dir., Pradman P. Kaul/Dir., Douglas M. Karp/Dir.

Owners: American International Group, Inc/14.49%, Mark Guirgis, Douglas M. Karp, Kingdon Capital Management, LLC/9.54%, Sedna Capital Management, LLC./6.44%, Paul K. Singh/6.04%, Paul G. Pizzani, AIG Global Sports and Entertainment Fund, L.P./7.25%, John G. Puente, Insiders/7.69%, John F. DePodesta, Tracy B. Lawson, Sean OSullivan RLT/11.39%, Pradman P. Kaul, AIG Global Emerging Markets Fund, L.L.C./6.55% *(17 Owners included in Index)*

Princeton National Bancorp Inc

606 S Main St., Princeton, IL, 61356; *PH:* 1-815-875-4444; *Fax:* 1-815-872-0247; *http://* www.pnbc-inc.com; *Email:* pnbc@citizens1st.com

General - Incorporation	DE	Stock - Price on:12/24/2007	$28.865
Employees	270	Stock Exchange	NDQ
Auditor	BKD, LLP	Ticker Symbol	PNBC
Stk Agt	NA	Outstanding Shares	3,340,000
Counsel	NA	E.P.S.	$1.852
DUNS No.	12-257-0591	Shareholders	NA

Business: The group's principal activities are to provide commercial banking and trust business services. It operates through its subsidiary, citizens first national bank. The services offered include commercial, real estate and agricultural lending, consumer deposit and financial services and trust and farm management services. The services are provided to individuals, businesses and governmental bodies. At 31-Dec-2003, it operates through fourteen offices located in the eleven communities in north central Illinois. The offices are located in princeton, depue, genoa, hampshire, henry, huntley, minooka, oglesby, Peru, sandwich and spring valley.

Primary SIC and add'l.: 6712 6021

CIK No: 0000707855

Subsidiaries: Citizens First National Bank

Officers: Tony J. Sorcic/Dir., CEO, Pres./$355,402.00, Lou Ann Birkey/VP - Investor Relations, Corp. Sec., Michael E. Smith/VP - Risk Management, Todd D. Fanning/CFO, Sr. VP, Treasurer/$142,559.00, James B. Miller/Exec. VP, Commercial Banking Officer/$191,941.00, Jacqualyn L. Funderberg/47/Sr. VP - Consumer Banking, Patrick Murray/Sr. VP - Financial Advisor/$171,935.00, Joyce Roggy/Sr. VP - Administrative Services, Jill Smith/Sr. VP - Human Resources

Directors: Tony J. Sorcic/Dir., CEO, Pres., Craig O. Wesner/66/Chmn., Donald E. Grubb/Dir., Ervin I. Pietsch/Dir., Stephen W. Samet/Dir., Daryl Becker/Dir., Thomas M. Longman/Dir., Willard Lee/Dir., Gary C. Bruce/55/Dir., Mark Janko/Dir., John R. Ernat/Dir., Sharon L. Covert/Dir.

Owners: Sharon L. Covert, Tony J. Sorcic/2.62%, Ervin I. Pietsch, Mark Janko, John R. Ernat, Wellington Management Company, LLP/5.10%, Tontine Partners, LP/5.09%, Craig O. Wesner, Thomas M. Longman, Daryl Becker, JESCO & CO/5.44%, Willard Lee, Gary C. Bruce, Donald E. Grubb, Stephen W. Samet

Financial Data: *Fiscal Year End:*12/31　　*Latest Annual Data:* 12/31/2006

Year		Sales		Net Income
2006		$63,771,000		$6,488,000
2005		$48,811,000		$7,574,000
2004		$38,034,000		$6,872,000
Curr. Assets:	$50,324,000	**Curr. Liab.:**	$920,213,000	**P/E Ratio:** 15.59
Plant, Equip.:	$28,670,000	**Total Liab.:**	$966,604,000	**Indic. Yr. Divd.:** $1.080
Total Assets:	$1,031,959,000	**Net Worth:**	$65,355,000	**Debt/ Equity:** 0.5575

Princeton Review Inc

2315 Broadway, New York, NY, 10024; *PH:* 1-212-874-8282; *Fax:* 1-212-874-0775; *http://* www.princetonreview.com

General - Incorporation	DE	Stock - Price on:12/24/2007	$4.93
Employees	565	Stock Exchange	NDQ
Auditor	Ernst & Young LLP	Ticker Symbol	REVU
Stk Agt	Continental Stock Transfer & Trust Co	Outstanding Shares	27,610,000
Counsel	Patterson, Belknap, Webb & Tyler	E.P.S.	-$0.57
DUNS No.	NA	Shareholders	NA

Business: The group's principal activity is to provide integrated classroom-based, print and online products and services that address the needs of students, parents, educators and educational institutions. The group operates through three divisions: test preparation services division provides test preparation courses, tutoring and admissions counseling service and receives royalties from its independent franchisees. Admissions services division, authors print and software titles published primarily by random house, operates review.com and embark.com Web sites and sells Web-based products to educational institutions. K-12 services division, authors workbooks and creates princeton review branded content for textbooks published by mcgraw-hill, operates homeroom.com subscription service, provides training and professional development services to educators.

Primary SIC and add'l.: 8299 7375

CIK No: 0001113668

Subsidiaries: Apply Technology, LLC, Princeton Review Management, LLC, Princeton Review Operations, LLC, Princeton Review Products, LLC, Princeton Review Publishing, LLC, The Princeton Review Canada, Inc.

Officers: Michael J. Perik/Dir., CEO, Pres., John S. Katzman/48/Founder, Chmn./$463,696.00, Mark Chernis/COO, Pres. - Test Preparation Division/$574,112.00, Harriet Brand/Contact - Investor Relations, Public Relations, Linda Nessim-Rubin/Exec. VP - Communications, Human Resources, Neal S. Winneg/Exec. VP, Sec., General Counsel, Stephen L. Cootey/40/Board Observer, Suellen Glasser/Ombudsman, Kevin Howell/Exec. VP, GM - K, 12 Services, Jay Rosner/Executive Dir., Robin Raskin/Contact - Investor Relations, Public Relations, Stephen Melvin/CFO

Directors: Michael J. Perik/Dir., CEO, Pres., John S. Katzman/48/Founder, Chmn., David Schiff/Member - Advisory Board, Kenneth Adelman/Member - Advisory Board, Bob Kiley/Member - Advisory Board, John C. Reid/56/Dir., Robert Maher/Member - Advisory Board, Floyd H. Flake/Member - Advisory Board, Gary Bitter/Member - Advisory Board, Arthur Taylor/Member - Advisory Board, Lew Ernst/Member - Advisory Board, Don Cameron/Member - Advisory Board, John Humins/Member - Advisory Board, Allan McLeod/Member - Advisory Board, Margaret McKenna/Member - Advisory Board *(30 Directors included in Index)*

Owners: Columbia Wanger Asset Management, L.P./9.21%, John C. Reid, Margot Lebenberg, Richard Sarnoff, Insiders/35.47%, Random House TPR, Inc./5.47%, Mark Chernis/2.86%, Andrew Bonanni, Wellington Management Company, LLP/11.59%, Robert E. Evanson, Stephen Quattrociocchi/1.03%, Bear, Stearns & Co., Inc./8.65%, Heartland Advisors, Inc./8.35%, Howard A. Tullman, John S. Katzman/31.63% *(17 Owners included in Index)*

Financial Data: *Fiscal Year End:*12/31　　*Latest Annual Data:* 12/31/2006

Year		Sales		Net Income
2006		$140,740,000		-$9,531,000
2005		$130,493,000		-$2,182,000
2004		$113,785,000		-$30,413,000
Curr. Assets:	$51,872,000	**Curr. Liab.:**	$54,079,000	
Plant, Equip.:	$16,209,000	**Total Liab.:**	$76,945,000	**Indic. Yr. Divd.:** NA
Total Assets:	$118,108,000	**Net Worth:**	$41,163,000	**Debt/ Equity:** NA

Principal Financial Group Inc

711 High St., Des Moines, IA, 50392; *PH:* 1-515-247-5111; *Fax:* 1-515-246-5475; *http://* www.principal.com

General - Incorporation	DE	Stock - Price on:12/24/2007	$58.34
Employees	15,289	Stock Exchange	NYSE
Auditor	Ernst & Young LLP	Ticker Symbol	PFG
Stk Agt	Principal Financial Group	Outstanding Shares	267,790,000
Counsel	Debevoise & Plimpton	E.P.S.	$3.99
DUNS No.	NA	Shareholders	NA

Business: The groups principle activity is to provide retirement savings, investment and insurance products and services. The groups products include life, health and disability insurances. The group operates from United States.

Primary SIC and add'l.: 6311 6211 6162

CIK No: 0001126328

Subsidiaries: Benefit Fiduciary Corporation, Boston Insurance Trust, Inc., BrasilPrev Seguros e Previdencia S.A., CCIP, LLC, Columbus Circle Investors, Delaware Charter Guarantee & Trust Company, Dental-Net, Inc., Distribuidora Principal Mexico, S.A. de C.V., Employers Dental Services, Inc., Equity FC, Ltd., Executive Benefit Services, Inc., HealthRisk Resource Group, Inc., Jf Molloy & Associates, Inc., Molloy Medical Management Company, Inc., Petula Associates, Ltd. 87 Subsidiaries included in the Index

Officers: Barry J. Griswell/Chmn., CEO/$16,848,920.00, James D. Devries/Sr. VP - Human Resources, Michael H. Gersie/CFO, Exec. VP/$3,868,504.00, Norman R. Sorensen/Sr. VP - International Asset Accumulation, Ralph C. Eucher/Sr. VP - Retirement, Investor Services, Ellen Z. Lamale/Sr. VP, Chief Actuary, Mary A. O'Keefe/Sr. VP, Chief Marketing Officer, Karen E. Shaff/Exec. VP, General Counsel, James P. McCaughan/Pres. - Global Asset Management/$4,321,588.00, Larry D. Zimpleman/Dir., COO, Pres./$4,506,267.00, Julia M. Lawler-Johnson/Chief Investment Officer, Sr. VP, Timothy J. Minard/Sr. VP - Retirement Distribution, Nora M. Everett/Sr. VP, Deputy General Counsel, Margaret W. Skinner/Sr. VP - Life, Health Segment, Joyce Nixson Hoffman/Sr. VP, Corp. Sec. *(24 Officers included in Index)*

Directors: Barry J. Griswell/Chmn., CEO, Sandra L. Helton/Dir., Gary E. Costley/Dir., Michael T. Dan/Dir., Arjun K. Mathrani/Dir., Richard L. Keyser/Dir., Larry D. Zimpleman/Dir., COO, Pres., Daniel C. Gelatt/Dir., William T. Kerr/Dir., Elizabeth E. Tallett/Dir., Therese M. Vaughan/Dir., Julia M. Lawler/48/Dir., Chief Investment Officer, Sr. VP, Jocelyn Carter-Miller/Dir., Betsy J. Bernard/Dir.

Owners: Northern Trust Corporation/7.00%, Barry J. Griswell, Richard L. Keyser, Larry D. Zimpleman, Therese M. Vaughan, Federico F. Pea, Elizabeth E. Tallett, James P. McCaughan, Gary E. Costley, Michael H. Gersie, Insiders/1.00%, John E. Aschenbrenner, Betsy J. Bernard, Charles S. Johnson, Jocelyn Carter-Miller *(20 Owners included in Index)*

Financial Data: *Fiscal Year End:*12/31　　*Latest Annual Data:* 12/31/2006

Year		Sales		Net Income
2006		$9,870,500,000		$1,064,300,000
2005		$9,007,700,000		$919,000,000
2004		$8,303,700,000		$825,600,000
Curr. Assets:	$2,843,100,000	**Curr. Liab.:**	$88,300,000	**P/E Ratio:** 15.85
Plant, Equip.:	$422,500,000	**Total Liab.:**	$135,797,300,000	**Indic. Yr. Divd.:** $0.800
Total Assets:	$143,658,100,000	**Net Worth:**	$7,860,800,000	**Debt/ Equity:** 0.1908

Prineville Bancorp

555 NW Third St., Prineville, OR, 97754; *PH:* 1-541-447-4106; *http://* www.cfbnk.com

General - Incorporation		Stock - Price on:12/24/2007	NA
Employees	NA	Stock Exchange	OTC
Auditor	NA	Ticker Symbol	PNVL
Stk Agt	NA	Outstanding Shares	1,180,000
Counsel	NA	E.P.S.	NA
DUNS No.	NA	Shareholders	NA

Business: The groups principal activities include offering comprehensive financial services to businesses, farmers, individuals, professionals and families. Services of the group include saving accounts, money markets, checking accounts, personal banking, private banking, Debit cards, Credit Cards, ATM and online customer help. The group operates from the United States.

Primary SIC and add'l.: 6021

CIK No:

Officers: Robin B. Freeman/Dir., CEO, Pres., John Hajovsky/CFO, Exec. VP, Myron Williams/Exec. VP, Chief Credit Officer, Robert W. St Yves/Dir. Emeritus - Community First Bank, Russ Spalding/Dir. Emeritus - Community First Bank, Beverly Clarno/Dir. Emeritus - Community First Bank, John Collins/Dir. Emeritus - Community First Bank, Andy Phillips/Exec. VP, Sr. Loan Officer

Directors: Robin B. Freeman/Dir., CEO, Pres., Stuart J. Shelk/Chmn., Robert Komlofske/Dir., Joe Bankofier/Dir., Mike Holland/Dir., Jeff Robberson/Dir., Peggy Morgan/Dir., Steven Forrester/Dir., James Dutchuk/Dir. Emeritus - Community First Bank, James A. Diegel/Dir.

Printlux.com Inc

1282 Vernon Dr., Vancouver, BC, V6A 4C9; ***PH:*** 1-604-254-6929; ***Fax:*** 1-604-254-7644;
http:// www.printlux.com; ***Email:*** plx@mindsharecommunications.com

General - Incorporation	Canada	**Stock**- Price on:12/24/2007	$0.14
Employees	NA	Stock Exchange	NA
Auditor	NA	Ticker Symbol	NA
Stk Agt	Computershare Trust Co of Canada	Outstanding Shares	NA
Counsel	NA	E.P.S	NA
DUNS No.	NA	Shareholders	NA

Business: The group's principal activity is providing up-to-the-minute innovations in print, promotional and warehouse management services. The company, with roots in a traditional bricks-and-mortar printing shop, takes printing orders online through its ePoise platform and fulfills them using its offset printing facility. The company also offers services in graphic design, digital prepress, offset printing, high speed document printing, post-press, customized shipping, inventory management, and warehousing. It opened its doors as Graffico Printers in 1990 as a commercial printer. The company introduced its Internet-enabled printing service and evolved into Printlux.com in March of 1999.

Primary SIC and add'l.: 2752 2759

CIK No: 0001297091

Printronix Inc

14600 Myford Rd., Irvine, CA, 92623; ***PH:*** 1-714-368-2300; ***Fax:*** 1-714-368-2600;
http:// www.printronix.com; ***Email:*** info@printronix.com

General - Incorporation	DE	**Stock**- Price on:12/24/2007	$13.05
Employees	673	Stock Exchange	NDQ
Auditor	BDO Seidman, LLP	Ticker Symbol	PTNX
Stk Agt	Mellon Investor Services LLC	Outstanding Shares	6,680,000
Counsel	Kirshman & Harris	E.P.S	$0.67
DUNS No.	06-617-7007	Shareholders	NA

Business: The group's principle activity is to design, develop, manufacture and market medium and high speed printing solutions and related supplies and services. The printers are used in critical applications where reliability and performance are crucial and industrial settings such as manufacturing plants, distribution centers, and front office and information technology department. The group has manufacturing and configuration sites located in the United States, Singapore, Holland and Mexico. It markets line matrix, thermal and fanfold laser and also provides professional services for systems integration and post-sales support with supplies, spares, repairs and maintenance capability. The group has 19 sales and support locations around the world.

Primary SIC and add'l.: 3577

CIK No: 0000311505

Subsidiaries: Printronix Asia Pte. Ltd., Printronix Australia Pty. Ltd., Printronix Deutschland GmbH, Printronix do Brasil, Printronix France S.a.r.l., Printronix Iberica, S.L., Printronix Latinoamericana, S.A. de C.V., Printronix Luxembourg Intl S.a.r.l., Printronix Luxembourg S.a.r.l., Printronix Nederland B.V., Printronix Osterreich GmbH, Printronix Printer (Shenzhen) Co., Ltd., Printronix Schweiz GmbH, Printronix Singapore Pte. Ltd., Printronix U.K. Ltd.

Officers: Robert A. Kleist/79/Dir., CEO, Pres./$328,458.00, Juli A. Mathews/VP - Human Resources, Assist. Corp. Sec., James B. McWilson/Sr. VP - Sales, The Americas, EMEA/$306,274.00, George L. Harwood/Sr. VP - Finance, IS, CFO, Corp. Sec./$291,842.00, David A. Sakai/Sr. VP - Worldwide Marketing, Theodore A. Chapman/Sr. VP - Engineering, Product Marketing, CTO/$279,905.00, Victor C. Fitzsimmons/Sr. VP - Worldwide Operations/$285,493.00, Albert Ching/VP - Asia Pacific Sales, Marketing, Claus Hinge/VP - Sales, Europe, William D. Mathewes/VP - Product Development

Directors: Robert A. Kleist/79/Dir., CEO, Pres., Bruce T. Coleman/Dir., John R. Dougery/Dir., Chris Whitney Halliwell/Dir., Erwin A. Kelen/Dir., Charles E. Turnbull/Dir.

Owners: Robert A. Kleist/17.50%, Royce & Associates LLC/7.30%, George L. Harwood/1.50%, Theodore A. Chapman/1.00%, Insiders/23.90%, AWM Investment Company Inc/6.80%, Charles E. Turnbull/0.10%, Dimensional Fund Advisors Inc./7.00%, Chris Whitney Halliwell/0.10%, C. Victor Fitzsimmons/1.50%, Erwin A. Kelen/0.60%, John R. Dougery/1.30%, James B. McWilson/0.60%, Rutabaga Capital Management LLC/9.80%, Bruce T. Coleman/0.30%

Financial Data: ***Fiscal Year End:***03/30 ***Latest Annual Data:*** 3/30/2007

Year	Sales	Net Income
2007	$128,416,000	$2,880,000
2006	$127,821,000	-$7,959,000
2005	$131,711,000	$1,939,000

Curr. Assets:	$77,743,000	**Curr. Liab.:**	$25,228,000	**P/E Ratio:**	25.10
Plant, Equip.:	$31,618,000	**Total Liab.:**	$39,744,000	**Indic. Yr. Divd.:**	$0.400
Total Assets:	$109,984,000	**Net Worth:**	$70,240,000	**Debt/ Equity:**	NA

Priority Healthcare Corp

250 Technology Pk., Lake Mary, FL, 32746; ***PH:*** 1-407-804-6700;
http:// www.priorityhealthcare.com

General - Incorporation	IN	**Stock**- Price on:12/24/2007	NA
Employees	NA	Stock Exchange	NA
Auditor	PricewaterhouseCoopers LLP	Ticker Symbol	NA
Stk Agt	Computershare Investor Services LLC	Outstanding Shares	NA
Counsel	Baker & Daniels	E.P.S	NA
DUNS No.	87-940-2170	Shareholders	NA

Business: The group's principal activities are the distribution of specialty pharmaceuticals and related medical supplies to the alternate site healthcare market. The group provides patient-specific, self-injectable biopharmaceuticals and disease treatment programs to individuals with chronic diseases, medical supplies to outpatient renal care centers and office-based physicians in oncology and other physician specialty markets. The group also offers value-added services to meet the specific needs by shipping refrigerated pharmaceuticals overnight in special packaging to maintain appropriate temperatures and offers automated order entry services and customized distribution for group accounts. Further, it also provides disease treatment programs for hepatitis, cancer, human growth deficiency, rheumatoid arthritis, infertility, pain management and others. On 18 sep 2003, the group acquired the operating assets of sinuspharmacy corporation.

Primary SIC and add'l.: 5122

CIK No: 0001037975

Subsidiaries: Aetna Specialty Pharmacy, LLC, Byfield Drug, Inc., Chesapeake Infusion, Inc., First Rx, Inc., Freco, Inc., HealthBridge Reimbursement and Product Support, Inc., Integrity Healthcare Services, Inc., Lynnfield Compounding Center, Inc., Lynnfield Drug, Inc., Matrix Oncology, LLC, Pharmacy Plus, Inc., PHF, Inc., PHRC, Inc., Priority Healthcare Corporation West, Priority Healthcare Distribution, Inc. 19 Subsidiaries included in the Index

Prism Software Corp

15500-C Rockfield Blvd., Irvine, CA, 92618; ***PH:*** 1-949-855-3100; ***Fax:*** 1-949-855-6341;
http:// prism-software.com; ***Email:*** sales@prism-software.com

General - Incorporation	DE	**Stock**- Price on:12/24/2007	$0.006
Employees	14	Stock Exchange	OTC
Auditor	Cacciamatta Accountancy Corp	Ticker Symbol	PSOF
Stk Agt	U.S. Stock Transfer Corp	Outstanding Shares	141,590,000
Counsel	NA	E.P.S	-$0.011
DUNS No.	16-128-8758	Shareholders	NA

Business: The group's principle activity is to provide enterprise document and content management solutions. Its products can transform to and from a wide variety of print and data formats such as hp pcl, adobe postscript and pdf, IBM afp/ ipds, ascii and ebcdic, tiff and windows gdi. Its customer base includes a number of organizations in different markets like financial services, health care, service bureau printing, government, education and manufacturing that use its solutions in managing high-volume, large scale document printing that resides on mainframes or disparate systems and needs to be intelligently redirected to appropriate output devices on the network. The company distributes its products throughout North America, South America and Europe through direct sales, resellers, value-added resellers and printer manufacturers. Its products include printconsole and printconsole conversion modules.

Primary SIC and add'l.: 7372 7379

CIK No: 0000908235

Financial Data: ***Fiscal Year End:***12/31 ***Latest Annual Data:*** 12/31/2005

Year	Sales	Net Income
2005	$1,229,000	-$1,460,000
2004	$736,000	-$1,374,000
2003	$491,000	-$5,254,000

Curr. Assets:	$167,000	**Curr. Liab.:**	$798,000		
Plant, Equip.:	$51,000	**Total Liab.:**	$12,074,000	**Indic. Yr. Divd.:**	NA
Total Assets:	$241,000	**Net Worth:**	-$11,832,000	**Debt/ Equity:**	NA

Private Bk Peninsula

505 Hamilton Ave., Ste. 110, Palo Alto, CA, 94301; ***PH:*** 1-650-843-2265; ***Fax:*** 1-650-289-9192;
http:// www.the-private-bank.com

General - Incorporation		**Stock**- Price on:12/24/2007	$15.9
Employees	NA	Stock Exchange	OTC
Auditor	NA	Ticker Symbol	PBPC
Stk Agt	NA	Outstanding Shares	1,860,000
Counsel	NA	E.P.S	NA
DUNS No.	NA	Shareholders	NA

Business: The groups principal activity is a locally owned and managed commercial Bank, distinguished by a primary emphasis on customized service to meet the financial needs of local individuals and businesses. Services of the group include commercial loans & lines of credit, commercial real estate loans, construction loans, personal checking, savings, and money market accounts, business checking and money market accounts, certificates of deposit and debit card.

Primary SIC and add'l.: 6022

CIK No:

Officers: Kenneth D. Brenner/Dir., CEO, Romeo C. Luz/Sr. VP - Lending, Steven Leen/Sr. VP, CFO, Nicole L. Bader/Sr. VP, Chief Credit Officer, Tracy G. Herrick/Dir., Chief Economist, Robert S. Holden/Dir., Pres., Chief Lending Officer, William W. Phillips/Dir., Exec. VP - Business Development, Susan J. Wells/VP, Relationship Mgr., Ann E. Wright/VP - Operations, Michael V. Hansen/Exec. VP - Technology, Asset Based Lending, Brian M. Palter/VP - Business Development, John T. Cavender/Contact, Stella J. Feng/VP, Relationship Mgr., Natasha Kurtova French/VP - Business Development, Teresa M. Link/VP, Relationship Mgr.

Directors: Kenneth D. Brenner/Dir., CEO, Mark D. Mordell/Chmn., Hugh P. Barton/Dir. Emeritus, Georgie L. Gleim/Dir., Kurt Hammerstrom/Dir., Lisa B. Hendrickson/Dir., Tracy G. Herrick/Dir., Chief Economist, Robert S. Holden/Dir., Pres., Chief Lending Officer, William W. Phillips/Dir., Exec. VP - Business Development, Roxy H. Rapp/Dir., Nancy Weeks Rossen/Dir. Emeritus, Clifford G. Rudolph/Dir., Richard A. Strock/Dir.

Private Media Group Inc

Carretera de Rub 22-26, Sant Cugat del Valls, Barcelona, 8190; ***PH:*** 34-935907070;
http:// www.prvt.com; ***Email:*** info@prvt.com

General - Incorporation	NV	**Stock**- Price on:12/24/2007	$2.18
Employees	137	Stock Exchange	NDQ
Auditor	BDO Audiberia Auditores	Ticker Symbol	PRVT
Stk Agt	Interwest Transfer Company, Inc.	Outstanding Shares	53,150,000
Counsel	NA	E.P.S	-$0.02
DUNS No.	NA	Shareholders	NA

Business: The group's principal activities are the acquisition, refinement and delivery of adult feature products and services, including a range of proprietary websites, digital versatile discs, unrated and adult feature magazines, videos and CD-roms. The group also distributes and licenses its proprietary products and services on the Internet, including magazines, videos, interactive services, adult novelty products and the private circle fashion line. All the products are oriented to the adult entertainment market. The group distributes its products in Sweden, Finland, Denmark, estonia, latvia, Poland, Russia, the United Kingdom, Ireland, Germany, the Netherlands, luxembourg, Belgium, the czech republic, slovenia, Austria, hungary, Switzerland, Italy, Greece, turkey, cyprus, France, Spain, Portugal, Canada, the United States, Mexico, Chile, Brazil, paraguay, uruguay, Argentina, South Africa and Japan.

Primary SIC and add'l.: 7812 2731 7375 2721

CIK No: 0001068084

Subsidiaries: Barbuda B.V., Ceresland S.L., Cine Craft, Ltd., Coldfair Holdings Limited, Fraserside Holdings Ltd., Milcap Media Group S.L., Milcap Publishing Group Italy Srl, Peach Entertainment Distribution AB, Private Benelux B.V., Private France SAS, Private Media Group Canada, Inc., Private Media Group Services S.L., Private North America, Ltd.

Officers: Berth H. Milton/Chmn., CEO, Pres., Johan Gillborg/CFO, Sec., Philip Christmas/VP, Javier Sanchez/Exec. VP - Production, Operations, Peter T. Cohen/COO

Directors: Berth H. Milton/Chmn., CEO, Pres., Bo Rodebrant/55/Dir., Lluis Torralba/40/Dir., Daniel Sanchez/39/Dir., Johan G. Carlberg/49/Dir.

Owners: Johan Gillborg, Bo Rodebrant, Johan G. Carlberg, Philip Christmas, Javier Snchez/1.40%, Lluis Torralba, Berth H. Milton/56.80%, Insiders/57.90%, Daniel Snchez

Financial Data: *Fiscal Year End:*12/31   *Latest Annual Data:* 12/31/2006

Year	Sales	Net Income
2006	$38,417,000	$630,000
2005	$32,673,000	$59,000
2004	$48,784,000	$326,000

Curr. Assets:	$41,400,000	*Curr. Liab.:*	$13,685,000	
Plant, Equip.:	$3,288,000	*Total Liab.:*	$13,859,000	*Indic. Yr. Divd.:* NA
Total Assets:	$74,823,000	*Net Worth:*	$60,964,000	*Debt/ Equity:* 0.0028

PrivateBancorp Inc

70 W Madison, Chicago, IL, 60602; *PH:* 1-312-683-7100; *Fax:* 1-312-683-7111; *http://* www.privatebancorp.com

General - Incorporation	DE	**Stock** - Price on:12/24/2007	$33.72
Employees	471	Stock Exchange	NDQ
Auditor	Ernst & Young LLP	Ticker Symbol	PVTB
Stk Agt	Illinois Stock Transfer Co	Outstanding Shares	22,070,000
Counsel	Jenner & Block	E.P.S.	$1.69
DUNS No.	NA	Shareholders	NA

Business: The group's principal activity is to provide commercial banking services, real estate services, wealth management services and individual banking services through seven banking locations. The commercial services offered include full range of lending products, lines of credit for working capital, term loans for equipment and other investment purposes, letters of credit and non-credit products including lockbox, cash concentration accounts and electronic funds transfer. Real estate services provide commercial, residential real estate and construction loans. Wealth management services include investment management, personal trust, retirement accounts and brokerage and investment services. Individual banking services provided includes interest bearing checking with credit line, money market deposit accounts and debit cards. The customers of the group are affluent individuals, professionals and entrepreneurs.

Primary SIC and add'l.: 6022 6712

CIK No: 0000889936

Subsidiaries: Bloomfield Hills Statutory Trust I, Lodestar Investment Counsel, LLC, Private Investment Limited Partnership I, PrivateBancorp Statutory Trust II, PrivateBancorp Statutory Trust III, The PrivateBank, The PrivateBank Michigan, The PrivateBank and Trust Company, The PrivateBank Mortgage Company, LLC, TrustCo, Company

Officers: Calvin R. Kleinmann/Chmn., CEO - Privatebank, Kansas City, in Formation, David T. Provost/Chmn., CEO - Privatebank, Michigan, Brian D. Schmitt/Chmn., CEO - Privatebank, Georgia, Robert M. Burch/Vice Chmn., MD - Privatebank, Michigan, Sanford B. Scott/Vice Chmn., MD - Privatebank, St. Louis, Gary S. Collins/Vice Chmn., MD - Privatebank, Trust Company/$657,839.00, Hugh H. McLean/Vice Chmn., MD - Privatebank, Trust Company/$657,065.00, Christina M. Ksoll/MD - Privatebank, Trust Company, Dennis L. Klaeser/CFO/$720,280.00, Lauren J. Henzel/MD, Sr. Trust Officer, MD, Sr. Trust Officer, David J. Hesselbein/MD - Privatebank, Trust Company, Martin L. Klauber/MD - Privatebank, Trust Company, Alan H. Kohn/MD - Privatebank, Trust Company, Christopher C. Hainey/MD - Privatebank, Trust Company, Wallace L. Head/MD, Dir. - Wealth Management, The Privatebank and Trust Company *(74 Officers included in Index)*

Directors: David T. Provost/Chmn., CEO - Privatebank, Michigan, Brian D. Schmitt/Chmn., CEO - Privatebank, Georgia, Calvin R. Kleinmann/Chmn., CEO - Privatebank, Kansas City, in Formation, Robert M. Burch/Vice Chmn., MD - Privatebank, Michigan, William R. Langley/Dir. Emeriti, Donald L. Beal/Dir., William J. Podl/Dir., Cheryl Mayberry McKissack/Dir., Michael B. Susman/Dir. Emeriti, William A. Castellano/Dir., Philip M. Kayman/Dir., William A. Goldstein/Dir., Caren L. Reed/Dir. Emeriti, Ralph B. Mandell/Dir., Richard C. Jensen/Dir. *(23 Directors included in Index)*

Owners: Dennis L. Klaeser, William A. Goldstein/1.48%, John B. Williams, Patrick F. Daly, Insiders/16.25%, Richard C. Jensen, Edward W. Rabin, Donald L. Beal, Philip M. Kayman, Cheryl Mayberry McKissack, Hugh H. McLean/1.62%, William J. Podl, Ralph B. Mandell/4.91%, Robert F. Coleman, Thomas F. Meagher *(20 Owners included in Index)*

Financial Data: *Fiscal Year End:*12/31   *Latest Annual Data:* 12/31/2006

Year	Sales	Net Income
2006	$280,657,000	$37,846,000
2005	$195,442,000	$33,420,000
2004	$128,279,000	$26,995,000

Curr. Assets:	$102,887,000	*Curr. Liab.:*	$3,567,084,000	*P/E Ratio:* 19.95
Plant, Equip.:	$21,413,000	*Total Liab.:*	$3,964,267,000	*Indic. Yr. Divd.:* $0.300
Total Assets:	$4,261,391,000	*Net Worth:*	$297,124,000	*Debt/ Equity:* 1.4521

Pro Pharmaceuticals Inc

7 Wells Ave., Newton, MA, 02459; *PH:* 1-617-559-0033; *Fax:* 1-617-928-3450; *http://* www.pro-pharmaceuticals.com

General - Incorporation	NV	**Stock** - Price on:12/24/2007	$0.699
Employees	8	Stock Exchange	AMEX
Auditor	Deloitte & Touche LLP	Ticker Symbol	PRW
Stk Agt	Continental Stock Transfer & Trust Co	Outstanding Shares	40,360,000
Counsel	NA	E.P.S.	-$0.019
DUNS No.	NA	Shareholders	NA

Business: The group's principle activity is to develop a biochemical technology that will focus on the existing drug therapies. The technology will reduce toxicity and improve efficacy of the existing drug therapies including cancer chemotherapies. In order to achieve that, the technology will combine the drugs with a number of carbohydrate compounds. The fundamental objective of this technology is to increase the body's tolerance to the drugs by enabling delivery of the drugs while protecting the healthy tissue. The company has selected the first group of drugs that include 5-fluorouracil, adriamycin, taxol, cytoxan and cisplatin for the upgradation programs. The company is in the development stage. The group operates from United States.

Primary SIC and add'l.: 8731

CIK No: 0001133416

Subsidiaries: Pro-Pharmaceuticals Securities Corp.

Officers: David Platt/Chmn., CEO, Pres., Member - Scientific Advisory Board/$356,749.00, Maureen E. Foley/COO/$266,856.00, Carl L. Lueders/CFO/$330,926.00, Anthony D. Squeglia/VP - Investor Relations, Anatole A. Klyosov/Chief Scientist, Member - Scientific Advisory Board/$274,983.00, Eliezer Zomer/Exec. VP - Manufacturing, Product Development, Member - Scientific Advisory Board/$308,678.00, Leslie R. Laufman/Member, Medical Member - Advisory Board, Bruce Silver/Member, Medical Member - Advisory Board

Directors: David Platt/Chmn., CEO, Pres., Member - Scientific Advisory Board, Henry J. Esber/Dir., Member - The Scientific Advisory Board, Anatole A. Klyosov/Chief Scientist, Member - Scientific Advisory Board, Irwin Joseph Goldstein/Member - Scientific Advisory Board, Steven Prelack/Dir., Mildred Christian/Dir., Member - Scientific Advisory Board, Jerald K. Rome/Dir., Dale H. Conaway/Dir., Member - Scientific Advisory Board, Edgar Ben-Josef/Member - Scientific, Medical Advisory Board, Zbigniew J. Witczak/Member - The Scientific Advisory Board, John S. MacDonald/Member - Medical Advisory Board, James T. Gourzis/79/Dir., Colin Neill/61/Dir.

Owners: Dale H. Conaway, Henry J. Esber, Mildred S. Christian, Maureen E. Foley/2.00%, Steven Prelack, Insiders/18.20%, Jerald K. Rome, Eliezer Zomer/1.50%, James C. Czirr/11.50%, Carl L. Lueders, Anatole Klyosov/2.60%, David Platt/11.30%

Financial Data: *Fiscal Year End:*12/31   *Latest Annual Data:* 12/31/2006

Year	Sales	Net Income
2006	NA	-$3,193,000
2005	NA	-$6,544,000
2004	NA	-$7,180,000

Curr. Assets:	$5,936,000	*Curr. Liab.:*	$5,989,000	
Plant, Equip.:	$112,000	*Total Liab.:*	$6,385,000	*Indic. Yr. Divd.:* NA
Total Assets:	$6,363,000	*Net Worth:*	-$22,000	*Debt/ Equity:* NA

Pro Tech Communications Inc

4492 Okeechobee Rd., Fort Pierce, FL, 34947; *PH:* 1-772-464-5100; *Fax:* 1-772-464-6644; *http://* www.protechcommunications.com; *Email:* info@protechcom.com

General - Incorporation	FL	**Stock** - Price on:12/24/2007	NA
Employees	9	Stock Exchange	OTC
Auditor	Eisner LLP	Ticker Symbol	PCTU
Stk Agt	American Stock Transfer & Trust Co.	Outstanding Shares	NA
Counsel	NA	E.P.S.	-$0.048
DUNS No.	79-009-8909	Shareholders	NA

Business: The group's principal activities are to design, develop, manufacture and market lightweight telecommunications headsets. The group is also into telecommunication integration business and call center operations business. The products of the group include the procom headset, the apollo headset, the apollo freedom series headset, the gemini amplifier, the usb adapter, the dsp intelligent microphone, the manager's headset, the apex, the astra, the active series headset and the trinity headset. These products are used by telephone operating companies, telephone system manufacturers, aerospace applications, personal computer manufacturers and government agencies. The operations of the group are carried out throughout the United States. The groups major customers are muzak corporation, mcdonalds corporation, 3m corporation and hello direct.

Primary SIC and add'l.: 7389 3661

CIK No: 0000945481

Subsidiaries: NCT Group, Inc, NCT Hearing

Officers: Joanna Lipper/Investor Relations Officer

Financial Data: *Fiscal Year End:*12/31   *Latest Annual Data:* 12/31/2005

Year	Sales	Net Income
2005	$1,261,000	-$2,062,000
2004	$1,195,000	-$1,390,000
2003	$1,179,000	-$974,000

Curr. Assets:	$564,000	*Curr. Liab.:*	$1,301,000	
Plant, Equip.:	$220,000	*Total Liab.:*	$5,126,000	*Indic. Yr. Divd.:* NA
Total Assets:	$3,204,000	*Net Worth:*	-$1,923,000	*Debt/ Equity:* NA

Pro-Dex Inc

151 E Columbine Ave., Santa Ana, CA, 92707; *PH:* 1-714-241-4411; *Fax:* 1-714-513-7755; *http://* www.pdex.com; *Email:* investor_relations@pro-dex.com

General - Incorporation	CO	**Stock** - Price on:12/24/2007	$1.5001
Employees	122	Stock Exchange	NDQ
Auditor	Moss Adams LLP	Ticker Symbol	PDEX
Stk Agt	Computershare Trust Co	Outstanding Shares	9,640,000
Counsel	NA	E.P.S.	$0.056
DUNS No.	84-937-0358	Shareholders	NA

Business: The group's principal activity is to develop and manufacture pneumatic, electric and battery powered rotary drive systems. It operates through two wholly owned subsidiaries micro motors, inc. And Oregon micro systems, inc. Micro motors, inc designs, develops and manufactures electric, air, and battery powered rotary drive systems for the medical device industry and for the dental industry. Oregon micro systems, inc designs and manufactures embedded multi-axis motion controllers used to regulate the motion of servo and stepper motors, predominantly for the semiconductor and medical analysis equipment industries. The group also designs and manufactures miniature pneumatic motors for industrial applications in the automotive, aerospace, apparel and entertainment industries.

Primary SIC and add'l.: 6719 5047 3823 3843 8021

CIK No: 0000788920

Subsidiaries: Pro-Dex Astromec, Inc.

Officers: Mark P. Murphy/48/Dir., CEO, Pres., Phillip S. Brown/46/VP - Engineering, Jeff J. Ritchey/45/CFO, Treasurer, Sec., Patrick L. Johnson/47/Exec. VP, Chief Business Development Officer, Rhea Gustafson/47/Pres. - Astromec, Richard L. Van Kirk/47/VP - Manufacturing

Directors: Mark P. Murphy/48/Dir., CEO, Pres., George J. Isaac/63/Dir., Michael A. Mesenbrink/61/Dir., Valerio L. Giannini/70/Dir., William L. Healey/63/Dir.

Owners: George J. Isaac/1.70%, Insiders/10.90%, Valerio L. Giannini, Michael A. Mesenbrink, First Wilshire Securities Management Inc./16.60%, Ronald G. Coss/13.40%, Jeffrey J. Ritchey/1.20%, Patrick Johnson/5.30%, Mark P. Murphy/1.70%

Financial Data: *Fiscal Year End:*06/30   *Latest Annual Data:* 6/30/2006

Year	Sales	Net Income
2006	$17,061,000	$827,000
2005	$13,834,000	$1,849,000
2004	$14,200,000	$1,120,000

Curr. Assets:	$9,757,000	Curr. Liab.:	$3,109,000	P/E Ratio:	25.00
Plant, Equip.:	$3,778,000	Total Liab.:	$5,256,000	Indic. Yr. Divd.:	NA
Total Assets:	$18,107,000	Net Worth:	$12,851,000	Debt/ Equity:	NA

Pro-Fac Cooperative Inc

PO Box 30682, Rochester, NY, 14603; **PH:** 1-585-218-4210; **Fax:** 1-585-218-4241; **http://** www.profaccoop.com

General - Incorporation	NY	**Stock**- Price on:12/24/2007	$15.5
Employees	NA	Stock Exchange	NDQ
Auditor	Freed Maxick & Battaglia, Cpas, P.C	Ticker Symbol	PFACP
Stk Agt	NA	Outstanding Shares	NA
Counsel	Harris Beach	E.P.S.	NA
DUNS No.	06-425-5938	Shareholders	NA

Business: The group's principal activities are to process and market crops grown by its members. It includes fruits, vegetables, beans, beets, cucumbers and popcorn. The distribution activities of the group are to deliver raw fruits and vegetables to its customers. On 19-Aug-2002, the company entered a termination agreement with bird eye foods pursuant to which, among other things, the marketing and facilitation agreement and the patronage income of 90% form birds eye foods was terminated. The birds eye foods agreed to pay a termination fee of 10 million per year for five years. At 28-Jun-2003 there are approximately 548 pro-fac members, consisting of individual growers or associations of growers located in New York, Delaware, Illinois, Michigan, Washington and Georgia.

Primary SIC and add'l.: 0115 5149 2032 5431

CIK No: 0000202932

Subsidiaries: Birds Eye Foods, Holdings LLC

Officers: Stephen R. Wright/GM, CEO, CFO, Sec., Peter Call/Chmn., Pres., Allan Overhiser/Dir., VP, Treasurer, David Mehalick/Assist. Treasurer, Assist. Sec., Kevin Murphy/Assist. Treasurer, Assist. Sec., VP, Member Relations, Thomas Willett/Assist. Treasurer, Chris Jagel/Assist. Sec., Steven D. Koinzan/60/Dir., VP, Shari Burgo/Assist. Treasurer, Assist. Sec. - Securities Coordinator

Directors: Peter Call/Chmn., Pres., Darell Sarff/Dir., Kenneth A. Dahlstedt/Dir., Kenneth Mattingly/Dir., James Vincent/Dir., Allan Overhiser/Dir., VP, Treasurer, William Lipinski/Dir., Joseph Herman/Dir., Cornelius D. Harrington/Dir., Charles R. Altemus/77/Dir., Robert Debadts/Dir., Bruce Fox/Dir., Paul Roe/Dir., Frank Stotz/Dir., Steven D. Koinzan/60/Dir., VP *(16 Directors included in Index)*

Owners: Bruce R. Fox/0.19%, Peter R. Call/2.29%, Kenneth A. Dahlstedt/0.42%, Stephen R. Wright/0.03%, James Vincent/0.16%, Paul E. Roe/1.41%, Kenneth A. Mattingly/0.72%, Darell Sarff/0.15%, Steven D. Koinzan/0.01%, Charles R. Altemus/0.05%, Bruce R. Fox/0.64%, Peter R. Call/0.21%, Robert DeBadts/0.01%, Peter R. Call/0.29%, James Vincent/0.08% *(42 Owners included in Index)*

Financial Data: Fiscal Year End:06/26   Latest Annual Data: 6/24/2006

Year	Sales	Net Income
2006	$36,000	-$2,184,000
2005	NA	$1,639,000
2004	NA	$9,104,000

Curr. Assets:	$12,601,000	Curr. Liab.:	$13,453,000		
Plant, Equip.:	NA	Total Liab.:	$14,453,000	Indic. Yr. Divd.:	NA
Total Assets:	$34,098,000	Net Worth:	$19,537,000	Debt/ Equity:	NA

Proassurance Corp

100 Brookwood Pl., Ste. 300, Birmingham, AL, 35209; **PH:** 1-205-877-4400; **Fax:** 1-205-868-4073; **http://** www.proassurance.com; **Email:** information@proassurance.com

General - Incorporation	DE	**Stock**- Price on:12/24/2007	$54.82
Employees	589	Stock Exchange	NYSE
Auditor	Ernst & Young LLP	Ticker Symbol	PRA
Stk Agt	Mellon Investor Services LLC	Outstanding Shares	33,340,000
Counsel	Burr & Forman	E.P.S.	$4.32
DUNS No.	NA	Shareholders	NA

Business: The group's principle activity is to provide professional and general liability insurance for physicians and surgeons, dentists, hospitals and others engaged in the delivery of health care. The group operates in two segments, namely professional liability insurance and personal lines insurance. The professional liability insurance segment provides professional and general liability insurance for providers of medical and other healthcare services and providers of legal services. This segment also includes accident and health and workers' compensation insurance. The personal lines segment provides private passenger automobile, homeowner, boat and umbrella insurance products primarily for educational employees and their families. The group's quarterly revenue for September 2007 was 178.62 millions of USD.

Primary SIC and add'l.: 6719 6324

CIK No: 0001127703

Subsidiaries: American Captive Corporation, American Insurance Management Corporation, E-Health Solutions Group, Inc., Healthcare Compliance Purchasing Group, LLC, IAO, Inc., Medical Assurance, Inc., Medical Insurance of Indiana Agency, Inc., MEEMIC Insurance Company, MEEMIC Insurance Services Corporation, MEMH Holdings, Inc., Mutual Assurance Agency of Ohio, Inc., National Capital Insurance Brokerage Ltd., National Capital Risk Services LLC, NCRIC Corporation, NCRIC Insurance Agency, Inc. 28 Subsidiaries included in the Index

Officers: Stancil W. Starnes/CEO, Victor T. Adamo/60/Vice Chmn., COO, Pres./$1,642,371.00, Howard H. Friedman/Co - Pres. - Professional Liability Group, Chief Underwriting Officer, Chief Actuary, Sr. VP/$1,091,090.00, Darryl K. Thomas/Co - Pres. - Professional Liability Group, Chief Claims Officer, Sr. VP, James J. Morello/Chief Acounting Officer, Treasurer, Sr. VP, Edward L. Rand/CFO, Sr. VP/$1,005,804.00, Jeffrey L. Bowlby/Sr. VP, Chief Marketing Officer - Professional Liability Group, Jeffrey P. Lisenby/Corp. Sec. - Legal Counsel, VP, Frank B. O'Neil/Sr. VP - Corporate Communications, Investor Relations, Hayes V. Whiteside/Sr. VP, Medical Dir.

Directors: Victor T. Adamo/60/Vice Chmn., COO, Pres., Derrill A. Crowe/Chmn., John J. McMahon/Dir., William J. Listwan/65/Dir., Wilfred W. Yeargan/Dir., Ann F. Putallaz/Dir., Robert E. Flowers/Dir., William H. Woodhams/Dir., Lucian F. Bloodworth/Dir., Paul R. Butrus/Dir., John P. North/Dir.

Owners: Paul R. Butrus/1.30%, Robert E. Flowers, Edward L. Rand, Insiders/9.20%, Wellington Management Company, LLP/5.60%, JPMorgan Chase & Co./7.30%, John P. North, Ann F. Putallaz, Lucian F. Bloodworth, T. Rowe Price Associates, Inc/7.20%, Howard H. Friedman, Wilfred W. Yeargan, Derrill A. Crowe/6.60%, William H. Woodhams, John J. McMahon *(17 Owners included in Index)*

Financial Data: Fiscal Year End:12/31   Latest Annual Data: 12/31/2006

Year	Sales	Net Income
2006	$737,598,000	$236,425,000
2005	$645,312,000	$113,457,000
2004	$794,553,000	$72,811,000

Curr. Assets:	$716,166,000	Curr. Liab.:	NA	P/E Ratio:	14.06
Plant, Equip.:	$23,135,000	Total Liab.:	$3,224,306,000	Indic. Yr. Divd.:	NA
Total Assets:	$4,342,853,000	Net Worth:	$1,118,547,000	Debt/ Equity:	0.1540

Probe Manufacturing Inc

25242 Arctic Ocean Dr., Lake Forest, CA, 92630; **PH:** 1-949-206-6868; **http://** www.probemi.com; **Email:** info@probemi.com

General - Incorporation	NV	**Stock**- Price on:12/24/2007	$0.45
Employees	60	Stock Exchange	OTC
Auditor	Jaspers + Hall, PC	Ticker Symbol	PMFI
Stk Agt	Integrity Stock Transfer, Inc.	Outstanding Shares	10,270,000
Counsel	Jeffrey Conrad	E.P.S.	$0.03
DUNS No.	NA	Shareholders	NA

Business: The groups principal activities include manufacturing electronics and providing services to original equipment manufacturers. Services of the group include surface mount and through hole assembly, cable assembly, mechanical assembly, and fully integrated box build systems for high complexity electronics. Customers of the group include industrial, automotive, semiconductor, medical, communication and military. The group operates through six segments namely industrial, military, automotive, communication, medical and semiconductor products. The group operates from the United States.

Primary SIC and add'l.: 3679

CIK No: 0001329606

Officers: Reza Zarif/Co - Founder, CEO, Pres., John Bennett/CFO, VP - Finance, Controller, Linwood J. Goddard/VP - Quality, Organizational Development

Directors: Reza Zarif/Co - Founder, CEO, Pres., Kambiz Mahdi/Co - Founder, Dir., Barrett Evans/Dir., Jeffrey Conrad/Dir.

Owners: Reza Zarif/20.97%, Dennis Benner/5.37%, Insiders/57.70%, Ashford Capital, LLC/8.09%, Jeffrey Conrad, eFund Capital Partners, LLC/15.50%, Kambiz Mahdi/18.66%, Barrett Evans/0.96%

Financial Data: Fiscal Year End:12/31   Latest Annual Data: 12/31/2006

| Year | Sales | Net Income |
| 2006 | $9,310,000 | $151,000 |

Curr. Assets:	$1,968,000	Curr. Liab.:	$2,101,000	P/E Ratio:	45.00
Plant, Equip.:	$318,000	Total Liab.:	$3,032,000	Indic. Yr. Divd.:	NA
Total Assets:	$2,286,000	Net Worth:	-$745,000	Debt/ Equity:	NA

Procentury Corp

465 Cleveland Ave., Westerville, OH, 43082; **PH:** 1-614-895-2000; **Fax:** 1-614-895-2707; **http://** www.procentury.com; **Email:** info@procentury.com

General - Incorporation	OH	**Stock**- Price on:12/24/2007	$17.16
Employees	310	Stock Exchange	NDQ
Auditor	KPMG LLP	Ticker Symbol	PROS
Stk Agt	National City Bank	Outstanding Shares	13,360,000
Counsel	Squire, Sanders & Dempsey LLP	E.P.S.	$1.63
DUNS No.	NA	Shareholders	NA

Business: The group's principal activity is to market and underwrite general liability, commercial property and multi-peril insurance for small and mid-sized businesses. It primarily write specialty excess and surplus lines insurance through a select group of general agents. The group operates in two segments; property and casualty lines includes general liability, multi-peril and commercial property. Surety lines includes specialty bonds, landfill bonds and bail bonds. The group markets their products through 83 agents. As of 31st dec 2003, it had 117 office locations throughout the United States.

Primary SIC and add'l.: 6331

CIK No: 0001273397

Subsidiaries: Century Surety Company (CSC), ProCentury Insurance Company (Subsidiary of CSC), ProCentury Risk Partners Insurance Company, ProFinance Holdings Statutory Trust II, ProFinance Statutory Trust I

Officers: Edward F. Feighan/Chmn., CEO, Pres., Erin Elizabeth West/CFO, Christopher John Timm/Exec. VP, Pres. - Century Insurance Group, Jeff Racz/Contact - Investor Relations

Directors: Edward F. Feighan/Chmn., CEO, Pres., Michael J. Endres/Dir., Robert F. Fix/Dir., Alan R. Weiler/Dir., Robert Jay Woodward/Dir., Press C. Southworth/Dir., Jeffrey A. Maffett/59/Dir.

Owners: Jeffrey A. Maffett, Goldman Sachs Asset Management, L.P./8.10%, Robert F. Fix, Press C. Southworth, T. Rowe Price Associates, Inc./9.10%, Greg D. Ewald, Edward F. Feighan/1.70%, Christopher J. Timm/2.10%, Robert J. Woodward, Stonehenge Opportunity Fund, LLC/6.60%, Dimensional FundAdvisors LP/5.60%, Erin E. West, Michael J. Endres, Wells Fargo& Company/12.20%, Insiders/5.10% *(16 Owners included in Index)*

Financial Data: Fiscal Year End:12/31   Latest Annual Data: 12/31/2006

Year	Sales	Net Income
2006	$238,881,000	$20,901,000
2005	$191,791,000	$10,241,000
2004	$158,800,000	$14,980,000

Curr. Assets:	$128,690,000	Curr. Liab.:	$18,998,000	P/E Ratio:	10.53
Plant, Equip.:	NA	Total Liab.:	$436,660,000	Indic. Yr. Divd.:	$0.160
Total Assets:	$579,048,000	Net Worth:	$142,388,000	Debt/ Equity:	0.2013

Procera Networks Inc

100 Cooper Ct., Los Gatos, CA, 95032; **PH:** 1-408-354-7200; **Fax:** 1-408-354-7211; **http://** www.proceranetworks.com

General - Incorporation	NV	**Stock**- Price on:12/24/2007	$3.179
Employees	41	Stock Exchange	OTC
Auditor	Burr, Pilger & Mayer LLP	Ticker Symbol	PRNW
Stk Agt	Pacific Stock Transfer Company	Outstanding Shares	68,930,000
Counsel	NA	E.P.S.	NA
DUNS No.	NA	Shareholders	NA

Business: The groups principle activity is develops intelligent network appliances that provide a non-intrusive, wire speed network overlay to protect, control and optimize internal IP-based networks. The group markets its product under the tradename include Procera's OptimIP(TM). The group operates from the United States, Australia, Asia, Europe, Canada and Middle East. The group's quarterly revenue for Sep'07 was 1.65 millions of USD.

Primary SIC and add'l.: 3669 3577

CIK No: 0001165231

Officers: Tom Williams/Dir., CEO, CFO, Douglas J. Glader/65/Dir., Pres., Sven Nowicki/Dir., Exec. VP, GM - EMEA, Alexander Havang/CTO, Gary J. Johnson/64/Sr. VP - Sales, Marketing, Jon Linden/VP - OEM, Major Accounting, EMEA, Albert Lopez/VP - Worldwide Marketing, GM - Asia Pacific, David Stepner/COO

Directors: Tom Williams/Dir., CEO, CFO, Douglas J. Glader/65/Dir., Pres., Sven Nowicki/Dir., Exec. VP, GM - EMEA, Scott McClendon/Dir., Tom Saponas/Dir., Staffan E.S. Hillberg/Dir., Mary M. Losty/Dir.

Owners: Mary Losty/2.40%, Thomas Saponas, Gary Johnson/1.40%, Thomas Williams/1.90%, Scott McClendon, Douglas Glader/5.60%, Sven Nowicki/3.90%, Staffan Hillberg, Insiders/15.50%

Financial Data: Fiscal Year End:01/31   Latest Annual Data: 12/31/2006

Year	Sales	Net Income
2006	$1,914,000	-$7,503,000

Curr. Assets:	$6,758,000	Curr. Liab.:	$1,347,000		
Plant, Equip.:	$6,331,000	Total Liab.:	$4,213,000	Indic. Yr. Divd.:	NA
Total Assets:	$17,503,000	Net Worth:	$13,290,000	Debt/ Equity:	NA

Procter & Gamble

1 Procter & Gamble Plz., Cincinnati, OH, 45202; **PH:** 1-513-983-1100; **Fax:** 1-513-983-9369; http:// www.pg.com

General - Incorporation	OH	Stock- Price on:12/24/2007	$61.88
Employees	138,000	Stock Exchange	NYSE
Auditor	Deloitte & Touche LLP	Ticker Symbol	PG
Stk Agt	Bank of New York	Outstanding Shares	3,150,000,000
Counsel	NA	E.P.S.	$2.92
DUNS No.	00-131-6827	Shareholders	NA

Business: The group's principle activity is to provide branded consumer goods product. The group's solutions include personnel and beauty care, winter skin care, Newscope(R) white mouthwash, and pet nutrition and mature skin therapy. The group products are sold under the brand names Pampers, Tide, Ariel, Always, Pantene, Bounty, Folgers, Pringles, Charmin, Downy, Iams, Crest, Actonel and Olay. The group operates from United States.

Primary SIC and add'l.: 2087 2045 2676 2844 2834 2841

CIK No: 0000080424

Subsidiaries: AB Tudor Hellesens, AG fr Aetherische Oele, Alejandro Llauro E. Hijos S.A.I.C., An-Pro Company, Anjali (HK)Corporation Limited, Arab Orient Holding, Atkinsons of London Ltd., B&C International Co. (BVI)Ltd., Baraca Planet, Sociedad Limitada, Beauty Center AG, Becruz, S.A. de C.V., Belcosa Distribuidora de Cosmticos Ltda., Belfam Industria Cosmetic S.A., Belmed Ltda., Belvedere USA Corp. 682 Subsidiaries included in the Index

Officers: Alan G. Lafley/61/Chmn., CEO, Pres./$27,736.00, Werner Geissler/55/Vice Chmn. - Global Operations, Group Pres. - Central, Eastern Europe, Middle East, Africa, Dimitri Panayotopoulos/57/Vice Chmn. - Global Household Care, Robert A. McDonald/55/Vice Chmn. - Global Operations, COO/$7,624.00, Robert A. Steele/53/Group Pres. - Household Care, Vice Chmn. - Global Health, Well, Being, Clayton C. Daley/57/Vice Chmn., CFO/$7,595.00, James J. Johnson/62/Chief Legal Officer - Procter, Gamble Company, Gilbert G. Cloyd/62/CTO, Filippo Passerini/51/Chief Information, Global Services Officer, Charlotte R. Otto/55/Global External Relations Officer, Jeffery K. Schomburger/46/Pres. - Global Wal*mart Team, Edward D. Shirley/52/Group Pres. - North America, Chris Peterson/GM - Investor Relations, John Chevalier/Dir. - Investor Relations, Nathalie Bidal/Assoc. Dir. (58 Officers included in Index)

Directors: Alan G. Lafley/61/Chmn., CEO, Pres., Robert A. McDonald/55/Vice Chmn. - Global Operations, COO, Clayton C. Daley/57/Vice Chmn., CFO, Bruce L. Byrnes/60/Vice Chmn., Norman R. Augustine/73/Dir., Scott D. Cook/56/Dir., Joseph T. Gorman/70/Dir., Charles R. Lee/68/Dir., Lynn M. Martin/68/Dir., James W. McNerney/59/Dir., Johnathan A. Rodgers/62/Dir., John F. Smith/70/Dir., Ralph Snyderman/68/Dir., Margaret C. Whitman/52/Dir., Ernesto Zedillo/56/Dir.

Owners: Susan E. Arnold, Employee Stock Ownership Trust/68.70%, Insiders/0.01%, James M. Kilts, James W. McNerney, Ernesto Zedillo, Charles R. Lee, Norman R. Augustine, Ralph Snyderman, Bruce L. Byrnes, Johnathan A. Rodgers, Scott D. Cook, Lynn M. Martin, A. G. Lafley, Susan E. Arnold (31 Owners included in Index)

Financial Data: Fiscal Year End:06/30   Latest Annual Data: 6/30/2006

Year	Sales	Net Income
2006	$68,222,000,000	$8,684,000,000
2005	$56,741,000,000	$7,257,000,000
2004	$51,407,000,000	$6,481,000,000

Curr. Assets:	$24,031,000,000	Curr. Liab.:	$30,717,000,000	P/E Ratio:	21.19
Plant, Equip.:	$19,540,000,000	Total Liab.:	$71,254,000,000	Indic. Yr. Divd.:	$1.400
Total Assets:	$138,014,000,000	Net Worth:	$66,760,000,000	Debt/ Equity:	NA

Procyon Corp

1300 S Highland Ave., Clearwater, FL, 33756; **PH:** 1-727-443-0530; **Fax:** 1-727-447-5617; http:// www.amerigel.com

General - Incorporation	CO	Stock- Price on:12/24/2007	$0.4
Employees	12	Stock Exchange	OTC
Auditor	Ferlita, Walsh & Gonzalez P.A	Ticker Symbol	PCYN
Stk Agt.	Computershare Investor Services LLC	Outstanding Shares	8,050,000
Counsel	NA	E.P.S.	$0.04
DUNS No.	83-861-7173	Shareholders	NA

Business: The group's principal activity is the development and marketing of proprietary medical products used to treat pressure ulcers, dermatitis, inflammation and other skin problems. The group conducts operations through its two wholly owned subsidiaries, amerx health care corp and sirius medical supply. Amerx health care corp develops and markets proprietary medical products used in the treatment of pressure ulcers, dermatitis, inflammation and other skin problems. Sirius medical supply operates as a full service mail order medical supply company selling primarily to medicare and medicaid customers. Major brands of the group include, amerigel(R) hydrogel wound dressing, amerigel preventive care lotion and amerigel wound wash. The products are sold through distributors to health care institutions and to retailers including national and regional chain stores and pharmacies.

Primary SIC and add'l.: 2834

CIK No: 0000812306

Subsidiaries: Amerx

Officers: Regina W. Anderson/61/Chmn., CEO, James B. Anderson/38/Dir., CFO

Directors: Regina W. Anderson/61/Chmn., CEO, Chester L. Wallack/67/Dir., Justice W. Anderson/31/Dir., James B. Anderson/38/Dir., CFO, Fred W. Suggs/62/Dir., Alan B. Crane/58/Dir., Jeffery S. Slowgrove/51/Dir., Michael T. Foley/70/Dir.

Owners: Chester L. Wallack, Alan B. Crane, Michael T. Foley, James B. Anderson, Justice W. Anderson, Regina W. Anderson, Fred W. Suggs, Jeffery S. Slowgrove, RMS Limited, Insiders

Financial Data: Fiscal Year End:06/30   Latest Annual Data: 6/30/2006

Year	Sales	Net Income
2006	$2,313,000	$342,000
2005	$2,198,000	$315,000
2004	$2,025,000	$258,000

Curr. Assets:	$839,000	Curr. Liab.:	$208,000	P/E Ratio:	8.00
Plant, Equip.:	$63,000	Total Liab.:	$217,000	Indic. Yr. Divd.:	NA
Total Assets:	$911,000	Net Worth:	$694,000	Debt/ Equity:	0.4258

Productivity Technologies Corp

3100 Copper Ave., Fenton, MI, 48430; **PH:** 1-810-714-0200; http:// www.atlastechnologies.com

General - Incorporation	DE	Stock- Price on:12/24/2007	$0.08
Employees	NA	Stock Exchange	OTC
Auditor	Follmer Rudzewicz	Ticker Symbol	PRAC
Stk Agt	Continental Stock Transfer & Trust Co	Outstanding Shares	NA
Counsel	NA	E.P.S.	NA
DUNS No.	NA	Shareholders	NA

Business: The group's principle activities are to manufacture automated industrial systems, machinery, equipment, electrical control panels and provide engineering services. The group operates with three manufacturing plants, sales and engineering offices. The operations are conducted through the subsidiaries, atlas technologies, inc. and westland control systems, inc. The products manufactured include metal stamp presses such as quick die change, flexible transfer, stacking and destacking automation equipment. The products are sold to automobile and automotive parts manufacturers, appliance manufacturers and manufacturers of garden and lawn equipment, office furniture, heating, ventilation and air conditioning equipment and aircraft. The major customers are ford motor company, dana corporation and bmw manufacturing ltd.

Primary SIC and add'l.: 3542

CIK No: 0000911787

Subsidiaries: Atlas Technologies GmbH, Atlas Technologies, Inc, WCS Acquisition Corp

Financial Data: Fiscal Year End:06/30   Latest Annual Data: 6/30/2004

Year	Sales	Net Income
2004	$28,155,000	$721,000
2002	$24,768,000	-$4,128,000
2001	$27,992,000	-$3,114,000

Curr. Assets:	$10,516,000	Curr. Liab.:	$12,460,000		
Plant, Equip.:	$5,569,000	Total Liab.:	$17,048,000	Indic. Yr. Divd.:	NA
Total Assets:	$20,350,000	Net Worth:	$3,301,000	Debt/ Equity:	1.1923

Professional Business Bank

199 S Los Robles Ave. No. 130, Pasadena, CA, 91101; **PH:** 1-626-395-7000; http:// www.probizbank.com; **Email:** customer_service@probizbank.com

General - Incorporation		Stock- Price on:12/24/2007	$19.7
Employees	39	Stock Exchange	NA
Auditor	NA	Ticker Symbol	NA
Stk Agt	U.S. Stock Transfer Corp	Outstanding Shares	NA
Counsel	NA	E.P.S.	NA
DUNS No.	NA	Shareholders	NA

Business: The groups principal activities include providing financial solutions for the clients. Services of the group include savings account, loans and mortgage, credit card facilities, Debit cards, ATM, Investment accounts and Internet banking. The group operates from the United States. In the year 2006, the groups total assets were $161,922,000.

Primary SIC and add'l.: 6029

CIK No:

Officers: Norman O. Broyer/Dir., CEO, Pres., Robert A. Hunt/Sr. VP, Branch Banking Administrator, Edwin J. Fix/Sr. VP, Chief Credit Officer, Michael W. McCall/Sr. VP, CFO

Directors: Norman O. Broyer/Dir., CEO, Pres., Elliot L. Shell/Dir., Walter H. Carleton/Dir., Larry D. Tashjian/Dir., James A. Asher/Dir., Joyce Gaines/Dir., William H. Baribault/Dir., Charles J. Gonzalez/Dir., Don Clark/Dir., Trude C. Taylor/Dir., James G. Ellis/Dir., William D. Truax/Dir., Glenn Yamada/Dir.

Professional Veterinary Products Ltd

10077 S 134th St., Omaha, NE, 68138; **PH:** 1-402-331-4440; **Fax:** 1-402-331-8655; http:// www.pvpl.com

General - Incorporation	NE	Stock- Price on:12/24/2007	NA
Employees	NA	Stock Exchange	NA
Auditor	Quick & McFarlin, P.C	Ticker Symbol	NA
Stk Agt	Dr. Lionel L. Reilly	Outstanding Shares	NA
Counsel	Baird, Holm, McEachen, Pedersen	E.P.S.	NA
DUNS No.	10-230-2700	Shareholders	NA

Business: The group's principal activity is to distribute animal health products to practicing veterinarians. It offers a broad array of prescription, non-prescription and sundry items to assist veterinarians in their practice. It also sells small quantity of feed additive type products. The group acts as a wholesale distributor primarily to shareholders. Shareholders are limited to the ownership of one share of stock and must be a licensed veterinarian or business entity comprised of licensed veterinarians. The group distributes approximately 18,000 different items including biologicals, pharmaceuticals, parasiticides, instruments and equipment. The group primarily sells branded products as marketed by the major animal health manufacturers and suppliers.

Primary SIC and add'l.: 5191 0742 5122

CIK No: 0000947425

Subsidiaries: Exact Logistics, LLC, ProConn, LLC

Officers: Lionel Reilly/CEO, Pres., Neal Soderquist/VP - Finance, CFO, Stephen J. Price/49/COO, Exec. VP, Chris McGonigle/PHR, VP - People, Jamie Meadows/VP - Supply Chain, Leon Thomas/VP - Technology

Directors: G. W. Buckaloo/61/Vice Chmn., Tom Latta/Dir., Scott Shuey/Dir., Steven Wright/Dir., Buddy Ray/Dir., William Swartz/Dir., Donald Janezic/62/Dir., Tom Wakefield/Dir., Sam Morris/Dir.

Owners: G. W. Buckaloo, Eileen Sam Holly Morris, Donald R. Fogle, Tom Latta, Scott A. Shuey, Buddy D. Ray, Thomas E. Wakefield, Vicky Wilkey, Insiders, William Swartz

Professionals Direct Inc

5211 Cascade Rd., S.e., Grand Rapids, MI, 49546; **PH:** 1-616-456-8899;
http:// www.professionalsdirect.com

General - Incorporation	MI	**Stock**- Price on:12/24/2007	$42
Employees	41	Stock Exchange	NA
Auditor	BDO Seidman LLP	Ticker Symbol	NA
Stk Agt	NA	Outstanding Shares	NA
Counsel	NA	E.P.S	$4.53
DUNS No.	NA	Shareholders	NA

Business: The group's principal activity is to provide insurance services through its wholly owned subsidiaries. The subsidiaries include professionals direct insurance company, professionals direct employer organization, inc., professionals direct finance, inc, professionals direct insurance services, inc and professionals direct statutory trust i. The group provides professional liability insurance to attorneys and law firms in Michigan and other states. It markets property and casualty insurance products and is also licensed to sell most types of life and health insurance. The group's other activities include underwriting, policy issuance, claims administration, providing accounting and information systems services to insurance companies and financing of premiums to customers.

Primary SIC and add'l.: 6311

CIK No: 0001158269

Subsidiaries: Professionals Direct Employer Organization, Inc., Professionals Direct Finance, Inc., Professionals Direct Insurance Company, Professionals Direct Insurance Services, Inc., Professionals Direct Statutory Trust I, Professionals Direct Statutory Trust II

Officers: Stephen M. Tuuk/54/Chmn., CEO, Pres., Stephen M. Westfield/46/VP - Finance, Principal Financial, Accounting Officer

Directors: Stephen M. Tuuk/54/Chmn., CEO, Pres., Blake W. Krueger/54/Dir., David W. Crooks/59/Dir., Thomas J. Ryan/60/Dir., Thomas F. Dickinson/51/Dir., Joseph A. Fink/65/Dir.

Owners: Tracy T. Larsen/1.80%, Stephen M. Westfield/3.00%, David W. Crooks/3.30%, Thomas J. Ryan/0.70%, Stephen M. Tuuk/5.00%, Insiders/20.20%, Joseph A. Fink/2.00%, Mary L. Ursul/4.40%

Financial Data: Fiscal Year End:12/31   Latest Annual Data: 12/31/2006

Year	Sales	Net Income
2006	$18,906,000	$1,628,000
2005	$17,491,000	$502,000
2004	$17,979,000	$531,000

Curr. Assets:	$28,200,000	Curr. Liab.:	$4,935,000	P/E Ratio:	9.27
Plant, Equip.:	$529,000	Total Liab.:	$56,886,000	Indic. Yr. Divd.:	NA
Total Assets:	$69,211,000	Net Worth:	$12,325,000	Debt/ Equity:	0.4941

Profile Technologies Inc

260 Cottage St., Ste. C, Littleton, NH, 03561; **PH:** 1-603-444-3388; **Fax:** 1-603-444-3362;
http:// www.profiletechnh.com; **Email:** email@profiletechnh.com

General - Incorporation	DE	**Stock**- Price on:12/24/2007	$1.1
Employees	4	Stock Exchange	OTC
Auditor	Peterson Sullivan PLLC	Ticker Symbol	PRTK
Stk Agt	NA	Outstanding Shares	12,730,000
Counsel	Ncguire Woods	E.P.S	-$0.14
DUNS No.	92-978-7547	Shareholders	NA

Business: The group's principle activities include research and development of high speed scanning process to test remotely buried, encased and insulated pipelines for corrosion. Its electromagnetic wave inspection process (emw) is nondestructive and noninvasive. It is a patented process of analyzing the waveforms of electrical impulses in a way that extracts point-to-point information along a segment of pipeline to illustrate the integrity of the entire pipeline. Its emw process is designed to detect external corrosion of pipelines which occurs under pipe insulation and on buried pipes. The company has developed two basic emw inspection techniques namely dual pulse or pulse propagation analyzer and single-pulse or calibration mark z. These techniques provide an assessment of the overall integrity of the pipe in question and the location and classification of electromagnetic anomalies. The customers of the company include large petrochemical, utility and petroleum companies. The group operates from United States.

Primary SIC and add'l.: 7389

CIK No: 0001014653

Officers: Henry E. Gemino/57/Dir., Co - Founder, CEO, CFO, Murphy Evans/76/Chmn., Pres., Robert C. Geib/37/COO, Philip L. Jones/65/Exec. VP

Directors: Henry E. Gemino/57/Dir., Co - Founder, CEO, CFO, Murphy Evans/76/Chmn., Pres., Charles Christenson/78/Dir., Richard L. Palmer/64/Dir.

Owners: Charles Christenson, Henry E. Gemino, Richard L. Palmer, Gale D. Burnett, Philip L. Jones, Insiders, Murphy Evans

Financial Data: Fiscal Year End:06/30   Latest Annual Data: 06/30/2007

Year	Sales	Net Income
2007	NA	-$1,825,000
2006	NA	-$1,232,000
2005	NA	-$1,147,000

Curr. Assets:	$865,000	Curr. Liab.:	$1,256,000		
Plant, Equip.:	$16,000	Total Liab.:	$1,256,000	Indic. Yr. Divd.:	NA
Total Assets:	$883,000	Net Worth:	-$373,000	Debt/ Equity:	NA

Progen Industries Ltd

16 Benson St., Toowong, Queensland, 4066; **PH:** 61-7384-23333; http:// www.progen.com.au

General - Incorporation	Australia	**Stock**- Price on:12/24/2007	$4.21
Employees	NA	Stock Exchange	NDQ
Auditor	Ernst & Young LLP	Ticker Symbol	PGLA
Stk Agt	Computershare Investor Services LLC	Outstanding Shares	44,320,000
Counsel	NA	E.P.S	NA
DUNS No.	75-869-0101	Shareholders	NA

Business: The group's principle activities are the discovery, research and development of potential biopharmaceutical therapeutics for the treatment of human diseases; import and distribution of biological and chemical reagents and kits for a select group of international companies; and provision of contracting services related to the process development, manufacture and quality assurance of biological products. Products include small molecule semi-synthetic oligosaccharides (short sugar chains) and glycomimetics with anti-angiogenic, anti-metastatic and anti-thrombotic properties which is being developed as both a cancer and cardiovascular product, high quality chemical and biological reagents such as acrylamide, agarose, biochemical reagents and buffers, dna/ rna modifying enzymes and streptavidin. Contracting services offered include the manufacture of biopoducts.

Primary SIC and add'l.: 8731 5169 2899 2836 5122 2834

CIK No: 0000943502

Officers: Justus Homburg/CEO, Stephen Chang/Exec. Chmn., Sarah Meibusch/VP - Business Development, Linton Burns/Company Sec., CFO, Anand Gautam/VP - Research, Development, James Garner/VP - Clinical, Medical Affairs, John Devlin/VP - Manufacturing Operations

Directors: Stephen Chang/Exec. Chmn., Malvin L. Eutick/Non Exec. Dir., John R. Zalcberg/Non Exec. Dir., Patrick Burns/Non Exec. Dir.

Owners: Northcape Capital Pty Ltd/6.02%, Justus T. Homburg, Linton W. P. Burns, Insiders/1.40%, Malvin L. Eutick, John R. Zalcberg, Stephen Chang/1.40%, Patrick O. Burns, Manifest Capital Management Pty Ltd/5.96%

Financial Data: Fiscal Year End:06/30   Latest Annual Data: 06/30/2007

Year	Sales	Net Income
2007	$723,000	-$16,723,000
2006	$677,000	-$5,227,000
2005	$1,076,000	-$4,548,000

Curr. Assets:	$12,029,000	Curr. Liab.:	$1,170,000		
Plant, Equip.:	$1,066,000	Total Liab.:	$1,367,000	Indic. Yr. Divd.:	NA
Total Assets:	$13,159,000	Net Worth:	$11,792,000	Debt/ Equity:	NA

Progenics Pharmaceuticals Inc

777 Old Saw Mill River Rd., Tarrytown, NY, 10591; **PH:** 1-914-789-2800; **Fax:** 1-914-789-2817;
http:// www.progenics.com; **Email:** info@progenics.com

General - Incorporation	DE	**Stock**- Price on:12/24/2007	$23
Employees	191	Stock Exchange	NDQ
Auditor	PricewaterhouseCoopers LLP	Ticker Symbol	PGNX
Stk Agt	American Stock Transfer & Trust Co.	Outstanding Shares	26,550,000
Counsel	Dewey Ballantine	E.P.S	-$0.67
DUNS No.	19-555-1247	Shareholders	NA

Business: The group's principle activities include developing and commercializing therapeutic products to treat the unmet medical needs of patients with debilitating conditions and life-threatening diseases. The company's programs are directed towards symptom management and supportive care for HIV infection and cancer. The products developed by the company include methylnaltrexone (mntx), pro 542, pro 140, provax, gmk vaccine and psma. The group operates from United States.

Primary SIC and add'l.: 8731 2834 2836

CIK No: 0000835887

Subsidiaries: Progenics Pharmaceuticals Nevada, Inc.

Officers: Paul J. Maddon/Founder, CEO, Chief Science Officer/$4,604,038.00, Nitya G. Ray/VP - Manufacturing, Walter M. Capone/VP - Commercial Development, Operations, Thomas A. Boyd/Sr. VP - Product Development/$1,043,197.00, Robert A. McKinney/CFO, Sr. VP - Finance, Operations, Treasurer/$774,499.00, Robert J. Israel/Sr. VP - Medical Affairs, Benedict Osorio/VP - Quality, Lynn M. Bodarky/42/VP - Marketing, Methylnaltrexone Brand Team, Richard W. Krawiec/VP - Corporate Affairs, Stephen P. Goff/Dir., Member - Scientific Advisory Board, William C. Olson/VP - Research, Development, Alton B. Kremer/VP - Clinical Research/$884,984.00, Mark R. Baker/Sr. VP, General Counsel/$1,048,960.00

Directors: Paul J. Maddon/Founder, CEO, Chief Science Officer, Kurt W. Briner/Co - Chmn., Paul F. Jacobson/Co - Chmn., Alan N. Houghton/Chmn. - Scientific Advisory Board, David B. Agus/Member - Scientific Advisory Board, Sherie L. Morrison/Member - Scientific Advisory Board, Robin A. Weiss/Member - Scientific Advisory Board, Samuel J. Danishefsky/Member - Scientific Advisory Board, Warren D.W. Heston/Member - Scientific Advisory Board, Philip O. Livingston/Member - Scientific Advisory Board, John Mendelsohn/Member - Scientific Advisory Board, David A. Scheinberg/Dir., Member - Scientific Advisory Board, Stephen P. Goff/Dir., Member - Scientific Advisory Board, Mark F. Dalton/Dir., Nicole S. Williams/Dir. *(20 Directors included in Index)*

Owners: Paul J. Maddon/6.40%, Mark F. Dalton/9.40%, Federated Investors, Inc./6.50%, Sectoral Asset Management Inc./8.90%, Alton B. Kremer, Mark R. Baker, Paul Tudor Jones/10.90%, Thomas A. Boyd, David A. Scheinberg, Kurt W. Briner, Paul F. Jacobson/1.10%, Insiders/21.00%, Stephen P. Goff, Robert A. McKinney, Charles A. Baker *(18 Owners included in Index)*

Financial Data: Fiscal Year End:12/31   Latest Annual Data: 12/31/2006

Year	Sales	Net Income
2006	$69,906,000	-$21,618,000
2005	$9,486,000	-$69,429,000
2004	$9,576,000	-$42,018,000

Curr. Assets:	$130,668,000	Curr. Liab.:	$38,841,000		
Plant, Equip.:	$11,387,000	Total Liab.:	$55,065,000	Indic. Yr. Divd.:	NA
Total Assets:	$165,911,000	Net Worth:	$110,846,000	Debt/ Equity:	NA

Proginet Corp

200 Garden City Plz., Ste. 220, Garden City, NY, 11530; **PH:** 1-516-535-3600;
Fax: 1-516-535-3601; http:// www.proginet.com; **Email:** info@proginet.com

General - Incorporation	DE	**Stock**- Price on:12/24/2007	$1.4
Employees	46	Stock Exchange	OTC
Auditor	BDO Seidman LLP	Ticker Symbol	PRGF
Stk Agt	Mellon Trust Co	Outstanding Shares	14,510,000
Counsel	NA	E.P.S	$0.04
DUNS No.	NA	Shareholders	NA

Business: The groups principle activity is to develop enterprise security software. The groups products include CyberFusion(R), CyberFusion Integration Suite(TM), SecurForce(R), SecurAccess(R), and SecurPass(R). The group provides services include project management, requirements analysis, security assessment, quick start installation programs, implementation and deployment, and control and compliance programs. The group operates from United States.

Primary SIC and add'l.: 7370

CIK No: 0000934868

Officers: Kevin M. Kelly/Dir., CEO, Pres., Arne H. Johnson/59/Sr. VP, Jack Gazzola/Sr. VP - Sales, Kevin Bohan/CIO, Debra A. Dimaria/CFO, Corp. Sec., Thomas C. Bauer/CTO, John W. Gazzola/54/Sr. VP - Sales

Directors: Kevin M. Kelly/Dir., CEO, Pres., John C. Daily/65/Chmn., George T. Hawes/Dir., Stephen Sternbach/Dir., William Loscalzo/Dir., Kelly Hyslop/Dir., Amit K. Basak/34/Dir., Stephen Kezirian/34/Dir.

Owners: John W. Gazzola/0.85%, Scot Cohen/9.95%, Kevin M. Kelly/6.43%, William Loscalzo/0.81%, Insiders/26.32%, Arne H. Johnson/1.27%, John C. Daily/2.57%, Kelly E. Hyslop/3.64%, John Mazzone/8.88%, The Red Oak Fund, LP/8.70%, George T. Hawes/5.79%, Stephen Sternbach/1.03%

Financial Data: Fiscal Year End:07/31 **Latest Annual Data:** 07/31/2007

Year	Sales	Net Income
2007	$9,377,000	$937,000
2006	$8,498,000	$585,000
2005	$7,899,000	-$489,000

Curr. Assets:	$3,142,000	**Curr. Liab.:**	$3,274,000	**P/E Ratio:**	23.33
Plant, Equip.:	$197,000	**Total Liab.:**	$3,439,000	**Indic. Yr. Divd.:**	NA
Total Assets:	$8,553,000	**Net Worth:**	$5,114,000	**Debt/ Equity:**	NA

Progress Energy Inc

410 S Wilmington St., Raleigh, NC, 27601; *PH:* 1-919-546-6111; *Fax:* 1-919-546-2920; *http://* www.progress-energy.com

General - Incorporation	NC	Stock - Price on:12/24/2007	$47.43
Employees	11,000	Stock Exchange	NYSE
Auditor	Deloitte & Touche LLP	Ticker Symbol	PGN
Stk Agt.... Computershare Investor Services LLC		Outstanding Shares	257,860,000
Counsel	One Equity Partners LLC	E.P.S.	$2.57
DUNS No.	NA	Shareholders	NA

Business: The groups principle activities include generating and distributing electricity and natural gas. The group operates from United States.

Primary SIC and add'l.: 5984 4923 4911 7389 8711 3743

CIK No: 0001094093

Subsidiaries: Carolina Power & Light Company d/b/a Progress Energy Carolinas, Inc., Florida Power Corporation d/b/a/ Progress Energy Florida, Inc., Florida Progress Corporation, Progress Capital Holdings, Inc., Progress Energy Service Company, LLC, Progress Fuels Corporation, Progress Telecom, LLC, Progress Telecommunications Corporation, Progress Ventures, Inc. d/b/a Progress Energy Ventures, Inc, PV Holdings, Inc., Strategic Resource Solutions Corp.

Officers: Robert B. McGehee/Chmn., CEO/$9,857,281.00, William D. Johnson/Chmn., CEO, Pres./$3,818,970.00, Peter M. Scott/CFO - Progress Energy, Inc, CEO, Pres. - Progress Energy Service Company/$4,197,537.00, Fred N. Day/64/CEO, Pres./$1,717,523.00, Jeffrey J. Lyash/CEO, Pres. - Progress Energy Florida, Lloyd M. Yates/CEO, Pres. - Progress Energy Carolinas, David J. Maxon/VP - North Central Region, Progress Energy Florida, Mitch Perry/VP - Finance, Progress Energy Carolinas, Tucker R. Mann/VP - Customer, Marketing Services, Progress Energy Carolinas, Progress Energy Florida, Bob Adrian/VP - Competitive Commercial Operations, Progress Ventures, Inc, Rodney E. Gaddy/VP - Corporate Services, Progress Energy Carolinas, Progress Energy Florida, Progress Energy Service Company, Robert F. Drennan/VP - Investor Relations, Progress Energy Service Company, Charles M. Gates/VP - Power Generation, Progress Energy Florida, Thomas R. Sullivan/Chief Risk Officer, VP, Treasurer - Treasury, Enterprise Risk Management, Progress Energy Service Company, Nancy H. Temple/VP - Corporate Communications, Progress Energy Service Company (54 Officers included in Index)

Directors: Robert B. McGehee/Chmn., CEO, Edwin B. Borden/Dir., Robert W. Jones/Dir., Charles W. Pryor/Dir., James E. Bostic/Dir., David L. Burner/Dir., Richard L. Daugherty/Dir., Harris E. Deloach/Dir., W. D. Frederick/Dir., Steven W. Jones/Dir., Marie E. McKee/Dir., John H. Mullin/Dir., Carlos A. Saladrigas/Dir., Theresa M. Stone/Dir., Alfred C. Tollison/Dir.

Owners: Theresa M. Stone, Peter M. Scott, David L. Burner, Alfred C. Tollison, Clayton S. Hinnant, Harris E. DeLoach, William D. Johnson, W. D. Frederick, Fred N. Day, Marie E. McKee, John H. Mullin, Richard L. Daugherty, Steven W. Jones, Insiders, Carlos A. Saladrigas (20 Owners included in Index)

Financial Data: Fiscal Year End:12/31 **Latest Annual Data:** 12/31/2006

Year	Sales	Net Income
2006	$9,570,000,000	$571,000,000
2005	$10,108,000,000	$697,000,000
2004	$9,772,000,000	$759,000,000

Curr. Assets:	$3,585,000,000	**Curr. Liab.:**	$2,818,000,000	**P/E Ratio:**	14.92
Plant, Equip.:	$15,732,000,000	**Total Liab.:**	$17,312,000,000	**Indic. Yr. Divd.:**	$2.460
Total Assets:	$25,701,000,000	**Net Worth:**	$8,379,000,000	**Debt/ Equity:**	NA

Progress Software Corp

14 Oak Pk. Dr., Bedford, MA, 01730; *PH:* 1-781-280-4000; *Fax:* 1-781-280-4095; *http://* www.progress.com

General - Incorporation	MA	Stock - Price on:12/24/2007	$33.17
Employees	1,661	Stock Exchange	NDQ
Auditor	Deloitte & Touche LLP	Ticker Symbol	PRGS
Stk Agt...... American Stock Transfer & Trust Co.		Outstanding Shares	41,020,000
Counsel	Goodwin Procter LLP	E.P.S.	$0.96
DUNS No.	10-885-4894	Shareholders	NA

Business: The group's principal activities are to develop, market and distribute software for the development, deployment, integration and management of business applications. The products include development tools, databases, application servers, messaging servers, application management tools and integration products for distributed and Web-based applications as well as for client/server and host/terminal applications. Progress, webspeed, objectstore and provision are registered trademarks of the group. The group competes in various markets with a number of entities including database vendors

offering development tools in conjunction with their database systems, such as IBM, microsoft corporation, oracle corporation and sybase, inc. The principal international markets served by the group, include Europe, Middle East and Africa (emea), Latin America and Asia. On 19-Dec-2002, the group acquired excelon corporation.

Primary SIC and add'l.: 7372 7379 7378 7373

CIK No: 0000876167

Subsidiaries: Actional Corporation, Actional Technologies, Ltd., Apama Inc., Apama Limited, DataDirect Technologies Corp., DataDirect Technologies GmbH, DataDirect Technologies KK, DataDirect Technologies Ltd., DataDirect Technologies NV, EasyAsk Corporation, NEON Systems Quebec, Inc., NEON Systems UK Ltd, NEON Systems, Inc., Object Design S.a.r.l., PeerDirect Company 59 Subsidiaries included in the Index

Officers: Joseph W. Alsop/Dir., Co - Founder, CEO, James D. Freedman/Sr. VP, General Counsel, John Stewart/Primary Investor Relations Officer, David H. Benton/VP, Corporate Controller, Principal Accounting Officer, Richard D. Reidy/Pres. - Datadirect Technologies, Larry R. Harris/VP, GM - Easyask Products, David G. Ireland/Pres. - Openedge Division, Sr. VP - Progress Field Operations, Peter G. Sliwkowski/VP - Products, Enterprise Infrastructure Division, Gordon Van Huizen/VP - Sonic, Actional Products, Greg O'Connor/VP - Corporate Development, Strategy, Norman R. Robertson/Sr. VP - Finance, Administration, CFO, Jeffrey P. Stamen/Sr. VP - Corporate Development, Strategy, Joseph A. Andrews/VP - Human Resources

Directors: Joseph W. Alsop/Dir., Co - Founder, CEO, Michael L. Mark/Chmn., Roger J. Heinen/Dir., Scott A. McGregor/Dir., Barry Bycoff/Dir., Charles Kane/Dir.

Owners: T. Rowe Price Associates, Inc./8.10%, FMR Corp./5.80%, Joseph W. Alsop/5.40%, David G. Ireland, Insiders/10.00%, Scott A. McGregor, Roger J. Heinen, Charles F. Kane, Barclays Global Investors, N.A./5.20%, Michael L. Mark, Amram Rasiel/1.40%, Norman R. Robertson, James D. Freedman, Richard D. Reidy/1.00%, Private Capital Management, L.P./7.80%

Financial Data: Fiscal Year End:11/30 **Latest Annual Data:** 05/31/2007

Year	Sales	Net Income
2007	NA	NA
2006	$447,063,000	$29,401,000
2005	$405,376,000	$46,257,000

Curr. Assets:	$360,139,000	**Curr. Liab.:**	$214,169,000	**P/E Ratio:**	43.64
Plant, Equip.:	$57,585,000	**Total Liab.:**	$225,675,000	**Indic. Yr. Divd.:**	NA
Total Assets:	$670,239,000	**Net Worth:**	$444,564,000	**Debt/ Equity:**	0.0035

Progressive Corp

6300 Wilson Mills Rd., Mayfield Village, OH, 44143; *PH:* 1-440-461-5000; *Fax:* 1-800-456-6590; *http://* www.progressive.com

General - Incorporation	OH	Stock - Price on:12/24/2007	$23.5
Employees	27,778	Stock Exchange	NYSE
Auditor	PricewaterhouseCoopers LLP	Ticker Symbol	PGR
Stk Agt	National City Bank	Outstanding Shares	736,220,000
Counsel	Baker & Hostetler	E.P.S.	$1.93
DUNS No.	04-841-5509	Shareholders	NA

Business: The group's principle activity is to provide insurance services. The groups services include home and property, and vehicle insurance. The group operates from United States.

Primary SIC and add'l.: 6331 6719

CIK No: 0000080661

Subsidiaries: 3841189 Canada, Inc., Bayside Underwriters Insurance Agency, Inc., Commercial Resource Services Company, Drive Insurance Holdings, Inc., Drive New Jersey Insurance Company, Drive Resource Services Company, Garden Sun Insurance Services, Inc., Greenberg Financial Insurance Services, Inc., Insurance Confirmation Services, Inc., Lakeside Insurance Agency, Inc., Midland Financial Group, Inc., Midland Risk Services, Inc., Mountain Laurel Assurance Company, National Continental Insurance Company, Pacific Motor Club 70 Subsidiaries included in the Index

Officers: Glenn M. Renwick/53/Dir., CEO, Pres./$5,434,879.00, Brian C. Domeck/49/CFO, VP, Thomas A. King/48/VP, Treasurer, Jeffrey W. Basch/50/VP, Chief Accounting Officer, Charles E. Jarrett/51/Chief Legal Officer, VP, Sec./$1,170,531.00, John A. Barbagallo/49/Group Pres. - Drive Business, William M. Cody/46/Chief Investment Officer/$1,341,054.00, Susan Patricia Griffith/Chief Human Resources Officer, Brian J. Passell/52/Group Pres. - Claims/$1,418,922.00, John P. Sauerland/44/Group Pres. - Direct Business, Brian A. Silva/55/Group Pres. - Commercial Auto Business, Raymond M. Voelker/45/CIO

Directors: Glenn M. Renwick/53/Dir., CEO, Pres., Peter B. Lewis/75/Chmn., Philip A. Laskawy/67/Dir., Norman S. Matthews/75/Dir., Patrick H. Nettles/65/Dir., Charles A. Davis/60/Dir., Stephen R. Hardis/73/Dir., Bernadine P. Healy/64/Dir., Abby F. Kohnstamm/55/Dir., Donald B. Shackelford/76/Dir., Bradley T. Sheares/51/Dir., Jeffrey D. Kelly/55/Dir.

Owners: Insiders/7.80%, Bernadine P. Healy, Abby F. Kohnstamm, Thomas W. Forrester, Ruane, Cunniff& Goldfarb Inc./10.30%, Stephen R. Hardis, Davis Selected Advisers, L.P./10.80%, Charles E. Jarrett, William M. Cody, The TCW Group, Inc./6.10%, Glenn M. Renwick, Brian J. Passell, Donald B. Shackelford, Norman S. Matthews, Patrick H. Nettles (20 Owners included in Index)

Financial Data: Fiscal Year End:12/31 **Latest Annual Data:** 12/31/2006

Year	Sales	Net Income
2006	$14,786,400,000	$1,647,500,000
2005	$14,303,400,000	$1,393,900,000
2004	$13,782,100,000	$1,648,700,000

Curr. Assets:	$3,608,300,000	**Curr. Liab.:**	$1,390,000,000	**P/E Ratio:**	11.52
Plant, Equip.:	$973,400,000	**Total Liab.:**	$12,635,500,000	**Indic. Yr. Divd.:**	$0.040
Total Assets:	$19,482,100,000	**Net Worth:**	$6,846,600,000	**Debt/ Equity:**	NA

Proguard Acquisition Corp

3040 E Commercial Blvd, Ft. Lauderdale, FL, 33308; *PH:* 1-954-491-0704

General - Incorporation	FL	Stock - Price on:12/24/2007	NA
Employees	NA	Stock Exchange	OTC
Auditor	Sherb & Co., LLP	Ticker Symbol	PGRD
Stk Agt	Cottonwood Stock Transfer	Outstanding Shares	2,780,000
Counsel	NA	E.P.S.	-$0.09
DUNS No.	NA	Shareholders	NA

Business: The groups principal activity is common stock purchase and sale agreement with Corrections Systems International, Inc. The group operates from the United States.

Primary SIC and add'l.: 7382

CIK No: 0001300662

Subsidiaries: Proguard Protection Services, Inc.

Officers: Frank R. Bauer/63/Dir., CEO, Pres., Norman H. Becker/70/Dir., Treasurer, CFO, Controller, Ricardo A. Rivera/37/Dir., VP, Sec.

Directors: Frank R. Bauer/63/Dir., CEO, Pres., Norman H. Becker/70/Dir., Treasurer, CFO, Controller, Ricardo A. Rivera/37/Dir., VP, Sec.

Owners: Frank R. Bauer/20.39%, Insiders/26.55%, Norman H. Becker/3.63%, Carmine Catizone/7.44%, Pasquale Catizone/3.43%, Frank R. Bauer/4.69%, Ricardo A. Rivera/2.53%, Plymouth Capital, Inc./5.41%

Financial Data: ***Fiscal Year End:*** 12/31 ***Latest Annual Data:*** 12/31/2006

Year	Sales	Net Income
2006	$11,000	-$114,000

Curr. Assets:	$454,000	**Curr. Liab.:**	$2,000		
Plant, Equip.:	NA	**Total Liab.:**	$2,000	**Indic. Yr. Divd.:**	NA
Total Assets:	$454,000	**Net Worth:**	$452,000	**Debt/ Equity:**	NA

ProLink Holdings Corp

410 S Benson Ln., Chandler, AZ, 85224; ***PH:*** 1-480-961-8800; ***Fax:*** 1-480-961-8537; ***http://*** www.goprolink.com; ***Email:*** sales@goprolink.com

General - Incorporation .... DE
Employees 117
Auditor .... Marchal & Cooper, LLP
Stk Agt .... American Stock Transfer & Trust Co.
Counsel .... NA
DUNS No. .... NA

Stock - Price on:12/24/2007 .... $1.25
Stock Exchange .... OTC
Ticker Symbol .... PLKH
Outstanding Shares 37,560,000
E.P.S .... -$0.28
Shareholders .... NA

Business: The groups principle activities include designing, manufacturing and selling electronic distance measurement and course management systems to golf course owners and operators. The group markets its products under the tradenames include ParView(R) and ProLink (R). The group operates from the United States.

Primary SIC and add'l.: 7372

CIK No: 0001072816

Subsidiaries: ProLink Solutions, LLC

Officers: Lawrence Bain/CEO - Prolink Solutions/$471,000.00, Andy Batkin/CEO - Prolink Media, Prolink Solutions, Dave M. Gomez/VP, General Counsel - Prolink Solutions/$164,889.00, Gerard L. Johnson/Sr. VP - Operations, Prolink Solutions, Dale Miller/Sr. VP - Sales, Prolink Solutions, John Godshall/CTO - Prolink Solutions, Scott Murr/VP - Finance, Prolink Solutions, Steven N. Tanis/VP - Engineering, Prolink Solutions, Jeffrey E. Cline/VP - Institutional Sales, Prolink Solutions, Chris Kager/Exec. VP - Prolink Media, Prolink Solutions, Pat Parenti/Sr. VP - International Sales, Prolink Solutions, Cameron Kohn/Contact - Press, Danny Lam/Pres. - Prolink Solutions/$1,658,170.00, David Rivers/Exec. VP - Prolink Solutions, Michael S. Browne/CFO, COO - Prolink Solutions *(17 Officers included in Index)*

Directors: William Fugazy/Vice Chmn. - Prolink Solutions, Steve Fisher/Chmn. - Prolink Solutions, Andrew L. Wing/52/Dir., Robert Ellin/41/Dir., Jay Wolf/34/Dir., Barry I. Regenstein/50/Dir.

Owners: Jay Wolf/14.90%, Christopher Wightman, Danny Lam/1.10%, William D. Fugazy/4.00%, Insiders/40.40%, Barry I. Regenstein, Charles Sherman, Ashford Capital Partners, LP/6.00%, Lawrence D. Bain/7.60%, Barry A. Sullivan, Dave M. Gomez, Trinad Capital Master Fund, Ltd./14.90%, Robert Ellin/14.90%, Steven D. Fisher/16.60%

Financial Data: ***Fiscal Year End:*** 12/31 ***Latest Annual Data:*** 12/31/2006

Year	Sales	Net Income
2006	$23,450,000	-$3,643,000
2005	$16,180,000	-$3,371,000
2004	NA	-$729,000

Curr. Assets:	$8,073,000	**Curr. Liab.:**	$12,302,000		
Plant, Equip.:	$5,260,000	**Total Liab.:**	$16,011,000	**Indic. Yr. Divd.:**	NA
Total Assets:	$16,602,000	**Net Worth:**	$590,000	**Debt/ Equity:**	NA

Prologic Mgmt Systems Inc

2708 E Columbia St., No. 110, Tucson, AZ, 85714; ***PH:*** 1-520-747-4100; ***http://*** www.prologic.com

General - Incorporation .... AZ
Employees 1
Auditor .... Epstein Weber & Conover, PLC
Stk Agt .... American Stock Transfer & Trust Co.
Counsel .... NA
DUNS No. 11-805-4238

Stock - Price on:12/24/2007 .... $0.03
Stock Exchange .... OTC
Ticker Symbol .... PRLO
Outstanding Shares .... NA
E.P.S .... NA
Shareholders .... NA

Business: The group's principal activities are to provide commercial systems integration and professional services firm, specializing in high-availability, fully integrated systems, providing systems integration services, networking services, security and database software for the commercial market. It operates through its wholly owned subsidiary, basis, inc. In fiscal 2004 company discontinued some of the activities.

Primary SIC and add'l.: 7379 7372 7373

CIK No: 0000938320

Subsidiaries: Arizona orporation

Financial Data: ***Fiscal Year End:*** 03/31 ***Latest Annual Data:*** 3/31/2006

Year	Sales	Net Income
2006	NA	-$176,000
2005	NA	$2,585,000
2004	NA	$7,019,000

Curr. Assets:	$0	**Curr. Liab.:**	$1,606,000		
Plant, Equip.:	NA	**Total Liab.:**	$1,606,000	**Indic. Yr. Divd.:**	NA
Total Assets:	$0	**Net Worth:**	-$2,333,000	**Debt/ Equity:**	NA

ProLogis

4545 Airport Way, Denver, CO, 80239; ***PH:*** 1-303-567-5000; ***Fax:*** 1-303-567-5605; ***http://*** www.prologis.com; ***Email:*** info@prologis.com

General - Incorporation .... MD
Employees 1,270
Auditor .... KPMG LLP
Stk Agt .... Computershare Trust Co
Counsel .... NA
DUNS No. .... NA

Stock - Price on:12/24/2007 .... $58.1
Stock Exchange .... NYSE
Ticker Symbol .... PLD
Outstanding Shares 256,600,000
E.P.S $3.49
Shareholders .... NA

Business: The groups principle activities include owning, managing and developing of industrial distribution facilities. In the year 2006, the group acquired 895 acres of land. The group operates from the United States, Europe, Asia and Mexico. The groups quarterly revenue for September 2007 was 3462.22 millions of USD.

Primary SIC and add'l.: 6798

CIK No: 0000899881

Subsidiaries: Allagash Property Trust, Bergstrom Partners LP, Brazos Property Trust, Cimmaron Property Trust, CSI/Frigo LLC, Deerfield Property Trust, Elkhorn Property Trust, International Industrial Investments Incorporated, International Rivercenter, Keystone Realty Services Incorporated, Korea Investments (1)Incorporated, Korea Investments (2)Incorporated, KPJV LLP, Macquarie-ProLogis Management LLC, Meridian Realty Partners, LP 112 Subsidiaries included in the Index

Officers: Jeffrey H. Schwartz/Chmn., CEO/$4,679,278.00, Robert J. Watson/CEO - Prologis European Properties, Edward S. Nekritz/General Counsel, Sec./$1,263,704.00, Gary E. Anderson/COO - Europe, Pres., Ming Z. Mei/Pres. - China, Walter C. Rakowich/Trustee, COO, Pres./$4,014,261.00, Ted R. Antenucci/Chief Investment Officer, Pres./$4,040,140.00, Dessa M. Bokides/48/CFO, Exec. VP/$2,337,128.00, Masato Miki/Co - Pres. - Japan, Mike Yamada/Co - Pres. - Japan, Paul Congleton/MD - North American Fund Management, Ranald A. Hahn/MD - Southern Europe, Kenneth Hall/MD - Global Development, United Kingdom, Larry H. Harmsen/MD - North American Capital Deployment, Eric D. Brown/Sr. VP, Regional Dir. - Operations *(46 Officers included in Index)*

Directors: Jeffrey H. Schwartz/Chmn., CEO, John Cutts/Vice Chmn. - Europe, Michael D. Steuert/Trustee, William D. Zollars/Trustee, Andre J. Teixeira/Trustee, Andrea M. Zulberti/Trustee, Walter C. Rakowich/Trustee, COO, Pres., Dane K. Brooksher/Trustee, Stephen L. Feinberg/Trustee, George L. Fotiades/Trustee, Christine Garvey/Trustee, Donald P. Jacobs/Trustee, Nelson C. Rising/Trustee

Owners: Edward S. Nekritz, Donald P. Jacobs, Insiders/1.69%, Stephen L. Feinberg, William D. Zollars, George L. Fotiades, Andrea M. Zulberti, Dane K. Brooksher, Walter C. Rakowich, Andr J. Teixeira, Michael D. Steuert, Jeffrey H. Schwartz, Nelson C. Rising, Christine N. Garvey, Dessa M. Bokides *(16 Owners included in Index)*

Financial Data: ***Fiscal Year End:*** 12/31 ***Latest Annual Data:*** 12/31/2006

Year	Sales	Net Income
2006	$2,463,909,000	$874,367,000
2005	$1,868,041,000	$396,163,000
2004	$598,139,000	$232,795,000

Curr. Assets:	$1,131,294,000	**Curr. Liab.:**	$794,866,000		
Plant, Equip.:	$12,702,416,000	**Total Liab.:**	$9,504,946,000	**Indic. Yr. Divd.:**	$1.840
Total Assets:	$15,903,525,000	**Net Worth:**	$6,398,579,000	**Debt/ Equity:**	1.3601

Prolong International Corp

6 Thomas, Irvine, CA, 92618; ***PH:*** 1-714-587-2700; ***http://*** www.prolong.com

General - Incorporation .... NV
Employees .... NA
Auditor .... Haskell & White LLP
Stk Agt .... Continental Stock Transfer & Trust Co
Counsel .... NA
DUNS No. 92-630-4403

Stock - Price on:12/24/2007 .... $0.003
Stock Exchange .... OTC
Ticker Symbol .... PRLI
Outstanding Shares .... NA
E.P.S .... NA
Shareholders .... NA

Business: The group's principle activity is to manufacture, sell and distribute a patented line of performance lubricants and automotive appearance products. The group markets a variety of products based on anti-friction metal treatment (afmt). The products of the group include prolong series of engine treatment, transmission treatment, gas/diesel fuel system treatment, super penetrating lubricant, and multi-purpose precision oil. The customers of the group include the consumer automotive, consumer household, industrial users and federal, state and local governments. The products are marketed in the United States, Canada, Mexico, Puerto Rico, Central America, China, Hong Kong, Japan, Thailand, sub-saharan Africa, Brazil, Chile, Germany, turkey, hungary and slovakia. The group distributes its products through automotive after market chain stores, mass merchandisers, independent distributors, direct response television sales and Internet.

Primary SIC and add'l.: 5172 2842 2851 2992

CIK No: 0001016965

Subsidiaries: Prolong International Holdings Ltd, Prolong International Ltd, Prolong Super Lubricants, Inc

Financial Data: ***Fiscal Year End:*** 12/31 ***Latest Annual Data:*** 09/30/2005

Year	Sales	Net Income
2005	NA	NA
2004	$7,910,000	-$2,855,000
2003	$8,351,000	-$2,206,000

Curr. Assets:	$2,348,000	**Curr. Liab.:**	$3,118,000		
Plant, Equip.:	$139,000	**Total Liab.:**	$5,230,000	**Indic. Yr. Divd.:**	NA
Total Assets:	$8,844,000	**Net Worth:**	$3,615,000	**Debt/ Equity:**	0.9640

Promotora Valle Hermosa Corp

1809 E Broadway St., Ste. 346, Oviedo, FL, 32765; ***PH:*** 1-800-377-2137; ***Fax:*** 1-877-231-0495; ***http://*** www.promotoravh.com; ***Email:*** promotoravh@earthlink.net

General - Incorporation .... FL
Employees .... NA
Auditor .... Wiener, Goodman & Co., P.c.
Stk Agt .... Pacific Stock Transfer Company
Counsel .... Goldberg Law Group
DUNS No. .... NA

Stock - Price on:12/24/2007 .... $0.055
Stock Exchange .... OTC
Ticker Symbol .... PVHI
Outstanding Shares .... NA
E.P.S .... NA
Shareholders .... NA

Business: The groups principle activity is engaged in the production and distribution of wines. The group operates from the United States.

Primary SIC and add'l.: 1520

CIK No: 0001093800

Subsidiaries: Maria Paz Housing Complex

Officers: Ramon E. Rosales/CEO, Maria Fernanda Rosales/34/Chmn., Pres./$19,500.00, Maria Gracia Rosales/29/Dir., CFO/$4,550.00, Fanny Patricia Marin/46/Dir., Sec., Treasurer

Directors: Maria Fernanda Rosales/34/Chmn., Pres., Maria Gracia Rosales/29/Dir., CFO, Fanny Patricia Marin/46/Dir., Sec., Treasurer

Owners: Ramon Rosales/7.00%, Maria Fernanda Rosales/25.00%, Maria Gracia Roasales/28.00%

Financial Data: Fiscal Year End:12/31 Latest Annual Data: 12/31/2006

Year	Sales	Net Income
2006	$881,000	-$23,000
2005	$13,337,000	-$18,000
2004	$12,529,000	$667,000

Curr. Assets:	$674,000	Curr. Liab.:	$1,368,000		
Plant, Equip.:	$347,000	Total Liab.:	$1,368,000	Indic. Yr. Divd.:	NA
Total Assets:	$1,021,000	Net Worth:	-$348,000	Debt/ Equity:	NA

Proquest Co

777 Eisenhower Pk.way, Ann Arbor, MI, 48106; *PH:* 1-734-761-4700; *http://* www.proquestcompany.com

General		Stock	
Incorporation	DE	Price on:12/24/2007	NA
Employees	2,414	Stock Exchange	NA
Auditor	KPMG LLP	Ticker Symbol	NA
Stk Agt	EquiServe Trust Co N.A	Outstanding Shares	NA
Counsel	NA	E.P.S	-$0.49
DUNS No.	00-506-9141	Shareholders	NA

Business: The group's principle activity is to publish information solutions for the education, automotive and power equipment markets. The company provides products and services through two business segments: information and learning and business solutions. The information and learning segment primarily serves the education market by collecting, organizing and publishing content from a wide range of sources including newspapers, periodicals and books. The business solutions segment is primarily engaged in the delivery in electronic form of comprehensive parts and service information to the automotive market. It also provides dealers in the power equipment (motorcycle, marine, recreational vehicle, lawn & garden and heavy equipment) market with management systems that enable them to manage their inventory, customer service and other aspects of their businesses. On 09-Jul-2004, the company acquired serials solutions, inc. The group operates from United States.

Primary SIC and add'l.: 3579 3572 7375 7389

CIK No: 0000215219

Subsidiaries: Bigchalk, Inc., Chadwyck-Healey Espana, SA, Copley Publishing Group, Inc., Homeworkcentral.com, Inc., LearningPage.com, Inc., Mediaseek Technologies, Inc., Norman Ross Publishing, Inc., ProQuest Alison Limited, ProQuest Alison, Gmbh, ProQuest Alison, Inc., ProQuest Alison, SA, ProQuest Alison, SARL, ProQuest Alison, SRL, ProQuest Business Solutions Inc., ProQuest Content Operations, Inc. 28 Subsidiaries included in the Index

Officers: Richard Surratt/CEO, Pres., David Asai/Sr. VP, CFO, Todd W. Buchardt/Sr. VP, General Counsel, Sec., Ron Klausner/Pres. - Voyager Expanded Learning, Andrew H. Wyszkowski/54/Pres.

Directors: William E. Oberndorf/Chmn., James P. Roemer/Dir., Gary L. Roubos/Dir., Frederick J. Schwab/Dir., Todd S. Nelson/Dir., Linda G. Roberts/Dir., Randy Best/Dir., David G. Brown/Dir.

Owners: Randy Best, Richard Surratt, James P. Roemer, David G. Brown, Gary L. Roubos, Insiders/14.80%, Todd S. Nelson, Keystone, Inc./9.00%, David A. Prichard, Alan W. Aldworth/1.20%, Kevin Gregory, William E. Oberndorf/12.00%, Ronald D. Klausner, Linda G. Roberts, Tweedy, Browne Company LLC/7.90% *(20 Owners included in Index)*

Financial Data: Fiscal Year End:01/01 Latest Annual Data: 12/31/2005

Year	Sales	Net Income
2005	$545,913,000	-$14,493,000
2004	$469,651,000	$49,821,000

Curr. Assets:	$196,374,000	Curr. Liab.:	$833,374,000		
Plant, Equip.:	$173,545,000	Total Liab.:	$969,804,000	Indic. Yr. Divd.:	NA
Total Assets:	$917,114,000	Net Worth:	-$52,690,000	Debt/ Equity:	NA

Prosofttraining

410 N 44th St., Ste. 600, Phoenix, AZ, 85008; *PH:* 1-602-794-4199; *http://* www.prosofttraining.com

General		Stock	
Incorporation	NV	Price on:12/24/2007	$0.006
Employees	48	Stock Exchange	OTC
Auditor	Hein & Assoc. LLP	Ticker Symbol	POSOQ
Stk Agt	Interwest Transfer Company, Inc.	Outstanding Shares	4,780,000
Counsel	NA	E.P.S	-$1.882
DUNS No.	92-986-1771	Shareholders	NA

Business: The group's principle activities are to develop content and certifications for individuals to develop and validate critical information and communications technology workforce skills. It creates and distributes a complete library of classroom and e-learning courses. Content revenue is derived from the sale of course materials in the form of books, CD-roms, self-study kits, assessment products, Internet-based course books, royalties and content licenses. The group's content is focused on training and education for job-role and vendor-specific certifications. It distributes the content through its computerprep division to individuals, schools, colleges, commercial training centers and corporations. The group's client includes entities such as the university of phoenix, new horizons, compusa, American express, IBM, lockheed martin, time warner cable, etc. The group distributes its content broadly in the United States, Canada, Europe, Middle East and Africa.

Primary SIC and add'l.: 8331

CIK No: 0001018693

Subsidiaries: ComputerPREP, Inc., Net Guru Technologies, Inc., Pro-Soft Development Corp., Prosoft Training Hong Kong Limited, ProsoftTraining Europe Limited, ProsoftTraining Solutions Singapore Pte Ltd, The Chapel Hill Group - Technology Consultants, Inc.

Officers: James A. Stanger/VP - Certification, Product Development, Karen M. Jensen/VP - Administration, Lindsay H. Miller/Sr. VP, GM

Financial Data: Fiscal Year End:07/31 Latest Annual Data: 7/31/2005

Year	Sales	Net Income
2005	$7,032,000	-$2,608,000
2004	$8,048,000	-$1,566,000
2003	$12,020,000	-$2,308,000

Curr. Assets:	$1,575,000	Curr. Liab.:	$1,160,000		
Plant, Equip.:	$123,000	Total Liab.:	$5,009,000	Indic. Yr. Divd.:	NA
Total Assets:	$8,500,000	Net Worth:	$3,491,000	Debt/ Equity:	NA

Prospect Capital Corp

Formerly: Prospect Energy Corp
10 E 40th St., New York, NY, 10016; *PH:* 1-212-448-0702; *http://* www.prospectstreet.com

General		Stock	
Incorporation	MD	Price on:12/24/2007	$18.41
Employees	NA	Stock Exchange	NDQ
Auditor	BDO Seidman, LLP	Ticker Symbol	PSEC
Stk Agt	American Stock Transfer & Trust Co.	Outstanding Shares	19,880,000
Counsel	NA	E.P.S.	$1.17
DUNS No.	NA	Shareholders	NA

Business: The groups principal activity is to lend to and invests in companies in the energy industry. The group operates from the United States. The assets of the group for the year 2006 were $138,480 (thousands).

Primary SIC and add'l.: 6211

CIK No: 0001287032

Officers: John Francis Barry/Chmn., CEO, Grier M. Eliasek/Dir., COO, Pres., William E. Vastardis/CFO, Chief Compliance Officer, Daria Becker/Investor Relation Officer, David L. Belzer/Professional, James A. Flores/Professional, Mark Hull/Professional, Kurt W. Rieke/Professional, Bart J. De Bie/Professional, Montgomery W. Cook/Professional, John S. Hopley/Professional, Eric K. Klaussmann/Professional, Robert S. Everett/Professional, Amir Friedman/Professional, Richard A. Hightower/Professional *(21 Officers included in Index)*

Directors: John Francis Barry/Chmn., CEO, Grier M. Eliasek/Dir., COO, Pres., William J. Gremp/Dir., Lee F. Liebolt/Dir., Walter V.E. Parker/Dir.

Owners: Walter V.E. Parker, William J. Gremp, William E. Vastardis, Insiders/2.20%, M. Grier Eliasek, Lee F. Liebolt, John F. Barry/2.10%

Financial Data: Fiscal Year End:06/30 Latest Annual Data: 06/30/2007

Year	Sales	Net Income
2007	$40,681,000	$16,728,000
2006	$21,207,000	$12,896,000
2005	$8,093,000	$8,751,000

Curr. Assets:	NA	Curr. Liab.:	NA	P/E Ratio:	11.40
Plant, Equip.:	NA	Total Liab.:	NA	Indic. Yr. Divd.:	NA
Total Assets:	NA	Net Worth:	NA	Debt/ Equity:	NA

Prospect Medical Holdings Inc

400 Corporate Pointe, Ste. 525, Culver City, CA, 90230; *PH:* 1-310-338-8677; *Fax:* 1-310-338-1109; *http://* www.prospectmedicalholdings.com

General		Stock	
Incorporation	DE	Price on:12/24/2007	$5.45
Employees	367	Stock Exchange	AMEX
Auditor	Ernst & Young LLP	Ticker Symbol	PZZ
Stk Agt	American Stock Transfer & Trust Co.	Outstanding Shares	7,940,000
Counsel	Stephan Oringher Richman T & M PC	E.P.S.	$0.50
DUNS No.	NA	Shareholders	NA

Business: The group's principal activity is to provide management services to affliated physician organizations that operate as independent physician associations ("IPAs") or medical clinics. The company's affiliated physician organizations enter into agreements with health maintenance organizations ("HMOs") to provide enrollees of the HMOs with a full range of medical services in exchange for fixed, prepaid monthly fees known as "capitation" payments.

Primary SIC and add'l.: 8011

CIK No: 0001063561

Subsidiaries: Antelope Valley Medical Associates, Inc, APAC Medical Group, Inc., Medical Corporation, Nuestra Familia Medical Group, Inc, Pegasus Medical Group, Inc, Pinnacle Health Resources, Prospect Health Source Medical Group, Inc, Prospect NWOC Medical Group, Inc, Prospect Professional Care Medical Group, Inc., Residential Funding Corporation, Santa Ana/Tustin Physicians Group, Inc, Sierra Medical Management, Inc, Sierra Primary Care Medical Group, StarCare Medical Group, Inc.

Officers: Catherine Dickson/Dir., CEO - Prospect Medical Systems, Jacob Y. Terner/Chmn., CEO, Michael A. Terner/VP - HMO Contracting, Prospect Medical Systems, Mike Heather/CFO, Devin Sullivan/Contact - Investor Relations, Stewart Kahn/Exec. VP, Sec., Linda Hodges/Exec. VP, Donna Vigil/VP - Finance, Terri Holmes/VP - Information Technology, Prospect Medical Systems, Rosa Catalano/VP - Medical Management, Prospect Medical Systems, Ria Berger/VP - Human Resources, Prospect Medical Systems

Directors: Jacob Y. Terner/Chmn., CEO, Catherine Dickson/Dir., CEO - Prospect Medical Systems, David Levinsohn/Dir., Jeereddi Prasad/60/Dir., Samuel S. Lee/42/Dir., Ken Schwartz/Dir., Joel S. Kanter/Dir., Gene Burleson/Dir., Glenn R. Robson/46/Dir.

Owners: Samuel S. Lee/8.30%, Jeereddi Prasad/3.50%, Joel S. Kanter/1.10%, Kenneth Schwartz/1.70%, Jacob Y. Terner/12.50%, Gene E. Burleson/1.30%, Kevin Kimberlin/6.10%, David& Alexa Topper Family Trust/8.30%, David A. Levinsohn/2.40%, Donna Vigil/0.70%, Mike Heather/2.60%, Catherine S. Dickson/1.40%, Richard N. Merkin/5.30%, Insiders/32.50%, Stewart R. Kahn/0.50%

Financial Data: Fiscal Year End:09/30 Latest Annual Data: 9/30/2006

Year	Sales	Net Income
2006	$135,796,000	$4,890,000
2005	$133,518,000	$4,073,000

Curr. Assets:	$24,768,000	Curr. Liab.:	$24,892,000	P/E Ratio:	10.90
Plant, Equip.:	$1,286,000	Total Liab.:	$32,773,000	Indic. Yr. Divd.:	NA
Total Assets:	$66,657,000	Net Worth:	$33,803,000	Debt/ Equity:	0.1720

Prosperity Bancshares Inc

4295 San Felipe, Houston, TX, 77027; *PH:* 1-713-693-9300; *Fax:* 1-713-693-9360; *http://* www.prosperitybanktx.com; *Email:* investor.relations@prosperitybanktx.com

General		Stock	
Incorporation	TX	Price on:12/24/2007	$34.45
Employees	908	Stock Exchange	NDQ
Auditor	Deloitte & Touche LLP	Ticker Symbol	PRSP
Stk Agt	Computershare Trust Co	Outstanding Shares	43,800,000
Counsel	Bracewell & Patterson	E.P.S.	$2.07
DUNS No.	83-111-7007	Shareholders	NA

Business: The group's principal activities are to offer a variety of traditional loans and deposit products to its customers and small and medium-sized businesses. It offers loans for automobiles and other consumer durables, home equity loans, debit cards, personal computer banking and other cash. It

also offers certificates of deposit, now accounts, savings accounts and overdraft protection at competitive rates. The group operates fifty one full-service banking offices with 29 located in the greater houston metropolitan area, eleven in eight contiguous counties situated south and southwest of houston, south Texas and eleven located in Dallas. In 2003 the group acquired abrams centre national bank and first state bank of north Texas and in 2004, village bank and trust and liberty bancshares inc.

Primary SIC and add'l.: 6712 6022

CIK No: 0001068851

Subsidiaries: First Capital (TX) Statutory Trust I, First Capital (TX) Statutory Trust II, MainCorp Leasing Co., Paradigm Capital Trust II, Prosperity Bank, Prosperity Holdings of Delaware, LLC, Prosperity Interim Corporation, Prosperity Statutory Trust II, Prosperity Statutory Trust III, Prosperity Statutory Trust IV

Officers: David Zalman/Chmn., CEO/$864,689.00, James D. Rollins/COO, Pres./$547,385.00, Randy D. Hester/Chief Lending Officer - Prosperity Bank, David Hollaway/CFO/$374,893.00, Chris A. Bagley/Chief Credit Officer - Prosperity Bank, Peter E. Fisher/General Counsel/$300,446.00, Dan Agnew/Pres. - Fort Bend County Banking Centers, Houston Area, Prosperity Bank, Mark Humphrey/Pres. - Clear Lake Banking Center, Houston Area, Prosperity Bank, Mike Meyer/Pres. - Austin Area, Central Texas Area, Prosperity Bank, Ray Armour/Pres. - North Austin Banking Centers, Central Texas Area, Prosperity Bank, Melvin Barta/Pres. - Schulenburg Banking Center, Central Texas Area, Prosperity Bank, Bobby Williamson/Pres. - Bryan, College Station Banking Centers, Central Texas Area, Prosperity Bank, Jonathan Kalich/Pres. - Fayette County Banking Centers, Central Texas Area, Prosperity Bank, David Weatherston/Pres. - Water Street Banking Center, South Texas Area, Prosperity Bank, Jay W. Porter/Pres. - North Houston Banking Centers, Houston Area, Prosperity Bank *(27 Officers included in Index)*

Directors: David Zalman/Chmn., CEO, H. E. Timanus/Vice Chmn., Gene Payne/Chmn. - Dallas, Fort Worth, Prosperity Bank, Steve Hipes/Chmn. - South Texas Area, Prosperity Bank, Eddie Safady/Chmn. - Austin Area, Central Texas Area, Prosperity Bank, Ned S. Holmes/63/Dir., James A. Bouligny/72/Dir., William H. Fagan/78/Dir., Michael D. Hunter/65/Dir., Reed S. Morian/62/Dir., Perry Mueller/74/Dir., Robert Steelhammer/67/Dir., Tracy T. Rudolph/68/Dir., Harrison Stafford/66/Dir., Don L. Stricklin/49/Dir.

Owners: Peter Fisher, David Hollaway, William H. Fagan/2.08%, Michael D. Hunter, David Zalman/1.48%, Leah Henderson, Ned S. Holmes/2.48%, James D. Rollins, Insiders/12.78%, S. Reed Morian, Harrison Stafford, James A. Bouligny, Perry Mueller, L. Don Stricklin, Tracy T. Rudolph *(17 Owners included in Index)*

Financial Data: *Fiscal Year End:*12/31 *Latest Annual Data:* 12/31/2006

Year	Sales	Net Income
2006	$265,721,000	$61,725,000
2005	$192,223,000	$47,860,000
2004	$134,827,000	$34,707,000

Curr. Assets:	$290,482,000	**Curr. Liab.:**	$3,781,354,000	**P/E Ratio:**	17.05
Plant, Equip.:	$66,906,000	**Total Liab.:**	$3,922,358,000	**Indic. Yr. Divd.:**	$0.500
Total Assets:	$4,586,769,000	**Net Worth:**	$664,411,000	**Debt/ Equity:**	0.1743

Prospero Minerals Corp

575 Madison Ave., 10th Fl., New York, NY, 10022; ***PH:*** 1-212-937-8442; ***Fax:*** 1-212-605-0222; ***http://*** www.prosperominerals.com; ***Email:*** info@prospero-minerals.com

General - Incorporation	NV	**Stock**- Price on:12/24/2007	NA
Employees	NA	Stock Exchange	OTC
Auditor	Lawrence Scharfman & Co., CPA P.C.	Ticker Symbol	PSPO
Stk Agt	NA	Outstanding Shares	NA
Counsel	NA	E.P.S	-$0.01
DUNS No.	NA	Shareholders	NA

Business: The groups principal activity is to conduct mineral exploration activities on the mineral properties in order to assess whether these claims possess commercially exploitable mineral deposits. The group designed to explore for commercially viable deposits of base and precious minerals, such as gold, diamonds, silver, lead, barium, mercury, copper, and zinc minerals. In March 2006, the group acquired Lobaye Gold SURL. The group operates from the United States.

Primary SIC and add'l.: 1400

CIK No: 0001243741

Subsidiaries: CMC Exploration Corporation

Officers: Etoile L. Pinder/CEO, Pres., Treasurer, Sec., David Reeve/54/Acting Chief Operations Mgr., Hubert L. Pinder/74/Dir., CFO

Directors: Hubert L. Pinder/74/Dir., CFO

Owners: Chris Roth/21.20%, Insiders/7.80%, Didier Llinas/7.80%

Financial Data: *Fiscal Year End:*12/31 *Latest Annual Data:* 3/31/2006

Year	Sales	Net Income
2006	NA	-$358,000
2005	NA	-$62,000
2004	NA	-$86,000

Curr. Assets:	$94,000	**Curr. Liab.:**	$283,000		
Plant, Equip.:	$424,000	**Total Liab.:**	$283,000	**Indic. Yr. Divd.:**	NA
Total Assets:	$518,000	**Net Worth:**	$235,000	**Debt/ Equity:**	NA

Protalex Inc

145 Union Sq. Dr., New Hope, PA, 18938; ***PH:*** 1-215-862-9720; ***Fax:*** 1-215-862-6614; ***http://*** www.protalex.com; ***Email:*** info@protalex.com

General - Incorporation	DE	**Stock**- Price on:12/24/2007	$1.3
Employees	10	Stock Exchange	OTC
Auditor	Grant Thornton LLP	Ticker Symbol	PRTX
Stk Agt	American Stock Transfer & Trust Co.	Outstanding Shares	28,600,000
Counsel	NA	E.P.S	-$0.33
DUNS No.	NA	Shareholders	NA

Business: The group's principle activity is to develop biopharmaceutical drugs used for the treatment of autoimmune and inflammatory diseases. The bioregulatory compounds are based on the principle of normalizing the activities of immune cells at a more basic level than traditional pharmaceutical agents, which act upon the end products of complex metabolic pathways. The company is in its development stage and currently has no products in the market.The group operates from United States.

Primary SIC and add'l.: 8731

CIK No: 0001099215

Subsidiaries: Protalex Delaware

Officers: Steven H. Kane/Dir., CEO, Pres./$691,138.00, Paula M. Jardieu/Member - Scientific Advisory Board, Marc L. Rose/VP, CFO, Treasurer, Corportate Sec./$444,630.00, Edward W. Bernton/Medical Dir.

Directors: Steven H. Kane/Dir., CEO, Pres., Kirk G. Raab/Chmn., Frank M. Dougherty/Dir., Eugene A. Bauer/Dir., Peter G. Tombros/Dir., Dinesh Patel/Dir., Carleton A. Holstrom/Dir., Thomas P. Stagnaro/Dir.

Owners: Marc L. Rose, Insiders/26.00%, Peter G. Tombros, Steven H. Kane/4.40%, Victor S. Sloan, Thomas P. Stagnaro/1.10%, vSpring SBIC, L.P./14.90%, Kirk G. Raab/2.50%, Eugene A. Bauer, Carleton A. Holstrom, John E. Doherty/10.80%, LB I Group/5.60%, Dinesh Patel/14.90%, Frank M. Dougherty/1.70%

Financial Data: *Fiscal Year End:*05/31 *Latest Annual Data:* 5/31/2006

Year	Sales	Net Income
2006	NA	-$6,104,000
2005	NA	-$5,568,000
2004	NA	-$2,989,000

Curr. Assets:	$17,817,000	**Curr. Liab.:**	$969,000		
Plant, Equip.:	$372,000	**Total Liab.:**	$972,000	**Indic. Yr. Divd.:**	NA
Total Assets:	$18,210,000	**Net Worth:**	$17,238,000	**Debt/ Equity:**	NA

Protection One Inc

1035 N 3rd St., Ste. 101, Lawrence, KS, 66044; ***PH:*** 1-785-856-5500; ***http://*** www.protectionone.com

General - Incorporation	DE	**Stock**- Price on:12/24/2007	NA
Employees	2,400	Stock Exchange	NDQ
Auditor	Deloitte & Touche LLP	Ticker Symbol	PONE
Stk Agt	Mellon Investor Services LLC	Outstanding Shares	NA
Counsel	Kirkland & Ellis LLP	E.P.S	-$1.23
DUNS No.	78-709-1222	Shareholders	NA

Business: The group's principle activity is to provide security alarm monitoring services that include sales, installation and related servicing of security alarm systems for residential and small business customers. The alarm monitoring systems developed by the group is designed to detect or react to various occurrences or conditions like intrusion or the presence of fire or smoke. These devices are connected to a computerized control panel, which gets activated by incoming alarm signals and telephone calls. The group also provides other services such as remote audio verification, repairing the systems after the expiry of the warranty period and wireless back up. The group serves approximately 1.2 million customers comprising of single family and multifamily residences, commercial and wholesale clients. The group's quarterly revenue for September 2007 was 93.52 millions of USD.

Primary SIC and add'l.: 1731 7382

CIK No: 0000916230

Subsidiaries: Network Multifamily Security Corporation, Protection One Alarm Monitoring, Inc., Security Monitoring Services, Inc. (d/b/a, CMS)

Officers: Richard Ginsburg/Dir., CEO, Pres./$2,634,732.00, Peter Pefanis/COO, Exec. VP/$1,626,133.00, Steve Williams/Pres. - Network Multifamily Corporation, Eric J. Griffin/Corp. Sec., VP, General Counsel/$340,380.00, Darius Nevin/CFO, Exec. VP/$1,699,978.00, Mack Sands/COO, Exec. VP, Nancy Roll/Mgr. - Executive Customer Relations, Paul Patterson/Dir. - Customer Operations, Joseph Sanchez/Sr. VP - Customer Operations/$313,410.00

Directors: Richard Ginsburg/Dir., CEO, Pres., Robert J. McGuire/71/Dir., David A. Tanner/Dir., Michael Weinstock/Dir., Steven Rattner/55/Dir., Henry Ormond/35/Dir.

Owners: Quadrangle Debt Recovery Advisors LP/23.32%, Peter J. Pefanis/1.03%, Darius G. Nevin/1.17%, Richard Ginsburg/1.79%, Insiders/4.05%, Joseph R. Sanchez, Raymond C. Kubacki, POI Acquisition, L.L.C./46.64%, Eric J. Griffin, Arlene M. Yocum, Robert J. McGuire

Financial Data: *Fiscal Year End:*12/31 *Latest Annual Data:* 12/31/2006

Year	Sales	Net Income
2006	$270,552,000	-$17,405,000
2005	$263,024,000	-$26,993,000
2004	$269,259,000	-$323,906,000

Curr. Assets:	$64,647,000	**Curr. Liab.:**	$69,637,000		
Plant, Equip.:	$22,430,000	**Total Liab.:**	$523,896,000	**Indic. Yr. Divd.:**	NA
Total Assets:	$443,953,000	**Net Worth:**	-$79,943,000	**Debt/ Equity:**	NA

Protective Life Corp

2801 Hwy. 280 S, Birmingham, AL, 35223; ***PH:*** 1-205-268-1000; ***Fax:*** 1-205-268-3196; ***http://*** www.protective.com

General - Incorporation	DE	**Stock**- Price on:12/24/2007	$48.51
Employees	2,743	Stock Exchange	NYSE
Auditor	PricewaterhouseCoopers LLP	Ticker Symbol	PL
Stk Agt	Bank of New York	Outstanding Shares	70,070,000
Counsel	NA	E.P.S	$4.18
DUNS No.	00-690-0476	Shareholders	NA

Business: The groups principle activity is to provide investment and insurance products. The company operates through five business segments namely life marketing, acquisitions, annuities, stable value products and asset protection. The group operates from United States.

Primary SIC and add'l.: 6311 6719 6321

CIK No: 0000355429

Subsidiaries: Empire General Life Assurance Corporation, Protective Life Insurance Company, West Coast Life Insurance Company

Officers: John D. Johns/Chmn., CEO, Pres./$2,333,703.00, Richard J. Bielen/Vice Chmn., CFO/$706,946.00, Carolyn King/Sr. VP - Acquisitions, Corporate Development, Scott Adams/Sr. VP, Chief Human Resources Officer, Carolyn M. Johnson/COO, Exec. VP, Gary Corsi/53/CFO, Exec. VP/$1,055,798.00, Andrew Martin/Pres. - Administration, First Protective, Deborah J. Long/Exec. VP, Sec., General Counsel/$601,059.00, Brent E. Griggs/Sr. VP - Asset Protection, Carl S. Thigpen/Exec. VP, Chief Investment Officer, Judy Wilson/Sr. VP - Stable Value Products, Steven G. Walker/Sr. VP, Controller, Chief Accounting Officer, Stephen R. Briggs/Exec. VP - Life, Annuity Division/$938,923.00

Directors: John D. Johns/Chmn., CEO, Pres., Richard J. Bielen/Vice Chmn., CFO, Vanessa Wilson/Dir., William A. Terry/Dir., Malcolm Portera/Dir., Corbin H. Day/Dir., John J. McMahon/Dir., James S.M. French/Dir., Michael W. Warren/Dir., Vanessa Leonard/Dir., Thomas L. Hamby/Dir., Charles D. McCrary/Dir., Dowd C. Ritter/Dir.

Owners: John J. McMahon, Allen W. Ritchie, Richard J. Bielen, EARNEST Partners, LLC/6.70%, Deborah J. Long, William A. Terry, Malcolm Portera, Corbin H. Day, Gary J. Cooper, Vanessa Wilson, Michael W. Warren, John D. Johns, Vanessa Leonard, Charles D. McCrary, Stephen R. Briggs *(22 Owners included in Index)*

Financial Data: Fiscal Year End: 12/31 Latest Annual Data: 12/31/2006

Year	Sales	Net Income
2006	$2,679,133,000	$281,561,000
2005	$2,109,204,000	$246,567,000
2004	$1,988,575,000	$234,580,000

Curr. Assets:	$6,379,476,000	Curr. Liab.:	$16,949,000	P/E Ratio:	11.55
Plant, Equip.:	$43,796,000	Total Liab.:	$37,482,219,000	Indic. Yr. Divd.:	$0.900
Total Assets:	$39,795,294,000	Net Worth:	$2,313,075,000	Debt/ Equity:	0.6267

Protective Life Insurance Co

2801 Hwy. 280 S, Birmingham, AL, 35223; *PH:* 1-205-268-1000; *Fax:* 1-800-866-3555; *http://* www.protective.com

General		Stock	
Incorporation	TN	Price on:12/24/2007	$48.68
Employees	2,743	Stock Exchange	NA
Auditor	PricewaterhouseCoopers LLP	Ticker Symbol	NA
Stk Agt	Bank of New York	Outstanding Shares	70,070,000
Counsel	NA	E.P.S	$4.18
DUNS No.	00-690-0476	Shareholders	NA

Business: The group's principle activity is to offer individual life insurance products, credit life and disability insurance products, guaranteed investment contracts, guaranteed funding agreements, and fixed and variable annuities. The group is a wholly owned subsidiary of protective life corporation. The group's activities are divided into three segments, namely, life insurance, retirement savings and investment products and specialty insurance products. The group markets these products through independent agents, insurance brokers, stockbrokers, financial institutions, company sales representatives and automobile dealers.

Primary SIC and add'l.: 6311 6321

CIK No: 0000310826

Subsidiaries: Protective Life Corporation (PLC)

Officers: John D. Johns/56/Chmn., CEO, Pres., Brent E. Griggs/52/Sr. VP - Asset Protection, Kevin J. Howard/48/Sr. VP, Chief Product Actuary - Life, Annuity, Steven G. Walker/48/Sr. VP, Controller, Chief Accounting Officer, Judy Wilson/49/Sr. VP - Stable Value Products, Carl S. Thigpen/51/Exec. VP, Chief Investment Officer, Deborah J. Long/54/Exec. VP, Sec., General Counsel, Wayne E. Stuenkel/54/Sr. VP, Chief Actuary, Stephen R. Briggs/58/Exec. VP - Life, Annuity, Dir., Carolyn King/57/Sr. VP - Acquisitions, Corporate Development, Scott D. Adams/43/Sr. VP, Chief Human Resources Officer, Richard J. Bielen/47/Exec. VP, Chief Investment Officer, Treasurer, Dir., Carolyn M. Johnson/47/COO, Exec. VP

Directors: John D. Johns/56/Chmn., CEO, Pres., Richard J. Bielen/47/Exec. VP, Chief Investment Officer, Treasurer, Dir.

Owners: EARNEST Partners, LLC/6.70%, John D. Johns, Deborah J. Long, Gary Corsi, Richard J. Bielen, Allen W. Ritchie, Barclays Global Investors, NA/5.40%, Insiders, Regions Financial Corporation/5.60%, Stephen R. Briggs

Financial Data: Fiscal Year End: 12/31 Latest Annual Data: 12/31/2006

Year	Sales	Net Income
2006	$2,679,133,000	$281,561,000
2005	$2,109,204,000	$246,567,000
2004	$1,988,575,000	$234,580,000

Curr. Assets:	$6,379,476,000	Curr. Liab.:	$16,949,000	P/E Ratio:	11.65
Plant, Equip.:	$43,796,000	Total Liab.:	$37,482,219,000	Indic. Yr. Divd.:	$0.900
Total Assets:	$39,795,294,000	Net Worth:	$2,313,075,000	Debt/ Equity:	0.6267

Protein Polymer Technologies Inc

10655 Sorrento Valley Rd., San Diego, CA, 92121; *PH:* 1-858-558-6064; *Fax:* 1-858-558-6477; *http://* www.ppti.com; *Email:* info@ppti.com

General		Stock	
Incorporation	DE	Price on:12/24/2007	$0.115
Employees	18	Stock Exchange	OTC
Auditor	Squar, Peterson, LLP	Ticker Symbol	PPTI
Stk Agt	Continental Stock Transfer & Trust Co	Outstanding Shares	67,810,000
Counsel	Paul, Hastings, Janofsky & Walker LLP	E.P.S	-$0.08
DUNS No.	36-444-6104	Shareholders	NA

Business: The group's principle activities include research, development, production and clinical testing of medical products based on its proprietary protein-based biomaterials technology. The products of the company are surgical repairs of tissue, surgical adhesives and sealants, soft tissue augmentation products, wound healing matrices, drug delivery formulations and surgical adhesion barriers. The company's operations have been directed primarily toward developing business strategies, raising capital, research and development activities, conducting clinical testing of the product candidates, exploring marketing channels and recruiting personnel. The company focuses on the development materials technology and products to be used in the surgical repair of tissue, surgical adhesives and sealants, soft tissue augmentation products, wound healing matrices, drug delivery formulations and surgical adhesion barriers. The group operates from United States.

Primary SIC and add'l.: 6794 2834

CIK No: 0000858155

Officers: William N. Plamondon/Chmn., CEO/$300,000.00, Joseph Nichols/Technical Advisor, Paul J. Jones/Technical Advisors, Daniel I.C. Wang/Technical Advisors, Barry Feiner/Legal Counsel, Erin Davis/43/Sec., Franco A. Ferrari/VP - Laboratory Operations, Polymer Production, Dir. - Molecular Genetics/$155,372.00, Edward J. Hartnett/Technical Advisors, James M. Anderson/Technical Advisors, Joseph Cappello/VP - Research, Development, CTO, Dir. - Polymer Research/$167,860.00, William J. Efcavitch/Technical Advisors, Radine G. Pobuda/Dir. - Quality Systems, Regulatory Affairs, Edward E. David/Technology Consultant, David A. Tirrell/Technical Advisors

Directors: William N. Plamondon/Chmn., CEO, Richard Adelson/Dir., Kerry L. Kuhn/Dir., James B. McCarthy/Dir., Allan Farber/Dir.

Owners: Redec & Associates, LLC/19.80%, Allan Farber/1.00%, Richard Adelson, James B. McCarthy, William N. Plamondon/2.30%, Johnson & Johnson Development Company/18.70%, Erin Davis, Franco A. Ferrari/2.20%, Kerry L. Kuhn/1.20%, Insiders/9.10%, Joseph Cappello/2.50%, Matthew Szulik/18.10%

Financial Data: Fiscal Year End: 12/31 Latest Annual Data: 12/31/2006

Year	Sales	Net Income
2006	$605,000	-$7,878,000
2005	$867,000	-$5,822,000
2004	$457,000	-$3,565,000

Curr. Assets:	$184,000	Curr. Liab.:	$5,130,000		
Plant, Equip.:	$228,000	Total Liab.:	$5,515,000	Indic. Yr. Divd.:	NA
Total Assets:	$962,000	Net Worth:	-$4,553,000	Debt/ Equity:	NA

Proteo Inc

2102 Business Ctr Dr., Ste. 130, Irvine, CA, 92626; *PH:* 1-949-253-4155; *http://* www.proteo.de

General		Stock	
Incorporation	NV	Price on:12/24/2007	$0.6
Employees	5	Stock Exchange	OTC
Auditor	Squar, Peterson, LLP	Ticker Symbol	PTEO
Stk Agt	Transfer Online, Inc.	Outstanding Shares	23,880,000
Counsel	NA	E.P.S	-$0.02
DUNS No.	NA	Shareholders	NA

Business: The group's principal activities are to develop, manufacture, promote and market pharmaceuticals and other biotech products. The group focuses on the development of pharmaceuticals based on human protein elafin which naturally occurs in human skin, lungs, and mammary glands. This human protein is useful in the treatment of cardiac infarction, serious injuries caused by accidents, post surgery damage to tissue and complications resulting from organ transplantations. The group is a development stage company.

Primary SIC and add'l.: 8731 2834

CIK No: 0001063104

Subsidiaries: German corporation, Proteo Biotech AG

Officers: Birge Bargmann/43/Dir., CEO, CFO, Pres.

Directors: Birge Bargmann/43/Dir., CEO, CFO, Pres., Oliver Wiedow/51/Chmn., Barbara Kahlke/44/Dir., Florian Wegner/Dir., Fred Fandrich/Member - Scientific Advisory Board, Jens-Michael Schroder/Member - Scientific Advisory Board, Jurgen Paal/Member - Scientific Advisory Board, Joerg Alte/47/Dir., Holger Pusch/51/Dir., Hartmut Weigelt/62/Dir.

Owners: Insiders, Oliver Wiedow, Barbara Kahlke, Holger Pusch, Joerg Alte, Birge Bargmann, Hartmut Weigelt

Financial Data: Fiscal Year End: 12/31 Latest Annual Data: 12/31/2006

Year	Sales	Net Income
2006	NA	-$650,000
2005	NA	-$1,132,000
2004	NA	-$640,000

Curr. Assets:	$409,000	Curr. Liab.:	$965,000		
Plant, Equip.:	$389,000	Total Liab.:	$965,000	Indic. Yr. Divd.:	NA
Total Assets:	$798,000	Net Worth:	-$171,000	Debt/ Equity:	NA

Protherics Plc

The Heath Business & Technical Pk., Runcorn, WA7 4QX; *PH:* 44-01928518000; *Fax:* 44-1928518002; *http://* www.protherics.com; *Email:* information@protherics.com

General		Stock	
Incorporation	England and Wales	Price on:12/24/2007	$11.6
Employees	190	Stock Exchange	NDQ
Auditor	PricewaterhouseCoopers LLP	Ticker Symbol	PTIL
Stk Agt	Neville Registrars Limited	Outstanding Shares	31,030,000
Counsel	NA	E.P.S	-$0.31
DUNS No.	NA	Shareholders	NA

Business: The groups principle activity is to provide immunotherapeutics and oncology services. The group products sold under the trade names CroFab(R), DigiFab(R), Voraxaze(TM) and ViperaTAb(TM). The groups operates through two segments namely sale, manufacture and development of pharmaceutical products and royalties arising from outlicensed technology. The group operates from the United Kingdom, the United States and Australia. The group's quarterly revenue for September 2007 was 14.82 millions of USD.

Primary SIC and add'l.: 2833 2834

CIK No: 0000945725

Subsidiaries: DeMontford Biopharma Limited, Enact Pharma Limited, Enzacta Limited, Enzacta R&D Limited, Genethics Limited, Kymed GB Limited, Polyclonal Antibodies Limited, Proteus Biotechnology Limited, Protherics Australasia pty Limited, Protherics Inc., Protherics Medicines Development Limited, Protherics Services pty Limited, Protherics UK Limited, Protherics Utah Inc., TAb (London) Limited 16 Subsidiaries included in the Index

Officers: Andrew John Heath/Executive Dir., CEO, Barrington Marshall Riley/59/Dir., Dir. - Finance, James Campbell Christie/Executive Dir., Operations Dir., John Robert Brown/Executive Dir., Dir. - Finance, Saul Komisar/Executive Dir., Pres., Ian Scoular/Dir. - Business Development, Nick Staples/Dir. - Corporate Affairs, Sally Waterman/Dir. - Research, Development, David Briscoe/Dir. - Marketing, Sales, Europe

Directors: Andrew John Heath/Executive Dir., CEO, Stuart Michael Wallis/Chmn., James Campbell Christie/Executive Dir., Operations Dir., Barrington Marshall Riley/59/Dir., Dir. - Finance, John Robert Brown/Executive Dir., Dir. - Finance, Garry Watts/Dir., Bryan Geoffrey Morton/Non Exec. Dir., Jacques Gonella/Non Exec. Dir.

Owners: S. M. Wallis, A. J. Heath, J. R. Brown, B. M. Riley, G. Watts/0.01%, J. C. Christie, J. Gonella/2.43%

Financial Data: Fiscal Year End: 03/31 Latest Annual Data: 03/31/2007

Year	Sales	Net Income
2007	$61,071,000	-$39,915,000
2006	$30,810,000	-$16,507,000
2005	$35,398,000	-$13,890,000

Curr. Assets:	$72,310,000	Curr. Liab.:	$29,222,000		
Plant, Equip.:	$14,108,000	Total Liab.:	$58,777,000	Indic. Yr. Divd.:	NA
Total Assets:	$104,625,000	Net Worth:	$45,847,000	Debt/ Equity:	NA

Protocall Technologies Inc

47 Mall Dr., Commack, NY, 11725; *PH:* 1-631-543-3655; *Fax:* 1-631-543-6944; *http://* www.protocall.com; *Email:* info@TitleMatch.com

General - Incorporation	NV	Stock - Price on:12/24/2007	$0.09
Employees	14	Stock Exchange	OTC
Auditor	Eisner LLP	Ticker Symbol	PCLI
Stk Agt	Holladay Stock Transfer, Inc.	Outstanding Shares	79,190,000
Counsel	GREENBERG TRAURIG, LLP	E.P.S	-$0.11
DUNS No.	NA	Shareholders	NA

Business: The groups principle activities include developing and commercializing of a proprietary system that enables retailers to produce fully packaged software, movie and television digital media products. The group operates from the United States.

Primary SIC and add'l.: 7389

CIK No: 0001171180

Subsidiaries: Precision Type, Inc., Protocall Software Delivery Systems, Inc.

Officers: Bruce Newman/Dir., Founder, CEO, Syd Dufton/Pres., Aaron Knoll/CTO, Brenda S. Newman/Sr. VP - Operations, Rights Management, Mary Litchhult/VP - Business Development

Directors: Bruce Newman/Dir., Founder, CEO, Peter Greenfield/Chmn.

Owners: Jeffrey Josef/6.06%, Peter Greenfield/13.19%, Bruce Newman/5.08%, Brenda Newman/4.19%, CIMOS, Inc/14.67%, Joachim R. Anzer/47.71%, Insiders/20.88%

Financial Data: Fiscal Year End:12/31 **Latest Annual Data:** 12/31/2006

Year	Sales	Net Income
2006	$1,071,000	-$5,989,000
2005	$506,000	-$5,154,000
2004	$206,000	-$6,939,000

Curr. Assets:	$317,000	Curr. Liab.:	$2,819,000		
Plant, Equip.	$96,000	Total Liab.:	$8,220,000	Indic. Yr. Divd.:	NA
Total Assets:	$875,000	Net Worth:	-$7,345,000	Debt/ Equity:	NA

ProtoKinetix Inc

885 Georgia St. W , Ste. 1500, Vancouver, BC, V6C 3E8; **PH:** 1-604-687-9887; http:// www.protokinetix.com

General - Incorporation	NV	Stock - Price on:12/24/2007	$0.39
Employees	NA	Stock Exchange	OTC
Auditor	Peterson Sullivan PLLC	Ticker Symbol	PKTX
Stk Agt	Transfer Online, Inc.	Outstanding Shares	NA
Counsel	NA	E.P.S	NA
DUNS No.	NA	Shareholders	NA

Business: The groups principal activity is owns rights to a family of synthetic anti freeze glycoproteins. The group markets its product under the trademark AAGP(TM). The group operates from the United States.

Primary SIC and add'l.: 8731

CIK No: 0001128189

Owners: Centrum Bank AG/10.90%, Fred C. Whittaker, John Todd/7.00%

Financial Data: Fiscal Year End:12/31 **Latest Annual Data:** 12/31/2006

Year	Sales	Net Income
2006	NA	-$1,968,000
2005	$2,000	-$5,096,000
2004	NA	-$5,388,000

Curr. Assets:	$613,000	Curr. Liab.:	$415,000		
Plant, Equip.:	$1,000	Total Liab.:	$415,000	Indic. Yr. Divd.:	NA
Total Assets:	$614,000	Net Worth:	$199,000	Debt/ Equity:	NA

Proton Laboratories Inc

1135 Atlantic Ave., Ste 101, Alameda, CA, 94501; **PH:** 1-510-865-6412; http:// www.protonlabs.com

General - Incorporation	WA	Stock - Price on:12/24/2007	$0.175
Employees	3	Stock Exchange	OTC
Auditor	Hansen, Barnett & Maxwell	Ticker Symbol	PLBI
Stk Agt	Holladay Stock Transfer, Inc.	Outstanding Shares	26,470,000
Counsel	Joel Seidner Esq	E.P.S	-$0.13
DUNS No.	NA	Shareholders	NA

Business: The group's principal activity is to sell and market residential and commercial functional water systems throughout the United States of America. The group's operations are located in alameda and California. The group acts as an exclusive importer and master distributor of functional water systems that are manufactured by matsushita electric corporation of America. The group formulates intellectual properties under licensing agreements, supplies consumer products, consults on projects utilizing functional water, facilitates between manufacturer and industry and acts as educators on the benefits of functional water.

Primary SIC and add'l.: 5499 4941

CIK No: 0001110781

Subsidiaries: BentleyCapitalCorp.com Inc., Water Science, Inc.

Officers: Edward E. Alexander/Chmn., CEO, CFO, Dir. - New Business Development, California Office, Gary A. Taylor/Dir., Pres. - Portland Office, Carl Halterman/VP - Technology Integration, Washington Office, H. Tanaka/VP - Technology, California Office, Victor Miranda/Operations Mgr., K. Hanaoka/Scientific Adviser, G. Fernandes/Scientific Adviser, Jean Wang/Dir. - Asian Sales, Joel Seidner/Legal Counsel - Houston, Texas

Directors: Edward E. Alexander/Chmn., CEO, CFO, Dir. - New Business Development, California Office, Gary A. Taylor/Dir., Pres. - Portland Office

Owners: Edward Alexander/28.10%, Gary Taylor/0.44%, Insiders/37.10%, Legacy Media, LLC/10.80%, Jed Astin/3.70%, Gregory Darragh/4.80%

Financial Data: Fiscal Year End:12/31 **Latest Annual Data:** 12/31/2006

Year	Sales	Net Income
2006	$143,000	-$1,717,000
2005	$328,000	-$982,000
2004	$380,000	-$966,000

Curr. Assets:	$154,000	Curr. Liab.:	$406,000		
Plant, Equip.:	$204,000	Total Liab.:	$677,000	Indic. Yr. Divd.:	NA
Total Assets:	$364,000	Net Worth:	-$312,000	Debt/ Equity:	NA

ProtoSource Corp

1 Bethlehem Plz., 4th Fl., Bethlehem, PA, 18018; **PH:** 1-610-332-2893; **Fax:** 1-610-954-8279; http:// www.protosource.com

General - Incorporation	CA	Stock - Price on:12/24/2007	$0.04
Employees	141	Stock Exchange	OTC
Auditor	Margolis & Co P.C	Ticker Symbol	PSCO
Stk Agt	Corporate Stock Transfer, Inc.	Outstanding Shares	NA
Counsel	NA	E.P.S	-$0.03
DUNS No.	60-813-2395	Shareholders	NA

Business: The group's principle activity is to provide dial-up Internet access, Web hosting services and Web development services to individuals, public agencies and businesses. On 13-Jan-2004, it acquired p2i newspaper inc. The merger with p2i newspaper at start of 2004 indicates protosource's long-term business strategy: to focus on the delivery of technologically sophisticated, database-driven, business-to-business services and solutions. The primary business is mining, management and databasing of print content for publishing industry and its distribution via Internet. Major clients include newspapers from tribune, mcclatchy and gannett publishing organizations, as well as retailers and government in North America and the UK. The group operates from United States.

Primary SIC and add'l.: 9999

CIK No: 0000932772

Subsidiaries: P2i Newspaper, Inc., P2i, Inc.

Officers: Peter A. Wardle/Dir., CEO, CFO, Pres., Thomas C. Butera/Dir., COO

Directors: Peter A. Wardle/Dir., CEO, CFO, Pres., Mark Blanchard/Non - Exec. Dir., Stewart Kalter/Non - Exec. Dir., Joseph Dimarino/Non - Exec. Dir., Thomas C. Butera/Dir., COO

Owners: Mark Blanchard, Insiders, Peter Wardle, Peter J. Pappas, Thomas Butera

Financial Data: Fiscal Year End:12/31 **Latest Annual Data:** 12/31/2006

Year	Sales	Net Income
2006	$2,641,000	-$304,000
2005	$1,939,000	-$496,000
2004	$1,640,000	-$1,028,000

Curr. Assets:	$402,000	Curr. Liab.:	$4,045,000		
Plant, Equip.:	$71,000	Total Liab.:	$4,715,000	Indic. Yr. Divd.:	NA
Total Assets:	$1,049,000	Net Worth:	-$3,666,000	Debt/ Equity:	NA

ProUroCare Medical Inc

One Carlson Pkwy., Ste. 124, Plymouth, MN, 55447; **PH:** 1-952-476-9093; **Fax:** 1-952-476-9340; http:// www.prourocare.com; **Email:** Inquiries@prourocare.com

General - Incorporation	NV	Stock - Price on:12/24/2007	$0.3
Employees	2	Stock Exchange	OTC
Auditor	Virchow, Krause & Company, LLP	Ticker Symbol	PRRC
Stk Agt	Interwest Transfer Company, Inc.	Outstanding Shares	15,830,000
Counsel	NA	E.P.S	NA
DUNS No.	NA	Shareholders	NA

Business: The groups principal activity is engaged in the business of developing and marketing innovative products for the detection and treatment of male urologic prostate disease. The group markets its product under the tradename ProUroScan(TM). The group operates from the United States.

Primary SIC and add'l.: 3841

CIK No: 0001222244

Subsidiaries: ProUroCare Inc.,

Officers: Richard C. Carlson/Dir., CEO, Richard B. Thon/CFO, Dick Thon/Contact - Investor Relation

Directors: Richard C. Carlson/Dir., CEO, Maurice R. Taylor/62/Chmn., Robert Rudelius/Dir., David F. Koenig/Dir., Alexander Nazarenko/Dir., Scott E. Smith/52/Dir.

Owners: CS Medical Technologies, LLC/12.30%, David Koenig/3.50%, Michael P. Grossman/2.40%, Profile, L.L.C./8.90%, Richard B. Thon/1.40%, Scott Smith/1.00%, Insiders/27.20%, Clement Nelson/13.40%, Maurice R. Taylor/10.60%, Richard C. Carlson/1.10%, Alex Nazarenko/21.40%

Financial Data: Fiscal Year End:12/31 **Latest Annual Data:** 12/31/2006

Year	Sales	Net Income
2006	NA	-$2,960,000
2005	NA	-$2,028,000
2004	NA	-$2,319,000

Curr. Assets:	$18,000	Curr. Liab.:	$1,238,000		
Plant, Equip.:	$4,000	Total Liab.:	$3,648,000	Indic. Yr. Divd.:	NA
Total Assets:	$595,000	Net Worth:	-$3,053,000	Debt/ Equity:	NA

Provectus Pharmaceuticals Inc

7327 Oak Ridge Hwy., Ste. A, Knoxville, TN, 37931; **PH:** 1-865-769-4011; **Fax:** 1-865-769-4013; http:// www.pvct.com; **Email:** info@pvct.com

General - Incorporation	NV	Stock - Price on:12/24/2007	$1.49
Employees	4	Stock Exchange	OTC
Auditor	BDO Seidman, LLP	Ticker Symbol	PVCT
Stk Agt	Atlas Stock Transfer Corp	Outstanding Shares	45,450,000
Counsel	NA	E.P.S	-$0.22
DUNS No.	NA	Shareholders	NA

Business: The groups principle activities include developing a portfolio of patented and proprietary technologies that support multiple products in the prescription drug, medical device and OTC products categories. In the year 2006, the groups patents at merger with Valley Pharmaceuticals, Inc. The group operates from the United States.

Primary SIC and add'l.: 3841 2834 2844

CIK No: 0000315545

Subsidiaries: Provectus Biotech, Inc., Provectus Devicetech, Inc, Provectus Pharmatech, Inc., Pure-ific Corporation, Xantech Pharmaceuticals, Inc.

Officers: Craig H. Dees/55/Chmn., CEO/$950,137.00, Peter R. Culpepper/Corporate Treasurer, Sec., CFO, Timothy Scott/49/Dir., Pres./$950,137.00, Eric A. Wachter/44/Dir., Sr. VP/$950,137.00, Damon Testaverde/Investment Advisor, Daniel Berg/Investor Relations Officer, Janet Vasquez/Contact - Public Relations

Directors: Craig H. Dees/55/Chmn., CEO, David Darst/Member - Advisory Board, Stuart Fuchs/60/Dir., Timothy Scott/49/Dir., Pres., Eric A. Wachter/44/Dir., Sr. VP, Gregory H. Bailey/Member - Advisory Board, Paul M. Goldfarb/Member - Advisory Board

Owners: Timothy C. Scott/5.60%, Stuart Fuchs/2.00%, Donald E. Adams/14.10%, Eric A. Wachter/7.00%, Peter R. Culpepper/2.30%, Craig H. Dees/5.70%, Gryffindor Capital Partners I, L.L.C./11.30%, Insiders/20.80%

Financial Data: Fiscal Year End:12/31   Latest Annual Data: 12/31/2006

Year	Sales	Net Income
2006	$1,000	-$8,871,000
2005	$7,000	-$11,764,000
2004	$32,000	-$4,345,000

Curr. Assets:	$7,311,000	Curr. Liab.:	$802,000		
Plant, Equip.:	$30,000	Total Liab.:	$802,000	Indic. Yr. Divd.:	NA
Total Assets:	$16,325,000	Net Worth:	$15,522,000	Debt/ Equity:	NA

Provida Pension Fund Administrator

Avenida Pedro De Valdivia 100, Santiago; *PH:* 56-26970040; *http://* www.bbvaprovida.cl

General - Incorporation	Chile	Stock - Price on:12/24/2007	$31.1
Employees	1,551	Stock Exchange	NYSE
Auditor	Delloitte Touche Tohmatsu	Ticker Symbol	PVD
Stk Agt.	NA	Outstanding Shares	22,090,000
Counsel	NA	E.P.S.	$3.83
DUNS No.	NA	Shareholders	NA

Business: The group's principal activities are the provision of various pension related services including collection of affiliated worker contributions, management of individual capitalization accounts for each affiliated worker, investment of funds into a single pension fund and payment of pension, life and disability benefits.

Primary SIC and add'l.: 6371

CIK No: 0000931588

Subsidiaries: Provida Internacional S.A.

Officers: Jorge Matuk Chijner/CEO, Mauricio Ayara Ahumada/Mgr. - Human Resources, Andres V. Schilling/General Counsel, Juan Carlos Reyes Madriaza/COO, Gabriel G. Gonzalez/Mgr. - Accounting, Consolidation Division, Joaquin C. Huerta/Chief Investment Officer, Carlo L. Rich/Chief Commercial Officer, Arnaldo E. Miranda/Auditor, Maria Paz Yancz Maclas/Mgr. - Planning, Control Division, Alexia Cornejo Moreno/Mgr. - Operating, Marketing Risk Division

Directors: Gustavo A. Lemaric/Vice Chmn., Gregorio Villalabeitiaa Galarraga/Chmn., Carlos Pla Royo/Dir., Alberto P. Cruz/Dir., Juan Prado Rey-Baltar/Dir., Ximena Rincon Gonzalez/Dir., Jose Antonio Viera Gallo/Dir.

Owners: BBVA Pensiones Chile S.A./51.62%, Mario Picero Castro, Juan Carlos, Carlo Ljubetic Rich, The Bank of New York/27.30%, Insiders

Financial Data: Fiscal Year End:12/31   Latest Annual Data: 12/31/2006

Year	Sales	Net Income
2006	$315,653,000	$84,518,000
2005	$265,274,000	$68,562,000
2004	$221,371,000	$61,465,000

Curr. Assets:	$31,937,000	Curr. Liab.:	$112,590,000		
Plant, Equip.:	$48,811,000	Total Liab.:	$172,431,000	Indic. Yr. Divd.:	NA
Total Assets:	$568,396,000	Net Worth:	$395,966,000	Debt/ Equity:	NA

Provide Commerce Inc

5005 Wateridge Vista Dr., San Diego, CA, 92121; *PH:* 1-858-638-4900; *http://* www.prvd.com

General - Incorporation	DE	Stock - Price on:12/24/2007	$33.73
Employees	NA	Stock Exchange	NDQ
Auditor	Ernst & Young LLP	Ticker Symbol	PRVD
Stk Agt	EquiServe Trust Co N.A	Outstanding Shares	NA
Counsel	NA	E.P.S.	NA
DUNS No.	NA	Shareholders	NA

Business: The group principal activities are providing an e-commerce marketplace for perishable goods that consistently delivers fresh, high-quality products direct from the supplier to the customer at competitive prices. The group platform combines an online storefront, proprietary supply chain management technology, established supplier relationships and an integrated logistical relationship with federal express corporation to bypass legacy supply chains of wholesalers, distributors and retailers. The group's trademarks are provide commercetm, proflowers(R) uptown primetm, cherry moon farmstm and freshness factor(r).

Primary SIC and add'l.: 5193 5421 7375

CIK No: 0001263756

Officers: William Strauss/49/Dir., COO, CEO, Pres., John Kuehn/Sr. VP - Planning, Logistics, Adam Fischer/VP - Planning, Forecasting, Mark Irace/VP - Marketing, Jonathan Sills/VP - Strategy, Product Development, Rex Bosen/VP - Finance, Accounting, Mark Sottosanti/Sr. VP - Planning, Logistics, Blake Bilstad/Sr. VP, General Counsel, Sec., Simon Leach/VP - Customer Retention, Bharat Gogia/VP - Information Systems, Greg Smith/VP - Merchandising, Marc Schneider/VP - Customer, Contact - Operations, Kent Olson/Corporate Development, Prana Gogia/VP - Information Systems, Anna Hansen/Sr. VP - Consumer Insights, Service (18 Officers included in Index)

Directors: William Strauss/49/Dir., COO, CEO, Pres., Joel T. Citron/45/Chmn., Jordanna Schutz/27/Dir., Peter J. McLaughlin/69/Dir., James M. Myers/49/Dir., Arthur B. Laffer/67/Dir., Marilyn R. Seymann/64/Dir., Joseph P. Kennedy/55/Dir., David E.R. Dangoor/58/Dir.

Providence & Worcester Railroad Co

75 Hammond St., Worcester, MA, 01610; *PH:* 1-508-755-4000; *Fax:* 1-508-753-5548; *http://* www.pwrr.com

General - Incorporation	RI	Stock - Price on:12/24/2007	$19.25
Employees	149	Stock Exchange	AMEX
Auditor	Deloitte & Touche LLP	Ticker Symbol	PWX
Stk Agt.	Computershare Investor Services LLC	Outstanding Shares	4,550,000
Counsel	NA	E.P.S.	$0.03
DUNS No.	00-150-3614	Shareholders	NA

Business: The group's principle activity is to provide regional freight railroad services in Massachusetts, Rhode Island, Connecticut and New York. The company, through its connecting carriers, services customers located throughout North America. The company currently has 545 miles of tracks and operates the double stack intermodal terminal facilities in new England in worcester, Massachusetts. The company also generates income through sale of properties, grants of easements and licenses and leases of land and tracks. In 2003, chemicals and plastics and construction aggregate were the two largest commodity groups transported by the company. It serves approximately 165 customers in Massachusetts, Rhode Island, Connecticut and New York. The group operates from United States.

Primary SIC and add'l.: 4731

CIK No: 0000831968

Officers: Robert H. Eder/Chmn., CEO/$475,621.00, Joe Martin/Accounting Representative, Jonathan Meindersma/Assist. General Counsel, Clarke Brown/Dir. - Purchasing, Excursions, Jeanne Blackman/Accounting Receivable, Denis Glaude/Supervisor, Communications, Signals, Carmella Rigoli/Administrative Assist., William Wentworth/Supervisor - Equipment, Mary Lou Murphy/Enginering, Thomas Lewis/Chief Engineer - Track, David Rutkowski/Chief Mechanical Officer, John Killoy/Locomotive Superintendent, James Cox/Car Shop Superintendent, Marie Angelini/Sec., General Counsel, Richard Fisher/Dir. - Rules, Safety (33 Officers included in Index)

Directors: Robert H. Eder/Chmn., CEO, James C. Garvey/Dir., Scott P. Conti/Dir., Pres., Richard W. Anderson/Dir., John J. Healy/Dir., Charles M. McCollam/Dir., Joseph J. Garrahy/Dir., Craig M. Scott/Dir., Frank W. Barrett/Dir.

Owners: Keeley Asset Management Corp./8.40%, Charles M. McCollam, Robert H. Eder/19.40%, Richard W. Anderson/4.40%, Robert H. Eder/18.60%, Steinberg Asset Management, LLC/10.30%, Craig M. Scott, James C. Garvey, David F. Fitzgerald, Joseph J. Garrahy, Robert H. Eder/92.60%, Frank W. Barrett, Scott P. Conti, John J. Healy, Frank K. Rogers (18 Owners included in Index)

Financial Data: Fiscal Year End:12/31   Latest Annual Data: 12/31/2006

Year	Sales	Net Income
2006	$29,824,000	$1,042,000
2005	$27,942,000	$1,258,000
2004	$26,490,000	$1,038,000

Curr. Assets:	$6,475,000	Curr. Liab.:	$4,150,000	P/E Ratio:	641.67
Plant, Equip.:	$88,549,000	Total Liab.:	$24,400,000	Indic. Yr. Divd.:	$0.160
Total Assets:	$95,024,000	Net Worth:	$70,624,000	Debt/ Equity:	NA

Providence Resources Inc

Airfield House, Airfield Pk., Donnybrook, Dublin; *PH:* 44-35312194074; *Fax:* 44-35312194006; *http://* www.providenceresources.com

General - Incorporation	TX	Stock - Price on:12/24/2007	$0.14
Employees	NA	Stock Exchange	OTC
Auditor	Chisholm, Bierwolf & Nilson, LLC	Ticker Symbol	PVRS
Stk Agt	NA	Outstanding Shares	NA
Counsel	NA	E.P.S.	NA
DUNS No.	NA	Shareholders	NA

Business: The groups principal activity is to own and operates one drilling rig and two well service rigs based in Young County, Texas. The group operates from the United States.

Primary SIC and add'l.: 1311

CIK No: 0001112064

Subsidiaries: PDX Drilling I, LLC, Providence Exploration, LLC, PRT Holdings, LLC

Officers: Tony O'Reilly/Dir., Chief Executive, Stephen Carroll/Dir., Dir. - Finance, Michael Graham/Dir., Company Sec., Tony Odone/COO, Barry Ridley/Commercial Mgr., John O'Sullivan/Exploration Mgr., Andrew Rawlinson/Sr. Operations Geologist, Fergus Roe/Operations CO - Ordinator, Susan Bishop/Mgr. Technical Processing - Cartography, Anne Marie Smyth/Project Geologist

Directors: Brian Hillery/Non Exec. Chmn., Tony O'Reilly/Dir., Chief Executive, Stephen Carroll/Dir., Dir. - Finance, Lex Gamble/Non Exec. Dir., Peter Kidney/Non Exec. Dir., James S.D. McCarthy/Non Exec. Dir., Philip Nolan/Non Exec. Dir., Michael Graham/Dir., Company Sec.

Owners: Insiders/14.04%, Nora Coccaro, Markus Mueller/13.72%, Nicolas Mathys/6.43%, Bo Thorwald Berglin/5.08%

Financial Data: Fiscal Year End:12/31   Latest Annual Data: 12/31/2006

Year	Sales	Net Income
2006	$26,000	-$6,762,000
2005	NA	-$945,000
2004	$75,000	-$312,000

Curr. Assets:	$2,265,000	Curr. Liab.:	$1,637,000		
Plant, Equip.:	$27,483,000	Total Liab.:	$5,527,000	Indic. Yr. Divd.:	NA
Total Assets:	$29,796,000	Net Worth:	$24,152,000	Debt/ Equity:	NA

Providence Service Corp

5524 E 4th St., Tucson, AZ, 85711; *PH:* 1-520-747-6600; *Fax:* 1-520-747-6605; *http://* www.provcorp.com; *Email:* businessinquiries@provcorp.com

General - Incorporation	DE	Stock - Price on:12/24/2007	$27.64
Employees	2,811	Stock Exchange	NDQ
Auditor	McGladrey & Pullen LLP	Ticker Symbol	PRSC
Stk Agt	Computershare Investor Services LLC	Outstanding Shares	11,570,000
Counsel	Blank Rome LLP	E.P.S.	$0.85
DUNS No.	NA	Shareholders	NA

Business: The group's principal activity is to provide home and community based social services to government sponsored clients under programs such as welfare, juvenile justice, medicaid and corrections. The group operates no beds, treatment facilities, hospitals, or group homes preferring to provide services in the client's own home or other community setting. The group also contracts with not-for-profit organizations to provide management services for a fee. The group operates primarily in Arizona, Delaware, Florida, Illinois, Indiana, Maine, Michigan, Nebraska, New Mexico, North Carolina, Ohio, Oklahoma, South Carolina, Tennessee, Texas, Virginia, and west Virginia. On 06-Jan-2004, the group acquired dockside services, inc.

Primary SIC and add'l.: 8322

CIK No: 0001220754

Subsidiaries: AlphaCare Resources, Inc., Camelot Care Corporation, Childrens Behavioral Health, Inc., Choices Group, Inc., College Community Services, Cypress Management Services, Inc., Dockside Services, Inc., Drawbridges Counseling Services, LLC, Family Preservation Services of Florida, Inc., Family Preservation Services of North Carolina, Inc., Family Preservation Services of Washington DC, Inc., Family Preservation Services of West Virginia, Inc., Family Preservation Services, Inc., Family-Based Strategies, Inc., Maple Star Nevada 28 Subsidiaries included in the Index

Officers: Fletcher Jay McCusker/Chmn., CEO, Fred D. Furman/Exec. VP, General Counsel, Craig A. Norris/COO, Michael N. Deitch/CFO, Mary J. Shea/Exec. VP - Program Services, Michelle Pitot/Dir. - Organizational Development, Michael Fidgeon/COO - Eastern Region, Tasha Walsh/VP - Clinical Services, Betty Dixon/VP - Development, Kate Blute/Dir. - Investor, Public Relations

Directors: Fletcher Jay McCusker/Chmn., CEO, Warren S. Rustand/Dir., Hunter Hurst/Dir., Kristi L. Meints/Dir., Richard Singleton/Dir., Steven I. Geringer/Dir.

Owners: Michael N. Deitch, Fred Furman, Deutsche Asset Management, Inc/6.80%, Next Century Growth Investors, LLC/8.10%, Fletcher Jay McCusker/1.00%, Warren S. Rustand, Craig A. Norris, Mary J. Shea, Richard Singleton, Kristi L. Meints, Hunter Hurst, Steven I. Geringer, Wasatch Advisors, Inc/11.70%, Bank of America/8.10%, William Boyd Dover *(19 Owners included in Index)*

Financial Data: ***Fiscal Year End:***12/31 ***Latest Annual Data:*** 12/31/2006

Year	Sales	Net Income
2006	$191,857,000	$9,381,000
2005	$145,708,000	$9,425,000
2004	$96,966,000	$7,085,000

Curr. Assets:	$95,733,000	***Curr. Liab.:***	$28,599,000	***P/E Ratio:***	33.30
Plant, Equip.:	$2,784,000	***Total Liab.:***	$33,279,000	***Indic. Yr. Divd.:***	NA
Total Assets:	$192,335,000	***Net Worth:***	$159,056,000	***Debt/ Equity:***	0.0040

Provident Community Bancshares Inc

Formerly: Union Financial Bancshares Inc
2700 Celn.se Rd., Rock Hill, SC, 29732; ***PH:*** 1-803-325-9400; ***http://*** www.provcombank.com

General - Incorporation	DE	***Stock***- Price on:12/24/2007	$21.2
Employees	72	Stock Exchange	NDQ
Auditor	Elliot Davis LLC	Ticker Symbol	NA
Stk Agt	Registrar & Transfer Co	Outstanding Shares	1,830,000
Counsel	Nelson Mullins Riley & Scarborough	E.P.S	$1.50
DUNS No.	76-585-6042	Shareholders	NA

Business: The group's principal activities are to attract deposits from the general public and originate mortgage loans, commercial real estate, construction and consumer loans. The deposit accounts includes now accounts, money market savings accounts, passbook and statement saving accounts, individual retirement accounts and certificate of deposit accounts. The operations of the group are carried through its main office and six full service banking centers and a lending and investment center, which is located in South Carolina. Provident financial services is a wholly-owned subsidiary of the bank that provides investment brokerage services.

Primary SIC and add'l.: 6035 6712

CIK No: 0000926164

Subsidiaries: Provident Community Bank, Union Financial Statutory Trust I

Officers: Dwight V. Neese/57/Dir., CEO, Pres./$394,851.00, Lud W. Vaughn/57/Exec. VP, COO - Provident Community Bank/$169,955.00, Wanda J. Wells/52/Shareholder Relation Officer, Sr. VP, Chief Administrative Officer, Corp. Sec. - Provident Community Bank, Richard Flake/59/CFO, Exec. VP/$242,979.00, Jeff M. Thompson/VP - Laurens Marketing Executive, Commercial Relationship Mgr. - Provident Community Bank, Susan D. Taylor/VP - Fairfield Marketing Executive - Provident Community Bank, Lori H. Patrick/VP - York County Consumer Marketing Executive - Provident Community Bank, Lisa Morris/VP - Union County Marketing Executive - Provident Community Bank, Brenda Billardello/VP, Marketing Dir. - Provident Community Bank, Henry G. Alexander/VP - Commercial Relationship Mgr. - Provident Community Bank, Mark Pack/Chief Credit Officer - Provident Community Bank, Carolyn Belue/VP, Operational Administration Mgr. - Provident Community Bank, Ed A. Brock/York County Marketing Pres., Sr. Commercial Relationship Mgr. - Provident Community Bank, Holly Coffer/Assist. VP - Human Resources Administrator - Provident Community Bank, Crystal Hamby/Consumer Marketing Executive Greenville County, Provident Community Bank

Directors: Dwight V. Neese/57/Dir., CEO, Pres., Carl L. Mason/Chmn., Louis M. Jordan/Dir., Philip C. Wilkins/Dir. - Provident Community Bank, Robert H. Breakfield/Dir. - Provident Community Bank, William M. Graham/Dir. - Provident Community Bank, Russell Smart/Dir. - Provident Community Bank, James W. Edwards/Dir. - Provident Community Bank

Owners: Robert H. Breakfield, Louis M. Jordan/6.90%, Lud W. Vaughn, Carl L. Mason/1.00%, William M. Graham/1.70%, Dwight V. Neese/4.30%, James W. Edwards, Jeffrey L. Gendell/8.90%, Richard H. Flake/3.00%, Philip C. Wilkins, Insiders/18.20%

Financial Data: ***Fiscal Year End:***12/31 ***Latest Annual Data:*** 12/31/2006

Year	Sales	Net Income
2006	$26,377,000	$2,803,000
2005	$21,804,000	$2,466,000
2004	$19,535,000	$2,156,000

Curr. Assets:	$11,841,000	***Curr. Liab.:***	$347,757,000	***P/E Ratio:***	14.52
Plant, Equip.:	$5,708,000	***Total Liab.:***	$361,663,000	***Indic. Yr. Divd.:***	$0.460
Total Assets:	$387,630,000	***Net Worth:***	$25,967,000	***Debt/ Equity:***	0.4661

Provident Financial Holdings Inc

3756 Central Ave., Riverside, CA, 92506; ***PH:*** 1-951-686-6060; ***Fax:*** 1-951-782-6134; ***http://*** www.myprovident.com

General - Incorporation	DE	***Stock***- Price on:12/24/2007	$24.82
Employees	266	Stock Exchange	NDQ
Auditor	Deloitte & Touche LLP	Ticker Symbol	PROV
Stk Agt	Registrar & Transfer Co	Outstanding Shares	6,500,000
Counsel	Breyer & Assocaite PC	E.P.S	$1.059
DUNS No.	95-935-5090	Shareholders	NA

Business: The group's principal activities are to provide community banking, mortgage banking, investment services and real estate operations. The services are provided to consumers and small to mid-sized businesses in the inland empire region of southern California. The group's operations primarily consist of accepting deposits from customers within the communities surrounding its full service offices and investing those funds in single-family, multi-family, commercial real estate, construction, commercial business, consumer and other loans. Mortgage banking activities consist of the origination and sale of mortgage loans secured by single-family residences and consumer loans. The group offers investment services and conducts real estate operations through its subsidiary, provident financial corporation. The business of the group is conducted through eleven banking offices located in California.

Primary SIC and add'l.: 6712 6035

CIK No: 0001010470

Subsidiaries: First Service Corporation., Profed Mortgage, Inc., Provident Financial Corp, Provident Savings Bank, F.S.B.

Officers: Craig G. Blunden/Chmn., CEO, Pres., Thomas Fenn/Chief Lending Officer, Sr. VP, Kathryn R. Gonzales/Sr. VP - Retail Banking, Donavon P. Ternes/CFO, Exec. VP, Lilian Brunner-Salter/CIO, Sr. VP, Richard L. Gale/Sr. VP - Mortgage Banking, Deborah Hill/VP - Human Resources, David S. Weiant/Chief Lending Officer, Sr. VP

Directors: Craig G. Blunden/Chmn., CEO, Pres., Bruce W. Bennett/Dir., Robert G. Schrader/Dir., William E. Thomas/Dir., Joseph P. Barr/Dir., Debbi H. Guthrie/Dir., Roy H. Taylor/Dir.

Owners: Thomas Fenn, Robert G. Schrader/3.03%, Joseph P. Barr, Dimensional Fund Advisors LP/9.07%, Roy H. Taylor, Craig G. Blunden/6.19%, Thomson Horstmann & Bryant, Inc./9.84%, Richard L. Gale/1.48%, Lilian Salter, Donavon P. Ternes/2.24%, William E. Thomas, Jeffrey L. Gendell/9.85%, Bruce W. Bennett, Provident Savings Bank, F.S.B./10.98%, Insiders/17.87% *(17 Owners included in Index)*

Financial Data: ***Fiscal Year End:***06/30 ***Latest Annual Data:*** 06/30/2007

Year	Sales	Net Income
2007	$118,529,000	$11,286,000
2006	$112,848,000	$20,540,000
2005	$99,913,000	$18,699,000

Curr. Assets:	$123,062,000	***Curr. Liab.:***	$940,049,000		
Plant, Equip.:	$6,860,000	***Total Liab.:***	$1,486,260,000	***Indic. Yr. Divd.:***	$0.720
Total Assets:	$1,622,470,000	***Net Worth:***	$136,210,000	***Debt/ Equity:***	4.8403

Provident Financial Services Inc

830 Bergen Ave., Jersey City, NJ, 07306; ***PH:*** 1-201-333-1000; ***Fax:*** 1-201-915-5480; ***http://*** www.providentbanknj.com

General - Incorporation	DE	***Stock***- Price on:12/24/2007	$16.87
Employees	795	Stock Exchange	NYSE
Auditor	KPMG LLP	Ticker Symbol	PFS
Stk Agt	Registrar & Transfer Co	Outstanding Shares	66,690,000
Counsel	NA	E.P.S	$0.85
DUNS No.	NA	Shareholders	NA

Business: The group's principal activity is to provide a full range of banking services to individual and corporate customers through branch offices in New Jersey. It attracts deposits from general public and originates commercial real estate loans, residential mortgage loans, mortgage warehouse loans, commercial business loans, construction loans and consumer loans. The group also sells loans, primarily long-term fixed-rate residential mortgages and invests in mortgage-backed securities, debt and equity securities and other permissible investments. The deposit products include savings, money market accounts and now accounts. The group's services are provided through 54 full-service banking offices in the New Jersey counties of hudson, bergen, essex, mercer, middlesex, monmouth, morris, ocean, somerset and union..

Primary SIC and add'l.: 6035 6712

CIK No: 0001178970

Subsidiaries: First Sentinel Capital Trust I, First Sentinel Capital Trust II, The Provident Bank

Officers: Paul M. Pantozzi/Chmn., CEO/$2,866,685.00, Kevin J. Ward/Vice Chmn., COO/$1,065,232.00, Kenneth J. Wagner/Sr. VP - Investor Relations, John F. Kuntz/General Counsel, Corp. Sec., Christopher Martin/Dir., Pres./$509,672.00, Linda A. Niro/Sr. VP, CFO/$532,657.00

Directors: Paul M. Pantozzi/Chmn., CEO, Kevin J. Ward/Vice Chmn., COO, Edward O'Donnell/Dir., Thomas E. Sheenan/Dir., John P. Mulkerin/Dir., John G. Collins/Dir., Carlos Hernandez/Dir., Geoffrey M. Connor/Dir., William T. Jackson/Dir., Jeffries Shein/Dir., Thomas W. Berry/Dir., Laura L. Brooks/Dir., Katharine Laud/Dir., Arthur McConnell/Dir., Frank L. Fekete/Dir. *(16 Directors included in Index)*

Owners: Christopher Martin, Thomas E. Sheenan, Paul M. Pantozzi/1.40%, Dimensional Fund Advisors LP/7.00%, Jeffries Shein/1.20%, Carlos Hernandez, Thomas W. Berry, Kevin J. Ward, Private Capital Management, L.P./9.50%, Donald W. Blum, Geoffrey M. Connor, Linda A. Niro, Insiders/7.30%, Arthur McConnell, Edward ODonnell *(21 Owners included in Index)*

Financial Data: ***Fiscal Year End:***12/31 ***Latest Annual Data:*** 12/31/2006

Year	Sales	Net Income
2006	$314,090,000	$53,685,000
2005	$305,683,000	$58,499,000
2004	$258,694,000	$49,301,000

Curr. Assets:	$113,762,000	***Curr. Liab.:***	$3,826,463,000	***P/E Ratio:***	20.08
Plant, Equip.:	$60,339,000	***Total Liab.:***	$4,723,808,000	***Indic. Yr. Divd.:***	$0.440
Total Assets:	$5,742,964,000	***Net Worth:***	$1,019,156,000	***Debt/ Equity:***	0.8212

Provident New York Bancorp

Formerly: Provident Bank
400 Rella Blvd., Montebello, NY, 10901; ***PH:*** 1-845-369-8040; ***http://*** www.providentbanking.com

General - Incorporation	DE	***Stock***- Price on:12/24/2007	$13.82
Employees	507	Stock Exchange	NDQ
Auditor	Crowe Chizek & Co. LLC	Ticker Symbol	PBNY
Stk Agt	Registrar & Transfer Co	Outstanding Shares	42,390,000
Counsel	Luse Gorman Pomerenk & Schick	E.P.S	$0.48
DUNS No.	NA	Shareholders	NA

Business: The group's principal activity is to provide financial services by accepting deposits and originating loans to individuals and businesses. It offers federal deposit insurance corporation insured savings and demand deposits to customers. It also originates one-to-four family residential and real estate loans, consumer loans, construction loans and commercial business loans. The deposits offered include demand, savings, now, money market accounts and certificates of deposits. The additional products and services offered include Internet banking services for consumers, investment management and trust services for companies and individuals, and mutual funds and annuities products for individuals. The business of the group is conducted through 18 branch offices and 25 ATMs throughout rockland county and orange counties, New York. On 14-Jan-2004, the group acquired ellenville national bank holding company, inc.

Primary SIC and add'l.: 6035 6712

CIK No: 0001070154

Subsidiaries: Hardenburgh Abstract Company of Orange County,Inc., Provest Services Corp. I, Provest Services Corp. II, Provident Municipal Bank, Provident REIT, Inc., Warsave Development Co., WSB Funding, Inc.

Officers: George Strayton/Dir., CEO, Pres., Paul Maisch/CFO, Exec. VP, Carl Capuano/Sr. VP, Commercial Lending Mgr., William Lamadore/Sr. VP - Commercial Loans, Corporate Services, Daniel G. Rothstein/Exec. VP, Chief Risk Officer, General Counsel, Corp. Sec., Stephen G. Dormer/Exec. VP, Assist. to The Office, Pres. - Commercial Lending, Strategic Planning, John J. Fitzpatrick/Sr. VP, Dir. - Management Information Systems, Richard Jones/Exec. VP - Business Services, John Carothers/Sr. VP, Chief Credit Officer, Alfred Friedman/Sr. VP, Chief Auditor

Directors: George Strayton/Dir., CEO, Pres., William F. Helmer/Chmn., Judith Hershaft/Dir., Donald T. McNelis/Dir., Thomas F. Jauntig/Dir., Victoria Kossover/Dir., Richard Nozell/Dir., Burt Steinberg/Dir., Dennis L. Coyle/Dir., Carl J. Rosenstock/Dir., William R. Sichol/Dir., Gary F. Zeh/Dir., Michael R. Kennedy/Dir., Thomas G. Kahn/Dir.

Owners: William R. Sichol, Daniel G. Rothstein, Thomas G. Kahn/2.60%, Stephen G. Dormer, Insiders/12.10%, Victoria Kossover, Michael R. Kennedy, Judith Hershaft, William F. Helmer/1.00%, George Strayton/1.90%, Richard O. Jones, Richard A. Nozell, Paul A. Maisch, Thomas F. Jauntig, Provident New York Bancorp/5.10% (20 Owners included in Index)

Financial Data: Fiscal Year End:09/30   Latest Annual Data: 09/30/2007

Year	Sales	Net Income
2007	$171,479,000	$19,627,000
2006	$152,768,000	$20,195,000
2005	$133,178,000	$21,242,000

Curr. Assets:	$70,521,000	Curr. Liab.:	$2,412,398,000	P/E Ratio:	29.40
Plant, Equip.:	$31,739,000	Total Liab.:	$2,436,051,000	Indic. Yr. Divd.:	$0.200
Total Assets:	$2,841,337,000	Net Worth:	$405,286,000	Debt/ Equity:	0.0237

Providential Holdings Inc

17011 Beach Blvd., Ste. 1230, Huntington Beach, CA, 92647; *PH:* 1-714-843-5450; *Fax:* 1-714-843-5452; *http://* phiglobal.com

General - Incorporation	NV	Stock- Price on:12/24/2007	NA
Employees	NA	Stock Exchange	OTC
Auditor	Kabani & Co, Inc	Ticker Symbol	PRVH
Stk Agt	Jersey Transfer & Trust Co	Outstanding Shares	NA
Counsel	NA	E.P.S.	$0.00
DUNS No.	09-608-7267	Shareholders	NA

Business: The group's principal activities are to provide financial services, merger and acquisition advisory and consulting services. The group also advises on importing and exporting of industrial and consumer goods and on emerging markets and technologies. The products and services of the group include liquid crystal displays (LCD's), information technology, identification technologies, mobile entertainment systems, industrial machinery and equipment, telecommunications and computer hardware and software. The group is a diversified holding company. On 17-Jan-2003, it acquired 46.5% of nettel global communications group. The group operates solely in the United States.

Primary SIC and add'l.: 7389

CIK No: 0000704172

Subsidiaries: Diva Entertainment, Inc, Providential Capital, Inc, Providential Energy Corporation., Providential Securities, Inc., Provimex, Inc., Touchlink Communications, Inc

Officers: Henry D. Fahman/Chmn., CEO, Acting CFO, Tam T. Bui/COO, CTO, Timothy Pham/VP - Business Development, Gene Bennett/Business Development Officer - Asia, Tina T. Phan/Dir., Sec., Treasurer

Directors: Henry D. Fahman/Chmn., CEO, Acting CFO, Tina T. Phan/Dir., Sec., Treasurer, Robert W. Stevenson/Dir., Thorman Hwinn/Dir.

Owners: Insiders/22.06%, Tina T. Phan/6.87%, Henry D. Fahman/14.91%, Thorman Hwinn

Financial Data: Fiscal Year End:06/30   Latest Annual Data: 06/30/2007

Year	Sales	Net Income
2007	$3,572,000	$34,000
2006	$4,119,000	$992,000
2005	$4,279,000	-$2,120,000

Curr. Assets:	$9,921,000	Curr. Liab.:	$3,116,000		
Plant, Equip.:	$2,000	Total Liab.:	$3,116,000	Indic. Yr. Divd.:	NA
Total Assets:	$9,922,000	Net Worth:	$6,806,000	Debt/ Equity:	NA

Proxim Corp

935 Stewart Dr., Sunnyvale, CA, 94085; *PH:* 1-408-731-2700; *http://* www.proxim.com

General - Incorporation	DE	Stock- Price on:12/24/2007	$0.008
Employees	353	Stock Exchange	OTC
Auditor	PricewaterhouseCoopers LLP	Ticker Symbol	PROXQ
Stk Agt	EquiServe Trust Co N.A	Outstanding Shares	33,780,000
Counsel	Wilson Sonsini Goodrich & Rosati	E.P.S.	-$4.416
DUNS No.	15-392-4972	Shareholders	NA

Business: The group's principle activities ar to provide broadband or high-speed wireless access products that enable service providers, businesses and other enterprises to deliver data, voice and video services. It operates in two segments: wireless wide area network ('wwan') and wireless local area network ('wlan'). The wwan product line includes point-to-point lynx, tsunami products and point-to-multipoint tsunami products. The wlan product line includes orinoco 802.11 access point and client card products. Products are marketed worldwide to service providers and enterprise customers, directly through its sales force and indirectly through distributors, system integrators, value-added resellers and OEMs, such as comstor, somera communications inc and tech data. Customers and partners include at&t wireless group, avaya, cingular wireless, dell computer, fujitsu, hewlett-packard, motorola, telefonica, telmex, verizon wireless, China mobile, China unicom, and t-mobile, usa.

Primary SIC and add'l.: 3669 4813

CIK No: 0001112263

Subsidiaries: Proxim Europe B.V., Proxim International Holdings, Inc., Proxim K.K. a/k/a Proxim Kabushiki Kaisha, Proxim Wireless Networks, Inc., WirelessHome Corporation

Officers: Robert E. Fitzgerald/Dir., CEO, Dana E. Wheeler/Sr. VP - Millimeter Wave Operations, Mark S. Bittner/Sr. VP - Sales, Americas, Gabriel Hebert/VP - Global Operations, Support, David L. Renauld/VP - Corporate Affairs, General Counsel, Sec., Pankaj Manglik/Dir., COO, Pres., Brian Sereda/CFO, Geoffrey L. Smith/Sr. VP - Business Development, Lionel Chmilewsky/Sr. VP - International

Directors: Robert E. Fitzgerald/Dir., CEO, Daniel A. Saginario/Chmn., John Gerdelman/Dir., Alan B. Howe/Dir., Pankaj Manglik/Dir., COO, Pres.

Financial Data: Fiscal Year End:12/31   Latest Annual Data: 12/31/2004

Year	Sales	Net Income
2004	$113,724,000	-$48,727,000
2003	$148,466,000	-$127,440,000
2002	$144,660,000	-$239,850,000

Curr. Assets:	$37,311,000	Curr. Liab.:	$54,158,000		
Plant, Equip.:	$5,981,000	Total Liab.:	$67,864,000	Indic. Yr. Divd.:	NA
Total Assets:	$63,607,000	Net Worth:	-$44,928,000	Debt/ Equity:	NA

Proxim Wireless

Formerly: YDI Wireless Inc

2115 Onel Dr., San Jose, CA, 95131; *PH:* 1-408-731-2700; *http://* www.tlxs.com

General - Incorporation	DE	Stock- Price on:12/24/2007	$1.4
Employees	240	Stock Exchange	NDQ
Auditor	Fitzgerald, Snyder & Co. P.C	Ticker Symbol	PRXM
Stk Agt	Registrar & Transfer Co	Outstanding Shares	21,550,000
Counsel	NA	E.P.S.	-$0.88
DUNS No.	NA	Shareholders	NA

Business: The group's principal activity is to provide broadband, or high-speed, wireless access products and access cards both in the United States and internationally. It offers a broad range of systems that enable service providers, businesses and other enterprises to create complete broadband wireless networks that connect end-users to the fiber backbone. The group has two primary product lines: high-speed point-to-point products and point-to-multipoint products. Point-to-point products includes our link cx and link ex and point-to-multipoint product includes etherant ii. The group operates in North America (us and Canada), Latin America (Mexico, central, South America and Caribbean), Asia-Pacific (China, Taiwan, Japan, other pacific territories, Australia, New Zealand), Europe (western, eastern, Russia), Middle East and Africa. On 13-May-2004 the group acquired karlnet inc, on 22-Jun-2004, terabeam corporation and on 25-Jun-2004, ricochet networks inc.

Primary SIC and add'l.: 3679 3663

CIK No: 0000712511

Subsidiaries: KarlNet, Inc., Proxim Europe B.V., Proxim Hong Kong Limited, Proxim International Operations, Inc., Proxim Wireless Corporation, Ricochet Networks, Inc., Terabeam Corporation, Terabeam International Holdings, Inc., Young Design, Inc.

Officers: Robert E. Fitzgerald/Dir., CEO/$747,744.00, Pankaj Manglik/COO, Pres./$736,133.00, David L. Renauld/VP - Corporate Affairs, General Counsel, Sec./$234,237.00, Brian J. Sereda/47/CFO, Treasurer/$175,572.00

Directors: Robert E. Fitzgerald/Dir., CEO, Daniel A. Saginario/Chmn., John Gerdelman/Dir., Robert A. Wiedemer/Dir., Alan B. Howe/Dir.

Owners: Robert E. Fitzgerald/14.40%, Patrick L. Milton, Lloyd I. Miller/6.30%, David L. Renauld, Pankaj Manglik, Concorde Equity II, LLC/10.70%, Daniel A. Saginario, Brian J. Sereda, Robert A. Wiedemer, Mobius Venture Capital/10.40%, Insiders/16.30%, John W. Gerdelman

Financial Data: Fiscal Year End:12/31   Latest Annual Data: 12/31/2006

Year	Sales	Net Income
2006	$75,384,000	-$23,163,000
2005	$58,982,000	-$11,160,000
2004	$22,897,000	-$1,346,000

Curr. Assets:	$27,385,000	Curr. Liab.:	$16,953,000		
Plant, Equip.:	$2,660,000	Total Liab.:	$19,041,000	Indic. Yr. Divd.:	NA
Total Assets:	$49,875,000	Net Worth:	$30,834,000	Debt/ Equity:	0.0657

Pruco Life Insurance Co

213 Washington St., Newark, NJ, 07102; *PH:* 1-973-802-6000; *http://* www.prudential.com

General - Incorporation	AZ	Stock- Price on:12/24/2007	NA
Employees	NA	Stock Exchange	NA
Auditor	PricewaterhouseCoopers LLP	Ticker Symbol	NA
Stk Agt	AIM Investment Services, Inc	Outstanding Shares	NA
Counsel	NA	E.P.S.	NA
DUNS No.	13-444-1658	Shareholders	NA

Business: The group's principal activity is to provide individual life insurance, variable life insurance, term life insurance, variable and fixed annuities and a non-participating guaranteed interest contract called prudential credit enhanced gic. These services are provided in the district of columbia, guam and in all states and territories except New York. The products include term life insurance, universal life insurance, variable and fixed annuities and guaranteed investment contracts. The group is a wholly owned subsidiary of the prudential insurance company of America.

Primary SIC and add'l.: 6311

CIK No: 0000777917

Subsidiaries: Pruco Life Insurance Company, Prudential Financial Inc., Prudential Insurance., The Prudential Insurance Company of America

Officers: Scott D. Kaplan/Dir., CEO, Pres., Thomas C. Castano/Attorney in Fact, Tucker I. Marr/Chief Financial, Accounting Officer

Directors: Scott D. Kaplan/Dir., CEO, Pres., James J. Avery/Dir., David R. Odenath/Dir., Bernard J. Jacob/Dir., Ronald Paul Joelson/Dir., Helen M. Galt/Dir.

Prudential Bancorp Inc of Pennsylvania

1834 Oregon Ave., Philadelphia, PA, 19145; *PH:* 1-215-755-1500; *Fax:* 1-215-755-7521; *http://* www.prudentialsavingsbank.com; *Email:* info@prudentialsavingsbank.com

General - Incorporation	PA	Stock- Price on:12/24/2007	$13.65
Employees	68	Stock Exchange	NDQ
Auditor	Deloitte & Touche LLP	Ticker Symbol	PBIP
Stk Agt	Registrar & Transfer Co	Outstanding Shares	11,760,000
Counsel	NA	E.P.S.	$0.31
DUNS No.	NA	Shareholders	NA

Business: The groups principal activity is to provide banking and financial services. The financial products of the group include real estate and construction loan, commercial loan and multi-family residential loan. The group operates from the United States. The assets of the group for the year 2006 were $472,381,338.

Primary SIC and add'l.: 6036 6712

CIK No: 0001302324

Subsidiaries: Prudential Savings Bank

Officers: Thomas A. Vento/Dir., CEO, Pres., Christopher J. Mercanti/VP - Treasurer, Jerome R. Balka/Dir., Counsel, Regina Wilson/VP, Sec., Salvatore Fratanduono/VP - Lending, Louis Diflavis/Assist. VP, Investment Specialist, Donna Schaefer/Assist. Sec., Joseph R. Corrato/Exec. VP, CFO, Chief Accounting Officer, David H. Krauter/VP, Chief Lending Officer, Maria Ann Botta/Assist. VP - Branch Operations, Nicholas A. Digianivittorio/Assist. Treasurer, Mary Jane King/Assist. Sec., Branch Mgr. - Broad St. Branch, Anastasia Brooks/Assist. Sec., Branch Mgr. - Drexel Hill Branch, Maddalena Sunseri/Assist. Sec., Branch Mgr. - Center City Branch, Kimberly Ann Dorner/Assist. Sec., Branch Mgr. - Pennsport Mall Branch *(19 Officers included in Index)*

Directors: Thomas A. Vento/Dir., CEO, Pres., Joseph W. Packer/Chmn., Jerome R. Balka/Dir., Counsel, A. J. Fanelli/Dir., John P. Judge/Dir., Francis V. Mulcahy/Dir.

Owners: Thomas A. Vento, Joseph W. Packer, John P. Judge, Joseph R. Corrato, Insiders/0.80%, Stilwell Value Partners I, L.P./9.90%, David H. Krauter, Prudential Mutual Holding Company/60.70%, A. J. Fanelli, Jerome R. Balka, Francis V. Mulcahy

Financial Data: **Fiscal Year End:**09/30 **Latest Annual Data:** 9/30/2006

Year	Sales	Net Income
2006	$25,480,000	$3,837,000
2005	$21,645,000	$3,392,000

Curr. Assets:	$16,623,000	**Curr. Liab.:**	$383,550,000	**P/E Ratio:**	44.03
Plant, Equip.:	$1,721,000	**Total Liab.:**	$384,933,000	**Indic. Yr. Divd.:**	$0.200
Total Assets:	$472,381,000	**Net Worth:**	$87,448,000	**Debt/ Equity:**	NA

Prudential Financial Inc

751 Broad St., Newark, NJ, 07102; ***PH:*** 1-973-802-6000; ***Fax:*** 1-973-802-4479; ***http://*** www.prudential.com

General - Incorporation	NJ	**Stock**- Price on:12/24/2007	$102.16
Employees	39,814	Stock Exchange	NYSE
Auditor	PricewaterhouseCoopers LLP	Ticker Symbol	PRU
Stk Agt	EquiServe Trust Co N.A	Outstanding Shares	465,000,000
Counsel	NA	E.P.S	$7.75
DUNS No.	NA	Shareholders	NA

Business: The group's principle activity is to provide life insurance services. The group's services include mutual funds, annuities, real estate brokerage franchises, institutional retirement and relocation services. The group operatesfrom United States.

Primary SIC and add'l.: 6311 6282

CIK No: 0001137774

Subsidiaries: 745 Property Investments, American Skandia Advisory Services, Inc., American Skandia Fund Services, Inc., American Skandia Information Services and Technology Corporation, American Skandia Investment Services Incorporated, American Skandia Life Assurance Corporation, American Skandia Marketing, Incorporated, American Skandia, Inc., ARL Holdings, Inc., Asian Infrastructure Mezzanine Capital Fund, Asset Disposition Trust, 1995-2, Bache Financial Derivatives, Ltd., Bache Financial Limited, Bache Overseas Funding Limited, Bache, S.A. de C.V. 311 Subsidiaries included in the Index

Officers: Art F. Ryan/65/Chmn., CEO, Pres., Susan L. Blount/50/Sr. VP, General Counsel, Robert Charles Golden/61/Exec. VP, Richard J. Carbone/60/CFO, Sr. VP/$4,967,877.00, Sharon C. Taylor/53/Sr. VP - Corporate Human Resources, Peter B. Sayre/Sr. VP, Controller, Principal Accounting Officer

Directors: Art F. Ryan/65/Chmn., CEO, Pres., John R. Strangfeld/54/Vice Chmn., Vivian L. Banta/57/Vice Chmn., Rodger A. Lawson/61/Vice Chmn., Mark B. Grier/55/Vice Chmn., William H. Gray/66/Dir., Constance J. Horner/66/Dir., James A. Unruh/66/Dir., Christine A. Poon/55/Dir., Gilbert Casellas/55/Dir., Frederic Becker/72/Dir., James G. Cullen/65/Dir., Karl J. Krapek/59/Dir., Jon F. Hanson/71/Dir., Gordon M. Bethune/66/Dir. *(16 Directors included in Index)*

Owners: National Union Fire Insurance/44.30%, Lexington Insurance Company/45.70%, Pacific LifeCorp/10.00%

Financial Data: **Fiscal Year End:**12/31 **Latest Annual Data:** 12/31/2006

Year	Sales	Net Income
2006	$32,488,000,000	$3,428,000,000
2005	$31,708,000,000	$3,540,000,000
2004	$28,348,000,000	$2,256,000,000

Curr. Assets:	$15,581,000,000	**Curr. Liab.:**	$28,860,000,000	**P/E Ratio:**	13.98
Plant, Equip.:	NA	**Total Liab.:**	$431,374,000,000	**Indic. Yr. Divd.:**	$1.150
Total Assets:	$454,266,000,000	**Net Worth:**	$22,892,000,000	**Debt/ Equity:**	0.7675

Prudential Plc

Jackson National Life, 1 Corporate Way, Lansing, MI, 48951; ***PH:*** 1-517-381-5500; ***Fax:*** 1-517-706-5517; ***http://*** www.prudential.co.uk; ***Email:*** marina.novis@prudential.co.uk

General - Incorporation	UK	**Stock**- Price on:12/24/2007	$29.96
Employees	23,248	Stock Exchange	NYSE
Auditor	Mark Tucker	Ticker Symbol	PUK
Stk Agt	Lloyds TSB Registrars	Outstanding Shares	2,440,000,000
Counsel	Cleary Gottlieb Steen & Hamilton	E.P.S	$0.93
DUNS No.	NA	Shareholders	NA

Business: The group's principal activity is the provision of financial services in Europe, the United States and Asia. The group operates through UK and Europe insurance operations, jackson national life and prudential Asia divisions. The UK and Europe insurance operation provides a range of financial products and services including annuities, corporate and individual pensions, with-profits bonds, savings and investment products and individual savings accounts to around seven million customers. Jackson national life offers fixed, equity-indexed and variable annuities, term and permanent life insurance and institutional products. Prudential Asia provides a comprehensive range of savings, protection and investment products tailored to the needs of each local market.

Primary SIC and add'l.: 6371 6726 6399 6321 6311

CIK No: 0001116578

Subsidiaries: Egg Banking plc, Jackson National Life Insurance Company, M&G Investment Management Limited, PCA Life Assurance Company Limited, Prudential Annuities Limited, Prudential Assurance Company Singapore (Pte) Limited, Prudential Retirement Income Limited, The Prudential Assurance Company Limited

Officers: Nick Prettejohn/Executive Dir., Marina Novis/Investor Relations Officer, Jon Bunn/Dir. - Public Relations, William Baldwin-Charles/Head - Group Media Relations, Claire Glover/Group Communications Assist., Damian Leeson/Dir. - Group Public Affairs, James Matthews/Dir. - Investor Relations, Mark Tucker/Dir., Group Chief Executive, Michael McLintock/Executive Dir., Sally Padget/Head - European Parliamentary Affairs, Barry Stowe/Executive Dir., James Wilcox/Contact - Head - Group Public Affairs UK, Asia, Tina Christou/Group Head - Property Public Affairs, Paulette King/PA to Dir. - Group Public Affairs, Duncan West/Group Public Affairs Mgr. *(19 Officers included in Index)*

Directors: David Clementi/Chmn., Philip Broadley/Dir., Group Dir. - Finance, Clark Manning/Executive Dir., James Ross/Sr. Non Exec. Dir., Mark Tucker/Dir., Group Chief Executive, Michael McLintock/Executive Dir., Bridget MacAskill/Non Exec. Dir., Keki Dadiseth/Dir., Nick Prettejohn/Executive Dir., Michael Garrett/Dir., Kathleen O'Donovan/Dir., Lord Turnbull/Dir., Barry Stowe/Executive Dir., Winfried Bischoff/Non Exec. Dir., Ann Godbehere/Non Exec. Dir.

Owners: Barry Stowe/0.00%, Mark Tucker/0.01%, James Ross/0.00%, Keki Dadiseth/0.00%, Michael McLintock/0.01%, Nick Prettejohn/0.00%, Roberto Mendoza/0.01%, Michael Garrett/0.00%, Bridget Macaskill/0.00%, Philip Broadley/0.00%, Lord Turnbull/0.00%, Clark Manning/0.00%, Kathleen O'Donovan/0.00%

Financial Data: **Fiscal Year End:**12/31 **Latest Annual Data:** 12/31/2005

Year	Sales	Net Income
2005	$70,452,994,000	$2,051,194,000
2004	$42,847,584,000	$175,321,000
2003	$23,993,744,000	$1,182,703,000

Curr. Assets:	$2,909,264,000	**Curr. Liab.:**	NA		
Plant, Equip.:	NA	**Total Liab.:**	NA	**Indic. Yr. Divd.:**	$0.460
Total Assets:	$2,909,264,000	**Net Worth:**	NA	**Debt/ Equity:**	NA

PS Business Parks Inc

701 Western Ave., Glendale, CA, 91201; ***PH:*** 1-818-244-8080; ***Fax:*** 1-818-242-0566; ***http://*** www.psbusinessparks.com; ***Email:*** info@psbusinessparks.com

General - Incorporation	CA	**Stock**- Price on:12/24/2007	$63.45
Employees	144	Stock Exchange	AMEX
Auditor	Ernst & Young LLP	Ticker Symbol	PSB
Stk Agt	American Stock Transfer & Trust Co.	Outstanding Shares	21,330,000
Counsel	NA	E.P.S	$0.78
DUNS No.	NA	Shareholders	NA

Business: The groups principle activities include acquiring, developing and operating commercial properties, primarily multi-tenant flex, office and industrial space. In the year 2006, the group acquired WesTech Business Park. The group operates from the United States. The groups quarterly revenue for September 2007 was 68.71 millions of USD.

Primary SIC and add'l.: 4225 6798

CIK No: 0000866368

Subsidiaries: American Office Park Properties, TPGP, Inc., AOPP Acquisition Corp. Two, Hernmore, Inc., Metro Park Gude, L.L.C., Metro Park I, L.L.C., Metro Park II, L.L.C., Metro Park III, L.L.C., Metro Park IV, L.L.C., Metro Park V, L.L.C., Miami International Commerce Center, Monroe Parkway, L.L.C., PS Business Parks, L.P., PS Rose Canyon, L.L.C., PSB Boca Commerce Park, L.L.C., PSB Wellington Commerce Park I, L.L.C. 27 Subsidiaries included in the Index

Officers: Joseph D. Russell/46/Dir., CEO, Pres./$1,666,284.00, John Petersen/COO, Exec. VP/$897,236.00, Edward A. Stokx/Exec. VP, CFO, Investor Relations Officer/$654,628.00, Brett Franklin/Sr. VP - Acquisitions, Dispositions/$672,492.00, Maria R. Hawthorne/Sr. VP - East Coast/$661,206.00, Coby Holley/VP - Pacific Northwest, Robin Mather/VP, Divisional VP - Southern California, William McFaul/VP - Maryland, Eddie F. Ruiz/VP, Dir. - Facilities, Viola I. Sanchez/VP - Southeast, David Vicars/VP - Midwest, Stuart Hutchison/Regional Mgr. - Southern California, Trenton Groves/VP, Corporate Controller, David Weinstein/Regional Mgr. - Northern California, Keith Summers/Regional Mgr. - Virginia *(17 Officers included in Index)*

Directors: Joseph D. Russell/46/Dir., CEO, Pres., Ronald L. Havner/48/Chmn., Vern O. Curtis/71/Dir., Wesley R. Burns/48/Dir., Arthur M. Friedman/70/Dir., Alan K. Pribble/63/Dir., James H. Kropp/Dir., Harvey Lenkin/69/Dir., Michael V. McGee/Dir., Robert Wesley Burns/Dir.

Owners: Alan K. Pribble, Insiders/2.10%, Wellington Management Company, LLP/7.50%, Public Storage, Inc/25.40%, Joseph D. Russell, Ronald L. Havner, Edward A. Stokx, Wesley R. Burns, T. Rowe Price Associates, Inc/5.30%, Vern O. Curtis, John W. Petersen, Brett M. Franklin, James H. Kropp, Harvey Lenkin, Arthur M. Friedman *(17 Owners included in Index)*

Financial Data: **Fiscal Year End:**12/31 **Latest Annual Data:** 12/31/2006

Year	Sales	Net Income
2006	$242,839,000	$64,580,000
2005	$220,248,000	$75,294,000
2004	$219,071,000	$62,143,000

Curr. Assets:	$68,362,000	**Curr. Liab.:**	$42,394,000	**P/E Ratio:**	78.33
Plant, Equip.:	$1,360,894,000	**Total Liab.:**	$109,442,000	**Indic. Yr. Divd.:**	$1.760
Total Assets:	$1,462,864,000	**Net Worth:**	$1,055,203,000	**Debt/ Equity:**	0.0635

Psb Bancorp Inc

1835 Market St., Philadelphia, PA, 19103; ***PH:*** 1-215-979-7900; ***http://*** www.firstpennbank.com

General - Incorporation	PA	**Stock**- Price on:12/24/2007	NA
Employees	154	Stock Exchange	NA
Auditor	Grant Thornton LLP	Ticker Symbol	NA
Stk Agt	Registrar & Transfer Co	Outstanding Shares	NA
Counsel	NA	E.P.S	NA
DUNS No.	03-901-9922	Shareholders	NA

Business: The group's principal activities are to attract deposits from the general public and invest those deposits in loans secured by residential mortgage loans, commercial real estate loans, commercial business loans, construction loans, student loans and mortgage-backed securities. The operations of the group are conducted through its subsidiary first penn bank. The group through its subsidiary offers residential and consumer loans with other community-banking services through 12 offices within southeastern Pennsylvania and southern New Jersey. The group offers a variety of deposits including demand, now, money market, savings and certificates of deposit.

Primary SIC and add'l.: 6022 6712

CIK No: 0001047537

Subsidiaries: First Penn Bank, Jade Abstract Company, Jade Insurance Company, PSA Financial Corp., PSA Service Corp., Transnational Mortgage Company

Owners: Anthony DiSandro/8.40%, Gary Polimeno, Vincent J. Fumo/17.50%, Insiders/27.80%, James F. Kenney, Rosanne Pauciello, James W. Eastwood/1.10%, Dennis P. Wesley, American Bank Incorporated/6.80%

PSB Group Inc

1800 E Twelve Mile Rd. , Madison Heights, MI, 48071; *PH:* 1-248-548-2900; *http://* www.psbnetbank.com; *Email:* admin@bankpeoples.com

General - Incorporation ... MI
Employees ... 161
Auditor ... Plante & Moran, PLLC
Stk Agt ... Registrar & Transfer Co
Counsel ... NA
DUNS No. ... NA

Stock - Price on:12/24/2007 ... $19
Stock Exchange ... OTC
Ticker Symbol ... PSBG
Outstanding Shares ... 3,070,000
E.P.S. ... $1.01
Shareholders ... NA

Business: The group's principal activities are to develop and market business process automation and management applications and collaborative solutions for program management and quote management. These software solutions enable manufacturers to rapidly automate key business processes. It is a holding company of peoples state bank inc the services of the group includes checking and savings accounts, time deposits, safe deposit facilities, commercial loans, real estate mortgage loans, installment loans, iras and night depository facilities. The various kinds of deposits accepted by the bank includes, demand, savings, money market demand and certificates accounts. The group provides full-service banking through 10 branch offices and four loan origination offices to the Michigan communities of wayne, oakland, macomb, and genesee counties.

Primary SIC and add'l.: 6712 6022

CIK No: 0001235091

Subsidiaries: Peoples State Bank, PSB Insurance Agency, Inc., PSB, Capital, Inc., Universal Mortgage Corporation

Officers: Michael J. Tierney/Dir., CEO, Pres./$236,017.00, Michael J. Banks/Sr. VP, Chief Lending Officer - Peoples State Bank, Maureen Zak/VP - Peoples State Bank, Jon Shamus/VP - Peoples State Bank, Catherine M. Revord/Sr. VP, Dir. - Human Resources - Peoples State Bank/$106,463.00, David A. Wilson/Sr. VP, CFO - Peoples State Bank/$148,948.00, David M. Borcherding/First VP - Peoples State Bank, Ellen George/VP - Peoples State Bank, Gary D. Forhan/Sr. VP - Marketing, Product Management, Peoples State Bank, Jeffrey L. Moore/Sr. VP, Chief Credit Officer - Peoples State Bank, Scott Whitford/VP - Peoples State Bank, Avis Karim/First VP - Peoples State Bank, Tami Janowicz/Sr. VP - Retail, Compliance, Peoples State Bank/$112,286.00, Vincent Szymborski/Sr. VP - Retail Banking, Peoples State Bank, Dounia Senawi/First VP - Peoples State Bank *(23 Officers included in Index)*

Directors: Michael J. Tierney/Dir., CEO, Pres., Longine V. Morawski/Vice Chmn., David L. Wood/Chmn., Sydney L. Ross/Dir., Edward H. Turner/Dir., Robert L. Cole/Dir., James Jacobs/Dir., Michael J. Kowalski/Dir.

Owners: Insiders/5.88%, Christopher S. Olson/9.44%, Edward H. Turner, Michael J. Kowalski, Michael J. Banks, David L. Wood/1.51%, Catherine M. Revord, Dr. Leon Fill Foundation/0.18%, Madison Holdings Limited Partnership/8.11%, Michael J. Tierney, Sydney L. Ross, Longine V. Morawski/1.05%, David A. Wilson, Tami Janowicz, Vincent J. Szymborski *(18 Owners included in Index)*

Financial Data: *Fiscal Year End:*12/31 *Latest Annual Data:* 12/31/2006

Year	Sales	Net Income
2006	$37,283,000	$2,888,000
2005	$33,823,000	$4,005,000
2004	$28,459,000	$4,218,000

Curr. Assets:	$16,726,000	**Curr. Liab.:**	$452,244,000	**P/E Ratio:**	18.81
Plant, Equip.:	$12,731,000	**Total Liab.:**	$452,988,000	**Indic. Yr. Divd.:**	$0.720
Total Assets:	$497,234,000	**Net Worth:**	$44,246,000	**Debt/ Equity:**	0.0168

PSB Holdings Inc

40 Main St., Putnam, CT, 06260; *PH:* 1-860-928-6501; *Fax:* 1-860-928-2147; *http://* www.putnamsavings.com

General - Incorporation ... Federal
Employees ... 88
Auditor ... Whittlesey & Hadley, P.C.
Stk Agt ... Registrar & Transfer Co
Counsel ... NA
DUNS No. ... NA

Stock - Price on:12/24/2007 ... $10.75
Stock Exchange ... NDQ
Ticker Symbol ... PSBH
Outstanding Shares ... 6,800,000
E.P.S. ... $0.29
Shareholders ... NA

Business: The groups principal activity is to provide banking and financial services.The financial products of the group include real estate and construction loan, commercial loan and multi-family residential loan. The assets of the group for the year 2006 were $474,417 (thousands).

Primary SIC and add'l.: 6712 6712 6035 6035

CIK No: 0001293211

Subsidiaries: PSB Realty, LLC, Putnam Savings Bank, Windham North Properties, LLC

Officers: Thomas A. Borner/Chmn., CEO, Robert J. Halloran/Dir., CFO, Pres., John F. Lafountain/Sr. VP, Sr. Retail Loan Officer, Anthony J. Serio/Sr. VP, Sr. Commercial Loan Officer, Barbara M. Goloski/Assist. VP, Branch Mgr. - Price Chopper, Phillis D. Jaeger/Assist. VP, Branch Mgr. - Danielson, Raymond R. Perry/Assist. VP - Investment Services, Laura A. Williams/VP, Operations Officer, Barbara A. Elliott/Assist. VP, Human Resources Officer, Donna M. Glaude/Branch Mgr. - Main Office, Brenda Engel/Branch Mgr. - Griswold, Gina Kolodnicki/Branch Mgr. - Gales Ferry, Janet D. Richmond/Branch Mgr. - Pomfret Center, Barbara L. McGarry/Corp. Sec., Richard L. Moore/Commercial Loan Officer *(26 Officers included in Index)*

Directors: Thomas A. Borner/Chmn., CEO, Maurice P. Beaulac/Dir., Charles W. Bentley/Dir., Paul M. Kelly/Dir., Robert J. Halloran/Dir., CFO, Pres., Richard A. Loomis/Dir., John P. Miller/Dir., Mary E. Patenaude/Dir., Charles H. Puffer/Dir.

Owners: Robert J. Halloran, Jitendra K. Sinha, John P. Miller, Putnam Bancorp, MHC, Thomas A. Borner, Mary E. Patenaude, Richard A. Loomis, Paul M. Kelly, Charles W. Bentley, Charles H. Puffer, Insiders

Financial Data: *Fiscal Year End:*06/30 *Latest Annual Data:* 06/30/2007

Year	Sales	Net Income
2007	$28,172,000	$1,924,000
2006	$21,873,000	$2,116,000
2005	$15,986,000	$1,269,000

Curr. Assets:	$10,364,000	**Curr. Liab.:**	$296,965,000	**P/E Ratio:**	43.00
Plant, Equip.:	$4,504,000	**Total Liab.:**	$425,505,000	**Indic. Yr. Divd.:**	NA
Total Assets:	$474,417,000	**Net Worth:**	$48,912,000	**Debt/ Equity:**	2.5162

PSB Holdings Inc WI

1905 Stewart Ave., Wausau, WI, 54401; *PH:* 1-715-842-2191; *http://* www.psbwi.com

General - Incorporation ... WI
Employees ... 138
Auditor ... Wipfli LLP
Stk Agt ... Registrar & Transfer Co
Counsel ... NA
DUNS No. ... NA

Stock - Price on:12/24/2007 ... $74.38
Stock Exchange ... OTC
Ticker Symbol ... PSBQ
Outstanding Shares ... 1,570,000
E.P.S. ... $2.15
Shareholders ... NA

Business: The groups principal activity is engaged as local community bank. Services of the group include personal banking, including checking accounts, savings and time accounts, installment, credit and debit cards, and other personal loans, as well as mortgage loans. The group offers both commercial and personal customers automated teller machines and online computer banking. In the year 2006, the groups total assets were $501,840 (thousands).

Primary SIC and add'l.: 6712

CIK No: 0000948368

Subsidiaries: Peoples State Bank, PSB Investments, Inc.

Officers: Peter W. Knitt/CEO, Pres./$197,823.00, Scott M. Cattanach/Sec., Treasurer/$129,279.00

Directors: Gordon P. Gullickson/79/Chmn., David K. Kopperud/62/Dir., Thomas R. Polzer/65/Dir., William M. Reif/65/Dir., Gordon P. Connor/70/Dir., Patrick L. Crooks/73/Dir., William J. Fish/57/Dir., Charles A. Ghidorzi/63/Dir., Thomas A. Riiser/72/Dir., John H. Sonnentag/65/Dir.

Owners: William J. Fish/1.18%, Charles A. Ghidorzi, Scott M. Cattanach, Thomas A. Riiser/1.11%, Gordon P. Gullickson, The Banc Fund Company, LLC/8.65%, John H. Sonnentag, Patrick L. Crooks/1.09%, William M. Reif, Lawrence Hanz/5.85%, Gordon P. Connor/1.24%, Thomas R. Polzer/1.26%, Peter W. Knitt, David K. Kopperud/1.33%, Insiders/8.26%

Financial Data: *Fiscal Year End:*12/31 *Latest Annual Data:* 12/31/2006

Year	Sales	Net Income
2006	$33,408,000	$3,427,000
2005	$29,232,000	$4,340,000
2004	$25,325,000	$3,526,000

Curr. Assets:	$28,006,000	**Curr. Liab.:**	$455,666,000	**P/E Ratio:**	34.60
Plant, Equip.:	$11,933,000	**Total Liab.:**	$467,393,000	**Indic. Yr. Divd.:**	$2.640
Total Assets:	$501,840,000	**Net Worth:**	$34,447,000	**Debt/ Equity:**	0.5680

PSI Corp

Formerly: Friendlyway Corp
1244 Main St., Linfield, PA, 19498; *PH:* 1-610-495-8413; *http://* www.friendlywayinc.com

General - Incorporation ... NV
Employees ... NA
Auditor ... Lopez, Blevins, Bork & Assoc. LLP
Stk Agt ... American Stock Transfer & Trust Co.
Counsel ... NA
DUNS No. ... 78-533-2800

Stock - Price on:12/24/2007 ... NA
Stock Exchange ... OTC
Ticker Symbol ... PSCP
Outstanding Shares ... NA
E.P.S. ... NA
Shareholders ... NA

Business: The group's principle activities include acquiring, operating and developing environmental contracting and consulting companies, and related businesses. All operating companies were disposed of or sold in prior years. Presently, the company is a non-operating shell corporation. The group operates from United States.

Primary SIC and add'l.: 9999

CIK No: 0000888702

Subsidiaries: Friendlyway Technologies, Inc

Officers: David Foni/CEO

Financial Data: *Fiscal Year End:*10/31 *Latest Annual Data:* 10/31/2005

Year	Sales	Net Income
2005	$2,006,000	-$2,269,000
2004	NA	-$294,000
2003	NA	-$133,000

Curr. Assets:	$631,000	**Curr. Liab.:**	$3,137,000		
Plant, Equip.:	$55,000	**Total Liab.:**	$3,431,000	**Indic. Yr. Divd.:**	NA
Total Assets:	$686,000	**Net Worth:**	-$2,745,000	**Debt/ Equity:**	NA

PSi Technologies Holdings Inc

Electronics Ave., FTI Special Economic Zone, Taguig City, Metro Manila; *PH:* 632-8384694; *Fax:* 632-8384648; *http://* www.psitechnologies.com; *Email:* fmcanlas@psitechnologies.com.ph

General - Incorporation ... Philippines
Employees ... 3,420
Auditor ... SyCip Gorres Velayo & Co
Stk Agt ... Bank of New York
Counsel ... H. G. Tiu Law Offices
DUNS No. ... NA

Stock - Price on:12/24/2007 ... $1.8
Stock Exchange ... NDQ
Ticker Symbol ... PSIT
Outstanding Shares ... 13,290,000
E.P.S. ... -$0.92
Shareholders ... NA

Business: The group's principal activities are the manufacturing of semiconductors and semiconductor packaging. It also provides test services for power and non-power applications. These are used in telecommunications and networking systems, computers and computer peripherals, consumer electronics, electronic office equipment, automotive systems and industrial products including plastics and hermetics.

Primary SIC and add'l.: 3674 3559

CIK No: 0001106714

Subsidiaries: Pacsem Realty, Inc., Pacsem Technologies Inc., PSi Technologies Chengdu Company Limited, PSi Technologies China Holdings Co., Ltd., PSi Technologies Laguna, Inc., PSi Technologies, Inc., PSitech Realty, Inc.

Officers: Arthur J. Young/Chmn., CEO, Hermenigilda B. Sancon/Dir. - Manufacturing, Alfredo M. Canlas/Dir. - Marketing, Sales, Cynthia E. Jose/Dir. - Key Accounting, Joel Jun D. Saberon/Dir. - Manufacturing, Ligaya Anza-Zipagang/Dir. - Reliability, Quality, Romil A. Acosta/Dir. - Supply Chain, Francis H. Suarez/48/CFO, Treasurer, Helen G. Tiu/Corp. Sec., Cesar A. Castillo/Dir. - Facilities, Gil Setijono Gilarsi/Dir. - Business Development, VP - Quality, Fernando B. Silva/MD - PSi Technologies Laguna, Inc, Thomas Moersheim/CTO, Hilarion V. Cajucom/CFO, Antonio L. Arboleda/Dir. - Human Resources Development *(18 Officers included in Index)*

Directors: Arthur J. Young/Chmn., CEO, Mandakini Puri/Dir., Romeo L. Bernardo/Dir., Robert F. De Ocampo/Dir., Patchara Samalapa/Dir., Kuppusamy Kanapathi/Dir., Brian A. Renaud/Dir.

Owners: Merrill Lynch Global Emerging Markets Partners, L.P./53.70%, Greathill Pte., Ltd./14.70%, Austin W. Marxe/10.30%, Arthur J. Young/1.24%

Financial Data: *Fiscal Year End:*12/31 *Latest Annual Data:* 12/31/2006

Year		Sales			Net Income
2006		$89,737,000			-$11,601,000
2005		$80,341,000			-$19,750,000
2004		$79,139,000			-$14,648,000
Curr. Assets:	$24,401,000	Curr. Liab.:	$37,793,000		
Plant, Equip.:	$36,099,000	Total Liab.:	$45,428,000	Indic. Yr. Divd.:	NA
Total Assets:	$61,777,000	Net Worth:	$16,350,000	Debt/ Equity:	NA

pSivida Ltd

400 Pleasant St., Watertown, MA, 02472; ***PH:*** 1-617-926-5000; ***Fax:*** 1-617-926-5050;
http:// www.psivida.com

General - Incorporation....Australia
Employees....55
Auditor....Deloitte Touche Tohmatsu
Stk Agt....NA
Counsel....NA
DUNS No.....NA

Stock- Price on:12/24/2007....$1.46
Stock Exchange....NDQ
Ticker Symbol....PSDV
Outstanding Shares....46,410,000
E.P.S....-$2.47
Shareholders....NA

Business: The group is composed of elemental silicon, one of the most abundant elements on the earth's crust, which is engineered to create a "honeycomb" structure of pores. These pores can be formed into a diverse array of shapes and sizes and can be filled with various drugs, genes and proteins. The group currently acquire BioSilicon from QinetiQ in the UK for use in internal and collaborative research. Our lead product, BrachySil, is currently manufactured in accordance with FDA guidelines by Hosokawa Micron. The group operates from United States.

Primary SIC and add'l.: 3826

CIK No: 0001314102

Subsidiaries: AION Diagnostics Limited, pSiMedica Limited, pSiOncology Pte. Limited, pSivida Inc.

Officers: Aaron Finlay/Company Sec., Paul Ashton/MD, Leigh Canham/Chief Scientific Officer - Psimedica Limited, Lori Freedman/VP - Corporate Affairs, General Counsel, Company Sec., Michael Soja/VP - Finance, CFO, Brian Leedman/VP - Investor Relations Psivida Limited, Katherine Woodthorpe/Non Exec. Dir.

Directors: David Mazzo/Non Exec. Chmn., Michael W. Rogers/Non Exec. Dir.

Owners: Gavin Rezos/2.22%, Aaron Finlay, David Mazzo, Michael Rogers, Paul Ashton/2.45%, Michael Soja, Lori Freedman, Roger Brimblecombe, Insiders/3.49%, Pfizer, Inc./12.80%

Financial Data: *Fiscal Year End:*06/30 *Latest Annual Data:* 6/30/2006

Year		Sales			Net Income
2006		$1,441,000			-$46,348,000
2005		$632,000			-$12,620,000
Curr. Assets:	$12,470,000	Curr. Liab.:	$17,495,000		
Plant, Equip.:	$2,292,000	Total Liab.:	$44,137,000	Indic. Yr. Divd.:	NA
Total Assets:	$170,151,000	Net Worth:	$126,014,000	Debt/ Equity:	NA

PSS World Medical Inc

4345 Spoint Blvd., Jacksonville, FL, 32216; ***PH:*** 1-904-332-3000; ***Fax:*** 1-904-332-3213;
http:// www.pssd.com

General - Incorporation....FL
Employees....3,304
Auditor....KPMG LLP
Stk Agt......American Stock Transfer & Trust Co.
Counsel....Willkie Farr & Gallagher LLP
DUNS No.....10-182-2682

Stock- Price on:12/24/2007....$18.68
Stock Exchange....NDQ
Ticker Symbol....PSSI
Outstanding Shares....67,200,000
E.P.S....$0.73
Shareholders....NA

Business: The group's principle activity is to market and distribute medical products through two segments namely, physician supply and elder care. The physician supply business distributes medical supplies, equipment and pharmaceuticals. These products are distributed to office-based physicians who specialize in family practice, general practice, internal medicine and pediatrics. Elder care business provides consistent and reliable service to the long-term and elder care industry. The products offered include medical supplies, incontinent supplies and personal care items, enteral feeding supplies and other supplies required by the long-term care patient. The group distributes all the products through its 46 full service distribution centers located in the United States of America. The group's quarterly revenue for September 2007 was 457.93 millions of USD.

Primary SIC and add'l.: 5047 5122

CIK No: 0000920527

Subsidiaries: Diagnostic Imaging, Inc., Gulf South Medical Supply, Inc, PSS World Medical, Inc

Officers: David A. Smith/Chmn., CEO, Pres./$2,034,891.00, Bradley J. Hilton/Sr. VP - Operations/$513,308.00, David M. Bronson/CFO, Exec. VP/$873,444.00, Gary A. Corless/COO, Exec. VP/$951,791.00, Robert C. Weiner/VP - Investor Relations, Jeffrey H. Anthony/Sr. VP - Corporate Development, David D. Klarner/VP, Treasurer, Mary M. Jennings/VP - Tax, Chief Compliance Officer, John F. Sasen/Exec. VP, Chief Marketing Officer/$801,141.00, Kevin P. English/Sr. VP - Finance, Thomas D'Innocenzi/VP - Global Sourcing, Steven J. Magiera/VP - Business Development, John G. Kammlade/VP - Internal Audit, Edward D. Dienes/Sr. VP - Sales, Physician Sales, Service, Billy Ray Clemons/VP - Sales, Gulf South Medical Supply *(16 Officers included in Index)*

Directors: David A. Smith/Chmn., CEO, Pres., Charles E. Adair/Dir., Alvin R. Carpenter/Dir., O' Neal T. Douglas/Dir., Melvin L. Hecktman/Dir., Delores P. Kesler/Dir., Stephen H. Rogers/Dir., Jeffrey C. Crowe/Dir.

Owners: Select Equity Group, Inc./9.90%, Delores P. Kesler, John F. Sasen, Gary A. Corless, Insiders/3.30%, Melvin L. Heckman, David M. Bronson, David A. Smith, Bradley J.Hilton, Alvin R. Carpenter, Stephen H. Rogers, Barclays Global Investors NA/5.20%, Charles E. Adair, T. ONeal Douglas

Financial Data: *Fiscal Year End:*03/31 *Latest Annual Data:* 3/30/2007

Year		Sales			Net Income
2007		$1,741,639,000			$50,481,000
2006		$1,619,417,000			$44,257,000
2005		$1,473,769,000			$38,972,000
Curr. Assets:	$417,813,000	Curr. Liab.:	$189,230,000	P/E Ratio:	26.69
Plant, Equip.:	$81,105,000	Total Liab.:	$369,540,000	Indic. Yr. Divd.:	NA
Total Assets:	$646,358,000	Net Worth:	$276,818,000	Debt/ Equity:	0.3956

Psychemedics Corp

125 Nagog Pk., Acton, MA, 01720; ***PH:*** 1-978-206-8220; ***Fax:*** 1-978-264-9236;
http:// www.psychemedics.com

General - Incorporation....DE
Employees....104
Auditor....BDO Seidman LLP
Stk Agt.....Computershare Investor Services LLC
Counsel.........Lynch, Brewer, Hoffman & Fink
DUNS No.....15-158-8647

Stock- Price on:12/24/2007....$20.04
Stock Exchange....AMEX
Ticker Symbol....PMD
Outstanding Shares....5,200,000
E.P.S....$0.94
Shareholders....NA

Business: The group's principle activity is to provide testing services for the detection of abused substances through the analysis from hair samples. It utilizes a patented technology for performing immunoassays on enzymatically dissolved hair samples. The technology is a testing service that screens for the presence of certain drugs of abuse in hair. The application of radioimmunoassay procedures using hair differs from the more widely used application of radioimmunoassay procedures using urine samples. The company's tests provide quantitative information that indicates the approximate amount of drug ingested as well as historical data, which can show a pattern of individual drug use over a period of time. The company provides commercial testing and confirmation by mass spectrometry using industry-accepted practices for cocaine, marijuana, pcp, methamphetamine, and opiates. The company operates solely in the domestic market. The group operates from United States.

Primary SIC and add'l.: 8071

CIK No: 0000806517

Officers: Raymond C. Kubacki/Chmn., CEO, Pres./$435,910.00, Michael Schaffer/VP - Laboratory Operations/$253,060.00, William Thistle/Sr. VP, General Counsel/$313,648.00, Harry F. Connick/82/Dir. - Private Investor

Directors: Raymond C. Kubacki/Chmn., CEO, Pres., Harry F. Connick/82/Dir. - Private Investor, Fred J. Weinert/60/Dir., Walter S. Tomenson/61/Dir.

Owners: Peter C. Monson, Fred J. Weinert/3.10%, Walter S. Tomenson, Insiders/10.20%, Raymond C. Kubacki/3.80%, Cortina Asset Management, LLC/12.20%, Michael I. Schaffer, Ashford Capital Management, Inc./6.50%, Harry F. Connick, Wayne H. Huizenga/11.30%, William R. Thistle/1.50%

Financial Data: *Fiscal Year End:*12/31 *Latest Annual Data:* 12/31/2006

Year		Sales			Net Income
2006		$23,425,000			$4,902,000
2005		$21,389,000			$4,049,000
2004		$18,937,000			$2,764,000
Curr. Assets:	$12,291,000	Curr. Liab.:	$1,757,000	P/E Ratio:	21.32
Plant, Equip.:	$747,000	Total Liab.:	$1,757,000	Indic. Yr. Divd.:	$0.600
Total Assets:	$13,261,000	Net Worth:	$11,504,000	Debt/ Equity:	NA

Psychiatric Solutions Inc

6640 Carothers Pkwy., Ste. 500, Franklin, TN, 37067; ***PH:*** 1-615-312-5700; ***Fax:*** 1-615-312-5711;
http:// www.psysolutions.com

General - Incorporation....DE
Employees....12,600
Auditor....Ernst & Young LLP
Stk Agt....StockTrans, Inc.
Counsel....NA
DUNS No.....36-452-5360

Stock- Price on:12/24/2007....$36.29
Stock Exchange....NDQ
Ticker Symbol....PSYS
Outstanding Shares....54,290,000
E.P.S....$1.20
Shareholders....NA

Business: The group's principal activity is to provide behavioral health care services. The group operates in two segments owned and leased facilities segment & management contract segment. The group operates 26 owned or leased patient behavioral health care facilities with approximately 3,200 beds in 15 states. The group through its management contract division, they manage 43 inpatient behavioral health care units for third parties & 11 inpatient behavioral health care facilities for government agencies. The group acquired two inpatient psychiatric facilities from brentwood behavioral health on 01-Mar-2004, two inpatient healthcare facilities from palmetto on 01-May-2004, four inpatient healthcare facilities from heartland on 01-Jun-2004, 78 bed inpatient healthcare facilities from piedmont on 11-Jun-2004 & 144 bed inpatient healthcare facilities from alliance behavioural on 30-Jun-2004.

Primary SIC and add'l.: 8093 9999 8063

CIK No: 0000829608

Subsidiaries: Aeries Healthcare Corporation, Aeries Healthcare of Illinois, Inc., Atlantic Shores Hospital, LLC, Behavioral Educational Services, Inc., Behavioral Healthcare LLC, BHC Alhambra Hospital, Inc., BHC Belmont Pines Hospital, Inc., BHC Canyon Ridge Hospital, LLC, BHC Cedar Crest RTC, Inc., BHC Cedar Vista Hospital, Inc., BHC Clinicas Del Este Hospital, Inc., BHC Fairfax Hospital, Inc., BHC Fort Lauderdale Hospital, Inc., BHC Fox Run Hospital, Inc., BHC Fremont Hospital, Inc. 162 Subsidiaries included in the Index

Officers: Joey A. Jacobs/Chmn., CEO, Pres./$4,273,068.00, Brent Turner/Exec. VP - Finance, Administration/$1,186,499.00, Chris Howard/Exec. VP, General Counsel, Sec./$860,738.00, Jack E. Polson/Exec. VP, Chief Accounting Officer/$1,181,171.00, Steven T. Davidson/Chief Development Officer, Terry Bridges/COO

Directors: Joey A. Jacobs/Chmn., CEO, Pres., Mark P. Clein/Dir., David M. Dill/Dir., William M. Petrie/Dir., Christopher Grant/Dir., William F. Carpenter/Dir., Richard D. Gore/Dir., Edward K. Wissing/Dir.

Owners: Richard D. Gore, Christopher L. Howard, William B. Rutherford, Edward K. Wissing, Jack E. Polson, Christopher Grant, William M. Petrie, Joey A. Jacobs/2.50%, Insiders/4.20%, Brent Turner, David M. Dill, AXA Financial, Inc./5.00%, Mark P. Clein, William F. Carpenter

Financial Data: *Fiscal Year End:*12/31 *Latest Annual Data:* 12/31/2006

Year		Sales			Net Income
2006		$1,026,490,000			$60,632,000
2005		$727,774,000			$27,154,000
2004		$487,190,000			$16,801,000
Curr. Assets:	$243,260,000	Curr. Liab.:	$139,973,000	P/E Ratio:	30.24
Plant, Equip.:	$543,806,000	Total Liab.:	$953,417,000	Indic. Yr. Divd.:	NA
Total Assets:	$1,581,196,000	Net Worth:	$627,779,000	Debt/ Equity:	1.1419

PT Indosat Tbk

Indosat Bldg, Jalan Medan Merdeka Barat 21, Jakarta, 10110; ***PH:*** 62-213802614;
http:// www.indosat.com

General - Incorporation	Indonesia	Stock- Price on:12/24/2007	$37.15
Employees	4,969	Stock Exchange	NYSE
Auditor	Purwantono, Sarwoko & Sandjaja	Ticker Symbol	IIT
Stk Agt	Bank of New York	Outstanding Shares	108,680,000
Counsel	NA	E.P.S	$1.90
DUNS No	72-869-4605	Shareholders	NA

Business: The group's principal activities are the provision of cellular services, fixed telecommunications and midi business. Cellular services cover prepaid (mentari and smart) and postpaid (matrix and bright) services and launched in 2003 mobile banking services, gprs, mms & sms facilities, and prepaid international roaming services. The group is the sole provider of idd business in the indonesian market through idd 001 & idd 008 services. Midi business offers data communications & multimedia services to the indonesian market. Frame relay service is covering 17 major cities in Indonesia and over 20 countries worldwide through indosat and lintasarta. Other services include international telephone services, telegrams, facsimile services, circuit leasing, video-links, TV links, integrated services digital network (isdn) and other data transmissions.

Primary SIC and add'l.: 4813 4822 7389 4812 4899 7379

CIK No: 0000929700

Subsidiaries: Acasia Communictions Sdn Bhd, ASEAN Cableship Pte. Ltd, Asean Telecom Holding Sdn Bhd, Camintel SA3, ICO Global Communication Ltd, Indosat Finance Company B.V, Indosat International Finance Company B.V, Indosat Singapore Pte Ltd, PT Aplikanusa Lintasarta, PT Artajasa Pembayaran Elektronis1, PT Broadband Multimedia Tbk, PT Indosat Mega Media, PT Multi Media Asia Indonesia, PT Padang Golf Bukit Sentul, PT Satelindo Multi Media 18 Subsidiaries included in the Index

Officers: Kaizad B. Heerjee/Dir., CEO, Deputy Pres., Wong Heang Tuck/Dir., CFO, Dir. - Finance., Wityasmoro Sih Handayanto/50/Dir. - Regional Sales, Johny Swandi Sjam/Dir., Pres., Wahyu Wijayadi/Dir., Corporate Services Dir., S. Wimbo S. Hardjito/52/Dir. - Corporate Services, Raymond Tan Kim Meng/Dir., Network Dir., Peter Seah Lim Huat/Pres. - Commisioner, Lim Ah Doo/Independent Commissioner, Lee Theng Kiat/Commisioner, Sio Tat Hiang/Commisioner, Sum Soon Lim/Commisioner, Farida Eva Riyanti Hutapea/58/Independent Commissioner, Setyanto P. Santosa/Commisioner, Soeprapto/Independent Commissioner (21 Officers included in Index)

Directors: Kaizad B. Heerjee/Dir., CEO, Deputy Pres., Wong Heang Tuck/Dir., CFO, Dir. - Finance., Johny Swandi Sjam/Dir., Pres., Wahyu Wijayadi/Dir., Corporate Services Dir., Raymond Tan Kim Meng/Dir., Network Dir., Joseph Chan Lam Seng/49/Dir., Guntur S. Siboro/Dir., Marketing Dir., Fadzri Sentosa/Dir. - Jabotabek, Corporate Sales Dir., Syakieb Ahmad Sungkar/Dir., Regional Sales Dir., Roy Kannan/Dir., Information Technology Dir.

Owners: ICL entities/40.81%, Government/14.29%, Government/100.00%, JP Morgan Chase Bank US Resident/7.41%

Financial Data: Fiscal Year End:12/31   Latest Annual Data: 12/31/2006

Year	Sales	Net Income
2006	$1,356,919,000	$194,128,000
2005	$1,179,022,000	$190,799,000
2004	$1,135,530,000	$207,187,000

Curr. Assets:	$628,097,000	Curr. Liab.:	$754,235,000		
Plant, Equip.:	$2,774,715,000	Total Liab.:	$2,222,202,000	Indic. Yr. Divd.:	$1.310
Total Assets:	$4,059,763,000	Net Worth:	$1,837,561,000	Debt/ Equity:	NA

PTS Products International Inc

3355 Spring Mountain Rd., Ste. 66, Las Vegas, NV, 89102; **PH:** 1-702-327-7266; **http://** www.ptspi.com; **Email:** peter@ptspi.com

General - Incorporation	NV	Stock- Price on:12/24/2007	$0.002
Employees	20	Stock Exchange	OTC
Auditor	Lynda R. Keeton Cpa	Ticker Symbol	PTSH
Stk Agt	Pacific Stock Transfer Company	Outstanding Shares	502,070,000
Counsel	NA	E.P.S	-$0.006
DUNS No	NA	Shareholders	NA

Business: The group's principal activity is to seek new business. In 2003, the group has purchased 100 flexiciser units under an arrangement whereby it will pay the actual manufactured cost of the units, will jointly market the product and divide profits equally with the manufacturer. If the group can sell the first order of unit, it intends to continue this business. The group develops two separate diagnostic tools: allergy testing device and chiropractic outcome-measuring instrument. The group holds the patents, trademarks and legal rights to manufacture and sell and lease its electronic allergy testing device and is continually striving to achieve refinement of its prototype. On 24-Nov-2003, the group acquired pts products international inc. And on 02-Jun-2004, it also acquired pts technologies inc.

Primary SIC and add'l.: 3841

CIK No: 0001080924

Subsidiaries: Disability Access Consultants, Inc, Elast Technologies, Global Links Card Services, Inc., Glove Box, Inc., PTS Products International, Inc, PTS Technologies,Inc

Officers: Peter Chin/Chmn., CEO, CFO

Directors: Peter Chin/Chmn., CEO, CFO

Owners: AWI, Inc./30.00%, Insiders, Peter Chin, Insiders/48.00%, Insiders/100.00%, Sandy Chin, Sandy Chin/7.00%, Majestic Safe-T-Products, LTD/100.00%, Barbara Thorpe/100.00%, Majestic Safe-T-Products, LTD/100.00%, Peter Chin/100.00%, Asmac Financial, Inc./1.00%, Peter Chin/48.00%

Financial Data: Fiscal Year End:12/31   Latest Annual Data: 12/31/2006

Year	Sales	Net Income
2006	$782,000	-$1,741,000
2005	$131,000	-$1,646,000
2004	$49,000	-$2,645,000

Curr. Assets:	$226,000	Curr. Liab.:	$665,000		
Plant, Equip.:	$205,000	Total Liab.:	$1,013,000	Indic. Yr. Divd.:	NA
Total Assets:	$1,344,000	Net Worth:	$330,000	Debt/ Equity:	7.8593

Public Media Works Inc

14759 Oxnard St., Van Nuys, CA, 91411; **PH:** 1-818-904-9029; **http://** www.publicmediaworks.com

General - Incorporation	DE	Stock- Price on:12/24/2007	$0.035
Employees	NA	Stock Exchange	OTC
Auditor	Burnham & Schumm P.C.	Ticker Symbol	PUBM
Stk Agt	Holladay Stock Transfer, Inc.	Outstanding Shares	38,490,000
Counsel	NA	E.P.S	-$0.24
DUNS No	NA	Shareholders	NA

Business: The groups principle activities include developing, producing, marketing and distributing of film and television projects for targeted, fan based audiences. The group operates from the United States.

Primary SIC and add'l.: 7812

CIK No: 0001108730

Subsidiaries: Public Media Works, Inc.

Officers: Corbin Bernsen/CEO, Pres., Mark Smith/CFO

Directors: George Mainas/63/Dir.

Owners: Michael Wittlin/14.28%, Thomas A. Szabo/8.53%, George Mainas/16.97%, Corbin Bernsen/15.85%, Insiders/32.84%

Financial Data: Fiscal Year End:02/28   Latest Annual Data: 02/28/2007

Year	Sales	Net Income
2007	$6,000	-$259,000

Curr. Assets:	$13,000	Curr. Liab.:	$1,380,000		
Plant, Equip.:	$6,000	Total Liab.:	$1,380,000	Indic. Yr. Divd.:	NA
Total Assets:	$336,000	Net Worth:	-$1,044,000	Debt/ Equity:	NA

Public Service Co of Colorado

1225 17th St., Denver, CO, 80202; **PH:** 1-303-571-7511; **http://** www.psco.com

General - Incorporation	CO	Stock- Price on:12/24/2007	NA
Employees	NA	Stock Exchange	NA
Auditor	Deloitte & Touche LLP	Ticker Symbol	NA
Stk Agt	U.S. Bank, N.A.,	Outstanding Shares	NA
Counsel	Kelly Stansfield & O'Donnell	E.P.S	NA
DUNS No	00-691-5953	Shareholders	NA

Business: The group's principle activities include generating, purchasing, transmiting, distributing and selling electricity; and purchases, transmits, distributes, sells and transports natural gas in Colorado. The group operates from United States.

Primary SIC and add'l.: 4923 4931

CIK No: 0000081018

Subsidiaries: 1480 Welton, Inc, Green and Clear Lakes Company, PSR Investments, Inc

Officers: Patricia K. Vincent/Dir., CEO, Pres., Gary R. Johnson/VP, General Counsel, Dir., Benjamin G.S Fowke/VP, CFO, Dir., Teresa S. Madden/VP, Controller, Paul J. Bonavia/VP, Dir.

Directors: Patricia K. Vincent/Dir., CEO, Pres., Richard C. Kelly/Chmn., Paul J. Bonavia/VP, Dir., Gary R. Johnson/VP, General Counsel, Dir., Benjamin G.S Fowke/VP, CFO, Dir.

Public Service Co of North Carolina Inc

1426 Main St., Columbia, SC, 29201; **PH:** 1-803-217-9000; **http://** www.psnc.com

General - Incorporation	SC	Stock- Price on:12/24/2007	NA
Employees	NA	Stock Exchange	NA
Auditor	Deloitte & Touche LLP	Ticker Symbol	NA
Stk Agt	First Union Nat'l Bank	Outstanding Shares	NA
Counsel	NA	E.P.S	NA
DUNS No	00-699-6607	Shareholders	NA

Business: The group's principle activities include distributing and selling natural gas; promotion, sale and installation of both new and replacement cooking, water heating, laundry, space heating, cooling and humidity control natural gas appliances and equipment; conversion and maintenance services for natural gas-fueled vehicles; and natural gas brokerage and supply services. The group operates from United States.

Primary SIC and add'l.: 4924

CIK No: 0000081025

Subsidiaries: PSNC Energy, Scana Corporation

Public Service Company of Oklahoma

1 Riverside Plz., Columbus, OH, 43215; **PH:** 1-614-716-1000; **Fax:** 1-614-716-1823; **http://** www.psoklahoma.com

General - Incorporation	NY	Stock- Price on:12/24/2007	$24.88
Employees	1,233	Stock Exchange	NYSE
Auditor	Deloitte & Touche LLP	Ticker Symbol	POH
Stk Agt	Medallion Program	Outstanding Shares	9,010,000
Counsel	NA	E.P.S	$1.47
DUNS No	00-790-7926	Shareholders	NA

Business: The group's principle activities include generating, transmiting and distributing electric power to approximately 505,000 retail customers in eastern and southwestern Oklahoma. The company also supplies electric power at wholesale to other utility companies, municipalities, rural electric cooperatives and other market participants. It provide services to natural gas and oil production, oil refining, steel processing, aircraft maintenance, paper manufacturing, timber products, glass, chemicals, cement, plastics, aerospace manufacturing, telecommunications and rubber goods manufacturing industries. The company is a wholly owned subsidiary of American electric power company inc. The group operates from United States.

Primary SIC and add'l.: 4911

CIK No: 0000081027

Officers: Carole Huff Hicks/Mgr. - Community Affairs, Tim Hushbeck/Mgr. - Community Affairs, Vic Brown/Mgr. - Community Affairs, Frank Phillips/Mgr. - Community Affairs, Stuart Solomon/COO, Pres. - PSO, Preston Kissman/VP - Distribution Operations, Bill McKamey/VP - External Affairs, Bobby Mouser/Dir. - Customer Services, Marketing, Alan Decker/Dir. - Regulatory Services, Andrea Chancellor/GM - Corporate Communications, David Sartin/Dir. - Business Operations, Steve Fate/Mgr. - System Liaison, Floyd Schulte/Mgr. - Safety, Health

Directors: Michael G. Morris/Dir., Nicholas K. Akins/47/Dir., Carl L. English/61/Dir., Thomas M. Hagan/63/Dir., John B. Keane/61/Dir., Holly K. Koeppel/49/Dir., Robert P. Powers/53/Dir., Susan Tomasky/Dir., Stephen P. Smith/Dir., Dennis E. Welch/Dir.

Financial Data: Fiscal Year End:12/31   Latest Annual Data: 12/31/2006

Year	Sales	Net Income
2006	$1,441,784,000	$36,860,000
2005	$1,304,078,000	$57,893,000
2004	$1,047,521,000	$37,542,000

Curr. Assets:	$378,050,000	**Curr. Liab.:**	$525,514,000	**P/E Ratio:**	10.41
Plant, Equip.:	$1,999,187,000	**Total Liab.:**	$1,993,608,000	**Indic. Yr. Divd.:**	NA
Total Assets:	$2,579,046,000	**Net Worth:**	$585,438,000	**Debt/ Equity:**	NA

Public Service Enterprise Group Inc

80 Pk. Plz., Newark, NJ, 07102; ***PH:*** 1-973-430-7000; ***Fax:*** 1-973-824-7056; ***http://*** www.pseg.com

General - Incorporation .... NJ
Employees 9,677
Auditor .... Deloitte & Touche LLP
Stk Agt .... Continental Stock Transfer & Trust Co
Counsel .... NA
DUNS No. 00-697-3812

Stock- Price on:12/24/2007 .... $87.85
Stock Exchange .... NYSE
Ticker Symbol .... PEG
Outstanding Shares 253,520,000
E.P.S .... NA
Shareholders .... NA

Business: The group's principle activities include generating, transmitting, distributing and marketing electric energy. The group operates through four segments anamely power, pse&g, global and resources.The group operates from United States.

Primary SIC and add'l.: 4911 4932 4931

CIK No: 0000788784

Subsidiaries: PSEG Energy Holdings LLC, PSEG Energy Resources & Trade LLC, PSEG Fossil LLC, PSEG Global International Holdings LLC, PSEG Global LLC, PSEG Power LLC, PSEG Resources LLC, Public Service Electric and Gas Company

Officers: Ralph Izzo/Chmn., CEO, Pres./$2,718,373.00, Edwin R. Selover/Exec. VP, General Counsel, Miriam E. Gilligan/56/VP - Finance, Treasurer - Energy Holdings, Thomas M. O'Flynn/CFO, Exec. VP/$2,285,923.00, Frank Cassidy/61/COO, Pres. - Power/$2,136,444.00, Michael J. Thomson/49/Pres. - Fossil, Eileen A. Moran/Pres., Morton A. Plawner/60/Treasurer, Edward J. Biggins/Sec., Stephen C. Byrd/Sr. VP - Finance, Business Development, Strategy, M, A, Pseg Services Corporation, David P. Falck/Sr. VP - Law, Pseg Services Corporation, Ralph Larossa/COO, Pres. - Public Service Electric, Gas Company, Elbert C. Simpson/COO, Pres. - Pseg Services Corporation, Patty Johnson/Contact - Media, Matthew McGrath/44/Pres. *(22 Officers included in Index)*

Directors: Ralph Izzo/Chmn., CEO, Pres., Albert R. Gamper/64/Dir., Caroline Dorsa/47/Dir., William V. Hickey/63/Dir., Conrad K. Harper/66/Dir., Thomas A. Renyi/61/Dir., Richard J. Swift/63/Dir., Ernest H. Drew/70/Dir., Shirley Ann Jackson/61/Dir.

Owners: Ernest H. Drew, James E. Ferland, Frank Cassidy, Robert J. Dougherty, Thomas A. Renyi, William V. Hickey, Insiders, Richard J. Swift, Thomas M. OFlynn, Franklin Resources, Inc./9.00%, Caroline Dorsa, Ralph Izzo, Conrad K. Harper, Capital Research and Management Company/7.90%, Albert R. Gamper *(16 Owners included in Index)*

Financial Data: **Fiscal Year End:**12/31 **Latest Annual Data:** 12/31/2006

Year	Sales	Net Income
2006	$12,164,000,000	$739,000,000
2005	$12,430,000,000	$661,000,000
2004	$10,996,000,000	$726,000,000

Curr. Assets:	$3,662,000,000	**Curr. Liab.:**	$3,406,000,000		
Plant, Equip.:	$13,002,000,000	**Total Liab.:**	$21,743,000,000	**Indic. Yr. Divd.:**	$2.340
Total Assets:	$28,570,000,000	**Net Worth:**	$6,747,000,000	**Debt/ Equity:**	1.5558

Public Service Enterprise Group Incorporated

80 Pk. Plz., Newark, NJ, 07102; ***PH:*** 1-973-430-7000; ***Fax:*** 1-973-824-7056; ***http://*** www.pseg.com

General - Incorporation .... NJ
Employees 9,677
Auditor .... Deloitte & Touche LLP
Stk Agt .... The Bank of New York
Counsel .... NA
DUNS No. 00-697-3812

Stock- Price on:12/24/2007 .... $87.36
Stock Exchange .... NYSE
Ticker Symbol .... PEG
Outstanding Shares 253,520,000
E.P.S $3.68
Shareholders .... NA

Business: The group owns and operates electric and gas transmission and distribution business. The group supplies electric and gas services in New Jersey. The group distributes electric energy and gas to residential, commercial and industrial customers.

Primary SIC and add'l.: 4931 4932

CIK No: 0000081033

Officers: Ralph Izzo/50/Chmn., CEO, Pres., William J. Metzger/VP, Assist. Controller - Power, Pseg Services Corporation, Morton A. Plawner/VP, Treasurer - Public Service Enterprise Group Incorporated, Public Service Enterprise Group Incorporated, Public Service Electric, Gas Company, Christopher McAuliffe/VP - Environment, Litigation, Employment, Pseg Services Corporation, Brian Smith/VP - Communications, Pseg Services Corporation, Michael S. Paszynsky/VP - Security, Claims, Pseg Services Corporation, Richard D. Quinn/VP - Compensation, Benefits, Pseg Services Corporation, Eric B. Svenson/VP - Environmental, Health, Safety, Pseg Services Corporation, James E. Ferland/65/CFO, David G. Seabrook/VP - Merger, Acquisitions, Holdings, Pseg Services Corporation, Stuart J. Black/VP - Internal Auditing Services, Pseg Services Corporation, Richard P. Bonnifield/VP - Legal Services, Pseg Services Corporation, Anne E. Hoskins/VP - Federal Affairs, Policy, Pseg Services Corporation, Shawn P. Leyden/VP - Corporate, Commercial, Pseg Services Corporation, Tamara L. Linde/VP - Regulatory, Pseg Services Corporation *(56 Officers included in Index)*

Directors: Ralph Izzo/50/Chmn., CEO, Pres., Caroline Dorsa/48/Dir., Ernest H. Drew/70/Dir., Albert R. Gamper/65/Dir., Conrad K. Harper/67/Dir., William V. Hickey/63/Dir., Shirley Ann Jackson/61/Dir., Thomas A. Renyi/Dir., Richard J. Swift/Dir.

Owners: Franklin Resources, Inc./9.00%, Ralph Izzo, Edwin R. Selover, James E. Ferland, Ralph A. LaRossa, Insiders, Conrad K. Harper, Caroline Dorsa, Patricia A. Rado, Albert R. Gamper, Capital Research and Management Company/7.90%, Robert E. Busch

Financial Data: **Fiscal Year End:**12/31 **Latest Annual Data:** 12/31/2006

Year	Sales	Net Income
2006	$12,164,000,000	$739,000,000
2005	$12,430,000,000	$661,000,000
2004	$10,996,000,000	$726,000,000

Curr. Assets:	$3,662,000,000	**Curr. Liab.:**	$3,406,000,000	**P/E Ratio:**	25.54
Plant, Equip.:	$13,002,000,000	**Total Liab.:**	$21,743,000,000	**Indic. Yr. Divd.:**	$2.340
Total Assets:	$28,570,000,000	**Net Worth:**	$6,747,000,000	**Debt/ Equity:**	1.5558

Public Service of New Hampshire

107 Selden St., Berlin, CT, 06037; ***PH:*** 1-800-286-5000; ***Fax:*** 1-860-665-5418; ***http://*** www.psnh.com; ***Email:*** psnhreq@psnh.com

General - Incorporation .... NH
Employees 5,869
Auditor .... Deloitte & Touche LLP
Stk Agt .... NA
Counsel .... NA
DUNS No. 00-697-1352

Stock- Price on:12/24/2007 .... $28.7
Stock Exchange .... NA
Ticker Symbol .... NA
Outstanding Shares 154,550,000
E.P.S $3.76
Shareholders .... NA

Business: The group's principle activity is to provide electric services to a variety of customers including residential, commercial and industrial. In addition to retail services, the company also provides wholesale services to 10 municipalities and utilities. The company is a wholly owned subsidiary of northeast utilities. The group operates from United States.

Primary SIC and add'l.: 4911

CIK No: 0000315256

Subsidiaries: CL&P Funding LLC, CL&P Receivables Corporation, E. S. Boulos Company, Holyoke Power and Electric Company, Holyoke Water Power Company, Mode 1 Communications, Inc., North Atlantic Energy Corporation, North Atlantic Energy Service Corporation, Northeast Generation Company, Northeast Generation Services Company, Northeast Nuclear Energy Company, Northeast Utilities (a Massachusetts business trust), Northeast Utilities Service Company, NU Enterprises, Inc., PSNH Funding LLC 29 Subsidiaries included in the Index

Officers: Martin Murray/Media Contact, Kathleen Lewis/Contact - Seacoast, Northern Division, Elizabeth Larocca/Contact - Southern Division, Sue Blothenburg/Contact - Western Central Division, Shirley M. Payne/56/VP - Accounting, Controller, John M. MacDonald/VP - Energy Delivery, Generation, Paul E. Ramsey/VP - Customer Services, Gary A. Long/COO, Pres.

Owners: Raymond P. Necci, David R. McHale, Leon J. Olivier, Gregory J. Butler, WMECO, CL&P, PSNH, Charles W. Shivery, Gary A. Long, Rodney O. Powell, Cheryl W. Grise

Financial Data: **Fiscal Year End:**12/31 **Latest Annual Data:** 12/31/2006

Year	Sales	Net Income
2006	$6,884,388,000	$470,578,000
2005	$7,397,390,000	-$253,488,000
2004	$6,686,699,000	$122,147,000

Curr. Assets:	$1,731,051,000	**Curr. Liab.:**	$1,363,835,000	**P/E Ratio:**	7.63
Plant, Equip.:	$6,242,186,000	**Total Liab.:**	$8,388,857,000	**Indic. Yr. Divd.:**	$0.800
Total Assets:	$11,303,236,000	**Net Worth:**	$2,798,179,000	**Debt/ Equity:**	1.5860

Public Storage Inc

701 Western Ave., Glendale, CA, 91201; ***PH:*** 1-818-244-8080; ***Fax:*** 1-818-553-2388; ***http://*** www.publicstorage.com

General - Incorporation .... CA
Employees 6,000
Auditor .... Ernst & Young LLP
Stk Agt .... Computershare Trust Co
Counsel .... NA
DUNS No. .... NA

Stock- Price on:12/24/2007 .... $82.905
Stock Exchange .... NYSE
Ticker Symbol .... PSA
Outstanding Shares 169,320,000
E.P.S .... NA
Shareholders .... NA

Business: The groups principle activities include acquiring, developing, owning and operating self-storage facilities. The group operates through three segments namely, domestic operations, European operations and domestic ancillary operations. In the year 2006, the group acquired 32 self-storage facilities. The group operates from the United States.

Primary SIC and add'l.: 4225 6798

CIK No: 0000318380

Subsidiaries: Connecticut Storage Fund, PS Co-Investment Partners, PS Illinois Trust, PS Insurance Company - Hawaii, Ltd, PS Orangeco, Inc, PS Partners VIII, Ltd, PS Partners, Ltd, PS Tennessee, LP, PS Texas Holdings, Ltd, PSA Institutional Partners, LP, PSAC Development Partners, LP, Public Storage Institutional Fund, Public Storage Institutional Fund III, Public Storage Pickup & Delivery, LP, Public Storage Properties IV, Ltd 24 Subsidiaries included in the Index

Officers: Ronald L. Havner/Vice Chmn., CEO, Pres., David F. Doll/Pres. - Real Estate Division, John S. Baumann/Sr. VP, Chief Legal Officer, Candace N. Krol/Sr. VP - Human Resources, John Reyes/Sr. VP, CFO, John E. Graul/Sr. VP

Directors: Ronald L. Havner/Vice Chmn., CEO, Pres., Wayne B. Hughes/Chmn., Harvey Lenkin/Trustee, Dann V. Angeloff/Trustee, William C. Baker/Trustee, John T. Evans/Trustee, Uri P. Harkham/Trustee, Gary E. Pruitt/Trustee, Daniel C. Staton/Trustee

Owners: John Reyes, David F. Doll, Tamara Hughes Gustavson/12.50%, Candace N. Krol, John T. Evans, John S. Baumann, William C. Baker, Wayne B. Hughes/11.50%, Ronald L. Havner, Harvey Lenkin, Dann V. Angeloff, Wayne B. Hughes/2.60%, Gary E. Pruitt, John E. Graul, Uri P. Harkham *(17 Owners included in Index)*

Financial Data: **Fiscal Year End:**12/31 **Latest Annual Data:** 12/31/2006

Year	Sales	Net Income
2006	$1,381,655,000	$314,026,000
2005	$1,060,961,000	$456,393,000
2004	$927,976,000	$366,213,000

Curr. Assets:	$555,584,000	**Curr. Liab.:**	$370,964,000		
Plant, Equip.:	$9,597,541,000	**Total Liab.:**	$2,182,248,000	**Indic. Yr. Divd.:**	$2.000
Total Assets:	$11,198,473,000	**Net Worth:**	$8,208,045,000	**Debt/ Equity:**	0.1350

Publicard Inc

75 Rockefeller Plz., 16th Fl., New York, NY, 10019; ***PH:*** 1-212-265-7013; ***Fax:*** 1-212-307-5781; ***http://*** www.publicard.com; ***Email:*** corporate@publicard.com

General - Incorporation .... PA
Employees 31
Auditor .... Deloitte & Touche LLP
Stk Agt .... Continental Stock Transfer & Trust Co
Counsel .... NA
DUNS No. 00-229-5152

Stock- Price on:12/24/2007 .... NA
Stock Exchange .... OTC
Ticker Symbol .... CARD
Outstanding Shares .... NA
E.P.S $0.251
Shareholders .... NA

Business: The group's principal activity is to provide products and solutions to facilitate secure access and transactions. It designs and develops smart card software and hardware solutions for campus environments that includes institutions such as corporate campuses, secondary schools and universities. The group also licenses smart card reader technology and the integrated circuit technology within readers to facilitate secure access to computers, networks and the Internet, as well as secure Internet transactions, by enabling the use of cryptographic and other security applications.

Primary SIC and add'l.: 3823 3829 7372

CIK No: 0000081050

Subsidiaries: Amazing! Smart Card Technologies, Inc., Blackwold, Inc., Boxsterview, Inc., Continental Distilling Corporation, Greystone Peripherals, Inc., Hanten Acquisition Co., Infineer Ltd., Infineer, Inc., Orr-Schelen-Mayeron & Associates, Inc., Publicker Chemical Corporation, Publicker Gasohol, Inc., Publicker, Inc., Redwold, Inc., Sagrocry, Inc.

Officers: Joseph E. Sarachek/Dir., CEO, Stephen A. Spitzer/35/Acting Principal Financial Officer

Directors: Joseph E. Sarachek/Dir., CEO, Harry I. Freund/Chmn., Jay S. Goldsmith/Vice Chmn., Clifford B. Cohn/Dir., L. G. Schafran/Dir., Emil Vogel/Dir.

Owners: Insiders/10.30%, Taube Hodson Stonex/11.00%, Harry I. Freund/4.10%, L. G. Schafran/1.10%, Emil Vogel, Clifford B. Cohn, Jay S. Goldsmith/5.00%

Financial Data: Fiscal Year End:12/31 Latest Annual Data: 12/31/2006

Year	Sales	Net Income
2006	$3,314,000	$6,267,000
2005	$3,617,000	-$2,031,000
2004	$4,395,000	-$4,859,000

Curr. Assets:	$1,377,000	Curr. Liab.:	$2,136,000		
Plant, Equip.:	$11,000	Total Liab.:	$2,352,000	Indic. Yr. Divd.:	NA
Total Assets:	$1,388,000	Net Worth:	-$964,000	Debt/ Equity:	NA

Publicis Groupe

133, Ave. Des Champs-elysees, Paris, 75008; ; *http://* www.publicis.fr

General - Incorporation	France	Stock- Price on:12/24/2007	$43.79
Employees	39,939	Stock Exchange	OTC
Auditor	Bruno Perrin , Isabelle Massa	Ticker Symbol	PUBGY
Stk Agt.	NA	Outstanding Shares	198,710,000
Counsel	NA	E.P.S.	$2.67
DUNS No.	NA	Shareholders	NA

Business: The group's principle activity is the provision of international advertising and communications services. The company operates through the following divisions: communications: advertising and other customer support services such as research, crisis management, public relations, financial advertising, design, in-house communications and recruitment advertising, direct marketing, sales promotions, and comprehensive graphic and artwork services.

Primary SIC and add'l.: 4899 7372 7311 5999

CIK No: 0001050952

Subsidiaries: Arc Integrated Marketing, Arc worldwide, Badillo Nazca S&S Inc, Bartle Bogle Hegarty, Beacon Communications, BMZ + more Management, Buhler and Partners, Burrell Communications, Capps Digital, Carr Noir, Challenger House, Chow Communications, Conill Advertising, Creators of Multi Media Art Ltd, Drugstore Champs Elyses 149 Subsidiaries included in the Index

Owners: Tateo Mataki, Elisabeth Badinter, Simon Badinter, Monique Bercault, Hlne Ploix, Michel Cicurel, Amaury de Seze, Grard Worms, Bertrand Siguier, Claudine Bienaim, Yutaka Narita, Lone Meyer, Sophie Dulac, Maurice Lvy, Felix G. Rohatyn *(18 Owners included in Index)*

Financial Data: Fiscal Year End:12/31 Latest Annual Data: 12/31/2006

Year	Sales	Net Income
2006	$5,790,836,000	$582,252,000
2005	$4,888,019,000	$467,838,000
2004	$5,218,830,000	$472,082,000

Curr. Assets:	$9,607,823,000	Curr. Liab.:	$9,180,046,000		
Plant, Equip.:	$604,697,000	Total Liab.:	$14,257,920,000	Indic. Yr. Divd.:	$0.570
Total Assets:	$18,411,584,000	Net Worth:	$4,059,923,000	Debt/ Equity:	NA

Publix Super Markets Inc

3300 Publix Corporate Pkwy., Lakeland, FL, 33811; *PH:* 1-863-688-1188; *Fax:* 1-863-284-5532; *http://* www.publix.com

General - Incorporation	FL	Stock- Price on:12/24/2007	$75
Employees	62,000	Stock Exchange	OTC
Auditor	KPMG LLP	Ticker Symbol	PUSH
Stk Agt.	NA	Outstanding Shares	NA
Counsel	NA	E.P.S.	$1.38
DUNS No.	00-692-2009	Shareholders	NA

Business: The group's principle activity is to provide supermarket services. The groups products include grocery, dairy, produce, deli, bakery, meat, seafood, housewares, and health and beauty care items. The group operates from United States.

Primary SIC and add'l.: 5461 5421 5451 5411

CIK No: 0000081061

Subsidiaries: Crispers, LLC, Lone Palm Golf Club, LLC, PTO, LLC, Publix Alabama, LLC, Publix Asset Management Company, Publix Tennessee, LLC, PublixDirect, LLC, Real Sub, LLC

Officers: Charles H. Jenkins/64/Dir., CEO/$912,785.00, Laurie S. Zeitlin/CIO, Sr. VP/$639,943.00, Brenda Reid/Mgr. - Media, Community Relations, William E. Crenshaw/57/Dir., Pres./$736,982.00, David P. Phillips/48/CFO, Treasurer/$594,599.00, Maria Brous/Dir. - Media, Community Relations, Shannon Patten/Mgr. - Media, Community Relations, Central FL, Dwaine Stevens/Mgr. - Media, Community Relations

Directors: Charles H. Jenkins/64/Dir., CEO, Howard M. Jenkins/56/Chmn., Vane E. McClurg/66/Dir., Sherrill W. Hudson/65/Dir., Carol Jenkins Barnett/51/Dir., Hoyt R. Barnett/64/Dir., Joan G. Buccino/70/Dir., William E. Crenshaw/57/Dir., Pres., Kelly E. Norton/69/Dir., Maria A. Sastre/52/Dir.

Owners: 401(k) Plan/5.63%, Joan G. Buccino, Hoyt R. Barnett, Sherrill W. Hudson, Charles H. Jenkins/1.17%, Kelly E. Norton, Insiders/12.46%, Carol Jenkins Barnett/5.81%, Howard M. Jenkins/2.90%, Vane E. McClurg, Laurie S. Zeitlin, David P. Phillips, Maria A. Sastre, William E. Crenshaw/1.11%, Employee Stock Ownership Plan/30.87%

Financial Data: Fiscal Year End:12/31 Latest Annual Data: 12/30/2006

Year	Sales	Net Income
2006	$21,819,725,000	$1,097,209,000
2005	$20,744,811,000	$989,156,000
2004	$18,686,371,000	$819,383,000

Curr. Assets:	$2,047,761,000	Curr. Liab.:	$1,811,273,000		
Plant, Equip.:	$3,047,881,000	Total Liab.:	$2,521,449,000	Indic. Yr. Divd.:	$0.200
Total Assets:	$6,727,223,000	Net Worth:	$4,205,774,000	Debt/ Equity:	NA

Puda Coal Inc New

426 Xuefu St., Taiyuan, Shanxi Province, 30006; *PH:* 954-493-8900; *http://* www.puda-coal.com

General - Incorporation	FL	Stock- Price on:12/24/2007	$2.46
Employees	NA	Stock Exchange	OTC
Auditor	Moore Stephens Ellis Foster Ltd.	Ticker Symbol	PUDC
Stk Agt	Fidelity Transfer Co	Outstanding Shares	NA
Counsel	NA	E.P.S.	NA
DUNS No.	NA	Shareholders	NA

Business: The groups principle activity is supplier of metallurgical coking coal to the industrial sector in the Peoples Republic of China. Services of the group include steel producers for the purpose of making the coke required for the steel manufacturing process. Specific customers of the group include Baotou Steel Group, Liulin Coal Cleaning Plant, Liulin Jinmei Coal, Jiangsu Yueda, Xiaoyi Jinyan Electricity, Shizhou Coal Gas, Lvliang Longteng Coke, Liulin Dongjiagou Coal Mine, Liulin Luojiapo Coal Mine. The group operates from China. The group's quarterly revenue for Sep'07 was 40.54 millions of USD.

Primary SIC and add'l.: 5050

CIK No: 0001162747

Subsidiaries: British Virgin Islands, Purezza Marketing, Inc.

Officers: Zhao Ming/Chmn., CEO, Zhao Yao/Dir., COO, Wenwei Tian/Dir. - Investor Relations

Directors: Zhao Ming/Chmn., CEO, Zhao Yao/Dir., COO

Owners: Keating Reverse Merger Fund, LLC/5.10%, Insiders/57.20%, Zhao Ming/57.20%

Financial Data: Fiscal Year End:12/31 Latest Annual Data: 12/31/2006

Year	Sales	Net Income
2006	$137,771,000	$1,354,000
2005	$51,710,000	$965,000
2004	NA	-$380,000

Curr. Assets:	$49,385,000	Curr. Liab.:	$12,936,000		
Plant, Equip.:	$9,870,000	Total Liab.:	$39,947,000	Indic. Yr. Divd.:	NA
Total Assets:	$62,984,000	Net Worth:	$23,037,000	Debt/ Equity:	1.0545

Puget Energy Inc

10885 NE 4th St., Ste. 1200, Bellevue, WA, 98004; *PH:* 1-425-454-6363; *Fax:* 1-425-424-6537; *http://* www.pse.com

General - Incorporation	WA	Stock- Price on:12/24/2007	$24
Employees	2,400	Stock Exchange	NYSE
Auditor	PricewaterhouseCoopers LLP	Ticker Symbol	PSD
Stk Agt	Mellon Investor Services LLC	Outstanding Shares	116,860,000
Counsel	NA	E.P.S.	$1.76
DUNS No.	NA	Shareholders	NA

Business: The groups principle activity is to provide energy services. The group operates from United States.

Primary SIC and add'l.: 4911 4923 4939

CIK No: 0000081100

Subsidiaries: InfrastruX Group, Inc., Puget Sound Energy, Inc.

Officers: Stephen P. Reynolds/Chmn., CEO, Pres., K. J. Harris/43/Sr. VP - Regulatory Policy, Energy Efficiency, Jennifer L. O'Connor/Sr. VP, General Counsel, Corp. Sec., Chief Ethics, Compliance Officer, Durga Dorsaisamy/Dir. - Investor Relations, D. E. Gaines/50/VP - Finance, Treasurer, James W. Eldredge/VP, Controller, Chief Accounting Officer, P. M. Wiegand/55/VP - Project Development, Contract Management, D. P. Brady/43/Sr. VP - Customer Service, Information Technology, CIO, P. K. Bussey/51/Sr. VP - Corporate Affairs, Donald E. Gaines/VP - Finance, Treasurer, Bertrand Valdman/44/Sr. VP - Finance, CFO, Eric M. Markell/CFO, Exec. VP, S. McLain/51/Sr. VP - Operations, M. D. Mellies/47/VP - Human Resources, C. E. Shirley/54/VP - Energy Efficiency Services

Directors: Stephen P. Reynolds/Chmn., CEO, Pres., Sally G. Narodick/Dir., Phyllis J. Campbell/Dir., Stephen E. Frank/Dir., Craig W. Cole/Dir., Kenneth P. Mortimer/Dir., Tomio Moriguchi/Dir., William S. Ayer/Dir., Herbert B. Simon/Dir., George W. Watson/Dir.

Financial Data: Fiscal Year End:12/31 Latest Annual Data: 12/31/2006

Year	Sales	Net Income
2006	$2,905,693,000	$219,216,000
2005	$2,573,210,000	$155,726,000
2004	$2,568,813,000	$55,022,000

Curr. Assets:	$821,365,000	Curr. Liab.:	$1,071,133,000	P/E Ratio:	13.64
Plant, Equip.:	$5,332,508,000	Total Liab.:	$4,948,121,000	Indic. Yr. Divd.:	$1.000
Total Assets:	$7,066,039,000	Net Worth:	$2,116,029,000	Debt/ Equity:	NA

Pulaski Financial Corp

12300 Olive Blvd. St., Louis, MO, 63141; *PH:* 1-314-878-2210; *Fax:* 1-314-878-7130; *http://* www.pulaskibankstl.com

General - Incorporation	MO	Stock- Price on:12/24/2007	$15.655
Employees	361	Stock Exchange	NDQ
Auditor	KPMG LLP	Ticker Symbol	PULB
Stk Agt	Registrar & Transfer Co	Outstanding Shares	9,980,000
Counsel	Kappel, Neill & Wolff	E.P.S.	$0.905
DUNS No.	04-897-8014	Shareholders	NA

Business: The group's principal activity is to accept deposits from the general public and use such funds to originate one-to four-family residential mortgage loans within its lending market area. The group is a community oriented financial institution that provides traditional financial services through five full service branches within st. Louis city metropolitan area. The group provides traditional retail banking services, one-to-four family residential mortgage loans and consumer loan products including home equity and personal loans. The group sells insurance products and annuities through pulaski service corporation.

Primary SIC and add'l.: 6035 6712

CIK No: 0001062438

Subsidiaries: Pulaski Bank, Pulaski Financial Statutory Trust I, Pulaski Financial Statutory Trust II, Pulaski Service Corporation

Officers: William A. Donius/Chmn., CEO, Ramsey K. Hamadi/CFO, Thomas W. Reeves/Pres., Brian Bjorkman/Pres. - Commercial Lending, Matthew Locke/Sr. VP - Kansas City, Lisa K. Simpson/Sr. VP - Human Resources, Rita Kuster/Sr. VP - Commercial Lending, Paul J. Milano/Treasurer, Controller, Helen Z. Liu/Exec. Assist. - Pulaski Bank, Mike Arneth/Contact - General Media Inquiries, Woody Wallace/Contact - General Media Inquiries, Tad Gage/Contact - General Media Inquiries

Directors: William A. Donius/Chmn., CEO, Leon A. Felman/Dir., Timothy K. Reeves/Dir., William M. Corrigan/Dir., Lee S. Wielansky/Dir., Stanley J. Bradshaw/Dir., Michael R. Hogan/Dir., Steven C. Roberts/Dir.

Owners: Leon A. Felman/7.23%, Stanley J. Bradshaw, William M. Corrigan, Ramsey K. Hamadi/1.13%, William A. Donius/5.13%, Christopher K. Reichert/1.85%, Lee S. Wielansky, Michael R. Hogan, Pulaski Bank Employee Stock Ownership Plan/6.11%, Insiders/16.56%, William A. Donius/5.13%, Timothy K. Reeves, Steven C. Roberts

Financial Data: Fiscal Year End:09/30 Latest Annual Data: 9/30/2006

Year	Sales	Net Income
2006	$66,677,000	$9,838,000
2005	$48,737,000	$7,479,000
2004	$32,792,000	$5,852,000

Curr. Assets:	$28,441,000	Curr. Liab.:	$852,116,000	P/E Ratio:	17.30
Plant, Equip.:	$20,930,000	Total Liab.:	$886,634,000	Indic. Yr. Divd.:	$0.340
Total Assets:	$962,460,000	Net Worth:	$75,827,000	Debt/ Equity:	0.2867

Pulte Homes Inc

100 Bloomfield Hills Pkwy., Ste. 300, Bloomfield Hills, MI, 48304; **PH:** 1-248-647-2750; **Fax:** 1-248-433-4598; **http://** www.pulte.com

General - Incorporation	MI	**Stock** - Price on:12/24/2007	$24.79
Employees	12,400	Stock Exchange	NYSE
Auditor	Ernst & Young LLP	Ticker Symbol	PHM
Stk Agt	EquiServe Trust Co N.A	Outstanding Shares	255,970,000
Counsel	NA	E.P.S.	$1.32
DUNS No.	18-620-8351	Shareholders	NA

Business: The groups principle activity is to provide home building and financial services. The group also provides mortgage-banking services. The group operates from United States, Mexico, Puerto Rico and Argentina.

Primary SIC and add'l.: 6035 6162 6719 1521 1531

CIK No: 0000822416

Subsidiaries: Asset Five Corp., Asset One Corp., Chandler Natural Resources Corporation, Chase Triple M, LLC, Chilean limited liability company, Clairmont, LLC ., Contractors Insurance Company of North America, Inc, Controladora PHC, S.A. de C.V, Corte Bella Golf Club, LLC., CP Sunridge, LLC., Del E. Webb Financial Corporation., Del Webb California Corp., Del Webb Commercial Properties Corporation, Del Webb Communities of Illinois, Inc., Del Webb Communities, Inc. 110 Subsidiaries included in the Index

Officers: Richard J. Dugas/Dir., CEO, Pres./$15,694,370.00, Robert P. Schafer/VP - Finance, Homebuilding Operations, West Region, David G. Schreiner/VP - Active Adult Development, Melanie Hearsch/Mgr. - Corporate Communications, Caryn Klebba/Mgr. - Corporate Communications, Julia Weston/Exec. Assist., Gregory M. Nelson/VP, Assist. Sec., Steven A. Burch/VP - Strategic Marketing, Steven C. Petruska/COO, Exec. VP/$11,514,310.00, Roger A. Cregg/CFO, Exec. VP/$7,314,944.00, Peter J. Keane/Sr. VP - Homebuilding Operations/$3,601,940.00, Jerry R. Batt/CIO, VP, Steven M. Cook/VP, General Counsel, Sec., Sean J. Degen/VP - Architectural Services, Vincent J. Frees/VP, Controller (23 Officers included in Index)

Directors: Richard J. Dugas/Dir., CEO, Pres., William J. Pulte/Chmn., William B. Smith/Dir., Patrick J. O'Leary/Dir., Alan E. Schwartz/Dir., Debra J. Kelly-Ennis/Dir., John J. Shea/Dir., David N. McCammon/Dir., Francis J. Sehn/Dir., Brian P. Anderson/Dir., Kent D. Anderson/Dir., Bernard W. Reznicek/Dir.

Owners: Francis J. Sehn, Bernard W. Reznicek, John J. Shea, Alan E. Schwartz, Kent D. Anderson, William B. Smith, Patrick J. OLeary, The TCW Group, Inc. on behalf of the TCW Business Unit/8.01%, Insiders/19.30%, Legg Mason Capital Management, Inc./10.09%, David N. McCammon, Peter J. Keane, Richard J. Dugas, Steven C. Petruska, William J. Pulte/16.49% (18 Owners included in Index)

Financial Data: Fiscal Year End:12/31 Latest Annual Data: 12/31/2006

Year	Sales	Net Income
2006	$14,274,408,000	$687,471,000
2005	$14,694,535,000	$1,491,913,000
2004	$11,711,216,000	$986,541,000

Curr. Assets:	$10,507,656,000	Curr. Liab.:	$3,061,566,000		
Plant, Equip.:	NA	Total Liab.:	$6,599,513,000	Indic. Yr. Divd.:	$0.160
Total Assets:	$13,176,874,000	Net Worth:	$6,577,361,000	Debt/ Equity:	0.5469

Puradyn DYN Filter Technologies Inc

2017 High Ridge Rd., Boynton Beach, FL, 33426; **PH:** 1-561-547-9499; **Fax:** 1-561-547-8629; **http://** www.puradyn.com; **Email:** info@puradyn.com

General - Incorporation	DE	**Stock** - Price on:12/24/2007	NA
Employees	28	Stock Exchange	OTC
Auditor	Webb & Co., P.A.	Ticker Symbol	PFTI
Stk Agt	Florida Atlantic Stock Transfer	Outstanding Shares	NA
Counsel	NA	E.P.S.	-$0.09
DUNS No.	78-563-5624	Shareholders	NA

Business: The group's principal activity is to design, manufacture and distribute oil purification systems under the trademark puradyn(r). The puradyn by-pass oil filtration system cleans oil by continually removing solid and liquid contaminants from the oil through filtration and evaporation process. The oil purification system extends the life of lubricating oil in gas and diesel engines and also hydraulic fluid used in industrial machinery. It is manufactured in six different sizes suitable for placement on engines or equipment with oil sump capacities ranging from 8 to 240 quarts. The group also manufactures and sells disposable replacement filter elements for the puradyn. The products of the group are marketed to various market segments including trucking, marine, agricultural, bus, recreational vehicle, generator, construction, mining, industrial and hydraulic applications. The group operates in the United States and the United Kingdom.

Primary SIC and add'l.: 3599

CIK No: 0001019787

Subsidiaries: Puradyn Filter Technologies, Ltd

Officers: Joseph V. Vittoria/Chmn., CEO, Kevin Davies/49/MD, Cindy L. Gimler/CFO, Kevin G. Kroger/Dir., COO, Pres., Alan J. Sandler/VP, Chief Administrative Officer, Sec., Kathryn A. Morris/Dir. - Corporate Communications, Rene Garcia/Transfer Agent

Directors: Joseph V. Vittoria/Chmn., CEO, Richard C. Ford/64/Vice Chmn., Alan J. Sandler/VP, Chief Administrative Officer, Sec., Kevin G. Kroger/Dir., COO, Pres., John S. Caldwell/Dir., Charles W. Walton/Dir., Forrest D. Hayes/Dir., Dominick Telesco/Dir.

Owners: Alan J. Sandler/1.10%, Richard C. Ford/12.20%, Dominick Telesco/7.40%, Kevin G. Kroger/3.70%, Charles W. Walton/1.20%, Joseph V. Vittoria/11.60%, Quantum Industrial Partners LDC/15.40%, Glenhill Capital Management, LP/14.70%, Insiders

Financial Data: Fiscal Year End:12/31 Latest Annual Data: 12/31/2006

Year	Sales	Net Income
2006	$3,073,000	-$2,653,000
2005	$2,475,000	-$3,191,000
2004	$2,472,000	-$3,588,000

Curr. Assets:	$2,000,000	Curr. Liab.:	$1,308,000		
Plant, Equip.:	$194,000	Total Liab.:	$7,147,000	Indic. Yr. Divd.:	NA
Total Assets:	$2,275,000	Net Worth:	-$4,872,000	Debt/ Equity:	NA

Purchase Point Media Corp

6950 Central Hwy., Pennsauken, NJ, 08109; **PH:** 1-212-481-1005

General - Incorporation	MN	**Stock** - Price on:12/24/2007	$0.037
Employees	NA	Stock Exchange	OTC
Auditor	Madsen & Associates, CPA's Inc.	Ticker Symbol	PPMC
Stk Agt	Signature Stock Transfer, Inc.	Outstanding Shares	NA
Counsel	NA	E.P.S.	NA
DUNS No.	NA	Shareholders	NA

Business: The groups principal activity is owns a patented grocery cart advertising display device called the last word(R) that attaches to supermarket shopping carts. The group also entered into a joint participation agreement with CBS Radio and TV wherein CBS will offer stores free advertising and then sell Radio, TV and the last word (TM) advertising to product manufactures who sell their products in the stores. The group operates from the United States, Canada, France, Germany and the United Kingdom.

Primary SIC and add'l.: 4899

CIK No: 0001001065

Officers: Steven A. Kempenich/37/Dir., CEO, Acting Sec., Steve Rubakh/47/Dir., Acting CFO, Pres.

Directors: Steven A. Kempenich/37/Dir., CEO, Acting Sec., Albert P. Folsom/69/Dir., Raymond A. Hatch/73/Dir., Michael F. Reuling/64/Dir., Steve Rubakh/47/Dir., Acting CFO, Pres.

Owners: Folsom Family Holdings/3.39%, Amtel Communications, Inc/3.39%, Raymond A. Hatch, Steve Rubakh/60.91%, Insiders/64.55%

Financial Data: Fiscal Year End:06/30 Latest Annual Data: 06/30/2007

Year	Sales	Net Income
2007	NA	-$444,000
2006	NA	-$237,000
2005	NA	-$711,000

Curr. Assets:	$202,000	Curr. Liab.:	$2,043,000		
Plant, Equip.:	$2,000	Total Liab.:	$2,043,000	Indic. Yr. Divd.:	NA
Total Assets:	$212,000	Net Worth:	-$1,831,000	Debt/ Equity:	NA

Purchasesoft Inc

7514 Girard Ave., Ste. 1440, La Jolla, CA, 92037; **PH:** 1-949-263-0910; **http://** www.purchasesoft.com; **Email:** Sales@purchasesoft.com

General - Incorporation	DE	**Stock** - Price on:12/24/2007	$0.0001
Employees	NA	Stock Exchange	OTC
Auditor	Gruber & Co., LLC	Ticker Symbol	PSFX
Stk Agt	Mendoza Berger & Co. LLP	Outstanding Shares	NA
Counsel	NA	E.P.S.	NA
DUNS No.	08-521-1589	Shareholders	NA

Business: The group designs, develops, markets and services purchasing and material management application software. The products of the group include electronic catalogs, requisitioning, e-mail enabled authorization, request for quotations, quotations and analyses. The activities also include purchasing, receiving, inventory, fixed asset and invoice management and advanced decision support. The group serves a broad range of customers from small and mid-sized businesses to fortune 2000 companies. The group acquired netshare solutions, gmbh on 09-Feb-2004 & computer information enterprises inc on 26-Feb-2004

Primary SIC and add'l.: 7372

CIK No: 0000727063

Officers: Steven A. Flagg/45/Chmn., CEO, Pres., Louis D. Rose/66/Dir. - Strategic Services, Stuart Williamson/58/VP - Support, Kevin A. Yanoscik/47/Dir., CFO, Werner Kuno Loechle/53/Dir., COO

Directors: Steven A. Flagg/45/Chmn., CEO, Pres., Kevin A. Yanoscik/47/Dir., CFO, Werner Kuno Loechle/53/Dir., COO, Louis Blatt/42/Member - Advisory Board

Owners: Anastasia Kostoff-Mann, HARRAHS INTERACTIVE INVESTMENT COMPANY/7.82%, CEDE & CO United States/12.41%

Financial Data: Fiscal Year End:05/31 Latest Annual Data: 5/31/2004

Year	Sales	Net Income
2004	$211,000	-$394,000
2001	$604,000	-$8,440,000
2000	$338,000	-$3,900,000

Curr. Assets:	$149,000	Curr. Liab.:	$736,000		
Plant, Equip.:	$7,000	Total Liab.:	$751,000	Indic. Yr. Divd.:	NA
Total Assets:	$258,000	Net Worth:	-$493,000	Debt/ Equity:	NA

Pure BioFuels Corp

9440 Little Santa Monica, Beverly Hills, CA, 90210; **PH:** 1-310-402-5916; **http://** www.purebiofuels.com; **Email:** info@purebiofuels.com

General - Incorporation	NV	**Stock**- Price on:12/24/2007	$0.97
Employees	11	Stock Exchange	OTC
Auditor	Dale Matheson Carr-hilton Labonte LLP	Ticker Symbol	PBOF
Stk Agt	Pacific Stock Transfer Company	Outstanding Shares	NA
Counsel	NA	E.P.S.	-$0.71
DUNS No.	NA	Shareholders	NA

Business: The groups principle activity is to sell a software product called MetaTraffic. The software is a web traffic analysis application that once installed on a website provides live traffic statistics on visitors at the website. The group operates from the United States.

Primary SIC and add'l.: 2869

CIK No: 0001283193

Subsidiaries: Metasun Software Corp

Officers: Luis Humberto Goyzueta Angobaldo/Founder, Dir., CEO/$270,000.00, Patrick F. Orlando/CTO, David Clifton/VP/$154,500.00, Carlos Alberto Pinto/Dir., COO, Steven S. Magami/Dir., Pres., Gustavo A. Goyzueta Angobaldo/CFO, Jp Bustamante Romero/Compliance Officer, Juan Manuel Oyakawa Kishimoto/Production Officer, Ursula De La Mata/Business Development Officer, Antonio Vila Benites/Project Development Officer, Dayana Bedoya Hart/Logistics Officer, Liliana Castillo/Quality Control, Environment Officer, Alberto Pinto/42/Dir., COO

Directors: Luis Humberto Goyzueta Angobaldo/Founder, Dir., CEO, Adam Roseman/Chmn., Steven S. Magami/Dir., Pres., Carlos Alberto Pinto/Dir., COO, Eric Reehl/Dir., Roger Ballentine/Member - Advisory Board, Shaine K. Tyson/Member - Advisory Board, Alberto Pinto/42/Dir., COO

Owners: Insiders/20.90%, Plainfield Asset Management LLC/14.70%, Adam Roseman/1.10%, David Clifton/4.80%, Luis Goyzueta/15.30%, Steven Magami, Alberto Pinto/2.00%, Gustavo Goyzueta/2.00%

Financial Data: *Fiscal Year End:*01/31 *Latest Annual Data:* 12/31/2006

Year	Sales	Net Income
2006	NA	-$1,076,000
2005	$150,000	-$33,000

Curr. Assets:	$1,314,000	*Curr. Liab.:*	$956,000		
Plant, Equip.:	$4,021,000	*Total Liab.:*	$1,556,000	*Indic. Yr. Divd.:*	NA
Total Assets:	$5,528,000	*Net Worth:*	$3,971,000	*Debt/ Equity:*	0.1958

Pure Bioscience

1725 Gillespie Way, Ste. 101, El Cajon, CA, 92020; *PH:* 1-619-596-8600; *Fax:* 1-619-596-8700; *http://* www.purebio.com

General - Incorporation	CA	**Stock**- Price on:12/24/2007	$3.53
Employees	12	Stock Exchange	OTC
Auditor	Mayer Hoffman Mccann, P.C	Ticker Symbol	PURE
Stk Agt	Computershare Trust Co	Outstanding Shares	24,800,000
Counsel	NA	E.P.S.	-$0.16
DUNS No.	NA	Shareholders	NA

Business: The group's principal activity is to manufacture and distribute water purifying, measuring and dispensing apparatus for pharmaceutical and consumer use. The group's principal product is fillmaster, a water purification, measuring and dispensing system used in pharmacies for the reconstitution of liquid oral antibiotics and other applications. The group also caters to the consumer market with its brand nutripure, a residential drinking water system. Other products of the group include scanmaster, nutripure elite filters, medifier and others. The group discontinued the operations of water treatment division in 2004.

Primary SIC and add'l.: 3589 7342

CIK No: 0001006028

Subsidiaries: EXCOA Nevada

Officers: Michael L. Krall/Chmn., CEO, Pres., Donna Singer/Dir., Exec. VP, Tommy G. Thompson/Dir., Sec., Andrew J. Buckland/CFO, Dennis B. Atchley/Corp. Sec.

Directors: Michael L. Krall/Chmn., CEO, Pres., Greg Barnhill/Dir., Dennis Brovarone/Dir., Gary Brownell/Dir., Donna Singer/Dir., Exec. VP, Tommy G. Thompson/Dir., Sec., Murray H. Gross/Dir.

Owners: Dennis Brovarone/3.98%, Gregory Barnhill/3.65%, Insiders/24.82%, Murray H. Gross, Donna Singer/4.45%, Tommy G. Thompson/2.29%, Michael L. Krall/8.03%, Gary Brownell/3.74%, Andrew J. Buckland/1.47%, Dennis Atchley/1.91%

Financial Data: *Fiscal Year End:*07/31 *Latest Annual Data:* 7/31/2006

Year	Sales	Net Income
2006	$200,000	-$3,683,000
2005	$156,000	-$317,000
2004	$263,000	-$2,308,000

Curr. Assets:	$5,067,000	*Curr. Liab.:*	$412,000		
Plant, Equip.:	$353,000	*Total Liab.:*	$412,000	*Indic. Yr. Divd.:*	NA
Total Assets:	$7,965,000	*Net Worth:*	$7,553,000	*Debt/ Equity:*	NA

Pure Cycle Corp

8451 Delaware St., Thornton, CO, 80260; *PH:* 1-303-292-3456; *Fax:* 1-303-292-3475; *http://* www.purecyclewater.com; *Email:* info@purecyclewater.com

General - Incorporation	DE	**Stock**- Price on:12/24/2007	$8.02
Employees	3	Stock Exchange	NDQ
Auditor	Ghp Horwath, P.C	Ticker Symbol	PCYO
Stk Agt	Computershare Investor Services LLC	Outstanding Shares	18,370,000
Counsel	NA	E.P.S.	-$0.37
DUNS No.	NA	Shareholders	NA

Business: The group's principle activity is to provide water to municipal water providers in denver metropolitan region and users in Nevada, Arizona and California. The group operates from United States.

Primary SIC and add'l.: 3581

CIK No: 0000276720

Officers: Mark W. Harding/CFO, Pres., Dir. - Principal Executive Office, Principal Financial Officer, Kevin B. McNeill/Controller, Scott E. Lehman/Corp. Sec., Engineer

Directors: Harrison H. Augur/Chmn., Mark W. Harding/CFO, Pres., Dir. - Principal Executive Office, Principal Financial Officer, Peter C. Howell/Dir., George M. Middlemas/Dir., Richard L. Guido/Dir., Mark D. Campbell/Dir., Arthur G. Epker/Dir.

Owners: Mark W. Harding/3.60%, TPC Ventures, LLC/6.10%, Trigran Investments, Inc./5.70%, George M. Middlemas, Insiders/8.30%, Peter C. Howell, Richard L. Guido, Mark D. Campbell/4.00%, Wellington Management Company, LLP/11.80%, Par Capital Management, Inc./13.00%, Harrison H. Augur, High Plains A&M, LLC/14.80%

Financial Data: *Fiscal Year End:*08/31 *Latest Annual Data:* 8/31/2006

Year	Sales	Net Income
2006	$272,000	-$793,000
2005	$235,000	-$1,051,000
2004	$205,000	-$1,976,000

Curr. Assets:	$3,121,000	*Curr. Liab.:*	$380,000		
Plant, Equip.:	$4,000	*Total Liab.:*	$54,170,000	*Indic. Yr. Divd.:*	NA
Total Assets:	$108,834,000	*Net Worth:*	$54,665,000	*Debt/ Equity:*	NA

PureDepth Inc

255 Shoreline Dr., Ste. 610, Redwood City, CA, 94065; *PH:* 1-303-858-1177; *Fax:* 1-650-632-0818; *http://* www.puredepth.com; *Email:* sales@puredepth.com

General - Incorporation	CO	**Stock**- Price on:12/24/2007	$1.7
Employees	NA	Stock Exchange	OTC
Auditor	Comiskey & Company	Ticker Symbol	PDEP
Stk Agt	TranShare Corporation	Outstanding Shares	66,160,000
Counsel	NA	E.P.S.	NA
DUNS No.	NA	Shareholders	NA

Business: The groups principle activities include buying and selling coins, precious metals, precious gem stones, jewelry and collectibles. The group markets its products under the tradenames include The Gold and Diamond Exchange," and "Colorado Coin". The group operates from the United States.

Primary SIC and add'l.: 3679

CIK No: 0001281108

Officers: Thomas L. Marcus/CEO, Mark Yahiro/Sr. VP - Marketing, Business Development, Jonathan McCaman/CFO, Kristin Bowman/Dir., Sr. VP - Corporate, Strategic Development, Thomas Credelle/Sr. VP - Worldwide Engineering, Development, Douglas Erickson/54/VP - Worldwide Sales

Directors: Thomas L. Marcus/CEO, John Floisand/Dir., Kristin Bowman/Dir., Sr. VP - Corporate, Strategic Development, Mark Kalow/Dir., John R. Stringer/Dir.

Owners: Lagunitas Partners LP/5.30%, Fred Angelopoulos/4.10%, David Hancock/3.00%, Kristin Bowman/2.90%, John Floisand, Mark Yahiro/2.20%, Insiders/11.70%, K One W One Limited/55.10%, Vision Opportunity Master Fund, Ltd./13.20%, Mark Kalow, Tom Marcus

PVC Container Corp

2 Industrial Way W, Eatontown, NJ, 07724; *PH:* 1-732-542-0060; *Fax:* 1-732-544-8007; *http://* www.pvcc.com

General - Incorporation	DE	**Stock**- Price on:12/24/2007	$2.35
Employees	550	Stock Exchange	OTC
Auditor	BDO Seidman LLP	Ticker Symbol	PVCO
Stk Agt	Registrar & Transfer Co	Outstanding Shares	NA
Counsel	Herbert S Meeker	E.P.S.	NA
DUNS No.	04-580-0315	Shareholders	NA

Business: The group's principal activities are to manufacture and market a line of plastic containers and related chemical compounds. The group has two reportable segments: plastic containers and polyvinyl chloride compound. The plastic containers segment manufactures custom designed pet, hdpe and pvc containers mainly for packaging of cosmetics, toiletries, foods, household lawn and garden chemicals and other industrial chemical products. The compound segment manufactures pvc compound used by the company as well as external customers. The external use of the pvc compound is for extruded profiles and accessories, furniture, molding and other indoor fixtures and molded electrical and electronic housings.

Primary SIC and add'l.: 3085 3087

CIK No: 0000081288

Subsidiaries: Airopak Corporation, Marpac Industries, Inc., Marpac Southwest, Inc, Novapak Corporation, Novatec Plastic Inc

Officers: William J. Bergen/CEO, Pres.

Financial Data: *Fiscal Year End:*06/30 *Latest Annual Data:* 6/30/2005

Year	Sales	Net Income
2005	$85,795,000	-$6,102,000
2004	$97,747,000	-$65,000
2003	$90,433,000	$873,000

Curr. Assets:	$31,032,000	*Curr. Liab.:*	$11,779,000		
Plant, Equip.:	$22,245,000	*Total Liab.:*	$40,237,000	*Indic. Yr. Divd.:*	NA
Total Assets:	$53,314,000	*Net Worth:*	$13,077,000	*Debt/ Equity:*	1.5538

PVF Capital Corp

30000 Aurora Rd., Solon, OH, 44139; *PH:* 1-440-248-7171; *Fax:* 1-440-914-3908; *http://* www.parkviewfederal.com

General - Incorporation	OH	**Stock**- Price on:12/24/2007	$13.1899
Employees	197	Stock Exchange	NDQ
Auditor	Crowe Chizek & Co. LLC	Ticker Symbol	PVFC
Stk Agt	National City Bank	Outstanding Shares	7,730,000
Counsel	Muldoon Murphy & Aguggia LLP	E.P.S.	$0.65
DUNS No.	02-409-8527	Shareholders	NA

Business: The group's principal activity is to attract deposits from the general public and invest these funds primarily in loans secured by first mortgages on real estate located in the bank's market area. The principal market area consists of portage, lake, geauga, cuyahoga, summit, stark, medina and lorain counties in Ohio. The group attracts deposits by offering a variety of deposit instruments, including checking accounts, money market accounts, regular savings accounts and certificates of deposit which range in maturity from seven days to four years. The group is a federally chartered savings bank and is a holding company for park view federal savings bank. It operates park view federal savings bank, pvf service corporation, pvf holding inc and mid pines land company. The group conducts its business through sixteen offices located in cuyahoga, summit, medina, lorain, lake and geauga counties in Ohio.

Primary SIC and add'l.: 6035 6712

CIK No: 0000928592

Subsidiaries: Mid Pines Land Co., Park View Federal Savings Bank, PVF Community Development Corp., PVF Holdings Inc., PVF Mortgage Corp., PVF Service Corporation
Officers: John R. Male/Chmn., CEO, Christine Misencik/Branch Mgr. - Avon Office, Mark Hansen/Branch Mgr. - Bedford Office, Richard Force/Branch Mgr. - Bainbridge Office, Lindsey Resnick/Branch Mgr. - Beachwood Office, Marguerite Krahe/Business Development, Ron Swentek/Branch Mgr. - Chardon Office, Sue Lawler Jantonio/Branch Mgr. - Mentor Office, Keith C. Swaney/Dir., COO, Pres., Treasurer, Michele Bahleda/Branch Mgr. - Aurora Office, Patricia Provenzano/Branch Mgr. - Solon Office, Barbara Stettnisch/Branch Mgr. - Strongsville Office, Raymond Olevero/Branch Mgr. - Mayfield Heights Office, Marelene Zampedro/Branch Mgr. - North Royalton Office, Jeffrey N. Male/59/VP, Sec. *(19 Officers included in Index)*
Directors: John R. Male/Chmn., CEO, Ronald D. Holman/Dir., Raymond J. Negrelli/Dir., Robert K. Healey/Dir., Stanley T. Jaros/Dir., Keith C. Swaney/Dir., COO, Pres., Treasurer, Gerald A. Fallon/Dir., Stuart D. Neidus/Dir.
Owners: Steven A. Calabrese/7.81%, Raymond J. Negrelli, Jeffrey N. Male/3.79%, Stanley T. Jaros, Robert K. Healey, Ronald D. Holman, Jeffrey L. Gendell/7.78%, Richard A. Barone/5.37%, Insiders/18.00%, Keith C. Swaney/3.11%, Stuart D. Neidus, Gerald A. Fallon, John R. Male/8.45%
Financial Data: Fiscal Year End:06/30 **Latest Annual Data:** 6/30/2006

Year	Sales	Net Income
2006	$57,714,000	$4,843,000
2005	$46,969,000	$5,584,000
2004	$45,239,000	$6,910,000

Curr. Assets:	$19,738,000	**Curr. Liab.:**	$797,233,000	**P/E Ratio:**	20.29
Plant, Equip.:	$12,850,000	**Total Liab.:**	$837,108,000	**Indic. Yr. Divd.:**	$0.300
Total Assets:	$906,081,000	**Net Worth:**	$68,973,000	**Debt/ Equity:**	0.5646

Pyramid Breweries Inc

91 S Royal Brougham Way, Seattle, WA, 98134; **PH:** 1-206-682-8322; **Fax:** 1-206-682-8420; **http://** www.pyramidbrew.com; **Email:** host@pyramidbrew.com

General - Incorporation	WA	**Stock** - Price on:12/24/2007	$3.47
Employees	480	Stock Exchange	NDQ
Auditor	Moss Adams LLP	Ticker Symbol	PMID
Stk Agt	Mellon Shareholder Services LLC	Outstanding Shares	9,160,000
Counsel. Heller Ehrman White & McAuliffe LLP		E.P.S	$0.01
DUNS No.	92-755-1283	Shareholders	NA

Business: The group's principle activities include marketing and selling crafts beers, soda, food, apparel and other items. It produces and markets over 20 styles of beer under the pyramid and thomas kemper brand names, also produces six premium sodas under the brand name of thomas kemper soda. It also operates restaurants adjacent to its breweries, under the pyramid alehouse brand name. In addition, the company produces old-fashioned, full-flavored, hand crafted sodas. The company has four breweries; two main breweries located in seattle, Washington and berkeley, California. The other two breweries are located in walnut creek and sacramento. In 2003, the company sold approximately 159,000 barrels of its beer and soda products. On 03-Aug-2004, the group acquired assets of portland brewing company. The group operates from United States.
Primary SIC and add'l.: 5813 2082 5812
CIK No: 0001001917
Subsidiaries: PBC Acquisition, LLC, Pyramid Gilman Street Property, LLC
Owners: Mark House/1.50%, George Hancock/12.30%, Kurt Dammeier/16.80%, Michael OBrien, Gary McGrath/1.80%, Scott Svenson, Scott Barnum/1.20%, Lee Andrews, Dimensional Fund Advisors LP/6.18%, Patrick Coll/1.40%, Insiders/36.20%
Financial Data: Fiscal Year End:12/31 **Latest Annual Data:** 12/31/2006

Year	Sales	Net Income
2006	$50,356,000	-$1,561,000
2005	$48,358,000	-$1,055,000
2004	$40,084,000	-$2,729,000

Curr. Assets:	$6,048,000	**Curr. Liab.:**	$7,468,000	**P/E Ratio:**	86.75
Plant, Equip.:	$26,716,000	**Total Liab.:**	$16,562,000	**Indic. Yr. Divd.:**	NA
Total Assets:	$34,040,000	**Net Worth:**	$17,478,000	**Debt/ Equity:**	0.4213

Pyramid Oil Co

PO Box 832, Bakersfield, CA, 93302; **PH:** 1-663-225-1000; **http://** www.pyramidoil.com; **Email:** info@PyramidOil.com

General - Incorporation	CA	**Stock** - Price on:12/24/2007	$3.45
Employees	13	Stock Exchange	AMEX
Auditor	Singer Lewak Greenbaum & Goldstein	Ticker Symbol	PDO
Stk Agt	U.S. Stock Transfer Corp	Outstanding Shares	3,740,000
Counsel	NA	E.P.S	$0.191
DUNS No.	00-486-8980	Shareholders	NA

Business: The group's principle activities include exploring, developing and producing crude oil and natural gas. The company acquires interests in land through acquisition and lease, drills and operates oil and gas wells to discover oil and gas. The company also participates in specific joint ventures with others in the development of oil and gas properties. Extracted crude oil and natural gas are sold to refineries and pipeline companies. The company operates 27 oil and gas leases in kern and santa barbara counties in California. Production operation mainly deals with pumping oil from wells into tanks and maintaining production facilities. The group operates from United States.
Primary SIC and add'l.: 1311
CIK No: 0000081318
Officers: John H. Alexander/60/Dir., CEO, Pres.
Directors: John H. Alexander/60/Dir., CEO, Pres., Michael D. Herman/50/Chmn., Thomas W. Ladd/59/Dir., Gary L. Ronning/65/Dir., John E. Turco/77/Dir.
Owners: John H. Alexander/1.99%, Michael D. Herman/55.66%, John E. Turco/4.90%, Insiders/62.55%
Financial Data: Fiscal Year End:12/31 **Latest Annual Data:** 12/31/2006

Year	Sales	Net Income
2006	$3,958,000	$949,000
2005	$3,761,000	$1,089,000
2004	$2,927,000	$612,000

Curr. Assets:	$2,797,000	**Curr. Liab.:**	$593,000	**P/E Ratio:**	18.06
Plant, Equip.:	$3,641,000	**Total Liab.:**	$1,586,000	**Indic. Yr. Divd.:**	NA
Total Assets:	$6,696,000	**Net Worth:**	$5,109,000	**Debt/ Equity:**	0.0007

Q Comm International Inc

1145 S 1680 W, Orem, UT, 84058; **PH:** 1-801-226-4222; **http://** www.qcomm.com

General - Incorporation	UT	**Stock** - Price on:12/24/2007	$0.21
Employees	45	Stock Exchange	NA
Auditor	Hansen, Barnett & Maxwell, P.c.	Ticker Symbol	NA
Stk Agt	American Stock Transfer & Trust Co.	Outstanding Shares	6,910,000
Counsel	NA	E.P.S	-$1.08
DUNS No.	NA	Shareholders	NA

Business: The group's principal activity is to market and sell prepaid telephone products through point of sale terminals. The qxpress is designed to replace the traditional distribution system for prepaid products, which consists of vouchers and hard cards that must be purchased by the retail merchant and that are subject to a number of problems, including loss, theft and inventory financing and management issues. Proprietary qxpress system includes the qxpress 200 terminals, a data center and the software and communication protocols that manage, operate and maintain the system and that enable the terminals to communicate with the data center. The group's operations are carried out in the United States of America.
Primary SIC and add'l.: 4813
CIK No: 0001102901
Subsidiaries: Point de Vente, Q Comm, Inc.
Financial Data: Fiscal Year End:12/31 **Latest Annual Data:** 12/31/2005

Year	Sales	Net Income
2005	$46,349,000	-$8,614,000
2004	$16,576,000	-$6,548,000
2003	$25,686,000	-$5,694,000

Curr. Assets:	$6,559,000	**Curr. Liab.:**	$1,764,000		
Plant, Equip.:	$1,322,000	**Total Liab.:**	$2,187,000	**Indic. Yr. Divd.:**	NA
Total Assets:	$8,884,000	**Net Worth:**	$6,697,000	**Debt/ Equity:**	0.0102

Q.E.P. Co Inc

1001 Broken Sound Pkwy. NW, Ste. A, Boca Raton, FL, 33487; **PH:** 1-561-994-5550; **Fax:** 1-866-435-8665; **http://** www.qep.com

General - Incorporation	DE	**Stock** - Price on:12/24/2007	$5.87
Employees	511	Stock Exchange	NDQ
Auditor	Grant Thornton LLP	Ticker Symbol	QEPC
Stk Agt	Computershare Trust Co	Outstanding Shares	3,440,000
Counsel	Holland & Knight LLP	E.P.S	$0.50
DUNS No.	03-824-2848	Shareholders	NA

Business: The group's principle activities are to manufacture, market and distribute specialty tools and flooring related products. The products of the group include adhesives, grouts, mortars, dry set powders, carpet seaming tape and an assortment of carpet installation tools. The group markets over 3,000 specialty tools and flooring related products under the brand names q.e.p.(TM), o'tool(tm), qset(TM) and roberts(tm), which are used primarily for surface preparation and installation of ceramic tile, carpet and wood flooring. These products are sold through four distribution channels: the group's sales staff; independent mfg. Representatives; an in-house telemarketing sales force; outside salaried and commissioned sales representatives. The group operates in the United States and 49 other countries throughout the world. The group's total revenue for year 2007 was 216.01 millions of USD.
Primary SIC and add'l.: 3425 3546 3423
CIK No: 0001017815
Subsidiaries: Boiardi Products Corporation, P.r.c.i. Sa, Q.e.p. Aust. Pty. Limited, Q.E.P. Chile Limitada, Q.e.p. Co. Aust. Pty. Limited, Q.E.P. Co. New Zealand Limited, Q.E.P. Co. U.K. Limited, Q.E.P. Stone Holdings Inc., Q.E.P. Zocalis Holding LLC, Q.E.P.-OTool, Inc., Roberts Capitol, Inc., Roberts Company Canada Limited, Roberts Germany GmbH, Roberts Holding International Inc., Roberts Mexicana, S.A. DE C.V. 17 Subsidiaries included in the Index
Officers: Lewis Gould/65/Chmn., CEO/$559,056.00, Susan J. Gould/62/Sec., Leonard Gould/39/Dir., Sr. VP/$251,338.00, James Brower/42/COO, Exec. VP/$264,006.00, Jamie L. Clingan/45/Sr. VP - International Marketing, Stuart F. Fleischer/56/CFO, Sr. VP, Treasurer/$255,109.00, Richard A. Brooke/60/Sr. VP/$195,327.00, Kenneth Weiss/42/Sr. VP - Commercial Sales
Directors: Lewis Gould/65/Chmn., CEO, Emil Vogel/65/Dir., Leonard Gould/39/Dir., Sr. VP, David W. Kreilein/50/Dir., Robert W. Muir/59/Dir.
Owners: Stuart Fleischer, Laura M. Holm, Emil Vogel/1.50%, Leonard Gould/1.00%, Insiders/50.90%, Robert W. Muir, David L. Kreilein, Susan J. Gould/11.60%, Lewis Gould/48.70%, Private Management Group, Inc./10.00%
Financial Data: Fiscal Year End:02/28 **Latest Annual Data:** 02/28/2007

Year	Sales	Net Income
2007	$216,006,000	-$5,573,000
2006	$212,314,000	$998,000
2005	$173,625,000	$3,955,000

Curr. Assets:	$65,003,000	**Curr. Liab.:**	$59,924,000		
Plant, Equip.:	$6,770,000	**Total Liab.:**	$64,873,000	**Indic. Yr. Divd.:**	NA
Total Assets:	$87,156,000	**Net Worth:**	$22,283,000	**Debt/ Equity:**	0.2220

QAD Inc

100 Innovation Pl., Santa Barbara, CA, 93018; **PH:** 1-805-684-6614; **Fax:** 1-805-565-4202; **http://** www.qad.com

General - Incorporation	DE	**Stock** - Price on:12/24/2007	$8.29
Employees	1,500	Stock Exchange	NDQ
Auditor	KPMG LLP	Ticker Symbol	QADI
Stk Agt	American Stock Transfer & Trust Co.	Outstanding Shares	32,580,000
Counsel	Nida & Maloney	E.P.S	$0.13
DUNS No.	03-956-1725	Shareholders	NA

Business: The group's principle activity is to provide collaborative commerce software applications for multi-national, large and mid-range manufacturing companies. The group serves the specific needs of the automotive, consumer products, electronics, food and beverage, industrial and medical industries. The maintenance technology strategy is focused on delivering collaborative solutions. Services ensures that the customers receive the right services from pre-installation, to implementation, to ongoing service and support. The products and services are marketed through direct and indirect sales channels and service organizations located throughout the world. The group has operations in the United States, Canada, Europe, the Middle East, Africa, Asia, Australia, South America, Central America and Mexico. The group's total revenue for year 2007 was 235.59 millions of USD.

Primary SIC and add'l.: 7372 7371

CIK No: 0001036188

Subsidiaries: QAD Asia Limited, QAD Australia Pty Ltd., QAD Bermuda Ltd., QAD Bilgisayar Yazilim Ltd. Sirketi, QAD Brasil Ltda., QAD Brazil Inc., QAD Canada ULC, QAD China Ltd., Qad Emea Holdings B.v., Qad Emea Limited, QAD Europe A. G., QAD Europe B.V., QAD Europe GmbH, QAD Europe Limited, QAD Europe NV/SA 38 Subsidiaries included in the Index

Officers: Karl F. Lopker/Dir., CEO/$1,091,656.00, Pamela M. Lopker/Chmn., Pres./$1,091,656.00, Daniel Lender/CFO, Exec. VP/$735,879.00, Roland B. Desilets/Exec. VP, General Counsel, Sec./$433,036.00

Directors: Karl F. Lopker/Dir., CEO, Pamela M. Lopker/Chmn., Pres., Peter R. Van Cuylenburg/Dir., Scott J. Adelson/Dir., Thomas J. O'Malia/Dir.

Owners: Barry A. Patmore, Daniel Lender/0.49%, Pamela M./55.97%, Scott J. Adelson/0.03%, Roland B. Desilets/0.12%, Thomas J. OMalia/0.01%, Peter R. vanCuylenburg, Vincent P. Niedzielski/0.03%, Insiders/56.50%

Financial Data: *Fiscal Year End:* 01/31   *Latest Annual Data:* 1/31/2007

Year	Sales	Net Income
2007	$235,587,000	$7,633,000
2006	$225,494,000	$20,742,000
2005	$231,206,000	$24,483,000

Curr. Assets:	$109,864,000	Curr. Liab.:	$97,113,000	P/E Ratio:	63.77
Plant, Equip.:	$43,884,000	Total Liab.:	$116,088,000	Indic. Yr. Divd.:	$0.100
Total Assets:	$188,687,000	Net Worth:	$71,936,000	Debt/ Equity:	0.2162

QC Holdings Inc

9401 Indian Creek Pkwy., Ste. 1500, Overland Park, KS, 66210; *PH:* 1-913-234-5000; *Fax:* 1-913-234-5500; *http://* www.qcholdings.com

General - Incorporation	KS	**Stock**- Price on:12/24/2007	$16.12
Employees	2,017	Stock Exchange	NDQ
Auditor	Grant Thornton LLP	Ticker Symbol	QCCO
Stk Agt	UMB Bank, N.A.	Outstanding Shares	19,510,000
Counsel	NA	E.P.S.	NA
DUNS No.	NA	Shareholders	NA

Business: The group's principal activity is to provide payday loans in the United States. It operates 295 stores with locations in Arizona, California, Colorado, Florida, Idaho, Illinois, Indiana, Kansas, Kentucky, Louisiana, Mississippi, Missouri, Nevada, New Mexico, North Carolina, Oregon, South Carolina, Utah, Virginia, Washington and Wisconsin, as of 31-Mar-2004. It also provides other consumer financial products and services, such as check cashing services, title loans, money transfers and money orders.

Primary SIC and add'l.: 6099

CIK No: 0001289505

Subsidiaries: Cash Title Loans, Inc., Financial Services of North Carolina, Inc., QC Advance, Inc., QC Financial Services of California, Inc., QC Financial Services of Texas, Inc., QC Financial Services, Inc., QC Properties, LLC

Officers: Don Early/Chmn., CEO, Mary Lou Andersen/Vice Chmn., Sec., Robert L. Albin/Sr. VP, Darrin J. Andersen/COO, Pres., Douglas E. Nickerson/CFO, Wayne S. Wood/45/VP - Operations, Eastern US, Michael O. Walrod/VP - Operations, Western US

Directors: Don Early/Chmn., CEO, Mary Lou Andersen/Vice Chmn., Sec., Richard B. Chalker/Dir., Mary V. Powell/Dir., Francis P. Lemery/Dir., Gerald F. Lamberti/Dir., Kevin A. Richardson/Dir.

Owners: Don Early, Murray A. Indick, Gerald F. Lamberti, Prides Capital Partners, L.L.C., Cumberland Associates LLC, Richard B. Chalker, Insiders, Mary Lou Andersen, Wayne S. Wood, Gregory L. Smith, Kevin A. Richardson, Douglas E. Nickerson, Mary V. Powell, Darrin J. Andersen, Francis P. Lemery

Financial Data: *Fiscal Year End:* 12/31   *Latest Annual Data:* 12/31/2006

Year -	Sales	Net Income
2006	$172,282,000	$9,209,000
2005	$152,878,000	$5,379,000
2004	$124,823,000	$18,479,000

Curr. Assets:	$80,445,000	Curr. Liab.:	$15,706,000	P/E Ratio:	32.24
Plant, Equip.:	$31,859,000	Total Liab.:	$19,230,000	Indic. Yr. Divd.:	NA
Total Assets:	$121,130,000	Net Worth:	$101,900,000	Debt/ Equity:	NA

QCR Holdings Inc

3551 7th St., Ste. 204, Moline, IL, 61265; *PH:* 1-309-736-3580; *Fax:* 1-309-743-7705; *http://* www.qcbt.com

General - Incorporation	DE	**Stock**- Price on:12/24/2007	$17.19
Employees	351	Stock Exchange	NDQ
Auditor	McGladrey & Pullen LLP	Ticker Symbol	QCRH
Stk Agt	Illinois Stock Transfer Co	Outstanding Shares	4,570,000
Counsel	NA	E.P.S.	$0.75
DUNS No.	80-821-0546	Shareholders	NA

Business: The group's principal activities are to provide full-service commercial and consumer banking and trust and asset management services. The group accept deposits from the public and invest those deposits in loans and securities. The group is a multi-bank holding company operates through four offices located in bettendorf and davenport, Iowa and in moline, Illinois. The group also engages in merchant credit card processing through its wholly owned subsidiary quad city bancard inc based in moline, Illinois.

Primary SIC and add'l.: 6712 6022

CIK No: 0000906465

Subsidiaries: Cedar Rapids Bank and Trust Company, M2 Lease Funds, LLC, QCR Holdings Statutory Trust II, QCR Holdings Statutory Trust III, QCR Holdings Statutory Trust IV, QCR Holdings Statutory Trust V, Quad City Bancard, Inc., Quad City Bank and Trust Company, Rockford Bank and Trust Company

Officers: Douglas M. Hultquist/CEO, Pres./$500,418.00, Larry J. Helling/Dir., Chief Lending Officer/$383,995.00, Jill A. Dekeyser/VP, Dir. - Human Resources, Todd A. Gipple/Dir., CFO, Exec. VP/$331,981.00, Shellee R. Showalter/VP, Dir. - Finance, Equity Compensation, Timothy R. Harding/Sr. VP, Dir. - Internal Audit, Shawna Graham/VP, Dir. - Risk Management, William M. Tank/Sr. VP, Chief Credit Officer, Michael J. Wyffels/CTO, VP, Victor J. Quinn/Exec. VP - Funds Management, Kathleen M. Francque/Sr. VP - Deposit Operations

Directors: Douglas M. Hultquist/CEO, Pres., Michael A. Bauer/Vice Chmn., Larry J. Helling/Dir., Chief Lending Officer, James J. Brownson/Dir., Joyce E. Bawden/Dir., Charles A. Ruhl/Dir., John K. Lawson/Dir., Patrick S. Baird/Dir., John A. Rife/Dir., John H. Harris/Dir., Todd A. Gipple/Dir., CFO, Exec. VP, Marc C. Slivken/Dir., Mark C. Kilmer/Dir., Edwin A. Maxwell/Dir., John H. Anderson/Dir. *(17 Directors included in Index)*

Owners: Larry J. Helling/1.10%, John A. Rife, Patrick S. Baird, Mark C. Kilmer, Banc Funds/8.20%, Douglas M. Hultquist/1.30%, Charles M. Peters, Todd A. Gipple/1.10%, Michael A. Bauer/1.20%, Ronald G. Peterson, John K. Lawson, James J. Brownson, Insiders/10.10%, Tontine/5.50%

Financial Data: *Fiscal Year End:* 12/31   *Latest Annual Data:* 12/31/2006

Year	Sales	Net Income
2006	$80,929,000	$2,802,000
2005	$58,761,000	$4,810,000
2004	$46,744,000	$5,217,000

Curr. Assets:	$54,113,000	Curr. Liab.:	$1,138,990,000	P/E Ratio:	30.16
Plant, Equip.:	$32,525,000	Total Liab.:	$1,199,430,000	Indic. Yr. Divd.:	$0.080
Total Assets:	$1,271,675,000	Net Worth:	$70,883,000	Debt/ Equity:	0.6677

Qiagen

19300 Germantown Rd., Germantown, MD, 20874; *PH:* 1-240-686-7700; *Fax:* 1-240-686-1618; *http://* www.qiagen.com; *Email:* qiagen@qiagen.com

General - Incorporation	Netherlands	**Stock**- Price on:12/24/2007	$17.95
Employees	1,954	Stock Exchange	NDQ
Auditor	Ernst & Young LLP	Ticker Symbol	QGEN
Stk Agt	American Stock Transfer & Trust Co.	Outstanding Shares	150,510,000
Counsel	Mintz Levin Cohn Ferris Glovsky Popeo	E.P.S.	$0.33
DUNS No.	48-984-0363	Shareholders	NA

Business: The group's principal activities are the production and distribution of technologies for the separation, purification and handling of nucleic acids such as dna and rna. The group's products are used in biological research, research institutions, diagnostic and therapeutic industries. The group has production and manufacturing facilities in Germany, the United States and Switzerland, and distribution subsidiaries in the United States, Switzerland, Japan, the United Kingdom, Canada, France, Australia and Italy.

Primary SIC and add'l.: 8071 3841 3826

CIK No: 0001015820

Subsidiaries: QIAGEN AG, QIAGEN AS, QIAGEN GmbH, QIAGEN Instruments AG, Qiagen K.k., QIAGEN Ltd., QIAGEN North American Holdings, Inc., QIAGEN Sciences, Inc., QIAGEN, Inc.

Officers: Peer M. Schatz/CEO, Metin Colpan/52/Supervisory Dir., Roland Sackers/CFO, Franz A. Wirtz/74/Supervisory Dir., Bernd Uder/Sr. VP - Global Sales, Joachim Schorr/Sr. VP - Global Research, Development, Heinrich Hornef/76/Supervisory Dir., Jochen Walter/Supervisory Dir., Michael Collasius/VP - Automated Systems, Douglas Liu/VP - Global Operations, Ulrich Schriek/VP - Corporate Business Development, Thomas Schweins/VP - Marketing, Strategy, Gerhard Sohn/VP - Global Human Resources, Solveigh Mahler/Dir. - Investor Relations, Public Relations, Thomas Theuringer/Public Relations Mgr. *(16 Officers included in Index)*

Directors: Detlev H. Riesner/65/Chmn., Erik Hornnaess/69/Member - Supervisory Board, Carsten P. Claussen/79/Member - Supervisory Board, Manfred Karobath/66/Member - Supervisory Board, Heino Von Prondzynski/59/Member - Supervisory Board, Werner Brandt/54/Member - Supervisory Board

Owners: Ming S. Liu/7.16%, Insiders/16.68%, Sing-Ching Lu/4.67%, Varoujan Amirkhanian/4.85%

Financial Data: *Fiscal Year End:* 12/31   *Latest Annual Data:* 12/31/2006

Year	Sales	Net Income
2006	$465,778,000	$70,539,000
2005	$398,395,000	$62,225,000
2004	$380,629,000	$48,705,000

Curr. Assets:	$683,191,000	Curr. Liab.:	$116,531,000	P/E Ratio:	14.03
Plant, Equip.:	$221,277,000	Total Liab.:	$645,847,000	Indic. Yr. Divd.:	NA
Total Assets:	$1,212,012,000	Net Worth:	$566,165,000	Debt/ Equity:	NA

Qiao Xing Universal Telephone Inc

Qiao Xing Bldg Wu Shi Industrial Zon, Huizhou City, Guangdong, 516023; *PH:* 86-7522820268; *Fax:* 86-7522820298; *http://* www.cosun-xing.com

General - Incorporation British Virgin Islands	**Stock**- Price on:12/24/2007	$12.5099
Employees	1,162	Stock Exchange	NDQ
Auditor	AC Nielsen & De CV Sucursal	Ticker Symbol	XING
Stk Agt	NA	Outstanding Shares	NA
Counsel	Andrew N. Bernstein	E.P.S.	NA
DUNS No.	NA	Shareholders	NA

Business: The group operates through its subsidiaries whose principle activity is to manufacture and sell telecommunication terminals and equipment, including corded and cordless telephone sets. The group operates from United States.

Primary SIC and add'l.: 3661 6719

CIK No: 0001051846

Subsidiaries: CEC Telecom Co., Ltd., Hui Zhou Qiao Xing Communication Industry Limited, Hui Zhou Qiao Xing Property Limited, Qiao Xing Communication Holdings, Ltd., Qiao Xing Mobile Communication Co. Ltd.

Officers: Rui Lin Wu/Chmn., CEO, Zhi Yang Wu/Vice Chmn., Sec., Albert Leung/CFO, Rick Xiao/Dir. - Investor Relations

Directors: Rui Lin Wu/Chmn., CEO, Zhi Yang Wu/Vice Chmn., Sec., Ze Yun Mu/Non Exec. Dir., Sonny Kwok Wing Hung/Non Exec. Dir., Yi Hong Zhang/Non Exec. Dir., Edward Tsai/51/Non Exec. Dir.

Owners: Insiders/23.90%, Galbo Enterprises Limited/5.30%, Rui Lin Wu/23.00%, Zhi Zhong Wu/1.00%, Wu Holdings Limited/23.00%

Financial Data: *Fiscal Year End:* 12/31   *Latest Annual Data:* 12/31/2006

Year	Sales	Net Income
2006	$412,759,000	-$2,541,000
2005	$356,166,000	$30,816,000
2004	$243,953,000	$2,764,000

Curr. Assets:	$442,063,000	**Curr. Liab.:**	$250,021,000	**P/E Ratio:**	14.03
Plant, Equip.:	$34,576,000	**Total Liab.:**	$295,734,000	**Indic. Yr. Divd.:**	NA
Total Assets:	$535,358,000	**Net Worth:**	$239,624,000	**Debt/ Equity:**	NA

Qimonda AG

Gustav-Heinemann-Ring 212, Munich, 81739; ; *http://* www.qimonda.com;
Email: investor.relations@qimonda.com

General - Incorporation Federal Republic of Germany **Stock**- Price on:12/24/2007 $16.06
Employees 11,802 Stock Exchange NYSE
Auditor KPMG LLP Ticker Symbol QI
Stk Agt Registrar Services GmbH Outstanding Shares 342,000,000
Counsel NA E.P.S -$1.07
DUNS No. NA Shareholders NA

Business: The groups principle activity is to manufacture memory products. The groups products marketed under the brand names TwinFlash(R), AENEON(R), Qimonda(TM) and RLDRAM(R). The group operates from the Germany. The group's quarterly revenue for Sept 2007 was 711.00 millions of USD.

Primary SIC and add'l.: 3674

CIK No: 0001369377

Subsidiaries: Infineon Technologies Flash Ltd., Qimonda (Melaka) Sdn. Bhd, Qimonda Asia Pacific Pte. Ltd., Qimonda Dresden GmbH& Co. oHG, Qimonda Flash GmbH, Qimonda Holding B.V, Qimonda Investment B.V, Qimonda Module (Suzhou) Co. Ltd., Qimonda North America Corp., Qimonda Portugal S.A., Qimonda Richmond, LLC, Qimonda Technologies (Suzhou) Co., Ltd

Officers: Kin Wah Loh/54/Chmn. - Management Board, CEO, Peter J. Fischl/Chmn. - Supervisory Board, Member - Management Board, Exec. VP, Thomas J. Seifert/45/Member - Management Board, COO, Michael Majerus/47/Member - Management Board, CFO, Steve Harrison/VP - Investor Relations, Andreas Schaller/Sr. Dir. - Investor Relations

Directors: Kin Wah Loh/54/Chmn. - Management Board, CEO, Peter J. Fischl/Chmn. - Supervisory Board, Member - Management Board, Exec. VP, Richard Previte/Dep. Chmn. - Supervisory Board, Yoshio Nishi/Member - Supervisory Board, Lothar Armbrecht/Member - Supervisory Board, Hans Grundbacher/Member - Supervisory Board, Thomas J. Seifert/45/Member - Management Board, COO, Michael Majerus/47/Member - Management Board, CFO, Johann Grundbacher/44/Member - Supervisory Board, Claus Weyrich/64/Member - Supervisory Board

Owners: Public Shareholders/22.53%, Infineon Technologies AG/28.44%, Infineon Technologies Investment B.V/49.03%

Financial Data: *Fiscal Year End:*09/30 *Latest Annual Data:* 09/30/2006

Year	Sales	Net Income
2006	$4,840,472,000	$93,891,000
2005	$3,403,560,000	$21,686,000

Curr. Assets:	$3,561,522,000	**Curr. Liab.:**	$1,876,555,000		
Plant, Equip.:	$2,639,104,000	**Total Liab.:**	$2,524,912,000	**Indic. Yr. Divd.:**	NA
Total Assets:	$7,436,437,000	**Net Worth:**	$4,911,525,000	**Debt/ Equity:**	NA

Qlogic Corp

26650 Aliso Viejo Pkwy., Aliso Viejo, CA, 92656; *PH:* 1-949-389-6000; *Fax:* 1-949-389-6009;
http:// www.qlogic.com; *Email:* support@qlogic.com

General - Incorporation DE **Stock**- Price on:12/24/2007 $16.84
Employees 973 Stock Exchange NDQ
Auditor KPMG LLP Ticker Symbol QLGC
Stk Agt Computershare Investor Services LLC Outstanding Shares 153,530,000
Counsel O'melveny & Myers E.P.S $0.66
DUNS No. 80-855-6617 Shareholders NA

Business: The group's principal activities are to design and supply semiconductor and board level input output products, full fabric switches and enclosure management semiconductors. The group simplifies the process of networking storage for original equipment manufacturers, resellers and system integrators with end-to-end storage area network. It produces controller chips, management enclosure chips, host bus adapters, fabric switches and management software, which are the backbone of storage networks for large corporations and small to medium-sized businesses. The products of the group include sanbladetm hbas, sanboxtm fibre channel switches and sansurfer tool kittm management software. The customers include cisco systems inc, dell computer corporation, emc corporation, fujitsu limited, hitachi limited, hewlett packard company, intel corporation, IBM corporation, quantum corp, sony, storage, technology corporation (storagetek), sun microsystems, inc. And many others.

Primary SIC and add'l.: 3672 3674

CIK No: 0000918386

Subsidiaries: QLGC Limited, QLogic (UK)Limited, QLogic Enclosure Management Products, Inc., QLogic International Ltd., QLogic Luxembourg S.a.r.l., QLogic Roseville, Inc., QLogic Switch Products Group, Inc., QLogic System Interconnect Group, Inc.

Officers: H. K. Desai/Chmn., CEO/$6,230,189.00, Anthony J. Massetti/Sr. VP, CFO, Jesse L. Parker/VP, GM - Network Solutions Group, Denis R. Maynard/Sr. VP - Worldwide Sales, Service/$1,261,877.00, Michael L. Hawkins/VP, General Counsel, Sec., Roger J. Klein/VP, GM - Host Solutions Group/$641,875.00, Jeff W. Benck/COO, Pres., Shishir Shah/VP, GM - Storage Solutions Group, Phil A. Felando/VP - Human Resources

Directors: H. K. Desai/Chmn., CEO, Jim Fiebiger/Dir., Larry Carter/Dir., Balakrishnan Iyer/Dir., George Wells/Dir., Joel Birnbaum/Dir., Carol Miltner/Dir.

Owners: Anthony J. Massetti, Carol L. Miltner, Roger J. Klein, Larry R. Carter, Balakrishnan S. Iyer, Joel S. Birnbaum, Denis R. Maynard, AMVESCAP PLC/5.60%, Janus Capital Management LLC/6.30%, Robert W. Miller, H.K. Desai/3.80%, James R. Fiebiger, Insiders/5.40%, George D. Wells

Financial Data: *Fiscal Year End:*04/02 *Latest Annual Data:* 4/1/2007

Year	Sales	Net Income
2007	$586,697,000	$105,418,000
2006	$494,077,000	$283,588,000
2005	$571,903,000	$157,596,000

Curr. Assets:	$939,519,000	**Curr. Liab.:**	$68,821,000		
Plant, Equip.:	$77,464,000	**Total Liab.:**	$70,157,000	**Indic. Yr. Divd.:**	NA
Total Assets:	$1,026,340,000	**Net Worth:**	$956,183,000	**Debt/ Equity:**	NA

QLT Inc

2579 Midpoint Dr., Fort Collins, CO, 80525; *PH:* 1-604-707-7000; *Fax:* 1-604-707-7001;
http:// www.qltinc.com; *Email:* corpcomm@qltinc.com

General - Incorporation Canada **Stock**- Price on:12/24/2007 $7.71
Employees 254 Stock Exchange NDQ
Auditor Deloitte & Touche LLP Ticker Symbol QLTI
Stk Agt Computershare Trust Co of Canada Outstanding Shares 75,340,000
Counsel Farris, Vaughan, Wills & Murphy E.P.S -$2.39
DUNS No. 24-368-6433 Shareholders NA

Business: The group's principal activities are development and commercialization of proprietary pharmaceutical products. The products of the group are used in the treatment of ocular, oncology, immunological and other diseases. The group offers photodynamic therapy, a field of medicine that uses photosensitizers, which are light-activated drugs, in the treatment of disease. The commercial products of the group include photosensitizers used in the treatment of vision loss and other ocular conditions in people over the age of 50. The products of the group are sold in Canada, the United States, Europe and other countries.

Primary SIC and add'l.: 2834 2836 2833 8731

CIK No: 0000827809

Subsidiaries: Qlt Usa, Inc.

Officers: Robert L. Butchofsky/Dir., CEO, Pres./$1,149,072.00, Daniel Wattier/VP - Marketing, Sales, Therese Hayes/VP - Investor Relations, Corporate Communications, Alain Curaudeau/Sr. VP - Portfolio, Project Management/$656,188.00, Cameron Nelson/VP - Finance, CFO/$574,743.00, Linda Lupini/Sr. VP - Human Resources, Organizational Development, Alexander R. Lussow/VP - Business Development, Sean Moriarty/Pres. - QLT USA, Inc, Tamara Hicks/Assoc. Dir. - Media, Investor Relations

Directors: Robert L. Butchofsky/Dir., CEO, Pres., Boyd C. Clarke/Chmn., Peter A. Crossgrove/Dir., Julia G. Levy/Founder, Dir. Emerita, Ian Massey/Dir., Alan C. Mendelson/Dir., Richard R. Vietor/Dir., Jack L. Wood/Dir., Bruce L.A. Carter/Dir., Philip B. Livingston/Dir.

Owners: Mackenzie Financial Corporation/12.50%, Robert L. Butchofsky, Cameron R. Nelson, Bruce Carter, Jana Partners LLC/11.60%, Duff E. Scott, Insiders/1.40%, Ronald D. Henriksen, Alan C. Mendelson, Peter A. Crossgrove, Jack L. Wood, Peter J. OCallaghan, Richard R. Vietor, Michael R. Duncan, Alain H. Curaudeau *(19 Owners included in Index)*

Financial Data: *Fiscal Year End:*12/31 *Latest Annual Data:* 12/31/2006

Year	Sales	Net Income
2006	$175,090,000	-$101,605,000
2005	$241,973,000	-$325,412,000
2004	$186,072,000	-$165,709,000

Curr. Assets:	$478,009,000	**Curr. Liab.:**	$154,980,000		
Plant, Equip.:	$50,497,000	**Total Liab.:**	$335,892,000	**Indic. Yr. Divd.:**	NA
Total Assets:	$639,106,000	**Net Worth:**	$303,214,000	**Debt/ Equity:**	0.5549

QMed Inc

25 Christopher Way, Eatontown, NJ, 07724; *PH:* 1-732-544-5544; *Fax:* 1-732-544-5404;
http:// www.qmedinc.com

General - Incorporation DE **Stock**- Price on:12/24/2007 $3.09
Employees 104 Stock Exchange NDQ
Auditor Amper, Politziner & Mattia P.C Ticker Symbol QMED
Stk Agt American Stock Transfer & Trust Co. Outstanding Shares 17,030,000
Counsel NA E.P.S -$1.086
DUNS No. 10-865-1787 Shareholders NA

Business: The group's principal activities are to develop, manufacture and market advanced medical devices, systems and integrated cardiovascular management systems. It also produces and markets medical systems that provide diagnostic interpretation of certain disease. This includes a line of ambulatory ischemic heart monitors, interpretative electrocardiographs, a system for the analysis of heart rate variability and a system for the measurement of venous blood flow.

Primary SIC and add'l.: 3845 8099

CIK No: 0000729213

Subsidiaries: Health e Monitoring, Inc, Heart Map, Inc., HeartMasters LLC, Interactive Heart Management Corp, Lakeshore Captive Insurance Company, Inc., QMedCare Dakota, LLC, QMedCare, Inc.

Officers: Jane A. Murray/COO, CEO, Pres., Richard I. Levin/Member - Advisory Board, Co - Founder - Cardiology Consultant, Glenn Alexander/41/VP - Finance, Controller, Principal Accounting Officer, Robert Mosby/VP - Corporate Strategy, Development, Teri J. Kraf/Sr. VP - Health Management Services, John Siegel/Sr. VP - Sales, Disease Management Field Services, William T. Schmitt/Sr. VP, CFO

Directors: Bruce F. Wesson/65/Chmn., Richard I. Levin/Member - Advisory Board, Co - Founder - Cardiology Consultant, Narinder P. Bhalla/Member - Advisory Board, Cardiology Consultant, Barry P. Rosenzweig/Member - Advisory Board, Cardiology Consultant, David Feldman/Dir., Bruce A. Campbell/59/Dir., Lucia L. Quinn/54/Dir., John J. Gargana/76/Dir., John P. Zanotti/39/Dir.

Owners: John Siegel/2.90%, Jane A. Murray/2.90%, Galen Partners III, L.P./22.90%, Richard I. Levin, Teri J. Kraf/10.50%, William T. Schmitt, Bruce Campbell, John W. Rohfritch, John P. Zanotti, Insiders/35.50%, Michael W. Cox/10.50%, David Feldman, John J. Gargana, Lucia L. Quinn, Bruce F. Wesson/23.20%

Financial Data: *Fiscal Year End:*11/30 *Latest Annual Data:* 11/30/2006

Year	Sales	Net Income
2006	$9,881,000	-$14,236,000
2005	$22,146,000	$3,886,000
2004	$15,577,000	-$1,739,000

Curr. Assets:	$16,251,000	**Curr. Liab.:**	$5,165,000		
Plant, Equip.:	$989,000	**Total Liab.:**	$5,796,000	**Indic. Yr. Divd.:**	NA
Total Assets:	$20,811,000	**Net Worth:**	$15,015,000	**Debt/ Equity:**	NA

QNB Corp

15 N 3rd St., Quakertown, PA, 18951; *PH:* 1-215-538-5600; *Fax:* 1-215-538-5765;
http:// www.qnb.com; *Email:* info@qnb.com

General - Incorporation	PA	Stock- Price on:12/24/2007	$23
Employees	138	Stock Exchange	OTC
Auditor	S. R. Snodgrass, A.C.	Ticker Symbol	QNBC
Stk Agt	Registrar & Transfer Co	Outstanding Shares	3,130,000
Counsel	NA	E.P.S.	$0.92
DUNS No.	13-109-7479	Shareholders	NA

Business: The group's principal activity is to provide commercial banking services through its wholly owned subsidiary, the quakertown national bank. It attracts deposits from the general public and uses these funds for purchasing investment securities and for providing commercial, residential mortgage, construction, home equity, business, consumer and student loans. The group serves residents and businesses of upper bucks, southern lehigh and northern montgomery counties in Pennsylvania through seven branch locations.

Primary SIC and add'l.: 6712 6021

CIK No: 0000750558

Subsidiaries: The Quakertown National Bank.

Officers: Thomas J. Bisko/Dir., CEO, Pres./$291,694.00, Robert C. Werner/COO, Exec. VP/$204,320.00, Bret H. Krevolin/CFO, Exec. VP/$183,795.00, Heather J. Gossler/44/Sr. VP - Retail Banking, Scott G. Orzechoski/Sr. VP, Commerical Lending Officer/$135,075.00, Mary Ann Smith/CIO/Sr. VP/$154,281.00, Jean Scholl/Contact - Investor Relations

Directors: Thomas J. Bisko/Dir., CEO, Pres., Dennis Helf/61/Chmn., Arden G. Link/68/Dir., Norman L. Baringer/Dir., Charles M. Meredith/72/Dir., Gary S. Parzych/52/Dir., Kenneth F. Brown/52/Dir., Anna Mae Papso/64/Dir., Henry L. Rosenberger/62/Dir., Edgar L. Stauffer/70/Dir., Bonnie L. Rankin/54/Dir.

Owners: Anna Mae Papso, Mary Ann Smith/1.01%, Bonnie L. Rankin, Norman L. Baringer, Kenneth F. Brown/4.64%, Scott G. Orzechoski, Robert C. Werner, Dennis Helf, Heather J. Gossler, Charles M. Meredith/1.71%, Bret H. Krevolin, Insiders/17.11%, Arden G. Link, Henry L. Rosenberger/1.05%, Edgar L. Stauffer/3.10% *(17 Owners included in Index)*

Financial Data: Fiscal Year End:12/31   Latest Annual Data: 12/31/2006

Year	Sales	Net Income
2006	$35,939,000	$5,420,000
2005	$32,261,000	$5,046,000
2004	$30,258,000	$6,203,000

Curr. Assets:	$26,977,000	Curr. Liab.:	$563,275,000	P/E Ratio:	25.00
Plant, Equip.:	$6,442,000	Total Liab.:	$564,129,000	Indic. Yr. Divd.:	$0.880
Total Assets:	$614,539,000	Net Worth:	$50,410,000	Debt/ Equity:	NA

Qnective Inc

Formerly: SoTech Inc
3702 S Virginia St., Ste. G12 - 401, Reno, NV, 89502;

General - Incorporation	NA	Stock- Price on:12/24/2007	NA
Employees	NA	Stock Exchange	NA
Auditor	Telford Sadovnick, PLLC	Ticker Symbol	NA
Stk Agt	NA	Outstanding Shares	NA
Counsel	NA	E.P.S.	$0.00
DUNS No.	NA	Shareholders	NA

Business: The groups principal activities include processing of developing and marketing the China Shoppers software. The group operates from China.

Primary SIC and add'l.: 8748

CIK No: 0001353637

Officers: Joe Hicks/Dir., CEO, CFO, Pres.

Directors: Joe Hicks/Dir., CEO, CFO, Pres.

Owners: Capella IV LLC/57.14%

Financial Data: Fiscal Year End:NA   Latest Annual Data: 12/31/2006

Year	Sales	Net Income
2006	NA	-$72,000

Curr. Assets:	NA	Curr. Liab.:	$6,000		
Plant, Equip.:	NA	Total Liab.:	$6,000	Indic. Yr. Divd.:	NA
Total Assets:	NA	Net Worth:	-$6,000	Debt/ Equity:	NA

QPC Lasers Inc

15632 Roxford St., Sylmar, CA, 91342; **PH:** 1-818-986-0000; **Fax:** 1-818-833-1538;
http:// www.qpc.cc; **Email:** info@qpclasers.com

General - Incorporation	NV	Stock- Price on:12/24/2007	$0.75
Employees	42	Stock Exchange	OTC
Auditor	Weinberg & Co., P.A	Ticker Symbol	QPCI
Stk Agt	Holladay Stock Transfer, Inc.	Outstanding Shares	38,560,000
Counsel	NA	E.P.S.	-$0.3
DUNS No.	NA	Shareholders	NA

Business: The groups principle activities include designing and manufacturing brightness lasers for a variety of commercial and military purposes. The group has developed multiple technology platforms. The group operates from the United States.

Primary SIC and add'l.: 3674

CIK No: 0001310753

Subsidiaries: Quintessence Photonics Corporation

Officers: Jeffrey Ungar/CEO, Pres., Founder, Dir., George M. Lintz/Founder, CFO, COO, Executive Vice Chmn., Thomas Stakelon/VP - Quality Control, Paul Rudy/Sr. VP - Marketing, Sales, Mayer Engel/Dir. - Worldwide Sales, Blima Tuller/VP - Finance, Chief Accounting Officer, Wentao Hu/VP - Engineering, Marie Dagresto/Contact - Investor Relation

Directors: Jeffrey Ungar/CEO, Pres., Founder, Dir., George M. Lintz/Founder, CFO, COO, Executive Vice Chmn., Merrill A. McPeak/Vice Chmn., Israel Ury/Dir., Robert Adams/Dir.

Owners: Finisar Corporation/17.50%, Jeffrey Ungar/11.60%, Paul Rudy, Merrill McPeak, Insiders/19.80%, George Lintz/6.80%, Robert Adams, Israel Ury, Wendell Lew/7.70%

Financial Data: Fiscal Year End:12/31   Latest Annual Data: 12/31/2006

Year	Sales	Net Income
2006	$3,073,000	-$18,693,000
2005	$4,000	-$16,000

Curr. Assets:	$3,347,000	Curr. Liab.:	$2,268,000		
Plant, Equip.:	$3,962,000	Total Liab.:	$8,667,000	Indic. Yr. Divd.:	NA
Total Assets:	$7,435,000	Net Worth:	-$1,231,000	Debt/ Equity:	NA

QSGI Inc

400 Royal Palm Way, Palm Beach, FL, 33480; **PH:** 1-561-835-9757; **Fax:** 1-561-835-9909;
http:// www.qsgi.com; **Email:** investorrelations@QSGI.com

General - Incorporation	DE	Stock- Price on:12/24/2007	$0.7
Employees	68	Stock Exchange	OTC
Auditor	Rubin Brown LLP	Ticker Symbol	QSGI
Stk Agt	American Stock Transfer & Trust Co.	Outstanding Shares	31,170,000
Counsel	NA	E.P.S.	-$0.02
DUNS No.	NA	Shareholders	NA

Business: The groups principle activity is data security and compliance services as well as data center hardware and data center maintenance services are geared towards both the users of business computing hardware i.e. desktops, laptops, related peripherals and servers as well as the users of enterprise class hardware i.e. mainframes, midrange processors, large storage, controllers. The group operates through three segments namely data security & compliance, data center hardware and data center maintenance. The group operates from the United States, the United Kingdom, Asia, Europe, Canada, Africa, Australia, South America and Middle East. The group's quarterly revenue for Sep '07 is 8.76 millions of USD.

Primary SIC and add'l.: 5932

CIK No: 0000027960

Officers: Marc Sherman/Chmn., CEO/$511,690.00, Edward L. Cummings/Dir., CFO/$278,670.00, Seth A. Grossman/Dir., COO, Pres./$390,655.00, Joel Owens/Exec. VP, Dir. - International Operations/$463,877.00, Jack Tull/Product Mgr. - Desktop Hardware, Matthew Perthes/Product Specialist - Desktop Hardware, Export Sales, Barry Hanburger/Product Mgr. - IBM Midrange, Storage Products, Mark Jacobson/Dir. - Sales, Chris Schoeller/VP - Data Security, Compliance Sales, Andy Kerr/Contact - Data Center Maintenance

Directors: Marc Sherman/Chmn., CEO, Edward L. Cummings/Dir., CFO, Seth A. Grossman/Dir., COO, Pres., Keith R. Elliot/Dir., Robert W. Vanhellemont/Dir., John F. Cunningham/Dir., Geoff Smith/Dir.

Owners: Joel L. Owens, Insiders/32.10%, Edward L. Cummings/8.10%, Geoffrey A. Smith, Robert W. VanHellemont, David A. Harris, Keith R. Elliott/1.20%, John F. Cunningham, Seth A. Grossman/7.40%, Marc Sherman/13.00%

Financial Data: Fiscal Year End:12/31   Latest Annual Data: 12/31/2006

Year	Sales	Net Income
2006	$46,409,000	-$485,000
2005	$36,386,000	-$1,266,000
2004	$22,080,000	$133,000

Curr. Assets:	$14,410,000	Curr. Liab.:	$6,870,000		
Plant, Equip.:	$410,000	Total Liab.:	$7,738,000	Indic. Yr. Divd.:	NA
Total Assets:	$24,179,000	Net Worth:	$12,220,000	Debt/ Equity:	NA

QSound Labs Inc

3115 12th St. NE, Ste. 400, Calgary, AB, T2E 7J2; **PH:** 1-403-291-2492; http:// www.qsound.com;
Email: info@qsound.com

General - Incorporation	Canada	Stock- Price on:12/24/2007	$4.43
Employees	25	Stock Exchange	NDQ
Auditor	KPMG LLP, Grant Thornton LLP	Ticker Symbol	QSND
Stk Agt	Computershare Investor Services LLC	Outstanding Shares	9,400,000
Counsel	Fulbright & Jaworski LLP	E.P.S.	-$0.18
DUNS No.	24-761-7806	Shareholders	NA

Business: The group's principle activities include developing and licensing sound imaging audio technology used in personal computer, multi-media and home video game industries; and develops and manufactures custom hearing aids. The group operates from United States.

Primary SIC and add'l.: 3679 3842

CIK No: 0000840518

Subsidiaries: including QSound Ltd., QCommerce Inc., QTelNet Inc.

Officers: David J. Gallagher/Dir., CEO, CFO, Pres., Joanna Varvos/Corp. Sec., Shawn Richards/Dir. - Business Development, Europe Sales, Jacques Lapointe/Dir. - Product Management, Marketing, Murray Bruce/Controller, Shigeru Matsuda/Contact - Japanese Sales, Kam Ching/Asia, Pacific Sales, Willis Liu/Mgr. - Technical Support, Asia, Pacific Technical Support

Directors: David J. Gallagher/Dir., CEO, CFO, Pres., Patty M. Chakour/Dir., Stanley E. McDougall/Dir., Tony Stelliga/Dir.

Owners: Tony D. Stelliga, David J. Gallagher/5.20%, KBW Partners/7.50%, Fred Kayne/7.10%, Joanna Varvos, Stanley E. McDougall, Patty M. Chakour

Financial Data: Fiscal Year End:12/31   Latest Annual Data: 12/31/2006

Year	Sales	Net Income
2006	NA	NA
2005	NA	NA
2004	NA	NA

Curr. Assets:	$2,719,000	Curr. Liab.:	$314,000		
Plant, Equip.:	$348,000	Total Liab.:	$399,000	Indic. Yr. Divd.:	NA
Total Assets:	$3,474,000	Net Worth:	$3,075,000	Debt/ Equity:	NA

QSR Music Technologies Inc

2011 Seward Ave., Naples, FL, 34109; **PH:** 1-239-597-5888; **Fax:** 1-239-597-3936;
http:// www.qrsmusic.com; **Email:** qrssupport@qrsinc.com

General - Incorporation	DE	Stock- Price on:12/24/2007	$0.76
Employees	60	Stock Exchange	OTC
Auditor	Altschuler, Melvoin & Glasser LLP	Ticker Symbol	QRSM
Stk Agt	American Registrar & Transfer Co	Outstanding Shares	9,780,000
Counsel	NA	E.P.S.	-$0.06
DUNS No.	NA	Shareholders	NA

Business: The group's principal activities are to manufacture and market pianomation(R) music instrument digital interface, story and clark pianos, sale of midi cds and floppy disks and music rolls for player pianos. The pianomation(R) midi system is a musical instrument digital interface equipped playback system for acoustic and digital pianos. The pianomation(R) product has an electronic processor and a mechanical assembly, which drives solenoid actuators, which receives signals from a CD player,

disk drive or personal computer. It also markets the playola system of portable piano automation. The group manufactures, imports and markets pianos under the story and clark trademark. The group has 6 United States trademark registrations namely qrs logo, qrs, hobart m. Cable, story and clark, pianomation and gulbransen. On 11-Dec-2002 the group acquired certain assets of gulbransen, inc.

Primary SIC and add'l.: 3931

CIK No: 0001126535

Subsidiaries: Church Services, Inc, QRS Music Technologies, QRS Music Technologies HK Limited

Officers: Thomas A. Dolan/48/CEO, Pres., Ann A. Jones/43/Dir., CFO, Sec., Treasurer

Directors: Richard A. Dolan/Chmn., Geoffry Matlin/Dir., Ann A. Jones/43/Dir., CFO, Sec., Treasurer, Richard Kurtz/Dir., Thomas Ogrady/Dir., Frank Seta/Dir.

Owners: Thomas Dolan/4.00%, Richard Dolan/58.00%, Ann Jones/2.00%, Insiders/62.00%, Geoffry Matlin

Financial Data: Fiscal Year End:06/30 **Latest Annual Data:** 6/30/2006

Year	Sales	Net Income
2006	$18,085,000	$168,000
2005	$20,247,000	$1,098,000
2004	$18,513,000	$1,463,000

Curr. Assets:	$10,907,000	Curr. Liab.:	$2,575,000		
Plant, Equip.:	$1,207,000	Total Liab.:	$3,253,000	Indic. Yr. Divd.:	NA
Total Assets:	$13,046,000	Net Worth:	$9,794,000	Debt/ Equity:	0.0648

Quadramed Corp

12110 Sunset Hills Rd., Ste. 600, Reston, VA, 20190; **PH:** 1-703-709-2300; **Fax:** 1-703-709-2490; **http://** www.quadramed.com; **Email:** investorrelations2@quadramed.com

General - Incorporation	DE	Stock- Price on:12/24/2007	$3.19
Employees	578	Stock Exchange	AMEX
Auditor	BDO Seidman LLP	Ticker Symbol	QD
Stk Agt	Computershare Investor Services LLC	Outstanding Shares	43,870,000
Counsel	Skadden, Arps	E.P.S	$0.18
DUNS No.	18-706-1957	Shareholders	NA

Business: The group's principal activities are to provide healthcare information technology products and services that help healthcare providers to deliver outstanding patient care with optimum efficiency. The group operates through its three segments: enterprise division, health information management software division and financial services division. The products of the group include Affinity Integration Enterprise Information System, Quantim Health Information Management Software, Master Person Index Software and Services, Clinical Outcome Practice Evaluator and electronic transaction services. It markets its products to veterans health administration facilities, specialty hospitals, hospital associations and physicians located in Columbia, Puerto Rico, and Canada. On 04-Aug-2004, the group acquired Tempus Software Inc.

Primary SIC and add'l.: 8742 7372

CIK No: 0001018833

Subsidiaries: QuadraMed Affinity Corporation, QuadraMed International Limited, QuadraMed International Pty. Limited, Tempus Software LLC

Officers: Keith B. Hagen/Dir., CEO, Pres./$1,626,112.00, Steven V. Russell/Sr. VP - Corporate Development/$357,668.00, Linda Baum/VP - Customer Services, Brook Carlon/Sr. VP - Human Resources, James R. Klein/Exec. VP - Product Management, CTO/$690,545.00, David L. Piazza/CFO, Exec. VP/$518,743.00, Joseph I. Bormel/Chief Medical Officer, VP - Clinical Product Management, James R. Milligan/Sr. VP - Sales, Government Programs/$559,498.00

Directors: Keith B. Hagen/Dir., CEO, Pres., Robert L. Pevenstein/61/Chmn., Robert W. Miller/Dir., James E. Peebles/Dir.

Owners: Joseph L. Feshbach, Keith B. Hagen/1.70%, James R. Milligan, Steven V. Russell, MacKay Shields LLC/33.20%, David L. Piazza, Lawrence P. English/4.20%, Zazove Associates LLC/18.00%, Cannell Capital LLC/8.20%, Insiders/7.10%, William K. Jurika/8.60%, North Run Advisors LLC/7.30%, Robert W. Miller, Robert L. Pevenstein, James R. Klein (17 Owners included in Index)

Financial Data: Fiscal Year End:12/31 **Latest Annual Data:** 12/31/2006

Year	Sales	Net Income
2006	$125,201,000	$11,945,000
2005	$122,313,000	-$3,938,000
2004	$130,456,000	-$41,829,000

Curr. Assets:	$78,758,000	Curr. Liab.:	$68,001,000		
Plant, Equip.:	$2,557,000	Total Liab.:	$73,727,000	Indic. Yr. Divd.:	NA
Total Assets:	$116,198,000	Net Worth:	$42,471,000	Debt/ Equity:	NA

Quadtech International Inc

Formerly: Meier Worldwide Intermedia Inc
300-1055 W Hastings St., Vancouver, BC, V6E 2E9; **PH:** 1-604-331-2511; **http://** www.quadtechint.com

General - Incorporation	NV	Stock - Price on:12/24/2007	$0.011
Employees	1	Stock Exchange	OTC
Auditor	Madsen & Assoc. CPAs, Inc	Ticker Symbol	QTII
Stk Agt	West Coast Stock Transfer	Outstanding Shares	28,930,000
Counsel	NA	E.P.S	-$0.016
DUNS No.	NA	Shareholders	NA

Business: The group's principle activity is to produce feature films for the local and international market; and provide multi-media interactive video services via Internet. The group operates from United States.

Primary SIC and add'l.: 7375 6719 7812

CIK No: 0001061316

Subsidiaries: Covenant Corporation

Officers: John Meier/Chmn., CEO, Pres., Roland J. Vetter/CFO, Tony Hines/Technical Team, Dennis Lusk/Technical Team, Steven Hill/Technical Team

Directors: John Meier/Chmn., CEO, Pres., Harry Evans/Dir., Benjamin Moglin/Member - Technical Advisory Board

Owners: Iloria Corporation Ltd/32.36%, John Meier/10.89%, Insiders, Harry Evans, Meier Entertainment Group Inc., Roland J. Vetter

Financial Data: Fiscal Year End:10/31 **Latest Annual Data:** 10/31/2006

Year	Sales	Net Income
2006	NA	-$2,397,000
2005	NA	-$364,000
2004	$81,000	-$395,000

Curr. Assets:	$0	Curr. Liab.:	$239,000		
Plant, Equip.:	NA	Total Liab.:	$239,000	Indic. Yr. Divd.:	NA
Total Assets:	$0	Net Worth:	-$238,000	Debt/ Equity:	NA

Quaker Chemical Corp

1 Quaker Pk., 901 Hector St., Conshohocken, PA, 19428; **PH:** 1-610-832-4000; **Fax:** 1-610-832-8682; **http://** www.quakerchem.com; **Email:** info@quakerchem.com

General - Incorporation	PA	Stock- Price on:12/24/2007	$24.2
Employees	1,287	Stock Exchange	NYSE
Auditor	PricewaterhouseCoopers LLP	Ticker Symbol	KWR
Stk Agt	PricewaterhouseCoopers LLP	Outstanding Shares	10,070,000
Counsel	Fox Rothschild O'brien & Frankel	E.P.S	$1.38
DUNS No.	00-235-0866	Shareholders	NA

Business: The group's principal activities are to develop, produce and market a broad range of formulated chemical specialty products for heavy industrial and manufacturing applications. The group operates in three segments: metalworking process chemicals segment provides products used as lubricants. Coatings segment provides temporary and permanent coatings for metal and concrete products and chemical milling maskants. Other chemical products segment provides other various chemical products. The products and services offered include rolling lubricants, corrosion preventives, metal finishing compounds, machining and grinding compounds, forming compounds, hydraulic fluids and technology for the removal of hydrogen sulfide. The group's customers include manufacturers of steel, automobiles, appliances, and durable goods. In Jul 2003, the group acquired eural s.r.l.

Primary SIC and add'l.: 2992 2869 2899

CIK No: 0000081362

Subsidiaries: AC Products, Inc., Epmar Corporation, Kelko Quaker Chemical, S.A., Nippon Quaker Chemical, Ltd., Q2 Technologies, LLC, Quaker Australia Holdings Pty. Limited, Quaker Automotive Italia, S.r.l., Quaker Chemical (Australasia) Pty. Limited, Quaker Chemical (China) Co. Ltd., Quaker Chemical B.V., Quaker Chemical Canada Limited, Quaker Chemical Corporation, Quaker Chemical Europe B.V., Quaker Chemical Holdings South Africa (Pty) Limited, Quaker Chemical Hungary Ltd. 28 Subsidiaries included in the Index

Officers: Ronald J. Naples/Chmn., CEO/$1,952,889.00, Jeffry D. Benoliel/VP, Sec., General Counsel, Neal E. Murphy/50/VP, Treasurer/$691,509.00, Frank R. Olah/General Tax Counsel, Tax Officer, Jan F. Nieman/VP, MD - Asia, Pacific, Wilbert Platzer/VP, MD - Europe/$531,950.00, Mark A. Featherstone/CFO, VP, Treasurer, Michael F. Barry/Sr. VP, MD - North America/$712,336.00, Mark A. Harris/Sr. VP - Global Strategy, Marketing/$590,334.00, Irene M. Kisleiko/Assist. Corp. Sec. - Contact - Investor Relations, Jose Luiz Bregolato/VP, MD - South America

Directors: Ronald J. Naples/Chmn., CEO, Jeffry D. Frisby/Dir., Joseph B. Anderson/Dir., Donald R. Caldwell/Dir., Robert E. Chappell/Dir., Edwin J. Delattre/Dir., William R. Cook/Dir., Patricia C. Barron/Corp. Dir., Robert H. Rock/Dir.

Owners: Edwin J. Delattre, William R. Cook, Mark A. Harris, Michael F. Barry, Patricia C. Barron, Donald R. Caldwell, Robert H. Rock, Joseph B. Anderson, Jeffry D. Frisby, Wilbert Platzer, Ronald J. Naples/7.60%, Insiders/11.80%, Dimensional Fund Advisors LP/7.90%, Ronald J. Naples Quaker Chemical Corporation/7.60%, Robert E. Chappell (17 Owners included in Index)

Financial Data: Fiscal Year End:12/31 **Latest Annual Data:** 12/31/2006

Year	Sales	Net Income
2006	$460,451,000	$11,667,000
2005	$424,033,000	$1,688,000
2004	$400,695,000	$8,974,000

Curr. Assets:	$186,241,000	Curr. Liab.:	$90,179,000	P/E Ratio:	18.91
Plant, Equip.:	$60,927,000	Total Liab.:	$242,516,000	Indic. Yr. Divd.:	$0.860
Total Assets:	$357,382,000	Net Worth:	$110,831,000	Debt/ Equity:	NA

Quaker Fabric Corp

941 Grinnell St., Fall River, MA, 02721; **PH:** 1-418-227-9897; **Fax:** 1-418-227-9899; **http://** www.quakerfabric.com; **Email:** info@victor.qc.ca

General - Incorporation	DE	Stock- Price on:12/24/2007	$1.14
Employees	1,008	Stock Exchange	OTC
Auditor	PricewaterhouseCoopers LLP	Ticker Symbol	QFAB
Stk Agt	EquiServe Trust Co N.A	Outstanding Shares	16,880,000
Counsel	Proskauer Rose	E.P.S	-$2.288
DUNS No.	00-104-5095	Shareholders	NA

Business: The group's principal activities are to design, manufacture and market woven upholstery fabrics and jacquard upholstery fabrics for residential furniture. It also develops and manufactures specialty yarns. The product line of the group consists of over 5,000 traditional, contemporary, transitional and country fabric patterns intended to meet the styling and design, color, texture, quality and pricing requirements of furniture manufacturers. The group introduces approximately 1,000 new products to the market annually. It has distribution centers in Mexico, North America, the Middle East, South America and Europe and serves over 3,000 furniture manufacturers worldwide.

Primary SIC and add'l.: 2281 2299

CIK No: 0000103341

Subsidiaries: Quaker Fabric Corporation of Fall River

Officers: Larry A. Liebenow/Dir., CEO, Pres./$710,551.00, Steven Schroeder/International Sales Mgr., Houssam Rayess/Contact - Sales, Middle East, Derek Joseph/Contact - South Africa Sales, Billy Desousa/Contact - Sales, Pacific Rim, Asia, Meno Liew/Contact - Southeast Asia Sales, Rodrigo Prieto/International Sales Mgr. - South, Central America

Directors: Larry A. Liebenow/Dir., CEO, Pres., Sangwoo Ahn/Chmn., Jerry I. Porras/Dir., Eriberto R. Scocimara/Dir.

Owners: Insiders/33.50%, Paul J. Kelly/1.60%, Larry A. Liebenow/20.90%, Sangwoo Ahn/3.40%, Duncan Whitehead/17.80%, Aegis Financial Corporation/12.20%, Eriberto R. Scocimara, Beatrice M. Spires/1.20%, Jerry I. Porras, Thomas Muzekari, Nortex Holdings, Inc./16.70%, Ingalls & Snyder, LLC/4.70%, Wells Fargo & Company/6.30%, Dimensional Fund Advisors LP/7.50%

Financial Data: Fiscal Year End:12/31 **Latest Annual Data:** 12/30/2006

Year	Sales	Net Income
2006	$151,664,000	-$37,632,000
2005	$224,684,000	-$26,256,000

Curr. Assets:	$78,444,000	Curr. Liab.:	$59,783,000		
Plant, Equip.:	$137,660,000	Total Liab.:	$78,698,000	Indic. Yr. Divd.:	NA
Total Assets:	$219,862,000	Net Worth:	$141,164,000	Debt/ Equity:	NA

QUALCOMM

5775 Morehouse Dr., San Diego, CA, 92121; *PH*: 1-858-587-1121; *Fax*: 1-858-658-2100;
http:// www.qualcomm.com; *Email*: corpcomm@qualcomm.com

General - Incorporation .... DE
Employees 11,200
Auditor .... PricewaterhouseCoopers LLP
Stk Agt..... Computershare Investor Services LLC
Counsel .... Gray, Cary, Ware & Freidenrich
DUNS No. 14-435-6508

Stock- Price on:12/24/2007 .... $43.17
Stock Exchange .... NDQ
Ticker Symbol .... QCOM
Outstanding Shares 1,670,000,000
E.P.S. $1.64
Shareholders .... NA

Business: The groups principle activities include designing, manufacturing and marketing digital wireless telecommunication products and services. The group also provides asset management and mobile applications. The group operates from United States.

Primary SIC and add'l.: 7373 3669

CIK No: 0000804328

Subsidiaries: Qualcomm (uk) Limited, Qualcomm Bangalore Design Center Private Limited, Qualcomm Cdma Technologies (korea) Y.h, Qualcomm Cdma Technologies Asia-pacific Pte. Ltd., Qualcomm Cdma Technologies Gmbh, Qualcomm Cdma Technologies, T.y.k, Qualcomm Communication Technologies Ltd, Qualcomm Flarion Technologies, Inc., Qualcomm Global Trading, Inc., Qualcomm Gt Holdings, Inc., Qualcomm India Private Limited, Qualcomm Mauritius Holdings Limited, Qualcomm Wireless Semi Conductor Technologies Limited, SnapTrack, Inc., Spike Technologies (India) Private Ltd 16 Subsidiaries included in the Index

Officers: Paul E. Jacobs/Dir., CEO, Joan Waltman/Pres. - Qualcomm Enterprise Services, Sanjay K. Jha/COO, Pres. - Qualcomm Cdma Technologies Group, William F. Davidson/Sr. VP - Global Marketing, Investor Relations, William E. Keitel/CFO, Exec. VP, Norm Fjeldheim/CIO, Sr. VP, Nancy Linke Patton/Sr. Dir. - Investor Relations, John Sinnott/Dir. - Investor Relations, John Batey/VP, GM - Qualcomm Mems Technologies, William Bold/Sr. VP - Government Affairs, Len J. Lauer/Exec. VP, Group Pres., Gina Lombardi/Pres. - Mediaflo USA, John Gilbert/VP - Investor Relations, Garrett Ponder/Investor Relations Analyst, Emily Kilpatrick/Contact - Corporate Communications *(36 Officers included in Index)*

Directors: Paul E. Jacobs/Dir., CEO, Irwin Mark Jacobs/Chmn., Richard C. Atkinson/Dir., Adelia A. Coffman/Dir., Donald G. Cruickshank/Dir., Raymond V. Dittamore/Dir., Duane A. Nelles/Dir., Peter M. Sacerdote/Dir., Brent Scowcroft/Dir., Marc I. Stern/Dir., Richard Sulpizio/Dir., Barbara T. Alexander/Dir., Robert E. Kahn/Dir., Sherry Lansing/Dir.

Owners: Raymond V. Dittamore, Brent Scowcroft, Peter M. Sacerdote, Diana Lady Dougan, Duane A. Nelles, Roberto Padovani, Donald G. Cruickshank, Marc I. Stern, Paul E. Jacobs, Richard Sulpizio, Barbara T. Alexander, Irwin Mark Jacobs/2.15%, Steven R. Altman, Insiders/3.40%, Adelia A. Coffman *(19 Owners included in Index)*

Financial Data: Fiscal Year End:09/25 Latest Annual Data: 07/01/2007

Year	Sales	Net Income
2007	NA	NA
2006	$7,526,000,000	$2,470,000,000
2005	$5,673,000,000	$2,143,000,000

Curr. Assets:	$8,821,000,000	Curr. Liab.:	$2,258,000,000	P/E Ratio:	26.32
Plant, Equip.:	$1,788,000,000	Total Liab.:	$2,660,000,000	Indic. Yr. Divd.:	$0.560
Total Assets:	$18,495,000,000	Net Worth:	$15,835,000,000	Debt/ Equity:	NA

Quality Distribution Inc

4041 Pk. Oaks Blvd., Ste. 200, Tampa, FL, 33610; *PH*: 1-813-630-5826; *Fax*: 1-813-630-1537;
http:// www.qualitydistribution.com; *Email*: info_qdi@qualitydistribution.com

General - Incorporation .... FL
Employees 1,228
Auditor .... PricewaterhouseCoopers LLP
Stk Agt .... Wachovia Bank N.A
Counsel .... NA
DUNS No. 93-112-1610

Stock- Price on:12/24/2007 .... $11.08
Stock Exchange .... NDQ
Ticker Symbol .... QLTY
Outstanding Shares 19,130,000
E.P.S. $0.50
Shareholders .... NA

Business: The group's principal activity is to operate bulk tank truck network in North America. The bulk tank truck market includes all items shipped by bulk tank truck carriers and consists of the shipping of chemicals, gasoline and food-grade products. The group transports a broad range of chemical products and provides customers with value-added services, including intermodal, transportation management, transloading, tank cleaning, dry-bulk hauling, leasing and other logistics services. The group utilizes third-party affiliate terminals and owner-operator drivers in our core bulk service network. The group is core carriers for many companies engaged in chemical processing including dow chemical company, procter & gamble company, e.i. Dupont and ppg industries and also provide services to each of the top 100 chemical producers in the world with U.S. Operations.

Primary SIC and add'l.: 4213

CIK No: 0000922863

Officers: Gerald L. Detter/63/Chmn., CEO/$2,165,137.00, Gary R. Enzor/COO, Pres./$618,383.00, Robert M. Bonnet/VP - Safety, Security, Diane Helland/Dir. - Investor Relations, Communication, Administration, Timothy B. Page/55/CFO, Sr. VP/$493,027.00, Virgil T. Leslie/53/Exec. VP - Sales/$298,717.00, Robert J. Millstone/64/Sr. VP, General Counsel, Sec./$377,175.00, Robert E. Warner/Sr. VP - Operations, Dennis R. Copeland/58/Sr. VP - Administration

Directors: Gerald L. Detter/63/Chmn., CEO, Robert H. Falk/Dir., Thomas R. Miklich/Dir., Robert E. Gadomski/Dir., Marc E. Becker/35/Dir., Joshua J. Harris/Dir., Richard B. Marchese/Dir., Donald C. Orris/Dir., Eric L. Press/Dir., Ali M. Rashid/Dir., Alan H. Schumacher/61/Dir., John J. Suydam/Dir.

Owners: Timothy B. Page, Thomas R. Miklich, Robert J. Millstone, Apollo Investment Fund III, L.P./55.04%, Insiders/4.28%, Donald C. Orris, Marc E. Becker, Richard B. Marchese, Ali M. Rashid, Federated Investors/5.79%, Cannell Capital LLC/6.27%, Virgil T. Leslie/1.12%, Gerald L. Detter, Eric L. Press, Gary R. Enzor *(19 Owners included in Index)*

Financial Data: Fiscal Year End:12/31 Latest Annual Data: 12/31/2006

Year	Sales	Net Income
2006	$730,159,000	$54,207,000
2005	$678,076,000	$11,873,000
2004	$622,015,000	-$10,557,000

Curr. Assets:	$133,475,000	Curr. Liab.:	$66,285,000	P/E Ratio:	4.36
Plant, Equip.:	$117,345,000	Total Liab.:	$384,266,000	Indic. Yr. Divd.:	NA
Total Assets:	$421,262,000	Net Worth:	$35,163,000	Debt/ Equity:	7.8556

Quality Systems Inc

18191 Von Karman Ave., Ste. 450, Irvine, CA, 92612; *PH*: 1-949-255-2600; *Fax*: 1-949-255-2605;
http:// www.qsii.com; *Email*: qsi@qsii.com

General - Incorporation .... CA
Employees 647
Auditor .... Grant Thornton LLP
Stk Agt .... U.S. Stock Transfer Corp
Counsel .... Rutan & Tucker
DUNS No. 07-954-2304

Stock- Price on:12/24/2007 .... $38.17
Stock Exchange .... NDQ
Ticker Symbol .... QSII
Outstanding Shares 27,120,000
E.P.S. $1.26
Shareholders .... NA

Business: The group's principal activity is to develop and market healthcare information systems. These systems automate medical and dental group practices, community health centers, physician hospital organizations, management service organizations and dental schools. The group operates through two divisions. The nextgen division develops and sells proprietary electronic medical records software and practice management systems under the nextgen(r)(4) name. The qsi division develops and markets dental practice management and medical practice management software suites. The group's software systems include general patient information, appointment scheduling, billing, insurance claims processing, treatment outcome studies, treatment planning, drug formularies, electronic patient records, dental charting and letter generation. It also provides its clients with hardware and software maintenance and support, system training and electronic claims submission services.

Primary SIC and add'l.: 7373 7372

CIK No: 0000708818

Subsidiaries: NextGen Healthcare Information Systems, Inc

Officers: Louis E. Silverman/49/Dir., CEO, Pres./$1,074,310.00, Gregory Flynn/50/Exec. VP - General Manage, QSI Division/$518,572.00, Paul Holt/42/CFO/$451,406.00

Directors: Louis E. Silverman/49/Dir., CEO, Pres., Sheldon Razin/70/Chmn., Founder, Patrick B. Cline/47/Dir., Ahmed Hussein/67/Dir., Vincent J. Love/67/Dir., Steven T. Plochcoki/56/Dir., Ibrahim Fawzy/65/Dir., Edwin Hoffman/70/Dir., Russell Pflueger/44/Dir.

Owners: Ibrahim Fawzy, Paul A. Holt, Ahmed Hussein/17.10%, Louis E. Silverman, FMR Corp./8.60%, Insiders/37.10%, Steven T. Plochocki, Sheldon Razin/19.00%, Patrick B. Cline, Vincent J. Love, Gregory Flynn

Financial Data: Fiscal Year End:03/31 Latest Annual Data: 3/31/2007

Year	Sales	Net Income
2007	$157,165,000	$33,232,000
2006	$119,287,000	$23,322,000
2005	$88,961,000	$16,109,000

Curr. Assets:	$133,098,000	Curr. Liab.:	$56,482,000	P/E Ratio:	31.55
Plant, Equip.:	$5,029,000	Total Liab.:	$59,435,000	Indic. Yr. Divd.:	$1.000
Total Assets:	$150,681,000	Net Worth:	$91,246,000	Debt/ Equity:	NA

Qualmark Corp

4580 Florence St., Denver, CO, 80238; *PH*: 1-303-254-8800; *Fax*: 1-303-254-8343;
http:// www.qualmark.com; *Email*: sales@qualmark.com

General - Incorporation .... CO
Employees 50
Auditor .... GHP Horwath, P.C
Stk Agt .... Computershare Investor Services LLC
Counsel .... NA
DUNS No. 78-212-3129

Stock- Price on:12/24/2007 .... $1.5
Stock Exchange .... OTC
Ticker Symbol .... QMRK
Outstanding Shares 8,810,000
E.P.S. $0.06
Shareholders .... NA

Business: The group's principal activity is to design, manufacture and market vibration and thermal chambers for quality control testing of various electronic devices. The group operates two business segments: equipment segment and the accelerated reliability test centers. The equipment segment manufactures and markets vibration and thermal chambers for quality control testing of various electronic devices. Accelerated reliability test centers segment operates service centers where vibration and thermal chambers are available to customers for daily rental. Industries manufacturing products like circuit boards, personal computers, flight navigation systems and cellular telephones use the group's systems to perform highly accelerated stress testing.

Primary SIC and add'l.: 8734 3823 3841

CIK No: 0001006691

Subsidiaries: C-corporation, QualMark Ling Corporation

Officers: Charles D. Johnston/Dir., CEO, Pres./$358,450.00, Anthony Scalese/CFO, Principal Accounting Officer/$181,200.00, Greg Leger/VP - Service, Engineering Ling Electronics/$187,100.00, Ralph Poplawsky/VP - Technical Services, CTO, Gary Larson/VP - Sales, Marketing, Andy Grimaldi/VP, GM - Ling Electronics

Directors: Charles D. Johnston/Dir., CEO, Pres., James L.D. Roser/Dir., William Sanko/Dir., Gerald Laber/Dir., Christopher Roser/Dir.

Owners: The Roser Partnership II, LTD/1.70%, Partners for Growth/9.40%, Gregory Leger, William Sanko/1.00%, Insiders/43.50%, The Roser Partnership III, SBIC, LP/37.20%, James L.D. Roser/39.40%, Anthony A. Scalese, Gerald Laber, Charles D. Johnston/2.40%

Financial Data: Fiscal Year End:12/31 Latest Annual Data: 12/31/2006

Year	Sales	Net Income
2006	$16,427,000	$1,151,000
2005	$14,845,000	$2,088,000
2004	$12,012,000	$1,502,000

Curr. Assets:	$8,209,000	Curr. Liab.:	$3,432,000	P/E Ratio:	15.00
Plant, Equip.:	$787,000	Total Liab.:	$5,088,000	Indic. Yr. Divd.:	NA
Total Assets:	$12,049,000	Net Worth:	$6,961,000	Debt/ Equity:	0.2337

Qualstar Corp

3990-B Heritage Oak Ct., Simi Valley, CA, 93063; *PH*: 1-805-583-7744; *Fax*: 1-805-583-7749;
http:// www.qualstar.com; *Email*: sales@qualstar.com

General - Incorporation .... CA
Employees 89
Auditor .... Ernst & Young LLP
Stk Agt .... Corporate Stock Transfer, Inc.
Counsel .... Stradling Yocca Carlson & Rauth
DUNS No. .... NA

Stock- Price on:12/24/2007 .... $3.5
Stock Exchange .... NDQ
Ticker Symbol .... QBAK
Outstanding Shares 12,250,000
E.P.S. .... -$0.2
Shareholders .... NA

Business: The group's principal activities are to design, develop, manufacture and sell automated magnetic tape libraries. These are used to store, retrieve and manage data primarily in network computing environments. Tape libraries include cartridge tape drives, storage arrays of tape cartridges and robotics

to move the tape cartridges from storage locations to the tape drives. The group offers tape libraries for multiple tape drive technologies including those using advanced intelligent tape, quarter inch cartridge tape drives and media. The applications of the product include automated backup, archiving, digital video and image management. On 11-Jul-2002, the group acquired the assets and intellectual properties of n2power incorporated, a privately held company which designs and produces small and efficient open-frame switching power supplies.

Primary SIC and add'l.: 3572

CIK No: 0000758938

Subsidiaries: Qualstar Sales and Service Corporation

Officers: William J. Gervais/Dir., CEO, Pres., Richard A. Nelson/Dir., VP - Engineering, Sec., David L. Griffith/VP - Operations, Robert K. Covey/VP - Marketing, Robert C. King/VP - Sales, Andrew Farina/CFO, VP, Bob Covey/VP - Marketing

Directors: William J. Gervais/Dir., CEO, Pres., Richard A. Nelson/Dir., VP - Engineering, Sec., Carl W. Gromada/Dir., Robert E. Rich/Dir., Stanley W. Corker/Dir., Robert A. Meyer/Dir.

Owners: Wellington Management/8.10%, Robert E. Rich/1.10%, Carl Gromada, Stanley W. Corker, Richard A. Nelson/15.60%, Insiders/42.00%, Wells Capital Management Inc./12.90%, William J. Gervais/23.90%, Robert K. Covey

Financial Data: Fiscal Year End:06/30 Latest Annual Data: 6/30/2006

Year	Sales	Net Income
2006	$21,731,000	-$1,692,000
2005	$25,144,000	-$1,647,000
2004	$31,530,000	-$731,000

Curr. Assets:	$27,374,000	Curr. Liab.:	$2,222,000		
Plant, Equip.:	$601,000	Total Liab.:	$2,222,000	Indic. Yr. Divd.:	NA
Total Assets:	$44,063,000	Net Worth:	$41,841,000	Debt/ Equity:	NA

Quanex Corp

1900 W Loop S, Ste. 1500, Houston, TX, 77027; **PH:** 1-713-961-4600; **Fax:** 1-713-439-1016; **http://** www.quanex.com; **Email:** inquiry@quanex.com

General - Incorporation	DE	Stock - Price on:12/24/2007	$49.64
Employees	4,200	Stock Exchange	NYSE
Auditor	Deloitte & Touche LLP	Ticker Symbol	NX
Stk Agt..... American Stock Transfer & Trust Co.		Outstanding Shares	37,100,000
Counsel	Fulbright & Jaworski LLP	E.P.S.	$3.41
DUNS No.	00-535-7249	Shareholders	NA

Business: The groups principle activity is to manufacture engineered materials and components for the vehicular products and building products industry. The groups products include MACSTEEL, MACSTEEL Animations, HOMESHIELD and Nichols Aluminum. The group operates from United States.

Primary SIC and add'l.: 1796 3647 3316 3312 3317 3351

CIK No: 0000276889

Subsidiaries: Besten Equipment,Inc., Colonial Craft,Inc., Imperial Products,Inc., Macsteel Monroe,inc., Mikron Industries,Inc., Nichols Aluminum-Alabama,Inc., Quanex Bar,Inc., Quanex Health Management Company,Inc., Quanex Manufacturing,Inc., Quanex OPI,Inc., Quanex Solutions,Inc., Quanex Steel,Inc., Quanex Technologies,Inc., Temroc Metals,Inc.

Officers: Raymond A. Jean/Chmn., CEO, Pres., John J. Mannion/VP, Treasurer, Michael R. Bayles/56/VP, Pres. - Building Products, Kevin P. Delaney/Sr. VP, General Counsel, Sec., Paul A. Hammonds/VP - Corporate Development, Brent L. Korb/VP, Controller, Thomas M. Walker/CFO, Sr. VP - Finance, Mark A. Marcucci/54/VP, Pres. - Macsteel

Directors: Raymond A. Jean/Chmn., CEO, Pres., Joseph J. Ross/Dir., Richard L. Wellek/Dir., Vincent R. Scorsone/Dir., Donald G. Barger/Dir., Susan F. Davis/Dir., Joseph D. Rupp/Dir.

Owners: Kevin P. Delaney/0.26%, Insiders/3.15%, Joseph J. Ross/0.17%, Donald G. Barger, Mark A. Marcucci/0.36%, Richard L. Wellek/0.12%, Barclays Global Investors, Lord Abbett& Co, Thomas M. Walker/0.14%, Joseph J. Rupp/0.02%, Susan F. Davis/0.18%, Artisan Partners Limited, Raymond A. Jean/1.76%

Financial Data: Fiscal Year End:10/31 Latest Annual Data: 10/31/2006

Year	Sales	Net Income
2006	$2,032,572,000	$160,183,000
2005	$1,969,007,000	$155,160,000
2004	$1,460,268,000	$54,467,000

Curr. Assets:	$450,609,000	Curr. Liab.:	$208,413,000	P/E Ratio:	13.98
Plant, Equip.:	$432,058,000	Total Liab.:	$443,637,000	Indic. Yr. Divd.:	$0.560
Total Assets:	$1,202,152,000	Net Worth:	$758,515,000	Debt/ Equity:	0.1606

Quanta Capital Holdings Ltd

22 Church St., Penthouse, Hamilton; **PH:** 441-294-6350; **http://** www.quantaholdings.com; **Email:** info@quantaholdings.com

General - Incorporation	Bermuda	Stock - Price on:12/24/2007	NA
Employees	79	Stock Exchange	NDQ
Auditor	PricewaterhouseCoopers LLP	Ticker Symbol	QNTA
Stk Agt	Bank of New York	Outstanding Shares	NA
Counsel	NA	E.P.S.	NA
DUNS No.	NA	Shareholders	NA

Business: The groups principle activity is to provide insurance and reinsurance services. The groups products include structured insurance and marine and aviation. The group operates from United States.

Primary SIC and add'l.: NA

CIK No: 0001264242

Subsidiaries: Environmental Strategies Consulting LLC, Events Analysis Corporation, QLT of Alabama, LLC, QLT of Buffalo LLC, Quanta 4000 Holding Company Ltd., Quanta 4000 Ltd., Quanta Capital Statutory Trust I, Quanta Capital Statutory Trust II, Quanta Europe Ltd., Quanta Indemnity Company, Quanta Insurance Agency Services Inc., Quanta Intermediary Services Inc., Quanta Life Reinsurance Ltd., Quanta Reinsurance Ltd., Quanta Reinsurance U.S. Ltd. 20 Subsidiaries included in the Index

Officers: Peter D. Johnson/CEO, Pres., Jonathan J.R. Dodd/CFO, Martha G. Bannerman/General Counsel

Directors: James J. Ritchie/Chmn., Robert Lippincott/Dep. Chmn., William H. Bolinder/Dir., John C. McKenna/Dir., Roland C. Baker/Dir., Robert B. Shapiro/Dir., Susan Fleming Cabrera/Dir.

Owners: James J. Ritchie, The Baupost Group LLC./9.93%, William H. Bolinder, Insiders, Morgan Stanley/5.51%, John C. McKenna, Donald Smith & Co., Inc./9.48%, Susan F. Cabrera, Robert Lippincott, Jonathan J.R. Dodd, Roland C. Baker, Robert B. Shapiro, Boston Partners Asset Management, LLC/9.44%, NWQ Investment Management Co. LLC/5.33%, Brandes Investment Partners LP/7.72%

Financial Data: Fiscal Year End:12/31 Latest Annual Data: 12/31/2006

Year	Sales	Net Income
2006	$258,483,000	-$62,904,000
2005	$431,111,000	-$105,952,000
2004	$287,155,000	-$54,581,000

Curr. Assets:	$419,944,000	Curr. Liab.:	$112,595,000		
Plant, Equip.:	$1,112,000	Total Liab.:	$925,892,000	Indic. Yr. Divd.:	NA
Total Assets:	$1,329,226,000	Net Worth:	$328,336,000	Debt/ Equity:	0.1858

Quanta Services Inc

1360 Post Oak Blvd., Ste. 2100, Houston, TX, 77056; **PH:** 1-713-629-7600; **Fax:** 1-713-629-7676; **http://** www.quantaservices.com; **Email:** headquarters@quantaservices.com

General - Incorporation	DE	Stock - Price on:12/24/2007	$30.13
Employees	12,021	Stock Exchange	NYSE
Auditor	PricewaterhouseCoopers LLP	Ticker Symbol	PWR
Stk Agt..... American Stock Transfer & Trust Co.		Outstanding Shares	119,510,000
Counsel	NA	E.P.S.	$0.39
DUNS No.	00-800-4165	Shareholders	NA

Business: The groups principle activity is to provide specialty contracting services, offering end-to-end network solutions to the electric power, gas, telecommunications, cable television and specialty services industries. Specific customers of the group include Alabama Power Company, American Electric Power, Alltel Corporation and CenterPoint Energy, Inc. In the year 2007 the group acquired InfraSource Services, Inc. The group operates from United States.

Primary SIC and add'l.: 4931

CIK No: 0001050915

Subsidiaries: Advanced Technologies and Installation Corporation, Allteck Line Contractors (USA), Inc., Allteck Line Contractors, Inc., Arby Construction, Inc., Austin Trencher, Inc., Bradford Brothers, Inc., Brown Engineering, CCLC, Inc., CMI Services, Inc., Colorado IM Electric, Conti Communications, Inc., Croce Electric Company, Inc., Crown Fiber Communications, Inc., DB Utilities, DE Conti Communications, Inc. 126 Subsidiaries included in the Index

Officers: John R. Colson/Chmn., CEO, Pres./$2,206,550.00, Derrick A. Jensen/37/VP, Controller, Chief Accounting Officer/$665,791.00, James H. Haddox/CFO/$1,135,973.00, John R. Wilson/Dir., Pres. - Electric Power, Gas Division/$1,016,509.00, Benadetto G. Bosco/50/Sr. VP - Business Development, Outsourcing, Darren B. Miller/48/VP - Information Technology, Administration, Nicholas M. Grindstaff/45/Treasurer, Kenneth W. Trawick/60/Pres. - Telecommunications, Cable Television Division/$1,062,550.00, Vincent A. Mercaldi/Corp. Sec., Tana L. Pool/48/VP, General Counsel, James F. ONeil/49/Sr. VP - Operations Integration, Audit, Joseph A. Avila/57/Exec. VP - Strategic Operations, Process

Directors: John R. Colson/Chmn., CEO, Pres., James R. Ball/Dir., Ralph R. Disibio/Dir., Vincent D. Foster/Dir., Bernard Fried/Dir., Louis C. Golm/Dir., Worthing F. Jackman/Dir., Bruce Ranck/Dir., Gary A. Tucci/Dir., John R. Wilson/Dir., Pres. - Electric Power, Gas Division, Pat Wood/Dir.

Owners: Parkhouse Family Irrevocable Trust, Friess Associates LLC, U.S. Trust Corporation, Jeffrey L. Gendell, Columbia Wanger Asset Management, L.P., James C. Thomas, Vincent D. Foster, William G. Parkhouse, James H. & Constance Haddox, FMR Corp., Steven P. Colmar, Sydney L. Thomas

Financial Data: Fiscal Year End:12/31 Latest Annual Data: 12/31/2006

Year	Sales	Net Income
2006	$2,131,038,000	$17,483,000
2005	$1,858,626,000	$29,557,000
2004	$1,626,510,000	-$9,194,000

Curr. Assets:	$990,629,000	Curr. Liab.:	$334,456,000	P/E Ratio:	77.26
Plant, Equip.:	$276,789,000	Total Liab.:	$910,074,000	Indic. Yr. Divd.:	NA
Total Assets:	$1,639,157,000	Net Worth:	$729,083,000	Debt/ Equity:	0.5335

Quantrx Biomedical Corp

100 S Main St. Ste. 300, Doylestown, PA, 18901; **PH:** 1-267-880-1595; **http://** www.quantrx.com; **Email:** ir@quantrx.com

General - Incorporation	NV	Stock - Price on:12/24/2007	$0.95
Employees	6	Stock Exchange	OTC
Auditor	Williams & Webster, P.S.	Ticker Symbol	QTXB
Stk Agt..... Computershare Investor Services LLC		Outstanding Shares	40,910,000
Counsel	NA	E.P.S.	-$0.26
DUNS No.	NA	Shareholders	NA

Business: The groups principle activity is biomedical that is committed to the research, development, acquisition and commercialization of medical diagnostic products. The group operates from the United States. The group's quarterly revenue for Sep '07 was 0.09 millions of USD.

Primary SIC and add'l.: 8731

CIK No: 0000820608

Officers: Walter W. Witoshkin/Chmn., CEO/$316,454.00, William H. Fleming/Dir., Chief Scientific Officer, Sec., Sasha Afanassiev/CFO, VP - Finance/$241,742.00, Cynthia E. Horton/VP - Diagnostics/$180,100.00, Michael Hogan/Founder, Chief Scientific Officer - Genomics USA

Directors: Walter W. Witoshkin/Chmn., CEO, William H. Fleming/Dir., Chief Scientific Officer, Sec., Evan Levine/42/Dir., Arthur Hull Hayes/Dir., Shalom Hirschman/Dir., Michael Hogan/Founder, Chief Scientific Officer - Genomics USA

Owners: Sasha Afanassiev/0.24%, Evan Levine/9.67%, Sherbrooke Partners, LLC/11.02%, Shalom Hirschman/1.24%, Matthew Balk/14.00%, William H. Fleming/1.20%, Arthur Hull Hayes, Mark Capital, LLC/7.17%, Walter W. Witoshkin/2.00%

Financial Data: Fiscal Year End:12/31 Latest Annual Data: 12/31/2006

Year	Sales	Net Income
2006	$91,000	-$7,693,000
2005	$56,000	-$1,093,000
2004	$66,000	-$20,000

Curr. Assets:	$1,837,000	Curr. Liab.:	$370,000		
Plant, Equip.:	$157,000	Total Liab.:	$747,000	Indic. Yr. Divd.:	NA
Total Assets:	$4,313,000	Net Worth:	$3,566,000	Debt/ Equity:	NA

Quantum Co Inc

123 High St., Dublin, OH, 43017; *PH:* 1-614-336-3590; *http://* www.quantumcompany.com; *Email:* quantum@rrcol.com

General - Incorporation	NV	*Stock*- Price on:12/24/2007	$3.1
Employees	NA	Stock Exchange	NA
Auditor	Chang G. Park, Cpa	Ticker Symbol	NA
Stk Agt	Holladay Stock Transfer, Inc.	Outstanding Shares	199,200,000
Counsel	NA	E.P.S.	-$0.33
DUNS No.	NA	Shareholders	NA

Business: The group's principial activity is to provide an online marketing portal. Online marketing portal is a site where users can go to find merchants who are marketing their business. The company has two E-shop subsidiaries that has developed an online marketing portal that is geared toward smaller business that cannot afford large marketing budgets to give them an advertising presence. E-shop charges the merchant a fee to put them in the online portal that E-shop promotes to the local community. The merchants have the ability to promote themselves on the portal by having an informational page, a link to their website, and a printable coupon. The marketing portal is fully operational. However, the company is currently determining what methods to use to attract retailers and consumers. To date no services have been provided.

Primary SIC and add'l.: 7389
CIK No: 0001106599
Subsidiaries: E-shop California, E-shop Nevada
Officers: Derek Jones/70/Chmn., CEO, CFO, Sec.
Directors: Derek Jones/70/Chmn., CEO, CFO, Sec.
Owners: Derek Jones

Financial Data: Fiscal Year End: 12/31 *Latest Annual Data:* 3/31/2007

Year	Sales	Net Income
2007	$1,016,174,000	-$64,094,000
2006	$834,287,000	-$41,479,000
2005	$794,168,000	-$3,496,000

Curr. Assets:	$386,461,000	*Curr. Liab.:*	$329,450,000		
Plant, Equip.:	$50,241,000	*Total Liab.:*	$871,388,000	*Indic. Yr. Divd.:*	NA
Total Assets:	$1,125,829,000	*Net Worth:*	$254,441,000	*Debt/ Equity:*	1.9552

Quantum Corp

1650 Technology Dr., Ste. 700, San Jose, CA, 95110; *PH:* 1-408-944-4000; *Fax:* 1-408-944-4040; *http://* www.quantum.com; *Email:* ir@quantum.com

General - Incorporation	DE	*Stock*- Price on:12/24/2007	$3.04
Employees	2,900	Stock Exchange	NYSE
Auditor	Ernst & Young LLP	Ticker Symbol	QTM
Stk Agt	Computershare Investor Services LLC	Outstanding Shares	199,200,000
Counsel	Wilson Sonsini Goodrich & Rosati	E.P.S.	-$0.37
DUNS No.	02-119-5540	Shareholders	NA

Business: The group's principal activity is to provide backup, archiving and recovery of critical data. It also designs, manufactures and services automated tape libraries used to manage, store and transfer data. The group operates through two segments: digital linear tape(dlt) group which design, develop, license, service, and market dlttape and super dlttape drives as well as media cartridges. Storage solutions group designs, develops, manufactures, services, and market tape automation systems and solutions. It has foreign operations in Europe and Asia. The group offers a broad line of tape automation systems, which are used to manage, store and transfer data in enterprises networked computing enviornments. The group's disk-based backup systems include enhanced backup systems.

Primary SIC and add'l.: 3572
CIK No: 0000709283
Subsidiaries: ATL Products UK Ltd., ATL Products UK Ltd., a United Kingdom corporation, Certance (US) Holdings, Inc., Certance (US) Holdings, Inc., a Delaware corporation, Certance Holding Corporation, a Delaware corporation, Certance Holding Corporation., Certance International, a Cayman Islands company, Certance International., Certance LLC, a Delaware limited liability company, Certance LLC., Duantum Storage UK Ltd., a United Kingdom corporation, M4 Data (Holdings) Ltd., Quantum Distribution (UK) Limited, Quantum Distribution (UK) Limited, a United Kingdom corporation, Quantum Distribution (UK) Limited. 45 Subsidiaries included in the Index
Officers: Richard E. Belluzzo/Chmn., CEO/$1,418,345.00, Jon Gacek/CFO, Exec. VP/$1,472,297.00, Shawn D. Hall/VP, General Counsel, Sec., Barbara Barrett/VP - Human Resources, Steve Dalton/Sr. VP - Engineering, Brad Cohen/Contact - Media Relations, Jenny Lee/Contact - Investor Relations, William C. Britts/49/Exec. VP - Sales, Marketing, Service, Bill Britts/Exec. VP - Sales, Marketing, Service/$1,468,310.00
Directors: Richard E. Belluzzo/Chmn., CEO, Michael A. Brown/Dir., Thomas S. Buchsbaum/Dir., Alan L. Earhart/Dir., Steven C. Wheelwright/Dir., Paul Auvil/Dir., Joseph A. Marengi/Dir., Bruce Pasternack/Dir., Dennis Wolf/Dir., Edward M. Esber/Dir., John Partridge/Dir., Elizabeth A. Fetter/Dir.
Owners: Steven C. Wheelwright, Elizabeth A. Fetter, Alan L. Earhart, John M. Partridge, Noonday Asset Management, L.P./6.19%, Anthony E. Carrozza, Insiders/4.45%, James L. Wold, Thomas S. Buchsbaum, Richard E. Belluzzo/2.08%, Elm Ridge Capital Management, LLC/5.21%, Edward M. Esber, NWQ Investment Management Company, LLC/18.69%, Edward J. Hayes, Howard L. Matthews *(20 Owners included in Index)*

Financial Data: Fiscal Year End: 03/31 *Latest Annual Data:* 03/31/2007

Year	Sales	Net Income
2007	$1,016,174,000	-$64,094,000
2006	$834,287,000	-$41,479,000
2005	$794,168,000	-$3,496,000

Curr. Assets:	$386,461,000	*Curr. Liab.:*	$329,450,000		
Plant, Equip.:	$50,241,000	*Total Liab.:*	$871,388,000	*Indic. Yr. Divd.:*	NA
Total Assets:	$1,125,829,000	*Net Worth:*	$254,441,000	*Debt/ Equity:*	NA

Quantum Energy Inc

PO Box 929, Penticton, BC, V2A 6J9; *PH:* 1-604-592-3577; *http://* www.quantumenergyinc.net

General - Incorporation	NV	*Stock*- Price on:12/24/2007	$0.33
Employees	NA	Stock Exchange	OTC
Auditor	Killman, Murrell & Co., P.c.	Ticker Symbol	QEGY
Stk Agt	NA	Outstanding Shares	NA
Counsel	NA	E.P.S.	NA
DUNS No.	NA	Shareholders	NA

Business: The groups principal activity is in oil and gas exploration and acquisitions. The group intends to acquire interest in the properties and working interests in the production owned by established oil and gas production companies, whether public or private, in the United States oil producing areas. The group operates from the United States.

Primary SIC and add'l.: 1311
CIK No: 0001295961
Officers: Shane Lowry/38/Dir., CEO, Pres., Sec., Treasurer, Andrea Bleasdale/Contact - Investor Relation
Directors: Shane Lowry/38/Dir., CEO, Pres., Sec., Treasurer
Owners: Caroline Schut/17.58%, Lorena Jensen/24.18%, Bruce Ellsworth/43.96%, Insiders/85.72%

Curr. Assets:	$385,000	*Curr. Liab.:*	$2,393,000		
Plant, Equip.:	$951,000	*Total Liab.:*	$2,775,000	*Indic. Yr. Divd.:*	NA
Total Assets:	$1,344,000	*Net Worth:*	-$1,431,000	*Debt/ Equity:*	NA

Quantum Fuel Systems Techs Worldwide Inc

17872 Cartwright Rd., Irvine, CA, 92614; *PH:* 1-949-399-4500; *Fax:* 1-949-399-4600; *http://* www.qtww.com

General - Incorporation	DE	*Stock*- Price on:12/24/2007	$2.18
Employees	702	Stock Exchange	NDQ
Auditor	Ernst & Young, LLP	Ticker Symbol	QTWW
Stk Agt	Mellon Investor Services LLC	Outstanding Shares	66,050,000
Counsel	Morrison & Foerster LLP	E.P.S.	-$1.66
DUNS No.	NA	Shareholders	NA

Business: The group's principle activities are to design, manufacture and supply integrated fuel systems to original equipment manufacturers (OEMs) for use in alternative fuel vehicles and fuel cell applications. The operations are classified into four segments: alternative fuels, fuel cell systems, advanced research and product development and corporate expenses. Alternative fuels division includes sale of compressed natural gas ('cng') and propane ('lpg') fuel storage, fuel delivery and electronic control systems to OEMs. Fuel cell systems division includes sale of fuel cell-related fuel storage, fuel delivery and electronic control systems to OEMs and hydrogen refueling systems. Advanced research and product development includes customer-funded research and development and company sponsored research and development. The group's revenues are generated in the United States, Japan, Germany and Korea. The group's total revenue for year 2007 was 146.68 millions of USD.

Primary SIC and add'l.: 3714 8731
CIK No: 0001166380
Subsidiaries: AmStar, LLC, Classic Acquisition Company, LLC, PowerTrain Integration, LLC, Starcraft Automotive Group, Inc., Starcraft Corporation, Starcraft de Mexico, S. de R.L. de C.V., Starcraft Southwest, Inc., Tarxien Automotive Products Limited, Tecstar Manufacturing Limited, Tecstar Partners, LLC, Tecstar, L.P., Wheel to Wheel Parts.com, LLC, Wheel to Wheel Powertrain, LLC, Wheel to Wheel, LLC
Officers: Alan P. Niedzwiecki/Dir., CEO, Pres./$1,647,117.00, Jeffrey P. Beitzel/Dir., COO/$1,071,595.00
Directors: Alan P. Niedzwiecki/Dir., CEO, Pres., Dale L. Rasmussen/Chmn., Thomas J. Tyson/Dir., Carl E. Sheffer/Dir., Jeffrey P. Beitzel/Dir., COO, Brian A. Runkel/Dir., Scott G. Samuelsen/Dir., Paul E. Grutzner/Dir.
Owners: Brian A. Runkel, Carl E. Sheffer, Brian W. Olson, Thomas J. Tyson, Douglass C. Goad/2.00%, Dale L. Rasmussen, Bradley J. Timon, Alan P. Niedzwiecki, Scott G. Samuelsen, Kenneth R. Lombardo, Paul E. Grutzner, Jeffrey P. Beitzel/2.80%, Insiders/11.10%, Richard C. Anderson/3.60%

Financial Data: Fiscal Year End: 04/30 *Latest Annual Data:* 04/30/2007

Year	Sales	Net Income
2007	$146,684,000	-$140,529,000
2006	$192,682,000	-$35,533,000
2005	$54,300,000	-$13,099,000

Curr. Assets:	$77,303,000	*Curr. Liab.:*	$50,868,000		
Plant, Equip.:	$23,717,000	*Total Liab.:*	$90,247,000	*Indic. Yr. Divd.:*	NA
Total Assets:	$282,309,000	*Net Worth:*	$191,593,000	*Debt/ Equity:*	0.4538

Quantum Group Inc

3420 FairLn. Farms Rd. , Ste 4, Wellington, FL, 33414; *PH:* 1-567-798-9800; *http://* www.thequantumgroupinc.com

General - Incorporation	NV	*Stock*- Price on:12/24/2007	NA
Employees	22	Stock Exchange	AMEX
Auditor	Daszkal Bolton LLP	Ticker Symbol	QGP
Stk Agt	Fidelity Transfer Co	Outstanding Shares	NA
Counsel	NA	E.P.S.	-$6.7
DUNS No.	NA	Shareholders	NA

Business: The group is a development stage company with no current revenues. As of 6-Feb-2004, management's efforts have been primarily in market research, business development, negotiations of various letters of intent and due diligence on potential acquisitions, joint ventures and licensing agreements. Its business model is to become a leading provider of services to the healthcare industry in three complementary areas. Those include: outsourcing for physicians, managed care organizations, healthcare facilities, physician associations; developing new technologies that will create a more effective and responsive healthcare system and providing leading edge healthcare services to consumers.

Primary SIC and add'l.: 6324
CIK No: 0001118847
Officers: Noel J. Guillama/Dir., CEO, Pres., Donald B. Cohen/Dir., Co - Founder, VP, CFO, Susan D. Guillama/Dir., VP, Chief Administrative Officer, Sec.

Directors: Noel J. Guillama/Dir., CEO, Pres., Donald B. Cohen/Dir., Co - Founder, VP, CFO, Lawrence B. Fisher/Dir., James D. Baker/Dir., Susan D. Guillama/Dir., VP, Chief Administrative Officer, Sec., Mark Haggerty/Dir., Peter Nauert/64/Dir., Michael Rosenbaum/Dir., Jose De La Torre/Dir., Alberto G. Del Valle/Dir., Gregg M. Steinberg/Dir.

Owners: Insiders, Mark Haggerty, Michael Rosenbaum, Professional Offshore Opportunity Fund, LLC/10.09%, Jose de la Torre, James D. Baker, Alberto Del Valle, Thomas Hartley/7.04%, Susan Darby Guillama/1.37%, Lion Gate Capital, Inc./5.57%, High Capital Funding LLC/19.21%, Lawrence Fisher, Gregg M. Steinberg/3.93%, Richard Adler/5.57%, Donald B. Cohen/3.35% *(16 Owners included in Index)*

Financial Data: *Fiscal Year End:*10/31 *Latest Annual Data:* 10/31/2006

Year	Sales	Net Income
2006	$95,000	-$4,673,000
2005	$1,000	-$1,854,000
2004	NA	-$1,120,000

Curr. Assets:	$685,000	*Curr. Liab.:*	$3,337,000		
Plant, Equip.:	$153,000	*Total Liab.:*	$3,455,000	*Indic. Yr. Divd.:*	NA
Total Assets:	$1,092,000	*Net Worth:*	-$2,363,000	*Debt/ Equity:*	NA

Quantum MRI Inc

4750 Paton St., Vancouver, BC, V6L 2J1; *PH:* 1-303-506-1633

General - Incorporation	WA	**Stock**- Price on:12/24/2007	$0.07
Employees	NA	Stock Exchange	OTC
Auditor	Manning Elliott LLP	Ticker Symbol	QTMR
Stk Agt.	NA	Outstanding Shares	NA
Counsel	NA	E.P.S.	NA
DUNS No.	NA	Shareholders	NA

Business: The groups principal activity is a battery operated incineration system that destroys a range of needles by passing an electric current through the needle thereby reducing the steel to ashes in a matter of seconds. The group operates from the United States.

Primary SIC and add'l.: 7389

CIK No: 0001123844

Subsidiaries: SETI Corp

Officers: Kelly Fielder/39/Dir., CEO, Treasurer, Gary Rushin/52/VP - Finance

Directors: Kelly Fielder/39/Dir., CEO, Treasurer

Owners: Spectrum Meditech Inc., Insiders/63.20%, Murray Atkins/18.20%, Kelly Fielder/63.00%

Financial Data: *Fiscal Year End:*03/31 *Latest Annual Data:* 03/31/2007

Year	Sales	Net Income
2007	NA	-$1,951,000

Curr. Assets:	$0	*Curr. Liab.:*	$1,902,000		
Plant, Equip.:	$2,000	*Total Liab.:*	$1,902,000	*Indic. Yr. Divd.:*	NA
Total Assets:	$2,000	*Net Worth:*	-$1,900,000	*Debt/ Equity:*	NA

Quartz Mountain Resources Ltd

800 W Pender St., Ste. 1020, Vancouver, BC, V6C 2V6; *PH:* 1-604-684-6365

General - Incorporation	Canada	**Stock**- Price on:12/24/2007	$0.5221
Employees	NA	Stock Exchange	OTC
Auditor	KPMG LLP	Ticker Symbol	QZMRF
Stk Agt.	Computershare Trust Co of Canada	Outstanding Shares	NA
Counsel	NA	E.P.S.	NA
DUNS No.	24-620-3665	Shareholders	NA

Business: The group's principle activity is to explore and develop mineral properties, primarily gold and silver properties. The group operates from United States.

Primary SIC and add'l.: 1041 1044 6719

CIK No: 0000811522

Subsidiaries: Delaware corporation, Nevada corporation, Quartz Mountain Gold Inc, Wavecrest Resources Inc

Officers: Rene G. Carrier/Pres., Dir. - North Vancouver, British Columbia, Canada, Jeffrey R. Mason/Principal Accounting Officer, Gordon J. Fretwell/Dir., Sec. - West Vancouver

Directors: Brian F. Causey/Dir., Gordon J. Fretwell/Dir., Sec. - West Vancouver, Barry T. Coughlan/Dir.

Owners: Estate of David S. Jennings/29.60%, Robert A. Dickinson/11.20%, Rene G. Carrier/1.12%

Financial Data: *Fiscal Year End:*07/31 *Latest Annual Data:* 7/31/2006

Year	Sales	Net Income
2006	NA	-$65,000
2005	NA	-$85,000
2004	NA	-$87,000

Curr. Assets:	$1,114,000	*Curr. Liab.:*	$17,000		
Plant, Equip.:	NA	*Total Liab.:*	$17,000	*Indic. Yr. Divd.:*	NA
Total Assets:	$1,114,000	*Net Worth:*	$1,097,000	*Debt/ Equity:*	NA

Quebecor World Inc

612 St-Jacques St., Montreal, QC, H3C 4M8; *PH:* 1-514-954-0101; *Fax:* 1-514-954-9624; *http://* www.quebecorworld.com

General - Incorporation	Canada	**Stock**- Price on:12/24/2007	$12.21
Employees	31,200	Stock Exchange	NYSE
Auditor	KPMG LLP	Ticker Symbol	IQW
Stk Agt.	Computershare Trust Co of Canada	Outstanding Shares	131,830,000
Counsel	NA	E.P.S.	-$2.94
DUNS No.	24-796-1865	Shareholders	NA

Business: The group's principle activities are to provide commercial print media services. The products provided by the group include magazines, inserts and circulars, books, catalogs, specialty printing and direct mail, dictionaries, digital pre-media, logistics, mail list technologies and other value-added services. The group operates in Europe, Latin America, the United States, Canada, France, the United Kingdom, Spain, Switzerland, Sweden, Finland, Austria, Belgium, Brazil, Chile, Argentina, Peru, columbia, Mexico and India. The group's quarterly revenue for September 2007 was 1,414.60 millions of USD.

Primary SIC and add'l.: 8999 2721 2759 2711 2732

CIK No: 0001003470

Subsidiaries: Quebecor Inc.

Officers: Wes William Lucas/Dir., CEO, Pres., Monique F. Leroux/Sr. Exec. VP, CFO - Desjardins, Guy Trahan/Pres. - Quebecor World Latin America, Antonio Fernandez/COO - Quebecor World Europe, Yvan Lesniak/Pres. - Operations, Quebecor World France, Tony Ross/VP - Communications, Louis Saint-Arnaud/Sr. VP - Legal Affairs, Corp. Sec., Julie Tremblay/VP - Human Resources, Jacques Mallette/CFO, Exec. VP, Kevin J. Clarke/Pres. - Book, Dir.y Publishing Services, Brian Freschi/Pres. - Catalog, Retail Insert, Sunday Magazine, Brad Nathan/Pres. - Quebecor World Logistics, Antonio Galasso/Pres. - North American Premedia, Pres. - Magazine, Catalog, Specialty Group, Michel Guichard/VP - Finance, Paul Jones/VP - International Sales - Europe *(32 Officers included in Index)*

Directors: Wes William Lucas/Dir., CEO, Pres., Brian Mulroney/Chmn., erik Peladeau/Vice Chmn., Jean Neveu/Dir., Pierre Karl Peladeau/Dir., Alain Rheaume/Dir., Robert Normand/Corp. Dir., Douglas Graeme Bassett/Dir., Michele Desjardins/Corp. Dir., Andre Caille/Corp. Dir., Reginald K. Brack/Corp. Dir., Robert Coallier/Dir.

Financial Data: *Fiscal Year End:*12/31 *Latest Annual Data:* 12/31/2006

Year	Sales	Net Income
2006	$6,086,300,000	$29,800,000
2005	$6,283,300,000	-$169,500,000
2004	$6,622,100,000	$141,500,000

Curr. Assets:	$939,400,000	*Curr. Liab.:*	$1,015,400,000		
Plant, Equip.:	$2,287,400,000	*Total Liab.:*	$3,791,000,000	*Indic. Yr. Divd.:*	$0.400
Total Assets:	$5,823,400,000	*Net Worth:*	$2,032,400,000	*Debt/ Equity:*	NA

Quepasa Corp

7550 E Redfield Rd., Scottsdale, AZ, 85260; *PH:* 1-480-348-2665; *Fax:* 1-480-951-0221; *http://* www.quepasa.com

General - Incorporation	NV	**Stock**- Price on:12/24/2007	$5.94
Employees	77	Stock Exchange	NDQ
Auditor	Perelson Weiner LLP	Ticker Symbol	QPSA
Stk Agt.	Corporate Stock Transfer, Inc.	Outstanding Shares	12,240,000
Counsel	NA	E.P.S.	NA
DUNS No.	NA	Shareholders	NA

Business: The group's principal activities are to provide Internet portal and on-line community services in both Spanish and English to the hispanic market. The group's quepasa.com Web site provides users with information and content centered around the Spanish language and offers traditional portal services including e-mail and news. The Web site allows individuals to quickly access content and features and also offers services in English. The group provides one-stop destination for identifying, selecting and accessing resources, services, content and information on the Web. The group's competitors include yahoo!espanol, America online Latin America and terra lycos.

Primary SIC and add'l.: 7375

CIK No: 0001078099

Subsidiaries: Quepasa.com de

Officers: Robert B. Stearns/55/Chmn., CEO/$1,225,829.00, Eric Rayman/Sr. VP - Sales, Marketing, Charles B. Mathews/CFO, Exec. VP/$90,000.00, Cynthia Martinez/Technical Assist. - Sales, Marketing, Douglas A. Gray/44/CTO

Directors: Robert B. Stearns/55/Chmn., CEO, Jeffrey S. Peterson/35/Dir., Lionel Sosa/58/Dir., Michael D. Matte/48/Dir., Alonso Ancira/55/Dir., Malcolm Jozoff/58/Dir., Jill Syverson-Stork/54/Dir.

Owners: Stephan F. Allen/12.20%, Robert B. Stearns/4.70%, Jeffrey S. Peterson/8.20%, Lionel Sosa/0.10%, Jill Syverson-Stork, Richard L. Scott/10.90%, Charles B. Mathews/2.70%, Mexicans& Americans Trading Together, Inc./24.50%, Alonso Ancira, Malcolm Jozoff/0.10%, Michael D. Matte/0.10%, Insiders/16.80%, Douglas A. Gray/0.80%

Financial Data: *Fiscal Year End:*12/31 *Latest Annual Data:* 03/31/2007

Year	Sales	Net Income
2007	NA	NA
2006	$395,000	-$13,606,000
2005	$765,000	-$2,959,000

Curr. Assets:	$14,501,000	*Curr. Liab.:*	$899,000		
Plant, Equip.:	$546,000	*Total Liab.:*	$899,000	*Indic. Yr. Divd.:*	NA
Total Assets:	$16,089,000	*Net Worth:*	$15,190,000	*Debt/ Equity:*	NA

Quest Capital Corp

550 Burrard St., Ste.1028, Bentall 5, Vancouver, BC, V6C 2B5; *PH:* 1-604-689-1428; *Fax:* 1-604-681-4692; *http://* www.questcapcorp.com

General - Incorporation	Canada	**Stock**- Price on:12/24/2007	NA
Employees	NA	Stock Exchange	AMEX
Auditor	PricewaterhouseCoopers LLP	Ticker Symbol	QCC
Stk Agt.	Computershare Trust Co	Outstanding Shares	NA
Counsel	NA	E.P.S.	NA
DUNS No.	NA	Shareholders	NA

Business: The groups principle activity is to provide mortgages to the real estate industry. The group also provides mortgage financing services. The group operates from Canada.

Primary SIC and add'l.: NA

CIK No: 0000832342

Subsidiaries: Quest Management Corp., Quest Securities Corporation, Viceroy Australia Pty Ltd., Viceroy Gold Corporation

Officers: Brian E. Bayley/Dir., CEO, Pres., Robert Buchan/Exec. Chmn., Murray A. Sinclair/Dir., MD, Derek Wasson/Sr. VP, Michael Atkinson/VP, Mark Monaghan/VP - Quest Capital, Narinder Nagra/CFO, Sandra Lee/Legal Assist., Corp. Sec., Ken Gordon/COO, Jeff Beaucage/VP - Originations, Pauline Pasetka/Controller

Directors: Brian E. Bayley/Dir., CEO, Pres., Robert Buchan/Exec. Chmn., Murray A. Sinclair/Dir., MD, Robert G. Atkinson/Dir., Michael Winn/Dir., Daniel Goodman/Dir., David W. Black/Dir., Michael Hannesson/Dir., Walter Traub/Dir., Dale Peniuk/Dir.

Quest Diagnostics Inc

1290 Wall St. W, Lyndhurst, NJ, 07071; *PH:* 1-201-393-5000; *Fax:* 1-201-729-8920; *http://* www.questdiagnostics.com

General - Incorporation	DE	Stock- Price on:12/24/2007	$51.8
Employees	41,000	Stock Exchange	NYSE
Auditor	PricewaterhouseCoopers LLP	Ticker Symbol	DGX
Stk Agt	National City Bank	Outstanding Shares	192,690,000
Counsel	NA	E.P.S.	$2.77
DUNS No.	05-635-4640	Shareholders	NA

Business: The group's principle activitiy is to provide diagnostic testing and related services. The group also provides anatomic pathology and testing services for clinical trials. The group operates from United States.

Primary SIC and add'l.: 8071 8099

CIK No: 0001022079

Subsidiaries: American Medical Laboratories, Incorporated, AML Inc., Analisis, S.A., APL Properties Limited Liability Company, Associated Clinical Laboratories, C&S Clinical Laboratory, Inc. (d/b/a Clinical Diagnostic Services), Central Plains Holdings, Inc., Central Plains Laboratories, LLC, Compunet Clinical Laboratories, Diagnostic Laboratory of Oklahoma LLC, Diagnostic Path Lab, Inc., Diagnostic Reference Services Inc., DPD Holdings, Inc., ExamOne Canada, Inc., Intellisys, Inc. 61 Subsidiaries included in the Index

Officers: Surya N. Mohapatra/Chmn., CEO, Pres./$9,076,699.00, Robert A. Hagemann/CFO, Sr. VP/$3,236,119.00, David M. Zewe/Sr. VP - Diagnostic Testing Operations/$2,137,088.00, Robert E. Peters/VP - Sales, Marketing/$1,591,477.00, Michael E. Prevoznik/Sr. VP, General Counsel/$1,868,426.00, Laure Park/VP - Investor Relations, Nancy Fitzsimmons/Dir. - Media Relations, Timothy Sharpe/VP - Compliance, Gladys Daniel/Dir. - Purchasing

Directors: Surya N. Mohapatra/Chmn., CEO, Pres., John B. Ziegler/Dir., Rosanne Haggerty/Dir., James F. Flaherty/Dir., John C. Baldwin/Dir., Jenne K. Britell/Dir., William F. Buehler/Dir., Gary M. Pfeiffer/Dir., Dan C. Stanzione/Dir., Gail R. Wilensky/Dir.

Owners: Daniel C. Stanzione, Robert A. Hagemann, John B. Ziegler, Jenne K. Britell, Robert E. Peters, Rosanne Haggerty, Michael E. Prevoznik, Gail R. Wilensky, David M. Zewe, William R. Grant, John C. Baldwin, Insiders/1.70%, Gary M. Pfeiffer, William F. Buehler, GlaxoSmithKline plc/18.90% *(16 Owners included in Index)*

Financial Data: Fiscal Year End:12/31   Latest Annual Data: 12/31/2006

Year	Sales	Net Income
2006	$6,268,659,000	$586,421,000
2005	$5,503,711,000	$546,277,000
2004	$5,126,601,000	$499,195,000

Curr. Assets:	$1,191,018,000	Curr. Liab.:	$1,150,870,000	P/E Ratio:	18.70
Plant, Equip.:	$752,357,000	Total Liab.:	$2,642,311,000	Indic. Yr. Divd.:	NA
Total Assets:	$5,661,482,000	Net Worth:	$3,019,171,000	Debt/ Equity:	0.4087

Quest Group International Inc

18 Technology, Ste. 130, Irvine, CA, 92618; *PH:* 1-949-336-7111; *http://* www.questgrp.net

General - Incorporation	NV	Stock- Price on:12/24/2007	$1.2
Employees	2	Stock Exchange	OTC
Auditor	Jones Simkins, P.C.	Ticker Symbol	QSTG
Stk Agt.	NA	Outstanding Shares	73,260,000
Counsel	NA	E.P.S.	$0.01
DUNS No.	NA	Shareholders	NA

Business: The groups principle activity is to develop and distribute a line of nutritional products that call the NeoSource products. The group operates from the United States and Japan.

Primary SIC and add'l.: 2833

CIK No: 0001174228

Officers: Harin Padma-Nathan/CEO, Craig Davis/Dir., Pres., Steven Gershick/CFO, Rosh Chandraratna/Chief Scientific Officer, Sharyar Baradaran/Dir., Sec.

Directors: Craig Davis/Dir., Pres., Sharyar Baradaran/Dir., Sec.

Owners: Insiders/38.50%, Hunter World Markets, Inc./8.90%, Parkash Gill/22.40%, Santa Monica Capital Partners II, LLC/12.90%, Sharyar Baradaran, Kurt Brendlinger/12.90%, Harin Padma-Nathan/2.50%

Financial Data: Fiscal Year End:09/30   Latest Annual Data: 9/30/2006

Year	Sales	Net Income
2006	$2,423,000	$193,000

Curr. Assets:	$383,000	Curr. Liab.:	$117,000		
Plant, Equip.:	$18,000	Total Liab.:	$119,000	Indic. Yr. Divd.:	NA
Total Assets:	$402,000	Net Worth:	$283,000	Debt/ Equity:	NA

Quest Minerals & Mining Corp

18b E 5th St., Paterson, NJ, 07524; *PH:* 1-973-684-0075

General - Incorporation	UT	Stock- Price on:12/24/2007	$0.0053
Employees	2	Stock Exchange	OTC
Auditor	Kempisty & Company CPAs, P.C.	Ticker Symbol	QMMG
Stk Agt.	Nevada Agency & Trust Company	Outstanding Shares	137,970,000
Counsel	NA	E.P.S.	-$0.145
DUNS No.	NA	Shareholders	NA

Business: The groups principle activity is coal producer in the world, other leading coal producers include India, South Africa, and Australia. The group operates from the United States. The group's quarterly revenue for Sep '07 was 0.04 millions of USD.

Primary SIC and add'l.: 1241

CIK No: 0001130126

Subsidiaries: E-Z Mining Co., Inc., Gwenco, Inc., Quest Energy, Ltd., Quest Marine Terminal, Ltd., Quest Minerals & Mining Ltd., Taylor Mining, Inc.

Officers: Eugene Chiaramonte/Pres., Principal Executive Officer, Principal Accounting Officer

Owners: Eugene Chiaramonte/12.00%, Insiders/12.00%

Financial Data: Fiscal Year End:12/31   Latest Annual Data: 12/31/2005

Year	Sales	Net Income
2005	$357,000	-$20,456,000
2004	$2,913,000	-$38,005,000
2003	NA	-$5,000

Curr. Assets:	$16,000	Curr. Liab.:	$7,106,000		
Plant, Equip.:	$406,000	Total Liab.:	$7,774,000	Indic. Yr. Divd.:	NA
Total Assets:	$10,263,000	Net Worth:	$2,489,000	Debt/ Equity:	NA

Quest Oil Corp

2038 Corte Del Nogal, Ste. 110, Carlsbad, CA, 92011; *PH:* 1-760-804-8844

General - Incorporation	NV	Stock- Price on:12/24/2007	NA
Employees	NA	Stock Exchange	OTC
Auditor	Malone & Bailey, PC	Ticker Symbol	QOIL
Stk Agt	Empire Stock Transfer Inc.	Outstanding Shares	NA
Counsel	The Baum Law Firm, PC	E.P.S.	-$0.003
DUNS No.	NA	Shareholders	NA

Business: The groups principle activity is acquiring and participating in exploration stage oil and gas properties around the globe. In the year 2005, the group acquired Wallstin Petroleum, LLC. The group operates from the United States and Canada.

Primary SIC and add'l.: 1311

CIK No: 0001089104

Subsidiaries: Petrostar Oil Services Inc, Quest Canada Corporation, Wallstin Petroleum LLC

Officers: James B. Panther/Dir., CEO, Pres., Phillip C. Scott/CFO

Directors: James B. Panther/Dir., CEO, Pres.

Financial Data: Fiscal Year End:03/31   Latest Annual Data: 3/31/2006

Year	Sales	Net Income
2006	$1,723,000	-$9,258,000
2005	NA	-$998,000
2004	$1,000	-$426,000

Curr. Assets:	$1,633,000	Curr. Liab.:	$538,000		
Plant, Equip.:	$1,871,000	Total Liab.:	$741,000	Indic. Yr. Divd.:	NA
Total Assets:	$6,964,000	Net Worth:	$6,223,000	Debt/ Equity:	NA

Quest Resource Corp

9520 N May, Ste. 300, Oklahoma City, OK, 73120; *PH:* 1-405-488-1304; *Fax:* 1-405-840-9897; *http://* www.qrcp.net

General - Incorporation	NV	Stock- Price on:12/24/2007	$11.73
Employees	265	Stock Exchange	NDQ
Auditor	Cawley & Gillespie & Assoc., Inc.	Ticker Symbol	QRCP
Stk Agt	UMB Bank	Outstanding Shares	22,220,000
Counsel	Quest Cherokee LLC	E.P.S.	-$2.67
DUNS No.	NA	Shareholders	NA

Business: The group's principal activities are to acquire, produce, transport, explore and develop natural gas (coal bed methane) in a ten county region. The group also owns and operates a gas gathering pipeline network of 600 miles in length within this basin. The group operates in three segments: pipeline transmission, oil and gas production, and oil and gas wells and pipeline development and servicing. As on 07-Nov-2002, the group acquired stp cherokee, inc.

Primary SIC and add'l.: 4923 1389 4932 4612 1311

CIK No: 0000775351

Subsidiaries: Bluestem Pipeline, LLC, J-W Gas Gathering, LLC, Ponderosa Gas Pipeline Company, Producers Service, Incorporated, Quest Cherokee Oilfield Services, LLC, Quest Cherokee, LLC, Quest Energy Service, Inc., Quest Oil & Gas Corporation, STP Cherokee, Inc

Officers: Jerry D. Cash/46/Chmn., CEO, Pres./$669,941.00, Richard Marlin/55/Exec. VP - Engineering/$602,711.00, David E. Grose/55/CFO/$666,545.00, David Bolton/39/Exec. VP - Land/$222,208.00, David C. Lawler/40/COO, Steven L. Hochstein/50/Exec. VP - Exploration, A&D

Directors: Jerry D. Cash/46/Chmn., CEO, Pres., James B. Kite/Dir., John C. Garrison/55/Dir., Jon H. Rateau/50/Dir., Malone N. Mitchell/46/Dir., William H. Damon/55/Dir.

Owners: David W. Bolton, James B. Kite/4.20%, John C. Garrison, Jon H. Rateau, Richard A. Hoover, William H. Damon, Wellington Management Company, LLP/7.30%, Insiders/14.20%, N. Malone Mitchell, Jerry D. Cash/7.80%, Richard Marlin, David Grose

Financial Data: Fiscal Year End:12/31   Latest Annual Data: 12/31/2006

Year	Sales	Net Income
2006	$60,251,000	-$48,478,000
2005	$48,893,000	-$31,941,000
2004	$30,011,000	-$393,000

Curr. Assets:	$70,676,000	Curr. Liab.:	$27,411,000		
Plant, Equip.:	$378,375,000	Total Liab.:	$261,515,000	Indic. Yr. Divd.:	NA
Total Assets:	$463,300,000	Net Worth:	$117,354,000	Debt/ Equity:	1.9828

Quest Software Inc

5 Polaris Way, Aliso Viejo, CA, 92656; *PH:* 1-949-754-8000; *Fax:* 1-949-754-8999; *http://* www.quest.com

General - Incorporation	CA	Stock- Price on:12/24/2007	$16.35
Employees	2,763	Stock Exchange	NDQ
Auditor	Deloitte & Touche LLP	Ticker Symbol	QSFT
Stk Agt	U.S. Stock Transfer Corp	Outstanding Shares	101,530,000
Counsel	Wilson Sonsini Goodrich & Rosati	E.P.S.	$0.39
DUNS No.	NA	Shareholders	NA

Business: The group's principle activity is to develop, sell and support software products. Such products improve the customers' ability to develop, deploy and manage their packaged and custom software applications and associated software infrastructure components such as databases, application servers and operating systems. The products are adopted for applications such as oracle financials peoplesoft, sap and siebel. The group also provides consulting, training and support services to its customers. It has research and development subsidiaries in Russia, Israel and Canada and sales subsidiaries in Europe, Canada, Australia, Japan and Latin America for marketing, distribution and support of products and services. The group's quarterly revenue for September 2007 was 152.15 millions of USD.

Primary SIC and add'l.: 7372 7375 7379

CIK No: 0001088033

Subsidiaries: 1397639 Ontario Ltd., 881229 Alberta Ltd., Active Concepts Pty. Ltd., Active Concepts, Inc., Aelita Software Corporation, Aelita Software Limited, AfterMail Limited, DB Associates IT Pty. Ltd., Discus Data Solutions, Inc., eCritical Corporation, Fastlane Technologies (UK) Limited, Fastlane Technologies Corporation, Fastlane Technologies GmbH, Fresh Dew Investments Limited, Imceda Software Australia Pty. Ltd. 56 Subsidiaries included in the Index

Officers: Vincent C. Smith/Chmn., CEO, Anthony Foley/Sr. VP - Worldwide Sales, Carrie Reber/Dir. - Product Public Relations, Lora Deeds/Public, Analyst Relations Active Dir.y, Identity Management, Sharepoint Solutions, Daphne Kent/Application Management Solutions, Rachel

Gross/Public, Analyst Relations, Database Management Solutions, Scott Davidson/Sr. VP, CFO, Johannes Ahrends/Oracle Expert, Mike Ault/Oracle Expert, Claudia Fernandez/SQL Server, DB2, Oracle, Sybase Expert, Steven Feuerstein/Oracle PL, SQL Expert, David Gugick/Microsoft SQL Server MVP, Guy Harrison/Oracle, Mysql Expert, Kevin Kline/Microsoft SQL Server MVP, Patrick O'Keeffe/SQL Server Expert *(28 Officers included in Index)*

Directors: Vincent C. Smith/Chmn., CEO, John H. Dirks/Dir., Kevin M. Klausmeyer/Dir., Raymond J. Lane/Dir., Jerry Murdock/Dir., Augustine L. Nieto/Dir., Paul Sallaberry/Dir.

Owners: Insiders/34.20%, Kingdon Capital Management, LLC/5.10%, FMR Corp./14.20%, Kevin M. Klausmeyer, Vincent C. Smith/32.10%, Jerry Murdock, Raymond J. Lane, Paul A. Sallaberry

Financial Data: *Fiscal Year End:* 12/31 *Latest Annual Data:* 12/31/2005

Year	Sales	Net Income
2005	$476,382,000	$41,798,000
2004	$389,463,000	$47,220,000
2003	$304,288,000	$21,516,000

Curr. Assets:	$338,582,000	**Curr. Liab.:**	$230,624,000	**P/E Ratio:**	41.92
Plant, Equip.:	$82,845,000	**Total Liab.:**	$277,640,000	**Indic. Yr. Divd.:**	NA
Total Assets:	$973,007,000	**Net Worth:**	$695,367,000	**Debt/ Equity:**	NA

Questar Assessment Inc

Formerly: Touchstone Applied Science Assoc Inc
4 Hardscrabble Hts., Brewster, NY, 10509; *PH:* 1-845-277-8100; *http://* www.tasa.com

General - Incorporation	DE	**Stock** - Price on:12/24/2007	NA
Employees	64	Stock Exchange	OTC
Auditor	Lazar Levine & Felix LLP	Ticker Symbol	QUSA
Stk Agt	American Stock Transfer & Trust Co.	Outstanding Shares	NA
Counsel	Rider, Weiner, Frankel	E.P.S	$0.18
DUNS No.	07-096-1024	Shareholders	NA

Business: The group's principal activity is to develop, publish and distribute proprietary instructional and assessment products to elementary and secondary schools, colleges and universities throughout the United States. The group's operations are carried out through two segments: assessment and instructional. The assessment segment designs, develops and evaluates assessment needs for schools, school districts and test and textbook publishers. The instructional segment designs, publishes and distributes 'consumable' student workbooks for grades k-6 and creates and publishes books, pamphlets and test preparation materials for teachers, students and parents.

Primary SIC and add'l.: 8748 2731 7372

CIK No: 0000726603

Subsidiaries: Achievement Data, Inc., Assessment and Evaluation Concepts Inc., Beck Evaluation and Testing Associates, Inc.

Officers: Andrew L. Simon/Chmn., CEO, Michael D. Beck/Dir., Sr. VP, Stephen H. Ivens/National Consultant, Midwest, Michigan, Minnesota, Wisconsin, Gary Nelson/Sales Representative - Connecticut, Massachusetts, Rhode Island, Michael Dorsey/VP - National Sales, Ed Hulefeld/Regional Sales Mgr. - Delaware, Maryland, New Jersey, Pennsylvania, Virginia, West Virginia, District, Columbia, Marty Winn/Regional Sales Mgr. - Arizona, California, Nevada, New Mexico, Oregon, Utah, Washington, Thomas J. Fitzgibbon/Consultant - Florida, Linda G. Straley/Dir., VP, Sec., Pasquale J. Devito/Sr. VP, James Williams/CFO, VP

Directors: Andrew L. Simon/Chmn., CEO, Steven R. Berger/Dir., Donald W. Hughes/Dir., Linda G. Straley/Dir., VP, Sec., Chris L. Nguyen/Dir., Thomas G. Struzzieri/Dir., Theodore Naegeli/Dir., Michael D. Beck/Dir., Sr. VP, David L. Warnock/Dir., Martin E. Maleska/Dir.

Owners: Midsouth Investor Fund L.P., Chris L. Nguyen, Donald W. Hughes, Andrew L. Simon, Steven R. Berger, Kevin Gruneich, David L. Warnock, Thomas G. Struzzieri, Cahill, Warnock Strategic, Linda G. Straley, Michael D. Beck, Theodore Naegeli, Camden Partners Strategic Fund III, L.P., Insiders

Financial Data: *Fiscal Year End:* 10/31 *Latest Annual Data:* 10/31/2006

Year	Sales	Net Income
2006	$23,686,000	-$1,125,000
2005	$11,687,000	$475,000
2004	$11,185,000	$823,000

Curr. Assets:	$10,827,000	**Curr. Liab.:**	$8,825,000		
Plant, Equip.:	$3,734,000	**Total Liab.:**	$22,019,000	**Indic. Yr. Divd.:**	NA
Total Assets:	$36,658,000	**Net Worth:**	$14,639,000	**Debt/ Equity:**	NA

Questar Corp

180 E 100 S St., Salt Lake City, UT, 84145; *PH:* 1-801-324-5000; *Fax:* 1-801-324-5483; *http://* www.questarcorp.com

General - Incorporation	UT	**Stock** - Price on:12/24/2007	$54.27
Employees	2,188	Stock Exchange	NYSE
Auditor	Ernst & Young LLP	Ticker Symbol	STR
Stk Agt	Corporate Stock Transfer	Outstanding Shares	172,410,000
Counsel	Skadden, Meagher & Flom LLP	E.P.S	$2.73
DUNS No.	12-120-8789	Shareholders	NA

Business: The groups principle activity is to deliver natural gas. The group operates through four business segments namely gas and oil exploration and production, midstream field services, interstate gas transportation and retail gas distribution. The group operates from United States.

Primary SIC and add'l.: 1321 1311 6719 3669 4922 4924

CIK No: 0000751652

Subsidiaries: natural gas-focused energy company, Public Utility Holding Company, Questar Employee Services, Inc, Questar Energy Trading Company, Questar Exploration and Production Company, Questar Gas Company, Questar Gas Management Company, Questar InfoComm, Inc, Questar Market Resources Company, Questar Market Resources, Inc, Questar Pipeline, Questar Pipeline Company, Wexpro Company

Officers: Keith O. Rattie/Chmn., CEO, Pres./$4,014,503.00, Charles B. Stanley/Dir., Exec. VP/$3,200,637.00, Ronald W. Jibson/VP - Operations, Management Questar Gas, Chad Jones/Dir. - Communication, Perry H. Richards/VP - Questar Gas Management Company, James R. Livsey/VP - Wexpro Company, Eric L. Dady/General Counsel - Management Questar Marketing Resources, David M. Curtis/VP, Controller, Kelly B. Maxfield/VP - Information Technology, Administration, Scott C. Brown/General Counsel, Shahab Saeed/COO, VP - Questar Infocomm, Lawrence A. Conti/VP - Operations, Gas Control, Management Questar Pipeline, Alan K. Allred/Exec. VP/$1,506,990.00, Allan R. Bradley/Sr. VP, Stephen E. Parks/CFO, Sr. VP/$1,432,570.00 *(28 Officers included in Index)*

Directors: Keith O. Rattie/Chmn., CEO, Pres., M. W. Scoggins/60/Dir., Harris H. Simmons/53/Dir., Charles B. Stanley/Dir., Exec. VP, James A. Harmon/72/Dir., Bruce A. Williamson/48/Dir., Phillips S. Baker/48/Dir., Teresa Beck/53/Dir., R. D. Cash/65/Dir., Richard L. Flury/60/Dir., Robert E. McKee/61/Dir., Gary G. Michael/67/Dir.

Owners: Alan K. Allred/0.18%, Thomas C. Jepperson/0.10%, Robert E. McKee, M. W. Scoggins, Teresa Beck, Phillips S. Baker, S. E. Parks/0.41%, R. D. Cash/0.85%, Harris H. Simmons, Charles B. Stanley/0.29%, Insiders/2.79%, Keith O. Rattie/0.66%, James A. Harmon, Gary G. Michael, Bruce A. Williamson *(16 Owners included in Index)*

Financial Data: *Fiscal Year End:* 12/31 *Latest Annual Data:* 12/31/2006

Year	Sales	Net Income
2006	$2,835,600,000	$444,100,000
2005	$2,724,888,000	$325,681,000
2004	$1,901,431,000	$229,301,000

Curr. Assets:	$753,400,000	**Curr. Liab.:**	$678,900,000	**P/E Ratio:**	20.79
Plant, Equip.:	$4,091,400,000	**Total Liab.:**	$2,859,200,000	**Indic. Yr. Divd.:**	$0.490
Total Assets:	$5,064,700,000	**Net Worth:**	$2,205,500,000	**Debt/ Equity:**	0.4322

Questar Gas Co

PO Box 45360, Salt Lake City, UT, 84145; *PH:* 1-803-324-5497; *http://* www.questarcorp.com

General - Incorporation	UT	**Stock** - Price on:12/24/2007	NA
Employees	NA	Stock Exchange	NA
Auditor	Ernst & Young LLP	Ticker Symbol	NA
Stk Agt	Wells Fargo Shareowner Services	Outstanding Shares	NA
Counsel	NA	E.P.S	NA
DUNS No.	00-793-9069	Shareholders	NA

Business: The group's principle activity is to distribute gas to customers in the major populated area of Utah and also serves customers in eastern, central and southwestern Utah. The company's distribution system consists of 90% of Utah's population and captures a market share of over 90% for furnace and water heaters. The distribution system and annual gas supply plan of the company is designed to handle day demand requirements. The company transports the gas through an affiliated company questar pipeline. The group operates from United States.

Primary SIC and add'l.: 4932 4923 5169 4924 4922

CIK No: 0000068589

Subsidiaries: Questar Corporation

Officers: Alan K. Allred/CEO, Pres., Ronald W. Jibson/VP - Operations, Shahab Saeed/VP, David M. Curtis/VP, Controller, Jim Grambihler/Contact - Natural Gas Vehicles, Carl B. Galbraith/Dir. - Community, Business Development, Brad L. Markus/Mgr. - Community, Business Development, Kelly B. Maxfield/VP - Information Technology, Administration, Craig Davis/Contact - Residential, Gene Valle/Contact - Residential, Brad Simons/Contact - Commercial, Industrial, Bruce Rickenbach/Contact - Commercial, Industrial, Sam Blundell/Contact - Commercial, Industrial, Stephanie Gallegos/Contact - Commercial, Industrial, Tom Willis/Contact - Commercial, Industrial *(20 Officers included in Index)*

Directors: Keith O. Rattie/Chmn., Harris H. Simmons/Dir., Teresa Beck/Dir., Gary G. Michael/Dir., Bruce A. Williamson/Dir.

Questar Pipeline Co

180 E 100 S St., Salt Lake City, UT, 84145; *PH:* 1-801-324-2400; *http://* www.questar.com

General - Incorporation	UT	**Stock** - Price on:12/24/2007	NA
Employees	NA	Stock Exchange	NA
Auditor	Ernst & Young LLP	Ticker Symbol	NA
Stk Agt	Wells Fargo Shareowner Services	Outstanding Shares	NA
Counsel	NA	E.P.S	NA
DUNS No.	09-202-7077	Shareholders	NA

Business: The group's principal activity is to transport natural gas in the rocky mountain states of Utah, Wyoming and Colorado. It also provides storage services in Utah and Wyoming. The group is a wholly owned subsidiary of questar regulated services company. It provides interruptible storage service at clay basin and allows firm storage service customers the right to release their injection and withdrawal rights to other parties.

Primary SIC and add'l.: 4922 4932 4924

CIK No: 0000764044

Officers: Allan R. Bradley/Dir., CEO, Pres., Stephen E. Parks/Sr. VP, CFO, Lawrence A. Conti/VP - Operations, Gas Control, Shahab Saeed/VP, COO - Questar Infocomm, David M. Curtis/VP, Controller, Principal Accounting Officer, Kelly B. Maxfield/VP - Information Technology, Administrative Services, Scott C. Brown/General Counsel, Chad Jones/Dir. - Communication

Directors: Allan R. Bradley/Dir., CEO, Pres., Keith O. Rattie/54/Chmn., Charles B. Stanley/49/Dir., Bruce A. Williamson/48/Dir., M. W. Scoggins/60/Dir., Phillips S. Baker/48/Dir., Teresa Beck/53/Dir., R. D. Cash/65/Dir., Richard L. Flury/60/Dir., James A. Harmon/72/Dir., Robert E. Mckee/61/Dir., Gary G. Michael/67/Dir., Harris H. Simmons/53/Dir.

Questcor Pharmaceuticals Inc

3260 Whipple Rd., Union City, CA, 94587; *PH:* 1-510-400-0700; *Fax:* 1-510-400-0799; *http://* www.questcor.com

General - Incorporation	CA	**Stock** - Price on:12/24/2007	$0.4798
Employees	70	Stock Exchange	AMEX
Auditor	Odenberg, Muranishi & Co. LLP	Ticker Symbol	QSC
Stk Agt	Computershare Trust Co	Outstanding Shares	69,040,000
Counsel	Latham & Watkins	E.P.S	$0.00
DUNS No.	79-757-5172	Shareholders	NA

Business: The group's principle activities include developing and marketing acute care and critical care hospital, specialty pharmaceutical and related healthcare products. The products of the company are glofil-125, inulin, ethamolin and dermaflo. Glofil and inulin are two injectable drugs to assess kidney function and its treatment. Ethamolin is an injectable drug to treat bleeding esophageal varices. Nutramax products are topical triple antibiotic wound care products. The customers of the company include large drug wholesalers and distributors and certain hospitals and treatment centers. In Jun 2003, the group acquired nascobal(R) an fda approved nasal gel formulation of cyanocobalamin usp from nastech. The group operates from United States.

Primary SIC and add'l.: 2834

CIK No: 0000891288

CIK No: 0000891288

Officers: Jim Fares/45/CEO, Pres./$682,100.00, Steve Cartt/Exec. VP - Commercial Development, George Stuart/VP - Finance, CFO/$370,968.00, Dave Medeiros/VP - Pharmaceutical Operations, Stephen L. Cartt/Exec. VP - Corporate Development/$421,410.00, David J. Medeiros/VP - Pharmaceutical Operations/$380,647.00, Steven C. Halladay/Sr. VP - Clinical, Regulatory Affairs

Directors: Neal C. Bradsher/Dir., Albert Hansen/53/Dir., Gregg Lapointe/49/Dir., Virgil D. Thompson/Dir., Don M. Bailey/Dir., David Young/Dir.

Owners: George M. Stuart, Albert Hansen/3.06%, David J. Medeiros/1.70%, Steven C. Halladay, Sigma-Tau Finanziaria SpA and its affiliates/20.02%, Eric J. Liebler, Insiders/13.98%, Special Situations Private Equity Fund, L.P. and its affiliates/5.85%, Virgil D. Thompson, David Young, Don M. Bailey, Broadwood Partners, L.P./5.03%, Stephen L. Cartt, Gregg Lapointe, James L. Fares/2.39% *(17 Owners included in Index)*

Financial Data: **Fiscal Year End:**12/31 **Latest Annual Data:** 12/31/2006

Year	Sales	Net Income
2006	$12,788,000	-$10,109,000
2005	$14,162,000	$7,392,000
2004	$18,404,000	-$832,000

Curr. Assets:	$23,984,000	**Curr. Liab.:**	$6,478,000		
Plant, Equip.:	$665,000	**Total Liab.:**	$13,538,000	**Indic. Yr. Divd.:**	NA
Total Assets:	$29,635,000	**Net Worth:**	$16,097,000	**Debt/ Equity:**	NA

Quick-Med Technologies Inc

3427 SW 42nd Way, Gainesville, FL, 32608; **PH:** 1-561-750-4202; **Fax:** 1-561-750-4203; **http://** www.quickmedtech.com; **Email:** info@quickmed-technologies.com

General - Incorporation	NV	**Stock**- Price on:12/24/2007	$0.75
Employees	8	Stock Exchange	OTC
Auditor	Daszkal Bolton LLP	Ticker Symbol	QMDT
Stk Agt	Continental Stock Transfer & Trust Co	Outstanding Shares	30,430,000
Counsel	NA	E.P.S.	-$0.07
DUNS No.	NA	Shareholders	NA

Business: The groups principle activity is life sciences company focused on developing proprietary, broad based technologies in medical and consumer healthcare markets. The group markets its products under the tradenames include MultiStat (TM) and NIMBUS(TM). The group operates from the United States.

Primary SIC and add'l.: 3841

CIK No: 0001088206

Officers: Ladd J. Greeno/CEO, Allan Lane/Chemist, Research Team, Albina Mikhaylova/Expert in Bio, Medical Engineering, Material Science, Scientific Team, David S. Lerner/Dir., Founder, Pres., Paul G. Cerjan/Dir., VP - Worldwide Military Affairs, Gerald M. Olderman/Dir., VP - Research, Development, Commercialization, Scientific Team, Gregory S. Schultz/Dir., VP - Laboratory, Clinical Research, Scientific Team, George E. Friel/Dir., VP - Chemical, Biological Affairs, Nam H. Nguyen/CFO, Roy D. Carr/Dir. - Research, Development Medical Devices, Natasha A. Sorobey/Corp. Sec. - Corporate, Investor Relations, Christopher D. Batich/Scientific Team, Expert in Bio, Medical Engineering, Material Science, William Toreki/Scientific Team, Expert in Polymer Chemistry, Bernd Liesenfeld/Scientific Team, Expert in Materials Science, Engineering, Susan Leander/Research Scientist *(19 Officers included in Index)*

Directors: Michael R. Granito/Chmn., David S. Lerner/Dir., Founder, Pres., Richard F. Caffrey/Dir., Paul G. Cerjan/Dir., VP - Worldwide Military Affairs, Gerald M. Olderman/Dir., VP - Research, Development, Commercialization, Scientific Team, Gregory S. Schultz/Dir., VP - Laboratory, Clinical Research, Scientific Team, George E. Friel/Dir., VP - Chemical, Biological Affairs

Owners: Gregory S. Schultz/2.90%, Michael R. Granito/36.00%, Gerald M. Olderman/2.40%, Richard F. Caffrey/0.40%, Cheryl L. Turnbull/0.10%, Nam H. Nguyen/2.80%, Insiders/82.70%, David S. Lerner/11.50%, Phronesis Partners, L.P./19.50%, Ladd J. Greeno/1.50%, Paul G. Cerjan/2.40%, Natasha A. Sorobey/1.90%, George E. Friel/1.40%

Financial Data: **Fiscal Year End:**06/30 **Latest Annual Data:** 6/30/2006

Year	Sales	Net Income
2006	$1,230,000	-$1,701,000
2005	$182,000	-$1,927,000
2004	$48,000	-$2,369,000

Curr. Assets:	$229,000	**Curr. Liab.:**	$245,000		
Plant, Equip.:	$16,000	**Total Liab.:**	$1,807,000	**Indic. Yr. Divd.:**	NA
Total Assets:	$526,000	**Net Worth:**	-$1,281,000	**Debt/ Equity:**	NA

Quicklogic Corp

1277 Orleans Dr., Sunnyvale, CA, 94089; **PH:** 1-408-990-4000; **Fax:** 1-408-990-4040; **http://** www.quicklogic.com; **Email:** info@quicklogic.com

General - Incorporation	DE	**Stock**- Price on:12/24/2007	$2.71
Employees	147	Stock Exchange	NDQ
Auditor	PricewaterhouseCoopers LLP	Ticker Symbol	QUIK
Stk Agt	PricewaterhouseCoopers LLP	Outstanding Shares	28,860,000
Counsel	NA	E.P.S.	-$0.48
DUNS No.	60-668-6269	Shareholders	NA

Business: The group's principle activities are to develop, market and support advanced field programmable gate array semiconductors (fpga), embedded standard product (esp) and associated software tools. The group also licenses quickworks and quicktools design software and sell programming hardware. The products are based on vialink technology, user-programmable platform and the associated software tools used for system design. The vialink technology provides high security, low power and design efficiency. The user-programmable platform facilitates full utilization of a device's logic cells, clocks and input/output pins. Software tools enable customers to efficiently implement their designs using the group's products. The customers of the group include IBM, motorola, samsung, sony and honeywell. The products are sold through a network of sales managers, independent sales representatives and electronics distributors in North America, Europe and Asia. The group's quarterly revenue for September 2007 was 9.03 millions of USD.

Primary SIC and add'l.: 3674 7372

CIK No: 0000882508

Subsidiaries: Q Aquisition Corporation, QuickLogic Canada Company, QuickLogic GmbH, QuickLogic International, Inc., QuickLogic Kabushiki Kaisha, QuickLogic Software (India) Private Ltd

Officers: Thomas E. Hart/Chmn., CEO, Pres./$662,628.00, Terry L. Barrette/VP - Operations/$268,789.00, Carl M. Mills/VP - Finance, CFO/$271,869.00, Timothy Saxe/CTO - Sr. Engineering Executive/$300,282.00, Catriona Meney/VP - Human Resources, Development/$149,732.00, Alan Tsun/VP - Advanced Solutions Development, Canadian Operations, Brian C. Faith/VP - Solutions Marketing, Ajith Dasari/VP - Worldwide Engineering, Andrew J. Pease/VP - Worldwide Sales, Andrea Vedanayagam/Dir. - Corporate Communications

Directors: Thomas E. Hart/Chmn., CEO, Pres., Nicholas Aretakis/Dir., Arturo Krueger/Dir., Gary H. Tauss/Dir., Michael J. Callahan/Dir., Christine Russell/Dir., Hide L. Tanigami/Dir.

Owners: Insiders/9.55%, State of Wisconsin Investment Board/5.74%, Michael J. Callahan, Andrew J. Pease, Gary H. Tauss, Thomas E. Hart/5.79%, Christine Russell, Dimensional Fund Advisors Inc./5.07%, Timothy Saxe/1.73%, Arturo Krueger, Terry L. Barrette, Catriona Meney, Carl M. Mills/1.05%

Financial Data: **Fiscal Year End:**01/01 **Latest Annual Data:** 12/31/2006

Year	Sales	Net Income
2006	$34,924,000	-$9,214,000
2004	$44,612,000	-$8,832,000

Curr. Assets:	$39,948,000	**Curr. Liab.:**	$11,249,000		
Plant, Equip.:	$5,480,000	**Total Liab.:**	$12,867,000	**Indic. Yr. Divd.:**	NA
Total Assets:	$50,235,000	**Net Worth:**	$37,368,000	**Debt/ Equity:**	0.0384

Quicksilver Resources Inc

777 W Rosedale St., Ste. 300, Fort Worth, TX, 76104; **PH:** 1-817-665-5000; **Fax:** 1-817-665-5004; **http://** www.qrinc.com

General - Incorporation	DE	**Stock**- Price on:12/24/2007	$48.4
Employees	488	Stock Exchange	NYSE
Auditor	Deloitte & Touche LLP	Ticker Symbol	KWK
Stk Agt	Mellon Investor Services LLC	Outstanding Shares	78,160,000
Counsel	Cantey & Hanger	E.P.S.	$1.25
DUNS No.	NA	Shareholders	NA

Business: The group's principal activity is to acquire, develop, explore, produce and sell natural gas, crude oil and natural gas liquid. It is also engaged in the gathering, processing and transmission of natural gas. The group pursues business through the acquisition and development of oil and gas mineral leases, gas gathering systems and producing natural gas and crude oil properties. It currently has an interest in natural gas and crude oil mineral leases, a pipeline transmission system, gas gathering and processing facilities and wells producing hydrocarbons that are located principally in the states of Michigan, Wyoming, Montana and Indiana as well as in Canada. The group holds and owns 5,100 producing wells and operates 41% of these wells.

Primary SIC and add'l.: 1311 1321 1382 4612

CIK No: 0001060990

Subsidiaries: Beaver Creek Pipeline, LLC, Cowtown Drilling, Inc.Texas, Cowtown Pipeline Funding, Inc., Cowtown Pipeline Management,Inc., GTG Pipeline Corporation, Mercury Michigan Inc., MGV Energy Inc., Terra Energy Ltd.

Officers: Glenn Darden/Dir., CEO, Pres./$978,292.00, John C. Cirone/Sr. Pres., General Counsel, Sec./$589,597.00, Marlu S. Hiller/VP, Treasurer, Dana W. Johnson/COO, Sr. VP - Quicksilver Resources Canada Inc, Anne D. Self/Dir., VP - Human Resources, Jeff Cook/Exec. VP - Operation, Philip W. Cook/Sr. VP, CFO/$581,350.00, William S. Buckler/VP - US Operations, Robert N. Wagner/VP - Reservoir Engineering, Wayne D. Blair/VP, Controller, Richard C. Buterbaugh/VP - Investor Relations, Corporate Planning, Stan G. Page/VP - US Operation, John C. Regan/VP - Controller, Chief Accounting Officer

Directors: Glenn Darden/Dir., CEO, Pres., Thomas F. Darden/Chmn., Anne D. Self/Dir., VP - Human Resources, Steven M. Morris/Dir., James A. Hughes/Dir., Mark J. Warner/Dir., Yandell W. Rogers/Dir., Byron W. Dunn/Dir.

Owners: Quicksilver Energy L.P., Steven M. Morris, Thomas F. Darden, Neuberger Berman Inc., John C. Cirone, Pennsylvania Management, LLC, Philip W. Cook, Yandell W. Rogers, Paul J. Cook, FMR Corp., Insiders, Anne Darden Self, James A. Hughes, Glenn Darden, Capital Research and Management Company *(16 Owners included in Index)*

Financial Data: **Fiscal Year End:**12/31 **Latest Annual Data:** 12/31/2006

Year	Sales	Net Income
2006	$390,362,000	$93,719,000
2005	$310,448,000	$87,434,000
2004	$179,729,000	$31,272,000

Curr. Assets:	$170,964,000	**Curr. Liab.:**	$199,389,000	**P/E Ratio:**	41.02
Plant, Equip.:	$1,679,280,000	**Total Liab.:**	$1,299,815,000	**Indic. Yr. Divd.:**	NA
Total Assets:	$1,882,912,000	**Net Worth:**	$575,666,000	**Debt/ Equity:**	1.8997

Quidel Corp

10165 McKellar Ct., San Diego, CA, 92121; **PH:** 1-858-552-1100; **Fax:** 1-858-546-8955; **http://** www.quidel.com; **Email:** ir@quidel.com

General - Incorporation	DE	**Stock**- Price on:12/24/2007	$15.32
Employees	266	Stock Exchange	NDQ
Auditor	Ernst & Young LLP	Ticker Symbol	QDEL
Stk Agt	American Stock Transfer & Trust Co.	Outstanding Shares	32,440,000
Counsel	Gibson, Dunn & Crutcher LLP	E.P.S.	$0.72
DUNS No.	09-702-0739	Shareholders	NA

Business: The group's principal activity is to develop, manufacture and market point-of-care rapid diagnostics for detection of human medical conditions and illness. The products of the group diagnose acute and chronic conditions focused on women's and family health. The products include quickvue, quickvue+, quickvue advance, ovuquick, conceive, cards, rapidvue, bluetest, metra, pyrilinks qus-2, alkphase-b, novocalcin, chondrex, rapignost, rapimat and femexam. These products are marketed to professionals for use in the physician offices and clinical laboratories through a network of national and regional distributors and through organizations that provide store brand products. The major customers of the group include cardinal healthcare corporation, sumitomo seiyaku biomedical co ltd and mckesson corporation.

Primary SIC and add'l.: 2835

CIK No: 0000353569

Subsidiaries: Litmus Concepts, Inc., Metra Biosystems, Inc., Osteo Sciences Corporation, Pacific Biotech, Inc

Officers: Caren L. Mason/Dir., CEO, Pres./$1,390,136.00, Robert J. Bujarski/Sr. VP, General Counsel, Corp. Sec./$471,266.00, Mark E. Paiz/COO/$812,662.00, Thomas J. Foley/CTO/$699,625.00, John M. Radak/CFO, Richard Tarbox/Sr. VP, Corporate Development Officer, Scot M. McLeod/Sr. VP - Operations

Directors: Caren L. Mason/Dir., CEO, Pres., Douglas S. Harrington/55/Dir., Mark A. Pulido/Dir., Thomas D. Brown/Dir., Mary Lake Polan/Dir., Rod F. Dammeyer/Dir., Jack W. Schuler/Dir.

Owners: Thomas D. Brown, Douglas S. Harrington, Entities affiliated with Larry N. Feinberg/9.90%, Jack W. Schuler/9.50%, Mark E. Paiz/1.10%, Paul E. Landers, Thomas J. Foley, Rod F. Dammeyer, Mary Lake Polan, Caren L. Mason/1.50%, Mark A. Pulido, Robert J. Bujarski, T. Rowe Price Associates, Inc./6.90%, Insiders/13.60%

Financial Data: *Fiscal Year End:*12/31 *Latest Annual Data:* 12/31/2006

Year	Sales	Net Income
2006	$106,015,000	$21,718,000
2005	$92,299,000	-$9,259,000
2004	$78,691,000	-$6,287,000

Curr. Assets:	$67,669,000	**Curr. Liab.:**	$14,606,000	**P/E Ratio:**	24.71
Plant, Equip.:	$20,058,000	**Total Liab.:**	$23,772,000	**Indic. Yr. Divd.:**	NA
Total Assets:	$127,048,000	**Net Worth:**	$103,276,000	**Debt/ Equity:**	NA

Quigley Corp

The Kells Bldg., 621 Shady Retreat Rd., Doylestown, PA, 18901; *PH:* 1-267-880-1100; *Fax:* 1-267-880-1153; *http://* www.quigleyco.com; *Email:* customercare@quigleyco.com

General - Incorporation	NV	**Stock**- Price on:12/24/2007	$5.11
Employees	132	Stock Exchange	NDQ
Auditor	Amper, Politziner & Mattia P.C	Ticker Symbol	QGLY
Stk Agt	American Stock Transfer & Trust Co.	Outstanding Shares	12,680,000
Counsel	Eastburn & Gray	E.P.S	-$0.23
DUNS No.	62-055-7298	Shareholders	NA

Business: The group's principal activities are to develop, manufacture, market and distribute cold remedy products to the consumer through over-the-counter market place. The group has 3 segments: cold remedy products, health and wellness and ethical pharmaceutical. The cold remedy products include cold-eeze and cold remedy lozenge. Health and wellness segment markets and sells a range of health and wellness products. Ethical pharmaceutical is involved in research and development activity to develop patent applications for potential pharmaceutical products. The trade names include cold-eeze(R), cold-eeze(R) sugar free, cold-eeze(R) bubble gum and zigg-eeze(tm).

Primary SIC and add'l.: 2834

CIK No: 0000868278

Subsidiaries: Darius International Inc., Innerlight Global Pte. LTD, Innerlight Inc, Quigley Manufacturing Inc., Quigley Pharma Inc.

Officers: Guy J. Quigley/Chmn., CEO, Pres./$957,060.00, George J. Longo/Dir., VP, CFO/$491,570.00, Charles A. Phillips/Dir., VP, COO/$716,209.00, Richard Rosenbloom/COO

Directors: Guy J. Quigley/Chmn., CEO, Pres., Jacqueline F. Lewis/Dir., Stephen W. Wouch/Dir., Rounsevelle W. Schaum/Dir., Terrence O. Tormey/Dir., George J. Longo/Dir., VP, CFO, Charles A. Phillips/Dir., VP, COO

Owners: Insiders/41.20%, STEPHEN W. WOUCH, CHARLES A. PHILLIPS/12.20%, TERRENCE O. TORMEY, ROUNSEVELLE W. SCHAUM, GUY J. QUIGLEY/27.00%, JACQUELINE F. LEWIS/1.00%, GEORGE J. LONGO/4.70%

Financial Data: *Fiscal Year End:*12/31 *Latest Annual Data:* 12/31/2006

Year	Sales	Net Income
2006	$42,125,000	-$1,748,000
2005	$53,658,000	$3,217,000
2004	$43,948,000	$453,000

Curr. Assets:	$29,793,000	**Curr. Liab.:**	$9,252,000		
Plant, Equip.:	$4,838,000	**Total Liab.:**	$9,252,000	**Indic. Yr. Divd.:**	NA
Total Assets:	$34,845,000	**Net Worth:**	$25,529,000	**Debt/ Equity:**	NA

Quiksilver Inc

15202 Graham St., Huntington Beach, CA, 92649; *PH:* 1-714-889-2200; *Fax:* 1-714-889-2315; *http://* www.quiksilver.com; *Email:* zqk@quiksilver.com

General - Incorporation	DE	**Stock**- Price on:12/24/2007	$14.28
Employees	9,200	Stock Exchange	NYSE
Auditor	Deloitte & Touche LLP	Ticker Symbol	ZQK
Stk Agt	American Stock Transfer & Trust Co.	Outstanding Shares	124,490,000
Counsel	Hewitt & O'neil	E.P.S	$0.54
DUNS No.	08-358-4029	Shareholders	NA

Business: The groups principle activities include designing, producing and distributing branded apparel, wintersports and golf equipment, footwear, accessories and related products. The groups products are sold under the brand names Dynastar, Look, Lange and Kerma. The group operates from United States.

Primary SIC and add'l.: 2339 2321 2311 3021 2325 2329

CIK No: 0000805305

Subsidiaries: Bakio SL, Caribbean Pty Ltd., Cariboo SARL, Cleveland Golf Asia YK, DC Australia Pty Ltd., DC Direct, Inc., DC Shoes International Ltd., DC Shoes, Inc., Echos Beach Caf SARL (renamed from DC Europe SARL), Emerald Coast SA (renamed from Gotcha SA), Escatade Ltd., Fidra, Inc., Groupe Rossignol KK, Haapiti SRL, Hawk Designs, Inc. 89 Subsidiaries included in the Index

Officers: Robert B. McKnight/Chmn., CEO, Charles S. Exon/Exec. VP - Business, Legal Affairs, Sec., General Counsel, Bernard Mariette/45/Dir., Pres., Steven L. Brink/CFO, Treasurer, Kelly Slater/36/Quiksilver Surf Team, Dane Reynolds/Quiksilver Surf Team, Fred Patacchia/Quiksilver Surf Team, Julian Wilson/Quiksilver Surf Team, Clay Marzo/Quiksilver Surf Team, Jeremy Flores/Quiksilver Surf Team, Danny Fuller/Quiksilver Surf Team, David H. Morgan/Exec. VP - Global Finance, Operations

Directors: Robert B. McKnight/Chmn., CEO, William M. Barnum/53/Dir., Michael H. Gray/Dir., Charles E. Crowe/52/Dir., Douglas K. Ammerman/56/Dir., Laurent Boix-Vives/81/Dir., Timothy M. Harmon/55/Dir., Bernard Mariette/45/Dir., Pres., Heidi J. Ueberroth/Dir.

Owners: Bernard Mariette/1.40%, PRIMECAP Management Company/6.80%, Robert B. McKnight/3.80%, Mazama Capital Management, Inc./11.70%, Steven L. Brink, Timothy M. Harmon, Charles S. Exon, FMR Corp./13.90%, Laurent Boix-Vives/2.00%, Charles E. Crowe, Michael H. Gray, Douglas K. Ammerman, David H. Morgan, William M. Barnum, Insiders/8.80%

Financial Data: *Fiscal Year End:*10/31 *Latest Annual Data:* 10/31/2006

Year	Sales	Net Income
2006	$2,362,288,000	$93,016,000
2005	$1,780,869,000	$107,120,000
2004	$1,266,939,000	$81,369,000

Curr. Assets:	$1,513,262,000	**Curr. Liab.:**	$881,405,000		
Plant, Equip.:	$439,078,000	**Total Liab.:**	$1,754,915,000	**Indic. Yr. Divd.:**	NA
Total Assets:	$2,641,528,000	**Net Worth:**	$886,613,000	**Debt/ Equity:**	NA

Quilmes Industrial (QUINSA) S.A

84, Grand Rue, Luxembourg, L-1660; ; *http://* www.quinsa.com

General - Incorporation	Grand Duchy Of Luxembourg	**Stock**- Price on:12/24/2007	$73.15
Employees	6,649	Stock Exchange	NYSE
Auditor	PricewaterhouseCoopers LLP	Ticker Symbol	LQU
Stk Agt	Bank of New York	Outstanding Shares	54,200,000
Counsel	NA	E.P.S	$3.47
DUNS No.	40-057-5296	Shareholders	NA

Business: The group's principal activities are the production and distribution of beer as well as soft drinks, hops and malt in Argentina, paraguay, uruguay, Bolivia and Chile under different brand names. Beer is produced under the quilmes brand in Argentina, the becker brand in Chile, the bremen, pilsen and baviera brands in paraguay and the pilsen and zillertal brands in uruguay. The group also imports and distributes other beers including the heineken, amstel, buckler and kaiser brands and also bottles coca-cola under license in paraguay.

Primary SIC and add'l.: 2086 2083 5149 5181 2082

CIK No: 0001010246

Subsidiaries: Agrega S.A., Aydecar S.A., CCBA S.A, Cerveceria Boliviana Nacional S.A., Cervecera Chile S.A., Cerveceria Paraguaya S.A., Cervecera y Maltera Quilmes S.A.I.C.A. y G., Colosas S.A., Compaa Salus S.A., Eco de los Andes S.A., Embotelladora 9 de Julio S.A.I.C.I. y F., Embotelladora Perla de Norte S.A.I.C.I.A. y F., Fbrica Paraguaya de Vidrios S.A., FNC S.A., Intergal S.A. 25 Subsidiaries included in the Index

Officers: Joao M. Giffoni Castro Neves/41/Dir., CEO, Pablo Gonzalez/40/VP - Logistics, Faustino Arias/47/VP - International Operations, Gustavo Castelli/49/CFO, Mariano Botas/45/VP - Corporate Affairs, Fernando Massuh/VP - People, Fernando Ragni/Head - Soft Drinks, Argentina, Hernan Redin/41/VP - Shared Business Services, Information Technology, Gustavo Troia/52/VP - Supply Chain, Adrian Gonzalez Fischer/45/VP - Sales, Distribution, Argentina, Jorge Mastroizzi/39/VP - Marketing, Argentina

Directors: Joao M. Giffoni Castro Neves/41/Dir., CEO, Alvaro Cardoso De Souza/60/Co - Chmn., Victorio Carlos De Marchi/70/Co - Chmn., Milton Seligman/57/Dir., Floreal Horacio Crespo/63/Dir., Fernando Martin Minaudo/39/Dir.

Financial Data: *Fiscal Year End:*12/31 *Latest Annual Data:* 12/31/2006

Year	Sales	Net Income
2006	$1,166,300,000	$164,600,000
2005	$954,300,000	$139,600,000
2004	$765,200,000	$99,900,000

Curr. Assets:	$535,200,000	**Curr. Liab.:**	$478,800,000		
Plant, Equip.:	$625,300,000	**Total Liab.:**	$946,300,000	**Indic. Yr. Divd.:**	$0.920
Total Assets:	$2,941,100,000	**Net Worth:**	$1,994,800,000	**Debt/ Equity:**	NA

Quinenco

Enrique Foster Sur 20, 14th Fl., Las Condes, Santiago; *PH:* 56-27507100; *Fax:* 56-27507101; *http://* www.quinenco.cl/gobierno/directores.html

General - Incorporation	Chile	**Stock**- Price on:12/24/2007	NA
Employees	13,666	Stock Exchange	NA
Auditor	PricewaterhouseCoopers	Ticker Symbol	NA
Stk Agt	NA	Outstanding Shares	NA
Counsel	NA	E.P.S	NA
DUNS No.	98-018-7553	Shareholders	NA

Business: The group principal activity is engaged in the investment in all types of personal and real, corporeal and incorporeal properties. It participates in the following business: financial services which provides financial consultations, investment banking and banking services. Food and beverages manufacture beer, wines, mineral water, carbonated drinks, and juices, pasta, edible oils and soups. Telecommunications sector provides telecommunication services such as domestic and international multi - carrier services, Internet, Web hosting, call waiting, voice mail, conference call, call blocking and isdn. Manufacturing sector manufactures cables, wires, tubes, steel sheets and aluminum profiles. Hotel and property sector develops properties and handles hotel operation. Brand names include cristal, royal guard, escudo, paulaner, budweiser, guinness, schneider, cordoba; salta, santa fe, lucchetti, napoli, talliani, romano, miraflores, oro, el dorado and dona sofia.

Primary SIC and add'l.: 1099 4899 3441 6211 2082 3990 6282

CIK No: 0001040649

Subsidiaries: Inversiones Rio Grande S.A., LQ Inversiones Financieras S.A., Madeco S.A., VTR S.A.

Officers: Francisco Perez MacKenna/48/CEO, Fernando Silva Lavin/58/Controller, Felipe Joannon Vergera/46/Business Development Mgr., Manuel Jose Noguera Ezaguire/Chief Legal Counsel, Luis Fernando Antunez Bories/CFO, Martin Rodriguez Guiraldes/45/Mgr. - Strategic Development

Directors: Andronico Luksic Craig/Vice Chmn., Guillermo Luksic Craig/Chmn., Juan Andres Fontaine Talavera/Dir., Gonzalo Duque Menendez/Dir., Hernan Buchi Buc/Dir., Jean-Paul Luksic Fontbona/Dir., Matko Maroevic Koljatic/Dir.

Quintana Maritime Ltd

Pandoras 13 & Kyprou St., Glyfada, 16674; ; *http://* www.quintanamaritime.com; *Email:* operations@quintanamaritime.com

General - Incorporation	Marshall Islands	**Stock**- Price on:12/24/2007	$15.52
Employees	53	Stock Exchange	NDQ
Auditor	Deloitte, Sofianos & Cambanis S.A	Ticker Symbol	QMAR
Stk Agt	Computershare Trust Co	Outstanding Shares	56,010,000
Counsel	NA	E.P.S	$0.47
DUNS No.	NA	Shareholders	NA

Business: The groups principal activity is to provide dry bulk marine transportation services. The groups service is dry bulk vessels transport a variety of cargoes including coal, iron ore and grain. The group operates from the United States. The net sale of the group for the year 2006 was $103,317 (thousands).

Primary SIC and add'l.: 4412

CIK No: 0001325098

Subsidiaries: Barbara Shipco LLC, Coal Age Shipco LLC, Coal Glory Shipco LLC, Coal Gypsy Shipco LLC, Coal Hunter Shipco LLC, Coal Pride Shipco LLC, Fearless Shipco LLC, Grain Express Shipco LLC, Grain Harvester Shipco LLC, Iron Anne Shipco LLC, Iron Beauty Shipco LLC, Iron Bill Shipco LLC, Iron Bradyn Shipco LLC, Iron Brooke Shipco LLC, Iron Fuzeyya Shipco LLC 31 Subsidiaries included in the Index

Officers: Stamatis Molaris/Dir., CEO, Pres., Nikos Frantzeskakis/Chief Commercial, Operations Officer, Paul J. Cornell/CFO, Michael Koutsouridis/Operations, Marine Mgr., Apostolos Apostolou/Technical Mgr., Dimos Iliopoulos/New Buildings, Drydockings Mgr., Dimitris Logothetis/Purchasing Mgr., Vassilis Koutsolakos/Financial Controller, Steve Putnam/General Counsel, Paul Lampoutis/Contact - Investor Relations, Media

Directors: Stamatis Molaris/Dir., CEO, Pres., Corbin J. Robertson/Chmn., Joseph R. Edwards/35/Dir., Gurpal Singh Grewal/Dir., James S. Nelson/Dir., Peter Costalas/Dir., Hans J. Mende/Dir., Corbin J. Robertson/37/Dir.

Owners: Insiders/16.50%, Quintana Maritime Partners, L.P./9.10%, Gurpal Singh Grewal, Steve Putman, FR X Offshore, L.P./6.90%, Joseph R. Edwards, Corbin J. Robertson/9.10%, Corbin J. Robertson, King Street Capital Management, L.L.C./7.20%, Paul J. Cornell, James S. Nelson, Hans J. Mende/4.30%, Stamatis Molaris/1.10%, Nikos Frantzeskakis, Peter Costalas

Financial Data: *Fiscal Year End:* 12/31 *Latest Annual Data:* 12/31/2006

Year		Sales		Net Income	
2006		$108,141,000		$12,744,000	
2005		$42,062,000		$5,528,000	
Curr. Assets:	$26,325,000	**Curr. Liab.:**	$57,922,000	**P/E Ratio:**	33.02
Plant, Equip.:	$1,014,362,000	**Total Liab.:**	$632,722,000	**Indic. Yr. Divd.:**	$0.960
Total Assets:	$1,057,440,000	**Net Worth:**	$424,718,000	**Debt/ Equity:**	1.6408

Quintek Technologies Inc

17951 Lyons Cir., Huntington Beach, CA, 92674; *PH:* 1-714-848-7741; *Fax:* 1-714-848-7701; *http://* www.quintek.com

General - Incorporation	CA	**Stock**- Price on:12/24/2007	$0.019
Employees	22	Stock Exchange	OTC
Auditor	Kabani & Co, Inc	Ticker Symbol	QTEK
Stk Agt	Interwest Transfer Company, Inc.	Outstanding Shares	163,520,000
Counsel	NA	E.P.S.	-$0.005
DUNS No.	NA	Shareholders	NA

Business: The group's principal activity is to develop, manufacture and distribute the q4300 technology used for recording digital images on aperture card media. The group's principal product is the q4400 desktop aperture card printer which is used by engineering departments to print directly to aperture cards from digital files without using chemicals for film development. The q4400 system is comprised of quinplot software package and the q4400 aperture card printer. Aperture cards are used by various industries which include construction, electronics, defense, automotive, machinery, amusement parks, ship building, oil refineries, utilities, railroads, government and aerospace. The customers of the group are large manufacturers or utility companies that produce complex, mechanical and electrical products in a variety of industries.

Primary SIC and add'l.: 7372

CIK No: 0001107714

Subsidiaries: Quintek Services, Inc., Sapphire Consulting Services

Officers: James Kernan/Chmn., CEO, Andrew Haag/CFO, James Tocha/Contact - East Coast Region, Teresa Kunz/Contact - Northwest Region

Directors: James Kernan/Chmn., CEO, Zubair Kazi/Member - Advisory Board, Gary Blum/Member - Advisory Board, Paul E. Himes/Member - Advisory Board, Roger Lents/Member - Advisory Board

Owners: Andrew Haag/10.22%, Robert Steele/32.81%, Andrew Haag/50.00%, Robert Steele/7.41%, Robert Steele/50.00%, Insiders/12.71%, Andrew Haag/32.81%, James Kernan/3.01%

Financial Data: *Fiscal Year End:* 06/30 *Latest Annual Data:* 6/30/2006

Year		Sales		Net Income	
2006		$2,307,000		-$2,946,000	
2005		$1,548,000		-$7,418,000	
2004		$299,000		-$999,000	
Curr. Assets:	$411,000	**Curr. Liab.:**	$3,860,000		
Plant, Equip.:	$297,000	**Total Liab.:**	$5,034,000	**Indic. Yr. Divd.:**	NA
Total Assets:	$812,000	**Net Worth:**	-$4,223,000	**Debt/ Equity:**	NA

Quipp Inc

4800 NW 157th St., Miami, FL, 33014; *PH:* 1-305-623-8700; *Fax:* 1-305-623-0980; *http://* www.quipp.com; *Email:* info@quipp.com

General - Incorporation	FL	**Stock**- Price on:12/24/2007	$7.25
Employees	106	Stock Exchange	NDQ
Auditor	KPMG LLP	Ticker Symbol	QUIP
Stk Agt	American Stock Transfer & Trust Co.	Outstanding Shares	1,460,000
Counsel	Morgan, Lewis & Bockius LLP	E.P.S.	-$3.18
DUNS No.	10-196-0458	Shareholders	NA

Business: The group's principal activities are to design, manufacture, install, service and market post-press material handling equipment to newspaper publishers. The products of the group include newspaper stackers, bottom wrapper, automatic cart loading system, newspaper conveyor systems, automatic palletizer system and other products including stream aligners, centering pacers, fold compressors, newspaper sensors and press production monitors. The group also sells products to original equipment manufacturers to compliment the product line and provide the customers a single source for integrated post-press material handling systems. Major trademarks of the group are 'quipp' and 'quipp gripp'. The group exports its products to the Far East countries, Canada, Latin America and other foreign countries. On 06-Mar-2003, the group acquired certain assets of usa leader inc.

Primary SIC and add'l.: 3554

CIK No: 0000796577

Subsidiaries: Newstec, Inc., Quipp Systems, Inc.

Officers: Michael S. Kady/Dir., CEO, Pres., Eric Bello/CFO, VP - Finance, John Connors/Pres. - Newstec, VP - Corporate Development, Quipp, Inc, Greg Verstrate/Contact - Sales, Product Information, United States, Southeast, Angel Arrabal/VP - Sales, Quipp Systems, Inc, Mohammed Jamil/VP - Customer Service, Quipp Systems, Inc, Christer A. Sjogren/Exec. VP - Quipp Systems, Inc, David Switalski/VP - Operations, Quipp Systems, Inc, Terry Connors/Contact - Sales, Product Information, United States, Northeast, David O'Neill/Contact - Sales, Product Information, United States, Central, Tim Dudley/Contact - Sales, Product Information, United States, Midwest, Terry Mason/Contact - Sales, Product Information, United States, Western

Directors: Cristina H. Kepner/62/Chmn., William A. Dambrackas/64/Dir., Lawrence J. Gibson/55/Dir., Arthur J. Rawl/65/Dir., Robert C. Strandberg/50/Dir., John D. Lori/40/Dir.

Owners: Angel Arrabal, Arthur J. Rawl, John Connors/1.60%, Insiders/25.50%, Michael S. Kady/1.40%, David W. Wright/10.10%, John D. Lori/9.90%, Robert C. Strandberg, Pyramid Trading Limited Partnership/11.00%, David Switalski, William A. Dambrackas, Cristina H. Kepner/1.80%, Mohammed Jamil, Lawrence J. Gibson, Boston Avenue Capital, LLC./7.70% *(20 Owners included in Index)*

Financial Data: *Fiscal Year End:* 12/31 *Latest Annual Data:* 12/31/2006

Year		Sales		Net Income	
2006		$26,414,000		-$3,294,000	
2005		$25,783,000		$254,000	
2004		$24,690,000		$486,000	
Curr. Assets:	$11,003,000	**Curr. Liab.:**	$6,780,000		
Plant, Equip.:	$2,161,000	**Total Liab.:**	$6,935,000	**Indic. Yr. Divd.:**	$0.200
Total Assets:	$16,062,000	**Net Worth:**	$9,127,000	**Debt/ Equity:**	0.0181

Quixote Corp

35 E Wacker Dr., Chicago, IL, 60601; *PH:* 1-312-467-6755; *Fax:* 1-312-467-1356; *http://* www.quixotecorp.com; *Email:* info@quixotecorp.com

General - Incorporation	DE	**Stock**- Price on:12/24/2007	$19.26
Employees	1,000	Stock Exchange	NDQ
Auditor	Grant Thornton LLP	Ticker Symbol	QUIX
Stk Agt	Computershare Trust Co	Outstanding Shares	9,020,000
Counsel	Holland & Knight LLP	E.P.S.	-$1.71
DUNS No.	05-057-5984	Shareholders	NA

Business: The group's principal activities are to develop, manufacture and market highway and transportation safety products to protect, direct and inform motorists and highway workers. These products include energy-absorbing highway crash cushions, flexible post delineators, electronic wireless measuring and sensing devices, weather information systems and forecasting services, variable message signs, highway advisory radios, intelligent intersection control devices and other highway and transportation safety devices. The group operates in domestic and international markets.

Primary SIC and add'l.: 2531 3993 6719 3089

CIK No: 0000032870

Subsidiaries: E-Tech Testing Services,Inc., Energy Absorption Systems (AL) LLC, Energy Absorption Systems (Europe),Inc., Energy Absorption Systems,Inc., Highway Information Systems,Inc., Nu-Metrics,Inc., Peek Traffic Corporation, Quixote Asia Pacific,Inc., Quixote Europe,Inc., Quixote Foreign Sales Corporation, Quixote Latin American, Inc., Quixote Middle East/Africa, Inc., Quixote Traffic Corporation, Quixote Transportation Safety (Asia Pacific) Pty Limited, Quixote Transportation Safety Mexico S. de R.L. de C.V. 22 Subsidiaries included in the Index

Officers: Leslie J. Jezuit/Chmn., CEO, Daniel P. Gorey/CFO, VP, Treasurer, Joan R. Riley/VP, General Counsel, Sec., Dir. - Investor Relations, Jeffery S. Held/VP - Corporate Development, James E. Connell/Pres. - Protect, Direct Group, Timothy M. O' Leary/Pres. - Intersection Control Group, Bruce C. Reimer/Pres. - Inform Group

Directors: Leslie J. Jezuit/Chmn., CEO, James H. Devries/Dir., Lawrence C. McQuade/Dir., Duane M. Tyler/Dir., Robert D. Van Roijen/Dir., Joseph M. Giglio/Dir.

Owners: Robert D. van Roijen/1.50%, Investment Counselors of Maryland/5.40%, Leslie J. Jezuit/2.90%, Joan R. Riley/1.20%, James H. DeVries/2.40%, Royce & Associates LLC/5.50%, FMR Corp./14.20%, Security Investors LLC/7.90%, Insiders/10.40%, Daniel P. Gorey/1.60%, Lawrence C. McQuade/1.20%, T. Rowe Price Associates, Inc./5.00%, Duane M. Tyler, Wellington Management Company, LLP/13.50%

Financial Data: *Fiscal Year End:* 06/30 *Latest Annual Data:* 6/30/2006

Year		Sales		Net Income	
2006		$161,134,000		-$10,102,000	
2005		$146,353,000		-$650,000	
2004		$150,290,000		-$17,027,000	
Curr. Assets:	$64,249,000	**Curr. Liab.:**	$26,121,000		
Plant, Equip.:	$17,660,000	**Total Liab.:**	$74,166,000	**Indic. Yr. Divd.:**	$0.380
Total Assets:	$119,374,000	**Net Worth:**	$45,208,000	**Debt/ Equity:**	NA

Quotemedia Inc

17100 E Shea Blvd., Ste. 230, Fountain Hills, AZ, 85268; *PH:* 1-480-905-7311; *http://* www.quotemedia.com; *Email:* contactus@quotemedia.com

General - Incorporation	NV	**Stock**- Price on:12/24/2007	$0.27
Employees	35	Stock Exchange	OTC
Auditor	Hein & Assoc. LLP	Ticker Symbol	QMCI
Stk Agt	Stalt, Inc.	Outstanding Shares	65,770,000
Counsel	NA	E.P.S.	-$0.022
DUNS No.	NA	Shareholders	NA

Business: The group's principal activities are that of a software developer and an application service provider. The group collects and delivers financial data content via the Internet. It develops and licenses Web-based software components that deliver cost effective, dynamic content to websites of potential customers. Quotestream(tm) is the group's Web-based streaming online portfolio management suite that delivers instant market data. The suite comprises of quotestream bronze, quotestream silver, quotestream gold, and quotestream professional. These deliver market indices, stock watch lists, static and interactive charts and both delayed and real-time streaming (dynamically updated) content in a small Web-delivered application that requires no downloads or user-resident software. The group's customers include brokerage firms, financial institutions, mutual fund companies, portals, public companies, Fortune 500 companies and individual investors.

Primary SIC and add'l.: 7379 7372 7375

CIK No: 0001101433

Subsidiaries: 1338768 Ontario Inc

Officers: Keith R. Guelpa/Dir., CEO, Co - Founder, Pres., Keith J. Randall/CFO, VP, Sec., Dave Shworan/Dir., Pres.

Directors: Keith R. Guelpa/Dir., CEO, Co - Founder, Pres., Robert J. Thompson/Chmn., Dave Shworan/Dir., Pres.

Owners: David M. Shworan/38.30%, Keith J. Randall/1.10%, Insiders/48.60%, Keith R. Guelpa/13.90%, Robert J. Thompson/2.40%

Financial Data: *Fiscal Year End:* 12/31 *Latest Annual Data:* 12/31/2006

Year	Sales	Net Income
2006	$3,743,000	-$595,000
2005	$2,466,000	$25,000
2004	$1,010,000	-$297,000

Curr. Assets:	$1,274,000	**Curr. Liab.:**	$1,071,000		
Plant, Equip.:	$482,000	**Total Liab.:**	$2,856,000	**Indic. Yr. Divd.:**	NA
Total Assets:	$1,950,000	**Net Worth:**	-$907,000	**Debt/ Equity:**	NA

Quovadx Inc

7600 E Orchard Rd., Ste. 300 S, Greenwood, CO, 80111; ***PH:*** 1-602-267-7500; ***http://*** www.quovadx.com

General - Incorporation	DE	**Stock**- Price on:12/24/2007	$3.13
Employees	365	Stock Exchange	NA
Auditor	Ernst & Young LLP	Ticker Symbol	NA
Stk Agt	Mellon Shareholder Services LLC	Outstanding Shares	42,240,000
Counsel	Wilson Sonsini Goodrich & Rosati	E.P.S	$0.18
DUNS No.	NA	Shareholders	NA

Business: The group's principle activity is to provide software and services to more than 20,000 enterprise customers which helps to develop, extend and integrate applications based on open standards. It generates revenue from three segments: software license, professional services and recurring revenue. The group's software and services offerings include an integrated suite of application development tools and vertical enterprise applications for companies in healthcare, financial services, software, telecommunications, public sector, manufacturing and life sciences. Rogue wave, sourcepro, stingray, cloverleaf, hostaccess, webaccel, insurenet, qdx and quovadx are the registered trademarks of the group.

Primary SIC and add'l.: 7375 7372

CIK No: 0001094561

Subsidiaries: CareScience, Inc, Confer Software, Inc, Healthcare.com Corporation, Quovadx Ltd, Rogue Wave Software, Inc, Royal Health Care of Long Island, LLC

Officers: Harvey A. Wagner/Dir., CEO, Pres., Russell Fleischer/CEO - Integration Solutions, Mike Epplen/Sr. VP - Sales, Marketing, Integration Solutions Division, Carolyn Jolley/Sr. VP - Services, Support, Integration Solutions Division, May Hu/Sr. VP - Research, Development, Integration Solutions Division, Juan C. Perez/VP, Controller, Principal Accounting Officer, Matthew T. Pullam/Exec. VP, CFO, Treasurer, Principal Financial Officer, Linda K. Wackwitz/Sec., Paul Bellamy/Sr. VP - International Operations, Integration Solutions Division

Directors: Harvey A. Wagner/Dir., CEO, Pres., Jeffrey M. Krauss/Chmn., Fred L. Brown/Dir., James A. Gilbert/Dir., James B. Hoover/Dir., Charles J. Roesslein/Dir.

Owners: Royce and Associates, L.L.C/5.55%, James B. Hoover/1.23%, Jeffrey M. Krauss, Harvey A. Wagner/2.41%, Afshin Cangarlu/1.30%, Trigran Investments, Inc./7.06%, James A. Gilbert, Cory Isaacson, Austin M. Marxe/5.35%, Insiders/8.91%, Matthew T. Pullam, Charles J. Roesslein, Lloyd I. Miller/6.54%, Heartland Advisors, Inc./14.21%, Thomas H. Zajac *(17 Owners included in Index)*

Financial Data: ***Fiscal Year End:***12/31 ***Latest Annual Data:*** 12/31/2006

Year	Sales	Net Income
2006	$84,120,000	-$13,115,000
2005	$83,103,000	-$2,888,000
2004	$82,801,000	-$24,231,000

Curr. Assets:	$48,629,000	**Curr. Liab.:**	$38,845,000	**P/E Ratio:**	17.39
Plant, Equip.:	$4,516,000	**Total Liab.:**	$43,403,000	**Indic. Yr. Divd.:**	NA
Total Assets:	$121,974,000	**Net Worth:**	$78,571,000	**Debt/ Equity:**	NA

Qwest Communications International Inc

1801 California St., Denver, CO, 80202; ***PH:*** 1-303-992-1400; ***Fax:*** 1-303-992-1724; ***http://*** www.qwest.com

General - Incorporation	DE	**Stock**- Price on:12/24/2007	$9.52
Employees	38,383	Stock Exchange	NYSE
Auditor	KPMG LLP	Ticker Symbol	Q
Stk Agt	Bank of New York	Outstanding Shares	1,850,000,000
Counsel	NA	E.P.S	$1.40
DUNS No.	14-872-1178	Shareholders	NA

Business: The groups principle activity is to provide local telecommunications and related services. The group operates through three segments namely wire line, wireless and other services. In the year 2006, the group acquired OnFiber Communications, Inc. The group operates from United States.

Primary SIC and add'l.: 6519 4813

CIK No: 0001037949

Subsidiaries: Qwest Capital Funding, Inc., Qwest Communications Corporation, Qwest Corporation, Qwest N. Limited Partnership, Qwest Services Corporation

Officers: Edward A. Mueller/61/Chmn., CEO, Richard C. Notebaert/60/Chmn., CEO/$16,490,490.00, Barry K. Allen/59/Exec. VP - Operations/$4,331,712.00, John W. Richardson/63/CFO, Exec. VP, Thomas E. Richards/Exec. VP - Business Markets Group, Shirley Bloomfield/Sr. VP - Federal Relations, Stephanie G. Comfort/Sr. VP - Corporate Strategy, Bob Tregemba/Exec. VP - Network Operations, Rich Baer/Exec. VP, General Counsel/$2,779,375.00, Steven R. Davis/Sr. VP - Public Policy, David Heller/Chief Ethics, Compliance Officer, VP - Risk Management, Paula Kruger/Exec. VP - Mass Markets/$1,808,439.00, Teresa Taylor/Chief Human Resources Officer, Exec. VP, Roland Thornton/Exec. VP - Wholesale Markets, Dan Yost/Exec. VP - Product

Directors: Edward A. Mueller/61/Chmn., CEO, Richard C. Notebaert/60/Chmn., CEO, Patrick J. Martin/Dir., James A. Unruh/Dir., Anthony Welters/Dir., Linda G. Alvarado/Dir., Charles L. Biggs/Dir., Dane K. Brooksher/Dir., Peter S. Hellman/Dir., David R. Hoover/Dir., Caroline Matthews/Dir., Wayne W. Murdy/Dir., Frank Popoff/Dir.

Owners: Linda G. Alvarado, Peter S. Hellman, David R. Hoover, Insiders, Paula Kruger, Wayne W. Murdy, Dane K. Brooksher, Richard N. Baer, State Street Bank and Trust Company, Trustee/6.20%, Barry K. Allen, Patrick J. Martin, Legg Mason Capital Management, Inc. and Legg Mason Value Trust, Inc./13.20%, Frank P. Popoff, Capital Research and Management Company and The Growth Fund of America, Inc./13.50%, Charles L. Biggs *(22 Owners included in Index)*

Financial Data: ***Fiscal Year End:***12/31 ***Latest Annual Data:*** 12/31/2006

Year	Sales	Net Income
2006	$13,923,000,000	$593,000,000
2005	$13,903,000,000	-$779,000,000
2004	$13,809,000,000	-$1,794,000,000

Curr. Assets:	$3,654,000,000	**Curr. Liab.:**	$5,160,000,000	**P/E Ratio:**	21.64
Plant, Equip.:	$14,579,000,000	**Total Liab.:**	$22,684,000,000	**Indic. Yr. Divd.:**	$0.080
Total Assets:	$21,239,000,000	**Net Worth:**	-$1,445,000,000	**Debt/ Equity:**	NA

R & B Inc

3400 E Walnut St., Colmar, PA, 18915; ***PH:*** 1-215-997-1800

General - Incorporation	PA	**Stock**- Price on:12/24/2007	$11
Employees	NA	Stock Exchange	NDQ
Auditor	KPMG LLP	Ticker Symbol	RBIN
Stk Agt	NA	Outstanding Shares	NA
Counsel	Barry D. Myers	E.P.S	NA
DUNS No.	09-371-5316	Shareholders	NA

Business: The group's principal activity is to supply automotive replacement parts, fasteners and service line products. The group designs, packages and markets over 70,000 different automotive replacement parts including window handles, headlamp aiming screws, power steering filler caps, pedal pads and carburetor pre-heater hoses. The products of the group are sold under the brand names motormite(R), dorman(R), champ(R), pik-a-nut(R), platinum parts tm, brakeware(R) and tru-torque(r). The group's products are sold primarily in the United States through automotive aftermarket retailers, national, regional and local warehouse distributors and specialty markets.

Primary SIC and add'l.: 5013 5015

CIK No: 0000868780

Subsidiaries: 1664403 Ontario Inc.(Hermoff), Allparts, Inc., Dorman Products of America, Ltd.(1), Motor Power Industries, Inc., RB Distribution, Inc., RB Management, Inc., Scan-Tech USA/Sweden, A.B.

Officers: Richard N. Berman/51/Chmn., CEO, Pres./$618,800.00, Steven L. Berman/48/Dir., Exec. VP, Sec., Treasurer/$618,800.00, Mathias J. Barton/48/Sr. VP, CFO/$329,865.00, Joseph M. Beretta/53/Sr. VP - Product/$329,105.00, Fred Frigo/51/Sr. VP - Operations, Thomas J. Knoblauch/52/VP, General Counsel, Assist. Sec., Donald J. Barry/45/Sr. VP - Sales, Trade Marketing/$314,850.00

Directors: Richard N. Berman/51/Chmn., CEO, Pres., Edgar W. Levin/Dir., John F. Creamer/Dir., George L. Bernstein/Dir., Steven L. Berman/48/Dir., Exec. VP, Sec., Treasurer, Paul R. Lederer/Dir.

Owners: Paul R. Lederer, Mathias J. Barton, Edgar W. Levin, Jordan S. Berman/7.70%, George L. Bernstein, Insiders/32.00%, Donald J. Barry, Dimensional Fund Advisors LP/6.80%, Columbia Management Advisors, LLC/7.20%, Steven L. Berman/15.20%, John F. Creamer, Joseph M. Beretta, Royce & Associates, LLC/10.30%, Richard N. Berman/14.20%, T. Rowe Price Small-Cap Value Fund, Inc/6.20%

R&G Financial Corp

290 Jess T. Piero Ave., Hato Rey, San Juan, PR, 00918; ***PH:*** 1-787-758-2424; ***Fax:*** 1-787-766-8175; ***http://*** www.rgonline.com

General - Incorporation	PR	**Stock**- Price on:12/24/2007	NA
Employees	NA	Stock Exchange	OTC
Auditor	PricewaterhouseCoopers LLP	Ticker Symbol	RGFC
Stk Agt	American Stock Transfer & Trust Co.	Outstanding Shares	NA
Counsel	Patton Boggs LLP	E.P.S	NA
DUNS No.	09-048-1664	Shareholders	NA

Business: The group's principal activities are to provide banking services through its subsidiaries. Its services include residential, commercial and personal loans and a wide range of deposit products. The group also provides private banking, trust and other financial services to its customers. Banking activities include commercial banking services, corporate and construction lending, consumer lending and credit cards. Mortgage banking activities include the origination, purchase, sale and servicing of mortgage loans on single-family residences. The group offers trust and investment services through its private banking department and its broker-dealer. It also acts as insurance agent for certain types of credit-related insurance. At 31-Dec-2003, the group operated 31 branch offices.

Primary SIC and add'l.: 6022 6712

CIK No: 0001016933

Subsidiaries: Continental Capital Corp, Puerto Rico commercial bank, R&G Mortgage Corp, R-G Crown Bank, R-G Premier Bank of Puerto Rico, The Mortgage Store of Puerto Rico, Inc.

Officers: Rolando Rodriguez/Dir., CEO, Pres., Victor Galan Fundora/Exec. VP - Production, Retail Mortgage Banking, Hector Secola/Exec. VP - Human Resources, Jose Antonio Diaz/Pres. - R, G Premier Bank, Jose Vigoreaux/Exec. VP, Dir. - Operations RG Premier Bank, Andres I. Perez/CFO, Exec. VP, Joanellie Vargas/Controller, Steven Velez/Pres. - R, G Mortgage, Jean Francois Dumazet/Pres. - R, G Insurance Corp, Victor M. Irizarry/Exec. VP, Chief Lending Officer, Melba Acosta/Exec. VP, Chief Administrative Officer, Carlos Mantaras/Exec. VP - Retail Banking - Consumer Lending, R, G Premier Bank

Directors: Rolando Rodriguez/Dir., CEO, Pres., Juan Agosto-Alicea/Chmn., Gilberto Rivera-Arreaga/Dir., Benigno R. Fernandez/Dir., Eduardo McCormack/Dir., Ileana M. Colon-Carlo/Dir., Melba Figueroa/Dir., Roberto Gorbea/Dir., Rafael Nin/Dir., Enrique Umpierre-Suarez/Dir., Laureno Carus Abarca/Dir.

Curr. Assets:	$429,592,000	**Curr. Liab.:**	$8,729,580,000		
Plant, Equip.:	$54,446,000	**Total Liab.:**	$9,343,012,000	**Indic. Yr. Divd.:**	NA
Total Assets:	$10,198,602,000	**Net Worth:**	$855,590,000	**Debt/ Equity:**	0.5940

R.G. Barry Corp

13405 Yarmouth Rd. NW, Pickerington, OH, 43147; ***PH:*** 1-614-729-7275; ***Fax:*** 1-614-729-7276; ***http://*** www.rgbarry.com; ***Email:*** footwear@rgbarry.com

General - Incorporation		**Stock**- Price on:12/24/2007	$12.8
Employees	200	Stock Exchange	AMEX
Auditor	NA	Ticker Symbol	DFZ
Stk Agt	Bank of New York	Outstanding Shares	10,110,000
Counsel	NA	E.P.S	$2.14
DUNS No.	NA	Shareholders	NA

Business: The groups principal activity is to develop and market accessories category footwear. The group marketed its products under the trade names Dearfoams(R), EZfeet(R) and Terrasoles(R). The group operates from the United States, France and China.

Primary SIC and add'l.: 5139 3142 3149

CIK No: 0000927693

Officers: Greg A. Tunney/Dir., CEO, Pres., Harry Miller/Sr. VP - Human Resources, Daniel D. Viren/Sr. VP - Finance, CFO, Sec., Glenn Evans/Sr. VP - Sourcing, Pam Gentile/Sr. VP - Sales, Pres. - Dearfoams Brands, Thomas Jz Konecki/Sr. VP - Sales, Licensing, Business Development, Lee F. Smith/Sr. VP - Design, Product Development, Jose G. Ibarra/VP, Treasurer, Michael Schatz/VP - Sourcing

Directors: Greg A. Tunney/Dir., CEO, Pres., Gordon Zacks/75/Chmn., Nicholas Dipaolo/66/Dir., David P. Lauer/66/Dir., Roger E. Lautzenhiser/54/Dir., Edward M. Stan/84/Dir., David L. Nichols/67/Dir., Janice E. Page/59/Dir., Thomas M. Von Lehman/59/Dir., Harvey A. Weinberg/71/Dir.

Financial Data: *Fiscal Year End:*NA *Latest Annual Data:* 7/1/2006

Year	Sales	Net Income
2006	$32,883,000	-$4,199,000
2005	$105,488,000	$8,048,000

Curr. Assets:	$34,809,000	**Curr. Liab.:**	$18,816,000		
Plant, Equip.:	$2,419,000	**Total Liab.:**	$31,448,000	**Indic. Yr. Divd.:**	NA
Total Assets:	$40,444,000	**Net Worth:**	$8,996,000	**Debt/ Equity:**	0.0079

R.H. Donnelley Corp

1001 Winstead Dr., Cary, NC, 27513; *PH:* 1-919-297-1600; *Fax:* 1-866-527-4550; *http://* www.rhdonnelley.com; *Email:* info@rhd.com

General - Incorporation .... DE
Employees 4,400
Auditor .... KPMG LLP
Stk Agt .... Bank of New York
Counsel .... NA
DUNS No. 04-997-7473

Stock- Price on:12/24/2007 .... $73.17
Stock Exchange .... NYSE
Ticker Symbol .... RHD
Outstanding Shares 71,000,000
E.P.S $0.12
Shareholders .... NA

Business: The group's principle activity is to market yellow pages advertising in the United States. The group sells advertising for more than 170 yellow pages directories with a total circulation of over 15 million. Together with the dontech partnership and sprint corporation, the group sells yellow pages advertising in Illinois, northwest Indiana, Nevada, Florida, Virginia and North Carolina. The group also provides pre-press publishing services for approximately 240 yellow pages directories. The acquisition transforms the group from a sales agent and pre-press vendor into a publisher of yellow pages directories. The group's quarterly revenue for September 2007 was 669.94 millions of USD.

Primary SIC and add'l.: 7319 2741 7379 7389

CIK No: 0000030419

Subsidiaries: Dex Media East LLC, Dex Media Service LLC, Dex Media West LLC, Dex Media, Inc, DonTech Holdings, LLC, R.H. Donnelley Inc, R.H. Donnelley Publishing & Advertising of Illinois Holdings, LLC, R.H. Donnelley Publishing & Advertising of Illinois Partnership, The DonTech II Partnership

Officers: David C. Swanson/Chmn., CEO/$7,106,787.00, Peter J. McDonald/COO, Pres./$3,757,608.00, Tyler D. Gronbach/Sr. VP - Corporate Communications, Administration, Jeffrey A. Smith/43/VP, Controller, Steven M. Blondy/CFO, Exec. VP/$2,957,821.00, Robert J. Bush/Sr. VP, General Counsel/$1,452,593.00, Al Duy/Sr. VP - Information Technology, Publishing Services, Maggie Lebeau/Sr. VP, Chief Marketing Officer, Gretchen Zech/Sr. VP - Human Resources, George F. Bednarz/Sr. VP - RHD Interactive/$1,376,908.00, Jenny L. Apker/50/VP, Treasurer

Directors: David C. Swanson/Chmn., CEO, Alan F. Schultz/Dir., Robert Kamerschen/Dir., Michael P. Connors/Dir., David M. Veit/Dir., Nancy E. Cooper/Dir., Thomas J. Reddin/Dir., Edwina D. Woodbury/Dir., Russell T. Lewis/Dir., Barry Lawson Williams/Dir.

Owners: Insiders/3.70%, Michael P. Connors, FMR Corp/8.10%, David M. Veit, David C. Swanson/1.70%, UBS AG/7.20%, Nancy E. Cooper, Barry Lawson Williams, Edwina Woodbury, Peter J. McDonald, Robert Kamerschen, Steven M. Blondy, Lord, Abbett& Co. LLC/9.10%, Robert J. Bush, George F. Bednarz *(20 Owners included in Index)*

Financial Data: *Fiscal Year End:*12/31 *Latest Annual Data:* 12/31/2006

Year	Sales	Net Income
2006	$1,895,921,000	-$237,704,000
2005	$956,631,000	$67,533,000
2004	$681,083,000	$70,312,000

Curr. Assets:	$1,532,225,000	**Curr. Liab.:**	$2,009,218,000		
Plant, Equip.:	$159,362,000	**Total Liab.:**	$14,326,712,000	**Indic. Yr. Divd.:**	NA
Total Assets:	$16,147,468,000	**Net Worth:**	$1,820,756,000	**Debt/ Equity:**	NA

R.R. Donnelley & Sons Co

111 S Wacker Dr., Chicago, IL, 60606; *PH:* 1-312-326-8000; *Fax:* 1-312-326-7156; *http://* www.rrdonnelley.com

General - Incorporation .... DE
Employees 53,000
Auditor .... Deloitte & Touche LLP
Stk Agt..... Computershare Investor Services LLC
Counsel .... NA
DUNS No. 00-511-9573

Stock- Price on:12/24/2007 .... $43.63
Stock Exchange .... NYSE
Ticker Symbol .... RRD
Outstanding Shares 220,100,000
E.P.S $1.11
Shareholders .... NA

Business: The groups principle activity is to provide printing services. The group also provide logistic and information services. In the year 2007, the group acquired Von Hoffmann. The group operates from United States.

Primary SIC and add'l.: 2731 7379 7375 2754

CIK No: 0000029669

Subsidiaries: Allentown S.H. Leasing Company, Asia Printers Group Ltd., Astron BPO Limited, Astron BSL Limited, Astron Business Process Solutions GmbH, Astron Business Services GmbH, Astron Business Services Sp. zo. o., Astron Cominformatic A.G., Astron Document Management (PVT) Limited, Astron Document Management Limited, Astron Document Services Limited, Astron Document Solutions Limited, Astron Lasercom Espana S.L., Astron Lasercom Italia S.R.L., Astron Lasercom S.A. 123 Subsidiaries included in the Index

Officers: Thomas J. Quinlan/45/Dir., CEO, Pres./$3,233,497.00, Suzanne S. Bettman/43/Exec. VP, General Counsel, Sec./$1,338,477.00, Miles McHugh/CFO/$613,845.00

Directors: Thomas J. Quinlan/45/Dir., CEO, Pres., Stephen M. Wolf/66/Chmn., Norman H. Wesley/58/Dir., Lionel H. Schipper/75/Dir., Judith H. Hamilton/63/Dir., Bide L. Thomas/72/Dir., Thomas S. Johnson/67/Dir., John C. Pope/59/Dir., Michael T. Riordan/57/Dir., Oliver R. Sockwell/64/Dir.

Owners: Capital Research and Management Company/10.70%, Judith H. Hamilton, John R. Paloian, Norman H. Wesley, Robert F. Cummings, Lord, Abbett & Co. LLC/5.50%, Lionel H. Schipper, Suzanne S. Bettman, Stephen M. Wolf, Thomas S. Johnson, Mark A. Angelson, Bide L. Thomas, Michael T. Riordan, Dean E. Cherry, Miles W. McHugh *(19 Owners included in Index)*

Financial Data: *Fiscal Year End:*12/31 *Latest Annual Data:* 12/31/2006

Year	Sales	Net Income
2006	$9,316,600,000	$400,600,000
2005	$8,430,200,000	$137,100,000
2004	$7,156,400,000	$178,300,000

Curr. Assets:	$2,517,000,000	**Curr. Liab.:**	$1,611,800,000	**P/E Ratio:**	22.37
Plant, Equip.:	$2,142,300,000	**Total Liab.:**	$5,511,100,000	**Indic. Yr. Divd.:**	$1.040
Total Assets:	$9,635,800,000	**Net Worth:**	$4,124,700,000	**Debt/ Equity:**	NA

Rackable Systems Inc

46600 Landing Pkwy., Fremont, CA, 94538; *PH:* 1-510-933-8300; *Fax:* 1-408-321-0293; *http://* www.rackable.com; *Email:* sales@rackable.com

General - Incorporation .... DE
Employees 286
Auditor .... Deloitte & Touche LLP
Stk Agt .... Company reincorp
Counsel .... NA
DUNS No. .... NA

Stock- Price on:12/24/2007 .... $12.41
Stock Exchange .... NDQ
Ticker Symbol .... RACK
Outstanding Shares 28,620,000
E.P.S .... -$1.76
Shareholders .... NA

Business: The groups principle activities include developing, marketing and selling server and storage systems. The products of the group include modular and rack mounted systems. The group products sold under the trade names Rackable Systems, Foundation Series, Scale Out Series, OmniStor, RapidScale and Roamer. for September 2006, the group acquired Terrascale Technologies, Inc. Specific customers of the group include Microsoft and Yahoo. The group operates from the United States, Ireland, China and other. The group's quarterly revenue for September 2007 was 87.24 millions of USD.

Primary SIC and add'l.: 3571 3572

CIK No: 0001316625

Subsidiaries: Rackable Asia Pacific Ltd., Rackable Systems Canada Acquisition ULC, Rackable Systems Holding Corp., Rackable Systems Limited, Terrascale Technologies Inc., Terrascale Technologies ULC

Officers: Mark Barrenechea/Dir., CEO, Pres., Todd Ford/41/Pres., Madhu Ranganathan/CFO, Dominic Martinelli/VP - Information Technology, Gautham Sastri/Exec. VP - Rapidscale, Giovanni Coglitore/Founder, CTO, William P. Garvey/43/General Counsel, VP - Corporate Development, Sec., Tony Gaughan/Sr. VP, Chief Products Officer, David Yoffie/Sr. VP - Manufacturing Operations, Service, Maurice Leibenstern/General Counsel, Corp. Sec., Sr. VP - Development

Directors: Mark Barrenechea/Dir., CEO, Pres., Thomas K. Barton/44/Dir., Charles M. Boesenberg/Dir., Gary A. Griffiths/Dir., Michael J. Maulick/Dir., Hagi Schwartz/Dir., Ronald D. Verdoorn/Dir., Giovanni Coglitore/Founder, CTO

Owners: Waddell& Reed Financial Inc/7.20%, Mark J. Barrenechea, Todd R. Ford/1.00%, Michael J. Maulick, Insiders/3.80%, Thomas Gallivan, FMR Corp./14.70%, Gary A. Griffiths, Madhu Ranganathan, Ronald D. Verdoorn, Franklin Resources, Inc./7.50%, Thomas K. Barton/2.10%, Hagi Schwartz, Robert Weisickle, Charles M. Boesenberg

Financial Data: *Fiscal Year End:*12/31 *Latest Annual Data:* 12/31/2006

Year	Sales	Net Income
2006	$360,376,000	$11,472,000
2005	$214,985,000	$8,512,000
2004	$109,743,000	-$55,390,000

Curr. Assets:	$355,395,000	**Curr. Liab.:**	$87,215,000		
Plant, Equip.:	$5,372,000	**Total Liab.:**	$91,081,000	**Indic. Yr. Divd.:**	NA
Total Assets:	$406,770,000	**Net Worth:**	$315,689,000	**Debt/ Equity:**	NA

Rada Electronic Industries Ltd

7 Giborei Israel St., Netanya, 42504; *PH:* 972-98921111; *http://* www.rada.com

General - Incorporation .... Israel
Employees 124
Auditor .... Kost Forer Gabbay & Kasierer
Stk Agt ..... American Stock Transfer & Trust Co.
Counsel .... NA
DUNS No. 60-002-4749

Stock- Price on:12/24/2007 .... NA
Stock Exchange .... NDQ
Ticker Symbol .... RADA
Outstanding Shares .... NA
E.P.S .... -$0.07
Shareholders .... NA

Business: The groups principle activities include development, manufacturing and marketing of advanced electronic and computerized equipment for military use, such as avionics, computerized group support equipment, automated test equipment and a portable ruggedized computer; distributes and sells electronic components, personal computers and aircraft parts. The group also provides testing, screening and repair services for the commercial aviation industry. The group operates from United States.

Primary SIC and add'l.: 5065 3812 3825 3577

CIK No: 0000761238

Subsidiaries: Beijing Huarui Aircraft Components Maintenance and Services Co.

Officers: Zvi Alon/CEO, Herzle Bodinger/Chmn., Pres., Steve Hoffman/Dir. - Manufacturing, Elan Sigal/CFO, Dov Sella/VP - Marketing, Sales, Yuval Dan-Gur/VP - Engineering, Avishay Ingber/Dir. - QA, Avi Mano/Dir. - Procurement, Tali Chen/Dir. - Corporate Development, Shlomo Perry/Dir. - Marketing

Directors: Herzle Bodinger/Chmn., Pres., Michael Letchinger/52/Dir., Adrian Berg/60/Dir., Roy Kui Chuen Chan/61/Dir., Ben Zion Gruber/49/Dir., Nurit Mor/64/Dir., Eli Akavia/59/Dir.

Owners: Howard P.L. Yeung/59.20%, Kenneth Yeung/5.20%, Ben Zion Gruber/1.00%, Smithfield Fiduciary LLC/6.20%, Insiders/5.70%, Iroquuois Capital LLP/5.40%, Dov Sella, Roy Kui Chuen Chan, Herzle Bodinger/1.10%, Zvi Alon, Elan Sigal, Adrian Berg/1.00%

Financial Data: *Fiscal Year End:*12/31 *Latest Annual Data:* 12/31/2006

Year	Sales	Net Income
2006	$13,037,000	-$2,000,000
2005	$13,421,000	-$2,329,000
2004	$14,160,000	$822,000

Curr. Assets:	$9,326,000	**Curr. Liab.:**	$8,816,000		
Plant, Equip.:	$3,359,000	**Total Liab.:**	$11,381,000	**Indic. Yr. Divd.:**	NA
Total Assets:	$17,455,000	**Net Worth:**	$6,074,000	**Debt/ Equity:**	NA

RADCOM Ltd

6 Forest Ave., Paramus, NJ, 07652; *PH:* 1-201-518-0033; *Fax:* 1-201-556-9030; *http://* www.radcom.com

General - Incorporation: Israel
Employees: 136
Auditor: Somekh Chaikin
Stk Agt: NA
Counsel: Weil, Gotshal & Manges LLP
DUNS No.: 60-012-1115

Stock - Price on:12/24/2007: $1.36
Stock Exchange: NDQ
Ticker Symbol: RDCM
Outstanding Shares: 16,280,000
E.P.S: -$0.574
Shareholders: NA

Business: The groups principle activities include development, manufacturing, marketing and support of innovative, high-performance, easy-to-use internetworking test and analysis equipment for data communications and telecommunications network. The group operates from United States.

Primary SIC and add'l.: 7373 7379

CIK No: 0001016838

Subsidiaries: Radcom (uk) Ltd., Radcom Equipment, Inc., RADCOM Investments (1996) Ltd.

Officers: David Ripstein/CEO, Pres., Michael Shilinger/VP - Operations, Avi Zamir/Pres. - Radcom Equipment, Inc, US Subsidiary, Uzi Yahav/VP - Business Development, Jonathan Burgin/CFO, Phil Barton/Marketing Contact, Shahaf Kieselstein/VP - Research & Development, Hanan Klainer/VP - Sales, Miki Shilinger/VP - Operations, Doron Milchtaich/CTO

Directors: Zohar Zisapel/Chmn., Rony Ross/Dir., Dan Barnea/Dir., Zohar Gilon/Dir.

Owners: Zohar Zisapel/22.10%, Yehuda Zisapel/12.40%, RAD Data Communications Ltd/1.10%

Financial Data: *Fiscal Year End:*12/31 *Latest Annual Data:* 12/31/2006

Year	Sales	Net Income
2006	$23,541,000	-$54,000
2005	$22,340,000	$1,527,000
2004	$16,055,000	-$1,678,000

Curr. Assets:	$24,158,000	**Curr. Liab.:**	$8,375,000		
Plant, Equip.:	$1,408,000	**Total Liab.:**	$12,380,000	**Indic. Yr. Divd.:**	NA
Total Assets:	$27,753,000	**Net Worth:**	$15,373,000	**Debt/ Equity:**	NA

Radian Group Inc

1601 Market St., Philadelphia, PA, 19103; ***PH:*** 1-215-231-1000; ***Fax:*** 1-215-854-1457; ***http://*** www.radiangroupinc.com

General - Incorporation: DE
Employees: 1,027
Auditor: Deloitte & Touche LLP
Stk Agt: Bank of New York
Counsel: NA
DUNS No.: 79-611-7851

Stock - Price on:12/24/2007: $57.86
Stock Exchange: NYSE
Ticker Symbol: RDN
Outstanding Shares: 80,240,000
E.P.S: $5.01
Shareholders: NA

Business: The group's principal activity is to provide mortgage insurance and risk management services. The group operates through three segments: mortgage insurance, mortgage services and financial guaranty. The mortgage insurance segment provides private mortgage insurance and risk management services to mortgage lending institutions. The mortgage services segment provides real estate information products and services to mortgage industry. The financial guaranty segment provides credit-related insurance coverage.

Primary SIC and add'l.: 6719 6351

CIK No: 0000890926

Subsidiaries: Amerin Guaranty Corporation, Amerin Re Corporation, Asset Recovery Solutions Group Inc, CMAC Investment Management Corporation, Commonwealth Mortgage Assurance Company of Texas, Credit Derivatives Limited, Enhance C-BASS Residual Finance Corporation, Enhance Financial Services Group Inc., Guaranty Risk Services, Inc., Radian Asset Assurance Inc., Radian Asset Assurance Limited, Radian Asset Securities Inc, Radian Capital, LLC, Radian Europe Limited, Radian Financial Products Limited 30 Subsidiaries included in the Index

Officers: S. A. Ibrahim/56/Dir., CEO, Robert E. Croner/Sr. VP - Human Resources, Mark A. Casale/Pres. - Radian Guaranty Inc, Lawrence Delgatto/CIO, Sr. VP, Rick Altman/Sr. VP - Corporate Planning, Jeff Cashmer/Sr. VP - International Mortgage, Radian Guaranty Inc, Jack Praschnik/Sr. VP, Head - Global Structured Products, MD - International Financial Guaranty Radian Asset Assurance Inc, John Deluca/Dir. - Marketing, Public Finance Group, Stephen D. Cooke/Pres. - Radian Asset Assurance Inc, Mona Zeehandelaar/Sr. VP - Investor Relations, Corporate Communications, Robert C. Quint/CFO, Exec. VP, Teresa Bryce/Exec. VP, General Counsel, Sec.

Directors: S. A. Ibrahim/56/Dir., CEO, Herbert Wende/70/Chmn., Howard B. Culang/60/Dir., Jan Nicholson/63/Dir., Stephen T. Hopkins/56/Dir., James W. Jennings/70/Dir., David C. Carney/69/Dir., Ronald W. Moore/62/Dir., Robert W. Richards/64/Dir., Anthony W. Schweiger/66/Dir.

Financial Data: *Fiscal Year End:*12/31 *Latest Annual Data:* 12/31/2006

Year	Sales	Net Income
2006	$1,327,946,000	$582,172,000
2005	$1,298,151,000	$522,854,000
2004	$1,364,053,000	$518,653,000

Curr. Assets:	$364,729,000	**Curr. Liab.:**	$197,634,000	**P/E Ratio:**	8.85
Plant, Equip.:	$33,937,000	**Total Liab.:**	$3,861,114,000	**Indic. Yr. Divd.:**	$0.080
Total Assets:	$7,928,671,000	**Net Worth:**	$4,067,557,000	**Debt/ Equity:**	0.1791

Radiant Logistics Inc

1227 120th Ave. Ne, Bellevue, WA, 98005; ***PH:*** 1-425-943-4599; ***Fax:*** 1-425-943-4598; ***http://*** www.radiant-logistics.com; ***Email:*** info@radiant-logistics.com

General - Incorporation: DE
Employees: 27
Auditor: Stonefield Josephson, Inc.
Stk Agt: NA
Counsel: NA
DUNS No.: NA

Stock - Price on:12/24/2007: $0.62
Stock Exchange: OTC
Ticker Symbol: RLGT
Outstanding Shares: 33,960,000
E.P.S: $0.01
Shareholders: NA

Business: The groups principal activities include managing freight transportation. The groups businesses increasingly strive to minimize inventory levels, perform manufacturing and assembly operations in lowest cost locations and distribute their products in numerous global markets. In January 2006, the group acquired Airgroup Corporation. The group operates from the United States.

Primary SIC and add'l.: 8742

CIK No: 0001171155

Subsidiaries: Airgroup Corporation

Officers: Bohn H. Crain/Chmn., CEO, CFO, Stephen M. Cohen/General Counsel, Sec., Treasurer, Member - Dir., William H. Moultrie/65/Pres., COO - Airgroup, Daniel Stegemoller/53/VP, COO - Airgroup, Rodney Eaton/53/VP, Chief Accounting Officer, Controller

Directors: Bohn H. Crain/Chmn., CEO, CFO, Stephen M. Cohen/General Counsel, Sec., Treasurer, Member - Dir.

Owners: SPH Investments, Inc./5.10%, Stephen M. Cohen/7.40%, Millennium Global High Yield Fund Limited/8.50%, Michael Garnick/5.30%, William H. Moultrie, Rodney Eaton, Dan Stegemoller, Insiders/31.20%, Bohn H. Crain/23.00%

Financial Data: *Fiscal Year End:*12/31 *Latest Annual Data:* 12/31/2005

Year	Sales	Net Income
2005	NA	-$149,000
2004	NA	-$25,000

Curr. Assets:	$5,292,000	**Curr. Liab.:**	$148,000	**P/E Ratio:**	14.42
Plant, Equip.:	NA	**Total Liab.:**	$148,000	**Indic. Yr. Divd.:**	NA
Total Assets:	$5,307,000	**Net Worth:**	$5,159,000	**Debt/ Equity:**	NA

Radiant Systems Inc

3925 Brookside Pkwy., Alpharetta, GA, 30022; ***PH:*** 1-770-576-6000; ***Fax:*** 1-770-754-7790; ***http://*** www.radiantsystems.com; ***Email:*** inquiries@radiantsystems.com

General - Incorporation: GA
Employees: 1,032
Auditor: Deloitte & Touche LLP
Stk Agt: Computershare Investor Services, LLC
Counsel: Smith, Gambrell & Russell
DUNS No.: 17-724-2435

Stock - Price on:12/24/2007: $13.01
Stock Exchange: NDQ
Ticker Symbol: RADS
Outstanding Shares: 31,100,000
E.P.S: $0.32
Shareholders: NA

Business: The group's principal activities are to develop, install and deliver technology solutions for retail and hospitality industries. Provides site management and enterprise management technology. The group operates through two segments: store systems and enterprise software systems. Store systems segment delivers site management systems including point-of-sale (pos), self-service kiosk and back-office systems designed specifically for the company's core vertical markets of petroleum and convenience store, food service and entertainment. Enterprise software systems segment delivers Web-based radiant 6e enterprise productivity software suite including functionality such as workforce and supply chain management to the broader retail markets both within and outside the company's core vertical markets. On 13-Jan-2004, the group acquired aloha technologies. On Jan 31, 2004, the group completed a tax-free split-off of enterprise, known as bluecube software.

Primary SIC and add'l.: 7372 7373

CIK No: 0000845818

Subsidiaries: Estorelink.Com, Inc., MenuLink Computer Solutions, Inc., Radiant Enterprise Software LLC, Radiant Hospitality Systems, Ltd., Radiant Systems Asia-Pacific Pty Ltd., Radiant Systems Central Europe, Inc., Radiant Systems International, Inc., Radiant Systems Retail Solutions Pte Ltd., Radiant Systems Retail Solutions, S.L., Radiant Systems s.r.o., Radiant Systems UK Limited, RADS Holding Corp., RetailEnterprise, LLC

Officers: John H. Heyman/Dir., CEO/$983,881.00, Alon Goren/Chmn., CTO/$597,387.00, Carlyle Taylor/Pres. - Hardware Division, Andrew S. Heyman/COO/$762,326.00, Mark E. Haidet/CFO/$464,525.00, Paul Langenbahn/Pres. - Hospitality Division, Chris Lybeer/Pres. - Retail, Entertainment Division, Mark Schoen/Pres. - Global Petroleum, Convenience Retail Division, Keith Hicks/VP - Human Resources

Directors: John H. Heyman/Dir., CEO, Alon Goren/Chmn., CTO, James S. Balloun/Dir., Alexander J. Douglas/Dir., Michael Z. Kay/Dir., William A. Clement/Dir., Donna A. Lee/Dir.

Owners: Insiders/20.00%, Alon Goren/15.30%, William A. Clement, Alex A. Porter/5.10%, Columbia Wanger Asset Management, L.P./10.00%, Michael Z. Kay, Mark E. Haidet, Alexander J. Douglas, James S. Balloun, Andrew S. Heyman/1.50%, John H. Heyman/2.50%

Financial Data: *Fiscal Year End:*12/31 *Latest Annual Data:* 12/31/2006

Year	Sales	Net Income
2006	$222,310,000	$18,357,000
2005	$172,042,000	$5,562,000
2004	$134,874,000	$4,188,000

Curr. Assets:	$88,044,000	**Curr. Liab.:**	$58,388,000		
Plant, Equip.:	$14,726,000	**Total Liab.:**	$82,684,000	**Indic. Yr. Divd.:**	NA
Total Assets:	$198,655,000	**Net Worth:**	$115,971,000	**Debt/ Equity:**	0.1610

Radiation Therapy Services Inc

2234 Colonial Blvd., Fort Myers, FL, 33907; ***PH:*** 1-239-931-7275; ***Fax:*** 1-239-931-7380; ***http://*** www.rtsx.com

General - Incorporation: FL
Employees: 1,240
Auditor: Ernst & Young LLP
Stk Agt: American Stock Transfer & Trust Co.
Counsel: NA
DUNS No.: NA

Stock - Price on:12/24/2007: $26.01
Stock Exchange: NDQ
Ticker Symbol: RTSX
Outstanding Shares: 23,480,000
E.P.S: $1.30
Shareholders: NA

Business: The group's principal activity is to provide radiation therapy services to cancer patients. The group owns, operates and manages treatment centers focused exclusively on providing comprehensive radiation treatment alternatives ranging from conventional external beam radiation to newer, technologically advanced options. The group currently provide radiation therapy in 41 free standing and 11 hospital based treatment centers. The treatment centers are clustered into 17 regional networks in eight states, including Alabama, Delaware, Florida, Kentucky, Maryland, Nevada, New York and North Carolina. The group conducts business under the name of its wholly owned subsidiary, 21st century oncology inc. On 23-Jun-2004, the group acquired the assets of devoto construction inc.

Primary SIC and add'l.: 7352 8099 8742

CIK No: 0001056904

Subsidiaries: 21st Century Oncology of Alabama, Inc., 21st Century Oncology of Kentucky, LLC, 21st Century Oncology of New Jersey, Inc., 21st Century Oncology, Inc., Ambergris, LLC, Arizona Radiation Therapy Management Services, Inc., Berlin Radiation Therapy Treatment Center, LLC, Bluegrass Regional Cancer Center, LLP, California Radiation Therapy Management Services, Inc., Devoto Construction of Southwest Florida, Inc., Faxton Leasing, LLC, Financial Services of Southwest Florida, LLC(surviving entity in merger with Financial Services of Southwest Florida, Inc.), Maryland Radiation Therapy Management Services, Inc., Naples PET, LLC, Nevada Radiation Therapy Management Services, Inc. 24 Subsidiaries included in the Index

Officers: Daniel E. Dosoretz/54/Dir., CEO, Pres., James H. Rubenstein/52/Dir., Dir. - Medical., Sec., David M. Koeninger/54/Exec. VP, Joseph Biscardi/38/Chief Accounting Officer, Corporate Controller, Nicholas Laudico/Investor Relations Officer, David N.T. Watson/42/CFO, Exec. VP

Directors: Daniel E. Dosoretz/54/Dir., CEO, Pres., Howard M. Sheridan/63/Chmn., Michael J. Katin/59/Dir., James H. Rubenstein/52/Dir., Dir. - Medical., Sec., Herbert F. Dorsett/74/Dir., Leo R. Doerr/67/Dir., Ronald E. Inge/51/Dir., Rabbi Solomon Agin/70/Dir., Janet Watermeier/55/Dir., Solomon Agin/70/Dir.

Owners: Michael J. Katin/4.20%, Daniel E. Dosoretz/16.00%, David N. T. Watson, Solomon Agin, Herbert F. Dorsett, Howard M. Sheridan/9.30%, James H. Rubenstein/10.80%, Leo Doerr, Ronald E. Inge, Insiders/40.50%

Financial Data: Fiscal Year End:12/31   **Latest Annual Data:** 12/31/2006

Year	Sales	Net Income
2006	$293,982,000	$30,323,000
2005	$227,250,000	$24,969,000
2004	$171,373,000	$9,188,000

Curr. Assets:	$87,538,000	**Curr. Liab.:**	$37,568,000	**P/E Ratio:**	19.41
Plant, Equip.:	$152,379,000	**Total Liab.:**	$257,181,000	**Indic. Yr. Divd.:**	NA
Total Assets:	$399,094,000	**Net Worth:**	$134,808,000	**Debt/ Equity:**	1.4166

Radica Games Ltd

6/f., 2-12 Au Pui Wan St., Ste. V, Fo Tan; ; http:// www.radicagames.com

General - Incorporation .... Bermuda	Stock- Price on:12/24/2007 .... $1.53
Employees 112	Stock Exchange .... NDQ
Auditor .... KPMG LLP	Ticker Symbol .... NA
Stk Agt .... U.S. Stock Transfer Corp	Outstanding Shares 8,730,000
Counsel .... NA	E.P.S. .... -$0.07
DUNS No. 66-278-3141	Shareholders .... NA

Business: The group's principle activities are the design, development, manufacture and distribution of a variety of electronic and mechanical handheld and tabletop games. It operates in two business segments: video games accessories ("Vga"), which includes video game controllers, steering wheels and other accessories and vga sourcing business; and games, which includes electronic and mechanical handheld and tabletop games. Electronic handheld and tabletop games areas include solitaire, hearts and gin rummy. Sports games include world class golf (TM) and football. It offers a broad line of electronic games including virtual fishing games such as sport bass fishin' (TM). The group operates in Hong Kong, United States, Canada, Europe, Asia-Pacific and other countries.

Primary SIC and add'l.: 3944

CIK No: 0000919642

Subsidiaries: Disc, Inc., Dongguan Radica Games Manufactory Co. Ltd, Leda Media Products Ltd, Radica (Macao Commercial Offshore) Limited, Radica Canada Ltd, Radica China Ltd, Radica Enterprises Ltd, Radica Europe Ltd, Radica Innovations (UK) Ltd (dormant), Radica Limited, Radica Technology (Shenzhen) Co. Ltd., Radica UK Ltd, RadMex S.A. de C.V.

Financial Data: Fiscal Year End:12/31   **Latest Annual Data:** 12/31/2006

Year	Sales	Net Income
2006	$13,037,000	-$2,000,000
2005	$13,421,000	-$2,329,000
2004	$14,160,000	$822,000

Curr. Assets:	$9,326,000	**Curr. Liab.:**	$8,816,000		
Plant, Equip.:	$3,359,000	**Total Liab.:**	$11,381,000	**Indic. Yr. Divd.:**	NA
Total Assets:	$17,455,000	**Net Worth:**	$6,074,000	**Debt/ Equity:**	NA

Radio One Inc

5900 Princess Garden Pkwy., 7th Fl., Lanham, MD, 20706; **PH:** 1-301-306-1111; **Fax:** 1-301-306-9426; http:// www.radio-one.com; **Email:** info@radio-one.com

General - Incorporation .... DE	Stock- Price on:12/24/2007 .... $7.15
Employees .... NA	Stock Exchange .... NDQ
Auditor .... Ernst & Young LLP	Ticker Symbol .... ROIA
Stk Agt ..... American Stock Transfer & Trust Co.	Outstanding Shares .... NA
Counsel .... Convigton & Burling	E.P.S. .... -$0.265
DUNS No. .... NA	Shareholders .... NA

Business: The group's principal activities are to acquire, operate and maintain radio broadcasting stations in the United States primarily targeting the african-american region. The group owns and operates 67 radio stations in 22 markets. The group also programs five channels on the xm satellite radio system. The group operates in Washington, dc baltimore, atlanta, philadelphia, detroit, st. Louis, cleveland and richmond. During 2004, the group acquired wsnj-FM, licensed to bridgeton, New Jersey, from New Jersey radio partners llc. On 16-Sep-2004, the group acquired assets of krts-FM.

Primary SIC and add'l.: 4832

CIK No: 0001041657

Subsidiaries: Bell Broadcasting Company, Blue Chip Broadcasting, Ltd, Charlotte Broadcasting, LLC, Hawes-Saunders Broadcast Properties, Inc, Home Plate Suite, LLC, New Mableton Broadcasting Corporation, Radio One Cable Holdings, Inc., Radio One Licenses, LLC, Radio One Media Holdings, LLC, Radio One of Atlanta, LLC, Radio One of Boston, Inc., Radio One of Charlotte, LLC, Radio One of Indiana, L.P, Radio One of Texas, L.P., Reach Media, Inc. 18 Subsidiaries included in the Index

Officers: Alfred C. Liggins/Dir., Pres., Treasurer, CEO/$1,186,552.00, Catherine L. Hughes/61/Chmn., Sec./$643,574.00, Leslie C. Bauer/CIO, Deborah A. Cowan/Sr. VP - Finance, John W. Mathews/VP - Engineering, Scott R. Royster/CFO, Exec. VP/$878,755.00, Barry Mayo/Pres. - Radio Divison, Alejandro A. Clabiorne/VP - Marketing, Linda J. Eckard-Vilardo/VP, Assist. Sec., Chief Administrative Officer/$866,669.00, Doug Abernethy/Regional VP, Bruce Demps/Regional VP, Jackie Kindall/VP - Human Resources, Mike Plantamura/VP, General Counsel, Gary Weiss/Regional VP, Rick Porter/Sr. VP, Regional Mgr. (20 Officers included in Index)

Directors: Alfred C. Liggins/Dir., Pres., Treasurer, CEO, Catherine L. Hughes/61/Chmn., Sec., Brian W. McNeill/Dir., Doyle B. Mitchell/Dir., Ronald E. Blaylock/Dir., Geoffrey D. Armstrong/Dir., Terry L. Jones/Dir., Ross L. Love/Dir.

Owners: Insiders/3.30%, Alfred C. Liggins/70.20%, Linda J. Vilardo, Insiders, Brian W. McNeill, Catherine L. Hughes/5.80%, The Vanguard Group/7.30%, Insiders/100.00%, Concordia Advisors/10.40%, Alfred C. Liggins, Terry L. Jones, Terry L. Jones, Alfred C. Liggins, Linda J. Vilardo, Scott R. Royster (33 Owners included in Index)

Financial Data: Fiscal Year End:12/31   **Latest Annual Data:** 12/31/2006

Year	Sales	Net Income
2006	$367,017,000	-$6,730,000
2005	$371,134,000	$50,530,000
2004	$319,761,000	$61,602,000

Curr. Assets:	$103,912,000	**Curr. Liab.:**	$72,307,000		
Plant, Equip.:	$53,945,000	**Total Liab.:**	$1,176,963,000	**Indic. Yr. Divd.:**	NA
Total Assets:	$2,195,210,000	**Net Worth:**	$1,018,267,000	**Debt/ Equity:**	0.9282

RadioShack Corp

Mail Stop CF3-201 300, RadioShack Circle, Fort Worth, TX, 76102; **PH:** 1-817-415-3011; **Fax:** 1-817-415-2647; http:// www.radioshack.com

General - Incorporation .... DE	Stock- Price on:12/24/2007 .... $33.87
Employees 40,000	Stock Exchange .... NYSE
Auditor .... PricewaterhouseCoopers LLP	Ticker Symbol .... RSH
Stk Agt .... Wells Fargo Shareowner Services	Outstanding Shares 135,560,000
Counsel .... NA	E.P.S. $1.15
DUNS No. .... NA	Shareholders .... NA

Business: The group's principle activity is to sell consumer electronic goods and services. The group also provides private label and third party branded products and services. The group's product line includes electronic parts and accessories, cellular, PCs and conventional telephones, audio and video equipment, direct-to-home (DTH) satellite systems and personal computers and related products. The group operates from United States, Puerto Rico and the Virgin Islands.

Primary SIC and add'l.: 5722 5999 5731 5064 3577

CIK No: 0000096289

Subsidiaries: Tandy Finance Corporation

Officers: Julian C. Day/56/Chmn., CEO/$3,525,322.00, Wesley V. Lowzinski/Sr. VP, General Merchandise Mgr., James F. Gooch/CFO, Exec. VP/$602,032.00, David S. Goldberg/Sr. VP, General Counsel, Corp. Sec., David P. Johnson/Sr. VP, Corporate Controller/$628,070.00

Directors: Julian C. Day/56/Chmn., CEO, Frank J. Belatti/60/Dir., Richard J. Hernandez/Dir., Eugene H. Lockhart/Dir., Jack L. Messman/68/Dir., William G. Morton/Dir., Thomas G. Plaskett/Dir., Edwina D. Woodbury/Dir., Daniel R. Feehan/Dir., Robert S. Falcone/Dir.

Owners: Jack L. Messman, Mark C. Hill, Thomas G. Plaskett, Edwina D. Woodbury, Eugene H. Lockhart, David P. Johnson, Insiders/1.00%, T. Rowe Price Associates, Inc./6.20%, William G. Morton, FMR Corp./14.99%, Frank J. Belatti, Gary M. Stone, Daniel R. Feehan, James F. Gooch, Leonard H. Roberts/2.50% (20 Owners included in Index)

Financial Data: Fiscal Year End:12/31   **Latest Annual Data:** 12/31/2006

Year	Sales	Net Income
2006	$4,777,500,000	$73,400,000
2005	$5,081,700,000	$267,000,000
2004	$4,841,200,000	$337,200,000

Curr. Assets:	$1,599,600,000	**Curr. Liab.:**	$984,200,000	**P/E Ratio:**	29.45
Plant, Equip.:	$386,300,000	**Total Liab.:**	$1,416,200,000	**Indic. Yr. Divd.:**	$0.250
Total Assets:	$2,070,000,000	**Net Worth:**	$653,800,000	**Debt/ Equity:**	0.4889

RadiSys Corp

5445 NE Dawson Creek Dr., Hillsboro, OR, 97124; **PH:** 1-503-615-1100; **Fax:** 1-503-615-1115; http:// www.radisys.com; **Email:** info@radisys.com

General - Incorporation .... OR	Stock- Price on:12/24/2007 .... $12.86
Employees 606	Stock Exchange .... NDQ
Auditor .... KPMG LLP	Ticker Symbol .... RSYS
Stk Agt .... Mellon Shareholder Services LLC	Outstanding Shares 21,950,000
Counsel .... NA	E.P.S. .... -$0.95
DUNS No. 18-107-4055	Shareholders .... NA

Business: The group's principal activities are to develop, produce and market computer system products for embedded computer applications in the manufacturing automation, medical, transportation, telecommunications, and test equipment marketplaces. It provides embedded systems for compute, data processing, and network-intensive applications within the commercial systems, service provider systems, and enterprise systems markets. The group designs and delivers a broad range of products at different levels of integration: complete turnkey systems; embedded subsystems and functional platforms; compute, i/o and packet processing blades; software, middleware, and microcode and semiconductors. The customers include OEMs such as aglient technologies, alcatel, applied materials, inc., avaya inc, and cisco systems inc.

Primary SIC and add'l.: 3823 7371

CIK No: 0000873044

Subsidiaries: Nihon RadiSys KK, RadiSys B.V., RadiSys GmbH, RadiSys Ireland Limited, RadiSys Israel Ltd., RadiSys Systems Technology (Shanghai) Co. Ltd., RadiSys Technology (Ireland) Limited, RadiSys UK Limited

Officers: Scott C. Grout/Dir., CEO, Pres./$1,402,885.00, Anthony Ambrose/VP, GM - Communications Networks, Wade Clowes/VP - Commercial Segment, Julia Harper/VP - Corporate Operations/$660,487.00, Glenn Splieth/VP - Human Resources, Brian Bronson/CFO/$433,092.00, George Shenoda/CTO, VP - Research, Development, Christian Lepiane/VP - Worldwide Sales, Corporate Marketing/$621,368.00, Peter Briscoe/Exec. VP, GM, Grant Henderson/VP - Product Marketing, Holly Stephens/Mgr. - Investor Relations, Finance

Directors: Scott C. Grout/Dir., CEO, Pres., Scott C. Gibson/Chmn., William W. Lattin/Dir., Lorene K. Steffes/Dir., Ken J. Bradley/Dir., Richard J. Faubert/Dir., Kevin C. Melia/Dir., Carl W. Neun/Dir.

Owners: Ken J. Bradley, Ronald J. Juvonen/8.71%, Christian A. Lepiane, Scott C. Grout/1.68%, Julia A. Harper, Kevin C. Melia, Lorene K. Steffes, Keith Lambert, Barclays Global Investors, NA./5.73%, Insiders/5.33%, Brown Capital Management, Inc./6.47%, Renaissance Technologies Corp./5.21%, The D3 Family Fund, L.P./10.79%, William W. Lattin, Carl W. Neun (19 Owners included in Index)

Financial Data: Fiscal Year End:12/31   **Latest Annual Data:** 12/31/2006

Year	Sales	Net Income
2006	$292,481,000	-$13,016,000
2005	$260,234,000	$15,958,000
2004	$245,824,000	$13,011,000

Curr. Assets:	$221,384,000	**Curr. Liab.:**	$59,809,000		
Plant, Equip.:	$11,075,000	**Total Liab.:**	$158,199,000	**Indic. Yr. Divd.:**	NA
Total Assets:	$381,654,000	**Net Worth:**	$223,455,000	**Debt/ Equity:**	0.4359

Radius Explorations Ltd

355 Burrard St., Ste. 830, Vancouver, BC, V6C 2G8; **PH:** 1-212-344-1600; http:// www.radiusgold.com

General - Incorporation	BC
Employees	NA
Auditor	Amisano Hanson
Stk Agt	Pacific Corporate Trust Co
Counsel	NA
DUNS No.	NA

Stock - Price on:12/24/2007	$0.677
Stock Exchange	OTC
Ticker Symbol	RDUFF
Outstanding Shares	NA
E.P.S.	NA
Shareholders	NA

Business: The group's principal activities are mining (non-oil-and-gas) exploration and development including gold explorations in Central America. The company is in early-stage exploration. It aims to discover new gold deposits and eventually aims to sell the ounces it discovers (or the company) to an established mining company. The company 14 different projects explores in three areas: Nicaragua, Guatemala and Mexico. In July 2004, Radius Gold was formed after the merger of Radius Explorations Ltd and PilaGold Inc. It trades on the TSX Venture Exchange (TSX-V) under the symbol RDU, and on the OTC BB under the symbol RDUFF.BB

Primary SIC and add'l.: 1000

CIK No: 0001113260

Subsidiaries: Corporacin Geolgica de Panam, Desarrollo Geologico Minerao, S.A., Exploraciones Minera de Guatemala, S.A., Exploraciones Mineras de Guatemala S.A, Geometalos Del Norte-Geonorte, Minerales de Nicaragua S.A., Minerales Sierra Pacifico S.A., Minerales Sierra Pacifico, S.A., Pavon (Cayman) Inc., Radius (Cayman) Inc., Radius (Cayman) Inc. and Pavon (Cayman) Inc., Radius Panam Corporation, Weltern Resources Corp, Recursos Del Cibao, S.A

Officers: Simon T. Ridgway/Dir., CEO, Pres., Ralph Rushton/VP - Corporate Development, Dir., Jock Slater/VP - Exploration, Cheryl Messier/CFO, Tim Osler/Sec., David Cass/VP - Exploration

Directors: Simon T. Ridgway/Dir., CEO, Pres., Ralph Rushton/VP - Corporate Development, Dir., Mario Szotlender/Dir., Craig Bow/Dir., Bradford J. Cooke/Dir., David P. Farrell/Dir., Nicholas Glass/Dir., Harmen J. Keyser/Dir.

Owners: Mario Szotlender/2.54%, Tim Osler/1.20%, David Cass/0.04%, Simon Ridgway/5.02%, Cheryl Messier/0.28%, Harmen Keyser/0.38%, David Farrell/0.28%, Insiders/10.96%, Nicholas Glass/0.37%, Ralph Rushton/0.63%, Craig Bow/0.28%, Bradford Cooke/0.28%

Financial Data: Fiscal Year End:12/31 Latest Annual Data: 12/31/2006

Year	Sales	Net Income
2006	NA	-$3,619,000
2005	NA	-$2,992,000
2004	NA	-$11,890,000

Curr. Assets:	$9,485,000	Curr. Liab.:	$192,000		
Plant, Equip.:	$284,000	Total Liab.:	$192,000	Indic. Yr. Divd.:	NA
Total Assets:	$9,769,000	Net Worth:	$9,577,000	Debt/ Equity:	NA

Radix Marine Inc

9119 Ridgetop Blvd, Ste 260, Silverdale, WA, 98383; **PH:** 1-360-692-6446;
http:// www.radixmarine.com

General - Incorporation	NV
Employees	NA
Auditor	Jonathon P. Reuben CPA
Stk Agt	Pacific Stock Transfer Company
Counsel	NA
DUNS No.	NA

Stock - Price on:12/24/2007	NA
Stock Exchange	OTC
Ticker Symbol	RDXM
Outstanding Shares	NA
E.P.S.	NA
Shareholders	NA

Business: The group's principal activity is to design, develop and construct naval undersea warfare combat vehicle prototype and gb-challenger class craft. It is part of an industry consortium which is under contract to the U.S. Navy for the spartan unmanned surface vehicle (usv) advanced concept technical demonstration (actd). The spartan actd is a four-year program for development of multi-mission patrol craft. The group also offers a manned, multi-mission craft called the gb challenger series. This craft can be reconfigured to perform a variety of military, safety, security, and environmental marine missions. The group intends to develop and market a complete line of manned and unmanned marine craft for the domestic and international market. On 30-Sep-2002, the group acquired integrated maritime platforms international inc.

Primary SIC and add'l.: 3731

CIK No: 0001030984

Financial Data: Fiscal Year End:06/30 Latest Annual Data: 06/30/2004

Year	Sales	Net Income
2004	$279,000	-$1,727,000
2003	$252,000	-$1,230,000
2002	$0	-$565,000

Curr. Assets:	$253,000	Curr. Liab.:	$992,000		
Plant, Equip.:	$486,000	Total Liab.:	$1,693,000	Indic. Yr. Divd.:	NA
Total Assets:	$1,616,000	Net Worth:	-$77,000	Debt/ Equity:	NA

Radview Software Ltd

14 Hamelacha St., Pk. Afek, Rosh Haayin, 48091; **PH:** 1-972-3-915-7060; **Fax:** 1-972-3-915-7683;
http:// www.radview.com; **Email:** info@radview.com

General - Incorporation	Israel
Employees	NA
Auditor	Kost Forer Gabbay & Kasierer
Stk Agt	Computershare Investor Services LLC
Counsel	Mintz Levin Cohn Ferris Et Al
DUNS No.	NA

Stock - Price on:12/24/2007	$0.09
Stock Exchange	OTC
Ticker Symbol	RDVWF
Outstanding Shares	NA
E.P.S.	NA
Shareholders	NA

Business: The group's principal activity is to develop and market software that measures the performance of Web applications. The products include webload, webrm and webft. Webload software ensures the performance of Web applications. Webrm software promotes the use of resources, facilitates collaboration and enables increased productivity by allowing technology staff to share testing technologies. Webft offers functional testing under real-world conditions. The group also provides services like customer support, maintenance and training. The customers of the group include American express, bank of America, british telecom, compaq, dell computer, fidelity investments, hewlett-packard, IBM, lucent technologies, mitsubishi, sap, toyota, sun microsystems and vanguard.

Primary SIC and add'l.: 7372

CIK No: 0001114999

Subsidiaries: RadView Software (UK) Ltd., RadView Software AB, RadView Software Gmbll, RadView Software, Inc.

Officers: Yochai Hacohen/Dir., CEO, Eran Witkon/VP - Product, Development, Ilan Kinreich/Dir., Founder, Chief Strategy Officer, Bill Spain/VP - Sales, Guy Spigelman/VP - Sales EMEA, Eli Sofer/CFO, Rafi Benami/VP, North America GM, Rami Goraly/VP - Marketing, Limor Stoller/39/VP - Finance

Directors: Yochai Hacohen/Dir., CEO, Jaron Lotan/Chmn., Shai Beilis/Dir., Ilan Kinreich/Dir., Founder, Chief Strategy Officer, David Assia/Dir., Eli Blatt/Dir., Hanna Lerman/Dir.

Owners: Yashir Hishtalmut Agah/0.10%, Shem Basum Ltd./3.90%, Fortissimo Capital Fund (Israel), L.P./60.10%, Yashir Gemel Klally/0.70%, Meitav Underwriting Ltd./1.70%, Shai Beilis/0.10%, Etgarim Pitzuim Madad/0.10%, Etgarim Gemel Klally/1.50%, Etgarim Hishtalmut Tasiot/0.10%, Perfect Central Compensation Fund/0.70%, Etgarim Pitzuim Klally/0.70%, Formula Ventures L.P./0.70%, Perfect Study Fund/6.50%, Fortissimo Capital Fund (Israel-DP), L.P./6.00%, Meitav Gemel Ltd./8.60% (28 Owners included in Index)

Financial Data: Fiscal Year End:12/31 Latest Annual Data: 12/31/2006

Year	Sales	Net Income
2006	$4,283,000	-$1,798,000
2005	$5,645,000	-$2,465,000
2004	$4,663,000	-$3,780,000

Curr. Assets:	$911,000	Curr. Liab.:	$2,895,000		
Plant, Equip.:	$102,000	Total Liab.:	$3,406,000	Indic. Yr. Divd.:	NA
Total Assets:	$1,367,000	Net Worth:	-$2,039,000	Debt/ Equity:	NA

Radvision Ltd

17-17 State Hwy. 208, Ste. 300, Fair Lawn, NJ, 07410; **PH:** 1-201-689-6300; **Fax:** 1-201-689-6301;
http:// www.radvision.com; **Email:** info@radvision.com

General - Incorporation	Israel
Employees	427
Auditor	Kost Forer Gabbay & Kasierer
Stk Agt	American Stock Transfer & Trust Co.
Counsel	Danziger, Klagsbald, Rosen & Co
DUNS No.	NA

Stock - Price on:12/24/2007	$21.36
Stock Exchange	NDQ
Ticker Symbol	RVSN
Outstanding Shares	22,310,000
E.P.S.	$0.71
Shareholders	NA

Business: The group's principle activities are the design, development and supply of products and technology that enable real-time voice, video and data communications over packet networks, including the Internet and other networks based on the Internet protocol. The company has over 250 clients including bosch, philips electronics, shanghai bell, nippon telegraph & telephone and siemens.

Primary SIC and add'l.: 4899 3669

CIK No: 0001105519

Subsidiaries: Radvision (hk) Ltd., Radvision (uk) Ltd., Radvision B.v., Radvision Communication Development (beijing) Co. Ltd., Radvision France S.a.r.l, Radvision Inc., Radvision Japan Kk

Officers: Boaz Raviv/CEO, Tsipi Kagan/CFO, Arnie Taragin/52/Corporate VP, General Counsel, Eli Doron/Pres., Chief Strategy Officer, Zeev Bikowsky/GM - Technology Business Unit, Alon Barnea/GM - Mobile, Service Provider Business Unit, Ron Bleakney/GM - Americas, Eitan Livne/GM - Asia Pacific, Dana Maor/VP - Human Resources, Ilan Givon/VP - Operations, Robert Rickwood/57/GM - Europe, Middle East, Africa, Philippe Besseyre Des Horts/GM - Europe, Middle East, Africa, EMEA, Rael Kolevsohn/VP, General Counsel

Directors: Zohar Zisapel/Chmn., Joseph Atsmon/Dir., Dan Barnea/Dir., Andreas Mattes/Dir., Efraim Wachtel/Dir., Liora Lev/Dir.

Owners: TimesSquare Capital Management, LLC/5.29%, Royce & Associates, LLC/5.50%, Clough Capital Partners L.P./5.21%, Zohar Zisapel/10.83%

Financial Data: Fiscal Year End:12/31 Latest Annual Data: 12/31/2006

Year	Sales	Net Income
2006	$91,023,000	$15,248,000
2005	$74,012,000	$14,690,000
2004	$64,236,000	$5,984,000

Curr. Assets:	$129,198,000	Curr. Liab.:	$25,537,000	P/E Ratio:	30.08
Plant, Equip.:	$3,609,000	Total Liab.:	$29,954,000	Indic. Yr. Divd.:	NA
Total Assets:	$182,559,000	Net Worth:	$152,605,000	Debt/ Equity:	NA

Radware Ltd

575 Corporate Dr., Ste. 205, Mahwah, NJ, 07430; **PH:** 1-201-512-9771; **Fax:** 1-201-512-9774;
http:// www.radware.com; **Email:** info@radware.com

General - Incorporation	Israel
Employees	475
Auditor	Kost Forer Gabbay & Kasierer
Stk Agt	American Stock Transfer & Trust Co.
Counsel	NA
DUNS No.	NA

Stock - Price on:12/24/2007	$14.4
Stock Exchange	NDQ
Ticker Symbol	RDWR
Outstanding Shares	19,420,000
E.P.S.	-$0.52
Shareholders	NA

Business: The groups principle activity is to develop, manufacture and sale of Internet traffic management solutions that enable continuous, high quality access, uninterrupted availability and optimal performance of Web sites and other Internet protocol services, applications and content. The group operates from USA, France, Germany, Sweden, the UK, the Netherlands, Australia, China, Italy, Japan, Singapore and Korea.

Primary SIC and add'l.: 7379 7373

CIK No: 0001094366

Subsidiaries: Nihon Radware KK, Radware Australia Pty. Ltd., Radware Canada Inc., Radware France, Radware GmbH, Radware Inc, Radware Korea Ltd., Radware Singapore Pte. Ltd., Radware Srl, Radware UK Limited

Officers: Roy Zisapel/37/CEO, Pres., Christopher McCleary/55/Exec. Chmn., Vered Raviv-Schwarz/39/General Counsel, Sec., Meir Moshe/54/CFO, Amir Peles/36/CTO, VP, Dennis S. Dobson/Investor Relations Contact, Larry Marino/51/Pres. - Radware Inc, Christine Aruza/40/VP - Corporate Marketing, Yuval Pemper/37/VP - Research, Development

Directors: Christopher McCleary/55/Exec. Chmn., Yehuda Zisapel/65/Dir., Hagen Hultzsch/67/Dir., Zohar Gilon/60/Dir., Orna Berry/59/Dir.

Owners: Meir Moshe/1.51%, Roy Zisapel/5.18%, FMR Corp./8.42%, P.A.W. Capital Corp./5.12%, Yehuda Zisapel/13.57%, Insiders/20.27%

Financial Data: Fiscal Year End:12/31 Latest Annual Data: 12/31/2006

Year	Sales	Net Income
2006	$81,410,000	-$1,280,000
2005	$77,584,000	$9,344,000
2004	$68,439,000	$13,780,000

Curr. Assets:	$166,716,000	Curr. Liab.:	$29,310,000	P/E Ratio:	30.08
Plant, Equip.:	$9,253,000	Total Liab.:	$33,254,000	Indic. Yr. Divd.:	NA
Total Assets:	$215,668,000	Net Worth:	$182,414,000	Debt/ Equity:	NA

Radyne Comstream Inc

3138 E Elwood St. , Phoenix, AZ, 85034; *PH:* 1-602-437-9620; *http://* www.radynecomstream.com

General - Incorporation	DE	*Stock*- Price on:12/24/2007	$9.86
Employees	343	Stock Exchange	NDQ
Auditor	KPMG LLP	Ticker Symbol	RADN
Stk Agt	Continental Stock Transfer & Trust Co	Outstanding Shares	18,400,000
Counsel	NA	E.P.S.	$0.62
DUNS No.	03-137-4952	Shareholders	NA

Business: The group's principal activities are to design, manufacture and sell products, systems and software used for the transmission and reception of data over satellite and cable communications networks. The products include satellite modulators and demodulators and earth stations, satellite broadcast receivers, frequency converters, ancillary products, equipment racks containing integrated modems and supporting equipment for data, audio and television communications and an integrated modem and router products. The major customers of the group are digital television users, international telecommunications providers, Internet service providers, financial information providers, systems integrators and the United States government. The group sells its products in the United States, Asia, Latin America, Europe, Canada and Africa.

Primary SIC and add'l.: 3669 7372

CIK No: 0000718573

Subsidiaries: Armer Communications Engineering Services Inc, Comstream Corporation, Tiernan Radyne ComStream Inc, Xicom Technology Europe Ltd, Xicom Technology Inc

Officers: Myron Wagner/Dir., CEO, COO, Pres./$1,592,376.00, Steven Eymann/56/CTO, Exec. VP/$469,261.00, Malcolm C. Persen/CFO, VP, Sec./$895,733.00, Garry D. Kline/VP, Corporate Controller, Assist. Sec., Brian Duggan/Pres., GM - Tiernan/$324,305.00, Walter Wood/Pres. - Xicom Technologies, Inc, GM/$489,825.00, Norm Larson/VP, GM, Radyne, Louis Dubin/VP - Sales, Marketing, David Koblinski/VP - Business Development, Rick Fleeter/Pres. - Aeroastro, Inc

Directors: Myron Wagner/Dir., CEO, COO, Pres., C. J. Waylan/Chmn., Robert C. Fitting/Dir., Dennis Elliott/Dir., James J. Spilker/Dir., Yip Loi Lee/Dir., William Keiper/Dir.

Owners: Myron Wagner, Putnam Investment/8.83%, Brian Duggan/1.68%, Dennis W. Elliott, Barclays Global Investors NA/5.51%, Robert C. Fitting/1.75%, C. J. Waylan, Malcolm C. Persen, Yip Loi Lee, Steven W. Eymann/1.97%, Insiders/8.32%, Royce & Associates/6.68%, James J. Spilker, Discovery Group I LLC/5.05%, Walter Wood *(16 Owners included in Index)*

*Financial Data: Fiscal Year End:*12/31   *Latest Annual Data:* 12/31/2006

Year		Sales		Net Income
2006		$134,209,000		$11,865,000
2005		$103,263,000		$10,686,000
2004		$56,578,000		$13,500,000
Curr. Assets:	$80,263,000	*Curr. Liab.:*	$17,991,000	*P/E Ratio:* 16.43
Plant, Equip.:	$3,822,000	*Total Liab.:*	$18,139,000	*Indic. Yr. Divd.:* NA
Total Assets:	$120,004,000	*Net Worth:*	$101,865,000	*Debt/ Equity:* NA

RAESystems

3775 N 1st St., San Jose, CA, 95134; *PH:* 1-408-952-8200; *Fax:* 1-408-952-8480; *http://* www.raesystems.com; *Email:* tech@raesystems.com

General - Incorporation	DE	*Stock*- Price on:12/24/2007	$2.35
Employees	791	Stock Exchange	AMEX
Auditor	BDO Seidman LLP	Ticker Symbol	RAE
Stk Agt	Interwest Transfer Company, Inc.	Outstanding Shares	59,300,000
Counsel	NA	E.P.S.	-$0.14
DUNS No.	NA	Shareholders	NA

Business: The group's principal activity is to manufacture atmospheric monitors, photo-ionization detectors, radiation detectors, gas detection tubes, sampling pumps and security monitoring devices. These products are used in weapons of mass destruction, detection of hazardous materials, toxic industrial chemicals, semiconductor waste, gamma rays, neutrons and other atmospheric contaminants and hazards, as well as in confined space entry monitoring programs all over the world. The group's products are marketed in the United States, Canada, western Europe, Mexico, Latin America, Japan and Singapore, as well as Beijing, shanghai and other petroleum-focused provinces in China. On 27-May-2004, the group acquired 64% stake in ke li heng security equipment co ltd (klh).

Primary SIC and add'l.: 7375 3829

CIK No: 0001084876

Subsidiaries: RAE France, RAE Systems (Asia) Limited, RAE Systems (Hong Kong) Limited, RAE Systems (Shanghai) Incorporated, RAE Systems Europe ApS, RAE Systems Inc., RAE United Kingdom Limited, Rae-klh (beijing) Co. Ltd, Renex Technology Limited

Officers: Robert I. Chen/Chmn., CEO, Pres./$349,377.00, George Mallinckrodt/RAE Systems Sales Dir. - Latin America, Mexico, Jesus Rubalcava/RAE Systems Regional Sales Mgr., Sana Qayyum/RAE Systems Regional Sales Mgr. - Internal Sales, Marketing, Administration, Alaa Ayoub/RAE Systems Regional Sales Mgr. - Middle East, Northern Africa O, G Industrial, Utilities Applications, Peter C. Hsi/Dir., CTO, VP/$207,630.00, Hong Tao Sun/VP - Engineering, Rudy Mui/VP - Marketing/$312,021.00, Gregory J. Vervais/VP, Chief Human Resources Officer, Robert Christopher Hameister/VP, Michael R. Ownby/Corp. Sec., Randall Gausman/CFO, VP/$53,456.00, Christopher Hameister/VP - Asia, Pacific, Europe, Middle East Business, Operations, Fei-Zhou Shen/VP - Worldwide Manufacturing, Michael Jorgensen/Regional Sales Mgr. - Africa, Australia, New Zealand, Dir. - Business Development Middle East, South Central Asia, South Pacific *(31 Officers included in Index)*

Directors: Robert I. Chen/Chmn., CEO, Pres., Sigrun Hjelmquist/Dir., Neil W. Flanzraich/Dir., Lyle Feisel/Dir., Peter C. Hsi/Dir., CTO, VP, James W. Power/Dir., Marvin A. Strait/Dir.

Owners: Lyle D. Feisel, Robert I. Chen/27.00%, Peter C. Hsi/5.00%, Wellington Management, LLP/7.00%, Kopp Investment Advisors, LLC/7.00%, Sigrun Hjelmquist, Marvin A. Strait, Neil W. Flanzraich/1.00%, Insiders/33.00%, Randall K. Gausman, FMR Corp./5.00%, Donald W. Morgan, Christopher Hameister, Rudy W. Mui

*Financial Data: Fiscal Year End:*12/31   *Latest Annual Data:* 12/31/2006

Year		Sales		Net Income
2006		$67,986,000		-$1,529,000
2005		$60,293,000		-$759,000
2004		$45,540,000		$2,335,000
Curr. Assets:	$60,279,000	*Curr. Liab.:*	$23,638,000	
Plant, Equip.:	$15,120,000	*Total Liab.:*	$29,079,000	*Indic. Yr. Divd.:* NA
Total Assets:	$89,753,000	*Net Worth:*	$56,179,000	*Debt/ Equity:* 0.0600

Railamerica Inc

5300 Broken Sound Blvd. Nw, Boca Raton, FL, 33487; *PH:* 1-561-994-6015; *http://* www.railamerica.com

General - Incorporation	DE	*Stock*- Price on:12/24/2007	NA
Employees	2,000	Stock Exchange	NYSE
Auditor	PricewaterhouseCoopers LLP	Ticker Symbol	RRA
Stk Agt	American Stock Transfer & Trust Co.	Outstanding Shares	NA
Counsel	Greenberg Traurig	E.P.S.	NA
DUNS No.	79-778-9716	Shareholders	NA

Business: The group's principal activity is to own and operate short line freight railroads in North America and regional freight railroad in Australia. It owns 47 railroads with approximately 11,900 miles in the United States, Australia and Canada. It operates 37 short line railroads properties and one tourist railroad in the United States. It also transports goods such as coal, lumber and forest products, agricultural and farm products and paper products. On 25-Jan-2004, the group acquired Central Michigan Railway Company.

Primary SIC and add'l.: 4011

CIK No: 0000887637

Subsidiaries: 3025619 Nova Scotia Limited, A & R Line, Inc., Alabama & Gulf Coast Railway LLC, American Rail Dispatching Center, Inc., Arizona & California Railroad Company, Bauxite & Northern Railway Company, California Northern Railroad Company, California Western Railroad, Inc., Cape Breton & Central Nova Scotia Railway Limited, Cascade and Columbia River Railroad Company, Central Oregon & Pacific Railroad, Inc., Central Railroad Company of Indianapolis, d/b/a Chicago, Ft. Wayne & Eastern Railroad, Central Western Railway Corporation, Connecticut Southern Railroad, Inc., Dakota Rail, Inc. 75 Subsidiaries included in the Index

Officers: Charles Swinburn/64/Dir., CEO, Michael E. Emmons/VP - Information Technology, Thomas C. Owen/Sr. VP - Business Development - Corporate Strategy, Daniel A. Hershman/VP - Litigation Counsel, Terry K. Forsman/Sr. VP - Human Resources, Todd N. Cecil/VP - Real Estate, Jan Polley/Pres. - Railamerica Operations East, Michael J. Howe/CFO, Exec. VP, Jim Ryan/Assist. GM - Cape Breton, Central Nova Scotia Railway, Roy Budgell/Marketing, Sales, Cape Breton, Central Nova Scotia Railway, Pete Jespersen/GM - Ventura County Railroad CO, Jose Ramos/Marketing, Sales, Ventura County Railroad CO, Sandy Franger/VP - Contracts - Interline Agreements, M. S. Linn/Sr. VP - Asset Management, Robert J. Rabin/Sr. VP, Corporate Controller *(96 Officers included in Index)*

Directors: Charles Swinburn/64/Dir., CEO, William G. Pagonis/64/Chmn., Richard Rampell/51/Dir., Donald D. Redfearn/53/Dir., Pres., Chief Administrative Officer, Sec., Ferd C. Meyer/64/Dir., Anne H. McNamara/Dir., Douglas R. Nichols/50/Dir., Harold R. Curtis/68/Dir.

Owners: Charles Swinburn, Keeley Asset Management Corp./7.98%, Richard Rampell, Anne McNamara, Dimensional FundAdvisors Inc./8.47%, Heartland Advisors/6.45%, Ferd C. Meyer, Donald D. Redfearn/1.35%, Harold R. Curtis, Douglas R. Nichols, Joe R. Conklin, Michael J. Howe, Scott G. Williams, William G. Pagonis, Highfields Capital Management LP/7.56% *(16 Owners included in Index)*

Rainbow Media Enterprises Inc

200 Jericho QuaDrangle, Jericho, NY, 11753; *PH:* 1-516-803-3000; *http://* www.rainbow-media.com

General - Incorporation	DE	*Stock*- Price on:12/24/2007	NA
Employees	NA	Stock Exchange	NA
Auditor	NA	Ticker Symbol	NA
Stk Agt	NA	Outstanding Shares	NA
Counsel	NA	E.P.S.	NA
DUNS No.	NA	Shareholders	NA

Business: The group's principal business includes three national 24-hour networks, a variety of on-demand programming services, a suite of 21 high-definition channels with the unique high-definition programming content known as VOOM(SM), and motion picture production and distribution. The business also includes Rainbow Network Communications, a full-service network programming origination and distribution company.

Primary SIC and add'l.: 4841

CIK No: 0001289606

Raindance Communications Inc

1157 Century Dr, Louisville, CO, 80027; *PH:* 1-800-878-7326; *http://* www.raindance.com

General - Incorporation	DE	*Stock*- Price on:12/24/2007	NA
Employees	NA	Stock Exchange	NA
Auditor	KPMG LLP	Ticker Symbol	NA
Stk Agt	Wells Fargo Bank Minnesota N.A	Outstanding Shares	NA
Counsel	Cooley Godward LLP	E.P.S.	NA
DUNS No.	NA	Shareholders	NA

Business: The group's principal activity is to provide remote communication services for everyday business meetings and events. The group's services are based on proprietary architecture that integrates traditional telephony technology with real-time interactive Web tools. Reservation less conferencing provides for automated reservation less audio conferencing with simple Web controls and presentation tools. Web conferencing pro allows users to integrate reservation less automated audio conferencing with advanced Web interactive tools over the Web such as application sharing and Web touring. Operator assisted conferencing provides operator assistance during high profile conferencing events and additional services such as call taping and transcription. Unlimited conferencing offers unlimited local toll access to our reservation less conferencing service for a fixed monthly rate. The group serves computer software, business services manufacturing and financial services markets.

Primary SIC and add'l.: 4899

CIK No: 0001046832

Officers: Don Detampel/CEO, Tom Hart/VP - Client Services, Brad Dupee/VP - Channel Sales, Neal Nicholas/VP - North American Sales, Kenneth Mesikapp/Sr. VP - Finance, Accounting, Peter Holst/38/COO, Pres., Bryce L. Ambraziunas/Sr. VP - Operations, Nicholas J. Cuccaro/CFO, Todd Vernon/43/Co - Founder, CTO, Stephanie A. Anagnostou/39/Sr. VP, General Counsel

Directors: Todd Vernon/43/Co - Founder, CTO

Rainier Pacific Financial Group Inc

1498 Pacific Ave., Ste. 400, Tacoma, WA, 98402; *PH:* 1-253-926-4038; *Fax:* 1-253-926-4090; *http://* www.rainierpac.com

General - Incorporation............................WA
Employees..171
Auditor ....Moss Adams LLP
Stk Agt.........................Computershare Trust Co
Counsel...NA
DUNS No. ....NA

Stock - Price on:12/24/2007 ....$18.06
Stock Exchange...NDQ
Ticker Symbol...RPFG
Outstanding Shares 5,990,000
E.P.S...$0.53
Shareholders...NA

Business: The group's principal activity is to provide full range of banking services through banking offices located in pierce county and south king county, Washington. The group offers a broad array of deposit and loan services through rainier pacific bank and offers automobile and homeowner's insurance, financial planning and non-FDIC insured mutual fund and investment services through the wholly owned subsidiary, support systems, inc. The group operates through 12 full-service banking offices, 19 automated teller machines, call center and Internet banking services.

Primary SIC and add'l.: 6712 6035

CIK No: 0001243800

Subsidiaries: Rainier Pacific Bank, Rainier Pacific Savings Bank

Officers: John A. Hall/Dir., CEO, Pres./$562,311.00, Joel G. Edwards/CFO, VP, Treasurer/$258,941.00, Victor J. Toy/Sr. VP, Corp. Sec./$347,286.00, Carolyn S. Middleton/Bank VP, Chief Lending Officer/$247,503.00, Dalen D. Harrison/VP/$245,078.00, Sandra K. Steffeney/VP, Richard D. Pickett/VP, Waylin L. McCurley/VP, David R. Webb/VP

Directors: John A. Hall/Dir., CEO, Pres., Edward J. Brooks/Chmn., Stephen M. Bader/Dir., Alan M. Somers/Dir., Alfred H. Treleven/Dir., Brian K. Knutson/Dir., Robert H. Combs/Dir., Charles E. Cuzzetto/Dir., Karyn R. Clarke/Dir.

Owners: Victor J. Toy/1.87%, Dalen D. Harrison, Edward J. Brooks/1.26%, Insiders/16.52%, Joel G. Edwards/1.45%, John A. Hall/2.59%, Rainier Pacific/9.80%, Brian E. Knutson/1.02%, Carolyn S. Middleton, Karyn R. Clarke, Robert H. Combs/1.02%, Private Capital Management, L.P./7.78%, Dimensional Fund Advisors LP/5.05%, Rainier Pacific Foundation/7.41%, Charles E. Cuzzetto (18 Owners included in Index)

Financial Data: Fiscal Year End:12/31   Latest Annual Data: 12/31/2006

Year	Sales	Net Income
2006	$63,104,000	$2,960,000
2005	$50,477,000	$2,693,000
2004	$48,069,000	$3,627,000

Curr. Assets:	$16,081,000	Curr. Liab.:	$463,073,000	P/E Ratio:	34.08
Plant, Equip.:	$34,383,000	Total Liab.:	$814,867,000	Indic. Yr. Divd.:	$0.260
Total Assets:	$902,697,000	Net Worth:	$87,830,000	Debt/ Equity:	3.8210

Raining Data Corp

25A Technology Dr., Irvine, CA, 92618; *PH:* 1-949-442-4400; *Fax:* 1-949-250-8187; *http://* www.rainingdata.com; *Email:* techinfo@rainingdata.com

General - Incorporation............................DE
Employees..131
Auditor ....KPMG LLP
Stk Agt.............................Registrar & Transfer Co
Counsel..........Wilson Sonsini Goodrich & Rosati
DUNS No. 18-764-3614

Stock - Price on:12/24/2007 ....$3.17
Stock Exchange...NDQ
Ticker Symbol...RDTA
Outstanding Shares 21,150,000
E.P.S...-$0.14
Shareholders...NA

Business: The group's principal activity is to design, develop, sell, and support four software product lines: multidimensional database management systems, rapid application development software tools, xml data management servers and the pick data provider for the net development environment. The products are sold to in-house corporate development teams, commercial application developers, system integrators, independent software vendors, value-added resellers and independent consultants. In addition to computer software products, the group provides continuing maintenance and customer service contracts as well as professional services, technical support and training.

Primary SIC and add'l.: 7372 7379

CIK No: 0000820738

Subsidiaries: Omnis Software, Inc, Pick Systems UK, Ltd, PickAX, Inc, Raining Data France, Raining Data Germany, Gmbh, Raining Data Holdings, Ltd, Raining Data UK, Ltd, Raining Data US, Inc

Officers: Carlton H. Baab/Dir., CEO, Pres., Klaus Schroedl/Contact - Training, Consulting, Keith Shimmin/Sales Mgr., Mandi Townsend/Contact - Sales, Mark Morley/Contact - Technical Support, Thomas G. Lim/CFO, VP - Finance, Sec., Bob Albo/VP - XML, Centric Business Solutions, John H. Bramley/VP - Product Development, Janet Cioffi/VP - Sales, Americas, Asia Pacific, Gail Lawrence/Inside Sales Representative, Alain Teboul/French Office Mgr., Robert Janovszky/Sales Mgr. - Pour L'europe du Sud, Anne Rougier/Finance, Administration Dir., Jean Lemonnier/Support at Assistance, Birgit Jaeger/Contact - Sales (18 Officers included in Index)

Directors: Carlton H. Baab/Dir., CEO, Pres., Richard W. Koe/Chmn., Gerald F. Chew/Dir., Douglas G. Marshall/Dir.

Owners: Richard W. Koe, Douglas G. Marshall, Astoria Capital Partners L.P., Rockport Group LP, Gerald F. Chew, Carlton H. Baab, Richard W. Smith, Robert W. Albo, Insiders, Philip and Debra Barrett Charitable Remainder Trust, Thomas Lim

Financial Data: Fiscal Year End:03/31   Latest Annual Data: 03/31/2007

Year	Sales	Net Income
2007	$18,744,000	-$2,958,000
2006	$20,294,000	-$1,624,000
2005	$21,483,000	-$921,000

Curr. Assets:	$13,037,000	Curr. Liab.:	$8,348,000		
Plant, Equip.:	$871,000	Total Liab.:	$30,040,000	Indic. Yr. Divd.:	NA
Total Assets:	$41,810,000	Net Worth:	$11,770,000	Debt/ Equity:	2.4451

Rainmaker Systems Inc

900 E Hamilton Ave., Ste. 400, Campbell, CA, 95008; *PH:* 1-408-626-3800; *Fax:* 1-408-369-0910; *http://* www.rmkr.com; *Email:* inquiries@rmkr.com

General - Incorporation............................CA
Employees..415
Auditor ....BDO Seidman LLP
Stk Agt.........................U.S. Stock Transfer Corp
Counsel...............................White S. Case LLC
DUNS No. 62-650-4781

Stock - Price on:12/24/2007 ....$7.19
Stock Exchange...NDQ
Ticker Symbol...RMKR
Outstanding Shares 18,690,000
E.P.S...$0.12
Shareholders...NA

Business: The group's principle activities are to provide sales, marketing, and e-commerce services for technology companies on an outsourced basis. In addition, the company's services also include customer database enhancement, crm technology integration and order management. The services to their technology clients are designed to increase the revenue from their support contracts and software

subscriptions and to enhance their customer relationships. Core services include professional telesales, direct marketing and hosted e-commerce. The customers of the company are hardware and software companies with significant installed customer bases and products that benefit from focused sales and marketing programs for support contracts, software subscriptions, or maintenance agreements. The group's quarterly revenue for September 2007 was 19.08 millions of USD.

Primary SIC and add'l.: 7389

CIK No: 0001094007

Subsidiaries: Rainmaker Service Contract Sales, Inc., Rainmaker Service Sales, Inc, Rainmaker Services, Inc., Sunset Direct, Inc.

Officers: Michael Silton/Dir., CEO/$654,685.00, Clinton Hauptmeier/39/GM - Lead Generation/$259,005.00, Steve Valenzuela/Sr. VP, CFO/$341,299.00, Robert Langer/52/GM - Service Sales/$264,201.00, Ritch Haselden/42/GM - Service Sales/$276,598.00, Ken Forbes/CTO, VP, Carmela Wong/VP - Marketing, Investor Relations Officer, Eric Anderson/VP - Worldwide Sales, Randy Lowe/VP - Business Development, Emeerging Markets, Doug Huggins/VP, GM - Client Services, Moe Bawa/VP, GM - Client Services, P. J. Stone/VP - Global Call Center Operations, Bill Davidheiser/VP - Engineering

Directors: Michael Silton/Dir., CEO, Alok Mohan/Non Exec. Chmn., Robert Leff/Dir., Mitchell Levy/Dir., Brad Peppard/Dir.

Owners: Alok Mohan/1.50%, Clinton Hauptmeier, Bradford Peppard, Mitchell Levy, Steve Valenzuela/1.30%, Michael Silton/10.00%, Robert Leff/1.10%, Diker GP, L.L.C./9.70%, Fort Mason Capital, LLC/5.00%, Ritch Haselden, Insiders/16.40%, Robert Langer

Financial Data: Fiscal Year End:12/31   Latest Annual Data: 06/30/2007

Year	Sales	Net Income
2007	NA	NA
2006	$48,921,000	$3,403,000
2005	$32,114,000	-$5,004,000

Curr. Assets:	$37,030,000	Curr. Liab.:	$31,828,000	P/E Ratio:	35.95
Plant, Equip.:	$4,293,000	Total Liab.:	$32,556,000	Indic. Yr. Divd.:	NA
Total Assets:	$54,258,000	Net Worth:	$21,702,000	Debt/ Equity:	0.0643

RAIT Financial Trust

1818 Market St., 28th Fl., Philadelphia, PA, 19103; *PH:* 1-215-861-7900; *Fax:* 1-215-861-7920; *http://* www.raitinvestmenttrust.com; *Email:* info@raitft.com

General - Incorporation ....MD
Employees..70
Auditor ....Grant Thornton LLP
Stk Agt...... American Stock Transfer & Trust Co.
Counsel...NA
DUNS No. ....NA

Stock - Price on:12/24/2007 ....$29.98
Stock Exchange...NYSE
Ticker Symbol...RAS
Outstanding Shares 63,690,000
E.P.S...-$3.4
Shareholders...NA

Business: The groups principle activity is to invest in real estate properties. The group also provides debt-financing options to the real estate industry. In the year 2006, the group acquired Taberna Realty Finance Trust. The group operates from the United States. The group's quarterly revenue for Sept 2007 was 247.37 millions of USD.

Primary SIC and add'l.: 6798

CIK No: 0001045425

Subsidiaries: 6006 Executive Boulevard, LLC, 901 King Street Associates, 990 Stewart Avenue Investors, LLC, Amarillo Dunhill, LLC, Bear Stearns ARM Trust 2005-7, Bear Stearns ARM Trust 2005-9, Braden Lakes Member, LLC, Broadstone I Partner, LLC, Buckner-Beckley, L.L.C., Chestnut Street Properties I LLC, Citigroup Mortgage Loan Trust 2005-11, Cornerstone Member, LLC, CWABS Trust 2005 HYB9, Diversified Historic Investors III: Lincoln Court Apartments Trust, E Pointe Properties I, Ltd. 90 Subsidiaries included in the Index

Officers: Daniel Gideon Cohen/Dir. - Trustee, CEO/$307,213.00, Mitchell Kahn/Co - Pres., Jack E. Salmon/CFO, Treasurer/$29,970.00, Plamen Mitrikov/Exec. VP - Asset Management, Ellen J. Distefano/Chief Accounting Officer/$450,367.00, Scott F. Schaeffer/COO, Pres./$1,174,006.00, Raphael Licht/Chief Administrative Officer, Chief Legal Officer, Sec., Kenneth R. Frappier/Chief Credit Officer/$846,606.00, Wade Vandegrift/Contact - Taberna Securities, LLC, Thomas Bogal/Contact - Taberna Securities, LLC, Howard Altschul/Contact - Taberna Securities, LLC, Tero Tiilikainen/Contact - Taberna Securities, LLC

Directors: Daniel Gideon Cohen/Dir. - Trustee, CEO, Betsy Z. Cohen/Chmn., Edward S. Brown/66/Dir., Trustee, Kristin S. Kim/Dir., Trustee, Daniel Promislo/74/Dir., Trustee, Murray Stempel/Dir., Trustee, Frank A. Farnesi/Dir., Trustee, Arthur Makadon/64/Dir., Trustee, John F. Quigley/Dir., Trustee

Owners: Aristeia Special Investments Master LP, Aristeia Partners LP, Aristeia International Limited, Merrill Lynch Financial Market/1.80%, Radcliffe SPC, Ltd. for and on behalf of the Class A Segregated Portfolio, DB RREEF Reflex Master Portfolio Ltd

Financial Data: Fiscal Year End:12/31   Latest Annual Data: 12/31/2006

Year	Sales	Net Income
2006	$102,282,000	$77,918,000
2005	$110,553,000	$78,027,000
2004	$99,073,000	$66,158,000

Curr. Assets:	$503,474,000	Curr. Liab.:	$129,441,000		
Plant, Equip.:	NA	Total Liab.:	$10,864,102,000	Indic. Yr. Divd.:	$1.840
Total Assets:	$12,060,506,000	Net Worth:	$1,196,404,000	Debt/ Equity:	NA

Ralcorp Holdings Inc

800 Market St., Ste. 2900, St. Louis, MO, 63101; *PH:* 1-314-877-7000; *Fax:* 1-314-877-7666; *http://* www.ralcorp.com; *Email:* investorrelations@ralcorp.com

General - Incorporation ....MO
Employees...6,500
Auditor ....PricewaterhouseCoopers LLP
Stk Agt.........................EquiServe Trust Co N.A
Counsel...NA
DUNS No. 82-640-9369

Stock - Price on:12/24/2007 ....$54.4
Stock Exchange...NYSE
Ticker Symbol...RAH
Outstanding Shares 27,040,000
E.P.S...$1.18
Shareholders...NA

Business: The groups principle activities include manufacturing, distributing and marketing store brand food products. The groups products include ready-to-eat and hot cereal products, store brand and value brand snack mixes and corn-based snacks. In the year 2007 the group acquired Bloomfield Bakers and Lovin Oven L.L.C. The group operates from United States.

Primary SIC and add'l.: 2052 2032 2043 2033 2068 2064

CIK No: 0001029506

Subsidiaries: Bakery Chef, LL.C, Bremner, Inc, Canadian Limited Partnership, Community Shops, Inc., Flavor House Products, Inc., Heritage Wafer, LLC, Lofthouse Bakery Products, Inc, Medallion Foods, Inc., National Oats Company, Nutcracker Brands, Inc., PL Financial Incorporated, RAH Canada Limited Partnership, Ralcorp Receivables Corporation, Ralston Food Sales, Inc, RH Financial Corporation 22 Subsidiaries included in the Index

Officers: Kevin J. Hunt/Dir., Co - CEO, Pres., David P. Skarie/Co - CEO, Pres., Charles G. Huber/44/Corporate VP, General Counsel, Sec., Thomas G. Granneman/59/Corporate VP, Controller, R. D. Wilkinson/58/Corporate VP

Directors: Kevin J. Hunt/Dir., Co - CEO, Pres., William P. Stiritz/73/Chmn., Joe R. Micheletto/72/Dir., David W. Kemper/58/Dir., Richard A. Liddy/73/Dir., Jack W. Goodall/70/Dir., Bill G. Armstrong/60/Dir., David R. Banks/71/Dir.

Owners: David R. Banks, William P. Stiritz/4.40%, Richard G. Scalise, Keeley Asset Management Corp./5.74%, Insiders/9.10%, Joe R. Micheletto/1.00%, Richard R. Koulouris, Bill G. Armstrong, Thomas G. Granneman, BAMCO, Inc./7.00%, Jack W. Goodall, Richard A. Liddy, David P. Skarie, Bank of New York Mellon Corporation/6.27%, Barclays Global Investors UK Holdings Limited/5.18% *(20 Owners included in Index)*

Financial Data: Fiscal Year End:09/30 Latest Annual Data: 09/30/2007

Year	Sales	Net Income
2007	$2,233,400,000	$31,900,000
2006	$1,850,200,000	$68,300,000
2005	$1,675,100,000	$71,400,000

Curr. Assets:	$386,400,000	Curr. Liab.:	$197,000,000	P/E Ratio: 43.52
Plant, Equip.:	$401,100,000	Total Liab.:	$1,031,100,000	Indic. Yr. Divd.: NA
Total Assets:	$1,507,500,000	Net Worth:	$476,400,000	Debt/ Equity: 1.5009

RAM Energy Resources Inc

5100 E Skelly Dr. Ste. 650, Tulsa, OK, 74135; *PH:* 1-918-663-2800; *http://* ramenergy.triadcentral.com

General - Incorporation	DE	Stock - Price on:12/24/2007	$5.4
Employees	100	Stock Exchange	NDQ
Auditor	BDO Seidman, LLP	Ticker Symbol	RAME
Stk Agt	Continental Stock Transfer & Trust Co	Outstanding Shares	41,150,000
Counsel	NA	E.P.S.	$0.05
DUNS No.	NA	Shareholders	NA

Business: The groups principle activities include acquiring, development, exploiting, exploring and producing oil and natural gas properties. In May 8, 2006, the group acquired Tremisis Energy Acquisition Corporation. The group operates from Texas, Louisiana and Oklahoma. The group's quarterly revenue for September 2007 was 18.43 millions of USD.

Primary SIC and add'l.: 1311

CIK No: 0001282648

Subsidiaries: Carmen Field Limited Partnership (CFLP), Magic Circle Energy Corporation

Officers: Larry E. Lee/Chmn., CEO, Pres., John M. Longmire/Sr. VP, CFO, Larry G. Rampey/Sr. VP - Operations, Drake N. Smiley/Sr. VP - Land - Exploration, John L. Cox/Sr. VP, Sec., Treasurer, Robert E. Phaneuf/VP - Corporate Development

Directors: Larry E. Lee/Chmn., CEO, Pres., Sean P. Lane/Dir., Gerald R. Marshall/Dir., John M. Reardon/Dir.

Owners: John M. Longmire, Larry E. Lee/31.00%, Sean P. Lane, Cumberland Associates, LLC/5.50%, Gerald R. Marshall, Robert E. Phaneuf, Larry G. Rampey, Britani Talley Bowman/28.00%, Rockbay Capital Management, LP/5.60%, John L. Cox, Insiders/32.00%, Drake N. Smiley, John M. Reardon

Financial Data: Fiscal Year End:12/31 Latest Annual Data: 12/31/2006

Year	Sales	Net Income
2006	$70,244,000	$5,048,000
2005	NA	$351,000
2004	NA	$65,000

Curr. Assets:	$15,712,000	Curr. Liab.:	$18,180,000	P/E Ratio: 108.00
Plant, Equip.:	$142,805,000	Total Liab.:	$189,620,000	Indic. Yr. Divd.: NA
Total Assets:	$161,725,000	Net Worth:	-$27,895,000	Debt/ Equity: NA

RAM Holdings Ltd

RAM Re House, Penthouse Ste., 46 Reid St., Hamilton; ; *http://* www.ramre.com; *Email:* Info@ramre.com

General - Incorporation	Bermuda	Stock - Price on:12/24/2007	$16.62
Employees	13	Stock Exchange	NDQ
Auditor	PricewaterhouseCoopers LLP	Ticker Symbol	RAMR
Stk Agt	Bank of New York	Outstanding Shares	27,230,000
Counsel	NA	E.P.S.	$0.69
DUNS No.	NA	Shareholders	NA

Business: The groups principal activity is to provide reinsurance services. The products of the group include public finance and structured finance. Specific customers of the group include Ambac Assurance Corporatio, Assured Guaranty Corp, CIFG IXIS Financial Guaranty North America, Inc and Financial Security Assurance Inc. The group operates from the United States. The assets of the group for the year 2006 were $494,960 (thousands).

Primary SIC and add'l.: 6351

CIK No: 0001352713

Subsidiaries: RAM Reinsurance Company Ltd.

Officers: Vernon M. Endo/Dir., CEO, Pres./$1,508,468.00, Richard Lutenski/CFO/$1,041,952.00, David K. Steel/Chief Risk Mgr./$897,323.00, James P. Gerry/MD/$1,574,463.00, Paul Wollmann/MD, Victoria W. Guest/General Counsel/$641,072.00

Directors: Vernon M. Endo/Dir., CEO, Pres., Steven J. Tynan/Chmn. - RAM Reinsurance Company, Edward F. Bader/Dir., Victor J. Bacigalupi/Dir., David L. Boyle/Dir., Allan S. Bufferd/Dir., Daniel C. Lukas/Dir., Mark F. Milner/Dir., Dirk A. Stuurop/Dir., Conrad Voldstad/Dir., Joan H. Dillard/Dir., Joseph Donovan/Dir.

Owners: Vernon M. Endo, Bank of America/5.00%, Richard Lutenski, Steven J. Tynan/9.10%, David K. Steel, Conrad P. Voldstad, Insiders/11.00%, The PMI Group, Inc./23.40%, American International Group, Inc./10.60%, Mary Ellen Pavlovsky, David L. Boyle, James P. Gerry, High Ridge Capital Partners Limited Partnership/8.90%, Allan S. Bufferd, Dirk A. Stuurop *(18 Owners included in Index)*

Financial Data: Fiscal Year End:12/31 Latest Annual Data: 12/31/2006

Year	Sales	Net Income
2006	$72,055,000	$41,053,000

Curr. Assets:	$58,419,000	Curr. Liab.:	$5,362,000	P/E Ratio: 10.86
Plant, Equip.:	$73,000	Total Liab.:	$257,636,000	Indic. Yr. Divd.: NA
Total Assets:	$711,903,000	Net Worth:	$379,267,000	Debt/ Equity: 0.1011

Rambus Inc

4440 El Camino Real, Los Altos, CA, 94022; *PH:* 1-650-947-5000; *Fax:* 1-650-947-5001; *http://* www.rambus.com; *Email:* info@rambus.com

General - Incorporation	DE	Stock - Price on:12/24/2007	$18.82
Employees	333	Stock Exchange	NDQ
Auditor	PricewaterhouseCoopers LLP	Ticker Symbol	RMBS
Stk Agt	Computershare Investor Services LLC	Outstanding Shares	102,760,000
Counsel	Wilson Sonsini Goodrich & Rosati	E.P.S.	-$0.11
DUNS No.	62-257-4903	Shareholders	NA

Business: The group's principal activities are to design, develop, license and market high-speed chip-connection technologies to enhance the performance and cost-effectiveness of computers, consumer electronics, communications systems and networking products. These solutions include multiple chip-to-chip interface products, which can be grouped into two major categories: memory interfaces and logic interfaces. The memory interface products provide an interface between memory chips and logic chips. The logic interface products provide an interface between two logic chips. The group sells its technology to customers in the Far East, North America and Europe. The major lisensees of the group include elpida, hitachi, ltd., intel, matsushita, mitsubishi electric corporation, nec corporation, oki electric industry co., ltd., renesas technology corporation, samsung and toshiba. Rambus, rdram, xdr, raser, raserx and redwood are registered trademarks of rambus inc.

Primary SIC and add'l.: 7373 7379

CIK No: 0000917273

Subsidiaries: Rambus, Rambus Chip Technologies Private Limited, Rambus Deutschland GmbH, Rambus K.K.

Officers: Harold Hughes/62/Dir., CEO, Pres., Laura Stark/Sr. VP - Platform Solutions, John T.C. Ho/VP - Engineering, Thomas Lavelle/Sr. VP, General Counsel, Martin Scott/Sr. VP - Engineering, Sharon Holt/Sr. VP - Worldwide Sales, Licensing, Marketing, Michael Schroeder/VP - Human Resources, Kevin Donnelly/Sr. VP - Engineering, Mark Horowitz/50/Dir., Chief Scientist, Tim Messegee/VP - Corporate Marketing, Eric Ries/VP, MD - Rambus Japan, John D. Danforth/Sr. Legal Advisor, Satish Rishi/Sr. VP, CFO, Udo Muerle/Dir. - Business Development, Europe, Craig Hample/Technical Dir. - Rambus Fellow *(18 Officers included in Index)*

Directors: Harold Hughes/62/Dir., CEO, Pres., Kevin Kennedy/53/Chmn., Penelope A. Herscher/48/Dir., Thomas J. Bentley/59/Dir., Michael P. Farmwald/54/Dir., Sunlin Chou/62/Dir., Bruce Dunlevie/51/Dir., Abraham Sofaer/70/Dir., David Shrigley/60/Dir., Mark Horowitz/50/Dir., Chief Scientist, Eric Ries/VP, MD - Rambus Japan

Owners: Samir A. Patel, Satish Rishi, Thomas J. Bentley, Penelope A. Herscher, Kevin Kennedy, Kevin S. Donnelly, Abraham D. Sofaer, David Shrigley, Robert K. Eulau, Bruce Dunlevie, Harold Hughes, Vanguard Horizon FundsVanguard Capital/4.98%, Insiders/6.90%, Sunlin Chou, Michael P. Farmwald/2.71% *(20 Owners included in Index)*

Financial Data: Fiscal Year End:12/31 Latest Annual Data: 12/31/2006

Year	Sales	Net Income
2006	$195,324,000	-$13,816,000
2005	$157,198,000	$33,677,000
2004	$144,874,000	$33,559,000

Curr. Assets:	$442,744,000	Curr. Liab.:	$218,438,000	P/E Ratio: 62.73
Plant, Equip.:	$26,019,000	Total Liab.:	$222,329,000	Indic. Yr. Divd.: NA
Total Assets:	$604,617,000	Net Worth:	$382,288,000	Debt/ Equity: 0.4707

Ramco-Gershenson Properties Trust

31500 Nwestern Hwy., Ste. 300, Farmington Hills, MI, 48334; *PH:* 1-248-350-9900; *Fax:* 1-248-350-9925; *http://* www.ramco-gershenson.com; *Email:* ir@ramco-gershenson.com

General - Incorporation	MD	Stock - Price on:12/24/2007	$36.5
Employees	133	Stock Exchange	NYSE
Auditor	Grant Thornton LLP	Ticker Symbol	RPT
Stk Agt	American Stock Transfer & Trust Co.	Outstanding Shares	17,960,000
Counsel	NA	E.P.S.	$3.07
DUNS No.	NA	Shareholders	NA

Business: The groups principle activities include owning, acquiring, manages and leasing community shopping centers. In the year 2006, the group acquired Ramco 450 LLC and Collins Pointe Plaza. The group operates from the United States. The groups quarterly revenue for Septmber 2007 was 37.75 millions of USD.

Primary SIC and add'l.: 6798

CIK No: 0000842183

Subsidiaries: 28th Street Kentwood Associates, Auburn Mile Association, Beacon Square Development LLC, Boca Mission, LLC, Chester Springs SC, L.L.C., Collins Pointe Holding LLC, Crofton 450 LLC, Double Rivers, LLC, East Town Plaza Holdings Corp., East Town Plaza, LLC, East Town SP, LLC, Jackson Acquisitions Development LLC, Jackson Crossing Limited Partnership, Linton Delray, LLC, Merchants 450 LLC 113 Subsidiaries included in the Index

Officers: Dennis E. Gershenson/Chmn., CEO, Pres.,Trustee/$1,034,905.00, Edward Wizner/VP - Development, Redevelopment, Alan D. Maximiuk/VP - Financial Services, Joseph W. Sutschek/VP - Development, Jode P. Balsiger/VP - Design - Construction, Peter J. Debenedictis/VP - Development, Redevelopment, Edward A. Eickhoff/VP - Development, Redevelopment, Walter G. Kile/VP, Controller, Richard J. Smith/CFO, Sec./$594,266.00, Fred A. Zantello/Exec. VP/$502,059.00, Thomas W. Litzler/Exec. VP - Development, New Business Initiatives/$514,391.00, Catherine Clark/Sr. VP - Acquisitions/$327,749.00, Michael J. Sullivan/Sr. VP - Asset Management, Laith Hermiz/VP - Development, Redevelopment, Russell W. Strassburg/VP - Information Services

Directors: Dennis E. Gershenson/Chmn., CEO, Pres.,Trustee, Stephen R. Blank/Trustee, Arthur Goldberg/Trustee, Robert A. Meister/Trustee, Joel M. Pashcow/Trustee, Mark K. Rosenfeld/Trustee, Michael A. Ward/Trustee, Joel D. Gershenson/Trustee

Owners: Robert A. Meister, Cohen& Steers, Inc. and related entity/9.10%, Richard J. Smith, Stephen R. Blank, Richard D. Gershenson/11.80%, Bruce Gershenson/11.80%, Thomas W. Litzler, Catherine J. Clark, Barclays Global Investors, N.A. and related entities/7.30%, Mark K. Rosenfeld, Frederick A. Zantello, Joel D. Gershenson/11.80%, Arthur H. Goldberg, Dennis E. Gershenson/11.20%, Joel M. Pashcow/1.30% *(18 Owners included in Index)*

Financial Data: Fiscal Year End:12/31 Latest Annual Data: 12/31/2006

Year	Sales	Net Income
2006	$153,249,000	$35,624,000
2005	$141,623,000	$18,493,000
2004	$131,895,000	$15,120,000

Curr. Assets:	$53,014,000	Curr. Liab.:	$36,815,000		
Plant, Equip.:	$897,975,000	Total Liab.:	$760,287,000	Indic. Yr. Divd.:	$1.850
Total Assets:	$1,064,870,000	Net Worth:	$304,583,000	Debt/ Equity:	NA

Ramtal Inc

80 Wall St., Ste. 815, New York, NY, 10005;

General - Incorporation	NY	**Stock**- Price on:12/24/2007	NA
Employees	NA	Stock Exchange	NDQ
Auditor	Michael T. Studer CPA P.C	Ticker Symbol	MPET
Stk Agt	Atlas Stock Transfer Corp	Outstanding Shares	NA
Counsel	NA	E.P.S.	NA
DUNS No.	NA	Shareholders	NA

Business: The group's principal activity is to engage in any lawful corporate undertaking, including, but not limited to, selected mergers and acquisitions. The group has been in the developmental stage since inception and its operations to date have been limited to issuing shares to its original shareholders and filing this registration statement. The group seeks, investigates and, if such investigation warrants, acquires an interest in a business entity which desires to seek the perceived advantages of a corporation which has a class of securities registered under the Exchange Act. The group does not restrict its search to any specific business, industry, or geographical location and may participate in a business venture of virtually any kind or nature.

Primary SIC and add'l.: 6770

CIK No: 0001314636

Ramtron International Corp

1850 Ramtron Dr., Colorado Springs, CO, 80921; **PH:** 1-719-481-7000; **Fax:** 1-719-481-9294; **http://** www.ramtron.com; **Email:** info@ramtron.com

General - Incorporation	DE	**Stock**- Price on:12/24/2007	$3.3
Employees	111	Stock Exchange	NDQ
Auditor	KPMG LLP	Ticker Symbol	RMTR
Stk Agt	Citibank N.A	Outstanding Shares	26,120,000
Counsel	Jones Day	E.P.S.	$0.02
DUNS No.	14-430-1439	Shareholders	NA

Business: The group's principle activities are to design, develop and market semiconductor memory and integrated products. The group, primarily has two product lines namely, ferroelectric nonvolatile random access memory products (fram) and enhanced dynamic random access memory (dram). Fram technology integrates ferroelectric materials with standard semiconductor chip design and manufacturing technology to provide nonvolatile memory products which are applicable to digital cameras, smart cards, utility meters, set-top boxes, optical networks, security systems, home and office electronics and industrial controls. Dram products address the access and retrieval speed limitations of conventional drams and the high costs and high power requirements associated with high-speed static random access memory. The group markets its products through both direct, retail and e-commerce sales channels. The group's quarterly revenue for September 2007 was 13.40 millions of USD.

Primary SIC and add'l.: 3572

CIK No: 0000849502

Subsidiaries: Ramtron Canada Inc., Ramtron K.K., Ramtron LLC

Officers: William W. Staunton/CEO, Eric A. Balzer/Dir., CFO, John Vinh/Semiconductor Analyst, John Zambakkides/Contant, Sales, Jamie Gauld/Customer Service, Sales Support Mgr., Craig Taylor/Marketing, Technical Support, Lee A. Brown/VP - Corporate, Investor Communications, Diane Ratliff/Human Resources Administrator, Andrew Franco/Contact - Sales, Terry Andrews/Dir. - European Sales, Alex Tsui/Dir. - Asia Pacific Sales, Hee-Jun Lee/South Korean Sales Mgr., Shoji Hayase/Dir. - Japan Sales, Catherine Cohen/Media Relations Mgr.

Directors: William G. Howard/Chmn., Eric A. Balzer/Dir., CFO, Theodore J. Coburn/Dir., Jack Saltich/Dir., William L. George/Dir.

Owners: Cortina Asset Management, LLC/9.50%, Eric A. Balzer/1.80%, Ashford Capital Management, Inc./9.50%, National Electrical Benefit Fund/9.40%, Insiders/7.60%, William G. Howard/1.40%, Jack L. Saltich, Theodore J. Coburn, William W. Staunton/3.40%, William L. George

Financial Data: Fiscal Year End:12/31 Latest Annual Data: 12/31/2006

Year	Sales	Net Income
2006	$40,481,000	$457,000
2005	$34,392,000	-$6,491,000
2004	$57,828,000	$3,602,000

Curr. Assets:	$17,988,000	Curr. Liab.:	$6,746,000		
Plant, Equip.:	$4,527,000	Total Liab.:	$15,385,000	Indic. Yr. Divd.:	NA
Total Assets:	$32,457,000	Net Worth:	$17,072,000	Debt/ Equity:	0.3100

Rancher Energy Corp

999 18th St. Ste. 1740, Denver, CO, 80202; **PH:** 1-303-629-1125; **http://** www.rancherenergy.com; **Email:** investors@rancherenergy.com

General - Incorporation	NV	**Stock**- Price on:12/24/2007	$0.9
Employees	NA	Stock Exchange	OTC
Auditor	Williams & Webster, P.S.	Ticker Symbol	RNCH
Stk Agt	Pacific Stock Transfer Company	Outstanding Shares	95,050,000
Counsel	NA	E.P.S.	NA
DUNS No.	NA	Shareholders	NA

Business: The groups principal activity is an independent energy company formed for the purpose of engaging in the development, production, and marketing of oil and gas. In June 2006, the group acquired the Broadview Dome Prospect. The group operates from the United States.

Primary SIC and add'l.: 1382

CIK No: 0001287900

Officers: John Works/Dir., CEO, Pres., Sec., Treasurer, Andrew Casazza/COO, Dan Foley/CFO, John Dobitz/Sr. VP - Engineering

Directors: John Works/Dir., CEO, Pres., Sec., Treasurer, Mark Worthey/Dir., William A. Anderson/68/Dir., Joseph P. McCoy/57/Dir., Patrick M. Murray/65/Dir., Myron M. Sheinfeld/78/Dir.

Owners: Andrew F. Casazza, Joseph P. McCoy, William A. Anderson, Myron M. Sheinfeld, Morgan Stanley & Co. for a/c Persistency Capital/6.21%, Mark Worthey, Insiders/3.59%, John Works/2.17%, Patrick M. Murray, Hound Performance/5.38%, John Dobitz, RAB Special Situations Fund Ltd./9.18%, Millennium Global Investments Limited/9.77%, SPGP/5.93%, Old Westbury Real Return Fund/9.73% (*16 Owners included in Index*)

Curr. Assets:	$5,584,000	Curr. Liab.:	$4,694,000		
Plant, Equip.:	$74,284,000	Total Liab.:	$5,720,000	Indic. Yr. Divd.:	NA
Total Assets:	$81,478,000	Net Worth:	$75,758,000	Debt/ Equity:	NA

Rancho Santa Monica Developments Inc

3104 Sunnyhurst Rd., North Vancouver, BC, V7K 2G3; **PH:** 1-604-537-5905

General - Incorporation	NV	**Stock**- Price on:12/24/2007	$1.01
Employees	NA	Stock Exchange	OTC
Auditor	Moore & Associates Chartered	Ticker Symbol	RSDV
Stk Agt	Pacific Stock Transfer Company	Outstanding Shares	NA
Counsel	NA	E.P.S.	NA
DUNS No.	NA	Shareholders	NA

Business: The groups principal activity is development of real estate and group have acquired real property located in solidaridad, on which group have constructed and provide management services for the apartment units being constructed on the adjoining property. The group operates from the United States and Canada.

Primary SIC and add'l.: 6552

CIK No: 0001313605

Officers: Graham G. Alexander/38/Dir., CEO, CFO, Pres., Sec., Treasurer, Angela Manetta/45/VP

Directors: Graham G. Alexander/38/Dir., CEO, CFO, Pres., Sec., Treasurer

Owners: Insiders/54.30%, Graham G. Alexander/52.90%, Angela Manetta

Financial Data: Fiscal Year End:11/30 Latest Annual Data: 11/30/2006

Year	Sales	Net Income
2006	NA	-$24,000
2005	NA	-$60,000

Curr. Assets:	$9,000	Curr. Liab.:	$37,000		
Plant, Equip.:	$175,000	Total Liab.:	$87,000	Indic. Yr. Divd.:	NA
Total Assets:	$174,000	Net Worth:	$86,000	Debt/ Equity:	0.6097

Rand Capital Corp

2200 Rand Bldg., Buffalo, NY, 14203; **PH:** 1-716-853-0802; **Fax:** 1-716-854-8480; **http://** www.randcapital.com

General - Incorporation	NY	**Stock**- Price on:12/24/2007	$3.47
Employees	4	Stock Exchange	NDQ
Auditor	Freed Maxick & Battaglia, CPAs, PC	Ticker Symbol	RAND
Stk Agt	Continental Stock Transfer & Trust Co	Outstanding Shares	5,720,000
Counsel	NA	E.P.S.	$1.33
DUNS No.	NA	Shareholders	NA

Business: The groups principal activity is to making investments in companies. The group operates from the United States. The assets of the group for the year 2006 were $29,463,944.

Primary SIC and add'l.: 6799

CIK No: 0000081955

Subsidiaries: Rand Capital Management, LLC, Rand Capital SBIC, L.P

Officers: Allen F. Grum/Dir., CEO, Pres./$214,521.00, Daniel P. Penberthy/Treasurer, Peter Grum/Pres., Elspeth Donaldson/Office Mgr.

Directors: Allen F. Grum/Dir., CEO, Pres., Reginald B. Newman/Chmn., Jayne K. Rand/Dir., Robert M. Zak/Dir., Erland E. Kailbourne/Dir., Ross B. Kenzie/Dir., Willis S. McLeese/Dir.

Owners: Allen F. Grum/1.30%, Erland E. Kailbourne, Jayne K. Rand/2.60%, Ross B. Kenzie/1.70%, Willis S. McLeese/13.90%, Insiders/28.90%, Robert M. Zak, Brown Advisory Holdings Inc./13.60%, Reginald B. Newman/7.80%, Daniel P. Penberthy

Financial Data: Fiscal Year End:12/31 Latest Annual Data: 12/31/2006

Year	Sales	Net Income
2006	$1,327,000	$8,166,000
2005	$737,000	-$411,000
2004	$784,000	-$211,000

Curr. Assets:	$4,843,000	Curr. Liab.:	$728,000	P/E Ratio:	2.43
Plant, Equip.:	$13,000	Total Liab.:	$12,682,000	Indic. Yr. Divd.:	NA
Total Assets:	$29,464,000	Net Worth:	$16,782,000	Debt/ Equity:	0.4701

Rand Logistics Inc

461 Fifth Ave., 25th Fl., New York, NY, 10017; **PH:** 1-212-644-3450

General - Incorporation	DE	**Stock**- Price on:12/24/2007	NA
Employees	NA	Stock Exchange	OTC
Auditor	Goldstein Golub Kessler LLP	Ticker Symbol	RLOG
Stk Agt	Continental Stock Transfer & Trust Co	Outstanding Shares	NA
Counsel	NA	E.P.S.	NA
DUNS No.	NA	Shareholders	NA

Business: The groups principle activity is to provide marine transportation services to dry bulk goods suppliers and purchasers operating in ports in the Great Lakes. In the year March 2006, the group acquired Lower Lakes Towing Ltd. The group operates from the United States. The group's quarterly revenue for Sep '07 was 28.88 millions of USD.

Primary SIC and add'l.: 4789

CIK No: 0001294250

Officers: Laurence S. Levy/52/Chmn., CEO/$1,176,580.00, Edward Levy/44/Pres./$929,728.00, Joseph W. McHugh/53/CFO

Directors: Laurence S. Levy/52/Chmn., CEO, Scott Bravener/44/Dir., Isaac Kier/55/Dir., Cabot H. Lodge/52/Dir., Jonathan Brodie/52/Dir.

Owners: Wellington Management Company, LLP, Cabot H. Lodge, MHR Advisors LLC, Kier Family, L.P., Isaac Kier, GMT Capital Corp., Rand Management LLC, Islandia, L.P., Jonathan Brodie, MHR Capital Partners Master Account LP, Hummingbird Management, LLC, Joseph W. McHugh, Edward Levy, Scott Bravener, David M. Knott (*17 Owners included in Index*)

Curr. Assets:	$24,706,000	*Curr. Liab.:*	$2,096,000	*P/E Ratio:*	29.58
Plant, Equip.:	NA	*Total Liab.:*	$6,841,000	*Indic. Yr. Divd.:*	NA
Total Assets:	$26,790,000	*Net Worth:*	$19,948,000	*Debt/ Equity:*	0.6407

Randgold Resources Ltd

La Motte Chambers, La Motte St, St. Helier, Jersey; *PH:* 44-1534735333; *Fax:* 44-1534735444; *http://* www.randgoldresources.com

General - Incorporation .... Channel Islands	*Stock*- Price on:12/24/2007 ....$22.21
Employees...702	Stock Exchange.....................................NDQ
Auditor .... PricewaterhouseCoopers LLP	Ticker Symbol...GOLD
Stk Agt.... Computershare Investor Services LLC	Outstanding Shares 68,850,000
Counsel...NA	E.P.S..$0.69
DUNS No..NA	Shareholders...NA

Business: The group's principle activity is the operation of an opencast mining activities and exploration. Employing a multi-disciplinary team, including specialists in geology, finance, mining engineering and metallurgy, the group is focusing its exploration and new business programmes on the key areas of southern mali and northern cote d'ivoire, western mali and more recently, senegal. All the group's mining and exploration activities are conducted in west Africa.

Primary SIC and add'l.: 1041

CIK No: 0001175580

Subsidiaries: Mining Investments (Jersey) Limited, Morila Limited, Randgold Resources (Burkina) Limited, Randgold Resources (Cte d'Ivoire) Limited, Randgold Resources (Mali) Limited, Randgold Resources (Senegal) Limited, Randgold Resources (Somilo) Limited, Randgold Resources Cte d'Ivoire SARL, Randgold Resources Mali Limited SARL, Randgold Resources Tanzania (T) Limited, Seven Bridges Trading 14 (Proprietary) Limited, Socit des Mines de Loulo SA, Socit des Mines de Morila SA

Officers: Mark D. Bristow/Dir., CEO, Mahamadou Samake/GM - Mali, Tania De Welzim/Group Financial Controller, Amadou Konta/GM - Loulo, Ngolo Sanogo/Financial Controller - Mali, John Steele/GM - Capital Projects, David H. Haddon/General Counsel, Sec., Lois Wark/Mgr. - Corporate Communications, Cartography, Graham Shuttleworth/Dir., CFO, Bill Houston/GM - Human Resources, Paul Harbidge/Exploration Mgr., Victor Matfield/Corporate Finance Mgr., Adrian Reynolds/GM - Exploration, Evaluation, Chris Prinsloo/Group Financial, Commercial Mgr.

Directors: Mark D. Bristow/Dir., CEO, Philippe Lietard/Chmn., Karl Voltaire/Dir., Bernard H. Asher/Sr. Non Exec. Dir., Robert I. Israel/Non Exec. Dir., Aubrey L. Paverd/Dir., Norborne P. Cole/Dir.

Owners: B. H. Asher, Wells Fargo & Company/8.69%, BNY (Nominees) Limited/82.38%, A. L. Paverd, K. Voltaire, R. I. Israel, N. P. Cole, P. Litard, D. M. Bristow/1.07%, Insiders/1.80%, R. A. Williams

*Financial Data: Fiscal Year End:*12/31 *Latest Annual Data:* 12/31/2005

Year	Sales	Net Income
2005	$155,282,000	$36,419,000
2004	$83,743,000	$16,888,000
2003	$116,505,000	$42,960,000

Curr. Assets:	$212,555,000	*Curr. Liab.:*	$93,682,000	*P/E Ratio:*	32.19
Plant, Equip.:	$275,819,000	*Total Liab.:*	$176,101,000	*Indic. Yr. Divd.:*	$0.090
Total Assets:	$505,069,000	*Net Worth:*	$328,968,000	*Debt/ Equity:*	1.9532

Range Resources Corp

777 Main St., Ste. 800, Fort Worth, TX, 76102; *PH:* 1-817-870-2601; *Fax:* 1-817-870-2316; *http://* www.rangeresources.com

General - Incorporation .... DE	*Stock*- Price on:12/24/2007 ....$40.74
Employees..644	Stock Exchange....................................NYSE
Auditor .... Ernst & Young LLP	Ticker Symbol..RRC
Stk Agt..... Computershare Investor Services LLC	Outstanding Shares 148,010,000
Counsel...NA	E.P.S..$1.31
DUNS No................................06-043-1467	Shareholders...NA

Business: The group's principal activities are to acquire, develop and explore oil and gas properties. At 31-Dec-2003, the group had 1,883 proven drilling locations and 252 proven recompletions. The group also provides financing to smaller oil and gas producers through a wholly-owned subsidiary, independent producer finance. It also provides transportation, processing and marketing services. The properties of the group are located in the southwest, gulf coast and appalachian regions of the United States. The customers include utilities, marketing companies and industrial users.

Primary SIC and add'l.: 1311 1380 6159 4925

CIK No: 0000315852

Subsidiaries: Domain Energy International Corporation (a), Energy Assets Operating Company, Great Lakes Energy Partners, LLC, Gulfstar Energy, Inc., Gulfstar Seismic, Inc., Ohio Interstate Gas Transmission Company, Pine Mountain Acquisition, Inc., Pine Mountain Oil & Gas, Inc., PMOG Holdings, Inc., Range Energy Finance Corporation, Range Energy I, Inc., Range Energy Services Company, Range Energy Ventures Corporation, Range Gas Company, Range Gathering & Processing Company 20 Subsidiaries included in the Index

Officers: John H. Pinkerton/Dir., CEO, Pres./$3,147,838.00, Steven L. Grose/Sr. VP - Appalachia, Rodney L. Waller/Sr. VP, Sec./$999,708.00, Roger S. Manny/Sr. VP, CFO/$1,209,898.00, Chad L. Stephens/Sr. VP - Corporate Development, Jeffrey L. Ventura/Dir., Exec. VP, COO/$2,105,101.00, Mark D. Whitley/Sr. VP - Permian - Engineering Technology/$1,434,789.00, Alan W. Farquharson/Sr. VP - Reservoir Engineering

Directors: John H. Pinkerton/Dir., CEO, Pres., Charles L. Blackburn/Chmn., Jonathan S. Linker/Dir., Jeffrey L. Ventura/Dir., Exec. VP, COO, Richard V. Eales/Dir., Kevin S. McCarthy/Dir., Allen Finkelson/Dir., Anthony V. Dub/Dir.

Owners: John H. Pinkerton/1.50%, Charles L. Blackburn, Roger S. Manny, FMR Corp./14.60%, Jeffrey L. Ventura, Allen Finkelson, Jonathan S. Linker, Kevin S. McCarthy, Insiders/3.60%, Mark D. Whitley, Anthony V. Dub, Richard V. Eales, Rodney L. Waller, Goldman Sachs Asset Management, L.P./10.90%

*Financial Data: Fiscal Year End:*12/31 *Latest Annual Data:* 12/31/2006

Year	Sales	Net Income
2006	$779,728,000	$158,702,000
2005	$535,957,000	$111,011,000
2004	$320,707,000	$42,231,000

Curr. Assets:	$320,337,000	*Curr. Liab.:*	$232,356,000	*P/E Ratio:*	31.10
Plant, Equip.:	$2,723,819,000	*Total Liab.:*	$1,931,513,000	*Indic. Yr. Divd.:*	$0.120
Total Assets:	$3,187,674,000	*Net Worth:*	$1,256,161,000	*Debt/ Equity:*	0.8733

Rank Group Plc

Statesman House, Stafferton Way, Maidenhead, SL6 1AY; *PH:* 01628-504000; *Fax:* 01628-504042; *http://* www.rank.com

General - Incorporation ....UK	*Stock*- Price on:12/24/2007 ....$3.8
Employees...NA	Stock Exchange.......................................OTC
Auditor ....PricewaterhouseCoopers LLP	Ticker Symbol..RANKF
Stk Agt ....CT Corporation System	Outstanding Shares ....NA
Counsel...NA	E.P.S...NA
DUNS No...........................49-426-1175	Shareholders...NA

Business: The group's principal activities are the provision of leisure and entertainment services to the film industry. Its leisure and entertainment activities include casinos and bingo clubs, hard rock cafes and global rights to the hard rock brand. The group also owns film processing and video and digital versatile disc duplication and distribution facilities. It operates primarily in the United Kingdom and North America, although it also has activities in continental Europe and other parts of the world. During 2003, the group acquired blue square ltd and distronics, an independent DVD and CD replicators in Europe and sold rank leisure machine services ltd and rank seasonal amusements ltd.

Primary SIC and add'l.: 5812 7011 7999 7812 7832

CIK No: 0001026291

Subsidiaries: Resorts USA

Officers: Ian Burke/51/Dir., Chief Executive, Peter Gill/52/Dir. - Finance, Pamela Coles/Dir., Company Sec., Martin Belsham/MD - Blue Square, Simon Wykes/MD - Mecca Bingo, Valentin Coruna/MD - Top Rank Espana, Peter McCann/MD - Grosvenor Casinos, Alan Armstrong/Compliance, Development Dir., Michele Jennings/Commercial Dir., Sue Waldock/Dir. - Human Resources

Directors: Peter Johnson/60/Chmn., Pamela Coles/Dir., Company Sec., Bill Shannon/58/Non Exec. Dir., John Warren/54/Non Exec. Dir., Ian Burke/51/Dir., Chief Executive, Brendan O'Neill/59/Non Exec. Dir., Peter Gill/52/Dir. - Finance, Richard Greenhalgh/63/Sr. Non Exec. Dir.

*Financial Data: Fiscal Year End:*12/31 *Latest Annual Data:* 12/31/2004

Year	Sales	Net Income
2004	$3,763,228,000	-$155,091,000
2003	$3,425,213,000	$139,612,000
2002	$2,366,650,000	$264,405,000

Curr. Assets:	$1,588,674,000	*Curr. Liab.:*	$895,484,000	*P/E Ratio:*	32.19
Plant, Equip.:	$1,421,060,000	*Total Liab.:*	$2,336,966,000	*Indic. Yr. Divd.:*	NA
Total Assets:	$4,005,787,000	*Net Worth:*	$1,668,821,000	*Debt/ Equity:*	NA

Rapid Link Inc

Formerly: Dial Thru International Corp
17383 Sunset Blvd., Ste. 350, Los Angeles, CA, 90272; *PH:* 1-310-566-1700

General - Incorporation .... DE	*Stock*- Price on:12/24/2007 ....NA
Employees...30	Stock Exchange.......................................NA
Auditor .... KBA Group LLP	Ticker Symbol...NA
Stk Agt .... Computershare Trust Co of Canada	Outstanding Shares 51,790,000
Counsel..............................Arter & Hadden	E.P.S..-$0.024
DUNS No...NA	Shareholders...NA

Business: The group's principal activity is to provide a wide variety of international and domestic dial thru and re-origination services. The services include international dial-thru, Internet voice and fax services. The group also provides e-commerce solutions and other value-added communication services, using its voice over Internet protocol network to effectively deliver the products to the end user. The group also offers new opportunities for existing Internet service providers (isps) who want to expand into voice services, private corporate networks seeking to lower long-distance costs and Web-enabled corporate call centers engaged in electronic commerce. The international operations of the group are located in western Europe, Africa and south east Asia.

Primary SIC and add'l.: 4813

CIK No: 0000913659

Subsidiaries: Dial Thru International Argentina S.A., Dial Thru International Corporation, South Africa, Dial Thru International Venezuela, C.A., Dial Thru, Inc, DTI Com, Inc, DTI Liqco, Inc, Rapid Link Telecommunications, GmbH

Officers: Christopher J. Canfield/47/CFO, Pres., Treasurer, Dir., Michael P. Prachar/38/COO

Directors: Christopher J. Canfield/47/CFO, Pres., Treasurer, Dir.

Owners: Robert M. Fidler, Apex Acquisitions, Inc./37.01%, Lawrence J. Vierra, John A. Jenkins/50.36%, Insiders/75.26%, David R. Hess

*Financial Data: Fiscal Year End:*10/31 *Latest Annual Data:* 10/31/2006

Year	Sales	Net Income
2006	$13,351,000	-$1,111,000
2005	$9,827,000	-$2,565,000
2004	$13,381,000	$707,000

Curr. Assets:	$1,651,000	*Curr. Liab.:*	$6,313,000		
Plant, Equip.:	$379,000	*Total Liab.:*	$10,796,000	*Indic. Yr. Divd.:*	NA
Total Assets:	$8,242,000	*Net Worth:*	-$2,554,000	*Debt/ Equity:*	NA

Raptor Networks Technology Inc

1241 E Dyer Rd., Ste. 150, Santa Ana, CA, 92705; *PH:* 1-949-623-9300; *Fax:* 1-949-623-9400; *http://* www.raptor-networks.com; *Email:* investor_relations@raptor-networks.com

General - Incorporation .... CO	*Stock*- Price on:12/24/2007 ....$1.43
Employees...26	Stock Exchange.......................................OTC
Auditor ....Comiskey & Co. P.C	Ticker Symbol...RPTN
Stk Agt ....First American Stock Transfer, Inc.	Outstanding Shares 58,900,000
Counsel...NA	E.P.S..-$0.6
DUNS No...NA	Shareholders...NA

Business: The group's principal activity is to provide edgar filing services. These services are provided to companies outsourcing the formatting and electronic filing of registration statements, periodic reports and other forms with the u. S. Securities and exchange commission. The group also provides integrated high-speed ethernet switching systems, which enable new emerging high bandwidth critical applications. The data network market areas include video, storage, Internet protocol telephony and technology refresh. The group markets its products in Europe and the United States. As on 17-Oct-2003, the group acquired raptor networks technologies inc.

Primary SIC and add'l.: 7379

CIK No: 0001163300

Officers: Tom Wittenschlaeger/Chmn., CEO, Pres., Bob Van Leyen/CFO, Sec./$201,110.00, Stephen Gropp/VP - Major Accounting, Mike Carwana/VP - Engineering, Product Development, Do A.C. Van Drunen/GM - Asia, Pacific, Ivo Meijer/GM - Europe

Directors: Tom Wittenschlaeger/Chmn., CEO, Pres., Larry L. Enterline/Dir., Ken R. Bramlett/Dir., Albert Wong/59/Dir., David T. Phillips/Member - Advisory Board, Paul R. Jones/Member - Advisory Board, Jerome P. Thode/Member - Advisory Board, James F. Sutter/Member - Advisory Board, Robert C. Bystedt/Member - Advisory Board, Omar A. El/Member - Advisory Board

Owners: Jamie Mieko Hamamoto, Brookstreet Securities Corporation/1.59%

Financial Data: Fiscal Year End:12/31   **Latest Annual Data:** 12/31/2006

Year	Sales	Net Income
2006	$849,000	-$17,100,000
2005	$289,000	-$13,391,000
2004	$54,000	-$20,575,000

Curr. Assets:	$2,631,000	**Curr. Liab.:**	$19,431,000	
Plant, Equip.:	$283,000	**Total Liab.:**	$19,431,000	**Indic. Yr. Divd.:** NA
Total Assets:	$3,113,000	**Net Worth:**	-$16,318,000	**Debt/ Equity:** NA

Raptor Pharmaceuticals Corp

9 Commercial Blvd, Ste. 200, Novato, CA, 94949; **PH:** 1-415-382-8111; **Fax:** 1-415-382-1368; **http://** www.raptorpharma.com; **Email:** info@raptorpharma.com

General - Incorporation	DE	**Stock** - Price on:12/24/2007	$0.63
Employees	5	Stock Exchange	OTC
Auditor	Burr, Pilger & Mayer LLP	Ticker Symbol	RPTP
Stk Agt	Nevada Agency & Trust Company	Outstanding Shares	32,340,000
Counsel	NA	E.P.S.	NA
DUNS No.	NA	Shareholders	NA

Business: The groups principal activities include research and development of a novel drug and drug targeting platform intended to initially treat a variety of brain disorders, neurodegenerative diseases, cancer and metabolic diseases through the proprietary use of a natural human protein known as the receptor associated protein. In May 2006, the group acquired Raptor Pharmaceutical Inc. The group operates from the United States.

Primary SIC and add'l.: 2834

CIK No: 0001203944

Officers: Christopher M. Starr/Co - Founder, Dir., CEO, Todd C. Zankel/Co - Founder, Chief Scientific Officer, Annie Verde/Sr. Mgr. - Accounting, Amanda Verde/Member - Research Team, Kim Tsuchimoto/CFO, Treasurer, Sec. - Investor Contact

Directors: Christopher M. Starr/Co - Founder, Dir., CEO, Raymond W. Anderson/Dir., Erich Sager/Dir., Todd C. Zankel/Co - Founder, Chief Scientific Officer, Simone Haslam/Founder, Sara Isbell/Founder, Guojun Bu/Member - Medical Scientific Advisory Board, William C. Mobley/Member - Medical Scientific Advisory Board, Rivka Sherman-Gold/Member - Medical Scientific Advisory Board, Sam Teichman/Member - Medical Scientific Advisory Board, Andres Lozano/Member - Medical Scientific Advisory Board

Owners: Todd C. Zankel/10.30%, Kim R. Tsuchimoto, Christopher M. Starr/10.30%, Insiders/24.90%, Raymond W. Anderson, Erich Sager/4.10%

Raser Technologies Inc

5152 N Edgewood Dr., Provo, UT, 84604; **PH:** 1-800-765-1200; **http://** www.rasertech.com; **Email:** info@rasertech.com

General - Incorporation	UT	**Stock** - Price on:12/24/2007	$9.4
Employees	NA	Stock Exchange	NYSE
Auditor	Hein & Assoc., LLP	Ticker Symbol	RZ
Stk Agt	Interwest Transfer Company, Inc.	Outstanding Shares	NA
Counsel	NA	E.P.S.	-$0.3
DUNS No.	NA	Shareholders	NA

Business: The group's principal activity is to develop advanced motor technology for broad applications, including the growing electric hybrid vehicle market. The group has developed several innovations in electric motors and controllers that increase torque and power, allowing reduced manufacturing costs and providing enhanced performance. The group in its development stage conducts operations in the state of Utah. On 14-Oct-2003, the group acquired raser technologies inc.

Primary SIC and add'l.: 7379

CIK No: 0001103078

Subsidiaries: Amp Resources, LLC, Power Acquisition Sub

Officers: Brent M. Cook/Dir., CEO/$221,200.00, Patrick Schwartz/Pres./$2,048,246.00, Timothy D. Fehr/CTO, Sr. VP, Martin F. Petersen/CFO

Directors: Brent M. Cook/Dir., CEO, Kraig T. Higginson/Chmn., Lee A. Daniels/Dir., James A. Herickhoff/Dir., Alan G. Perriton/Dir., Reynold Roeder/Dir., Barry Markowitz/Dir.

Owners: Kraig T. Higginson/17.40%, Brent M. Cook/1.50%, William Dwyer, Ned Warner/10.90%, Barry G. Markowitz, Jack Kerlin/9.60%, Alan G. Perriton, Lee A. Daniels, John Ritter, Patrick J. Schwartz, Reynold Roeder, James A. Herickhoff, Insiders/20.30%, Sergei Kolomeitsev

Financial Data: Fiscal Year End:12/31   **Latest Annual Data:** 12/31/2006

Year	Sales	Net Income
2006	$123,000	-$18,489,000
2005	$332,000	-$8,933,000
2004	$30,000	-$6,976,000

Curr. Assets:	$9,954,000	**Curr. Liab.:**	$695,000	**P/E Ratio:** 27.10
Plant, Equip.:	$879,000	**Total Liab.:**	$695,000	**Indic. Yr. Divd.:** NA
Total Assets:	$11,405,000	**Net Worth:**	$10,710,000	**Debt/ Equity:** NA

Raven Gold Corp

2470 St. Rose Pkwy., Ste. 304, Henderson, NV, 89074; **PH:** 1-604-484-3701; **http://** www.ravengold.com

General - Incorporation	NV	**Stock** - Price on:12/24/2007	NA
Employees	NA	Stock Exchange	OTC
Auditor	Moore & Assoc., Chartered	Ticker Symbol	RVNG
Stk Agt	Continental Stock T & T Co.	Outstanding Shares	NA
Counsel	NA	E.P.S.	NA
DUNS No.	NA	Shareholders	NA

Business: The groups principal activity is in the business of the acquisition, and exploration of mineral properties with a view to exploiting any mineral deposits. In April 2005, the group acquired the mining rights to two claims collectively known as the Big Mike Border Gold property located in the Skeeena Mining District of British Columbia, Canada. The group operates from the United States and Canada.

Primary SIC and add'l.: 1000

CIK No: 0001332052

Officers: Blair Naughty/Dir., CEO, Pres., David Peterson/Sr. Advisor, Bashir Virji/CFO

Directors: Blair Naughty/Dir., CEO, Pres., Gary Haukeland/Dir., Michael Sandidge/Dir., Lawrence Stevenson/Dir., David Michaud/Dir.

Financial Data: Fiscal Year End:04/30   **Latest Annual Data:** 4/30/2006

Year	Sales	Net Income
2006	NA	-$51,000

Curr. Assets:	$322,000	**Curr. Liab.:**	$2,103,000	
Plant, Equip.:	$1,625,000	**Total Liab.:**	$2,103,000	**Indic. Yr. Divd.:** NA
Total Assets:	$2,447,000	**Net Worth:**	$344,000	**Debt/ Equity:** NA

Raven Industries Inc

205 E 6th St., Sioux Falls, SD, 57117; **PH:** 1-605-336-2750; **Fax:** 1-605-335-0268; **http://** www.ravenind.com; **Email:** raveninfo@ravenind.com

General - Incorporation	SD	**Stock** - Price on:12/24/2007	$35.06
Employees	910	Stock Exchange	NDQ
Auditor	PricewaterhouseCoopers LLP	Ticker Symbol	RAVN
Stk Agt	Wells Fargo Bank, N.A.	Outstanding Shares	18,090,000
Counsel	NA	E.P.S.	$1.52
DUNS No.	00-725-7348	Shareholders	NA

Business: The group's principal activity is to manufacture specialized products for industrial, recreation, agriculture and military/aerospace markets. The group operates in four business segments: electronic systems, flow controls, engineered films and aerostar. The electronic systems segment provides a variety of assemblies and controls to the United States department of defense and other military contractors. Assemblies manufactured by this segment include communication, environmental control, computer and other products. Flow control segment manufactures devices for precision farming applications and marine navigation. Engineered films segment produces rugged reinforced plastic sheeting for industrial, construction and agricultural applications and high altitude balloons for public and commercial research. Aerostar segment produces and markets custom-shaped advertising inflatables that have a number of uses including parade floats and advertising media.

Primary SIC and add'l.: 3699 3672 3089 3081 3069 0711 3829

CIK No: 0000082166

Subsidiaries: Aerostar International, Inc., GTH, Inc. (formerly known as Glasstite, Inc.), Raven Industries Canada, Inc., Raven Industries GmbH

Officers: Ron Moquist/CEO, Pres./$452,830.00, Thomas Iacarella/CFO, VP/$285,972.00, Karen M. Iversen/Finance Executive Assist., David R. Bair/Division VP - Electronic Systems Division/$278,086.00, James D. Groninger/Division VP - Engineered Films Division/$268,732.00

Directors: Kevin T. Kirby/53/Dir.

Owners: Insiders/12.10%, Mark L. West, Kevin T. Kirby, T. Rowe Price Associates, Inc./13.20%, Cynthia H. Milligan, David R. Bair, Anthony W. Bour, Mark E. Griffin, Conrad J. Hoigaard, Barbara K. Ohme, Thomas Iacarella, Daniel A. Rykhus, Thomas S. Everist, Ronald M. Moquist/5.10%, David A. Christensen/3.50% *(16 Owners included in Index)*

Financial Data: Fiscal Year End:01/31   **Latest Annual Data:** 1/31/2007

Year	Sales	Net Income
2007	$217,529,000	$25,441,000
2006	$204,528,000	$24,262,000
2005	$168,086,000	$17,891,000

Curr. Assets:	$73,219,000	**Curr. Liab.:**	$16,464,000	**P/E Ratio:** 23.53
Plant, Equip.:	$36,264,000	**Total Liab.:**	$21,496,000	**Indic. Yr. Divd.:** $0.440
Total Assets:	$119,764,000	**Net Worth:**	$98,268,000	**Debt/ Equity:** NA

Raven Moon Entertainment Inc

2005 Tree Fork Ln., Ste. 101, Longwood, FL, 32750; **PH:** 1-407-774-4462; **Fax:** 1-407-774-4464; **http://** www.ravenmoon.net

General - Incorporation	FL	**Stock** - Price on:12/24/2007	NA
Employees	3	Stock Exchange	OTC
Auditor	Richard L. Brown & Co P.A	Ticker Symbol	RVEN
Stk Agt	Florida Atlantic Stock Transfer, Inc.	Outstanding Shares	NA
Counsel	NA	E.P.S.	-$0.001
DUNS No.	NA	Shareholders	NA

Business: The group's principal activity is to produce, develop, promote, sell and distribute family values and christian-oriented video entertainment products. It also develops and produces children's television programs and videos, CD music production, Internet websites focused on the entertainment industry and music publishing and talent management. The group also distributes plush toys. The products of the group are marked worldwide.

Primary SIC and add'l.: 7812

CIK No: 0001058056

Subsidiaries: JB Toys, LLC, Raven Animation, Inc, Raven Moon Home Video Products, LLC

Officers: Joey Difrancesco/Chmn., CEO

Directors: Joey Difrancesco/Chmn., CEO, Janice K. Battenberg/Dir., Robert J. McCarthy/Dir., Larry Oakley/Dir., Kristi Neher Davvison/Member - Advisory Board, Mary Beth Beth Leidman/Member - Advisory Board, James H. Rosenfield/Member - Advisory Board

Owners: Lawrence C. Oakley, Insiders/42.16%, Joseph DiFrancesco/77.79%, Jacques Danon/4.18%, Robert J.McCarthy, Janice K. Battenberg, Joseph DiFrancesco/42.16%, Insiders/77.79%

Financial Data: Fiscal Year End:12/31   **Latest Annual Data:** 12/31/2006

Year	Sales	Net Income
2006	$7,000	-$12,346,000
2005	$10,000	-$7,614,000
2004	$2,000	-$10,643,000

Curr. Assets:	$115,000	**Curr. Liab.:**	$6,328,000		
Plant, Equip.:	NA	**Total Liab.:**	$6,938,000	**Indic. Yr. Divd.:**	NA
Total Assets:	$115,000	**Net Worth:**	-$6,823,000	**Debt/ Equity:**	NA

Raymond James Financial Inc

880 Carillon Pkwy., St. Petersburg, FL, 33716; ***PH:*** 1-727-567-1000; ***Fax:*** 1-727-567-8915; ***http://*** www.rjf.com; ***Email:*** investorrelations@raymondjames.com

General - Incorporation .... FL
Employees .... NA
Auditor .... KPMG LLP
Stk Agt .... Heritage Trust Co
Counsel .... Paul L. Matecki
DUNS No. 07-759-2889

Stock- Price on:12/24/2007 .... $32.32
Stock Exchange .... NYSE
Ticker Symbol .... RJF
Outstanding Shares 119,080,000
E.P.S $1.93
Shareholders .... NA

Business: The groups principle activity is to provide financial services. The group operates through eight business segments namely private client group, capital markets, asset management, RJbank, emerging markets, stock loan/borrow, proprietary capital and certain corporate activities combined in the other segment. The group operates from United States.

Primary SIC and add'l.: 6719 6282 6035 6211

CIK No: 0000720005

Subsidiaries: Eagle Asset Management, Inc, Heritage Asset Management, Inc., Raymond James & Associates, Inc., Raymond James Bank, FSB, Raymond James Financial Services, Inc, Raymond James Ltd.

Officers: Peter Bailey/CEO, Pres. - Raymond James Ltd, Thomas A. James/Chmn., CEO, Richard G. Averitt/Chmn., CEO - Raymond James Financial Services, Richard K. Riess/Exec. VP, Asset Management CEO - Eagle Asset Management, Raymond James Financial, Chet Helck/COO, Pres., Jeffrey E. Trocin/Exec. VP - Equity Capital Markets, Raymond James, Associates, George Catanese/49/Sr. VP, Chief Risk Officer, Angela M. Biever/MD - Consumer Internet Intel Capital, Jeffrey P. Julien/CFO, Sr. VP - Finance - Fixed Income Department, Thomas R. Tremaine/51/Exec. VP - Operations, Administration, Raymond James, Associates, Timothy J. Eitel/CIO, Sr. VP, Paul L. Matecki/53/Sr. VP, General Counsel, Dir. - Compliance, RJF, Dennis Zank/Pres. - Raymond James, Associates, Jennifer C. Ackart/44/Controller, Chief Accounting Officer, C. Van Sayler/Sr. VP, Mgr. - Fixed Income Department, Raymond James, Associates

Directors: Thomas A. James/Chmn., CEO, Richard G. Averitt/Chmn., CEO - Raymond James Financial Services, Francis S. Godbold/64/Vice Chmn., Hardwick Simmons/Dir., Wick Simmons/Dir., William H. Habermeyer/65/Dir., Paul W. Marshall/65/Dir., Paul C. Reilly/53/Dir., Kenneth A. Shields/Dir.

Owners: Insiders/14.03%, Shelley G. Broader, Francis S. Godbold, Paul C. Reilly, Earnest Partners LLC/8.26%, Jeffrey E. Trocin, William H. Habermeyer, Hardwick Simmons, Robert P. Saltzman, Robert A. James Trust/6.25%, Paul W. Marshall, Private Capital Management L.P./9.44%, Thomas A. James/12.23%, Chet Helck, Angela M. Biever *(19 Owners included in Index)*

Financial Data: ***Fiscal Year End:***09/30 ***Latest Annual Data:*** 9/30/2006

Year	Sales	Net Income
2006	$2,632,757,000	$214,342,000
2005	$2,156,997,000	$151,046,000
2004	$1,829,776,000	$127,575,000

Curr. Assets:	$10,144,813,000	**Curr. Liab.:**	$14,027,565,000	**P/E Ratio:**	16.75
Plant, Equip.:	$4,294,630,000	**Total Liab.:**	$14,266,684,000	**Indic. Yr. Divd.:**	$0.400
Total Assets:	$16,254,168,000	**Net Worth:**	$1,757,814,000	**Debt/ Equity:**	NA

Rayonier Inc

50 N Laura St., Jacksonville, FL, 32202; ***PH:*** 1-904-357-9100; ***Fax:*** 1-904-357-9101; ***http://*** www.rayonier.com

General - Incorporation .... NC
Employees 2,000
Auditor .... Deloitte & Touche LLP
Stk Agt .... Bank of New York
Counsel .... NA
DUNS No. .... NA

Stock- Price on:12/24/2007 .... $45
Stock Exchange .... NYSE
Ticker Symbol .... RYN
Outstanding Shares 77,420,000
E.P.S $2.41
Shareholders .... NA

Business: The groups principle activities include owning, leasing and managing 2.7 million acres of timberland and real estate properties. The group operates through three segments namely, timber, real estate and performance fibers. In the year 2006, the group acquired 228,000 acres of timberland in six states. The group operates from the United States.

Primary SIC and add'l.: 0811 6519 6798 2823 6531

CIK No: 0000052827

Subsidiaries: Forestal Rayonier Chile Ltd, Matariki Forestry Group, Matariki Forests, Rayonier Australia Pty Ltd., Rayonier Canterbury, LLC, Rayonier China Limited, Rayonier Distribution Corp., Rayonier Far East Ltd., Rayonier Foreign Sales Corporation, Rayonier Forest Management, Inc., Rayonier Forest Operations, LLC, Rayonier Forest Resources, L.P., Rayonier HB Limited, Rayonier Industries Ltd., Rayonier International Financial Services Limited 34 Subsidiaries included in the Index

Officers: Lee W. Nutter/64/Chmn., CEO, Pres./$5,667,740.00, Paul G. Boynton/43/Sr. VP - Performance Fibers/$1,673,214.00, Timothy H. Brannon/60/Sr. VP - Forest Resources, Wood Products/$2,555,133.00, Edwin W. Frazier/50/Sr. VP - Administration, Corp. Sec./$1,664,979.00, Carl E. Kraus/60/Sr. VP - Finance, Rayonier/$611,466.00, Charles Margiotta/55/Sr. VP - Business Development, Hans E. Vanden Noort/49/Chief Accounting Officer, Sr. VP/$1,009,380.00, Michael R. Herman/45/VP, General Counsel, Charles H. Hood/58/VP - Corporate Affairs

Directors: Lee W. Nutter/64/Chmn., CEO, Pres., Thomas I. Morgan/54/Dir., Carl S. Sloane/71/Dir., Lee M. Thomas/63/Dir., David C. Brown/56/Dir., James H. Hance/63/Dir., Richard D. Kincaid/46/Dir., Paul G. Kirk/70/Dir., Ronald Townsend/66/Dir., Larkin V. Martin/45/Dir.

Owners: Carl E. Kraus, JPMorgan Chase& Co./5.00%, Timothy H. Brannon, Insiders/2.96%, Arnhold and S. Bleichroeder Advisers, LLC/8.64%, Hans E. NoortVanden, Katherine D. Ortega, Lee M. Thomas, Paul G. Kirk, Carl S. Sloane, James H. Hance, Paul G. Boynton, Thomas I. Morgan, Lee W. Nutter/1.16%, David C. Brown *(19 Owners included in Index)*

Financial Data: ***Fiscal Year End:***12/31 ***Latest Annual Data:*** 12/31/2006

Year	Sales	Net Income
2006	$1,229,807,000	$176,418,000
2005	$1,180,708,000	$182,839,000
2004	$1,206,996,000	$156,901,000

Curr. Assets:	$298,554,000	**Curr. Liab.:**	$193,337,000	**P/E Ratio:**	18.67
Plant, Equip.:	$1,481,293,000	**Total Liab.:**	$1,046,620,000	**Indic. Yr. Divd.:**	$2.000
Total Assets:	$1,962,882,000	**Net Worth:**	$916,262,000	**Debt/ Equity:**	0.7243

Raytec Corp

7015 SW McEwan Rd., Lake Oswego, OR, 97035; ***PH:*** 1-503-620-2073; ***http://*** www.raytek.com; ***Email:*** support@raytek.com

General - Incorporation .... NV
Employees .... NA
Auditor .... Amisano Hanson
Stk Agt .... Transfer Online, Inc.
Counsel .... NA
DUNS No. .... NA

Stock- Price on:12/24/2007 .... NA
Stock Exchange .... NA
Ticker Symbol .... NA
Outstanding Shares .... NA
E.P.S .... NA
Shareholders .... NA

Business: The group's principle activity is to focus on perishable food and agricultural product management. The group also manufacture, develop and market perishable control systems for the grocery industry. The group also develops antimicrobial products for food safety applications. The company provides its customers worldwide with performance products, related services and innovative solutions to all three key issues relating to perishable management including shrink reduction, quality assurance and food safety. The company provide service, including installation, maintenance and emergency service, of their installed products. The company's other products include water filtration and purification equipment. The group uses innovative technologies such as SANI-T-BAG, ShrinkGUARD, OdorGUARD. SANI-T-BAG, an innovative delivery system for clorine dioxide. ShrinkGuard, an innovative system for perishable foods. The group operates from United States.

Primary SIC and add'l.: 3585

CIK No: 0001305522

Subsidiaries: Raytec Development Corp.

Raytheon Co

870 Winter St., Waltham, MA, 02451; ***PH:*** 1-781-522-3000; ***Fax:*** 1-781-522-3001; ***http://*** www.raytheon.com

General - Incorporation .... DE
Employees 80,000
Auditor .... PricewaterhouseCoopers LLP
Stk Agt ..... American Stock Transfer & Trust Co.
Counsel .... NA
DUNS No. 00-133-9159

Stock- Price on:12/24/2007 .... $56.33
Stock Exchange .... NYSE
Ticker Symbol .... RTN
Outstanding Shares 443,860,000
E.P.S $5.25
Shareholders .... NA

Business: The group principle activity is to provide defense and aerospace systems. The group operates from United States.

Primary SIC and add'l.: 3721 3812 8711 4899 3679

CIK No: 0001047122

Subsidiaries: ARC Development Corporation, ARC Dry Creek, Inc., ARC Financial Services Corporation

Officers: William H. Swanson/Chmn., CEO/$17,231,510.00, James E. Schuster/CEO, Exec. VP - Raytheon Aircraft Company/$4,412,803.00, Michael D. Keebaugh/VP, Pres. - Intelligence, Information Systems, Daniel L. Smith/VP, Pres. - Integrated Defense Systems, Pamela A. Wickham/VP - Corporate Affairs - Communications, Richard A. Goglia/VP, Corporate Development Treasurer, Jay B. Stephens/Sr. VP, General Counsel, Sec./$4,161,368.00, William J. Lynn/VP - Government Operations - Strategy, Greg Smith/VP - Investor Relations, Richard R. Yuse/VP, Pres. - Raytheon Technical Services Company LLC, Michael J. Wood/VP, Chief Accounting Officer, John D. Harris/VP - Contracts - Supply Chain, Lawrence J. Harrington/VP - Internal Audit, Rebecca R. Rhoads/CIO, VP, Colin Schottlaender/VP, Pres. - Network Centric Systems *(24 Officers included in Index)*

Directors: William H. Swanson/Chmn., CEO, Vernon E. Clark/63/Dir., Barbara M. Barrett/57/Dir., John M. Deutch/69/Dir., Frederic M. Poses/65/Dir., William R. Spivey/61/Dir., Ronald L. Skates/Dir., Michael C. Ruettgers/65/Dir., Linda G. Stuntz/53/Dir.

Owners: Insiders, William R. Spivey, Vernon E. Clark, Linda G. Stuntz, Michael C. Ruettgers, Ferdinand Colloredo-Mansfeld, Barbara M. Barrett, Jay B. Stephens, William H. Swanson, John M. Deutch, Louise L. Francesconi, Frederic M. Poses, Ronald L. Skates, James E. Schuster, David C. Wajsgras

Financial Data: ***Fiscal Year End:***12/31 ***Latest Annual Data:*** 12/31/2006

Year	Sales	Net Income
2006	$20,291,000,000	$1,283,000,000
2005	$21,894,000,000	$871,000,000
2004	$20,245,000,000	$417,000,000

Curr. Assets:	$9,517,000,000	**Curr. Liab.:**	$6,715,000,000	**P/E Ratio:**	10.73
Plant, Equip.:	$2,131,000,000	**Total Liab.:**	$14,225,000,000	**Indic. Yr. Divd.:**	$1.020
Total Assets:	$25,491,000,000	**Net Worth:**	$11,101,000,000	**Debt/ Equity:**	0.2928

Razor Resources Inc

650 W.41st Ave., Vancouver, BC, V5Z 4M4; ***PH:*** 1-604-267-0111

General - Incorporation .... NV
Employees .... NA
Auditor .... Fazzari & Partners LLP
Stk Agt .... Empire Stock Transfer Inc.
Counsel .... Day Pitney LLP
DUNS No. .... NA

Stock- Price on:12/24/2007 .... $1.6
Stock Exchange .... OTC
Ticker Symbol .... RZRR
Outstanding Shares .... NA
E.P.S .... NA
Shareholders .... NA

Business: The groups principle activities include exploring the acquisition of mineral claims and exploring of mineral claim property. The group has not conducted any exploration on sole mineral property asset known as the Mahatta property located southwest of Port Alice, British Columbia on Vancouver Island. The group operates from the United States.

Primary SIC and add'l.: 1000

CIK No: 0001333614

Officers: Bing Wong/73/Dir., Pres., Principal Exec. Officer, Principal Financial Officer, Principal Accounting Officer, Treasurer, Sec., Rong Xin Yang/37/Dir., Financial Officer, Sec.

Directors: Bing Wong/73/Dir., Pres., Principal Exec. Officer, Principal Financial Officer, Principal Accounting Officer, Treasurer, Sec., Rong Xin Yang/37/Dir., Financial Officer, Sec., Drew Simpson/57/Dir.

Owners: Rong Xin Yang/9.32%, Drew Simpson/9.32%, Insiders/70.33%, Raymond Wei Ming Xu/2.05%, Bing Wong/46.62%

RBC Bearings Inc

1 Tribology Ctr., Oxford, CT, 06478; **PH:** 1-203-267-7001; **Fax:** 1-203-267-5000; http:// www.rbcbearings.com

General - Incorporation	DE	**Stock** - Price on:12/24/2007	$40.38
Employees	1,745	Stock Exchange	NDQ
Auditor	Ernst & Young LLP	Ticker Symbol	ROLL
Stk Agt	LaSalle Bank N.A	Outstanding Shares	21,500,000
Counsel	NA	E.P.S.	NA
DUNS No.	NA	Shareholders	NA

Business: The groups principle activities include manufacturing and marketing engineered precision plain, roller and ball bearings. Customers served by the group include industrial and aerospace and defense. The groups operates through four segments namely plain bearings, roller bearings, ball bearings and other. The group operates from the United States. The group's quarterly revneue for September 2007 was 78.23 millions of USD.

Primary SIC and add'l.: 3562

CIK No: 0001324948

Subsidiaries: Industrial Tectonics Bearings Corporation, J. Bovagnet SA, RBC Aircraft Products, Inc., RBC De Mexico S DE RL DE CV, RBC France SAS, RBC Linear Precision Products, Inc., RBC Nice Bearings, Inc., RBC Oklahoma, Inc., RBC Precision ProductsBremen, Inc., RBC Precision ProductsPlymouth, Inc., RBC Southwest Products, Inc., Roller Bearing Company of America, Inc., Schaublin Holding SA, Schaublin SA, Tyson Bearing Company, Inc.

Officers: Michael J. Hartnett/Chmn., CEO, Pres./$2,054,463.00, Daniel A. Bergeron/CFO, VP/$444,155.00, Phillip H. Beausoleil/GM - Industrial Tectonics Bearings, Transport Dynamics/$422,987.00, Thomas C. Crainer/GM - Heim Bearings, RBC Torrington, CT Plant, Schaublin SA/$448,679.00, Richard J. Edwards/VP, GM - RBC Division/$375,777.00, Thomas M. Burigo/Corporate Controller, Thomas J. Williams/Corporate General Counsel, Sec.

Directors: Michael J. Hartnett/Chmn., CEO, Pres., Richard R. Crowell/Dir., Amir Faghri/Dir., William P. Killian/Dir., Alan B. Levine/Dir., Thomas J. O'Brien/Dir.

Owners: Michael J. Hartnett/4.60%, William P. Killian, Alan B. Levine, Daniel A. Bergeron, Thomas J. OBrien, Richard R. Crowell, Thomas C. Crainer, Phillip H. Beausoleil, Richard J. Edwards, Westfield Capital Management Company, LLC/9.07%, Amir Faghri, Insiders/5.40%, T. Rowe Price Associates, Inc./6.08%

Financial Data: Fiscal Year End:04/01 Latest Annual Data: 3/31/2007

Year		Sales		Net Income
2007		$306,062,000		$28,479,000
2006		$274,509,000		$12,439,000
2005		$243,016,000		$7,260,000
Curr. Assets:	$158,991,000	Curr. Liab.:	$38,335,000	P/E Ratio: 30.13
Plant, Equip.:	$55,343,000	Total Liab.:	$257,928,000	Indic. Yr. Divd.: NA
Total Assets:	$250,169,000	Net Worth:	-$7,759,000	Debt/ Equity: 0.3514

RC2 Corp

1111 W 22nd St., Ste. 320, Oak Brook, IL, 60523; **PH:** 1-630-573-7200; **Fax:** 1-630-573-7575; http:// www.rc2corp.com

General - Incorporation	DE	**Stock** - Price on:12/24/2007	$40.52
Employees	777	Stock Exchange	NDQ
Auditor	KPMG LLP	Ticker Symbol	RCRC
Stk Agt	First National Bank of Boston	Outstanding Shares	21,180,000
Counsel	NA	E.P.S.	$1.30
DUNS No.	62-155-5952	Shareholders	NA

Business: The group's principal activities are to produce and market collectibles and toys. The group's product line includes automotive, high performance and racing vehicle replicas, agricultural, construction and outdoor sports vehicle replicas, sports trading cards, racing apparel and souvenirs, pre-teen vehicles and role play activity toys and collectible figures. The products are sold through more than 20,000 retail outlets located in North America, Europe and Asia-Pacific. The major customers are wal-Mart and john deere dealer network and the major brands include racing champions (R), ertl collectibles (R), britains (R), American muscle (TM), amt (R), outdoor sportsman (TM), w. Britain (R), press pass(R) and joyride studios (r). On 04-Mar- 2003, the group acquired learning curve international inc.

Primary SIC and add'l.: 3944 5092 5131 3949

CIK No: 0001034239

Subsidiaries: Acre 689 Limited, Bondco 988 Limited, DiecastExpress.com, Inc., Green's Racing Souvenirs, Inc., Lci (h.k.) Limited, Learning Curve Canada Holdco, Inc., Learning Curve International, Inc., Racing Champions International Limited, Racing Champions Worldwide Limited, Rc2 (h.k.) Limited, RC2 Australia Pty. Ltd., RC2 Brands, Inc., RC2 Canada Corporation, RC2 Deutschland GmbH, RC2 South, Inc. 17 Subsidiaries included in the Index

Officers: Curtis W. Stoelting/Dir., CEO/$1,377,978.00, Jody L. Taylor/CFO, Sec./$707,378.00, Peter J. Henseler/Pres./$1,362,237.00, Gregory J. Kilrea/COO/$501,056.00, John W. Donaldson/Exec. VP

Directors: Curtis W. Stoelting/Dir., CEO, Robert E. Dods/Chmn., Boyd L. Meyer/Vice Chmn., Peter K.K. Chung/Dir., Linda A. Huett/63/Dir.

Owners: Boyd L. Meyer, Peter K.K. Chung, Peter J. Henseler/1.10%, Greg Kilrea, Robert E. Dods, Dimensional Fund Advisors LP/6.50%, Columbia Wanger Asset Management, L.P./5.40%, Curtis W. Stoelting/1.90%, Thomas M. Collinger, John S. Bakalar, Barclays Global Investors, NA/7.50%, Michael J. Merriman, Daniel M. Wright, John J. Vosicky, Jody L. Taylor (20 Owners included in Index)

Financial Data: Fiscal Year End:12/31 Latest Annual Data: 12/31/2006

Year		Sales		Net Income
2006		$518,829,000		$34,094,000
2005		$504,445,000		$53,130,000
2004		$381,425,000		$33,978,000
Curr. Assets:	$236,968,000	Curr. Liab.:	$107,365,000	P/E Ratio: 31.17
Plant, Equip.:	$38,991,000	Total Liab.:	$162,714,000	Indic. Yr. Divd.: NA
Total Assets:	$614,640,000	Net Worth:	$451,926,000	Debt/ Equity: NA

RCM Technologies Inc

2500 McClellan Ave., Ste. 350, Pennsauken, NJ, 08109; **PH:** 1-856-486-1777; **Fax:** 1-856-488-8833; http:// www.rcmt.com; **Email:** info@rcmt.com

General - Incorporation	NV	**Stock** - Price on:12/24/2007	$8.26
Employees	2,534	Stock Exchange	NDQ
Auditor	Grant Thornton LLP	Ticker Symbol	RCMT
Stk Agt	American Stock Transfer & Trust Co.	Outstanding Shares	11,940,000
Counsel	Morgan, Lewis & Bockius LLP	E.P.S.	$0.60
DUNS No.	08-477-0619	Shareholders	NA

Business: The group's principal activity is to provide business and technology solutions through the adaptation and deployment of advanced information technology and engineering services. The group's operations are conducted through three business segments: information technology, professional engineering and commercial services. The information technology segment offers responsive, timely and comprehensive business and information technology consulting and solutions to support the entire system applications development and implementation process. The professional engineering segment provides personnel to perform project engineering, computer aided design and other managed task technical services. The commercial services segment provides specialty health care professionals and general support services. The group operates in the United States and Canada. The major customers include 3m, adp, bristol myers squibb, bruce power lp, entergy, flightsafety international and IBM.

Primary SIC and add'l.: 7376 7363 7379

CIK No: 0000700841

Officers: Leon Kopyt/63/Chmn., CEO, Pres./$644,479.00, Dan White/Sr. VP - Engineering Services, Cindy Sypher/Division Mgr. - Technical Services, New Opportunites, Peter Lindsay/Chief Engineer, Erika Wilkins/Human Resources Specialist, Gord Leighton/QA Mgr., Juan Laverde/Dir. - Finance, Angela He/Mgr. - Accounting, Rocco Campanelli/Exec. VP/$335,526.00, Kevin D. Miller/41/Sr. VP/$273,910.00, John Pringle/55/Sr. VP, James Schappert/49/Sr. VP/$265,310.00, Vicki Swisher/Mgr. - Pickering Operations, Catherine Clarke/Engineering Design Analysis, Josephine Chen/Mgr. - Risk Management Engineering (19 Officers included in Index)

Directors: Leon Kopyt/63/Chmn., CEO, Pres., Stanton Remer/58/Dir., CFO, Exec. VP, Treasurer, Sec., Lawrence Needleman/66/Dir., Norman S. Berson/81/Dir., Robert B. Kerr/65/Dir.

Owners: Leon Kopyt/5.20%, Heartland Advisors, Inc./13.30%, Stanton Remer/1.70%, John Pringle, David Gilfor, Christopher Giunta, Insiders/11.00%, Kevin D. Miller/1.70%, Norman S. Berson, Robert B. Kerr, Frank Bocassi, Columbia Wanger Asset Management, L.P./15.70%, Dimensional Fund Advisors LP/6.90%, Rocco Campanelli

Financial Data: Fiscal Year End:12/31 Latest Annual Data: 12/30/2006

Year		Sales		Net Income
2006		$201,920,000		$6,356,000
2005		$180,618,000		$3,536,000
Curr. Assets:	$64,116,000	Curr. Liab.:	$31,084,000	P/E Ratio: 14.00
Plant, Equip.:	$4,021,000	Total Liab.:	$31,084,000	Indic. Yr. Divd.: NA
Total Assets:	$106,773,000	Net Worth:	$75,689,000	Debt/ Equity: NA

RCN Corp

196 Van Buren St., Ste. 300, Herndon, VA, 20170; **PH:** 1-703-434-8200; **Fax:** 1-703-434-8290; http:// www.rcn.com; **Email:** sales@rcn.com

General - Incorporation	DE	**Stock** - Price on:12/24/2007	$18.5
Employees	1,800	Stock Exchange	NDQ
Auditor	Friedman LLP	Ticker Symbol	RCNI
Stk Agt	Mellon Investor Services LLC	Outstanding Shares	37,720,000
Counsel	NA	E.P.S.	-$3.87
DUNS No.	96-624-3164	Shareholders	NA

Business: The group's principal activity is to deliver bundled communications services to residential customers over the broadband network. The services include local and long distance telephone, video programming (including digital cable TV) and data services to residential customers over the predominantly owned network. The group operates in Boston, New York city, the philadelphia suburbs, Chicago, san francisco along with a few communities in los angeles. It offers one-stop shopping for phone, cable television and cable modem Internet services to residential customers. Resilink and essentials are the brand names of various bundled services.

Primary SIC and add'l.: 7379 4841 4813 4822

CIK No: 0001041858

Subsidiaries: RCN Telecom Services of Massachusetts, Inc, RCN-BecoCom LLC, Starpower Communications, LLC

Officers: Peter D. Aquino/Dir., CEO, Pres./$4,541,307.00, Benjamin R. Preston/Sr. VP, General Counsel, Michael T. Sicoli/CFO, Exec. VP/$1,823,734.00, Richard Ramlall/Sr. VP - Strategic - External Affairs/$662,494.00, John D. Filipowicz/49/Sr. VP, GM/$657,276.00, P. K. Ramani/50/Sr. VP, Chief Service Officer, Leslie Sears/42/Sr. VP, Controller

Directors: Peter D. Aquino/Dir., CEO, Pres., James F. Mooney/Chmn., Michael E. Katzenstein/Dir., Lee S. Hillman/Dir., Benjamin C. Duster/Dir., Daniel Tseung/Dir., Theodore H. Schell/Dir.

Owners: Michael E. Katzenstein, Daniel Tseung, Theodore H. Schell, Leslie J. Sears, The Altar Rock Fund L.P./19.03%, PK Ramani, David E. Shaw/5.30%, JGD Management Corp./8.60%, Jana Partners LLC/6.60%, James F. Mooney/1.50%, Benjamin R. Preston, Peter D. Aquino/1.10%, Insiders/4.20%, Lee S. Hillman, Benjamin C. Duster (19 Owners included in Index)

Financial Data: Fiscal Year End:12/31 Latest Annual Data: 12/31/2006

Year		Sales		Net Income
2006		$585,476,000		-$11,856,000
2005		$560,964,000		-$136,112,000
2004		$486,831,000		$1,059,058,000
Curr. Assets:	$235,596,000	Curr. Liab.:	$162,022,000	
Plant, Equip.:	$613,572,000	Total Liab.:	$405,445,000	Indic. Yr. Divd.: NA
Total Assets:	$975,381,000	Net Worth:	$569,936,000	Debt/ Equity: 0.3548

Reader's Digest Association Inc

Readers Digest Rd., Pleasantville, NY, 10570; **PH:** 1-914-238-1000; http:// www.readersdigest.com

General - Incorporation	DE	**Stock**- Price on:12/24/2007	NA
Employees	4,300	Stock Exchange	NA
Auditor	Ernst & Young LLP	Ticker Symbol	NA
Stk Agt	Mellon Investor Services LLC	Outstanding Shares	NA
Counsel	NA	E.P.S.	NA
DUNS No.	00-132-5935	Shareholders	NA

Business: The groups principle activity is to publish magazines. The group markets books including Reader's Digest Select Editions, how-to guides and cookbooks. The group operates from United States.

Primary SIC and add'l.: 5735 2721 2731 7812

CIK No: 0000858558

Subsidiaries: 3634116 Canada Inc., Allrecipes.com, Inc., Ardee Music Publishing, Inc., Asian Qualiproducts Services, Limited, Books Are Fun, Ltd., Caribe Condor S.A. de C.V., Christmas Angel Productions, Inc., Corporativo Readers Digest Mexico S. de R.L. de CV, Das Beste aus Readers Digest AG/Selection du Readers Digest SA/Selzione dal Readers, Det Beste A/S, Digest SA, Distrimedia Services B.V., Editura Readers Digest SRL, EFundraising.com Corporation Incorporated/Corporation eFundraising.com Incorporee, Euroseleccoes - Publicacoes E Artigos Promocionais, Lda. 119 Subsidiaries included in the Index

Officers: Eric W. Schrier/CEO, Pres., Michael S. Geltzeiler/CFO, Sr. VP, Jeffrey S. Spar/CIO, Sr. VP, Michael A. Brennan/Sr. VP, Pres. - Latin America, Asia, Pacific, Thomas D. Gardner/Exec. VP, Pres. - RD International, Clifford H.R. Dupree/VP, Assist. Sec., Assoc. General Counsel, Michael A. Brizel/Sr. VP, General Counsel, Albert L. Perruzza/Sr. VP - Global Operations - Business Redesign, Richard E. Clark/Sr. VP - Investor Relations, Global Communications, Lisa Cribari/VP - Global Human Resources, Amy Krause/National Dir. - Online Sales

Directors: Thomas O. Ryder/Chmn.

Reading International Inc

500 Citadel Dr., Ste. 300, Commerce, CA, 90040; **PH:** 1-213-235-2240; **Fax:** 1-213-235-2229; http:// www.readingrdi.com

General - Incorporation	NV	**Stock**- Price on:12/24/2007	$9.35
Employees	1,451	Stock Exchange	AMEX
Auditor	Deloitte & Touche LLP	Ticker Symbol	RDI
Stk Agt	U.S. Stock Transfer Corp	Outstanding Shares	22,490,000
Counsel	NA	E.P.S.	$0.13
DUNS No.	11-426-1399	Shareholders	NA

Business: The group's principal activities are to develop, own and operate cinemas in the United States, Australia, New Zealand and Puerto Rico, cinema based entertainment-themed retail centers in Australia and New Zealand and 'off broadway' style live theaters in the United States. The group also develops, owns and operates commercial real estate in Australia, New Zealand and the United States.

Primary SIC and add'l.: 7999 6512

CIK No: 0000716634

Subsidiaries: AHGP, Inc., AHLP, Inc., Angelika Film Centers (Dallas), Inc., Angelika Film Centers (Plano), LP, Angelika Film Centers LLC, Australia Country Cinemas Pty Ltd, Bayou Cinemas LP, Big 4 Farming LLC, Burwood Developments Pty Ltd, Citadel 57th Street, LLC, Citadel Agriculture, Inc., Citadel Cinemas, Inc., Citadel Realty, Inc., Cliveden Ltd, Copenhagen Courtenay Central Ltd 80 Subsidiaries included in the Index

Officers: James J. Cotter/Chmn., CEO, Pres./$889,000.00, Margaret Cotter/Dir., Pres. - Live Theaters, USA, Ellen M. Cotter/COO - Domestic Cinemas, Brett Marsh/Dir. - Domestic Real Estate, USA, Andrzej Matyczynski/CFO/$273,000.00, Craig S. Tompkins/Chief Legal Officer/$444,500.00, Wayne Smith/Executive Dir. - Pacific Operations, Australia, New Zealand/$287,000.00, Robert F. Smerling/Pres. - Domestic Cinemas, USA/$368,000.00, Ian Sands/Operations Dir. - Pacific Cinemas, Australia, New Zealand, John Willey/Development Dir. - Pacific Real Estate, Australia, New Zealand

Directors: James J. Cotter/Chmn., CEO, Pres., Margaret Cotter/Dir., Pres. - Live Theaters, USA, Alfred Villasenor/Dir., Eric Barr/Dir., James J. Cotter/Dir., William D. Gould/Dir., Edward L. Kane/Dir., Gerard P. Laheney/Dir.

Owners: Pacific Assets Management LLC/8.90%, James J. Cotter/71.10%, Insiders/29.10%, Margaret Cotter/2.30%, Dimensional Fund Advisors/4.00%, Eric Barr, William D. Gould, Gerard P. Laheney, James J. Cotter/2.60%, James J. Cotter/19.40%, Edward L. Kane, Margaret Cotter/2.70%, Alfred Villaseor, Edward L. Kane, Insiders/71.90% (19 Owners included in Index)

Financial Data: Fiscal Year End:12/31 Latest Annual Data: 12/31/2006

Year	Sales	Net Income
2006	$106,125,000	$3,856,000
2005	$101,070,000	$989,000
2004	$102,982,000	-$8,463,000

Curr. Assets:	$30,291,000	**Curr. Liab.:**	$37,288,000	**P/E Ratio:**	33.39
Plant, Equip.:	$212,421,000	**Total Liab.:**	$178,969,000	**Indic. Yr. Divd.:**	NA
Total Assets:	$289,231,000	**Net Worth:**	$107,659,000	**Debt/ Equity:**	NA

Ready Mix Inc

3430 E Flamingo Rd., Ste. 100, Las Vegas, NV, 89121; **PH:** 1-702-433-2090; **Fax:** 1-702-433-0189; http:// www.readymixinc.com

General - Incorporation	NV	**Stock**- Price on:12/24/2007	$13.005
Employees	30	Stock Exchange	AMEX
Auditor	Sample Of Cooper LLP	Ticker Symbol	RMX
Stk Agt	Corporate Stock Transfer, Inc.	Outstanding Shares	3,810,000
Counsel	NA	E.P.S.	$0.56
DUNS No.	NA	Shareholders	NA

Business: The groups principle activity is to supply construction materials. The group products include ready mix concrete, sand and grave. Customers of the group include subcontractors, prime contractors, homebuilders, commercial and industrial property developers. The group's quarterly revenue for September 2007 was 19.09 millions of USD.

Primary SIC and add'l.: 1442 3273 1446

CIK No: 0001317405

Officers: Bradley E. Larson/Dir., CEO, Robert R. Morris/Dir., Pres., Robert A. Deruiter/VP - Arizona, Kenneth D. Nelson/Dir., VP, Clint Tryon/CFO, Sec., Treasurer, Lenny Remmert/Nevada Sales Mgr., Kristi Lattin/Arizona Sales Mgr.

Directors: Bradley E. Larson/Dir., CEO, Robert R. Morris/Dir., Pres., Kenneth D. Nelson/Dir., VP, Charles E. Cowan/61/Dir., Charles R. Norton/66/Dir., Don A. Patterson/53/Dir., Dan H. Stewart/55/Dir.

Owners: Robert R. Morris, Don A. Patterson, Kenneth D. Nelson, Dan H. Stewart, Insiders, Bulldog Investors, Clint Tryon, Meadow Valley Corporation, Charles E. Cowan, Robert A. De Ruiter, Bradley E. Larson, Charles R. Norton

Financial Data: Fiscal Year End:12/31 Latest Annual Data: 12/31/2006

Year	Sales	Net Income
2006	$83,589,000	$3,339,000
2005	$67,734,000	$2,486,000
2004	$59,136,000	$2,440,000

Curr. Assets:	$20,066,000	**Curr. Liab.:**	$9,662,000		
Plant, Equip.:	$25,481,000	**Total Liab.:**	$19,556,000	**Indic. Yr. Divd.:**	NA
Total Assets:	$47,023,000	**Net Worth:**	$27,467,000	**Debt/ Equity:**	NA

Reality Wireless Networks Inc

7235 N Creek Loop, Gig Harbor, WA, 98335; **PH:** 1-253-853-3632; http:// www.realitynetworks.com; **Email:** sjc98335@hotmail.com

General - Incorporation	NV	**Stock**- Price on:12/24/2007	NA
Employees	NA	Stock Exchange	OTC
Auditor	Salberg & Co P.A	Ticker Symbol	SAHN
Stk Agt	Pacific Stock Transfer Company	Outstanding Shares	NA
Counsel	NA	E.P.S.	NA
DUNS No.	NA	Shareholders	NA

Business: The group provides fixed, wireless, high-speed and broadband Internet access services to residential homes and small businesses. It provides this service as an alternative to digital subscriber line or cable Internet access service. The group offers its Internet access service via wireless networking technologies that utilize the unlicensed 2.4 ghz ism and 5 ghz unii spectrum bands. The group provides these services in southern California. On 17-Nov-2003, the group acquired orange soda inc.

Primary SIC and add'l.: 7372 7371

CIK No: 0001088537

Financial Data: Fiscal Year End:09/30 Latest Annual Data: 09/30/2004

Year	Sales	Net Income
2004	$60,000	-$7,486,000
2003	$112,000	-$3,893,000
2002	$182,000	-$2,222,000

Curr. Assets:	NA	**Curr. Liab.:**	$2,356,000		
Plant, Equip.:	NA	**Total Liab.:**	$2,382,000	**Indic. Yr. Divd.:**	NA
Total Assets:	$38,000	**Net Worth:**	-$2,344,000	**Debt/ Equity:**	NA

Realnetworks Inc

2601 Elliott Ave., Ste. 1000, Seattle, WA, 98121; **PH:** 1-206-674-2700; **Fax:** 1-206-674-2699; http:// www.realnetworks.com; **Email:** advertising@real.com

General - Incorporation	WA	**Stock**- Price on:12/24/2007	$8.25
Employees	1,594	Stock Exchange	NDQ
Auditor	KPMG LLP	Ticker Symbol	RNWK
Stk Agt	Mellon Investor Services LLC	Outstanding Shares	154,250,000
Counsel	NA	E.P.S.	$0.49
DUNS No.	83-610-1485	Shareholders	NA

Business: The group's principal activity is to provide network-delivered digital media services and the technology that enables digital media creation, distribution and consumption. It is at the center of the intersection between technology and digital content. The group develops and markets software products and services designed to enable users of personal computers and other consumer electronic devices to send and receive audio, video and other multimedia services using the Internet and other digital networks. The group's products and services include the real.com and realone.com network of Web sites, the real broadcast network and realplayer goldpass subscription service, which offers subscribers an all-in-one package of premium software, services and exclusive content.in aug 2003, the group acquired listen. On 30-Jan-2004, the group acquired gamehouse inc.

Primary SIC and add'l.: 7379 7372

CIK No: 0001046327

Subsidiaries: Aegisoft Corp., Audio Mill, Inc., GameHouse, Inc., Mr. Goodliving Ltd., Multipoint, Inc., NetZip, Inc., RealNetworks Australia Pty. Limited, RealNetworks Digital Music of California, Inc., RealNetworks E-Commerce LLC, RealNetworks GmbH, RealNetworks Hong Kong, Limited, RealNetworks Investments LLC, RealNetworks K.K., RealNetworks Korea, Ltd., RealNetworks Ltd. 24 Subsidiaries included in the Index

Officers: Robert Glaser/Chmn., CEO/$3,757,203.00, Michael Eggers/Sr. VP, CFO/$535,558.00, Savino Ferrales/Sr. VP - Human Resources, John Giamatteo/Exec. VP - Worldwide Technology Products, Solutions International Operations/$1,752,632.00, Robert Kimball/Sr. VP - Legal, Business Affairs, General Counsel, Corp. Sec./$1,245,796.00, Dan Sheeran/Sr. VP - Corporate Partnerships, Business Development/$885,007.00, Carla Stratfold/Sr. VP - North America Sales, Harold Zeitz/Sr. VP - Games, Media Software, Services

Directors: Robert Glaser/Chmn., CEO, Eric Benhamou/Dir., Edward Bleier/Dir., James Breyer/Dir., Jonathan D. Klein/Dir., Kalpana Raina/Dir., Jeremy Jaech/Dir.

Owners: Robert Glaser/33.70%, James W. Breyer, Goldman Sachs Asset Management, L.P./9.40%, Kalpana Raina, John Giamatteo, Daniel Sheeran, Jonathan D. Klein, Insiders/35.00%, Jeremy Jaech, Edward Bleier, Roy Goodman, Entities deemed to be affiliated with Barclays GlobalInvestors,/5.70%, Michael Eggers, Robert Kimball, Eric A. Benhamou

Financial Data: Fiscal Year End:12/31 Latest Annual Data: 12/31/2006

Year	Sales	Net Income
2006	$395,261,000	$145,216,000
2005	$325,059,000	$312,345,000
2004	$266,719,000	-$22,997,000

Curr. Assets:	$769,195,000	**Curr. Liab.:**	$185,070,000		
Plant, Equip.:	$47,743,000	**Total Liab.:**	$333,650,000	**Indic. Yr. Divd.:**	NA
Total Assets:	$1,303,416,000	**Net Worth:**	$969,766,000	**Debt/ Equity:**	0.1069

Realogy Corp

One Campus Dr., Parsippany, NJ, 07054; **PH:** 1-973-407-2000; http:// www.realogy.com

General - Incorporation	DE	**Stock** - Price on:12/24/2007	NA
Employees	NA	Stock Exchange	NA
Auditor	Deloitte& Touche LLP	Ticker Symbol	NA
Stk Agt	The Bank of New York	Outstanding Shares	NA
Counsel	NA	E.P.S.	NA
DUNS No.	NA	Shareholders	NA

Business: The group operates through its subsidiaries whose principle activity is to invest in real estate properties. The group operates through four segments namely, real estate franchise services, company owned real estate brokerage services, relocation services and title, and settlement services. In the year 2006, the group acquired 111 brokerage companies and 19 real estate companies. The group operates from the United States.

Primary SIC and add'l.: 6531 6541

CIK No: 0001355001

Subsidiaries: A Market Place, Inc., Advantage Title& Insurance, LLC, AFS Mortgage, Allmon, Tiernan& Ely, Inc., Alpha Referral Network, Inc., American TitleCompany of Houston, APEX Real Estate Information Services Alabama, L.L.C., APEX Real Estate Information Services, LLC, APEX Real Estate Information Services, LLP, Apple Ridge Funding LLC, Apple Ridge Services Corporation, Associated Client Referral Corp., Associates Investments, Associates Realty Network, Associates Realty, Inc. 249 Subsidiaries included in the Index

Officers: Henry R. Silverman/Chmn., CEO, Alexander E. Perriello/CEO, Pres. - Realogy Franchise Group, Kevin J. Kelleher/CEO, Pres. - Cartus Corporation, Bruce Zipf/CEO, Pres. - NRT LLC, Donald J. Casey/CEO, Pres. - Title Resource Group LLC, Richard A. Smith/Vice Chmn., Pres., Anthony E. Hull/CFO, Exec. VP, Treasurer, David J. Weaving/Chief Administrative Officer, Exec. VP, Christopher R. Cade/40/Chief Accounting Officer, Sr. VP, Controller, Patteson C. Cardwell/44/Exec. VP, General Counsel, Marilyn Wasser/Exec. VP, General Counsel, Corp. Sec., Mark Panus/Sr. VP - Corporate Communications

Directors: Henry R. Silverman/Chmn., CEO, Richard A. Smith/Vice Chmn., Pres., Martin L. Edelman/66/Dir., Kenneth Fisher/49/Dir., Cheryl D. Mills/42/Dir., Robert W. Pittman/54/Dir., Robert F. Smith/75/Dir., Robert E. Nederlander/74/Dir.

Owners: Anthony E. Hull, Bruce Zipf, Richard A. Smith, Alexander E. Perriello, Apollo Funds/98.90%, Insiders/1.10%

Realty Income Corp

220 W Crest St., Escondido, CA, 92025; **PH:** 1-760-741-2111; **Fax:** 1-760-741-2235; http:// www.realtyincome.com

General - Incorporation	MD	**Stock** - Price on:12/24/2007	$26.45
Employees	70	Stock Exchange	NYSE
Auditor	KPMG LLP	Ticker Symbol	O
Stk Agt	Bank of New York	Outstanding Shares	101,020,000
Counsel	NA	E.P.S.	$1.14
DUNS No.	NA	Shareholders	NA

Business: The groups principle activities include owning, leasing, retailing and managing real estate properties. The group operates through 30 segments. In the year 2006, the group acquired 322 properties. The group operates from the United States. The groups quarterly revenue for September 2007 was 74.09 millions of USD.

Primary SIC and add'l.: 6798

CIK No: 0000726728

Subsidiaries: 1008 Whitlock Ave, LLC, 1453 Montgomery Hwy, LLC, 1735 Cobb Parkway SE, LLC, 2035 W Spring St, LLC, 2205 Riverside Pkwy, LLC, 2237 Capital Circle NE, LLC, 2921 Ross Clark Cir, LLC, 3113 Gulf Breeze Pkwy, LLC, 316 Commons Dr, LLC, 3527 Old Norcross Rd, LLC, 3904 Pepperell Pkwy, LLC, 406 Grayson Hwy, LLC, 4081 US Highway 231, LLC, 4095 Pleasant Hill, LLC, 4675 Center Point Rd, LLC 36 Subsidiaries included in the Index

Officers: Thomas A. Lewis/Vice Chmn., CEO/$2,136,103.00, Steve Burchett/Assoc. VP - Sr. Legal Counsel, Richard G. Collins/Exec. VP - Portfolio Management, Realty Income/$539,427.00, Kim S. Kundrak/Sr. VP, Tere H. Miller/VP - Investor Relations, Corporate Communications, Erik O. Valderhaug/Legal Counsel, Gregory J. Fahey/VP, Controller, Mayra Flores/Sr. Paralegal Assist., Carolyn Clemmer/Sr. Paralegal, Gail Ferrell/Paralegal, Donna Harms/Paralegal, Sue Busch/Legal Department Assist. Coordinator, Christy Anderson/Sr. Legal Department Coordinator, Steve Perraud/Financial Relations Mgr., David Butterfield/Investor Outreach Mgr. *(43 Officers included in Index)*

Directors: Thomas A. Lewis/Vice Chmn., CEO, William E. Clark/Chmn., Kathleen R. Allen/Dir., Donald R. Cameron/Dir., Roger P. Kuppinger/Dir., Michael D. Mckee/Dir., Ronald L. Merriman/Dir., Willard H. Smith/Dir., Mark Manheimer/Dir., Gregory T. McLaughlin/Dir.

Owners: Gary M. Malino/0.30%, Roger P. Kuppinger/0.10%, Willard H. Smith, Donald R. Cameron/0.10%, Kathleen R. Allen, Michael R. Pfeiffer/0.10%, William E. Clark, Thomas A. Lewis/0.50%, Michael D. McKee/0.10%, Insiders/2.50%, Paul M. Meurer/0.10%, Richard G. Collins/0.10%, Ronald L. Merriman

Financial Data: Fiscal Year End:12/31 Latest Annual Data: 12/31/2006

Year	Sales		Net Income
2006	$240,100,000		$110,781,000
2005	$196,676,000		$99,119,000
2004	$175,555,000		$103,397,000

Curr. Assets:	$16,526,000	**Curr. Liab.:**	$42,100,000	**P/E Ratio:**	23.20
Plant, Equip.:	$2,485,544,000	**Total Liab.:**	$970,516,000	**Indic. Yr. Divd.:**	$1.530
Total Assets:	$2,546,508,000	**Net Worth:**	$1,575,992,000	**Debt/ Equity:**	0.6155

Receivable Acquisition & Management Corp

140 Broadway Fl 46, New York, NY, 10005; **PH:** 1-212-858-7590; http:// www.ramcoglobal.com; **Email:** info@ramcoglobal.com

General - Incorporation	DE	**Stock** - Price on:12/24/2007	$0.06
Employees	NA	Stock Exchange	OTC
Auditor	Bagell, Levine & Company, LLC	Ticker Symbol	RCVA
Stk Agt	American Stock Transfer & Trust Co.	Outstanding Shares	17,100,000
Counsel	NA	E.P.S.	NA
DUNS No.	NA	Shareholders	NA

Business: The groups principle activity is in the business of acquiring and collecting portfolios of performing, sub performing and non performing consumer and commercial receivables. The group operates from the United Kingdom. The group's quarterly revenue for June '07 was 0.06 millions of USD.

Primary SIC and add'l.: 6153

CIK No: 0000733337

Subsidiaries: Feminique Corporation

Officers: Max Khan/CEO, Pres., Karin Bautz/Investor Relations Contact

Directors: Gobind Sahney/Chmn., Steven T. Lowe/Dir.

Owners: Gobind Sahney/5.80%, Insiders/25.45%, Max Khan/19.31%, Claudia DiNatale/29.56%, Mehtab Sultana/8.66%, Steven Lowe, Lisa Sahney Trust/11.59%

Curr. Assets:	$449,000	**Curr. Liab.:**	$199,000		
Plant, Equip.:	NA	**Total Liab.:**	$199,000	**Indic. Yr. Divd.:**	NA
Total Assets:	$1,017,000	**Net Worth:**	$819,000	**Debt/ Equity:**	NA

Reclamation Consulting & Applications Inc

940 Calle Amanecer, Unit E, San Clemente, CA, 92673; **PH:** 1-949-542-7440; http:// www.rca-inc.com; **Email:** info@rca-inc.com

General - Incorporation	CO	**Stock** - Price on:12/24/2007	$0.24
Employees	8	Stock Exchange	OTC
Auditor	Corbin & Co LLP	Ticker Symbol	RCAA
Stk Agt	Computershare Ltd.	Outstanding Shares	49,070,000
Counsel	NA	E.P.S.	-$0.19
DUNS No.	92-694-7185	Shareholders	NA

Business: The group's principal activities are to develop, produce and market alderox(tm) line of products including asa-12(TM), kr7(TM) and proprietary applicator systems. Asa-12(TM) is an asphalt/concrete release agent that allows asphalt to slide easily from truck beds. Kr7(TM) is a concrete release agent that allows concrete to easily release from concrete molds and form. The group markets its products under the trade names alderox(tm) and asa-12t.

Primary SIC and add'l.: 3569 5169

CIK No: 0001100091

Subsidiaries: Aquadynamic Technologies, Inc

Officers: Michael Davies/Dir., CEO, Sec., Gordon Davies/Dir., Pres., Paul Hughes/38/CFO, COO

Directors: Michael Davies/Dir., CEO, Sec., Gordon Davies/Dir., Pres.

Owners: Gordon W. Davies, Sally Holden, Paul Hazell, Insiders, Michael C. Davies, John Benjamin, Paul Hughes

Financial Data: Fiscal Year End:06/30 Latest Annual Data: 6/30/2006

Year	Sales		Net Income
2006	$96,000		-$7,215,000
2005	$243,000		-$3,703,000
2004	$289,000		-$2,543,000

Curr. Assets:	$137,000	**Curr. Liab.:**	$2,253,000		
Plant, Equip.:	$45,000	**Total Liab.:**	$3,778,000	**Indic. Yr. Divd.:**	NA
Total Assets:	$1,139,000	**Net Worth:**	-$2,638,000	**Debt/ Equity:**	NA

RecycleNet

175 E 400 S, Ste. 900, Salt Lake City, UT, 84111; **PH:** 1-801-531-0404; **Fax:** 1-801-531-0707; http:// www.recycle.net

General - Incorporation	UT	**Stock** - Price on:12/24/2007	$0.04
Employees	NA	Stock Exchange	OTC
Auditor	Hansen, Barnett & Maxwell	Ticker Symbol	GARM
Stk Agt	Atlas Stock Transfer Corp	Outstanding Shares	77,110,000
Counsel	NA	E.P.S.	$0.00
DUNS No.	NA	Shareholders	NA

Business: The group's principle activities are to design Internet sites, Internet advertising and Internet trading of consumable recyclable goods. The group has developed and implemented a broad range of software solutions including site management, sales management, search, customer interaction and transaction processing systems using a combination of proprietary custom designed technologies and commercially available license technologies. It also provides Internet hosting facilities and redundant high speed Internet connectivity. The group has developed its own content and Web site management tools to facilitate the maintenance and updating of its Web sites. The group's quarterly revenue for September 2007 was 0.23 millions of USD.

Primary SIC and add'l.: 7375

CIK No: 0001084662

Officers: Paul Roszel/Chmn., Dir. - Recycling Operations, Richard R. Ivanovick/CFO, Keith A. Deck/Dir., Officer

Directors: Paul Roszel/Chmn., Dir. - Recycling Operations, Keith A. Deck/Dir., Officer

Owners: Inter-Continental Recycling, Inc/50.04%, Keith A. Deck/1.05%, Insiders/9.83%, Inter-Continental Recycling, Inc/95.86%, Inter-Continental Recycling, Inc/3.46%, Inter-Continental Recycling, Inc/1.12%, Insiders/1.12%, Richard R. Ivanovick/5.32%

Financial Data: Fiscal Year End:12/31 Latest Annual Data: 12/31/2006

Year	Sales		Net Income
2006	$1,150,000		$122,000
2005	$918,000		-$59,000
2004	$738,000		$10,000

Curr. Assets:	$366,000	**Curr. Liab.:**	$181,000		
Plant, Equip.:	$32,000	**Total Liab.:**	$181,000	**Indic. Yr. Divd.:**	NA
Total Assets:	$513,000	**Net Worth:**	$332,000	**Debt/ Equity:**	NA

Red Hat Inc

1801 Varsity Dr., Raleigh, NC, 27606; **PH:** 1-919-754-3700; **Fax:** 1-919-754-3701; http:// www.redhat.com

General - Incorporation	DE	**Stock** - Price on:12/24/2007	$23.72
Employees	1,800	Stock Exchange	NYSE
Auditor	PricewaterhouseCoopers LLP	Ticker Symbol	RHT
Stk Agt	Mellon Investor Services LLC	Outstanding Shares	193,180,000
Counsel	Hale & Dorr LLP	E.P.S.	$0.29
DUNS No.	NA	Shareholders	NA

Business: The group's principal activity is to provide an enterprise operating system and related systems management services based on open source technology. These services are provided for information technology infrastructure requirements of large enterprises. The group developed an enterprise operating system, red hat enterprise linux as and added two additional versions to it namely, red hat enterprise linux es and red hat enterprise linux ws. It also provides a red hat enterprise linux operating system, which is suitable from a price and functionality perspective for the application areas of the information technology infrastructure of the large enterprise. Red hat network provides an integrated management service that allows red hat enterprise linux technologies to be updated, configured, and provisioned and the performance of these technologies to be monitored in an automated fashion.

Primary SIC and add'l.: 7372 7371

CIK No: 0001087423

Subsidiaries: Red Hat AB, Red Hat Asia Pacific Pty. Ltd., Red Hat Asia Pte. Ltd., Red Hat BV, Red Hat Canada Limited, Red Hat Financial Holdings, Inc., Red Hat GmbH, Red Hat India Pvt. Ltd., Red Hat Ireland Ltd., Red Hat K.K., Red Hat Professional Consulting, Inc., Red Hat S.A.R.L., Red Hat S.L., Red Hat S.p.A., Red Hat Software Services (Beijing) Co., Ltd. 18 Subsidiaries included in the Index

Officers: Matthew J. Szulik/Chmn., CEO, Pres./$5,230,983.00, Alex Pinchev/58/Exec. VP - Worldwide Sales/$2,427,393.00, Charlie Peters/CFO, Exec. VP/$1,742,935.00, Paul J. Cormier/Exec. VP - Engineering/$1,496,737.00, Michael R. Cunningham/Exec. VP, General Counsel, Delisa Alexander/VP - Human Capital, Lee Congdon/VP - Global Information Technology, Linda Brewton/Mgr. - Investor Relations, Nicholas Van Wyk/VP - Operations, Sr. Transformation Executive, Michael Chen/VP - Corporate Marketing, Brian Stevens/CTO, VP - Engineering, Dion Cornett/VP - Investor Relations, Tom Rabon/Exec. VP - Corporate Affairs, Michael Tiemann/VP - Open Source Affairs

Directors: Matthew J. Szulik/Chmn., CEO, Pres., Marye Anne Fox/60/Dir., William S. Kaiser/52/Dir., Hugh H. Shelton/66/Dir., Steve W. Albrecht/61/Dir., Narendra Kumar Gupta/59/Dir.

Owners: Matthew J. Szulik/2.62%, Narendra K. Gupta, Eugene J. McDonald, Paul J. Cormier, UBS AG/8.61%, Joanne Rohde, Mazama Capital Management, Inc./6.61%, Wellington Management Company, LLP/6.70%, Steve W. Albrecht, Alex Pinchev, William S. Kaiser, Insiders/3.82%, Marye Anne Fox, Charles E. Peters, T. Rowe Price Associates, Inc./11.43% *(17 Owners included in Index)*

Financial Data: *Fiscal Year End:* 02/28 *Latest Annual Data:* 2/28/2007

Year	Sales	Net Income
2007	$400,624,000	$59,907,000
2006	$278,330,000	$79,685,000
2005	$196,466,000	$45,426,000

Curr. Assets:	$1,007,065,000	**Curr. Liab.:**	$300,363,000		
Plant, Equip.:	$45,258,000	**Total Liab.:**	$964,618,000	**Indic. Yr. Divd.:**	NA
Total Assets:	$1,785,854,000	**Net Worth:**	$821,236,000	**Debt/ Equity:**	0.6940

Red Lion Hotels Corp

Formerly: WestCoast Hospitality Corp

201 W N River Dr., Ste. 100, Spokane, WA, 99201; *PH:* 1-509-459-6100; *http://* www.redlion.com

General - Incorporation	WA	**Stock**- Price on:12/24/2007	$12.21
Employees	3,178	Stock Exchange	NYSE
Auditor	BDO Seidman LLP	Ticker Symbol	NA
Stk Agt	American Stock Transfer & Trust Co.	Outstanding Shares	19,190,000
Counsel	Riddell William	E.P.S.	NA
DUNS No.	06-003-8056	Shareholders	NA

Business: The group's principal activity is to operate hotels, entertainment and real estate operations in the western United States. The group also provides hospitality and entertainment engaged in the ownership, management, franchising and development of mid-scale, full service hotels under our westcoast, ticketswest and red lion brands. The group operates through four segments: hotels and restaurants, franchise, central service and development, entertainment and real estate. At 30-Jun-2004, the hotel system contained 68 hotels located in 12 states and one Canadian province and also owned and operates in 48 of these hotels, consisting of 27 owned hotels, 15 leased hotels and six third-party owned hotels. The remaining 23 hotels were owned and operated by third-party franchisees. On 13-Jan-2004, the group acquired red lion hotel yakima gateway and red lion hotel bellevue.

Primary SIC and add'l.: 7011 7922 6519

CIK No: 0001052595

Subsidiaries: North River Drive Company, Red Lion Hotels Franchising, Inc., Red Lion Hotels Holdings, Inc., Red Lion Hotels Management, Inc., Red Lion Properties, Inc., TicketsWest.com, Inc., WestCoast Hotel Properties, Inc., Whc805, LLC

Officers: Arthur M. Coffey/Dir., CEO, Pres./$845,436.00, Anupam Narayan/Exec. VP, Chief Investment Officer/$449,099.00, Anthony F. Dombrowik/Sr. VP, Corporate Controller, Jack G. Lucas/VP, Pres. - Ticketswest, John M. Taffin/Exec. VP - Hotel Operations/$330,717.00, Thomas L. McKeirnan/Sr. VP, General Counsel, Sec./$238,310.00, David Barbieri/CIO, VP, Krisann Hatch/VP - Human Resources, Shannon Kapek/VP - Financial Analysis

Directors: Arthur M. Coffey/Dir., CEO, Pres., Donald Barbieri/Chmn., Jon E. Eliassen/Dir., Richard Barbieri/Dir., Peter Stanton/Dir., Ronald Taylor/Dir., Ryland P. Davis/Dir.

Owners: John M. Taffin, Richard L. Barbieri/1.10%, Donald K. Barbieri/8.50%, Heather H. Barbieri/8.50%, Arthur M. Coffey, Dimensional Fund Advisors Inc./6.90%, Ronald R. Taylor, Wells Fargo & Company/7.70%, Jon E. Eliassen, Anupam Narayan, Ryland P. Skip Davis, Thomas L. McKeirnan, WM Advisors, Inc./7.10%, Peter F. Stanton, Insiders/11.20% *(16 Owners included in Index)*

Financial Data: *Fiscal Year End:* 12/31 *Latest Annual Data:* 12/31/2006

Year	Sales	Net Income
2006	$170,368,000	-$575,000
2005	$165,048,000	$4,495,000
2004	$163,143,000	-$6,285,000

Curr. Assets:	$53,646,000	**Curr. Liab.:**	$32,287,000	**P/E Ratio:**	555.00
Plant, Equip.:	$249,860,000	**Total Liab.:**	$167,647,000	**Indic. Yr. Divd.:**	NA
Total Assets:	$351,438,000	**Net Worth:**	$183,791,000	**Debt/ Equity:**	0.6205

Red Robin Gourmet Burgers Inc

6312 S Fiddler's Green Cir., Ste. 200N, Greenwood Village, CO, 80111; *PH:* 1-303-846-6000; *Fax:* 1-303-846-6048; *http://* www.redrobin.com; *Email:* relations@redrobin.com

General - Incorporation	DE	**Stock**- Price on:12/24/2007	$38.87
Employees	21,535	Stock Exchange	NDQ
Auditor	Deloitte & Touche LLP	Ticker Symbol	RRGB
Stk Agt	American Stock Transfer & Trust Co.	Outstanding Shares	16,740,000
Counsel	O'melveny & Myers	E.P.S.	$1.76
DUNS No.	NA	Shareholders	NA

Business: The group's principal activity is to own and operate a chain of casual dining restaurants. The menu focused by this chain of restaurants is the gourmet burger, which is made of beef, chicken, veggie, pot roast, pork, fish and turkey and serve in various recipes. The group offers a wide selection of toppings for these burgers inclusive of fresh guacamole, roasted green chilies, honey mustard dressing, grilled pineapple, crispy onion straws, sauteed mushrooms and a choice of six different cheeses. The group also offers salads, soups, appetizers, other entrees such as carnitas fajitas and pastas, desserts and non-alcoholic beverages. The group currently owns and operates 118 restaurants in 14 states with an additional 107 restaurants operating under franchise or license agreements in 22 states and two Canadian provinces.

Primary SIC and add'l.: 5812

CIK No: 0001171759

Subsidiaries: Red Robin International, Inc., Red Robin West, Inc

Officers: Dennis B. Mullen/Chmn., CEO, Annita M. Menogan/VP, Sec., Chief Legal Officer, Susan Lintonsmith/Sr. VP, Chief Marketing Officer, Katie Scherping/CFO, Michael E. Woods/Sr. VP, Chief Knowledge Officer, Todd A. Brighton/Chief Development Officer, Sr. VP, Eric C. Houseman/COO, Pres.

Directors: Dennis B. Mullen/Chmn., CEO, James T. Rothe/Dir., Richard J. Howell/Dir., Edward T. Harvey/Dir., Gary J. Singer/Dir., Benjamin D. Graebel/Dir., Taylor J. Simonton/Dir.

Owners: Wellington Management Company, LLP/6.20%, Gary J. Singer, T. Rowe Price Associates, Inc./9.50%, Dennis B. Mullen, Columbia Wanger Asset Management, L.P./7.00%, Richard J. Howell, Katherine L. Scherping, James T. Rothe, Michael J. Snyder/6.60%, Insiders/3.80%, FMR Corp./14.50%, Magnetar Capital Partners LP/7.90%, Michael E. Woods, Eric C. Houseman, Benjamin D. Graebel *(20 Owners included in Index)*

Financial Data: *Fiscal Year End:* 12/25 *Latest Annual Data:* 12/31/2006

Year	Sales	Net Income
2006	$618,721,000	$29,362,000
2005	$486,023,000	$27,386,000
2004	$409,064,000	$23,381,000

Curr. Assets:	$29,283,000	**Curr. Liab.:**	$70,162,000	**P/E Ratio:**	22.21
Plant, Equip.:	$351,736,000	**Total Liab.:**	$207,065,000	**Indic. Yr. Divd.:**	NA
Total Assets:	$450,598,000	**Net Worth:**	$243,533,000	**Debt/ Equity:**	0.4639

Red Rock Pictures Holding Inc

8228 Sunset Blvd., First Fl., Los Angeles, CA, 90046; *PH:* 1-301-474-1219; *Fax:* 1-323-474-1219; *http://* www.redrockpics.com; *Email:* info@redrockpics.com

General - Incorporation	NV	**Stock**- Price on:12/24/2007	$1.86
Employees	NA	Stock Exchange	OTC
Auditor	Dntw Chartered Accountants, LLP	Ticker Symbol	RRPH
Stk Agt	Integrity Stock Transfer, Inc.	Outstanding Shares	NA
Counsel	NA	E.P.S.	NA
DUNS No.	NA	Shareholders	NA

Business: The groups principal activity is in the mineral exploration. The group engaged in the finance, production, and distribution and marketing of filmed entertainment products, including theatrical motion pictures, television programs, home video products, and digitally delivered entertainment and media.

Primary SIC and add'l.: 7819

CIK No: 0001329957

Officers: Robert L. Levy/Chmn., CEO, Barry Layne/Pres., David Kane/CFO

Directors: Robert L. Levy/Chmn., CEO, Daniel S. Laikin/Dir., Reno R. Rolle/Dir., John Whitesell/Dir.

Owners: Robert Levy/2.43%, Insiders/2.43%, National Lampoon, Inc./19.46%

Redback Networks Inc

300 Holger Way, San Jose, CA, 95134; *PH:* 1-408-750-5000; *http://* www.redback.com

General - Incorporation	DE	**Stock**- Price on:12/24/2007	$25.02
Employees	505	Stock Exchange	NA
Auditor	PricewaterhouseCoopers LLP	Ticker Symbol	NA
Stk Agt	U.S. Stock Transfer Corp	Outstanding Shares	NA
Counsel	NA	E.P.S.	NA
DUNS No.	NA	Shareholders	NA

Business: The group's principal activity is to provide advanced telecommunications networking equipment. These systems enable carriers and service providers to rapidly deploy high-speed access and services to the Internet and corporate networks. The group's product lines consist of the smstm family of subscriber management systems and the smartedge(R) router and service gateway systems combine networking hardware and software. The group's products are designed to enable our customers to create regional and national networks that support major broadband access technologies. The main products of the group include sms 500, sms 1800, sms 1800 sl, sms 10000 and sms 10000 sl. The group markets its products in North America, Europe and Asia. The group's customers include both end-user customers and resellers like sbc communications and british telecom. On 03-Nov-2003, the group filed for bankruptcy proceedings under chapter 11 and emerged from such proceedings on 02-Jan-2004.

Primary SIC and add'l.: 7379 7373 7372

CIK No: 0001081290

Subsidiaries: 610380 B.c. Inc., 610381 B.c. Inc., Merlin Systems, Inc., Redback Networks Brazil Ltda., Redback Networks Canada Inc., Redback Networks de Mexico, Redback Networks GmbH, Redback Networks International, Inc., Redback Networks KK, Redback Networks Korea, Inc., Redback Networks Research, Redback Networks SARL, Redback Networks Spain, S.L., Redback Networks Systems Canada, Inc.

Officers: Kevin A. Denuccio/Dir., CEO, Pres., Georges Antoun/Sr. VP - World Wide Field Operations, Ebrahim Abbasi/Sr. VP - Operations, Information Technology, Customer Service, Scott Marshall/Sr. VP - Engineering, Product Management

Directors: Kevin A. Denuccio/Dir., CEO, Pres.

Redcell Power Corp

598-999 Canada Pl., Vancouver, BC, V6C 3E1; *PH:* 1-604-629-2461

General - Incorporation	DE	*Stock* - Price on:12/24/2007	NA
Employees	NA	Stock Exchange	NA
Auditor	MacKay LLP	Ticker Symbol	NA
Stk Agt	NA	Outstanding Shares	NA
Counsel	NA	E.P.S.	NA
DUNS No.	NA	Shareholders	NA

Business: The group's principle activities include marketing and distributing portable power batteries. Power batteries include alkaline, photo lithium, watch, calculator, hearing aid and cordless and telephone batteries. The group operates from United States.

Primary SIC and add'l.: 5199

CIK No: 0001079548

Subsidiaries: RedCell Batteries Inc

Officers: Kelly Fielder/Dir., CEO, Acting CFO, Pres.

Directors: Kelly Fielder/Dir., CEO, Acting CFO, Pres.

Reddi Brake Supply Corp

1175 E 400 S, Ste. 900, Salt Lake City, UT, 84111; *PH:* 1-801-269-8535

General - Incorporation	NV	*Stock* - Price on:12/24/2007	$0.5
Employees	NA	Stock Exchange	OTC
Auditor	Madsen & Associates, CPA's Inc.	Ticker Symbol	RDDI
Stk Agt	NA	Outstanding Shares	4,640,000
Counsel	NA	E.P.S.	NA
DUNS No.	NA	Shareholders	NA

Business: The groups principal activity is engaging professional firms specializing in business acquisitions or reorganizations. The group operates from the United States.

Primary SIC and add'l.: 5013

CIK No: 0000867687

Subsidiaries: RBSC, Inc.

Officers: Alexander H. Walker/CEO, Michael J. Zwebner/56/Chmn., Pres., Ronald S. Friend/53/Dir., Sec., Treasurer

Directors: Michael J. Zwebner/56/Chmn., Pres., Ronald S. Friend/53/Dir., Sec., Treasurer, Paul Holm/55/Dir.

Owners: Port Universal Corporation/3.40%, Timotha Ann Kent/14.40%, Paul Holm, Michael Zwebner/4.20%, Alexander H. Walker/14.40%, Ronald S. Friend, Insiders/7.70%, Amanda Cardinalli/14.40%, Alexander H. Walker/46.70%

Reddy Ice Holdings Inc

8750 N Central Expwy., Ste. 1800, Dallas, TX, 75231; *PH:* 1-214-526-6740; *Fax:* 1-214-443-5357; *http://* www.reddyice.com; *Email:* information@reddyice.com

General - Incorporation	DE	*Stock* - Price on:12/24/2007	$30.13
Employees	1,600	Stock Exchange	NYSE
Auditor	Deloitte & Touche LLP	Ticker Symbol	FRZ
Stk Agt	American Stock Transfer & Trust Co.	Outstanding Shares	21,810,000
Counsel	NA	E.P.S.	$0.55
DUNS No.	NA	Shareholders	NA

Business: The groups principle activities include manufacturing and distributing of packaged ice. The group operates through two segments namely, ice products and non-ice products. The group acquired 10 businesses in the year 2006 and 2 businesses in the year 2005. The group operates from the United States.

Primary SIC and add'l.: 2097

CIK No: 0001268984

Subsidiaries: Reddy Ice Corporation

Officers: Jimmy C. Weaver/CEO, Pres., Steven J. Janusek/CFO, Exec. VP, Sec., Ben D. Key/Exec. VP - Sales, Marketing, Graham D. Davis/Sr. VP - Central Operations, Thomas L. Dann/Sr. VP - Western Operations, Joseph A. Geloso/Sr. VP - Eastern Operations, Raymond D. Booth/COO, Exec. VP, Mark A. Steffek/VP - Finance, Treasurer

Directors: William P. Brick/Chmn., Theodore J. Host/Dir., Michael S. McGrath/Dir., Tracy L. Noll/Dir., Robert N. Verdecchio/Dir.

Owners: Michael S. McGrath, Jimmy C. Weaver/1.00%, Wachovia Corporation/5.10%, Steven J. Janusek, Robert N. Verdecchio, Shamrock Activist Value Funds/6.40%, Raymond D. Booth, Ben D. Key, Theodore J. Host, Insiders/3.30%, Tracy L. Noll, Noonday Asset Management, L.P./9.90%, Thornburg Asset Management/7.60%, William P. Brick/1.00%

*Financial Data: Fiscal Year End:*12/31 *Latest Annual Data:* 12/31/2006

Year		Sales		Net Income
2006		$346,038,000		$14,661,000
2005		$319,772,000		-$12,116,000
2004		$285,727,000		$16,551,000
Curr. Assets:	$80,951,000	*Curr. Liab.:*	$41,628,000	*P/E Ratio:* 23.20
Plant, Equip.:	$230,242,000	*Total Liab.:*	$442,624,000	*Indic. Yr. Divd.:* $1.680
Total Assets:	$610,272,000	*Net Worth:*	$167,648,000	*Debt/ Equity:* NA

RedEnvelope Inc

149 New Montgomery St., San Francisco, CA, 94105; *PH:* 1-415-371-9100; *Fax:* 1-415-371-1134; *http://* www.redenvelope.com

General - Incorporation	DE	*Stock* - Price on:12/24/2007	$6.78
Employees	210	Stock Exchange	NDQ
Auditor	Deloitte & Touche LLP	Ticker Symbol	REDE
Stk Agt	American Stock Transfer & Trust Co.	Outstanding Shares	9,630,000
Counsel	NA	E.P.S.	-$1.35
DUNS No.	NA	Shareholders	NA

Business: The group's principle activity is to operate as an Internet and catalog retailer of upscale gifts. The company publishes full-color catalogs. The company's Website www.redenvelope.com allows customers to shop for gifts by occasion, recipient, lifestyle and price, and, depending on the season, features between approximately 650 and 850 different gift items. The company offers a wide variety of products in numerous product categories, including flowers and plants, jewelry, men's and women's accessories, gift baskets, gourmet foods, personal care, sports and games, gadget and tools, baby and kids, home and garden, office, and bar, wine and cigar accessories. The group operates from United States.

Primary SIC and add'l.: 7375 5947 5999

CIK No: 0001236038

Officers: John Pound/53/Executive Chmn., Frank Buettner/52/COO, Pres., Christopher E. Nordquist/42/Chief Administrative Officer, General Counsel, William T. Gochnauer/61/Interim CFO, Scott Sanborn/38/Chief Marketing Officer

Directors: John Pound/53/Executive Chmn., Joseph C. Gandolfo/Dir., Gregory Shove/Dir., Daniel R. Lyle/Dir., Michael E. Dunn/Dir., Karen Edwards/Dir., Scott Galloway/Dir.

Owners: Christopher E. Nordquist, John Pound/9.30%, CCM Master Qualified Fund, Ltd./7.80%, Karen Edwards, Integrity Brands Fund, L.P./9.00%, Michael E. Dunn, Wellington Management Co./14.10%, Glenhill Advisors, LLC/12.20%, Insiders/18.30%, Ken Constable, Stephens Investment Management, L.L.C./8.80%, Scott Galloway/3.90%, Joseph C. Gandolfo, Daniel R. Lyle, Fine Capital Partners/13.70% *(17 Owners included in Index)*

*Financial Data: Fiscal Year End:*04/30 *Latest Annual Data:* 04/01/2007

Year		Sales		Net Income
2007		$121,273,000		-$3,535,000
2006		$113,175,000		-$5,622,000
2005		$101,418,000		-$5,153,000
Curr. Assets:	$38,108,000	*Curr. Liab.:*	$15,070,000	
Plant, Equip.:	$7,587,000	*Total Liab.:*	$16,234,000	*Indic. Yr. Divd.:* NA
Total Assets:	$46,268,000	*Net Worth:*	$30,034,000	*Debt/ Equity:* 0.0137

Redhand International Inc

277 W 11th St., Apt. 2f, New York, NY, 10014; *PH:* 1-212-924-3548

General - Incorporation	NV	*Stock* - Price on:12/24/2007	$0.12
Employees	NA	Stock Exchange	NA
Auditor	Michael Pollack, CPA	Ticker Symbol	NA
Stk Agt	NA	Outstanding Shares	NA
Counsel	NA	E.P.S.	NA
DUNS No.	NA	Shareholders	NA

Business: The group's principle activity is to operates in pool hall and restaurant industries. It is currently doing business as westchester sports grill. It provides dining, including alcoholic beverages, and entertainment services to its customers. Entertainment services include live bands and appropriate dancing areas; sports entertainment including video games, billiard tables, and television monitors showing sports events and news. The customers of the company include the residential, university, commercial, and tourist communities.The group operates from United States.

Primary SIC and add'l.: 5812

CIK No: 0001070512

*Financial Data: Fiscal Year End:*12/31 *Latest Annual Data:* 12/31/2004

Year		Sales		Net Income
2004		NA		-$35,000
2002		$215,000		-$35,000
2001		$325,000		-$15,000
Curr. Assets:	NA	*Curr. Liab.:*	$36,000	
Plant, Equip.:	NA	*Total Liab.:*	$36,000	*Indic. Yr. Divd.:* NA
Total Assets:	NA	*Net Worth:*	-$36,000	*Debt/ Equity:* NA

Redhook Ale Brewery Inc

14300 NE 145th St., Ste. 210, Woodinville, WA, 98072; *PH:* 1-425-483-3232; *Fax:* 1-425-485-0761; *http://* www.redhook.com; *Email:* redhook@redhook.com

General - Incorporation	WA	*Stock* - Price on:12/24/2007	$7.25
Employees	134	Stock Exchange	NDQ
Auditor	Moss Adams LLP	Ticker Symbol	HOOK
Stk Agt	Mellon Investor Services LLC	Outstanding Shares	8,320,000
Counsel	Riddell Williams	E.P.S.	-$0.01
DUNS No.	01-146-9848	Shareholders	NA

Business: The group's principle activity is to provide various styles and flavors of crafted beer in the United States. The company produces nine distinctive brands of beer: redhook e.s.b, redhook India pale ale, redhook hefe-weizen, blackhook porter, double black stout, redhook blonde ale, winterhook and redhook nut brown ale. The products are directly sold to consumers in draft and bottles at restaurants, bars and liquor stores, supermarkets, warehouse clubs and convenience stores. The group operates from United States.

Primary SIC and add'l.: 2082

CIK No: 0000892222

Officers: Paul S. Shipman/Chmn., CEO/$384,500.00, David J. Mickelson/COO, Pres./$247,750.00, Gerard C. Prial/VP - Sales, Eastern Operations/$207,590.00, Allen L. Triplett/VP - Brewing/$207,590.00, Jay T. Caldwell/CFO, Treasurer/$63,778.00

Directors: Paul S. Shipman/Chmn., CEO, Frank H. Clement/Dir., Anthony J. Short/Dir., John W. Glick/Dir., David R. Lord/Dir., John D. Rogers/Dir., Michael Loughran/Dir.

Owners: Gerard C. Prial/1.50%, Dimensional FundAdvisors LP/8.30%, Paul S. Shipman/3.60%, Michael Loughran, David J. Mickelson/2.10%, John D. Rogers, Frank H. Clement/3.40%, David R. Lord, Insiders/12.00%, Allen L. Triplett/1.60%, Busch Investment Corporation/33.20%

*Financial Data: Fiscal Year End:*12/31 *Latest Annual Data:* 12/31/2006

Year		Sales		Net Income
2006		$35,714,000		$516,000
2005		$31,099,000		-$1,200,000
2004		$33,372,000		-$954,000
Curr. Assets:	$15,414,000	*Curr. Liab.:*	$7,104,000	*P/E Ratio:* 103.57
Plant, Equip.:	$58,076,000	*Total Liab.:*	$13,149,000	*Indic. Yr. Divd.:* NA
Total Assets:	$73,841,000	*Net Worth:*	$60,692,000	*Debt/ Equity:* 0.0695

Rediff.com India Ltd

43 W 24th St., New York, NY, 10010; *PH:* 1-212-929-1727; *Fax:* 1-212-627-9503; *http://* www.rediff.com; *Email:* investor@rediff.co.in

General - Incorporation	India	**Stock**- Price on:12/24/2007	$18.4
Employees	274	Stock Exchange	NDQ
Auditor	Deloitte Haskins & Sells	Ticker Symbol	REDF
Stk Agt	Citibank N.A	Outstanding Shares	29,090,000
Counsel	Sullivan & Cromwell	E.P.S	$0.18
DUNS No.	NA	Shareholders	NA

Business: The group's principal activity is to provide Internet products and services to consumers and businesses throughout India and the global Indian community in the United States. The group's websites consists of interest specific channels relevant to Indian interests. The channels include cricket, finance, movies, astrology, contest, home decor, women, a range of community features and products such as free and paid e-mail, chat, instant messaging, blogs, matchmaker, astrology services, 'rediff on palm' and wireless short messaging services. The group also publishes a weekly newspaper, India abroad, in the United States and Canada and provides prepaid long distance communication services primarily to the Indian community in the United States and Canada.

Primary SIC and add'l.: 7379 7311

CIK No: 0001103783

Subsidiaries: Rediff Holdings, Inc., Rediff.com, Inc

Officers: Ajit Balakrishnan/60/Chmn., MD, Joy Basu/47/CFO

Directors: Ajit Balakrishnan/60/Chmn., MD, Diwan Arun Nanda/64/Dir., Sunil N. Phatarphekar/44/Dir., Ashok Narasimhan/60/Dir., Pulak Prasad/40/Dir., Sridar Iyengar/61/Dir., Rashesh C. Shah/45/Dir.

Owners: Draper-India International/15.00%, Rediffusion Holdings Private Limited/15.00%, Ajit Balakrishnan/24.00%, Insiders/48.00%, Diwan Arun Nanda/24.00%, Queenswood Investments Ltd/14.00%

Financial Data: *Fiscal Year End:*03/31 *Latest Annual Data:* 03/31/2007

Year	Sales	Net Income
2007	$28,676,000	$6,963,000
2006	$18,701,000	$1,213,000
2005	$12,627,000	-$1,428,000

Curr. Assets:	$60,652,000	**Curr. Liab.:**	$7,239,000	**P/E Ratio:**	32.19
Plant, Equip.:	$5,532,000	**Total Liab.:**	$7,240,000	**Indic. Yr. Divd.:**	NA
Total Assets:	$74,110,000	**Net Worth:**	$66,870,000	**Debt/ Equity:**	NA

Redpoint Bio Corp

Formerly: Robcor Properties Inc

12890 Hilltop Rd., Argyle, NJ, 76226; *PH:* 1-972-233-0300

General - Incorporation	FL	**Stock**- Price on:12/24/2007	$2.45
Employees	NA	Stock Exchange	OTC
Auditor	Malone & Bailey, PC	Ticker Symbol	RPBC
Stk Agt	Securities Transfer Corp	Outstanding Shares	NA
Counsel	NA	E.P.S	NA
DUNS No.	NA	Shareholders	NA

Business: The groups principle activity is to own and operate real property interests while also seeking to identify a privately held operating group desiring to become a publicly held company by merging through a reverse merger or acquisition. The group operates from the United States.

Primary SIC and add'l.: 8731

CIK No: 0001328003

Subsidiaries: Robcor, LLC

Officers: Timothy P. Halter/41/Dir., CEO, CFO, Pres., Michael Heitz/56/Exec. VP

Directors: Timothy P. Halter/41/Dir., CEO, CFO, Pres.

Owners: SF Capital Partners Ltd., Insiders, NJTC Venture Fund SBIC, L.P., Leif Kjaergaard, Cargill, Incorporated, S.R. One, Limited, Scott M. Horvitz, Danisco Venture A/S, Michael A. Roth, Robert Chefitz, Matthew Rhodes Kropf, Robert W. Bryant, RK Ventures Group, LLC, Brian J. Stark, James Gunton *(19 Owners included in Index)*

Financial Data: *Fiscal Year End:*12/31 *Latest Annual Data:* 12/31/2006

Year	Sales	Net Income
2006	$99,000	-$26,000
2005	$88,000	-$54,000

Curr. Assets:	NA	**Curr. Liab.:**	$50,000		
Plant, Equip.:	$933,000	**Total Liab.:**	$870,000	**Indic. Yr. Divd.:**	NA
Total Assets:	$935,000	**Net Worth:**	$65,000	**Debt/ Equity:**	NA

Redwood Capital Bank

402 G St., Eureka, CA, 95501; *PH:* 1-707-444-9800; *http://* www.redwoodcapitalbank.com

General - Incorporation		**Stock**- Price on:12/24/2007	NA
Employees	NA	Stock Exchange	OTC
Auditor	NA	Ticker Symbol	RDWO
Stk Agt	NA	Outstanding Shares	NA
Counsel	NA	E.P.S	NA
DUNS No.	NA	Shareholders	NA

Business: The groups principle activity is to provide recruiting services. The groups service area includes the research and development, engineering, marketing, sales, information technology and manufacturing industries. The group operates from United States.

Primary SIC and add'l.: 6029

CIK No:

Redwood Trust Inc

1 Belvedere Pl., Ste. 300, Mill Valley, CA, 94941; *PH:* 1-415-389-7373; *Fax:* 1-415-381-1773; *http://* www.redwoodtrust.com; *Email:* investorrelations@redwoodtrust.com

General - Incorporation	MD	**Stock**- Price on:12/24/2007	$52.0799
Employees	91	Stock Exchange	NYSE
Auditor	Grant Thornton LLP	Ticker Symbol	RWT
Stk Agt	Computershare Investor Services LLC	Outstanding Shares	27,360,000
Counsel	NA	E.P.S	$4.39
DUNS No.	NA	Shareholders	NA

Business: The groups principal activity is to provide residential and commercial real estate loans. The group operates from the United States.

Primary SIC and add'l.: 6798 6798

CIK No: 0000930236

Subsidiaries: Acacia CDO 10, Ltd, Acacia CDO 4, Ltd., Acacia CDO 5, Ltd., Acacia CDO 6, Ltd., Acacia CDO 7, Ltd., Acacia CDO 8, Ltd., Acacia CDO 9, Ltd, Acacia CDO CRE 1, Ltd., Cypress Trust, Inc., Madrona LLC, Madrona Residential Funding LLC, Redwood Asset Management, Inc., Redwood Capital Trust I, Redwood Mortgage Funding, Inc., RWT Holdings, Inc. 23 Subsidiaries included in the Index

Officers: George E. Bull/59/Chmn., CEO/$5,266,722.00, Douglas B. Hansen/49/Dir., Pres., Founder/$4,883,989.00, Martin S. Hughes/49/CFO/$2,121,318.00, Harold F. Zagunis/49/VP/$1,305,420.00, Brett D. Nicholas/38/VP/$2,543,954.00, Andrew I. Sirkis/45/VP/$1,925,806.00, Lauren Morgensen/Investor Relations Officer

Directors: George E. Bull/59/Chmn., CEO, Douglas B. Hansen/49/Dir., Pres., Founder, Richard D. Baum/60/Dir., Thomas C. Brown/58/Dir., Mariann Byerwalter/46/Dir., Greg H. Kubicek/50/Dir., Georganne C. Proctor/50/Dir., Charles J. Toeniskoetter/62/Dir., David L. Tyler/69/Dir.

Owners: Insiders/5.70%, Richard D. Baum, Douglas B. Hansen/1.38%, George E. Bull/2.88%, Mariann Byerwalter, Andrew I. Sirkis, Harold F. Zagunis, Greg H. Kubicek, Martin S. Hughes, David L. Tyler, Thomas C. Brown, Charles J. Toeniskoetter, Brett D. Nicholas, Georganne C. Proctor

Financial Data: *Fiscal Year End:*12/31 *Latest Annual Data:* 12/31/2006

Year	Sales	Net Income
2006	$885,160,000	$127,532,000
2005	$959,951,000	$199,872,000
2004	$655,320,000	$232,635,000

Curr. Assets:	$355,369,000	**Curr. Liab.:**	$86,137,000	**P/E Ratio:**	11.86
Plant, Equip.:	$12,402,000	**Total Liab.:**	$12,027,783,000	**Indic. Yr. Divd.:**	$3.000
Total Assets:	$13,030,473,000	**Net Worth:**	$1,002,690,000	**Debt/ Equity:**	12.9146

Reebok International Ltd

1895 J W Foster Blvd., Canton, MA, 02021; *PH:* 1-781-401-5000; *http://* www.reebok.com

General - Incorporation	MA	**Stock**- Price on:12/24/2007	NA
Employees	NA	Stock Exchange	NA
Auditor	Ernst & Young LLP	Ticker Symbol	NA
Stk Agt	Ernest & Young LLP	Outstanding Shares	NA
Counsel	NA	E.P.S	NA
DUNS No.	09-745-3682	Shareholders	NA

Business: The group's principal activities are to design and market sports and fitness products, including footwear, apparel and accessories. It also designs and markets casual footwear, apparel and accessories for non-athletic use. It operates under four brands: the reebok brand, the rockport brand, ralph lauren and polo footwear brands and the greg norman brand. The reebok brand designs, produces and markets sport, fitness and casual footwear, apparel and accessories under the brand name reebok and weebok. Rockport designs, produces, markets and distributes comfort footwear under the rockport brand for men and women. Ralph lauren footwear markets ralph lauren and polo ralph lauren footwear products. Greg norman collections produce men's and women's apparel and accessories, which are marketed under the greg norman name and logo. It has operations in the United Kingdom, Europe and other countries. On 30-Jun-2004, the group acquired the hockey company holdings, inc.

Primary SIC and add'l.: 3021 3149 2329 3143 2331

CIK No: 0000770949

Subsidiaries: Ralph Lauren Footwear Co., Inc., The Rockport Company, LLC

Reed Elsevier Plc

1-3 Strand, London, WCZN 5EH; *PH:* 44-02079307077; *Fax:* 44-02071665799; *http://* www.reedelsevier.com

General - Incorporation	England And Wales	**Stock**- Price on:12/24/2007	$51.23
Employees	NA	Stock Exchange	NYSE
Auditor	Deloitte & Touche LLP	Ticker Symbol	RUK
Stk Agt	Bank of New York	Outstanding Shares	312,400,000
Counsel	Reed Smith LLP	E.P.S	$2.30
DUNS No.	21-024-4596	Shareholders	NA

Business: The group's principal activity is that of a holding company. The group's principal investments are its direct 50% shareholding in reed elsevier group plc and 39% shareholding in reed elsevier finance bv, which are engaged in publishing and information activities, and financing activities, respectively.

Primary SIC and add'l.: 2721 2731 7375 2741 6719

CIK No: 0000929869

Subsidiaries: Academic Press , Butterworths Australia (5), Dott. A. Giuffr Editore Spa (40%), Elsevier B.V., Elsevier Finance SA, Elsevier Health Sciences (2), Elsevier Inc., Elsevier Limited, Elsevier Properties SA, Elsevier Reed Finance B.V., Elsevier Risks SA, Elsevier Swiss Holdings S, Endeavor Information Systems, Inc., Excerpta Medica Medical Communications B.V., Excerpta Medica, Inc 53 Subsidiaries included in the Index

Officers: Crispin Davis/58/Dir., CEO, Mark Armour/53/Dir., CFO, Nick Baker/49/Chief Strategy Officer, Ian Fraser/Dir. - Human Resources, Mark Popolano/CTO, Patrick Kerr/Contact - Media, Shira Tabachnikoff/Contact - Media, Ence, Medical, David Ruth/Media Contact - Science, Medical, Ylann Schemm/Media Contact - Science, Medical, David Kurt/Contact - Media, Rick Blake/Contact - Media, Russell Schweiss/Contact - Media, Salina Le Bris/Contact - Media, Tim Haigh/Contact - Media, Reed Business Information UK, Annemiek Kraaijvanger/Contact - Media, Reed Business Information NL *(18 Officers included in Index)*

Directors: Crispin Davis/58/Dir., CEO, Jan Hommen/65/Chmn., Mark Armour/53/Dir., CFO, Robert Polet/52/Non Exec. Dir., Dien D. Boer-Kruyt/Non Exec. Dir., Erik Engstrom/45/Dir., Strauss Zelnick/Non Exec. Dir., Mark Elliott/58/Non Exec. Dir., Lisa Hook/50/Non Exec. Dir., Andrew Prozes/62/Dir., Patrick Tierney/62/Dir., Gerard Van De Aast/50/Dir., David Reid/61/Non Exec. Dir., Lord Sharman/65/Non Exec. Dir., Rolf Stomberg/67/Non Exec. Dir.

Owners: FMR Corporation/7.95%, The Capital Group Companies, Inc/8.26%, Legal & General Group plc/3.93%, Prudential plc/4.11%, Insiders

Financial Data: *Fiscal Year End:*12/31 *Latest Annual Data:* 12/31/2006

Year	Sales	Net Income
2006	NA	$395,738,000
2005	NA	$323,510,000
2004	$9,451,900,000	$865,043,000

Curr. Assets:	$1,829,799,000	**Curr. Liab.:**	$97,955,000	**P/E Ratio:**	32.19
Plant, Equip.:	NA	**Total Liab.:**	$97,955,000	**Indic. Yr. Divd.:**	$1.300
Total Assets:	$3,434,302,000	**Net Worth:**	$3,336,347,000	**Debt/ Equity:**	NA

Refac Optical Group

5 Harmon Dr., Blackwood, NJ, 08012; **PH:** 1-856-228-0077; *http://* www.refac.com

General - Incorporation	DE	Stock - Price on:12/24/2007	NA
Employees	5	Stock Exchange	NA
Auditor	Grant Thornton LLP	Ticker Symbol	NA
Stk Agt	American Stock Transfer & Trust Co.	Outstanding Shares	NA
Counsel	Skadden, Meagher & Flom LLP	E.P.S.	NA
DUNS No.	04-122-7562	Shareholders	NA

Business: The group is in the business of new product development, graphic design and communications, brand and trademark licensing, technology and patent licensing and the manufacture and marketing of consumer electronic products. The company acquires from its clients the rights to license others to manufacture, use or sell throughout the world or in specific markets in accordance with related to technical know-how. The company also operates facility for exploiting idle patents, unused or abandoned products and technological developments. The company's operations are carried on in the United States, Europe and Asia.

Primary SIC and add'l.: 6794 8748 3679

CIK No: 0000082788

Subsidiaries: OptiCare Merger Sub, Inc, USV Merger Sub, Inc.

Reflect Scientific Inc

970 Terra Bella Ave., Mountain View, CA, 94043; **PH:** 1-650-960-0300; *http://* www.reflectscientific.com; **Email:** businessdevelopment@reflectscientific.com

General - Incorporation	UT	Stock - Price on:12/24/2007	$1.35
Employees	NA	Stock Exchange	OTC
Auditor	HJ & Assoc., LLC	Ticker Symbol	RSCF
Stk Agt	Atlas Stock Transfer Corp	Outstanding Shares	NA
Counsel	NA	E.P.S.	-$0.08
DUNS No.	NA	Shareholders	NA

Business: The group's principal activity is to manufacture and distribute unique laboratory consumables, disposables such as filtration and purification products. The group also manufactures customized sample handling vials, electronic wiring assemblies, high temperature silicone, graphite and vespel/graphite sealing components. Original equipment manufacturers (OEM) uses the products of the group in the chemical analysis industries primarily in the field of gas/liquid chromatography. Chromatography is a laboratory technique for separating a mixture of compounds into its individual components. On 31-Dec-2003, the company acquired reflect scientific inc.

Primary SIC and add'l.: 7375

CIK No: 0001103090

Subsidiaries: Mountain View

Officers: Kim Boyce/Dir., CEO, Pres., Thomas Tait/52/Dir., VP, Kevin Cooksy/45/Sec., Treasurer, John Hammerman/Dir. - Business Development, Marketing, Brian Smithgall/51/GM - Image Labs, Eric Pierson/46/GM - Miralogix, John Dain/GM - All Temp Engineering, Nicholas Henneman/51/Dir. - Manufacturing Cryometrix

Directors: Kim Boyce/Dir., CEO, Pres., Thomas Tait/52/Dir., VP, Craig D. Morrison/64/Dir.

Owners: Craig D. Morrison, Insiders, Nicholas J. Henneman, Kevin Cooksy, Tom Tait, Dain Family Revocable Trust, Kim Boyce

Financial Data: Fiscal Year End:12/31   **Latest Annual Data:** 12/31/2006

Year	Sales	Net Income
2006	$2,573,000	-$979,000
2005	$2,241,000	$38,000
2004	$2,103,000	$43,000

Curr. Assets:	$1,039,000	**Curr. Liab.:**	$270,000		
Plant, Equip.:	$211,000	**Total Liab.:**	$332,000	**Indic. Yr. Divd.:**	NA
Total Assets:	$6,342,000	**Net Worth:**	$6,010,000	**Debt/ Equity:**	NA

Reg Technologies Inc

1103-11871 Horseshoe Way, Richmond, BC, V7A 5H5; **PH:** 1-604-278-5996; *http://* www.regtech.com; **Email:** info@regtech.com

General - Incorporation	Canada	Stock - Price on:12/24/2007	$0.48
Employees	NA	Stock Exchange	OTC
Auditor	Smythe Ratcliffe LLP	Ticker Symbol	REGRF
Stk Agt	Computershare Trust Co	Outstanding Shares	NA
Counsel	NA	E.P.S.	NA
DUNS No.	24-861-4034	Shareholders	NA

Business: The group's principal activity is to develop axial vane type rotary engine and other applications. Its products include rand cam/direct charge engine and other randcam applications such as compressors and pumps. The group's subsidiary rand energy group inc which controls regi us inc own the us marketing and intellectual rights.

Primary SIC and add'l.: 3511 3519

CIK No: 0000925541

Subsidiaries: Rand Energy Group Inc, Regi U.s., Inc.

Officers: John G. Robertson/Dir., Pres., Sec., James Vandeberg/Dir., CFO, Jennifer Lorette/Dir., VP - Administration, Robert Brooks/Advisor, Brian Cherry/VP - Radmax Technology, Robert Grisar/VP - Engineering, Lynn Petersen/VP - Marketing

Directors: John G. Robertson/Dir., Pres., Sec., James Vandeberg/Dir., CFO, Susanne M. Robertson/Dir., Jennifer Lorette/Dir., VP - Administration

Owners: John G. Robertson/11.16%, James Vandeberg, Jennifer Lorette, Susanne Robertson/19.57%

Financial Data: Fiscal Year End:04/30   **Latest Annual Data:** 04/30/2007

Year	Sales	Net Income
2007	NA	-$619,000
2006	NA	-$1,085,000
2005	NA	-$351,000

Curr. Assets:	$448,000	**Curr. Liab.:**	$112,000		
Plant, Equip.:	NA	**Total Liab.:**	$112,000	**Indic. Yr. Divd.:**	NA
Total Assets:	$448,000	**Net Worth:**	$336,000	**Debt/ Equity:**	NA

Regal Bancorp Inc MA

10123 Reisterstown Rd. , Owings Mills, MD, 21117; **PH:** 1-410-363-1772; **Fax:** 1-410-363-3567; *http://* www.regalbank.com

General - Incorporation	MD	Stock - Price on:12/24/2007	$37.5
Employees	NA	Stock Exchange	OTC
Auditor	NA	Ticker Symbol	RGBM
Stk Agt	NA	Outstanding Shares	NA
Counsel	NA	E.P.S.	NA
DUNS No.	NA	Shareholders	NA

Business: The groups principal activities include providing second to none customer service in every facet of business. The groups services provide products for the entrepreneur, including lines of credit, commercial loans, saving accounts, mortgage and credit cards. The group operates from the United States.

Primary SIC and add'l.: 6036

CIK No: 0000865430

Officers: Bradley G. Sanner/Pres., CEO - Regal Bank, Trust, Jamie H. Gronning/Exec. VP - Business Development, Regal Bank, Trust, Sandra P. Horton/VP - Technology, Regal Bank, Trust, Matthew D. Vinson/VP - Loan Administration, Regal Bank, Trust, Deborah P. Goldberg/Regional VP - Baltimore County West, Regal Bank, Trust, Gene Pryor/Regional VP - Carroll County, Regal Bank, Trust, Donald Marshall/VP - Wholesale Correspondent Lending, Regal Bank, Trust, Kimberly L. Mercer/VP - Administration, Security, Corp. Sec. - Regal Bank, Trust, Kelli A. Dell/Assist. VP, Branch Officer - Regal Bank, Trust, Ryan Frieman/Assist. VP, Branch Officer - Regal Bank, Trust, Dave Hyder/Assist. VP - Wholesale Correspondent Lending, Regal Bank, Trust, Patty S. Palmer/Assist. VP, Branch Officer - Regal Bank, Trust, Tammy L. Tucker/Assist. VP - Compliance, Internal Audit Mgr. - Regal Bank, Trust, Arthur C. Brock/Assist. VP, Controller - Regal Bank, Trust, Rene A. Arevalo/Technology Officer - Regal Bank, Trust *(20 Officers included in Index)*

Regal Beloit Corp

200 State St., Beloit, WI, 53511; **PH:** 1-608-364-8800; **Fax:** 1-608-364-8818; *http://* www.regal-beloit.com; **Email:** finance@regal-beloit.com

General - Incorporation	WI	Stock - Price on:12/24/2007	$48.13
Employees	13,600	Stock Exchange	NYSE
Auditor	Deloitte & Touche LLP	Ticker Symbol	RBC
Stk Agt	Computershare Investor Services LLC	Outstanding Shares	31,960,000
Counsel	NA	E.P.S.	$3.45
DUNS No.	00-611-1751	Shareholders	NA

Business: The group's principle activity is to manufacture commercial and industrial electric motors, heating, ventilation and air conditioning, electric motors, electric generators and controls, and mechanical motion control products. The group opertaes from United States.

Primary SIC and add'l.: 3714 3594 3545 3621 3566

CIK No: 0000082811

Subsidiaries: Capacitores Components de Mexico S deRLde CV, Changzhou Modern Technologies, LTD., Changzhou REGAL-BELOIT Sinya Motor Co. Ltd., Compania Armadora S. de R.L. de C.V., Costruzioni Meccaniche Legnanesi, GE Holmes Industries, GE Holmes Industries, LLC, GEMI Motors India PVT. Limited, Hub City, Inc., LEESON Canada, an Alberta Limited Partnership, LEESON Electric Corporation, Marathon Electric Far East Pte. Ltd., Marathon Electric Manufacturing Corporation, Marathon Electric Manufacturing of Mexico, S. DE R.L. DE C.V., Marathon Redevelopment Corp. 30 Subsidiaries included in the Index

Officers: Henry W. Knueppel/60/Chmn., CEO, Mark J. Gliebe/47/Dir., COO, Pres., David A. Barta/CFO, VP, David E. Eisenreich/64/VP, Pres. - Industrial Power Transmission, Power Generation, Paul J. Jones/VP, General Counsel, Sec., Terry Colvin/VP - Corporate Human Resources

Directors: Henry W. Knueppel/60/Chmn., CEO, Frederick G. Kasten/68/Dir., Christopher L. Doerr/57/Dir., Mark J. Gliebe/47/Dir., COO, Pres., Stephen N. Graff/73/Dir., Dean A. Foate/48/Dir., Curtis W. Stoelting/46/Dir., Thomas J. Fischer/59/Dir., Carol N. Skornicka/65/Dir., Rakesh Sachdev/52/Dir.

Owners: Christopher L. Doerr, Thomas J. Fischer, Dimensional Fund Advisors LP/6.71%, Dean A. Foate, David A. Barta, Curtis W. Stoelting, Mark J. Gliebe, Stephen N. Graff, David L. Eisenreich, James L. Packard, Barclays Global Investors, NA/5.11%, Insiders, Frederick G. Kasten, Henry W. Knueppel, AXA Financial, Inc./7.29% *(16 Owners included in Index)*

Financial Data: Fiscal Year End:12/31   **Latest Annual Data:** 12/30/2006

Year	Sales	Net Income
2006	$1,619,545,000	$109,806,000
2005	$1,428,707,000	$69,557,000
2004	$756,557,000	$30,435,000

Curr. Assets:	$487,280,000	**Curr. Liab.:**	$218,791,000	**P/E Ratio:**	14.03
Plant, Equip.:	$244,329,000	**Total Liab.:**	$683,510,000	**Indic. Yr. Divd.:**	$0.600
Total Assets:	$1,342,554,000	**Net Worth:**	$647,996,000	**Debt/ Equity:**	0.4175

Regal Entertainment Group

7132 Regal Ln., Knoxville, TN, 37918; **PH:** 1-865-922-1123; **Fax:** 1-865-922-3188; *http://* www.regalcinemas.com

General - Incorporation	DE	Stock - Price on:12/24/2007	$22.34
Employees	24,049	Stock Exchange	NYSE
Auditor	KPMG LLP	Ticker Symbol	RGC
Stk Agt	Wells Fargo Shareowner Services	Outstanding Shares	152,730,000
Counsel	NA	E.P.S.	$2.17
DUNS No.	NA	Shareholders	NA

Business: The group's principle activity is to operate as a motion picture exhibitor in the theatre circuit in the United States. As on 25-Sep-2003, the group operates diverse theatre circuit in the United States consisting of 6,061 screens in 555 theatres in 39 states. The group has a geographically diverse circuit that includes theatres in 41 of the top 50 U.S. Demographic market areas as well as prime locations in growing suburban markets. The group's size, reach and quality of the theatre circuit provide an exceptional platform to realize economies of scale in the theatre operations and capitalize upon high-Margin ancillary revenue opportunities. The group's quarterly revenue for September 2007 was 752.90 millions of USD.

Primary SIC and add'l.: 7832 6719

CIK No: 0001168696

Subsidiaries: A 3 Theatres of San Antonio, Ltd., A 3 Theatres of Texas,Inc., Act III Cinemas,Inc., Act III Inner Loop Theatres,Inc., Act III Theatres,Inc., CDP Limited Liability Company, Eastgate Theatre,Inc., Edwards Theatres,Inc., Florence Theatre Corporation, Frederick Plaza Cinemas,Inc., General American Theatres,Inc., Green Hills Commons, LLC, Hoyts Cinemas Corporation, Interstate Theatres Corporation, Morgan Edwards Theatre Corporation 55 Subsidiaries included in the Index

Officers: Michael L. Campbell/Chmn., CEO, Amy E. Miles/CFO, Exec. VP, Treasurer, Peter B. Brandow/Exec. VP, General Counsel, Sec., Gregory W. Dunn/COO, Pres., Donald De Laria/VP - Investor Relations

Directors: Michael L. Campbell/Chmn., CEO, Thomas D. Bell/Dir., Stephen A. Kaplan/Dir., Lee M. Thomas/Dir., Jack Tyrrell/Dir., Nestor R. Weigand/Dir., Alex Yemenidjian/Dir., Charles E. Brymer/Dir., David H. Keyte/Dir.

Owners: Lee M. Thomas, Nestor R. Weigand, Thomas D. Bell, Amy E. Miles, Anschutz Company/48.80%, Gregory W. Dunn, Anschutz Company/100.00%, Michael L. Campbell, Insiders/1.60%, Alex Yemenidjian, David H. Keyte, Peter B. Brandow, Jack Tyrrell

Financial Data: *Fiscal Year End:*12/29 *Latest Annual Data:* 12/28/2006

Year	Sales	Net Income
2006	$2,598,100,000	$86,300,000
2005	$2,516,700,000	$91,800,000
2004	$2,468,000,000	$82,500,000

Curr. Assets:	$321,100,000	**Curr. Liab.:**	$644,200,000	**P/E Ratio:**	11.46
Plant, Equip.:	$1,934,700,000	**Total Liab.:**	$2,471,400,000	**Indic. Yr. Divd.:**	$1.200
Total Assets:	$2,542,400,000	**Net Worth:**	$69,000,000	**Debt/ Equity:**	NA

Regal One Corpn New

9517 DuxburyLn., Los Angeles, CA, 90034; *PH:* 1-310-838-4645; *http://* www.regal1.com

General - Incorporation	FL	Stock - Price on:12/24/2007	$0.05
Employees	NA	Stock Exchange	OTC
Auditor	George Brenner, CPA	Ticker Symbol	RONE
Stk Agt	OTR Transfer Agency	Outstanding Shares	3,630,000
Counsel	NA	E.P.S.	$0.11
DUNS No.	NA	Shareholders	NA

Business: The groups principal activity is investing in, coaching and bringing public biomedical companies that meet the investment criteria of the Company. The group believes that it reached compliance with BDC operating requirements. The group operates from the United States.

Primary SIC and add'l.: 8742

CIK No: 0000845385

Subsidiaries: O2 Technology, Inc

Officers: Malcolm R. Currie/Chmn., CEO, Richard A. Hull/COO, Pres., Richard Abruscato/Acting CFO, Allen Gelbard/Business Development, William J. Resinnger/Business Development, Christopher Dieterich/Legal, Raul Silvestre/Legal

Directors: Malcolm R. Currie/Chmn., CEO, Carl Perry/Dir., Neil Williams/Dir.

Owners: AB Investments LLC/26.25%, C.B. Family Trust/9.57%, Aaron Grunfeld/8.20%, Robert B. Kay/8.90%, Malcolm Currie/13.83%, Insiders/13.83%

Financial Data: *Fiscal Year End:*12/31 *Latest Annual Data:* 12/31/2006

Year	Sales	Net Income
2006	$2,479,000	$1,699,000
2005	NA	-$222,000
2004	NA	-$1,646,000

Curr. Assets:	$1,203,000	**Curr. Liab.:**	$1,741,000		
Plant, Equip.:	NA	**Total Liab.:**	$1,741,000	**Indic. Yr. Divd.:**	NA
Total Assets:	$2,744,000	**Net Worth:**	$1,003,000	**Debt/ Equity:**	NA

Regalito Copper Corp

Formerly: Lumina Copper Corp
625 Howe St., Ste. 1550, Vancouver, BC, V6C 2T6; *PH:* 1-604-681-7474; *http://* www.luminacopper.com

General - Incorporation	Canada	Stock - Price on:12/24/2007	NA
Employees	NA	Stock Exchange	NA
Auditor	Grant Thornton LLP	Ticker Symbol	NA
Stk Agt	Pacific Corporate Trust Co	Outstanding Shares	NA
Counsel	NA	E.P.S.	NA
DUNS No.	NA	Shareholders	NA

Business: The groups principle activities include acquiring and developing copper exploration property and other exploration mineral properties. In March 2006, the group merged with Pan Pacific Copper Co., Ltd. The group operates from United States.

Primary SIC and add'l.: NA

CIK No: 0001239197

Subsidiaries: Minera Lumina Copper Chile Sa

Regan Holding Corp

2090 Marina Ave., Petaluma, CA, 94954; *PH:* 1-707-778-8638; *http://* www.legacynet.com

General - Incorporation	CA	Stock - Price on:12/24/2007	NA
Employees	NA	Stock Exchange	NA
Auditor	Burr, Pilger & Mayer, LLP	Ticker Symbol	NA
Stk Agt	Computershare Investor Services LLC	Outstanding Shares	NA
Counsel	NA	E.P.S.	NA
DUNS No.	61-723-9363	Shareholders	NA

Business: The group's principle activity is to design, market and administer life insurance and annuity products of American national insurance company, il annuity and insurance company and transamerica life insurance and annuity company. The group offers and sells variable annuity and life insurance products, mutual funds, debt and equity securities and conducts estate-planning seminars for producers. The group also builds legacy marketing's sales network on a multi-level structure in which producers may sponsor other producers.

Primary SIC and add'l.: 6411 6211 6719

CIK No: 0000870069

Subsidiaries: Imagent Online, LLC, Legacy Advisory Services, Inc., Legacy Financial Services, Legacy Marketing Group, Prospectdigital, LLC, Values Financial Network

Officers: Lynda L. Regan/59/Chmn., Founder, CEO, John W. Abbott/50/CIO, Preston R. Pitts/56/Dir., CFO, COO, Pres.

Directors: Lynda L. Regan/59/Chmn., Founder, CEO, Preston R. Pitts/56/Dir., CFO, COO, Pres., Ute Scott-Smith/48/Dir., Daniel J. Speight/51/Dir., Donald Ratajczak/65/Dir.

Owners: Ute Scott-Smith/1.70%, Lynda L. Regan/48.40%, J. Daniel Speight, Insiders/57.70%, John W. Abbott, Donald Ratajczak, R. Preston Pitts/6.40%

Regen Biologics Inc

411 Hackensack Ave., Hackensack, NJ, 07601; *PH:* 1-201-651-5140; *Fax:* 1-201-651-5141; *http://* www.regenbio.com; *Email:* info@regenbio.com

General - Incorporation	DE	Stock - Price on:12/24/2007	$0.44
Employees	20	Stock Exchange	OTC
Auditor	Ernst & Young LLP	Ticker Symbol	RGBI
Stk Agt	Computershare Trust Co	Outstanding Shares	103,890,000
Counsel	NA	E.P.S.	-$0.118
DUNS No.	18-944-9226	Shareholders	NA

Business: The group's principal activities are to design, develop, manufacture and market minimally invasive human implants and medical devices for the repair and regeneration of damaged human tissue. The group developed a proprietary collagen based matrix technology, which has been clinically proven to regenerate lost or damaged tissue. This technology produces a scaffold, which promotes the natural re-growth of tissue into the implanted matrix. The group chose to initially adapt this technology in the orthopedic area, which offers a substantial unmet need and large market size.

Primary SIC and add'l.: 7373 8099 7379

CIK No: 0000883697

Subsidiaries: DBA ReGen Biologics, Inc., RBio, Inc., ReGen Biologics AG

Officers: Gerald E. Bisbee/Chmn., CEO, Pres./$669,923.00, Juan Carlos Monllau/Scientific Advisor, Paolo Bulgheroni/Scientific Advisor, Steven P. Arnoczky/Scientific Advisor, Brion D. Umidi/Sr. VP, CFO/$313,552.00, Shu-Tung Li/Scientific Advisor, John Dichiara/Sr. VP - Clinical, Regulatory Affairs/$294,781.00, Mininder S. Kocher/Scientific Advisor, Thomas L. Smestad/Consultant, Charles P. Ho/Scientific Advisor, Stephen V. Harris/Dir. - Manufacturing, William G. Rodkey/VP - Scientific Affairs/$265,394.00

Directors: Gerald E. Bisbee/Chmn., CEO, Pres., Robert G. McNeil/Dir., Alan W. Baldwin/Dir., William R. Timken/Dir., Abhi Acharya/Dir., Richard J. Steadman/Dir.

Owners: Alan W. Baldwin, Abhi Acharya, Insiders, William R. Timken, Brion D. Umidi, Richard J. Steadman, Gerald E. Bisbee, Robert G. McNeil, Iridian Asset Management LLC, William Rodkey, John Dichiara, Stockholders Agreement Group, Sanderling Ventures, Gagnon

Financial Data: *Fiscal Year End:*12/31 *Latest Annual Data:* 12/31/2006

Year	Sales	Net Income
2006	$586,000	-$12,657,000
2005	$570,000	-$11,731,000
2004	$504,000	-$6,781,000

Curr. Assets:	$8,569,000	**Curr. Liab.:**	$1,338,000		
Plant, Equip.:	$321,000	**Total Liab.:**	$9,175,000	**Indic. Yr. Divd.:**	NA
Total Assets:	$9,031,000	**Net Worth:**	-$10,598,000	**Debt/ Equity:**	NA

Regency Affiliates Inc

729 Se Federal Hwy, Ste 307, Stuart, FL, 34994; *PH:* 1-212-644-3450; *http://* www.regencyaffiliates.com

General - Incorporation	DE	Stock - Price on:12/24/2007	NA
Employees	3	Stock Exchange	OTC
Auditor	Rosenberg Rich Baker Berman & Co	Ticker Symbol	RAFI
Stk Agt	Transfer Online, Inc.	Outstanding Shares	NA
Counsel	NA	E.P.S.	$0.20
DUNS No.	18-864-4157	Shareholders	NA

Business: The group's owns aggregate stone used for railroad ballast, road construction, construction along shorelines and decorative uses. It operates through its subsidiaries national resource development corporation (nrdc). Nrdc owns 70 million short tons of previously quarried and stockpiled rock. On 30-Jun-2004, the group acquired 50% membership interest in mesc capital llc.

Primary SIC and add'l.: 5531 2499

CIK No: 0000099249

Subsidiaries: Iron Mountain Resources, Inc., National Resource Development Corporation, Regency Power Corporation, Rustic Crafts International, Inc., Security Land and Development Company Limited Partnership

Officers: Laurence S. Levy/Chmn., CEO, Pres., Carol Zelinski/53/Sec., Neil N. Hasson/CFO

Directors: Laurence S. Levy/Chmn., CEO, Pres., Errol Glasser/54/Dir.

Owners: Michael J. Meagher, Laurence S. Levy, Errol Glasser, Raffles Associates, L.P., Neil N. Hasson, Insiders, Royalty Holdings, LLC

Financial Data: *Fiscal Year End:*12/31 *Latest Annual Data:* 12/31/2005

Year	Sales	Net Income
2005	NA	-$819,000
2004	NA	-$2,265,000
2003	NA	-$2,318,000

Curr. Assets:	$10,240,000	**Curr. Liab.:**	$474,000		
Plant, Equip.:	$4,000	**Total Liab.:**	$474,000	**Indic. Yr. Divd.:**	NA
Total Assets:	$18,317,000	**Net Worth:**	$17,843,000	**Debt/ Equity:**	NA

Regency Centers Corp

1 Independent Dr., Ste. 114, Jacksonville, FL, 32202; *PH:* 1-904-598-7000; *Fax:* 1-904-634-3428; *http://* www.regencycenters.com; *Email:* irinfo@regencycenters.com

General - Incorporation	FL	Stock - Price on:12/24/2007	$74.38
Employees	499	Stock Exchange	NYSE
Auditor	KPMG LLP	Ticker Symbol	REG
Stk Agt	Wachovia First Union Corp	Outstanding Shares	69,480,000
Counsel	NA	E.P.S.	NA
DUNS No.	NA	Shareholders	NA

Business: The groups principle activities include owning, operating and developing high-quality community and neighborhood shopping centers. In the year 2006, the group acquired six shopping centers. The group operates from the United States. The groups quarterly revenue for september 2007 was 116.98 millions of USD.

Primary SIC and add'l.: 6798

CIK No: 0000910606

Subsidiaries: 1488-2978 SC GP, LLC, 1488-2978 SC, L.P., 4S Regency Partners, LLC, Alameda Bridgeside Shopping Center, LLC, Allenbeth Associates Limited Partnership, Amherst Street Shopping Center, LLC, Applegate Ranch, LLC, AZCO Partners, Bammel Center, LLC, Bammel North Houston Center, Ltd., Bartram Park Center, LLC, Belleview Square, LLC, Bordeaux Development, LLC, Buckwalter-Bluffton, LLC, Capitol Place I Investment Limited Partnership 359 Subsidiaries included in the Index

Officers: Martin E. Stein/Chmn., CEO/$4,974,703.00, Mary Lou Fiala/Dir., COO, Pres./$3,006,946.00, Whitney B. Kantor/V P, Marketing, Mkt Research, Michael R. Kinsella/V P, Regional Officer, Peter J. Knoedler/V P, Investments, Patrick P. Krejs/V P, Regional Officer, Frank R. Kroner/V P, Information Technology, Michael D. Leonard/V P, Investments, Paul C. Maxwell/V P, Investments, David A. McNulty/V P, Investments, Kathy D. Miller/V P, Tax, Thomas C. Paul/V P, Internal Audit, Celia R. Paulk/V P, Corporate Accounting, Scott R. Prigge/V P, GM - Property Operation, Bruce R. Qualls/V P, Investments *(66 Officers included in Index)*

Directors: Martin E. Stein/Chmn., CEO, Mary Lou Fiala/Dir., COO, Pres., Raymond L. Bank/51/Dir., Ronald C. Blankenship/55/Dir., A. R. Carpenter/63/Dir., Dix J. Druce/57/Dir., Douglas S. Luke/60/Dir., John C. Schweitzer/60/Dir., Thomas G. Wattles/53/Dir., Terry N. Worrell/60/Dir., Bruce M. Johnson/Dir., MD, CFO, Joan W. Newton/Dir.

Owners: Barclays Global Investors, NA/5.40%, Mary Lou Fiala, A. R. Carpenter, Terry N. Worrell, Bruce M. Johnson, Brian M. Smith, Douglas S. Luke, John C. Schweitzer, Thomas G. Wattles, The Vanguard Group, Inc/5.70%, Raymond L. Bank, Deutsche Bank AG/15.20%, Morgan Stanley/13.90%, Insiders/2.80%, Ronald C. Blankenship *(17 Owners included in Index)*

Financial Data: Fiscal Year End:12/31 **Latest Annual Data:** 12/31/2006

Year		Sales			Net Income
2006		$420,338,000			$218,511,000
2005		$396,946,000			$162,647,000
2004		$391,948,000			$136,327,000
Curr. Assets:	$101,208,000	**Curr. Liab.:**	$151,457,000		
Plant, Equip.:	$3,040,154,000	**Total Liab.:**	$1,734,572,000	**Indic. Yr. Divd.:**	$2.640
Total Assets:	$3,671,785,000	**Net Worth:**	$1,853,317,000	**Debt/ Equity:**	0.9004

Regency Energy Partners LP

1700 Pacific Ave., Ste. 2900, Dallas, TX, 75201; *PH:* 1-214-750-1771; *Fax:* 1-214-750-1749; *http://* www.regencyenergy.com

General - Incorporation	DE	**Stock**- Price on:12/24/2007	$25.25
Employees	284	Stock Exchange	NDQ
Auditor	Deloitte & Touche LLP	Ticker Symbol	RGNC
Stk Agt	American Stock Transfer & Trust Co.	Outstanding Shares	47,680,000
Counsel	NA	E.P.S	-$0.05
DUNS No.	NA	Shareholders	NA

Business: The groups principle activities include gathering, processing, marketing and transporting natural gas. The groups operates through two segments namely gathering and processing, and transportation. In the year 2005, the group acquired TexStar Field Services, L.P. The group operates from the United States. The group's quarterly revenue for September 2007 was 285.44 millions of USD.

Primary SIC and add'l.: 4922 4923

CIK No: 0001338613

Subsidiaries: Gulf States Transmission Corporation, Palafox Joint Venture, Regency Eastex Newline LP, Regency Eastex Protreat I LP, Regency Eastex Protreat II LP, Regency Energy Finance Corp., Regency Field Services LP, Regency FN GP LLC, Regency Frio Newline LLC, Regency FS GP LLC, Regency FS LP, Regency Gas Company Ltd., Regency Gas Gathering and Processing LLC, Regency Gas Marketing GP LLC, Regency Gas Marketing LP 37 Subsidiaries included in the Index

Officers: James W. Hunt/Chmn., CEO, Pres., Stephen L. Arata/Exec. VP, CFO - Regency, William E. Joor/Exec. VP, Sec., Shannon Ming/Dir. - Investor Relations, Alvin Suggs/Sr. VP, General Counsel, Richard Moncrief/COO, Exec. VP, Durell J. Johnson/VP - Operations, Engineering, Charles M. Davis/Sr. VP - Corporate Development, Lawrence B. Connors/VP - Finance, James A. Scott/Sr. VP - Gas Supply, Business Development, James M. Richter/VP - Human Resources, Christofer D. Rozzell/VP - Corporate Development

Directors: James W. Hunt/Chmn., CEO, Pres., Mark T. Mellana/Dir., Brian P. Ward/Dir., Dean A. Fuller/Dir., Otis J. Winters/Dir., James Burgoyne/Dir., Daniel Castagnola/Dir., Paul Halas/Dir.

Owners: HM5/GP LLC/29.50%, Jack D. Furst, Edward J. Herring, Gary W. Luce, William E. Joor, J. Otis Winters, James W. Hunt, Michael L. Williams, Joe Colonnetta, Robert D. Kincaid, Jason H. Downie, Alvin Suggs, Stephen L. Arata, A. Dean Fuller, Insiders/31.80%

Financial Data: Fiscal Year End:12/31 **Latest Annual Data:** 12/31/2006

Year		Sales			Net Income
2006		$896,865,000			-$7,244,000
2005		$692,603,000			-$11,224,000
Curr. Assets:	$120,074,000	**Curr. Liab.:**	$135,314,000		
Plant, Equip.:	$734,034,000	**Total Liab.:**	$800,428,000	**Indic. Yr. Divd.:**	NA
Total Assets:	$1,013,085,000	**Net Worth:**	$212,657,000	**Debt/ Equity:**	3.1256

Regeneration Technologies Inc

11621 Research Cir., Alachua, FL, 32615; *PH:* 1-386-418-8888; *Fax:* 1-386-418-0342; *http://* www.rtix.com

General - Incorporation	DE	**Stock**- Price on:12/24/2007	$10.95
Employees	416	Stock Exchange	NDQ
Auditor	Deloitte & Touche LLP	Ticker Symbol	RTIX
Stk Agt	Deloitte & Touche LLP	Outstanding Shares	29,640,000
Counsel	Fulbright & Jaworski LLP	E.P.S	-$0.21
DUNS No.	NA	Shareholders	NA

Business: The group's principal activities are to process and distribute human musculoskeletal and other comprehensive healing and natural tissue products. Surgeons use these tissues to repair and promote the healing of a wide variety of bone and other tissue defects, including spinal vertebrae repair, musculoskeletal reconstruction, fracture repair, repairs to the jaw and related tissues, urinary incontinence and heart valve disorders. These allografts are made from bone, cartilage, tendon, ligament and other soft tissues recovered from deceased tissue donors primarily through a national network of organ and tissue recovery agencies. The group is also a processor of conventional allografts, which are allografts that are not tooled, by the processor for a specific surgical use. The group's products are supplied to hospitals. The products of the groups' are marketed in 50 states and in 10 countries.

Primary SIC and add'l.: 3842

CIK No: 0001100441

Officers: Brian K. Hutchison/Chmn., CEO, Pres./$1,728,549.00, Thomas F. Rose/CFO, VP/$553,929.00, Joseph W. Condon/VP - Operations/$383,154.00, Tara Zerby/VP - Xenograft Technologies, Caroline A. Hartill/VP - Quality Assurance, Regulatory Affairs, Chief Scientific Officer/$442,934.00, Beverly Bliss/VP - RTI Donor Services, Lennox K. Archibald/Medical Dir., Carolyn Shaffer/VP - Human Resources, Organizational Development, Roger W. Rose/Exec. VP/$728,304.00, Wendy Crites Wacker/Dir. - Corporate Communications

Directors: Brian K. Hutchison/Chmn., CEO, Pres., Peter F. Gearen/Dir., Michael J. Odrich/Dir., Phillip R. Chapman/Dir., David J. Simpson/Dir., Julianne M. Bowler/Dir., Gregory P. Rainey/Dir.

Owners: David J. Simpson, Frontier Capital Management Co., Inc./6.60%, Caroline A. Hartill, Thomas F. Rose, Brian K. Hutchison/4.00%, Michael J. Odrich/5.90%, LeRoy C. Kopp/6.90%, LB I Group Inc./5.60%, Joseph W. Condon, Peter F. Gearen, Philip R. Chapman, Gregory P. Rainey, HealthCor Management, L.P./5.30%, Roger W. Rose, Gagnon Securities LLC/12.70% *(17 Owners included in Index)*

Financial Data: Fiscal Year End:12/31 **Latest Annual Data:** 12/31/2006

Year		Sales			Net Income
2006		$73,970,000			-$11,125,000
2005		$75,199,000			-$5,551,000
2004		$92,703,000			$6,155,000
Curr. Assets:	$73,301,000	**Curr. Liab.:**	$16,517,000		
Plant, Equip.:	$41,047,000	**Total Liab.:**	$19,918,000	**Indic. Yr. Divd.:**	NA
Total Assets:	$129,808,000	**Net Worth:**	$109,890,000	**Debt/ Equity:**	NA

Regeneron Pharmaceuticals Inc

777 Old Saw Mill River Rd., Tarrytown, NY, 10591; *PH:* 1-914-347-7000; *Fax:* 1-914-347-2113; *http://* www.regeneron.com

General - Incorporation	NY	**Stock**- Price on:12/24/2007	$18.32
Employees	573	Stock Exchange	NDQ
Auditor	PricewaterhouseCoopers LLP	Ticker Symbol	REGN
Stk Agt	American Stock Transfer & Trust Co.	Outstanding Shares	65,960,000
Counsel	Skadden, Meagher & Flom LLP	E.P.S	-$1.91
DUNS No.	19-487-3139	Shareholders	NA

Business: The group's principal activities are to discover and develop pharmaceutical products for the treatment of serious medical conditions. The product pipeline includes product candidates for the treatment of obesity, rheumatoid arthritis and other inflammatory conditions, cancer and related disorders, allergies, asthma, and other diseases and disorders. The group has formed collaborations to advance other research and development efforts. It is conducting research with the procter & gamble company in muscle diseases and also collaborating with medarex, inc. To discover, develop, and commercialize certain human antibodies as therapeutics. In partnership with amgen inc., the group has development rights to neurotrophin-3, or nt-3, a clinical compound for the treatment of constipating conditions, although there are no ongoing development activities for nt-3 at this time.

Primary SIC and add'l.: 2834 8731

CIK No: 0000872589

Officers: Leonard S. Schleifer/Dir., CEO, Pres./$3,395,103.00, Stuart A. Kolinski/42/VP, General Counsel, Sec., William G. Roberts/50/VP - Regulatory Development, Peter Powchik/51/Sr. VP - Clinical Development, Murray A. Goldberg/Exec. VP - Finance, Administration, CFO, Treasurer, Assist. Sec./$1,234,158.00, George D. Yancopoulos/Dir., Exec. VP, Pres. - Regeneron Research Laboratories, Chief Scientific Officer/$2,495,235.00, Randall G. Rupp/Sr. VP - Manufacturing, Process Sciences/$1,055,116.00, Neil Stahl/Sr. VP - Preclinical Development, Biomoleculer Science/$1,328,045.00, Robert J. Terifay/48/Sr. VP - Commercial

Directors: Leonard S. Schleifer/Dir., CEO, Pres., Roy P. Vagelos/Chmn., Charles A. Baker/Dir., Joseph L. Goldstein/Dir., Member - Scientific Advisory Board, George L. Sing/Dir., Eric M. Shooter/Dir., Arthur F. Ryan/Dir., George D. Yancopoulos/Dir., Exec. VP, Pres. - Regeneron Research Laboratories, Chief Scientific Officer, Michael S. Brown/Dir., Member - Scientific Advisory Board, Alfred G. Gilman/Dir., Member - Scientific Advisory Board

Owners: Michael S. Brown, Charles A. Baker/2.70%, Joseph L. Goldstein, Charles A. Baker, Alfred G. Gilman, Joseph L. Goldstein/2.30%, Eric M. Shooter/3.40%, Leonard S. Schleifer/75.40%, Arthur F. Ryan, Insiders/90.70%, Randall G. Rupp, Alfred G. Gilman/3.40%, Leonard S. Schleifer/4.70%, Eric M. Shooter, Insiders/13.20% *(22 Owners included in Index)*

Financial Data: Fiscal Year End:12/31 **Latest Annual Data:** 06/30/2007

Year		Sales			Net Income
2007		NA			NA
2006		$63,447,000			-$102,337,000
2005		$66,193,000			-$95,446,000
Curr. Assets:	$469,984,000	**Curr. Liab.:**	$45,014,000		
Plant, Equip.:	$49,353,000	**Total Liab.:**	$368,466,000	**Indic. Yr. Divd.:**	NA
Total Assets:	$585,090,000	**Net Worth:**	$216,624,000	**Debt/ Equity:**	1.0168

Regenerx Biopharmaceuticals Inc

3 Bethesda Metro Ctr., Ste. 630, Bethesda, MD, 20814; *PH:* 1-301-280-1992; *Fax:* 1-301-280-1996; *http://* www.regenerx.com; *Email:* info@regenerx.com

General - Incorporation	DE	**Stock**- Price on:12/24/2007	$2.1
Employees	10	Stock Exchange	AMEX
Auditor	Reznick Group P.C	Ticker Symbol	RGN
Stk Agt	American Stock Transfer & Trust Co.	Outstanding Shares	46,550,000
Counsel	NA	E.P.S	-$0.2
DUNS No.	07-126-2505	Shareholders	NA

Business: The group's principle activities include research and development of new pharmaceutical products for the treatment of human diseases. The company is currently focusing of commercialization of thymosin beta4, a 43 amino acid peptide. This product is used for the treatment of injured tissues and non healing wounds to enable more rapid repair and tissue generation. The company's new pharmaceutical products are used for the treatment of diseases or conditions that arise as a result of immune system disorders, including chronic viral infections, cancer and auto immune disease. The group operates from United States.

Primary SIC and add'l.: 8731 2834

CIK No: 0000707511

Subsidiaries: Sigma-Tau, S.p.A.

Officers: J. J. Finkelstein/Dir., CEO, Pres./$391,490.00, Allan L. Goldstein/Chmn., Chief Scientific Advisor, David Crockford/VP - Clinical, Regulatory Affairs/$285,573.00, Neil C. Lyons/CFO, Treasurer/$317,615.00

Directors: J. J. Finkelstein/Dir., CEO, Pres., Allan L. Goldstein/Chmn., Chief Scientific Advisor, Albert Rosenfeld/Dir. Emeritus, Joseph C. McNay/Dir., Mauro Bove/Dir., Thompson L. Bowles/Dir., Richard J. Hindin/Dir.

Owners: Rick Hindin/3.70%, J. J. Finkelstein/4.30%, Allan Goldstein/4.80%, Joseph McNay/3.20%, Sigma - Tau/37.00%, Insiders/15.80%

Financial Data: Fiscal Year End:12/31 **Latest Annual Data:** 12/31/2006

Year	Sales	Net Income
2006	$272,000	-$8,267,000
2005	NA	-$5,455,000
2004	NA	-$3,326,000

Curr. Assets:	$17,436,000	Curr. Liab.:	$1,249,000		
Plant, Equip.:	$53,000	Total Liab.:	$1,249,000	Indic. Yr. Divd.:	NA
Total Assets:	$17,502,000	Net Worth:	$16,252,000	Debt/ Equity:	NA

ReGenesis Community Health Center

250 NNo. 3rd Ave., Ste 310, Delray Beach, FL, 33494; **PH:** 1-864-582-2411;
http:// www.regenesischc.org; **Email:** info@regenesischc.org

General - Incorporation ....FL	Stock- Price on:12/24/2007 ....NA
Employees..NA	Stock Exchange....................................NA
Auditor ....Webb & Co P.A	Ticker Symbol.......................................NA
Stk Agt....... Olde Monmouth Stk Trnsfer Co. Inc.	Outstanding Shares ....NA
Counsel..NA	E.P.S...NA
DUNS No. ....NA	Shareholders..NA

Business: The group's priciple activity is to engage in lawful corporate undertaking including, but not limited to a selected merger and/or acquisition with a private company operating as a cosmetic and non-surgical cosmetic center. The company has been in the developmental stage since inception and have no operations to date other than issuing shares to their original shareholders. The group operates from United States.

Primary SIC and add'l.: 6770

CIK No: 0001317971

Officers: Anne Invernale/51/Dir., CEO, CFO, Pres.

Directors: Anne Invernale/51/Dir., CEO, CFO, Pres.

Owners: Insiders/90.91%, Anne Invernale/90.91%

Regent Communications Inc

2000 Fifth Third Ctr., 511 Walnut St., Cincinnati, OH, 45202; **PH:** 1-513-651-1190;
Fax: 1-513-651-1195; http:// www.regentcomm.com

General - Incorporation ....DE	Stock- Price on:12/24/2007 ....$3.34
Employees..890	Stock Exchange...................................NDQ
Auditor ....Deloitte & Touche LLP	Ticker Symbol.....................................RGCI
Stk Agt.....Computershare Investor Services LLC	Outstanding Shares 38,700,000
Counsel...........................Graydon, Head & Ritchey	E.P.S...-$0.76
DUNS No. ....NA	Shareholders..NA

Business: The group's principal activity is to provide radio broadcasting services. It acquires, develops and operates radio stations in mid-sized and small markets. The group owns and operates 54 FM and 20 AM radio stations in 16 markets in California, Colorado, Illinois, Indiana, Kentucky, Louisiana, Michigan, Minnesota, New York, Pennsylvania and Texas. On 25-Feb-2003, it acquired 12 radio stations from brill media company llc.

Primary SIC and add'l.: 4899 6719 4832

CIK No: 0000913015

Subsidiaries: Livingston County Broadcasters, Inc., Regent Broadcasting Management, LLC, Regent Broadcasting Midwest, LLC, Regent Broadcasting of Albany, Inc., Regent Broadcasting of Chico, Inc., Regent Broadcasting of Duluth, Inc., Regent Broadcasting of El Paso, Inc., Regent Broadcasting of Erie, Inc., Regent Broadcasting of Evansville/Owensboro, Inc., Regent Broadcasting of Flagstaff, Inc., Regent Broadcasting of Flint, Inc., Regent Broadcasting of Ft. Collins, Inc., Regent Broadcasting of Grand Rapids, Inc., Regent Broadcasting of Kingman, Inc., Regent Broadcasting of Lafayette, Inc. 46 Subsidiaries included in the Index

Officers: William L. Stakelin/Dir., CEO, Pres./$668,776.00, Jonathan Lesko/Investor Relations Contact, Fred L. Murr/Sr. VP - Operations, Michael J. Grimsley/Regional VP, Robert A. Moody/VP - Programming, Robert Allen/VP - Finance, Accounting, David J. Remund/VP - Engineering, Matthew A. Yeoman/VP - Operations, Robert J. Ausfeld/Regional VP, Anthony Vasconcellos/CFO, Exec. VP/$498,471.00

Directors: William L. Stakelin/Dir., CEO, Pres., William P. Sutter/Chmn., Timothy M. Mooney/Dir., Andrew L. Lewis/Dir., John H. Wyant/Dir.

Owners: Andrew L. Lewis, Dimensional Fund Advisors LP/9.05%, Riley Investment Management LLC/6.54%, Insiders/13.81%, T. Rowe Price Associates, Inc./8.58%, William L. Stakelin/4.00%, William P. Sutter, Blue Chip Venture Company, Ltd./8.40%, Timothy M. Mooney, John H. Wyant/8.52%, Weiss, Peck & Greer Investments, a division of Robeco USA, L.L.C./7.68%, Anthony A. Vasconcellos/1.48%

Financial Data: Fiscal Year End:12/31 **Latest Annual Data:** 12/31/2006

Year	Sales	Net Income
2006	$85,033,000	-$26,596,000
2005	$85,600,000	-$6,639,000
2004	$84,187,000	$13,235,000

Curr. Assets:	$22,721,000	Curr. Liab.:	$9,311,000		
Plant, Equip.:	$36,753,000	Total Liab.:	$232,485,000	Indic. Yr. Divd.:	NA
Total Assets:	$451,645,000	Net Worth:	$219,160,000	Debt/ Equity:	0.9854

REGI U.S. Inc

11780 Hammersmith Way, Richmond, BC, V7A 5E9; **PH:** 1-604-278-5996; **Fax:** 1-604-278-3409;
http:// www.regtech.com; **Email:** info@regtech.com

General - Incorporation ....OR	Stock- Price on:12/24/2007 ....$1.1
Employees..NA	Stock Exchange...................................OTC
Auditor ....Smythe Ratcliffe LLP	Ticker Symbol....................................RGUS
Stk Agt ....Nevada Agency & Trust Company	Outstanding Shares ....NA
Counsel....................................Mr. Vandeberg	E.P.S...NA
DUNS No. ....NA	Shareholders..NA

Business: The group's principle activities include developing and exploiting axial vane type rotary engines. The group operates from United States.

Primary SIC and add'l.: 3714

CIK No: 0000922330

Officers: John G. Robertson/Chmn., CEO, Pres., James Vandeberg/Dir., CFO, Brian Cherry/VP - Radmax Technology, Jennifer Lorette/Dir., VP - Administration, Robert Brooks/Advisor, Robert Grisar/VP - Engineering, Lynn Petersen/VP - Marketing

Directors: John G. Robertson/Chmn., CEO, Pres., James Vandeberg/Dir., CFO, Susanne M. Robertson/Dir., Jennifer Lorette/Dir., VP - Administration

Owners: John G. Robertson/37.31%, Robert Grisar, James McCann/11.20%, James Vandeberg, Lynn Petersen, Insiders/35.86%, Rand Energy Group Inc./11.20%, Jennifer Lorette

Financial Data: Fiscal Year End:04/30 **Latest Annual Data:** 4/30/2006

Year	Sales	Net Income
2006	NA	-$7,779,000
2005	NA	-$585,000
2004	NA	-$610,000

Curr. Assets:	$300,000	Curr. Liab.:	$200,000		
Plant, Equip.:	NA	Total Liab.:	$200,000	Indic. Yr. Divd.:	NA
Total Assets:	$300,000	Net Worth:	$100,000	Debt/ Equity:	NA

Regions Financial Corp

1900 5th Ave. N, Birmingham, AL, 35203; **PH:** 1-205-944-1300; **Fax:** 1-901-580-3915;
http:// www.regions.com

General - Incorporation ....DE	Stock- Price on:12/24/2007 ....$34.14
Employees..35,900	Stock Exchange..................................NYSE
Auditor ....Ernst & Young LLP	Ticker Symbol...RF
Stk Agt ....Computershare Ltd.	Outstanding Shares 704,710,000
Counsel..NA	E.P.S...$2.42
DUNS No. 08-654-2222	Shareholders..NA

Business: The groups principle activity is to provide banking services. The groups services include mortgage banking, insurance brokerage, credit life insurance, leasing, and commercial accounts. The group operates from United States.

Primary SIC and add'l.: NA

CIK No: 0001281761

Subsidiaries: Albrecht & Associates, Inc., Athletic Resource Management, Inc., Capital Factors Holdings, Inc., Capital Factors, Inc., Capital Tempfunds, Inc., CF Funding Corporation, CF Investor Corporation, CF One, Inc., CF Two LLC, CID Holding Company, Credit Source, Inc., Cumberland Securities Company, Inc., EFC Holdings Corporation, EquiFirst Corporation, EquiFirst Mortgage Corporation of Minnesota 116 Subsidiaries included in the Index

Officers: Douglas G. Edwards/CEO, Pres. - Morgan Keegan, Company Inc/$3,181,408.00, Dowd C. Ritter/CEO, Pres./$18,433,990.00, Jackson W. Moore/Exec. Chmn./$29,190,350.00, Charles W. Mayer/53/Sr. Exec. VP - Registrant, Regions Bank, Richard D. Horsley/65/Dir., Head - Transaction, Integration, Registrant, Regions Bank, VP - Regions Agency, Inc, Dir. - Regions Life Insurance Co, EFC Holdings Corp/$16,141,220.00, O. B. Grayson Hall/Sr. Exec. VP - General Banking Group, David C. Gordon/59/Exec. VP - Operations - Technology, Bryan D. Jordan/CFO, Sr. Exec. VP/$2,148,547.00, Candice W. Bagby/Sr. Exec. VP - Consumer Services Group, David B. Edmonds/Sr. Exec. VP - Human Resources Group, Timothy G. Laney/Sr. Exec. VP - Business Services, William C. Wells/Chief Risk Officer, Sr. Exec. VP - Risk Management Group, Alton E. Yother/CFO, Exec. VP - Finance Group

Directors: Jackson W. Moore/Exec. Chmn., Allen B. Morgan/Vice Chmn. - Regions Financial Corporation, George W. Bryan/Dir., David J. Cooper/Dir., Richard D. Horsley/65/Dir., Head - Transaction, Integration, Registrant, Regions Bank, VP - Regions Agency, Inc, Dir. - Regions Life Insurance Co, EFC Holdings Corp, Spence L. Wilson/Dir., Harry W. Witt/Dir., Claude B. Nielsen/Dir., Jorge M. Perez/Dir., John R. Roberts/Dir., Lee J. Styslinger/Dir., Samuel W. Bartholomew/Dir., Earnest W. Deavenport/Dir., Don Defosset/Dir., Martha R. Ingram/Dir. *(19 Directors included in Index)*

Owners: Lee J. Styslinger, John R. Roberts, Susan W. Matlock, Spence L. Wilson, Charles D. McCrary, Insiders/2.53%, Robert R. Waller, Allen B. Morgan, Bryan D. Jordan, George W. Bryan, Harry W. Witt, David J. Cooper, Martha R. Ingram, Richard D. Horsley, Samuel E. Upchurch *(28 Owners included in Index)*

Financial Data: Fiscal Year End:12/31 **Latest Annual Data:** 12/31/2006

Year	Sales	Net Income
2006	$7,756,362,000	$1,353,145,000
2005	$6,142,699,000	$1,000,544,000
2004	$4,610,039,000	$823,765,000

Curr. Assets:	$7,396,885,000	Curr. Liab.:	$110,895,040,000	P/E Ratio:	14.11
Plant, Equip.:	$2,398,494,000	Total Liab.:	$122,667,567,000	Indic. Yr. Divd.:	$1.440
Total Assets:	$143,369,021,000	Net Worth:	$20,701,454,000	Debt/ Equity:	0.4230

Regis Corp

7201 Metro Blvd., Minneapolis, MN, 55439; **PH:** 1-952-947-7777; **Fax:** 1-952-947-7600;
http:// www.regiscorp.com

General - Incorporation ....MN	Stock- Price on:12/24/2007 ....$38.58
Employees..59,000	Stock Exchange..................................NYSE
Auditor ....PricewaterhouseCoopers LLP	Ticker Symbol.....................................RGS
Stk Agt ....Wells Fargo Bank, N.A.	Outstanding Shares 44,300,000
Counsel..NA	E.P.S...$2.11
DUNS No. 04-670-9747	Shareholders..NA

Business: The groups principle activity is to operate hair and retail product salons. The group owns hair clubs for men and women, provides hair restoration services and operates beauty schools. The group operates from United States.

Primary SIC and add'l.: 7231 6794 3999

CIK No: 0000716643

Subsidiaries: Hair Club

Officers: Darryll Porter/CEO, Pres. - Hair Club Men, Women, Paul D. Finkelstein/Chmn., CEO, Pres./$4,728,105.00, Gordon Nelson/Exec. VP - Fashion, Education, Marketing/$1,200,777.00, Kris Bergly/COO, Exec. VP, Eric A. Bakken/Sr. VP, General Counsel, Randy L. Pearce/Sr. Exec. VP, Chief Financial, Administrative Officer/$1,278,638.00, Mark Kartarik/Sr. VP, Pres. - Franchise Division/$954,518.00, John C. Briggs/Sr. VP, Pres. - Smartstyle Family Hair Salons, Raymond Duke/Sr. VP, International MD - UK, Norma Knudsen/COO - Trade Secret Division, Exec. VP - Merchandising, Lynn Hempe/Sr. VP, Chief Merchandising Officer, David Bortnem/COO - Mastercuts, Diane Calta/COO - Supercuts, Amy Edwards/COO - Promenade Salon Concepts, John Exline/COO - Smartstyle Family Hair Salons *(17 Officers included in Index)*

Directors: Paul D. Finkelstein/Chmn., CEO, Pres., Myron Kunin/Vice Chmn., David B. Kunin/Dir., Thomas L. Gregory/Dir., Van Zandt Hawn/Dir., Susan Hoyt/Dir., Rolf F. Bjelland/Dir.

Owners: Mark Kartarik, Susan S. Hoyt, The TCW Group, Inc./5.27%, David B. Kunin, Zandt Van Hawn, Paul D. Finkelstein/1.42%, Mellon Financial Corporation/5.11%, Myron Kunin/2.31%, Randy L. Pearce, Thomas L. Gregory, Gordon B. Nelson, Rolf F. Bjelland, Insiders/6.18%

Financial Data: **Fiscal Year End:**06/30 **Latest Annual Data:** 6/30/2006

Year	Sales	Net Income
2006	$2,430,864,000	$109,578,000
2005	$2,194,294,000	$64,631,000
2004	$1,923,143,000	$104,218,000

Curr. Assets:	$525,064,000	**Curr. Liab.:**	$538,632,000	**P/E Ratio:**	18.28
Plant, Equip.:	$494,085,000	**Total Liab.:**	$1,218,806,000	**Indic. Yr. Divd.:**	$0.160
Total Assets:	$2,132,114,000	**Net Worth:**	$913,308,000	**Debt/ Equity:**	NA

Register Com Inc

575 Eighth Ave, 11th Fl., New York, NY, 10018; ***PH:*** 1-212-798-9100; ***http://*** www.register.com

General - Incorporation	DE	**Stock**- Price on:12/24/2007	NA
Employees	NA	Stock Exchange	NA
Auditor	PricewaterhouseCoopers LLP	Ticker Symbol	NA
Stk Agt	PricewaterhouseCoopers LLP	Outstanding Shares	NA
Counsel	Brobeck, Phleger & Harrison	E.P.S	NA
DUNS No.	NA	Shareholders	NA

Business: The group's principal activity is to provide Internet domain name registration and other online products and services such as Web hosting, email, domain name forwarding and advertising. The Internet domain name registration system consists of two principal functions: a registry maintains a master database of domain names, and their corresponding Internet protocol (ip) addresses, registered in a particular top level domain. A registrar acts as an intermediary between the registry and the businesses and consumers, referred to as registrants, seeking to register domain names. The group offers its products and services indirectly through global partner network (gpn) of companies, which include Internet service providers, Web-hosting companies, telecom carriers, Web portals and other e-businesses.

Primary SIC and add'l.: 7375

CIK No: 0001091284

Subsidiaries: Net Searchers International (France) Sarl, Net Searchers International (Italy) Srl, Net Searchers International Limited, RCOM Canada, Corp., Register.com (UK) Holdings Limited, Register.com (UK) Limited, Register.com Europe PLC, Register.com Sarl, Rlom (it) Srl, RPI, Inc.

Rehabcare Group Inc

7733 Forsyth Blvd., 23rd Fl., St. Louis, MO, 63105; ***PH:*** 1-314-863-7422; ***Fax:*** 1-314-863-0769; ***http://*** www.rehabcare.com; ***Email:*** info@rehabcare.com

General - Incorporation	DE	**Stock**- Price on:12/24/2007	$14.47
Employees	6,800	Stock Exchange	NYSE
Auditor	Ernst & Young, LLP	Ticker Symbol	RHB
Stk Agt	Chase Mellon Shareholder Services LLC	Outstanding Shares	17,470,000
Counsel	NA	E.P.S	$0.46
DUNS No.	11-421-4281	Shareholders	NA

Business: The group's principal activity is to offer temporary healthcare staffing and therapy program management services for hospitals and skilled nursing facilities. The healthcare staffing industry provides staffing of nurses, physicians and other allied healthcare professionals such as physical and occupational therapists, speech/language pathologists, respiratory therapists, radiological technicians, advanced practice professionals, pharmacists, and medical and surgical specialized technicians. The therapy program management consists of managing of hospital based inpatient acute rehabilitation and skilled nursing units, outpatient therapy programs and contract therapy programs.on 02-Feb-2004, the group sold it's healthcare staffing division and on 03-Feb-2004, the group acquired cpr therapies llc and on 02-Mar-2004, American vitalcare, inc. And managed alternative care, inc and on 03-May-2004, phase 2 consulting.

Primary SIC and add'l.: 8099 7363

CIK No: 0000812191

Subsidiaries: American VitalCare, Inc., Clear Lake Rehabilitation Hospital, LLC, Lafayette Specialty Hospital, LLC, Managed Alternative Care, Inc., Phase 2 Consulting, Inc., RehabCare Group East, Inc., RehabCare Group Management Services, Inc., RehabCare Group of Amarillo, L.P., RehabCare Group of Arlington, L.P., RehabCare Group of California, Inc., RehabCare Group of Texas, L.P., RehabCare Group of Virginia, LLC, RehabCare Hospital Holdings, LLC, RehabCare Texas Holdings, Inc., Salt Lake Physical Therapy Associates, Inc. 18 Subsidiaries included in the Index

Officers: John H. Short/Dir., CEO, Pres./$1,248,186.00, Don Adam/Chief Development Officer, Sr. VP, Kenneth Adams/Sr. VP - Medical Affairs, Chief Medical Officer, Michael Garcia/Chief Human Resources Officer, Tom Davis/Exec. VP - Freestanding Hospitals Division/$578,845.00, Peter Doerner/Group Sr. VP, David Groce/Sr. VP, General Counsel, Corp. Sec./$337,711.00, Pat Henry/Exec. VP - Operations/$573,105.00, Sean Maloney/Sr. VP - Clinical Research, Development, Alan Sauber/Sr. VP - Government, Regulatory Affairs, Jay Shreiner/Sr. VP, CFO/$385,978.00, Dave Totaro/Sr. VP - Marketing - Communications, Mary Pat Welc/Sr. VP - Operations

Directors: John H. Short/Dir., CEO, Pres., Harry E. Rich/Chmn., Colleen Conway-Welch/Dir., Theodore M. Wight/Dir., Anthony S. Piszel/Dir., Suzan L. Rayner/Dir., Larry Warren/Dir.

Owners: Insiders/5.26%, Anthony S. Piszel, Suzan L. Rayner, Tom E. Davis/1.24%, Wells Fargo & Company/7.96%, Patricia M. Henry, Harry E. Rich, John H. Short/1.77%, Franklin Resources, Inc./5.63%, FMR Corp./7.35%, Barclays Global Investors, NA/5.27%, Theodore M. Wight, Colleen Conway-Welch, Larry Warren, Snow Capital Management, L.P./10.36% *(18 Owners included in Index)*

Financial Data: **Fiscal Year End:**12/31 **Latest Annual Data:** 12/31/2006

Year	Sales	Net Income
2006	$614,793,000	$7,280,000
2005	$454,266,000	-$16,982,000
2004	$383,846,000	$23,181,000

Curr. Assets:	$178,115,000	**Curr. Liab.:**	$92,133,000		
Plant, Equip.:	$31,833,000	**Total Liab.:**	$217,431,000	**Indic. Yr. Divd.:**	NA
Total Assets:	$428,296,000	**Net Worth:**	$210,779,000	**Debt/ Equity:**	0.4806

Reinhold Industries Inc

12827 E Imperial Hwy, Santa Fe Springs, CA, 90670; ***PH:*** 1-562-944-3281; ***http://*** www.reinhold-ind.com

General - Incorporation	DE	**Stock**- Price on:12/24/2007	NA
Employees	117	Stock Exchange	NA
Auditor	Ernst & Young LLP	Ticker Symbol	NA
Stk Agt	Continental Stock Transfer & Trust Co	Outstanding Shares	NA
Counsel	Petillon & Hansen	E.P.S	NA
DUNS No.	04-190-8609	Shareholders	NA

Business: The group's principal activity is to manufacture advanced custom composite components, sheet molding compounds and rubber rollers for a variety of applications in the United States and Europe. The operating segments of the group consist of five; the aerospace segment which manufactures structural and ablative composite components mainly for subcontractors of the U.S. Defense industry. Compositair segment manufactures commercial aircraft seatbacks and other commercial products. The commercial segment business unit manufactures compression molded smc (sheet molding compound) products for lighting, water filtration and other various commercial and aerospace applications. The np aerospace segment produces products for law enforcement, lighting, military, automotive and commercial aircraft. Bingham segment manufactures rubber rollers for graphic arts and industrial applications. The group markets its products in the United States and Europe.

Primary SIC and add'l.: 3728 3069

CIK No: 0000862255

Officers: Micheal T. Furry/CEO, Pres.

Reinsurance Group of America Inc

1370 Timberlake Manor Pkwy., Chesterfield, MO, 63017; ***PH:*** 1-636-736-7000; ***Fax:*** 1-636-736-7145; ***http://*** www.rgare.com; ***Email:*** investrelations@rgare.com

General - Incorporation	MO	**Stock**- Price on:12/24/2007	$61.18
Employees	978	Stock Exchange	NYSE
Auditor	Deloitte & Touche LLP	Ticker Symbol	RGA
Stk Agt	Chase Mellon Shareholder Services LLC	Outstanding Shares	61,890,000
Counsel	NA	E.P.S	$4.86
DUNS No.	80-775-8511	Shareholders	NA

Business: The group's principal activity is to provide life reinsurance, international life and disability on a direct and reinsurance basis and non-traditional business including asset-intensive products and financial reinsurance. The non-traditional business includes asset-intensive and financial reinsurance. The asset-intensive products primarily include reinsurance of corporate-owned life insurance and annuities. The group has operations in the United States, Canada, Latin America, Europe, Argentina, South Africa and other places.

Primary SIC and add'l.: 6311

CIK No: 0000898174

Subsidiaries: General American Argentina Seguros de Vida, Reinsurance Company of Missouri, RGA Americas Reinsurance Company, RGA Asia Pacific Pty Limited, RGA Australian Holdings Pty, Limited, RGA Capital Limited, RGA Capital Trust I, RGA Financial Group, LLC, RGA Global Reinsurance Company, Ltd, RGA Holdings Limited, RGA International Corporation, RGA International Reinsurance Company, RGA Life Reinsurance Company of Canada, RGA Reinsurance (UK) Limited, RGA Reinsurance Company 23 Subsidiaries included in the Index

Officers: Greig A. Woodring/CEO, Pres./$4,809,730.00, David B. Atkinson/CEO, COO, Exec. VP, Pres. - RGA Reinsurance Company/$2,000,982.00, Alain Neemeh/CEO, Pres. - RGA Life Reinsurance Company, Canada, Graham S. Watson/Sr. Exec. VP, Chief Marketing Officer, CEO - RGA Inernational/$3,700,661.00, Mike Stein/COO, Exec. VP - US Division, RGA Reinsurance Company, Paul A. Schuster/Sr. Exec. VP - US Division, RGA Reinsurance Company/$1,702,533.00, James E. Sherman/Exec. VP, General Counsel, Sec., Paul Nitsou/COO, Exec. VP, Pres. - RGA International, Jack B. Lay/CFO, Sr. Exec. VP/$1,737,983.00, Robert M. Musen/Exec. VP - RGA Reinsurance Company, Brendan J. Galligan/Exec. VP - Asia Pacific Operations, RGA International, John Laughlin/Exec. Vice Rresident, RGA Financial Markets

Directors: Steven A. Kandarian/Chmn. - RGA, Joseph A. Reali/55/Dir., William J. Bartlett/58/Dir., Cliff J. Eason/60/Dir., Stuart I. Greenbaum/71/Dir., Alan C. Henderson/62/Dir., Georgette A. Piligian/43/Dir.

Owners: Jack B. Lay, Graham Watson, David B. Atkinson, William J. Bartlett, Barclay's Global Investors, NA/5.50%, Alan C. Henderson, Stuart Greenbaum, Insiders/1.55%, Greig A. Woodring, Wellington Management Company, LLP/5.50%, MetLife, Inc./52.50%, Paul A. Schuster, Cliff J. Eason

Financial Data: **Fiscal Year End:**12/31 **Latest Annual Data:** 12/31/2006

Year	Sales	Net Income
2006	$5,193,691,000	$288,210,000
2005	$4,584,765,000	$224,180,000
2004	$4,038,919,000	$221,891,000

Curr. Assets:	$1,559,586,000	**Curr. Liab.:**	$29,384,000	**P/E Ratio:**	12.64
Plant, Equip.:	NA	**Total Liab.:**	$16,062,752,000	**Indic. Yr. Divd.:**	$0.360
Total Assets:	$19,036,837,000	**Net Worth:**	$2,815,384,000	**Debt/ Equity:**	0.6760

Reis Inc

Formerly: Wellsford Real Properties Inc

530 Fifth Ave., New York, NY, 10036; ***PH:*** 1-212-921-1122; ***http://*** www.wellsford.com

General - Incorporation	MD	**Stock**- Price on:12/24/2007	$9.44
Employees	12	Stock Exchange	NA
Auditor	Ernst& Young LLP	Ticker Symbol	NA
Stk Agt	NA	Outstanding Shares	NA
Counsel	NA	E.P.S	$0.11
DUNS No.	NA	Shareholders	NA

Business: The group operates through its subsidiaries whose principle activity is to provide banking services. The group financial products include acquire, develop, finance and operate real properties and invest in private and public real estate companies. The group operates through three segments namely commercial property activities, debt and equity activities and residential activities. The group operates from the United States.

Primary SIC and add'l.: 7389

CIK No: 0001038222

Subsidiaries: Beekman Holdings, Inc., Beekman Housing Ventures, LLC, Clairborne Fordham Tower, LLC, Claverack Housing Ventures, LLC, Creamer Vitale Wellsford L.L.C., East Lyme Housing Ventures, LLC, Gold Peak at Palomino Park L.L.C., Green River at Palomino Park L.L.C., OrchardsII Ventures LLC, Palomino Park Owners Association, Palomino Park Public Improvements Corp., Palomino Park Telecom L.L.C., Park at Highlands L.L.C., Parkside Caf at Palomino Park, Inc., Red Canyon at Palomino Park L.L.C. 27 Subsidiaries included in the Index

Officers: Lloyd Lynford/52/CEO, Pres., Greg Williams/Contact - Product Management, Jonathan Garfield/Dir., Exec. VP, William Sander/COO - Reis Services, LLC, Mark P. Cantaluppi/37/CFO, VP, Michael Richardson/Sr. VP - Sales, Marketing, Sam Chandan/Chief Economist, Sr. VP - Economic Research, David Geib/Contact - Client Services, Christopher Johnston/Contact - Client Services, Denesha Kelly/Contact - Client Services, Juliet Leibon/Contact - Client Services, Kevin Varley/Contact - Product Management

Directors: Jeffrey H. Lynford/Chmn., James J. Burns/68/Vice Chmn., Bonnie R. Cohen/65/Dir., Douglas Crocker/67/Dir., Meyer Frucher/61/Dir., Mark S. Germain/57/Dir., Edward Lowenthal/63/Dir., Jonathan Garfield/Dir., Exec. VP, Michael J. Del/Dir., Christian M. Mitchell/Dir.

Owners: S. Muoio& Co. LLC/7.70%, James J. Burns, Mark P. Cantaluppi, Jeffrey H. Lynford/13.80%, Meyer S. Frucher, Edward Lowenthal/1.60%, Bonnie R. Cohen, Caroline Hunt TrustEstate/5.00%, Davidson Kempner Partners/10.50%, Mark S. Germain/2.70%, William H. Darrow, Insiders/24.00%, David M. Strong/3.30%, Douglas Crocker/1.40%

Financial Data: ***Fiscal Year End:***12/31 ***Latest Annual Data:*** 12/31/2006

Year	Sales	Net Income
2006	NA	$1,026,000
2004	$27,649,000	-$32,703,000
2003	$35,602,000	-$45,859,000

Curr. Assets:	$44,217,000	***Curr. Liab.:***	$8,139,000		
Plant, Equip.:	$41,159,000	***Total Liab.:***	$50,882,000	***Indic. Yr. Divd.:***	NA
Total Assets:	$108,477,000	***Net Worth:***	$57,596,000	***Debt/ Equity:***	NA

Reliability Inc

15720 Pk. Row, Ste. 500, Houston, TX, 77084; ***PH:*** 1-281-492-0550; ***Fax:*** 1-281-492-0615; ***http://*** www.relinc.com; ***Email:*** info01@relinc.com

General - Incorporation	TX	***Stock***- Price on:12/24/2007	$0.25
Employees	4	Stock Exchange	OTC
Auditor	Fitts, Roberts & Co., P.c.	Ticker Symbol	REAL
Stk Agt	Computershare Trust Co	Outstanding Shares	9,340,000
Counsel	Winstead Sechrest & Minick	E.P.S	-$0.32
DUNS No.	04-292-3847	Shareholders	NA

Business: The group's principal activities are to design, manufacture, market and support equipments used to test and condition integrated circuits. The group operates through three segments: testing products, testing services and power sources. The testing products segment designs, manufactures and markets systems that utilize burn-in and test technology within the same product. The testing services segment provides burn-in and other related services to its customers. The power sources segment designs, manufactures and markets power sources, primarily a line of dc-to-dc power converters which convert direct current voltage into a higher or lower voltage. The group operates in the United States and Singapore. Intel corporation, alliance semiconductor corporation and advanced micro devices, inc are some of the groups customers. In Jul 2003, the group acquired ezy-load product line.

Primary SIC and add'l.: 3629 3825

CIK No: 0000034285

Subsidiaries: Reliability Singapore Pte Ltd.

Officers: James Tolan/CEO - Medallion, Inc, Larry Edwards/66/Chmn., CEO, Pres., Thomas L. Langford/Dir. - Reliability Incorporated, Consultant, Medallion Electric, Inc, Matthew Masaracchio/VP, GM - Medallion Electric, Inc, Alex Katz/Dir. - Reliability Incorporated, Consultant, Medallion Electric, Inc, Ronald Masaracchio/VP - Medallion Electric, Inc, James M. Harwell/53/Exec. VP, Acting CFO, Sec., Mark E. Spoor/COO, Pres. - Medallion Electric, Inc

Directors: Larry Edwards/66/Chmn., CEO, Pres., David C. Kurland/Dir., Philip Uhrhan/Dir., Lee C. Cooke/Dir.

Owners: Minerva Group, L.P./7.92%, Thomas L. Langford/1.11%, Insiders/16.39%, James M. Harwell/4.30%, Jay Gottlieb/5.94%, Fidelity Management & Research Company/7.28%, Lee C. Cooke, Philip Uhrhan/0.42%, Larry Edwards/10.21%

Financial Data: ***Fiscal Year End:***12/31 ***Latest Annual Data:*** 12/31/2006

Year	Sales	Net Income
2006	$237,000	-$178,000
2005	$2,900,000	-$3,484,000
2004	$3,187,000	-$4,913,000

Curr. Assets:	$1,503,000	***Curr. Liab.:***	$278,000		
Plant, Equip.:	$1,002,000	***Total Liab.:***	$278,000	***Indic. Yr. Divd.:***	NA
Total Assets:	$2,505,000	***Net Worth:***	$2,227,000	***Debt/ Equity:***	NA

Reliance Steel & Aluminum Co

350 S Grand Ave., Ste. 5100, Los Angeles, CA, 90071; ***PH:*** 1-213-687-7700; ***Fax:*** 1-213-687-8792; ***http://*** www.rsac.com

General - Incorporation	CA	***Stock***- Price on:12/24/2007	$57.46
Employees	8,600	Stock Exchange	NYSE
Auditor	Ernst & Young LLP	Ticker Symbol	RS
Stk Agt	American Stock Transfer & Trust CO.	Outstanding Shares	76,230,000
Counsel	Arter & Hadden	E.P.S	$5.28
DUNS No.	00-690-8636	Shareholders	NA

Business: The group's principle activity is to provide metal processing services. The group also sells metal products. The groups products include galvanized, hot-rolled and cold-finished steel, stainless steel, aluminum, brass, copper, titanium and alloy steel. The group operates from United States. In the year 2007, the group acquired Clayton Metals, Inc. and Metalweb plc.

Primary SIC and add'l.: 3312 3366 5051

CIK No: 0000861884

Subsidiaries: Allegheny Steel Distributors Inc., Aluminum and Stainless Inc., American Metals Corporation, American Steel LLC, AMI Metals Inc., CCC Steel Inc., Central Plains Steel Co., Chapel Steel Corp., Chatham Steel Corporation, Durrett Sheppard Steel Co. Inc., Liebovich Bros. Inc., Lusk Metals, Pacific Metal Company, PDM Steel Service Centers Inc., Phoenix Corporation 23 Subsidiaries included in the Index

Officers: David H. Hannah/Dir., CEO/$3,334,480.00, Gregg J. Mollins/Dir., COO, Pres./$2,526,755.00, Karla R. Lewis/CFO, Exec. VP/$1,741,828.00, James P. MacBeth/Sr. VP - Carbon Steel Operations/$1,960,300.00, William K. Sales/Sr. VP - Non - Ferrous Operations/$1,745,634.00, Yvette M. Schiotis/Sec., Stephen E. Almond/Pres. - Phoenix Corporation, Thomas A. Compton/Pres. - Precision Strip, Inc, Terry L. Wilson/Pres. - Service Steel Aerospace Corp, Jerry D. Pearson/Pres. - Siskin Steel, Supply Company, Inc, Daniel T. Yunetz/Pres. - Toma Metals, Inc, Daniel A. Mangan/Pres. - Valex Corp, Craig Sauer/Pres. - Viking Materials, Inc, Kim P. Feazle/Investor Relations Officer, Kay Rustand/VP, General Counsel *(30 Officers included in Index)*

Directors: David H. Hannah/Dir., CEO, Joe D. Crider/Non - Exec. Chmn., Franklin R. Johnson/Dir., Richard J. Slater/Dir., Douglas M. Hayes/Dir., Mark V. Kaminski/Dir., Leslie A. Waite/Dir., Thomas W. Gimbel/Dir., Gregg J. Mollins/Dir., COO, Pres.

Owners: David H. Hannah, Mark V. Kaminski, Insiders/13.57%, Douglas M. Hayes, Karla R. Lewis, Joe D. Crider, FMR Corp./5.90%, James P. MacBeth, William K. Sales, Franklin R. Johnson, Leslie A. Waite, Richard J. Slater, Gregg J. Mollins

Financial Data: ***Fiscal Year End:***12/31 ***Latest Annual Data:*** 12/31/2006

Year	Sales	Net Income
2006	$5,748,376,000	$354,507,000
2005	$3,370,722,000	$205,437,000
2004	$2,947,202,000	$169,728,000

Curr. Assets:	$1,675,389,000	***Curr. Liab.:***	$550,739,000	***P/E Ratio:***	10.50
Plant, Equip.:	$742,672,000	***Total Liab.:***	$1,866,529,000	***Indic. Yr. Divd.:***	$0.320
Total Assets:	$3,614,173,000	***Net Worth:***	$1,746,398,000	***Debt/ Equity:***	0.6822

Reliant Energy Inc

1000 Main St., Houston, TX, 77002; ***PH:*** 1-713-497-3000; ***Fax:*** 1-713-488-5925; ***http://*** www.reliant.com

General - Incorporation	DE	***Stock***- Price on:12/24/2007	$26.27
Employees	3,524	Stock Exchange	NYSE
Auditor	KPMG LLP	Ticker Symbol	RRI
Stk Agt	Computershare Investor Services LLC	Outstanding Shares	341,620,000
Counsel	NA	E.P.S	$0.25
DUNS No.	NA	Shareholders	NA

Business: The groups principle activity is to provide electricity and energy services. The group operates from United States.

Primary SIC and add'l.: 4931 6799 4911

CIK No: 0001126294

Subsidiaries: CapTrades GP, LLC, CapTrades, LP, Conemaugh Fuels, LLC, Keystone Fuels, LLC, MidWest Ash Disposal, Inc., OPOS MidAtlantic, Inc., Orion Power Atlantic, Inc., Orion Power Capital, LLC, Orion Power Development Company, Inc., Orion Power Holdings, Inc., Orion Power Marketing and Supply, Inc., Orion Power Midwest GP, Inc., Orion Power Midwest LP, LLC, Orion Power Midwest, L.P., Orion Power New York GP, Inc. 64 Subsidiaries included in the Index

Officers: Mark M. Jacobs/Dir., CEO, Pres./$3,624,557.00, Michael L. Jines/Sr. VP, General Counsel, Corp. Sec./$1,647,350.00, Thomas C. Livengood/52/Sr. VP, Controller, Matthew R. Benner/Sr. VP - Retail Marketing, Operations, Karen D. Taylor/Sr. VP - Human Resources, Chief Diversity Officer, Brian Landrum/COO, Exec. VP/$3,168,489.00, Suzanne L. Kupiec/Sr. VP, Chief Risk Officer, Jerry J. Langdon/56/Exec. VP - Public, Regulatory Affairs, Corporate Compliance Officer/$1,785,301.00, Dave Freysinger/Sr. VP - Generation Operations, Rogers Herndon/Sr. VP - Commercial Operations, Origination, Carla J. Mitcham/Sr. VP - Smart Energy, Dennis Barber/Dir. - Investor Relations

Directors: Mark M. Jacobs/Dir., CEO, Pres., Steven L. Miller/Dir., Joel V. Staff/Dir., William E. Barnett/Dir., Donald J. Breeding/Dir., Kirbyjon H. Caldwell/Dir., Laree E. Perez/Dir., William L. Transier/Dir., Sarah M. Barpoulis/Dir., Evan J. Silverstein/Dir.

Owners: William E. Barnett, Steven L. Miller, Insiders, Michael L. Jines, Kinetics Asset Management,Inc./7.00%, Kirbyjon H. Caldwell, Horizon Asset Management,Inc./9.90%, Brian Landrum, Laree E. Perez, William L. Transier, Evan J. Silverstein, Trafelet Capital Management, L.P./5.20%, Mark M. Jacobs, Donald J. Breeding, Joel V. Staff *(19 Owners included in Index)*

Financial Data: ***Fiscal Year End:***12/31 ***Latest Annual Data:*** 12/31/2006

Year	Sales	Net Income
2006	$10,877,385,000	-$327,812,000
2005	$9,711,995,000	-$330,556,000
2004	$8,735,538,000	-$29,370,000

Curr. Assets:	$3,173,249,000	***Curr. Liab.:***	$2,693,243,000	***P/E Ratio:***	131.35
Plant, Equip.:	$5,741,995,000	***Total Liab.:***	$6,617,260,000	***Indic. Yr. Divd.:***	NA
Total Assets:	$10,567,133,000	***Net Worth:***	$3,949,873,000	***Debt/ Equity:***	NA

Reliant Home Warranty Corp

350 Bay St., Ste. 250, Toronto, ON, M5H 2S6; ***PH:*** 1-416-445-9500; ***http://*** www.relianthwc.com

General - Incorporation	FL	***Stock***- Price on:12/24/2007	$2.42
Employees	NA	Stock Exchange	NA
Auditor	SF Partnership, LLP	Ticker Symbol	NA
Stk Agt	Florida Atlantic Stock Transfer, Inc.	Outstanding Shares	NA
Counsel	NA	E.P.S	NA
DUNS No.	NA	Shareholders	NA

Business: The groups principle activity is to offer a wide range of products and services to consumers through the medium of videotape. The group operates from the United States.

Primary SIC and add'l.: 6162

CIK No: 0001108028

Officers: Boyd Soussana/Dir., CEO, Pres., Paul Burden/Chief Finacila Officer, Dir., Steven Hamilton/54/Sr. VP - Investor Relations

Directors: Boyd Soussana/Dir., CEO, Pres., Paul Burden/Chief Finacila Officer, Dir., John Roberts/74/Dir.

Curr. Assets:	$328,000	***Curr. Liab.:***	$1,819,000		
Plant, Equip.:	NA	***Total Liab.:***	$1,819,000	***Indic. Yr. Divd.:***	NA
Total Assets:	$791,000	***Net Worth:***	-$1,029,000	***Debt/ Equity:***	NA

Reliv International Inc

136 Chesterfield Industrial Blvd., Chesterfield, MO, 63005; ***PH:*** 1-636-537-9715;
Fax: 1-636-537-9753; ***http://*** www.reliv.com; ***Email:*** intlinfo@relivinc.com

General - Incorporation	DE	**Stock**- Price on:12/24/2007	$10.22
Employees	246	Stock Exchange	NDQ
Auditor	Ernst & Young LLP	Ticker Symbol	RELV
Stk Agt	American Stock Transfer & Trust Co.	Outstanding Shares	16,200,000
Counsel	NA	E.P.S	$0.44
DUNS No.	15-209-9479	Shareholders	NA

Business: The group's principle activities are to produce a line of food products including nutritional supplements, weight management products, functional foods, sports nutrition and a line of skin care products. The nutritional supplements include vitamins, minerals, dietary supplements, herbs and compounds derived there from. The functional foods are products designed to influence specific functions of the body. These products are sold by subsidiaries of the group to a sales force of independent distributors who sell products directly to consumers. The group and its subsidiaries sell products to distributors throughout the United States, Australia, Canada, New Zealand, Mexico, the United Kingdom, Ireland, the Philippines, Malaysia and Singapore. The group's quarterly revenue for September 2007 was 25.12 millions of USD.

Primary SIC and add'l.: 2844 2099 5499

CIK No: 0000768710

Subsidiaries: Nutrition 2000, Inc., Reliv Australia Pty, Reliv Canada Company, Reliv Europe, Inc, Reliv Germany, GmbH, Reliv International Sdn. Bhd, Reliv New Zealand, Limited, Reliv Now de Mexico, S. de R.L. de C.V, Reliv Philippines, Inc., Reliv Singapore Pte Ltd, Reliv U.K. Limited, Reliv World Corporation, Reliv, Inc.

Officers: Robert L. Montgomery/Chmn., CEO, Pres., Co - Founder/$1,274,899.00, Carl W. Hastings/Vice Chmn., Chief Scientific Officer/$594,261.00, Jennie Santhuff/Dir. - Distributor Services, Sue Stone/MD - Rhonda Wright, Bennett, Distributor Relations, Stephen M. Merrick/Dir., Sr. VP - International Development, General Counsel/$360,225.00, Scott R. Montgomery/COO, Exec. VP/$381,000.00, Ryan Montgomery/Exec. VP - Worldwide Sales, Steve Hastings/Sr. VP - North American Sales, Steven D. Albright/CFO, VP/$334,772.00, Paul Lim/GM - Reliv Malaysia, Singapore, Javier Ramirez/National Sales Mgr. - Reliv Mexico, US Hispanic Sales, Mark Lewis/National Sales Mgr. - Reliv Canada, Fred Cameron/VP - International Development, Don Gibbons/Sr. VP - International Sales, Michael Tan/National Sales Mgr. - Reliv Malaysia, Singapore
(21 Officers included in Index)

Directors: Robert L. Montgomery/Chmn., CEO, Pres., Co - Founder, Carl W. Hastings/Vice Chmn., Chief Scientific Officer, Stephen M. Merrick/Dir., Sr. VP - International Development, General Counsel, Sandra S. Montgomery/Co - Founder, Patrick G. Doherty/Dir., Denis St John/Dir., Donald L. McCain/Dir., John B. Akin/Dir., Robert M. Henry/Dir., Michael D. Smith/Dir.

Owners: Denis St. John, John B. Akin, Robert L. Montgomery/22.14%, Robert M. Henry, Ryan A. Montgomery, Stephen M. Merrick/3.42%, Donald L. McCain/2.21%, Steven G. Hastings, Carl W. Hastings/3.79%, Scott R. Montgomery, Insiders/32.72%, Steven D. Albright

Financial Data: ***Fiscal Year End:***12/31 ***Latest Annual Data:*** 12/31/2006

Year	Sales	Net Income
2006	$117,467,000	$7,898,000
2005	$113,565,000	$7,521,000
2004	$96,982,000	$5,387,000

Curr. Assets:	$24,845,000	**Curr. Liab.:**	$8,615,000	**P/E Ratio:**	23.23
Plant, Equip.:	$9,435,000	**Total Liab.:**	$9,548,000	**Indic. Yr. Divd.:**	$0.100
Total Assets:	$37,282,000	**Net Worth:**	$27,734,000	**Debt/ Equity:**	NA

RELM Wireless Corp

7100 Technology Dr., West Melbourne, FL, 32904; ***PH:*** 1-321-984-1414; ***Fax:*** 1-321-984-0168; ***http://*** www.relm.com; ***Email:*** info@relm.com

General - Incorporation	NV	**Stock**- Price on:12/24/2007	$5.12
Employees	92	Stock Exchange	AMEX
Auditor	BDO Seidman, LLP	Ticker Symbol	RWC
Stk Agt	American Stock Transfer & Trust Co.	Outstanding Shares	13,340,000
Counsel	Morris Brown	E.P.S	NA
DUNS No.	NA	Shareholders	NA

Business: The groups principal activities include designing, manufacturing and marketing wireless communications products. The groups products include two-way land mobile radios, repeaters, base stations, and related components subsystems. The group marketed its products under the trade names BK Radio, RELM, and RELM/BK. Specific customers of the group include United States Forest Service (USFS) and the DOI. The groups net sale in the year 2006 was $32,445 (thousand).

Primary SIC and add'l.: 3663 3679

CIK No: 0000002186

Officers: David P. Storey/CEO, Pres./$606,902.00, William P. Kelly/CFO, Exec. VP/$425,694.00

Directors: Warren N. Romine/Dir., John Wellhausen/Dir.

Owners: Wentworth, Hauser & Violich, Inc./5.10%, Ralph R. Whitney, Donald F.U. Goebert/12.20%, Randolph K. Piechocki, George N. Benjamin, Harold B. Cook/1.00%, David P. Storey/4.50%, John Wellhausen, James C. Gale, William P. Kelly/1.60%, Insiders/19.40%

Financial Data: ***Fiscal Year End:***12/31 ***Latest Annual Data:*** 12/31/2006

Year	Sales	Net Income
2006	$32,445,000	$3,427,000
2005	$28,519,000	$10,292,000
2004	$20,656,000	$7,877,000

Curr. Assets:	NA	**Curr. Liab.:**	NA		
Plant, Equip.:	NA	**Total Liab.:**	NA	**Indic. Yr. Divd.:**	NA
Total Assets:	NA	**Net Worth:**	NA	**Debt/ Equity:**	NA

REMEC Inc

9404 Chesapeake Dr., San Diego, CA, 92123; ***PH:*** 1-858-842-3356; ***http://*** www.remec.com; ***Email:*** investorrelations@remec.com

General - Incorporation	CA	**Stock**- Price on:12/24/2007	$1.5
Employees	4	Stock Exchange	OTC
Auditor	Squar, Milner, Raehl & Williamson	Ticker Symbol	REMC
Stk Agt	Mellon Investor Services LLC	Outstanding Shares	NA
Counsel	Milberg Weiss Bershad & Schulman	E.P.S	NA
DUNS No.	10-316-1188	Shareholders	NA

Business: The group's principal activities are carried out through two groups: the commercial group and the defense and space group. The commercial group develops and manufactures high frequency subsystems used in the transmission of voice, video and data traffic over fixed access and mobile wireless communication networks. The defense and space group provides a broad spectrum of radio frequencies, microwave and guidance products for systems integrated by prime contractors in military and space applications. It also develops and manufacture wireless communications equipment used in the defense industry, including communications equipment integrated into electronic systems for tactical aircraft, ships, ground systems, satellites, missile systems and smart weapons. On 01-Jun-2003 himark & on 10-Nov-2003 paradigm wireless systems inc.

Primary SIC and add'l.: 3823

CIK No: 0000769874

Subsidiaries: Chelton Microwave, Chelton Microwave Corporation, Chelton REMEC Defense & Space, Inc., RDS Acquisition Corp.

Officers: David F. Wilkinson/CFO, Donald J. Wilkins/Corporate Compliance Officer, Richard A. Sackett/Dir., Pres., General Counsel, Sec.

Directors: Andre R. Horn/Chmn., Thomas A. Corcoran/Dir., Jeffrey M. Nash/Dir., William H. Gibbs/Dir., Mark D. Dankberg/Dir., Richard A. Sackett/Dir., Pres., General Counsel, Sec.

Owners: Morgan Stanley/8.18%, Andre R. Horn/1.08%, Mark D. Dankberg/1.18%, Millenco, L.P./9.05%, Kellogg Capital Group, LLC/10.66%, Option Opportunities Company/6.67%, Insiders/4.36%, S. Muoio& Co. LLC/8.41%, Jeffrey M. Nash, SACC Partners LP and Affiliates/6.31%, William H. Gibbs, Thomas A. Corcoran, David F. Wilkinson, Richard A. Sackett

Financial Data: ***Fiscal Year End:***01/31 ***Latest Annual Data:*** 1/31/2005

Year	Sales	Net Income
2005	$423,911,000	-$90,781,000
2004	$384,535,000	-$49,408,000
2003	$246,588,000	-$63,794,000

Curr. Assets:	$186,806,000	**Curr. Liab.:**	$107,806,000		
Plant, Equip.:	$71,967,000	**Total Liab.:**	$110,418,000	**Indic. Yr. Divd.:**	$0.750
Total Assets:	$274,923,000	**Net Worth:**	$164,505,000	**Debt/ Equity:**	NA

Remedent USA Inc

Xavier De Cocklaan 42, Deurle, 9831; ***PH:*** 011-3293-217080; ***http://*** www.remedent.be

General - Incorporation	NV	**Stock**- Price on:12/24/2007	$1.75
Employees	NA	Stock Exchange	OTC
Auditor	Ria Verheyen	Ticker Symbol	REMI
Stk Agt	MDB Capital Group LLC	Outstanding Shares	NA
Counsel	NA	E.P.S	NA
DUNS No.	NA	Shareholders	NA

Business: The group's principle activity is to distribute high technology professional dental equipment. The group's principal product is remecure cl-15, a high-speed dental curing light that is sourced from a contract manufacturer in France. The group operates through two subsidiaries namely, remedent professional inc and remedent nv. It holds 22% of remedent nv, a belgian manufacturer of professional dental equipment. Remedent professional inc is the wholly owned United States-based sales organisation for equipment manufactured by remedent nv.

Primary SIC and add'l.: 5047 7389

CIK No: 0001078037

Subsidiaries: Remedent Asia Pte. Ltd, Remedent N.V. Remedent Professional, Inc., Remedent Professional Holdings, Inc, Remedent Professional, Inc.

Officers: Robin List/CEO - Europe, Frederik Braet/Area Mgr. - Europe, Jo Lejeune/International Sales Mgr. OTC - Europe, Philippe Van Acker/Dir. - Finance, Yves Dossche/Technical Mgr. - Europe, Griet Van Bastelaere/International Sales Mgr. Dental - Asia, N, S America, Els Quet/Management Assist. - Europe, Tim Verhaeghe/Head Regulatory Affairs, Business Development Mgr. OTC, Katrien De Vogelaere/Project Mgr. - Europe, Ellen Christiaen/Mgr. - International Sales, Marketing, Evelyne Jacquemyns/Dental Consultant, Stacey Ammons/Operations Mgr. - USA, Andrew Soh/Regional GM - Asia, Koen Steyaert/COO, Emelie De Decker/Customer Service Coordinator

Directors: Guy De Vreese/Chmn.

Owners: Austin W. Marxe and David M. Greenhouse/35.63%, Philippe Van Acker, Jon D. Gruber/10.14%, Insiders/35.99%, Paul J. Solit/12.13%, Fred Kolsteeg, Stephen Ross/2.78%, Special Situations Cayman Fund LP/6.64%, Robin List/4.20%, Lagunitas Partners LP/7.22%, Special Situations Private Equity Fund, L.P./27.30%, Guy De Vreese/28.37%, Potomac Capital Partners LP/5.21%

Financial Data: ***Fiscal Year End:***03/31 ***Latest Annual Data:*** 03/31/2007

Year	Sales	Net Income
2007	$6,676,000	-$1,496,000
2006	$7,394,000	-$3,887,000
2005	$7,072,000	-$103,000

Curr. Assets:	$4,579,000	**Curr. Liab.:**	$3,045,000		
Plant, Equip.:	$317,000	**Total Liab.:**	$3,106,000	**Indic. Yr. Divd.:**	NA
Total Assets:	$5,063,000	**Net Worth:**	$1,957,000	**Debt/ Equity:**	0.2736

RemedyTemp Inc

101 Enterprise, Sliso Viejo, CA, 92656; ***PH:*** 1-949-425-7600; ***http://*** www.remedystaff.com

General - Incorporation	CA	**Stock**- Price on:12/24/2007	NA
Employees	NA	Stock Exchange	NA
Auditor	PricewaterhouseCoopers LLP	Ticker Symbol	NA
Stk Agt	American Stock Transfer & Trust Co.	Outstanding Shares	NA
Counsel	Gibson, Dunn & Crutcher LLP	E.P.S	NA
DUNS No.	07-252-1453	Shareholders	NA

Business: The group's principle activities are to provide clerical, light industrial, information technology and financial temporary staffing services. These services are catered to industrial, service and technology companies, professional organizations and governmental agencies. It has invested significant human and financial resources to provide its clients with premium temporary workers and unique value-added services. The group's primary proprietary technologies designed are market analysis profiling sourcing, human performance technology, i/search 2000 and employee data gathering and evaluation. The group provides its services in 37 states through a network of 238 offices. Its trademarks are: remedy(R), remedy temporary services(R), remedytemp(R), remedy technical(R), caller access(R), intellisearch(R), intelligent staffing(R), hire intelligence(R), edge(R), vsm(R), hpt(R), the intelligent temporary(R), remedy logistics group(R), remx technology group(r).

Primary SIC and add'l.: 7363

CIK No: 0001013467

Officers: Stephen D. Sorensen/Chmn., CEO, Irwin Much/Pres. - Franchise Division, Paul J. Sorensen/Pres. - Select Staffing, Melissa J. Porter/Chief Sales Officer, Mark R. McComb/COO, Richard K. Hulme/Chief Administrative Officer

Directors: Stephen D. Sorensen/Chmn., CEO

Remote Dynamics Inc

200 Chisholm Pl., Ste. 120, Plano, TX, 75075; *PH:* 1-972-395-5579; *Fax:* 1-972-423-1620; *http://* www.remotedynamics.com; *Email:* info@remotedynamics.com

General - Incorporation	DE	**Stock** - Price on:12/24/2007	$0.002
Employees	19	Stock Exchange	OTC
Auditor	Chisholm, Bierwolf & Nilson, LLC	Ticker Symbol	REDI
Stk Agt	Mellon Investor Services LLC	Outstanding Shares	65,060,000
Counsel	NA	E.P.S.	NA
DUNS No.	NA	Shareholders	NA

Business: The group's principal activities are to develop and implement mobile communications solutions for long-haul truck fleets, service vehicle fleets and other mobile-asset fleets, including integrated voice, data and position location services. The group provides mobile communications services through a wireless enhanced services network, which utilizes patented technology developed and owned by the group. The group provides services through contracts with certain telecommunications companies and 66 cellular carriers. The group's products and services are classified into two operating categories: minorplanet vehicle management information (vmi(tm)) and nsc systems. Nsc systems includes three separate product and service categories: truck fleet mobile communications, sbc service vehicles and mobile asset tracking. The group holds 42 United States and 16 foreign patents that cover certain key features of its network.

Primary SIC and add'l.: 4812

CIK No: 0000944400

Subsidiaries: HighwayMaster of Canada LLC, RD Technologies, Inc.

Officers: Gary Hallgren/CEO, Greg Jones/Sr. VP - Operations, Justin Gibbs/Controller

Directors: David Walters/Chmn., Keith Moore/Dir., Dennis Ackerman/Dir., Marshall G. Saffer/Dir., Phillip K. Hunter/Dir.

Owners: Insiders, Bounce Mobile Systems, Inc., David Walters, Insiders, David Walters, Dennis Ackerman, Bounce Mobile Systems, Inc.

Financial Data: *Fiscal Year End:* 08/31 *Latest Annual Data:* 8/31/2006

Year	Sales	Net Income
2006	$5,906,000	-$18,155,000
2005	$16,372,000	-$15,663,000

Curr. Assets:	$2,669,000	Curr. Liab.:	$8,354,000		
Plant, Equip.:	$2,237,000	Total Liab.:	$10,676,000	Indic. Yr. Divd.:	NA
Total Assets:	$11,158,000	Net Worth:	-$4,368,000	Debt/ Equity:	NA

Remote Knowledge Inc

3657 Briar Pk. Dr. Ste. 100, Houston, TX, 77042; *PH:* 1-281-599-4800; *http://* www.rkiq.com; *Email:* ir@rkiq.com

General - Incorporation	DE	**Stock** - Price on:12/24/2007	$0.65
Employees	17	Stock Exchange	OTC
Auditor	Hein & Associates LLP	Ticker Symbol	RKNW
Stk Agt	Computershare Investor Services LLC	Outstanding Shares	15,710,000
Counsel	NA	E.P.S.	-$0.43
DUNS No.	NA	Shareholders	NA

Business: The groups principle activities include developing, delivering and supporting proprietary communications and data management products. The groups technology platforms supply in motion high speed Internet and voice services, advanced search applications to provide content. The group operates from the United States.

Primary SIC and add'l.: 3661

CIK No: 0001059099

Officers: Randy S. Bayne/44/Dir., CEO, Pres., Henry Houston/68/Dir., CFO, Exec. VP, Mark Van Eman/VP - Operations

Directors: Randy S. Bayne/44/Dir., CEO, Pres., Richard C. Webb/74/Chmn., Henry Houston/68/Dir., CFO, Exec. VP, Dan Granader/59/Dir., Steve Phelps/48/Dir., William H. Moody/68/Dir.

Owners: Henry Houston, Alan Granader, Neil Granader, Harry L. Bayne, Randy S. Bayne, Robert Duncan, William H. Moody, Mark Sullivan, Richard C. Webb, Dan Granader, George Ball, Insiders, Don A. Sanders, Steve Phelps, Ben Morris

Financial Data: *Fiscal Year End:* 12/31 *Latest Annual Data:* 12/31/2006

Year	Sales	Net Income
2006	$32,000	-$7,225,000
2005	$7,000	-$8,248,000
2004	$44,000	-$4,565,000

Curr. Assets:	$611,000	Curr. Liab.:	$5,620,000	P/E Ratio:	14.42
Plant, Equip.:	$387,000	Total Liab.:	$7,462,000	Indic. Yr. Divd.:	NA
Total Assets:	$998,000	Net Worth:	-$6,464,000	Debt/ Equity:	NA

Remotemdx Inc

150 W Civic Ctr. Dr., Ste. 400, Salt Lake City, UT, 84070; *PH:* 1-801-974-9474; *Fax:* 1-801-451-6281; *http://* www.remotemdx.com

General - Incorporation		**Stock** - Price on:12/24/2007	$1.46
Employees	97	Stock Exchange	OTC
Auditor	Hansen, Barnett and Maxwell	Ticker Symbol	RMDX
Stk Agt	American Stock Transfer & Trust Co.	Outstanding Shares	113,930,000
Counsel	NA	E.P.S.	-$0.36
DUNS No.	NA	Shareholders	NA

Business: The groups principal activity is to provide personal security services utilizing two or three way voice communications, patented wireless location technology and systems that focus on offender monitoring and tracking, personal security, senior supervision and health monitoring. The group operates from the United States.

Primary SIC and add'l.: 4899 4812 3812 3829 7382 4822 7375 5065 5063

CIK No: 0001284891

Officers: David Derrick/Chmn., CEO, James Dalton/Pres., Vice Chmn., Randy E. Olshen/Pres. Securealert - Inc., Michael Acton/CFO, Sec., Treasurer, Bruce G. Derrick/CTO

Directors: David Derrick/Chmn., CEO, James Dalton/Pres., Vice Chmn., Peter McCall/Dir., Robert Childers/Dir.

Financial Data: *Fiscal Year End:* 09/30 *Latest Annual Data:* 9/30/2006

Year	Sales	Net Income
2006	$1,070,000	-$23,798,000
2005	$862,000	-$10,984,000
2004	$1,118,000	-$6,407,000

Curr. Assets:	$8,661,000	Curr. Liab.:	$6,251,000		
Plant, Equip.:	$3,483,000	Total Liab.:	$6,251,000	Indic. Yr. Divd.:	NA
Total Assets:	$12,192,000	Net Worth:	$2,351,000	Debt/ Equity:	NA

Remy International Inc

2902 Enterprise Dr., Anderson, IN, 46013; *PH:* 1-765-778-6499; *http://* www.delcoremy.com

General - Incorporation	DE	**Stock** - Price on:12/24/2007	$71.85
Employees	NA	Stock Exchange	OTC
Auditor	Ernst & Young LLP	Ticker Symbol	REMYF
Stk Agt	American Stock Transfer & Trust Co.	Outstanding Shares	NA
Counsel	NA	E.P.S.	NA
DUNS No.	82-488-7400	Shareholders	NA

Business: The group's principle activities include manufacturing and remanufacturing of original equipment manufacturer and aftermarket electrical, powertrain/drivetrain and related components for automobiles and light trucks, medium and heavy duty trucks and other heavy duty vehicles, with products like starter motors, alternators, engines, transmissions, torque convertors, traction control systems and fuel systems. The group operates from United States.

Primary SIC and add'l.: 3519 3694 3714

CIK No: 0001046859

Subsidiaries: Ballantrae Corporation, Central Precision Limited, Delco Remy International (Europe) GmbH, Electro Diesel Rebuild bvba, Electro-Rebuild Tunisie S.A.R.L., Franklin Power Products, Inc., HSG I, Inc., HSG II, Inc., International Fuel Systems, Inc., IPower Technologies LLC, M. & M. Knopf Auto Parts, LLC, Magnum Power Products, LLC, Marine Corporation of America, Nabco, Inc., Power Investments Marine, Inc. 59 Subsidiaries included in the Index

Renaissance Learning Inc

2911 Peach St., Wisconsin Rapids, WI, 54495; *PH:* 1-715-424-3636; *Fax:* 1-715-424-4242; *http://* www.renlearn.com

General - Incorporation	WI	**Stock** - Price on:12/24/2007	$12.23
Employees	1,059	Stock Exchange	NDQ
Auditor	Deloitte & Touche LLP	Ticker Symbol	RLRN
Stk Agt	Piper Jaffray	Outstanding Shares	29,050,000
Counsel	Godfrey & Kahn	E.P.S.	$0.25
DUNS No.	18-922-1526	Shareholders	NA

Business: The group's principal activity is to provide learning information systems software and school information programs to pre-kindergarten through senior high schools in the United States and Canada. The computer-based learning information systems consist of computer software and the related training designed to improve student academic performance. This is done by increasing the quality, quantity and timeliness of performance data available to educators and by facilitating increased student practice of essential skills. The major products include star reading, accelerated math, star math, perfect copy, surpass and star early literacy. In addition to the learning information system products, the group provides professional development training for educators through reading renaissance, math renaissance, school renaissance and other training programs.

Primary SIC and add'l.: 7372 8999

CIK No: 0001030484

Subsidiaries: Advantage Learning Systems India Private Limited, Renaissance Learning Australia Proprietary Limited, Renaissance Learning of Canada Co., Renaissance Learning UK Limited, RL Asset Management, Inc., RL Investments, Inc.

Owners: Insiders/70.70%, Mary T. Minch, Steven A. Schmidt, Judith Ames Paul/35.20%, Steven C. Bell/5.10%, Harold E. Jordan, Addison L. Piper, Terrance D. Paul/35.20%, Judith A. Ryan, John H. Grunewald, Gordon H. Gunnlaugsson

Financial Data: *Fiscal Year End:* 12/31 *Latest Annual Data:* 12/31/2006

Year	Sales	Net Income
2006	$111,528,000	$11,993,000
2005	$116,283,000	$24,751,000
2004	$114,048,000	$22,702,000

Curr. Assets:	$49,994,000	Curr. Liab.:	$34,712,000		
Plant, Equip.:	$11,811,000	Total Liab.:	$38,140,000	Indic. Yr. Divd.:	$0.280
Total Assets:	$117,711,000	Net Worth:	$79,571,000	Debt/ Equity:	0.0388

RenaissanceRe Holdings Ltd

Renaissance House, 8-20 East Brdway, Pembroke; ; *http://* www.renre.com

General - Incorporation	Bermuda	**Stock** - Price on:12/24/2007	$59.47
Employees	218	Stock Exchange	NYSE
Auditor	Willkie Farr & Gallagher LLP	Ticker Symbol	RNR
Stk Agt	Mellon Investor Services LLC	Outstanding Shares	72,260,000
Counsel	Wilkie Farr & Gallagher	E.P.S.	NA
DUNS No.	NA	Shareholders	NA

Business: The group's principal activities are to provide insurance and reinsurance coverage for natural and man-made catastrophes. The coverage protects against natural catastrophes such as earthquakes and hurricanes and other natural calamities and man-made catastrophes such as winter storms, freezes, floods, fires, tornadoes and explosions. The activities are carried out through two segments: reinsurance operations and individual risk operations. The reinsurance segment provides property catastrophe reinsurance and specialty reinsurance to selected insurers and reinsurers on a worldwide basis. The individual risk segment provides insurance for commercial and homeowners' catastrophe-exposed property business, and also provides reinsurance on a quota share basis.

Primary SIC and add'l.: 6719 6331

CIK No: 0000913144

Subsidiaries: DaVinci Reinsurance Ltd., DaVinciRe Holdings Ltd., Glencoe Group Holdings Ltd., Glencoe Insurance Ltd., Glencoe U.S. Holdings Inc., Renaissance Investment Holdings Ltd., Renaissance Investment Management Company Limited, Renaissance Reinsurance Ltd., Renaissance Underwriting Managers Ltd., Stonington Insurance Company

Officers: William J. Ashley/CEO, Pres. - Glencoe Group Holdings Ltd, Neill A. Currie/Dir., CEO/$5,928,570.00, Fred R. Donner/CFO, Exec. VP/$1,444,458.00, Kevin J. O'Donnell/Sr. VP/$2,834,722.00, Stephen H. Weinstein/39/Sr. VP, Chief Compliance Officer, General Counsel, Sec., John D. Nichols/Exec. VP/$2,716,797.00, Peter C. Durhager/Sr. VP, Chief Administrative Officer, William I. Riker/Dir., Pres./$6,899,256.00, Mark A. Wilcox/40/Sr. VP, Chief Accounting Officer, Corporate Controller, Todd R. Fonner/Sr. VP, Chief Risk Officer, Chief Investment Officer, David Lilly/Investor Contact

Directors: Neill A. Currie/Dir., CEO, James W. MacGinnitie/Chmn., Scott E. Pardee/Dir., Brian R. Hall/Dir., Nicholas L. Trivisonno/Dir., Edmund B. Greene/Dir., William I. Riker/Dir., Pres., Jean D. Hamilton/Dir., Thomas A. Cooper/Dir., William F. Hecht/Dir., Henry Klehm/Dir., Ralph B. Levy/Dir.

Owners: John D. Nichols, William I. Riker/1.70%, Brian R. Hall, AXA/9.97%, Orbis Investment Management Limited/5.00%, Insiders/4.50%, Thomas A. Cooper, Scott E. Pardee, Neill A. Currie, Pzena Investment Management, LLC/6.30%, Jean D. Hamilton, FMR Corp./9.90%, Fred R. Donner, Edmund B. Greene, John M. Lummis *(21 Owners included in Index)*

Financial Data: *Fiscal Year End:*12/31 *Latest Annual Data:* 12/31/2006

Year	Sales	Net Income
2006	$1,840,737,000	$797,110,000
2005	$1,655,907,000	-$246,763,000
2004	$1,567,992,000	$164,242,000

Curr. Assets:	$3,480,345,000	**Curr. Liab.:**	$395,083,000		
Plant, Equip.:	NA	**Total Liab.:**	$3,838,245,000	**Indic. Yr. Divd.:**	$0.880
Total Assets:	$7,769,026,000	**Net Worth:**	$3,280,497,000	**Debt/ Equity:**	0.1362

Renasant Corp

209 Troy St., Tupelo, MS, 38802; *PH:* 1-662-680-1001; *Fax:* 1-662-680-1234;
http:// www.renasantbank.com; *Email:* info@renasant.com

General - Incorporation	MS	Stock- Price on:12/24/2007	$24.79
Employees	813	Stock Exchange	NDQ
Auditor	Horne LLP	Ticker Symbol	RNST
Stk Agt	Registrar & Transfer Co	Outstanding Shares	15,560,000
Counsel	NA	E.P.S.	$1.74
DUNS No.	NA	Shareholders	NA

Business: The groups principle activity is to provide financial services. The groups services include qualified retirement plans, profit sharing and other employee benefit plans, personal trusts and estates. The products of the group include commercial, financial and agricultural loans and commercial mortgage. The groups operates through four segments namely Mississippi community bank, Tennessee community bank, Alabama community bank and insurance agency. In January 1, 2005, the group acquired Heritage Financial Holding Corporation. The group operates from the United States. The group's quarterly net income for September 2007 was 8.30 millions of USD.

Primary SIC and add'l.: 6411 6036 6712 6022 6282 6029 6163 6162

CIK No: 0000715072

Subsidiaries: Heritage Financial Statutory Trust I, PHC Statutory Trust I, PHC Statutory Trust II, Primeco, Inc., Renasant Bank, Renasant Insurance, Inc.

Officers: Robinson E. McGraw/Chmn., CEO, Pres., Stephen M. Corban/Sr. Exec. VP - General Counsel, James W. Gray/CIO, Sr. Exec. VP, Stuart R. Johnson/Sr. Exec. VP, CFO, Harold H. Livingston/Sr. Exec. VP, Chief Credit Officer, Larry R. Mathews/Sr. Exec. VP, Dir. - Sales, Marketing, Claude H. Springfield/Sr. Exec. VP, Chief Credit Policy Officer, Mitchell C. Waycaster/Sr. Exec. VP, Chief Administrative Officer, Scott J. Cochran/Pres. - Renasant Mississippi, Rick R. Hart/Dir., Pres. - Renasant Tennessee, Michael D. Ross/Pres. - Renasant Alabama, Francis J. Cianciola/Dir., Exec. VP

Directors: Robinson E. McGraw/Chmn., CEO, Pres., Larry J. Young/Vice Chmn., Joe H. Trulove/Dir., Eugene B. Gifford/Dir. Emeritus, Richard L. Heyer/Dir., Neal A. Holland/Dir., Harold B. Jeffreys/Dir., Jack C. Johnson/Dir., Niles J. McNeel/Dir., Theodore S. Moll/Dir., John W. Smith/Dir., George H. Booth/Dir., Walter L. Bourland/Dir. Emeritus, A. M. Edwards/Dir. Emeritus, Robert C. Leake/Dir. Emeritus *(26 Directors included in Index)*

Owners: Joe H. Trulove, Harold B. Jeffreys/1.29%, Francis J. Cianciola, Jack C. Johnson, William M. Beasley, Neal A. Holland/1.40%, Stuart R. Johnson, Theodore S. Moll, Richard L. Heyer, Frank B. Brooks, James W. Gray, Insiders/8.81%, Mitchell C. Waycaster, Marshall H. Dickerson, Niles J. McNeel *(22 Owners included in Index)*

Financial Data: *Fiscal Year End:*12/31 *Latest Annual Data:* 12/31/2006

Year	Sales	Net Income
2006	$200,236,000	$27,125,000
2005	$168,605,000	$24,209,000
2004	$110,332,000	$18,443,000

Curr. Assets:	$98,201,000	**Curr. Liab.:**	$2,253,177,000	**P/E Ratio:**	14.25
Plant, Equip.:	$41,350,000	**Total Liab.:**	$2,358,652,000	**Indic. Yr. Divd.:**	$0.640
Total Assets:	$2,611,356,000	**Net Worth:**	$252,704,000	**Debt/ Equity:**	NA

Renewable Energy Resources Inc

Formerly: Internal Hydro International Inc
607a W Martin Luther King Blvd, Tampa, FL, 33603; *PH:* 1-818-981-1796;
http:// www.internalhydro.com

General - Incorporation	FL	Stock- Price on:12/24/2007	NA
Employees	3	Stock Exchange	NA
Auditor	Baumann, Raymondo & Co., P.A	Ticker Symbol	NA
Stk Agt	Island Stock Transfer	Outstanding Shares	NA
Counsel	NA	E.P.S.	-$0.018
DUNS No.	NA	Shareholders	NA

Business: The group's principle activity is to seek business opportunities relating to home building and home buying through acquisition, joint venture and developing such businesses. It includes mortgage broking, mortgage originations and lending, construction lending and other services that would benefit prospective home buyers. On 29-Dec-2003, the group abandoned the above business plans. On 02-Jan-2004, it merged with internal command international inc. The group intends to generate and

distribute electricity through alternative power system a patented technology that uses water pressure flow. Ec iv, utilizes wastewater, fluid or gas flow from any source where flow pressure is present and yet wasted to create electricity. The system is noiseless and emission free. The group operates from United States.

Primary SIC and add'l.: 9999 1521 6719 8741 6531

CIK No: 0001108064

Officers: Kenneth Brown/CEO, Pres., Craig Huffman/Chmn., Interim CEO, Acting Principal Financial Officer, Edward R. Hart/COO, Ezra Smith/VP

Directors: Craig Huffman/Chmn., Interim CEO, Acting Principal Financial Officer, Wade Kenyon/67/Dir., Mark Pena/Dir., Anthony Pecoraro/Dir., Tony Council/51/Dir., Michael Scionti/39/Dir., James A. Thomas/Dir.

Owners: Kevin Pickard, Craig Huffman, Mercatus & Partners LTD FBO, John P. Gordon, James A. Thomas, John F. Simonetti, Insiders, Dan Simonetti, Edward R. Hart

Financial Data: *Fiscal Year End:*12/31 *Latest Annual Data:* 06/30/2007

Year	Sales	Net Income
2007	NA	-$850,000
2006	NA	-$535,000
2005	NA	-$2,813,000

Curr. Assets:	$7,000	**Curr. Liab.:**	$241,000		
Plant, Equip.:	$14,000	**Total Liab.:**	$1,148,000	**Indic. Yr. Divd.:**	NA
Total Assets:	$200,000	**Net Worth:**	-$948,000	**Debt/ Equity:**	NA

Renovis Inc

2 Corporate Dr., South San Francisco, CA, 94080; *PH:* 1-650-266-1400; *Fax:* 1-650-266-1460;
http:// www.renovis.com

General - Incorporation	DE	Stock- Price on:12/24/2007	$3.52
Employees	111	Stock Exchange	NDQ
Auditor	Ernst & Young LLP	Ticker Symbol	NA
Stk Agt	Wells Fargo Shareowner Services	Outstanding Shares	29,580,000
Counsel	NA	E.P.S.	-$1.24
DUNS No.	NA	Shareholders	NA

Business: The group's principal activity is to develop drugs to treat neurological diseases and disorders. It's research and development programmes focus on major medical needs in the areas of pain, trauma, stroke and neurodegenerative diseases. The group's main product is cerovive, a drug for acute ischemic stroke. The group is developing two clinical candidates for the treatment of pain: ren-1654, an oral drug for neuropathic pain in clinical trials and ren-213, an intravenous drug for post-operative pain. It operates in the United States and Europe.

Primary SIC and add'l.: 2834 8731

CIK No: 0001118361

Officers: Corey S. Goodman/Dir., CEO, Pres./$2,597,470.00, Marlene F. Perry/Sr. VP - Human Resources/$613,606.00, John C. Doyle/39/Sr. VP - Corporate Development, CFO/$1,014,555.00, Alan C. Mendelson/Sec., George F. Fraley/VP - Legal Affairs, Assoc. General Counsel, Jeff Farrow/VP - Finance, Chief Accounting Officer, Michael G. Kelly/Sr. VP - Research, Development/$1,294,735.00

Directors: Corey S. Goodman/Dir., CEO, Pres., Jeffrey M. Friedman/Chmn. - Medical, Member - Scientific Advisory Board, John P. Walker/Chmn., Bruce L.A. Carter/Dir., Nancy M. Crowell/Dir., Anthony B. Evnin/Dir., John H. Friedman/Dir., Judith A. Hemberger/Dir., Carla Shatz/Member - Medical Scientific Advisory Board, Edward E. Penhoet/Dir., Eric M. Gordon/Member - Scientific Advisory Board, William Catterall/Member - Medical Scientific Advisory Board, Kenneth W. Bair/Member - Medical Scientific Advisory Board, Robert C. Malenka/Member - Medical Scientific Advisory Board, Wade S. Smith/Member - Medical Scientific Advisory Board *(16 Directors included in Index)*

Owners: Corey S. Goodman/1.79%, Edward E. Penhoet/4.04%, Bruce L.A. Carter, John C. Doyle, Michael G. Kelly, Tito A. Serafini, John P. Walker, Anthony B. Evnin/4.58%, Marlene F. Perry, Entities affiliated with RA Capital Management, LLC/5.49%, Entities affiliated with Biotechnology Value Fund, L.P./7.95%, Insiders/15.90%, Dushyant Pathak, Nancy M. Crowell, John H. Friedman/2.44% *(16 Owners included in Index)*

Financial Data: *Fiscal Year End:*12/31 *Latest Annual Data:* 12/31/2006

Year	Sales	Net Income
2006	$10,428,000	-$28,376,000
2005	$6,647,000	-$31,980,000
2004	$2,625,000	-$39,941,000

Curr. Assets:	$100,035,000	**Curr. Liab.:**	$10,531,000		
Plant, Equip.:	$7,052,000	**Total Liab.:**	$14,215,000	**Indic. Yr. Divd.:**	NA
Total Assets:	$107,301,000	**Net Worth:**	$93,086,000	**Debt/ Equity:**	0.0289

Renovo Holdings

The Manchester Incubator Bldg., 48 Grafton St., Manchester, M13 9XX; *PH:* 407-599-2886;
Fax: 44-1616067333; *http://* www.renovo.com; *Email:* info@renovo.com

General - Incorporation	NV	Stock- Price on:12/24/2007	$0.0015
Employees	NA	Stock Exchange	OTC
Auditor	Jaspers + Hall, PC	Ticker Symbol	RNVO
Stk Agt	NA	Outstanding Shares	499,850,000
Counsel	NA	E.P.S.	-$0.001
DUNS No.	NA	Shareholders	NA

Business: The groups principal activity is seeking to establish Renovo in the Florida restoration market, with the ability to expedite the recovery process, with eventual capability of responding to loss and restoration across the United States. The group operates from the United States.

Primary SIC and add'l.: 5960

CIK No: 0001143451

Officers: Mark Ferguson/Co - Founder, CEO, John Hutchison/Chief Medical Officer, Sharon O'Kane/Co - Founder, Executive Dir. - Research, Development, Simon Bielecki/Head - Communications, Andrew Kay/Executive Dir. - Commercial, Robin Cridland/Executive Dir. - Finance, Business Development, Company Sec., Stephen W. Carnes/43/Dir., Pres., Sec., Treasurer

Directors: Mark Ferguson/Co - Founder, CEO, Rodger Pannone/Chmn., David Ebsworth/Non Exec. Dir., David Feigal/Non Exec. Dir., Arthur Rosenthal/Non Exec. Dir., Sharon O'Kane/Co - Founder, Executive Dir. - Research, Development, Andrew Kay/Executive Dir. - Commercial, Robin Cridland/Executive Dir. - Finance, Business Development, Company Sec., Barrie Thorpe/Sr. Non

Exec. Dir., Lord Leslie Turnberg/Non Exec. Dir., Mike Longaker/Member - Scientific Advisory Board, Gus McGrouther/Member - Scientific Advisory Board, Tom Mustoe/Member - Scientific Advisory Board, Carl Peck/Member - Scientific Advisory Board, Greg Schultz/Member - Scientific Advisory Board *(18 Directors included in Index)*

Owners: Stephen W. Carnes/52.00%, Insiders/52.00%

Financial Data: *Fiscal Year End:*12/31   *Latest Annual Data:* 12/31/2006

Year	Sales	Net Income
2006	NA	-$421,000
2005	NA	-$435,000
2004	NA	-$1,099,000

Curr. Assets:	NA	Curr. Liab.:	$1,094,000		
Plant, Equip.:	NA	Total Liab.:	$1,094,000	Indic. Yr. Divd.:	NA
Total Assets:	NA	Net Worth:	-$1,094,000	Debt/ Equity:	NA

Rent A Center Inc

5700 Tennyson Pkwy., Ste. 100, Plano, TX, 75024; *PH:* 1-972-801-1100; *Fax:* 1-972-943-0113; *http://* www.rentacenter.com

General - Incorporation	DE	**Stock** - Price on:12/24/2007	$26.79
Employees	19,740	Stock Exchange	NDQ
Auditor	Grant Thornton LLP	Ticker Symbol	RCII
Stk Agt	JPMorgan Service Center	Outstanding Shares	70,360,000
Counsel	Winstead Sechrest & Minick	E.P.S.	$1.12
DUNS No.	61-275-9738	Shareholders	NA

Business: The groups principle activity is to operate retail stores. The groups products include home electronics, appliances, computers, furniture and accessories. The group operates from United States.

Primary SIC and add'l.: 5712 5064

CIK No: 0000933036

Subsidiaries: ColorTyme, Inc, Rent-A-Centre, Ltd

Officers: Mark E. Speese/Chmn., CEO/$2,362,094.00, Robert F. Bloom/CEO, Pres. - Colortyme, Inc, Mitchell E. Fadel/Dir., COO, Pres./$857,043.00, Robert D. Davis/CFO, Sr. VP - Finance, Treasurer/$515,743.00, Christopher A. Korst/Sr. VP, General Counsel, Sec./$388,985.00, Theodore V. Demarino/Sr. VP - Operations, David G. Ewbank/Sr. VP - Operations, Edward C. Ford/Sr. VP - Operations, Kevin Hollaway/Sr. VP - Operations, Michael J. Kelly/Sr. VP - Operations, Michael P. Kilbane/Sr. VP - Operations, Fred G. Mattox/Sr. VP - Operations, Michael R. McNamara/Sr. VP - Operations, Charles J. White/Sr. VP - Operations, David E. West/Sr. VP - Operational Services/$356,168.00 *(39 Officers included in Index)*

Directors: Mark E. Speese/Chmn., CEO, Mitchell E. Fadel/Dir., COO, Pres., Laurence M. Berg/Dir., Mary Elizabeth Burton/Dir., Peter P. Copses/Dir., Michael J. Gade/Dir., J. V. Lentell/Dir., Jeffery M. Jackson/Dir., Leonard H. Roberts/Dir.

Owners: Michael J. Gade, Pzena Investment Management, LLC/10.90%, Mary Elizabeth Burton, Mark E. Speese/3.70%, Insiders/4.70%, Christopher A. Korst, Mitchell E. Fadel, Leonard H. Roberts, J. V. Lentell, Robert D. Davis, David E. West, Hotchkis and Wiley Capital Management, LLC/6.50%, Barclays Global Investors, NA/5.60%, Peter P. Copses

Financial Data: *Fiscal Year End:*12/31   *Latest Annual Data:* 12/31/2006

Year	Sales	Net Income
2006	$2,433,908,000	$103,092,000
2005	$2,339,107,000	$135,738,000
2004	$2,313,255,000	$155,855,000

Curr. Assets:	$1,183,257,000	Curr. Liab.:	$504,719,000	P/E Ratio:	23.92
Plant, Equip.:	$220,499,000	Total Liab.:	$1,797,997,000	Indic. Yr. Divd.:	NA
Total Assets:	$2,740,956,000	Net Worth:	$942,959,000	Debt/ Equity:	1.2630

Rent Way Inc

One Rentway Pl., Erie, PA, 16505; *PH:* 1-814-455-5378; *http://* www.rentway.com

General - Incorporation	PA	**Stock** - Price on:12/24/2007	NA
Employees	NA	Stock Exchange	NA
Auditor	Ernst & Young LLP	Ticker Symbol	NA
Stk Agt	American Stock Transfer & Trust Co.	Outstanding Shares	NA
Counsel	Hodgson Russ	E.P.S.	NA
DUNS No.	01-872-6489	Shareholders	NA

Business: The group's principal activity is to operate stores that rent durable household products. The group operates in two segments- the rental-purchase industry and through dpi, the prepaid local phone service industry. The products include home entertainment equipment, furniture, major appliances, computers and jewelry to customers under full-service rental-purchase agreements that generally allow the customers to obtain ownership of the merchandise at the conclusion of an agreed upon rental period. It also provides prepaid local phone service to consumers on a monthly basis through its majority-owned subsidiary, dpi teleconnect, llc. As of 30-Jun-2004, the group operated 753 rental-purchase stores in 33 states.

Primary SIC and add'l.: 7359

CIK No: 0000893046

Subsidiaries: dPi Teleconnect LLC

Rentech Inc

10877 Wilshire Blvd., Ste. 710, Los Angeles, CA, 90024; *PH:* 1-310-571-9800; *Fax:* 1-310-571-9799; *http://* www.rentechinc.com

General - Incorporation	CO	**Stock** - Price on:12/24/2007	$2.3202
Employees	177	Stock Exchange	AMEX
Auditor	Ehrhardt Keefe Steiner & Hottman P.C	Ticker Symbol	RTK
Stk Agt	Computershare Trust Co	Outstanding Shares	162,750,000
Counsel	Brega & Winters	E.P.S.	-$0.331
DUNS No.	14-948-8496	Shareholders	NA

Business: The group's principal activity is to convert gases made from carbon-bearing material into liquid hydrocarbon, including high grade diesel fuel, naphtha and waxes. The group has developed and owns a patented and proprietary process for the conversion of synthesis gas produced from natural gas, coal, refinery bottoms, industrial off-gas and other hydrocarbon feedstock into clean, sulfur-free and aromatic-free alternative fuels, naphthas and waxes. The rentech gtl technology is licensed to oil and gas companies, operators of industrial gas plants, owners of other carbon-bearing feedstocks and other members of the energy industry.

Primary SIC and add'l.: 3822 2869 2851 1389 6794

CIK No: 0000868725

Subsidiaries: Petroleum Mud Logging, Inc., Rentech Development Corporation, Rentech Services Corporation, Sand Creek Energy, LLC

Officers: Hunt D. Ramsbottom/Dir., CEO, Pres., Douglas M. Miller/COO, Merrick I. Kerr/CFO, Geoffrey S. Flagg/Chief Accounting Officer, Richard O. Sheppard/Sr. VP - Project Development, Richard T. Penning/Exec. VP - Commercial Affairs, Thomas S. Sayles/Sr. VP - Corporate Communications, Government Affairs, Harold A. Wright/CTO, Sr. VP, Debra L. Harshman/Chief Accounting Officer, Colin Morris/General Counsel, Sec., Julie Dawoodjee/Dir. - Investor Relations

Directors: Hunt D. Ramsbottom/Dir., CEO, Pres., Dennis L. Yakobson/Chmn., Edward M. Stern/Dir., Thomas L. Bury/Dir., Michael F. Ray/Dir., Erich W. Tiepel/Dir., Halbert S. Washburn/Dir., Michael S. Burke/Dir.

Owners: Ronald C. Butz, M.A.G. Capital, LLC/8.30%, Merrill Lynch & Co., Inc./10.20%, Dennis L. Yakobson, Wellington Management Company, LLP/9.70%, Thomas L. Bury, Hunt D. Ramsbottom/1.50%, Richard O. Sheppard, Edward M. Stern, BlackRock, Inc./12.30%, Halbert S. Washburn, Insiders/4.50%, Michael F. Ray, Geoffrey S. Flagg, David C. Callaham/7.00% *(17 Owners included in Index)*

Financial Data: *Fiscal Year End:*09/30   *Latest Annual Data:* 9/30/2006

Year	Sales	Net Income
2006	$44,517,000	-$38,648,000
2005	$7,185,000	-$14,359,000
2004	$8,773,000	-$7,211,000

Curr. Assets:	$81,487,000	Curr. Liab.:	$15,966,000		
Plant, Equip.:	$63,085,000	Total Liab.:	$74,102,000	Indic. Yr. Divd.:	NA
Total Assets:	$150,686,000	Net Worth:	$76,585,000	Debt/ Equity:	1.0887

Rentrak Corp

7700 NE Ambassador Pl., Portland, OR, 97220; *PH:* 1-503-284-7581; *Fax:* 1-503-331-2734; *http://* www.rentrak.com; *Email:* sales@rentrak.com

General - Incorporation	OR	**Stock** - Price on:12/24/2007	$14.49
Employees	213	Stock Exchange	NDQ
Auditor	Grant Thornton LLP	Ticker Symbol	RENT
Stk Agt	U.S. Stock Transfer Corp	Outstanding Shares	10,730,000
Counsel	Miller Nash	E.P.S.	$0.52
DUNS No.	05-002-0122	Shareholders	NA

Business: The group's principle activities are to collect, process, analyze and present rental and sales information regarding videocassettes, digital videodiscs and video games. These are leased to home video specialty stores and other retailers by way of its pay per transaction system (ppt). The ppt system, home video specialty stores and other retailers that rent to consumers, including grocery stores and convenience stores, lease units, and other media for a low initial fee share a portion of each retail rental transaction with the group. The group's quarterly revenue for September 2007 was 22.87 millions of USD.

Primary SIC and add'l.: 7841 7379 8741 5735

CIK No: 0000800458

Subsidiaries: Sony Pictures Home Entertainment, Inc, SuperComm, Inc

Officers: Paul A. Rosenbaum/Chmn., CEO/$673,006.00, Christopher Roberts/Sr. VP - Sales, Marketing, Tracey Kilpatrick/Transaction Processing Mgr., Glen Merison/Dir. - Sales, Steve Buck/Dir. - Business Relations, Matt Hemeon/Contact - Canada, George Georgiadis/SCM Project Dir., Marty Graham/Pres. - PPT Division, Brad Hackley/VP - Home Video Essentials, Ron Giambra/Sr. VP - Theatrical/$317,776.00, Kenneth Papagan/Pres., Chief Strategy Officer/$402,873.00, Cathy Hetzel/Pres. - AMI Division, Amir Yazdani/Exec. VP - Information Technology, CIO/$325,950.00, Timothy Erwin/VP - Sales, Customer Relations, Mark Thoenes/CFO, Exec. VP/$341,003.00

Directors: Paul A. Rosenbaum/Chmn., CEO, Cecil D. Andrus/Dir., Judith G. Allen/Dir., George H. Kuper/Dir., Stanford C. Stoddard/Dir., Ralph R. Shaw/Dir., Tom Allen/55/Dir.

Owners: Paul Rosenbaum/4.80%, Cecil Andrus, Tom Allen, Judith Allen, Amir Yazdani/1.70%, Ralph Shaw, Ronald Giambra, George Kuper, Insiders/10.40%, Kenneth Papagan, Mark Cuban/5.90%, Stanford Stoddard, Mark Thoenes

Financial Data: *Fiscal Year End:*03/31   *Latest Annual Data:* 3/31/2007

Year	Sales	Net Income
2007	$105,998,000	$6,048,000
2006	$93,394,000	$4,466,000
2005	$98,538,000	$5,242,000

Curr. Assets:	$54,623,000	Curr. Liab.:	$16,468,000	P/E Ratio:	27.87
Plant, Equip.:	$5,097,000	Total Liab.:	$18,806,000	Indic. Yr. Divd.:	NA
Total Assets:	$60,372,000	Net Worth:	$41,566,000	Debt/ Equity:	NA

Replidyne Inc

1450 Infinite Dr., Louisville, CO, 80027; *PH:* 1-303-996-5500; *Fax:* 1-303-996-5599; *http://* www.replidyne.com; *Email:* contact@replidyne.com

General - Incorporation	DE	**Stock** - Price on:12/24/2007	$5.6
Employees	85	Stock Exchange	NDQ
Auditor	KPMG LLP	Ticker Symbol	RDYN
Stk Agt	American Stock Transfer & Trust Co.	Outstanding Shares	27,010,000
Counsel	NA	E.P.S.	$0.80
DUNS No.	NA	Shareholders	NA

Business: The groups principle activities include discovering, developing, in licensing and commercializing innovative anti infective products. The group operates from United States.

Primary SIC and add'l.: 2834

CIK No: 0001180145

Officers: Kenneth J. Collins/Co - Founder, Dir., CEO, Pres., Roger M. Echols/Chief Medical Officer, Nebojsa Janjic/Co - Founder, Chief Scientific Officer, Sec., Peter W. Letendre/Chief Commercial Officer, Donald J. Morrissey/Sr. VP - Corporate Development, Mark L. Smith/CFO, Treasurer, Jill B. Clark/Exec. Dir. - Human Resources, Administration

Directors: Kenneth J. Collins/Co - Founder, Dir., CEO, Pres., Nebojsa Janjic/Co - Founder, Chief Scientific Officer, Sec., Kirk K. Calhoun/Dir., Ralph Christoffersen/Dir., Geoffrey Duyk/Dir., Christopher D. Earl/Dir., Augustine Lawlor/Dir., Daniel J. Mitchell/Dir., Henry Wendt/Dir., Edward Brown/Dir.

Owners: Daniel J. Mitchell, Roger M. Echols, OZ Master Fund, Ltd., HealthCare Ventures VI, L.P., Morgenthaler Partners VII, L.P., D. E. Shaw Meniscus Portfolios, L.L.C., Kenneth J. Collins, TPG Biotechnology Partners, L.P. and its affiliates, Duquesne Capital Management LLC and its affiliates, Kirk K. Calhoun, Peter W. Letendre, Ralph E. Christoffersen, Sequel Limited Partnership III and its affiliates, Mark Smith, Perseus-Soros BioPharmaceutical Fund, LP *(20 Owners included in Index)*

Financial Data: Fiscal Year End: 12/31 Latest Annual Data: 12/31/2006

Year	Sales	Net Income
2006	$15,988,000	-$29,249,000
2005	$441,000	-$33,669,000
2004	$834,000	-$19,239,000

Curr. Assets:	$132,280,000	Curr. Liab.:	$64,133,000		
Plant, Equip.:	$3,170,000	Total Liab.:	$64,189,000	Indic. Yr. Divd.:	NA
Total Assets:	$135,561,000	Net Worth:	$71,372,000	Debt/ Equity:	NA

Repligen Corp

41 Seyon St., Bldg. 1, Ste. 100, Waltham, MA, 02453; *PH:* 1-781-250-0111; *Fax:* 1-781-250-0115; *http://* www.repligen.com; *Email:* info@repligen.com

General - Incorporation	DE	Stock - Price on:12/24/2007	$3.74
Employees	45	Stock Exchange	NDQ
Auditor	Ernst & Young LLP	Ticker Symbol	RGEN
Stk Agt	American Stock Transfer & Trust Co.	Outstanding Shares	30,480,000
Counsel	Testa, Hurwitz & Thibeault	E.P.S.	-$0.03
DUNS No.	01-330-8119	Shareholders	NA

Business: The group's principal activity is to develop therapeutic products for debilitating pediatric diseases. The major products of the group include secretin for autism, ctla4-ig for stem cell transportation and uridine for mitochondrial diseases. These products are synthetic forms of naturally occurring substances that may correct improperly regulated biological processes with minimal toxicity or side effects. The customers of the group include chromatography, diagnostics, biopharmaceutical companies and laboratory researchers.

Primary SIC and add'l.: 2834 2836 8731

CIK No: 0000730272

Officers: Walter C. Herlihy/Dir., CEO, Pres./$540,353.00, James R. Rusche/Sr. VP - Research, Development/$321,252.00, Daniel P. Witt/VP - Operations/$269,027.00, Daniel W. Muehl/45/CFO, Sec./$369,163.00, Laura Whitehouse Pew/VP - Marketing Development, Melissa M. Payer/Sales, Marketing Associate

Directors: Walter C. Herlihy/Dir., CEO, Pres., Alexander Rich/83/Co - Founder, Co - Chmn., Paul Schimmel/67/Co - Founder, Co - Chmn., Thomas F. Ryan/Dir., Karen A. Dawes/Dir., Robert J. Hennessey/Dir.

Owners: Thomas F. Ryan, Insiders/9.39%, Paul Schimmel/2.55%, Robert J. Hennessey, James R. Rusche, Ronald L. Chez/5.14%, Alexander Rich/1.75%, Daniel P. Witt, Xmark Opportunity Partners, LLC/5.50%, BVF Inc./6.69%, Walter C. Herlihy/2.60%, Karen Dawes, Daniel W. Muehl

Financial Data: Fiscal Year End: 03/31 Latest Annual Data: 3/31/2007

Year	Sales	Net Income
2007	$14,074,000	-$889,000
2006	$12,911,000	$697,000
2005	$9,360,000	-$2,984,000

Curr. Assets:	$25,731,000	Curr. Liab.:	$3,337,000		
Plant, Equip.:	$3,145,000	Total Liab.:	$3,537,000	Indic. Yr. Divd.:	NA
Total Assets:	$29,076,000	Net Worth:	$25,538,000	Debt/ Equity:	NA

Repro Med Systems Inc

24 Carpenter Rd., Chester, NY, 10918; *PH:* 1-845-469-2042; *Fax:* 1-845-469-5518; *http://* www.repro-med.com; *Email:* info@repro-med.com

General - Incorporation	NY	Stock - Price on:12/24/2007	$0.13
Employees	20	Stock Exchange	OTC
Auditor	Meyler & Co. LLC	Ticker Symbol	REPR
Stk Agt	Continental Stock Transfer & Trust Co	Outstanding Shares	28,760,000
Counsel	NA	E.P.S.	-$0.01
DUNS No.	04-840-3299	Shareholders	NA

Business: The group's principle activities include designing and manufacturing medical devices. The company's product mixes include emergency medical products, contract manufacturing, infusion therapy, gynecological instruments and male impotency treatment. Emergency medical products consists of res-q-vac hand powered emergency suction pump and plus reusable silicone resuscitators. Contract manufacturing develops portable, hand-operated suction pump. The infusion systems group includes freedom60 syringe infusion pump for ambulatory infusions. Gynecological instruments include the masterson endometrial biopsy kit and the thermal cautery system. The company markets the restore kit, including pro-long constriction rings for the treatment of impotency. The group operates from United States.

Primary SIC and add'l.: 3841 3845

CIK No: 0000704440

Subsidiaries: Repro-Med Europe

Officers: Andrew Sealfon/Co - Founder, Chmn., CEO, Pres., Principal Financial Officer

Directors: Andrew Sealfon/Co - Founder, Chmn., CEO, Pres., Principal Financial Officer, Ray Spagnoli/Dir., Remo Spagnoli/78/Dir.

Owners: Nathan Blumberg/1.00%, Paul Mark Baker/4.00%, Andrew I. Sealfon/20.00%, Remo Spagnoli/6.00%

Financial Data: Fiscal Year End: 02/28 Latest Annual Data: 2/28/2007

Year	Sales	Net Income
2007	$1,735,000	-$255,000
2006	$1,746,000	-$218,000
2005	$1,560,000	-$401,000

Curr. Assets:	$814,000	Curr. Liab.:	$659,000		
Plant, Equip.:	$221,000	Total Liab.:	$1,784,000	Indic. Yr. Divd.:	NA
Total Assets:	$1,138,000	Net Worth:	-$646,000	Debt/ Equity:	NA

Repros Therapeutics Inc

Formerly: Zonagen Inc

2408 Timberloch Pl, Ste. b-7, The Woodlands, TX, 77380; *PH:* 1-281-719-3400; *http://* www.reprosrx.com

General - Incorporation	DE	Stock - Price on:12/24/2007	$13.04
Employees	8	Stock Exchange	NDQ
Auditor	PricewaterhouseCoopers LLP	Ticker Symbol	RPRX
Stk Agt	Computershare Trust Co	Outstanding Shares	12,770,000
Counsel	Andrews & Kurch LLP	E.P.S.	-$1.34
DUNS No.	61-298-9426	Shareholders	NA

Business: The group's principal activity is to develop pharmaceutical products for the reproductive system, including sexual dysfunction, vaccine adjuvants, fertility and female health as well as urological applications, specifically prostate cancer. The major products are vasomax(R), vasofem(tm), bimexes(tm) and erxin(tm). Vasomax(R) is a disintegrating oral formulation of phentolamine for the treatment of med. Vasofem(tm) is being developed by the group to treat female sexual dysfunction (fsd). Bimexes(tm) is a second generation, multi-component oral therapy for med that acts on multiple physiological pathways. The sexual dysfunction products incorporate phentolamine, an alpha-adrenergic blocker, as the active agent. Erxin(tm) is a multi-component injection therapy, which includes phentolamine.

Primary SIC and add'l.: 8731 2834

CIK No: 0000897075

Officers: Joseph S. Podolski/60/Dir., CEO, Pres./$459,649.00, Louis Ploth/54/Dir., VP - Business Development, CFO, Sec./$283,847.00, Ronald Wiehle/59/VP - Research, Development

Directors: Joseph S. Podolski/60/Dir., CEO, Pres., Daniel F. Cain/62/Chmn., David Poorvin/61/Dir., Jean L. Fourcroy/78/Dir., Jeffrey R. Harder/Dir., Louis Ploth/54/Dir., VP - Business Development, CFO, Sec., Nola Masterson/61/Dir.

Owners: David Poorvin, Joseph S. Podolski/3.70%, Efficacy Biotech Master Fund Ltd/7.90%, Jean L. Fourcroy, Andre van As, Louis Ploth/2.30%, Jeffrey R. Harder, Insiders/7.60%, Daniel F. Cain, Nola E. Masterson

Financial Data: Fiscal Year End: 12/31 Latest Annual Data: 12/31/2006

Year	Sales	Net Income
2006	$596,000	-$14,195,000
2005	$634,000	-$7,391,000
2004	$257,000	-$3,697,000

Curr. Assets:	$6,961,000	Curr. Liab.:	$4,059,000		
Plant, Equip.:	$65,000	Total Liab.:	$4,059,000	Indic. Yr. Divd.:	NA
Total Assets:	$7,849,000	Net Worth:	$3,790,000	Debt/ Equity:	NA

Repsol YPF

Pasco De La Castellana 278-280, Madrid, 28046; *PH:* 212-450-4950; *http://* www.repsolypf.com

General - Incorporation	Spain	Stock - Price on:12/24/2007	$38.63
Employees	36,931	Stock Exchange	NYSE
Auditor	PricewaterhouseCoopers LLP	Ticker Symbol	REP
Stk Agt	Bank of New York	Outstanding Shares	1,220,000,000
Counsel	King & Spalding LLP	E.P.S.	NA
DUNS No.	46-221-3091	Shareholders	NA

Business: The group's principal activities are the exploration, development and production of crude oil and natural gas. It's activities include the transport of petroleum products, liquefied petroleum gas (lpg) and natural gas; petroleum refining; production of a wide range of petrochemicals and marketing of petroleum products, petroleum derivatives, petrochemicals, lpg and natural gas.

Primary SIC and add'l.: 1311 2911 5541 1321 4924 5169 5984

CIK No: 0000847838

Subsidiaries: A&C Pipeline Holding, A.I.E. Ciudad Sanitaria Vall d Hebrn, Adicor, S.A., Adm. Servicios Energa Mxico, S.A. de CV, AECS Hospital Bellvitge AIE, AECS Hospital Trias i Pujol AIE, AESA Construcciones y Servicios, AESA Construcciones y Servicios Bolivia, Agragas, S.P.A., Air Miles Espaa, S.A., Alberto Pasqualini REFAP, S.A., Aplicaciones y Proyectos energticos, S.A., Argentine Private Development Company (APDC), Asfalnor, S.A., Asfaltos Espaoles, S.A. 335 Subsidiaries included in the Index

Officers: Antonio Brufau Niubo/60/Chmn., CEO, Jaume Giro Ribas/44/Group MD, ED - Communication, Head - Chmn.s Office, Enrique Locutura/Group MD, ED - LNG, Pedro Fernandez Frial/Trustee, Group MD, ED - Downstream, Jorge Segrelles Garcia/MD, Fernando Ramirez Mazarredo/Group MD, ED - Finance, Corporate Services, Miguel Martinez San Martin/Group MD, COO, Cristina Sanz Mendiola/Group MD, ED - Corporate Resources, Alejandro Plaza Mayor/Dir. - Investor Relations, Laura Rejon/Front Office Mgr., Investor Relations Officer, Vidal Larrad Cuadrillero/Mgr. - Back Office, Investor Relations Officer, Teresa Gil Aldea/Investor Relations Officer, Clara Velasco Alvarez/Investor Relations Officer, Amalio Graino Bertrand/GM - Madrid, Francisco J. Garcia/Dir. - Crude, Madrid *(34 Officers included in Index)*

Directors: Antonio Brufau Niubo/60/Chmn., CEO, Alfonso Ballestero Aguilar/Chmn. - Madrid, Jorge Mercader Miro/65/Vice Chmn., Luis Fernando Del Rivero Asensio/59/Vice Chmn., Luis Carlos Croissier Batista/58/Dir., Luis Suarez De Lezo Mantilla/57/Group MD, ED - Legal Affairs, Sec., Enrique Helguera De La Villa/Dir., Trustee, Sec., Angel Durandez Adeva/65/Dir., Jose Manuel Loureda Mantinan/69/Dir., Manuel Raventos Negra/61/Dir., Angel Castineira Fernandez/Trustee, Antonio Hernandez-gil Alvarez-Cienfuegos/55/Dir., Carmelo De Las Morenas Lopez/68/Dir., Luis Suarez D. Mantilla/General Counsel, Sec., Pedro Fernandez Frial/Trustee, Group MD, ED - Downstream *(20 Directors included in Index)*

Owners: Jos Manuel Loureda Mantin/0.00%, Luis Surez de Lezo Mantilla, Henri Philippe Reichstul, Paulina Beato Blanco, Manuel Ravents Negra, PEMEX Internacional Espaa, S.A., Javier Echenique Landiribar/0.00%, Luis Fernando Del Rivero Asensio, Juan Abell Gallo/0.01%, Artur Carulla Font, Jorge Mercader Mir, La Caixa/9.10%, Carmelo de las Morenas Lpez/0.00%, Antonio Brufau Niub/0.00%, Sacyr Vallehermoso/20.01%

Financial Data: Fiscal Year End: 12/31 Latest Annual Data: 12/31/2006

Year	Sales	Net Income
2006	$72,722,124,000	$3,923,932,000
2005	$60,457,698,000	$3,388,568,000
2004	$56,880,472,000	$2,651,029,000

Curr. Assets:	$18,369,334,000	Curr. Liab.:	$13,302,023,000		
Plant, Equip.:	$31,254,142,000	Total Liab.:	$36,709,621,000	Indic. Yr. Divd.:	NA
Total Assets:	$61,098,203,000	Net Worth:	$24,388,582,000	Debt/ Equity:	NA

Republic Airways Holdings Inc

8909 Purdue Rd., Ste. 300, Indianapolis, IN, 46268; ***PH:*** 1-317-484-6000; ***Fax:*** 1-317-484-6040; ***http://*** www.republicairways.com; ***Email:*** marketing@rjet.com

General - Incorporation .... DE
Employees 3,700
Auditor .... Deloitte & Touche LLP
Stk Agt...... American Stock Transfer & Trust Co.
Counsel .... NA
DUNS No. .... NA

Stock- Price on:12/24/2007 .... $21.25
Stock Exchange .... NDQ
Ticker Symbol .... RJET
Outstanding Shares 41,330,000
E.P.S $1.85
Shareholders .... NA

Business: The group's principle activity is to opertate scheduled passenger airline. It's a holding company that operates chautauqua airlines inc and republic airline inc. The chautauqua is a regional airline offering, as of Mar 31, 2004, scheduled passenger service on approxilately 525 flights daily to 64 cities in 27 states, Canada and the bahamas pursuant to code-share agreements with amr corp, the parent of American airlines, us airways, inc and delta air lines inc. The group operates from United States.

Primary SIC and add'l.: NA

CIK No: 0001159154

Subsidiaries: Chautauqua Airlines, Inc, Republic Airline Inc., Shuttle America Corporation

Officers: Bryan Bedford/Chmn., CEO, Pres./$1,262,440.00, Lars-Eric Arnell/VP - Corporate Development, Warren Wilkinson/VP - Government Affairs, Corporate Communications, Hal Cooper/Exec. VP, CFO, Treasurer, Sec., Jerry Balsano/VP - Customer Service, Donald Olvey/VP - Safety, Jeffrey Jones/VP - Marketing Planning, Development, Wayne C. Heller/Dir., Exec. VP, COO/$764,738.00, Beth Taylor/VP, Controller, Timothy Dooley/VP - Financial Planning, Analysis, Jeff Domrese/VP - Maintenance, Technical Operations, Thomas Duffy/VP - Technical Services, Paul Kinstedt/VP - Systems Operations Control

Directors: Bryan Bedford/Chmn., CEO, Pres., Wayne C. Heller/Dir., Exec. VP, COO, Joseph M. Jacobs/Dir., Douglas J. Lambert/Dir., Jay L. Maymudes/Dir., Robert H. Cooper/Dir., Arthur H. Amron/Dir., Mark E. Landesman/Dir., Mark L. Plaumann/Dir., Lawrence J. Cohen/Dir., Charles E. Davidson/Dir.

Owners: Mark L. Plaumann, Orbis Investment Management Limited Orbis Asset Management Limited, Wexford Capital LLC, Robert H. Cooper, Lawrence J. Cohen, Jay L. Maymudes, Yale M. Fergang, Douglas J. Lambert, WexAir LLC, Joseph M. Jacobs, Insiders, Charles E. Davidson, Dimensional Fund Advisors LP, Wayne C. Heller, Mark E. Landesman *(20 Owners included in Index)*

Financial Data: ***Fiscal Year End:***12/31 ***Latest Annual Data:*** 12/31/2006

Year	Sales	Net Income
2006	$1,143,078,000	$79,510,000
2005	$905,021,000	$60,654,000
2004	$646,324,000	$38,852,000

Curr. Assets:	$263,104,000	***Curr. Liab.:***	$203,045,000		
Plant, Equip.:	$1,889,717,000	***Total Liab.:***	$1,849,612,000	***Indic. Yr. Divd.:***	NA
Total Assets:	$2,358,441,000	***Net Worth:***	$508,829,000	***Debt/ Equity:***	3.4676

Republic Bancorp Inc/KY

601 W Market St., Louisville, KY, 40202; ***PH:*** 1-502-584-3600; ***Fax:*** 1-502-584-3753; ***http://*** www.republicbank.com; ***Email:*** info@republicbank.com

General - Incorporation .... KY
Employees 722
Auditor .... Crowe Chizek & Co. LLC
Stk Agt..... Computershare Investor Services LLC
Counsel .... NA
DUNS No. 02-665-7296

Stock- Price on:12/24/2007 .... $16.84
Stock Exchange .... NDQ
Ticker Symbol .... NA
Outstanding Shares .... NA
E.P.S $1.27
Shareholders .... NA

Business: The group's principle activities are to accept deposits and originate loans to individuals and businesses. The group provides commercial banking services through 26 centers in north central and central Kentucky through its principal subsidiaries namely republic bank & trust company and republic bank & trust company of Indiana. The group accepts checking, savings, money market certificate of deposits, individual retirement accounts and other time deposit accounts. The group also originates residential, commercial and construction real estate loans, commercial loans, consumer loans and home equity loans. Apart from all these, the group also provides services such as investment management, trust services, life, long term care and title insurance sales, item processing and other financial services.

Primary SIC and add'l.: 6022 6712

CIK No: 0000921557

Subsidiaries: Republic Bancorp Capital Trust, Republic Bank & Trust Company, Republic Bank & Trust Company of Indiana, Republic Capital LLC, Republic Invest Co.

Officers: Steven Trager/Dir., CEO, Pres./$456,904.00, Gary Pierce/VP, COO - Republic Bank, Trust Company, Kevin Sipes/CFO, Exec. VP/$420,042.00, David Vest/48/Exec. VP, Chief Lending Officer, Chief Deposit Officer/$443,295.00, Pam Liddle/Banking Center Supervisor, Julie Bombik/Banking Center Supervisor, Justin Duell/Business Banking Officer, Val Claycomb/Banking Center Mgr. - Republic Bank, Trust Company, Robin Shadrick/Banking Center Supervisor - Republic Bank, Trust Company, Chris Rooks/Banking Center Supervisor - Republic Bank, Trust Company, Julie Moore/Banking Center Mgr. - Republic Bank, Trust Company, Freda Wilson/Banking Center Supervisor - Republic Bank, Trust Company, Aaron Geiser/Banking Center Supervisor - Republic Bank, Trust Company, Denice Leamer/Banking Center Supervisor - Republic Bank, Trust Company, Scott Smith/VP, Business Lending Mgr. - Republic Bank, Trust Company *(102 Officers included in Index)*

Directors: Steven Trager/Dir., CEO, Pres., Bernard M. Trager/Founder, Chmn., Scott A. Trager/55/Vice Chmn., Susan Stout Tamme/Dir., Michael T. Rust/Dir., Charles E. Anderson/Dir., Pres., Henry M. Altman/71/Dir., Sandra Metts Snowden/62/Dir., Wayne R. Stratton/60/Dir.

Owners: Henry M. Altman, Charles E. Anderson, Scott A. Trager, Jaytee Properties, Kevin Sipes, Sheldon Gilman, Jaytee Properties, Steven E. Trager, Bernard M. Trager, Kevin Sipes, Michael T. Rust, Bernard M. Trager, Susan Stout Tamme, Insiders, Sheldon Gilman *(25 Owners included in Index)*

Financial Data: ***Fiscal Year End:***12/31 ***Latest Annual Data:*** 12/31/2006

Year	Sales	Net Income
2006	$208,240,000	$28,351,000
2005	$186,122,000	$35,065,000
2004	$159,560,000	$32,501,000

Curr. Assets:	$81,613,000	***Curr. Liab.:***	$2,741,180,000	***P/E Ratio:***	13.26
Plant, Equip.:	$36,560,000	***Total Liab.:***	$2,809,439,000	***Indic. Yr. Divd.:***	$0.440
Total Assets:	$3,046,787,000	***Net Worth:***	$237,348,000	***Debt/ Equity:***	0.1687

Republic First Bancorp Inc

Two Liberty, 50 S 16th St., Ste. 2400, Philadelphia, PA, 19102; ***PH:*** 1-215-735-4422; ***Fax:*** 1-215-735-0508; ***http://*** www.rfbkonline.com

General - Incorporation .... PA
Employees 147
Auditor .... Beard Miller Co. LLP
Stk Agt .... NA
Counsel .... NA
DUNS No. 36-445-6731

Stock- Price on:12/24/2007 .... $9.8
Stock Exchange .... NDQ
Ticker Symbol .... FRBK
Outstanding Shares 10,450,000
E.P.S $0.84
Shareholders .... NA

Business: The group's principal activities are to provide banking services including credit and depositary services. The group operates through its two wholly owned subsidiaries, republic first bank and first bank of Delaware. The lending products of the group include commercial, real estate, construction loans, automobiles loans, home improvement loans, mortgages, home equity and consumer loans. The group accepts time, demand, and money market accounts and savings deposits. The group operates throughout the greater philadelphia and Delaware area through its offices and branches in philadelphia, montgomery counties and new castle county.

Primary SIC and add'l.: 6712 6022

CIK No: 0000834285

Subsidiaries: Republic First Bank

Officers: Harry D. Madonna/Chmn., CEO/$716,641.00, Denise Tinney/Corp. Sec., Louis J. Decesare/Dir., Pres./$391,952.00, Paul Frenkiel/CFO, Exec. VP/$148,516.00, Paul A. Verdi/45/Exec. VP, Chief Retail Banking Officer, Randy McGarry/COO, Exec. VP/$163,369.00

Directors: Harry D. Madonna/Chmn., CEO, Robert J. Coleman/Dir., Lyle W. Hall/Dir., Harris Wildstein/Dir., William W. Batoff/Dir., Louis J. Decesare/Dir., Pres., Neal I. Rodin/Dir., Steven J. Shotz/Dir., Barry L. Spevak/Dir.

Owners: Harris Wildstein/7.00%, Louis J. DeCesare, Paul A. Verdi, Lyle W. Hall, Randy McGarry, Robert J. Coleman/1.50%, Paul Frenkiel/1.00%, Insiders/23.60%, Harry D. Madonna/6.50%, Neal I. Rodin/1.80%, Barry L. Spevak, William W. Batoff/1.30%, Steven J. Shotz/3.80%

Financial Data: ***Fiscal Year End:***12/31 ***Latest Annual Data:*** 12/31/2006

Year	Sales	Net Income
2006	$66,385,000	$10,118,000
2005	$48,995,000	$8,893,000
2004	$49,924,000	$8,940,000

Curr. Assets:	$88,497,000	***Curr. Liab.:***	$919,720,000	***P/E Ratio:***	11.67
Plant, Equip.:	$6,220,000	***Total Liab.:***	$934,090,000	***Indic. Yr. Divd.:***	NA
Total Assets:	$1,008,824,000	***Net Worth:***	$74,734,000	***Debt/ Equity:***	0.0827

Republic Property Trust

13861 Sunrise Valley Dr., Ste. 410, Herndon, VA, 20171; ***PH:*** 1-703-880-2900; ***http://*** www.republicpropertytrust.com

General - Incorporation .... MD
Employees 76
Auditor .... Ernst & Young LLP
Stk Agt .... LaSalle Bank N.A
Counsel .... NA
DUNS No. .... NA

Stock- Price on:12/24/2007 .... $12.37
Stock Exchange .... NYSE
Ticker Symbol .... RPB
Outstanding Shares 26,090,000
E.P.S .... NA
Shareholders .... NA

Business: The group's principle activities include owning, operating, acquiring and developing Class A office properties. In the 2007, the group acquired 127,000 square foot office property. The group operates from the United States.

Primary SIC and add'l.: 6798

CIK No: 0001335686

Subsidiaries: Presidents Park I LLC, Presidents Park II LLC, Presidents Park III LLC, Republic WPB LLC, Republic 20th Street LLC, Republic Park LLC, Republic Property Limited Partnership, Republic Property TRS, LLC, RKB Corporate Oaks LLC, RKB CP IV LLC, RKB Dulles Tech LLC, RKB Lakeside LLC, RKB Lakeside Manager LLC, RKB Pender LLC, RKB Willowwood LLC 23 Subsidiaries included in the Index

Officers: Mark R. Keller/CEO - Trustee, Michael J. Green/CFO, Exec. VP

Directors: Mark R. Keller/CEO - Trustee, Richard L. Kramer/Chmn., Steven A. Grigg/Trustee, John S. Chalsty/Trustee, Gregory H. Leisch/Trustee, Ronald D. Paul/Trustee, Ronald J. Kramer/Trustee

Owners: Wesley Capital Management, LLC/8.40%, Ronald J. Kramer, Gary R. Siegel/2.20%, Ronald D. Paul, High Rise Capital Advisors, L.L.C/8.60%, Michael C. Jones, Nuveen Asset Management/7.60%, Security Capital Research& Management Incorporated/15.30%, Insiders/13.50%, Mark R. Keller/1.20%, Gregory H. Leisch, Michael J. Green, Davidson Kempner Capital Management LLC/5.00%, Peter J. Cole, Steven A. Grigg *(17 Owners included in Index)*

Curr. Assets:	$21,331,000	***Curr. Liab.:***	$10,728,000		
Plant, Equip.:	$551,752,000	***Total Liab.:***	$384,152,000	***Indic. Yr. Divd.:***	NA
Total Assets:	$596,468,000	***Net Worth:***	$186,813,000	***Debt/ Equity:***	NA

Republic Services Inc

110 SE 6th St., 28th Fl., Fort Lauderdale, FL, 33301; ***PH:*** 1-954-769-2400; ***Fax:*** 1-954-769-2664; ***http://*** www.republicservices.com

General - Incorporation .... DE
Employees 13,000
Auditor .... Ernst & Young LLP
Stk Agt .... Wachovia Bank N.A
Counsel .... NA
DUNS No. 02-013-8298

Stock- Price on:12/24/2007 .... $30.8
Stock Exchange .... NYSE
Ticker Symbol .... RSG
Outstanding Shares 193,570,000
E.P.S $1.40
Shareholders .... NA

Business: The group's principle activity is to provide services in the domestic non-hazardous solid waste industry. Customers served by the group include commercial, industrial, municipal and residential customers. The group operates from United States.

Primary SIC and add'l.: 4953 4212

CIK No: 0001060391

Subsidiaries: 623 Landfill, Inc., A-Best Disposal, Inc., Ace Disposal Services, Inc., ADAJ Corporation, Anderson Refuse Co., Inc., Anderson Solid Waste, Inc., Arc Disposal Company, Inc., Ariana, LLC, Astro Waste Services, Inc., Atlas Transport, Inc., Barker Brothers Waste Incorporated, Barker Brothers, Inc., Bay Collection Services, Inc., Bay Environmental Management, Inc., Bay Landfills, Inc. 155 Subsidiaries included in the Index

Officers: James E. O'Connor/Chmn., CEO/$5,341,147.00, Jerry S. Clark/VP, Controller, Tim Benter/VP, Assoc. General Counsel, Tom Miller/Regional VP - Southwest Region, Edward A. Lang/VP - Finance, Treasurer, Kenneth M. Baylor/VP - Employee, Labor Relations, Will Flower/VP - Communications, Matthew E. Davies/VP - Environmental Engineering, Compliance, Andy Gray/Mgr. - Corporate Accounting, Nancy Bretas/Mgr. - Corporate Communications, Bill Halnon/CIO, VP, Bob Shepard/Regional VP - Southern Region, Craig J. Nichols/VP - Human Resources, Michael J. Cordesman/COO, Pres./$2,529,472.00, Brian A. Bales/VP - Corporate Development *(25 Officers included in Index)*

Directors: James E. O'Connor/Chmn., CEO, Harris W. Hudson/64/Vice Chmn., Ramon A. Rodriguez/Dir., Michael W. Wickham/Dir., Lee W. Nutter/Dir., John W. Croghan/Dir., Allan C. Sorensen/Dir.

Owners: Tod C. Holmes, Michael W. Wickham, James E. OConnor, Allan C. Sorensen, Michael J. Cordesman, Ramon A. Rodriguez, Cascade Investment, L.L.C/14.10%, John W. Croghan, Insiders, Lee W. Nutter, David A. Barclay, Harris W. Hudson

Financial Data: Fiscal Year End:12/31 Latest Annual Data: 12/31/2006

Year	Sales	Net Income
2006	$3,070,600,000	$279,600,000
2005	$2,863,900,000	$253,700,000
2004	$2,708,100,000	$237,900,000

Curr. Assets:	$393,400,000	Curr. Liab.:	$602,200,000	P/E Ratio:	21.39
Plant, Equip.:	$2,163,800,000	Total Liab.:	$3,007,300,000	Indic. Yr. Divd.:	$0.680
Total Assets:	$4,429,400,000	Net Worth:	$1,422,100,000	Debt/ Equity:	1.1064

ResCare Inc

9901 Linn Sta. Rd., Louisville, KY, 40223; *PH:* 1-502-394-2100; *Fax:* 1-502-394-2206; *http://* www.rescare.com

General - Incorporation	KY	**Stock** - Price on:12/24/2007	$19.83
Employees	37,000	Stock Exchange	NDQ
Auditor	KPMG LLP	Ticker Symbol	RSCR
Stk Agt	National City Bank	Outstanding Shares	28,630,000
Counsel	NA	E.P.S.	$1.20
DUNS No.	07-022-6105	Shareholders	NA

Business: The group's principal activities are to provide residential, therapeutic, job training, educational and support services to populations with special needs, including persons with developmental and other disabilities to youth with special needs and to adults who are experiencing barriers to employment. The group has three reportable operating segments: disabilities services, youth services and training services. The disabilities service segment provides services to individuals with mental retardation or other developmental disabilities. The youth services segment addresses the specific needs of at-risk and troubled youths to enable each youth to be a more productive member of the community. The training services segments provides educational and vocational skills training, to enable disadvantaged youths to become responsible working adults.

Primary SIC and add'l.: 8331 8361 8052

CIK No: 0000776325

Subsidiaries: Alternative Youth Services, Inc., Arbor E&T, LLC, Capital TX Investments, Inc., CATX Properties, Inc., CNC/Access, Inc., Community Advantage, Inc., Community Alternatives Illinois, Inc., Community Alternatives Indiana, Inc., Community Alternatives Kentucky, Inc., Community Alternatives Missouri, Inc., Community Alternatives Nebraska, Inc., Community Alternatives Texas Partner, Inc., Community Alternatives Virginia, Inc., Creative Networks, LLC, Normal Life, Inc. 37 Subsidiaries included in the Index

Officers: Ralph G. Gronefeld/49/CEO, Pres./$2,193,015.00, David W. Miles/CFO/$468,323.00, Katherine W. Gilchrist/55/Public Accountant/$421,257.00, Vincent Doran/Pres. - Employment, Training Services Group/$574,385.00, Paul G. Dunn/Pres. - Rescares Arbor E, T Operations/$608,055.00, David S. Waskey/General Counsel, Chief Compliance Officer, Nina P. Seigle/Chief People Officer, Nel Taylor/Chief Communications Officer, Julie Caldwell/Dir. - Human Resources, Barbara Winters/VP - Northern Region, Bob Bond/Sr. Regional Dir., George Watts/CIO, Michael J. Reibel/Sr. VP - Support Services, Richard Tinsley/Chief Development Officer, Kelley Abell/Chief Government Relations Officer *(25 Officers included in Index)*

Directors: Ronald G. Geary/Chmn., Jay Naeem/Exec. Dir., Julie Roberts/Exec. Dir., Geoff Harris/Exec. Dir., Halsey E. Sandford/Dir., Olivia F. Kirtley/Dir., Steven S. Reed/Dir., William E. Brock/Dir., David Braddock/Dir., Robert E. Hallagan/Dir., Robert M. Le Blanc/Dir., Shane McFall/Exec. Dir., Dave Folkner/Exec. Dir., Cindy Buckler/Exec. Dir., John Walburn/Exec. Dir.

Owners: FMR Corporation/12.00%, Vincent F. Doran, Dimensional Fund Advisors LP/5.30%, Insiders/3.10%, David W. Miles, William E. Brock, David Braddock, Steven S. Reed, Ronald G. Geary/1.60%, Onex Corporation/25.50%, Bank of America Corporation/12.60%, Paul G. Dunn, Amalgamated Gadget, L.P./5.90%, Katherine W. Gilchrist, Robert E. Hallagan *(19 Owners included in Index)*

Financial Data: Fiscal Year End:12/31 Latest Annual Data: 12/31/2006

Year	Sales	Net Income
2006	$1,302,118,000	$36,696,000
2005	$1,088,770,000	$21,222,000
2004	$1,009,016,000	$21,507,000

Curr. Assets:	$236,291,000	Curr. Liab.:	$126,371,000	P/E Ratio:	16.53
Plant, Equip.:	$75,606,000	Total Liab.:	$374,418,000	Indic. Yr. Divd.:	NA
Total Assets:	$726,056,000	Net Worth:	$351,477,000	Debt/ Equity:	0.5808

Research Frontiers Inc

240 Crossways Pk. Dr., Woodbury, NY, 11797; *PH:* 1-516-364-1902; *Fax:* 1-516-364-3798; *http://* www.refr-spd.com; *Email:* info@smartglass.com

General - Incorporation	DE	**Stock** - Price on:12/24/2007	$13
Employees	11	Stock Exchange	NDQ
Auditor	BDO Seidman LLP	Ticker Symbol	REFR
Stk Agt	Continental Stock Transfer & Trust Co	Outstanding Shares	15,350,000
Counsel	Ostrolenk, Faber, Gerb & Soffen, LLP	E.P.S.	-$0.287
DUNS No.	00-291-1857	Shareholders	NA

Business: The group's principal activity is to develop and market technology and devices to control the flow of light. These devices are referred to as 'light valves' or suspended particle devices (SPDs). SPD technology is made by a flexible light-control film invented by RFI, allows the user to instantly and precisely control the shading of glass/plastic manually or automatically. The group's products includes spd-smart windows, sunshades, skylights, interior partitions for homes and buildings, automotive windows, sunroofs, sun-visors, sunshades, rear-view mirrors, instrument panels, navigation systems, aircraft windows, eyewear products and flat panel displays for electronic products. Spd-smart light control film is used in architectural, automotive, marine, aerospace, filmmakers and appliance applications. The group holds 438 patents and patent applications and 29 licensees through out the world.

Primary SIC and add'l.: 5065 3679 8731

CIK No: 0000793524

Subsidiaries: SPD Enterprises, Inc, SPD Inc., Taliq Corp

Officers: Robert L. Saxe/Chmn., CEO, Michael R. Lapointe/VP - Marketing, Joseph M. Harary/Dir., COO, Pres., General Counsel, Patricia A. Bryant/Mgr. - Investor Relations, Gregory M. Sottile/Dir. - Marketing Development

Directors: Robert L. Saxe/Chmn., CEO, Robert M. Budin/Dir., Victor F. Keen/Dir., Albert P. Malvino/Dir., Joseph M. Harary/Dir., COO, Pres., General Counsel

Owners: Michael R. LaPointe/0.83%, Robert M. Budin/1.62%, Victor F. Keen/2.44%, Albert P. Malvino/1.50%, Joseph M. Harary/3.05%, Insiders/15.97%, Robert L. Saxe/8.79%

Financial Data: Fiscal Year End:12/31 Latest Annual Data: 12/31/2006

Year	Sales	Net Income
2006	$163,000	-$3,304,000
2005	$139,000	-$3,748,000
2004	$201,000	-$4,263,000

Curr. Assets:	$3,126,000	Curr. Liab.:	$259,000		
Plant, Equip.:	$103,000	Total Liab.:	$259,000	Indic. Yr. Divd.:	NA
Total Assets:	$3,252,000	Net Worth:	$2,993,000	Debt/ Equity:	NA

Research In Motion Ltd

Research In Motion, 295 Phillip St., Waterloo, ON, 75039; *PH:* 1-972-650-6126; *Fax:* 1-972-650-2006; *http://* www.rim.net; *Email:* investor_relations@rim.com

General - Incorporation	ON	**Stock** - Price on:12/24/2007	$170.6
Employees	6,254	Stock Exchange	NDQ
Auditor	Ernst & Young LLP	Ticker Symbol	RIMM
Stk Agt	Computershare Investor Services LLC	Outstanding Shares	185,900,000
Counsel	NA	E.P.S.	$1.87
DUNS No.	NA	Shareholders	NA

Business: The group's principal activities are to design, manufacture and market innovative wireless solutions for the mobile communications market. The group provides seamless access to time-sensitive information including e-mail, messaging, Internet and intranet-based applications. The group's technology enables a broad array of third party developers and manufacturers in North America and around the world to enhance their products and services with wireless connectivity.

Primary SIC and add'l.: 3663 7379 3660

CIK No: 0001070235

Subsidiaries: Metals Co., Ltd., Neomax Co., Ltd, Research In Motion Corporation, Research In Motion UK Limited, RIM Finance, LLC, SYNNEX Corporation

Officers: James L. Balsillie/Co - CEO Research In Motion, Mike Lazaridis/Pres., Co - CEO, Larry Conlee/COO, Don Morrison/COO, Douglas E. Fregin/Dir., VP - Operations, Dennis Kavelman/CFO, David Werezak/VP - Enterprise Business Unit, Mark Guibert/VP - Corporate Marketing, Robin Bienfait/CIO, Brian Bidulka/Chief Accounting Officer

Directors: James Estill/Dir., Douglas Wright/Dir., Douglas E. Fregin/Dir., VP - Operations, John E. Richardson/Dir., Kendall Cork/Dir., Barbara Stymiest/Dir., John Wetmore/Dir.

Financial Data: Fiscal Year End:03/04 Latest Annual Data: 03/03/2007

Year	Sales	Net Income
2007	$3,037,103,000	$631,572,000
2006	$2,065,845,000	$382,078,000
2005	$1,350,447,000	$213,387,000

Curr. Assets:	$1,256,579,000	Curr. Liab.:	$278,680,000		
Plant, Equip.:	$326,313,000	Total Liab.:	$313,389,000	Indic. Yr. Divd.:	NA
Total Assets:	$2,312,156,000	Net Worth:	$1,998,767,000	Debt/ Equity:	NA

Reserve Petroleum Co

6801 N Brd.way Ste. 300, Oklahoma City, OK, 73116; *PH:* 1-405-848-7551

General - Incorporation	DE	**Stock** - Price on:12/24/2007	$200
Employees	8	Stock Exchange	OTC
Auditor	Murrell, Hall, McIntosh & Co., PLLP	Ticker Symbol	RSRV
Stk Agt	NA	Outstanding Shares	NA
Counsel	NA	E.P.S.	$28.49
DUNS No.	05-693-8822	Shareholders	NA

Business: The group's principle activities are the exploration and development of oil and natural gas properties. The company owns non-producing mineral interests located in the states of Oklahoma and Texas. The company sells its oil and gas on the spot market or has sales contracts that are based on the spot market price. The company also derives income from its investments in partnerships.

Primary SIC and add'l.: 1382

CIK No: 0000083350

Officers: Mason McLain/81/Chmn., Principal Executive Officer, Pres./$72,149.00, James L. Tyler/60/VP, Sec., Treasurer, Principal Financial, Accounting Officer, Kyle L. McLain/53/Dir., Mgr. - Production, Cameron R. McLain/49/Dir., Mgr. - Exploration, Robert T. McLain/78/Dir., VP

Directors: Mason McLain/81/Chmn., Principal Executive Officer, Pres., Robert T. McLain/78/Dir., VP, William M. Smith/49/Dir., Doug Fuller/50/Dir., Kyle L. McLain/53/Dir., Mgr. - Production, Cameron R. McLain/49/Dir., Mgr. - Exploration, Robert L. Savage/60/Dir., Marvin E. Harris/56/Dir.

Owners: Mason McLain/10.44%, Robert L. Savage/0.78%, Insiders/29.88%, Cameron R. McLain/3.95%, Kyle L. McLain/3.95%, Norma Moe/7.34%, Jerry L. Crow/3.30%, Robert T. McLain/7.46%

Financial Data: Fiscal Year End:12/31 Latest Annual Data: 12/31/2006

Year	Sales	Net Income
2006	$9,933,000	$4,275,000
2005	$8,523,000	$3,812,000
2004	$4,265,000	$1,749,000

Curr. Assets:	$11,754,000	**Curr. Liab.:**	$689,000	**P/E Ratio:**	7.02
Plant, Equip.:	$5,128,000	**Total Liab.:**	$1,521,000	**Indic. Yr. Divd.:**	$6.000
Total Assets:	$17,650,000	**Net Worth:**	$16,129,000	**Debt/ Equity:**	0.0131

Residential Capital Corp

8400 Normandale Lake Blvd, Ste. 250, Minneapolis, MN, 55437; ***PH:*** 1-952-857-8700; ***http://*** www.rescapholdings.com; ***Email:*** investorrelations@rescapholdings.com

General - Incorporation	DE	**Stock**- Price on:12/24/2007	NA
Employees	NA	Stock Exchange	NA
Auditor	PricewaterhouseCoopers LLP	Ticker Symbol	NA
Stk Agt	NA	Outstanding Shares	NA
Counsel	NA	E.P.S	NA
DUNS No.	NA	Shareholders	NA

Business: The group's principle activity is to provide residential mortgage services. The area of operation includes New York, New Jersey and Connecticut. The group specialize in financing for 1-4 family properties, co-ops, condos, and mixed use properties. Since the companies inception in 1987, it has established itself as a major participant in the mortgage industry. The group represents a host of lending institutions to ensure clients obtain the lowest possible rate and points for the specific loan of their choice. The company explains the subtleties of the various mortgage programs so that each client can make an educated, informed decision. The group pre-qualify each client prior to beginning the mortgage process. The group operates from United States.

Primary SIC and add'l.: 6162

CIK No: 0001332815

Subsidiaries: General Motors Acceptance Corporation, GMAC Mortgage Group, Inc., GMAC Residential Holding Corp., Gmac-rfc Holding Corp.

Officers: Bruce J. Paradis/CEO, Jim Jones/Dir., CEO, Ronald J. Kravit/Dir. - Managing Principal, Paul Bossidy/Dir. - Sr. Operating Consultant, Bill Casey/Treasurer, Luke Hayden/Sr. MD - Capital Markets, Residential Finance Group, James R. Giertz/Dir., CFO, Sanjiv Khattri/Dir., CFO, Linda Zukauckas/Dir., Controller, Chief Accounting Officer, Gregory B. Schultz/Pres. - Business Capital Group, Christopher J. Nordeen/Pres. - International Business Group, David A. Marple/General Counsel, Robert D. Isom/COO - Residential Finance Group, Residential Capital Corporation

Directors: Jim Jones/Dir., CEO, Michael E. Rossi/Chmn., Eric A. Feldstein/Chmn., Thomas Jacob/Dir., Thomas C. Melzer/Dir., Ronald J. Kravit/Dir. - Managing Principal, Paul Bossidy/Dir. - Sr. Operating Consultant, James R. Giertz/Dir., CFO, Sanjiv Khattri/Dir., CFO, David C. Walker/Dir., Linda Zukauckas/Dir., Controller, Chief Accounting Officer

Resin Systems Inc

400, 2421 - 37th Ave. NE, Calgary, AB, T2E 6Y7; ***PH:*** 1-403-219-8000; ***Fax:*** 1-403-219-8001; ***http://*** www.grouprsi.com

General - Incorporation	AB	**Stock**- Price on:12/24/2007	$1.48
Employees	NA	Stock Exchange	OTC
Auditor	KPMG LLP	Ticker Symbol	RSSYF
Stk Agt	Computershare Trust Co	Outstanding Shares	NA
Counsel	NA	E.P.S	NA
DUNS No.	NA	Shareholders	NA

Business: The groups principle activity is to develop composite products. The groups products include utility poles and roller tube. The group operates from Canada.

Primary SIC and add'l.: NA

CIK No: 0001130646

Subsidiaries: Resin Systems International Ltd

Officers: Paul Giannelia/Dir., CEO, Pres., Mark Warren/CTO, Robert Schaefer/CFO, Corp. Sec., Scott Terhune/Sr. VP - Production, Cheryl Fitzpatrick/Sr. VP - Sales, Marketing, Laurien Abel/Contact - Investor, Public Relationsinvestor, Public Relations

Directors: Wilmot Matthews/Chmn., David A. Williams/Dir., Dwayne Hunka/Dir., Zsolt Feketekuty/Dir., Brian Felesky/Dir., James Gray/Dir.

Financial Data: ***Fiscal Year End:***12/31 ***Latest Annual Data:*** 12/31/2006

Year	Sales	Net Income
2006	$4,060,000	-$35,836,000
2005	$910,000	-$17,552,000
2004	$304,000	-$11,682,000

Curr. Assets:	$4,003,000	**Curr. Liab.:**	$6,428,000		
Plant, Equip.:	$9,215,000	**Total Liab.:**	$21,483,000	**Indic. Yr. Divd.:**	NA
Total Assets:	$7,087,000	**Net Worth:**	-$14,395,000	**Debt/ Equity:**	NA

Resmed Inc

14040 Danielson St., Poway, CA, 92064; ***PH:*** 1-858-746-2438; ***Fax:*** 1-858-777-5677; ***http://*** www.resmed.com; ***Email:*** reception@resmed.com

General - Incorporation	DE	**Stock**- Price on:12/24/2007	$42.9
Employees	2,500	Stock Exchange	NYSE
Auditor	KPMG LLP	Ticker Symbol	RMD
Stk Agt	American Stock Transfer & Trust Co.	Outstanding Shares	77,840,000
Counsel	Latham & Watkins	E.P.S	$0.83
DUNS No.	75-114-9311	Shareholders	NA

Business: The group's principal activities are to develop, manufacture and distribute medical equipment. This equipment is used for the treatment, diagnosis and management of sleep disordered breathing or sdb. Sdb includes obstructive sleep apnea and other respiratory disorders that occur during sleep. The products of the group include flow generators, diagnostic products, mask systems, headgear and other accessories. The group operates in the United States, Australia, United Kingdom, France, Germany, Sweden, Switzerland and Singapore. The group acquired servo magnetics inc on 14-May-2002.

Primary SIC and add'l.: 6719 3841

CIK No: 0000943819

Subsidiaries: AudioCodes Argentina SA, AudioCodes Brasil Equipamentos de Voz sobre IP Ltda, AudioCodes Europe Limited, AudioCodes France SAS, AudioCodes Germany GmbH, AudioCodes Inc, AudioCodes India Private Limited, AudioCodes Korea Co. Ltd., AudioCodes National Inc., AudioCodes Russ Ltd, AudioCodes USA Inc, Hoefner Medizintechnik GmbH, MAP Beteiligungs GmbH, MAP Medische Techniek voor Arts en Patient BV, MAP Medizin-Technologie GmbH 48 Subsidiaries included in the Index

Officers: Peter C. Farrell/Chmn., CEO, Founder/$2,377,319.00, Hillary Theakston/Dir. - Investor Relations, Kieran T. Gallahue/Pres./$1,228,339.00, Keith Serzen/COO - Americas/$1,000,620.00, David Pendarvis/Sr. VP - Organizational Development/$826,997.00, Caroline Carr/VP - Global Customer Operations, Paul Eisen/Sr. VP - Asia Pacific, Brett A. Sandercock/41/CFO/$671,693.00, Robert Douglas/48/COO - Sydney, Lasse Beijer/COO - Europe

Directors: Peter C. Farrell/Chmn., CEO, Founder, Barry J. Make/Member - Medical Advisory Board, Nicholas Hill/Member - Medical Advisory Board, Gary W. Pace/Dir., Helmut Teschler/Member - Medical Advisory Board, Michael Coppola/Member - Medical Advisory Board, Anthony N. Demaria/Member - Medical Advisory Board, Michael A. Quinn/Dir., Richard Sulpizio/Dir., Neil J. Douglas/Member - Medical Advisory Board, Tucker B. Woodson/Member - Medical Advisory Board, Jonathan R.L. Schwartz/Member - Medical Advisory Board, Ralph Pascualy/Member - Medical Advisory Board, John Wareham/Dir., Terence M. Davidson/Mmeber - Medical Advisory Board *(19 Directors included in Index)*

Owners: Insiders/4.50%, Kieran Gallahue, T. Rowe Price Associates, Inc./7.30%, Donagh McCarthy, Keith Serzen, Peter C. Farrell/2.00%, Brett Sandercock, William Blair& Company LLC/5.30%, Ronald Taylor, Christopher G. Roberts, Gary W. Pace, Richard Sulpizio, Michael A. Quinn, John Wareham, David Pendarvis

Financial Data: ***Fiscal Year End:***06/30 ***Latest Annual Data:*** 6/30/2006

Year	Sales	Net Income
2006	$606,996,000	$88,211,000
2005	$425,505,000	$64,785,000
2004	$339,338,000	$57,284,000

Curr. Assets:	$510,284,000	**Curr. Liab.:**	$129,000,000	**P/E Ratio:**	50.47
Plant, Equip.:	$245,376,000	**Total Liab.:**	$269,073,000	**Indic. Yr. Divd.:**	NA
Total Assets:	$1,007,221,000	**Net Worth:**	$738,148,000	**Debt/ Equity:**	0.1098

Resolve Staffing Inc

3235 Omni Dr., Cincinnati, OH, 45245; ***PH:*** 1-513-943-4243; ***Fax:*** 1-513-943-4908; ***http://*** www.resolvestaffing.com; ***Email:*** ir@resolvestaffing.com

General - Incorporation	NV	**Stock**- Price on:12/24/2007	$1.15
Employees	10,000	Stock Exchange	OTC
Auditor	PKF	Ticker Symbol	RSFF
Stk Agt	Florida Atlantic Stock Transfer, Inc.	Outstanding Shares	NA
Counsel	NA	E.P.S	-$0.43
DUNS No.	NA	Shareholders	NA

Business: The group's principal activity is to provide human resource services focusing on the professional, clerical, administrative and light industrial staffing market in west central Florida. The group operates through its subsidiary integra. Integra recruits, trains and deploys temporary personnel and provides payroll administration to its clients providing its services to business in the manufacturing, distribution, hospitality, and construction industries. The group provides certain other services including screening, recruiting, training, workforce deployment, loss prevention and safety training, pre-employment testing and assessment, background searches, compensation program design, customized personnel management reports, job profiling, description, application, turnover tracking, analysis, drug testing policy administration, affirmative action plans, opinion surveys and follow-up analysis, exit interviews and follow-up analysis.

Primary SIC and add'l.: 7363 7361

CIK No: 0001106207

Subsidiaries: Integra Staffing, Inc

Officers: Ronald Heineman/50/Dir., CEO, Scott Horne/46/CFO, Steve Ludders/55/COO, Tom Lawry/46/Controller, Treasurer, Steve Roux/40/Exec. VP

Directors: Ronald Heineman/50/Dir., CEO, Donald E. Quarterman/39/Dir., William A. Brown/49/Dir., William Walton/72/Dir.

Owners: Scott Horne/1.60%, Bill Walton/20.72%, Ronald Heineman/41.38%, Steve Roux/1.60%, Steve Ludders/0.26%, Bill Brown/12.24%, Insiders/77.00%

Financial Data: ***Fiscal Year End:***12/31 ***Latest Annual Data:*** 03/31/2007

Year	Sales	Net Income
2007	NA	NA
2006	NA	NA
2005	NA	NA

Curr. Assets:	$19,462,000	**Curr. Liab.:**	$41,107,000		
Plant, Equip.:	$1,344,000	**Total Liab.:**	$57,432,000	**Indic. Yr. Divd.:**	NA
Total Assets:	$57,812,000	**Net Worth:**	$380,000	**Debt/ Equity:**	NA

Resource America Inc

712 Fifth Ave., 10th Fl., New York, NY, 10019; ***PH:*** 1-212-506-3870; ***Fax:*** 1-215-546-5388; ***http://*** www.resourceamerica.com

General - Incorporation	DE	**Stock**- Price on:12/24/2007	$24.11
Employees	224	Stock Exchange	NDQ
Auditor	Grant Thornton LLP	Ticker Symbol	REXI
Stk Agt	American Stock Transfer & Trust Co.	Outstanding Shares	17,610,000
Counsel	Michael Yecies	E.P.S	$0.23
DUNS No.	04-615-7046	Shareholders	NA

Business: The group's principal activity is to use industry specific expertise to generate and administer investment opportunities for itself and for outside investors in the energy, real estate and financial services sectors. The group operates in five segments: energy, real estate finance, leasing, financial services and other activities. In the energy segment, the group drills for and sells natural gas and transports natural gas from wells it owns and operates to interstate pipelines and in some cases, to end-users. In real estate finance segment, it manages a portfolio of real estate loans whose underlying properties are located in the mid Atlantic region of the United States. In leasing segment, the group focused on expansion of operation through sponsorship of equipment leasing program. Financial service segment, functioned as investment entity to acquire securities of small mid-sized regional banks and bank holding companies.

Primary SIC and add'l.: 1311 6159 6153 6211

CIK No: 0000083402

Subsidiaries: ABB Associates I, Inc., ABB Associates II, Inc., Apidos Capital Management, LLC, Axios Capital Management, LLC, Chadwick Securities, Inc., Chesterfield Mortgage Investors, Inc., CP/GP, Inc., Deerfield RPI, LLC, FLI Holdings, Inc., Ischus Capital Management, LLC, Ischus II LLC, LEAF Asset Management, Inc., LEAF Capital Management, Inc., LEAF Financial Corporation, LEAF Fund I, LLC 109 Subsidiaries included in the Index

Officers: Jonathan Z. Cohen/Dir., CEO, Pres., Michael S. Yecies/Sr. VP, Chief Legal Officer, Sec., Steven J. Kessler/CFO, Sr. VP, Thomas Elliott/Sr. VP - Finance, David E. Bloom/Sr. VP, Crit S. Dement/Sr. VP, Shivan Govindan/Sr. Principal, Resource Financial Institutions Group, Inc, Rob Reynolds/Chief Investment Officer, Sr. Portfolio Mgr. - Resource Europe Management, Ltd, Alan F. Feldman/Sr. VP, Vikram M. Lokur/Dir. - Resource Financial Fund Management, Miles Herman/Dir., COO, Pres. - Leaf Financial Corporation, Jeffrey D. Blomstrom/Pres. - Resource Financial Fund Management, Rffm, Christopher D. Allen/MD - Rffm, Gretchen L. Bergstresser/Pres., Sr. Portfolio Mgr. - Apidos Capital Management, LLC, John Stelwagon/MD - Apidos Capital Management *(20 Officers included in Index)*

Directors: Jonathan Z. Cohen/Dir., CEO, Pres., Edward E. Cohen/Chmn., Andrew M. Lubin/Dir., Michael J. Bradley/Dir., Hersh Kozlov/Dir., Carlos C. Campbell/Dir., Kenneth A. Kind/Dir., John S. White/Dir., Miles Herman/Dir., COO, Pres. - Leaf Financial Corporation

Owners: Michael J. Bradley, Kenneth A. Kind, Carlos C. Campbell, Jonathan Z. Cohen/8.86%, Alan F. Feldman/2.43%, Edward E. Cohen/13.59%, Michael S. Yecies, Steven J. Kessler/1.25%, John S. White, Kenneth H. Shubin Stein/8.98%, Thomas C. Elliott, Andrew M. Lubin, Insiders/25.03%, Hersh Kozlov, Leon G. Cooperman/6.11%

Financial Data: Fiscal Year End:09/30　Latest Annual Data: 9/30/2006

Year	Sales	Net Income
2006	$78,824,000	$19,870,000
2005	$51,605,000	$16,458,000
2004	$214,841,000	$18,409,000

Curr. Assets:	$56,367,000	**Curr. Liab.:**	$28,368,000	**P/E Ratio:**	25.11
Plant, Equip.:	$10,837,000	**Total Liab.:**	$214,089,000	**Indic. Yr. Divd.:**	$0.280
Total Assets:	$416,753,000	**Net Worth:**	$193,062,000	**Debt/ Equity:**	NA

Resource Capital Corp

712 5th Ave., 10th Fl., New York, NY, 10019; **PH:** 1-212-506-3870; **Fax:** 1-212-245-6372; **http://** www.resourcecapitalcorp.com; **Email:** pschreiber@resourceamerica.com

General - Incorporation	MD	**Stock** - Price on:12/24/2007	$15.99
Employees	NA	Stock Exchange	NYSE
Auditor	Grant Thornton LLP	Ticker Symbol	RSO
Stk Agt	American Stock Transfer & Trust Co.	Outstanding Shares	NA
Counsel	NA	E.P.S.	$0.52
DUNS No.	NA	Shareholders	NA

Business: The groups principle activity is to invest in the financial fund management, real estate and commercial finance sectors. The group operates from the United States. The groups quarterly revenue for September 2007 was 74.09 millions of USD.

Primary SIC and add'l.: 6798

CIK No: 0001332551

Subsidiaries: Apidos CDO I, Apidos CDO III, Ischus CDO II, Ltd., RCC Commercial, Inc., RCC Real Estate SPE II, LLC, RCC Real Estate SPE, LLC, RCC Real Estate, Inc., Resource Capital Funding II, LLC, Resource Capital Funding, LLC, Resource Real Estate CDO 2006-1, Ltd., Resource Real Estate Funding CDO 2006-1 Investor, LLC, Resource TRS, Inc.

Officers: Jonathan Z. Cohen/Dir., CEO, Pres., Christopher D. Allen/36/Sr. VP - Commercial Lending, Gretchen Bergstresser/43/Sr. VP - Syndicated Loans, Jeffrey D. Blomstrom/37/Sr. VP - CDO Structuring, David E. Bloom/41/Sr. VP - Real Estate Investments, John R. Boyt/32/VP, Dir. - Loan Originations, David J. Bryant/42/CFO, Sr. VP, Crit Dement/53/Sr. VP - Equipment Leasing, Thomas C. Elliott/34/Sr. VP - Finance, Operations, Alan F. Feldman/Sr. VP - Real Estate Investments, Kevin M. Finkel/35/VP - Real Estate Investments, Steven J. Kessler/63/Sr. VP - Finance, Pamela Schreiber/64/VP - Investor Relations, Andrew P. Shook/37/Sr. VP - Rmbs, Cmbs, Victor Wang/45/VP, Dir. - Asset Management *(16 Officers included in Index)*

Directors: Jonathan Z. Cohen/Dir., CEO, Pres., Edward E. Cohen/Chmn., Walter T. Beach/Dir., William B. Hart/Dir., Gary Ickowicz/Dir., Murray S. Levin/Dir., Sherrill P. Neff/Dir.

Owners: David J. Bryant, Gary Ickowicz, Omega Advisors, Inc./11.05%, Kensington Investment Group, Inc./5.13%, Steven J. Kessler, Jeffrey D. Blomstrom, Murray S. Levin, David E. Bloom, William B. Hart, Insiders/7.33%, Walter T. Beach/4.05%, Resource America, Inc./8.11%, Jonathan Z. Cohen/1.61%, Sherrill P. Neff, Edward E. Cohen/1.07%

Financial Data: Fiscal Year End:12/31　Latest Annual Data: 12/31/2006

Year	Sales	Net Income
2006	$137,228,000	$15,606,000
2005	$61,698,000	$10,908,000

Curr. Assets:	$47,913,000	**Curr. Liab.:**	$138,253,000	**P/E Ratio:**	14.67
Plant, Equip.:	NA	**Total Liab.:**	$1,485,278,000	**Indic. Yr. Divd.:**	$1.640
Total Assets:	$1,802,829,000	**Net Worth:**	$317,551,000	**Debt/ Equity:**	4.2396

Resource Finance & Investment Ltd

10 Rte. de l'aeroport, Geneva 15, 1215; **PH:** 41-227990800; **http://** www.resource-finance.com

General - Incorporation	Bermuda	**Stock** - Price on:12/24/2007	$0.52
Employees	NA	Stock Exchange	OTC
Auditor	Staley, Okada & Partners	Ticker Symbol	RFIVF
Stk Agt	NA	Outstanding Shares	NA
Counsel	NA	E.P.S.	NA
DUNS No.	NA	Shareholders	NA

Business: The groups principal activity is in the exploration, development and production from properties, including the construction of extraction and processing facilities and commencement of operations. In the year 2005, the group acquired Cadillac West Explorations Inc. The group operates from Canada.

Primary SIC and add'l.: 1499 1061 1031

CIK No: 0000877090

Subsidiaries: Dynamex Resources Corporation, Oregon Resources Corporation,

Officers: Philip Garratt/Dir., CEO, Pres., Cheryl Wilson/Dir., VP, Nicholas Plumbridge/Dir., Mgr. - Investor Relations, Charles S. Smith/Advisor, Jay O. Gatten/Advisor, Boyce Moodie/Advisor, Gannett Fleming/Advisor, Dorian E. Kuper/Advisor, Kuper Consulting LLC, Tom H. Kuper/Advisor, Kuper Consulting LLC, Daryl Hoyt/Advisor, James J. Dingman/Advisor, Marc Lakmaaker/Investor Relations, North America, Daniel F. Smith/COO - Oregon Resources Corporation, George N. Gabriel/CFO - Oregon Resources Corporation, Todd Lessard/Dir. - Engineering, Processing, Oregon Resources Corporation *(16 Officers included in Index)*

Directors: Philip Garratt/Dir., CEO, Pres., Michael Brickell/Chmn., Cheryl Wilson/Dir., VP, Isaac Moss/Dir., Nicholas Plumbridge/Dir., Mgr. - Investor Relations

Owners: Philip Garratt/5.30%, RAB Special Situation (Master) Fund Limited/11.00%, Insiders/5.50%, Nick Plumbridge

Financial Data: Fiscal Year End:12/31　Latest Annual Data: 12/31/2005

Year	Sales	Net Income
2005	NA	-$1,548,000
2004	NA	-$663,000
2003	NA	-$463,000

Curr. Assets:	$5,211,000	**Curr. Liab.:**	$1,370,000		
Plant, Equip.:	$2,537,000	**Total Liab.:**	$3,974,000	**Indic. Yr. Divd.:**	NA
Total Assets:	$8,827,000	**Net Worth:**	$4,853,000	**Debt/ Equity:**	NA

Resources Connection Inc

695 Town Ctr. Dr., Ste. 600, Costa Mesa, CA, 92626; **PH:** 1-714-430-6400; **Fax:** 1-714-428-6090; **http://** www.resourcesglobal.com; **Email:** corp@resources-us.com

General - Incorporation	DE	**Stock** - Price on:12/24/2007	$32.32
Employees	3,607	Stock Exchange	NDQ
Auditor	PricewaterhouseCoopers LLP	Ticker Symbol	RECN
Stk Agt	American Stock Transfer & Trust Co.	Outstanding Shares	49,020,000
Counsel	NA	E.P.S.	$1.06
DUNS No.	NA	Shareholders	NA

Business: The group's principal activity is to provide professional services to clients on a project-by-project basis. It provides human resources management services, such as compensation program design and implementation and information technology services, transitions of management information systems and internal audit services. The group assists with discrete projects that require specialized professional expertise in accounting and finance, such as mergers and acquisitions due diligence, financial analyses, corporate reorganizations and tax-related projects. It also assists the clients with periodic needs, such as budgeting and forecasting, audit preparation and public reporting.

Primary SIC and add'l.: 8742 8721

CIK No: 0001084765

Subsidiaries: RC Holdings I, LLC, RC Holdings II, LLC, RC Management Group, LLC, RCG, LP, RCTC, RCTC LLC, RECN of Texas, LP, Resources Audit Solutions, LLC, Resources Connection Australia Pty Ltd., Resources Connection LLC, Resources Connection LLCDBA RCTC Resources Connection LLC, Resources Connection Ltd., Resources Connection Mexico S DE RL DE CV, Resources Global Enterprise Consulting Co., Resources Global Professional K.K. 28 Subsidiaries included in the Index

Officers: Donald B. Murray/61/Chmn., CEO, Pres./$2,293,526.00, Stephen J. Giusto/Dir., CFO, Exec. VP - Corporate Development, Sec., Principal Financial Officer, Principal Accounting Officer/$938,403.00, Robert A. Pisano/65/Dir. - Resources Connection, Karen M. Ferguson/44/Dir., Exec. VP/$948,403.00, Kate W. Duchene/45/Chief Legal Officer, Exec. VP - Human Relations, Assist. Sec./$938,842.00, Anthony Cherbak/54/Exec. VP - Operations/$925,276.00

Directors: Donald B. Murray/61/Chmn., CEO, Pres., Stephen J. Giusto/Dir., CFO, Exec. VP - Corporate Development, Sec., Principal Financial Officer, Principal Accounting Officer, Thomas D. Christopoul/44/Dir., Karen M. Ferguson/44/Dir., Exec. VP, Neil Dimick/58/Dir., Jolene Sykes Sarkis/58/Dir., Robert F. Kistinger/55/Dir.

Owners: Neil Dimick, Jolene Sykes Sarkis, Robert Kistinger, Anthony Cherbak, Robert A. Pisano, T. Rowe Price Associates, Inc./11.73%, Stephen J. Giusto/1.29%, Wellington Management Company, LLP/11.23%, Lone Pine/5.42%, Insiders/7.44%, TimesSquare Capital Management, LLC/5.55%, Kate W. Duchene, Donald B. Murray/4.45%, AXA Assurances I.A.R.D. Mutuelle/5.53%, Thomas Christopoul *(16 Owners included in Index)*

Financial Data: Fiscal Year End:05/31　Latest Annual Data: 05/31/2007

Year	Sales	Net Income
2007	$735,891,000	$54,765,000
2006	$633,843,000	$60,597,000
2005	$537,636,000	$56,056,000

Curr. Assets:	$227,728,000	**Curr. Liab.:**	$66,614,000	**P/E Ratio:**	30.21
Plant, Equip.:	$26,725,000	**Total Liab.:**	$81,175,000	**Indic. Yr. Divd.:**	NA
Total Assets:	$398,611,000	**Net Worth:**	$317,436,000	**Debt/ Equity:**	NA

Respironics Inc

1010 Murry Ridge Ln., Murrysville, PA, 15668; **PH:** 1-724-387-5200; **Fax:** 1-724-387-5010; **http://** www.respironics.com

General - Incorporation	DE	**Stock** - Price on:12/24/2007	$43.94
Employees	4,700	Stock Exchange	NDQ
Auditor	Ernst & Young LLP	Ticker Symbol	RESP
Stk Agt	Mellon Investor Services LLC	Outstanding Shares	73,640,000
Counsel	Steven P. Fulton	E.P.S.	$1.56
DUNS No.	08-072-8314	Shareholders	NA

Business: The group's principal activity is to develop, manufacture and market medical devices used by patients suffering from sleeping and respiratory disorders. The group' products are classified into three major categories namely: homecare, hospital and respiratory. The homecare products include airway pressure devices used at home for treatment of sleep apnea, respiratory devices, portable ventilation products, home oxygen products, and infant management and developmental care products. The hospital products segment includes therapeutic devices that control and assist a patient's ventilation and cardio-respiratory monitoring products. Respiratory drug delivery products include those used both at home and in hospital settings. On 01-Jul-2004, the group acquired western biomedical technologies and on 01-Feb-2004, it acquired profile therapeutics plc.

Primary SIC and add'l.: 3845 3841

CIK No: 0000780434

Subsidiaries: Ambulatory Resource Centres Investment Company, Inc., Ambulatory Resource Centres of Florida, Inc., Ambulatory Resource Centres of Massachusetts, Inc., Ambulatory Resource Centres of Texas, Inc., Ambulatory Resource Centres of Washington, Inc., Ambulatory Resource Centres of Wilmington, Inc., Ambulatory Surgery Center of Cool Springs, LLC, Ambulatory Surgery Center of Worcester, LLC, ARC Development Corporation, ARC Dry Creek, Inc., ARC Financial Services Corporation, ARC Kentucky, LLC, ARC New Hartford, Inc., ARC of Bellingham, L.P., ARC of Georgia, LLC 26 Subsidiaries included in the Index

Officers: John L. Miclot/Dir., CEO, Pres., Gerald E. McGinnis/Chmn., Advanced Technology Officer, Steven P. Fulton/VP, General Counsel, Susan A. Lloyd/VP - Respiratory Drug Delivery, Craig B. Reynolds/Dir., Exec. VP, COO, Derek Smith/Pres. - Hospital Group, Donald J. Spence/Pres. - Sleep, Home Respiratory Group, Daniel J. Bevevino/CFO, VP, Geoffrey C. Waters/Pres. - International Group, David P. White/Chief Medical Officer

Directors: John L. Miclot/Dir., CEO, Pres., Gerald E. McGinnis/Chmn., Advanced Technology Officer, Douglas A. Cotter/Dir., Craig B. Reynolds/Dir., Exec. VP, COO, Terry J. Dewberry/Dir., Donald H. Jones/Dir., Joseph C. Lawyer/Dir., James W. Liken/Dir., Candace L. Littell/Dir., Mylle H. Mangum/Dir., Sean C. McDonald/Dir., John C. Miles/Dir.

Owners: Douglas A. Cotter/0.07%, Donald J. Spence/0.06%, James W. Liken/0.19%, Mylle H. Mangum/0.06%, Gerald E. McGinnis/1.50%, Donald H. Jones/0.12%, John L. Miclot/0.62%, Sean C. McDonald/0.10%, Insiders/4.33%, Candace L. Littell/0.08%, Craig B. Reynolds/0.41%, Joseph C. Lawyer/0.07%, John C. Miles, Daniel J. Bevevino/0.38%, Fidelity Management Trust (FMC) Company/9.85% *(17 Owners included in Index)*

Financial Data: *Fiscal Year End:*06/30 *Latest Annual Data:* 6/30/2006

Year	Sales	Net Income
2006	$1,046,141,000	$99,893,000
2005	$911,497,000	$84,356,000
2004	$759,550,000	$65,020,000

Curr. Assets:	$776,278,000	**Curr. Liab.:**	$239,151,000	**P/E Ratio:**	26.47
Plant, Equip.:	$155,953,000	**Total Liab.:**	$293,258,000	**Indic. Yr. Divd.:**	NA
Total Assets:	$1,226,820,000	**Net Worth:**	$933,562,000	**Debt/ Equity:**	NA

Response Biomedical Corp

8081 Lougheed Hwy., Burnaby, BC, V5A 1W9; *PH:* 1-604-456-6010; *http://* www.responsebio.com

General - Incorporation	Canada	**Stock**- Price on:12/24/2007	$0.99
Employees	NA	Stock Exchange	OTC
Auditor	Ernst & Young LLP	Ticker Symbol	RPBIF
Stk Agt	Computershare Trust Co	Outstanding Shares	NA
Counsel	NA	E.P.S	NA
DUNS No.	NA	Shareholders	NA

Business: The group's principle activity is to engage in the research, development and commercialisation of diagnostic technologies for the medical point-of-care and onsite environmental testing markets.The company provides a diagnostic with an immunoassay platform called RAMP tests commercially for three cardiac markers used in the early detection of heart attack, environmental detection of West Nile virus and biodefense applications including the detection of anthrax, ricin, small pox and botulinum toxin. RAMP is used by healthcare professionals and in physicians' offices, medical clinics, hospital emergency departments and laboratories worldwide. The company has received regulatory clearance from Health Canada and the US Food and Drug Administration to market its RAMP Cardiac Marker Tests for detecting myoglobin, troponin I and CK-MB to assist in the rapid diagnosis of heart attack or acute myocardial infarction. The company has achieved CE Mark and its Quality Management Sy The group operates from United States.

Primary SIC and add'l.: 8734

CIK No: 0000806888

Subsidiaries: Response Biomedical Inc., Response Development Inc.

Officers: William J. Radvak/45/Dir., CEO, Pres., Reed Simmons/VP - Manufacturing, Robert Pilz/VP - Finance, Duane A. Morris/COO, Joanne Stephenson/VP - Business Development, Paul Harris/VP - Research, Development

Directors: William J. Radvak/45/Dir., CEO, Pres., Richard Bastiani/Chmn., Anthony F. Holler/Dir., Stephen Kahn/Member - Scientific Advisory Board, Ian Webb/Dir., Wayne S. Kay/Dir., William F. Peacock/Member - Scientific Advisory Board, Robert H. Christenson/Member - Scientific Advisory Board, Todd Patrick/Dir., Richard K. Bear/Dir.

Owners: Insiders/3.90%, Robert G. Pilz, Anthony F. Holler/1.20%, Reed W. Simmons, Ian A. Webb, Todd R. Patrick/1.20%, Paul C. Harris, William J. Radvak, Brian G. Richards

Financial Data: *Fiscal Year End:*12/31 *Latest Annual Data:* 12/31/2006

Year	Sales	Net Income
2006	$3,793,000	-$7,986,000
2005	$2,994,000	-$7,229,000

Curr. Assets:	$9,754,000	**Curr. Liab.:**	$1,805,000		
Plant, Equip.:	$1,356,000	**Total Liab.:**	$1,898,000	**Indic. Yr. Divd.:**	NA
Total Assets:	$11,127,000	**Net Worth:**	$9,229,000	**Debt/ Equity:**	NA

Restoration Hardware Inc

15 Koch Rd., Ste. J, Corte Madera, CA, 94925; *PH:* 1-415-924-1005; *Fax:* 1-415-927-9133; *http://* www.restorationhardware.com

General - Incorporation	DE	**Stock**- Price on:12/24/2007	$5.89
Employees	2,100	Stock Exchange	NDQ
Auditor	Deloitte & Touche LLP	Ticker Symbol	RSTO
Stk Agt	Computershare Investor Services LLC	Outstanding Shares	38,780,000
Counsel	Morrison & Foerster LLP	E.P.S	-$0.6
DUNS No.	87-863-1423	Shareholders	NA

Business: The group's principle activity is the distribution of home furnishings, decorative and functional hardware and related merchandise. The group's products include furniture and lighting, discovery items, accessories and books, hardware and housewares. In addition, the group operates a direct-to-customer sales channel, which includes both catalog and Internet. The group's trademark is 'restoration hardware'. The group's total revenue for year 2007 was 712.81 millions of USD.

Primary SIC and add'l.: 5710 5719 5251

CIK No: 0000863821

Subsidiaries: Restoration Hardware Canada Inc, RHG Management, LLC, The Michaels Furniture Company, Inc.

Officers: Gary Friedman/Chmn., CEO, Pres./$1,095,738.00, Chris Newman/Sr. VP, CFO, Sec./$1,024,337.00, Ken Dunaj/COO/$1,358,276.00, Bonnie Orofino/Chief Merchandising Officer/$636,944.00, Vivian MacDonald/VP, Corporate Controller/$285,057.00, Ian Sears/Chief Marketing Officer, GM - RH Direct

Directors: Gary Friedman/Chmn., CEO, Pres., Robert Camp/Dir., Raymond Hemmig/Dir., Glenn Krevlin/Dir., Ann Rhoades/Dir., Robert C. Hamer/Dir., Michael T. Young/Dir.

Owners: Ann M. Rhoades, Robert E. Camp, Bonnie McConnell-Orofino, Palo Alto Investors, LLC/7.60%, Ken Dunaj, Robert C. Hamer, Vardon Capital, LLC/8.60%, Tiger Consumer Management, LLC/7.10%, Reservoir Capital Partners, L.P/6.50%, Glenn J. Krevlin/13.00%, Insiders/23.40%, Michael T. Young, Gary G. Friedman/8.70%, Vivian Macdonald, Raymond C. Hemmig *(16 Owners included in Index)*

Financial Data: *Fiscal Year End:*01/28 *Latest Annual Data:* 2/3/2007

Year	Sales	Net Income
2007	$712,810,000	$3,252,000
2006	$581,657,000	-$29,307,000
2005	$525,823,000	$1,704,000

Curr. Assets:	$220,414,000	**Curr. Liab.:**	$110,588,000		
Plant, Equip.:	$87,961,000	**Total Liab.:**	$224,259,000	**Indic. Yr. Divd.:**	NA
Total Assets:	$316,367,000	**Net Worth:**	$92,108,000	**Debt/ Equity:**	1.6180

Restore Medical Inc

2800 Patton Rd., St. Paul, MN, 55113; *PH:* 1-651-634-3111; *Fax:* 1-651-634-3088; *http://* www.restoremedical.com; *Email:* info@restoremedical.com

General - Incorporation	DE	**Stock**- Price on:12/24/2007	$2.05
Employees	67	Stock Exchange	NDQ
Auditor	KPMG LLP	Ticker Symbol	REST
Stk Agt	Wells Fargo Shareowner Services	Outstanding Shares	15,680,000
Counsel	Dorsey and Whitney	E.P.S	-$2.48
DUNS No.	NA	Shareholders	NA

Business: The groups principal activities include developing, manufacturing and marketing medical device system. The group products sold under the trade name Pillar(R). The group operates from the United States, Asia Pacific, Europe and other. Of the net sale in the year 2006, the United States accounted for $4,580, Asia Pacific $570, Europe $487 and other $249 (thousands).

Primary SIC and add'l.: 3841 3841 3842

CIK No: 0001350620

Officers: Robert J. Paulson/Dir., CEO, Pres., Christopher R. Geyen/Sr. VP, CFO, Craig G. Palmer/Sr. VP - US Sales, Michael R. Kujak/VP - Marketing, David L. Bremseth/VP - Clinical, Regulatory, Quality Affairs, Paul J. Buscemi/VP - Research, Development, John P. Sopp/VP - Operations, Philip E. Radichel/VP - Information Systems, Luc C. Hoogstraten/MD - Netherlands, Jenefer Pardy/Contact - Canada, Nuno Nicola/Contact - Portugal, Scarlet Candela/Contact - Chile, Bernhard Neuwirth/Contact - Germany, Aharon Shimon/Contact - Israel

Directors: Robert J. Paulson/Dir., CEO, Pres., Mark B. Knudson/Chmn., Luke B. Evnin/Dir., Stephen Kraus/Dir., John G. Schulte/Dir., Howard P. Liszt/Dir., Richard J. Nigon/Dir.

Owners: General Electric Pension Trust/5.60%, Mark B. Knudson/10.60%, John Schulte, Howard Liszt, Robert J. Paulson/1.40%, Insiders/39.40%, Luke Evnin/27.60%, MPM Capital Funds/27.60%, Paul J. Buscemi, Bessemer Venture Partners/8.90%, Royce& Associates, LLC/7.00%, Magnetar Financial LLC/8.80%, John J. Foster, Edward W. Numainville

Financial Data: *Fiscal Year End:*12/31 *Latest Annual Data:* 12/31/2006

Year	Sales	Net Income
2006	$5,886,000	-$13,030,000
2005	$4,854,000	-$7,021,000
2004	$945,000	-$7,554,000

Curr. Assets:	$25,980,000	**Curr. Liab.:**	$4,320,000		
Plant, Equip.:	$539,000	**Total Liab.:**	$7,197,000	**Indic. Yr. Divd.:**	NA
Total Assets:	$26,765,000	**Net Worth:**	$19,568,000	**Debt/ Equity:**	0.1403

Retail Ventures Inc

3241 Westerville Rd., Columbus, OH, 43224; *PH:* 1-614-471-4722; *Fax:* 1-614-478-2253; *http://* www.retailventuresinc.com

General - Incorporation	OH	**Stock**- Price on:12/24/2007	$16.29
Employees	7,422	Stock Exchange	NYSE
Auditor	Deloitte & Touche LLP	Ticker Symbol	RVI
Stk Agt	National City Bank	Outstanding Shares	47,280,000
Counsel	Bellinger & Dewolf	E.P.S	$2.55
DUNS No.	NA	Shareholders	NA

Business: The groups principle activity is to operate retail stores. The groups products include mens, womens and childrens apparel, accessories, jewelry, shoes, home fashions, electronics and seasonal items. The group operates through three business segments namely Value City Department Stores LLC, DSW Inc. and Filenes Basement, Inc. The group operates from United States.

Primary SIC and add'l.: 5331 5311 5661

CIK No: 0000874444

Subsidiaries: Carlyn Advertising Agency, Inc., DSW Inc., DSW Shoe Warehouse, Inc., Filenes Basement, Inc., GB Retailers, Inc., Gramex Retail Stores, Inc., J.S. Overland Delivery, Inc., Retail Ventures Imports, Inc., Retail Ventures Jewelry, Inc., Retail Ventures Licensing, Inc., Retail Ventures Services, Inc., Value City Department Stores Charitable Foundation, Value City Department Stores LLC, Value City Department Stores Services, Inc., Value City of Michigan, Inc.

Officers: Heywood Wilansky/Dir., CEO, Pres./$7,576,861.00, Steven E. Miller/49/Sr. VP, Controller/$548,396.00, James A. McGrady/CFO, Treasurer, Sec./$1,001,161.00, Julia A. Davis/47/Exec. VP, General Counsel/$601,155.00, Jed L. Norden/57/Exec. VP, Chief Administrative Officer/$1,720,815.00

Directors: Heywood Wilansky/Dir., CEO, Pres., Jay L. Schottenstein/Chmn., Henry L. Aaron/74/Dir., Ari Deshe/Dir., Jon P. Diamond/Dir., Elizabeth M. Eveillard/Dir., Lawrence J. Ring/Dir., Harvey L. Sonnenberg/Dir., James L. Weisman/69/Dir.

Owners: Jay L. Schottenstein, Cerberus Partners, L.P., Geraldine Schottenstein, Ari Deshe, Schottenstein Stores, Jon P. Diamond

Financial Data: *Fiscal Year End:*01/28 *Latest Annual Data:* 2/3/2007

Year	Sales	Net Income
2007	$3,067,658,000	-$150,913,000
2006	$2,913,371,000	-$183,418,000
2005	$2,739,631,000	-$19,448,000

Curr. Assets:	$887,947,000	**Curr. Liab.:**	$613,508,000		
Plant, Equip.:	$279,909,000	**Total Liab.:**	$1,037,169,000	**Indic. Yr. Divd.:**	NA
Total Assets:	$1,267,217,000	**Net Worth:**	$91,620,000	**Debt/ Equity:**	3.4336

Retalix Ltd

6200 Tennyson Pkwy., Ste. 150, Plano, TX, 75024; *PH:* 1-469-241-8400; *Fax:* 1-469-241-0771; *http://* www.retalix.com; *Email:* info@retalix.com

General - Incorporation	Israel
Employees	1,500
Auditor	Kesselman & Kesselman
Stk Agt	American Stock Transfer & Trust Co.
Counsel	NA
DUNS No.	60-010-4467

Stock - Price on:12/24/2007	$19.51
Stock Exchange	NDQ
Ticker Symbol	RTLX
Outstanding Shares	19,670,000
E.P.S.	$0.23
Shareholders	NA

Business: The group's principle activities are the provision of integrated enterprise-wide software solutions for the retail food industry worldwide, including supermarkets, convenience stores and restaurants. The operations supported by the products include data capture and communications at the point-of-sale terminal or checkout; front office activities, such as cash management and credit authorizations; back office activities, such as employee scheduling and inventory control; and enterprise-wide activities, such as pricing strategy, supplier management and data mining and analysis. To date, the company's products have been installed in more than 20,000 stores and restaurants in 44 countries. The group's quarterly revenue for Sep '07 was 58.06 millions of USD.

Primary SIC and add'l.: 7373 7372 7379

CIK No: 0001064060

Subsidiaries: BASS Inc., Cell-Time Ltd., DemanDX Ltd., IREX - Israel Retail Exchange Ltd., Kohav Orion Advertising and Information Ltd., M.P.S. Millennium Pos Solution S.r.l, OMI International Inc., P.O.S. (Restaurant Solutions) Ltd., Palm Point Ltd., Retail College StoreNext Ltd., Retail Control Systems Inc., Retalix (UK) Limited, Retalix Australia PTY Ltd., Retalix France SARL, Retalix Holdings Inc. 25 Subsidiaries included in the Index

Officers: Barry Shaked/Chmn., CEO, Pres., Avinoam Bloch/COO, Yosi Kan/CTO, Danny Moshaioff/CFO, Exec. VP, Saul Simon/Exec. VP - Customer Marketing Solutions, Motti Gadish/Dir. - Corporate Communications, Investor Relations, Leslie Wolf-Creutzfeldt/Contact - The Global Consulting Group, Eli Spirer/Exec. VP - Operations, Moti Lichi/VP - Fuel, Convenience Store Solutions, Alon Goetz/Exec. VP - Grocery Solutions, Yoni Stutzen/Exec. VP - International Sales, Gil Roth/VP - Analytics, Optimization Solutions, Reuben Halevi/Exec. VP - Product Development, COO, Ray Carlin/Exec. VP - Sales, Marketing, Ofer Nimtsovich/Exec. VP - Customer Services, Retalix USA, Inc

Directors: Barry Shaked/Chmn., CEO, Pres., Ian O'Reilly/Dir., Sigal Hoffman/Dir., Amnon Lipkin-Shahak/Dir., Brian Cooper/Dir., David Bresler/External Dir., Louis Berman/Dir.

Owners: Barry Shaked/5.00%, Brian Cooper/3.90%, Insiders/0.10%

Financial Data: Fiscal Year End:12/31 Latest Annual Data: 12/31/2006

Year	Sales	Net Income
2006	$203,744,000	$1,278,000
2005	$187,371,000	$14,621,000
2004	$122,954,000	$4,837,000

Curr. Assets:	$120,817,000	Curr. Liab.:	$52,158,000		
Plant, Equip.:	$11,180,000	Total Liab.:	$68,123,000	Indic. Yr. Divd.:	NA
Total Assets:	$279,174,000	Net Worth:	$211,051,000	Debt/ Equity:	NA

Retractable Technologies Inc

511 Lobo Ln., Little Elm, TX, 75068; *PH:* 1-972-294-1010; *Fax:* 1-972-294-3600; *http://* www.vanishpoint.com; *Email:* rti@vanishpoint.com

General - Incorporation	TX
Employees	146
Auditor	CF & Co. LLP
Stk Agt	American Registrar & Transfer Co
Counsel	NA
DUNS No.	NA

Stock - Price on:12/24/2007	$2.55
Stock Exchange	AMEX
Ticker Symbol	RVP
Outstanding Shares	23,740,000
E.P.S.	-$0.296
Shareholders	NA

Business: The group's principal activities are to design, develop, manufacture and market patented safety needle devices for the healthcare industry. The main patented product is the vanishpoint(R) product that includes 3cc syringes, 1cc tuberculin, insulin, and allergy antigen syringes; 5 abd 10cc syringes; a blood collection tube holder, small tube adapter, a dental syringe, a self retracting iv catheter introducer and a full displacement syringe. The group has an exclusive license granted for the patent rights for a worldwide exclusive license to manufacture, market, sell and distribute products until the expiration of the last of the patents. Acute care hospitals, alternate care facilities, clinics, emergency centers, surgical centers are some of the customers of the group. The products are distributed in the United States and its territories through general line and specialty distributors.

Primary SIC and add'l.: 3841

CIK No: 0000946563

Officers: Thomas J. Shaw/Chmn., CEO, Pres./$400,000.00, Kathryn M. Duesman/Executive Dir. - Global Health, Russell B. Kuhlman/VP - Sales/$169,208.00, Michele M. Larios/VP, General Counsel/$409,564.00, Lawrence G. Salerno/Dir. - Operations, Douglas W. Cowan/CFO, VP, Treasurer/$348,502.00, Judy Ni Zhu/Research, Development Mgr., John R. Maday/Production Mgr., James A. Hoover/Dir. - Quality Assurance, Steven R. Wisner/Exec. VP/$305,117.00, John W. Fort/Dir. - Accounting, Jules Millogo/Medical Dir.

Directors: Thomas J. Shaw/Chmn., CEO, Pres., Russell B. Kuhlman/VP - Sales

Owners: Insiders/20.40%, Thomas J. Shaw/47.30%, Michele M. Larios/1.00%, Marwan Saker/15.20%, Lillian E. Salerno/1.00%, Clarence Zierhut, Jimmie Shiu/1.60%, Steven R. Wisner/1.00%, Marwan Saker/1.80%, Suzanne M. August/11.70%, Signia Capital Management, LLC/5.00%, Thomas J. Shaw/3.40%, Marco Laterza, Insiders/51.20%, Douglas W. Cowan/1.00% (18 Owners included in Index)

Financial Data: Fiscal Year End:12/31 Latest Annual Data: 12/31/2006

Year	Sales	Net Income
2006	$25,325,000	-$3,869,000
2005	$24,235,000	-$1,238,000
2004	$21,522,000	$54,691,000

Curr. Assets:	$57,781,000	Curr. Liab.:	$6,891,000		
Plant, Equip.:	$12,212,000	Total Liab.:	$11,085,000	Indic. Yr. Divd.:	NA
Total Assets:	$70,795,000	Net Worth:	$59,710,000	Debt/ Equity:	0.0718

Reunion Industries Inc

11 Stanwix St., Ste. 1400, Pittsburgh, PA, 15222; *PH:* 1-412-281-2111; *Fax:* 1-412-281-4747; *http://* www.reunionindustries.com

General - Incorporation	DE
Employees	354
Auditor	Mahoney Cohen & Co. CPA, P.C
Stk Agt	Registrar & Transfer Co
Counsel	NA
DUNS No.	00-690-9857

Stock - Price on:12/24/2007	NA
Stock Exchange	OTC
Ticker Symbol	RUNI
Outstanding Shares	NA
E.P.S.	-$0.15
Shareholders	NA

Business: The group's principal activities are to manufacture high volume, precision plastic products and to provide engineered plastic services. Oneida division, designs and produces injection molded parts and provides secondary services such as hot stamping, welding, printing, painting and assembly of such products. In addition, the group designs and builds custom molds at its tools shops in order to produce component parts for specific customers.

Primary SIC and add'l.: 3443 3089 3499

CIK No: 0001003429

Subsidiaries: Buttes Drilling-C Company, Reunion Industries, Inc., Reunion Titan, Inc., Shanghai Klemp Metals Products Company

Owners: John G. Poole, The John Grier Poole Family Limited Partnership, Jack T. Croushore, Kimball J. Bradley, Stanwich Financial Services Corp., Charles E. Bradley, Jesse Poole, Joseph C. Lawyer, Thomas N. Amonett, David E. Jackson, Insiders, John M. Froehlich, The Charles E. Bradley, Sr. Familiy Limited partnership, Thomas L. Cassidy, LC Capital Master Fund, Ltd.

Financial Data: Fiscal Year End:12/31 Latest Annual Data: 12/31/2006

Year	Sales	Net Income
2006	$59,490,000	$5,387,000
2005	$49,727,000	-$2,420,000
2004	$68,650,000	-$162,000

Curr. Assets:	$23,592,000	Curr. Liab.:	$62,892,000		
Plant, Equip.:	$6,532,000	Total Liab.:	$66,949,000	Indic. Yr. Divd.:	NA
Total Assets:	$44,418,000	Net Worth:	-$23,029,000	Debt/ Equity:	NA

Reuters Group Plc

3 Times Sq., New York, NY, 10036; *PH:* 1-646-223-4000; *Fax:* 1-646-223-4009; *http://* about.reuters.com; *Email:* miriam.mckay@reuters.com

General - Incorporation	England And Wales
Employees	16,134
Auditor	PricewaterhouseCoopers LLP
Stk Agt	Morgan ADR Service Center
Counsel	NA
DUNS No.	51-032-7760

Stock - Price on:12/24/2007	$74.79
Stock Exchange	NDQ
Ticker Symbol	RTRSY
Outstanding Shares	207,070,000
E.P.S.	$3.01
Shareholders	NA

Business: The group's principle activity is the provision of information and software applications tailored for professionals in the financial services, media and corporate markets. In Jan 2004, the group's segment is re-aligned into four customer segments. Institutional sales and trading, focuses on sales and trading end-users dealing in the foreign exchange, fixed income, equities, commodities and energy related markets. Asset management and research, focuses on supporting end-users such as portfolio managers, wealth managers, investment bankers and research analysts. Enterprise, focuses on enterprise information distribution systems, risk and enterprise information products (eip). Media, focuses on wholesale media business, serving the needs of newspapers, television and cable networks, radio stations, websites and consumers.

Primary SIC and add'l.: 4899 7383 6211 7389 7375

CIK No: 0001056084

Subsidiaries: Instinet Group, Radianz, Reuters AG, Reuters America Holdings Inc, Reuters America LLC, Reuters Australia Pty Limited, Reuters BV, Reuters Canada Limited, Reuters Europe SA, Reuters Finance PLC, Reuters Group Overseas Holdings Ltd, Reuters Holdings Limited, Reuters Hong Kong Limited, Reuters International Holdings SARL, Reuters Investments (2002) Limited 27 Subsidiaries included in the Index

Officers: Chris Ahearn/Pres. - Reuters Media, John Alcantara/Global Head - Service Operations, Lee Ann Daly/Chief Marketing Officer

Directors: Nandan Nilekani/Dir.

Owners: Fidelity International Limited*/6.50%, Capital Group of Companies, Inc./3.10%, AMVESCAP plc/4.90%, Lawton Fitt, Ken Olisa, David Grigson, Barclays PLC/3.10%, Insiders, Dick Olver, Legal & General Investment Management/3.50%, Schroders Plc/7.80%, ValueAct Capital Master Fund L.P./6.60%, BlackRock Inc.**/3.80%, Niall FitzGerald, Tom Glocer (19 Owners included in Index)

Financial Data: Fiscal Year End:12/31 Latest Annual Data: 12/31/2006

Year	Sales	Net Income
2006	$5,027,051,000	$597,526,000
2005	$4,229,726,000	$681,437,000
2004	$5,748,974,000	$845,777,000

Curr. Assets:	$1,187,215,000	Curr. Liab.:	$1,788,658,000		
Plant, Equip.:	$724,867,000	Total Liab.:	$3,424,506,000	Indic. Yr. Divd.:	$1.280
Total Assets:	$3,975,014,000	Net Worth:	$550,507,000	Debt/ Equity:	NA

Revlon Consumer Products Corp

237 Pk. Ave., New York, NY, 10017; *PH:* 1-212-527-5230; *http://* www.revlon.com

General - Incorporation	DE
Employees	6,800
Auditor	KPMG LLP
Stk Agt	American Stock Transfer & Trust Co.
Counsel	NA
DUNS No.	78-882-0165

Stock - Price on:12/24/2007	NA
Stock Exchange	NA
Ticker Symbol	NA
Outstanding Shares	NA
E.P.S.	NA
Shareholders	NA

Business: The group's principal activities are to manufacture and market cosmetics and skin care, fragrances and personal care products. The products of the group under cosmetics and skin care product line include lip makeup, nail color, nail care products, eye and face makeup and skin care products such as lotions, cleansers, creams, toners and moisturizers. Fragrances include perfumes, eau de toilettes, colognes, and body sprays. Personal care line of products consists of hair care, antiperspirant hypo allergenic personal care products. The customers of the group include large mass volume retailers, chain drug stores, department stores and other specialty stores inclusive of perfumeries. The operations are conducted in the United States of America, Australia, Canada, Mexico and South Africa. The trademarks of the group include revlon, colorstay, moondrops, super lustrous, ultima ii and colorsilk.

Primary SIC and add'l.: 2844

CIK No: 0000890547

Subsidiaries: Acn 000 189 186 Pty Limited, Almay, Inc., CEIL Comercio e Distribuidora Ltda., Cendico B.V., Charles of the Ritz Group Ltd., Charles Revson Inc., Cosmetics & More Inc., Deutsche Revlon GmbH, European Beauty Products S.L., Europenne de Produits de Beaut, S.A.S., New Revlon Argentina S.A., North America Revsale Inc, PPI Two, Productos Cosmeticos de Revlon, S.A., Promethean Insurance Limited 60 Subsidiaries included in the Index

Officers: David L. Kennedy/Dir., CEO, Pres., Robert K. Kretzman/Exec. VP - Human Resources, Chief Legal Officer, General Counsel, Carl Kooyoomjian/Exec. VP - Technical Affairs, Worldwide Operations, Karl Obrecht/Exec. VP - North American Sales, Chris Elshaw/Sr. VP, MD - Europe, Alan T. Ennis/CFO, Exec. VP, Arthur Franson/Sr. VP - Worldwide Manufacturing, Graeme Howard/Sr. VP, MD - Asia Pacific, Neil Scancarella/Exec. VP, Chief Science Officer, Mark M. Sexton/Sr. VP - General Tax Counsel, Simon Worraker/Sr. VP, MD - Latin America, Edward A. Mammone/Sr. VP, Corporate Controller, Chief Accounting Officer, Abbe F. Goldstein/Sr. VP - Investor Relations, Corporate Communications

Directors: David L. Kennedy/Dir., CEO, Pres., Ronald O. Perelman/Chmn., Paul J. Bohan/Dir., Barry F. Schwartz/Dir., Alan S. Bernikow/Dir., Donald G. Drapkin/Dir., Kenneth L. Wolfe/Dir., Linda Gosden Robinson/Dir., Kathi P. Seifert/Dir., Meyer Feldberg/Dir., Howard Gittis/Dir., Edward J. Landau/Dir., Debra L. Lee/Dir.

Revlon Inc

237 Pk. Ave., New York, NY, 10017; **PH:** 1-212-527-4000; **Fax:** 1-212-527-4995; http:// www.revloninc.com

General - Incorporation	DE	Stock - Price on:12/24/2007	$1.39
Employees	6,000	Stock Exchange	NYSE
Auditor	KPMG LLP	Ticker Symbol	REV
Stk Agt..... American Stock Transfer & Trust Co.		Outstanding Shares	508,440,000
Counsel	NA	E.P.S.	-$0.34
DUNS No.	00-126-5818	Shareholders	NA

Business: The group's principal activities are to manufacture, market and sell an extensive array of cosmetics and skin care fragrances and personal care products. The group's products are marketed under brands: revlon, colorstay, revlon age defying, almay and ultima in cosmetics; moon drops, eterna 27, ultima and jeanne gatineau in skin care; charlie and fire & ice in fragrances; and flex, outrageous,mitchum, colorstay, colorsilk, jean nate, bozzano and colorama in personal care products. Each brand is marketed with a distinct and uniform global image, including packaging and advertising, while retaining the flexibility to tailor products to local and regional preferences. The products are sold in more than 100 countries across five continents.

Primary SIC and add'l.: 2844

CIK No: 0000887921

Subsidiaries: Acn 000 189 186 Pty Limited, Almay Inc, CEIL Comercio e Distribuidora Ltda., Cendico B.V., Charles of the Ritz Group Ltd., Charles Revson Inc., Cosmetics & More Inc., Deutsche Revlon GmbH, European Beauty Products S.L., Europenne de Produits de Beaut, New Revlon Argentina S.A., North America Revsale Inc., PPI Two Corporation, Productos Cosmeticos de Revlon, Promethean Insurance Limited 61 Subsidiaries included in the Index

Officers: David L. Kennedy/Dir., CEO, Pres./$1,587,967.00, Carl Kooyoomjian/Exec. VP - Technical Affairs, Worldwide Operations, Edward A. Mammone/Sr. VP, Corporate Controller, Chief Accounting Officer, Abbe F. Goldstein/Sr. VP - Investor Relations, Corporate Communications, Robert K. Kretzman/Exec. VP - Human Resources, Chief Legal Officer, General Counsel/$1,336,537.00, Karl Obrecht/Exec. VP - North American Sales, Chris Elshaw/Sr. VP, MD - Europe, Alan T. Ennis/CFO, Exec. VP/$290,678.00, Arthur Franson/Sr. VP - Worldwide Manufacturing, Graeme Howard/Sr. VP, MD - Asia Pacific, Neil Scancarella/Exec. VP, Chief Science Officer, Mark M. Sexton/Sr. VP - General Tax Counsel, Simon Worraker/Sr. VP, MD - Latin America

Directors: David L. Kennedy/Dir., CEO, Pres., Ronald O. Perelman/Chmn., Alan S. Bernikow/Dir., Paul J. Bohan/Dir., Meyer Feldberg/Dir., Howard Gittis/Dir., Edward J. Landau/Dir., Debra L. Lee/Dir., Linda Gosden Robinson/Dir., Kathi P. Seifert/Dir., Kenneth L. Wolfe/Dir.

Owners: FMR Corp./13.16%, Robert K. Kretzman, Paul J. Bohan, Ronald O. Perelman/57.45%, Alan S. Bernikow, Insiders/100.00%, Insiders/57.87%, David L. Kennedy, Kenneth L. Wolfe, Jack L. Stahl/1.19%, Thomas E. McGuire, Alan T. Ennis, Debra L. Lee, Kathi P. Seifert, Edward J. Landau (19 Owners included in Index)

Financial Data: Fiscal Year End:12/31   Latest Annual Data: 12/31/2006

Year	Sales	Net Income
2006	$1,331,400,000	-$251,300,000
2005	$1,332,300,000	-$83,700,000
2004	$1,297,200,000	-$142,500,000

Curr. Assets:	$488,000,000	Curr. Liab.:	$377,200,000		
Plant, Equip.:	$115,300,000	Total Liab.:	$2,161,700,000	Indic. Yr. Divd.:	NA
Total Assets:	$931,900,000	Net Worth:	-$1,229,800,000	Debt/ Equity:	NA

Rewards Network Inc

2 N Riverside Plz., Ste. 950, Chicago, IL, 60606; **PH:** 1-312-521-6767; **Fax:** 1-312-521-6769; http:// www.rewardsnetwork.com; **Email:** info@rewardsnetwork.com

General - Incorporation	DE	Stock - Price on:12/24/2007	$3.89
Employees	410	Stock Exchange	AMEX
Auditor	KPMG LLP	Ticker Symbol	IRN
Stk Agt..... American Stock Transfer & Trust Co.		Outstanding Shares	27,120,000
Counsel	NA	E.P.S.	-$0.71
DUNS No.	NA	Shareholders	NA

Business: The group's principal activity is to provide dining reward programs. The members of the group are offered dining savings and reward programs at restaurants throughout the United States. The group operates numerous other private-label and co-branded dining programs where members earn a different reward, like airline miles, loyalty points or cash back. The partners of the group include nine airlines, bankcard issuers and players in the loyalty marketing industry and other corporations. The group has approximately 10,830 participating restaurants in over 55 metropolitan markets in more than 40 states.

Primary SIC and add'l.: 7389

CIK No: 0000078536

Subsidiaries: FFA Acquisition Corporation, iDine Media Group Inc., Restaurant Cash California LLC, Restaurant Cash LLC, Rewards Network Canada GP Corporation, Rewards Network Canada LP, Rewards Network Establishment Services Inc, Rewards Network International, Inc., Rewards Network Services Inc., RTR Funding LLC, TMNI International Inc.

Officers: Ronald L. Blake/Dir., CEO, Pres./$3,401,468.00, Christopher J. Locke/CFO, Sr. VP, Treasurer/$401,784.00, Roya Behnia/Sr. VP, General Counsel, Sec., Chief Privacy Officer/$159,402.00, Megan E. Flynn/41/Sr. VP - Business Development/$408,053.00, Robert S. Wasserman/48/Exec. VP - Sales - Marketing, Operations/$576,156.00

Directors: Ronald L. Blake/Dir., CEO, Pres., Donald J. Liebentritt/57/Chmn., Harold I. Shain/Dir., Raymond A. Gross/Dir., Adam M. Aron/Dir., Peter C.B. Bynoe/Dir., Philip F. Handy/Dir., Nils E. Larsen/Dir., John A. Ward/Dir., Frank E. Wood/Dir., Karen I. Bremer/49/Dir.

Owners: Philip F. Handy, Karen I. Bremer, Ronald L. Blake/1.10%, Megan E. Flynn, Harold I. Shain, Bryan R. Adel, Donald J. Liebentritt, The State Teachers Retirement Board of Ohio/13.70%, Frank E. Wood, Adam M. Aron, Raymond A. Gross, Insiders/4.00%, Peter C.B. Bynoe, Christopher J. Locke, Halmostock Limited Partnership/1.80% (19 Owners included in Index)

Financial Data: Fiscal Year End:12/31   Latest Annual Data: 3/31/2007

Year	Sales	Net Income
2007	NA	NA
2006	NA	NA
2005	$289,935,000	-$621,000

Curr. Assets:	$182,446,000	Curr. Liab.:	$36,489,000		
Plant, Equip.:	$8,712,000	Total Liab.:	$121,842,000	Indic. Yr. Divd.:	NA
Total Assets:	$206,579,000	Net Worth:	$84,737,000	Debt/ Equity:	NA

Rex Stores Corp

2875 Needmore Rd., Dayton, OH, 45414; **PH:** 1-937-276-3931; **Fax:** 1-937-276-8643; http:// www.rexstores.com; **Email:** investors@rexstores.com

General - Incorporation	DE	Stock - Price on:12/24/2007	$19.66
Employees	818	Stock Exchange	NYSE
Auditor	Deloitte & Touche LLP	Ticker Symbol	RSC
Stk Agt .... American Registrar & Transfer Co		Outstanding Shares	10,610,000
Counsel	NA	E.P.S.	NA
DUNS No.	11-288-6817	Shareholders	NA

Business: The group's principal activity is the retailing of consumer electronics and home appliances. The group offers a broad selection of brand name products and product categories. The products include big screen and standard-sized televisions, video and audio equipment, camcorders and major household appliances including washers, dryers, dishwashers, refrigerators, freezers, ovens and other. The group operates 249 stores in 37 states under the 'rex' trade name, serving over 200 small to medium-sized towns and communities.

Primary SIC and add'l.: 5722 3631 5731

CIK No: 0000744187

Subsidiaries: AVA Acquisition Corp., Kelly & Cohen Appliances, Inc.(1), Rex Acquisition, LLC, Rex Alabama, Inc., REX Investment, LLC, Rex Kansas, Inc., Rex Radio and Television, Inc., rexstores.com, Inc., Stereo Town, Inc.

Owners: Zafar A. Rizvi/2.80%, Robert Davidoff/2.80%, Advisory Research, Inc./6.00%, Mervyn L. Alphonso, David S. Harris, Insiders/34.10%, Charles A. Elcan, Douglas L. Bruggeman/2.00%, Lawrence Tomchin/5.10%, David Fuchs/1.60%, Keith B. Magby/1.00%, FMR Corp./13.30%, Stuart A. Rose/23.60%, Edward M. Kress/1.30%, Dimensional Fund Advisors LP/9.40% (16 Owners included in Index)

Financial Data: Fiscal Year End:01/31   Latest Annual Data: 1/31/2007

Year	Sales	Net Income
2007	$347,334,000	$11,351,000
2006	$396,032,000	$28,269,000
2005	$391,300,000	$27,549,000

Curr. Assets:	$136,006,000	Curr. Liab.:	$47,915,000		
Plant, Equip.:	$124,778,000	Total Liab.:	$92,976,000	Indic. Yr. Divd.:	NA
Total Assets:	$335,208,000	Net Worth:	$230,789,000	Debt/ Equity:	0.0860

Rexahn Pharmaceuticals Inc

9620 Medical Ctr. Dr., Rockville, MD, 20850; **PH:** 1-240-268-5300; http:// www.rexahn.com; **Email:** info@rexahn.com

General - Incorporation	DE	Stock - Price on:12/24/2007	$1.55
Employees	15	Stock Exchange	OTC
Auditor	Lazar, Levine & Felix, LLP	Ticker Symbol	RXHN
Stk Agt ...... Olde Monmouth Stk Trnsfer Co. Inc.		Outstanding Shares	50,330,000
Counsel	NA	E.P.S.	-$0.1
DUNS No.	NA	Shareholders	NA

Business: The groups principal activity is focusing on oncology drugs and groups research and development focuses on three therapeutic areas that affect the lives of many people cancer, diseases of the central nervous system namely anxiety, depression and sexual dysfunction. The group operates from the United States.

Primary SIC and add'l.: 2834

CIK No: 0001228627

Officers: Chang H. Ahn/Chmn., CEO, Founder, Tae Heum Jeong/Dir., CFO, Sec.

Directors: Chang H. Ahn/Chmn., CEO, Founder, David M. McIntosh/Dir., Charles Beever/Dir., Kwang Soo Cheong/Dir., Michelle Y. Kang/Dir., Tae Heum Jeong/Dir., CFO, Sec., Freddie Ann Hoffman/Dir.

Owners: Kwang Soo Cheong, Chang H. Ahn/29.61%, Rexgene Biotech Co., Ltd./9.52%, David McIntosh, Tae Heum Jeong/2.09%, Charles Beever, Michele Y. Kang, KT&G Corporation/4.97%, Young-Soon Park/6.69%, Insiders/38.84%, Chong Kun Dang Pharmaceutical Corp./5.96%

Financial Data: Fiscal Year End:12/31   Latest Annual Data: 12/31/2006

Year	Sales	Net Income
2006	$75,000	-$6,486,000
2005	$266,000	-$6,350,000
2004	$60,000	-$280,000

Curr. Assets:	$4,517,000	Curr. Liab.:	$575,000		
Plant, Equip.:	$150,000	Total Liab.:	$1,775,000	Indic. Yr. Divd.:	NA
Total Assets:	$4,989,000	Net Worth:	$3,214,000	Debt/ Equity:	NA

Rexam Plc

8770 W Bryn Mawr Ave., Chicago, IL, 60631; **PH:** 1-773-399-3000; **Fax:** 1-773-399-3354; http:// www.rexam.com; **Email:** investor.relations@rexam.com

General - Incorporation		Stock - Price on:12/24/2007	$49.51
Employees	NA	Stock Exchange	NA
Auditor	PricewaterhouseCoopers LLP	Ticker Symbol	NA
Stk Agt	Mellon Trust Co	Outstanding Shares	NA
Counsel	NA	E.P.S.	NA
DUNS No.	NA	Shareholders	NA

Business: The groups principal activity is to provide packaging solutions. The products of the group include plastic containers, glass bottles and vials, lipstick cases, compacts, and plastic tubs. Specific customers of the group include Anheuser-Busch, Coca Cola and Carlsberg. The group opeartes from Europe, the Americas and Asia.

Primary SIC and add'l.: 3085 3411 3089

CIK No: 0000800016

Officers: Leslie Van De Walle/52/CEO, Bill Barker/59/Group Dir. - Beverage Cans, Graham Chipchase/45/Group Dir. - Plastic Packaging, David Robbie/45/Dir. - Finance, Tomas Sjolin/Sector Dir. - Beverage Can Europe, Asia, Harry Barto/Sector Dir. - Beverage Can North America, Andre Balbi/Sector Dir. - Beverage Can South America, Paul Martin/Group IM Dir., Rudolph Kalveks/Group Corporate Development Dir., David Gibson/Company Sec., Roger Bellis/Group Dir. - Human Resources, Jonathan Thornton/Group Communications Dir.

Directors: Rolf Borjesson/65/Chmn., Carl Symon/62/Non Exec. Dir., Michael Buzzacott/61/Non Exec. Dir., Noreen Doyle/60/Non Exec. Dir., Wolfgang K. Meusburger/54/Non Exec. Dir., Jean-Pierre Rodier/61/Non Exec. Dir.

Financial Data: Fiscal Year End: 12/31 **Latest Annual Data:** 12/31/2005

Year	Sales	Net Income
2005	$5,570,230,000	$383,738,000
2004	$6,059,157,000	$231,192,000
2002	$4,951,178,000	-$194,132,000

Curr. Assets:	NA	Curr. Liab.:	NA		
Plant, Equip.:	NA	Total Liab.:	NA	Indic. Yr. Divd.:	NA
Total Assets:	NA	Net Worth:	NA	Debt/ Equity:	NA

Reynolds & Reynolds Co

One Reynolds Way, Dayton, OH, 45430; **PH:** 1-937-485-2000; **http://** www.reyrey.com

General - Incorporation	OH	Stock - Price on:12/24/2007	NA
Employees	NA	Stock Exchange	NA
Auditor	Deloitte & Touche LLP	Ticker Symbol	NA
Stk Agt	Wells Fargo Bank, N.A.	Outstanding Shares	NA
Counsel	Coolidge Wall Womsley & Lombard	E.P.S.	NA
DUNS No.	00-427-7430	Shareholders	NA

Business: The group's principle activities are carried out through four segments: software solutions, transformation solutions, documents and the financial services segment. Software solutions segment consists of the software solutions and the info-structure services business units. This segment provides integrated computer systems products and related services. Transformation solutions segment provides specialized training, Web services and customer relationship management. Documents segment manufactures and distributes printed business forms to automotive retailers. The financial services segment provides financing, principally for sales of the computer systems.

Primary SIC and add'l.: 6159 2761 7372 7379

CIK No: 0000083588

Subsidiaries: Formcraft Holdings, Inc., Incadea, GmbH, L.s.i., LLC, Networkcar, Inc., Reyna Capital Corporation, Reyna Funding, LLC, Reynolds & Reynolds Netherlands B.V., Reynolds and Reynolds (Canada) Limited, Reynolds and Reynolds Austria GmbH, Reynolds and Reynolds Company France GmbH, Reynolds and Reynolds Dealer Services S.L., Reynolds and Reynolds GmbH, Reynolds and Reynolds Holdings, Inc., Reynolds and Reynolds Italy Srl., Reynolds and Reynolds Limited 21 Subsidiaries included in the Index

Officers: Thomas Schwartz/Contact - Media Inquiries

Reynolds American Inc

401 N Main St., Winston-Salem, NC, 27102; **PH:** 1-336-741-2000; **Fax:** 1-336-741-4238; **http://** www.reynoldsamerican.com

General - Incorporation	NC	Stock - Price on:12/24/2007	$61.96
Employees	7,500	Stock Exchange	NYSE
Auditor	KPMG LLP	Ticker Symbol	RAI
Stk Agt	Bank of New York	Outstanding Shares	295,000,000
Counsel	NA	E.P.S.	$4.04
DUNS No.	NA	Shareholders	NA

Business: The groups principle activities include manufacturing and marketing cigarettes. The group operates from United States.

Primary SIC and add'l.: NA

CIK No: 0001275283

Subsidiaries: Cigarette Manufacturers Supplies Inc., FHS, Inc., Gallaher Reynolds Equipment Company, GMB, Inc., Huu-wa-ka, LLC, Lane Limited, Northern Brands International, Inc., Quezon Holdings, B.V., R. J. Reynolds Gallaher International Sarl, R. J. Reynolds Global Products, Inc., R. J. Reynolds Smoke Shop, Inc, R. J. Reynolds Tobacco (CI), Co., R. J. Reynolds Tobacco B.V., R. J. Reynolds Tobacco C.V., R. J. Reynolds Tobacco Co. 32 Subsidiaries included in the Index

Officers: Susan M. Ivey/Chmn., CEO, Pres./$8,169,922.00, Richard M. Sanders/CEO, Pres. - Santa Fe Natural Tobacco Company, Inc, Daniel M. Delen/CEO, Pres. - RJ Reynolds Tobacco Company, Bill Rosson/CEO, Pres. - Conwood Company, LLC, Conwood Sales Co, LLC, Mark D. Smith/VP - Communications, Santa Fe Natural Tobacco Company, Inc, Nadyne T. Brown/VP - Human Resources, Santa Fe Natural Tobacco Company, Inc, Rusty Gaston/VP - Information Technology, Santa Fe Natural Tobacco Company, Inc, Michael O. Johnson/Sr. VP, General Counsel, Sec. - Santa Fe Natural Tobacco Company, Inc, Michael A. Little/Sr. VP - Manufacturing, Santa Fe Natural Tobacco Company, Inc, Melanie S. Barbee/VP - Marketing, Sales, Santa Fe Natural Tobacco Company, Inc, Rudy W. Cook/VP - Product Development, Santa Fe Natural Tobacco Company, Inc, Donald I. Lamonds/CIO, Exec. VP - RJ Reynolds Tobacco Company, Gavin D. Little/Exec. VP - Consumer, Trade Marketing, RJ Reynolds Tobacco Company, John E. Franzino/Sr. VP - Finance, Accounting, CFO, Treasurer - Santa Fe Natural Tobacco Company, Inc, Folan P. McDara/Sec. *(41 Officers included in Index)*

Directors: Susan M. Ivey/Chmn., CEO, Pres., Nana Mensah/Dir., Neil R. Withington/Dir., Antonio Monteiro De Castro/Dir., Betsy S. Atkins/Dir., H.G. L. Powell/Dir., Joseph P. Viviano/Dir., Thomas C. Wajnert/Dir., John T. Chain/Dir., Martin D. Feinstein/Dir., John J. Zillmer/Dir.

Owners: Jeffrey A. Eckmann, Nana Mensah, Thomas C. Wajnert, H.G L. Powell, Susan M. Ivey, Lynn J. Beasley, John T. Chain, Insiders, AMVESCAP PLC, Tommy J. Payne, Charles A. Blixt, INVESCO Asset Management Limited, British American Tobacco p.l.c, Capital Research and Management Company, Joseph P. Viviano *(17 Owners included in Index)*

Financial Data: Fiscal Year End: 12/31 **Latest Annual Data:** 12/31/2006

Year	Sales	Net Income
2006	$8,510,000,000	$1,210,000,000
2005	$8,256,000,000	$1,042,000,000
2004	$6,437,000,000	$688,000,000

Curr. Assets:	$4,935,000,000	Curr. Liab.:	$4,092,000,000	P/E Ratio:	15.34
Plant, Equip.:	$1,062,000,000	Total Liab.:	$11,135,000,000	Indic. Yr. Divd.:	$3.000
Total Assets:	$18,178,000,000	Net Worth:	$7,043,000,000	Debt/ Equity:	0.6177

RF Industries

7610 Miramar Rd., Bldg. 6000, San Diego, CA, 92126; **PH:** 1-858-549-6340; **Fax:** 1-858-549-6345; **http://** www.rfindustries.com; **Email:** rfi@rfindustries.com

General - Incorporation	NV	Stock - Price on:12/24/2007	$5.66
Employees	87	Stock Exchange	NDQ
Auditor	J. H. Cohn LLP	Ticker Symbol	RFIL
Stk Agt	Continental Stock Transfer & Trust Co	Outstanding Shares	3,320,000
Counsel	NA	E.P.S.	$0.29
DUNS No.	02-185-2181	Shareholders	NA

Business: The group's principle activities are to design, manufacture and sell communication equipment primarily to the radio and other professional communication related industries. The group operates through two divisions: the rf connector division and the neulink division. The rf connector division designs, manufactures and distributes coaxial connectors used in radio frequency (rf) wireless and digital transmission communication applications. The rf neulink division designs and manufactures, through outside contractors, wireless data products commonly known as rf data links and wireless modems. The group exports to customers in South America, Canada, Mexico, Europe, Australia and the Middle East. The group's quarterly revenue for September 2007 was 4.31 millions of USD.

Primary SIC and add'l.: 3678 3669

CIK No: 0000740664

Officers: Howard F. Hill/67/Dir., CEO, Victor H. Powers/CFO

Directors: Howard F. Hill/67/Dir., CEO, Robert Jacobs/56/Dir., John R. Ehret/70/Dir., Marvin H. Fink/71/Dir., Linde Kester/62/Dir., William L. Reynolds/71/Dir.

Owners: Walrus Partners, LLC/9.40%, Marvin Fink, Insiders/14.20%, Linde Kester/2.70%, Howard H. Hill/9.20%, William L. Reynolds, Robert Jacobs, Hytek International, Ltd./13.60%, John R. Ehret

Financial Data: Fiscal Year End: 10/31 **Latest Annual Data:** 10/31/2006

Year	Sales	Net Income
2006	$15,188,000	$1,541,000
2005	$13,152,000	$445,000
2004	$11,227,000	$1,224,000

Curr. Assets:	$14,574,000	Curr. Liab.:	$1,764,000	P/E Ratio:	16.17
Plant, Equip.:	$376,000	Total Liab.:	$1,855,000	Indic. Yr. Divd.:	$0.080
Total Assets:	$15,319,000	Net Worth:	$13,464,000	Debt/ Equity:	NA

RF Micro Devices Inc

7628 Thorndike Rd., Greensboro, NC, 27409; **PH:** 1-336-664-1233; **Fax:** 1-336-931-7454; **http://** www.rfmd.com

General - Incorporation	NC	Stock - Price on:12/24/2007	$6.27
Employees	3,252	Stock Exchange	NDQ
Auditor	Ernst & Young LLP	Ticker Symbol	RFMD
Stk Agt	First Union Shareholder Services	Outstanding Shares	194,220,000
Counsel	NA	E.P.S.	NA
DUNS No.	NA	Shareholders	NA

Business: The groups principal activities include designing and manufacturing radio frequency components and system solutions. The products of the group include power amplifiers, transmit modules, cellular transceivers and transceiver modules. The group products sold under the trade name Optimum Technology Matching(R). Specific customers of the group include Nokia Corporation, Motorola, Inc., Samsung Electronics Co., Ltd., LG Electronics, Inc., Sony Ericsson Mobile Communications and BenQ Corporation. The group operates from the United States and International. Of the sale in the year 2006, the United States accounted for $113,200 and International $657,047 (thousands).

Primary SIC and add'l.: 3674 3679

CIK No: 0000911160

Subsidiaries: OOO Neosilicon, RF Micro Devices (Beijing) Co. Ltd., RF Micro Devices (Canada) ULC, RF Micro Devices (Denmark) ApS, RF Micro Devices (Finland) Oy, RF Micro Devices (Holland) B.V., RF Micro Devices (Korea) YH, RF Micro Devices (Taiwan) B.V., RF Micro Devices Export, Inc., RF Micro Devices International, Inc., RF Micro Devices UK Ltd, RF Micro Devices, Svenska AB, RFMD Infrastructure Product Group, Inc., RFMD WPAN, Inc., RFMD, LLC

Officers: Robert A. Bruggeworth/Dir., CEO, Pres., William J. Pratt/Dir., CTO, Corporate VP, Powell T. Seymour/Corporate VP - Strategic Operations, Assist. Sec., Jerry D. Neal/Exec. VP - Marketing, Strategic Development, William A. Priddy/CFO, Corporate VP - Administration, Sec., Steven E. Creviston/Corporate VP - Cellular Products Group, Gary J. Grant/Corporate VP - Quality Assurance, Forrest J. Moore/CIO, Corporate VP - Information Technology, James D. Stilson/Corporate VP - Operations, Suzanne B. Rudy/VP, Corporate Treasurer, Compliance Officer, Assist. Sec., Barry D. Church/VP, Corporate Controller, Gregory J. Thompson/VP - Sales

Directors: Robert A. Bruggeworth/Dir., CEO, Pres., Albert E. Paladino/Chmn., Daniel A. Dileo/Dir., William J. Pratt/Dir., CTO, Corporate VP, Jeffery R. Gardner/Dir., Jack Harding/Dir., David A. Norbury/Dir., Erik H. Van Der Kaay/Dir., Walter H. Wilkinson/Dir., John R. Harding/Dir.

Owners: Jerry D. Neal, Erik H. van der Kaay, William A. Priddy, Putnam, LLC and affiliates/4.97%, Robert A. Bruggeworth, Insiders/4.12%, William J. Pratt, Walter H. Wilkinson, Steven E. Creviston, Barclays Global Investors, N.A./11.95%, Mazama Capital Management, Inc/11.82%, John R. Harding, David A. Norbury, Daniel A. DiLeo, Jeffery R. Gardner *(16 Owners included in Index)*

Financial Data: Fiscal Year End: 04/01 **Latest Annual Data:** 3/31/2007

Year	Sales	Net Income
2007	$1,023,615,000	$83,416,000
2006	$770,247,000	$16,330,000
2005	$634,204,000	-$66,045,000

Curr. Assets:	$580,439,000	Curr. Liab.:	$113,216,000		
Plant, Equip.:	$373,455,000	Total Liab.:	$369,967,000	Indic. Yr. Divd.:	NA
Total Assets:	$1,089,634,000	Net Worth:	$719,667,000	Debt/ Equity:	0.3414

RF Monolithics Inc

4441 Sigma Rd., Dallas, TX, 75244; ***PH:*** 1-972-233-2903; ***Fax:*** 1-972-387-8148; ***http://*** www.rfm.com; ***Email:*** info@rfm.com

General - Incorporation	DE	**Stock**- Price on:12/24/2007	$5.599
Employees	205	Stock Exchange	NDQ
Auditor	McGladrey & Pullen LLP	Ticker Symbol	RFMI
Stk Agt	EquiServe Trust Co N.A	Outstanding Shares	9,170,000
Counsel	Cooley Godward LLP	E.P.S	-$0.72
DUNS No.	09-681-7002	Shareholders	NA

Business: The group's principal activities are to designs, develops, manufacture and market a broad range of radio frequency component and module products. The products are produced in two groups low power products and communication products. The low power products include low power components and virtual wire, short range radio products. The communication products include frequency control modules and filters. The products are in the range of 50 megahertz to 2.4 gigahertz, which is based on surface acoustic wave technology. The products are manufactured to perform specific functions and integrated modules to meet system performance requirements. The products are used in automotive, consumer, computer, industrial and telecommunication industries. The group's facilities are at located in Dallas, Texas. The group also contracts manufacturing operations from the Philippines, Taiwan and Japan. The group exports products to France, Germany, Asia and other foreign countries.

Primary SIC and add'l.: 3679 3829 7389

CIK No: 0000922204

Subsidiaries: Aleier, Inc., Cirronet, Inc.

Officers: David M. Kirk/Dir., CEO, Pres., Joseph E. Andrulis/Sr. VP, Group Mgr. - Wireless Solutions Group, James P. Farley/VP, Controller, Darrell L. Ash/Sr. VP - Technology, Harley E. Barnes/CFO, David B. Crawford/VP - Sales, Robert J. Kansy/VP - Engineering, Jon S. Prokop/VP - Operations, Robert M. Gemmell/Pres. - Cirronet

Directors: David M. Kirk/Dir., CEO, Pres., Michael R. Bernique/Chmn., Dean C. Campbell/Dir., Francis J. Hughes/Dir., William L. Eversole/Dir.

Owners: Insiders/17.50%, David M. Kirk/2.60%, David B. Crawford/1.00%, Robert M. Gemmell/2.60%, Michael R. Bernique/1.50%, Austin W. Marxe/10.80%, Harley E. Barnes/1.00%, Dean C. Campbell/2.10%, Francis J. Hughes/1.20%, William L. Eversole, Joseph E. Andrulis

Financial Data: ***Fiscal Year End:***08/31 ***Latest Annual Data:*** 8/31/2006

Year	Sales	Net Income
2006	$54,162,000	$581,000
2005	$46,222,000	$484,000
2004	$48,506,000	$2,237,000

Curr. Assets:	$23,081,000	**Curr. Liab.:**	$5,513,000		
Plant, Equip.:	$6,275,000	**Total Liab.:**	$5,624,000	**Indic. Yr. Divd.:**	NA
Total Assets:	$30,400,000	**Net Worth:**	$24,776,000	**Debt/ Equity:**	0.1987

RFMD

7628 Thorndike Rd., Greensboro, NC, 27409; ***PH:*** 1-336-664-1233; ***Fax:*** 1-336-931-7454; ***http://*** www.rfmd.com

General - Incorporation	NC	**Stock**- Price on:12/24/2007	$6.34
Employees	3,252	Stock Exchange	NDQ
Auditor	Ernst & Young LLP	Ticker Symbol	NA
Stk Agt	Wachovia Bank N.A	Outstanding Shares	194,220,000
Counsel	NA	E.P.S	$0.39
DUNS No.	62-775-5010	Shareholders	NA

Business: The group's principal activity is to design, develop, manufacture and market proprietary radio frequency integrated circuits. These integrated circuits are used in cellular phones, base stations, wireless local area networks (wlans), cable television modems, and global positioning systems (gps). The group's products include amplifiers, mixers, modulators or demodulators and single chip transmitters, receivers and transceivers. The customers of the group are original equipment manufacturers and original design manufacturers. The major customers of the group are nokia corporation, motorola inc and samsung electronics co ltd. The products are marketed in the United States, China, Europe, Korea, Taiwan, central and South America, Japan, Canada and Singapore markets. On 24-May-2004, the group acquired silicon wave inc.

Primary SIC and add'l.: 3674 3559 3669

CIK No: 0000911160

Subsidiaries: OOO Neosilicon, RF Micro Devices (Beijing) Co. Ltd., RF Micro Devices (Canada) ULC, RF Micro Devices (Denmark) ApS, RF Micro Devices (Finland) Oy, RF Micro Devices (Holland) B.V., RF Micro Devices (Korea) YH, RF Micro Devices (Taiwan) B.V., RF Micro Devices Export, Inc., RF Micro Devices International, Inc., RF Micro Devices UK Ltd, RF Micro Devices, Svenska AB, RFMD Infrastructure Product Group, Inc., Rfmd Wpan, Inc., RFMD, LLC

Officers: Robert A. Bruggeworth/Dir., CEO, Pres./$3,870,704.00, Powell T. Seymour/Corporate VP - Strategic Operations, Sec., Gary J. Grant/Corporate VP - Quality Assurance, Jerry D. Neal/Exec. VP - Marketing, Strategic Development/$1,742,213.00, Steven E. Creviston/Corporate VP - Cellular Products Group/$1,783,885.00, William J. Pratt/Dir., CTO, Corporate VP/$1,744,760.00, William A. Priddy/CFO, Corporate VP - Administration, Sec./$1,810,520.00, James D. Stilson/Corporate VP - Operations, Forrest J. Moore/Corporate VP - Information Technology, CIO, Gregory J. Thompson/VP - Sales, Barry D. Church/46/VP, Corporate Controller, Principal Accounting Officer, Suzanne B. Rudy/VP, Corporate Treasurer, Compliance Officer, Assist. Sec.

Directors: Robert A. Bruggeworth/Dir., CEO, Pres., Albert E. Paladino/Chmn., David A. Norbury/Dir., Erik H. Van Der Kaay/Dir., John R. Harding/53/Dir., Jeffery R. Gardner/Dir., William J. Pratt/Dir., CTO, Corporate VP, Daniel A. Dileo/Dir., Walter H. Wilkinson/Dir.

Owners: William J. Pratt, William A. Priddy, Jeffery R. Gardner, Daniel A. DiLeo, Steven E. Creviston, Albert E. Paladino, Barclays Global Investors, N.A. and affiliates/12.02%, David A. Norbury, State Street Bank and Trust Company, Trustee/5.50%, Robert A. Bruggeworth, John R. Harding, Putnam, LLC and affiliates/5.00%, Walter H. Wilkinson, Erik H. van der Kaay, Jerry D. Neal *(17 Owners included in Index)*

Financial Data: ***Fiscal Year End:***04/01 ***Latest Annual Data:*** 3/31/2007

Year	Sales	Net Income
2007	$1,023,615,000	$83,416,000
2006	$770,247,000	$16,330,000
2005	$634,204,000	-$66,045,000

Curr. Assets:	$580,439,000	**Curr. Liab.:**	$113,216,000	**P/E Ratio:**	14.74
Plant, Equip.:	$373,455,000	**Total Liab.:**	$369,967,000	**Indic. Yr. Divd.:**	NA
Total Assets:	$1,089,634,000	**Net Worth:**	$719,667,000	**Debt/ Equity:**	0.3414

RG America

1507 Capital Ave., Ste 101, Plano, TX, 75074; ***PH:*** 1-972-919-4774; ***http://*** www.rgamerica.com; ***Email:*** info@rgamerica.com

General - Incorporation	NV	**Stock**- Price on:12/24/2007	$0.1298
Employees	36	Stock Exchange	OTC
Auditor	Whitley Penn	Ticker Symbol	RGMI
Stk Agt	NA	Outstanding Shares	29,250,000
Counsel	NA	E.P.S	-$0.366
DUNS No.	NA	Shareholders	NA

Business: The group's principal activities include fee-based services that address clients' risk management needs for their real estate assets. It offers three main types of services namely a full-service risk management program designed for the multi-family housing industry; a general lines insurance agency specializing in placing business related insurance for a variety of customers; and a multi-family housing and commercial real estate restoration division. In Dec 2003 the group acquired restoration group America 2003 and its wholly owned subsidiaries rg insurance services inc., rg risk management inc., rg restoration inc., and restoration group America inc.

Primary SIC and add'l.: 6159

CIK No: 0001088401

Subsidiaries: CTFD Marine, Inc, CTFD, Inc, Invvision Funding Inc, Practical Business Solutions 2000, Inc, Restoration Group America, 2003, Inc, Restoration Group America, Inc, RG Florida GC, Inc, RG Florida SC, Inc, RG Industries, Inc, RG Insurance Services, Inc, RG Restoration, Inc, RG Risk Management, Inc, RG Roofing, Inc, Total Professional Restoration, Inc, Urban Logic, Inc

Officers: Bruce A. Hall/51/CEO, CFO, Kevin L. Dahlberg/45/Exec. VP, James A. Rea/40/Dir., COO, Pres.

Directors: Edward P. Rea/67/Chmn., Michael A. Jenkins/66/Dir., Paul S. Johnson/74/Dir., James A. Rea/40/Dir., COO, Pres.

Owners: Rea Brothers, Ltd./9.13%, Jerod Yates/9.86%, Brandon Hawk/8.47%, BHDH Family LP/9.42%, JAAVBR, LP/9.87%, Bryan Cauthen/8.47%, J 2 Family LP/9.85%, Paul S. Johnson, Michael A. Jenkins, Edward P. Rea/9.47%, Insiders/20.48%, James A. Rea/11.01%

Financial Data: ***Fiscal Year End:***12/31 ***Latest Annual Data:*** 12/31/2006

Year	Sales	Net Income
2006	$20,373,000	-$9,857,000
2005	$20,624,000	$2,069,000
2004	$5,100,000	-$2,283,000

Curr. Assets:	$14,038,000	**Curr. Liab.:**	$17,401,000		
Plant, Equip.:	$952,000	**Total Liab.:**	$17,404,000	**Indic. Yr. Divd.:**	NA
Total Assets:	$15,042,000	**Net Worth:**	-$2,362,000	**Debt/ Equity:**	NA

RG Global Lifestyles Inc

30021 Tomas Ste. 200, Rcho Sta Marg, CA, 92688; ***PH:*** 1-949-888-9550; ***Fax:*** 1-949-666-5151; ***http://*** www.rgglife.com; ***Email:*** info@rgglife.com

General - Incorporation	CA	**Stock**- Price on:12/24/2007	NA
Employees	3	Stock Exchange	OTC
Auditor	Beckstead and Watts, LLP	Ticker Symbol	RGBL
Stk Agt	Computershare Investor Services LLC	Outstanding Shares	
Counsel	NA	E.P.S	-$0.6
DUNS No.	NA	Shareholders	NA

Business: The groups principle activity is manufacture and sale of natural supplements, health and beauty aid products for the nutraceutical industry. The group operates from the United States and Vietnam. The group's revenue for Sep '07 was 0.54 millions of USD.

Primary SIC and add'l.: 3585

CIK No: 0000932136

Subsidiaries: Aquair, Inc.,

Officers: Grant King/57/CEO/$2,364,375.00, William C. Hitchcock/CFO/$1,247,774.00, Karim J. Murray/Information Technology Consulting, Project Management, Juzer Jangbarwala/CTO/$1,279,548.00, Steve Ritchie/64/Management Member

Directors: Joseph Murray/37/Dir., David Koontz/55/Dir.

Owners: Steve Ritchie, Joseph Murray/14.10%, Grant King/3.90%, Budy Hartono/10.70%, William Hitchcock/3.80%, Louis Knickerbocker/26.40%, Juzer Jangbarwala/2.10%

Financial Data: ***Fiscal Year End:***12/31 ***Latest Annual Data:*** 12/31/2000

Year	Sales	Net Income
2000	$30,345,000	-$3,394,000

Curr. Assets:	$11,580,000	**Curr. Liab.:**	$10,212,000		
Plant, Equip.:	$2,527,000	**Total Liab.:**	$19,644,000	**Indic. Yr. Divd.:**	NA
Total Assets:	$18,142,000	**Net Worth:**	-$1,502,000	**Debt/ Equity:**	NA

RGC Resources Inc

519 Kimball Ave. NE, Roanoke, VA, 24016; ***PH:*** 1-540-777-4427; ***Fax:*** 1-540-777-2636; ***http://*** www.rgcresources.com

General - Incorporation	VA	**Stock**- Price on:12/24/2007	$28.31
Employees	135	Stock Exchange	NDQ
Auditor	Brown, Edwards & Co., L.l.p.	Ticker Symbol	RGCO
Stk Agt	Agent & Dividend Reinvestment Agent	Outstanding Shares	2,160,000
Counsel	NA	E.P.S	$1.75
DUNS No.	NA	Shareholders	NA

Business: The group's principal activities are selling and distributing of natural gas to approximately 57,700 customers in roanoke, Virginia, bluefield, west Virginia and the surrounding areas. The group also sells and distributes propane to approximately 18,100 customers in western Virginia and southern west Virginia. The group provides information system services to software providers in the utility industry. The group operates in four segments. Gas utilities provides energy services. Propane operation delivers propane gas and related services. Energy marketing sells natural gas to industrial transportation customers. Other services includes appliance services, mapping services and information system services. Approximately 90.1% of the group's customers are residential, 9.8% are small commercial users and the remaining percentage is made up of large industrial customers.

Primary SIC and add'l.: 4922 4924 6719 1321

CIK No: 0001069533

Subsidiaries: Bluefield Gas Company, Diversified Energy Company, RGC Ventures of Virginia, Inc., Roanoke Gas Company

Officers: John B. Williamson/Chmn., CEO, Pres., Howard T. Lyon/VP, Treasurer, Controller, Dale P. Lee/VP, Sec.

Directors: John B. Williamson/Chmn., CEO, Pres., Abney S. Boxley/Dir., Allen J. Layman/Dir., Frank S. Smith/Dir., Frank T. Ellett/Dir., Maryellen F. Goodlatte/Dir., Nancy H. Agee/Dir., George W. Logan/Dir., Raymond D. Smoot/Dir.

Owners: George W. Logan, John S. DOrazio, Abney S. Boxley, Insiders/6.46%, Howard T. Lyon, Maryellen F. Goodlatte, Frank T. Ellett, John B. Williamson/1.83%, Nancy H. Agee, Frank S. Smith, Jane N. OKeeffe, Raymond D. Smoot, Dale P. Lee, Allen J. Layman

Financial Data: ***Fiscal Year End:***09/30 ***Latest Annual Data:*** 09/30/2007

Year	Sales	Net Income
2007	$89,901,000	$3,806,000
2006	$107,798,000	$3,512,000
2005	$121,648,000	$3,507,000

Curr. Assets:	$35,140,000	***Curr. Liab.:***	$29,839,000	***P/E Ratio:***	13.33
Plant, Equip.:	$79,040,000	***Total Liab.:***	$74,167,000	***Indic. Yr. Divd.:***	$1.220
Total Assets:	$114,663,000	***Net Worth:***	$40,495,000	***Debt/ Equity:***	0.6824

Rhapsody Acquisition Corp

10 E 53rd St., 35th Fl., New York, NY, 10022; ***PH:*** 1-212-319-7676

General - Incorporation	DE	***Stock***- Price on:12/24/2007	$7.42
Employees	NA	Stock Exchange	OTC
Auditor	BDO Seidman, LLP	Ticker Symbol	RPSD
Stk Agt	Continental Stock T & T Co.	Outstanding Shares	NA
Counsel	NA	E.P.S	$0.09
DUNS No.	NA	Shareholders	NA

Business: The groups principal activity is searching for prospective target businesses to acquire. The group operates from the United States.

Primary SIC and add'l.: 7389

CIK No: 0001361538

Officers: Eric S. Rosenfeld/50/Chmn., CEO, Pres., David D. Sgro/31/CFO, Arnaud Ajdler/32/Dir., Sec., Joel Greenblatt/Special Advisor

Directors: Eric S. Rosenfeld/50/Chmn., CEO, Pres., Arnaud Ajdler/32/Dir., Sec., Leonard B. Schlemm/55/Dir., Jon Bauer/50/Dir., Colin D. Watson/66/Dir.

Owners: Fir Tree, Inc./9.20%, Jon Bauer, Brahman Capital Corp./6.30%, Insiders/16.90%, Millennium Management, L.L.C./10.60%, Colin D. Watson, Arnaud Ajdler, Leonard B. Schlemm, Eric S. Rosenfeld/13.80%, Dorset Management Corporation/6.10%

Financial Data: ***Fiscal Year End:***12/31 ***Latest Annual Data:*** 03/31/2007

Year	Sales	Net Income
2007	NA	$351,000

Curr. Assets:	$40,501,000	***Curr. Liab.:***	$455,000		
Plant, Equip.:	NA	***Total Liab.:***	$8,436,000	***Indic. Yr. Divd.:***	NA
Total Assets:	$40,501,000	***Net Worth:***	$32,065,000	***Debt/ Equity:***	NA

Rhodia

Cn 7500 , 8 Cedar Brook Dr., Cranbury, NJ, 08512; ***PH:*** 1-609-860-4000; ***http://*** www.rhodia.com; ***Email:*** rhodia.communication-corporate@eu.rhodia.com

General - Incorporation	France	***Stock***- Price on:12/24/2007	$48.88
Employees	17,077	Stock Exchange	OTC
Auditor	PricewaterhouseCoopers LLP	Ticker Symbol	RHAYY
Stk Agt	Citibank N.A	Outstanding Shares	100,310,000
Counsel	NA	E.P.S	$1.10
DUNS No.	76-455-849	Shareholders	NA

Business: The group's principal activities are the research and production of speciality chemicals. Fine organics: life science chemicals, pharmaceutical ingredients, diphenols and aromas, intermediates; consumer specialities: rhodia food, hpcii, phosphates; industrial specialities: tire and rubber, silicones, paper, paint and construction materials; polyamides: engineering plastics, fibres, industrial yarns, textile yarns, polyamide intermediates; services & specialities: eco services, acetow, rare earths.

Primary SIC and add'l.: 2821 4953 2834 2899 3011 2823 2824

CIK No: 0001062814

Subsidiaries: A TRPP, Rhodia S.A, Rhne-Poulenc, Wuxi Chemicals Co. Ltd

Officers: Jean-Pierre Clamadieu/Dir., CEO, Jacques Kheliff/55/Dir., Group VP - Sustainable Development, Marchos De Marchi/Pres. - Latin America Zone, Michel Ybert/57/Pres. - Asia Pacific Zone, Eric Noyrez/Pres. - Silcea Enterprise, Nicolas Beniere/Group VP - Industrial, Marc Chollet/Group VP - Strategy, Lucia Dumas/Group VP - Corporate Communications, Pascal Juery/Group VP - Purchasing, Bernard Chambon/61/Group Exec. VP - Human Resources, Communications, Sustainable Development, Gilles Auffret/61/COO, Jean-Pierre Labroue/46/Group Exec. VP, General Counsel, Corp. Sec., Pascal Bouchiat/48/Group Exec. VP, CFO, Laurent Schmitt/50/Pres. - Polyamide Enterprise, Mike De Ruosi/51/Pres. - Novecare Enterprise *(21 Officers included in Index)*

Directors: Jean-Pierre Clamadieu/Dir., CEO, Yves Rene Nanot/Chmn., Aldo Cardoso/Dir., Jacques Kheliff/55/Dir., Group VP - Sustainable Development, Pascal Colombani/Dir., Jerome Contamine/Dir., Michel De Fabiani/Dir., Olivier Legrain/Dir., Pierre Levi/Dir., Francis Mer/Dir., Hubertus Sulkowski/Dir.

Owners: Olivier Legrain, Michel de Fabiani, Pierre Lvi, Yves Ren Nanot, Aldo Cardoso, Pascal Colombani, Jacques Kheliff, Jean-Pierre Clamadieu, Jrme Contamine

Financial Data: ***Fiscal Year End:***12/31 ***Latest Annual Data:*** 12/31/2006

Year	Sales	Net Income
2006	$6,946,098,000	$19,805,000
2005	$6,567,498,000	-$763,938,000
2004	$7,205,396,000	-$1,043,766,000

Curr. Assets:	$3,541,045,000	***Curr. Liab.:***	$2,839,965,000		
Plant, Equip.:	$2,323,728,000	***Total Liab.:***	$7,632,655,000	***Indic. Yr. Divd.:***	NA
Total Assets:	$6,638,468,000	***Net Worth:***	-$1,027,193,000	***Debt/ Equity:***	NA

Rica Foods Inc

95 Merrick Way, Ste 507, Coral Gables, FL, 33134; ***PH:*** 1-305-476-1757; ***http://*** www.ricafoods.com

General - Incorporation	NV	***Stock***- Price on:12/24/2007	$0.0001
Employees	NA	Stock Exchange	OTC
Auditor	Stonefield Josephson, Inc	Ticker Symbol	RCFO
Stk Agt	Mr. Oconitrillo	Outstanding Shares	NA
Counsel	NA	E.P.S	NA
DUNS No.	19-970-8785	Shareholders	NA

Business: The group's principal activities are to produce and sell fresh and frozen poultry, processed chicken products, commercial eggs and concentrate for livestock and domestic animals production and distribution of animal feeds. The operations of the group are principally conducted through two wholly owned companies, corporacion pipasa sa and corporacion as de oros sa. The group operates 28 fried chicken quick service restaurants in Costa Rica called restaurantes as and don amado. The group's main brand names for broiler chicken, chicken parts, mixed cuts and chicken breasts are mimados(tm), dogpro(tm) kan kan(tm), and ascan(tm), pipasa and as de oros. Chicken by-products include sausages, bologna, chicken nuggets, chicken patties, frankfurters and pate. The group also distributes commercial eggs, fertile eggs and recycling material.

Primary SIC and add'l.: 0251 0252 5144 5812 2099 6719 2015

CIK No: 0000789881

Financial Data: ***Fiscal Year End:***09/30 ***Latest Annual Data:*** 9/30/2004

Year	Sales	Net Income
2004	$138,512,000	-$3,397,000
2003	$127,905,000	-$799,000
2002	$130,665,000	$3,063,000

Curr. Assets:	$29,627,000	***Curr. Liab.:***	$24,010,000		
Plant, Equip.:	$39,076,000	***Total Liab.:***	$60,944,000	***Indic. Yr. Divd.:***	NA
Total Assets:	$80,603,000	***Net Worth:***	$19,658,000	***Debt/ Equity:***	1.2949

Richardson Electronics Ltd

40W267 Keslinger Rd., LaFox, IL, 60147; ***PH:*** 1-630-208-3637; ***Fax:*** 1-630-208-2550; ***http://*** www.rell.com; ***Email:*** info@rell.com

General - Incorporation	DE	***Stock***- Price on:12/24/2007	$9.38
Employees	1,268	Stock Exchange	NDQ
Auditor	Ernst & Young, LLP	Ticker Symbol	RELL
Stk Agt	LaSalle Bank N.A	Outstanding Shares	16,360,000
Counsel	NA	E.P.S	$2.33
DUNS No.	02-547-8371	Shareholders	NA

Business: The group's principal activity is to provide engineered solutions, which serves the radio frequency and wireless communications, industrial power conversion, security and display systems markets. The services are provided to customers through product manufacturing, systems integration, prototype design, testing and logistics. The products include radio frequency and microwave components, power semiconductors, electron tubes, microwave generators, data display monitors and electronic security products and systems. The products are used to control, switch or amplify electrical power or signals, or as display, recording or alarm devices in a variety of industrial, communication and security applications. The trade names are amperex, capture, cetron, national and rf gain.

Primary SIC and add'l.: 3679 3671 3674

CIK No: 0000355948

Subsidiaries: AAR Aircraft & Engine Sales & Leasing, AAR Aircraft Services, Inc., AAR Allen Services, Inc., AAR Engine Services, Inc, AAR International, Inc., AAR Manufacturing Group, Inc, AAR Parts Trading, Inc., AAR Services, Inc.

Officers: Edward J. Richardson/Chmn., CEO, Pres./$1,338,632.00, Kathleen M. McNally/Sr. VP - Marketing Operations And Customer Support, Wendy Diddell/Exec. VP - Corporate Development/$732,475.00, Brad R. Knechtel/Exec. VP - Supply Chain Management, Bart Petrini/Exec. VP, GM - Electron Device Group, Michael Bauer/Sr. VP, Chief Human Resources Officer, Kyle C. Badger/Exec. VP, General Counsel, Sec., Dan Fujii/Interim CFO, Corporate Controller, John Denatale/56/CIO, William G. Seils/Assist. Sec., Robert J. Heise/VP, GM - Display Systems Group, Gregory J. Peloquin/Exec. VP, GM - RF, Wireless, Power Division/$350,426.00

Directors: Edward J. Richardson/Chmn., CEO, Pres., Harold L. Purkey/Dir., Samuel Rubinovitz/Dir., Jacques Bouyer/Dir., Scott Hodes/Dir., John R. Peterson/Dir., Ad Ketelaars/Dir., Arnold R. Allen/Dir.

Owners: Gregory J. Peloquin, Lee Munder Investments, Ltd/5.45%, T. Rowe Price Associates, Inc/8.27%, Royce& Associates, LLC/9.10%, Wendy Diddell, Edward J. Richardson/16.71%, Arnold R. Allen, David J. DeNeve, David J. Gilmartin, Ad Ketelaars, Harold L. Purkey, John R. Peterson, Arnold R. Allen, Insiders/99.59%, Samuel Rubinovitz *(26 Owners included in Index)*

Financial Data: ***Fiscal Year End:***05/28 ***Latest Annual Data:*** 6/3/2006

Year	Sales	Net Income
2006	$637,940,000	-$2,642,000
2005	$578,724,000	-$16,017,000
2004	$520,069,000	$6,033,000

Curr. Assets:	$255,329,000	***Curr. Liab.:***	$97,098,000	***P/E Ratio:***	4.08
Plant, Equip.:	$33,375,000	***Total Liab.:***	$211,059,000	***Indic. Yr. Divd.:***	$0.160
Total Assets:	$309,299,000	***Net Worth:***	$98,240,000	***Debt/ Equity:***	NA

Richmont Mines Inc

110 Ave. Principale, Rouyn-Noranda, PQ, J9X 4P2; ***PH:*** 1-819-797-2465; ***http://*** www.richmont-mines.com; ***Email:*** jnormandeau@richmont-mines.com

General - Incorporation	QC	***Stock***- Price on:12/24/2007	$2.87
Employees	305	Stock Exchange	AMEX
Auditor	KPMG LLP	Ticker Symbol	RIC
Stk Agt	Computershare Trust Co	Outstanding Shares	24,250,000
Counsel	NA	E.P.S	$0.423
DUNS No.	24-502-2389	Shareholders	NA

Business: The group's principle activity is to acquire, explore and develop mining properties, principally gold. The group operates in two Canadian provinces: quebec and newfoundland. The group's mining properties consist of nugget pond mine and mill, hammerdown mine, francoeur mine, camflo mill and louvem mines. The group's quarterly revenue for September 2007 was 5.33 millions of CAD.

Primary SIC and add'l.: 1041 1081

CIK No: 0001023996

Subsidiaries: Camflo Mill Inc., Louvem Mines Inc.

Officers: Martin Rivard/Dir., CEO, Pres., Luc Dorofte/Mine Captain, Beaufor Mine, Jacques Daigneault/Sr. Geologist, Denis Bellemare/Chief Engineer - Projects, Julie Normandeau/Contact - Investor Relations, Laurent Chevalier/Chief Accountant - Beaufor Mine, Nicole Veilleux/Dir. - Finance, Marcel St-Pierre/Mine Captain, East Amphi Property, Helene Lapointe/Dir. - Human

Resources, Christine Lapointe/Controller, Stephane Tremblay/Health, Safety, Training Coordinator, Beaufor, East Amphi Mines, Camflo Mill, Operations Quebec Division, Stephanie Lee/Dir., Sec., Richard Dubuc/Chief Geologist - Beaufor Mine, Jules Riopel/Dir. - Geology, Exploration, Marcel Beaudoin/Mgr. - Mine, Beaufor Mine *(18 Officers included in Index)*

Directors: Martin Rivard/Dir., CEO, Pres., Jean-Guy Rivard/Chmn., Denis Arcand/Vice Chmn., Rejean Houle/Dir., Raynald Vezina/Dir., Stephanie Lee/Dir., Sec.

Financial Data: **Fiscal Year End:**12/31 **Latest Annual Data:** 12/31/2006

Year	Sales	Net Income
2006	$30,998,000	-$9,494,000
2005	$18,571,000	-$23,558,000
2004	$32,914,000	$509,000

Curr. Assets:	$23,226,000	**Curr. Liab.:**	$5,059,000		
Plant, Equip.:	$13,511,000	**Total Liab.:**	$11,408,000	**Indic. Yr. Divd.:**	NA
Total Assets:	$39,957,000	**Net Worth:**	$28,549,000	**Debt/ Equity:**	NA

Rick's Cabaret International Inc

10959 Cutten Rd., Houston, TX, 77066; ***PH:*** 1-281-397-6730; ***Fax:*** 1-281-820-1445; ***http://*** www.ricks.com; ***Email:*** ir@ricks.com

General		**Stock**	
Incorporation	TX	Price on:12/24/2007	$9.2044
Employees	560	Stock Exchange	NDQ
Auditor	Whitley Penn	Ticker Symbol	RICK
Stk Agt	American Stock Transfer & Trust Co.	Outstanding Shares	6,120,000
Counsel	NA	E.P.S.	$0.49
DUNS No.	92-788-1383	Shareholders	NA

Business: The group's principal activity is to own and operate adult nightclubs that offer live adult entertainment, restaurant and bar operations. The group owns and operates six adult nightclubs in houston, austin and san antonio, Texas, minneapolis and Minnesota. It operates the nightclubs under the name rick's cabaret and xtc. It also operates premiere adult entertainment Internet Web sites in two categories: online entertainment and online auctions of adult products and erotica. The online entertainment sites are www.dancerdorm.com, www.amateurdan.com, and www.xxxpassword.com. The online adult auction Web sites are www.naughtybids.com, www.pornauction.com, www.xxxauctionville.com, www.xxxbids.com, www.xxxgayauction.com, and www.allgayauction.com. On 12-Jun-2003, the group acquired taurus entertainment companies inc.

Primary SIC and add'l.: 7375 7999

CIK No: 0000935419

Subsidiaries: Bobby's Novelty, Inc., Broadstreets Cabaret, Inc., Citation Land LLC, Peregrine Enterprises, Inc, RCI Billing, Inc., RCI Dating Services, Inc., RCI Debit Services, Inc., RCI Entertainment (Ft. Worth), Inc., RCI Entertainment (Minnesota), Inc., RCI Entertainment (New York), Inc., RCI Entertainment (North Carolina), Inc., RCI Entertainment (San Antonio), Inc., RCI Entertainment Texas, Inc., RCI Holdings, Inc., RCI Internet Holding, Inc. 22 Subsidiaries included in the Index

Officers: Eric Langan/38/CEO, Pres./$430,901.00, Travis Reese/VP, Dir. - Technology, Information Systems CIO/$197,816.00, Allan Priaulx/Contact - Investor, Media Relations, Phillip Marshall/58/CFO

Directors: Robert L. Watters/Founder, Allan Bergstrom/Dir., Steven L. Jenkins/Dir.

Owners: Alan Bergstrom/0.30%, Robert L. Watters/0.60%, Eric S. Langan/15.30%, Burlingame Asset Management/Blair Sanford/6.20%, E. S. Langan. L.P./7.70%, Estate of Ralph McElroy/14.00%, Insiders/17.30%, JLF Asset Management/Jeff Feinberg/13.20%, Steven L. Jenkins/0.10%, Travis Reese/1.00%

Financial Data: **Fiscal Year End:**09/30 **Latest Annual Data:** 9/30/2006

Year	Sales	Net Income
2006	$24,487,000	$1,753,000
2005	$14,824,000	-$215,000
2004	$15,960,000	$775,000

Curr. Assets:	$1,688,000	**Curr. Liab.:**	$3,952,000	**P/E Ratio:**	30.68
Plant, Equip.:	$17,424,000	**Total Liab.:**	$16,694,000	**Indic. Yr. Divd.:**	NA
Total Assets:	$30,603,000	**Net Worth:**	$13,908,000	**Debt/ Equity:**	0.4386

Ricoh Co Ltd

5 Dedrick Pl., West Caldwell, NJ, 07006; ***PH:*** 1-973-882-2000; ***Fax:*** 1-973-882-5840; ***http://*** www.ricoh.com

General		**Stock**	
Incorporation	Japan	Price on:12/24/2007	$116
Employees	NA	Stock Exchange	OTC
Auditor	KPMG Azsa & Co	Ticker Symbol	RICOF
Stk Agt	Chuo Mitsui Trust & Banking Co Ltd	Outstanding Shares	NA
Counsel	NA	E.P.S.	NA
DUNS No.	69-054-9118	Shareholders	NA

Business: The group's principal activities are manufacturing and distributing office automation equipment, including copiers, facsimile machines, data processing equipment, printers and related supplies. The operations of the group are divided into two segments: office equipment and other business. The office equipment segment is sub-divided into copiers & related supplies and communication & information systems. The copiers segment includes digital copiers, multi functional printers and software. The communications & information segment includes printers, scanners, CD-recordable and CD-re writable drives, fax machines, personal computers, software & services. The other business segment includes electronic devices & photographic equipment. The group's brands include ricoh, gestetner, lanier & savin. The group manufactures its products in Japan, the United States, the UK, France & China.

Primary SIC and add'l.: 3577 3661 3861

CIK No: 0000317891

Subsidiaries: San-Ai Co., Ltd., Tohoku Ricoh Co., Ltd.

Officers: Shiroh Kondoh/Representative Dir., CEO, Pres., Katsumi Yoshida/Dir., Corporate Exec. VP, Kiyoshi Sakai/Dir., Corporate Exec. VP, Kohji Tomizawa/Corporate Auditor, Shigekazu Iijima/Corporate Auditor, Kenji Matsuishi/Corporate Auditors, Takehiko Wada/Corporate Auditors, Kazuo Togashi/Corporate Sr. VP, Takashi Nakamura/Dir., Corporate Exec. VP, Thomas Salierno/Group Executive Officer, Hiroshi Hamada/Principal Advisor, Satoshi Itoh/66/Substitute Corporate Auditor, Kazunori Azuma/Dir., Corporate Exec. VP, Masayuki Matsumoto/Dir., Corporate Exec. VP, Zenji Miura/Dir., Corporate Exec. VP *(49 Officers included in Index)*

Directors: Shiroh Kondoh/Representative Dir., CEO, Pres., Masamitsu Sakurai/Chmn., Takaaki Wakasugi/Dir., Koichi Endo/Dir., Corporate Exec. VP, Katsumi Yoshida/Dir., Corporate Exec. VP, Takashi Nakamura/Dir., Corporate Exec. VP, Kazunori Azuma/Dir., Corporate Exec. VP, Masayuki Matsumoto/Dir., Corporate Exec. VP, Zenji Miura/Dir., Corporate Exec. VP, Kiyoshi Sakai/Dir., Corporate Exec. VP, Takuya Goto/Dir.

Owners: Norihisa Goto, Yoshimasa Matsuura, Sadahiro Arikawa, Kiyoto Nagasawa, Yutaka Ebi, Shiroh Sasaki, Hiroshi Tsuruga, Hisashi Takata, Hiroshi Adachi, Norio Tanaka, Susumu Ichioka, The Master Trust Bank of Japan, Ltd./9.06%, Kohji Sawa, Makoto Hashimoto, Japan Trustee Services Bank, Ltd./5.38% *(20 Owners included in Index)*

Financial Data: **Fiscal Year End:**03/31 **Latest Annual Data:** 03/31/2007

Year	Sales	Net Income
2007	$17,533,263,000	$946,814,000
2006	$16,368,291,000	$829,547,000
2005	$16,954,280,000	$777,037,000

Curr. Assets:	$8,919,172,000	**Curr. Liab.:**	$5,846,394,000		
Plant, Equip.:	$2,292,675,000	**Total Liab.:**	$8,786,736,000	**Indic. Yr. Divd.:**	NA
Total Assets:	$17,446,009,000	**Net Worth:**	$8,207,222,000	**Debt/ Equity:**	NA

Ridgefield Acquisition Corp

900 Third Ave, Ste. 201, New York, NY, 10022; ***PH:*** 1-303-368-0401

General		**Stock**	
Incorporation	CO	Price on:12/24/2007	$1.5
Employees	1	Stock Exchange	OTC
Auditor	Carlin, Charron & Rosen LLP	Ticker Symbol	RDGA
Stk Agt	Atlas Stock Transfer Corp	Outstanding Shares	1,140,000
Counsel	NA	E.P.S.	-$0.12
DUNS No.	10-849-4055	Shareholders	NA

Business: The group's principal activity is to develop prototype micro-robotic device to manipulate organic tissues on an extremely small scale. The group is in development stage and currently seeking to arrange for a merger, acquisition, business combination or other arrangement to pursue its operations.

Primary SIC and add'l.: 9999

CIK No: 0000812152

Subsidiaries: Bio-Medical Automation, Inc.

Owners: Steven N. Bronson/75.60%, Kenneth Schwartz/2.80%, Leonard Hagan/1.30%, RAM Capital/8.80%, Insiders/79.80%

Financial Data: **Fiscal Year End:**12/31 **Latest Annual Data:** 12/31/2006

Year	Sales	Net Income
2006	$14,000	-$139,000
2005	$8,000	-$39,000
2004	$29,000	-$48,000

Curr. Assets:	$435,000	**Curr. Liab.:**	$8,000		
Plant, Equip.:	NA	**Total Liab.:**	$8,000	**Indic. Yr. Divd.:**	NA
Total Assets:	$435,000	**Net Worth:**	$428,000	**Debt/ Equity:**	NA

Ridgewood Energy K Fund Llc

1314 King St., Wilmington, DE, 19801; ***PH:*** 1-302-888-7444

General		**Stock**	
Incorporation	DE	Price on:12/24/2007	NA
Employees	NA	Stock Exchange	NA
Auditor	Deloitte & Touche, LLP	Ticker Symbol	NA
Stk Agt	NA	Outstanding Shares	NA
Counsel	NA	E.P.S.	NA
DUNS No.	NA	Shareholders	NA

Business: The group's principle activity is to operate natural gas projects. The group's projects located in the U.S. waters of the Gulf of Mexico, although the Fund would consider investments in oil prospect in the Gulf of Mexico. Ridgewood Energy Corporation ("Ridgewood Energy"), a Delaware corporation, is the Manager. As the Manager, Ridgewood Energy has direct and exclusive control over the management and control of Fund operations. The group operates from United States.

Primary SIC and add'l.: 1381

CIK No: 0001285480

Officers: Robert E. Swanson/60/Chmn., CEO, Pres., Greg W. Tabor/47/Exec. VP, Dir. - Business Development, Kathleen P. McSherry/42/CFO, Sr. VP, Daniel V. Gulino/47/Sr. VP, General Counsel, Robert L. Gold/48/Exec. VP, Adrien Doherty/55/Exec. VP

Directors: Robert E. Swanson/60/Chmn., CEO, Pres.

Ridgewood Energy L Fund LLC

1314 King St. , Wilmington, DE, 19801; ***PH:*** 1-800-942-5550; ***http://*** www.ridgewoodenergy.com; ***Email:*** info@ridgewoodenergy.com

General		**Stock**	
Incorporation	DE	Price on:12/24/2007	NA
Employees	NA	Stock Exchange	NA
Auditor	Deloitte & Touche, LLP	Ticker Symbol	NA
Stk Agt	NA	Outstanding Shares	NA
Counsel	NA	E.P.S.	NA
DUNS No.	NA	Shareholders	NA

Business: The group is a liability company formed to acquire interests primarily in natural gas projects located in the U.S. waters of the Gulf of Mexico, although the Fund would also consider investments in oil projects in the Gulf of Mexico.

Primary SIC and add'l.: 1381

CIK No: 0001295714

Officers: Robert E. Swanson/60/Chmn., CEO, Pres., Robert L. Gold/Exec. VP, Greg W. Tabor/47/Exec. VP, Dir. - Business Development, Kathleen P. McSherry/CFO, Sr. VP, Daniel V. Gulino/Sr. VP, General Counsel, Adrian Doherty/Exec. VP, Kenneth D. Webb/Mgr. - Geoscience, Randy A. Bennett/Land Mgr., Harvey J. Dupuy/Mgr. - Engineering, Operations, Mirna Valdes/VP - Investor Relations

Directors: Robert E. Swanson/60/Chmn., CEO, Pres.

Ridgewood Energy M Fund LLC

1314 King St., Wilmington, DE, 19801; ***PH:*** 1-302-888-7444

General - Incorporation	DE	Stock - Price on:12/24/2007	NA
Employees	NA	Stock Exchange	NA
Auditor	Deloitte & Touche, LLP	Ticker Symbol	NA
Stk Agt.	NA	Outstanding Shares	NA
Counsel	NA	E.P.S.	NA
DUNS No.	NA	Shareholders	NA

Business: The group's main activity is to acquire interest primarily in natural gas projects. The area of operation includes the U.S. waters of the Gulf of Mexico, although the fund would consider investments in oil projects in the Gulf of Mexico.

Primary SIC and add'l.: 1381

CIK No: 0001302834

Officers: Robert E. Swanson/60/Chmn., CEO, Pres., Adrien Doherty/55/Exec. VP, Kathleen P. McSherry/42/CFO, Sr. VP, Daniel V. Gulino/47/Sr. VP, General Counsel, Greg W. Tabor/47/Exec. VP, Dir. - Business Development, Robert L. Gold/48/Exec. VP

Directors: Robert E. Swanson/60/Chmn., CEO, Pres.

Owners: Insiders, Robert E. Swanson

Rigel Pharmaceuticals Inc

1180 Veterans Blvd., South San Francisco, CA, 94080; *PH:* 1-650-624-1100; *Fax:* 1-650-624-1101; *http://* www.rigel.com; *Email:* communications@rigel.com

General - Incorporation	DE	Stock - Price on:12/24/2007	$9.4
Employees	152	Stock Exchange	NDQ
Auditor	Ernst & Young LLP	Ticker Symbol	RIGL
Stk Agt.	Wells Fargo Shareowner Services	Outstanding Shares	30,210,000
Counsel	Cooley Godward LLP	E.P.S.	-$2.44
DUNS No.	NA	Shareholders	NA

Business: The group's principle activity is to develope novel, small-molecule drug. Its business model is to develop a portfolio of drug candidates through phase ii clinical research, after which the company intends to seek commercialization partners for clinical evaluation, regulatory approval and marketing. The company's lead product research programs focus on: mast cell activation to treat immunologic diseases such as asthma/allergy and autoimmune disorders; an antiviral agent to treat hepatitis c, and ubiquitin ligases, a new class of cancer drug target. The company has begun clinical testing of its first product, for allergic rhinitis, and plans to follow this with two additional drugs in the clinic by the end of 2003. The company's approach to drug discovery is based on advanced, proprietary functional genomics techniques that allow it to directly identify targets that regulate disease pathways and are also suitable for drug modulation. The group operates from United States.

Primary SIC and add'l.: 8731

CIK No: 0001034842

Officers: James M. Gower/Chmn., CEO/$2,499,327.00, Ryan Maynard/CFO, VP/$774,148.00, Robin Cooper/Sr. VP - Pharmaceutical Sciences, Jim Welch/Investor Relations Officer/$934,165.00, Elliott B. Grossbard/Sr. VP - Medical Development/$1,504,844.00, Raul R. Rodriguez/COO, Exec. VP/$1,609,880.00, Donald G. Payan/Co - Founder, Dir., Exec. VP, Chief Scientific Officer/$1,644,950.00, Dolly Vance/Sr. VP, General Counsel, Corp. Sec.

Directors: James M. Gower/Chmn., CEO, Donald G. Payan/Co - Founder, Dir., Exec. VP, Chief Scientific Officer, Walter H. Moos/Dir., Peter S. Ringrose/Dir., Jean Deleage/Dir., Gary A. Lyons/Dir., Hollings C. Renton/Dir., Stephen A. Sherwin/Dir., Bradford S. Goodwin/Dir.

Owners: Elliott B. Grossbard/1.30%, Donald G. Payan/2.00%, Entities Affiliated with James E. Flynn/6.10%, Walter H. Moos, Raul Rodriguez/1.50%, Oppenheimer Funds, Inc./8.60%, Bradford S. Goodwin, Great Point Partners, LLC/6.10%, FMR Corporation/9.20%, Hollings C. Renton, Insiders/9.60%, Peter S. Ringrose, James H. Welch, James M. Gower/2.60%, Stephen A. Sherwin (20 Owners included in Index)

Financial Data: Fiscal Year End:12/31   Latest Annual Data: 12/31/2006

Year	Sales	Net Income
2006	$33,473,000	-$37,637,000
2005	$16,526,000	-$45,256,000
2004	$4,733,000	-$56,255,000

Curr. Assets:	$108,014,000	Curr. Liab.:	$11,238,000		
Plant, Equip.:	$2,975,000	Total Liab.:	$26,011,000	Indic. Yr. Divd.:	NA
Total Assets:	$113,240,000	Net Worth:	$87,229,000	Debt/ Equity:	0.0152

Rightnow Technologies Inc

136 Enterprise Blvd., Bozeman, MT, 59718; *PH:* 1-406-522-4200; *Fax:* 1-406-522-4227; *http://* www.rightnow.com

General - Incorporation	DE	Stock - Price on:12/24/2007	$16.24
Employees	658	Stock Exchange	NDQ
Auditor	KPMG LLP	Ticker Symbol	RNOW
Stk Agt.	U.S. Stock Transfer Corp	Outstanding Shares	32,960,000
Counsel	Dorsey & Whitney LLP	E.P.S.	-$0.54
DUNS No.	NA	Shareholders	NA

Business: The group's principal activity is to provide software solutions designed to optimize customer service operations for businesses of all sizes. The group's solution supports multiple communication channels, including Web, interactive voice, e-mail, chat, telephone and proactive outbound e-mail communications. The group offers its solutions through a multi-tenant, hosted on-demand model that reduces the cost and risk associated with deploying traditional enterprise crm software. The group operates in the United States, Europe and Asia-Pacific.

Primary SIC and add'l.: 7372

CIK No: 0001111247

Officers: Greg R. Gianforte/47/Chmn., Founder, CEO, Pres./$394,833.00, Alan A. Rassaby/VP - Legal, Risk Management, General Counsel, Sec./$320,028.00, Susan J. Carstensen/CFO, VP - Finance, Administration, Treasurer/$366,435.00, Mike Myer/VP - Development, CTO, Jason Mittelstaedt/VP - Marketing/$386,506.00, Scott Creighton/VP - Business Development, Steve Daines/VP, GM - Asia, Pacific, Jeff Davison/VP - Finance, Operations, Michael Saracini/VP, GM - Americas, Joseph Brown/VP, GM - Europe, Middle East, Africa, EMEA, Laef Olson/CIO

Directors: Greg R. Gianforte/47/Chmn., Founder, CEO, Pres., William J. Lansing/49/Dir., Roger L. Evans/62/Dir., Richard E. Allen/51/Dir., Margaret L. Taylor/56/Dir., Gregory M. Avis/49/Dir., Thomas W. Kendra/Dir.

Owners: Insiders/43.80%, Alan A. Rassaby, Peter P. Dunning, William J. Lansing, Gregory M. Avis, Jason Mittelstaedt, Richard E. Allen, Entities affiliated with Greylock/13.40%, Jay Rising, Susan J. Carstensen, Margaret L. Taylor, Roger L. Evans, Michael A. Myer/1.30%, Susan Gianforte/24.70%, Schroder Investment Management North America Inc./6.20% (17 Owners included in Index)

Financial Data: Fiscal Year End:12/31   Latest Annual Data: 12/31/2006

Year	Sales	Net Income
2006	$110,388,000	-$5,008,000
2005	$87,148,000	$7,693,000
2004	$61,764,000	$3,449,000

Curr. Assets:	$134,039,000	Curr. Liab.:	$83,665,000		
Plant, Equip.:	$10,073,000	Total Liab.:	$130,768,000	Indic. Yr. Divd.:	NA
Total Assets:	$178,242,000	Net Worth:	$47,474,000	Debt/ Equity:	NA

Rim Semiconductor Co

Formerly: New Visual Corp

5920 FRIARS Rd. , Ste 104, San Diego, CA, 92108; *PH:* 1-503-257-6700; *http://* www.rimsemi.com; *Email:* info@rimsemi.com

General - Incorporation	UT	Stock - Price on:12/24/2007	NA
Employees	NA	Stock Exchange	NA
Auditor	Marcum & Kliegman LLP	Ticker Symbol	NA
Stk Agt.	Continental Stock Transfer & Trust Co	Outstanding Shares	NA
Counsel	Baker & McKenzie LLP	E.P.S.	-$0.035
DUNS No.	80-865-6359	Shareholders	NA

Business: The group's principal activity is to develop new content telecommunications technologies. The group operates in two segments: telecommunications and entertainment. The telecommunications segment develops semiconductor technology that allows data to be transmitted at greater speeds over longer distances using regular copper telephone wire. Its technology is designed to increase the capacity of the copper telephone network, allowing telephone companies to provide enhanced video, data and voice services over the existing copper telecommunications infrastructure. The entertainment segment produces motion pictures, films and videos. Artisan pictures distribute the films mainly in the United States and Canada.

Primary SIC and add'l.: 7372 7812 3674

CIK No: 0001026595

Subsidiaries: NV Entertainment, Inc.

Officers: Brad Ketch/Dir., CEO, Pres., Ray Willenberg/Chmn., Exec. VP, Walter Chen/Member - Technical Advisory Board, Michael Propp/Member - Technical Team, Laurie Evans/Contact

Directors: Brad Ketch/Dir., CEO, Pres., Ray Willenberg/Chmn., Exec. VP, Jack Peckham/Dir., David Tan/Dir., David J. Greaves/Member - Technical Advisory Board, Thomas Cooper/Dir., David Wojcik/Member - Technical Advisory Board

Owners: Boon Tiong Tan, Thomas J. Cooper, David Wojcik, Insiders/7.52%, Brad Ketch/2.95%, Jack L. Peckham, Ray Willenberg/3.43%

Financial Data: Fiscal Year End:10/31   Latest Annual Data: 10/31/2006

Year	Sales	Net Income
2006	$62,000	-$15,966,000
2005	$40,000	-$4,690,000
2004	$288,000	-$5,506,000

Curr. Assets:	$2,400,000	Curr. Liab.:	$10,013,000		
Plant, Equip.:	$65,000	Total Liab.:	$11,492,000	Indic. Yr. Divd.:	NA
Total Assets:	$10,012,000	Net Worth:	-$1,480,000	Debt/ Equity:	NA

Rim Semiconductor Company

305 Ne 102nd Ave. Ste. 105, Portland, OR, 97220; *PH:* 1-503-257-6700; *Fax:* 1-503-633-6622; *http://* www.rimsemi.com; *Email:* info@rimsemi.com

General - Incorporation	UT	Stock - Price on:12/24/2007	$0.078
Employees	14	Stock Exchange	OTC
Auditor	Marcum & Kliegman LLP	Ticker Symbol	RSMI
Stk Agt.	Olde Monmouth Stk Trnsfer Co. Inc	Outstanding Shares	435,140,000
Counsel	Munck Butrus, P.C.	E.P.S.	-$0.035
DUNS No.	NA	Shareholders	NA

Business: The group's principal activity is developing transmission technology products to enable data to be transmitted across copper telephone wire at speeds and over distances that exceed those offered by leading DSL technology providers. The group markets its products under the tradenames include Powerstream(TM) and Cupria(TM). The group operates from the United States.

Primary SIC and add'l.: 3674

CIK No: 0001026595

Subsidiaries: NV Entertainment Inc

Officers: Ray Willenberg/Chmn., CEO, Pres., David Wojcik/Sr. VP - Sales, Marketing, Walter Chen/Member - Technical Advisory Board, an Active Leader in The Development - Cupria, Michael Propp/Co - Founder Adaptive Networks, David J. Greaves/Member - Technical Advisory Board, Tom Moxon/Chief Science Advisor, Keith Chipperfield/Dir. - Engineering

Directors: Ray Willenberg/Chmn., CEO, Pres., Brad Ketch/Dir., Thomas Cooper/Dir., David Tan/Dir.

Owners: David Wojcik, Jack L. Peckham, Boon Tiong Tan, Thomas J. Cooper, Brad Ketch/2.95%, Ray Willenberg/3.43%, Insiders/7.52%

Financial Data: Fiscal Year End:10/31   Latest Annual Data: 10/31/2006

Year	Sales	Net Income
2006	$62,000	-$15,966,000
2005	$40,000	-$4,690,000
2004	$288,000	-$5,506,000

Curr. Assets:	$2,400,000	Curr. Liab.:	$10,013,000		
Plant, Equip.:	$65,000	Total Liab.:	$11,492,000	Indic. Yr. Divd.:	NA
Total Assets:	$10,012,000	Net Worth:	-$1,480,000	Debt/ Equity:	NA

Rimage Corp

7725 Washington Ave. S, Minneapolis, MN, 55439; *PH:* 1-952-944-8144; *Fax:* 1-952-944-7808; *http://* www.rimage.com

General - Incorporation	MN	Stock- Price on:12/24/2007	$34.26
Employees	205	Stock Exchange	NDQ
Auditor	KPMG LLP	Ticker Symbol	RIMG
Stk Agt	Wells Fargo Shareowner Services	Outstanding Shares	10,100,000
Counsel	Dorsey & Whitney LLP	E.P.S.	$1.42
DUNS No.	15-177-2530	Shareholders	NA

Business: The group's principal activities are to design, manufacture and sell CD recordable (CD-r) and DVD recordable (DVD-r) publishing systems required for producing discs with customized digital content on an on-demand basis. The group's publishing systems, which include equipment to handle a full range of low to high production volumes, incorporate robotics, software and custom printing technology for disc labeling. The group focuses its CD-r and DVD-r publishing solutions on a set of vertical markets with special needs for customized, on-demand digital information such as digital photography, banking and finance, government, business offices, and medical imaging. The CD-r production systems provide turnkey pre mastering, recording and label printing in a single machine that may be used alone or on a network. The perfect image(R) CD printer and autoprinter are fast and unattended systems for professional quality color printing on the surface of both CD's and DVD's.

Primary SIC and add'l.: 7379 3577 3572

CIK No: 0000892482

Subsidiaries: Rimage Europe GmbH, Rimage Japan

Officers: Bernard P. Aldrich/Dir., CEO, Pres./$526,590.00, David J. Suden/Dir., CTO/$343,310.00, Manuel M. Almeida/COO/$381,455.00, Konrad Rotermund/MD - Rimage Europe, Thomas R. Cuffari/VP - Business Development, Photo, William J. Farmer/Sr. VP - Engineering, Maureen A. Hayes/VP - Information Systems, Pamela V. Lampert/VP - Human Resources/$200,099.00, Yoshi Oyamada/VP - Business Development, Asia, Pacific, Kevin L. Stagg/VP - Software Engineering, Jerry J. Weyandt/VP - Services, Luke T. Wigger/VP - Americas Channel Sales, Robert M. Wolf/CFO/$259,219.00, Richard G. Cinquina/Equity Marketing Partners

Directors: Bernard P. Aldrich/Dir., CEO, Pres., James L. Reissner/Chmn., Philip D. Hotchkiss/Dir., Lawrence M. Benveniste/Dir., Thomas F. Madison/Dir., Steven M. Quist/Dir., David J. Suden/Dir., CTO

Owners: Lawrence M. Benveniste, James L. Reissner/1.10%, Steven M. Quist, Robert M. Wolf, Insiders/7.00%, Royce & Associates, LLC/8.90%, Pamela V. Lampert, Philip D. Hotchkiss, Bernard P. Aldrich/1.90%, Munder Capital Management/4.90%, David J. Suden/1.10%, Thomas F. Madison, Manuel M. Almeida

Financial Data: *Fiscal Year End:*12/31 *Latest Annual Data:* 12/31/2006

Year		Sales		Net Income
2006		$103,252,000		$13,084,000
2005		$95,410,000		$11,368,000
2004		$70,848,000		$9,072,000

Curr. Assets:	$70,116,000	Curr. Liab.:	$16,163,000	P/E Ratio:	26.15
Plant, Equip.:	$3,626,000	Total Liab.:	$16,883,000	Indic. Yr. Divd.:	NA
Total Assets:	$112,359,000	Net Worth:	$95,476,000	Debt/ Equity:	NA

Rimfire Minerals Corp

700 W Pender St., Ste. 700, Vancouver, BC, V6C 1G8; *PH:* 1-604-669-6660; *http://* www.rimfire.bc.ca; *Email:* info@rimfire.bc.ca

General - Incorporation	BC	Stock- Price on:12/24/2007	NA
Employees	NA	Stock Exchange	NA
Auditor	Hay & Watson	Ticker Symbol	NA
Stk Agt	Pacific Corporate Trust Co	Outstanding Shares	NA
Counsel	Province Of British Columbia	E.P.S.	NA
DUNS No.	NA	Shareholders	NA

Business: The groups principle activity is to invest in precious metals exploration projects. The group operates from United States and Western Canada.

Primary SIC and add'l.: 9999

CIK No: 0001135347

Subsidiaries: Breakwater Resources Ltd., Rimfire Alaska, Ltd

Officers: David A. Caulfield/Dir., CEO, Pres., Dorothy Miller/CFO, Mark E. Baknes/VP - Exploration, Jason S. Weber/Mgr. - Corporate Communications, Robert A. Duncan/Mgr. - Exploration, Mike Roberts/Sr. Geologist, Wesley A. Hodson/GIS Specialist - Geologist, Ahnna Pildysh/Community Relations, Marketing Coordinator, Dan Lui/Project Geologist

Directors: David A. Caulfield/Dir., CEO, Pres., Henry Awmack/Chmn., Ian J. Talbot/Dir., Bipin Ghelani/Dir., Jack H.L. Miller/Dir., Gary Paulson/Dir.

Owners: Ian J. Talbot, Jack H.L. Miller, Gary P. Paulson, Mark E. Baknes, Bipin Ghelani, The Canadian Depository, David A. Caulfield, Depository Trust Company, Henry J. Awmack

Rinker Group Ltd

Level 8, Tower B, 799 Pacific Hwy., Chatswood, NSW 2067; ; *http://* www.rinker.com.au

General - Incorporation	Australia	Stock- Price on:12/24/2007	$78.84
Employees	14,358	Stock Exchange	NA
Auditor	Deloitte Touche Tohmatsu	Ticker Symbol	NA
Stk Agt	JP Morgan Chase Bank, N.A.	Outstanding Shares	179,010,000
Counsel	NA	E.P.S.	$4.34
DUNS No.	NA	Shareholders	NA

Business: The group's principal activities are carried out through the following divisions: rinker materials include the manufacture and supply of heavy building materials such as crushed and sized aggregates, cements, concrete, concrete block, asphalt, concrete pipe, gypsum, pre-stressed concrete products and polyethylene pipe. Rinker operates in Florida, Arizona and 29 other states in the United States. Readymix business include the production of heavy building materials in Australia and China. Readymix products include quarry concrete, hard rock, sand and gravel and engineering, technical advice and literature services such as analysis of hardened concrete, quality control and statistical analysis, mix design and evaluation of raw materials. On 01-Apr-2003, the group acquired rinker materials (tianjin) co ltd and excel concrete pty ltd on 02-Jun-2003. It operates in North America, Asia, New Zealand and Australia.

Primary SIC and add'l.: NA

CIK No: 0001228028

Subsidiaries: Acn 065 064 502 Pty Ltd., ALC Las Vegas Mining Claims, LLC, American Limestone West, LLC, ARC Management Company,Inc., ARC Materials Corporation, Ave Maria Rinker Materials, LLC, BettaformConstructions Pty Ltd, Birchtown Holdings,Inc., Broadway& Frame Premix Concrete Pty Ltd, Excel Concrete (NSW) Pty Ltd, Excel Concrete Pty Ltd, FCS Las Vegas Mining Claims, LLC, Florida Crushed Stone Company, Fort Calhoun Stone Company, Guernsey Stone Company 70 Subsidiaries included in the Index

Officers: Bob Beattie/National Concrete Improvement Mgr. - Beenleigh QLD, John Bush/Environmental Products Mgr. - Melbourne VIC, Debra Jackson/Human Resources Mgr. - Country East, Chatswood NSW, Andrew Wright/Production Mgr. - Toowoomba QLD, Peter Hewson/Trainee Quarry Mgr. - Canberra ACT, Karmen Coath/SAP, Information Technology Training Mgr. - Milton QLD, John Mak/Production Mgr. - Artarmon NSW

Financial Data: *Fiscal Year End:*03/31 *Latest Annual Data:* 3/31/2006

Year		Sales		Net Income
2006		$5,108,400,000		$738,100,000
2005		$4,312,400,000		$437,600,000
2004		$3,706,200,000		$345,900,000

Curr. Assets:	$1,325,900,000	Curr. Liab.:	$686,200,000		
Plant, Equip.:	$1,923,900,000	Total Liab.:	$1,799,400,000	Indic. Yr. Divd.:	$3.580
Total Assets:	$4,535,100,000	Net Worth:	$2,735,700,000	Debt/ Equity:	NA

Rio Narcea Gold Mines Ltd

C/secundino Roces Riera, 3?2, Centro De Empresas Asipo I, Parque Empresarial De Asipo, Cays Llanera, Asturias, 33428; *PH:* 34-985733300; *http://* www.rionarcea.com; *Email:* info@rngm.com

General - Incorporation	Canada	Stock- Price on:12/24/2007	$5.13
Employees	417	Stock Exchange	NA
Auditor	Ernst & Young LLP	Ticker Symbol	NA
Stk Agt	Computershare Trust Company of Canada	Outstanding Shares	165,250,000
Counsel	Mr. Colilla	E.P.S.	$0.57
DUNS No.	NA	Shareholders	NA

Business: The groups principle activities include exploration and production of gold. The group operates from United States.

Primary SIC and add'l.: 1041

CIK No: 0001098506

Officers: Chris I. Von Christierson/60/Chmn., CEO, Juan H. Abello/Consejo de Administracion, David Baril/51/COO, Eugene Spiering/VP - Exploracion, Alberto Lavandeira/51/Pres., John W. Hick/VP - del Consejo de Administracion y Consejero Delegado, Javier Colilla/48/Sr. VP - Corporate, Omar Gomez/34/CFO, Michelle Roth/Investor Relations

Directors: Chris I. Von Christierson/60/Chmn., CEO, David N. Murray/62/Dir., Eric Schwitzer/56/Dir., Anthony H. Bloom/68/Dir., John W. Hick/VP - del Consejo de Administracion y Consejero Delegado, Hugh R. Snyder/71/Dir., Rupert Pennant-Rea/59/Dir., Cliff J. Davis/64/Dir.

Financial Data: *Fiscal Year End:*12/31 *Latest Annual Data:* 12/31/2006

Year		Sales		Net Income
2006		$225,694,000		$73,502,000
2005		$105,500,000		-$39,977,000
2004		$71,971,000		-$43,308,000

Curr. Assets:	$114,468,000	Curr. Liab.:	$84,321,000		
Plant, Equip.:	$227,274,000	Total Liab.:	$153,702,000	Indic. Yr. Divd.:	NA
Total Assets:	$385,983,000	Net Worth:	$231,934,000	Debt/ Equity:	NA

Rio Tinto Ltd

120 Collins St., Melbourne, Victoria, 3000; *PH:* 61-0392833333; *Fax:* 61-0392833707; *http://* www.riotinto.com; *Email:* nigel.jones@riotinto.com

General - Incorporation	Australia	Stock- Price on:12/24/2007	$56.6
Employees	NA	Stock Exchange	OTC
Auditor	PricewaterhouseCoopers LLP	Ticker Symbol	RTOLF
Stk Agt	JP Morgan Chase Bank, N.A.	Outstanding Shares	NA
Counsel	Shannon Crompton	E.P.S.	NA
DUNS No.	75-335-1972	Shareholders	NA

Business: The group's principal activities are the exploration and extraction of mineral resources such as coal, iron ore, gold, nickel, uranium and copper; production of salt and alumina; aluminium smelting; refining and marketing of talc, borates and nonferrous metal; and bauxite mining.

Primary SIC and add'l.: 3295 1021 3334 1099 1041 1011 5052

CIK No: 0000887028

Subsidiaries: Argyle Diamonds Limited, Australian Coal Holdings Pty Limited, Comalco Aluminium Limited, Hamersley Holdings Limited, Kelian Pty Limited, Kennecott Energy and Coal Company, Kennecott Holdings Corporation, Kennecott Land Company, Kennecott Minerals Holdings Company, Kennecott Utah Copper Corporation, North IOC Holdings Pty Limited, North Limited, Pacific Aluminium Pty Limited, Palabora Holdings Limited, Peko-Wallsend Pty Limited 43 Subsidiaries included in the Index

Officers: Tom Albanese/50/Dir., CEO, Charles Lenegan/56/MD - Rio Tinto Australia, Melbourne, Eric Finlayson/Head - Exploration, London, Jason Combes/Investor Contact - North America, David Ovington/Investor Contact - Rio Tinto plc, Dave Skinner/Investor Contact - Rio Tinto Limited, Ben Mathews/41/Company Sec., Global Head - Secretarial Services, Hugo Bague/Head - Human Resources, London, Sam Walsh/58/Chief Executive - Iron Ore, Perth, Andrew Vickerman/Head - Communication, External Relations, London, Oscar Groeneveld/54/Chief Executive - Aluminium, Brisbane, Bret Clayton/45/Chief Executive - Copper, London, Keith Johnson/46/Group Executive, Business Resources, London, Michael Merton/Head - Global Business Services, London, Grant Thorne/Group Executive, Technology, Innovation, Brisbane *(21 Officers included in Index)*

Directors: Tom Albanese/50/Dir., CEO, Paul Skinner/63/Chmn., Rod Eddington/58/Non Exec. Dir., Guy Elliott/52/Dir., Dir. - Finance, Dick Evans/61/Dir., Yves Fortier/73/Non Exec. Dir., Paul Tellier/69/Non Exec. Dir., Ashton Calvert/62/Non Exec. Dir., Richard Sykes/65/Non Exec. Dir., Richard Goodmanson/60/Non Exec. Dir., David Mayhew/67/Non Exec. Dir., Lord Kerr/66/Non Exec. Dir., David Clementi/52/Non Exec. Dir., Vivienne Cox/48/Non Exec. Dir., Michael Fitzpatrick/55/Non Exec. Dir. *(16 Directors included in Index)*

Owners: Australian Foundation Investment Company Limited, Westpac Financial Services Limited, Argo Investments Limited, Citicorp Nominees Pty Limited/2.22%, AMP Life Limited, Suncorp Custodian Services Pty Limited, Westpac Custodian Nominees Pty Limited/7.26%, J P Morgan Nominees Australia Limited/7.92%, Citicorp Nominees Pty Limited, Citicorp Nominees Pty Limited, RBC Dexia Investor Services Australia Nominees Pty Ltd, Citicorp Nominees Pty Limited, National Nominees Limited/8.46%, Cogent Nominees Pty Limited/1.38%, Tinto Holdings Australia Pty Limited/37.45% *(20 Owners included in Index)*

Rio Tinto Plc

5 Aldermanbury Sq., London, EC2V 7HR; *PH:* 44-0-2077812000; *Fax:* 44-0-2077811800;
http:// www.riotinto.com; *Email:* nigel.jones@riotinto.com

General - Incorporation	UK	*Stock* - Price on:12/24/2007	$303.93
Employees	35,245	Stock Exchange	NYSE
Auditor	PricewaterhouseCoopers LLP	Ticker Symbol	RTP
Stk Agt	NA	Outstanding Shares	327,360,000
Counsel	NA	E.P.S.	$21.01
DUNS No.	21-024-8928	Shareholders	NA

Business: The group's principle activity is the exploration and extraction of minerals in Australia, New Zealand, North America and many parts of the world. The group is the combination of rio tinto plc and rio tinto ltd, structure as a single economic entity. The group's interests in mining include copper, gold, iron ore, coal, aluminum, borates, and titanium dioxide feedstock. The group also mines diamonds, silver, zinc, lead, bauxite, nickel, molybdenum, salt, talc, tin and uranium.

Primary SIC and add'l.: 1011 1021 1041 1099 1479 5052

CIK No: 0000863064

Subsidiaries: Argyle Diamonds Limited, Australian Coal Holdings Pty Limited, Comalco Aluminium Limited, Hamersley Holdings Limited, Kelian Pty Limited, Kennecott Energy and Coal Company, Kennecott Holdings Corporation, Kennecott Land Company, Kennecott Minerals Holdings Company, Kennecott Utah Copper Corporation, North IOC Holdings Pty Limited, North Limited, Pacific Aluminium Pty Limited, Palabora Holdings Limited, Peko-Wallsend Pty Limited 43 Subsidiaries included in the Index

Officers: Oscar Groeneveld/54/Chief Executive - Aluminium Group, Andrew Vickerman/Head - Communication, External Relations, London, Stephen Consedine/46/Company Sec. - Melbourne, Anette Lawless/51/Company Sec., Preston Chiaro/54/Chief Executive - Energy, London, Sam Walsh/58/Chief Executive - Iron Ore, Perth, Tom Albanese/Executive Dir., Chief Executive - London, Leigh Clifford/60/Dir., Chief Executive, Guy Elliott/Executive Dir., Dir. - Finance, London, Bret Clayton/45/Chief Executive - Copper, London, Michael Merton/Head - Global Business Services, London, Grant Thorne/Group Executive, Technology, Innovation, Brisbane, Nigel Jones/Investor Contact, David Ovington/Investor Contact, Dick Evans/Executive Dir., Chief Executive - Rio Tinto Alcan, Montreal *(23 Officers included in Index)*

Directors: Paul Skinner/Chmn., David Clementi/52/Non Exec. Dir., Andrew Gould/61/Non Exec. Dir., Tom Albanese/Executive Dir., Chief Executive - London, Leigh Clifford/60/Dir., Chief Executive, Guy Elliott/Executive Dir., Dir. - Finance, London, Ashton Calvert/62/Non Exec. Dir., Vivienne Cox/48/Non Exec. Dir., Rod Eddington/58/Non Exec. Dir., Michael Fitzpatrick/55/Non Exec. Dir., David Mayhew/67/Non Exec. Dir., Richard Sykes/65/Non Exec. Dir., Dick Evans/Executive Dir., Chief Executive - Rio Tinto Alcan, Montreal, Yves Fortier/73/Non Exec. Dir., Richard Goodmanson/Non Exec. Dir. *(17 Directors included in Index)*

Owners: Barclays PLC/4.02%, Legal & General plc/3.13%, The Capital Group Companies, Inc/3.90%

Financial Data: Fiscal Year End:12/31 Latest Annual Data: 12/31/2006

Year	Sales	Net Income
2006	$22,465,000,000	$6,649,000,000
2005	$19,033,000,000	$4,969,000,000
2003	$9,228,000,000	$1,508,000,000

Curr. Assets:	$6,875,000,000	Curr. Liab.:	$5,780,000,000		
Plant, Equip.:	$22,306,000,000	Total Liab.:	$16,363,000,000	Indic. Yr. Divd.:	$4.160
Total Assets:	$37,154,000,000	Net Worth:	$20,791,000,000	Debt/ Equity:	NA

Rio Vista Energy Partners LP

820 Gessner Rd., Ste. 1285, Houston, TX, 77024; *PH:* 1-713-467-8235; *Fax:* 1-760-772-8588;
http:// www.riovistaenergy.com

General - Incorporation	DE	*Stock* - Price on:12/24/2007	$9.8875
Employees	15	Stock Exchange	NDQ
Auditor	Burton McCumber & Cortez LLP	Ticker Symbol	RVEP
Stk Agt	Computershare Investor Services LLC	Outstanding Shares	1,910,000
Counsel	NA	E.P.S.	$1.579
DUNS No.	NA	Shareholders	NA

Business: The group's principal activity is to purchase, transport, and sell liquefied petroleum (LPG). It owns and operates terminal facilities in Texas, the United States and in Tamaulipas, Mexico, as well as approximately 23 miles of pipelines, which connect these facilities. The primary market of this company's LPG is the northeastern region of Mexico, which includes the sates of Coahuila, Nuevo Leon, and Tamaulipas. The company was a wholly owned subsidiary of Penn Octane until September 30, 2004, when Penn Octane completed a series of transactions involving the transfer of substantially all of its owned pipeline and terminal assets in Texas and Matamoros, Mexico and certain immaterial liabilities to the Rio Vista Operating Partnership L.P.

Primary SIC and add'l.: 5172

CIK No: 0001260828

Subsidiaries: Penn Octane de Mexico, S. de R.L. de C.V., Penn Octane International, LLC, Rio Vista Operating GP LLC, Rio Vista Operating Partnership L.P., Tergas, S. de R.L. de C.V., Termatsal, S. de R.L. de C.V.

Officers: Ian T. Bothwell/48/Acting CEO, Acting Pres., VP, CFO, Treasurer, Assist. Sec., Richard R. Canney/53/Chmn., Mgr., Murray J. Feiwell/Board Of Mgr.

Directors: Richard R. Canney/53/Chmn., Mgr., Douglas G. Manner/52/Member - Board of Managers

Owners: Douglas G. Manner, Insiders/4.45%, Murray J. Feiwell, Jerry L. Lockett, Charles C. Handly, Jerome B. Richte/26.60%, Richard R. Canney, Ian T. Bothwell, Swank Group, LLC, Swank Energy Income/22.87%

Financial Data: Fiscal Year End:12/31 Latest Annual Data: 12/31/2006

Year	Sales	Net Income
2006	$908,000	$3,298,000
2005	$120,892,000	-$2,161,000
2004	$35,181,000	-$63,000

Curr. Assets:	$6,441,000	Curr. Liab.:	$2,116,000	P/E Ratio:	6.26
Plant, Equip.:	$10,704,000	Total Liab.:	$2,116,000	Indic. Yr. Divd.:	$1.000
Total Assets:	$17,156,000	Net Worth:	$15,040,000	Debt/ Equity:	NA

Ripple Lake Diamonds Inc

595 Howe St., Ste 305, Vancouver, BC, V6C 2T5; *PH:* 1-604-484-8264; *http://* www.ripplelake.com

General - Incorporation	Canada	*Stock* - Price on:12/24/2007	$0.09
Employees	NA	Stock Exchange	OTC
Auditor	James Stafford, Inc	Ticker Symbol	RLLKF
Stk Agt	Pacific Corporate Trust Co	Outstanding Shares	NA
Counsel	DuMoulin Black	E.P.S.	NA
DUNS No.	NA	Shareholders	NA

Business: The group's principal activity is diamond exploration. The company has recently assembled and acquired 2 highly prospective Canadian diamond exploration properties in Ontario and Nunavut. Ripple Lake completed a successful Initial Public Offering in January 2005 following a highly successful Phase One exploration program at both properties. Based on the encouraging Phase One results, the Company has expanded the claim areas at both properties. The Company has now commenced its summer 2005 exploration program. Current exploration activities include additional detailed sampling and aero magnetic surveys to determine drill targets at both properties.

Primary SIC and add'l.: 8880

CIK No: 0001321847

Officers: George Cavey/VP - Exploration, Dir., Timothy Crowhurst/Dir., Pres., Ming Wong/CFO

Directors: George Cavey/VP - Exploration, Dir., Timothy Crowhurst/Dir., Pres., William Schmidt/Dir.

Owners: Richard Genovese/8.95%, Robert Lipsett/11.23%, Firebird Global Master Fund, Ltd./5.73%, Timothy Crowhurst/6.38%

Financial Data: Fiscal Year End:06/30 Latest Annual Data: 6/30/2006

Year	Sales	Net Income
2006	$2,000	-$1,812,000
2005	$2,000	-$2,845,000

Curr. Assets:	$346,000	Curr. Liab.:	$43,000	P/E Ratio:	6.26
Plant, Equip.:	$428,000	Total Liab.:	$43,000	Indic. Yr. Divd.:	NA
Total Assets:	$775,000	Net Worth:	$732,000	Debt/ Equity:	NA

Rising Sun Bancorp MD

Ctr. Sq., Rising Sun, MD, 21911; *PH:* 1-301-658-5504

General - Incorporation	MD	*Stock* - Price on:12/24/2007	$15.8
Employees	NA	Stock Exchange	OTC
Auditor	NA	Ticker Symbol	RSAM
Stk Agt	Registrar & Transfer Co	Outstanding Shares	NA
Counsel	NA	E.P.S.	NA
DUNS No.	NA	Shareholders	NA

Business: The groups principal activities include providing banking and financial services. The group offers a complete array of checking and savings accounts, along with money management products that will satisfy any individual or business banking customers needs. The group operates from the United States.

Primary SIC and add'l.: 6021

CIK No: 0000869582

Financial Data: Fiscal Year End:12/31 Latest Annual Data: 12/31/2002

Year	Sales	Net Income
2002	$7,258,000	$910,000

Curr. Assets:	$5,135,000	Curr. Liab.:	$93,714,000		
Plant, Equip.:	$2,918,000	Total Liab.:	$99,373,000	Indic. Yr. Divd.:	NA
Total Assets:	$109,398,000	Net Worth:	$10,025,000	Debt/ Equity:	0.4727

Risk George Industries Inc A

802 S Elm St., Kimball, NE, 69145; *PH:* 1-308-235-4645; *Fax:* 1-308-235-2609;
http:// www.grisk.com; *Email:* gri@megavision.com

General - Incorporation	CO	*Stock* - Price on:12/24/2007	$7.21
Employees	275	Stock Exchange	OTC
Auditor	Mason Russell West, LLC	Ticker Symbol	RISKA
Stk Agt	NA	Outstanding Shares	5,340,000
Counsel	NA	E.P.S.	$0.59
DUNS No.	NA	Shareholders	NA

Business: The groups principle activities include designing, manufacturing, and selling of computer keyboards, push button switches, burglar alarm components and systems, pool alarms, thermostats, EZ Duct wire covers and water sensors. The group operates from the United States.

Primary SIC and add'l.: 3669

CIK No: 0000084112

Subsidiaries: GRI Telemark Corp., R&D Labs

Owners: Ken R. Risk/55.28%

Financial Data: Fiscal Year End:04/30 Latest Annual Data: 10/31/2007

Year	Sales	Net Income
2007	$3,007,000	$755,000
2006	$14,254,000	$2,732,000
2005	$13,113,000	$2,515,000

Curr. Assets:	$24,413,000	Curr. Liab.:	$586,000	P/E Ratio:	14.42
Plant, Equip.:	$926,000	Total Liab.:	$704,000	Indic. Yr. Divd.:	$0.170
Total Assets:	$25,570,000	Net Worth:	$24,866,000	Debt/ Equity:	NA

RiT Technologies Ltd

900 Corporate Dr., Mahwah, NJ, 07430; *PH:* 1-201-512-1970; *Fax:* 1-201-512-1286;
http:// www.rittech.com; *Email:* mkt@rit.co.il

General - Incorporation	Israel	*Stock* - Price on:12/24/2007	$1.46
Employees	128	Stock Exchange	NDQ
Auditor	Somekh Chaikin	Ticker Symbol	RITT
Stk Agt	American Stock Transfer & Trust Co.	Outstanding Shares	14,640,000
Counsel	NA	E.P.S.	-$0.37
DUNS No.	NA	Shareholders	NA

Business: The groups principle activities include development, manufacturing and selling of premise wiring products and local loop connectivity management systems. The group operates from United States.

Primary SIC and add'l.: 3669

CIK No: 0001041844

Subsidiaries: RiT Tech (1997) Ltd., RiT Technologies, Inc.

Officers: Doron Zinger/CEO, Pres., Simona Green/VP - Finance, Hila Hubsch/General Counsel, Guy Shapira/VP - Research & Development, Avi Kovarsky/Sr. VP - Sales, Zafi Shatz/VP - Human Resources, Raphael Ben Asher/VP - Operations, Oded Nachmoni/VP - Marketing - Product Strategy, Ely Cohen/VP - Business Development

Directors: Yehuda Zisapel/Chmn., Israel Frieder/Dir., Meir Barel/Dir., Hagen Hultzsch/Dir., Liora Katzenstein/Dir.

Owners: Meir Barel/5.24%, Insiders/22.34%, Yehuda Zisapel/17.10%, Zohar Zisapel/12.72%, Austin W. Marxe/21.31%

Financial Data: Fiscal Year End:12/31 **Latest Annual Data:** 12/31/2006

Year	Sales	Net Income
2006	$25,092,000	-$1,722,000
2005	$27,852,000	$1,403,000
2004	$18,427,000	-$2,975,000

Curr. Assets:	$19,041,000	**Curr. Liab.:**	$8,195,000		
Plant, Equip.:	$801,000	**Total Liab.:**	$10,593,000	**Indic. Yr. Divd.:**	NA
Total Assets:	$21,761,000	**Net Worth:**	$11,168,000	**Debt/ Equity:**	NA

Rita Medical Systems Inc

967 N Shoreline Blvd., Mountain View, CA, 94013; **PH:** 1-650-385-8500; http:// www.ritamedical.com

General - Incorporation	DE	**Stock**- Price on:12/24/2007	NA
Employees	221	Stock Exchange	NA
Auditor	Stonefield Josephson, Inc	Ticker Symbol	NA
Stk Agt	U.S. Stock Transfer Corp	Outstanding Shares	NA
Counsel	Cravath, Swaine & Moore LLP	E.P.S.	NA
DUNS No.	NA	Shareholders	NA

Business: The group's principle activities are to develop, manufacture and market invasive products to treat patients with solid cancerous or benign tumors. The group's products use radiofrequency energy to heat tissue to a high enough temperature to ablate it, or cause cell death. The group's products include radiofrequency generators and disposable needle electrode devices. Disposable devices consist of needle shaped electrodes containing curved wire arrays that are deployed into the targeted body tissue. Radio frequency generators employ an internal computer to assist the physician in safely and effectively controlling the delivery of radiofrequency during the ablation. The group's products are distributed in the United States through direct sales force and internationally through distribution partners.

Primary SIC and add'l.: 3845

CIK No: 0001056421

Subsidiaries: Horizon Medical Products, Inc, RITA Medical Systems France, S.A.R.L., RITA Medical Systems Netherlands, BV

Officers: Joseph M. Devivo/Dir., CEO, Pres., Mario Martinez/Exec. VP - Operations, GM, Darrin Uecker/CTO, Juan J. Soto/Exec. VP - Global Sales, Michael D. Angel/CFO

Directors: Joseph M. Devivo/Dir., CEO, Pres.

Owners: Entities Affiliated with Kopp Investment Advisors, LLC/10.00%, Entities Affiliated with SF Capital Partners, Ltd./5.50%, Entities Affiliated with Atlas Master Fund, Ltd./10.00%, Joseph DeVivo/1.90%, Wesley Johnson, Steve LaPorte, Thomas Dugan, Tocqueville Asset Management, L.P./5.00%, Scott Halsted/3.90%, James Brands, Vincent Bucci, John Soto, Mario Martinez, Insiders/8.00%, Darrin Uecker *(17 Owners included in Index)*

Ritchie Bros. Auctioneers Inc

3901 Faulkner Dr., Lincoln, NE, 68516; **PH:** 1-402-421-3631; **Fax:** 1-402-421-1738; http:// www.rbauction.com; **Email:** csg@rbauction.com

General - Incorporation	Canada	**Stock**- Price on:12/24/2007	$60.53
Employees	821	Stock Exchange	NYSE
Auditor	KPMG LLP	Ticker Symbol	RBA
Stk Agt	KPMG LLP	Outstanding Shares	34,680,000
Counsel	NA	E.P.S.	$1.97
DUNS No.	20-098-7212	Shareholders	NA

Business: The group sells, through public auctions, a broad range of industrial equipment, including equipment used in the construction, transportation, mining, forestry, petroleum and agricultural industries. The international used equipment market includes both mobile and stationary equipment and trucks and trailers produced by manufacturers such as caterpillar, hitachi, ingersoll rand, john deere, kenworth, komatsu, mack and volvo for the construction, mining, forestry, petroleum, agriculture and transportation industries. Industrial equipment includes crawler tractors, excavators, and loader backhoes and wheel loaders. Operational activities of the group are located in more than 90 locations in north and Central America, Europe, Asia, Australia, Africa and the Middle East.

Primary SIC and add'l.: 5012 5084

CIK No: 0001046102

Subsidiaries: Ritchie Bros. Auctioneers (America) Inc., Ritchie Bros. Auctioneers (Canada) Ltd., Ritchie Bros. Auctioneers B.V., Ritchie Bros. Holdings (America) Inc., Ritchie Bros. Holdings Inc., Ritchie Bros. Holdings Ltd., Ritchie Bros. Properties Inc., Ritchie Bros. Properties Ltd.

Officers: Peter J. Blake/Dir., CEO, Robert S. Armstrong/CFO, Corp. Sec., Randall J. Wall/COO, Pres., Robert K. MacKay/Pres. - United States, Asia, Australia, Guylain Turgeon/Sr. VP, MD - European Operations, Bob Armstrong/VP - Finance, CFO

Directors: Peter J. Blake/Dir., CEO, Charles E. Croft/Chmn., Eric Patel/Dir., Beverley A. Briscoe/Dir., Russell C. Cmolik/Dir.

Financial Data: Fiscal Year End:12/31 **Latest Annual Data:** 12/31/2006

Year	Sales	Net Income
2006	$261,040,000	$57,218,000
2005	$212,633,000	$53,580,000
2004	$182,257,000	$34,899,000

Curr. Assets:	$228,067,000	**Curr. Liab.:**	$133,698,000		
Plant, Equip.:	$285,091,000	**Total Liab.:**	$185,590,000	**Indic. Yr. Divd.:**	$0.960
Total Assets:	$554,227,000	**Net Worth:**	$368,637,000	**Debt/ Equity:**	NA

Rite Aid Corp

30 Hunter Ln., Camp Hill, PA, 17011; **PH:** 1-717-761-2633; **Fax:** 1-717-975-5871; http:// www.riteaid.com

General - Incorporation	DE	**Stock**- Price on:12/24/2007	$6.06
Employees	37,638	Stock Exchange	NYSE
Auditor	Deloitte & Touche LLP	Ticker Symbol	RAD
Stk Agt	Computershare Investor Services LLC	Outstanding Shares	538,410,000
Counsel	NA	E.P.S.	-$0.22
DUNS No.	01-457-8892	Shareholders	NA

Business: The group's principle activity is to operate retail drugstores. The group operates from United States.

Primary SIC and add'l.: 5912

CIK No: 0000084129

Subsidiaries: 112 Burleigh Avenue Norfolk, LLC, 1515 West State Street Boise, Idaho, LLC, 1740 Associates, LLC, 3581 Carter Hill Road - Montgomery Corp., 39/41 Hightstown Road, LLC, 4042 Warrensville Center Road - Warrensville Ohio,Inc., 5277 Associates,Inc., 537 Elm Street Corporation, 5600 Superior Properties,Inc., 657-659 Broad St. Corp., 764 South Broadway-Geneva, Ohio, LLC, 912 Elmwood Avenue - Buffalo, LLC, Ann& Government Streets - Mobile, Alabama, LLC, Apex Drug Stores,Inc., Broadview and Wallings-Broadview Heights Ohio,Inc. 107 Subsidiaries included in the Index

Officers: Mary F. Sammons/61/Chmn., CEO, Pres./$4,270,966.00, Matt Miles/Sr. VP - Central Division, Jon Olson/Sr. VP - Southern Division, Jerry Mark Debruin/49/Exec. VP - Pharmacy/$1,181,658.00, Philip J. Keough/Sr. VP - Pharmacy Operations, Kevin Twomey/CFO, Exec. VP/$1,062,180.00, Mark De Bruin/Exec. VP - Pharmacy, Douglas E. Donley/45/Chief Accounting Officer, Sr. VP, Robert J. Easley/49/COO, Pierre Legault/48/Chief Administrative Officer, Brian Fiala/Exec. VP - Store Operations, Tim Burger/Sr. VP - Northeast Division, Jerry Cardinale/Sr. VP - Category Management, Tom Reichert/Sr. VP - Mid Atlantic Division, Theresa Nichols/Group VP - Benefits, Compensation *(33 Officers included in Index)*

Directors: Mary F. Sammons/61/Chmn., CEO, Pres., Michel Coutu/Non - Exec. Co - Chmn., Andre Belzile/Dir., Francois J. Coutu/Dir., Michael N. Regan/Dir., Robert G. Miller/64/Dir., Joseph B. Anderson/64/Dir., John G. Danhakl/Dir., Marcy Syms/56/Dir., Michael A. Friedman/64/Dir., Alfred M. Gleason/Dir., Robert A. Mariano/58/Dir., Stuart M. Sloan/Dir., Jonathan D. Sokoloff/50/Dir., George G. Golleher/60/Dir. *(17 Directors included in Index)*

Owners: Tudor Investment Corp./5.65%, Stuart M. Sloan, Mark C. Panzer, Kevin Twomey, John G. Danhakl/8.23%, Philip G. Satre, Green Equity Investors III, L.P./8.22%, Alfred M. Gleason, Mary F. Sammons/1.64%, Jonathan D. Sokoloff/8.34%, Insiders/12.65%, James P. Mastrian, Thornburg Investment Management Inc./5.23%, Robert G. Miller/1.61%, Marcy Syms *(21 Owners included in Index)*

Financial Data: Fiscal Year End:03/04 **Latest Annual Data:** 3/4/2006

Year	Sales	Net Income
2006	$17,270,968,000	$1,273,006,000
2005	$16,816,439,000	$302,478,000
2004	$16,600,449,000	$83,379,000

Curr. Assets:	$2,884,812,000	**Curr. Liab.:**	$2,143,324,000	**P/E Ratio:**	303.00
Plant, Equip.:	$1,717,022,000	**Total Liab.:**	$5,381,450,000	**Indic. Yr. Divd.:**	NA
Total Assets:	$6,988,371,000	**Net Worth:**	$1,606,921,000	**Debt/ Equity:**	NA

Rival Technologies Inc

3155 E Patrick Ln., Ste. 1, Las Vegas, NV, 89120; **PH:** 1-866-601-1340; **Fax:** 1-604-684-0526; http:// www.rvti.com; **Email:** info@rivaltechnologiesinc.com

General - Incorporation	NV	**Stock**- Price on:12/24/2007	$0.63
Employees	NA	Stock Exchange	OTC
Auditor	Dohan & Co	Ticker Symbol	RVTI
Stk Agt	Computershare Trust Co	Outstanding Shares	46,610,000
Counsel	NA	E.P.S.	-$0.01
DUNS No.	NA	Shareholders	NA

Business: The groups principle activities include acquiring and developing technologies related to diesel engines and oil and gas. The group operates from United States.

Primary SIC and add'l.: NA

CIK No: 0001176337

Subsidiaries: CWI Technology, Tracker Capital Corp, Tru Oiltech

Officers: G. A. Constable/CEO, Pres. - TRU Oiltech, Robin J. Harvey/CEO, Pres., Anatoly Mezheritsky/Managing Engineer - CWI Technology

Owners: Rockridge Capital Corp./28.40%, Robin J. Harvey

Financial Data: Fiscal Year End:12/31 **Latest Annual Data:** 12/31/2006

Year	Sales	Net Income
2006	NA	-$467,000
2005	NA	-$1,195,000
2004	NA	-$647,000

Curr. Assets:	$362,000	**Curr. Liab.:**	$22,000		
Plant, Equip.:	$3,000	**Total Liab.:**	$22,000	**Indic. Yr. Divd.:**	NA
Total Assets:	$369,000	**Net Worth:**	$347,000	**Debt/ Equity:**	NA

River City Bank (Mechanicsville VA)

6127 Mechanicsville Tpke., Mechanicsville, VA, 23111; **PH:** 1-804-569-0422; **Fax:** 1-804-569-0423; http:// www.rcbank.com

General - Incorporation		**Stock**- Price on:12/24/2007	$9.75
Employees	NA	Stock Exchange	NDQ
Auditor	NA	Ticker Symbol	RCBK
Stk Agt	NA	Outstanding Shares	1,800,000
Counsel	NA	E.P.S.	NA
DUNS No.	NA	Shareholders	NA

Business: The groups principal activity is to provide personal and commercial banking services. The products of the group include credit cards, cars, vacations, boats, and other recreational vehicles loan and MasterCard. The groups services include commercial and consumer banking. The group operates from the United States.

Primary SIC and add'l.: 6022 6712

CIK No:

Officers: Jeanne Reaves/Dir., CEO, Pres., Anker Christensen/Sr. VP, CFO, Keith Reppart/Sr. VP, Sales Mgr., Victoria Dolan/VP - Human Resources, Wendy Duer/Sr. VP - Marketing, Richard M. Healy/Sr. VP, Consumer Banking Mgr., Jon Roberts/Sr. VP, Dir. - Technology, Patrick McHone/Sr. VP, Commercial Real Estate Mgr., Steve Eskew/Sr. VP - Risk Management

Directors: Jeanne Reaves/Dir., CEO, Pres., Jon S. Kelly/Chmn., Shawn L. Devlin/Dir., William R. Parker/Dir., James L. Welch/Dir., John Mesic/Dir., Michael Newell/Dir., Donald K. Hansen/Dir., Joseph F. Gwerder/Dir., Steve Pleau/Dir.

River Hawk Aviation Inc

Formerly: Viva International Inc
954 Business Pk. Dr., Ste.4, Traverse, MI, 49686; *PH:* 1-231-946-4343; *http://* www.flyviva.com

General - Incorporation	DE	**Stock** - Price on:12/24/2007	NA
Employees	8	Stock Exchange	NA
Auditor	Kempisty & Co	Ticker Symbol	NA
Stk Agt	Interstate Transfer Company	Outstanding Shares	NA
Counsel	NA	E.P.S.	NA
DUNS No.	NA	Shareholders	NA

Business: The group's principle activity is to provide passenger and cargo airline services. The group has four wholly owned subsidiaries - viva airlines, ct industries inc, hardyston distributors inc and universal filtration industries inc. Viva airlines inc is a development stage company that will provide passenger and cargo services to various destinations from its commercial hub in santo domingo, Dominican Republic. The other three subsidiaries are all inactive. On 08-Jan-2003, it sold 80 % of its subsidiary harvey westbury corp to a former officer and subsequently spun-off the remaining 20% interest to its shareholders. As at 31-Dec-2003, it is yet to commence flight operations. During the year 2003, it acquired viva airlines inc. The group operates from United States.
Primary SIC and add'l.: 4512
CIK No: 0001088734
Subsidiaries: Eastern Caribbean Airlines Corporation, Viva Airlines, Inc
Officers: Calvin Humphrey/60/Chmn., CEO
Directors: Calvin Humphrey/60/Chmn., CEO, Roger Larreur/42/Dir., James Paquette/59/Dir.
Owners: Robert J. Scott, Calvin Humphrey, Cambridge Partners, LLC, Robert Scott, David M. Otto, David M. Otto, Insiders

River Valley Bancorp

430 Clifty Dr., Madison, IN, 47250; *PH:* 1-812-273-4949; *Fax:* 1-812-273-4944;
http:// www.rvfbank.com

General - Incorporation	IN	**Stock** - Price on:12/24/2007	$17.48
Employees	77	Stock Exchange	NDQ
Auditor	BKD LLP	Ticker Symbol	RIVR
Stk Agt	Fifth Third Bank	Outstanding Shares	1,620,000
Counsel	Lonnie D. Collins	E.P.S.	$1.29
DUNS No.	86-137-6036	Shareholders	NA

Business: The group's principal activity is to accept deposits from the general public and use such funds to originate consumer, commercial and residential loans. The group is a savings and loan holding company for river valley financial bank. At 31-Dec-2003, it operates through five full-service offices located in jefferson county, Indiana. The subsidiaries of the group are river valley financial bank and madison first service corporation.
Primary SIC and add'l.: 6035 6712
CIK No: 0001015593
Subsidiaries: Madison First Service Corporation, River Valley Financial Bank, River Valley Statutory Trust I, RVFB Holdings, Inc., RVFB Investments, Inc., RVFB Portfolio, LLC.
Officers: Matthew Forrester/CEO, Pres./$204,836.00, John Muessel/VP, Trust Officer, Bob Schoenstein/Assist. VP, Mary Ellen Wehner/Commercial Loan Operations Mgr., Sheri Furnish/Loan Officer - Madison, IN Office, Deanna Liter/VP - Data Services, Sandy Stilwell/Customer Service Mgr. - Main Office, Anthony Brandon/Exec. VP/$117,755.00, Mary Ellen McClelland/Executive Sec., Vickie Grimes/VP Controller, VP - Finance, Teresa Smith/Data Processing Mgr., Rick Nelson/Carrollton, KY Branch Mgr., Linda Stark/Trust Administrator, Loy Skirvin/VP - Human Resources, Larry C. Fouse/62/Treasurer/$74,845.00 *(32 Officers included in Index)*
Directors: Robert W. Anger/70/Dir., Michael J. Hensley/52/Dir., Fred W. Koehler/Dir., Sue L. Livers/Dir., Charles J. McKay/55/Dir.
Owners: River Valley Financial Bank, as Trustee/8.90%, Charles J. McKay/2.00%, Michael J. Hensley/1.30%, Fred W. Koehler/3.70%, Insiders/18.20%, Lillian Sue Livers, Matthew P. Forrester/3.30%, Jeffrey L. Gendell/8.70%, Wellington Management Company, LLP/5.60%, Robert W. Anger/1.40%, Mary E. Davee/7.30%

Financial Data: Fiscal Year End:12/31   Latest Annual Data: 12/31/2006

Year	Sales	Net Income
2006	$21,416,000	$1,945,000
2005	$18,798,000	$2,086,000
2004	$16,063,000	$2,347,000

Curr. Assets:	$14,142,000	**Curr. Liab.:**	$220,943,000	**P/E Ratio:**	13.87
Plant, Equip.:	$7,813,000	**Total Liab.:**	$318,102,000	**Indic. Yr. Divd.:**	$0.800
Total Assets:	$342,249,000	**Net Worth:**	$24,147,000	**Debt/ Equity:**	3.8718

Riverbed Technology Inc

199 Fremont St., San Francisco, CA, 94105; *PH:* 1-415-247-8800; *Fax:* 1-415-247-8801;
http:// www.riverbed.com; *Email:* info@riverbed.com

General - Incorporation	DE	**Stock** - Price on:12/24/2007	$43.99
Employees	325	Stock Exchange	NDQ
Auditor	Ernst& Young LLP	Ticker Symbol	RVBD
Stk Agt	Mellon Investor Services LLC	Outstanding Shares	69,130,000
Counsel	NA	E.P.S.	$0.11
DUNS No.	NA	Shareholders	NA

Business: The groups principle activity is to develop an innovative and comprehensive solution. The products of the group include caching and WAN optimization. The group products sold under the trade names Interceptor(TM), Riverbed(R) and Steelhead(R). The group operates from domestic and international. The group's quarterly revenue for September 2007 was 63.31millions of USD.
Primary SIC and add'l.: 3577 3577 3669 7372 7372 3669
CIK No: 0001357326

Subsidiaries: Riverbed Technology AG, Riverbed Technology Australia Ltd., Riverbed Technology BV, Riverbed Technology Canada Ltd., Riverbed Technology GmbH, Riverbed Technology India Ltd., Riverbed Technology International, Inc., Riverbed Technology KK, Riverbed Technology Korea, Inc., Riverbed Technology Ltd., Riverbed Technology Pte. Ltd., Riverbed Technology S.A.R.L., Riverbed Technology South Africa (Proprietary) Limited, Riverbed Technology SRL, Riverbed Technology, S.r.l.
Officers: Jerry M. Kennelly/Chmn., CEO, Steve McCanne/Dir., CTO, Eric Wolford/Sr. VP - Marketing - Business Development, Randy S. Gottfried/CFO, David M. Peranich/Sr. VP - Worldwide Sales, Gordon Chaffee/VP - Engineering, Stephen R. Smoot/VP - Technical Operations, Mark Stuart Day/Chief Scientist, Harold E. Irvine/CIO, Brett A. Nissenberg/General Counsel, VP - Corporate - Legal Affairs
Directors: Jerry M. Kennelly/Chmn., CEO, Steve McCanne/Dir., CTO, Michael R. Kourey/Dir., Stanley J. Meresman/Dir., Christopher J. Schaepe/Dir., James R. Swartz/Dir., Mark A. Floyd/Dir.
Owners: David M. Peranich, James R. Swartz/2.30%, Stanley J. Meresman, Randy S. Gottfried, Mark A. Floyd, Jerry M. Kennelly/7.70%, Entities affiliated with Lightspeed Venture Partners/9.90%, Blake G. Modersitzki, FMR Corp./12.30%, Eric Wolford, Michael R. Kourey, Insiders/28.80%, Steven McCanne/7.50%, Christopher J. Schaepe/10.10%

Financial Data: Fiscal Year End:12/31   Latest Annual Data: 12/31/2006

Year	Sales	Net Income
2006	$90,207,000	-$15,845,000
2005	$22,941,000	-$17,426,000
2004	$2,562,000	-$9,827,000

Curr. Assets:	$140,485,000	**Curr. Liab.:**	$39,166,000		
Plant, Equip.:	$7,718,000	**Total Liab.:**	$41,789,000	**Indic. Yr. Divd.:**	NA
Total Assets:	$150,769,000	**Net Worth:**	$108,980,000	**Debt/ Equity:**	NA

Riverbend Holdings Inc

826 Barracks St., New Orleans, LA, 70116; *PH:* 1-504-524-2433

General - Incorporation	CO	**Stock** - Price on:12/24/2007	NA
Employees	NA	Stock Exchange	NA
Auditor	Coulter & Justus, P.C	Ticker Symbol	NA
Stk Agt	NA	Outstanding Shares	NA
Counsel	NA	E.P.S.	NA
DUNS No.	NA	Shareholders	NA

Business: The group's principle activity is to provide local, long distance and prepaid calling card telecommunication services. The group also provides data and Internet services. The group operates from United States.
Primary SIC and add'l.: 7389
CIK No: 0001302672
Subsidiaries: Riverbend Telecom, Inc.

Rivergreen Bank ME

36 Portland Rd., Kennebunk, ME, 04043; *PH:* 1-207-985-9222; *Fax:* 1-207-985-8382;
http:// www.rivergreenbank.com

General - Incorporation		**Stock** - Price on:12/24/2007	$18
Employees	NA	Stock Exchange	OTC
Auditor	NA	Ticker Symbol	RVGR
Stk Agt	NA	Outstanding Shares	NA
Counsel	NA	E.P.S.	NA
DUNS No.	NA	Shareholders	NA

Business: The groups principal activities include providing banking services as community banking. Services of the group include checking accounts, savings accounts, certificates of deposit, installment loans, real estate mortgage loans, commercial loans, traveler's checks, safe deposit boxes, night depository and automated teller services. The group operates from the United States.
Primary SIC and add'l.: 6022
CIK No:
Officers: Noel B. Graydon/CEO, Pres., Terrance L. Beers/COO, Exec. VP, Scott Boyer/Sr. VP - Credit Administrations, Betsy G. Buzulchuck/Sr. VP - Deposit Operations, Human Resources, David N. Moravick/Sr. VP, Bank Mgr. - Saco, Charles Jerram/Sr. VP - Commercial Lender, York, Bonnie G. Sylvestre/VP, Bank Mgr. - Kennebunk, Aaron J. Cannan/VP - Commercial Lending, Melissa A. Cookson/VP - Loan Operations, Carri L. Brown/CFO, Exec. VP, Shelli Berry/Assist. VP - Human Resources, Donna Desaulnier/VP, Bank Secrecy Act Officer, Susan Elliston/Assist. VP - Kennebunk Branch, Matthew Fernandez/Assist. VP, Assistant Controller, Donald Godfrey/VP - Commercial Lender *(52 Officers included in Index)*
Directors: Ronald D. Bourque/Dir., Marc R. Brunelle/Dir., Lawrence C. Brackley/Corporate Clerk, Dir., Karen Forbes Darling/Dir., Timothy M. Dietz/Dir., James M. Faulkner/Dir., Frances M. Harrison/Dir., Peter M. Martin/Dir., Michael Scarks/Dir., Douglas R. Stockbridge/Dir., Drew E. Swenson/Dir., King H. Weinstein/Dir.

Riverview Bancorp Inc

Riverview Ctr., Vancouver, WA, 98687; *PH:* 1-360-693-6650; *Fax:* 1-360-693-6275;
http:// www.riverviewbank.com

General - Incorporation	WA	**Stock** - Price on:12/24/2007	$14.04
Employees	255	Stock Exchange	NDQ
Auditor	Deloitte & Touche LLP	Ticker Symbol	RVSB
Stk Agt	U.S. Stock Transfer Corp	Outstanding Shares	11,630,000
Counsel	NA	E.P.S.	$1.02
DUNS No.	03-078-0985	Shareholders	NA

Business: The group's principal activities are to attract deposits from the general public and invest such deposits in various consumer-based real estate loans, other consumer and commercial loans, investment securities and mortgage-backed securities. It originates residential construction loans, business loans and consumer loans. The group is a bank holding company, which operates through its subsidiary, riverview savings bank. The banking activities are conducted through 13 branch offices in camas, washougal, stevenson, white salmon, battle ground, goldendale, vancouver (six branch offices) and longview, Washington. The group also operates a trust and financial services company, riverview asset management corporation, located in downtown vancouver, Washington. On 18-Jul-2003, it acquired today's bancorp inc.
Primary SIC and add'l.: 6712 6035
CIK No: 0001041368

Subsidiaries: Riverview Asset Management Corp, Riverview Community Bank, Riverview Services, Inc.

Officers: Patrick Sheaffer/Chmn., CEO/$373,402.00, John A. Karas/Exec. VP, Trust Company CEO/$284,789.00, James D. Baldovin/Sr. VP - Retail Banking, David A. Dahlstrom/Exec. VP, Chief Credit Officer/$221,628.00, Ronald A. Wysaske/Dir., COO, Pres./$360,753.00, Ronald L. Dobyns/Sr. VP, CFO/$175,119.00, Terry Long/Sr. VP - Operations, Technology, Scott Miller/Sr. VP - Marketing, Krista Holland/Sr. VP - Human Resources

Directors: Patrick Sheaffer/Chmn., CEO, Edward R. Geiger/Vice Chmn., Paul L. Runyan/Dir., Jerry C. Olson/Dir., Ronald A. Wysaske/Dir., COO, Pres., Gary R. Douglass/Dir., Michael D. Allen/Dir.

Owners: Insiders/11.30%, Patrick Sheaffer/4.71% Jerry C. Olson, Edward R. Geiger, Dimensional Fund Advisors LP/5.67%, Banc Fund V L.P/5.43%, Riverview Community Bank/6.98%, John A. Karas, Michael D. Allen, Robert K. Leick, Ronald L. Dobyns, Paul L. Runyan/2.15%, David A. Dahlstrom, Gary R. Douglass, Ronald A. Wysaske/1.86%

Financial Data: *Fiscal Year End:*03/31 , *Latest Annual Data:* 3/31/2007

Year	Sales	Net Income
2007	$70,334,000	$11,606,000
2006	$56,066,000	$9,738,000
2005	$37,659,000	$6,529,000

Curr. Assets:	$35,245,000	**Curr. Liab.:**	$709,804,000	**P/E Ratio:**	13.76
Plant, Equip.:	$21,402,000	**Total Liab.:**	$720,139,000	**Indic. Yr. Divd.:**	$0.400
Total Assets:	$820,348,000	**Net Worth:**	$100,209,000	**Debt/ Equity:**	0.1014

Riviera Holdings Corp

2901 Las Vegas Blvd. S, Las Vegas, NV, 89109; *PH:* 1-702-734-5110; *Fax:* 1-702-794-9442; *http://* www.theriviera.com

General - Incorporation	NV	Stock - Price on:12/24/2007	$37.33
Employees	1,500	Stock Exchange	AMEX
Auditor	Deloitte & Touche LLP	Ticker Symbol	RIV
Stk Agt	American Registrar & Transfer Co	Outstanding Shares	12,460,000
Counsel	Dechert, Price & Rhoads	E.P.S.	$0.33
DUNS No.	80-729-0101	Shareholders	NA

Business: The group's principal activity is to operate hotels and casinos through its subsidiaries: riviera operating corporation (riviera las vegas), riviera gaming management inc and riviera black hawk inc. The company operates mainly in the gaming, hotel, restaurant and entertainment segments. Through its las vegas operations, the company offers value-oriented experience by providing a variety of hotel rooms, restaurants and entertainment with some of las vegas' popular shows. Through its new subsidiary, riviera black hawk, it offers a variety of non-gaming amenities like parking facilities for vehicles with convenient and free self-park and valet options; a 252-seat casual buffet styled restaurant; and an entertainment center. Gaming management provides services like assisting new venue licensee applicants in designing and planning their gaming operations.

Primary SIC and add'l.: 9999 7021 7011

CIK No: 0000899647

Subsidiaries: Riviera Black Hawk, Riviera Hotel & Casino, Riviera Operating Corporation

Officers: William L. Westerman/76/Chmn., CEO, Pres./$1,244,363.00, Tullio J. Marchionne/53/Sec., General Counsel/$332,512.00, Mark B. Lefever/43/Treasurer, CFO/$233,039.00

Directors: William L. Westerman/76/Chmn., CEO, Pres., Jeffrey A. Silver/62/Dir., James N. Land/78/Dir., Vincent L. Divito/48/Dir., Paul A. Harvey/70/Dir.

Owners: High Desert Gaming, LLC/5.60%, Brett Torino and related parties/3.40%, Vincent L. DiVito, Insiders/3.70%, Triple Five Investco LLC, Dominion Financial LLC and Syd Ghermezian/9.50%, Barry Sternlicht and related parties/6.00%, William L. Westerman, Desert Rock Enterprises LLC, the Derek J. Stevens Trust and the Gregory J. Stevens Trust/8.40%, Tullio J. Marchionne, Robert A. Vannucci/2.30%, James N. Land, Jeffrey A. Silver, D.E. Shaw & Co., L.P. and related parties/9.80%, Flag Luxury Properties, LLC/6.70%, Paul A. Harvey *(18 Owners included in Index)*

Financial Data: *Fiscal Year End:*12/31   *Latest Annual Data:* 12/31/2006

Year	Sales	Net Income
2006	$200,944,000	-$335,000
2005	$202,227,000	-$3,999,000
2004	$220,519,000	-$2,086,000

Curr. Assets:	$34,142,000	**Curr. Liab.:**	$25,235,000	**P/E Ratio:**	113.12
Plant, Equip.:	$171,320,000	**Total Liab.:**	$244,216,000	**Indic. Yr. Divd.:**	NA
Total Assets:	$213,682,000	**Net Worth:**	-$30,534,000	**Debt/ Equity:**	NA

Riviera Tool Co

5460 Executive Pkwy, Grand Rapids, MI, 49512; *PH:* 1-616-698-2100; *http://* www.rivieratool.com; *Email:* rivsales@rivieratool.com

General - Incorporation	MI	Stock - Price on:12/24/2007	NA
Employees	140	Stock Exchange	OTC
Auditor	Deloitte & Touche LLP	Ticker Symbol	RIVT
Stk Agt	Stock Transfer & Trust Co	Outstanding Shares	NA
Counsel	NA	E.P.S.	-$0.36
DUNS No.	10-163-3568	Shareholders	NA

Business: The group's principle activities include designing and manufacturing complex die systems used in the production of sheet metal stamped parts and assemblies for the automotive industry. The stamping systems are used to form automobile and truck body parts such as hoods, fenders, doors, door frames, structural components and bumpers. The company's dies are used in the high-speed production of sheet metal stamped parts and assemblies. The dies manufactured by the company generally include automation features, adding to the complexity of design and construction. Original equipment manufacturers are developing organizational structures involving internal design and engineering personnel as well as supplier representatives which they are using to develop new car models. The company's main customers are daimlerchrysler ag, ford motor company, general motors corporation and their tier one suppliers of sheet metal stamped parts and assemblies. The group operates from United States.

Primary SIC and add'l.: 3465

CIK No: 0001018349

Officers: Kenneth K. Rieth/48/Chmn., CEO, Pres., Peter C. Canepa/49/CFO, Treasurer, Sec., Brian Rieth/45/VP, GM, Thomas J. Winters/66/VP - Sales

Directors: Kenneth K. Rieth/48/Chmn., CEO, Pres., Dann J. Engels/51/Dir., Jay S. Baron/42/Dir., James V. Gillette/52/Dir.

Owners: Peter C. Canepa/0.80%, Insiders/18.70%, Kenneth K. Rieth/17.40%, James V. Gillette, Thomas J. Winters/0.50%

Financial Data: *Fiscal Year End:*08/31   *Latest Annual Data:* 08/31/2006

Year	Sales	Net Income
2006	$24,041,000	-$1,639,000
2005	$19,274,000	-$2,502,000
2004	$24,689,000	-$8,241,000

Curr. Assets:	$11,124,000	**Curr. Liab.:**	$7,037,000		
Plant, Equip.:	$10,049,000	**Total Liab.:**	$19,050,000	**Indic. Yr. Divd.:**	NA
Total Assets:	$21,543,000	**Net Worth:**	$2,493,000	**Debt/ Equity:**	NA

RLI Corp

9025 N Lindbergh Dr., Peoria, IL, 61615; *PH:* 1-309-692-1000; *Fax:* 1-309-692-1068; *http://* www.rlicorp.com

General - Incorporation	IL	Stock - Price on:12/24/2007	$56.51
Employees	649	Stock Exchange	NYSE
Auditor	KPMG LLP	Ticker Symbol	RLI
Stk Agt	Wells Fargo Shareowner Services	Outstanding Shares	23,960,000
Counsel	NA	E.P.S.	$6.78
DUNS No.	03-841-1591	Shareholders	NA

Business: The group's principal activity is to underwrite selected property and casualty insurance products through its subsidiaries. The commercial property coverage insurance includes earthquake, wind, flood and collapse coverage. It writes coverage for a wide range of commercial and industrial risks such as office buildings, apartments, condominiums, certain industrial and mercantile structures, buildings under construction and movable equipment. The casualty segment includes liability products where loss and related settlement expenses must be estimated, as the ultimate disposition of claims may take several years to fully develop. The surety segment offers a selection of small and medium-size commercial products related to the statutory requirement for bonds on construction and energy-related projects.

Primary SIC and add'l.: 6719 6331

CIK No: 0000084246

Subsidiaries: Mt. Hawley Insurance Company, RLI Aviation, Inc., RLI Indemnity Company, RLI Insurance Agency Ltd., RLI Insurance Company, RLI Insurance Ltd., RLI Underwriting Services, Inc., Safe Fleet Insurance Services, Inc., Underwriters Indemnity General Agency, Inc.

Officers: Jonathan E. Michael/Dir., CEO, Pres./$3,453,186.00, Donald J. Driscoll/VP - Claim, Carol J. Denzer/CIO, Aaron H. Jacoby/VP - Corporate Development, Michael J. Stone/COO, Pres./$1,886,480.00, Joseph E. Dondanville/Sr. VP, CFO/$1,366,664.00, Kevin McDonough/VP - West Coast Property, John E. Robison/Treasurer, Seth A. Davis/VP - Internal Audit, Jeffrey D. Fick/VP - Human Resources/$514,374.00, Daniel O. Kennedy/VP, General Counsel, Corp. Sec./$612,173.00, Craig W. Kliethermes/VP - Actuarial Services, James S. Davis/RLI Underwriter, Exec. VP, Target Marketing Specialist, Roy C. Die/VP - Surety, David A. Dunn/RLI Underwriter *(34 Officers included in Index)*

Directors: Jonathan E. Michael/Dir., CEO, Pres., Gerald D. Stephens/Chmn., Gerald I. Lenrow/Dir., Jordan W. Graham/Dir., Robert O. Viets/Dir., Edward F. Sutkowski/Dir., Charles M. Linke/Dir., Richard H. Blum/Dir., Barbara R. Allen/Dir., John T. Baily/Dir., Lynn F. McPheeters/Dir.

Owners: Barbara R. Allen, Joseph E. Dondanville/1.10%, Insiders/12.10%, Jeffrey D. Fick, Lynn F. McPheeters, Robert O. Viets, Gerald I. Lenrow, Jonathan E. Michael/2.20%, Charles M. Linke, Daniel O. Kennedy, Edward F. Sutkowski, Richard H. Blum, Jordan W. Graham, John T. Baily, Michael J. Stone/1.20% *(18 Owners included in Index)*

Financial Data: *Fiscal Year End:*12/31   *Latest Annual Data:* 12/31/2006

Year	Sales	Net Income
2006	$632,708,000	$134,639,000
2005	$569,302,000	$107,134,000
2004	$578,800,000	$73,036,000

Curr. Assets:	$868,453,000	**Curr. Liab.:**	$93,364,000	**P/E Ratio:**	8.33
Plant, Equip.:	$20,590,000	**Total Liab.:**	$2,014,776,000	**Indic. Yr. Divd.:**	$0.880
Total Assets:	$2,771,296,000	**Net Worth:**	$756,520,000	**Debt/ Equity:**	0.1304

RMD Technologies Inc

308 W 5th St. , Holtville, CA, 92250; *PH:* 1-760-356-2039; *http://* www.rmdrecycling.com; *Email:* info@RMDRecycling.com

General - Incorporation	CA	Stock - Price on:12/24/2007	NA
Employees	NA	Stock Exchange	OTC
Auditor Child, Van Wagoner & Bradshaw, PLLC		Ticker Symbol	NA
Stk Agt	NA	Outstanding Shares	NA
Counsel	NA	E.P.S.	NA
DUNS No.	NA	Shareholders	NA

Business: The group's principal activity is to provide full service recycler of computers, monitors, and electronic equipment. The company provides certified e-waste recycling services and certified data destruction. The company was formed to provide businesses and consumers with technology disposal and recycling services using proper, environmentally safe procedures. The company has grown to offer computer pickup and disposal services throughout the nation. The company pioneered "Responsible Technology" to correctly handle obsolete computers and monitors— without sending them to landfills.

Primary SIC and add'l.: 7389

CIK No: 0001312112

Officers: Patrick A. Galliher/47/Dir., CFO, Principal Executive Officer, Pres., Treasurer, Suzanne E. Galliher/41/Dir., VP, Sec.

Directors: Patrick A. Galliher/47/Dir., CFO, Principal Executive Officer, Pres., Treasurer, Suzanne E. Galliher/41/Dir., VP, Sec.

Owners: Suzanne E. Galliher/17.04%, John Fleming/17.04%, Insiders/68.16%, Patrick A. Galliher/51.12%, Sichenzia Ross Friedman Ference LLP/8.52%

RNS Software Inc

2197 W 2nd Ave., Ste. 103, Vancouver, BC, V6K 1H7; *PH:* 1-604-789-2410

General - Incorporation	NV	Stock - Price on:12/24/2007	NA
Employees	NA	Stock Exchange	OTC
Auditor	Dale Matheson Carr-Hilton LaBonte LLP	Ticker Symbol	RNSW
Stk Agt	Interwest Transfer Company, Inc.	Outstanding Shares	NA
Counsel	NA	E.P.S.	NA
DUNS No.	NA	Shareholders	NA

Business: The groups principal activity is business of developing and marketing a search engine optimization software package named SEOdoctor. Product allows a clients website to have key identifier words embedded in the home page which in turn would interact with search engines and result in the clients website receiving a higher profile / ranking in searches. The group operates from the United States.

Primary SIC and add'l.: 7372

CIK No: 0001341319

Officers: Livio Susin/52/Dir., CEO, CFO, Pres., Sec., Treasurer

Directors: Livio Susin/52/Dir., CEO, CFO, Pres., Sec., Treasurer

Owners: Ferruccio Susin/9.58%, Insiders/76.67%, Livio Susin/76.67%, Gail Lorraine Jellema/9.58%

Roadhouse Grill Inc

2703-a Gateway Dr., Pompano Beach, FL, 33069; **PH:** 1-954-957-2600;
http:// www.roadhousegrill.com

General - Incorporation	FL	Stock - Price on:12/24/2007	$0.41
Employees	2,893	Stock Exchange	OTC
Auditor	Rachlin Cohen & Holtz, LLP	Ticker Symbol	GRLL
Stk Agt	American Stock Transfer & Trust Co.	Outstanding Shares	29,220,000
Counsel	NA	E.P.S.	-$0.41
DUNS No.	79-819-125	Shareholders	NA

Business: The group's principal activities are to operate, franchise and license full service casual dining restaurants. The restaurants offer a diverse, moderately priced lunch and dinner menu, highlighting exhibition cooking of steaks and other grilled entrees. The restaurant also features daily fresh baked yeast rolls, appetizers and homemade ice cream. The casual dining restaurants are targeted towards singles, couples, families and senior citizens. As of 25-Apr-2004, group owned 69 roadhouse grill restaurants located in Alabama, Arkansas, Florida, Georgia, Louisiana, Mississippi, New York, North Carolina, Ohio, and South Carolina. The group also has three franchised restaurants in Malaysia, one franchised restaurant in brasilia, Brazil, one franchised restaurant in las vegas, Nevada, one franchised restaurant in cincinnati, Ohio, and four joint venture restaurants in Italy.

Primary SIC and add'l.: 5813 5812

CIK No: 0001019376

Subsidiaries: Roadhouse Grill of Georgia, Inc., Roadhouse Grill of New York, Inc., Roadhouse Grill of North Miami, Inc., Roadhouse Grill of South Carolina, Inc., Roadhouse Grill Property, L.C., Roadhouse Grill-Commercial, Inc.

Officers: Ayman Sabi/44/Dir., CEO, CFO, Pres., Alain K.K. Lee/50/Dir., Exec. VP, Corp. Sec., Mark Rogers/44/VP - Operations

Directors: Ayman Sabi/44/Dir., CEO, CFO, Pres., Ronald J. Buck/44/Dir., Nathan D. Benn/45/Dir., Alain K.K. Lee/50/Dir., Exec. VP, Corp. Sec., Francis Lee/50/Dir.

Owners: Ayman Sabi/9.50%, Tonto Capital Partners, G.P./9.50%, Berjaya Group Limited/66.50%

Financial Data: Fiscal Year End:04/24 **Latest Annual Data:** 04/30/2006

Year	Sales	Net Income
2006	$115,995,000	-$10,721,000
2005	$129,207,000	-$2,441,000
2001	$168,055,000	-$15,856,000

Curr. Assets:	$2,511,000	Curr. Liab.:	$25,188,000		
Plant, Equip.:	$19,368,000	Total Liab.:	$33,406,000	Indic. Yr. Divd.:	NA
Total Assets:	$25,108,000	Net Worth:	-$8,298,000	Debt/ Equity:	NA

Robbins & Myers Inc

51 Plum St., Ste. 260, Dayton, OH, 45440; **PH:** 1-937-458-6600; **Fax:** 1-937-458-6614;
http:// www.robn.com

General - Incorporation	OH	Stock - Price on:12/24/2007	$47.16
Employees	3,271	Stock Exchange	NYSE
Auditor	Ernst & Young LLP	Ticker Symbol	RBN
Stk Agt	National City Bank	Outstanding Shares	17,090,000
Counsel	Thompson Hine & Flory	E.P.S.	$2.96
DUNS No.	00-428-3990	Shareholders	NA

Business: The group's principal activity is to design, manufacture and market highly engineered, application-critical equipment and systems for the pharmaceutical, energy and industrial markets worldwide. The pharmaceutical segment includes primary processing equipment including glass-lined reactors and storage vessels, secondary processing, dosing, filling, printing and security equipment. The energy segment includes hydraulic drilling power sections, down-hole pumps and a broad line of ancillary equipment, such as rod guides, rod and tubing rotators, wellhead systems, pipeline closure products and valves. The industrial segment includes progressing cavity pump products, mixing and turbine agitation equipment and fluoropolymer-lined products and accessories. The group's brand names include pfaudler, moyno, chemineer, laetus, frymakoruma, siebler, hapa and hercules. The group operates in the United States, Europe, South America and Asia.

Primary SIC and add'l.: 3559 3491 3561 3594 3443 5084

CIK No: 0000084290

Subsidiaries: Bosspak Pty Limited, Chemineer, Asia, Ptd. Ltd., Chemineer, Inc., Dalian Moyno Pump Co., Ltd., Dioptec Scan Limited, Edlon, Inc., Fryma S.a.r.l., FrymaKoruma AG, FrymaKoruma GmbH, Glasteel Parts and Services, Inc., GMM Pfaudler Limited, Ingeniere Pharmaceutique Modulaire S.A., Moyno de Mexico, S.A. de C.V., Moyno, Inc., Pfaudler Equipamentos Industriais Ltda. 63 Subsidiaries included in the Index

Officers: Peter C. Wallace/52/Dir., CEO, Pres., Kevin J. Brown/Controller - Principal, Accounting Officer, Saeid Rahimian/VP, Pres. - Fluid Management Group, Joseph M. Rigot/Corp. Sec., General Counsel, Gary L. Brewer/VP, Pres. - Process Solutions Group, Christopher M. Hix/CFO, VP, Michael J. McAdams/Treasurer

Directors: Peter C. Wallace/52/Dir., CEO, Pres., Thomas P. Loftis/62/Chmn., William D. Manning/72/Dir., Dale L. Medford/56/Dir., Daniel W. Duval/70/Dir., David T. Gibbons/62/Dir., Stephen F. Kirk/57/Dir., Andrew Lampereur/44/Dir.

Owners: David T. Gibbons, Stephen F. Kirk, Saeid Rahimian, William D. Manning, Dale L. Medford, Barclays Global Investors UK Holdings Limited/5.90%, Daniel W. Duval, Peter C. Wallace, AXA/6.70%, Kevin J. Brown, Andrew G. Lampereur, Christopher M. Hix, M.H.M. & Co., Ltd./17.40%, Thomas P. Loftis, Insiders/2.40% (16 Owners included in Index)

Financial Data: Fiscal Year End:08/31 **Latest Annual Data:** 8/31/2006

Year	Sales	Net Income
2006	$625,389,000	-$19,587,000
2005	$604,773,000	-$262,000
2004	$585,758,000	$9,770,000

Curr. Assets:	$284,121,000	Curr. Liab.:	$165,820,000	P/E Ratio:	19.25
Plant, Equip.:	$127,030,000	Total Liab.:	$348,251,000	Indic. Yr. Divd.:	$0.260
Total Assets:	$698,323,000	Net Worth:	$338,379,000	Debt/ Equity:	NA

Robert Half International Inc

2884 Sand Hill Rd., Menlo Park, CA, 94025; **PH:** 1-650-234-6000; **Fax:** 1-650-234-6999;
http:// www.rhii.com; **Email:** investor.relations@rhi.com

General - Incorporation	DE	Stock - Price on:12/24/2007	$35.75
Employees	13,400	Stock Exchange	NYSE
Auditor	PricewaterhouseCoopers LLP	Ticker Symbol	RHI
Stk Agt	Mellon Investor Services LLC	Outstanding Shares	166,250,000
Counsel	NA	E.P.S.	$1.74
DUNS No.	04-325-6403	Shareholders	NA

Business: The group's principle activity is to provide professional staffing and consulting services. The group provides staffing services in finance, accounting, technology, legal, administrative, marketing and creative industries. The group operates from United States, Australia, France, Germany, Ireland, Canada, Brazil, Singapore, Spain and Japan.

Primary SIC and add'l.: 7361 7389 8721 7363 8744

CIK No: 0000315213

Subsidiaries: Atlantic Temporaries, Inc., BMK Resources, Inc., BMK Services, Inc., Cooperative Resources, Inc., Golden State Temporaries, Inc., Jersey Temporaries, Inc., Monarch Staffing, L.P., OfficeTeam Inc., Protiviti B.V., Protiviti Co., Protiviti GmbH, Protiviti Holdings Inc., Protiviti Hong Kong Co. Ltd., Protiviti Inc., Protiviti Japan Co., Ltd. 53 Subsidiaries included in the Index

Officers: Harold M. Messmer/Chmn., CEO/$13,041,870.00, Keith M. Waddell/Vice Chmn., CFO, Pres./$8,299,871.00, Paul F. Gentzkow/COO, Pres. - Staffing Services/$6,930,874.00, Robert W. Glass/Exec. VP - Corporate Development/$2,187,672.00, Steven Karel/Sr. VP, Sec., General Counsel/$1,644,507.00, Michael Buckley/Exec. VP, Chief Administrative Officer, Treasurer, Reesa M. Staten/Sr. VP - Corporate Communications, Paula Streit/VP, Controller - Field Accounting, Elena West/Sr. VP - Marketing, Evelyn Crane-Oliver/Assoc. General Counsel, Assist. Sec.

Directors: Harold M. Messmer/Chmn., CEO, Keith M. Waddell/Vice Chmn., CFO, Pres., Andrew S. Berwick/Dir., Frederick P. Furth/Dir., Edward W. Gibbons/Dir., Thomas J. Ryan/Dir., Stephen J. Schaub/Dir.

Owners: Insiders/11.60%, Harold M. Messmer/2.80%, Thomas J. Ryan/0.20%, FMR Corp./12.70%, Michael C. Buckley/0.10%, Stephen J. Schaub/1.70%, Andrew S. Berwick, Barclays Global Investors, N.A./17.40%, Keith M. Waddell/1.80%, Edward W. Gibbons/0.50%, Frederick P. Furth/2.80%, Paul F. Gentzkow/1.20%, Capital Research and Management Company/9.40%, Steven Karel/0.20%, Robert W. Glass/0.40%

Financial Data: Fiscal Year End:12/31 **Latest Annual Data:** 12/31/2006

Year	Sales	Net Income
2006	$4,013,546,000	$283,178,000
2005	$3,338,439,000	$237,870,000
2004	$2,675,696,000	$140,604,000

Curr. Assets:	$1,112,355,000	Curr. Liab.:	$402,740,000	P/E Ratio:	20.55
Plant, Equip.:	$132,081,000	Total Liab.:	$416,350,000	Indic. Yr. Divd.:	$0.400
Total Assets:	$1,459,021,000	Net Worth:	$1,042,671,000	Debt/ Equity:	0.0036

Roberts Realty Investors Inc

450 Nridge Pk.way, Ste. 302, Atlanta, GA, 30350; **PH:** 1-770-394-6000

General - Incorporation	GA	Stock - Price on:12/24/2007	$7.687
Employees	10	Stock Exchange	AMEX
Auditor	Deloitte & Touche, LLP	Ticker Symbol	RPI
Stk Agt	American Stock Transfer & Trust Co.	Outstanding Shares	5,810,000
Counsel	NA	E.P.S.	-$0.96
DUNS No.	NA	Shareholders	NA

Business: The groups principle activities include developing, constructing, and managing multifamily apartment communities, neighborhood retail centers, and one office building. The group operates through four segments namely multifamily, retail/office, the land and corporate. In the year 2005, the group acquired Spectrum Shopping Center and 14.5 acres of undeveloped land on Westside Parkway. The group operates from the United States. The group's quarterly revenue for September 2007 was 2.03 millions of USD.

Primary SIC and add'l.: 6513 6798

CIK No: 0001011109

Subsidiaries: Roberts Bassett LLC, Roberts Grand Pavilion LLC, Roberts Spectrum LLC

Owners: Charles S. Roberts/37.80%, Ben A. Spalding, Dennis H. James/2.10%, Insiders/45.00%, James M. Goodrich/4.90%, Jarell Jones, Charles R. Elliott

Financial Data: Fiscal Year End:12/31 **Latest Annual Data:** 12/31/2006

Year	Sales	Net Income
2006	$8,057,000	-$3,858,000
2005	$5,879,000	$1,256,000
2004	$5,577,000	$36,986,000

Curr. Assets:	$4,824,000	Curr. Liab.:	$1,056,000		
Plant, Equip.:	$125,128,000	Total Liab.:	$90,469,000	Indic. Yr. Divd.:	NA
Total Assets:	$131,767,000	Net Worth:	$41,298,000	Debt/ Equity:	1.8866

Robocom Systems International Inc

1111 Rte. 110, Farmingdale, NY, 11735; **PH:** 1-631-753-2180; **Fax:** 1-631-249-2831;
http:// www.robocom.com; **Email:** sales@robocom.com

General - Incorporation	NY	Stock - Price on:12/24/2007	$0.25
Employees	NA	Stock Exchange	OTC
Auditor	Eisner & Lubin LLP	Ticker Symbol	RIMS
Stk Agt	Continental Stock Transfer & Trust Co	Outstanding Shares	4,840,000
Counsel	NA	E.P.S.	-$0.026
DUNS No.	07-628-6152	Shareholders	NA

Business: The group's principal activities are to develop, market and support advanced warehouse management software solutions that enable companies to realize significant cost savings by automating their warehouse operations and providing inventory visibility throughout the supply chain. The group's primary product, rims(tm), is a client-configurable software solution that enables a company's warehouse to respond to a customer order with greater accuracy and in a more timely manner, thereby turning the warehouse into a competitive advantage. Rims operates in an open system environment and interfaces with and an organization's existing information systems. The group also provides installation, training, implementation support and maintenance services and resells related hardware.

Primary SIC and add'l.: 7378 7379 7376 3577

CIK No: 0001039757

Officers: Irwin Balaban/76/Chmn., CEO, Pres., Brian /Support Team, Christine /Support Team, Sue /Support Team, Judith /Support Team, Terri /Support Team, Paul /Support Team, Todd /Support Team, Hugo /Support Team

Directors: Irwin Balaban/76/Chmn., CEO, Pres., Robert B. Friedman/69/Dir., Herbert Goldman/77/Co - Founder, Dir., Lawrence B. Klein/74/Dir.

Owners: Robert B. Friedman/3.26%, Irwin Balaban/22.52%, Insiders/62.37%, Herbert Goldman/20.36%, Steven N. Bronson/8.61%, Lawrence B. Klein/15.38%

Financial Data: Fiscal Year End:05/31 **Latest Annual Data:** 05/31/2007

Year	Sales	Net Income
2007	NA	-$119,000
2006	NA	$883,000
2005	$3,568,000	$503,000

Curr. Assets:	$3,324,000	**Curr. Liab.:**	$75,000		
Plant, Equip.:	NA	**Total Liab.:**	$75,000	**Indic. Yr. Divd.:**	$0.570
Total Assets:	$3,324,000	**Net Worth:**	$3,249,000	**Debt/ Equity:**	NA

Rochdale Mining Corp

3430 E Sunrise Dr., Ste. 120, Tucson, AZ, 85718; **PH:** 1-520-299-0390

General - Incorporation	NV	**Stock** - Price on:12/24/2007	NA
Employees	NA	Stock Exchange	OTC
Auditor	NA	Ticker Symbol	RHDC
Stk Agt	Pacific Stock Transfer Company	Outstanding Shares	NA
Counsel	NA	E.P.S.	NA
DUNS No.	NA	Shareholders	NA

Business: The group principal activity is in the acquisition and exploration of mineral resources. The group operates from the United States and Canada

Primary SIC and add'l.: 1000

CIK No: 0001329484

Officers: Harold W. Gardner/52/Dir., CEO, Pres., Principal Exec. Officer, David Rambaran/Sec., David Hackman/66/Dir., VP - Exploration, Sec., Jas Butalia/Dir., CFO

Directors: Harold W. Gardner/52/Dir., CEO, Pres., Principal Exec. Officer, Paul D. Brock/44/Dir., David Hackman/66/Dir., VP - Exploration, Sec., Jas Butalia/Dir., CFO, Terence Schorn/74/Dir.

Owners: Insiders/6.80%, Agosto Corporation Limited/9.00%, Integrity Capital Group, LLC/32.30%, Paul D. Brock/1.20%, Harold W. Gardner/5.70%, West Peak Ventures of Canada Limited/5.70%

Rochester Gas & Electric Corp

52 Farm View Dr., New Gloucester, ME, 04260; **PH:** 1-207-688-6300

General - Incorporation	NY	**Stock** - Price on:12/24/2007	$25.12
Employees	1,016	Stock Exchange	NA
Auditor	PricewaterhouseCoopers LLP	Ticker Symbol	NA
Stk Agt	First National Bank	Outstanding Shares	34,510,000
Counsel	NA	E.P.S.	$2.25
DUNS No.	NA	Shareholders	NA

Business: The group operates through its subsidiaries whose principle activity is to provide electric energy and natural gas services. The group operates from the United States.

Primary SIC and add'l.: 4924 5984 4923 4931 4932 4911

CIK No: 0000084557

Subsidiaries: Central Maine Power Company, Connecticut Natural Gas Corporation, Energetix, Inc., Energy East Enterprises, Inc., Energy East Management Corporation, Maine Electric Power Co., Inc., Maine Natural Gas Corporation, New York State Electric & Gas Corporation, NORVARCO, Rochester Gas and Electric Corporation, The Berkshire Gas Company, The Energy Network, Inc., The Southern Connecticut Gas Company

Officers: James P. Laurito/51/Dir., CEO, Pres., Joseph J. Syta/Principal Financial, Accounting Officer, VP, Controller, Treasurer

Directors: James P. Laurito/51/Dir., CEO, Pres., Wesley W. Von Schack/63/Dir., Robert E. Rude/54/Dir.

Financial Data: Fiscal Year End:12/31 **Latest Annual Data:** 12/31/2006

Year	Sales	Net Income
2006	$1,116,293,000	$82,295,000
2005	$1,105,526,000	$78,989,000
2004	$1,034,057,000	$70,317,000

Curr. Assets:	$365,401,000	**Curr. Liab.:**	$250,529,000	**P/E Ratio:**	14.67
Plant, Equip.:	$1,558,042,000	**Total Liab.:**	$1,877,800,000	**Indic. Yr. Divd.:**	NA
Total Assets:	$2,480,390,000	**Net Worth:**	$602,590,000	**Debt/ Equity:**	NA

Rochester Medical Corp

1 Rochester Medical Dr., Stewartville, MN, 55976; **PH:** 1-507-533-9600; **Fax:** 1-507-533-9740; **http://** www.rocm.com; **Email:** info@rocm.com

General - Incorporation	MN	**Stock** - Price on:12/24/2007	$15.39
Employees	213	Stock Exchange	NDQ
Auditor	Mcgladrey & Pullen, LLP	Ticker Symbol	ROCM
Stk Agt	Wells Fargo Shareowner Services	Outstanding Shares	11,660,000
Counsel	NA	E.P.S.	$2.78
DUNS No.	60-544-0718	Shareholders	NA

Business: The group's principle activities include developing, manufacturing and marketing innovative urinary continence and urine drainage care products for the extended care and acute care markets. Extended care products include a line of male external catheters for managing male urinary incontinence and a line of intermittent catheters for managing both male and female urinary retention. It also includes the femsoft(R) insert, a soft, liquid-filled, conformable urethral insert for managing female stress urinary incontinence in adult females. Acute care products include a line of standard foley catheters and its release-nf(R) catheter; an antibacterial foley catheter to reduce the incidence of hospital acquired urinary tract infection. The products are marketed under the name rochester medical (r). The significant customers of the company are convatec, hollister, maersk and mentor. The group operates from United States.

Primary SIC and add'l.: 3841

CIK No: 0000868368

Officers: Anthony J. Conway/Chmn., CEO, Pres., Sec., Martyn R. Sholtis/Corporate VP, Dara Lynn Horner/VP - Marketing, Philip J. Conway/Founder, VP - Production Technologies, David A. Jonas/CFO, Treasurer

Directors: Anthony J. Conway/Chmn., CEO, Pres., Sec., Philip J. Conway/Founder, VP - Production Technologies, Benson Smith/Dir., Darnell L. Boehm/Dir., Roger W. Schnobrich/Dir., Peter R. Conway/Dir.

Owners: Philip J. Conway/4.70%, Peter R. Conway/6.90%, Insiders/24.60%, Scott R. Asen/8.40%, Anthony J. Conway/9.10%, Townsend Group Investments, Inc./6.20%, David A. Jonas/1.60%, Darnell L. Boehm, Robert W. Schnobrich, Dara Lynn Horner/1.30%, Martyn R. Sholtis, Benson Smith

Financial Data: Fiscal Year End:09/30 **Latest Annual Data:** 09/30/2007

Year	Sales	Net Income
2007	$32,663,000	$34,050,000
2006	$21,666,000	$1,959,000
2005	$15,942,000	$934,000

Curr. Assets:	$12,507,000	**Curr. Liab.:**	$4,843,000	**P/E Ratio:**	5.38
Plant, Equip.:	$8,239,000	**Total Liab.:**	$12,856,000	**Indic. Yr. Divd.:**	NA
Total Assets:	$35,952,000	**Net Worth:**	$23,097,000	**Debt/ Equity:**	0.1159

Rochester Resources Ltd

Formerly: Hilton Resources Ltd
1305 - 1090 W Georgia St., Vancouver, BC, V6E 3V7; **PH:** 1-604-685-9316; **Fax:** 1-604-683-1585; **http://** www.rochesterresourcesltd.com

General - Incorporation	Canada	**Stock** - Price on:12/24/2007	$1.711
Employees	NA	Stock Exchange	OTC
Auditor	D&H Group LLP	Ticker Symbol	RCTFF
Stk Agt	Computershare Trust Co	Outstanding Shares	NA
Counsel	NA	E.P.S.	-$0.023
DUNS No.	NA	Shareholders	NA

Business: The groups principle activities include acquiring, exploring and developing gold and silver mineral properties. The group operates from Canada.

Primary SIC and add'l.: 1381 1382

CIK No: 0001099957

Subsidiaries: Minera Nayarit S.A. de C.V.

Officers: Alfredo Parra Davila/CEO, Pres., Harvey Lim/Sec., Jose Manual Silva/CFO, Eduardo Luna/Consulting Dir., Joseph M. Keane/Consulting Dir., Lindsay R. Bottomer/Consulting Dir.

Directors: Nick Demare/Chmn., Douglas F. Good/Dir., Marc Cernovitch/35/Dir.

Owners: Burlingame Equity Investors LP/8.10%, Harvey Lim/0.23%, Eduardo Luna/0.31%, Jose Manuel Silva/0.62%, Joseph Keane/0.70%, Lindsay Bottomer/0.33%, Nick DeMare/5.12%, Alfredo Parra/12.63%, Marc Cernovitch/0.62%

Financial Data: Fiscal Year End:05/31 **Latest Annual Data:** 5/31/2006

Year	Sales	Net Income
2006	NA	-$1,258,000
2005	NA	-$723,000
2004	NA	-$542,000

Curr. Assets:	$1,976,000	**Curr. Liab.:**	$1,259,000		
Plant, Equip.:	$1,272,000	**Total Liab.:**	$6,390,000	**Indic. Yr. Divd.:**	NA
Total Assets:	$21,455,000	**Net Worth:**	$15,065,000	**Debt/ Equity:**	NA

Rock of Ages Corp

772 Graniteville Rd., Graniteville, VT, 05654; **PH:** 1-802-476-3121; **Fax:** 1-802-476-3110; **http://** www.rockofages.com; **Email:** info@rockofages.com

General - Incorporation	DE	**Stock** - Price on:12/24/2007	$5
Employees	582	Stock Exchange	NDQ
Auditor	KPMG LLP	Ticker Symbol	ROAC
Stk Agt	American Stock Transfer & Trust Co.	Outstanding Shares	7,400,000
Counsel	Skadden, Meagher & Flom LLP	E.P.S.	-$0.08
DUNS No.	NA	Shareholders	NA

Business: The group's principle activity is the manufacture and retail of granite products, primarily granite memorials used in cemeteries. The group owns and operates 10 active quarry properties and 6 manufacturing and sawing facilities in North America, principally in Vermont and the province of quebec. The group markets and distributes its memorials on a retail basis through approximately 82 company-owned retail sales outlets and sells memorials wholesale to approximately 70 independent authorized rock of ages retailers in the United States and Canada. The group markets its memorials at four quality and price points under four separate brand names: rock of ages signature, rock of ages sealmark, golden rule by rock of ages and stone eternal by rock of ages. The group also sells non-branded memorials. The group's quarterly revenue for September 2007 was 21.48 millions of USD.

Primary SIC and add'l.: 3281 6553 5999 1411

CIK No: 0000084581

Subsidiaries: Carolina Quarries, Inc., Kabushiki Kaisha Rock of Ages Asia, Keith Monument Company LLC, Max Mining & Resources S.a.r.L., Pennsylvania Granite Corporation, Rock of Ages Canada, Inc., Rock of Ages Kentucky Cemeteries, LLC, Rock of Ages Memorials, Inc., Sioux Falls Monument Co.

Officers: Kurt M. Swenson/Chmn., CEO, Pres./$614,085.00, Donald Labonte/COO, Pres. - Manufacturing Division/$311,430.00, Douglas S. Goldsmith/COO, Pres. - Quarries Division/$216,065.00, Michael B. Tule/Sr. VP, General Counsel, Sec., Nancy Rowden

Brock/51/CFO, Sr. VP/$217,986.00, Rich Urbach/COO, Pres. - Retail Division/$184,756.00, Peter Friberg/VP - Wholesale Sales, Robert Campo/VP - Sales, Marketing, John Rose/Dir. - Manufacturing, Customer Service, Michael J. Caputo/Dir. - Precision Granite Products, Todd Paton/Dir. - Tourism, Paul Hutchins/Dir. - Human Resources, Laura Plude/CFO

Directors: Kurt M. Swenson/Chmn., CEO, Pres., Pamela G. Sheiffer/Dir., Frederick E. Webster/Dir., James L. Fox/Dir., Charles M. Waite/Dir., Richard C. Kimball/Dir.

Owners: Richard C. Kimball/2.40%, Kevin C. Swenson/37.40%, James L. Fox, Richard C. Kimball/1.10%, Pamela G. Sheiffer, Charles M. Waite/1.00%, Charles M. Waite/1.10%, Robert L. Pope/3.30%, Dimensional Fund Advisors, Inc/6.00%, Donald Labonte, Kevin C. Swenson/18.00%, Insiders/24.30%, Lord Abbett & Co., LLC/5.10%, Estate of Douglas M. Schair/12.20%, Kurt M. Swenson/20.00% *(18 Owners included in Index)*

Financial Data: *Fiscal Year End:*12/31 *Latest Annual Data:* 12/31/2006

Year	Sales	Net Income
2006	$80,964,000	-$5,365,000
2005	$89,506,000	-$16,143,000
2004	$86,594,000	-$3,221,000

Curr. Assets:	$45,219,000	Curr. Liab.:	$46,995,000		
Plant, Equip.:	$46,263,000	Total Liab.:	$61,887,000	Indic. Yr. Divd.:	NA
Total Assets:	$94,388,000	Net Worth:	$32,501,000	Debt/ Equity:	0.0077

Rock Tenn Co

504 Thrasher St., Norcross, GA, 30071; *PH:* 1-770-448-2193; *Fax:* 1-678-291-7666; *http://* www.rocktenn.com; *Email:* investorrel@rocktenn.com

General - Incorporation	GA	**Stock** - Price on:12/24/2007	$32.97
Employees	9,500	Stock Exchange	NYSE
Auditor	Ernst & Young LLP	Ticker Symbol	RKT
Stk Agt.... Computershare Investor Services LLC		Outstanding Shares	40,080,000
Counsel	Womble Carlyle Sandridge & Rice	E.P.S.	$2.07
DUNS No.	00-328-9725	Shareholders	NA

Business: The groups principle activity is to provide paperboard and marketing and packaging solutions for the consumer product industry. The group operates through four business segments namely packaging products, paperboard, merchandising displays, and corrugated packaging. In the year 2007 the group acquired Fold-Pak. The group operates from United States.

Primary SIC and add'l.: 2653 2679 2631

CIK No: 0000230498

Subsidiaries: 9124-1232 Quebec Inc., 9124-1232 Quebec Inc. Quebec, Canada, Alliance Display, LLC, Alliance Rock-Tenn Mexico, S. de R.L. de., Alliance Services Mexico, S. de R.L. de, Dominion Paperboard Products Ltd., Groupe Cartem Wilco Inc., GSD Packaging, LLC, Ling Industries, Inc., Ling Quebec, Inc., PCPC, Inc., Rock-Tenn Canada Holdings II, Inc., Rock-Tenn Canada Holdings, Inc., Rock-Tenn Company of Canada, Rock-Tenn Company of Illinois, Inc. 33 Subsidiaries included in the Index

Officers: James A. Rubright/Chmn., CEO, James L. Einstein/Exec. VP, GM Alliance Division, Stephen A. Meadows/Chief Accounting Officer, Robert B. McIntosh/Sr. VP, General Counsel, Sec., Steven C. Voorhees/CFO, Exec. VP, David E. Dreibelbis/Exec. VP, GM - Paperboard Division, Michael E. Kiepura/Exec. VP, GM - Folding Carton Division

Directors: James A. Rubright/Chmn., CEO, John W. Spiegel/Dir., James E. Young/Dir., Russell M. Currey/Dir., James W. Johnson/Dir., Stephen G. Anderson/Dir., John D. Hopkins/Dir., L. L. Gellerstedt/Dir., Stephen G. Felker/Dir., Robert B. Currey/Dir., Hyatt J. Brown/Dir.

Owners: Michael E. Kiepura, James L. Einstein, Robert B. Currey, James E. Young, James A. Rubright/1.77%, Russell M. Currey/2.48%, Stephen G. Anderson/1.18%, Stephen G. Felker, Insiders/10.17%, Steven C. Voorhees, Hyatt J. Brown/2.37%, Dimensional FundAdvisors Inc./8.18%, David E. Dreibelbis, John D. Hopkins, John W. Spiegel *(16 Owners included in Index)*

Financial Data: *Fiscal Year End:*09/30 *Latest Annual Data:* 9/30/2006

Year	Sales	Net Income
2006	$2,138,100,000	$28,700,000
2005	$1,733,481,000	$17,614,000
2004	$1,581,261,000	$17,648,000

Curr. Assets:	$485,600,000	Curr. Liab.:	$306,000,000	P/E Ratio:	15.48
Plant, Equip.:	$850,600,000	Total Liab.:	$1,256,600,000	Indic. Yr. Divd.:	$0.400
Total Assets:	$1,784,000,000	Net Worth:	$508,600,000	Debt/ Equity:	NA

Rockelle Corp

162 Miller Pl. Rd., Miller Place, NY, 11764; *PH:* 1-631-244-9841; *Fax:* 1-631-244-9842; *http://* www.rockellecorp.com

General - Incorporation	DE	**Stock** - Price on:12/24/2007	$0.1
Employees	NA	Stock Exchange	OTC
Auditor	Gately & Associates, LLC	Ticker Symbol	RKLC
Stk Agt	Olde Monmouth Stk Trnsfer Co. Inc.	Outstanding Shares	36,430,000
Counsel	NA	E.P.S.	-$0.092
DUNS No.	NA	Shareholders	NA

Business: The groups principle activities include building, owning, operating, and franchise of various types of quick service food establishments. The group operates from the United States. The group's revenue for Sep '07 was 0.02 millions of USD.

Primary SIC and add'l.: 5812

CIK No: 0001265850

Subsidiaries: Rockelle Riverhead Corp

Officers: Gerard A. Stephan/54/Chmn., CEO, Pres.

Directors: Gerard A. Stephan/54/Chmn., CEO, Pres., Warren Rothouse/46/Dir., Michael Stephan/55/Dir., Gerard Stephan/28/Dir.

Owners: Gerard Stephan, Carmella F. Stephan/5.40%, Michael Stephan, Insiders/55.00%, Gerard Stephan/49.60%

Financial Data: *Fiscal Year End:*12/31 *Latest Annual Data:* 12/31/2006

Year	Sales	Net Income
2006	$166,000	-$1,548,000
2005	$156,000	-$689,000

Curr. Assets:	$171,000	Curr. Liab.:	$1,125,000	P/E Ratio:	14.42
Plant, Equip.:	$1,043,000	Total Liab.:	$1,244,000	Indic. Yr. Divd.:	NA
Total Assets:	$2,095,000	Net Worth:	$851,000	Debt/ Equity:	NA

Rocketinfo Inc

3101 W Coast Hwy., Ste. 210, Newport Beach, CA, 92663; *PH:* 1-949-548-0223; *http://* www.rocketinfo.com; *Email:* investors@rocketinfo.com

General - Incorporation	DE	**Stock** - Price on:12/24/2007	$0.18
Employees	11	Stock Exchange	OTC
Auditor	Moore & Assoc. Chartered	Ticker Symbol	RKTI
Stk Agt.... Computershare Investor Services LLC		Outstanding Shares	46,330,000
Counsel	NA	E.P.S.	-$0.05
DUNS No.	NA	Shareholders	NA

Business: The group's principle activity is to acquire high quality oil and gas properties. This includes primarily proved producing and proved undeveloped reserves. The company also intends to explore low-risk development drilling and work-over opportunities with experienced, strong operators. The company will attempt to finance oil and gas operations through a combination of privately placed debt and/or equity. On 04-Aug-2004, the company acquired rocked technologies inc. The group operates from United States.

Primary SIC and add'l.: 1381 1311

CIK No: 0001085203

Subsidiaries: Rocket Technologies Inc

Officers: William Ganz/Dir., CEO, Pres., Philip W. Bode/Dir. - Sr. Business, Communication Consultant, Dan Bode/VP - Business Development, Cindy Rivera/General Office Mgr., Carol Laws/Accounting, Compliance, Paul Eagland/CFO, Martin Thornell/54/Dir. - Research, Camila Maz/39/Dir., Sec., Treasurer, Kyle Rose/Customer Service Mgr., Danny Doan/Software Developer, Phil Chin/Software Developer, Alena Perez/Advertising Intern, Brad Fellers/Sr. Accounting Mgr., Jay Rivera/Administrative Office Assist., Katie A. Leary/Accounting Executive *(17 Officers included in Index)*

Directors: William Ganz/Dir., CEO, Pres., Philip Graves/53/Dir., Ray Welt/Dir., Camila Maz/39/Dir., Sec., Treasurer, Philip W. Bode/Dir. - Sr. Business, Communication Consultant

Owners: Insiders/14.42%, Daren DeJean, Ray Welt, Martin Thornell, Maria C. Maz/8.02%, Cadaques, SA/5.01%, Bill Ganz/3.90%, Philip Graves, Ricardo Requena/8.31%

Financial Data: *Fiscal Year End:*12/31 *Latest Annual Data:* 12/31/2006

Year	Sales	Net Income
2006	$342,000	-$2,165,000
2005	$211,000	-$2,333,000
2004	$84,000	-$2,230,000

Curr. Assets:	$55,000	Curr. Liab.:	$519,000		
Plant, Equip.:	$82,000	Total Liab.:	$519,000	Indic. Yr. Divd.:	NA
Total Assets:	$4,124,000	Net Worth:	$3,605,000	Debt/ Equity:	NA

Rockford Corp

600 S Rockford Dr., Tempe, AZ, 85281; *PH:* 1-480-967-3565; *Fax:* 1-480-967-8132; *http://* www.rockfordcorp.com

General - Incorporation	AZ	**Stock** - Price on:12/24/2007	$2.39
Employees	256	Stock Exchange	NDQ
Auditor	Ernst & Young LLP	Ticker Symbol	ROFO
Stk Agt	EquiServe Trust Co N.A	Outstanding Shares	9,400,000
Counsel	Steptoe & Johnson	E.P.S.	-$0.82
DUNS No.	NA	Shareholders	NA

Business: The group's principal activities are to design, manufacture and distribute high performance audio systems for the mobile, professional and home theater audio markets. The products offered by the group include digital and analog amplifiers, speakers, source units, CD changers, digital media players and accessories. The products are primarily marketed in the worldwide mobile audio aftermarket to consumers who want to improve the audio systems in their cars, trucks, boats and airplanes. Rockford fosgate, lightning audio, mb quart, q-logic, installedge.com and omnifi are the brand names through which the products are marketed.

Primary SIC and add'l.: 3651

CIK No: 0000828064

Subsidiaries: Audio Innovations, Inc, MB Quart Shanghai, Inc, Rockford (Europe) Elektronik Vertriebs GmbH, Rockford Foreign Sales Corporation, Rockford Sales.Com, Inc, Rockford Singapore Corporation

Officers: Gary W. Suttle/Dir., CEO, Pres./$569,349.00, Richard G. Vasek/VP - Finance, CFO, Sec./$346,163.00, William R. Jackson/VP - Sales, Marketing/$389,792.00, Mark W. Matson/VP - Global Operations/$248,710.00, Jacqueline M. Mott/VP - Human Resources, Facilities/$235,224.00, James C. Strickland/VP - Engineering

Directors: Gary W. Suttle/Dir., CEO, Pres., Jerry E. Goldress/Chmn., Nicholas G. Bartol/Dir., John P. Lloyd/Dir., Timothy C. Bartol/Dir., Ralph B. Godfrey/Dir.

Owners: Nicholas G. Bartol, Daeg Capital Management, LLC, Insiders, Monument Investors Limited Partnership, Jacqueline M. Mott, Jerry E. Goldress, Ralph B. Godfrey, Boulder Investors Limited Partnership, Richard G. Vasek, Austin W. Marxe, SKIRITAI Capital LLC, Franklin Advisers, Inc., Gary W. Suttle, Mark W. Matson, John P. Lloyd *(20 Owners included in Index)*

Financial Data: *Fiscal Year End:*12/31 *Latest Annual Data:* 12/31/2006

Year	Sales	Net Income
2006	$102,776,000	-$8,847,000
2005	$135,682,000	-$4,087,000
2004	$169,555,000	-$38,855,000

Curr. Assets:	$40,852,000	Curr. Liab.:	$24,373,000		
Plant, Equip.:	$2,487,000	Total Liab.:	$34,310,000	Indic. Yr. Divd.:	NA
Total Assets:	$44,555,000	Net Worth:	$10,245,000	Debt/ Equity:	1.0810

Rockport Healthcare Group Inc

50 Briar Hollow Ln., Ste. 515W, Houston, TX, 77027; *PH:* 1-713-621-9424; *Fax:* 1-713-621-9492; *http://* www.rockporthealthcare.com

General - Incorporation	DE	**Stock** - Price on:12/24/2007	NA
Employees	NA	Stock Exchange	OTC
Auditor	Thomas Leger & Co., LLP	Ticker Symbol	RPHL
Stk Agt	Computershare Trust Co	Outstanding Shares	NA
Counsel	NA	E.P.S.	NA
DUNS No.	NA	Shareholders	NA

Business: The group's principle activity is developing, operating and managing networks consisting of health care providers and medical suppliers that serve employees with work-related injuries and illnesses. The group offers access to a comprehensive health care network at a local, state or national level for its clients and their customers. The groups provides its preferred provider organization (ppo) as rockport united network sm.

Primary SIC and add'l.: 8099

CIK No: 0000919606

Subsidiaries: Rockport Community Network, Inc, Rockport Group of Texas, Inc, Rockport Preferred, Inc

Owners: Gregory H. Neer, George Bogle/5.20%, Mark C. Neer, Larry K. Hinson/1.10%, Eric H. Kolstad, Harry M. Neer/5.50%, Insiders/53.00%, John K. Baldwin/45.40%

Rockport National Bancorp Inc

16 Main St., Rockport, MA, 01966; *PH:* 1-978-546-3411

General - Incorporation	MA	Stock - Price on:12/24/2007	$74
Employees	NA	Stock Exchange	OTC
Auditor	NA	Ticker Symbol	RPOR
Stk Agt	NA	Outstanding Shares	NA
Counsel	NA	E.P.S.	NA
DUNS No.	NA	Shareholders	NA

Business: The groups principal activities include providing banking and financial services. The group offers a complete array of checking and savings accounts, along with money management products that will satisfy any individual or business banking customers needs. The group operates from the United States.

Primary SIC and add'l.: 6712

CIK No: 0001083331

Rockville Financial Inc

25 Pk. St., Rockville, CT, 06066; *PH:* 1-860-291-3600; *Fax:* 1-860-291-3666; *http://* www.sbr.com

General - Incorporation	CT	Stock - Price on:12/24/2007	$15.22
Employees	189	Stock Exchange	NDQ
Auditor	Deloitte & Touche LLP	Ticker Symbol	RCKB
Stk Agt	Registrar & Transfer Co	Outstanding Shares	19,570,000
Counsel	NA	E.P.S.	$0.37
DUNS No.	NA	Shareholders	NA

Business: The groups principal activity is to provide financial services. The products of the group include residential, commercial real estate, commercial business and consumer loans. The group operates from the United States. The assets of the group for the year 2006 were $1,232,836 (thousands).

Primary SIC and add'l.: 6712 6099 6036

CIK No: 0001311131

Subsidiaries: Rockville Bank, Rockville Financial Services, Inc., SBR Investment Corp., Inc, SBR Mortgage Company

Officers: William J. McGurk/66/Dir., CEO, Pres./$2,618,674.00, Joseph F. Jeamel/68/Dir., Exec. VP/$1,408,074.00, Gregory A. White/43/Sr. VP, CFO, Treasurer/$272,791.00, Judy L. Keppner/49/Sec., Kathleen M. Svendsen/Investment Executive, Rockville Bank, Sarah Maskill/Investment Executive, Rockville Bank, Wayne L. Stanley/Investment Executive, Rockville Bank

Directors: William J. McGurk/66/Dir., CEO, Pres., Betty R. Sullivan/Chmn., Michael A. Bars/52/Dir., David A. Engelson/64/Dir., Perry C. Chilberg/59/Dir., Joseph F. Jeamel/68/Dir., Exec. VP, Raymond H. Lefurge/58/Dir., Stuart E. Magdefrau/53/Dir., Thomas S. Mason/68/Dir., Peter F. Olson/69/Dir., Pamela J. Guenard/Dir.

Owners: Betty R. Sullivan, Insiders/1.98%, Peter F. Olson, Stuart E. Magdefrau, Charles J. DeSimone, William J. McGurk, Thomas S. Mason, Michael A. Bars, Raymond H. Lefurge, Kristen A. Johnson, Joseph F. Jeamel, Perry C. Chilberg, Rosemarie Novello Papa, David A. Engelson, Rockville Financial MHC, Inc./54.61% (17 Owners included in Index)

Financial Data: Fiscal Year End:12/31   Latest Annual Data: 12/31/2006

Year	Sales	Net Income
2006	$68,577,000	$6,854,000
2005	$52,676,000	$3,426,000

Curr. Assets:	$26,854,000	Curr. Liab.:	$1,072,452,000	P/E Ratio:	41.14
Plant, Equip.:	$12,624,000	Total Liab.:	$1,077,772,000	Indic. Yr. Divd.:	$0.160
Total Assets:	$1,232,836,000	Net Worth:	$155,064,000	Debt/ Equity:	0.0190

Rockwell Automation Inc

1201 S 2nd St., Milwaukee, WI, 53204; *PH:* 1-414-382-2000; *Fax:* 1-414-382-4444; *http://* www.rockwellautomation.com

General - Incorporation	DE	Stock - Price on:12/24/2007	$68.99
Employees	23,000	Stock Exchange	NYSE
Auditor	Deloitte & Touche LLP	Ticker Symbol	ROK
Stk Agt	Mellon Investor Services LLC	Outstanding Shares	157,750,000
Counsel	NA	E.P.S.	$9.23
DUNS No.	96-194-1531	Shareholders	NA

Business: The group's principle activity is to provide industrial automation power, control and information solutions. The group operates from United States.

Primary SIC and add'l.: 3669 3812 3829 3679

CIK No: 0001024478

Subsidiaries: Allen-Bradley Company, Allen-Bradley Technical Services, Inc., Anorad Corporation, Anorad Europe BV, Anorad Israel Ltd., ATW Properties Pty.) Ltd., Black Gauntlet Limited, Breter S.r.L., Dodge de Mexico S.A. de C.V., EJA Engineering Ltd., EJA Limited, Federal Pacific Electric Co., GEPA Gesellschaft fur ProzeBautomation und PC-Anwendungen mbH, Goss Processing Systems, Inc., Grupo Industrias Reliance S.A. de C.V. 100 Subsidiaries included in the Index

Officers: Keith D. Nosbusch/Chmn., CEO, Pres., John D. Cohn/Sr. VP - Strategic Development, Communications, David M. Dorgan/44/VP, Controller, Susan Schmitt/Sr. VP - Human Resources, Theodore D. Crandall/52/CFO, Sr. VP, Scott Summerville/Pres. - Asia Pacific Region, Marty Thomas/Sr. VP - Operations, Engineering Services, Steven W. Etzel/VP, Treasurer, Steve

Eisenbrown/Sr. VP - Architecture, Software, Jordi Andreu/Pres. - European Region, Sujeet Chand/Sr. VP - Advanced Technology, CTO, Randall Hoeflein/VP - Continuous Improvement, Douglas M. Hagerman/Sr. VP, General Counsel, Sec., John P. McDermott/Sr. VP - Global Sales, Marketing, John M. Miller/41/VP, Chief Intellectual Property Counsel (19 Officers included in Index)

Directors: Keith D. Nosbusch/Chmn., CEO, Pres., Barry C. Johnson/Dir., Bruce M. Rockwell/Dir., Betty C. Alewine/Dir., Verne G. Istock/Dir., David B. Speer/Dir., Joseph F. Toot/Dir., Kenneth F. Yontz/Dir., William T. McCormick/Dir.

Owners: Joseph F. Toot, MassachusettsFinancialServicesCompany/7.00%, Verne G. Istock, Bruce M. Rockwell, Steven A. Eisenbrown, Betty C. Alewine, Barry C. Johnson, William T. McCormick, James V. Gelly, Kenneth F. Yontz, Joseph D. Swann, Douglas M. Hagerman, Theodore D. Crandall, Keith D. Nosbusch, John P. McDermott (17 Owners included in Index)

Financial Data: Fiscal Year End:09/30   Latest Annual Data: 09/30/2007

Year	Sales	Net Income
2007	$5,003,900,000	$1,487,800,000
2006	$5,561,400,000	$607,000,000
2005	$5,003,200,000	$540,000,000

Curr. Assets:	$2,188,000,000	Curr. Liab.:	$1,293,300,000		
Plant, Equip.:	$671,600,000	Total Liab.:	$2,817,200,000	Indic. Yr. Divd.:	$1.160
Total Assets:	$4,735,400,000	Net Worth:	$1,918,200,000	Debt/ Equity:	0.1871

Rockwell Collins Inc

400 Collins Rd. NE, Cedar Rapids, IA, 52498; *PH:* 1-319-295-1000; *Fax:* 1-319-295-1523; *http://* www.rockwellcollins.com; *Email:* collins@rockwellcollins.com

General - Incorporation	DE	Stock - Price on:12/24/2007	$71.04
Employees	18,600	Stock Exchange	NYSE
Auditor	Deloitte & Touche LLP	Ticker Symbol	COL
Stk Agt	Mellon Investor Services LLC	Outstanding Shares	167,340,000
Counsel	Gary R. Chadick	E.P.S.	$3.16
DUNS No.	NA	Shareholders	NA

Business: The groups principle activity is to provide designing, production and support of communications and aviation electronics for military and commercial customers. The group provides services include equipment repair and overhaul, service parts, field service engineering, training, technical information services. The group operates from United States.

Primary SIC and add'l.: 3812 3669

CIK No: 0001137411

Subsidiaries: Anzus, Inc., Intertrade Limited, K Systems, Inc., Kaiser Optical Systems, Inc., NLX Holding Corporation, Rockwell Collins Aerospace& Electronics, Inc., Rockwell Collins Danmark ApS, Rockwell Collins Deutschland GmbH, Rockwell Collins Deutschland Holdings GmbH, Rockwell Collins Deutschland Services GmbH, Rockwell Collins ElectroMechanical Systems, Inc., Rockwell Collins European Holdings S. r.l., Rockwell Collins Government Systems (Canada), Inc., Rockwell Collins International Financing LIMITED, Rockwell Collins International Holdings LIMITED 20 Subsidiaries included in the Index

Officers: Clayton M. Jones/Chmn., CEO, Pres., Dave Gosch/Media Inquiries, Gregory S. Churchill/COO, Exec. VP - Government Systems, Ken Estelle/VP, GM - Technical Service Solutions, Ken Schreder/VP, GM - Simulation, Training Solutions, Melanie Richert/Community Relations, Charitable Contributions, Cheri Kampman/Contact - K-12 Partnership, Volunteer Programs, Jenny Becker/Community Relations, Education Programs, Pam J. Tvrdy/Media Inquiries, Dan Crookshank/Investor Relations Officer, Tom Hobson/State Government, Public Affairs, Sherry Mendel/Corporate Brand Management, Marsha A. Schulte/VP - Finance, Controller, Phil J. Jasper/VP, GM - Integrated Systems, Jeffrey A. Standerski/VP, GM - Air Transport Systems (31 Officers included in Index)

Directors: Clayton M. Jones/Chmn., CEO, Pres., Joseph F. Toot/Dir., Michael P.C. Carns/Dir., Cheryl L. Shavers/Dir., Donald R. Beall/Dir., Anthony J. Carbonec/Dir., Mark Donegan/Dir., Andrew J. Policano/Dir., Chris A. Davis/Dir.

Owners: Robert K. Ortberg, Joseph F. Toot, Cheryl L. Shavers, Chris A. Davis, Robert M. Chiusano, Michael P.C. Carns, Andrew J. Policano, Gary R. Chadick, Donald R. Beall, Insiders/2.00%, Gregory S. Churchill, Patrick E. Allen, Mark Donegan, Clayton M. Jones, Ralph E. Eberhart (16 Owners included in Index)

Financial Data: Fiscal Year End:09/30   Latest Annual Data: 9/30/2006

Year	Sales	Net Income
2006	$3,863,000,000	$477,000,000
2005	$3,445,000,000	$396,000,000
2004	$2,930,000,000	$301,000,000

Curr. Assets:	$2,169,000,000	Curr. Liab.:	$1,459,000,000	P/E Ratio:	22.48
Plant, Equip.:	$607,000,000	Total Liab.:	$2,177,000,000	Indic. Yr. Divd.:	$0.640
Total Assets:	$3,750,000,000	Net Worth:	$1,573,000,000	Debt/ Equity:	NA

Rockwell Diamonds Inc

Formerly: Rockwell Ventures Inc
Level 0, Wilds View, Isle Of Houghton, Cnr. Carse Ogowrie & Boundary Rd, Houghton Estate, Johannesburg, 2198; ; *http://* www.rockwellventures.com

General - Incorporation	Canada	Stock - Price on:12/24/2007	NA
Employees	NA	Stock Exchange	OTC
Auditor	Davidson & Co LLP	Ticker Symbol	RDIAF
Stk Agt	Computershare Investor Services	Outstanding Shares	NA
Counsel	Gordon Fretwell	E.P.S.	NA
DUNS No.	NA	Shareholders	NA

Business: The group's principal activity is the exploration of mineral properties. The group's properties are located in Canada and Chile.

Primary SIC and add'l.: 1090

CIK No: 0001095847

Subsidiaries: 549949 Bc Ltd., Minera Ricardo Resources Inc. S.A.

Officers: John Bristow/Dir., CEO, Pres., Gordon J. Fretwell/Dir., Sec. - Attorneys, Dominique De La Roche/Dir., CFO

Directors: John Bristow/Dir., CEO, Pres., David Copeland/Chmn., Dominique De La Roche/Dir., CFO, Patrick Bartlett/Dir., Gordon J. Fretwell/Dir., Sec. - Attorneys, Rene Carrier/Dir., Douglas Silver/Dir., Scott D. Cousens/Dir., Dennis Mark Bristow/Dir.

Owners: Insiders/84.30%, Scott D. Cousens/2.50%, Rene G. Carrier/0.30%, Douglas B. Silver/0.20%, D. Mark Bristow/1.50%, John W. Bristow/0.30%, Fortis Global Custody Services/5.00%, Dominique de la Roche/0.20%, David Copeland/1.00%, Gordon Fretwell/0.60%

Financial Data: *Fiscal Year End:*08/31 *Latest Annual Data:* 05/31/2007

Year	Sales	Net Income
2007	$9,415,000	-$5,932,000
2006	NA	-$1,410,000
2005	NA	-$1,183,000

Curr. Assets:	$52,813,000	*Curr. Liab.:*	$27,891,000		
Plant, Equip.:	$41,740,000	*Total Liab.:*	$54,556,000	*Indic. Yr. Divd.:*	NA
Total Assets:	$121,273,000	*Net Worth:*	$66,717,000	*Debt/ Equity:*	NA

Rockwell Medical Technologies Inc

30142 Wixom Rd., Wixom, MI, 48393; *PH:* 1-248-960-9009; *Fax:* 1-248-960-9119;
http:// www.rockwellmed.com; *Email:* invest@rockwellmed.com

General - Incorporation	MI	Stock - Price on:12/24/2007	$5.4
Employees	200	Stock Exchange	NDQ
Auditor	Plante & Moran, PLLC	Ticker Symbol	RMTI
Stk Agt	American Registrar & Transfer Co	Outstanding Shares	11,510,000
Counsel	NA	E.P.S.	-$0.322
DUNS No.	93-372-1433	Shareholders	NA

Business: The group's principal activity is to manufacture and distribute hemodialysis concentrates, dialysis kits and other ancillary hemodialysis products to hemodialysis providers. The group has licensed an iron maintenance therapy for dialysis patients utilizing water soluble iron in dialysate. The ancillary products include on-off kits, sterile subclavian dressing change trays, arterial and venous blood tubing lines, fistula needles, intravenous administration sets, transducer protectors and dialyzers. The group's principal suppliers include archer daniels midland co., ashland inc., cargill inc., church & dwight co. Inc., morton salt company and nipro medical corporation.

Primary SIC and add'l.: 2835 3841 3845 2833

CIK No: 0001041024

Subsidiaries: Luitpold Inc, Minntech Corporation (Minntech)., Rockwell Transportation Inc, Vifor International, Ltd

Officers: Robert L. Chioini/44/Founder, Chmn., CEO, Pres./$294,345.00, Thomas E. Klema/VP, CFO, Sec., Treasurer/$160,216.00

Directors: Robert L. Chioini/44/Founder, Chmn., CEO, Pres., Kenneth L. Holt/55/Dir., Ronald D. Boyd/45/Dir., Patrick J. Bagley/43/Dir.

Owners: Kenneth L. Holt/1.50%, Ronald D. Boyd/1.40%, Insiders/26.80%, Thomas E. Klema/7.20%, Patrick J. Bagley/1.80%, Thomas G. Berlin/7.20%, Robert L. Chioini/18.50%

Financial Data: *Fiscal Year End:*12/31 *Latest Annual Data:* 03/31/2007

Year	Sales	Net Income
2007	$9,474,000	-$1,647,000
2006	$28,639,000	-$4,575,000
2005	$27,695,000	$77,000

Curr. Assets:	$9,059,000	*Curr. Liab.:*	$4,453,000		
Plant, Equip.:	$2,588,000	*Total Liab.:*	$4,779,000	*Indic. Yr. Divd.:*	NA
Total Assets:	$13,153,000	*Net Worth:*	$8,374,000	*Debt/ Equity:*	0.0471

Rockwood Holdings Inc

100 Overlook Ctr., Princeton, NJ, 08540; *PH:* 1-609-514-0300; *Fax:* 1-609-514-8720;
http:// www.rockwoodspecialties.com

General - Incorporation	DE	Stock - Price on:12/24/2007	$34.96
Employees	9,525	Stock Exchange	NYSE
Auditor	Deloitte & Touche LLP	Ticker Symbol	ROC
Stk Agt	American Stock Transfer & Trust Co.	Outstanding Shares	73,790,000
Counsel	NA	E.P.S.	$2.772
DUNS No.	NA	Shareholders	NA

Business: The groups principal activities include developing, manufacturing and marketing chemical materials. The group operates through six segments namely, specialty chemicals, performance additives, titanium dioxide pigments, advanced ceramics, specialty compounds and electronics. The group operates from the United States.

Primary SIC and add'l.: 2819 2851 2899 2865

CIK No: 0001315695

Subsidiaries: Aachener Chemische Werke Gesellschaft fr glastechnische Produckte und Verfahren GmbH, Advantis Technologies, Inc., Agena Resinas e Colas Ltda., Alberti & Co. GmbH, AlphaGary (Canada) Limited, AlphaGary Corporation, AlphaGary Limited, AM Craig Ltd., Ardrox Ltd., ArdroxAgena Quimica Ltda., BAE Vermgensverwaltungs GmbH, BCI Pensions Trustees Ltd., Bedec Tir S.A., Bonder Iran S.S.K. (a), Brent Europe Ltd. 166 Subsidiaries included in the Index

Officers: Seifi Ghasemi/Chmn., CEO, Stephen B. Ainscough/CEO, Pres. - Viance LLC, Thomas J. Riordan/Sr. VP - Law, Administration, Andrew M. Ross/Pres. - Rockwood Color Pigments, Services, Robert J. Zatta/CFO, Sr. VP, Stephen M. D'Onfro/Pres. - Advantis Technologies, Monika Engel-Bader/Pres. - Chemetall, Robert Gingue/Pres. - Specialty Compounds Segment, Wolf-Dieter Griebler/Pres. - Sachtleben Chemie, Timothy McKenna/VP - Investor Relations, Communications, Andreas Gruenewald/Dir. - Financial Planning, Controlling, Simon Jones/VP - Tax, J. H. Overkamp/Corporate Treasurer, Udo Pinger/General Counsel - Europe, James T. Sullivan/Corporate Controller *(20 Officers included in Index)*

Directors: Seifi Ghasemi/Chmn., CEO, Brian F. Carroll/Dir., Kent J. Masters/Dir., Sheldon R. Erikson/Dir., Todd A. Fisher/Dir., Perry Golkin/Dir., Douglas L. Maine/Dir., Cynthia A. Niekamp/Dir., Susan Schnabel/Dir.

Owners: Wells Fargo Bank, N.A., KKR, Seifi Ghasemi, Thomas J. Riordan, Perry Golkin, Insiders, Brian F. Carroll, Sheldon R. Erikson, DLJMB, Todd A. Fisher, Douglas L. Maine, Robert J. Zatta, Cynthia A. Niekamp

Financial Data: *Fiscal Year End:*12/31 *Latest Annual Data:* 12/31/2006

Year	Sales	Net Income
2006	$2,975,200,000	$103,000,000
2005	$3,121,200,000	$95,800,000
2004	$1,743,500,000	-$216,100,000

Curr. Assets:	$1,479,900,000	*Curr. Liab.:*	$854,500,000	*P/E Ratio:*	13.24
Plant, Equip.:	$1,374,900,000	*Total Liab.:*	$4,099,300,000	*Indic. Yr. Divd.:*	NA
Total Assets:	$5,219,800,000	*Net Worth:*	$1,120,500,000	*Debt/ Equity:*	1.8825

Rocky Mountain Chocolate Factory Inc

265 Turner Dr., Durango, CO, 81303; *PH:* 1-970-259-0554; *Fax:* 1-970-259-5895;
http:// www.rmcf.com

General - Incorporation	CO	Stock - Price on:12/24/2007	$16.03
Employees	235	Stock Exchange	NDQ
Auditor	Ehrhardt Keefe Steiner & Hottman P.C	Ticker Symbol	RMCF
Stk Agt	Computershare Trust Co	Outstanding Shares	6,070,000
Counsel	Thompson & Knight	E.P.S.	$0.74
DUNS No.	02-208-3893	Shareholders	NA

Business: The group's principle activity is to manufacture extensive line of premium chocolate candies and other confectionery products. It operates through two segments: franchising and manufacturing. The products of the group are sold through franchisees and at group owned stores. The group's revenues are currently derived from three principal sources namely: sale of chocolates and other confectionery products manufactured by the group; the collection of initial franchise fees and royalties from franchisees' sales; and sales at group-owned stores of chocolates and other confectionery products. The group's total revenue for year 2007 was 31.57 millions of USD.

Primary SIC and add'l.: 6794 9999 2064

CIK No: 0000785815

Officers: Franklin E. Crail/66/Chmn., Pres., Principal Executive Officer/$277,454.00, Gregory L. Pope/42/Sr. VP - Franchise Support, Development/$221,000.00, Jay B. Haws/58/VP - Creative Services/$188,000.00, Virginia M. Perez/70/Corp. Sec., Edward L. Dudley/45/Sr. VP - Sales, Marketing/$225,000.00, Bryan J. Merryman/48/Dir., CFO, COO, Treasurer/$310,000.00, William K. Jobson/52/CIO

Directors: Franklin E. Crail/66/Chmn., Pres., Principal Executive Officer, Fred M. Trainor/69/Dir., Lee N. Mortenson/72/Dir., Gerald A. Kien/76/Dir., Clyde W. Engle/65/Dir., Bryan J. Merryman/48/Dir., CFO, COO, Treasurer

Owners: Lee N. Mortenson/0.35%, Jay B. Haws/1.08%, Bryan J. Merryman/2.10%, Gerald A. Kien/1.32%, Gregory L. Pope/2.14%, Edward L. Dudley/1.46%, Hodges Capital Management, Inc./14.39%, Clyde Wm. Engle/1.04%, Franklin E. Crail/11.06%, Fred M. Trainor/2.70%, Insiders/23.00%

Financial Data: *Fiscal Year End:*02/28 *Latest Annual Data:* 2/28/2007

Year	Sales	Net Income
2007	$31,573,000	$4,745,000
2006	$28,074,000	$4,065,000
2005	$24,524,000	$3,317,000

Curr. Assets:	$10,759,000	*Curr. Liab.:*	$3,256,000		
Plant, Equip.:	$5,754,000	*Total Liab.:*	$3,942,000	*Indic. Yr. Divd.:*	$0.400
Total Assets:	$18,456,000	*Net Worth:*	$14,515,000	*Debt/ Equity:*	NA

Rocky Mountain Fudge Company Inc

4596 Russell St., Salt Lake City, UT, 84117; *PH:* 1-801-230-1807

General - Incorporation	NV	Stock - Price on:12/24/2007	$0.6
Employees	NA	Stock Exchange	OTC
Auditor	Moore & Assoc., LLP	Ticker Symbol	RMFD
Stk Agt	NA	Outstanding Shares	NA
Counsel	NA	E.P.S.	$0.00
DUNS No.	NA	Shareholders	NA

Business: The groups principle activity is engage in the business of manufacturing and retailing fudge candy. The group operates from the United States. The group's revenue for Aug '07 was 7.55 millions of USD.

Primary SIC and add'l.: 2064

CIK No: 0001347078

Subsidiaries: Wasatch Candy Company, Inc.

Officers: Ronald Moulton/72/Dir., CEO, Pres., Steven D. Moulton/45/Dir., VP, Treasurer, Vallerie Moulton/68/Dir., Sec.

Directors: Ronald Moulton/72/Dir., CEO, Pres., Steven D. Moulton/45/Dir., VP, Treasurer, Vallerie Moulton/68/Dir., Sec.

Owners: Vallerie Moulton/32.00%, Steven Moulton/16.00%, Insiders/64.00%, Ronald Moulton/16.00%, Diane Moulton/8.00%, Traci Baird/8.00%

Financial Data: *Fiscal Year End:*12/31 *Latest Annual Data:* 12/31/2006

Year	Sales	Net Income
2006	$10,000	-$23,000

Curr. Assets:	$38,000	*Curr. Liab.:*	$26,000		
Plant, Equip.:	NA	*Total Liab.:*	$26,000	*Indic. Yr. Divd.:*	NA
Total Assets:	$38,000	*Net Worth:*	$12,000	*Debt/ Equity:*	NA

Rocky Mountain Minerals Inc

2480 N Tolemac Way, Prescott, AZ, 86305; *PH:* 1-928-778-1450; *Fax:* 1-928-771-1667;
http:// www.rockymountainminerals.com; *Email:* info@rockymountainminerals.com

General - Incorporation	WY	Stock - Price on:12/24/2007	$0.025
Employees	NA	Stock Exchange	OTC
Auditor	Causey Demgen & Moore Inc	Ticker Symbol	RMMI
Stk Agt	Computershare Trust Co	Outstanding Shares	100,710,000
Counsel	NA	E.P.S.	$0.00
DUNS No.	61-025-8659	Shareholders	NA

Business: The group's principle activities include acquireing, developing, exploring and operating mineral properties. The company is a development stage company. The company's business activities involve the construction and operation of ore mill facilities. The company also provides clearance of trails and exploratory drilling and mining, full-scale mining, backgrading, reseeding and fertilizing. In 2003, the company acquired 25% interest in two oil and gas leases in the nw shelf, offshore Australia. The group operates from United States.

Primary SIC and add'l.: 1099

CIK No: 0000312583

Officers: Mark A. Muzzin/CEO, CFO, Melanie F. Hill/Company Sec.

Directors: Geoffrey E. Albers/Chmn., Peter Sterling/Dir., Ray W. Hill/Dir., John Rubel/Dir., David Bruce Hill/65/Dir.

Owners: Don Knaute/5.38%, Ernest Geoffrey Albers/25.86%, Richard Bain/5.29%, William Ray Hill/9.13%, David Bruce Hill/12.72%, Insiders/35.03%

Financial Data: *Fiscal Year End:* 10/31 *Latest Annual Data:* 10/31/2006

Year	Sales	Net Income
2006	$1,000	-$28,000
2005	NA	-$399,000
2004	NA	-$53,000

Curr. Assets:	$48,000	*Curr. Liab.:*	$46,000		
Plant, Equip.:	$150,000	*Total Liab.:*	$69,000	*Indic. Yr. Divd.:*	$0.370
Total Assets:	$306,000	*Net Worth:*	$237,000	*Debt/ Equity:*	0.1069

Rocky Shoes & Boots Inc

39 E Canal St., Nelsonville, OH, 45764; *PH:* 1-614-753-1951; *http://* www.rockyboots.com

General - Incorporation	OH	**Stock**- Price on:12/24/2007	$16.69
Employees	1,325	Stock Exchange	NDQ
Auditor	Deloitte & Touche LLP	Ticker Symbol	RCKY
Stk Agt	Fifth Third Bank	Outstanding Shares	5,470,000
Counsel	Porter Wright Morris & Arthur LLP	E.P.S.	$0.64
DUNS No.	07-942-1384	Shareholders	NA

Business: The group's principle activity is to design, manufacture and market men's and women's footwear. The group markets its products under the trademark rocky(r). The group maintains a nationwide network of company sales representatives who sell their products primarily through independent shoe, sporting goods, specialty and uniform stores and catalogs throughout the United States. The product lines of the group consist of rugged outdoor, occupational and casual footwear. Rugged outdoor footwear consists of all season sport/hunting boots that are waterproof and insulated and a line of rubber footwear. This product category includes work/steel toe footwear designed for industrial, construction and manufacturing workers. The group operates in waterloo, ontario outside of the United States. The group's quarterly revenue for September 2007 was 82.31 millions of USD.

Primary SIC and add'l.: 3143 3149 3144

CIK No: 0000895456

Subsidiaries: Durango Boot Company LLC, EJ Asia Limited, EJ Footwear LLC, Five Star Enterprises Ltd., Georgia Boot LLC, Georgia Boot Properties LLC, HM Lehigh Safety Shoe Co. LLC, Lehigh Safety Shoe Co. LLC, Lehigh Safety Shoe Properties LLC, Lifestyle Footwear, Inc., Northlake Boot Company LLC, Rocky Canada, Inc.

Owners: James E. McDonald/1.10%, Glenn E. Corlett, James L. Stewart, Patrick J.Campbell, Curtis A. Loveland/1.60%, Harley E. Rouda, Mike Brooks/6.80%, Thomas R. Morrison, Courtney G.Haning, Michael L. Finn, Lotsoff Capital Management/8.50%, Insiders/12.40%, FMR Corp./10.00%, WS Capital, L.L.C./6.80%, David Sharp/1.20%

Financial Data: *Fiscal Year End:* 12/31 *Latest Annual Data:* 12/31/2006

Year	Sales	Net Income
2006	$263,491,000	$4,819,000
2005	$296,023,000	$13,014,000
2004	$132,249,000	$8,594,000

Curr. Assets:	$157,216,000	*Curr. Liab.:*	$21,647,000	*P/E Ratio:*	26.08
Plant, Equip.:	$24,350,000	*Total Liab.:*	$142,228,000	*Indic. Yr. Divd.:*	NA
Total Assets:	$246,356,000	*Net Worth:*	$104,128,000	*Debt/ Equity:*	0.7838

Rodinia Minerals Inc

600 - 595 Howe St., Vancouver, BC, V6C 2T5; *PH:* 1-604-685-6465; *http://* www.rodiniaminerals.com; *Email:* info@rodiniaminerals.com

General - Incorporation	Canada	**Stock**- Price on:12/24/2007	NA
Employees	NA	Stock Exchange	NA
Auditor	Manning Elliott LLP	Ticker Symbol	NA
Stk Agt	Pacific Corporate Trust Co	Outstanding Shares	NA
Counsel	NA	E.P.S.	NA
DUNS No.	NA	Shareholders	NA

Business: The group's principle activity is to explore mining properties. The Workman Creek Project, is located in Gila County, Arizona. The group is well funded, with C$310,650 in cash on its balance sheet as of September 30, 2004 (most recent data available); this cash was augmented by Rodinias recent completion of a C$1.3 million private placement. This should be sufficient capital to finance the two phase exploration and development plan that the Company is pursuing at its Workman Creek Project. Additionally, The group operates from United States.

Primary SIC and add'l.: 1000

CIK No: 0001331123

Subsidiaries: Donnybrook Platinum Resources Inc.

Officers: Donald Morrison/Dir., CEO, Pres., Ken Thorsen/Dir., VP - Exploration, Robert Pirooz/Dir. - Inside Legal Counsel Lumina, Pan American Silverfor Lumina, Pan American Silver, Donald Mosher/Dir., VP - Corporate Communications

Directors: Donald Morrison/Dir., CEO, Pres., Ken Thorsen/Dir., VP - Exploration, Robert Pirooz/Dir. - Inside Legal Counsel Lumina, Pan American Silverfor Lumina, Pan American Silver, Donald Mosher/Dir., VP - Corporate Communications

Roebling Financial Corp Inc New

Delaware Ave. Rr 130, Roebling, NJ, 08554; *PH:* 1-609-499-9400; *http://* www.roeblingbank.com

General - Incorporation	NJ	**Stock**- Price on:12/24/2007	$11.8
Employees	36	Stock Exchange	OTC
Auditor	NA	Ticker Symbol	RBLG
Stk Agt	Registrar & Transfer Co	Outstanding Shares	1,710,000
Counsel	NA	E.P.S.	NA
DUNS No.	NA	Shareholders	NA

Business: The groups principle activity is to provide financial services including based community bank. Services of the group include loan servicing includes collecting and remitting loan payments, accounting for principle and interest, making inspections as required of mortgaged premises, contacting delinquent mortgagors, supervising foreclosures and property dispositions in the event of unremedied defaults, and generally administering the loans. The group operates from the United States. The group's quarterly revenue for Sep '07 is 0.10 millions of USD.

Primary SIC and add'l.: 6712

CIK No: 0001293283

Subsidiaries: Roebling Bank

Officers: Frank J. Travea/Pres., CEO - Roebling Bank, John J. Ferry/Chmn. - Roebling Bank, John A. Lavecchia/Vice Chmn. - Roebling Bank, Joan K. Geary/Sec. - Roebling Bank, Mark V. Dimon/Treasurer - Roebling Bank, Jan A. Summers/Sr. VP, CFO, COO - Roebling Bank, George N. Nyikita/Dir. - Roebling Bank, Robert R. Semptimphelter/Dir. - Roebling Bank, John Clawges/Sr. VP, Sr Lending Officer - Roebling Bank, Bonnie Horner/VP - Lending Division, Roebling Bank, Cindy Pawlyzyn/Assist. Branch Mgr. - Roebling, NJ, Roebling Bank, Rose Stevenson/Assist. Branch Mgr. - Roebling, NJ, Roebling Bank, Gladys Emery/Assist. Branch Mgr. - New Egypt, NJ, Roebling Bank, Charles Maffetone/Assist. Branch Mgr. - Westampton, NJ, Roebling Bank, Charmi Shah/Assist. Branch Mgr. - Delran, NJ, Roebling Bank

Owners: Kenneth R. Abercrom/5.00%, Roebling Bank Employee Stock/7.80%, Mark V. Dimon/5.90%, John J. Ferry/5.10%, Lance S. Gad/7.70%

Rofin Sinar Technologies Inc

40984 Concept Dr., Plymouth, MI, 48170; *PH:* 1-734-455-5400; *Fax:* 1-734-455-2741; *http://* www.rofin-sinar.com; *Email:* info@rofin-ham.de

General - Incorporation	DE	**Stock**- Price on:12/24/2007	$68.11
Employees	1,490	Stock Exchange	NDQ
Auditor	KPMG LLP	Ticker Symbol	RSTI
Stk Agt	Bank of New York	Outstanding Shares	15,540,000
Counsel	NA	E.P.S.	$1.74
DUNS No.	96-066-1775	Shareholders	NA

Business: The group's principal activities are to design, develop, engineer, manufacture and market laser-based products. These products are primarily used for cutting, welding and marking a wide range of materials in the machine tool, automotive and semiconductor/electronics industries. The products include laser marking products and lasers for cutting and welding. Laser marking products include powerline/starmark series, combiline/starmark systems and multiscan. Laser cutting and welding products consists of starweld, starcut series and perfolas systems. These products are manufactured and tested in the United States, Germany, the United Kingdom and other Europe and Asian countries. In 2003, the group acquired an additional 37% of the share capital of rofin-Marubeni laser corporation, atsugi-shi, Japan. In 2004, the group acquired 90% of the common stock of optoskand ab, gothenburg, Sweden, through its wholly owned subsidiary, prc laser corp and jersey and lee laser inc.

Primary SIC and add'l.: 3699

CIK No: 0001019361

Subsidiaries: Carl Baasel Lasertechnik GmbH & Co. KG, CBL Verwaltungsgesellschaft mbH, DILAS Diodenlaser GmbH, Lee Laser, Inc., Optoskand AB, PMB Elektronik GmbH, PRC Laser Corporation, PRC Laser Europe N.V., Rasant-Alcotec Beschichtungstechnik GmbH, Rofin-Baasel Benelux B.V., Rofin-Baasel China Co., Ltd., Rofin-Baasel Espana S.L., Rofin-Baasel France S.A., Rofin-Baasel Italiana S.r.l., Rofin-Baasel Japan Corp. 25 Subsidiaries included in the Index

Officers: Gunther Braun/50/Dir., CEO, Pres., Ingrid Mittelstaedt/43/CFO, Exec. VP - Finance, Administration, Treasurer, Walter Volkmar/64/General Mgr. - Rofin, Sinar Laser Gmbh Marking Division, Louis Molnar/54/COO - Macro Division, Thomas Merk/45/COO

Directors: Gunther Braun/50/Dir., CEO, Pres., Peter Wirth/61/Chmn., William R. Hoover/78/Dir., Ralph E. Reins/67/Dir., Stephen D. Fantone/53/Dir., Carl F. Baasel/66/Dir., Gary K. Willis/62/Dir., Daniel J. Smoke/58/Dir.

Owners: Lou Molnar, Gunther Braun, Gary K. Willis, Stephen Fantone, Daniel J. Smoke, Ralph E. Reins, Carl F. Baasel, Peter Wirth, Insiders/2.00%, Thomas Merk

Financial Data: *Fiscal Year End:* 09/30 *Latest Annual Data:* 9/30/2006

Year	Sales	Net Income
2006	$420,890,000	$49,623,000
2005	$375,191,000	$37,975,000

Curr. Assets:	$387,556,000	*Curr. Liab.:*	$104,897,000		
Plant, Equip.:	$36,254,000	*Total Liab.:*	$140,294,000	*Indic. Yr. Divd.:*	NA
Total Assets:	$501,521,000	*Net Worth:*	$358,440,000	*Debt/ Equity:*	0.0642

Rogers Communications Inc

333 Bloor St. E, 10th Fl., Toronto, ON, M4W 1G9; *PH:* 1-416-935-7777; *http://* www.rogers.com

General - Incorporation	BC	**Stock**- Price on:12/24/2007	NA
Employees	21,000	Stock Exchange	NYSE
Auditor	KPMG LLP	Ticker Symbol	RCI
Stk Agt	Computershare Trust Co of Canada	Outstanding Shares	NA
Counsel	NA	E.P.S.	$0.88
DUNS No.	20-164-9068	Shareholders	NA

Business: The group's principle activities are divided into three segments: wireless segment offering wireless voice services, paging, cellular services, digital pcs and data communications; cable systems offering cable television services, high-speed Internet access and operating video stores and media segment offering publishing services, radio and television broadcasting and teleshopping. The group's wireless service operates under the brand name Rogers AT&T Wireless. The group's quarterly revenue for September 2007 was 2,611.00 millions of USD.

Primary SIC and add'l.: 4833 4812 4832 4841

CIK No: 0000733099

Subsidiaries: Blue Jays Holdco Inc., Rogers Broadcasting Limited, Rogers Cable Inc., Rogers Media Inc, Rogers Publishing Limited, Rogers Telecom Inc., Rogers Wireless Communications Inc

Officers: Edward Rogers/Dir., CEO, Pres., Nadir H. Mohamed/Dir., COO, Pres. - Communications Group, Melinda M. Rogers/Dir., VP - Strategy, Development, Anthony P. Viner/Sr. VP - Media, William W. Linton/CFO, VP - Finance, John R. Gossling/VP - Financial Operations, Kevin P. Pennington/Sr. VP, Chief Human Resources Officer, Robert W. Bruce/Sr. VP - Communications Group, David J. Watt/VP - Business Economics, Ronan D. McGrath/Pres. - Rogers Shared Operations, CIO, Kenneth G. Engelhart/VP - Regulatory, Bruce M. Mann/VP - Investor Relations, Jan L. Innes/VP - Communications, Graeme H. McPhail/VP, Assoc. General Counsel, Lorraine M. Daly/VP, Treasurer *(42 Officers included in Index)*

Directors: Edward Rogers/Dir., CEO, Pres., Philip B. Lind/Vice Chmn., Alan D. Horn/Chmn., Christopher J.C. Wansbrough/74/Dir., Peter C. Godsoe/Dir., Colin D. Watson/65/Dir., Melinda M. Rogers/Dir., VP - Strategy, Development, David R. Peterson/Dir., Loretta A. Rogers/Dir., John A. Tory/Dir., Charles W.D. Birchall/Dir., John H. Clappison/Dir., Thomas I. Hull/Dir., Nadir H. Mohamed/Dir., COO, Pres. - Communications Group, William T. Schleyer/Dir. *(16 Directors included in Index)*

Financial Data: *Fiscal Year End:* 12/31 *Latest Annual Data:* 12/31/2006

Year	Sales	Net Income
2006	$7,583,888,000	$669,318,000
2005	$6,419,688,000	-$268,207,000
2004	$4,656,529,000	-$224,700,000

Curr. Assets:	$1,487,945,000	Curr. Liab.:	$2,141,818,000		
Plant, Equip.:	$5,776,729,000	Total Liab.:	$8,499,481,000	Indic. Yr. Divd.:	$0.500
Total Assets:	$11,792,010,000	Net Worth:	$3,292,530,000	Debt/ Equity:	NA

Rogers Corp

1 Technology Dr., Rogers, CT, 06263; *PH:* 1-860-774-9605; *Fax:* 1-860-779-5509;
http:// www.rogerscorporation.com

General - Incorporation	MA	Stock- Price on:12/24/2007	$40.84
Employees	2,500	Stock Exchange	NYSE
Auditor	Ernst & Young LLP	Ticker Symbol	ROG
Stk Agt.	Registrar & Transfer Co	Outstanding Shares	17,670,000
Counsel	NA	E.P.S.	$1.55
DUNS No.	00-114-1167	Shareholders	NA

Business: The group's principal activity is to manufacture and sell specialty polymer composite materials and components for targeted applications. The group has three business segments: printed circuit materials, polymer materials and components and high performance foams. Printed circuit materials include printed circuit board laminates for high frequency circuits, flexible printed circuit board laminates for flexible circuits and polyester based industrial laminates. Polymer materials and components include elastomer components, composite materials, high performance moldable composites and power distribution bus bars. Performance foams includes urethane foams and silicon foams. On 31-Jan-2004, the group acquired kf inc., a korean manufacturer of liquid level sensing devices for the automotive market.

Primary SIC and add'l.: 3086 3672 3643
CIK No: 0000084748
Subsidiaries: KF, Inc., Rogers (Shanghai) International Trading Co. Ltd., Rogers (Shanghai) International Trading Co. Ltd. - Shenzen Branch, Rogers (U.K.) Ltd., Rogers China, Inc., Rogers Circuit Materials Incorporated, Rogers GmbH, Rogers Induflex N.V., Rogers Japan Inc., Rogers KF, Inc., Rogers Korea, Inc, Rogers L-K Corp., Rogers N.V., Rogers S.A., Rogers Southeast Asia, Inc. 22 Subsidiaries included in the Index
Officers: Robert D. Wachob/60/Dir., CEO, Pres./$2,744,416.00, Dennis M. Loughran/VP - Finance, CFO/$842,448.00, Robert C. Daigle/VP - Research, Development, CTO/$671,694.00, John A. Richie/VP - Human Resources/$805,846.00, Paul B. Middleton/Corporate Controller/$452,150.00, Robert M. Soffer/VP, Treasurer, Sec., Frank J. Gillern/VP - Advanced Circuit Materials Division/$841,085.00, William Tryon/Mgr. - Investor, Public Relations
Directors: Robert D. Wachob/60/Dir., CEO, Pres., Gregory B. Howey/65/Dir., Leonard R. Jaskol/71/Dir., Leonard M. Baker/73/Dir., Charles M. Brennan/66/Dir., Walter E. Boomer/69/Dir., Carol R. Jensen/56/Dir., Eileen S. Kraus/69/Dir., Robert G. Paul/66/Dir., Carl J. Hsu/Dir.
Owners: Dennis M. Loughran, Westport Asset Management, Inc./7.30%, Carol R. Jensen, Robert C. Daigle, Paul B. Middleton, Gregory B. Howey, Insiders/9.00%, Barclays Global Investors NA/5.80%, Walter E. Boomer, Lord, Abbett & Co. LLC/13.10%, Capital Research and Management Company/8.00%, Charles M. Brennan, Edward L. Diefenthal, Robert D. Wachob/1.91%, Leonard R. Jaskol *(21 Owners included in Index)*

Financial Data: *Fiscal Year End:*01/01 **Latest Annual Data:** 12/31/2006

Year	Sales	Net Income
2006	$454,562,000	$46,456,000
2005	$365,002,000	$40,098,000

Curr. Assets:	$272,554,000	Curr. Liab.:	$82,143,000	P/E Ratio:	16.47
Plant, Equip.:	$141,728,000	Total Liab.:	$123,725,000	Indic. Yr. Divd.:	NA
Total Assets:	$480,902,000	Net Worth:	$357,177,000	Debt/ Equity:	NA

Rohm & Haas Co

100 Independence Mall W, Philadelphia, PA, 19106; *PH:* 1-215-592-3000; *Fax:* 1-215-592-3377;
http:// www.rohmhass.com

General - Incorporation	DE	Stock- Price on:12/24/2007	$53.7
Employees	15,800	Stock Exchange	NYSE
Auditor	PricewaterhouseCoopers LLP	Ticker Symbol	ROH
Stk Agt.	Computershare Trust Co	Outstanding Shares	216,750,000
Counsel	NA	E.P.S.	$3.26
DUNS No.	00-229-2043	Shareholders	NA

Business: The groups principle activity is to provide innovative technology. In the year 2007, the group acquired Eastman Kodak Company's Light Management Films business. The group operates from United States.
Primary SIC and add'l.: 2821 2865 2891 2899 2851
CIK No: 0000084792
Subsidiaries: Acima AG fur Chemische Industrie, AgroFresh Inc., Bee Chemical Company, Beijing Eastern Rohm and Haas Company, Limited, Canadian Brine Limited, Canadian Salt Company Limited, Canadian Salt Finance Company, Canadian Salt Holding Company, Charles Lennig & Company LLC, CVD Incorporated, Ecuatoriana de Sal Y Productos Quimicos C.A., GLC Trucking Co., Inc., Glendale Salt Development LLC, Inagua General Store, Limited, Inagua Transports, Incorporated 154 Subsidiaries included in the Index
Officers: Raj L. Gupta/Chmn., CEO, Pres./$8,739,156.00, James C. Swanson/VP, GM - Paint, Coatings Materials, NAR, Gray Wirth/VP, Dir. - European Region, Philip G. Lewis/VP, Dir. - Environmental Health, Safety, EHS, Sustainable Development, Robert A. Lonergan/Exec. VP, General Counsel, Corp. Sec./$1,962,525.00, Gary S. Calabrese/CTO, VP, Pierre R. Brondeau/Exec. VP/$3,047,493.00, Michael G. Hamilton/VP, Business Unit Dir. - Global Powder Coatings, Anne M. Wilms/CIO, Exec. VP, Thomas D. MacPhee/VP, Dir. - Corporate Development, Strategy, Geoffrey B. Hurwitz/VP, Dir. - Government Relations, Sam Shoemaker/VP, Business Unit Dir. - CMP Technologies, Rohm, Haas Electronic Materials, Thomas L. Archibald/VP, Dir. - Engineering, Operations, Walter W. Becky/VP, Guillermo Novo/VP, Business Dir. - Process Chemicals, New Platforms *(39 Officers included in Index)*
Directors: Raj L. Gupta/Chmn., CEO, Pres., Thomas W. Haas/52/Dir., Ronaldo H. Schmitz/69/Dir., Richard L. Keyser/Dir., Marna C. Whittington/Dir., Gilbert S. Omenn/Dir., George M. Whitesides/Dir., Gary L. Rogers/Dir., Sandra O. Moose/Dir., David W. Haas/Dir., Rick J. Mills/66/Dir., William J. Avery/67/Dir.
Owners: G. S. Omenn, R. L. Keyser, G. M. Whitesides, A. E. Barton, J. M. Croisetiere, M. C. Whittington, J. P. Montoya, R. L. Gupta, P. R. Brondeau, D. W. Haas, R. H. Schmitz, Insiders, Dodge & Cox/7.82%, R. A. Lonergan, W. J. Avery *(22 Owners included in Index)*
Financial Data: *Fiscal Year End:*12/31 **Latest Annual Data:** 12/31/2006

Year	Sales		Net Income
2006	$8,230,000,000		$735,000,000
2005	$7,994,000,000		$637,000,000
2004	$7,300,000,000		$497,000,000

Curr. Assets:	$3,411,000,000	Curr. Liab.:	$1,988,000,000	P/E Ratio:	16.47
Plant, Equip.:	$2,669,000,000	Total Liab.:	$5,400,000,000	Indic. Yr. Divd.:	$1.480
Total Assets:	$9,553,000,000	Net Worth:	$4,031,000,000	Debt/ Equity:	0.4695

Rollins Inc

2170 Piedmont Rd. NE, Atlanta, GA, 30324; *PH:* 1-404-888-2000; *Fax:* 1-404-888-2662;
http:// www.rollinscorp.com; *Email:* investorrelations@rollinscorp.com

General - Incorporation	DE	Stock- Price on:12/24/2007	$22.96
Employees	8,400	Stock Exchange	NYSE
Auditor	Grant Thornton LLP	Ticker Symbol	ROL
Stk Agt.	Computershare Investor Services LLC	Outstanding Shares	67,120,000
Counsel	NA	E.P.S.	$0.90
DUNS No.	00-691-9088	Shareholders	NA

Business: The group's principal activity is to provide pest and termite control services to both residential and commercial customers in North America. The group's services are performed through contract that specifies the pricing arrangement with the customer. Orkin inc, a wholly owned subsidiary of the group provides customized services from over 400 locations to approximately 1.6 million customers. Orkin serves customers in the United States, Canada and Mexico providing essential pest control services and protection against termite damage, rodents and insects. The customers of the group include homes and businesses, including hotels, food service establishments, food manufacturers, retailers and transportation companies. On 03-May-2004, the group acquired western pest services and affiliates.
Primary SIC and add'l.: 7342
CIK No: 0000084839
Subsidiaries: 3094488 Nova Scotia Company ULC, 615345 Nb,inc., Canada Limited Partnership, Dettelbach Pesticide Corporation, IFC Company Holdings,Inc., IFC Properties, LLC, Kinro Investments,Inc., Orkin Expansion,Inc., Orkin International,Inc., Orkin S.A de C.V., Orkin Systems, Inc, Orkin,Inc., Orkin-IFC Properties LLC, PCO Holdings, Inc, PCO Services Corporation 22 Subsidiaries included in the Index
Officers: Gary W. Rollins/62/Inside Dir., CEO, COO, Pres./$2,552,379.00, Michael W. Knottek/62/Sr. VP, Sec./$608,393.00, Harry J. Cynkus/CFO, Treasurer/$594,862.00, Glen W. Rollins/41/VP/$910,564.00, Chris McGill/Human Resources Mgr. - Corporate Recruiter
Directors: Gary W. Rollins/62/Inside Dir., CEO, COO, Pres., Randall R. Rollins/75/Chmn., Henry B. Tippie/80/Dir., Wilton Looney/87/Dir., James B. Williams/74/Dir., Bill J. Dismuke/70/Dir., Thomas J. Lawley/Dir.
Owners: Wilton Looney, James B. Williams, Glen Rollins, Harry J. Cynkus, Insiders, Bill J. Dismuke, Henry B. Tippie, Michael W. Knottek, Gary W. Rollins, Randall Rollins, Mario Gabelli
Financial Data: *Fiscal Year End:*12/31 **Latest Annual Data:** 12/31/2006

Year	Sales	Net Income
2006	$858,878,000	$57,809,000
2005	$802,417,000	$52,773,000
2004	$750,884,000	$52,055,000

Curr. Assets:	$151,073,000	Curr. Liab.:	$185,206,000	P/E Ratio:	25.51
Plant, Equip.:	$72,141,000	Total Liab.:	$241,716,000	Indic. Yr. Divd.:	$0.300
Total Assets:	$453,175,000	Net Worth:	$211,459,000	Debt/ Equity:	0.0045

Roma Financial Corp

2300 Rte 33, Robbinsville, NJ, 08691; *PH:* 1-609-223-8300; http:// www.romabank.com

General - Incorporation	USA	Stock- Price on:12/24/2007	$16.47
Employees	140	Stock Exchange	NDQ
Auditor	Beard Miller Company LLP	Ticker Symbol	ROMA
Stk Agt.	NA	Outstanding Shares	32,730,000
Counsel	NA	E.P.S.	$0.19
DUNS No.	NA	Shareholders	NA

Business: The groups principal activity is to provide and financial and financial services. The products of the group include commercial, consumer and real estate mortgage loan. The group operates from the United States. The assets of the group for the year 2006 were $876,081 (thousands).
Primary SIC and add'l.: 6029
CIK No: 0001355823
Subsidiaries: General Abstract & Title Agency, Roma Bank, Roma Capital Investment Corporation
Officers: Peter A. Inverso/Dir., CEO, Pres./$622,377.00, Maurice T. Perilli/Chmn., Exec. VP/$445,090.00, Sharon L. Lamont/CFO/$104,288.00, Margaret T. Norton/Sr. VP, Sec./$360,175.00, Barry J. Zadworny/Sr. VP - Compliance/$229,462.00, Madhusudhan Kotta/Sr. VP, Treasurer - Investments, Keith C. Pericoloso/Sr. VP - Operations/$183,260.00, Gilda C. Picerno/Regional VP, Robert W. Sumner/VP - Information Technology, Peter Villa/First VP - Commercial Lending, Pamela Craig/Regional VP
Directors: Peter A. Inverso/Dir., CEO, Pres., Maurice T. Perilli/Chmn., Exec. VP, Simon H. Belli/Dir., Louis A. Natale/Dir., Rudolph A. Palombi/Dir., Michele N. Siekerka/Dir., Robert H. Rosen/Dir.
Owners: Stilwell Value LLC/6.00%, Stilwell Associates, L.P./6.00%, Joseph Stilwell/6.00%, Stilwell Value Partners VI, L.P./6.00%, Stilwell Partners, L.P./6.00%
Financial Data: *Fiscal Year End:*12/31 **Latest Annual Data:** 12/31/2006

Year	Sales	Net Income
2006	$44,329,000	$5,248,000
2005	$37,548,000	$7,535,000
2004	$32,719,000	$7,612,000

Curr. Assets:	$69,299,000	Curr. Liab.:	$633,835,000		
Plant, Equip.:	$30,669,000	Total Liab.:	$641,427,000	Indic. Yr. Divd.:	$0.060
Total Assets:	$876,081,000	Net Worth:	$234,654,000	Debt/ Equity:	0.0234

Rome Bancorp Inc

100 W Dominick St., Rome, NY, 13440; *PH:* 1-315-336-7300; *Fax:* 1-315-336-5440;
http:// www.romesavings.com; *Email:* investorrelations@romesavings.com

General - Incorporation .... DE
Employees 99
Auditor .... Crowe Chizek & Co. LLC
Stk Agt .... Registrar & Transfer Co
Counsel .... Thacher Proffitt & Wood LLP
DUNS No. .... NA

Stock- Price on:12/24/2007 .... $12.41
Stock Exchange .... NDQ
Ticker Symbol .... ROME
Outstanding Shares 8,420,000
E.P.S. $0.30
Shareholders .... NA

Business: The group's principal activities are to provide community banking services through its wholly owned subsidiary, the rome savings bank. The deposits offered by the group include regular savings deposits that consist of passbook and statement savings accounts, interest-bearing demand accounts, non-interest-bearing demand accounts, money market and time deposits. It offers residential real estate mortgage loans, commercial real estate loans, consumer and commercial loans. The services are provided through the four offices located in oneida county, New York.

Primary SIC and add'l.: 6712 6035

CIK No: 0001088144

Subsidiaries: 100 On the Mall Corporation, Clocktower Insurance Agency Incorporated, RSB Capital, Inc., RSB Properties, Inc.

Officers: Charles M. Sprock/Chmn., CEO, Pres. - Rome Savings Bank/$1,390,105.00, Susan Hert/Branch Mgr. - Lee Branch, Rome Savings Bank, Mary Faith E. Messenger/VP, Controller - Rome Savings Bank, Sandra L. Reader/VP - Consumer Loans, Rome Savings Bank, Francis C. Thalmann/VP - Branch Administration, Rome Savings Bank, David C. Nolan/Exec. VP, CFO - Rome Savings Bank/$581,875.00, Christine G. Ruben/Assist. VP, Human Resources Officer - Rome Savings Bank, Karin M. Reiss/Loan Officer - Rome Savings Bank, Deniece M. Zeller/Loan Officer - Rome Savings Bank, Albert Casab/Loan Officer - Rome Savings Bank, Mary K. Chmielewski/Administrative Assist., Branch Mgr. - Chestnut Street, Rome Savings Bank, Deborah L. Curtis/Branch Mgr. - New Hartford, Rome Savings Bank, Karen Wells/Branch Mgr. - West Rome, Rome Savings Bank, Pamela S. Barber/Deposit Mgr. - Rome Savings Bank, Bruce D. Fraser/VP - Security, Human Resources, Compliance, Rome Savings Bank *(30 Officers included in Index)*

Directors: Charles M. Sprock/Chmn., CEO, Pres. - Rome Savings Bank, John A. Reinhardt/Dir. - Rome Savings Bank, David C. Grow/Dir. - Rome Savings Bank, Dale A. Laval/Dir. - Rome Savings Bank, Michael Jay Valentine/Dir. - Rome Savings Bank, Bruce R. Engelbert/Dir. - Rome Savings Bank, Kirk B. Hinman/Dir. - Rome Savings Bank

Owners: Insiders/17.90%, David C. Nolan/1.60%, Bruce R. Engelbert/1.20%, David C. Grow/1.20%, Employee Stock Ownership Plan Trust of Rome/7.92%, Michael J. Valentine/1.60%, Dale A. Laval, Charles M. Sprock/3.90%, Kirk B. Hinman/3.20%, Anton V. Schutz/5.37%

Financial Data: Fiscal Year End:12/31 Latest Annual Data: 12/31/2006

Year	Sales	Net Income
2006	$19,353,000	$2,488,000
2005	$18,561,000	$3,402,000
2004	$16,270,000	$2,400,000

Curr. Assets:	$8,952,000	**Curr. Liab.:**	$196,005,000	**P/E Ratio:**	30.27
Plant, Equip.:	$6,072,000	**Total Liab.:**	$221,728,000	**Indic. Yr. Divd.:**	$0.320
Total Assets:	$298,759,000	**Net Worth:**	$77,031,000	**Debt/ Equity:**	0.3062

Ronco Corp

61 Moreland Rd., Simi Valley, CA, 93065; *PH:* 1-805-433-1030; *Fax:* 1-805-433-1033; *http://* www.ronco.com; *Email:* customerservice@roncoweb.com

General - Incorporation .... DE
Employees .... NA
Auditor Mahoney Cohen & Company, CPA, P.C.
Stk Agt .... Corporate Stock Transfer, Inc.
Counsel .... NA
DUNS No. .... NA

Stock- Price on:12/24/2007 .... NA
Stock Exchange .... OTC
Ticker Symbol .... RNCP
Outstanding Shares .... NA
E.P.S .... NA
Shareholders .... NA

Business: The groups principle activity is a developer, marketer and distributor of consumer products for the kitchen and home branded. Products of the group include kitchen products and household products. The group operates from the United States.

Primary SIC and add'l.: 3631 3634 3639 5091 5961 5963

CIK No: 0000869498

Subsidiaries: Ronco Marketing Corporation

Officers: Paul Kabashima/CEO, Ronald C. Stone/CFO

Directors: Harold D. Kahn/Dir., Thomas J. Lykos/Dir., John S. Reiland/Dir.

Owners: LBI Group, Inc./6.20%, Sanders Opportunity Fund (Institutional), L.P./8.00%, Sanders Morris Harris, Inc., Copper Beech Equity Partners LLC, The Quaker Investment Trust -/5.90%, Apogee Fund, L.P./1.50%, Tom and Nancy Juda Living Trust/2.10%, Renaissance US Growth Investment Trust PLC, Renaissance US Growth Investment Trust PLC/2.10%, Heartland Group, Inc.,, Paul Wallace, Sandor Capital Master Fund, L.P./1.10%, Bookbend & Co./12.40%, The Quaker Investment Trust -, Insiders *(47 Owners included in Index)*

Curr. Assets:	$11,293,000	**Curr. Liab.:**	$24,160,000		
Plant, Equip.:	$1,185,000	**Total Liab.:**	$24,373,000	**Indic. Yr. Divd.:**	NA
Total Assets:	$28,239,000	**Net Worth:**	$3,865,000	**Debt/ Equity:**	2.3665

Ronson Corp

Corporate Pk. III, Campus Dr., Somerset, NJ, 08875; *PH:* 1-732-563-7888; *Fax:* 1-732-563-2246; *http://* www.ronsoncorp.com

General - Incorporation .... NJ
Employees 95
Auditor .... Demetrius & Co LLC
Stk Agt .... Registrar & Transfer Co
Counsel .... Poter, Wright, Morris & Arthur
DUNS No. 00-214-8500

Stock- Price on:12/24/2007 .... $1.71
Stock Exchange .... NDQ
Ticker Symbol .... RONC
Outstanding Shares 4,820,000
E.P.S. .... -$0.08
Shareholders .... NA

Business: The group's principle activity is to manufacture and market consumer products and to provide aviation services to the general public and government agencies. The group's consumer products consists of consumer packaged products and flame products including ronsonol lighter fluid and multi-fill butane fuel injectors, flints, wicks for lighters and windproof lighters. The group's aviation services segment includes air charter, air cargo, cargo handling, avionics, management aviation, flight training, new and used aircraft sales, aircraft repairs, aircraft fueling, storage and office rental. The consumer products are distributed through food brokers, distributors, drug chains and hardware representatives. The group markets its products in the United States, Canada, Mexico and other countries. The group's quarterly revenue for September 2007 was 6.61 millions of USD.

Primary SIC and add'l.: 3999 4581

CIK No: 0000084919

Subsidiaries: Ronson Aviation, Inc., Ronson Consumer Products Corporation (RCPC), Ronson Corporation of Canada Ltd., Ronsonol lighter fluid

Officers: Louis V. Aronson/CEO, Pres., Justin P. Walder/Sec., Daryl K. Holcomb/CFO, VP, Controller, Erwin M. Ganz/Treasurer

Directors: Robert A. Aronson/Dir., Barbara L. Collins/55/Dir., Edward E. David/83/Dir., Paul H. Einhorn/Dir., Leo I. Motiuk/63/Dir., Gerard J. Quinnan/80/Dir.

Owners: Carl W. Dinger/11.60%, Gerard J. Quinnan, Barbara L. Collins, Insiders/32.60%, Steel Partners/9.50%, Louis V. Aronson/27.70%, Robert A. Aronson, Edward E. David, Justin P. Walder/1.70%, Leo I. Motiuk, Daryl K. Holcomb/1.30%, Erwin M. Ganz/1.00%

Financial Data: Fiscal Year End:12/31 Latest Annual Data: 12/31/2006

Year	Sales	Net Income
2006	$29,244,000	$67,000
2005	$26,563,000	-$333,000
2004	$28,483,000	$193,000

Curr. Assets:	$6,196,000	**Curr. Liab.:**	$7,074,000		
Plant, Equip.:	$5,772,000	**Total Liab.:**	$11,094,000	**Indic. Yr. Divd.:**	NA
Total Assets:	$14,720,000	**Net Worth:**	$3,626,000	**Debt/ Equity:**	1.0210

ROO Group Inc

228 E 45th St., 8th Fl., New York, NY, 10017; *PH:* 1-212-661-4111; *Fax:* 1-646-619-4074; *http://* www.roo.com; *Email:* enquiries@rooemail.com

General - Incorporation .... DE
Employees 140
Auditor .... Moore Stephens, P.C
Stk Agt .... Continental Stock Transfer & Trust Co
Counsel .... Wolf & Marcus LLP
DUNS No. .... NA

Stock- Price on:12/24/2007 .... $1.89
Stock Exchange .... OTC
Ticker Symbol .... RGRP
Outstanding Shares 38,370,000
E.P.S. .... -$0.91
Shareholders .... NA

Business: The group's principal activities are to provide the aggregation of video content, media management, online advertising, hosting and content delivery. The group, through its operating subsidiary roo media corporation, is a digital media company which provides products and solutions to a global base of clients that enable the broadcast of topical video content from their Internet websites, www.rootv.com. The group also operates a global network of individual destination portals under the brand roo TV that enables the end users in different regions around the world to view video content over the Internet. On 03-Dec-2003, the group acquired roo media corporation. On 30-Apr-2004 and 01-Jun-2004, the group acquired the reality group pty ltd and undercover media pty ltd respectively.

Primary SIC and add'l.: 7375

CIK No: 0001076700

Subsidiaries: Factory212 Pty. Ltd., ROO Broadcasting Limited, ROO Media (Australia) Pty Ltd., ROO Media Corporation, ROO TV Pty Ltd., Virilitec Industries

Officers: Robert Petty/Chmn., CEO, Robin Smyth/Exec. Dir., CFO, Tristan Place/VP - Sales, Strategic Partnerships, Australasia, Steve Quinn/COO, Pres., Paula Balzer/Chief Marketing Officer, Rick Gell/Chief Content Officer, Bert Solivan/GM, Exec. VP - ROO Media US, Tony Martin/Sr. VP, ROO Media Europe, Lou Kerner/46/CFO

Directors: Robert Petty/Chmn., CEO, Doug Chertok/Dir., Scott Ackerman/Dir., Simon Bax/Dir., Stephen Palley/Dir.

Owners: Simon Bax, Stephen Quinn/5.00%, Insiders/71.06%, Douglas Chertok, Cobble Creek Consulting, Inc./10.00%, Rubin Irrevocable Family Trust/10.00%, Insiders/75.00%, 033 Asset Management/6.72%, Robin Smyth/51.00%, Stephen Quinn/2.10%, Lewis Asset Management, Corp./6.12%, Wellington Management Company, LLP/17.51%, Robert Petty/6.50%, Rubin Irrevocable Family Trust, Ashford Capital Partners, L.P/12.26% *(21 Owners included in Index)*

Financial Data: Fiscal Year End:12/31 Latest Annual Data: 12/31/2006

Year	Sales	Net Income
2006	$9,768,000	-$14,625,000
2005	$6,619,000	-$8,957,000
2004	$3,937,000	-$4,226,000

Curr. Assets:	$16,496,000	**Curr. Liab.:**	$4,703,000		
Plant, Equip.:	$948,000	**Total Liab.:**	$4,909,000	**Indic. Yr. Divd.:**	NA
Total Assets:	$20,610,000	**Net Worth:**	$15,790,000	**Debt/ Equity:**	0.0223

RoomLinX

2150 - W 6th Ave., Unit N, Broomfield, CO, 80020; *PH:* 1-305-544-1111; *Fax:* 1-303-544-1110; *http://* www.roomlinx.com; *Email:* sales@roomlinx.com

General - Incorporation .... NV
Employees .... NA
Auditor .... Eisner LLP
Stk Agt .... Registrar & Transfer Co
Counsel .... NA
DUNS No. .... NA

Stock- Price on:12/24/2007 .... $0.025
Stock Exchange .... OTC
Ticker Symbol .... RMLX
Outstanding Shares .... NA
E.P.S. .... NA
Shareholders .... NA

Business: The group's principal activity is to provides wired networking solutions and wireless fidelity networking solutions also known as wi-fi, for high speed Internet access to hotels, convention centers, corporate apartments and special events locations.

Primary SIC and add'l.: 7379 7336 8748 7375

CIK No: 0001021096

Financial Data: Fiscal Year End:12/31 Latest Annual Data: 12/31/2004

Year	Sales	Net Income
2004	$2,009,000	-$12,176,000
2003	$1,057,000	-$449,000

Curr. Assets:	$143,000	**Curr. Liab.:**	$746,000		
Plant, Equip.:	$142,000	**Total Liab.:**	$746,000	**Indic. Yr. Divd.:**	NA
Total Assets:	$300,000	**Net Worth:**	-$446,000	**Debt/ Equity:**	NA

Roper Industries Inc

6901 Professional Pkwy. E, Ste. 200, Sarasota, FL, 34240; *PH:* 1-941-556-2601; *Fax:* 1-941-556-2670; *http://* www.roperind.com

General - Incorporation............................ DE
Employees 6,900
Auditor ....PricewaterhouseCoopers LLP
Stk Agt..................................Wachovia Bank N.A
Counsel....................................David B. Liner
DUNS No. 00-326-4850

Stock - Price on:12/24/2007 ....$55.76
Stock Exchange...NYSE
Ticker Symbol...ROP
Outstanding Shares 88,280,000
E.P.S...$2.39
Shareholders..NA

Business: The groups principle activity is to produce engineered products. The groups products include energy systems and controls, scientific and industrial imaging products and software, and radio frequency products The group operates through four business segments namely industrial technology, energy systems and controls, scientific and industrial imaging, and RF technology. The group operates from United States.

Primary SIC and add'l.: 3625 3594 3823 3492

CIK No: 0000882835

Subsidiaries: Abel Equipos, S.A, Abel GmbH & Co KG, Abel Pumpen GmbH, Abel Pumps, L.P., Acton Research Corporation, Ai Cambridge Ltd., Amot Controls Corporation, Amot Controls GmbH, Amot Controls Ltd., Amot/Metrix Investment Company, Amtech Systems (Hong Kong), Ltd., Amtech Systems Corporation, Amtech World Corporation, Antek Instruments GmbH, CCC Services, Inc. 105 Subsidiaries included in the Index

Officers: Brian D. Jellison/Chmn., CEO, Pres./$8,703,227.00, Will Nigel Crocker/VP, David B. Liner/VP, General Counsel, Sec., Timothy J. Winfrey/VP - Energy Systems, Controls/$1,286,932.00, Benjamin W. Wood/VP - Scientific, Industrial Imaging/$1,158,775.00, John Humphrey/42/CFO, VP/$1,360,525.00, Nigel W. Crocker/53/VP - Instrumentation/$1,150,522.00, Richard A. Canada/VP - Human Resources, Paul J. Soni/VP, Controller

Directors: Brian D. Jellison/Chmn., CEO, Pres., John F. Fort/Dir., Lawrence W. Banks/Dir., David W. Devonshire/Dir., Robert D. Johnson/Dir., William J. Prezzano/67/Dir., Christopher Wright/Dir., Donald J. Calder/70/Dir., Richard Wallman/57/Dir.

Owners: David W. Devonshire, Franklin Resources, Inc./6.20%, Richard F. Wallman, Brian D. Jellison/1.40%, Robert D. Johnson, Wilbur J. Prezzano, Donald G. Calder, T. Rowe Price Associates, Inc./11.90%, Lawrence W. Banks, Nigel W. Crocker, Benjamin W. Wood, John F. Fort, Neuberger Berman Inc./6.10%, Timothy J. Winfrey, Christopher Wright (17 Owners included in Index)

Financial Data: Fiscal Year End:12/31   Latest Annual Data: 12/31/2006

Year	Sales	Net Income
2006	$1,700,734,000	$193,324,000
2005	$1,453,731,000	$153,175,000
2004	$969,764,000	$93,852,000

Curr. Assets:	$627,495,000	Curr. Liab.:	$587,649,000	P/E Ratio:	23.33
Plant, Equip.:	$107,003,000	Total Liab.:	$1,508,520,000	Indic. Yr. Divd.:	$0.260
Total Assets:	$2,995,359,000	Net Worth:	$1,486,839,000	Debt/ Equity:	0.4862

Rosedale Decorative Products Ltd

184 Ct.land Ave., Concord, ON, L4K 4L3; *PH:* 1-905-669-8909

General - Incorporation......................Canada
Employees ....NA
Auditor ....SF Partnership LLP
Stk Agt...... Continental Stock Transfer & Trust Co
Counsel..NA
DUNS No. ....NA

Stock - Price on:12/24/2007 ....$0.05
Stock Exchange..OTC
Ticker Symbol...ROSD
Outstanding Shares ....NA
E.P.S..NA
Shareholders..NA

Business: The group's principal activities are to design, manufacture and market wallpapers and decorative fabrics. The group's products include wallpaper and wallpaper borders, designer fabrics, area rugs, ceiling panels and paint. The group operates through its wholly owned subsidiaries rosedale wallcoverings and fabrics inc and ontario paint and wallpaper limited. Majority of the group's operations is carried on in the United States and Canada. The group also operates a retail paint and wallpaper store in toronto.

Primary SIC and add'l.: 5231 2679 2259

CIK No: 0001051357

Subsidiaries: 1010037 Ontario Inc., 521305 Ontario Inc., Ontario Paint & Wallpaper Limited, Rosedale Wallcoverings & Fabrics Inc.

Financial Data: Fiscal Year End:12/31   Latest Annual Data: 12/31/2004

Year	Sales	Net Income
2004	$8,359,000	-$1,993,000
2002	$21,194,000	$164,000
2001	$17,781,000	-$889,000

Curr. Assets:	$5,564,000	Curr. Liab.:	$6,658,000		
Plant, Equip.:	$2,272,000	Total Liab.:	$6,668,000	Indic. Yr. Divd.:	NA
Total Assets:	$7,876,000	Net Worth:	$1,208,000	Debt/ Equity:	0.2753

Rosetta Genomics Ltd

675 U.S. Hwy 1, Ste. B119, North Brunswick, NJ, 08902; *PH:* 1-732-246-9900;
Fax: 1-732-246-9988; *http://* www.rosettagenomics.com;
Email: investor.relations@rosettagenomics.com

General - Incorporation......................Israel
Employees 41
Auditor ....NA
Stk Agt...... American Stock Transfer & Trust Co.
Counsel..NA
DUNS No. ....NA

Stock - Price on:12/24/2007 ....$7.1
Stock Exchange..NDQ
Ticker Symbol...ROSG
Outstanding Shares 8,870,000
E.P.S..-$0.97
Shareholders..NA

Business: The groups principal activity is to provide diagnostic and therapeutic product. The group operates from the United States.

Primary SIC and add'l.: 2834 8731

CIK No: 0001362959

Subsidiaries: Rosetta Genomics Inc.

Officers: Amir Avniel/CEO, Pres., Isaac Bentwich/Founder, Dir., Chief Architect, Tamir Kazaz/CFO, Corp. Sec., Dalia Cohen/Exec. VP, Head - Global Research, Development, Ranit Aharonov/Exec. VP - Diagnostics, Intellectual Property, Ayelet Chajut/VP - Therapeutics, Zvi Bentwich/Chief Scientist

Directors: Yoav Z. Chelouche/Chmn., Aaron J. Ciechanover/Chmn. - Scientific Advisory Board, Eithan Galun/Member - Scientific Advisory Board, Isaac Bentwich/Founder, Dir., Chief Architect, Robert Langer/Member - Scientific Advisory Board, Alexander Rich/Member - Scientific Advisory Board, Michael Sela/Member - Scientific Advisory Board, Moshe Many/Dir., Joshua Rosensweig/Dir., Nathan Hod/Dir., Simcha Sadan/Dir., Gerald Dogon/External Dir., Tali Yaron-Eldar/External Dir., Eithan Rubinstein/Member - Scientific Advisory Board

Owners: Isaac Bentwich/16.00%, Simcha Sadan, Highbridge International LLC/6.50%, Tamir Kazaz, Joshua Rosensweig, Insiders/19.60%, Moshe Many, Yoav Chelouche/1.00%, Ranit Aharonov, Nathan Hod, Amir Avniel/5.50%

Financial Data: Fiscal Year End:12/31   Latest Annual Data: 12/31/2006

Year	Sales	Net Income
2006	NA	-$7,607,000
2005	NA	-$5,843,000
2004	NA	-$2,982,000

Curr. Assets:	$12,684,000	Curr. Liab.:	$1,543,000		
Plant, Equip.:	$461,000	Total Liab.:	$2,144,000	Indic. Yr. Divd.:	NA
Total Assets:	$13,243,000	Net Worth:	$11,099,000	Debt/ Equity:	NA

Rosetta Resources Inc

717 Texas, Ste. 2800, Houston, TX, 77002; *PH:* 1-713-335-4000; *Fax:* 1-713-335-4197;
http:// www.rosettaresources.com; *Email:* info@rosettaresources.com

General - Incorporation .... DE
Employees 135
Auditor ....PricewaterhouseCoopers LLP
Stk Agt...... American Stock Transfer & Trust Co.
Counsel..NA
DUNS No. ....NA

Stock - Price on:12/24/2007 ....$24.23
Stock Exchange..NDQ
Ticker Symbol...ROSE
Outstanding Shares 50,770,000
E.P.S..NA
Shareholders..NA

Business: The groups principle activities include exploring, developing, producing and acquiring oil and natural gas. The products of the group include Crude Oil and natural gas. Specific customer of the group is Calpine Energy Services. The group operates from the United States. The group's quarterly revenue for September 2007 was 89.72 milions of USD.

Primary SIC and add'l.: 1381 1311 2999 1321 1321 1311 2999 1381

CIK No: 0001340282

Subsidiaries: Rosetta Resources Holdings, LLC, Rosetta Resources Offshore, LLC, Rosetta Resources Operating GP, LLC, Rosetta Resources Operating LP

Officers: Randy L. Limbacher/CEO, Pres., Denise D. Bednorz/VP, Controller, Edward E. Seeman/VP - Northern Division/$369,707.00, Teri Greer/Contact - Investor Relations, Chad J. Driskill/VP - Marketing, Business Development, Michael J. Rosinski/Exec. VP, CFO, Treasurer/$516,513.00, Charles F. Chambers/Exec. VP - Corporate Development/$503,811.00, Michael H. Hickey/VP, General Counsel/$508,294.00, John M. Thibeaux/VP - Southern Division, Gerald L. Maxwell/VP - Human Resources

Directors: Henry D. Houston/Chmn., Donald D. Patteson/Dir., Richard W. Beckler/Dir., Louis G. Graziadio/Dir., Josiah O. Low/Dir.

Owners: John M. Thibeaux, U.S. Trust Excelsior Value and Restructuring Fund/5.40%, Michael H. Hickey, Denise D. Bednorz, Capital Research and Management Company/8.90%, Edward E. Seeman, Josiah O. Low, Charles F. Chambers, Henry D. Houston, Insiders, Michael J. Rosinski, First Pacific Advisors, LLC/17.00%, Louis G. Graziadio, Donald D. Patteson, Jackie C. Driskill (18 Owners included in Index)

Financial Data: Fiscal Year End:12/31   Latest Annual Data: 12/31/2006

Year	Sales	Net Income
2006	$271,763,000	$44,608,000
2005	$113,104,000	$17,535,000

Curr. Assets:	$131,452,000	Curr. Liab.:	$100,760,000		
Plant, Equip.:	$1,082,610,000	Total Liab.:	$397,116,000	Indic. Yr. Divd.:	NA
Total Assets:	$1,219,405,000	Net Worth:	$822,289,000	Debt/ Equity:	0.3164

Ross Stores Inc

4440 Rosewood Dr., Pleasanton, CA, 94588; *PH:* 1-925-965-4400; *Fax:* 1-925-965-4388;
http:// www.rossstores.com; *Email:* investor.relations@ros.com

General - Incorporation .... DE
Employees 13,300
Auditor ....Deloitte & Touche LLP
Stk Agt..................................Bank of New York
Counsel.............Gray, Cary, Ware & Freidenrich
DUNS No. 02-908-9711

Stock - Price on:12/24/2007 ....$30.95
Stock Exchange..NDQ
Ticker Symbol...ROST
Outstanding Shares 138,640,000
E.P.S...$1.77
Shareholders..NA

Business: The group's principle activity is to operate off price retail apparel and home accessories stores. The group operates from United States.

Primary SIC and add'l.: 5632 5611 5651 5641 5094 5661

CIK No: 0000745732

Officers: Michael Balmuth/Vice Chmn., CEO, Pres./$8,169,693.00, Barbara Rentler/Exec. VP - Merchandising/$2,010,192.00, James S. Fassio/Exec. VP - Property Development, Construction, Store Design/$1,976,389.00, Gary L. Cribb/COO, Exec. VP, Art Roth/Sr. VP - Merchandise Control, Michael L. Wilson/Sr. VP - Distribution, Transportation, Jennifer Vecchio/Sr. VP, General Merchandise Mgr., Mary Walter/Sr. VP - Stores, Michael B. OSullivan/Exec. VP, Chief Administrative Officer, Mark Lehocky/Sr. VP, General Counsel, Robert J. Bernard/Sr. VP, General Merchandise Mgr., Bernie Brautigan/Sr. VP, General Merchandise Mgr., Terri Mann/Sr. VP, General Merchandise Mgr., Michael K. Kobayashi/CIO, Sr. VP, Jane D. Marvin/Sr. VP - Human Resources (20 Officers included in Index)

Directors: Michael Balmuth/Vice Chmn., CEO, Pres., Norman A. Ferber/Chmn., Stuart G. Moldaw/Chmn. Emeritus, Michael J. Bush/Dir., George P. Orban/Dir., Donald H. Seiler/Dir., Gunnar K. Bjorklund/Dir., Sharon D. Garrett/Dir.

Owners: Stuart G. Moldaw, Lisa Panattoni, Donald H. Seiler, Michael Balmuth, Barbara Rentler, Capital Research and Management Company/9.10%, Insiders/2.90%, Gunnar K. Bjorklund, James S. Fassio, Sharon D. Garrett, George P. Orban/1.00%, John G. Call, Michael J. Bush, AMVESCAP PLC/6.60%, Norman A. Ferber (16 Owners included in Index)

Financial Data: Fiscal Year End:01/28   Latest Annual Data: 2/3/2007

Year	Sales	Net Income
2007	$5,570,210,000	$241,634,000
2006	$4,944,179,000	$199,632,000
2005	$4,239,990,000	$169,902,000

Curr. Assets:	$1,514,956,000	**Curr. Liab.:**	$1,083,257,000	**P/E Ratio:**	17.49
Plant, Equip.:	$748,233,000	**Total Liab.:**	$1,448,761,000	**Indic. Yr. Divd.:**	$0.300
Total Assets:	$2,358,591,000	**Net Worth:**	$909,830,000	**Debt/ Equity:**	NA

Rotech Healthcare Inc NEW

2600 Technology Dr., Ste. 300, Orlando, FL, 32804; ***PH:*** 1-407-822-4600; ***Fax:*** 1-407-297-6217; ***http://*** www.rotech.com; ***Email:*** corporate@rotech.com

General - Incorporation	DE	**Stock**- Price on:12/24/2007	$1.22
Employees	4,900	Stock Exchange	NDQ
Auditor	Deloitte & Touche LLP	Ticker Symbol	ROHI
Stk Agt	NA	Outstanding Shares	25,510,000
Counsel	NA	E.P.S.	-$5.07
DUNS No.	NA	Shareholders	NA

Business: The groups principle activity is to provide home medical equipment and related products and services. The groups services include Medicare and Medicaid. The products of the group include oxygen concentrators, liquid oxygen systems, portable oxygen systems, ventilator therapy systems and nebulizer equipment. The group operates from the United States. The group's quarterly revenue for September 2007 was 140.93 millions of USD.

Primary SIC and add'l.: 3821 3841 5047 3842 3845

CIK No: 0001175108

Subsidiaries: A-1 Medical Equipment, Inc., Abba Medical Equipment, Inc., Acadia Home Care, Allied Medical Supply, Inc., Always Medical Equipment, Inc., Andy Boyds InHome Medical, Inc., West, Andy Boyds InHome Medical/InHome Medical Inc., Anniston Health& Sickroom Supplies, Inc., Berkeley Medical Equipment, Inc., Best Care Medical Supply, Inc., Beta Medical Equipment, Inc., Cambria Medical Supply, Inc., Camden Medical Supply, Inc., Care Medical Supplies, Inc., Centennial Medical Equipment, Inc. 122 Subsidiaries included in the Index

Officers: Philip L. Carter/Dir., CEO, Pres., Michael R. Dobbs/COO, Steven P. Alsene/CFO, Treasurer, Rebecca L. Myers/Chief Legal Officer, Corp. Sec.

Directors: Philip L. Carter/Dir., CEO, Pres., Arthur J. Reimers/Chmn., Edward L. Kuntz/Dir., James H. Bloem/Dir., Arthur Siegel/Dir., Jason B. Mudrick/Dir.

Owners: Edward L. Kuntz, Michael R. Dobbs/1.60%, Arthur Siegel, Steve P. Alsene, Insiders/5.23%, Philip L. Carter/2.94%, James H. Bloem, Arthur J. Reimers

Financial Data: ***Fiscal Year End:***12/31 ***Latest Annual Data:*** 12/31/2006

Year	Sales	Net Income
2006	$498,751,000	-$534,099,000
2005	$533,182,000	$5,546,000
2004	$535,329,000	$36,010,000

Curr. Assets:	$104,181,000	**Curr. Liab.:**	$72,311,000		
Plant, Equip.:	$148,153,000	**Total Liab.:**	$456,073,000	**Indic. Yr. Divd.:**	NA
Total Assets:	$497,133,000	**Net Worth:**	$35,717,000	**Debt/ Equity:**	33.5898

Rotoblock Corp

1715 Cook St. , Ste. 205, Vancouver, BC, V5Y 3J6; ***PH:*** 1-604-872-1234; ***http://*** www.rotoblock.com

General - Incorporation	NV	**Stock**- Price on:12/24/2007	$0.036
Employees	3	Stock Exchange	OTC
Auditor	James Stafford, Inc	Ticker Symbol	ROTB
Stk Agt	Holladay Stock Transfer, Inc.	Outstanding Shares	30,270,000
Counsel	Lang Michener	E.P.S.	-$0.03
DUNS No.	NA	Shareholders	NA

Business: The groups principal activity is engage in the development and licensing of an Oscillating Piston Engine. The group operates from the United States.

Primary SIC and add'l.: 8731

CIK No: 0001289441

Subsidiaries: Rotoblock Inc

Officers: Matthias Heinze/53/Dir., CEO, Pres., Peter H. Scholl/Engineer, Wilfred L. Chipman/Chief Scientist, Lang Michener/Legal Counsel, Otto Baartman/Engineer, Thomas M. Howard/60/CFO, Principal Accounting Officer, Dir., Mariya Petrovska/Dir., Sec., Tony R. Collins/36/VP - Corporate Development, Technology

Directors: Matthias Heinze/53/Dir., CEO, Pres., Thomas M. Howard/60/CFO, Principal Accounting Officer, Dir., Ching Chen Chan/Dir., Steve Schneider/46/Dir., Mariya Petrovska/Dir., Sec.

Owners: Autodistributors/12.00%, Matthias Heinze/1.00%, Ching Chen Chan/1.00%, Marlin Financial/7.00%, Insiders/2.00%

Financial Data: ***Fiscal Year End:***04/30 ***Latest Annual Data:*** 04/30/2007

Year	Sales	Net Income
2007	NA	-$864,000
2006	NA	-$2,767,000
2005	NA	-$306,000

Curr. Assets:	$269,000	**Curr. Liab.:**	$40,000		
Plant, Equip.:	NA	**Total Liab.:**	$40,000	**Indic. Yr. Divd.:**	NA
Total Assets:	$378,000	**Net Worth:**	$338,000	**Debt/ Equity:**	NA

Rotonics Manufacturing Inc

17022 S Figueroa St. , Gardena, CA, 90248; ***PH:*** 1-310-538-4932; ***http://*** www.rotocast.com

General - Incorporation	DE	**Stock**- Price on:12/24/2007	NA
Employees	429	Stock Exchange	NA
Auditor	Windes & McClaughry Acc. Corp	Ticker Symbol	NA
Stk Agt	American Stock Transfer & Trust Co.	Outstanding Shares	NA
Counsel	E. Paul Tonkovich	E.P.S.	NA
DUNS No.	00-521-2048	Shareholders	NA

Business: The group's principal activities are manufacturing and market plastic containers for commercial, agricultural, pharmaceutical, point of purchase display, medical waste, refuse, marine health care and residential use. It has ten manufacturing locations in North America. The group also has custom plastic products for a variety of industries, using the roto-molding process and on a small scale, injection molding and dip molding process. Roto-molding is a process for molding plastic resin by rotating a mold in a heated environment while the plastic resin powder placed inside the mold melts and evenly coats the inner wall of the mold. The injection molding process varies in that the plastic resin is first heated to a molten state and then injected under pressure into a mold. The group operates solely in the domestic market. The trade names are rmi-c, rmi-d, and rmi-f.

Primary SIC and add'l.: 3089

CIK No: 0000801873

Subsidiaries: Plastech International, Inc., Rotational Molding, Inc.

Owners: Bill Allen, Marc L. Berman/1.10%, Sherman McKinniss/45.70%, Larry DeDonato/1.20%, Insiders/50.80%, Douglas W. Russell, Paul E. Tonkovich, Jules Sandford, Linn Derickson/8.70%, Larry L. Snyder/1.00%

Roundys Supermarkets Inc

875 E Wisconsin Ave., Milwaukee, WI, 53202; ***PH:*** 1-414-231-5000; ***http://*** www.roundys.com; ***Email:*** customercare@roundys.com

General - Incorporation	WI	**Stock**- Price on:12/24/2007	NA
Employees	NA	Stock Exchange	NA
Auditor	Ernst & Young LLP	Ticker Symbol	NA
Stk Agt	NA	Outstanding Shares	NA
Counsel	NA	E.P.S.	NA
DUNS No.	00-794-7195	Shareholders	NA

Business: The group's principal activity is the wholesale distribution of food and nonfood products to supermarkets and warehouse food stores. The products are supplied to stores and supermarkets located at Illinois, Wisconsin, Michigan, Indiana, Ohio, Missouri, Kentucky, Arkansas, Pennsylvania, Minnesota, Tennessee and west Virginia. As of Jan 3, 2004, the company operated 115 company-ownedretail grocery stores primarily under the pick 'n save, copps and rainbow foods banners. In 2003, the group acquired seven kohl's grocery stores and 32 rainbow foods stores.

Primary SIC and add'l.: 9999 8742 5141 5411

CIK No: 0000314423

Subsidiaries: Badger Assurance, Ltd., Holt Public Storage, Inc., I.T.A., Inc., Jondex Corp., Kee Trans, Inc., Mega Marts, Inc., Midland Grocery of Michigan, Inc., Ropak, Inc., Scot Lad Foods, Inc., The Copps Corporation, Ultra Mart Foods, Inc.

Officers: Robert A. Mariano/Chmn., CEO, Jane Voichick/Dir. - Roundys Foundation, Donald S. Rosanova/Exec. VP - Operations, Vivian King/Dir. - Public Affairs, John Boyle/Group VP - Information Technology, Business Process Excellence, Darren W. Karst/CFO, Exec. VP, Edward G. Kitz/Group VP - Legal, Risk, Treasury, Ronald Cooper/Group VP - Sales, Marketing, Michael J. Schmitt/Group VP - Real Estate, Robin Michel/Group VP - Procurement, Merchandising, Gary Fryda/Group VP - Retail Operations, Customer Satisfaction, Colleen Stenholt/Group VP - Human Resources

Directors: Robert A. Mariano/Chmn., CEO, Geraldo H. Gonzalez/Dir. - Roundys Foundation, Flamont T. Butler/Dir. - Roundys Foundation

Rowan Cos Inc

2800 Post Oak Blvd., Ste. 5450, Houston, TX, 77056; ***PH:*** 1-713-621-7800; ***Fax:*** 1-713-960-7660; ***http://*** www.rowancompanies.com; ***Email:*** ir@rowancompanies.com

General - Incorporation	DE	**Stock**- Price on:12/24/2007	$40.69
Employees	5,160	Stock Exchange	NYSE
Auditor	Deloitte & Touche LLP	Ticker Symbol	RDC
Stk Agt	Computershare Trust Co	Outstanding Shares	110,640,000
Counsel	NA	E.P.S.	$3.26
DUNS No.	00-793-0050	Shareholders	NA

Business: The group's principal activities are to provide contract drilling and aviation services. The group also manufactures and sells heavy equipment. The group operates through three segments: drilling, manufacturing and aviation. The drilling segment includes contract drilling of oil and gas wells, both onshore and offshore. The manufacturing segment manufactures and markets heavy equipment for the mining and transportation, alloy steel and drilling industries. The aviation segment provides helicopter and fixed-wing aircraft services.

Primary SIC and add'l.: 1382 3559 4522

CIK No: 0000085408

Subsidiaries: Atlantic Maritime Services, Inc., LeTourneau, Inc., Rowan Drilling Company, Inc., Rowan International, Inc., Rowandrill, Inc.

Officers: D. F. McNease/Chmn., CEO, Pres./$3,860,185.00, Dan C. Eckermann/VP - Manufacturing, CEO, Pres. - Letourneau Technologies, Inc, Melanie Trent/Corp. Sec., Special Assist. to The CEO, Kevin Bartol/VP - Strategic Planning, Terry Woodall/VP - Human Resources, Mike Dowdy/VP - Engineering, George C. Jones/Compliance Officer, Greg Hatfield/Controller, David Russell/Exec. VP - Drilling Operations/$1,277,615.00, John L. Buvens/Exec. VP - Legal/$1,272,893.00, William C. Provine/VP - Investor Relations, William H. Wells/CFO, VP - Finance/$1,187,723.00, Mark A. Keller/Exec. VP - Business Development/$1,279,519.00

Directors: D. F. McNease/Chmn., CEO, Pres., R. G. Croyle/Dir., Lord Moynihan/52/Dir., William T. Fox/62/Dir., Graham Hearne/70/Dir., H. E. Lentz/Dir., Dexter P. Peacock/66/Dir., John R. Huff/62/Dir., Frederick R. Lausen/70/Dir., Robert E. Kramek/Dir.

Owners: Graham Hearne, M. A. Keller, Lord Moynihan, Dexter P. Peacock, D. F. McNease, William T. Fox, W. H. Wells, John R. Huff, Insiders, J. L. Buvens, Frederick R. Lausen, D. P. Russell, H. E. Lentz, R. G. Croyle

Financial Data: ***Fiscal Year End:***12/31 ***Latest Annual Data:*** 12/31/2006

Year	Sales	Net Income
2006	$1,510,734,000	$318,246,000
2005	$1,068,782,000	$229,800,000
2004	$708,501,000	-$1,273,000

Curr. Assets:	$1,102,849,000	**Curr. Liab.:**	$516,706,000	**P/E Ratio:**	12.48
Plant, Equip.:	$2,133,226,000	**Total Liab.:**	$1,561,352,000	**Indic. Yr. Divd.:**	$0.400
Total Assets:	$3,435,398,000	**Net Worth:**	$1,874,046,000	**Debt/ Equity:**	0.2590

Royal & Sun Alliance Insurance Group Plc

9th Fl., One Plantation Pl., 30 Fenchurch St., London, EC3M 3BD; ; ***http://*** www.royalsunalliance.com

General		Stock	
Incorporation	UK	Price on:12/24/2007	NA
Employees	NA	Stock Exchange	NA
Auditor	PricewaterhouseCoopers LLP	Ticker Symbol	NA
Stk Agt	NA	Outstanding Shares	NA
Counsel	NA	E.P.S.	NA
DUNS No.	NA	Shareholders	NA

Business: The group's principal activities are the provision of life assurance, commercial and personal assurance, and offers personal finance products and services in the United Kingdom, the United States of America, continental Europe, Australia, New Zealand, Middle East, Africa and Asia-Pacific. The group also operates estate agency chain in the United Kingdom. During 2002, the group acquired trekroner forsikring in Denmark.

Primary SIC and add'l.: 6321 6719 6311 6726 6331

CIK No: 0001126313

Subsidiaries: 1185215 Ontario Limited, 2763303 Canada Limited, 3342484 Canada Limited, 571721 Alberta Ltd, 721811 Ontario Inc., 788325 Ontario Inc, 800989 Ontario Inc, 815168 Ontario Inc., 821458 Ontario Inc, 859834 Ontario Inc, 924431 Ontario Inc, Agilerus Investment Management Limited, Agilon Financial Inc., Aktsam Forsakringskonsult AB, Allen & Harris (Newbury) Limited 281 Subsidiaries included in the Index

Officers: Paul Whittaker/CEO - Emerging Markets, Andy Haste/Dir., Group Chief Executive, George Culmer/Dir., CFO, Bridget McIntyre/Dir., UK Chief Executive, Neil MacMillan/Group Dir. - Audit, Risk, Mark Chambers/General Counsel, Group Company Sec., Tony Latham/Group Dir. - Global Relations, Simon Lee/Chief Executive - International Businesses, Orlagh Hunt/Group Dir. - Human Resources, Clare Salmon/Group Strategy, Marketing, Customer Dir., David Weymouth/Group Operations, Information Technology Dir., Shona Cotterill/Group Head - Investor Relations, Wendy Hardy/Investor Relations Advisor, Catherine Friedrich/Investor Relations Assist.

Directors: John Napier/Chmn., Bridget McIntyre/Dir., UK Chief Executive, Malcolm Le May/Dir., George Culmer/Dir., CFO, Noel Harwerth/Dir., John Maxwell/Dir., Edward Lea/Dir., Andy Haste/Dir., Group Chief Executive

Royal Ahold

Piet Heinkade 167 - 173, 1019 GM Amsterdam, Netherlands, 1507; **PH:** 31-0205095100; **Fax:** 31-0205095110; **http://** www.ahold.com; **Email:** ahold-human-resources@ahold.com

General		Stock	
Incorporation	Netherlands	Price on:12/24/2007	NA
Employees	NA	Stock Exchange	NA
Auditor	Deloitte Accountants B.V	Ticker Symbol	NA
Stk Agt	National City Bank Corp Trust Ops	Outstanding Shares	NA
Counsel	NA	E.P.S.	NA
DUNS No.	40-717-0315	Shareholders	NA

Business: The group's principal activity is to provide food primarily through retail trade outlets, along with complementary food service activities. As of dec 2002, the group operated or serviced 5,606 stores, including 790 franchise stores and 450 associated stores, with the majority of the franchise stores & associated stores located in the Netherlands. The store format primarily used by the group is the supermarket, along with operating or servicing hypermarkets, discount stores, specialty stores, cash and carry stores and convenience stores, operating primarily in Europe and the United States, with some operations in Latin America and Asia-Pacific. Some stores operated by the group include albert heijn, stop & shop, giant-landover and giant carlisle.

Primary SIC and add'l.: 2011 5921 6512 5411 5499 5441 5141

CIK No: 0000869425

Subsidiaries: Ahold Americas Holdings, Inc., Ahold Belgi N.V., Ahold Brazil B.V., Ahold Central Europe, s.r.o., Ahold Central Holdings, Inc., Ahold Coffee Company B.V., AHOLD Czech Republic, a.s., Ahold Finance Company N.V., Ahold Finance U.S.A., LLC, Ahold Financial Services, LLC, Ahold Information Services, Inc., Ahold Insurance N.V., Ahold Investment N.V., Ahold Lease U.S.A., Inc, Ahold Nederland B.V. 47 Subsidiaries included in the Index

Officers: Anders Moberg/58/CEO, Pres., Kenneth Bengtsson/Pres., CEO - ICA AB1, Johan Boeijenga/Pres., CEO - Albert, Hypernova, Bert Roetert/Pres., CEO - Schuitema NV, Luis Palha/CEO - Jeronimo Martins Retail1, Jose Alvarez/Pres., CEO - Stop, Shop, Giant, Landover, Carl Schlicker/Pres., CEO - Giant, Carlisle, Tops, Enrique Boerboom/Corp. Sec., Marielle Reints/Deputy Corp. Sec., Caro Bamforth/Dir. - Media Relations, Paul Aliker/59/Sr. VP, Chief Business Control Officer - Ahold, Peter Zoutendijk/GM - Gall, Barry F. Scher/VP - Public Affairs, Communications, Ahold USA, Ellen Van Den Haak/Mgr. - Digital Communications, Sjoerd Holleman/Analyst - Investor Relations *(30 Officers included in Index)*

Directors: Rene Dahan/67/Chmn. - Supervisory Board, Jan H.M. Hommen/65/Vice Chmn., Tom De Swaan/62/Vice Chmn. - Supervisory Board, Judith Sprieser/55/Member - Supervisory Board, Stephanie M. Shern/60/Member - Supervisory Board, Karen De Segundo/62/Member - Supervisory Board, Derk C. Doijer/59/Member - Supervisory Board, Myra Hart/68/Member - Supervisory Board

Royal Bancshares of Pennsylvania Inc

732 Montgomery Ave., Narberth, PA, 19072; **PH:** 1-610-668-4700; **Fax:** 1-610-668-1185; **http://** www.royalbankpa.com; **Email:** info@royalbankamerica.com

General		Stock	
Incorporation	PA	Price on:12/24/2007	$21.84
Employees	162	Stock Exchange	NDQ
Auditor	Beard Miller Co. LLP	Ticker Symbol	RBPAA
Stk Agt	StockTrans, Inc.	Outstanding Shares	13,410,000
Counsel	NA	E.P.S.	$1.44
DUNS No.	88-499-6356	Shareholders	NA

Business: The group's principal activity is to provide commercial banking services to individuals and corporate customers through sixteen banking offices. The group accepts demand deposits, money market deposit accounts, savings deposits, super now and time deposits. The group lends commercial loans, commercial mortgage loans, residential mortgage loans (including home equity lines of credit), construction loans, real estate tax liens and installment loans. The other services provided by the group include safe deposit boxes, collections, Internet banking and bill payment, drive-up, ATM and night depository facilities. The service areas of the group are montgomery, chester, bucks, Delaware, berks and philadelphia counties, southern New Jersey and Delaware in the vicinity of wilmington.

Primary SIC and add'l.: 6712 6022

CIK No: 0000922487

Subsidiaries: Crusader Servicing Corporation, Royal Bancshares Capital Trust I, Royal Bancshares Capital Trust II, Royal Bank America Leasing, LP, Royal Bank America., Royal Investments America, LLC, Royal Investments of Delaware, Inc., Royal Real Estate of Pennsylvania, Inc.

Officers: Joseph P. Campbell/Dir., CEO, Pres./$1,106,398.00, Linda Tabas Stempel/Dir. - Investor Relations, James J. McSwiggan/Dir., COO, Risk Assessment Officer/$661,499.00, George McDonough/52/Corp. Sec., Gregg J. Wagner/CFO

Directors: Joseph P. Campbell/Dir., CEO, Pres., Robert R. Tabas/Chmn., John M. Decker/Dir., Daniel M. Tabas/Dir., Edward R. Tepper/Dir., Howard Wurzak/Dir., Anthony J. Micale/Dir., Mitchell L. Morgan/Dir., Linda Tabas Stempel/Dir. - Investor Relations, Albert Ominsky/Dir., Carl M. Cousins/Dir., James J. McSwiggan/Dir., COO, Risk Assessment Officer, Gregory T. Reardon/Dir., Murray Stempel/Dir., Patrick J. McCormick/Dir. *(16 Directors included in Index)*

Owners: Linda Tabas Stempel/0.45%, Edward B. Tepper/0.32%, Richard Tabas, Howard Wurzak/0.82%, Evelyn R. Tabas, Daniel M. Tabas, Evelyn R. Tabas/14.44%, Mitchell L. Morgan/0.30%, George McDonough/0.07%, Anthony J. Micale/0.13%, James J. McSwiggan/0.58%, Joseph P. Campbell/1.89%, Daniel M. Tabas/32.78%, John M. Decker/0.60%, Richard Tabas *(27 Owners included in Index)*

Financial Data: *Fiscal Year End:*12/31 *Latest Annual Data:* 12/31/2006

Year	Sales	Net Income
2006	$104,977,000	$21,568,000
2005	$101,286,000	$32,053,000
2004	$80,701,000	$20,033,000

Curr. Assets:	$98,930,000	Curr. Liab.:	$870,111,000	P/E Ratio:	14.96
Plant, Equip.:	$50,280,000	Total Liab.:	$1,189,907,000	Indic. Yr. Divd.:	$1.150
Total Assets:	$1,356,311,000	Net Worth:	$163,254,000	Debt/ Equity:	1.4848

Royal Bank of Canada

1 Liberty Plz., New York, NY, 10006; **PH:** 1-212-858-7100; **Fax:** 1-212-428-2329; **http://** www.rbc.com

General		Stock	
Incorporation	Canada	Price on:12/24/2007	$52.96
Employees	70,000	Stock Exchange	NYSE
Auditor	Deloitte & Touche LLP	Ticker Symbol	RY
Stk Agt	Computershare Trust Co of Canada	Outstanding Shares	1,280,000,000
Counsel	NA	E.P.S.	$4.23
DUNS No.	24-828-6577	Shareholders	NA

Business: The group's principle activities are to provide banking services and other financial services. Financial services include deposit accounts, investments and mutual funds, financial planning and advice, credit and debit cards, business and personal loans and residential and commercial mortgages. The group also provides insurance services which include a wide range of creditor, life, health, travel, home, auto and reinsurance products and services. These services are provided to individuals, small and medium-sized businesses and mid market commercial clients in Canada, the U.S., the Caribbean and the bahamas.

Primary SIC and add'l.: 6021 8741 6211 6411

CIK No: 0001000275

Subsidiaries: 4111494 Canada Inc., 4145348 Canada Corp., 4145356 Canada Ltd., 6024530 Canada Inc., Business Mens Assurance Company of America, CBRM, Inc., Church Street Management, Inc., Conlark Inc., Finance Corporation of Bahamas Limited, Investment Holdings (Cayman) Limited, Liberty Life Insurance Company, Prism Financial Corporation, R.B.C. Holdings (Bahamas) Limited, RBC Action Direct Inc., RBC Alternative Assets, Inc. 62 Subsidiaries included in the Index

Officers: Gordon M. Nixon/Dir., CEO, Pres., William W. Moriarty/Vice Chmn., Head - Global Research Division, Doug McGregor/Co - Pres., MD, Head - Global Investment Banking, Equity Markets, Kirby Gavelin/MD, Head - Equity Capital Markets, Mark Hughes/MD, Head - Global Credit, Bruce MacDonald/Head - Wholesale Global Technology, Operations, Troy Maxwell/MD, CFO, Adrian Bell/MD, Head - International Bonds, John W. Burbidge/MD, COO - Europe, Asia, Bryan B.K. Osmar/MD, Richard V. Pilosof/MD, Head - Global Debt Markets, Mark Standish/Co - Pres., MD, Head - Global Markets, Anne Sutherland/MD, Head - National Client Group, Richard Tavoso/MD - Global Arbitrage, Trading, Jackie Braden/Contact - Media Relation, Corporate Communication *(48 Officers included in Index)*

Directors: Gordon M. Nixon/Dir., CEO, Pres., David P. O'Brien/Chmn., Jamie R. Anderson/Dep. Chmn., Michael Norris/Dep. Chmn., Bruce Rothney/Dep. Chmn., Jean Pierre Ouellet/Vice Chmn., Andrew G. Scace/Vice Chmn., Wm. G. Sembo/Vice Chmn., William W. Moriarty/Vice Chmn., Head - Global Research Division, Michael H. McCain/Dir., Jacques Lamarre/Dir., Brandt C. Louie/Dir., Robert B. Peterson/70/Dir., Pedro J. Reinhard/Dir., Kathleen P. Taylor/Dir. *(23 Directors included in Index)*

Owners: John M. Plunk, Ray W. Barnes, Edgar W. Welden, Dan M. David, William Britt Sexton/1.00%, James R. Thompson, Bobby A. Bradley, John D. Johns, Drayton Nabers, Stancil W. Starnes, William D. Montgomery, Insiders/17.30%, John J. McMahon/3.30%, Phillip C. McWane/6.20%, Richard Murray *(19 Owners included in Index)*

Financial Data: *Fiscal Year End:*10/31 *Latest Annual Data:* 10/31/2006

Year	Sales	Net Income
2006	$32,162,954,000	$4,212,548,000
2005	$24,995,490,000	$2,970,249,000
2004	$20,206,454,000	$2,330,535,000

Curr. Assets:	$394,639,000	Curr. Liab.:	$79,849,000	P/E Ratio:	24.83
Plant, Equip.:	$15,673,000	Total Liab.:	$92,633,000	Indic. Yr. Divd.:	$2.070
Total Assets:	$676,630,000	Net Worth:	$583,997,000	Debt/ Equity:	NA

Royal Bank of Scotland Group Plc (The)

1 Citizens Plz., Providence, RI, 02903; **PH:** 1-401-456-7000; **Fax:** 1-401-456-7819; **http://** www.rbs.com; **Email:** economics@rbs.co.uk

General		Stock	
Incorporation	UK	Price on:12/24/2007	$24.26
Employees	NA	Stock Exchange	NYSE
Auditor	Deloitte & Touche LLP	Ticker Symbol	RBS-PP
Stk Agt	NA	Outstanding Shares	NA
Counsel	NA	E.P.S.	NA
DUNS No.	21-451-3087	Shareholders	NA

Business: The group's principal activities are retail banking, insurance and other financial services which includes leasing, installment financing, hire purchase, custody, credit card, confirming house, factoring, invoice discounting, provision of mezzanine finance and provision of development capital. In addition to the provision of a full range of banking services under the the royal bank of Scotland and natwest brands, the enlarged group also includes a number of other major financial services brands: direct line: one of the UK's private motor insurers and a leader in the delivery of financial services; citizens

financial group: based in Rhode Island usa-the second largest bank in new England; ulster bank: based in northern Ireland and with a strong position in the republic of Ireland; and coutts group: the international private banking and manages the wealth of 70,000 high net worth clients from 38 offices around the world.

Primary SIC and add'l.: 6331 6211 6021 6159

CIK No: 0000844150

Subsidiaries: Citizens Financial Group, Inc., Coutts & Co, Greenwich Capital Markets, Inc., National Westminster Bank Plc, RBS Insurance Group Limited, Ulster Bank Limited

Officers: Monica McCormack/Mgr. - Media Relations, Tesco Personal Finance, Debbie Milsom/Public Relations Mgr. - One Accounting, First Active Mortgages, Britain, Rob Davies/Media Relations Consultant, The One Accounting, First Active Mortgages, Britain, Julie Hurcomb/Head - Corporate Marketing, Nick Gill/Mgr. - Media Relations, Coutts Group, Claire Lilley/Mgr. - Communications, RBS International, Vicki Hudson/Assist. Mgr. - RBS International, Annabelle Flambard/Assist. Mgr. - Communications, RBS International, Shaun Gamble/Mgr. - Media Relations, Corporate Markets, Ila Kotecha/Mgr. - Media Relations, Corporate Markets, Peter Ward/Sr. VP, Head - Corporate Communications, RBS Greenwich Capital, Emmanuel Prado/CM - France, Corporate Markets, Europe, Raffaella Parapetti/CM - Italy, Christine Kortyka/CM - Germany, Olivia De La Lama/CM - Spain *(60 Officers included in Index)*

Directors: Tom McKillop/64/Chmn., Joe MacHale/56/Non - Exec. Dir., Fred Goodwin/49/Exec. Dir., Guy Whittaker/51/Exec. Dir., Group Dir. - Finance, Lawrence Fish/63/Exec. Dir., Gordon Pell/58/Exec. Dir., Chief Exec. - Retail Markets, Steve Robson/64/Non - Exec. Dir., Peter Sutherland/61/Non - Exec. Dir., Johnny Cameron/53/Exec. Dir., Chief Exec. - Corporate Markets, Mark Fisher/47/Exec. Dir., Chief Exec. - Manufacturing, Colin Buchan/53/Non - Exec. Dir., Jim Currie/66/Non - Exec. Dir., Bill Friedrich/59/Non - Exec. Dir., Archie Hunter/64/Non - Exec. Dir., Charles Koch/61/Non - Exec. Dir. *(17 Directors included in Index)*

Curr. Assets:	$22,749,069,000	***Curr. Liab.:***	$1,139,218,610,000		
Plant, Equip.:	$34,540,892,000	***Total Liab.:***	$1,628,413,716,000	***Indic. Yr. Divd.:***	NA
Total Assets:	$1,706,928,566,000	***Net Worth:***	$78,514,851,000	***Debt/ Equity:***	NA

Royal Bodycare Inc

2301 Crown Ct., Irving, TX, 75038; ***PH:*** 1-972-893-4000; ***http://*** www.rbcnow.com

General - Incorporation	NV	***Stock***- Price on:12/24/2007	$0.69
Employees	70	Stock Exchange	OTC
Auditor	Lane Gorman Trubitt LLP	Ticker Symbol	RBCL
Stk Agt	Fidelity Transfer Co	Outstanding Shares	20,190,000
Counsel	Gardere, Wynne Sewell LLP	E.P.S.	$0.04
DUNS No.	13-003-5017	Shareholders	NA

Business: The group's principal activity is to market nutritional supplements and personal care products. The products include herbal formulas, vitamins, minerals, antioxidants, fitness, weight management programs and hair and skin products. All of these products are marketed under our royal bodycare trade name. These products are procured from unaffiliated manufacturers and suppliers and are manufactured according to the company's specifications. The trademarks of the group include royal bodycare(R) and the names of certain key products such as microhydrin(r). The group operates in domestic as well as foreign markets.

Primary SIC and add'l.: 5122

CIK No: 0000830052

Subsidiaries: BizAdigm, Inc., MPM Medical, Inc., RBC Life Sciences Canada, Inc., RBC Life Sciences Korea Co., Ltd., RBC Life Sciences USA, Inc.

Officers: Clinton Howard/CEO, Chmn. - Scientific Advisor/$375,351.00, Wayne R. Holbrook/53/Dir., Pres./$320,623.00, Trevor Scofield/VP - International Operations, Dennis N. Windsor/48/VP - Sales, Marketing/$205,618.00, Steven E. Brown/VP - Dir., CFO/$225,632.00, Kenneth L. Sabot/62/Dir., Sr. VP - Operations/$238,215.00, Don Clark/CIO, Jerry Lee Phelps/VP - Science, Technology, Scientific Advisor, Albert Zehr/Scientific Advisor, Leonard Smith/Scientific Advisor, Kimberly Purdy Lloyd/Scientific Advisor, Debi Drake/Scientific Advisor, Carolyn Marocco/Scientific Advisor

Directors: Clinton Howard/CEO, Chmn. - Scientific Advisor, Wayne R. Holbrook/53/Dir., Pres., Joseph P. Philipp/58/Dir., Ike J. Guest/69/Dir., Kenneth L. Sabot/62/Dir., Sr. VP - Operations, Paul R. Miller/66/Dir.

Owners: Insiders, Ike J. Guest, Dennis N. Windsor, Steven E. Brown, Clinton H. Howard, Wayne R. Holbrook, My Garden, Ltd., Kenneth L. Sabot, Leonid Lapp, Joseph P. Philipp

Financial Data: ***Fiscal Year End:***12/31 ***Latest Annual Data:*** 12/31/2006

Year	***Sales***	***Net Income***
2006	$21,697,000	$436,000
2005	$19,361,000	$592,000
2004	$18,266,000	$537,000

Curr. Assets:	$6,933,000	***Curr. Liab.:***	$4,999,000		
Plant, Equip.:	$3,584,000	***Total Liab.:***	$8,033,000	***Indic. Yr. Divd.:***	NA
Total Assets:	$13,515,000	***Net Worth:***	$5,483,000	***Debt/ Equity:***	0.4639

Royal Caribbean Cruises Ltd

1050 Caribbean Way, Miami, FL, 33132; ***PH:*** 1-305-539-6000; ***Fax:*** 1-305-539-0562; ***http://*** www.royalcaribbean.com

General - Incorporation	Liberia	***Stock***- Price on:12/24/2007	$41.19
Employees	42,271	Stock Exchange	NYSE
Auditor	PricewaterhouseCoopers LLP	Ticker Symbol	RCL
Stk Agt	Wachovia Bank N.A	Outstanding Shares	212,460,000
Counsel	Bradley Stein	E.P.S.	$2.49
DUNS No.	07-699-3526	Shareholders	NA

Business: The group's principal activity is to offer shipboard services and amenities. The group operates two brands, celebrity cruises and royal Caribbean international. The celebrity cruises primarily serves the premium segment. It operates through ten cruise ships with 16,454 berths and offers various cruise itineraries that range from 2 to 16 nights. The royal Caribbean international serves the volume cruise vacation sector that is categorized as the contemporary and premium segment. It operates through 18 cruise ships with 41,994 berths, offering various cruise itineraries that range from 2 to 14 nights and call on destinations throughout the world. The ships operate worldwide and call on destinations in Alaska, the bahamas, the baltic, Bermuda, California, Canada, the Caribbean, Europe, the galapagos islands, Hawaii, Mexico, new England, the panama canal, scandinavia and South America.

Primary SIC and add'l.: 4481

CIK No: 0000884887

Subsidiaries: Adventure of the Seas Inc., Blue Sapphire Marine Inc., Cape Liberty Cruise Port LLC, Celebrity Cruise Lines Inc., Celebrity Cruises Holdings Inc., Celebrity Cruises Inc., Constellation Inc., Cruise Mar Investment Inc., Cruise Mar Shipping Holdings Ltd., doing business as Celebrity Cruises, Enchantment of the Seas Inc., Esker Marine Shipping Inc., Explorer of the Seas Inc., Fantasia Cruising Inc., Galapagos Cruises Inc. 43 Subsidiaries included in the Index

Officers: Richard D. Fain/59/Chmn., CEO - Royal Caribbean Cruises Ltd/$5,963,419.00, Lyan Sierra-Caro/Acct Executive, Corporate Communications, Adam M. Goldstein/Pres. - Royal Caribbean International/$2,014,676.00, Brian Rice/CFO, Exec. VP/$1,745,012.00, Harri Kulovaara/Exec. VP - Maritime/$1,318,531.00, Craig Milan/Pres. - Royal Celebrity Tours, Susan Hooper/Sr. VP, MD - Europe, Middle East, Africa, Lisa Bauer/Sr. VP - North American Sales, Royal Caribbean International, Alice Norsworthy/Sr. VP - Marketing, Royal Caribbean International, Michael Bayley/Sr. VP - Hotel Operations, Royal Caribbean International, William Wright/Sr. VP - Marine Operations, Royal Caribbean International, Mike Sutten/CIO, Bradley H. Stein/Sec.

Directors: Richard D. Fain/59/Chmn., CEO - Royal Caribbean Cruises Ltd, Arne Alexander Wilhelmsen/42/Dir., Bernard W. Aronson/61/Dir., Arvid Grundekjoen/52/Dir., William L. Kimsey/65/Dir., Laura Laviada/57/Dir., Gert W. Munthe/51/Dir., Eyal Ofer/57/Dir., Thomas J. Pritzker/57/Dir., William K. Reilly/68/Dir., Bernt Reitan/60/Dir.

Owners: Bernard W. Aronson, Thomas J. Pritzker, Insiders, Eyal Ofer, Laura Làviada, Harri U. Kulovaara, Osiris Holdings Inc., William L. Kimsey, Daniel J. Hanrahan, A. Wilhelmsen AS, William K. Reilly, Arne Alexander Wilhelmsen, Barclays Global Investors, NA, Arvid Grundekjoen, Cruise Associates *(21 Owners included in Index)*

Financial Data: ***Fiscal Year End:***12/31 ***Latest Annual Data:*** 12/31/2006

Year	***Sales***	***Net Income***
2006	$5,229,584,000	$633,922,000
2005	$4,903,174,000	$715,956,000
2004	$4,555,375,000	$474,691,000

Curr. Assets:	$501,904,000	***Curr. Liab.:***	$1,872,368,000	***P/E Ratio:***	16.54
Plant, Equip.:	$11,429,106,000	***Total Liab.:***	$7,301,513,000	***Indic. Yr. Divd.:***	$0.600
Total Assets:	$13,393,088,000	***Net Worth:***	$6,091,575,000	***Debt/ Equity:***	0.7949

Royal Financial Inc

9226 S Commercial Ave., Chicago, IL, 60617; ***PH:*** 1-773-768-4800; ***http://*** www.royalsavingsbank.com

General - Incorporation	DE	***Stock***- Price on:12/24/2007	$15.95
Employees	47	Stock Exchange	OTC
Auditor	Crowe, Chizek and Company LLC	Ticker Symbol	RYFL
Stk Agt	Registrar & Transfer Co	Outstanding Shares	2,570,000
Counsel	NA	E.P.S.	NA
DUNS No.	NA	Shareholders	NA

Business: The group operates through its subsidiaries whose principle activities include operating as a capitalized and profitable community savings bank dedicated to providing quality customer service. The services of the group include commercial loan products, such as commercial real estate loans, multi family real estate loans, and to a lesser extent, commercial loans. The group operates from the United States. The group's quarterly revenue for Jun '07 was 4.28 millions of USD.

Primary SIC and add'l.: 6036

CIK No: 0001303531

Subsidiaries: Royal Savings Bank

Owners: PL Capital Group/9.70%, Andrew Morua, Donald A. Moll/2.20%, John T. Dempsey, James A. Fitch, Leonard Szwajkowski, Royal Financial, Inc. Employee Stock Ownership Plan Trust/8.20%, Insiders/7.50%, Rodolfo Serna, Peter C. Rolewicz, Alan W. Bird/1.60%, Barbara K. Minster/1.20%, Philip J. Timyan/9.10%

Curr. Assets:	$21,905,000	***Curr. Liab.:***	$99,430,000		
Plant, Equip.:	$5,934,000	***Total Liab.:***	$100,970,000	***Indic. Yr. Divd.:***	NA
Total Assets:	$132,632,000	***Net Worth:***	$31,662,000	***Debt/ Equity:***	NA

Royal Gold Inc

1660 Wynkoop St., Ste. 1000, Denver, CO, 80202; ***PH:*** 1-303-573-1660; ***Fax:*** 1-303-595-9385; ***http://*** www.royalgold.com; ***Email:*** info@royalgold.com

General - Incorporation	DE	***Stock***- Price on:12/24/2007	$24.77
Employees	13	Stock Exchange	NDQ
Auditor	PricewaterhouseCoopers LLP	Ticker Symbol	RGLD
Stk Agt	Computershare Trust Co	Outstanding Shares	28,610,000
Counsel	Hogan & Hartson LLP	E.P.S.	NA
DUNS No.	04-268-8416	Shareholders	NA

Business: The group's principal activity is to acquire and manage precious metals royalties. The group seeks to acquire existing royalties or to finance projects that are in production or near production in exchange for royalty interests. The group also explores and develops properties that may contain precious metals and obtains royalty and other interests upon transferring the operating interests to other mining companies. Its principal mineral property interests are royalties over the mining complex that includes the pipeline and south pipeline gold mines operated by the cortez joint venture. The group owns a royalty on all of the properties held by yamana resources, inc. In santa cruz province, Argentina, a portion of the mule canyon mine operated by newmont mining corporation and an exploration-stage project in Nevada. In fiscal 2003, the group acquired high desert mineral resources.

Primary SIC and add'l.: 1041

CIK No: 0000085535

Subsidiaries: Calgom Mining, Inc., Denver Mining Finance Company, Environmental Strategies, Inc., Greek American Exploration Ltd., High Desert Mineral Resources, Inc., Mono County Mining Company, RG Russia, Inc., Royal Camp Bird, Inc., Royal Crescent Valley, Inc., Royal Gold Pty, Ltd., Royal Kanaka Creek Corporation, Royal Trading Company, Sofia Minerals Ltd.

Officers: Tony Jensen/CEO, Pres., Stanley Dempsey/Executive Chmn., Stefan L. Wenger/CFO, Karen P. Gross/VP, Corp. Sec., William Heissenbuttel/VP - Corporate Development, Bruce Kirchhoff/General Counsel

Directors: Stanley Dempsey/Executive Chmn., John W. Goth/Dir., Oden S. Howell/Dir., Merritt E. Marcus/Dir., James W. Stuckert/Dir., Donald Worth/Dir., Craig M. Haase/Dir.

Owners: Karen P. Gross, Stanley Dempsey/2.40%, Craig M. Haase, John W. Goth, Donald Worth, Stefan L. Wenger, FMR Corp./6.70%, Insiders/13.67%, James W. Stuckert/6.20%, Oden S. Howell/1.90%, Merritt E. Marcus/1.30%, William Heissenbuttel, Tony Jensen

Financial Data: ***Fiscal Year End:***06/30 ***Latest Annual Data:*** 6/30/2006

Year	Sales	Net Income
2006	$28,380,000	$11,350,000
2005	$25,302,000	$11,454,000
2004	$21,353,000	$8,872,000

Curr. Assets:	$84,776,000	Curr. Liab.:	$3,324,000		
Plant, Equip.:	NA	Total Liab.:	$10,601,000	Indic. Yr. Divd.:	$0.260
Total Assets:	$172,260,000	Net Worth:	$161,660,000	Debt/ Equity:	0.3948

Royal Group Inc

Formerly: Royal Group Technologies Ltd
1 Royal Gate Blvd., Woodbridge, ON, L4L 8Z7; *PH:* 1-905-264-0701;
http:// www.royalgrouptech.com

General - Incorporation	Canada	Stock - Price on:12/24/2007	$13.08
Employees	NA	Stock Exchange	NA
Auditor	KPMG LLP	Ticker Symbol	NA
Stk Agt	Computershare Trust Co	Outstanding Shares	NA
Counsel	Davies, Ward, Phillips & Vineberg LLP	E.P.S.	NA
DUNS No.	20-557-3363	Shareholders	NA

Business: The group's principle activity is to provide extrusion of polyvinyl chloride building products; the product segment includes custom (window) profiles, exterior cladding, outdoor products, window coverings and pipe fittings. The support segment prodives materials, machinery, and distibution, R&D and property management services primarily for the products segment. Effective December 2004 the company changed its fiscal year end from September to December. The group operates from United States.

Primary SIC and add'l.: 3084 3088 3089
CIK No: 0001047693
Subsidiaries: VinylTech, Inc.

Royal Invest International Corp

Formerly: BusinessWay International Corp
1350 Ave. Of The Americas, 24th Fl, New York, NY, 10019; *PH:* 1-203-557-3845;
http:// www.businessway.com

General - Incorporation	DE	Stock - Price on:12/24/2007	NA
Employees	NA	Stock Exchange	OTC
Auditor	Meyler & Co. LLC	Ticker Symbol	RIIC
Stk Agt	Interwest Transfer Company, Inc.	Outstanding Shares	NA
Counsel	NA	E.P.S.	-$0.14
DUNS No.	NA	Shareholders	NA

Business: The group's principal activities are to manufacture and distributing the cor-bit line of computers. The group operates in three divisions, the personal computers manufacturing, retail store operations and franchising and business-to-business Internet software programming and b2b research and development. The personal computers manufacturing and assembler division operated by cor-bit peripherals inc sells personal computers to businesswy's independent franchise retail stores operations. The Internet software research development (b2b) manufacture and developed an Internet-based software, business-to-business model, data base search software and an access-based inventory management software link.

Primary SIC and add'l.: 3571 7372 5045
CIK No: 0001079574
Subsidiaries: 3423336 Canada Ltd., Puritan Securities, Inc.
Officers: Jerry Gruenbaum/Chmn., CEO, Nathan Lapkin/Dir., Pres.
Directors: Jerry Gruenbaum/Chmn., CEO, Nathan Lapkin/Dir., Pres.
Owners: Jerry Gruenbaum, Muermans Vast Goed Roermond BV, Grassy Knoll Associates, LLC, Fabrice Zambito, Pinnacle Associates, LLC, Amstel Holdings BV Ltd, Nathan Lapkin
Financial Data: Fiscal Year End: 07/31 *Latest Annual Data:* 07/31/2005

Year	Sales	Net Income
2005	$25,000	-$374,000
2004	NA	-$248,000

Curr. Assets:	NA	Curr. Liab.:	$380,000		
Plant, Equip.:	NA	Total Liab.:	$380,000	Indic. Yr. Divd.:	NA
Total Assets:	NA	Net Worth:	-$380,000	Debt/ Equity:	NA

Royal KPN N.V.

494 8th Ave., 23rd Fl., New York, NY, 10001; *PH:* 1-212-560-9898; *Fax:* 1-212-560-0770;
http:// www.kpn.com

General - Incorporation		Stock - Price on:12/24/2007	$16.75
Employees	NA	Stock Exchange	NYSE
Auditor	NA	Ticker Symbol	KPN
Stk Agt	Morgan ADR Service Center	Outstanding Shares	NA
Counsel	NA	E.P.S.	$1.14
DUNS No.	NA	Shareholders	NA

Business: The groups principle activity is to provide technology services. The groups services include mobile telephony, internet and TV services. The group operates through four segments namely, voice, connectivity, integrated and managed solutions, and EnterCom. The group operates from the Netherlands.

Primary SIC and add'l.: 4813
CIK No: 0001001474
Subsidiaries: BASE N.V./S.A., E-Plus Mobilfunk GmbH & Co.KG, Infonet Nederland B.V., KPN B.V., KPN Consumer Internet and Media Services B.V., KPN EuroRings B.V., KPN HotSpots B.V., KPN Mobile Holding B.V., KPN Mobile International B.V., KPN Mobile N.V., KPN Telecom Retail B.V., KPN Telecommerce B.V., Sympac B.V., Telfort B.V., XS4ALL Holding B.V.
Officers: A. J. Scheepbouwer/64/Chmn., CEO, M.h M. Smits/47/Dir., CFO, Stan P. Miller/50/Dir., MD - Mobile International, Baptiest Coopmans/43/Dir.t, MD - Consumer Marketing, Eric Hageman/Dir. Head - Investor Relations, Frank Theunis/Investor Relations Officer, Wouter Ligteringen/Investor Relations Officer, Martijn Meijering/Investor Relations Analyst, Christiaan Schieven/Investor Relations Analyst

Directors: A. J. Scheepbouwer/64/Chmn., CEO, A. H.J. Risseeuw/72/Chmn. - Supervisory Board, D. G. Eustace/72/Vice Chmn. - Supervisory Board, D. I. Jager/65/Member - Supervisory Board, Baptiest Coopmans/43/Dir.t, MD - Consumer Marketing, M.h M. Smits/47/Dir., CFO, Eelco Blok/51/Dir., Stan P. Miller/50/Dir., MD - Mobile International, J. B.M. Streppel/59/Member - Supervisory Board, M. Bischoff/66/Member - Supervisory Board, Ir M.E. Van Lier Lels/49/Member - Supervisory Board, C. M. Colijn-Hooijmans/Member - Supervisory Board
Owners: M.H. M. Smits, E. Blok, D. I. Jager, H. J. Risseeuw, A. J. Scheepbouwer
Financial Data: Fiscal Year End: 12/31 *Latest Annual Data:* 12/31/2006

Year	Sales	Net Income
2006	$15,918,857,000	$2,071,551,000
2005	$14,136,998,000	$1,627,366,000
2004	$16,511,969,000	$2,836,588,000

Curr. Assets:	$4,037,477,000	Curr. Liab.:	$5,081,835,000	P/E Ratio:	13.24
Plant, Equip.:	$10,060,686,000	Total Liab.:	$22,154,634,000	Indic. Yr. Divd.:	$0.600
Total Assets:	$28,473,590,000	Net Worth:	$6,318,956,000	Debt/ Equity:	NA

Royal Quantum Group Inc

251 MidPk. Blvd. SE , Ste.145, Calgary, AB, T2X 1S3; *PH:* 1-403-288-4321; *Fax:* 1-403-201-5792;
http:// www.royalquantum.com

General - Incorporation		Stock - Price on:12/24/2007	$0.29
Employees	NA	Stock Exchange	OTC
Auditor	NA	Ticker Symbol	RYQG
Stk Agt	Pacific Stock Transfer Company	Outstanding Shares	38,260,000
Counsel	NA	E.P.S.	NA
DUNS No.	NA	Shareholders	NA

Business: The groups principal activity committed to the acquisition and development of small to medium size businesses. The group operates from the United States.

Primary SIC and add'l.: 7389
CIK No:
Officers: Ron Ruskowsky/Dir., CEO, CFO, Pres., Roger Janssen/Dir., VP, Corp. Sec., Phil Van Angeren/Dir., Exploration Mgr.
Directors: Ron Ruskowsky/Dir., CEO, CFO, Pres., Roger Janssen/Dir., VP, Corp. Sec., Phil Van Angeren/Dir., Exploration Mgr.
Financial Data: Fiscal Year End: NA *Latest Annual Data:* 12/31/2006

Year	Sales	Net Income
2006	NA	-$399,000
2005	NA	-$169,000
2004	$34,000	-$1,786,000

Curr. Assets:	$0	Curr. Liab.:	$426,000		
Plant, Equip.:	$2,000	Total Liab.:	$459,000	Indic. Yr. Divd.:	NA
Total Assets:	$2,000	Net Worth:	-$457,000	Debt/ Equity:	NA

Royal Standard Minerals Inc

1 Main St., Manhattan, NV, 89022; *PH:* 1-604-662-8184; *http://* www.royal-standard.com;
Email: info@royal-standard.com

General - Incorporation	Canada	Stock - Price on:12/24/2007	$0.58
Employees	NA	Stock Exchange	OTC
Auditor	McCarney Greenwood LLP	Ticker Symbol	RYSMF
Stk Agt	Computer share & Trust Co.	Outstanding Shares	78,280,000
Counsel	Gary Sugar	E.P.S.	-$0.053
DUNS No.	NA	Shareholders	NA

Business: The group's principle activities include acquiring and exploring gold and precious metals. The group operates from United States.

Primary SIC and add'l.: 1041
CIK No: 0001027162
Subsidiaries: Investment Group Inc., Manhattan Mining Co, Pinon Exploration Corporation, Sharpe Resources Corporation, Southeastern Resources Inc, Standard Energy Inc.
Officers: Roland M. Larsen/Dir., CEO, Pres., Kimberly R. Koerner/Dir., Treasurer, Samuel Gulko/CFO
Directors: Roland M. Larsen/Dir., CEO, Pres., Mackenzie I. Watson/Dir., James C. Dunlop/Dir., Kimberly R. Koerner/Dir., Treasurer, Edward G. Thompson/Member - Advisory Board, Robert N. Granger/Member - Advisory Board, John D. Harvey/Member - Advisory Board
Owners: Kimberly L. Koerner, Roland M. Larsen, Sprott Asset Management/16.90%, Mackenzie I. Watson
Financial Data: Fiscal Year End: 01/31 *Latest Annual Data:* 01/31/2007

Year	Sales	Net Income
2007	NA	-$8,454,000
2006	NA	-$1,611,000
2005	$19,000	-$9,416,000

Curr. Assets:	$1,445,000	Curr. Liab.:	$222,000		
Plant, Equip.:	$5,070,000	Total Liab.:	$354,000	Indic. Yr. Divd.:	NA
Total Assets:	$6,646,000	Net Worth:	$6,293,000	Debt/ Equity:	NA

Royale Energy Inc

7676 Hazard Ctr. Dr., Ste. 1500, San Diego, CA, 92108; *PH:* 1-619-881-2800; *Fax:* 1-619-881-2899;
http:// www.royl.com; *Email:* ir@royl.com

General - Incorporation	CA	Stock - Price on:12/24/2007	$3.99
Employees	30	Stock Exchange	NDQ
Auditor	Sprouse & Anderson LLP	Ticker Symbol	ROYL
Stk Agt	Computershare Trust Co	Outstanding Shares	7,920,000
Counsel	Sheinfeld, Maley & Kay	E.P.S.	-$0.54
DUNS No.	11-858-8888	Shareholders	NA

Business: The group's principal activity is to produce and market oil and natural gas. The group operates in two operating segments: turnkey drilling services and oil and gas exploration. The group acquires oil and gas lease interests, proved reserves and provides drilling services for both exploratory and development wells. The group owns wells and leases in major geological basins located mainly in California.

Primary SIC and add'l.: 1381 1311

CIK No: 0000864839

Officers: Donald H. Hosmer/Dir., CEO, Pres., Co - Founder, Chanda Idano/Dir. - Marketing, Public Relations, Ronald Lipnick/Controller, Stephen M. Hosmer/CFO, Exec. VP, Sec., Steven Heraty/Dir. - Investor Relations, William G. Donaldson/Chief Engineer, Mohamed Abdel-Rahman/Chief Geologist

Directors: Donald H. Hosmer/Dir., CEO, Pres., Co - Founder, Harry E. Hosmer/Chmn., George M. Watters/Dir., Len Kemp/Dir., Oscar Hildebrandt/Dir., Gilbert C.L. Kemp/74/Dir., Gary Grinsfelder/Dir., Tony Hall/Dir.

Owners: Stephen M. Hosmer/14.71%, George M. Watters, Donald H. Hosmer/12.51%, Harry E. Hosmer/9.93%, Gilbert C. L. Kemp, Insiders/41.32%, Oscar A. Hildebrandt

Financial Data: **Fiscal Year End:** 12/31 **Latest Annual Data:** 12/31/2006

Year	Sales	Net Income
2006	$24,896,000	-$2,650,000
2005	$25,643,000	$1,186,000
2004	$25,944,000	$2,193,000

Curr. Assets:	$13,182,000	**Curr. Liab.:**	$12,410,000		
Plant, Equip.:	$20,526,000	**Total Liab.:**	$18,167,000	**Indic. Yr. Divd.:**	$0.050
Total Assets:	$33,715,000	**Net Worth:**	$15,548,000	**Debt/ Equity:**	0.1229

Royalite Petroleum Co Inc

Formerly: Worldbid Corp

810 Peace Portal Dr., Ste. 201, Blaine, WA, 78733; *PH:* 1-360-201-0400; *http://* www.worldbid.com

General		**Stock**	
Incorporation	NV	Price on:12/24/2007	NA
Employees	NA	Stock Exchange	OTC
Auditor	Sarna & Co.	Ticker Symbol	RYPE
Stk Agt	Pacific Stock Transfer Company	Outstanding Shares	NA
Counsel	O'Neill & CompanyGary Dunn	E.P.S.	NA
DUNS No.	NA	Shareholders	NA

Business: The group's principal activity is to provide electronic commerce via the Internet through an online Website. The activities of the group are carried out by worldbid Canada corporation. The group owns and operates an international business-to-business and government-to-business facilitation service. The services of the group combines proprietary software with the power of the Internet to bring buyers and sellers together from around the world for interactive trade. It has designed worldbid.com Internet Web site to enable companies throughout the world to procure, source or buy and tender or sell products and services nationally and internationally.

Primary SIC and add'l.: 7372 7375 7389

CIK No: 0001080399

Subsidiaries: Worldbid Canada Corporation

Officers: Michael L. Cass/54/Dir., CEO, Pres., Gary Dunn/Corporate Lawyer, Intellectual Property Rights, Internet Law, Howard Thomson/CFO, Treasurer, Dir., Paul Wagorn/Dir., COO

Directors: Michael L. Cass/54/Dir., CEO, Pres., William Charles Tao/49/Dir., Howard Thomson/CFO, Treasurer, Dir., Paul Wagorn/Dir., COO

Owners: William Charles Tao/1.10%, Michael L. Cass/8.10%, Logan Anderson/5.10%, Insiders/14.80%, US Global Investors Global Resources fund/6.10%, Ian K. Matheson/7.70%, Harold C. Moll/8.70%, Howard Thomson

RPC Inc

2801 Buford Hwy., Ste. 520, Atlanta, GA, 30329; *PH:* 1-404-321-2140; *Fax:* 1-404-321-5483; *http://* www.rpc.net; *Email:* irdept@rpc.net

General		**Stock**	
Incorporation	DE	Price on:12/24/2007	$16.7
Employees	2,000	Stock Exchange	NYSE
Auditor	Grant Thornton LLP	Ticker Symbol	RES
Stk Agt	Computershare Investor Services LLC	Outstanding Shares	97,910,000
Counsel	NA	E.P.S.	NA
DUNS No.	11-827-2517	Shareholders	NA

Business: The group's principal activity is to provide oilfield services and equipment to oil and gas companies engaged in the exploration, production and development of oil and gas properties. The services and equipment provided include snubbing services, coiled tubing services, pressure pumping services, nitrogen services, firefighting and well control, the rental of drill pipe and other specialized oilfield equipment, and marine services. The group operates through two business segments, namely technical services and support services. Technical services include group's oilfield service lines that utilize people and equipment to perform value-added completion, production and maintenance services. Support services include group's oilfield service lines that primarily provide equipment for customer use or services to assist customer operations. On 1-Apr-2003, the group acquired bronco oilfield services inc.

Primary SIC and add'l.: 1389 4226

CIK No: 0000742278

Subsidiaries: Bronco Oilfield Services, Inc., Cudd Pressure Control, Inc., Cudd Pumping Services, Inc., International Training Services, Inc., Patterson Services, Inc., Patterson Truck Line, Inc., RPC Crane Liquidation, LLC, RPC Energy de Mexico, RPC Energy International, Inc., RPC Energy Services (Chengdu) Ltd., RPC Energy Services of Canada, Ltd, RPC Investment Company, RPC Waste Management Services, Inc., Well Control School de Venezuela, SA

Officers: Richard A. Hubbell/63/Inside Dir., CEO, Pres./$1,649,790.00, Jim Landers/VP - Corporate Finance, Ben M. Palmer/47/CFO, VP, Treasurer/$632,120.00, Linda H. Graham/71/Inside Dir., VP, Sec./$320,320.00, Natasha Coleman/Investor Relations, Corporate Mgr. - Communications

Directors: Richard A. Hubbell/63/Inside Dir., CEO, Pres., Randall R. Rollins/76/Chmn., Linda H. Graham/71/Inside Dir., VP, Sec., James A. Lane/64/Outside Affiliated Dir., Wilton Looney/87/Dir., Gary W. Rollins/63/Dir., Henry B. Tippie/80/Dir., James B. Williams/74/Dir., Bill J. Dismuke/Dir.

Owners: Ben M. Palmer, Insiders/67.40%, Gary W. Rollins/62.00%, Richard A. Hubbell/1.50%, Linda H. Graham

Financial Data: **Fiscal Year End:** 12/31 **Latest Annual Data:** 12/31/2006

Year	Sales	Net Income
2006	$596,630,000	$110,794,000
2005	$427,643,000	$66,484,000
2004	$339,792,000	$34,773,000

Curr. Assets:	$182,254,000	**Curr. Liab.:**	$70,952,000	**P/E Ratio:**	14.40
Plant, Equip.:	$262,797,000	**Total Liab.:**	$139,020,000	**Indic. Yr. Divd.:**	$0.200
Total Assets:	$474,307,000	**Net Worth:**	$335,287,000	**Debt/ Equity:**	0.2211

RPM International Inc

2628 Pearl Rd., Medina, OH, 44258; *PH:* 1-330-273-5090; *Fax:* 1-330-225-8743; *http://* www.rpminc.com; *Email:* info@rpminc.com

General		**Stock**	
Incorporation	DE	Price on:12/24/2007	$23.05
Employees	9,213	Stock Exchange	NYSE
Auditor	Ernst & Young, LLP	Ticker Symbol	RPM
Stk Agt	National City Bank	Outstanding Shares	120,890,000
Counsel	Calfee, Halter & Griswold	E.P.S.	$1.69
DUNS No.	00-415-5651	Shareholders	NA

Business: The groups principle activity is to manufacture coatings, sealants and specialty chemicals for maintenance and improvement applications. The groups products include waterproofing products, fluorescent colorants and pigments and fiberglass reinforced plastic grating. The groups products are sold under various brand names including STONHARD, TREMCO and ZINSSER. The group operates through two business segments namely the consumer and industrial segment. The group operates from United States.

Primary SIC and add'l.: 2891 2851

CIK No: 0000110621

Subsidiaries: A/D Fire Protection Systems Corp., Agpro (N.Z.) Limited, American Emulsions Co., Inc., Bondex International, Inc., Bondo Corporation, BPAG, Inc., Carboline Company, Carboline Dubai Corporation, Carboline International Corporation, Chemical Coatings, Inc., Chemical Specialties Manufacturing Corporation, Chemrite Equipment Systems (Pty.) Ltd., DAP Holdings, LLC, DAP Products Inc., Day-Glo Color Corp. 79 Subsidiaries included in the Index

Officers: Frank C. Sullivan/CEO, Pres./$3,706,068.00, Keith R. Smiley/VP, Treasurer, Assist. Sec., Paul G. Hoogenboom/Sr. VP - Manufacturing, Operations, CIO/$1,320,296.00, Ronald A. Rice/COO, Exec. VP/$1,686,521.00, Lonny R. Dirusso/VP - Information Technology, Stephen J. Knoop/Sr. VP - Corporate Development, Matt Ratajczak/VP - Global Taxes, Robert L. Matejka/VP, Controller/$1,258,790.00, Kelly P. Tompkins/Exec. VP, Chief Administrative Officer/$1,712,493.00, Ernest Thomas/CFO, Sr. VP, Edward W. Moore/VP, General Counsel, Sec., Kathie M. Rogers/Mgr. - Investor Relations

Directors: Thomas C. Sullivan/Chmn., James A. Karman/Dir., Charles A. Ratner/Dir., Jerry Sue Thornton/Dir., Joseph P. Viviano/Dir., Frederick R. Nance/54/Dir., David A. Daberko/63/Dir., Edward B. Brandon/Dir., Donald K. Miller/Dir., William B. Summers/Dir., William A. Papenbrock/Dir., Max D. Amstutz/Dir., Bruce Carbonari/Dir.

Owners: Thomas C. Sullivan/0.20%, Charles A. Ratner, Insiders/2.10%, Joseph P. Viviano, Frank C. Sullivan/0.80%, William B. Summers, William A. Papenbrock, Barclays Global Investors, NA/5.30%, Donald K. Miller, Bruce A. Carbonari, Paul G. P. Hoogenboom/0.10%, Robert L. Matejka/0.20%, Ronald A. Rice/0.20%, Jerry Sue Thornton, Edward B. Brandon *(18 Owners included in Index)*

Financial Data: **Fiscal Year End:** 05/31 **Latest Annual Data:** 05/31/2007

Year	Sales	Net Income
2007	$3,338,764,000	$208,289,000
2006	$3,008,338,000	-$76,205,000
2005	$2,555,735,000	$105,032,000

Curr. Assets:	$1,369,218,000	**Curr. Liab.:**	$713,500,000	**P/E Ratio:**	14.05
Plant, Equip.:	$444,692,000	**Total Liab.:**	$2,054,277,000	**Indic. Yr. Divd.:**	$0.760
Total Assets:	$2,980,218,000	**Net Worth:**	$925,941,000	**Debt/ Equity:**	NA

RPM Technologies Inc

9981 W 190th St. , Ste. C, Mokena, IL, 60448; *PH:* 1-708-479-0057

General		**Stock**	
Incorporation	DE	Price on:12/24/2007	$0.17
Employees	NA	Stock Exchange	OTC
Auditor	Frank L. Sassetti & Co.	Ticker Symbol	RPMM
Stk Agt	Securities Transfer Corp	Outstanding Shares	NA
Counsel	NA	E.P.S.	NA
DUNS No.	NA	Shareholders	NA

Business: The groups principle activities include developing, producing through subcontract manufacturing, marketing and selling plastic pallets and other material handling products. Specific customers of the group include Toyota, Goodyear, Dow Chemical, Exxon Mobil, the United States Department of Defense, the National Guard, the United States Department of Forestry,Wm.Wrigley Jr. Company, Kraft and Sara Lee. The group operates from the United States, Canada and South America.

Primary SIC and add'l.: 3089 2448

CIK No: 0001099150

Owners: David Lade, Randy Zych/8.69%, Insiders/15.41%, Charles Foerg/7.48%

Financial Data: **Fiscal Year End:** 12/31 **Latest Annual Data:** 12/31/2006

Year	Sales	Net Income
2006	$2,928,000	-$1,596,000
2005	$2,862,000	-$1,046,000
2003	$1,492,000	-$711,000

Curr. Assets:	$1,725,000	**Curr. Liab.:**	$2,616,000		
Plant, Equip.:	$718,000	**Total Liab.:**	$4,561,000	**Indic. Yr. Divd.:**	NA
Total Assets:	$3,246,000	**Net Worth:**	-$1,315,000	**Debt/ Equity:**	NA

RRSat Global Communications Network Ltd

111 Brigham St., Ste. 15c, Hudson, MA, 01749; *PH:* 1-978-310-4054; *Fax:* 1-978-310-4056; *http://* www.rrsat.com; *Email:* info@rrsat.com

General		**Stock**	
Incorporation	Israel	Price on:12/24/2007	$17.8
Employees	NA	Stock Exchange	NDQ
Auditor	NA	Ticker Symbol	RRST
Stk Agt	American Stock Transfer & Trust Co.	Outstanding Shares	17,240,000
Counsel	NA	E.P.S.	$0.58
DUNS No.	NA	Shareholders	NA

Business: The groups principal activity is to provide transmission services. The groups services include Uplink, Downlink and Turnaround services using Teleports, Flyaway and Transportable Uplink and Downlink systems. The group operates from the United States.

Primary SIC and add'l.: 3663 4841 4899

CIK No: 0001375829

Officers: David Rival/61/Dir., CEO, Gil Efron/42/CFO, Lior Rival/VP - Sales, Marketing, Ziv Mor/Dir. - Engineering

Directors: David Rival/61/Dir., CEO, Gilad Ramot/57/Chmn., David Assia/Dir., Amit Ben-Yehuda/Dir., Yigal Berman/Dir., Avi Kurzweil/Dir., Vered Levy-Ron/Dir., Alexander Milner/Dir., Ron Oren/Dir.

Owners: Kardan Communications Ltd./24.55%, David Rivel/14.00%, Del-Ta Engineering Equipment Ltd./35.30%, Insiders/14.00%

Financial Data: ***Fiscal Year End:***12/31 ***Latest Annual Data:*** 12/31/2006

Year	Sales	Net Income
2006	$43,284,000	$7,305,000
2005	$31,311,000	$4,245,000
2004	$23,767,000	$5,170,000

Curr. Assets:	$65,037,000	**Curr. Liab.:**	$10,762,000		
Plant, Equip.:	$12,452,000	**Total Liab.:**	$15,788,000	**Indic. Yr. Divd.:**	NA
Total Assets:	$79,133,000	**Net Worth:**	$63,345,000	**Debt/ Equity:**	NA

RS Group of Cos Inc

200 Yorkland Blvd., Ste 200, Toronto, ON, M2J 5C1; ***PH:*** 1-416-394223; ***http://*** www.rsgc.com; ***Email:*** info@rsgc.com

General		Stock	
Incorporation	FL	Price on:12/24/2007	$0.003
Employees	NA	Stock Exchange	OTC
Auditor	Rotenberg Meril Solomon	Ticker Symbol	RSGC
Stk Agt	Interwest Transfer Company, Inc.	Outstanding Shares	NA
Counsel	Fasken Martineau	E.P.S	NA
DUNS No.	NA	Shareholders	NA

Business: The group's principal activity is to provide pass-through risk solution for various credit related products. The group, through its wholly owned subsidiary, has introduced rentshieldtm, a residential rental guarantee program being offered to North America's residential real estate market. The objective of this program is to reduce the financial risk inherent in property management. The rentshieldtm product facilitates the landlord's receipt of rents by electronic payment. The group also provides rentshieldtm express, which includes credit verification and background checks to help landlords select qualified tenants. The entire program may be accessed by customers through an Internet based network. The group's mortgage default insurance is a credit insurance product sold to mortgage companies to facilitate their offer of higher-than-average-risk mortgages. The group has operations in North America & Canada.

Primary SIC and add'l.: 6411

CIK No: 0001200202

Subsidiaries: RS Group of Companies, Inc.

Officers: John Hamilton/Chmn., CEO, David Sanderson/CFO, Patterson J. McBaine/Mgr.

Directors: John Hamilton/Chmn., CEO, Stephen Stonhill/Dir.

Financial Data: ***Fiscal Year End:***12/31 ***Latest Annual Data:*** 12/31/2005

Year	Sales	Net Income
2005	$31,501,000	$565,000
2004	$16,322,000	-$250,000
2003	$58,000	-$2,251,000

Curr. Assets:	$3,745,000	**Curr. Liab.:**	$4,993,000		
Plant, Equip.:	$803,000	**Total Liab.:**	$5,342,000	**Indic. Yr. Divd.:**	NA
Total Assets:	$19,171,000	**Net Worth:**	$13,830,000	**Debt/ Equity:**	NA

RSA Security Inc

174 Middlesex TpkE, Bedford, MA, 01730; ***PH:*** 1-781-515-5000; ***Fax:*** 1-781-515-5010; ***http://*** www.rsasecurity.com

General		Stock	
Incorporation	DE	Price on:12/24/2007	$17.99
Employees	31,100	Stock Exchange	NA
Auditor	Deloitte & Touche LLP	Ticker Symbol	NA
Stk Agt	Deloitte & Touche LLP	Outstanding Shares	2,100,000,000
Counsel	Hale & Dorr LLP	E.P.S	$0.61
DUNS No.	NA	Shareholders	NA

Business: The group's principal activity is to provide electronic security solutions. The group provides interoperable solutions for establishing online identities, access rights and privileges for people, applications and devices. The operations of the group are conducted through two segments: e-security solutions and rsa capital segment. E-security solutions segment sells enterprise solutions and developer solutions through our four product lines: rsa securid authentication, rsa keon digital certificates and smart card solutions, rsa bsafe developer tools, and rsa cleartrust Web access management software. Rsa capital segment consists of the investment activities.

Primary SIC and add'l.: 7372 3577 6799

CIK No: 0000932064

Subsidiaries: 3-G International, Inc., ASR Securities Corp., Cyota Israel Ltd., Cyota, Inc., RSA Investments Inc., RSA Partners I, L.P., RSA Security (S) PTE Ltd., RSA Security Australia Pty Ltd., RSA Security B.V., RSA Security France SARL, RSA Security GmbH, RSA Security Holding Limited, RSA Security Holdings Inc., RSA Security Ireland Limited, RSA Security Japan Ltd. 25 Subsidiaries included in the Index

Officers: Arthur W. Coviello/Dir., CEO, Pres., Jim Melvin/VP - Marketing, Security Solutions, Rick Welch/Sr. VP, GM - Developer Solutions Division, Dennis Hoffman/VP - General Manage, Data Security Group, Chief Strategy Officer, Vivian M. Vitale/Sr. VP - Human Resources, Gerard Wilson/CIO, Sr. VP, William L. McQuaide/Sr. VP - Enterprise Products Division, James Bandanza/VP - Worldwide Sales, Field Operations, Charles F. Kane/Sr. VP - Finance, CFO, Robert P. Nault/Sr. VP, General Counsel, Sec., John Worrall/VP, GM - Information, Event Management Group, Christopher Young/Sr. VP - Consumer Division, Bret Hartman/CTO

Directors: Arthur W. Coviello/Dir., CEO, Pres., Charles Stuckey/65/Chmn. Emeritus, James K. Sims/Chmn., Robert P. Badavas/Dir., Orson Swindle/Dir., Joseph B. Lassiter/Dir., Richard A. Demillo/Dir., Richard L. Earnest/Dir., Gloria Larson/Dir., William Harris/Dir.

Financial Data: ***Fiscal Year End:***12/31 ***Latest Annual Data:*** 12/31/2006

Year	Sales	Net Income
2006	$11,155,090,000	$1,223,982,000
2005	$9,663,955,000	$1,133,165,000
2004	$8,229,488,000	$871,189,000

Curr. Assets:	$6,520,587,000	**Curr. Liab.:**	$3,881,104,000	**P/E Ratio:**	29.49
Plant, Equip.:	$2,035,559,000	**Total Liab.:**	$8,240,540,000	**Indic. Yr. Divd.:**	NA
Total Assets:	$18,566,247,000	**Net Worth:**	$10,325,707,000	**Debt/ Equity:**	0.3542

RTG Ventures Inc

10125 W Colonial Dr, Ste. 212, Ocoee, FL, 34761;

General		Stock	
Incorporation	FL	Price on:12/24/2007	$0.029
Employees	NA	Stock Exchange	OTC
Auditor	Sherb & Co. LLP	Ticker Symbol	RTGV
Stk Agt	National Stock Transfer, Inc.	Outstanding Shares	NA
Counsel	NA	E.P.S	NA
DUNS No.	NA	Shareholders	NA

Business: The groups principle activity is to promote championship gaming events. The group operates from United States.

Primary SIC and add'l.: NA

CIK No: 0001127475

Subsidiaries: MJWC, Inc.

Officers: Linda Perry/CEO, Barrington J. Fludgate/CFO

Owners: Silverlake Holdings Inc./15.88%, Insiders/45.35%, Linda Perry/15.44%, Lancer Corporation/14.03%

Financial Data: ***Fiscal Year End:***08/31 ***Latest Annual Data:*** 8/31/2006

Year	Sales	Net Income
2006	NA	-$134,000
2005	NA	-$619,000
2004	NA	-$2,435,000

Curr. Assets:	NA	**Curr. Liab.:**	$305,000		
Plant, Equip.:	NA	**Total Liab.:**	$305,000	**Indic. Yr. Divd.:**	NA
Total Assets:	NA	**Net Worth:**	-$305,000	**Debt/ Equity:**	NA

RTI International Metals Inc

1000 Warren Ave., Niles, OH, 44446; ***PH:*** 1-330-544-7700; ***Fax:*** 1-330-544-7701; ***http://*** www.rti-intl.com

General		Stock	
Incorporation	OH	Price on:12/24/2007	$78.61
Employees	1,362	Stock Exchange	NYSE
Auditor	PricewaterhouseCoopers LLP	Ticker Symbol	RTI
Stk Agt	National City Bank	Outstanding Shares	23,060,000
Counsel	NA	E.P.S	$4.09
DUNS No.	04-522-4347	Shareholders	NA

Business: The group's principal activities are to produce titanium mill products and fabricated metal parts. The group conducts business in two segments: titanium group and the fabrication and distribution group. The titanium group melts and produces a complete range of titanium mill products, which are further processed by its customers for use in a variety of aerospace and industrial applications. The fabrication and distribution group's products are used primarily in the aerospace, oil and gas, geothermal energy production and chemical process industries, and a number of other industrial applications. The fabrication and distribution group also operates a number of distribution centers specializing in high temperature and corrosion resistant alloys including titanium, stainless steel and nickel-based products. The group operates in the United States, England, France and Korea.

Primary SIC and add'l.: 3499 3339 3356

CIK No: 0001068717

Subsidiaries: BowSteel Corporation, BowSteel of Texas Corporation, Claro Precision, Inc., Earthline Technologies, Inc., Etca G.p., LLC, Etca L.p., Inc., Extrusion Technology Corporation of America, Galt Alloys, Inc., NATI Gas Company, New Century Metals Southeast, Inc., New Century Metals, Inc., Pierce-Spafford Metals Company, Inc., Reamet, S.A., RMI Delaware, Inc., RMI Metals, Inc. 32 Subsidiaries included in the Index

Officers: Dawne S. Hickton/Vice Chmn., CEO/$921,835.00, William T. Hull/CFO, Sr. VP, Treasurer/$625,532.00, Michael C. Wellham/Dir., COO, Pres./$357,141.00, Stephen R. Giangiordano/Exec. VP/$510,419.00, Chad Whalen/VP, General Counsel, Richard E. Leone/Mgr. - Investor Relations

Directors: Dawne S. Hickton/Vice Chmn., CEO, Robert M. Hernandez/Chmn., Edith E. Holiday/Dir., James A. Williams/Dir., Charles C. Gedeon/Dir., Daniel I. Booker/Dir., Ronald L. Gallatin/62/Dir., Craig R. Andersson/Dir., Donald P. Fusilli/Dir., Michael C. Wellham/Dir., COO, Pres.

Owners: Gordon L. Berkstresser, Craig R. Andersson, Michael C. Wellham, Edith E. Holiday, Ronald L. Gallatin, Dawne S. Hickton, James A. Williams, Stephen R. Giangiordano, Donald P. Fusilli, John H. Odle, William T. Hull, Charles C. Gedeon, Rainer Investment Management, Inc./7.10%, Daniel I. Booker, Timothy G. Rupert *(18 Owners included in Index)*

Financial Data: ***Fiscal Year End:***12/31 ***Latest Annual Data:*** 12/31/2006

Year	Sales	Net Income
2006	$505,389,000	$75,700,000
2005	$346,906,000	$38,935,000
2004	$214,591,000	-$2,957,000

Curr. Assets:	$467,154,000	**Curr. Liab.:**	$101,443,000	**P/E Ratio:**	19.55
Plant, Equip.:	$102,470,000	**Total Liab.:**	$181,732,000	**Indic. Yr. Divd.:**	NA
Total Assets:	$643,913,000	**Net Worth:**	$462,181,000	**Debt/ Equity:**	0.0297

RTW Inc

PO Box 390327, Minneapolis, MN, 55439; ***PH:*** 1-952-893-0403; ***Fax:*** 1-952-893-3700; ***http://*** www.rtwi.com; ***Email:*** ir@rtwi.com

General		Stock	
Incorporation	MN	Price on:12/24/2007	$8.24
Employees	168	Stock Exchange	NDQ
Auditor	Ernst & Young LLP	Ticker Symbol	RTWI
Stk Agt	Wells Fargo Bank Minnesota N.A	Outstanding Shares	5,170,000
Counsel	Rider Bennett Egan & Arundel LLP	E.P.S	$0.42
DUNS No.	14-851-5299	Shareholders	NA

Business: The group's principle activities are to provide comprehensive management products and services to insured and self-insured employers for their workers' compensation programs. The group operates two proprietary management systems: rtw solution(R) and the ID15(R) system. The rtw solutions are designed to lower employers' workers' compensation costs and return injured employees to work as soon as possible. The ID15 systems are designed to identify those injured employees who are likely to get stuck in the workers compensation system. The group also uses management techniques, including designated health care providers, medical fee schedule review, utilization review and doctor peer review, to control medical costs. The operations are carried on in the United States. The group's quarterly revenue for September 2007 was 12.99 millions of USD.

Primary SIC and add'l.: 6331

CIK No: 0000915781

Subsidiaries: American Compensation Insurance Company, Bloomington Compensation Insurance Company

Officers: Jeffrey B. Murphy/Dir., CEO, Pres./$449,373.00, Thomas J. Byers/52/Exec. VP - Sales, Marketing/$257,505.00, David M. Dietz/VP - Business Development/$215,539.00, Keith D. Krueger/COO/$225,981.00, Alfred L. Latendresse/CFO, Exec. VP, Treasurer, Sec./$258,231.00, Patricia M. Sheveland/VP - Case, Claims Management/$214,271.00

Directors: Jeffrey B. Murphy/Dir., CEO, Pres., John O. Goodwyne/Chmn., Gregory D. Koschinska/Dir., William J. Deters/Dir., David C. Prosser/Dir., John W. Prosser/Dir., Lyron L. Bentovim/Dir.

Owners: Jeffrey B. Murphy/4.40%, Patricia M. Sheveland, Keith D. Krueger/1.10%, Dimensional Fund Advisors, Inc./9.20%, Lyron L. Bentovim/9.10%, David C. Prosser/8.30%, First Wilshire Securities Management, Inc./8.80%, U.S. Bancorp/7.80%, Insiders/32.80%, William J. Deters/1.00%, John O. Goodwyne, Gregory D. Koschinska, David M. Dietz, Alfred L. LaTendresse/2.20%, John W. Prosser/6.90%

Financial Data: Fiscal Year End: 12/31   **Latest Annual Data:** 12/31/2006

Year	Sales	Net Income
2006	$53,872,000	$3,288,000
2005	$59,011,000	$5,998,000
2004	$58,857,000	$9,941,000

Curr. Assets:	$95,258,000	**Curr. Liab.:**	$7,325,000	**P/E Ratio:**	19.62
Plant, Equip.:	$1,570,000	**Total Liab.:**	$167,084,000	**Indic. Yr. Divd.:**	NA
Total Assets:	$218,439,000	**Net Worth:**	$51,355,000	**Debt/ Equity:**	NA

Rub A Dub Soap Inc

2591 Dallas Pkwy Ste. 102, Frisco, TX, 75034; **PH:** 1-469-633-0100; **http://** www.rubadubsoap.com; **Email:** order@rubadubsoap.com

General - Incorporation	NV	**Stock**- Price on:12/24/2007	$10
Employees	NA	Stock Exchange	OTC
Auditor	Sherb & Co., LLP	Ticker Symbol	RUBD
Stk Agt	NA	Outstanding Shares	NA
Counsel	NA	E.P.S.	NA
DUNS No.	NA	Shareholders	NA

Business: The groups principal activity is online retailer of handmade, natural, vegetable based soaps and gift baskets in the development stage. The group operates from the United States.

Primary SIC and add'l.: 6799

CIK No: 0001169138

Officers: Kevin B. Halter/47/Dir., CEO, Pres., Pam J. Halter/53/Dir., CFO, Sec., Treasure

Directors: Kevin B. Halter/47/Dir., CEO, Pres., Pam J. Halter/53/Dir., CFO, Sec., Treasure

Owners: Halter Capital Corporation, Kevin B. Halter, Insiders

Financial Data: Fiscal Year End: 05/31   **Latest Annual Data:** 05/31/2007

Year	Sales	Net Income
2007	NA	-$31,000
2006	NA	-$72,000
2005	$2,000	-$33,000

Curr. Assets:	NA	**Curr. Liab.:**	NA		
Plant, Equip.:	NA	**Total Liab.:**	NA	**Indic. Yr. Divd.:**	NA
Total Assets:	NA	**Net Worth:**	NA	**Debt/ Equity:**	NA

Rubicon Minerals Corp

800 W Pender St., Ste. 1540, Vancouver, BC, V6C 2V6; **PH:** 1-604-623-3333; **Fax:** 1-604-623-3355; **http://** www.rubiconminerals.com

General - Incorporation	BC	**Stock** - Price on:12/24/2007	$1.9294
Employees	8	Stock Exchange	AMEX
Auditor	Devisser Gray	Ticker Symbol	RBY
Stk Agt	Computershare Investor Services LLC	Outstanding Shares	77,460,000
Counsel	Davis & Company LLP	E.P.S.	-$0.019
DUNS No.	NA	Shareholders	NA

Business: The groups principle activity is to provide exploration services for gold and base metal deposits. The group operates from Canada.

Primary SIC and add'l.: 9999

CIK No: 0001057791

Subsidiaries: Africo Resources Ltd, Toquima Minerals Corporation

Officers: David W. Adamson/Dir., CEO, Pres., Robert G. Lewis/CFO, Bill Cavalluzzo/VP - Investor Relations, Matthew C. Wunder/VP - Exploration, Michael J. Vande Guchte/Mgr. - Corporate Development, William Cavalluzzo/VP - Investor Relations Ontario, Canada

Directors: David W. Adamson/Dir., CEO, Pres., Garfield J. MacVeigh/Chmn., Philip Martin/Dir., Chris Bradbrook/Dir., Kevin Sherkin/Dir., John Brodie/Dir., David R. Reid/Dir.

Financial Data: Fiscal Year End: 12/31   **Latest Annual Data:** 12/31/2006

Year	Sales	Net Income
2006	NA	-$2,955,000
2005	NA	-$6,602,000
2004	NA	-$5,193,000

Curr. Assets:	$10,727,000	**Curr. Liab.:**	$838,000		
Plant, Equip.:	$77,000	**Total Liab.:**	$3,547,000	**Indic. Yr. Divd.:**	NA
Total Assets:	$15,359,000	**Net Worth:**	$11,812,000	**Debt/ Equity:**	NA

Rubio's Restaurants Inc

1902 Wright Pl., Ste. 300, Carlsbad, CA, 92008; **PH:** 1-760-929-8226; **Fax:** 1-760-929-8203; **http://** www.rubios.com

General - Incorporation	DE	**Stock** - Price on:12/24/2007	$10.88
Employees	3,300	Stock Exchange	NDQ
Auditor	KPMG LLP	Ticker Symbol	RUBO
Stk Agt	U.S. Stock Transfer Corp	Outstanding Shares	9,820,000
Counsel	Heller Ehrman White & McAuliffe LLP	E.P.S.	-$0.35
DUNS No.	NA	Shareholders	NA

Business: The group's principal activity is to provide restaurant services in southwestern United States. At 15-Mar-2004, they own and operate 145 quick-service Mexican restaurants that offer traditional Mexican cuisine combined with fresh seafood indicative of the baja region of Mexico. The group's restaurants are located in California, Arizona, Nevada, Colorado, Oregon and Utah. The food items are prepared on-site and made-to-order. The menu feature includes burritos, soft-shell tacos and quesadillas made with marinated, chargrilled chicken breast and lean steak.

Primary SIC and add'l.: 5813 5812 6794

CIK No: 0001082423

Officers: Daniel E. Pittard/58/CEO, Pres./$341,572.00, Lawrence A. Rusinko/VP - Marketing/$561,663.00, Carl Arena/54/VP - Development/$207,764.00, Gerry Leneweaver/VP - People Services/$258,141.00, Frank Henigman/CFO

Directors: Ralph Rubio/Co - Founder, Chmn., William R. Bensyl/Dir., Timothy J. Ryan/68/Dir., Kyle Anderson/Dir., Craig Andrews/Dir., Jack W. Goodall/Dir., Loren C. Pannier/66/Dir.

Owners: Royce and Associates/8.70%, Brightleaf Capital LLC/5.20%, Craig S. Andrews, Alex Meruelo Living Trust/5.00%, Loren C. Pannier, Ralph Rubio/9.70%, Jack W. Goodall/1.20%, Insiders/30.40%, Lawrence A. Rusinko, Rosewood Capital, L.P./15.90%, Carl Arena, Kyle A. Anderson/15.90%, John Fuller/1.50%, Daniel E. Pittard, Timothy J. Ryan

Financial Data: Fiscal Year End: 12/25   **Latest Annual Data:** 12/31/2006

Year	Sales	Net Income
2006	$152,268,000	-$3,461,000
2005	$140,757,000	-$228,000
2004	$137,400,000	$3,040,000

Curr. Assets:	$15,841,000	**Curr. Liab.:**	$17,304,000		
Plant, Equip.:	$36,909,000	**Total Liab.:**	$27,003,000	**Indic. Yr. Divd.:**	NA
Total Assets:	$67,505,000	**Net Worth:**	$40,502,000	**Debt/ Equity:**	NA

Ruby Tuesday Inc

150 W Church Ave., Maryville, TN, 37801; **PH:** 1-865-379-5700; **Fax:** 1-865-379-6826; **http://** www.rubytuesday.com; **Email:** investorrelations@rubytuesday.com

General - Incorporation	GA	**Stock**- Price on:12/24/2007	NA
Employees	16,500	Stock Exchange	NYSE
Auditor	KPMG LLP	Ticker Symbol	RT
Stk Agt	Bank of New York	Outstanding Shares	NA
Counsel	NA	E.P.S.	$1.45
DUNS No.	00-690-1102	Shareholders	NA

Business: The group's principal activity is to own and operate ruby tuesday(R) casual dining restaurants. The group offers franchises for the ruby tuesday concept in domestic and international markets through both our franchise partnership program and traditional franchising. As of 1-Jun-2004, the group owned and operated 484 casual dining restaurants, located in 26 states and the district of columbia. The franchise partnerships operated 209 restaurants located in 18 states. The traditional franchisees operated seven domestic and 36 international restaurants located in Kentucky and the Asian pacific region, India, Puerto Rico, Canada, Mexico, ice land, eastern Europe, and central and South America.

Primary SIC and add'l.: 6794 5812

CIK No: 0000068270

Officers: Sandy Beall/Founder, Chmn., CEO, Pres., Shannon Hepp/VP - Investor Relations, Planning, Ramona Seale/Contact - Institutional Inquiries, Rhonda Sallas/Contact - Shareholder Inquiries, Mark Young/Sr. VP - Marketing, Scarlett May/VP, General Counsel, Sec., Margie Duffy/Sr. VP, CFO/$1,254,430.00, Rob Leboeuf/Sr. VP, Chief People Officer, Kimberly Grant/Exec. VP/$1,385,817.00, Nick Ibrahim/CTO, Sr. VP/$1,379,220.00, Rick Johnson/Sr. VP/$1,251,001.00, Kurt Juergens/Sr. VP - Real Estate Development, Mark Ingram/Pres. - Franchise Development

Directors: Sandy Beall/Founder, Chmn., CEO, Pres., Donald Ratajczak/65/Dir., Kevin T. Clayton/45/Dir., James A. Haslam/54/Dir., Stephen I. Sadove/57/Dir., Clarie L. Arnold/61/Dir., Samuel E. Beall/58/Dir., Bernard Lanigan/60/Dir.

Owners: John B. McKinnon, Capital Research and Management Company/6.20%, Stephen I. Sadove, Bernard Lanigan, James A. Haslam, Kimberly Grant, Westport Asset Management, Inc./5.74%, Claire L. Arnold, Lord Abbett & Co. LLC/8.67%, Kevin T. Clayton, Nicolas N. Ibrahim, Donald Ratajczak, Richard A. Johnson, Marguerite N. Duffy, Samuel E. Beall/4.46% *(17 Owners included in Index)*

Financial Data: Fiscal Year End: 06/06   **Latest Annual Data:** 6/6/2006

Year	Sales	Net Income
2006	$1,306,240,000	$100,977,000
2005	$1,110,294,000	$102,298,000
2004	$1,041,359,000	$109,847,000

Curr. Assets:	$78,340,000	**Curr. Liab.:**	$107,998,000		
Plant, Equip.:	$984,127,000	**Total Liab.:**	$644,410,000	**Indic. Yr. Divd.:**	$0.500
Total Assets:	$1,171,568,000	**Net Worth:**	$527,158,000	**Debt/ Equity:**	NA

Ruddick Corp

301 S Tryon St., Ste. 1800, Charlotte, NC, 28202; **PH:** 1-704-372-5404; **Fax:** 1-704-372-6409; **http://** www.ruddickcorp.com

General - Incorporation	NC	**Stock**- Price on:12/24/2007	$30.75
Employees	12,800	Stock Exchange	NYSE
Auditor	KPMG LLP	Ticker Symbol	RDK
Stk Agt	American Stock Transfer & Trust Co.	Outstanding Shares	48,010,000
Counsel	Helms Mulliss & Wicker	E.P.S.	$1.54
DUNS No.	04-727-9351	Shareholders	NA

Business: The groups principle activity is to operate supermarkets. The groups products include meat and seafood, bakery items, wines and non-food items including health and beauty care, floral and other products. The group operates from United States.

Primary SIC and add'l.: 5411 2281

CIK No: 0000085704

Subsidiaries: A&E Iplik Sanayi ve Ticaret Anonim Sirketi, American & Efird (Bangladesh) Ltd., American & Efird (G.B.) Limited, American & Efird (H.K.) Limited, American & Efird (Haiti), S.A., American & Efird (Malaysia) SDN. BHD., American & Efird (Polska) Sp. z o.o., American & Efird (South Africa) (Proprietary) Ltd., American & Efird Canada Inc., American & Efird de Mexico, S.A. de C.V, American & Efird Enterprises, Inc., American & Efird International B.V., American & Efird Italia S.p.A., American & Efird Mills (S) Pte. Ltd., American & Efird, Inc. 45 Subsidiaries included in the Index

Officers: Thomas W. Dickson/Chmn., CEO, Pres., Ronald H. Volger/VP, Treasurer, John B. Woodlief/CFO, VP - Finance, Douglas J. Yacenda/Sec., Jesse B. Libensperger/Assist. Treasurer, Assist. Sec.

Directors: Thomas W. Dickson/Chmn., CEO, Pres., Anna Spangler Nelson/Dir., Edwin B. Borden/Dir., John R. Belk/Dir., Bailey W. Patrick/Dir., Robert H. Spilman/Dir., James E.S. Hynes/Dir., Stuart R. Dickson/Dir., Alan T. Dickson/Dir., Isaiah Tidwell/Dir., John P. Derham Cato/Dir., Harold C. Stowe/Dir.

Owners: John B. Woodlief, John P. Derham Cato, Frederick J. Morganthall, Alan T. Dickson/4.10%, Isaiah Tidwell, T. Rowe Price Trust Company/12.90%, John R. Belk, Bailey W. Patrick, Edwin B. Borden, Fred A. Jackson, Robert H. Spilman, Southeastern Asset Management, Inc./10.10%, Thomas W. Dickson, Harold C. Stowe, James E. S. Hynes *(18 Owners included in Index)*

Financial Data: *Fiscal Year End:*09/02 *Latest Annual Data:* 10/1/2006

Year	Sales	Net Income
2006	$3,265,856,000	$72,336,000
2005	$2,964,655,000	$68,598,000
2004	$2,868,597,000	$64,659,000

Curr. Assets:	NA	**Curr. Liab.:**	NA	**P/E Ratio:**	19.97
Plant, Equip.:	NA	**Total Liab.:**	NA	**Indic. Yr. Divd.:**	$0.440
Total Assets:	NA	**Net Worth:**	NA	**Debt/ Equity:**	0.3293

Rudolph Technologies Inc

PO Box 1000, One Rudolph Rd., Flanders, NJ, 07836; ***PH:*** 1-973-691-1300; ***http://*** www.rudolphtech.com

General - Incorporation	DE	**Stock**- Price on:12/24/2007	$17.1
Employees	620	Stock Exchange	NDQ
Auditor	KPMG LLP	Ticker Symbol	RTEC
Stk Agt	American Stock Transfer & Trust Co.	Outstanding Shares	29,090,000
Counsel	Wilson Sonsini Goodrich & Rosati	E.P.S	$0.94
DUNS No.	NA	Shareholders	NA

Business: The group's principal activities are to design, develop and manufacture high-performance process control metrology and defect inspection systems used in semiconductor device manufacturers. The group provides full-fab solutions through a family of stand-alone systems and integrated modules for both transparent and opaque thin film measurements and macro-defect detection. The group's thin film measurement proprietary systems measure the thickness and other properties of thin films applied during various steps in the manufacture of integrated circuits, enabling semiconductor device manufacturers to improve yields and reduce overall production costs. Also includes macro-defect inspection proprietary systems detect and classify defects in semiconductor wafers. The group's system support in variety of applications in diffusion, etch, lithography, cvd, pvd, cmp and macro-defect detection.

Primary SIC and add'l.: 3674 3823

CIK No: 0001094392

Subsidiaries: ISOA, Inc. (dba Yield Metrology Group), Rudolph Technologies Europe, B.V., Rudolph Technologies Japan KK

Officers: Paul F. McLaughlin/Chmn., CEO/$970,855.00, Steven R. Roth/Sr. VP - Finance, Administration, CFO/$392,097.00, Robert M. Loiterman/48/Sr. VP, GM - Metrology Business Unit/$419,458.00, Nathan H. Little/56/Companys Exec. VP, GM - Inspection Business Unit/$399,177.00, Ajay Khanna/48/VP - International Accounting, Mayson D. Brooks/49/VP - Global Sales, George Collins/59/VP - New Business Development, Robert Dicrosta/60/VP - Global Customer Support, Robert A. Koch/46/VP, General Counsel, John R. Kurdock/63/VP - Manufacturing, Metrology, Assist. GM, Ardelle R. Johnson/53/VP - Corporate Marketing, Jeffrey T. Nelson/52/VP - Manufacturing, Inspection, Michael P. Plisinski/38/VP, GM - Data Analysis, Review Business Unit/$415,663.00

Directors: Paul F. McLaughlin/Chmn., CEO, Daniel H. Berry/Dir., Paul Craig/Dir., Thomas G. Greig/Dir., Carl E. Ring/Dir., Richard F. Spanier/Dir., Aubrey C. Tobey/Dir., Jeff L. Odell/Dir., Michael W. Wright/Dir., John R. Whitten/Dir.

Owners: John R. Whitten, Michael P. Plisinski, Robert M. Loiterman, Liberty Partners Holdings/6.29%, FMR Corp./14.92%, Paul Craig, Aubrey C. Tobey, Carl E. Ring, Mazama Capital Management, Inc./5.24%, Paul F.McLaughlin/2.51%, Thomas G. Greig/6.34%, Daniel H. Berry, Jeff L. ODell, Steven R. Roth, Michael W. Wright *(19 Owners included in Index)*

Financial Data: *Fiscal Year End:*12/31 *Latest Annual Data:* 12/31/2006

Year	Sales	Net Income
2006	$201,168,000	$12,706,000
2005	$82,918,000	$4,977,000
2004	$84,248,000	$6,752,000

Curr. Assets:	$236,744,000	**Curr. Liab.:**	$36,304,000	**P/E Ratio:**	16.60
Plant, Equip.:	$16,882,000	**Total Liab.:**	$47,610,000	**Indic. Yr. Divd.:**	NA
Total Assets:	$440,486,000	**Net Worth:**	$392,876,000	**Debt/ Equity:**	NA

Rumson-Fair Haven Bank

500 Broad St., Shrewsbury, NJ, 07702; ***PH:*** 1-732-933-3875; ***Fax:*** 1-732-933-0461; ***http://*** www.rfhbank.com

General - Incorporation		**Stock**- Price on:12/24/2007	$10.25
Employees	NA	Stock Exchange	OTC
Auditor	Beard Miller Company LLP	Ticker Symbol	RFHB
Stk Agt	Registrar & Transfer Co	Outstanding Shares	2,210,000
Counsel	NA	E.P.S	NA
DUNS No.	NA	Shareholders	NA

Business: The groups principal activities include providing banking services as community banking. Services of the group include checking accounts, savings accounts, certificates of deposit, installment loans, real estate mortgage loans, commercial loans, traveler's checks, safe deposit boxes, night depository and automated teller services. The group operates from the United States.

Primary SIC and add'l.: 6099

CIK No:

Officers: Robert E. Davis/Dir., CEO, Pres., Dennis J. Flanagan/Dir., Exec. VP, CFO, Lillian Palumbo/Assist. Treasurer, Lauren M. Flanagan/Branch Mgr. - Shrewsbury, Peter Leyman/Branch Mgr. - Fair Haven, Alexandra Smith/Branch Mgr. - Rumson, Raymond C. Leahy/Sr. VP - Commercial Lending, Thomas Sannelli/Sr. VP, Karen M. Birmingham/VP - Operations, John Lauricella/VP - Lending, Diane McCormick/VP, Syed Murtaza/Assist. VP, Edward Gough/Assist. Treasurer, Richard Klimko/Assist. Treasurer

Directors: Robert E. Davis/Dir., CEO, Pres., William J. Barrett/Chmn., Joseph Castelluci/Dir., Stephen A. Tyler/Dir., Thomas I. Unterberg/Dir., Van R. Whisnand/Dir., Christopher Abruzzo/Member - Advisory Board, Warren S. Beebe/Member - Advisory Board, Michael V. Benedetto/Member - Advisory Board, Michael A. Bruno/Member - Advisory Board, Jack A. Callahan/Member - Advisory Board, Dennis M. Crawford/Member - Advisory Board, Dennis Donato/Member - Advisory Board, Peter S. Falvo/Member - Advisory Board, Ron Gillaspie/Member - Advisory Board *(31 Directors included in Index)*

Rural Cellular Corp

3905 Dakota St. SW, Alexandria, MN, 56308; ***PH:*** 1-320-762-2000; ***Fax:*** 1-320-808-2181; ***http://*** www.rccwireless.com

General - Incorporation	MN	**Stock**- Price on:12/24/2007	$38.6
Employees	1,057	Stock Exchange	NDQ
Auditor	Deloitte & Touche LLP	Ticker Symbol	RCCC
Stk Agt	Wells Fargo Shareowner Services	Outstanding Shares	15,560,000
Counsel	Moss & Barnett P.A	E.P.S	-$7.37
DUNS No.	79-472-4054	Shareholders	NA

Business: The group's principal activities are to provide wireless communication services in the midwest, south, northeast and northwest areas of the United States. The group through wireless communication systems provide caller ID, short message service, numeric paging, visual message notification, group ring, add-a-line, voicemail regional personal toll-free number, nationwide calling option and voice activated dialing. The group also offer the customers regional calling plans and roaming packages that allow the customers to pay home usage rates while traveling within specified regional zones, both within and outside of the cellular service areas. As of 31-Dec-2003, the group's network covered a total population of approximately 6.3 million and served approximately 660,000 voice customers, excluding wholesale customers.

Primary SIC and add'l.: 5063 4812

CIK No: 0000869561

Subsidiaries: Alexandria Indemnity, Inc., RCC Atlantic Licenses, LLC, RCC Atlantic, Inc., RCC Minnesota, Inc., RCC Transport, Inc., TLA Spectrum, LLC, Wireless Alliance, LLC

Officers: Richard P. Ekstrand/58/Dir., Pres., CEO - Unicel/$1,157,967.00, Scott G. Donlea/Sr. VP - Network, Product Development, Unicel, Elizabeth L. Kohler/VP - Legal Services, Unicel, Anthony J. Bolland/Dir. - Unicel, Jeffrey A. Hitland/Sr. VP - Sales, Marketing, Unicel, Paul Finnegan/Dir. - Unicel, Wesley E. Schultz/Dir., Exec. VP, CFO - Unicel/$805,157.00, Don C. Swenson/Dir. - Unicel, Karen C. Henrikson/VP - Human Resources, Unicel, George W. Wikstrom/Dir. - Unicel, George M. Revering/Dir. - Unicel, David J. Del Zoppo/VP - Finance, Accounting, Unicel/$284,477.00, Ann K. Newhall/57/Dir., Exec. VP, COO, Sec./$802,928.00, William D. Finley/VP, Controller - Unicel, John D. Foote/VP - Customer Operations, Unicel *(19 Officers included in Index)*

Directors: Richard P. Ekstrand/58/Dir., Pres., CEO - Unicel, James V. Continenza/45/Dir., Jacques Leduc/45/Dir., Wesley E. Schultz/Dir., Exec. VP, CFO - Unicel, Ann K. Newhall/57/Dir., Exec. VP, COO, Sec.

Owners: Kingdon Capital Management, LLC/7.00%, Anthony J. Bolland/5.10%, North Holdings, Inc., Don C. Swenson, Garden Valley Telephone Co., North Holdings, Inc./8.20%, Boston Ventures Management, Inc./5.10%, Paul J. Finnegan/7.40%, George M. Revering, Insiders/18.80%, Eric Semler/8.00%, Madison Dearborn Partners/7.40%, Insiders/8.20%, Telephone& Data Systems, Inc./33.30%, James V. Continenza *(29 Owners included in Index)*

Financial Data: *Fiscal Year End:*12/31 *Latest Annual Data:* 12/31/2006

Year	Sales	Net Income
2006	$564,460,000	-$116,041,000
2005	$544,935,000	-$64,122,000
2004	$504,817,000	-$58,941,000

Curr. Assets:	$261,434,000	**Curr. Liab.:**	$101,227,000		
Plant, Equip.:	$211,978,000	**Total Liab.:**	$1,964,146,000	**Indic. Yr. Divd.:**	NA
Total Assets:	$1,384,648,000	**Net Worth:**	-$765,156,000	**Debt/ Equity:**	NA

Rural/Metro Corp

9221 E Via de Ventura, Scottsdale, AZ, 85258; ***PH:*** 1-480-994-3886; ***http://*** www.ruralmetro.com; ***Email:*** feedback@ruralmetro.com

General - Incorporation	DE	**Stock**- Price on:12/24/2007	$6.5
Employees	7,800	Stock Exchange	NDQ
Auditor	PricewaterhouseCoopers LLP	Ticker Symbol	RURL
Stk Agt	Computershare Trust Services	Outstanding Shares	24,680,000
Counsel	Greenberg Traurig	E.P.S	-$0.09
DUNS No.	05-145-2183	Shareholders	NA

Business: The group's principal activities are to provide diversified emergency services, which includes medical transportation, fire protection and other related services in 26 states. The emergency services are provided to patients on both a fee-for-service basis and a non-refundable subscription fee basis. The group's two operating segments are medical transportation and related services and fire and other. The medical transportation and related services includes emergency ambulance services provided to individuals, fire districts, municipalities, as well as non-emergency ambulance services provided to individuals requiring either advanced or basic levels of medical supervision during transport. The fire and other includes a variety of fire protection services including fire prevention, suppression, training, alarm monitoring, dispatch, fleet and billing services.

Primary SIC and add'l.: 7389 4119 8082 9224

CIK No: 0000906326

Subsidiaries: Aid Ambulance at Vigo County, Inc., Ambulance Transport Systems, Inc, American Limousine Service, Inc., Beacon Transportation, Inc., Choice American Ambulance Service, Inc., Coastal EMS, Inc., Corning Ambulance Service Inc., Donlock, Ltd., E.M.S. Ventures, Inc., Eastern Ambulance Service, Inc., Eastern Paramedics, Inc., EMS Ventures of South Carolina, Inc., Gold Cross Ambulance Service of Pa., Inc., Gold Cross Ambulance Services, Inc., Keefe& Keefe Ambulette, Ltd. 105 Subsidiaries included in the Index

Officers: Jack E. Brucker/Dir., CEO, Pres., Louis G. Jekel/Vice Chmn., Sec., Kristine B. Ponczak/44/CFO, Sr. VP, Treasurer, Sec., Kurt M. Krumperman/57/Sr. VP - Federal Affairs, Strategic Initiatives, Gregory A. Barber/50/VP, Controller, Principal Accounting Officer, Brian O. Allery/42/VP - Risk, Insurance, Safety, National Purchasing, Real Estate

Directors: Jack E. Brucker/Dir., CEO, Pres., Cor J. Clement/Chmn., Louis G. Jekel/Vice Chmn., Sec., Mary Anne Carpenter/Dir., Robert E. Wilson/Dir., Henry G. Walker/Dir., Conrad A. Conrad/Dir.

Owners: Kristine B. Ponczak, Mary Anne Carpenter, Barry Landon, Cor J. Clement, Accipiter Entities/14.96%, Jack E. Brucker/2.31%, Louis G. Jekel, Robert E. Wilson, Conrad A. Conrad, Henry G. Walker, Kurt M. Krumperman, Epoch Investment Partners, Inc./9.88%, FMR Corp./14.87%, Insiders/3.92%, Stadium Capital Management, LLC/11.37%

Financial Data: *Fiscal Year End:* 06/30 *Latest Annual Data:* 06/30/2007

Year	Sales	Net Income
2007	$467,611,000	-$1,009,000
2006	$450,899,000	$3,490,000
2005	$531,084,000	$88,331,000

Curr. Assets:	$114,709,000	**Curr. Liab.:**	$73,926,000	**P/E Ratio:**	108.33
Plant, Equip.:	$45,970,000	**Total Liab.:**	$390,595,000	**Indic. Yr. Divd.:**	NA
Total Assets:	$296,388,000	**Net Worth:**	-$96,272,000	**Debt/ Equity:**	NA

Rurban Financial Corp

401 Clinton St., Defiance, OH, 43512; *PH:* 1-419-783-8950; *Fax:* 1-419-784-4085; *http://* www.rurbanfinancial.net

General - Incorporation	OH	**Stock** - Price on:12/24/2007	$12.52
Employees	216	Stock Exchange	NDQ
Auditor	BKD LLP	Ticker Symbol	RBNF
Stk Agt	Computershare Investor Services LLC	Outstanding Shares	5,030,000
Counsel	NA	E.P.S	$0.60
DUNS No.	12-179-6833	Shareholders	NA

Business: The group's principle activities are to provide banking and data processing services. It operates through 3 segments: banking, data processing and other. Banking segment includes revenues from loans like commercial, agricultural and mortgages, investments, deposits, and financial services. Data processing provides data processing services principally to banks and earns revenues through service fees. Other segment includes trust and financial services to customers nationwide and rurban life, its subsidiary, which provides insurance products to customers of the group's subsidiary banks. Other commercial banking services include checking and now accounts, passbook savings and money market accounts, certificates of deposits, trust services and other banking services.

Primary SIC and add'l.: 6712 6021

CIK No: 0000767405

Subsidiaries: RFCBC, Inc., Rurban Operations Corp., Rurban Statutory Trust I, Rurban Statutory Trust II, Rurbanc Data Services, Inc, The Exchange Bank, The State Bank and Trust Company

Officers: Henry R. Thiemann/CEO, Pres. - Rfcbc, Inc/$216,676.00, Kenneth A. Joyce/Dir., CEO, Pres./$399,284.00, Mark A. Klein/CEO, Pres. - State Bank, Trust Company/$224,212.00, Craig A. Kuhlman/Pres. - Reliance Financial Services, David A. Bell/Exec. VP, Trust Support Mgr. - Reliance Financial Services, David L. Schnepp/Regional Pres. - State Bank, Trust Company, William C. Brandt/Exec. VP, Rdsi Banking Systems Officers, Jon A. Brenneman/Exec. VP, Chief Marketing Officer - Rdsi Banking Systems, Jonathan R. Gathman/Exec. VP - Sr. Lender, The State Bank, Trust Company, Thomas A. Buis/Dir., Independent Consultant, Duane L. Sinn/CFO, Exec. VP/$147,472.00, James M. Bremer/CIO, Exec. VP - Rdsi Banking Systems, Valda L. Colbart/Assist. VP, Investor Relations Officer, Keeta J. Diller/VP, Corp. Sec., Gary A. Saxman/COO, Exec. VP - Rdsi Banking Systems

Directors: Kenneth A. Joyce/Dir., CEO, Pres., Steven D. Vandemark/Chmn., Michael J. Walz/Dir., Rita A. Kissner/Dir., John Fahl/Dir., John R. Compo/Dir., Thomas M. Callan/Dir., Thomas L. Sauer/Dir., Thomas A. Buis/Dir., Independent Consultant, Richard L. Hardgrove/Dir., Robert A. Fawcett/Dir.

Owners: John Fahl, Insiders/7.13%, Thomas L. Sauer, Duane L. Sinn, Thomas M. Callan, Kenneth A. Joyce/1.43%, Robert A. Fawcett, Mark A. Klein, Michael J. Walz, Henry R. Thiemann, Steven D. VanDemark, John R. Compo/1.09%, Thomas A. Buis, Richard L. Hardgrove, Rita A. Kissner

Financial Data: *Fiscal Year End:* 12/31 *Latest Annual Data:* 12/31/2006

Year	Sales	Net Income
2006	$55,221,000	$2,760,000
2005	$39,330,000	$673,000
2004	$36,718,000	$2,734,000

Curr. Assets:	$25,762,000	**Curr. Liab.:**	$470,050,000	**P/E Ratio:**	20.87
Plant, Equip.:	$15,532,000	**Total Liab.:**	$499,051,000	**Indic. Yr. Divd.:**	$0.280
Total Assets:	$556,007,000	**Net Worth:**	$56,955,000	**Debt/ Equity:**	0.4008

Rush Enterprises Inc

555 IH 35 S, Ste. 500, New Braunfels, TX, 78130; *PH:* 1-830-626-5200; *Fax:* 1-830-626-5310; *http://* www.rushenterprises.com

General - Incorporation	TX	**Stock** - Price on:12/24/2007	$22.6
Employees	2,912	Stock Exchange	NDQ
Auditor	Ernst & Young LLP	Ticker Symbol	RUSHB
Stk Agt	American Stock Transfer & Trust Co.	Outstanding Shares	25,380,000
Counsel	Fulbright & Jaworski LLP	E.P.S	NA
DUNS No.	06-212-4110	Shareholders	NA

Business: The groups principle activity is to operate heavy- and medium-duty truck dealerships. The group also provides construction equipment. The group operates from United States.

Primary SIC and add'l.: 7513 6159 5511

CIK No: 0001012019

Subsidiaries: AiRush,Inc., International General Agency, Los Cuernos,Inc., Rush Accessories Corp., Rush Administrative Services,Inc., Rush Equipment Centers of Texas,Inc., Rush GMC Truck Center of El Paso,Inc., Rush GMC Truck Center of Phoenix,Inc., Rush GMC Truck Center of San Diego,Inc., Rush GMC Truck Center of Tucson,Inc., Rush Retail Centers,Inc., Rush Truck Center of Albuquerque,Inc., Rush Truck Center of New Mexico,Inc., Rush Truck Centers of Alabama,Inc., Rush Truck Centers of Arizona,Inc. 24 Subsidiaries included in the Index

Officers: W. M. Rush/Dir., CEO, Pres./$1,914,654.00, J. M. Lowe/Sr. VP - Corporate Development, Derrek Weaver/Chief Compliance Officer, VP - Legal Affairs, David C. Orf/Sr. VP - Marketing, Fleets, Specialized Equipment Sales/$591,053.00, James E. Thor/Sr. VP - Retail Sales, Martin A. Naegelin/Exec. VP/$609,100.00, Daryl J. Gorup/Sr. VP - Dealership Operations/$606,516.00, Richard D. Hall/VP - Insurance, Scott Anderson/Sr. VP - Finance, Insurance, Steven L. Keller/CFO, VP

Directors: W. M. Rush/Dir., CEO, Pres., Marvin W. Rush/Chmn., Harold D. Marshall/Dir., Thomas A. Akin/Dir., Ronald J. Krause/Dir., John D. Rock/Dir.

Owners: W. M. Rush, W. M. Rush, Marvin W. Rush, Daryl J. Gorup, Ronald J. Krause, Thomas A. Akin, Martin A. Naegelin, Munder Capital Management/15.70%, David C. Orf, Wasatch Advisors, Inc./6.30%, Lord, Abbett & Co. LLC/17.20%, Insiders/34.60%, Martin A. Naegelin, John D. Rock, Ronald J. Krause *(22 Owners included in Index)*

Rush Financial Technologies Inc

100 S Wacker Dr., Ste. 1550, Chicago, IL, 60606; *PH:* 1-866-866-6546; *http://* www.rushfintech.com

General - Incorporation	TX	**Stock** - Price on:12/24/2007	$0.2
Employees	95	Stock Exchange	OTC
Auditor	KBA Group LLP	Ticker Symbol	TNFG
Stk Agt	UMB Bank, N.A.	Outstanding Shares	271,860,000
Counsel	NA	E.P.S	-$0.16
DUNS No.	NA	Shareholders	NA

Business: The group's principal activities are to offer insurance and investment products to clients through a network of agents and representatives. The group did business as rushtrade group offering real-time technology development and direct-access online brokerage. The group's products include rushtrade direct, a level i browser-based product and rushtrade direct pro, a level ii software-based product. Both the products provide customers or other users and licensees of the rushtrade software with real-time quotes and charts, fast and reliable access to multiple exchanges, ecns or market maker participants and other advanced decision support and portfolio management tools. Rushtrade software services offers licensing of the rushtrade direct access software and other arrangements and is in development stage. On 27-Feb-2004, the group acquired lostview development corporation.

Primary SIC and add'l.: 6211 6719 6321 6411 7372

CIK No: 0000884892

Subsidiaries: LostView Development Corporation, Rush Group Technologies, Inc., Rushmore Insurance Services, Inc., Rushmore Securities Corporation, RushTrade Securities, Inc., RushTrade.com, Inc.

Owners: Mary Patricia Kane/1.00%, Jerald G. Kallas/1.80%, Wellington Management Co./17.30%, Gayle C. Tinsley, Charles B. Brewer, Insiders/3.20%, Michael G. Nolan, Steve B. Watson, Russell N. Crawford, PAR Investment Partners, L.P./10.60%, Bernay Box and Bonanza Master Fund, Ltd./42.30%, Forest Hill Capital/12.30%

Financial Data: *Fiscal Year End:* 12/31 *Latest Annual Data:* 12/31/2006

Year	Sales	Net Income
2006	$37,536,000	-$1,082,000
2005	$2,346,000	-$3,180,000
2004	$2,200,000	-$2,497,000

Curr. Assets:	$274,852,000	**Curr. Liab.:**	$244,867,000		
Plant, Equip.:	$615,000	**Total Liab.:**	$264,113,000	**Indic. Yr. Divd.:**	NA
Total Assets:	$294,719,000	**Net Worth:**	$30,606,000	**Debt/ Equity:**	0.5253

Russ Berrie and Company Inc

111 Bauer Dr., Oakland, NJ, 07436; *PH:* 1-201-337-9000; *http://* www.russberrie.com; *Email:* sales@russberrie.com

General - Incorporation	NJ	**Stock** - Price on:12/24/2007	$18.92
Employees	1,034	Stock Exchange	NYSE
Auditor	KPMG LLP	Ticker Symbol	RUS
Stk Agt	Registrar & Transfer Co	Outstanding Shares	21,080,000
Counsel	NA	E.P.S	$0.21
DUNS No.	01-158-6153	Shareholders	NA

Business: The group's principal activities are to design, manufacture and market a variety of gift products to retail stores. Its core product line includes around 7,100 gift items and home decor products and non core product line around 1,000 functional consumer products. This product line encompasses seasonal and everyday products that focus on theme or concept groupings such as collectible heirloom bears, stuffed animals, wedding, anniversary, baby gifts, tabletop accessories, home decor, home and garden accessories, glass, porcelain and ceramic gifts, contemporary lifestyle gifts, bath toys, developmental toys, feeding utensils and bowls, pacifiers, bottles, bibs, soft toys, mobiles and feeders. The products are marketed under the trade names and trademark russ(R) and russhome(TM) . It serves its customers in England, Holland, Belgium, Ireland, Spain, Germany, Austria, Canada, France and Australia. On 02-Aug-2004, the group sold bright of America, inc.

Primary SIC and add'l.: 5945 5947 5092 3942 3949

CIK No: 0000739878

Subsidiaries: Amrams Distributing Ltd., Kids Line Australia Pty Ltd., Kids Line, LLC, Russ Australia Pty Limited, Russ Berrie & Co. (West), Inc., Russ Berrie (Benelux) B.V., Russ Berrie (Deutschland) GmbH, Russ Berrie (Holdings) Limited, Russ Berrie (Ireland) Limited, Russ Berrie (sterreich) GmbH, Russ Berrie (U.K.) Limited, Russ Berrie and Company Investments, Inc., Russ Berrie and Company Properties, Inc., Russ Berrie and Company, Inc., Russ Berrie Espaa, S.L. 21 Subsidiaries included in the Index

Officers: Michael Levin/CEO, Pres. - Kidsline LLC, Andrew R. Gatto/Dir., CEO, Pres./$965,529.00, Teresa Chan/VP - Far East Operations, Y. B. Lee/Sr. VP - Design, Development, Far East, Pres. - Korean Operations, Chris Robinson/Pres. - International Division, Russ Berrie, UK LTD, Fritz Hirsch/Pres. - Sassy Inc, Thomas J. Sancetta/VP - Sales Administration, Anthony P. Cappiello/Exec. VP, Chief Administrative Officer/$538,461.00, Jeffrey A. Bialosky/Exec. VP - Sales/$423,442.00, Marc S. Goldfarb/Sr. Vice Persident, General Counsel, Corp. Sec./$420,934.00, Arline Wall/Sr. VP - Product Development, Marketing, James J. O'Reardon/CFO, VP/$316,826.00

Directors: Andrew R. Gatto/Dir., CEO, Pres., Raphael Benaroya/Vice Chmn., Michael Zimmerman/Chmn., Mario Ciampi/Dir., Charles Klatskin/Dir., Frederick J. Horowitz/Dir., Lauren Krueger/Dir., Salvatore M. Salibello/Dir., Daniel Posner/Dir., Joseph Kling/Dir., Lauren Robertsen/Dir., Elliott Wahle/Dir., Carl Epstein/Dir., William A. Landman/56/Dir.

Owners: Michael Zimmerman/20.90%, Insiders/23.00%, Salvatore Salibello, Anthony Cappiello, Carl Epstein, Jeffrey Bialosky, Raphael Benaroya, Charles Klatskin

Financial Data: *Fiscal Year End:* 12/31 *Latest Annual Data:* 12/31/2006

Year	Sales	Net Income
2006	$294,769,000	-$9,436,000
2005	$290,156,000	-$35,099,000
2004	$265,959,000	-$20,000,000

Curr. Assets:	$132,084,000	**Curr. Liab.:**	$86,212,000		
Plant, Equip.:	$13,993,000	**Total Liab.:**	$113,103,000	**Indic. Yr. Divd.:**	NA
Total Assets:	$303,767,000	**Net Worth:**	$190,664,000	**Debt/ Equity:**	NA

Russel Metals Inc

1900 Minnesota Ct., Ste 210, Mississauga, ON, L5N 3C9; *PH:* 1-905-819-7777; *http://* www.russelmetals.com; *Email:* info@russelmetals.com

General - Incorporation......................Canada	Stock - Price on:12/24/2007 ....$29.3249
Employees ....NA	Stock Exchange...OTC
Auditor ....Deloitte & Touche LLP	Ticker Symbol..RUSMF
Stk Agt.............................Mellon Trust Co	Outstanding Shares ....NA
Counsel..NA	E.P.S...NA
DUNS No. 20-008-4853	Shareholders...NA

Business: The group's principle activity is to provide specialized metal processing service to satisfy specifications established by end users. The company's network of service centers carries a full line of metal products in a wide range of sizes, shapes and specifications, including carbon hot rolled and cold finished steel, pipe and tubular products, stainless steel and aluminum. The company purchases these products primarily from producers in North America and packages them for end users who typically require products in quantities that are smaller than the economic minimum order available from producers. The customers of the company include machinery and equipment manufacturing, construction, shipbuilding and mining and petroleum industries. The service center network includes 45 Canadian and 5 us locations.

Primary SIC and add'l.: 3316 3312

CIK No: 0000903657

Subsidiaries: Fedmet Corp., Fedmet Enterprises Corporation, Fedmet International Corporation, Fil (us) Inc., Pioneer Steel & Tube Corp., RMI Holdings LLC, Russel Metals Corp., Russel Metals Williams Bahcall Inc., Sunbelt Group L.P., Thunder Bay Terminals Ltd., Triumph Tubular & Supply Ltd., Wirth Steel, a General Partnership

Officers: Edward M. Siegel/Dir., CEO, Pres., William M. O'Reilly/Sec. - Davies Ward Phillips, Vineberg LLP, Toronto, Lesley M.S. Coleman/VP, Controller - Mississauga, Marion E. Britton/VP, Chief Accounting Officer, Assist. Sec., Brian R. Hedges/CFO, Exec. VP, Elaine G. Toomey/Assist. Sec. - Mississauga, Paula Evans Nash/Mgr. - Compensation, Benefits

Directors: Edward M. Siegel/Dir., CEO, Pres., Anthony F. Griffiths/Chmn., Alain Benedetti/Dir., Robbert Hartog/Dir., Lise Lachapelle/Dir., James F. Dinning/Dir., Carl R. Fiora/Corp. Dir., John W. Robinson/Dir., Alice D. Laberge/Dir.

Russell Corp

755 Lee St., Alexander City, AL, 35011; **PH:** 1-256-500-4000; **http://** www.russellcorp.com

General - Incorporation...........................DE	Stock - Price on:12/24/2007 ....NA
Employees ....NA	Stock Exchange...NA
Auditor ....Ernst & Young LLP	Ticker Symbol...NA
Stk Agt.............................Suntrust Bank	Outstanding Shares ....NA
Counsel..NA	E.P.S...NA
DUNS No. 00-339-5902	Shareholders...NA

Business: The group's principal activity is to design, manufacture and market a variety of apparel products. These products include fleece, t-shirts, casual shirts, jackets, athletic shorts, socks and camouflage attire for men, women, boys and girls. The group also supplies team uniforms and other related apparel to colleges, high schools, other organized sports teams and league baseball teams. These products are sold under brand names russell athletic(R), jerzees(R), mossy oak(R), cross creek(R), moving comfort(R), discus(R), bike(R), spalding(R), dudley(R) and sherrin(r). The group's products are sold in the United States, Canada and 70 other countries. In 2003, the group acquired the majority of the assets of bike athletic company and sporting goods business of spalding sports worldwide inc.

Primary SIC and add'l.: 2329 2331 2326 2339

CIK No: 0000085812

Subsidiaries: Alexander City Flying Service, Inc., American Sportswear, S.A., Athletic de Camargo S.A. de C.V., Brooks Sports Gmbh, Brooks Sports Limited, Brooks Sports, Inc., Citygate Textiles Limited, Cross Creek Apparel, LLC, Cross Creek de Honduras, S. de R.L., Cross Creek Holdings, Inc., Cumberland Asset Management, Inc., DeSoto Mills, LLC, Eagle R Holdings Limited, Frontier Yarns, LLC, Jerzees Apparel, LLC 56 Subsidiaries included in the Index

RussOil Corp

Formerly: Cassidy Media Inc
415 Madison Ave., 15th Fl., New York, NY, 10017; **PH:** 1-646-673-8427

General - Incorporation...........................CA	Stock - Price on:12/24/2007 ....NA
Employees ....NA	Stock Exchange...OTC
Auditor ....Wolinetz, Lafazan & Co., P.c.	Ticker Symbol...RUSOE
Stk Agt.............................Island Stock Transfer	Outstanding Shares ....NA
Counsel..NA	E.P.S...NA
DUNS No. ....NA	Shareholders...NA

Business: The groups principal activity is to provide online marketing. The group products include web site development, internet commercials and flash banners, presentations. The group operates through three segments namely media, affiliate marketing, and technology.

Primary SIC and add'l.: 7310

CIK No: 0001369092

Officers: Kimberly A. Hennessey/36/Dir., CEO, CFO, Pres., Nicole Gagne/31/Sec.

Directors: Kimberly A. Hennessey/36/Dir., CEO, CFO, Pres.

Owners: Nicole Gagne/4.20%, Kimberly A. Hennessey/66.70%, Insiders/70.90%

Financial Data: Fiscal Year End:09/30 Latest Annual Data: 12/31/2006

Year	Sales	Net Income
2006	NA	-$101,000

Curr. Assets:	NA	Curr. Liab.:	$9,000		
Plant, Equip.:	NA	Total Liab.:	$26,000	Indic. Yr. Divd.:	NA
Total Assets:	NA	Net Worth:	-$26,000	Debt/ Equity:	NA

Ruth's Chris Steak House Inc

500 International Pkwy., Ste. 100, Heathrow, FL, 32746; **PH:** 1-407-333-7440; **Fax:** 1-407-833-9625; **http://** www.ruthschris.com

General - Incorporation...........................DE	Stock - Price on:12/24/2007 ....$17.42
Employees 3,827	Stock Exchange...NDQ
Auditor ....KPMG LLP	Ticker Symbol..RUTH
Stk Agt......American Stock Transfer & Trust Co.	Outstanding Shares 23,190,000
Counsel..NA	E.P.S...$1.05
DUNS No. ....NA	Shareholders...NA

Business: The groups principle activity is to provide restaurants services. The groups services include veal, lamb, poultry and seafood dishes. The products of the group include shrimp, mushrooms stuffed with crabmeat, shrimp remoulade, Louisiana seafood gumbo, onion soup au gratin, crabtini and seven salads. The group operates from the United States. The group's quarterly revenue for September 2007 was 70.22 millions of USD.

Primary SIC and add'l.: 5812

CIK No: 0001324272

Subsidiaries: R. F. Inc., R.C. Equipment, Inc., RCSH Holdings, Inc., RCSH Management, Inc., RCSH Operations, Inc., RCSH Operations, LLC, RCSH Promotions, LLC, Ruths Chris Steak House #15, Inc., Ruths Chris Steak House Boston LLC, Ruths Chris Steak House Dallas, L.P., Ruths Chris Steak House Franchise, Inc., Ruths Chris Steak House Texas, LP

Officers: Craig S. Miller/Chmn., CEO, Pres., Geoffrey D.K. Stiles/Exec. VP - Operations, COO, Thomas J. Pennison/Sr. VP - Finance, CFO, Thomas E. O'Keefe/Sr. VP, General Counsel, David L. Cattell/Sr. VP - Development, Construction, Chief Development Officer, Sarah C. Jackson/49/Sr. VP - Human Resources

Directors: Craig S. Miller/Chmn., CEO, Pres., Robin P. Selati/Dir., Carla R. Cooper/Dir., Alan Vituli/Dir., Bannus B. Hudson/Dir.

Owners: Craig S. Miller/2.60%, Rainier Investment Management, Inc/5.40%, Thomas J. Pennison, Madison Dearborn/17.80%, Geoffrey D. K. Stiles, Thomas E. OKeefe, Alan Vituli, KDI Capital Partners, LLC/6.90%, Insiders/22.00%, Carla R. Cooper, Robin P. Selati/17.80%, David L. Cattell, Bannus Hudson, FMR Corp/8.40%

Financial Data: Fiscal Year End:12/25 Latest Annual Data: 12/31/2006

Year	Sales	Net Income
2006	$271,479,000	$23,790,000
2005	$214,537,000	$10,933,000
2004	$192,197,000	$2,442,000

Curr. Assets:	$26,353,000	Curr. Liab.:	$59,304,000		
Plant, Equip.:	$105,092,000	Total Liab.:	$141,742,000	Indic. Yr. Divd.:	NA
Total Assets:	$209,720,000	Net Worth:	$67,978,000	Debt/ Equity:	NA

Ryans Restaurant Group Inc

405 Lancaster Ave, Greer, SC, 29652; **PH:** 1-864-879-1000; **http://** www.ryansinc.com

General - Incorporation ....SC	Stock - Price on:12/24/2007 ....NA
Employees ....NA	Stock Exchange...NA
Auditor ....KPMG LLP	Ticker Symbol...NA
Stk Agt......American Stock Transfer & Trust Co.	Outstanding Shares ....NA
Counsel......Wyche, Burgess, Freeman & Parham	E.P.S...NA
DUNS No. 09-132-9268	Shareholders...NA

Business: The group's principal activity is to own and operate restaurants located principally in the southern and midwestern United States. The group's restaurants are family-oriented restaurants serving a variety of foods from centrally located scatter bars collectively known as the mega bar(R) buffet as well as grilled entrees such as charboiled steaks, hamburgers, chicken and seafood. The mega bar(R) includes fresh and pre-made salad items, soups, cheeses, a variety of hot meats and vegetables and hot yeast rolls prepared and baked daily on site. The group's bakery bar feature hot and fresh-from-the-oven cookies, brownies and other bakery products and various dessert selections, such as ice cream, frozen yogurt, fresh fruit, cakes, cobblers and several dessert toppings. The restaurants also offer a variety of non-alcoholic beverages. At 31-Dec-2003, the group owned and operated 334 restaurants.

Primary SIC and add'l.: 5812

CIK No: 0000355622

Subsidiaries: Big R Procurement Company, LLC, Fire Mountain Restaurants, Inc.

Owners: Roe H. Hatlen, Robert M. Rosenberg, Caxton-Iseman Investments L.P., Frederick J. Iseman, Glenn D. Drasher, Michael R. Andrews, Insiders, Sentinel Capital PartnersII, L.P., Fred P. Williams, Mario O. Lee, Thomas H. Mitchell, David S. Lobel

Ryanair Holdings Plc

C/o Ryanair Limited, Dublin Airport, Dublin; **PH:** 44-8444440; **http://** www.ryanair.ie

General - Incorporation ....Ireland	Stock - Price on:12/24/2007 ....$37.99
Employees 3,453	Stock Exchange...NDQ
Auditor ....KPMG LLP	Ticker Symbol..RYAAY
Stk Agt.............................Bank of Ireland	Outstanding Shares 309,330,000
Counsel..NA	E.P.S...$2.44
DUNS No. 98-620-6019	Shareholders...NA

Business: The group's principal activity is the operation of low fares airline business. The group plans to continue to develop this activity by expanding its low fares formula on new and existing routes. The group operates in 150 routes with 72 aircrafts.

Primary SIC and add'l.: 7514 4512 4522

CIK No: 0001038683

Subsidiaries: Darley Investments Limited, Ryanair Limited, Ryanair.com Limited

Officers: Michael Cawley/Deputy CEO, COO, Michael O'Leary/Dir., CEO, Howard Millar/Dir. - Finance, David O'Brien/Dir. - Flight Operations, Ray Conway/Chief Pilot, Jim Callaghan/Sec., Caroline Green/Head - Customer Service, Edward Wilson/Dir. - Personnel, In, Flight, Michael Hickey/Dir. - Engineering

Directors: Michael O'Leary/Dir., CEO, David Bonderman/Chmn., Kyran McLaughlin/Dir., Michael Horgan/Dir., Anthony T. Ryan/Dir., Klaus Kirchberger/Dir., Emmanuel Faber/Dir., Paolo Pietrogrande/Dir., James R. Osborne/Dir.

Owners: Michael O'Leary/4.30%, Gilder Gagnon Howe & Co LLC/6.20%, Fidelity Investments/5.90%, Capital Group Companies Inc/11.90%, Wellington Investment Management/6.00%, Chieftain Capital Management Inc/3.60%, Bank of Ireland Asset Management Ltd./4.10%

Financial Data: Fiscal Year End:03/31 Latest Annual Data: 03/31/2007

Year	Sales	Net Income
2007	$2,982,899,000	$577,778,000
2006	$2,043,899,000	$380,191,000
2005	$1,726,334,000	$366,058,000

Curr. Assets:	$2,479,960,000	Curr. Liab.:	$1,021,475,000		
Plant, Equip.:	$3,058,836,000	Total Liab.:	$3,190,761,000	Indic. Yr. Divd.:	NA
Total Assets:	$5,630,654,000	Net Worth:	$2,439,892,000	Debt/ Equity:	NA

Ryder System Inc

11690 NW 105th St., Miami, FL, 33178; *PH:* 1-305-500-3726; *Fax:* 1-305-500-3203; *http://* www.ryder.com

General - Incorporation	FL	**Stock**- Price on:12/24/2007	$52.18
Employees	28,600	Stock Exchange	NYSE
Auditor	Pricewaterhousecoopers LLP	Ticker Symbol	R
Stk Agt	Computershare Investor Services LLC	Outstanding Shares	61,150,000
Counsel	NA	E.P.S	$4.04
DUNS No.	00-692-2827	Shareholders	NA

Business: The group's principle activity is to provide transportation and logistic services. The group operates through three segments namely fleet management solutions, supply chain solutions and dedicated contract carriage. The group operates from Canada, Latin America, Europe and Asia.

Primary SIC and add'l.: 7513 8742 4213

CIK No: 0000085961

Subsidiaries: 1318359 Ontario Limited, Ascent Logistics (Taiwan) Company Ltd., Associated Ryder Capital Services, Inc., CRTS Logistica Automotiva S.A., Far East Freight, Inc., Globe Master Insurance Company, Logicair Limited, Mitchell Self Drive Limited, Network Vehicle Central, Inc., Phaseking Limited, Road Master, Limited, RSI Acquisition Corp., RSI Holding B.V., RSI Purchase Corp., RTI Argentina, S.A. 106 Subsidiaries included in the Index

Officers: Gregory T. Swienton/Chmn., CEO/$4,898,710.00, Mark T. Jamieson/54/CFO, Exec. VP/$1,309,255.00, Bobby J. Griffin/Pres. - International Operations/$1,237,586.00, Robert E. Sanchez/CFO, Exec. VP, Thomas S. Renehan/Exec. VP - Sales, Marketing, US Fleet Management Solutions, Gregory F. Greene/Chief Human Resources Officer, Exec. VP, Robert D. Fatovic/Exec. VP, Chief Legal Officer, Corp. Sec., Anthony G. Tegnelia/Pres. - US Fleet Management Solutions/$1,696,551.00, Vicki A. O'Meara/Pres. - US Supply Chain Solutions/$1,851,107.00, David P. Bouchard/MD - International, Art A. Garcia/46/Sr. VP, Controller

Directors: Gregory T. Swienton/Chmn., CEO, Hansel E. Tookes/Dir., Abbie J. Smith/Dir., Lynn M. Martin/Dir., Eugene A. Renna/Dir., Christine A. Varney/Dir., John M. Berra/Dir., Follin E. Smith/Dir., Patrick L. Hassey/Dir., David I. Fuente/Dir., Luis P. Nieto/52/Dir.

Owners: Follin E. Smith, David I. Fuente, Gregory T. Swienton/1.23%, Daniel H. Mudd, John M. Berra, Abbie J. Smith, Patrick L. Hassey, Hansel E. Tookes, Eugene A. Renna, Christine A. Varney, Lynn M. Martin, Anthony G. Tegnelia, Bobby J. Griffin, Insiders/1.97%, Vicki A. OMeara

Financial Data: *Fiscal Year End:*12/31 *Latest Annual Data:* 12/31/2006

Year		Sales		Net Income	
2006		$6,306,643,000		$248,959,000	
2005		$5,740,847,000		$226,929,000	
2004		$5,150,278,000		$215,609,000	
Curr. Assets:	$1,261,816,000	**Curr. Liab.:**	$1,267,622,000	**P/E Ratio:**	12.92
Plant, Equip.:	$5,008,300,000	**Total Liab.:**	$5,108,144,000	**Indic. Yr. Divd.:**	$0.840
Total Assets:	$6,828,923,000	**Net Worth:**	$1,720,779,000	**Debt/ Equity:**	1.4461

Ryerson Tull Inc

2621 W 15th Pl., Chicago, IL, 60608; *PH:* 1-773-762-2121; *http://* www.ryersontull.com

General - Incorporation	DE	**Stock**- Price on:12/24/2007	$38.66
Employees	5,700	Stock Exchange	NA
Auditor	Ernst & Young, LLP	Ticker Symbol	NA
Stk Agt	Bank of New York	Outstanding Shares	26,520,000
Counsel	NA	E.P.S	$2.81
DUNS No.	00-132-5422	Shareholders	NA

Business: The group's principle activity is to provide process metals and other materials. The group's products include stainless, carbon and alloy, and aluminum. The group operates from United States.

Primary SIC and add'l.: 3441 3399

CIK No: 0000790528

Subsidiaries: Integris Metals, Inc., J. M. Tull Metals Company, Inc., Joseph T. Ryerson & Son, Inc., Ryerson Americas, Inc. f/k/a Ryerson Tull International, Inc., Ryerson Procurement Corporation f/k/a Ryerson Tull Procurement Corporation

Officers: Neil S. Novich/Chmn., CEO, Pres., Terence R. Rogers/VP - Finance, Treasurer, Jay M. Gratz/CFO, Exec. VP, Lily L. May/VP, Controller, Chief Accounting Officer, Gary J. Niederpruem/Exec. VP, Darell R. Zerbe/CIO, VP, Stephen E. Makarewicz/Pres. - Ryerson South, William Korda/VP - Human Resources, James M. Delaney/Pres. - Global Accounting, Virginia M. Dowling/VP, Corp. Sec., Deputy General Counsel, Anita J. Pickens/Exec. VP, Louise M. Turilli/VP, General Counsel

Directors: Neil S. Novich/Chmn., CEO, Pres., Jameson A. Baxter/Dir., Anru D. Williams/Dir., Jerry K. Pearlman/Dir., Richard G. Cline/Dir., James A. Henderson/Dir., Gregory P. Josefowicz/Dir., Martha Miller De Lombera/Dir., Russell M. Flaum/Dir., Dennis J. Keller/Dir., James R. Kackley/Dir.

Owners: Richard G. Cline, M. Louise Turilli, Darell R. Zerbe, William Korda, Virginia M. Dowling, Neil S. Novich/2.14%, Gary J. Niederpruem, Lily L. May, James A. Henderson, Jay M. Gratz, Martha Miller de Lombera, Anr D. Williams, Russell M. Flaum, Gregory P. Josefowicz, Insiders/6.53% *(23 Owners included in Index)*

Financial Data: *Fiscal Year End:*12/31 *Latest Annual Data:* 12/31/2006

Year		Sales		Net Income	
2006		$5,908,900,000		$71,800,000	
2005		$5,780,500,000		$98,100,000	
2004		$3,302,000,000		$54,500,000	
Curr. Assets:	$1,873,600,000	**Curr. Liab.:**	$453,500,000	**P/E Ratio:**	13.76
Plant, Equip.:	$401,100,000	**Total Liab.:**	$1,888,600,000	**Indic. Yr. Divd.:**	$0.200
Total Assets:	$2,537,300,000	**Net Worth:**	$648,700,000	**Debt/ Equity:**	1.2099

Ryland Group Inc (The)

24025 Pk. Sorrento, Ste. 400, Calabasas, CA, 91302; *PH:* 1-818-223-7500; *Fax:* 1-818-223-7667; *http://* www.ryland.com; *Email:* investors@ryland.com

General - Incorporation	MD	**Stock**- Price on:12/24/2007	$40.85
Employees	2,810	Stock Exchange	NYSE
Auditor	Ernst & Young LLP	Ticker Symbol	RYL
Stk Agt	American Stock Transfer & Trust Co.	Outstanding Shares	42,050,000
Counsel	NA	E.P.S	-$1.05
DUNS No.	02-258-5913	Shareholders	NA

Business: The group's principle activity is to provide homebuilding and mortgage financing services. The group's services include design, construction and sale, title insurance, settlement, escrow and homeowners insurance brokerage services. The homebuilding services attached single-family homes to active adults seeking retirement housing. The financial services provide mortgage-related products and services. The groups mortgage financing services include conventional, federal housing administration and veterans administration mortgages. The group operates from United States.

Primary SIC and add'l.: 6411 1531 6162

CIK No: 0000085974

Subsidiaries: Ryland Homes of California, Inc., Ryland Organization Company, The Ryland Corporation

Officers: Chad R. Dreier/Chmn., CEO, Pres./$31,435,080.00, Drew P. MacKintosh/VP - Investor Relations, Renu L. Mentch/VP - Tax, Kipling W. Scott/COO, Exec. VP/$4,969,255.00, Peter G. Skelly/Pres. - North Region, Ryland Homes, Ken L. Trainer/Pres. - Texas Region, Ryland Homes, William M. Butler/Pres. - West Region, Ryland Homes, Eric E. Elder/Sr. VP - Marketing, Robert J. Cunnion/Sr. VP - Human Resources, Gordon A. Milne/CFO, Exec. VP/$4,604,660.00, Valerie S. Zook/VP - Compensation, Benefits, David L. Fristoe/Sr. VP, Controller, Chief Accounting Officer, Larry T. Nicholson/COO/$4,876,096.00, Daniel G. Schreiner/Sr. VP/$3,613,501.00, Jennifer Painter/VP, Assist. General Counsel *(20 Officers included in Index)*

Directors: Chad R. Dreier/Chmn., CEO, Pres., Roland A. Hernandez/Dir., Ned Mansour/Dir., Paul J. Varello/Dir., William L. Jews/Dir., Robert E. Mellor/Dir., Norman J. Metcalfe/65/Dir., John O. Wilson/Dir., Leslie M. Frecon/54/Dir., Daniel T. Bane/Dir., Charlotte St. Martin/62/Dir.

Owners: LMM LLC/16.30%, PBK Holdings, Inc./7.10%, Norman J. Metcalfe, Charlotte St. Martin, Leslie M. Frecon, Ned Mansour, Daniel G. Schreiner, Insiders, Chad R. Dreier, Robert E. Mellor, Paul J. Varello, FMR Corp./14.50%, Baillie Gifford & Co./6.30%, Tremblant Capital Group/6.70%, Roland A. Hernandez *(22 Owners included in Index)*

Financial Data: *Fiscal Year End:*12/31 *Latest Annual Data:* 06/30/2007

Year		Sales		Net Income	
2007		NA		$142,895,000	
2006		$4,757,216,000		$359,942,000	
2005		$4,817,566,000		$447,052,000	
Curr. Assets:	$2,986,522,000	**Curr. Liab.:**	$773,665,000	**P/E Ratio:**	18.00
Plant, Equip.:	$76,887,000	**Total Liab.:**	$1,723,782,000	**Indic. Yr. Divd.:**	$0.480
Total Assets:	$3,416,697,000	**Net Worth:**	$1,511,166,000	**Debt/ Equity:**	0.6969

S&T Bank

800 Philadelphia St., Indiana, PA, 15701; *PH:* 1-724-349-0599; *Fax:* 1-724-465-1417; *http://* www.stbank.com; *Email:* Compliance@stbank.net

General - Incorporation	PA	**Stock**- Price on:12/24/2007	$33.3
Employees	790	Stock Exchange	NDQ
Auditor	Ernst & Young LLP	Ticker Symbol	STBA
Stk Agt	Ernest & Young LLP	Outstanding Shares	24,800,000
Counsel	NA	E.P.S	$2.23
DUNS No.	06-875-1148	Shareholders	NA

Business: The group's principal activity is to provide banking services through its wholly owned subsidiaries. The services provided include accepting time and demand deposit accounts, originating secured and unsecured commercial and consumer loans. The group also provides letters of credit and offers discount brokerage services, personal financial planning and credit card services. The group operates through a branch network of 49 offices located in armstrong, blair, allegheny, jefferson, butler, cambria, clarion, clearfield, Indiana and westmoreland counties of Pennsylvania.

Primary SIC and add'l.: 6035 6141 6022 6712 6153 6162

CIK No: 0000719220

Subsidiaries: 9th Street Holdings, Inc., Commonwealth Trust Credit Life Insurance Company, Evergreen Insurance Associates, LLC, S&T Bancholdings, Inc., S&T Insurance Group, LLC, S&T Professional Resources Group, LLC, S&T Settlement Services, LLC, Stewart Capital Advisors, LLC

Officers: James C. Miller/62/Chmn., CEO, Tony E. Kallsen/40/Exec. VP, Loan Administration Group Mgr., Lisa K. Wymer/VP, Trust Operations Mgr., Connie M. Reed/Trust Operations Supervisor, Darren A. Bonson/VP - Financial Advisor, Dirk W. Johnson/Assist. VP - Financial Advisor, Kristain Krecota/Assist. VP - Financial Advisor, Toni Heming/Registered Representative, Dorothy P. Mattern/VP, Relationship Mgr., Karen J. Hackman/VP, Relationship Mgr., Bonnie J. Confer/VP, Relationship Mgr., Dennis E. Hunt/VP, Relationship Mgr., Christine D. Bondra/Assist. VP, Relationship Mgr., Jeffrey M. Russo/VP, Divisional Sales Mgr., Steven P. Leach/VP - Financial Advisor *(40 Officers included in Index)*

Directors: James C. Miller/62/Chmn., CEO, James V. Milano/48/Dir., Myles D. Sampson/63/Dir., Charles A. Spadafora/66/Dir., John J. Delaney/66/Dir., Ruth M. Grant/76/Dir. Emeritus, Alan Papernick/70/Dir., Christine J. Olson/51/Dir., Frank W. Jones/62/Dir., William J. Gatti/66/Dir., Michael J. Donnelly/50/Dir., Jeffrey D. Grube/54/Dir., James L. Carino/75/Dir., Samuel Levy/69/Dir., Joseph A. Kirk/68/Dir. *(18 Directors included in Index)*

Owners: Insiders/8.20%, David L. Krieger, Frank W. Jones, William J. Gatti, Michael J. Donnelly, Todd D. Brice, Ruth M. Grant/1.10%, James L. Carino/1.20%, Ariel Capital Management, LLC, Thomas A. Brice, Alan Papernick, Robert E. Rout, Charles A. Spadafora, John J. Delaney, Edward C. Hauck *(23 Owners included in Index)*

Financial Data: *Fiscal Year End:*12/31 *Latest Annual Data:* 12/31/2006

Year		Sales		Net Income	
2006		$245,092,000		$53,336,000	
2005		$209,690,000		$58,243,000	
2004		$182,840,000		$54,358,000	
Curr. Assets:	$59,980,000	**Curr. Liab.:**	$2,753,327,000	**P/E Ratio:**	16.32
Plant, Equip.:	$35,700,000	**Total Liab.:**	$2,999,492,000	**Indic. Yr. Divd.:**	$1.240
Total Assets:	$3,338,543,000	**Net Worth:**	$339,051,000	**Debt/ Equity:**	0.7531

S.Y. Bancorp Inc

1040 E Main St., Louisville, KY, 40206; *PH:* 1-502-582-2571; *Fax:* 1-501-625-1041; *http://* www.syb.com

General - Incorporation	KY	**Stock**- Price on:12/24/2007	$24.12
Employees	437	Stock Exchange	NDQ
Auditor	KPMG LLP	Ticker Symbol	SYBT
Stk Agt	Stock Yards Bank & Trust Co	Outstanding Shares	14,350,000
Counsel	NA	E.P.S	$1.62
DUNS No.	36-194-2212	Shareholders	NA

Business: The group's principal activities are to provide commercial and retail banking services; trust and investment management services and mortgage banking services through its subsidiary, stock yards bank & trust company. The group's commercial and personal banking activities include checking, savings and time deposit accounts; secured and unsecured loans; letter of credit and safe deposit boxes. The lending activities include commercial loans, industrial loans, real estate loans, and consumer loans. At 31-Dec-2003, the bank had twenty one full service-banking locations in louisville and southern Indiana and one loan production office in indianapolis, Indiana.

Primary SIC and add'l.: 6712 6022

CIK No: 0000835324

Subsidiaries: S.Y. Bancorp Capital Trust I, Stock Yards Bank & Trust Company

Officers: David P. Heintzman/Chmn., CEO, Pres. - Executive Office/$914,790.00, Kathy C. Thompson/Dir., Sr. Exec. VP - Investment Management, Trust/$509,185.00, James A. Hillebrand/Exec. VP - Private Banking/$254,565.00, Carolyn Sachse/Sr. VP - Mortgage Lending, Philip S. Poindexter/Exec. VP - Commercial Lending/$240,849.00, Nancy B. Davis/Exec. VP - Shareholder Relations, Sec., Treasurer, CFO/$315,238.00, Judy S. Sprowls/Sr. VP - Retail Banking, Gregory A. Hoeck/Exec. VP - Retail Banking, Phillip S. Smith/Exec. VP - Credit Administration, Steve Smith/VP - Brokerage Center

Directors: David P. Heintzman/Chmn., CEO, Pres. - Executive Office, Kathy C. Thompson/Dir., Sr. Exec. VP - Investment Management, Trust, James E. Carrico/Dir., Bruce P. Madison/Dir., Norman Tasman/Dir., David H. Brooks/Dir., Charles R. Edinger/Dir., Carl G. Herde/Dir., Nicholas X. Simon/Dir., Robert L. Taylor/Dir., Richard A. Lechleiter/Dir.

Owners: Insiders/11.70%, Fidelity Management and Research/6.70%, Stock Yards Bank & Trust Company/6.60%

Financial Data: Fiscal Year End:12/31 Latest Annual Data: 12/31/2006

Year	Sales	Net Income
2006	$115,009,000	$22,896,000
2005	$99,465,000	$21,644,000
2004	$85,216,000	$18,912,000
Curr. Assets:	$66,595,000	**Curr. Liab.:** $1,288,757,000
Plant, Equip.:	$27,289,000	**Total Liab.:** $1,288,877,000 **Indic. Yr. Divd.:** $0.640
Total Assets:	$1,426,321,000	**Net Worth:** $137,444,000 **Debt/ Equity:** NA

S1 Corp

3500 Lenox Rd. , Ste. 200, Atlanta, GA, 30326; **PH:** 1-404-923-3500; **Fax:** 1-404-923-6727; **http://** www.s1.com

General - Incorporation	DE	**Stock** - Price on:12/24/2007	$7.9299
Employees	1,380	Stock Exchange	NDQ
Auditor	PricewaterhouseCoopers LLP	Ticker Symbol	SONE
Stk Agt	American Stock Transfer & Trust Co.	Outstanding Shares	61,650,000
Counsel	Hogan & Hartson LLP	E.P.S.	$0.00
DUNS No.	04-101-0856	Shareholders	NA

Business: The group's principal activity is to provide software solutions for financial organizations including banks, credit unions, investment firms and insurance companies on a global basis. The group's software solutions automate the channels by which financial institutions interact with their customers. These channels support person-to-person interaction such as talking to a teller in a bank branch or working with an insurance agent or to a customer support representative over the phone. The group also offers customer interaction technology solutions that allow organizations to automate, integrate and personalize interactions with the customers.

Primary SIC and add'l.: 7371 7373 7375 7372 7374

CIK No: 0001063254

Subsidiaries: FICS America, Inc, FICS Group Holdings, Inc, FICS Group N.V, Financial Integrated Contact Solutions SA (Proprietary) Limited, FRS Belgium NV/SA, FRS France SARL, FRS Hong Kong, FRS Luxembourg, FRS Netherlands, FRS Singapore, FRS Spain SL, Frs U.k. Ltd, Mosaic Software Holdings (UK) Ltd, Mosaic Software Ltd, Mosaic Software, Inc 33 Subsidiaries included in the Index

Officers: Johann Dreyer/Dir., CEO, Pres./$1,589,146.00, Craig Saks/COO - Fundamo, Rachel Van Eyk/Contact, Greg Orenstein/Sr. VP - Corporate Development, John Stone/CFO/$351,959.00, Meigan Putnam/56/Sr. VP/$2,122,834.00, Jan Kruger/Group Pres. - Postilion/$1,300,253.00, Neil Underwood/38/Sr. VP/$1,407,209.00, Dean Jordaan/Sr. VP - Product Strategy - Postilion, Pierre Naude/Sr. VP, GM - Postilion Americas, Postilion, Mitchell Elegbe/MD - Interswitch, Albert Oosthuizen/VP - Product Development, Postilion, Malik Velani/Product Mgr. - Postilion

Directors: Johann Dreyer/Dir., CEO, Pres., John W. Spiegel/Chmn., Thomas P. Johnson/Dir., Jeffrey C. Smith/Dir., Edward Terino/Dir., Ram Gupta/Dir., Gregory J. Owens/Dir., Douglas M. Ivester/Dir.

Owners: John Stone, Wellington Management Company, LLP/7.19%, Douglas M. Ivester, Gregory J. Owens, Johann J. Dreyer, Ramius Capital Group, LLC and related entities/10.50%, John W. Spiegel, Meigan Putnam, Thomas P. Johnson, Dimensional FundAdvisors LP/9.56%, Insiders/12.07%, Jan Kruger, Ram Gupta, Jeffrey C. Smith/10.50%, Neil Underwood

Financial Data: Fiscal Year End:12/31 Latest Annual Data: 12/31/2006

Year	Sales	Net Income
2006	$192,310,000	$17,902,000
2005	$204,068,000	-$1,057,000
2004	$241,043,000	$15,570,000
Curr. Assets:	$150,719,000	**Curr. Liab.:** $67,492,000 **P/E Ratio:** 18.44
Plant, Equip.:	$12,137,000	**Total Liab.:** $83,576,000 **Indic. Yr. Divd.:** NA
Total Assets:	$307,805,000	**Net Worth:** $224,229,000 **Debt/ Equity:** 0.0140

S2C Global Systems Inc

1650-1188 W Georgia, Vancouver, BC, V6E 4A2; **PH:** 1-604-629-2461; **http://** www.s2cglobal.com; **Email:** sales@s2cglobal.com

General - Incorporation	NV	**Stock** - Price on:12/24/2007	$0.1
Employees	NA	Stock Exchange	OTC
Auditor	MacKay LLP	Ticker Symbol	STWG
Stk Agt	Colonial Stock Transfer Co Inc	Outstanding Shares	NA
Counsel	NA	E.P.S.	NA
DUNS No.	NA	Shareholders	NA

Business: The group's principal activity is to manufacture, promote and market distribution system for prepackaged 5-gallon bottled water. The company has established a specific mechanical system, the "Aquaduct System", related to the operation and promotion of the prepackaged water distribution system. Currently, the company is in the final development stages to bring its distribution system to market. The company will enter into a variety of profit sharing, rental and distribution agreements for the Aquaduct with retailers across North America. Once its first bulk merchandising system has become fully established in the North American market, the company will position itself globally as a leader in bulk item retailing.

Primary SIC and add'l.: 5140

CIK No: 0001338629

Officers: Roderick C. Bartlett/55/Dir., CEO, Pres., Harlod Forzley/Dir., CFO, John Balanko/Corporate Finance, Peter Miele/Marketing, Chris Haugen/Contact - Technology, Trevor Reber/Operations

Directors: Roderick C. Bartlett/55/Dir., CEO, Pres., Alejandro Bautista/Dir., Harlod Forzley/Dir., CFO, Mark D. Lambert/Dir., Tina Vanderheyden/Dir., Craig Robson/Member - Advisory Board, Des Biali/Member - Advisory Board, Stephen C. Millen/Member - Advisory Board

Owners: Mark Lambert, Insiders/16.24%, Tina VanderHayden, Harold Forzley/5.17%, Alejandro Bautista/2.16%, Roderick Bartlett/8.58%

Financial Data: Fiscal Year End:12/31 Latest Annual Data: 12/31/2006

Year	Sales	Net Income
2006	NA	-$713,000
Curr. Assets:	$5,000	**Curr. Liab.:** $662,000
Plant, Equip.:	$233,000	**Total Liab.:** $662,000 **Indic. Yr. Divd.:** NA
Total Assets:	$238,000	**Net Worth:** -$424,000 **Debt/ Equity:** NA

S3 Investment Co Inc

43180 Business Pk. Dr., Ste. 202, Temecula, CA, 92590; **PH:** 1-951-677-8073; **http://** www.s3investments.com; **Email:** investors@s3investments.com

General - Incorporation	CA	**Stock** - Price on:12/24/2007	NA
Employees	21	Stock Exchange	OTC
Auditor	Chisholm Bierwolf & Nilson LLC	Ticker Symbol	SIVC
Stk Agt	Transfer Online, Inc.	Outstanding Shares	NA
Counsel	NA	E.P.S.	NA
DUNS No.	NA	Shareholders	NA

Business: The group's principal activity is to develop, market and sell enterprise compliance and risk management software solutions enabling clients to ensure that privacy, e business and security policies remain aligned with regulatory requirements, and an organization's business strategies and performance goals. The group ceased business of distribution of natural foods and supplements in fiscal 2003. On Apr 16, 2003 the group acquired securesoft systems, inc.

Primary SIC and add'l.: 7372

CIK No: 0001161647

Subsidiaries: Securesoft Systems, Inc

Officers: Jim Bickel/Chmn., CEO

Directors: Jim Bickel/Chmn., CEO, Gary Nerison/Dir., Manhong Liu/Dir.

Owners: Insiders/100.00%, Insiders/72.00%, Chris Bickel, James Bickel/55.00%, Insiders, James Bickel/100.00%, Chris Bickel/17.00%

Curr. Assets:	$1,467,000	**Curr. Liab.:** $1,047,000
Plant, Equip.:	$16,000	**Total Liab.:** $1,047,000 **Indic. Yr. Divd.:** NA
Total Assets:	$2,650,000	**Net Worth:** $1,017,000 **Debt/ Equity:** NA

Saba Software Inc

2400 Bridge Pkwy., Redwood Shores, CA, 94065; **PH:** 1-650-581-2500; **Fax:** 1-650-581-2581; **http://** www.saba.com; **Email:** info@saba.com

General - Incorporation	DE	**Stock** - Price on:12/24/2007	$5.2
Employees	516	Stock Exchange	NDQ
Auditor	Ernst & Young LLP	Ticker Symbol	SABA
Stk Agt	Mellon Investor Services LLC	Outstanding Shares	28,760,000
Counsel	NA	E.P.S.	-$0.27
DUNS No.	NA	Shareholders	NA

Business: The group's principle activity is to provide human capital development and management solutions. It is designed to increase organizational performance through the implementation of a management system for aligning, developing and managing people. It also helps large enterprises to efficiently manage regulatory compliance, increase sales and channel readiness, increase speed of customer acquisition and increase visibility into organizational performance. The group also provides consulting services, customer support and education services. The group operates in the United States, Australia, Canada, France, Germany, India and the United Kingdom. The customers of the group include global organizations in the automotive, communications, computer and electronics, consumer package goods, financial services, government and software and transportation industries. The group's total revenue for year 2007 was 99.87 millions of USD.

Primary SIC and add'l.: 7379 7372

CIK No: 0001070380

Subsidiaries: Centra RTP, Inc., Centra Software Australia Pty Ltd, Centra Software Europe Limited, Centra Software Securities Corporation, Centra Software Southern Europe SAS, Centra Software, LLC, Graduate Group Ltd., Human Performance Technologies, Inc., Saba Software (Bermuda) Ltd., Saba Software (Canada) Inc., Saba Software (UK) Ltd., Saba Software GmbH, Saba Software India Private Limited, Saba Software International, Inc., Saba Software K.K. 24 Subsidiaries included in the Index

Officers: Bobby Yazdani/Chmn., CEO/$815,067.00, Don Bosworth/Pres. - Saba North America, Public Sector, Kazuo Hosoi/VP - Saba North East Asia, Alun Cope-Morgan/Pres. - Saba Europe, Middle East, Africa, Juan Cuadros/VP - Saba Latin America, Peter Williams/Exec. VP - Corporate Development/$423,700.00, Gabi Schindler/Chief Marketing Officer, Mike Martini/CFO, Terry Dyckman/Chief Human Capital Officer, Tina Weinfurther/Sr. VP - Saba Corporate Strategy, Amar Dhaliwal/Sr. VP - Product Operations Group

Directors: Bobby Yazdani/Chmn., CEO, Clifton T. Weatherford/Dir., Joe E. Kiani/Dir., Douglas M. Ferguson/Dir., Lawrence D. Lenihan/Dir., Dow R. Wilson/Dir.

Owners: Lawrence D. Lenihan/9.60%, Douglas M. Ferguson, Peter E. Williams/1.10%, Clifton T. Weatherford, Dow R. Wilson, Mark D. Frost, Entities Affiliated with Pequot Capital Management, Inc./9.60%, Bobby Yazdani/6.60%, ZF Partners LP/6.60%, Diker GP, LLC/9.00%, Joe E. Kiani, Insiders/17.50%, Diker Management, LLC/9.60%

Financial Data: Fiscal Year End:05/31 Latest Annual Data: 05/31/2007

Year	Sales	Net Income
2007	$99,867,000	-$7,974,000
2006	$71,147,000	-$6,931,000
2005	$42,210,000	-$3,416,000

Curr. Assets:	$45,231,000	**Curr. Liab.:**	$47,866,000		
Plant, Equip.:	$2,172,000	**Total Liab.:**	$55,187,000	**Indic. Yr. Divd.:**	NA
Total Assets:	$107,034,000	**Net Worth:**	$51,847,000	**Debt/ Equity:**	0.0597

Sabine Royalty Trust

Trust Div., Bank of America Plz., 17th Fl., 901 Main St., Dallas, TX, 75202; ***PH:*** 1-214-209-2400; ***Fax:*** 1-214-209-2431; ***http://*** www.sbr-sabineroyalty.com

General - Incorporation	TX	**Stock**- Price on:12/24/2007	$42.35
Employees	NA	Stock Exchange	NYSE
Auditor	Deloitte & Touche LLP	Ticker Symbol	SBR
Stk Agt	Mellon Investor Services LLC	Outstanding Shares	14,580,000
Counsel	Thompson & Knight, LLC	E.P.S	$3.86
DUNS No.	NA	Shareholders	NA

Business: The groups principle activity is to invest in real estate properties. The group operates from the United States and New Mexico. The groups quarterly revenue for Septmber 2007 was 16.80 millions of USD.

Primary SIC and add'l.: 6792

CIK No: 0000710752

Officers: Ron E. Hooper/Sr. VP

Financial Data: Fiscal Year End:12/31 ***Latest Annual Data:*** 12/31/2006

Year	Sales	Net Income
2006	$61,958,000	$59,831,000
2005	$54,770,000	$52,681,000
2004	$42,390,000	$40,588,000

Curr. Assets:	$4,445,000	**Curr. Liab.:**	$372,000	**P/E Ratio:**	13.24
Plant, Equip.:	NA	**Total Liab.:**	$372,000	**Indic. Yr. Divd.:**	$4.480
Total Assets:	$5,370,000	**Net Worth:**	$4,998,000	**Debt/ Equity:**	NA

Sabre Holdings Corp

3150 Sabre Dr. Md 9105, Southlake, TX, 76092; ***PH:*** 1-682-605-1551; ***http://*** www.sabre.com

General - Incorporation	DE	**Stock**- Price on:12/24/2007	NA
Employees	8,800	Stock Exchange	NA
Auditor	Ernst & Young LLP	Ticker Symbol	NA
Stk Agt	NA	Outstanding Shares	NA
Counsel	NA	E.P.S	NA
DUNS No.	96-140-9331	Shareholders	NA

Business: The groups principle activity is to retail travel products and provides distribution and technology solutions for the travel industry. The group also provides airline ticket booking, rental cars, hotel reservations, and cruise/tour packages services. The group operates from United States.

Primary SIC and add'l.: 7372 7375 6719 4729

CIK No: 0001020265

Subsidiaries: 4less Limited, All-Hotels Limited, All-Hotels.com Limited, all-hotels.cominc., all-hotelsinc., Articulate Solutions Limited, Auto Holidays, Autos Europe Limited, Broomco, Cordex Computer Services Limited, Danube Travel Limited, Destination Australia Limited, Destination Malaysia Limited, Destination USA Limited, Drive America Limited 81 Subsidiaries included in the Index

Officers: Sam Gilliland/Chmn., CEO, Jeffery M. Jackson/CFO, Exec. VP, Thomas Klein/Exec. VP, Group Pres. - Sabre Travel Network, Sabre Airline Solutions, Michelle Peluso/Exec. VP, David A. Schwarte/Exec. VP, General Counsel, Al Comeaux/Sr. VP - Corporate Communications

Directors: Sam Gilliland/Chmn., CEO, Pamela B. Strobel/Dir., Richard G. Lindner/Dir., Glenn W. Marschel/Dir., Royce S. Caldwell/Dir., Bob L. Martin/Dir., Mary Alice Taylor/Dir., Richard L. Thomas/Dir., Christopher J. Fraleigh/Dir., Ronald V. Waters/Dir.

Owners: Pamela B. Strobel, Mark Miller, Thomas Klein, Royce S. Caldwell, Insiders/1.96%, Richard L. Thomas, Mary Alice Taylor, Michelle Peluso, Richard G. Lindner, Glenn W. Marschel, Jeffery M. Jackson, Michael S. Gilliland, John S. Stow, Bob L. Martin, David A. Schwarte

Saddlebrook Resorts Inc

5700 Saddlebrook Way, Wesley Chapel, FL, 33543; ***PH:*** 1-813-973-1111; ***Fax:*** 1-813-973-1312; ***http://*** www.saddlebrookresort.com

General - Incorporation	FL	**Stock**- Price on:12/24/2007	NA
Employees	NA	Stock Exchange	NA
Auditor	PricewaterhouseCoopers LLP	Ticker Symbol	NA
Stk Agt	NA	Outstanding Shares	NA
Counsel	NA	E.P.S	NA
DUNS No.	09-738-1404	Shareholders	NA

Business: The group's principle activity is to operate resort, which contains condominium units that have been sold to third parties or to affiliates of the company. The majority of the condominium units are hotel accommodations that participate in the rental pool. Other resort facilities of the company include two 18 hole golf courses, 45 tennis courts, three swimming pools, three restaurants, a convention facility with approximately 82,000 square feet of meeting and function space, a health spa, a fitness center, shops and other facilities necessary for the operation of a resort. The company operates as a wholly-owned subsidiary of saddlebrook holdings, inc. The group operates from United States.

Primary SIC and add'l.: 7997 7011 7999

CIK No: 0000313151

Officers: Johnnie Giffin/Leisure Travel Dir., Tom Wilkie/Leisure Travel Dir., Eva Colon/Mgr. - Catering, Conference Services, Jamie Cuffe/Mgr. - Catering, Conference Services, John Spitz/Concierge, Floor Mgr. Convention Groups, Annette Turer/Leisure Travel Dir., Yvonne Bohannon/Dir. - Group Activities, Spa Sales, Doug Pollard/Assoc. Dir. - Catering, Conference Services, Kristen Kachurak/Dir. - Catering, Conference Services, Nicole Briggs/Social Catering Mgr., Dick Boehning/Chief Marketing Officer, Mark Marker/VP - Sales, Kristen Boehning/Dir. - Southeast, Western Region Sales, Ed Danon/Dir. - Mid Atlantic Sales, Sean Dempsey/Dir. - Executive Group Sales *(18 Officers included in Index)*

Sadia

Rua Fortunato Ferraz 659 - V. Anastacio, Sao Paulo; ***PH:*** 55-1136493552; ***http://*** www.sadia.com; ***Email:*** grm@sadia.com.br

General - Incorporation	Brazil	**Stock**- Price on:12/24/2007	$46.35
Employees	45,381	Stock Exchange	NYSE
Auditor	KPMG LLP	Ticker Symbol	SDA
Stk Agt	Concordia CVMCC	Outstanding Shares	67,710,000
Counsel	Greenberg Traurig LLP	E.P.S	$5.06
DUNS No.	NA	Shareholders	NA

Business: The group's principal activities are the production, marketing, sale and distribution of processed products, such as refrigerated pizza and pasta, frozen food, breaded products, industrialized pork and poultry products. It also produces chickens, turkeys and pork for both the domestic and international markets.

Primary SIC and add'l.: 0213 2099 2038 2015

CIK No: 0001130968

Subsidiaries: Sadia Concrdia S.A., Sadia Frigobrs S.A.

Officers: Gilberto Tomazoni/CEO, Alexandre D. Campos/Dir. - International Sales, Flavio L. Favero/Regional Production Dir., Ronaldo K. Muller/Regional Production Dir., Welson Teixeira Junior/Dir. - Investor Relations, Control, Administration, Information Technology, Luiz Gonzaga Murat Junior/55/CFO, Dir. - Investor Relations, Alfredo Felipe Da Luz Sobrinho/Corporate Relations, Dir. - Legal Affairs, Paulo Francisco Alexandre Striker/54/Dir. - Logistics, Ricardo Fernando Thomas Fernandez/Dir. - Grain Purchase, Sergio Carvalho Mandin Fonseca/Commercial Dir., Jose Nestor Conceicao Hopf/Sec., Adriano Lima Ferreira/Dir. - Finance, Artemio Listoni/Dir. - Beef Activity, Eduardo Nunes De Noronha/Dir. - Management, Human Resources, Jose Augusto Lima De Sa/Dir. - International Relations *(23 Officers included in Index)*

Directors: Alcides L. Tapias/Vice Chmn., Eduardo Fontana DAvila/Vice Chmn., Walter F. Filho/Chmn., Diva Helena Furlan/Dir., Marcelo Fontana/Dir., Luiza Helena Trajano Inacio Rodrigues/Dir., Everaldo Nigro Dos Santos/Dir., Francisco Silverio Morales Cespede/Dir., Vicente F. Campos/Dir., Norberto Fatio/64/Dir., Jose Marcos Konder Comparato/Dir.

Owners: PREVI Caixa de Prev. dos Func. do Banco do Brasil/0.69%, Dodge & Cox/10.27%, Oppenheimer Funds Inc. Foreign Investment Fund/8.86%, Sunflower Participacs S.A./13.99%, Administradora e Comercial Old Ltda/9.99%, Fundao Attilio F. X. Fontana/9.73%, PREVI Caixa de Prev. dos Func. do Banco do Brasil/13.93%, Administradora e Comercial Old Ltda/0.01%

Financial Data: Fiscal Year End:12/31 ***Latest Annual Data:*** 12/31/2006

Year	Sales	Net Income
2006	$3,202,728,000	$169,067,000
2005	$3,143,745,000	$259,164,000
2004	$2,678,958,000	$184,248,000

Curr. Assets:	$2,311,531,000	**Curr. Liab.:**	$1,169,099,000		
Plant, Equip.:	$1,010,470,000	**Total Liab.:**	$2,554,152,000	**Indic. Yr. Divd.:**	NA
Total Assets:	$3,769,842,000	**Net Worth:**	$1,215,690,000	**Debt/ Equity:**	NA

Saehan Bancorp

3580 Wilshire Blvd., Ste. 1500, Los Angeles, CA, 90010; ***PH:*** 1-213-388-5550; ***Fax:*** 1-213-637-9899; ***http://*** www.saehanbank.com

General - Incorporation		**Stock**- Price on:12/24/2007	$11.5
Employees	NA	Stock Exchange	OTC
Auditor	NA	Ticker Symbol	SAEB
Stk Agt	Mellon Investor Services LLC	Outstanding Shares	11,090,000
Counsel	NA	E.P.S	-$0.02
DUNS No.	NA	Shareholders	NA

Business: The group operates through its subsidiary whose principal activity is to provide banking and financial services to the customers. Services of the group include checking accounts, savings accounts, certificates of deposit, installment loans, real estate mortgage loans, commercial loans, traveler's checks, safe deposit boxes, night depository and automated teller services. The group operates from the United States.

Primary SIC and add'l.: 6712 6022

CIK No:

Officers: Benjamin Hong/Dir., CEO, Pres., Daniel Kim/Sr. VP, CFO, Young Oh/Sr. VP, Chief Credit Officer, Young Lee/COO, Sr. VP, Annie Ahn/Sr. VP, Chief Administration Officer

Directors: Benjamin Hong/Dir., CEO, Pres., Hae Ryong Kim/Vice Chmn., Kee W. Ha/Chmn., Dong Soo Han/Dir., Dong Kie Lee/Dir., Il Young Kim/Dir., In Pyoung Kim/Dir., Peter Choi/Dir., Hui Taek Chong/Dir., Daewoong Chung/Dir., Myung Joon Kim/Dir., Myungja Kim/Dir., Soon K. Kim/Dir., Don Rhee/Dir., Pyung Sun Kim/Dir.

Financial Data: Fiscal Year End:NA ***Latest Annual Data:*** 12/31/2002

Year	Sales	Net Income
2002	$19,736,000	$3,182,000
2001	$20,088,000	$2,424,000
2000	$16,042,000	$2,206,000

Curr. Assets:	$25,573,000	**Curr. Liab.:**	$236,691,000		
Plant, Equip.:	$1,981,000	**Total Liab.:**	$239,193,000	**Indic. Yr. Divd.:**	NA
Total Assets:	$263,611,000	**Net Worth:**	$24,418,000	**Debt/ Equity:**	NA

Safe Technologies International Inc

123 NW 13 St., Ste. 30408, Boca Raton, FL, 33432; ***PH:*** 1-561-832-2700; ***http://*** www.safetechnologies.com; ***Email:*** investorrelations@safetechnologies.com

General - Incorporation	DE	**Stock**- Price on:12/24/2007	$0.0011
Employees	NA	Stock Exchange	OTC
Auditor	Baum & Co. P.A	Ticker Symbol	SFAD
Stk Agt	United Stock Transfer, Inc.,	Outstanding Shares	932,630,000
Counsel	NA	E.P.S	$0.00
DUNS No.	NA	Shareholders	NA

Business: The group's principal activity is to provide a broad range of Internet and technology based services. The group has one active subsidiary: Internet associates international, inc (iai). Iai is an Internet marketing and Web site development firm involved in the development, marketing, and hosting of Web sites. Iai specializes in designing and developing Web sites. This allows business customers to tap into the e-commerce platform, combining innovative Web design and programming with traditional marketing and advertising elements. The group operates entirely in the domestic market.

Primary SIC and add'l.: 7375 7379

CIK No: 0000829117

Subsidiaries: Connect.ad Services, Inc., Connect.ad, Inc., Internet Associates International, Inc., Total Micro Computers, Inc.

Officers: Randi Swatt/48/Dir., Acting CEO, Acting Chief Financial, Valda Reinbergs/56/Dir., Sec.

Directors: Randi Swatt/48/Dir., Acting CEO, Acting Chief Financial, Valda Reinbergs/56/Dir., Sec., Bruce E. Taylor/53/Dir.

Owners: Ruth Deutsch/24.20%, Insiders/2.00%, Valda Reinbergs, Universal Equity Holdings LLC/24.10%, Randi Swatt/1.10%, Franklin Frank/24.20%

Financial Data: Fiscal Year End:12/31 Latest Annual Data: 03/31/2007

Year	Sales	Net Income
2007	NA	NA
2006	NA	NA
2005	$30,000	-$253,000

Curr. Assets:	$14,000	Curr. Liab.:	$1,404,000		
Plant, Equip.:	NA	Total Liab.:	$1,404,000	Indic. Yr. Divd.:	NA
Total Assets:	$15,000	Net Worth:	-$1,389,000	Debt/ Equity:	NA

Safe Travel Care Inc

2011 San Elijo Ave., Ste. A, Cardiff, CA, 92007; **PH:** 1-760-634-3056; http:// www.safetravelcare.com

General - Incorporation	NV	**Stock** - Price on:12/24/2007	NA
Employees	NA	Stock Exchange	NA
Auditor	Gruber & Co., LLC	Ticker Symbol	NA
Stk Agt	American Registrar & Transfer Co	Outstanding Shares	NA
Counsel	NA	E.P.S.	NA
DUNS No.	NA	Shareholders	NA

Business: The group's principal activity is to provide travel protection services with specialization in the development, marketing and sale of travel insurance products and services to the north American traveler. The products of the group are the "Secure" and "Secure Plus" travel protection insurance plans. The travel protection plans focus on worldwide emergency medical evacuation and 24-hour emergency assistance with such essentials as trip cancellation reimbursement, travel delay, baggage delay, lost baggage compensation, medical/dental expense coverage, flight insurance, and accidental death benefits for a nominal cost per travel day.

Primary SIC and add'l.: 7389 7375

CIK No: 0001080398

Officers: John Michael Tastad/CEO, Thomas Black/44/Pres./$65,000.00, James J. Fahrner/CFO

Directors: Jeffrey W. Flannery/51/Chmn.

Owners: Jeffrey W. Flannery/100.00%, Insiders/100.00%

Curr. Assets:	$2,333,000	Curr. Liab.:	$4,375,000		
Plant, Equip.:	$80,000	Total Liab.:	$4,387,000	Indic. Yr. Divd.:	NA
Total Assets:	$5,441,000	Net Worth:	$1,055,000	Debt/ Equity:	NA

Safeco Corp

Safeco Plz., Seattle, WA, 98185; **PH:** 1-206-545-5000; **Fax:** 1-206-545-5995; http:// www.safeco.com

General - Incorporation	WA	**Stock** - Price on:12/24/2007	$62.2
Employees	7,208	Stock Exchange	NYSE
Auditor	Ernst & Young LLP	Ticker Symbol	SAF
Stk Agt	Bank of New York	Outstanding Shares	106,180,000
Counsel	NA	E.P.S.	$7.36
DUNS No.	00-794-2675	Shareholders	NA

Business: The group's principle activity is to provide insurance services. The groups services include property and casualty, surety and life insurance. The group operates from United States.

Primary SIC and add'l.: 6311 6331 6351 6519

CIK No: 0000086104

Subsidiaries: American Economy Insurance Company, American States Insurance Company, American States Insurance Company of Texas, American States Lloyds Insurance Company, American States Preferred Insurance Company, Emerald City Insurance Agency, Inc., F.B. Beattie & Company, Inc., First National Insurance Company of America, General America Corporation, General America Corporation of Texas, General Insurance Company of America, Insurance Company of Illinois, Safecare Company, Inc., Safeco Financial Institution Solutions, Inc., Safeco General Agency, Inc. 24 Subsidiaries included in the Index

Officers: Paula Rosput Reynolds/Dir., CEO, Pres./$6,141,333.00, Arthur Chong/Exec. VP, Chief Legal Officer/$1,893,871.00, Eric R. Martinez/Exec. VP - Claims, Customer Care, Procurement, Kris L. Hill/41/VP, Controller, Mike Hughes/Exec. VP - Insurance Operations/$1,208,249.00, William Jenks/CIO, Ross Kari/CFO, Exec. VP/$1,761,897.00, Allie Mysliwy/Exec. VP, Chief Business Services Officer/$1,625,971.00, Teresa J. Dalenta/43/Sr. VP - Claims, Customer Care, Kim Garland/Pres. - Open Seas Insurance

Directors: Paula Rosput Reynolds/Dir., CEO, Pres., Joseph W. Brown/Non - Exec. Chmn., Peter Currie/Dir., Judith Runstad/Dir., Joshua Green/Dir., John Hamlin/Dir., Charles R. Rinehart/Dir., William G. Reed/Dir., Maria Eitel/Dir., Gary Locke/Dir., Kerry Killinger/Dir., Robert Cline/Dir.

Owners: Robert S. Cline, Insiders/2.82%, Allie R. Mysliwy, Judith M. Runstad, Joshua Green/2.42%, Ross J. Kari, Michael H. Hughes, William G. Reed, Arthur Chong, Michael E. LaRocco, Paula Rosput Reynolds, Joseph W. Brown

Financial Data: Fiscal Year End:12/31 Latest Annual Data: 12/31/2006

Year	Sales	Net Income
2006	$6,289,900,000	$880,000,000
2005	$6,351,100,000	$691,100,000
2004	$6,195,400,000	$562,400,000

Curr. Assets:	$1,877,900,000	Curr. Liab.:	NA	P/E Ratio:	8.12
Plant, Equip.:	$130,400,000	Total Liab.:	$10,271,100,000	Indic. Yr. Divd.:	$1.600
Total Assets:	$14,199,000,000	Net Worth:	$3,927,900,000	Debt/ Equity:	0.3060

Safeguard Scientifics Inc

435 Devon Pk. Dr., Blvd. 800, Wayne, PA, 19087; **PH:** 1-610-293-0600; **Fax:** 1-610-293-0601; http:// www.safeguard.com

General - Incorporation	PA	**Stock** - Price on:12/24/2007	$2.75
Employees	1,264	Stock Exchange	NYSE
Auditor	KPMG LLP	Ticker Symbol	SFE
Stk Agt	Mellon Investor Services LLC	Outstanding Shares	120,920,000
Counsel	Morgan, Lewis & Bockius LLP	E.P.S.	$0.18
DUNS No.	00-194-2283	Shareholders	NA

Business: The group's principal activity is to create long-term shareholder value by taking controlling interests primarily in information technology and healthcare life sciences companies. The group also develops and operates emerging technology companies through its extensive network of partner companies and private equity funds. These resources include capital, management and operational expertise. Safeguard's existing strategic subsidiaries focus on financial services, healthcare and pharmaceutical, manufacturing, retail and distribution, and telecommunications. It operates through three segments: strategic companies, non-strategic companies, and compucom.

Primary SIC and add'l.: 8742 7373 8711 5045

CIK No: 0000086115

Subsidiaries: Acsis, Inc., Alliance Consulting Group Associates, Inc., Alliance Holdings, Inc., Alliance IT Consulting India Private Limited, Bonfield Fund Management, L.P., Bonfield Partners Capital, L.P., Bonfield VII, Ltd., ChromaServices, Inc., Clarient Diagnostic Services, Inc., Clarient, Inc., Laureate Pharma, Inc., Mantas, Inc., Mensamind, Inc., Pacific Title and Art Studio, Inc., Safeguard 2000 Capital, L.P. 28 Subsidiaries included in the Index

Officers: Peter J. Boni/Dir., CEO, Pres./$2,718,814.00, John E. Shave/VP - Investor Relations, Corporate Communications, Michael J. Pellini/VP - Life Sciences Group, Jim P. O'Connell/Sr. Associate, James A. Datin/Exec. VP, MD - Life Sciences/$1,516,302.00, Stephen Zarrilli/Acting CFO, Acting Sr. VP, Acting Chief Administrative Officer/$40,577.00, Raymond J. Land/Sr. VP, Chief Administrative Officer, CFO, Brian J. Sisko/Sr. VP, General Counsel, John A. Loftus/Exec. VP, MD - Information Technology/$1,655,526.00, Steven J. Feder/Sr. VP, General Counsel/$881,425.00, Kevin L. Kemmerer/Sr. VP - Information Technology Group, Gary J. Kurtzman/VP - Life Sciences, Erik B. Rasmussen/VP - Information Technology Group, Mark Mitchell/Sr. Associate, Technology

Directors: Peter J. Boni/Dir., CEO, Pres., Robert E. Keith/Chmn., Julie A. Dobson/Dir., Andrew E. Lietz/Dir., Todd Hewlin/Member - Advisory Board, Technology Advisors, Phil Moyer/Member - Advisory Board, Technology Advisors, Michael J. Cody/Dir., Robert J. Rosenthal/Dir., George MacKenzie/Dir., George D. McClelland/Dir., Jack L. Messman/Dir., John W. Poduska/Dir., John J. Roberts/Dir., Rick Bennett/Member - Advisory Board, Information Technology, Stephen M. Goodman/Member - Advisory Board, Information Technology *(28 Directors included in Index)*

Owners: Christopher J. Davis, George MacKenzie, Andrew E. Lietz, John W. Poduska, Jack L. Messman, Julie A. Dobson, Peter J. Boni/1.10%, George D. McClelland, James A. Datin, Robert E. Keith, John A. Loftus, Insiders/3.50%, Steven J. Feder

Financial Data: Fiscal Year End:12/31 Latest Annual Data: 12/31/2006

Year	Sales	Net Income
2006	$198,060,000	$46,030,000
2005	$186,216,000	-$32,070,000
2004	$156,709,000	-$54,820,000

Curr. Assets:	$214,986,000	Curr. Liab.:	$78,092,000	P/E Ratio:	9.17
Plant, Equip.:	$44,889,000	Total Liab.:	$223,988,000	Indic. Yr. Divd.:	NA
Total Assets:	$443,381,000	Net Worth:	$211,881,000	Debt/ Equity:	0.6649

Safenet Inc

4690 Millennium Dr., Belcamp, MD, 21017; **PH:** 1-410-931-7500; http:// www.safenet-inc.com

General - Incorporation	DE	**Stock** - Price on:12/24/2007	NA
Employees	1,043	Stock Exchange	NA
Auditor	Ernst & Young LLP	Ticker Symbol	NA
Stk Agt	American Stock Transfer & Trust Co.	Outstanding Shares	NA
Counsel	Venable, Baetjer & Howard LLP	E.P.S.	NA
DUNS No.	10-148-2511	Shareholders	NA

Business: The group's principal activities are to design, manufacture and market enterprise network security solutions using encryption technology. The security technology provides selective access to computer networks, prevents electronic eavesdropping or alteration during electronic data transmission and provides message authentication. The group's products include safenet/smart card, safenet/security center, secure modems, secure dial access systems, frame relay encryptors, etc. The products of the group are used in electronic commerce applications by financial institutions, government agencies and large corporations to secure data transmissions on private and public computer networks. During the year, the group acquired cylink corporation, raquia networks inc and ssh communications security corporation. On 15-Mar-2004, the group acquired rainbow technologies, inc.

Primary SIC and add'l.: 3661 7373

CIK No: 0000850313

Subsidiaries: 353 Patent LLC, Caro Kann Corporation, Cylink Communications B.V., Cylink France SARL, Cylink International Corporation, Datakey Corporation, Digital Spread Spectrum Technologies, Inc., DMDSecure.com BV, IAS, LLC, IRE Secure Solutions, Inc., iVea Corporation, MediaSentry, Inc., Mykotronx, Inc., Nihon SafeNet KK, Pijnenburg Securealink USA, Inc. 43 Subsidiaries included in the Index

Officers: Ian Edward Dix/Chief Marketing Officer, Prakash Panjwani/Sr. VP - Operations, GM - Commercial Security Division, Chris Fedde/COO, Pres., Phil Saunders/Sr. VP - Worldwide Sales, Donna St Germain/Public Relation, Kevin Hicks/General Counsel, Sec., John W. Frederick/Sr. VP, CFO, Jim Summers/Sr. VP, GM - Government Solutions Division, Diane Smith/VP - Human Resources

Directors: Alex Slusky/Dir., Chris Nicholson/Dir., David Fishman/Dir.

Owners: Chris S. Fedde, Shelley A. Harrison, Steve Lesem, Insiders/7.80%, Dimensional FundAdvisors LP/7.90%, Walter W. Straub/2.70%, Phil Saunders, Prakash Panjwani, Andrew E. Clark, Kenneth A. Mueller, Thomas A. Brooks, Carole D. Argo/1.10%, Bruce R. Thaw/1.40%, Arthur L. Money, Carter J. Beese *(18 Owners included in Index)*

Safetek International Inc

5509 11th Ave., Brooklyn, NY, 11219; **PH:** 1-972-35613468; http:// www.safetekinternational.com

General - Incorporation	DE	**Stock** - Price on:12/24/2007	NA
Employees	NA	Stock Exchange	OTC
Auditor	Sherb & Co. LLP	Ticker Symbol	SFIN
Stk Agt	Securities Transfer Corp	Outstanding Shares	NA
Counsel	NA	E.P.S.	-$0.032
DUNS No.	NA	Shareholders	NA

Business: The group is seeking additional financing and is looking for merger or acquisition. The group has no business and does not provide any services. The group has suspended substantially all operating activities in 2000.

Primary SIC and add'l.: 9999

CIK No: 0000833080

Subsidiaries: Life Sciences Ltd, Oriens Life Sciences

Financial Data: Fiscal Year End:12/31   Latest Annual Data: 12/31/2005

Year	Sales	Net Income
2005	NA	-$2,929,000
2004	NA	-$125,000
2001	$2,000	-$663,000

Curr. Assets:	$512,000	Curr. Liab.:	$2,305,000		
Plant, Equip.:	$15,000	Total Liab.:	$3,466,000	Indic. Yr. Divd.:	NA
Total Assets:	$595,000	Net Worth:	-$3,103,000	Debt/ Equity:	NA

Safety Components International Inc

804 Green Valley Rd., Ste. 300, Greensboro, NC, 27408; **PH:** 1-336-379-6220; *http://* www.safetycomponents.com

General - Incorporation	DE	Stock - Price on:12/24/2007	$6.5
Employees	8,700	Stock Exchange	NA
Auditor	KPMG LLP	Ticker Symbol	NA
Stk Agt.	Continental Stock Transfer & Trust Co	Outstanding Shares	17,480,000
Counsel. Shereff Friedman Hoffman & Goodman		E.P.S.	-$5.68
DUNS No.	82-519-8484	Shareholders	NA

Business: The group's principal activity is to supply automotive airbag, cushions and technical fabrics. It also manufactures value-added technical fabrics used in a variety of niche industrial and commercial applications such as ballistics material for luggage, filtration, aircraft escape slides, military tents and fire service apparel. It sells airbag fabric domestically and cushions worldwide to the major airbag module integrators that outsource such products. The group's automotive products include passenger, driver and side impact airbag cushions and side protection curtains. The major customers of the group include autoliv, takata-petri and trw. The group's operations are conducted in North America and Europe.

Primary SIC and add'l.: 2399 3714

CIK No: 0000918964

Officers: Joseph L. Gorga/Dir., CEO, Pres., Gary L. Smith/Dir., Exec. VP, CFO, John V. Rainey/VP - Manufacturing, Steve Ramey/Environmental Managment Representative, Katerina Kolarova/Quality Mgr., Hector Obergon/Program, Sales Dir., Larry Harbin/Customer Quality Affairs Mgr., Regina Stancell/Customer Quality Affairs Assist., Samir M. Gabriel/VP, Controller, Vick Crowley/Treasurer, Stephen B. Duerk/Pres., William F. Nelli/Principal Financial, Accounting Officer, David Baksa/GM, Nick Borrelli/Quality Assurance Mgr., Uwe Zimmermann/GM *(23 Officers included in Index)*

Directors: Joseph L. Gorga/Dir., CEO, Pres., Gary L. Smith/Dir., Exec. VP, CFO, Stephen W. Bosworth/Dir., David L. Wax/Dir., Pamela K. Wilson/Dir.

Owners: Kenneth T. Kunberger, Insiders/98.00%, Thomas E. McKenna, John L. Bakane, Joseph L. Gorga, Insiders/82.00%, Wilbur L. Ross, Jr. and Affiliated Entities/98.00%, Wilbur L. Ross, Jr. and Affiliated Entities/82.00%, Gary L. Smith, Stephen W. Bosworth

Financial Data: Fiscal Year End:12/31   Latest Annual Data: 03/31/2007

Year	Sales	Net Income
2007	NA	$19,023,000
2006	$720,916,000	-$50,055,000
2005	$220,114,000	$3,543,000

Curr. Assets:	$306,920,000	Curr. Liab.:	$103,428,000		
Plant, Equip.:	$163,344,000	Total Liab.:	$305,546,000	Indic. Yr. Divd.:	NA
Total Assets:	$492,813,000	Net Worth:	$168,220,000	Debt/ Equity:	1.0274

Safety Insurance Group Inc

20 Custom House St., Boston, MA, 02110; **PH:** 1-617-951-0600; **Fax:** 1-617-603-4837; *http://* www.safetyinsurance.com

General - Incorporation	DE	Stock - Price on:12/24/2007	$41.65
Employees	579	Stock Exchange	NDQ
Auditor	PricewaterhouseCoopers LLP	Ticker Symbol	SAFT
Stk Agt.	Computershare Investor Services LLC	Outstanding Shares	16,230,000
Counsel	NA	E.P.S.	$6.59
DUNS No.	NA	Shareholders	NA

Business: The group's principal activity is to provide personal automobile insurance in Massachusetts. In addition, the group offers a portfolio of insurance products, including commercial automobile, homeowners, dwelling fire, umbrella and business owner policies. The group operates exclusively in Massachusetts through its insurance company subsidiaries, safety insurance company or safety insurance and safety indemnity insurance company. The group has relationships with 548 independent insurance agents in 758 locations throughout Massachusetts. The product lines of the group are private passenger automobile, commercial automobile, homeowners, business owners policies, commercial package policies, personal umbrella, dwelling fire, commercial umbrella, inland marine and watercraft.

Primary SIC and add'l.: 6719 6331

CIK No: 0001172052

Subsidiaries: Safety Indemnity Insurance Company, Safety Insurance Company, Whiteshirts Asset Management Corporation, Whiteshirts Management Corporation

Officers: David F. Brussard/Chmn., CEO, Pres., David E. Krupa/VP - Property Claims, Edward N. Patrick/VP - Underwriting, Daniel D. Loranger/VP - Management Information Systems, CIO, William J. Begley/VP, CFO, Sec., Robert J. Kerton/VP - Casualty Claims, James D. Berry/VP - Insurance Operations, George M. Murphy/41/VP - Marketing

Directors: David F. Brussard/Chmn., CEO, Pres., Richard A. Caputo/42/Dir., Frederic H. Lindeberg/67/Dir., Peter J. Manning/69/Dir., David K. McKown/70/Dir.

Owners: Edward N. Patrick/1.20%, William J. Begley, David E. Krupa, Richard A. Caputo/1.00%, Daniel D. Loranger/1.70%, JZ Equity Partners PLC/7.40%, Barclays Global Investors, N.A./6.90%, Insiders/8.30%, David K. McKown, Moody, Aldrich and Sullivan LLC/6.10%, Peter J. Manning, Frederic H. Lindeberg, David F. Brussard/2.80%

Financial Data: Fiscal Year End:12/31   Latest Annual Data: 12/31/2006

Year	Sales	Net Income
2006	$680,712,000	$111,941,000
2005	$671,457,000	$95,182,000
2004	$636,440,000	$44,990,000

Curr. Assets:	$311,042,000	Curr. Liab.:	$76,513,000		
Plant, Equip.:	NA	Total Liab.:	$859,400,000	Indic. Yr. Divd.:	$1.000
Total Assets:	$1,355,748,000	Net Worth:	$496,348,000	Debt/ Equity:	0.0085

Safeway Stores

5918 Stoneridge Mall Rd., Pleasanton, CA, 94588; **PH:** 1-925-467-3000; **Fax:** 1-925-467-3321; *http://* www.safeway.com

General - Incorporation	DE	Stock - Price on:12/24/2007	$35.35
Employees	207,000	Stock Exchange	NYSE
Auditor	Deloitte & Touche LLP	Ticker Symbol	SWY
Stk Agt.	EquiServe Trust Co N.A	Outstanding Shares	441,600,000
Counsel	NA	E.P.S.	$2.01
DUNS No.	00-913-7209	Shareholders	NA

Business: The group's principle activity is to provide food and drug retail stores. The group also provides gift, prepaid, sports and entertainment cards. The group operates from United States.

Primary SIC and add'l.: 5912

CIK No: 0000086144

Subsidiaries: AOL Express, Inc., APR Forwarders, Inc., Avia Partners, Inc., Blackhawk (Macao Offshore Commercial) Ltd., Blackhawk Developments, Inc., Blackhawk Marketing (HK) Limited, Blackhawk Marketing Holdings (Canada), Inc., Blackhawk Marketing Holdings Ltd., Blackhawk Marketing Services (Canada) Ltd., Blackhawk Marketing Services, Inc., Blackhawk Marketing, LLC, Blackhawk Network, LLC, Blackhawk Properties, Inc., Canada Safeway Holdings Limited, Canada Safeway Liquor Stores Limited 121 Subsidiaries included in the Index

Officers: Steven A. Burd/58/Chmn., CEO, Pres./$7,003,993.00, Russell M. Jackson/Sr. VP - Human Resources, David R. Stern/Sr. VP - Planning, Business Development, David T. Ching/CIO, Sr. VP, Robert A. Gordon/Sr. VP - Sec., General Counsel Chief Governance Officer, Kenneth M. Shachmut/Sr. VP - Strategic Initiatives, Health Initiatives, Reengineering, Robert L. Edwards/CFO, Exec. VP/$3,036,887.00, Brian C. Cornell/Exec. VP, Chief Marketing Officer/$5,052,377.00, Larree M. Renda/Exec. VP, Chief Strategist, Administrative Officer/$3,007,800.00, Bruce L. Everette/Exec. VP - Retail Operations/$3,046,196.00, David F. Bond/Sr. VP - Finance, Control, Chief Accounting Officer, Donald P. Wright/Sr. VP - Real Estate, Engineering, Melissa C. Plaisance/Sr. VP - Finance, Investor Relations, Jerry Tidwell/Sr. VP - Supply Operations

Directors: Steven A. Burd/58/Chmn., CEO, Pres., Paul Hazen/66/Dir., Janet E. Grove/57/Dir., Mohan Gyani/56/Dir., Robert I. MacDonnell/70/Dir., Douglas F. MacKenzie/48/Dir., Rebecca A. Stirn/55/Dir., William Y. Tauscher/58/Dir., Raymond G. Viault/63/Dir.

Owners: Bruce L. Everette, Janet E. Grove, Robert I. MacDonnell, Raymond G. Viault, Brandes Investment Partners, LP/8.00%, Douglas J. Mackenzie, William Y. Tauscher, AXA Financial, Inc./11.50%, Robert L. Edwards, Brian C. Cornell, Steven A. Burd/1.40%, Mohan Gyani, FMR Corp./11.70%, Rebecca A. Stirn, Larree M. Renda *(17 Owners included in Index)*

Financial Data: Fiscal Year End:12/31   Latest Annual Data: 12/30/2006

Year	Sales	Net Income
2006	$40,185,000,000	$870,600,000
2005	$38,416,000,000	$561,100,000

Curr. Assets:	$3,702,400,000	Curr. Liab.:	$4,263,900,000	P/E Ratio:	17.50
Plant, Equip.:	$9,097,100,000	Total Liab.:	$10,837,200,000	Indic. Yr. Divd.:	$0.280
Total Assets:	$15,756,900,000	Net Worth:	$4,919,700,000	Debt/ Equity:	NA

Saflink Corp

12413 Willows Rd. NE, Ste. 300, Kirkland, WA, 98034; **PH:** 1-425-278-1100; **Fax:** 1-425-278-1300; *http://* www.saflink.com; **Email:** info@saflink.com

General - Incorporation	DE	Stock - Price on:12/24/2007	NA
Employees	122	Stock Exchange	OTC
Auditor	KPMG LLP	Ticker Symbol	SFLK
Stk Agt.	U.S. Stock Transfer Corp	Outstanding Shares	NA
Counsel	Baker & McKenzie LLP	E.P.S.	-$0.203
DUNS No.	79-120-0587	Shareholders	NA

Business: The group's principal activity is to provide network security software solutions to protect the safety of information assets and track network access by authorized personnel. The products offered by the group are used to protect business and personal information and to replace passwords and personal identification numbers in order to safeguard and simplify access to electronic systems. The group's products are divided into two groups: enterprise network products and stand-alone workstation products. The enterprise network products include safsolution enterprise edition, saf2000 for the enterprise, safmodule for nmas, safaccess for etrust sso. Safsolution windows workstation edition, is the only stand-alone workstation product. The products are marketed to customers in healthcare, pharmaceuticals, education, government and financial services sectors. On 22nd mar 2004, the group acquired ssp solutions inc.

Primary SIC and add'l.: 7371 7376 7379

CIK No: 0000847555

Subsidiaries: Spartan Acquisition Corporation, SSP-Litronic

Officers: Steven M. Oyer/Dir., Interim CEO, Jeffrey T. Dick/CFO

Directors: Steven M. Oyer/Dir., Interim CEO, Trevor Neilson/Vice Chmn., Richard P. Kiphart/Dir., Lincoln D. Faurer/Dir., Glenn L. Argenbright/Dir., Gordon E. Fornell/Dir., Asa Hutchinson/Dir.

Financial Data: Fiscal Year End:12/31   Latest Annual Data: 12/31/2006

Year	Sales	Net Income
2006	$4,161,000	-$120,114,000
2005	$7,116,000	-$47,037,000
2004	$6,398,000	-$15,937,000

Curr. Assets:	$2,484,000	Curr. Liab.:	$8,805,000		
Plant, Equip.:	$420,000	Total Liab.:	$8,805,000	Indic. Yr. Divd.:	NA
Total Assets:	$3,454,000	Net Worth:	-$5,351,000	Debt/ Equity:	NA

Saga Communications Inc

73 Kercheval Ave., Ste. 201, Grosse Pointe Farms, MI, 48236; **PH:** 1-313-886-7070; **Fax:** 1-313-886-7150; *http://* www.sagacommunications.com; **Email:** by@sagacom.com

General - Incorporation .... DE	Stock- Price on:12/24/2007 ....$10
Employees 922	Stock Exchange...NYSE
Auditor .... Ernst & Young LLP	Ticker Symbol..SGA
Stk Agt............................ EquiServe Trust Co N.A	Outstanding Shares 20,200,000
Counsel............................Edwards & Angell	E.P.S...$0.57
DUNS No. 79-807-3136	Shareholders..NA

Business: The group's principal activities are to acquire, develop and operate radio and television stations. The group's stations employ a variety of programming formats, including classic hits, adult contemporary, album oriented rock, news/talk, country and classical. The group operates through two segments: radio and television. The group owns or operates five television stations and three low power television stations serving three markets, three radio networks, and fortynine FM and twentyseven AM radio stations serving twentyone markets including columbus, Ohio, norfolk, Virginia, manchester, New Hampshire and milwaukee, Wisconsin. During 2003, the group acquired wwit-AM, woxl-AM, wodb-FM, winq-FM, wjza-FM & wjzk-FM radio stations.

Primary SIC and add'l.: 4833 4832

CIK No: 0000886136

Subsidiaries: Franklin Communications, Inc., Lakefront Communications, LLC, Saga Air, LLC, Saga Broadcasting, LLC, Saga Communications of Arkansas, LLC, Saga Communications of Charlottesville, LLC, Saga Communications of Illinois, LLC, Saga Communications of Iowa, LLC, Saga Communications of Michigan, LLC, Saga Communications of Milwaukee, LLC, Saga Communications of New England, LLC, Saga Communications of New Hampshire, LLC, Saga Communications of North Carolina, LLC, Saga Communications of South Dakota, LLC, Saga Communications of Tuckessee, LLC 17 Subsidiaries included in the Index

Officers: Edward K. Christian/Chmn., CEO, Pres./$1,247,318.00, Samuel D. Bush/CFO, Sr. VP, Treasurer/$475,441.00, Michelle Novak/Programming Coordinator, Research Dir., Catherine A. Bobinski/VP, Chief Accounting Officer, Corporate Controller, Steven J. Goldstein/Exec. VP, Group Program Dir./$606,459.00, Warren S. Lada/Sr. VP - Operations/$474,036.00, Marcia K. Lobaito/Sr. VP, Dir. - Business Affairs/$245,687.00, Greg Urbiel/Dir. - Engineering, Larry Downes/Dir. - Integrated Media

Directors: Edward K. Christian/Chmn., CEO, Pres., Steven J. Goldstein/Exec. VP, Group Program Dir.

Owners: Insiders/0.33%, Donald Schwall/0.11%, Jay Kister/1.00%, Kelly Black/0.06%, Munjit Johal/0.06%, Jan Wallace/0.27%

Financial Data: Fiscal Year End:12/31 Latest Annual Data: 12/31/2006

Year		Sales		Net Income
2006		$142,946,000		$12,448,000
2005		$140,790,000		$10,566,000
2004		$134,644,000		$15,842,000
Curr. Assets:	$38,939,000	Curr. Liab.:	$17,322,000	P/E Ratio: 17.61
Plant, Equip.:	$73,658,000	Total Liab.:	$186,405,000	Indic. Yr. Divd.: NA
Total Assets:	$322,641,000	Net Worth:	$136,236,000	Debt/ Equity: 0.9607

Sagemark Cos Ltd

1285 Ave Of The Americas, New York, NY, 10019; PH: 1-212-554-4219

General - Incorporation .... NY	Stock- Price on:12/24/2007 ....$0.71
Employees 32	Stock Exchange..OTC
Auditor ....Moore Stephens, P.C	Ticker Symbol..SKCO
Stk Agt..... American Stock Transfer & Trust Co.	Outstanding Shares 7,660,000
Counsel...NA	E.P.S...-$0.3
DUNS No. 00-147-6100	Shareholders..NA

Business: The group's principal activity is to acquire, organize and operate positron emission tomography centers. The centers use diagnostic procedures that detect cancer in the human body. The group has a positron emission tomography center in wichita, Kansas. The group currently owns and operates pet centers in wichita, Kansas and parsipanny, New Jersey. The pet procedures requires the use of flouro-deoxy-glucose and positron emission tomography scanning equipment.

Primary SIC and add'l.: 3845 8062 6719

CIK No: 0000089041

Subsidiaries: Bethesda PET Management LLCMaryland, Hialeah PET Management LLC Florida, Morris County PET Management LLC New Jersey, P.E.T. Management of Queens, LLC New York, Premier Cyclotron International Corp. Delaware, Premier P.E.T. Imaging International, Inc. Delaware, Premier P.E.T. Imaging of Arlington Heights, Inc. Illinois, Premier P.E.T. Imaging of New Jersey, Inc. New Jersey, Premier P.E.T. Imaging of Wichita, LLC Kansas, Premier P.E.T. of Long Island, LLCNew York, Premier PET Imaging of D.C. and Maryland, Inc. Maryland, Premier PET Imaging of Jacksonville, LLCFlorida, SIS Capital Corp. Delaware, Suffolk PET Management LLC New York

Owners: Elizabeth Farrell Longton, Bocara Corp./7.00%, Edward Arnold/10.00%, George W. Mahoney/1.00%, Insiders/22.00%, Edward D. Bright/1.00%, Tara Capital, Inc./8.00%, Pamels Corp./5.00%, Michael Fagien/3.00%, Theodore B. Shapiro/4.00%, Stephen A. Schulman/8.00%, Robert L. Blessey/7.00%

Financial Data: Fiscal Year End:12/31 Latest Annual Data: 12/31/2006

Year		Sales		Net Income
2006		$10,391,000		-$1,815,000
2005		$7,701,000		-$1,822,000
2004		$6,222,000		-$818,000
Curr. Assets:	$5,999,000	Curr. Liab.:	$8,138,000	
Plant, Equip.:	$10,498,000	Total Liab.:	$14,701,000	Indic. Yr. Divd.: NA
Total Assets:	$23,366,000	Net Worth:	$6,679,000	Debt/ Equity: 1.0713

Sagient Research Systems Inc

3655 Nobel Dr, Ste. 540, San Diego, CA, 92122; PH: 1-858-623-1600; http:// www.sagientresearch.com

General - Incorporation .... DE	Stock- Price on:12/24/2007 ....$0.15
Employees ....NA	Stock Exchange..OTC
Auditor .... Peterson & Co. LLP	Ticker Symbol..SRYS
Stk Agt.............Corporate Stock Transfer, Inc.	Outstanding Shares ....NA
Counsel...NA	E.P.S...NA
DUNS No. ....NA	Shareholders..NA

Business: The group's principal activity is to maintain an online auction environment for public companies to offer securities to select institutional investors at substantial savings over secondary public offering or traditional private placement. The group is a technology oriented financial services firm, which produces and markets proprietary financial data through advanced technology platforms. The data

products are distributed through advanced technology platform on a subscription basis to analysts, investment bankers, institutional investors and other financial professionals. The group provides agency trading, independent research and investment banking services for institutional investors through its wholly owned subsidiary, dp securities, inc. The group's placementtracker.com is the proprietary data-oriented research product.

Primary SIC and add'l.: 7389 7375

CIK No: 0001065191

Subsidiaries: DP Securities, Inc., PCS Securities, Inc.

Officers: Brian M. Overstreet/Co - Founder, CEO, Pres., Henry Hoa Duong/COO, Robert F. Kyle/Exec. VP

Directors: Brian M. Overstreet/Co - Founder, CEO, Pres., Robert F. Kyle/Exec. VP

Financial Data: Fiscal Year End:12/31 Latest Annual Data: 12/31/2004

Year		Sales		Net Income
2004		$2,775,000		-$871,000
2003		$2,127,000		-$1,460,000
2002		$18,525,000		-$25,238,000
Curr. Assets:	$478,000	Curr. Liab.:	$3,811,000	
Plant, Equip.:	$301,000	Total Liab.:	$3,811,000	Indic. Yr. Divd.: NA
Total Assets:	$783,000	Net Worth:	-$3,029,000	Debt/ Equity: NA

SAIA Inc

Formerly: SCS Transportation Inc

11465 Johns Creek Pk.way, Ste. 400, Duluth, GO, 30097; PH: 1-770-232-5067; http:// www.saia.com

General - Incorporation .... DE	Stock- Price on:12/24/2007 ....$26.41
Employees 8,400	Stock Exchange..NDQ
Auditor .... KPMG LLP	Ticker Symbol...SAIA
Stk Agt .... Mellon Investor Services LLC	Outstanding Shares 14,260,000
Counsel...NA	E.P.S...$1.50
DUNS No. ....NA	Shareholders..NA

Business: The group's principal activity is to provide trucking transportation and supply chain solutions to the retail, petrochemical and manufacturing industries. The group offers regional, interregional and national less-than-truckload and selected truckload services across the United States through its two wholly-owned regional transportation subsidiaries, saia motor freight line, inc. And jevic transportation, inc. Saia is a multi-regional less-than-truckload carrier that serves the south, southwest, pacific northwest and the west. Jevic is less-than-truckload ground transportation services provider that also offers selected truckload services throughout the continental United States and Canada. On 16-Feb-2004, the group acquired clark bros transfer, inc.

Primary SIC and add'l.: 4789 6719 4213

CIK No: 0001177702

Subsidiaries: Jevic Transportation, Inc., Saia Motor Freight Line, Inc

Officers: Richard D. O'Dell./Dir., CEO, Pres./$999,161.00, Jim Darby/VP - Finance, CFO, Rick O'Dell/Pres., Sally Buchholz/VP - Marketing - Customer Service, Mark Robinson/VP - Information Technology, CIO/$401,028.00, Anthony D. Albanese/Sr. VP - Sales, Operations/$623,679.00, Renee McKenzie/Treasurer, Tony Albanese/Sr. VP - Sales - Operations, Reuben Gegenheimer/VP - Human Resources, Mike Burger/VP - Maintenance, Properties

Directors: Richard D. O'Dell/Dir., CEO, Pres., Linda J. French/59/Dir., Douglas W. Rockel/48/Dir., John J. Holland/55/Dir., James A. Olson/Dir., Jeffrey C. Ward/Dir., William F. Martin/58/Dir., Bjorn E. Olsson/60/Dir.

Owners: John J. Holland, Goldman Sachs Asset Management, L.P./7.85%, James A. Olson, Dimensional Fund Advisors LP/8.72%, Jeffrey C. Ward, Insiders/4.72%, David J. Letke, Barclays Global Investors/8.32%, Herbert A. Trucksess/3.32%, James J. Bellinghausen, Anthony Albanese, James A. Darby, Richard D. ODell, Bjorn E. Olsson, Douglas W. Rockel (18 Owners included in Index)

Financial Data: Fiscal Year End:12/31 Latest Annual Data: 12/31/2006

Year		Sales		Net Income
2006		$874,738,000		-$20,681,000
2005		$1,098,031,000		$27,459,000
2004		$982,270,000		$19,259,000
Curr. Assets:	$133,684,000	Curr. Liab.:	$126,641,000	
Plant, Equip.:	$314,832,000	Total Liab.:	$284,245,000	Indic. Yr. Divd.: NA
Total Assets:	$487,400,000	Net Worth:	$203,155,000	Debt/ Equity: 0.5957

SAIC Inc

10260 Campus Point Dr., San Diego, CA, 92121; PH: 1-858-826-6000; Fax: 1-858-826-6800; http:// www.saic.com

General - Incorporation .... DE	Stock- Price on:12/24/2007 ....$18.16
Employees 44,100	Stock Exchange..NYSE
Auditor ....Deloitte & Touche LLP	Ticker Symbol...SAI
Stk Agt .... Mellon Investor Services LLC	Outstanding Shares 416,330,000
Counsel...NA	E.P.S...NA
DUNS No. ....NA	Shareholders..NA

Business: The groups principle activities include scientific, engineering, systems integration and technical services and solutions. The group operates from the United States. The group's quarterly revenue for September 2007 was 2365.00 millions of USD.

Primary SIC and add'l.: 7376 8741 7389 8742 7373 8748 7371 8744 8733 7379 9661 8711

CIK No: 0001336920

Officers: Ken C. Dahlberg/Chmn., CEO, Mark W. Sopp/CFO, Exec. VP, Donald H. Foley/Exec. VP - Special Projects, Arnold L. Punaro/Exec. VP - Government Affairs, Communications, Support Operations, William A. Roper/Exec. VP, Douglas E. Scott/Exec. VP, General Counsel, Sec., Theoren P. Smith/53/CTO, Exec. VP, John H. Warner/67/Exec. VP, Deborah H. Alderson/Pres. - Defense Solutions Group, Larry J. Peck/Exec. VP - Homeland Security, Lawrence B. Prior/COO, John R. Hartley/42/Sr. VP, Corporate Controller, Steven P. Fisher/47/Treasurer, Sr. VP, Greg Henson/Dir. Business Development, Sr. VP, Brian F. Keenan/Exec. VP - Human Resources (23 Officers included in Index)

Directors: Ken C. Dahlberg/Chmn., CEO, W. H. Demisch/Dir., M. E. John/Dir., J. P. Jumper/Dir., J. A. Drummond/Dir., J. J. Hamre/Dir., A. K. Jones/Dir., H. M.J. Kraemer/Dir., E. J. Sanderson/Dir., L. A. Simpson/Dir., Joseph P. Walkush/Dir., Exec. VP - Strategic Initiatives, A. T. Young/Dir.

Owners: D.H. Foley, L.J. Peck, A.K. Jones, K.C. Dahlberg, Vanguard Fiduciary Trust Company/4.40%, J. H. Warner, Mason Capital Management LLC/7.90%, E. J. Sanderson, K.C. Dahlberg, D.H. Foley, A.T. Young, Insiders, J.P. Walkush, G. T. Singley, TIAA-CREF Investment Management, LLC/6.00% (31 Owners included in Index)

Financial Data: Fiscal Year End:01/31 Latest Annual Data: 1/31/2007

Year	Sales		Net Income
2007	$8,294,000,000		$391,000,000
Curr. Assets:	$2,945,000,000	Curr. Liab.: $1,663,000,000	P/E Ratio: 18.92
Plant, Equip.:	$387,000,000	Total Liab.: $3,022,000,000	Indic. Yr. Divd.: NA
Total Assets:	$4,558,000,000	Net Worth: $1,536,000,000	Debt/ Equity: NA

Saifun Semiconductors Ltd

2350 Mission College Blvd., Ste. 1070, Santa Clara, CA, 95054; **PH:** 1-408-982-5888; **Fax:** 1-408-982-5890; **http://** www.saifun.com; **Email:** info@saifun.com

General - Incorporation	Israel	Stock - Price on:12/24/2007	$11.23
Employees	232	Stock Exchange	NDQ
Auditor	Kost, Forer, Gabbay & Kassierer	Ticker Symbol	SFUN
Stk Agt	American Stock Transfer & Trust Co.	Outstanding Shares	31,480,000
Counsel	NA	E.P.S.	$0.49
DUNS No.	NA	Shareholders	NA

Business: The groups principle activities include designing and manufacturing Flash, EEPROM and Embedded NVM. Specific customers of the group include Macronix International Co., Ltd and Infineon Technologies AG. The group operates from the United States, Germany, Taiwan, Japan, China and Israel. The group's quarterly revenue for September 2007 was 8.90 millions of USD.

Primary SIC and add'l.: 3674

CIK No: 0001297627

Subsidiaries: Saifun (BVI) Limited, Saifun Semiconductors USA, Inc., Saifun Ventures Ltd, Tulip Semiconductor Holdings (2005) Ltd., Tulip Semiconductor Ltd., Tulip Semiconductors L.P.

Officers: Boaz Eitan/Chmn., Founder, CEO, Igal Shany/CFO, Meir Janai/VP - Quality, Ramy Langer/54/VP - Business Development, Eduardo Maayan/Exec. VP - Business Development, Ron Eliyahu/VP - Research, Development

Directors: Boaz Eitan/Chmn., Founder, CEO, George Hervey/Dir., Matty Karp/Dir., Kenneth Levy/Dir., Ida Keidar Malits/Dir., Kobi Rozengarten/Dir., Yossi Sela/Dir.

Owners: Insiders/39.80%, Ida Keidar-Malits, Yossi Sela, Matty Karp/3.00%, Eduardo Maayan, Kenneth Levy, Kobi Rozengarten/1.30%, Boaz Eitan/34.80%, Igal Shany, Meir Janai, IDB Holding Corporation Ltd./8.60%, Argos Capital Appreciation Master Fund LP/4.80%, George Hervey, Ramy Langer

Financial Data: Fiscal Year End:12/31 Latest Annual Data: 12/31/2006

Year	Sales		Net Income
2006	$62,777,000		$34,995,000
2005	$78,601,000		$44,507,000
2004	$32,239,000		-$37,904,000
Curr. Assets:	$181,812,000	Curr. Liab.: $10,157,000	
Plant, Equip.:	$3,403,000	Total Liab.: $13,891,000	Indic. Yr. Divd.: NA
Total Assets:	$250,178,000	Net Worth: $236,287,000	Debt/ Equity: NA

Saigon National Bank

15606 Brookhurst St., Westminster, CA, 92683; **PH:** 1-714-338-8700; **http://** www.saigonnational.com

General - Incorporation		Stock - Price on:12/24/2007	$8
Employees	NA	Stock Exchange	OTC
Auditor	NA	Ticker Symbol	SAGN
Stk Agt	NA	Outstanding Shares	NA
Counsel	NA	E.P.S.	NA
DUNS No.	NA	Shareholders	NA

Business: The groups principal activities include providing locally owned community bank devoted to serving the financial needs of the Vietnamese business community. Services of the group include checking accounts, savings accounts, certificates of deposit, installment loans, real estate mortgage loans, commercial loans, traveler's checks, safe deposit boxes, night depository and automated teller services. The group operates from Southern California.

Primary SIC and add'l.: 6021

CIK No:

Officers: John J. Kennedy/Dir., CEO, Pres., Michael Mullarky/Exec. VP, CCO, Roy Painter/CFO, Exec. VP, Michael Maher/Sr. VP, Mgr.

Directors: John J. Kennedy/Dir., CEO, Pres., Hieu Tran/Chmn., Loc P. Huynh/Vice Chmn., Ban Duc Nguyen/Vice Chmn., James Avery/Dir., Kiem Nguyen/Dir., Andrew Chien/Dir., Binh Ho/Dir., Dat Phan/Dir., Thanh Phung/Dir., Lee Ross/Dir., Kim Tran/Dir.

Saks Inc

750 Lakeshore Pkwy., Birmingham, AL, 35211; **PH:** 1-205-940-4000; **http://** www.saksincorporated.com; **Email:** janine_bolin@saksinc.com

General - Incorporation	TN	Stock - Price on:12/24/2007	$21.18
Employees	12,320	Stock Exchange	NYSE
Auditor	PricewaterhouseCoopers LLP	Ticker Symbol	SKS
Stk Agt	Bank of New York	Outstanding Shares	142,360,000
Counsel	Charles J. Hansen	E.P.S.	-$0.1
DUNS No.	00-894-2252	Shareholders	NA

Business: The groups principle activity is to operate departmental stores. The groups products include fashion apparel, shoes, accessories, jewelry, cosmetics and gifts. The group operates from United States.

Primary SIC and add'l.: 5961 5311

CIK No: 0000812900

Subsidiaries: Cafe SFA - Minneapolis, Inc., Club Libby Lu, Inc., CPSIS, Inc., Fifth Floor Restaurant at SFA LLC, Jackson Leasing, LLC, Jackson Office Properties, Inc., Merchandise Credit, LLC, New York City Saks, LLC, Parisian Stores, Inc., Saks Direct, Inc., Saks Fifth Avenue Distribution Company, Saks Fifth Avenue Food Corporation, Saks Fifth Avenue of Texas, Inc., Saks Fifth Avenue Texas, L.P., Saks Fifth Avenue, Inc. 29 Subsidiaries included in the Index

Officers: Stephen I. Sadove/56/Dir., CEO/$14,139,350.00, Douglas E. Coltharp/46/CFO, Exec. VP, Kevin Wills/CFO, Exec. VP/$1,889,194.00, Marc J. Metrick/34/Group Sr. VP, Chief Strategy Officer, Terron E. Schaefer/63/Sr. VP - Marketing, Robert T. Wallstrom/42/Pres. - Off Fifth, Group Sr. VP, Julia Bentley/49/Sr. VP - Investor Relations, Communications, Corp. Sec., James A. Coggin/65/Pres., Chief Administrative Officer/$4,826,545.00, Charles J. Hansen/60/Exec. VP, General Counsel, Ronald L. Frasch/Pres., Chief Merchandising Officer/$2,873,437.00, Michael Brizel/Exec. VP, General Counsel, Christine A. Morena/52/Exec. VP - Human Resources, Carolyn R. Biggs/60/Exec. VP - Stores, Store Visual, Planning, Construction, Denise Incandela/43/Pres. - Saks Direct, Group Sr. VP, Thomas G. Matthews/53/Group Sr. VP - Asset Protection, Store Operations, Ethics, Compliance

Directors: Stephen I. Sadove/56/Dir., CEO, Ronald De Waal/56/Vice Chmn., Brad R. Martin/56/Chmn., Marguerite W. Kondracke/62/Dir., Michael S. Gross/46/Dir., Nora P. McAniff/49/Dir., Warren C. Neel/69/Dir., Christopher J. Stadler/43/Dir., Stanton J. Bluestone/73/Dir., Robert B. Carter/48/Dir., Donald E. Hess/59/Dir.

Owners: Nora P. McAniff, FMR Corp./10.55%, Donald E. Hess, Brad R. Martin, Inmobiliaria Carso, S.A. de C.V./7.81%, AXA Financial, Inc./6.83%, Christopher J. Stadler, Insiders/2.57%, Stanton J. Bluestone, Michael S. Gross, Robert B. Carter, Ronald de Waal, Warren C. Neel, Marsico Capital Management LLC/10.27%, Julius W. Erving (20 Owners included in Index)

Financial Data: Fiscal Year End:01/28 Latest Annual Data: 2/3/2007

Year	Sales		Net Income
2007	$2,940,003,000		$53,742,000
2006	$5,953,352,000		$22,348,000
2005	$6,437,277,000		$61,085,000
Curr. Assets:	$1,250,841,000	Curr. Liab.: $862,780,000	
Plant, Equip.:	$1,099,331,000	Total Liab.: $1,448,164,000	Indic. Yr. Divd.: NA
Total Assets:	$2,544,303,000	Net Worth: $1,096,139,000	Debt/ Equity: 0.4105

Salamon Group Inc

302-1028 Alberni St., Vancouver, BC, V6E 1A3; **PH:** 1-212-559-2011; **http://** www.salamongroup.com

General - Incorporation	NV	Stock - Price on:12/24/2007	NA
Employees	NA	Stock Exchange	OTC
Auditor	Kmj	Corbin & Co. LLP	Ticker Symbol	SLMU
Stk Agt	Signature Stock Transfer, Inc.	Outstanding Shares	NA
Counsel	NA	E.P.S.	NA
DUNS No.	NA	Shareholders	NA

Business: The group has completed development of the Technology and products containing the Technology. Now it is seeking licensees to manufacture and market the finished product.

Primary SIC and add'l.: 3621

CIK No: 0001274211

Officers: John E. Salamon/61/Dir., CEO, CFO, Pres., Sec., Treasurer

Directors: John E. Salamon/61/Dir., CEO, CFO, Pres., Sec., Treasurer, Bruce Larway/54/Dir.

Owners: John E. Salamon, Bruce Larway, Calgary, AB, White & Lee Investments, Officers and directors as a group

Salem Communications Corp

4880 Santa Rosa Rd., Camarillo, CA, 93012; **PH:** 1-805-987-0400; **Fax:** 1-805-384-4520; **http://** www.salem.cc

General - Incorporation	DE	Stock - Price on:12/24/2007	$12.04
Employees	1,171	Stock Exchange	NDQ
Auditor	Ernst & Young LLP	Ticker Symbol	SALM
Stk Agt	Bank of New York	Outstanding Shares	23,850,000
Counsel	Gibson, Dunn & Crutcher LLP	E.P.S.	$0.47
DUNS No.	10-307-5636	Shareholders	NA

Business: The group's principal activity is to own and operate radio stations in metropolitan markets in the United States. The group owns and operates 92 radio stations, including 58 stations in 22 of the top 25 markets. The group also owns salem radio network(R) which is a developer, producer and syndicator of religious and family issues oriented talk, news and music programming with over 1,600 affiliated radio stations. The group also owns complementary Internet and publishing businesses. It also owns and operates srn news network (snn), salem music network (smn), reach satellite network (rsn) and salem radio representatives (srr) which produce and distribute talk, news and music programming to radio stations in the U.S. The group owns and operates oneplace, llc which provides on-demand audio streaming and related services and ccm communications, inc. (ccm) which publishes magazines that follow the christian music industry. On 02-Aug-2004, it acquired christianjobs.com.

Primary SIC and add'l.: 4899 4832

CIK No: 0001050606

Subsidiaries: Salem Communications Acquisition Corporation AcquisitionCo, Salem Communications Corporation

Officers: Edward G. Atsinger/Dir., CEO/$2,175,588.00, Greg R. Anderson/Pres. - Salem Radio Network, Evan D. Masyr/CFO, Sr. VP, Eric H. Halvorson/Dir., COO, Pres., Joe D. Davis/Pres. - Radio Division/$786,962.00, David A.R. Evans/Pres. - New Business Development, Interactive, Publishing/$1,344,461.00, James R. Cumbee/Pres. - Non - Broadcast Media, Jonathan L. Block/VP, General Counsel, Sec., Eric Jones/Primary Investor Relations Officer, Robert C. Adair/Sr. VP - Operations/$463,793.00

Directors: Edward G. Atsinger/Dir., CEO, Stuart W. Epperson/Chmn., Eric H. Halvorson/Dir., COO, Pres., Richard A. Riddle/Dir., Roland S. Hinz/Dir., Judge Paul Pressler/Dir., Denny Weinberg/Dir., David Davenport/Dir., Paul Pressler/77/Dir.

Owners: Edward C. Atsinger/5.97%, Richard A. Riddle, Paul Pressler, Nancy A. Epperson, Robert C. Adair, Columbia Wanger Asset Management, L.P./18.11%, Edward G. Atsinger/23.73%, Brown Brothers Harriman & Co./7.04%, Stuart W. Epperson/22.76%, Joe D. Davis, Nancy A. Epperson/15.77%, Dennis M. Weinberg, Gamco Investors, Inc., et al/5.24%, Roland S. Hinz, Insiders/46.94% (22 Owners included in Index)

Financial Data: Fiscal Year End:12/31 Latest Annual Data: 09/30/2007

Year	Sales		Net Income
2007	$174,228,000		$7,987,000
2006	$227,769,000		$18,999,000
2005	$211,839,000		$12,662,000
Curr. Assets:	$40,595,000	Curr. Liab.: $27,295,000	P/E Ratio: 15.05
Plant, Equip.:	$128,713,000	Total Liab.: $448,548,000	Indic. Yr. Divd.: NA
Total Assets:	$686,264,000	Net Worth: $237,716,000	Debt/ Equity: 1.4504

Salesforce.com Inc

1 Market St., Ste. 300, San Francisco, CA, 94105; *PH:* 1-415-901-7000; *Fax:* 1-415-901-7040; *http://* www.salesforce.com; *Email:* info@salesforce.com

General - Incorporation	DE	Stock - Price on:12/24/2007	$41.65
Employees	2,070	Stock Exchange	NYSE
Auditor	Ernst & Young LLP	Ticker Symbol	CRM
Stk Agt	Computershare Investor Services LLC	Outstanding Shares	115,500,000
Counsel	NA	E.P.S.	$0.09
DUNS No.	NA	Shareholders	NA

Business: The group's principle activity is to provide customer relationship management service to businesses of all sizes and industries. These services help customers sales force automation; customer service and support; marketing automation; document management; analytics and custom application development. The group markets its services on a subscription basis, primarily through our direct sales efforts and also indirectly through partners. The group operates in the United States, Europe and Asia-Pacific regions. The group's total revenue for year 2007 was 497.10 millions of USD.

Primary SIC and add'l.: 7374 7389

CIK No: 0001108524

Subsidiaries: 1338768 Ontario Inc, 1342077 Ontario Inc, African Metals Ltd, Aluminium Consortium Venezuela B.V., Angola Mining Finance Ltd, Angola Mining Services Ltd, Angola Technical Services Ltd, Atlas Steels Company Ltd, Auvernier Limited (in liquidation), Baniettor Mining (Pty) Ltd, BHP Billiton (BVI) Ltd, BHP Billiton (RA) Limited (in liquidation), BHP Billiton (UK) Limited, BHP Billiton Aluminium Ltd, BHP Billiton Aluminium Projects (Pty) Ltd 21 Subsidiaries included in the Index

Officers: Marc Benioff/Chmn., CEO/$10.00, Parker Harris/Exec. VP - Technology, Jim Steele/Pres. - Worldwide Sales, Distribution/$1,632,745.00, Kenneth I. Juster/Exec. VP - Law, Policy, Corporate Strategy/$1,561,304.00, Steve Cakebread/CFO/$1,736,579.00, John Freeland/Pres. - Worldwide Operations/$1,447,933.00, Bill Dewes/51/Chief Accounting Officer, Sr. VP

Directors: Marc Benioff/Chmn., CEO, Alan Hassenfeld/Dir., Craig Ramsey/Dir., Larry Tomlinson/Dir., Stratton Sclavos/Dir., Craig Conway/Dir., Sanford Robertson/Dir., Shirley Young/Dir., Maynard Webb/Dir.

Owners: Craig Ramsey, Jim Steele, Sanford R. Robertson, Turner Investment Partners, Inc./5.09%, Kenneth Juster, Insiders/19.24%, Shirley Young, Larry Tomlinson, Craig Conway, FMR Corp./12.80%, Stratton Sclavos, Alan Hassenfeld, The TCW Group, Inc./13.48%, Marc Benioff/15.48%, Steve Cakebread (16 Owners included in Index)

*Financial Data: Fiscal Year End:*01/31   *Latest Annual Data:* 1/31/2007

Year	Sales	Net Income
2007	$497,098,000	$481,000
2006	$309,857,000	$28,474,000
2005	$176,375,000	$7,346,000
Curr. Assets:	$419,096,000	Curr. Liab.: $376,999,000	P/E Ratio:4165.00
Plant, Equip.:	$30,155,000	Total Liab.: $378,407,000	Indic. Yr. Divd.: NA
Total Assets:	$664,832,000	Net Worth: $281,791,000	Debt/ Equity: NA

Salestactix Inc

2755 Bristol St., Costa Mesa, CA, 92626; *PH:* 1-949-248-5461; *http://* www.salestactix.com

General - Incorporation	DE	Stock - Price on:12/24/2007	NA
Employees	2	Stock Exchange	OTC
Auditor	Cacciamatta Accountancy Corporation	Ticker Symbol	STCXE
Stk Agt	Fidelity Transfer Co	Outstanding Shares	NA
Counsel	NA	E.P.S.	-$0.18
DUNS No.	NA	Shareholders	NA

Business: The group produces and sells a line of premium skin care products to physicians and mail order. The group has developed its own line of dermatologist-formulated skin care products including moisturizers, cleaners, sunscreens, and anti-aging emollients with glycolic acid. The group's products are sold under the name of rejuvenage, which is trademarked in United States and United Kingdom, and name of bladium, which is trademarked in United States. As of 01-Jan-2004, the company has discontinued its business activities and operations.

Primary SIC and add'l.: 2844

CIK No: 0000822370

Officers: Leonard J. Brandt/CEO, Principal Executive Officer, George Carpenter/Pres., Horace Hertz/CFO - Principal Financial, Accounting Officer

Directors: David B. Jones/Dir., Jerome Vaccaro/Dir., Kevin R. Keating/Dir., Henry T. Harbin/Dir.

Owners: Scott Absher/5.20%, Insiders/81.20%, Silas Philip, Richardson & Patel/75.50%

*Financial Data: Fiscal Year End:*12/31   *Latest Annual Data:* 12/31/2006

Year	Sales	Net Income
2006	NA	-$436,000
2005	NA	-$21,000
2004	NA	-$266,000
Curr. Assets:	$112,000	Curr. Liab.: $330,000	
Plant, Equip.:	NA	Total Liab.: $330,000	Indic. Yr. Divd.: NA
Total Assets:	$112,000	Net Worth: -$217,000	Debt/ Equity: NA

Salisbury Bancorp Inc

5 Bissell St., Lakeville, CT, 06039; *PH:* 1-860-435-9801; *Fax:* 1-860-435-0631; *http://* www.salisbury-bank.com

General - Incorporation	CT	Stock - Price on:12/24/2007	$33.6
Employees	118	Stock Exchange	AMEX
Auditor	Shatswell, MacLeod & Co. P.C	Ticker Symbol	SAL
Stk Agt	Registrar & Transfer Co	Outstanding Shares	1,680,000
Counsel	NA	E.P.S.	$2.22
DUNS No.	NA	Shareholders	NA

Business: The group's principal activities are to provide general, commercial and mortgage banking and trust services through its offices located in canaan, lakeville, salisbury and sharon in Connecticut. The group originates loans for consumers and business purposes. The group also offers safe deposit rentals, foreign exchange transfer services and other ancillary services to businesses and individuals. The group is engaged in the business of attracting deposits from the general public and investing those deposits in residential and commercial real estate, consumer and small business loans. The group's products and services are all of a nature of commercial bank and trust company. The group acquired canaan national bancorp in 2004.

Primary SIC and add'l.: 6712 6022

CIK No: 0001060219

Subsidiaries: Salisbury Bank and Trust Company

Officers: John F. Perotti/Chmn., CEO, Heather Ongley/Sr. Mortgage Processor, Underwriter, Mortgage Loan Origination, Diane Farrell/Sr. VP - Marketing, Roberta Reed/Sr. VP - Marketing, Joseph Law/VP - Loan Administration, Loan Origination, Diane E.R. Johnstone/Sr. VP, Trust Officer - Trust, Investment Services, Lana J. Morrison/VP, Sec. - Loan Origination, Betsy Summerville/Sr. VP, Retail Banking Officer - Operations, Retail Banking, Darrel Long/VP - Operations, Operations, Retail Banking, Missy Hanlon/Mortgage Servicing Officer - Loan Administration, Lisa Riley/Mgr. - Loan Servicing, Jerry Baldwin/Exec. VP - Commercial Lending, New Business Development, Sarah O'Connell/Mortgage Originator, Georgann Farnum/Egremont Office Branch Mgr. - Operations, Retail Banking, Karen S. Ralph/Assist. VP - Credit Administration, Loan Administration (42 Officers included in Index)

Directors: John F. Perotti/Chmn., CEO, Michael A. Varet/66/Dir., Richard J. Cantele/48/COO, Pres., Louis E. Allyn/60/Dir., John R.H. Blum/78/Presiding Dir., Louise F. Brown/64/Dir., Holly J. Nelson/54/Dir., Nancy F. Humphreys/66/Dir., Robert S. Drucker/66/Dir.

Owners: Insiders/7.04%, Louise F. Brown/0.16%, Robert S. Drucker/0.45%, John F. Foley/0.44%, Louis E. Allyn, John F. Perotti/0.67%, Nancy F. Humphreys/0.10%, Holly J. Nelson/0.09%, Richard J. Cantele, Michael A. Varet/3.93%, John R. H. Blum/0.95%

*Financial Data: Fiscal Year End:*12/31   *Latest Annual Data:* 12/31/2006

Year	Sales	Net Income
2006	$28,312,000	$4,254,000
2005	$25,681,000	$4,561,000
2004	$21,306,000	$4,019,000
Curr. Assets:	$14,241,000	Curr. Liab.: $402,259,000	P/E Ratio: 14.18
Plant, Equip.:	$6,136,000	Total Liab.: $405,990,000	Indic. Yr. Divd.: $1.080
Total Assets:	$450,340,000	Net Worth: $44,349,000	Debt/ Equity: NA

Saliva Diagnostic Systems Inc

2294 Nostrand Ave., Brooklyn, NY, 11210; *PH:* 1-917-853-6440; *Fax:* 1-212-937-3801; *http://* www.salv.com; *Email:* help@salv.com

General - Incorporation	DE	Stock - Price on:12/24/2007	$0.17
Employees	5	Stock Exchange	OTC
Auditor	Lazar Levine & Felix LLP	Ticker Symbol	SSUR
Stk Agt	American Stock Transfer & Trust Co.	Outstanding Shares	37,380,000
Counsel	NA	E.P.S.	$0.10
DUNS No.	NA	Shareholders	NA

Business: The group's principle activities include developing, manufacturing and marketing of medical collection devices and rapid immunoassays for use in the detection of infectious diseases. The company's products fall into two categories: rapid immunoassays and medical specimen collection devices. The company has developed four rapid tests utilizing immunochromatography for the detection of antibodies to selected pathogens, including HIV and helicobacter pylori. Rapid immunoassays products include sero-strip HIV, hema-strip HIV and saliva-strip HIV. Medical specimen collection device includes omni sal(r). This product is a patented saliva collection device currently sold to several commercial companies for use with their laboratory assays for the detection of HIV infection, drugs-of-abuse and cigarette smoking. The company markets its products in the United States, the United Kingdom, Canada and Africa. The group operates from United States.

Primary SIC and add'l.: 3841 6794

CIK No: 0000885534

Officers: Steven M. Peltzman/61/Chmn., CEO, Bruce D. Pattison/61/Dir., COO, Pres., Leo Ehrlich/50/Dir., CFO, Sec., Moshe Bodner/Sales, Marketing

Directors: Steven M. Peltzman/61/Chmn., CEO, Bruce D. Pattison/61/Dir., COO, Pres., Leo Ehrlich/50/Dir., CFO, Sec., Richard Woodrich/62/Dir., Joseph Levi/49/Dir.

Owners: Leo Ehrlich/10.30%, Steve Peltzman, Joe Levi, Bruce Pattison, Helenka Bodner/48.00%, Jules Nordlicht/7.00%, Chaim Ravad/9.10%, Richard Woodrich, Insiders/11.80%

*Financial Data: Fiscal Year End:*12/31   *Latest Annual Data:* 12/31/2006

Year	Sales	Net Income
2006	$900,000	-$5,332,000
2005	$756,000	-$2,561,000
2004	$1,399,000	-$280,000
Curr. Assets:	$333,000	Curr. Liab.: $992,000	
Plant, Equip.:	$42,000	Total Liab.: $5,599,000	Indic. Yr. Divd.: NA
Total Assets:	$514,000	Net Worth: -$5,085,000	Debt/ Equity: NA

Salix Pharmaceuticals Ltd

1700 Perimeter Pk. Dr., Morrisville, NC, 27560; *PH:* 1-919-862-1000; *Fax:* 1-919-228-4265; *http://* www.salix.com

General - Incorporation	DE	Stock - Price on:12/24/2007	$12.63
Employees	240	Stock Exchange	NDQ
Auditor	Ernst & Young LLP	Ticker Symbol	SLXP
Stk Agt	Computershare Investor Services LLC	Outstanding Shares	47,160,000
Counsel	Wyrick Robbins Yates & Ponton	E.P.S.	$0.85
DUNS No.	79-310-8036	Shareholders	NA

Business: The group's principal activities are to develop and market prescription pharmaceutical products for the treatment of gastrointestinal disease that affect digestive tract. The group uses third-party manufacturers to produce material for use in clinical trials and for commercial product. The group's first marketed product, colazal is approved by the food and administration for the treatment of mildly to moderately active ulcerative colitis and the first new oral therapy approved by the fda for this indication. In Nov 2003, the group acquired the right to sell 25, 75 and 100 milligram dosage strengths of azathioprine tablets in North America under the brand name azasan. Azasan is a drug that suppresses immune system responses and is indicated for preventing rejection of kidney transplants and treatment of severe arthritis. The group currently markets colazal and two dosage strengths of azasan.

Primary SIC and add'l.: 2834 8731

CIK No: 0001009356

Subsidiaries: Chong Kun Dang Pharmaceutical Corporation., Glycyx Pharmaceuticals, Ltd, Omnichem s.a.

Officers: Carolyn J. Logan/CEO, Pres./$1,017,361.00, Adam C. Derbyshire/Sr. VP - Finance, Administration, CFO/$512,988.00, Randy W. Hamilton/Founder - Business Development Advisor, Lorin K. Johnson/Founder, Chief Scientific Liaison, William P. Forbes/VP - Research, Development, Chief Development Officer/$404,456.00, Michael G. Freeman/Executive Dir. - Investor Relations, Corporate Communications

Directors: John F. Chappell/Chmn., Thomas W. D'Alonzo/Dir., Randy W. Hamilton/Founder - Business Development Advisor; Lorin K. Johnson/Founder, Chief Scientific Liaison, Richard A. Franco/Dir., William Harral/Dir., William P. Keane/Dir.

Owners: Insiders/5.56%, Lord, Abbett & Co. LLC/5.95%, David N. Taylor, William P. Keane, Carolyn J. Logan/2.06%, EARNEST Partners, LLC/5.14%, William Harral, Putnam, LLC d/b/a Putnam Investments/5.88%, Richard A. Franco, Adam C. Derbyshire, John F. Chappell/1.80%, Wellington Management Company, LLP/13.77%, William P. Forbes, Thomas W. DAlonzo

Financial Data: Fiscal Year End:12/31   Latest Annual Data: 12/31/2006

Year	Sales	Net Income
2006	$208,533,000	$31,510,000
2005	$154,903,000	-$60,585,000
2004	$105,496,000	$6,839,000

Curr. Assets:	$170,125,000	Curr. Liab.:	$44,980,000	P/E Ratio:	18.04
Plant, Equip.:	$3,866,000	Total Liab.:	$45,572,000	Indic. Yr. Divd.:	NA
Total Assets:	$323,123,000	Net Worth:	$277,551,000	Debt/ Equity:	0.0553

Sally Beauty Holdings Inc

3001 Colorado Blvd., Denton, TX, 76210; **PH:** 1-940-898-7500; **Fax:** 1-940-898-7927; *http://* www.sallybeauty.com

General - Incorporation	DE	**Stock**- Price on:12/24/2007	$9.72
Employees	15,800	Stock Exchange	NYSE
Auditor	KPMG LLP	Ticker Symbol	SBH
Stk Agt	NA	Outstanding Shares	180,320,000
Counsel	NA	E.P.S.	$0.24
DUNS No.	NA	Shareholders	NA

Business: The groups principle activity is to supply professional beauty products. The groups products include hair care products, styling appliances, skin and nail care products, and other beauty items. The group operates through two segments namely, Sally Beauty Supply and Beauty Systems Group. In the year 2006, the group acquired Salon Success. The group operates from the United States and the United Kingdom.

Primary SIC and add'l.: 2844

CIK No: 0001368458

Subsidiaries: Armstrong McCall Holdings L.L.C., Armstrong McCall Holdings, Inc., Armstrong McCall Management, L.C., Armstrong McCall, L.P., Arnolds, Inc., Beauty Holding LLC, Beauty Systems Group (Canada), Inc., Beauty Systems Group LLC, Beyond the Zone, Inc., Brentwood Beauty Laboratories International, Inc., Coloresse, Inc., D&G Haselock Limited, Diorama Services Company, LLC, Energy of Beauty, Inc., Esthetician Services Inc. 65 Subsidiaries included in the Index

Officers: Gary G. Winterhalter/Dir., CEO, Pres., Richard W. Dowd/Sr. VP - Distribution, CIO, John R. Golliher/Pres. - Beauty Systems Group, Bennie L. Lowery/Sr. VP, General Merchandise Mgr. - Beauty Systems Group, Neil B. Riemer/Pres. - Armstrong Mccall, David L. Rea/Sr. VP, CFO, Treasurer, Raal H. Roos/Sr. VP, General Counsel, Sec., Michael G. Spinozzi/Pres. - Sally Beauty Supply, Jan Roberts/Contact - Media Relations, Sandy Martin/Investor Relations Officer

Directors: Gary G. Winterhalter/Dir., CEO, Pres., James G. Berges/Chmn., Kathleen J. Affeldt/Dir., Marshall E. Eisenberg/Dir., Donald J. Gogel/Dir., Robert R. McMaster/Dir., Walter L. Metcalfe/Dir., John A. Miller/Dir., Martha Miller De Lombera/Dir., Edward W. Rabin/Dir., Richard J. Schnall/Dir.

Owners: John R. Golliher, John A. Miller, Bennie L. Lowery, Insiders/1.21%, Kathleen J. Affeldt, CDR Investors/47.60%, Gary T. Robinson, O.S.S. Capital Management LP and affiliates/5.09%, David L. Rea, Martha Miller de Lombera, Marshall E. Eisenberg, Carol L. Bernick/6.96%, Edward W. Rabin, Raal H. Roos, Neil B. Riemer (20 Owners included in Index)

Financial Data: Fiscal Year End:09/30   Latest Annual Data: 09/30/2007

Year	Sales	Net Income
2007	$2,513,772,000	$44,492,000
2006	$2,373,100,000	$110,193,000

Curr. Assets:	$770,289,000	Curr. Liab.:	$291,182,000		
Plant, Equip.:	$142,735,000	Total Liab.:	$332,874,000	Indic. Yr. Divd.:	NA
Total Assets:	$1,338,841,000	Net Worth:	$1,005,967,000	Debt/ Equity:	NA

Salomon Smith Barney Fairfield Futures Fund LP

731 Lexington Ave., 25th Fl, New York, NY, 10022; **PH:** 1-212-559-2011

General - Incorporation	NY	**Stock**- Price on:12/24/2007	NA
Employees	NA	Stock Exchange	NA
Auditor	KPMG LLP	Ticker Symbol	NA
Stk Agt	NA	Outstanding Shares	NA
Counsel	NA	E.P.S.	NA
DUNS No.	NA	Shareholders	NA

Business: The group is a limited partnership organized on March 25, 2002 under the partnership laws of the State of New York. The Partnership commenced trading operations on June 5, 2002. The group operates from United States.

Primary SIC and add'l.: 6221

CIK No: 0001170406

Officers: Jason C. Shapiro/Dir., Pres., Jennifer Magro/Dir., CFO, Jerry Pascucci/Dir., Pres., Ihor Rakowsky/Dir., Sec.

Directors: Jason C. Shapiro/Dir., Pres., David J. Vogel/Dir., Shelley Ullman/Dir., Jennifer Magro/Dir., CFO, Jerry Pascucci/Dir., Pres., Ihor Rakowsky/Dir., Sec., Steve Ciampi/Dir., Raymond Nolte/Dir., Daryl Dewbrey/Dir.

Owners: David J. Vogel, Keystone District Council

Salon Media Group Inc

101 Spear St., Ste. 203, San Francisco, CA, 94105; **PH:** 1-415-645-9200; **Fax:** 1-415-645-9204; *http://* www.salon.com; **Email:** investor@salon.com

General - Incorporation	DE	**Stock**- Price on:12/24/2007	NA
Employees	NA	Stock Exchange	OTC
Auditor	Burr, Pilger & Mayer LLP	Ticker Symbol	SLNM
Stk Agt	Computershare Investor Services LLC	Outstanding Shares	NA
Counsel	Morrison & Foerster LLP	E.P.S.	-$1.1
DUNS No.	NA	Shareholders	NA

Business: The group's principal activity is in the provision of online news and information. The group produces a total network of eight primary subject specific websites and two online communities - the well and table talk. The group offers award-winning journalism from breaking news and in-depth analysis to provocative commentary on politics, technology, culture and entertainment. The group also provides audio streaming Website.

Primary SIC and add'l.: 7375

CIK No: 0001084332

Subsidiaries: MP3Lit.com, Inc, The Well, LLC

Officers: Christopher Neimeth/CEO/$356,572.00, Max Garrone/Editor, Scott Rosenberg/Sr. Editor, Technology, Walter Shapiro/Washington Bureau Chief, Kerry Lauerman/Editorial Dir. - New York, Gary Kamiya/Writer at Large, Editorial, Jeanne Carstensen/Managing Editor, Ruth Henrich/Assoc. Managing Editor, Gail Ann Williams/Dir. - Communities, Bob Watts/Art Dir., Mignon Khargie/Illustrator, Design, Zach Trenholm/Contributing Illustrator, Jerry Palmisano/Programmer, Louis Bennett/Web Engineer, Nico Raffo/Web Engineer (60 Officers included in Index)

Directors: Robert McKay/Dir., James H. Rosenfield/Dir., Robert Ellis/Dir., David Talbot/Founder, John Warnock/Dir., George Hirsch/Dir., Elizabeth Hambrecht/Dir., Deepak Desai/49/Dir.

Owners: Octavia LLC, Conrad Lowry, Robert McKay, David Talbot, Robert Ellis, Shea Ventures LLC, Constellation Venture Capital, Elizabeth Hambrecht, Nancy & Timothy Armstrong, John Warnock, Wenner Media LLC, Deepak Desai, James Rosenfield, Adobe Systems Incorporated, Harvey Gamm (21 Owners included in Index)

Financial Data: Fiscal Year End:03/31   Latest Annual Data: 03/31/2007

Year	Sales	Net Income
2007	$7,748,000	-$1,566,000
2006	$6,516,000	-$1,122,000
2005	$6,628,000	-$518,000

Curr. Assets:	$1,889,000	Curr. Liab.:	$1,554,000		
Plant, Equip.:	$115,000	Total Liab.:	$1,639,000	Indic. Yr. Divd.:	NA
Total Assets:	$5,605,000	Net Worth:	$3,966,000	Debt/ Equity:	NA

Salton Inc

1955 Field Ct., Lake Forest, IL, 60045; **PH:** 1-847-803-4600; **Fax:** 1-847-803-1211; *http://* www.saltoninc.com

General - Incorporation	DE	**Stock**- Price on:12/24/2007	$1.79
Employees	984	Stock Exchange	OTC
Auditor	Grant Thornton, LLP	Ticker Symbol	SFPI
Stk Agt	UMB Bank, N.A.	Outstanding Shares	15,360,000
Counsel	Sonnenschein Nath & Rosenthal LLP	E.P.S.	-$6.05
DUNS No.	19-430-2212	Shareholders	NA

Business: The group's principal activities are to design, market, manufacture and distribute a broad range of branded, high quality small appliances, home decor and personal care products. Its product mix includes a broad range of small kitchen and home appliances, tabletop products, time products, lighting products, picture frames and personal care and wellness products. Small appliances include heating appliances, motor driven appliances, beverage makers, cookware and floor care. Home decor consist of tabletop products, picture frames, time and lighting products. Personal care and wellness include health equipment, massagers, hair care, beauty, oral health care and relaxation items. The group markets and sells its products in North America, Europe, Asia, Australia, New Zealand and South Africa. Its customers are mass merchandisers, department stores, specialty stores, mail order catalogs and retailers.

Primary SIC and add'l.: 3231 3263 3873 3999 3639 3634

CIK No: 0000878280

Subsidiaries: Icebox LLC, Salton Australia Pty Ltd., Salton Europe PLC, Salton Hong Kong Ltd., Salton International CV, Salton S.a.r.l., Salton UK, Salton/Toastmaster Logistics LLC, Toastmaster, Inc.

Officers: William M. Lutz/48/Interim CEO, CFO, David C. Sabin/Chmn., Sec., William B. Rue/COO, Pres., Ken Sgro/Investor Relations Officer

Directors: David C. Sabin/Chmn., Sec., Leonhard Dreimann/60/Dir., Jason B. Mudrick/33/Dir., Daniel J. Stubler/64/Dir., Bruce J. Walker/64/Dir., Steven Oyer/53/Dir., Lester Lee/48/Dir.

Owners: Harbinger Capital Partners Master Fundl, Ltd./17.70%, David C. Sabin/3.90%, William Lutz, Insiders/7.10%, Angelo, Gordon& Co., L.P./5.00%, Leonhard Dreimann/7.00%, Bruce J. Walker, Dimensional FundAdvisors Inc./7.50%, Centre PartnersII LLC/5.70%, Contrarian Capital Management, L.L.C./16.80%, William B. Rue/2.70%, Steven Oyer

Financial Data: Fiscal Year End:07/02   Latest Annual Data: 06/30/2007

Year	Sales	Net Income
2007	$523,301,000	-$91,156,000
2006	$635,960,000	-$67,967,000
2005	$1,071,012,000	-$51,787,000

Curr. Assets:	$561,874,000	Curr. Liab.:	$255,770,000		
Plant, Equip.:	$81,152,000	Total Liab.:	$697,461,000	Indic. Yr. Divd.:	NA
Total Assets:	$854,552,000	Net Worth:	$133,576,000	Debt/ Equity:	NA

Samaritan Pharmaceuticals Inc

101 Convention Ctr. Dr., Ste. 310, Las Vegas, NV, 89109; **PH:** 1-702-735-7001; **Fax:** 1-702-737-7016; *http://* www.samaritanpharma.com

General - Incorporation	NV	**Stock**- Price on:12/24/2007	$0.23
Employees	15	Stock Exchange	AMEX
Auditor	Sherb & Co. LLP	Ticker Symbol	LIV
Stk Agt	Securities Transfer Corp	Outstanding Shares	159,420,000
Counsel	NA	E.P.S.	-$0.19
DUNS No.	NA	Shareholders	NA

Business: The group's principal activity is to engage in research and development of novel therapeutic and diagnostic products. These products help to treat chronic debilitating diseases such as alzheimer's, cancer, central nervous system disorders, cardiovascular disease, HIV and Parkinson's disease. The group is in its development stage and none of its proprietary products has reached a commercial stage. It operates solely in the domestic market.

Primary SIC and add'l.: 2834 8731

CIK No: 0001057377

Subsidiaries: Samaritan Ireland Pharmaceuticals, Limited, Steroidogenesis Inhibitors, Inc.

Officers: Janet Greeson/Chmn., CEO, Pres./$493,233.00, Eugene Boyle/Dir., CFO/$330,835.00, Tom Lang/Chief Drug Development Officer/$339,378.00, Kristi Eads/VP - Business Development, Corp. Sec., George Weaver/Regulatory Affairs, Drug Development/$148,489.00, Vassilios Papadopoulos/47/Chief Scientist - Key Consultant, Christos Dakas/MD - Samaritan Europe, In, Licensing Europe/$152,686.00, Dianne Thompson/Controller, Richard Brown/Investor Relations, Barrie G. Fuller/Operations Investor Relations

Directors: Janet Greeson/Chmn., CEO, Pres., Erasto R.C. Saldi/Dir., Thomas H. Winn/Dir., Laurent Lecanu/Dir., Cynthia C. Thompson/Dir., Eugene Boyle/Dir., CFO, Julio Garcia/Dir., Welter Holden/Dir.

Owners: Eugene J. Boyle/6.00%, Thomas H. Winn, Welter "Budd" Holden/1.60%, Insiders/21.40%, Thomas Lang, Janet R. Greeson/10.90%, Laurent Lecanu, Kristi C. Eads, Cynthia C. Thompson, George Weaver, Vassilios Papadopoulos/1.10%, Douglas D. Bessert/2.90%, Christos Dakas, Erasto R.C. Saldi

Financial Data: Fiscal Year End:12/31   Latest Annual Data: 12/31/2006

Year	Sales	Net Income
2006	$32,000	-$7,573,000
2005	$257,000	-$5,558,000
2004	NA	-$4,864,000

Curr. Assets:	$1,074,000	Curr. Liab.:	$1,520,000		
Plant, Equip.:	$128,000	Total Liab.:	$1,520,000	Indic. Yr. Divd.:	NA
Total Assets:	$2,499,000	Net Worth:	$980,000	Debt/ Equity:	NA

Samex Mining Corp

No. 301 32920 Ventura Ave., Abbotsford, BC, V2S 6J3; *PH:* 1-604-870-9920; *http://* www.samex.com; *Email:* 4info@samex.com

General - Incorporation ..... BC	Stock- Price on:12/24/2007 ..... $0.73
Employees ..... NA	Stock Exchange ..... OTC
Auditor ..... Dale Matheson Carr-Hilton Labonte	Ticker Symbol ..... SMXMF
Stk Agt ..... Computershare Trust Co	Outstanding Shares ..... NA
Counsel ..... NA	E.P.S. ..... NA
DUNS No. 25-528-7187	Shareholders ..... NA

Business: The group's principal activity is to acquire and explore mineral resource properties. The group currently owns or has interests in mineral exploration properties in the altiplano region of Bolivia, including the walter property.

Primary SIC and add'l.: 1044 1031 1041

CIK No: 0000766504

Subsidiaries: Bolivex S.A., Emibol S.A., Empresa Minera Boliviana S. A., Minas Bolivex S.A., Minera Samex Chile S.A., Samex International Ltd., Samex S.A., South American Mining & Exploration Corp

Officers: Jeffrey Dahl/46/Dir., CEO, Pres., Allen Leschert/Dir., Counsel, Larry McLean/Dir., VP - Operations, Robert E. Kell/Dir., VP - Exploration, Brenda McLean/56/Corp. Sec.

Directors: Jeffrey Dahl/46/Dir., CEO, Pres., Peter J. Dahl/67/Chmn., Larry McLean/Dir., VP - Operations, Patricio Kyllmann/Dir., Robert E. Kell/Dir., VP - Exploration, Allen Leschert/Dir., Counsel

Owners: Larry D. McLean/0.61%, Brenda McLean/0.34%, Patricio G. Kyllmann/0.20%, Peter J. Dahl/0.83%, Allen D. Leschert/0.54%, Robert E. Kell/0.73%, Jeffrey P. Dahl/0.54%

Financial Data: Fiscal Year End:11/30   Latest Annual Data: 12/31/2005

Year	Sales	Net Income
2005	NA	-$2,475,000
2004	NA	-$3,287,000
2003	NA	-$1,180,000

Curr. Assets:	$1,207,000	Curr. Liab.:	$58,000		
Plant, Equip.:	$97,000	Total Liab.:	$58,000	Indic. Yr. Divd.:	NA
Total Assets:	$1,303,000	Net Worth:	$1,245,000	Debt/ Equity:	NA

San Diego Gas & Electric Co

8326 Century Pk. Ct, San Diego, CA, 92123; *PH:* 1-619-696-2000; *http://* www.sdge.com

General - Incorporation ..... CA	Stock- Price on:12/24/2007 ..... $24.8
Employees ..... NA	Stock Exchange ..... OTC
Auditor ..... Deloitte & Touche LLP	Ticker Symbol ..... SDOGI
Stk Agt ..... NA	Outstanding Shares ..... NA
Counsel ..... NA	E.P.S. ..... NA
DUNS No. 00-691-1457	Shareholders ..... NA

Business: The group's principle activities include generating, purchasing and distributing electric energy; and purchases and distributes natural gas. The group operates from United States.

Primary SIC and add'l.: 4931 4923

CIK No: 0000086521

Subsidiaries: SDG&E Funding LLC

Officers: Debra L. Reed/CEO, Pres., David L. Geier/VP - Electric Transmission, Distribution, Anne Shen Smith/Sr. VP - Customer Services/$1,043,330.00, Pamela J. Fair/VP - Customer Operations, Lee Schavrien/Sr. VP - Regulatory Affairs/$837,379.00, Lad Lorenz/VP - Regulatory Affairs, Michael R. Niggli/COO/$2,930,639.00, Dennis V. Arriola/Sr. VP, CFO/$1,090,900.00, Matt Burkhart/VP - Electric, Gas Procurement, Eugene Mitchell/Regional VP - External Affairs, Margot A. Kyd/VP - Supply Management, Michelle M. Mueller/VP - Customer Services, Mass Markets, Robert M. Schlax/VP, Controller, Bret J. Lane/VP - Environmental, Safety, Facilities, Chief Environmental Officer, Davis W. Smith/Sr. VP, General Counsel *(21 Officers included in Index)*

Directors: Edwin A. Guiles/Chmn., Mark A. Snell/Dir.

Owners: Insiders, Lee M. Stewart, James P. Avery, Michael R. Niggli, Debra L. Reed, Mark A. Snell, Anne S. Smith, Dennis V. Arriola, Lee Schavrien

Financial Data: Fiscal Year End:12/31   Latest Annual Data: 12/31/2006

Year	Sales	Net Income
2006	$2,785,000,000	$242,000,000
2005	$2,512,000,000	$267,000,000
2004	$2,274,000,000	$213,000,000

Curr. Assets:	NA	Curr. Liab.:	NA		
Plant, Equip.:	NA	Total Liab.:	NA	Indic. Yr. Divd.:	NA
Total Assets:	NA	Net Worth:	NA	Debt/ Equity:	0.9644

San Diego Trust Bank CA

2550 5th Ave. Ste. 1010, San Diego, CA, 92103; *PH:* 1-619-525-1700; *http://* www.sandiegotrust.com; *Email:* info@sandiegotrust.com

General - Incorporation ..... NA	Stock- Price on:12/24/2007 ..... $32.95
Employees ..... NA	Stock Exchange ..... OTC
Auditor ..... NA	Ticker Symbol ..... SDBK
Stk Agt ..... NA	Outstanding Shares ..... NA
Counsel ..... NA	E.P.S. ..... NA
DUNS No. ..... NA	Shareholders ..... NA

Business: The groups principal activities include providing banking and financial services. Services of the group include checking accounts, savings accounts, certificates of deposit, installment loans, real estate mortgage loans, commercial loans, traveler's checks, safe deposit boxes, night depository and automated teller services. The group operates from the United States.

Primary SIC and add'l.: 6712

CIK No:

Officers: Michael E. Perry/Chmn., CEO, Pres., Toby Reschan/Dir., Sr. Exec. VP, COO, John Penrith/Exec. VP - Real Estate Industries Group, Joe Simmons/Exec. VP, Chief Credit Officer, William Lamison/Sr. VP, Commercial Lending Officer, Nasrin Rostami/Sr. VP - Operations, Risk Management, John Jeffries/Sr. VP, CFO, Mary Purviance/Sr. VP, Mgr.

Directors: Michael E. Perry/Chmn., CEO, Pres., Brian H. Gowland/Vice Chmn., Larry L. Willette/Chmn. Emeritus, Claudette G. Wilson/Dir., James R. St. John/Dir., Richard H. Wesselink/Dir., William E. Cole/Dir., Toby Reschan/Dir., Sr. Exec. VP, COO, Christopher J. Coseo/Dir., Daniel D. Herde/Dir., James W. Ledwith/Dir., Michael A. Morton/Dir.

San Holdings Inc

9800 Pyramid Ct., Ste. 130, Englewood, CO, 80112; *PH:* 1-303-660-3933; *Fax:* 1-303-814-0693; *http://* www.sanz.com

General - Incorporation ..... CO	Stock- Price on:12/24/2007 ..... $0.064
Employees 133	Stock Exchange ..... OTC
Auditor ..... Grant Thornton LLP	Ticker Symbol ..... SANZ
Stk Agt ..... Computershare Investor Services LLC	Outstanding Shares 96,950,000
Counsel ..... NA	E.P.S. ..... -$0.266
DUNS No. 18-854-6964	Shareholders ..... NA

Business: The group's principal activity is to provide sophisticated enterprise-level data storage and data management solutions to commercial and government clients. It focuses on the design, delivery and management of data storage systems that are built using a network architecture. The products and services of the group include storage solutions that the group design and deliver as a customized project to meet a client's specific needs, storage-related consulting services and a proprietary storage-related software product that facilitates data access and management for geospatial imagery users. Storage area network (san) and network attached storage (nas) systems are secondary, high-speed computer networks dedicated to data storage and backup functions. On 01-Apr-2003, the group acquired solunet storage holding corp and indirectly its operating subsidiary solunet storage inc.

Primary SIC and add'l.: 7372 3572

CIK No: 0000799097

Subsidiaries: Colorado corporation, Solunet Storage, Inc

Officers: Todd A. Oseth/Chmn., CEO, Pres., David Rosenthal/CFO, Robert Antoniazzi/VP - Solutions, Kevin Burns/VP - Marketing - Business Development, Richard Hoffman/VP - Sales

Directors: Todd A. Oseth/Chmn., CEO, Pres., Kevin J. Calhoun/Dir., Case H. Kuehn/55/Dir., Kent J. Lund/Dir., Clarence E. Terry/Dir., Steve M. Liff/Dir., Daryl C. Hollis/Dir., George R. Rea/Dir., Michael T. Gillen/Dir., Eric S. Nelson/Dir.

Owners: George R. Rea, Sun Solunet, LLC, Insiders, John Jenkins, Marc J. Leder, Robert C. Ogden, Kent J. Lund, Rodger R. Krouse, Daryl C. Hollis

Financial Data: Fiscal Year End:12/31   Latest Annual Data: 12/31/2006

Year	Sales	Net Income
2006	$58,745,000	-$32,957,000
2005	$59,115,000	-$15,803,000
2004	$66,158,000	-$6,750,000

Curr. Assets:	$18,127,000	Curr. Liab.:	$25,199,000		
Plant, Equip.:	$472,000	Total Liab.:	$32,013,000	Indic. Yr. Divd.:	NA
Total Assets:	$22,155,000	Net Worth:	-$9,858,000	Debt/ Equity:	NA

San Jose Water Company

374 W Santa Clara St., San Jose, CA, 95196; *PH:* 1-408-279-7800; *Fax:* 1-408-279-7917; *http://* www.sjwater.com; *Email:* customer_service@sjwater.com

General - Incorporation ..... CA	Stock- Price on:12/24/2007 ..... $29.42
Employees 357	Stock Exchange ..... NYSE
Auditor ..... KPMG LLP	Ticker Symbol ..... NA
Stk Agt ..... American Stock Transfer & Trust Co.	Outstanding Shares 18,310,000
Counsel ..... NA	E.P.S. $1.91
DUNS No. 00-691-3644	Shareholders ..... NA

Business: The group's principal activities are to produce, purchase, store, purify, distribute and sell water. The group provides nonregulated water related services under agreements with municipalities. The nonregulated services include full water system operations, billings and cash remittances. The group provides water service to customers in portions of the cities of cupertino and san jose and in the cities of campbell, monte sereno, saratoga and the town of los gatos and santa clara.

Primary SIC and add'l.: 6552 4941

CIK No: 0000766829

Officers: Richard W. Roth/Dir., CEO, Pres./$1,311,057.00, Angela Yip/CFO, Treasurer/$441,382.00, Suzy Papazian/Corp. Sec. - Attorney, George Belhumeur/Sr. VP - Operations/$626,740.00, Scott R. Yoo/COO/$589,127.00, Dana Drysdale/VP - Information Systems, Andrea J. Elliott/Controller, Richard J. Pardini/VP, Chief Engineer

Directors: Richard W. Roth/Dir., CEO, Pres., Drew Gibson/Chmn., Philip J. Dinapoli/Dir., Mark L. Cali/Dir., Douglas R. King/Dir., George E. Moss/Dir., Charles J. Toeniskoetter/Dir., Frederick R. Ulrich/Dir., Robert A. Van Valer/Dir.

Owners: Mario J. Gabelli/6.50%, Drew Gibson, Robert A. VanValer, Roscoe Moss/11.70%, Philip J. DiNapoli, Scott R. Yoo, Richard W. Roth, Mark L. Cali, Frederick R. Ulrich, Douglas R. King, George E. Moss/16.70%, Angela Yip, Insiders/17.70%, George J. Belhumeur, Charles J. Toeniskoetter *(16 Owners included in Index)*

Financial Data: ***Fiscal Year End:*** 12/31 ***Latest Annual Data:*** 12/31/2006

Year	Sales	Net Income
2006	$189,238,000	$38,581,000
2005	$180,105,000	$21,840,000
2004	$166,911,000	$19,786,000

Curr. Assets:	$59,475,000	***Curr. Liab.:***	$37,246,000	***P/E Ratio:***	15.40
Plant, Equip.:	$546,811,000	***Total Liab.:***	$477,682,000	***Indic. Yr. Divd.:***	$0.610
Total Assets:	$705,864,000	***Net Worth:***	$228,182,000	***Debt/ Equity:***	0.8644

San Juan Basin Royalty Trust

Compass Bank, Trust Department, 2525 Ridgmar Blvd., Ste. 100, Fort Worth, TX, 76116; ***PH:*** 1-866-809-4553; ***Fax:*** 1-817-735-0936; ***http://*** www.sjbrt.com; ***Email:*** sjt@compassbank.com

General - Incorporation	TX	***Stock*** - Price on:12/24/2007	$33.06
Employees	NA	Stock Exchange	NYSE
Auditor	Weaver and Tidwell, LLP	Ticker Symbol	SJT
Stk Agt	Computershare Investor Services LLC	Outstanding Shares	46,610,000
Counsel	NA	E.P.S	$2.44
DUNS No.	NA	Shareholders	NA

Business: The groups principle activity is to invest in real estate properties. The group operates from the United States. The groups quarterly revenue for September 2007 was 37.65 millions of USD.

Primary SIC and add'l.: 6792

CIK No: 0000319655

Officers: Lee Ann Anderson/VP, Sr. Trust Officer, Kaye Wilke/Investor Relations Officer

Owners: Compass Bank

Financial Data: ***Fiscal Year End:*** 12/31 ***Latest Annual Data:*** 12/31/2006

Year	Sales	Net Income
2006	$137,519,000	$135,867,000
2005	$154,026,000	$151,560,000
2004	$111,102,000	$109,391,000

Curr. Assets:	$4,658,000	***Curr. Liab.:***	$4,543,000		
Plant, Equip.:	NA	***Total Liab.:***	$4,658,000	***Indic. Yr. Divd.:***	$2.080
Total Assets:	$26,481,000	***Net Worth:***	$21,823,000	***Debt/ Equity:***	NA

San Luis Trust Bank FSB

1001 Marsh St., San Luis Obispo, CA, 93401; ***PH:*** 1-805-541-9200; ***Fax:*** 1-805-541-9230; ***http://*** www.sanluistrustbank.com

General - Incorporation		***Stock*** - Price on:12/24/2007	$10
Employees	NA	Stock Exchange	OTC
Auditor	NA	Ticker Symbol	SNLS
Stk Agt	NA	Outstanding Shares	NA
Counsel	NA	E.P.S	NA
DUNS No.	NA	Shareholders	NA

Business: The groups principal activity is to serve all of customers lending and deposit needs. The group offers a broad base of financial products and services, need equity line of credit, a construction loan or simply to find the best rates in town. Services of the group include maximum ATM withdrawal per day, bank letter re account info, cashier's checks, check cashing, non customers closing account within 90 days of opening, collections incoming, no charge, collections outgoing and courier service.

Primary SIC and add'l.: 6029

CIK No:

Officers: Bradley J. Lyon/Dir., CEO, Pres., Casey Appell/Exec. VP, CCA, Eric Wells/Sr. VP, Doug Bradley/VP - Operations, Rick Mosbrucker/Assist. VP - Loan Administration, Brian Rober/VP, Controller, Paul White/AVP - Consumer Lender, Lupe Meraz/Consumer Lender, Jonna Phillips/VP, Julie Scherz/Loan Officer, Joe Brundage/Executive Assist., Zakiya Upshur/Credit Analyst, Derek Rosenstrauch/Credit Analyst, Jin Kim/Credit Analyst, Katrina Boswell/Credit Analyst *(33 Officers included in Index)*

Directors: Bradley J. Lyon/Dir., CEO, Pres., James H. Avery/Dir., Jonathan M. Hastings/Dir., Daniel L. Helbert/Dir., John A. Ronca/Dir., Bill Smith/Dir., Kenneth Rosenblum/Dir.

SAND Technology Inc

754A Lexington Ave., Kenilworth, NJ, 07033; ***PH:*** 1-732-214-2707; ***Fax:*** 1-732-750-4849; ***http://*** www.sand.com

General - Incorporation	Canada	***Stock*** - Price on:12/24/2007	$0.41
Employees	NA	Stock Exchange	OTC
Auditor	Deloitte & Touche LLP	Ticker Symbol	SNDTF
Stk Agt	Continental Stock Transfer & Trust Co	Outstanding Shares	NA
Counsel	NA	E.P.S	NA
DUNS No.	24-367-7150	Shareholders	NA

Business: The group's principle activities include designing, developing, marketing and supporting software products that enable users to retrieve information from large amounts of data, products known as the nucleus product suite, which are designed to provide an efficient and cost-effective way to make inquiries of large databases. The group operates from United States.

Primary SIC and add'l.: 5045 6719 7372 7378 3571 6794 7379

CIK No: 0000753050

Subsidiaries: Sand Technology Corporation, Sand Technology Ireland Limited, STSI Licensing, LLC

Officers: Arthur G. Ritchie/Chmn., CEO, Haydn Lewis/MD - Northern Europe, Gilles Therrien/VP - Finance, Administration, CFO, Georges Dube/Dir., Sec., Roland Markowski/MD - Central Europe, Linda Arens/VP - Marketing, Alliances, Richard Grondin/VP - Research & Development and Deployment, Robin Carr/VP - Sales, North America

Directors: Arthur G. Ritchie/Chmn., CEO, Martin Shindler/Dir., George Wicker/Dir., Georges Dube/Dir., Sec., Marc Malouin/Dir., Wayne Musselman/Dir., Douglas S. Pryde/Dir.

Owners: Estate of Jerome Shattner/8.20%, Arthur G. Ritchie/18.30%

Financial Data: ***Fiscal Year End:*** 07/31 ***Latest Annual Data:*** 7/31/2006

Year	Sales	Net Income
2006	$4,842,000	-$3,647,000
2005	$4,984,000	-$6,020,000
2004	$4,024,000	-$5,364,000

Curr. Assets:	$2,645,000	***Curr. Liab.:***	$2,096,000	***P/E Ratio:***	16.77
Plant, Equip.:	$205,000	***Total Liab.:***	$2,217,000	***Indic. Yr. Divd.:***	NA
Total Assets:	$3,045,000	***Net Worth:***	$828,000	***Debt/ Equity:***	NA

Sanders Morris Harris Group Inc

600 Travis, Ste. 3100, Houston, TX, 77002; ***PH:*** 1-713-224-3100; ***Fax:*** 1-713-224-1101; ***http://*** www.smhgroup.com

General - Incorporation	TX	***Stock*** - Price on:12/24/2007	$12.69
Employees	547	Stock Exchange	NDQ
Auditor	KPMG LLP	Ticker Symbol	SMHG
Stk Agt	Computershare Investor Services LLC	Outstanding Shares	24,720,000
Counsel	NA	E.P.S	$0.33
DUNS No.	NA	Shareholders	NA

Business: The group's principal activities are to provide financial services, which include institutional, prime and retail brokerage, investment and merchant banking, trust related services, asset management and investment management services. The group serves a diverse group of institutional, corporate and individual clients. On 02-May-2003, the group acquired 50% ownership interest in the salient companies and 23.15% profits interest in the endowment fund and on Apr 1, 2004, it acquired a 69% interest in charlotte capital.

Primary SIC and add'l.: 6211

CIK No: 0001071341

Subsidiaries: Charlotte Capital, LLC, Corporate Opportunities Fund, Corporate Opportunities Fund, L.P., Edelman Business Services, LLC, Edelman Financial Services, LLC, Edelman Mortgage Services, LLC, Environmental Opportunities, Environmental Opportunities Fund II, Environmental Opportunities Fund II, L.P., Environmental Opportunities Fund, L.P., Fund II Mgt. Co. LLC, Institutional, L.P., Life Sciences Opportunities Fund II (Institutional), L.P., Life Sciences Opportunities Fund II, L.P., Life Sciences Opportunity Fund 36 Subsidiaries included in the Index

Officers: Ben T. Morris/Dir., CEO/$568,701.00, Pamela Caloway/Assist. Corp. Sec., Rick Berry/Principal Financial Officer/$335,136.00, Robert E. Garrison/Pres./$350,000.00

Directors: Ben T. Morris/Dir., CEO, George L. Ball/Chmn., Don A. Sanders/Vice Chmn., Scott McClelland/Dir., Albert W. Niemi/Dir., Richard E. Bean/Dir., Nolan Ryan/Dir., Charles W. Duncan/Dir., Blair W. Waltrip/Dir.

Owners: Don A. Sanders/13.10%, Dan S. Wilford, Ben T. Morris/4.30%, T. Rowe Price Associates, Inc./5.50%, Richard E. Bean, Philip C. Timon/Endowment Capital, L.P/7.30%, Robert E. Garrison/1.40%, Nolan Ryan, Charles W. Duncan, George L. Ball/4.60%, Rick Berry, Scott B. McClelland, Insiders/25.90%, Albert W. Niemi, John T. Unger *(18 Owners included in Index)*

Financial Data: ***Fiscal Year End:*** 12/31 ***Latest Annual Data:*** 12/31/2006

Year	Sales	Net Income
2006	$166,748,000	$3,406,000
2005	$127,292,000	$10,674,000
2004	$121,532,000	$12,414,000

Curr. Assets:	$98,969,000	***Curr. Liab.:***	$46,390,000		
Plant, Equip.:	$12,323,000	***Total Liab.:***	$49,982,000	***Indic. Yr. Divd.:***	$0.180
Total Assets:	$282,042,000	***Net Worth:***	$219,936,000	***Debt/ Equity:***	0.0025

Sanderson Farms Inc

127 Flynt Rd., Laurel, MS, 39441; ***PH:*** 1-601-649-4030; ***Fax:*** 1-601-426-1461; ***http://*** www.sandersonfarms.com

General - Incorporation	MS	***Stock*** - Price on:12/24/2007	$43.95
Employees	8,700	Stock Exchange	NDQ
Auditor	Ernst & Young LLP	Ticker Symbol	SAFM
Stk Agt	Mellon Investor Services LLC	Outstanding Shares	20,130,000
Counsel	NA	E.P.S	$1.88
DUNS No.	09-604-3708	Shareholders	NA

Business: The group's principal activity is to produce, process, market and distribute fresh and frozen chicken products. The food items include frozen entrees such as chicken and dumplings, lasagna, seafood gumbo, shrimp creole and corn dogs. The ice pack, chill pack and frozen chicken are sold in whole, cut-up and boneless form under the brand name sanderson farms(r). The products are sold primarily to retailers and distributors located in the southeastern, southwestern and western United States. The group also sells chicken products to governmental agencies, fast food operators and to customers who resell the products outside of the continental United States.

Primary SIC and add'l.: 0251 2099 0252 2015

CIK No: 0000812128

Subsidiaries: Sanderson Farms, Inc (Production Division), Sanderson Farms, Inc. (Foods Division), Sanderson Farms, Inc. (Processing Division)

Officers: Joe F. Sanderson/Chmn., CEO, Lampkin Butts/Dir., COO, Pres., James A. Grimes/Sec., Chief Accounting Officer, Mike Cockrell/Dir., Treasurer, CFO, Bob Billingsley/Dir. - Development, Doug Lee/Dir. - Processing, Neil Morgan/Dir. - Sales, Randy Pettus/Dir. - Production, John Rice/Dir. - Technical Services, Robin Robinson/Dir. - Organization Development, Corporate Communication, Brian Romano/Dir. - Administration, Bob Rosa/Chief Financial Analyst

Directors: Joe F. Sanderson/Chmn., CEO, John H. Baker/66/Dir., Charles W. Ritter/Dir., Phil K. Livingston/Dir., Lampkin Butts/Dir., COO, Pres., Robert Khayat/Dir., Dianne Mooney/Dir., Beverly Wade Hogan/Dir., Gail Jones Pittman/Dir., Mike Cockrell/Dir., Treasurer, CFO, John Bierbusse/Dir., Rowan H. Taylor/83/Dir., Fred Banks/Dir., Toni Cooley/Dir.

Owners: Lampkin Butts/9.65%, John Bierbusse, Artisan Partners Limited Partnership/12.62%, John H. Baker, Gail Jones Pittman, Michael D. Cockrell, Rowan H. Taylor, Charles W. Ritter, Beverly Hogan, Robin Robinson/9.34%, Joe F. Sanderson/6.60%, James A. Grimes, Phil K. Livingston, Insiders/16.73%, NFJ Investment Group L.P/5.15% *(16 Owners included in Index)*

Financial Data: Fiscal Year End:10/31 Latest Annual Data: 10/31/2006

Year	Sales	Net Income
2006	$1,047,930,000	-$11,501,000
2005	$1,006,185,000	$70,638,000
2004	$1,052,297,000	$91,428,000

Curr. Assets:	$207,201,000	Curr. Liab.:	$79,152,000	P/E Ratio:	23.38
Plant, Equip.:	$390,690,000	Total Liab.:	$195,827,000	Indic. Yr. Divd.:	$0.480
Total Assets:	$600,373,000	Net Worth:	$404,546,000	Debt/ Equity:	0.3765

Sandisk Corp

601 McCarthy Blvd., Milpitas, CA, 95035; *PH:* 1-408-801-1000; *Fax:* 1-408-801-8657; *http://* www.sandisk.com

General - Incorporation	DE	Stock- Price on:12/24/2007	$48.24
Employees	2,586	Stock Exchange	NDQ
Auditor	Ernst & Young LLP	Ticker Symbol	SNDK
Stk Agt	Computershare Trust Co	Outstanding Shares	228,210,000
Counsel	Brobeck, Phleger & Harrison	E.P.S.	$0.34
DUNS No.	36-240-7041	Shareholders	NA

Business: The groups principle activity is to supply flash memory data storage products. The groups products are used in a variety of products including digital cameras, mobile phones, universal serial bus drives and gaming consoles. Customers served by the group include the pharmaceutical, biotechnology, chemical, technology, clinical, food processing and consumer product industries. The group operates from United States.

Primary SIC and add'l.: 3679 3674

CIK No: 0001000180

Subsidiaries: SanDisk (Cayman) Limited, SanDisk B.V., SanDisk Equipment YK, SanDisk GmbH, SanDisk Hong Kong Limited, SanDisk India Device Design Centre, Ltd, SanDisk International Limited, SanDisk Israel Ltd, SanDisk Korea Ltd, (YH), SanDisk Limited, SanDisk Manufacturing Limited, SanDisk Scotland Limited, SanDisk Secure Content Solutions, Inc., SanDisk Secure Content Solutions, Ltd., SanDisk Sweden AB 16 Subsidiaries included in the Index

Officers: Eli Harari/Chmn., CEO, Founder/$9,969,490.00, Nelson Chan/Exec. VP - Consumer Products Business, Corporate Marketing/$5,962,987.00, Sanjay Mehrotra/Dir., COO, Pres./$5,800,381.00, Judy Bruner/Exec. VP - Administration, CFO/$3,842,405.00, Yoram Cedar/Exec. VP - Handset Business, Corporate Engineering/$3,184,215.00, Randhir Thakur/Exec. VP - Technology, Worldwide Operations/$3,347,781.00

Directors: Eli Harari/Chmn., CEO, Founder, Irwin Federman/Vice Chmn., Steven J. Gomo/Dir., Sanjay Mehrotra/Dir., COO, Pres., Eddy W. Hartenstein/Dir., Catherine P. Lego/Dir., Michael Marks/Dir., James D. Meindl/Dir.

Owners: Sanjay Mehrotra, James D. Meindl, Steven J. Gomo, Eddy W. Hartenstein, Judy Bruner, Delaware Management Holdings/5.49%, Randhir Thakur, Irwin Federman, Nelson Chan, Eli Harari/2.26%, Entities Controlled by ClearBridge Advisors, LLC/6.97%, Insiders/3.28%, Michael E. Marks, Entities Controlled by Capital Group International, Inc/14.43%, Catherine P. Lego *(16 Owners included in Index)*

Financial Data: Fiscal Year End:01/01 Latest Annual Data: 12/31/2006

Year	Sales	Net Income
2006	$3,257,525,000	$198,896,000
2005	$1,777,055,000	$266,616,000

Curr. Assets:	$4,241,861,000	Curr. Liab.:	$896,447,000		
Plant, Equip.:	$317,965,000	Total Liab.:	$2,193,673,000	Indic. Yr. Divd.:	NA
Total Assets:	$6,967,783,000	Net Worth:	$4,768,134,000	Debt/ Equity:	0.2554

Sands Regent (The)

345 N Arlington Ave, Reno, NV, 89501; *PH:* 1-702-348-2210; *http://* www.sandsregency.com

General - Incorporation	NV	Stock- Price on:12/24/2007	NA
Employees	1,239	Stock Exchange	NDQ
Auditor	Deloitte & Touche LLP	Ticker Symbol	SNDS
Stk Agt	U.S. Stock Transfer Corp	Outstanding Shares	NA
Counsel	Latham & Watkins	E.P.S.	NA
DUNS No.	12-180-8943	Shareholders	NA

Business: The group's principal activity is the ownership and operation of the sands regency casino/hotel in reno, Nevada. The casino/hotel has approximately 29,000 square feet of gaming space and 836 hotel rooms, including 29 suites of various sizes. The complex includes a tony roma's restaurant, a pizza hut, an arby's restaurant, a coffee house/deli-style restaurant and an original mels diner restaurant. The facilities include cocktail lounges, a health club and almost 12,000 square feet of convention and meeting space, which can seat up to 950 people. The casino offers 19 table games, blackjack tables, craps tables, roulette, three-card poker table and approximately 651 slot machines. On 04-Jun-2002, the group acquired gold ranch casino and rv resort and on 1-May-2004, rail city casino.

Primary SIC and add'l.: 5399 7011 7021 5947 5812

CIK No: 0000753899

Subsidiaries: Dayton Gaming, inc., Last Chance, Inc, Plantation Investments, Inc., Zante, Inc.

Officers: Ferenc B. Szony/52/Dir., CEO, Pres., Robert Medeiros/42/COO, Exec. VP, Cornelius T. Klerk/53/CFO, Laura Corl/Motorcoach Sales Associate, Linda D. Hope/Regional Sales Mgr., Ken Matsuzaki/Sales Mgr., Lisa Miolini/Marketing Mgr.

Directors: Ferenc B. Szony/52/Dir., CEO, Pres., Jon N. Bengtson/63/Chmn., Louis J. Phillips/69/Dir., Larry Tuntland/67/Dir., David R. Grundy/57/Dir., Douglas M. Hayes/63/Dir., Pete Cladianos/48/Dir.

Owners: Cornelius Klerk, Jon N. Bengtson, Insiders/8.78%, Louis J. Phillips, Larry Tuntland, Deborah Lundgren/10.60%, Doug Hayes, Pete Cladianos, Pete Cladianos/11.96%, Robert J. Medeiros/1.89%, David Belding/9.90%, David R. Grundy, Ferenc B. Szony/3.63%

Sandston Corp

40950 Woodward Ave., Ste. 304, Bloomfield Hills, MI, 48304; *PH:* 1-248-723-3007; *http://* www.nematron.com; *Email:* info@nematron.com

General - Incorporation	MI	Stock- Price on:12/24/2007	$0.12
Employees	NA	Stock Exchange	OTC
Auditor	Plante & Moran, PLLC	Ticker Symbol	SDON
Stk Agt	Registrar & Transfer Co	Outstanding Shares	10,800,000
Counsel	NA	E.P.S.	$0.00
DUNS No.	06-880-6041	Shareholders	NA

Business: The group's principal activities are to design, manufacture and market factory automation products, including computer hardware and software. The group's industrial computers and terminals are called industrial control computers and industrial workstations, which are ruggedized computers with built-in displays, keyboards or other forms of operator interface. The group has four products used in industrial and factory automation workplace and are sold under the trade namesopencontroltm, hyperkernel(R), paragon(TM) and flopro(r). The products are mainly sold in the United States and France.

Primary SIC and add'l.: 7373 3571

CIK No: 0000892832

Subsidiaries: Interface Systems, Inc.

Officers: Daniel J. Dorman/45/Chmn., CEO, Principal Financial Officer, Pres., Richard A. Walawender/47/Dir., Corp. Sec.

Directors: Daniel J. Dorman/45/Chmn., CEO, Principal Financial Officer, Pres., Lawrence J. Defiore/47/Dir., Richard A. Walawender/47/Dir., Corp. Sec.

Owners: Walawender Holdings, LLC/1.80%, Daniel J. Dorman/48.60%, Lawrence J. De Fiore, Living Trust/3.70%, Patricia A. Dorman/5.50%

Financial Data: Fiscal Year End:12/31 Latest Annual Data: 12/31/2006

Year	Sales	Net Income
2006	NA	-$14,000
2005	NA	$3,124,000
2004	NA	$3,124,000

Curr. Assets:	$100,000	Curr. Liab.:	$1,000		
Plant, Equip.:	NA	Total Liab.:	$1,000	Indic. Yr. Divd.:	NA
Total Assets:	$100,000	Net Worth:	$100,000	Debt/ Equity:	NA

Sandy Spring Bancorp Inc

17801 Georgia Ave., Olney, MD, 20832; *PH:* 1-301-774-6400; *Fax:* 1-301-260-0044; *http://* www.sandyspringbank.com

General - Incorporation	MD	Stock- Price on:12/24/2007	$33.4
Employees	676	Stock Exchange	NDQ
Auditor	McGladrey & Pullen LLP	Ticker Symbol	SASR
Stk Agt	American Stock Transfer & Trust Co.	Outstanding Shares	15,740,000
Counsel	NA	E.P.S.	$2.10
DUNS No.	03-582-4218	Shareholders	NA

Business: The group's principal activity is to provide commercial, retail banking and trust services. The group is a bank holding concern and operates through its wholly owned subsidiary, sandy spring bank. The services provided by the group include lending of commercial and real estate loans and acceptance of demand, money market, savings and time deposits. The customers of the group include individuals and businesses. The group offers its services through 30 community offices and 45 ATMs located in anne arundel, frederick, howard, montgomery and prince george's counties in Maryland.

Primary SIC and add'l.: 6021 6712

CIK No: 0000824410

Subsidiaries: Sandy Spring Bank, Sandy Spring Capital Trust II, Sandy Spring Insurance Corporation, The Equipment Leasing Corporation, West Financial Services, Inc.

Officers: Hunter R. Hollar/Dir. - Sandy Spring Bank, Pres., CEO - Sandy Spring Bancorp, Bank/$1,067,909.00, Drew W. Stabler/Chmn. - Sandy Spring Bank, Louis R. Caceres/Exec. VP - Sandy Spring Bank/$377,874.00, Ronald E. Kuykendall/Exec. VP, General Counsel, Sec. - Sandy Spring Bancorp, Bank, Daniel J. Schrider/Exec. VP, Chief Credit Officer - Sandy Spring Bank/$368,391.00, Frank H. Small/Exec. VP, Chief Operating Offier - Sandy Spring Bancorp, Bank/$842,640.00, Sara E. Watkins/Exec. VP - Sandy Spring Bank, Philip J. Mantua/Exec. VP, CFO - Sandy Spring Bancorp, Bank/$347,174.00, John Chirtea/Dir. - Sandy Spring Bank, Mark E. Friis/Dir. - Sandy Spring Bak, Susan D. Goff/Dir. - Sandy Spring Bak, Solomon Graham/Dir. - Sandy Spring Bak, Gilbert L. Hardesty/Dir. - Sandy Spring Bak, Pamela A. Little/Dir. - Sandy Spring Bak, Charles F. Mess/Dir. - Sandy Spring Bak *(22 Officers included in Index)*

Directors: Robert L. Mitchell/71/Dir., Robert L. Orndorff/Dir. - Sandy Spring Bank

Owners: Gilbert L. Hardesty, Insiders/5.84%, Robert L. Orndorff/1.17%, Pamela A. Little, Marshall H. Groom, Solomon Graham, Susan D. Goff, Philip J. Mantua, John Chirtea, Drew W. Stabler, Craig A. Ruppert, Charles F. Mess, Daniel J. Schrider, Lewis R. Schumann, Louis R. Caceres *(20 Owners included in Index)*

Financial Data: Fiscal Year End:12/31 Latest Annual Data: 12/31/2006

Year	Sales	Net Income
2006	$192,338,000	$32,871,000
2005	$159,069,000	$33,098,000
2004	$140,159,000	$14,367,000

Curr. Assets:	$122,097,000	Curr. Liab.:	$2,335,872,000	P/E Ratio:	15.90
Plant, Equip.:	$47,756,000	Total Liab.:	$2,372,680,000	Indic. Yr. Divd.:	$0.920
Total Assets:	$2,610,457,000	Net Worth:	$237,777,000	Debt/ Equity:	0.1571

Sangamo Biosciences Inc

Point Richmond Tech Ctr. II, 501 Canal Blvd., Ste. A100, Richmond, CA, 94804; *PH:* 1-510-970-6000; *Fax:* 1-510-236-8951; *http://* www.sangamo.com; *Email:* info@sangamo.com

General - Incorporation	DE	Stock- Price on:12/24/2007	$8.4682
Employees	75	Stock Exchange	NDQ
Auditor	Ernst & Young LLP	Ticker Symbol	SGMO
Stk Agt	Computershare Investor Services LLC	Outstanding Shares	35,070,000
Counsel	Brobeck, Phleger & Harrison	E.P.S.	-$0.66
DUNS No.	NA	Shareholders	NA

Business: The group's principal activities are to conduct research, develop and commercialize transcription factors for regulation of gene expression. The group's gene recognition-tm- technology platform is a proprietary technology enabling the engineering of a class of transcription factors known as zinc finger dna-binding proteins (zfps). Universal gene recognition enables the technology, which is widely applicable to pharmaceutical discovery, development of human therapeutics, clinical diagnostics and plant agricultural and industrial biotechnology. The group intends to commercialize its technology on its applications. The group operates only in domestic market.

Primary SIC and add'l.: 8731

CIK No: 0001001233

Subsidiaries: Dow Chemical Corporation

Officers: Edward O. Lanphier/Founder, CEO, Pres./$1,095,246.00, Eric T. Rhodes/VP - Business Development, David G. Ichikawa/Sr. VP - Business Development/$489,615.00, Edward Rebar/Sr. Dir. - Technology, Dale Ando/VP - Therapeutic Development, Chief Medical Officer/$572,486.00, Ely Benaim/VP - Clinical Affairs, Elizabeth Wolffe/Contact - Corporate Communications, Philip D. Gregory/VP - Research/$428,423.00, Sean Brennan/Sr. Dir. - Intellectual Property, Greg S. Zante/VP - Finance, Administration/$387,207.00

Directors: Edward O. Lanphier/Founder, CEO, Pres., Carl O. Pabo/Chmn. - Scientific Advisory Board, William G. Gerber/Dir., Ward H. Wolff/Dir., John W. Larson/Dir., Michael Gilman/Member - Scientific Advisory Board, Aaron Klug/Member - Scientific Advisory Board, Michael C. Wood/Dir., Barrie Carter/Member - Scientific Advisory Board, Kevin Struhl/Member - Scientific Advisory Board, Judith Campisi/Member - Scientific Advisory Board, Steven J. Mento/Dir., Gabor M. Rubanyi/Member - Scientific Advisory Board, Margaret A. Liu/Dir.

Owners: Dale G. Ando, Insiders/15.60%, Philip D. Gregory, Ward H. Wolff, Kopp Investment Advisors, LLC/8.80%, David M. Greenhouse/6.00%, Edward O. Lanphier/8.80%, Edwards Lifesciences Corporation/5.30%, John W. Larson/1.20%, William G. Gerber, Michael C. Wood/3.80%, Margaret A. Liu, Gregory S. Zante, David G. Ichikawa, Steven J. Mento

Financial Data: Fiscal Year End:12/31 Latest Annual Data: 12/31/2006

Year	Sales	Net Income
2006	$7,885,000	-$17,864,000
2005	$2,484,000	-$13,293,000
2004	$1,315,000	-$13,818,000

Curr. Assets:	$55,056,000	Curr. Liab.:	$5,200,000		
Plant, Equip.:	$675,000	Total Liab.:	$7,075,000	Indic. Yr. Divd.:	NA
Total Assets:	$55,780,000	Net Worth:	$48,705,000	Debt/ Equity:	NA

Sangui Biotech International Inc

1393 N Bennett Cir., Farmington, UT, 84025; *PH:* 1-49-2302915200; *Fax:* 1-49-2302915191; *http://* www.sanguibiotech.com; *Email:* info@sangui.de

General - Incorporation	CO	Stock - Price on:12/24/2007	$0.07
Employees	NA	Stock Exchange	OTC
Auditor	HJ & Assoc. LLC	Ticker Symbol	SGBI
Stk Agt	NA	Outstanding Shares	NA
Counsel	NA	E.P.S.	NA
DUNS No.	NA	Shareholders	NA

Business: The group's principal activity is to conduct research, develop, manufacture and marketing of medical products. The group develops haemoglobin-based artificial oxygen carriers, products thereof and an anti-aging cosmetic based on the oxygen carriers. The group also develops a long-term implantable glucose sensor, its by-products and sensors. During fiscal 2003, the group discontinued sangui usa and sangui Singapore.

Primary SIC and add'l.: 3841 2834

CIK No: 0001104280

Subsidiaries: GlukoMediTech AG, Sangui Biotech Singapore Pte Ltd., Sangui BioTech, Inc, SanguiBioTech AG

Owners: Insiders/4.30%, Joachim Fleing, Wolfgang Barnikol/3.90%

Financial Data: Fiscal Year End:06/30 Latest Annual Data: 12/31/2006

Year	Sales	Net Income
2006	$736,789,000	$43,169,000
2005	$570,922,000	$79,806,000
2004	$477,169,000	$84,459,000

Sanguine Corp

101 E Green St. Ste. 6, Pasadena, CA, 91105; *PH:* 1-626-405-0079; *http://* www.sanguine-corp.com; *Email:* info@sanguine-corp.com

General - Incorporation	NV	Stock - Price on:12/24/2007	$0.11
Employees	2	Stock Exchange	OTC
Auditor	HJ Associates & Consultants, LLP	Ticker Symbol	SGNC
Stk Agt	Continental Stock Transfer & Trust Co	Outstanding Shares	84,090,000
Counsel	NA	E.P.S.	$0.01
DUNS No.	NA	Shareholders	NA

Business: The groups principle activity is development of a synthetic red blood cell product called "PHER-O2." The group operates from the United States.

Primary SIC and add'l.: 2836

CIK No: 0000926287

Officers: Thomas C. Drees/Founder, Chmn., CEO, Pres., James A.M. Shapiro/Dir. - Clinical Islet Transplant Program, Steven P. Miller/Executive Dir. - Strategic Development, Craig Morrison/Dir., VP - Surgical Applications, David Nelson/Dir., CFO, Sec., Treasurer, Leonard Burningham/Corporate Counsel, Michael Dancy/Investor Contact

Directors: Thomas C. Drees/Founder, Chmn., CEO, Pres., John Dillberger/Member - Medical Advisory Board, Cass L. Terry/Member - Medical Advisory Board, Herbert J. Meiselman/Member - Medical, Applications Member - Advisory Board, Craig Morrison/Dir., VP - Surgical Applications, Robert Kwun/Member - Medical Advisory Board, David Nelson/Dir., CFO, Sec., Treasurer

Owners: Thomas C. Drees/48.70%, Edward L. Kunkel, Insiders/49.70%, David E. Nelson

Financial Data: Fiscal Year End:12/31 Latest Annual Data: 12/31/2006

Year	Sales	Net Income
2006	$6,000	-$617,000
2005	$1,000	-$338,000
2004	$15,000	$908,000

Curr. Assets:	$30,000	Curr. Liab.:	$408,000		
Plant, Equip.:	$1,000	Total Liab.:	$408,000	Indic. Yr. Divd.:	NA
Total Assets:	$31,000	Net Worth:	-$377,000	Debt/ Equity:	NA

Sanmina Sci Corp

2700 N 1st St., San Jose, CA, 95134; *PH:* 1-408-964-3555; *Fax:* 1-408-964-3636; *http://* www.sanmina-sci.com; *Email:* info@sanmina-sci.com

General - Incorporation	DE	Stock - Price on:12/24/2007	$3.43
Employees	40,903	Stock Exchange	NDQ
Auditor	KPMG LLP	Ticker Symbol	NA
Stk Agt	Wells Fargo Shareowner Services	Outstanding Shares	529,880,000
Counsel	Wilson Sonsini Goodrich & Rosati	E.P.S.	-$2.15
DUNS No.	79-877-8395	Shareholders	NA

Business: The groups principle activity is to provide customized and integrated electronics manufacturing services. Customers served by the group include defense and aerospace, medical and automotive industries. Specific customers of the group include IBM and HP. The group operates from United States.

Primary SIC and add'l.: 8741 3672 3674

CIK No: 0000897723

Subsidiaries: Ambulatory Resource Centres Investment Company, Inc., Ambulatory Resource Centres of Florida, Inc., Ambulatory Resource Centres of Massachusetts, Inc., Ambulatory Resource Centres of Texas, Inc., Ambulatory Resource Centres of Washington, Inc., Ambulatory Resource Centres of Wilmington, Inc., Ambulatory Surgery Center of Cool Springs, LLC, Ambulatory Surgery Center of Worcester, LLC, ARC Development Corporation, ARC Dry Creek, Inc., ARC Financial Services Corporation, ARC Kentucky, LLC, ARC New Hartford, Inc., ARC of Bellingham, L.P., ARC of Georgia, LLC 121 Subsidiaries included in the Index

Officers: Jure Sola/Chmn., CEO, David White/CFO, Exec. VP, Dennis Young/Exec. VP - Worldwide Sales, Marketing, Hari Pillai/Pres. - Global EMS Operations, Joseph R. Bronson/Dir., COO, Pres., Walt Hussey/Pres. - Technology Components Group, Michael Tyler/Exec. VP, General Counsel, Corp. Sec., Paige Bombino/Investor Relations Officer, Michael Kovacs/Dir. - Corporate Marketing, Ulrike Winter/Dir. - Marketing Communications, Public Relations Europe

Directors: Jure Sola/Chmn., CEO, Eugene A. Sapp/Dir., Mario Rosati/Dir., Peter Simone/Dir., Alain Couder/Dir., Wayne Shortridge/Dir., Jackie Ward/Dir., Neil Bonke/Dir., Joseph R. Bronson/Dir., COO, Pres., Joseph Licata/Dir.

Owners: Eugene A. Sapp, Peter J. Simone, Dennis Young, Jure Sola/1.62%, Brandes Investment Partners, LP. and certain affiliated entities/5.30%, Alain Couder, Insiders/2.73%, AXA Financial, Inc. and certain affiliated entities/12.51%, David White, Columbia Wanger Asset Management, LP/10.15%, Joseph G. Licata, Joseph R. Bronson, Hari Pillai, Michael Tyler, Barclays Global Investors, NA/5.87% (19 Owners included in Index)

Financial Data: Fiscal Year End:10/01 Latest Annual Data: 09/29/2007

Year	Sales	Net Income
2007	$10,384,254,000	-$1,134,657,000
2006	$10,955,421,000	-$141,557,000
2005	$11,734,674,000	-$1,006,002,000

Curr. Assets:	$3,491,003,000	Curr. Liab.:	$1,974,249,000		
Plant, Equip.:	$620,132,000	Total Liab.:	$3,591,867,000	Indic. Yr. Divd.:	NA
Total Assets:	$5,862,430,000	Net Worth:	$2,270,563,000	Debt/ Equity:	0.4315

Sanofi Aventis

55 Corporate Dr., Bridgewater, NJ, 08807; *PH:* 1-908-981-5000; *http://* www.sanofi-synthelabo.com

General - Incorporation	France	Stock - Price on:12/24/2007	$40.63
Employees	100,289	Stock Exchange	NYSE
Auditor	Platinum Equities LLP	Ticker Symbol	SNY
Stk Agt	Bank of New York	Outstanding Shares	2,700,000,000
Counsel	Jean-pierre Kerjouan	E.P.S.	$2.16
DUNS No.	NA	Shareholders	NA

Business: The group's principal activities are the research, production and distribution of pharmaceuticals through the following therapeutic areas: central nervous system, cardiovascular/thrombosis, oncology and internal medicine. It has operations in more than one hundred countries worldwide.

Primary SIC and add'l.: 2835 2834

CIK No: 0001121404

Subsidiaries: Aventis Inc., Aventis Pharma SA, Aventis Pharmaceuticals Inc., Hoechst GmbH, Sanofi-aventis Amerique du Nord S.N.C., Sanofi-aventis Deutschland Gmbh, Sanofi-aventis Europe S.A.S., Sanofi-Pasteur Inc, Sanofi-Synthlabo SAS

Officers: Jean-Francois Dehecq/68/Chmn., CEO, Jean-Claude Armbruster/Sr. VP, Advisor to The Chmn. Employee Relations, Christian Lajoux/Sr. VP - Pharmaceutical Operations, France, Antoine Ortoli/Sr. VP - Pharmaceutical Operations, Intercontinental, Philippe Peyre/Sr. VP - Corporate Affairs, Pierre Chancel/Sr. VP - Global Marketing, Gilles Lhernould/Sr. VP - Industrial Affairs, Jean-Claude Leroy/Exec. VP - Finance, Legal, Hanspeter Spek/Exec. VP - Pharmaceutical Operations, Gerard Le Fur/57/Dir., Sr. Exec. VP, Heinz-Werner Meier/Sr. VP - Human Resources, Sr. VP - Pharmaceutical Operations Germany, Marie-Helene Laimay/Sr. VP - Audit, Internal Control Assessment, David Williams/58/Sr. VP, Marc Cluzel/Sr. VP - Scientific, Medical Affairs, Laurence Debroux/CFO, Sr. VP (22 Officers included in Index)

Directors: Jean-Francois Dehecq/68/Chmn., CEO, Jurgen Dormann/67/Vice Chmn., Rene Barbier De La Serre/67/Dir., Robert Castaigne/61/Dir., Thierry Desmarest/61/Dir., Jean-Rene Fourtou/68/Dir., Igor Landau/63/Dir., Bruno Weymuller/58/Dir., Lord Douro/61/Dir., Hubert Markl/68/Dir., Klaus Pohle/69/Dir., Serge Kampf/72/Dir., Jean-Marc Bruel/71/Dir., Christian Mulliez/46/Dir., Gerard Van Kemmel/67/Dir. (17 Directors included in Index)

Owners: Treasury shares/0.64%, Public/74.49%, LOral/10.52%, - of which held by sanofi-aventis/0.61%, Employees/1.23%, Insiders/100.00%

Financial Data: Fiscal Year End:12/31 Latest Annual Data: 12/31/2006

Year	Sales	Net Income
2006	$38,934,327,000	$5,326,090,000
2005	$33,770,797,000	$2,608,049,000
2004	$20,524,669,000	-$5,000,526,000

Curr. Assets:	$18,106,594,000	Curr. Liab.:	$13,522,513,000		
Plant, Equip.:	$8,200,383,000	Total Liab.:	$41,606,614,000	Indic. Yr. Divd.:	$0.990
Total Assets:	$102,370,781,000	Net Worth:	$60,764,167,000	Debt/ Equity:	NA

Sanpaolo IMI SpA

Piazza San Carlo 156, Turin, 10121; ; *http://* www.sanpaolo.it

General - Incorporation	Italy	Stock - Price on:12/24/2007	NA
Employees	43,476	Stock Exchange	NYSE
Auditor	PricewaterhouseCoopers LLP	Ticker Symbol	NA
Stk Agt	NA	Outstanding Shares	NA
Counsel	NA	E.P.S.	NA
DUNS No.	NA	Shareholders	NA

Business: The groups principle activity is to provide banking services including corporate banking, personal financial services. The group also provides asset management, mortgage banking, medium-long term lending, real estate, treasury, brokerage and equity investment. The group operates from United States.

Primary SIC and add'l.: 6159 6162 6211 6282 6021

CIK No: 0000939187

Subsidiaries: Banca OPI S.p.A., Sanpaolo IMI S.p.A.

Officers: Mario Greco/CEO, Alfonso Iozzo/Dir., MD, Pietro Modiano/GM, Piero Luongo/53/Head - General, Legal Affairs Division, as Board Sec.

Directors: Orazio Rossi/Dep. Chmn., Enrico Salza/Chmn., Mario Sarcinelli/Dir., Pio Bussolotto/Dir., Gian Guido Sacchi Morsiani/Dir., Anthony Orsatelli/Dir., Alberto Tazzetti/Dir., Maurizio Barracco/Dir., Alfonso Iozzo/Dir., MD, Ettore Gotti Tedeschi/Dir., Iti Mihalich/Dir., Jose Manuel Varela/Dir., Alfredo Saenz Abad/Dir., Giuseppe Fontana/Dir., Leone Sibani/Dir. *(17 Directors included in Index)*

Santa Clara Valley

1500 Warburton Ave., Santa Clara, CA, 95050; **PH:** 1-408-615-2200; **Fax:** 1-408-241-6771; *http://* www.siliconvalleypower.com; **Email:** info@siliconvalleypower.com

General - Incorporation		Stock - Price on:12/24/2007	$17.5
Employees	NA	Stock Exchange	OTC
Auditor	NA	Ticker Symbol	SCVE
Stk Agt	NA	Outstanding Shares	NA
Counsel	NA	E.P.S.	NA
DUNS No.	NA	Shareholders	NA

Business: The groups principle activity is to provide electricity to the residential and industrial sectors. The group is also research and development facilities, manufacturing plants, and mission-critical servers. The group operates from United States.

Primary SIC and add'l.: 6029

CIK No:

Officers: Debby Barry/Sr. VP - Dark Fiber Leasing Services

Santa Cruz CTY BK CA

325 Soquel Ave., Santa Cruz, CA, 95062; **PH:** 1-831-457-5000; **Fax:** 1-831-457-5001; *http://* www.sccountybank.com

General - Incorporation		Stock - Price on:12/24/2007	$23.75
Employees	NA	Stock Exchange	OTC
Auditor	NA	Ticker Symbol	SCZC
Stk Agt	Stock Transfer & Trust Co	Outstanding Shares	1,650,000
Counsel	NA	E.P.S.	NA
DUNS No.	NA	Shareholders	NA

Business: The groups principal activities include locally owned and operated full service commercial bank. Services of the group include checking accounts, savings accounts, certificates of deposit, installment loans, real estate mortgage loans, commercial loans, traveler's checks, safe deposit boxes, night depository and automated teller services. The group operates from the United States.

Primary SIC and add'l.: 6022

CIK No:

Officers: David Heald/Dir., CEO, Pres.

Directors: George R. Gallucci/Chmn., William J. Hansen/Vice Chmn., Kenneth R. Chappell/Dir., Tila Guerrero/Dir., Steven G. John/Dir., Thomas N. Griffin/Dir., Gary A. Reece/Dir.

Santa Fe Energy Trust

221 W Sixth St., Austin, TX, 78701; **PH:** 1-800-852-1422

General - Incorporation	TX	Stock - Price on:12/24/2007	$24.35
Employees	NA	Stock Exchange	NYSE
Auditor	KPMG LLP	Ticker Symbol	NA
First National Bank Of Texas, N.A.		Outstanding Shares	6,300,000
Counsel	NA	E.P.S.	$3.90
DUNS No.	NA	Shareholders	NA

Business: The groups principle activities include acquiring, investing, operating and developing oil and gas properties. The group operates from the United States.

Primary SIC and add'l.: 6792

CIK No: 0000893486

Officers: Mike Ulrich/VP

Financial Data: *Fiscal Year End:*12/31 *Latest Annual Data:* 12/31/2005

Year	Sales	Net Income
2005	$26,109,000	$25,205,000
2004	$20,364,000	$19,595,000
2003	$22,193,000	$21,383,000

Curr. Assets:	$93,000	Curr. Liab.:	NA	P/E Ratio:	6.24
Plant, Equip.:	NA	Total Liab.:	NA	Indic. Yr. Divd.:	NA
Total Assets:	$4,940,000	Net Worth:	$4,940,000	Debt/ Equity:	NA

Santa Fe Financial Corp

5840 Interface Dr., Ann Arbor, MI, 48103; **PH:** 1-734-214-2000; **Fax:** 1-734-994-8074; *http://* www.staffware.com

General - Incorporation	NV	Stock - Price on:12/24/2007	$17.85
Employees	3	Stock Exchange	OTC
Auditor	Burr, Pilger & Mayer LLP	Ticker Symbol	SFEF
Stk Agt	Computershare Trust Co	Outstanding Shares	1,240,000
Counsel	NA	E.P.S.	-$1.81
DUNS No.	05-283-5626	Shareholders	NA

Business: The group's principal activity is to purchase and manage real estate operations. The real estate properties include the land, improvements and leaseholds at 750 kearny street, san francisco. The group's operations also include a controlling interest in a 27-unit multi-family apartment complex and a 3-unit apartment building located in los angeles, California. The group's other investments include income-producing instruments, equity and debt securities which may include real estate based companies and real estate investment trust, cash and securities assets and other investments.

Primary SIC and add'l.: 6719 6513 6159

CIK No: 0000086759

Subsidiaries: 614 Acanto Properties, Inc., Crateo Inc, Intergroup Woodland Village, Inc, Portsmouth Square, Inc.

Officers: John V. Winfield/61/Chmn., CEO, Pres., Michael G. Zybala/56/VP, Sec., General Counsel, David T. Nguyen/35/Treasurer, Controller, Serving as CFO

Directors: John V. Winfield/61/Chmn., CEO, Pres., John C. Love/68/Dir., William J. Nance/63/Dir.

Owners: John V. Winfield, Insiders, Guinness Peat Group plc, The InterGroup Corporat John V. Winfield as a group, The InterGroup Corporation

Financial Data: *Fiscal Year End:*06/30 *Latest Annual Data:* 6/30/2006

Year	Sales	Net Income
2006	$441,000	-$602,000
2005	$440,000	-$2,300,000
2004	$415,000	$2,695,000

Curr. Assets:	$262,000	Curr. Liab.:	$8,033,000		
Plant, Equip.:	$4,547,000	Total Liab.:	$13,473,000	Indic. Yr. Divd.:	NA
Total Assets:	$29,988,000	Net Worth:	$11,904,000	Debt/ Equity:	4.1954

Santa Lucia Bancorp CA

7480 El Camino Real, Atascadero, CA, 93422; **PH:** 1-805-466-7087; **Fax:** 1-805-466-0402; *http://* www.santaluciabank.com

General - Incorporation	CA	Stock - Price on:12/24/2007	$27
Employees	88	Stock Exchange	OTC
Auditor	Vavrinek, Trine, Day & Co.,LLP	Ticker Symbol	SLBA
Stk Agt	U.S. Stock Transfer Corp	Outstanding Shares	1,930,000
Counsel	NA	E.P.S.	$1.69
DUNS No.	NA	Shareholders	NA

Business: The group operates through its subsidiaries whose principal activities include commercial banking business. Services of the group include information and perform over the telephone, an Internet banking system named EZLink, which offers online banking and computer bill payment, home equity lines of credit, business equipment leasing, and home mortgage loans and the group introduced its new health savings account. In December 2006, the groups total assets were $240.7 (millions).

Primary SIC and add'l.: 6022

CIK No: 0001355607

Subsidiaries: Santa Lucia Bank

Officers: Larry H. Putnam/Dir., CEO, Pres./$273,214.00, John C. Hansen/Dir., CFO, COO, Pres./$234,523.00, Jim Cowan/Exec. VP, Credit Administrator/$148,208.00, Melodee Fontana/VP, Operations Administrator, Sharon Satterthwaite/VP, Controller, Kristie Keller/Assist. VP - Central Operations, Teri Davis/VP, Loan Officer, Jim Kelley/VP, Loan Officer, Larry Womack/VP, Assist. Credit Administrator, Kim Donaldson/Assist. VP, Operations Officer, Robert Covarrubias/VP, Mgr. - Paso Robles Office, Cheryl Mumford/Assist. VP, Operations Officer, Paso Robles Officer, Ryun McCrory/Assist. VP - Loan Officer - Paso Robles Office, Darren Barnes/Loan Officer, Paso Robles Officer, Mike McKenzie/VP, Mgr. - Arroyo Grande Office *(23 Officers included in Index)*

Directors: Larry H. Putnam/Dir., CEO, Pres., Douglas C. Filipponi/Vice Chmn., Jerry W. Decou/Chmn., John C. Hansen/Dir., CFO, COO, Pres., Khatchik H. Achadjian/Dir., Jack D. Stinchfield/Dir., Jean Hawkins/Dir., Paul G. Moerman/Dir., Stanley R. Cherry/Dir.

Owners: Khatchik H. Achadjian, Jean Hawkins/5.60%, Larry H. Putnam/4.60%, Douglas C. Filipponi/6.00%, Stanley R. Cherry/5.80%, Paul G. Moerman/3.40%, Jerry W. DeCou/4.70%, Jack D. Stinchfield/2.60%, Insiders/33.80%, John C. Hansen/1.50%, Trust for the Santa Lucia Bank/7.75%

Financial Data: *Fiscal Year End:*12/31 *Latest Annual Data:* 12/31/2006

Year	Sales	Net Income
2006	$18,037,000	$3,388,000

Curr. Assets:	$13,347,000	Curr. Liab.:	$214,446,000		
Plant, Equip.:	$9,258,000	Total Liab.:	$221,601,000	Indic. Yr. Divd.:	$0.400
Total Assets:	$240,738,000	Net Worth:	$19,137,000	Debt/ Equity:	NA

Santander BanCorp

207 Ponce de Leon Ave., Hato Rey, PR, 00917; **PH:** 1-787-777-4100; **Fax:** 1-787-766-1437; *http://* www.santandernet.com

General - Incorporation	Puerto Rico	Stock - Price on:12/24/2007	$17.34
Employees	1,591	Stock Exchange	NYSE
Auditor	Deloitte & Touche LLP	Ticker Symbol	SBP
Stk Agt	Mellon Investor Services LLC	Outstanding Shares	46,640,000
Counsel	NA	E.P.S.	-$0.52
DUNS No.	NA	Shareholders	NA

Business: The group's principal activities are that of a commercial bank, providing banking services through its wholly owned subsidiary, banco santander Puerto Rico. The group operates in three segments: retail banking, mortgage banking and investments. Retail banking segment is composed principally of branch-based banking, including middle market, commercial, construction, agricultural, leasing, consumer and other branch-based and specialized divisions. Mortgage banking involves the origination and servicing of residential mortgage loans. The investment segment handles the investment portfolio comprised mostly of government securities, mortgage backed securities and interest bearing deposits as well as all trading and derivative activities. The group is also engaged in insurance activities. The group operates through a network of 66 branches in Puerto Rico and 139 ATMs. In 2003, the group acquired santander securities corporation.

Primary SIC and add'l.: 6712 6021 6321 6799

CIK No: 0001099958

Subsidiaries: Banco Santander Puerto Rico, Santander Asset Management provides portfolio management and advisory services, Santander Insurance Agency, Santander International Bank, Santander Mortgage Corporation, Santander Securities Corporation

Officers: Jose R. Gonzalez/Vice Chmn., CEO, Pres./$1,304,986.00, Luis Cintron/VP - Real Estate Assets, Jose Gordon Santoni/51/First Sr. VP - Credit Administration, Carlos Manuel Garcia/Dir., Sr. Exec. VP, COO/$995,848.00, Juan M. Diaz Soultaire/Sr. VP - Investor Relations, Sarbanes, Oxley,

Basel Officer, Roberto Cordova/Exec. VP - Wholesale Banking, Evelyn Vega Sella/Sr. VP - Corporate Communications, Ivonna J. Pacheco/First Sr. VP - Human Resources, Maria Leticia Garcia/VP, Bank Controller, Jose alvarez Giraldez/Exec. VP - Operations, Information Technology, Luis Roig Hostas/MD, CFO, Juan C. Batlle/Pres. - Santander Asset Management Corporation, Frank Serra/COO, Sr. VP, Dennis Williams/Sr. VP, Chief Investment Officer, Mario E. Delgado/Pres. - Island Finance Division (56 Officers included in Index)

Directors: Jose R. Gonzalez/Vice Chmn., CEO, Pres., Gonzalo De Las Heras/Chmn., Maria Calero/Dir., Exec. VP, Chief Accounting Officer, Stephen Ferriss/Dir., Victor Arbulu-Crousillat/Dir., Carlos Manuel Garcia/Dir., Sr. Exec. VP, COO, Jesus Zabalza/Dir., Roberto H. Valentin/Dir., Rafael S. Bonilla/Dir., Sec., Sr. VP - Legal, Compliance

Owners: Insiders, Laura Vzquez, Mara Calero, Jos Santoni, James Rodrguez, Roberto H. Valentn, Carlos M. Garca, Ivonna Pacheco, Jos R. Gonzlez, Banco Santander Central Hispano, S.A.

Financial Data: Fiscal Year End:12/31 Latest Annual Data: 12/31/2006

Year	Sales	Net Income
2006	$736,789,000	$43,169,000
2005	$570,922,000	$79,806,000
2004	$477,169,000	$84,459,000
Curr. Assets: $517,570,000	**Curr. Liab.:** $8,073,737,000	**P/E Ratio:** 19.48
Plant, Equip.: $62,472,000	**Total Liab.:** $8,608,948,000	**Indic. Yr. Divd.:** $0.640
Total Assets: $9,188,168,000	**Net Worth:** $579,220,000	**Debt/ Equity:** NA

Santarus Inc

10590 W Ocean Air Dr., Ste. 200, San Diego, CA, 92130; **PH:** 1-858-314-5700; **Fax:** 1-858-314-5701; http:// www.santarus.com; **Email:** contact@santarus.com

General - Incorporation	DE	**Stock** - Price on:12/24/2007	$5.17
Employees	338	Stock Exchange	NDQ
Auditor	Ernst & Young LLP	Ticker Symbol	SNTS
Stk Agt	American Stock Transfer & Trust Co.	Outstanding Shares	50,750,000
Counsel	NA	E.P.S.	-$0.99
DUNS No.	NA	Shareholders	NA

Business: The group's principal activities are to develop and market proprietary pharmaceutical products with new formulations, enhanced delivery systems and expanded indications. Its focus is development and commercialization of next generation proton pump inhibitor or ppi products which are frequently prescribed drugs for the treatment of many upper gastrointestinal, or gi, diseases and disorders. The group's product candidates are rapinex powder-for-suspension, rapinex capsule and rapinex chewable tablet, are proprietary immediate-release formulations of omeprazole which are intended to treat or prevent a variety of upper gi diseases and disorders including heartburn, gastroesophageal reflux disease, or gerd, erosive esophagitis, or ee, upper gi bleeding and peptic ulcer diseases. The other two product candidates that provide an alternative formulations of immediate-release omeprazole are rapinex capsule and rapinex chewable tablet.

Primary SIC and add'l.: 8731 2834

CIK No: 0001172480

Officers: Gerald T. Proehl/Dir., CEO, Pres., David E. Ballard/52/VP - Clinical Research, Medical Affairs, Maria Bedoya/VP - Regulatory Affairs, Quality Assurance, Michael D. Step/Sr. VP - Corporate Development, William C. Denby/Sr. VP - Commercial Operations, Martha L. Hough/54/VP - Finance, Investor Relations, E. D. Ballard/VP - Clinical Research, Medical Affairs, Thomas J. Joyce/48/VP - Marketing, National Accounting, Warren E. Hall/Sr. VP - Manufacturing, Product Development, Debra P. Crawford/Sr. VP, CFO, Treasurer, Sec., Blake A. Boland/47/VP - Sales, Julie A. Demeules/Sr. VP - Human Resources, Jonathan M. Hee/49/VP - Commercial Affairs, Carey J. Fox/39/VP, General Counsel

Directors: Gerald T. Proehl/Dir., CEO, Pres., David F. Hale/Chmn., Benjamin D. Gold/Member - Medical Advisory Board, Michael E. Herman/Dir., Joshua J. Ofman/Member - Medical Advisory Board, Ted W. Love/Dir., Daniel D. Burgess/Dir., Michael G. Carter/Dir., Brian G. Feagan/Member - Medical Advisory Board, Stephan Targan/Member - Medical Advisory Board, Donald O. Castell/Member - Medical Advisory Board, Loren A. Laine/Member - Medical Advisory Board, M. Brian Fennerty/Member - Medical Advisory Board, Kent Snyder/Dir., William J. Sandborn/Member - Medical Advisory Board

Owners: St. Paul Companies, Inc./8.60%, David F. Hale, Insiders/5.80%, Debra P. Crawford, William Blair & Company, L.L.C./13.70%, Westfield Capital Management Co. LLC/14.40%, Daniel D. Burgess, Warren E. Hall, William C. Denby, Ted W. Love, Michael E. Herman, Kent Snyder, Julie A. DeMeules, Gerald T. Proehl/1.90%, Michael G. Carter

Financial Data: Fiscal Year End:12/31 Latest Annual Data: 12/31/2006

Year	Sales	Net Income
2006	$49,242,000	-$56,466,000
2005	$26,524,000	-$64,986,000
2004	$1,348,000	-$81,495,000
Curr. Assets: $90,890,000	**Curr. Liab.:** $31,880,000	
Plant, Equip.: $334,000	**Total Liab.:** $47,324,000	**Indic. Yr. Divd.:** NA
Total Assets: $93,628,000	**Net Worth:** $46,305,000	**Debt/ Equity:** NA

Santos Ltd

10111 Richmond Ave., Ste. 500, Houston, TX, 77042; **PH:** 1-713-986-1700; **Fax:** 1-713-986-4200; http:// www.santos.com

General - Incorporation		**Stock** - Price on:12/24/2007	$49.89
Employees	NA	Stock Exchange	NDQ
Auditor	NA	Ticker Symbol	STOSY
Stk Agt	Citibank N.A	Outstanding Shares	NA
Counsel	NA	E.P.S.	NA
DUNS No.	NA	Shareholders	NA

Business: The groups principal activities include exploring and producing oil and gas. The group operates from Australia and the United States.

Primary SIC and add'l.: 1311 3533 1321 1382 1389 1381

CIK No: 0000800861

Officers: John Charles Ellice-Flint/57/MD, Jon Young/Exec. VP - Corporate Projects, John Anderson/VP - Strategic Projects, Peter Wasow/CFO, James Baulderstone/General Counsel, Company Sec., Martyn Eames/VP - Corporate - People

Directors: Stephen Gerlach/62/Dir., Kenneth Charles Borda/55/Dir., Kenneth Alfred Dean/55/Dir., Roy Alexander Franklin/54/Dir., Richard Michael Harding/58/Dir., Judith Sloan/53/Dir., Trevor Brown/Dir., Rick Wilkinson/Dir., Mark MacFarlane/Dir.

Financial Data: Fiscal Year End:12/31 Latest Annual Data: 12/31/2006

Year	Sales	Net Income
2006	$2,160,235,000	$507,836,000
2005	$1,807,655,000	$556,409,000
2004	$1,170,852,000	$296,360,000
Curr. Assets: $837,053,000	**Curr. Liab.:** $775,014,000	
Plant, Equip.: $4,507,061,000	**Total Liab.:** $2,799,963,000	**Indic. Yr. Divd.:** NA
Total Assets: $5,448,459,000	**Net Worth:** $2,648,496,000	**Debt/ Equity:** NA

Sapiens International Corp

4000 Ctr.Green Way, Ste. 100, Cary, NC, 27513; **PH:** 1-919-405-1500; **Fax:** 1-919-405-1700; http:// www.sapiens.com; **Email:** usa@sapiens.com

General - Incorporation	Netherlands	**Stock** - Price on:12/24/2007	$3.07
Employees	364	Stock Exchange	NDQ
Auditor	Kost Forer Gabbay & Kasierer	Ticker Symbol	SPNS
Stk Agt	Meespierson Intertrust	Outstanding Shares	14,850,000
Counsel	NA	E.P.S.	-$0.13
DUNS No.	85-545-2025	Shareholders	NA

Business: The group's principle activity is the provision of business software solutions. Its products support insurance claims processing, loan/mortgage management and other business solutions. The company operates through its worldwide subsidiaries. The group's quarterly revenue for Sep '07 was 10.53 millions of USD.

Primary SIC and add'l.: 7372

CIK No: 0000885740

Subsidiaries: Sapiens, Sapiens (UK) Limited, Sapiens Americas Corporation, Sapiens Deutschland GmbH, Sapiens France S.A.S, Sapiens International Corporation, Sapiens Israel Software Systems Ltd, Sapiens Japan Co, Sapiens Technologies (1982) Ltd

Officers: Roni Al-Dor/CEO, Pres., Manabu Okada/MD - Japan, Roni Giladi/CFO, Rami Doron/COO, Martin Greenberg/VP, Product Mgr. - Property, Casualty, Reinsurance, Michael Vaccarello/VP - Sales, Marketing, Americas, Elior Brin/52/CFO, Exec. VP, Michaella Kudish/VP - Technologies, Sagi Schliesser/VP - Research & Development

Directors: Eli Reifman/Dir., Hadas Gazit Kaiser/Dir., Guy Bernstein/Dir., Uzi Netanel/Dir., Yacov Elinav/Dir., Ron Zuckerman/Dir., Gad Goldstein/Dir., Naamit Salomon/Dir., Ido Schechter/Dir.

Owners: Gad Goldstein, Roni Al Dor, Magnum Technology Limited, Insiders/56.00%, Eli Reifman, Ron Zuckerman, Highbridge International LLC, F.I.D. Holdings Ltd., Formula Systems (1985) Ltd.

Financial Data: Fiscal Year End:12/31 Latest Annual Data: 12/31/2006

Year	Sales	Net Income
2006	$44,311,000	-$3,825,000
2005	$39,404,000	-$9,099,000
2004	$47,804,000	-$4,842,000
Curr. Assets: $15,839,000	**Curr. Liab.:** $28,455,000	**P/E Ratio:** 19.48
Plant, Equip.: $1,495,000	**Total Liab.:** $41,690,000	**Indic. Yr. Divd.:** NA
Total Assets: $45,619,000	**Net Worth:** $3,929,000	**Debt/ Equity:** NA

Sapient Corp

25 1st St., Cambridge, MA, 02141; **PH:** 1-617-621-0200; **Fax:** 1-617-621-1300; http:// www.sapient.com

General - Incorporation	DE	**Stock** - Price on:12/24/2007	$7.6
Employees	4,952	Stock Exchange	NDQ
Auditor	PricewaterhouseCoopers LLP	Ticker Symbol	SAPE
Stk Agt	American Stock Transfer & Trust Co.	Outstanding Shares	123,680,000
Counsel	NA	E.P.S.	$0.04
DUNS No.	79-016-6219	Shareholders	NA

Business: The group's principal activity is to provide business and technology consultancy that helps large companies to achieve measurable business results. The group delivers business value to the clients by understanding the key business problems they face and by solving those problems. The group operates through five segments: financial services, technology and communications, consumer and transportation, automotive,consumer and energy, public services. The group currently has offices in cambridge, Massachusetts, New York, jersey city, san francisco, Chicago, atlanta, Dallas, los angeles, Washington D.C., dusseldorf, london, Munich, new delhi and toronto. The group owns 50% of the voting stock of a consulting joint venture in milan.

Primary SIC and add'l.: 7378 7372 7375

CIK No: 0001008817

Subsidiaries: HWT, Inc., Sapient Australia Pty. Ltd., Sapient Canada Inc., Sapient Corporation Private Limited, Sapient GmbH, Sapient Government Services, Inc., Sapient Limited, Sapient Netherlands, B.V., Sapient Securities Corporation

Officers: Alan J. Herrick/Dir., CEO, Pres./$912,625.00, Preston B. Bradford/Sr. VP, Chief Operations, Administrative Officer, Jane E. Owens/55/Sr. VP, General Counsel, Alan M. Wexler/44/Sr. VP, MD - North America/$637,235.00, Gaston Legorburu/Sr. VP, Chief Creative Officer, Joseph S. Tibbetts/Sr. VP, CFO, Stephen P. Sarno/41/VP, Corporate Controller, Chief Accounting Officer

Directors: Alan J. Herrick/Dir., CEO, Pres., Jeffrey M. Cunningham/55/Chmn., Dennis H. Chookaszian/64/Dir., Darius W. Gaskins/68/Dir., Gary S. McKissock/65/Dir., Jane E. Owens/55/Sr. VP, General Counsel, Stuart J. Moore/46/Dir., Bruce D. Parker/60/Dir., Hermann Buerger/Dir., Stephen P. Sarno/41/VP, Corporate Controller, Chief Accounting Officer, James M. Benson/61/Dir.

Owners: Joseph S. Tibbetts, Stuart J. Moore/17.10%, Paul E. George/6.60%, Alan M. Wexler, Dennis H. Chookaszian, Alan J. Herrick, Scott J. Krenz, Insiders/19.60%, Christian Oversohl, Darius W. Gaskins, Hermann Buerger, Bruce D. Parker, Wellington Management Company, LLP/13.50%, Sheeroy D. Desai, Samuel C. Sichko/12.70% (19 Owners included in Index)

Financial Data: Fiscal Year End:12/31 Latest Annual Data: 12/31/2006

Year	Sales	Net Income
2006	$421,643,000	$3,136,000
2005	$333,038,000	$25,698,000
2004	$266,036,000	$22,819,000
Curr. Assets: $257,600,000	**Curr. Liab.:** $108,701,000	**P/E Ratio:** 190.00
Plant, Equip.: $27,623,000	**Total Liab.:** $127,087,000	**Indic. Yr. Divd.:** NA
Total Assets: $342,064,000	**Net Worth:** $214,497,000	**Debt/ Equity:** NA

Sappi Ltd

225 Franklin St., Boston, MA, 02110; ***PH:*** 1-617-423-7300; ***Fax:*** 1-617-423-5494;
http:// www.sappi.com

General - Incorporation	South Africa	**Stock**- Price on:12/24/2007	$19.38
Employees	15,199	Stock Exchange	NYSE
Auditor	Deloitte & Touche LLP	Ticker Symbol	SPP
Stk Agt	Bank of New York	Outstanding Shares	227,900,000
Counsel	Cravath, Swaine & Moore LLP	E.P.S	$0.33
DUNS No.	64-477-5264	Shareholders	NA

Business: The group's principal activity is the manufacturing and selling of pulp, paper and wood products. The group conducts its business through sappi fine paper and sappi forest products. Sappi fine paper produces a range of uncoated graphic and business paper, coated and uncoated speciality paper and casting release paper used in the manufacture of artificial leather and textured polyurethane applications. Sappi forest products owns and manages about 540,000 hectares of plantations and produces dissolving pulp, newsprint and kraft packaging paper, bleached and unbleached paper pulp, and beneficiates wood into timber products. The group operates in the southern Africa, North America and Europe.

Primary SIC and add'l.: 2679 2421 2611

CIK No: 0001072483

Subsidiaries: Jiangxi Chenming Paper Co Ltd, Lignin Insurance Co. Ltd., S.D. Warren Company, Sappi Alfeld GmbH, Sappi Austria Produktions GmbH& Co KG, Sappi Cloquet LLC, Sappi Ehingen GmbH, Sappi Esus Beteiligungs-verwaltungs GmbH, Sappi Europe SA, Sappi Holding GmbH, Sappi International SA, Sappi Lanaken NV, Sappi Lanaken Press Paper NV, Sappi Maastricht BV, Sappi Management Services (Pty) Ltd. 20 Subsidiaries included in the Index

Officers: Jan Labuschagne/CEO - Sappi Forest Products, Wayne Rau/CEO - Sappi Trading, Ralph Boettger/Dir., CEO, Berry Wiersum/CEO - Sappi Fine Paper Europe, Mark Gardner/CEO, Pres. - Sappi Fine Paper North America, Dinga Mncube/MD - Sappi Fine Paper South Africa, Wikus Van Zyl/Group Mgr. - Investor Relations, Stephen Blyth/Group Financial Mgr., Roland Agar/Group Internal Audit Mgr., Jorg Passler/Group Treasurer, Ria Sanz/Group Corporate Counsel, Rudolf Thummer/Group Head - Technology, Lucia Swartz/Group Head - Human Resources, Robert Hope/Group Head - Strategic Development, Henri Kirsten/Dir. - Finance, Sappi Trading *(48 Officers included in Index)*

Directors: Ralph Boettger/Dir., CEO, Eugene Van As/68/Chmn., Klaas D. Kluis/Dir., Mark Richard Thompson/Dir., Exec. Dir. - Finance, Meyer Feldberg/Non - Exec. Dir., Nigel Rudd/Dir., James Edward Healey/Non - Exec. Dir., Jock McKenzie/Dir., Karen R. Osar/Dir., Helmut Claus-Jurgen Mamsch/Dir., Deenadayalen Konar/Dir., Bridgette Radebe/Dir., Franklin Abraham Sonn/Dir., David Charles Brink/Non - Exec. Dir.

Owners: First National Nominees/24.60%, ABSA Nominees/12.30%, Standard Bank Nominees/23.10%, Industrial Development Corporation of South Africa Limited/6.70%, Insiders/0.30%, Nedcor Bank Nominees Limited/26.10%

Financial Data: ***Fiscal Year End:***02/10 ***Latest Annual Data:*** 10/1/2006

Year	Sales	Net Income
2006	$4,941,000,000	-$116,000,000
2005	$5,018,000,000	-$332,000,000
2004	$4,728,000,000	$52,000,000

Curr. Assets:	$1,376,000,000	**Curr. Liab.:**	$1,485,000,000	**P/E Ratio:**	19.48
Plant, Equip.:	$3,937,000,000	**Total Liab.:**	$3,827,000,000	**Indic. Yr. Divd.:**	$0.300
Total Assets:	$5,406,000,000	**Net Worth:**	$1,579,000,000	**Debt/ Equity:**	NA

Sara Lee Corp

3500 Lacey Rd., Downers Grove, IL, 60515; ***PH:*** 1-630-598-8100; ***Fax:*** 1-630-598-8482;
http:// www.saralee.com

General - Incorporation	MD	**Stock**- Price on:12/24/2007	$17.76
Employees	109,000	Stock Exchange	NYSE
Auditor	PricewaterhouseCoopers LLP	Ticker Symbol	SLE
Stk Agt	Sara Lee Corp	Outstanding Shares	734,580,000
Counsel	NA	E.P.S	$0.53
DUNS No.	00-521-3962	Shareholders	NA

Business: The groups principle activities include manufacturing and marketing food and beverages. The groups products include baked goods, processed meats, coffee and tea, beverage systems, intimate apparel, underwear, and activewear. The group's products are marketed under the trade names Ambi pur,Hillshire farm and jimmey dean. The group operates from United States.

Primary SIC and add'l.: 2013 2879 2051 2844 2251 2099 2095

CIK No: 0000023666

Subsidiaries: 2476230 Malta Limited, A/s Blumoller, ABCI SASU, Agepal Sarl, Alimentares Lda., Allsohl GmbH, Aoste Argentina, Aoste Belgique B.v., Aoste Espana S.a., Aoste Export Snc, Aoste Food Service Sa, Aoste Holding Snc, Aoste Libre Service Pretranche Snc, Aoste Management Sasu, Aoste Sb Gmbh 375 Subsidiaries included in the Index

Officers: Adriaan Nuhn/55/CEO, Exec. VP - Sara Lee International/$3,039,264.00, Brenda C. Barnes/Chmn., CEO/$8,692,394.00, Stephen J. Cerrone/Exec. VP - Human Resources, Roderick A. Palmore/Exec. VP, General Counsel, Sec./$3,085,185.00, Vincent H. Janssen/Exec. VP, Thomas B. Hansson/Sr. VP - Strategic Planning, Corporate Development, Frank Van Oers/Exec. VP, Jon Harris/Sr. VP - Global Communications, Mike Cummins/Dir. - Corporate Communications, James W. Nolan/Exec. VP, Christopher J. Fraleigh/Exec. VP/$2,114,088.00, L. M. De Kool/Exec. VP, Chief Financial, Administrative Officer/$4,637,231.00

Directors: Brenda C. Barnes/Chmn., CEO, Ian Prosser/Dir., Laurette T. Koellner/Dir., Jonathan P. Ward/Dir., Cees J.A. Van Lede/Dir., Virgis W. Colbert/Dir., Christopher B. Begley/Dir., Norman R. Sorensen/Dir., Rozanne L. Ridgway/Dir., James S. Crown/Dir.

Owners: Insiders, James S. Crown, L.M. de Kool, Brenda C. Barnes, Willie D. Davis, Jonathan P. Ward, Virgis W. Colbert, Capital Group International, Inc./5.60%, Christopher B. Begley, Laurette T. Koellner, Brandes Investment Partners, L.P./5.90%, Adriaan Nhn, Cornelis J.A. van Lede, Roderick A. Palmore, Sir Ian Prosser *(18 Owners included in Index)*

Financial Data: ***Fiscal Year End:***07/02 ***Latest Annual Data:*** 7/1/2006

Year	Sales	Net Income
2006	$15,944,000,000	$555,000,000
2005	$19,254,000,000	$719,000,000
2004	$19,566,000,000	$1,272,000,000

Curr. Assets:	$5,746,000,000	**Curr. Liab.:**	$5,423,000,000	**P/E Ratio:**	33.51
Plant, Equip.:	$3,271,000,000	**Total Liab.:**	$11,860,000,000	**Indic. Yr. Divd.:**	$0.400
Total Assets:	$14,883,000,000	**Net Worth:**	$2,948,000,000	**Debt/ Equity:**	NA

Sasol Ltd

900 Threadneedle, Houston, TX, 77079; ***PH:*** 1-281-588-3000; ***Fax:*** 1-281-588-3144;
http:// www.sasol.com; ***Email:*** sasol.internet@sasol.com

General - Incorporation	South Africa	**Stock**- Price on:12/24/2007	$37.85
Employees	30,368	Stock Exchange	NYSE
Auditor	KPMG Inc	Ticker Symbol	SSL
Stk Agt	Puglisi & Associates	Outstanding Shares	625,200,000
Counsel	NA	E.P.S	$3.95
DUNS No.	64-463-2069	Shareholders	NA

Business: The group's principal activity is the production of oil and gas with substantial chemical interests. These core interests are supported by coal-mining operations in South Africa, where coal is converted into synfuels and chemicals through proprietary fischer-tropsch technologies. The group has chemical manufacturing and marketing operations in Europe, Asia and the Americas. Chemical portfolios include polymers, solvents, surfactants, waxes and nitrogenous products. The group also refines crude oil into liquid fuels in South Africa.

Primary SIC and add'l.: 6726 2821 4925 1231 2911 2869 1321

CIK No: 0000314590

Subsidiaries: Pipeline Investments Company (Pty) Limited, Sasol Chemical Holdings International (Pty) Limited, Sasol Chemical Industries ltd, Sasol Chemicals Europe ltd, Sasol Chemicals Pacific ltd, Sasol Financing (Pty) Limited, Sasol Financing International plc, Sasol Gas Holdings (Pty), Sasol Gas Limited, Sasol Investment Company (Pty) Limited., Sasol Mining (Pty) Limited, Sasol Oil (Pty) Limited, Sasol Oil International Limited, Sasol Petroleum International (Pty) Limited, Sasol Synfuels (Pty) Limited 17 Subsidiaries included in the Index

Officers: Pat Davies/Dir., CEO, Nolitha Fakude/43/Executive Dir., Johannes Albertus Botha/Group GM, Abraham De Klerk/Group GM, Nereus Louis Joubert/Group GM, Company Sec., Giullean Johann Strauss/Group GM, Cavan Hill/Group Mgr. - Investor Relations, Hubert Naude/Mgr. - Investor Relations, Leon Lotz/Agronomist, Free State, Northern Cape, Arnold Otto/Marketing Mgr. - Mpumalanga, Handro Swart/Mgr. - Agronomical Services, Bertus Pretorius/Marketing Mgr. - Western Cape, Bheki Khumalo/Contact - Group Corporate Affairs Mgr., Lawrence Patrick Adrian Davies/57/Chief Executive, Benny Mokaba/Executive Dir. *(29 Officers included in Index)*

Directors: Pat Davies/Dir., CEO, Henk Dijkgraaf/Non Exec. Dir., Hixonia Nyasulu/Dir., Mandla Gantsho/Non Exec. Dir., Pieter Cox/Non Exec. Dir., Benny Mokaba/Executive Dir., Nolitha Fakude/43/Executive Dir., Anshu Jain/Non Exec. Dir., Tom Wixley/Dir., Hendrik George Dijkgraaf/61/Dir., Sam Montsi/Non Exec. Dir., Jurgen Schrempp/Non Exec. Dir., Brian Connellan/Non Exec. Dir., Elisabeth Bradley/Non Exec. Dir., Imogen Mkhize/Non Exec. Dir.

Owners: Elisabeth Bradley, Brian Connellan, Pat Davies, Tom Wixley, Pieter Cox

Financial Data: ***Fiscal Year End:***06/30 ***Latest Annual Data:*** 6/30/2006

Year	Sales	Net Income
2006	$7,973,000,000	$1,456,000,000
2005	$10,203,948,000	$1,469,029,000
2004	$9,480,142,000	$858,887,000

Curr. Assets:	$4,386,000,000	**Curr. Liab.:**	$2,600,000,000	**P/E Ratio:**	19.48
Plant, Equip.:	$6,180,000,000	**Total Liab.:**	$5,570,000,000	**Indic. Yr. Divd.:**	$1.630
Total Assets:	$12,099,000,000	**Net Worth:**	$6,529,000,000	**Debt/ Equity:**	NA

Satcon Technology Corp

27 Drydock Ave., Boston, MA, 02210; ***PH:*** 1-617-897-2400; ***Fax:*** 1-617-897-2401;
http:// www.satcon.com

General - Incorporation	DE	**Stock**- Price on:12/24/2007	$1.18
Employees	195	Stock Exchange	NDQ
Auditor	Vitale, Caturano & Co., Ltd.	Ticker Symbol	SATC
Stk Agt	American Registrar & Transfer Co	Outstanding Shares	42,800,000
Counsel	Hale & Dorr LLP	E.P.S	-$0.35
DUNS No.	15-725-7502	Shareholders	NA

Business: The group's principal activities are to develop enabling technologies for the emerging digital power marketplace that include ups systems, distributed power generation and power quality markets. The group operates through three segments: applied technology, power systems and electronics. The products include power conversion systems, power electronics systems, digital control software, high performance motors and vibration test systems, hybrid microcircuits, rf components, thin film substrates and amplifiers. The group manufactures power and energy management products that will convert, store and manage electricity for the businesses and consumers that require high-quality, uninterruptible power supply.

Primary SIC and add'l.: 8731 3699 3674

CIK No: 0000889423

Subsidiaries: Ling Electronics, Ltd., SatCon Applied Technology, Inc, SatCon Electronics, Inc, SatCon Power Systems Canada, Ltd., SatCon Power Systems, Inc

Officers: David B. Eisenhaure/Dir., CEO, Pres./$326,995.00, Edward Wagner/VP - Engineering, Jim O'Rourke/VP - Motors, Leo Casey/CTO, VP, Bill O'Donnell/Pres. - Satcon Applied Technology, Inc, Clemens Van Zeyl/Pres. - Satcon Power Systems Canada, Ltd/$293,832.00, Dave O'Neil/VP - Finance, Treasurer/$248,707.00, Daniel E. Gladkowski/57/VP - Administration, Sec., John W. Peacock/Controller, Chief Accounting Officer

Directors: David B. Eisenhaure/Dir., CEO, Pres., Andrew R. Muir/Dir., Marshall J. Armstrong/Dir., Joseph E. Levangie/Dir., John M. Carroll/Dir., James L. Kirtley/Dir., Daniel R. Dwight/Dir.

Owners: David E. O'Neil, William J. O'Donnell, Insiders/23.80%, Andrew R. Muir, Joseph E. Levangie, David J. Prend/8.80%, Marshall J. Armstrong, Daniel E. Gladkowski, John M. Carroll, RockPort Capital PartnersII, L.P./8.80%, James L. Kirtley, Philip J. Deutch/8.80%, Clemens van Zeyl, David B. Eisenhaure/6.70%, Daniel R. Dwight *(16 Owners included in Index)*

Financial Data: ***Fiscal Year End:***09/30 ***Latest Annual Data:*** 12/31/2006

Year	Sales	Net Income
2006	$33,757,000	-$19,778,000
2005	$35,955,000	-$10,246,000
2004	$34,158,000	-$10,958,000

Curr. Assets:	$20,937,000	**Curr. Liab.:**	$9,544,000		
Plant, Equip.:	$3,663,000	**Total Liab.:**	$10,005,000	**Indic. Yr. Divd.:**	NA
Total Assets:	$27,732,000	**Net Worth:**	$15,602,000	**Debt/ Equity:**	NA

Satelinx Inc

Formerly: Vectoria Inc

809 Deslauriers, Ville St. Lauent, QC, H4N 1X3; *PH:* 1-514-332-2523; *http://* www.vectoria.ca

General - Incorporation	NV	Stock - Price on:12/24/2007	$0.16
Employees	NA	Stock Exchange	OTC
Auditor	Schwartz Levitsky Feldman LLP	Ticker Symbol	VTRR
Stk Agt	NA	Outstanding Shares	NA
Counsel	NA	E.P.S	NA
DUNS No.	NA	Shareholders	NA

Business: The group's principal activity was to provide Internet protocol telephony services by developing telephony network infrastructure. The products and services were provided to small and medium size business. The group's Internet protocol voice offered full integration of voice, data, Internet and video over existing Internet protocol network. During the year 2002, it sold its Internet access services business. It presently has no business and is seeking a suitable acquisition.

Primary SIC and add'l.: 7375

CIK No: 0001082706

Subsidiaries: Satelinx Tracking Systems Inc, Satelinx Tracking Systems Inc., Ville St. Lauent, Quebec, Canada

Satellite Newspapers Corp

Bank of America Building, 980 Post Rd. E, 2nd Fl., Westport, CT, 06880; *PH:* 1-203-401-8089; *Fax:* 1-305-858-1495; *http://* www.satellitenewspapers.com; *Email:* Sales@satellitenewspapers.com

General - Incorporation	NV	Stock - Price on:12/24/2007	$0.0008
Employees	NA	Stock Exchange	OTC
Auditor	Meyler & Company, LLC	Ticker Symbol	SNWP
Stk Agt	Signature Stock Transfer, Inc.	Outstanding Shares	423,480,000
Counsel	NA	E.P.S	-$0.619
DUNS No.	NA	Shareholders	NA

Business: The groups principle activities include providing global access to detailed information from content publishers via multiple output devices. The group operates from the United States and China.

Primary SIC and add'l.: 2750

CIK No: 0001061688

Officers: Roy Piceni/40/Chmn., CEO, Pres., Randy Hibma/36/Dir., CFO

Directors: Roy Piceni/40/Chmn., CEO, Pres., Randy Hibma/36/Dir., CFO

Owners: Roy Piceni/58.01%, Insiders/58.01%

Financial Data: Fiscal Year End:12/31 Latest Annual Data: 12/31/2006

Year	Sales	Net Income
2006	NA	-$5,240,000
2005	$1,672,000	-$2,617,000
2004	$1,091,000	-$8,205,000

Curr. Assets:	$1,000	Curr. Liab.:	$3,903,000		
Plant, Equip.:	NA	Total Liab.:	$3,903,000	Indic. Yr. Divd.:	NA
Total Assets:	$1,000	Net Worth:	-$3,901,000	Debt/ Equity:	NA

Satellite Security

5101 Summit Bridge Rd. , Middletown, DE, 19709; *PH:* 1-302-376-0241; *http://* www.satsecurity.com; *Email:* sales@satsecurity.com

General - Incorporation	NV	Stock - Price on:12/24/2007	$0.023
Employees	17	Stock Exchange	OTC
Auditor	Tauber & Balser, P.C.	Ticker Symbol	SLTS
Stk Agt	American Registrar & Transfer Co	Outstanding Shares	110,980,000
Counsel	NA	E.P.S	$6.57
DUNS No.	NA	Shareholders	NA

Business: The groups principle activity is engaged in providing asset tracking services, through use of the global positioning system and various communications platforms, for asset security and logistic control. The groups solutions generally involve the sale of a GPS tracking device and subsequent monitoring of that device. The group operates from the United States.

Primary SIC and add'l.: 9995

CIK No: 0001084088

Subsidiaries: Satellite Security Systems, Inc.,

Officers: Zirk Engelbrecht/51/Chmn., CEO

Directors: Zirk Engelbrecht/51/Chmn., CEO

Owners: Kenneth Dixon/2.56%, Stephen Hallock/12.40%, Zirk Engelbrecht/16.67%, Insiders/16.67%, John Phillips/2.55%, Marcy Miller/13.52%

Financial Data: Fiscal Year End:12/31 Latest Annual Data: 12/31/2006

Year	Sales	Net Income
2006	$1,515,000	-$5,335,000
2005	$1,227,000	-$1,778,000
2004	$2,437,000	-$6,613,000

Curr. Assets:	$443,000	Curr. Liab.:	$5,183,000		
Plant, Equip.:	$15,000	Total Liab.:	$5,960,000	Indic. Yr. Divd.:	NA
Total Assets:	$829,000	Net Worth:	-$5,131,000	Debt/ Equity:	NA

Satyam Computer Services Ltd

1 Gatehall Dr., Ste. 301, Parsippany, NJ, 07054; *PH:* 1-973-656-0650; *Fax:* 1-973-656-0653; *http://* www.satyam.com

General - Incorporation	India	Stock - Price on:12/24/2007	$25.72
Employees	39,018	Stock Exchange	NYSE
Auditor	V.P. Rama Rao	Ticker Symbol	SAY
Stk Agt	NA	Outstanding Shares	333,600,000
Counsel	NA	E.P.S	$0.90
DUNS No.	65-032-0716	Shareholders	NA

Business: The group's principal activities are to provide information technology services, Internet services and develop software products. The ranges of services include consulting, systems design, software development, system integration and application maintenance. The group provides its services to a wide range of industries including insurance, banking and financial services, manufacturing, telecommunications, transportation and engineering services. The group has offshore development centers located throughout India. It also has offsite centers located in the United States, UK, Japan, Singapore, Australia, China, Malaysia, Hong Kong, Germany and dubai. The group has a global customer base of 300 customers, which includes 101 Fortune 500 companies.

Primary SIC and add'l.: 6726 7372 7371

CIK No: 0001106056

Officers: Rama Raju/Co - Founder, CEO, V. Murali/43/Dir., Sr. VP - Commercial, Contract, Michael Vodicka/Program Dir., John Willett/CIO - Qantas, Virender Aggarwal/Dir., Sr. VP, Subramanian D. /48/Dir., Sr. VP - Vertical Business Unit, Violet Yeo/Contact - Australia, New Zealand, Priti Thakker/Contact - US, Canada, Deepak Nangia/Country Mgr. - ANZ Satyam, Lincoln Hunter/Deputy General Counsel, Qantas, Hari T. /43/Dir., Sr. VP - Human Resources, Jayaraman G. /52/Sr. VP - Corporate Governance, Company Sec., Shailesh Shah/47/Dir., Sr. VP - Corporate Strategy Group, A. S. Murty/49/Dir., Sr. VP - Leadership Development Group, Joseph Abraham/55/Dir., Sr. VP - Vertical Business Unit, Retail *(25 Officers included in Index)*

Directors: Rama Raju/Co - Founder, CEO, Ramalinga B. Raju/Chmn., Virender Aggarwal/Dir., Sr. VP, Subramanian D. /48/Dir., Sr. VP - Vertical Business Unit, V. P. Rama-Rao/Dir., Mangalam Srinivasan/Dir., Krishna G. Palepu/Dir., Vinod K. Dham/57/Dir., Rammohan M. Rao/Dir., V. Murali/43/Dir., Sr. VP - Commercial, Contract, T. R. Prasad/Dir., V. S. Raju/Dir., Hari T. /43/Dir., Sr. VP - Human Resources, Shailesh Shah/47/Dir., Sr. VP - Corporate Strategy Group, A. S. Murty/49/Dir., Sr. VP - Leadership Development Group *(23 Directors included in Index)*

Owners: Insiders/0.39%, FMR Corp/8.95%, SRSR Holdings Private Limited/8.38%, Ram Mynampati/0.14%

Financial Data: Fiscal Year End:03/31 Latest Annual Data: 3/31/2007

Year	Sales	Net Income
2007	$1,461,400,000	$298,400,000
2006	$1,096,300,000	$249,400,000
2005	$793,597,000	$153,760,000

Curr. Assets:	$609,200,000	Curr. Liab.:	$211,200,000	P/E Ratio:	19.48
Plant, Equip.:	$163,100,000	Total Liab.:	$253,100,000	Indic. Yr. Divd.:	$0.150
Total Assets:	$1,624,100,000	Net Worth:	$1,371,000,000	Debt/ Equity:	NA

Sauer Danfoss Inc

250 Pkwy. Dr., Ste. 270, Lincolnshire, IL, 60069; *PH:* 1-515-239-6000; *Fax:* 1-515-239-6318; *http://* www.sauer-danfoss.com

General - Incorporation	DE	Stock - Price on:12/24/2007	$29.22
Employees	9,200	Stock Exchange	NYSE
Auditor	KPMG LLP	Ticker Symbol	SHS
Stk Agt	Wells Fargo Bank, N.A.	Outstanding Shares	48,130,000
Counsel	NA	E.P.S	$0.75
DUNS No.	60-735-6649	Shareholders	NA

Business: The groups principle activity is to supply engineered hydraulic and electronic systems and components. The groups products include orbital motors, hydrostatics, electric drives and steering products. Customers served by the group include the agriculture, construction, road building and material handling industries. The group operates from United States.

Primary SIC and add'l.: 3594 3492 3566

CIK No: 0000865734

Subsidiaries: Custom Design Electronics of Sweden AB, Daikin-Sauer-Danfoss Manufacturing Ltd., Hydro-Gear Limited Partnership, Hydro-Gear,Inc., Integrated Control Technologies Ltd., Merkur Hydraulika a.s., Oy Sauer-Danfoss AB, Sauer-Danfoss (Almhult) AB, Sauer-Danfoss (Berching) GmbH, Sauer-Danfoss (Bologna) SpA, Sauer-Danfoss (Kaiserslautern) GmbH, Sauer-Danfoss (Swindon) Ltd., Sauer-Danfoss (US) Company, Sauer-Danfoss a.s., Sauer-Danfoss A/S 40 Subsidiaries included in the Index

Officers: Ole Steen Andersen/Dir., CEO, Pres. - Sauer, Danfoss Inc, Jorgen M. Clausen/Chmn., CEO, Pres. - Danfoss A S, David J. Anderson/Dir., CEO, Pres./$2,083,149.00, Hans J. Cornett/Exec. VP, Chief Marketing Officer/$907,007.00, Thomas K. Kittel/Exec. VP, Pres. - Propel Division/$746,343.00, Kenneth D. McCuskey/VP, Chief Accounting Officer, Sec., Kathy Laczniak/Investor Relations Administrator, John N. Langrick/Dir. - Finance Europe, Wolfgang Schramm/Exec. VP, Pres. - Controls Division, Charles M. Cohrs/Treasurer, Karl J. Schmidt/CFO, Exec. VP/$995,088.00, James R. Wilcox/62/Exec. VP, Pres. - Work Function Division/$1,475,069.00, Ronald C. Hanson/VP - Human Resources, Finn H. Lyhne/VP - Electric Drives, Henrik Krabsen/Exec. VP, Pres. - Work Function Division *(16 Officers included in Index)*

Directors: Ole Steen Andersen/Dir., CEO, Pres. - Sauer, Danfoss Inc, Jorgen M. Clausen/Chmn., CEO, Pres. - Danfoss A S, David J. Anderson/Dir., CEO, Pres., Sven Murmann/Vice Chmn., Joseph F. Loughrey/Dir., Nicola Keim/47/Dir., Klaus H. Murmann/Dir., Johannes F. Kirchhoff/Dir., Hans Kirk/Dir., Steven H. Wood/Dir.

Owners: Karl J. Schmidt, Hans Kirk, Hans J. Cornett, Danfoss A/S, Sven Murmann, Jrgen Clausen, Johannes F. Kirchhoff, Steven H. Wood, Nicola Keim, James R. Wilcox, Ole Steen Andersen, Klaus H. Murmann, Sauer Holding GmbH, Danfoss Murmann Holding A/S, Hannelore Murmann *(19 Owners included in Index)*

Financial Data: Fiscal Year End:12/31 Latest Annual Data: 12/31/2006

Year	Sales	Net Income
2006	$1,739,088,000	$53,748,000
2005	$1,547,816,000	$38,715,000
2004	$1,404,159,000	$33,186,000

Curr. Assets:	$605,305,000	Curr. Liab.:	$437,962,000	P/E Ratio:	36.99
Plant, Equip.:	$503,977,000	Total Liab.:	$789,716,000	Indic. Yr. Divd.:	$0.720
Total Assets:	$1,309,155,000	Net Worth:	$465,991,000	Debt/ Equity:	0.3945

Saul Centers Inc

7501 Wisconsin Ave., Ste. 1500, Bethesda, MD, 20814; *PH:* 1-301-986-6200; *Fax:* 1-301-986-6079; *http://* www.saulcenters.com

General - Incorporation	MD	Stock - Price on:12/24/2007	$45.38
Employees	60	Stock Exchange	NYSE
Auditor	Ernst & Young LLP	Ticker Symbol	BFS
Stk Agt	Continental Stock Transfer & Trust Co	Outstanding Shares	17,570,000
Counsel	NA	E.P.S	$1.60
DUNS No.	NA	Shareholders	NA

Business: The groups principle activities include owning, management and developing of income-producing properties. In the year 2006, the group acquired Smallwood Village Center. The group operates from the United States.

Primary SIC and add'l.: 6798

CIK No: 0000907254

Subsidiaries: Avenel VI Inc., Briggs Chaney Plaza, LLC, Kentlands Lot 1, LLC, Saul Holdings Limited Partnership, Saul Monocacy, LLC, Saul QRS, Inc., Saul Subsidiary I Limited Partnership, Saul Subsidiary II Limited Partnership, Smallwood Village Center, LLC

Officers: Francis B. Saul/75/Chmn., CEO/$227,710.00, Francis B. Saul/46/Dir., Pres., Thomas H. McCormick/Sr. VP, General Counsel, Scott V. Schneider/CFO, Sr. VP, Treasurer, Sec./$422,383.00, John F. Collich/Sr. VP - Retail Development/$373,707.00, Christopher H. Netter/Sr. VP - Leasing/$413,513.00, Charles W. Sherren/Sr. VP - Property Management, Robert Wulff/Sr. VP - Acquisitions, Development, William F. Anhut/VP - Finance, Richard R. Meiburger/VP, Controller, Kenneth D. Shoop/VP, Chief Accounting Officer, William S. Hoy/Sr. VP - Construction

Directors: Francis B. Saul/75/Chmn., CEO, Philip D. Caraci/69/Vice Chmn., Gilbert M. Grosvenor/76/Dir., Francis B. Saul/46/Dir., Pres., John E. Chapoton/71/Dir., Philip C. Jackson/79/Dir., David B. Kay/51/Dir., Paul X. Kelley/79/Dir., Charles R. Longsworth/78/Dir., Patrick F. Noonan/65/Dir., James W. Symington/80/Dir., John R. Whitmore/74/Dir.

Owners: Insiders/39.00%, Patrick F. Noonan, Charles R. Longsworth, Scott V. Schneider, Paul X. Kelley, John F. Collich, David B. Kay, John R. Whitmore, Philip C. Jackson, John E. Chapoton, Francis B. Saul, Francis B. Saul/35.40%, James W. Symington, Christopher H. Netter, Philip D. Caraci *(16 Owners included in Index)*

Financial Data: ***Fiscal Year End:***12/31 ***Latest Annual Data:*** 12/31/2006

Year	Sales	Net Income
2006	$137,978,000	$32,680,000
2005	$127,015,000	$29,227,000
2004	$112,842,000	$26,174,000

Curr. Assets:	$41,309,000	**Curr. Liab.:**	$27,967,000		
Plant, Equip.:	$627,651,000	**Total Liab.:**	$568,446,000	**Indic. Yr. Divd.:**	$1.880
Total Assets:	$700,537,000	**Net Worth:**	$132,091,000	**Debt/ Equity:**	NA

Savannah Bancorp Inc

25 Bull St., Savannah, GA, 31401; ***PH:*** 1-912-629-6486; ***Fax:*** 1-912-232-3733;
http:// www.savb.com

General		***Stock***	
Incorporation	GA	Price on:12/24/2007	$25.18
Employees	195	Stock Exchange	NDQ
Auditor	BDO Seidman LLP	Ticker Symbol	SAVB
Stk Agt	Registrar & Transfer Co	Outstanding Shares	5,830,000
Counsel	Ellis Painter Ratteree Bart LLP	E.P.S.	$1.67
DUNS No.	61-506-7568	Shareholders	NA

Business: The group's principle activity is to provide full range of deposit services, medium-term commercial, personal and mortgage services through five full service offices located in savannah, boulevard, west chatham, whitemarsh island & medical arts shopping center in Georgia. The group is a multi-bank holding company for bryan bank & trust and the savannah bank, national association. The group offers cash management services, non-cash deposit courier service, safe deposit boxes, traveler's checks and direct deposit of payroll, u.s savings bonds, official bank checks and automatic draft for various accounts. The trust department offers a full array of trust services, including investment management, personal trusts, custodial accounts, estate administration and employee benefit administration.

Primary SIC and add'l.: 6022 6712

CIK No: 0000860519

Subsidiaries: Bryan Bank & Trust Georgia, Harbourside Community Bank, FSB, SAVB Capital Trust 1, SAVB Capital Trust 2, SAVB Properties, LLC, The Savannah Bank

Officers: John C. Helmken/44/Dir., CEO, Pres./$231,093.00, Robert B. Briscoe/55/CFO/$154,854.00, Stephen R. Stramm/57/Exec. VP - Lending/$189,211.00

Directors: John C. Helmken/44/Dir., CEO, Pres., Wiley J. Ellis/66/Chmn., James E. Burnsed/68/Vice Chmn., Clifford H. Dales/48/Dir., James Toby Roberts/62/Dir., Berryman W. Edwards/65/Dir., Carlton L. Gill/66/Dir., Lane M. Morrison/61/Dir., Robert T. Thompson/67/Dir., Robert H. Demere/59/Dir., Russell W. Carpenter/67/Dir., Curtis J. Lewis/54/Dir., Charles E. Izlar/55/Dir., Aaron M. Levy/66/Dir., James W. Royal/58/Dir.

Owners: Robert H. Demere/1.26%, James E. Burnsed/1.79%, Charles E. Izlar/0.03%, Lane M. Morrison/1.27%, Carlton L.Gill/1.96%, Robert T. Thompson/1.46%, James W. Royal/1.34%, Russell W. Carpenter/0.90%, John C. Helmken/1.57%, Berryman W. Edwards, Wiley J. Ellis/1.54%, Aaron M. Levy/0.93%, Archie H. Davis/2.87%, Clifford H. Dales/0.13%, Curtis J. Lewi/1.51% *(17 Owners included in Index)*

Financial Data: ***Fiscal Year End:***12/31 ***Latest Annual Data:*** 12/31/2006

Year	Sales	Net Income
2006	$59,492,000	$10,002,000
2005	$46,752,000	$9,040,000
2004	$32,807,000	$5,736,000

Curr. Assets:	$47,297,000	**Curr. Liab.:**	$747,511,000	**P/E Ratio:**	14.90
Plant, Equip.:	$6,910,000	**Total Liab.:**	$776,940,000	**Indic. Yr. Divd.:**	$0.480
Total Assets:	$843,514,000	**Net Worth:**	$66,574,000	**Debt/ Equity:**	NA

Savannah Electric & Power Co

600 Bay St. E, Savannah, GA, 31401; ***PH:*** 1-912-644-7171

General		***Stock***	
Incorporation	GA	Price on:12/24/2007	$23.11
Employees	NA	Stock Exchange	NYSE
Auditor	Deloitte & Touche LLP	Ticker Symbol	SVJ
Stk Agt	Bank of New York	Outstanding Shares	NA
Counsel	Bouhan, Williams & Levy	E.P.S.	NA
DUNS No.	00-692-6539	Shareholders	NA

Business: The group's principle activities include generating and supplying power. The group operates from United States.

Primary SIC and add'l.: 4911

CIK No: 0000086940

Subsidiaries: Alabama Power Capital Trust IV, Alabama Power Capital Trust V, Alabama Power Capital Trust VI, Alabama Power Capital Trust VII, Alabama Power Capital Trust VIII, Alabama Power Company, Alabama Property Company, Georgia Power Capital Trust IV, Georgia Power Capital Trust IX, Georgia Power Capital Trust V, Georgia Power Capital Trust VI, Georgia Power Capital Trust VII, Georgia Power Capital Trust VIII, Georgia Power Capital Trust X, Georgia Power Capital Trust XI 38 Subsidiaries included in the Index

Financial Data: ***Fiscal Year End:***12/31 ***Latest Annual Data:*** 12/31/2005

Year	Sales	Net Income
2005	$444,994,000	$32,633,000
2004	$356,960,000	$25,732,000
2002	$299,552,000	$22,880,000

Curr. Assets:	$133,136,000	**Curr. Liab.:**	$162,141,000		
Plant, Equip.:	$661,863,000	**Total Liab.:**	$631,344,000	**Indic. Yr. Divd.:**	NA
Total Assets:	$912,801,000	**Net Worth:**	$281,457,000	**Debt/ Equity:**	NA

Save The World Air Inc

5125 Lankershim Blvd, North Hollywood, CA, 91601; ***PH:*** 1-818-487-8000;
http:// www.savetheworldair.com; ***Email:*** info@stwa.com

General		***Stock***	
Incorporation	NV	Price on:12/24/2007	NA
Employees	NA	Stock Exchange	NA
Auditor	Weinberg & Company, P.A.	Ticker Symbol	NA
Stk Agt	Nevada Agency & Trust Company	Outstanding Shares	NA
Counsel	NA	E.P.S.	-$0.19
DUNS No.	NA	Shareholders	NA

Business: The groups principle activities include acquiring new technologies, developing products using groups technologies, conducting scientific tests regarding groups technologies and prototype products, and initiating sales and marketing efforts. The group has taken actions within the United States and internationally to secure intellectual property rights to the ZEFS and CAT MATE devices. The group operates from the United States.

Primary SIC and add'l.: 3714

CIK No: 0001103795

Officers: Charles R. Blum/70/Dir., CEO, Pres., John Richard Bautista/COO, Exec. VP, Eugene E. Eichler/Dir., Interim CFO, Charles Dargen/CFO

Directors: Charles R. Blum/70/Dir., CEO, Pres., Joseph Helleis/70/Chmn., Joseph J. Brown/Dir., Eugene E. Eichler/Dir., Interim CFO, Cecil Bond Kyte/37/Dir., Bruce H. Mckinnon/Dir., John F. Price/Dir., Steven Bolio/63/Dir., Nathan Shelton/61/Dir., Dennis M. Kenneally/Dir.

Owners: Joseph Helleis/1.20%, Cecil B. Kyte/5.00%, Insiders/16.10%, Leodis C. Matthews/6.60%, John Bautista/1.10%, Joette M. Dell/8.40%, John F. Price/1.40%, Bruce H. McKinnon/3.20%, Eugene E. Eichler/4.50%, John Brown/1.00%

Financial Data: ***Fiscal Year End:***12/31 ***Latest Annual Data:*** 12/31/2006

Year	Sales	Net Income
2006	$30,000	-$10,182,000
2005	NA	-$3,115,000
2004	NA	-$6,803,000

Curr. Assets:	$347,000	**Curr. Liab.:**	$1,570,000		
Plant, Equip.:	$322,000	**Total Liab.:**	$1,570,000	**Indic. Yr. Divd.:**	NA
Total Assets:	$673,000	**Net Worth:**	-$897,000	**Debt/ Equity:**	NA

Savi Media Group Inc

9852 W Katella Ave. No. 363, Anahiem, CA, 92804; ***PH:*** 1-714-740-0601;
http:// www.savimediagroup.com

General		***Stock***	
Incorporation	NV	Price on:12/24/2007	NA
Employees	NA	Stock Exchange	OTC
Auditor	Ham, Langston & Brezina LLP	Ticker Symbol	SVMI
Stk Agt	Pacific Stock Transfer Company	Outstanding Shares	NA
Counsel	Frank Longo	E.P.S.	$0.006
DUNS No.	NA	Shareholders	NA

Business: The group has discontinued both its energy marketing and biotechnology activities. The group intends to acquire companies operating in the entertainment industry and develop into an independent multimedia entertainment company. The group is in development stage and currently has no significant operations. The group has not yet generated revenue from new business activities and is devoting substantially all of its efforts to business planning and the search for sources of capital to fund its efforts.

Primary SIC and add'l.: 7812 3944

CIK No: 0001096637

Officers: Greg Sweeney/Dir., CEO, Pres., Serge Monros/Chmn., Chief Technicial Officer, Rudy Rodriguez/Dir., COO, Steve Botkin/CIO, Phil Scott/CFO, Frank Longo/Legal General Counsel

Directors: Greg Sweeney/Dir., CEO, Pres., Serge Monros/Chmn., Chief Technicial Officer, Philip Pisanelli/57/Dir., Alexander P. Haig/Member - Strategic Advisory Board, John Dunlap/Member - Strategic Advisory Board, Richard Maas/Member - Strategic Advisory Board, Alexander M. Haig/Member - Strategic Advisory Board, Rudy Rodriguez/Dir., COO

Owners: His Devine Vehicle/50.00%, New Creation Outreach, Inc., Kathy Procopio, Rudy Rodriguez, Insiders, Cornell Capital, Alexander M. Haig/10.17%, Alexander P. Haig/10.17%, Alexander M. Haig, Phil Pisanell, Cyrus Incorporated/8.04%, Serge Monros, New Creation Outreach, Inc./50.00%, Steve Botkin, G & K Automotive *(23 Owners included in Index)*

Financial Data: ***Fiscal Year End:***12/31 ***Latest Annual Data:*** 12/31/2006

Year	Sales	Net Income
2006	NA	-$22,871,000
2005	NA	-$138,426,000
2004	$197,000	-$106,418,000

Curr. Assets:	$1,000	**Curr. Liab.:**	$21,313,000		
Plant, Equip.:	$202,000	**Total Liab.:**	$21,313,000	**Indic. Yr. Divd.:**	NA
Total Assets:	$290,000	**Net Worth:**	-$21,023,000	**Debt/ Equity:**	NA

Savient Pharmaceuticals Inc

1 Tower Ctr., 14th Fl., East Brunswick, NJ, 08816; ***PH:*** 1-732-418-9300; ***Fax:*** 1-732-418-0570;
http:// www.savientpharma.com; ***Email:*** information@savient.com

General		***Stock***	
Incorporation	DE	Price on:12/24/2007	$13.11
Employees	67	Stock Exchange	NDQ
Auditor	Grant Thornton LLP	Ticker Symbol	SVNT
Stk Agt	American Registrar & Transfer Co	Outstanding Shares	53,100,000
Counsel	NA	E.P.S.	-$0.78
DUNS No.	10-111-3025	Shareholders	NA

Business: The group's principle activity is to develop, manufacture and market pharmaceutical products for unmet medical needs in both niche and larger market segments. The group distributes its products on a worldwide basis primarily through a direct sales force in the United States, the United

Kingdom and Israel. . The group's major products are oxandrin (R), bio-tropin tm, delatestryl (R), biolon (R), mircette (R), silkis(R) and bio-hep-b (r). The group maintaining worldwide approximately 409 issued patents either owned or exclusively licensed including 63 patents issued in the United States, 16 patents issued by the European patent office, which in turn resulted in the issuance of 160 national patents in Europe, and 17 patents issued in Israel. The group's quarterly revenue for September 2007 was 2.58 millions of USD.

Primary SIC and add'l.: 2834 8731

CIK No: 0000722104

Subsidiaries: Acacia Biopharma Limited, Myelos Corporation, Rosemont Pharmaceuticals Limited

Officers: Christopher G. Clement/Dir., CEO, Pres./$1,459,160.00, Philip K. Yachmetz/Exec. VP, Chief Business Officer/$918,204.00, Paul Hamelin/Sr. VP - Commercial Operations/$559,216.00, Brian J. Hayden/Sr. VP, CFO, Treasurer/$496,512.00, Zebulun D. Horowitz/Sr. VP, Chief Medical Officer/$903,329.00, Robert Lamm/Sr. VP - Quality, Regulatory Affairs

Directors: Christopher G. Clement/Dir., CEO, Pres., Stephen O. Jaeger/Chmn., Virgil Thompson/Dir., Herbert J. Conrad/Dir., Alan L. Heller/Dir., Joseph Klein/Dir., Lee S. Simon/Dir.

Owners: PHILIP K. YACHMETZ, Palo Alto Investors/17.50%, Alan Heller, Paul Hamelin, Zebulun D. Horowitz, Christopher G. Clement, Herbert Conrad, Insiders/4.80%, Stephen O. Jaeger, Faye Wattleton, Lee Simon, Virgil Thompson, David Tendler, Joseph Klein, Barclays Global Investors, N.A/7.60% *(16 Owners included in Index)*

Financial Data: Fiscal Year End: 12/31 **Latest Annual Data:** 12/31/2006

Year	Sales	Net Income
2006	$47,514,000	$60,325,000
2005	$87,794,000	$5,968,000
2004	$123,895,000	-$27,515,000

Curr. Assets:	$194,858,000	**Curr. Liab.:**	$20,164,000	**P/E Ratio:**	15.24
Plant, Equip.:	$1,139,000	**Total Liab.:**	$20,207,000	**Indic. Yr. Divd.:**	NA
Total Assets:	$197,893,000	**Net Worth:**	$177,686,000	**Debt/ Equity:**	NA

Savvis Communications Corp

1 Savvis Pk.way, Town & Country, MO, 63017; **PH:** 1-314-628-7000; **http://** www.savvis.net

General - Incorporation	DE	**Stock** - Price on: 12/24/2007	$49.78
Employees	2,166	Stock Exchange	NDQ
Auditor	Ernst & Young LLP	Ticker Symbol	NA
Stk Agt	Mellon Investor Services LLC	Outstanding Shares	52,730,000
Counsel	Hogan & Hartson LLP	E.P.S.	$4.53
DUNS No.	NA	Shareholders	NA

Business: The group's principal activity is to provide outsourced network, computing, application services and Internet-related services. The products are sold under the trade names: managed ip, high bandwidth Internet access and managed hosting. The managed ip service business provides managed data networking services to corporate customers. It offers managed Internet solutions and Internet access. It also provides equipment, installation and technical support to manage the circuit. The managed hosting provides reliable, high-performance Internet connectivity, data center security, scalability and the ability to monitor performance at the site. These services are provided to medium and large businesses, multinational corporations, and Internet service provider. The group operates in America, Europe and Asian countries. On 5-Mar-2004, it acquired cable and wireless usa inc, cable and wireless Internet services inc and certain assets of cable and wireless America.

Primary SIC and add'l.: 7375 7379 7389

CIK No: 0001058444

Subsidiaries: SAVVIS Argentina, S.A., SAVVIS Australia Pty. Ltd., SAVVIS Bermuda Ltd., SAVVIS Communications Chile, S.A., SAVVIS Communications Corporation, SAVVIS Communications International, Inc., SAVVIS Communications KK, SAVVIS Communications Private Limited, SAVVIS do Brasil Ltda., SAVVIS Europe B.V., SAVVIS Federal Systems, Inc., SAVVIS France S.A.S., SAVVIS Germany GmbH, SAVVIS Hong Kong Limited, SAVVIS Italia S.r.l. 30 Subsidiaries included in the Index

Officers: Philip J. Koen/Dir., CEO/$5,918,142.00, Jonathan C. Crane/Dir., Pres./$3,006,807.00, Jeffrey H. Von Deylen/Dir., CFO/$1,840,008.00, Richard Warley/MD - International/$1,246,756.00, James Mori/MD - US Sales, Timothy Caulfield/MD - Global Operations/$906,460.00, Margaret Hohl/Sr. VP - Global Human Resources, Matthew Fanning/MD - Business Development, Michael Tardif/Sr. VP - Product Engineering, Development, Mary Ann Altergott/Sr. VP - Global Human Resources, Eugene Defelice/Sr. VP, General Counsel, Sec., Bryan Doerr/CTO, Bill Fathers/Sr. VP - Development, Engineering, James Whitemore/Chief Marketing Officer, Elizabeth Corse/Dir. - Investor Relations

Directors: Philip J. Koen/Dir., CEO, James E. Ousley/Chmn., Jonathan C. Crane/Dir., Pres., Jeffrey H. Von Deylen/Dir., CFO, Thomas E. McInerney/Dir., John D. Clark/Dir., Clyde A. Heintzelman/Dir., James P. Pellow/Dir., Patrick J. Welsh/Dir.

Owners: Thomas E. McInerney, Jonathan C. Crane, James E. Ousley, Philip J. Koen, Welsh, Carson, Anderson & Stowe, Patrick J. Welsh, James P. Pellow, Richard S. Warley, Insiders, Timothy Caulfield, Clyde A. Heintzelman, John D. Clark, Jeffrey H. Von Deylen

Financial Data: Fiscal Year End: 12/31 **Latest Annual Data:** 12/31/2006

Year	Sales	Net Income
2006	$763,971,000	-$43,958,000
2005	$667,012,000	-$69,069,000
2004	$616,823,000	-$148,798,000

Curr. Assets:	$165,249,000	**Curr. Liab.:**	$140,086,000	**P/E Ratio:**	11.66
Plant, Equip.:	$284,437,000	**Total Liab.:**	$605,354,000	**Indic. Yr. Divd.:**	NA
Total Assets:	$467,019,000	**Net Worth:**	-$138,335,000	**Debt/ Equity:**	NA

Saxon Capital Inc

4860 Cox Rd. Ste. 300, Glen Allen, VA, 23060; **PH:** 1-804-967-7400; **https://** www.saxonmortgage.com

General - Incorporation	MD	**Stock** - Price on: 12/24/2007	$18.85
Employees	NA	Stock Exchange	NA
Auditor	Deloitte & Touche LLP	Ticker Symbol	NA
Stk Agt	American Stock Transfer & Trust Co.	Outstanding Shares	NA
Counsel	NA	E.P.S.	NA
DUNS No.	NA	Shareholders	NA

Business: The group's principal activity is to originate, purchase, securitize and service primarily non-conforming residential mortgage loans. The group originates or purchases mortgage loans through three separate origination channels. Wholesale channel originates or purchases loans through the group's network of approximately 3,000 brokers throughout the country. Retail channel originates mortgage loans directly to borrowers through the group's wholly-owned subsidiary, America's moneyline, which has a retail branch network of 20 locations. Correspondent channel purchases mortgage loans from approximately 400 correspondents following a complete re-underwriting of each mortgage loan.

Primary SIC and add'l.: 6162

CIK No: 0001279493

Subsidiaries: Saxon Advance Receivables Company, Inc., Saxon Asset Securities Company, Saxon Capital Holdings, Inc., Saxon Funding Management, Inc., Saxon Holding, Inc., Saxon Mortgage Services, Inc., Saxon Mortgage, Inc., Saxon Securities and Certificates, Inc., SCI Services, Inc., TRS Securities and Certificates, Inc.

Sba Communications Corp

5900 Broken Sound Pkwy. NW, Boca Raton, FL, 33487; **PH:** 1-561-995-7670; **Fax:** 1-561-998-3448; **http://** www.sbasite.com

General - Incorporation	FL	**Stock** - Price on: 12/24/2007	$33.26
Employees	615	Stock Exchange	NDQ
Auditor	Ernst & Young LLP	Ticker Symbol	SBAC
Stk Agt	EquiServe Trust Co N.A	Outstanding Shares	102,800,000
Counsel	NA	E.P.S.	NA
DUNS No.	NA	Shareholders	NA

Business: The group's principal activity is to operate wireless communication towers in the United States and Puerto Rico. The group operates principally in three business segments: site development construction, site development consulting and site leasing. The site development segment offers assistance in developing own networks, designing a network, acquiring locations to place antennas and, obtaining zoning approvals, building towers and installing antennas. The site leasing segment leases antenna space on towers and other structures. As on 31-Dec-2003 the group owned 3,093 towers. The major customers include at&t wireless, bechtel corporation, cingular wireless, general dynamics, nextel, sprint pcs, t-mobile and verizon wireless.

Primary SIC and add'l.: 8741 4899

CIK No: 0001034054

Subsidiaries: BowSteel Corporation, BowSteel of Texas Corporation, Claro Precision, Inc., Earthline Technologies, Inc., Etca G.p., LLC, Etca L.p., Inc., Extrusion Technology Corporation of America, Galt Alloys, Inc., NATI Gas Company, New Century Metals, Inc.

Officers: Jeffrey A. Stoops/Dir., CEO, Pres./$1,802,598.00, Anthony J. MacAione/Sr. VP, CFO/$653,238.00, Kurt L. Bagwell/COO, Sr. VP/$869,356.00, Thomas P. Hunt/Sr. VP, General Counsel/$917,029.00, Pamela J. Kline/VP - Capital Markets, Reid Boynton/Regional VP - North East, Brendan Cavanagh/VP, Chief Accounting Officer, Jim D. Williamson/Regional VP - Southeast, William J. Bates/VP - Business Development, Jorge Grau/CIO, VP, Michael S. Romesburg/VP - Tower Development, Jason V. Silberstein/VP - Property Management/$617,174.00, David Tribble/VP - Construction Services, Jo Carol Walton/VP - Human Resources

Directors: Jeffrey A. Stoops/Dir., CEO, Pres., Steven E. Bernstein/47/Chmn., Brian C. Carr/46/Dir., Duncan H. Cocroft/Dir., Philip L. Hawkins/Dir., Jack Langer/Dir., Steven E. Nielsen/Dir.

Owners: Goldman, Sachs& Co./8.00%, Jeffrey A. Stoops/2.20%, Jack Langer, Brian C. Carr, Anthony J. Macaione, Steven E. Nielsen, Richard B. Worley/6.20%, Steven E. Bernstein, Thomas P. Hunt, Duncan H. Cocroft, Philip L. Hawkins, T. Rowe Price Associates, Inc./7.70%, Jason V. Silberstein, Kurt L. Bagwell, Insiders/3.90%

Financial Data: Fiscal Year End: 12/31 **Latest Annual Data:** 12/31/2006

Year	Sales	Net Income
2006	$351,102,000	-$133,448,000
2005	$259,991,000	-$94,709,000
2004	$231,482,000	-$147,280,000

Curr. Assets:	$127,607,000	**Curr. Liab.:**	$58,354,000		
Plant, Equip.:	$1,105,942,000	**Total Liab.:**	$1,660,371,000	**Indic. Yr. Divd.:**	NA
Total Assets:	$2,046,292,000	**Net Worth:**	$385,921,000	**Debt/ Equity:**	8.1974

Sbarro Inc

401 Brdhollow Rd. , Melville, NY, 11747; **PH:** 1-800-456-4837; **http://** www.sbarro.com; **Email:** generalcomments@sbarro.com

General - Incorporation	NY	**Stock** - Price on: 12/24/2007	NA
Employees	NA	Stock Exchange	NA
Auditor	BDO Seidman LLP	Ticker Symbol	NA
Stk Agt	NA	Outstanding Shares	NA
Counsel	Parker Chapin Flattau & Klimpl	E.P.S.	NA
DUNS No.	09-878-7849	Shareholders	NA

Business: The group's principle activities include developing and operating of a family oriented cafeteria style Italian restaurants under the "Sbarro" and "Sbarro The Italian Eatery" names. The group operates from United States.

Primary SIC and add'l.: 5812

CIK No: 0000766004

Officers: Peter Beaudrault/Chmn., CEO, Pres., Anthony Missano/Pres. - Sbarro Business Development, Anthony J. Puglisi/CFO, VP, Stuart M. Steinberg/General Counsel, John Brisco/Pres. - Franchise Development

Directors: Peter Beaudrault/Chmn., CEO, Pres.

Owners: MidOcean/74.40%, Insiders/4.90%, Anthony Missano, Aktiva Investments International NV/12.00%, Anthony Puglisi, Peter Beaudrault/3.30%

SBD International Inc

6464 NW 5th Way, Ft. Lauderdale, FL, 33309; **PH:** 1-954-489-2962; **Fax:** 1-954-489-2962; **http://** www.sbdinternational.net; **Email:** info@sbdinternational.net

General - Incorporation	FL	**Stock** - Price on: 12/24/2007	NA
Employees	NA	Stock Exchange	OTC
Auditor	Bagell, Levine & Company, LLC	Ticker Symbol	SBDN
Stk Agt	Island Stock Transfer	Outstanding Shares	NA
Counsel	NA	E.P.S.	NA
DUNS No.	NA	Shareholders	NA

Business: The groups principle activity is engage in several contracts for construction projects in Thailand. In June 2005, the group acquired a property in Chiefland from Munch LLc.

Primary SIC and add'l.: 9995

CIK No: 0001106643
Subsidiaries: Integral Inc.
Officers: C. M. Nurse/Chmn., CEO, Pres.
Directors: C. M. Nurse/Chmn., CEO, Pres.
Owners: Insiders/48.00%, Scarborough Ltd./2.00%, Star Invest Group, Zono Plc/45.00%, C. M. Nurse, C. M. Nurse/48.00%

SBE Inc

4550 Norris Canyon Rd., San Ramon, CA, 94583; **PH:** 1-510-355-2000; **http://** www.sbei.com

General - Incorporation .... DE	Stock- Price on:12/24/2007 ....$2.39
Employees...37	Stock Exchange..NA
Auditor .... BDO Seidman LLP	Ticker Symbol...NA
Stk Agt........... American Registrar & Transfer Co	Outstanding Shares ....NA
Counsel....................... Goley Godward	E.P.S...NA
DUNS No. 00-912-7531	Shareholders...NA

Business: The group's principal activities are to design, market and support network communications solutions for original equipment manufacturers in the embedded and enterprise-level information technology computing markets. The principal products of the group include vmebus, wan adapters, LAN adapters, storage network interface cards and intelligent communications controllers. The vmebus product line provides connectivity between a mini-computer system and a local or wide area network. Wan adapter products are focused on the need for wide area network connectivity to communicate across switched telephone networks or satellites. Lan adapter products are focused on LAN connectivity using high speed ethernet technology. Storage network interface cards provide interface used by personal computers. The intelligent communications controllers provide communication solutions to the telecommunication market.

Primary SIC and add'l.: 7371 3669
CIK No: 0000087050
Officers: Mikael Hagman/40/CEO, Pres., Kenneth G. Yamamoto/52/Dir., Pres., David W. Brunton/VP - Finance, CFO, Leo Fang/36/Exec. VP, Nelson Abal/50/VP - Sales, Kirk Anderson/VP - Operations
Directors: Ronald J. Ritchie/65/Chmn., John Reardon/44/Dir., Marion M. Stuckey/66/Dir., John Derrico/Dir., Kenneth G. Yamamoto/52/Dir., Pres.
Owners: AIGH Investment Partners LLC/19.20%, John Reardon/0.30%, Susan Major/0.20%, Insiders/31.30%, Johan Ihrfelt/0.10%, David Brunton/0.50%, Per Bystedt/16.50%, Serwello AB/6.20%, Tommy Hallberg/0.50%, Mikael Hagman/1.40%, Magnus Goertz/8.80%, Thomas Eriksson/5.30%

Financial Data: Fiscal Year End:10/31 Latest Annual Data: 10/31/2006

Year	Sales	Net Income
2006	$6,127,000	-$16,183,000
2005	$8,056,000	-$4,230,000
2004	$11,066,000	-$1,679,000

Curr. Assets:	$2,993,000	Curr. Liab.:	$1,292,000		
Plant, Equip.:	$508,000	Total Liab.:	$1,547,000	Indic. Yr. Divd.:	NA
Total Assets:	$4,868,000	Net Worth:	$3,321,000	Debt/ Equity:	0.0580

SBT Bancorp Inc CT

760 Hopmeadow St., Simsbury, CT, 06070; **PH:** 1-860-408-5493

General - Incorporation ....CT	Stock- Price on:12/24/2007 ....$30
Employees...NA	Stock Exchange..OTC
Auditor ... Shatswell, MacLeod & Company, P.C.	Ticker Symbol...SBTB
Stk Agt...... American Stock Transfer & Trust Co.	Outstanding Shares ....NA
Counsel.....................Day, Berry & Howard, LLP	E.P.S..$1.14
DUNS No. ....NA	Shareholders...NA

Business: The groups principle activity is an investment in the bank, which is a community oriented financial institution providing a variety of banking and investment services. The services of the group include commercial loans, term real estate loans, construction loans, SBA loans and various types of consumer loans, accepting checking, savings, and time deposits. The group operates from the United States.

Primary SIC and add'l.: 6719
CIK No: 0001354174
Subsidiaries: SBT Investment Services, Inc., The Simsbury Bank & Trust Company Inc.
Officers: Martin J. Geitz/52/Dir., CEO, Pres., Jane F. Von Holzhausen/63/Dir., Sec., Anthony F. Bisceglio/60/CFO, Exec. VP, Terry L. Boulton/52/Sr. VP, Chief Retail Banking Officer, Paul R. Little/47/Chief Lending Officer, Sr. VP
Directors: Martin J. Geitz/52/Dir., CEO, Pres., Robert J. Bogino/65/Vice Chmn., Lincoln S. Young/73/Chmn., David W. Sessions/57/Dir., Jane F. Von Holzhausen/63/Dir., Sec., George B. Odlum/68/Dir., James T. Fleming/52/Dir., Edward J. Guarco/54/Dir., Barry R. Loucks/65/Dir., Penny R. Woodford/63/Dir.
Owners: David W. Sessions/1.80%, Barry R. Loucks/1.60%, Penny R. Woodford, Robert J. Bogino/3.10%, Jane F. Von Holzhausen/1.30%, Terry L. Boulton, Gary R. Kevorkian/1.90%, Insiders/17.20%, Edward J. Guarco, Lincoln S. Young/2.10%, Martin J. Geitz/1.60%, James T. Fleming, Anthony F. Bisceglio/1.20%, George B. Odlum/1.50%

Financial Data: Fiscal Year End:12/31 Latest Annual Data: 12/31/2006

Year	Sales	Net Income
2006	$12,292,000	$717,000

Curr. Assets:	$16,701,000	Curr. Liab.:	$200,030,000		
Plant, Equip.:	$1,552,000	Total Liab.:	$200,927,000	Indic. Yr. Divd.:	$0.440
Total Assets:	$217,047,000	Net Worth:	$16,119,000	Debt/ Equity:	NA

Scailex Corp Ltd

Formerly: Scitex Corp Ltd
16 Shenkar St., Entrance B, Herzliya Pituach, 46733; **PH:** 972-99610900; **Fax:** 972-99610912; **http://** www.scailex.com

General - Incorporation ....Israel	Stock- Price on:12/24/2007 ....$9.15
Employees...32	Stock Exchange..OTC
Auditor ....Brightman, Almagor & Co	Ticker Symbol...SCIXF
Stk Agt ..... American Stock Transfer & Trust Co.	Outstanding Shares 38,180,000
Counsel........................Goldfarb, Levy, Eran & Co	E.P.S...NA
DUNS No. 60-002-6561	Shareholders...NA

Business: The groups principle activities include designing, development, manufacture, marketing and support of primarily industrial ink jet digital printing solutions. The group also provides digital preprint and Internet imagery. The group operates from United States.

Primary SIC and add'l.: 3577 5045
CIK No: 0000315816
Subsidiaries: Jemtex InkJet Printing Ltd., Scailex Vision (Tel Aviv) Ltd.
Officers: Yahel Shachar/CEO, Shachar Rachim/36/CFO, Moshe Cohen/56/Internal Auditor
Directors: Eran Schwartz/43/Chmn., Yoav Biran/68/Dir., Dror Barzilai/55/Dir., Irit Ben-Ami/47/Dir., Arie Ovadia/59/Dir., Mordechai Peled/48/Dir., Arie Silverberg/60/Dir., Shalom Singer/61/Dir., Arie Zief/62/Dir.
Owners: Tao Tsuot Ltd., Suny Electronics Ltd., Ilan Ben Dov, Israel Petrochemical Enterprises Ltd.

Financial Data: Fiscal Year End:12/31 Latest Annual Data: 12/31/2006

Year	Sales	Net Income
2006	NA	$22,543,000
2005	NA	$106,138,000
2004	$128,185,000	$47,253,000

Curr. Assets:	$296,187,000	Curr. Liab.:	$22,502,000	P/E Ratio:	19.48
Plant, Equip.:	$12,000	Total Liab.:	$34,538,000	Indic. Yr. Divd.:	NA
Total Assets:	$319,572,000	Net Worth:	$285,034,000	Debt/ Equity:	NA

Scana Corp

1426 Main St., Columbia, SC, 29201; **PH:** 1-803-217-9000; **Fax:** 1-803-217-8119; **http://** www.scana.com

General - Incorporation ....SC	Stock- Price on:12/24/2007 ....$38.92
Employees...5,683	Stock Exchange..NYSE
Auditor ....Deloitte & Touche LLP	Ticker Symbol...SCG
Stk Agt ....SCANA Corp	Outstanding Shares 116,660,000
Counsel..NA	E.P.S..$2.52
DUNS No. 10-190-4845	Shareholders...NA

Business: The group's principle activities include generating, transmitting, distributing and marketing electricity and natural gas to wholesale and retail customers. The group operates in six segments include electric operations, gas distribution, gas transmission, retail gas marketing, energy marketing and other. Electric operations segment generates, transmits and distributes electricity. Gas distribution segment purchases and sells natural gas primarily to retail customers. Gas transmission segment purchases and transmits natural gas to distribution companies. Retail gas marketing segment markets natural gas. Energy marketing segment markets electricity and natural gas to industrial, large commercial and wholesale customers. The group operates from United States.

Primary SIC and add'l.: 4922 4911 4813 6719 4924 1321
CIK No: 0000754737
Subsidiaries: Primesouth, Inc., Public Service Company of North Carolina, Incorporated, Scana Communications, Inc., Scana Energy Marketing, Inc., Scana Services, Inc., Scg Pipeline, Inc., Servicecare, Inc., South Carolina Electric & Gas Company, South Carolina Fuel Company, Inc., South Carolina Generating Company, Inc., South Carolina Pipeline Corporation
Officers: William B. Timmerman/60/Chmn., CEO, Pres./$549,479.00, Sarena D. Burch/50/Sr. VP - Fuel Procurement, Asset Management, Paul V. Fant/55/COO, Pres. - Carolina Gas Transmission, Francis P. Mood/69/Sr. VP, General Counsel, Assist. Sec./$600,208.00, Kevin B. Marsh/51/COO, Pres. - South Carolina Electric, Gas Company/$395,663.00, Jimmy Addison/CFO, Sr. VP/$272,068.00, Joseph C. Bouknight/54/Sr. VP - Human Resources, George J. Bullwinkel/58/COO, Pres. - Scana Energy Marketing, Inc/$391,812.00, Stephen A. Byrne/47/Sr. VP - Generation - Nuclear, Fossil Hydro, South Carolina Electric, Gas Company/$307,433.00, Mark R. Cannon/Risk Management Officer, Treasurer, Carlette L. Walker/Corporate Compliance, Internal Auditing Officer, James E. Swan/Controller, Lynn M. Williams/Corp. Sec., Felicia Rhue Howard/Mgr. - Community, Economic Development, Local Government, Project Development, David Mottel/Contact - Aiken Region (23 Officers included in Index)
Directors: William B. Timmerman/60/Chmn., CEO, Pres., Bill L. Amick/Dir., John A. Warren/Dir. Emeriti, Benjamin A. Hagood/Dir. Emeriti, Elaine T. Freeman/Dir. Emeriti, William T. Cassels/Dir. Emeriti, James B. Edwards/Dir. Emeriti, Henry Ponder/Dir. Emeriti, James A. Bennett/Dir., William C. Burkhardt/Dir. Emeriti, Sharon A. Decker/Dir., Maybank D. Hagood/Dir., Hayne W. Hipp/Dir., Lynne M. Miller/Dir., Maceo K. Sloan/Dir. (20 Directors included in Index)
Owners: Insiders, W. B. Timmerman, S. A. Decker, B. L. Amick, W. H. Hipp, G. J. Bullwinkel, F. P. Mood, K. B. Marsh, SCANA Corporation/9.60%, D. M. Hagood, M. K. Sloan, J. A. Bennett, Barclays Entities/5.04%, H. C. Stowe, W. C. Burkhardt (19 Owners included in Index)

Financial Data: Fiscal Year End:12/31 Latest Annual Data: 12/31/2006

Year	Sales	Net Income
2006	$4,563,000,000	$310,000,000
2005	$4,777,000,000	$320,000,000
2004	$3,885,000,000	$257,000,000

Curr. Assets:	$1,376,000,000	Curr. Liab.:	$1,405,000,000	P/E Ratio:	15.44
Plant, Equip.:	$7,195,000,000	Total Liab.:	$6,865,000,000	Indic. Yr. Divd.:	$1.760
Total Assets:	$9,817,000,000	Net Worth:	$2,952,000,000	Debt/ Equity:	0.9880

Scanner Technologies Corp

14505 21st Ave. N, Ste. 220, Minneapolis, MN, 55447; **PH:** 1-763-476-8271; **Fax:** 1-763-476-0364; **http://** www.scannertech.com; **Email:** sales@scannertech.com

General - Incorporation ....NM	Stock- Price on:12/24/2007 ....$0.2
Employees...20	Stock Exchange..OTC
Auditor .Lurie Besikof Lapidus & Company LLP	Ticker Symbol..SCNI
Stk Agt .... Standard Registrar & Transfer Co Inc.	Outstanding Shares 12,240,000
Counsel...NA	E.P.S...-$0.15
DUNS No. ....NA	Shareholders...NA

Business: The groups principle activities include developing and marketing vision inspection products that are used in the semiconductor industry for the inspection of integrated circuits. Products of the group include Integrated circuits, which designed to be assembled to circuit substrates or printed

circuit boards. Specific customers of the group include Integration Technology Ltd. HTL Co. Japan Ltd., Kanematsu USA Inc., Yamatake & Co., Ltd. and STATS ChipPAC, Inc. The group operates from the United States, Japan, Singapore and Malaysia. The group's quarterly revenue for Sep '07 was 0.47 millions of USD.

Primary SIC and add'l.: 3559

CIK No: 0000217222

Subsidiaries: Scanner Technologies Corporation International

Owners: Elaine E. Beaty, Betsy Brenden Radtke, Elwin M. Beaty, David P. Mork, Michael A. Thorsland, Insiders

Financial Data: ***Fiscal Year End:***12/31 ***Latest Annual Data:*** 12/31/2006

Year	Sales	Net Income
2006	$2,497,000	-$1,084,000
2005	$1,596,000	-$1,893,000
2004	$5,834,000	$1,053,000

Curr. Assets:	$1,864,000	**Curr. Liab.:**	$240,000		
Plant, Equip.:	$14,000	**Total Liab.:**	$240,000	**Indic. Yr. Divd.:**	NA
Total Assets:	$1,984,000	**Net Worth:**	$1,744,000	**Debt/ Equity:**	NA

Scansource Inc

6 Logue Ct., Greenville, SC, 29615; ***PH:*** 1-864-288-2432; ***Fax:*** 1-864-288-1165; ***http://*** www.scansource.com; ***Email:*** sales@scansource.com

General - Incorporation....SC | ***Stock***- Price on:12/24/2007....$33.78
Employees....916 | Stock Exchange....NDQ
Auditor....Ernst & Young LLP | Ticker Symbol....SCSC
Stk Agt......American Stock Transfer & Trust Co. | Outstanding Shares....25,730,000
Counsel....Alston & Bird LLP | E.P.S....$1.71
DUNS No.....78-041-2177 | Shareholders....NA

Business: The groups principle activity is to distribute point-of-sale and automatic identification and data capture systems and solutions. The groups products include cash drawers, check readers, keyboards and labels. The group operates from United States.

Primary SIC and add'l.: 5085 5084

CIK No: 0000918965

Subsidiaries: 4100 Quest, LLC, Logue Court Properties, LLC, Netpoint International, Inc., Outsourcing Unlimited, Inc., Partner Services, Inc. f/k/a ChannelMax, Inc., ScanSource Canada, Inc., ScanSource de Mexico S de RL de CV, ScanSource EDC Limited, ScanSource Europe (Italia) Sede Secondaria, ScanSource Europe Limited, ScanSource Europe SPRL, ScanSource France SARL, ScanSource Germany GmbH, ScanSource Netherlands, ScanSource Properties, LLC 17 Subsidiaries included in the Index

Officers: Michael L. Baur/Dir., CEO, Richard P. Cleys/CFO, VP, Xavier Cartiaux/MD - Scansource Europe, Elias Botbol/Pres. - Scansource Latin America, John Black/Pres. - Catalyst Telecom, Clay Sorensen/Pres. - Paracon, John Gaillard/Pres. - Scansource Security Distribution, Jill Phillips/Pres. - T2 Supply, Robert S. McLain/48/VP - Marketing, Scott Benbenek/Pres. - Worldwide Operations, Andrea Meade/Exec. VP - Operations, Corporate Development

Directors: Michael L. Baur/Dir., CEO, James G. Foody/78/Chmn., Steven R. Fischer/63/Dir., Michael J. Grainger/56/Dir., John P. Reilly/60/Dir.

Owners: Michael J. Grainger, First Pacific Advisors, LLC/8.60%, John P. Reilly, Insiders/4.00%, FMR Corp./11.20%, Andrea D. Meade, James G. Foody, Lord, Abbett & Co. LLC/11.80%, Michael L. Baur/2.30%, Scott R. Benbenek, Eaton Vance Management/5.40%, Kayne Anderson Rudnick Investment Management, LLC/7.00%, Richard P. Cleys, Steven R. Fischer, T. Rowe Price Associates, Inc./5.30% *(17 Owners included in Index)*

Financial Data: ***Fiscal Year End:***06/30 ***Latest Annual Data:*** 06/30/2007

Year	Sales	Net Income
2007	$1,986,927,000	$42,626,000
2006	$1,665,600,000	$39,816,000
2005	$1,469,094,000	$35,732,000

Curr. Assets:	$567,086,000	**Curr. Liab.:**	$302,990,000	**P/E Ratio:**	19.99
Plant, Equip.:	$27,098,000	**Total Liab.:**	$337,703,000	**Indic. Yr. Divd.:**	NA
Total Assets:	$613,219,000	**Net Worth:**	$274,606,000	**Debt/ Equity:**	0.4153

SCBT Financial Corp

520 Gervais St., Columbia, SC, 29201; ***PH:*** 1-803-771-2265; ***Fax:*** 1-803-531-0524; ***http://*** www.scbandt.com

General - Incorporation....SC | ***Stock***- Price on:12/24/2007....$36.19
Employees....634 | Stock Exchange....NDQ
Auditor....J. W. Hunt And Co LLP | Ticker Symbol....SCBT
Stk Agt....SunTrust Bank | Outstanding Shares....9,190,000
Counsel....NA | E.P.S....$2.26
DUNS No.....00-792-0127 | Shareholders....NA

Business: The group's principal activities are to provide general banking and consumer finance services. The investment products include annuities, mutual funds, loans for businesses, agriculture, real estate, personal use, home improvement and automobiles, credit cards, home equity lines of credit. The other services include providing safe deposit boxes, bank money orders, wire transfer services, asset management services, discount brokerage services and use of ATM facilities. The group through its subsidiaries provides a variety of deposits including checking accounts, now accounts, savings and other time deposits of various types. The group provides these services through its 33 full service offices in 18 South Carolina towns.

Primary SIC and add'l.: 6021 6712

CIK No: 0000764038

Subsidiaries: SCBT Capital Trust I, SCBT Capital Trust II, SCBT Capital Trust III, South Carolina Bank and Trust of the Piedmont, N.A., South Carolina Bank and Trust, N.A., SunBank, N.A.

Officers: Robert R. Hill/CEO, Pres./$598,954.00, Thomas S. Camp/Pres. - SCBT Piedmont/$342,298.00, Richard C. Mathis/CRO/$335,177.00, Jay Reagan/Assist. VP - Wealth Management, Shields M. Cochran/Sr. VP - Wealth Management, West Summers/Sr. VP, Dir. - Investments, Wealth Management, Ann Snelling/Sr. VP, Trust Mgr. - Wealth Management, Joe E. Burns/CCO, James C. Hunter/Sec., John C. Pollok/CFO, COO, Sr. Exec. VP/$431,226.00, John F. Windley/Pres. - SCBT/$321,463.00, Mark Benson/Assist. VP - Wealth Management, Michelle Allison/Sr. VP - Wealth Management, Doug G. Holman/VP, Relationship Mgr., Trust Officer - Wealth Management, Steve Olsson/Contact - Beaufort Region, Mortgage *(71 Officers included in Index)*

Directors: Robert R. Horger/57/Chmn., Harry M. Mims/66/Dir., Susie H. Vanhuss/68/Dir., Dewall A. Waters/64/Dir., James W. Roquemore/53/Dir., John W. Williamson/59/Dir., Cathy Cox Yeadon/58/Dir., Colden R. Battey/72/Dir., Dalton B. Floyd/69/Dir., Oswald M. Fogle/63/Dir., Dwight W. Frierson/51/Dir., Caine R. Halter/46/Dir., Thomas E. Suggs/58/Dir., Luther J. Battiste/58/Dir., Ralph W. Norman/54/Dir.

Owners: Thomas S. Camp, Cathy Cox Yeadon, Caine R. Halter, Dalton B. Floyd, Harry M. Mims, Colden R. Battey/1.00%, John F. Windley, Robert R. Horger, Richard C. Mathis, Ralph W. Norman, Insiders/7.50%, James W. Roquemore, Thomas E. Suggs, Susie H. VanHuss, Dewall A. Waters *(23 Owners included in Index)*

Financial Data: ***Fiscal Year End:***12/31 ***Latest Annual Data:*** 12/31/2006

Year	Sales	Net Income
2006	$158,356,000	$19,805,000
2005	$118,148,000	$16,655,000
2004	$90,559,000	$14,016,000

Curr. Assets:	$78,406,000	**Curr. Liab.:**	$1,909,820,000	**P/E Ratio:**	16.53
Plant, Equip.:	$48,904,000	**Total Liab.:**	$2,016,525,000	**Indic. Yr. Divd.:**	NA
Total Assets:	$2,178,413,000	**Net Worth:**	$161,888,000	**Debt/ Equity:**	0.8427

Schawk Inc

1695 River Rd., Des Plaines, IL, 60018; ***PH:*** 1-847-827-9494; ***Fax:*** 1-847-827-1264; ***http://*** www.schawk.com; ***Email:*** information@schawk.com

General - Incorporation....DE | ***Stock***- Price on:12/24/2007....$19.19
Employees....3,500 | Stock Exchange....NYSE
Auditor....Ernst & Young LLP | Ticker Symbol....SGK
Stk Agt.....EquiServe Trust Co N.A | Outstanding Shares....26,770,000
Counsel....Vedder, Price, Kaufman & Kammholz | E.P.S....$1.04
DUNS No.....00-520-0662 | Shareholders....NA

Business: The group's principal activity is to provide digital imaging graphic services for the consumer products industry in North America and Asia. Digital imaging graphic arts serves consumer products packaging, advertising and promotional markets. The facilities produce conventional, electronic and desktop color separations, creative design, art production, electronic retouching, conventional and digital platemaking and digital press proofs. They are produced for the three main printing processes used in the graphic arts industry: lithography, flexography and gravure. The group operates in the United States, Canada, queretaro, Mexico, Japan, Singapore, Malaysia, China and a network of global affiliations in Australia, Europe and Asia. On 01-Jan-2004, the group acquired virtualcolor division of fort dearborn company.

Primary SIC and add'l.: 7336

CIK No: 0000719164

Subsidiaries: 9108-2859 Quebec, Inc., Anthem Design & Consulting (Shenzhen) Co. Ltd., Anthem Design Singapore Pte. Ltd., Anthem Group, Inc., Cactus Imaging Centres, Inc., Clyde Gravure Ltd., Dulip Ltd, Gallions Estates Ltd, Laserscan Technology (M)Sdn. Bhd., Miramar Equipment, Inc., Reprographic Wace Group GMBH, Riddington and Co. Ltd., Ripley and Co. Ltd, Ripley Group Ltd., Ripley Roll Lable Ltd. 51 Subsidiaries included in the Index

Officers: David A. Schawk/Dir., CEO, Pres./$1,463,840.00, Chuck Dale/Sr. VP - Global Operations, Ronald J. Vittorini/Corporate Counsel, VP - Legal Affairs, Assist. Sec., James J. Patterson/Sr. VP, CFO/$608,160.00, Alex A. Sarkisian/Dir., COO, Exec. VP/$750,932.00, Anne Marie Pagliacci/Exec. VP, Group MD - Anthem Worldwide, Jennifer Erfurth/Global VP - Human Resources

Directors: David A. Schawk/Dir., CEO, Pres., Clarence W. Schawk/Chmn., Alex A. Sarkisian/Dir., COO, Exec. VP, John T. McEnroe/54/Dir., Judith W. McCue/58/Dir., Hollis W. Rademacher/70/Dir., Leonard S. Caronia/Dir., Michael G. O'Rourke/39/Dir.

Owners: Westfield Capital Management Company, LLC, Schawk 2006 GRAT, Judith W. McCue, Cathy Ann Schawk, Marilyn G. Schawk, J.P. Morgan Chase & Co., David A. Schawk, Hollis W. Rademacher, Insiders, James J. Patterson, Myron M. Kaplan, Clarence W. Schawk, John T. McEnroe, Alex A. Sarkisian, Michael G. ORourke *(16 Owners included in Index)*

Financial Data: ***Fiscal Year End:***12/31 ***Latest Annual Data:*** 12/31/2006

Year	Sales	Net Income
2006	$548,406,000	$28,388,000
2005	$614,520,000	$30,472,000
2004	$238,345,000	$22,678,000

Curr. Assets:	$180,130,000	**Curr. Liab.:**	$90,437,000	**P/E Ratio:**	16.98
Plant, Equip.:	$82,227,000	**Total Liab.:**	$269,318,000	**Indic. Yr. Divd.:**	$0.130
Total Assets:	$538,246,000	**Net Worth:**	$268,928,000	**Debt/ Equity:**	NA

Scheid Vineyards Inc

305 Hilltown Rd., Salinas, CA, 93908; ***PH:*** 1-831-455-9990; ***Fax:*** 1-831-455-9998; ***http://*** www.scheidvineyards.com

General - Incorporation....DE | ***Stock***- Price on:12/24/2007....$35.58
Employees....150 | Stock Exchange....OTC
Auditor....Moss Adams LLP | Ticker Symbol....SVIN
Stk Agt......American Stock Transfer & Trust Co. | Outstanding Shares....1,020,000
Counsel.........Jeffer, Mangels, Butler & Marmaro | E.P.S....$4.29
DUNS No.....15-984-2913 | Shareholders....NA

Business: The group's principal activity is to produce premium varietal wine grapes on an independent basis. The group operates approximately 5,600 acres of wine grape vineyards on the central coast of California. The group currently produces 17 varieties of premium wine grapes, primarily chardonnay, cabernet sauvignon, merlot, pinot noir, sauvignon blanc and syrah. The group sells the majority of its wine grape production under long-term grape purchase contracts. On a smaller scale, the group also sells a portion of its grapes pursuant to an acreage contract whereby the winery client purchases the entire grape production from specified acreage for a set price per acre. The group converts a small portion of its grapes to premium bulk wine, which is sold pursuant to wine purchase agreements or on the bulk wine market.

Primary SIC and add'l.: 0762 2084 0172

CIK No: 0001039213

Subsidiaries: Scheid Vineyards California Inc.

Officers: Scott D. Scheid/CEO, Pres., Heidi M. Scheid/Sr. VP, Michael S. Thomsen/CFO, Kurt J. Gollnick/COO, Sr. VP

Directors: Alfred G. Scheid/Chmn., Founder, John L. Crary/Dir., Robert P. Hartzell/Dir.

Financial Data: ***Fiscal Year End:***12/31 ***Latest Annual Data:*** 12/31/2005

Year	Sales	Net Income
2005	$31,209,000	$4,407,000
2004	$23,624,000	$1,335,000
2003	$26,356,000	$3,040,000

Curr. Assets:	$19,411,000	**Curr. Liab.:**	$5,199,000	**P/E Ratio:**	8.29
Plant, Equip.:	$69,964,000	**Total Liab.:**	$47,908,000	**Indic. Yr. Divd.:**	NA
Total Assets:	$89,925,000	**Net Worth:**	$42,017,000	**Debt/ Equity:**	NA

Schering Plough Corp

2000 Galloping Hill Rd., Kenilworth, NJ, 07033; *PH:* 1-908-298-4000; *Fax:* 1-908-298-7653; *http://* www.sch-plough.com

General - Incorporation .... NJ
Employees 33,500
Auditor .... Deloitte & Touche LLP
Stk Agt .... Bank of New York
Counsel .... NA
DUNS No. 05-455-4290

Stock- Price on:12/24/2007 .... $30.56
Stock Exchange .... NYSE
Ticker Symbol .... NA
Outstanding Shares 1,490,000,000
E.P.S $1.02
Shareholders .... NA

Business: The groups principle activities include manufacturing and developing pharmaceutical and diagnostic substance. The group operates from United States.

Primary SIC and add'l.: 5912 2840 2834

CIK No: 0000310158

Subsidiaries: AESCA Pharma GmbH, Avondale Chemical Co., Ltd., Beneficiadora e Industrializadora S.A. de C.V., Brazil Holdings Ltd., DNAX Research Institute of Molecular& Cellular Biology, Inc., DNAX Research, Inc., Essex Chemie A.G, Essex Italia S.p.A., Essex Pharma GmbH, Garden Insurance Co., Ltd., Integrated Therapeutics Group, Inc., S-P Holding GmbH, Scherico, Ltd., Schering Bermuda Ltd, Schering Canada Inc. 55 Subsidiaries included in the Index

Officers: Fred Hassan/Chmn., CEO/$29,657,930.00, Stanley F. Barshay/Chmn. - Consumer Health Care, Ian McInnes/Sr. VP - Global Supply Chain, Thomas P. Koestler/Exec. VP, Pres. - Schering, Plough Research Institute/$5,497,127.00, Alex Kelly/VP - Investor Relations, Ron C. Cheeley/Sr. VP - Global Human Resources, William J. Creelman/52/VP - Tax, John B. Landis/Sr. VP - Pharmaceutical Sciences, Margriet Gabriel-Regis/Sr. VP - Specialty Care Customer Group Global Pharmaceutical Business, John M. Carroll/VP - Global Internal Audits, James S. MacDonald/Exec. VP - Preclinical Development, Michael J. Dubois/Sr. VP - Global Licensing, Strategic Alliances, Lisa W. Deberardine/VP - Strategic Planning, Financial Forecasting, Franceso Granata/Group VP - Eucan Region I, David A. Piacquad/Sr. VP - Business Development *(50 Officers included in Index)*

Directors: Fred Hassan/Chmn., CEO, Jack L. Stahl/Dir., Thomas J. Colligan/Dir., Robert C. Kidder/Dir., Hans W. Becherer/Dir., Robert F.W. Van Oordt/Dir., Arthur F. Weinbach/Dir., Antonio M. Perez/Dir., Carl E. Mundy/Dir., Patricia F. Russo/Dir., Philip Leder/Dir., Eugene R. McGrath/Dir., Kathryn C. Turner/Dir.

Owners: Capital Research and Management Company/6.70%, C. Robert Kidder, Thomas Koestler, Robert J. Bertolini, Insiders, Fred Hassan, Carl E. Mundy, Raul E. Kohan, Cecil B. Pickett, Carrie S. Cox, Arthur F. Weinbach, Robert F.W. van Oordt, Philip Leder, Patricia F. Russo, Eugene R. McGrath *(20 Owners included in Index)*

Financial Data: *Fiscal Year End:*12/31 *Latest Annual Data:* 12/31/2006

Year	Sales	Net Income
2006	$10,594,000,000	$1,143,000,000
2005	$9,508,000,000	$269,000,000
2004	$8,272,000,000	-$947,000,000

Curr. Assets:	$10,423,000,000	**Curr. Liab.:**	$4,162,000,000	**P/E Ratio:**	29.96
Plant, Equip.:	$4,365,000,000	**Total Liab.:**	$8,163,000,000	**Indic. Yr. Divd.:**	$0.260
Total Assets:	$16,071,000,000	**Net Worth:**	$7,908,000,000	**Debt/ Equity:**	0.2941

Schiff Nutrition International Inc

Formerly: Weider Nutrition International Inc
2002 S 5070 W, Salt Lake City, UT, 84104; *PH:* 1-801-975-5000; *http://* www.weider.com

General - Incorporation .... DE
Employees 382
Auditor .... Deloitte & Touche LLP
Stk Agt .... Bank of New York
Counsel .... NA
DUNS No. 95-837-6105

Stock- Price on:12/24/2007 .... $6.49
Stock Exchange .... NYSE
Ticker Symbol .... WNI
Outstanding Shares 26,640,000
E.P.S $0.42
Shareholders .... NA

Business: The group's principal activities are to develop, manufacture, market, distribute and sell branded and private label vitamins, nutritional supplements and sports nutrition products. The group is organized into three business units: the Schiff specialty unit markets a complete line of specialty supplements, vitamins, and minerals under the Schiff brand as well as private label products. The active nutrition unit develops and markets sports nutrition, nutritional bar and weight management products primarily under weider and tiger's milk brands. The Haleko unit develops, manufactures, and markets nutrition products primarily under the Multipower and Multaben brands. The group operates in the United States, Germany and South America.

Primary SIC and add'l.: 2087 5136 2834 9999

CIK No: 0001022368

Subsidiaries: Coppal Research, Inc., Haleko Management GmbH, Schiff Nutrition Group, Inc., Weider Nutrition (WNI) Limited, Weider Nutrition BV, Weider Nutrition GmbH, Weider Nutrition Italia SrL, WNG Holdings (International) Limited, Inc.

Officers: Bruce J. Wood/Dir., CEO, Pres./$1,878,307.00, Thomas H. Elitharp/Exec. VP - Operations, Support Services/$823,400.00, Daniel A. Thomson/Exec. VP - Business Development, General Counsel, Corp. Sec./$626,361.00, Joseph W. Baty/CFO, Exec. VP/$942,064.00

Directors: Bruce J. Wood/Dir., CEO, Pres., Eric Weider/Chmn., George F. Lengvari/Vice Chmn., Ronald L. Corey/Dir., Brian P. McDermott/Dir., Roger H. Kimmel/Dir., H. F. Powell/Dir.

Owners: Eric Weider/1.60%, Brian P. McDermott, Weider Health and Fitness/100.00%, Bruce J. Wood/5.10%, Roger H. Kimmel/1.40%, Insiders/14.90%, H. F. Powell/1.20%, Ronald L. Corey/1.10%, Joseph W. Baty/2.20%, GAMCO INVESTORS Inc./22.10%, Daniel A. Thomson/1.40%, Thomas H. Elitharp/1.70%

Financial Data: *Fiscal Year End:*05/31 *Latest Annual Data:* 05/31/2007

Year	Sales	Net Income
2007	$172,656,000	$12,436,000
2006	$178,372,000	$15,839,000
2005	$239,854,000	$6,569,000

Curr. Assets:	$113,828,000	**Curr. Liab.:**	$23,312,000	**P/E Ratio:**	14.11
Plant, Equip.:	$13,287,000	**Total Liab.:**	$24,108,000	**Indic. Yr. Divd.:**	NA
Total Assets:	$131,615,000	**Net Worth:**	$107,507,000	**Debt/ Equity:**	NA

Schlumberger Ltd

5599 San Felipe, Ste. 100, Houston, TX, 77056; *PH:* 1-713-513-2000; *Fax:* 1-713-513-2006; *http://* www.slb.com

General - Incorporation .... Netherlands
Employees 70,000
Auditor .... PricewaterhouseCoopers LLP
Stk Agt .... Computershare Trust Co
Counsel .... NA
DUNS No. 00-185-4546

Stock- Price on:12/24/2007 .... $85.51
Stock Exchange .... NYSE
Ticker Symbol .... SLB
Outstanding Shares 1,180,000,000
E.P.S $3.71
Shareholders .... NA

Business: The group's principal activity is to provide global oilfield and information services. It operates through three business segments. The schlumberger oilfield services segment supplies products, services and technical solutions to the oil and gas exploration and production industry. The westerngeco segment provides comprehensive worldwide reservoir imaging, monitoring, development services and multiclient seismic library. Westerngeco is 70% owned by schlumberger and 30% owned by baker hughes. The other segment comprises the axalto (cards and point-of-sale terminals), electricity meters, business continuity, infodata, telecom software products, water services, essentis and payphones activities. The group operates in over 100 countries in North America, Latin America, Europe, west Africa, cis, Middle East and Asia. In 2004, the group discontinued its schlumberger sema business, infodata business and telecom billing software business.

Primary SIC and add'l.: 8748 1382 1389 1381 8713

CIK No: 0000087347

Subsidiaries: Dowell Schlumberger Corporation, Schlumberger Antilles N.V., Schlumberger B.V., Schlumberger Canada Limited, Schlumberger Holdings Limited, Schlumberger Middle East S.A., Schlumberger Offshore Services N.V.(Limited), Schlumberger Oilfield Holdings Limited, Schlumberger Oilfield UK Plc, Schlumberger Overseas S.A., Schlumberger Plc, Schlumberger SA, Schlumberger Seaco Inc., Schlumberger Surenco S.A., Schlumberger Technology Corporation 20 Subsidiaries included in the Index

Officers: Andrew Gould/61/Chmn., CEO/$17,531,000.00, Antonio Campo/Pres. - Latin America, Jeff Spath/Pres. - Reservoir Management Group, Dalton Boutte/Pres. - Westerngeco/$3,122,761.00, Anne Devanneaux/Corporate Communications, Europe, Sami Iskander/Pres. - Drilling, Measurements, Satish Pai/Pres. - Europe, Africa/$2,914,371.00, Imran Kizilbash/Pres. - Reservoir Characterization Group, Bill Coates/Pres. - North America, Zaki Selim/Pres. - Middle East, Asia, Mario Ruscev/Pres. - Testing, Charles Woodburn/Pres. - Wireline, Belgacem Chariag/Pres. - Well Services, Patrick Schorn/Pres. - Completions, Don Sweet/Pres. - Artificial Lift *(39 Officers included in Index)*

Directors: Andrew Gould/61/Chmn., CEO, Michael E. Marks/57/Dir., Philippe Camus/59/Dir., Nikolay Kudryavtsev/57/Dir., Leo Rafael Reif/57/Dir., Didier Primat/63/Dir., Adrian Lajous/64/Dir., Tony Isaac/66/Dir., Nicolas Seydoux/68/Dir., Jamie S. Gorelick/57/Dir., Tore I. Sandvold/60/Dir., Rana Talwar/59/Dir., Linda Gillespie Stuntz/53/Dir.

Owners: Jean-Marc Perraud, Adrian Lajous, Chakib Sbiti, John Deutch, FMR Corp./7.90%, Michael E. Marks, Rana Talwar, Mark Corrigan, Insiders, Didier Primat, Satish Pai, Tony Isaac, Dalton Boutte, Linda Gillespie Stuntz, Andr Lvy-Lang *(20 Owners included in Index)*

Financial Data: *Fiscal Year End:*12/31 *Latest Annual Data:* 12/31/2006

Year	Sales	Net Income
2006	$19,230,478,000	$3,709,851,000
2005	$14,716,951,000	$2,206,967,000
2004	$11,608,863,000	$1,223,870,000

Curr. Assets:	$9,185,662,000	**Curr. Liab.:**	$6,454,795,000	**P/E Ratio:**	23.05
Plant, Equip.:	$5,576,041,000	**Total Liab.:**	$12,412,255,000	**Indic. Yr. Divd.:**	$0.700
Total Assets:	$22,832,138,000	**Net Worth:**	$10,419,883,000	**Debt/ Equity:**	0.4066

Schmitt Industries Inc

2765 NW Nicolai St., Portland, OR, 97210; *PH:* 1-503-227-7908; *Fax:* 1-503-223-1258; *http://* www.schmitt-ind.com

General - Incorporation .... OR
Employees 37
Auditor .... Grant Thornton LLP
Stk Agt .... Interwest Transfer Company, Inc.
Counsel .... NA
DUNS No. 61-775-3686

Stock- Price on:12/24/2007 .... $8.51
Stock Exchange .... NDQ
Ticker Symbol .... SMIT
Outstanding Shares 2,660,000
E.P.S $0.43
Shareholders .... NA

Business: The group's principal activities are to design, assemble, market and distribute computer-controlled balancing equipment and precision laser measurement systems. The group's activities are carried out through two segments: balancer and measurement. Balancer segment designs, assembles and markets computer-controlled balancing equipment that consists of computer control unit, sensor, spindle-mounting adapter and balanced head. Measurement segment designs, manufactures and markets precision laser measurement systems and operates a precision laser light scatter measurement laboratory. The group has operations in the United States, Canada, Mexico, Germany, United Kingdom and Asia.

Primary SIC and add'l.: 3699 3545

CIK No: 0000922612

Subsidiaries: Schmitt Europe, Ltd., Schmitt Measurement Systems, Inc.

Owners: Timothy D.J. Hennessy, Michael S. McAfee, Wayne A. Case/3.80%, Maynard E. Brown, David M. Hudson, Insiders/8.90%, Linda M. Case/3.80%, Shufro, Rose & Co. LLC/5.20%, Carlo J. Cannell/6.70%, Nicusa Capital Partners/5.50%, David W. Case/4.20%, Walter Brown Pistor/19.10%

Financial Data: *Fiscal Year End:*05/31 *Latest Annual Data:* 05/31/2007

Year	Sales	Net Income
2007	$11,882,000	$1,285,000
2006	$11,503,000	$1,350,000
2005	$10,530,000	$1,608,000

Curr. Assets:	$8,956,000	**Curr. Liab.:**	$1,106,000	**P/E Ratio:**	18.11
Plant, Equip.:	$1,209,000	**Total Liab.:**	$1,112,000	**Indic. Yr. Divd.:**	NA
Total Assets:	$10,927,000	**Net Worth:**	$9,814,000	**Debt/ Equity:**	NA

Schnitzer Steel Industries Inc

3200 NW Yeon Ave., Portland, OR, 97296; *PH:* 1-503-224-9900; *Fax:* 1-503-321-2648; *http://* www.schn.com; *Email:* ir@schn.com

General - Incorporation OR
Employees 3,252
Auditor PricewaterhouseCoopers LLP
Stk Agt Wells Fargo Bank, N.A.
Counsel Benesch Friedlander Coplan Aronoff
DUNS No. 02-775-4084

Stock- Price on:12/24/2007 $50.49
Stock Exchange NDQ
Ticker Symbol SCHN
Outstanding Shares 29,480,000
E.P.S $4.32
Shareholders NA

Business: The groups principle activity is to recycle ferrous and non-ferrous metals. The group also recycles used and salvaged vehicles and manufacture finished steel products. The group operates in three business segments namely the metals recycling business, the auto parts business, and the steel manufacturing business. The group operates from United States.

Primary SIC and add'l.: 5093 3312 5015

CIK No: 0000912603

Subsidiaries: Apache Truck Leasing, Inc., B. Rovner & Co., Inc., Cascade Steel Rolling Mills, Inc, Cherry City Metals, LLC, Crawford Street Corporation, Edman Corp., FerMar, LLC, General Metals of Alaska, Inc., General Metals of Tacoma, Inc., GLA Real Estate Holdings, LLC, GreenLeaf Auto Recyclers, LLC, H. Finkelman, Inc., Joint Venture Operations, Inc., Karileen, LLC, Levis Iron and Metal, Inc. 58 Subsidiaries included in the Index

Officers: John D. Carter/Dir., CEO, Pres., Gary A. Schnitzer/66/Exec. VP, Tom Zelenka/Contact - Environmental, Public Affairs, Gregory J. Witherspoon/62/CFO, VP, Richard D. Peach/45/VP, Deputy CFO, Chief Accounting Officer, Tamara L. Lundgren/51/COO, Exec. VP, Donald W. Hamaker/56/Pres. - Metals Recycling Business, Thomas D. Klauer/54/Pres. - Auto Parts Business, Jeffrey Dyck/45/Pres. - Steel Manufacturing Business, Richard C. Josephson/60/VP, General Counsel, Sec.

Directors: John D. Carter/Dir., CEO, Pres., Kenneth M. Novack/Chmn., Robert S. Ball/Dir., Ralph R. Shaw/Dir., Scott Lewis/Dir., Jean S. Reynolds/Dir., Jill Schnitzer Edelson/Dir., William A. Furman/Dir., Mark L. Palmquist/Dir., William D. Larsson/Dir., Judith Johansen/Dir.

Owners: Marilyn S. Easly, Insiders, M&G Investment Management Ltd./10.10%, MANUEL SCHNITZER FAMILY GROUP,, GILBERT SCHNITZER FAMILY GROUP,, Carol S. Lewis, Scott Lewis, AXA Rosenberg Investment Management LLC/5.40%, Mardi S. Schnitzer, Robert S. Ball, Marilyn S. Easly, Gregory J. Witherspoon, Dimensional Fund Advisors Inc./7.00%, Mardi S. Schnitzer, Gary Schnitzer *(40 Owners included in Index)*

Financial Data: *Fiscal Year End:*08/31 *Latest Annual Data:* 08/31/2007

Year	Sales	Net Income
2007	$2,572,265,000	$131,334,000
2006	$1,854,715,000	$143,068,000
2005	$853,078,000	$146,867,000

Curr. Assets:	$440,392,000	**Curr. Liab.:**	$151,112,000	**P/E Ratio:**	10.77
Plant, Equip.:	$312,907,000	**Total Liab.:**	$305,466,000	**Indic. Yr. Divd.:**	$0.070
Total Assets:	$1,044,698,000	**Net Worth:**	$734,099,000	**Debt/ Equity:**	0.2191

Scholastic Corp

557 Broadway, New York, NY, 10012; ***PH:*** 1-212-343-6100; ***Fax:*** 1-212-343-6934; ***http://*** www.scholastic.com; ***Email:*** investor_relations@scholastic.com

General - Incorporation DE
Employees 9,500
Auditor Ernst & Young LLP
Stk Agt Mellon Investor Services LLC
Counsel Coudert Brothers
DUNS No. 00-150-3580

Stock- Price on:12/24/2007 $35.6
Stock Exchange NDQ
Ticker Symbol SCHL
Outstanding Shares 42,860,000
E.P.S $2.54
Shareholders NA

Business: The groups principle activity is to publish books for children. The group also operates school-based book clubs and book fairs, and school-based and direct-to-home continuity programs. The group operates through four segments namely children's book publishing and distribution, educational publishing, media, licensing and advertising, and international. The group operates from United States.

Primary SIC and add'l.: 2731 2721 2741 7812

CIK No: 0000866729

Subsidiaries: 524 Films LLC, Bookshelf Publishing Australia Pty. Ltd., BTBCAT, Inc., Caribe Grolier, Inc., Catteshall Ltd.(50% owned), Chicken House Publishing Ltd., Children's Music Library, Inc., Federated Credit Corp., Georgetown Studios, Inc., Grolier (Malaysia) SDN BHD, Grolier (New York) Incorporated, Grolier Credit Services (U.K.) Limited, Grolier Direct Marketing Pty. Ltd., Grolier Incorporated, Grolier Interactive Inc. 72 Subsidiaries included in the Index

Officers: Richard Robinson/Chmn., CEO, Pres./$1,730,684.00, Margery W. Mayer/Exec. VP, Pres. - Scholastic Education/$816,921.00, Judith A. Newman/Exec. VP, Pres. - Book Clubs, Lisa Holton/Exec. VP, Pres. - Book Fairs, Trade/$789,779.00, Karen Proctor/VP - Community Affairs, Government Relations, Maureen OConnell/Exec. VP, Chief Administrative Officer, CFO/$362,946.00, Cynthia Augustine/Sr. VP - Human Resources, Employee Services, Devereux Chatillon/Sr. VP, General Counsel, Sec., Seth D. Radwell/Exec. VP, Pres. - e, Scholastic, Beth Ford/Sr. VP - Global Operations, Information Technology, Richard M. Spaulding/Dir., Exec. VP - Strategic Marketing, Heather J. Myers/Sr. VP - Strategic Planning, Business Development, Alan Boyko/Pres. - Book Fairs, Greg Worrell/Pres. - Scholastic Classroom, Library Group, Francie Alexander/Sr. VP - Scholastic Education, Chief Academic Officer *(19 Officers included in Index)*

Directors: Richard Robinson/Chmn., CEO, Pres., Ramon C. Cortines/Dir., James W. Barge/53/Dir., Augustus Oliver/Dir., Peter M. Mayer/Dir., John G. McDonald/Dir., Richard M. Spaulding/Dir., Exec. VP - Strategic Marketing, Rebeca M. Barrera/Dir., Andrew S. Hedden/Dir., John L. Davies/Dir., Mae Jemison/Dir.

Owners: Scholastic Corporation/6.30%, Mary Sue Robinson Morrill/8.70%, Barbara Robinson Buckland, Barbara Robinson Buckland/6.70%, Florence L. Robinson/1.30%, Scholastic Corporation, William W. Robinson, Dimensional Fund Advisors LP/6.50%, William W. Robinson/6.90%, Florence L. Robinson, T. Rowe Price Associates, Inc./8.60%, Mary Sue Robinson Morrill, Richard Robinson, Richard Robinson/17.30%

Financial Data: *Fiscal Year End:*05/31 *Latest Annual Data:* 05/31/2007

Year	Sales	Net Income
2007	$2,179,100,000	$60,900,000
2006	$2,283,800,000	$68,600,000
2005	$2,079,900,000	$64,300,000

Curr. Assets:	$1,078,900,000	**Curr. Liab.:**	$689,000,000	**P/E Ratio:**	25.07
Plant, Equip.:	$397,000,000	**Total Liab.:**	$1,002,900,000	**Indic. Yr. Divd.:**	NA
Total Assets:	$2,052,200,000	**Net Worth:**	$1,049,300,000	**Debt/ Equity:**	0.3412

School Specialty Inc

W6316 Design Dr., Greenville, WI, 54942; ***PH:*** 1-920-734-5712; ***Fax:*** 1-920-882-5863; ***http://*** www.schoolspecialty.com

General - Incorporation WI
Employees 2,800
Auditor Deloitte & Touche LLP
Stk Agt American Stock Transfer & Trust Co.
Counsel Godfrey & Kahn
DUNS No. 00-614-4026

Stock- Price on:12/24/2007 $35.79
Stock Exchange NDQ
Ticker Symbol SCHS
Outstanding Shares NA
E.P.S $1.33
Shareholders NA

Business: The group's principal activity is marketing of supplemental educational supplies to schools and teachers for pre-kindergarten through twelfth grade. The group operates through two segments: traditional and specialty. Traditional segment consists of consumables (classroom supplies, instructional materials, educational games, art supplies and school forms), school furniture and indoor and outdoor equipment. The specialty segment offers product lines for specific educational disciplines, such as art, industrial arts, physical education, sciences, and early childhood. This segment also supplies student academic planners. Specialty businesses include the following brands such as childcraft, classroomdirect, sax arts and crafts, frey scientific, sportime,teacher's video and brodhead garrett.

Primary SIC and add'l.: 5712 7375 5943

CIK No: 0001055454

Subsidiaries: Amalgamated Widgets, Inc., Bird-in-Hand Woodworks, Inc., Califone International, Inc., Childcraft Education Corp., ClassroomDirect.com, LLC, Delta Education, LLC, Frey Scientific, Inc., Global Video, LLC, New School, Inc., Premier Agendas, Inc., Premier School Agendas, Ltd., Select Agendas, Corp., Sportime, LLC

Officers: David J. Vander Zanden/Dir., CEO, Pres./$775,665.00, Ronald E. Suchodolski/Exec. VP - Childcraft Education Corp, Joseph Elliott/Exec. VP - School Specialty Science, Paul Deal/Exec. VP - Supply Chain, Rachel P. McKinney/Chief Human Resources Officer, Exec. VP, Terrell Anderson/Exec. VP - School Specialty Publishing, Richmond Holden/Exec. VP - Educators Publishing Service, Kevin L. Bachler/VP, Interim CFO, Peter S. Savitz/Exec. VP - Sportime, Roger Smith/Exec. VP - Classroom Direct, Herman Nell/CIO, Exec. VP, Stephen Korte/Exec. VP - School Specialty Publishing/$519,678.00, Greg Cessna/Exec. VP - Essentials/$600,048.00, John Thoreson/Exec. VP - Sax Arts - Crafts, David Rust/Exec. VP - School Specialty Visual Media *(20 Officers included in Index)*

Directors: David J. Vander Zanden/Dir., CEO, Pres., Terry L. Lay/Chmn., Edward Emma/Dir., Jonathan J. Ledecky/Dir., Jacqueline F. Woods/Dir., Jacqueline A. Dout/Dir., Herbert L. Trucksess/Dir.

Owners: Dimensional Fund Advisors LP/6.10%, David J. Vander Zanden/2.10%, David G. Gomach, Terry L. Lay, Jonathan J. Ledecky/4.30%, Cramer Rosenthal McGlynn, LLC/6.70%, Mary M. Kabacinski, T. Rowe Price Associates, Inc./6.60%, Steven F. Korte, MSD Capital, L.P./13.20%, Insiders/6.90%, Herbert A. Trucksess, Gregory D. Cessna, Edward C. Emma, EARNEST Partners, LLC/12.10%

Financial Data: *Fiscal Year End:*04/29 *Latest Annual Data:* 04/28/2007

Year	Sales	Net Income
2007	$1,043,152,000	$18,046,000
2006	$1,015,729,000	$61,000
2005	$1,002,507,000	$43,001,000

Curr. Assets:	$249,470,000	**Curr. Liab.:**	$134,957,000	**P/E Ratio:**	36.90
Plant, Equip.:	$73,264,000	**Total Liab.:**	$340,060,000	**Indic. Yr. Divd.:**	NA
Total Assets:	$884,605,000	**Net Worth:**	$544,545,000	**Debt/ Equity:**	NA

Schweitzer Mauduit International Inc

100 N Point Ctr. E, Ste. 600, Alpharetta, GA, 30022; ***PH:*** 1-770-569-4271; ***Fax:*** 1-770-569-4209; ***http://*** www.schweitzer-mauduit.com; ***Email:*** investors@swm-us.com

General - Incorporation DE
Employees 3,541
Auditor Deloitte & Touche LLP
Stk Agt American Registrar & Transfer Co
Counsel NA
DUNS No. 92-978-5616

Stock- Price on:12/24/2007 $31.77
Stock Exchange NYSE
Ticker Symbol SWM
Outstanding Shares 15,710,000
E.P.S -$0.23
Shareholders NA

Business: The group's principal activity is to produce specialty papers and supply fine papers to the tobacco industry. The activities of the group are broadly classified into two segments: tobacco products and non-tobacco products. The tobacco products segment includes cigarette, plug wrap and tipping papers used to wrap various parts of a cigarette, reconstituted tobacco leaf for use as filler in cigarettes, reconstituted tobacco wrappers and binders for cigars and paper products used in cigarette packaging. The non-tobacco products segment includes lightweight printing and writing papers, coated papers for packaging and labeling applications, business forms, furniture laminates, battery separator paper, drinking straw wrap, filter papers and other specialized papers. The group has operations in north and South America, western and eastern Europe and Asia. On 12-Feb-2004, the group, through its subsidiary, acquired p.t. Kimsari paper Indonesia.

Primary SIC and add'l.: 2621 2679

CIK No: 0001000623

Subsidiaries: LTR Industries S.A., Luna Rio Landholding Corporation, Malaucne Industries S.N.C., P.t. Pdm Indonesia, Papèteries de Malaucne S.A.S, Papeteries de Mauduit S.A.S, Papeteries de Saint-Girons S.A.S., PDM Industries S.N.C., PDM Philippines Industries, Inc., Saint-Girons Industries S.N.C., Schweitzer-Mauduit Canada, Inc., Schweitzer-Mauduit do Brasil, S.A., Schweitzer-Mauduit France S.A.R.L., Schweitzer-Mauduit Holding S.A.R.L., Schweitzer-Mauduit Industries S.A.R.L. 17 Subsidiaries included in the Index

Officers: Wayne H. Deitrich/Chmn., CEO, Clifford J. Bienert/VP - US Operations, William R. Foust/VP - Administration, Wayne L. Grunewald/Controller, Otto R. Herbst/Pres. - Americas, Widjaja Jiemy/Pres. - Southeast Asian Operations, Paul C. Roberts/VP - Strategic Planning, Implementation, John W. Rumely/General Counsel, Sec., Peter J. Thompson/CFO, Treasurer, Frederic Villoutreix/Dir., COO, Michel Fievez/Pres. - European Operations

Directors: Wayne H. Deitrich/Chmn., CEO, Laurent G. Chambaz/60/Dir., Claire L. Arnold/61/Dir., K. C. Caldabaugh/61/Dir., Manuel J. Iraola/60/Dir., Richard D. Jackson/71/Dir., Leonard J. Kujawa/Dir., Larry B. Stillman/66/Dir., Frederic Villoutreix/Dir., COO, Robert F. McCullough/Dir.

Owners: Laurent G. Chambaz, Dimensional Fund Advisors LP/7.12%, Insiders/5.60%, Barclays Global Investors Japan/5.42%, Otto R. Herbst, Wayne H. Deitrich/3.05%, Pzena Investment Management, LLC/8.04%, Thomas A. Russo/11.10%, Paul C. Roberts, Robert F. McCullough, Larry B. Stillman, Gardner Russo/11.60%, Manuel J. Iraola, Claire L. Arnold, Widjaja Jiemy *(21 Owners included in Index)*

Financial Data: *Fiscal Year End:*12/31 *Latest Annual Data:* 12/31/2006

Year	Sales	Net Income
2006	$655,200,000	-$800,000
2005	$669,800,000	$19,400,000
2004	$657,500,000	$36,400,000

Curr. Assets:	$235,600,000	**Curr. Liab.:**	$166,500,000		
Plant, Equip.:	$416,800,000	**Total Liab.:**	$377,000,000	**Indic. Yr. Divd.:**	$0.600
Total Assets:	$696,600,000	**Net Worth:**	$304,000,000	**Debt/ Equity:**	0.2736

SCI Engineered Materials Inc

Formerly: Superconductive Components Inc
2839 Charter St., Columbus, OH, 43228; ***PH:*** 1-614-486-0261;
http:// www.superconductivecomp.com

General - Incorporation	OH	**Stock**- Price on:12/24/2007	$7
Employees	21	Stock Exchange	OTC
Auditor	Hausser + Taylor LLC	Ticker Symbol	SCCI
Stk Agt	NA	Outstanding Shares	3,470,000
Counsel	Porter Wright Morris & Arthur LLP	E.P.S	$0.12
DUNS No.	NA	Shareholders	NA

Business: The group's principal activities are to develop, manufacture and market products incorporating high temperature superconductive (hts) materials. . The operations are carried out through two divisions: the sci division and the tmi division. The tmi division manufactures and markets source materials, both ceramics and metals, for the thin film vacuum deposition industry. The sci division produces and markets various high temperature superconductive products, which include both superconducting and non-superconducting products. The group's catalogue lists 208 products. The group also has an operating Website www.sciengineeredmaterials.com in 2003. The group sold its product to 363 customers in 2003.

Primary SIC and add'l.: 3253

CIK No: 0000830616

Officers: Daniel Rooney/Chmn., CEO, Pres./$232,487.00, Gerald S. Blaskie/CFO, VP, Mike Barna/VP - Sales/$209,904.00, Scott Campbell/VP - Technology/$135,362.00

Directors: Daniel Rooney/Chmn., CEO, Pres., Robert H. Peitz/Dir., Walter J. Doyle/Dir., Edward W. Ungar/Dir., Robert J. Baker/Dir.

Owners: Berlin Capital Growth L.P., Laura Shunk, Robert H. Peitz, Daniel Funk, Scott Campbell, Ingeborg Funk Childrens Trust, Insiders, Mid South Investor Fund L.P., Thomas G. Berlin, Lake Street Fund L.P., Curtis A. Loveland, Robert J. Baker, Windcom Investments SA, Edward W. Ungar, Walter J. Doyle *(17 Owners included in Index)*

Financial Data: ***Fiscal Year End:***12/31 ***Latest Annual Data:*** 12/31/2006

Year	Sales	Net Income
2006	$8,046,000	$302,000
2005	$3,457,000	-$333,000
2004	$2,173,000	-$1,100,000

Curr. Assets:	$1,902,000	**Curr. Liab.:**	$677,000	**P/E Ratio:**	58.33
Plant, Equip.:	$1,104,000	**Total Liab.:**	$822,000	**Indic. Yr. Divd.:**	NA
Total Assets:	$3,327,000	**Net Worth:**	$2,504,000	**Debt/ Equity:**	0.0726

Sciclone Pharmaceuticals Inc

950 Tower Ln., Ste. 900, Foster City, CA, 94404; ***PH:*** 1-650-358-3456; ***Fax:*** 1-650-358-3469;
http:// www.sciclone.com; ***Email:*** investorrelations@sciclone.com

General - Incorporation	DE	**Stock**- Price on:12/24/2007	$2.5
Employees	166	Stock Exchange	NDQ
Auditor	Ernst & Young LLP	Ticker Symbol	SCLN
Stk Agt	Mellon Investor Services LLC	Outstanding Shares	46,090,000
Counsel	Gray, Cary, Ware & Freidenrich	E.P.S	-$0.17
DUNS No.	78-593-9141	Shareholders	NA

Business: The group's principal activity is to develop and commercialize therapeutics for the treatment of life-threatening diseases. The group's lead product, zadaxin, is in two phase 3 hepatitis c clinical trials in the United States, a phase 3 hepatitis b clinical trial in Japan, a phase 2 malignant melanoma clinical trial in Europe and two phase 2 liver cancer trials in the United States. Zadaxin has been approved for sale in over 30 countries and is currently marketed in China and selected countries in Asia, Latin America and the Middle East. The group's other drug development opportunities include scv-07, an orally available therapy to treat viral and infectious diseases, as well as products to address the protein-based disorder that causes cystic fibrosis.

Primary SIC and add'l.: 2834

CIK No: 0000880771

Subsidiaries: Sciclone Do Brasil Produtos Farmaceuticos Ltda, Sciclone Japan K.k., Sciclone Pharmaceuticals International Holding Ltd, Sciclone Pharmaceuticals International Limited, Sciclone Pharmaceuticals Italy Srl

Officers: Friedhelm Blobel/Dir., CEO, Pres./$1,998,132.00, Randy J. McBeath/VP - Marketing, Israel Rios/Chief Medical Officer, Sriram Vemuri/Sr. VP - Product Development, Manufacturing, Hans P. Schmid/MD - Sciclone Pharmaceuticals International, Ltd/$456,096.00, Cynthia W. Tuthill/Sr. VP - Scientific Affairs, Chief Scientific Officer, Richard A. Waldron/CFO, Exec. VP/$496,541.00

Directors: Friedhelm Blobel/Dir., CEO, Pres., John D. Baxter/Dir., Chmn., Sciclone's Scientific Advisory Board, Dean S. Woodman/Chmn., Rolf H. Henel/Dir., Jon S. Saxe/Dir., Jules Dienstag/Member - Hepatitis Advisory Board, Ira D. Lawrence/Dir., Richard J. Hawkins/Dir., Michael Karin/Member - Hepatitis Advisory Board, Willis Maddrey/Member - Hepatitis Advisory Board, John McHutchison/Member - Hepatitis Advisory Board, Eugene Schiff/Member - Hepatitis Advisory Board, Teresa L. Wright/Member - Hepatitis Advisory Board

Owners: Sigma-Tau and Affiliates/19.30%, Richard A. Waldron/1.30%, Hans P. Schmid, Rolf H. Henel, Insiders/5.50%, Richard J. Hawkins, Alfred R. Rudolph, John D. Baxter/1.20%, Jon S. Saxe, Ira D. Lawrence, Dean S. Woodman

Financial Data: ***Fiscal Year End:***12/31 ***Latest Annual Data:*** 12/31/2006

Year	Sales	Net Income
2006	$32,662,000	$727,000
2005	$28,334,000	-$7,713,000
2004	$24,396,000	-$13,278,000

Curr. Assets:	$60,741,000	**Curr. Liab.:**	$7,882,000		
Plant, Equip.:	$297,000	**Total Liab.:**	$7,950,000	**Indic. Yr. Divd.:**	NA
Total Assets:	$62,584,000	**Net Worth:**	$54,634,000	**Debt/ Equity:**	NA

Sciele Pharma Inc

Formerly: First Horizon Pharmaceutical Corp
Five Concourse Pkwy., Ste. 1800, Atalanta, GA, 30328; ***PH:*** 1-678-341-1436;
http:// www.horizonpharm.com

General - Incorporation	DE	**Stock**- Price on:12/24/2007	$23.75
Employees	782	Stock Exchange	NA
Auditor	BDO Seidman LLP	Ticker Symbol	NA
Stk Agt	LaSalle Bank N.A	Outstanding Shares	35,260,000
Counsel	Arnall Golden Gregory	E.P.S	$1.42
DUNS No.	NA	Shareholders	NA

Business: The group's principal activity is to market brand name prescription drugs. The group intends to develop new patentable formulations, use new delivery methods and seek regulatory approval for new indications of existing drugs. The main products of the group include nisoldipine, nitrolingual pumpspray, prenate advance and prenate gt, ponstel, furadantin, tanafed dp and tanafed dmx, robinul and robinul forte. The group sells its products to cardiologists, obstetricians and gynecologists, pediatricians, gastroenterologists and primary care physicians. The products of the group are sold under the tradenames mescolor, protuss, zoto-hc (and an associated design), defen, zebutal, prenate gt and furadantin.

Primary SIC and add'l.: 5122

CIK No: 0001106773

Subsidiaries: First Horizon Pharmaceutical (Cyprus) Limited, First Horizon Pharmaceutical Cayman Limited, First Horizon Pharmaceutical Ireland Limited

Officers: Patrick P. Fourteau/Dir., CEO, Pres./$3,392,398.00, Joseph T. Schepers/Primary Investor Relations Officer, Leslie Zacks/Exec. VP - Legal, Compliance/$645,286.00, Darrell Borne/Exec. VP, CFO, Sec., Treasurer/$1,572,144.00, Edward Schutter/Exec. VP, Chief Commercial Officer/$466,490.00, Larry M. Dillaha/Chief Medical Officer, Exec. VP/$363,140.00

Directors: Patrick P. Fourteau/Dir., CEO, Pres., Pierre Lapalme/Chmn., Jerry N. Ellis/Dir., William J. Robinson/Dir., Jon S. Saxe/Dir., Patrick J. Zenner/Dir., Jerry C. Griffin/Dir.

Owners: Jerry N. Ellis, William J. Robinson, JPMorgan Chase & Co/6.30%, Pierre Lapalme, Paradigm Capital Management, Inc./5.30%, Darrell Borne, John N. Kapoor/6.80%, Insiders/4.10%, Patrick J. Zenner, Ed Schutter, Larry Dillaha, Jerry C. Griffin, Jon S. Saxe, Leslie Zacks, Patrick P. Fourteau/2.30% *(17 Owners included in Index)*

Financial Data: ***Fiscal Year End:***12/31 ***Latest Annual Data:*** 12/31/2006

Year	Sales	Net Income
2006	$293,181,000	$45,244,000
2005	$216,358,000	$39,209,000
2004	$151,967,000	$26,554,000

Curr. Assets:	$269,067,000	**Curr. Liab.:**	$37,839,000	**P/E Ratio:**	17.59
Plant, Equip.:	$9,142,000	**Total Liab.:**	$202,182,000	**Indic. Yr. Divd.:**	NA
Total Assets:	$590,005,000	**Net Worth:**	$387,823,000	**Debt/ Equity:**	0.3709

Science Applications International Corp

10260 Campus Point Dr., San Diego, CA, 92121; ***PH:*** 1-858-826-6000; ***http://*** www.saic.com

General - Incorporation	DE	**Stock**- Price on:12/24/2007	NA
Employees	NA	Stock Exchange	NA
Auditor	Houlihan Lokey Howard	Ticker Symbol	NA
Stk Agt	Mellon Investor Services LLC	Outstanding Shares	NA
Counsel	Douglas E. Scott	E.P.S	NA
DUNS No.	05-478-1240	Shareholders	NA

Business: The group's principal activities are to provide professional and technical services. These services involve the application of scientific expertise to provide solutions to complex technical problems for government and commercial customers. The group's operating segments are regulated, non-regulated telecommunications and non-regulated other. Regulated segment provides technical services and products through contractual arrangements either as a prime contractor or subcontractor, primarily for departments and agencies of the U.S. Government. Non-regulated telecommunications and the non-regulated other segments provide technical services and products primarily to customers in commercial markets. On 19-Dec-2003, the group acquired exploranium g.s. Limited, on 25-Jul-2003, opta limited and on 09-Aug-2004, trios associates, inc.

Primary SIC and add'l.: 8731 8711

CIK No: 0000353394

Subsidiaries: AMSEC Corporation, AMSEC LLC, AMSEC Subsidiary Holding Corp., ANXeBusiness Corp., AOT Holding Corp., Bull, Inc., Campus Point Realty Corporation, e-Banc Holding Corp., Eagan, McAllister Associates, Inc., EAI Corporation, Energy& Environmental Solutions, LLC, Hicks& Associates, Inc., InQuirion Pty Limited, JMD Development Corporation, Machinexpert Holding Corp. 37 Subsidiaries included in the Index

Officers: Ken C. Dahlberg/Chmn., CEO, Mark W. Sopp/CFO, Exec. VP, Douglas E. Scott/Sr. VP, General Counsel, Sec., Larry J. Peck/Exec. VP - Homeland Security, Donald H. Foley/Dir., Exec. VP, Chief Engineering, Technology Officer, Arnold Punaro/Exec. VP - Government Affairs, Communications, Support Operations GM - Washington Operations, Joseph P. Walkush/Exec. VP - Strategic Initiatives, Grant L. Clark/Sr. VP, Dir. - Contracts, Chief Deputy Counsel, Greg Henson/Sr. VP, Dir. - Business Development, Brian F. Keenan/Exec. VP - Human Resources, Joseph W. Craver/Pres. - Infrastructure, Logistics, Product Solutions Group, Deborah H. Alderson/Pres. - Defense Solutions Group, Lawrence B. Prior/Pres. - Intelligence, Security Group, Theoren P. Smith/CTO, Exec. VP, Charles F. Koontz/Pres. - Information Technology, Network Solutions Group

Directors: Ken C. Dahlberg/Chmn., CEO, W. H. Demisch/Dir., Jere A. Drummond/Dir., John J. Hamre/Dir., A. K. Jones/Dir., H.M. J. Kraemer/Dir., E. J. Sanderson/Dir., Louis A. Simpson/Dir., A. T. Young/Dir., Donald H. Foley/Dir., Exec. VP, Chief Engineering, Technology Officer, Robert J. Beyster/Founder, J. P. Jumper/Dir., M. E. John/Dir.

Scientific Energy Inc

731 Lexington Ave., 25th Fl, New York, NJ, 10022; ***PH:*** 1-212-559-2011

General - Incorporation	UT	**Stock**- Price on:12/24/2007	NA
Employees	NA	Stock Exchange	OTC
Auditor	Child, Van Wagoner & Bradshaw, PLLC	Ticker Symbol	SCGY
Stk Agt	Interstate Transfer Company	Outstanding Shares	NA
Counsel	NA	E.P.S	NA
DUNS No.	NA	Shareholders	NA

Business: The group proposes to develop and manufacture various energy generation devices and energy efficient mechanisms for use in existing portable electronic devices, including portable laptop computers, handheld devices, cellular phones, and other electronic devices. In addition, it is developing technology that would assist industrial concerns and consumers in various applications to reduce energy consumption. The company is based in Salt Lake City, Utah.

Primary SIC and add'l.: 6794

CIK No: 0001276531

Officers: Stanley Chan/54/Chmn., CEO, CFO, Pres.

Directors: Stanley Chan/54/Chmn., CEO, CFO, Pres.

Owners: Insiders/48.60%, Stanley Chan/48.60%

Financial Data: Fiscal Year End:12/31 Latest Annual Data: 12/31/2006

Year	Sales	Net Income
2006	NA	-$36,000
2005	NA	-$44,000

Curr. Assets:	$369,000	Curr. Liab.:	$0		
Plant, Equip.:	$1,000	Total Liab.:	$0	Indic. Yr. Divd.:	NA
Total Assets:	$371,000	Net Worth:	$371,000	Debt/ Equity:	NA

Scientific Games Corp

750 Lexington Ave., 25th Fl., New York, NY, 10022; *PH:* 1-212-754-2233; *Fax:* 1-212-754-2372; *http://* www.scientificgames.com

General - Incorporation	DE	Stock- Price on:12/24/2007	$35.02
Employees	5,500	Stock Exchange	NDQ
Auditor	Deloitte & Touche LLP	Ticker Symbol	SGMS
Stk Agt	American Stock Transfer & Trust Co.	Outstanding Shares	92,540,000
Counsel	NA	E.P.S.	$0.75
DUNS No.	80-673-0115	Shareholders	NA

Business: The group's principal activities are to supply instant tickets, systems and services to lotteries and supply of wagering systems and services to pari-mutuel operators. It operates under four-business groups: lottery group, pari-mutuel group, venue management group and telecom products group. Lottery group provides integrated lottery service, on-line lottery systems, instant tickets and related facilities management, cooperative services and programs to lottery authorities. Pari-mutuel group provides systems and services to horse and greyhound racetracks, off-track betting operations, casinos, jai alai frontons. Venue management group is licensed operator for all pari-mutuels wagering in the Netherlands. Telecom products manufactures prepaid phone cards. During the year 2003, the group acquired mdi entertainment, inc.

Primary SIC and add'l.: 4812 7376 7948 7999 7993

CIK No: 0000750004

Subsidiaries: Autotote Canada Inc., Autotote Dominicana Inc., Autotote Enterprises, Inc., Autotote Europe GmbH, Autotote Gaming, Inc., Autotote Interactive, Inc., Autotote Panama, Inc., BlitzlosLtd., Honsel Printpool GmbH, Knightway Promotions Limited, MDI Entertainment, LLC, NASRIN Services LLC, Scientific Connections India Private Limited, Scientific Connections Limited, Scientific Connections SDN BHD 53 Subsidiaries included in the Index

Officers: Lorne A. Weil/Chmn., CEO/$6,533,126.00, Michael R. Chambrello/COO, Pres./$3,344,135.00, William J. Huntley/VP, Pres. Sports - Gaming Technology, Dewayne E. Laird/60/CFO, VP/$1,833,095.00, Ira H. Raphaelson/54/VP, General Counsel, Sec./$1,778,896.00, Steven M. Saferin/59/VP, Pres. - Properties, Robert C. Becker/49/VP, Treasurer, Sally L. Conkright/55/VP - Administration, Chief Human Resources Officer, Larry A. Potts/VP, Chief Compliance Officer, Dir. - Security, Stephen L. Gibbs/VP, Chief Accounting Officer, James Metcalfe/VP - Tax, Steve W. Beason/CTO, VP, Pres. - Lottery Systems Group, David Pye/VP - Corporate Development, Brooks Pierce/VP, Pres. Racing, Edward Furey/Press Contact

Directors: Lorne A. Weil/Chmn., CEO, Joseph R. Wright/Dir., Gerald J. Ford/Dir., Michael J. Regan/Dir., Eric M. Turner/Dir., Barry F. Schwartz/Dir., Ronald O. Perelman/Dir., Peter A. Cohen/Dir.

Owners: Lorne A. Weil/2.50%, Gerald J. Ford, RS Investment Management Co. LLC/6.95%, Barry F. Schwartz, DeWayne E. Laird, Ira H. Raphaelson, Eric M. Turner, Insiders/31.76%, Martin E. Schloss, Ronald O. Perelman/28.06%, Brian G. Wolfson, Howard Gittis, Michael J. Regan, Joseph R. Wright, Michael R. Chambrello *(17 Owners included in Index)*

Financial Data: Fiscal Year End:12/31 Latest Annual Data: 12/31/2006

Year	Sales	Net Income
2006	$897,230,000	$66,761,000
2005	$781,683,000	$75,319,000
2004	$725,495,000	$65,742,000

Curr. Assets:	$344,702,000	Curr. Liab.:	$194,023,000	P/E Ratio:	46.69
Plant, Equip.:	$450,660,000	Total Liab.:	$1,231,532,000	Indic. Yr. Divd.:	NA
Total Assets:	$1,759,610,000	Net Worth:	$528,078,000	Debt/ Equity:	1.7293

Scientific Industries Inc

70 Orville Dr., Bohemia, NY, 11716; *PH:* 1-631-567-4700; *http://* www.scientificindustries.com; *Email:* info@scientificindustries.com

General - Incorporation	DE	Stock- Price on:12/24/2007	$3.25
Employees	17	Stock Exchange	OTC
Auditor	Nussbaum Yates & Wolpow, P.C	Ticker Symbol	SCND
Stk Agt	Continental Stock Transfer & Trust Co	Outstanding Shares	1,130,000
Counsel	NA	E.P.S.	$0.20
DUNS No.	00-121-1119	Shareholders	NA

Business: The group's principal activities are to manufacture and market laboratory equipment. The laboratory equipment consists of vortex mixer, the vortex-genie 2 and related accessories. The customers include hospital and research laboratories, clinics, pharmaceutical manufacturers, medical device manufacturers and other related industries. The products are distributed and marketed through a network of domestic and foreign laboratory equipment dealers. The group also markets its products through attendance of trade shows, advertising in trade publications, brochures and catalogs, and its Website. The latest products manufactured include the roto-shake genie (registered trademark), a multi-purpose rotator/rocker; and the enviro-genie (trademark), a multi-functional benchtop refrigerated incubator.

Primary SIC and add'l.: 3821

CIK No: 0000087802

Officers: Helena R. Santos/44/CEO, Pres., Treasurer, Robert P. Nichols/47/Exec. VP, Sec.

Directors: Joseph G. Cremonese/72/Chmn., Arthur M. Borden/88/Dir., James S. Segasture/72/Dir., Joseph I. Kesselman/83/Dir., Roger B. Knowles/83/Dir., Grace S. Morin/60/Dir.

Owners: Joseph I. Kesselman/5.50%, James S. Segasture/16.30%, Grace S. Morin/9.90%, Lowell A. Kleiman/12.20%, Arthur M. Borden/5.20%

Financial Data: Fiscal Year End:06/30 Latest Annual Data: 6/30/2006

Year	Sales	Net Income
2006	$3,465,000	$322,000
2005	$3,593,000	$305,000
2004	$3,533,000	$249,000

Curr. Assets:	$3,234,000	Curr. Liab.:	$773,000	P/E Ratio:	16.25
Plant, Equip.:	$247,000	Total Liab.:	$781,000	Indic. Yr. Divd.:	$0.070
Total Assets:	$4,137,000	Net Worth:	$3,356,000	Debt/ Equity:	NA

Scientific Learning Corp

300 Frank H. Ogawa Plz., Ste. 600, Oakland, CA, 94612; *PH:* 1-510-444-3500; *Fax:* 1-510-444-3580; *http://* www.scientificlearning.com; *Email:* customerservice@scilearn.com

General - Incorporation	DE	Stock- Price on:12/24/2007	$6.58
Employees	195	Stock Exchange	NDQ
Auditor	Ernst & Young LLP	Ticker Symbol	SCIL
Stk Agt	Continental Stock Transfer & Trust Co	Outstanding Shares	17,080,000
Counsel	Cooley Godward LLP	E.P.S.	$0.03
DUNS No.	93-910-6852	Shareholders	NA

Business: The group's principle activity is to develop and market proprietary training software and other educational products and services. It offers training programs that build the language and reading skills that are the foundation for learning. The company has designed a product 'fast forword', which is designed to help children, adolescents and adults with language comprehension. The company's products include fast forword, slc lesson, reword, progresstracker, reading edge and crosstrain. The company provides services through brainconnection.com, which offers an interactive Web site, conferences for educators and online professional development. Its products are delivered through a variety of distribution channels, including sales to public schools, speech and language professionals in private practice and direct-to-consumer channels. The group's quarterly revenue for September 2007 was 11.35 millions of USD.

Primary SIC and add'l.: 8299 7371

CIK No: 0001042173

Officers: Robert C. Bowen/Chmn., CEO/$475,869.00, Sherrelle Jiggitts Walker/Chief Education Officer, Glenn G. Chapin/VP - K, 12 Sales/$340,703.00, Steven L. Miller/Sr. VP - Research, Linda L. Carloni/VP, General Counsel, Corp. Sec./$274,685.00, Jane A. Freeman/Sr. VP, CFO/$335,105.00, William M. Jenkins/Sr. VP - Product Development/$277,918.00, James R. Bray/VP - Business Development, Government Affairs, Mary Anne Petrillo/Dir. - Marketing, Jessica J. Lindl/VP - Marketing, Gillian M. McCormack/VP - Operations, John Hopkins/Sales Assistance, Public Schools in Canada, Shelley Weisbrich/Sales Assistance, Private, Independent Schools in The US, Canada, Martha Burns/Sales Assistance, Professionals in Private Practice in The US, Canada

Directors: Robert C. Bowen/Chmn., CEO, Michael A. Moses/Vice Chmn., David W. Smith/Dir., Lance R. Odden/Dir., Carleton A. Holstrom/Dir., Michael M. Merzenich/Dir., Joseph Boyd Martin/Dir., Paula A. Tallal/Dir., Edward Vermont Blanchard/Dir., Rodman W. Moorhead/Dir., Ajit M. Dalvi/Dir.

Owners: William M. Jenkins/1.20%, Trigran Investments, Inc./10.50%, Glenn G. Chapin, David W. Smith, Warburg, Pincus Ventures, LP/49.20%, Carleton A. Holstrom/1.90%, Edward Vermont Blanchard/1.20%, Ajit M. Dalvi, Insiders/65.10%, Paula A. Tallal/3.60%, Joseph B. Martin, Linda L. Carloni, Jane A. Freeman/1.50%, Michael M. Merzenich/2.90%, Robert C. Bowen/6.30%

Financial Data: Fiscal Year End:12/31 Latest Annual Data: 12/31/2006

Year	Sales	Net Income
2006	$40,998,000	$208,000
2005	$40,319,000	$5,597,000
2004	$30,976,000	-$693,000

Curr. Assets:	$24,433,000	Curr. Liab.:	$20,482,000		
Plant, Equip.:	$941,000	Total Liab.:	$25,266,000	Indic. Yr. Divd.:	NA
Total Assets:	$26,283,000	Net Worth:	$1,017,000	Debt/ Equity:	NA

Scientific Technologies Inc

6550 Dumbarton Cir., Fremont, CA, 94555; *PH:* 1-510-471-9717; *http://* www.sti.com

General - Incorporation	OR	Stock- Price on:12/24/2007	$10.68
Employees	NA	Stock Exchange	NDQ
Auditor	BDO Seidman LLP	Ticker Symbol	STIZ
Stk Agt	Mellon Investor Services LLC	Outstanding Shares	NA
Counsel	Wilson Sonsini Goodrich & Rosati	E.P.S.	NA
DUNS No.	05-461-3583	Shareholders	NA

Business: The group's principal activities are to design, manufacture and distribute electrical and electronic industrial controls such as machine safety and automation sensing products. The group's product lines include safety light curtains, safety interlock switches, safety relays, profiling scanners, factory automation sensors, controls, fiber optics, power monitoring, non-contract ultrasonic sensors and controllers. The group's products are supplied to industrial automation, commercial and defense customers. The group operates through two business segments: safety products and automation products. Safety products consist of optical guarding products used to safeguard personnel in manufacturing environments against injury caused by robots and moving machinery. Automation products include photoelectric and fiber optic sensors used for detecting objects in factory automation applications.

Primary SIC and add'l.: 3679 3699

CIK No: 0000708250

Subsidiaries: Applied Electro Technology International, Dunn Sales Incorporated, Lundahl Instruments, Inc, PSI-Tronix Technologies Incorporated, STI Scientific Technologies GmbH

Scientific-Atlanta Inc

5030 Sugarloaf Pk.way, Lawrenceville, GA, 30044; *PH:* 1-770-903-5000; *http://* www.sciatl.com

General - Incorporation	GA	Stock- Price on:12/24/2007	$27.05
Employees	49,926	Stock Exchange	NA
Auditor	Ernst & Young LLP	Ticker Symbol	NA
Stk Agt	Computershare Investor Services LLC	Outstanding Shares	6,070,000,000
Counsel	NA	E.P.S.	$1.17
DUNS No.	00-326-5022	Shareholders	NA

Business: The group's principal activity is to provide broadband transmission networks, digital interactive subscriber systems, content distribution networks and worldwide customer service and support for the cable television industry. It produces a wide variety of products for the cable television industry which comprised of digital interactive set-tops, high-speed cable modems, integrated computer systems and software, rf electronics and optical communications products. Scientific-atlanta, the scientific-atlanta logo, explorer, powervu, prisma, gainmaker and continuum are the registered trademarks of the group. The operations of the group are conducted in juarez, Mexico, kortrijk and Belgium. The customers of the group include aol time warner inc, cablevision systems, comcast corporation, charter communications inc, cox communications inc, adelphia communications corporation and their subsidiaries.

Primary SIC and add'l.: 3663

CIK No: 0000087777

Subsidiaries: Sammex, L.p., Scientific-Atlanta Financial Enterprises

Officers: James F. McDonald/CEO, Lawrence J. Bradner/Sr. VP, Pres. - Scicare Broadband Services, Luis Avila/VP - Corporate Strategic Planning, Dean Rockwell/VP, GM - Digital Media Networks, John A. Buckett/VP - Corporate Development, Robert C. McIntyre/CTO, Sr. VP, Allen H. Ecker/Exec. VP, Brian C. Koenig/60/Sr. VP - Human Resources, George Stromeyer/VP, MD, Dwight B. Duke/Corporate Sr. VP, David B. Davies/VP - Strategy, Product Marketing Subscriber Networks, Mark Palazzo/VP, GM - Access Networks, Bill Katherman/VP, MD - Asia Pacific Region, Patrick M. Tylka/57/Sr. VP, Pres. - Worldwide Sales, Michael Harney/Sr. VP, Pres. - Subscriber Networks *(17 Officers included in Index)*

Financial Data: **Fiscal Year End:**07/01 **Latest Annual Data:** 7/29/2006

Year	Sales	Net Income
2006	$28,484,000,000	$5,580,000,000
2005	$24,801,000,000	$5,741,000,000
2004	$22,045,000,000	$4,401,000,000

Curr. Assets:	$14,343,000,000	**Curr. Liab.:**	$8,703,000,000	**P/E Ratio:**	23.12
Plant, Equip.:	$3,290,000,000	**Total Liab.:**	$9,678,000,000	**Indic. Yr. Divd.:**	NA
Total Assets:	$35,594,000,000	**Net Worth:**	$25,826,000,000	**Debt/ Equity:**	0.2271

Scion-Cardiovascular Inc

14256 SW 119th Ave., Miami, FL, 33186; *PH:* 1-305-259-8880; *http://* www.scioncv.com

General - Incorporation	FL	**Stock**- Price on:12/24/2007	NA
Employees	NA	Stock Exchange	NA
Auditor	Berenfeld Spritzer Shechter & Sheer	Ticker Symbol	NA
Stk Agt	NA	Outstanding Shares	NA
Counsel	Wu & Kao PLLC	E.P.S.	NA
DUNS No.	NA	Shareholders	NA

Business: The group's principle activity is to develop and manufacture patented and patent pending devices designed to facilitate minimally invasive surgical procedures in interventional cardiology and radiology. The group's devices are designed to make these procedures easier for the doctor to perform, and safer for the patient, by reducing required time in the operating room, speeding up the recovery time, and assisting in eliminating debris that could cause complications. The company is a latter-stage medical device business with a creative corporate culture that encourages its employees to explore product innovations that are intended to improve patient outcomes. Sci-Pro, Clo-Sur P.A.D., Sci-Pro.

Primary SIC and add'l.: 3841

CIK No: 0001328782

Officers: Lorraine O'Toole/Contact - Training Schedule or Organize a Training Seminar

SCM Microsystems Inc

41740 Christy St., Fremont, CA, 94538; *PH:* 1-510-360-2300; *Fax:* 1-510-360-0211; *http://* www.scmmicro.com; *Email:* scmsales@scmmicro.com

General - Incorporation	DE	**Stock**- Price on:12/24/2007	$3.6
Employees	156	Stock Exchange	NDQ
Auditor	Deloitte & Touche LLP	Ticker Symbol	NA
Stk Agt	American Stock Transfer & Trust Co.	Outstanding Shares	15,730,000
Counsel	Wilson Sonsini Goodrich & Rosati	E.P.S.	$0.31
DUNS No.	85-966-6471	Shareholders	NA

Business: The group's principal activities are to design, develop and market hardware, software and silicon solutions that enable users to conveniently and securely access digital content and services that have been protected through digital encryptions. The group operates through three segments: digital TV, PC security and flash media interface. Digital TV offers conditional access modules that provide secure, removable decryption for digital pay-TV broadcasts. Pc security offers smart card reader technology that enables secure access to pcs, networks and physical facilities. Flash media interface provides digital media readers and asics that are used to transfer digital content to and from various flash media. The group sells products to digital TV operators, conditional access providers, government contractors, systems integrators, large enterprises, computer manufacturers, smart card readers, photographic equipment manufacturers and banks and other financial institutions.

Primary SIC and add'l.: 7372 3679

CIK No: 0001036044

Subsidiaries: ARC Development Corporation, ARC Dry Creek, Inc., ARC Financial Services Corporation, ARC Kentucky, LLC, ARC New Hartford, Inc., ARC of Bellingham, L.P., ARC of Georgia, LLC, ARC Worcester Center, L.P.

Officers: Robert Schneider/Dir., CEO/$760,135.00, Felix Marx/Dir., CEO, Annika Oelsner/Contact - Media, Europe, Asia, Manfred Mueller/VP - Sales, Stephan Rohaly/CFO, Sec./$305,245.00, Darby Dye/Contact - Investor Relations, US

Directors: Robert Schneider/Dir., CEO, Felix Marx/Dir., CEO, Werner Karl Koepf/Chmn., Hagen Hultzsch/Dir., Manuel Cubero/45/Dir., Ng Poh Chuan/Dir., Steven Humphreys/Dir., Simon Turner/Dir.

Owners: Werner Koepf, Manuel Cubero, Steven Humphreys, Manfred Mueller, Hagen Hultzsch, Stephan Rohaly, Royce& Associates, LLC/10.00%, Insiders/7.10%, Dimensional FundAdvisors, Inc./7.40%, Simon Turner, Robert Schneider/5.00%

Financial Data: **Fiscal Year End:**12/31 **Latest Annual Data:** 12/31/2006

Year	Sales	Net Income
2006	$33,613,000	$1,042,000
2005	$48,721,000	-$12,435,000
2004	$49,084,000	-$18,663,000

Curr. Assets:	$47,901,000	**Curr. Liab.:**	$15,934,000	**P/E Ratio:**	11.61
Plant, Equip.:	$1,457,000	**Total Liab.:**	$16,037,000	**Indic. Yr. Divd.:**	NA
Total Assets:	$51,355,000	**Net Worth:**	$35,318,000	**Debt/ Equity:**	0.0044

Scopus Video Networks Ltd

3 Independence Way, 1st Fl., Princeton, NJ, 08540; *PH:* 1-609-987-8090; *Fax:* 1-609-987-8095; *http://* www.scopus.net; *Email:* info@scopus.net

General - Incorporation	Israel	**Stock**- Price on:12/24/2007	$4.71
Employees	250	Stock Exchange	NDQ
Auditor	Brightman Almagor & Co.	Ticker Symbol	SCOP
Stk Agt	Bank of New York	Outstanding Shares	13,450,000
Counsel	Gross, Kleinhendler	E.P.S.	-$0.25
DUNS No.	NA	Shareholders	NA

Business: The groups principle activities include developing, marketing and supporting digital video networking products. The products of the group include intelligent video gateways, encoders, decoders and network management. The group operates from North and South America, Asia and the Pacific and, Europe, the Middle East and Africa. The group's quarterly revenue for September 2007 was 15.18 millions of USD.

Primary SIC and add'l.: 3661 3663

CIK No: 0001342575

Subsidiaries: Scopus Video Networks Inc.

Officers: Yaron Simler/Dir., CEO, Eitan Koter/Pres., Moshe Eisenberg/CFO, Ovadia Cohen/VP - Business Development, Marketing Communications, Moshe Rousso/VP - Research & Development, Ronit Kalujny/VP - Operations, Sharon Witzrabin/VP - Human Resources, Ehud Helft/Investor Contact, Kenny Green/Investor Contact, Zeev Gelbart/Investor Contact, Shlomo Arbiv/VP - Finance, Shimon Shanor/VP - Sales

Directors: Yaron Simler/Dir., CEO, David Mahlab/Chmn., Yoel Gat/Dir., Jackie Goren/Dir., Michael Anghel/Dir., Louis Silver/Dir., Izhak Tamir/Dir., Orit Leitman/Dir.

Owners: Vertex Israel II/8.20%, S Squared Technology/5.40%, David Mahlab/4.70%, Optibase Ltd./22.60%, Insiders/10.80%, Kern Capital Management, LLC/9.10%, Pitango Venture Capital Fund III/12.40%, Yoel Gat/3.60%, Yaron Simler/1.70%, Genesis Partners II/6.50%, AWM Investment Company Inc./8.30%

Financial Data: **Fiscal Year End:**12/31 **Latest Annual Data:** 12/31/2006

Year	Sales	Net Income
2006	$47,272,000	-$3,792,000
2005	$44,791,000	-$3,850,000
2004	$35,051,000	-$2,941,000

Curr. Assets:	$52,960,000	**Curr. Liab.:**	$12,984,000		
Plant, Equip.:	$2,928,000	**Total Liab.:**	$14,645,000	**Indic. Yr. Divd.:**	NA
Total Assets:	$56,164,000	**Net Worth:**	$41,519,000	**Debt/ Equity:**	NA

Scor

1, Avenue Du General De Gaulle, La Defense Cedex, Paris, 92074; *PH:* 33 1 46 98 7000 ; *Fax:* 33-4767-0409; *http://* www.hbfuller.com; *Email:* scor@scor.com

General - Incorporation	France	**Stock**- Price on:12/24/2007	NA
Employees	994	Stock Exchange	OTC
Auditor	Ernst & Young LLP	Ticker Symbol	SCRYY
Stk Agt	Bank of New York	Outstanding Shares	NA
Counsel	NA	E.P.S.	NA
DUNS No.	38-181-3229	Shareholders	NA

Business: The groups principle activity is to provide provision of insurance and reinsurance. The group also provides credit, surety and political risks; large industrial risks; alternative reinsurance including securitisation and coverage of derivative risks. The group operates from United States.

Primary SIC and add'l.: 6321 6331 6311 6722

CIK No: 0001023027

Subsidiaries: Commercial Risk Partners Ltd., IRP Holdings Limited, SCOR (UK)Group Ltd., SCOR Canada Reinsurance Company, SCOR Deutschland Rckversicherungs-Actien-Gesellschaft, SCOR Financial Services Limited, SCOR Italia Riassicurazioni S.p.A., SCOR Life US Re Insurance Company, SCOR Reinsurance Asia Pacific Pte. Ltd., SCOR Reinsurance Company, Scor U.s. Corp., SCOR VIE

Officers: Gilles Meyer/50/Deputy CEO - Scor Global Life, Dir. - Business Unit 1, Scor Global Life, Uwe Eymer/66/CEO - Scor Global Life, Benjamin Gentsch/48/Deputy CEO - DE, Scor Global P&C, CEO - DE, Scor Switzerland, Victor Peignet/50/CEO - Scor Global P, C, Henry Klecan/Pres., CEO - Canada, Denis Kessler/55/Chmn., CEO - Scor SE, France, Yves Corcos/CEO - United States, Alessandra Zorza/Mgr. - Italy, Annie Laforet/Dir., Exec. VP - Belgium, Scor Services Belux, Andre Smet/Assist. VP, Marketing Dir. - Belgium, Yvan Besnard/Deputy MD - France, Godefroy De Colombe/Dir. - Public Affairs, Miguel Alferieff/MD - Spain, Jean-Luc Besson/62/Chief Risk Officer, Patrick Thourot/59/COO - Scor SE *(71 Officers included in Index)*

Directors: Denis Kessler/55/Chmn., CEO - Scor SE, France, Herbert Schimetschek/69/Dir., Allan Chapin/66/Dir., Carlo Acutis/69/Dir., Claude Tendil/62/Dir., Jean Simonnet/71/Dir., Andre Levy-Lang/70/Dir., Daniel Havis/52/Dir., Antonio Borges/58/Dir., Luc Rouge/56/Dir., Helman Le Pas De Secheval/42/Dir., Daniel Valot/63/Dir., Georges Chodron De Courcel/57/Dir.

Financial Data: **Fiscal Year End:**12/31 **Latest Annual Data:** 12/31/2005

Year	Sales	Net Income
2005	$2,944,418,000	$195,426,000
2004	$3,480,584,000	$337,007,000
2003	$4,722,688,000	-$724,539,000

Curr. Assets:	$5,160,430,000	**Curr. Liab.:**	$561,405,000		
Plant, Equip.:	$97,121,000	**Total Liab.:**	$14,363,219,000	**Indic. Yr. Divd.:**	NA
Total Assets:	$16,379,068,000	**Net Worth:**	$2,015,849,000	**Debt/ Equity:**	NA

Scor Holding (Switzerland) Ltd

Formerly: Converium Holding

General Guisan-quai 26, Zrich, CH-8002; ; *http://* www.converium.com

General - Incorporation	Switzerland	**Stock**- Price on:12/24/2007	$9.05
Employees	514	Stock Exchange	NYSE
Auditor	PricewaterhouseCoopers Ltd	Ticker Symbol	CHR
Stk Agt	Bank of New York	Outstanding Shares	293,010,000
Counsel	Christian Felderer	E.P.S.	NA
DUNS No.	NA	Shareholders	NA

Business: The group's principal activity is the provision of all major types of reinsurance services, such as property and casualty, general accident, health and life as well as financial. The group also offers catastrophe-excessive-of-loss reinsurance. In addition the company offers "Non Traditional" products to help customers manage capital and risk.

Primary SIC and add'l.: 6321 6399 6331 6311

CIK No: 0001162586

Subsidiaries: Converium AG, Converium Finance (Bermuda) Ltd, Converium Finance S.A., Converium Holding (UK)Ltd, Converium Holdings (North America) Inc., Converium Insurance (North America) Inc., Converium Insurance (UK)Ltd, Converium IP Management Ltd, Converium London Management Ltd, Converium Reinsurance (North America) Inc., Converium Rckversicherung (Deutschland) AG, Converium Underwriting Ltd

Officers: Inga Beale/45/CEO, Christoph Ludemann/52/Head - Life, Health Reinsurance, Paolo De Martin/39/CFO, Markus Krall/Chief Risk Officer, Sylvie VanViet/47/Head - Strategy, Development, Christopher Wing/40/CFO, Jakob Eugster/56/Head - Standard Property, Casualty Reinsurance, Frank Schaar/Head - Standard Property, Casualty Reinsurance, Andreas Zdrenyk/49/COO, Christian Felderer/54/General Counsel - Operations, Terry G. Clarke/63/MD, Dir., Benjamin Gentsch/48/Head - Specialty Lines

Directors: Rudolf Kellenberger/63/Vice Chmn., Markus Dennler/52/Chmn., Lennart Blecher/53/Dir., Detlev Bremkamp/Dir., Harald Wiedmann/63/Dir., Denis Kessler/56/Dir., Jean-Luc Besson/60/Dir., Victor Peignet/50/Dir., Gilles Meyer/50/Dir., Georges Chodron De Courcel/58/Dir., Jurg Marty/64/Dir., Friedrich J. Sauerlander/66/Dir., Derrell J. Hendrix/55/Dir.

Scores Holding Co Inc

533-535 W 27th St., New York, NY, 10001; *PH:* 1-212-868-4900; *Fax:* 1-212-868-4414; *http://* www.scoresholdings.com

General - Incorporation	UT	**Stock**- Price on:12/24/2007	$0.011
Employees	4	Stock Exchange	OTC
Auditor	Sherb & Co. LLP	Ticker Symbol	SCRH
Stk Agt	Atlas Stock Transfer Corp	Outstanding Shares	165,190,000
Counsel	NA	E.P.S	-$0.019
DUNS No.	NA	Shareholders	NA

Business: The group's principal activity is to operate an adult entertainment nightclub in newyork. The group was a full service Internet company which was closed in Mar 2002. The nightclub is scheduled to open in the third quarter of 2003.

Primary SIC and add'l.: 5813

CIK No: 0000831489

Subsidiaries: Sunrise Web Development, Inc., West Entertainment Inc.

Officers: Curtis R. Smith/39/CFO - Principal Executive, Financial Officer, Elda Auerbach/44/Sec.

Owners: Richard K. Goldring/46.10%, Elliot Osher/8.80%, William Osher/8.80%, Insiders/54.90%

Financial Data: *Fiscal Year End:*12/31 *Latest Annual Data:* 12/31/2006

Year	Sales	Net Income
2006	$1,976,000	-$2,664,000
2005	$1,569,000	$319,000
2004	$1,339,000	-$112,000

Curr. Assets:	$395,000	**Curr. Liab.:**	$238,000		
Plant, Equip.:	NA	**Total Liab.:**	$258,000	**Indic. Yr. Divd.:**	NA
Total Assets:	$675,000	**Net Worth:**	$417,000	**Debt/ Equity:**	NA

Scott's Liquid Gold Inc

4880 Havana St., Denver, CO, 80239; *PH:* 1-303-373-4860; *Fax:* 1-303-576-6151; *http://* www.scottsliquidgold.com

General - Incorporation	CO	**Stock**- Price on:12/24/2007	$0.89
Employees	88	Stock Exchange	OTC
Auditor	Ehrhardt Keefe Steiner & Hottman P.C	Ticker Symbol	SLGD
Stk Agt	Wells Fargo Shareowner Services	Outstanding Shares	10,530,000
Counsel	NA	E.P.S	-$0.24
DUNS No.	00-707-2176	Shareholders	NA

Business: The group's principal activity is to manufacture and market household and skin care products. It operates in two segments: household products and skin care products. The group's household products consist of scott's liquid gold(R) for wood, a wood preservative and cleaner and touch of scent (R), an aerosol room air freshener. The group's skin care products are sold primarily under the name alpha hydrox (r). It also manufactures injection-molded components consisting of plastic caps for touch of scent and scott's liquid gold and dispensers for touch of scent.

Primary SIC and add'l.: 2842 2844

CIK No: 0000088000

Subsidiaries: Advertising Promotions Incorporated, Colorado Product Concepts, Inc., Neoteric Cosmetics, Inc., SLG Chemicals, Inc., SLG Plastics, Inc.

Officers: Mark E. Goldstein/Chmn., CEO, Pres./$435,513.00, Jeffry B. Johnson/Dir., CFO, Treasurer/$202,038.00, Brian L. Boberick/Controller, Jeffrey R. Hinkle/Dir., VP - Marketing, Sales/$232,473.00, Dennis P. Passantino/Dir., VP - Operations, Corp. Sec./$197,410.00

Directors: Mark E. Goldstein/Chmn., CEO, Pres., Jeffry B. Johnson/Dir., CFO, Treasurer, Jeffrey R. Hinkle/Dir., VP - Marketing, Sales, Dennis P. Passantino/Dir., VP - Operations, Corp. Sec., Carl A. Bellini/Dir., Dennis H. Field/Dir., Gerald J. Laber/Dir.

Owners: Scotts Liquid Gold-Inc./11.40%, Jeffry B. Johnson/2.20%, Mark E. Goldstein/26.10%, Dennis H. Field/0.70%, Gerald J. Laber/0.90%, Carl A. Bellini/0.90%, Dennis P. Passantino/2.10%, Yorktown Avenue Capital, LLC/13.60%, Insiders/33.40%, Jeffrey R. Hinkle/3.30%

Financial Data: *Fiscal Year End:*12/31 *Latest Annual Data:* 12/31/2006

Year	Sales	Net Income
2006	$16,144,000	-$3,587,000
2005	$24,139,000	-$198,000
2004	$22,647,000	-$903,000

Curr. Assets:	$7,107,000	**Curr. Liab.:**	$3,369,000		
Plant, Equip.:	$13,160,000	**Total Liab.:**	$8,245,000	**Indic. Yr. Divd.:**	NA
Total Assets:	$20,327,000	**Net Worth:**	$12,083,000	**Debt/ Equity:**	NA

Scottish Re Group Ltd

13840 Ballantyne Corporate Pl., Ste. 500, Charlotte, NC, 28277; *PH:* 1-704-542-9192; *Fax:* 1-704-542-5744; *http://* www.scottishannuity.com; *Email:* info@scottishre.com

General - Incorporation	Cayman Islands	**Stock**- Price on:12/24/2007	$5.04
Employees	399	Stock Exchange	NYSE
Auditor	Ernst & Young LLP	Ticker Symbol	SCT
Stk Agt	Computershare Investor Services LLC	Outstanding Shares	68,000,000
Counsel	NA	E.P.S	-$6.11
DUNS No.	NA	Shareholders	NA

Business: The group's principle activity is to reinsure life insurance, annuities and annuity-type products. The activities of the group are carried out through three segments: life reinsurance, wealth management and other. The life reinsurance segment underwrites life insurance, annuities and annuity-type products through life insurance companies and other financial institutions located in the United States as well as worldwide. The wealth management division writes variable life insurance and variable annuity products for high net worth individuals and families. The other division comprises of revenues and expenses not related to life reinsurance or wealth management segments. The group has operations in Bermuda, the Cayman Islands, Ireland, the United Kingdom and the United States. During 2003, the group discontinued its wealth management division in Luxembourg. The group's quarterly revenue for Sep '07 was 500.04 millions of USD.

Primary SIC and add'l.: 6311

CIK No: 0001064122

Subsidiaries: Orkney Holdings, LLC, Orkney Re, Inc., Scottish Annuity & Life Holdings (Bermuda) Limited, Scottish Annuity & Life Insurance Company (Bermuda) Limited, Scottish Annuity & Life Insurance Company (Cayman) Ltd., Scottish Annuity & Life International Insurance Company(Bermuda) Ltd., Scottish Financial (Luxembourg) S.a.r.l., Scottish Holdings (Barbados) Ltd., Scottish Holdings, Inc., Scottish Re (Dublin) Limited, Scottish Re (U.S.), Inc., Scottish Re Capital Markets, Inc., Scottish Re Group Limited, Scottish Re Holdings Limited, Scottish Re Life (Bermuda) Limited 25 Subsidiaries included in the Index

Officers: Clifford J. Wagner/Pres., CEO - Scottish Holdings, Inc/$688,111.00, George Zippel/Dir., CEO, Pres., David R. Howell/CEO - Scottish Re Holdings Limited/$822,203.00, Andrew Linfoot/Dir. - Asia, Scottish Annuity, Life Insurance Company Ltd, Joan M. Paulter/VP - Treaties, Scottish Re, US, Inc, Andre Hermans/Sr. Mgr. - Underwriting, Claims Services, Scottish Annuity, Life Insurance Company Ltd, Manic Lefebvre/Sr. Mgr. - Actuarial Services, Scottish Annuity, Life Insurance Company Ltd, Paul Goldean/Chief Administrative Officer/$702,751.00, Thomas A. McAvity/Exec. VP, Chief Investment Strategist, Jolene Loh/Sr. Mgr. - Business Development, Scottish Annuity, Life Insurance Company Ltd, Warren Copp/Chief Underwriter Scottish Re International Business, Duncan Hayward/CFO - Scottish Re ltd, David Heeney/Chief Marketing Officer UK - Ireland, Scottish Re ltd, Alex King/Head - Protection Marketing, Scottish Re ltd, George Scott/Legal Counsel - Scottish Re ltd *(34 Officers included in Index)*

Directors: George Zippel/Dir., CEO, Pres., Michael C. French/Chmn., Bill Caulfield-Browne/Vice Chmn., Oscar R. Scofield/Chmn. - Scottish Re, US, Inc, Jeffrey P. Hughes/Dir., Michael Austin/Dir., Glenn S. Schafer/Dir., Lenard B. Tessler/Dir., Larry Port/Dir., Michael Rollings/Dir., William G. Caulfeild-Browne/Dir., Jean-Claude Damerval/Dir., Norman Lamont/Dir., Hazel Rollins O'Leary/Dir., Robert M. Chmely/Dir. *(22 Directors included in Index)*

Owners: Dean Miller, Clifford Wagner, Paul Goldean, Jeffrey Hughes, Insiders, Investor Group/68.70%, David Howell, Robert Joyal, Hugh McCormick, CMBP II (Cayman) Ltd./13.60%

Financial Data: *Fiscal Year End:*12/31 *Latest Annual Data:* 12/31/2006

Year	Sales	Net Income
2006	$2,451,500,000	-$366,714,000
2005	$2,297,329,000	$130,197,000
2004	$811,817,000	$71,391,000

Curr. Assets:	$1,716,791,000	**Curr. Liab.:**	$167,612,000		
Plant, Equip.:	NA	**Total Liab.:**	$12,370,970,000	**Indic. Yr. Divd.:**	NA
Total Assets:	$13,436,072,000	**Net Worth:**	$1,057,192,000	**Debt/ Equity:**	3.4787

Scotts Miracle-Gro Co

Formerly: Scotts Co

14111 Scottslawn Rd., Marysville, OH, 43041; *PH:* 1-937-644-0011; *http://* www.scotts.com

General - Incorporation	OH	**Stock**- Price on:12/24/2007	$44.42
Employees	5,720	Stock Exchange	NYSE
Auditor	Deloitte & Touche LLP	Ticker Symbol	SMG
Stk Agt	National City Bank	Outstanding Shares	63,570,000
Counsel	NA	E.P.S	$1.64
DUNS No.	04-184-3434	Shareholders	NA

Business: The groups principle activity is to supply fertilizers and grass seed. Customers served by the group include home improvement centers, mass merchandisers, warehouse clubs and large hardware chains. The group operates from United States.

Primary SIC and add'l.: 2873 3524 2874 6719

CIK No: 0000825542

Subsidiaries: ASEF BV, Corwen Home and Garden Limited, EG Systems, Inc., Hyponex Corporation, Levington Group Ltd., Miracle-Gro Lawn Products, Inc., OM Scott International Investments Ltd., OMS Investments, Inc., Rod McLellan Company, Sanford Scientific, Inc., Scotts Australia Pty Ltd., Scotts Benelux BVBA, Scotts Canada Ltd., Scotts Celaflor GmbH & Co. KG, Scotts Celaflor HGmbH 53 Subsidiaries included in the Index

Officers: James Hagedorn/Chmn., CEO, Denise S. Stump/Exec. VP - Global Human Resources, Dave Evans/CFO, Exec. VP, Barry W. Sanders/Exec. VP - Global Technologies, Operations, Rich Martinez/Chief Environmental Officer

Directors: James Hagedorn/Chmn., CEO, Mark R. Baker/Dir., Gordon F. Brunner/Dir., Arnold W. Donald/Dir., Joseph P. Flannery/Dir., Katherine Hagedorn Littlefield/Dir., Thomas N. Kelly/Dir., Karen G. Mills/Dir., Patrick J. Norton/Dir., Stephanie M. Shern/Dir., John S. Shiely/Dir., Nancy G. Mistretta/Dir.

Owners: Insiders, Karen G. Mills, Arnold W. Donald, EARNEST Partners, LLC, Gordon F. Brunner, David M. Aronowitz, Thomas N. Kelly, Hagedorn Partnership, L.P., Patrick J. Norton, John S. Shiely, Morgan Stanley and affiliated institutional, Barry W. Sanders, Christopher L. Nagel, Joseph P. Flannery, David C. Evans *(21 Owners included in Index)*

Financial Data: *Fiscal Year End:*09/30 *Latest Annual Data:* 9/30/2006

Year	Sales	Net Income
2006	$2,697,100,000	$132,700,000
2005	$2,369,300,000	$100,600,000
2004	$2,096,100,000	$100,900,000

Curr. Assets:	$942,000,000	**Curr. Liab.:**	$496,200,000	**P/E Ratio:**	27.09
Plant, Equip.:	$367,600,000	**Total Liab.:**	$1,135,900,000	**Indic. Yr. Divd.:**	$0.500
Total Assets:	$2,217,600,000	**Net Worth:**	$1,081,700,000	**Debt/ Equity:**	4.7577

Scout Exploration Inc

3550 Quesnel Dr., Vancouver, BC, V6L 2W6; *PH:* 1-604-738-9442;
http:// www.scoutexploration.com

General - Incorporation	NV	Stock- Price on:12/24/2007	$0.59
Employees	NA	Stock Exchange	OTC
Auditor	MacKay LLP	Ticker Symbol	SCXN
Stk Agt	NA	Outstanding Shares	NA
Counsel	NA	E.P.S.	NA
DUNS No.	NA	Shareholders	NA

Business: The groups principal activities include conducting mineral exploration activities on the property in order to assess whether it does possess economic reserves of gold, silver and other ores. The group operates from the United States.

Primary SIC and add'l.: 1000

CIK No: 0001371474

Officers: Kathleen Scalzo/Dir., Pres., Treasurer, CEO, Principal Accounting Officer, Jason Walsh/Sec.

Directors: Kathleen Scalzo/Dir., Pres., Treasurer, CEO, Principal Accounting Officer, Shane Ivancoe/Dir.

Owners: Kassel Enterprises Inc./11.00%, Insiders/18.60%, Kathleen Scalzo/5.10%, Heath Ellingham/2.70%, Celltech Professional Services/3.40%, Mark Hague/2.70%, D.A. Huston and Assoc./4.10%, 667981 BC Ltd./2.70%, Jason Walsh/2.50%, Iscis Holdings Ltd/9.30%, Shane Ivancoe/11.00%, Jim Pettit/2.70%

*Financial Data: Fiscal Year End:*09/30 *Latest Annual Data:* 9/30/2006

Year	Sales	Net Income
2006	NA	-$85,000

Curr. Assets:	$31,000	Curr. Liab.:	$29,000		
Plant, Equip.:	NA	Total Liab.:	$29,000	Indic. Yr. Divd.:	NA
Total Assets:	$31,000	Net Worth:	$2,000	Debt/ Equity:	NA

Scpie Holdings Inc

1888 Century Pk. E., Ste. 800, Los Angeles, CA, 90067; *PH:* 1-310-551-5900; *Fax:* 1-310-551-5928; *http://* www.scpie.com; *Email:* investor@scpie.com

General - Incorporation	DE	Stock- Price on:12/24/2007	$25.5
Employees	120	Stock Exchange	NYSE
Auditor	Ernst & Young LLP	Ticker Symbol	SKP
Stk Agt	Mellon Investor Services LLC	Outstanding Shares	9,570,000
Counsel	Latham & Watkins	E.P.S.	$1.61
DUNS No.	07-492-5926	Shareholders	NA

Business: The group's principal activity is to provide medical malpractice insurance and related liability insurance products to physicians, healthcare facilities and other healthcare industry. The group's insurance business is organized into two segments: direct healthcare liability insurance and assumed reinsurance operations. Direct healthcare liability insurance represents professional liability insurance for physicians, oral and maxillofacial surgeons, hospitals and other healthcare providers. Assumed reinsurance represents the book of assumed worldwide reinsurance of professional, commercial and personal liability coverage, commercial and residential property risks, accident and health coverage and marine coverage.

Primary SIC and add'l.: 6351

CIK No: 0001013609

Subsidiaries: American Healthcare Indemnity Company, American Healthcare Specialty Insurance Company, Lloyds of London, SCPIE Indemnity Company, SCPIE Insurance Services, Inc, SCPIE Underwriting Limited

Officers: Donald J. Zuk/Dir., CEO, Pres./$1,054,477.00, Howard Bender/VP - Communications

Directors: Donald J. Zuk/Dir., CEO, Pres., Mitchell S. Karlan/Chmn., Henry L. Stoutz/Dir., William A. Renert/Dir., Wendell L. Moseley/Dir., Ronald H. Wender/Dir., Jack E. McCleary/Dir., Willis T. King/Dir., Kaj Ahlmann/Dir., Marshall S. Geller/Dir., Joseph D. Stilwell/46/Dir.

Owners: Wendell L. Moseley, The Stilwell Group/9.85%, SuNOVA, L.P./5.24%, Joseph P. Henkes/1.11%, Dimensional Fund Advisors LP/6.37%, Insiders/9.38%, Jack E. McCleary, Henry L. Stoutz, William A. Renert, Mitchell S. Karlan, Robert B. Tschudy/1.07%, Donald J. Zuk/2.78%, Ronald H. Wender, Barclays Global Investors, LTD/6.02%, Ronald L. Goldberg *(17 Owners included in Index)*

*Financial Data: Fiscal Year End:*12/31 *Latest Annual Data:* 12/31/2006

Year	Sales	Net Income
2006	$143,909,000	$12,280,000
2005	$151,455,000	$3,468,000
2004	$157,322,000	-$7,886,000

Curr. Assets:	$227,165,000	Curr. Liab.:	NA		
Plant, Equip.:	$1,733,000	Total Liab.:	$478,865,000	Indic. Yr. Divd.:	NA
Total Assets:	$685,509,000	Net Worth:	$206,644,000	Debt/ Equity:	NA

Scrap China Corp

175 E 400 S, Ste 900, Salt Lake City, UT, 84111; ; *http://* www.scrapchina.com

General - Incorporation	UT	Stock- Price on:12/24/2007	NA
Employees	NA	Stock Exchange	NA
Auditor	Hansen, Barnett & Maxwell	Ticker Symbol	NA
Stk Agt	Atlas Stock Transfer Corp	Outstanding Shares	NA
Counsel	NA	E.P.S.	NA
DUNS No.	NA	Shareholders	NA

Business: The group is in the process of setting up a base of operations in China to obtain all necessary permits and licenses required to import scrap materials into China. The Company will then formulate its business plan and project finance requirements. The seed capital has been provided by the parent company, RecycleNet Corporation. The group operates from United States.

Primary SIC and add'l.: 5090

CIK No: 0001336388

Officers: Paul Roszel/Chmn., CEO, Pres., Richard R. Ivanovick/CFO

Directors: Paul Roszel/Chmn., CEO, Pres., Keith A. Deck/Dir.

Owners: Paul Roszel/3.46%, Richard R. Ivanovick/5.32%, Inter-Continental/50.04%, Keith A. Deck/1.05%

SE Financial Corp PA

1901 E Passyunk Ave. 3, Philadelphia, PA, 19148; *PH:* 1-215-468-1700; *http://* www.stedmondsfsb.com

General - Incorporation	PA	Stock- Price on:12/24/2007	NA
Employees	NA	Stock Exchange	OTC
Auditor	NA	Ticker Symbol	SEFL
Stk Agt	Registrar & Transfer Co	Outstanding Shares	NA
Counsel	NA	E.P.S.	-$0.05
DUNS No.	NA	Shareholders	NA

Business: The groups principle activities include providing traditional retail banking services. The services of the group include lending products one to four family residential mortgage, multi family mortgage loans, commercial real estate mortgage loans, construction loans, home equity loans, savings account loans and other consumer loans. The group operates from the United States.

Primary SIC and add'l.: 6035

CIK No: 0001277138

Officers: Pamela M. Cyr/Pres., CEO - St. Edmonds Federal Savings Bank, Marcy C. Panzer/Chmn. - St. Edmonds Federal Savings Bank, Christopher J. Jacobsen/Exec. VP, COO - St. Edmonds Federal Savings Bank, Charles Frederick Miller/Exec. VP, Chief Lending, Credit Officer - St. Edmonds Federal Savings Bank, Charles M. Cahn/Dir. - St. Edmonds Federal Savings Bank, Megan L. Mahoney/Dir. - St. Edmonds Federal Savings Bank, David M. Rosenberg/Dir. - St. Edmonds Federal Savings Bank, Susanne Spinell Shuster/Dir. - St. Edmonds Federal Savings Bank, Samuel Barsky/Sec., Dir. - St. Edmonds Federal Savings Bank, Andrew A. Hines/Dir. - St. Edmonds Federal Savings Bank, William J. Parker/Dir. - St. Edmonds Federal Savings Bank, William F. Saldutti/Dir. - St. Edmonds Federal Savings Bank, John Durso/Mgr. - Ardmore Office, St. Edmonds Federal Savings Bank, Helen T. Demarco/Mgr. - Passyunk Avenue Office, St. Edmonds Federal Savings Bank, Kelly Czechowicz/Mgr. - Washington Township Office, St. Edmonds Federal Savings Bank *(16 Officers included in Index)*

*Financial Data: Fiscal Year End:*10/31 *Latest Annual Data:* 10/31/2006

Year	Sales	Net Income
2006	$10,029,000	-$262,000
2005	$7,545,000	$756,000
2004	$5,703,000	$742,000

Curr. Assets:	$3,511,000	Curr. Liab.:	$139,354,000		
Plant, Equip.:	$5,409,000	Total Liab.:	$151,536,000	Indic. Yr. Divd.:	NA
Total Assets:	$175,514,000	Net Worth:	$23,979,000	Debt/ Equity:	NA

Sea Breeze Power Corp

333 Seymour St., Ste 1400, Vancouver, BC, V6B 5A6; *PH:* 1-604-689-2991; *http://* www.seabreezepower.com; *Email:* info@seabreezepower.com

General - Incorporation	BC	Stock- Price on:12/24/2007	$0.5084
Employees	NA	Stock Exchange	OTC
Auditor	Morgan & Co	Ticker Symbol	SBEZF
Stk Agt	Pacific Corporate Trust Co	Outstanding Shares	NA
Counsel	NA	E.P.S.	NA
DUNS No.	NA	Shareholders	NA

Business: The group's current principal activity is planning, permitting, obtaining environmental assessments, designing and financing renewable energy sites and it proposes to construct and operate renewable energy projects in the future. The company is currently developing large-scale wind farms on the coast of British Columbia in northern Vancouver Island for power generation. It has eight projects in various stages of development. The company is also developing underwater electricity transmission lines, as well as pursuing other renewable energy opportunities, such as hydro, energy storage, and direct current transmission projects. Sea Breeze is participating in a transmission project in the Pacific Northwest that will link Washington State's Olympic Peninsula in the US to Vancouver Island.

Primary SIC and add'l.: 4911

CIK No: 0001278145

Subsidiaries: Harrison Lake Hydro Inc, Powerhouse Developments Inc, Powerhouse Electric Corp, Sea Breeze Energy Inc, Sea Breeze Management Services Inc, Sea Breeze Pacific Regional Transmission System, Inc, Sea Breeze Power Projects Inc.

Officers: Paul B. Manson/Dir., Pres., Jan Campfens/CFO, Resja Campfens/VP - Environmental Affairs, Sam Kenny/Contact - Info, Mike Wise/Project Mgr. - Technical Consultant

Directors: Henry P. Anderson/Dir., Mark Hoffman/Dir., Paul B. Manson/Dir., Pres., Charles Eckberg/Dir., Ken Puryear/Dir., Carol Edwards/Member - Advisory Board, Bent Jorgensen/Member - Advisory Board, Roy McAlister/Member - Advisory Board

Seaboard Corp

9000 W 67th St., Shawnee Mission, KS, 66202; *PH:* 1-913-676-8800; *Fax:* 1-913-676-8872; *http://* www.seaboardcorp.com; *Email:* seaboard@seaboardcorp.com

General - Incorporation	DE	Stock- Price on:12/24/2007	$2430
Employees	10,363	Stock Exchange	AMEX
Auditor	KPMG LLP	Ticker Symbol	SEB
Stk Agt	UMB Bank, N.A.	Outstanding Shares	1,260,000
Counsel	Sullivan & Worcester LLP	E.P.S.	$182.32
DUNS No.	00-104-2472	Shareholders	NA

Business: The groups principle activity is to process and produce pork. The group also provides ocean transportation. The group operates through six business segments namely pork, commodity trading and milling, marine, sugar and citrus, power and other businesses. The group operates from United States.

Primary SIC and add'l.: 4499 0133 0213 3699 3612 5153 2084

CIK No: 0000088121

Subsidiaries: Agencia Maritima del Istmo, S.A., Agencias Generales Conaven, C.A., Almacenadora Conaven, S.A., Boyar Estates S.A., Cape Fear Railways, Inc., Cayman Freight Shipping Services, Lt, Chestnut Hill Farms Honduras,S. de R.L. de C.V., Delta Packaging Company Ltd., Desarrollo Industrial Bioacuatico,S.A., Eureka Chickens Limited, Franquicias Azucareras S.A., H&O Shipping Limited, Ingenio y Refineria San Martin del Tabacal S.R.L., InterAfrica Grains Ltd., JacintoPort International LP 60 Subsidiaries included in the Index

Officers: Rodney K. Brenneman/CEO - Pork/$1,941,927.00, Steven J. Bresky/Chmn., CEO, Pres./$2,862,700.00, David M. Dannov/CEO - Commodity Trading, Milling/$672,415.00, Edward A. Gonzalez/CEO - Marine/$1,134,481.00, Richard A. Watt/CEO - Sugar, Citrus, Armando G. Rodriguez/CEO - Power, Adriana N. Hoskins/Assist. Treasurer, James L. Gutsch/VP - Engineering,

David A. Adamsen/Dir., VP, David M. Becker/VP, General Counsel, Sec., Robert L. Steer/CFO, Sr. VP, Treasurer/$2,274,868.00, David S. Oswalt/VP - Taxation, Business Development, Barry E. Gum/VP - Finance, Treasurer, John A. Virgo/VP, Corporate Controller, Chief Accounting Officer, Ralph L. Moss/VP - Government Affairs

Directors: Steven J. Bresky/Chmn., CEO, Pres., David A. Adamsen/Dir., VP, Douglas W. Baena/Dir., Kevin M. Kennedy/Dir., Joseph E. Rodrigues/Dir.

Owners: Kevin M. Kennedy, Douglas W. Baena, Insiders, David M. Dannov, Seaboard Flour, Steven J. Bresky, Harry H. Bresky, Joseph E. Rodrigues, David A. Adamsen

Financial Data: *Fiscal Year End:*12/31 *Latest Annual Data:* 12/31/2006

Year	Sales	Net Income
2006	$2,707,397,000	$258,689,000
2005	$2,688,894,000	$266,662,000
2004	$2,683,980,000	$168,096,000

Curr. Assets:	$1,196,569,000	**Curr. Liab.:**	$389,242,000	**P/E Ratio:**	13.33
Plant, Equip.:	$637,813,000	**Total Liab.:**	$719,023,000	**Indic. Yr. Divd.:**	$3.000
Total Assets:	$1,961,433,000	**Net Worth:**	$1,203,307,000	**Debt/ Equity:**	0.1084

Seabridge Gold Inc

106 Front St. E, Ste. 400, Toronto, ON, M5A 1E1; *PH:* 1-416-367-9292; *http://* www.seabridgegold.net; *Email:* info@seabridgegold.net

General - Incorporation	Canada	**Stock**- Price on:12/24/2007	$18.9
Employees	7	Stock Exchange	AMEX
Auditor	KPMG LLP	Ticker Symbol	SA
Stk Agt	Computershare Investor Services LLC	Outstanding Shares	34,670,000
Counsel	DuMoulin Black	E.P.S.	-$0.166
DUNS No.	NA	Shareholders	NA

Business: The groups principle activity is to provide mineral exploration services. The group operates from Canada.

Primary SIC and add'l.: 6799

CIK No: 0001231346

Subsidiaries: N.W.T. Limited, Nevada corporation, Pacific Intermountain Gold Inc., Seabridge Gold Corporation

Officers: Rudi P. Fronk/Dir., CEO, Pres., William E. Threlkeld/Sr. VP, Roderick Chisholm/CFO, Sec.

Directors: Rudi P. Fronk/Dir., CEO, Pres., James S. Anthony/Chmn., William M. Calhoun/Dir., Henry Fenig/62/Dir. - Toronto, Ontario, Eliseo Gonzalez-Urien/Dir., Frederick A. Banfield/Dir., Thomas C. Dawson/Dir., Louis J. Fox/Dir.

Owners: Louis Fox/0.95%, Frederick Banfield/0.71%, Insiders/12.04%, William Calhoun/0.53%, Roderick Chisholm/0.52%, Thomas Dawson/0.23%, Rudi Fronk/4.04%, Eliseo Gonzalez-Urien/0.22%, William Threlkeld/0.99%, Henry Fenig/0.38%

Financial Data: *Fiscal Year End:*12/31 *Latest Annual Data:* 12/31/2006

Year	Sales	Net Income
2006	NA	-$12,152,000
2005	NA	-$4,399,000
2004	NA	-$5,539,000

Curr. Assets:	$5,882,000	**Curr. Liab.:**	$373,000		
Plant, Equip.:	$49,000	**Total Liab.:**	$1,686,000	**Indic. Yr. Divd.:**	NA
Total Assets:	$52,553,000	**Net Worth:**	$50,867,000	**Debt/ Equity:**	NA

SeaBright Insurance Holdings Inc

2101 4th Ave., Ste. 1600, Seattle, WA, 98121; *PH:* 1-206-269-8504; *Fax:* 1-206-269-8903; *http://* www.sbic.com

General - Incorporation	DE	**Stock** - Price on:12/24/2007	$17.24
Employees	178	Stock Exchange	NDQ
Auditor	KPMG LLP	Ticker Symbol	SEAB
Stk Agt	Computershare Investor Services LLC	Outstanding Shares	20,800,000
Counsel	NA	E.P.S.	$1.794
DUNS No.	NA	Shareholders	NA

Business: The groups principle activity is to provide workers compensation insurance.Customers served by the group include Maritime employers and construction industry. The groups service is claim. The group operates from the United States. The group's quarterly revenue for September 2007 was 66.73 millions of USD.

Primary SIC and add'l.: 6331

CIK No: 0001267201

Subsidiaries: PointSure Insurance Services, Inc., SeaBright Insurance Company

Officers: John G. Pasqualetto/Chmn., CEO, Pres., Richard Gergasko/Exec. VP, Joseph De Vita/Sr. VP, CFO, Richard Seelinger/Sr. VP - Policyholder Services, Marc Miller/Sr. VP, Chief Medical Officer, Drue Wax/General Counsel, Sr. VP, Corp. Sec., Jeff Wanamaker/Sr. VP - Underwriting, James L. Borland/CIO, VP

Directors: John G. Pasqualetto/Chmn., CEO, Pres., Peter Y. Chung/Dir., William M. Feldman/Dir., Mural R. Josephson/Dir., George M. Morvis/Dir., Joseph A. Edwards/Dir., Michael D. Rice/Dir.

Owners: Wells Fargo & Company/7.70%, Peter Y. Chung, Joseph S. De Vita, Richard W. Seelinger, Drue D. Wax, Joseph A. Edwards, George M. Morvis, William M. Feldman, Mural R. Josephson, Eubel Brady & Suttman Asset Management, Inc./8.10%, John G. Pasqualetto/1.60%, Insiders/5.00%, Skyline Asset Management, LP/5.30%, Richard J. Gergasko

Financial Data: *Fiscal Year End:*12/31 *Latest Annual Data:* 12/31/2006

Year	Sales	Net Income
2006	$205,927,000	$33,229,000
2005	$172,250,000	$18,292,000
2004	$86,669,000	$7,206,000

Curr. Assets:	$49,717,000	**Curr. Liab.:**	$40,172,000	**P/E Ratio:**	9.61
Plant, Equip.:	$1,241,000	**Total Liab.:**	$365,149,000	**Indic. Yr. Divd.:**	NA
Total Assets:	$614,275,000	**Net Worth:**	$249,126,000	**Debt/ Equity:**	0.0461

SeaChange International

50 Nagog Pk., Acton, MA, 01720; *PH:* 1-978-897-0100; *Fax:* 1-978-897-0132; *http://* www.schange.com

General - Incorporation	DE	**Stock**- Price on:12/24/2007	$7.83
Employees	811	Stock Exchange	NDQ
Auditor	Grant Thornton, LLP	Ticker Symbol	SEAC
Stk Agt	Mellon Investor Services LLC	Outstanding Shares	29,390,000
Counsel	Testa, Hurwitz & Thibeault	E.P.S.	-$0.29
DUNS No.	80-749-9595	Shareholders	NA

Business: The group's principal activity is to develop, manufacture and market systems called video storage servers. The group operates in three segments namely broadband systems, broadcast systems and services. The broadband systems segment includes digital advertising and video-on-demand products, that digitally manage, store and distribute digital video for cable system operators and telecommunications companies. The broadcast systems segment includes products for the storage, archival, on-air playback of advertising and other video programming for the broadcast television industry. The service segment includes installation, training, product maintenance and technical support for the other segments. Major customers of the group are cable system operators, broadcast and telecommunications companies.

Primary SIC and add'l.: 7319 3663

CIK No: 0001019671

Subsidiaries: ON Demand Group, Limited vvv, Royal Bank of Scotland Group plc, Software development and professional services revenues

Officers: William C. Styslinger/61/Chmn., CEO, Pres./$548,966.00, Andrew Thomas Birchall/62/Sr. VP, Simone Sassoli/Europe, Middle East, Africa, Cable, Telcos Operators, Yefim Nivoro/Key Sales Contact - Latin America, The Caribbean, Jim Sheehan/Public Relations Contact, Anthony William Kelly/45/Sr. VP, Maria Duquette/VP - Customer Services, Chris West/Asia Pacific, Worldwide Broadcast Sales, Yvette M. Kanouff/41/Chief Strategy Officer/$739,033.00, Steven M. Davi/43/Sr. VP - Software Engineering/$421,722.00, Tom Rosenstein/VP - Product Marketing, Alliances, William L. Fiedler/Treasurer, Sec., Sr. VP - Finance, Administration/$230,455.00, Kevin M. Bisson/45/CFO, Treasurer, Sec., Sr. VP - Finance, Administration/$473,843.00, Zheng Gao/Pres. - Seachange China, ZQ Interactive, Marcello Dellepiane/Key Sales Contact - Europe, Middle East, Africa, Broadcast *(21 Officers included in Index)*

Directors: William C. Styslinger/61/Chmn., CEO, Pres., Martin R. Hoffmann/75/Dir., Thomas F. Olson/58/Dir., Mary P. Cotton/49/Dir., Carmine Vona/69/Dir.

Owners: Thomas F. Olson, Insiders/13.30%, Yvette M. Kanouff, William C. Styslinger/7.50%, Mary Palermo Cotton, Martin R. Hoffmann, David J. Greene and Company, LLC/7.10%, Ira Goldfarb, William L. Fiedler, Kevin M. Bisson, Wellington Management Company, LLP/12.30%, Carmine Vona, Columbia Wanger Asset Management, L.P./7.00%, Steven M. Davi, Dimensional Fund Advisors LP/8.30%

Financial Data: *Fiscal Year End:*01/31 *Latest Annual Data:* 1/31/2007

Year	Sales	Net Income
2007	$161,334,000	-$8,174,000
2006	$126,264,000	-$12,317,000
2005	$157,303,000	$9,938,000

Curr. Assets:	$99,575,000	**Curr. Liab.:**	$41,016,000		
Plant, Equip.:	$30,720,000	**Total Liab.:**	$42,137,000	**Indic. Yr. Divd.:**	NA
Total Assets:	$199,296,000	**Net Worth:**	$157,159,000	**Debt/ Equity:**	NA

Seacoast Banking Corp of Florida

815 Colorado Ave., Stuart, FL, 34994; *PH:* 1-772-287-4000; *Fax:* 1-772-288-6012; *http://* www.seacoastcorp.com

General - Incorporation	FL	**Stock**- Price on:12/24/2007	$22.11
Employees	534	Stock Exchange	NDQ
Auditor	KPMG LLP	Ticker Symbol	SBCF
Stk Agt	Continental Stock Transfer & Trust Co	Outstanding Shares	19,120,000
Counsel	NA	E.P.S.	$0.71
DUNS No.	11-296-3608	Shareholders	NA

Business: The group's principal activities are to provide a wide range of deposit accounts, consumer and commercial loans, retail banking and trust and asset management services as well as securities and annuity products. The operations of the group are conducted through its subsidiary first national bank and trust company of the treasure coast. The group operates through 28 banking offices in stuart, palm city, jensen beach, hutchinson island, hobe sound, vero beach, sebastian, port st. Lucie and ft. Pierce. The group also offers PC/Internet banking from personal computers. The Internet service allows customers to access transactional information on their deposit accounts, review loan and deposit balances, transfer funds between linked accounts and make loan payments from a deposit account, 24 hours a day.

Primary SIC and add'l.: 6022 6712

CIK No: 0000730708

Subsidiaries: Big O RV Resort, Inc., Century National Bank, First National Bank & Trust Company of the Treasure Coast, FNB Brokerage Services, Inc., FNB Insurance Services, Inc., FNB Property Holdings, Inc., FNB RE Services, Inc., SBCF Capital Trust I, SBCF Statutory Trust II, South Branch Building, Inc.

Officers: Dennis S. Hudson/Chmn., CEO/$863,267.00, Douglas A. Gilbert/Dir., COO, Pres./$957,661.00, Jean O. Strickland/Sr. Exec. VP/$539,994.00, William C. Curtis/Sr. Exec. VP, Chief Banking Officer/$455,388.00, William R. Hahl/CFO, Exec. VP

Directors: Dennis S. Hudson/Chmn., CEO, Dale M. Hudson/Vice Chmn., Edwin E. Walpole/Dir., Jeffrey C. Bruner/Dir., Jeffrey S. Furst/Dir., Thomas E. Rossin/Dir., Michael T. Crook/Dir., John H. Crane/Dir., Christopher E. Fogal/Dir., Stephen E. Bohner/Dir., Douglas A. Gilbert/Dir., COO, Pres., John R. Santarsiero/Dir., Thomas H. Thurlow/Dir.

Owners: Stephen E. Bohner, William R. Hahl, Insiders/22.36%, Thomas H. Thurlow, T. Michael Crook, Dennis S. Hudson/7.38%, Dale M. Hudson/8.47%, Dennis S. Hudson/7.04%, Douglas A. Gilbert, C. William Curtis, Edwin E. Walpole/1.29%, Jeffrey C. Bruner, Thomas E. Rossin, John H. Crane, Jeffrey S. Furst *(18 Owners included in Index)*

Financial Data: *Fiscal Year End:*12/31 *Latest Annual Data:* 12/31/2006

Year	Sales	Net Income
2006	$164,087,000	$23,854,000
2005	$119,045,000	$20,759,000
2004	$86,259,000	$14,922,000

Curr. Assets:	$92,215,000	**Curr. Liab.:**	$2,097,494,000	**P/E Ratio:**	20.28
Plant, Equip.:	$37,070,000	**Total Liab.:**	$2,177,010,000	**Indic. Yr. Divd.:**	$0.640
Total Assets:	$2,389,435,000	**Net Worth:**	$212,425,000	**Debt/ Equity:**	NA

Seacoast Commerce Bank

296 H St., Chula Vista, CA, 91910; *PH:* 1-619-476-7776; *Fax:* 1-619-476-7770; *http://* www.seacoastcommercebank.com; *Email:* info@sccombank.com

General - Incorporation	......	Stock - Price on:12/24/2007	......$10.75
Employees	NA	Stock Exchange	OTC
Auditor	NA	Ticker Symbol	SCCB
Stk Agt.	U.S. Stock Transfer Corp	Outstanding Shares	NA
Counsel	NA	E.P.S.	NA
DUNS No.	NA	Shareholders	NA

Business: The groups principal activities include providing banking and financial services as community banking. Services of the group include checking accounts, savings accounts, certificates of deposit, installment loans, real estate mortgage loans, commercial loans, traveler's checks, safe deposit boxes, night depository and automated teller services. The group operates from the United States.

Primary SIC and add'l.: 6029

CIK No:

Officers: Richard M. Sanborn/Dir., CEO, Pres., John Lucas/Investor Relations, Esteban Castrejon/VP - Commercial Lending, Real Estate Loan Officer, James Biddle/Investor Relations, Mark A. Nugent/Exec. VP, Chief Credit Officer, Toni Flannagan/CFO, Exec. VP, Beatriz Orozco/Assist. VP, Operations Officer, Mary Rankin/VP, Ron Perry/Sr. VP, SBA Loan Department Mgr., Gregory G. Dingens/Investor Relations

Directors: Richard M. Sanborn/Dir., CEO, Pres., Bruce A. Nunes/Chmn., Robert Dephilippis/Dir., Mark I. Greene/Dir., William S. Schairer/Dir., Allan W. Arendsee/Dir., Richard S. Levenson/Dir., Ronald A. Bedell/Dir.

Seacor Holdings Inc

2200 Eller Dr., Fort Lauderdale, FL, 33316; **PH:** 1-954-523-2200; **Fax:** 1-954-524-9185; **http://** www.seacorholdings.com

General - Incorporation	DE	Stock - Price on:12/24/2007	$93.03
Employees	4,994	Stock Exchange	NYSE
Auditor	Ernst & Young LLP	Ticker Symbol	CKH
Stk Agt.	American Stock Transfer & Trust Co.	Outstanding Shares	24,180,000
Counsel	NA	E.P.S.	$8.57
DUNS No.	NA	Shareholders	NA

Business: The group's principal activities are to provide offshore marine services and environmental services. The offshore marine services segment charters vessels to owners and operators of offshore drilling rigs and production platforms, both domestically and internationally. The vessels deliver cargo and personnel to offshore installations, handle anchors for drilling rigs and other marine equipment, support offshore construction and maintenance work and provide standby safety support. The environmental service business provides contractual oil spill response and other professional services to those who store, transport, produce or handle petroleum and certain non-petroleum oils. The group has operations in the United States, gulf of Mexico, offshore west Africa, the north sea, the Far East, Latin America and mediterranean.

Primary SIC and add'l.: 4491 4499

CIK No: 0000859598

Subsidiaries: Arctic Leasing LLC, Boston Putford Offshore Safety Ltd., Bruce Marine Limited, Congo Seacor Marine SA, Delaware Tanker Holding I,Inc., Delaware Tanker Holding II,Inc., Delaware Tanker Holding III,Inc., Delaware Tanker Holding IV,Inc., Delaware Tanker Holding V,Inc., Energy Logistics,Inc., Era FBO LLC, Era Helicopters (Mexico) LLC, Era Helicopters, LLC, Era Leasing LLC, F2B Investments Inc. 220 Subsidiaries included in the Index

Officers: Charles Fabrikant/Chmn., CEO, Pres./$6,136,578.00, Randall Blank/Sr. VP, John Gellert/Sr. VP/$2,046,331.00, Dick Fagerstal/Sr. VP - Corporate Development, Treasurer/$877,023.00, Alice Gran/Sr. VP, General Counsel, Andrew Strachan/VP, Richard Ryan/Sr. VP, CFO, MD MD - Seacor Marine, International Ltd/$678,951.00, Matthew Cenac/VP, Chief Accounting Officer, James A.F. Cowderoy/48/Sr. VP, Tim McKeand/VP - Investor Relations Contact

Directors: Charles Fabrikant/Chmn., CEO, Pres., Andrew R. Morse/Dir., Michael E. Gellert/Dir., Stephen Stamas/Dir., Richard M. Fairbanks/67/Dir., Pierre De Demandolx/Dir., John C. Hadjipateras/57/Dir., Steven J. Wisch/Dir., Oivind Lorentzen/Dir., Christopher Regan/Dir., Steven Webster/Dir.

Owners: Steven J. Wisch, Steven Webster, Richard Ryan, John C. Hadjipateras, Porter Felleman/9.43%, Goldman Sachs Asset Management, L.P./8.96%, Randall Blank, Stephen Stamas, Richard M. Fairbanks, Charles Fabrikant/4.72%, Dick Fagerstal, FMR Corporation/7.83%, Oivind Lorentzen, Pierre de Demandolx, John Gellert (18 Owners included in Index)

Financial Data: Fiscal Year End:12/31   Latest Annual Data: 12/31/2006

Year	Sales	Net Income
2006	$1,323,445,000	$234,394,000
2005	$972,004,000	$170,709,000
2004	$491,860,000	$19,889,000

Curr. Assets:	$938,369,000	Curr. Liab.:	$295,509,000	P/E Ratio:	11.33
Plant, Equip.:	$1,770,210,000	Total Liab.:	$1,689,010,000	Indic. Yr. Divd.:	NA
Total Assets:	$3,252,982,000	Net Worth:	$1,557,078,000	Debt/ Equity:	0.6170

Seagate Technology

920 Disc Dr., Scotts Valley, CA, 95066; **PH:** 1-831-438-6550; **Fax:** 1-831-429-6356; **http://** www.seagate.com

General - Incorporation	Cayman Islands	Stock - Price on:12/24/2007	$21.38
Employees	60,000	Stock Exchange	NYSE
Auditor	Ernst & Young LLP	Ticker Symbol	STX
Stk Agt.	Computershare Trust Co	Outstanding Shares	543,680,000
Counsel	NA	E.P.S.	$0.65
DUNS No.	NA	Shareholders	NA

Business: The groups principle activity is to provide advanced digital storage solutions. The groups products include desktop, laptop and external storage. The groups services include data migration and data archiving. The group operates from United States.

Primary SIC and add'l.: NA

CIK No: 0001137789

Subsidiaries: ActionFront Data Recovery (Netherlands) B.V., ActionFront Data Recovery Inc., ActionFront Data Recovery Labs Inc., Beijing Representative Office, Cork Branch, India Liaison Office, Limavady Northern Ireland Branch, Maxtor (Gibraltar) Limited, Maxtor (Japan) Ltd., Maxtor Asia Pacific Limited, Maxtor Corporation, Maxtor Disc Drives Pty Limited, Maxtor Europe Limited, Maxtor Europe S.r.l., Maxtor Global Ltd. 64 Subsidiaries included in the Index

Officers: William D. Watkins/Dir., CEO/$3,405,851.00, Dave Wickersham/COO, Pres., Jaroslaw Glembocki/Sr. VP - Heads, Media/$1,537,860.00, Robert Whitmore/CTO, Exec. VP, Pat King/Sr. VP, GM - Consumer Electronics, Dave Mosley/Sr. VP - Global Disc Storage Operations, David Wickersham/COO, Pres./$3,040,203.00, Todd Abbott/Exec. VP - Sales, Marketing, Customer Service, Brian Dexheimer/Exec. VP, Chief - Sales, Marketing Officer/$2,803,996.00, Sherman Black/Sr. VP, GM - Enterprise Compute Business, Jim Chirico/Exec. VP - Global Disc Storage Operations, James Druckrey/Sr. VP, GM - Branded Solutions, Jerry Glembocki/Sr. VP - Heads, Media, William Hudson/Exec. VP, General Counsel, Corp. Sec., Phil Pollok/Sr. VP - New Business Initiatives (18 Officers included in Index)

Directors: William D. Watkins/Dir., CEO, Stephen J. Luczo/Chmn., Frank J. Biondi/Dir., William W. Bradley/Dir., James A. Davidson/Dir., Donald E. Kiernan/Dir., David F. Marquardt/Dir., Lydia M. Marshall/Dir., C. S. Park/Dir., Gregorio Reyes/Dir., John W. Thompson/Dir.

Owners: Charles C. Pope, Frank J. Biondi, William W. Bradley, David F. Marquardt, Gregorio Reyes, Affiliates of Franklin Resources, Inc./10.64%, C. S. Park, Donald E. Kiernan, Insiders/4.61%, Lydia M. Marshall, John W. Thompson, Jaroslaw S. Glembocki, Brian S. Dexheimer, Affiliates of Legg Mason, Inc/5.73%, David A. Wickersham (21 Owners included in Index)

Financial Data: Fiscal Year End:07/01   Latest Annual Data: 6/30/2006

Year	Sales	Net Income
2006	$9,206,000,000	$840,000,000
2005	$7,553,000,000	$707,000,000
2004	$6,224,000,000	$529,000,000

Curr. Assets:	$2,461,000,000	Curr. Liab.:	$1,248,000,000	P/E Ratio:	32.89
Plant, Equip.:	$1,301,000,000	Total Liab.:	$2,087,000,000	Indic. Yr. Divd.:	$0.400
Total Assets:	$3,942,000,000	Net Worth:	$1,855,000,000	Debt/ Equity:	0.3920

Sealed Air Corp

200 Riverfront Blvd., Elmwood Park, NJ, 07407; **PH:** 1-201-791-7600; **Fax:** 1-201-703-4205; **http://** www.sealedaircorp.com

General - Incorporation	DE	Stock - Price on:12/24/2007	$31.18
Employees	17,400	Stock Exchange	NYSE
Auditor	KPMG LLP	Ticker Symbol	SEE
Stk Agt	Mellon Investor Services LLC	Outstanding Shares	161,550,000
Counsel	NA	E.P.S.	$1.92
DUNS No.	78-223-5980	Shareholders	NA

Business: The group's principle activities include manufacturing and selling food protective and specialty packaging products. The group also manufactures and sells adhesive tapes, solar collectors, recycled kraft paper, loose-fill polystyrene packaging, covers for swimming pools, elimination and neutralization of static electricity. The group's trademarks are Cryovac, Dri-Loc, Cell-Aire, Cellu-Cushion and Korrvu. The group operates from United States, North America, Europe, Latin America and Asia-Pacific.

Primary SIC and add'l.: 2672 2621 3089 2671 3433

CIK No: 0001012100

Subsidiaries: Beleggingsmaatschappij 't Hagelkruus b.v., Ciras CV, CPI Packaging, Inc., Cryovac (Foshan Gaoming) Co., Ltd., Cryovac (Malaysia) Sdn. Bhd., Cryovac (Philippines) Inc., Cryovac (Singapore) Pte. Ltd., Cryovac (Thailand) Limited, Cryovac Australia Pty. Ltd., Cryovac Brasil Ltda., Cryovac Chile Holdings, LLC, Cryovac China Holdings I, Inc., Cryovac Far East Holdings, LLC, Cryovac Holdings II, LLC, Cryovac International Holdings, Inc. 129 Subsidiaries included in the Index

Officers: William V. Hickey/63/Dir., CEO, Pres./$1,992,497.00, Jeffrey S. Warren/Controller, Katherine H. White/VP, General Counsel, Sec., David B. Crosier/Sr. VP/$1,074,185.00, Tod S. Christie/49/Treasurer, David H. Kelsey/CFO, Sr. VP/$1,082,973.00, Robert A. Pesci/Sr. VP/$805,470.00, James P. Mix/56/VP, Manuel Mondragon/58/VP, Hugh L. Sargant/VP, Ruth Roper/53/VP, Jonathan B. Baker/54/VP/$609,711.00, Christopher C. Woodbridge/VP, Cheryl Fells Davis/55/VP, Karl R. Deily/50/VP (19 Officers included in Index)

Directors: William V. Hickey/63/Dir., CEO, Pres., Hank Brown/67/Dir., Michael Chu/59/Dir., Lawrence R. Codey/63/Dir., Charles F. Farrell/77/Dir., Jacqueline B. Kosecoff/58/Dir., Kenneth P. Manning/66/Dir., William J. Marino/64/Dir., Dermot T.J. Dunphy/75/Dir.

Owners: William V. Hickey, William J. Marino, David H. Kelsey, Kenneth P. Manning, Jonathan B. Baker, Lawrence R. Codey, Stuart K. J. Prosser, Insiders/1.80%, Hank Brown, Charles F. Farrell, Capital Research and Management Company and The Growth Fund of America, Inc./15.80%, David B. Crosier, Jacqueline B. Kosecoff, Michael Chu, Robert A. Pesci (17 Owners included in Index)

Financial Data: Fiscal Year End:12/31   Latest Annual Data: 12/31/2006

Year	Sales	Net Income
2006	$4,327,900,000	$274,100,000
2005	$4,085,100,000	$255,800,000
2004	$3,798,100,000	$215,600,000

Curr. Assets:	$1,756,700,000	Curr. Liab.:	$1,406,100,000		
Plant, Equip.:	$970,100,000	Total Liab.:	$3,366,100,000	Indic. Yr. Divd.:	NA
Total Assets:	$5,020,900,000	Net Worth:	$1,654,800,000	Debt/ Equity:	1.0190

Sealife Corp

5601 W Slauson Ave., Culver City, CA, 90230; **PH:** 1-310-338-9757; **Fax:** 1-310-338-9762; **http://** www.sealifemarine.com

General - Incorporation	DE	Stock - Price on:12/24/2007	$0.08
Employees	4	Stock Exchange	OTC
Auditor	Pollard-Kelley Auditing Services, Inc	Ticker Symbol	SLIF
Stk Agt	National City Bank	Outstanding Shares	39,990,000
Counsel	NA	E.P.S.	-$0.109
DUNS No.	NA	Shareholders	NA

Business: The group's principal activity is painting of marine vessels. The products are marketed under the brand name of sealife 1000tm. The sealife 1000 product is competitive, as it protects hulls of ships longer than other normal paints. It does not require a primer coat and is environmentally friendly. Sealife 1000 is anti-foul coating authorized to be labeled environmentally compatible by the us environment protection agency ('epa'). The other products of the group include sealife 2000tm and sealife 3000tm which are in the research and development stage. On 20-Dec-2002, the group acquired sealife corp and changed its name from integrated enterprises inc.

Primary SIC and add'l.: 2851

CIK No: 0000749753

Subsidiaries: ProTerra Technologies, Inc., SeaLife Marine Products, Inc.

Officers: Robert A. McCaslin/Dir., CFO, Pres.

Directors: Robert A. McCaslin/Dir., CFO, Pres.

Financial Data: Fiscal Year End:12/31   Latest Annual Data: 12/31/2005

Year	Sales	Net Income
2005	$163,000	-$3,359,000
2004	$27,000	-$1,807,000

Curr. Assets:	$443,000	**Curr. Liab.:**	$326,000		
Plant, Equip.:	NA	**Total Liab.:**	$641,000	**Indic. Yr. Divd.:**	NA
Total Assets:	$1,989,000	**Net Worth:**	$1,348,000	**Debt/ Equity:**	NA

Sealy Corp

1 Office Pkwy. at Sealy Dr., Trinity, NC, 27370; *PH:* 1-336-861-3500; *Fax:* 1-336-861-3501; *http://* www.sealy.com

General - Incorporation DE; Employees 6,233; Auditor Deloitte & Touche LLP; Stk Agt NC Bank Shareholder Srvcs Ops; Counsel NA; DUNS No. NA

Stock- Price on:12/24/2007 $16.56; Stock Exchange NYSE; Ticker Symbol ZZ; Outstanding Shares 91,450,000; E.P.S. $0.87; Shareholders NA

Business: The groups principle activities include manufacturing and marketing bedding products. The groups products are mattresses and mattress foundations. The groups products marketed under the brand names Sealy, Sealy Posturepedic, Stearns & Foster, SpringFree and Reflexions. The group operates through two segments namely, the Americas and Europe. The group operates from the United States, Brazil, Spain, Italy, France and Mexico.

Primary SIC and add'l.: 2515 3999 6794

CIK No: 0000748015

Subsidiaries: Advanced Sleep Products, Brandwein& Company, Gestion Centurion,Inc., Mattress Holding SAS, Mattress Holdings International B.V., Mattress Holdings International LLC, North American Bedding Company, Ohio-Sealy Mattress Manufacturing Co., Ohio-Sealy Mattress Manufacturing Co.,Inc., Sapsa Bedding GmbH, Sapsa Bedding SAS, Sapsa Bedding SL, Sapsa Bedding Sprl (Belgium), Sapsa Bedding Sprl (Holland), Sapsa Bedding Srl 50 Subsidiaries included in the Index

Officers: David J. McIlquham/Chmn., CEO, Pres., Jeffrey C. Claypool/Sr. VP - Human Resources, Lawrence J. Rogers/Pres. - Sealy International Group, Kenneth L. Walker/Sr. VP, General Counsel, Sec., Jeffrey C. Ackerman/CFO, Exec. VP, Alfred R. Boulden/Sr. VP - Field Sales, Charles L. Dawson/Sr. VP - National Accounting, Michael G. Hofmann/Sr. VP - Operations, Phillip Dobbs/Sr. VP - Marketing, Mark Boehmer/Investor Relations Officer

Directors: David J. McIlquham/Chmn., CEO, Pres., Steven Barnes/Dir., Brian F. Carroll/Dir., James W. Johnston/Dir., Dean B. Nelson/Dir., Paul Norris/Dir., Scott M. Stuart/Dir., Gary E. Morin/Dir., Richard Roedel/Dir.

Owners: Jeffery C. Akerman, KKR Millenium GP LLC, Marc C. Cahodes, Brian F. Carroll, James W. Johnston, Lawrence J. Rogers, Philip Dobbs, Insiders, Farallon Capital Management LLC, James B. Hirshorn, David J. McIlquham, Gary E. Morin

Financial Data: *Fiscal Year End:*11/30 *Latest Annual Data:* 11/26/2006

Year	Sales	Net Income
2006	$1,582,843,000	$73,967,000
2005	$1,469,574,000	$68,479,000
2004	$1,314,020,000	-$40,067,000

Curr. Assets:	$300,019,000	**Curr. Liab.:**	$255,204,000	**P/E Ratio:**	17.43
Plant, Equip.:	$164,179,000	**Total Liab.:**	$1,355,272,000	**Indic. Yr. Divd.:**	$0.300
Total Assets:	$898,503,000	**Net Worth:**	-$456,769,000	**Debt/ Equity:**	NA

Seamless Wi-Fi Inc

800 N Rainbow Blvd, Las Vegas, NV, 89107; *PH:* 1-775-588-2387; *Fax:* 1-775-588-2499; *http://* www.slwf.net; *Email:* info@slwf.biz

General - Incorporation NV; Employees 3; Auditor Kempisty & Company CPAs, P.C.; Stk Agt American Stock Transfer & Trust Co.; Counsel NA; DUNS No. NA

Stock- Price on:12/24/2007 $0.0009; Stock Exchange OTC; Ticker Symbol SLWF; Outstanding Shares 3,550,000,000; E.P.S. $0.001; Shareholders NA

Business: The groups principle activity is to provide Wireless Internet access at business locations. The group operates through three segments namely seamless sky fi, seamless peer 2 peer software and seamless internet products and services. In January 2005, the group acquired the assets of Seamless P2P, LLC and in March 2006, Vercel Corporation. The group operates from the United States and Canada. The group's quarterly revenue for Sep '07 was 0.01 millions of USD.

Primary SIC and add'l.: 7372

CIK No: 0000880584

Subsidiaries: SEAMLESS INTERNET, INC., SEAMLESS PEER 2 PEER, INC., SEAMLESS SKYY-FI, INC.

Officers: Albert Reda/Dir., CEO, CFO, Pres., Ken Reda/Pres. - Seamless P2P, John Domerego/Dir., Pres. - Seamless Internet, Mildred Carroll/Sec., Philip Siegel/Pres.

Directors: Albert Reda/Dir., CEO, CFO, Pres., John Domerego/Dir., Pres. - Seamless Internet, Matt Sebal/Dir.

Owners: Insiders/13.20%, Matt Sebal, John Domerego, Albert R. Reda/13.10%

Financial Data: *Fiscal Year End:*06/30 *Latest Annual Data:* 06/30/2007

Year	Sales	Net Income
2007	$43,000	$3,210,000
2006	$39,000	-$6,368,000
2005	$2,000	-$3,914,000

Curr. Assets:	$375,000	**Curr. Liab.:**	$1,575,000		
Plant, Equip.:	$51,000	**Total Liab.:**	$1,575,000	**Indic. Yr. Divd.:**	NA
Total Assets:	$4,993,000	**Net Worth:**	$3,418,000	**Debt/ Equity:**	NA

Searchhelp Inc

6800 Jericho Tpke., Ste. 208E, Syosset, NY, 11791; *PH:* 1-516-922-4765; *Fax:* 1-516-624-0638; *http://* www.searchhelp.com; *Email:* info@searchhelp.com

General - Incorporation DE; Employees 9; Auditor Lazar Levine & Felix LLP; Stk Agt American Stock Transfer & Trust Co.; Counsel NA; DUNS No. NA

Stock- Price on:12/24/2007 $0.25; Stock Exchange OTC; Ticker Symbol SHLP; Outstanding Shares 38,380,000; E.P.S. -$0.11; Shareholders NA

Business: The group's principal activities are to develop software intended to keep children safe while online and provide turnkey solutions for both local communities and media companies. It's more expanded purpose will be to seek out emerging capabilities, products and services that exhibit great promise of improving family safety and well being. The company is initially focusing its marketing efforts on its s.p.i.k.e. Software product. Spike software/browser reflects the searchhelp philosophy in helping parents and families deal with the increasingly complex and threatening aspects of child Internet usage. Spike remote sentry addresses the same child computer usage issues and reflects the reality that families face of needing to monitor children when the parent is away from home.

Primary SIC and add'l.: 7319 7371

CIK No: 0001163573

Subsidiaries: Amber Alert Agent, Inc, Digital ID Services, Inc, E-Top-Pics, Inc, FamilySafe, Inc., Indoor Air Quality Services, Inc

Officers: William Bozsnyak/Founder, Chmn., CEO, Brian O'Connor/COO, Exec. VP - Marketing, John Caruso/CFO, Paul J. Pollack/Contact - Investor Relations

Directors: William Bozsnyak/Founder, Chmn., CEO, David M. Barnes/Dir.

Owners: Joseph Carrizzo/8.43%, David M. Barnes, Brian P. OConnor/6.56%, John Caruso, Insiders/22.85%, Debbie Seaman/7.02%, William Bozsnyak/15.73%

Financial Data: *Fiscal Year End:*12/31 *Latest Annual Data:* 12/31/2006

Year	Sales	Net Income
2006	$319,000	-$3,952,000
2005	$1,723,000	-$3,780,000
2004	$1,000	-$1,200,000

Curr. Assets:	$588,000	**Curr. Liab.:**	$2,345,000		
Plant, Equip.:	$109,000	**Total Liab.:**	$3,926,000	**Indic. Yr. Divd.:**	NA
Total Assets:	$2,476,000	**Net Worth:**	-$1,450,000	**Debt/ Equity:**	NA

Searchlight Minerals Corp

2441 W Horizon Ridge Pkwy., Ste. 120, Henderson, NV, 89052; *PH:* 1-702-939-5247; *Fax:* 1-702-939-5249; *http://* www.searchlightminerals.com; *Email:* info@searchlightminerals.com

General - Incorporation NV; Employees 6; Auditor Kyle L. Tingle, CPA. LLC; Stk Agt Pacific Stock Transfer Company; Counsel NA; DUNS No. NA

Stock- Price on:12/24/2007 $3.45; Stock Exchange OTC; Ticker Symbol SRCH; Outstanding Shares 91,380,000; E.P.S. -$0.06; Shareholders NA

Business: The groups principal activity is in an exploration stage company engaged in the acquisition and development of mineral properties. The group operates from the United States.

Primary SIC and add'l.: 7389

CIK No: 0001084226

Officers: Ian R. McNeil/36/Dir., CEO, Pres./$179,642.00, Carl S. Ager/33/Dir., VP, Sec., Treasurer/$151,642.00, Melvin L. Williams/47/CFO

Directors: Ian R. McNeil/36/Dir., CEO, Pres., Carl S. Ager/33/Dir., VP, Sec., Treasurer, Robert D. McDougal/75/Dir., Harry B. Crockett/67/Dir.

Owners: Insiders/13.52%, Carl S. Ager/1.36%, Gerald A. Lembas/5.52%, Robert D. McDougal, Harry B. Crockett/9.76%, Ian K. Matheson/15.24%, Nanominerals Corp./17.51%, Centrum Bank AG/5.34%, Melvin L. Williams, Ian R. McNeil/1.36%

Financial Data: *Fiscal Year End:*12/31 *Latest Annual Data:* 12/31/2006

Year	Sales	Net Income
2006	NA	-$3,652,000
2005	NA	-$1,722,000
2004	NA	-$590,000

Curr. Assets:	$3,790,000	**Curr. Liab.:**	$1,583,000		
Plant, Equip.:	$157,000	**Total Liab.:**	$1,583,000	**Indic. Yr. Divd.:**	NA
Total Assets:	$5,021,000	**Net Worth:**	$3,438,000	**Debt/ Equity:**	0.0359

Sears Holdings Corp

3333 Beverly Rd., Hoffman Estates, IL, 60179; *PH:* 1-847-286-2500; *Fax:* 1-847-286-8351; *http://* www.searshc.com

General - Incorporation DE; Employees 352,000; Auditor Deloitte & Touche LLP; Stk Agt Computershare Trust Co; Counsel NA; DUNS No. NA

Stock- Price on:12/24/2007 $172.12; Stock Exchange NDQ; Ticker Symbol SHLD; Outstanding Shares 152,490,000; E.P.S. $8.11; Shareholders NA

Business: The groups principal activity is to provide broad line retailer services. The group products sold under the trade names KENMORE(R), CRAFTSMAN(R), DIEHARD(R) and LANDS END(R). The groups operates through three segments namely Kmart, Sears Domestic and Sears Canada. The group operates from the Canada and the United States. Of the total assets in the year 2006, Kmart accounted for $7,750, Sears Domestic $19,209 and Sears Canada $3,107 (thousands).

Primary SIC and add'l.: 5399 5331 7532 5311 7534 5961 7538 3714 5963

CIK No: 0001310067

Subsidiaries: KCD IP, LLC, Kmart Corporation, Kmart Holding Corporation, Kmart Management Corporation, Lands End, Inc., LRFG, LLC, Sears Brands, LLC, Sears Canada, Inc, Sears Financial Holdings Corporation, Sears Holdings Management Corporation, Sears Reinsurance Company Ltd, Sears, Roebuck and Co.

Officers: Aylwin B. Lewis/Dir., CEO, Pres., William C. Crowley/50/Dir., CFO, Chief Administrative Officer, Exec. VP, Karen A. Austin/46/CIO, Exec. VP, Mark C. Good/51/Exec. VP, GM - Home Services, William R. Harker/35/Sr. VP, General Counsel, Corp. Sec., Bruce W. Johnson/56/Exec. VP - Supply Chain, Operations, Robert D. Luse/45/Sr. VP - Human Resources, Maureen A. McGuire/56/Chief Marketing Officer, Exec. VP, William K. Phelan/45/VP, Controller, Chief Accounting Officer, Peter J. Whitsett/42/Sr. VP - Merchandising, Corwin M. Yulinsky/53/Exec. VP - Strategy, Customer Insight, Allen R. Ravas/52/Sr. VP - Finance, Treasurer, John C. Walden/48/Exec. VP, Chief Customer Officer

Directors: Aylwin B. Lewis/Dir., CEO, Pres., Edward S. Lampert/45/Chmn., Donald J. Carty/Dir., William C. Crowley/50/Dir., CFO, Chief Administrative Officer, Exec. VP, Richard C. Perry/53/Dir., Steven T. Mnuchin/45/Dir., Ann N. Reese/54/Dir., Thomas J. Tisch/53/Dir., Emily Scott/Dir.

Owners: T. Tisch/2.70%, M. McGuire, A. Reese, A. Lewis, R. Perry/1.80%, Insiders/47.50%, A. Lacy, S. Mnuchin, Legg Mason Capital Management, Inc/8.10%, ESL Investments, Inc./42.50%

Financial Data: *Fiscal Year End:*01/28 *Latest Annual Data:* 2/3/2007

Year	Sales	Net Income
2007	$53,012,000,000	$1,490,000,000
2006	$49,124,000,000	$858,000,000
2005	$19,701,000,000	$1,106,000,000

Curr. Assets:	$15,406,000,000	Curr. Liab.:	$10,052,000,000		
Plant, Equip.:	$9,132,000,000	Total Liab.:	$17,352,000,000	Indic. Yr. Divd.:	NA
Total Assets:	$30,066,000,000	Net Worth:	$12,714,000,000	Debt/Equity:	0.2067

Seaspan Corp

Unit 2, 7th Fl., 141 Connaught Rd. W, Bupa Centre; *PH:* 852-25401686; *Fax:* 852-25401686; *http://* www.seaspancorp.com; *Email:* info@seaspancorp.com

General - Incorporation .... Marshall Islands	**Stock** - Price on:12/24/2007 ....$32.42		
Employees 1	Stock Exchange.................................NYSE		
Auditor .... KPMG LLP	Ticker Symbol.......................................SSW		
Stk Agt..... American Stock Transfer & Trust Co.	Outstanding Shares 47,570,000		
Counsel...NA	E.P.S...$0.32		
DUNS No. ....NA	Shareholders.......................................NA		

Business: The groups principle activities include owning and operating a fleet of 23 containerships. In the year 2005, the group acquired ten containerships. The group operates from the United States. The groups quarterly revenue for September 2007 was 54.17 millions of USD.

Primary SIC and add'l.: 4412 4449 4731 4491

CIK No: 0001332639

Officers: Gerry Wang/45/Dir., CEO, Kevin M. Kennedy/48/CFO, Sec., Graham Porter/Dir., MD

Directors: Gerry Wang/45/Dir., CEO, Kyle Washington/37/Chmn., David Korbin/Dir., Peter Lorange/Dir., Peter S. Shaerf/Dir., Milton K. Wong/Dir., Barry R. Pearl/Dir., Graham Porter/Dir., MD

Owners: Neuberger & Berman L.P./14.20%

Financial Data: *Fiscal Year End:*12/31 *Latest Annual Data:* 12/31/2006

Year	Sales	Net Income
2006	$118,489,000	$35,564,000
2005	$34,803,000	$14,329,000

Curr. Assets:	$96,655,000	Curr. Liab.:	$11,167,000	P/E Ratio:	17.43
Plant, Equip.:	$1,198,782,000	Total Liab.:	$590,201,000	Indic. Yr. Divd.:	$1.790
Total Assets:	$1,315,272,000	Net Worth:	$725,071,000	Debt/Equity:	NA

Seattle Genetics Inc

21823 30th Dr. SE, Bothell, WA, 98021; *PH:* 1-425-527-4000; *Fax:* 1-425-527-4001; *http://* www.seattlegenetics.com; *Email:* contact@seagen.com

General - Incorporation .... DE	**Stock** - Price on:12/24/2007 ....$10.01		
Employees 151	Stock Exchange.................................NDQ		
Auditor .... PricewaterhouseCoopers LLP	Ticker Symbol......................................SGEN		
Stk Agt.................. Mellon Investor Services LLC	Outstanding Shares 57,010,000		
Counsel.......................Venture Law Group	E.P.S...-$0.77		
DUNS No. ....NA	Shareholders.......................................NA		

Business: The group's principal activity is to develop monoclonal antibody-based therapeutic products for the treatment of cancer and immunologic diseases. Its diverse portfolio of product candidates includes sgn-30 and sgn-15 in phase ii clinical development and sgn-40 in phase i clinical trials. In addition, it has three product candidates currently in preclinical development, sgn-35, sgn-75 and sgn-17/19. The product candidates are based on three technologies: genetically engineered monoclonal antibodies, monoclonal antibody-drug conjugates (adcs) and antibody-directed enzyme prodrug therapy (adept).

Primary SIC and add'l.: 2834 2836 8731

CIK No: 0001060736

Officers: Clay B. Siegall/Dir., CEO, Pres./$999,500.00, Morris Z. Rosenberg/VP - Development/$593,514.00, Todd E. Simpson/CFO/$808,622.00, Jonathan Drachman/Sr. Medical Dir., Iqbal S. Grewal/VP - Preclinical Therapeutics, Peter D. Senter/VP - Chemistry, Paul J. Carter/VP - Antibody Technologies, Eric L. Dobmeier/Chief Business Officer/$680,883.00, Eric Sievers/Sr. Medical Dir., Thomas C. Reynolds/Chief Medical Officer

Directors: Clay B. Siegall/Dir., CEO, Pres., Oliver Press/Member - Scientific Advisory Board, Felix J. Baker/Dir., Marc E. Lippman/Dir., Member - Scientific Advisory Board, David W. Gryska/52/Dir., Srinivas Akkaraju/Dir., Daniel F. Hoth/Dir., Franklin M. Berger/Dir., John P. McLaughlin/Dir., Daniel G. Welch/Dir., Bruce R. Blazar/Member - Scientific Advisory Board, Michael A. Caligiuri/Member - Scientific Advisory Board, Richard A. Flavell/Member - Scientific Advisory Board, Albert F. Lobuglio/Member - Scientific Advisory Board, William J. Murphy/Member - Scientific Advisory Board

Owners: Clay B. Siegall/3.10%, Todd E. Simpson, David W. Gryska, Daniel F. Hoth, Marc E. Lippman, Pamela A. Trail, Bill & Melinda Gates Foundation/5.30%, Felix Baker/15.40%, FMR Corporation/7.70%, Srinivas Akkaraju/7.90%, Eric L. Dobmeier, Douglas G. Southern, Morris Z. Rosenberg, Franklin M. Berger, Jonathan Gallen/7.80% *(16 Owners included in Index)*

Financial Data: *Fiscal Year End:*12/31 *Latest Annual Data:* 12/31/2006

Year	Sales	Net Income
2006	$10,005,000	-$36,015,000
2005	$9,757,000	-$29,433,000
2004	$6,701,000	-$35,439,000

Curr. Assets:	$85,429,000	Curr. Liab.:	$8,549,000		
Plant, Equip.:	$7,794,000	Total Liab.:	$9,461,000	Indic. Yr. Divd.:	NA
Total Assets:	$97,695,000	Net Worth:	$88,234,000	Debt/Equity:	NA

Seawright Holdings Inc

600 Cameron St., Alexandria, VA, 22314; *PH:* 1-703-340-1629; *http://* www.seawrightsprings.com

General - Incorporation .... DE	**Stock** - Price on:12/24/2007 ....$1.77		
Employees 1	Stock Exchange.................................OTC		
Auditor ... Russell Bedford Stefanou Mirchandani	Ticker Symbol......................................SWRI		
Stk Agt .... Oxford Transfer & Registrar	Outstanding Shares 10,400,000		
Counsel...NA	E.P.S...-$0.24		
DUNS No. ....NA	Shareholders.......................................NA		

Business: The groups principle activity is selling natural spring water under the Seawright Springs label while aggressively pursuing the bulk sale of natural spring water produced. In June 2005, the group acquired from Quibell, glass bottle. The group operates from the United States.

Primary SIC and add'l.: 2086

CIK No: 0001132887

Subsidiaries: SEAWRIGHT SPRINGS, LLC

Officers: Joel P. Sens/43/Dir., CEO, Pres., Treasurer, Sec., Jake Rubin/Contact - Media

Directors: Jeffrey Sens/43/Dir.

Owners: Joel Sens/37.06%, Jeffrey Sens, Insiders/37.07%

Financial Data: *Fiscal Year End:*12/31 *Latest Annual Data:* 12/31/2006

Year	Sales	Net Income
2006	$3,000	-$1,785,000
2005	$3,000	-$1,116,000
2004	NA	-$454,000

Curr. Assets:	$411,000	Curr. Liab.:	$1,767,000		
Plant, Equip.:	$2,110,000	Total Liab.:	$3,509,000	Indic. Yr. Divd.:	NA
Total Assets:	$2,775,000	Net Worth:	-$734,000	Debt/Equity:	NA

Securac Corp

68, 4620 Manilla Rd. SE, Calgary, AB, T2G 4B7; *PH:* 1-403-225-0403; *http://* www.securac.net; *Email:* findoutmore@securac.net

General - Incorporation .... NV	**Stock** - Price on:12/24/2007 ....NA		
Employees ....NA	Stock Exchange.................................OTC		
Auditor .... Chisholm, Bierwolf & Nilson, LLC	Ticker Symbol......................................SECU		
Stk Agt ..... American Stock Transfer & Trust Co.	Outstanding Shares ....NA		
Counsel...NA	E.P.S...NA		
DUNS No. ....NA	Shareholders.......................................NA		

Business: The groups principle activities include developing and commercializing of enterprise governance, risk and compliance software and services. The group markets its product under the tradename Acertus(TM). In January 2005, the group acquired Risk Governance, Inc. Specific customers of the group include Research in Motion, Coca Cola HBC, Teekay Shipping Corporation, PepsiCo, DeBeers Canada Inc., Cisco Systems, BMO Financial, the Ontario Ministry of Transportation, and the Canada Border Service Agency. The group operates from the United States and Canada.

Primary SIC and add'l.: 7371

CIK No: 0000775926

Subsidiaries: Risk Governance Inc., Securac Inc.

Officers: Terry W. Allen/Dir., CEO - Securac INC, Paul J. Hookham/Dir., CFO - Securac Inc., Howard W. Enns/COO - Securac Inc., Rob Foss/VP - Technology Solutions, Securac Inc., Anton Wootliff/CTO - Securac Inc., Terry Hoffman/MD - Physical Risk Practice, Securac Inc., Lindsay John Cox/MD - European Operations, VP - Strategic Marketing - Business Development, Securac INC, Gerri Masciangelo/VP - Professional Services, Support, Securac INC, Todd Behrens/VP - Product Management, Strategy, Securac INC, Rick A. Preston/VP - Investor Relations, Public Affairs, Securac INC, Susan Boily/Corporate Communications, Investor Relations, Securac Inc

Financial Data: *Fiscal Year End:*12/31 *Latest Annual Data:* 12/31/2005

Year	Sales	Net Income
2005	$1,172,000	-$8,438,000
2004	$602,000	-$2,727,000
2003	NA	-$9,000

Curr. Assets:	$348,000	Curr. Liab.:	$2,286,000		
Plant, Equip.:	$33,000	Total Liab.:	$2,292,000	Indic. Yr. Divd.:	NA
Total Assets:	$1,596,000	Net Worth:	-$695,000	Debt/Equity:	NA

Secure Computing Corp

4810 Harwood Rd., San Jose, CA, 95124; *PH:* 1-408-979-6100; *http://* www.sctc.com

General - Incorporation .... DE	**Stock** - Price on:12/24/2007 ....$7.39		
Employees 885	Stock Exchange.................................NDQ		
Auditor .... Ernst & Young LLP	Ticker Symbol......................................SCUR		
Stk Agt .... Wells Fargo Bank, N.A.	Outstanding Shares 67,230,000		
Counsel...NA	E.P.S...-$0.96		
DUNS No. 60-619-3803	Shareholders.......................................NA		

Business: The group's principal activities are to design, develop and market computer software products and services. The products and services provide secure access control for all users engaged in the business over public network, including the Internet, intranets and extranets. The group operates in two segments: products and services and advance technology. The products and services segment markets a range of solutions that provide risk-free, personalized access control across any public. The advance technology segment develops new technologies and products that meet the emerging needs of both the departments of defense and the commercial sector. The customers of the group include industries such as manufacturing and retail, school systems and Internet service providers, international organizations and foreign governments.on 14-Oct-2003 the group acquired n2h2, inc. The group discontinued operations of advance technology division in oct 2003

Primary SIC and add'l.: 7372 8742 8731 7371 3577 7373

CIK No: 0001001916

Officers: John McNulty/Chmn., CEO, Pres., Mary K. Budge/Sr. VP, Sec., General Counsel, Timothy McGurran/COO, Pres., Tim Steinkopf/Sr. VP, CFO, Stephen M. Puricelli/Dir., Private Investor, Vincent M. Schiavo/Sr. VP - Worldwide Sales, Ker Gibbs/VP - Asia Pacific, Jay Goldlist/VP, GM - Enterprise Security Division, James F. Jordan/Dir., Private Investor, Mike Gallagher/Sr. VP - Product Development, Paul Judge/CTO, Atri Chatterjee/Sr. VP - Marketing, Paul Henry/VP - Technology Evangelism, Scott Montgomery/VP - Product Management

Directors: John McNulty/Chmn., CEO, Pres., Jay Chaudhry/Vice Chmn., Robert J. Frankenberg/Dir., Alexander Zakupowsky/Dir., James F. Jordan/Dir., Private Investor, Richard L. Scott/Dir., Stephen M. Puricelli/Dir., Private Investor, Eric P. Rundquist/Dir., Cary J. Davis/Dir.

Owners: Cary Davis/8.90%, Mary Budge, Vincent Schiavo, Michael Gallagher, Robert J. Frankenberg, Timothy Steinkopf, John McNulty/2.10%, Eric P. Rundquist, Alexander Zakupowsky, Jay Chaudhry/7.10%, Warburg Pincus Private Equity IX, L.P./8.90%, Stephen M. Puricelli, Insiders/26.70%, James Jordan, Richard Scott/5.20%

Financial Data: *Fiscal Year End:* 12/31 *Latest Annual Data:* 12/31/2006

Year	Sales	Net Income
2006	$176,697,000	-$27,398,000
2005	$109,175,000	$21,374,000
2004	$93,378,000	$12,835,000

Curr. Assets:	$90,368,000	Curr. Liab.:	$118,872,000		
Plant, Equip.:	$14,300,000	Total Liab.:	$314,387,000	Indic. Yr. Divd.:	NA
Total Assets:	$724,128,000	Net Worth:	$409,741,000	Debt/ Equity:	0.1800

Secure Technologies Group Inc

21634 Club Villa Terr, Boca Raton, FL, 33433; *PH:* 1-778-549-5665; *http://* www.securtecgroup.com

General		Stock	
Incorporation	DE	Price on:12/24/2007	$0.01
Employees	NA	Stock Exchange	OTC
Auditor	Lewis S. Schiller	Ticker Symbol	SCTC
Stk Agt	American Stock Transfer & Trust Co.	Outstanding Shares	NA
Counsel	NA	E.P.S	-$1.13
DUNS No.	03-047-2815	Shareholders	NA

Business: The group's principle activity is to market and sell security products. The products offered include the gil 2001 portal control system and the secured card solutions software program. The gil 2001 portal control system includes embedded defensive countermeasures for piggybacked entry, weapons or credentials pass back, run back breeches and protection against forced entry. The secured card solutions software program enables colleges and universities to link access control of their recreation facilities with the university ID card, process memberships, issue recreation equipment and obtain utilization reports for multiple recreation facilities. The group operates mainly in the United States.

Primary SIC and add'l.: 7382

CIK No: 0000316618

Subsidiaries: Granite Technologies Acquisition Corp., Secured Portal Systems, Inc., Secured Systems Group, Inc.

Financial Data: *Fiscal Year End:* 12/04 *Latest Annual Data:* 10/31/2006

Year	Sales	Net Income
2006	$22,147,800,000	$1,693,800,000
2005	$21,930,500,000	$1,446,800,000
2004	$26,000	-$5,232,000

Curr. Assets:	$10,000	Curr. Liab.:	$5,155,000		
Plant, Equip.:	NA	Total Liab.:	$9,351,000	Indic. Yr. Divd.:	NA
Total Assets:	$10,000	Net Worth:	-$9,341,000	Debt/ Equity:	NA

Securecare Technologies Inc

3755 Capital of Texas Hwy. S, Ste. 106E, Austin, TX, 78704; *PH:* 1-888-447-3707; *Fax:* 1-866-734-7706; *http://* www.securecaretech.com

General		Stock	
Incorporation	NV	Price on:12/24/2007	NA
Employees	4	Stock Exchange	OTC
Auditor	KBA Group LLP	Ticker Symbol	SCUC
Stk Agt	Fidelity Transfer Co	Outstanding Shares	NA
Counsel	NA	E.P.S	-$33.44
DUNS No.	NA	Shareholders	NA

Business: The group's principal activity is to provide electronic transmittal, processing and data storage services for the healthcare industry. The group's technology solutions are Web service applications that are designed to provide secure workflow and data exchange between health care professionals. The products include securecare(tm) for e-signature and secure transmission of patient data, net.care(tm) for assessment accuracy and verification, and facts2000(TM) for forecasting and monitoring of nursing home cash flow. The group also provides digital certificate and e-signature technology that enable health care organizations to manage workflow processes easily and securely without the paper shuffle typically associated with their business. The group's solutions connect physicians, home health agencies and nursing homes via electronic medical record products and services. The group markets its services to customers throughout the United States.

Primary SIC and add'l.: 7379 7372

CIK No: 0000018530

Officers: Dennis J. Nasto/Dir., CEO, Richard F. Corlin/Chmn., Chief Medical Officer, Edward Hill/Physician Advisor, Neil S. Burley/CFO, VP, Mary T. Herald/Physician Advisor, Eugene Fry/Chief Compliance Officer, VP - Product, Technology Development

Directors: Dennis J. Nasto/Dir., CEO, Richard F. Corlin/Chmn., Chief Medical Officer, Robert R. McMillan/Dir., Allen J. Stamy/Dir., Laszlo J. Meszaros/Dir.

Owners: Richard F. Corlin/3.00%, Neil Burley/1.00%, Gene Fry/1.00%, Allen Stamy, Insiders/6.00%, Gryphon Opportunities Fund I, LLC/62.00%, Dennis Nasto/1.00%

Financial Data: *Fiscal Year End:* 12/31 *Latest Annual Data:* 12/31/2006

Year	Sales	Net Income
2006	$245,000	-$20,353,000
2005	$387,000	-$2,985,000
2004	$211,000	-$2,271,000

Curr. Assets:	$154,000	Curr. Liab.:	$1,084,000		
Plant, Equip.:	$45,000	Total Liab.:	$1,122,000	Indic. Yr. Divd.:	NA
Total Assets:	$199,000	Net Worth:	-$923,000	Debt/ Equity:	NA

Secured Digital Applications Inc

230 Pk. Ave., 10th Fl., New York, NY, 07663; *PH:* 1-212-551-1747; *Fax:* 1-212-808-3020; *http://* www.digitalapps.net

General		Stock	
Incorporation	DE	Price on:12/24/2007	$0.064
Employees	20	Stock Exchange	OTC
Auditor	GHP Horwath, P.C	Ticker Symbol	SDGL
Stk Agt	Registrar & Transfer Co	Outstanding Shares	130,250,000
Counsel	NA	E.P.S	$0.007
DUNS No.	NA	Shareholders	NA

Business: The group's principal activity is to provide network facilities and services for synchronous wireless broadband applications. These services include distance learning, live news coverage, remote video surveillance, emergency field services and on site progress monitoring. The group operates through two divisions. Application division includes application development, broadband network operation, delivery of value added applications and services, sale of devices that utilize broadband networks and the sale of biometric security devices. Material handling division includes industrial moving, packing and unpacking industrial equipment, land transportation and secured logistics, as well as the sale, rental and servicing of material handling equipment. The group has operations in Malaysia and the United States of America. On 09-Dec-2003, the group acquired 80% interest in asiaco material handling, 67% interest in asiaco logistic and 60% interest in asiaco services.

Primary SIC and add'l.: 7372 7353 4731

CIK No: 0000940516

Subsidiaries: Armor Multi Services Sdn Bhd, Armor Multi Systems Sdn Bhd (AMS), China Sea Trade Company, Inc., Digital Image ID Sdn Bhd, Eystar Distribution Sdn Bhd, Gallant Focus (M) Sdn Bhd, Gallant IT Holdings Sdn Bhd (GIH), Gallant Service Centre (M) Sdn Bhd (GSC), Gallant Zone (M) Sdn Bhd, Innospective Sdn Bhd, Perwimas Telecommunications Sdn Bhd, SDA Worldwide, Inc., Secured Digital Applications (M) Sdn Bhd (SDAM), Secured Shipping Sdn Bhd

Officers: Patrick Soon-hock Lim/Chmn., CEO, Pres., Soong Kwong Choon/Consultant, Ismail Talib/Dir. - US Operations, Valerie Hoi-fah Looi/Dir., Corp. Sec., Raghuram Bayaneni/Information Technology Consultant, Chee Hong Leong/Dir. - Corporate Finance, Krishna Pande/Advisory Panel, Fixed Wireless Access, Yahaya Ibrahim/Advisory Panel, Distance Learning, Mohd Nor Awang/Advisory Panel, Telemedicine, Steven Yong/Chief Accounting Officer, Kelvin Ng/Finance Mgr., Head - BPO Services Division, Sharon Teh/Assist., Mgr.

Directors: Patrick Soon-hock Lim/Chmn., CEO, Pres., Valerie Hoi-fah Looi/Dir., Corp. Sec., Mustaffar Yacob/Dir., Chee Hong Leong/Dir. - Corporate Finance

Owners: Voon-Fui Yong, Wan Abdul Razak bin Muda, Insiders/38.25%, Patrick Soon-Hock Lim/34.52%, Valerie Hoi-Fah Looi/4.22%

Financial Data: *Fiscal Year End:* 12/31 *Latest Annual Data:* 12/31/2006

Year	Sales	Net Income
2006	$36,946,000	$657,000
2005	$28,307,000	$127,000
2004	$20,438,000	$1,232,000

Curr. Assets:	$8,570,000	Curr. Liab.:	$1,172,000	P/E Ratio:	8.00
Plant, Equip.:	$993,000	Total Liab.:	$1,489,000	Indic. Yr. Divd.:	NA
Total Assets:	$10,168,000	Net Worth:	$8,499,000	Debt/ Equity:	NA

Secured Diversified Investment Ltd

5205 E Lincoln Dr., Paradise Valley, AZ, 85253; *PH:* 1-949-851-1069

General		Stock	
Incorporation	NV	Price on:12/24/2007	$1.01
Employees	3	Stock Exchange	OTC
Auditor	Kabani & Co, Inc	Ticker Symbol	SDVF
Stk Agt	Fidelity Transfer Co	Outstanding Shares	NA
Counsel	NA	E.P.S	NA
DUNS No.	NA	Shareholders	NA

Business: The group's principal activities are to own interest in real estate properties, shopping centers and hotels. The group owns shopping centers in dickinson, North Dakota; las vegas, Nevada; and orange, California and a hotel in dickinson, North Dakota. On 19-Nov-2003, the group acquired the remaining 50% interest in spencer springs, llc.

Primary SIC and add'l.: 7812 7819

CIK No: 0000013156

Subsidiaries: Diversified Commercial Brokers, LLC, Diversified Commercial Mortgage, Inc., Nationwide Commercial Brokers, Inc.

Officers: Jan Wallace/53/Dir., CEO, Pres., Munjit Johal/52/CFO

Directors: Jan Wallace/53/Dir., CEO, Pres., Peter Richman/41/Dir., Jay Kister/33/Dir.

Owners: Kelly Black/6.20%, Jay Kister, Munjit Johal/6.10%, Donald Schwall/12.30%, Jan Wallace/27.30%, Insiders/32.90%

Financial Data: *Fiscal Year End:* 12/31 *Latest Annual Data:* 3/31/2007

Year	Sales	Net Income
2007	NA	$90,000
2006	NA	$98,000
2005	$549,000	$794,000

Curr. Assets:	$85,000	Curr. Liab.:	$185,000		
Plant, Equip.:	$1,555,000	Total Liab.:	$1,471,000	Indic. Yr. Divd.:	NA
Total Assets:	$1,651,000	Net Worth:	$90,000	Debt/ Equity:	NA

Secured Financial Network Inc

101 Ne 3rd Ave., Ste. 1500, Ft. Lauderdale, FL, 33301; *PH:* 1-954-332-3793

General		Stock	
Incorporation	NV	Price on:12/24/2007	$0.04
Employees	2	Stock Exchange	OTC
Auditor	Sherb & Co., LLP	Ticker Symbol	SFNL
Stk Agt	First American Stock Transfer, Inc.	Outstanding Shares	34,630,000
Counsel	NA	E.P.S	-$0.068
DUNS No.	NA	Shareholders	NA

Business: The group's principle activities include researching and developing an innovative acne therapy system(tm). The company's products offer the benefits over typical acne treatment products: reduced irritation, moisture retention properties, maintenance of skin's natural pH balance and skin healing qualities. The company has acquired the rights to use the registered trademark 'zit stick' (r). On 22-Mar-2004, the company acquired h bana ltd. The group operates from United States.

Primary SIC and add'l.: 8731 2844 2834

CIK No: 0001100394

Officers: Jeffrey L. Schultz/57/Dir., CEO, Pres., Michael Fasci/49/Chmn., CFO, Pres., Stephen F. Burg/Dir., Sec.

Directors: Jeffrey L. Schultz/57/Dir., CEO, Pres., Michael Fasci/49/Chmn., CFO, Pres., Caesar Berger/Dir., Stephen F. Burg/Dir., Sec.

Owners: Jeffrey L. Schultz/16.80%, Stephen F. Burg/0.20%, Michael Fasci/3.30%, Insiders/65.20%, HEB, LLC/15.20%, Brian Corday/17.10%

Financial Data: *Fiscal Year End:* 12/31 *Latest Annual Data:* 6/30/2006

Year	Sales	Net Income
2006	$311,000	-$564,000
2005	$2,130,000	-$2,758,000

Curr. Assets:	$6,000	Curr. Liab.:	$2,790,000		
Plant, Equip.:	$3,000	Total Liab.:	$2,790,000	Indic. Yr. Divd.:	NA
Total Assets:	$9,000	Net Worth:	-$2,781,000	Debt/ Equity:	NA

Secured Services Inc

1155 N Service Rd. W, Unit 8, Oakville, ON, L6M 3E3; *PH:* 1-866-419-3900;
http:// www.secured-services.com

General - Incorporation	DE	Stock - Price on:12/24/2007	$0.006
Employees	62	Stock Exchange	OTC
Auditor	J. H. Cohn LLP	Ticker Symbol	SSVC
Stk Agt.	American Stock Transfer & Trust Co.	Outstanding Shares	18,410,000
Counsel	NA	E.P.S.	-$0.68
DUNS No.	NA	Shareholders	NA

Business: The group's principal activity is to provide security software solutions. The software ensures that only those people or business processes that are entitled to access corporate resources and applications to access them. It helps companies to manage user population, that needs to access those resources and applications. The group's product includes identiprise, which provides identity and access management to a broad range of technology environments. It also offers various levels of consulting and support services that identifies and manages security issues and practices. The software products are generally sold on a perpetual license basis. The group also provides services to customers with project management, architecture and design, custom development services and training. The group mainly operates in the United States.

Primary SIC and add'l.: 7379 7372 7371
CIK No: 0000851943
Subsidiaries: Secured Services Canada, Inc., SSI Minnesota Corp., SSI Operating Corp.
Officers: Dale Quick/Dir., CEO, Pres., John Lund/CFO, Ken Hetzer/Contact - Media Relations
Directors: Dale Quick/Dir., CEO, Pres., King Moore/Dir.
Owners: Vasco Data Security International, Inc/3.90%, Toucan Capital Fund II L.P., The Dubreuil Family Trust, Kendall T. Hunt, Michael Faber, Shawn Kreloff, King T. Moore, Dale Quick, 033 Asset Management, LLC, Insiders, NextPoint Partners II L.P., Vasco Data Security International, Inc.

Financial Data: Fiscal Year End:12/31 Latest Annual Data: 12/31/2004

Year	Sales	Net Income
2004	$2,194,000	-$5,757,000
2003	$1,024,000	-$1,016,000
2002	$363,000	-$598,000

Curr. Assets:	$2,538,000	Curr. Liab.:	$1,915,000		
Plant, Equip.:	$147,000	Total Liab.:	$2,181,000	Indic. Yr. Divd.:	NA
Total Assets:	$7,156,000	Net Worth:	$4,975,000	Debt/ Equity:	1.9741

SecureLogic Corp

43 Hemelacha St., Netanya, 42505; *PH:* 866-838-1102

General - Incorporation	NV	Stock - Price on:12/24/2007	$0.1
Employees	NA	Stock Exchange	OTC
Auditor	Brightman Almagor & Co.	Ticker Symbol	SLGI
Stk Agt.	Pacific Stock Transfer Company	Outstanding Shares	NA
Counsel	NA	E.P.S.	NA
DUNS No.	NA	Shareholders	NA

Business: The group's principal activity is to provide software products that served the consumer, small business and corporate enterprise market. The group operates through three segments namely baggage handling systems, WMS and software, and maintenance services and support. The group operates from the United States.

Primary SIC and add'l.: 7389 7372 3661 3669 7379
CIK No: 0001098875
Subsidiaries: ChainLogic, Ltd., SecureLogic, Inc., SecureLogic, Ltd., SpaceLogic, Ltd.
Officers: Gary Koren/59/Chmn., CEO, Pres., Shalom Dolev/51/Dir., VP - Security Systems, Tomer Nahum/36/CFO
Directors: Gary Koren/59/Chmn., CEO, Pres., Shalom Dolev/51/Dir., VP - Security Systems, Cathal Flynn/69/Dir., Sean Deson/44/Dir., Paul Goodman/46/Dir., Iftach Yeffet/50/Dir., Michael Klein/55/Dir.
Owners: Shalom Dolev/6.50%, Iftach Yeffet/6.70%, Tony Gross/6.60%, Sean Deson/3.60%, Michael Klein/13.40%, Gary Koren/30.40%, Cathal Flynn, Insiders/73.70%, Paul Goodman

Financial Data: Fiscal Year End:12/31 Latest Annual Data: 12/31/2006

Year	Sales	Net Income
2006	$1,297,000	-$1,963,000
2005	$807,000	-$4,750,000
2004	NA	$5,995,000

Curr. Assets:	$1,391,000	Curr. Liab.:	$1,414,000		
Plant, Equip.:	$136,000	Total Liab.:	$2,183,000	Indic. Yr. Divd.:	NA
Total Assets:	$1,869,000	Net Worth:	-$314,000	Debt/ Equity:	NA

Security Bank Corp

4219 Forsyth Rd., Macon, GA, 31210; *PH:* 1-478-722-6200; *Fax:* 1-478-722-6229;
http:// www.securitybank.net

General - Incorporation	GA	Stock - Price on:12/24/2007	NA
Employees	422	Stock Exchange	NDQ
Auditor	McNair, Middlebrooks & Co. LLP	Ticker Symbol	SBKC
Stk Agt	Registrar & Transfer Co	Outstanding Shares	NA
Counsel	NA	E.P.S.	$0.96
DUNS No.	19-482-3951	Shareholders	NA

Business: The group's principal activities are to offer a variety of community banking services to its customers in the United States. The group operates through 23 banking and mortgage production offices, with the majority of its business being drawn from bibb, houston and jones counties in the state of Georgia. It provides a range of retail and commercial banking products and services, including checking, savings and money market accounts; certificates of deposit; credit cards; individual retirement accounts; safe-deposit boxes; money orders; electronic funds transfer services; travelers' checks and automatic teller machine access. The group's lending activities include mortgage, commercial and consumer loans to local borrowers. The group operates through its subsidiaries namely security bank of bibb county, security bank of houston county and security bank of jones county.

Primary SIC and add'l.: 6712 6022
CIK No: 0000925464
Subsidiaries: Rivoli Bank & Trust, Rivoli Bank and Trust Statutory Trust I, Security Bank of Bibb County (a), Security Bank of Houston County, Security Bank of Jones County, Security Bank of North Metro, Statutory Trust I, Statutory Trust II
Officers: Averett H. Walker/Dir., CEO, Pres./$810,242.00, Linda L. Cassidy/Sec., Richard A. Collinsworth/COO, Exec. VP/$576,405.00, James R. McLemore/CFO, Exec. VP/$363,768.00
Directors: Averett H. Walker/Dir., CEO, Pres., Alford C. Bridges/Chmn., Edward M. Beckham/Vice Chmn., Richard W. White/Dir., Frank H. Childs/Dir., Robert M. Stalnaker/Dir., Thad G. Childs/Dir., Larry C. Walker/Dir., Benjamin W. Griffith/Dir., John W. Ramsey/Dir., Timothy Kevin Reece/Dir., Robert T. Mullis/Dir., Ruthie G. McMichael/Dir., Joe E. Timberlake/Dir., James R. Williams/Dir. *(18 Directors included in Index)*
Owners: Frank C. Winn/2.87%, David J. McDade/3.21%, William C. Lumpkin/11.12%, Insiders/58.94%, James E. Daniell/2.92%, Larry W. Jackson/19.82%, William H. Harrison/1.08%, Phil D. Miller/1.36%, Carl E. Carr/7.34%, Joel R. Tidwell/3.50%, Tom D. Richey/1.14%, Jack F. Gamel/5.02%, Richard W. Kinsey/4.34%, Jimmy R. Smith/7.71%, Paul T. Price *(16 Owners included in Index)*

Financial Data: Fiscal Year End:12/31 Latest Annual Data: 12/31/2006

Year	Sales	Net Income
2006	$166,045,000	$23,392,000
2005	$94,801,000	$16,185,000
2004	$68,759,000	$12,319,000

Curr. Assets:	$159,815,000	Curr. Liab.:	$2,021,844,000		
Plant, Equip.:	$43,417,000	Total Liab.:	$2,187,663,000	Indic. Yr. Divd.:	$0.350
Total Assets:	$2,494,071,000	Net Worth:	$306,407,000	Debt/ Equity:	NA

Security Bank of CA

3403 Tenth St., Ste. 100, Riverside, CA, 92501; *PH:* 1-877-461-7262; *Fax:* 1-951-368-2271;
http:// www.securitybankca.com

General - Incorporation		Stock - Price on:12/24/2007	$20
Employees	NA	Stock Exchange	OTC
Auditor	NA	Ticker Symbol	SBOC
Stk Agt	U.S. Stock Transfer Corp	Outstanding Shares	NA
Counsel	NA	E.P.S.	NA
DUNS No.	NA	Shareholders	NA

Business: The groups principal activities include providing banking and financial services. Services of the group include checking accounts, savings accounts, certificates of deposit, installment loans, real estate mortgage loans, commercial loans, traveler's checks, safe deposit boxes, night depository and automated teller services. The group operates from the United States.

Primary SIC and add'l.: 6022
CIK No:
Officers: James A. Robinson/Chmn., CEO, Ernie Hwang/Vice Chmn., Chief Lending Officer, Kristine Chung/Exec. VP, SBA Mgr., Michael Vanderpool/Dir., COO, Pres., Pam Fortin/CIO, Sr. VP, Jamie Robinson/Sr. VP, Commercial Team Mgr., Timothy Streeter/Exec. VP, Chief Credit Officer, Thomas Ferrer/Sr. VP, CFO, Russell Burch/Dir., Pres. - Burchco
Directors: James A. Robinson/Chmn., CEO, Ernie Hwang/Vice Chmn., Chief Lending Officer, Tim Hanigan/Founder, Joseph Tavaglione/Dir., Bruce Varner/Dir., Barry J. Aronoff/Dir., Gerald B. Bashaw/Dir., Russell Burch/Dir., Pres. - Burchco, Ernest Castro/Dir., Ayad Fargo/Dir., Nicholas H. Goldware/Dir., Amy Harrison/Dir., Steve Kienle/Dir., Walter T. McDonald/Dir., Michael Vanderpool/Dir., COO, Pres. *(29 Directors included in Index)*

Security Bus BK CA

701 B St., Ste. 100, San Diego, CA, 92101; *PH:* 1-619-231-8500; *Fax:* 1-619-237-4200;
http:// www.securitybusinessbank.com; *Email:* contacts@securitybusinessbank.com

General - Incorporation		Stock - Price on:12/24/2007	$19.85
Employees	NA	Stock Exchange	OTC
Auditor	NA	Ticker Symbol	NA
Stk Agt	NA	Outstanding Shares	1,780,000
Counsel	NA	E.P.S.	NA
DUNS No.	NA	Shareholders	NA

Business: The groups principal activities include providing banking services as community banking. Services of the group include checking accounts, savings accounts, certificates of deposit, installment loans, real estate mortgage loans, commercial loans, traveler's checks, safe deposit boxes, night depository and automated teller services. The group operates from the United States.

Primary SIC and add'l.: 6029
CIK No:
Officers: Paul F. Rodeno/Dir., CEO, Pres., Pamela Maes/Sr. VP, CFO, Steve Espino/Exec. VP, Sr. Lending Officer, Claire Fitzpatrick/Exec. VP - Cashier, Gail Jensen-Bigknife/Exec. VP, Chief Credit Officer, Chris J. Burr/Sr. VP - Commercial Lending, Thomas E. Welch/Sr. VP - SBA Lending, Brian J. Smith/Sr. VP - Commercial Lending, Kim Tronerud-Coy/VP - Commercial Lending, Ricardo MacEdo/VP - Commercial Lending, Sean O'Neill/VP - Commercial Lending, Colette McLoughlin/VP - SBA Lender, Jeanine Baggett/VP - SBA Lender, Greg M. Cody/Dir. - Private Investor, Nicholas Zillges/Sr. VP - Cash Management
Directors: Paul F. Rodeno/Dir., CEO, Pres., Robert P. Keller/Chmn., Gordon R. Carrier/Dir., Greg M. Cody/Dir. - Private Investor, Dennis S. Cruzan/Dir., Bruce A. Millimaki/Dir., Gail Stoorza-Gill/Dir.

Security Capital Assurance Ltd

One Bermudiana Rd., Hamilton; *PH:* 4412947448; *http://* www.scafg.com

General - Incorporation	Bermuda	Stock - Price on:12/24/2007	$30.45
Employees	160	Stock Exchange	NYSE
Auditor	Pricewaterhousecoopers LLP	Ticker Symbol	SCA
Stk Agt	Bank of New York	Outstanding Shares	65,300,000
Counsel	NA	E.P.S.	$2.03
DUNS No.	NA	Shareholders	NA

Business: The group operates through subsidiaries whose principle activity is to provide financial guaranty insurance, reinsurance and other credit enhancement products. The group operates through two segments namely, financial guarantee insurance and financial guarantee reinsurance. The group operates from the United States.

Primary SIC and add'l.: 6351

CIK No: 0001358164

Subsidiaries: SCA Administrative Holdings US Inc., SCA Bermuda Administrative Ltd, SCA Holdings US Inc., XL Capital Assurance (U.K.) Limited, XL Capital Assurance Inc. ("XLCA"), XL Financial Administrative Services, XL Financial Assurance Ltd, XL Portfolio Advisors Inc., XLCA Admin LLC, XLCDS LLC

Officers: Paul S. Giordano/Dir., CEO, Pres., David P. Shea/CFO, Exec. VP, Edward B. Hubbard/Exec. VP, Pres., COO - XL Capital Assurance Inc, Michael E. Rego/Exec. VP - Financial Guarantee Reinsurance, Richard P. Heberton/MD, Chief Credit Officer - XL Capital Assurance Inc , Tom W. Currie/Sr. VP, Chief Risk Officer, Claude L. Leblanc/Exec. VP - Corporate Development, Strategy, Security Capital Assurance, T. Wynne Morriss/Sr. VP, Head - Origination, XL Capital Assurance Inc., Orlando Rivera/MD, Head - Human Resources, Kirstin Romann Gould/Sec.

Directors: Paul S. Giordano/Dir., CEO, Pres., Michael P. Esposito/Chmn., Grant E. Gibbons/Dir., Richard P. Heberton/MD, Chief Credit Officer - XL Capital Assurance Inc , Bruce G. Hannon/Dir., Mary R. Hennessy/Dir., Robert M. Lichten/Dir., Brian M. Ohara/Dir., Coleman D. Ross/Dir., Alan Z. Senter/Dir.

Owners: XL Insurance (Bermuda) Ltd/46.05%, Legg Mason Capital Management, Inc./10.84%

Financial Data: *Fiscal Year End:*12/31 *Latest Annual Data:* 12/31/2006

Year	Sales			Net Income
2006		$238,639,000		$117,355,000
Curr. Assets:	$585,984,000	**Curr. Liab.:**	$101,855,000	**P/E Ratio:** 12.58
Plant, Equip.:	NA	**Total Liab.:**	$1,130,294,000	**Indic. Yr. Divd.:** $0.080
Total Assets:	$2,496,814,000	**Net Worth:**	$1,366,520,000	**Debt/ Equity:** NA

Security Capital Corp

Three Pickwick Plz., Ste. 310, Greenwich, CT, 06830; *PH:* 1-203-625-0770;
http:// www.securitycapitalcorporation.com

General - Incorporation	DE	**Stock**- Price on:12/24/2007	$67.85
Employees	NA	Stock Exchange	NA
Auditor	McGladrey & Pullen LLP	Ticker Symbol	NA
Stk Agt	Bank of New York	Outstanding Shares	NA
Counsel	NA	E.P.S	NA
DUNS No.	05-294-4659	Shareholders	NA

Business: The group's principle activities are to provide various services to corporations and their employees and franchising of educational child care centers. It operates through two segments: the employer cost containment and health services segment provides services to employers and their employees relating to industrial health and safety, industrial medical care, workers' compensation insurance and the direct and indirect costs associated therewith. The educational services segment is engaged in the franchising of educational child care centers with related activities in operations advisory, real estate and site selection services.

Primary SIC and add'l.: 6324 8351

CIK No: 0000314340

Subsidiaries: Caronia Corporation, CMI Barron Risk Management Services,Inc., CMI Management Company, CompManagement, CompManagement Disability Services Company, CompManagement Health Systems,Inc., CompManagement Integrated Disability Services Inc., CompManagement of Virginia,Inc., CompManagement,Inc., Integrated Claims Strategies,Inc., KRAMMCO,Inc., Managed Care Holdings Corporation, Octagon Risk Services,Inc., Primrose Holdings,Inc., Primrose School Franchising Company, PS-Bentwater,Inc. 17 Subsidiaries included in the Index

Financial Data: *Fiscal Year End:*12/31 *Latest Annual Data:* 03/31/2007

Year	Sales	Net Income
2007	$3,283,000	-$1,321,000
2006	$2,793,000	-$920,000

Security Devices International Inc

120 Adelaide Str. W, Ste. 2500, Toronto, ON, M5H 1T1; *PH:* 1-416-787-1871;
http:// www.lektrox.com; *Email:* info@lektrox.com

General - Incorporation	DE	**Stock**- Price on:12/24/2007	$3.15
Employees	NA	Stock Exchange	OTC
Auditor	Schwartz Levitsky Feldman LLP	Ticker Symbol	SDEV
Stk Agt	Transfer Online, Inc.	Outstanding Shares	NA
Counsel	NA	E.P.S	NA
DUNS No.	NA	Shareholders	NA

Business: The groups principal activities include developing wireless electric ammunition for use in military, homeland security, law enforcement, and professional and home security applications. The group operates from the United States.

Primary SIC and add'l.: 3690

CIK No: 0001354866

Officers: Sheldon Kales/CEO, Ilan Shalev/Project Mgr., Haim Danon/Engineering Mgr., Yoav Paz/Chief Medical Consultant, Emanuel Mendes/Consultant Product Development, Natan Blaunstein/58/Dir., VP - Research, Development, Chief Scientist, Mark Friedman/Patent Attorneys, Rakesh Malhotra/CFO, William J. Lacey/Corporate Advisor

Directors: Emanuel Mendes/Consultant Product Development, Natan Blaunstein/58/Dir., VP - Research, Development, Chief Scientist, Boaz Dor/Dir., Gregory Sullivan/Dir.

Owners: Boaz Dor/8.90%, Insiders/32.60%, Gregory Sullivan/2.80%, Dror Shachar/8.40%, Sheldon Kales/21.00%

Financial Data: *Fiscal Year End:*11/30 *Latest Annual Data:* 11/30/2006

Year	Sales			Net Income
2006		NA		-$1,661,000
Curr. Assets:	$1,468,000	**Curr. Liab.:**	$108,000	
Plant, Equip.:	NA	**Total Liab.:**	$108,000	**Indic. Yr. Divd.:** NA
Total Assets:	$1,468,000	**Net Worth:**	$1,360,000	**Debt/ Equity:** NA

Security Federal Corp

238 Richland Ave. W, Aiken, SC, 29801; *PH:* 1-803-641-3000

General - Incorporation	SC	**Stock**- Price on:12/24/2007	$24.5
Employees	159	Stock Exchange	OTC
Auditor	Elliott Davis LLC	Ticker Symbol	SFDL
Stk Agt	Security Federal Corp	Outstanding Shares	2,610,000
Counsel	Breyer & Assocaite PC	E.P.S	$1.60
DUNS No.	03-909-3042	Shareholders	NA

Business: The group's principal activity is to accept savings deposits from the general public and the origination of mortgage loans to enable to purchase or refinance one- to four-family residential real estate. The group is a federally chartered stock savings bank, which is head quartered in alien, South Carolina and has 01 branch offices in alien and lexington counties. The group also makes loans secured by multi-family residential, commercial real estate, consumer and commercial loans. In addition, the group originates construction loans and loans for the acquisition, development and construction of residential subdivisions and commercial projects.

Primary SIC and add'l.: 6035 6712

CIK No: 0000818677

Subsidiaries: Security Federal Insurance, Inc., Security Federal Investments, Security Federal Trust

Owners: Gasper L. Toole/4.05%, Thomas L. Moore, Clifton T. Weeks/11.76%, Thomas W. Weeks/7.56%, William Clyburn, Robert E. Scott/8.61%, Roy G. Lindburg/2.00%, Chris J. Verenes, Harry O. Weeks/3.10%, Insiders/28.95%, Timothy W. Simmons/6.71%, Robert E. Alexander

Financial Data: *Fiscal Year End:*03/31 *Latest Annual Data:* 03/31/2007

Year	Sales			Net Income
2007		$45,958,000		$4,127,000
2006		$35,247,000		$3,813,000
2005		$28,294,000		$3,505,000
Curr. Assets:	$16,901,000	**Curr. Liab.:**	$610,592,000	**P/E Ratio:** 15.31
Plant, Equip.:	$11,663,000	**Total Liab.:**	$621,076,000	**Indic. Yr. Divd.:** NA
Total Assets:	$658,678,000	**Net Worth:**	$37,602,000	**Debt/ Equity:** 0.2890

Security Intelligence Technologies Inc

145 Huguenot St., New Rochelle, NY, 10801; *PH:* 1-914-654-8700; *Fax:* 1-914-654-1302;
http:// www.secintel.com

General - Incorporation	FL	**Stock**- Price on:12/24/2007	$0.008
Employees	38	Stock Exchange	OTC
Auditor	Demetrius & Co LLC	Ticker Symbol	SITG
Stk Agt	Corporate Stock Transfer, Inc.	Outstanding Shares	93,580,000
Counsel	NA	E.P.S	-$0.034
DUNS No.	NA	Shareholders	NA

Business: The group's principal activities are to design, assemble, market and sell security and surveillance products and systems. The products include covert audio and video intercept, electronic countermeasures, radio communication, explosive contraband detection, biological and chemical masks and protective clothing, lie detection and global positioning systems. These products are used for tracking, locating and recovering vehicles and fleet management. The group's products and services are used by military, law enforcement and security personnel in the public and private sectors, as well as governmental agencies, multinational corporations and non-governmental organizations. The operations are carried on in the United States.

Primary SIC and add'l.: 7382

CIK No: 0001117258

Owners: Insiders/53.80%, Ben Jamil/50.90%, Chris R. Decker/5.70%, Michael D. Farkas/5.40%, Tom Felice/1.00%

Financial Data: *Fiscal Year End:*06/30 *Latest Annual Data:* 6/30/2006

Year	Sales			Net Income
2006		$2,400,000		-$3,052,000
2005		$2,736,000		-$9,781,000
2004		$3,013,000		-$4,999,000
Curr. Assets:	$676,000	**Curr. Liab.:**	$9,254,000	
Plant, Equip.:	$5,000	**Total Liab.:**	$9,748,000	**Indic. Yr. Divd.:** NA
Total Assets:	$699,000	**Net Worth:**	-$9,049,000	**Debt/ Equity:** NA

Security Land & Development Corp

512 B Wheeler Executive Ctr., Augusta, GA, 30909; *PH:* 1-706-736-6334

General - Incorporation	GA	**Stock**- Price on:12/24/2007	NA
Employees	NA	Stock Exchange	NA
Auditor	Elliot Davis LLC	Ticker Symbol	NA
Stk Agt	NA	Outstanding Shares	NA
Counsel	NA	E.P.S	NA
DUNS No.	05-623-3539	Shareholders	NA

Business: The group's principal activity is the acquisition of developed and undeveloped real estate for investment purposes or to be developed and leased as income producing property. The group's activities are conducted in Georgia where it has acquired properties in the richmond and columbia counties. The properties include a retail strip center on Washington road in augusta, leased to publix supermarkets inc that operates it as a retail food supermarket. The other properties include a commercial property on Washington road in augusta, a development property on belair road and north belair road extension in evans, a commercial property on old evans road in evans and a residential property on stanley drive, currently leased as a single family residence.

Primary SIC and add'l.: 6519 6512

CIK No: 0000088572

Subsidiaries: Royal Palms Motel, Inc., SLDC, LLC

Officers: Greenlee T. Flanagin/58/Dir., CEO, Pres., John C. Bell/59/Dir., VP, Gregory B. Scurlock/59/Dir., Sec., Treasurer

Directors: Greenlee T. Flanagin/58/Dir., CEO, Pres., Stewart W. Flanagin/59/Chmn., David M. Alalof/65/Dir., John C. Bell/59/Dir., VP, Gregory B. Scurlock/59/Dir., Sec., Treasurer, Robert M. Flanagin/49/Dir.

Owners: Stewart W. Flanagin/9.30%, Robert Flanagin/10.00%, John C. Bell/7.10%, Ann Flanagin Smith/7.80%, David M. Alalof/2.00%, Greenlee T. Flanagin/10.40%, Greenlee T. Flanagin/5.50%

Security National Financial Corp

5300 S 360 W, Ste. 250, Salt Lake City, UT, 84123; **PH:** 1-801-264-1060; **Fax:** 1-801-265-9882; **http://** www.securitynational.com; **Email:** contact@securitynational.com

General - Incorporation	UT	**Stock**- Price on:12/24/2007	$5.64
Employees	530	Stock Exchange	NDQ
Auditor	Hansen, Barnett & Maxwell	Ticker Symbol	SNFCA
Stk Agt	Zions First National Bank	Outstanding Shares	13,320,000
Counsel	Henriod & Nielsen	E.P.S.	$0.41
DUNS No.	07-301-3799	Shareholders	NA

Business: The group's principal activities are to provide mortgage loans, life insurance and cemetery and mortuary services. Under insurance services, the group provides services in selected lines of life insurance, annuity products and accident and health insurance. These products are marketed in 36 states through independent licensed insurance agents. The group operates five cemeteries in Utah and one in California, in addition to eight mortuaries in Utah and five in Arizona. The group is also into pre-need selling of funeral, cemetery and cremation services. Under mortgage loan services, the group originates and underwrites residential and commercial loans for new construction and existing homes and real estate projects. On 16-Mar-2004, the group acquired paramount security life insurance company.

Primary SIC and add'l.: 6162 6321 7261 6311

CIK No: 0000318673

Subsidiaries: California Memorial Estates, Inc., Cottonwood Mortuary, Inc., Crystal Rose Funeral Home, Inc., Deseret Memorial, Inc., Greer-Wilson Funeral Home, Inc., Holladay Cottonwood Memorial Foundation, Holladay Memorial Park, Inc., Insuradyne Corporation, Memorial Estates, Inc., Memorial Insurance Company of America, Memorial Mortuary, Paradise Chapel Funeral Home, Inc., Paramount Security Life Insurance Company), Security National Capital, Inc., Security National Funding 21 Subsidiaries included in the Index

Officers: George R. Quist/Chmn., Founder, CEO/$272,033.00, Robert G. Quist/First VP, Sec./$155,803.00, Stephen M. Sill/CFO, VP, Treasurer/$144,707.00, Christie Q. Overbaugh/Sr. VP - Internal Operations, Scott M. Quist/Dir., COO, Pres., Randall MacKey/Legal Counsel, Joeseph L. Henriod/Legal Counsel

Directors: George R. Quist/Chmn., Founder, CEO, Charles L. Crittenden/Dir., Norman G. Wilbur/Dir., Robert G. Hunter/Dir., Craig H. Moody/Dir., Lynn J. Beckstead/Dir., Scott M. Quist/Dir., COO, Pres.

Owners: Stephen M. Sill/0.50%, George R. and Shirley C. Quist Family Partnership, Ltd./27.80%, George R. Quist/6.90%, Charles L. Crittenden, Insiders/53.20%, Craig H. Moody, Robert G. Hunter, Lynn J. Beckstead/1.10%, Norman G. Wilbur, Employee Stock Ownership Plan/15.70%, Associated Investors/5.40%, Christie Q. Overbaugh/1.40%, Robert G. Quist/2.60%, Scott M. Quist/12.60%

Financial Data: Fiscal Year End:12/31 Latest Annual Data: 12/31/2006

Year		Sales		Net Income
2006		$152,531,000		$5,124,000
2005		$129,950,000		$3,488,000
2004		$117,198,000		$2,122,000
Curr. Assets:	$30,543,000	**Curr. Liab.:**	$18,407,000	**P/E Ratio:** 8.29
Plant, Equip.:	$22,805,000	**Total Liab.:**	$322,146,000	**Indic. Yr. Divd.:** NA
Total Assets:	$377,395,000	**Net Worth:**	$52,971,000	**Debt/ Equity:** NA

Security With Advanced Technology Inc

10855 Dover St., Ste. 1000, Loveland, CO, 80021; **PH:** 1-303-439-0372; **Fax:** 1-303-439-0414; **http://** www.swat-systems.com; **Email:** ir@shiftwatch.com

General - Incorporation	CO	**Stock**- Price on:12/24/2007	$3.8
Employees	NA	Stock Exchange	NDQ
Auditor	BDO Seidman, LLP	Ticker Symbol	SWAT
Stk Agt	Corporate Stock Transfer, Inc.	Outstanding Shares	5,980,000
Counsel	NA	E.P.S.	-$3.02
DUNS No.	NA	Shareholders	NA

Business: The groups principle activity is to develop digital technology. The group products sold under the trade names ShiftWatch(R)LE, ShiftWatch(R)FS, ShiftWatch(R)VCC and Tapestream(TM). Specific customer of the group is Kansas City Area Transit Authority. The group operates from the United States. The group's quarterly revenue for September 2007 was 0.42 millions of USD.

Primary SIC and add'l.: 3663 7382 5063

CIK No: 0001216199

Officers: Scott G. Sutton/43/Dir., CEO, Pres., Gregory Pusey/55/Chmn., Sec., Jeffrey G. McGonegal/57/CFO, Ben Cook/Dir. - Division X, Michael Cox/VP - Engineering, Corey Holland/Dir. - Technology Division, Greg Milan/VP - Sales, Thomas Muenzberg/VP - Finance

Directors: Scott G. Sutton/43/Dir., CEO, Pres., Gregory Pusey/55/Chmn., Sec., Thomas R. Marinelli/56/Dir., Barry C. Loder/49/Dir., Gail Schoettler/64/Dir., Robert J. Williams/67/Dir.

Owners: Insiders/25.40%, Vision Opportunity Master Fund, Ltd./37.70%, Barry C. Loder, Jeffrey G. McGonegal/1.60%, Robert J. Williams, The Peierls Foundation, Inc./21.50%, Gregory Pusey/8.70%, Gail Schoettler, Thomas R. Marinelli/2.10%, Scott G. Sutton/11.70%

Financial Data: Fiscal Year End:12/31 Latest Annual Data: 12/31/2006

Year		Sales		Net Income
2006		$296,000		-$9,347,000
2005		$109,000		-$4,193,000
2004		$269,000		-$1,326,000
Curr. Assets:	$3,941,000	**Curr. Liab.:**	$1,215,000	
Plant, Equip.:	$201,000	**Total Liab.:**	$1,282,000	**Indic. Yr. Divd.:** NA
Total Assets:	$8,933,000	**Net Worth:**	$7,651,000	**Debt/ Equity:** NA

Sedona Corp

1003 W 9th Ave., 2nd Fl., King of Prussia, PA, 19406; **PH:** 1-610-337-8400; **Fax:** 1-610-337-8490; **http://** www.sedonacorp.com; **Email:** info@sedonacorp.com

General - Incorporation	PA	**Stock**- Price on:12/24/2007	$0.26
Employees	14	Stock Exchange	OTC
Auditor	McGladrey & Pullen LLP	Ticker Symbol	SDNA
Stk Agt	StockTrans, Inc.	Outstanding Shares	91,880,000
Counsel	NA	E.P.S.	-$0.03
DUNS No.	06-437-0802	Shareholders	NA

Business: The group's principle activity is to develop, market, service and support enterprise-wide Internet customer relationship management (crm) application solutions. The group's flagship application solution is intarsia(tm). This is a fully integrated and customized crm application solution priced specifically to bring a comprehensive and seamlessly integrated set of customer relationship management components to small and mid-sized financial service organizations. Intarsia enables financial service organizations to create an effective marketing, sales and services environment for customers, partners and suppliers. Intarsia provides financial service organizations with a consolidated view of their customer relationships and enables their customers to have a complete view of the financial service organizations' businesses. The group's quarterly revenue for September 2007 was 0.35 millions of USD.

Primary SIC and add'l.: 7372 7371

CIK No: 0000764843

Officers: Marco A. Emrich/Dir., CEO, Pres., Anita Primo/CFO, VP, Timothy Rimlinger/CTO, VP

Directors: Marco A. Emrich/Dir., CEO, Pres., David R. Vey/Chmn., Jack A. Pellicci/Dir., David C. Bluestone/Dir., Scott C. Edelman/Dir., Roger W. Scearce/Dir., Victoria V. Looney/Dir.

Owners: Insiders/44.76%, Scott C. Edelman, Victoria V. Looney, Marco A. Emrich/1.61%, David C. Bluestone, Roger W. Scearce, David R. Vey/46.08%, Timothy A. Rimlinger, Anita M. Primo, Jack A. Pellicci

Financial Data: Fiscal Year End:12/31 Latest Annual Data: 12/31/2006

Year		Sales		Net Income
2006		$1,415,000		-$2,252,000
2005		$723,000		-$2,894,000
2004		$1,087,000		-$2,922,000
Curr. Assets:	$424,000	**Curr. Liab.:**	$4,552,000	
Plant, Equip.:	$19,000	**Total Liab.:**	$8,804,000	**Indic. Yr. Divd.:** NA
Total Assets:	$716,000	**Net Worth:**	-$8,088,000	**Debt/ Equity:** NA

Sei Investments Co

1 Freedom Valley Dr., Oaks, PA, 19456; **PH:** 1-610-676-1000; **Fax:** 1-610-676-2995; **http://** www.seiinvestments.com

General - Incorporation	PA	**Stock**- Price on:12/24/2007	$58.39
Employees	2,230	Stock Exchange	NDQ
Auditor	PricewaterhouseCoopers LLP	Ticker Symbol	SEIC
Stk Agt	American Registrar & Transfer Co	Outstanding Shares	99,110,000
Counsel	Morgan, Lewis & Bockius LLP	E.P.S.	$1.33
DUNS No.	06-437-8086	Shareholders	NA

Business: The group's principal activity is to provide asset management and products and services that enable the clients to establish asset allocation strategies and gain access to investment managers. The group operates in five segments: private banking and trust provides investment processing solutions, fund processing solutions and investment management programs to banks and trust institutions. Investment advisors provide investment management programs and solutions to affluent investors. Enterprises provide retirement investment and business solutions to pension plan sponsors, hospitals, etc. Money manager provides solutions to us based investment managers and mutual fund companies. Investment in new businesses provides investment management, fund and investment processing solutions outside the United States.

Primary SIC and add'l.: 6282 7373 6211

CIK No: 0000350894

Subsidiaries: Lartington Limited, SEI Advanced Capital Management, Inc., SEI Asset Korea Co., Ltd., SEI Capital Limited, SEI European Services Limited, SEI Franchise, Inc., SEI Funds, Inc., SEI Global Capital Investments, Inc., SEI Global Holdings (Cayman) Inc., SEI Global Investments Corporation, SEI Global Nominee Ltd., SEI Global Services, Inc., SEI Insurance Group, Inc., SEI Investments (Asia), Limited, SEI Investments (France) Company 37 Subsidiaries included in the Index

Officers: Al West/Chmn., CEO/$870,024.00, Edward D. Loughlin/Exec. VP/$1,029,619.00, James V. Morris/Sr. VP - Retirement Solutions, Carolyn McLaurin/Sr. VP - Foundation, Endowment Group, Michael Cagnina/MD - Multiemployer Plans, Paul F. Klauder/VP, MD - Corporate Marketing

Directors: Al West/Chmn., CEO

Owners: Scott J. Vassalluzzo/5.48%, Edward D. Loughlin, Thomas W. Smith/7.37%, Alfred P. West/19.15%, Wayne M. Withrow, Dennis McGonigle, Howard D. Ross, Henry H. Porter, Sarah W. Blumenstein, Richard B. Lieb, Insiders/35.77%, Carmen V. Romeo/1.87%, Robert F. Crudup, William M. Doran/4.81%, Kathryn M. McCarthy *(17 Owners included in Index)*

Financial Data: Fiscal Year End:12/31 Latest Annual Data: 12/31/2006

Year		Sales		Net Income
2006		$1,175,749,000		$236,990,000
2005		$773,007,000		$188,344,000
2004		$692,269,000		$169,021,000
Curr. Assets:	$586,473,000	**Curr. Liab.:**	$196,127,000	**P/E Ratio:** 24.23
Plant, Equip.:	$130,732,000	**Total Liab.:**	$339,813,000	**Indic. Yr. Divd.:** $0.140
Total Assets:	$1,079,705,000	**Net Worth:**	$630,512,000	**Debt/ Equity:** NA

Sekoya Holdings Ltd

Ste. 366-916 W Brd.way, Vancouver, BC, V5Z 1K7; **PH:** 1-604-269-6622

General - Incorporation	NV	**Stock**- Price on:12/24/2007	NA
Employees	NA	Stock Exchange	NA
Auditor	Gordon K.W. Gee	Ticker Symbol	NA
Stk Agt	Empire Stock Transfer Inc.	Outstanding Shares	NA
Counsel	NA	E.P.S.	NA
DUNS No.	NA	Shareholders	NA

Business: The groups principal activity is to create and develop the initial phase of website. The group operates from China.

Primary SIC and add'l.: 6199

CIK No: 0001347004

Officers: Shirley Wong/43/Dir., Pres., Principal Exec. Officer, Principal Financial Officer, Principal Accounting Officer, Treasurer, Sec.

Directors: Shirley Wong/43/Dir., Pres., Principal Exec. Officer, Principal Financial Officer, Principal Accounting Officer, Treasurer, Sec.

Owners: Insiders/82.58%, Shirley Wong/82.58%

Selas Corp of America

1260 Red Fox Rd., Arden Hills, MN, 55112; **PH:** 1-651-636-9770; **Fax:** 1-651-636-9503; **http://** www.selas.com; **Email:** sales@selas.com

General - Incorporation	PA	**Stock**- Price on:12/24/2007	$6.85
Employees	561	Stock Exchange	NDQ
Auditor	Virchow, Krause & Co. LLP	Ticker Symbol	NA
Stk Agt	Mellon Investor Services LLC	Outstanding Shares	5,710,000
Counsel	Drinker Biddle & Reath LLP	E.P.S	$0.248
DUNS No.	00-234-5767	Shareholders	NA

Business: The group operates through miniature medical and electronics products segment which designs and manufactures micro miniature components, systems and molded plastic parts primarily for the hearing instrument manufacturing industry and also for the electronics, telecommunications, computer and medical equipment industries. The targeted customers include medical product manufacturers of portable and lightweight battery powdered devices, large ac-powered units and a variety of sensors. The group operates in the unites states, France, Germany, Japan, Canada, China, Portugal and Singapore.

Primary SIC and add'l.: 3714 3423 3567 3845

CIK No: 0000088790

Subsidiaries: Resistance Technology, Inc., RTI Electronics, Inc., RTI Tech PTE LTD

Officers: Mark S. Gorder/61/Dir., CEO, Pres./$371,288.00, Scott Longval/31/CFO, Treasurer/$122,198.00, Christopher D. Conger/47/VP - Research, Development/$172,551.00, Michael P. Geraci/49/VP - Sales, Marketing/$175,296.00, Dennis L. Gonsior/49/VP - Operations/$163,808.00

Directors: Mark S. Gorder/61/Dir., CEO, Pres., Michael J. McKenna/Chmn., Robert N. Masucci/Dir., Nicholas A. Giordano/Dir.

Owners: Steven M. Binnix, Estate of Siggi B. Wilzig/5.90%, The Trust Company of New Jersey/8.10%, Robert N. Masucci/1.70%, Moreton Bay Capital, LLC/7.00%, Mark S. Gorder/7.90%, Scott Longval, Nicholas A. Giordano/1.30%, Amivest Capital Management/7.90%, Dimensional Fund Advisors LP/5.70%, Christopher D. Conger, Mario J. Gabelli/6.40%, Insiders/13.40%, Michael J. McKenna/1.90%, Dennis L. Gonsior *(16 Owners included in Index)*

Financial Data: *Fiscal Year End:*12/31 *Latest Annual Data:* 12/31/2006

Year	Sales	Net Income
2006	$51,726,000	$1,163,000
2005	$44,455,000	$1,529,000
2004	$35,183,000	$148,000

Curr. Assets:	$18,786,000	**Curr. Liab.:**	$10,341,000	**P/E Ratio:**	27.62
Plant, Equip.:	$6,774,000	**Total Liab.:**	$18,674,000	**Indic. Yr. Divd.:**	NA
Total Assets:	$34,281,000	**Net Worth:**	$15,607,000	**Debt/ Equity:**	0.3447

Select Comfort Corp

9800 59th Ave., N, Minneapolis, MN, 55442; *PH:* 1-763-551-7000; *Fax:* 1-763-551-7826; *http://* www.selectcomfort.com; *Email:* info@selectcomfort.no

General - Incorporation	MN	**Stock**- Price on:12/24/2007	$16.38
Employees	2,853	Stock Exchange	NDQ
Auditor	KPMG LLP	Ticker Symbol	SCSS
Stk Agt	Wells Fargo Shareowner Services	Outstanding Shares	49,300,000
Counsel	Oppenheimer Wolff & Donnelly	E.P.S	$0.73
DUNS No.	17-730-2858	Shareholders	NA

Business: The group's principal activities are to develop, manufacture and market adjustable-firmness beds and other sleep related products. It offers four different sleep number bed models featuring patented single or dual air chamber. The products are sold under the trademarks select comfort, sleep number, the sleep number bed by select comfort, the sleep number store by select comfort, comfort club and sleep better on air. Sleep number mattresses are enclosed by comfortable, durable belgian damask covering for comfort and durability. In addition, the group offers a line of accessory products including specialty pillows, mattress pads, comforters, sheets and bed frames. As on 03-Jan-2004, the group operated 344 retail stores. The products are sold to customers through retail, direct marketing, e-commerce, wholesale channel furniture retailers and the qvc shopping channel.

Primary SIC and add'l.: 2515

CIK No: 0000827187

Subsidiaries: Select Comfort Canada Holding Inc., Select Comfort Canada ULC, Select Comfort Direct Corporation, Select Comfort Retail Corporation, Select Comfort SC Corporation, Select Comfort Wholesale Corporation, selectcomfort.com corporation

Officers: William R. McLaughlin/Chmn., CEO/$3,181,370.00, Mark A. Kimball/Sr. VP - Legal, General Counsel, Sec., Kathryn V. Roedel/Sr. VP - Global Supply Chain/$858,459.00, Ernest Park/CIO, Sr. VP, Scott F. Peterson/Sr. VP - Human Resources/$752,150.00, Wendy L. Schoppert/Sr. VP - International, Keith C. Spurgeon/Sr. VP - Sales, James C. Raabe/Sr. VP, CFO/$675,878.00

Directors: William R. McLaughlin/Chmn., CEO, Thomas J. Albani/Dir., Christopher P. Kirchen/Dir., David T. Kollat/Dir., Christine M. Day/Dir., Jean-Michel Valette/Dir., Stephen L. Gulis/Dir., Brenda J. Lauderback/Dir., Michael A. Peel/Dir., Ervin R. Shames/Dir.

Owners: Douglas J. Collier, Michael A. Peel, Scott F. Peterson, Christopher P. Kirchen, Jean-Michel Valette, Barclays Global Investors, NA/6.70%, Stephen L. Gulis, Brenda J. Lauderback, Lord, Abbett & Co. LLC/8.90%, David T. Kollat, Royce & Associates, LLC/5.40%, Ervin R. Shames, William R. McLaughlin/3.50%, James C. Raabe, Thomas J. Albani *(20 Owners included in Index)*

Financial Data: *Fiscal Year End:*12/31 *Latest Annual Data:* 12/30/2006

Year	Sales	Net Income
2006	$806,038,000	$47,183,000
2005	$691,066,000	$43,767,000

Curr. Assets:	$105,056,000	**Curr. Liab.:**	$94,898,000	**P/E Ratio:**	22.44
Plant, Equip.:	$53,866,000	**Total Liab.:**	$107,487,000	**Indic. Yr. Divd.:**	NA
Total Assets:	$228,834,000	**Net Worth:**	$121,347,000	**Debt/ Equity:**	NA

Selectica Inc

1740 Technology Dr., Ste. 450, San Jose, CA, 95110; *PH:* 1-408-570-9700; *Fax:* 1-408-570-9705; *http://* www.selectica.com

General - Incorporation	DE	**Stock**- Price on:12/24/2007	$1.94
Employees	170	Stock Exchange	NDQ
Auditor	Armanino McKenna LLP	Ticker Symbol	SLTC
Stk Agt	U.S. Stock Transfer Corp	Outstanding Shares	30,560,000
Counsel	NA	E.P.S	-$0.54
DUNS No.	NA	Shareholders	NA

Business: The group's principle activities are to develop and market interactive selling system software and services for electronic commerce, sales force automation and build-to-order applications. The software and services enable companies to efficiently sell complex products and services over intranets, extranets and the Internet. It allows companies to use the Internet platform to deploy selling applications to many points of contact including personal computers, in-store kiosks and mobile devices. The products offered by the group include ace enterprise, ace mobile, ace enterprise manager, ace pricer, ace application data manager, ace quoter, ace studio, ace repository and ace connector products. The major customers include asea brown boveri (abb), applied bio systems, bell Canada, cisco, dell, general electric, fireman's fund insurance company, hitachi, juniper networks, rockwell automation and tellabs. The group's total revenue for year 2007 was 14.72 millions of USD.

Primary SIC and add'l.: 7379 7373 7372

CIK No: 0001090908

Subsidiaries: LoanMarket Resources, Inc., Selectica Australia Pty Ltd., Selectica Canada, Inc., Selectica France Sorl, Selectica GmbH, Selectica India Private Limited, Selectica Japan, K.K., Selectica Mexico S. de R.L. de C.V., Selectica Scandinavia AB, Selectica U.K. Limited, Wakely Acquisition Corp.

Officers: Robert Jurkowski/Chmn., CEO, Bill Roeschlein/CFO, VP, Terry Nicholson/COO - Contract Management Solutions, Steven Goldner/VP - Engineering, James Dias/VP - Worldwide Marketing, Sales, Santosh Srinivasan/VP - Solutions Engineering, Joe Longo/VP - Professional Services, Stephen Bennion/VP, GM - Configuration, Pricing, Quoting Solutions, Doug Bell/VP - Marketing, Sumit Bando/CTO - Contract Management Solutions, Tony Rossi/Contact - Investor Relations

Directors: Robert Jurkowski/Chmn., CEO, James Arnold/Dir.

Owners: Terry Nicholson, James Arnold, Brenda Zawatski, Steve Goldner, Insiders/1.10%, Steele Partners II, L.P./9.00%, Lloyd I. Miller/6.70%, Bill Roeschlein, Dimensional Fund Advisors, Inc./9.50%, Bank of America Corporation/6.25%

Financial Data: *Fiscal Year End:*03/31 *Latest Annual Data:* 3/31/2006

Year	Sales	Net Income
2006	$23,433,000	-$17,507,000
2005	$31,120,000	-$14,653,000
2004	$40,024,000	-$8,846,000

Curr. Assets:	$59,795,000	**Curr. Liab.:**	$10,552,000		
Plant, Equip.:	$1,992,000	**Total Liab.:**	$13,723,000	**Indic. Yr. Divd.:**	NA
Total Assets:	$63,636,000	**Net Worth:**	$49,913,000	**Debt/ Equity:**	NA

Selective Insurance Group Inc

40 Wantage Ave., Branchville, NJ, 07890; *PH:* 1-973-948-3000; *Fax:* 1-973-948-0292; *http://* www.selective.com

General - Incorporation	NJ	**Stock**- Price on:12/24/2007	$26.33
Employees	2,100	Stock Exchange	NDQ
Auditor	KPMG LLP	Ticker Symbol	SIGI
Stk Agt	EquiServe Trust Co N.A	Outstanding Shares	54,860,000
Counsel	NA	E.P.S	$2.59
DUNS No.	00-697-1816	Shareholders	NA

Business: The group's principal activity is to provide property and casualty insurance products and diversified insurance services and products. The group operates from United States.

Primary SIC and add'l.: 6719 6331 6351

CIK No: 0000230557

Subsidiaries: SelecTech, LLC, Selective Auto Insurance Company of New Jersey, Selective HR Solutions, Inc., Selective Insurance Company of America, Selective Insurance Company of New England, Selective Insurance Company of New York, Selective Insurance Company of South Carolina, Selective Insurance Company of the Southeast, Selective Technical Administrative Resources, Inc., Selective Way Insurance Company, SRM Insurance Brokerage, LLC, Wantage Avenue Holding Company Inc.

Officers: Gregory E. Murphy/Chmn., CEO, Pres./$5,067,039.00, Richard F. Connell/CEO, CIO, Sr. Exec. VP/$1,268,134.00, Kerry A. Guthrie/Exec. VP, Chief Investment Officer, Sharon R. Cooper/Sr. VP - Corporate Communication, Victor N. Daley/Exec. VP - Human Resources, Dale A. Thatcher/CFO, Exec. VP/$1,052,946.00, Michael H. Lanza/Sr. VP, General Counsel, Ronald J. Zaleski/Exec. VP, Chief Actuary/$1,019,460.00, Jamie Ochiltree/Sr. Exec. VP - Insurance Operations/$1,492,977.00, Jennifer Diberardino/VP, Assist. Treasurer, Robyn Turner/Corporate Counsel

Directors: Gregory E. Murphy/Chmn., CEO, Pres., Paul D. Bauer/Dir., Marston W. Becker/Dir., David A. Brown/Dir., John C. Burville/Dir., William M. Kearns/Dir., Joan M. Lamm-Tennant/Dir., Griffin S. McClellan/Dir., Ronald L. Okelley/Dir., John F. Rockart/Dir., William M. Rue/Dir., Brian J. Thebault/Dir.

Owners: Ronald J. Zaleski, Joan M. Lamm-Tennant, Becker W. Marston, Richard F. Connell, Dale A. Thatcher, Insiders/4.10%, William M. Rue, Jamie Ochiltree, Gregory E. Murphy, Dimensional Fund Advisors LP/7.67%, Griffin S. McClellan, Paul D. Bauer, Barclays Global Investors, NA and Affiliates/5.28%, William M. Kearns, Thebault J. Brian *(19 Owners included in Index)*

Financial Data: *Fiscal Year End:*12/31 *Latest Annual Data:* 12/31/2006

Year	Sales	Net Income
2006	$1,807,867,000	$163,574,000
2005	$1,671,012,000	$148,493,000
2004	$1,571,536,000	$128,639,000

Curr. Assets:	$992,982,000	**Curr. Liab.:**	$149,374,000	**P/E Ratio:**	10.17
Plant, Equip.:	$59,004,000	**Total Liab.:**	$3,690,478,000	**Indic. Yr. Divd.:**	$0.480
Total Assets:	$4,767,705,000	**Net Worth:**	$1,077,227,000	**Debt/ Equity:**	0.3483

SEMCO Energy Inc

PO Box 5004, Port Huron, MI, 48060; *PH:* 1-866-473-6261; *Fax:* 1-810-987-7638; *http://* www.semcoenergy.com

General - Incorporation	MI	**Stock**- Price on:12/24/2007	$7.77
Employees	569	Stock Exchange	NA
Auditor	PricewaterhouseCoopers LLP	Ticker Symbol	NA
Stk Agt	National City Bank	Outstanding Shares	35,520,000
Counsel	NA	E.P.S	$0.34
DUNS No.	08-971-2079	Shareholders	NA

Business: The group's principal activities are to provide natural gas and associated services and products to commercial, residential and industrial customers. The group operates solely in the domestic market. The group operates through four business segments: gas distribution, which distributes and transports natural gas to residential, commercial and industrial customers. Construction services, which installs underground natural gas mains and service lines. It also provides underground construction services to the telecommunications and water supply industries. Information technology services that provide it infrastructure outsourcing services and other it services. Propane, pipeline and storage consist of three pipelines and a gas storage facility, which is located in Michigan.

Primary SIC and add'l.: 4911 8999 4922 4923

CIK No: 0000277158

Subsidiaries: Alaska Pipeline Company, Hotflame Gas, Inc., NORSTAR Pipeline Company, Inc., SEMCO Energy Ventures, Inc., SEMCO Gas Storage Company, SEMCO Information Technology, Inc., SEMCO Pipeline Company

Officers: George A. Schreiber/Dir., CEO, Pres., Peter F. Clark/Sr. VP, General Counsel, Eugene N. Dubay/Sr. VP - Operations, Sherry L. Abbott/Corp. Sec., Michael V. Palmeri/CFO, Sr. VP, Treasurer, Steven W. Warsinske/VP, Controller, Thomas Connelly/Dir. - Investor Relations

Directors: George A. Schreiber/Dir., CEO, Pres., Donald W. Thomason/Chmn., John T. Ferris/Dir., Edwina Rogers/Dir., John Van Roden/Dir., Ben A. Stevens/Dir., Harvey I. Klein/Dir., Paul F. Naughton/Dir., Charles H. Podowski/Dir., Thomas W. Sherman/Dir.

Financial Data: Fiscal Year End:12/31 Latest Annual Data: 12/31/2006

Year	Sales	Net Income
2006	$640,501,000	$10,414,000
2005	$615,102,000	$12,275,000
2004	$508,336,000	-$5,183,000

Curr. Assets:	$234,501,000	Curr. Liab.:	$171,630,000	P/E Ratio:	22.85
Plant, Equip.:	$590,890,000	Total Liab.:	$764,558,000	Indic. Yr. Divd.:	NA
Total Assets:	$1,031,571,000	Net Worth:	$267,013,000	Debt/ Equity:	1.8486

Semiconductor Manufacturing Intl Corp

4378 Enterprise St., Fremont, CA, 94538; **PH:** 1-510-492-2020; **Fax:** 1-510-651-1242; http:// www.smics.com

General - Incorporation	Cayman Islands	Stock - Price on:12/24/2007	$6.86
Employees	9,773	Stock Exchange	NYSE
Auditor	Deloitte Touche Tohmatsu	Ticker Symbol	SMI
Stk Agt	Computershare Investor Services LLC	Outstanding Shares	369,410,000
Counsel	NA	E.P.S.	-$0.05
DUNS No.	NA	Shareholders	NA

Business: The groups principle activity is to provide integrated circuit (IC) manufacturing service at 0.35 micron to 65 nanometer and finer line technologies. The groups services include libraries and EDA. The group operates from United States.

Primary SIC and add'l.: NA

CIK No: 0001267482

Subsidiaries: Semiconductor Manufacturing International (Beijing) Corporation, Semiconductor Manufacturing International (Shanghai) Corporation, Semiconductor Manufacturing International (Tianjin) Corporation, SemiconductorManufacturingInternational (Chengdu) Corporation

Officers: Richard Ru-gin Chang/Executive Dir., Founder, CEO, Pres., Marco Mora/COO, Morning Wu/Acting CFO, Chief Accounting Officer, Qualified Accountant, Anne Wai Yui Chen/Company Sec. - Hong Kong Representative, Compliance Officer, Akio Kawabata/VP - Marketing, Toshiaki Ikoma/CTO

Directors: Richard Ru-gin Chang/Executive Dir., Founder, CEO, Pres., Yang Yuan Wang/Chmn., Ta-Lin Hsu/Dir., Henry Shaw/Dir., Tsuyoshi Kawanishi/Dir., Lip-Bu Tan/Dir., Albert Yu/Dir., Jiang Shang Zhou/Dir., Zheng Gang Wang/Non Exec. Dir.

Owners: SIIC Asset Management Co. Ltd., SIIC CM Development Funds Limited, Albert Y. C. Yu, Ta-Lin Hsu, Richard Ru Gin Chang, SIHL Treasury Limited, SIIC Treasury (B.V.I.) Limited, S.I. Technology Production Holdings Limited

Financial Data: Fiscal Year End:12/31 Latest Annual Data: 12/31/2006

Year	Sales	Net Income
2006	$1,465,323,000	-$44,109,000
2005	$1,171,319,000	-$111,534,000
2004	$974,665,000	$89,745,000

Curr. Assets:	$1,049,666,000	Curr. Liab.:	$677,362,000	P/E Ratio:	8.00
Plant, Equip.:	$3,244,401,000	Total Liab.:	$1,533,872,000	Indic. Yr. Divd.:	NA
Total Assets:	$4,541,292,000	Net Worth:	$3,007,420,000	Debt/ Equity:	NA

Seminis Inc

1905 Lirio Ave., Saticoy, CA, 93004; ; http:// www.seminis.com

General - Incorporation	DE	Stock - Price on:12/24/2007	NA
Employees	NA	Stock Exchange	NA
Auditor	PricewaterhouseCoopers LLP	Ticker Symbol	NA
Stk Agt	NA	Outstanding Shares	NA
Counsel	Cahill Gordon & Reindel LLP	E.P.S.	NA
DUNS No.	NA	Shareholders	NA

Business: The group's principal activities are to develop, produce and market vegetable and fruit seeds throughout the world. It develops seeds designed to reduce the need for chemicals, increase crop yield, reduce spoilage, offer longer shelf life and create tastier foods with better nutrition. The group is a majority-owned subsidiary of savia, s.a. De c.v. The group produces more than 60 species and 4,000 vegetable and fruit seed products. The seeds are marketed through three full-line brands: asgrow, petoseed and royal sluis and five specialty and regional brands. The product lines marketed under these brands cover most species of vegetables and fruits including beans, beets, broccoli, Brussels sprouts, cabbage, carrots, cauliflower, celery, Chinese cabbage, cucumbers, eggplant, leeks, lettuce, melons, onions, peas, peppers, pumpkin, radish, spinach, squash, sweet corn, tomatoes and watermelon. The seeds are marketed in over 120 countries.

Primary SIC and add'l.: 0181

CIK No: 0001078259

Officers: Juliet Ream/General Counsel, Kerry Preete/Pres., Marlin Edwards/VP - Research, Development, Ibrahim El Menschawi/VP - Strategy, Marketing, Aldo Noseda/VP - Information Technology, Jorge Christlieb/VP - Asia, Dieter Holtz/VP - Europe, Middle East, Africa, EMEA, Andy Kuchan/CFO, Bill Hallman/VP - Supply, Delivery Chain, Nancy Wolfe/VP - Human Resources, Glenn Stith/VP - Americas

Semitool Inc

655 W Reserve Dr., Kalispell, MT, 59901; **PH:** 1-406-752-2107; **Fax:** 1-406-752-5522; http:// www.semitool.com

General - Incorporation	MT	Stock - Price on:12/24/2007	$9.85
Employees	NA	Stock Exchange	NDQ
Auditor	Grant Thornton, LLP	Ticker Symbol	SMTL
Stk Agt	Bank of Boston	Outstanding Shares	32,080,000
Counsel	Morrison & Foerster LLP	E.P.S.	$0.16
DUNS No.	09-620-0175	Shareholders	NA

Business: The group's principle activities are to design, develop, manufacture and service wet chemical processing equipment for use in the fabrication of semiconductor devices. The primary suites of tools of the group include electrochemical deposition systems for electroplating copper, gold, solder and other metals; cleaning, stripping and etching systems; and wafer container cleaning tools. The equipment is utilized in semiconductor fabrication front-end and back-end processes, including wafer level packaging. The customers of the group include major semiconductor device and wafer level packaging manufacturers worldwide. International sales are carried on in Europe, Japan, Asia and other countries. The group's total revenue for year 2007 was 215.22 millions of USD.

Primary SIC and add'l.: 7372 3559

CIK No: 0000934550

Subsidiaries: Rhetech, Inc., Semitool (Asia) Pte Ltd., Semitool Austria GmbH, Semitool Europe Ltd., Semitool France SARL, Semitool Halbleitertechnik Vertriebs GmbH, Semitool Israel, Limited, Semitool Italia SRL, Semitool Japan Inc., Semitool Korea, Inc.

Officers: Larry Viano/CFO, VP, Geoff High/Investor Relations Officer

Owners: C. Richard Deininger, Charles P. Grenier, Larry A. Viano, Timothy C. Dodkin, Donald P. Baumann, Insiders/32.10%, Dana R. Scranton, Ladeine A. Thompson/30.80%, Daniel J. Eigeman, Wells Fargo & Company/8.80%, Howard E. Bateman, Larry E. Murphy, Royce & Associates, LLC/9.00%, Steven C. Stahlberg

Financial Data: Fiscal Year End:09/30 Latest Annual Data: 9/30/2006

Year	Sales	Net Income
2006	$243,218,000	$9,836,000
2005	$190,373,000	$10,050,000
2004	$139,627,000	$7,354,000

Curr. Assets:	$178,413,000	Curr. Liab.:	$63,550,000	P/E Ratio:	29.85
Plant, Equip.:	$44,610,000	Total Liab.:	$71,372,000	Indic. Yr. Divd.:	NA
Total Assets:	$232,396,000	Net Worth:	$161,024,000	Debt/ Equity:	0.0618

Semotus Solutions Inc

718 University Ave., Ste. 202, Los Gatos, CA, 95032; **PH:** 1-408-399-6120; **Fax:** 1-408-395-5404; http:// www.semotus.com; **Email:** info@semotus.com

General - Incorporation	NV	Stock - Price on:12/24/2007	$0.066
Employees	23	Stock Exchange	AMEX
Auditor	LL Bradford & Co	Ticker Symbol	DLK
Stk Agt	Computershare Investor Services LLC	Outstanding Shares	34,950,000
Counsel	Taliesin Durant	E.P.S.	-$1.18
DUNS No.	95-846-6005	Shareholders	NA

Business: The group's principle activities are to provide enterprise application software connecting employees to critical business systems, information and processes. The software helps mobile employees make better and faster decisions, increase customer satisfaction and improve efficiencies in their business processes for shorter sales and service cycles. The products include quotexpress, companynewsx and commodityxpress that serve vertical markets as workforce automation with the hiplinkxs family of products and services and financial services with the global market pro and equity market pro products and services. These products form the core of the enterprise software marketing strategy with wireless and mobile features available in the software. Its registered trademarks are 'semotus', 'quotexpress', 'mailxpress', 'net2wireless' and 'simkin'. The group's total revenue for year 2007 was 1.62 millions of USD.

Primary SIC and add'l.: 7375 7372

CIK No: 0000832370

Subsidiaries: Clickmarks, Inc., Expand Beyond Corporation, Semotus Systems, Corp., WizShop.com, Inc.

Officers: Anthony N. Lapine/66/Chmn., CEO/$235,392.00, Taliesin Durant/General Counsel, Corp. Sec., Pamela B. Lapine/Pres./$150,800.00, Charles Dargan/53/CFO, Vladimir Soskov/Chief, Technology Officer/$110,419.00

Directors: Anthony N. Lapine/66/Chmn., CEO, Mark Williams/Dir., Robert Lanz/Dir., Laurence Murray/Dir.

Owners: Southridge Partners LP/9.99%, Robert Lanz, Insiders/10.30%, Mark Williams, Pamela LaPine/7.50%, Vladimir Soskov, Anthony LaPine/7.50%, Laurence W. Murray

Financial Data: Fiscal Year End:03/31 Latest Annual Data: 03/31/2007

Year	Sales	Net Income
2007	$1,621,000	-$2,063,000
2006	$2,433,000	-$1,434,000
2005	$1,806,000	-$654,000

Curr. Assets:	$1,601,000	Curr. Liab.:	$1,097,000		
Plant, Equip.:	$3,000	Total Liab.:	$1,097,000	Indic. Yr. Divd.:	NA
Total Assets:	$5,019,000	Net Worth:	$3,922,000	Debt/ Equity:	NA

Sempra Energy

101 Ash St., San Diego, CA, 92101; **PH:** 1-619-696-2000; **Fax:** 1-619-696-2374; http:// www.sempra.com

General - Incorporation	CA	Stock - Price on:12/24/2007	$62.03
Employees	14,061	Stock Exchange	NYSE
Auditor	Deloitte & Touche LLP	Ticker Symbol	SRE
Stk Agt	Computershare Trust Co	Outstanding Shares	263,810,000
Counsel	NA	E.P.S.	$5.25
DUNS No.	02-271-5540	Shareholders	NA

Business: The groups principle activity is to provide electric and natural gas services. The group operates through four segments namely Southern California Gas, San Diego Gas & Electric, Sempra Energy Trading and Sempra Energy Resources. The group operates from United States.

Primary SIC and add'l.: 4924 4939 4911

CIK No: 0001032208

Subsidiaries: Chilquinta Energia, S.A., Luz del Sur, S.A.A., San Diego Gas & Electric Company, Sempra Energy Financial, Sempra Energy Global Enterprises, Sempra Energy International, Sempra Energy Resources, Sempra Energy Trading Corp., Sempra Metals Group Limited, Sodigas Pampeana S.A., Sodigas Sur S.A., Southern California Gas Company

Officers: Donald E. Felsinger/Chmn., CEO/$12,175,680.00, Michael W. Allman/CEO, Pres. - Sempra Generation, Darcel L. Hulse/CEO, Pres. - Sempra LNG, Steven J. Prince/Chmn., CEO - Sempra Commodities, George S. Liparidis/CEO, Pres. - Sempra Pipelines, Storage, Debra L. Reed/CEO, Pres. - San Diego Gas, Electric, SDG, E, Randall B. Peterson/VP, Chief Compliance Officer, Mark A. Snell/CFO, Exec. VP/$2,791,301.00, Thomas S. Sayles/VP - Federal, State Affairs, Amy Chiu/VP - Audit Services, Steven D. Davis/VP - Communications, Community Partnerships, Monica Haas/VP - Corporate Planning, William J. Ichord/VP - Government Relations, Jeff Martin/VP - Investor Relations, Mike Morgan/VP - International Affairs *(31 Officers included in Index)*

Directors: Donald E. Felsinger/Chmn., CEO, Steven J. Prince/Chmn., CEO - Sempra Commodities, Carlos Ruiz Sacristan/Dir., Richard G. Newman/Dir., William C. Rusnack/Dir., William P. Rutledge/Dir., William G. Ouchi/Dir., Neal E. Schmale/Dir., COO, Pres., James G. Brocksmith/Dir., Richard A. Collato/Dir., Wilford D. Godbold/Dir., William D. Jones/Dir.

Owners: Insiders, Donald E. Felsinger, Richard G. Newman, Richard A. Collato, James G. Brocksmith, William C. Rusnack, Javade Chaudhri, Neal E. Schmale, Edwin A. Guiles, Mark A. Snell, William G. Ouchi, Wilford D. Godbold, William D. Jones, William P. Rutledge

Financial Data: **Fiscal Year End:**12/31 **Latest Annual Data:** 12/31/2006

Year	Sales	Net Income
2006	$11,761,000,000	$1,406,000,000
2005	$11,737,000,000	$920,000,000
2004	$9,410,000,000	$895,000,000

Curr. Assets:	$12,016,000,000	**Curr. Liab.:**	$10,349,000,000	**P/E Ratio:**	11.82
Plant, Equip.:	$13,964,000,000	**Total Liab.:**	$21,259,000,000	**Indic. Yr. Divd.:**	$1.240
Total Assets:	$28,949,000,000	**Net Worth:**	$7,511,000,000	**Debt/ Equity:**	0.5863

Semtech Corp

200 Flynn Rd., Camarillo, CA, 93012; ***PH:*** 1-805-498-2111; ***Fax:*** 1-805-498-3804; ***http://*** www.semtech.com

General - Incorporation	DE	**Stock**- Price on:12/24/2007	$17.61
Employees	689	Stock Exchange	NDQ
Auditor	Ernst & Young LLP	Ticker Symbol	SMTC
Stk Agt	Mellon Investor Services LLC	Outstanding Shares	62,880,000
Counsel	NA	E.P.S.	$0.42
DUNS No.	00-847-9941	Shareholders	NA

Business: The group's principal activities are to manufacture, design and distribute analog and mixed-signal semiconductors for commercial applications. The products are principally sold to customers in the communications, computer and industrial markets. The group's semiconductor industry is divided into analog and digital semiconductor products. Analog semiconductors condition and regulate functions such as temperature, speed, sound and electrical current. Digital semiconductors process binary information, such as that used by computers. Mixed-signal devices incorporate both analog and digital functions into a single chip and enable digital electronics to interface with the outside world. The customers of the group are original equipment manufacturers and their suppliers, including agilent, cisco, compal electronics, dell, hewlett packard, IBM, intel, lucky goldstar, microsoft, motorola, quanta com. The group has its operations in the United States, Asia-Pacific & Europe.

Primary SIC and add'l.: 3674 3679

CIK No: 0000088941

Subsidiaries: Semtech (International) AG, Semtech Corpus Christi Corporation, Semtech Corpus Christi, S.A. de C.V., Semtech France SARL, Semtech Germany GmbH, Semtech Limited, Semtech Neuchtel SA, Semtech New York Corporation, Semtech San Diego Corporation, Semtech Switzerland GmbH

Officers: Mohan Maheswaran/Dir., CEO, Pres./$1,749,099.00, Clay Beltran/VP - Worldwide Operations, Alain Dantec/Sr. VP - Advanced Communications, Sensing Products, Kevin P. Caffey/VP - Quality, Reliability, Suzanna Fabos/General Counsel, Sec., Mark Drucker/Sr. VP - Test, Measurement Products, Clemente Beltran/VP - Worldwide Operations, Resat N. Necar/VP - Marketing - Power Management, Jeffrey Pohlman/Sr. VP - Protection Products/$748,457.00, Michael Wilson/Sr. VP - Power Management Products/$697,086.00, Lawrence A. King/VP - Engineering, Portable Products/$654,437.00, Terry Sears/Mgr. - Marketing Communications, Emeka Chukwu/CFO, VP, Ken Barry/VP - Human Resources, James Kim/VP - Worldwide Sales, Marketing

Directors: Mohan Maheswaran/Dir., CEO, Pres., Rockell N. Hankin/Chmn., Glen M. Antle/Dir., John L. Piotrowski/Dir., James P. Burra/Dir., Dean W. Baker/Dir., Bruce C. Edwards/Dir., Wildford Dean Baker/Dir., James T. Schraith/Dir., James T. Lindstrom/Dir.

Owners: T. Rowe Price Associates, Inc/6.70%, James T. Schraith, Wellington Management Company, LLP/5.70%, Rockell N. Hankin, Jeffrey T. Pohlman, Glen M. Antle, John D. Poe/2.10%, Lawrence A. King, Insiders/6.40%, Capital Research and Management Company and SMALLCAP World Fund, Inc./8.00%, Alan Bennett, James P. Burra, Michael J. Wilson, Mohan R. Maheswaran, John L. Piotrowski *(18 Owners included in Index)*

Financial Data: **Fiscal Year End:**01/29 **Latest Annual Data:** 1/28/2007

Year	Sales	Net Income
2007	$252,538,000	$31,128,000
2006	$239,338,000	$41,951,000
2005	$253,612,000	$58,888,000

Curr. Assets:	$250,434,000	**Curr. Liab.:**	$29,018,000	**P/E Ratio:**	41.93
Plant, Equip.:	$55,674,000	**Total Liab.:**	$33,559,000	**Indic. Yr. Divd.:**	NA
Total Assets:	$457,925,000	**Net Worth:**	$424,366,000	**Debt/ Equity:**	NA

SendTec Inc

877 Executive Ctr. Dr. W, Ste. 300, St. Petersburg, FL, 33702; ***PH:*** 1-727-576-6630; ***Fax:*** 1-727-576-4864; ***http://*** www.sendtec.com

General - Incorporation	DE	**Stock**- Price on:12/24/2007	$0.27
Employees	131	Stock Exchange	OTC
Auditor	Marcum & Kliegman LLP	Ticker Symbol	SNDN
Stk Agt	American Stock Transfer & Trust Co.	Outstanding Shares	51,900,000
Counsel	Haynes and Boone, LLP	E.P.S.	-$0.78
DUNS No.	NA	Shareholders	NA

Business: The groups principle activity is in the exploration engage in the business of mineral exploration. In June 2005, the group completed a reverse merger with RelationServe, Inc. The group operates from the United States. The group's quarterly revenue for Sep '07 was 7.36 millions of USD.

Primary SIC and add'l.: 7389 7319 7331 8748 7379

CIK No: 0001296001

Subsidiaries: Friendsand, Inc., RelationServe Access, Inc., SendTec Acquisition Corp

Officers: Paul Soltoff/Chmn., CEO/$373,725.00, Eric Obeck/Pres./$435,401.00, Donald Gould/CFO/$272,220.00, Steven Morvay/MD, Exec. VP - Client Services, Daniel Hall/Sr. VP, Corp. Sec., General Counsel

Directors: Paul Soltoff/Chmn., CEO, Anthony Abate/Dir., Robert G. Beauregard/Dir., Vincent Addonisio/Dir., Robert F. Hussey/Dir.

Owners: SDS Capital Group SPC, Ltd./10.50%, Shawn McNamara, Insiders/16.50%, Eric Obeck/5.30%, Alexandra Global Master Fund/9.60%, MHB Trust/9.60%, Vincent Addonisio, LB I Group Inc./8.80%, Leslie T. Altavilla Revocable Trust/5.20%, Robert G. Beauregard, Fursa Alternative Strategies LLC/9.00%, Donald Gould/4.20%, Stratum Wealth Management, LLC/8.70%, Anthony Abate, Paul Soltoff/6.30% *(16 Owners included in Index)*

Financial Data: **Fiscal Year End:**12/31 **Latest Annual Data:** 12/31/2006

Year	Sales	Net Income
2006	$35,863,000	-$42,511,000
2005	$11,303,000	-$2,788,000

Curr. Assets:	$15,890,000	**Curr. Liab.:**	$13,543,000	**P/E Ratio:**	30.12
Plant, Equip.:	$1,352,000	**Total Liab.:**	$34,412,000	**Indic. Yr. Divd.:**	NA
Total Assets:	$58,413,000	**Net Worth:**	$24,001,000	**Debt/ Equity:**	NA

Seneca Foods Corp

3736 S Main St., Marion, NY, 14505; ***PH:*** 1-315-926-8100; ***Fax:*** 1-315-926-8300; ***http://*** www.senecafoods.com; ***Email:*** foundation@senecafoods.com

General - Incorporation	NY	**Stock**- Price on:12/24/2007	$26.83
Employees	2,811	Stock Exchange	NDQ
Auditor	BDO Seidman LLP	Ticker Symbol	SENEA
Stk Agt	NA	Outstanding Shares	7,580,000
Counsel	Jaeckle Fleischmann & Mugel	E.P.S.	NA
DUNS No.	00-220-7322	Shareholders	NA

Business: The group's principle activity is to process and sell vegetables and fruits. The group operates in two segments: food and non-food segment. The food segment includes canned vegetable, frozen vegetable and fruit products. The group processes canned and frozen vegetables for pillsbury under the green giant brand name. The non-food segment provides trade sales of cans and ends. The products are sold to retail and institutional markets under branded labels of libby's, blue boy, aunt nellie's farm kitchen and seneca. The group's total revenue for year 2007 was 1,024.85 millions of USD.

Primary SIC and add'l.: 4522 2033 2099 2037

CIK No: 0000088948

Subsidiaries: Marion Foods, Inc., Seneca Foods International, Ltd., Seneca Snack Company

Officers: Kraig H. Kayser/Dir., CEO, Pres./$548,009.00, Susan W. Stuart/Dir. - Marketing Consultant, Jeffrey L. Van Riper/51/Sec., Controller, Paul L. Palmby/46/COO/$253,542.00, Carl A. Cichetti/50/CIO/$179,548.00, Dean E. Erstad/45/Sr. VP - Sales, John D. Exner/46/General Counsel, Roland E. Breunig/56/CFO/$128,002.00, Cynthia L. Fohrd/45/Chief Administrative Officer

Directors: Kraig H. Kayser/Dir., CEO, Pres., Arthur S. Wolcott/Chmn., Brymer G. Humphreys/Dir., Susan W. Stuart/Dir. - Marketing Consultant, Thomas Paulson/Dir., Arthur H. Baer/Dir., Andrew M. Boas/Dir., Robert T. Brady/Dir., Douglas F. Brush/Dir.

Owners: Insiders, Kraig H. Kayser/41.30%, Kraig H. Kayser/42.68%, Franklin Resources, Inc./5.93%, Carl Marks Management Company, LP/32.86%, Kraig H. Kayser, Arnhold and S. Bleichroeder Advisers, LLC/5.20%, Arthur H. Baer, Philip G. Paras, Thomas Paulson, Arthur S. Wolcott/52.26%, The Pillsbury Company/3.69%, Susan W. Stuart/12.65%, T. Rowe Price Associates, Inc./2.98%, Nancy A. Marks/6.95% *(58 Owners included in Index)*

Financial Data: **Fiscal Year End:**03/31 **Latest Annual Data:** 3/31/2007

Year	Sales	Net Income
2007	$1,024,853,000	$32,067,000
2006	$883,823,000	$21,993,000
2005	$864,274,000	$7,907,000

Curr. Assets:	$451,439,000	**Curr. Liab.:**	$116,984,000	**P/E Ratio:**	10.20
Plant, Equip.:	$172,235,000	**Total Liab.:**	$353,144,000	**Indic. Yr. Divd.:**	NA
Total Assets:	$626,715,000	**Net Worth:**	$273,571,000	**Debt/ Equity:**	0.7690

Seneca-Cayuga Bancorp Inc

19 Cayuga St., Seneca Falls, NY, 13148; ***PH:*** 1-315-568-5855; ***http://*** www.senecafallssavings.com

General - Incorporation	Federal	**Stock**- Price on:12/24/2007	$9.25
Employees	53	Stock Exchange	OTC
Auditor	Beard Miller Co. LLP	Ticker Symbol	SCAY
Stk Agt	Registrar & Transfer Co	Outstanding Shares	2,380,000
Counsel	NA	E.P.S.	$0.12
DUNS No.	NA	Shareholders	NA

Business: The groups principal activity is operating as a conservative thrift institution soliciting deposits and making primarily residential mortgage loans in the Northern Finger Lakes region of New York State. The group operates through two segments namely community banking franchise and its insurance agency. The group operates from the United States. In the year 2006, the groups total assets were $152,766 (thousands).

Primary SIC and add'l.: 6035

CIK No: 0001356261

Subsidiaries: Seneca Falls Savings Bank, Seneca-Cayuga Personal Services, LLC (d/b/a Royce & Rosenkrans, Inc.

Officers: Robert E. Kernan/CEO, Pres., Menzo D. Case/CFO, Exec. VP, Robert Rosenkrans/60/Managing Officer - Seneca, Cayuga Personal Services, LLC

Directors: Bradford M. Jones/55/Vice Chmn., Marilyn Bero/70/Dir., Herbert R. Holden/66/Dir., Frank Nicchi/55/Dir., Gerald MacAluso/55/Dir., August P. Sinicropi/59/Dir., Vincent P. Sinicropi/52/Dir., David Swenson/61/Dir.

Owners: Herbert R. Holden, Robert E. Kernan, David Swenson, Vincent P. Sinicropi, Gerald Macaluso, Seneca Falls Savings Bank/55.00%, August P. Sinicropi, Bradford M. Jones, Menzo D. Case, Robert Rosenkrans, Insiders/59.20%, Marilyn Bero

Financial Data: **Fiscal Year End:**12/31 **Latest Annual Data:** 12/31/2006

Year	Sales	Net Income
2006	$9,797,000	$81,000

Curr. Assets:	$7,860,000	**Curr. Liab.:**	$114,420,000		
Plant, Equip.:	$4,518,000	**Total Liab.:**	$134,042,000	**Indic. Yr. Divd.:**	NA
Total Assets:	$152,766,000	**Net Worth:**	$18,724,000	**Debt/ Equity:**	NA

Senesco Technologies Inc

303 George St., Ste. 420, New Brunswick, NJ, 08901; *PH:* 1-732-296-8400; *Fax:* 1-732-296-9292; *http://* www.senesco.com; *Email:* info@senesco.com

General - Incorporation	DE	*Stock*- Price on:12/24/2007	$1.15
Employees	5	Stock Exchange	AMEX
Auditor	Goldstein Golub Kessler LLP	Ticker Symbol	SNT
Stk Agt	American Stock Transfer & Trust Co.	Outstanding Shares	17,470,000
Counsel	NA	E.P.S.	-$0.17
DUNS No.	NA	Shareholders	NA

Business: The group's principal activity is to research, develop and commercially exploit significant platform technology. This technology involves the identification and characterization of genes that control the aging of all flowers, fruits and vegetables and the programmed cell death of mammalian cells. It also extends the shelf life of perishable plant products, produce leafy crops, increase crop production in horticultural and agronomic crops and reduce the harmful effects of environmental stress. The group's technology is designed to confer positive traits on fruits, flowers, vegetables, forestry species and agronomic crops. It has isolated and characterized the senescence-induced lipase gene, deoxyhypusine synthase (dhs) gene and factor 5a gene in certain species of plants. The competitors are paradigm genetics, aventis crop science, mendel biotechnology, bionova holding corporation, renessen llc, exelixis plant sciences, inc. And eden bioscience.

Primary SIC and add'l.: 8731

CIK No: 0001035354

Subsidiaries: Senesco, Inc

Officers: Bruce C. Galton/Dir., CEO, Pres., Sascha P. Fedyszyn/VP - Corporate Development, Sec., Richard Dondero/VP - Research, Development, John E. Thompson/Dir., Exec. VP - Research, Development, Joel Brooks/CFO, Treasurer

Directors: Bruce C. Galton/Dir., CEO, Pres., Alan B. Bennett/Chmn. - Scientific Advisory Board, Rudolf Stalder/67/Chmn., John E. Thompson/Dir., Exec. VP - Research, Development, Christopher Forbes/Dir., Thomas C. Quick/53/Dir., Charles A. Dinarello/Member - Scientific Advisory Board, John N. Braca/50/Dir., David Rector/61/Dir., Jack Van Hulst/Dir., James W. Mier/Member - Scientific Advisory Board

Owners: Thomas C. Quick, Joel P. Brooks, Rudolf Stalder, John E. Thompson, John N. Braca, Jack Van Hulst, Stanford International Bank Limited, Christopher Forbes, Stanford Venture Capital Holdings, Richard Dondero, Bruce C. Galton, YA Global Investments, L.P., Sascha P. Fedyszyn, YA Global Investments, L.P., Heartland Advisors, Inc. *(17 Owners included in Index)*

*Financial Data: Fiscal Year End:*06/30   *Latest Annual Data:* 06/30/2007

Year	Sales	Net Income
2007	$300,000	-$3,252,000
2006	$67,000	-$3,315,000
2005	$125,000	-$2,189,000

Curr. Assets:	$1,308,000	*Curr. Liab.:*	$449,000		
Plant, Equip.:	$10,000	*Total Liab.:*	$583,000	*Indic. Yr. Divd.:*	NA
Total Assets:	$3,535,000	*Net Worth:*	$2,952,000	*Debt/ Equity:*	NA

Senetek Plc

831 Latour Ct., Ste. A, Napa, CA, 94558; *PH:* 1-707-226-3900; *Fax:* 1-707-259-6241; *http://* www.senetekplc.com; *Email:* ir@senetek.net

General - Incorporation	England And Wales	*Stock*- Price on:12/24/2007	$0.295
Employees	NA	Stock Exchange	OTC
Auditor	Macias Gini & Co LLP	Ticker Symbol	SNKTY
Stk Agt	Bank of New York	Outstanding Shares	NA
Counsel	Baker & Mckenzie LLP	E.P.S.	NA
DUNS No.	28-976-5232	Shareholders	NA

Business: The group's principal activity is the development and marketing of proprietary products that fulfill unmet consumer needs related to aging. The group comprises two segments: dermatological/skin care compounds: addressing photo aging and other skin care needs. Biopharmaceuticals: addressing sexual dysfunction.

Primary SIC and add'l.: 2834

CIK No: 0000789944

Subsidiaries: Carm Cosmeceutical Sciences Inc., Senetek Asia Limited, Senetek Denmark ApS, corporations, Senetek Drug Delivery Technologies Inc.

Officers: Frank J. Massino/Chmn., CEO, William O'Kelly/CFO

Directors: Frank J. Massino/Chmn., CEO, Rodger Bogardus/Dir., Kerry Dukes/Dir., Claudio Franceschi/Member - Scientific Advisory Board, Jan Fahrenkrug/Member - Scientific Advisory Board, Gerald Weinstein/Member - Scientific Advisory Board, Hartmut Porst/Member - Scientific Advisory Board, John Walker/Member - Scientific Advisory Board, Brian Clark/Member - Scientific Advisory Board, Anthony Linnane/Member - Scientific Advisory Board, Anthony Williams/Dir.

Owners: Anthony Williams, Kerry Dukes, Insiders/6.10%, Rodger Bogardus, Frank J. Massino/4.70%, William OKelly

*Financial Data: Fiscal Year End:*12/31   *Latest Annual Data:* 12/31/2006

Year	Sales	Net Income
2006	$8,431,000	$1,883,000
2005	$5,871,000	-$1,739,000
2004	$7,550,000	$566,000

Curr. Assets:	$5,390,000	*Curr. Liab.:*	$3,828,000		
Plant, Equip.:	$210,000	*Total Liab.:*	$7,886,000	*Indic. Yr. Divd.:*	NA
Total Assets:	$6,915,000	*Net Worth:*	-$971,000	*Debt/ Equity:*	NA

Senior High Income Portfolio Inc

800 Scudders Mill Rd., Plainsboro, NJ, 08536; *PH:* 1-609-282-5284

General - Incorporation	MD	*Stock*- Price on:12/24/2007	NA
Employees	NA	Stock Exchange	NYSE
Auditor	NA	Ticker Symbol	NA
Stk Agt	Bank of New York	Outstanding Shares	NA
Counsel	NA	E.P.S.	NA
DUNS No.	NA	Shareholders	NA

Business: The groups principal activity is to invest in real estate properties. The group operates from the United States.

Primary SIC and add'l.: 7389

CIK No: 0000896665

Officers: Alice A. Pellegrino/Sec., Vincent B. Tritto/Sec.

Senior Housing Properties Trust

400 Ctr. St., Newton, MA, 02458; *PH:* 1-617-796-8350; *Fax:* 1-617-796-8349; *http://* www.snhreit.com; *Email:* info@snhreit.com

General - Incorporation	MD	*Stock*- Price on:12/24/2007	$22.56
Employees	NA	Stock Exchange	NYSE
Auditor	Ernst & Young LLP	Ticker Symbol	SNH
Stk Agt	Wells Fargo Shareowner Services	Outstanding Shares	83,650,000
Counsel	NA	E.P.S.	$0.98
DUNS No.	NA	Shareholders	NA

Business: The groups principle activities include operating, leasing and acquiring real estate properties and healthcare properties. The group operates from the United States.

Primary SIC and add'l.: 6798

CIK No: 0001075415

Subsidiaries: CCC Alpha Investments Trust, CCC Delaware Trust, CCC Financing I Trust, CCC Financing Limited, L.P., CCC Investments I, L.L.C., CCC Leisure Park Corporation, CCC of Kentucky Trust, CCC Ohio Healthcare Trust, CCC Pueblo Norte Trust, CCC Retirement Communities II, L.P., CCC Retirement Partners Trust, CCC Retirement Trust, CCC Senior Living Corporation, CCCP Senior Living LLC, CCDE Senior Living LLC 119 Subsidiaries included in the Index

Officers: David J. Hegarty/COO, Pres./$96,779.00, William J. Sheehan/Dir. - Internal Audit, Compliance, Tim A. Bonang/Mgr. - Investor Relations, Richard A. Doyle/Treasurer, CFO, Katie Johnston/Investor Relations Analyst

Directors: Barry M. Portnoy/Founder, Managing Trustee, Frank J. Bailey/Trustee, John L. Harrington/Trustee, Frederick N. Zeytoonjian/Trustee, Adam D. Portnoy/Managing Trustee

Owners: John R. Hoadley, John L. Harrington, Adam P. Portnoy, Morgan Stanley/7.90%, David J. Hegarty, Frank J. Bailey, Frederick N. Zeytoonjian, Cohen & Steers, Inc./6.40%, Gerard M. Martin, The Vanguard Group, Inc./5.70%, Insiders, Barry M. Portnoy

*Financial Data: Fiscal Year End:*12/31   *Latest Annual Data:* 12/31/2006

Year	Sales	Net Income
2006	$179,806,000	$66,101,000
2005	$163,187,000	$63,912,000
2004	$148,523,000	$56,742,000

Curr. Assets:	$17,887,000	*Curr. Liab.:*	$13,318,000	*P/E Ratio:*	23.02
Plant, Equip.:	$1,537,851,000	*Total Liab.:*	$565,308,000	*Indic. Yr. Divd.:*	$1.360
Total Assets:	$1,584,774,000	*Net Worth:*	$1,019,466,000	*Debt/ Equity:*	0.3548

Senior Optician Service Inc

18610 E 32nd Ave., Greenacres, WA, 99016; *PH:* 1-509-891-8373

General - Incorporation	MN	*Stock*- Price on:12/24/2007	$0.1
Employees	NA	Stock Exchange	OTC
Auditor	Gruber & Co., LLC	Ticker Symbol	SOSV
Stk Agt	NA	Outstanding Shares	5,850,000
Counsel	NA	E.P.S.	$0.00
DUNS No.	NA	Shareholders	NA

Business: The group's principle activity is to focus primarily on specialty eyewear sales and service for home or faculty bound senior citizens. The company will initially offer its services to retail optician center in richfield, Minnesota. The services will be principally marketed to individuals in homebound residential situations, assisted living facilities and temporary and permanent residence facilities for senior citizens. The company plans to use an interactive Website server to use at various nurses stations at assisted living facilities and other temporary and permanent residence facilities for senior citizens. The nursing stations will then request products, services and schedule on-site optician appointments for the facility residents.

Primary SIC and add'l.: 3827 5995

CIK No: 0001101423

Officers: Patrick Downey/67/Dir., CEO, CFO, Pres., Donald Hill/65/Dir., Pres., Sandra Hill/59/Sec., Treasurer, Bradley Peterson/59/VP

Directors: Patrick Downey/67/Dir., CEO, CFO, Pres., Donald Hill/65/Dir., Pres.

Owners: Gregory M. Wilson, Insiders, Kaniksu Financial, Patrick Downey

*Financial Data: Fiscal Year End:*03/12   *Latest Annual Data:* 03/31/2007

Year	Sales	Net Income
2007	NA	-$27,000
2006	NA	-$62,000
2005	NA	-$23,000

Curr. Assets:	NA	*Curr. Liab.:*	$107,000		
Plant, Equip.:	NA	*Total Liab.:*	$107,000	*Indic. Yr. Divd.:*	NA
Total Assets:	NA	*Net Worth:*	-$107,000	*Debt/ Equity:*	NA

Senomyx Inc

4767 Nexus Ctr. Dr., San Diego, CA, 92121; *PH:* 1-858-646-8300; *Fax:* 1-858-404-0752; *http://* www.senomyx.com; *Email:* info@senomyx.com

General - Incorporation	DE	*Stock*- Price on:12/24/2007	$14.66
Employees	112	Stock Exchange	NDQ
Auditor	Ernst & Young LLP	Ticker Symbol	SNMX
Stk Agt	Mellon Investor Services LLC	Outstanding Shares	30,330,000
Counsel	NA	E.P.S.	-$0.74
DUNS No.	NA	Shareholders	NA

Business: The group's principle activities include discovering and developing fragrance and flavor molecules for use in a wide range of consumer products. The group operates from United States.

Primary SIC and add'l.: 8731

CIK No: 0001123979

Officers: Kent Snyder/Dir., CEO, Pres./$2,114,418.00, Mark J. Zoller/Exec. VP - Discovery, Development, Chief Scientific Officer/$680,640.00, John Poyhonen/Sr. VP, Chief Financial, Business Officer/$773,625.00, Harry J. Leonhardt/51/Sr. VP, General Counsel, Corp. Sec./$755,909.00, Sharon Wicker/Sr. VP - Commercialization, Chief Strategy Officer/$621,819.00, Donald S. Karanewsky/Sr. VP - Discovery, Tony Rogers/VP - Finance, Treasury, Gwen Rosenberg/VP - Investor Relations, Corporate Communications, Albert Zlotnik/VP - Biology

Directors: Kent Snyder/Dir., CEO, Pres., Lubert Stryer/Chmn. - Scientific Advisory Board, Mark Leschly/Chmn., Charles Zuker/Member - Scientific Advisory Board, Emmanuel A. Theodorakis/Member - Scientific Advisory Board, Roger Tsien/Member - Scientific Advisory Board, Harold McGee/Member - Scientific Advisory Board, Jean-Philippe Pin/Member - Scientific Advisory Board, Peter H. Seeberger/Member - Scientific Advisory Board, Charles Stevens/Member - Scientific Advisory Board, Stephen A. Block/Dir., Denis Baylor/Member - Scientific Advisory Board, Stephen J. Benkovic/Member - Scientific Advisory Board, Simon Campbell/Member - Scientific Advisory Board, Catherine Dulac/Member - Scientific Advisory Board *(22 Directors included in Index)*

Owners: Insiders/5.20%, Michael E. Herman, Jay M. Short, Dennis F. OBrien, T. Rowe Price Associates, Inc./12.40%, Sharon Wicker, Mark Zoller, Mark Leschly, John Poyhonen, Kent Snyder/2.60%, Harry J. Leonhardt, Stephen A. Block, Christopher J. Twomey, AXA Financial, Inc./7.70%

Financial Data: *Fiscal Year End:*12/31 *Latest Annual Data:* 06/30/2007

Year	Sales	Net Income
2007	NA	NA
2006	$12,230,000	-$23,057,000
2005	$9,385,000	-$19,830,000

Curr. Assets:	$75,343,000	Curr. Liab.:	$9,888,000		
Plant, Equip.:	$14,839,000	Total Liab.:	$20,705,000	Indic. Yr. Divd.:	NA
Total Assets:	$90,182,000	Net Worth:	$69,477,000	Debt/ Equity:	NA

Sense Technologies Inc

2535 N Carleton Ave., Grand Island, NE, 68803; *PH:* 1-308-381-1355; *Fax:* 1-308-381-6557; *http://* www.sensetech.com

General		Stock	
Incorporation	YT	Price on:12/24/2007	NA
Employees	NA	Stock Exchange	OTC
Auditor	Amisano Hanson	Ticker Symbol	SNSG
Stk Agt	Pacific Corporate Trust Co	Outstanding Shares	NA
Counsel	NA	E.P.S.	-$0.03
DUNS No.	NA	Shareholders	NA

Business: The group's principle activities include manufacturing, distributing, marketing and sublicensing world-wide technology to produce the guardian alert(TM) backing awareness system for motor vehicles utilizing microwave radar technology. The group operates from United States.

Primary SIC and add'l.: 3679 6794

CIK No: 0001077638

Officers: Bruce E. Schreiner/Dir., CEO, CFO, Pres., James N. Morton/Corp. Sec., Stephanie Burchfield/Contact - Media Relations, Bev Hummel/Sec.

Directors: Bruce E. Schreiner/Dir., CEO, CFO, Pres., James R. Iman/Dir., Cynthia L. Schroeder/Dir., Robert Doviak/Dir.

Owners: First Americans Insurance Service Inc./5.92%, Steve Sommers/7.43%, Cynthia L. Schroeder, Insiders/3.04%, James Iman, Bruce E. Schreiner/2.60%

Financial Data: *Fiscal Year End:*02/28 *Latest Annual Data:* 02/28/2007

Year	Sales	Net Income
2007	$98,000	-$1,225,000
2006	$75,000	-$1,490,000
2005	$47,000	-$499,000

Curr. Assets:	$165,000	Curr. Liab.:	$1,541,000		
Plant, Equip.:	$55,000	Total Liab.:	$1,541,000	Indic. Yr. Divd.:	NA
Total Assets:	$399,000	Net Worth:	-$1,142,000	Debt/ Equity:	NA

Sensient Technologies Corp

777 E Wisconsin Ave., Milwaukee, WI, 53202; *PH:* 1-414-271-6755; *Fax:* 1-414-347-3785; *http://* www.sensient-tech.com; *Email:* corporate.communications@sensient-tech.com

General		Stock	
Incorporation	WI	Price on:12/24/2007	$26.09
Employees	3,582	Stock Exchange	NYSE
Auditor	Ernst & Young, LLP	Ticker Symbol	SXT
Stk Agt	Wells Fargo Shareowner Services	Outstanding Shares	47,010,000
Counsel	NA	E.P.S.	$1.59
DUNS No.	00-608-8884	Shareholders	NA

Business: The group's principal activities are carried out through two segments: flavors and fragrances group and the color group. The flavors and fragrances group manufactures and supplies flavors, ingredient systems and aroma chemicals to the dairy, food processing, beverage, personal care and household products industries worldwide. The color group makes synthetic and natural colors for domestic and international producers of beverages, bakery products, processed foods, confections, cosmetics and pharmaceuticals. The group also produces and distributes chili powder, paprika, chili pepper and dehydrated vegetables. The group's plants are located in California, Illinois, Indiana, Michigan, Ohio, Wisconsin, Belgium, Canada, France, Germany, Italy, Mexico, New Jersey, Pennsylvania, the Netherlands, Spain and the United Kingdom. In aug 2003, the group acquired formulabs iberica sa.

Primary SIC and add'l.: 2038 2099 2087

CIK No: 0000310142

Subsidiaries: Sensient Colors Inc, Sensient Dehydrated Flavors Company, Sensient Flavors Inc

Officers: Kenneth P. Manning/Chmn., CEO, Pres./$6,471,187.00, John Collopy/Assist. Treasurer, James Clarke/Assist. General Counsel, Richard J. Malin/Assist. Controller, Stephen J. Rolfs/VP, Controller, Chief Accounting Officer, Ho-Seung Yang/VP - Marketing, Technology, John L. Hammond/Chief Administrative Officer, VP, Sec., General Counsel/$1,276,850.00, Ralph G. Pickles/Pres. - Flavors, Fragrances Group/$1,583,608.00, Richard Carney/VP - Administration/$1,189,091.00, Peter Bradley/Pres. - Color Group, Richard F. Hobbs/CFO, VP, Treasurer/$1,780,665.00

Directors: Kenneth P. Manning/Chmn., CEO, Pres., Hank Brown/68/Dir., Fergus M. Clydesdale/71/Dir., James A.D. Croft/70/Dir., William V. Hickey/63/Dir., Peter M. Salmon/58/Dir., Essie Whitelaw/60/Dir., Elaine R. Wedral/63/Dir.

Owners: Peter M. Salmon, Richard Carney, James A.D. Croft, Gabelli Asset Management Inc./11.88%, Insiders, Fergus M. Clydesdale, Dimensional Fund Advisors LP/6.86%, Elaine R. Wedral, Kenneth P. Manning, Richard F. Hobbs, John L. Hammond, Essie Whitelaw, Hank Brown, Barclays Global Investors, NA/5.29%, William V. Hickey *(17 Owners included in Index)*

Financial Data: *Fiscal Year End:*12/31 *Latest Annual Data:* 06/30/2007

Year	Sales	Net Income
2007	$304,310,000	$21,233,000
2006	$272,760,000	$15,367,000
2005	$1,023,930,000	$44,195,000

Curr. Assets:	$551,702,000	Curr. Liab.:	$260,610,000	P/E Ratio:	17.16
Plant, Equip.:	$391,456,000	Total Liab.:	$749,963,000	Indic. Yr. Divd.:	$0.720
Total Assets:	$1,454,067,000	Net Worth:	$704,104,000	Debt/ Equity:	0.6089

Sensor System Solutions Inc

45 Pk.er Ave., Ste A, Irvine, CA, 92618; *PH:* 1-949-855-6688; *http://* www.acsensor.com; *Email:* info@corp3s.com

General		Stock	
Incorporation	NV	Price on:12/24/2007	NA
Employees	17	Stock Exchange	OTC
Auditor	Weinberg & Co. P.A	Ticker Symbol	SSYO
Stk Agt	Worldwide Stock Transfer LLC	Outstanding Shares	NA
Counsel	NA	E.P.S.	-$0.045
DUNS No.	NA	Shareholders	NA

Business: The group's principal activity is to operate instant photo booths and related products. It operates 16 instant photo booths and provides related products in public access areas primarily in Germany. Of the instant photo booths that are installed, 4 are located in shopping centers and 12 are located in various city government buildings. The group's existing customers are government and municipal agencies, malls and shopping centers.

Primary SIC and add'l.: 7221

CIK No: 0001111872

Subsidiaries: Automotive Systems, Inc, Spectre Holdings, Inc., Spectre Merger Sub, Inc.

Officers: Michael Young/Chmn., Founder, CEO - Investor Relations, Jay Liang/GM, Jacek Beben/Sr. Staff Engineer, Roger G. Sullivan/VP - Sales, Marketing, James P. Owens/CFO

Directors: Michael Young/Chmn., Founder, CEO - Investor Relations, Hanlin Chen/Dir.

Owners: Michael Young/14.00%, Future Front International Co. Ltd./19.00%, Insiders/14.00%

Financial Data: *Fiscal Year End:*12/31 *Latest Annual Data:* 12/31/2005

Year	Sales	Net Income
2005	$1,325,000	-$2,729,000
2004	$661,000	-$3,662,000
2003	$293,000	-$425,000

Curr. Assets:	$752,000	Curr. Liab.:	$2,757,000		
Plant, Equip.:	$234,000	Total Liab.:	$2,786,000	Indic. Yr. Divd.:	NA
Total Assets:	$1,090,000	Net Worth:	-$1,696,000	Debt/ Equity:	NA

Sentex Sensing Technology Inc

1801 E 9th St., Cleveland, OH, 44114; *PH:* 1-216-687-0289; *Fax:* 1-216-687-0298; *http://* www.sentextech.com

General		Stock	
Incorporation	NJ	Price on:12/24/2007	$0.028
Employees	NA	Stock Exchange	OTC
Auditor	Hausser + Taylor LLC	Ticker Symbol	SNTX
Stk Agt	Cotinental Stock Transfer	Outstanding Shares	199,850,000
Counsel	NA	E.P.S.	-$0.003
DUNS No.	05-143-0858	Shareholders	NA

Business: The group's principal activity is to buy, sell and trade in information technology equipment, primarily computer equipment. It acquires unneeded, older computer equipment and resells that equipment to certain consumers on a global basis. The group is an asset manager and computer dealer and is fully integrated with complete demanufacturing and some recycling capability.

Primary SIC and add'l.: 7377 7379 7378

CIK No: 0000729599

Subsidiaries: Regency Technologies, LLC

Officers: Robert S. Kendall/69/Chmn., CEO, Treasurer, William R. Sprow/69/CFO, Controller, Henrik Rubinstein/Dir., Pres., Maryann Kusa/Investor Relations Department

Directors: Robert S. Kendall/69/Chmn., CEO, Treasurer, Henrik Rubinstein/Dir., Pres.

Owners: Balmoral Financial Services Company/7.50%, Insiders/58.60%, Viewpoint Technology, Inc./6.00%, CPS Capital, Limited/24.00%, Robert S. Kendall/24.00%, 1st Management Finance, Inc./34.60%

Financial Data: *Fiscal Year End:*11/30 *Latest Annual Data:* 11/30/2006

Year	Sales	Net Income
2006	$21,000	-$579,000
2005	$159,000	-$377,000
2004	$3,915,000	-$781,000

Curr. Assets:	NA	Curr. Liab.:	$8,272,000		
Plant, Equip.:	NA	Total Liab.:	$8,272,000	Indic. Yr. Divd.:	NA
Total Assets:	$1,900,000	Net Worth:	-$6,372,000	Debt/ Equity:	NA

Sentigen Holding Corp

445 Marshall St., Phillipsburg, NJ, 08865; *PH:* 1-908-454-7774; *http://* www.sentigen.com

General		Stock	
Incorporation	DE	Price on:12/24/2007	$25.55
Employees	NA	Stock Exchange	NA
Auditor	Deloitte & Touche LLP	Ticker Symbol	NA
Stk Agt	American Stock Transfer & Trust Co.	Outstanding Shares	NA
Counsel	NA	E.P.S.	NA
DUNS No.	61-326-0975	Shareholders	NA

Business: The group's principal activities are to provide contract research and development services and products such as cell culture media, reagents and other research products to companies engaged in the drug discovery process. It also conducts scientific research to develop environmentally sound approaches to prevent insect crop damage and the spread of human diseases by impacting insect behavior. The group's customers include manufacturers in the biotechnology and pharmaceutical industries, hospitals, universities and research institutions.

Primary SIC and add'l.: 2835 8731 2836 6719

CIK No: 0000864890

Subsidiaries: Cell & Molecular Technologies, Inc., Sentigen Biosciences, Inc

Officers: Joseph K. Pagano/Chmn., CEO, Pres., Kevin J. Lee/VP - Research, Thomas J. Livelli/Dir., Pres., Scott G. Segler/CFO

Directors: Joseph K. Pagano/Chmn., CEO, Pres., Thomas J. Livelli/Dir., Pres., Frederick R. Adler/Dir., Gerald Greenwald/Dir., Joel M. Pearlberg/Dir., Samuel A. Rozzi/Dir., Bruce Slovin/Dir., Arnold B. Pollard/Dir.

Sentinel Sec Lif Ins

2121 S State St., Salt Lake City, UT, 84115; **PH:** 1-801-484-8514; **http://** www.sentinellife.org

General - Incorporation	NA	**Stock**- Price on:12/24/2007	$62
Employees	NA	Stock Exchange	OTC
Auditor	NA	Ticker Symbol	SENI
Stk Agt.	NA	Outstanding Shares	NA
Counsel	NA	E.P.S.	NA
DUNS No.	NA	Shareholders	NA

Business: The groups principle activity is to provide recruiting services. The groups service area includes the research and development, engineering, marketing, sales, information technology and manufacturing industries. The group operates from United States.

Primary SIC and add'l.: 6311

CIK No:

Officers: Earl L. Tate/Pres.

SentiSearch Inc

1482 E Valley Rd., Santa Barbara, CA, 93108; **PH:** 1-805-684-1830

General - Incorporation	DE	**Stock**- Price on:12/24/2007	$0.18
Employees	NA	Stock Exchange	OTC
Auditor	Raich Ende Malter & Co. LLP	Ticker Symbol	SSRC
Stk Agt.	NA	Outstanding Shares	7,690,000
Counsel	NA	E.P.S.	-$0.06
DUNS No.	NA	Shareholders	NA

Business: The groups principal activities include entering into a license agreement with Columbia for an exclusive worldwide right to the Columbia License. The group entered into a contribution agreement with Sentigen pursuant to which Sentigen transferred all of its olfaction intellectual property, including the Columbia License. The group operates from the United States.

Primary SIC and add'l.: 6794

CIK No: 0001380024

Subsidiaries: Sentigen Biosciences, Inc. (Sentigen Biosciences)

Owners: D. H. Blair Investment Banking Corp./14.75%, Thomas J. Livelli/1.55%, Joseph K. Pagano/17.89%, Insiders/27.93%, Frederick R. Adler/8.49%

Financial Data: Fiscal Year End:12/31   Latest Annual Data: 12/31/2006

Year	Sales	Net Income
2006	NA	-$438,000

Curr. Assets:	$68,000	Curr. Liab.:	$39,000		
Plant, Equip.:	NA	Total Liab.:	$39,000	Indic. Yr. Divd.:	NA
Total Assets:	$177,000	Net Worth:	$138,000	Debt/ Equity:	NA

Sento Corp

600 E Timpanogos Cir., Bldg. H, Orem, UT, 84097; **PH:** 1-801-431-9200; **Fax:** 1-801-532-2173; **http://** www.sento.com

General - Incorporation	UT	**Stock**- Price on:12/24/2007	$1.48
Employees	1,603	Stock Exchange	NA
Auditor	Ernst & Young LLP	Ticker Symbol	NA
Stk Agt.	American Stock Transfer & Trust Co.	Outstanding Shares	4,130,000
Counsel	Stoel Rives LLP	E.P.S.	-$1.74
DUNS No.	16-154-8284	Shareholders	NA

Business: The group's principle activities are to design, implement and manage high-tech solutions for customer acquisition, customer care, technical support and help-desk functions. It uses advanced systems, including client and server-based database and reporting systems, Internet, local area networks, multi-user systems, computer-telephony integration, crm and integrated voice response technologies, for providing the services. The group provides international and domestic support services to original equipment manufacturers, software publishers, hardware system manufacturers and other entities requiring mid-level to high-end technical services. It helps the clients reduce headcount, eliminate unnecessary capital expenditures and improve the experience for the customer. The group operates in Ireland, Scotland, South Africa and India.

Primary SIC and add'l.: 7376 7379

CIK No: 0000004317

Subsidiaries: Sento BV, Sento SAS, Sento Technical Services Corporation, Xtrasource Acquisitions, Inc

Officers: Kim Cooper/Chmn., CEO, Pres., Thomas Tyler/Sr. VP - Marketing, Sales, Stephen W. Fulling/Sr. VP, Chief Information, Technology Officer, Richard Steiner/VP - Quality, Training, Michael Williams/COO, MD, Bart Van Eunen/VP - European Business Development

Directors: Kim Cooper/Chmn., CEO, Pres., Phillip J. Windley/Dir., Richard Dyer/Dir., Eric Olafson/Dir., Lloyd C. Mahaffey/Dir., Dave McGinn/Dir.

Owners: Great Gable Master Fund, Ltd./18.00%, Barclays Global Investors, Na./5.00%, Plutus Transeo Fund, LP/19.00%, Insiders/11.00%, Phillip J. Windley, Anthony J. Sansone, Thomas Rooney/9.00%, Tom Tyler, Richard E. Dyer, Patrick F. ONeal/4.00%, Brian Maloy, Kim A. Cooper, Eric Olafson/1.00%, David B. McGinn, Stephen W. Fulling (16 Owners included in Index)

Financial Data: Fiscal Year End:03/31   Latest Annual Data: 3/31/2006

Year	Sales	Net Income
2006	$51,129,000	-$154,000
2005	$31,786,000	-$1,798,000
2004	$21,396,000	-$1,465,000

Curr. Assets:	$13,992,000	Curr. Liab.:	$10,454,000		
Plant, Equip.:	$7,068,000	Total Liab.:	$14,268,000	Indic. Yr. Divd.:	NA
Total Assets:	$23,315,000	Net Worth:	$9,047,000	Debt/ Equity:	0.4015

Sentry Technology Corp

1881 Lakeland Ave., Ronkonkoma, NY, 11779; **PH:** 1-631-739-2000; **Fax:** 1-631-739-2118; **http://** www.sentrytechnology.com; **Email:** sentry@sentrytechnology.com

General - Incorporation	DE	**Stock**- Price on:12/24/2007	$0.06
Employees	71	Stock Exchange	OTC
Auditor	SF Partnership LLP	Ticker Symbol	SKVY
Stk Agt	American Stock Transfer & Trust Co.	Outstanding Shares	120,740,000
Counsel	Stroock & Stroock & Lavan	E.P.S.	-$0.02
DUNS No.	96-751-0033	Shareholders	NA

Business: The group's principal activities are to design, sell, install and service radio frequency and electro-magnetic electronic article surveillance systems and closed circuit television solutions. The CCTV products are marketed under the trade name SentryVision SmartTrack.

Primary SIC and add'l.: 7382 3663 3669

CIK No: 0001030708

Subsidiaries: Custom Security Industries Inc, Sentry Technology Canada Inc

Officers: Peter L. Murdoch/Chmn., CEO, Pres., Joan E. Miller/VP - Finance, Principal Financial, Accounting Officer, Treasurer

Directors: Peter L. Murdoch/Chmn., CEO, Pres., Robert D. Furst/Dir., Jonathan G. Granoff/Dir.

Owners: Insiders/65.90%, Peter L. Murdoch/51.20%, Robert D. Furst/16.80%, Jonathan G. Granoff, Joan E. Miller

Financial Data: Fiscal Year End:12/31   Latest Annual Data: 12/31/2006

Year	Sales	Net Income
2006	$12,135,000	-$2,304,000
2005	$13,570,000	-$1,690,000
2004	$16,665,000	$31,000

Curr. Assets:	$6,181,000	Curr. Liab.:	$4,905,000		
Plant, Equip.:	$609,000	Total Liab.:	$6,949,000	Indic. Yr. Divd.:	NA
Total Assets:	$8,834,000	Net Worth:	$648,000	Debt/ Equity:	NA

Sepracor Inc

84 Waterford Dr., Marlborough, MA, 01752; **PH:** 1-508-481-6700; **Fax:** 1-508-357-7499; **http://** www.sepracor.com; **Email:** info@sepracor.com

General - Incorporation	DE	**Stock**- Price on:12/24/2007	$43.82
Employees	2,470	Stock Exchange	NDQ
Auditor	PricewaterhouseCoopers LLP	Ticker Symbol	SEPR
Stk Agt	Computershare Trust	Outstanding Shares	106,430,000
Counsel	Douglas E. Reedich	E.P.S.	$1.65
DUNS No.	13-166-1746	Shareholders	NA

Business: The group's principal activities are to discover, develop and commercialization of innovative pharmaceutical compounds. The pharmaceutical compounds are directed towards serving unmet medical needs. The group's drug development program has yielded an extensive portfolio of pharmaceutical compounds for treatment in two major therapeutic areas, respiratory and central nervous system disorders. The group has operations in the United States and Canada.

Primary SIC and add'l.: 2834 8731

CIK No: 0000877357

Subsidiaries: Sepracor Canada Holdings, Inc, Sepracor Canada Limited, Sepracor Research & Development Trust, Sepracor Securities Corporation, Sepracor, N.V.

Officers: Adrian Adams/Dir., CEO, Pres., Timothy J. Barberich/Exec. Chmn./$7,966,493.00, Mark H.N. Corrigan/Exec. VP - Research, Development/$3,024,550.00, David P. Southwell/CFO, Exec. VP - Corporate Planning, Development, Licensing/$3,587,306.00, Douglas E. Reedich/50/Sr. VP - Legal Affairs, Andrew I. Koven/Exec. VP, General Counsel, Corp. Sec., Robert F. Scumaci/Exec. VP - Corporate Finance, Administration, Technical Operations/$2,689,196.00

Directors: Adrian Adams/Dir., CEO, Pres., Timothy J. Barberich/Exec. Chmn., James W. O'Shea/Vice Chmn., James G. Andress/Dir., Robert J. Cresci/Dir., Timothy J. Rink/Dir., Alan A. Steigrod/Dir., Digby W. Barrios/Dir., James F. Mrazek/Dir.

Owners: Digby W. Barrios, Mark H. N. Corrigan, Insiders/5.30%, T. Rowe Price Associates, Inc./10.50%, William J. OShea, PRIMECAP Management Company/6.70%, James F. Mrazek, FMR Corp. and related entities/15.40%, Caxton International Limited and related entities/7.10%, Robert J. Cresci, Robert F. Scumaci, Alan A. Steigrod, James G. Andress, Capital Group International,Inc./5.50%, David P. Southwell (17 Owners included in Index)

Financial Data: Fiscal Year End:12/31   Latest Annual Data: 12/31/2006

Year	Sales	Net Income
2006	$1,196,534,000	$184,562,000
2005	$820,928,000	$3,927,000
2004	$380,877,000	-$295,658,000

Curr. Assets:	$1,221,028,000	Curr. Liab.:	$680,112,000	P/E Ratio:	26.56
Plant, Equip.:	$72,811,000	Total Liab.:	$1,401,625,000	Indic. Yr. Divd.:	NA
Total Assets:	$1,493,793,000	Net Worth:	$92,168,000	Debt/ Equity:	5.0843

Sequa Corp

200 Pk. Ave., New York, NY, 10166; **PH:** 1-212-986-5500; **Fax:** 1-212-370-1969; **http://** www.sequa.com

General - Incorporation	DE	**Stock**- Price on:12/24/2007	$112.24
Employees	10,155	Stock Exchange	NA
Auditor	KPMG LLP	Ticker Symbol	NA
Stk Agt	Bank of New York	Outstanding Shares	11,390,000
Counsel	NA	E.P.S.	$5.64
DUNS No.	00-137-4727	Shareholders	NA

Business: The groups principle activity is to provide technology solutions for the aerospace, automotive, metal coating, specialty chemicals, industrial machinery and other products industries. The group operates from United States.

Primary SIC and add'l.: 3764 5199 3479 3634 2396 3728

CIK No: 0000095301

Subsidiaries: After Six, Inc., ARC Automotive Italia S.r.l., ARC Automotive, Inc., Atlantic Research Corporation, Casco Electronics GmbH, Casco IMOS Italia S.r.l., Casco Investors Corporation, Casco Products Corporation, Chromalloy American Corporation, Chromalloy Castings Tampa Corporation, Chromalloy Component Services, Inc., Chromalloy Gas Turbine Corporation, Chromalloy Gas Turbine Europa, B.V., Chromalloy Gas Turbine France, Chromalloy Heavy Industrial Turbine, Limited. 36 Subsidiaries included in the Index

Officers: Martin Weinstein/Vice Chmn., CEO/$1,831,161.00, Donna Costello/VP, Controller, Steven R. Lowson/VP, Michael Blickensderfer/VP - Taxes, James P. Langelotti/VP, Treasurer, Linda G. Kyriakou/VP - Corporate Communications, Robert L. Iuliucci/VP - Environmental, Safety, Health, Robert D. Devito/VP - Corporate Development, Strategy, Diane C. Bunt/Sec., Mitchell D. Bittman/Assist. Sec., Gerard M. Dombek/Sr. VP - Metal Coating/$701,466.00, Steven Schaus/VP - Operational Excellence, Robert F. Ellis/Sr. VP - Specialty Chemicals/$979,878.00, John J. Dowling/Sr. VP - Legal, Kenneth J. Binder/CFO, Exec. VP (16 Officers included in Index)

Directors: Martin Weinstein/Vice Chmn., CEO, Gail A. Binderman/Chmn., Michael I. Sovern/Dir., Mark A. Alexander/Dir., Robert F. Weinberg/Dir., Richard S. Lefrak/Dir., Gerald S. Gutterman/Dir., Stanley R. Zax/70/Dir., Fred R. Sullivan/Dir., Gerald Tsai/79/Dir., Edward E. Barr/Dir.

Owners: Donna Costello, Fred R. Sullivan, Robert F. Weinberg, Richard S. LeFrak, Fred R. Sullivan, Insiders/28.37%, Kenneth Binder, Gail Binderman, Gail Binderman, John J. Dowling, Insiders/61.51%, Mark E. Alexander/61.30%, Robert F. Ellis, Robert F. Weinberg, Mark E. Alexander/25.66% (19 Owners included in Index)

Financial Data: Fiscal Year End:12/31   Latest Annual Data: 12/31/2006

Year	Sales	Net Income
2006	$2,183,816,000	$65,606,000
2005	$1,997,558,000	$27,323,000
2004	$1,864,063,000	$19,227,000

Curr. Assets:	$1,158,040,000	Curr. Liab.:	$443,484,000	P/E Ratio:	19.90
Plant, Equip.:	$455,541,000	Total Liab.:	$1,257,046,000	Indic. Yr. Divd.:	NA
Total Assets:	$2,031,604,000	Net Worth:	$745,070,000	Debt/ Equity:	0.9915

Sequenom Inc

3595 John Hopkins Ct., San Diego, CA, 92121; **PH:** 1-858-202-9000; **Fax:** 1-858-202-9001; http:// www.sequenom.com

General - Incorporation	DE	**Stock**- Price on:12/24/2007	$4.64
Employees	123	Stock Exchange	NDQ
Auditor	Ernst & Young LLP	Ticker Symbol	SQNM
Stk Agt	American Stock Transfer & Trust Co.	Outstanding Shares	40,120,000
Counsel	Cooley Godward LLP	E.P.S.	-$0.53
DUNS No.	NA	Shareholders	NA

Business: The group's principle activity is to provide the genetic analysis products and services. The products of the group include MassARRAY(R) system for nucleic acid analysis. The customers of the group include clinical research and clinical marker validation, molecular medicine, diagnostic service laboratories, and animal testing laboratories. The group operates in the United States, Europe and Asia. The group's quarterly revenue for September 2007 was 9.84 millions of USD.

Primary SIC and add'l.: 2835 8731

CIK No: 0001076481

Subsidiaries: Gemini Genomics, (UK) Ltd., Gemini Genomics, Ltd., Sequenom GmbH, SequenomGemini, Ltd.

Officers: Harry Stylli/CEO, Pres./$1,172,017.00, Charles R. Cantor/Chief Scientific Officer/$422,211.00, Clarke Neumann/VP, General Counsel/$313,242.00, Elizabeth Dragon/Sr. VP - R & D/$301,984.00, Micheal Monke/Sr. VP - Sales, Marketing, Paul Hawran/CFO, Larry Myres/VP - Operations, Clarke Neuman/VP, General Counsel

Directors: Harry F. Hixson/69/Chmn., Ronald M. Lindsay/60/Dir., Ernst Gunter Afting/65/Dir., Larry E. Lenig/59/Dir., Patrick G. Enright/46/Dir.

Owners: Siemens Venture Capital GMBH/9.33%, ComVest Investment Partners II LLC/18.33%, LB I Group Inc./14.64%, Insiders/20.48%, Clarke Neumann, Charles R. Cantor, Paul Hawran, Ernst-Gunter Afting, Ronald M. Lindsay, Harry F. Hixson, Pequot Private Equity Fund IV/16.62%, Elizabeth A. Dragon, Stephens Investment Management/5.50%, Larry F. Lenig/18.37%, Harry Stylli/1.31% (17 Owners included in Index)

Financial Data: Fiscal Year End:12/31   Latest Annual Data: 12/31/2006

Year	Sales	Net Income
2006	$28,496,000	-$17,577,000
2005	$19,421,000	-$26,537,000
2004	$22,449,000	-$34,625,000

Curr. Assets:	$34,408,000	Curr. Liab.:	$10,757,000		
Plant, Equip.:	$4,528,000	Total Liab.:	$14,431,000	Indic. Yr. Divd.:	NA
Total Assets:	$39,881,000	Net Worth:	$25,450,000	Debt/ Equity:	NA

Sequiam Corp

300 Sunport Ln, Orlando, Florida, 32809; **PH:** 1-407-541-0773; **Fax:** 1-407-240-1431; http:// www.sequiam.com; **Email:** information@sequiam.com

General - Incorporation	CA	**Stock**- Price on:12/24/2007	$0.18
Employees	13	Stock Exchange	OTC
Auditor	Tedder, James, Worden & Assoc. P.A	Ticker Symbol	SQUM
Stk Agt	Pacific Stock Transfer Company	Outstanding Shares	84,700,000
Counsel	NA	E.P.S.	-$0.071
DUNS No.	NA	Shareholders	NA

Business: The group's principal activity is to develop, market and support a portfolio of Internet and print enterprise software products. It provides application service provider hosting of Internet-enabled solutions, Internet service provider including Internet access and hosting, consulting, application integration and custom Web development and software development services. The group operates in two segments: information management and safety and security. The information management segment includes Internet remote print suite of software products and interactive Web-based technologies. The safety and security segment sells the biovault (TM), a secure safe intended for personal firearms that uses fingerprint recognition technology to open instead of a traditional key. On 03-May-2003 the group acquired smart biometrics inc , on 01-Jun-2003 telepartners inc and fingerprint detection technologies inc on 11-Sep-2003.

Primary SIC and add'l.: 7379 7375

CIK No: 0001123606

Subsidiaries: Biometric Security (PTY) LTD. (a/k/a Secure Biometrics.co.za), Constellation Biometrics Corporation, Fingerprint Detection Technologies, Inc., Sequiam Biometrics, Inc., Sequiam Education, Inc., Sequiam Software, Inc., Sequiam Sports, Inc.

Officers: Nicholas H. Vandenbrekel/Chmn., CEO, Pres., Founder, Kevin Henderson/Pres. - Sequiam Biometrics, Alan McGinn/CTO, VP, Mark L. Mroczkowski/Dir., CFO, Exec. VP, Treasurer, Corp Sec., Phil Dumas/VP - Product Development, Douglas R. Dillman/Controller

Directors: Nicholas H. Vandenbrekel/Chmn., CEO, Pres., Founder, Mark L. Mroczkowski/Dir., CFO, Exec. VP, Treasurer, Corp Sec., James C. Stanley/Dir.

Owners: Insiders, Nicholas H. VandenBrekel, Mark L. Mroczkowski, Biometrics Investors, LLC, Walter H. Sullivan

Financial Data: Fiscal Year End:12/31   Latest Annual Data: 12/31/2006

Year	Sales	Net Income
2006	$1,688,000	-$5,201,000
2005	$626,000	-$5,431,000
2004	$265,000	-$5,847,000

Curr. Assets:	$1,658,000	Curr. Liab.:	$7,020,000		
Plant, Equip.:	$920,000	Total Liab.:	$8,211,000	Indic. Yr. Divd.:	NA
Total Assets:	$3,718,000	Net Worth:	-$4,493,000	Debt/ Equity:	NA

Seracare Life Sciences Inc

375 W St., West Bridgewater, MA, 02379; **PH:** 1-508-580-1900; **Fax:** 1-508-580-2202; http:// www.seracare.com

General - Incorporation	CA	**Stock**- Price on:12/24/2007	NA
Employees	242	Stock Exchange	OTC
Auditor	KPMG LLP	Ticker Symbol	SRLS
Stk Agt	Computershare Trust Co	Outstanding Shares	NA
Counsel	NA	E.P.S.	NA
DUNS No.	NA	Shareholders	NA

Business: The group's principal activities are to manufacture plasma-based diagnostic products and distribute therapeutic products. The group operates through two divisions: diagnostics division and therapeutics division. Diagnostic products are used to diagnose specific patient conditions, including infectious disease and blood type and therapeutic products are used as exciepients in the manufacture of vaccines. The group's products also include non-human blood products that are used for cell culture, research and for in vitro diagnostic use. The products are marketed to both domestic and international manufacturers of therapeutic and diagnostic products. The customers of the group includes pharmaceutical companies, researchers and disgnostic test makers. On 16-Jul- 2003, the group acquired biomedical resources, inc.

Primary SIC and add'l.: 2836 2834 2835

CIK No: 0001156295

Subsidiaries: BioMedical Resources, Inc, Boston Biomedica, Inc, Genomics Collaborative, Inc, SeraCare BioBank

Officers: Susan L.N. Vogt/CEO, Pres., Gregory A. Gould/CFO, Kathleen W. Benjamin/VP - Human Resources, Ron Dilling/VP - Operations, Mark M. Manak/Chief Scientific Officer, Kathi Shea/VP - Bioservices Operation, David M. Olsen/VP - Corporate Quality, Bill Smutny/VP - Sales, Marketing

Curr. Assets:	$40,932,000	Curr. Liab.:	$17,009,000		
Plant, Equip.:	$7,423,000	Total Liab.:	$43,365,000	Indic. Yr. Divd.:	NA
Total Assets:	$89,128,000	Net Worth:	$45,764,000	Debt/ Equity:	NA

Serefex Corp

4328 Corporate Sq. Blvd, Ste. C, Naples, FL, 34104; **PH:** 1-239-262-1610; http:// www.serefex.com; **Email:** info@serefex.com

General - Incorporation	DE	**Stock**- Price on:12/24/2007	$0.05
Employees	2	Stock Exchange	OTC
Auditor	Lake & Assoc. CPA's LLC	Ticker Symbol	SFXC
Stk Agt	Equity Transfer Services Inc	Outstanding Shares	159,760,000
Counsel	NA	E.P.S.	-$0.002
DUNS No.	NA	Shareholders	NA

Business: The group's primary activity is producing magnetic ancillary product lines including, paper and tapes, and computer telecommunication products. The products offered by the group are Chat-N-Mouse(TM) optical mouse with a built in microphone, tracking wheel and zoom button functions, Fridge Tape(TM) adhesively backed magnetic tape, Fridge Pic(TM) magnetic photo paper, Fridge Notes(TM) magnetically backed dry eraser sheets, Locker Tape(TM) adhesively backed self unwinding magnetic tape, and Heavy Duty Fridge Tape(TM) adhesively backed industrial strength magnetic tape. The group operates in the United States.

Primary SIC and add'l.: 7372

CIK No: 0000773937

Officers: Brian Dunn/Dir., CEO, Pres., Sec., Don Gunther/Advisor to Dir., Robert C. Marconi/Advisor to Dir., Shawn William/VP - Operations, Ben M. Jones/Advisor to Dir., Todd Bartlett/CFO, Treasurer, James Fligg/Advisor to Dir.

Directors: Brian Dunn/Dir., CEO, Pres., Sec., Terrence P. Monahan/Dir.

Owners: Don Gunther/12.70%, Shawn M. Williams/0.90%, Insiders/13.70%, Ben M. Jones/17.20%, Terrence P. Monahan/2.00%, Brian S. Dunn/10.10%, Todd A. Bartlett/0.80%, Robert C. Marconi/5.60%

Financial Data: Fiscal Year End:12/31   Latest Annual Data: 12/31/2006

Year	Sales	Net Income
2006	$358,000	-$546,000
2005	$346,000	-$895,000
2004	$5,000	-$715,000

Curr. Assets:	$328,000	Curr. Liab.:	$44,000		
Plant, Equip.:	$12,000	Total Liab.:	$44,000	Indic. Yr. Divd.:	NA
Total Assets:	$536,000	Net Worth:	$492,000	Debt/ Equity:	NA

Serena Software Inc

2755 Campus Dr., 3rd Fl., San Mateo, CA, 94403; **PH:** 1-650-522-6600; http:// www.serena.com; **Email:** info@serena.com

General - Incorporation .... DE
Employees .... NA
Auditor .... KPMG LLP
Stk Agt .... Mellon Investor Services LLC
Counsel .... Wilson Sonsini Goodrich & Rosati
DUNS No. 12-016-9321

Stock- Price on:12/24/2007 .... $24
Stock Exchange .... NDQ
Ticker Symbol .... SRNA
Outstanding Shares .... NA
E.P.S .... NA
Shareholders .... NA

Business: The group's principle activity of the group is to provide enterprise change management software and services to enterprise applications. The products are used to manage and control application change for organizations whose business operations are dependent on managing information technology, or it. These application architectures contain a mainframe application utilizing data in a mainframe database, a middle-tier of Unix, Linux or Window NT servers, and a Web browser client or Web service interface. At 31-Jan-2004, our products have been installed in over 3,600 customer sites worldwide and our customers include 46 of the Fortune 50 companies such as American Express, UBS AG, Duke Energy, Capital One, Bank of America, Caterpillar, Safeway, General Electric, IBM, Metlife, Prudential, and SBC Communications. On 05-Jun-2003, the group acquired Teamshare(R) Inc and on 23-Apr- 2004, Merant. PLC. The group operates from United States.

Primary SIC and add'l.: 7376 7372

CIK No: 0001073967

Subsidiaries: Apptero, Inc, Merant BV, Merant Holdings, Merant Inc., Merant Limited, Merant SA, Merant Trustees Limited, Serena Holdings Limited, SERENA Software (UK) Limited, SERENA Software Benelux BVBA, SERENA Software Canada Limited, Serena Software Europe Limited, SERENA Software France SARL, SERENA Software GmbH, SERENA Software International FSC, Inc 18 Subsidiaries included in the Index

Officers: Jeremy Burton/CEO, Pres., Peter Sianchuk/VP - Worldwide Customer Support, Michael R. Steinharter/Sr. VP - Worldwide Field Operations, Rene Bonvanie/Sr. VP - Worldwide Marketing, Partner Programs, Online Services, Robert I. Pender/CFO, Sr. VP - Finance, Administration, Carl Theobald/Sr. VP - Research, Development, Matthew Dimaria/46/Sr. VP - Worldwide Marketing, Edward Malysz/Sr. VP, General Counsel

Directors: David Roux/Chmn., Douglas D. Troxel/Dir., John Joyce/Dir., Hollie Moore/Dir., Elizabeth Hackenson/Dir.

Owners: Hollie J. Moore, Matthew DiMaria, David J. Roux, Carl Theobald, Insiders, Silver Lake funds, Edward Malysz, John R. Joyce, Douglas D. Troxel, Robert I. Pender

Serino 1 Corp

Formerly: Serion 1 Corp
3163 Kennedy Blvd., Jersy City, NJ, 07306; *PH:* 1-201-217-4137

General - Incorporation .... NJ
Employees .... NA
Auditor .... Moore & Assoc., Chartered
Stk Agt .... Jersey Transfer & Trust Co
Counsel .... NA
DUNS No. .... NA

Stock- Price on:12/24/2007 .... NA
Stock Exchange .... NA
Ticker Symbol .... NA
Outstanding Shares .... NA
E.P.S .... NA
Shareholders .... NA

Business: The group's principle activity is to provide a method for a foreign or domestic private company to become a reporting ("public") company whose securities are qualified for trading in the United States secondary market. The group operates from United States.

Primary SIC and add'l.: 9995

CIK No: 0001331612

Officers: Michael Jordan Friedman/30/Chmn., CEO, CFO, Pres., Dominick M. Cingari/33/Dir., COO

Directors: Michael Jordan Friedman/30/Chmn., CEO, CFO, Pres., Dominick M. Cingari/33/Dir., COO, Richard J. Verdiramo/43/Dir., Jay Odintz/47/Dir.

Owners: Dominick Cingari/13.74%, Illuminate, Inc./25.06%, Michael Jordan Friedman/31.66%, Jay Odintz/1.87%, Marcia Roberts/15.30%, Insiders/47.27%

Serino 2 Corp

3163 Kennedy Blvd., Jersy City, NJ, 07306; *PH:* 1-201-217-4137

General - Incorporation .... NJ
Employees .... NA
Auditor .... Gately & Assoc. LLC
Stk Agt .... Jersey Transfer & Trust Co
Counsel .... NA
DUNS No. .... NA

Stock- Price on:12/24/2007 .... NA
Stock Exchange .... NA
Ticker Symbol .... NA
Outstanding Shares .... NA
E.P.S .... NA
Shareholders .... NA

Business: The group's principle activity is to engage in any lawful corporate undertaking, including, but not limited to, selected mergers and acquisitions. We have been in the developmental stage since inception and have no operations to date other than issuing shares to our original shareholder. The group operates from United States.

Primary SIC and add'l.: 6770

CIK No: 0001331613

Serino 3 Corp

3163 Kennedy Blvd., Jersy City, NJ, 07306; *PH:* 1-201-217-4137

General - Incorporation .... NJ
Employees .... NA
Auditor .... Sf Partnership, LLP
Stk Agt .... Jersey Transfer & Trust Co
Counsel .... NA
DUNS No. .... NA

Stock- Price on:12/24/2007 .... NA
Stock Exchange .... NA
Ticker Symbol .... NA
Outstanding Shares .... NA
E.P.S .... NA
Shareholders .... NA

Business: The groups principle activity is to provide critical intelligence for the business, investor, and legal communities. The operates from United States.

Primary SIC and add'l.: 6770

CIK No: 0001331615

Serino 4 Corp

3163 Kennedy Blvd., Jersy City, NJ, 07306; *PH:* 1-201-217-4137

General - Incorporation .... NJ
Employees .... NA
Auditor .... Gately & Assoc. LLC
Stk Agt .... Jersey Transfer & Trust Co
Counsel .... NA
DUNS No. .... NA

Stock- Price on:12/24/2007 .... NA
Stock Exchange .... NA
Ticker Symbol .... NA
Outstanding Shares .... NA
E.P.S .... NA
Shareholders .... NA

Business: The group's principle activity is to engage in any lawful corporate undertaking, including, but not limited to, selected mergers and acquisitions. The group operates from United States.

Primary SIC and add'l.: 6770

CIK No: 0001331616

Officers: John Forsythe/Pres.

Owners: Vincent L. Verdiramo/100.00%

Serino 5 Corp

3163 Kennedy Blvd., Jersy City, NJ, 07306; *PH:* 1-201-217-4137

General - Incorporation .... NJ
Employees .... NA
Auditor .... Gately & Assoc. LLC
Stk Agt .... Jersey Transfer & Trust Co
Counsel .... NA
DUNS No. .... NA

Stock- Price on:12/24/2007 .... NA
Stock Exchange .... NA
Ticker Symbol .... NA
Outstanding Shares .... NA
E.P.S .... NA
Shareholders .... NA

Business: The group's principal activity is to issue shares to the original shareholders. The group is in the developmental stage since inception.

Primary SIC and add'l.: 6770

CIK No: 0001331617

Serion 6 Corp

3163 Kennedy Blvd., Jersy City, NJ, 07306; *PH:* 1-201-217-4137

General - Incorporation .... NJ
Employees .... NA
Auditor .... Gately & Assoc. LLC
Stk Agt .... NA
Counsel .... NA
DUNS No. .... NA

Stock- Price on:12/24/2007 .... NA
Stock Exchange .... NA
Ticker Symbol .... NA
Outstanding Shares .... NA
E.P.S .... NA
Shareholders .... NA

Business: The group's activities include but not limited to selecting mergers and acquisitions. The company has been in the developmental stage since inception. The company has no operations to date other than issuing shares to its original shareholders.

Primary SIC and add'l.: 6770

CIK No: 0001331618

Serono

15 Bis, Chemin Des Mines, Case Postale 54, Switzerland, CH-1211; ; *http://* www.serono.com

General - Incorporation .... Switzerland
Employees 4,750
Auditor .... PricewaterhouseCoopers S.P.A
Stk Agt .... Bank of New York
Counsel .... Shaw Pittman
DUNS No. .... NA

Stock- Price on:12/24/2007 .... NA
Stock Exchange .... NA
Ticker Symbol .... NA
Outstanding Shares .... NA
E.P.S .... NA
Shareholders .... NA

Business: The group's principal activities are the research, development, production and marketing of prescription pharmaceuticals. The group's products are organized into the following therapeutic areas: reproductive health provides treatment of infertility disorders. Neurology segment provides treatment in for relapsing-remitting multiple sclerosis. Growth and metabolism provides treatment of aids wasting and growth hormone deficiencies.

Primary SIC and add'l.: 2836 2834 8731

CIK No: 0001117399

Subsidiaries: Applied Research Systems ARS Holding N.V., Ares Trading S.A., Ares Trading Uruguay S.A., Horizon North SA, Horizon South SA, Industria Farmaceutica Serono S.p.A., Inter-Lab Ltd., InterPharm Industries (1991) Ltd, InterPharm Laboratories Ltd., Istituto di Ricerche Biomediche Antoine Marxer RBM S.p.A., Istituto Farmacologico Serono Nederland B.V., Laboratoires Serono S.A., Lockshield lLtd, Serono (Thailand) Co., Ltd., Serono 92 Limited 51 Subsidiaries included in the Index

Officers: Ernesto Bertarelli/Vice Chmn., MD, CEO, Jacques Theurillat/Dir., Sr. Exec. VP - Strategic Corporate Development, Deputy CEO, Roland Baumann/Sr. Exec. VP, Group Compliance Officer, Head - Corporate Administration, Fereydoun Firouz/Pres. - Serono, Inc, Roberto Gradnik/Sr. Exec. VP - Europe, Stuart Grant/CFO, Anders Harfstrand/Sr. Exec. VP - International, Franck Latrille/Sr. Exec. VP - Global Product Development, Francois Naef/Sr. Exec. VP, Head - Group Human Resources, Legal Department, Timothy Wells/Sr. Exec. VP - Research

Directors: Ernesto Bertarelli/Vice Chmn., MD, CEO, Jacques Theurillat/Dir., Sr. Exec. VP - Strategic Corporate Development, Deputy CEO, Georges Muller/Chmn., Pierre E. Douaze/Dir., Patrick L. Gage/Dir., Bernard Mach/Dir., Sergio Marchionne/Dir., Alberto Togni/Dir.

Financial Data: **Fiscal Year End:** 12/31 **Latest Annual Data:** 06/30/2007

Year	Sales	Net Income
2007	$1,268,872,000	$63,430,000
2006	$1,179,267,000	$62,520,000
2005	$881,770,000	$57,723,000

Curr. Assets:	$506,673,000	**Curr. Liab.:**	$209,588,000		
Plant, Equip.:	$36,685,000	**Total Liab.:**	$222,229,000	**Indic. Yr. Divd.:**	NA
Total Assets:	$847,684,000	**Net Worth:**	$625,455,000	**Debt/ Equity:**	NA

Service 1st Bancorp

2800 W March Ln., Ste. 120, Stockton, CA, 95219; *PH:* 1-209-956-7800; *Fax:* 1-209-956-9633; *http://* www.service1stbank.com; *Email:* yourbank@service1stbank.com

General - Incorporation	CA	**Stock**- Price on:12/24/2007	$14.25
Employees	47	Stock Exchange	OTC
Auditor	Vavrinek, Trine, Day & Co. LLP	Ticker Symbol	SVCF
Stk Agt	Stock Transfer Co	Outstanding Shares	2,390,000
Counsel	NA	E.P.S	$0.30
DUNS No.	NA	Shareholders	NA

Business: The group's principal activity is to provide savings and loan holding services. The depositary products consist of fixed-term certificates, regular savings, money market, individual retirement accounts and checking accounts. Loans offered include home equity, multi-family and commercial real estate loans, mortgage-backed securities, and construction and land loans. The group functions through three subsidiaries: Severn Savings Bank, FSB, Louis Hyatt, Inc., and SBI Mortgage Company. The primary area of operations is Anne Arundel county, Maryland where the group operates two full branches.

Primary SIC and add'l.: 6712 6022

CIK No: 0001225078

Subsidiaries: Service 1st Bank

Officers: John O. Brooks/Chmn., CEO, Gina Manley/VP - Mgr. - Lodi, Tom Vander Ploeg/Exec. VP, Chief Credit Officer, Dana Bagley/Assist. VP - Relationship Mgr. - Stockton, Heather Barth/Credit Specialist - Note Department, Jessica Bowers/Relationship Mgr. - Tracy, Holly Cambra/Assist. VP - Operations Officer - Tracy, Tawnie Ellwanger/Loan Processor, Comercial Capital, Julie Evans/VP, Compliance Officer, Becky Stokes/Assist. VP, Executive Administrative Assistant, Matt Klinker/VP, Mgr. - Information Systems, Robin Park/VP, Note Department Mgr., Bryan R. Hyzdu/68/Dir., Pres., Steve Mizuno/Sr. VP - Mgr. - Tracy, Shannon Reinard/Exec. VP, Operations Mgr. - Service 1st Bank *(41 Officers included in Index)*

Directors: John O. Brooks/Chmn., CEO, Bryan R. Hyzdu/68/Dir., Pres., Dean Andal/Dir., Eugene Gini/Dir., Robert D. Lawrence/Dir., Frances C. Mizuno/Dir., Richard R. Paulsen/Dir., Toni Marie Raymus/Dir., Michael K. Repetto/Dir., Anthony F. Souza/Dir., Al Van Veldhuizen/Dir., Donald L. Walters/Dir.

Owners: Albert Van Veldhuizen/1.34%, Dean F. Andal/1.16%, Toni Marie Raymus/1.76%, John O. Brooks/2.21%, Robert E. Bloch/1.20%, Robert D. Lawrence/2.87%, Patrick Carman/1.54%, Frances C. Mizuno/1.39%, Shannon Reinard/0.76%, Insiders/27.59%, Anthony F. Souza/3.90%, Bryan R. Hyzdu/2.38%, Richard R. Paulsen/1.75%, Michael K. Repetto/1.36%, Donald L. Walters/1.45% *(16 Owners included in Index)*

Financial Data: *Fiscal Year End:*12/31 *Latest Annual Data:* 12/31/2006

Year	Sales	Net Income
2006	$13,532,000	$847,000
2005	$9,166,000	$1,423,000
2004	$7,167,000	$1,414,000

Curr. Assets:	$20,122,000	**Curr. Liab.:**	$201,098,000	**P/E Ratio:**	47.50
Plant, Equip.:	$1,389,000	**Total Liab.:**	$210,253,000	**Indic. Yr. Divd.:**	NA
Total Assets:	$227,220,000	**Net Worth:**	$16,967,000	**Debt/ Equity:**	0.5320

Service Bancorp Inc

81 Main St., Medway, MA, 02053; *PH:* 1-508-533-4343; *Fax:* 1-508-533-1245; *http://* www.stratabank.com

General - Incorporation	MA	**Stock**- Price on:12/24/2007	$33.75
Employees	96	Stock Exchange	OTC
Auditor	Wolf & Co. P.C	Ticker Symbol	SERC
Stk Agt	Continental Stock Transfer & Trust Co	Outstanding Shares	1,650,000
Counsel	NA	E.P.S	$0.47
DUNS No.	NA	Shareholders	NA

Business: The group's principal activities are to provide banking and other financial services to individuals and small businesses. The services of the group include deposit products like savings, checking and term certificate accounts and lending activities like mortgage, consumer and commercial loans. It also purchases and sells securities through non-bank subsidiaries. The services are provided through eight full-service banking offices located in norfolk, worcester and middlesex counties.

Primary SIC and add'l.: 6712 6035

CIK No: 0001063939

Subsidiaries: Franklin Village Security Corporation, Medway Security Corporation, Service Capital Trust I, Strata Bank

Officers: Pamela J. Montpelier/45/Dir., CEO, Pres./$312,355.00, Dana S. Philbrook/CFO/$165,562.00, Paul T. Carey/48/Exec. VP, Sr. Loan Officer/$185,075.00, Amy M. Costello/35/Exec. VP - Retail Banking, Support Operations, Philip Purcell/Sr. VP, Commercial Loan Officer, Lori Patel/Commercial Loan Officer, Wayne A. Janelle/Commercial Loan Officer, Dale Lawrence/Strata Mortgage Center Experts, Jack Fraser/Strata Mortgage Center Experts

Directors: Pamela J. Montpelier/45/Dir., CEO, Pres., Eugene R. Liscombe/62/Chmn., James W. Murphy/73/Dir., Eugene G. Stone/Dir., Kelly A. Verdolino/48/Dir., John E. Brabazon/43/Dir., John J. Burns/51/Dir., David L. Porter/58/Dir., Stephen B. Lincoln/64/Dir., Paul V. Kenney/45/Dir., Lawrence E. Novick/68/Dir., Michael J. Sheehan/Dir., Richard Giusti/64/Dir., John T. Hasenjaeger/Dir., Thomas R. Howie/65/Dir. *(16 Directors included in Index)*

Owners: Paul V. Kenney/0.20%, Amy M. Costello/0.30%, Kenneth C.A. Isaacs/1.00%, Kelly A. Verdolino/1.00%, Kenneth R. Lehman and Joan Abercrombie Lehman/11.40%, Richard Giusti/0.70%, Dana S. Philbrook/0.50%, Lawrence E. Novick/0.40%, John T. Hasenjaeger, Paul T. Carey/0.60%, Eric D. Hovde/5.00%, Thomas R. Howie/0.20%, Service Bancorp, MHC/55.00%, Eugene R. Liscombe/0.10%, Pamela J. Montpelier/0.90% *(17 Owners included in Index)*

Financial Data: *Fiscal Year End:*06/30 *Latest Annual Data:* 06/30/2007

Year	Sales	Net Income
2007	$26,346,000	$1,248,000
2006	$22,753,000	$1,870,000
2005	$18,921,000	$2,117,000

Curr. Assets:	$10,509,000	**Curr. Liab.:**	$268,719,000	**P/E Ratio:**	45.00
Plant, Equip.:	$3,591,000	**Total Liab.:**	$374,496,000	**Indic. Yr. Divd.:**	NA
Total Assets:	$402,166,000	**Net Worth:**	$27,670,000	**Debt/ Equity:**	3.7030

Service Corp International

1929 Allen Pkwy., Houston, TX, 77019; *PH:* 1-713-522-5141; *Fax:* 1-713-525-5586; *http://* www.sci-corp.com

General - Incorporation	TX	**Stock**- Price on:12/24/2007	$13.1
Employees	14,454	Stock Exchange	NYSE
Auditor	PricewaterhouseCoopers LLP	Ticker Symbol	NA
Stk Agt	Bank of New York	Outstanding Shares	293,980,000
Counsel	NA	E.P.S	$0.19
DUNS No.	04-575-6715	Shareholders	NA

Business: The groups principle activity is to provide funeral, cremation and cemetery services. The groups business brands include a variety of choices, from the simplest funeral arrangements to elegant ceremonies requiring intricate planning and unique features or events. The group operates from United States.

Primary SIC and add'l.: 7261 6553

CIK No: 0000089089

Subsidiaries: 3052761 Canada Inc. (Dormant), 3056269 Nova Scotia Company, 3056271 Nova Scotia Company, Affiliated Family Funeral Service, Inc., Affiliated Family funeral Service, Inc. (MA Corp), AFFS Boston, Inc., AFFS North, Inc., AFFS Norwood, Inc., AFFS Quincy, Inc., AFFS South Coast East, Inc., AFFS South Coast West, Inc., AFFS West, Inc., AKH Luxco S.C.A., Auman funeral Home, Inc., Aumans, Inc. 238 Subsidiaries included in the Index

Officers: Thomas L. Ryan/Dir., CEO, Pres./$4,520,105.00, Anthony L. Coelho/Dir. - Consultant, Eric D. Tanzberger/CFO, Sr. VP, Treasurer/$1,105,039.00, Sumner J. Waring/Sr. VP - Major Marketing Operations, Elisabeth G. Nash/VP - Process, Technology, James M. Shelger/58/Sr. VP, General Counsel, Sec./$1,863,174.00, Stephen M. Mack/Sr. VP - Middle Marketing Operations, Jane D. Jones/VP - Human Resources, Alan R. Buckwalter/Dir. - Consultant, Daniel J. Garrison/Sr. VP - Operations Support, Jeffrey I. Beason/VP, Corporate Controller, Harris E. Loring/57/VP, Treasurer, Gregory T. Sangalis/Sr. VP, General Counsel, Sec., Philip C. Jacobs/Sr. VP, Chief Marketing Officer, Donald R. Robinson/VP - Supply Chain Management *(18 Officers included in Index)*

Directors: Thomas L. Ryan/Dir., CEO, Pres., Robert L. Waltrip/Chmn., Founder, Anthony L. Coelho/Dir. - Consultant, A. J. Foyt/Dir., Alan R. Buckwalter/Dir. - Consultant, Victor L. Lund/Dir., Blair W. Waltrip/Dir., Malcolm S. Gillis/Dir., John W. Mecom/Dir., Clifton H. Morris/Dir., Edward E. Williams/Dir.

Owners: FMR Corp., Fidelity Management & Research Company/15.30%, R. L. Waltrip/2.70%, Thomas L. Ryan, Southeastern Asset Management, Inc.,/5.80%, Barrow, Hanley, Mewhinney & Strauss, Inc./10.70%, Michael R. Webb, Vanguard Windsor Funds/10.00%, Insiders/5.80%, James M. Shelger, Eric D. Tanzberger

Financial Data: *Fiscal Year End:*12/31 *Latest Annual Data:* 12/31/2006

Year	Sales	Net Income
2006	$1,747,295,000	$56,511,000
2005	$1,715,737,000	-$127,941,000
2004	$1,860,862,000	$114,128,000

Curr. Assets:	$238,337,000	**Curr. Liab.:**	$407,947,000	**P/E Ratio:**	68.95
Plant, Equip.:	$3,485,912,000	**Total Liab.:**	$4,698,685,000	**Indic. Yr. Divd.:**	$0.120
Total Assets:	$9,729,389,000	**Net Worth:**	$1,594,775,000	**Debt/ Equity:**	1.0695

Servidyne Inc

Formerly: Abrams Industries Inc
1945 The Exchange, Se, Ste. 300, Altanta, GA, 30339; *PH:* 1-770-953-0304; *http://* www.abramsproperties.com

General - Incorporation	GA	**Stock**- Price on:12/24/2007	$4.5
Employees	79	Stock Exchange	NA
Auditor	Deloitte & Touche LLP	Ticker Symbol	NA
Stk Agt	Suntrust Bank	Outstanding Shares	3,530,000
Counsel	NA	E.P.S	$0.67
DUNS No.	00-692-4617	Shareholders	NA

Business: The group's principal activities are divided into four segments: construction of retail and commercial projects, real estate, energy and facilities solutions and energy services . Construction activities consist primarily of new construction, expansion and remodeling of retail store buildings, banks, shopping centers, warehouses and distribution centers and other commercial buildings. The real estate segment activities include investments in shopping centers and office properties in the southeast and midwest. Energy and facilities solutions provides energy services and maintenance and service request solutions. Energy services segment implements energy saving lighting programs and other energy related services that reduce energy consumption. The group acquired wheatstone energy group, inc on 19-Dec-2003, itendant, inc on 16-Apr-2004 & building performance engineers, inc in fiscal 2005.

Primary SIC and add'l.: 6512 8741 1540

CIK No: 0000001923

Subsidiaries: Abrams Construction, Inc., Abrams Power, Inc., Abrams Properties, Inc., Abrams-Columbus Limited Partnership, ABRI Facility Services, Inc., AFC Real Estate, Inc., AI North Fort Myers, LLC, Benncoff, LLC, Chipjax, LLC, Merchants Crossing of Jackson, Inc., Merchants Crossing of North Fort Myers, Inc., Merchants Crossing, Inc., Prestley Mill, LLC, Servidyne Systems, LLC, The Wheatstone Energy Group, LLC

Officers: Alan R. Abrams/Chmn., CEO, Pres., Todd Jarvis/CEO, Pres. - Servidyne Systems, LLC, Joel Lowery/Exec. VP - Sales, Marketing, Barry Abramson/Sr. VP, Rick Paternostro/VP - Operations, Mark J. Thomas/CFO, Melinda S. Garrett/Dir., VP, Sec., Andrew J. Abrams/Dir., Exec. VP, Jim Gieselman/VP - Engineering Services, Jim Dore/VP - Services Sales, Jo Mundy/VP - Accounting Management, Michael Chudecke/VP - Business Development

Directors: Alan R. Abrams/Chmn., CEO, Pres., Robert T. McWhinney/Dir., Melinda S. Garrett/Dir., VP, Sec., David L. Abrams/Dir., Andrew J. Abrams/Dir., Exec. VP, Samuel E. Allen/Dir., Gilbert L. Danielson/Dir.

Owners: Melinda S. Garrett, Abrams Partners, L.P., Andrew J. Abrams, Robert T. McWhinney, Mark J. Thomas, Insiders, Ann U. Abrams, Gilbert L. Danielson, Kandu Partners L.P., Alan R. Abrams, Samuel E. Allen, Todd M. Jarvis, David L. Abrams

Financial Data: *Fiscal Year End:*04/30 *Latest Annual Data:* 4/30/2006

Year	Sales	Net Income
2006	$18,690,000	$526,000
2005	$22,795,000	$1,800,000
2004	$39,082,000	-$1,850,000

Curr. Assets:	$13,236,000	**Curr. Liab.:**	$4,584,000		
Plant, Equip.:	$23,494,000	**Total Liab.:**	$31,464,000	**Indic. Yr. Divd.:**	$0.140
Total Assets:	$52,410,000	**Net Worth:**	$20,947,000	**Debt/ Equity:**	1.0582

Servotronics Inc

1110 Maple St., Elma, NY, 14059; *PH:* 1-716-655-5990; *Fax:* 1-716-655-6012; *http://* www.servotronics.com; *Email:* info@servotronics.com

General - Incorporation .... DE
Employees 234
Auditor ...... Freed Maxick & Battaglia, Cpas, P.C
Stk Agt. .... EquiServe Trust Co N.A
Counsel .... Jaeckle Fleischmann & Mugel
DUNS No. 00-210-5245

Stock - Price on:12/24/2007 .... $10.02
Stock Exchange .... AMEX
Ticker Symbol .... SVT
Outstanding Shares 1,960,000
E.P.S. $0.57
Shareholders .... NA

Business: The group's principal activity is to design, manufacture and sell advanced technology products. These products consist of control components and consumer products consisting of knives and various types of cutlery. It operates in two business segments, the advanced technology and the consumer products. The advanced technology group designs manufactures and sells servo-control components for government and commercial applications. The consumer products also designs manufactures and sells a variety of cutlery products for use by consumers and government agencies. The group's reportable segments are strategic business units that offer different products and services.

Primary SIC and add'l.: 3621 3452 3421 3594

CIK No: 0000089140

Subsidiaries: 87 South Main Corp., G.N. Metal Products, Inc., King Cutlery, Inc., MRO Corporation, Ontario Knife Company, Queen Cutlery Company, Servotronics, Inc., SVT Management, Inc., Tsv Elma, Inc., TSV Franklinville, Inc.

Officers: Nicholas D. Trbovich/Founder, Chmn., CEO, Pres./$487,098.00

Directors: Nicholas D. Trbovich/Founder, Chmn., CEO, Pres.

Owners: Donald W. Hedges/3.10%, William H. Duerig/3.00%, Cari L. Jaroslawsky, Servotronics, Inc./33.60%, Nicholas D. Trbovich/23.10%, Raymond C. Zielinski/2.70%, Nicholas D. Trbovich/5.90%, Harvey Houtkin/15.10%, Insiders/47.60%, Michael D. Trbovich/1.40%

Financial Data: *Fiscal Year End:* 12/31 *Latest Annual Data:* 12/31/2006

Year	Sales	Net Income
2006	$24,548,000	$1,096,000
2005	$23,126,000	$1,363,000
2004	$22,113,000	$734,000

Curr. Assets:	$16,299,000	Curr. Liab.:	$3,045,000	P/E Ratio:	17.58
Plant, Equip.:	$5,940,000	Total Liab.:	$8,190,000	Indic. Yr. Divd.:	NA
Total Assets:	$22,638,000	Net Worth:	$14,448,000	Debt/ Equity:	0.3189

SES Solar Inc

Rte. de Saint-Julien 129, 1228 Plan-Les-Ouates, Geneva; *PH:* 41-0228841484; *Fax:* 41-0228841480; *http://* www.sessolar.com; *Email:* info@societe-energie-solaire.com

General - Incorporation .... DE
Employees .... NA
Auditor .... Wyss/ Christian Feller
Stk Agt. .... Interwest Transfer Company, Inc.
Counsel .... NA
DUNS No. .... NA

Stock - Price on:12/24/2007 .... $0.6
Stock Exchange .... OTC
Ticker Symbol .... SESI
Outstanding Shares .... NA
E.P.S. .... NA
Shareholders .... NA

Business: The groups principal activities include operating of an Internet based auction website over which users can advertise and buying and selling goods and services for a fee. The group operates from the United States.

Primary SIC and add'l.: 4931

CIK No: 0001078858

Officers: Jean-Christophe Hadorn/Dir., CEO, Sandrine Crisafulli/CFO, COO

Directors: Jean-Christophe Hadorn/Dir., CEO, Michael D. Noonan/Dir., Christiane Erne/Dir., Daniel Erne/Dir., John Veltheer/Dir.

Owners: Insiders/66.20%, Christiane Ern/66.10%, SG Private Banking (Suisse) S.A./9.28%, Jean-Christophe Hadorn/3.30%, John Veltheer

Financial Data: *Fiscal Year End:* 12/31 *Latest Annual Data:* 12/31/2006

Year	Sales	Net Income
2006	$129,000	-$1,240,000
2005	NA	-$60,000
2004	$0	-$87,000

Curr. Assets:	$6,546,000	Curr. Liab.:	$863,000		
Plant, Equip.:	$342,000	Total Liab.:	$1,658,000	Indic. Yr. Divd.:	NA
Total Assets:	$7,308,000	Net Worth:	$5,650,000	Debt/ Equity:	NA

Severn Bancorp Inc

200 Westgate Cir., Ste. 200, Annapolis, MD, 21401; *PH:* 1-410-260-2000; *Fax:* 1-410-841-6296; *http://* www.severnbank.com; *Email:* info@severn.hpwsb.com

General - Incorporation .... MD
Employees 121
Auditor .... Beard Miller Co. LLP
Stk Agt. .... Registrar & Transfer Co
Counsel .... NA
DUNS No. .... NA

Stock - Price on:12/24/2007 .... $17.08
Stock Exchange .... NDQ
Ticker Symbol .... SVBI
Outstanding Shares 10,070,000
E.P.S. $1.40
Shareholders .... NA

Business: The group's principal activity is to provide savings and loan holding services. The depositary products consist of fixed-term certificates, regular savings, money market, individual retirement accounts and checking accounts. Loans offered include home equity, multi-family and commercial real estate loans, mortgage-backed securities, and construction and land loans. The group functions through three subsidiaries: Severn Savings Bank, FSB, Louis Hyatt, Inc., and SBI Mortgage Company. The primary area of operations is Anne Arundel county, Maryland where the group operates two full branches.

Primary SIC and add'l.: 6712 6035

CIK No: 0000868271

Subsidiaries: Crownsville Holdings I, LLC, Homeowners Title and Escrow Corporation, HS West, LLC, le Development Corporation, Louis Hyatt, Inc., SBI Mortgage Company, Severn Financial Services Corporation, Severn Savings Bank, FSB., SSB Realty Holdings II, LLC, SSB Realty Holdings, LLC

Officers: Alan J. Hyatt/Chmn., CEO, Pres./$483,822.00, Melvin E. Meekins/Dir., Exec. VP/$505,509.00, Scott S. Kirkley/55/Dir., Exec. VP, Sec., Treasurer/$349,415.00, Thomas G. Bevivino/CFO, Exec. VP/$238,781.00

Directors: Alan J. Hyatt/Chmn., CEO, Pres., Albert W. Shields/63/Dir., Melvin Hyatt/75/Dir., Melvin E. Meekins/Dir., Exec. VP, Scott S. Kirkley/55/Dir., Exec. VP, Sec., Treasurer, Louis Dipasquale/85/Dir., Keith Stock/55/Dir., Ronald P. Pennington/68/Dir., Theodore T. Schultz/68/Dir.

Owners: Melvin E. Meekins/5.82%, Albert W. Shields/0.78%, Louis DiPasquale/2.27%, Alan J. Hyatt/15.72%, Ronald P. Pennington/1.39%, Theodore T. Schultz/0.61%, Insiders/34.01%, Thomas G. Bevivino/0.04%, Scott S. Kirkley/4.21%, Keith Stock/1.25%, Louis Hyatt/10.39%, Melvin Hyatt/1.96%

Financial Data: *Fiscal Year End:* 12/31 *Latest Annual Data:* 12/31/2006

Year	Sales	Net Income
2006	$74,042,000	$15,748,000
2005	$59,883,000	$14,554,000
2004	$48,231,000	$12,931,000

Curr. Assets:	$28,319,000	Curr. Liab.:	$649,855,000	P/E Ratio:	12.20
Plant, Equip.:	$31,381,000	Total Liab.:	$825,474,000	Indic. Yr. Divd.:	$0.240
Total Assets:	$911,916,000	Net Worth:	$86,442,000	Debt/ Equity:	1.9093

Sew Cal Logo Inc

207 W 138 St., Los Angeles, CA, 90061; *PH:* 1-310-352-3300; *Fax:* 1-310-352-3370; *http://* www.sewcal.com; *Email:* sales@sewcal.com

General - Incorporation .... NV
Employees 65
Auditor .... Moore & Associates, Chartered
Stk Agt .... First American Stock Transfer, Inc.
Counsel .... NA
DUNS No. .... NA

Stock - Price on:12/24/2007 .... $0.0031
Stock Exchange .... OTC
Ticker Symbol .... SEWC
Outstanding Shares 17,760,000
E.P.S. .... NA
Shareholders .... NA

Business: The groups principle activity is supplier of wardrobe as well as promotional and cast and crew items for feature films and television, to the major motion picture studios. In the year 2005 the group acquired a branded line of Surf and Sports Wear items named Pipeline Posse. The group operates from the United States. The group's quarterly revenue for Sep '07 was 0.45 millions of USD.

Primary SIC and add'l.: 2300

CIK No: 0001281984

Owners: Richard L. Songer/14.78%, Novian & Novian LLP/5.71%, Lori Heskett/3.98%, Insiders/24.47%

SGL Carbon

Rheingaustrasse 182-184, Wiesbaden, 65203; *PH:* 49-6116029100; *Fax:* 49-6116029305; *http://* www.sglcarbon.com; *Email:* cpc@sglcarbon.de

General - Incorporation .... Germany
Employees 5,249
Auditor .... Ernst & Young
Stk Agt .... JP Morgan Chase Bank, N.A.
Counsel .... NA
DUNS No. 31-619-0842

Stock - Price on:12/24/2007 .... $14.45
Stock Exchange .... OTC
Ticker Symbol .... SGGGY
Outstanding Shares 190,910,000
E.P.S. $0.42
Shareholders .... NA

Business: The group's principal activity is to manufacture carbon, graphite and composite materials. The group operates in four divisions: carbon and graphite: develops graphite electrodes designed for industrial steel production in electric arc furnaces; graphite specialties: supplies products made of isostatically pressed, extruded, die and vibration-molded graphite, carbon/carbon, felt, graphite foils and laminated sheets, carbon and graphite yarns for a variety of applications; corrosion protection: manufactures a complete range of products and services for industrial corrosion protection and SGL Technologies: develops new business opportunities based on the group's competencies for high technology materials, processes and applications. The group has operations in Europe, North, Central and South America.

Primary SIC and add'l.: 3823 3295 3674 1629 2891 3561 3624

CIK No: 0001015111

Subsidiaries: Gelter Ringsdorff S.A., HITCO Carbon Composites, Inc, M.g.p. LLC, SGL Brakes GmbH, SGL Canada Inc., SGL Carbon Beteiligung GmbH, SGL Carbon Far East Ltd, SGL Carbon GmbH, SGL Carbon GmbH & Co, SGL Carbon Holding GmbH, SGL Carbon Holdings S.L., SGL Carbon Japan Ltd., SGL Carbon LLC, SGL Carbon Ltd, SGL Carbon Polska S.A 23 Subsidiaries included in the Index

Officers: Robert J. Koehler/Chmn., CEO, Armin Bruch/Chmn. - Carbon Graphite Business Area, Gerd Wingefeld/Chmn. - Specialties Business Area, Christian Pagel/Head - Corporate Business Systems Effective, Vanessa Rau/Assist. Corporate Communications, Investor Relations, Joachim Heins-Bunde/Group Coordination, Corporate Planning, Jan Verdenhalven/MD - SGL Technologies, Wilhelm Hauf/Group Coordination, Accounting, Helmut Muhlbradt/Group Coordination, Human Resources, Legal, Gunter Piechowski/Site Mgr., Human Resources Mgr., Britta Dottger/Group Coordination, Treasury, Sten Daugaard/Dir., CFO, Raj Roychowdhury/Head - Investor Relations, Daniela Rink/Mgr. - Investor Relations

Directors: Robert J. Koehler/Chmn., CEO, Sten Daugaard/Dir., CFO, Theodore H. Breyer/Dir., Hariolf Kottmann/Dir., Hans-Werner Zorn/Member - Supervisory Board, Max Dietrich Kley/Member - Supervisory Board, Claus Hendricks/Member - Supervisory Board, Hubert Lienhard/Member - Supervisory Board, Jacques Loppion/Member - Supervisory Board, Heinz Will/Member - Supervisory Board, Michael Pfeiffer/Member - Supervisory Board, Heinz-Gunter Piechowski/Member - Supervisory Board, Josef Scherer/Member - Supervisory Board, Andrew H. Simon/Member - Supervisory Board, Utz-Hellmuth Felcht/Member - Supervisory Board *(16 Directors included in Index)*

Owners: Hermes Investment Management Limited/2.90%, Fidelity Investments International UK Ltd./4.90%, Fidelity Management & Research Co/10.10%

Financial Data: *Fiscal Year End:* 12/31 *Latest Annual Data:* 12/31/2005

Year	Sales	Net Income
2005	$1,260,900,000	$26,900,000
2004	$1,263,707,000	-$121,022,000
2003	$1,319,300,000	-$61,000,000

Curr. Assets:	$711,300,000	Curr. Liab.:	$373,100,000		
Plant, Equip.:	$412,900,000	Total Liab.:	$1,099,000,000	Indic. Yr. Divd.:	NA
Total Assets:	$1,454,100,000	Net Worth:	$353,600,000	Debt/ Equity:	NA

SGX Pharmaceuticals Inc

10505 Roselle St., San Diego, CA, 92121; *PH:* 1-858-558-4850; *Fax:* 1-858-558-4859; *http://* www.sgxpharma.com

Shannon International Inc

General - Incorporation	DE	Stock - Price on:12/24/2007	$5.29
Employees	124	Stock Exchange	NDQ
Auditor	Ernst & Young LLP	Ticker Symbol	SGXP
Stk Agt	U.S. Stock Transfer Corp	Outstanding Shares	15,330,000
Counsel	NA	E.P.S.	-$1.24
DUNS No.	NA	Shareholders	NA

Business: The groups principle activities include discovering, developing and commercializing cancer therapeutics. The group operates from the United States. The group's quarterly revenue for September 2007 was 7.59 millions of USD.

Primary SIC and add'l.: 2834

CIK No: 0001125603

Officers: Michael Grey/Dir., CEO, Pres./$1,579,001.00, Jason Spark/Contact - Media, Siegfried Reich/VP - Drug Discovery/$497,338.00, Terry Rugg/Chief Medical Officer, VP - Development, Stephen K. Burley/Chief Scientific Officer, Sr. VP - Research/$957,367.00, Kristine Figueroa/Sr. Dir. - Human Resources, Todd W. Myers/CFO/$469,424.00, Annette North/VP - Legal Affairs, Corp. Sec./$496,782.00

Directors: Michael Grey/Dir., CEO, Pres., Christopher S. Henney/Chmn., Louis C. Bock/Dir., Karin Eastham/Dir., Jean-Francois Formela/Dir., Vijay Lathi/Dir.

Owners: Annette North, Todd W. Myers, Karin Eastham, Louis C. Bock, BAVP, L.P., Insiders, Atlas Venture FundIV, L.P., Jean-Francois Formela, Index Ventures Associates I Limited, Stephen K. Burley, Siegfried Reich, Biotechnology Value Fund, L.P., Sprout Capital VIII, L.P., Vijay Lathi, Christopher Henney *(16 Owners included in Index)*

Financial Data: Fiscal Year End:12/31   Latest Annual Data: 12/31/2006

Year	Sales	Net Income
2006	$27,780,000	-$28,052,000
2005	$21,636,000	-$29,391,000
2004	$27,297,000	-$18,752,000

Curr. Assets:	$39,025,000	Curr. Liab.:	$21,762,000		
Plant, Equip.:	$5,435,000	Total Liab.:	$34,851,000	Indic. Yr. Divd.:	NA
Total Assets:	$48,464,000	Net Worth:	$13,613,000	Debt/ Equity:	NA

Shadow Marketing Inc

7116 Pioneer Way, Ste. C, Gig Harbor, WA, 98335; *PH:* 1-253-851-1164; *Fax:* 1-253-851-1165; *http://* www.shadowmarketinginc.com

General - Incorporation	NV	Stock - Price on:12/24/2007	NA
Employees	NA	Stock Exchange	OTC
Auditor	Michael T. Studer CPA P.C.	Ticker Symbol	SDWM
Stk Agt	Island Stock Transfer	Outstanding Shares	NA
Counsel	NA	E.P.S.	NA
DUNS No.	NA	Shareholders	NA

Business: The groups principal activities include involving in the publication of "Up & Over" magazine, which contains articles focusing on purchase, training and care of sports horses. The group operates from the United States.

Primary SIC and add'l.: 5146 2092 0912 0913

CIK No: 0001343750

Officers: Greg Fedun/40/Dir., CEO, Pres., Christopher Paterson/42/Dir., Sec., Treasurer, Principal Financial Officer, Francis Powers/Corporate Controller, Terrie Ulmer/Contact - Accounting, David Stafford/Pres., Brian Hodkinson/Contact - Sales, Todd Houk/Contact - Sales

Directors: Greg Fedun/40/Dir., CEO, Pres., Christopher Paterson/42/Dir., Sec., Treasurer, Principal Financial Officer

Owners: Christopher Paterson/26.86%, Greg Fedun/26.86%, Insiders/53.72%

Financial Data: Fiscal Year End:06/30   Latest Annual Data: 06/30/2007

Year	Sales	Net Income
2007	NA	-$8,000

Curr. Assets:	$0	Curr. Liab.:	$22,000		
Plant, Equip.:	NA	Total Liab.:	$22,000	Indic. Yr. Divd.:	NA
Total Assets:	$0	Net Worth:	-$21,000	Debt/ Equity:	NA

Shamir Optical Industry Ltd

29800 Agoura Rd., Ste. 102, Agoura Hills, CA, 91301; *PH:* 1-818-889-6292; *Fax:* 1-818-889-6293; *http://* www.shamir.co.il; *Email:* Shamir_opt@shamir.co.il

General - Incorporation	Israel	Stock - Price on:12/24/2007	$10
Employees	NA	Stock Exchange	NDQ
Auditor	Kost, Forer, Gabbay & Kassierer	Ticker Symbol	SHMR
Stk Agt	American Stock Transfer & Trust Co.	Outstanding Shares	16,260,000
Counsel	NA	E.P.S.	$0.49
DUNS No.	NA	Shareholders	NA

Business: The groups principle activities include developing, designing, manufacturing and marketing progressive lenses. The products of the group include frames, spectacle lenses, contact lenses and optical accessories. The group operates from Israel, The United States, Europe, Asia and other.

Primary SIC and add'l.: 3851

CIK No: 0001317362

Subsidiaries: Alpha Optik GmbH, Altra Optica Espana SL, Altra Optica Lda., Altra Trading GmbH, Aspect Optics Ltd, Cambridge Optical Group Limited, E-vision LLC, E. S. P. Optics Ltd., Eyal Optical Industries (1995) Ltd., Eyal Optics Holdings A.C.S. Ltd., Inray Ltd., Interoptic SARL, JMH Holding Ltd., P.D.A. Advanced Optics Systems Ltd., Shamir Insight, Inc. 17 Subsidiaries included in the Index

Officers: Giora Ben-Zeev/65/Dir., CEO, Pres., Raanan Naftalovich/CEO - Shamir Insight Inc, Giora Salz/CEO, Pres. - Eyal Optical Industry, Eyal Hayardeny/Exec. VP, VP - Business Development, Rami Ben-Zeev/VP - Business Management, Dan Katzman/CTO, VP, Dagan Avishai/Exec. VP, VP - Marketing, Yagen Moshe/CFO, Ron Sonnenschein/GM - Altra Optic

Directors: Giora Ben-Zeev/65/Dir., CEO, Pres., Uzi Tzur/68/Chmn., Efrat Cohen/40/Dir., Ami Samuels/49/Dir., Zeev Feldman/56/Dir., Guy Vaadia/44/Dir., Joseph Tzur/55/Dir.

Owners: Dan Katzman/2.23%, FIBI Investment House Ltd./8.37%, Royce & Associates, LLC/7.38%, Kibbutz Shamir/59.64%

Financial Data: Fiscal Year End:12/31   Latest Annual Data: 12/31/2006

Year	Sales	Net Income
2006	$97,280,000	$6,460,000
2005	$80,364,000	$8,105,000
2004	$71,269,000	$8,812,000

Curr. Assets:	$98,496,000	Curr. Liab.:	$38,556,000		
Plant, Equip.:	$28,368,000	Total Liab.:	$67,193,000	Indic. Yr. Divd.:	NA
Total Assets:	$146,996,000	Net Worth:	$79,803,000	Debt/ Equity:	NA

Shanda Interactive Entertainment Ltd

No. 1 Intelligen Office Bldg, No. 690 Bibo Rd, Pudong New Area, Shanghai, 201203; *PH:* 8621-50504740; *Fax:* 8621-50274740-8088; *http://* www.shanda.com.cn; *Email:* info@shanda.com.cn

General - Incorporation	Cayman Islands	Stock - Price on:12/24/2007	$27.52
Employees	2,392	Stock Exchange	NDQ
Auditor	PricewaterhouseCoopers	Ticker Symbol	SNDA
Stk Agt	Bank of New York	Outstanding Shares	71,580,000
Counsel	Simpson Thacher & Bartlett LLP	E.P.S.	$2.50
DUNS No.	NA	Shareholders	NA

Business: The groups principle activity is to provide portfolio of diversified entertainment content, including multi-player online role-playing and casual online games. The groups products include network personal computer game platform and a variety of cartoons. The group operates from United States.

Primary SIC and add'l.: NA

CIK No: 0001278308

Subsidiaries: AB Qualitrol AKM, ABEK LLC, AC Intermediate Co., ACC Motion GmbH, ACCU-Sort Asia Pacific PTE.LTD, Accu-sort Europe Gmbh, Accu-sort Systems Australia Pty.ltd, Accu-sort Systems, Inc., ACME-Cleveland Corporation, Advanced Motion Controls AB, Aeronautique Systems BIP SAS, Alltec Angewandte Laserlicht Technologie GmbH, Alltec Italia S.r.l., Alltec UK Ltd., American Precision Industries, Inc. 19 Subsidiaries included in the Index

Officers: Tianqiao Chen/Chmn., CEO, Jun Tang/Dir., Pres., Acting CFO, Jingying Wang/Sr. VP, Yanmei Zhang/Sr. VP, Hai Ling/Sr. VP, Haibin Qu/Executive Sr. VP, Danian Chen/Dir., Executive Sr. VP, Qunzhao Tan/Dir., CTO, Executive Sr. VP, Xiangdong Zhang/Sr. VP, Daniel Zhang/35/Dir., VP, CFO, Donald Chan/Sr. VP, Jianwu Liang/VP, Jisheng Zhu/VP, Yu Diana Li/VP, Maggie Yun Zhou/Mgr. - Investor Relations *(16 Officers included in Index)*

Directors: Tianqiao Chen/Chmn., CEO, Jun Tang/Dir., Pres., Acting CFO, Danian Chen/Dir., Executive Sr. VP, Qunzhao Tan/Dir., CTO, Executive Sr. VP, Qianqian Luo/Dir., Chengyu Xiong/Dir., Jingsheng Huang/Dir., Yong Zhang/Dir., Bruno Wu/Dir.

Owners: Haibin Qu, Cisco Systems, Inc, Qianqian Luo, AXA Group, Danian Chen, Tianqiao Chen, Jun Tang, Skyline Media Limited, Qunzhao Tan

Financial Data: Fiscal Year End:12/31   Latest Annual Data: 12/31/2006

Year	Sales	Net Income
2006	$211,874,000	$67,772,000
2005	$235,014,000	$20,481,000
2004	$156,917,000	$73,640,000

Curr. Assets:	$471,459,000	Curr. Liab.:	$348,946,000		
Plant, Equip.:	$44,713,000	Total Liab.:	$349,318,000	Indic. Yr. Divd.:	NA
Total Assets:	$658,895,000	Net Worth:	$309,577,000	Debt/ Equity:	NA

Shandong Zhouyuan Seed & Nursery Co Ltd

Formerly: Pingchuan Pharmaceutical Inc
238 Jianxindong St., Laizhou; *PH:* 86-451-827-13712

General - Incorporation	NC	Stock - Price on:12/24/2007	NA
Employees	NA	Stock Exchange	OTC
Auditor	Kempisty & Co	Ticker Symbol	SZSN
Stk Agt	Florida Atlantic Stock Transfer, Inc.	Outstanding Shares	NA
Counsel	NA	E.P.S.	NA
DUNS No.	NA	Shareholders	NA

Business: The group's principal activity is to produce antibiotics, medicine in capsule form, traditional Chinese medicine and other products. The group also produces medical intermediates and pharmaceutical preparations, as well as medical instruments and health care food and other related products. These products are marketed in all of the provinces of China, and in the municipalities and autonomous regions in China. The group also has an active export business, particularly to Russia.

Primary SIC and add'l.: 8731 2834

CIK No: 0001121282

Subsidiaries: Heilongjiang Pingchuan, Pingchuan Pharmaceutical, Inc

Officers: Wang Zhigang/45/Dir., CEO, Sanncy Zeng/38/Dir., CFO

Directors: Wang Zhigang/45/Dir., CEO, Sanncy Zeng/38/Dir., CFO, Wang Zhicheng/41/Dir., Daoqi Jiang/65/Dir., Chi Ming Chan/46/Dir.

Owners: Wang Zhigang/4.60%, Hu Zhanwu/9.10%, Wang Zhicheng, Insiders/4.70%

Financial Data: Fiscal Year End:12/31   Latest Annual Data: 12/31/2006

Year	Sales	Net Income
2006	$425,000	-$348,000
2005	$274,000	-$136,000
2004	$39,000	-$193,000

Curr. Assets:	$473,000	Curr. Liab.:	$2,572,000		
Plant, Equip.:	$1,778,000	Total Liab.:	$3,002,000	Indic. Yr. Divd.:	NA
Total Assets:	$3,636,000	Net Worth:	$634,000	Debt/ Equity:	NA

Shannon International Inc

Formerly: Shannon International Resources Inc
715 - 5th Ave., SW, Ste 2000, Calgary, AB, T2P 2X6; *PH:* 1-902-487225; *http://* www.shannon-intl.com; *Email:* info@shannon-intl.com

General - Incorporation	NV	Stock - Price on:12/24/2007	$0.009
Employees	NA	Stock Exchange	OTC
Auditor	Miller & McCollom	Ticker Symbol	SHIR
Stk Agt	Pacific Stock Transfer Company	Outstanding Shares	NA
Counsel	NA	E.P.S.	NA
DUNS No.	NA	Shareholders	NA

Business: The group's principle activities include acquiring, developing and producing oil and gas properties in the province of prince edward island, Canada. The company has expanded its focus to include software investments. Currently, the company holds 25% working interest in one permit (96-06) and a

further five percent working interest in six additional permits ((96-04, 96-05, 96-07, 96-08, 96-09, 96-10) grants the exclusive right to carry out geological-geophysical work and exploratory drilling for all petroleum, natural gas and coalbed methane gas in the areas of the permits. The group operates from United States.

Primary SIC and add'l.: 1311

CIK No: 0001081047

Subsidiaries: Logical Sequence Incorporated, Shannon Investments Ltd.

Officers: William J. Clements/Dir., CFO, CEO, Pres., Blair Coady/CEO, Pres.

Directors: William J. Clements/Dir., CFO, CEO, Pres., Dennis Brovarone/Dir.

Owners: Insiders/9.50%, William J. Clements/6.50%, Dennis Brovarone/6.00%

Financial Data: Fiscal Year End:06/30   Latest Annual Data: 6/30/2006

Year	Sales	Net Income
2006	$965,000	-$2,271,000
2005	$908,000	-$1,281,000
2004	NA	-$900,000

Curr. Assets:	$148,000	Curr. Liab.:	$2,800,000		
Plant, Equip.:	$658,000	Total Liab.:	$2,828,000	Indic. Yr. Divd.:	NA
Total Assets:	$807,000	Net Worth:	-$6,718,000	Debt/ Equity:	NA

Sharp Holding Corp

5120 Woodway, Ste 9029, Houston, TX, 77056; *PH:* 1-713-960-9100; *http://* www.sharpholding.com

General - Incorporation	DE	Stock- Price on:12/24/2007	$0.0015
Employees	26	Stock Exchange	OTC
Auditor	Ham, Langston & Brezina LLP	Ticker Symbol	SHAR
Stk Agt.	American Stock Transfer & Trust Co.	Outstanding Shares	NA
Counsel	NA	E.P.S.	NA
DUNS No.	NA	Shareholders	NA

Business: The group's principal activity is to develop software solutions that are utilized to provide marketing solutions for Fortune 500 companies. The group designs software with unique customization and personalization features to maximize technology and customer benefits. In addition, the group provides innovative marketing solutions to strategic partners for bundled delivery in conjunction with its redistribution partners. The contents of its offerings are targeted at helping those partners retain customers and strengthen their Internet brand presence. The group's trademarks are hack tracertm, it's your nettm and desktop malltm.

Primary SIC and add'l.: 7372 7373 7379

CIK No: 0001101588

Subsidiaries: Celebrity Entertainment Group, Inc., Sharp Technology, Inc.

Financial Data: Fiscal Year End:12/31   Latest Annual Data: 12/31/2004

Year	Sales	Net Income
2004	$68,000	-$2,734,000
2003	$83,000	-$1,526,000
2002	$375,000	-$979,000

Curr. Assets:	$78,000	Curr. Liab.:	$5,156,000		
Plant, Equip.:	$56,000	Total Liab.:	$5,224,000	Indic. Yr. Divd.:	NA
Total Assets:	$331,000	Net Worth:	-$4,893,000	Debt/ Equity:	NA

Sharpe Resources Corp

3258 Mob Neck Rd., Heathsville, VA, 22473; *PH:* 1-804-580-8107; *Fax:* 1-804-580-4132; *http://* www.sharpe-resources.com; *Email:* srcinfo@sharpe-resources.com

General - Incorporation	Canada	Stock- Price on:12/24/2007	$0.065
Employees	NA	Stock Exchange	OTC
Auditor	McCarney Greenwood LLP	Ticker Symbol	SHGPF
Stk Agt.	Gary Sugar LLP	Outstanding Shares	NA
Counsel	Sugar Moretti	E.P.S.	NA
DUNS No.	NA	Shareholders	NA

Business: The group's principle activity is to produces oil and gas . The group operates from United States.

Primary SIC and add'l.: 1311

CIK No: 0001024696

Subsidiaries: Sharpe Energy Company

Officers: Roland M. Larsen/Dir., CEO, Pres. - Houston, Kimberly A. Koerner/Dir., Corp. Sec. - Brambleton, Virginia

Directors: Roland M. Larsen/Dir., CEO, Pres. - Houston, James Dunlop/Dir., Kimberly A. Koerner/Dir., Corp. Sec. - Brambleton, Virginia, Troy Koerner/Dir.

Owners: Roland M. Larsen Richmond, Virginia/11.30%, Troy Koerner Brambleton, Virginia, CDS & Co. (2) Toronto, Ontario/51.85%, Kimberley Koerner Brambleton, Virginia

Financial Data: Fiscal Year End:12/31   Latest Annual Data: 12/31/2006

Year	Sales	Net Income
2006	$29,000	-$349,000
2005	$18,000	$289,000
2004	$109,000	-$195,000

Curr. Assets:	$461,000	Curr. Liab.:	$831,000		
Plant, Equip.:	NA	Total Liab.:	$831,000	Indic. Yr. Divd.:	NA
Total Assets:	$461,000	Net Worth:	-$370,000	Debt/ Equity:	NA

Sharper Image Corp

350 The Embarcadero, 6th Fl., San Francisco, CA, 94105; *PH:* 1-415-445-6000; *http://* www.sharperimage.com

General - Incorporation	DE	Stock- Price on:12/24/2007	$12.26
Employees	2,500	Stock Exchange	NDQ
Auditor	Deloitte & Touche LLP	Ticker Symbol	SHRP
Stk Agt.	Mellon Investor Services LLC	Outstanding Shares	15,130,000
Counsel	Robert Wallach	E.P.S.	-$4.27
DUNS No.	05-461-2601	Shareholders	NA

Business: The group's principle activity is to sell innovative and entertaining products through its retail stores, catalog, Internet and other marketing channels throughout the United States. The group has stores and catalog operations which operate internationally through licensees. The three primary sales

channels are the Sharper Image stores, the Sharper Image catalog and the Internet. The incentive and gift merchandise certificates are sold to the client companies, who in turn distribute them under their programs. The group operates 109 image stores in 31 states and the District of Columbia and licensees operates three stores internationally and two airport stores in the United States. The group's total revenue for year 2007 was 525.25 millions of USD.

Primary SIC and add'l.: 7375 5947 5961

CIK No: 000811696

Officers: Steven A. Lightman/Dir., CEO, Pres., Daniel W. Nelson/Sr. VP - Finance, Controller, Interim CFO/$303,333.00, Rebecca Roedell/CFO

Directors: Steven A. Lightman/Dir., CEO, Pres., Jerry W. Levin/Chmn., Michael S. Koeneke/Dir., Howard M. Leibman/Dir., George B. James/Dir., Morton E. David/Dir., Howard Gross/Dir., William R. Fields/Dir., Jason G. Bernzweig/Dir., Peter A. Feld/Dir., Marc J. Leder/Dir.

Owners: William L. Feroe, Jerry W. Levin, Wells Fargo& Company, Insiders, Jeffrey P. Forgan, Dimensional Fund Advisors LP, George B. James, Howard M. Liebman, William Fields, Richard J. Thalheimer, David M. Meyer, Daniel W. Nelson, Marc J. Leder, Sun Capital Securities, Morton E. David *(22 Owners included in Index)*

Financial Data: Fiscal Year End:01/31   Latest Annual Data: 01/31/2007

Year	Sales	Net Income
2007	$525,251,000	-$59,894,000
2006	$668,993,000	-$16,136,000
2005	$760,003,000	$14,650,000

Curr. Assets:	$132,082,000	Curr. Liab.:	$110,751,000		
Plant, Equip.:	$86,140,000	Total Liab.:	$140,828,000	Indic. Yr. Divd.:	NA
Total Assets:	$263,994,000	Net Worth:	$123,166,000	Debt/ Equity:	NA

Sharps Compliance Corp

9220 Kirby Dr., Ste. 500, Houston, TX, 77054; *PH:* 1-713-432-0300; *Fax:* 1-713-432-0555; *http://* www.sharpsinc.com; *Email:* sharps@sharpsinc.com

General - Incorporation	DE	Stock- Price on:12/24/2007	$3
Employees	26	Stock Exchange	OTC
Auditor	UHY LLP	Ticker Symbol	SCOM
Stk Agt	Registrar & Transfer Co	Outstanding Shares	11,810,000
Counsel	NA	E.P.S.	$0.06
DUNS No.	62-166-7948	Shareholders	NA

Business: The group's principal activity is to develop solutions for improving safety and efficiency related to the proper disposal of medical waste by industry and consumers. Disposal solutions include disposal by mail system, IV poles, asset return boxes, needle disposal system, disposable coolers, linen recovery system, biohazard spill clean-up kit and disposal system, and online imaging & tracking solutions. Environmental services include destruction and disposal of medical sharps waste, confidential documents, pharmaceutical products, and non-hazardous industrial waste. The group also offers consulting services. The group operates in 6 market segments including healthcare, agriculture, retail, hospitality, professional, industrial, and pharmaceutical.

Primary SIC and add'l.: 3842

CIK No: 0000898770

Subsidiaries: dba Sharps Compliance,Inc., dba Sharps Environmental Services of Texas Inc, Sharps Compliance, Inc, Sharps e-Tools, Sharps e-Tools.com, Inc, Sharps Environmental Services, Inc, Sharps Manufacturing, Inc, Sharps Safety, Inc.

Officers: Burton J. Kunik/Chmn., CEO, Pres., Mark Iske/Sr. VP - Operations, David P. Tusa/Exec. VP, CFO - Business Development, David C. Mayfield/Sr. VP - Sales, Marketing

Directors: Burton J. Kunik/Chmn., CEO, Pres.

Owners: John W. Dalton/11.50%, Herb Schneider/5.70%, Insiders/42.20%, Burton J. Kunik/19.70%, David P. Tusa/2.90%, Philip C. Zerrillo/2.70%, John R. Grow/0.60%, Parris H. Holmes/11.10%, Ramsay Gillman/4.90%, Gardner F. Parker/2.00%

Financial Data: Fiscal Year End:06/30   Latest Annual Data: 06/30/2007

Year	Sales	Net Income
2007	$11,956,000	$785,000
2006	$10,563,000	$382,000
2005	$9,001,000	-$193,000

Curr. Assets:	$1,656,000	Curr. Liab.:	$1,656,000	P/E Ratio:	50.00
Plant, Equip.:	$473,000	Total Liab.:	$1,939,000	Indic. Yr. Divd.:	NA
Total Assets:	$2,190,000	Net Worth:	$252,000	Debt/ Equity:	NA

Shaw Communications Inc

630 3rd Ave. SW, Ste. 900, Calgary, AB, T2P 4L4; *PH:* 1-403-750-4500; *Fax:* 1-403-750-4501; *http://* www.shaw.ca

General - Incorporation	Canada	Stock- Price on:12/24/2007	$42.95
Employees	8,200	Stock Exchange	NYSE
Auditor	Ernst & Young LLP	Ticker Symbol	SJR
Stk Agt	Ernest & Young LLP	Outstanding Shares	216,740,000
Counsel	NA	E.P.S.	$2.14
DUNS No.	20-636-5447	Shareholders	NA

Business: The group's principle activities are to provide cable television and other communication services. The services provided by the group include direct to home, satellite services, telecommunications and Internet access. The group's quarterly revenue for August 2007 was 715.47 millions of CAd.

Primary SIC and add'l.: 4899 7375 4813 4841

CIK No: 0000932872

Officers: Jim Shaw/Dir., CEO, Jr Shaw/Exec. Chmn., Peter J. Bissonnette/Pres., Bradley S. Shaw/Dir., Sr. VP - Operations, Douglas J. Black/Corp. Sec., Rhonda Bashnick/VP - Finance, Ken C.C. Stein/Sr. VP - Corporate, Regulatory Affairs, Louis Desrochers/Honorary Sec., Michael Davella/Sr. VP - Planning, Steve Wilson/Sr. VP, CFO

Directors: Jim Shaw/Dir., CEO, Jr Shaw/Exec. Chmn., Donald F. Mazankowski/Dir., Lynda Haverstock/Dir., Gregory John Keating/Dir., Bradley S. Shaw/Dir., Sr. VP - Operations, James F. Dinning/Dir., Michael W. Obrien/Dir., Carl E. Vogel/Dir., George F. Galbraith/Dir., Ronald V. Joyce/Dir., Jc Sparkman/Dir., Willard H. Yuill/Dir., Adrian Burns/Dir., Harold A. Roozen/Dir. *(16 Directors included in Index)*

Financial Data: Fiscal Year End:08/31   Latest Annual Data: 8/31/2006

Year	Sales	Net Income
2006	$2,219,504,000	$419,321,000
2005	$1,855,135,000	$142,466,000
2004	$1,577,282,000	$61,521,000

Curr. Assets:	$192,238,000	**Curr. Liab.:**	$535,494,000			
Plant, Equip.:	$2,030,676,000	**Total Liab.:**	$5,155,836,000	**Indic. Yr. Divd.:**	$0.940	
Total Assets:	$6,585,599,000	**Net Worth:**	$1,429,763,000	**Debt/ Equity:**	NA	

Shaw Group Inc (The)

4171 Essen Ln., Baton Rouge, LA, 70809; *PH:* 1-225-932-2500; *Fax:* 1-225-987-3328;
http:// www.shawgrp.com; *Email:* ir@shawgrp.com

General - Incorporation	LA	**Stock** - Price on:12/24/2007	$45.49
Employees	22,000	Stock Exchange	NYSE
Auditor	KPMG LLP	Ticker Symbol	SGR
Stk Agt	Wachovia Bank N.A	Outstanding Shares	80,760,000
Counsel	Gary P. Graphia	E.P.S.	-$0.03
DUNS No.	18-003-8382	Shareholders	NA

Business: The group's principle activity is to provide engineering, construction and maintenance services to the power, process, and environmental and infrastructure industries. The group provides project-related services, including design, engineering, construction, procurement, maintenance, technology and consulting services. The group also manufactures and distributes stainless, alloy and carbon steel pipe fittings. The group operates from United States, Canada, the Asia/Pacific Rim, Europe, South America and the Middle East.

Primary SIC and add'l.: 3494 3498 8999

CIK No: 0000914024

Subsidiaries: ACL Piping, Inc., Aiton & Co Limited, American Plastic Pipe and Supply, LLC, Arlington Avenue E Venture, LLC, Associated Valve, Inc., B.F. Shaw, Inc., Badger Technologies, LLC, Badger Technology Holdings, LLC, Benicia North Gateway II, LLC, C.B.P. Engineering Corp., Camden Road Venture, LLC, Chimento Wetlands, LLC, Coastal Estuary Services, LLC, Cojafex B.V., Eagle Industries, Inc. 185 Subsidiaries included in the Index

Officers: J. M. Bernhard/Chmn., CEO, Pres., Dirk J. Wild/Chief Accounting Officer, Sr. VP, David P. Barry/Pres. - Nuclear Division, Power Group, Ron D. McCall/Pres. - Maintenance Division, David L. Chapman/Pres. - Fabrication, Manufacturing Group, Richard F. Gill/Exec. VP, Robert L. Belk/Exec. VP, Gary P. Graphia/Exec. VP - Corporate Development, Strategy, Cliff S. Rankin/General Counsel, Corp. Sec., Lou Pucher/Pres. - Energy, Chemicals Group, Ronald W. Oakley/Pres. - Environmental, Infrastructure Group, Monty Glover/Pres. - Fossil Division, Power Group

Directors: J. M. Bernhard/Chmn., CEO, Pres., Lane L. Grigsby/Dir., Daniel A. Hoffler/Dir., Michael J. Mancuso/Dir., Albert D. McAlister/Dir., Charles E. Roemer/Dir., James F. Barker/Dir., David W. Hoyle/Dir., Thos. E. Capps/Dir.

Owners: Jeffrey L. Gendell/9.45%, Insiders/5.08%, Ronald W. Oakley, FMR Corp./14.06%, David W. Hoyle, Charles E. Roemer, James F. Barker, Ziff Asset Management, L.P./7.64%, Lane L. Grigsby, Albert D. McAlister, Daniel A. Hoffler, David L. Chapman, Robert L. Belk, Monty R. Glover, Dirk J. Wild *(16 Owners included in Index)*

Financial Data: Fiscal Year End:08/31 **Latest Annual Data:** 8/31/2006

Year	Sales	Net Income
2006	$4,775,615,000	$50,850,000
2005	$3,265,916,000	$16,376,000
2004	$3,076,945,000	-$28,975,000

Curr. Assets:	$1,678,660,000	**Curr. Liab.:**	$1,040,659,000		
Plant, Equip.:	$175,431,000	**Total Liab.:**	$1,272,519,000	**Indic. Yr. Divd.:**	NA
Total Assets:	$2,529,134,000	**Net Worth:**	$1,243,207,000	**Debt/ Equity:**	0.9522

Shearson Financial Network Inc

2470 St. Rose Pkwy No. 314, Henderson, NV, 89074; *PH:* 1-702-868-7900;
http:// www.shearsonhomeloans.com

General - Incorporation	NV	**Stock** - Price on:12/24/2007	$0.004
Employees	39	Stock Exchange	OTC
Auditor	Pollard-kelley Auditing Services, Inc	Ticker Symbol	SHSN
Stk Agt	Continental Stock Transfer & Trust Co	Outstanding Shares	316,120,000
Counsel	NA	E.P.S.	-$0.536
DUNS No.	NA	Shareholders	NA

Business: The groups principle activities include selling specialty coffee beans, brewed coffee and espresso based beverages through company owned and franchised retail locations. The group operates from the United States. The group's quarterly revenue for Sep '07 was 1.13 millions of USD.

Primary SIC and add'l.: 6162

CIK No: 0001138173

Subsidiaries: Allstate Home Loans, Inc, Shearson Home Loans

Officers: Michael A. Barron/57/Chmn., CEO/$300,000.00, Lee Shorey/CFO/$90,000.00, Joseph A. Cosio-Barron/58/Pres./$300,000.00, Wanda Witoslawski/43/Controller

Directors: Michael A. Barron/57/Chmn., CEO

Owners: Theresa Carlise, Joseph Cosio-Barron/3.60%, Eclipse Holding Corporation/7.00%, Keith Fink/12.20%, Greg Shanberg/17.70%, Insiders/6.70%, Michael A. Barron/2.40%, Lee Shorey

Financial Data: Fiscal Year End:12/31 **Latest Annual Data:** 12/31/2006

Year	Sales	Net Income
2006	$8,533,000	$2,757,000
2005	$6,826,000	-$10,930,000
2004	$6,566,000	-$11,188,000

Curr. Assets:	$21,471,000	**Curr. Liab.:**	$23,096,000	**P/E Ratio:**	6.07
Plant, Equip.:	$1,417,000	**Total Liab.:**	$24,349,000	**Indic. Yr. Divd.:**	NA
Total Assets:	$30,783,000	**Net Worth:**	$6,434,000	**Debt/ Equity:**	NA

Sheervision Inc

4030 Palos Verdes Dr. N, Ste. 104, Rolling Hills Estates, CA, 90274; *PH:* 1-310-265-8918;
Fax: 1-310-265-8919; *http://* www.sheervision.com; *Email:* customerservice@sheervision.com

General - Incorporation	DE	**Stock** - Price on:12/24/2007	$0.5
Employees	24	Stock Exchange	OTC
Auditor	Miller Ellin & Company, LLP	Ticker Symbol	SVSO
Stk Agt	Fidelity Transfer Co	Outstanding Shares	12,280,000
Counsel	NA	E.P.S.	-$0.1
DUNS No.	NA	Shareholders	NA

Business: The groups principle activities include design and sell proprietary surgical loupes and light systems to the dental, medical and veterinary markets. The group operates from the United States and Asia.

Primary SIC and add'l.: 3841 3842

CIK No: 0001096187

Subsidiaries: Sheervision, Inc.

Officers: Suzanne Lewsadder/Chmn., CEO, Treasurer, Jeffrey Lewsadder/Dir., Pres., Sec., Suzanne Puente/CFO, Terri Wiest/61/National Sales Dir. - Dental Hygiene, Martin Chaput/40/Online Marketing Mgr.

Directors: Suzanne Lewsadder/Chmn., CEO, Treasurer, Jeffrey Lewsadder/Dir., Pres., Sec., Shemiran Hart/Dir., Sharon Biddle/Dir., David Frankel/Dir.

Owners: Jeffrey Lewsadder/72.60%, Sharon Biddle, David Frankel, Insiders/73.00%

Financial Data: Fiscal Year End:08/31 **Latest Annual Data:** 08/31/2006

Year	Sales	Net Income
2006	$2,981,000	-$2,349,000
2005	NA	-$80,000
2004	$7,000	-$76,000

Curr. Assets:	$1,542,000	**Curr. Liab.:**	$363,000		
Plant, Equip.:	$101,000	**Total Liab.:**	$363,000	**Indic. Yr. Divd.:**	NA
Total Assets:	$1,643,000	**Net Worth:**	$1,280,000	**Debt/ Equity:**	NA

Sheffield Pharmaceuticals Inc

3985 Research Pk. Dr., Ann Arbor, MI, 48108; *PH:* 1-734-332-7800

General - Incorporation	DE	**Stock** - Price on:12/24/2007	NA
Employees	8	Stock Exchange	OTC
Auditor	Berman & Co., P.A.	Ticker Symbol	PPXP
Stk Agt	Standard Registrar & Transfer Co Inc.	Outstanding Shares	NA
Counsel	McDermott Will & Emery	E.P.S.	NA
DUNS No.	80-747-6676	Shareholders	NA

Business: The group's principal activity is to develop proprietary drugs using pulmonary delivery technologies. The group is in development stage. The group develops nine respiratory and systemic (non-respiratory) therapies to be delivered through the group's metered solution inhaler and aerosol drug delivery system. The products of the group are respiratory drugs, which are used in the treatment of respiratory diseases such as asthma, chronic obstructive pulmonary diseases and cystic fibrosis. The group is developing a range of products to treat respiratory and systemic diseases in its proprietary pulmonary delivery systems, including the premaire(R) delivery system ('premaire') and tempo(tm) inhaler ('tempo'). The group acquires in-license portfolio of pulmonary delivery technologies to meet the market opportunity.

Primary SIC and add'l.: 8731 2834

CIK No: 0000894158

Officers: Steve H. Kanzer/44/Chmn., CEO, Charles L. Bisgaier/54/Dir., Pres., Joseph A. Rudick/51/Dir., Chief Medical Officer, John S. Althaus/54/VP - Advanced Technology

Directors: Steve H. Kanzer/44/Chmn., CEO, Nicholas Stergis/33/Vice Chmn., Jeff Wolf/44/Dir., Daniel J. Dorman/45/Dir., James S. Kuo/43/Dir., Charles L. Bisgaier/54/Dir., Pres., Jeffrey J. Kraws/43/Dir., Joseph A. Rudick/51/Dir., Chief Medical Officer

Owners: Charles Bisgaier, Accredited Venture Capital, LLC, Ridgeback Capital Investment Ltd., Insiders, Steve H. Kanzer, James S. Kuo, Jeffrey Wolf, Firebird Capital, Jeffrey J. Kraws, Daniel J. Dorman, Nicholas Stergis, Joseph A. Rudick

Shell Canada Ltd

400 4th Ave Sw, Calgary, AB, T2P 0J4,; *PH:* 1-403-691-3111; *http://* www.shell.ca/hom

General - Incorporation	Canada	**Stock** - Price on:12/24/2007	NA
Employees	NA	Stock Exchange	NA
Auditor	PricewaterhouseCoopers LLP	Ticker Symbol	NA
Stk Agt	Mellon Trust Co	Outstanding Shares	NA
Counsel	NA	E.P.S.	NA
DUNS No.	20-175-2268	Shareholders	NA

Business: The group's principle activities of the group are classified into three divisions: resources which includes exploration, production and marketing activities for crude oil, bitumen, natural gas, natural gas liquids and sulphur in the foothills area of alberta, and an in-situ oil sands project in peace river, alberta; oil products includes manufacturing, distribution and sales of refined petroleum products across Canada. Refineries in montreal, quebec, sarnia, ontario, and fort saskatchewan, alberta convert crude oil into gasoline, diesel fuel, aviation fuels, solvents, lubricants, asphalt and heavy fuel oils; and corporate and other which includes controllership, financing, administration and general corporate facility management, and also oil sands, a joint venture agreement in which the group holds 60% interest in the athabasca oil sands project in northern alberta.

Primary SIC and add'l.: 1311 2819 2911

CIK No: 0000702983

Officers: Clive Mather/CEO, Pres., Ian H. Kilgour/Sr. VP - Exploration, Production, Donna Tarka/Controller, Richard W. Riegert/Assoc. General Counsel - E, P, Assist. Sec., Celina Doyle/Contact - Athabasca Oil Sands Project, Community Relations, Muskeg River Mine, Margit Phillips/Contact - Athabasca Oil Sands Project, Community Relations, Scotford Upgrader, Doug Thibault/Contact - Propane, Butane Pricing Information, LPG Marketing Rep, West, Bruce Graham/Contact - Propane, Butane Pricing Information, East Prices, LPG Marketing Rep, East, Terri Leclair/Contact - Surplus Equipment Sales, Investment Recovery Coordinator, Graham Boje/VP, Rob W.P. Symonds/VP - Foothills, Ramzi R. Fawaz/VP, David R. Collyer/Dir., VP, Greg Guidry/Dir., Sr. VP - Exploration, Production, Brian E. Straub/Dir., Sr. VP - Oil Sands *(34 Officers included in Index)*

Directors: Rob J. Routs/Chmn., Kerry L. Hawkins/67/Dir., Nancy C. Southern/51/Dir., Derek H. Burney/68/Dir., Ida J. Goodreau/56/Dir., Raymond Royer/69/Dir., Ronald W. Osborne/61/Dir., Brian E. Straub/Dir., Sr. VP - Oil Sands, Adrian W. Loader/Dir., Pres., David W. Kerr/64/Dir., Marvin E. Odum/50/Dir., Greg Guidry/Dir., Sr. VP - Exploration, Production, David R. Collyer/Dir., VP

Shells Seafood Restaurants Inc

16313 N Dale Mabry Hwy., Ste. 100, Tampa, FL, 33618; *PH:* 1-813-961-0944;
Fax: 1-813-960-9059; *http://* www.shellsseafood.com; *Email:* talktoshells@shellsseafood.com

General - Incorporation	DE
Employees	600
Auditor	Kirkland, Russ, Murphy & Tapp P.A
Stk Agt	Continental Stock Transfer & Trust Co
Counsel	Fulbright & Jaworski LLP
DUNS No.	84-706-7683

Stock - Price on:12/24/2007	$0.22
Stock Exchange	OTC
Ticker Symbol	SHLL
Outstanding Shares	18,870,000
E.P.S.	-$0.19
Shareholders	NA

Business: The group's principal activity is to own, manage and operate 28 full service, casual dining seafood restaurants in Florida under the name shells. The group owns 23 shells restaurants, a 51% ownership interest in one shells restaurant and manages four additional shells restaurants pursuant to contractual arrangements. The restaurants feature a wide selection of seafood items, including shrimp, oysters, clams, scallops, lobster, crab, crawfish, and daily fresh fish specials, cooked to order in a variety of ways. The restaurants also offer a wide selection of signature pasta dishes, appetizers, salads, desserts and full bar service.

Primary SIC and add'l.: 5812

CIK No: 0000935066

Officers: Leslie J. Christon/CEO, Pres./$333,685.00, Warren R. Nelson/CFO, Exec. VP/$188,852.00, Guy C. Kathman/VP - Operations/$157,015.00, Christopher R. Ward/VP - Purchasing/$138,693.00

Directors: Philip R. Chapman/46/Dir., Michael R. Golding/75/Dir., Gary L. Herman/44/Dir., Christopher D. Illick/69/Dir., Jay A. Wolf/35/Dir.

Owners: Warren R. Nelson, James R. Adler, Frederick R. Adler, Leslie J. Christon, Guy C. Kathman, Banyon Investment, LLC, Trinad Capital Master Fund, Ltd., Pequot Capital Management, Inc., Christopher R. Ward, Michael R. Golding, Robert Ellin, Insiders, Lagunitas Partners, LP, Gary L. Herman, Bruce Galloway (19 Owners included in Index)

Financial Data: Fiscal Year End:01/01 Latest Annual Data: 12/31/2006

Year	Sales	Net Income
2006	$47,830,000	-$3,003,000
2005	$41,564,000	-$1,343,000

Curr. Assets:	$1,695,000	Curr. Liab.:	$6,141,000		
Plant, Equip.:	$9,171,000	Total Liab.:	$8,976,000	Indic. Yr. Divd.:	NA
Total Assets:	$13,837,000	Net Worth:	$4,339,000	Debt/ Equity:	0.3761

Shelron Group Inc

29 Broadway Ave., New York, NY, 10006; PH: 1-212-836-4041; http:// www.shelron.com; Email: info@activshopper.com

General - Incorporation	DE
Employees	1
Auditor	Rotenberg Meril Solomon
Stk Agt	Securities Transfer Corp
Counsel	NA
DUNS No.	NA

Stock - Price on:12/24/2007	$0.007
Stock Exchange	OTC
Ticker Symbol	SHRN
Outstanding Shares	410,690,000
E.P.S.	-$0.002
Shareholders	NA

Business: The group's principal activity is to develop enterprise application integration products, which integrates independent business software applications to unify a variety of information and services. The group is in the development stage. The group intends to market its products and services to medium to large-sized enterprises in the United States, Europe and Israel.

Primary SIC and add'l.: 7375 7373

CIK No: 0001125903

Subsidiaries: TTTTickets Holding Corp

Officers: Eliron Yaron/39/Chmn., CEO, Founder, Joel Gering/Investor Relations Officer

Directors: Eliron Yaron/39/Chmn., CEO, Founder, Yossi Levi/27/Dir., Issac Maizel/27/Dir.

Owners: Insiders/28.89%, Eliron Yaron/52.00%, Insiders/52.00%, Joseph Corso/21.72%, Eliron Yaron/7.17%

Financial Data: Fiscal Year End:12/31 Latest Annual Data: 12/31/2006

Year	Sales	Net Income
2006	$1,115,000	-$918,000
2005	$374,000	-$1,477,000
2004	$7,000	-$646,000

Curr. Assets:	$660,000	Curr. Liab.:	$279,000		
Plant, Equip.:	$83,000	Total Liab.:	$279,000	Indic. Yr. Divd.:	NA
Total Assets:	$795,000	Net Worth:	$517,000	Debt/ Equity:	NA

Shenandoah Telecommunications Co

500 Shentel Way, Edinburg, VA, 22824; PH: 1-540-984-4141; Fax: 1-540-984-8192; http:// www.shentel.com; Email: resumes@shentel.net

General - Incorporation	VA
Employees	356
Auditor	KPMG LLP
Stk Agt	NA
Counsel	NA
DUNS No.	05-673-0450

Stock - Price on:12/24/2007	$48.14
Stock Exchange	NDQ
Ticker Symbol	SHEN
Outstanding Shares	7,780,000
E.P.S.	$0.71
Shareholders	NA

Business: The group's principle activities are to provide regulated and unregulated telecommunication services through its nine wholly owned subsidiaries. The services provided by the group include: telephone service and wireless personal communications service under the brand name 'sprint', cellular telephone, cable television, unregulated communications equipment sales and services, Internet access and paging services. The group provides integrated telecommunication products and services in the northern shenandoah valley and surrounding areas. The group operates in harrisonburg, Virginia, harrisburg, Pennsylvania, altoona and northern Virginia. The group also leases towers and operates and maintains an interstate fiber optic network. The group's quarterly revenue for September 2007 was 35.42 millions of USD.

Primary SIC and add'l.: 4899 4813 4812 6719 4841

CIK No: 0000354963

Subsidiaries: Converged Service of West Virginia, Inc., NTC Communications, LLC, Shenandoah Cable Television Company, Shenandoah Long Distance Company, Shenandoah Mobile Company, Shenandoah Network Company, Shenandoah Personal Communications Company, Shenandoah Telephone Company, ShenTel Communications Company, Shentel Converged Services, Inc., Shentel Management Company, ShenTel Service Company, Shentel Wireless Company

Officers: Christopher E. French/Chmn., CEO, Pres./$767,781.00, David E. Ferguson/VP - Customer Services, Jonathan R. Spencer/VP, General Counsel, Corp. Sec., Earle A. MacKenzie/CFO, COO, Exec. VP/$649,565.00, David K. MacDonald/VP - Operations/$346,281.00, William L. Pirtle/VP - Sales, Laurence F. Paxton/55/VP - Information Systems

Directors: Christopher E. French/Chmn., CEO, Pres., Douglas C. Arthur/Vice Chmn., James E. Zerkel/Dir., Richard Koontz/Dir., Dale S. Lam/Dir., William Truban/Dir., Tracy Fitzsimmons/Dir., Ken L. Burch/Dir., Jonelle St. John/Dir.

Owners: Earle A. MacKenzie, Insiders/5.54%, William A. Truban, William L. Pirtle, Ken L. Burch/1.09%, Dale S. Lam, Wachovia Corporation/5.16%, James E. Zerkel, David K. MacDonald, Richard L. Koontz, Tracy Fitzsimmons, David E. Ferguson, Christopher E. French/3.97%

Financial Data: Fiscal Year End:12/31 Latest Annual Data: 12/31/2006

Year	Sales	Net Income
2006	$169,195,000	$17,922,000
2005	$146,391,000	$10,735,000
2004	$120,974,000	$10,243,000

Curr. Assets:	$30,863,000	Curr. Liab.:	$21,280,000	P/E Ratio:	27.83
Plant, Equip.:	$155,644,000	Total Liab.:	$72,531,000	Indic. Yr. Divd.:	$0.480
Total Assets:	$207,720,000	Net Worth:	$135,189,000	Debt/ Equity:	NA

Shengtai Pharmaceutical Inc

Formerly: West Coast Car Co

Changda Rd. E, Development District, Changle County, Shandong, 262400; PH: 86-536-6295728; http:// west-coast-car-company.ebizautos.com

General - Incorporation	DE
Employees	NA
Auditor	Moore Stephens Wurth F & T LLP
Stk Agt	Interwest Transfer Company, Inc.
Counsel	NA
DUNS No.	NA

Stock - Price on:12/24/2007	NA
Stock Exchange	OTC
Ticker Symbol	SGTI
Outstanding Shares	NA
E.P.S.	NA
Shareholders	NA

Business: The group's is a pre-owned retail automobile dealership in Southern California. The company commenced its operations in Temecula, California in November 2004. As of August 30, 2005 we have bought and sold a 1997 Porsche Boxter car and 2005 Nissan Altima. At this time there are no vehicles in inventory.

Primary SIC and add'l.: 5500

CIK No: 0001295079

Officers: Qingtai Liu/50/Chmn., CEO, Yizhao Zhang/CFO, Tim Bonnell/Customer Service, Rob Howe/Mgr.

Directors: Qingtai Liu/50/Chmn., CEO, Yongqiang Wang/39/Dir., Chris W. Wang/37/Dir., Changxin Li/Dir., Winfred Lee/Dir.

Owners: China Private Equity Partners Co., Limited/7.90%, Insiders/41.15%, Qingtai Liu/41.15%, Pope Investments LLC/19.67%

Financial Data: Fiscal Year End:12/30 Latest Annual Data: 12/31/2006

Year	Sales	Net Income
2006	NA	-$65,000

Curr. Assets:	$2,000	Curr. Liab.:	$124,000		
Plant, Equip.:	NA	Total Liab.:	$124,000	Indic. Yr. Divd.:	NA
Total Assets:	$2,000	Net Worth:	-$122,000	Debt/ Equity:	NA

SHEP Technologies Inc

595 Howe St., Ste 504, Vancouver, BC, V6C 2T5; PH: 1-604-689-1515; http:// www.infinitebang.com; Email: info@shepinc.com

General - Incorporation	Canada
Employees	NA
Auditor	Davidson & Co LLP
Stk Agt	Montreal Trust Co of Can (Vancouver)
Counsel	NA
DUNS No.	NA

Stock - Price on:12/24/2007	$0.006
Stock Exchange	OTC
Ticker Symbol	STLOF
Outstanding Shares	NA
E.P.S.	NA
Shareholders	NA

Business: The group's principal activity is to develop and market stored hydraulic energy propulsion system, which is designed for wide ranging applications in the global transportation industry. The system uses electronics, a patented hydraulic motor and a proprietary accumulator to capture kinetic energy otherwise lost during vehicle braking. The system uses the recovered energy for vehicle acceleration during the low speed acceleration phase. The use of recovered energy will decrease in fuel consumption in transportation vehicles. On 26-Sep-2003, the group acquired shep technologies (UK) limited.

Primary SIC and add'l.: 3714

CIK No: 0001135443

Subsidiaries: SHEP Limited, SHEP Technologies (UK) Limited

Financial Data: Fiscal Year End:12/31 Latest Annual Data: 12/31/2004

Year	Sales	Net Income
2004	NA	-$1,905,000
2003	NA	-$3,292,000
2002	$31,000	-$1,126,000

Curr. Assets:	$95,000	Curr. Liab.:	$1,554,000		
Plant, Equip.:	$34,000	Total Liab.:	$1,554,000	Indic. Yr. Divd.:	NA
Total Assets:	$129,000	Net Worth:	-$1,424,000	Debt/ Equity:	NA

Sherwin Williams Co

101 Prospect Ave Nw, Cleveland, OH, 44115; PH: 1-216-566-2200; http:// www.sherwin-williams.com

General - Incorporation	OH
Employees	30,767
Auditor	Ernst & Young LLP
Stk Agt	Bank of New York
Counsel	NA
DUNS No.	00-420-6397

Stock - Price on:12/24/2007	$66.94
Stock Exchange	NYSE
Ticker Symbol	NA
Outstanding Shares	131,890,000
E.P.S.	$4.38
Shareholders	NA

Business: The groups principle activity is to provide aluminum oxide. The group operates from United States.

Primary SIC and add'l.: 5231 2851 3429 6512

CIK No: 0000089800

Subsidiaries: Coatings S. R. L., Compania Sherwin-Williams, S.A. de C.V., Contract Transportation Systems Co., Eurofinish S.r.l., Foreign Subsidiaries, Omega Specialty Products & Services LLC, Productos Quimicos Y Pinturas, S.A. de C.V., Quetzal Pinturas, S.A. de C.V., Ronseal

(Ireland) Limited, Ronseal Limited, Sherwin-Williams (Caribbean) N.V., Sherwin-Williams (Shanghai) Paints Company Limited, Sherwin-Williams (West Indies) Limited, Sherwin-Williams Argentina I.y C.S.A., Sherwin-Williams Automotive Europe S.p.A. 32 Subsidiaries included in the Index

Officers: Christopher M. Connor/Chmn., CEO, Alexander Zalesky/Pres., GM - International Division Global Group, Sean P. Hennessy/CFO, Sr. VP - Finance/$2,250,837.00, Thomas E. Hopkins/Sr. VP - Human Resources, Richard M. Weaver/VP - Administration, Robert J. Wells/VP - Corporate Communications, Public Affairs, Robert J. Davisson/Pres., GM - Southeastern Division Paint Stores Group, Timothy J. Drouilhet/Pres., GM - Eastern Division, Paint Stores Group, Conway G. Ivy/66/Sr. VP - Corporate Planning, Development, Thomas W. Seitz/Sr. VP - Strategic Excellence Initiatives/$2,110,832.00, John L. Ault/VP, Corporate Controller, Cheri M. Phyfer/Pres. - General Manger South Western Division Paint Stores Group, Cynthia D. Brogan/VP, Treasurer, Michael T. Cummins/VP - Taxes, Assist. Sec., Mark J. Dvoroznak/VP - Corporate Audit, Loss Prevention *(24 Officers included in Index)*

Directors: Christopher M. Connor/Chmn., CEO, Daniel E. Evans/Dir., Susan J. Kropf/Dir., Robert W. Mahoney/Dir., Malachi A. Mixon/Dir., Curtis E. Moll/Dir., Richard K. Smucker/Dir., David F. Hodnik/Dir., Gary E. McCullough/Dir., Arthur F. Anton/Dir., James C. Boland/Dir.

Owners: S. J. Kropf, S. P. Hennessy, D. E. Evans, R. K. Smucker, C. M. Connor/1.16%, J. G. Morikis, J. C. Boland, T. W. Seitz, C. E. Moll, A. F. Anton, L. E. Stellato, Insiders/2.42%, G. E. McCullough, D. F. Hodnik, A. M. Mixon *(16 Owners included in Index)*

Financial Data: *Fiscal Year End:*12/31 *Latest Annual Data:* 12/31/2006

Year	Sales	Net Income
2006	$7,809,759,000	$576,058,000
2005	$7,190,661,000	$463,258,000
2004	$6,113,789,000	$393,254,000

Curr. Assets:	$2,450,281,000	**Curr. Liab.:**	$2,074,815,000	**P/E Ratio:**	15.28
Plant, Equip.:	$828,781,000	**Total Liab.:**	$3,002,727,000	**Indic. Yr. Divd.:**	$1.260
Total Assets:	$4,995,087,000	**Net Worth:**	$1,992,360,000	**Debt/ Equity:**	0.1523

Shiloh Industries Inc

880 Steel Dr., Valley City, OH, 44280; ***PH:*** 1-330-558-2600; ***Fax:*** 1-330-558-2666; ***http://*** www.shiloh.com

General - Incorporation	DE	**Stock**- Price on:12/24/2007	$13.18
Employees	1,990	Stock Exchange	NDQ
Auditor	Grant Thornton, LLP	Ticker Symbol	SHLO
Stk Agt	Computershare Investor Services LLC	Outstanding Shares	16,350,000
Counsel	NA	E.P.S	$0.58
DUNS No.	80-995-3136	Shareholders	NA

Business: The group's principal activity is to manufacture blanks and stamped components for industrial uses. The automotive, light truck, heavy truck and other industrial markets use the products of the group. The group also builds modular assemblies, which include components used in the structural and powertrain systems of a vehicle. The stampings are principally used as components in mufflers, seat frames, structural rails, window lifts, heat shields, vehicle brakes and other structural body components. The structural systems include bumper beams, door impact beams, steering column supports, chassis components and structural underbody modules. The other activities of the group include designing, engineering and manufacturing of precision tools, dies and welding and assembly equipment for use in its operations.

Primary SIC and add'l.: 3714 3544 3545 3312

CIK No: 0000904979

Subsidiaries: C & H Design Company, Greenfield Die& Manufacturing Corp., Jefferson Blanking Inc., Liverpool Coil Processing, Incorporated, Medina Blanking, Inc., Sectional Stamping, Inc., Shiloh Automotive, Inc., Shiloh Corporation, Shiloh de Mexico S.A. de C.V., Shiloh Incorporated, Shiloh Industries, Inc. Dickson Manufacturing Division, Shiloh International S.A. de C.V., The Sectional Die Company, VCS Properties, LLC

Officers: Theodore K. Zampetis/Dir., CEO, Pres., James F. Keys/Exec. VP - Research, Advanced Technology, Worldwide Standard Products Company, David J. Hessler/Dir., Sec., Stephen Graham/CFO

Directors: Theodore K. Zampetis/Dir., CEO, Pres., Curtis E. Moll/Chmn., David J. Hessler/Dir., Sec., Cloyd J. Abruzzo/Dir., Dieter Kaesgen/Dir., George G. Goodrich/Dir., Robert King/Dir., John J. Tanis/Dir., Gary A. Oatey/Dir.

Owners: Theodore K. Zampetis, Dieter Kaesgen, James F. Keys, David J. Hessler, Gary A. Oatey, Tontine Capital Partners, L.P., John J. Tanis, Stephen E. Graham, Cloyd J. Abruzzo, MTD Holdings Inc, Curtis E. Moll, Anthony M. Parente, Insiders, George G. Goodrich, Dimensional Fund Advisers, Inc.

Financial Data: *Fiscal Year End:*10/31 *Latest Annual Data:* 10/31/2007

Year	Sales	Net Income
2007	$590,414,000	$9,550,000
2006	$620,375,000	$7,118,000
2005	$634,579,000	$26,752,000

Curr. Assets:	$140,255,000	**Curr. Liab.:**	$119,240,000		
Plant, Equip.:	$199,845,000	**Total Liab.:**	$205,847,000	**Indic. Yr. Divd.:**	NA
Total Assets:	$341,110,000	**Net Worth:**	$135,263,000	**Debt/ Equity:**	0.7782

Shiming U.S. Inc

Formerly: Argenta Systems Inc

12/f, Shanxi Zhengquan Bldg., Gaoxin 2nd Rd., Shanxi Province, V6E 2N7; ***PH:*** 86-852-282-30000; ***http://*** www.argentasystems.com

General - Incorporation	NV	**Stock**- Price on:12/24/2007	NA
Employees	NA	Stock Exchange	NA
Auditor	Gruber & Co., LLC	Ticker Symbol	NA
Stk Agt	Nevada Agency & Trust Company	Outstanding Shares	NA
Counsel	NA	E.P.S	NA
DUNS No.	NA	Shareholders	NA

Business: The groups principle activity is to determine feasibility of marketing the Vitamineralherb.com products in various markets. The group operates from the United States.

Primary SIC and add'l.: 3679

CIK No: 0001091294

Officers: Chunan Liu/50/Dir., CFO

Directors: Chunan Liu/50/Dir., CFO

Owners: Genrong Qu, Insiders, Rui Wang, Shiming Wang, Shaanxi Meixian Shiming Non-Ferrous Metallurgy Co., Ltd., Nairang Liu, Cunhu Yang

Financial Data: *Fiscal Year End:*12/31 *Latest Annual Data:* 12/31/2006

Year	Sales	Net Income
2006	$5,533,000	$2,504,000
2005	$0	-$110,000

Curr. Assets:	$19,979,000	**Curr. Liab.:**	$719,000		
Plant, Equip.:	$2,750,000	**Total Liab.:**	$873,000	**Indic. Yr. Divd.:**	NA
Total Assets:	$28,123,000	**Net Worth:**	$27,249,000	**Debt/ Equity:**	NA

Shinhan Financial Group Co Ltd

800 3rd Ave., 32nd Fl., New York, NY, 10022; ***PH:*** 1-212-371-8000; ***Fax:*** 1-212-371-8875; ***http://*** www.shinhangroup.com

General - Incorporation	Korea	**Stock**- Price on:12/24/2007	$127
Employees	14,414	Stock Exchange	NYSE
Auditor	KPMG Samjong Accounting Corp	Ticker Symbol	SHG
Stk Agt	Korean Securities Depository	Outstanding Shares	190,780,000
Counsel	NA	E.P.S	NA
DUNS No.	NA	Shareholders	NA

Business: The group's principal activity is the provision of financial services which include commercial and trust banking, trade-related and other products to small and medium-sized enterprises, large corporations and individuals. Other services include retail and institutional brokerage, equity and bond underwriting, beneficiary certificate distribution, commercial paper underwriting and proprietary trading, management of investment trusts where the investment products currently consist of money market and fixed-income funds, financing and general, in-alliance (with manufacturers), shipping and retail operating leases, loans and factoring services primarily to its leasing customers, consulting services of global standards to domestic corporate customers and high quality Internet financial services.

Primary SIC and add'l.: NA

CIK No: 0001263043

Subsidiaries: Good Morning Shinhan Securities Co., Ltd., Good Morning Shinhan Securities Europe Ltd., Good Morning Shinhan Securities USA Inc., Jeju Bank, SH Asset Management Co., Ltd., SH&C Life Insurance Co., Ltd., Shinhan Asia Limited, Shinhan Bank, Shinhan Bank (Deutschland) GmbH, Shinhan Bank America, Shinhan BNP Paribas Investment Trust Co., Ltd., Shinhan Capital Co., Ltd., Shinhan Card Co., Ltd., Shinhan Credit Information Co., Ltd., Shinhan Data System 20 Subsidiaries included in the Index

Officers: In Ho Lee/65/Dir., CEO, Pres., Jae Woo Lee/56/Deputy Pres. - Business Management Team, General Affairs Team, Credit Card Business Support Team, Sang Hoon Shin/Dir., Pres., Buhmsoo Choi/51/Deputy CFO, Pres. - Finance Management Team, Investor Relations Team, Strategic Planning Team, Public Relations Team, Jae Woon Yoon/55/Deputy Pres. - Synergy Management Team, Information, Technology Planning Team, Audit, Compliance Team, Risk Management Team

Directors: In Ho Lee/65/Dir., CEO, Pres., Eung Chan Ra/70/Chmn., Young Woo Kim/56/Dir., Philippe Reynieix/59/Dir., Yong Woong Yang/60/Dir., Shee Yul Ryoo/70/Dir., Sang Hoon Shin/Dir., Pres., Sung Bin Chun/55/Dir., Si Jong Kim/71/Dir., Pyung Joo Kim/Dir., Sang Yoon Lee/66/Dir., Yoon Soo Yoon/62/Dir., Byung Hun Park/80/Dir., Young Hoon Choi/80/Dir., Haeng Nam Chung/67/Dir.

Owners: Korea Deposit Insurance Corporation/5.86%, Korea National Pension Fund/3.17%, NTC-GOV SPORE/1.12%, SSB-ARTISAN/1.12%, Citibank, N.A./2.00%, BNP Paribas Group/9.06%, Euro-Pacific Growth Fund/3.20%, Shinhan Bank/1.87%, Daekyo/1.40%, Shinhan Financial Group Employee Stock Ownership Association/1.24%, Fidelity Investment Trust/1.01%, Capital World Growth and Income Fund/2.68%

Financial Data: *Fiscal Year End:*12/31 *Latest Annual Data:* 12/31/2006

Year	Sales	Net Income
2006	$14,100,254,000	$1,617,331,000
2005	$10,189,322,000	$1,738,768,000
2004	$9,546,627,000	$1,417,128,000

Curr. Assets:	$22,829,371,000	**Curr. Liab.:**	$128,904,140,000		
Plant, Equip.:	$2,306,817,000	**Total Liab.:**	$181,887,449,000	**Indic. Yr. Divd.:**	NA
Total Assets:	$192,864,720,000	**Net Worth:**	$10,977,272,000	**Debt/ Equity:**	NA

Ship Finance International Ltd

14 Par-La-Ville Rd. , Par-la-Ville Pl., Hamilton; ***PH:*** 1-441-2959500; ***Fax:*** 1-441-2953494; ***http://*** www.shipfinance.bm

General - Incorporation	Bermuda	**Stock**- Price on:12/24/2007	$29.52
Employees	1	Stock Exchange	NYSE
Auditor	Moore Stephens, P.C	Ticker Symbol	SFL
Stk Agt	Mellon Investor Services LLC	Outstanding Shares	72,740,000
Counsel	NA	E.P.S	$2.78
DUNS No.	NA	Shareholders	NA

Business: The groups principle activity is to operate vessels and offshore-related assets. Specific customers of the group include Frontline, Horizon Lines Inc., Golden Ocean, Seadrill, and SCAN Geophyisical ASA. The group operates from United States.

Primary SIC and add'l.: NA

CIK No: 0001289877

Officers: Lars Solbakken/CEO - Ship Finance Management AS, Ole B. Hjertaker/CFO - Ship Finance Management AS

Directors: Craig H. Stevenson/54/Chmn., Paul Leand/Dir., Tor Olav Troim/Dir., Kate Blankenship/Dir.

Owners: Farahead Investments Inc./16.50%, Hemen Holding Ltd./24.92%, Insiders

Financial Data: *Fiscal Year End:*12/31 *Latest Annual Data:* 12/31/2005

Year	Sales	Net Income
2005	$437,510,000	$209,546,000
2004	$492,069,000	$262,659,000

Curr. Assets:	$307,153,000	**Curr. Liab.:**	$173,655,000		
Plant, Equip.:	$246,549,000	**Total Liab.:**	$1,953,147,000	**Indic. Yr. Divd.:**	$2.160
Total Assets:	$2,553,677,000	**Net Worth:**	$600,530,000	**Debt/ Equity:**	NA

Shire Plc

725 Chesterbrook Blvd., Wayne, PA, 19087; ***PH:*** 1-484-595-8800; ***Fax:*** 1-484-595-8200; ***http://*** www.shire.com

vd., Wayne, PA, 19087; *PH:* 1-484-595-8800; *Fax:* 1-484-595-8200; *http://* www.shire.com

General - Incorporation ....England and Wales	*Stock*- Price on:12/24/2007 ....$72.02
Employees...NA	Stock Exchange..NDQ
Auditor ....Deloitte & Touche LLP	Ticker Symbol.......................................SHPGY
Stk Agt..................Morgan ADR Service Center	Outstanding Shares 185,130,000
Counsel..NA	E.P.S..-$9.03
DUNS No...NA	Shareholders..NA

Business: The groups principle activity is to provide pharmaceutical product and services. The groups operates through two segments namely pharmaceutical products and royalties. The products of the group include DAYTRANA, ELAPRASE, PENTASA, REPLAGAL and AGRYLIN. The group operates from the United Kingdom and North America. The group's quarterly revenue for September 608.70 millions of USD.

Primary SIC and add'l.: 2834

CIK No: 0000936402

Subsidiaries: Shire BioChem, Inc., Shire Deutschland GmbH & Co. KG, Shire Development, Inc., Shire France S A, Shire Human Genetic Therapies AB, Shire Human Genetic Therapies, Inc, Shire International Licensing BV, Shire Italia SpA, Shire LLC, Shire Pharmaceutical Contracts Limited, Shire Pharmaceuticals Development Limited, Shire Pharmaceuticals Group Limited, Shire Pharmaceuticals Iberica S.L., Shire Pharmaceuticals Ireland Limited, Shire Pharmaceuticals Limited 20 Subsidiaries included in the Index

Officers: Matthew Emmens/Dir., CEO, Angus Russell/Dir., CFO, Brian Martin/Dir., GM, Leonhard Terp/MD, Jose Antonio Senz De Broto/MD - Shire Pharmaceuticals Iberica, SL, Spain, Juan Lopez De San Roman/Marketing, Sales Dir., Matt Cabrey/Sr. Mgr. - Corporate Communications, Claude Perron/VP, GM, Tony Ooi/MD, Jessica Mann/Sr. VP - Global Corporate Communications, Clea Rosenfeld/VP - Investor Relations, John Freeman/MD - Shire Pharmaceutical Limited, Tim Tustin/MD - Export, Vincent Lucet/GM - Shire France SA, France, Gian Piero Reverberi/GM - Shire Italia SpA, Italy *(19 Officers included in Index)*

Directors: Matthew Emmens/Dir., CEO, James Cavanaugh/Chmn., Brian Martin/Dir., GM, David Mott/Non Exec. Dir., Angus Russell/Dir., CFO, Barry Price/Sr. Non Exec. Dir., Robin Buchanan/Non Exec. Dir., David Kappler/Non Exec. Dir., Patrick Langlois/Non Exec. Dir., Kate Nealon/Non Exec. Dir., Jeffrey Leiden/Non Exec. Dir.

Owners: Fidelity International Limited/5.00%, Matthew Emmens, Tatjana May, David Kappler, James Cavanaugh, Angus Russell, Kate Nealon, Robin Buchanan, Insiders, James Grant, Greg Flexter, Barry Price

Financial Data: Fiscal Year End:12/31 Latest Annual Data: 12/31/2006

Year	Sales	Net Income
2006	$1,796,500,000	$278,200,000
2005	$1,599,316,000	-$410,843,000
2004	$1,363,207,000	$269,007,000

Curr. Assets:	$1,810,300,000	*Curr. Liab.:*	$1,332,000,000		
Plant, Equip.:	$292,800,000	*Total Liab.:*	$1,384,100,000	*Indic. Yr. Divd.:*	$0.130
Total Assets:	$3,326,400,000	*Net Worth:*	$1,942,300,000	*Debt/ Equity:*	NA

Shoe Carnival Inc

8233 Baumgart Rd., Evansville, IN, 47725; *PH:* 1-812-867-6471; *Fax:* 1-812-867-4570; *http://* www.shoecarnival.com; *Email:* info@shoecarnival.com

General - Incorporation ....IN	*Stock*- Price on:12/24/2007 ....$28.75
Employees..1,800	Stock Exchange..NDQ
Auditor ....Deloitte & Touche LLP	Ticker Symbol..NA
Stk Agt.....Computershare Investor Services LLC	Outstanding Shares 13,020,000
Counsel...............................Baker & Daniels	E.P.S..$1.72
DUNS No...09-539-1173	Shareholders..NA

Business: The group's principle activity is to sell footwear and related products through retail stores. The group provides athletic and non-athletic footwear for women, men, and children. The group's stores also carry complementary accessories such as handbags, wallets, shoe care items and socks. As of January 2006, the group operated 263 stores in 23 states in the Midwest, South and Southeast regions of the United States. The group's total revenue for year 2007 was 681.66 millions of USD.

Primary SIC and add'l.: 5661

CIK No: 0000895447

Subsidiaries: SCHC, Inc., SCLC, Inc, Shoe Carnival Ventures, LLC

Officers: Mark L. Lemond/Dir., CEO, Pres./$1,221,351.00, Wayne J. Weaver/Chmn., Executive Officer/$300,000.00, Steven D. Meyer/Sr. VP - Store Operations, Terry L. Clements/VP - Information Services, Thomas V. Welden/VP - Distribution, Kathy A. Yearwood/VP, Controller, Myrna G. Reiss/VP - Marketing, David A. Kapp/VP - Planning, Analysis, Sec., Tucker Robinson/Assist. VP - Buyer Men's Athletics, Bruce C. Boehmer/VP - Loss Prevention, David M. Groff/VP - Administration, Business Development, Kirk V. Light/VP - Store Planning, Real Estate, Timothy T. Baker/Exec. VP - Store Operations/$621,790.00, Sean M. Georges/VP - Human Resources, Clifton E. Sifford/Exec. VP, General Merchandise Mgr./$613,358.00 *(18 Officers included in Index)*

Directors: Mark L. Lemond/Dir., CEO, Pres., Wayne J. Weaver/Chmn., Executive Officer, Gerald W. Schoor/Dir., Kent A. Kleeberger/Dir., William E. Bindley/Dir.

Owners: Timothy T. Baker, Dimensional Fund Advisors LP/7.80%, Barclays Global Investors, NA/9.60%, Wayne J. Weaver/28.10%, Insiders/33.70%, Clifton E. Sifford, Kerry W. Jackson, FMR Corp./12.40%

Financial Data: Fiscal Year End:01/28 Latest Annual Data: 2/3/2007

Year	Sales	Net Income
2007	$681,662,000	$23,764,000
2006	$655,638,000	$18,790,000
2005	$590,186,000	$12,529,000

Curr. Assets:	$237,142,000	*Curr. Liab.:*	$84,928,000	*P/E Ratio:*	16.72
Plant, Equip.:	$74,020,000	*Total Liab.:*	$101,213,000	*Indic. Yr. Divd.:*	NA
Total Assets:	$311,162,000	*Net Worth:*	$209,949,000	*Debt/ Equity:*	NA

Shoe Pavilion Inc

13245 Riverside Dr., Ste. 450, Sherman Oaks, CA, 91423; *PH:* 1-818-907-9975; *Fax:* 1-818-907-8017; *http://* www.shoepavilion.com; *Email:* internet@shoepavilion.com

General - Incorporation ....DE	*Stock*- Price on:12/24/2007 ....$3.14
Employees..512	Stock Exchange..NDQ
Auditor ....Deloitte & Touche LLP	Ticker Symbol..NA
Stk Agt.....................Mellon Investor Services LLC	Outstanding Shares 9,540,000
Counsel...............Shepherd, Mullin, Rechter Et Al	E.P.S..-$0.174
DUNS No. 02-131-7664	Shareholders..NA

Business: The group principal activity is to operate independent off-price shoe stores, which offer a broad selection of women's and men's designer label and branded merchandise. As at 03-Jan-2004, the group operated 85 retail stores including its Internet store in the states of California, Washington and Oregon. It offers quality designer and name brand footwear under 75 brand names such as converse, anne klein 2, reebok, skechers and nine west diesel, fila, ralph lauren, rockport, steve madden, vans and via spiga. The group purchases inventories from domestic and international vendors and independent resellers. The stores operate under the trade names shoe pavilion and shoe pavilion designer shoe warehouse.

Primary SIC and add'l.: 5661

CIK No: 0001051009

Subsidiaries: Shoe Pavilion Corporation

Officers: Dmitry Beinus/56/Chmn., CEO, Pres./$566,480.00, Robert R. Hall/VP, COO/$189,020.00, Michael P. McHugh/CFO, Exec. VP

Directors: Dmitry Beinus/56/Chmn., CEO, Pres., Peter G. Hanelt/63/Dir., Ann Iverson/63/Dir., Randy Katz/54/Dir., Mark J. Miller/56/Dir.

Owners: Randy Katz, Insiders/32.20%, Jack Roth/10.20%, Dmitry Beinus/30.00%, Peter G. Hanelt, Royce & Associates, LLC/11.50%, Ann Iverson, Mark J. Miller, Robert R. Hall/1.20%, Bruce L. Ross

Financial Data: Fiscal Year End:12/31 Latest Annual Data: 12/30/2006

Year	Sales	Net Income
2006	$131,305,000	$1,865,000
2005	$102,510,000	$2,633,000

Curr. Assets:	$43,846,000	*Curr. Liab.:*	$20,525,000		
Plant, Equip.:	$5,948,000	*Total Liab.:*	$26,034,000	*Indic. Yr. Divd.:*	NA
Total Assets:	$52,205,000	*Net Worth:*	$26,171,000	*Debt/ Equity:*	0.0082

Shopko Stores Inc

700 Pilgrim Way, Green Bay, WI, 54304; *PH:* 1-920-497-2211; *http://* www.shopko.com

General - Incorporation ....WI	*Stock*- Price on:12/24/2007 ....NA
Employees...NA	Stock Exchange...NA
Auditor ....Deloitte & Touche LLP	Ticker Symbol..NA
Stk Agt ....Wells Fargo Shareowner Services	Outstanding Shares ....NA
Counsel..NA	E.P.S..NA
DUNS No...02-325-2638	Shareholders..NA

Business: The group's principal activity is to provide general merchandise and retail health services through shopko retail and pamida retail stores. At 31-Jan-2004, the group had 141 shopko retail stores operating in 15 midwest, pacific northwest and western mountain states and 218 pamida retail stores operating in 16 midwest, north central and rocky mountain states. The group offer services to meet the customer's need for home, family basics, casual apparel and seasonal products along with retail health, such as jewelry, cosmetics, small appliances, home textiles, electronics, sporting goods, candy, snack foods, furniture and other health care products

Primary SIC and add'l.: 5912 5311

CIK No: 0000878314

Subsidiaries: P.M. Place Stores Company, Pamida Foundation, Pamida Transportation Company, Pamida, Inc., Penn-Daniels, Incorporated, Places Associates Expansion, LLC, ShopKo Foundation, Inc., ShopKo Properties, Inc., ShopKo Ventures - Duluth, Inc., SKO Holdings, Inc., SKO Optical Manufacturing, Inc., SVS Trucking, Inc.

Officers: Michael R. MacDonald/Chmn., CEO

Directors: Michael R. MacDonald/Chmn., CEO

Shopsmith Inc

6530 Poe Ave., Dayton, OH, 45414; *PH:* 1-937-898-6070; *Fax:* 1-937-890-5197; *http://* www.shopsmith.com; *Email:* resume@shopsmith.com

General - Incorporation ....OH	*Stock*- Price on:12/24/2007 ....$0.2
Employees...NA	Stock Exchange.......................................OTC
Auditor ....Crowe Chizek & Co. LLC	Ticker Symbol.......................................SSMH
Stk Agt ....Crowe Chizek & Co. LLC	Outstanding Shares ....NA
Counsel.....................Thompson Hine & Flory	E.P.S..NA
DUNS No...05-754-3530	Shareholders..NA

Business: The group's principal activities are to manufacture and market power woodworking tools designed primarily for the home workshop. The product, shopsmith mark v is a compact power woodworking tool that performs the functions of five separate tools: a table saw, a wood lathe, a disc sander, a horizontal boring machine and a vertical drill press. The other products manufactured include mark v accessories such as a lathe duplicator that allows a woodworker to duplicate original turnings and a dust collector which is used for dust free woodworking. The power woodworking tools are marketed under the brand name shopsmith. The group distributes its products directly to consumers through demonstration programs, telephone solicitation, mail order and Internet. The group has operations in the United States, Canada and the United Kingdom.

Primary SIC and add'l.: 3546 5251 3423 5961

CIK No: 0000089925

Subsidiaries: Jefferson City Tool Company, Shopsmith Woodworking Centers Ltd. Co., Shopsmith Woodworking Promotions, Inc.

Officers: Robert Folkerth/Pres.

Directors: John Folkerth/Chmn.

Financial Data: Fiscal Year End:04/02 Latest Annual Data: 4/2/2005

Year	Sales	Net Income
2005	$13,359,000	-$771,000
2004	$13,793,000	$130,000
2003	$15,336,000	$100,000

Curr. Assets:	$3,810,000	*Curr. Liab.:*	$2,679,000		
Plant, Equip.:	$2,658,000	*Total Liab.:*	$5,053,000	*Indic. Yr. Divd.:*	NA
Total Assets:	$7,049,000	*Net Worth:*	$1,996,000	*Debt/ Equity:*	NA

Shore Bancshares Inc

18 E Dover St., Easton, MD, 21601; *PH:* 1-410-822-1400; *Fax:* 1-410-820-4238; *http://* www.shbi.net

General - Incorporation	MD	Stock - Price on:12/24/2007	$28.49
Employees	285	Stock Exchange	NDQ
Auditor	Stegman & Co	Ticker Symbol	SHBI
Stk Agt	Registrar & Transfer Co	Outstanding Shares	8,380,000
Counsel	NA	E.P.S.	$1.60
DUNS No.	NA	Shareholders	NA

Business: The group's principal activity is to provide commercial and consumer banking services through 12 branches and 16 ATM's. These services are provided to individuals, businesses and other organizations in kent, queen anne's, caroline, talbot and dorchester counties in Maryland. The group accepts commercial checking, savings, certificate of deposit and overnight investment sweep accounts. The commercial lending portfolio includes working capital loans, lines of credit, term loans, account receivable financing, real estate acquisition development, construction loans and letters of credit. The consumer loans provided by the group include mortgage loans, home improvement, installment personal loans, credit cards, automobile and other financing. Other services include merchant credit card clearing, direct deposit of payroll, Internet and telephone banking, discount brokerage and mutual funds. On 01-Apr-2004, the group acquired midstate bancorp, inc.

Primary SIC and add'l.: 6712 6021

CIK No: 0001035092

Subsidiaries: Centreville National Bank of Maryland, Elliott Wilson Insurance, LLC, Mubell Finance, LLC, Shore Pension Services, LLC., The Avon-Dixon Agency, LLC, The Felton Bank, The Talbot Bank of Easton, Maryland, Wye Financial Services, LLC

Officers: Moorhead W. Vermilye/Dir., CEO, Pres., Susan E. Leaverton/Treasurer/$209,290.00, Lloyd L. Beatty/Dir., Exec. VP, COO/$315,500.00, Carol I. Brownawell/Sec.

Directors: Moorhead W. Vermilye/Dir., CEO, Pres., Christopher F. Spurry/Chmn., Lloyd L. Beatty/Dir., Exec. VP, COO, Thomas H. Evans/Dir., W. Edwin Kee/Dir., Mark M. Freestate/Dir., Herbert L. Andrew/Dir., Blenda W. Armistead/Dir., Richard C. Granville/Dir., Winfield F. Trice/Dir., Walter Edwin Kee/Dir., Neil R. Lecompte/Dir., Paul M. Bowman/Dir., Jerry F. Pierson/Dir., William W. Duncan/Dir.

Owners: Lloyd L. Beatty, William W. Duncan, Christopher F. Spurry, Richard C. Granville/1.76%, Daniel T. Cannon, Mark M. Freestate, Neil R. LeCompte, Edwin W. Kee, Jerry F. Pierson, Blenda W. Armistead, Herbert L. Andrew/1.05%, Susan E. Leaverton, Insiders/6.08%, Thomas H. Evans, Moorhead W. Vermilye/1.98% *(17 Owners included in Index)*

Financial Data: Fiscal Year End:12/31   Latest Annual Data: 12/31/2006

Year	Sales		Net Income
2006	$70,810,000		$13,554,000
2005	$58,882,000		$12,888,000
2004	$49,172,000		$10,198,000
Curr. Assets:	$85,138,000	Curr. Liab.:	$805,772,000
Plant, Equip.:	$16,371,000	Total Liab.:	$834,321,000 Indic. Yr. Divd.: $0.640
Total Assets:	$945,649,000	Net Worth:	$111,327,000 Debt/ Equity: 0.2381

Shore Community Bank

1216 Rte. 37 E, Toms River, NJ, 08753; *PH:* 1-732-240-5800; *http://* www.shorecommunitybank.com

General - Incorporation		Stock - Price on:12/24/2007	$12.75
Employees	NA	Stock Exchange	OTC
Auditor	NA	Ticker Symbol	SHRC
Stk Agt	Registrar & Transfer Co	Outstanding Shares	NA
Counsel	NA	E.P.S.	NA
DUNS No.	NA	Shareholders	NA

Business: The groups principal activities include providing banking and financial services. Services of the group include checking accounts, savings accounts, certificates of deposit, installment loans, real estate mortgage loans, commercial loans, traveler's checks, safe deposit boxes, night depository and automated teller services. The group operates from the United States.

Primary SIC and add'l.: 6022

CIK No:

Officers: Theodore D. Bessler/Dir., CEO, Pres., Philip Garfinkel/Dir., Corp. Sec., Gary L. Green/Counsel, Carmine Derosa/Residential Mortgage Specialist - Mortgage Lending, Robert T. English/Exec. VP, CFO, COO, Vincent Dalessandro/Sr. VP, Sr. Loan Officer, James Feeney/VP, Lending Officer, Oliva Mele/VP, Branch Administrator, Security Officer, Dawn Tortoriello/VP, Lending Officer, Samaris Tassinaro/Assist. VP, Lending Officer, George Fisher/VP, Business Development Officer, Paul Orzechowski/VP - SBA Lending, Diana Doyle/Assist. VP, Branch Mgr., Phyllis Martin/Assist. VP, Branch Mgr., Rosemary Cardone/Assist. VP, Controller *(21 Officers included in Index)*

Directors: Theodore D. Bessler/Dir., CEO, Pres., Zev Rosen/Chmn., Leonard Silidker/Dir., Harry Jay Levin/Dir., David Rosen/Dir., Earl F. Sutton/Dir., Daniel J. Vitale/Dir., Louis Amato/Member - Advisory Board, Richard J. Banach/Member - Advisory Board, Jerry Boisseau/Dir., Howard Butensky/Dir., Dennis Cirone/Dir., Rosanne Citta/Dir., Harry Disbrow/Dir., Philip Garfinkel/Dir., Corp. Sec. *(47 Directors included in Index)*

Shore Financial Corp

25020 Shore Pkwy., Onley, VA, 23418; *PH:* 1-757-787-1335; *Fax:* 1-757-789-3745; *http://* www.shorebank.com

General - Incorporation	VA	Stock - Price on:12/24/2007	$13.05
Employees	87	Stock Exchange	NDQ
Auditor	Goodman & Co. LLP	Ticker Symbol	SHBK
Stk Agt	Fulton Financial Advisors	Outstanding Shares	2,500,000
Counsel	Leclair Ryan	E.P.S.	$1.075
DUNS No.	09-655-9471	Shareholders	NA

Business: The group's principle activity is to provide banking services through its subsidiary shore investments inc. It provides checking, cash management, credit card merchant services, employee benefits and sweep accounts. The lending activities include loan options including operating lines of credit, equipment loans and real estate loans. In addition, the group provides non-deposit investment products including stocks, bonds, mutual funds and insurance products. It operates through seven banking offices and six ATMs. The group also delivers its services through the Internet and telephone. The banking offices are located on the eastern shore of Virginia and Maryland, including the counties of accomack, northampton, salisbury and wicomico county.

Primary SIC and add'l.: 6712 6022

CIK No: 0001045690

Subsidiaries: Shore Investments, Inc.

Officers: Scott C. Harvard/Dir., CEO, Pres./$256,343.00, Lynn M. Badger/Investor Relations Contact, Steven M. Belote/Sr. VP, CFO/$119,227.00, Anderson J. Duer/Sr. VP - Lending/$113,108.00, Brenda L. Payne/Sr. VP - Operations

Directors: Scott C. Harvard/Dir., CEO, Pres., Henry P. Custis/Chmn., Page D. Elmore/Dir., Dixon L. Leatherbury/Dir., Terrell E. Boothe/Dir., Richard F. Hall/Dir., Lloyd J. Kellam/Dir.

Owners: J. Anderson Duer, Terrell E. Boothe/1.00%, Insiders/19.10%, Henry P. Custis/7.20%, L. Dixon Leatherbury/1.90%, Steven M. Belote, Richard F. Hall/2.30%, Scott C. Harvard/3.80%, D. Page Elmore, Lloyd J. Kellam

Financial Data: Fiscal Year End:12/31   Latest Annual Data: 12/31/2006

Year	Sales		Net Income
2006	$18,504,000		$2,933,000
2005	$15,230,000		$2,675,000
2004	$12,617,000		$2,353,000
Curr. Assets:	$9,470,000	Curr. Liab.: $233,336,000	P/E Ratio: 12.14
Plant, Equip.:	$7,044,000	Total Liab.: $234,550,000	Indic. Yr. Divd.: $0.280
Total Assets:	$260,676,000	Net Worth: $26,126,000	Debt/ Equity: NA

Shotgun Energy Corp

Formerly: Avalon Energy Corp
1288 Alberni St., No. 809, Vancouver, BC, V6E4R8; *PH:* 1-604-664-0499; *http://* www.avalonenergy.ws

General - Incorporation	NV	Stock - Price on:12/24/2007	$0.072
Employees	NA	Stock Exchange	NA
Auditor	L.I. Bradford & Co., LLC	Ticker Symbol	NA
Stk Agt	Int Registrar and Transfer Agency	Outstanding Shares	NA
Counsel	NA	E.P.S.	NA
DUNS No.	NA	Shareholders	NA

Business: The groups principle activity is to explore minerals and natural gas. The group operates from the United States and Canada.

Primary SIC and add'l.: 1382

CIK No: 0000746631

Officers: Robert Klein/Dir., CEO, Pres., Carlton Parfitt/Dir., CFO, Sec.

Directors: Robert Klein/Dir., CEO, Pres., Carlton Parfitt/Dir., CFO, Sec., Jack M. Ashton/Member - Advisory Board, Patrick T. Webb/Member - Advisory Board, Robert Milam/Member - Advisory Board

Owners: Carlton Parfitt, Insiders, Cede & Co/65.98%, Robert Klein

Financial Data: Fiscal Year End:12/31   Latest Annual Data: 12/31/2006

Year	Sales		Net Income
2006	NA		-$738,000
2005	NA		-$1,951,000
2004	NA		-$1,678,000
Curr. Assets:	$373,000	Curr. Liab.: $147,000	
Plant, Equip.:	$1,066,000	Total Liab.: $147,000	Indic. Yr. Divd.: NA
Total Assets:	$1,675,000	Net Worth: $1,528,000	Debt/ Equity: NA

Shuffle Master Inc

1106 Palms Airport Dr., Las Vegas, NV, 89119; *PH:* 1-702-897-7150; *Fax:* 1-702-897-2284; *http://* www.shufflemaster.com; *Email:* shfl@shufflemaster.com

General - Incorporation	MN	Stock - Price on:12/24/2007	$17.5
Employees	550	Stock Exchange	NDQ
Auditor	Deloitte & Touche LLP	Ticker Symbol	SHFL
Stk Agt	Wells Fargo Bank, N.A.	Outstanding Shares	35,220,000
Counsel	Larkin, Hoffman, Daly & Lindgren	E.P.S.	$0.44
DUNS No.	78-373-4411	Shareholders	NA

Business: The group's principle activities are to develop, manufacture and market technology-based products for the gaming industry. The group operates two reportable segments namely, utility products and entertainment products. Utility products include shufflers, chip sorting machines and ITS product lines. Entertainment products include proprietary table games, table master products and shuffle up. The group's quarterly revenue for July 2007 was 45.13 millions of USD.

Primary SIC and add'l.: 3999 7372 3944

CIK No: 0000718789

Subsidiaries: CARD Casinos Austria Research and Development Limited, CARD LLC, CARD-Australasia Limited, Gaming Products Pty Ltd, Shuffle Master Australasia Holdings Pty Ltd, Shuffle Master Australasia Pty Ltd, Shuffle Master Australia Pty Ltd, Shuffle Master GMBH, Shuffle Master GMBH & Co KG (dba CARD), Shuffle Master Holding GMBH, Shuffle Master Holding GMBH & Co Financing Consulting-KEG, Shuffle Master International Limited, Shuffle Master International, Inc., Shuffle Master Management-Services GMBH, Shuffle Master of Mississippi, Inc. 17 Subsidiaries included in the Index

Officers: Mark L. Yoseloff/Chmn., CEO, Pedro Gonzalez/Accounting Exec. - Americas, Nile Konicek/Accounting Exec. - Americas, Matt Pijnappels/Accounting Exec. - Americas, Kate Reinhart/Accounting Exec. - Americas, Kyle Samuels/Accounting Exec. - Americas, Chris Harbison/Accounting Exec. - Americas, Ken Swanson/Accounting Exec. - Americas, Steve Venuto/Sr. Sales Executive - Americas, Maurits Vander Cruyssen/Sales Consultant Canada, Alexander Grohs/Dir. - Sales, Europe, Africa, Richard L. Baldwin/Sr. VP, CFO, Georg Fekete/Product Dir. - Europe, Africa, Wolfgang Scheidl/Product Mgr. - Europe, Africa, Roland Schultz/Sales Contact - Europe, Africa *(31 Officers included in Index)*

Directors: Mark L. Yoseloff/Chmn., CEO, Garry W. Saunders/Dir., Louis Castle/Dir., Todd D. Jordan/Dir., Phil Peckman/Dir.

Owners: Transamerica Investment Management, LLC/6.45%, Kayne Anderson Rudnick Investment Management, LLC/5.69%, FMR Corp./7.65%, Insiders/6.10%, Columbia Wanger Asset Management, L.P./8.46%, Paul C. Meyer, Louis Castle, Garry W. Saunders, Richard Baldwin, Todd Jordan, Mark L. Yoseloff/3.80%, Brooke R. Dunn, Baron Capital Group,Inc./8.10%, Ken Robson

Financial Data: Fiscal Year End:10/31   Latest Annual Data: 10/31/2006

Year	Sales		Net Income
2006	$162,991,000		$5,093,000
2005	$112,860,000		$29,180,000
2004	$84,783,000		$24,144,000
Curr. Assets:	$89,396,000	Curr. Liab.: $108,291,000	P/E Ratio: 39.77
Plant, Equip.:	$21,061,000	Total Liab.: $272,658,000	Indic. Yr. Divd.: NA
Total Assets:	$305,207,000	Net Worth: $32,549,000	Debt/ Equity: NA

Shumate Industries Inc

12060 Fm 3083, Conroe, TX, 77301; *PH:* 1-936-539-9533; *http://* www.shumateinc.com

General - Incorporation	DE	**Stock** - Price on:12/24/2007	$1.88
Employees	83	Stock Exchange	OTC
Auditor	Malone & Bailey, PC	Ticker Symbol	SHMT
Stk Agt	American Registrar & Transfer Co	Outstanding Shares	20,020,000
Counsel	NA	E.P.S.	-$0.31
DUNS No.	NA	Shareholders	NA

Business: The group operates through its subsidiaries whose principle activities include contract machining and manufacturing, and·a valve product line. The group markets its products under the tradename Hemiwedge(R). The group operates from the United States.

Primary SIC and add'l.: 3498 3496 3441 3444 3494 3469

CIK No: 0001085254

Subsidiaries: Hemiwedge Valve Corporation, Shumate Machine Works, Inc.

Officers: Larry C. Shumate/55/Chmn., CEO, Pres./$231,770.00, Russell T. Clark/42/Dir., VP, COO/$177,770.00, Matthew C. Flemming/39/Dir., CFO, Exec. VP, Treasurer, Sec./$234,450.00, Gunter Maurer/VP - Manufacturing, Stan Allen/VP - Technology, Business Development

Directors: Larry C. Shumate/55/Chmn., CEO, Pres., Russell T. Clark/42/Dir., VP, COO, Matthew C. Flemming/39/Dir., CFO, Exec. VP, Treasurer, Sec., Francis X. Marshik/81/Dir., Steven B. Erikson/40/Dir., Leo B. Womack/65/Dir., Kenton Chickering/72/Dir., Frank Jungers/81/Dir.

Owners: Kenton Chickering, Steven B. Erikson, Stillwater National Bank & Trust Company/12.19%, Whalehaven Capital Fund, Ltd./5.34%, Insiders/28.97%, Matthew C. Flemming/6.80%, Frank X. Marshik/2.12%, Francis Jungers/2.30%, Larry C. Shumate/9.02%, Leo B. Womack, Russell T. Clark/7.30%

Financial Data: *Fiscal Year End:*12/31   *Latest Annual Data:* 12/31/2006

Year		Sales		Net Income
2006		$7,720,000		-$1,309,000
2005		$4,965,000		$1,978,000
2004		$3,417,000		$1,184,000
Curr. Assets:	$3,194,000	Curr. Liab.:	$2,855,000	
Plant, Equip.:	$2,303,000	Total Liab.:	$5,790,000	Indic. Yr. Divd.: NA
Total Assets:	$5,909,000	Net Worth:	$118,000	Debt/ Equity: NA

Shutterfly Inc

2800 Bridge Pkwy., Ste. 101, Redwood City, CA, 94065; *PH:* 1-650-610-5200; *Fax:* 1-650-654-1299; *http://* www.shutterfly.com; *Email:* irinquiries@shutterfly.com

General - Incorporation	DE	**Stock** - Price on:12/24/2007	$22.92
Employees	275	Stock Exchange	NDQ
Auditor	Pricewaterhousecoopers LLP	Ticker Symbol	SFLY
Stk Agt	Mellon Investor Services LLC	Outstanding Shares	24,010,000
Counsel	NA	E.P.S.	$0.41
DUNS No.	NA	Shareholders	NA

Business: The groups principle activity is to selling photo based products. The products of the group include greeting cards, personalized calendars and photo books. In June 2005, the group acquired Memory Matrix, Inc. The group operates from the United States of America. The group's quarterly revenue for September 2007 was 32.60 millions of USD.

Primary SIC and add'l.: 7384 7379 7375

CIK No: 0001125920

Subsidiaries: Memory Matrix, Inc

Officers: Jeffrey T. Housenbold/Dir., CEO, Pres./$742,312.00, Stephen E. Recht/CFO/$458,901.00, Andy Young/Chief Marketing Officer, Jeannine Smith/Sr. VP - Operations/$313,157.00, Kathryn Olson/Chief Marketing Officer, Dwayne Black/Sr. VP - Operations, Stanford Au/Sr. VP - Technology/$389,655.00, Doug Galen/Sr. VP - Business, Corporate Development/$370,078.00, Doug Appleton/VP - Legal, Bjorn Hansen/VP - Manufacturing Operations, Jeffrey Whitehead/CIO, VP - Internet Operations, Judith McGarry/Investor Relations Officer, Peter Elarde/VP - Product Marketing, Janice Gaub/VP - Consumer Marketing, John Kaelle/VP - Finance *(20 Officers included in Index)*

Directors: Jeffrey T. Housenbold/Dir., CEO, Pres., Philip A. Marineau/Chmn., Stephen J. Killeen/Dir., Nancy J. Schoendorf/Dir., Jim White/Dir., Patricia A. House/53/Dir., Pat House/Dir., Eric Keller/Dir.

Owners: Douglas J. Galen/1.00%, Jeannine M. Smith Thomas/2.00%, Mohr, Davidow Ventures/17.00%, Eric J. Keller, Nancy J. Schoendorf/17.00%, James H. Clark/29.90%, James N. White/5.00%, Stephen J. Killeen, Insiders/32.50%, Stanford S. Au, Stephen E. Recht/1.30%, Jeffrey T. Housenbold/5.40%, Sutter Hill Ventures/6.70%, Philip A. Marineau, Patricia A. House

Financial Data: *Fiscal Year End:*12/31   *Latest Annual Data:* 12/31/2006

Year		Sales		Net Income
2006		$123,353,000		$5,798,000
2005		$83,902,000		$28,932,000
2004		$54,499,000		$3,709,000
Curr. Assets:	$128,597,000	Curr. Liab.:	$26,432,000	P/E Ratio: 55.90
Plant, Equip.:	$30,919,000	Total Liab.:	$28,834,000	Indic. Yr. Divd.: NA
Total Assets:	$180,160,000	Net Worth:	$151,326,000	Debt/ Equity: 0.0052

Si Financial Group Inc

803 Main St., Willimantic, CT, 06226; *PH:* 1-860-423-4581; *Fax:* 1-860-423-0319; *http://* www.savingsinstitute.com

General - Incorporation	US	**Stock** - Price on:12/24/2007	$12
Employees	225	Stock Exchange	NDQ
Auditor	Mcgladrey & Pullen, LLP	Ticker Symbol	SIFI
Stk Agt	Registrar & Transfer Co	Outstanding Shares	12,420,000
Counsel	NA	E.P.S.	$0.21
DUNS No.	NA	Shareholders	NA

Business: The groups principle activity is to provide financial services. The group provides services include insurance, trust and investment services. The group originates deposits from one- to four-family residential, multi-family and commercial real estate, commercial business and consumer loans. The group operates from United States.

Primary SIC and add'l.: NA

CIK No: 0001292580

Subsidiaries: 803 Financial Corp., Savings Institute Bank and Trust Company, SI Capital Trust I, SI Mortgage Company, SI Realty Company, Inc.

Officers: Rheo A. Brouillard/Dir., CEO, Pres., Brian J. Hull/CFO, Exec. VP, Sandra M. Mitchell/VP, Corp. Sec., Michael J. Moran/59/Sr. VP, Sr. Credit Officer, Sonia M. Dudas/57/Sr. VP, Sr. Trust Officer, Laurie L. Gervais/43/VP, Dir. - Human Resources

Directors: Rheo A. Brouillard/Dir., CEO, Pres., Henry P. Hinckley/Chmn., Robert O. Gillard/Dir., Roger Engle/Dir., Donna M. Evan/Dir., Robert C. Cushman/Dir., Steven H. Townsend/Dir., Mark D. Alliod/Dir., Michael R. Garvey/Dir.

Owners: Insiders/3.60%, Roger Engle, SI Bancorp, MHC/58.70%, Henry P. Hinckley, Brian J. Hull, Mark D. Alliod, Rheo A. Brouillard, Sonia M. Dudas, Donna M. Evan, Steven H. Townsend, Robert C. Cushman, Robert O. Gillard, Michael J. Moran, Laurie L. Gervais, Michael R. Garvey

Financial Data: *Fiscal Year End:*12/31   *Latest Annual Data:* 12/31/2006

Year		Sales		Net Income
2006		$49,319,000		$2,778,000
2005		$40,215,000		$3,397,000
2004		$32,954,000		$1,288,000
Curr. Assets:	$29,932,000	Curr. Liab.:	$655,940,000	P/E Ratio: 57.14
Plant, Equip.:	$10,512,000	Total Liab.:	$674,651,000	Indic. Yr. Divd.: $0.160
Total Assets:	$757,037,000	Net Worth:	$82,386,000	Debt/ Equity: 0.2069

SI International Inc

12012 Sunset Hills Rd., Ste. 800, Reston, VA, 20190; *PH:* 1-703-234-7000; *Fax:* 1-703-234-7500; *http://* www.si-intl.com; *Email:* investors@si-intl.com

General - Incorporation	DE	**Stock** - Price on:12/24/2007	$32.5
Employees	4,300	Stock Exchange	NDQ
Auditor	Ernst & Young LLP	Ticker Symbol	SINT
Stk Agt	American Stock Transfer & Trust Co.	Outstanding Shares	13,110,000
Counsel	Austin Brown & Wood	E.P.S.	$1.59
DUNS No.	NA	Shareholders	NA

Business: The group's principal activities are to provide information technology and network solutions primarily to the federal government. The group combines the technological and industrial expertise to provide a full spectrum of state-of-the-practice solutions and services, from design and development to implementation and operations, to assist the clients in achieving their missions.the group also provides its services to a small number of commercial entities. The areas of services of the group include software development, systems consulting, esolutions, information security, learning solutions, systems engineering, and network solutions mission-critical outsourcing. The clients of the group include the U.S. Air force space command, U.S. Army, the department of state, the immigration and naturalization service and the intelligence community. On 21-Jan-2004, the group acquired matcom international corp.

Primary SIC and add'l.: 7375 7372

CIK No: 0001143363

Subsidiaries: Bridge Technology Corporation, MATCOM International Corporation, Shenandoah Electronic Intelligence, Inc., SI International Application Development, Inc., SI International Consulting, Inc., SI International Engineering, Inc., SI International Learning, Inc, SI International SEIT, Inc., SI International Technology Services, Inc., SI International Telecom Corporation, Zen Technology, Inc.

Officers: Bradford S. Antle/CEO, Pres./$745,417.00, Ray J. Oleson/Exec. Chmn./$510,578.00, Marc Tommer/Sr. VP - Finance, Accounting, Lee Stratton/Sr. VP - Human Resources, Doug Berry/VP - Civilian Agency Programs, Esther Burgess/VP - GSA, Gwac Programs, Alliant PMO, Lisa Douds/VP - Systems Services Division, Andy Ganias/VP, Controller, Alan Hill/VP - Corporate Communications, Investor Relations, Francis Moody/VP - Business Process Outsourcing, Earl Pedersen/VP - Enterprise Applications, E, Government, Patricia Pickett/Sr. VP - Business Development, Jack Reilly/VP - Internal Audits, William Smithson/VP - Financial Systems, Thomas B. Pettit/Sr. VP - Applications Development Business Unit *(45 Officers included in Index)*

Directors: Ray J. Oleson/Exec. Chmn., Maureen Baginski/Dir., Walter J. Culver/Dir., Dennis J. Reimer/Dir., Edward H. Sproat/Dir., Thomas R. Marsh/Dir., James E. Crawford/Dir., Walter C. Florence/Dir., John Stenbit/Dir., Charles A. Bowsher/Dir.

Owners: Marylynn Stowers, Maureen A. Baginski, John P. Stenbit, James E. Crawford, Neuberger Berman Inc./5.80%, Insiders/8.10%, Thomas E. Lloyd, Ray J. Oleson/2.50%, Harry D. Gatanas, Edward H. Sproat, Leslee H. Gault, R. Thomas Marsh, Dennis J. Reimer, Wells Fargo& Co/7.80%, FMR Corp/14.00% *(21 Owners included in Index)*

Financial Data: *Fiscal Year End:*12/31   *Latest Annual Data:* 12/30/2006

Year		Sales		Net Income
2006		$461,970,000		$20,153,000
2005		$397,919,000		$16,937,000
2004		$262,306,000		$10,877,000
Curr. Assets:	$134,341,000	Curr. Liab.:	$58,318,000	P/E Ratio: 20.83
Plant, Equip.:	$5,908,000	Total Liab.:	$167,826,000	Indic. Yr. Divd.: NA
Total Assets:	$335,695,000	Net Worth:	$167,869,000	Debt/ Equity: 0.2830

Siberian Energy Group Inc

275 Madison Ave., 6th Fl., New York, NY, 10016; *PH:* 1-212-828-3011; *http://* www.siberianenergy.com

General - Incorporation	NV	**Stock** - Price on:12/24/2007	$1.58
Employees	21	Stock Exchange	OTC
Auditor	Lumsden & McCormick, LLP	Ticker Symbol	SIBN
Stk Agt	American Stock Transfer & Trust Co.	Outstanding Shares	15,030,000
Counsel	NA	E.P.S.	-$0.15
DUNS No.	NA	Shareholders	NA

Business: The groups principle activity is seeking opportunities for investment in and/or acquisition of small to medium companies in Russia, specifically in the oil and gas industry. In December 2006, the group acquired oil and gas related geological information on the Karabashki zone of Khanty-Mansiysk Autonomous district from Key Brokerage, LLC. The group operates from Russia.

Primary SIC and add'l.: 1381

CIK No: 0001301299

Subsidiaries: KONDANEFTEGAZ, LLC, SIBERIAN ENERGY GROUP, Zauralneftegez Limited

Officers: David Zaikin/Founder, Chmn., CEO, Elena Pochapski/Dir., CFO, Vladimir Eret/COO, Technical Dir., Vladimir Orlov/Representative, Moscow

Directors: David Zaikin/Founder, Chmn., CEO, Tim Peara/Vice Chmn., Elena Pochapski/Dir., CFO, Oleg Zhuravlev/Dir.

Owners: Vladimir Eret/2.00%, Oleg V. Zhuravlev/2.40%, Tim Peara/3.60%, Elena Pochapski/5.20%, David Zaikin/9.10%, Sergey Potapov/2.00%, Insiders/21.90%, Victor Repin/15.00%

Financial Data: *Fiscal Year End:*12/31 *Latest Annual Data:* 12/31/2006

Year	Sales	Net Income
2006	$360,000	-$3,080,000
2005	$446,000	-$882,000
2004	NA	-$834,000

Curr. Assets:	$117,000	**Curr. Liab.:**	$1,884,000		
Plant, Equip.:	$2,703,000	**Total Liab.:**	$1,884,000	**Indic. Yr. Divd.:**	NA
Total Assets:	$2,819,000	**Net Worth:**	$935,000	**Debt/ Equity:**	NA

Sibling Entertainment Group Holdings Inc

Formerly: Sona Development Corp
2610-1066 W Hastings St., Vancouver, BC, V6E 3X2; *PH:* 1-604-602-1717

General - Incorporation	NV	Stock- Price on:12/24/2007	NA
Employees	NA	Stock Exchange	OTC
Auditor	Dale Matheson Carr-Hilton LaBonte LLP	Ticker Symbol	SIBE
Stk Agt	Interwest Transfer	Outstanding Shares	NA
Counsel	NA	E.P.S	NA
DUNS No.	NA	Shareholders	NA

Business: The groups principal activities include involving in the development of alternative energy products. The group operates from the United States.

Primary SIC and add'l.: 7990

CIK No: 0001099728

Officers: Nora Coccaro/51/Dir., CEO, CFO, Principal Accounting Officer

Directors: Nora Coccaro/51/Dir., CEO, CFO, Principal Accounting Officer, Mitchell Maxwell/55/Chmn., Victoria Maxwell/44/Dir., James Cardwell/47/Dir., Richard Bernstein/54/Dir.

Owners: Michael Baybak/31.23%, Insiders/1.53%, Nora Coccaro/1.53%

Curr. Assets:	$0	**Curr. Liab.:**	$233,000		
Plant, Equip.:	NA	**Total Liab.:**	$233,000	**Indic. Yr. Divd.:**	NA
Total Assets:	$0	**Net Worth:**	-$233,000	**Debt/ Equity:**	NA

Siboney Corp

PO Box 221029, 325 N Kirkwood Rd., Ste. 300, St. Louis, MO, 63122; *PH:* 1-314-822-3163; *Fax:* 1-314-822-3197; *http://* www.siboney.com

General - Incorporation	MD	Stock- Price on:12/24/2007	$0.13
Employees	46	Stock Exchange	OTC
Auditor	RubinBrown LLP	Ticker Symbol	SBON
Stk Agt	Registrar & Transfer Co	Outstanding Shares	16,920,000
Counsel	Thompson Coburn LLP	E.P.S	-$0.05
DUNS No.	00-696-8457	Shareholders	NA

Business: The group's principal activities are to publish and distribute educational software products through its wholly owned subsidiary siboney learning group. It publishes educational software in math, reading, language arts and science for students and teachers in grade kindergarten through adult. The software enables students to master key skills, which are stressed on standardized tests and in textbooks. The group publishes over 200 titles for macintosh, windows, dos and apple ii operating systems. The group offers distinct product lines: gamco educational software, orchard teacher's choice software, teacher support software, inc and educational activities software.

Primary SIC and add'l.: 7372

CIK No: 0000090057

Subsidiaries: Siboney Learning Group, Inc

Officers: Timothy J. Tegeler/Dir., Chmn., CEO/$89,291.00, William D. Edwards/Dir., Exec. VP, CFO, COO/$226,145.00, Rebecca M. Braddock/Dir., VP, Sec., Rubin Brown/Accountant

Directors: Timothy J. Tegeler/Dir., Chmn., CEO, William D. Edwards/Dir., Exec. VP, CFO, COO, Rebecca M. Braddock/Dir., VP, Sec., Lewis B. Shepley/Dir., John J. Riffle/Dir., Jerome W. Thomasson/Dir.

Owners: Lewis B. Shepley/4.87%, Jerome W. Thomasson/1.53%, William D. Edwards/3.41%, Rebecca M. Braddock/2.86%, Timothy J. Tegeler/18.49%, U.S. Bancorp/7.37%, Insiders/31.21%, John J. Riffle/1.67%

Financial Data: *Fiscal Year End:*12/31 *Latest Annual Data:* 12/31/2006

Year	Sales	Net Income
2006	$6,296,000	-$1,013,000
2005	$7,545,000	-$1,236,000
2004	$10,183,000	$101,000

Curr. Assets:	$1,505,000	**Curr. Liab.:**	$779,000		
Plant, Equip.:	$132,000	**Total Liab.:**	$3,348,000	**Indic. Yr. Divd.:**	NA
Total Assets:	$6,023,000	**Net Worth:**	$2,676,000	**Debt/ Equity:**	1.0797

Siclone Industries Inc

378 N Main, Ste. 124, Layton, UT, 84041; *PH:* 1-801-497-9075

General - Incorporation	DE	Stock- Price on:12/24/2007	$0.0001
Employees	NA	Stock Exchange	OTC
Auditor	Child, Van Wagoner & Bradshaw, PLLC	Ticker Symbol	SICL
Stk Agt	NA	Outstanding Shares	NA
Counsel	NA	E.P.S	NA
DUNS No.	NA	Shareholders	NA

Business: The groups principal activity is intends to seek, investigate, and if warranted, acquire an interest in a business opportunity. The group operates from the United States.

Primary SIC and add'l.: 6770

CIK No: 0001083446

Officers: Paul Adams/49/Dir., CEO, Pres.

Directors: Paul Adams/49/Dir., CEO, Pres.

Owners: Business Growth Funding, Inc./2.50%, Minnie Merchants, Inc./2.50%, Venture Resources, Inc./2.50%, Brad S. Shepherd/42.80%

Financial Data: *Fiscal Year End:*12/31 *Latest Annual Data:* 12/31/2006

Year	Sales	Net Income
2006	NA	-$27,000
2005	NA	-$13,000
2004	NA	-$10,000

Curr. Assets:	$0	**Curr. Liab.:**	$82,000		
Plant, Equip.:	NA	**Total Liab.:**	$82,000	**Indic. Yr. Divd.:**	NA
Total Assets:	$0	**Net Worth:**	-$82,000	**Debt/ Equity:**	NA

Siebel Systems Inc

2207 Bridgepointe Pk.way, San Mateo, CA, 94404; *PH:* 1-650-477-5000; *http://* www.oracle.com

General - Incorporation	DE	Stock- Price on:12/24/2007	NA
Employees	NA	Stock Exchange	NA
Auditor	KPMG LLP	Ticker Symbol	NA
Stk Agt	Mellon Investor Services LLC	Outstanding Shares	NA
Counsel	Cooley Godward LLP	E.P.S	NA
DUNS No.	80-885-6512	Shareholders	NA

Business: The group's principal activity is to provide business applications software for the front office. The group also provides implementation, training and customer support services. Customers of the group include Accenture Ltd, Cisco Systems Inc, IBM Corp, Microsoft Corp and Unisys Corp. The group operates in Argentina, Australia, Austria, Belgium, Brazil, Canada, China, Columbia, Czech Republic, Denmark, Finland, France, Germany, India, Ireland, Italy, Japan, Korea, Mexico, Netherlands, Norway, Portugal, Singapore, South Africa, Spain, Sweden, Switzerland, the United Kingdom and the United States.

Primary SIC and add'l.: 7372 7373

CIK No: 0001006835

Subsidiaries: BankFrame Eontec Inc., Comercial Siebel Systems Chile Limitada, Corporate Training Systems Limited, Do-Holding B.V., Do-Opleidingstechnologie B.V., edocs Asia-Pacific Pty Ltd, edocs Europe Netherlands B.V., edocs Europe UK Ltd, edocs International, Inc., edocs Soultions, Inc., edocs, Inc., edocs, Inc., Malaysia Representative Office, Eontec Australia Pty Ltd, Eontec B.V., Eontec Financial Solutions Limited 94 Subsidiaries included in the Index

Siebert Financial Corp

885 3rd Ave., 17th Fl., New York, NY, 10022; *PH:* 1-212-644-2400; *Fax:* 1-212-486-2784; *http://* www.siebertnet.com

General - Incorporation	NY	Stock- Price on:12/24/2007	$4.1
Employees	90	Stock Exchange	NDQ
Auditor	Eisner LLP	Ticker Symbol	SIEB
Stk Agt	Eisner LLP	Outstanding Shares	22,210,000
Counsel	NA	E.P.S	$0.14
DUNS No.	00-697-9157	Shareholders	NA

Business: The group's principle activity is to provide discount brokerage services to customers, investment banking services to institutional clients and trading securities. The group operates through its wholly owned subsidiary, muriel siebert & co., inc. The group acts as senior manager, co-manager or otherwise participating in the underwriting or sales syndicates of municipal, corporate debt and equity, government agency and mortgage/asset backed securities issues. The group currently maintains seven retail discount brokerage offices in the United States. The group's quarterly revenue for September 2007 was 7.45 millions of USD.

Primary SIC and add'l.: 6211 6282

CIK No: 0000065596

Subsidiaries: Muriel Siebert & Co., Inc., National Financial Services Corp, Siebert Womans Financial Network, Inc

Officers: Muriel F. Siebert/75/Chairwoman, Dir., CEO, Pres., Jeanne M. Rosendale/43/Exec. VP, General Counsel/$445,000.00, Ameen Esmail/49/Dir., Exec. VP/$270,000.00, Joseph M. Ramos/49/CFO, Exec. VP/$336,250.00, Daniel Iesu/48/Sec./$200,000.00

Directors: Muriel F. Siebert/75/Chairwoman, Dir., CEO, Pres., Ameen Esmail/49/Dir., Exec. VP, Patricia L. Francy/62/Dir., Leonard M. Leiman/76/Dir., Jane H. Macon/61/Dir., Robert P. Mazzarella/61/Dir., Nancy S. Peterson/74/Dir.

Owners: Nancy S. Peterson, Insiders/90.00%, Muriel F. Siebert/89.90%, Jeanne M. Rosendale, Robert P. Mazzarella, Leonard M. Leiman, Daniel Iesu, Patricia L. Francy, Jane H. Macon, Ameen Esmail

Financial Data: *Fiscal Year End:*12/31 *Latest Annual Data:* 12/31/2006

Year	Sales	Net Income
2006	$32,619,000	$3,425,000
2005	$31,172,000	$1,863,000
2004	$28,104,000	$533,000

Curr. Assets:	$36,374,000	**Curr. Liab.:**	$6,460,000	**P/E Ratio:**	24.12
Plant, Equip.:	$510,000	**Total Liab.:**	$6,460,000	**Indic. Yr. Divd.:**	$0.200
Total Assets:	$46,869,000	**Net Worth:**	$40,409,000	**Debt/ Equity:**	NA

SIELOX Inc

Formerly: Dynabazaar Inc
170 E Ninth Ave., Runnemede, NJ, 08078; *PH:* 1-856-861-4579; *http://* www.fairmarket.com

General - Incorporation	DE	Stock- Price on:12/24/2007	$0.27
Employees	NA	Stock Exchange	NA
Auditor	Rothstein, Kass & Co, P.C	Ticker Symbol	NA
Stk Agt	Computershare Investor Services LLC	Outstanding Shares	23,690,000
Counsel	NA	E.P.S	-$0.01
DUNS No.	NA	Shareholders	NA

Business: The group's principle activity is to provide online auction and promotions technology that enables marketer to market excess inventory. It offers a wide range of service, technology and expertise to help large merchants maximize yield on clearance, excess and off-lease inventory and to realize process efficiencies. The services are used in four primary areas: retail and discount clearance, promotions and interactive marketing, business-to-business surplus and outsourced auctions and e-commerce to portals and other Web communities. The customers of the group include retailers, distributors and manufacturers as well as Internet portals and other Web communities engaged in e-commerce. On sep 4, 2003 the group sold all of its operating assets to ebay inc. The group provided services to certain retained customers in the United States and United Kingdom until dec 31, 2003. The group's quarterly revenue for Sep'07 was 6.43 millions of USD.

Primary SIC and add'l.: 7372 7389

CIK No: 0001053676

Owners: Lloyd I. Miller/12.00%, Raymond Steele, Sebastian E. Cassetta, Insiders/12.53%, James Mitarotonda/11.03%, Jay Gottlieb/8.44%, Rory J. Cowan, Melvyn Brunt, Barington Capital Group, L.P./15.69%

Financial Data: Fiscal Year End:12/31   Latest Annual Data: 12/31/2006

Year	Sales	Net Income
2006	$7,613,000	-$386,000
2005	NA	$1,256,000
2004	NA	-$1,962,000

Curr. Assets:	$9,225,000	Curr. Liab.:	$2,350,000		
Plant, Equip.:	$92,000	Total Liab.:	$4,575,000	Indic. Yr. Divd.:	NA
Total Assets:	$14,535,000	Net Worth:	$9,960,000	Debt/ Equity:	NA

Siemens

Citicorp Ctr., 153 E. 53rd St., New York, NY, 10022; *PH:* 1-212-258-4000; *Fax:* 1-212-767-0580; *http://* www.siemens.de

General - Incorporation ....Germany	Stock- Price on:12/24/2007 ....$141.91
Employees...475,000	Stock Exchange...NYSE
Auditor . KPMG Deutsche Treuhand Gesellschaft	Ticker Symbol...SI
Stk Agt...NA	Outstanding Shares 896,220,000
Counsel..NA	E.P.S..$4.54
DUNS No..NA	Shareholders..NA

Business: The group's principal activities are divided in eight divisions: information and communication: networks, mobile phones and business services; automation and control: automation and drives, industrial solutions and services; power: power generation, transmission and distribution; transportation: products and systems for railway and automotive industries; medical: healthcare products, solutions and services; osram: lighting sources and electronic controls; financing: services for financing, investment, treasury, fund management and insurance; real estate: development, management and leasing. Vdo automotive: integrated, and electromechanical systems and modules used in automotive applications. Building technologies: temperature, safety, electrical and security regulation systems for industrial property. Business services: information and communication systems with maintenance and support services. Industrial services: facilities systems and contracting services.

Primary SIC and add'l.: 4911 3641 3823 3571 3661 3845 6531

CIK No: 0001135644

Subsidiaries: AS Siemens, BSH Bosch und Siemens Hausgerte GmbH, CTI Molecular Imaging, Inc., DP Siemens Ukraine, Framatome ANP S.A.S., Fujitsu Siemens Computers (Holding) B.V., Grupo Siemens S.A. de C.V., National & German Electrical & Electronic Services Co., OOO Siemens, OSRAM Argentina S.A.C.I., OSRAM de Mxico S.A. de C.V., OSRAM do Brasil Lampadas Eltricas Ltda., OSRAM GmbH, OSRAM Ltd., OSRAM Pte. Ltd. 83 Subsidiaries included in the Index

Officers: Peter Loscher/CEO, Pres., Ralf P. Thomas/Corporate VP, Controller, Peter Y. Solmssen/MD, Jurgen Radomski/MD, Klaus Wucherer/64/MD, Joe Kaeser/51/Head - Corporate Finance, Eduardo Montes/57/MD, Thomas Rackow/56/Member - Supervisory Board, Industrial Mgr., Hermann Requardt/Head - Corporate Technology, Rudi Lamprecht/MD, Jorn Roggenbuck/Head - Media Relations, Anne Beck/Press Officer, Astrid Heinz/Press Officer, Janine Krebs/Trainee, Rosemarie Reiche/Press Assist. (18 Officers included in Index)

Directors: Gerhard Cromme/65/Chmn. - Supervisory Board, Erich R. Reinhardt/Sr. VP, Member - Managing Board, Ralf Heckmann/Member - Supervisory Board, Heinrich Hiesinger/Member - Managing Board, Berthold Huber/Member - Supervisory Board, Bettina Haller/49/Member - Supervisory Board, Michael Mirow/70/Member - Supervisory Board, Dieter Scheitor/58/Member - Supervisory Board, John David Coombe/63/Member - Supervisory Board, Albrecht Schmidt/70/Member - Supervisory Board, Lothar Adler/59/Member - Supervisory Board, Peter Von Siemens/71/Member - Supervisory Board, Industrial Mgr., Birgit Grube/63/Member - Supervisory Board, Wolfgang Muller/60/Member - Supervisory Board, Heinz Hawreliuk/61/Member - Supervisory Board (22 Directors included in Index)

Financial Data: Fiscal Year End:09/30   Latest Annual Data: 9/30/2006

Year	Sales	Net Income
2006	$110,797,960,000	$3,848,270,000
2005	$90,896,136,000	$2,708,390,000
2004	$92,688,428,000	$4,198,706,000

Curr. Assets:	$65,484,037,000	Curr. Liab.:	$49,428,642,000		
Plant, Equip.:	$15,316,954,000	Total Liab.:	$77,352,392,000	Indic. Yr. Divd.:	$1.470
Total Assets:	$115,426,542,000	Net Worth:	$37,183,453,000	Debt/ Equity:	NA

Siena Technologies Inc

Formerly: Network Installation Corp
5625 S Arville St., Ste. Elas, NV, 89118; *PH:* 1-702-889-8777;
http:// www.networkinstallationcorp.net

General - Incorporation ....NV	Stock- Price on:12/24/2007 ....$0.1
Employees..48	Stock Exchange...NA
Auditor ....Jaspers & Hall, P.C	Ticker Symbol...NA
Stk Agt............ Pacific Stock Transfer Company	Outstanding Shares 42,160,000
Counsel..NA	E.P.S...-$0.05
DUNS No..NA	Shareholders..NA

Business: The group's principal activities are to design and install specialty communication systems for data, voice, video and telecom. The services rendered by the group include the installation of data, voice, video and telecom networks, the sale of networking products that are installed and to consult services in the assessment of existing networks. The operations of the group are conducted through its subsidiary network installation holdings inc. The customers include the university of California - los angeles, university of southern California, wells fargo and safeway. On 26-May-2003, the group acquired network installation corporation & on 01-Mar-2004, the group acquired del mar systems.

Primary SIC and add'l.: 3672

CIK No: 0001069778

Subsidiaries: Installation Holdings, Inc, Kelley Communication Company, Inc, Kelley Technologies

Officers: Jeffrey R. Hultman/68/Dir., CEO, Christopher Pizzo/39/Dir., CFO

Directors: Jeffrey R. Hultman/68/Dir., CEO, Christopher Pizzo/39/Dir., CFO, Michael Kelley/67/Dir.

Owners: Insiders/34.90%, Christopher G. Pizzo/1.00%, Dutchess Group/7.70%, Jeffrey R. Hultman, Gary Elliston/20.71%, James Michael Kelley/35.70%

Financial Data: Fiscal Year End:12/31   Latest Annual Data: 12/31/2006

Year	Sales	Net Income
2006	$18,758,000	-$590,000
2005	$5,932,000	-$15,534,000
2004	$1,890,000	-$4,168,000

Curr. Assets:	$2,562,000	Curr. Liab.:	$6,027,000		
Plant, Equip.:	$1,022,000	Total Liab.:	$13,909,000	Indic. Yr. Divd.:	NA
Total Assets:	$10,934,000	Net Worth:	-$2,974,000	Debt/ Equity:	NA

Sierra Bancorp

86 N Main St., Porterville, CA, 93257; *PH:* 1-559-782-4900; *Fax:* 1-559-782-4994; *http://* www.sierrabancorp.com

General - Incorporation ....CA	Stock- Price on:12/24/2007 ....$27.87
Employees..288	Stock Exchange..NDQ
Auditor ....Vavrinek, Trine, Day & Co. LLP	Ticker Symbol...BSRR
Stk Agt ....................U.S. Stock Transfer Corp	Outstanding Shares 9,760,000
Counsel..NA	E.P.S...$2.01
DUNS No..NA	Shareholders..NA

Business: The group's principal activity is to provide community and retail banking services. The group offers a wide range of services, which include checking, interest bearing transaction, savings, time and certificates of deposit, retirement accounts, agricultural loans, credit card loans, construction and real estate loans. The group operates seventeen full service branch offices and three credit centres. The branch offices are located in California city and porterville, visalia, tulare and tehachapi counties and credit centres in fresno and porterville counties.

Primary SIC and add'l.: 6022 6712

CIK No: 0001130144

Subsidiaries: Bank of the Sierra, Sierra Capital Trust I, Sierra Statutory Trust II

Officers: James C. Holly/Dir., CEO, Pres./$824,791.00, James F. Gardunio/Sr. VP, Chief Credit Officer/$342,660.00, Kevin J. McPhaill/Exec. VP, Chief Banking Officer/$182,260.00, Diane L. Rotondo/Sec., Kenneth R. Taylor/CFO, Exec. VP/$257,136.00

Directors: James C. Holly/Dir., CEO, Pres., Morris A. Tharp/Chmn., Gregory A. Childress/Dir., Albert L. Berra/Dir., Robert L. Fields/Dir., Gordon T. Woods/Dir., Vincent L. Jurkovich/Dir., Robert H. Tienken/Dir.

Owners: Ron Foster/7.70%, Patricia L. Childress/6.00%

Financial Data: Fiscal Year End:12/31   Latest Annual Data: 12/31/2006

Year	Sales	Net Income
2006	$91,990,000	$19,190,000
2005	$73,787,000	$16,194,000
2004	$62,414,000	$13,346,000

Curr. Assets:	$65,708,000	Curr. Liab.:	$1,050,848,000	P/E Ratio:	14.67
Plant, Equip.:	$20,796,000	Total Liab.:	$1,124,703,000	Indic. Yr. Divd.:	$0.640
Total Assets:	$1,215,074,000	Net Worth:	$90,371,000	Debt/ Equity:	NA

Sierra Health Services Inc

2724 N Tenaya Way, Las Vegas, NV, 89128; *PH:* 1-702-242-7000; *Fax:* 1-702-242-9711; *http://* www.sierrahealth.com; *Email:* investorrelations@sierrahealth.com

General - Incorporation ....NV	Stock- Price on:12/24/2007 ....$41.5
Employees...2,900	Stock Exchange...NYSE
Auditor ....Deloitte & Touche LLP	Ticker Symbol...SIE
Stk Agt .... Wells Fargo Shareowner Services	Outstanding Shares 55,970,000
Counsel..............Morgan, Lewis & Bockius LLP	E.P.S...$1.87
DUNS No. 12-086-8807	Shareholders..NA

Business: The groups principle activity is to provide healthcare services. The group provides family healthcare including home care services. The group operates from United States.

Primary SIC and add'l.: 6324 8099

CIK No: 0000754009

Subsidiaries: Behavioral Healthcare Options, Inc., CII Financial, Inc., Family Health Care Services, Family Home Hospice, Inc., Health Plan of Nevada, Inc., Northern Nevada Health Network, Inc., Sierra Health and Life Insurance Company, Inc., Sierra Health Holdings, Inc., Sierra Health-Care Options, Inc., Sierra Home Medical Products, Inc., Sierra Medical Management, Inc. and Subsidiaries, Sierra Military Health Services, LLP, Texas Health Choice, L.C., Sierra Nevada Administrators, Inc., Southwest Medical Associates, Inc., Southwest Realty, Inc.

Officers: Anthony M. Marlon/Chmn., CEO, Pres., Marc R. Briggs/CFO, Sr. VP, Treasurer, Laurence S. Howard/Sr. VP - Program Office, Robert L. Schaich/VP - Information Technology, CIO, Donald J. Giancursio/Sr. VP - Sales, Marketing, Darren G.D. Sivertsen/Sr. VP - Operations, Scott G. Cassano/VP - Provider Relations, Joseph A. Kaufman/VP - Medical Affairs, Chief Medical Officer, William R. Godfrey/Exec. VP - Administrative Services, Marie H. Soldo/Exec. VP - Government Affairs, Special Projects, Frank E. Collins/Sr. VP - Legal, Administration, Sec., Michael A. Montalvo/VP - Customer Service, Daniel A. Kruger/VP - Human Resources, Jonathon W. Bunker/COO, Pres., Kathleen M. Marlon/VP - Workers Compensation Operations (17 Officers included in Index)

Directors: Anthony M. Marlon/Chmn., CEO, Pres., Charles L. Ruthe/73/Dir., William J. Raggio/Dir. Emeritus, Michael E. Luce/56/Dir., Albert L. Greene/57/Dir., Thomas Y. Hartley/73/Dir., Anthony L. Watson/60/Dir.

Owners: Paul H. Palmer, Frank E. Collins, Albert L. Greene, Anthony L. Watson, Charles L. Ruthe, UnitedHealth Group Incorporated/8.00%, Insiders/9.20%, Thomas Y. Hartley, Jonathon W. Bunker, Anthony M. Marlon/8.00%, Michael E. Luce, Donald J. Giancursio, Putnam, LLC dba Putnam Investments/6.40%

Financial Data: Fiscal Year End:12/31   Latest Annual Data: 12/31/2006

Year	Sales	Net Income
2006	$1,718,892,000	$140,471,000
2005	$1,385,036,000	$120,017,000
2004	$1,575,435,000	$122,737,000

Curr. Assets:	$543,953,000	Curr. Liab.:	$402,953,000	P/E Ratio:	22.19
Plant, Equip.:	$71,893,000	Total Liab.:	$592,694,000	Indic. Yr. Divd.:	NA
Total Assets:	$809,412,000	Net Worth:	$216,718,000	Debt/ Equity:	0.3224

Sierra Monitor Corp

1991 Tarob Ct., Milpitas, CA, 95035; ***PH:*** 1-408-262-6611; ***Fax:*** 1-408-262-9042; ***http://*** www.sierramonitor.com; ***Email:*** sales@sierramonitor.com

General - Incorporation	CA	**Stock**- Price on:12/24/2007	$2.1
Employees	48	Stock Exchange	OTC
Auditor	Squar, Milner, Raehl & Williamson	Ticker Symbol	SRMC
Stk Agt	U.S. Stock Transfer Corp	Outstanding Shares	11,080,000
Counsel	NA	E.P.S	$0.06
DUNS No.	02-120-0571	Shareholders	NA

Business: The group's principle activities incluude designing and developing hazardous gas monitoring devices for the protection of personnel and facilities in industrial work places. It develops various industrial instruments used to monitor and control environments and to enable communication between industrial devices, such as gas detection systems, programmable logic controllers and various analytical systems and sensing devices. Products manufactured are sold primarily to oil and gas drilling and refining companies, chemical plants, waste-water treatment plants, telecommunications companies, parking garages, landfill rehabilitation projects and building automation projects. The group operates from United States.

Primary SIC and add'l.: 3829

CIK No: 0000100625

Officers: Gordon R. Arnold/CEO, Sec., CFO/$190,476.00, Stephen R. Ferree/Dir. - Marketing, Michael C. Farr/VP - Operations/$174,589.00, Edward K. Hague/VP - Engineering/$254,566.00, Tamara S. Allen/Controller

Directors: Robert C. Marshall/Dir., Jay T. Last/Dir., Richard C. Kramlich/72/Dir.

Owners: Edward K. Hague/6.20%, Gordon R. Arnold/11.10%, Insiders/60.30%, Jay T. Last/18.20%, Richard C. Kramlich/20.00%, Robert C. Marshall/2.90%, Shires Income plc./14.00%, Michael C. Farr/1.50%

Financial Data: **Fiscal Year End:**12/31 **Latest Annual Data:** 12/31/2006

Year	Sales	Net Income
2006	$10,855,000	$468,000
2005	$8,816,000	-$231,000
2004	$9,126,000	-$186,000

Curr. Assets:	$4,736,000	**Curr. Liab.:**	$1,327,000	**P/E Ratio:**	35.00
Plant, Equip.:	$135,000	**Total Liab.:**	$1,327,000	**Indic. Yr. Divd.:**	NA
Total Assets:	$5,056,000	**Net Worth:**	$3,729,000	**Debt/ Equity:**	NA

Sierra Pacific Power Co

6100 Neil Rd., Reno, NV, 89520; ***PH:*** 1-775-834-3600; ***http://*** www.sierrapacific.com

General - Incorporation	NV	**Stock**- Price on:12/24/2007	$18.06
Employees	3,212	Stock Exchange	NA
Auditor	Deloitte & Touche LLP	Ticker Symbol	NA
Stk Agt	Wells Fargo Shareholder Services	Outstanding Shares	221,250,000
Counsel	NA	E.P.S	$1.32
DUNS No.	00-697-1006	Shareholders	NA

Business: The group's principal activities are to transmit, generate, purchase and sell electric energy and natural gas. The group is a wholly owned subsidiary of Sierra Pacific Resources. The customers of the group include residential, commercial, industrial and public sectors. Major industries served include gaming/recreation, mining, warehousing/manufacturing, offices, health care, education, military bases and other governmental entities. Electric service is provided to Las Vegas and surrounding Clark County, northern Nevada and the Lake Tahoe area of California. Natural gas services are provided in the Reno-Sparks area of Nevada.

Primary SIC and add'l.: 4923 4924 4911

CIK No: 0000090144

Subsidiaries: Canyon Fuel Company, LLC, NEICO, Nevada Electric Investment Company (NEICO), NPC, NVP Capital III (Trust), Pinnacle West Energy Corporation (PWEC), Sierra Pacific Power Company, SPPC, Tuscarora Gas Pipeline Company (TGPC)

Officers: Michael W. Yackira/Dir., CEO, Stephen R. Wood/Dir., Corporate Sr. VP - Administration, SPR, Jeffrey L. Ceccarelli/Corporate Sr. VP - Service Delivery, Operations, Roberto R. Denis/Corporate Sr. VP - Energy Supply, SPR, Tony F. Sanchez/Corporate Sr. VP - SPR, Charlie Basso/Ely Energy Centercommunity Representative, David Sims/Project Issues, Ely Energy Centre, John E. Brown/Dir., Controller, Paul J. Kaleta/Corporate Sr. VP, General Counsel, Corp. Sec. - SPR, William D. Rogers/Corporate Sr. VP, CFO, Treasurer - SPR, Britta Carlson/Mgr. - Investor Relations

Directors: Michael W. Yackira/Dir., CEO, Walter M. Higgins/Chmn., Donald L. Shalmy/Dir., Glenn Christenson/Dir., Brian J. Kennedy/Dir., Joseph B. Anderson/Dir., John E. Brown/Dir., Controller, Mary O. Simmons/Dir., Stephen R. Wood/Dir., Corporate Sr. VP - Administration, SPR, Mary Lee Coleman/Dir., Krestine M. Corbin/Dir., Theodore J. Day/Dir., Jerry E. Herbst/Dir., John F. O'Reilly/Dir., Phil Satre/Dir. *(17 Directors included in Index)*

Financial Data: **Fiscal Year End:**12/31 **Latest Annual Data:** 12/31/2006

Year	Sales	Net Income
2006	$3,355,950,000	$279,792,000
2005	$3,030,219,000	$86,137,000
2004	$2,823,839,000	$32,471,000

Curr. Assets:	$933,207,000	**Curr. Liab.:**	$576,074,000	**P/E Ratio:**	13.68
Plant, Equip.:	$6,103,658,000	**Total Liab.:**	$6,209,779,000	**Indic. Yr. Divd.:**	$0.320
Total Assets:	$8,832,076,000	**Net Worth:**	$2,622,297,000	**Debt/ Equity:**	1.5696

Sierra Pacific Resources

6100 Neil Rd., Reno, NV, 89511; ***PH:*** 1-775-834-4011; ***Fax:*** 1-775-834-4202; ***http://*** www.sierrapacificresources.com

General - Incorporation	NV	**Stock**- Price on:12/24/2007	$17.75
Employees	3,212	Stock Exchange	NYSE
Auditor	Deloitte & Touche LLP	Ticker Symbol	SRP
Stk Agt	Deloitte & Touche LLP	Outstanding Shares	221,250,000
Counsel	NA	E.P.S	$1.32
DUNS No.	12-180-9347	Shareholders	NA

Business: The groups principle activity is to provide energy services. The group operates through three business segments namely NPC electric, SPPC electric and SPPC natural gas service. The group operates from United States.

Primary SIC and add'l.: 4911 9999 4922

CIK No: 0000741508

Subsidiaries: Arch Coal Company, Canyon Fuel Company, LLC, GPSF-B, NEICO, Nevada Electric Investment Company, NPC, Pion Pine Corp, Pion Pine Investment Co., Sierra Pacific Power Company, TransCanada PipeLines, Ltd.

Officers: Walter M. Higgins/Chmn., CEO, Pres./$5,571,013.00, Jeffrey L. Ceccarelli/Corporate Sr. VP - Service Delivery, Operations/$1,272,899.00, Michael W. Yackira/Dir., COO, Pres./$1,465,408.00, Donald L. Shalmy/Corporate Sr. VP - Policy, External Affairs, Pres. - Nevada Power Company, Roberto R. Denis/Corporate Sr. VP - Energy Supply/$1,253,800.00, John E. Brown/Controller, Britta Carlson/Mgr. - Investor Relations, Paul J. Kaleta/Corporate Sr. VP, General Counsel, Corp. Sec./$1,263,004.00, Stephen R. Wood/Corporate Sr. VP - Administration, Mary O. Simmons/VP - Rates, Regulations, William D. Rogers/Corporate CFO, Sr. VP, Treasurer, Grant Sims/Mgr. - Economic Development, Bradley E. Woodring/Economic Development Exec., Tony F. Sanchez/Corporate Sr. VP

Directors: Walter M. Higgins/Chmn., CEO, Pres., Krestine M. Corbin/Dir., James R. Donnelley/72/Dir., Jerry E. Herbst/Dir., Mary Lee Coleman/Dir., Joseph B. Anderson/Dir., Glenn Christenson/Dir., Brian J. Kennedy/Dir., Clyde T. Turner/Dir., Michael W. Yackira/Dir., COO, Pres., Phil Satre/Dir., Theodore J. Day/Dir., John F. OReilly/Dir., Donald D. Snyder/Dir.

Owners: Donald D. Snyder, Michael W. Yackira, Joseph B. Anderson, Roberto Denis, Theodore J. Day, Insiders, Canyon Capital Advisors LLC/6.40%, Walter M. Higgins, Clyde T. Turner, Kinetics Asset Management, Inc./6.60%, Jeffrey L. Ceccarelli, Krestine M. Corbin, Jerry E. Herbst, Philip G. Satre, Mary L. Coleman *(18 Owners included in Index)*

Financial Data: **Fiscal Year End:**12/31 **Latest Annual Data:** 12/31/2006

Year	Sales	Net Income
2006	$3,355,950,000	$279,792,000
2005	$3,030,219,000	$86,137,000
2004	$2,823,839,000	$32,471,000

Curr. Assets:	$933,207,000	**Curr. Liab.:**	$576,074,000	**P/E Ratio:**	13.45
Plant, Equip.:	$6,103,658,000	**Total Liab.:**	$6,209,779,000	**Indic. Yr. Divd.:**	$0.320
Total Assets:	$8,832,076,000	**Net Worth:**	$2,622,297,000	**Debt/ Equity:**	1.5696

Sierra Wireless Inc

13811 Wireless Way, Richmond, BC, V6V 3A4; ***PH:*** 1-604-231-1100; ***http://*** www.sierrawireless.com; ***Email:*** privacy@SierraWireless.com

General - Incorporation	Canada	**Stock**- Price on:12/24/2007	$25.33
Employees	268	Stock Exchange	NDQ
Auditor	KPMG LLP	Ticker Symbol	SWIR
Stk Agt	Computershare Investor Services LLC	Outstanding Shares	25,730,000
Counsel	Blake, Cassels & Graydon LLP	E.P.S	$0.88
DUNS No.	NA	Shareholders	NA

Business: The group's principle activities are to develop, manufacture, market, sell and support a broad range of single and multi-mode wireless data modems. The group also enables software for use with handheld computing devices, notebook computers and vehicle-based or monitoring applications. The group's quarterly revenue for September 2007 was 111.52 millions of USD.

Primary SIC and add'l.: 3577 3571 3578

CIK No: 0001111863

Subsidiaries: Sierra Wireless (Asia-Pacific) Limited, Sierra Wireless (UK) Limited, Sierra Wireless America,Inc.

Officers: Jason W. Cohenour/CEO, Pres., David McLennan/CFO, Sec., Steve Burrington/VP - Worldwide Systems Engineering, Rich Winters/VP - Supply Chain, Dan Schieler/Sr. VP - Worldwide Sales, James B. Kirkpatrick/CTO, Peter Ciceri/Dir. - Management Consultant, Evan Jones/VP - Engineering, Trent Punnett/Sr. VP - Marketing, Corporate Development, Mike Ardelan/VP - North American Enterprise, OEM Sales, Jim Lahey/VP - EMEA, Pat Watson/VP - Human Resources, Mike O'Brien/VP - Carrier and Distribution Sales, Americas, Jin Pak/VP - Sales, Asia Pacific, Central, Latin America, Stephen Blaine/VP - Engineering *(23 Officers included in Index)*

Directors: Charles E. Levine/Chmn., Kent Thexton/Dir., Peter Ciceri/Dir. - Management Consultant, Gregory D. Aasen/Dir., David B. Sutcliffe/Corp. Dir., Paul G. Cataford/Dir., Jane Rowe/Dir.

Financial Data: **Fiscal Year End:**12/31 **Latest Annual Data:** 12/31/2006

Year	Sales	Net Income
2006	$221,285,000	$9,796,000
2005	$107,144,000	-$36,468,000
2004	$211,205,000	$24,920,000

Curr. Assets:	$169,472,000	**Curr. Liab.:**	$57,631,000		
Plant, Equip.:	$13,400,000	**Total Liab.:**	$58,776,000	**Indic. Yr. Divd.:**	NA
Total Assets:	$211,608,000	**Net Worth:**	$152,832,000	**Debt/ Equity:**	NA

SIFCO Industries Inc

970 E 64th St., Cleveland, OH, 44103; ***PH:*** 1-216-881-8600; ***Fax:*** 1-216-432-6281; ***http://*** www.sifco.com; ***Email:*** info@sifco.com

General - Incorporation	OH	**Stock**- Price on:12/24/2007	$18.52
Employees	390	Stock Exchange	AMEX
Auditor	Grant Thornton LLP	Ticker Symbol	SIF
Stk Agt	National City Corp	Outstanding Shares	5,230,000
Counsel	Squire, Sanders & Dempsey LLP	E.P.S	$1.273
DUNS No.	00-415-4407	Shareholders	NA

Business: The group's principal activities are to produce and sell a variety of metalworking processes, services and products to meet the specific design requirements of its customers. The group operates through three segments: turbine component services and repair group, aerospace component manufacturing group and metal finishing group. Turbine component services and repair group repairs and remanufacture jet engine and heavy industrial turbine engine components. Aerospace component manufacturing group manufactures medium sized forged parts in various alloys. Metal finishing group provides a specialized electrochemical finishing processes for anodizing and electropolishing. The operations of the group are carried in the United States, the United Kingdom, Ireland and France.

Primary SIC and add'l.: 3471 3724 3462

CIK No: 0000090168

Subsidiaries: SIFCO Custom Machining Company, SIFCO Exports, Limited, SIFCO Holdings, Inc., SIFCO Irish Holdings, Limited, SIFCO Research and Development, Limited, SIFCO Selective Plating (UK), Limited, SIFCO Selective Plating France, SARL, SIFCO Turbine Components Limited

Officers: Jeffrey P. Gotschall/60/Chmn., CEO, Frank A. Cappello/50/VP - Finance, CFO, Remigijus H. Belzinskas/Corporate Controller, Daniel G. Berick/Sec.

Directors: Jeffrey P. Gotschall/60/Chmn., CEO, Hudson D. Smith/57/Dir., Charles P. Miller/70/Dir., Alayne L. Reitman/44/Dir., Douglas J. Whelan/69/Dir., Frank N. Nichols/68/Dir.

Owners: Jeffrey P. Gotschall/2.80%, Frank N. Nichols, Alayne L. Reitman, Janice Carlson/37.89%, Dimensional Fund Advisors, LP/5.53%, Tontine Capital Management, LLC/9.50%, Douglas J. Whelan, Hudson D. Smith/2.16%, Frank A. Cappello, Charles P. Miller, Insiders/5.98%

Financial Data: Fiscal Year End:09/30   Latest Annual Data: 9/30/2006

Year	Sales	Net Income
2006	$86,989,000	$960,000
2005	$80,968,000	-$196,000
2004	$87,393,000	-$5,946,000

Curr. Assets:	$32,237,000	Curr. Liab.:	$17,226,000	P/E Ratio:	16.10
Plant, Equip.:	$14,059,000	Total Liab.:	$23,592,000	Indic. Yr. Divd.:	NA
Total Assets:	$48,775,000	Net Worth:	$25,183,000	Debt/ Equity:	NA

Sify Technologies Ltd

Formerly: Sify Ltd

2880 Lakeside Dr., Ste. 205, Santa Clara, CA, 95054; **PH:** 1-408-748-1000; **Fax:** 1-408-748-1009; **http://** www.sifycorp.com

General - Incorporation	India	Stock- Price on:12/24/2007	$8.85
Employees	1,910	Stock Exchange	NDQ
Auditor	KPMG LLP	Ticker Symbol	SIFY
Stk Agt.	Citibank N.A	Outstanding Shares	42,500,000
Counsel	NA	E.P.S.	-$0.02
DUNS No.	NA	Shareholders	NA

Business: The group's principal activities are to provide integrated end-to-end Internet solutions. The group operates through four segments: corporate network/ data services, which provides private network services, messaging services and Web hosting businesses; Internet access services, which provides dial-up Internet access and public Internet access through cyber cafes; online portal services and content offerings and other services such as development of e-learning software.

Primary SIC and add'l.: 7379 7375

CIK No: 0001094324

Subsidiaries: IndiaWorld Communications Limited, Sify Americas Inc., Sify Communications Limited , Sify International Inc., Sify Networks Private Limited

Officers: Raju Vegesna/MD, CEO, Rahul Swarup/Pres. - Enterprise Solutions, Ajith K.N. /39/Head - Human Resources, David Appasamy/Chief Communication Officer, Arvind Mathur/Sr. VP - International Business, K. N. Ajith/Head - Human Resources, Venkata Rao Mallineni/Advisor, Business Strategy, S. Gopalakrishnan/41/Pres., Bhaskar Sayyaparaju/CTO, Pijush Kanti Das/54/CFO, Pres., V. Sivaramakrishnan/Pres. - Consumer Marketing, Suri Venkat/COO, V. M. Kumar/Sr. VP - International Business, C. V.S. Suri/COO, P. J. Nath/Executive Pres. - Enterprise Solutions (16 Officers included in Index)

Directors: T. H. Chowdary/76/Dir., C. B. Mouli/61/Dir., S. K. Rao/64/Dir., P. S. Raju/55/Dir., S. R. Sukumara/63/Dir.

Owners: Infinity Capital Ventures, LP/42.23%, Raju Vegesna/41.83%

Financial Data: Fiscal Year End:03/31   Latest Annual Data: 3/31/2006

Year	Sales	Net Income
2006	$105,256,000	-$3,355,000
2005	$82,839,000	-$7,051,000
2004	$64,544,000	-$8,555,000

Curr. Assets:	$108,547,000	Curr. Liab.:	$57,189,000		
Plant, Equip.:	$37,825,000	Total Liab.:	$63,983,000	Indic. Yr. Divd.:	NA
Total Assets:	$164,748,000	Net Worth:	$100,765,000	Debt/ Equity:	NA

SIGA Technologies Inc

420 Lexington Ave., Ste. 408, New York, NY, 10170; **PH:** 1-212-672-9100; **Fax:** 1-212-697-3130; **http://** www.siga.com; **Email:** info@siga.com

General - Incorporation	DE	Stock- Price on:12/24/2007	$3.41
Employees	44	Stock Exchange	NDQ
Auditor	PricewaterhouseCoopers LLP	Ticker Symbol	SIGA
Stk Agt.	American Stock Transfer & Trust Co.	Outstanding Shares	33,010,000
Counsel	NA	E.P.S.	-$0.29
DUNS No.	93-265-1516	Shareholders	NA

Business: The group's principal activities are to discover, develop and commercialize vaccines, antibiotics and novel anti-infectives for the prevention and treatment of infectious diseases. It is developing a certain commensal bacteria (commensals) as a means to deliver mucosal vaccines. Commensals are harmless bacteria that naturally inhabit the body's surfaces with different commensals inhabiting different mucosal surfaces. It is also developing veterinary vaccines and surface protein expression system. Its anti-infective programs are aimed at the increasingly serious problem of drug resistance and are designed to block the ability of bacteria to attach to human tissue. The group has research and development activities in Oregon state university and at the university of California, los angeles. On 23-May-2003, the group acquired all of the assets of plexus vaccine inc and assumed certain liabilities.

Primary SIC and add'l.: 8731 2834

CIK No: 0001010086

Subsidiaries: MacAndrews & Forbes Holdings Inc., Quest Diagnostics, Inc.

Officers: Eric Rose/Chmn., CEO, Thomas N. Konatich/CFO, VP/$350,833.00, Dennis E. Hruby/Chief Scientific Officer/$403,666.00, John R. Odden/53/VP - Business Development

Directors: Eric Rose/Chmn., CEO, Thomas E. Constance/Dir., Adnan M. Mjalli/Dir., Mehmet C. Oz/Dir., Judy S. Slotkin/Dir., James J. Antal/Dir., Paul G. Savas/Dir., Michael Weiner/Dir., Steven L. Fasman/Dir., Scott M. Hammer/Dir.

Owners: Dennis E. Hruby/1.80%, Mehmet C. Oz, Scott M. Hammer, Thomas E. Constance, Thomas N. Konatich/1.60%, Eric A. Rose/2.40%, Insiders/8.10%, James J. Antal, Paul G. Savas, TransTech Pharma, Inc./15.00%, Bernard L. Kasten/4.80%, Adnan M. Mjalli, MacAndrews & Forbes Inc./15.90%, Steven L. Fasman, Michael A. Weiner (17 Owners included in Index)

Financial Data: Fiscal Year End:12/31   Latest Annual Data: 12/31/2006

Year	Sales	Net Income
2006	$7,258,000	-$9,899,000
2005	$8,477,000	-$2,288,000
2004	$1,839,000	-$9,373,000

Curr. Assets:	$11,398,000	Curr. Liab.:	$2,050,000		
Plant, Equip.:	$1,320,000	Total Liab.:	$6,746,000	Indic. Yr. Divd.:	NA
Total Assets:	$14,028,000	Net Worth:	$7,282,000	Debt/ Equity:	NA

Sigma Aldrich Corp

3050 Spruce St., St. Louis, MO, 63103; **PH:** 1-314-771-5765; **Fax:** 1-314-286-7874; **http://** www.sigmaaldrich.com

General - Incorporation	DE	Stock- Price on:12/24/2007	$42.34
Employees	7,299	Stock Exchange	NDQ
Auditor	KPMG LLP	Ticker Symbol	SIAL
Stk Agt ... Computershare Investor Services LLC		Outstanding Shares	131,320,000
Counsel	NA	E.P.S.	$2.20
DUNS No.	07-992-8354	Shareholders	NA

Business: The groups principle activities include developing, manufacturing, purchasing and distributing a range of biochemicals and organic chemicals for scientific and genomic research, biotechnology, pharmaceutical development, the diagnosis of disease and as key components in pharmaceutical and other high-technology manufacturing industries. The group operates from United States.

Primary SIC and add'l.: 2834 2835 2869 5169 2899

CIK No: 0000090185

Subsidiaries: Aldrich Chemical Company, Inc., Aldrich Chemical Foreign Holding LLC, Chemical Trade, Limited, KL Acquisition Corp, MedChem, Limited, Proligo Australia Pty. Ltd., Proligo Chemie GmbH, Proligo France SAS, Proligo International GmbH, Proligo Japan KK, Proligo Singapore Pte. Ltd., SAF-LAB, SAFC Biosciences Limited, SAFC Biosciences Pty. Ltd., SAFC Biosciences, Inc. 86 Subsidiaries included in the Index

Officers: Jai P. Nagarkatti/61/Dir., CEO, Pres./$1,932,293.00, Frank Wicks/Pres. - Safc/$968,505.00, Rich Keffer/General Counsel, Sec., David Smoller/Pres. - Research Biotech, Karen Miller/Controller, Kirk Richter/Treasurer, Gerrit Van Den Dool/VP - Sales, Steven M. Paul/57/Dir., Exec. VP - Science, Technology, Gilles Cottier/Pres. - Research Essentials, Michael R. Hogan/CFO, Chief Administrative Officer/$1,071,807.00, Dave Julien/Pres. - Research Specialties/$925,467.00, Doug Rau/VP - Human Resources, Carl Turza/CIO, Steve Walton/VP - Quality, Safety, Shahed I. Yousaf/48/Pres. - Research Biotech

Directors: Jai P. Nagarkatti/61/Dir., CEO, Pres., David R. Harvey/68/Chmn., Nina V. Fedoroff/Dir., Steven M. Paul/57/Dir., Exec. VP - Science, Technology, Dean D. Spatz/62/Dir., Timothy R.G. Sear/70/Dir., Barrett Toan/59/Dir., Lee W. McCollum/57/Dir., Avi Nash/53/Dir., William C. O'Neil/72/Dir., Pedro J. Reinhard/61/Dir.

Owners: Dean D. Spatz, Lee W. McCollum, Avi M. Nash, Barrett A. Toan, David W. Julien, Pedro J. Reinhard, Insiders, Jai P. Nagarkatti, William C. ONeil, AMVESCAP PLC, Timothy R.G. Sear, Franklin D. Wicks, Michael R. Hogan, Nina V. Fedoroff, Steven M. Paul (17 Owners included in Index)

Financial Data: Fiscal Year End:12/31   Latest Annual Data: 12/31/2006

Year	Sales	Net Income
2006	$1,797,500,000	$276,800,000
2005	$1,666,500,000	$258,300,000
2004	$1,409,200,000	$232,900,000

Curr. Assets:	$1,112,900,000	Curr. Liab.:	$442,600,000	P/E Ratio:	19.25
Plant, Equip.:	$645,100,000	Total Liab.:	$923,400,000	Indic. Yr. Divd.:	$0.460
Total Assets:	$2,334,300,000	Net Worth:	$1,410,900,000	Debt/ Equity:	0.1444

Sigma Designs Inc

1221 California Cir., Milpitas, CA, 95035; **PH:** 1-408-262-9003; **Fax:** 1-408-957-9740; **http://** www.sigmadesigns.com; **Email:** ir@sdesigns.com

General - Incorporation	CA	Stock- Price on:12/24/2007	$25.3
Employees	180	Stock Exchange	NDQ
Auditor	Armanino Mckenna LLP	Ticker Symbol	SIGM
Stk Agt	Computershare Investor Services	Outstanding Shares	23,770,000
Counsel	Wilson Sonsini Goodrich & Rosati	E.P.S.	$0.48
DUNS No.	06-474-8635	Shareholders	NA

Business: The group's principle activities are to develop, manufacture and market multimedia computer devices and products. It sells the products to computer manufacturers, distributors, value-added resellers and corporate customers. The group develops system solutions for convergence products including streaming video, DVD playback, Internet connectivity and personal video recording. It provides digital video decoding solutions for applications in full-screen full-motion video streaming and digital versatile disk or DVD playback. The group's mpeg-2 chips and add-in boards enables applications such as DVD title creation, DVD decoding, streaming video and ip multicasting. It has a research and development office in France and sales offices in Hong Kong, Japan, Korea and Taiwan. The group's total revenue for year 2007 was 91.22 millions of USD.

Primary SIC and add'l.: 7373 3674 3572 3577

CIK No: 0000790715

Subsidiaries: Blue7 Communications

Officers: Thinh Q. Tran/Chmn., CEO, Co - Founder/$1,104,639.00, Kit Tsui/VP - Planning, Administration/$311,889.00, Kenneth Lowe/VP - Business Development, Strategic Marketing, Investor Relations/$304,020.00, Jacques Martinella/VP - Engineering/$371,597.00, Silvio Perich/Sr. VP - Worldwide Sales/$496,277.00, Hung Nguyen/GM, VP - Wireless Products Division, Thomas E. Gay/CFO, Edward McGregor/Contact, Mark Kent/48/Sec.

Directors: Thinh Q. Tran/Chmn., CEO, Co - Founder, William J. Almon/Dir., Julien Nguyen/Dir., Lung C. Tsai/Dir.

Owners: Lung C. Tsai, Thinh Q. Tran/4.30%, Julien Nguyen, Kenneth Lowe, Insiders/6.00%, Silvio Perich, Entities associated with Galleon Management, L.L.C./4.10%, Jacques Martinella, Kit Tsui, William J. Almon

Financial Data: Fiscal Year End:01/28   Latest Annual Data: 2/3/2007

Year	Sales	Net Income
2007	$91,218,000	$6,244,000
2006	$33,320,000	$1,884,000
2005	$31,437,000	$1,840,000

Curr. Assets:	$61,533,000	Curr. Liab.:	$22,749,000	P/E Ratio:	52.71
Plant, Equip.:	$3,364,000	Total Liab.:	$23,112,000	Indic. Yr. Divd.:	NA
Total Assets:	$76,084,000	Net Worth:	$52,972,000	Debt/ Equity:	NA

SigmaTel Inc

1601 S MoPac Expwy., Ste. 100, Austin, TX, 78746; **PH:** 1-512-381-3700; **Fax:** 1-512-744-1700; **http://** www.sigmatel.com; **Email:** corporate@sigmatel.com

General - Incorporation: DE
Employees: 407
Auditor: PricewaterhouseCoopers LLP
Stk Agt: Computershare Investor Services LLC
Counsel: NA
DUNS No.: NA

Stock - Price on:12/24/2007: $3.05
Stock Exchange: NDQ
Ticker Symbol: SGTL
Outstanding Shares: 35,810,000
E.P.S: -$3.3
Shareholders: NA

Business: The group's principal activities are to design, develop, and market fabless semiconductor products. The products are proprietary, analog-intensive, mixed-signal integrated circuits used for a variety of products in the consumer electronics and computing markets. These products are used in portable compressed audio players, such as mp3 players, notebook and desktop pcs, DVD players, digital televisions, set-top boxes, universal serial bus and storage devices. The group provides customers complete, system-level solutions that include highly integrated ics, customizable firmware and software, software development tools, reference designs and applications support. The products of the group are marketed to direct and indirect customers including both original equipment manufacturers (OEMs) and odms.

Primary SIC and add'l.: 5065 3679 3674 3572

CIK No: 0001043639

Subsidiaries: Oasis Semiconductor (Cayman) Limited, Oasis Semiconductor (Hong Kong) Limited, Oasis Semiconductor, Inc, Protocom Corporation, SigmaTel Asia, Limited, SigmaTel Caymans, SigmaTel International Holdings, Inc, SigmaTel Japan Y.K., SigmaTel Korea, Ltd, SigmaTel Singapore Holdco Pte. Ltd, SigmaTel Singapore SMS Pte. Ltd, SigmaTel UK Limited

Officers: Phil Pompa/CEO, Pres./$691,549.00, Melissa Bixby/VP - Human Resources, Daniel P. Mulligan/41/Sr. VP - Technology, Strategy/$398,775.00, Scott R. Schaefer/VP - Finance, CFO/$196,199.00, Barry Bumgardner/VP, General Counsel, Steve Beatty/Sr. VP - Product Lines, Operations/$679,963.00, Kevin Beadle/49/Sr. VP - Sales, Marketing, Martha Aviles/Contact - Media, Investor Relations

Directors: William P. Osborne/Chmn., Kenneth P. Lawler/48/Dir., Alexander M. Davern/Dir., Robert T. Derby/Dir., John A. Hime/Dir.

Owners: Insiders, Ronald P. Edgerton/2.10%, Robert T. Derby, Daniel P. Mulligan, Ross A. Goolsby, Phillip E. Pompa, William P. Osborne, Scott R. Schaefer, Stephan L. Beatty, Alexander M. Davern, Renaissance Technologies Corp./5.70%, FMR Corp./9.80%

Financial Data: *Fiscal Year End:*12/31 *Latest Annual Data:* 12/31/2006

Year	Sales	Net Income
2006	$159,365,000	-$109,024,000
2005	$324,457,000	$35,879,000
2004	$194,805,000	$52,556,000

Curr. Assets:	$143,146,000	**Curr. Liab.:**	$34,577,000		
Plant, Equip.:	$13,301,000	**Total Liab.:**	$39,839,000	**Indic. Yr. Divd.:**	NA
Total Assets:	$173,391,000	**Net Worth:**	$133,552,000	**Debt/ Equity:**	0.0514

Sigmatron International Inc

2201 Landmeier Rd., Elk Grove Village, IL, 60007; ***PH:*** 1-847-956-8000; ***Fax:*** 1-847-640-4528; ***http://*** www.sigmatronintl.com

General - Incorporation: DE
Employees: 2,140
Auditor: BDO Seidman LLP
Stk Agt: Grant Thornton LLP
Counsel: D'ancona & Pflaum
DUNS No.: 82-562-2327

Stock - Price on:12/24/2007: $9.25
Stock Exchange: NDQ
Ticker Symbol: SGMA
Outstanding Shares: 3,790,000
E.P.S: $0.58
Shareholders: NA

Business: The group's principal activity is to provide electronic manufacturing services. These services include manufacture of printed circuit board assemblies and completely assembled electronic products. The services rendered range from assembly of individual components to the assembly and testing of box-build electronic products. The group offers automatic and manual assembly and testing of original equipment manufacturers products. It also includes material sourcing and procurement, design, manufacturing and test engineering support, warehousing and shipment services and assistance in obtaining approval from government and other regulatory agencies. The customers are in consumer electronics, gaming, fitness, industrial electronics, telecommunications, automotive and home appliance industries. The group operates in the United States, China and Taiwan. On 4th-Aug-2004 the group acquired 37.5% interest in smt unlimited.

Primary SIC and add'l.: 3679 3672 3674

CIK No: 0000915358

Subsidiaries: AbleMex S.A. de C.V., Standard Components de Mexico, S.A.

Officers: Gary R. Fairhead/56/Dir., CEO, Pres./$188,213.00, Franklin D. Sove/74/Chmn., Dir. - Investor Relations, Daniel P. Camp/VP - Operations, Wujiang, Suzhou, China/$183,406.00, Frank Magallanes/Mexico Sales Mgr., Keith Wheaton/VP - Customer Service, Sales, Marketing Contact, Leo Rullamas/GM - Sales, Marketing Contact, Linda K. Blake/CFO, VP - Finance, Treasurer, Sec./$162,710.00, Greg A. Fairhead/Exec. VP - Operations, Assist., Sec./$219,934.00, Stephen H. McNulty/VP - Sales, James Henderson/Dir. - Operations, Elk Grove Village, Illinois, Raj Upadhyaya/Exec. VP - Operations, Hayward, California/$259,530.00, Yousef Heidari/VP - Engineering, Hayward, California, Hom-Ming Chang/VP - Test Engineering, Hayward, California

Directors: Gary R. Fairhead/56/Dir., CEO, Pres., Franklin D. Sove/74/Chmn., Dir. - Investor Relations, Thomas W. Rieck/63/Dir., John P. Chen/54/Dir., Carl A. Zemenick/63/Dir., Dilip S. Vyas/60/Dir.

Owners: Gary R. Fairhead/2.80%, Thomas W. Rieck, Zeff Holding Company, LLC/5.50%, Gregory A. Fairhead/1.80%, Linda K. Blake/1.00%, Dilip S. Vyas, Raj B. Upadhyaya, Insiders/9.60%, John P. Chen, Fidelity Low-Price Stock Fund/9.80%, Daniel P. Camp/1.30%, John P. Sheehan/1.30%, Tang Foundation for the Research of Traditional Chinese Medicine/6.60%, Carl A. Zemenick, Cyrus Tang Foundation/10.50% *(17 Owners included in Index)*

Financial Data: *Fiscal Year End:*04/30 *Latest Annual Data:* 04/30/2007

Year	Sales	Net Income
2007	$165,909,000	$1,698,000
2006	$124,786,000	$1,882,000
2005	$106,077,000	$4,699,000

Curr. Assets:	$55,363,000	**Curr. Liab.:**	$21,029,000		
Plant, Equip.:	$30,544,000	**Total Liab.:**	$51,045,000	**Indic. Yr. Divd.:**	NA
Total Assets:	$98,940,000	**Net Worth:**	$47,895,000	**Debt/ Equity:**	0.6886

Signalife Inc

531 S Main St., Ste. 301, Greenville, SC, 29601; ***PH:*** 1-864-233-2300; ***Fax:*** 1-864-233-2100; ***http://*** www.signalife.com; ***Email:*** info@signalife.com

General - Incorporation: DE
Employees: 13
Auditor: Elliott Davis, LLC
Stk Agt: Atlas Stock Transfer Corp
Counsel: NA
DUNS No.: NA

Stock - Price on:12/24/2007: $0.869
Stock Exchange: AMEX
Ticker Symbol: SGN
Outstanding Shares: 45,710,000
E.P.S: -$0.341
Shareholders: NA

Business: The groups principle activities include researching, developing and marketing medical devices. The group products include Fidelity 100 Monitor System, Holter Monit, Fidelity 200 Event Recording System and Cardiac Vest. The group operates from the United States.

Primary SIC and add'l.: 3841 3845 3841

CIK No: 0000810365

Subsidiaries: Memonitor,Inc.

Officers: Pamela Bunes/45/Dir., CEO, Pres./$607,233.00, Budimir S. Drakulic/CTO, Chief Scientist/$207,021.00, Kevin Kading/Investor Relation Officer, John Woodbury/Securities Counsel, Kevin F. Pickard/44/Interim CFO

Directors: Pamela Bunes/45/Dir., CEO, Pres., Ellsworth Roston/Dir., Jennifer Black/Dir., Lowell T. Harmison/Dir., Norma Provencio/Dir., Rowland Perkins/Dir., Mitchell W. Krucoff/Member - Advisory Board, Andrea Natale/Member - Advisory Board, Michael M. Laks/Member - Advisory Board, Melvin J. Hinich/Member - Advisory Board, Jay A. Johnson/Dir., Robert E. Windom/Dir., Steven Joseph Phillps/Dir., Charles H. Harrison/65/Dir., Jesse S. Rosas/49/Dir.

Owners: Budimir S. Drakulic, Trellus Management Co./9.90%, Ellsworth Roston/1.90%, Jay A. Johnson, Rowland Perkins, John Viney/100.00%, Jennifer Black, Insiders/3.50%, Lowell T. Harmison, YA Global Investments, L.P./9.90%, Robert E. Windom, Tracey Hampton/43.70%, Charles H. Harrison

Financial Data: *Fiscal Year End:*12/31 *Latest Annual Data:* 12/31/2006

Year	Sales	Net Income
2006	$190,000	-$11,716,000
2005	NA	-$8,661,000
2004	NA	-$6,966,000

Curr. Assets:	$3,644,000	**Curr. Liab.:**	$1,576,000		
Plant, Equip.:	$280,000	**Total Liab.:**	$1,576,000	**Indic. Yr. Divd.:**	NA
Total Assets:	$4,520,000	**Net Worth:**	$2,945,000	**Debt/ Equity:**	NA

Signature Bank

565 5th Ave., New York, NY, 10017; ***PH:*** 1-646-822-1500; ***http://*** www.signatureny.com

General - Incorporation: NY
Employees: 347
Auditor: NA
Stk Agt: NA
Counsel: NA
DUNS No.: NA

Stock - Price on:12/24/2007: $34.19
Stock Exchange: NDQ
Ticker Symbol: SBNY
Outstanding Shares: 29,670,000
E.P.S: NA
Shareholders: NA

Business: The group's principal activity is to provide talented, passionate, and dedicated financial professionals an environment in which they can conduct their practice to the maximum benefit of their clients. The result for clients is a special feeling they associate with Signature professionals and, ultimately, the Signature brand: the experience of being financially well cared for. The group securities provide full banking, brokerage, and insurance capabilities under one roof. With a "best of breed" approach to selecting our products. The group is a New York-based full service commercial bank with 18 private client offices located in the New York metropolitan area. The group serves the needs of privately owned business clients, their owners and senior managers. Group offers a wide variety of business and personal banking products and services through the bank as well as investment, brokerage, asset management and insurance products and services through our subsidiary.

Primary SIC and add'l.: 6022

CIK No: 0001288784

Officers: Joseph J. Depaolo/Dir., CEO, Pres., Mark T. Sigona/COO, Exec. VP, Michael J. Merlo/Exec. VP, Chief Credit Officer, Michael Sharkey/CTO, Sr. VP, Eric R. Howell/Sr. VP, CFO, Investor Contact, Susan J. Lewis/Media Contact, Michael Schwartz/Community Development

Directors: Joseph J. Depaolo/Dir., CEO, Pres., John Tamberlane/Vice Chmn., Scott A. Shay/Chmn., Yacov Levy/Dir., Alfred B. Delbello/Dir., Kathryn A. Byrne/Dir., Ann F. Kaplan/Dir., Jeffrey W. Meshel/Dir., Alfonse M. D'Amato/Dir.

Signature Eyewear Inc

498 N Oak St., Inglewood, CA, 90302; ***PH:*** 1-310-330-2700; ***Fax:*** 1-310-330-2765; ***http://*** www.signatureeyewear.com; ***Email:*** comments@signatureeyewear.com

General - Incorporation: CA
Employees: 102
Auditor: Grobstein, Horwath & Company LLP
Stk Agt: American Stock Transfer & Trust Co.
Counsel: NA
DUNS No.: NA

Stock - Price on:12/24/2007: $0.85
Stock Exchange: OTC
Ticker Symbol: SEYE
Outstanding Shares: 6,860,000
E.P.S: $0.14
Shareholders: NA

Business: The groups principal activities include designing, marketing and distributing prescription eyeglass frames and sunglasses. The group operates from the United States.

Primary SIC and add'l.: 5048 3851

CIK No: 0001036292

Officers: Michael Prince/CEO

Owners: Kevin D. Seifert, Bluebird Finance Limited/100.00%, Drew Miller/1.50%, Bluebird Finance Limited/16.50%, Michael Prince/15.70%, Richard M. Torre/28.00%, Ted Pasternack/2.80%, Insiders/50.60%, Raul Khantzis, Craig N. Springer/9.80%, Edward Meltzer/1.60%

Financial Data: *Fiscal Year End:*10/31 *Latest Annual Data:* 10/31/2006

Year	Sales	Net Income
2006	$23,162,000	$683,000
2005	$25,050,000	$1,606,000
2004	$23,609,000	-$371,000

Curr. Assets:	$9,019,000	**Curr. Liab.:**	$7,200,000	**P/E Ratio:**	6.07
Plant, Equip.:	$495,000	**Total Liab.:**	$12,903,000	**Indic. Yr. Divd.:**	NA
Total Assets:	$10,233,000	**Net Worth:**	-$2,670,000	**Debt/ Equity:**	NA

Signature Leisure Inc

100 Candace Dr., Ste 100, Maitland, FL, 32751; *PH:* 1-407-599-2886;
http:// www.valdeconnections.com; *Email:* info@signatureleisure.com

General - Incorporation	CO	*Stock* - Price on:12/24/2007	$0.021
Employees	1	Stock Exchange	OTC
Auditor	Cordovano & Honeck LLP	Ticker Symbol	SGLS
Stk Agt	Corporate Stock Transfer, Inc.	Outstanding Shares	231,280,000
Counsel	NA	E.P.S	$0.00
DUNS No.	NA	Shareholders	NA

Business: The group's principle activities are to sell matted and framed photographs located in longmont, Colorado. Photographs are sold at art shows and via the Internet. During the year 2003, the company changed its business from sales of photographs to providing services to hair salon, spa and modeling industries. The group is in the process of developing a business plan to address operations, services, sales and marketing in the hair salon, spa and modeling industries.

Primary SIC and add'l.: 5946 7384

CIK No: 0001135194

Subsidiaries: E Cubed Technology, Inc., Parker Productions, Inc.

Officers: Steven W. Carnes/Chmn., Pres., Andra Espinoza/Consultant, Evan Weybright/VP - Operations, Edward R. Miers/Special Advisor, Consultant

Directors: Steven W. Carnes/Chmn., Pres.

Owners: Stephen W. Carnes/45.00%

Financial Data: Fiscal Year End:12/31   Latest Annual Data: 12/31/2006

Year	Sales	Net Income
2006	$81,000	-$2,291,000
2005	$102,000	-$1,619,000
2004	$229,000	-$1,903,000

Curr. Assets:	$91,000	*Curr. Liab.:*	$432,000		
Plant, Equip.	$2,000	*Total Liab.:*	$432,000	*Indic. Yr. Divd.:*	NA
Total Assets:	$101,000	*Net Worth:*	-$331,000	*Debt/ Equity:*	NA

Signet Group Plc

Zenith House, The Hyde, London, NW9 6EW; *PH:* 44-8709090301; *http://* www.signetgroupplc.com

General - Incorporation	UK	*Stock* - Price on:12/24/2007	$21.83
Employees	16,836	Stock Exchange	NYSE
Auditor	KPMG Audit Plc	Ticker Symbol	SIG
Stk Agt	NA	Outstanding Shares	NA
Counsel	Weil, Gotshal & Manges LLP	E.P.S	NA
DUNS No.	21-024-2640	Shareholders	NA

Business: The group's principal activity is retailing of jewellery, watches and gifts with branches throughout the United Kingdom and the United States. It currently operates 1,660 speciality retail jewellery stores. These include 1,050 stores in the United States in 45 states and 610 stores in the United Kingdom.

Primary SIC and add'l.: 5947 5944

CIK No: 0000832988

Subsidiaries: Signet Group QUEST Limited

Officers: Liam O'Sullivan/36/Group Treasurer, Walker Boyd/55/Dir., Group Dir. - Finance, Terry Burman/62/Dir., Group Chief Executive, Tim Jackson/Contact - Investor Relations, Mark Jenkins/50/Group Company Sec., Mark Light/47/Dir., Chief Executive - US, Robert Anderson/49/Dir., Chief Executive - UK, Tom Buchanan/Contact - Financial Public Relations, UK, Mahmoud Siddig/Contact - Financial Public Relations, US, Nina Flintham/Contact - Media, David Bouffard/Contact - Media, Wendel Verbeek/Contact - Financial Public Relations

Directors: Malcolm Williamson/69/Chmn., Mark Light/47/Dir., Chief Executive - US, Robert Walker/63/Dir., Dale W. Hilpert/65/Dir., Walker Boyd/55/Dir., Group Dir. - Finance, Terry Burman/62/Dir., Group Chief Executive, Russell Walls/64/Dir., Brook Land/59/Dir., Robert Anderson/49/Dir., Chief Executive - UK, Robert Blanchard/63/Dir.

Financial Data: Fiscal Year End:01/28   Latest Annual Data: 2/3/2007

Year	Sales	Net Income
2007	$3,725,060,000	$264,445,000
2006	$3,118,568,000	$235,276,000
2005	$3,048,472,000	$259,641,000

Curr. Assets:	$2,369,187,000	*Curr. Liab.:*	$621,565,000		
Plant, Equip.:	$470,847,000	*Total Liab.:*	$1,217,551,000	*Indic. Yr. Divd.:*	$0.720
Total Assets:	$3,442,710,000	*Net Worth:*	$2,225,159,000	*Debt/ Equity:*	0.2040

Signet International Holdings Inc

205 Worth Ave., Ste. 316, Palm Beach, FL, 33480; *PH:* 1-561-832-2000

General - Incorporation	DE	*Stock* - Price on:12/24/2007	NA
Employees	NA	Stock Exchange	OTC
Auditor	S. W. Hatfield, CPA	Ticker Symbol	SIGN
Stk Agt	NA	Outstanding Shares	NA
Counsel	NA	E.P.S	NA
DUNS No.	NA	Shareholders	NA

Business: The groups principle activity is to launch a gaming and entertainment television network. The group operates from United States.

Primary SIC and add'l.: 6770

CIK No: 0001317833

Subsidiaries: Signet Entertainment Corporation, Signet International Holdings, Inc.

Officers: Ernesto W. Letiziano/61/Dir., CEO, CFO, Pres., S. W. Hatfield/Principal Accountant

Directors: Ernesto W. Letiziano/61/Dir., CEO, CFO, Pres.

Owners: Grad Richard/9.78%, Ernest W. Letiziano/50.00%, Ernest W. Letiziano/24.38%, Thomas Donaldson/20.00%, Hope E. Hillabrand/30.00%, Letiziano Ernest W./24.38%, Donaldson Thomas/14.65%, Hillabrand Hope E./12.21%

Silgan Holdings Inc

4 Landmark Sq, Stamford, CT, 06901; *PH:* 1-203-975-7110; *http://* www.silgan.com

General - Incorporation	DE	*Stock* - Price on:12/24/2007	$57.01
Employees	8,600	Stock Exchange	NDQ
Auditor	Ernst & Young LLP	Ticker Symbol	SLGN
Stk Agt	Bank of New York	Outstanding Shares	37,630,000
Counsel	NA	E.P.S	$3.30
DUNS No.	17-827-7612	Shareholders	NA

Business: The groups principle activity is to manufacture metal and plastic consumer goods packaging products. The groups products include steel, aluminum and custom designed plastic containers, tubes and closures, and metal, composite and plastic vacuum closures. The group also provides metal, composite and plastic vacuum closures for food and beverage products. The group operates from United States.

Primary SIC and add'l.: 3089 3411 3085

CIK No: 0000849869

Subsidiaries: Aim Packaging, Inc., Alcoa Inc.s North American aluminum roll-on closure business, Amcor White Cap, LLC(Silgan Closures LLC), Amoco Container Company, Campbell Soup Companys steel container manufacturing business, Clearplass Containers, Inc., Del Monte Corporations U.S. can manufacturing operations, Express Plastic Containers Limited, Finger Lakes Packaging Company, Inc., a subsidiary of Birds Eye Foods, Inc., Food Metal and Specialty business of American National Can Company, Fort Madison Can Company of The Dial Corporation, Fortune Plastics Inc., Monsanto Companys plastic container business, Nestl Food Companys metal container manufacturing division, Pacific Coast Producers can manufacturing operations 20 Subsidiaries included in the Index

Officers: Anthony J. Allott/Dir., CEO, Pres./$2,494,080.00, Glenn A. Paulson/Exec. VP/$559,309.00, Russell F. Gervais/Pres. - Silgan Plastics Corporation/$792,255.00, Kimberly I. Ulmer/40/VP, Controller, Frank W. Hogan/Sr. VP, General Counsel, Sec., James D. Beam/Pres. - Silgan Containers Corporation/$997,964.00, Malcolm E. Miller/VP, Treasurer, Robert B. Lewis/CFO, Exec. VP/$864,293.00, Anthony P. Andreacchi/VP - Tax

Directors: Anthony J. Allott/Dir., CEO, Pres., Philip R. Silver/Non - Exec. Chmn., Greg D. Horrigan/Non - Exec. Chmn., William J. Cennings/Dir., Jeffrey C. Crow/Dir., Edward A. Lapekas/Dir., John W. Alden/Dir.

Owners: Greg D. Horrigan/15.15%, James D. Beam, Russell F. Gervais, Jeffrey C. Crowe, R. Philip Silver/18.21%, Anthony J. Allott, John W. Alden, Insiders/35.06%, William C. Cennings, Robert B. Lewis, Edward A. Lapekas, Glenn A. Paulson

Financial Data: Fiscal Year End:12/31   Latest Annual Data: 12/31/2006

Year	Sales	Net Income
2006	$2,667,519,000	$104,016,000
2005	$2,495,551,000	$87,550,000
2004	$2,420,445,000	$84,145,000

Curr. Assets:	$717,752,000	*Curr. Liab.:*	$432,964,000		
Plant, Equip.:	$894,647,000	*Total Liab.:*	$1,641,839,000	*Indic. Yr. Divd.:*	$0.640
Total Assets:	$2,008,379,000	*Net Worth:*	$366,540,000	*Debt/ Equity:*	2.3763

Silicom Ltd

6 Forest Ave., Paramus, NJ, 07652; *PH:* 1-201-843-1175; *Fax:* 1-201-843-1457;
http:// www.silicom.co.il

General - Incorporation	Israel	*Stock* - Price on:12/24/2007	$18.82
Employees	55	Stock Exchange	NDQ
Auditor	Somekh Chaikin	Ticker Symbol	SILC
Stk Agt	NA	Outstanding Shares	5,360,000
Counsel	NA	E.P.S	$0.93
DUNS No.	60-008-5914	Shareholders	NA

Business: The groups principle activities include designing, manufacturing, marketing and support of modular, miniature connectivity products that combine hardware and software to enable portable computers to interface with local area networks. The group operates from United States.

Primary SIC and add'l.: 3577

CIK No: 0000916793

Subsidiaries: Silicom Connectivity Solutions, Inc

Officers: Eran Gilad/CFO

Owners: Bjurman, Barry & Associates/6.16%, Avi Eizenmann/4.38%, Yehuda Zisapel/12.46%, Zohar Zisapel/12.19%, Robert Sussman/11.65%, Insiders/16.99%

Financial Data: Fiscal Year End:12/31   Latest Annual Data: 12/31/2006

Year	Sales	Net Income
2006	$16,118,000	$2,599,000
2005	$10,876,000	$1,322,000
2004	$4,559,000	-$1,240,000

Curr. Assets:	$12,885,000	*Curr. Liab.:*	$3,452,000		
Plant, Equip.:	$379,000	*Total Liab.:*	$4,672,000	*Indic. Yr. Divd.:*	NA
Total Assets:	$17,853,000	*Net Worth:*	$13,181,000	*Debt/ Equity:*	NA

Silicon Graphics Inc

1140 E Arques Ave., Sunnyvale, CA, 94085; *PH:* 1-650-960-1980; *Fax:* 1-650-933-0316;
http:// www.sgi.com

General - Incorporation	DE	*Stock* - Price on:12/24/2007	$27.84
Employees	1,738	Stock Exchange	NDQ
Auditor	KPMG LLP	Ticker Symbol	SGIC
Stk Agt	EquiServe Trust Co N.A	Outstanding Shares	11,130,000
Counsel	NA	E.P.S	$1.69
DUNS No.	02-403-9778	Shareholders	NA

Business: The group's principal activities are to provide products, services and solutions for use in high-performance computing, visualization and storage. The group focuses on three segments: server segment, visual workstation segment and global services segment. The server segment's current products include visualization systems, high-performance servers and integrated storage solutions. The visual workstation segment's current products include the silicon graphics fuel and silicon graphics tezro workstations. The global services segment supports computer hardware and software products and provides professional services to help customers realize the full value of their information technology investments. The group operates in the United States, Europe and other parts of the world. The trademarks of the group are silicon graphics, sgi, o2, octane, onyx, origin, failsafe, irix, altix, opengl and reality center.

Primary SIC and add'l.: 7373 7378 3575 3571

CIK No: 0000802301

Subsidiaries: Alias Systems NV, Cray Financial Corporation, Cray Research (Canada) Inc., Cray Research (Israel), Ltd., Cray Research America Latina Ltd., Cray Research Asia/Pacific, Inc., Cray Research Eastern Europe Ltd., Cray Research India Ltd., Cray Research International, Inc., Cray Research Limited, Cray Research, LLC, Korea Silicon Graphics Ltd., MIPS Computer Systems Federal, Inc., MIPS HR Systems, Inc., ParaGraph International, Inc. 52 Subsidiaries included in the Index

Officers: Robert Ewald/Dir., CEO, Barry J. Weinert/VP, General Counsel, Tim Butchart/VP - Sales, EMEA, Bill Trestrail/VP - SGI Asia Pacific, Dennis W. Daniels/Sr. VP - Human Resources, Eng Lim Goh/CTO, Sr. VP, Kathy A. Lanterman/CFO, Sr. VP, Corporate Controller, Dave Parry/Sr. VP, Product GM, David A. Barr/Chief Accounting Officer, Corporate Controller

Directors: Robert Ewald/Dir., CEO, Kevin Katari/Chmn., Joanne O. Isham/Dir., Eugene I. Davis/Dir., Anthony Grillo/Dir., Anthony R. Muller/Dir., James A. McDivitt/Dir., Robert R. Bishop/Dir., Chun Won Yi/Dir.

Owners: Morgan Stanley/7.20%, Dennis McKenna, Whippoorwill Associates, Incorporated/8.10%, Symphony Asset Management LLC/9.30%, James A. McDivitt, Chun Won Yi, Insiders/1.40%, Eng Lim Goh, Barry J. Weinert, Kevin D. Katari, Watershed Asset Management L.L.C./13.60%, Robert H. Ewald, David Parry, Anthony Grillo, Quadrangle Debt Recovery Advisors LP/27.80% *(18 Owners included in Index)*

Financial Data: *Fiscal Year End:* 06/24 *Latest Annual Data:* 6/30/2006

Year	Sales		Net Income
2006	$518,805,000		-$146,194,000
2005	$729,965,000		-$76,008,000
2004	$842,002,000		-$45,770,000

Curr. Assets:	$261,009,000	*Curr. Liab.:*	$316,666,000		
Plant, Equip.:	$47,749,000	*Total Liab.:*	$710,512,000	*Indic. Yr. Divd.:*	NA
Total Assets:	$380,058,000	*Net Worth:*	-$330,454,000	*Debt/ Equity:*	0.7054

Silicon Image Inc

1060 E Arques Ave., Sunnyvale, CA, 94085; *PH:* 1-408-616-4000; *Fax:* 1-408-830-9530; *http://* www.siimage.com; *Email:* investor@siliconimage.com

General - Incorporation	DE	**Stock** - Price on: 12/24/2007	$8.61
Employees	442	Stock Exchange	NDQ
Auditor	Deloitte & Touche LLP	Ticker Symbol	SIMG
Stk Agt	Mellon Investor Services LLC	Outstanding Shares	87,760,000
Counsel	Fenwick & West LLP	E.P.S.	$0.43
DUNS No.	NA	Shareholders	NA

Business: The group's principle activities are to design, develop and market semiconductor solutions for communications applications. The group offers a variety of products including transmitters, receivers, controllers, video processors, storage semiconductors and a series of redundant array of independent disks, controller boards and storage subsystems. It offers products in three markets: personal computing, consumer electronics and storage. The products of the group's are sold to distributors and original equipment manufacturers throughout the world through a direct sales force with field offices located in North America, Taiwan and Europe, and indirectly through a network of distributors and manufacturer's representatives located throughout North America, Asia and Europe. The group's quarterly revenue for September 2007 was 86.28 millions of USD.

Primary SIC and add'l.: 3674

CIK No: 0001003214

Subsidiaries: CMD Technology Inc., DVDO, Inc., HDMI Licensing, LLC, Silicon Image KK, Silicon Image, UK, Simplay Labs, LLC, Slice Acquisition Corp., TWN Acquisition Corp., Zillion Technologies, LLC

Officers: Steve Tirado/Dir., CEO, Pres./$3,674,954.00, Rob Valiton/43/VP - Worldwide Sales/$1,497,165.00, Eric C. Almgren/VP - Business Development, Intellectual Property Licensing, Robert Freeman/CFO/$943,680.00, Brett Gaines/VP - Strategic Business Development, Paul Dal Santo/COO, Noland Granberry/Chief Accounting Officer, Corporate Controller, Edward Lopez/Chief Legal Officer, Jurgen Ruprecht/VP - Systems Development, Sal Cobar/VP - Worldwide Sales, Doug Haslam/VP - Human Resources, Duane J. Northcutt/CTO/$1,245,732.00, Peter Rado/VP - Worldwide Operations, Quality, John H.J. Shin/VP - Engineering/$1,002,148.00, Dale Zimmerman/VP - Worldwide Marketing *(17 Officers included in Index)*

Directors: Steve Tirado/Dir., CEO, Pres., Peter Hanelt/Chmn., William George/Dir., John Hodge/Dir., Masood Jabbar/Dir., William J. Raduchel/Dir.

Owners: Masood Jabbar, Barclays Global Investors/5.68%, Robert Freeman, William Raduchel, John Hodge, Duane J.Northcutt, The Vanguard Group/4.97%, Steve Tirado/1.08%, Peter Hanelt, Insiders/2.62%, John Shin, William George, Rob Valiton, David Hodges

Financial Data: *Fiscal Year End:* 12/31 *Latest Annual Data:* 12/31/2006

Year	Sales		Net Income
2006	$294,958,000		$42,465,000
2005	$212,399,000		$49,549,000
2004	$173,159,000		-$324,000

Curr. Assets:	$336,551,000	*Curr. Liab.:*	$74,471,000	*P/E Ratio:*	18.32
Plant, Equip.:	$18,431,000	*Total Liab.:*	$75,009,000	*Indic. Yr. Divd.:*	NA
Total Assets:	$380,231,000	*Net Worth:*	$305,222,000	*Debt/ Equity:*	NA

Silicon Laboratories Inc

400 W Cesar ChAve.z, Austin, TX, 78701; *PH:* 1-512-416-8500; *Fax:* 1-512-464-9444; *http://* www.silabs.com

General - Incorporation	DE	**Stock** - Price on: 12/24/2007	$35.32
Employees	742	Stock Exchange	NDQ
Auditor	Ernst & Young LLP	Ticker Symbol	SLAB
Stk Agt	American Stock Transfer & Trust Co.	Outstanding Shares	54,770,000
Counsel	Andrews & Kurch LLP	E.P.S.	$3.06
DUNS No.	NA	Shareholders	NA

Business: The group's principal activity is to design and develop proprietary, analog-intensive, mixed-signal integrated circuits (ics) for the communications industry. These circuits are marketed for various communications industries. The group provides ics that can be incorporated into communications devices, such as wireless phones and modems, as well as cable and satellite set-top boxes, personal computer modems, voice over Internet protocol on data networks, voice over digital subscriber line modems, personal video recorders, telephone equipment and optical network equipment. The customers include agere systems, broadcom, echostar, PC-tel, samsung, smart link, sony, Texas instruments, thomson and wavecom. The group also has international markets in Europe and the Pacific Rim region.

Primary SIC and add'l.: 3674

CIK No: 0001038074

Subsidiaries: Silicon Laboratories Asia Pacific, Limited, Silicon Laboratories FRANCE, Silicon Laboratories GmbH, Silicon Laboratories International Pte. Ltd., Silicon Laboratories Italy S.r.l., Silicon Laboratories Sweden AB, Silicon Laboratories Technology, LLC, Silicon Laboratories UK Limited, Silicon Laboratories Y.K., Silicon Labs CP,Inc., Silicon Labs HV,Inc., Silicon Labs Isolation,Inc.

Officers: Necip Sayiner/Dir., CEO, Pres./$3,235,839.00, Douglas Holberg/VP - Technology, William G. Bock/57/Sr. VP, CFO/$240,543.00, David Bresemann/VP, Derrell Coker/VP, Gary R. Gay/57/VP - Worldwide Sales/$798,529.00, Mark Downing/VP - Strategy, Business Development, Kurt Hoff/VP - Worldwide Sales, Tyson Tuttle/VP, Paul V. Walsh/43/VP - Finance/$427,187.00, Jon Ivester/VP - Worldwide Operations

Directors: Necip Sayiner/Dir., CEO, Pres., Nav Sooch/Chmn., William Wood/52/Dir., Ted R. Enloe/69/Dir., Berry H. Cash/Dir., Larry G. Walker/Dir., David R. Welland/Dir.

Owners: Gary R. Gay, Russell J. Brennan, Ted R. Enloe, Navdeep S. Sooch/2.83%, Laurence G. Walker, William P. Wood, Entities deemed to be affiliated with Franklin Resources, Inc./7.44%, Entities deemed to be affiliated with Capital Group International, Inc./7.73%, Jonathan D. Ivester, Entities deemed to be affiliated with AXA Assurances I.A.R.D. Mutuelle/10.54%, Harvey B. Cash, Paul V. Walsh, David R. Welland/4.51%, Necip Sayine, Insiders/10.27% *(16 Owners included in Index)*

Financial Data: *Fiscal Year End:* 12/31 *Latest Annual Data:* 12/30/2006

Year	Sales		Net Income
2006	$464,597,000		$31,158,000
2005	$425,689,000		$47,506,000

Curr. Assets:	$476,841,000	*Curr. Liab.:*	$107,537,000	*P/E Ratio:*	11.54
Plant, Equip.:	$32,584,000	*Total Liab.:*	$114,955,000	*Indic. Yr. Divd.:*	NA
Total Assets:	$613,003,000	*Net Worth:*	$498,048,000	*Debt/ Equity:*	0.0726

Silicon Motion Technology Corp

2125 Zanker Rd., San Jose, CA, 95131; *PH:* 1-408-501-5300; *Fax:* 1-408-467-9390; *http://* www.siliconmotion.com.tw; *Email:* IR@siliconmotion.com

General - Incorporation	Cayman Islands	**Stock** - Price on: 12/24/2007	$25.37
Employees	361	Stock Exchange	NDQ
Auditor	Deloitte & Touche LLP	Ticker Symbol	SIMO
Stk Agt	Butterfield Bank (Cayman) Limited	Outstanding Shares	31,150,000
Counsel	NA	E.P.S.	$1.09
DUNS No.	NA	Shareholders	NA

Business: The groups principle activities include designing, developing and marketing semiconductor solutions. The products of the group include USB 2.0 controller, flash memory controller, portable audio ocs and multimedia display processors. Specific customers of the group include Lexar Media, Samsung, Sony and STMicroelectronics. The group operates from Taiwan, the United States, Japan and other. The group's quarterly revenue for September 2007 was 1497.49 millions of USD.

Primary SIC and add'l.: 3679 3674

CIK No: 0001329394

Subsidiaries: Silicon Motion, Inc

Officers: Wallace C. Kou/Dir., CEO, Pres., Jason Chiang/VP, Special Assist. to CEO, Frank Chang/Sr. Dir. - Research, Development, Ken Chen/VP - Operations, Riyadh Lai/CFO

Directors: Wallace C. Kou/Dir., CEO, Pres., James Chow/Chmn., Tsung-Ming Chung/Dir., C. S. Ho/Dir., Lie-Chun Liu/Dir., Yung-Chien Wang/Dir., Henry Chen/Dir.

Owners: Yung-Chien Wang, Ken Chen, Brandywine Global Investment Management, LLC/11.40%, Wallace C. Kou/1.70%, Tsung-Ming Chung, James Chow/1.80%, Frank Chang, Lien-chun Liu, Henry Chen, C. S. Ho

Financial Data: *Fiscal Year End:* 12/31 *Latest Annual Data:* 12/31/2005

Year	Sales		Net Income
2005	$81,906,000		$20,528,000
2004	$68,872,000		$8,519,000
2003	$26,812,000		$3,236,000

Curr. Assets:	$151,862,000	*Curr. Liab.:*	$29,412,000		
Plant, Equip.:	$9,799,000	*Total Liab.:*	$29,475,000	*Indic. Yr. Divd.:*	NA
Total Assets:	$169,644,000	*Net Worth:*	$140,169,000	*Debt/ Equity:*	NA

Silicon Mountain Holdings Inc

Formerly: Z-Axis Corp
4755 Walnut St., Boulder, CO, 80301; *PH:* 1-303-938-1155; *http://* www.zaxis.com

General - Incorporation	CO	**Stock** - Price on: 12/24/2007	$0.14
Employees	19	Stock Exchange	NA
Auditor	Ehrhardt Keefe Steiner & Hottman P.C	Ticker Symbol	NA
Stk Agt	Computershare Trust Co	Outstanding Shares	3,830,000
Counsel	NA	E.P.S.	-$0.44
DUNS No.	10-848-5319	Shareholders	NA

Business: The group's principle activities include developing and producing computer generated video graphics and other presentation materials. The products of the company are computer generated graphics, live action video, photographs, graphic artwork, document presentation, special effects and presentation exhibit boards. The company also provides consulting and presentation services which includes analysis of complex litigation issues, design of demonstrative evidence, production of such evidence and courtroom presentation. The litigation support customers are law firms, corporations and insurance companies. Vupoint, a product of the company, is a courtroom presentation system used by trial teams, outside counsel and in-house attorneys. The group operates from United States.

Primary SIC and add'l.: 7372 7384

CIK No: 0000723928

Subsidiaries: Silicon Mountains

Officers: Rudolph A. Cates/37/Dir., CEO, Pres., Shaun Hanner/39/COO, Stephanie Kelso/Pres., Heidi Oneil/Dir. - Finance, Administration, Juan C. Perez/42/CFO

Directors: Rudolph A. Cates/37/Dir., CEO, Pres., John Blackman/65/Chmn., Stephanie Kelso/Pres., Mark Crossen/59/Dir., Mickey Fain/52/Dir., Steven King/52/Dir., Chong Man Lee/48/Dir., Camillo Martino/46/Dir., Eric A. Wittenberg/50/Dir.

Owners: Mickey Fain, Eric Wittenburg, John Blackman/3.24%, Mark Crossen/41.60%, Patrick Hanner/11.88%, Rudolph A. Cates/24.47%, Roger Haston/8.13%, Chong Man Lee, Insiders/70.94%

Financial Data: *Fiscal Year End:* 03/31 *Latest Annual Data:* 03/31/2007

Year	Sales	Net Income
2007	$3,226,000	-$327,000
2006	$2,945,000	-$425,000
2005	$3,487,000	$8,000

Curr. Assets:	$984,000	**Curr. Liab.:**	$778,000		
Plant, Equip.:	$99,000	**Total Liab.:**	$895,000	**Indic. Yr. Divd.:**	NA
Total Assets:	$1,448,000	**Net Worth:**	$552,000	**Debt/ Equity:**	NA

Silicon Storage Technology Inc

1171 Sonora Ct., Sunnyvale, CA, 94086; ***PH:*** 1-408-735-9110; ***Fax:*** 1-408-735-9036; ***http://*** www.sst.com; ***Email:*** quality@sst.com

General - Incorporation CA
Employees 631
Auditor PricewaterhouseCoopers LLP
Stk Agt American Stock Transfer & Trust Co.
Counsel Cooley Godward LLP
DUNS No. 61-819-2074

Stock- Price on:12/24/2007 $3.75
Stock Exchange NDQ
Ticker Symbol SSTI
Outstanding Shares 103,560,000
E.P.S. $0.25
Shareholders NA

Business: The group's principal activity is to supply flash memory semiconductor devices. The group offers these products to digital consumer, networking, wireless communications and Internet computing markets. The group operates through four segments: standard memory product group, application specific product group, special product group and technology licensing. The major customers of the group include apple, dell, intel, lg electronics, motorola, panasonic, samsung, sanyo, siemens, sony and others. The group operates in the United States, Europe, Japan, Korea, Taiwan, China and other Asian countries. On 13-Sep-2004, the group acquired majority stake in emosyn llc.

Primary SIC and add'l.: 3674 6794

CIK No: 0000855906

Subsidiaries: Memtech SSD, Corporation, S.t.i., LLC, SimpleTech Cayman Limited, SimpleTech Europe, SimpleTech Europe, BV, SimpleTech Global Limited, SimpleTech Hong Kong Limited, STEC, Inc.

Officers: Bing Yeh/Chmn., CEO, Pres., Chen Tsai/Sr. VP - Worldwide Backend Operations, Paul Lui/Sr. VP - Standard, Special Product Group, Pres. - SST, Michael Briner/Sr. VP - Application Specific Product Group, Jack K. Lai/VP - Administration, Corporate Development, Sec., Derek Best/Sr. VP - Sales, Marketing, Yaw Wen Hu/Dir., COO, Exec. VP, James Boyd/CFO, Sr. VP - Finance

Directors: Bing Yeh/Chmn., CEO, Pres., Yasushi Chikagami/Dir., Ronald Chwang/Dir., Tsuyoshi Taira/Dir., Yaw Wen Hu/Dir., COO, Exec. VP, Terry Nickerson/Dir.

Financial Data: **Fiscal Year End:**12/31 **Latest Annual Data:** 12/31/2005

Year	Sales	Net Income
2005	$430,899,000	-$29,838,000
2004	$449,198,000	$23,929,000
2003	$295,041,000	-$65,167,000

Curr. Assets:	$277,078,000	**Curr. Liab.:**	$95,377,000		
Plant, Equip.:	$19,415,000	**Total Liab.:**	$98,004,000	**Indic. Yr. Divd.:**	NA
Total Assets:	$477,837,000	**Net Worth:**	$379,833,000	**Debt/ Equity:**	NA

Siliconware Precision Industries Co Ltd

1735 Technology Dr., Ste. 300, San Jose, CA, 95110; ***PH:*** 1-408-573-5500; ***Fax:*** 1-408-573-5530; ***http://*** www.spil.com.tw; ***Email:*** info@spil.com.tw

General - Incorporation Taiwan
Employees 12,971
Auditor PricewaterhouseCoopers LLP
Stk Agt China Trust Commercial Bank
Counsel Lee & Li
DUNS No. NA

Stock- Price on:12/24/2007 $11.13
Stock Exchange NDQ
Ticker Symbol SPIL
Outstanding Shares 543,290,000
E.P.S. $0.07
Shareholders NA

Business: The group's principal activities are the manufacture, assembly and provision of testing and turnkey services of integrated circuits. Other activities include the manufacture and process of electronic accessories and provision of investment and agency services. Operations are carried out in Taiwan, the british virgin islands, the cayman islands and the United States of America.

Primary SIC and add'l.: 3674 3672

CIK No: 0001111759

Subsidiaries: Siliconware Investment Company Ltd., Siliconware Technology (Suzhou) Limited, Siliconware U.S.A. Inc., Spil (b.v.i.) Holding Limited, SPIL (Cayman) Holding Limited

Officers: Chi-Wen W. Tsai/Vice Chmn., CEO, Pres., Johnson Tien/Sr. VP - Marketing, Sales Group, Eva Chen/Dir., CFO, Y. J. Chang/Sr. VP - Manufacturing Group, Michael Chang/VP - Hsinchu Branch, Carl Chen/VP - Manufacturing Group, Jack Chen/VP - North America Customer Service, Johnson Tai/VP - Bumping, Testing Taichung, C. S. Hsiao/VP - Research, Development Center, Yu Hu Liu/VP - Chang Hua Site, Jas Hsieh/VP - Quality, Reliability Center

Directors: Chi-Wen W. Tsai/Vice Chmn., CEO, Pres., Bough Lin/Chmn., Eva Chen/Dir., CFO, Wen-Chung Lin/Dir., Yen-Chun Chang/Dir., Jing-Shan Aur/Dir., Ing-Dar Liu/Dir., Hsiu-Li Liu/Dir., Wen-Lung Lin/Dir., Wen-Jung Lin/Dir., Jerome Tsai/Dir., Wen-Lung Cheng/Dir., Fu-Mei Tang/Dir., Teresa Wang/Dir.

Owners: Citibank in Custody for Citigroup Global Markets Ltd./1.50%, Kuming Investment Company Ltd./1.85%, Chi-Wen Tsai/1.26%, HSBC in Custody for Goldman Sachs International Company/1.23%, Siliconware Investment Company Ltd./1.19%, Citibank/19.64%, Government of Singapore Investment Corp. PFE. Ltd./1.57%, Sanford C. Bemstein & Co. Delaware Business Trust-Emerging Market Value Series/1.34%, Insiders/6.88%, Wen-Lung Lin/1.09%, Bough Lin/1.50%

Financial Data: **Fiscal Year End:**12/31 **Latest Annual Data:** 12/31/2006

Year	Sales	Net Income
2006	$1,752,866,000	$258,158,000
2005	$1,325,850,000	$121,076,000
2004	$1,110,654,000	$115,537,000

Curr. Assets:	$887,445,000	**Curr. Liab.:**	$347,662,000		
Plant, Equip.:	$1,032,076,000	**Total Liab.:**	$580,271,000	**Indic. Yr. Divd.:**	$0.370
Total Assets:	$2,570,425,000	**Net Worth:**	$1,990,154,000	**Debt/ Equity:**	NA

Silver Dragon Resources Inc

5160 Yonge St., Ste. 803, Toronto, ON, M2N 6L9; ***PH:*** 1-416-223-8500; ***Fax:*** 1-416-223-8507; ***http://*** www.silverdragonresources.com; ***Email:*** info@silverdragonresources.com

General - Incorporation DE
Employees NA
Auditor SF Partnership, LLP
Stk Agt Signature Stock Transfer, Inc.
Counsel NA
DUNS No. NA

Stock- Price on:12/24/2007 $1.09
Stock Exchange OTC
Ticker Symbol SDRG
Outstanding Shares NA
E.P.S. NA
Shareholders NA

Business: The groups principal activities include developing and marketing electric automobiles. In April 2005, the group acquired Sino Silver Corp. The group operates from the United States.

Primary SIC and add'l.: 1040

CIK No: 0001017290

Subsidiaries: California Electric Automobile Co., Inc., Sanhe Sino-Top Resources and Technologies, Ltd., Silver Dragon Mining De Mexico, S.A. De C.V.

Officers: Marc M. Hazout/Dir., CEO, Pres., Colin P. Sutherland/Dir., CFO, Manuel Chan/Dir., VP - Operations - China, Sri Siva-Kumaran/Corporate Controller, Alessandro M. Motta/Dir. - Investor Relations, Information Technology, Jennifer Ouaknine/Corporate Administration, Lourdes Nunez/Administration - Mexico, Rosario Reyes/Administrative Superintendent, Mexico, Douglas R. Wood/Project Mgr. - Cerro Las Minitas, Mexico, Juan Carlos Gonzalez/GM - Cerro Las Minitas, Mexico, Tony Yu/Operations Mgr. - China, Ava Li/Assist. Operations Mgr. - China, Tiebing Liu/Geologist, China, Hao Xu/Project Mgr. - China

Directors: Marc M. Hazout/Dir., CEO, Pres., Colin P. Sutherland/Dir., CFO, Manuel Chan/Dir., VP - Operations - China, Terry Christopher/Dir.

Owners: ALPHA CAPITAL ANSTALT, Marc Hazout/26.20%, Insiders/26.20%, HELLER CAPITAL INVESTMENTS LLC, DRAGONFLY CAPITAL PARTNERS LLC

Financial Data: **Fiscal Year End:**12/31 **Latest Annual Data:** 12/31/2006

Year	Sales	Net Income
2006	NA	-$8,236,000
2005	NA	-$543,000
2004	NA	-$399,000

Curr. Assets:	$4,000,000	**Curr. Liab.:**	$393,000		
Plant, Equip.:	$249,000	**Total Liab.:**	$393,000	**Indic. Yr. Divd.:**	NA
Total Assets:	$11,118,000	**Net Worth:**	$10,614,000	**Debt/ Equity:**	NA

Silver Falls Bank OR

19245 Molalla Ave., Oregon City, OR, 97045; ***PH:*** 1-503-518-8808; ***Fax:*** 1-503-518-8828; ***http://*** www.silverfallsbank.com

General - Incorporation
Employees NA
Auditor NA
Stk Agt Registrar & Transfer Co
Counsel NA
DUNS No. NA

Stock- Price on:12/24/2007 $38
Stock Exchange OTC
Ticker Symbol SVFL
Outstanding Shares NA
E.P.S. NA
Shareholders NA

Business: The groups principal activities include providing banking and financial services. Services of the group include checking accounts, savings accounts, certificates of deposit, installment loans, real estate mortgage loans, commercial loans, traveler's checks, safe deposit boxes, night depository and automated teller services. The group operates from the United States.

Primary SIC and add'l.: 6029

CIK No:

Silver Pearl Enterprises Inc

1541 E Interstate 30, Rockwall, TX, 75087; ***PH:*** 1-972-722-3352

General - Incorporation NV
Employees 2
Auditor The Hall Group, Cpas
Stk Agt Signature Stock Transfer, Inc.
Counsel NA
DUNS No. NA

Stock- Price on:12/24/2007 $0.15
Stock Exchange OTC
Ticker Symbol SVPE
Outstanding Shares 5,700,000
E.P.S. -$0.06
Shareholders NA

Business: The groups principle activity is a retailer of home and commercial furniture and related accessories. Products of the group include sofas, love seats, mirrors, occasional tables, lamps, rugs, bed frames, bureaus and dressers, pictures, and assorted home and business ornamental accessories. The group operates from the United States.

Primary SIC and add'l.: 7389

CIK No: 0001326396

Officers: Denise D. Smith/Dir., CEO, CFO, Pres.

Directors: Denise D. Smith/Dir., CEO, CFO, Pres.

Owners: TriPoint Capital Advisors, LLC/8.43%, Art Xpectations, LLC/7.02%, Progressive Capital Markets, LLC/6.32%, Denise D. Smith/70.21%, Insiders/70.21%

Financial Data: **Fiscal Year End:**12/31 **Latest Annual Data:** 12/31/2006

Year	Sales	Net Income
2006	$98,000	-$345,000

Curr. Assets:	$75,000	**Curr. Liab.:**	$44,000		
Plant, Equip.:	$53,000	**Total Liab.:**	$44,000	**Indic. Yr. Divd.:**	NA
Total Assets:	$199,000	**Net Worth:**	$155,000	**Debt/ Equity:**	NA

Silver River Ventures Inc

1615 Golden Aspen Dr., Ste. 101, Ames, IA, 50010; ***PH:*** 1-515-233-8333; ***http://*** www.bioforcenano.com

General - Incorporation NV
Employees 23
Auditor Chisholm, Bierwolf & Nilson, LLC
Stk Agt StockTrans, Inc.
Counsel NA
DUNS No. NA

Stock- Price on:12/24/2007 $1.01
Stock Exchange OTC
Ticker Symbol BFNH
Outstanding Shares 24,100,000
E.P.S. -$0.18
Shareholders NA

Business: The groups principle activities include developing and marketing nanotech tools and solutions for the life sciences through instruments, consumables, and applications. The groups technology is introduced as the Nano enabler(TM) system. The group operates from United States.

Primary SIC and add'l.: 1400

CIK No: 0001310488

Subsidiaries: BioForce, Silver River Acquisitions, Inc.

Officers: Eric Henderson/51/Chmn., CEO, Pres., Sec., Kerry M. Frey/62/Dir., COO, Curtis Mosher/37/VP - Research, Development, Gregory D. Brown/46/Dir., CFO, Treasurer, Michael Lynch/31/Dir. - Nano Enabler, TM Products, Saju Nettikadan/39/Dir. - Nanoapplications Development Group

Directors: Eric Henderson/51/Chmn., CEO, Pres., Sec., Nancy A. Ah Chong/Dir., Kerry M. Frey/62/Dir., COO, Jean-Jacques Sunier/46/Dir., Larry Gold/66/Dir., Gregory D. Brown/46/Dir., CFO, Treasurer

Owners: FCPR SGAM Biotechnology Fund/27.10%, Alma & Gabriel Elias/8.80%, Eric R. Henderson/15.60%, Harvey Kaye/7.00%, Jean-Jacques Sunier/0.20%, Edward F. Cowle/3.50%, Kerry M. Frey/0.60%, Insiders/16.90%, Larry Gold/0.20%

Financial Data: Fiscal Year End:12/31   Latest Annual Data: 12/31/2006

Year	Sales	Net Income
2006	$415,000	-$3,974,000
2005	NA	-$19,000

Curr. Assets: -	$3,874,000	Curr. Liab.:	$840,000		
Plant, Equip.:	$538,000	Total Liab.:	$1,119,000	Indic. Yr. Divd.:	NA
Total Assets:	$5,061,000	Net Worth:	$3,942,000	Debt/ Equity:	0.0764

Silver Screen Studios Inc

233 Peachtree St. , Ste. 1225, Atlanta, GA, 30303; *PH:* 1-404-222-7344; *http://* www.silverscreenstudiogroup.com

General - Incorporation	GA	Stock- Price on:12/24/2007	$0.007
Employees	NA	Stock Exchange	NA
Auditor	Norman H. Ross, P.C	Ticker Symbol	NA
Stk Agt	NA	Outstanding Shares	398,230,000
Counsel	NA	E.P.S.	-$0.003
DUNS No.	NA	Shareholders	NA

Business: The group's principal activity are to develop, produce and distribute a broad range of music, motion picture and other filmed entertainment content through their operating subsidiaries. The group also intends to establish a music publishing division, a television production division and a producer/artist management division.

Primary SIC and add'l.: 9999

CIK No: 0001262456

Subsidiaries: Greenlight Productions, Inc., SSSG Acquisition Corp.

Officers: Barry Thomas/50/Dir., CEO

Directors: Barry Thomas/50/Dir., CEO

Financial Data: Fiscal Year End:12/31   Latest Annual Data: 12/31/2006

Year	Sales	Net Income
2006	NA	-$731,000
2005	NA	-$78,000
2004	NA	-$1,276,000

Curr. Assets:	$4,000	Curr. Liab.:	NA		
Plant, Equip.:	$20,000	Total Liab.:	NA	Indic. Yr. Divd.:	NA
Total Assets:	$24,000	Net Worth:	$24,000	Debt/ Equity:	NA

Silver Standard Resources Inc

999 W Hastings St., Ste. 1180, Vancouver, BC, V6C 2W2; *PH:* 1-604-689-3846; *http://* www.silver-standard.com; *Email:* invest@silverstandard.com

General - Incorporation	Canada	Stock- Price on:12/24/2007	NA
Employees	16	Stock Exchange	NDQ
Auditor	PricewaterhouseCoopers LLP	Ticker Symbol	SSRI
Stk Agt	Computershare Trust Company of Canada	Outstanding Shares	NA
Counsel	NA	E.P.S.	-$0.34
DUNS No.	20-115-9365	Shareholders	NA

Business: The group's principal activity is to acquire, explore and develop silver mineral properties primarily in Australia, Argentina, Chile and the United States. The group has interests in three advanced silver-dominant projects: a 100% owned bowdens project in Australia, the manantal espejo project in Argentina and the el asiento project in Bolivia. The group acquired 43.4% interest in sunshine Argentina inc on 27-Jun-2002.

Primary SIC and add'l.: 1044 1041

CIK No: 0000921638

Subsidiaries: Black Hawk Mining Inc., Coastal Capital Partners L.P., Pacific Rim Mining Corp., Silver Standard Australia Pty. Ltd

Officers: Robert A. Quartermain/Dir., CEO, Pres., George Paspalas/Sr. VP - Operations, Tom S.Q. Yip/CFO, VP - Finance, Michael Robb/67/VP - Project Development, Kenneth C. McNaughton/VP - Exploration, Ross A. Mitchell/59/VP - Finance, Joseph Ovsenek/Sr. VP - Corporate, Linda J. Sue/Corp. Sec., Paul W. Lafontaine/Dir. - Investor Relations, Jonathan N. Singh/Corporate Controller, Ron Burk/Chief Geologist, Max H. Holtby/Sr. Geologist

Directors: Robert A. Quartermain/Dir., CEO, Pres., Gordon R.E. Davis/Dir., John R. Brodie/Dir., David L. Johnston/Dir., William Meyer/Dir., Peter W. Tomsett/Dir.

Owners: K. McNaughton/0.23%, R. A. Quartermain/1.28%, J. Ovsenek/0.36%, M. Robb/0.13%, R. Mitchell/0.21%

Financial Data: Fiscal Year End:12/31   Latest Annual Data: 12/31/2006

Year	Sales	Net Income
2006	NA	-$9,478,000
2005	NA	-$22,806,000
2004	NA	-$63,003,000

Curr. Assets:	$244,898,000	Curr. Liab.:	$4,601,000		
Plant, Equip.:	$6,975,000	Total Liab.:	$6,606,000	Indic. Yr. Divd.:	NA
Total Assets:	$254,817,000	Net Worth:	$248,211,000	Debt/ Equity:	NA

Silver Star Energy Inc

9595 Wilshire Blvd, Ste. 900, Beverly Hills, CA, 90212; *PH:* 1-310-477-2211; *http://* www.silverstarenergy.com; *Email:* ir@silverstarenergy.com

General - Incorporation	NV	Stock- Price on:12/24/2007	$0.024
Employees	NA	Stock Exchange	OTC
Auditor	Robison, Hill & Co.	Ticker Symbol	SVSE
Stk Agt	NA	Outstanding Shares	96,220,000
Counsel	Chris Dieterich Law Offices	E.P.S.	$0.02
DUNS No.	NA	Shareholders	NA

Business: The groups principle activities include identifying, acquiring and developing working interests in underdeveloped oil and gas projects that do not meet the requirements of larger producers and developers. In August 2005, the group acquired Kansas oil and gas play. The group operates from the United States. The group's quarterly revenue for Sep '07 was 0.05 millions of USD.

Primary SIC and add'l.: 1382

CIK No: 0001216964

Officers: Robert McIntosh/Dir., CEO, Pres., David Naylor/Dir., CFO, Treasurer, Richard Johnson/Engineering Consultant

Directors: Robert McIntosh/Dir., CEO, Pres., David Naylor/Dir., CFO, Treasurer

Owners: Robert McIntosh/6.13%, Sak Narwal/12.16%, Naomi Patricia Johnson/8.63%, Insiders/6.13%

Financial Data: Fiscal Year End:12/31   Latest Annual Data: 12/31/2006

Year	Sales	Net Income
2006	$2,401,000	$1,781,000
2005	$1,678,000	-$5,544,000
2004	NA	-$1,118,000

Curr. Assets:	$747,000	Curr. Liab.:	$4,351,000		
Plant, Equip.:	$4,050,000	Total Liab.:	$4,690,000	Indic. Yr. Divd.:	NA
Total Assets:	$4,995,000	Net Worth:	$305,000	Debt/ Equity:	NA

Silver State Bancorp

170 S Green Valley Pkwy., Henderson, NV, 89012; *PH:* 1-702-433-8300; *Fax:* 1-702-968-8517; *http://* www.silverstatebank.com

General - Incorporation		Stock- Price on:12/24/2007	$22.8
Employees	536	Stock Exchange	NDQ
Auditor	NA	Ticker Symbol	SSBX
Stk Agt	Mellon Investor Services LLC	Outstanding Shares	17,400,000
Counsel	NA	E.P.S.	$1.71
DUNS No.	NA	Shareholders	NA

Business: The groups principal activity is to serve all of customers lending and deposit needs. Services of the group include purchase or construct a building, buy machinery and equipment, purchase an existing business, augment working capital, refinance debt and balloon payments, start a franchise or a new business.

Primary SIC and add'l.: 6712 6022

CIK No: 0001362719

Officers: Corey L. Johnson/50/Dir., CEO, Pres./$604,287.00, Michael Threet/38/CFO, COO, Corp. Sec./$242,309.00, Douglas E. French/50/Exec. VP - Commercial Real Estate Lending, Silver State Bank, Calvin D. Regan/42/Pres. - Silver State Bank, Thomas J. Russell/58/Exec. VP, Credit Administrator - Silver State Bank, Kirk Viau/42/Sr. VP, Chief Risk Officer

Directors: Corey L. Johnson/50/Dir., CEO, Pres., Bryan S. Norby/51/Chmn., Brian M. Collins/45/Dir., Brian Cruden/47/Dir., Alan Knudson/57/Dir., Craig McCall/51/Dir., Thomas Nicholson/71/Dir., Phillip C. Peekman/59/Dir.

Owners: Craig A. McCall/1.57%, Thomas T. Nicholson/16.43%, Brian W. Cruden/1.11%, Phillip C. Peekman/1.62%, Corey L. Johnson/2.01%, Brian M. Collins/4.74%, Insiders/35.49%, Bryan S. Norby/2.70%, Alan Knudson, Thomas J. Russell, Estate of Ronald C. Yanke/16.10%, Calvin D. Regan/1.40%, Douglas E. French/1.90%, Michael J. Threet/1.04%

Financial Data: Fiscal Year End:NA   Latest Annual Data: 12/31/2002

Year	Sales	Net Income
2002	$24,084,000	$2,245,000
2001	$24,302,000	$1,892,000
2000	$22,217,000	$2,208,000

Curr. Assets:	$17,810,000	Curr. Liab.:	$303,567,000		
Plant, Equip.:	$13,555,000	Total Liab.:	$357,933,000	Indic. Yr. Divd.:	NA
Total Assets:	$379,889,000	Net Worth:	$21,956,000	Debt/ Equity:	NA

Silver Wheaton Corp

666 Burrard St., Ste. 3400, Vancouver, BC, V6C 2X8; *PH:* 1-604-684-9648; *http://* www.silverwheaton.com; *Email:* info@silverwheaton.com

General - Incorporation	BC	Stock- Price on:12/24/2007	$11.856
Employees	9	Stock Exchange	NYSE
Auditor	Deloitte & Touche LLP	Ticker Symbol	SLW
Stk Agt	Mellon Trust Co	Outstanding Shares	221,280,000
Counsel	NA	E.P.S.	$0.40
DUNS No.	NA	Shareholders	NA

Business: The group's activities include mining with 100% of its revenue from silver production and it expects to sell approximately 9.5 million ounces of silver in 2005. The company is debt free, unhedged and seeking further acquisitions. The group's quarterly revenue for Sep '07 was 39.60 millions of USD.

Primary SIC and add'l.: 1040

CIK No: 0001323404

Subsidiaries: Wheaton Trading (Caymans) Ltd

Officers: Peter Barnes/Dir., CEO, Pres., Nolan Watson/CFO, Randy Smallwood/Exec. VP - Corporate Development, David Awram/Investor Relation Officer

Directors: Peter Barnes/Dir., CEO, Pres., Eduardo Luna/Chmn., Wade D. Nesmith/Dir., John Brough/Dir., Peter R. Gillin/Dir., Lawrence Bell/Dir., Douglas Holtby/Dir.

Financial Data: Fiscal Year End:12/31   Latest Annual Data: 12/31/2006

Year	Sales	Net Income
2006	$158,541,000	-$90,753,000
2005	$70,895,000	$25,291,000

Curr. Assets:	$61,347,000	Curr. Liab.:	$21,354,000		
Plant, Equip.:	NA	Total Liab.:	$297,242,000	Indic. Yr. Divd.:	NA
Total Assets:	$702,399,000	Net Worth:	$405,157,000	Debt/ Equity:	NA

Silverado Financial Inc

1475 S Bascom Ave., Ste 210, Campbell, CA, 95008; *PH:* 1-408-371-2301;
http:// www.silveradofinancial.com; *Email:* info@silveradofinancial.com

General - Incorporation	NV	Stock - Price on:12/24/2007	$0.0025
Employees	100	Stock Exchange	OTC
Auditor	Sallmann, Yang & Alameda	Ticker Symbol	SLVO
Stk Agt	Nevada Agency & Trust Company	Outstanding Shares	19,640,000
Counsel	NA	E.P.S	-$0.026
DUNS No.	NA	Shareholders	NA

Business: The group's principal activity is to provide first and second mortgage products to borrowers in California. It conducts this activity through its operating subsidiary, realty capital corporation. The group provides mortgage products designed for borrowers who satisfy the credit, documentation or other underwriting standards prescribed by conventional mortgage lenders and loan buyers, such as fannie mae and freddie mac as well as those who do not. The group operates offices located in campbell and pleasanton, California. In 2003, the group originated 100% of its loans in California. Of the loans originated, 65% were refinances of existing mortgages and 35% were for the purchase of residential property. On 09-May-2003, the group acquired realty capital corporation. On 09-May-2004, it acquired lendingtech.com inc.

Primary SIC and add'l.: 6162 6159

CIK No: 0001032405

Subsidiaries: Financial Software Inc. (FSI), Silverado Mortgage Corporation (SMC)

*Financial Data: Fiscal Year End:*12/31   *Latest Annual Data:* 12/31/2004

Year	Sales	Net Income
2004	$903,000	-$993,000
2003	$116,000	-$938,000
2002	$8,000	-$403,000

Curr. Assets:	$55,000	Curr. Liab.:	$467,000		
Plant, Equip.:	$744,000	Total Liab.:	$467,000	Indic. Yr. Divd.:	NA
Total Assets:	$822,000	Net Worth:	$355,000	Debt/ Equity:	1.8190

Silverado Gold Mines Ltd

1111 W Georgia St., Ste. 505, Vancouver, BC, V6E 4M3; *PH:* 1-604-689-1535;
Fax: 1-604-682-3519; *http://* www.silverado.com; *Email:* pr@silverado.com

General - Incorporation	BC	Stock - Price on:12/24/2007	$0.09
Employees	NA	Stock Exchange	OTC
Auditor	Berkovits, Lago & Co LLP	Ticker Symbol	SLGLF
Stk Agt	Computershare Trust Co	Outstanding Shares	NA
Counsel	Key & Mehringer	E.P.S	NA
DUNS No.	24-293-3950	Shareholders	NA

Business: The group's principal activity is to acquire, explore and develop mineral properties and low rank coal water fuel technology as a replacement for oil fried boilers and utility generators. The group's exploration and development activities are managed and conducted by affiliated companies, tri-con mining ltd., tri-con mining inc. And tri-con mining Alaska inc. The group holds interests in four groups of mineral properties in Alaska: the nolan gold project, ester dome property, marshall dome property and hammond property.

Primary SIC and add'l.: 1041 1099

CIK No: 0000731727

Subsidiaries: Silverado Green Fuel Inc.

Officers: Garry Anselmo/Chmn., CEO, CFO, COO, Pres., Roger C. Burggraf/Environment, Safety Administrator - Land Man, Alaska, John R. MacKay/75/Corp. Sec., Gilbert A. Dobbs/71/Mining Superintendent, Karsten Eden/VP - Exploration, Daniel L. Basketfield/VP - Environmental Engineering, Warrack G. Willson/VP - Fuel Technology Division - Silverado Green Fuel INC

Directors: Garry Anselmo/Chmn., CEO, CFO, COO, Pres., James F. Dixon/60/Dir., Stuart C. McCulloch/72/Dir.

Owners: James F. Dixon/1.50%, Insiders/10.00%, John R. Mackay/0.80%, Stuart McCulloch/1.20%, Garry L. Anselmo/6.40%

*Financial Data: Fiscal Year End:*11/30   *Latest Annual Data:* 11/30/2006

Year	Sales	Net Income
2006	NA	-$7,683,000
2005	NA	-$3,394,000
2004	NA	-$4,304,000

Curr. Assets:	$4,031,000	Curr. Liab.:	$1,341,000		
Plant, Equip.:	$1,054,000	Total Liab.:	$2,110,000	Indic. Yr. Divd.:	NA
Total Assets:	$5,085,000	Net Worth:	$2,975,000	Debt/ Equity:	NA

Silvergraph International Inc

11919 Burke St., Santa Fe Springs, CA, 90670; *PH:* 1-562-696-3656; *Fax:* 1-562-696-0090;
http:// www.silvergraph.com

General - Incorporation	NV	Stock - Price on:12/24/2007	$1.09
Employees	11	Stock Exchange	OTC
Auditor	Weinberg & Co., P.A	Ticker Symbol	SVGI
Stk Agt	NA	Outstanding Shares	36,020,000
Counsel	NA	E.P.S	-$0.05
DUNS No.	NA	Shareholders	NA

Business: The groups principal activity is to seek, investigate, and, if warranted, acquire an interest in a business opportunity. The groups merger, exchange of, may make the groups acquisition of a business opportunity stock, or otherwise. The group operates from the United States.

Primary SIC and add'l.: 7330

CIK No: 0001115975

Officers: James R. Simpson/CEO, William W. Lee/Pres., Gary Freeman/CFO, James R. Martin/Exec. VP - Sales, Marketing

Directors: Gary R. Martin/58/Dir., Evan Levine/42/Dir.

Owners: James R. Simpson, Gary R. Martin, Gary Freeman, Insiders, William W. Lee, Hock-Simpson, LLC, Robert J. Neborsky, M.D. Inc. Combination Retirement Trust, Lions Head Capital, LLC, Mark Capital, LLC, James R. Martin, Evan Levine, Winosaco, LLC

*Financial Data: Fiscal Year End:*12/31   *Latest Annual Data:* 12/31/2006

Year	Sales	Net Income
2006	$868,000	-$1,135,000
2005	NA	-$5,000

Curr. Assets:	$378,000	Curr. Liab.:	$754,000		
Plant, Equip.:	$221,000	Total Liab.:	$1,100,000	Indic. Yr. Divd.:	NA
Total Assets:	$660,000	Net Worth:	-$440,000	Debt/ Equity:	NA

Silverleaf Resorts Inc

1221 River Bend Dr., Ste. 120, Dallas, TX, 75247; *PH:* 1-214-631-1166; *Fax:* 1-214-637-0585;
http:// www.silverleafresorts.com; *Email:* info@silverleafresorts.com

General - Incorporation	TX	Stock - Price on:12/24/2007	$19.5
Employees	2,157	Stock Exchange	AMEX
Auditor	BDO Seidman LLP	Ticker Symbol	SVL
Stk Agt	Chase Mellon Shareholder Services LLC	Outstanding Shares	NA
Counsel	NA	E.P.S.	NA
DUNS No.	01-556-0402	Shareholders	NA

Business: The group's principle activities are to market and sell one-week annual and biennial vacation intervals and provide financial services for the purchase of vacation intervals. In addition the group has in-house sales, marketing, financing, and property management capabilities and coordinates all aspects of the operation of the 19 existing owned or managed resorts and the development of any new timeshare resort, including site selection, design, and construction. Vacation intervals are marketed to individuals primarily through direct mail and telephone solicitation. The group's quarterly revenue for September 2007 was 67.53 millions of USD.

Primary SIC and add'l.: 7997 6531 6141

CIK No: 0001033032

Subsidiaries: Silverleaf Finance I, Inc., Silverleaf Finance II, Inc

Officers: Robert E. Mead/Chmn., CEO/$3,668,279.00, Robert G. Levy/VP - Resort Operations, Darla Cordova/VP - Employee, Marketing Services, Edward L. Lahart/Exec. VP - Operations, Sandra G. Cearley/Sec., Michael D. Jones/VP - Information Services, Herman Jay Hankamer/VP - Resort Development, Lelori Marconi/VP - Preview Center Marketing, Sharon K. Brayfield/Pres./$511,856.00, Joe W. Conner/COO/$309,375.00, David T. Oconnor/Exec. VP - Sales/$1,188,902.00, Harry J. White/CFO, Treasurer/$329,063.00, Barbara L. Lewis/VP - Financial Services, Michael P. Lowrey/VP - Call Center Operations, Thomas J. Morris/Sr. VP - Capital Markets *(16 Officers included in Index)*

Directors: Robert E. Mead/Chmn., CEO, Richard J. Budd/Dir., James B. Francis/Dir., Herbert B. Hirsch/Dir., Rebecca Janet Whitmore/Dir.

Owners: Bonanza Capital, Ltd./5.69%, Robert E. Mead/24.73%, Sharon K. Brayfield/1.63%, Grace Brothers, Ltd./16.18%, Herbert B. Hirsch, Andreeff Equity Advisors, L.L.C./5.48%, Harry J. White/1.16%, David T. OConnor/1.86%, Rebecca Janet Whitmore, Richard J. Budd, Joe W. Conner, James B. Francis, Insiders/31.83%

Curr. Assets:	$31,408,000	Curr. Liab.:	$22,638,000		
Plant, Equip.:	$176,004,000	Total Liab.:	$326,338,000	Indic. Yr. Divd.:	NA
Total Assets:	$474,530,000	Net Worth:	$148,192,000	Debt/ Equity:	NA

Silverstar Holdings Ltd

1900 Glades Rd., Ste. 435, Boca Raton, FL, 33431; *PH:* 1-561-479-0040; *Fax:* 1-561-479-0757;
http:// www.silverstarholdings.com; *Email:* clive@silverstarholdings.com

General - Incorporation	Bermuda	Stock - Price on:12/24/2007	$1.85
Employees	12	Stock Exchange	NDQ
Auditor	Rachlin Cohen & Holtz LLP	Ticker Symbol	SSTR
Stk Agt	NA	Outstanding Shares	10,200,000
Counsel	NA	E.P.S.	-$0.56
DUNS No.	NA	Shareholders	NA

Business: The group operates through its subsidiaries whose principle activity is to operate sports-themed websites, specialized in subscription based nascar, college football and basketball and other fantasy sports games, and student sports, specializes in media products and marketing programs focusing on the high school athletic market; and operates wireless, a start-up company that develops wireless broadband products. The group operates from United States.

Primary SIC and add'l.: 4899 7372 7375 6719

CIK No: 0001003390

Subsidiaries: Fantasy Sports, Inc., First South Africa Management Corp, First South African Holdings (Pty), Ltd, Silverstar Holdings, Inc, Strategy First, Inc.

Officers: Clive Kabatznik/CEO, Pres.

Owners: Douglas A. Brisotti, Insiders, Cornelius J. Roodt, Clive P. Kabatznik, Michael Levy, Edward Roffman

*Financial Data: Fiscal Year End:*06/30   *Latest Annual Data:* 06/30/2007

Year	Sales	Net Income
2007	$19,794,000	-$2,407,000
2006	$3,316,000	-$1,979,000
2005	$2,299,000	$159,000

Curr. Assets:	$13,162,000	Curr. Liab.:	$3,587,000		
Plant, Equip.:	$78,000	Total Liab.:	$6,137,000	Indic. Yr. Divd.:	NA
Total Assets:	$17,538,000	Net Worth:	$11,400,000	Debt/ Equity:	0.2395

Simclar Inc

2230 W 77th St., Hialeah, FL, 33016; *PH:* 1-305-556-9210; *Fax:* 1-305-364-1350;
http:// www.simclar.com

General - Incorporation	FL	Stock - Price on:12/24/2007	$5.86
Employees	780	Stock Exchange	NDQ
Auditor	Battelle & Battelle LLP	Ticker Symbol	SIMC
Stk Agt	Continental Stock Transfer & Trust Co	Outstanding Shares	6,470,000
Counsel	NA	E.P.S.	$0.55
DUNS No.	08-413-0400	Shareholders	NA

Business: The group's principle activity is contract manufacturing of electronic and electro-mechanical products, providing advanced electronics manufacturing services (EMS) to original equipment manufacturers (OEMs) in the data processing, telecommunications, instrumentation and food preparation equipment industries. The principal custom-designed products of the group include complex printed circuit boards (PCBs), conventional and molded cables, wire harnesses and electro-mechanical

assemblies. The group also provides OEMs with value-added, turnkey contract manufacturing services and total systems assembly and integration. The group's manufacturing and assembly operations are located in Florida, Texas, Massachusetts, Missouri, Ohio and Mexico. The group's quarterly revenue for September 2007 was 33.15 millions of USD.

Primary SIC and add'l.: 3699 3679

CIK No: 0000764039

Subsidiaries: Simclar (Mexico), Inc., Simclar (North America), Inc., Simclar de Mexico, S.A. de C.V., Simclar Interconnect Technologies, Inc., Techdyne (Europe) Limited

Officers: Samuel J. Russell/63/Chmn., CEO/$120,000.00, Barry Pardon/56/Dir., Pres./$166,793.00, Marshall W. Griffin/50/CFO, Treasurer, Sec./$115,672.00, Edward L. McGrath/62/VP, GM

Directors: Samuel J. Russell/63/Chmn., CEO, John Ian Durie/51/Dir., Barry Pardon/56/Dir., Pres., Christina Margaret Janet Russell/63/Dir., Graeme A. Manson/48/Dir., Patrick Lacchia/39/Dir., Kenneth M. MacKay/62/Dir.

Owners: John Ian Durie, Insiders, Simclar Group Limited, Samuel J. Russell, Barry Pardon, Christina M. J. Russell

Financial Data: *Fiscal Year End:*12/31 *Latest Annual Data:* 12/31/2006

Year	Sales	Net Income
2006	$116,031,000	$2,863,000
2005	$61,005,000	$947,000
2004	$53,582,000	$2,342,000

Curr. Assets:	$42,831,000	**Curr. Liab.:**	$28,595,000	**P/E Ratio:**	10.65
Plant, Equip.:	$9,924,000	**Total Liab.:**	$45,942,000	**Indic. Yr. Divd.:**	NA
Total Assets:	$63,864,000	**Net Worth:**	$17,922,000	**Debt/ Equity:**	0.7148

Simmons Bedding Co

One Concourse Pkwy, Ste 800, Atlanta, GA, 30328; *PH:* 1-770-512-7700; *http://* www.simmonsco.com; *Email:* international@simmons.com

General - Incorporation	DE	**Stock**- Price on:12/24/2007	NA
Employees	NA	Stock Exchange	NA
Auditor	PricewaterhouseCoopers LLP	Ticker Symbol	NA
Stk Agt	NA	Outstanding Shares	NA
Counsel	NA	E.P.S	NA
DUNS No.	03-820-4020	Shareholders	NA

Business: The group's principle activities include manufacturing and distributing a broad range of mattresses, box springs, bedding frames and sleep accessories. The group operates from United States.

Primary SIC and add'l.: 2515

CIK No: 0001014022

Subsidiaries: Dreamwell, Ltd., Revezbien Establishment, SC Holdings, Inc., Simmons Capital Management, LLC, Simmons Caribbean Bedding, Inc., Simmons Contract Sales, LLC, Simmons I.P., Inc., Simmons International Limited, Simmons Juvenile Company, LLC, Sleep Country USA, Inc., The Simmons Manufacturing Co., LLC, Windsor Bedding Co., LLC, World of Sleep Outlets, LLC

Simmons First National Corp

501 Main St., Pine Bluff, AR, 71601; *PH:* 1-870-541-1000; *Fax:* 1-870-541-1154; *http://* www.simmonsfirst.com

General - Incorporation	AR	**Stock**- Price on:12/24/2007	$28.42
Employees	1,134	Stock Exchange	NDQ
Auditor	BKD LLP	Ticker Symbol	SFNC
Stk Agt	National City Bank	Outstanding Shares	14,130,000
Counsel	NA	E.P.S	$1.94
DUNS No.	10-364-9554	Shareholders	NA

Business: The group's principal activity is to provide guaranteed student loans, mortgage banking services and commercial banking services to individuals and businesses. The group also provides a wide range of loans to commercial, agricultural and financial institution industry. The consumer services include checking, savings and time deposits, credit card and other consumer services. The group provides real estate loans for construction, single family residential and other commercial. Other services include personal and corporate trust services, investment management, securities and investment services. The banking subsidiaries of the group conduct their operations through 79 offices located in 45 communities in Arkansas. The group purchased nine financial centers from union planters bank, n.a. The locations include clinton, marshall, mountain view, fairfield bay, leslie and bee branch. On 19-Mar-2004, the group acquired alliance bancorporation, inc.

Primary SIC and add'l.: 6712 6021

CIK No: 0000090498

Subsidiaries: Simmons First Bank of El Dorado, Simmons First Bank of Jonesboro, Simmons First Bank of Northwest Arkansas, Simmons First Bank of Russellville, Simmons First Investment Group, Inc, Simmons First Investment Group, Inc., Simmons First National Bank, Simmons First National Corporation

Officers: Thomas J. May/61/Chmn., CEO/$1,071,391.00, Steve Trusty/CEO, Pres. - Simmons First, Hot Springs, Ronnie Twyford/Exec. VP - Operations, Simmons First, Hot Springs, David L. Bartlett/COO, Pres./$483,499.00, Marty D. Casteel/Exec. VP/$209,937.00, Rick Harris/Sr. VP - Lending, Simmons First, Hot Springs, Cindy Baswell/VP - Administration, Simmons First, Hot Springs, Tommie Jones/Sr. VP, HR Dir./$153,750.00, Linda Hogaboom/Contact - Malvern Avenue Branch, Robert A. Fehlman/CFO, Exec. VP/$255,694.00, John L. Rush/73/Sec., Lori Lemm/Contact - West Grand Branch, Cynthia Reed/Contact - Highway 7 South Branch, Nancy Hall/Contact - Albert Pike Branch

Directors: Thomas J. May/61/Chmn., CEO, George A. Makris/51/Dir., Steven A. Cosse/60/Dir., Harry L. Ryburn/72/Dir., Robert Lee Shoptaw/Dir., Stanley Eldon Reed/Dir., William E. Clark/64/Dir., Henry F. Trotter/70/Dir., Scott W. McGeorge/64/Dir.

Owners: Insiders/3.49%, William E. Clark, Robert L. Shoptaw, Steven A. Cosse, George A. Makris, Robert A. Fehlman, Employee Stock Ownership Trust/8.15%, Marty D. Casteel, Stanley E. Reed, Harry L. Ryburn, Thomas J. May/1.89%, David L. Bartlett, Scott W. McGeorge, Henry F. Trotter, Tommie K. Jones

Financial Data: *Fiscal Year End:*12/31 *Latest Annual Data:* 12/31/2006

Year	Sales	Net Income
2006	$197,309,000	$27,481,000
2005	$175,557,000	$26,962,000
2004	$156,911,000	$24,446,000

Curr. Assets:	$177,612,000	**Curr. Liab.:**	$2,309,086,000	**P/E Ratio:**	14.65
Plant, Equip.:	$69,866,000	**Total Liab.:**	$2,392,397,000	**Indic. Yr. Divd.:**	$0.720
Total Assets:	$2,651,413,000	**Net Worth:**	$259,016,000	**Debt/ Equity:**	0.3188

Simon Property Group Inc

225 W Washington St., Indianapolis, IN, 46204; *PH:* 1-317-636-1600; *Fax:* 1-317-263-2318; *http://* www.shopsimon.com; *Email:* ircontact@simon.com

General - Incorporation	DE	**Stock**- Price on:12/24/2007	$97.02
Employees	2,700	Stock Exchange	NYSE
Auditor	Ernst& Young LLP	Ticker Symbol	SPG
Stk Agt	Mellon Investor Services LLC	Outstanding Shares	223,390,000
Counsel	NA	E.P.S	$2.37
DUNS No.	NA	Shareholders	NA

Business: The groups principal activities include owning, developing and management of retail real estate, regional malls, premium outlet centers and lifestyle centers. In the year 2006, the group acquired Mall of Georgia. The group operates from the United States.

Primary SIC and add'l.: 6798

CIK No: 0001063761

Subsidiaries: CPG Partners, L.P., Kravco Simon Company, Kravco Simon Investments, L.P., M.S. Management Associates, Inc., Marigold Indemnity, Ltd., Rosewood Indemnity, Ltd., Shopping Center Associates, Simon Brand Ventures, LLC, Simon Business Network, LLC, Simon Capital Limited Partnership, Simon Global Limited, Simon Management Associates, LLC, Simon Property Group (Illinois), L.P., Simon Property Group (Texas), L.P., Simon Property Group Administrative Services Partnership, L.P. 19 Subsidiaries included in the Index

Officers: David Simon/Chmn., CEO/$3,096,156.00, Leslie T. Chao/CEO - Premium Outlet Centers, Chelsea, Michael J. Clarke/CFO, Co - Pres. - Premium Outlet Centers, Chelsea, John R. Klein/Co - Pres., Vicki Hanor/Exec. VP - Leasing, Richard S. Sokolov/Dir., COO, Pres., Hans C. Mautner/Dir., Pres. - International Division, Advisory Dir., David Bloom/Dir., Advisory Dir., James M. Barkley/Sec., General Counsel/$1,896,301.00, John Dahl/Chief Accounting Officer, Sr. VP, Carl Dieterle/Exec. VP - Development, Arthur W. Spellmeyer/Exec. VP - Development, Stephen E. Sterrett/CFO, Exec. VP/$1,820,399.00, Andrew Juster/Sr. VP, Treasurer, Gary Lewis/Pres. - Leasing, Sr. Exec. VP/$1,673,402.00 *(24 Officers included in Index)*

Directors: David Simon/Chmn., CEO, Herbert Simon/Chmn. Emeritus, Melvin Simon/Chmn. Emeritus, Albert J. Smith/Dir., Richard S. Sokolov/Dir., COO, Pres., Pieter S. Van Den Berg/Dir., Denise M. Debartolo York/Dir., Hans C. Mautner/Dir., Pres. - International Division, Advisory Dir., David Bloom/Dir., Advisory Dir., Reuben S. Leibowitz/Dir., Fredrick W. Petri/Dir., Birch Bayh/Dir., Melvyn E. Bergstein/Dir., Linda Bynoe/Dir., Karen N. Horn/Dir.

Owners: Melvin Simon& Associates,Inc/13.80%, Barclays Global Investors/5.10%, The Vanguard Group,Inc/6.00%, Morgan Stanley/5.40%, Edward J. DeBartolo/6.50%

Financial Data: *Fiscal Year End:*12/31 *Latest Annual Data:* 12/31/2006

Year	Sales	Net Income
2006	$3,332,154,000	$563,840,000
2005	$3,166,853,000	$475,749,000
2004	$2,641,751,000	$342,993,000

Curr. Assets:	$1,309,488,000	**Curr. Liab.:**	$1,109,190,000	**P/E Ratio:**	23.02
Plant, Equip.:	$18,257,833,000	**Total Liab.:**	$18,104,813,000	**Indic. Yr. Divd.:**	$3.360
Total Assets:	$22,084,455,000	**Net Worth:**	$3,979,642,000	**Debt/ Equity:**	NA

Simon Worldwide Inc

5200 W Century Blvd., Los Angeles, CA, 90045; *PH:* 1-310-417-4660; *http://* www.nitromed.com

General - Incorporation	DE	**Stock**- Price on:12/24/2007	$0.39
Employees	4	Stock Exchange	OTC
Auditor	BDO Seidman LLP	Ticker Symbol	SWWI
Stk Agt	American Stock Transfer & Trust CO.	Outstanding Shares	16,670,000
Counsel	Wilmer Cutler Pickering Hale and Dorr	E.P.S	-$0.19
DUNS No.	03-081-9759	Shareholders	NA

Business: The group's principal activity is to design, manufacture and sell custom screen-printed sports apparel and accessories such as t-shirts, pullovers, jackets, sports bags and caps designed to enhance corporate identity and build brand awareness. The group is a full-service promotional marketing agency, which specializes in the design and development of high-impact promotional products and programs. The group's products include screen-printed t-shirts, sweatshirts, sports bags, embroided shirts and caps.

Primary SIC and add'l.: 3949 5699

CIK No: 0000864264

Officers: Greg Mays/61/Dir., CFO/$499,467.00

Directors: Joseph W. Bartlett/74/Dir., Allan I. Brown/67/Dir., Terrence J. Wallock/63/Dir., Joseph Anthony Kouba/60/Dir., Greg Mays/61/Dir., CFO, Ira Tochner/46/Dir., Erika Paulson/34/Dir.

Owners: Insiders/7.70%, Joseph W. Bartlett, Eric Stanton/6.70%, Gregory P. Shlopak/6.40%, Greg Mays, J. Anthony Kouba, Patrick D. Brady/7.10%, Allan I. Brown/6.80%, Hazelton Capital Limited/6.80%, Everest Special Situations Fund L.P./12.90%, Terrence Wallock, H. Ty Warner/5.90%, Yucaipa and affiliates/19.40%

Financial Data: *Fiscal Year End:*12/31 *Latest Annual Data:* 12/31/2006

Year	Sales	Net Income
2006	NA	-$1,918,000
2005	NA	-$3,162,000
2004	NA	$20,636,000

Curr. Assets:	$18,009,000	**Curr. Liab.:**	$1,445,000		
Plant, Equip.:	NA	**Total Liab.:**	$1,445,000	**Indic. Yr. Divd.:**	NA
Total Assets:	$26,590,000	**Net Worth:**	-$7,236,000	**Debt/ Equity:**	NA

SimpleTech Inc

3001 Daimler St., Santa Ana, CA, 92705; *PH:* 1-800-367-7330; *http://* www.simpletech.com

General - Incorporation	CA	**Stock**- Price on:12/24/2007	$6.41
Employees	631	Stock Exchange	NDQ
Auditor	PricewaterhouseCoopers LLP	Ticker Symbol	NA
Stk Agt	American Stock Transfer & Trust Co.	Outstanding Shares	49,860,000
Counsel	NA	E.P.S	$0.48
DUNS No.	NA	Shareholders	NA

Business: The group's principal activities are to design, manufacture and market custom and open-standard memory solutions based on flash memory and dynamic random access memory or dram technologies. The group operates in three segments: consumer, OEM and xiran. The consumer segment markets open-standard memory storage products such as flash cards, dram modules, usb mini drives and hard disk drives, which are used primarily as upgrades in consumer electronic devices and computing systems. The OEM segment markets customized memory solutions for newly manufactured systems. The xiran segment develops advanced board-level solutions that optimize server performance for networked storage applications, including ip storage.

Primary SIC and add'l.: 3577 3679

CIK No: 0001102741

Subsidiaries: Memtech SSD, Corporation, S.t.i., LLC, SimpleTech Cayman Limited, SimpleTech Europe, SimpleTech Europe, BV, SimpleTech Global Limited, SimpleTech Hong Kong Limited, STEC, Inc.

Officers: Manouch Moshayedi/Chmn., CEO/$535,600.00, Mark Moshayedi/46/Dir., COO, Pres., CTO, Sec./$423,300.00, Dan Moses/Dir., CFO, Exec. VP/$354,500.00

Directors: Manouch Moshayedi/Chmn., CEO, Dan Moses/Dir., CFO, Exec. VP, Michael F. Ball/Dir., Mark Moshayedi/46/Dir., COO, Pres., CTO, Sec., James J. Peterson/Dir., Rajat Bahri/43/Dir., Vahid Manian/Dir.

Owners: James J. Peterson, Manouch Moshayedi/14.60%, Insiders/37.50%, Mark Moshayedi/22.30%, Michael F. Ball, Vahid Manian, Mike Moshayedi/13.80%, Dan Moses, Rajat Bahri, FMR Corp./14.30%

Financial Data: Fiscal Year End:12/31 Latest Annual Data: 12/31/2006

Year	Sales	Net Income
2006	$352,110,000	$21,851,000
2005	$261,988,000	$5,573,000
2004	$275,432,000	$4,689,000

Curr. Assets:	$188,275,000	Curr. Liab.:	$40,642,000	P/E Ratio:	14.24
Plant, Equip.:	$11,864,000	Total Liab.:	$40,642,000	Indic. Yr. Divd.:	NA
Total Assets:	$206,656,000	Net Worth:	$166,014,000	Debt/Equity:	NA

Simpson Manufacturing Co Inc

5956 W Las Positas Blvd., Pleasanton, CA, 94588; **PH:** 1-925-560-9000; **Fax:** 1-925-847-1603; **http://** www.simpsonmfg.com

General - Incorporation	DE	Stock- Price on:12/24/2007	$32.49
Employees	2,678	Stock Exchange	NYSE
Auditor	PricewaterhouseCoopers LLP	Ticker Symbol	SSD
Stk Agt	Computershare Trust Co	Outstanding Shares	48,410,000
Counsel	NA	E.P.S.	$1.87
DUNS No.	00-915-6449	Shareholders	NA

Business: The group's principal activities are to design, engineer and manufacture wood-to-wood, wood-to-concrete and wood-to-masonry connectors and pre-fabricated shearwalls. The group also offers a full line of adhesive, mechanical anchors and powder actuated tools for concrete, masonry and steel. The connector products enhances the safety and durability of the structures in which they are installed and also contributes to structural integrity and resistance to seismic, wind and other forces. The products of the group are marketed to the residential construction, light industrial and commercial construction. The group has 15 manufacturing locations in the United States, Canada, France, Denmark and England. In may 2003, the group acquired mga construction hardware & steel fabricating limited and mga connectors limited. During Apr 2004, the group acquired atf furrer holzgmbh.

Primary SIC and add'l.: 3449

CIK No: 0000920371

Subsidiaries: ATF GmbH, Quik Drive Australia Pty. Limited, Simpson Dura-Vent Company, Inc, Simpson France EURL, Simpson Manufacturing Cyprus Limited, Simpson Strong-Tie, Simpson Strong-Tie Australia, Inc, Simpson Strong-Tie Canada, Limited, Simpson Strong-Tie Company Inc, Simpson Strong-Tie Company Inc., Simpson Strong-Tie France SCI, Simpson Strong-Tie GmbH, Simpson Strong-Tie International, Inc, Simpson Strong-Tie Japan, Inc, Simpson Strong-Tie Mexico 17 Subsidiaries included in the Index

Officers: Thomas J. Fitzmyers/Dir., CEO, Pres./$3,193,062.00, Stephen B. Lamson/55/Dir., VP/$1,921,787.00, Stephen P. Eberhard/Executive Officer, Michael J. Herbert/CFO, Treasurer, Sec./$1,273,835.00, Phillip T. Kingsfather/Executive Officer/$1,029,445.00

Directors: Thomas J. Fitzmyers/Dir., CEO, Pres., Barclay Simpson/Chmn., Barry Lawson Williams/Dir., Earl F. Cheit/Dir., Stephen B. Lamson/55/Dir., VP, Robin Greenway MacGillivray/Dir., Peter N. Louras/Dir., Jennifer A. Chatman/Dir., Gary M. Cusumano/Dir.

Owners: Neuberger Berman, LLC/7.70%, Thomas J. Fitzmyers/1.20%, Michael J. Herbert, U.S. Trust Corporation/5.50%, Fidelity Management and Research Company/9.90%, Barclay Simpson/22.00%, Phillip T. Kingsfather, Jennifer A. Chatman, Peter N. Louras, Stephen B. Lamson, Earl F. Cheit, Insiders/23.80%, Barry Lawson Williams, Robin G. MacGillivray, ClearBridge Advisors, LLC/5.70% *(16 Owners included in Index)*

Financial Data: Fiscal Year End:12/31 Latest Annual Data: 12/31/2006

Year	Sales	Net Income
2006	$863,180,000	$102,496,000
2005	$846,256,000	$98,394,000
2004	$698,053,000	$81,508,000

Curr. Assets:	$479,338,000	Curr. Liab.:	$80,255,000	P/E Ratio:	17.37
Plant, Equip.:	$197,180,000	Total Liab.:	$82,459,000	Indic. Yr. Divd.:	$0.400
Total Assets:	$735,334,000	Net Worth:	$652,875,000	Debt/Equity:	0.0005

Simtek Corp

4250 Buckingham Dr., Ste. 100, Colorado Springs, CO, 80907; **PH:** 1-719-531-9444; **Fax:** 1-719-531-9481; **http://** www.simtek.com; **Email:** resumes@simtek.com

General - Incorporation	CO	Stock- Price on:12/24/2007	NA
Employees	52	Stock Exchange	NDQ
Auditor	Hein & Assoc. LLP	Ticker Symbol	SMTK
Stk Agt	Equity Transfer Services Inc	Outstanding Shares	NA
Counsel	NA	E.P.S.	-$0.06
DUNS No.	17-921-0075	Shareholders	NA

Business: The group's principle activities are to design, develop, produce and market nonvolatile semiconductor memories and programmed semiconductor logic products. It also provides electronics engineering research and development contracts. The products are used in commercial electronic equipment markets such as industrial control systems, office automation, medical instrumentation,

telecommunication systems, cable television and numerous military systems including communications, radar, sonar and smart weapons. The group has four sales and marketing offices, located in Colorado, Georgia ,windsor and Hong Kong. The group's quarterly revenue for September 2007 was 8.70 millions of USD.

Primary SIC and add'l.: 3674 6794

CIK No: 0000817516

Subsidiaries: Q-DOT, Simtek GMBH

Officers: Harold Blomquist/Chmn., CEO, Pres./$1,120,319.00, David Still/VP - Engineering, Ronald Sartore/Dir., Exec. VP/$190,901.00, Brian Alleman/CFO, VP/$405,132.00, Steve Hayes/VP - Worldwide Sales, Grant Hulse/VP - Worldwide Marketing, Chris McComb/VP - Worldwide Operations, Bernd Junghans/MD - Simtek Gmbh, Jeremy Cowx/MD - Apac Sales

Directors: Harold Blomquist/Chmn., CEO, Pres., Ronald Sartore/Dir., Exec. VP, Robert Keeley/Dir., Robert Pearson/Dir., Tom Surrette/Dir., Alfred Stein/Dir., John Hillyard/Dir., Philip Black/Dir.

Owners: John Hillyard, Big Bend XXVII Investments, L.P./9.57%, Insiders/3.65%, Toibb Investment LLC/6.93%, Crestview Capital Master LLC/16.47%, Brian Alleman, SF Capital Partners, Ltd/6.58%, Robert Keeley, Alfred Stein, Cypress Semiconductor Corporation/16.97%, Ronald Sartore, Renaissance Capital Growth & Income Fund III, Inc./6.64%, Renaissance US Growth Investment Trust PLC/6.64%, Robert Pearson, Harold A. Blomquist/1.85% *(16 Owners included in Index)*

Financial Data: Fiscal Year End:12/31 Latest Annual Data: 12/31/2006

Year	Sales	Net Income
2006	$30,630,000	-$2,007,000
2005	$10,385,000	-$5,785,000
2004	$14,902,000	-$3,670,000

Curr. Assets:	$18,742,000	Curr. Liab.:	$6,914,000		
Plant, Equip.:	$1,239,000	Total Liab.:	$9,134,000	Indic. Yr. Divd.:	NA
Total Assets:	$28,242,000	Net Worth:	$19,108,000	Debt/Equity:	NA

Simtrol Inc

520 Guthridge Ct., Ste. 250, Norcross, GA, 30092; **PH:** 1-678-533-1200; **Fax:** 1-770-441-1823; **http://** www.simtrol.com; **Email:** info@simtrol.com

General - Incorporation	DE	Stock- Price on:12/24/2007	$1.4
Employees	9	Stock Exchange	OTC
Auditor	Marcum & Kliegman LLP	Ticker Symbol	SMRL
Stk Agt	SunTrust Bank	Outstanding Shares	6,230,000
Counsel	NA	E.P.S.	-$0.92
DUNS No.	61-760-3089	Shareholders	NA

Business: The group's principal activities are to design, manufacture, market and support software based audiovisual control systems and videoconferencing products that operate on PC platforms. The primary product of the group, ongoertm is software that allows a control system to manage and control a wide variety of devices. The group offers component-technology development to support the integration of complex devices and custom user interface creation. The customers include audiovisual systems integrators, medium sized corporations, state, local and federal government agencies and health care facilities.

Primary SIC and add'l.: 7373 7372

CIK No: 0000846775

Subsidiaries: Quality Software Associates, Inc, Videoconferencing Systems, Inc

Officers: Richard W. Egan/43/Dir., CEO, Pres./$179,519.00, Stephen N. Samp/43/CFO, Sec./$157,394.00, Michael L. Miller/46/CTO, George W. Moring/42/CIO, William G. Joyce/43/Exec. VP - Operations, Matthew A. Finger/34/Dir. - Business Development, Barry S. Saltzman/46/Sr. VP - Channel Operations, Richard T. Eaton/59/Sr. VP - Sales

Directors: Richard W. Egan/43/Dir., CEO, Pres., Dallas S. Clement/43/Chmn., Edward S. Redstone/79/Dir., Larry M. Carr/65/Dir., Adam D. Senter/51/Dir., Julia B. North/60/Dir., Thomas J. Stallings/60/Dir.

Owners: Richard W. Egan, Steve Gorlin, Jarrett Gorlin, Larry M. M. Carr, Adam D. Senter, Donald B. Gasgarth, Vikas Group, Inc., Stephen N. Samp, Dallas S. Clement, Rakesh Ranchod, Oliver M. Cooper, Vestal Venture Capital, Edward S. Redstone, Julia B. North, Thomas J. Stallings *(25 Owners included in Index)*

Financial Data: Fiscal Year End:12/31 Latest Annual Data: 12/31/2006

Year	Sales	Net Income
2006	$225,000	-$1,462,000
2005	$125,000	-$1,366,000
2004	$566,000	-$899,000

Curr. Assets:	$99,000	Curr. Liab.:	$1,961,000		
Plant, Equip.:	$17,000	Total Liab.:	$2,013,000	Indic. Yr. Divd.:	NA
Total Assets:	$286,000	Net Worth:	-$1,727,000	Debt/Equity:	NA

Simulations Plus Inc

42505 10th St. W, Lancaster, CA, 93534; **PH:** 1-661-723-7723; **Fax:** 1-661-723-5524; **http://** www.simulations-plus.com; **Email:** info@simulations-plus.com

General - Incorporation	CA	Stock- Price on:12/24/2007	$10.4
Employees	33	Stock Exchange	AMEX
Auditor	Rose, Snyder & Jacobs LLP	Ticker Symbol	SLP
Stk Agt	Don Maddalon Integrity Stock Transfer	Outstanding Shares	7,720,000
Counsel	Luce, Forward, Hamilton & Scripps	E.P.S.	$0.08
DUNS No.	95-969-1809	Shareholders	NA

Business: The group's principal activity is to design and develop computer software. It also manufactures augmentative communication devices and computer access products that provide a voice for those who cannot speak and allow physically disabled persons to operate a standard computer. In addition, the group designs and develops pharmaceutical simulation software to promote cost-effective solutions to a number of problems in pharmaceutical research and in the education of pharmacy and medical students. It also develops and sells interactive, educational software programs that simulate science experiments conducted in high school science classes. The group markets its products in the United States, Australia, New Zealand, Canada, England, Norway, Finland, the Netherlands, France, Israel, Japan and Malaysia.

Primary SIC and add'l.: 7373 7372

CIK No: 0001023459

Subsidiaries: Words+, Inc.

Officers: Walter S. Woltosz/Chmn., CEO, Pres., Ronald F. Creeley/VP - Marketing, Sales, Michael B. Bolger/Founding Scientist, Virginia E. Woltosz/Dir., Sec., Treasurer, Momoko A. Beran/CFO

Directors: Walter S. Woltosz/Chmn., CEO, Pres., Richard R. Weiss/Dir., David Z. D'Argenio/Dir., Virginia E. Woltosz/Dir., Sec., Treasurer

Owners: David Z. Argenio, Virginia E. Woltosz/41.71%, Jeffrey A. Dahlen/1.46%, Insiders/52.45%, Richard R. Weiss, Ronald F. Creeley/4.48%

Financial Data: Fiscal Year End:08/31 Latest Annual Data: 08/31/2007

Year	Sales	Net Income
2007	$8,858,000	$1,466,000
2006	$5,855,000	$676,000
2005	$4,753,000	$262,000

Curr. Assets:	$3,895,000	Curr. Liab.:	$845,000	P/E Ratio:	65.00
Plant, Equip.:	$96,000	Total Liab.:	$845,000	Indic. Yr. Divd.:	NA
Total Assets:	$6,513,000	Net Worth:	$5,669,000	Debt/ Equity:	NA

Sin Holdings Inc

3225 S Garrison, Unit 21, Lakewood, CO, 80227; *PH:* 1-303-763-7307; *http://* www.senior-inet.com; *Email:* info@senior-inet.com

General - Incorporation	CO	Stock - Price on:12/24/2007	$2.05
Employees	NA	Stock Exchange	OTC
Auditor	Comiskey & Company	Ticker Symbol	SNHI
Stk Agt	Corporate Stock Transfer, Inc.	Outstanding Shares	7,280,000
Counsel	NA	E.P.S.	$0.00
DUNS No.	NA	Shareholders	NA

Business: The groups principle activity is owns and operates www.senior inet.com , a web portal for senior resources. The groups portal lists service providers categorically by geographic location, allowing users to access information quickly and efficiently. The group operates from the United States.

Primary SIC and add'l.: 2741

CIK No: 0001140414

Subsidiaries: Senior-Inet, Inc.

Officers: Steve S. Sinohui/59/Dir., Pres., Sec., Treasurer

Directors: Steve S. Sinohui/59/Dir., Pres., Sec., Treasurer

Owners: Steve Sinohui, Desert Bloom Investments, Inc., Desert Bloom Investments, Inc., Steve Sinohui

Financial Data: Fiscal Year End:12/31 Latest Annual Data: 12/31/2006

Year	Sales	Net Income
2006	$2,000	-$22,000
2005	$2,000	-$10,000

Curr. Assets:	$6,000	Curr. Liab.:	$26,000		
Plant, Equip.:	NA	Total Liab.:	$74,000	Indic. Yr. Divd.:	NA
Total Assets:	$11,000	Net Worth:	-$63,000	Debt/ Equity:	NA

Sina Corp

1468 Nan Jing Rd. W, United Plz., Ste. 1802, Shanghai, 200040; *PH:* 86-2162895678; *Fax:* 86-2162793803; *http://* www.sina.com

General - Incorporation	Cayman Islands	Stock - Price on:12/24/2007	$40.9
Employees	1,900	Stock Exchange	NDQ
Auditor	PricewaterhouseCoopers Zhong Tian	Ticker Symbol	SINA
Stk Agt	American Stock Transfer & Trust Co.	Outstanding Shares	54,540,000
Counsel	Orrick, Herrington & Sutcliffe LLP	E.P.S.	$0.88
DUNS No.	NA	Shareholders	NA

Business: The group's principal activity is the provision of online media and value added services. The group operates a branded network of websites which provide an array of services including online portals, premium email, wireless short messaging, search, classified information, online games, e-commerce, e-learning and enterprise e-solutions. Operations of the group are carried out in Hong Kong, the United States of America, China and Taiwan.

Primary SIC and add'l.: 7371 5045 7372 7379

CIK No: 0001094005

Subsidiaries: Beijing Davidhill Internet Technology Co., Ltd., Beijing New Media Information Technology Co., Ltd., Beijing SINA Information Technology Co., Ltd., Beijing Sina Interactive Game Technology Co.Ltd., Beijing SINA Internet Technology Service Co., Ltd., Crillion Corp., Davidhill Capital Inc., Fayco Network Technology Development (Shenzhen) Co. Ltd., Magic King Assets Ltd., Memestar Limited, Rich Sight Investment Limited, Shanghai SINA Technology Service Co. Ltd., SINA.com (Hong Kong) Limited, SINA.com Online, SINA.com Technology (China) Co. Ltd. 16 Subsidiaries included in the Index

Officers: Charles Chao/Dir., CEO, Pres., Herman Yu/CFO, Tong Chen/Exec. VP, Chief Editor, Bin Wang/VP, GM - Sina Mobile, Hong Du/Sr. VP - Sales, Marketing

Directors: Charles Chao/Dir., CEO, Pres., Yongji Duan/Chmn., Yan Wang/Vice Chmn., Pehong Chen/Dir., Xiaotao Chen/Dir., Hurst Lin/Dir., Lip-Bu Tan/Dir., Ter Fung Tsao/Dir., Songyi Zhang/Dir., Yi-Chen Zhang/Dir.

Owners: Insiders/7.10%, Ter Fung Tsao, Lip-Bu Tan, Yan Wang, Hurst Lin, Song-Yi Zhang, Gilder, Gagnon, Howe & Co. LLC/5.40%, Xiaotao Chen, Yongji Duan/4.70%, Stephen F. Mandel/6.90%, Pehong Chen, FMR Corp./5.80%, Charles Chao, Herman Yu, Benjamin Tsiang *(17 Owners included in Index)*

Financial Data: Fiscal Year End:12/31 Latest Annual Data: 12/31/2006

Year	Sales	Net Income
2006	$212,854,000	$39,916,000
2005	$193,552,000	$43,115,000
2004	$199,987,000	$65,996,000

Curr. Assets:	$418,112,000	Curr. Liab.:	$150,996,000	P/E Ratio:	52.44
Plant, Equip.:	$27,101,000	Total Liab.:	$150,996,000	Indic. Yr. Divd.:	NA
Total Assets:	$538,809,000	Net Worth:	$387,813,000	Debt/ Equity:	NA

Sinclair Broadcast Group Inc

10706 BeAve.r Dam Rd., Hunt Valley, MD, 21030; *PH:* 1-410-568-1500; *Fax:* 1-410-568-1533; *http://* www.sbgi.net; *Email:* comments@sbgi.net

General - Incorporation	MD	Stock - Price on:12/24/2007	$15.12
Employees	2,786	Stock Exchange	NDQ
Auditor	Ernst & Young LLP	Ticker Symbol	SBGI
Stk Agt	Mellon Investor Services LLC	Outstanding Shares	87,200,000
Counsel	NA	E.P.S.	$0.39
DUNS No.	17-551-6384	Shareholders	NA

Business: The group's principal activity is to own, operate and provide programming services to television stations. The group provides these services to 62 television stations in 39 markets throughout the United States. The television stations of the group are affiliated with 20 stations of fox, 19 with the wb, eight with abc, six with upn, four with nbc and three with cbs. Through it's wholly-owned subsidiary, sinclair ventures, the group owns equity interests in Internet-related companies including g1440, an Internet development and integration company. The group has an equity interest in and a strategic alliance with acrodyne communications inc, a manufacturer of transmitters and other television broadcast equipment.

Primary SIC and add'l.: 4832 4833

CIK No: 0000912752

Subsidiaries: Acrodyne Communications, Inc., Acrodyne Industries, Inc., Allegiance Capital L.P., Birmingham WABM-TV) Licensee, Inc., Builder 1440, LLC, Channel 33, Inc., ChesapeakeTelevisionLicensee,LLC, G1440 Holdings, Inc., G1440, LLC, Highwoods Joint Venture, I1440, LLC, KABBLicensee,LLC, KBSILicenseeL.P., KDNLLicensee,LLC, KDSM,LLC 105 Subsidiaries included in the Index

Officers: David D. Smith/Chmn., CEO, Pres./$1,024,951.00, Duncan J. Smith/Dir., VP, Sec., Thomas I. Waters/VP - Purchasing, Joe Defeo/VP - News, Donald H. Thompson/VP - Human Resources, Steven M. Marks/COO - Television Group/$1,118,328.00, Barry M. Faber/VP, General Counsel/$527,385.00, Lucy A. Rutishauser/VP - Corporate Finance, Treasurer/$258,587.00, Nat S. Ostroff/VP - New Technology, Gregg Seigel/VP - National Sales, William M. Butler/VP - Group Programming, Promotions, Darren Shapiro/VP - New Business Sales, David B. Amy/CFO, Exec. VP/$563,784.00, Delbert R. Parks/VP - Operations, Engineering, Frederick G. Smith/Dir., VP *(17 Officers included in Index)*

Directors: David D. Smith/Chmn., CEO, Pres., Martin R. Leader/Dir., Robert E. Smith/Dir., Duncan J. Smith/Dir., VP, Sec., Lawrence E. McCanna/Dir., Basil A. Thomas/Dir., Frederick G. Smith/Dir., VP, Daniel C. Keith/Dir.

Owners: Insiders/82.30%, Frederick G. Smith/20.00%, Insiders/93.20%, Duncan J. Smith/27.70%, Steven M. Marks, Dimensional Fund Advisors LP, Earnest Partners, LLC, Frederick G. Smith/17.70%, Morgan Stanley, Basil A. Thomas, GAMCO Investors, Inc./1.00%, David D. Smith/25.40%, David D. Smith/22.40%, Lucy A. Rutishauser, Duncan J. Smith/24.30% *(23 Owners included in Index)*

Financial Data: Fiscal Year End:12/31 Latest Annual Data: 12/31/2006

Year	Sales	Net Income
2006	$715,138,000	$53,977,000
2005	$692,067,000	$185,932,000
2004	$708,279,000	$24,022,000

Curr. Assets:	$291,365,000	Curr. Liab.:	$285,946,000	P/E Ratio:	38.77
Plant, Equip.:	$274,962,000	Total Liab.:	$2,005,268,000	Indic. Yr. Divd.:	$0.600
Total Assets:	$2,272,598,000	Net Worth:	$266,645,000	Debt/ Equity:	5.2614

Singing Machine Co Inc

6601 Lyons Rd., Bldg. A-7, Coconut Creek, FL, 33073; *PH:* 1-954-596-1000; *Fax:* 1-954-596-2000; *http://* www.singingmachine.com

General - Incorporation	DE	Stock - Price on:12/24/2007	$0.63
Employees	30	Stock Exchange	AMEX
Auditor	Berkovits, Lago & Co LLP	Ticker Symbol	SMD
Stk Agt	Continental Stock Transfer & Trust Co	Outstanding Shares	25,470,000
Counsel	NA	E.P.S.	$0.04
DUNS No.	06-232-6988	Shareholders	NA

Business: The group's principal activity is to produce, distribute, market and sell consumer karaoke audio equipment, accessories and recordings. The product line of the group consist of 34 different models of karaoke machines featuring CD plus graphics player sound enhancement, graphic equalizers, echo tape record/playback features and video cassette recorders. It markets its products under the trademark the singing machine(R) through various national and international trade shows, department stores, mass merchandisers, direct mail catalogs and showrooms, music and record stores, national chains, specialty stores and warehouse clubs. It markets its products in the United States, Asia, Canada, Central America and South America.

Primary SIC and add'l.: 7372 3652 3651

CIK No: 0000923601

Subsidiaries: International SMC (HK) Ltd, SMC Limidata

Officers: Anton Handal/CEO, Danny Zheng/CFO, Alicia Haskamp/Sr. VP - Sales, Product Development

Directors: Josef A. Bauer/Chmn., Stewart A. Merkin/Dir., Harvey Judkowitz/Dir., Bernard S. Appel/Dir., Carol Lau/Chairwoman, Peter Hon/Dir., Yat Tung Lau/Dir.

Owners: Gentle Boss Investments Ltd/6.29%, Danny Zheng, Joseph Bauer/4.00%, Yat Tung Lau, Insiders/5.24%, Stewart Merkin, Koncept International Ltd/53.55%, Bernard Appel, Alicia Haskamp, Carol Lau, Harvey Judkowitz, Peter Hon, Yi Ping Chan, Marc Goldberg

Financial Data: Fiscal Year End:03/31 Latest Annual Data: 03/31/2007

Year	Sales	Net Income
2007	$26,732,000	$739,000
2006	$32,306,000	-$1,905,000
2005	$38,210,000	-$3,592,000

Curr. Assets:	$3,912,000	Curr. Liab.:	$8,186,000	P/E Ratio:	15.75
Plant, Equip.:	$514,000	Total Liab.:	$8,186,000	Indic. Yr. Divd.:	NA
Total Assets:	$4,524,000	Net Worth:	-$3,662,000	Debt/ Equity:	NA

Sino Gas International Holdings Inc

The Farmhouse, 558 Lime Rock Rd., Lime Rock, CT, 06039; *PH:* 1-860-435-7000

General - Incorporation	UT	Stock - Price on:12/24/2007	$3.95
Employees	246	Stock Exchange	OTC
Auditor	Samuel H. Wong & Co., LLP	Ticker Symbol	SGAS
Stk Agt	Fidelity Transfer Co	Outstanding Shares	14,920,000
Counsel	NA	E.P.S.	$0.31
DUNS No.	NA	Shareholders	NA

Business: The groups principle activities include in the development of natural gas distribution systems in small and medium sized cities in China, as well as the distribution of natural gas to residential, commercial and industrial customers. The group operates through two segments namely construction and installation of gas facilities, and sales of gas to that customers. In April 2006, the group acquired Beijing Gas. The group operates from China.

Primary SIC and add'l.: 7389

CIK No: 0001326364

Subsidiaries: Beijing Chenguang Gas Ltd., Co., Beijing Gas, Beijing Zhong Ran Xiang Ke Gas Technology Ltd., Changli Gas Co. Ltd., Hengshui Gas Co. Ltd., Jin Zhou Wei Ye Gas Ltd., Lang Fang Development Zone Wei Ye Dangerous Goods Transportation Ltd., Lin Zhang County Wei Ye Gas Ltd., Long Yao County Zhong Ran Wei Ye Gas Ltd., Ning Jing Wei Ye Gas Ltd., Pegasus Tel, Inc, Pei County Wei Ye Gas Ltd., Shen Zhou Wei Ye Gas Ltd., Si Hong Wei Ye Gas Ltd., Si Shui Wei Ye Gas Ltd. 20 Subsidiaries included in the Index

Officers: Liu Yu Chuan/44/Chmn., CEO, Pres., Zhou Zhi Cheng/44/COO, Zhong Zhi Min/Marketing Dir., Bian Shu Kui/44/VP, Chief Engineer, Chen Fang/35/Dir., CFO

Directors: Liu Yu Chuan/44/Chmn., CEO, Pres., Chen Fang/35/Dir., CFO, Chen Guo Wei/52/Dir., Sun Quan Dong/42/Dir., John D. Kuhns/57/Dir.

Owners: John Kuhns, Liu Yuchuan, Vision Opportunity Master Fund, Ltd., T. Rowe Price Small-Cap Value Fund, Inc., Insiders, Chen Fang, Sun Quandong, Leading King Investment Limited, Zhong Zhimin, Vision Opportunity Master Fund, Ltd./88.30%, Bian Shukui, Eloten Group Ltd.

Financial Data: *Fiscal Year End:*12/31 *Latest Annual Data:* 12/31/2006

Year	Sales	Net Income
2006	$10,871,000	$5,166,000
2005	$8,000	-$48,000

Curr. Assets:	$15,249,000	**Curr. Liab.:**	$8,476,000	**P/E Ratio:**	6.07
Plant, Equip.:	$15,237,000	**Total Liab.:**	$8,476,000	**Indic. Yr. Divd.:**	NA
Total Assets:	$33,883,000	**Net Worth:**	$25,407,000	**Debt/ Equity:**	NA

SINO-American Development Corp

Formerly: Xerion EcoSolutions Group Inc
1427 W Valley Blvd., Ste. 101, Alhambra, CA, 91803; *PH:* 1-310-208-1182

General - Incorporation	CO	**Stock**- Price on:12/24/2007	NA
Employees	150	Stock Exchange	NA
Auditor ..... Murrell, Hall, McIntosh & Co., PLLP		Ticker Symbol	NA
Stk Agt	Signature Stock Transfer, Inc.	Outstanding Shares	NA
Counsel	NA	E.P.S.	NA
DUNS No.	88-330-9296	Shareholders	NA

Business: The group's principal activity is to develop gold extraction technology for the mining industry. The group is in the development stage.

Primary SIC and add'l.: 2899

CIK No: 0001000686

Subsidiaries: City Home Development Corporation, SINO - American Development Corporation, Town House (Wuhan) Land Limited, Town House Land (USA) Corporation, Town House Land Limited, Town House Miami Corporation

Officers: Silas Phillips/36/Dir., Pres., Treasurer, Sec., Principal Executive Officer, Principal Financial Officer

Directors: Fang Zhong/45/Dir., Fang Weijun/43/Dir., Fang Weifeng/41/Dir., Hu Min/Dir., Silas Phillips/36/Dir., Pres., Treasurer, Sec., Principal Executive Officer, Principal Financial Officer

Owners: Mark Abdou/6.66%, Nimish Patel/7.49%, Erick E. Richardson/55.45%

Financial Data: *Fiscal Year End:*12/31 *Latest Annual Data:* 12/31/2005

Year	Sales	Net Income
2005	$6,377,000	-$749,000
2004	NA	-$103,000
2003	NA	-$667,000

Curr. Assets:	$8,337,000	**Curr. Liab.:**	$14,851,000		
Plant, Equip.:	$15,884,000	**Total Liab.:**	$15,102,000	**Indic. Yr. Divd.:**	NA
Total Assets:	$24,221,000	**Net Worth:**	$8,766,000	**Debt/ Equity:**	0.4588

Sino-Biotics Inc

501 S Johnstone Ave., Ste. 501, Bartlesville, OK, 74003; *PH:* 1-918-336-1773

General - Incorporation	DE	**Stock**- Price on:12/24/2007	$0.02
Employees	1	Stock Exchange	OTC
Auditor	Malone & Bailey, PC	Ticker Symbol	SINO
Stk Agt	Corporate Stock Transfer, Inc.	Outstanding Shares	29,970,000
Counsel	NA	E.P.S.	$0.00
DUNS No.	NA	Shareholders	NA

Business: The groups principal activity is seeking acquisition or merger candidates with operating businesses and is seeking to complete an acquisition or merger with one of these candidates during its current fiscal year. The group operates from the United States.

Primary SIC and add'l.: 2851

CIK No: 0001110396

Officers: David Lennox/70/Chmn., CEO, Pres. Treasure, Sec.

Directors: David Lennox/70/Chmn., CEO, Pres. Treasure, Sec.

Owners: Venture Fund I/50.73%, David Lennox

Financial Data: *Fiscal Year End:*09/30 *Latest Annual Data:* 12/31/2001

Year	Sales	Net Income
2001	$919,000	-$1,314,000

Curr. Assets:	$190,000	**Curr. Liab.:**	$550,000		
Plant, Equip.:	$74,000	**Total Liab.:**	$561,000	**Indic. Yr. Divd.:**	NA
Total Assets:	$264,000	**Net Worth:**	-$298,000	**Debt/ Equity:**	NA

SinoFresh HealthCare Inc

516 Paul Morris Dr., Englewood, FL, 34223; *PH:* 1-941-681-3100; *Fax:* 1-941-681-3149;
http:// www.sinofresh.com

General - Incorporation	FL	**Stock**- Price on:12/24/2007	$0.12
Employees	6	Stock Exchange	OTC
Auditor	Moore Stephens Lovelace, P.A.	Ticker Symbol	SFSH
Stk Agt	American Stock Transfer & Trust Co.	Outstanding Shares	16,910,000
Counsel	The Otto Law Group, PLLC	E.P.S.	-$0.29
DUNS No.	NA	Shareholders	NA

Business: The groups principle activities include the research, development and marketing of novel therapies to treat inflammatory and infectious diseases and disorders of the upper respiratory system. The group markets its product under the tradename SinoFresh(TM) Nasal Mist. The group operates from the United States.

Primary SIC and add'l.: 2834

CIK No: 0001171596

Subsidiaries: SinoFresh Acquisition Corp, SinoFresh Corporation

Officers: Charles Fust/Chmn., CEO, Scott M. Klein/CFO, Michael Stampar/DO, Chief Medical Officer, William Wilferth/VP - Quality Assurance

Directors: Charles Fust/Chmn., CEO, Raymond J. Fonseca/Member - Medical Advisory Board, Richard Goldfarb/Member - Medical Advisory Board, William J. Kelvie/Member - Medical Advisory Board, Seth I. Rosenberg/Member - Medical Advisory Board, James A. Stankiewicz/Member - Medical Advisory Board, Jur T. Strobos/Member - Medical Advisory Board, Michael Weintraub/Member - Medical Advisory Board

Owners: David N. Macrae, David N. Macrae Trust, Gamma Opportunity Capital Partners, LP, Scott M. Klein, Insiders, Bluegrass Growth Fund, LTD, Stacey Maloney-Fust, Charles Fust Family LTD Partnership, Bushido Capital Growth Fund, LP, Charles A. Fust, P. Robert DuPont, DCOFI Master LDC, Bluegrass Growth Fund, LP, Stephen Bannon, Asset Managers International, LTD *(16 Owners included in Index)*

Financial Data: *Fiscal Year End:*12/31 *Latest Annual Data:* 12/31/2006

Year	Sales	Net Income
2006	$1,084,000	-$4,963,000
2005	$2,939,000	-$1,834,000
2004	$3,565,000	-$3,706,000

Curr. Assets:	$234,000	**Curr. Liab.:**	$4,537,000	**P/E Ratio:**	6.07
Plant, Equip.:	$48,000	**Total Liab.:**	$4,551,000	**Indic. Yr. Divd.:**	NA
Total Assets:	$2,346,000	**Net Worth:**	-$2,205,000	**Debt/ Equity:**	NA

Sinopec Shanghai Petrochemical Co Ltd

48 Jinyi Rd., Jinshan District, Shanghai, 200540; *PH:* 86-2157941941; *Fax:* 86-2157942267;
http:// www.spc.com.cn; *Email:* spc@spc.com.cn

General - Incorporation	China	**Stock**- Price on:12/24/2007	$68.28
Employees	22,922	Stock Exchange	NYSE
Auditor	KPMG LLP	Ticker Symbol	SHI
Stk Agt	Bank of New York	Outstanding Shares	71,970,000
Counsel	Zhang Jingming	E.P.S.	$4.50
DUNS No.	NA	Shareholders	NA

Business: The group's principal activity is the processing of crude oil into petrochemical products for sale. Other activities include investment management; trading in, import and export of petrochemical products; import and export of equipment and production of vinyl acetate, polypropylene compound and acrylic fibre products. Specific products of the group are petroleum, resins and plastics, synthetic fibres, intermediate petrochemicals and others. Petroleum products has crude oil distillation facilities used to produce vacuum and atmospheric gas oils used as feedstocks of the group's downstream processing facilities. Resins and plastics produce primarily polyester chips, low density polyethylene resins films, polypropylene resins and pva granules. Synthetic fibres produces primarily polyester and acrylic fibres primarily used in the textile and apparel industries. Intermediate petrochemicals produces ethylene and benzene. The group's operations are carried out in prc.

Primary SIC and add'l.: 1321 2824 2869 2911 2821 2865

CIK No: 0000908732

Subsidiaries: China Jinshan Associated Trading Corporation, Shanghai Golden Conti Petrochemical Company Limited, Shanghai Golden Phillips Petrochemical Company Limited, Shanghai Golden Way Petrochemical Company Limited, Shanghai Jinchang Engineering Plastics Company Limited, Shanghai Jindong Petrochemical Industrial Company Limited, Shanghai Jinhua Industrial Company Limited, Shanghai Petrochemical Enterprise Development Company Limited, Shanghai Petrochemical Investment Development Company Limited, Zhejiang Jin Yong Acrylic Fiber Company Limited

Officers: Rong Guangdao/50/Chmn., Pres., Du Chongjun/51/Vice Chmn., VP, Yin Yongli/68/Independent Supervisor, Zhang Chenghua/52/Supervisor, Zhang Jingming/50/Sec., Li Honggen/52/Dir., VP, Wang Yanjun/47/Supervisor, Geng Limin/53/External Supervisor, Lu Xiangyang/55/External Supervisor, Wu Haijun/43/Executive Dir., VP, Zhang Jianping/45/VP, Tang Chengjian/52/VP, Shi Wei/46/Executive Dir., VP, Gao Jinping/39/Executive Dir., Han Zhihao/54/Executive Dir., CFO *(16 Officers included in Index)*

Directors: Rong Guangdao/50/Chmn., Pres., Du Chongjun/51/Vice Chmn., VP, Chen Xinyuan/41/Dir., Han Zhihao/54/Executive Dir., CFO, Jiang Zhiquan/55/Dir., Zhou Yunnong/64/Dir., Sun Chiping/48/Dir., Wu Haijun/43/Executive Dir., VP, Li Honggen/52/Dir., VP, Dai Jinbao/52/Dir., Lei Dianwu/43/Dir., Xiang Hanyin/51/Dir., Shi Wei/46/Executive Dir., VP, Gao Jinping/39/Executive Dir.

Owners: HKSCC nominees Ltd., Insiders, China Petroleum & Chemical Corporation, Chongjun Du, Rong Guangdao

Financial Data: *Fiscal Year End:*12/31 *Latest Annual Data:* 12/31/2006

Year	Sales	Net Income
2006	$6,435,674,000	$108,973,000
2005	$5,678,054,000	$231,641,000
2004	$4,760,486,000	$500,914,000

Curr. Assets:	$969,590,000	**Curr. Liab.:**	$901,252,000	**P/E Ratio:**	52.44
Plant, Equip.:	$2,030,490,000	**Total Liab.:**	$1,082,350,000	**Indic. Yr. Divd.:**	$0.520
Total Assets:	$3,526,235,000	**Net Worth:**	$2,443,885,000	**Debt/ Equity:**	NA

Sinovac Biotech Ltd

39 Shangdi Xi Rd. , Haidian District, Beijing, 100085; *PH:* 86-1082890088; *http://* www.sinovac.com

General - Incorporation	West Indies	**Stock**- Price on:12/24/2007	$2.64
Employees	252	Stock Exchange	AMEX
Auditor	Ernst & Young LLP	Ticker Symbol	SVA
Stk Agt	Jensen, Barristers & Solicitors	Outstanding Shares	40,120,000
Counsel	NA	E.P.S	$0.15
DUNS No.	NA	Shareholders	NA

Business: The groups principle activities include researching, developing, commercializing, and selling human vaccines for infectious illnesses such as Hepatitis A and Hepatitis B, influenza and SARS. The groups products include Healive(R) and Anflu. The group operates from United States.

Primary SIC and add'l.: NA

CIK No: 0001084201

Subsidiaries: Sinovac Biotech Co., Ltd., Tangshan Yian Biological Engineering Co., Ltd

Officers: Weidong Yin/44/Chmn., CEO, Pres., Sec., Jinling Qin/63/Acting CFO, Nan Wang/42/Vice GM, Jiansan Zhang/Vice GM, Xuejie Gong/Sr. Mgr., Changju Fu/In Charge - Sales, Marketing, Business Dept, Wang Jingning/Sr. Mgr., Mgr. - Human Resources Department

Directors: Weidong Yin/44/Chmn., CEO, Pres., Sec., Simon Anderson/Dir., Xianping Wang/48/Dir., Yuk Lam Lo/60/Dir., Chup Hung Mok/51/Dir., Cathy Mok Chup Hung/49/Dir., Lo Yuk Lam/59/Dir.

Owners: Jiansan Zhang, Weidong Yin/15.27%, Lily Wang/10.69%, Simon Anderson, Nan Wang, Jinling Qin, Xianping Wang/1.25%, Sanjay Motwani/6.46%, Changjun Fu

Financial Data: *Fiscal Year End:*12/31 *Latest Annual Data:* 12/31/2006

Year	Sales	Net Income
2006	$15,355,000	-$696,000
2005	$8,608,000	-$5,111,000
2004	$6,454,000	-$4,667,000

Curr. Assets:	$21,740,000	**Curr. Liab.:**	$11,864,000	**P/E Ratio:**	52.44
Plant, Equip.:	$13,027,000	**Total Liab.:**	$17,764,000	**Indic. Yr. Divd.:**	NA
Total Assets:	$37,009,000	**Net Worth:**	$19,245,000	**Debt/ Equity:**	NA

Sirenza Microdevices Inc

303 S Technology Ct., Broomfield, CO, 80021; *PH:* 1-303-327-3030; *Fax:* 1-303-410-7088; *http://* www.sirenza.com

General - Incorporation	DE	**Stock**- Price on:12/24/2007	$11.97
Employees	839	Stock Exchange	NA
Auditor	Ernst & Young LLP	Ticker Symbol	NA
Stk Agt	Mellon Investor Services LLC	Outstanding Shares	51,480,000
Counsel	Morrison & Foerster LLP	E.P.S	$0.15
DUNS No.	NA	Shareholders	NA

Business: The group's principle activities are to design and supply radio frequency components for the commercial communications, consumer, and aerospace, defense and homeland security equipment markets. The group operates through three business segments namely, amplifier division, which includes amplifier, power amplifier, power module, transceiver, discrete and active antenna product lines; signal source division including voltage controlled oscillator, phase-locked loop and other multi-component modules products; and aerospace & defense (A&D) division, which draws products from the amplifier and signal source divisions for specific applications in the aerospace & defense and homeland security end-markets. The group's manufacturing facility is located at Colorado. The group has two customers, Avnet and Motorola.

Primary SIC and add'l.: 3674

CIK No: 0001103777

Subsidiaries: ISG Broadband Inc, Olin Acquisition Corporation, Penguin Acquisition Corporation, Sirenza Microdevices, Sirenza Microdevices Limited, Xemod Incorporated

Officers: Robert Van Buskirk/Dir., CEO, Pres./$1,389,116.00, Joseph H. Johnson/CTO, VP, Susan Ocampo/Treasurer, Norman Hilgendorf/Pres. - Smdi Segment/$381,048.00, Gerald Hatley/VP, Controller, Chief Accounting Officer, Greg Baker/VP - International Sales, Gerald Quinnell/Exec. VP - Corporate Business Development/$542,632.00, John Pelose/VP - Engineering, Product Development, Charles R. Bland/CFO, VP - Finance, Administration/$490,953.00, Clay B. Simpson/VP, General Counsel/$359,811.00, Tim Schamberger/VP - Americas Sales, Chris Menicou/VP - Quality, Reliability, Kathryn Zuber/VP - Human Resources

Directors: Robert Van Buskirk/Dir., CEO, Pres., John Ocampo/Chmn., John Bumgarner/Dir., Casimir Skrzypczak/Dir., Gil Van Lunsen/Dir., Christopher J. Crespi/Dir., John Zucker/Dir.

Owners: Charles Bland, John Ocampo and Susan Ocampo/22.70%, Norm Hilgendorf, Cortina Asset Management, LLC/5.00%, Gerald Quinnell, Gil Van Lunsen, Trivium Capital Management LLC/7.50%, John Bumgarner, Chris Crespi, Insiders/25.30%, Clay Simpson, Robert Van Buskirk/1.70%, Casimir Skrzypczak

Financial Data: *Fiscal Year End:*12/31 *Latest Annual Data:* 12/31/2006

Year	Sales	Net Income
2006	$136,578,000	$7,595,000
2005	$64,178,000	$1,392,000
2004	$61,256,000	$280,000

Curr. Assets:	$77,584,000	**Curr. Liab.:**	$27,277,000	**P/E Ratio:**	85.50
Plant, Equip.:	$15,345,000	**Total Liab.:**	$40,871,000	**Indic. Yr. Divd.:**	NA
Total Assets:	$211,592,000	**Net Worth:**	$170,721,000	**Debt/ Equity:**	0.0028

Sirf Technology Holdings Inc

217 Devcon Dr., San Jose, CA, 95112; *PH:* 1-408-467-0410; *Fax:* 1-408-467-0420; *http://* www.sirf.com; *Email:* ir@sirf.com

General - Incorporation	DE	**Stock**- Price on:12/24/2007	$21.22
Employees	445	Stock Exchange	NDQ
Auditor	Ernst & Young LLP	Ticker Symbol	SIRF
Stk Agt	Bank of New York	Outstanding Shares	52,970,000
Counsel	Pillsbury Winthrop Shaw Pittman LLP	E.P.S	$0.28
DUNS No.	83-557-3452	Shareholders	NA

Business: The group's principle activity is to supply GPS semiconductors and software products for mobile consumer and commercial applications. The group markets and sells their products in four target platforms namely, wireless handheld, automotive, portable computing devices and dedicated or embedded consumer and commercial devices. The group's mail direct customers are Motorola's iDEN group,Microsoft, Hewlett Packard, Dell, Palm and Medion. The group operates in the United States as well as in the Asia-Pacific Region. The group's quarterly revenue for September 2007 was 91.16 millions of USD.

Primary SIC and add'l.: 3669

CIK No: 0001163943

Subsidiaries: ImpulseSoft, Pvtd., SiRF Technology (Germany), SiRF Technology (India) Pvtd., SiRF Technology, A. B, SiRF Technology, Inc., SiRF Technology, K.K.

Officers: Michael L. Canning/CEO, Pres./$875,402.00, Kanwar Chadha/Founder, Dir., VP - Marketing/$691,959.00, Jim Basiji/VP - Engineering, Joseph M. Lavalle/VP - Sales/$521,856.00, Atul Shingal/VP - Operations/$500,522.00, Geoffrey Ribar/CFO/$1,114,991.00, Jim Murphy/VP - Human Resources, Sanjai Kohli/CTO, Geoff Ribar/Investor Relations

Directors: Diosdado P. Banatao/Chmn., James M. Smaha/72/Dir., Moiz M. Beguwala/61/Dir., Kanwar Chadha/Founder, Dir., VP - Marketing, Mohanbir Gyani/56/Dir., Stephen C. Sherman/64/Dir., Sam S. Srinivasan/63/Dir.

Owners: FMR Corp./10.40%, Michael L. Canning/1.90%, Diosdado P. Banatao/7.80%, OppenheimerFunds, Inc./5.50%, Joseph LaValle, Kanwar Chadha/2.50%, Geoffrey Ribar, Atul P. Shingal, Moiz M. Beguwala, Janus Capital Management LLC/6.70%, Insiders/12.70%, Mohanbir Gyani, James M. Smaha, Sam S. Srinivasan, Stephen C. Sherman

Financial Data: *Fiscal Year End:*12/31 *Latest Annual Data:* 12/31/2006

Year	Sales	Net Income
2006	$247,680,000	$2,400,000
2005	$165,070,000	$30,040,000
2004	$117,368,000	$30,723,000

Curr. Assets:	$223,710,000	**Curr. Liab.:**	$38,349,000	**P/E Ratio:**	75.79
Plant, Equip.:	$8,469,000	**Total Liab.:**	$39,320,000	**Indic. Yr. Divd.:**	NA
Total Assets:	$366,663,000	**Net Worth:**	$327,343,000	**Debt/ Equity:**	0.0041

SiriCOMM Inc

2900 Davis Blvd, Ste 130, Joplin, MO, 65804; *PH:* 1-417-626-9971; *http://* www.siricomminc.net; *Email:* support@siricomm.com

General - Incorporation	DE	**Stock**- Price on:12/24/2007	$0.19
Employees	26	Stock Exchange	OTC
Auditor	BKD LLP	Ticker Symbol	SIRC
Stk Agt	American Stock Transfer & Trust Co.	Outstanding Shares	25,270,000
Counsel	NA	E.P.S	-$0.32
DUNS No.	61-983-4914	Shareholders	NA

Business: The group's principle activity is to develop broadband wireless software and network infrastructure solutions for the commercial transportation industry and government. The company's unique virtual private network solution integrates multiple technologies including satellite communications, wi-fi wireless networking and productivity enhancing software. These solutions enable an ultra high-speed, open-architecture data network for its software applications and Internet access. The software solutions are designed to help trucking companies of any size to significantly reduce operating costs, improve productivity, enhance safety, and strengthen security. The group operates from United States.

Primary SIC and add'l.: 4899

CIK No: 0000851199

Subsidiaries: SiriCOMM, Inc

Officers: Mark Grannell/45/Dir., CEO, Pres., John Hillring/Chief Accounting Officer, Kory S. Dillman/Exec. VP - Internet - Software Development, David N. Mendez/Dir., Exec. VP - Sales, Marketing, John Burton/VP - Marketing, Sales, Matthew McKenzie/Sec.

Directors: Mark Grannell/45/Dir., CEO, Pres., William P. Moore/62/Dir., David N. Mendez/Dir., Exec. VP - Sales, Marketing, Terry W. Thompson/57/Dir., Richard P. Landis/61/Dir., Steven W. Fox/50/Dir.

Owners: Insiders/64.29%, Terry W. Thompson/1.48%, William P. Moore/30.22%, Steven W. Fox/5.25%, Robert J. Smith/7.28%, Matthew McKenzie/0.30%, Quest Capital Alliance LLC/5.25%, David N. Mendez/4.21%, Mark L. Grannell/0.60%

Financial Data: *Fiscal Year End:*09/30 *Latest Annual Data:* 9/30/2006

Year	Sales	Net Income
2006	$1,058,000	-$7,209,000
2005	$194,000	-$3,240,000
2004	NA	-$2,778,000

Curr. Assets:	$1,018,000	**Curr. Liab.:**	$1,245,000		
Plant, Equip.:	$3,239,000	**Total Liab.:**	$1,471,000	**Indic. Yr. Divd.:**	NA
Total Assets:	$5,073,000	**Net Worth:**	$3,308,000	**Debt/ Equity:**	0.0014

Sirius Satellite Radio Inc

1221 Ave. of the Americas, 36th Fl., New York, NY, 10020; *PH:* 1-212-584-5100; *Fax:* 1-212-584-5200; *http://* www.sirius.com

General - Incorporation	DE	**Stock**- Price on:12/24/2007	$2.85
Employees	772	Stock Exchange	NDQ
Auditor	Thacher & Bartlett LLP	Ticker Symbol	SIRI
Stk Agt	Bank of New York	Outstanding Shares	1,460,000,000
Counsel	NA	E.P.S	-$0.48
DUNS No.	NA	Shareholders	NA

Business: The groups principle activity is to provide satellite radio services. The groups services include subscription music services, free peer to peer music services and free streaming of digital content via the Internet. The products of the group include Digital Radio, XM Radio, Wireless Phone Providers and Traditional AM/FM Radio. The group products sold under the trade name SIRIUS. The group operates from the United States.

Primary SIC and add'l.: 4899 4832 4899

CIK No: 0000908937

Subsidiaries: Earth Station Ecuador Cia. Ltda, Satellite CD Radio, Inc, Sirius Asset Management Company LLC, Sirius Entertainment Promotions LLC, Spend LLC

Officers: Mel Karmazin/Dir., CEO/$31,217,250.00, Scott Greenstein/Pres. - Entertainment, Sports/$7,088,244.00, James E. Meyer/Pres. - Operations, Sales/$5,627,601.00, Patrick L. Donnelly/Exec. VP, General Counsel/$1,380,927.00, David J. Frear/CFO, Exec. VP/$2,464,062.00, Andreas Lazar/Sr. VP - Business Development, John H. Schultz/Sr. VP - Human Resources, Adrienne E. Calderone/Sr. VP, Corporate Controller

Directors: Mel Karmazin/Dir., CEO, Joseph P. Clayton/Chmn., Leon D. Black/Dir., Lawrence F. Gilberti/Dir., James P. Holden/Dir., Warren N. Lieberfarb/Dir., Michael J. McGuiness/Dir., James F. Mooney/Dir.

Owners: Leon D. Black, Insiders/2.60%, James P. Holden, Joseph P. Clayton, James F. Mooney, James E. Meyer, Patrick L. Donnelly, Apollo Investment FundIV, L.P./6.60%, Michael J. McGuiness, Lawrence F. Gilberti, Mel Karmazin/1.30%, Scott A. Greenstein, Warren N. Lieberfarb, David J. Frear

Financial Data: Fiscal Year End:12/31 Latest Annual Data: 12/31/2006

Year	Sales	Net Income
2006	$637,235,000	-$1,104,867,000
2005	$242,245,000	-$862,997,000
2004	$66,854,000	-$712,162,000

Curr. Assets:	$617,266,000	Curr. Liab.:	$875,065,000		
Plant, Equip.:	$810,389,000	Total Liab.:	$2,047,599,000	Indic. Yr. Divd.:	NA
Total Assets:	$1,658,528,000	Net Worth:	-$389,071,000	Debt/ Equity:	NA

Sirona Dental Systems Inc

Formerly: Schick Technologies Inc
30-30 47th Ave, Ste. 500, Long Island, NY, 11101; *PH:* 1-718-937-5765; *http://* www.schicktech.com

General - Incorporation	DE	Stock - Price on:12/24/2007	$37
Employees	1,978	Stock Exchange	NA
Auditor	Pmg Deutsche Treuh&-gesellschaft	Ticker Symbol	NA
Stk Agt	American Stock Transfer & Trust Co.	Outstanding Shares	54,730,000
Counsel	Dorsey & Whitney LLP	E.P.S	NA
DUNS No.	79-691-2350	Shareholders	NA

Business: The group's principal activity is to design, develop and manufacture innovative digital radiographic imaging systems and devices for the dental and medical markets. The dental devices include the cdr(R), computed dental radiography, imaging system that uses an intra-oral sensor to produce instant, full size, high-resolution dental X-ray images on a color computer monitor. The group also manufactures and sells the cdrcam(R) 2000, an intra-oral camera that fully integrates with the cdr system and the cdrpan(tm), a digital panoramic imaging device. The group manufactures and markets the accudexa(R) bone densitometer, a low-cost and easy-to-operate device for the assessment of bone mineral density and fracture risk. The products are based primarily on its proprietary active-pixel sensor (aps) imaging technology. The products are marketed primarily in the United States and Europe.

Primary SIC and add'l.: 3844 3845

CIK No: 0001014507

Subsidiaries: Schick Technologies, Inc

Officers: Jost Fischer/52/Chmn., CEO, Pres., Simone Blank/44/Dir., CFO, Exec. VP, Michael Stone/Pres., Ronald Rosner/Dir. - Finance, Administration, Jeff Slovin/COO - US Operations, Exec. VP - Sirona, Ari Neugroschl/VP - MIS, Will Autz/VP - Manufacturing, Stan Mandelkern/VP - Engineering

Directors: Jost Fischer/52/Chmn., CEO, Pres., Simone Blank/44/Dir., CFO, Exec. VP, Timothy P. Sullivan/50/Dir., Timothy D. Sheehan/35/Dir., David K. Beecken/61/Dir., Nicholas W. Alexos/44/Dir.

Owners: Insiders, William K. Hood, Jeffrey T. Slovin, Sirona Holdings Luxco S.C.A. and certain affiliates, Arthur D. Kowaloff

Financial Data: Fiscal Year End:03/31 Latest Annual Data: 9/30/2006

Year	Sales	Net Income
2006	$520,604,000	$755,000
2005	$52,418,000	$12,072,000

Curr. Assets:	$225,651,000	Curr. Liab.:	$123,886,000		
Plant, Equip.:	$61,042,000	Total Liab.:	$1,052,895,000	Indic. Yr. Divd.:	NA
Total Assets:	$1,541,004,000	Net Worth:	$487,846,000	Debt/ Equity:	0.9996

Sirva Inc

700 Oakmont Ln., Westmont, IL, 60559; *PH:* 1-630-570-3000; *Fax:* 1-630-468-4761; *http://* www.sirva.com

General - Incorporation	DE	Stock - Price on:12/24/2007	$2.43
Employees	4,000	Stock Exchange	NA
Auditor	Ernst & Young, LLP	Ticker Symbol	NA
Stk Agt	NA	Outstanding Shares	73,960,000
Counsel	NA	E.P.S	-$0.75
DUNS No.	NA	Shareholders	NA

Business: The groups principle activity is to relocate industry solutions including transferring corporate and government employees and moving individual consumers. The group operates through four segments namely, global relocation services, moving services North America, moving services Europe and Asia Pacific, and corporate. The group operates from the North America, Europe and Asia Pacific.

Primary SIC and add'l.: 4231 6531 4213 4731

CIK No: 0001181232

Subsidiaries: Allied International N.A.,Inc., Allied Pickfords Pty. Ltd., Allied Van Lines,Inc., CMS Holding, LLC, Executive Relocation Corporation, Meridian Mobility Resources, NAVL LLC, North American International Holding Corporation, North American Van Lines,Inc., Pickfords 1999 Limited, SIRVA (Asia Pacific) Pty. Ltd., SIRVA Holdings Limited, SIRVA Ireland, SIRVA Mortgage,Inc., SIRVA Relocation LLC 18 Subsidiaries included in the Index

Officers: Robert W. Tieken/Dir., CEO, Pres., John Springer/VP - Investor Relations, Daniel P. Mullin/Chief Accounting Officer, Kevin D. Pickford/MD, Pres. - Europe, James J. Bresingham/CFO, Sr. VP, Timothy P. Callahan/Sr. VP - Global Sales/$432,453.00, Douglas V. Gathany/VP, Treasurer - Investor Relations, Rene C. Gibson/Sr. VP - Human Resources, Michael B. McMahon/Pres. - Global Relocation Services/$480,585.00, Eryk J. Spytek/Sr. VP, General Counsel, Sec.

Directors: Robert W. Tieken/Dir., CEO, Pres., John R. Miller/Chmn., Jeremy MacKenzie/Dir., Joseph A. Smialowski/Dir., Kelly J. Barlow/Dir., Frederic F. Brace/Dir., Robert J. Dellinger/Dir., Thomas E. Ireland/Dir., Laban P. Jackson/65/Dir., Peter H. Kamin/Dir.

Owners: Michael B. McMahon, Jeremy Mackenzie, John R. Miller, Timothy P. Callahan, Clayton, Dubilier& Rice Fund V Limited Partnership/23.10%, Robert J. Dellinger, Joseph A. Smialowski, MLF Offshore Portfolio Company, L.P./14.28%, Insiders/2.07%, Robert W. Tieken, ValueAct Capital Master Fund, L.P./28.89%, Robert S. Pitts/5.41%, Brian P. Kelley/1.16%, Clayton, Dubilier& Rice Fund VI Limited Partnership/9.60%, Kevin D. Pickford *(17 Owners included in Index)*

Financial Data: Fiscal Year End:12/31 Latest Annual Data: 12/31/2006

Year	Sales	Net Income
2006	$3,865,300,000	-$54,600,000
2005	$3,681,200,000	-$265,400,000
2004	$3,475,942,000	-$69,063,000

Curr. Assets:	$799,800,000	Curr. Liab.:	$765,000,000		
Plant, Equip.:	$86,600,000	Total Liab.:	$1,360,400,000	Indic. Yr. Divd.:	NA
Total Assets:	$1,419,200,000	Net Worth:	$58,800,000	Debt/ Equity:	6.6013

Sitestar Corp

7109 Timberlake Rd., Ste. 201, Lynchburg, VA, 24502; *PH:* 1-434-239-4272; *Fax:* 1-818-332-4213; *http://* www.sitestar.com

General - Incorporation	NV	Stock - Price on:12/24/2007	$0.118
Employees	24	Stock Exchange	OTC
Auditor	Bagell, Josephs, Levine & Co. LLC	Ticker Symbol	SYTE
Stk Agt	Pacific Stock Transfer Company	Outstanding Shares	88,060,000
Counsel	NA	E.P.S	$0.009
DUNS No.	NA	Shareholders	NA

Business: The group's principal activities are to provide Internet access and enhanced products and services to small and medium sized enterprises. The products and services include Internet access services, Web design and hosting services, e-commerce solutions, online marketing consulting and management of mission critical Internet applications. Internet-based businesses have created on-line marketplaces for conducting business-to-business electronic commerce. These Internet locations bring buyers and sellers together in a central marketplace and provide services such as procurement management, financial settlement and quality assurance.

Primary SIC and add'l.: 6719 7375 7372 3577

CIK No: 0001096934

Subsidiaries: Advanced Internet Services, Inc., FRE Enterprises, Inc, Neocom Microspecialists, Inc

Officers: Frank Erhartic/Dir., CEO, Pres., Julie Erhartic/Dir., Sec., Daniel Judd/Dir., CFO, Controller, Michael Collado/VP - Marketing, Business Development

Directors: Frank Erhartic/Dir., CEO, Pres., Julie Erhartic/Dir., Sec., Daniel Judd/Dir., CFO, Controller

Owners: Frank Erhartic/27.92%, Insiders/27.92%

Financial Data: Fiscal Year End:12/31 Latest Annual Data: 12/31/2006

Year	Sales	Net Income
2006	$5,597,000	$992,000
2005	$3,680,000	$640,000
2004	$3,134,000	$83,000

Curr. Assets:	$324,000	Curr. Liab.:	$1,454,000	P/E Ratio:	9.08
Plant, Equip.:	$274,000	Total Liab.:	$2,332,000	Indic. Yr. Divd.:	NA
Total Assets:	$4,045,000	Net Worth:	$1,713,000	Debt/ Equity:	NA

Siteworks Inc

2534 N Miami Ave, Miami, FL, 33127; *PH:* 1-305-573-9339; *http://* www.siteworksinc.net

General - Incorporation	FL	Stock - Price on:12/24/2007	NA
Employees	NA	Stock Exchange	OTC
Auditor	Bagell, Josephs, Levine & Co. LLC	Ticker Symbol	SBDNE
Stk Agt	Integrity Stock Transfer, Inc.	Outstanding Shares	NA
Counsel	NA	E.P.S	NA
DUNS No.	NA	Shareholders	NA

Business: The groups principle activity is to provide contracting services. The groups services include excavation, grading, storm drain, onsite & offsite improvements. The groups servicing areas include commercial, industrial, private and public works construction. The group operates from United States.

Primary SIC and add'l.: NA

CIK No: 0001106643

Subsidiaries: Integral Inc., S B D International, Siteworks Building and Development Co.

Officers: Carl M. Nurse/Chmn., CEO, CFO, Pres., Sheryl E. Payne/Pres., Sec., CFO - RMO, William H. Payne/VP, William J. Mercier/General Superintendant, Field Operations, Patrick M. Reilly/Construction Supervisor, Safety Mgr.

Directors: Carl M. Nurse/Chmn., CEO, CFO, Pres.

Owners: Star Invest Group/0.00%, Zono Plc/45.00%, Insiders/0.00%, Scarborough Ltd./2.00%, C. M. Nurse/0.00%, C. M. Nurse/48.00%

Siti Sites Com Inc

594 Brd.way, Ste. 1001, New York, NY, 10012; *PH:* 1-212-965-0013

General - Incorporation	DE	Stock - Price on:12/24/2007	NA
Employees	1	Stock Exchange	NA
Auditor	Cooper & McCann LLP	Ticker Symbol	NA
Stk Agt	NA	Outstanding Shares	NA
Counsel	NA	E.P.S	NA
DUNS No.	11-335-7289	Shareholders	NA

Business: The group's principal activity is to develop websites for marketing news and services. The group operated hungrybands.com, newmediamusic.com, newyorkexpo.com & tropia.com websites. These websites related entirely to the music industry

Primary SIC and add'l.: 7375

CIK No: 0000812551

Owners: Lawrence M. Powers/46.10%, Insiders/46.60%, Toni Ann Tantillo, John Iannitto/9.30%, Barclay V. Powers/16.10%, Robert Ingenito/18.40%

Siuslaw Financial Group Inc

777 Oregon Coast Hwy 101, Florence, OR, 97439; *PH:* 1-541-997-3486; *http://* www.clicksvb.com

General - Incorporation		Stock - Price on:12/24/2007	$15.75
Employees	NA	Stock Exchange	OTC
Auditor	NA	Ticker Symbol	SFGP
Stk Agt	NA	Outstanding Shares	4,280,000
Counsel	NA	E.P.S	NA
DUNS No.	NA	Shareholders	NA

Business: The groups principal activity is chartered for the purpose of fulfilling the need for banking services in the small rural town of Mapleton, Oregon, located in Western Lane County. Services of the group include checking accounts, savings accounts, certificates of deposit, installment loans, real estate mortgage loans, commercial loans, traveler's checks and safe deposits.

Primary SIC and add'l.: 6712

CIK No:

Sivault Systems Inc

500 Fifth Ave., Ste 1650, New York, NY, 10110; *PH:* 1-212-935-5760; *http://* www.sivault.com; *Email:* investorrelations@sivault.com

General - Incorporation	NV
Employees	NA
Auditor	Miller Ellin & Co. LLP
Stk Agt	Interwest Transfer Company, Inc.
Counsel	NA
DUNS No.	NA

Stock- Price on:12/24/2007	NA
Stock Exchange	OTC
Ticker Symbol	SVTLQ
Outstanding Shares	NA
E.P.S.	-$0.573
Shareholders	NA

Business: The group's principal activities are to develop, market and distribute biometrics technologies specific to the security applications of banking and financial transactions. The products of the group include dynamic gesture recognition technology (grt) and dynamic signature verification (dsv). The group provides security interfaces that offers a wide array of end-to-end solutions targeted towards the specific multi-trillion dollar banking and financial transaction market segments. On 14-Jul-2004, the group acquired sivault analytics inc.

Primary SIC and add'l.: 3577 4813 7372

CIK No: 0011101046

Subsidiaries: Crossvue, Inc., eMedRx, Inc., Lightec Communications, Inc.

*Financial Data: Fiscal Year End:*06/30   *Latest Annual Data:* 06/30/2005

Year	Sales	Net Income
2005	$1,602,000	-$23,900,000
2004	$7,131,000	-$3,407,000
2003	$1,147,000	-$13,578,000

Curr. Assets:	$705,000	Curr. Liab.:	$9,780,000		
Plant, Equip.:	$70,000	Total Liab.:	$9,796,000	Indic. Yr. Divd.:	NA
Total Assets:	$8,143,000	Net Worth:	-$1,654,000	Debt/ Equity:	NA

Six Flags Inc

1540 Broadway, 15th Fl., New York, NY, 10036; *PH:* 1-212-652-9403; *Fax:* 1-212-354-3089; *http://* www.sixflags.com; *Email:* guestrelations@sftp.com

General - Incorporation	DE
Employees	2,500
Auditor	KPMG LLP
Stk Agt	Bank of New York
Counsel	NA
DUNS No.	06-227-3669

Stock- Price on:12/24/2007	$6.45
Stock Exchange	NYSE
Ticker Symbol	SIX
Outstanding Shares	94,680,000
E.P.S.	-$2.72
Shareholders	NA

Business: The group's principal activities are the ownership and operation of theme amusement and water parks. The group's theme parks offer a complete family-oriented entertainment experience through a broad selection of state-of-the-art and traditional thrill rides, water attractions, themed areas, concerts and shows, restaurants, game venues and merchandise outlets. In 2004, the group discontinued and sold substantially all of the assets used in the operation of six flags world of adventure near cleveland, Ohio.

Primary SIC and add'l.: 7999 7996

CIK No: 0000701374

Subsidiaries: AstroWorld GP LLC, AstroWorld LP, AstroWorld LP LLC, Aurora Campground, Inc., Darien Lake Management Company Inc., Darien Lake Theme Park and Camping Resort, Inc., Elitch Gardens L.P., Enchanted Parks, Inc., Fiesta Texas Hospitality LLC, Fiesta Texas, Inc., Flags Beverages, Inc., Frontier City Partners Limited Partnership, Frontier City Properties, Inc., Funtime Inc., Funtime Parks, Inc. 88 Subsidiaries included in the Index

Officers: Mark Shapiro/38/Dir., CEO, Pres./$3,990,601.00, James M. Coughlin/56/General Counsel, John E. Bement/55/Sr. VP, John Odum/50/Sr. VP - Park Strategy, Management, Walter S. Hawrylak/60/Sr. VP - Administration, Kyle Bradshaw/44/Sr. VP - Finance, Chief Accounting Officer, Randy Gerstenblatt/48/Sr. VP - Corporate Alliances, Wendy Goldberg/44/Sr. VP - Communications, Michael Israel/41/Sr. VP - Information Services, William Prip/40/Sr. VP - Corporate Finance, Treasurer, Angelina M. Vieira/38/Sr. VP - Entertainment, Marketing, Jeff Speed/CFO, Exec. VP/$2,508,470.00, Mark Quenzel/Exec. VP - Park Strategy, Management/$1,504,030.00, Mike Antinoro/Exec. VP - Entertainment, Marketing, Louis Koskovolis/Exec. VP - Corporate Alliances/$1,353,832.00 (16 Officers included in Index)

Directors: Mark Shapiro/38/Dir., CEO, Pres., Daniel M. Snyder/Chmn., Robert J. McGuire/67/Dir., Dwight Schar/Dir., Jack F. Kemp/72/Dir., Harvey Weinstein/55/Dir., Charles Elliott Andrews/Dir., Perry Rogers/Dir., Mark E. Jennings/44/Dir.

Owners: Jack Kemp, Cascade Investment, L.L.C./11.30%, Jeffrey R. Speed, Louis S. Koskovolis, Perry Rogers, Mark Jennings, Dimensional Fund Advisors LP/8.40%, Charles Elliott Andrews, Mark Shapiro, Mark Quenzel, Andrew M. Schleimer, Dwight C. Schar, Robert J. McGuire, Daniel M. Snyder/12.30%, Citigroup Inc./10.50% (23 Owners included in Index)

*Financial Data: Fiscal Year End:*12/31   *Latest Annual Data:* 12/31/2006

Year	Sales	Net Income
2006	$945,665,000	-$305,618,000
2005	$1,089,682,000	-$110,938,000
2004	$1,037,692,000	-$464,809,000

Curr. Assets:	$132,875,000	Curr. Liab.:	$291,421,000		
Plant, Equip.:	$1,936,225,000	Total Liab.:	$2,476,984,000	Indic. Yr. Divd.:	NA
Total Assets:	$3,187,616,000	Net Worth:	$376,140,000	Debt/ Equity:	10.5228

Sixx Holdings Inc

3878 Oak Lawn, Ste. 500, Dallas, TX, 75219; *PH:* 1-214-855-8800

General - Incorporation	DE
Employees	175
Auditor	KPMG LLP
Stk Agt	American Stock Transfer & Trust Co.
Counsel	NA
DUNS No.	60-929-0226

Stock- Price on:12/24/2007	$4.55
Stock Exchange	OTC
Ticker Symbol	SIXX
Outstanding Shares	NA
E.P.S	NA
Shareholders	NA

Business: The group's principal activity is to own and operate full service restaurants under the name patrizio that offer Italian-style cuisine and alcoholic beverages. It owns and operates two upscale Italian restaurants patrizio i, located in Dallas, Texas and patrizio ii, located in plano, Texas. The subsidiaries are patrizio restaurant, inc. And patrizio north, inc. The group utilizes local advertising, which emphasizes the restaurants as New York style trattorias featuring eighteenth century Italian paintings, an antique European bar and beautiful old world rugs with everything prepared with the freshest of ingredients. The group operates in the United States.

Primary SIC and add'l.: 5813 5812

CIK No: 0000832407

Subsidiaries: Patrizio Restaurant, Inc.

*Financial Data: Fiscal Year End:*12/31   *Latest Annual Data:* 12/31/2005

Year	Sales	Net Income
2005	$7,870,000	$454,000
2004	$7,622,000	$1,121,000
2003	$7,455,000	$217,000

Curr. Assets:	$2,289,000	Curr. Liab.:	$551,000		
Plant, Equip.:	$600,000	Total Liab.:	$577,000	Indic. Yr. Divd.:	NA
Total Assets:	$3,471,000	Net Worth:	$2,894,000	Debt/ Equity:	NA

SJW Corp

374 W Santa Clara St., San Jose, CA, 95113; *PH:* 1-408-279-7800; *Fax:* 1-408-279-7934; *http://* sjwadmin.vwh.net

General - Incorporation	CA
Employees	357
Auditor	KPMG LLP
Stk Agt	American Stock Transfer & Trust Co.
Counsel	NA
DUNS No.	NA

Stock- Price on:12/24/2007	$30.39
Stock Exchange	NA
Ticker Symbol	NA
Outstanding Shares	18,310,000
E.P.S.	$1.97
Shareholders	NA

Business: The groups principle activities include production, purchasing, storing, purification, distributing and retail sale of water. The group operates from the United States.

Primary SIC and add'l.: 3589 4941 7521 6552 7521 3589 6552 4941

CIK No: 0000766829

Subsidiaries: Crystal Choice Water Service LLC, San Jose Water Company, SJW Land Company

Officers: Richard W. Roth/Dir., CEO, Pres., Palle Jensen/VP, Chief Regulatory Affairs San Jose Water Company, Angela Yip/CFO, Treasurer, Suzy Papazian/Corp. Sec. - Attorney, George Belhumeur/Sr. VP - Operations - San Jose Water Company, Scott R. Yoo/COO - San Jose Water Company, Dana Drysdale/VP - Information Systems San Jose Water Company, Andrea J. Elliott/Controller - San Jose Water Company

Directors: Richard W. Roth/Dir., CEO, Pres., George E. Moss/Vice Chmn., Charles J. Toeniskoetter/Dir., Frederick R. Ulrich/Dir., Robert A. Van Valer/Dir., Mark L. Cali/Dir., Philip J. Dinapoli/Dir., Douglas R. King/Dir.

Owners: Robert A. Van Valer, George J. Belhumeur, Douglas R. King, Frederick R. Ulrich, Scott R. Yoo, Richard W. Roth, Mark L. Cali, Nancy O. Moss, Mario J. Gabelli, Roscoe Moss, Insiders, Drew Gibson, Angela Yip, George E. Moss, Philip J. DiNapoli (16 Owners included in Index)

*Financial Data: Fiscal Year End:*12/31   *Latest Annual Data:* 12/31/2006

Year	Sales	Net Income
2006	$189,238,000	$38,581,000
2005	$180,105,000	$21,840,000
2004	$166,911,000	$19,786,000

Curr. Assets:	$59,475,000	Curr. Liab.:	$37,246,000		
Plant, Equip.:	$546,811,000	Total Liab.:	$477,682,000	Indic. Yr. Divd.:	NA
Total Assets:	$705,864,000	Net Worth:	$228,182,000	Debt/ Equity:	NA

SK Telecom Co Ltd

11, Euljiro2-Ga, Jung-gu, Seoul; *PH:* 82-261007836; *http://* www.sktelecom.com; *Email:* press@sktelecom.com

General - Incorporation	Korea
Employees	6,646
Auditor	Deloitte Anjin LLC
Stk Agt	Kookmin Bank
Counsel	NA
DUNS No.	68-783-5116

Stock- Price on:12/24/2007	$27.48
Stock Exchange	NYSE
Ticker Symbol	SKM
Outstanding Shares	NA
E.P.S.	$2.29
Shareholders	NA

Business: The group's principal activity is the provision of nationwide cellular telephone communication services in the republic of Korea. Brands and products include speed 0ii0io, ting, ttl, uto, cara, leaderclub, Jun, nate and moneta.

Primary SIC and add'l.: 5731 4812

CIK No: 0001015650

Subsidiaries: Centurion IT Investment Association, Global Credit & Information Corp., IMM Cinema Fund, PAXNet Co., Ltd., Seoul Records, Inc., SK Capital Co., Ltd., SK Communications Co., Ltd., SK Telecom China Co., Ltd., SK Telecom International Inc., SK Telecom USA Holdings, Inc., SK Teletech Co., Ltd., SK Telink Co., Ltd., SK Wyverns Baseball Club Co., Ltd., SK-KTB Music Investment Fund, SLD Telecom PTE Ltd. 19 Subsidiaries included in the Index

Officers: Shin Bae Kim/Representative Dir., CEO, Pres., Chief Growth Officer, Joint Representative Dir., Bang Hyung Lee/Dir., Exec. VP, Sung Min Ha/Dir., Sr. VP, CFO, Head - Corporate Center

Directors: Shin Bae Kim/Representative Dir., CEO, Pres., Chief Growth Officer, Joint Representative Dir., Jung Nam Cho/Vice Chmn., Bang Hyung Lee/Dir., Exec. VP, Sung Min Ha/Dir., Sr. VP, CFO, Head - Corporate Center, Dae Sik Kim/Dir., Yong Woon Kim/Dir., Dae Gyu Byun/Dir., Seung Taik Yang/Dir., Jae Seung Yoon/Dir., Sang Chin Lee/Dir., Hyun Jin Im/Dir., Dal Sup Shim/Dir.

Owners: Bang Hyung Lee, Shin Bae Kim, Jae Seung Yoon, Sung Min Ha, POSCO/3.22%, SK Networks/1.49%, SK Group/25.80%, SK Corporation/24.31%, Dae Kyu Byun, Insiders

*Financial Data: Fiscal Year End:*12/31   *Latest Annual Data:* 12/31/2006

Year	Sales	Net Income
2006	$12,130,775,000	$2,068,582,000
2005	$10,721,820,000	$2,027,550,000
2004	$10,570,615,000	$1,553,076,000

Curr. Assets:	$5,130,358,000	Curr. Liab.:	$3,529,258,000	P/E Ratio:	52.44
Plant, Equip.:	$4,958,069,000	Total Liab.:	$7,885,725,000	Indic. Yr. Divd.:	NA
Total Assets:	$19,698,052,000	Net Worth:	$11,812,327,000	Debt/ Equity:	NA

SKECHERS USA

228 Manhattan Beach Blvd., Manhattan Beach, CA, 90266; *PH:* 1-310-318-3100; *Fax:* 1-310-318-5019; *http://* www.skechers.com; *Email:* info@skechers.com

General - Incorporation	DE	Stock - Price on:12/24/2007	$30.86
Employees	1,982	Stock Exchange	NYSE
Auditor	KPMG LLP	Ticker Symbol	SKX
Stk Agt	American Stock Transfer & Trust Co.	Outstanding Shares	45,520,000
Counsel	Kirkpatrick & Lockhart	E.P.S.	$1.66
DUNS No.	NA	Shareholders	NA

Business: The group's principal activity is to design, develop and distribute footwear for men, women and children under the skechers brand. The group operates through two segments wholesale and retail segment. Wholesale segment sells footwear directly to department stores and specialty retail stores and retail segment owns retail stores both domestically and on a smaller scale, internationally. The products of the group include four types of footwear: casuals, classics, outdoor and comfort (for men only). The group's products are sold in the United States through a wide range of department stores and specialty stores, network of own retail stores and e-commerce Web site. The group's product line currently consists of over 1,500 active styles that are organized in 15 distinct collections. The groups consumers are style-conscious 12- to 24-year-old men and women attracted to youthful brand image and fashion forward designs.

Primary SIC and add'l.: 7372 9999 5139 3149

CIK No: 0001065837

Subsidiaries: 310 Global Brands, Inc., Duncan Investments, LLC, Skechers By Mail, Inc., Skechers Collection LLC, Skechers EDC SPRL, Skechers International, Skechers International II, Skechers S.a.r.l., Skechers Sport LLC, Skechers U.S.A., Inc. II, Skechers USA Benelux B.V., Skechers USA Canada Inc., Skechers USA Deutschland GmbH, Skechers USA France SAS, Skechers USA Iberia, S.L. 19 Subsidiaries included in the Index

Officers: Robert Greenberg/Chmn., CEO/$2,530,396.00, Michael Greenberg/Dir., Pres./$1,737,666.00, David Weinberg/Dir., Exec. VP, COO/$1,519,464.00, Fred Schneider/CFO/$840,070.00, Philip Paccione/General Counsel, Exec. VP - Business Affairs, Corp. Sec., Mark Nason/Exec. VP - Production Development/$1,392,400.00

Directors: Robert Greenberg/Chmn., CEO, Michael Greenberg/Dir., Pres., David Weinberg/Dir., Exec. VP, COO, Jeffrey Greenberg/Dir., Morton D. Erlich/Dir., Geyer Kosinski/Dir., Richard Siskind/Dir., Jennifer Clay/Dir. - Public Relations

Owners: Jeffrey Greenberg/5.10%, Geyer Kosinski, Insiders/28.00%, Mark Nason, Wellington Management Company, LLP/11.30%, Robert Greenberg/76.50%, David Weinberg, Michael Greenberg/2.90%, Robert Greenberg/23.90%, Philip Paccione, Frederick Schneider, Morton D. Erlich, Michael Greenberg/6.80%, FMR Corp./8.80%, Insiders/88.40% (*17 Owners included in Index*)

Financial Data: Fiscal Year End:12/31 **Latest Annual Data:** 12/31/2006

Year	Sales	Net Income
2006	$1,205,368,000	$70,994,000
2005	$1,013,105,000	$44,717,000
2004	$926,036,000	$23,553,000

Curr. Assets:	$631,948,000	Curr. Liab.:	$181,161,000	P/E Ratio:	17.81
Plant, Equip.:	$87,645,000	Total Liab.:	$287,966,000	Indic. Yr. Divd.:	NA
Total Assets:	$737,053,000	Net Worth:	$449,087,000	Debt/ Equity:	0.0297

SKF Inc

Se-415 50, Gteborg; **PH:** 46-313371000; **Fax:** 46-313372832; **http://** www.skf.com

General - Incorporation	Sweden	Stock - Price on:12/24/2007	NA
Employees	NA	Stock Exchange	NA
Auditor	Thomas Thiel	Ticker Symbol	NA
Stk Agt	NA	Outstanding Shares	NA
Counsel	NA	E.P.S.	NA
DUNS No.	35-488-9727	Shareholders	NA

Business: The group's principle activities are to supply products, solutions and services in the rolling bearing and sealing businesses. The group's operations include technical support, maintenance services, condition monitoring and training. Industrial division is responsible for sales to industrial customers and for the product development and production of a wide range of bearings (spherical, cylindrical and angular contact bearings) . Automotive division's products include bearings, seals and related products for the automotive industry world-wide. Electrical division manufactures deep groove ball bearings and electrical components. Service division is responsible for sales to the industrial aftermarket. Skf aerospace produces bearings, seals and components for aircraft engines. Steel division produces special steels and steel components for bearing industry.

Primary SIC and add'l.: 3053 3312 3562

CIK No: 0000777504

Subsidiaries: AB Compania Sudamericana SKF, AB S.A. des Roulements Billes Sudois SKF, AB SKF-Agenturer, AB Svenska Kullagerfabriken, Altus Engineering Inc., Apex Dynamics Healthcare Products, terfrskringsaktiebolaget SKF, Atlas Ball Company, Atlas Management Inc., Bagaregrden 16:7 KB, Barseco (Pty) Ltd., Beijing Nankou SKF Railway Bearings Co. Ltd., Berger Vogel S.r.L., BFW Coupling Services Ltd., Brunei Opus Co. Ltd. 191 Subsidiaries included in the Index

Officers: Tom Johnstone/53/Dir., CEO, Pres., Alan Begg/54/Sr. VP - Group Technology Development, Quality, Tommy G. Klein/61/Sr. VP - Group Business, Development, Six Sigma, Lars G. Malmer/65/Sr. VP - Group Communication, Giuseppe Donato/64/Sr. VP, Eva Hansdotter/46/Sr. VP - Human Resources, Sustainability, Tore Bertilsson/57/Exec. VP - AB SKF, CFO, Phil Knights/60/Pres. - Service Division, Henrik Lange/47/Pres. - Industrial Division, Tryggve Sthen/56/Pres. - Automotive Division, Carina Bergfelt/48/General Counsel, Bo-Inge Stensson/47/Sr. VP - Group Demand Chain, Marita Bjork/50/Head - Investor Relations, Anna Alte/Assist. - Investor Relations, Monica Svensson/Sec. Investor Relations - SKF Group Headquarters

Directors: Tom Johnstone/53/Dir., CEO, Pres., Anders Scharp/74/Chmn., Goran Johansson/63/Dir., Eckhard Cordes/58/Dir., Hans-Olov Olsson/67/Dir., Lennart Larsson/60/Dir., Vito H. Baumgartner/68/Dir., Kennet Carlsson/46/Dep. Dir., Lena Treschow Torell/Dir., Leif ostling/63/Dir., Ulla Litzen/52/Dir., Jeanette Stenborg/41/Dep. Dir., Clas Ake Hedstrom/69/Dir., Winnie Kin Wah Fok/52/Dir.

SkillSoft

107 NE Blvd., Nashua, NH, 03062; **PH:** 1-603-324-3000; **Fax:** 1-603-324-3009; **http://** www.skillsoft.com; **Email:** information@skillsoft.com

General - Incorporation	Ireland	Stock - Price on:12/24/2007	$9.25
Employees	999	Stock Exchange	NDQ
Auditor	Ernst & Young LLP	Ticker Symbol	SKIL
Stk Agt	Computershare Inv Srvs (Ireland) Ltd	Outstanding Shares	111,010,000
Counsel	WilmerHale	E.P.S.	$0.26
DUNS No.	60-851-6464	Shareholders	NA

Business: The group's principle activity is to provide comprehensive e-learning solutions to businesses and government organizations. The group provides Web-based training resources that cover a variety of professional effectiveness, business and information technology topics. The solutions are designed to address training issues that support customers' business objectives and to provide a system of continuous support to working employees. The group offers a range of support and services to customers through professional services organizations. The group also provides installation, implementation consulting and technical support to customers. The group's total revenue for year 2007 was 225.17 millions of USD.

Primary SIC and add'l.: 7379 8299

CIK No: 0000940181

Subsidiaries: Books24x7.com, Inc., CBT Technology Limited, SkillSoft Asia Pacific PTE Ltd, SkillSoft Asia Pacific Pty Ltd, SkillSoft Canada Limited, SkillSoft Corporation, SkillSoft Deutschland GmbH, SkillSoft Finance Limited, SkillSoft France SARL, SkillSoft Ireland Ltd, SkillSoft New Zealand Ltd, SkillSoft UK Limited, SmartCertify Direct, Inc., SmartForce Benelux B.V., SmartForce Business Skills Ltd

Officers: Chuck Moran/Dir., CEO, Pres., Greg Priest/Chmn., Chief Strategy Officer, Tom McDonald/CFO, Exec. VP - Operations/$1,016,627.00, Jerry Nine/Founder, COO/$1,168,112.00, Mark Townsend/Exec. VP - Technology/$925,491.00, Colm Darcy/Exec. VP - Content Development/$614,561.00, Lee Ritze/Sr. VP - Marketing, Kevin Young/VP, MD - EMEA, Glenn Nott/VP, MD - Asia Pacific, John Ambrose/Sr. VP - Strategy, Corporate Development, Emerging Business, Anthony P. Amato/43/VP - Finance, Chief Accounting Officer

Directors: Chuck Moran/Dir., CEO, Pres., Greg Priest/Chmn., Chief Strategy Officer, Stewart K.P. Gross/Dir., Ferdinand Von Prondzynski/Dir., James S. Krzywicki/Dir., Jerry Nine/Founder, COO, William F. Meagher/69/Dir., Howard P. Edelstein/53/Dir.

Owners: Jerald A. Nine/1.30%, Thomas J. McDonald/1.10%, Howard P. Edelstein, Columbia Wanger Asset Management, L.P./20.00%, Colm M. Darcy, William F. Meagher, Westfield Capital Management Company LLC/8.70%, Charles E. Moran/2.80%, Mark A. Townsend/1.30%, James S. Krzywicki, Capital Group Companies, Inc./5.10%, Stewart K.P. Gross, Cramer Rosenthal McGlynn, LLC/7.30%, Insiders/6.90%, Ferdinand von Prondzynski

Financial Data: Fiscal Year End:01/31 **Latest Annual Data:** 1/31/2007

Year	Sales	Net Income
2007	$225,172,000	$24,153,000
2006	$215,567,000	$35,215,000
2005	$212,300,000	-$20,113,000

Curr. Assets:	$240,770,000	Curr. Liab.:	$202,636,000	P/E Ratio:	35.58
Plant, Equip.:	$9,672,000	Total Liab.:	$205,041,000	Indic. Yr. Divd.:	NA
Total Assets:	$342,970,000	Net Worth:	$137,929,000	Debt/ Equity:	NA

Skinny Nutritional Corp

Formerly: Creative Enterprises International Inc
3 Bala Plz. E, Ste. 117, Bala Cynwyd, PA, 19004; **PH:** 1-610-784-2000; **http://** www.creativepi.com

General - Incorporation	NV	Stock - Price on:12/24/2007	NA
Employees	12	Stock Exchange	OTC
Auditor	Connolly, Grady & Cha P.C	Ticker Symbol	SKNY
Stk Agt	Fidelity Transfer Co.	Outstanding Shares	NA
Counsel	NA	E.P.S.	-$0.049
DUNS No.	NA	Shareholders	NA

Business: The groups principle activities include marketing and distribution company of consumer products. The group operates from United States.

Primary SIC and add'l.: 5141

CIK No: 0001176325

Subsidiaries: Creative Enterprises, Inc.

Officers: Donald J. McDonald/55/Dir., CEO, Pres., Kenneth P. Brice/61/Dir., CFO, Michael Reis/63/Dir., Interim COO

Directors: Donald J. McDonald/55/Dir., CEO, Pres., Michael Salaman/45/Chmn., Kenneth P. Brice/61/Dir., CFO, Michael Reis/63/Dir., Interim COO

Owners: Yehuda Dachs/9.30%, Michael Reis, Donald J. McDonald, Charles Hallinan/6.60%, Michael Salaman/10.10%, Kenneth Brice, Insiders/12.10%

Financial Data: Fiscal Year End:12/31 **Latest Annual Data:** 12/31/2006

Year	Sales	Net Income
2006	$628,000	-$2,303,000
2005	$514,000	-$3,430,000

Curr. Assets:	$225,000	Curr. Liab.:	$3,635,000		
Plant, Equip.:	$6,000	Total Liab.:	$3,635,000	Indic. Yr. Divd.:	NA
Total Assets:	$231,000	Net Worth:	-$3,404,000	Debt/ Equity:	NA

Skins Inc

255 Newburyport Tpke, Rowley, MA, 01969; **PH:** 1-978-948-7915; **http://** www.skinsfootwear.com

General - Incorporation	NV	Stock - Price on:12/24/2007	$1.43
Employees	5	Stock Exchange	OTC
Auditor	Mahoney Cohen & Co., CPA, P.C.	Ticker Symbol	SKNN
Stk Agt	Nevada Agency & Trust Company	Outstanding Shares	36,820,000
Counsel	NA	E.P.S.	-$0.178
DUNS No.	NA	Shareholders	NA

Business: The groups principal activities include developing, marketing and supporting a voice interface software platform for the Chinese languages. The groups software will allow other software programmers and engineers to develop voice interface applications for the Chinese languages based on the software platform. The group operates from the United States.

Primary SIC and add'l.: 5812

CIK No: 0001300744

Officers: Mark Klein/CEO, Pres., Dennis Walker/VP - Sales, Kobi Levi/Sr. Designer, Deborah Gargiulo/CFO, Antonio Pavan/VP, Coo, Natalie Rivera/Production Mgr.

Directors: Michael J. Rosenthal/Chmn., Stephen Hochberg/Dir., Steve Reimer/Dir., Bill Priakos/Member - Advisory Board, Mark Itzkowitz/Member - Advisory Board, Frank Zambrelli/Dir.

Owners: Joshua Hermelin/8.40%, Steve Reimer, Mark Klein/23.80%, Antonio Pavan, Stephen Hochberg/1.20%, Insiders/27.80%, Geoffrey Dubey/7.60%, Michael J. Rosenthal/2.40%

Financial Data: *Fiscal Year End:*03/31 *Latest Annual Data:* 12/31/2006

Year	Sales	Net Income
2006	NA	-$4,100,000
2005	NA	-$77,000

Curr. Assets:	$28,000	**Curr. Liab.:**	$62,000		
Plant, Equip.:	NA	**Total Liab.:**	$62,000	**Indic. Yr. Divd.:**	NA
Total Assets:	$28,000	**Net Worth:**	-$34,000	**Debt/ Equity:**	NA

Skinvisible Inc

6320 S Sandhill Rd., Ste. 10, Las Vegas, NV, 89120; *PH:* 1-702-433-7154; *Fax:* 1-702-433-7192; *http://* www.skinvisible.com; *Email:* info@skinvisible.com

General - Incorporation	NV	**Stock**- Price on:12/24/2007	$0.325
Employees	6	Stock Exchange	OTC
Auditor	Sarna & Co	Ticker Symbol	SKVI
Stk Agt	Mellon Trust Co	Outstanding Shares	64,710,000
Counsel	NA	E.P.S.	-$0.02
DUNS No.	NA	Shareholders	NA

Business: The group's principal activity is to develop and manufacture innovative topical polymer-based delivery systems, technologies and formulations. The manufacturing process consists of proprietary polymer-based delivery systems or product formulations, which incorporates the delivery systems and additional ingredients including active agents for specific applications. The group offers skincare solutions for the healthcare, food service, industrial, cosmetic and salon industries, as well as for personal use in the retail marketplace.

Primary SIC and add'l.: 8731 2834

CIK No: 0001085277

Subsidiaries: Manloc Laboratories, Inc., Skinvisible International, Inc., Skinvisible Pharmaceuticals Inc.

Officers: Terry Howlett/Chmn., CEO, Pres., James A. Roszell/Chemist

Directors: Terry Howlett/Chmn., CEO, Pres., Jost Steinbruchel/Dir., Greg McCartney/Dir.

Owners: Greg McCartney/0.50%, Jost Steinbruchel/4.90%, Insiders/17.70%, Terry Howlett/12.30%

Financial Data: *Fiscal Year End:*12/31 *Latest Annual Data:* 12/31/2006

Year	Sales	Net Income
2006	$691,000	-$2,098,000
2005	$850,000	-$1,031,000
2004	$520,000	-$805,000

Curr. Assets:	$106,000	**Curr. Liab.:**	$1,150,000		
Plant, Equip.:	$30,000	**Total Liab.:**	$1,150,000	**Indic. Yr. Divd.:**	NA
Total Assets:	$887,000	**Net Worth:**	-$263,000	**Debt/ Equity:**	NA

Sky Financial Group Inc

221 S Church St., Bowling Green, OH, 43402; *PH:* 1-419-327-6300; *http://* www.skyfi.com

General - Incorporation	OH	**Stock**- Price on:12/24/2007	$27.21
Employees	4,369	Stock Exchange	NA
Auditor	Deloitte & Touche LLP	Ticker Symbol	NA
Stk Agt	Bank of New York	Outstanding Shares	117,880,000
Counsel	NA	E.P.S.	$1.69
DUNS No.	18-407-5372	Shareholders	NA

Business: The group's principal activities are carried out through three divisions: community banking, financial service affiliates and sky financial solutions. The community banking segment provides services to businesses and consumers through a regional structure. The financial service affiliates segment includes businesses relating to trust and investment management, insurance agency operations and other financial related services. It also includes non-conforming mortgage lending, broker operations and collection activities. The group's operates through 230 banking centers and 200 ATMs. On 05-Jan-2004 the group acquired, spencer-patterson agency inc, on 08-Jan-2004, second bancorp incorporated & on 01-Apr-2004, eob inc.

Primary SIC and add'l.: 6712 6021

CIK No: 0000855876

Subsidiaries: Access Partners LLC, Belmont Financial Network Inc, Celaris Brokerage LLC, First Western Capital Trust I, Freedom Financial Life Insurance Company, M&E Investment Group, Inc., Metropolitan Savings Service Corporation, Mid Am Capital Trust I, Prospect Trust I, Second Bancorp Capital Trust I, Second National Capital Corporation, Second National Financial Company LLC, Second National Loan Servicing Company, Sky Capital LLC, Sky Capital Management, Inc. 21 Subsidiaries included in the Index

Officers: Marty E. Adams/Chmn., CEO, Pres., Zahid Afzal/45/CTO, Division Exec. VP

Directors: Marty E. Adams/Chmn., CEO, Pres., Gregory C. Spangler/Dir., Gregory L. Ridler/Dir., Robert C. Duvall/Dir., Jonathan A. Levy/Dir., Thomas J. Oshane/Dir., Emerson J. Ross/Dir., George N. Chandler/Dir., Marylouise Fennell/Dir., Joseph N. Tosh/Dir., Gerard P. Mastroianni/Dir., Fred H. Johnson/Dir., James D. Hilliker/Dir., Raymond John Wean/Dir., John R. Wean/59/Dir.

Owners: John B. Gerlach, Daniel B. Benhase, James W. Nelson, Wm. J. Lhota, Kathleen H. Ransier, Donald R. Kimble, David P. Lauer, Thomas E. Hoaglin, David L. Porteous, Michael J. Endres, Karen A. Holbrook, Gene E. Little, Insiders/3.02%, Don M. Casto, Ronald C. Baldwin *(17 Owners included in Index)*

Financial Data: *Fiscal Year End:*12/31 *Latest Annual Data:* 12/31/2006

Year	Sales	Net Income
2006	$1,253,585,000	$190,338,000
2005	$1,041,606,000	$182,563,000
2004	$865,360,000	$194,355,000

Curr. Assets:	$914,441,000	**Curr. Liab.:**	$15,510,152,000	**P/E Ratio:**	16.10
Plant, Equip.:	$206,145,000	**Total Liab.:**	$15,845,446,000	**Indic. Yr. Divd.:**	$1.000
Total Assets:	$17,726,094,000	**Net Worth:**	$1,880,648,000	**Debt/ Equity:**	0.5954

Sky Petroleum Inc

Frost Bank Tower, 401 Congress Ave., Ste. 1540, Austin, TX, 78701; *PH:* 1-512-687-3427; *http://* www.skypetroleum.com; *Email:* info@skypetroleum.com

General - Incorporation	NV	**Stock**- Price on:12/24/2007	$0.5001
Employees	3	Stock Exchange	OTC
Auditor	Backstead And Watts, LLP	Ticker Symbol	SKPIE
Stk Agt	Pacific Stock Transfer Company	Outstanding Shares	58,790,000
Counsel	NA	E.P.S.	-$0.24
DUNS No.	NA	Shareholders	NA

Business: The groups principal activity is to identify opportunities to either make direct property acquisitions or to fund exploration or development of oil and natural gas properties. The group operates from the United States.

Primary SIC and add'l.: 1382

CIK No: 0001183276

Subsidiaries: Bekata Limited, Sastaro Limited

Officers: Brent D. Kinney/65/Dir., CEO, Michael D. Noonan/Dir., CEO, Sec., Shafiq Ur-Rahman/57/Mgr. - Finance, Administration, Ian Baron/Dir., VP - Exploration - Production, Mike Churchill/59/CFO

Directors: Brent D. Kinney/65/Dir., CEO, Michael D. Noonan/Dir., CEO, Sec., Peter Cockcroft/Dir., Ian Baron/Dir., VP - Exploration - Production, Karim Jobanputra/Dir., Nigel McCue/Dir.

Owners: Insiders/4.79%, Sheikh Hamad Bin Jassen Bin Jaber Al Thani/24.93%, Daniel Meyer/4.29%, Metage Capital Limited/8.59%, Michael Noonan

Financial Data: *Fiscal Year End:*12/31 *Latest Annual Data:* 12/31/2006

Year	Sales	Net Income
2006	$2,408,000	-$10,415,000
2005	NA	-$6,024,000
2004	$0	-$20,000

Curr. Assets:	$7,503,000	**Curr. Liab.:**	$136,000		
Plant, Equip.:	$17,706,000	**Total Liab.:**	$136,000	**Indic. Yr. Divd.:**	NA
Total Assets:	$25,213,000	**Net Worth:**	$25,078,000	**Debt/ Equity:**	NA

Skybridge Wireless Inc

6565 Spencer St., Ste. 205, Las Vegas, NV, 89119; *PH:* 1-702-897-8704; *http://* www.sbtginc.com

General - Incorporation	NV	**Stock**- Price on:12/24/2007	NA
Employees	NA	Stock Exchange	NA
Auditor	LL Bradford & Co	Ticker Symbol	NA
Stk Agt	Pacific Stock Transfer Company	Outstanding Shares	NA
Counsel	NA	E.P.S.	NA
DUNS No.	NA	Shareholders	NA

Business: The group's principal activity is to develop a business supplying high-speed fixed wireless Internet access to businesses and communities in the metropolitan markets. It is in the development stage and considering other services and products to pursue which may complement its business and meet the needs or demands of business customers. During sep-2003, the group acquired net service corporation.

Primary SIC and add'l.: 7375

CIK No: 0001081172

Subsidiaries: SkyBridge Wireless, Inc.

SkyePharma Plc

105 Piccadilly, London, W1J 7NJ; *PH:* 44-2074911777; *Fax:* 44-2074913338; *http://* www.skyepharma.com

General - Incorporation	UK	**Stock**- Price on:12/24/2007	$25.55
Employees	445	Stock Exchange	NDQ
Auditor	PricewaterhouseCoopers LLP	Ticker Symbol	SKYE
Stk Agt	Bank of New York	Outstanding Shares	NA
Counsel	Stringer Saul, Sullivan & Cromwell	E.P.S.	NA
DUNS No.	29-184-5683	Shareholders	NA

Business: The group's principal activities are the research and development, manufacture and sale of prescription pharmaceutical products. The group's five platform technologies are oral, injectable, inhalation, topical and solubilisation. Products include Paxil CR, Xatral OD, Uroxatral, Madopar DR, Coruno, Nifedipine, Diclofenac, Requip, Zileuton, Statin NK - 104, Altace, Foradil, Certihaler, Pulmicort HFA, Formoterol HFA, Qab 149, Formoterol Combi, Depocyt, Depomorphine, Psoraxine, Depobupivacaine, HGH, Interferon Alpha-2B, Solaraze, Multiple, Fenofibrate, Propofol IDD-D, and Busulfan.

Primary SIC and add'l.: 5122 8734 2834

CIK No: 0001018117

Subsidiaries: Jago Holding AG, Jagotec AG, Krypton Limited, SkyePharma (Jersey) Ltd, SkyePharma AB, SkyePharma AG, SkyePharma Canada Inc., SkyePharma Holding AG, SkyePharma Holding Inc., SkyePharma Inc., SkyePharma Production SAS, SkyePharma US Inc

Officers: Frank Condella/CEO, Ken Cunningham/COO, Jean-Marc Chevalier/Contact - Contract Manufacturing Questions, Peter Grant/Dir. - Finance, Lorraine Jones/Head - Business Development

Directors: David Ebsworth/Non Exec. Dir., Alan Bray/Dir., Argeris N. Karabelas/Non Exec. Dir., Stephen Harris/Non Exec. Dir., Jean-Charles Tschudin/Non Exec. Dir.

Skyflyer Inc

Friedrich-List-Allee 10, Wegberg, 41844; *PH:* 360-927-7354; *Fax:* 49-2432893629; *http://* www.skyflyertec.de; *Email:* info@skyflyer-tec.com

General - Incorporation	NV	**Stock**- Price on:12/24/2007	$0.17
Employees	1	Stock Exchange	OTC
Auditor	Davidson & Company LLP	Ticker Symbol	SKFL
Stk Agt	NA	Outstanding Shares	103,200,000
Counsel	NA	E.P.S.	$0.00
DUNS No.	NA	Shareholders	NA

Business: The groups principal activity is engage in the business of acquiring and exploring mineral properties in order to focus resources on developing technology and business. The group operates from the United States.

Primary SIC and add'l.: 1000

CIK No: 0001312402

Subsidiaries: Skyflyer Technology GmbH

Officers: Rolf G. Horchler/CEO, Sec., Dieter Wagels/CEO - Skyflyer Technology Gmbh, John Boschert/38/Sec., Treasurer

Owners: Inventa Holding GmbH/69.80%

Financial Data: Fiscal Year End:10/31   Latest Annual Data: 10/31/2006

Year	Sales	Net Income
2006	NA	-$227,000
2005	NA	-$42,000

Curr. Assets:	$34,000	**Curr. Liab.:**	$152,000		
Plant, Equip.:	$27,000	**Total Liab.:**	$307,000	**Indic. Yr. Dvd.:**	NA
Total Assets:	$104,000	**Net Worth:**	-$203,000	**Debt/ Equity:**	NA

Skyline Corp

2520 By-Pass Rd., Elkhart, IN, 46515; **PH:** 1-574-294-6521; **Fax:** 1-574-293-7574; **http://** www.skylinecorp.com

General - Incorporation	IN	**Stock**- Price on:12/24/2007	$32.03
Employees	2,800	Stock Exchange	NYSE
Auditor	Crowe Chizek & Co. LLC	Ticker Symbol	SKY
Stk Agt	Computershare Investor Services LLC	Outstanding Shares	8,390,000
Counsel	Barnes & Thornburg	E.P.S.	$0.17
DUNS No.	00-507-0669	Shareholders	NA

Business: The group's principal activities are to design, produce and distribute manufactured housing and recreational vehicles. Manufactured housing consists of mobile homes and multi-sectional homes. Recreational vehicles consist of travel trailers, including park models and fifth wheels. The group's recreational vehicles are sold under the nomad, layton and aljo trademarks for travel trailers and fifth wheels. The principal buyers continue to be young married couples and senior citizens. The customers of recreational vehicles are primarily vacationing middle- income families, retired couples traveling around the country and sportsmen pursuing four-season hobbies. During fiscal year 2004, the group produced 7,723 manufactured homes. The group operates solely in the domestic market.

Primary SIC and add'l.: 1521 3792 2452 2451 1522

CIK No: 0000090896

Subsidiaries: Homette Corporation, Layton Homes Corp, Skyline Corporation, Skyline Homes Inc

Officers: James R. Weigand/CFO/$244,500.00, Bruce G. Page/58/VP - Operations

Owners: David T. Link, William H. Lawson, Barclays Global Investors/6.80%, John C. Firth, Charles W. Chambliss, Third Avenue Management LLC/11.40%, Terrence M. Decio, Jerry Hammes, Dimensional Fund Advisors LP/7.60%, Andrew J. Mckenna, Arthur J. Decio/17.60%, Ronald F. Kloska, GAMCO Investors, Inc./10.40%, T. Rowe Price Associates, Inc./10.00%, Christopher R. Leader (18 Owners included in Index)

Financial Data: Fiscal Year End:05/31   Latest Annual Data: 05/31/2007

Year	Sales	Net Income
2007	$365,473,000	$2,593,000
2006	$508,543,000	$14,292,000
2005	$454,324,000	$5,452,000

Curr. Assets:	$204,375,000	**Curr. Liab.:**	$40,150,000	**P/E Ratio:**	48.53
Plant, Equip.:	$34,069,000	**Total Liab.:**	$50,649,000	**Indic. Yr. Dvd.:**	$0.720
Total Assets:	$248,403,000	**Net Worth:**	$197,754,000	**Debt/ Equity:**	NA

Skylynx Communications Inc

15 Paradise Plz., Sarasota, FL, 34239; **PH:** 1-941-955-1700; **http://** www.skylynx.com

General - Incorporation	DE	**Stock**- Price on:12/24/2007	NA
Employees	NA	Stock Exchange	OTC
Auditor	Cordovano & Honeck LLP	Ticker Symbol	SKYC
Stk Agt	NA	Outstanding Shares	NA
Counsel	NA	E.P.S.	NA
DUNS No.	NA	Shareholders	NA

Business: The group's principal activities is to provide Internet related services. The group provides logistics needs to the commercial fleet industry with special focus on emergency medical services (ems), police and fire department fleets. As a marketing driven company with a unique technological base, its goal is to provide first response groups with a low cost, highly reliable tracking, monitoring and data networking system that maximises vehicle and personnel utilization and enhances homeland security.on 04-Dec-2003, the group acquired interim corporate resources.

Primary SIC and add'l.: 7359 7375 6719 1389

CIK No: 0001061354

Subsidiaries: Founders Industries, Inc, Rover TelCom Corporation, Simpco, SkyLynx Communications de Costa Rica, S.A

Officers: Bryan K. Shobe/CEO, Melissa Shobe/Director Investor Relations

Financial Data: Fiscal Year End:06/30   Latest Annual Data: 06/30/2005

Year	Sales	Net Income
2005	$471,000	-$2,561,000
2004	$339,000	-$3,575,000
2003	$418,000	-$871,000

Curr. Assets:	$83,000	**Curr. Liab.:**	$1,722,000		
Plant, Equip.:	$27,000	**Total Liab.:**	$1,975,000	**Indic. Yr. Dvd.:**	NA
Total Assets:	$212,000	**Net Worth:**	-$1,762,000	**Debt/ Equity:**	NA

Skystar Bio-pharmaceutical Co

Formerly: Cyber Group Network Corp

Rm. 10601, Jiezuo Plz., No. 4, Fenghui Rd. S, Gaoxin, XIAN; **PH:** 86-4076-454433; **http://** www.cybergroupnetwork.com

General - Incorporation	NV	**Stock**- Price on:12/24/2007	$1.38
Employees	NA	Stock Exchange	OTC
Auditor	Moore Stephens Wurth F & T LLP	Ticker Symbol	SKBI
Stk Agt	Pacific Stock Transfer Company	Outstanding Shares	NA
Counsel	NA	E.P.S.	NA
DUNS No.	NA	Shareholders	NA

Business: The group's principal activity is to develop computer security technology and Internet accesses devices. The group has developed ppirt (password protection information retrieval technology), a computer software program designed to protect customer's valuable information from hackers and thieves. The electronic snitching device (e-snitch) is an electronic tracking tool that can locate missing/stolen computers within fifty feet of their location.

Primary SIC and add'l.: 7372

CIK No: 0001076939

Subsidiaries: Skystar Cayman

Owners: Wei Wen, Xinya Zhang, Insiders, Upform Group Limited, Weibing Lu, Scott R. Cramer, Renaissance US Growth Investment Trust PLC, Premier RENN US Emerging Growth Fund Limited, US Special Opportunities Trust PLC

Financial Data: Fiscal Year End:12/31   Latest Annual Data: 12/31/2006

Year	Sales	Net Income
2006	$9,796,000	$1,175,000
2005	$5,939,000	$1,468,000
2004	NA	-$274,000

Curr. Assets:	$999,000	**Curr. Liab.:**	$1,538,000		
Plant, Equip.:	$10,911,000	**Total Liab.:**	$2,500,000	**Indic. Yr. Dvd.:**	NA
Total Assets:	$12,247,000	**Net Worth:**	$9,747,000	**Debt/ Equity:**	0.0063

Skyterra Communications Inc

10802 Pk.ridge Blvd., Reston, VA, 20191; **PH:** 1-703-390-1899; **Fax:** 1-703-390-1893; **http://** www.skyterracom.com; **Email:** info@skyterracom.com

General - Incorporation	DE	**Stock**- Price on:12/24/2007	$8.2
Employees	132	Stock Exchange	OTC
Auditor	Ernst & Young, LLP	Ticker Symbol	SKYT
Stk Agt	American Stock Transfer & Trust Co.	Outstanding Shares	102,410,000
Counsel	NA	E.P.S.	-$0.93
DUNS No.	NA	Shareholders	NA

Business: The group's principle activity is to provide mobile digital voice and data communications services via satellite in North America through its subsidiary mobile satellite venture, l.p. The group's satellite voice and data services supports two-way circuit-switched voice, facsimile and data communication services and the satellite dispatch service allows voice communications among users in a customer-defined group using a push-to-talk device. Customer base of the group includes oil and gas pipeline companies, utilities and telecommunications companies with outside maintenance fleets, state and local public safety organizations, and public service organizations who need to seamlessly link resources on a nationwide basis. In 2003, the group acquired electronic system products inc.

Primary SIC and add'l.: 4899 6719 4813

CIK No: 0000756502

Subsidiaries: Hughes Communications, Inc

Officers: Alexander H. Good/CEO, Pres., Robert C. Lewis/Sr. VP, General Counsel, Sec., Scott MacLeod/CFO, Exec. VP, Treasurer, James A. Wiseman/VP, Corporate Controller

Directors: Jeffrey M. Killeen/Dir., Jeffrey A. Leddy/Dir., William F. Stasior/Dir., Aaron J. Stone/Dir., Andrew D. Africk/Dir., Michael Weiner/Dir.

Owners: Andrew D. Africk, Jeffrey Leddy, Jennifer A. Manner, Alexander H. Good/2.00%, Robert C. Lewis, Scott Macleod, Monish Kundra, Marc J. Rowan, Donald H. Gips, Eric A. Swank, Peter D. Karabinis, Aaron J. Stone, Drew Caplan, Gary M. Parsons/1.40%, Randy S. Segal

Financial Data: Fiscal Year End:12/31   Latest Annual Data: 12/31/2006

Year	Sales	Net Income
2006	$34,854,000	-$57,100,000
2005	$615,000	$59,325,000
2004	$2,127,000	$17,166,000

Curr. Assets:	$453,776,000	**Curr. Liab.:**	$21,112,000		
Plant, Equip.:	$110,263,000	**Total Liab.:**	$525,716,000	**Indic. Yr. Dvd.:**	NA
Total Assets:	$767,047,000	**Net Worth:**	-$119,943,000	**Debt/ Equity:**	NA

Skywest Inc

444 S River Rd., St. George, UT, 84790; **PH:** 1-435-634-3000; **Fax:** 1-435-634-3105; **http://** www.skywest.com

General - Incorporation	UT	**Stock**- Price on:12/24/2007	$26.86
Employees	8,792	Stock Exchange	NDQ
Auditor	Ernst & Young LLP	Ticker Symbol	SKYW
Stk Agt	Zions First National Bank	Outstanding Shares	64,530,000
Counsel	NA	E.P.S.	$2.26
DUNS No.	06-797-3032	Shareholders	NA

Business: The groups principle activity is to operate airlines. The group also provides freight services. The group operates from United States.

Primary SIC and add'l.: 7514 4522 4512

CIK No: 0000793733

Subsidiaries: Atlantic Southeast Airlines, Inc. (ASA), SkyWest Airlines

Officers: Jerry C. Atkin/Chmn., CEO/$1,532,408.00, Michael J. Kraupp/VP - Finance, Treasurer, Amber Hunter/Dir. - Communications, Development, Ronald B. Reber/COO, Pres. - Skywest Airlines/$962,438.00, Bradford R. Holt/VP - Flight Operations, Marissa Snow/Mgr. - Corporate Communications, Sonya Wolford/VP - Inflight Operations, Bryan T. Labrecque/COO, Pres./$450,629.00, Bradford R. Rich/CFO, Exec. VP, Treasurer/$926,382.00, Necia Clark-Mantle/VP - People Department, Michael H. Gibson/VP - Maintenance, James B. Jensen/VP - Information Technology, Steven L. Hart/VP - Marketing Development, Russell A. Childs/COO, Pres. - Skywest Airlines, Eric D. Christensen/VP - Planning, Corp. Sec. (17 Officers included in Index)

Directors: Jerry C. Atkin/Chmn., CEO, Mervyn K. Cox/Dir., Ian M. Cumming/Dir., Steven F. Udvar-Hazy/Dir., Ralph J. Atkin/Dir., Steve W. Albrecht/Dir., Henry J. Eyring/Dir., Robert G. Sarver/Dir., Margaret S. Billson/Dir., James L. Welch/Dir.

Owners: Jerry C. Atkin/3.70%, Henry J. Eyring, Insiders/5.50%, Barclays Global Investor/5.70%, Steve W. Albrecht, Bradford R. Rich, Steven F. Udvar-Hazy, Margaret S. Billson, Orbis Holding LTD/6.70%, Mervyn K. Cox, Bryan T. LaBrecque, Ronald B. Reber, Ralph J. Atkin, Robert G. Sarver, Ian M. Cumming

Financial Data: Fiscal Year End:03/31   Latest Annual Data: 12/31/2006

Year	Sales	Net Income
2006	$3,114,656,000	$145,806,000
2005	$1,964,048,000	$112,267,000
2004	$1,156,044,000	$81,952,000

Curr. Assets:	$1,095,454,000	**Curr. Liab.:**	$408,431,000	**P/E Ratio:**	11.88
Plant, Equip.:	$2,558,453,000	**Total Liab.:**	$2,553,126,000	**Indic. Yr. Divd.:**	$0.120
Total Assets:	$3,731,419,000	**Net Worth:**	$1,178,293,000	**Debt/ Equity:**	1.4564

Skyworks Solutions Inc

20 Sylvan Rd., Woburn, MA, 01801; *PH:* 1-781-376-3000; *http://* www.skyworksinc.com

General - Incorporation	DE	**Stock**- Price on:12/24/2007	NA
Employees	4,000	Stock Exchange	NDQ
Auditor	KPMG LLP	Ticker Symbol	SWKS
Stk Agt	American Stock Transfer & Trust Co.	Outstanding Shares	159,900,000
Counsel	NA	E.P.S	$0.36
DUNS No.	00-103-0311	Shareholders	NA

Business: The group's principal activities are to design, develop, manufacture and market proprietary semiconductor products and system solutions for manufacturers of wireless products. The semiconductor products segment designs and manufacture gallium arsenide integrated circuits, other discrete semiconductors and multi-chip modules. The group offers front-end modules, rf subsystems and cellular systems to top wireless handset and infrastructure customers. The group's major customers are samsung electronics co. And motorola, inc.

Primary SIC and add'l.: 3674 3679

CIK No: 0000004127

Subsidiaries: Company, Limited, Skyworks Communications Technology Development (Shanghai), Skyworks Semiconductor, Skyworks Solutions Canada, Limited, Skyworks Solutions Company, Limited, Skyworks Solutions India Private Limited, Skyworks Solutions Korea Limited, Skyworks Solutions Limited, Skyworks Solutions Limited, Denmark Representative Office, Skyworks Solutions Mauritius, Limited, Skyworks Solutions Oy, Skyworks Solutions Worldwide, Inc., Skyworks Solutions Worldwide, Inc., Beijing Representative Office, Skyworks Solutions Worldwide, Inc., Hong Kong Branch, Skyworks Solutions Worldwide, Inc., Singapore Representative Office 20 Subsidiaries included in the Index

Officers: David J. Aldrich/51/Dir., CEO, Pres., Mark V. Tremallo/52/VP, General Counsel, Sec., Liam K. Griffin/42/Sr. VP - Sales, Marketing, Gregory L. Waters/47/Exec. VP, Nien-Tsu Shen/54/VP - Quality, George M. Levan/62/VP - Human Resources, Stan Swearingen/48/VP, GM - Linear Products, Bruce J. Freyman/48/VP - Worldwide Operations, Thomas S. Schiller/37/VP - Corporate Development, Donald W. Palette/51/CFO, VP, Donald W. Palette/CFO

Directors: David J. Aldrich/51/Dir., CEO, Pres., Dwight W. Decker/58/Chmn., Balakrishnan S. Iyer/52/Dir., David P. McGlade/47/Dir., Moiz M. Beguwala/62/Dir., Kevin L. Beebe/49/Dir., Timothy R. Furey/50/Dir., David J. McLachlan/70/Dir., Thomas C. Leonard/73/Dir., Robert A. Schriesheim/48/Dir.

Owners: Fidelity Management & Research Company/11.10%, Kevin D. Barber, Thomas C. Leonard, Balakrishnan S. Iyer, Kevin L. Beebe, Insiders/4.10%, Gregory L. Waters, Allan M. Kline, Liam K. Griffin, Dwight W. Decker, David J. McLachlan, David J. Aldrich/1.20%, Moiz M. Beguwala, Timothy R. Furey, David P. McGlade

Financial Data: *Fiscal Year End:*09/30 *Latest Annual Data:* 12/29/2006

Year		Sales			Net Income
2006		$196,030,000			$12,037,000
Curr. Assets:	$495,982,000	**Curr. Liab.:**	$158,235,000		
Plant, Equip.:	$150,838,000	**Total Liab.:**	$395,279,000	**Indic. Yr. Divd.:**	NA
Total Assets:	$1,187,843,000	**Net Worth:**	$792,564,000	**Debt/ Equity:**	NA

SL Green Realty Corp

420 Lexington Ave., New York, NY, 10170; *PH:* 1-212-594-2700; *Fax:* 1-212-216-1785; *http://* www.slgreen.com

General - Incorporation	MD	**Stock**- Price on:12/24/2007	$135.6
Employees	814	Stock Exchange	NYSE
Auditor	Ernst& Young LLP	Ticker Symbol	SLG
Stk Agt	NA	Outstanding Shares	59,410,000
Counsel	NA	E.P.S	$9.71
DUNS No.	NA	Shareholders	NA

Business: The groups principle activities include management, acquiring, financing, developing, constructing and leasing real estate properties. The group operates through two segments namely, office real estate and structured finance investments. In the year 2006, the group acquired 521 Fifth Avenue and 609 Fifth Avenue. The group operates from the United States.The group's quarterly revenue for sept 2007 was 259.21 millions of USD.

Primary SIC and add'l.: 6798

CIK No: 0001040971

Subsidiaries: 1250 Broadway SPE Corp., 1515 Promote LLC, 1515 SLG Optionee LLC, 1515 SLG Private REIT LLC, 300 Main Lessee LLC, 399 Knollwood Lessee LLC, 750 Third Owner LLC, Belmont Insurance Company, eEmerge, Inc, GKK Manager LLC, GKK Manager Member Corp., Greater New York Property LLC, Green 110 East 42nd LLC, Green 1221 Interest Owner LLC, Green 1250 Broadway Acquisition LLC 82 Subsidiaries included in the Index

Officers: Marc Holliday/41/CEO/$16,806,870.00, Gregory F. Hughes/CFO, COO/$6,017,287.00, Andrew Mathias/Pres., Chief Investment Officer/$9,939,232.00, Andrew S. Levine/Chief Legal Officer/$1,722,745.00

Directors: Stephen L. Green/Chmn., John H. Alschuler/60/Dir., John S. Levy/72/Dir., Edwin Thomas Burton/65/Dir.

Owners: Gregory F. Hughes, Deutsche Bank AG/4.90%, AMVESCAP PLC/4.50%, Insiders/4.30%, John H. Alschuler, Andrew S. Levine, Stephen L. Green/3.10%, John S. Levy, ING Groep N.V./5.80%, Marc Holliday, Andrew Mathias, Edwin Thomas Burton, Stichting Pensioenfonds ABP/3.40%, EARNEST Partners, LLC/4.40%, The Vanguard Group, Inc./5.20%

Financial Data: *Fiscal Year End:*12/31 *Latest Annual Data:* 12/31/2006

Year		Sales			Net Income
2006		$552,277,000			$220,719,000
2005		$440,182,000			$157,419,000
2004		$348,988,000			$209,430,000
Curr. Assets:	$411,128,000	**Curr. Liab.:**	$189,106,000		
Plant, Equip.:	$2,775,723,000	**Total Liab.:**	$2,237,344,000	**Indic. Yr. Divd.:**	$2.800
Total Assets:	$4,632,227,000	**Net Worth:**	$2,394,883,000	**Debt/ Equity:**	NA

Sl Industries Inc

520 Fellowship Rd., Ste. A114, Mt. Laurel, NJ, 08054; *PH:* 1-856-727-1500; *Fax:* 1-856-727-1683; *http://* www.slpdq.com; *Email:* slinfo@slindustries.com

General - Incorporation	NJ	**Stock**- Price on:12/24/2007	$17.5
Employees	1,900	Stock Exchange	AMEX
Auditor	Grant Thornton LLP	Ticker Symbol	SLI
Stk Agt	American Stock Transfer & Trust Co.	Outstanding Shares	NA
Counsel	David Nuzzo	E.P.S	$0.86
DUNS No.	00-234-4083	Shareholders	NA

Business: The group's principal activity is to design, manufacture and market power electronics, power motion, power protection equipment teleprotection and specialized communication equipment. The group operates through four business segments: condor dc power supplies, teal electronics, sl montevideo technology and rfl electronics. Condor produces a wide range of standard and custom power supply products. Power supplies are also used in drive systems for electric equipment and other motion control systems. Teal designs and manufactures customized power conditioning and power distribution units. Sl-mti designs and manufactures intelligent, high power density precision motors. Rfl designs and manufactures teleprotection products/systems used to protect electric utility transmission lines and apparatus by isolating faulty transmission lines from a transmission grid. The group has operations in California, Minnesota and New Jersey.

Primary SIC and add'l.: 3694 3612 3621 3825

CIK No: 0000089270

Subsidiaries: AFBS, Inc., Apolo Tool & Die Manufacturing, Inc., AUS Corporation, Bon L Aluminum LLC, Bon L Campo Limited Partnership, Bon L Canada Inc., Bon L Holdings Corporation, Bon L Manufacturing Company, Capital Square Insurance Company, El Campo GP, LLC, Guangzhou Tredegar Film Products Limited, Idlewood Properties, Inc., Molecumetics Institute, Ltd.(1), Molecumetics, Ltd., PROMEA Engineering srl 38 Subsidiaries included in the Index

Officers: James Taylor/CEO, Pres./$491,224.00, Steven R. Gilliatt/Pres. - RFL Electronics, Inc, David R. Nuzzo/CFO, VP - Finance, Administration, Treasurer, Corp. Sec., Alan Pelan/Pres. - SL Montevideo Technology, Inc

Directors: Warren G. Lichtenstein/Chmn., Glen Kassan/Vice Chmn., Dwane J. Baumgardner/Dir., James A. Risher/Dir., James R. Henderson/Dir., Avrum Gray/Dir., Mark E. Schwarz/Dir.

Owners: Avrum Gray, Insiders, The Gabelli Funds, Dwane J. Baumgardner, Mark E. Schwarz, James R. Henderson, Steel Partners II, L.P., James C. Taylor, Warren G. Lichtenstein, David R. Nuzzo

Financial Data: *Fiscal Year End:*12/31 *Latest Annual Data:* 12/31/2006

Year		Sales			Net Income
2006		$176,773,000			$3,553,000
2005		$126,873,000			$7,147,000
2004		$118,804,000			$8,672,000
Curr. Assets:	$56,797,000	**Curr. Liab.:**	$29,286,000	**P/E Ratio:**	20.35
Plant, Equip.:	$12,132,000	**Total Liab.:**	$56,124,000	**Indic. Yr. Divd.:**	NA
Total Assets:	$106,543,000	**Net Worth:**	$50,419,000	**Debt/ Equity:**	0.3099

Slade's Ferry Bancorp

PO Box 390, Somerset, MA, 02726; *PH:* 1-508-643—7537; *Fax:* 1-508-675-1751; *http://* www.sladesferry.com

General - Incorporation	MA	**Stock**- Price on:12/24/2007	$16.08
Employees	111	Stock Exchange	NDQ
Auditor	Wolf & Co., P.C	Ticker Symbol	SFBC
Stk Agt	Registrar & Transfer Co	Outstanding Shares	4,060,000
Counsel	Peter G. Collias	E.P.S	$0.91
DUNS No.	07-569-7128	Shareholders	NA

Business: The group's principal activities are to provide a broad range of banking activities, including demand, savings, time deposits, related personal and commercial checking account services, real estate mortgages, commercial and installment lending. It also provides payroll services, money orders, traveler's checks, visa, mastercard, safe deposit rentals, automatic teller machines and cash management services. The group offers a full range of commercial, installment, student and real estate loans. The group provides commercial and financial services through its eleven banking offices located in fairhaven, fall river, new bedford, seekonk, somerset and swansea, Massachusetts and a loan production office in warwick, Rhode Island. The group competes with other banks, financial institutions and credit unions, including major banks and bank holding companies which have numerous offices and affiliates.

Primary SIC and add'l.: 6022 6712

CIK No: 0000857499

Subsidiaries: Slades Ferry Realty Trust, Slades Ferry Trust Company

Officers: Mary Lynn D. Lenz/Dir., CEO, Pres./$477,121.00, Deborah A. McLaughlin/CFO, COO/$236,591.00, Peter G. Collias/Corp. Sec., Manuel J. Tavares/Sr. VP - Slade's Ferry Trust Company/$195,355.00, Cecilia Viveiros/Assist. Corp. Sec., Dennis Wyatt/Sr. VP, James Rizzo/Sr. VP, Susan Wilbur/Sr. VP, Gary Vierra/Sr. VP

Directors: Mary Lynn D. Lenz/Dir., CEO, Pres., William J. Piccerelli/Dir., Joan Parkos Moran/56/Dir., Majed Mouded/66/Dir., Lawrence J. Oliveira/63/Dir., David F. Westgate/67/Dir., Melvyn A. Holland/70/Dir., Jean F. MacCormack/61/Dir., Shaun O'Hearn/62/Dir., Carl Ribeiro/61/Dir., William J. Sullivan/68/Dir., Anthony F. Cordeiro/46/Dir., Scott W. Costa/52/Dir., Paul Downey/Dir.

Owners: Carl Ribeiro, Mary Lynn D. Lenz/1.16%, Melvyn A. Holland, Francis A. Macomber/3.10%, William J. Sullivan/1.45%, Manuel J. Tavares, Peter G. Collias, Anthony F. Cordeiro, Shaun OHearn, Paul C. Downey, William J. Piccerelli, Insiders/13.75%, Lawrence J. Oliveira/1.33%, Deborah A. McLaughlin, Joan Parkos Moran *(19 Owners included in Index)*

Financial Data: *Fiscal Year End:*12/31 *Latest Annual Data:* 12/31/2006

Year		Sales			Net Income
2006		$36,264,000			$3,619,000
2005		$31,239,000			$4,020,000
2004		$26,617,000			$3,617,000
Curr. Assets:	$24,766,000	**Curr. Liab.:**	$427,147,000	**P/E Ratio:**	17.67
Plant, Equip.:	$5,587,000	**Total Liab.:**	$556,515,000	**Indic. Yr. Divd.:**	$0.360
Total Assets:	$607,760,000	**Net Worth:**	$51,245,000	**Debt/ Equity:**	2.7578

Slm Corp

12061 Bluemont Way, Reston, VA, 20190; *PH:* 1-703-810-3000; *Fax:* 1-703-984-5042; *http://* www.salliemae.com

General - Incorporation DE
Employees 11,000
Auditor PricewaterhouseCoopers LLP
Stk Agt Bank of New York
Counsel NA
DUNS No. 16-000-2218

Stock- Price on:12/24/2007 $57.7
Stock Exchange NYSE
Ticker Symbol SLM
Outstanding Shares 411,420,000
E.P.S. $1.73
Shareholders NA

Business: The groups principle activity is to provide student loans and administrator of college savings plans. The groups products include federal and private students loans. The group operates from United States.

Primary SIC and add'l.: 6111

CIK No: 0001032033

Subsidiaries: Arrow Global Ltd.

Officers: Charles Elliott Andrews/CEO/$1,558,599.00, Karen Kotowski/Sr. VP - Application Development, Robert C. Ballard/Sr. VP - Servicing, June M. McCormack/Exec. VP - Servicing, Technology, Sales Marketing/$1,834,835.00, Paul Mayer/Sr. VP - Corporate Development, Rob Meck/Sr. VP - Debt Management, Joni Reich/Sr. VP - Administration, Jonathan E. Kroehler/Sr. VP - Product Development, Marketing, Robert Lavet/Sr. VP, General Counsel, Dennis Wentworth/Sr. VP - Higher Education Sales, Bill Rachal/Sr. VP - Corporate Finance, Renee R. Mang/Sr. VP - Servicing, J. Lance Franke/Sr. VP - Corporate Finance, Jerry Maher/Sr. VP - Financial Institution Sales Guarantor Business Development, Robert S. Autor/CIO, Exec. VP *(18 Officers included in Index)*

Directors: Thomas J. Fitzpatrick/59/Vice Chmn., Albert L. Lord/Chmn., Ann Torre Bates/Dir., Charles L. Daley/Dir., William M. Diefenderfer/62/Dir., Diane Suitt Gilleland/61/Dir., Earl A. Goode/Dir., Ronald F. Hunt/64/Dir., Benjamin J. Lambert/71/Dir., Barry A. Munitz/66/Dir., Alexander A. Porter/69/Dir., Wolfgang Schoellkopf/75/Dir., Steven L. Shapiro/Dir., Barry L. Williams/63/Dir.

Owners: Capital Group International, Inc./11.60%, The TCW Group, Inc., on behalf of the TCW Business Unit/5.20%, Barrow, Hanley, Mewhinney & Strauss, Inc./6.60%

Financial Data: *Fiscal Year End:*12/31 *Latest Annual Data:* 12/31/2006

Year	Sales	Net Income
2006	$9,139,996,000	$1,156,956,000
2005	$6,581,470,000	$1,382,284,000
2004	$5,266,885,000	$1,913,270,000

Curr. Assets:	$9,386,139,000	**Curr. Liab.:**	$3,528,263,000	**P/E Ratio:**	23.17
Plant, Equip.:	NA	**Total Liab.:**	$111,766,575,000	**Indic. Yr. Divd.:**	$0.360
Total Assets:	$116,135,732,000	**Net Worth:**	$4,360,042,000	**Debt/ Equity:**	26.0627

SLS International Inc

1650 W Jackson St., Ozark, MO, 65721; *PH:* 1-417-883-4549; *Fax:* 1-417-883-2723; *http://* www.slsloudspeakers.com

General - Incorporation DE
Employees 52
Auditor Weaver & Martin LLC
Stk Agt Standard Registrar & Transfer Co Inc.
Counsel Freeborn & Peters LLP
DUNS No. NA

Stock- Price on:12/24/2007 NA
Stock Exchange OTC
Ticker Symbol SLSZ
Outstanding Shares NA
E.P.S. -$0.231
Shareholders NA

Business: The group's principle activities include manufacturing and selling loudspeakers through dealer networks. The company's product lines consist of professional contractor speaker system, the universal soldier speaker system and the home theater speaker system. Professional speaker system consists of eighteen different models of speaker systems, each model consisting of a speaker cabinet and components of woofers and ribbon drivers. Commercial loudspeakers consist of lower cost speakers with twelve models of different size that are sold in music stores for orchestras and disc jockeys. Home theatre systems consist of four models that use the smallest unit of professional contractor loudspeaker system as their basis. The company is currently re-packaging certain models of its professional contractor sound systems for the cinema and movie theater market. On 12-Mar-2004, the company acquired evenstar inc. The group operates from United States.

Primary SIC and add'l.: 3651

CIK No: 0001121785

Subsidiaries: Evenstar Mergersub, Inc.

Officers: John Gott/Chmn., CEO, Mike Maples/CFO, COO, Tom Tyson/VP - Sales, Engineering, Ed Moist/VP - Operations, Accounting, Tom Harrison/Dir. - Engineering, Bob R. Adams/Dir. - Technical Communications, Garth Showalter/Customer Service, Micah Collins/Customer Service, Don Stroh/Dir. - Sales, Consumer Products, Jeff Lowry/Eastern Regional Sales Mgr.

Directors: John Gott/Chmn., CEO

Financial Data: *Fiscal Year End:*12/31 *Latest Annual Data:* 12/31/2005

Year	Sales	Net Income
2005	$4,015,000	-$10,004,000
2004	$2,041,000	-$8,600,000
2003	$968,000	-$3,979,000

Curr. Assets:	$5,578,000	**Curr. Liab.:**	$1,856,000		
Plant, Equip.:	$4,925,000	**Total Liab.:**	$1,863,000	**Indic. Yr. Divd.:**	NA
Total Assets:	$10,613,000	**Net Worth:**	$8,750,000	**Debt/ Equity:**	NA

SM&A

4695 MacArthur Ct., 8th Fl., Newport Beach, CA, 92660; *PH:* 1-949-975-1550; *Fax:* 1-949-975-1624; *http://* www.smawins.com; *Email:* info@smawins.com

General - Incorporation CA
Employees 330
Auditor BDO Seidman, LLP
Stk Agt U.S. Stock Transfer Corp
Counsel NA
DUNS No. 18-763-9836

Stock- Price on:12/24/2007 $7.05
Stock Exchange NDQ
Ticker Symbol WINS
Outstanding Shares 18,730,000
E.P.S. $0.32
Shareholders NA

Business: The group's principle activity is to provide business capture services and high-value program support services. The integrated proposal management services are offered through a proprietary proposal management strategy and process. The team of employees and consultants provide program management, systems engineering, and expert support to major industrial customers in the aerospace, defense and information technology sectors. The group also provides systems engineering, program planning and other high-value technical support services to such high priority national programs as the joint strike fighter program and America's missile defense efforts. The major clients of the group are lockheed martin corp, raytheon company, the boeing company, accenture ltd and general dynamics.

Primary SIC and add'l.: 8741

CIK No: 0001050031

Subsidiaries: Sm&a-international, Inc., SM&A-WEST, Steven Myers & Associates, Inc, Steven Myers Holding Inc

Officers: Cynthia A. Davis/51/Dir., CEO, Kevin L. Keiners/47/Exec. VP - Operations, Sr. VP - Program Services Operations, Cathy L. McCarthy/60/COO, Pres./$1,055,465.00, Timothy G. Bauman/Exec. VP - Sales, Marketing/$517,863.00, Steve D. Handy/40/CFO, Sr. VP, Corp. Sec./$333,928.00, Robert Gurin/VP, Gail Sandford/Assoc., John Covington/Assoc., Robert Mullen/Assoc., Thomas A. Eide/41/Sr. VP - Consulting Operations/$403,185.00

Directors: Cynthia A. Davis/51/Dir., CEO, Dwight L. Hanger/Chmn., William C. Bowes/Dir., Christopher J. Lewis/Dir., Joseph B. Reagan/Dir., Robert J. Untracht/Dir., Robert Rodin/Dir., John P. Stenbit/Dir.

Owners: Sarbit Asset Management, Inc/5.04%, Heartland Advisors, Inc/5.17%, Dwight L. Hanger, Kevin L. Reiners, Cynthia A. Davis, Timothy G. Bauman, Steve D. Handy, Steven S. Myers/17.51%, Robert J. Untracht, Christopher J. Lewis/1.90%, Robert Rodin, William C. Bowes, Thomas A. Eide, Cathy L. McCarthy/2.18%, Royce & Associates, Inc., LLC/11.80% *(19 Owners included in Index)*

Financial Data: *Fiscal Year End:*12/31 *Latest Annual Data:* 12/31/2006

Year	Sales	Net Income
2006	$71,788,000	$3,631,000
2005	$76,711,000	$7,081,000
2004	$68,954,000	$9,692,000

Curr. Assets:	$31,773,000	**Curr. Liab.:**	$3,386,000	**P/E Ratio:**	28.20
Plant, Equip.:	$3,446,000	**Total Liab.:**	$4,030,000	**Indic. Yr. Divd.:**	NA
Total Assets:	$35,626,000	**Net Worth:**	$31,596,000	**Debt/ Equity:**	NA

Small Business Company

138 Victoria St., Level 6, Christchurch; *PH:* 858-481-5600; *http://* www.tsbc.co.nz

General - Incorporation DE
Employees NA
Auditor Moore & Associates, Chartered
Stk Agt Island Stock Transfer
Counsel NA
DUNS No. NA

Stock- Price on:12/24/2007 $0.33
Stock Exchange OTC
Ticker Symbol SBCO
Outstanding Shares NA
E.P.S. NA
Shareholders NA

Business: The groups principle activities include producing limited revenues in proof of concept beta testing and business development consulting services. The group also develops, packages and will market business improvement solutions for small business owners in the form of books, cds, and business coaching. The group will market these products through the Internet. The group operates from the United States.

Primary SIC and add'l.: 8742

CIK No: 0001285936

Officers: Stuart Schreiber/62/Dir., CEO, Pres., Treasurer, CFO, David Larson/57/Chmn., VP, COO, Sec., Dave Howell/Writer, Kate Guthrie/Design, Susan Tabbit/Writer, Rachelle Benson/Writer, Dennis Jarret/Writer, Ian McBride/Content Editor, Joe Kearns/Information Technology Mgr., Bruce Young/Content Developer, Michael Henderson/Developer, Fe Armstrong/Project Mgr., Geof Franks/Project Leader, Liz Hogg/Game, Mike Bell/Lead Developer

Directors: Stuart Schreiber/62/Dir., CEO, Pres., Treasurer, CFO, David Larson/57/Chmn., VP, COO, Sec., Peter Barca/53/Dir.

Owners: Insiders/68.02%, David Larson/34.01%, Paul Ferandell/6.20%, Stuart Schreiber/34.01%

Curr. Assets:	$18,000	**Curr. Liab.:**	$32,000		
Plant, Equip.:	$4,000	**Total Liab.:**	$343,000	**Indic. Yr. Divd.:**	NA
Total Assets:	$22,000	**Net Worth:**	-$321,000	**Debt/ Equity:**	NA

Small World Kids Inc

5711 Buckingham Pkwy., Culver City, CA, 90230; *PH:* 1-310-645-9680; *Fax:* 1-310-410-9606; *http://* www.smallworldkids.net; *Email:* info@smallworldtoys.com

General - Incorporation NV
Employees 59
Auditor Stonefield Josephson, Inc
Stk Agt Colonial Stock Transfer Co Inc
Counsel NA
DUNS No. NA

Stock- Price on:12/24/2007 NA
Stock Exchange OTC
Ticker Symbol SMWK
Outstanding Shares NA
E.P.S. NA
Shareholders NA

Business: The groups principle activities include developing, manufacturing, marketing and distributing educational and development toys. The group markets and distributes toys for infant, pre-school, early learning, imaginative play and active play categories. The group's products sold under the brand name IQ Baby, IQ Preschool, Ryans Room, Gertie Ball, Small World Living, Puzzibilities, All About Baby, Neurosmith and Imagiix. The group operates from United States.

Primary SIC and add'l.: NA

CIK No: 0001157564

Subsidiaries: Fashion Angels Enterprises, Inc, Small World Kids, Inc.

Officers: Debra Fine/Chmn., CEO, Pres., Eddy Goldwasser/Founder - Advisor, John J. Nelson/COO, Robert Rankin/CFO, Sec., Charles Messman/Contact - Investor Relations, Marie Dagresto/Contact - Investor Relations

Directors: Debra Fine/Chmn., CEO, Pres., John Matise/Dir., Lane Nemeth/Dir., David Swartz/Dir., Bob Lautz/Dir., Eddy Goldwasser/Founder - Advisor, Shelley Singhal/Dir., Gary Adelson/Dir., Alex Gerstenzang/54/Dir., Eric Manlunus/39/Dir.

Owners: Debra L. Fine/39.70%, C.E. Unterberg, Towbin Capital Partners 1, L.P., Eric Manlunus, Frontera Group, LLC, Lane Nemeth, Gamma Opportunity Capital Partners LP Class C, Gamma Opportunity Capital Partners LP Class A, St. Cloud Capital Partners, LP, Gary Adelson, Trinad Capital Master Fund Ltd, Sid Marshall, Inc., Robert Rankin, Insiders, Bushido Capital Master Fund, Hong Kong Credit Union *(23 Owners included in Index)*

Curr. Assets:	$12,290,000	**Curr. Liab.:**	$8,092,000		
Plant, Equip.:	$333,000	**Total Liab.:**	$21,274,000	**Indic. Yr. Divd.:**	NA
Total Assets:	$20,172,000	**Net Worth:**	-$1,103,000	**Debt/ Equity:**	NA

Smart & Final Inc

600 Citadel Dr., City Of Commerce, CA, 90040; *PH:* 1-323-869-7500; *http://* www.smartandfinal.com

General - Incorporation............................. DE
Employees..1,957
Auditor .... Ernst & Young LLP
Stk Agt................. Mellon Investor Services LLC
Counsel..NA
DUNS No. 00-690-9048

Stock - Price on:12/24/2007 ....NA
Stock Exchange...NA
Ticker Symbol...NA
Outstanding Shares ....NA
E.P.S..NA
Shareholders..NA

Business: The group's principal activity is to offer food items, supplies and equipment to small foodservice businesses and other business customer groups. The group operates through 219 non-membership warehouse grocery stores. These stores operate under the banners "Smart & Final" and "United Grocers Cash & Carry" ("Cash & Carry"). Stores under the smart & final banner include 173 stores primarily located in California with others in Arizona and Nevada. The cash & carry stores operate 46 stores in Washington, Oregon, northern California and Idaho. During 2003, the group sold Florida stores businesses and foodservice operations in Florida and northern California.

Primary SIC and add'l.: 5142 5143 5182 5111 5141

CIK No: 0000875751

Subsidiaries: American Foodservice Distributors, Inc, AmeriFoods Trading Company, Casino Frozen Foods, Inc., Casino USA, Inc., H L Holding Corporation, Port Stockton Food Dist., Inc., Smart & Final de Mexico, Smart & Final del Noroeste, Smart & Final Oregon, Inc., Smart & Final Stores Corporation

Officers: Etienne Snollaerts/Dir., CEO, Pres., Richard N. Phegley/Sr. VP, CFO, Richard A. Link/VP, Controller, Chief Accounting Officer

Directors: Etienne Snollaerts/Dir., CEO, Pres., Ross E. Roeder/Chmn., Hakim L. Aouani/Dir., Thierry Bourgeron/Dir., Timm F. Crull/Dir., David L. Meyers/Dir., Joel-Andre Ornstein/Dir., Stephen E. Watson/Dir.

Owners: Casino Guichard-Perrachon S.A./54.90%, Stephen E. Watson, Richard N. Phegley, David L. Meyers, Jol-Andr Ornstein, Insiders/7.30%, Zeke Duge, Dimensional Fund Advisors LP/5.20%, Ross E. Roeder/1.00%, Norah Morley, Donald G. Alvarado, Timm F. Crull, Etienne Snollaerts/1.60%, Reed Conner& Birdwell LLC/7.00%

Financial Data: Fiscal Year End:01/01   Latest Annual Data: 06/30/2007

Year	Sales	Net Income
2007	$229,769,000	-$6,589,000
2006	$249,541,000	-$4,878,000
2005	$135,166,000	-$1,460,000

Curr. Assets:	$29,183,000	**Curr. Liab.:**	$29,015,000		
Plant, Equip.:	$10,017,000	**Total Liab.:**	$39,811,000	**Indic. Yr. Divd.:**	NA
Total Assets:	$43,925,000	**Net Worth:**	$4,114,000	**Debt/ Equity:**	NA

Smart Energy Solutions Inc

511 E Main St., Sanford, NC, 27332; *PH:* 1-919-777-5999; *http://* www.smgy.net

General - Incorporation............................NV
Employees...7
Auditor ....Chisholm, Bierwolf & Nilson, LLC
Stk Agt.............Manhattan Transfer Registrar Co
Counsel..NA
DUNS No. ....NA

Stock - Price on:12/24/2007 ....$0.54
Stock Exchange...OTC
Ticker Symbol...SMGY
Outstanding Shares 76,890,000
E.P.S..-$0.09
Shareholders..NA

Business: The groups principle activities include manufacturing and selling involved in the battery brain products. The group operates from the United States.

Primary SIC and add'l.: 8742

CIK No: 0001086082

Subsidiaries: Smart Energy Solutions

Officers: Pete Mateja/CEO, Aharon Levinas/Dir., CTO, Ed Braniff/CFO, Andrew Knowles/VP - Sales, Marketing

Directors: Joseph Bahat/76/Chmn., Amir Uziel/Dir., Aharon Levinas/Dir., CTO, Jacob Enoch/Dir., Tamir Levinas/Dir., Michael Ben-Ari/48/Dir., Guy Moshe/56/Dir.

Owners: Joseph Bahat, Peter Mateja/2.20%, Aharon Y. Levinas/15.70%, Michael Ben-Ari/7.70%, Jacob Enoch, Edward Braniff/1.10%, Tamir Levinas/3.00%, Insiders/30.00%, Moshe Guy, EGFE, Ltd./6.60%

Financial Data: Fiscal Year End:12/31   Latest Annual Data: 12/31/2006

Year	Sales	Net Income
2006	$1,819,000	-$5,328,000
2005	$151,000	-$2,207,000
2004	NA	$108,000

Curr. Assets:	$2,644,000	**Curr. Liab.:**	$1,317,000	**P/E Ratio:**	30.12
Plant, Equip.:	$55,000	**Total Liab.:**	$1,317,000	**Indic. Yr. Divd.:**	NA
Total Assets:	$2,766,000	**Net Worth:**	$1,448,000	**Debt/ Equity:**	NA

Smart Modular Technologies (WWH) Inc

4211 Starboard Dr., Fremont, CA, 94538; *PH:* 1-510-623-1231; *Fax:* 1-510-623-1434; *http://* www.smartm.com; *Email:* info@smartm.com

General - Incorporation.........Cayman Islands
Employees..1,317
Auditor ....KPMG LLP
Stk Agt..........................Computershare Trust Co
Counsel..NA
DUNS No. ....NA

Stock - Price on:12/24/2007 ....$14.51
Stock Exchange...NDQ
Ticker Symbol......................................SMOD
Outstanding Shares 59,760,000
E.P.S..$0.83
Shareholders..NA

Business: The groups principal activities include designing, manufacturing, and distributing electronic subsystem. The products of the group include Flash Memory Cards and Modules, eFlashTools and FlashTools, and DRAM Modules. Specific customers of the group include Cisco Systems and Hewlett-Packard. The group operates from the United States of America, North and Latin America, Europe and Asia. Of the net sale in the year 2006, United States of America accounted for $444,277, North and Latin America $87,512, Europe $58,730 and ASIA $116,887 (thousands).

Primary SIC and add'l.: 3572 3679 7372 8711 3672 3577 3674

CIK No: 0001326973

Subsidiaries: ConXtra, Inc., Estecom Co. Ltd., Modular Brasil Participaes Ltda., SMART Modular Technologies (CI), Inc., SMART Modular Technologies (DE), Inc., SMART Modular Technologies (Deutschland) GmbH, SMART Modular Technologies (DH), Inc., SMART Modular Technologies (Europe) Limited, SMART Modular Technologies (Foreign Holdings), Inc., SMART Modular Technologies (Global), Inc., SMART Modular Technologies (Puerto Rico) Inc., SMART Modular Technologies Indstria de Componentes Eletrnicos Ltda., SMART Modular Technologies Sdn. Bhd., SMART Modular Technologies, Inc.

Officers: Iain MacKenzie/Dir., CEO, Pres., Jim Goudreau/Regional Sales Mgr., Todd Levy/Global Accounting Dir., Oliver Rodrigues/Sales Mgr., Chad Wood/Regional Sales Mgr., Kevin Toohey/Regional Sales Mgr., Bryan Heinze/Regional Sales Mgr., Bob Walts/Regional Sales Mgr., Nick Longhurst/Dir. - Sales, Jack A. Pacheco/Sr. VP, CFO, Alan Marten/VP, GM - Memory Business Unit, Wayne Eisenberg/VP - Worldwide Sales, Alex Melo/Smart Brazil, Channel Sales, Richard Seow/Dir. - Sales, Janet Leong/Business Development Mgr. *(22 Officers included in Index)*

Directors: Iain MacKenzie/Dir., CEO, Pres., Ajay Shah/Chmn., Dipanjan Deb/Dir., Eugene Frantz/Dir., C. S. Park/Dir., Mukesh Patel/Dir., Clifton Thomas Weatherford/Dir., Harry W. McKinney/Dir., Scott D. Mercer/Dir.

Owners: TPG Advisors IV, Inc/6.50%, Francisco Partners, G.P., LLC/16.20%, Jack A. Pacheco, Iain MacKenzie/1.50%, AIM Trimark Investments/6.50%, TPG Advisors III, Inc/4.30%, WestRiver Capital, L.L.C., T(3) Advisors II, Inc./5.40%, Century Capital Management, Inc./6.70%, Ajay Shah/7.10%, Mukesh Patel, Wayne Eisenberg, Patel Family Partners, L.P., Clifton Thomas Weatherford, Shah Capital Partners, L.P./7.10% *(21 Owners included in Index)*

Financial Data: Fiscal Year End:08/25   Latest Annual Data: 8/31/2006

Year	Sales	Net Income
2006	$707,406,000	$32,306,000
2005	$607,299,000	$26,196,000
1998	$714,651,000	$51,483,000

Curr. Assets:	$377,705,000	**Curr. Liab.:**	$196,674,000	**P/E Ratio:**	18.14
Plant, Equip.:	$25,971,000	**Total Liab.:**	$279,561,000	**Indic. Yr. Divd.:**	NA
Total Assets:	$426,456,000	**Net Worth:**	$146,895,000	**Debt/ Equity:**	0.4523

Smart Online Inc

2530 Meridian Pkwy Fl 2, Durham, NC, 27713; *PH:* 1-919-765-5000; *Fax:* 1-919-765-5020; *http://* www.smartonline.com; *Email:* corporate@smartonline.com

General - Incorporation ....
Employees..56
Auditor ....Sherb & Co., LLP
Stk Agt.............Continental Stock Transfer & Trust Co
Counsel..NA
DUNS No. ....NA

Stock - Price on:12/24/2007 ....$2.28
Stock Exchange...OTC
Ticker Symbol......................................SOLN
Outstanding Shares 17,870,000
E.P.S..-$0.31
Shareholders..NA

Business: The groups principle activities include developing and marketing Internet delivered software service software applications and data resources for small businesses with one to one hundred employees. The groups solutions are designed to automate and streamline business processes, reduce operating costs and improve internal controls. In October 2005, the group acquired Computility, Inc. The group operates from the United States.

Primary SIC and add'l.: 7372

CIK No: 0001113513

Subsidiaries: Smart Commerce, Inc.

Officers: Dennis Michael Nouri/55/Co - Founder, Dir., CEO, Pres./$216,461.00, Nicholas Sinigaglia/CFO/$125,530.00, Henry Nouri/52/Exec. VP/$196,461.00, Anil Kamath/CTO, Thomas Furr/Chief Strategy Officer/$160,030.00, Gary Mahieu/40/COO, VP - Smart Commerce, Inc/$150,000.00, Jay Trepanier/COO, Mike Stuart/39/VP - Sales, Brian Donaghy/40/VP - Product Strategy

Directors: Dennis Michael Nouri/55/Co - Founder, Dir., CEO, Pres., Jeffrey W. Lerose/63/Chmn., Shlomo Elia/65/Dir., Philippe Pouponnot/38/Dir., James C. Meese/66/Dir., David E. Colburn/61/Dir.

Owners: Nicholas A. Sinigaglia, Shlomo Elia, Thomas Furr/2.40%, Magnetar Capital Master Fund, Ltd./13.20%, Atlas Capital SA/13.10%, Insiders/19.40%, Gary Mahieu, Doron Roethler/11.20%, James Meese, Scott Whitaker, Philippe Pouponnot, Henry Nouri/8.40%, Michael Nouri/5.90%, Jeffrey W. LeRose, Herald Investment Trust, PLC/6.60%

Financial Data: Fiscal Year End:12/31   Latest Annual Data: 12/31/2006

Year	Sales	Net Income
2006	$3,645,000	-$5,024,000
2005	$2,702,000	-$15,591,000
2004	$1,003,000	-$2,672,000

Curr. Assets:	$925,000	**Curr. Liab.:**	$4,771,000		
Plant, Equip.:	$180,000	**Total Liab.:**	$5,607,000	**Indic. Yr. Divd.:**	NA
Total Assets:	$7,433,000	**Net Worth:**	$1,826,000	**Debt/ Equity:**	NA

Smart-tek Solutions Inc

433 Town Ctr., Ste. 316, Corte Madera, CA, 94925; *PH:* 1-604-628-8161; *Fax:* 1-902-482-5083; *http://* www.smart-teksolutions.com; *Email:* info@smart-teksolutions.com

General - Incorporation ....NV
Employees..26
Auditor .... Weinberg & Company, P.A.
Stk Agt................. Corporate Stock Transfer, Inc.
Counsel..NA
DUNS No. ....NA

Stock - Price on:12/24/2007 ....$0.15
Stock Exchange...OTC
Ticker Symbol...STTK
Outstanding Shares 73,250,000
E.P.S..-$0.04
Shareholders..NA

Business: The groups principle activities include designing, selling, installing and servicing the latest in security technology with proven electronic hardware and software products. In April 2005, the group acquired Smart tek Communications Inc. The group operates from the United States.

Primary SIC and add'l.: 7381

CIK No: 0000947011

Subsidiaries: Smart-tek Communications, Inc

Officers: Perry Law/46/Dir., CEO, CFO, Pres., Stephen Platt/VP - Smart - tek Communications

Directors: Perry Law/46/Dir., CEO, CFO, Pres.

Owners: Insiders/100.00%, Dublin Asset Protection A.G./6.83%, Perry Law/100.00%, Farthingham Capital Corporation/5.46%, Essex Property Management/12.29%

Financial Data: Fiscal Year End:06/30   Latest Annual Data: 06/30/2006

Year	Sales	Net Income
2006	$2,219,000	-$640,000
2005	$321,000	-$286,000
2004	NA	-$162,000

Curr. Assets:	$824,000	**Curr. Liab.:**	$2,251,000		
Plant, Equip.:	$16,000	**Total Liab.:**	$2,251,000	**Indic. Yr. Divd.:**	NA
Total Assets:	$1,291,000	**Net Worth:**	-$960,000	**Debt/ Equity:**	NA

SmarTire Systems Inc

13151 Vanier Pl., Ste. 150, Richmond, BC, V6V 2J1; **PH:** 1-604-276-9884;
http:// www.smartire.com; **Email:** info@smartire.com

General - Incorporation	Canada	**Stock**- Price on:12/24/2007	$0.0099
Employees	NA	Stock Exchange	OTC
Auditor	Bdo Dunwoody ,LLP	Ticker Symbol	SMTR
Stk Agt	Pacific Corporate Trust Co	Outstanding Shares	NA
Counsel	Clark, Wilson	E.P.S.	NA
DUNS No.	24-855-5856	Shareholders	NA

Business: The group's principal activities are to develop and distribute tire monitoring systems designed for improved vehicles safety, performance, reliability and fuel efficiency. The group operates in United States and Europe.

Primary SIC and add'l.: 3011 5014

CIK No: 0001057293

Subsidiaries: SmarTire Europe Limited, SmarTire Technologies Inc., SmarTire USA Inc.

Officers: Dave Warkentin/CEO, Pres., Greg Tooke/VP - Product, Supply Chain, Jeff Finkelstein/CFO, Shawn Lammers/VP - Engineering, Peter Moore/Contact - Walek, Associates

Directors: Martin Gannon/Dir., William Cronin/Dir., David Warkentin/Dir., George O'Leary/Dir.

Owners: Shawn Lammers, Martin Gannon, TAIB Bank B.S.C./4.99%, William Cronin, George O'Leary, Insiders/3.92%, Jeff Finkelstein, Staraim Enterprises Limited/4.90%, Xentennial Holdings Limited/4.90%, YA Global Investments LP/4.90%, Certain Wealth, Ltd./4.99%, Greg Tooke, Starome Investments Limited/4.90%, David Warkentin

Financial Data: Fiscal Year End:07/31 **Latest Annual Data:** 7/31/2006

Year	Sales	Net Income
2006	$3,456,000	-$28,829,000
2005	$1,463,000	-$16,120,000
2004	$1,658,000	-$10,987,000

Curr. Assets:	$5,007,000	**Curr. Liab.:**	$3,872,000		
Plant, Equip.:	$780,000	**Total Liab.:**	$35,098,000	**Indic. Yr. Divd.:**	NA
Total Assets:	$7,554,000	**Net Worth:**	-$28,026,000	**Debt/ Equity:**	NA

SmartPros Ltd

12 Skyline Dr., Hawthorne, NY, 10532; **PH:** 1-914-345-2620; **Fax:** 1-914-345-2660;
http:// corporate.smartpros.com; **Email:** info@smartpros.com

General - Incorporation	DE	**Stock**- Price on:12/24/2007	$6.65
Employees	70	Stock Exchange	AMEX
Auditor	Holtz Rubenstein Reminick LLP	Ticker Symbol	PED
Stk Agt	American Stock Transfer & Trust Co.	Outstanding Shares	4,880,000
Counsel	NA	E.P.S.	$0.39
DUNS No.	NA	Shareholders	NA

Business: The groups principal activity is to provide learning solutions for accounting/finance, legal and engineering professionals. In the year 2006, the group acquired Sage International Group Inc. The group operates from the United States.

Primary SIC and add'l.: 8331 7375

CIK No: 0001289863

Subsidiaries: Skye Multimedia Ltd, Working Values, Ltd.

Officers: Allen S. Greene/Chmn., CEO, Jack Fingerhut/Dir., Pres., Stanley Wirtheim/CFO, Joseph Fish/CTO, Joseph W. Higgins/Sr. VP - Sales, Shane Gillispie/VP - Marketing, eCommerce, Mark R. Luciano/VP - Engineering, Channel Partners, David Gebler/Pres. - Working Values, Sr. VP - Smartpros, Seth Oberman/Pres. - Skye Multimedia Ltd, Steve Henn/Pres. - Legal, Karen S. Stolzar/59/Sec.

Directors: Allen S. Greene/Chmn., CEO, John J. Gorman/Dir., Jack Fingerhut/Dir., Pres., Martin H. Lager/Dir., Joshua A. Weinreich/Dir., Leonard J. Stanley/54/Dir.

Owners: Allen S. Greene/6.20%, Gail Grollman/5.10%, Bruce Judson, Martin H. Lager, Joshua A. Weinreich/4.60%, Jack Fingerhut/3.30%, Insiders/16.00%, John J. Gorman, Stephen J. Clearman/9.70%, David M. Gebler, Peter St. Geams/12.40%

Financial Data: Fiscal Year End:12/31 **Latest Annual Data:** 12/31/2006

Year	Sales	Net Income
2006	$12,462,000	$1,511,000
2005	$10,430,000	$669,000
2004	$10,151,000	$711,000

Curr. Assets:	$9,632,000	**Curr. Liab.:**	$4,966,000	**P/E Ratio:**	17.05
Plant, Equip.:	$438,000	**Total Liab.:**	$5,086,000	**Indic. Yr. Divd.:**	NA
Total Assets:	$13,385,000	**Net Worth:**	$8,299,000	**Debt/ Equity:**	NA

Smarts Oil & Gas Inc

4128 Merriman Loop, Howell, MI, 48443; **PH:** 1-248-321-0121; *http://* www.smartsoilandgas.com

General - Incorporation	NV	**Stock**- Price on:12/24/2007	$0.17
Employees	2	Stock Exchange	OTC
Auditor	Robert L. White & Assoc., Inc.	Ticker Symbol	DYNI
Stk Agt	Florida Atlantic Stock Transfer, Inc.	Outstanding Shares	24,910,000
Counsel	NA	E.P.S.	-$0.001
DUNS No.	NA	Shareholders	NA

Business: The groups principal activity is to pursue an interest in the burgeoning oil and gas market. The group's initial entry into the market was the acquisition of several leases located in northern Louisiana. The group has also acquired leases in Texas and continues to pursue any opportunity to acquire other attractive oil and gas areas that can add value to the group. The group operates from the United States.

Primary SIC and add'l.: 8742

CIK No: 0001349922

Officers: Brian Ramsey/32/CEO, Scott Masse/CEO, Don Quarterman/CFO, Jim Gorney/Contact - Investor Relations

Directors: Daniel Seifer/32/Chmn., Eddie McGarraugh/62/Dir.

Owners: Don Quarterman/1.60%, Insiders/51.80%, Daniel Seifer/49.79%

Financial Data: Fiscal Year End:12/31 **Latest Annual Data:** 12/31/2006

Year	Sales	Net Income
2006	NA	-$37,000

Curr. Assets:	$64,000	**Curr. Liab.:**	NA		
Plant, Equip.:	$546,000	**Total Liab.:**	NA	**Indic. Yr. Divd.:**	NA
Total Assets:	$609,000	**Net Worth:**	$609,000	**Debt/ Equity:**	NA

SmartVideo Technologies Inc

1650 Oakbrook Dr., Ste. 405, Norcross, GA, 30093; **PH:** 1-770-729-8777;
http:// www.smartvideo.com

General - Incorporation		**Stock**- Price on:12/24/2007	NA
Employees	NA	Stock Exchange	OTC
Auditor	NA	Ticker Symbol	UVUM
Stk Agt	Continental Stock Transfer & Trust Co	Outstanding Shares	NA
Counsel	NA	E.P.S.	NA
DUNS No.	NA	Shareholders	NA

Business: The groups principal activities include providing interactive media solutions for consumers on the go. The group established market in the delivery of high quality mobile video, uVuMobile(TM) offers advertising based solutions across all new media platforms, including mobile and the Internet, that enable broadcasters and media companies to connect to consumers. The group markets its product include uVuMobile(TM). The group operates from the United States.

Primary SIC and add'l.: 4899

CIK No: 0001324332

Officers: William J. Loughman/52/CEO, Pres., CFO, Tracy Caswell/General Counsel, Tony Novia/Sr. VP - Programming, Distribution, Scott Hughes/CTO

Directors: Glenn H. Singer/48/Chmn., Michael E. Criden/48/Dir., Herman Rush/Member - Advisory Board, Joseph Indelli/Member - Advisory Board, Peter Sealey/Member - Advisory Board, James Rosenfield/Member - Advisory Board, Frederick Pierce/Member - Advisory Board, James D. Tate/Member - Advisory Board, Robert Rubin/Member - Advisory Board, Robert L. Friedman/Member - Advisory Board

Curr. Assets:	$4,487,000	**Curr. Liab.:**	$9,641,000		
Plant, Equip.:	$1,541,000	**Total Liab.:**	$10,782,000	**Indic. Yr. Divd.:**	NA
Total Assets:	$6,692,000	**Net Worth:**	-$4,091,000	**Debt/ Equity:**	NA

Smedvig ASA

Finnestadveien 28, Stavanger; **PH:** 47-51509900; *http://* www.smedvig.no;
Email: business.development@smedvig.no

General - Incorporation	Norway	**Stock**- Price on:12/24/2007	NA
Employees	NA	Stock Exchange	NA
Auditor	KPMG As	Ticker Symbol	NA
Stk Agt	CT Corporation	Outstanding Shares	NA
Counsel	NA	E.P.S.	NA
DUNS No.	51-766-3506	Shareholders	NA

Business: The group's principle activity of the group is offshore drilling contracting. The compnay operates through the following divisions: mobile units; mobile deep water drilling rigs; tender rigs; operator of self erecting tender rigs; well services; contracts for drilling maintenance, modification and well abandonment of fixed installations.

Primary SIC and add'l.: 1381 8711 1389

CIK No: 0001021232

Subsidiaries: AS Smedvig Prodrill, Smedvig Asia Ltd, Smedvig Offshore AS, Smedvig Rig AS

Smith & Nephew Plc

1450 Brooks Rd., Memphis, TN, 38116; **PH:** 1-901-396-2121; **Fax:** 1-901-396-9929;
http:// www.smith-nephew.com

General - Incorporation	UK	**Stock**- Price on:12/24/2007	$61.83
Employees	8,830	Stock Exchange	NYSE
Auditor	Ernst & Young LLP	Ticker Symbol	SNN
Stk Agt	Bank of New York	Outstanding Shares	188,600,000
Counsel	Ashurst Morris Crisp	E.P.S.	$2.29
DUNS No.	21-027-2498	Shareholders	NA

Business: The group's principle activities are the development and marketing of medical devices in the sectors of orthopaedics, endoscopy and advanced wound management. Orthopaedic products comprise reconstructive joint implants, trauma products and associated clinical therapies. The endoscopy sector develops and commercialises a range of endoscopic techniques, educational programmes and value-added services for surgeons to treat and repair soft tissues, articulating joints, spinal discs and vascular structures. The advanced wound management sector supplies a range of products and clinical support services for the treatment of chronic and acute skin wounds. Each of the three global business units manages its sales in ten international markets namely, the us, Canada, the UK, Germany, Japan, Australia, France, Italy, New Zealand and Ireland.

Primary SIC and add'l.: 3845 3842 3841

CIK No: 0000845982

Subsidiaries: Smith& Nephew (Europe) BV, Smith& Nephew (Malaysia) Sdn Bhd, Smith& Nephew (Overseas) Limited, Smith& Nephew (Pty) Limited, Smith& Nephew A/S, Smith& Nephew AB, Smith& Nephew AG, Smith& Nephew BV, Smith& Nephew Deutschland (Holdings) GmbH, Smith& Nephew Endoscopy KK, Smith& Nephew Farnham Limited, Smith& Nephew France SAS, smith& Nephew FZE Limited, Smith& Nephew GmbH, Smith& Nephew Healthcare Sdn Bhd 39 Subsidiaries included in the Index

Officers: David J. Illingworth/54/Dir., CEO, Joseph M. Devivo/41/Pres. - Orthopaedic Reconstruction, Michael Frazzette/46/Endoscopy Pres., Jim Ralston/61/Chief Legal Officer, Peter Hooley/60/Dir. - Finance, Paul M. Williams/Group Dir. - Human Resources, Peter W. Huntley/47/Group Dir. - Indirect Markets, Paul R. Chambers/63/Company Sec., Peter Arnold/46/Group Dir. - Technology, Christopher O'Donnell/Chief Executive, Adrian Hennah/50/Dir., CFO, Mark Augusti/42/Pres. - Orthopaedic Trauma, Clinical Therapies, Sarah Byrne-Quinn/44/Group Dir. - Strategy, Business Development, Scott Flora/Pres. - Orthopaedic Reconstruction, Joe Woody/42/Pres. - Advanced Wound Management, Incoming *(18 Officers included in Index)*

Directors: David J. Illingworth/54/Dir., CEO, John Buchanan/64/Chmn., Adrian Hennah/50/Dir., CFO, Pam Kirby/54/Non Exec. Dir., Rolf Stomberg/67/Non Exec. Dir., Richard De Schutter/67/Non Exec. Dir., Brian Larcombe/54/Non Exec. Dir., Warren Knowlton/61/Non Exec. Dir.

Owners: Brian Larcombe, David Illingworth, Pamela J. Kirby, Dudley G. Eustace, Rolf W. H. Stomberg, Christopher ODonnell, Christopher ODonnell, John Buchanan, Warren D. Knowlton, Peter Hooley, Richard De Schutter

Financial Data: Fiscal Year End:12/31 **Latest Annual Data:** 12/31/2006

Year	Sales	Net Income
2006	$2,779,000,000	$709,000,000
2005	$2,421,166,000	$321,790,000
2004	$2,405,360,000	$274,348,000

Curr. Assets:	$1,645,000,000	**Curr. Liab.:**	$816,000,000	**P/E Ratio:**	52.44
Plant, Equip.:	$637,000,000	**Total Liab.:**	$1,057,000,000	**Indic. Yr. Divd.:**	$0.670
Total Assets:	$3,284,000,000	**Net Worth:**	$2,227,000,000	**Debt/ Equity:**	NA

Smith & Wesson Holding Corp

2100 Roosevelt Ave., Springfield, MA, 01104; ***PH:*** 1-413-781-8300; ***Fax:*** 1-413-747-3317; ***http://*** www.smith-wesson.com; ***Email:*** qa@smith-wesson.com

General - Incorporation............................NV
Employees...832
Auditor.............................BDO Seidman LLP
Stk Agt...........Interwest Transfer Company, Inc.
Counsel...NA
DUNS No...NA

Stock- Price on:12/24/2007 ....$16.38
Stock Exchange...NDQ
Ticker Symbol...SWHC
Outstanding Shares 39,700,000
E.P.S...$0.34
Shareholders...NA

Business: The group's principal activities are to manufacture and distribute handguns, which includes revolvers and pistols. The group currently offers 72 different standard models of handguns in a wide variety of caliber, finish, size, composition, ammunition capacity, barrel lengths and other features. The group provides services like forging, heat treating, finishing, and plating. The group sells its products in Europe, Asia and Latin America. The group's major trademarks are airlite, heritage series, the sigma series, chiefs special, shorty, lady smith, bodyguard, mountain gun, mountain lite, magnum, lex mdc, s&w performance center. In fiscal 2004, the group discontinued crossings catalog business and smith & wesson advanced technology or swat division.

Primary SIC and add'l.: 3462 3429 3484

CIK No: 0001092796

Subsidiaries: Smith & Wesson Corp., Smith & Wesson Distributing, Inc., Smith & Wesson Firearms Training Centre GmbH, Smith & Wesson, Inc.

Officers: Michael F. Golden/Dir., CEO, Pres./$1,369,331.00, Kenneth W. Chandler/VP - Operations/$553,532.00, Thomas L. Taylor/VP - Marketing/$491,235.00, Ann B. Makkiya/Corporate Counsel, Sec., John A. Kelly/CFO/$534,497.00, Leland A. Nichols/COO/$761,511.00, Elizabeth Sharp/Investor Relations Officer

Directors: Michael F. Golden/Dir., CEO, Pres., Barry M. Monheit/61/Chmn., Robert L. Scott/62/Vice Chmn., Colton R. Melby/Dir., John B. Furman/Dir., Mitchell A. Saltz/Dir., Jeffrey D. Buchanan/Dir., Marie I. Wadecki/Dir., David M. Stone/Dir.

Owners: Leland A. Nichols, Mitchell A. Saltz/7.37%, Kenneth W. Chandler, Thomas L. Taylor, Ann B. Makkiya, Marie I. Wadecki, Barry M. Monheit/1.55%, Insiders/22.68%, John A. Kelly/1.18%, Robert L. Scott, Michael F. Golden, Colton R. Melby/10.65%, David M. Stone, John B. Furman, Jeffrey D. Buchanan

Financial Data: ***Fiscal Year End:***04/30 ***Latest Annual Data:*** 04/30/2007

Year	Sales	Net Income
2007	$236,552,000	$12,962,000
2006	$160,049,000	$8,702,000
2005	$125,788,000	$5,249,000

Curr. Assets:	$53,163,000	**Curr. Liab.:**	$31,695,000	**P/E Ratio:**	52.84
Plant, Equip.:	$28,182,000	**Total Liab.:**	$53,365,000	**Indic. Yr. Divd.:**	NA
Total Assets:	$94,698,000	**Net Worth:**	$41,333,000	**Debt/ Equity:**	2.3466

Smith & Wollensky Restaurant Group Inc

114 1st Ave., New York, NY, 10021; ***PH:*** 1-212-838-2061; ***http://*** www.smithandwollensky.com

General - Incorporation............................DE
Employees...1,676
Auditor.............................BDO Seidman LLP
Stk Agt......American Stock Transfer & Trust Co.
Counsel...........Paul, Hastings, Janofsky & Walker LLP
DUNS No...NA

Stock- Price on:12/24/2007 ....$10.89
Stock Exchange...NA
Ticker Symbol...NA
Outstanding Shares 8,600,000
E.P.S..-$0.55
Shareholders...NA

Business: The group's principal activity is to develop, own, operate and manage a high-end, high-volume diversified portfolio of restaurants in the United States. The group offers a high quality food, menus, which include seafood, lobsters, fish, veal, lamb, poultry and freshly baked bread. The group also offers desserts such as pecan pie, cheesecake, specialized confections and an extensive wine selection and customer service accompanied by attractive design and decor. The group provides its customers to view the chefs in action from the kitchen table in a glass-enclosed area inside of the main kitchen and offers outdoor dining except the restaurant located in philadelphia. The trademarks of the group are maloney and porcelli and wine week. At 29-Dec-2003, the group operated 16 restaurants, eleven of which were owned and five of which were managed.

Primary SIC and add'l.: 8741 5812

CIK No: 0001137047

Subsidiaries: Atlantic& Pacific Grill Associates, LLC, Dallas S&W, L.P., Houston S&W, L.P., La Cite Associates, LLC, Moe D.c., LLC, MOC of Miami, LLC, Mrs.Parks Sub, LLC, New York RGI Sub, LLC, Parade 59 Restaurant, LLC, Restaurant Group Management Services, LLC, S&W Chicago, LLC, S&w D.c., LLC, S&W New Orleans, LLC, S&W of Boston, LLC, S&W of Dallas LLC 22 Subsidiaries included in the Index

Officers: Alan N. Stillman/Founder, Chmn., CEO, Allison Good/VP - Marketing, Communications, Mark Hamwi/Corporate Controller, Christy Canterbury/Dir. - National Wine, Eli Levy/Regional Dir. - Operations, Opening Coordinator, Mark Levine/VP, Internal Auditor, Kevin Dillon/Regional Dir. - NYC, Kevin Zraly/VP - Wine, Eugene I. Zuriff/Pres., Samuel Goldfinger/CFO

Directors: Alan N. Stillman/Founder, Chmn., CEO, Richard Mandell/Dir., Jacob Berman/Dir., Robert D. Villency/Dir., Joseph E. Porcelli/55/Dir.

Owners: Walter F. Harrison, Alan N. Stillman/16.50%, Eugene I. Zuriff, SJ Strategic Investments LLC, LaGrange Capital Partners Offshore Fund, Ltd., Robert D. Villency, Richard A. Mandell, LaGrange Capital Administration, L.L.C., LaGrange Capital Partners, L.P., Kevin Dillon, Robert D. Villency, Jacob Berman, Lewis M. Eisenberg, Granum Capital Management, L.L.C., Frank LaGrange Johnson *(26 Owners included in Index)*

Financial Data: ***Fiscal Year End:***01/02 ***Latest Annual Data:*** 1/1/2007

Year	Sales	Net Income
2007	$124,820,000	-$4,233,000
2006	$126,441,000	-$3,076,000
2005	$124,324,000	-$2,040,000

Curr. Assets:	$10,624,000	**Curr. Liab.:**	$19,067,000		
Plant, Equip.:	$76,584,000	**Total Liab.:**	$48,949,000	**Indic. Yr. Divd.:**	NA
Total Assets:	$99,128,000	**Net Worth:**	$50,751,000	**Debt/ Equity:**	0.2447

Smith A O Corp

11270 W Pk. Pl., Milwaukee, WI, 53224; ***PH:*** 1-414-359-4000; ***Fax:*** 1-414-359-4064; ***http://*** www.aosmith.com

General - Incorporation............................DE
Employees...NA
Auditor.........................Ernst & Young LLP
Stk Agt...........Wells Fargo Shareowner Services
Counsel...NA
DUNS No...NA

Stock- Price on:12/24/2007 ....$41
Stock Exchange..OTC
Ticker Symbol...SAOSA
Outstanding Shares ....NA
E.P.S...NA
Shareholders...NA

Business: The groups principle activities include manufacturing water heating equipment and electric motors, serving a diverse mix of residential, commercial and industrial end markets. The group operates through two operating segments namely water products and electrical products. The group operates from the United States, Mexico, China and Canada. The group's quarterly revenue for Sep '07 was 553.50 millions of USD.

Primary SIC and add'l.: 3621

CIK No: 0000091142

Subsidiaries: A. O. Smith (China) Investment Co., Ltd., A. O. Smith (China) Water Heater Co., Ltd., A. O. Smith Electric Motors (Ireland) Ltd., A. O. Smith Electrical Products (Changzhou) Co., Ltd., A. O. Smith Electrical Products (S.E.A.) Pte Ltd., A. O. Smith Electrical Products (Shenzhen) Co., Ltd., A. O. Smith Electrical Products (Suzhou) Co., Ltd., A. O. Smith Electrical Products (Taizhou) Co., Ltd., A. O. Smith Electrical Products (Yueyang) Co., Ltd., A. O. Smith Electrical Products Limited, A. O. Smith Electrical Products Limited Liability Company, A. O. Smith Enterprises Ltd., A. O. Smith Holdings (Barbados) SRL, A. O. Smith Holdings (Ireland) Ltd., A. O. Smith International Corporation 38 Subsidiaries included in the Index

Officers: Paul W. Jones/Chmn., CEO, Christopher L. Mapes/Exec. VP, Pres. - EPC, Ajita Rajendra/Exec. VP, Pres. - WPC, Terry M. Murphy/CFO, Exec. VP, Ronald E. Massa/Exec. VP - Corporate Technology and Global Supply Chain, Mark A. Petrarca/Sr. VP - Human Resources, Public Affairs, Michael J. Cole/Pres. - A O Smith China Investment Co LTD, Randall S. Bednar/CIO, Sr. VP, John J. Kita/Sr. VP - Corporate Finance, Controller, Steve W. Rettler/Sr. VP - Corporate Development, James F. Stern/Exec. VP, General Counsel, Sec., Charles J. Bishop/66/Sr. VP - Corporate Technology

Directors: Paul W. Jones/Chmn., CEO, Ronald D. Brown/Dir., William F. Buehler/Dir., William P. Greubel/Dir., Robert J. O'Toole/Dir., Bruce M. Smith/Dir., Mark D. Smith/Dir., Idelle K. Wolf/Dir., Gene C. Wulf/Dir., Gloster B. Current/Dir.

Owners: Christopher L. Mapes, William F. Buehler, Idelle K. Wolf, Robert J. OToole/3.56%, Ronald D. Brown, Bruce M. Smith, Ronald E. Massa, Insiders/8.38%, Paul W. Jones, Gene C. Wulf, Mark D. Smith, Ajita G. Rajendra

Smith Barney Potomac Futures Fund LP

731 Lexington Ave 25th Fl, New York, NY, 10022; ***PH:*** 1-212-559-2011

General - Incorporation............................NY
Employees...NA
Auditor.......................................KPMG LLP
Stk Agt...NA
Counsel...NA
DUNS No...NA

Stock- Price on:12/24/2007 ....NA
Stock Exchange...NA
Ticker Symbol...NA
Outstanding Shares ....NA
E.P.S...NA
Shareholders...NA

Business: The groups principle activity is to provide brokerage and clearing services. The group also trades in commodity interests, including futures contracts, options and forward contracts. The group operates from United States.

Primary SIC and add'l.: 6221

CIK No: 0001043565

Officers: Daniel R. McAuliffe/Dir., CFO, Ihor Rakowsky/Dir., Sec., Jerry Pascucci/Dir., Pres.

Directors: David J. Vogel/Dir., Daniel R. McAuliffe/Dir., CFO, Shelley Ullman/Dir., Jennifer Magro/Dir., Ihor Rakowsky/Dir., Sec., Jerry Pascucci/Dir., Pres., Steven Ciampi/Dir., Raymond Nolte/Dir., Daryl Dewbrey/Dir.

Smith International Inc

PO Box 60068, Houston, TX, 77205; ***PH:*** 1-281-443-3370; ***Fax:*** 1-281-233-5199; ***http://*** www.smith.com; ***Email:*** info@smith.com

General - Incorporation............................DE
Employees...17,377
Auditor.........................Deloitte & Touche LLP
Stk Agt....................EquiServe Trust Co N.A
Counsel...NA
DUNS No.............................00-838-3382

Stock- Price on:12/24/2007 ....$59.72
Stock Exchange..NYSE
Ticker Symbol...SII
Outstanding Shares 200,480,000
E.P.S...$3.09
Shareholders...NA

Business: The group's principle activities are to manufacture and distribute products and services to the oil and gas exploration and production industry. The oilfield products and services segment consists of three business units: m-i, smith bits and smith services. M-i provides drilling and completion fluid systems and services, solids-control equipment and waste-management services. Smith bits manufactures and sells three-cone and diamond drill bits. Smith services manufactures and markets products and services used for drilling, workover, well completion and well re-entry operations. The distribution segment includes the wilson business unit, which markets pipes, valves, fittings, mill, safety and other maintenance products to energy and industrial markets. In August 2005, Smith Services acquired certain operating assets of Tubular Technology, Inc. and associated companies In November 2005, Smith Services acquired certain operating assets of Nunez Oil Field Pipe, Ltd. The group's quarterly revenue for Sep '07 was 2,245.06 millions of USD.

Primary SIC and add'l.: 3533 1381 3532

CIK No: 0000721083

Subsidiaries: CE Franklin Ltd., Chem-Tech, Inc., Omega II Insurance Ltd., S.I. Nederland B.V., Sii Megadiamond, Inc., Smith (Bermuda) Ltd., Smith Internacional de Venezuela, C.A., Smith International (North Sea) Ltd., Smith International Acquisition Corp., Smith International Australia (Pty) Ltd., Smith International Canada Ltd., Smith International Deutschland GmbH, Smith International Development Corporation, Smith International do Brasil Ltda., Smith International France, S.A.R.L. 18 Subsidiaries included in the Index

Officers: Doug Rock/Chmn., CEO, COO, Pres./$8,692,932.00, Jerry W. Neely/Advisory Dir., Margaret K. Dorman/CFO, Sr. VP, Treasurer/$1,970,425.00, Malcolm W. Anderson/Sr. VP - Human Resources, Richard E. Chandler/Sr. VP, General Counsel, Corp. Sec., Donald McKenzie/Operating Officer/$2,479,644.00, John J. Kennedy/Operating Officer/$1,759,725.00, Michael D. Pearce/Operating Officer, Bryan L. Dudman/Operating Officer/$1,777,023.00, Peter J. Pintar/VP - Corporate Strategy - Business Development, Joseph S. Rinando/VP, Corporate Controller, Geraldine D. Wilde/VP - Tax, Assist. Treasurer

Directors: Doug Rock/Chmn., CEO, COO, Pres., James R. Gibbs/Dir., Clyde G. Buck/Dir., Loren K. Carroll/Dir., Dod A. Fraser/Dir., Robert Kelley/Dir., John Yearwood/Dir.

Owners: John Yearwood, Doug Rock, Loren K. Carroll, Jerry W. Neely, Bryan L. Dudman, Robert Kelley, John Kennedy, James R. Gibbs, Donald McKenzie, Dod A. Fraser, Margaret K. Dorman, Clyde G. Buck, Insiders/1.50%

Financial Data: ***Fiscal Year End:***12/31 ***Latest Annual Data:*** 12/31/2006

Year	Sales	Net Income
2006	$7,333,559,000	$502,006,000
2005	$5,579,003,000	$302,305,000
2004	$4,419,015,000	$182,451,000

Curr. Assets:	$3,271,027,000	***Curr. Liab.:***	$1,379,468,000	***P/E Ratio:***	21.71
Plant, Equip.:	$887,044,000	***Total Liab.:***	$2,426,424,000	***Indic. Yr. Divd.:***	$0.400
Total Assets:	$5,335,475,000	***Net Worth:***	$1,986,937,000	***Debt/ Equity:***	NA

Smith Micro Software Inc

51 Columbia, Ste. 200, Aliso Viejo, CA, 92656; ***PH:*** 1-949-362-5800; ***Fax:*** 1-949-362-2300; ***http://*** www.smithmicro.com

General - Incorporation	DE	***Stock***- Price on:12/24/2007	$14.0699
Employees	128	Stock Exchange	NDQ
Auditor	Singer Lewak Greenbaum & Goldstein	Ticker Symbol	SMSI
Stk Agt	C.E. Unterberg Towbin LLC	Outstanding Shares	29,630,000
Counsel	Brobeck, Phleger & Harrison	E.P.S.	$0.21
DUNS No.	11-351-1190	Shareholders	NA

Business: The group's principal activities are to develop and sell ecommerce and communications software for personal and business use. It also provides Internet consulting and hosting services. The group operates in two businesses segments - software products and services. The products segment includes products developed for the Internet and broadband technologies, products that enable ecommerce, Internet communications, video conferencing, wireless communications, general system utility products and network fax along with traditional computer telephony. The services segment provides ebusiness consulting services Web site hosting and order fulfillment services.

Primary SIC and add'l.: 7372 7379

CIK No: 0000948708

Subsidiaries: pcs, stf

Officers: William W. Smith/Chmn., CEO, Pres./$900,331.00, David P. Sperling/CTO, VP/$447,497.00, Bruce T. Quigley/VP - Multi Operational Programs, Jonathan Kahn/Sr. VP, GM Compression - Consumer/$427,150.00, Darryl Lovato/VP - Advanced Technology, Robert Elliott/VP, Chief Marketing Officer, Andrew C. Schmidt/CFO/$614,553.00, Jeff Costello/VP - Sales Consumer - Small Business, Rick W. Wyand/Sr. VP - Sales Wireless Telcom - OEM, Chris Lippincott/VP - Operations/$398,348.00, William R. Wyand/Sr. VP - Sales Wireless Telcom - OEM/$484,990.00, David Przeracki/VP - Registered In - House Counsel, Mark McMillan/Exec. VP - Sales

Directors: William W. Smith/Chmn., CEO, Pres., Samuel Gulko/Dir., Thomas G. Campbell/Dir., William C. Keiper/Dir., Gregory Szabo/Dir., Ted L. Hoffman/Dir.

Owners: Andrew C. Schmidt, David P. Sperling, William W. Smith/9.02%, William C. Keiper, Insiders/11.10%, Gregory J. Szabo, FMR Corp./10.20%, Christopher g. Lippincott, William W. Wyand, Ted L. Hoffman, Thomas G. Campbell, Samuel Gulko, Jonathan Kahn

Financial Data: ***Fiscal Year End:***12/31 ***Latest Annual Data:*** 06/30/2007

Year	Sales	Net Income
2007	$24,826,000	$3,472,000
2006	$54,469,000	$8,956,000
2005	$20,258,000	$4,724,000

Curr. Assets:	$103,769,000	***Curr. Liab.:***	$4,969,000		
Plant, Equip.:	$417,000	***Total Liab.:***	$4,969,000	***Indic. Yr. Divd.:***	NA
Total Assets:	$131,026,000	***Net Worth:***	$126,057,000	***Debt/ Equity:***	NA

Smith Midland Corp

5119 Catlett Rd., Midland, VA, 22728; ***PH:*** 1-540-439-3266; ***Fax:*** 1-540-439-1232; ***http://*** www.smithmid.com; ***Email:*** info@smithmidland.com

General - Incorporation	DE	***Stock***- Price on:12/24/2007	$2.11
Employees	114	Stock Exchange	OTC
Auditor	BDO Seidman LLP	Ticker Symbol	SMID
Stk Agt	Computershare Trust Co	Outstanding Shares	4,640,000
Counsel	NA	E.P.S.	-$0.03
DUNS No.	88-471-8289	Shareholders	NA

Business: The group's principal activities are to invent, develop, manufacture, market, lease, license, sell and install precast concrete products. The group's products include Easi-Set Slenderwall(TM) prefabricated construction panels, Easi-Set Sierra Wall(TM) precast concrete walls, Easi-Set J-J Hooks(TM) highway safety barriers, Easi-Set Precast Buildings, Easi-Span(TM) expandable precast concrete buildings, and Easi-Set underground utility vaults. For the year ended December 31, 2005, Slenderwall(TM) accounted for 205% increase, Soundwall(TM) 101%, Easi-Set 24%, utility products 12%, and barrier rentals 47%.

Primary SIC and add'l.: 3272

CIK No: 0000924719

Subsidiaries: Easi-Set Industries

Officers: Rodney I. Smith/Chmn., CEO, Pres./$493,713.00, Ashley B. Smith/46/Dir., VP - Sales, Marketing/$123,635.00, Wesley A. Taylor/60/Dir., VP - Administration/$119,980.00, Steve Ott/41/VP - Engineering Smith, Midland Corp, Virginia, Alan D. Shutt/CFO

Directors: Rodney I. Smith/Chmn., CEO, Pres., Ashley B. Smith/46/Dir., VP - Sales, Marketing, Wesley A. Taylor/60/Dir., VP - Administration, Andrew G. Kavounis/83/Dir.

Owners: Lawrence R. Crews, AL Frank Asset Management, Inc./14.70%, Rodney I. Smith/14.60%, Wesley A. Taylor, Insiders/18.20%, Ashley B. Smith/3.10%, Andrew G. Kavounis

Financial Data: ***Fiscal Year End:***12/31 ***Latest Annual Data:*** 12/31/2006

Year	Sales	Net Income
2006	$29,362,000	-$816,000
2005	$23,791,000	$1,351,000
2004	$22,115,000	$492,000

Curr. Assets:	$10,711,000	***Curr. Liab.:***	$5,910,000		
Plant, Equip.:	$3,730,000	***Total Liab.:***	$10,049,000	***Indic. Yr. Divd.:***	NA
Total Assets:	$14,655,000	***Net Worth:***	$4,606,000	***Debt/ Equity:***	0.7708

Smithfield Foods Inc

200 Commerce St., Smithfield, VA, 23430; ***PH:*** 1-757-365-3000; ***Fax:*** 1-757-365-3017; ***http://*** www.smithfieldfoods.com; ***Email:*** information@smithfieldfoods.com

General - Incorporation	VA	***Stock***- Price on:12/24/2007	$31.99
Employees	52,500	Stock Exchange	NYSE
Auditor	Ernst & Young LLP	Ticker Symbol	SFD
Stk Agt	Computershare Investor Services LLC	Outstanding Shares	112,090,000
Counsel	NA	E.P.S.	$1.38
DUNS No.	00-311-0913	Shareholders	NA

Business: The groups principle activities include hog producing and pork processing. The group's product line includes leaner fresh pork products as well as lower-fat and lower-salt processed meats. The group operates from United States.

Primary SIC and add'l.: 2011 2013

CIK No: 0000091388

Subsidiaries: 814 Americas, Inc., ADA Premium Beef Co., Inc., Agri Plus S.a., AGRI Sp. z o.o., Agrotorvis S.R.L., Animex Fish Sp. z o.o., Animex Grupa Drobiarska Sp. z o.o., ANIMEX Holding Sp. z o.o., Animex Pasze Sp. z o.o., Animex Sp. z o.o., Animex-Krakowskie Zaklady Pierzarskie Sp. z o.o., ANIMEX-Opoloskie Zaklady Drobiarskie S.A., Animpol S.A., Bacon Business Acquisition Sub Inc., Beef Production LLC 156 Subsidiaries included in the Index

Officers: Larry C. Pope/53/Dir., CEO, Pres./$4,807,907.00, Morten Jensen/53/CEO - Central, Eastern Europe, Joseph W. Luter/43/Pres. - Smithfield Packing Company, Incorporated, Jerry H. Godwin/61/Pres. - Murphy, Brown, LLC/$2,281,899.00, Robert G. Hofmann/58/Pres. - North Side Foods Corp, Robert W. Manly/55/Exec. VP/$1,229,026.00, George H. Richter/63/Pres. - Farmland Foods, Inc/$3,336,995.00, Michael D. Flemming/59/VP - Sr. Counsel, William G. Otis/51/Pres. - Patrick Cudahy Incorporated, Jeffrey M. Luckman/49/VP - Livestock Procurement, Richard J.M. Poulson/69/Exec. VP/$2,639,686.00, Henry L. Morris/65/VP - Operations, Douglas P. Anderson/61/VP - Rendering, Dennis H. Treacy/53/VP - Environmental, Corporate Affairs, Vernon T. Turner/44/Corporate Tax Dir. *(28 Officers included in Index)*

Directors: Larry C. Pope/53/Dir., CEO, Pres., Joseph W. Luter/Chmn., Paul S. Trible/61/Dir., Paul J. Fribourg/54/Dir., Michael J. Zimmerman/57/Dir., John T. Schwieters/68/Dir., Melvin O. Wright/80/Dir., Frank S. Royal/68/Dir., Carol T. Crawford/65/Dir., Ray A. Goldberg/81/Dir., Robert L. Burrus/73/Dir., Wendell H. Murphy/69/Dir.

Owners: Richard J.M. Poulson, Frank S. Royal, Joseph W. Luter/3.90%, Paul J. Fribourg/6.30%, Robert L. Burrus, Ray A. Goldberg, Insiders/13.60%, Jerry H. Godwin, Robert W. Manly, Tradewinds Global Investors, LLC/8.10%, Lazard Asset Management LLC/6.40%, Wendell H. Murphy, Larry C. Pope, Daniel G. Stevens, John T. Schwieters *(18 Owners included in Index)*

Financial Data: ***Fiscal Year End:***04/30 ***Latest Annual Data:*** 4/30/2006

Year	Sales	Net Income
2006	$11,403,600,000	$172,700,000
2005	$11,354,200,000	$296,200,000
2004	$9,267,000,000	$227,100,000

Curr. Assets:	$2,023,600,000	***Curr. Liab.:***	$967,000,000	***P/E Ratio:***	21.47
Plant, Equip.:	$1,761,000,000	***Total Liab.:***	$3,183,300,000	***Indic. Yr. Divd.:***	NA
Total Assets:	$4,813,700,000	***Net Worth:***	$1,617,200,000	***Debt/ Equity:***	1.3244

Smithtown Bancorp

100 Motor Pkwy., Ste. 160, Hauppauge, NY, 11788; ***PH:*** 1-631-360-9300; ***Fax:*** 1-631-360-9373; ***http://*** www.bankofsmithtown.com; ***Email:*** investorinfo@bankofsmithtown.net

General - Incorporation	NY	***Stock***- Price on:12/24/2007	$23.38
Employees	188	Stock Exchange	NDQ
Auditor	Crowe Chizek & Co. LLC	Ticker Symbol	SMTB
Stk Agt	NA	Outstanding Shares	9,800,000
Counsel	NA	E.P.S.	$1.47
DUNS No.	00-699-4420	Shareholders	NA

Business: The group's principal activities are the provision of commercial and consumer financial services. The group also provides trust and estate administration, fiduciary and investment advisory services and acts as a bond and coupons paying agent for local municipalities. The group operates through 10 branch offices located in smithtown, commack, hauppauge, kings park, centereach, lake grove, northport and east setauket. The services of the group are provided to individuals, businesses and municipalities. On 31-Aug-2004, the group acquired seigerman-mulvey co.

Primary SIC and add'l.: 6022 6712

CIK No: 0000747345

Subsidiaries: Bank of Smithtown

Officers: Bradley E. Rock/Chmn., CEO, Pres./$1,472,394.00, Stacy L. Germano/VP, Trust Officer, Sharon Wittschen/VP - Commerical Lending, Anita M. Florek/CFO, Exec. VP/$317,191.00, Jeanne Quortrup/Mgr., Robert Gallagher/Mgr., Bonnie Luisi/Mgr., Patricia Guidi/Sr. VP - Operations, Ann Marie Tarantino/VP - Compliance, Deborah L. McElroy/VP - Human Resources, Patricia C. Delaney/Dir., General Counsel, John A. Romano/Exec. VP, Chief Retail Officer/$319,018.00, Karen Neale/Mgr., Robert Staron/VP - Loan Department, Richard T. Ritchie/Mgr. *(38 Officers included in Index)*

Directors: Bradley E. Rock/Chmn., CEO, Pres., Barry M. Seigerman/Dir., Sanford C. Scheman/Dir., Patrick A. Given/Dir., Hyukmun Kwon/Dir., Manny M. Schwartz/Dir., Augusta Kemper/Dir., Patricia C. Delaney/Dir., General Counsel, Robert W. Scherdel/Dir., Patricia Hoffman/Dir.

Owners: Barry M. Seigerman, Hyukmun Kwon, Robert W. Scherdel, Patrick A. Given, Sanford C. Scheman/1.01%, Thomas J. Stevens, Manny Schwartz, Bradley E. Rock/1.28%, John A. Romano, Robert J. Anrig, Insiders/12.68%, Augusta Kemper/6.27%, Anita M. Florek, Edith Hodgkinson/6.34%, Patricia C. Delaney

Financial Data: ***Fiscal Year End:***12/31 ***Latest Annual Data:*** 12/31/2006

Year	Sales	Net Income
2006	$77,138,000	$13,967,000
2005	$56,813,000	$11,066,000
2004	$41,050,000	$10,011,000

Curr. Assets:	$36,845,000	**Curr. Liab.:**	$892,672,000	**P/E Ratio:**	15.90
Plant, Equip.:	$27,570,000	**Total Liab.:**	$981,417,000	**Indic. Yr. Divd.:**	$0.160
Total Assets:	$1,048,224,000	**Net Worth:**	$66,807,000	**Debt/ Equity:**	0.7574

Smithway Motor Xpress Corp

PO Box 404, Fort Dodge, IA, 50501; *PH:* 1-515-576-7418; *Fax:* 1-515-576-8794; *http://* www.smxc.com

General - Incorporation....NV | **Stock**- Price on:12/24/2007....$10.58
Employees....1,036 | Stock Exchange....NA
Auditor....KPMG LLP | Ticker Symbol....NA
Stk Agt....UMB Bank, N.A. | Outstanding Shares....4,990,000
Counsel....Scudder Law Firm | E.P.S....$0.45
DUNS No....06-277-6083 | Shareholders....NA

Business: The group's principle activity is to provide nationwide transportation of diversified freight, concentrating primarily in flatbed operations. It operates over short-to-medium traffic routes, serving shippers located predominantly between the Rocky Mountains in the west and the Appalachian mountains in the east and in eight Canadian provinces. The group's network consists of its headquarters in Fort Dodge, Iowa and 10 terminals, field offices, and independent agencies. The group operates satellite-based tracking and communication units in all of its tractors. The group provides its customers electronic data interchange computer link or the Internet and with the aid of satellite communication, obtain location updates of in-transit freight, expected delivery times and account payment instructions.

Primary SIC and add'l.: 4213

CIK No: 0000941914

Subsidiaries: East West Motor Express Inc, New Horizons Leasing Inc, Smithway Motor Xpress Inc, SMSD Acquisition Corp

Officers: Larry G. Owens/Chmn., CEO, Pres., Sec. Officer, Chad A. Johnson/VP, Vehicle Operations Officer, Thomas J. Witt/47/Sr. VP - Sales, Operations, Douglas C. Sandvig/CFO, Sr. VP, Treasurer

Directors: Larry G. Owens/Chmn., CEO, Pres., Sec. Officer, Marlys L. Smith/Dir., Herbert D. Ihle/Dir., Labh S. Hira/Dir., Terry G. Christenberry/Dir.

Owners: Labh S. Hira, Douglas C. Sandvig, Chad A. Johnson, Larry G. Owens/5.30%, Terry G. Christenberry, Dimensional Fund Advisors LP/4.70%, Herbert D. Ihle, Insiders/28.70%, Marlys L. Smith/21.80%, Mesirow Financial Investment Management/7.20%

Financial Data: *Fiscal Year End:*12/31 *Latest Annual Data:* 12/31/2006

Year	Sales	Net Income
2006	$228,762,000	$4,282,000
2005	$220,386,000	$4,241,000
2004	$189,001,000	$2,241,000

Curr. Assets:	$26,676,000	**Curr. Liab.:**	$24,687,000	**P/E Ratio:**	23.51
Plant, Equip.:	$72,834,000	**Total Liab.:**	$69,646,000	**Indic. Yr. Divd.:**	NA
Total Assets:	$101,565,000	**Net Worth:**	$31,919,000	**Debt/ Equity:**	1.2412

Smitten Press Local Lore & Legends Inc

108 Royal St., New Orleans, LA, 70130; *PH:* 1-772-334-7129; *http://* www.smittenpress.com

General - Incorporation....ON | **Stock**- Price on:12/24/2007....$0.1
Employees....NA | Stock Exchange....OTC
Auditor....Salberg & Co P.A | Ticker Symbol....SPLIE
Stk Agt....NA | Outstanding Shares....NA
Counsel....NA | E.P.S....NA
DUNS No....NA | Shareholders....NA

Business: The group's principal activity is publishing and distributing of the Local Lore and Legends series of magazines. The group has reactivated its business with the focus on refining its business plan, refining its business plan, preparing to sell products through rack jobbers, or persons who set up and maintain newspaper-style boxes, as well as from its website.

Primary SIC and add'l.: 5900

CIK No: 0001315718

Officers: Robert Cox/CEO, CFO, Michael T. Williams/Dir., Pres.

Directors: Storey G. Badger/Dir., Michael T. Williams/Dir., Pres.

Owners: Robert L. Cox, The Estate of Richard Smitten

Financial Data: *Fiscal Year End:*12/31 *Latest Annual Data:* 12/31/2006

Year	Sales	Net Income
2006	NA	-$162,000

Curr. Assets:	$3,000	**Curr. Liab.:**	$399,000		
Plant, Equip.:	NA	**Total Liab.:**	$399,000	**Indic. Yr. Divd.:**	NA
Total Assets:	$3,000	**Net Worth:**	-$396,000	**Debt/ Equity:**	NA

SMTC Corp

635 Hood Rd., Markham, ON, L3R 4N6; *PH:* 1-905-479-1810; *http://* www.smtc.com; *Email:* info@smtc.com

General - Incorporation....DE | **Stock**- Price on:12/24/2007....$5.42
Employees....1,300 | Stock Exchange....NDQ
Auditor....KPMG LLP | Ticker Symbol....SMTX
Stk Agt....Chase Mellon Shareholder Services LLC | Outstanding Shares....14,650,000
Counsel....Ropes & Gray LLP | E.P.S....$0.82
DUNS No....NA | Shareholders....NA

Business: The group's principal activities are to provide advanced electronic manufacturing services to the electronic industry and original equipment manufacturers worldwide. The group's services include product designing, procurement, prototyping, assembly, test, comprehensive supply chain management, packaging, global distribution and after-sale support. These services are provided through eight manufacturing and technology centers located in the United States, Canada, Europe and Mexico. The group has relationships with over 50 original equipment manufacturers. The customers include IBM and alcatel. During 2003, the group discontinued appleton facility.

Primary SIC and add'l.: 3679

CIK No: 0001108320

Subsidiaries: 940862 Ontario Inc., HTM Holdings, Inc., Qualtron, Inc., Radio Componentes de Mexico, S.A. de S.V., SMTC Corporation, SMTC de Chihuahua S.A. de C.V., SMTC Ireland Company, SMTC Manufacturing Corporation of California, SMTC Manufacturing Corporation of Canada, SMTC Manufacturing Corporation of Colorado, SMTC Manufacturing Corporation of Massachusetts, SMTC Manufacturing Corporation of North Carolina, SMTC Manufacturing Corporation of Texas, SMTC Manufacturing Corporation of Wisconsin, SMTC Mex Holdings, Inc. 18 Subsidiaries included in the Index

Officers: John E. Caldwell/Dir., CEO, Pres./$1,091,851.00, Jane Todd/Sr. VP - Finance, CFO/$369,440.00, David Price/VP, GM - Enclosure Systems Division, Carl Munio/VP, GM - San Jose, Don Simpson/Sr. VP - Manufacturing - Engineering/$302,505.00, Betsy Smith/VP - Human Resources, Steve Hoffrogge/Sr. VP - Business Development/$576,949.00, Steve Dutton/VP - Global Sales, Catherine Copplestone/VP, GM - Chihuahua, Paul Blom/Sr. VP - Supply Chain

Directors: John E. Caldwell/Dir., CEO, Pres., Wayne McLeod/Chmn., Ian Loring/Dir., Blair Hendrix/Dir., Stephen Adamson/Dir., Thomas Cowan/Dir., William Brock/Dir.

Owners: Stephen Adamson/4.75%, John Caldwell/2.32%, Steven G. Hoffrogge, William Brock, Caisse de dpt et placement du Qubec/17.41%, Jane Todd, Bain Capital Funds/5.24%, Thomas Cowan, Wayne McLeod, Don G. Simpson, Red Oak Capital/7.76%, Insiders/7.77%

Financial Data: *Fiscal Year End:*12/31 *Latest Annual Data:* 12/31/2006

Year	Sales	Net Income
2006	$262,782,000	$10,461,000
2005	$228,766,000	-$112,000
2004	$244,596,000	$618,000

Curr. Assets:	$89,291,000	**Curr. Liab.:**	$71,245,000	**P/E Ratio:**	7.32
Plant, Equip.:	$24,804,000	**Total Liab.:**	$92,071,000	**Indic. Yr. Divd.:**	NA
Total Assets:	$115,962,000	**Net Worth:**	$23,891,000	**Debt/ Equity:**	0.6828

Smurfit Stone Container Corp

150 N Michigan Ave., Chicago, IL, 60601; *PH:* 1-312-346-6600; *Fax:* 1-312-580-2272; *http://* www.smurfit.com

General - Incorporation....DE | **Stock**- Price on:12/24/2007....$13.4
Employees....25,200 | Stock Exchange....NDQ
Auditor....Ernst & Young LLP | Ticker Symbol....SSCC
Stk Agt....Mellon Investor Services LLC | Outstanding Shares....255,020,000
Counsel....NA | E.P.S....-$0.07
DUNS No....09-253-3678 | Shareholders....NA

Business: The groups principle activity is to manufacture paperboard and paper-based packaging. The groups products include containerboard, kraft paper, solid-bleached sulfate, market pulp, folding cartons, coated and recycled boxboard. The group operates from United States.

Primary SIC and add'l.: 2672 2657 6719 2674 2653 2673 2631

CIK No: 0000919226

Subsidiaries: 3083527 Nova Scotia Company, 605681 N.b. Inc., 639647 British Columbia Ltd., Aspamill Inc., Associated Paper Mills (Ontario) Limited, Atlanta& Saint Andrews Bay Railroad Co., B.C. Shipper Supplies Ltd., Cameo Container Corporation, Cascapedia Booming Co. Ltd., CCA de Baja California S.A. de C.V., Celgar Investments,Inc., CIMIC Packaging Paper Co. Ltd., Clayton Partners Ltd, Dalton Paper Products,Inc., Dongguan Stone Millennium Paper& Packaging Industries, Ltd. 83 Subsidiaries included in the Index

Officers: Patrick J. Moore/Chmn., CEO, Pres./$7,478,757.00, Steven C. Strickland/56/Sr. VP - Sales, Container Division, Brian Gardner/Contact - Treasury, Bonds, John L. Knudsen/51/Sr. VP - Manufacturing, Container Division, Joseph V. Leblanc/VP - Research, Development, Charles A. Hinrichs/CFO, Sr. VP/$1,647,631.00, Paul K. Kaufmann/Sr. VP, Corporate Controller, Ronald D. Hackney/Sr. VP - Human Resources, Craig A. Hunt/Sr. VP, General Counsel, Sec., M. C. Jackson/Sr. VP - Containerboard Mill, Forest Resources Division/$1,379,437.00, Thomas A. Pagano/61/Sr. VP - Corporate Development/$1,693,227.00, Jeffrey S. Beyersdorfer/VP, Treasurer, Mathew J. Blanchard/VP, GM - Board Sales, Michael R. Oswald/Sr. VP, GM - Recycling Division, Mark R. O'Bryan/Sr. VP - Strategic Initiatives *(22 Officers included in Index)*

Directors: Patrick J. Moore/Chmn., CEO, Pres., James R. Boris/Dir., William T. Lynch/Dir., Jerry K. Pearlman/Dir., Thomas A. Reynolds/Dir., James J. O'Connor/Dir., Connie K. Duckworth/Dir., Alan E. Goldberg/Dir., William D. Smithburg/Dir., Eugene C. Sit/Dir.

Owners: William T. Lynch, Thomas A. Pagano, Mack C. Jackson, Deutsche Bank AG/7.11%, James R. Boris, FMR Corp./8.85%, Patrick J. Moore, Insiders/1.40%, Alan E. Goldberg, Thomas A. Reynolds, Steven J. Klinger, Eugene C. Sit, Charles A. Hinrichs, AXA/13.35%, William D. Smithburg *(20 Owners included in Index)*

Financial Data: *Fiscal Year End:*12/31 *Latest Annual Data:* 12/31/2006

Year	Sales	Net Income
2006	$7,157,000,000	-$59,000,000
2005	$8,396,000,000	-$327,000,000
2004	$8,291,000,000	-$46,000,000

Curr. Assets:	$926,000,000	**Curr. Liab.:**	$1,067,000,000		
Plant, Equip.:	$3,774,000,000	**Total Liab.:**	$5,970,000,000	**Indic. Yr. Divd.:**	NA
Total Assets:	$7,777,000,000	**Net Worth:**	$1,807,000,000	**Debt/ Equity:**	2.0998

Smurfit-Stone Container Enterprises Inc

150 N Michigan Ave., Chicago, IL, 60601; *PH:* 1-312-346-6600; *http://* www.smurfit-stone.com

General - Incorporation....DE | **Stock**- Price on:12/24/2007....$12.86
Employees....25,200 | Stock Exchange....NA
Auditor....Ernst & Young LLP | Ticker Symbol....NA
Stk Agt....Mellon Investor Services LLC | Outstanding Shares....255,020,000
Counsel....NA | E.P.S....-$0.07
DUNS No....00-521-3400 | Shareholders....NA

Business: The group's principle activities include producing and selling commodity pulp, paper and packaging products. The group operates from United States.

Primary SIC and add'l.: 2620 2670 2650

CIK No: 0000094610

Subsidiaries: Smurfit-Stone Container Corporation

Officers: Patrick J. Moore/Chmn., CEO, Paul K. Kaufmann/Sr. VP, Corporate Controller, Charles A. Hinrichs/Sr. VP, CFO, John Haudrich/Analyst, Investors Contact - Dir. - Investor Relations, Brian Gardner/Treasury, Bond, Mathew J. Blanchard/VP, GM - Board Sales, Tom Lange/Dir. - Public Relations, Brian Peura/Analyst, Investors Contact, Shirley Staggs/Analyst, Investors Conatct, Jeffrey S. Beyersdorfer/VP, Treasurer, Ronald D. Hackney/Sr. VP - Human Resources, Craig A. Hunt/Sr. VP, General Counsel, Sec., M. C. Jackson/Sr. VP - Containerboard Mill, Forest Resources Division, Steven J. Klinger/COO, Pres., Joseph V. Leblanc/VP - Research, Development *(17 Officers included in Index)*

Directors: Patrick J. Moore/Chmn., CEO, Eugene C. Sit/Dir., James R. Boris/Dir., Connie K. Duckworth/Dir., Alan E. Goldberg/Dir., William T. Lynch/Dir., James J. Oconnor/Dir., Jerry K. Pearlman/Dir., Thomas A. Reynolds/Dir., William D. Smithburg/Dir.

Owners: Deutsche Bank AG/7.10%, Mack C. Jackson, Connie K. Duckworth, FMR Corp./8.90%, Eugene C. Sit, Insiders/1.40%, William T. Lynch, Jerry K. Pearlman, William D. Smithburg, James R. Boris, Thomas A. Reynolds, James J. OConnor, Patrick J. Moore/0.60%, Wellington Management Company, LLP/9.80%, Alan E. Goldberg (20 Owners included in Index)

Financial Data: Fiscal Year End:12/31   Latest Annual Data: 12/31/2006

Year	Sales	Net Income
2006	$7,157,000,000	-$59,000,000
2005	$8,396,000,000	-$327,000,000
2004	$8,291,000,000	-$46,000,000

Curr. Assets:	$926,000,000	**Curr. Liab.:**	$1,067,000,000		
Plant, Equip.:	$3,774,000,000	**Total Liab.:**	$5,970,000,000	**Indic. Yr. Divd.:**	NA
Total Assets:	$7,777,000,000	**Net Worth:**	$1,807,000,000	**Debt/ Equity:**	2.0998

Snap-on Inc

2801 80th St., Kenosha, WI, 53143; **PH:** 1-262-656-5200; **Fax:** 1-262-656-5577; http:// www.snapon.com

General - Incorporation	DE	**Stock**- Price on:12/24/2007	$52.37
Employees	12,400	Stock Exchange	NYSE
Auditor	Deloitte & Touche LLP	Ticker Symbol	SNA
Stk Agt	EquiServe Trust Co N.A	Outstanding Shares	57,970,000
Counsel	NA	E.P.S.	$2.52
DUNS No.	00-609-0294	Shareholders	NA

Business: The groups principle activities include manufacturing and marketing tools, diagnostics and equipment solutions. The groups product line includes hand and power tools, information and management systems, shop equipment and other solutions for vehicle manufacturers, dealerships and repair centers. Customers served by the group include the government, agriculture and construction industries. The group operates from United States.

Primary SIC and add'l.: 3460 3423 7539 3540 7538

CIK No: 0000091440

Subsidiaries: IDSC Holdings LLC, Mitchell Repair Information Company, LLC, SB Tools S.a.r.l, Snap-on Global Holdings, Inc., Snap-on Holdings AB, Snap-on Tools Canada, Ltd., Snap-on Tools Company LLC, Snap-on Tools International, LLC

Officers: Jack D. Michaels/Chmn., CEO, Pres./$5,156,795.00, Donald E. Broman/60/Pres. - Industrial Worldwide, Iain Boyd/VP - Human Resources, Bennett L. Brenton/VP - Innovation, David R. Ellingen/49/Pres. - Snap, on Diagnostics, Mitchell, Andrew R. Ginger/VP, Chief Marketing Officer, Mike Gentile/Pres. - Hand Tools, Govind K. Arora/VP - Worldwide Strategic Sourcing, Susan F. Marrinan/56/VP, Sec., Chief Legal Officer/$1,184,444.00, Blaine A. Metzger/51/Sr. VP - Finance, Accounting, Snap, on Tools Company, LLC, Jeanne M. Moreno/51/CIO, VP, Martin M. Ellen/53/CFO, Sr. VP - Finance/$2,000,262.00, Mark S. Pezzoni/54/Pres. - Power, Special Tools, Richard V. Caskey/58/Pres. - Merchandise Products, Gary S. Henning/56/VP - Operations Development (28 Officers included in Index)

Directors: Jack D. Michaels/Chmn., CEO, Pres., Arthur L. Kelly/Dir., Lars Nyberg/Dir., Bruce S. Chelberg/Dir., Karen L. Daniel/Dir., Roxanne J. Decyk/Dir., John F. Fiedler/Dir., Edward H. Rensi/Dir., Richard F. Teerlink/Dir., Dudley W. Lehman/Dir., James P. Holden/Dir.

Owners: John F. Fiedler, Lars Nyberg, Susan F. Marrinan, Nicholas T. Pinchuk, Jack D. Michaels, Edward H. Rensi, Dudley W. Lehman, Insiders, Bruce S. Chelberg, Roxanne J. Decyk, Martin M. Ellen, Thomas J. Ward, Karen L. Daniel, Alan T. Biland, Richard F. Teerlink (16 Owners included in Index)

Financial Data: Fiscal Year End:12/31   Latest Annual Data: 12/30/2006

Year	Sales	Net Income
2006	$2,522,400,000	$100,100,000
2005	$2,362,200,000	$92,900,000

Curr. Assets:	$1,072,900,000	**Curr. Liab.:**	$506,100,000	**P/E Ratio:**	20.78
Plant, Equip.:	$295,500,000	**Total Liab.:**	$1,046,200,000	**Indic. Yr. Divd.:**	$1.080
Total Assets:	$2,008,400,000	**Net Worth:**	$962,200,000	**Debt/ Equity:**	0.4609

SNRG Corp

Formerly: Texen Oil & Gas Inc

14300 Nsight Blvd., Ste. 227, Scottsdale, AZ, 85260; **PH:** 1-480-991-2040

General - Incorporation	NV	**Stock**- Price on:12/24/2007	$0.025
Employees	NA	Stock Exchange	NA
Auditor	Epstein Weber & Conover, PLC	Ticker Symbol	NA
Stk Agt	Pacific Stock Transfer Company	Outstanding Shares	184,220,000
Counsel	NA	E.P.S.	$0.001
DUNS No.	NA	Shareholders	NA

Business: The group's principal activities are to explore, exploit, develop, produce and acquire natural gas and crude oil. The operations are conducted through subsidiary corporations. The group owns interests in 47 gross wells (15 wells net) in fields located in waller, victoria and dewitt counties of Texas region. It also owns interests in 4,871.7 net acres in Texas. In fiscal 2003, the group acquired Texas brookshire partners inc, brookshire drilling service llc, yegua inc, Texas gohlke partners inc and bwc minerals llc. The oil and gas products are sold primarily to domestic pipelines and refineries.

Primary SIC and add'l.: 1382

CIK No: 0001102944

Subsidiaries: BWC Minerals, LLC, Texas Brookshire Partners, Inc., Texas Gohlke Partners, Inc., Yegua, Inc.

Financial Data: Fiscal Year End:12/31   Latest Annual Data: 12/31/2005

Year	Sales	Net Income
2005	$484,000	$34,000
2004	$588,000	-$3,564,000

Curr. Assets:	$493,000	**Curr. Liab.:**	$2,549,000	**P/E Ratio:**	25.00
Plant, Equip.:	$4,660,000	**Total Liab.:**	$2,549,000	**Indic. Yr. Divd.:**	NA
Total Assets:	$5,153,000	**Net Worth:**	$2,604,000	**Debt/ Equity:**	NA

Socket Communications Inc

39700 Eureka Dr., Newark, CA, 94560; **PH:** 1-510-933-3000; **Fax:** 1-510-933-3030; http:// www.socketcom.com

General - Incorporation	DE	**Stock**- Price on:12/24/2007	$0.85
Employees	83	Stock Exchange	NDQ
Auditor	Moss Adams LLP	Ticker Symbol	SCKT
Stk Agt	American Stock Transfer & Trust Co.	Outstanding Shares	31,910,000
Counsel	Wilson Sonsini Goodrich & Rosati	E.P.S.	-$0.13
DUNS No.	79-036-3956	Shareholders	NA

Business: The group's principle activity is to develop and market connection solutions for handheld computers. The products include a family of low power battery friendly PC card adapters for peripheral connections, ethernet network connectivity, mobile data collection and wireless communications. The digital phone cards connect mobile computers to over one hundred data-enabled digital mobile phones, the peripheral connection cards connect computer peripherals to mobile computers, the data collection cards connect bar code wands and bar code laser scanners to mobile computers, the ethernet cards connect a mobile computer to a corporate ethernet network, allowing location-independent operation of mobile device. The group also recognizes revenues from funded engineering services and from the sale of interface chips to original equipment manufacturers. The group's quarterly revenue for Sep '07 was 5.42 millions of USD.

Primary SIC and add'l.: 3577

CIK No: 0000944075

Officers: Kevin J. Mills/46/CEO, Pres./$322,201.00, Mike L. Gifford/49/Exec. VP/$260,193.00, David W. Dunlap/CFO, Sec./$255,580.00, Leonard L. Ott/CTO, VP - Engineering, Interim, Kevin T. Scheier/51/VP - Sales, Solutions, Americas/$246,856.00, Peter K. Phillips/48/VP - Marketing, Robert J. Miller/57/VP - Engineering/$243,546.00, Tim Miller/VP - Worldwide Operations, Tom Noggle/VP - Engineering, Lee A. Baillif/47/VP, Controller, Robert C. Zink/Sr. VP - Worldwide Sales, Marketing, Jim Byers/Investor Relations Officer

Directors: Charlie Bass/66/Chmn., Gianluca Rattazzi/55/Dir., Enzo Torresi/63/Dir., Peter Sealey/67/Dir., Leon Malmed/70/Dir.

Owners: Gianluca Rattazzi, David W. Dunlap/1.70%, Insiders/22.20%, Enzo Torresi/1.00%, Kevin T. Scheier, Lee A. Baillif, Leon Malmed, Kevin J. Mills/2.60%, Peter K. Phillips, Micheal L. Gifford/2.10%, Charlie Bass/6.10%, Peter Sealey, Tim I. Miller, Robert J. Miller/2.20%, Leonard L. Ott/1.40%

Financial Data: Fiscal Year End:12/31   Latest Annual Data: 12/31/2006

Year	Sales	Net Income
2006	$24,981,000	-$2,912,000
2005	$25,034,000	-$167,000
2004	$26,130,000	$338,000

Curr. Assets:	$11,347,000	**Curr. Liab.:**	$6,886,000		
Plant, Equip.:	$742,000	**Total Liab.:**	$7,036,000	**Indic. Yr. Divd.:**	NA
Total Assets:	$22,787,000	**Net Worth:**	$15,751,000	**Debt/ Equity:**	0.0043

Sodexho Alliance

9801 Washingtonian Blvd., Gaithersburg, Maryland, 20878; **PH:** 1-33-130857203; http:// www.sodexho.com

General - Incorporation	France	**Stock**- Price on:12/24/2007	$73.04
Employees	NA	Stock Exchange	OTC
Auditor	PricewaterhouseCoopers LLP	Ticker Symbol	SDXAY
Stk Agt	Societe Generale	Outstanding Shares	155,910,000
Counsel	NA	E.P.S.	$3.06
DUNS No.	NA	Shareholders	NA

Business: The groups principle activity is to food and management services, remote site management, on-site clubs and retail outlets; service vouchers and cards and leisure services. The group operates from United States.

Primary SIC and add'l.: 7389 8744 5812 7999 4489

CIK No: 0001169715

Officers: Pierre Henry/Group COO, CEO - Service Vouchers, Cards, Michel Landel/Group CEO, Clodine Pincemin/Group Sr. VP - Communications - Sustainable Development, Damien Verdier/Group Sr. VP - Marketing, Rick Brockland/Pres. - Education USA, Food, Facilities Management Services, Steven Pangburn/Group Internal Audit, Sian Herbert-Jones/Group CFO, Philip Jansen/Group COO, Nicolas Japy/Group COO, Elisabeth Carpentier/Group Exec. VP, Group Chief Human Resources Officer, Christophe Solas/Pres. - China, Food, Facilities Management Services, Roberto Cirillo Cirillo/Group Sr. VP - Strategic Planning, Rohini Anand/Sr. VP, Group Chief Diversity Officer, Sylvia Metayer/Sr. VP, Group Financial Controller, Pierre Benaich/Investor Relations Contact (21 Officers included in Index)

Directors: Pierre Bellon/78/Chmn., Remi Baudin/78/Vice Chmn., Patricia Bellinger/47/Dir., Robert Baconnier/68/Dir., Astrid Bellon/39/Dir., Bernard Bellon/73/Dir., Francois-Xavier Bellon/43/Dir., Sophie Clamens/47/Dir., Paul Jeanbart/69/Dir., Charles Milhaud/65/Dir., Francois Perigot/82/Dir., Nathalie Szabo/44/Dir., Peter Thompson/62/Dir., Mark H.J. Tompkins/68/Dir.

Financial Data: Fiscal Year End:08/31   Latest Annual Data: 8/31/2006

Year	Sales	Net Income
2006	$16,421,114,000	$320,775,000
2005	$14,269,020,000	$189,488,000
2004	$13,901,930,000	$203,696,000

Curr. Assets:	$4,642,256,000	**Curr. Liab.:**	$4,775,698,000	**P/E Ratio:**	52.44
Plant, Equip.:	$551,733,000	**Total Liab.:**	$7,934,690,000	**Indic. Yr. Divd.:**	$1.060
Total Assets:	$10,012,029,000	**Net Worth:**	$2,077,339,000	**Debt/ Equity:**	NA

SoftBrands Inc

2 Meridian Crossings, Ste. 800, Minneapolis, MN, 55423; **PH:** 1-612-851-1500; **Fax:** 1-612-851-1560; http:// www.softbrands.com; **Email:** info@softbrands.com

General - Incorporation	DE	**Stock**- Price on:12/24/2007	$2.09
Employees	875	Stock Exchange	AMEX
Auditor	PricewaterhouseCoopers LLP	Ticker Symbol	SBN
Stk Agt	Wells Fargo Shareowner Services	Outstanding Shares	41,280,000
Counsel	NA	E.P.S.	NA
DUNS No.	NA	Shareholders	NA

Business: The group is a global leader in providing next-generation enterprise software for businesses in the hospitality and manufacturing sectors. With more than 4,000 customers in over 60 countries, the group has established a worldwide infrastructure for distribution, development, and support of enterprise software. The company worldwide headquarters are in Minneapolis, Minnesota. It has locations in United States, Latin America, United Kingdom, Africa, Australia, China, and India.

Primary SIC and add'l.: 7372

CIK No: 0001311926

Subsidiaries: AremisSoft Corporation

Officers: Randal B. Tofteland/Dir., Pres., CEO - Softbrands, Ralf Suerken/Sr. VP, GM - Manufacturing, Steven J. Vantassel/Sr. VP, GM - Hospitality, Gregg A. Waldon/Sr. VP, CFO, Susan Eich/Corporate Communications, Invester Relations

Directors: Randal B. Tofteland/Dir., Pres., CEO - Softbrands, George H. Ellis/58/Chmn., Dann V. Angeloff/Dir., Jeffrey Vorholt/Dir., Douglas W. Lewis/63/Dir., Elaine Wetmore/45/Dir., John Hunt/Dir.

Owners: Randal B. Tofteland/2.50%, Dann V. Angeloff, Insiders/7.90%, Capital Resource Partners IV, L.P./19.90%, Info-Quest SA/9.90%, Jeffrey Vorholt, Steven J. VanTassel, Ralf Suerken, John Hunt/22.30%, Kellogg Capital Group LLC/9.10%, George H. Ellis/4.00%, W. Douglas Lewis, Elaine Wetmore

Financial Data: Fiscal Year End:09/30   Latest Annual Data: 9/30/2006

Year	Sales	Net Income
2006	$69,289,000	-$16,218,000
2005	$70,781,000	$7,344,000

Curr. Assets:	$25,617,000	Curr. Liab.:	$36,382,000		
Plant, Equip.:	$2,787,000	Total Liab.:	$56,519,000	Indic. Yr. Divd.:	NA
Total Assets:	$75,047,000	Net Worth:	$18,528,000	Debt/ Equity:	1.0795

SofTech Inc

2 Highwood Dr., Tewksbury, MA, 01876; *PH:* 1-978-640-6222; *Fax:* 1-978-858-0440; *http://* www.softech.com; *Email:* info@softech.com

General - Incorporation	MA	Stock - Price on:12/24/2007	$0.1
Employees	62	Stock Exchange	OTC
Auditor	Vitale, Caturano & Co. Ltd	Ticker Symbol	SOFT
Stk Agt	Computershare Investor Services LLC	Outstanding Shares	12,210,000
Counsel	NA	E.P.S.	-$0.11
DUNS No.	05-348-0349	Shareholders	NA

Business: The group's principle activities are to develop, market, distribute and support cad/cam and product data management computer solutions. The group also provides hardware and a full array of service offerings in order to provide complete solutions to customers' mechanical and engineering problems. The services provided include hardware and software maintenance, installation, training, consulting, product designs and placement services. The products are cadra, designgateway, prospector, tooldesigner, expertcad, and expertcam, which are marketed to the plastic injection mold and tool and die industries. The group has sales offices in Europe and customer support offices in France, Germany and Italy. The competitors are parametric technology corporation, dassault, eds, autodesk and solidworks. The group's quarterly revenue for Aug '07 was 2.72 millions of USD.

Primary SIC and add'l.: 7379 7372 7371 7373

CIK No: 0000354260

Subsidiaries: Adra Systems Sarl, Adra Systems Srl, Information Decisions, Inc., SofTech GmbH, Workgroup Technology Corporation

Officers: Jean Croteau/Pres., Victor G. Bovey/51/VP - Engineering, Amy McGuire/CFO

Directors: William D. Johnston/61/Chmn., Timothy L. Tyler/54/Dir., Barry Bedford/50/Dir., Frederick A. Lake/Dir., Ronald A. Elenbaas/55/Dir., Michael Elliston/46/Dir.

Owners: William Johnston/44.50%, Joseph P. Mullaney/1.40%, Insiders/46.60%, Jean Croteau, Timothy L. Tyler, Victor G. Bovey, Frederick Lake, Ronald Elenbaas

Financial Data: Fiscal Year End:05/31   Latest Annual Data: 5/31/2006

Year	Sales	Net Income
2006	$12,478,000	-$1,332,000
2005	$12,120,000	-$1,425,000
2004	$12,294,000	-$1,853,000

Curr. Assets:	$3,020,000	Curr. Liab.:	$5,378,000		
Plant, Equip.:	$225,000	Total Liab.:	$18,538,000	Indic. Yr. Divd.:	NA
Total Assets:	$9,844,000	Net Worth:	-$8,694,000	Debt/ Equity:	NA

Softnet Technology Corp

485 RtE 1 S, Bldg. C, Ste. 350A, Iselin, NJ, 08830; *PH:* 1-908-212-1780; *Fax:* 1-908-212-1757; *http://* www.softnettechnology.com

General - Incorporation	NV	Stock - Price on:12/24/2007	$0.011
Employees	NA	Stock Exchange	OTC
Auditor	Bagell, Josephs, Levine & Co. LLC	Ticker Symbol	STTC
Stk Agt	Interwest Transfer Company, Inc.	Outstanding Shares	364,050,000
Counsel	NA	E.P.S.	-$0.017
DUNS No.	NA	Shareholders	NA

Business: The group's principle activities are the design, development and manufacture of biometrical time clocks and easy to use complete solutions using the available technologies. Its wholly owned subsidiaries, solutions technology inc and zingo sales ltd conduct the group's activities. Both the subsidiaries were acquired during the year 2002. Solutions technology inc manufactures the clocks that are used for tracking employees' time and attendance. It has developed the secureticme biometric ID system to solve the time and attendance needs of companies. Zingo sales is developing fixed based and hand held electronic bingo units for bingo halls. The group's quarterly revenue for Sep '07 was 2.39 millions of USD.

Primary SIC and add'l.: 3579 3578

CIK No: 0000051387

Subsidiaries: Clickese.com Inc., Indigo Technology Services, Inc., Net Centric Solutions, Inc, STI

Officers: James Booth/57/Chmn., CEO, Pres., Sec., Treasurer/$163,000.00, Kevin Holt/54/Dir., COO/$901,400.00

Directors: James Booth/57/Chmn., CEO, Pres., Sec., Treasurer, Darren Tietsworth/50/Dir., Dennis Goett/59/Dir., Kevin W. Remley/46/Dir.

Owners: Darren Tietsworth/0.14%, Kevin W. Remley/0.41%, Dennis Goett/0.14%, Kevin Holt/4.81%, Integrated Capital Partners, Inc./9.34%, Insiders/5.32%, James Booth/0.27%

Financial Data: Fiscal Year End:12/31   Latest Annual Data: 12/31/2006

Year	Sales	Net Income
2006	$6,213,000	-$7,334,000
2005	$514,000	-$3,800,000
2004	$344,000	-$3,259,000

Curr. Assets:	$585,000	Curr. Liab.:	$1,242,000		
Plant, Equip.:	$123,000	Total Liab.:	$1,242,000	Indic. Yr. Divd.:	NA
Total Assets:	$729,000	Net Worth:	-$513,000	Debt/ Equity:	NA

Sohu.com Inc

No.1 Pk., Zhongguancun E Rd., Haidian District, Beijing, 100084; *PH:* 86-1062726666; *http://* www.sohu.com

General - Incorporation	DE	Stock - Price on:12/24/2007	$28.83
Employees	1,971	Stock Exchange	NDQ
Auditor	PricewaterhouseCoopers	Ticker Symbol	SOHU
Stk Agt	Bank of New York	Outstanding Shares	36,830,000
Counsel	Timothy B. Bancroft-Goulston & Storrs	E.P.S.	$0.68
DUNS No.	NA	Shareholders	NA

Business: The group's principle activity is to provide Internet portal with e-commerce services, Web-based communications and community services in China. These services include online directory, which contained over 300,000 Chinese language Web listings and search engines. The group generates its revenues primarily through the sale of advertisements, promotions and sponsorships to advertisers and merchants. The group operates through its subsidiaries in China, Hong Kong and the United States of America. It has sales and marketing offices in Beijing, shanghai, guangzhou and Hong Kong. The group's qaurterly revenue for Sep '07 was 51.52 millions of USD.

Primary SIC and add'l.: 7375 7319

CIK No: 0001104188

Subsidiaries: All Honest International Limited, Beijing Sohu Interactive Software Co., Ltd., Beijing Sohu New Era Information Technology Co., Ltd., Go2Map Inc., Go2Map Software (Beijing) Co., Ltd, Kylie Enterprises Limited, Marvel Hero Limited, Sogou Inc., Sogou.com Limited, Sohu ITC Information Technology (Beijing) Co., Ltd., Sohu.com (Hong Kong) Ltd., Sohu.com (Search) Limited, Sohu.com Limited

Officers: Charles Zhang/Chmn., Founder, CEO/$768,849.00, Carol Yu/CFO, Co - Pres./$1,019,531.00, Belinda Wang/Co - Pres., Chief Marketing Officer/$394,378.00, Yu Gong/COO/$455,535.00, Chen Luming/VP - Olympic Project, Xiaochuan Wang/VP, Head - Research & Development, Research and Development Center, Gang Fang/VP - Products, Erin Sheng/Mgr. - Investor Relations, Corporate Communications

Directors: Charles Zhang/Chmn., Founder, CEO, Edward Roberts/Dir., Charles Huang/Dir., Dave Qi/Dir., Shi Wang/Dir., Jianjun Wang/Dir., Zhonghan Deng/40/Dir.

Owners: Charles Zhang/23.24%, Edward Roberts/2.25%, Dave (Belinda) Qi Wang, Charles Huang, Gong Yu, Photon Group Limited/21.52%, Shi Wang, Insiders/26.18%, Carol Yu, Xin Wang

Financial Data: Fiscal Year End:12/31   Latest Annual Data: 12/31/2006

Year	Sales	Net Income
2006	$134,236,000	$25,885,000
2005	$108,348,000	$29,781,000
2004	$103,209,000	$35,637,000

Curr. Assets:	$159,484,000	Curr. Liab.:	$97,575,000	P/E Ratio:	45.05
Plant, Equip.:	$21,453,000	Total Liab.:	$97,628,000	Indic. Yr. Divd.:	NA
Total Assets:	$253,591,000	Net Worth:	$155,963,000	Debt/ Equity:	NA

Soil Biogenics Ltd

595 Burrard St., Vancouver, BC, V7X 1A2; *PH:* 1-604-687-4432; *Fax:* 1-604-687-4709; *http://* www.soilbiogenics.com; *Email:* info@soilbiogenics.com

General - Incorporation		Stock - Price on:12/24/2007	$0.7
Employees	NA	Stock Exchange	OTC
Auditor	NA	Ticker Symbol	SOBGF
Stk Agt	Interwest Transfer Company, Inc.	Outstanding Shares	NA
Counsel	NA	E.P.S.	NA
DUNS No.	NA	Shareholders	NA

Business: The groups principle activity is in the business of bio organic fertilizer production and distribution in the Russia Federation. The group operates from Russia.

Primary SIC and add'l.: 2874

CIK No: 0001049576

Subsidiaries: Biogrunt, Biopotok-Piksa, Piksa Inter LLC, Piksa Research and Production Association LLC, Soil Biogenics Ltd, Soil Biogenics S.L.

Officers: Agustin Gomez De Segura/Dir., CFO, CEO, Pres., Vladimir Bashkin/Advisory Counsel, Victor Rubio/Advisory Counsel

Directors: Agustin Gomez De Segura/Dir., CFO, CEO, Pres., Alexander Becker/Dir.

Owners: Alexander Becker/6.69%, Redbridge Minerals (Overseas) Ltd./6.42%, Norbex Holdings Ltd./6.42%, Kastalia Ltd./8.66%, Alexei Y. Sementsow/7.42%

Financial Data: Fiscal Year End:NA   Latest Annual Data: 12/31/2005

Year	Sales	Net Income
2005	$1,818,000	-$12,000
2004	$1,810,000	$209,000
2003	$369,000	-$347,000

Curr. Assets:	$3,263,000	Curr. Liab.:	$1,068,000		
Plant, Equip.:	$95,000	Total Liab.:	$1,068,000	Indic. Yr. Divd.:	NA
Total Assets:	$3,396,000	Net Worth:	$2,329,000	Debt/ Equity:	NA

Solar Energy Ltd

145 - 925 W Georgia St., Vancover, BC, V6C 3L2; *PH:* 1-604-669-4771; *Fax:* 1-604-669-4731; *http://* www.solarenergylimited.com; *Email:* info@SolarEnergyLimited.com

General - Incorporation	DE	Stock - Price on:12/24/2007	$0.56
Employees	NA	Stock Exchange	OTC
Auditor	Williams & Webster, P.S	Ticker Symbol	SLREE
Stk Agt	Madison Stock Transfer, Inc.	Outstanding Shares	NA
Counsel	NA	E.P.S.	NA
DUNS No.	NA	Shareholders	NA

Business: The groups principal activities include developing cost effective solutions for global issues related to water, energy and pollution. In August 2005, the group acquired Planktos, Inc. and D2Fusion Inc. The group operates from the United States.

Primary SIC and add'l.: 4931

CIK No: 0001058322

Subsidiaries: D2Fusion, Inc., Hydro-Air Technologies, Planktos, Inc.,, Renewable Energy Ltd, Sunspring Inc

Officers: Andrew Wallace/58/Dir., CEO, CFO, Principal Accounting Officer

Directors: Andrew Wallace/58/Dir., CEO, CFO, Principal Accounting Officer, William Sherban/75/Dir., Toby Thatcher/29/Dir.

Owners: Baycove Capital Corp./9.10%, Insiders, Andrew Wallace, Central Shipping Investment, Inc./7.10%, Russ George/18.00%, William Sherban

Financial Data: Fiscal Year End:12/31 Latest Annual Data: 12/31/2006

Year	Sales	Net Income
2006	NA	-$1,609,000
2005	NA	-$6,603,000
2004	NA	-$91,000

Curr. Assets:	$230,000	Curr. Liab.:	$532,000		
Plant, Equip.:	NA	Total Liab.:	$1,594,000	Indic. Yr. Divd.:	NA
Total Assets:	$235,000	Net Worth:	-$1,359,000	Debt/ Equity:	NA

Solar EnerTech Corp

1600 Adams Dr., Menlo Park, CA, 94025; ; *http://* www.solarenertech.com; *Email:* investors@solarenertech.com

General - Incorporation	NV	Stock- Price on:12/24/2007	$1.5
Employees	48	Stock Exchange	OTC
Auditor	Malone & Bailey, PC	Ticker Symbol	SOEN
Stk Agt	Empire Stock Transfer Inc.	Outstanding Shares	78,810,000
Counsel	DLA Piper US	E.P.S.	-$0.38
DUNS No.	NA	Shareholders	NA

Business: The groups principal activities include manufacturing and distribution of PV Cells and established a marketing, purchasing and distribution arm. The group operates from the United States.

Primary SIC and add'l.: 3674

CIK No: 0001307873

Officers: Leo Shi Young/Dir., CEO, Pres., Shi Jian Yin/VP, Dir., COO, Zhong Quan Ma/CTO, April Zhong/Sr. VP, Yuhong Zhang/Dir. - Solar Energy Productions, Bill Zima/Investor Relations, Anthea Chung/CFO

Directors: Leo Shi Young/Dir., CEO, Pres., Shi Jian Yin/VP, Dir., COO, Fang Xie/Dir.

Owners: Insiders/28.11%, Ming Wai Anthea Chung, Leo Shi Young/21.29%, Jean Blanchard/33.94%, Frank Fang Xie/1.87%, Shi Jian Yin/4.44%, Donald Morgan

Financial Data: Fiscal Year End:09/30 Latest Annual Data: 09/30/2006

Year	Sales	Net Income
2006	NA	-$27,888,000

Curr. Assets:	$2,840,000	Curr. Liab.:	$3,323,000		
Plant, Equip.:	$809,000	Total Liab.:	$3,323,000	Indic. Yr. Divd.:	NA
Total Assets:	$4,221,000	Net Worth:	$898,000	Debt/ Equity:	NA

Solar Thin Films Inc

Formerly: American United Global Inc
Koerberki t 36, Budapest, 1112; *PH:* 36-124-82880

General - Incorporation	DE	Stock- Price on:12/24/2007	NA
Employees	NA	Stock Exchange	OTC
Auditor	Russell Bedford Stefanou Mirchandani	Ticker Symbol	SLTN
Stk Agt	NA	Outstanding Shares	NA
Counsel	NA	E.P.S.	NA
DUNS No.	13-740-6013	Shareholders	NA

Business: The group intends to focus it's business strategy on acquisitions of operating businesses in various sectors. Currently, the group's primary business interest is its 13% ownership of the common stock of western power and equipment corp (western). Western markets, rents and services various types of construction, industrial and agricultural equipment. The group operates through 15 facilities in Nevada, Oregon, Washington, California and Alaska. The group sells its products to contractors, governmental agencies and other customers primarily for use in the construction of residential and commercial buildings, roads, levees, dams and other projects.

Primary SIC and add'l.: 7353 9999 6719 5082

CIK No: 0000859792

Subsidiaries: Acquisition Corp., Lifetime Acquisition Corp., Merger

Officers: Csaba Toro/41/Dir., CEO

Directors: Csaba Toro/41/Dir., CEO, Zoltan Kiss/73/Chmn.

Owners: Joseph Gregory Kiss/9.20%, Zoltan Kiss/19.80%, Csaba Toro/3.70%, Maria Gabriella Kiss/10.60%, Insiders/28.70%, Michael Metter, Rubin Family Irrevocable Trust/12.30%, Laszlo Farkas/6.00%

Financial Data: Fiscal Year End:12/31 Latest Annual Data: 12/31/2006

Year	Sales	Net Income
2006	$2,427,000	$2,859,000
2005	NA	$602,000
2004	NA	-$2,296,000

Curr. Assets:	$6,090,000	Curr. Liab.:	$4,976,000		
Plant, Equip.:	$629,000	Total Liab.:	$8,076,000	Indic. Yr. Divd.:	NA
Total Assets:	$7,225,000	Net Worth:	-$806,000	Debt/ Equity:	NA

Solectron Corp

847 Gibraltar Dr, Milpitas, CA, 95035; *PH:* 1-408-957-8500; *http://* www.solectron.com

General - Incorporation	DE	Stock- Price on:12/24/2007	$3.83
Employees	44,500	Stock Exchange	NA
Auditor	KPMG LLP	Ticker Symbol	NA
Stk Agt	Computershare Investor Services LLC	Outstanding Shares	909,210,000
Counsel	Wilson Sonsini Goodrich & Rosati	E.P.S	$0.08
DUNS No.	08-701-1003	Shareholders	NA

Business: The groups principle activity is to provide supply-chain and product life-cycle services to original equipment manufacturers around the world. The group operates from United States.

Primary SIC and add'l.: 7379 7373 8711 7371

CIK No: 0000835541

Subsidiaries: Acn 080 683 003 Pty Limited, Blue Star Engineering Ltd., C-MAC do Brasil Ltd., C-MAC Holdings Ltd., C-MAC Invotronics Inc., C-MAC Kanata Inc., C-MAC Microcircuits GmbH, C-MAC Wongs Industries Holdings Ltd., Danayai ve Ticaret AS [aka Solectron Turkey], Distribuidora Solectron Chile Limitada, Marplace (Number 382) Limited, Morino Electroplating (S)Pte. Ltd., Navox Corporation, Percentage, PT Solectron Technology Indonesia 100 Subsidiaries included in the Index

Officers: Paul Tufano/55/Exec. VP, Interim CEO, Dave Purvis/56/CTO, Exec. VP, Marty Neese/46/Exec. VP - Operations, Douglas Britt/43/Exec. VP - Sales, Accounting Management, Paulett H. Eberhart/Corp. Dir., Heinz Fridrich/Corp. Dir., William R. Graber/Corp. Dir., Wesley M. C. Scott/Corp. Dir., Cyril Yansouni/Corp. Dir., Todd Duchene/44/Exec. VP, General Counsel, Sec., Craig London/62/Exec. VP - Solectron Global Services, Kevin O'Connor/49/Exec. VP, Chief Administrative Officer, Roop Lakkaraju/Sr. VP, Interim CFO

Directors: William A. Hasler/Chmn., Richard A. D'Amore/Dir., Paul R. Low/Dir.

Owners: Douglas Britt, Insiders/1.60%, AXA/14.00%, Capital Research and Management Company/5.90%, TCW Group, Inc./5.90%, Richard A. DAmore, Paul R. Low, Cyril Yansouni, William R. Graber, David Purvis, Warren Ligan, Craig London, Wesley C.M. Scott, FMR Corp./11.50%, Heinz Fridrich (18 Owners included in Index)

Financial Data: Fiscal Year End:08/26 Latest Annual Data: 8/25/2006

Year	Sales	Net Income
2006	$10,560,700,000	$133,200,000
2005	$10,441,100,000	$3,400,000
2004	$11,638,300,000	-$168,900,000

Curr. Assets:	$4,666,400,000	Curr. Liab.:	$2,159,100,000	P/E Ratio:	47.88
Plant, Equip.:	$726,600,000	Total Liab.:	$3,438,200,000	Indic. Yr. Divd.:	NA
Total Assets:	$5,817,000,000	Net Worth:	$2,378,800,000	Debt/ Equity:	0.2516

Solexa Inc

25861 Industrial Blvd., Hayward, CA, 94545; *PH:* 1-510-670-9300; *http://* www.lynxgen.com

General - Incorporation	DE	Stock- Price on:12/24/2007	NA
Employees	118	Stock Exchange	NA
Auditor	Ernst & Young LLP	Ticker Symbol	NA
Stk Agt	Computershare Investor Services LLC	Outstanding Shares	NA
Counsel	NA	E.P.S.	NA
DUNS No.	79-717-9611	Shareholders	NA

Business: The group's principal activities are to develop and apply technologies for the discovery of gene expression patterns and genomic variations. These technologies are based on the group's proprietary cloning procedure, megaclone. The group through its megaclone technology develops and commercializes processes that are aimed at handling and/or analyzing the dna molecules or fragments in biological samples. The technologies developed based on the megaclone include massively parallel signature sequencing technology, megasort technology and megatype technology. These are used in the pharmaceutical, biotechnology and agricultural industries. The group operates in North America, Asia and Europe.

Primary SIC and add'l.: 8731 7375 8099

CIK No: 0000913275

Subsidiaries: Lynx Therapeutics, GmbH, Solexa Limited

Solitario Resources Corp

4251 Kipling St., Ste. 390, Wheat Ridge, CO, 80033; *PH:* 1-303-534-1030; *Fax:* 1-303-534-1809; *http://* www.solitarioresources.com

General - Incorporation	CO	Stock- Price on:12/24/2007	$4.78
Employees	NA	Stock Exchange	AMEX
Auditor	Solomon Pearl Blum Heymann & Stich	Ticker Symbol	XPL
Stk Agt	Computershare Investor Services LLC	Outstanding Shares	29,610,000
Counsel	Solomon, Blum Heymann & Stich, LLP	E.P.S.	-$0.076
DUNS No.	NA	Shareholders	NA

Business: The groups principal activity is to acquire base metal properties. The group operates from the United States, Canada and Brazil.

Primary SIC and add'l.: 1021 1031 1044 1041

CIK No: 0000917225

Subsidiaries: Altoro Gold (BVI) Corp, Altoro Gold Corp., Altoro Mineracao, Ltd, Compania Minera Andes del Sur S.A, Minera Altoro (BVI) Ltd, Minera Altoro Brazil (BVI) Corp, Minera Andes (BVI) Corp., Minera Bongara S.A, Minera Solitario Peru, S.A, Minera Soloco, S.A., Mineracao Solitario Brazil, Ltd

Officers: Christopher E. Herald/Dir., CEO/$571,203.00, James R. Maronick/CFO/$352,773.00, Walter H. Hunt/Pres. - South American Operations/$424,856.00

Directors: Christopher E. Herald/Dir., CEO, Steven A. Webster/Chmn., Mark E. Jones/Vice Chmn., John Hainey/Dir., Leonard Harris/Dir., Brian Labadie/Dir.

Owners: Walter H. Hunt/1.70%, Insiders/13.90%, Newmont Mining Corporation of Canada/9.10%, Christopher E. Herald/3.10%, Sprott Securities/16.10%, James R. Maronick/2.30%, Steven A. Webster/4.00%, John Hainey, Mark E. Jones/1.60%, Brian Labadie, Leonard Harris

Financial Data: Fiscal Year End:12/31 Latest Annual Data: 12/31/2006

Year	Sales	Net Income
2006	NA	-$3,183,000
2005	NA	-$2,080,000
2004	NA	-$2,925,000

Curr. Assets:	$6,387,000	Curr. Liab.:	$1,832,000		
Plant, Equip.:	$2,687,000	Total Liab.:	$5,994,000	Indic. Yr. Divd.:	NA
Total Assets:	$25,038,000	Net Worth:	$19,044,000	Debt/ Equity:	NA

Solitron Devices Inc

3301 Electronics Way, West Palm Beach, FL, 33407; *PH:* 1-561-848-4311; *Fax:* 1-561-863-5946; *http://* www.solitrondevices.com; *Email:* sales@solitrondevices.com

General - Incorporation	DE	Stock- Price on:12/24/2007	$1.7
Employees	85	Stock Exchange	OTC
Auditor	Deleon & Co P.A	Ticker Symbol	SODI
Stk Agt	Berkovits, Lago & Co. LLP	Outstanding Shares	2,260,000
Counsel	NA	E.P.S.	$0.28
DUNS No.	00-147-9187	Shareholders	NA

Business: The group's principal activity is to design, develop, manufacture and market solid state semiconductor components and related devices. The group's products consist of control hybrid, junction and power mosfets, power transistor and field effect transistors. The semiconductor products classified as active electronic components control and direct the flow of electrical current by means of control signal such as voltage or current. Active electronic components include bipolar transistors and mos transistors. The products are sold to the us government, defense and aerospace markets. The products are exported to Europe, Canada and Latin America, Far East and Middle East.

Primary SIC and add'l.: 3674

CIK No: 0000091668

Subsidiaries: Solitron Specialty Products, Inc.

Officers: Jesse Quinn/Dir. - Operations

Owners: Steven T. Newby/11.40%, Insiders/29.75%, John Stayduhar Revocable Trust/12.62%, Shevach Saraf/28.74%, Joseph Schlig, Jacob Davis, Alexander C. Toppan/7.61%

Financial Data: Fiscal Year End:02/28 **Latest Annual Data:** 2/28/2007

Year	Sales		Net Income
2007	$7,760,000		$432,000
2006	$8,342,000		$1,941,000
2005	$8,055,000		$448,000
Curr. Assets:	$6,991,000	Curr. Liab.:	$1,812,000	P/E Ratio:	6.54
Plant, Equip.:	$489,000	Total Liab.:	$1,980,000	Indic. Yr. Divd.:	NA
Total Assets:	$7,533,000	Net Worth:	$5,553,000	Debt/ Equity:	NA

Solomon Technologies Inc

7375 Benedict Ave., Benedict, MD, 20612; **PH:** 1-727-859-4447;
http:// www.solomontechnologies.com; **Email:** info@solomontechnologies.com

General - Incorporation	DE	Stock - Price on:12/24/2007	$0.33
Employees	51	Stock Exchange	OTC
Auditor	UHY LLP	Ticker Symbol	SOLM
Stk Agt	Computershare Trust Co	Outstanding Shares	36,060,000
Counsel	NA	E.P.S	-$0.46
DUNS No.	NA	Shareholders	NA

Business: The group's principal activity is to develop and sell fully integrated electric power drive systems called as 'st electric propulsion systems' for marine applications. Its development of a patented technology 'electric wheel' and related proprietary technologies consisting of two shaftless, brushless, direct current permanent magnet electric motors connected by a planetary gear-set driving an output power shaft, all within a single, self-contained sealed housing. The principal market for the group is the recreational displacement hull component of the marine industry.

Primary SIC and add'l.: 3621

CIK No: 0001240722

Officers: Gary G. Brandt/49/CEO, Gary M. Laskowski/54/Chmn., VP, Peter W. De Vecchis/59/Pres., Michael Damelio/50/Dir., VP, Samuel F. Occhipinti/61/CFO

Directors: Gary M. Laskowski/54/Chmn., VP, Michael Damelio/50/Dir., VP, Jonathan D. Betts/47/Dir., Duane L. Crisco/47/Dir., David J. Parcells/49/Dir.

Owners: Gary M. Laskowski/3.40%, Thomas A. Kell, Jonathan D. Betts/3.70%, Peter W. DeVecchis, Duane L. Crisco, Kenneth M. Przysiecki, Samuel F. Occhipinti, Michael A. DAmelio/12.70%, D. Shannon LeRoy, Insiders/21.60%, Gary G. Brandt

Financial Data: Fiscal Year End:12/31 **Latest Annual Data:** 12/31/2006

Year	Sales		Net Income
2006	$2,279,000		-$16,263,000
2005	$69,000		-$6,633,000
2004	$370,000		-$6,358,000
Curr. Assets:	$2,889,000	Curr. Liab.:	$6,915,000		
Plant, Equip.:	$105,000	Total Liab.:	$6,915,000	Indic. Yr. Divd.:	NA
Total Assets:	$7,790,000	Net Worth:	$875,000	Debt/ Equity:	NA

Solstice Resorts Inc

Formerly: DTLL Inc
628 Harbor View Ln., Petoskey, MN, 49770; **PH:** 1-206-339-9221; *http://* solsticeresorts.com

General - Incorporation	MN	Stock - Price on:12/24/2007	$0.4
Employees	NA	Stock Exchange	NA
Auditor	Most & Co., LLP	Ticker Symbol	NA
Stk Agt	NA	Outstanding Shares	25,800,000
Counsel	NA	E.P.S	-$0.35
DUNS No.	NA	Shareholders	NA

Business: The group's principle activity is to seek merger candidates or asset purchase transactions. It previously manufactured and marketed dental related products. On Mar 20, 2003, the group's shareholders approved the sale of substantially all its assets to drai, llc, and ceased its business operations as of the close of business on Mar 20, 2003. The group operates from United States.

Primary SIC and add'l.: 9999

CIK No: 0000356767

Officers: Dual Cooper/61/Dir., CEO, Pres., Dennis Piotrowski/67/Dir., CFO

Directors: Dual Cooper/61/Dir., CEO, Pres., Dennis Piotrowski/67/Dir., CFO, William Thompson/68/Dir.

Owners: John & Kelly Paulsen JTE/5.00%, Dhru Desai/5.00%, Rotate Black, LLC/48.00%, Dennis Piotrowski/4.00%, Dual Cooper/8.00%

Financial Data: Fiscal Year End:12/31 **Latest Annual Data:** 12/31/2006

Year	Sales		Net Income
2006	NA		-$5,971,000
2005	NA		-$1,469,000
2004	NA		-$581,000
Curr. Assets:	$74,000	Curr. Liab.:	$408,000		
Plant, Equip.:	NA	Total Liab.:	$512,000	Indic. Yr. Divd.:	NA
Total Assets:	$1,634,000	Net Worth:	$1,122,000	Debt/ Equity:	0.0987

Soltera Mining Corp

Formerly: Atlin Mineral Exploration Corp
1005-289 Drake St., Vancouver, BC, V6B5Z5; **PH:** 1-604-732-1304

General - Incorporation	NV	Stock - Price on:12/24/2007	NA
Employees	NA	Stock Exchange	OTC
Auditor	Manning Elliott LLP	Ticker Symbol	SLTA
Stk Agt	Empire Stock Transfer Inc.	Outstanding Shares	NA
Counsel	NA	E.P.S	NA
DUNS No.	NA	Shareholders	NA

Business: The groups principal activity is to explore minerals and natural gas. The group operates from the United States and Canada.

Primary SIC and add'l.: 1081

CIK No: 0001348610

Officers: Nadwynn Sing/48/Dir., CEO, CFO, Pres., Sec., Treasurer

Directors: Nadwynn Sing/48/Dir., CEO, CFO, Pres., Sec., Treasurer

Owners: Nadwynn Sing/58.70%, Insiders/58.70%

Financial Data: Fiscal Year End:10/31 **Latest Annual Data:** 10/31/2006

Year	Sales		Net Income
2006	NA		-$31,000
Curr. Assets:	$27,000	Curr. Liab.:	$1,000		
Plant, Equip.:	NA	Total Liab.:	$1,000	Indic. Yr. Divd.:	NA
Total Assets:	$27,000	Net Worth:	$26,000	Debt/ Equity:	NA

Solutia Inc

575 Maryville Ctr. Dr., St. Louis, MO, 63141; **PH:** 1-314-674-1000; **Fax:** 1-314-674-1585;
http:// www.solutia.com; **Email:** info@solutia.com

General - Incorporation	DE	Stock - Price on:12/24/2007	$0.27
Employees	5,100	Stock Exchange	OTC
Auditor	Deloitte & Touche LLP	Ticker Symbol	SOLUQ
Stk Agt	American Stock Transfer & Trust Co.	Outstanding Shares	104,460,000
Counsel	NA	E.P.S	-$0.95
DUNS No.	04-085-3731	Shareholders	NA

Business: The groups principle activities include manufacturing and marketing chemical-based materials for consumer and industrial applications. The group operates through two business segments namely performance products and integrated nylon segments. The groupss products include laminated safety glass and after-market applications and specialties, including water treatment chemicals, heat transfer fluids and aviation hydraulic fluid. The groups nylon products include polymers and fibers. In the year 2007 the group acquired Akzo Nobel. The group operates from United States.

Primary SIC and add'l.: 2821 2819

CIK No: 0001043382

Subsidiaries: AMCIS AG, CarboGen AG., CPFilms Inc., CPFilms Vertriebs GmbH, Monchem International, Inc., Monchem, Inc, Solchem Netherlands C.V., Solutia Brasil Ltda., Solutia Canada Inc, Solutia Chemical Co., Ltd., Suzhou, Solutia Chemicals Iberica S.L., Solutia Chemicals India Private Limited, Solutia Europe S.A./N.V., Solutia Greater China, Inc, Solutia International Trading (Shanghai) Co., Ltd. 28 Subsidiaries included in the Index

Officers: Jeffry N. Quinn/Chmn., CEO, Pres., James R. Voss/Sr. VP - Business Operations, Max W. McCombs/VP - Environment, Safety, Health, Kent J. Davies/Sr. VP, Luc De Temmerman/Sr. VP, Jonathon P. Wright/Sr. VP, Robert T. Debolt/VP - Strategy, Rosemary L. Klein/Sr. VP, General Counsel, Corp. Sec., James M. Sullivan/CFO, Sr. VP, Timothy J. Spihlman/VP, Controller

Directors: Jeffry N. Quinn/Chmn., CEO, Pres., Paul H. Hatfield/72/Dir., Robert H. Jenkins/64/Dir., Frank A. Metz/74/Dir., Patrick J. Mulcahy/64/Dir., Sally G. Narodick/62/Dir., John B. Slaughter/73/Dir.

Owners: Ardsley Advisory Partners/6.99%

Financial Data: Fiscal Year End:12/31 **Latest Annual Data:** 12/31/2006

Year	Sales		Net Income
2006	$2,905,000,000		$11,000,000
2005	$2,825,000,000		$8,000,000
2004	$2,697,000,000		-$316,000,000
Curr. Assets:	$848,000,000	Curr. Liab.:	$1,124,000,000		
Plant, Equip.:	$795,000,000	Total Liab.:	$3,472,000,000	Indic. Yr. Divd.:	NA
Total Assets:	$2,055,000,000	Net Worth:	-$1,417,000,000	Debt/ Equity:	NA

Solution Technology International Inc

685 Mosser Rd., Ste. 11, McHenry, MD, 21541; **PH:** 1-301-387-6900; *http://* www.stius.com;
Email: sales-info-americas@stius.com

General - Incorporation	DE	Stock - Price on:12/24/2007	$0.0042
Employees	4	Stock Exchange	OTC
Auditor	Herman, Lagor, Hopkins & Meeks, P.A.	Ticker Symbol	STNL
Stk Agt	American Stock Transfer & Trust Co.	Outstanding Shares	54,670,000
Counsel	NA	E.P.S	-$0.08
DUNS No.	NA	Shareholders	NA

Business: The groups principle activity is to market a web based, multi language, multi currency software solution to the domestic and international insurance and reinsurance industry. The group markets its product under the tradename SurSITE(R). The group operates from the United States.

Primary SIC and add'l.: 5734

CIK No: 0001000285

Officers: Dan L. Jonson/Dir., CEO, Pres., Michael H. Pollack/CFO, Krishna K. Natarajan/Program Mgr. - Application Architect

Directors: Dan L. Jonson/Dir., CEO, Pres., Michael B. Shor/Dir., Mark D. Spaeth/Dir., Andrew J. Larsen/Member - Advisory Board

Owners: Michael B. Shor/3.30%, Dan L. Jonson/31.30%, Mark Spaeth

Financial Data: Fiscal Year End:12/31 **Latest Annual Data:** 12/31/2006

Year	Sales		Net Income
2006	NA		-$1,622,000
2005	NA		-$2,329,000
2004	$940,000		-$736,000
Curr. Assets:	$64,000	Curr. Liab.:	$5,569,000		
Plant, Equip.:	$27,000	Total Liab.:	$7,146,000	Indic. Yr. Divd.:	NA
Total Assets:	$547,000	Net Worth:	-$6,600,000	Debt/ Equity:	NA

Solvay Bank Corp NY

1537 Milton Ave, Solvay, NY, 13209; *PH:* 1-315-468-1661

General - Incorporation		Stock - Price on:12/24/2007 ....$52
Employees...NA		Stock Exchange..OTC
Auditor ....NA		Ticker Symbol...SOBS
Stk Agt...NA		Outstanding Shares ....NA
Counsel...NA		E.P.S...NA
DUNS No..NA		Shareholders..NA

Business: The groups principle activity is to provide recruiting services. The groups service area includes the research and development, engineering, marketing, sales, information technology and manufacturing industries. The group operates from United States.

Primary SIC and add'l.: 6022

CIK No: 0000809754

Financial Data: Fiscal Year End:NA   *Latest Annual Data:* 12/31/2002

Year	Sales	Net Income
2002	$26,169,000	$4,332,000
2001	$27,086,000	$3,629,000
2000	$26,214,000	$3,304,000

Curr. Assets:	$59,167,000	Curr. Liab.:	$373,970,000		
Plant, Equip.:	$4,682,000	Total Liab.:	$376,314,000	Indic. Yr. Divd.:	NA
Total Assets:	$409,925,000	Net Worth:	$33,611,000	Debt/ Equity:	NA

Somanetics Corp

1653 E Maple Rd., Troy, MI, 48083; *PH:* 1-248-689-3050; *Fax:* 1-248-689-4272; *http://* www.somanetics.net

General - Incorporation ....MI		Stock - Price on:12/24/2007 ....$18.69
Employees..84		Stock Exchange..NDQ
Auditor ....Deloitte & Touche LLP		Ticker Symbol..SMTS
Stk Agt..... American Stock Transfer & Trust Co.		Outstanding Shares 13,180,000
Counsel........ Honigman Miller Schwartz & Cohn		E.P.S..$0.85
DUNS No.............................05-247-5951		Shareholders..NA

Business: The group's principle activities include developing, manufacturing and marketing invos cerebral oximeter, the non-invasive patient monitoring systems. The system continuously measures the changes in the blood oxygen level in the brain. Invos analyzes various characteristics of human blood and tissue by measuring and analyzing low-intensity visible and near-infrared light transmitted into portions of the body. The cerebral oximeter is a relatively inexpensive, portable and easy-to-use monitoring system placed at a patient's bedside in hospital critical care areas, especially operating rooms, recovery rooms, intensive care units and emergency rooms. The company also develops correstore system for use in cardiac repair and reconstruction including heart surgeries called surgical ventricular restoration. The products of the company are marketed to cardiac, cardiovascular and vascular surgeons, neurosurgeons and anesthesiologists in the United States, Europe and Japan. The group operates from United States.

Primary SIC and add'l.: 3845

CIK No: 0000704328

Subsidiaries: FMR Corp

Officers: Bruce J. Barrett/Dir., CEO, Pres./$627,619.00, Ronald A. Widman/VP - Medical Affairs, Mary Ann Victor/VP - Communications, Administration, Sec./$267,626.00, William M. Iacona/CFO, VP, Controller, Treasurer/$244,414.00, Richard S. Scheuing/VP - Research, Development, Pamela A. Winters/VP - Operations, Dominic J. Spadafore/VP - Sales, Marketing/$257,534.00

Directors: Bruce J. Barrett/Dir., CEO, Pres., James I. Ausman/Dir., Daniel S. Follis/Dir., Robert R. Henry/Dir., Richard R. Sorensen/Dir.

Owners: Mary Ann Victor/1.30%, MFC Global Investment Management (U.S.), LLC/5.20%, Dominic J. Spadafore/1.00%, James E. Flynn/5.60%, William M. Iacona, Daniel S. Follis, FMR Corp./14.80%, Insiders/10.70%, Bruce J. Barrett/5.40%, James I. Ausman, Robert R. Henry/2.10%

Financial Data: Fiscal Year End:11/30   *Latest Annual Data:* 11/30/2006

Year	Sales	Net Income
2006	$28,701,000	$10,400,000
2005	$20,509,000	$7,751,000
2004	$12,609,000	$8,707,000

Curr. Assets:	$60,173,000	Curr. Liab.:	$2,205,000	P/E Ratio:	23.96
Plant, Equip.:	$2,124,000	Total Liab.:	$2,205,000	Indic. Yr. Divd.:	NA
Total Assets:	$92,423,000	Net Worth:	$90,218,000	Debt/ Equity:	NA

Somanta Pharmaceuticals Inc

19200 Von Karman Ave., Irvine, CA, 92612; *PH:* 1-949-477-8090; *Fax:* 1-949-706-3698; *http://* www.somanta.com; *Email:* a.coelho@somanta.com

General - Incorporation ....DE		Stock - Price on:12/24/2007 ....$0.25
Employees..4		Stock Exchange...OTC
Auditor ....Stonefield Josephson, Inc.		Ticker Symbol..SMPM
Stk Agt..... American Stock Transfer & Trust Co.		Outstanding Shares 14,290,000
Counsel...NA		E.P.S..-$0.09
DUNS No..NA		Shareholders..NA

Business: The groups principal activity is engaged in the development of drugs primarily for the treatment of cancer. The group is in license substances designed for anti cancer therapy in order along the regulatory and clinical pathway towards commercial approval. In January 2006, the group acquired Somanta Incorporated. The group operates from the United States.

Primary SIC and add'l.: 2834

CIK No: 0000888671

Subsidiaries: Somanta Incorporated, Somanta Limited

Officers: Agamemnon A. Epenetos/Dir., CEO, Pres., Terrance J. Bruggeman/Executive Chmn., Acting CFOs

Directors: Agamemnon A. Epenetos/Dir., CEO, Pres., Terrance J. Bruggeman/Executive Chmn., Acting CFOs, Michael R.D. Ashton/Dir., Jeffrey B. Davis/Dir., John R. Gibson/56/Dir., Kathleen H. Van Sleen/Dir.

Owners: Whalehaven Capital Fund Limited, Whalehaven Capital Fund Limited, Walbrook Trustees, Alpha Capital AG, SCO Capital Partners LLC, SCO Capital Partners LLC, XMark JV Investment Partners, LLC, Jeffrey B. Davis, Alpha Capital AG, John R. Gibson, Jeffrey B. Davis, XMark Opportunity Fund, L.P., XMark Opportunity Fund Ltd., XMark Opportunity Fund, L.P., XMark JV Investment Partners, LLC *(17 Owners included in Index)*

Financial Data: Fiscal Year End:04/30   *Latest Annual Data:* 04/30/2007

Year	Sales	Net Income
2007	$1,000	-$7,496,000

Curr. Assets:	$49,000	Curr. Liab.:	$8,245,000	P/E Ratio:	30.12
Plant, Equip.:	$17,000	Total Liab.:	$8,245,000	Indic. Yr. Divd.:	NA
Total Assets:	$67,000	Net Worth:	-$8,177,000	Debt/ Equity:	NA

Somaxon Pharmaceuticals Inc

3721 Valley Ctr. Dr., Ste. 500, San Diego, CA, 92130; *PH:* 1-858-480-0400; *Fax:* 1-858-509-1761; *http://* www.somaxon.com; *Email:* info@somaxon.com

General - Incorporation ....DE		Stock - Price on:12/24/2007 ....$13.1
Employees..37		Stock Exchange..NDQ
Auditor ....PricewaterhouseCoopers LLP		Ticker Symbol..SOMX
Stk Agt ..... American Stock Transfer & Trust Co.		Outstanding Shares 18,170,000
Counsel...NA		E.P.S..-$1.48
DUNS No..NA		Shareholders..NA

Business: The groups principal activities include developing, manufacturing and marketing proprietary product candidates for the treatment of diseases and disorders in the fields of psychiatry and neurology. The products of the group include SILENOR(TM), Nalmefene and Acamprosate. The group operates from the United States.

Primary SIC and add'l.: 2836 2834 2833 3845

CIK No: 0001339455

Officers: Kenneth M. Cohen/Dir., CEO, Pres., Susan E. Dube/Sr. VP - Corporate Development, Jeffrey W. Raser/Sr. VP - Sales, Marketing, Philip Jochelson/Sr. VP, Chief Medical Officer, Meg M. McGilley/CFO, VP, Matthew W. Onaitis/VP, General Counsel, Brian T. Dorsey/VP - Product Development, Robert L. Jones/VP - Human Resources, James L'Italien/Sr. VP - Regulatory Affairs, Quality Assurance

Directors: Kenneth M. Cohen/Dir., CEO, Pres., David F. Hale/Chmn., Terrell A. Cobb/Dir., Cam L. Garner/Dir., Scott L. Glenn/Dir., Jesse I. Treu/Dir., Daniel K. Turner/Dir., Kurt Von Emster/Dir., Kurt C. Wheeler/Dir., Michael L. Eagle/Dir.

Owners: Jeffrey W. Raser, David F. Hale, Jesse I. Treu, Funds affiliated with Montreux Equity Partners LLC, Meg M. McGilley, Scott L. Glenn, Funds affiliated with Domain Associates, L.L.C., Insiders, Kenneth M. Cohen, Philip Jochelson, Kurt von Emster, Susan E. Dub, Funds affiliated with MPM Capital, L.P., Terrell A. Cobb, Prospect Venture PartnersIII, LP *(22 Owners included in Index)*

Financial Data: Fiscal Year End:12/31   *Latest Annual Data:* 12/31/2006

Year	Sales	Net Income
2006	NA	-$46,410,000
2005	NA	-$38,487,000
2004	NA	-$13,598,000

Curr. Assets:	$58,429,000	Curr. Liab.:	$7,095,000	P/E Ratio:	18.14
Plant, Equip.:	$263,000	Total Liab.:	$7,095,000	Indic. Yr. Divd.:	NA
Total Assets:	$59,452,000	Net Worth:	$52,357,000	Debt/ Equity:	NA

Somera Communications Inc

301 S Npoint Dr., Coppell, TX, 75019; *PH:* 1-972-304-5660; *http://* www.somera.com

General - Incorporation ....DE		Stock - Price on:12/24/2007 ....NA
Employees...NA		Stock Exchange..NDQ
Auditor ....PricewaterhouseCoopers LLP		Ticker Symbol..SMRA
Stk Agt ....Mellon Investor Services LLC		Outstanding Shares ....NA
Counsel.......... Wilson Sonsini Goodrich & Rosati		E.P.S...NA
DUNS No.............................92-930-4657		Shareholders..NA

Business: The group's principal activities are to provide telecommunication operators with equipment sourcing and services. The group offers customers with a combination of new and redeployed equipment from various manufacturers to enable them stretch capital budgets and make fast multi-vendor purchases from a single cost-effective source. The new equipment consists of telecommunications equipment purchased from original equipment manufacturers or distributors. The redeployed equipment consists of equipment removed from operators' existing telecommunications network and equipment purchased from reseller group's offices which is located in Amsterdam, the Netherlands and Singapore. In 2002, the group acquired Compass Telecom Inc.

Primary SIC and add'l.: 5065 7389 4812

CIK No: 0001094243

Subsidiaries: Somera Communications B.V., Somera Communications France SARL, Somera Communications GmbH, Somera Communications Ltd., Somera Communications Ltda., Somera Communications Pte. Ltd., Somera Communications Sales, Inc.

Somerset Hills Bancorp

155 Morristown Rd., Bernardsville, NJ, 07924; *PH:* 1-908-221-0100; *Fax:* 1-908-221-1514; *http://* www.bankofsomersethills.com

General - Incorporation ....NJ		Stock - Price on:12/24/2007 ....$12.39
Employees..82		Stock Exchange..NDQ
Auditor ....Crowe Chizek & Co. LLC		Ticker Symbol..SOMH
Stk Agt ....Registrar & Transfer Co.		Outstanding Shares 4,750,000
Counsel...NA		E.P.S..$0.47
DUNS No..NA		Shareholders..NA

Business: The group's principal activity is to provide commercial banking services and personal and business checking accounts and time deposits, money market accounts and regular savings accounts. The group has two reportable segments namely, community banking and mortgage banking. The group's lending activities are oriented to the small-to-medium sized business, high net worth individuals, professional practices and consumer and retail customers living and working in the group's market area of Somerset and Morris counties in New Jersey.

Primary SIC and add'l.: 6712 6022

CIK No: 0001189396

Subsidiaries: Somerset Hills Bank, Somerset Hills Investment Holdings Inc, Somerset Hills Title Group LLC, Somerset Hills Wealth Management Services LLC, Sullivan Financial Services Inc

Officers: Stewart E. McClure/Vice Chmn., CEO, COO, Pres./$301,535.00, Matt Losapio/Assist. VP, Assistant Branch Mgr. Mendham Office, Maryjo Niziolek/Assist. Treasurer - Accounting Department, Daniel F. Dunn/Assist. VP, Sales Mgr. Summit Office, Kimberly Ryan/VP, Branch Mgr. Morristown Office, Jessalyn Mahan/Assist. Sec. - Operations, Joyce Henion/Assist. VP, Assistant Branch Manger Long Valley Office, Mark M. Schirm/CTO, Sr. VP - Operations, Rose Ferdinand/Assist. VP - Madison Office, Jeanne G. Hagen/VP - Human Resources, Investor Relations, Edward M. Stahl/Sr. VP - Branch Administration, Sales, James M. Nigro/Sr. VP, Sr. Loan Officer, Peter A. Longo/Sr. VP - Installment Lending, Scott L. Schachter/Sr. VP - Commercial Lending, Roberta A. Costain/VP - Main Office *(32 Officers included in Index)*

Directors: Stewart E. McClure/Vice Chmn., CEO, COO, Pres., Thompson H. McDaniel/Vice Chmn., Edward B. Deutsch/Chmn., Desmond V. Lloyd/Dir., Cornelius E. Golding/Dir., Jerome J. Graham/Dir., Gerald M. Sedam/Dir., Gerald B. O'Connor/Dir., Gerard Riker/Dir., Exec. VP, CFO, Treasurer, Paul F. Lozier/Dir., Thomas J. Marino/Dir.

Owners: Desmond V. Lloyd, Thomas J. Marino, Cornelius E. Golding, Stewart E. McClure/3.28%, Jerome J. Graham, Gerald B. OConnor, Thompson H. McDaniel/1.81%, Edward B. Deutsch/2.34%, Gerard Riker/1.27%, Gerald M. Sedam/2.65%, Paul F. Lozier, Insiders/12.51%

Financial Data: **Fiscal Year End:**12/31 **Latest Annual Data:** 12/31/2006

Year	Sales	Net Income
2006	$18,651,000	$2,198,000
2005	$14,546,000	$2,115,000
2004	$11,047,000	$1,359,000

Curr. Assets:	$30,070,000	**Curr. Liab.:**	$250,952,000	**P/E Ratio:**	26.36
Plant, Equip.:	$6,295,000	**Total Liab.:**	$251,532,000	**Indic. Yr. Divd.:**	$0.160
Total Assets:	$289,428,000	**Net Worth:**	$37,896,000	**Debt/ Equity:**	NA

Somerset International Group Inc

90 Washington Valley Rd., Bedminster, NJ, 07921; ***PH:*** 1-908-719-8909; ***http://*** www.somersetinternational.com; ***Email:*** info@somersetinternational.com

General - Incorporation	DE	**Stock**- Price on:12/24/2007	$0.1
Employees	20	Stock Exchange	OTC
Auditor	WithumSmith & Brown, P.C	Ticker Symbol	SOSI
Stk Agt	American Stock Transfer & Trust Co.	Outstanding Shares	7,040,000
Counsel	NA	E.P.S.	-$0.2
DUNS No.	07-522-6274	Shareholders	NA

Business: The group's principle activity is looking out for opportunities to maximize the value of tangible and intangible assets. The group operates from United States.

Primary SIC and add'l.: 3823

CIK No: 0000350524

Officers: John X. Adiletta/58/Chmn., CEO, CFO, Pres.

Directors: John X. Adiletta/58/Chmn., CEO, CFO, Pres.

Owners: John X. Adiletta/13.80%, William Farley/23.50%, Insiders/13.80%

Financial Data: **Fiscal Year End:**12/31 **Latest Annual Data:** 12/31/2006

Year	Sales	Net Income
2006	$1,740,000	-$1,137,000
2005	$1,540,000	-$1,037,000
2004	$1,000	-$1,222,000

Curr. Assets:	$493,000	**Curr. Liab.:**	$2,341,000		
Plant, Equip.:	$9,000	**Total Liab.:**	$2,655,000	**Indic. Yr. Divd.:**	NA
Total Assets:	$3,628,000	**Net Worth:**	-$2,731,000	**Debt/ Equity:**	NA

Sona Mobile Holdings Corp

Formerly: Perfectdata Corp
245 Pk. Ave., New York, NY, 10167; ***PH:*** 1-212-486-8887; ***http://*** www.perfectdata.com

General - Incorporation	DE	**Stock**- Price on:12/24/2007	$0.42
Employees	30	Stock Exchange	OTC
Auditor	Horwath Orenstein LLP	Ticker Symbol	SNMB
Stk Agt	U.S. Stock Transfer Corp	Outstanding Shares	57,780,000
Counsel	Millard Pilchowski Holweger Child	E.P.S.	-$0.1
DUNS No.	04-036-7914	Shareholders	NA

Business: The group's principal activities are to design, assemble and market cleaning and maintenance products for home, office and computer environments. The consumable cleaning and preventive maintenance products of the group are designed to eliminate or minimize contamination in and around computer and office automation equipment. The group operates under the trademark 'perfectdata' and the principal selling product is the perfectduster ecoduster line of compressed gas dusters. The group also sells CD and tape drive cleaners, CD player cleaners, static control products, laser and inkjet printer cleaners, fax and copy machine cleaners and a variety of premoistened cleaning wipes for specific equipment. The group's products are sold to more than 120 customers including office product distributors and dealers, stationery and computer retail stores and large warehouse in the United States, Canada and other countries.

Primary SIC and add'l.: 3589 3577 2842

CIK No: 0000719662

Subsidiaries: Sona Innovations Inc., Sona Innovations, Inc., Sona Mobile, Inc

Officers: Shawn Kreloff/45/Chmn., CEO, Pres./$1,032,269.00, Lance Yu/38/CTO, Sr. VP/$185,417.00, Stephen Fellows/42/VP, CFO - Corporate Secreta/$254,631.00

Directors: Shawn Kreloff/45/Chmn., CEO, Pres., Robert P. Levy/77/Dir., Jeffrey Branman/52/Dir.

Owners: John Bush/9.70%, Shawn Kreloff/7.50%, Robert P. Levy, Jeffrey M. Branman, Insiders/10.60%, Lance Yu/2.30%, Steven L. Martin/8.30%, ShuffleMaster, Inc./8.20%, Stephen Fellows

Financial Data: **Fiscal Year End:**12/31 **Latest Annual Data:** 12/31/2006

Year	Sales	Net Income
2006	$398,000	-$8,486,000
2005	NA	-$893,000

Curr. Assets:	$1,282,000	**Curr. Liab.:**	$335,000		
Plant, Equip.:	NA	**Total Liab.:**	$335,000	**Indic. Yr. Divd.:**	NA
Total Assets:	$1,282,000	**Net Worth:**	$947,000	**Debt/ Equity:**	NA

Sonesta International Hotels Corp

116 Huntington Ave., Boston, MA, 02116; ***PH:*** 1-617-421-5400; ***Fax:*** 1-617-421-5402; ***http://*** www.sonesta.com

General - Incorporation	NY	**Stock**- Price on:12/24/2007	$31
Employees	1,074	Stock Exchange	NDQ
Auditor	Ernst & Young LLP	Ticker Symbol	SNSTA
Stk Agt	American Stock Transfer & Trust Co.	Outstanding Shares	3,700,000
Counsel	NA	E.P.S.	-$0.91
DUNS No.	00-194-5922	Shareholders	NA

Business: The group's principle activities are to own and operate hotels in Boston, Massachusetts, key biscayne, Florida, new orleans and Louisiana. The group operates in two segments: owned and leased hotels and management activities. The owned and leased hotels segment includes revenues from room, food and beverage, parking and telephone receipts from hotel guests. The management activities segment includes the operations of hotels and resorts under management agreements, and fees from hotels to which the group has granted licenses. The group has entered into master franchise agreements for Brazil, Peru and Italy, and currently licenses six hotels in Peru, and four hotels, including a 10th century castle, in Italy. The group's quarterly revenue for Sep '07 was 20.14 millions of USD.

Primary SIC and add'l.: 7021 7011 7521 5812

CIK No: 0000091741

Subsidiaries: Anguilla Hotel Management, Inc., Brewster Wholesale Corporation, Charterhouse of Cambridge Trust, Florida Sonesta Corporation, Hotel Corporation of America, Hotel Corporation of America (Bermuda) Limited, Hotel Corporation of Georgia, Key Biscayne Land Corporation, Newo Aruba N.V., P.R. By Design, Inc., Port Royal Company, Limited, Royal Sonesta, Inc., Sonesta Charitable Foundation, Inc., Sonesta Coconut Grove, Inc., Sonesta Costa Rica, S.A. 26 Subsidiaries included in the Index

Officers: Stephanie Sonnabend/CEO, Pres./$419,649.00, Peter Sonnabend/Vice Chmn., CEO/$415,907.00, Roger Sonnabend/82/Exec. Chmn./$572,275.00, Paul Sonnabend/76/Exec. VP/$433,837.00, Kathy Sonnabend Rowe/Sr. VP - Food, Beverage, Carol Beggs/47/VP - Technology, Dale Scharlat/Exec. Dir. - Regional Sales, New York Sales Office ~ Northeast Region, Kim Rodrigue/Exec. Dir. - Regional Sales, Washington DC Sales Office ~ Mid, Atlantic Region, Patti Sonnabend Wagner/Dir. - Corporate Accounting, Boy Van Riel/49/VP, Treasurer/$245,971.00, Jacqueline Sonnabend/Exec. VP, Stephen Sonnabend/76/Dir., Sr. VP, Antonella Sacchero/Sales Mgr. - Europe, Brian Fitzgerald/GM, George Lanzillo/Rooms Division Dir. *(28 Officers included in Index)*

Directors: Peter Sonnabend/Vice Chmn., CEO, Jean C. Tempel/65/Dir., Stephen Sonnabend/76/Dir., Sr. VP, George S. Abrams/76/Dir., Sally O'Connor/Dir., Norman Shostak/Dir., James Trombino/Dir., Charles J. Clark/59/Dir., Vernon R. Alden/84/Dir., Stephen Clark/Dir., Kim Earle/Dir., Peter Hanley/Dir., Anne-Marie Laderoute-Cuthbert/Dir., Leila MacFeeley/Dir., Margaret Moynihan/Dir. *(20 Directors included in Index)*

Owners: Charles J. Clark, Stephen Sonnabend/2.50%, Vernon R. Alden, Stephanie Sonnabend/6.90%, George S. Abrams, Roger P. Sonnabend/4.50%, Peter J. Sonnabend/5.60%, Jean C. Tempel, Joseph L. Bower

Financial Data: **Fiscal Year End:**12/31 **Latest Annual Data:** 12/31/2006

Year	Sales	Net Income
2006	$98,832,000	-$3,523,000
2005	$88,125,000	$4,668,000
2004	$89,907,000	-$4,602,000

Curr. Assets:	$35,616,000	**Curr. Liab.:**	$11,074,000		
Plant, Equip.:	$38,400,000	**Total Liab.:**	$119,057,000	**Indic. Yr. Divd.:**	$0.200
Total Assets:	$126,428,000	**Net Worth:**	$7,371,000	**Debt/ Equity:**	5.4515

Songzai International Holding Group Inc

5237 Farago Ave., Temple City, CA, 91780; ***PH:*** 1-954-975-5643; ***http://*** www.songzaigroup.com; ***Email:*** info@songzaigroup.com

General - Incorporation	NV	**Stock**- Price on:12/24/2007	$0.05
Employees	348	Stock Exchange	OTC
Auditor	Jimmy C.H. Cheung & Co	Ticker Symbol	SGZI
Stk Agt	Interwest Transfer Company, Inc.	Outstanding Shares	NA
Counsel	NA	E.P.S.	$0.00
DUNS No.	NA	Shareholders	NA

Business: The group's principal activity is to provide permanent placement and recruiting services in the fields of accounting and finance, information technology, administrative, office and general management areas. The group operates primarily in the greater metropolitan Kansas city, Missouri area. The group was formed for the purpose of acquiring substantially all of the assets and the assumption of certain liabilities of blair consulting group inc. The group has currently no ongoing business operations and is attempting to identify and acquire or merge with other businesses. On 16-Dec-2003, the group acquired harbin yong heng . In September , 2004, the group acquired a 75% interest in Heilongjiang Tong Gong Kuang Ye You Xian Gong Si an operational coal mine located near Heihe City in the PRC.

Primary SIC and add'l.: 7361 6719

CIK No: 0001145761

Subsidiaries: Heilongjiang Tong Gong Kuang, Ye You Xian Gong Si

Officers: Hongwen Li/51/Chmn., CEO, Feng Shan Chi/Chief General Engineer, Hongjun Li/CFO, Pres., Dian Sheng Xing/GM

Directors: Hongwen Li/51/Chmn., CEO

Owners: Hongwen Li/100.00%, Insiders/100.00%, Hongwen Li/16.00%, Hongjun Li/6.00%, Insiders/22.00%

Financial Data: **Fiscal Year End:**12/31 **Latest Annual Data:** 12/31/2006

Year	Sales	Net Income
2006	$3,835,000	$647,000
2005	$3,170,000	$726,000
2004	$820,000	-$320,000

Curr. Assets:	$1,880,000	**Curr. Liab.:**	$1,675,000		
Plant, Equip.:	$5,530,000	**Total Liab.:**	$1,675,000	**Indic. Yr. Divd.:**	NA
Total Assets:	$7,638,000	**Net Worth:**	$5,964,000	**Debt/ Equity:**	NA

Sonic Automotive Inc

6415 Idlewild Rd., Ste. 109, Charlotte, NC, 28212; ***PH:*** 1-704-566-2400; ***Fax:*** 1-704-536-4665; ***http://*** www.sonicautomotive.com

General - Incorporation .... DE	**Stock**- Price on:12/24/2007 .... $29.91
Employees 11,200	Stock Exchange .... NYSE
Auditor .... Deloitte & Touche LLP	Ticker Symbol .... SAH
Stk Agt...... American Stock Transfer & Trust Co.	Outstanding Shares 43,050,000
Counsel .... NA	E.P.S $2.11
DUNS No. 09-736-4715	Shareholders .... NA

Business: The groups principle activity is to provide automotive retailer ship. The group also provide vehicle maintenance, paint and warranty services. The group operates from United States.

Primary SIC and add'l.: 6141 5511 7532 7515

CIK No: 0001043509

Subsidiaries: AnTrev, LLC, Arngar, Inc., Autobahn, Inc., Avalon Ford, Inc., Capitol Chevrolet and Imports, Inc., Casa Ford of Houston, Inc., Cobb Pontiac Cadillac, Inc., Cornerstone Acceptance Corporation, FA Service Corporation, FAA Auto Factory, Inc., FAA Beverly Hills, Inc., FAA Capitol N, Inc., FAA Concord H, Inc., FAA Concord N, Inc., FAA Concord T, Inc. 270 Subsidiaries included in the Index

Officers: Bruton O. Smith/Chmn., CEO/$2,787,888.00, David P. Cosper/Vice Chmn., CFO/$1,287,372.00, Stephen K. Coss/Sr. VP, General Counsel, Sec., Mark J. Iuppenlatz/48/Exec. VP - Corporate Development/$1,704,851.00, Scott B. Smith/Dir., Pres., Chief Strategic Officer/$2,245,046.00

Directors: Bruton O. Smith/Chmn., CEO, David P. Cosper/Vice Chmn., CFO, Robert L. Rewey/Dir., David C. Vorhoff/Dir., William R. Brooks/Dir., William P. Benton/Dir., Jeffrey C. Rachor/Dir., William I. Belk/Dir., Victor H. Doolan/Dir., Robert H. Heller/Dir., Scott B. Smith/Dir., Pres., Chief Strategic Officer

Owners: Wasatch Advisors, Inc./5.10%, Sonic Financial Corporation, Robert H. Heller, Insiders, William I. Belk, Goldman Sachs Asset Management, L.P./9.00%, Insiders/7.40%, Jeffrey C. Rachor/1.50%, William P. Benton, Dimensional Fund Advisors LP/8.20%, Bruton O. Smith/3.00%, FMR Corp./9.90%, Victor H. Doolan, Barclays Global Investors, NA./5.50%, Mark J. Iuppenlatz *(22 Owners included in Index)*

Financial Data: **Fiscal Year End:**12/31 **Latest Annual Data:** 12/31/2006

Year	Sales	Net Income
2006	$7,972,074,000	$81,117,000
2005	$7,884,842,000	$91,861,000
2004	$7,394,937,000	$86,071,000

Curr. Assets:	$1,613,132,000	**Curr. Liab.:**	$1,431,693,000	**P/E Ratio:**	15.83
Plant, Equip.:	$220,551,000	**Total Liab.:**	$2,220,924,000	**Indic. Yr. Divd.:**	$0.480
Total Assets:	$3,124,764,000	**Net Worth:**	$903,840,000	**Debt/ Equity:**	0.6542

Sonic Corp

300 Johnny Bench Dr., Oklahoma City, OK, 73104; ***PH:*** 1-405-225-5000; ***Fax:*** 1-405-280-7696; ***http://*** www.sonicdrivein.com

General - Incorporation .... DE	**Stock**- Price on:12/24/2007 .... $22.21
Employees 332	Stock Exchange .... NDQ
Auditor .... Ernst & Young LLP	Ticker Symbol .... SONC
Stk Agt............ UMB Bank, N.A.	Outstanding Shares 66,750,000
Counsel.......... Phillips, McFall, McCaffrey Et Al	E.P.S $0.91
DUNS No. 07-121-8739	Shareholders .... NA

Business: The group's principal activities are to operate and franchise a chain of quick-service drive-in restaurants in the United States and Mexico. The restaurants offer made-to-order hamburgers, sandwiches and also feature signature items such as extra-long cheese coneys, hand-battered onion rings, tater tots, specialty soft drinks including cherry limeades and slushes and frozen desserts. The group also leases signs and real estate. Sonic industries inc. And sonic restaurants, inc. Are the two operating subsidiaries. Sonic industries inc. Serves as the franchisor of the sonic restaurant chain, as well as the administrative services center. Sonic restaurants, inc. Develops and operates the group-owned restaurants. At 31-Aug-2003, the group operated 2,706 restaurants consisting of 2,209 franchised units and 497 company-owned units.

Primary SIC and add'l.: 6794 5812

CIK No: 0000868611

Subsidiaries: America's Drive-in Corp., Sonic Community Development, Inc., Sonic IndustriesInc., Sonic Property Development, LLC, Sonic Restaurants,Inc., Sonic Technology Fund, LLC, Sonic Value Card, LLC, SPOTlight, LLC.

Officers: Clifford J. Hudson/53/Chmn., CEO, Renee G. Shaffer/CIO, VP, Stephen C. Vaughan/CFO, VP, Paige S. Bass/VP, General Counsel, Jeffry D. Carper/VP - Field Marketing, Claudia San Pedro/VP - Investor Relations, Treasurer, Terry D. Harryman/Controller, Anne Burkett/Principal, Internal Auditor, Mitchell W. Gregory/Sr. VP - Concept Development, Distribution, Andrew G. Ritger/Sr. VP - Development, Carolyn C. Cummins/VP - Compliance, Sec., Alan Cantrell/VP - SRI Field Finance, Robert J. Geresi/VP - SRI Operations, Keith O. Jossell/VP - Franchise Finance, William T. Pierquet/VP - SRI Development *(27 Officers included in Index)*

Directors: Clifford J. Hudson/53/Chmn., CEO, Troy N. Smith/Chmn. Emeritus, Frank E. Richardson/Dir., Michael J. Maples/65/Dir., Larry J. Nichols/Dir., Federico F. Pena/60/Dir., H. E. Rainbolt/Dir., Leonard Lieberman/Dir., Dean E. Werries/Dir. Emeritus, Robert M. Rosenberg/Dir.

Owners: Barclays Global Investors, NA/5.60%, T. Rowe Price Associates, Inc./6.80%, H. E. Rainbolt, Stephen C. Vaughan, Clifford J. Hudson/2.69%, Larry J. Nichols, Michael J. Maples, Scott W. McLain, Insiders/8.45%, FMR LLC/12.30%, Federico F. Pea, Earnest Partners, LLC/10.00%, Frank E. Richardson/3.37%, Michael A. Perry, Leonard Lieberman *(17 Owners included in Index)*

Financial Data: **Fiscal Year End:**08/31 **Latest Annual Data:** 08/31/2007

Year	Sales	Net Income
2007	$770,469,000	$64,192,000
2006	$693,262,000	$78,705,000
2005	$623,066,000	$75,381,000

Curr. Assets:	$42,510,000	**Curr. Liab.:**	$78,095,000	**P/E Ratio:**	24.96
Plant, Equip.:	$477,054,000	**Total Liab.:**	$241,759,000	**Indic. Yr. Divd.:**	NA
Total Assets:	$638,018,000	**Net Worth:**	$391,693,000	**Debt/ Equity:**	NA

Sonic Environmental Solutions Inc

8765 Ash St., Unit 7, Vancouver, BC, V6P 6T3; ; ***http://*** www.sesi.ca

General - Incorporation .... BC	**Stock**- Price on:12/24/2007 .... NA
Employees .... NA	Stock Exchange .... NA
Auditor .... Staley, Okada & Partners	Ticker Symbol .... NA
Stk Agt............ Pacific Corporate Trust Co	Outstanding Shares .... NA
Counsel .... Goodmans LLP	E.P.S .... NA
DUNS No. .... NA	Shareholders .... NA

Business: The group's activity is to market its sonic generator technology. The group serves markets including the environmental markets. The group is in the process of commercializing its patented sonic generator. The group works in co-operation with environmental management and handling companies local to each contaminated site and provides a complete on-site package treatment plant. The group provides on-site treatment and destruction of PCB.

Primary SIC and add'l.: 3825

CIK No: 0001270778

Subsidiaries: Contech PCB Containment Technology Inc., SESI Sysmtem Inc., Sonic Environmental Solutions Corp

Officers: Adam R. Sumel/Dir., CEO, Pres., Co - Founder, Cathy Hume/CEO - CHF, Investor Relations, Lisa Sharp/CFO, Larry Rodricks/VP - Remediation Services, Claudio Arato/Mgr. - Project Engineering, Richard Ilich/Dir., Sec., Co - Founder, Paul Austin/VP - Sales, Marketing, James Hill/Exec. VP

Directors: Adam R. Sumel/Dir., CEO, Pres., Co - Founder, David E. Coe/Chmn., Richard Ilich/Dir., Sec., Co - Founder, Roderick O. McElroy/Dir., Timothy J. Mason/Member - Technical & Advisory Board, Donald Nyberg/Member - Technical & Advisory Board, Jim McKinley/Member - Technical & Advisory Board, Paul Tinari/Member - Technical & Advisory Board, Klaus H. Oehr/Member - Technical & Advisory Board, Lorrie Hunt/Member - Technical & Advisory Board

Owners: Douglas B. Forster/5.00%, RAB Special Situations Master Fund Ltd./17.24%

Sonic Foundry Inc

222 W Washington Ave., Ste. 775, Madison, WI, 53703; ***PH:*** 1-608-443-1600; ***Fax:*** 1-608-443-1601; ***http://*** www.sonicfoundry.com

General - Incorporation .... MD	**Stock**- Price on:12/24/2007 .... $2.29
Employees 72	Stock Exchange .... NDQ
Auditor .... Grant Thornton LLP	Ticker Symbol .... SOFO
Stk Agt .... Continental Stock Transfer & Trust Co	Outstanding Shares 35,500,000
Counsel .... McBreen & Kopko	E.P.S .... -$0.18
DUNS No. 87-875-8200	Shareholders .... NA

Business: The group's principal activities are provide a variety of rich media communications technology and services including webcasting and Web presentation products. The group's high-performance webcasting and Web presentation solutions are trusted by Fortune 500 companies, education institutions and government agencies for a variety of critical communication needs. The group's products are also used for media analysis, distance learning, and content publishing applications. In fiscal 2003, the group disposed media services and desktop software division.

Primary SIC and add'l.: 7379 7371 7372

CIK No: 0001029744

Subsidiaries: International Image Services, Inc, Sonic Foundry Media Systems, Inc

Officers: Rimas P. Buinevicius/45/Chmn., CEO, Rob Schatz/Investor Contact, Kenneth A. Minor/46/CFO, Sec., Monty R. Schmidt/44/Founder, Dir., CTO, Darrin T. Coulson/43/COO

Directors: Rimas P. Buinevicius/45/Chmn., CEO, David C. Kleinman/72/Dir., Arnold B. Pollard/65/Dir., Frederick H. Kopko/53/Dir., Paul S. Peercy/67/Dir., Gary R. Weis/61/Dir., Monty R. Schmidt/44/Founder, Dir., CTO

Owners: Insiders/20.60%, Kenneth A. Minor/1.10%, Monty R. Schmidt/9.40%, David C. Kleinman, Darrin T. Coulson, Rimas P. Buinevicius/6.80%, Gary R. Weis, Arnold B. Pollard/1.50%, Frederick H. Kopko/1.10%, Paul S. Peercy

Financial Data: **Fiscal Year End:**09/30 **Latest Annual Data:** 09/30/2007

Year	Sales	Net Income
2007	$16,737,000	-$6,370,000
2006	$12,564,000	-$3,483,000
2005	$8,342,000	-$4,169,000

Curr. Assets:	$6,990,000	**Curr. Liab.:**	$4,792,000		
Plant, Equip.:	$2,294,000	**Total Liab.:**	$5,311,000	**Indic. Yr. Divd.:**	NA
Total Assets:	$16,912,000	**Net Worth:**	$11,601,000	**Debt/ Equity:**	0.0029

Sonic Innovations Inc

2795 E Cottonwood Pkwy., Ste. 660, Salt Lake City, UT, 84121; ***PH:*** 1-801-365-2800; ***Fax:*** 1-801-365-3000; ***http://*** www.sonici.com

General - Incorporation .... DE	**Stock**- Price on:12/24/2007 .... $8.88
Employees 639	Stock Exchange .... NDQ
Auditor .... KPMG LLP	Ticker Symbol .... SNCI
Stk Agt ..... American Stock Transfer & Trust Co.	Outstanding Shares 26,380,000
Counsel .... NA	E.P.S .... -$0.01
DUNS No. .... NA	Shareholders .... NA

Business: The group's principal activities are to design, manufacture and market advanced digital hearing aids for hearing impaired consumers. The group has developed patented digital signal processing (dsp) technologies and embedded them in the smallest single-chip dsp platform. The group's branded products are sold directly to more than 1,700 hearing care professionals in the United States and through a network of distributors throughout Europe, Japan, Australia and Canada. In may 2003, the group acquired sanomed handelsgesellschaft mbh.

Primary SIC and add'l.: 3841 3842

CIK No: 0001105982

Subsidiaries: Hearing Aid Specialists Pty Limited, Hoertoestelcentrum Sneek B.V., Hoorcomfort B.V., ME Management Services Pty Ltd., Omni Sonic Innovations ApS, Sanomed Handelsges mbH, Sonic Innovations A/S, Sonic Innovations Canada Ltd., Sonic Innovations GmbH, Sonic Innovations Hrgerte GmbH, Sonic Innovations Ltd., Sonic Innovations Pty Ltd., StarMedical B.V., Tympany, Inc., Wenger Hrgerte AG

Officers: Samuel L. Westover/Dir., CEO, Pres./$889,328.00, Michael Halloran/CFO, VP/$309,211.00, Jeffrey R. Geigel/VP - North America, Christie R. Mitchell/VP - Manufacturing Operations, Victor Bray/VP, Chief Audiology Officer/$275,499.00, Jerry Dabell/VP - Research, Development/$303,415.00, Brent H. Shimada/VP - Administration, General Counsel/$306,308.00, Richard V. Scott/VP - Worldwide Marketing, Scott O. Lindeman/43/VP, Corporate Controller

Directors: Samuel L. Westover/Dir., CEO, Pres., Andrew G. Raguskus/Chmn., James M. Callahan/Dir., Lewis S. Edelheit/Dir., Craig L. McKnight/Dir., Cherie M. Fuzzell/Dir., Kevin J. Ryan/Dir., Lawrence C. Ward/Dir., Robert W. Miller/Dir.

Owners: Samuel L. Westover/1.10%, Coghill Capital Management, L.L.C./9.60%, Jerry L. DaBell, Victor H. Bray, Morgan Stanley/6.60%, Stephen L. Wilson, T. Rowe Price Associates, Inc./8.20%, Robert W. Miller, Lewis S. Edelheit, James M. Callahan, Insiders/6.40%, Brent H. Shimada, Kevin J. Ryan/1.10%, Michael M. Halloran, Craig L. McKnight *(18 Owners included in Index)*

Financial Data: *Fiscal Year End:*12/31 *Latest Annual Data:* 12/31/2006

Year	Sales	Net Income
2006	$105,492,000	-$1,580,000
2005	$105,041,000	-$19,608,000
2004	$98,534,000	$411,000

Curr. Assets:	$60,829,000	**Curr. Liab.:**	$32,472,000	**P/E Ratio:**	296.00
Plant, Equip.:	$8,265,000	**Total Liab.:**	$42,417,000	**Indic. Yr. Divd.:**	NA
Total Assets:	$108,321,000	**Net Worth:**	$65,904,000	**Debt/ Equity:**	NA

Sonic Solutions

101 Rowland Way, Ste. 110, Novato, CA, 94945; ***PH:*** 1-415-893-8000; ***Fax:*** 1-415-893-8008; ***http://*** www.sonic.com; ***Email:*** info@sonic.com

General - Incorporation	CA	**Stock**- Price on:12/24/2007	$12.43
Employees	637	Stock Exchange	NDQ
Auditor	BDO Seidman, LLP	Ticker Symbol	SNIC
Stk Agt	Mellon Investor Services LLC	Outstanding Shares	26,010,000
Counsel	Heller Ehrman White & McAuliffe LLP	E.P.S	$0.65
DUNS No.	18-057-2539	Shareholders	NA

Business: The group's principal activities are to develop and market computer based tools that enable the creation of digital audio and video titles in the CD-audio and DVD-video formats. These tools are also used for recording data files on CD recordable disks and for backing up the information contained on hard disks attached to computers. The products include professional audio and video products, desktop products and technology products. Professional products consist of advanced DVD-video creation tools used by high-end professional customers. Desktop products include software-only DVD-video creation tools and DVD-video playback software used by lower end professionals, enthusiasts and consumers. Technology products include software that the group licenses to other companies for inclusion in the products. The group's markets include North America, France, Germany, UK, Japan, Europe and Pacific Rim. On 13-Feb-2004, the group acquired interactual technologies inc.

Primary SIC and add'l.: 7373

CIK No: 0000916235

Subsidiaries: InterActual Technologies, Inc., Live Picture S.A.R.L., MGI Software Corp., OLI V R Corporation Ltd., Roxio UK, Ltd., Sonic IP, Inc., Sonic Software (Shanghai) Co., Ltd, Sonic Solutions International, Inc., Sonic Solutions Japan, KK

Officers: Dave Habiger/CEO, Pres., Clay Leighton/CFO, Exec. VP, Mark Ely/Exec. VP - Strategy

Directors: Robert J. Doris/Chmn., Robert M. Greber/Dir., Mary C. Sauer/Dir., Peter J. Marguglio/Dir., Warren R. Langley/Dir.

Owners: Insiders/14.00%, Robert J. Doris/5.00%, Munder Capital Management/8.00%, Mark Ely/1.00%, David C. Habiger/2.00%, Clay A. Leighton/2.00%, Mary C. Sauer/2.00%, EARNEST Partners, LLC/6.00%, R. Warren Langley, Unicredito Italiano S.p.A./5.00%, Mazama Capital Management, Inc./8.00%, Peter J. Marguglio/1.00%, Robert M. Greber

Financial Data: *Fiscal Year End:*03/31 *Latest Annual Data:* 3/31/2006

Year	Sales	Net Income
2006	$148,676,000	$19,927,000
2005	$90,627,000	$8,542,000
2004	$56,853,000	$11,084,000

Curr. Assets:	$92,561,000	**Curr. Liab.:**	$39,937,000	**P/E Ratio:**	19.12
Plant, Equip.:	$4,833,000	**Total Liab.:**	$70,314,000	**Indic. Yr. Divd.:**	NA
Total Assets:	$209,471,000	**Net Worth:**	$139,157,000	**Debt/ Equity:**	NA

Sonicwall Inc

1143 Borregas Ave., Sunnyvale, CA, 94089; ***PH:*** 1-408-745-9600; ***Fax:*** 1-408-745-9300; ***http://*** www.sonicwall.com; ***Email:*** info@sonicwall.com

General - Incorporation	CA	**Stock**- Price on:12/24/2007	$8.72
Employees	436	Stock Exchange	NDQ
Auditor	Armanino Mckenna LLP	Ticker Symbol	SNWL
Stk Agt	Computershare Trust Co	Outstanding Shares	64,710,000
Counsel	Latham & Watkins	E.P.S	$0.09
DUNS No.	NA	Shareholders	NA

Business: The group's principal activity is to design, develop, manufacture and sell Internet security infrastructure products designed to provide secure Internet access. The products of the group enable secure Internet-based connectivity for distributed organizations and process secure transactions for enterprises and service providers. The security appliances provide robust, reliable, easy-to-use and affordable Internet security and virtual private network functionalities. The product line provides a comprehensive integrated security including firewall, vpn, anti-virus, content filtering and secure sockets layer encryption and decryption functionality. This helps users to get affordable secure Internet communications and conduct secure Internet transactions. The products of the group include sonicwall soho, sonicwall dmz, sonicwall pro, sonicwall pro-vx, sonicwall tele2 and sonicwall xprs2.

Primary SIC and add'l.: 7373 7372

CIK No: 0001093885

Subsidiaries: SonicWALL B.V.

Officers: Matthew Medeiros/Dir., CEO, Pres./$2,643,386.00, John Dilullo/VP - Worldwide Sales/$815,106.00, Robert D. Selvi/CFO/$902,876.00, Dawn Thompson/VP - Human Resources, Robert B. Knauff/46/VP - Finance, Corporate Controller, Chief Accounting Officer/$522,468.00, Steve Franzese/VP - Worldwide Marketing, John Gmuender/VP - Engineering, Douglas Brockett/VP, GM, Joe Levy/CTO, Boris Yanovsky/VP - Security Services, Applications, Patrick Sweeney/VP - Network Security Business Unit, Marvin Blough/VP - EMEA Sales, Frederick M. Gonzalez/58/VP, General Counsel, Corp. Sec./$484,896.00

Directors: Matthew Medeiros/Dir., CEO, Pres., John Shoemaker/Chmn., Keyur A. Patel/42/Dir., Cary H. Thompson/Dir., Edward F. Thompson/Dir., Charles Berger/Dir., David W. Garrison/Dir., Charles D. Kissner/Dir.

Owners: David W. Garrison, Keyur A. Patel, Matthew Medeiros/3.90%, Robert B. Knauff, John C. Shoemaker, Charles Berger, Insiders/5.80%, Barclays Global Investors, NA/6.50%, Frederick M. Gonzalez, Robert D. Selvi, BlackRock, Inc./8.30%, Charles D. Kissner, Goldman Sachs Asset Management, L.P./6.60%, Edward F. Thompson, Dimensional FundAdvisors LP/7.50% *(16 Owners included in Index)*

Financial Data: *Fiscal Year End:*12/31 *Latest Annual Data:* 12/31/2006

Year	Sales	Net Income
2006	$175,538,000	-$10,753,000
2005	$135,324,000	$6,276,000
2004	$125,649,000	-$313,000

Curr. Assets:	$274,481,000	**Curr. Liab.:**	$91,954,000		
Plant, Equip.:	$4,085,000	**Total Liab.:**	$98,223,000	**Indic. Yr. Divd.:**	NA
Total Assets:	$416,291,000	**Net Worth:**	$318,068,000	**Debt/ Equity:**	NA

Sono Tek Corp

2012 RtE 9W, Milton, NY, 12547; ***PH:*** 1-845-795-2020; ***Fax:*** 1-845-795-2720; ***http://*** www.sono-tek.com

General - Incorporation	NY	**Stock**- Price on:12/24/2007	$1.12
Employees	44	Stock Exchange	OTC
Auditor	Sherb & Co. LLP	Ticker Symbol	SOTK
Stk Agt	American Stock Transfer & Trust Co.	Outstanding Shares	14,360,000
Counsel	NA	E.P.S	$0.04
DUNS No.	02-065-0602	Shareholders	NA

Business: The group's principal activity is to develop, manufacture and sell ultrasonic liquid atomizing nozzles. The ultrasonic nozzle systems atomize low to medium viscosity liquids by converting electrical energy into mechanical motion in the form of high frequency (ultrasonic) vibrations which break liquids into minute drops that can be applied to surfaces at low velocity. The group has diversified its product offerings to provide coating systems to medical device manufacturers and to provide components for coating systems for surface acoustic wave wafers used in sensors. The group markets its products in the United States, western Europe, Far East and other foreign countries.

Primary SIC and add'l.: 3823 3699

CIK No: 0000806172

Subsidiaries: Sono-Tek Cleaning Systems

Officers: Christopher L. Coccio/Chmn., CEO/$210,675.00, Stephen J. Bagley/CFO/$116,780.00, Vincent F. Demaio/VP - Manufacturing Operations, Harvey L. Berger/69/Dir., CTO, Stephen R. Harshbarger/VP - Sales, Marketing/$147,718.00, Claudine Y. Corda/Sec., Joseph Riemer/Dir., Pres., Steve Harshbarger/VP - Sales, Marketing, Vincent Whipple/Regional Sales Mgr., Lui Abarca/Dir. - International Marketing Development, Anita Ennest/Assoc. - Sales, Robb Engle/Mgr. - Service

Directors: Christopher L. Coccio/Chmn., CEO, Edward J. Handler/Dir., Joseph Riemer/Dir., Pres., Samuel Schwartz/Dir., Philip Strasburg/Dir., Harvey L. Berger/69/Dir., CTO, Donald F. Mowbray/Dir.

Owners: Stephen R. Harshbarger, Norwood Venture Corporation/7.55%, Philip A. Strasburg, Edward J. Handler, Harvey L. Berger/2.68%, Stephen J. Bagley, Christopher L. Coccio/6.54%, Donald F. Mowbray, Insiders/21.80%, Herbert Spiegel/5.27%, Samuel Schwartz/10.92%

Financial Data: *Fiscal Year End:*02/28 *Latest Annual Data:* 2/28/2007

Year	Sales	Net Income
2007	$6,886,000	$544,000
2006	$6,871,000	$1,043,000
2005	$5,804,000	$795,000

Curr. Assets:	$2,110,000	**Curr. Liab.:**	$1,323,000	**P/E Ratio:**	37.33
Plant, Equip.:	$58,000	**Total Liab.:**	$2,086,000	**Indic. Yr. Divd.:**	NA
Total Assets:	$2,673,000	**Net Worth:**	$587,000	**Debt/ Equity:**	0.0121

Sonoco Products Co

1 N 2nd St., Hartsville, SC, 29550; ***PH:*** 1-843-383-7000; ***Fax:*** 1-843-383-7008; ***http://*** www.sonoco.com

General - Incorporation	SC	**Stock**- Price on:12/24/2007	$43.544
Employees	17,700	Stock Exchange	NYSE
Auditor	PricewaterhouseCoopers LLP	Ticker Symbol	SON
Stk Agt	Bank of New York	Outstanding Shares	100,000,000
Counsel	Haynsworth, Sinkler & Boyd	E.P.S	$1.95
DUNS No.	00-335-4230	Shareholders	NA

Business: The groups principle activity is to provide industrial and consumer packaging solutions. The groups products include coasters, beverage insulators, composite reels and fiber mining tubes. The group also provides paper mill services. The group operates from United States.

Primary SIC and add'l.: 2621 3082 2655 3085 2679 2652

CIK No: 0000091767

Subsidiaries: 1190138 Ontario Inc, Ahlstrom Cores BV, Beteiligungen Sonoco Deutschland Vermogensverwaltungsgesellschaft mbh, Cap Liners Ltd, Capseals Liners Ltd, Capseals Ltd, Colombiana PM, Convex Mold, Inc., Crellin BV, Crellin Europe BV, Engraph Puerto Rico, Inc., Georgia Paper Tube, Inc., Grove Paper Mill Co Ltd, Gunther of America, Inc., Gunther USA, Inc. 149 Subsidiaries included in the Index

Officers: Harris E. Deloach/63/Chmn., CEO, Pres./$8,433,610.00, Kevin P. Mahoney/51/VP - Corporate Planning, Cynthia A. Hartley/59/Sr. VP - Human Relations/$1,851,750.00, Jim C. Bowen/57/Sr. VP/$1,929,350.00, Ritchie L. Bond/51/Staff VP, Treasurer, Bernard W. Campbell/58/VP - Information Services, Chief Information Officer, Charles L. Sullivan/64/Exec. VP/$3,357,824.00, Jack M. Sanders/54/VP - Global Industrial Products, Charles J. Hupfer/61/CFO, Sr. VP, Corp. Sec./$2,591,975.00, Eddie L. Smith/56/VP - Industrial Products, Paper, Europe, Rodger D. Fuller/46/VP - Rigid Paper, Plastics, NA, Marty F. Pignone/49/VP, GM - Paper, NA

Directors: Harris E. Deloach/63/Chmn., CEO, Pres., James M. Micali/60/Dir., Marc D. Oken/60/Dir., Thomas E. Whiddon/55/Dir., Philippe Rollier/65/Dir., Edgar H. Lawton/47/Dir., Pamela Lewis Davies/51/Dir., Charles J. Bradshaw/71/Dir., Bernard L.M. Kasriel/61/Dir., John E. Linville/62/Dir., James L. Coker/67/Dir., John H. Mullin/66/Dir., Caleb C. Fort/46/Dir., Fitz L.H. Coker/72/Dir.

Owners: Barclays Global Investors, Ltd/10.22%, Insiders/5.00%, H. E. DeLoach/1.20%

Financial Data: *Fiscal Year End:*12/31 *Latest Annual Data:* 12/31/2006

Year	Sales	Net Income
2006	$3,656,839,000	$195,081,000
2005	$3,528,574,000	$161,877,000
2004	$3,155,433,000	$151,229,000

Curr. Assets:	$942,798,000	**Curr. Liab.:**	$659,824,000	**P/E Ratio:**	22.68
Plant, Equip.:	$1,019,594,000	**Total Liab.:**	$1,697,610,000	**Indic. Yr. Divd.:**	$1.040
Total Assets:	$2,916,678,000	**Net Worth:**	$1,219,068,000	**Debt/ Equity:**	0.6172

Sonoma Valley Bancorp

202 W Napa St., Sonoma, CA, 95476; ***PH:*** 1-707-935-3200; ***Fax:*** 1-707-935-3899; ***http://*** www.sonomavalleybank.com; ***Email:*** svb@sonomavlybnk.com

General - Incorporation	CA	Stock- Price on:12/24/2007	$28.52
Employees	49	Stock Exchange	OTC
Auditor	Richardson & Co	Ticker Symbol	SBNK
Stk Agt	American Stock Transfer & Trust Co.	Outstanding Shares	2,280,000
Counsel	NA	E.P.S.	$1.83
DUNS No.	NA	Shareholders	NA

Business: The group's principal activity is to provide banking services to small to medium-sized commercial businesses, professionals and upper middle to high-income individuals and families. The services offered by the group include demand deposits, and savings and time deposit accounts. Special merchant and business services include coin, night depository, and courier, on line cash management and merchant teller. The group's main branch is located in Sonoma and operates branch offices in Glen Ellen, California.

Primary SIC and add'l.: 6712 6022

CIK No: 0001120427

Subsidiaries: Sonoma Valley Bank

Officers: Mel Switzer/CEO, Pres./$682,638.00, Mary Dieter/COO, Exec. VP, Paco Villasenor/VP, Mgr., Sean C. Cutting/38/Loan Professional/$395,540.00, Suzanne Brangham/Sec., Brian Melland/Loan Professional, Vicki Rogers/Loan Professional, Becky Elster/Loan Professional, Teri Thomas/Loan Professional, Veronica Ordaz/Loan Professional

Directors: Bob Nicholas/Chmn., Harry Weise/Dir., Dale Downing/Dir., Angelo Sangiacomo/Dir., Robert Hitchcock/Dir., Valerie Pistole/Dir.

Owners: Insiders/27.04%, Angelo C. Sangiacomo/1.76%, Suzanne Brangham/1.20%, Mel Switzer/3.79%, Robert B. Hitchcock/4.93%, Dale T. Downing/2.52%, Robert J. Nicholas/4.81%

Financial Data: **Fiscal Year End:**12/31 **Latest Annual Data:** 12/31/2006

Year	Sales	Net Income
2006	$19,474,000	$3,992,000
2005	$15,671,000	$3,349,000
2004	$13,268,000	$2,908,000

Curr. Assets:	$9,124,000	Curr. Liab.:	$238,649,000	P/E Ratio:	16.58
Plant, Equip.:	$949,000	Total Liab.:	$251,250,000	Indic. Yr. Divd.:	$0.600
Total Assets:	$277,654,000	Net Worth:	$26,404,000	Debt/ Equity:	NA

Sonomawest Holdings Inc

2064 Hwy. 116 N, Sebastopol, CA, 95472; *PH:* 1-707-824-2534; *Fax:* 1-707-829-4630; *http://* www.sonomawestholdings.com

General - Incorporation	CA	Stock- Price on:12/24/2007	$26.5
Employees	6	Stock Exchange	OTC
Auditor	Macias Gini & Oconnell LLP	Ticker Symbol	SWHI
Stk Agt	Grant Thornton LLP	Outstanding Shares	1,190,000
Counsel	NA	E.P.S.	$0.30
DUNS No.	00-911-3226	Shareholders	NA

Business: The group's principal activity is to lease industrial properties located in sebastopol, California. The properties are leased out to multiple tenants with leases varying in length from month-to-month to ten years. The group's rental operations include industrial and agricultural property, which is rented to third parties.

Primary SIC and add'l.: 6531

CIK No: 0000102588

Officers: Walker R. Stapleton/Dir., CEO, CFO, Pres., Mike Babbini/Real Estate Mgr., Gwendolyn Toney/Controller

Directors: Walker R. Stapleton/Dir., CEO, CFO, Pres., David J. Bugatto/44/Dir., Robert W.C. Davies/34/Dir., David Janke/35/Dir.

Owners: Wendy S. Reyes/8.28%, Dorothy W. Stapleton/6.30%, David J. Bugatto/2.32%, Craig R. Stapleton/48.00%, Walker R. Stapleton/9.88%, Insiders/13.00%, Robert W.C. Davies, David A. Janke

Financial Data: **Fiscal Year End:**06/30 **Latest Annual Data:** 6/30/2006

Year	Sales	Net Income
2006	$2,667,000	$846,000
2005	$2,289,000	$4,000
2004	$2,050,000	$62,000

Curr. Assets:	$4,289,000	Curr. Liab.:	$1,084,000	P/E Ratio:	82.81
Plant, Equip.:	$1,412,000	Total Liab.:	$2,556,000	Indic. Yr. Divd.:	NA
Total Assets:	$8,473,000	Net Worth:	$5,917,000	Debt/ Equity:	NA

Sonoran Energy Inc

11300 W Olympic Blvd, Ste. 800, Los Angeles, CA, 90064; *PH:* 1-480-963-8800; *http://* www.sonoranenergy.com; *Email:* investors@sonoranenergy.com

General - Incorporation	WA	Stock- Price on:12/24/2007	$0.37
Employees	NA	Stock Exchange	OTC
Auditor	Epstein Weber & Conover, PLC	Ticker Symbol	SNRN
Stk Agt	Nevada Agency & Trust Company	Outstanding Shares	115,670,000
Counsel	NA	E.P.S.	-$0.07
DUNS No.	NA	Shareholders	NA

Business: The group's principle activity is to identify, acquire and develop oil and gas projects. The group operates in two reportable segments namely, oil and gas, and consulting services. The group acquired Scottsdale Oil Field Services Ltd. in June 2005. The group has a working interest in six oil and gas properties located within the state of California. The group's quarterly revenue for Oct '07 was 0.50 millions of USD.

Primary SIC and add'l.: 1381 1311

CIK No: 0001101661

Officers: Peter Rosenthal/Dir., CEO, Pres., Bill McFie/VP, Brian Rafferty/Dir., MD, Taylor Rafferty/Investor Relations Officer, Dana Johnston/Dir. - Investor Relations, Andrew Williams/CFO

Directors: Peter Rosenthal/Dir., CEO, Pres., Khaldoun Awamleh/49/Dir., Mehdi Varzi/Dir., Charles Waterman/Dir., Brad Farrow/Dir., Robert M. King/Dir., Brian Rafferty/Dir., MD

Owners: Mehdi Varzi, Frank Smith, Rasheed Rafidi/2.29%, Charles Waterman, Insiders/4.27%, Brad Farrow, Bill McFie/2.03%, David Mackertich, Peter Rosenthal/2.16%, Ala Nuseibeh/2.27%, Khaldoun Awamleh/1.00%, CUBUS APS/30.87%

Financial Data: **Fiscal Year End:**04/30 **Latest Annual Data:** 4/30/2006

Year	Sales	Net Income
2006	$1,938,000	-$10,130,000
2005	$519,000	-$7,429,000
2004	$291,000	-$4,829,000

Curr. Assets:	$5,745,000	Curr. Liab.:	$5,825,000		
Plant, Equip.:	$22,646,000	Total Liab.:	$7,386,000	Indic. Yr. Divd.:	NA
Total Assets:	$29,653,000	Net Worth:	$22,267,000	Debt/ Equity:	0.0467

Sonosite Inc

21919 30th Dr. SE, Bothell, WA, 98021; *PH:* 1-425-951-1200; *Fax:* 1-425-951-1201; *http://* www.sonosite.com

General - Incorporation	WA	Stock- Price on:12/24/2007	$30.61
Employees	550	Stock Exchange	NDQ
Auditor	KPMG LLP	Ticker Symbol	SONO
Stk Agt	Computershare Investor Services LLC	Outstanding Shares	16,600,000
Counsel	Orrick, Herrington & Sutcliffe LLP	E.P.S.	$0.50
DUNS No.	01-443-8860	Shareholders	NA

Business: The group's principal activities are to develop high-performance, hand-carried ultrasound imaging systems for use in a variety of clinical applications and settings. The products of the group include sonosite titantm system, for general imaging and cardiology applications, the sonosite 180plustm system, for general ultrasound imaging, the sonoheart elite, configured for cardiovascular applications. Its ilook 25 and ilook 15 imaging tools provides visual guidance for physicians and nurses while performing vascular access procedures and other examinations. The products are used in the fields of medical specialties such as radiology, obstetrics, gynecology, emergency medicine, surgery, cardiology, internal medicine and vascular medicine. Sonosite(R), the stylized sonosite logo, ilook(R), sonoheart(R), sonoknowledge(R), sitestand(R), sitepack(R) and sitecharge(R) are the registered trademarks of the group. On 27-May-2004, the group acquired sonometric health, inc.

Primary SIC and add'l.: 3841 3829 3845

CIK No: 0001055355

Subsidiaries: SonoSite (Asia) Limited, SonoSite Australasia Pty Limited, SonoSite Canada, Inc., SonoSite China Medical Ltd., SonoSite France SARL, SonoSite GmbH, SonoSite Iberica, S.L., SonoSite Japan KK, SonoSite, Ltd.

Officers: Kevin M. Goodwin/Dir., CEO, Pres./$1,115,902.00, Kathy Surace-Smith/VP, General Counsel, Corp. Sec./$454,499.00, Graham D. Cox/VP - International/$558,586.00, Marla R. Koreis/VP - Human Resources, Anne M. Bugge/VP - Corporate Affairs, John Lowell/VP - Operations, Daina L. Graham/VP - Regulatory Affairs, Quality Assurance, Dieter Schwartmann/VP - Europe, Juin-Jet Hwang/CTO, Lee Dunbar/VP - Premium Products Engineering, Jim Gilmore/VP - Research, Development, David Levesque/VP - Global Learning, David G. Willis/VP - Competitive Strategy, Innovation, Thomas J. Dugan/Sr. VP - Global Marketing, US Sales/$778,459.00, Michael J. Schuh/CFO/$384,220.00 *(16 Officers included in Index)*

Directors: Kevin M. Goodwin/Dir., CEO, Pres., Kirby L. Cramer/Non - Exec. Chmn., Carmen L. Diersen/Dir., Edward V. Fritzky/Dir., Paul V. Haack/Dir., Jacques Souquet/Dir., Steven R. Goldstein/Dir., William G. Parzybok/Dir., Jeffrey Pfeffer/Dir., Robert G. Hauser/Dir.

Owners: Jeffrey Pfeffer, BlackRock, Inc./6.95%, Kirby L. Cramer, Kevin M. Goodwin/1.01%, Edward V. Fritzky, Graham D. Cox, Insiders/4.99%, Rainier Investment Management, Inc./5.28%, Thomas Dugan, Jacques Souquet, Paul V. Haack, Robert G. Hauser, Kathryn Surace-Smith, Michael J. Schuh, Steven R. Goldstein *(17 Owners included in Index)*

Financial Data: **Fiscal Year End:**12/31 **Latest Annual Data:** 12/31/2006

Year	Sales	Net Income
2006	$171,083,000	$7,231,000
2005	$147,491,000	$5,436,000
2004	$115,817,000	$22,972,000

Curr. Assets:	$173,570,000	Curr. Liab.:	$25,162,000	P/E Ratio:	69.57
Plant, Equip.:	$10,185,000	Total Liab.:	$30,479,000	Indic. Yr. Divd.:	NA
Total Assets:	$211,510,000	Net Worth:	$181,031,000	Debt/ Equity:	NA

Sonus Networks Inc

7 Technology Pk. Dr., Westford, MA, 01886; *PH:* 1-978-614-8100; *Fax:* 1-978-614-8101; *http://* www.sonusnet.com; *Email:* ir@sonusnet.com

General - Incorporation	DE	Stock- Price on:12/24/2007	$8.57
Employees	719	Stock Exchange	NDQ
Auditor	Deloitte & Touche LLP	Ticker Symbol	SONS
Stk Agt	American Stock Transfer & Trust Co.	Outstanding Shares	252,510,000
Counsel	Bingham Dana Ltd	E.P.S.	$0.14
DUNS No.	NA	Shareholders	NA

Business: The group's principal activity is to provide voice infrastructure products for the new public network. The products of the group include carrier-class switching equipment and software that help voice services to be delivered over packet-based networks. The voice infrastructure products include the gsx9000-tm- open services switch, the insignus-tm- softswitch and the sonus insight-tm- management system. The customers of the group include long distance carriers, local exchange carriers, Internet service providers, cable operators, international telephone companies and carriers that provide services to other carriers. The group operates in the United States, Europe and Asia.

Primary SIC and add'l.: 7373 3661 3679

CIK No: 0001105472

Subsidiaries: Nihon Sonus Networks K.K., Sonus International,Inc., Sonus Networks (HK) Limited, Sonus Networks EURL, Sonus Networks GmbH, Sonus Networks India Private Limited, Sonus Networks Limited, Sonus Networks Pte. Ltd., Sonus Networks Pty. Ltd., Sonus Networks s.r.o., Sonus Securities Corporation, telecom technologies, inc., Westford Networks Mexico, S. de R.L. de C.V.

Officers: Hassan Ahmed/Chmn., CEO, Jeff Mayersohn/VP - Professional, Support Services, Charles Gray/VP, General Counsel, Chuba Udokwu/VP - Worldwide Engineering, James F. Collier/VP - Worldwide Sales, Richard Gaynor/CFO, Jocelyn Philbrook/VP - Corporate Marketing, Investor Relations, Mohammed Shanableh/VP - Worldwide Sales, Gale England/VP - Internal Operations, Matt Dillon/VP - Global Services, Bob Dye/VP - Corporate Strategy, Vikram Saksena/CTO

Directors: Hassan Ahmed/Chmn., CEO, Howard E. Janzen/54/Dir., John P. Cunningham/70/Dir., Paul J. Severino/Dir., Brian H. Thompson/Dir., Ed Anderson/Dir.

Owners: Paul J. Severino, Senate Limited/21.27%, Albert A. Notini, FMR Corp./13.77%, H. Brian Thompson, Howard E. Janzen, Ellen B. Richstone, Hassan M. Ahmed/3.64%, Wellington Management Company, LLP/11.46%, John P. Cunningham, Edward T. Anderson, Insiders/4.53%

Financial Data: **Fiscal Year End:**12/31 **Latest Annual Data:** 12/31/2006

Year	Sales	Net Income
2006	$279,483,000	$102,854,000
2005	$194,610,000	$8,368,000
2004	$170,738,000	$24,477,000

Curr. Assets:	$434,014,000	**Curr. Liab.:**	$121,817,000	**P/E Ratio:**	122.43
Plant, Equip.:	$38,100,000	**Total Liab.:**	$157,071,000	**Indic. Yr. Divd.:**	NA
Total Assets:	$589,604,000	**Net Worth:**	$432,533,000	**Debt/ Equity:**	NA

Sonus Pharmaceuticals Inc

22026 20th Ave. SE, Bothell, WA, 98021; *PH:* 1-425-487-9500; *Fax:* 1-425-489-0626; *http://* www.sonuspharma.com

General - Incorporation	DE	**Stock**- Price on:12/24/2007	$5.67
Employees	61	Stock Exchange	NDQ
Auditor	Ernst & Young LLP	Ticker Symbol	SNUS
Stk Agt	U.S. Stock Transfer Corp	Outstanding Shares	36,860,000
Counsel	Stradling Yocca Carlson & Rauth	E.P.S	-$0.597
DUNS No.	78-581-2371	Shareholders	NA

Business: The group's principal activity is to develop oncology drugs, like TOCOSOL Paclitaxel & TOCOSOL Camptothecin, that provide therapeutic alternatives for cancer patients. It has developed the TOCOSOL (TM) drug delivery technology platform to formulate injectable drugs that target cancer, diabetes, bacterial infections and cardiovascular disease. In October 2005, the Company entered into a collaboration and license agreement with Schering AG, a German corporation, and granted an exclusive, worldwide license to its TOCOSOL Paclitaxel anti-cancer product. The company's facility is located in Bothell, Washington.

Primary SIC and add'l.: 2834 8731 6794 2835

CIK No: 0000949858

Officers: Michael A. Martino/Dir., CEO, Pres./$932,037.00, Neile A. Grayson/VP - Strategic Planning, Corporate Development, Elaine Waller/VP - Regulatory Affairs, Quality Assurance, Alan Fuhrman/Dir., Sr. VP, CFO/$471,267.00, Lynn Gold/VP - Research, Process Development, Ingrid Rasch/VP - Human Resources, Dean R. Kessler/VP - Preclinical Development, Pamela Dull/Dir. - Investor Relations, Richard Daifuku/Acting Chief Medical Officer, VP - Preclinical, Clinical Research, K. C. Schaaf/Dir., General Counsel - Stradling Yocca Carlson, Rauth, Tom D'Orazio/VP - Strategic Marketing, Craig Eudy/VP, Controller, Wayne Rebich/VP - Financial Planning, Business Processes

Directors: Michael A. Martino/Dir., CEO, Pres., Robert E. Ivy/Chmn., Alan Fuhrman/Dir., Sr. VP, CFO, George W. Dunbar/Dir., Dwight Winstead/Dir., Michelle Burris/Dir., K. C. Schaaf/Dir., General Counsel - Stradling Yocca Carlson, Rauth

Owners: George W. Dunbar, Alan Fuhrman, Dwight Winstead, Atlas Master Fund, Ltd./9.10%, Insiders/5.10%, Robert E. Ivy, Schering Berlin Venture Corporation/13.20%, Michael A. Martino/2.80%, Michelle G. Burris, Michael B. Stewart

Financial Data: *Fiscal Year End:*12/31 *Latest Annual Data:* 12/31/2006

Year	Sales	Net Income
2006	$22,392,000	-$23,551,000
2005	$8,254,000	-$21,097,000
2004	NA	-$16,311,000

Curr. Assets:	$66,846,000	**Curr. Liab.:**	$19,910,000		
Plant, Equip.:	$1,186,000	**Total Liab.:**	$25,451,000	**Indic. Yr. Divd.:**	NA
Total Assets:	$68,493,000	**Net Worth:**	$43,042,000	**Debt/ Equity:**	NA

Sony Corp

550 Madison Ave., New York, NY, 10022; *PH:* 1-212-833-6800; *Fax:* 1-212-833-6956; *http://* www.sony.net

General - Incorporation	Japan	**Stock**- Price on:12/24/2007	$54.15
Employees	158,500	Stock Exchange	NYSE
Auditor	Pricewaterhousecoopers Aarata	Ticker Symbol	SNE
Stk Agt	UFJ Trust Bank Ltd	Outstanding Shares	1,000,000,000
Counsel	NA	E.P.S	$2.02
DUNS No.	69-055-3649	Shareholders	NA

Business: The group's principal activities are to develop, design, manufacture and sell electronic equipment, instruments and devices for consumer and industrial markets. The group also manufactures and markets home-use game consoles and software. The group operates through six segments: electronics: manufactures and sells audio-visual, informational and communicative equipment, instruments and devices; game: develops and sells playstation and playstation 2 game consoles and related software; music: manufactures and distributes recorded music in all commercial formats and musical genres; pictures: develops, produces and manufactures image-based software; financial services: represents insurance-related underwriting business and other segment: consists of various operating activities including Internet-related services and advertising agency.

Primary SIC and add'l.: 3944 3652 6159 7812 3651

CIK No: 0000313838

Subsidiaries: Aiwa Co., Ltd., DeNA Co., Ltd., SMEJ, Sony Capital Corporation, Sony Communication Network Corporation, Sony Computer Entertainment America Inc., Sony Electronics Inc, Sony Finance International Inc, Sony Life, Sony Magnescale Inc., Sony Pictures Entertainment Inc

Officers: Howard Stringer/Chmn., CEO, Ryoji Chubachi/Dir., Pres., Electronics CEO, Nobuyuki Oneda/CFO, Exec. VP, Keiji Kimura/Exec. VP, Officer in Charge - Technology Strategies, Intellectual Property, Electronics Business Strategies, Katsumi Ihara/Dir., Executive Deputy Pres., Officer in Charge - Semiconductor, Component Group, Nicole Seligman/Exec. VP, General Counsel, Yutaka Nakagawa/Executive Deputy Pres., Officer in Charge - Semiconductor, Component Group

Directors: Howard Stringer/Chmn., CEO, Ryoji Chubachi/Dir., Pres., Electronics CEO, Peter Bonfield/Dir., Katsumi Ihara/Dir., Executive Deputy Pres., Officer in Charge - Semiconductor, Component Group, Yoshihiko Miyauchi/Dir., Sakie T. Fukushima/Dir., Yoshiaki Yamauchi/Dir., Fueo Sumita/Dir., Yotaro Kobayashi/Dir., Fujio Cho/Dir., Ned Lautenbach/64/Dir., Akishige Okada/Dir., Ryuji Yasuda/Dir., Hirobumi Kawano/Dir.

Owners: Insiders

Financial Data: *Fiscal Year End:*03/31 *Latest Annual Data:* 03/31/2007

Year	Sales	Net Income
2007	$70,513,408,000	$1,073,788,000
2006	$63,541,206,000	$1,050,736,000
2005	$66,584,429,000	$1,523,693,000

Curr. Assets:	$32,040,954,000	**Curr. Liab.:**	$27,201,938,000	**P/E Ratio:**	45.05
Plant, Equip.:	$11,802,650,000	**Total Liab.:**	$62,933,159,000	**Indic. Yr. Divd.:**	$0.200
Total Assets:	$90,165,901,000	**Net Worth:**	$27,232,742,000	**Debt/ Equity:**	NA

Sopheon Plc

3050 Metro Dr., Ste. 200, Minneapolis, MN, 55425; *PH:* 1-952-851-7500; *Fax:* 1-952-851-7599; *http://* www.sopheon.com

General - Incorporation	UK	**Stock**- Price on:12/24/2007	$0.01
Employees	NA	Stock Exchange	OTC
Auditor	Ernst & Young LLP	Ticker Symbol	SOPEF
Stk Agt	NA	Outstanding Shares	NA
Counsel	LondonBriggs and Morgan	E.P.S	NA
DUNS No.	NA	Shareholders	NA

Business: The group's principle activity is the provision of software and services that enable organisations to access internal and external information and knowledge more efficiently. The group has also focused its activities increasingly within the market represented by major corporations and their information and process requirements for product development and research and development.

Primary SIC and add'l.: 7373 7379

CIK No: 0001109418

Officers: Andy Michuda/Executive Dir., CEO, Huub Rutten/VP - Product Research, Design, Paul Heller/CTO, Arif Karimjee/Dir., CFO

Directors: Andy Michuda/Executive Dir., CEO, Barry Mence/Chmn., Arif Karimjee/Dir., CFO, Stuart Silcock/Non Exec. Dir., Daniel Metzger/Non Exec. Dir., Bernard Al/Non Exec. Dir.

Financial Data: *Fiscal Year End:*12/31 *Latest Annual Data:* 12/31/2004

Year	Sales	Net Income
2004	$8,329,000	-$7,103,000

Curr. Assets:	$5,996,000	**Curr. Liab.:**	$3,811,000	**P/E Ratio:**	45.05
Plant, Equip.:	$212,000	**Total Liab.:**	$3,811,000	**Indic. Yr. Divd.:**	NA
Total Assets:	$6,208,000	**Net Worth:**	$2,397,000	**Debt/ Equity:**	NA

Sorell Inc

Formerly: NetMeasure Technology Inc

Buk-ri 35, Nama-Myun, Yongin City, Gyeonggi-do; *PH:* 82-313-298700; *http://* www.sorell.co

General - Incorporation	NV	**Stock**- Price on:12/24/2007	NA
Employees	NA	Stock Exchange	NA
Auditor	SF Partnership LLP	Ticker Symbol	NA
Stk Agt	Manhattan Transfer Registrar Co	Outstanding Shares	NA
Counsel	Cutler Law Group	E.P.S	NA
DUNS No.	NA	Shareholders	NA

Business: The group's principal activities are to acquire, develop and market technologies that assist network administrators in improving the efficiency, reliability and recoverability of Internet protocol networks. The group is a development stage company. Previously it was primarily involved in product development of probenet, a software package intended to run on multiple windows nt servers to monitor, alert and manage corporate ip networks which is a distributed network measurement software product. The subsidiary of the group is netmeasure technology (Canada) inc.

Primary SIC and add'l.: 5045 7372

CIK No: 0001073090

Subsidiaries: S-Cam Co., Ltd.

Sorl Auto Parts Inc

1169 YuMeng Rd., Ruian Economic Development Zone, Ruian, Zhejiang, 325200; ; *http://* www.sorl.cn

General - Incorporation	DE	**Stock**- Price on:12/24/2007	$7.09
Employees	1,621	Stock Exchange	NDQ
Auditor	Rotenberg & Co., LLP	Ticker Symbol	SORL
Stk Agt	Continental Stock Transfer & Trust Co	Outstanding Shares	18,270,000
Counsel	Troy & Gould	E.P.S	NA
DUNS No.	NA	Shareholders	NA

Business: The groups principle activities include manufacturing and distributing automotive air brake valves. The products of the group include clutch servo, rl351 series air dryer, relay valves and hand brake valves. The group products sold under the trade name SORL. Specific customers of the group include Dongfeng Axle Co., Ltd., Liuzhou Special Auto Manufacturing Co., Ltd and Beiqi Foton Motor Co., Ltd. The group operates from the United States and China. The group's quarterly revenue for September 2007 was 29.70 millions of USD.

Primary SIC and add'l.: 3714

CIK No: 0000714284

Subsidiaries: Fairford Holdings Limited, Ruili Group Ruian Auto Parts Co. Ltd.

Officers: Xiao Ping Zhang/45/Chmn., CEO/$50,000.00, Xiao Feng Zhang/40/Dir., COO, Jung Kang Chang/Dir., VP - International Sales, Jason Zhang/Deputy GM, Zong Yun Zhou/CFO/$20,000.00, Christopher Chu/Mgr. - Accounting, Richard Cai/Investor Relations Officer

Directors: Xiao Ping Zhang/45/Chmn., CEO, Xiao Feng Zhang/40/Dir., COO, Jung Kang Chang/Dir., VP - International Sales, Li Min Zhang/Dir., Zhi Zhong Wang/63/Dir., Yi Guang Huo/65/Dir., Jiang Hua Feng/42/Dir.

Owners: Xiao Feng Zhang/6.20%, Insiders/55.90%, Shu Ping Chi/6.20%, Xiao Ping Zhang/49.70%

Financial Data: *Fiscal Year End:*12/31 *Latest Annual Data:* 12/31/2006

Year	Sales	Net Income
2006	$84,898,000	$7,698,000
2005	$64,183,000	$4,950,000
2004	$46,815,000	$4,807,000

Curr. Assets:	$54,370,000	**Curr. Liab.:**	$7,175,000	**P/E Ratio:**	12.89
Plant, Equip.:	$16,312,000	**Total Liab.:**	$13,511,000	**Indic. Yr. Divd.:**	NA
Total Assets:	$70,880,000	**Net Worth:**	$57,369,000	**Debt/ Equity:**	NA

Sotheby's Holdings Inc

1334 York Ave., New York, NY, 10021; *PH:* 1-212-606-7000; *http://* www.sothebys.com

General - Incorporation	MI	Stock - Price on:12/24/2007	$48.38
Employees	1,497	Stock Exchange	NYSE
Auditor	Deloitte & Touche LLP	Ticker Symbol	BID
Stk Agt	Mellon Investor Services LLC	Outstanding Shares	66,080,000
Counsel	NA	E.P.S.	$2.65
DUNS No.	87-433-2687	Shareholders	NA

Business: The group's principle activities are the auction of fine arts, antiques, offering property, decorative art, jewelry and collectibles. The group operates in two segments: auction segment includes purchase and resale of art and other collectibles and the brokering of art and collectible purchases and sales through private treaty sales. Finance segment provides collectors and dealers with financing secured by works of art that the group either has in its possession or permits the borrower to possess. It conducts its financing activities through its wholly-owned direct and indirect subsidiaries. The group operates in North America, Europe and Asia. The group's quarterly revenue for Sep '07 was 85.06 millions of USD.

Primary SIC and add'l.: 6141 6153 7389

CIK No: 0000823094

Subsidiaries: Smith & Wesson Corp., Smith & Wesson Distributing, Inc., Smith & Wesson Firearms Training Centre GmbH, Smith & Wesson, Inc.

Officers: William F. Ruprecht/Dir., CEO, Pres./$8,774,398.00, Robin G. Woodhead/Dir., Exec. VP, CEO. - Sotheby's International/$1,658,798.00, Philipp Herzog Von Wurttemberg/Vice Chmn. - Sothebys Europe, MD - Sothebys Germany, Helyn Goldenberg/Chmn. - Sotheby's Midwest, Dir.- Fine Arts, Midwest, Jack Rosewitz/Dep. Chmn. - Capetown, South Africa, Hestia Den Dunnen/Sec. to Chmn. & Dep. Chmn., Bina Genovese/Mgr. - Cape Town Office, Rui Zhang/Resident Representative, Beijing, China, Walter Cheah/Consultant - Kuala Lumpur, Malaysia, Jie Wang/Deputy Dir., MD - Shanghai, Chief Representative - Shanghai, Beijing Office, Winnie Chang/MD - Taipei, Taiwan, Adela MacKinlay De Casal/Pres. - Art Advisory Services, Buenos Aires, Argentina, Charles Hignett/Consultant - Somerset, England, Lord Philip Cranworth/Contact - Suffolk, England, William Lucy/Contact - Sussex, South, East *(130 Officers included in Index)*

Directors: William F. Ruprecht/Dir., CEO, Pres., Robin G. Woodhead/Dir., Exec. VP, CEO. - Sotheby's International, Michael I. Sovern/Chmn., David Ober/Chmn. - Southeast, Alan Gotlieb/Chmn. - Canada, Mark Kretschmer/Chmn. - Capetown, South Africa, Walter J.P. Curley/Chmn. - Advisory Board, Alexis Gregory/Dep. Chmn. - Advisory Board, Carroll Petrie/Member - Advisory Board, Edward Gibbs/Dir., Head - Department, Islamic Art, Middle East, Gulf Region, Juan Abello/Member - Advisory Board, Alice Y.T. Cheng/Member - Advisory Board, William Cottingham/Dir., Exec. VP - Boston, Massachusetts, Lisa Hubbard/Exec. Dir. - International Jewelry, Michael Blakenham/Dir. *(35 Directors included in Index)*

Owners: FMR Corp/0.07%, Apex Capital, LLC/0.05%, Mitchell Zuckerman, Dennis M. Weibling, Michael Blakenham, George Bailey, Mellon Financial Corporation/0.07%, William S. Sheridan, Robin G. Woodhead, Michael I. Sovern, Allen Questrom, Rainier Investment Management/0.06%, Donald M. Stewart, Steven B. Dodge, Robert S. Taubman *(17 Owners included in Index)*

Financial Data: Fiscal Year End:12/31 Latest Annual Data: 12/31/2006

Year	Sales	Net Income
2006	$664,809,000	$107,049,000
2005	$513,508,000	$61,602,000
2004	$496,720,000	$86,679,000

Curr. Assets:	$1,047,827,000	Curr. Liab.:	$789,191,000	P/E Ratio:	18.26
Plant, Equip.:	$226,522,000	Total Liab.:	$1,175,478,000	Indic. Yr. Divd.:	$0.600
Total Assets:	$1,477,165,000	Net Worth:	$301,687,000	Debt/ Equity:	0.8909

Sound Banking Company

5039 Executive Dr., Morehead City, NC, 28557; **PH:** 1-252-727-5558; **Fax:** 1-252-727-5559; **http://** www.soundbanking.net; **Email:** soundbank@soundbanking.com

General - Incorporation		Stock - Price on:12/24/2007	$21.5
Employees	NA	Stock Exchange	OTC
Auditor	NA	Ticker Symbol	SNBN
Stk Agt	SunTrust Bank	Outstanding Shares	NA
Counsel	NA	E.P.S.	NA
DUNS No.	NA	Shareholders	NA

Business: The groups principal activities include providing banking and financial services. Services of the group include checking accounts, savings accounts, certificates of deposit, installment loans, real estate mortgage loans, commercial loans, traveler's checks, safe deposit boxes, night depository and automated teller services. The group operates from the United States.

Primary SIC and add'l.: 6029

CIK No:

Officers: Phillip S. Collins/Dir., CEO, Pres., Richard McIntyre/Exec. VP, Chief Lending Officer, Al Nelson/CFO, Sr. VP, Jody Smith/VP, Business Development Officer, John Aldredge/VP, Controller, Linda Ireland/VP - Operations, Compliance Officer, Greg Powell/VP, Business Development Officer, Bill Weinhold/VP, Business Development Officer, Sam O'Berry/VP, Business Development Officer, Mark Gatlin/VP, Business Development Officer, Desiree M. Ericksen/Information Technology, Security Officer, Shea Byrd/Retail Banking Officer, Beverly Daniel/Banking Officer, Traci Ellingsworth/Loan Administrator, Jessica Etheridge/Loan Administrator *(35 Officers included in Index)*

Directors: Phillip S. Collins/Dir., CEO, Pres., Jeffrey K. Moore/Chmn., Rodney K. Knowles/Dir., Dean K. Wagaman/Dir., Leslie N. Ipock/Dir., Malcolm C. Garland/Dir., Bill Blackmon/Dir., Chris Chadwick/Dir., L. A. Fredeen/Dir., John M. Harris/Dir., Randy Ramsey/Dir., Danny Varner/Dir., Dan Reitz/Member - Advisory Board, Brad Jones/Member - Advisory Board, Wes Collins/Member - Advisory Board *(46 Directors included in Index)*

Sound Health Solutions Inc

Formerly: Vista Medical Technologies Inc
2101 Faraday Ave., Carlsbad, CA, 92008; **PH:** 1-760-603-9120; **http://** www.ivow.com

General - Incorporation	DE	Stock - Price on:12/24/2007	$0.08
Employees	24	Stock Exchange	NA
Auditor	J. H. Cohn LLP	Ticker Symbol	NA
Stk Agt	EquiServe Trust Co N.A	Outstanding Shares	3,470,000
Counsel	Brobeck, Phleger & Harrison	E.P.S.	-$1.061
DUNS No.	83-628-3283	Shareholders	NA

Business: The group's principal activities are to develop, manufacture and market products that provide information to doctors performing minimally invasive general surgical, cardiac surgical and other selected microsurgical procedures. It also develops and sponsors training and support programs for medical personnel, which enhance the adoption of procedures incorporating use of our visualization

technology. The group's product lines include oprc advanced visualization and information system for general surgery and other complex endoscopic procedures and the series 8000 advanced visualization and information system, for use in cardiac surgery. The principal customers consist of original equipment manufacturers and distribution partners. On 15-Apr-2004 the group discontinued visualization technology business.

Primary SIC and add'l.: 3845 3842

CIK No: 0001035181

Subsidiaries: Sound Health Solutions, Inc., VOW Solutions, Inc.

Officers: Richard Gomberg/CFO

Directors: John R. Lyon/Chmn., Scott R. Pancoast/Dir., Bill Dugdale/Dir.

Financial Data: Fiscal Year End:12/31 Latest Annual Data: 12/31/2005

Year	Sales	Net Income
2005	$1,288,000	-$2,690,000
2004	$1,651,000	-$3,604,000
2003	$2,489,000	-$2,049,000

Curr. Assets:	$1,694,000	Curr. Liab.:	$1,216,000		
Plant, Equip.:	$253,000	Total Liab.:	$1,268,000	Indic. Yr. Divd.:	NA
Total Assets:	$3,748,000	Net Worth:	$2,479,000	Debt/ Equity:	0.0064

Sound Revolution Inc

1511 40th Ave. W, Vancouver, BC, V6M 1V7; **PH:** 1-604-780-3914; **Fax:** 1-604-408-5177; **http://** www.soundrevolution.net; **Email:** info@soundrevolution.net

General - Incorporation	DE	Stock - Price on:12/24/2007	$0.23
Employees	NA	Stock Exchange	OTC
Auditor	Peterson Sullivan PLLC	Ticker Symbol	SRVN
Stk Agt	Holladay Stock Transfer, Inc.	Outstanding Shares	NA
Counsel	NA	E.P.S.	NA
DUNS No.	NA	Shareholders	NA

Business: The groups principal activities include developing software to assist artists in maintaining, developing and communicating with their customers through email and the Internet. The group operates from the United States.

Primary SIC and add'l.: 8748

CIK No: 0001300867

Subsidiaries: Charity Tunes Inc,, Sound Revolution Recordings Inc

Officers: Robin Ram/CEO, Pres., Penny Green/Chmn., CFO, Sandra Wong/Dir. - Marketing, Nick Ostveen/Dir. - Technology

Directors: Penny Green/Chmn., CFO, Garry Newman/Dir., Robert Lanni/Member - Advisory Board, John Mulvihill/Member - Advisory Board, Susanne Milka/Dir.

Owners: Robin Ram/1.30%, Insiders/73.76%, Heather Remillard/8.83%, Penny Green/72.45%

Source Capital Inc

11400 W Olympic Blvd., Ste.1200, Los Angeles, CA, 90064; **PH:** 1-310-473-0225

General - Incorporation		Stock - Price on:12/24/2007	$69.19
Employees	NA	Stock Exchange	NYSE
Auditor	NA	Ticker Symbol	SOR
Stk Agt	Mellon Investor Services LLC	Outstanding Shares	8,580,000
Counsel	NA	E.P.S.	$2.72
DUNS No.	NA	Shareholders	NA

Business: The groups principal activity is to invest in business services and supplies, durable goods producers, retailing, energy, technology, healthcare, transportation, entertainment, financial, consumer durable goods and real estate investment trusts. The group operates from the United States.

Primary SIC and add'l.: 6722

CIK No: 0000091847

Officers: Eric S. Ende/63/Dir., Pres., Chief Investment Officer, Sherry Sasaki/53/Sec.

Directors: Willard H. Altman/72/Dir., Thomas P. Merrick/70/Dir., David Rees/84/Dir., Paul G. Schloemer/79/Dir., Lawrence J. Sheehan/75/Dir., Eric S. Ende/63/Dir., Pres., Chief Investment Officer

Financial Data: Fiscal Year End:12/31 Latest Annual Data: 12/31/2006

Year	Sales	Net Income
2006	$33,114,000	$28,029,000
2005	$85,267,000	$80,367,000
2004	$96,771,000	$92,164,000

Curr. Assets:	$552,000	Curr. Liab.:	$638,000		
Plant, Equip.:	NA	Total Liab.:	$638,000	Indic. Yr. Divd.:	$4.000
Total Assets:	$611,124,000	Net Worth:	$610,486,000	Debt/ Equity:	NA

Source Direct HL NEW

4323 Commerce Cir., Idaho Falls, ID, 83401; **PH:** 1-877-529-4114; **Fax:** 1-208-529-3054; **http://** www.simplywow.com

General - Incorporation	NV	Stock - Price on:12/24/2007	$0.32
Employees	7	Stock Exchange	OTC
Auditor	HJ & Assoc., LLC	Ticker Symbol	SODH
Stk Agt	Action Stock Transfer Corp	Outstanding Shares	8,190,000
Counsel	NA	E.P.S.	-$0.5
DUNS No.	NA	Shareholders	NA

Business: The groups principle activity is production of cleaning products. The group markets its products under the tradenames include Wow(R), Stain Pen(R) and Tuff Buff(R).

Primary SIC and add'l.: 2842

CIK No: 0001083661

Subsidiaries: Source Direct Holdings, Inc

Officers: Deren Z. Smith/39/Dir., Pres., Kevin Arave/51/Dir., Sec., Treasurer

Directors: Deren Z. Smith/39/Dir., Pres., Kevin Arave/51/Dir., Sec., Treasurer, Timothy Hooten/53/Dir.

Owners: Kevin Arave/21.10%, Timothy Hooten/4.40%, Insiders/43.90%, Deren Smith/18.30%

Financial Data: Fiscal Year End:06/30 Latest Annual Data: 6/30/2006

Year	Sales	Net Income
2006	$361,000	-$1,310,000
2005	$258,000	-$1,573,000
2004	$22,000	-$539,000

Curr. Assets:	$1,024,000	Curr. Liab.:	$350,000		
Plant, Equip.:	$814,000	Total Liab.:	$1,114,000	Indic. Yr. Divd.:	NA
Total Assets:	$1,933,000	Net Worth:	$820,000	Debt/ Equity:	NA

Source Interlink Cos Inc

27500 Riverview Ctr. Blvd., Ste. 400, Bonita Springs, FL, 34134; *PH:* 1-239-949-4450; *Fax:* 1-239-949-7623; *http://* www.sorc-info.com; *Email:* sales@sourceinterlink.com

General - Incorporation	DE	**Stock** - Price on:12/24/2007	$5.26
Employees	3,400	Stock Exchange	NDQ
Auditor	BDO Seidman LLP	Ticker Symbol	SORC
Stk Agt	Mellon Investor Services LLC	Outstanding Shares	52,310,000
Counsel	NA	E.P.S.	-$0.5
DUNS No.	55-637-0831	Shareholders	NA

Business: The group's principle activities include marketing and merchandising of entertainment products. The group's products include digital versatile discs, music compact discs, magazines, books and related items. The group operates from United States.

Primary SIC and add'l.: 2541 7389 2542 5192

CIK No: 0000943605

Subsidiaries: AEC Direct, Inc., Alliance Entertainment Corporation, Brand Manufacturing Corp, Chas. Levy Circulating Co., LLC., David E. Young, Inc., International Periodical Distributors, Inc., Primary Source, Inc., Source Home Entertainment, Inc., Source Interlink Canada, Inc., Source Interlink Companies, Inc, Source Interlink International, Inc., Source Mid-Atlantic News, LLC., Source-Chestnut Display Systems, Inc, Source-Huck Store Fixtures Company, Source-MYCO, Inc. 22 Subsidiaries included in the Index

Officers: James R. Gillis/55/Dir., Interim Co - CEO, COO, Pres., Douglas J. Bates/Sec., Jason Flegel/Exec. VP - Operations, Alan Tuchman/Exec. VP, Marc Fierman/CFO, Steven R. Parr/49/Pres. - Source Interlink Media

Directors: James R. Gillis/55/Dir., Interim Co - CEO, COO, Pres., Michael R. Duckworth/Chmn., Ariel Z. Emanuel/47/Dir., George A. Schnug/63/Dir., Gray Davis/65/Dir., Allan R. Lyons/67/Dir., David R. Jessick/55/Dir., Gregory Mays/62/Dir., Terrence Wallock/63/Dir.

Owners: George A. Schnug, David R. Jessick, Terrence J. Wallock, Insiders/3.70%, Wells Fargo& Company/6.40%, New Mountain Vantage Advisers, L.L.C/8.80%, AEC Associates, L.L.C/33.80%, Allan R. Lyons, Michael R. Duckworth, Aron S. Katzman, Peninusla Capital Management, L.P/5.60%, James R. Gillis/1.20%, Steven R. Parr, Ariel Z. Emanuel, Gov Gray Davis *(21 Owners included in Index)*

Financial Data: *Fiscal Year End:*01/31 *Latest Annual Data:* 1/31/2007

Year	Sales	Net Income
2007	$1,854,845,000	-$24,656,000
2006	$1,527,451,000	$12,879,000
2005	$356,644,000	$12,082,000

Curr. Assets:	$413,485,000	Curr. Liab.:	$383,962,000		
Plant, Equip.:	$67,915,000	Total Liab.:	$570,584,000	Indic. Yr. Divd.:	NA
Total Assets:	$1,010,031,000	Net Worth:	$439,447,000	Debt/ Equity:	0.3358

Source Petroleum Inc

620, 304 8th Ave. SW, Calgary, AB, T2P-1C1; *PH:* 1-403-444-2893; *Fax:* 1-403-444-0066; *http://* www.source-petroleum.com; *Email:* info@source-petroleum.com

General - Incorporation	NV	**Stock** - Price on:12/24/2007	$0.68
Employees	NA	Stock Exchange	OTC
Auditor	Peterson Sullivan PLLC	Ticker Symbol	SOPO
Stk Agt	Empire Stock Transfer Inc.	Outstanding Shares	NA
Counsel	NA	E.P.S.	NA
DUNS No.	NA	Shareholders	NA

Business: The groups principal activity is in the mineral exploration. The group acquired twenty five mineral claims in southwestern Alaska via staking which group believes are prospective for gold and copper. The group operates from the United States.

Primary SIC and add'l.: 1040

CIK No: 0001314363

Subsidiaries: 1245147 Alberta Ltd.

Officers: Hussein Charanek/39/Dir., CEO, CFO, Pres., Scott G. Rogers/36/Dir., Sec.

Directors: Hussein Charanek/39/Dir., CEO, CFO, Pres., Scott G. Rogers/36/Dir., Sec.

Owners: Insiders/15.87%, Hussein Charanek/15.38%, Scott Rogers

Financial Data: *Fiscal Year End:*12/31 *Latest Annual Data:* 12/31/2006

Year	Sales	Net Income
2006	$7,000	-$2,031,000
2005	NA	-$88,000

Curr. Assets:	$1,407,000	Curr. Liab.:	$360,000		
Plant, Equip.:	$45,752,000	Total Liab.:	$360,000	Indic. Yr. Divd.:	NA
Total Assets:	$50,838,000	Net Worth:	$50,478,000	Debt/ Equity:	NA

SOURCECORP

3232 Mckinney Ave, Ste. 900, Dallas, TX, 75204; *PH:* 1-214-953-7555; *http://* www.srcp.com

General - Incorporation	DE	**Stock** - Price on:12/24/2007	NA
Employees	NA	Stock Exchange	NDQ
Auditor	Deloitte & Touche LLP	Ticker Symbol	SRCP
Stk Agt	American Stock Transfer & Trust Co.	Outstanding Shares	NA
Counsel	Locke Liddell & Sapp LLP	E.P.S.	NA
DUNS No.	93-203-7344	Shareholders	NA

Business: The group's principal activity is to provide business process outsourcing solutions to industries such as financial services, government, legal, healthcare and transportation. The group operates in two segments: information management and distribution and healthcare, regulatory and legal compliance. The information management and distribution provides electronic imaging services, analog services, data capture and database management, Internet repository services and print and mail services.

The healthcare, regulatory and legal compliance provides services like processing a request for a patient's medical records, off-site active storage of a healthcare institutions medical records, online delivery of images of selected medical records and document and data conversion services for healthcare institutions. On 04-May-2004, the group acquired keypoint consulting llc.

Primary SIC and add'l.: 7389 7363 2759 7331

CIK No: 0000936931

Subsidiaries: ALS Acquisition Corp., American Economics Group,Inc., Associate Record Technician Services Acquisition Corp., Deliverex Acquisition Corp., Doctex Acquisition Corp., Economic Research Services,Inc, Economic Research Services,Inc.(1)(a), Edle Enterprises of Puerto Rico,Inc, Edle Enterprises of Puerto Rico,Inc.(2), Fastrieve,Inc., Glo-X,Inc., Glo-X,Inc.(3), Image Entry Acquisition Corp., Image Entry Federal SystemsInc., Image Entry Federal SystemsInc.(4)(c) 85 Subsidiaries included in the Index

Officers: Ed H. Bowman/Dir., CEO, Pres., Charles S. Gilbert/Sr. VP, General Counsel, Corp. Sec., Kerry Walbridge/Pres. - Business Process Solutions Division, Ralph D. Burns/VP - Corporate Development, Barry L. Edwards/CFO, Exec. VP, Dave Delgado/Pres. - Legal Claims, Regulatory Division, Dan H. Sawyers/Chief Accounting Officer

Directors: Ed H. Bowman/Dir., CEO, Pres.

SourceForge Inc

Formerly: VA Software Corp
650 Castro St., Ste. 450, Mountain View, CA, 94041; *PH:* 1-650-694-2100; *http://* www.vasoftware.com

General - Incorporation	DE	**Stock** - Price on:12/24/2007	$4.23
Employees	121	Stock Exchange	NDQ
Auditor	BDO Seidman LLP	Ticker Symbol	NA
Stk Agt	Computershare Investor Services LLC	Outstanding Shares	67,880,000
Counsel	Wilson Sonsini Goodrich & Rosati	E.P.S.	$0.13
DUNS No.	NA	Shareholders	NA

Business: The group's principal activity is to provide application software products and related osdn products and services. The group develops, markets and supports sourceforge enterprise edition, which is a proprietary software designed for corporate and public-sector information technology and software engineering organizations. Sourceforge provides development intelligence to its customers by combining software development tools with the ability to track, measure and report on software project activity in real-time. The group owns and manages a network of Web sites, collectively known as osdn, which are widely used by the information technology and software development communities. The group also sells consumer goods and digital animations through the Internet. Major customer of the group is intel corporation.

Primary SIC and add'l.: 7379 7372 3571 3572

CIK No: 0001096199

Subsidiaries: ThinkGeek, Inc

Officers: Ali Jenab/Dir., CEO, Pres., Patricia Morris/Sr. VP, CFO, Richard Marino/Group Pres. - Ostg, Jeff Bates/VP - Editorial Operations, Caroline Offutt/GM - Thinkgeek, Mike Rudolph/VP - Sourceforgenet Marketplace, Jay Seirmarco/VP, GM, Sourceforgenet Corp. Sec., General Counsel - VA Software Corporation, Andrew Zeiger/VP - Media Sales

Directors: Ali Jenab/Dir., CEO, Pres., Ram Gupta/Chmn., Robert M. Neumeister/Dir., Andrew Anker/Dir., Carl Redfield/Dir., David B. Wright/Dir., Scott E. Howe/Dir.

Owners: Darryll E. Dewan/1.30%, Carl Redfield, Patricia S. Morri, Ali Jenab/3.20%, Insiders/5.30%, Andrew Zeiger, Andrew Anker, Trivium Capital Management LLC/10.10%, James Jay Seirmarco, David B. Wright, Ram Gupta, Scott E. Howe, Robert M. Neumeister, Richard J. Marino, FMR Corporation/12.10%

Financial Data: *Fiscal Year End:*07/31 *Latest Annual Data:* 7/31/2006

Year	Sales	Net Income
2006	$43,632,000	$10,962,000
2005	$32,887,000	-$4,694,000
2004	$29,261,000	-$7,640,000

Curr. Assets:	$59,406,000	Curr. Liab.:	$8,141,000	P/E Ratio:	32.54
Plant, Equip.:	$627,000	Total Liab.:	$13,834,000	Indic. Yr. Divd.:	NA
Total Assets:	$63,212,000	Net Worth:	$49,378,000	Debt/ Equity:	NA

South American Minerals Inc

76 BeAve.r St., 26Th Fl., New York, NY, 10005; *PH:* 1-212-668-0842; *http://* www.southamericanminerals.com; *Email:* info@southamericanminerals.com

General - Incorporation	NV	**Stock** - Price on:12/24/2007	$0.18
Employees	NA	Stock Exchange	OTC
Auditor	NA	Ticker Symbol	SAMM
Stk Agt	American Stock Transfer & Trust Co.	Outstanding Shares	NA
Counsel	NA	E.P.S.	NA
DUNS No.	NA	Shareholders	NA

Business: The group operates through its subsidiaries whose principle activity is to engage in dredging for alluvial placer gold on the Konawaruk River in Guyana, South America on our own behalf and on behalf of the Venture in which we currently hold a 65% interest. The group operates from United States.

Primary SIC and add'l.: 1040

CIK No: 0001304668

South Carolina Electric & Gas Co

1426 Main St., Columbia, SC, 29201; *PH:* 1-803-217-9000; *http://* www.scana.com

General - Incorporation	SC	**Stock** - Price on:12/24/2007	NA
Employees	NA	Stock Exchange	NYSE
Auditor	Deloitte & Touche LLP	Ticker Symbol	SCG
Stk Agt	SCANA Corp	Outstanding Shares	NA
Counsel	NA	E.P.S.	NA
DUNS No.	00-791-9517	Shareholders	NA

Business: The group's principal activities are generation and sale of electricity. The group is a public utility company and a wholly owned subsidiary of scana corporation. The group serves wholesale and retail customers. The group operates in two segments: electric operations and gas distribution. Under electric operations segment, the group generates, transmits and distributes electricity to 24 counties

covering more than 15,000 square miles in the central, southern and southwestern portions of South Carolina. The electricity is provided to industrial, commercial and residential customers. Under gas distribution segment the group purchases and sells natural gas primarily at retail to 33 counties in South Carolina covering 22,000 square miles.

Primary SIC and add'l.: 4922 4911 4923 4931

CIK No: 0000091882

Subsidiaries: SCANA Corporation, South Carolina corporation

Officers: William B. Timmerman/61/Chmn., CEO, P. V. Fant/55/Sr. VP - Transmission Services, Kevin B. Marsh/51/COO, Pres., Jimmy E. Addison/Sr. VP, CFO, VP - Finance, James E. Swan/Principal Accounting Officer, Controller, S. D. Burch/50/Sr. VP - Fuel Procurement, Asset Management, Francis P. Mood/69/Sr. VP, General Counsel, Assist. Sec., J. C. Bouknight/Sr. VP - Human Resources, Stephen A. Byrne/48/Sr. VP - Generation - Nuclear, Fossil Hydro

Directors: William B. Timmerman/61/Chmn., CEO, James A. Bennett/46/Dir., William C. Burkhardt/Dir., Bill L. Amick/Dir., Sharon A. Decker/Dir., Maybank D. Hagood/Dir., Hayne W. Hipp/Dir., Lynne M. Miller/56/Dir., Maceo K. Sloan/58/Dir., Harold C. Stowe/Dir., Smedes G. York/Dir.

Owners: H. C. Stowe, G. S. York, S. A. Byrne, S. A. Decker, W. B. Timmerman, L. M. Miller, J. A. Bennett, Insiders, B. L. Amick, K. B. Marsh, W. C. Burkhardt, M. K. Sloan, J. E. Addison, F. P. Mood, D. M. Hagood (17 Owners included in Index)

South Financial Group Inc

The S Financial Group, Greenville, SC, 29602; **PH:** 1-864-255-7900; **Fax:** 1-864-239-2280; **http://** www.theSgroup.com

General - Incorporation	SC	**Stock**- Price on:12/24/2007	$23.49
Employees	2,618	Stock Exchange	NDQ
Auditor	KPMG LLP	Ticker Symbol	TSFG
Stk Agt	Registrar & Transfer Co	Outstanding Shares	74,150,000
Counsel	NA	E.P.S.	NA
DUNS No.	15-420-9571	Shareholders	NA

Business: The group's principal activity is to provide a full range of financial services including asset management, insurance, investments, mortgage services. The group provides services which includes commercial and consumer banking services like deposit accounts, secured and unsecured loans, cash management programs, trust functions, safe deposit services and certain insurance and brokerage services. It conducts business through 134 branch offices, of which 76 are in South Carolina, 24 in North Carolina and 34 are in Florida. On 16-Jul-2004, the group acquired cnb Florida bancshares, inc and Florida banks, inc.

Primary SIC and add'l.: 6351 6712 6162 6021

CIK No: 0000797871

Subsidiaries: American Pensions, Inc., Bowditch Insurance Corporation, Carolina First Bank, Carolina First Community Development Corporation, Carolina First Mortgage Loan Trust, Carolina First Mortgage Loan Trust II, Carolina First Securities, Inc., CF Investment Company, Citrus REIT Corporation, CNB Properties, Inc., Flaresco, Inc., Floreit, Inc., Florida Banks Capital Trust I, Florida Banks Capital Trust II, Florida Banks Statutory Trust I 40 Subsidiaries included in the Index

Officers: Mack I. Whittle/Chmn., CEO, Pres./$3,654,155.00, Andrew B. Cheney/58/Exec. VP, Chmn. - Mercantile Bank/$1,024,638.00, Timothy K. Schools/38/Exec. VP/$809,484.00, Michael W. Sperry/Exec. VP - Credit Policy, Risk Management, Mary A. Jeffrey/Exec. VP, Corp. Dir. - Human Resources, J. W. Davis/Dir., Pres., John C. Dubose/Exec. VP - Technology, Financial Services/$3,921,296.00, Kendall L. Spencer/Pres. - Mercantile Bank, Keith D. Williamson/Exec. VP, General Auditor, William P. Crawford/Exec. VP, General Counsel, Christopher T. Holmes/Exec. VP, Dir. - Retail Banking, Maurice J. Spagnoletti/Carolina First Bank, South Carolina, James W. Terry/60/Exec. VP - Corporate Banking/$2,885,269.00, James R. Gordon/42/CFO, Exec. VP, Lynn H. Harton/Exec. VP, Chief Risk, Credit Officer

Directors: Mack I. Whittle/Chmn., CEO, Pres., Earle H. Russell/Dir., William S. Hummers/Dir., William R. Timmons/Dir., David C. Wakefield/Dir., Jon W. Pritchett/Dir., Darla D. Moore/Dir., Samuel H. Vickers/Dir., J. W. Davis/Dir., Pres., Claymon C. Grimes/Dir., Dexter M. Hagy/Dir., Challis M. Lowe/Dir., Charles B. Schooler/Dir., John C.B. Smith/Dir., Edward J. Sebastian/Dir. (16 Directors included in Index)

Owners: John C.B. Smith, William P. Brant, Edward J. Sebastian, James W. Terry, Samuel H. Vickers, J. W. Davis, Mack I. Whittle, Charles B. Schooler, Andrew B. Cheney, Dexter M. Hagy, William R. Timmons, Claymon C. Grimes, David C. Wakefield, William S. Hummers, Timothy K. Schools (17 Owners included in Index)

Financial Data: Fiscal Year End:12/31   Latest Annual Data: 06/30/2007

Year	Sales	Net Income
2007	NA	NA
2006	$992,251,000	$112,866,000
2005	$809,507,000	$69,821,000

Curr. Assets:	$435,354,000	**Curr. Liab.:**	$11,354,399,000	**P/E Ratio:**	16.78
Plant, Equip.:	$219,163,000	**Total Liab.:**	$12,648,484,000	**Indic. Yr. Divd.:**	$0.720
Total Assets:	$14,210,516,000	**Net Worth:**	$1,562,032,000	**Debt/ Equity:**	0.5182

South Jersey Gas Co

1 S Jersey Plz., Folsom, NJ, 08037; **PH:** 1-609-561-9000; **Fax:** 1-609-561-8225; **http://** www.sjindustries.com; **Email:** investorrelations@sjindustries.com

General - Incorporation	NJ	**Stock**- Price on:12/24/2007	NA
Employees	NA	Stock Exchange	NA
Auditor	Deloitte & Touche LLP	Ticker Symbol	NA
Stk Agt	NA	Outstanding Shares	NA
Counsel	NA	E.P.S.	NA
DUNS No.	05-140-9605	Shareholders	NA

Business: The group's principle activity is to purchase, transmit and sell natural gas to residential, commercial and industrial customers. The company is a wholly owned subsidiary of south jersey industries and serves natural gas throughout the counties of Atlantic, cape may, cumberlan

Primary SIC and add'l.: 4923

CIK No: 0001035216

Subsidiaries: SJG Capital Trust

Officers: Edward J. Graham/Chmn., CEO, Pres., Richard H. Walker/Sr. VP, General Counsel, Sec., David A. Kindlick/CFO, Sr. VP

Directors: Edward J. Graham/Chmn., CEO, Pres., Shirli M. Billings/Dir., Frederick R. Raring/Dir., William J. Hughes/Dir., Sheila Hartnett-Devlin/Dir.

South Jersey Industries Inc

1 S Jersey Plz., Folsom, NJ, 08037; **PH:** 1-609-561-9000; **Fax:** 1-609-561-8225; **http://** www.sjindustries.com

General - Incorporation	NJ	**Stock**- Price on:12/24/2007	$34.9
Employees	611	Stock Exchange	NYSE
Auditor	Deloitte & Touche LLP	Ticker Symbol	SJI
Stk Agt	Wachovia Bank N.A	Outstanding Shares	29,470,000
Counsel	Cozen O'Connor	E.P.S.	$2.24
DUNS No.	05-140-9498	Shareholders	NA

Business: The group's principal activities are to acquire and develop utility and non-utility lines of business. The group provides a variety of energy related products and services through its wholly owned subsidiaries. It acquires and markets natural gas and electricity to retail end users and provides total energy management services to commercial and industrial customers. The group markets wholesale natural gas storage, commodity and transportation in the mid-Atlantic and southern states. It also develops and plans to operate energy-related projects in southern New Jersey. The subsidiary service territory includes 112 municipalities throughout Atlantic, Cape May and Salem Counties and portions of Burlington, Camden and Gloucester Counties. The subsidiary serves 288,008 residential, commercial and industrial customers.

Primary SIC and add'l.: 4931 1442 4922

CIK No: 0000091928

Subsidiaries: AC Landfill Energy, LLC, Energy & Minerals, Inc., Marina Energy LLC, R&T Group, Inc., SJ EnerTrade, Inc., SJI Services, LLC, South Jersey Energy Company, South Jersey Energy Service Plus, LLC, South Jersey Energy Solutions, LLC, South Jersey Fuel, Inc, South Jersey Gas Company, South Jersey Industries, Inc., South Jersey Resources Group, LLC, WC Landfill Energy, LLC

Officers: Edward J. Graham/Chmn., CEO, Pres./$989,923.00, Stephen H. Clark/Treasurer, David Robbins/Treasurer - SJE, David A. Kindlick/CFO, VP/$596,301.00, Thomas S. Kavanaugh/Controller - SJG, Kenneth Lynch/Assist. VP - Financial Reporting, Risk Management, Michael J. Renna/40/VP/$327,304.00, Ken Depriest/Contact - South Jersey Resources Group, LLC, Albert V. Ruggiero/59/VP/$594,738.00, Jeffrey E. Dubois/49/VP, Kittye Bedinger/Contact - South Jersey Resources Group, LLC, Richard H. Walker/57/VP, General Counsel, Sec./$487,822.00

Directors: Edward J. Graham/Chmn., CEO, Pres., Shirli M. Billings/67/Dir., Thomas A. Bracken/60/Dir., Sheila Hartnett-Devlin/49/Dir., Frederick R. Raring/70/Dir., Helen R. Bosley/60/Dir., William J. Hughes/75/Dir., Herman D. James/64/Dir., Keith S. Campbell/53/Dir., Cary W. Edwards/63/Dir.

Owners: Barclays Global Investors/6.00%, Sheila Hartnett-Devlin, David A. Kindlick, Dimensional Fund Advisors, Inc./8.30%, Richard H. Walker, Keith S. Campbell, Herman D. James, Richard J. Jackson, Edward J. Graham, William J. Hughes, Shirli M. Billings, Thomas A. Bracken, Frederick R. Raring, Insiders/1.20%, Cary W. Edwards (18 Owners included in Index)

Financial Data: Fiscal Year End:12/31   Latest Annual Data: 12/31/2006

Year	Sales	Net Income
2006	$931,428,000	$71,432,000
2005	$920,982,000	$47,919,000
2004	$819,076,000	$42,293,000

Curr. Assets:	$371,724,000	**Curr. Liab.:**	$422,794,000		
Plant, Equip.:	$920,005,000	**Total Liab.:**	$1,129,996,000	**Indic. Yr. Divd.:**	$1.080
Total Assets:	$1,573,032,000	**Net Worth:**	$443,036,000	**Debt/ Equity:**	0.7832

South Shore Resources Inc

Formerly: FirstBingo.com
PO Box 663, Times Sq., Leeward Hwy. Providenciales, Caicos Islands; **PH:** 41-628-13335; **http://** www.firstbingo.com

General - Incorporation	NV	**Stock**- Price on:12/24/2007	$0.45
Employees	NA	Stock Exchange	NA
Auditor	Williams & Webster, P.S	Ticker Symbol	NA
Stk Agt	Transfer Online, Inc.,	Outstanding Shares	NA
Counsel	NA	E.P.S.	NA
DUNS No.	NA	Shareholders	NA

Business: The group is a development stage company. The group develops and produces a game called trivia bingo. Trivia bingo will be played over the Internet and will be free to all participants. Trivia bingo will be divided into two divisions. One division will be an Internet trivia bingo game played on the Internet and other division will be a television game show. The group has recently completed the development of a beta version of its Internet trivia bingo game and trivia bingo is now operational on the Internet. The group's Web site will allow the customers to review all terms, rules and conditions applicable to trivia bingo and other uses at the site.

Primary SIC and add'l.: 7375

CIK No: 0001120285

Subsidiaries: WorldWide-Exclusive Limited.

Officers: Michael Kabin/53/Dir., Sec., CEO, Richard L. Wachter/55/Dir., CFO, Pres.

Directors: Michael Kabin/53/Dir., Sec., CEO, Richard L. Wachter/55/Dir., CFO, Pres.

Owners: Insiders/57.28%, Richard L. Wachter/57.28%

Financial Data: Fiscal Year End:12/31   Latest Annual Data: 12/31/2006

Year	Sales	Net Income
2006	NA	-$774,000
2005	$1,000	-$984,000
2004	$0	-$549,000

Curr. Assets:	$195,000	**Curr. Liab.:**	$756,000		
Plant, Equip.:	$3,000	**Total Liab.:**	$758,000	**Indic. Yr. Divd.:**	NA
Total Assets:	$230,000	**Net Worth:**	-$528,000	**Debt/ Equity:**	NA

South Street Financial Corp

155 W S St., Albemarle, NC, 28001; **PH:** 1-704-982-9184; **Fax:** 1-704-983-1308; **http://** www.homesavingsbank.org; **Email:** dsmith@SSt.financial.com

General - Incorporation	NC	**Stock**- Price on:12/24/2007	NA
Employees	48	Stock Exchange	OTC
Auditor	Dixon Hughes PLLC	Ticker Symbol	SSFC
Stk Agt	Dixon Hughes PLLC	Outstanding Shares	NA
Counsel	Brooks, Pierce Et Al	E.P.S.	$0.44
DUNS No.	95-982-4434	Shareholders	NA

Business: The group's principal activity is to accept retail deposits from the general public and use such deposits to lend mortgage loans secured by real estate. The group operates through its subsidiary, Home Savings Bank of Albemarle Inc. SSB. The financial services provided by the group include demand deposits, certificates of deposit, real-estate mortgage loans, non-residential loans, consumer loans and commercial loans. The group offers mortgage loans secured by residential real property, including one-to-four family residential real estate loans, home equity line of credit loans and other subordinate lien loans.

Primary SIC and add'l.: 6712 6035

CIK No: 0001014964

Subsidiaries: Park Ridge Associates, LLC, South Street Development Corporation

Officers: Ronald R. Swanner/Dir., CEO, Pres./$326,269.00, David L. Smith/Sec./$134,394.00, Christopher F. Cranford/CFO, Treasurer/$127,893.00, Cris D. Turner/VP/$144,027.00, Melody M. Goins/54/VP/$130,228.00, Sheila S. Barbee/Sr. VP, Sec. - Home Savings Bank, Larry L. Hatley/Sr. VP - Home Savings Bank, Carolyn B. Clontz/Assist. VP - Home Savings Bank, Paul Childress/Advisory Dir., Sam Griffin/Advisory Dir., Eddie Julian/Advisory Dir., Josh Morton/Advisory Dir., Wayne Sasser/Advisory Dir., Steve Surratt/Advisory Dir., Terry Whitley/Advisory Dir. *(30 Officers included in Index)*

Directors: Ronald R. Swanner/Dir., CEO, Pres., Banks J. Garrison/Dir., Caldwell A. Holbrook/Dir., Joel A. Huneycutt/Dir., Douglas D. Stokes/Dir., Greg E. Underwood/Dir.

Owners: Christopher F. Cranford, Cris D. Turner, Insiders/26.66%, Melody M. Goins, Ronald R. Swanner/3.28%, Douglas Dwight Stokes/16.06%, David L. Smith/1.27%, Caldwell A. Holbrook/15.46%, Joel A. Huneycutt/16.16%, Carl M. Hill/7.42%, Banks J. Garrison/14.30%, Greg E. Underwood/15.37%

Financial Data: *Fiscal Year End:*12/31 *Latest Annual Data:* 12/31/2006

Year	Sales	Net Income
2006	$16,589,000	$1,277,000
2005	$13,519,000	$1,580,000
2004	$11,320,000	$1,089,000

Curr. Assets:	$22,739,000	Curr. Liab.:	$246,598,000		
Plant, Equip.:	$6,695,000	Total Liab.:	$251,598,000	Indic. Yr. Divd.:	$0.400
Total Assets:	$276,986,000	Net Worth:	$25,388,000	Debt/ Equity:	NA

South Texas Oil Co

6330 McLeod Dr., Ste 1, Las Vegas, NV, 89123; *PH:* 1-702-262-2061; *http://* www.nutekoil.com

General - Incorporation	NV	Stock- Price on:12/24/2007	$9.17
Employees	5	Stock Exchange	NDQ
Auditor	Causey Demgen & Moore Inc.	Ticker Symbol	STXX
Stk Agt	Transfer Online, Inc.	Outstanding Shares	13,510,000
Counsel	NA	E.P.S	-$0.12
DUNS No.	NA	Shareholders	NA

Business: The groups principle activities include acquiring, developing and operating energy properties. The groups operating properties include Ann Burns, Burns, Davidson, Foster, Jane Burns, Shell, Smith and Talley. The group operates from United States.

Primary SIC and add'l.: NA

CIK No: 0001288946

Officers: Murray N. Conradie/Chmn., CEO, Pres., Edward Shaw/Dir., COO, Rickey Cooksey/CFO

Directors: Murray N. Conradie/Chmn., CEO, Pres., Conrad Humbke/Dir.

Owners: Jason F. Griffith/2.80%, Edward Shaw/2.09%, Insiders/13.70%, Murray N. Conradie/8.82%

Financial Data: *Fiscal Year End:*12/31 *Latest Annual Data:* 12/31/2006

Year	Sales	Net Income
2006	$640,000	-$733,000
2005	$292,000	-$1,021,000

Curr. Assets:	$1,322,000	Curr. Liab.:	$67,000		
Plant, Equip.:	$3,163,000	Total Liab.:	$544,000	Indic. Yr. Divd.:	NA
Total Assets:	$4,486,000	Net Worth:	$3,942,000	Debt/ Equity:	0.2470

Southcoast Financial Corp

534 Johnnie Dodds Blvd., Mount Pleasant, SC, 29464; *PH:* 1-843-884-0504; *Fax:* 1-843-884-2886; *http://* www.southcoastbank.com; *Email:* investor@sentigen.com

General - Incorporation	SC	Stock- Price on:12/24/2007	$20.26
Employees	115	Stock Exchange	NDQ
Auditor	Elliott Davis LLP	Ticker Symbol	SOCB
Stk Agt	NA	Outstanding Shares	6,260,000
Counsel	NA	E.P.S	$0.73
DUNS No.	NA	Shareholders	NA

Business: The group's principal activity is to provide commercial bank services including deposit and loan services. Other services of the group include residential mortgage loan origination services, safe deposit boxes, business courier service, night depository service, telephone banking, VISA and MasterCard brand credit cards, tax deposits, travelers checks and 24-hour automated teller machines. The group has eight locations in the Greater Charleston market, including offices in Charleston, North Charleston, Mt. Pleasant, Johns Island, Moncks Corner, Summerville and Goose Creek.

Primary SIC and add'l.: 6022 6712

CIK No: 0001083689

Subsidiaries: Southcoast Community Bank

Officers: Wayne L. Pearson/60/Chmn., CEO, Pres., William B. Seabrook/51/Exec. VP/$239,148.00, Paul D. Hollen/59/Dir., COO, Exec. VP/$301,259.00, Robert A. Daniel/57/Exec. VP/$237,194.00, William C. Heslop/32/CFO, Sr. VP/$83,646.00

Directors: Wayne L. Pearson/60/Chmn., CEO, Pres., Robert M. Scott/64/Dir., James H. Sexton/58/Dir., James P. Smith/53/Dir., William A. Coates/58/Dir., Tommy B. Baker/62/Dir., Stephen F. Hutchinson/61/Dir., Paul D. Hollen/59/Dir., COO, Exec. VP

Owners: Tommy B. Baker, Robert A. Daniel, James P. Smith/1.15%, Paul D. Hollen/1.99%, Insiders/10.64%, Stephen F. Hutchinson, Wayne L. Pearson/2.34%, William B. Seabrook, James H. Sexton, William A. Coates/1.38%, Robert M. Scott/1.34%, Goldman Sachs Asset Management, L.P./5.80%

Financial Data: *Fiscal Year End:*12/31 *Latest Annual Data:* 12/31/2006

Year	Sales	Net Income
2006	$35,247,000	$4,840,000
2005	$26,614,000	$4,189,000
2004	$19,295,000	$2,982,000

Curr. Assets:	$38,212,000	Curr. Liab.:	$312,734,000	P/E Ratio:	32.16
Plant, Equip.:	$25,126,000	Total Liab.:	$403,053,000	Indic. Yr. Divd.:	NA
Total Assets:	$481,856,000	Net Worth:	$78,803,000	Debt/ Equity:	1.4010

SouthCrest Financial Group Inc

600 N Glynn St., Ste. B, Fayetteville, GA, 30214; *PH:* 1-770-461-2781

General - Incorporation	GA	Stock- Price on:12/24/2007	$24
Employees	187	Stock Exchange	OTC
Auditor	Mauldin & Jenkins,Crtfd Pub. Acct.	Ticker Symbol	SCSG
Stk Agt	NA	Outstanding Shares	NA
Counsel	NA	E.P.S	NA
DUNS No.	NA	Shareholders	NA

Business: The group operates through its subsidiaries whose principal activities include providing banking and financial services to customers. Services of the group include consumer loans, real estate loans, and commercial loans as well as maintaining deposit accounts such as checking accounts, money market accounts, and a variety of certificates of deposit. The group operates from the United States.

Primary SIC and add'l.: 6021

CIK No: 0001279756

Subsidiaries: Bank of Upson, Peachtree Bank, The First National Bank of Polk County

Owners: Daniel W. Brinks/3.30%, Robert Cravey/5.50%, Harvey N. Clapp/2.40%, Michael D. McRae, Douglas J. Hertha, Joan Cravey/1.30%, Larry T. Kuglar/2.50%, Warren Patrick, Harold W. Wyatt/3.80%, Insiders/18.80%, Richard T. Bridges, Zack D. Cravey/5.10%

Financial Data: *Fiscal Year End:*12/31 *Latest Annual Data:* 12/31/2006

Year	Sales	Net Income
2006	$34,788,000	$5,774,000
2005	$29,088,000	$4,844,000
2004	$19,175,000	$3,857,000

Curr. Assets:	$34,311,000	Curr. Liab.:	$467,787,000		
Plant, Equip.:	$15,324,000	Total Liab.:	$475,474,000	Indic. Yr. Divd.:	$0.500
Total Assets:	$544,017,000	Net Worth:	$67,555,000	Debt/ Equity:	0.0113

Southeast Airport Group

Bosque De Alisos No. 47a - 4th Floor, Bosques De Las Lomas, 5120; *PH:* 52-5552840400; *http://* www.asur.com.mx

General - Incorporation	Mexico	Stock- Price on:12/24/2007	NA
Employees	NA	Stock Exchange	NYSE
Auditor	PricewaterhouseCoopers S.C	Ticker Symbol	NA
Stk Agt	NA	Outstanding Shares	NA
Counsel	NA	E.P.S	NA
DUNS No.	NA	Shareholders	NA

Business: The group's principle activities are the administration, operation and development of a group of nine airports in the southeast region of Mexico. The airports are located in the following cities: cancun, cozumel, merida, huatulco, oaxaca, veracruz, villahermosa, tapachula and minatitlan. It charges fees based on passenger traffic and the right to operate in its shopping areas. It also obtains rents and other revenues from the commercial activities that take place in their airports, such as the leasing of premises to restaurants and stores.

Primary SIC and add'l.: 3812 4581

CIK No: 0001123452

Subsidiaries: Aeropuerto de Cancun, S. A. de C. V., Aeropuerto de Cozumel, S. A. de C. V., Aeropuerto de Huatulco, S. A. de C. V., Aeropuerto de Merida, S. A. de C. V., Aeropuerto de Minatitlan, S. A. de C. V., Aeropuerto de Oaxaca, S. A. de C. V., Aeropuerto de Tapachula, S. A. de C. V., Aeropuerto de Veracruz, S. A. de C. V., Aeropuerto de Villahermosa, S. A. de C. V., Servicios Aeroportuarios del Sureste, S. A. de C. V.

Officers: Fernando Chico Pardo/Chmn., CEO, Adolfo Castro Rivas/44/Chief Financial, Strategic Planning Officer, Claudio Gongora/Chief Legal Counsel, Francisco Cuellar/Dir. - New Business Development, Gabriel Gurmendez/Dir. - Cancun Airport, Hector J. Navarrete/Dir. - Regional Airports, Manuel Gutierrez/Chief Commercial Officer

Directors: Fernando Chico Pardo/Chmn., CEO, Valentin Diez Morodo/Dir., Ricardo Guajardo Touche/Dir., George J. Vojta/Dir., Francisco Garza Zambrano/Dir., Alejandro Soberon Kuri/Dir., Rasmus Christiansen/Dir.

Owners: , ITA, through Bancomext/7.60%, Agrupacion Aeroportuaria Internacional II, S.A. de C.V.

Southeastern Bank Financial Corp

3530 Wheeler Rd., Augusta, GA, 30909; *PH:* 1-706-738-6990; *Fax:* 1-706-737-3106; *http://* www.georgiabankandtrust.com

General - Incorporation	GA	Stock- Price on:12/24/2007	$35.75
Employees	298	Stock Exchange	OTC
Auditor	Crowe Chizek & Co. LLC	Ticker Symbol	SBFC
Stk Agt	Georgia Bank & Trust Co	Outstanding Shares	5,430,000
Counsel	NA	E.P.S	$2.11
DUNS No.	19-996-6656	Shareholders	NA

Business: The group's principal activities are to provide wide range of lending services, acceptance of deposits and other services. The operations of the group are conducted through its wholly-owned subsidiary, Georgia bank & trust company of augusta. The group provides residential real estate, commercial real estate, construction and development, commercial and consumer loans to individuals, small and medium sized businesses and professionals. The group also accepts non-interest bearing demand, interest checking, money market, savings and time deposits. The group conducts its business through seven banking offices located in richmond and columbia counties.

Primary SIC and add'l.: 6022 6712

CIK No: 0000880116

Subsidiaries: Georgia Bank & Trust Company of Augusta, Southeastern Bank Financial Statutory Trust I

Officers: Daniel R. Blanton/Dir., CEO, Pres./$613,614.00, Susie W. Miville/VP, Controller, Pierce J. Blanchard/Exec. VP - Business Development, Robert C. Osborne/Exec. VP - Wealth Management, Jay B. Forrester/Group VP - Retail Banking, Angela J. Morales/Sr. VP - Retail Bank Operations, Jerry T. Rogers/VP - Investment Department, Frankie M. Wright/VP - Human Resources, Susan A. Wright/VP - Mortgage Lending, Savannah, Mark D. Allen/Assist. VP, Business

Development Officer, June B. Applewhite/Assist. VP, Office Mgr., Joe H. Attaway/Assist. VP, Facilities Mgr., Denise F. Bargeron/VP - Deposit Operations, Ricardo R. Bonner/Assist. VP, Business Development Officer, Dorothey G. Cunningham/Assist. VP - Audit, Compliance *(80 Officers included in Index)*

Directors: Daniel R. Blanton/Dir., CEO, Pres., Robert W. Pollard/Chmn., Grey B. Murray/Dir., Larry S. Prather/Dir., Milton Ruben/Dir., James W. Smith/Dir., Randolph R. Smith/Dir., Edward J. Tarver/Dir., Jane W. Howington/Dir., Warren A. Daniel/Dir., William J. Badger/Dir., James G. Blanchard/Dir., Braye C. Boardman/Dir., Marshall W. Brown/Dir., William P. Copenhaver/Dir. *(19 Directors included in Index)*

Owners: Levi A. Pollard/6.79%, Randolph R. Smith/5.08%, Daniel R. Blanton/8.00%, Warren A. Daniel, Ronald L. Thigpen/1.27%, Larry S. Prather, Edward G. Meybohm/4.76%, William J. Badger/1.28%, RWP, Sr., Enterprises, LLLP/17.02%, John W. Trulock, Robert W. Pollard/8.25%, Darrell R. Rains, Insiders/30.18%

Financial Data: Fiscal Year End:12/31   Latest Annual Data: 12/31/2006

Year	Sales	Net Income
2006	$79,619,000	$11,160,000
2005	$59,740,000	$9,954,000
2004	$47,914,000	$8,704,000

Curr. Assets:	$46,894,000	Curr. Liab.:	$941,278,000	P/E Ratio:	16.94
Plant, Equip.:	$23,403,000	Total Liab.:	$962,278,000	Indic. Yr. Divd.:	$0.520
Total Assets:	$1,041,202,000	Net Worth:	$78,924,000	Debt/ Equity:	0.2555

Southeastern Banking Corp

1010 Nway, Darien, GA, 31305; *PH:* 1-912-437-4141; *Fax:* 1-912-437-2294; *http://* www.southeasternbank.com

General - Incorporation	GA	**Stock** - Price on:12/24/2007	$28.7
Employees	164	Stock Exchange	OTC
Auditor	Mauldin & Jenkins LLC	Ticker Symbol	SEBC
Stk Agt	NA	Outstanding Shares	3,210,000
Counsel	NA	E.P.S	$2.04
DUNS No.	04-386-2663	Shareholders	NA

Business: The group's principal activities are to provide commercial and financial services to individuals, corporate and government customers. It provides traditional deposits, insurance services, official check services, wire transfers and safe deposit box rentals. Deposit services provided by the group includes time certificates plus now, money market, savings and individual retirement accounts. Credit services include commercial and installment loans, long-term mortgage origination, credit cards and standby letters of credit. It also provides insurance agent and investment brokerage services. At 31-Dec-2003, it operates through fifteen full-service banking offices located in southeast Georgia and northeast Florida and one loan production office.

Primary SIC and add'l.: 6022 6712
CIK No: 0000353386
Subsidiaries: Southeastern Bank
Officers: Cornelius P. Holland/Dir., CEO, Pres./$319,889.00, Alyson G. Beasley/Dir., VP, Treasurer/$147,605.00, John C. Houser/44/Exec. VP - Southeastern Bank/$186,997.00
Directors: Cornelius P. Holland/Dir., CEO, Pres., David H. Bluestein/Dir., Alyson G. Beasley/Dir., VP, Treasurer, Leslie H. Blair/68/Dir., Wade A. Strickland/68/Dir., Alva J. Hopkins/Dir.
Owners: Insiders/28.24%, Wade A. Strickland, William Downey/5.71%, Alyson G. Beasley/25.76%, David H. Bluestein, Lanier R. Miles, Cornelius P. Holland, Alva J. Hopkins/1.07%, John C. Houser, Leslie H. Blair

Financial Data: Fiscal Year End:12/31   Latest Annual Data: 12/31/2006

Year	Sales	Net Income
2006	$30,242,000	$6,575,000
2005	$26,485,000	$6,475,000
2004	$24,634,000	$5,803,000

Curr. Assets:	$23,410,000	Curr. Liab.:	$351,635,000	P/E Ratio:	13.93
Plant, Equip.:	$9,843,000	Total Liab.:	$358,116,000	Indic. Yr. Divd.:	$1.000
Total Assets:	$410,302,000	Net Worth:	$52,186,000	Debt/ Equity:	NA

Southern Banc Co Inc

221 S 6th St., Gadsden, AL, 35901; *PH:* 1-256-543-3860; *Fax:* 1-256-543-3864; *http://* www.sobanco.com; *Email:* services@sobanco.com

General - Incorporation	DE	**Stock** - Price on:12/24/2007	$13.75
Employees	31	Stock Exchange	OTC
Auditor	KPMG LLP	Ticker Symbol	SRNN
Stk Agt	NA	Outstanding Shares	NA
Counsel	Inzer, Haney & McWhorter	E.P.S	$0.13
DUNS No.	07-896-2065	Shareholders	NA

Business: The group's principal activities are to provide financial services through its four banking offices. The group is an independent community-oriented savings institution providing quality customer service. It offers banking services through its holding bank, the southern bank company that operates in four banking offices located in gadsden, albertville, guntersville and centre, Alabama. The group's lending activities consists of the origination of loans secured by mortgages on one-to-four-family residences and a variety of consumer loans in the group's market area. The group also makes limited amounts of non-residential real estate loans. The group attracts deposits principally from within its market area by offering a variety of deposit instruments, including regular checking, passbook, statement savings accounts and certificates of deposit, which range in term from seven days to ten years.

Primary SIC and add'l.: 6712 6035
CIK No: 0000946453
Subsidiaries: First Service Corporation, The Southern Bank Company

Financial Data: Fiscal Year End:06/30   Latest Annual Data: 6/30/2006

Year	Sales	Net Income
2006	$5,269,000	$235,000
2005	$5,503,000	$650,000
2004	$5,242,000	$577,000

Curr. Assets:	$6,240,000	Curr. Liab.:	$87,420,000	P/E Ratio:	105.77
Plant, Equip.:	$1,046,000	Total Liab.:	$87,710,000	Indic. Yr. Divd.:	$0.350
Total Assets:	$102,649,000	Net Worth:	$14,940,000	Debt/ Equity:	NA

Southern California Edison Co

2244 Walnut Grove Ave., Rosemead, CA, 91770; *PH:* 1-626-302-1212; *Fax:* 1-626-302-2517; *http://* www.sce.com

General - Incorporation	CA	**Stock** - Price on:12/24/2007	NA
Employees	NA	Stock Exchange	AMEX
Auditor	PricewaterhouseCoopers LLP	Ticker Symbol	NA
Stk Agt	Wells Fargo Shareowner Services	Outstanding Shares	NA
Counsel	NA	E.P.S	NA
DUNS No.	00-690-8818	Shareholders	NA

Business: The group's principle activities include producing and supplying electric energy for customers in central and southern California. The group operates from United States.

Primary SIC and add'l.: 4911
CIK No: 0000092103
Officers: Alan J. Fohrer/56/Chmn., CEO/$4,834,294.00, Polly L. Gault/54/Sr. VP - Public Affairs, Cecil R. House/46/VP - Operations Support, Chief Procurement Officer, Barbara J. Parsky/60/VP - Corporate Communications, John R. Fielder/Pres./$2,498,726.00
Directors: Alan J. Fohrer/56/Chmn., CEO, Ronald L. Olson/65/Dir., John E. Bryson/63/Dir., Luis G. Nogales/63/Dir., Charles B. Curtis/67/Dir., Robert H. Smith/71/Dir., France A. Cordova/60/Dir., Bradford M. Freeman/65/Dir., Richard T. Schlosberg/63/Dir., Thomas C. Sutton/64/Dir., James M. Rosser/68/Dir., Vanessa C.L. Chang/55/Dir., Brett White/48/Dir.
Owners: John E. Bryson, Robert H. Smith, Mahvash Yazdi, James M. Rosser, Thomas R. McDaniel, Richard T. Schlosberg, Thomas M. Noonan, Insiders/1.25%, Alan J. Fohrer, Luis G. Nogales, Theodore F. Craver, Charles B. Curtis, Thomas C. Sutton, France A. Crdova, Bradford M. Freeman *(17 Owners included in Index)*

Southern California Gas Co

555 W 5th St., Los Angeles, CA, 90013; *PH:* 1-213-244-1200; *Fax:* 1-213-244-3897; *http://* www.socalgas.com

General - Incorporation	CA	**Stock** - Price on:12/24/2007	NA
Employees	NA	Stock Exchange	NA
Auditor	Deloitte & Touche LLP	Ticker Symbol	NA
Stk Agt	NA	Outstanding Shares	NA
Counsel	NA	E.P.S	NA
DUNS No.	00-690-8826	Shareholders	NA

Business: The group's principal activity is to distribute and transport natural gas in southern California as well as parts of central California. The group offers two basic utility services: sale of natural gas and transportation of natural gas. Natural gas service of the group is also provided on a wholesale basis to the distribution systems of the city of long beach and san diego gas and electric company. The group also provides storage services to utility electric generation and large industrial and commercial customers. Core customers of the group are primarily residential and small commercial and industrial customers, without alternative fuel capability. The noncore customers consist primarily of utility electric generation, wholesale, large commercial, industrial and off-system customers.

Primary SIC and add'l.: 4923
CIK No: 0000092108
Subsidiaries: Ecotrans OEM Corporation, Southern California Gas Company, Southern California Gas Tower
Officers: Debra L. Reed/51/Chmn., CEO, Pres./$2,210,909.00, Michael R. Niggli/Dir., COO/$2,930,639.00, Dennis Arriola/CFO, Sr. VP/$1,090,900.00, Chris J. Baker/VP, Chief Information Technology Officer, Pamela J. Fair/VP - Customer Operations, James P. Harrigan/VP - Gas Acquisition, Margot A. Kyd/VP - Supply Management, Bret J. Lane/VP - Environmental, Safety, Facilities, Chief Environmental Officer, Lad Lorenz/VP - Regulatory Affairs, Richard M. Morrow/VP - Customer Services, Major Markets, Michelle M. Mueller/VP - Customer Services, Mass Markets, Lee Schavrien/Sr. VP - Regulatory Affairs/$837,379.00, Eugene Mitchell/Regional VP - External Affairs, Robert M. Schlax/VP, Controller, Anne Shen Smith/Sr. VP - Customer Services *(19 Officers included in Index)*
Directors: Debra L. Reed/51/Chmn., CEO, Pres., Mark A. Snell/Dir., Michael R. Niggli/Dir., COO
Owners: James P. Avery, Mark A. Snell, Anne S. Smith, Lee Schavrien, Insiders, Debra L. Reed, Michael R. Niggli, Lee M. Stewart, Dennis V. Arriola

Southern California Water Co

Formerly: Golden State Water CO
630 E Foothill Blvd, San Dimas, CA, 91773; *PH:* 1-909-394-3600; *http://* www.aswater.com; *Email:* investorinfo@aswater.com

General - Incorporation	CA	**Stock** - Price on:12/24/2007	$35.28
Employees	557	Stock Exchange	NA
Auditor	PricewaterhouseCoopers LLP	Ticker Symbol	NA
Stk Agt	Chase Mellon Shareholder Services LLC	Outstanding Shares	NA
Counsel	NA	E.P.S	$1.44
DUNS No.	00-690-8859	Shareholders	NA

Business: The group's principal activities are purchasing, production, distribution, sale of water and distribution of electricity. The group's other activities include providing wastewater treatment, customer billing, 24-hour customer support, and meter reading services. The group has three principal business units namely, water, electric distribution and contracted services. The group operates through California.

Primary SIC and add'l.: 4911 6719 4941
CIK No: 0000092116
Subsidiaries: American States Utility Services, Inc, California Cities Water Company, Inc., Chaparral City Water Company, Fort Bliss Water Services Company, Golden State Water Company, Old Dominion Utility Services, Inc., Terrapin Utility Services, Inc.

Financial Data: Fiscal Year End:12/31   Latest Annual Data: 12/31/2006

Year	Sales	Net Income
2006	$268,629,000	$23,081,000
2005	$236,197,000	$26,766,000
2004	$228,005,000	$18,541,000

Curr. Assets:	$64,436,000	Curr. Liab.:	$85,903,000	P/E Ratio:	24.50
Plant, Equip.:	$760,578,000	Total Liab.:	$653,221,000	Indic. Yr. Divd.:	$0.940
Total Assets:	$936,955,000	Net Worth:	$283,734,000	Debt/ Equity:	0.9394

Southern Co

30 Ivan Allen Jr. BlvdNW, Atlanta, GA, 30308; **PH:** 1-404-506-5000; **http://** www.southernco.com

General - Incorporation	DE	**Stock**- Price on:12/24/2007	$35.25
Employees	26,091	Stock Exchange	NYSE
Auditor	Deloitte & Touche LLP	Ticker Symbol	SO
Stk Agt	SCS Stockholder Services	Outstanding Shares	751,810,000
Counsel	NA	E.P.S	$2.27
DUNS No.	00-692-5341	Shareholders	NA

Business: The groups principle activities include acquiring, developing and operating power production and delivery facilities. The group operates in two segments: electric utilities and other. The group operates from United States.

Primary SIC and add'l.: 6719 4899 4911

CIK No: 0000092122

Subsidiaries: Alabama Power Capital Trust IV, Alabama Power Capital Trust V, Alabama Power Capital Trust VI, Alabama Power Capital Trust VII, Alabama Power Capital Trust VIII, Alabama Power Company, Alabama Property Company, Georgia Power Capital Trust IV, Georgia Power Capital Trust IX, Georgia Power Capital Trust V, Georgia Power Capital Trust VI, Georgia Power Capital Trust VII, Georgia Power Capital Trust VIII, Georgia Power Capital Trust X, Georgia Power Capital Trust XI 37 Subsidiaries included in the Index

Officers: Barnie J. Beasley/CEO, Pres. - Southern Nuclear, David M. Ratcliffe/60/Chmn., CEO, Pres./$7,854,264.00, Robert G. Dawson/CEO, Pres. - Southernline Wireless, Southern Telecom, Susan N. Story/48/CEO, Pres. - Gulf Power, Anthony J. Topazi/CEO, Pres. - Mississippi Power, James Barnie Beasley/56/CEO, Pres. - Southern Nuclear, Ron W. Hinson/Controller, Chief Accounting Officer, Principal Accounting Officer, William Paul Bowers/51/Exec. VP - SCS, Chris Bell/VP - Southern Wholesale Energy, Francis M. Fisher/59/VP - Customer Operations, Bernard P. Jacob/53/VP - External Affairs, Corporate Services, Ronnie R. Labrato/54/CFO, VP, Penny M. Manuel/45/VP, Sr. Production Officer, Phil Saunders/Sr. VP - Operations, Generation Services, Ed Day/Exec. VP - Engineering, Construction Services, Southern Company Generation *(39 Officers included in Index)*

Directors: David M. Ratcliffe/60/Chmn., CEO, Pres., Francis S. Blake/59/Dir., Zack T. Pate/Dir., Thomas F. Chapman/Dir., Dorrit J. Bern/58/Dir., Donald M. James/59/Dir., Juanita P. Baranco/59/Dir., William G. Smith/55/Dir., Neal J. Purcell/67/Dir., Ledon C. Anchors/67/Dir., William C. Cramer/55/Dir., Fred C. Donovan/67/Dir., William A. Pullum/60/Dir., Winston E. Scott/57/Dir., Bill Habermeyer/Dir. *(24 Directors included in Index)*

Owners: Juanita Powell Baranco, Francis S. Blake, Donald M. James, Michael D. Garrett, Thomas A. Fanning, Charles D. McCrary, David M. Ratcliffe, Thomas F. Chapman, Zack T. Pate, Dorrit J. Bern, William H. Habermeyer, Gerald J. St. P, William G. Smith, Insiders, Paul W. Bowers *(16 Owners included in Index)*

Financial Data: *Fiscal Year End:*12/31 *Latest Annual Data:* 12/31/2006

Year	Sales	Net Income
2006	$14,356,000,000	$1,573,000,000
2005	$13,554,000,000	$1,591,000,000
2004	$11,902,000,000	$1,532,000,000

Curr. Assets:	$4,019,000,000	**Curr. Liab.:**	$6,353,000,000	**P/E Ratio:**	15.67
Plant, Equip.:	$32,231,000,000	**Total Liab.:**	$30,743,000,000	**Indic. Yr. Divd.:**	$1.610
Total Assets:	$42,858,000,000	**Net Worth:**	$12,115,000,000	**Debt/ Equity:**	1.0320

Southern Community Bancshares Inc

325 2nd St. SE, Cullman, AL, 35055; **PH:** 1-256-734-4863; **Fax:** 1-256-737-8900; **http://** www.firstfederalcullman.com; **Email:** customerservice@southerncommunitybank.com

General - Incorporation	GA	**Stock**- Price on:12/24/2007	$13.16
Employees	95	Stock Exchange	OTC
Auditor	Mauldin & Jenkins LLC	Ticker Symbol	SNCB
Stk Agt	NA	Outstanding Shares	2,590,000
Counsel	NA	E.P.S	$0.91
DUNS No.	NA	Shareholders	NA

Business: The group's principal activity is to provide banking services in its primary market area of Fayette county and the surrounding countries. The group operates through its wholly owned commercial bank, southern community bank. The group's office is located in Georgia. As of December 31, 2005, the group had total assets of $334 million, an increase of 23% over December 31, 2004. The group's primary interest-earning assets as of December 31, 2005 were loans, which made up 81% of total interest-earning assets, and loan to deposit ratio was 97% as of December 31, 2005.

Primary SIC and add'l.: 6021 6712

CIK No: 0001171017

Subsidiaries: SCBI Capital Trust, Southern Community Bank

Officers: Gary D. McGaha/69/Dir., CEO, Pres., Lynn Reed/Contact - Human Resources Department, Leslye L. Grindle/CFO, Investor Relations Officer, Fred L. Faulkner/Chief Lending Officer, Sr. VP, Tina Stroud/Sr. VP, Branch Administrator

Directors: Gary D. McGaha/69/Dir., CEO, Pres., Thomas D. Reese/Chmn., Robert B. Dixon/Vice Chmn., James Stan Cameron/Dir., George Ronald Davis/Dir., Richard J. Dumas/Dir., William Wayne Leslie/Dir., William Mike Strain/Dir., Jackie L. Mask/Dir.

Owners: Thomas D. Reese/7.03%, George R. Davis/3.94%, Gary D. McGaha/1.53%, James S. Cameron/4.01%, Jackie L. Mask/2.98%, Richard J. Dumas/7.47%, Insiders/39.01%, William M. Strain/3.13%, Tina Stroud/0.01%, William Wayne Leslie/3.72%, Robert B. Dixon/5.94%, Leslye L. Grindle/0.09%, Fred L. Faulkner/1.52%

Financial Data: *Fiscal Year End:*12/31 *Latest Annual Data:* 12/31/2006

Year	Sales	Net Income
2006	$28,973,000	$2,496,000
2005	$19,973,000	$1,867,000
2004	$14,184,000	$1,680,000

Curr. Assets:	$19,517,000	**Curr. Liab.:**	$349,204,000	**P/E Ratio:**	14.46
Plant, Equip.:	$9,373,000	**Total Liab.:**	$361,886,000	**Indic. Yr. Divd.:**	NA
Total Assets:	$386,334,000	**Net Worth:**	$24,449,000	**Debt/ Equity:**	0.4350

Southern Connecticut Bancorp Inc

215 Church St., New Haven, CT, 06510; **PH:** 1-203-782-1100; **Fax:** 1-203-787-5056; **http://** www.scbancorp.com; **Email:** info@scbancorp.com

General - Incorporation	CT	**Stock**- Price on:12/24/2007	$7.4
Employees	43	Stock Exchange	AMEX
Auditor	McGladrey & Pullen LLP	Ticker Symbol	SSE
Stk Agt	Registrar & Transfer Co	Outstanding Shares	2,940,000
Counsel	NA	E.P.S	-$0.011
DUNS No.	NA	Shareholders	NA

Business: The group's principle activity is to provide full range of banking services to commercial and consumer customers. The group accepts deposits and offers loans to small to medium-sized businesses, professionals, individuals and their employees. The group's loan products include commercial and business loans, personal loans, mortgage loans, home equity loans, automobile loans and education loans. The kinds of deposits accepted by the group include checking accounts, money market accounts, savings accounts, a variety of certificates of deposits and ira accounts. The other services provided include, cashier's checks, traveler's checks, bank by mail, direct deposit and u. S. Savings bonds. The group is associated with a shared network of automated teller machines that its customers are able to use throughout Connecticut and other regions. The operations are conducted through 16 branches in the new haven market.

Primary SIC and add'l.: 6022 6712

CIK No: 0001137046

Subsidiaries: SCB Capital, Inc.

Officers: Joseph V. Ciaburri/Chmn., CEO/$258,872.00, Carl R. Borrelli/Dir., Treasurer, Michael M. Ciaburri/Dir., COO, Pres./$184,800.00, John Howard Howland/43/Exec. VP, Chief Administrative Officer/$142,183.00, Carlota I. Grate/54/CFO, Anthony M. Avellani/VP, Chief Accounting Officer

Directors: Joseph V. Ciaburri/Chmn., CEO, Elmer F. Laydon/Vice Chmn., Michael M. Ciaburri/Dir., COO, Pres., Dianna Atwood Johnson/Dir., Carl R. Borrelli/Dir., Treasurer, Alphonse F. Spadaro/Dir., Joshua H. Sandman/Dir., Juan Miguel Salas-Romer/Dir., Janette J. Parker/Dir., Alfred J. Ranieri/Dir., James Wherry/Dir.

Owners: John Howard Howland, Juan Miguel Salas-Romer/3.20%, Louis A. Lubrano, Michael M. Ciaburri/2.67%, Joshua H. Sandman/1.15%, Alphonse F. Spadaro/1.25%, Carl R. Borrelli/2.39%, Alfred J. Ranieri/2.05%, Joseph V. Ciaburri/5.27%, James D. Wherry, Carlota I. Grate, Insiders/21.22%, Elmer F. Laydon/5.81%, Wellington Management Company, LLP/8.63%

Financial Data: *Fiscal Year End:*12/31 *Latest Annual Data:* 03/31/2007

Year	Sales	Net Income
2007	NA	NA
2006	$7,884,000	-$118,000
2005	$5,809,000	-$278,000

Curr. Assets:	$35,278,000	**Curr. Liab.:**	$102,743,000		
Plant, Equip.:	$4,425,000	**Total Liab.:**	$103,931,000	**Indic. Yr. Divd.:**	NA
Total Assets:	$124,263,000	**Net Worth:**	$20,332,000	**Debt/ Equity:**	NA

Southern First Bancshares Inc

Formerly: Greenville First Bancshares Inc

100 Verdae Blvd., Ste. 100, Greenville, SC, 29607; **PH:** 1-864-679-9000; **http://** www.greenvillefirst.com

General - Incorporation	SC	**Stock**- Price on:12/24/2007	$20.6
Employees	68	Stock Exchange	NDQ
Auditor	Elliot Davis LLC	Ticker Symbol	SFST
Stk Agt	SunTrust Bank	Outstanding Shares	2,940,000
Counsel	Smith Helms Mulliss & Moore	E.P.S	$1.15
DUNS No.	NA	Shareholders	NA

Business: The group's principal activities are to provide both deposit and lending services. The group operates through its subsidiary, greenville first bank, a national commercial bank. The lending services provided includes real estate, commercial and equity line consumer loans to individuals and small to medium sized businesses and professional firms. The deposit services provided by the company include checking, commercial, savings accounts, money market accounts, certificate of deposits and retirement accounts such as iras. Other services provided by the group includes ATMs, safe deposit boxes, traveller's checks, direct deposit, U.S. Savings bonds, and banking by mail. The group operates through its main office located in greenville county, South Carolina.

Primary SIC and add'l.: 6712 6021

CIK No: 0001090009

Subsidiaries: Greenville First Bank, N.A., Greenville Statutory Trust I, Greenville Statutory Trust II

Officers: Art Seaver/Dir., CEO, Diane Totman/Contact, Miranda Breazeale/Contact, Lisa Perrin/Contact, Rebekah Webb/Contact, Rob Reeves/VP, Debbie Tucker/Assist. VP, Client Officer, Carolyn Herbert/Sr. VP, Allison Whitman/Contact, Rebekah Blake/Contact, Lesley Griffeth/Assist. VP, Client Officer, Blake Taylor/VP, Karen Mills/VP - Parkway Office, Edith Smith/Contact, Lori Pond/Contact *(31 Officers included in Index)*

Directors: Art Seaver/Dir., CEO, Jimmy Orders/Chmn., Trip Johnstone/Dir., Bill Sturgis/Dir., William B. Sturgis/73/Dir., Andy Cajka/Dir., Mark Cothran/Dir., Leighton Cubbage/Dir., Anne Ellefson/Dir., Dave Ellison/Dir., Fred Gilmer/Dir., Sr. VP, Tee Hooper/Dir.

Owners: Justin F. Strickland, Arthur R. Seaver/4.10%, Fred Gilmer/2.01%, Anne S. Ellefson/0.36%, William B. Sturgis/1.99%, Mark A. Cothran/2.43%, Fred Gilmer/1.31%, Tecumseh Hooper/1.15%, Rudolph G. Johnstone, Leighton M. Cubbage/6.69%, Edward J. Terrell, Andrew B. Cajka, David G. Ellison/0.60%, James B. Orders/1.99%, James M. Austin/1.96% *(16 Owners included in Index)*

Financial Data: *Fiscal Year End:*12/31 *Latest Annual Data:* 12/31/2006

Year	Sales	Net Income
2006	$31,674,000	$3,901,000
2005	$22,495,000	$2,514,000
2004	$14,729,000	$2,013,000

Curr. Assets:	$18,960,000	**Curr. Liab.:**	$461,357,000	**P/E Ratio:**	16.61
Plant, Equip.:	$7,463,000	**Total Liab.:**	$474,760,000	**Indic. Yr. Divd.:**	NA
Total Assets:	$509,344,000	**Net Worth:**	$34,583,000	**Debt/ Equity:**	0.3761

Southern Michigan Bancorp Inc

51 W Pearl St., Coldwater, MI, 49036; **PH:** 1-517-279-5500; **Fax:** 1-517-278-8469; **http://** www.smb-t.com

General - Incorporation	MI	Stock - Price on:12/24/2007	$23.3
Employees	NA	Stock Exchange	OTC
Auditor	Crowe Chizek & Co. LLC	Ticker Symbol	SOMC
Stk Agt.	NA	Outstanding Shares	1,680,000
Counsel	NA	E.P.S.	$2.29
DUNS No.	NA	Shareholders	NA

Business: The groups principal activities include providing community banking and financial services. Services of the group include checking accounts, savings accounts, certificates of deposit, installment loans, real estate mortgage loans, commercial loans, traveler's checks, safe deposit boxes, night depository and automated teller services. The group operates from the United States.

Primary SIC and add'l.: 6022 6712

CIK No: 0000703699

Officers: John H. Castle/Chmn., CEO, Danice L. Chartrand/Sr. VP, CFO, Sec., Treasurer - Principal Financial, Accounting Officer

Directors: John H. Castle/Chmn., CEO, Kurt G. Miller/Dir., Marcia Albright/Dir., Kenneth H. Cole/Dir., Gary H. Hart/Dir., Nolan E. Hooker/Dir., Gregory J. Hull/Dir., Thomas E. Kolassa/Dir., Donald J. Labrecque/Dir., Freeman E. Riddle/Dir., Dean Calhoun/Dir., Brain McConnell/Dir., James T. Grohalski/Honorary Dir., William E. Galliers/Honorary Dir., Harvey Randall/Honorary Dir. *(18 Directors included in Index)*

Financial Data: Fiscal Year End:12/31 Latest Annual Data: 12/31/2003

Year	Sales	Net Income
2003	$22,662,000	$3,263,000
2002	$22,892,000	$1,033,000
2001	$25,755,000	$2,744,000

Curr. Assets:	$18,241,000	Curr. Liab.:	$265,792,000		
Plant, Equip.:	$6,792,000	Total Liab.:	$295,229,000	Indic. Yr. Divd.:	$0.800
Total Assets:	$321,587,000	Net Worth:	$26,358,000	Debt/ Equity:	NA

Southern Missouri Bancorp Inc

531 Vine St., Poplar Bluff, MO, 63901; *PH:* 1-573-778-1800; *Fax:* 1-573-686-2920; *http://* www.smbtonline.com

General - Incorporation	MO	Stock - Price on:12/24/2007	NA
Employees	88	Stock Exchange	NDQ
Auditor	BKD LLP	Ticker Symbol	SMBC
Stk Agt.	Registrar & Transfer Co	Outstanding Shares	2,240,000
Counsel	NA	E.P.S.	$1.33
DUNS No.	87-432-8131	Shareholders	NA

Business: The group's principal activities are to attract deposits from the general public and providing one to four family residential mortgage loans. The group also provides mortgage loans secured by commercial real estate and commercial non-mortgage business loans and consumer loans. It provides banking services through its main office in poplar bluff and seven other full service branch facilities in poplar bluff, van buren, dexter, kennett, doniphan and qulin, Missouri.

Primary SIC and add'l.: 6035 6712

CIK No: 0000916907

Subsidiaries: Southern Missouri Bank and Trust Co.

Officers: Greg A. Steffens/Dir., CEO, Pres./$204,312.00, Samuel H. Smith/Dir., Sec., Kimberly A. Capps/COO, William D. Hribovsek/Chief Lending Officer/$148,974.00, Matthew T. Funke/CFO, Lorna Brannum/Investor Relations Officer

Directors: Greg A. Steffens/Dir., CEO, Pres., James W. Tatum/Chmn., Douglas L. Bagby/Vice Chmn., Sammy A. Schalk/Dir., Charles R. Moffitt/Dir., Charles R. Love/Dir., Rebecca McLane Brooks/Dir., Samuel H. Smith/Dir., Sec., Ronald D. Black/Dir.

Owners: Jeffrey L. Gendell/9.24%, Donald R. Crandell/8.43%, Charles R. Moffitt, Rebecca M. Brooks, Greg A. Steffens/5.39%, Sammy A. Schalk/1.45%, Samuel H. Smith/4.09%, Charles R. Love, Ronnie D. Black, Insiders/17.19%, Douglas L. Bagby, Southern Missouri Bancorp, Inc./7.28%, James W. Tatum/4.02%

Financial Data: Fiscal Year End:06/30 Latest Annual Data: 06/30/2007

Year	Sales	Net Income
2007	$25,756,000	$2,928,000
2006	$22,507,000	$2,784,000
2005	$19,598,000	$104,000

Curr. Assets:	$8,322,000	Curr. Liab.:	$316,913,000		
Plant, Equip.:	$8,931,000	Total Liab.:	$324,130,000	Indic. Yr. Divd.:	NA
Total Assets:	$350,684,000	Net Worth:	$26,554,000	Debt/ Equity:	0.2524

Southern National Bancorp of Virginia Inc

1770 Timberwood Blvd., Ste. 100, Charlottesville, VA, 22911; *PH:* 1-434-973-5242; *Fax:* 1-434-973-5717; *http://* www.sonabank.com; *Email:* customerservice@sonabank.com

General - Incorporation	VA	Stock - Price on:12/24/2007	$13.5
Employees	50	Stock Exchange	NDQ
Auditor	NA	Ticker Symbol	SONA
Stk Agt.	NA	Outstanding Shares	6,800,000
Counsel	NA	E.P.S.	$0.30
DUNS No.	NA	Shareholders	NA

Business: The groups principal activity is to provide banking and financial services. The groups services include s Telephone banking, weep accounts, zero balance accounts, web lockbox services and night depository. The products of the group include Lockbox, Business debit cards and SONA In House. The group operates from the United States. The total assets of the group for the year 2006 were $290,574 (thousands).

Primary SIC and add'l.: 6712 6022

CIK No: 0001325670

Subsidiaries: Sonabank, National Association

Officers: Georgia S. Derrico/Chmn., CEO/$207,083.00, Roderick R. Porter/Vice Chmn., COO, Pres./$160,416.00, William H. Stevens/Exec. VP - Credit/$170,000.00, William H. Lagos/Sr. VP, CFO/$120,083.00

Directors: Georgia S. Derrico/Chmn., CEO, Roderick R. Porter/Vice Chmn., COO, Pres., Neil J. Call/Dir., Michael A. Gaffney/Dir., Robin R. Shield/Dir., John J. Forch/Dir., Charles A. Kabbash/Dir., Fred Bollerer/Dir.

Owners: Roderick R. Porter/5.94%, Georgia S. Derrico/5.94%, Endurance General Partners, LP/6.38%, William H. Stevens, Robin R. Shield, Neil J. Call/1.25%, William H. Lagos, John J. Forch, Insiders/11.35%, Carl R. Varblow/8.44%, Michael A. Gaffney/1.24%, Charles A. Kabbash

Financial Data: Fiscal Year End:12/31 Latest Annual Data: 12/31/2006

Year	Sales	Net Income
2006	$11,047,000	$1,009,000

Curr. Assets:	$8,126,000	Curr. Liab.:	$220,837,000	P/E Ratio:	45.00
Plant, Equip.:	$3,499,000	Total Liab.:	$222,347,000	Indic. Yr. Divd.:	NA
Total Assets:	$290,574,000	Net Worth:	$68,227,000	Debt/ Equity:	NA

Southern Natural Gas Co

El Paso Bldg., 1001 Louisiana St., Houston, TX, 77002; *PH:* 1-205-325-3800; *http://* premier.sonetpremier.com

General - Incorporation	DE	Stock - Price on:12/24/2007	NA
Employees	NA	Stock Exchange	NA
Auditor	Ernst & Young, LLP	Ticker Symbol	NA
Stk Agt.	NA	Outstanding Shares	NA
Counsel	NA	E.P.S.	NA
DUNS No.	00-690-0518	Shareholders	NA

Business: The group's principle activity is to provide interstate transportation and storage of natural gas. The company is a wholly owned subsidiary of el paso energy corporation. The company conducts business activities through an interstate natural gas pipeline system, storage facilities and a liquefied natural gas (lng) terminalling facility. The company's interstate pipeline system extends from natural gas fields in Alabama, Louisiana, Mississippi, Texas and the gulf of Mexico to markets in Alabama, Florida, Georgia, Louisiana, Mississippi, South Carolina and Tennessee, including the metropolitan areas of atlanta and birmingham. The company provides natural gas transportation services for their distribution customers, primarily for residential and commercial end use, industrial customers, electric generation companies, gas producers, other gas pipelines and gas marketing and trading companies. The group operates from United States.

Primary SIC and add'l.: 4922

CIK No: 0000092232

Officers: James C. Yardley/Chmn., Pres., Norman G. Holmes/Dir., Sr. VP, Chief Commercial Officer, Daniel B. Martin/Dir., Sr. VP, John R. Sult/Sr. VP, CFO, Controller

Directors: James C. Yardley/Chmn., Pres., Norman G. Holmes/Dir., Sr. VP, Chief Commercial Officer, Daniel B. Martin/Dir., Sr. VP

Owners: Norman G. Holmes, John R. Sult, ElPaso Corporation/100.00%, James C. Yardley, Daniel B. Martin, Insiders

Southern Sauce Company Inc

5705 Kavanaugh Blvd., Little Rock, FL, 72207; *PH:* 1-501-663-3338; *https://* www.sauceco.net

General - Incorporation	FL	Stock - Price on:12/24/2007	$0.3
Employees	NA	Stock Exchange	OTC
Auditor	Sherb & Co., LLP	Ticker Symbol	SSAU
Stk Agt.	Florida Atlantic Stock Transfer, Inc.	Outstanding Shares	2,930,000
Counsel	NA	E.P.S.	$0.00
DUNS No.	NA	Shareholders	NA

Business: The groups principle activity is in food business based on proprietary recipes for barbecue sauces and other condiments for the retail market.

Primary SIC and add'l.: 5149

CIK No: 0001327364

Officers: Robert E. Jordan/52/Dir., CEO, Pres., Francis A. Rebello/57/Dir., Treasurer, Sec.

Directors: Robert E. Jordan/52/Dir., CEO, Pres., Francis A. Rebello/57/Dir., Treasurer, Sec., Anand Kumar/63/Dir., Todd W. Rowley/49/Dir., Bob Bova/48/Dir.

Owners: Todd W. Rowley, Insiders/10.90%, David E. Jordan/37.80%, Robert E. Jordan/4.10%, Francis A. Rebello/4.10%, Bob Bova, Anand Kumar

Financial Data: Fiscal Year End:12/31 Latest Annual Data: 12/31/2006

Year	Sales	Net Income
2006	$3,000	-$47,000

Curr. Assets:	$5,000	Curr. Liab.:	$15,000		
Plant, Equip.:	NA	Total Liab.:	$15,000	Indic. Yr. Divd.:	NA
Total Assets:	$6,000	Net Worth:	-$9,000	Debt/ Equity:	NA

Southern Star Energy Inc

307 - 1178 Hamilton St., Vancouver, BC, V6B 2S2; *PH:* 1-604-307-4274; *Fax:* 1-604-484-2403; *http://* www.ssenergyinc.com; *Email:* info@ssenergyinc.com

General - Incorporation	NV	Stock - Price on:12/24/2007	NA
Employees	NA	Stock Exchange	OTC
Auditor	Dale Matheson Carr-hilton Labonte LLP	Ticker Symbol	SSEY
Stk Agt.	Pacific Stock Transfer Company	Outstanding Shares	NA
Counsel	NA	E.P.S.	NA
DUNS No.	NA	Shareholders	NA

Business: The groups principle activities include selling a software product called LinkSurge and providing website development and online marketing services. The group operates through two segments namely consulting and software. The group operates from the United States.

Primary SIC and add'l.: 1311

CIK No: 0001341315

Subsidiaries: Surge Enterprises, Inc

Officers: Eric Boehnke/Dir., CEO, Bruce L. Ganer/VP - Exploration, Development, Larry L. Keller/Consulting Engineer, Hilda Kouvelis/CFO, Mike Newport/Operations Mgr., John Cunningham/Contact - Investor Relations, David W. Gibbs/Dir., Pres.

Directors: Eric Boehnke/Dir., CEO, David W. Gibbs/Dir., Pres.

Owners: Eric Boehnke/28.50%, Troy Mutter/53.60%, Frank Hollmann/19.90%, Insiders/28.50%

Financial Data: Fiscal Year End:05/31 Latest Annual Data: 05/31/2007

Year	Sales	Net Income
2007	NA	-$1,850,000

Curr. Assets:	$1,001,000	Curr. Liab.:	$730,000		
Plant, Equip.:	$2,797,000	Total Liab.:	$1,568,000	Indic. Yr. Divd.:	NA
Total Assets:	$3,808,000	Net Worth:	$2,240,000	Debt/ Equity:	NA

Southern Union Co

5444 Westheimer Rd., Houston, TX, 77056; **PH:** 1-713-989-2000; **Fax:** 1-713-989-1121;
http:// www.southernunionco.com

General - Incorporation	DE	Stock - Price on:12/24/2007	$33.5
Employees	2,312	Stock Exchange	NYSE
Auditor	PricewaterhouseCoopers LLP	Ticker Symbol	SUG
Stk Agt	EquiServe Trust Co N.A	Outstanding Shares	119,840,000
Counsel	Fleischman & Walsh	E.P.S.	$0.54
DUNS No.	00-792-8013	Shareholders	NA

Business: The group's principle activity is to operate assets in the regulated and unregulated natural gas industry. The group also provides transportation, storage and distribution of natural gas. The group operates through three business segments namely the transportation and storage segment, gathering and processing and the distribution segment. The group operates from United States.

Primary SIC and add'l.: 4922 4932 4924

CIK No: 0000203248

Subsidiaries: CCE Acquisition, LLC, Pan Gas Storage, LLC, Panhandle Eastern Pipe Line Company, LP, Trunkline Gas Company, LLC, Trunkline LNG Company, LLC, Trunkline LNG Holdings, LLC

Officers: George L. Lindemann/Chmn., CEO, Pres./$10,842,340.00, Richard N. Marshall/50/CFO, Sr. VP/$449,762.00, Jack Walsh/VP - Investor Relations, Robert M. Kerrigan/VP, Assist. General Counsel, Sec., Monica M. Gaudiosi/45/Sr. VP, Assoc. General Counsel/$882,784.00, Mitchell R. Roper/49/Pres. - Southern Union Gas Services, Robert J. Hack/45/COO - Missouri Gas Energy, John Barnett/Dir. - External Affairs, Eric D. Herschmann/Sr. Exec. VP/$8,304,584.00, Robert O. Bond/48/Sr. VP - Pipeline Operations/$1,047,553.00

Directors: George L. Lindemann/Chmn., CEO, Pres., Franklin W. Denius/82/Chmn. Emeritus, Adam M. Lindemann/Dir., George Rountree/73/Dir., Herbert H. Jacobi/72/Dir., Kurt A. Gitter/69/Dir., Thomas N. McCarter/77/Dir., David Brodsky/69/Dir., Allan D. Scherer/76/Dir.

Owners: George Rountree, David Brodsky, Robert O. Bond, Allan D. Scherer, Richard N. Marshall, Monica M. Gaudiosi, Insiders/10.30%, Herbert H. Jacobi, Julie H. Edwards, Eric D. Herschmann, Kurt A. Gitter, Adam M. Lindemann/2.70%, George L. Lindemann/6.56%, Thomas N. McCarter, Frank W. Denius *(16 Owners included in Index)*

Financial Data: Fiscal Year End:12/31 Latest Annual Data: 12/31/2006

Year	Sales	Net Income
2006	$2,340,144,000	$64,131,000
2005	$2,019,430,000	$20,683,000
2004	$1,799,774,000	$114,025,000

Curr. Assets:	$690,859,000	Curr. Liab.:	$1,200,824,000	P/E Ratio:	62.04
Plant, Equip.:	$4,584,427,000	Total Liab.:	$4,732,382,000	Indic. Yr. Divd.:	$0.400
Total Assets:	$6,782,790,000	Net Worth:	$2,050,408,000	Debt/ Equity:	1.4385

SouthFirst Bancshares Inc

126 N Norton Ave., Sylacauga, AL, 35150; **PH:** 1-256-245-4365; **Fax:** 1-256-245-6341;
http:// www.southfirst.com

General - Incorporation	DE	Stock - Price on:12/24/2007	NA
Employees	51	Stock Exchange	OTC
Auditor	Jones & Kirkpatrick P.C	Ticker Symbol	SZBI
Stk Agt	Registrar & Transfer Co	Outstanding Shares	NA
Counsel	Sirote & Permutt	E.P.S.	NA
DUNS No.	95-836-5074	Shareholders	NA

Business: The group's principal activities are to attract deposits from the general public and invest those deposits with funds in mortgage loans and construction loans. The group's deposit services include now accounts, money market accounts, passbook savings accounts and certificates of deposit. The group also invests the deposits in mortgage-backed securities, secured mortgage obligations and investment securities. The group serves through its main office located in sylacauga, branch offices located in talladega, clanton and centreville and a loan production office in hoover, Alabama.

Primary SIC and add'l.: 6035 6712

CIK No: 0000925963

Subsidiaries: SouthFirst Bank (federally chartered, SouthFirst Financial Services, Inc, SouthFirst Mortgage, Inc.

Financial Data: Fiscal Year End:09/30 Latest Annual Data: 09/30/2005

Year	Sales	Net Income
2005	$11,008,000	$34,000
2004	$10,360,000	-$528,000
2003	$11,178,000	$116,000

Curr. Assets:	$6,570,000	Curr. Liab.:	$102,461,000		
Plant, Equip.:	$4,901,000	Total Liab.:	$128,714,000	Indic. Yr. Divd.:	$0.400
Total Assets:	$139,138,000	Net Worth:	$10,424,000	Debt/ Equity:	NA

Southridge Enterprises Inc

3625 N Hall St., Ste. 900, Dallas, FL, 75219; **PH:** 1-954-564-5482;
http:// www.southridgeethanol.com; **Email:** info@southridgeethanol.com

General - Incorporation	NV	Stock - Price on:12/24/2007	$0.115
Employees	NA	Stock Exchange	OTC
Auditor	Robison, Hill & Co	Ticker Symbol	SORD
Stk Agt	Pacific Stock Transfer Company	Outstanding Shares	NA
Counsel	Clark Wilson LLP	E.P.S.	-$0.02
DUNS No.	NA	Shareholders	NA

Business: The groups principal activity is a renewable energy with a mission to become an ethanol producer in the southeastern region. In the year 2006, the group acquired an industrial plant facility located in Quitman County, Mississippi. The group operates from the United States.

Primary SIC and add'l.: 5031

CIK No: 0001303361

Subsidiaries: Southridge Environmental Inc, Southridge Ethanol Inc, Southridge Exploration Inc.

Owners: Insiders/37.05%, Alex Smid/37.05%, Insiders/37.05%

Financial Data: Fiscal Year End:08/31 Latest Annual Data: 08/31/2006

Year	Sales	Net Income
2006	NA	-$28,000
2005	NA	-$45,000

Curr. Assets:	$8,000	Curr. Liab.:	$25,000		
Plant, Equip.:	NA	Total Liab.:	$25,000	Indic. Yr. Divd.:	NA
Total Assets:	$8,000	Net Worth:	-$18,000	Debt/ Equity:	NA

SouthShore Community Bank

5998 Us Hwy. 41 N, Ste A, Apollo Beach, FL, 33572; **PH:** 1-813-649-9400; **Fax:** 1-813-865-4680;
http:// www.southshorecommunitybank.com

General - Incorporation		Stock - Price on:12/24/2007	$10.05
Employees	NA	Stock Exchange	OTC
Auditor		Ticker Symbol	SSHC
Stk Agt	Registrar & Transfer Co	Outstanding Shares	NA
Counsel	NA	E.P.S.	NA
DUNS No.		Shareholders	NA

Business: The groups principle activity is to provide personal and business banking services, loans, and additional services. The groups personal banking services include checking, money market, savings, certificate of deposits, debit card, and financial calculators. The group operates from United States.

Primary SIC and add'l.: 6021

CIK No:

Officers: Larry R. Tracy/Dir., CEO, Pres., Glenda L. Spencer/Dir. - Investor, Marianne Van Vliet/Assist. VP - Branch Operations, Susan C. Hubbard/COO, Sr. VP, Viet H. Tran/Sr. VP, CFO, Linda K. Sullivan/Loan Administrative Assist., Debra A. Monk/Customer Relations Representative, Alicia M. Meade/Teller, Sue R. Dougherty/Administrative Assist., Jeanne S. Sherrard/VP - Commercial Lender, Charlotte K. Clark/VP, Branch Mgr.

Directors: Larry R. Tracy/Dir., CEO, Pres., Robert A. Tronu/Dir., Crispin G. Stout/Dir., Mary E. Sultenfuss/Dir., G. R. Greenwell/Dir., Ronald A. Knight/Dir., Thomas H. Looker/Dir., Harold E. Ott/Dir., Robert G. Phillips/Dir., Gary F. Queen/Dir., Jack Sizemore/Dir., Glenda L. Spencer/Dir. - Investor

Southside Bancshares Inc

1201 S Beckham Ave., Tyler, TX, 75701; **PH:** 1-903-531-7111; **Fax:** 1-903-592-3692;
http:// www.Sside.com

General - Incorporation	TX	Stock - Price on:12/24/2007	$22.13
Employees	460	Stock Exchange	NDQ
Auditor	PricewaterhouseCoopers LLP	Ticker Symbol	SBSI
Stk Agt	Computershare Trust Co	Outstanding Shares	13,010,000
Counsel	NA	E.P.S.	NA
DUNS No.	NA	Shareholders	NA

Business: The group operates through its subsidiaries whose principle activity is to provide financial services. The groups services include consumer and commercial loans, deposit accounts, trust services, safe deposit services and brokerage. The products of the group include ATM and debit card. The group operates from the United States. The assets of the group for the year 2006 were $1,890,976 (thousands).

Primary SIC and add'l.: 6712 6022

CIK No: 0000705432

Subsidiaries: Red File #1, Inc., Southside Bank, Southside Delaware Financial Corporation, Southside Statutory Trust III

Officers: B. G. Hartley/Chmn., CEO/$558,576.00, Lee R. Gibson/CFO, Exec. VP/$330,077.00, Sam Dawson/Dir., Pres., Sec./$513,569.00, Jeryl W. Story/Sr. Exec. VP/$373,173.00, Susan Hill/Investor Relations

Directors: B. G. Hartley/Chmn., CEO, Robbie N. Edmonson/Vice Chmn., Sam Dawson/Dir., Pres., Sec., Herbert C. Buie/Dir., Melvin B. Lovelady/Dir., Paul W. Powell/Dir., Alton Cade/Dir., Michael D. Gollob/Dir., Joe Norton/Dir., William Sheehy/Dir.

Owners: Alton Cade, Lee R. Gibson, Michael D. Gollob, William Sheehy, Melvin B. Lovelady, Sam Dawson/1.20%, Insiders/12.40%, Joe Norton/1.30%, Robbie N. Edmonson, Paul W. Powell, B. G. Hartley/2.10%, Jeryl Story/1.10%, Herbert C. Buie/3.50%, First National Bank Group, Inc./5.10%

Financial Data: Fiscal Year End:12/31 Latest Annual Data: 12/31/2006

Year	Sales	Net Income
2006	$120,433,000	$15,002,000
2005	$100,929,000	$14,592,000
2004	$88,903,000	$16,099,000

Curr. Assets:	$65,122,000	Curr. Liab.:	$1,611,996,000		
Plant, Equip.:	$32,641,000	Total Liab.:	$1,780,372,000	Indic. Yr. Divd.:	$0.480
Total Assets:	$1,890,976,000	Net Worth:	$110,604,000	Debt/ Equity:	1.3561

Southwall Technologies Inc

3788 Fabian Way, Palo Alto, CA, 94303; **PH:** 1-650-798-1200; **Fax:** 1-650-798-1403;
http:// www.southwall.com

General - Incorporation	DE	Stock - Price on:12/24/2007	$1.075
Employees	140	Stock Exchange	OTC
Auditor	Burr, Pilger & Mayer, LLP	Ticker Symbol	SWTX
Stk Agt	Computershare Trust Co	Outstanding Shares	27,140,000
Counsel	Choate, Hall & Stewart	E.P.S.	-$0.1
DUNS No.	09-598-9869	Shareholders	NA

Business: The group's principle activities are to design, develop, manufacture and market sputtered thin-film coatings on flexible substrates for energy conservation and electronic applications. The products include transparent solar-control films, anti-reflective films, transparent conductive films, energy control films and various other coatings. The group supplies its products for use in electronic display products, automotive glass products and architectural glass products. The major customers of the group are mitsui chemicals, saint gobain sekurit, pilkington plc and v-kool. The group markets its products to OEMs in the United States, Japan, France, Germany and Asia through direct sales and sales representatives. The group's quarterly revenue for September 2007 was 9.25 millions of USD.

Primary SIC and add'l.: 3081

CIK No: 0000813619

Subsidiaries: Southwall Europe GmbH

Officers: Eugene R. Goodson/73/Dir., CEO, Pres./$156,992.00, Bruce Lang/VP - Marketing, Business Development, Jill Clardy/Dir. - Sales Operations, Customer Service, Roween Nacionales/Investor Relations, Dennis Capovilla/COO, Pres./$355,172.00, Mike Vargas/VP - Administration, Human Resources, Sicco W. T. Westra/57/VP - Business Development, Sylvia Kamenski/55/VP - Finance, Sec./$209,906.00, John Meade/Sales Officer, Mgr. - Automotive Sales, North America, Yukinori Asakawa/Sales Officer - Display Sales, Peter Buettrich/Sales Officer, Dir. - Automotive Sales Europe, Africa, Raimond Starmans/Sales Officer, Mgr. - Sales, Marketing, Middle East, India, Peter Kater/Sales Officer, Mgr. - Automotive Sales Asia Pacific, Yisheng Dai/Sales Officer - China Business Development Manage

Directors: Eugene R. Goodson/73/Dir., CEO, Pres., George Boyadjieff/69/Chmn., Jami K. Dover Nachtsheim/49/Dir., William A. Berry/70/Dir., Andre R. Horn/79/Dir., Peter E. Salas/53/Dir.

Owners: Needham & Company, LLC/7.40%, Needham Capital Management/5.80%, Insiders/7.70%, Dennis Capovilla/1.50%, Needham Capital Management, L.L.C./31.90%, Neil Bergstrom, Peter E. Salas, Eugene R. Goodson, Thomas G. Hood/3.20%, Needham Investment Management, LLC/5.30%, George Boyadjieff/1.70%, Dolphin Direct Equity Partners, L.P./21.80%, Sylvia Kamenski, Andre R. Horn, Wolfgang Heinze/1.40% *(17 Owners included in Index)*

Financial Data: ***Fiscal Year End:***12/31 ***Latest Annual Data:*** 12/31/2006

Year	Sales	Net Income
2006	$40,209,000	-$5,510,000
2005	$54,754,000	$3,320,000
2004	$57,573,000	-$185,000

Curr. Assets:	$16,003,000	**Curr. Liab.:**	$12,317,000		
Plant, Equip.:	$17,232,000	**Total Liab.:**	$23,655,000	**Indic. Yr. Divd.:**	NA
Total Assets:	$35,501,000	**Net Worth:**	$7,036,000	**Debt/ Equity:**	1.1523

Southwest Airlines Co

2702 Love Field Dr., Dallas, TX, 75235; ***PH:*** 1-214-792-4000; ***Fax:*** 1-214-792-5015; ***http://*** www.southwest.com

General - Incorporation	TX	**Stock**- Price on:12/24/2007	$14.57
Employees	32,664	Stock Exchange	NYSE
Auditor	Ernst & Young LLP	Ticker Symbol	LUV
Stk Agt	Continental Stock Transfer & Trust Co	Outstanding Shares	780,830,000
Counsel	NA	E.P.S.	$0.65
DUNS No.	05-532-9262	Shareholders	NA

Business: The groups principle activity is to provide airline services. The group operates from United States.

Primary SIC and add'l.: 4512 4731

CIK No: 0000092380

Subsidiaries: API Terminal, Inc., Southwest ABQ RES Center, Inc., Southwest Jet Fuel Co., TranStar Airlines Corporation, Triple Crown Insurance Ltd.

Officers: Gary C. Kelly/Vice Chmn., CEO/$1,405,883.00, James A. Ruppel/VP - Customer Relations - Rapid Rewards, Daryl Krause/Sr. VP - Inflight - Fleet Services, Deborah Ackerman/VP, General Counsel, Joe Harris/VP - Labor - Employee Relations, Chris Wahlenmaier/VP - Ground Operations, Mike Hafner/VP - Inflight Services, Ellen Torbert/VP - Reservations, Ginger C. Hardage/Sr. VP - Corporate Communications, Laura H. Wright/Sr. VP - Finance, CFO/$663,985.00, Lori Rainwater/VP - Internal Audit, Kerry Schwab/CTO, VP, Colleen C. Barrett/Dir., Pres., Corp. Sec./$1,256,935.00, Jeff Lamb/Sr. VP - Chief People, Administration Officer, Linda B. Rutherford/VP - Public Relations - Community Affairs *(33 Officers included in Index)*

Directors: Gary C. Kelly/Vice Chmn., CEO, Herbert D. Kelleher/Chmn., Travis C. Johnson/Dir., Louis Caldera/Dir., William P. Hobby/Dir., Nancy Loeffler/Dir., Colleen C. Barrett/Dir., Pres., Corp. Sec., David Biegler/Dir., Webb C. Crockett/Dir., William H. Cunningham/Dir., John T. Montford/Dir.

Owners: Gary C. Kelly, Nancy B. Loeffler, William P. Hobby, Insiders, William H. Cunningham, Louis E. Caldera, Capital Research and Management Company/11.00%, John T. Montford, Laura Wright, The Growth Fund of America, Inc./5.70%, T. Rowe Price Associates, Inc./7.70%, Webb C. Crockett, PRIMECAP Management Company/6.00%, Ron Ricks, David W. Biegler *(18 Owners included in Index)*

Financial Data: ***Fiscal Year End:***12/31 ***Latest Annual Data:*** 12/31/2006

Year	Sales	Net Income
2006	$9,086,000,000	$499,000,000
2005	$7,584,000,000	$548,000,000
2004	$6,530,000,000	$313,000,000

Curr. Assets:	$2,601,000,000	**Curr. Liab.:**	$2,887,000,000	**P/E Ratio:**	22.42
Plant, Equip.:	$10,094,000,000	**Total Liab.:**	$7,011,000,000	**Indic. Yr. Divd.:**	$0.020
Total Assets:	$13,460,000,000	**Net Worth:**	$6,449,000,000	**Debt/ Equity:**	0.2374

Southwest Bancorp Inc

608 S Main St., Stillwater, OK, 74074; ***PH:*** 1-405-372-2230; ***Fax:*** 1-405-742-1805; ***http://*** www.oksb.com

General - Incorporation	OK	**Stock**- Price on:12/24/2007	$24.54
Employees	429	Stock Exchange	NDQ
Auditor	Ernst & Young LLP	Ticker Symbol	OKSB
Stk Agt	Computershare Investor Services LLC	Outstanding Shares	14,290,000
Counsel	Hert & Baker	E.P.S.	$1.60
DUNS No.	12-258-2687	Shareholders	NA

Business: The group's principal activity is the provision of consumer and commercial banking services through its banking subsidiary, stillwater national bank and trust company. The group offers a wide variety of commercial and consumer lending and deposit services. The commercial loans offered include commercial real estate loans, working capital and other commercial loans, construction loans and small business administration guaranteed loans. Consumer lending services include government-guaranteed student loans, residential real estate loans and mortgage banking services and personal lines of credit and other installment loans. The deposit and personal banking services include business mail processing, commercial checking, certificates of deposit, money market accounts, now accounts, savings accounts and automatic teller machine access.

Primary SIC and add'l.: 6021 6712

CIK No: 0000914374

Subsidiaries: BNS, Inc., Business Consulting Group, Inc., Cash Source, Inc, CRK Properties, Inc., Grand Hill Investments, LLC, Healthcare Strategic Support, Inc., OKSB Statutory Trust I, SBI Capital Trust II, SNB Bank of Wichita, SNB Insurance Agency, Inc., SNB Real Estate Holdings, Inc., Snb Reit, Inc., Stillwater National Bank & Trust Company, Stillwater National Building Corporation, Stillwater Properties, Inc 16 Subsidiaries included in the Index

Officers: Rick J. Green/Vice Chmn., CEO, Pres./$881,730.00, Kerby E. Crowell/CFO, Exec. VP, Sec./$435,823.00

Directors: Rick J. Green/Vice Chmn., CEO, Pres., Robert B. Rodgers/Chmn., Joe Berry Cannon/Dir., Thomas D. Berry/Dir., David S. Crockett/Dir., James M. Johnson/Dir., Linford R. Pitts/Dir., James E. Berry/Dir., John Cohlmia/Dir., Berry J. Harrison/Dir., David P. Lambert/Dir., Russell W. Teubner/Dir.

Owners: David P. Lambert, Berry J. Harrison, Kerby E. Crowell, Kimberly G. Sinclair, Rick Green/1.15%, David S. Crockett, Robert B. Rodgers/2.24%, Joe Berry Cannon, Insiders/10.96%, Russell W. Tuebner, Linford R. Pitts, James M. Johnson, Thomas D. Berry, Charles H. Westerheide, James E. Berry/1.83% *(18 Owners included in Index)*

Financial Data: ***Fiscal Year End:***12/31 ***Latest Annual Data:*** 12/31/2006

Year	Sales	Net Income
2006	$186,536,000	$25,997,000
2005	$154,750,000	$21,014,000
2004	$118,870,000	$18,629,000

Curr. Assets:	$81,887,000	**Curr. Liab.:**	$1,780,007,000	**P/E Ratio:**	14.69
Plant, Equip.:	$23,691,000	**Total Liab.:**	$1,973,118,000	**Indic. Yr. Divd.:**	$0.370
Total Assets:	$2,170,628,000	**Net Worth:**	$197,510,000	**Debt/ Equity:**	0.9340

Southwest Casino Corp

2001 Killebrew Dr., Ste. 306, Minneapolis, MN, 55425; ***PH:*** 1-952-853-9990

General - Incorporation	NV	**Stock**- Price on:12/24/2007	$0.58
Employees	150	Stock Exchange	OTC
Auditor	Eide Bailly LLP	Ticker Symbol	SWCC
Stk Agt	Interwest Transfer Company, Inc.	Outstanding Shares	27,290,000
Counsel	NA	E.P.S.	$0.021
DUNS No.	NA	Shareholders	NA

Business: The groups principle activities include developing and developing casinos, and gaming facilities. The group operates The Cornerstone of Cripple Creek Casino. The group operates from United States.

Primary SIC and add'l.: NA

CIK No: 0001170848

Subsidiaries: Gold Rush I, LLC, North Metro Harness Initiative, LLC, Southwest Casino and Hotel Corp., Southwest Casino Deadwood, LLC, Southwest Charitable Enterprises, LLC, Southwest Entertainment,Inc., Southwest Missouri Gaming, LLC, SW Missouri, LLC

Officers: James B. Druck/CEO, Dir., Tracie Wilson/CFO, Thomas E. Fox/Pres., Jeffrey S. Halpern/VP - Government Affairs, Sec., Brian L. Foster/VP - Native American Operations, GM - Lucky Star Properties, Michael Hirsch/GM - Colorado Casinos, Thomas Snook/General Counsel

Directors: James B. Druck/CEO, Dir., David H. Abramson/Dir., Gus A. Chafoulias/Dir., Jim Holmes/Dir., Gregg P. Schatzman/Dir.

Owners: Gus A. Chafoulias/2.10%, Jim Holmes, James B. Druck/7.40%, Insiders/27.80%, Jeffrey S. Halpern/7.30%, Tracie L. Wilson, Thomas E. Fox/10.40%, Brian L. Foster, Gregg P. Schatzman, David H. Abramson

Financial Data: ***Fiscal Year End:***12/31 ***Latest Annual Data:*** 12/31/2006

Year	Sales	Net Income
2006	$21,475,000	$1,157,000
2005	$20,713,000	$566,000
2004	$20,209,000	-$4,358,000

Curr. Assets:	$2,572,000	**Curr. Liab.:**	$3,803,000	**P/E Ratio:**	29.00
Plant, Equip.:	$10,854,000	**Total Liab.:**	$11,298,000	**Indic. Yr. Divd.:**	NA
Total Assets:	$18,855,000	**Net Worth:**	$7,557,000	**Debt/ Equity:**	NA

Southwest Community Bank

5810 El Camino Real, Carlsbad, CA, 92008; ; ***http://*** www.swcbank.com

General - Incorporation	CA	**Stock**- Price on:12/24/2007	NA
Employees	NA	Stock Exchange	NA
Auditor	Vavrinek, Trine, Day & Co. LLP	Ticker Symbol	NA
Stk Agt	Wells Fargo Bank Minnesota N.A	Outstanding Shares	NA
Counsel	NA	E.P.S.	NA
DUNS No.	NA	Shareholders	NA

Business: The groups principle activity is to provide banking services. The group receives interest from loans and investment securities. The group operates from United States.

Primary SIC and add'l.: NA

CIK No: 0001275873

Subsidiaries: Fds Liquidation Corporation, Southwest Community Statutory Trust I

Southwest Gas Corp

5241 Spring Mountain Rd., Las Vegas, NV, 89193; ***PH:*** 1-702-876-7011; ***Fax:*** 1-702-364-3180; ***http://*** www.swgas.com

General - Incorporation	CA	**Stock**- Price on:12/24/2007	$35.74
Employees	4,902	Stock Exchange	NYSE
Auditor	PricewaterhouseCoopers LLP	Ticker Symbol	SWX
Stk Agt	NA	Outstanding Shares	42,160,000
Counsel	NA	E.P.S.	$2.03
DUNS No.	00-697-0917	Shareholders	NA

Business: The groups principle activity is to delivering gas to residential, commercial, and industrial customers. The group operates through two business segments namely natural gas operations and construction services. The group operates from United States.

Primary SIC and add'l.: 1623 4924

CIK No: 0000092416

Subsidiaries: Black Mountain Gas Company, Northern Pipeline Construction Co., Paiute Pipeline Company, Southwest Gas Capital II, III, IV, Southwest Gas Transmission Company, Utility Financial Corp.

Officers: Jeffrey W. Shaw/49/Dir., CEO/$1,748,652.00, George C. Biehl/Dir., CFO, Exec. VP, Corp. Sec./$1,127,692.00, A. Romero/VP - Southern Neveda Division, Christina A. Palacios/Sr. VP - Central Arizona Division, Roy R. Centrella/VP, Controller - CAO, Edward A. Janov/Sr. VP - Finance, Robyn Clayton/Contact - Media Relations, Kenneth J. Kenny/VP, Treasurer, James P.

Kane/Pres./$1,200,801.00, Thomas R. Sheets/Sr. VP, Legal Aff General Counsel/$775,777.00, Dudley J. Sondeno/Sr. VP, Chief Knowledge - Tech Off/$705,729.00, Garth Andrews/Contact - Media Relations, Libby Howell/Contact - Media Relations, Cynthia Messina/Contact - Media, Nevada California, J. Hester/Sr. VP - Reg Affairs, Energy Resources *(23 Officers included in Index)*

Directors: Jeffrey W. Shaw/49/Dir., CEO, Leroy C. Hanneman/Chmn., Richard M. Gardner/Dir., Thomas E. Chestnut/Dir., Manuel J. Cortez/Dir., Carolyn M. Sparks/Dir., Terrance L. Wright/Dir., Stephen C. Comer/58/Dir., George C. Biehl/Dir., CFO, Exec. VP, Corp. Sec., James J. Kropid/Dir., Michael O. Maffie/Dir., Anne L. Mariucci/Dir., Michael J. Melarkey/Dir.

Owners: GAMCO/5.87%, Barclays/9.60%, Carolyn M. Sparks, Thomas R. Sheets, Thomas E. Chestnut, Terrence L. Wright, George C. Biehl, Michael J. Melarkey, James J. Kropid, Jeffrey W. Shaw, Manuel J. Cortez, Thomas Y. Hartley, Lord Abbett/5.69%, T. Rowe Price/6.48%, Anne L. Mariucci *(21 Owners included in Index)*

Financial Data: *Fiscal Year End:*12/31 *Latest Annual Data:* 12/31/2006

Year	Sales	Net Income
2006	$2,024,758,000	$83,860,000
2005	$1,714,283,000	$43,823,000
2004	$1,477,060,000	$56,775,000

Curr. Assets:	$501,624,000	**Curr. Liab.:**	$496,064,000	**P/E Ratio:**	17.61
Plant, Equip.:	$2,804,346,000	**Total Liab.:**	$2,583,540,000	**Indic. Yr. Divd.:**	$0.860
Total Assets:	$3,484,965,000	**Net Worth:**	$901,425,000	**Debt/ Equity:**	1.3814

Southwest Georgia Financial Corp

201 1st St. SE, Moultrie, GA, 31768; *PH:* 1-229-985-1120; *Fax:* 1-229-985-0251; *http://* www.sgfc.com

General - Incorporation	GA	**Stock** - Price on:12/24/2007	$19.55
Employees	114	Stock Exchange	AMEX
Auditor	Thigpen, Jones, Seaton & Co. P.C	Ticker Symbol	SGB
Stk Agt	American Stock Transfer & Trust Co.	Outstanding Shares	2,600,000
Counsel	NA	E.P.S.	NA
DUNS No.	83-506-9774	Shareholders	NA

Business: The group's principal activity is to offer banking services. The group is community oriented and offers banking services to individuals and businesses in colquitt county, baker county, thomas county and other surrounding counties of southwest Georgia. The group offers consumer and commercial checking accounts, now accounts, savings accounts, certificates of deposit, lines of credit, master card and visa accounts and money transfers. The group finances commercial and consumer transactions, makes secured and unsecured loans and provides a variety of other banking services. The group also acts as a trust department, performing corporate, pension and personal trust services. The group offers property and casualty insurance, life, health and disability insurance through southwest Georgia insurance services inc. On 01-Mar-2004, the group acquired first bank holding company and its subsidiary, sylvester banking company.

Primary SIC and add'l.: 6022 6712

CIK No: 0000315849

Subsidiaries: Southwest Georgia Bank

Officers: Dewitt Drew/51/Dir., CEO, Pres./$263,582.00, Barbara Weeks/Personal Lines Customer Service Representative, Jenny Dollar/Contact - Agent, Randall L. Webb/59/Sr. VP, Geraldine Ferrone Luff/61/Sr. VP, Paul D. Bell/38/Sr. VP, Robert M. Carlton/66/Sr. VP, Morris I. Bryant/66/Sr. VP, George R. Kirkland/Sr. VP, Treasurer/$106,675.00, Larry Blanton/Sr. VP, Dir. - Insurance, Dennard Robison/Sr. Accounting Representative, Greg Costin/Contact - Agent, Keith Parker/Contact - Agent, Vicky Suber/Assist. Cashier - Personal Lines Supervisor, Kathy Fulford/Assist. VP - Commercial Lines Supervisor *(24 Officers included in Index)*

Directors: Dewitt Drew/51/Dir., CEO, Pres., Richard L. Moss/56/Vice Chmn., Michael J. McLean/61/Chmn., Cecil H. Barber/43/Dir., Roy Reeves/48/Dir., Johnny R. Slocumb/55/Dir., Broughton C. Williams/71/Dir., John H. Clark/Dir., Lane M. Wear/56/Dir., Marcus R. Wells/50/Dir.

Owners: Johnny R. Slocumb/1.79%, DeWitt Drew, Insiders/23.78%, Michael McLean/3.47%, Cecil H. Barber/1.27%, George R. Kirkland/1.24%, Richard L. Moss, David J. Dyer, Georgia Financial Corporation/12.60%, John H. Clark, John J. Cole/1.98%, Roy H. Reeves/1.02%, Broughton C. Williams, Marcus R. Wells

Financial Data: *Fiscal Year End:*12/31 *Latest Annual Data:* 12/31/2006

Year	Sales	Net Income
2006	NA	NA
2005	NA	NA
2004	NA	NA

Curr. Assets:	$12,385,000	**Curr. Liab.:**	$241,709,000		
Plant, Equip.:	$6,579,000	**Total Liab.:**	$260,560,000	**Indic. Yr. Divd.:**	$0.560
Total Assets:	$288,516,000	**Net Worth:**	$27,957,000	**Debt/ Equity:**	1.2676

Southwest Water Co

One Wilshire Bldg., 624 S. Grand Ave., Ste. 2900, Los Angeles, CA, 90017; *PH:* 1-213-929-1800; *Fax:* 1-213-929-1888; *http://* www.southwestwater.com; *Email:* swwc@swwc.com

General - Incorporation	DE	**Stock** - Price on:12/24/2007	$13.06
Employees	1,500	Stock Exchange	NDQ
Auditor	KPMG LLP	Ticker Symbol	SWWC
Stk Agt	Mellon Investor Services LLC	Outstanding Shares	24,060,000
Counsel	Latham & Watkins	E.P.S.	$0.40
DUNS No.	00-277-8694	Shareholders	NA

Business: The group's principal activities are to provide a range of services including water production and distribution, wastewater collection and treatment, public works services, utility sub metering and customer billing services. The group operates in two segments: services group and utility group operations. The services group operates and manages water and wastewater treatment facilities owned by cities, public agencies, municipal utility districts and private entities. The utility group supplies water for residential, business, industrial and public authority use for fire protection services. The services group is subject to environmental standards, not regulated in its pricing, marketing or rates of return. The utility group is governed by the regulatory bodies of the respective states and by the federal government.

Primary SIC and add'l.: 4941 4952

CIK No: 0000092472

Subsidiaries: Aqua Services, LP, AquaSource Services I, LLC, AquaSource Services II, LLC, CDC Maintenance,Inc., CHA Utilities, LLC., CHA Utility Company, LTD., ECO Capistrano Valley,Inc., ECO Resources,Inc., Hornsby Bend Utility Company, Inverness Utility Company,Inc., Metro-h2o Utilities,inc., Mid-Tex Utility Company,Inc., Midway Water Utilities,Inc., Monarch Utilities I, LP, Monarch Utilities, LLC 32 Subsidiaries included in the Index

Officers: Mark A. Swatek/Chmn., CEO/$1,350,868.00, Anton C. Garnier/Executive Vice Chmn./$502,338.00, James E. Mann/VP, Controller/$293,800.00, Cheryl L. Clary/CFO/$448,611.00, Michael O. Quinn/Pres. - Southwest Water Company Utility Group/$503,255.00, Walter J. Bench/Treasurer, Delise L. Keim/VP - Corporate Communications, Stephen C. Held/Pres. - Southwest Water Company Services Group, David B. Stanton/Exec. VP - Corporate Development, William K. Dix/VP, General Counsel, Mark Rodriguez/VP - Human Resources, Marlea A. Tichy/VP - Business Planning

Directors: Mark A. Swatek/Chmn., CEO, Anton C. Garnier/Executive Vice Chmn., William D. Jones/Dir., Donovan D. Huennekens/Dir., Maureen A. Kindel/Dir., Richard G. Newman/Dir., Frederick H. Christie/Dir., Linda Griego/Dir., Thomas Iino/Dir.

Owners: Linda Griego, Anton C. Garnier, Pictet Asset Management SA, James C. Castle, James E. Mann, Richard G. Newman, Frederick H. Christie, AMVESCAP PLC, Peter J. Moerbeek, Fisher Investments, Michael O. Quinn, Insiders, William D. Jones, Donovan D. Huennekens, Mark A. Swatek

Financial Data: *Fiscal Year End:*12/31 *Latest Annual Data:* 12/31/2006

Year	Sales	Net Income
2006	$224,182,000	$9,399,000
2005	$203,181,000	$2,399,000
2004	$187,952,000	$4,534,000

Curr. Assets:	$48,257,000	**Curr. Liab.:**	$35,830,000	**P/E Ratio:**	32.65
Plant, Equip.:	$389,625,000	**Total Liab.:**	$325,166,000	**Indic. Yr. Divd.:**	$0.230
Total Assets:	$491,693,000	**Net Worth:**	$166,527,000	**Debt/ Equity:**	0.8073

Southwestern Electric Power Co

428 Travis St., Shreveport, LA, 71156; *PH:* 1-888-216-3523; *http://* www.swepco.com

General - Incorporation	DE	**Stock** - Price on:12/24/2007	NA
Employees	NA	Stock Exchange	NA
Auditor	Deloitte & Touche LLP	Ticker Symbol	NA
Stk Agt	NA	Outstanding Shares	NA
Counsel	NA	E.P.S.	NA
DUNS No.	00-694-8764	Shareholders	NA

Business: The group's principle activities include generating, selling, purchasing, transmitting and distributing electric power to approximately 431,000 customers in northeastern Texas, northwestern Louisiana and western Arkansas. The company also sells electric power at wholesale to other utilities, municipalities and rural electric cooperatives. Among the principal industries served by the company are natural gas and oil production, petroleum refining, manufacturing of pulp and paper, chemicals, food processing and metal refining. The territory served by the company also includes several military installations, colleges and universities. The group operates from United States.

Primary SIC and add'l.: 4911

CIK No: 0000092487

Officers: Thomas P. Brice/Dir. - Business Operations Support, Brett Mattison/Dir. - Customer Services, Marketing, Albert M. Smoak/VP - Distribution Region Operations, Mike Young/GM - Corporate Communications, Johnie L. Wise/Dir. - Regulatory Services, Stacy L. Bankston/System Liaison Mgr., Tom Russell/Safety, Health Mgr., Brian Bond/VP - External Affairs, Venita McCellon-Allen/COO, Pres.

Owners: Stephen P. Smith, Holly K. Koeppel, Nicholas K. Akins, John B. Keane, Thomas M. Hagan, Venita McCellon-Allen, Carl L. English, Susan Tomasky, Michael G. Morris, Dennis E. Welch, Insiders

Southwestern Energy Co

2350 N Sam Houston Pkwy., E, Ste. 125, Houston, TX, 77032; *PH:* 1-281-618-4700; *Fax:* 1-281-618-4818; *http://* www.swn.com

General - Incorporation	AR	**Stock** - Price on:12/24/2007	$49.17
Employees	1,278	Stock Exchange	NYSE
Auditor	PricewaterhouseCoopers LLP	Ticker Symbol	SWN
Stk Agt	Computershare Trust Co	Outstanding Shares	169,900,000
Counsel	Cleary Gottlieb Steen & Hamilton	E.P.S.	NA
DUNS No.	00-690-2936	Shareholders	NA

Business: The group's principal activities are gas and oil exploration and production of natural gas, transmission and marketing and natural gas distribution. The group operates in four segments: exploration and production, natural gas distribution, marketing and transportation and other. The exploration and production segment explores, develops and produces natural gas and crude oil, with operations located in Arkansas, Oklahoma, Texas, New Mexico, and Louisiana. The natural gas distribution segment distributes and transmits natural gas to residential, commercial and industrial customers in northern Arkansas. Marketing and transportation segment provides marketing and transportation services. The other segment deals with commercial real estate operations.

Primary SIC and add'l.: 6719 1382 4789 1381 1311 4923 6552

CIK No: 0000007332

Subsidiaries: A.W. Realty Company, Arkansas Western Gas Company, DeSoto Drilling, Inc., DeSoto Gas Gathering Company, Diamond M Production Company, Overton Partners, L.P., SEECO, Inc., Southwestern Energy Pipeline Company, Southwestern Energy Production Company, Southwestern Energy Services Company, Southwestern Midstream Services Company

Officers: Harold M. Korell/Chmn., CEO, Pres./$4,717,909.00, Richard F. Lane/Exec. VP/$2,202,691.00, Mark K. Boling/Exec. VP, General Counsel, Sec./$1,378,818.00, Greg D. Kerley/CFO, Exec. VP/$2,242,865.00, Alan N. Stewart/Pres. - Arkansas Western Gas Company, Gene A. Hammons/Pres. - Southwestern Midstream Services Company, Dee W. Hency/30/VP - Administration, CIO, Timothy J. O'Donnell/VP - Human Resources, Treasurer, Stanley T. Wilson/Controller, Chief Accounting Officer, Alan J. Stubblefield/Sr. VP - Southwestern Energy Production Company, John D. Thaeler/Sr. VP - Seeco, Inc/$1,076,130.00, Alan R. Clemens/VP - Geosciences, Desoto Planning, Southwestern Energy Production Company, Seeco, Inc, Jim R. Dewbre/VP - Land, Southwestern Energy Production Company, Seeco, Inc, John C. Gargani/VP - Economic Planning, Acquisitions, Southwestern Energy Production Company, Seeco, Inc, Charles V. Stevens/Sr. VP - Arkansas Western Gas Company *(20 Officers included in Index)*

Directors: Harold M. Korell/Chmn., CEO, Pres., Lewis E. Epley/Dir., Robert L. Howard/Dir., Vello A. Kuuskraa/Dir., Kenneth R. Mourton/Dir., Charles E. Scharlau/Dir.

Owners: Lewis E. Epley, Robert L. Howard, John D. Thaeler, Richard F. Lane, Harold M. Korell/1.82%, Capital Research and Management Company and The Growth Fund of America, Inc./8.80%, Vello A. Kuuskraa, Stephen F. Mandel/5.60%, Kenneth R. Mourton, Charles E. Scharlau, Greg D. Kerley, Mark K. Boling, Insiders/5.06%

Financial Data: *Fiscal Year End:*12/31 *Latest Annual Data:* 12/31/2006

Year	Sales	Net Income
2006	$763,112,000	$162,636,000
2005	$676,329,000	$147,760,000
2004	$477,137,000	$103,576,000

Curr. Assets:	$323,836,000	**Curr. Liab.:**	$378,860,000	**P/E Ratio:**	54.03
Plant, Equip.:	$2,016,500,000	**Total Liab.:**	$944,426,000	**Indic. Yr. Divd.:**	NA
Total Assets:	$2,379,069,000	**Net Worth:**	$1,434,643,000	**Debt/ Equity:**	0.2267

Southwestern Public Service Co

3370 NACOGDOCHES Rd. , Ste.168, SAN ANTONIO, TX, 78217; ***PH:*** 1-210-590-9563; ***Fax:*** 1-210-590-9563; ***http://*** www.swps.com; ***Email:*** sales@swps.net

General - Incorporation ... NM
Employees ... NA
Auditor ... Deloitte & Touche LLP
Stk Agt ... NA
Counsel ... Hinkle Cox Enton Coffield Hensley
DUNS No. ... 00-736-9713

Stock- Price on:12/24/2007 ... NA
Stock Exchange ... NA
Ticker Symbol ... NA
Outstanding Shares ... NA
E.P.S ... NA
Shareholders ... NA

Business: The group's principle activities including generating, transmitting, distributing and marketing electric energy. The company has two wholly-owned subsidiaries; utility engineering corporation, whose operations include engineering design and construction management, and quixx corporation which has invested in a waste-to-energy cogeneration facility in North Carolina, holding certain nonutility assets and pursuing nonutility projects. Electric service is provided through an interconnected system to a population of about one million in a 52,000 square-mile area of the panhandle and south plains of Texas, eastern and southeastern New Mexico, the Oklahoma panhandle and southwestern Kansas. The group operates from United States.

Primary SIC and add'l.: 8711 4911

CIK No: 0000092521

Subsidiaries: Xcel Energy

Officers: David L. Eves/CEO, Patricia K. Vincent/Dir., VP, Teresa S. Madden/VP, Controller, Principal Accounting Officer, Gary R. Johnson/Dir., VP, General Counsel, Benjamin G.S. Fowke/Dir., VP, CFO, Principal Financial Officer, Paul J. Bonavia/Dir., VP

Directors: Richard C. Kelly/Chmn., Gary R. Johnson/Dir., VP, General Counsel, Benjamin G.S. Fowke/Dir., VP, CFO, Principal Financial Officer, Paul J. Bonavia/Dir., VP, Patricia K. Vincent/Dir., VP

Southwestern Resources Corp

PO Box 10102, Vancouver, BC, V7Y 1C6; ***PH:*** 1-604-669-2525; ***http://*** www.swgold.com; ***Email:*** info@swgold.com

General - Incorporation ... BC
Employees ... NA
Auditor ... Deloitte & Touche LLP
Stk Agt ... Computershare Trust Co
Counsel ... NA
DUNS No. ... NA

Stock- Price on:12/24/2007 ... NA
Stock Exchange ... NA
Ticker Symbol ... NA
Outstanding Shares ... NA
E.P.S ... NA
Shareholders ... NA

Business: The group's principle activities include acquiring, evaluating, exploring and developing mineral properties, especially with potential to host gold, silver, base metals and diamonds. The company is in development stage. The operations are conducted either directly or through agreements with third parties. The group operates from Peru, Chile, China and Argentina.

Primary SIC and add'l.: 1041 1099 1044 1499

CIK No: 0001095075

Subsidiaries: Canadian Southwestern Gold Inc, Exploraciones Clloausyo S.A.C., Mineral del Suroeste S.A.C., Peru Zinc Corporation, Southwest Minerals Inc, Southwestern Gold Corporation, Southwestern Gold(Chain) Inc, Wari Minerals Inc, Yunnan Gold Mountain Mining Company Ltd

Officers: Timo Jauristo/CEO, Interim Pres., VP - Corporate Development, Dir., John G. Paterson/Dir., CEO, Pres., Javier E. Salas/Dir. - Exploration, Peru, Parkash K. Athwal/VP - Finance, CFO, Thomas W. Beattie/VP - Corporate Affairs, Corp. Sec., Tan Shundao/GM - China, Alex Losada/VP - Exploration, Giovanni N. Susin/VP - Finance, Stan Myers/Dir. - Exploration, Latin America, Dumoulin Black/Solicitor

Directors: Timo Jauristo/CEO, Interim Pres., VP - Corporate Development, Dir., John G. Paterson/Dir., CEO, Pres., David W. Black/Chmn., James Hume/Dir., William D. McCartney/Dir.

Sovereign Bank

1500 Market St., Philadelphia, PA, 19102; ***PH:*** 1-610-320-8400; ***Fax:*** 1-610-320-8448; ***http://*** www.sovereignbank.com; ***Email:*** info@sovereignbank.com

General - Incorporation ... PA
Employees ... 10,949
Auditor ... Ernst & Young LLP
Stk Agt ... Mellon Investor Services LLC
Counsel ... Stevens & Lee
DUNS No. ... 08-162-6947

Stock- Price on:12/24/2007 ... $22.32
Stock Exchange ... NYSE
Ticker Symbol ... SOV
Outstanding Shares ... 476,930,000
E.P.S ... $0.51
Shareholders ... NA

Business: The group's principle activity is to provide baking services. The groups personal services include personal banking home, online banking with billpay, checking, savings and CDs, credit cards, education loans, mortgages, wealth management, insurance, and tool and planning. The group operates from United States.

Primary SIC and add'l.: 6712 6035

CIK No: 0000811830

Subsidiaries: 1130 Abstract, Inc., 201 Associates, Inc, 70 Quincy Avenue, LLC, CBL Service Corporation, Compass REIT Corp, Compass REIT Holding, Inc., First Essex Capital Statutory Trust II, First Essex Capital Trust I, First Essex Capital, Inc., First Essex Securities Corp, ML Capital Trust I, PBE Companies, LLC, Seacoast Capital Trust I, Seacoast Capital Trust II, Sov Apex Co. 48 Subsidiaries included in the Index

Officers: Joseph P. Campanelli/Dir., CEO, Pres./$3,621,598.00, Mark R. McCollom/CFO/$740,138.00, Stacey Weikel/Sr. VP, Dawn B. Heart/Lead Specialist, Thomas D. Cestare/Chief Accounting Officer, Exec. VP, Robert M. Rose/56/Credit Risk Management Officer, Exec. VP/$389,041.00, Salvatore J. Rinaldi/Chief - Staff, Dir. - Administration, Ed Shultz/Sr. VP, Dir. - Corporate Communications, Ellen Molle/VP, Mgr. - Communications, Boston, MA, Carl Brown/VP, Mgr. - Communications, Reading, PA

Directors: Joseph P. Campanelli/Dir., CEO, Pres., James J. Lynch/58/Vice Chmn., Michael P. Ehlerman/Non - Exec. Chmn., Cameron C. Troilo/69/Dir., Brian Hard/61/Dir., Daniel K. Rothermel/70/Dir., Marian L. Heard/67/Dir., Andrew C. Hove/73/Dir., Juan Rodriguez Inciarte/55/Dir., Maria Fiorini Ramirez/60/Dir., Ralph V. Whitworth/52/Dir., Gonzalo De Las/68/Dir., Alberto Sanchez/44/Dir.

Owners: Maria Fiorini Ramirez, Joseph P. Campanelli, Brian Hard, Ralph V. Whitworth/6.70%, Cameron C. Troilo, Relational Investors, LLC/6.70%, Lawrence M. Thompson, Robert M. Rose, Michael P. Ehlerman, Jay S. Sidhu/1.00%, Insiders, James J. Lynch, Mark R. McCollom, William J. Moran, Marian L. Heard *(18 Owners included in Index)*

Financial Data: **Fiscal Year End:**12/31 **Latest Annual Data:** 12/31/2006

Year	Sales	Net Income
2006	$4,923,940,000	$136,911,000
2005	$3,565,251,000	$676,160,000
2004	$2,706,442,000	$453,552,000

Curr. Assets:	$2,227,018,000	**Curr. Liab.:**	$52,384,554,000	**P/E Ratio:**	43.76
Plant, Equip.:	$605,707,000	**Total Liab.:**	$80,997,450,000	**Indic. Yr. Divd.:**	$0.320
Total Assets:	$89,641,849,000	**Net Worth:**	$8,644,399,000	**Debt/ Equity:**	2.2038

Sovereign Exploration Associates International Inc

503 Washington Ave., Ste. 2D, Newtown, PA, 18940; ***PH:*** 1-781-246-7512; ***Fax:*** 1-781-245-7774; ***http://*** www.sea-int.com

General - Incorporation ... UT
Employees ... 7
Auditor .. Baumann, Raymondo & Company P.A.
Stk Agt ... Transfer Online, Inc.
Counsel ... NA
DUNS No. ... NA

Stock- Price on:12/24/2007 ... $0.85
Stock Exchange ... OTC
Ticker Symbol ... SVXA
Outstanding Shares ... 29,120,000
E.P.S ... NA
Shareholders ... NA

Business: The groups principal activities include devoting to the continued exploration, discovery and recovery of shipwrecks of historic and intrinsic value. In December 2005, the group acquired Sea Quest. The group operates from the United States.

Primary SIC and add'l.: 1389 8731

CIK No: 0001019852

Subsidiaries: Artifact Recovery & Conservation Inc., Historic Discoveries, Inc., Sea Quest, Inc., Sea Research Inc., Sovereign Exploration Associates International of Spain, Inc.

Officers: Robert D. Baca/CEO, Founder, Barry Gross/Founder, Sr. VP - Sovereign Exploration Associates International, Inc

Directors: Robert D. Baca/CEO, Founder, Barry Gross/Founder, Sr. VP - Sovereign Exploration Associates International, Inc

Owners: Kevin J. Conner, Sea Hunt, Inc., Peter Knollenberg, Barry Gross, Robert McKinnon, Robert D. Baca, Curtis R. Sprouse, Martin Thorp, Donald G. Conrad, Sovereign Marine Explorations, Inc., Insiders, James Caven, John J. Barr

Financial Data: **Fiscal Year End:**06/30 **Latest Annual Data:** 6/30/2006

Year	Sales	Net Income
2006	$543,000	-$4,915,000
2005	$208,000	-$1,345,000
2004	$885,000	$177,000

Sovran Self Storage Inc

6467 Main St., Buffalo, NY, 14221; ***PH:*** 1-716-633-1850; ***Fax:*** 1-716-633-3397; ***http://*** www.sovranss.com; ***Email:*** info@sovranss.com

General - Incorporation ... MD
Employees ... 961
Auditor ... Ernst & Young LLP
Stk Agt ..... American Stock Transfer & Trust Co.
Counsel ... NA
DUNS No. ... NA

Stock- Price on:12/24/2007 ... $51.01
Stock Exchange ... NYSE
Ticker Symbol ... SSS
Outstanding Shares ... 20,590,000
E.P.S ... $1.76
Shareholders ... NA

Business: The groups principle activity is to provide inexpensive storage place to residential and commercial users. In the year 2006, the group acquired 42 properties. The group operates from the United States.

Primary SIC and add'l.: 4225 6798

CIK No: 0000944314

Subsidiaries: Iskalo Land Holdings, Locke Leasing, Locke Sovran I L.L.C., Locke Sovran I Manager Inc., Locke Sovran II L.L.C., Locke Sovran II Manager Inc., Sovran Acquisition Limited Partnership, Sovran Cameron, Sovran Congress, Sovran DeGaulle, Sovran Granbury, Sovran Grapevine, Sovran Holdings Inc., Sovran Huebner, Sovran Jones Road 22 Subsidiaries included in the Index

Officers: Robert J. Attea/Chmn., CEO/$932,775.00, Kenneth F. Myszka/Dir., COO, Pres./$849,968.00, David L. Rogers/Dir., CFO/$825,337.00, Joan Brickell/Dir. - Audits, Kevin Driscoll/Controller, Andrew Gregoire/VP - Finance, Sandra Herberger/VP - Administration, Legal Compliance, Edward Killeen/Exec. VP - Sales, Operations, Jennifer Kozub/Dir. - Human Resources, Jeffrey Myszka/Regional VP, Robert Myszka/VP - Joint Ventures, Michael Nowicki/Regional VP, David Paolini/VP - Information Technologies, Diane Piegza/VP - Corporate Communications, Paul Powell/Exec. VP - Real Estate *(19 Officers included in Index)*

Directors: Robert J. Attea/Chmn., CEO, Kenneth F. Myszka/Dir., COO, Pres., David L. Rogers/Dir., CFO, Charles E. Lannon/Dir., John E. Burns/Dir., Michael A. Elia/Dir., Anthony P. Gammie/Dir.

Owners: FMR Corp/12.30%, The Vanguard Group, Inc/5.80%, Cohen& Steers, Inc/7.90%, Deutsche Bank AG/8.50%

Financial Data: **Fiscal Year End:**12/31 **Latest Annual Data:** 12/31/2006

Year	Sales	Net Income
2006	$166,295,000	$36,610,000
2005	$138,305,000	$34,790,000
2004	$123,286,000	$32,004,000

Curr. Assets:	$49,933,000	**Curr. Liab.:**	$28,033,000		
Plant, Equip.:	$988,061,000	**Total Liab.:**	$522,299,000	**Indic. Yr. Divd.:**	$2.520
Total Assets:	$1,053,210,000	**Net Worth:**	$530,911,000	**Debt/ Equity:**	NA

Soyo Group Inc

1420 S Vintage Ave., Ontario, CA, 91761; *PH:* 1-909-292-2500; *Fax:* 1-909-937-0783;
http:// www.soyogroup.com; *Email:* informacion@soyogroupla.com

General - Incorporation	NV	Stock - Price on:12/24/2007	$0.52
Employees	36	Stock Exchange	OTC
Auditor	Vasquez & Co. LLP	Ticker Symbol	SOYO
Stk Agt.	Transfer Corp	Outstanding Shares	49,030,000
Counsel	NA	E.P.S.	$0.05
DUNS No.	NA	Shareholders	NA

Business: The group's principal activity is to distribute computer components and peripherals to distributors and retailers in north, central and South America and Taiwan. The group does not manufacture the products the products it distributes these products are supplied by soyo Taiwan located in Taipei, Taiwan. The group distributes for soyo(R) branded products in the United States and Latin America. Its products are motherboards, flash memory drives and international multimedia reader/ writer and usb ports.

Primary SIC and add'l.: 5045

CIK No: 0001108955

Subsidiaries: SOYO Computer, Inc, SOYO,Inc.

Officers: Ming Tung Chok/47/Dir., CEO, Pres., Nancy Chu/51/Dir., CFO, Sec., Edward O'Brien/Dir. - Marketing

Directors: Nancy Chu/51/Dir., CFO, Sec., Paul F. Risberg/46/Dir., Chung Chin Keung/42/Dir., Zhi Yang Wu/39/Dir.

Owners: Paul F. Risberg/0.02%, Zhi Yang Wu/0.01%, Insiders/53.50%, Chung Chin Keung/0.01%, Urmston Capital/20.50%, Ming Tung Chok/24.48%, Nancy Chu/28.98%

Financial Data: Fiscal Year End:12/31 Latest Annual Data: 12/31/2006

Year	Sales		Net Income
2006	$56,759,000		$679,000
2005	$38,263,000		$540,000
2004	$32,426,000		-$3,920,000
Curr. Assets:	$26,218,000	Curr. Liab.:	$20,302,000	P/E Ratio:	26.00
Plant, Equip.:	$552,000	Total Liab.:	$24,037,000	Indic. Yr. Divd.:	NA
Total Assets:	$26,769,000	Net Worth:	$2,732,000	Debt/ Equity:	NA

Soyodo Group Holdings Inc

1390 Monterey Pass Rd., Monterey Park, CA, 91754; *PH:* 1-323-261-1888

General - Incorporation	DE	Stock - Price on:12/24/2007	$0.2
Employees	NA	Stock Exchange	OTC
Auditor	Jaspers + Hall, PC	Ticker Symbol	SOYD
Stk Agt	Mountain Share Transfer	Outstanding Shares	8,190,000
Counsel	NA	E.P.S.	-$0.01
DUNS No.	NA	Shareholders	NA

Business: The groups principal activities include commencing a chain of member only stores in locations with large Chinese immigrant populations, offering Chinese culture related merchandise such as books, pre recorded CDs, stationery, gifts, and sports goods. The group operates from the United States.

Primary SIC and add'l.: 9995

CIK No: 0001103640

Officers: Song Ru-Hua/46/Chmn., Pres., Principal Executive Officer, Zhao Xiao-Zhong/45/Treasurer - Principal Financial, Accounting Officer, Zhang Hao/32/Dir., Sec., VP

Directors: Song Ru-Hua/46/Chmn., Pres., Principal Executive Officer, Zhang Hao/32/Dir., Sec., VP, Fang Ye/48/Dir., Song Pei-Kun/Dir., Yi Geng-Po/39/Dir.

Owners: Fang Ye/4.07%, Yi Geng-Po/1.64%, Song Pei-Kun/8.14%, Zhang Hao, Song Ru-Hua/78.10%, Insiders/92.19%

Financial Data: Fiscal Year End:12/31 Latest Annual Data: 12/31/2006

Year	Sales		Net Income
2006	$2,845,000		-$427,000
2005	$895,000		-$435,000
2004	NA		-$27,000
Curr. Assets:	$3,000	Curr. Liab.:	$497,000		
Plant, Equip.:	NA	Total Liab.:	$497,000	Indic. Yr. Divd.:	NA
Total Assets:	$3,000	Net Worth:	-$494,000	Debt/ Equity:	NA

Spacedev Inc

13855 Stowe Dr., Poway, CA, 92064; *PH:* 1-858-375-2000; *Fax:* 1-858-375-1000;
http:// www.spacedev.com

General - Incorporation	CO	Stock - Price on:12/24/2007	$0.72
Employees	174	Stock Exchange	OTC
Auditor	PKF	Ticker Symbol	SPDV
Stk Agt	Continental Stock Transfer & Trust Co	Outstanding Shares	29,630,000
Counsel	NA	E.P.S.	-$0.05
DUNS No.	NA	Shareholders	NA

Business: The group's principal activities are to commercially develop low-cost satellites, subsystems and to provide engineering technical services to major aerospace companies. The group provides smaller spacecraft and compatible small hybrid propulsion space systems to international, government and commercial enterprises. The products include microsatellites & nanosatellites, bd-ii spacecraft bus, motv (maneuvering and orbital transfer vehicle), hybrid propulsion and launch vehicle systems. The subsystem products include mfc (miniature flight computer), ms-vos (micro space vehicle operating system), PC-ds (power conditioning and distribution system) and mst. The group also provides mission analysis and design, spacecraft and subsystem design, microsatellite and nanosatellite launches and mission control and operations services.

Primary SIC and add'l.: 3764 3761

CIK No: 0001031833

Subsidiaries: Monoceros Acquisition Corp., SpaceDev, Inc.

Officers: Mark N. Sirangelo/47/Vice Chmn., CEO/$317,730.00, Richard Slansky/51/Dir., CFO, Pres., Corp. Sec./$322,335.00, Frank MacKlin/VP - Engineering, David Streich/VP - Human Resources, Scott Tibbitts/Dir., MD/$243,245.00, Jon Evans/VP - Business Development, Harrison Yelton/VP - Satellite Systems, Charlie Hodges/VP - Electromechanical Business, Mark Bailey/Dir. - Marketing

Directors: Mark N. Sirangelo/47/Vice Chmn., CEO, James Benson/63/Founder, Chmn., Richard Slansky/51/Dir., CFO, Pres., Corp. Sec., Curt Blake/Dir., Howell M. Estes/66/Dir., Wesley Huntress/Dir., Scott McClendon/Dir., Robert Walker/65/Dir., Scott Tibbitts/Dir., MD, General Howell Estes/Dir.

Owners: Susan C. Benson/21.48%, Scott McClendon, Robert S. Walker, Scott F. Tibbitts/2.40%, Howell M. Estes, Wesley T. Huntress, Insiders/42.93%, Mark N. Sirangelo/6.79%, Richard B. Slansky/7.05%, Curt Dean Blake, James W. Benson/20.48%, Laurus Master Fund, LLC/9.99%

Financial Data: Fiscal Year End:12/31 Latest Annual Data: 12/31/2006

Year	Sales		Net Income
2006	$32,556,000		-$952,000
2005	$9,005,000		$501,000
2004	$4,891,000		-$3,027,000
Curr. Assets:	$9,637,000	Curr. Liab.:	$8,200,000		
Plant, Equip.:	$3,793,000	Total Liab.:	$9,115,000	Indic. Yr. Divd.:	NA
Total Assets:	$26,131,000	Net Worth:	$17,016,000	Debt/ Equity:	0.0195

Spacehab Inc

12130 Hwy 3, Bldg 1, Webster, TX, 77598; *PH:* 1-713-558-5000; *http://* www.spacehab.com

General - Incorporation	WA	Stock - Price on:12/24/2007	$0.8
Employees	231	Stock Exchange	NDQ
Auditor	PMB Helin Donovan, LLP	Ticker Symbol	SPAB
Stk Agt	American Stock Transfer & Trust Co.	Outstanding Shares	12,990,000
Counsel	NA	E.P.S.	-$13.21
DUNS No.	14-843-4657	Shareholders	NA

Business: The group's principal activities are to develop, own and operate pressurized habitat modules that provide space-based laboratory research facilities and cargo services. The group also offers an unpressurized cargo carrier system. The group operates in four business segments: flight services, government services, astrotech and smi. Flight services provide access to the modules and integration and support services. Sgs provides support services to nasa . Astrotech provides payload-processing facilities to serve the satellite manufacturing and launch services industry. Smi develops space themed commercial business activities. The group owns and operates four pressurized laboratories and logistics supply modules, which enhance the capabilities of the space shuttle fleet.

Primary SIC and add'l.: 3728

CIK No: 0001001907

Subsidiaries: Space Media, Inc

Officers: Thomas B. Pickens/Dir., CEO, Brian K. Harrington/Sr. VP - Finance, CFO, Richard N. Fitts/VP - Government Services, Roscoe M. Moore/Exec. VP, Chief Strategic, Technical Officer, James D. Royston/Pres., Michael Bowker/COO, Peter J. Paceley/VP - Flight Services, Don M. White/VP, GM - Astrotech, James D. Baker/VP - On, Orbit Manufacturing, Brian N. Harris/VP - Business Development, Eva Decardenas/Media, Public, Investor Relations Contact, Suzanne Todd/Contact - Executive, Board Communications

Directors: Thomas B. Pickens/Dir., CEO, Barry A. Williamson/Chmn., Mark Adams/Dir., Myron J. Goins/Dir.

Owners: Lanphier Capital Management, Inc., SMH Capital Advisors, Inc./47.30%, Nicholas Morgan, Thomas B. Pickens, Astrium GmbH, James D. Royston, Roscoe M. Moore, Barry Williamson, Brian K. Harrington, Bruce & Co., Inc./9.20%, Plainfield Asset Management/12.60%, Insiders, TQA Special Opportunities Master Fund Ltd., Lanphier Capital Management, Inc./14.00%, Plainfield Asset Management *(18 Owners included in Index)*

Financial Data: Fiscal Year End:06/30 Latest Annual Data: 06/30/2007

Year	Sales		Net Income
2007	$52,762,000		-$16,292,000
2006	$50,746,000		-$12,397,000
2005	$59,401,000		$5,249,000
Curr. Assets:	$20,675,000	Curr. Liab.:	$17,922,000		
Plant, Equip.:	$61,637,000	Total Liab.:	$82,641,000	Indic. Yr. Divd.:	NA
Total Assets:	$85,450,000	Net Worth:	$2,809,000	Debt/ Equity:	12.6900

Span America Medical Systems Inc

70 Commerce Ctr., Greenville, SC, 29615; *PH:* 1-864-288-8877; *Fax:* 1-864-288-8692;
http:// www.spanamerica.com

General - Incorporation	SC	Stock - Price on:12/24/2007	$20.58
Employees	289	Stock Exchange	NDQ
Auditor	Elliot Davis LLC	Ticker Symbol	SPAN
Stk Agt	Elliot Davis LLC	Outstanding Shares	2,740,000
Counsel	Wyche, Burgess, Freeman & Parham	E.P.S.	$1.37
DUNS No.	07-370-4413	Shareholders	NA

Business: The group's principle activities include manufacturing and distributing polyurethane foam patient positioners. It operates through two segments namely medical and custom products. The medical segment consists of polyurethane foam mattress overlays, therapeutic replacement mattresses, patient positioners and seating products. The custom products segment consists of convoluted and geo-cut mattress overlays and designed pillows for consumers and foam packaging and cushioning materials for industries. The company's products are marketed to health care settings like acute care hospitals, long term care facilities, home health care providers. The products of the company are also sold to markets such as photographic film, durable goods, electronics, automotive and sports equipment industries. The group operates from United States.

Primary SIC and add'l.: 3069 2515

CIK No: 0000718924

Officers: James D. Ferguson/Dir., CEO, Pres., Clyde A. Shew/VP - Medical Sales, Marketing, Robert E. Ackley/VP - Operations, Richard C. Coggins/Dir., CFO, Treasurer, Sec., Wanda J. Totton/VP - Quality Control, James R. O'Reagan/VP - Research & Development and Engineering

Directors: James D. Ferguson/Dir., CEO, Pres., Thomas D. Henrion/Chmn., Robert H. Dick/Dir., Richard C. Coggins/Dir., CFO, Treasurer, Sec., Thomas F. Grady/Dir., Guy R. Guarch/Dir., Robert B. Johnston/Dir., Linda D. Norman/Dir., Peter S. Nyberg/Dir.

Owners: Jerry Zucker/8.50%, Douglas E. Kennemore/8.00%, Thomas D. Henrion/5.30%, Richard C. Coggins/2.20%, Robert H. Dick, James D. Ferguson/3.40%, Thomas F. Grady/1.40%, Guy R. Guarch, Robert B. Johnston/8.60%, Linda Norman, Peter S. Nyberg, Robert E. Ackley/1.10%, James R. OReagan, Clyde A. Shew/1.30%, Farnam Street Partners, L.P./9.30% *(19 Owners included in Index)*

Financial Data: Fiscal Year End:10/01 Latest Annual Data: 9/30/2006

Year	Sales	Net Income
2006	$51,557,000	$3,055,000
2005	$48,439,000	$2,439,000
2004	$49,929,000	$1,985,000

Curr. Assets:	$18,186,000	**Curr. Liab.:**	$4,848,000	**P/E Ratio:**	15.02
Plant, Equip.:	$8,132,000	**Total Liab.:**	$6,495,000	**Indic. Yr. Divd.:**	$0.320
Total Assets:	$31,012,000	**Net Worth:**	$24,517,000	**Debt/ Equity:**	NA

Spanish Broadcasting System Inc

2601 S Bayshore Dr., Ste. PH II, Coconut Grove, FL, 33133; ***PH:*** 1-305-441-6901; ***Fax:*** 1-305-446-5148; ***http://*** www.spanishbroadcasting.com

General - Incorporation	DE	**Stock**- Price on:12/24/2007	$4.37
Employees	656	Stock Exchange	NDQ
Auditor	KPMG LLP	Ticker Symbol	SBSA
Stk Agt	Wachovia Bank N.A	Outstanding Shares	64,780,000
Counsel	NA	E.P.S	-$0.15
DUNS No.	10-112-9252	Shareholders	NA

Business: The group's principal activity is to own and operate Spanish language FM and AM radio stations serving los angeles, New York, Puerto Rico, miami, Chicago, san francisco, Dallas and san antonio markets. The group operates 27 FM radio stations and 1 AM radio station. The group also operates another AM radio station under a brokerage agreement. The target market of the group is the hispanic population in the United States of America.

Primary SIC and add'l.: 4832

CIK No: 0000927720

Subsidiaries: Alarcon Holdings, Inc., Cadena Estereotempo, Inc., JuJu Media, Inc., KLAX Licensing, Inc., KLEY Licensing, Inc., KPTI Licensing, Inc., KRZZ Licensing, LLC, KSAH Licensing, Inc., KXOL Licensing, Inc., KZAB Licensing, Inc., KZBA Licensing, Inc., Mega Media Holdings, Inc., Portorican American Broadcasting, Inc., SBS Bay Area, LLC, SBS Funding, Inc. 49 Subsidiaries included in the Index

Officers: Raul Alarcon/Chmn., CEO, Pres./$2,376,852.00, William Tanner/Dir., Exec. VP - Programming, Marko Radlovic/Dir., COO, Exec. VP/$902,491.00, Joseph A. Garcia/CFO/$688,890.00, Jose Molina/Investor Relations Officer, Cynthia Hudson-Fernandez/45/Chief Creative Officer, Exec. VP/$314,231.00

Directors: Raul Alarcon/Chmn., CEO, Pres., Pablo Raul Alarcon/Chmn. Emeritus, Jack Langer/Dir., Raul Alarcon/Dir., Jason L. Shrinsky/Dir., William Tanner/Dir., Exec. VP - Programming, Marko Radlovic/Dir., COO, Exec. VP, Jose A. Villamil/Dir., Antonio S. Fernandez/Dir., Dan Mason/Dir.

Owners: Columbia Wanger Asset Management, L.P./7.80%, Lehman Brothers Holdings/5.60%, Ral Alarcn/95.60%, Joseph A. Garca/1.20%, Insiders/3.40%, Goldman Sachs Group/5.00%, Antonio S. Fernandez, Jose A. Villamil, CBS Corporation/22.10%, Jason L. Shrinsky, Insiders/100.00%, Pablo Ral Alarcn/4.40%, Ral Alarcn/1.60%, Dan Mason, Marko Radlovic *(16 Owners included in Index)*

Financial Data: ***Fiscal Year End:***12/31 ***Latest Annual Data:*** 12/31/2006

Year	Sales	Net Income
2006	$176,931,000	$49,870,000
2005	$169,832,000	-$35,270,000
2004	$156,443,000	$28,018,000

Curr. Assets:	$102,417,000	**Curr. Liab.:**	$28,638,000		
Plant, Equip.:	$28,022,000	**Total Liab.:**	$516,814,000	**Indic. Yr. Divd.:**	NA
Total Assets:	$929,740,000	**Net Worth:**	$322,994,000	**Debt/ Equity:**	NA

Spansion Inc

915 DeGuigne Dr., Sunnyvale, CA, 94088; ***PH:*** 1-408-962-2500; ***Fax:*** 1-408-616-8174; ***http://*** www.spansion.com

General - Incorporation	DE	**Stock**- Price on:12/24/2007	$11.41
Employees	9,465	Stock Exchange	NDQ
Auditor	Ernst& Young LLP	Ticker Symbol	SPSN
Stk Agt	Computershare Investor Services LLC	Outstanding Shares	134,880,000
Counsel	O'Melveny & Meyers, LLP	E.P.S	-$1.31
DUNS No.	NA	Shareholders	NA

Business: The groups principle activities include designing, developing, manufacturing, marketing and selling Flash memory solutions. The products of the group include PL Family, WS and NS Families, MS Family and CD Family. Specific customers of the group include Fujitsu and AMD. The group operates from North America, China, Korea, Europe and others. The group's quarterly revenyue for September 2007 was 611.07 millions of USD.

Primary SIC and add'l.: 3572 3674

CIK No: 0001322705

Subsidiaries: Cerium Laboratories LLC, Spansion (China) Co. Limited, Spansion (EMEA) SAS, Spansion (Kuala Lumpur) Sdn. Bhd, Spansion (Penang) Sdn.Bhd., Spansion (Thailand) Limited, Spansion Holdings (Singapore) Pte. Ltd., Spansion International, Inc., Spansion Japan Limited, Spansion LLC, Spansion Technology, Inc.

Officers: Bertrand Cambou/Dir., CEO, Pres., Michael Van Buskirk/CTO, Corporate VP - Worldwide Engineering, Anne Salin/Contact - Spansion Public Relations, EMEA, Koichi Wakamatsu/Contact - Spansion Public Relations, Korea, Bob Okunski/Investor Relations Officer, Michele Landry/Contact - Spansion Public Relations, Courtney Brigham/Contact - Spansion Public Relations, Dario Sacomani/CFO, Exec. VP, Clyde Charles Stiteler/Corporate VP - Final Manufacturing Operations, Sylvia Summers/55/Exec. VP - Consumer Smart Card, Industrial Division, Masao Taguchi/Pres. - Spansion Japan, Exec. VP, Chief Scientist, Nikki Tanis/Corporate VP - Corporate Marketing, Communications, Hans Wildenberg/Exec. VP - Media Storage Division, Masanobu Yoshida/Corporate VP - Wireless Solutions Division, Joy Wu/Contact - Spansion Public Relations, China *(33 Officers included in Index)*

Directors: Bertrand Cambou/Dir., CEO, Pres., David K. Chao/Dir., Robert L. Edwards/Dir., Patti S. Hart/Dir., David E. Roberson/Dir., Hector De J. Ruiz/62/Dir., John M. Stich/Dir., Gilles Delfassy/Dir., Donald L. Lucas/Dir.

Owners: FMR Corp./12.40%, Fujitsu Limited/100.00%, David E. Roberson, T. Rowe Price Associates, Inc./3.70%, Sylvia Summers, Fujitsu Limited/13.60%, David K. Chao, Patti S. Hart, Insiders, AMD Investments, Inc./100.00%, John M. Stich, James E. Doran, Bertrand F. Cambou, Thomas T. Eby, Donald Smith & Co., Inc./9.60% *(16 Owners included in Index)*

Financial Data: ***Fiscal Year End:***12/31 ***Latest Annual Data:*** 12/31/2006

Year	Sales	Net Income
2006	$2,579,274,000	-$147,763,000
2005	$2,002,805,000	-$304,116,000

Curr. Assets:	$1,775,070,000	**Curr. Liab.:**	$690,043,000		
Plant, Equip.:	$1,735,694,000	**Total Liab.:**	$1,703,957,000	**Indic. Yr. Divd.:**	NA
Total Assets:	$3,549,717,000	**Net Worth:**	$1,845,760,000	**Debt/ Equity:**	0.5650

Spantel Communications Inc

Spantel 2000 S.A.U.A. 82344748, Avenida Myramar 35, Fuengirola, Malaga, 29640; ***PH:*** 1-902 02 02 02; ***Fax:*** 1-952 19 87 85; ***http://*** www.span-tel.com

General - Incorporation	FL	**Stock**- Price on:12/24/2007	NA
Employees	NA	Stock Exchange	OTC
Auditor	Staley, Okada & Partners	Ticker Symbol	SPAL
Stk Agt	Computershare Trust Co	Outstanding Shares	NA
Counsel	NA	E.P.S	-$0.052
DUNS No.	80-361-6945	Shareholders	NA

Business: The group's principle activity is to provide discount long distance telephone services. The customers of the group include small to medium enterprises, larger corporations, governmental entities, educational institutions and residential customers. The services provided by the group include post payment telephone services, prepayment telephone services, direct access, switch and phone set, telephone cards and technical services. The ancillary proprietary products and services of the group include spansurf.com(R), spantecnica(R) and spanpower(r). The spansurf.com(R) is a free Internet service provider and portal. The spantecnica(R) provides in-house technical support and equipment sales and installations of telephone equipment and end user systems. The spanpower(R) provides residential electricity to one-kilowatt market.

Primary SIC and add'l.: 4813 4899 7375 7379

CIK No: 0000932818

Subsidiaries: Spantel 2000 S.A., Spantel Communications, Inc.

Financial Data: ***Fiscal Year End:***12/31 ***Latest Annual Data:*** 12/31/2005

Year	Sales	Net Income
2005	$18,811,000	-$1,126,000
2004	$19,932,000	$75,000
2003	$16,447,000	$1,289,000

Curr. Assets:	$4,809,000	**Curr. Liab.:**	$7,736,000		
Plant, Equip.:	$733,000	**Total Liab.:**	$8,026,000	**Indic. Yr. Divd.:**	NA
Total Assets:	$7,081,000	**Net Worth:**	-$944,000	**Debt/ Equity:**	NA

Spar Group Inc

555 White Plains Rd., Ste. 250, Tarrytown, NY, 10591; ***PH:*** 1-914-332-4100; ***Fax:*** 1-914-332-0741; ***http://*** www.sparinc.com

General - Incorporation	DE	**Stock**- Price on:12/24/2007	NA
Employees	2,765	Stock Exchange	NDQ
Auditor	Gureli Yeminli Mali Musavirlik	Ticker Symbol	NA
Stk Agt	U.S. Stock Transfer Corp	Outstanding Shares	18,930,000
Counsel	Jenkens & Gilchrist	E.P.S	-$0.22
DUNS No.	14-813-1907	Shareholders	NA

Business: The group's principal activity is to provide merchandising and marketing services throughout the United States and Canada. It operates in two divisions, the merchandising services division and the international division. The merchandising services division provides merchandising services, product demonstrations, product sampling, database marketing, teleservices and marketing research to manufacturers and retailers with product distribution primarily in mass merchandisers, drug chains and grocery stores in the United States. The international division provides merchandising services in Japan, Canada and turkey.

Primary SIC and add'l.: 7389

CIK No: 0001004989

Subsidiaries: Pacific Indoor Display Co, Inc, PIA Merchandising Co, Inc, PIA Merchandising Limited, Pivotal Field Services, Inc, Pivotal Sales Company, Retail Resources, Inc, SGRP Meridian (Pty), Ltd, SPAR Acquisition, Inc, SPAR All Store Marketing Services, Inc, SPAR Bert Fife, Inc, SPAR Canada Company, SPAR Canada, Inc, SPAR China Ltd, SPAR FM Japan, Inc, SPAR Group International, Inc 29 Subsidiaries included in the Index

Officers: Charles Cimitile/CFO/$279,684.00

Owners: Lorrence T. Kellar, Richard J. Riordan/6.40%, Patricia Franco, Jack W. Partridge, Heartland Advisors, Inc./6.50%, Robert G. Brown/45.80%, William H. Bartels/28.10%, Kori G. Belzer, Charles Cimitile, Jerry B. Gilbert, Insiders/79.90%, Robert O. Aders

Financial Data: ***Fiscal Year End:***12/31 ***Latest Annual Data:*** 12/31/2006

Year	Sales	Net Income
2006	$57,316,000	-$621,000
2005	$51,586,000	$878,000
2004	$51,370,000	-$12,268,000

Curr. Assets:	$14,683,000	**Curr. Liab.:**	$13,045,000		
Plant, Equip.:	$901,000	**Total Liab.:**	$13,549,000	**Indic. Yr. Divd.:**	NA
Total Assets:	$18,077,000	**Net Worth:**	$4,528,000	**Debt/ Equity:**	NA

Spare Backup Inc

72-757 Fred Waring Dr., Palm Desert, CA, 92260; ***PH:*** 1-760-779-0251; ***http://*** sparebackup.com; ***Email:*** info@sparebackup.com

General - Incorporation	DE	**Stock**- Price on:12/24/2007	$0.8
Employees	24	Stock Exchange	OTC
Auditor	Sherb & Co., LLP	Ticker Symbol	SPBU
Stk Agt	Holladay Stock Transfer, Inc.	Outstanding Shares	67,880,000
Counsel	NA	E.P.S	-$0.31
DUNS No.	NA	Shareholders	NA

Business: The groups principal activities include developer and marketer of a line of software products specifically designed for the small business and home business users. The groups products designed and developed especially for the small office or home environment, automatically and efficiently backs up all data on selected laptop or desktop computers. The group operates from the United States.

Primary SIC and add'l.: 7372

CIK No: 0001103577

Officers: Cery Perle/CEO, Alton Hoover/53/VP - Engineering, Ivor A. Newman/VP - Operations, Edward L. Hagan/35/Dir., Sec., Richard Rocaberte/VP - Product Development, Robert Schatz/Investor Contact

Directors: Edward L. Hagan/35/Dir., Sec., Richard Galterio/43/Dir.

Owners: Insiders/15.80%, First Capital Holdings International, Inc./3.40%, Langley Park Investment Trust, PLC/3.40%, Edward L. Hagan/2.40%, Richard Galterio/1.30%, Brookstreet Securities Corporation./5.20%, Cery B. Perle/12.10%

Financial Data: Fiscal Year End:12/31 Latest Annual Data: 12/31/2006

Year	Sales	Net Income
2006	$73,000	-$14,478,000
2005	$24,000	-$7,832,000
2004	$11,000	-$14,258,000

Curr. Assets:	$1,019,000	Curr. Liab.:	$12,871,000		
Plant, Equip.:	$489,000	Total Liab.:	$12,878,000	Indic. Yr. Divd.:	NA
Total Assets:	$1,583,000	Net Worth:	-$11,294,000	Debt/ Equity:	NA

Spark Networks Plc

8383 Wilshire Blvd., Ste. 800, Beverly Hills, CA, 90211; **PH:** 1-323-658-3000; *http://* www.spark.net

General - Incorporation	UK	**Stock**- Price on:12/24/2007	$5.44
Employees	200	Stock Exchange	AMEX
Auditor	Ernst & Young LLP	Ticker Symbol	LOV
Stk Agt	BNY Mellon Shareowner Services	Outstanding Shares	30,740,000
Counsel	NA	E.P.S.	$0.18
DUNS No.	NA	Shareholders	NA

Business: The group's principal activity is to provide online personals services in the United States and around the world. The company's web sites enable adults to meet online and participate in a community, become friends, date, form a long-term relationship or marry. It provides this opportunity through the many features on its web sites, such as detailed profiles, onsite email centers, real-time chat rooms and instant messaging services. The company is ranked as the third largest provider of online personals services in the United States in terms of total unique visitors.

Primary SIC and add'l.: 7389

CIK No: 0001314475

Subsidiaries: Doyoudo, Inc., Duplo AB, Entreprises MatchNet Canada, Inc., JDate Limited, MatchNet (Israel) Limited, MatchNet, Ltd, SocialNet, Inc, VAP AG

Officers: Adam Berger/Chmn., CEO, Mark Thompson/CFO/$731,866.00, Gregory R. Liberman/COO, Pres./$502,541.00, Joshua A. Kreinberg/General Counsel, Corp. Sec., Greg Franchina/CIO

Directors: Adam Berger/Chmn., CEO, David E. Siminoff/43/Chmn., Michael Brown/43/Dir., Jonathan Bulkeley/Dir., Benjamin Derhy/Dir., Christopher S. Gaffney/45/Dir., Michael A. Kumin/Dir., Laura B. Lauder/47/Dir., Tom Stockham/Dir.

Owners: Absolute Return Europe Fund, Adam S. Berger, Jonathan B. Bulkeley, Joshua A. Kreinberg, Benjamin A. Derhy, David Siminoff, Insiders, Gregory R. Liberman, Mark G. Thompson, Capital Research and Management Company, FM Fund Management Limited, Great Hill Investors, LLC, Michael A. Brown, Christopher S. Gaffney, Alon Carmel

Financial Data: Fiscal Year End:12/31 Latest Annual Data: 12/31/2006

Year	Sales	Net Income
2006	$68,853,000	$6,563,000
2005	$65,511,000	-$1,438,000
2004	$65,052,000	-$11,627,000

Curr. Assets:	$25,606,000	Curr. Liab.:	$11,880,000	P/E Ratio:	41.85
Plant, Equip.:	$2,306,000	Total Liab.:	$21,800,000	Indic. Yr. Divd.:	NA
Total Assets:	$51,626,000	Net Worth:	$29,826,000	Debt/ Equity:	NA

Sparta Commercial Services Inc

462 Seventh Ave., 20th Fl., New York, NY, 10018; **PH:** 1-212-239-2666; *http://* www.spartacommercial.com; **Email:** headquarters@spartacommercial.com

General - Incorporation	NV	**Stock**- Price on:12/24/2007	$0.05
Employees	15	Stock Exchange	OTC
Auditor	Russell Bedford Stefanou Mirchandani	Ticker Symbol	SRCO
Stk Agt	Executive Registrar & Transfer, Inc.	Outstanding Shares	123,220,000
Counsel	NA	E.P.S.	-$0.03
DUNS No.	NA	Shareholders	NA

Business: The groups principle activity is to provide commercial banking services. The group sales contracts of new and used motorcycles, scooters, and ada test and verification system (ATVs). The Companys products include SPARTA Flex Lease, SPARTA Purchase Plus and SPARTA Sport Loan. The group operates from United States.

Primary SIC and add'l.: 6552 1311 3662 1799 5063

CIK No: 0000318299

Subsidiaries: Sparta Commercial Services, LLC

Officers: Anthony L. Havens/54/Chmn., CEO, Pres., Richard P. Trotter/64/COO, David Collins/Investor Relations Contact, Carol Young/Investor Relations Contact, Sandra L. Ahman/44/Dir., VP, Sec., Anthony W. Adler/68/Exec. VP, Principal Financial Officer

Directors: Anthony L. Havens/54/Chmn., CEO, Pres., Kristian Srb/53/Dir., Jeffrey Bean/54/Dir., Sandra L. Ahman/44/Dir., VP, Sec.

Owners: Kristian Srb/26.90%, Jeffrey Bean, Anthony L. Havens/26.10%, Richard P. Trotter, Insiders/55.00%, Sandra L. Ahman, Anthony W. Adler/1.60%

Financial Data: Fiscal Year End:04/30 Latest Annual Data: 4/30/2006

Year	Sales	Net Income
2006	$169,000	-$5,957,000
2005	$66,000	-$2,580,000
2004	NA	-$1,772,000

Curr. Assets:	$1,510,000	Curr. Liab.:	$1,164,000		
Plant, Equip.:	$789,000	Total Liab.:	$2,516,000	Indic. Yr. Divd.:	NA
Total Assets:	$3,056,000	Net Worth:	$539,000	Debt/ Equity:	NA

Sparta Inc

25531 Commerctr Dr., Ste 120, Lake Forest, CA, 92630; **PH:** 1-949-768-8161; *http://* www.sparta.com

General - Incorporation	DE	**Stock**- Price on:12/24/2007	NA
Employees	NA	Stock Exchange	NA
Auditor	Ernst & Young LLP	Ticker Symbol	NA
Stk Agt	NA	Outstanding Shares	NA
Counsel	NA	E.P.S.	NA
DUNS No.	03-826-7076	Shareholders	NA

Business: The group's principal activity is to provide scientific, engineering and technical services as contractors and subcontractors, primarily for the U.S. Military services and other agencies of the U.S. Department of defense. The group analyzes complex technological, strategic and tactical issues necessary to define the requirements for new tactical and strategic weapons and defense systems. The group also develops engineering solutions to accommodate conflicting technological, schedule, and budgetary requirements and assists in the design, integration, evaluation and testing of software and hardware components. The group also manufactures composite parts for aircraft and missile systems. The activities also include research and development for laser systems, distributed interactive computer simulations, software development, advanced signal processing, information security, advanced materials and production technology and marine instrumentation.

Primary SIC and add'l.: 3728 8711

CIK No: 0000875623

Subsidiaries: St Sparta, Inc.

Officers: Bob Sepucha/CEO, Ray Gretlein/CIO, James S. Hansen/Officer - Systems Acquisition Support Operation, Missile Defense Sector, David Schreiman/CFO/$398,165.00, Maureen Baginski/Pres. - National Security Systems Sector, Paul Oppenheim/Mgr. - Operations, Composite Products, Troy A. Crites/Pres. - Mission Systems Sector/$561,216.00, Randy N. Morgan/Pres. - Missile Defense Sector/$463,160.00, James W. Snaman/Officer - Systems Acquisition Support Operation, Missile Defense Sector, Dorothy H. Hoffmann/52/VP, Dir. - Strategic Planning, Douglas R. Price/Officer - Applied Comm Tech Operation, National Security Systems Sector, Bifford J. Lyons/Officer - Advanced Systems, Technology Operation, Missile Defense Sector, Carl F. Muckenhirn/Officer - Information Systems Security Operation, National Security Systems Sector, Peter D. Schofield/Officer - Technology, Acquisition Support Operation, Missile Defense Sector, Jody L. Chiaro/Dir. - Human Resources (21 Officers included in Index)

Directors: Wayne R. Winton/72/Chmn., William E. Cook/59/Dir., Rockell N. Hankin/61/Dir., John L. Piotrowski/74/Dir., Gerald A. Zionic/65/Dir.

Owners: Gerald A. Zionic, John L. Piotrowski, Randy N. Morgan, Wayne R. Winton/4.00%, David E. Schreiman, William E. Cook, Troy A. Crites, Insiders/8.76%, Robert C. Sepucha/1.87%, Rockell N. Hankin

Spartan Motors Inc

1100 Reynolds Rd., Charlotte, MI, 48813; **PH:** 1-517-543-6400; **Fax:** 1-517-543-9269; *http://* www.spartanmotors.com

General - Incorporation	MI	**Stock**- Price on:12/24/2007	$32.49
Employees	1,079	Stock Exchange	NDQ
Auditor	Ernst & Young LLP	Ticker Symbol	SPAR
Stk Agt	American Stock Transfer & Trust Co.	Outstanding Shares	21,470,000
Counsel	NA	E.P.S.	$0.65
DUNS No.	06-017-8811	Shareholders	NA

Business: The group's principal activities are to design, engineer and manufacture custom heavy-duty chassis. The chassis consist of frame assembly, engine transmission, electrical system, running gear (wheels, tires, axles, suspension and brakes) for fire trucks and some specialty chassis applications. The group is organized into two principal groups, the chassis group and the emergency vehicle team (evteam). The chassis group consists of spartan motors chassis. Chassis customers are original equipment manufacturers who complete their heavy-duty vehicle product by mounting the body or apparatus on the company's chassis. The group discontinued carpenter segment in 2003.

Primary SIC and add'l.: 3711 3792 3713

CIK No: 0000743238

Subsidiaries: Crimson Fire Aerials, Inc., Crimson Fire, Inc., Road Rescue, Inc., Spartan de Mexico S.A. de C.V., Spartan Motors Chassis, Inc.

Officers: John E. Sztykiel/Dir., CEO, Pres./$839,259.00, William F. Foster/Dir., VP/$293,497.00, Richard J. Schalter/Dir., Pres./$836,010.00, James W. Knapp/CFO, Sec., Treasurer/$501,536.00, Jim Knapp/Shareholder Information Contact - Sec., Treasurer

Directors: John E. Sztykiel/Dir., CEO, Pres., David R. Wilson/Chmn., George Tesseris/Dir., Kenneth Kaczmarek/Dir., William F. Foster/Dir., VP, Charles E. Nihart/Dir., Richard J. Schalter/Dir., Pres.

Owners: F. Foster/6.32%, Insiders/10.98%, David R. Wilson, William F. Foster/6.32%, George Tesseris, Richard J. Schalter, Munder Capital Management/7.08%, James L. Logan, John E. Sztykiel/2.15%, Bear Stearns Asset Management, Inc./8.64%, Kenneth Kaczmarek, Charles E. Nihart, First Manhattan Co./5.88%, James W. Knapp

Financial Data: Fiscal Year End:12/31 Latest Annual Data: 12/31/2006

Year	Sales	Net Income
2006	$445,378,000	$16,828,000
2005	$343,007,000	$8,292,000
2004	$312,270,000	$5,882,000

Curr. Assets:	$157,977,000	Curr. Liab.:	$61,894,000	P/E Ratio:	34.94
Plant, Equip.:	$29,659,000	Total Liab.:	$87,467,000	Indic. Yr. Divd.:	$0.160
Total Assets:	$190,648,000	Net Worth:	$103,180,000	Debt/ Equity:	0.1854

Spartan Stores Inc

850 76th St. SW, Grand Rapids, MI, 49518; **PH:** 1-616-878-2000; **Fax:** 1-616-878-8561; *http://* www.spartanstores.com

General - Incorporation	MI	**Stock**- Price on:12/24/2007	$31.55
Employees	4,000	Stock Exchange	NDQ
Auditor	Deloitte & Touche LLP	Ticker Symbol	SPTN
Stk Agt	Trust and Asset Management	Outstanding Shares	21,670,000
Counsel	Warner, Norcross & Judd	E.P.S.	$1.18
DUNS No.	00-695-9613	Shareholders	NA

Business: The groups principle activity is to operate supermarkets and drugstores. The groups products include dry groceries, produce, dairy products, meat, deli, bakery, frozen food, seafood, floral products, general merchandise, pharmacy, and health and beauty care products. The group operates from United States.

Primary SIC and add'l.: 5146 5194 6552 5145 5147 5143 5141

CIK No: 0000877422

CIK No: 0000877422

Subsidiaries: Family Fare, LLC, Jfw Distributing Company, Llj Distributing Company, Market Development Corporation, Seaway Food Town, Inc., Si Insurance Agency, Inc., Spartan Insurance Company Ltd., Spartan Stores Distribution, LLC, Spartan Stores Fuel, LLC, Spartan Stores Holding, Inc, Uwg Company

Officers: Craig Sturken/Chmn., CEO, Pres./$1,977,711.00, Dennis Eidson/54/COO, Exec. VP/$842,294.00, Mark Eriks/Exec. VP - Support - Services, Thomas A. Van Hall/VP - Finance/$406,712.00, Theodore C. Adornato/Exec. VP - Retail Operations, Dave Des Couch/VP - Information Technology, David M. Staples/44/CFO, Exec. VP/$777,601.00, Alex J. Deyonker/Exec. VP, General Counsel, Sec., Derek Jones/39/Exec. VP - Supply Chain

Directors: Craig Sturken/Chmn., CEO, Pres., Kenneth T. Stevens/Dir., Elizabeth A. Nickels/Dir., James F. Wright/Dir., Frank M. Gambino/Dir., Shan M. Atkins/Dir., Timothy J. ODonovan/Dir., Frederick Morganthall/Dir.

Owners: Insiders/2.80%, Timothy J. O'Donovan, Dennis Eidson, Theodore C. Adornato, David M. Staples, Elizabeth A. Nickels, Frank M. Gambino, Craig C. Sturken/1.10%, Frederick S. Morganthall, James F. Wright, Thomas A. Van Hall, Barclays Global Investors, NA/11.40%, Kenneth T. Stevens, Shan M. Atkins

Financial Data: Fiscal Year End:03/25   Latest Annual Data: 3/31/2007

Year	Sales		Net Income
2007	$2,370,428,000		$25,160,000
2006	$2,039,926,000		$18,172,000
2005	$2,043,187,000		$18,826,000

Curr. Assets:	$185,195,000	**Curr. Liab.:**	$157,982,000	**P/E Ratio:**	26.74
Plant, Equip.:	$143,213,000	**Total Liab.:**	$314,758,000	**Indic. Yr. Divd.:**	$0.200
Total Assets:	$487,499,000	**Net Worth:**	$172,741,000	**Debt/ Equity:**	0.7434

Spartech Corp

120 S Central Ave., Ste. 1700, Clayton, MO, 63105; **PH:** 1-314-721-4242; **Fax:** 1-314-721-1447; **http://** www.spartech.com

General - Incorporation	DE	Stock - Price on:12/24/2007	$27.01
Employees	3,425	Stock Exchange	NYSE
Auditor	Ernst & Young LLP	Ticker Symbol	SEH
Stk Agt	Mellon Investor Services LLC	Outstanding Shares	32,130,000
Counsel	NA	E.P.S.	NA
DUNS No.	08-692-6250	Shareholders	NA

Business: The group's principal activities are to produce engineered thermoplastic material, polymeric compounds and molded and profile products for a wide spectrum of equipment manufacturers and other customers. The group operates in 47 manufacturing facilities and is organized into three segments. The custom sheet and rollstock segment extrudes plastic sheet, custom rollstock, laminates, and cell cast acrylic sheet.. The color and specialty compounds segment manufactures custom-designed plastic alloys, compounds, color concentrates, and calendered film. Molded and profile products segment manufactures injection molded products, complete thermoplastic wheels and tires, and profile extruded products.

Primary SIC and add'l.: 2821 2820 3081

CIK No: 0000077597

Subsidiaries: Alchem Plastics Corporation, Alchem Plastics, Inc., Alshin Tire Corporation, Anjac-Doron Plastics, Inc., Atlas Alchem Plastics, Inc., Franklin-Burlington Plastics, Inc., Industrias Spartech de Mexico, S.R.L. de C.V., Polymer Extruded Products, Inc., Spartech Canada, Inc., Spartech CMD, LLC, Spartech de Mexico, S.A. de C.V., Spartech FCD, LLC, Spartech Industries Florida, Inc., Spartech Industries, Inc., Spartech Plastics, Inc. 23 Subsidiaries included in the Index

Officers: George A. Abd/43/Dir., CEO, Pres., Randy C. Martin/44/Dir., Exec. VP - Corporate Development, CFO, Darrel Betz/Human Resources, Phil Karig/Purchasing, Supply Chain Management, Nick Chou/Sales, China, Tim Dawsey/Product Development Center, Angelo Acocella/Spartech Polycast, Chad Tomsheck/Spartech Polycom, Alam Shah/Polycom Material Development Center, Joe Herres/Calendaring, Converting Group, Sandra Nunes-Paiz/Spartech PEP, Korad Film, Sandy Engleman/Spartech Contract Manufacturing Division, Tom Myer/Spartech Industries, Molded Wheels

Directors: George A. Abd/43/Dir., CEO, Pres., Jackson W. Robinson/64/Chmn., Craig A. Wolfanger/48/Dir., Edward J. Dineen/Dir., Lloyd E. Campbell/Dir., Richard B. Scherrer/59/Dir., Victoria M. Holt/49/Dir., Ralph B. Andy/62/Dir., Walter J. Klein/60/Dir., Randy C. Martin/44/Dir., Exec. VP - Corporate Development, CFO, Pamela F. Lenehan/54/Dir.

Owners: Walter J. Klein, Phillip M. Karig, Columbia Wanger Asset Management, L.P./9.20%, Jackson W. Robinson, Michael L. Marcum, Victoria M. Holt, Pamela F. Lenehan, Lloyd E. Campbell, Dimensional Fund Advisors, Inc./6.30%, Ralph B. Andy, Darrell W. Betz, Randy C. Martin, George A. Abd, Jeffrey D. Fisher, Craig A. Wolfanger (18 Owners included in Index)

Curr. Assets:	$352,276,000	**Curr. Liab.:**	$217,480,000	**P/E Ratio:**	20.31
Plant, Equip.:	$324,025,000	**Total Liab.:**	$671,591,000	**Indic. Yr. Divd.:**	NA
Total Assets:	$1,110,871,000	**Net Worth:**	$439,280,000	**Debt/ Equity:**	NA

Sparton Corp

2400 E Ganson St., Jackson, MI, 49202; **PH:** 1-517-787-8600; **Fax:** 1-517-787-1822; **http://** www.sparton.com; **Email:** corporatecommunications@sparton.com

General - Incorporation	OH	Stock - Price on:12/24/2007	$7.3
Employees	1,200	Stock Exchange	NYSE
Auditor	BDO Seidman LLP	Ticker Symbol	SPA
Stk Agt	Illinois Stock Transfer Co	Outstanding Shares	9,800,000
Counsel	NA	E.P.S.	-$0.69
DUNS No.	00-535-6548	Shareholders	NA

Business: The group's principal activity is to design and manufacture electronic and electromechanical products and assemblies. Its products and services include 'box build' products, microprocessor-based systems, transducers, printed circuit boards and assemblies, sensors and electromechanical devices. These products are sold to original equipment manufacturers and other customers in the telecommunications, medical, scientific instrumentation, electronics, aerospace, and other industries and engineering services. The group also develops and manufactures sonobuoys, anti-submarine warfare (asw) devices, used by the us navy and other free-world countries.

Primary SIC and add'l.: 3679 3812

CIK No: 0000092679

Subsidiaries: Astro Instrumentation, Inc., Sparton Electronics Florida, Inc., Sparton of Canada, Limited, Sparton Technology, Inc., Spartronics Vietnam Co., LTD, Spartronics, Inc.

Officers: David W. Hockenbrocht/Dir., CEO, Pres./$410,813.00, Richard L. Langley/Dir., CFO/$206,381.00

Directors: David W. Hockenbrocht/Dir., CEO, Pres., Bradley O. Smith/Chmn., David P. Molfenter/Dir., James N. Deboer/Dir., Peter W. Slusser/Dir., Richard L. Langley/Dir., CFO, James D. Fast/Dir., William I. Noecker/Dir., Douglas R. Schrank/Dir., Lynda J.-s. Yang/Dir.

Owners: Douglas E. Johnson, Jens-Erik Fabricious-Olsen, Dimensional Fund Advisors, LP/5.80%, Judith A. Sare/7.40%, Lawndale Capital Management, Inc./9.10%, John J. Smith Trust/11.00%, Royce & Associates, LLC/5.00%, David W. Hockenbrocht/5.20%, Richard L. Langley, Bradley O. Smith/11.60%, Insiders/29.70%

Financial Data: Fiscal Year End:06/30   Latest Annual Data: 6/30/2006

Year	Sales		Net Income
2006	$170,805,000		$98,000
2005	$167,157,000		$8,112,000
2004	$161,004,000		-$2,043,000

Curr. Assets:	$99,598,000	**Curr. Liab.:**	$31,401,000		
Plant, Equip.:	$17,599,000	**Total Liab.:**	$53,207,000	**Indic. Yr. Divd.:**	NA
Total Assets:	$150,058,000	**Net Worth:**	$96,850,000	**Debt/ Equity:**	0.1500

Spatialight Inc

5 Hamilton Landing, Ste. 100, Novato, CA, 94949; **PH:** 1-415-883-1693; **Fax:** 1-415-883-3363; **http://** www.spatialight.com; **Email:** ir@spatialight.com

General - Incorporation	NY	Stock - Price on:12/24/2007	NA
Employees	122	Stock Exchange	OTC
Auditor	Odenberg, Muranishi & Co. LLP	Ticker Symbol	SPLT
Stk Agt	American Stock Transfer & Trust Co.	Outstanding Shares	NA
Counsel	NA	E.P.S.	-$14.462
DUNS No.	78-041-0114	Shareholders	NA

Business: The group's principal activity is to design and manufacture microdisplays for applications such as high definition television, computer monitors, video projectors and other applications used in wireless communication devices, defense, aerospace, portable games and digital assistants. These products are referred to as liquid crystal on silicon, liquid crystal displays, active matrix liquid crystal displays and spatial light modulators. The group sells its products directly as well as through original equipment manufacturers.

Primary SIC and add'l.: 3577 3679

CIK No: 0000881468

Subsidiaries: SpatiaLight Korea, Inc., SpatiaLight Technologies, Inc

Officers: David Hakala/Chmn., CEO, Sec. Treasurer, Michael S. Jin/CTO, Dir., Jerilyn Kessel/49/Dir., Financial Consultant, Strategist

Directors: David Hakala/Chmn., CEO, Sec. Treasurer, Claude Piaget/Dir., Michael S. Jin/CTO, Dir., Robert Munro/77/Dir., Jerilyn Kessel/49/Dir., Financial Consultant, Strategist, Volkan H. Ozguz/Dir., Young Hwan Kim/Dir.

Owners: Robert A. Olins/18.30%, Robert C. Munro, Wellington Management Company, LLP/6.70%, Herbert Ehrenthal, Don S. Suh, Michael S. Jin, Lawrence J. Matteson, Claude Piaget, David F. Hakala, Insiders/3.50%, Adele Becker/5.80%, Jerilyn Kessel

Financial Data: Fiscal Year End:12/31   Latest Annual Data: 12/31/2006

Year	Sales		Net Income
2006	$474,000		-$20,397,000
2005	$238,000		-$14,025,000
2004	$1,161,000		-$9,367,000

Curr. Assets:	$1,003,000	**Curr. Liab.:**	$13,897,000		
Plant, Equip.:	$5,206,000	**Total Liab.:**	$15,085,000	**Indic. Yr. Divd.:**	NA
Total Assets:	$6,246,000	**Net Worth:**	-$8,839,000	**Debt/ Equity:**	NA

Spatializer Audio Laboratories Inc

2060 E Ave.nida de Los Arboles, D190, Thousand Oaks, CA, 91362; **PH:** 1-408-453-4180; **http://** www.spatializer.com; **Email:** info@spatializer.com

General - Incorporation	DE	Stock - Price on:12/24/2007	$0.041
Employees	2	Stock Exchange	OTC
Auditor	Ramirez International	Ticker Symbol	SPAZ
Stk Agt	Computershare Investor Services LLC	Outstanding Shares	65,000,000
Counsel	NA	E.P.S.	$0.014
DUNS No.	17-365-5010	Shareholders	NA

Business: The group's principal activities are to develop, license and market advanced audio signal processing technologies and products for consumer electronics, entertainment and multimedia computing. The products include digital versatile discs for personal computers, home entertainment and PC gaming. The group's subsidiary desper products, inc. Develops audio signal technologies to simulate the effect of multi-speaker sonic environment. The technologies have been incorporated in products offered by toshiba, panasonic, jvc, samsung, sanyo and sharp.

Primary SIC and add'l.: 3679

CIK No: 0000890821

Subsidiaries: Desper Products, Inc.

Officers: Henry R. Mandell/Chmn., Principal Executive Officer, Principal Financial Officer, Sec.

Directors: Henry R. Mandell/Chmn., Principal Executive Officer, Principal Financial Officer, Sec., Carlo Civelli/Dir.

Owners: Henry R. Mandell/3.30%, Insiders/12.00%, Greggory A. Schneider/10.00%, Carlo Civelli/8.60%, Jay Gottlieb/20.90%

Financial Data: Fiscal Year End:12/31   Latest Annual Data: 12/31/2006

Year	Sales		Net Income
2006	$333,000		-$353,000
2005	$1,192,000		-$82,000
2004	$1,106,000		-$157,000

Curr. Assets:	$329,000	**Curr. Liab.:**	$87,000	**P/E Ratio:**	8.20
Plant, Equip.:	$3,000	**Total Liab.:**	$87,000	**Indic. Yr. Divd.:**	NA
Total Assets:	$464,000	**Net Worth:**	$377,000	**Debt/ Equity:**	NA

Speaking Roses International Inc

404 Ironwood Dr., Salt Lake City, UT, 84115; **PH:** 1-801-433-3900; **Fax:** 1-801-677-7677; **http://** www.speakingroses.com; **Email:** boardofdirectors@speakingroses.com

General - Incorporation	UT	Stock - Price on:12/24/2007	NA
Employees	NA	Stock Exchange	OTC
Auditor	Tanner LC	Ticker Symbol	SRII
Stk Agt	Interwest Transfer Company, Inc.	Outstanding Shares	NA
Counsel	NA	E.P.S.	-$0.17
DUNS No.	NA	Shareholders	NA

Business: The groups principal activity is to create products that express and evoke the emotions of life's special events with personalized floral messages. The group operates from the United States.

Primary SIC and add'l.: 6770

CIK No: 0000884321

Subsidiaries: Speaking Roses Development Corporation

Officers: Alan K. Farrell/40/CEO, Pres., David Nichols/50/Controller, Acting CFO, Rene Rodriguez/35/Dir., VP - Production, Operations

Directors: Roland N. Walker/52/Chmn., Terrell A. Lassetter/77/Dir., Robert E. Warfield/67/Dir., Rene Rodriguez/35/Dir., VP - Production, Operations

Owners: Kenneth D. Redding, Alan K. Farrell, John W. Winterholler, Ted Lloyd, Blaine Harris/10.24%, Roland N. Walker/24.60%, Rene Rodriguez/14.65%, Terry Isom/2.35%, Insiders, Robert E. Warfield/1.43%, Steven F. Hanson/9.11%, Terrell A. Lassetter/1.63%

Financial Data: *Fiscal Year End:*12/31 *Latest Annual Data:* 12/31/2006

Year	Sales	Net Income
2006	$1,601,000	-$6,266,000
2005	$1,297,000	-$4,493,000
2004	$1,691,000	-$2,900,000

Curr. Assets:	$294,000	Curr. Liab.:	$2,026,000		
Plant, Equip.:	$299,000	Total Liab.:	$6,175,000	Indic. Yr. Divd.:	NA
Total Assets:	$1,092,000	Net Worth:	-$5,083,000	Debt/ Equity:	NA

Spear & Jackson Inc

12012 Sshore Blvd., Ste. 103, Wellington, FL, 33414; *PH:* 1-561-793-7233; *http://* www.spear-and-jackson.com

General - Incorporation	NV	Stock - Price on:12/24/2007	$1.47
Employees	589	Stock Exchange	NA
Auditor	Sherb & Co., LLP	Ticker Symbol	NA
Stk Agt	Pacific Stock Transfer Company	Outstanding Shares	5,740,000
Counsel	NA	E.P.S.	-$0.61
DUNS No.	NA	Shareholders	NA

Business: The group's principal activity is to design, manufacture and market a line of multi-bit screwdrivers known as the megapro screwdrivers. These screwdriver products incorporate a patented retracting cartridge that can hold multiple screwdriver bits. The group is licensed to sell screwdriver products incorporating the patented cartridge design in the United States and Canada. The screwdriver products are sold to both the industrial and commercial tools market and to the retail market. The industrial and commercial tools market includes electrical, plumbing, industrial and contractor supply stores. The retail market is characterized by large, nation-wide retailers and big box home center stores.

Primary SIC and add'l.: 3423 3549

CIK No: 0001107206

Subsidiaries: Bowers Eclipse Equipment Shanghai Co. Limited, Bowers Group plc, Bowers Metrology (UK) Limited, Bowers Metrology Limited, Coventry Gauge Limited, CV Instruments Europe BV, CV Instruments Limited, Eclipse Magnetics Limited, James Neill Canada, Inc, James Neill Holdings Limited, James Neill USA, Inc., James Neill USA, Inc. Illinois, Magnacut Limited, Markbalance plc, Mega Tools Ltd 26 Subsidiaries included in the Index

Officers: Patrick Dyson/51/CFO, Lewis Hon Ching Ho/46/Chief Administrative Officer, Dir., Principal Executive Officer, Andy Yan Wai Poon/36/Dir., Sec., Maria Yuen Man Lam/37/Corporate Controller, Dir.

Directors: Lewis Hon Ching Ho/46/Chief Administrative Officer, Dir., Principal Executive Officer, Andy Yan Wai Poon/36/Dir., Sec., Maria Yuen Man Lam/37/Corporate Controller, Dir.

Owners: United Pacific Industries Limited/61.78%, Loeb Loeb Arbitrage Fund/6.70%

Financial Data: *Fiscal Year End:*09/30 *Latest Annual Data:* 9/30/2006

Year	Sales	Net Income
2006	$96,993,000	-$6,479,000
2005	$100,698,000	$3,095,000
2004	$101,179,000	$436,000

Curr. Assets:	$52,588,000	Curr. Liab.:	$20,155,000		
Plant, Equip.:	$15,594,000	Total Liab.:	$61,419,000	Indic. Yr. Divd.:	NA
Total Assets:	$83,260,000	Net Worth:	$21,841,000	Debt/ Equity:	NA

Special Devices Inc

14370 White Sage Rd., Moorpark, CA, 93021; *PH:* 1-805-553-1200; *Fax:* 1-805-553-1211; *http://* www.specialdevices.com; *Email:* general.info@specialdevices.com

General - Incorporation	DE	Stock - Price on:12/24/2007	NA
Employees	NA	Stock Exchange	NA
Auditor	PricewaterhouseCoopers LLP	Ticker Symbol	NA
Stk Agt	NA	Outstanding Shares	NA
Counsel	Gibson, Dunn & Crutcher LLP	E.P.S.	NA
DUNS No.	00-826-2529	Shareholders	NA

Business: The group's principle activities include designs and manufactures highly reliable pyrotechnic devices. The group operates through two main divisions viz., automotive products and aerospace division. The company's products are used by the automotive industry as initiators in airbag systems and the aerospace industry, primarily in tactical missile systems, spacecraft launch vehicles, propellants, explosives and military aircraft crew ejection systems. Production of the company's products consists of fabricating and assembling the hardware components and separately preparing the pyrotechnic charge. The customers for the company's products are the us government and others.

Primary SIC and add'l.: 3699 3764

CIK No: 0000875525

Subsidiaries: Scot, Incorporated

Officers: Christopher Hunter/CEO, Pres., Harry Rector/CFO, Nicholas J. Bruge/VP, GM - World Wide Automotive, Thomas R. Cessario/VP - Human Resources - Regulatory Affairs, Mike Rowland/VP, GM Defense - Aerospace, Gerald J. Shipp/VP, GM - Worldwide Mining, Blasting

Specialized Health Products Intl Inc

585 W 500 S, Bountiful, UT, 84010; *PH:* 1-801-298-3360; *Fax:* 1-801-298-1759; *http://* www.shpi.com

General - Incorporation	DE	Stock - Price on:12/24/2007	$0.78
Employees	NA	Stock Exchange	OTC
Auditor	PricewaterhouseCoopers LLP	Ticker Symbol	SHPI
Stk Agt	Colonial Stock Transfer Co Inc	Outstanding Shares	67,340,000
Counsel	Blackburn & Stoll	E.P.S.	$0.02
DUNS No.	87-304-4861	Shareholders	NA

Business: The group's principal activity is to design, develop, manufacture and license healthcare products. The group develops safety syringes, phlebotomy devices, safety catheter inserters, safety lancets and other medical devices. It incorporates safety needle technologies for syringes that include passive, automatic and manual safety needle retraction and needle shielding. Safety steel needle products are used for small needle access for fluid infusion and blood collection devices. The products manufactured by the group minimize the risk of accidental needle sticks, which are a leading cause of the spread of blood-borne diseases such as human immunodeficiency virus and autoimmunodeficiency syndrome and hepatitis b virus and hepatitis c virus. The group operates mainly in the United States.

Primary SIC and add'l.: 3841

CIK No: 0000790228

Subsidiaries: Safety Syringe Corporation, Specialized Health Products, Inc.

Officers: Jeffrey M. Soinski/Dir., CEO, Pres., Guy Jordan/Chmn., Donald Solomon/Dir., VP, Treasurer/$124,559.00, Donald Solomon/Dir., VP, COO, CTO/$462,231.00, Paul S. Evans/VP - Business Development, General Counsel, Sec./$398,606.00

Directors: Jeffrey M. Soinski/Dir., CEO, Pres., Guy Jordan/Chmn., Donald Solomon/Dir., VP, COO, CTO, Bob Walker/Dir., Stuart Randle/Dir., David Jahns/Dir., Steve Shapiro/Dir., Vincent Papa/58/Dir., Ralph Balzano/71/Dir.

Owners: David W. Jahns/23.00%, Jeffrey M. Soinski/2.60%, Donald D. Solomon/1.00%, Guy J. Jordan, Vincent J. Papa, Stephen I. Shapiro, Stuart A. Randle, Insiders/29.60%, David A. Green, Paul S. Evans/1.10%, Robert R. Walker, Ralph Balzano

Financial Data: *Fiscal Year End:*12/31 *Latest Annual Data:* 12/31/2006

Year	Sales	Net Income
2006	$13,269,000	$385,000
2005	$6,982,000	-$2,759,000
2004	$5,765,000	-$344,000

Curr. Assets:	$11,635,000	Curr. Liab.:	$4,162,000	P/E Ratio:	39.00
Plant, Equip.:	$1,282,000	Total Liab.:	$4,334,000	Indic. Yr. Divd.:	NA
Total Assets:	$16,624,000	Net Worth:	$12,290,000	Debt/ Equity:	NA

Specialty Laboratories Inc

2211 Michigan Ave., Santa Monica, CA, 90404; *PH:* 1-310-828-6543; *http://* www.specialtylabs.com

General - Incorporation	CA	Stock - Price on:12/24/2007	NA
Employees	NA	Stock Exchange	NA
Auditor	Ernst & Young LLP	Ticker Symbol	NA
Stk Agt	NA	Outstanding Shares	NA
Counsel	NA	E.P.S.	NA
DUNS No.	NA	Shareholders	NA

Business: The group's principal activities are to develop and perform esoteric clinical laboratory tests, which are called assays. The group offers more than 3,500 clinical esoteric assays, many of which have been developed through the group's internal research and development efforts. Esoteric assays are complex, comprehensive or unique tests used to diagnose, evaluate and monitor patients. These assays are performed on sophisticated instruments by highly skilled personnel and are offered by a limited number of clinical laboratories. The major customers of the group are hospitals, independent clinical laboratories and physicians. Genotypr tm, analyzer (R), datapassport(R) and data passportmd tm, outreach express(TM) and taro(TM) are trademarks of the group.

Primary SIC and add'l.: 8071

CIK No: 0001123333

Subsidiaries: Specialty Laboratories Asia Pte., Ltd., Specialty Laboratories International Ltd.

Officers: Jin Wang/Dir. - Laboratory, Cabrini Delaney/Mgr. - Clinical Trials Division, Christopher Lockhart/Dir. - Laboratory

Directors: Michael C. Dugan/Dir.

Specialty Underwriters' Alliance Inc

222 S Riverside Plz., Chicago, IL, 60606; *PH:* 1-312-277-1600; *Fax:* 1-312-277-1800; *http://* www.suainsurance.com; *Email:* administration@suainsurance.com

General - Incorporation	DE	Stock - Price on:12/24/2007	$7.79
Employees	83	Stock Exchange	NDQ
Auditor	PricewaterhouseCoopers LLP	Ticker Symbol	SUAI
Stk Agt	American Stock Transfer & Trust Co.	Outstanding Shares	15,400,000
Counsel	NA	E.P.S.	$0.80
DUNS No.	NA	Shareholders	NA

Business: The groups principle activity is to provide commercial property and casualty insurance. The groups services include reinsurance, underwriting, claims control and monitoring rate adequacy. The group operates from the United States. The group's quarterly revenue for September 2007 was 42.90 millions of USD.

Primary SIC and add'l.: 6331 6351

CIK No: 0001297568

Subsidiaries: SUA Insurance Company

Officers: Courtney C. Smith/Chmn., CEO, Pres., Peter E. Jokiel/Dir., CFO, Exec. VP, Treasurer, William S. Loder/Sr. VP, Chief Underwriting Officer, Gary J. Ferguson/Sr. VP, Chief Claims Officer, Scott Goodreau/VP, Chief Actuarial Officer, Scott Charbonneau/VP, Chief Actuarial Officer, Dan Rohan/VP, Controller, Barry G. Cordeiro/CIO, VP

Directors: Courtney C. Smith/Chmn., CEO, Pres., Peter E. Jokiel/Dir., CFO, Exec. VP, Treasurer, Robert E. Dean/Dir., Raymond C. Groth/Dir., Paul A. Philp/Dir., Robert H. Whitehead/Dir., Russell E. Zimmermann/Dir.

Owners: Scott W. Goodreau, FMR Corp./7.88%, Wells Fargo& Company/10.78%, Courtney Smith/1.03%, Robert E. Dean, Bares Capital Management/8.59%, Russell E. Zimmermann, Robert H. Whitehead, Peter E. Jokiel/1.01%, Insiders/3.99%, Gary J. Ferguson, Dreman Value Management, LLC/6.18%, Raymond C. Groth, Paul A. Philp, William S. Loder

Financial Data: *Fiscal Year End:* 12/31 *Latest Annual Data:* 12/31/2006

Year	Sales	Net Income
2006	$117,253,000	$8,408,000
2005	$30,165,000	-$17,996,000
2004	$280,000	-$8,155,000

Curr. Assets:	$174,776,000	Curr. Liab.:	$7,945,000	P/E Ratio:	9.62
Plant, Equip.:	$8,643,000	Total Liab.:	$249,315,000	Indic. Yr. Divd.:	NA
Total Assets:	$363,297,000	Net Worth:	$113,982,000	Debt/ Equity:	NA

Spectralink Corp

5755 Central Ave., Boulder, CO, 80301; *PH:* 1-303-440-5330; *Fax:* 1-303-440-5331; *http://* www.spectralink.com; *Email:* info@spectralink.com

General - Incorporation	DE	Stock - Price on:12/24/2007	$25.55
Employees	459	Stock Exchange	NDQ
Auditor	KPMG LLP	Ticker Symbol	SLNK
Stk Agt	EquiServe Trust Co N.A	Outstanding Shares	NA
Counsel	Ireland, Stapleton, Pryor & Pascoe	E.P.S.	NA
DUNS No.	61-687-1828	Shareholders	NA

Business: The group's principle activities are to design, manufacture and sell workplace wireless telephone systems. These systems complement existing telephone systems by providing mobile communications in a building or campus environment. The group's product portfolio consists of two categories differentiated by the wireless technology implemented: the link wireless telephone systemtm (link wts) and net link wireless telephones. Link wts uses a proprietary radio infrastructure in the 902-928 mhz radio band. The netlink products operate over ieee 802.11-compliant wireless local area networks in the 2400-2483 mhz frequency band using Internet protocol (ip) technology. The group sells its products through direct, distributor and original equipment manufacturers sales forces in the United States, Canada, Australia, United Kingdom, Mexico, Europe and Asia-pacific.

Primary SIC and add'l.: 3663

CIK No: 0000894268

Subsidiaries: SpectraLink Denmark ApS, SpectraLink International Corporation

Owners: John H. Elms/2.00%, Carolyn A. Smyth, Gerald J. Laber, Masood Garahi, Ronald Juvonen/5.10%, Ernest J. Sampias, Anthony V. Carollo, AMVESCAP PLC/11.40%, Werner Schmcking, Insiders/5.10%, Ole Lysgaard Madsen, Carl D. Carman, Lord, Abbett & Co./9.70%, John A. Kelley

Spectranetics Corp

96 Talamine Ct., Colorado Springs, CO, 80907; *PH:* 1-719-633-8333; *Fax:* 1-719-633-2248; *http://* www.spectranetics.com

General - Incorporation	DE	Stock - Price on:12/24/2007	$11.26
Employees	311	Stock Exchange	NDQ
Auditor	Ehrhardt Keefe Steiner & Hottman P.C	Ticker Symbol	SPNC
Stk Agt	Wells Fargo Shareowner Services	Outstanding Shares	31,140,000
Counsel	NA	E.P.S.	$0.19
DUNS No.	15-104-7370	Shareholders	NA

Business: The group's principal activities are to develop, manufacture and market a proprietary excimer laser system for the removal of tissue, specifically addressing multiple cardiovascular disorders. The group's products include cvx-300-laser unit, disposable laser devices and vitesse-tm-laser catheter. The cvx-300-laser unit is a proprietary excimer laser designed specifically for use in cardiovascular applications. The disposable laser devices is an integral part of the excimer laser system. The group markets in Canada, Mexico, South America, the Pacific Rim and Australia.

Primary SIC and add'l.: 3841 3845 3842

CIK No: 0000789132

Subsidiaries: Europe Medical segment is a marketing and sales

Officers: John G. Schulte/Dir., CEO, Pres./$887,016.00, Guy A. Childs/CFO, VP/$301,360.00, Jonathan W. McGuire/COO/$762,445.00, Lawrence E. Martel/VP - Operations, Kelly W. Elliott/VP - Clinical Affairs, Regulatory Submissions/$314,212.00, Stephen D. Okland/VP - Sales, Marketing/$575,432.00, Larry Adighije/VP - Business Development, Strategy, Don Fletcher/VP - Quality Assurance, Regulatory Compliance, Shar Matin/VP, MD - Spectranetics, BV, Wade A. Bowe/37/VP - Product Development, Catheter Manufacturing

Directors: John G. Schulte/Dir., CEO, Pres., Emile J. Geisenheimer/Chmn., John R. Fletcher/Dir., Craig M. Walker/Dir., Joseph M. Ruggio/Dir., Martin T. Hart/Dir., David G. Blackburn/Dir.

Owners: Craig M. Walker/1.10%, Arbor Capital Management, LLC/5.20%, Kelly Elliott, Deerfield Capital, L.P. and affiliates/6.10%, Will McGuire, John R. Fletcher, Joseph M. Ruggio, David G. Blackburn, Steve Okland, Emile J. Geisenheimer/1.30%, Guy A. Childs, Martin T. Hart, John G. Schulte/2.50%

Financial Data: *Fiscal Year End:* 12/31 *Latest Annual Data:* 12/31/2006

Year	Sales	Net Income
2006	$63,490,000	-$1,447,000
2005	$43,212,000	$1,038,000
2004	$34,708,000	$2,952,000

Curr. Assets:	$65,755,000	Curr. Liab.:	$13,203,000	P/E Ratio:	59.26
Plant, Equip.:	$16,176,000	Total Liab.:	$13,206,000	Indic. Yr. Divd.:	NA
Total Assets:	$91,494,000	Net Worth:	$78,288,000	Debt/ Equity:	NA

SpectraScience Inc New

11568 Sorrento Valley Rd. , San Diego, CA, 92121; *PH:* 1-858-847-0200; *http://* www.spectrascience.com; *Email:* info@spectrascience.com

General - Incorporation	MN	Stock - Price on:12/24/2007	$1.02
Employees	3	Stock Exchange	OTC
Auditor	J.H. Cohn LLP	Ticker Symbol	SCIE
Stk Agt	Wells Fargo Shareowner Services	Outstanding Shares	40,650,000
Counsel	NA	E.P.S.	-$0.03
DUNS No.	NA	Shareholders	NA

Business: The groups principal activities include endoscopy of the colon screening for colon cancer and are currently in a clinical trial of a product using the same technology for detecting esophageal cancer. The products of the group approved by the United States Food and Drug Administration. The group operates from the United States.

Primary SIC and add'l.: 3845

CIK No: 0000727672

Officers: James Hitchin/65/Chmn., CEO, CFO, Pres.

Directors: James Hitchin/65/Chmn., CEO, CFO, Pres., Chester E. Sievert/Dir., Mark McWilliams/Dir., Rand P. Mulford/Dir., Merrill A. Biel/Member - Medical Scientific Advisory Board, Douglas M. Hawkins/Member - Medical Scientific Advisory Board, Jose Jessurun/Member - Medical Scientific Advisory Board, Stanley J. Pappelbaum/Dir., Tommy Thompson/Dir., John Pappajohn/Dir.

Owners: Rand P. Mulford/1.90%, Stanley J. Pappelbaum, Chester E. Sievert/2.30%, Insiders/30.10%, Mark D. McWilliams/1.60%, Jim Hitchin/24.00%

Financial Data: *Fiscal Year End:* 12/31 *Latest Annual Data:* 12/31/2006

Year	Sales	Net Income
2006	NA	-$1,311,000
2005	NA	-$912,000
2004	NA	$17,000

Curr. Assets:	$350,000	Curr. Liab.:	$67,000		
Plant, Equip.:	NA	Total Liab.:	$67,000	Indic. Yr. Divd.:	NA
Total Assets:	$593,000	Net Worth:	$526,000	Debt/ Equity:	NA

Spectrasource Corp

14900 Westheimer, Ste. X, Houston, TX, 77082; *PH:* 1-281-902-5200; *http://* www.spectrasource.net; *Email:* info@spectrasource.net

General - Incorporation	NV	Stock - Price on:12/24/2007	$0.06
Employees	NA	Stock Exchange	OTC
Auditor	Eric C. Yartz	Ticker Symbol	SPCC
Stk Agt	First American Stock Transfer, Inc.	Outstanding Shares	NA
Counsel	NA	E.P.S.	NA
DUNS No.	18-610-1937	Shareholders	NA

Business: The group's principal activities are to provide products and services to the telecommunications market, commercial business applications, building owners. The group also caters to residential and commercial builders and developers and the general consumer market. These products and services include fiber optics, structured cabling, electrical components, lighting, ceiling fans, and associated hardware. On 30-Aug-2002 the group acquired home structure sound.

Primary SIC and add'l.: 5063 5047 3845

CIK No: 0000830318

Subsidiaries: Builders Lighting & Hardware, Inc., Connect Source Communications, Inc., Gulf Coast Fan & Light, Inc.

Officers: Charles Sheffield/Dir., CEO, Pres., Pieter De Buck/Exec. VP, Leon D. Hogg/Dir., Corp. Sec., Brook Zewdie/VP, Controller

Directors: Charles Sheffield/Dir., CEO, Pres., Leon D. Hogg/Dir., Corp. Sec., Geary Broadnax/Dir., William Sherrill/Dir., Michael Newman/Dir.

Financial Data: *Fiscal Year End:* 09/30 *Latest Annual Data:* 9/30/2004

Year	Sales	Net Income
2004	$9,065,000	-$57,000
2003	$7,999,000	$20,000
2002	$6,648,000	$229,000

Curr. Assets:	$2,281,000	Curr. Liab.:	$1,540,000		
Plant, Equip.:	$383,000	Total Liab.:	$3,088,000	Indic. Yr. Divd.:	NA
Total Assets:	$3,500,000	Net Worth:	$412,000	Debt/ Equity:	3.4611

Spectre Gaming Inc

14200 23rd Ave., Ste 2690, Plymouth, MN, 55447; *PH:* 1-763-553-7601; *Fax:* 1-763-559-1761; *http://* www.spectregaming.com; *Email:* info@spectregaming.net

General - Incorporation	MN	Stock - Price on:12/24/2007	$0.2
Employees	15	Stock Exchange	OTC
Auditor	Virchow, Krause & Co. LLP	Ticker Symbol	SGMG
Stk Agt	American Stock Transfer & Trust Co.	Outstanding Shares	18,460,000
Counsel	NA	E.P.S.	-$0.98
DUNS No.	NA	Shareholders	NA

Business: The group's principle activities include designing and developing networks, software and content that provides customers with a comprehensive gaming system. The services are provided mainly to the native American classes and charitable gaming markets. These games are classified under three categories: class i gaming includes traditional native American social and ceremonial games. Class i gaming is regulated at the native American tribe level. Class ii gaming includes bingo and if played at the same location where bingo is offered, pull-tabs and other games similar to bingo. Class iii gaming includes slot machines and most table games. The group operates from United States.

Primary SIC and add'l.: 7374 7372

CIK No: 0000891389

Officers: Bradly D. Olah/Dir., CEO, Pres., Russell C. Mix/Compliance Consultant, Kevin M. Greer/CFO, David Norris/46/COO, Pres.

Directors: Bradly D. Olah/Dir., CEO, Pres., Kenneth W. Brimmer/Chmn., N. D. Witcher/Dir., Robert Bonev/Dir., Namon D. Witcher/69/Dir., Charley Price/76/Dir.

Owners: Insiders/18.60%, Wayne W. Mills/11.30%, Kevin M. Greer, Bradley D. Olah/13.00%, Kenneth Brimmer/1.10%, White Pine Capital, LLC/7.30%, Perkins Capital Management, Inc/19.80%, Namon D. Witcher, Russell Mix/4.70%, Robert Bonev

Financial Data: *Fiscal Year End:* 12/31 *Latest Annual Data:* 12/31/2006

Year	Sales	Net Income
2006	$550,000	-$13,138,000
2005	NA	-$10,121,000
2004	$83,000	-$4,394,000

Curr. Assets:	$1,828,000	Curr. Liab.:	$12,367,000		
Plant, Equip.:	$7,362,000	Total Liab.:	$13,237,000	Indic. Yr. Divd.:	NA
Total Assets:	$9,480,000	Net Worth:	-$3,756,000	Debt/ Equity:	NA

Spectrum Brands Inc

6 Concourse Pkwy., Ste. 3300, Atlanta, GA, 30328; *PH:* 1-770-829-6200; *http://* www.spectrumbrands.com

General - Incorporation WI
Employees 8,400
Auditor KPMG LLP
Stk Agt Mellon Investor Services LLC
Counsel NA
DUNS No. 00-195-1946

Stock- Price on:12/24/2007 $6.78
Stock Exchange NYSE
Ticker Symbol SPC
Outstanding Shares 52,460,000
E.P.S -$11.72
Shareholders NA

Business: The groups principle activity is to provide consumer products. The group operates from United States.

Primary SIC and add'l.: 3691 3648

CIK No: 0001028985

Subsidiaries: Rayovac (UK) Limited, Rayovac Europe GmbH, ROV Holding, Inc., ROVCAL, Inc., Spectrum Brands Lux S.A.R.L, Tetra Holding GmbH, United Industries Corporation, United Pet Group, Inc., VARTA Consumer Batteries GmbH& Co. KGaA

Officers: Kent J. Hussey/62/Dir., CEO, David R. Lumley/Co - COO, Pres. - Global Batteries, Personal Care, Home, Garden, Remy E. Burel/57/Pres. - Europe, Rest, World, Hartmut Junghahn/45/Exec. VP - Latin America, John A. Heil/Co - COO, Pres. - Global Pet Supplies, Kenneth V. Biller/60/Pres. - Global Operations, James T. Lucke/Sec., Amy J. Yoder/Pres. - Home, Garden, Anthony L. Genito/CFO, Sr. VP, Nancy O'Donnell/VP - Investor Relations

Directors: Kent J. Hussey/62/Dir., CEO, John D. Bowlin/57/Chmn., Thomas R. Shepherd/78/Dir., Scott A. Schoen/49/Dir., Charles A. Brizius/38/Dir., David A. Jones/58/Dir., John S. Lupo/61/Dir., Barbara S. Thomas/58/Dir., William P. Carmichael/64/Dir.

Owners: Kenneth V. Biller, Adage Capital Partners, Anthony L. Genito, David R. Lumley, John S. Lupo, Insiders, Prentice Capital Management, LP, John D. Bowlin, John A. Heil, Charles A. Brizius, David A. Jones, GLG Partners LP, Scott A. Schoen, Thomas R. Shepherd, Artis Capital Management, L.P. *(24 Owners included in Index)*

Financial Data: *Fiscal Year End:*09/30 *Latest Annual Data:* 09/30/2007

Year	Sales	Net Income
2007	$1,994,522,000	-$596,713,000
2006	$2,551,752,000	-$433,972,000
2005	$2,359,447,000	$46,832,000

Curr. Assets:	$959,815,000	**Curr. Liab.:**	$562,613,000		
Plant, Equip.:	$311,839,000	**Total Liab.:**	$3,097,103,000	**Indic. Yr. Divd.:**	NA
Total Assets:	$3,549,320,000	**Net Worth:**	$452,217,000	**Debt/ Equity:**	12.5062

Spectrum Control Inc

8061 Avonia Rd., Fairview, PA, 16415; ***PH:*** 1-814-474-1571; ***Fax:*** 1-814-474-3110;
http:// www.spectrumcontrol.com

General - Incorporation PA
Employees 1,548
Auditor Ernst & Young LLP
Stk Agt Mellon Investor Services LLC
Counsel NA
DUNS No. 04-576-4453

Stock- Price on:12/24/2007 $14.09
Stock Exchange NDQ
Ticker Symbol SPEC
Outstanding Shares 13,330,000
E.P.S $0.64
Shareholders NA

Business: The group's principal activities are to design, manufacture and market a broad range of control products and systems. It operates in three segments: signal integrity products, power integrity products and management systems and frequency control products. The signal integrity products segment designs and manufactures a broad range of low pass electromagnetic interference filters, filtered arrays and specialty ceramic capacitors. The power integrity products and management systems segment designs and manufactures power integrity products and power management systems. The frequency control products segment designs and manufactures ceramic resonators, bandpass filters and patch antennas. The products are used in various industries including telecommunications, aerospace, military, medical and industrial control equipment. It has operations in the United States, Mexico, Germany, China and other foreign countries. On 27-Feb-2004, it acquired salisbury engineering, inc.

Primary SIC and add'l.: 3679 3678 3674 3675

CIK No: 0000092769

Subsidiaries: Spectrum Control (Hong Kong) Limited, Spectrum Control de Mexico, Spectrum Control Electronics (Dongguan) Co., Ltd., Spectrum Control GmbH, Spectrum Control Technology, Inc., Spectrum Control, Inc, Spectrum Engineering International, Inc., Spectrum FSY Microwave, Inc., Spectrum Microwave, Inc., Spectrum SEI Microwave, Inc., Spectrum Sensors and Controls, Inc.

Officers: Richard A. Southworth/Dir., CEO, Pres., Brian F. Ward/Sr. VP, Business Mgr. - Spectrum Sensors, Controls, John P. Freeman/Dir., Sr. VP, CFO, Michael Tantimonaco/VP - Mexican Operations, Lawrence G. Howanitz/Sr. VP, Business Mgr. - Spectrum Signal, Power Integrity, Jeffrey S. Peters/VP - Information Technology, Robert J. McKenna/Sr. VP - New Business, Resource Development

Directors: Richard A. Southworth/Dir., CEO, Pres., Gerald A. Ryan/Chmn., Scott D. Krentzman/Dir., John P. Freeman/Dir., Sr. VP, CFO, Thomas J. Gruenwald/Dir., James F. Toohey/Dir., Melvin Kutchin/Dir., Paul S. Bates/Dir., Edwin R. Bindseil/Dir., John M. Petersen/Dir.

Owners: Brian F. Ward, Robert J. McKenna, SnowCapitalManagementLP/9.18%, John M. Petersen/3.19%, Insiders/11.40%, Gerald A. Ryan/1.21%, Fidelity Management & Research/7.43%, James F. Toohey/1.81%, John P. Freeman, Richard A. Southworth/1.48%, Melvin Kutchin, QuakerCapitalManagement/11.07%, Lawrence G. Howanitz, Thomas J. Gruenwald, Edwin R. Bindseil/1.17% *(18 Owners included in Index)*

Financial Data: *Fiscal Year End:*11/30 *Latest Annual Data:* 11/30/2006

Year	Sales	Net Income
2006	$125,672,000	$5,871,000
2005	$98,354,000	$4,605,000
2004	$80,477,000	$4,166,000

Curr. Assets:	$52,462,000	**Curr. Liab.:**	$20,654,000	**P/E Ratio:**	22.02
Plant, Equip.:	$24,236,000	**Total Liab.:**	$30,608,000	**Indic. Yr. Divd.:**	NA
Total Assets:	$119,207,000	**Net Worth:**	$88,599,000	**Debt/ Equity:**	0.0117

Spectrum Laboratories Inc

18617 Broadwick St., Rancho Dominguez, CA, 90220; ***PH:*** 1-310-885-4600; ***Fax:*** 1-310-885-4666;
http:// www.spectrapor.com; ***Email:*** customerservice@spectrumlabs.com

General - Incorporation DE
Employees NA
Auditor Stonefield Josephson, Inc
Stk Agt American Stock Transfer & Trust Co.
Counsel NA
DUNS No. 05-485-5119

Stock- Price on:12/24/2007 NA
Stock Exchange OTC
Ticker Symbol SPTM
Outstanding Shares NA
E.P.S NA
Shareholders NA

Business: The group's principal activities are to develop and sell proprietary tabular membranes and membrane devices. The group also markets dialysis membranes and other sterile tamper proof specialty surgical products. The group's products include laboratory products, original equipment manufacturing and operating room disposable products. The group's customers include pharmaceutical and medical device manufacturers, laboratories and research institutes.

Primary SIC and add'l.: 3826 3842

CIK No: 0000319013

Subsidiaries: SLI Acquisition Corp., Spectrum Chromatography, Inc., Spectrum Europe B.V.

Officers: Roy T. Eddleman/Chairma, CEO, Anthony MacDonald/Pres., Brian Watts/CFO, VP - Finance, William Martin/VP - Manufacturing, Bob Adamson/VP - Sales, Marketing, Jesus F. Martinez/Chief Science Officer, David Goldberg/VP - Quality Assurance, Regulatory Affairs

Directors: Roy T. Eddleman/Chairma, CEO

Spectrum Organic Products Inc

5341old Redwood Hwy., Floorpetaluma, CA, 94954; ***PH:*** 1-707-778-8900;
http:// www.spectrumnaturals.com

General - Incorporation CA
Employees NA
Auditor Grant Thornton LLP
Stk Agt Corporate Stock Transfer, Inc.
Counsel NA
DUNS No. 17-549-6025

Stock- Price on:12/24/2007 $0.7
Stock Exchange OTC
Ticker Symbol SPOP
Outstanding Shares NA
E.P.S NA
Shareholders NA

Business: The group's principal activity is to manufacture, pack and sell nutritional supplements, organic and natural food products, cooking and nutritional oils, condiments, dressings and spreads on a wholesale basis to distributors, grocery and club store chains. The group's natural and organic food product lines include olive oils and other culinary oils, salad dressings, condiments and butter-substitutes. Nutritional supplement products include organic flax oils, evening primrose oil, borage oil, norwegian fish oil and other essential fatty acids in both liquid and capsule forms. The spectrum ingredients include organic and non organic culinary oils, organic vinegar and nutritional oils offered to other manufacturers for use in their products. Products are offered in over 6,000 health food stores nationwide and 2,000 grocery stores located throughout United States and Canada.

Primary SIC and add'l.: 2079 2035

CIK No: 0001034992

Spectrum Pharmaceuticals Inc

157 Technology Dr., Irvine, CA, 92618; ***PH:*** 1-949-788-6700; ***Fax:*** 1-949-788-6706;
http:// www.spectrumpharm.com; ***Email:*** info@spectrumpharm.com

General - Incorporation DE
Employees 50
Auditor Kelly & Co
Stk Agt U.S. Stock Transfer Corp
Counsel NA
DUNS No. 79-088-8002

Stock- Price on:12/24/2007 $6.6
Stock Exchange NDQ
Ticker Symbol SPPI
Outstanding Shares 25,670,000
E.P.S -$0.88
Shareholders NA

Business: The group's principal activities are to acquire, develop and commercialise proprietary and generic drug products, primarily for the treatment of cancer and related disorders. The group operates in two divisions: oncology and general drug. The oncology division acquires rights to clinical-stage oncology drug candidates and either alone, or through alliances with other companies, develop and eventually commercialize those drugs. The general drug division sells generic versions of drugs whose patent protection expires in the near term.

Primary SIC and add'l.: 8731 2834

CIK No: 0000831547

Subsidiaries: NeoGene Technologies, Inc., NeoJB LLC, Spectrum Pharmaceuticals GmbH

Officers: Rajesh C. Shrotriya/Chmn., CEO, Pres./$2,389,077.00, William Pedranti/VP, General Counsel, Shyam Kumaria/VP - Finance/$579,209.00, Luigi Lenaz/Chief Scientific Officer/$1,071,226.00, Ashok Gore/Sr. VP - Pharmaceutical Operations, Regulatory Compliance, Russell L. Skibsted/Sr. VP, Chief Business Officer, Daniel Pertschuk/VP - Medical Affairs, Enrico Mihich/Member - Scientific Advisory Board, Herbert M. Pinedo/Member - Scientific Advisory Board, Hagop Kantarjian/Member - Scientific Advisory Board, Kenneth A. Foon/Member - Scientific Advisory Board, Anthony Tolcher/Member - Scientific Advisory Board, Daniel D. Von Hoff/Member - Scientific Advisory Board

Directors: Rajesh C. Shrotriya/Chmn., CEO, Pres., Stuart M. Krassner/Dir., Julius Vida/Dir., Anthony E. Maida/Dir., Richard Fulmer/Dir., Mitchell P. Cybulski/Dir.

Owners: Mehta Dilip, Rockmore Investment Master Fund, Ltd., Shrotriya Rajesh/5.60%, Sands Brothers Venture Capital Funds I-IV LLC, Rockmore Investment Master Fund, Ltd./28.24%, Joseph Edelman/9.61%, Insiders/8.80%, Portside Growth and Opportunity Fund/60.00%, Portside Growth and Opportunity Fund, Fulmer Richard, Kumaria Shyam, Sands Brothers Venture Capital Funds I-IV LLC/11.76%, Maida Anthony, Vida Julius, Krassner Stuart *(16 Owners included in Index)*

Financial Data: *Fiscal Year End:*12/31 *Latest Annual Data:* 12/31/2006

Year	Sales	Net Income
2006	$5,673,000	-$23,284,000
2005	$577,000	-$18,642,000
2004	$258,000	-$12,286,000

Curr. Assets:	$52,287,000	**Curr. Liab.:**	$6,233,000		
Plant, Equip.:	$625,000	**Total Liab.:**	$7,288,000	**Indic. Yr. Divd.:**	NA
Total Assets:	$53,117,000	**Net Worth:**	$45,829,000	**Debt/ Equity:**	NA

Spectrum Sciences & Software Hldgs Corp

2677 Prosperity Ave., Ste. 300, Fairfax, VA, 22031; ***PH:*** 1-703-641-1100;
http:// www.spectrumholdingscorp.com

General - Incorporation	DE	Stock- Price on:12/24/2007	$0.39
Employees	170	Stock Exchange	OTC
Auditor	Grant Thornton, LLP	Ticker Symbol	HNIN
Stk Agt	Signature Stock Transfer, Inc.	Outstanding Shares	41,770,000
Counsel	NA	E.P.S.	-$0.24
DUNS No.	10-181-8995	Shareholders	NA

Business: The group's principle activity is to provide engineering, scientific and technological support services. It also provides specialized and standard ground support equipment for the United States department of defense and other governmental and commercial contractors. The company operates in three divisions: management services, manufacturing division and engineering and information technology services. The management services division operates and maintains military training ranges and associated infrastructure and assets. The manufacturing division focuses on the design, development, manufacturing, and systems integration of aerospace ground support equipment. The engineering and information technology services division provides services such as hazard analysis, modeling and simulation, range planning, air space planning, and environmental analyses. The group operates from United States.

Primary SIC and add'l.: 3724 7389 3761 3443

CIK No: 0001229195

Subsidiaries: Coast Engine and Equipment Company, Inc., Horne Engineering Services, LLC, M&M Engineering, Ltd., M&M Offshore Limited (a wholly owned subsidiary of M&M Engineering Ltd.), Spectrum Sciences and Software, Inc.

Officers: Darryl K. Horne/Chmn., CEO, Pres., Dwight Howard/COO, Michael M. Megless/Dir., CFO, Robert L. Suthard/COO, Vic Deleenheer/Division Mgr. - Coast Engine, Equipment Company

Directors: Darryl K. Horne/Chmn., CEO, Pres., Kelvin D. Armstrong/Dir., Karl H. Heer/Dir., Kenneth L. Johnson/Dir., Michael M. Megless/Dir., CFO, John A. Moore/Dir., Francis X. Ryan/Dir., Michael J. Bayer/Member - Corporate Advisory Board, Christopher D. Brady/Member - Corporate Advisory Board, Michael J. Driver/Member - Corporate Advisory Board, Gregory L. Frank/Member - Corporate Advisory Board, James E. Thomas/Member - Corporate Advisory Board, Evan Auld-Susott/Dir.

Owners: Darryl K. Horne/11.70%, Kenneth L. Johnson, Insiders/14.60%, Francis X. Ryan, Kelvin D. Armstrong/1.20%, Michael M. Megless, Trevor Foster/6.70%, John A. Moore, Karl Heer/1.10%

Financial Data: Fiscal Year End:12/31   Latest Annual Data: 12/31/2006

Year	Sales	Net Income
2006	$28,256,000	-$8,594,000
2005	$53,698,000	-$3,986,000
2004	$11,134,000	-$40,307,000

Curr. Assets:	$10,124,000	Curr. Liab.:	$3,621,000		
Plant, Equip.:	$5,737,000	Total Liab.:	$5,547,000	Indic. Yr. Divd.:	NA
Total Assets:	$30,064,000	Net Worth:	$24,517,000	Debt/ Equity:	0.0839

Spectrum Signal Processing Inc

2700 Production Way, Ste. 300, Burnaby, BC, V5A 4X1; **PH:** 1-604-421-5422;
http:// www.spectrumsignal.com

General - Incorporation	BC	Stock- Price on:12/24/2007	NA
Employees	NA	Stock Exchange	NA
Auditor	KPMG LLP	Ticker Symbol	NA
Stk Agt	Computershare Investor Services LLC	Outstanding Shares	NA
Counsel	Clark, Wilson	E.P.S.	NA
DUNS No.	24-724-0658	Shareholders	NA

Business: The group's principal activities are to design and develop high-density digital signal processing products for the wireless and voice over packet infrastructure markets. The signal processing technology transmits signals for wireless and voice over packet applications. These applications include voice-processing gateways that convert voice and data signals and the acquisition, processing and transmission of wireless signals. The products of the group are marketed to major commercial, industrial and defense customers in the United States and other countries.

Primary SIC and add'l.: 3661 7379 4812 3669

CIK No: 0000884455

Subsidiaries: Spectrum Signal Processing (UK) Limited, Spectrum Signal Processing (USA) Inc

Officers: Mark Briggs/VP - Marketing, Mike Farley/Pres. - USA, Mark Murray/Contact - USA, Keith Larose/Contact - Canada, Chris Sleaford/Contact - Canada, Brian Smith/Contact - USA, Chris Vandewinckel/Contact - USA, Douglas Atterbury/VP - Engineering, Elena A. Kinakin/40/VP - Finance, CFO, Sec.

Owners: ELENA A. KINAKIN, LEONARD G. PUCKER/1.01%, THE K2 PRINCIPAL FUND L.P./5.28%, LEVITICUS PARTNERS/14.64%, PASCAL E. SPOTHELFER/3.56%, MATTHEW MOHEBBI, JULES M.J. MEUNIER, MARTIN B. CARSKY, MARK A. BRIGGS, BRENT A. FLICHEL/2.00%, IRVING G. EBERT, DAVID E. SCOTT

Spectrx Inc

4955 Avalon Ridge Pkwy., Ste. 300, Norcross, GA, 30071; **PH:** 1-770-242-8723;
Fax: 1-770-242-8639; **http://** www.spectrx.com

General - Incorporation	DE	Stock- Price on:12/24/2007	NA
Employees	NA	Stock Exchange	OTC
Auditor	Eisner LLP	Ticker Symbol	SPRX
Stk Agt	SunTrust Bank	Outstanding Shares	NA
Counsel	Jones, Day, Reavis & Pogue	E.P.S.	-$0.1
DUNS No.	80-074-3106	Shareholders	NA

Business: The group's principal activities are to develop, manufacture and market insulin delivery, minimally-invasive fluid sampling procedures and cancer detection products. The insulin delivery and glucose monitoring activities are marketed under brand name simplechoice, which includes insulin pump disposables and a non-invasive interstitial fluid based continuous glucose monitoring development program. The group has collaborative agreements with medical device companies in helping, developing, commercialising and selling these products.

Primary SIC and add'l.: 8731

CIK No: 0000924515

Subsidiaries: Guided Therapeutics, Inc, Sterling Medivations, Inc

Officers: Mark L. Faupel/Dir., CEO, Acting CFO, Pres./$163,731.00, Richard L. Fowler/Sr. VP - Engineering, Bill Wells/Dir. - Communications

Directors: Mark L. Faupel/Dir., CEO, Acting CFO, Pres., John E. Imhoff/59/Dir., William Zachary/Dir., Mark A. Samuels/Dir., Michael C. James/Dir., Ronald W. Hart/Dir.

Owners: Opaline International, Inc., Barry Kurokawa, Bob Bowie, Mark A. Samuels, William E. Zachary, Susan Imhoff, Chestnut Ridge Partners, Easton Hunt Capital Partners, L.P., Dolphin Offshore Partners, LP, Dolores Maloof, SF Capital Partners, Sagamore Hill Hub Fund, Ltd., John Imhoff, ProMed Management Entities, Kuekenhof Equity Fund, LLP *(26 Owners included in Index)*

Financial Data: Fiscal Year End:12/31   Latest Annual Data: 12/31/2006

Year	Sales	Net Income
2006	$977,000	-$4,948,000
2005	$983,000	-$2,199,000
2004	$1,073,000	-$9,239,000

Curr. Assets:	$622,000	Curr. Liab.:	$10,658,000		
Plant, Equip.:	$568,000	Total Liab.:	$12,582,000	Indic. Yr. Divd.:	NA
Total Assets:	$1,241,000	Net Worth:	-$11,341,000	Debt/ Equity:	NA

SpeechSwitch Inc

750 State Rte. 34, Matawan, NJ, 07747; **PH:** 1-732-441-7700; **Fax:** 1-732-441-9895;
http:// www.speechswitch.com; **Email:** information@speechswitch.com

General - Incorporation	NJ	Stock- Price on:12/24/2007	$0.0012
Employees	3	Stock Exchange	OTC
Auditor	Bagell, Levine & Company, LLC	Ticker Symbol	SSWC
Stk Agt	NA	Outstanding Shares	46,000,000
Counsel	NA	E.P.S.	-$0.03
DUNS No.	NA	Shareholders	NA

Business: The groups principal activity is to develop technology and believes that the transition to an independent group will provide with access to capital. The group should provide needed financial resources to potentially penetrate the market and distribute the product. The group operates from the United States.

Primary SIC and add'l.: 7372

CIK No: 0001307989

Officers: Bruce R. Knef/Dir., CEO, Pres.

Directors: Bruce R. Knef/Dir., CEO, Pres., Jerome R. Mahoney/Chmn.

Owners: Insiders/100.00%, Jerome R. Mahoney, Jerome R. Mahoney/100.00%, Insiders

Financial Data: Fiscal Year End:12/31   Latest Annual Data: 12/31/2006

Year	Sales	Net Income
2006	$254,000	-$646,000
2005	$144,000	-$768,000

Curr. Assets:	$279,000	Curr. Liab.:	$1,810,000		
Plant, Equip.:	NA	Total Liab.:	$1,810,000	Indic. Yr. Divd.:	NA
Total Assets:	$288,000	Net Worth:	-$1,522,000	Debt/ Equity:	NA

Speedemissions Inc

1015 Tyrone Rd. Ste. 220, Tyrone, GA, 30290; **PH:** 1-770-306-7667;
http:// www.speedemissions.com; **Email:** info@speedemissions.com

General - Incorporation	FL	Stock- Price on:12/24/2007	$0.26
Employees	103	Stock Exchange	OTC
Auditor	Tauber & Balser, P. C.	Ticker Symbol	SPMI
Stk Agt	Interwest Transfer Company, Inc.	Outstanding Shares	3,030,000
Counsel	NA	E.P.S.	-$0.48
DUNS No.	NA	Shareholders	NA

Business: The groups principle activities include operating 35 vehicle emissions testing and safety inspection centers in three separate markets. The group operates from Atlanta, Georgia; Houston, Texas; and Salt Lake City, Utah, and four mobile units in the Atlanta, Georgia area.

Primary SIC and add'l.: 4785

CIK No: 0001158419

Subsidiaries: Speedemissions, Inc

Officers: Rich A. Parlontieri/CEO, Pres./$359,292.00, Randy M. Dickerson/COO, Exec. VP, Michael Shanahan/CFO/$141,596.00

Directors: Bradley A. Thonpson/44/Dir., Ernest A. Childs/61/Dir., John Bradley/49/Dir., Michael E. Guirlinger/59/Dir.

Owners: GCA Strategic Investment Fund Ltd/72.50%, Insiders, Global Capital Funding Group, LP/27.50%, GCA Strategic Investment Fund Ltd., Michael E. Guirlinger, Global Capital Funding Group, L.P., Barron Partners LP/100.00%, Richard A. Parlontieri

Financial Data: Fiscal Year End:12/31   Latest Annual Data: 12/31/2006

Year	Sales	Net Income
2006	$9,480,000	-$1,332,000
2005	$6,952,000	-$3,551,000
2004	$2,868,000	-$2,972,000

Curr. Assets:	$545,000	Curr. Liab.:	$976,000		
Plant, Equip.:	$1,229,000	Total Liab.:	$1,090,000	Indic. Yr. Divd.:	NA
Total Assets:	$8,935,000	Net Worth:	$7,845,000	Debt/ Equity:	NA

Speedus Corp

9 Desbrosses St., Ste. 402, New York, NY, 10013; **PH:** 1-888-773-3669; **Fax:** 1-212-937-5230;
http:// www.speedus.com; **Email:** investor@speedus.com

General - Incorporation	DE	Stock- Price on:12/24/2007	$0.71
Employees	21	Stock Exchange	NDQ
Auditor	PricewaterhouseCoopers LLP	Ticker Symbol	SPDE
Stk Agt	EquiServe Trust Co N.A	Outstanding Shares	15,970,000
Counsel	Willkie Farr & Gallagher LLP	E.P.S.	-$1.04
DUNS No.	88-452-8241	Shareholders	NA

Business: The group's principal activities are to invest in diverse businesses. During the year 2003, the group acquired a controlling interest in zargis medical corp to develop a service solution, targeted at primary care physicians, for the early screening and detection of valvular and congenital heart disease. On 06-May-2002, the group acquired controlling interest in f&b gudtfood, the creator and operator of the 'chic and quick' cafe, which operates a store in manhattan. The group has developed and launched

an online cell phone store, 007phones, which it licenses to a third party. It owns a fixed wireless spectrum in the New York city metropolitan area that it may commercialize in the future to support high-speed, or broadband, Internet access service. It also owns a portfolio of patents that allow for high-speed wireless communications. On 28-Jul-2003, the group acquired 68.9% interest in zargis medical corp.

Primary SIC and add'l.: 4841 7375 6719 5812

CIK No: 0001002520

Subsidiaries: CellularVision Technology, telecommunication

Officers: Shant S. Hovnanian/Chmn., CEO, Pres., Thomas M. Finn/Sec., Treasurer, CFO, John Kallassy/Exec. VP

Directors: Shant S. Hovnanian/Chmn., CEO, Pres.

Owners: Christpher Vizas, Thomas M. Finn, Jeffrey Najarian, William F. Leimkuhler, Insiders/47.40%, XO Holdings, Inc./11.10%, Shant S. Hovnanian/26.00%, Vahak S. Hovnanian/16.20%, John Kallassy/2.70%

Financial Data: *Fiscal Year End:*12/31 *Latest Annual Data:* 12/31/2006

Year	Sales	Net Income
2006	$846,000	-$5,615,000
2005	$1,038,000	-$5,468,000
2004	$917,000	$6,004,000

Curr. Assets:	$15,692,000	*Curr. Liab.:*	$1,034,000		
Plant, Equip.:	$528,000	*Total Liab.:*	$1,034,000	*Indic. Yr. Divd.:*	NA
Total Assets:	$17,136,000	*Net Worth:*	$16,102,000	*Debt/ Equity:*	NA

Speedway Motorsports Inc

5555 Concord Pkwy. S, Concord, NC, 28027; *PH:* 1-704-455-3239; *Fax:* 1-704-455-2168; *http://* www.speedwaymotorsports.com

General - Incorporation	DE	***Stock***- Price on:12/24/2007	$39.97
Employees	793	Stock Exchange	NYSE
Auditor	Deloitte & Touche LLP	Ticker Symbol	TRK
Stk Agt	Wachovia Bank Corporate Trust Group	Outstanding Shares	43,790,000
Counsel	NA	E.P.S	$1.99
DUNS No.	87-893-8893	Shareholders	NA

Business: The group's principal activity is to promote, market and sponsor motorsports activities in the United States. The group owns and operates atlanta motor speedway (ams), bristol motor speedway (bms),infineon raceway, las vegas motor speedway (lvms),lowe's motor speedway(lms), Texas motor speedway (tms) . It also owns, operates and sanctions the legends car and bandolero car circuits for which the group manufactures and sells smaller-scale, modified cars and parts through its subsidiary, 600 racing inc. Through finish line events subsidiary, it provides event food, beverage, and souvenir merchandising services. The group broadcasts substantially all of the nascar winston cup and busch series racing events and also other events, at each of the speedways over proprietary radio performance racing network.

Primary SIC and add'l.: 4833 7948

CIK No: 0000934648

Subsidiaries: 600 Racing, Inc., Atlanta Motor Speedway, LLC, Bristol Motor Speedway, LLC, Charlotte Motor Speedway, LLCa/k/a Lowes Motor Speedway at Charlotte (LMS), INEX Corporation, Jim Russell Group, Inc., Las Vegas Motor Speedway, LLC(LVMS), Motorsports by Mail, LLC, Nevada Speedway, LLCd/b/a Las Vegas Motor Speedway, Oil-Chem Research Corporation, SMI Systems, LLC, SMI Trackside, LLC(a subsidiary of THC), SMISC Holdings, Inc, Speedway Funding, LLC, Speedway Media, LLCd/b/a Racing Country USA 23 Subsidiaries included in the Index

Officers: Bruton O. Smith/79/Chmn., CEO/$2,050,000.00, William R. Brooks/56/Dir., Exec. VP, CFO/$1,232,598.00, H. A. Wheeler/67/Dir., COO, Pres./$1,186,133.00, Marcus G. Smith/32/Dir., Exec. VP - National Sales, Marketing/$1,111,986.00

Directors: Bruton O. Smith/79/Chmn., CEO, Marcus G. Smith/32/Dir., Exec. VP - National Sales, Marketing, William R. Brooks/56/Dir., Exec. VP, CFO, William P. Benton/82/Dir., Mark M. Gambill/55/Dir., H. A. Wheeler/67/Dir., COO, Pres., Tom E. Smith/64/Dir., James P. Holden/54/Dir., Robert L. Rewey/67/Dir.

Owners: Robert L. Rewey, Bruton O. Smith, American Century Companies, Inc., H. A. Wheeler, Sonic Financial Corporation, Insiders, William P. Benton, Marcus G. Smith, James P. Holden, William R. Brooks, Tom E. Smith, Mark M. Gambill

Financial Data: *Fiscal Year End:*12/31 *Latest Annual Data:* 12/31/2006

Year	Sales	Net Income
2006	$567,365,000	$111,222,000
2005	$544,068,000	$108,135,000
2004	$446,519,000	$73,654,000

Curr. Assets:	$203,041,000	*Curr. Liab.:*	$159,460,000	*P/E Ratio:*	16.65
Plant, Equip.:	$1,066,941,000	*Total Liab.:*	$769,434,000	*Indic. Yr. Divd.:*	$0.340
Total Assets:	$1,589,523,000	*Net Worth:*	$820,089,000	*Debt/ Equity:*	0.5092

Spescom Software Inc

10052 Mesa Ridge Ct., Ste. 100, San Diego, CA, 92121; *PH:* 1-858-625-3000; *http://* www.spescomsoftware.com

General - Incorporation	CA	***Stock***- Price on:12/24/2007	NA
Employees	38	Stock Exchange	NA
Auditor	Singer Lewak Greenbaum & Goldstein	Ticker Symbol	NA
Stk Agt	Mellon Investor Services LLC	Outstanding Shares	NA
Counsel	NA	E.P.S	NA
DUNS No.	02-238-6049	Shareholders	NA

Business: The group's principal activities are to develop, market and support integrated suite of collaborative document, configuration and records management software solutions. These products enable customers to create, capture, store, manage, share and distribute critical business information across an enterprise. The group's product include eb which consists of a core platform that contains functionality usually provided by multiple applications in a single fully integrated environment. This includes documents/content management, imaging, workflow and records management and collaborative workspace management. The customers of the group include utility, transportation, manufacturing and petrochemical industries and local governments. The group operates mainly in the United States and Europe.

Primary SIC and add'l.: 7372

CIK No: 0000813747

Subsidiaries: Spescom Ltd.

Officers: Alan Kiraly/47/Dir., CEO, Pierre De Wet/VP - Operations, John W. Low/Dir., CFO, Sec., Glenn Cox/VP - Sales, Marketing, Ben Martin/Dir. - EMEA, Michael D. Stout/Executive Advisor, Nuclear

Directors: Alan Kiraly/47/Dir., CEO, Michael Silverman/Chmn., John W. Low/Dir., CFO, Sec., Ross Hamilton/Dir., Hilton Isaacman/Dir., Jim Myers/Dir., Larry Unruh/Dir.

Owners: M.A.G. Capital, LLC, Forest Securities Limited, Michael Silverman, Alan Kiraly, Glenn Cox, John W. Low, Insiders, Hilton Isaacman, Spescom Ltd., Pierre de Wet, James P. Myers, Larry D. Unruh, Ross D. Hamilton

Financial Data: *Fiscal Year End:*09/30 *Latest Annual Data:* 02/03/2007

Year	Sales	Net Income
2007	$2,940,003,000	$53,742,000
2006	$7,006,000	-$1,022,000
2005	$5,825,000	-$3,548,000

Curr. Assets:	$1,139,000	*Curr. Liab.:*	$8,921,000		
Plant, Equip.:	$131,000	*Total Liab.:*	$9,601,000	*Indic. Yr. Divd.:*	NA
Total Assets:	$1,723,000	*Net Worth:*	-$7,878,000	*Debt/ Equity:*	NA

Spherion Corp

2050 Spectrum Blvd., Fort Lauderdale, FL, 33309; *PH:* 1-954-308-7600; *Fax:* 1-954-308-7666; *http://* www.spherion.com; *Email:* help@spherion.com

General - Incorporation	DE	***Stock***- Price on:12/24/2007	$10.09
Employees	273,000	Stock Exchange	NYSE
Auditor	Deloitte & Touche LLP	Ticker Symbol	SFN
Stk Agt	Bank of New York	Outstanding Shares	56,390,000
Counsel	NA	E.P.S	$0.97
DUNS No.	05-303-2074	Shareholders	NA

Business: The group's principle activity is to provide temporary staffing services, managed services and permanent placement services. It operates in two basic segments: staffing services and professional services. The staffing services operating segment include clerical and light industrial temporary staffing, managed services and permanent placement. The professional services operating segment includes temporary staffing and permanent placement of employees that specialize in information technology, finance and accounting, legal and administrative skill sets. The group's quarterly revenue for September 2007 was 495.17 millions of USD.

Primary SIC and add'l.: 7363 7361

CIK No: 0000914536

Subsidiaries: 3736008 Canada Inc., 6063721 Canada Inc., Comtex Information Systems,Inc., Human Resource Capital Group Inc., NorCross Holdings LLC, NorCross Teleservices L.P., Norrell Corporation, Norrell Resources Corporation, Norrell Services, Ltd, Norrell Temporary Services,Inc., RTO Insurance Limited, Spherion (Europe) Inc., Spherion Assessment Inc., Spherion Atlantic Enterprises LLC, Spherion Atlantic Operations LLC 26 Subsidiaries included in the Index

Officers: Roy G. Krause/Dir., CEO, Pres./$1,574,044.00, Mark W. Smith/CFO, Sr. VP/$677,483.00, Lisa G. Iglesias/Sr. VP, General Counsel, Sec./$498,769.00, William J. Grubbs/Exec. VP/$988,799.00, Teri L. Miller/Investor Relations Officer, John D. Heins/Sr. VP, Chief Human Resources Officer, Randy Atkinson/Investor Relations Officer

Directors: Roy G. Krause/Dir., CEO, Pres., James J. Forese/Chmn., David R. Parker/Dir., William F. Evans/Dir., Steven S. Elbaum/Dir., Ian J. Morrison/Dir., Michael A. Victory/Dir., Anne Szostak/Dir., Barbara Pellow/Dir.

Owners: Goldman Sachs Asset Management, L.P./7.40%, Mark W. Smith, James J. Forese, Barbara Pellow, Hotchkis and Wiley Capital Management, LLC/6.40%, Dimensional Fund Advisors LP./9.41%, William F. Evans, Lisa G. Iglesias, Donald Smith & Co., Inc./6.14%, Steven S. Elbaum, William Grubbs, David R. Parker, Daruma Asset Management, Inc./6.40%, Barclays/5.74%, Ian J. Morrison *(20 Owners included in Index)*

Financial Data: *Fiscal Year End:*01/01 *Latest Annual Data:* 12/31/2006

Year	Sales	Net Income
2006	$1,933,059,000	$54,682,000
2004	$2,032,715,000	$35,829,000

Curr. Assets:	$381,202,000	*Curr. Liab.:*	$173,933,000	*P/E Ratio:*	10.62
Plant, Equip.:	$87,291,000	*Total Liab.:*	$222,245,000	*Indic. Yr. Divd.:*	NA
Total Assets:	$693,387,000	*Net Worth:*	$471,142,000	*Debt/ Equity:*	0.0047

Spherion Pacific Enterprises LLC

2050 Spectrum Blvd., Fort Lauderdale, FL, 33309; *PH:* 1-954-308-7600; *http://* www.spherion.com; *Email:* help@spherion.com

General - Incorporation	DE	***Stock***- Price on:12/24/2007	NA
Employees	NA	Stock Exchange	NA
Auditor	Rose, Snyder & Jacobs	Ticker Symbol	NA
Stk Agt	Bank of New York	Outstanding Shares	NA
Counsel	Foley & Lardner LLP	E.P.S	NA
DUNS No.	NA	Shareholders	NA

Business: The group is presently exploring opportunities to effect an acquisition by merger, exchange, issuance of securities or similar business combinations. Earlier the group was into manufacturing and delivery of custom broadband wireless networking equipment for business and residential customers. The group sold substantially all its assets and liabilities to p-com inc during 2003.

Primary SIC and add'l.: 3669

CIK No: 0001014343

Owners: Trellus Small Cap Opportunity Fund LP/12.60%, Trinad Capital Master Fund, Ltd./4.70%, Roy Bingham, S. M. Hassan, Jason Brown/9.10%, Trellus Partners II LP/12.60%, Douglas Lioon/2.00%, Peter Meehan, Andrew Jacobs, Wendy Tenenberg, Vicis Capital Master Fund, LLC/4.80%, Trellus Offshore Fund Ltd/12.60%, Trellus Small Cap Opportunity Offshore Fund Ltd/12.60%, Dave Smith, Trellus Partners LP/12.60% *(17 Owners included in Index)*

Curr. Assets:	$1,655,000	*Curr. Liab.:*	$8,549,000		
Plant, Equip.:	$2,148,000	*Total Liab.:*	$9,278,000	*Indic. Yr. Divd.:*	NA
Total Assets:	$5,277,000	*Net Worth:*	-$4,001,000	*Debt/ Equity:*	0.2798

Spherix Inc

12051 Indian Creek Ct., Beltsville, MD, 20705; *PH:* 1-301-419-3900; *Fax:* 1-301-210-4909; *http://* www.spherixinc.com; *Email:* info@spherix.com

General - Incorporation .... DE
Employees 344
Auditor .... Grant Thornton LLP
Stk Agt...... American Stock Transfer & Trust Co.
Counsel .... NA
DUNS No. 04-398-4988

Stock - Price on:12/24/2007 .... $2.11
Stock Exchange .... NDQ
Ticker Symbol .... SPEX
Outstanding Shares 14,250,000
E.P.S. .... -$0.016
Shareholders .... NA

Business: The group's principal activity is to provide information and biotechnology services. The group operates in two business segments; biospherix and infospherix. The biospherix division is its biotechnology research and development arm, which develops proprietary products and services for economic commercial applications. The commercial information services division, government information service division and information technology division are collectively referred to as infospherix. The commercial information services division and government information service division operate information center services providing consulting, information management and materials management to the public and reservation and tourism solutions. The group's major trademarks are spherix, reserveworld, flycracker, and naturlose.

Primary SIC and add'l.: 7375 8731

CIK No: 0000012239

Subsidiaries: InfoSpherix Incorporated

Officers: Richard C. Levin/Dir., CEO, CFO, Pres., Claire L. Kruger/CEO, Dir. - Health Sciences, Gilbert V. Levin/Chmn., Exec. Officer Science, Robert L. Clayton/45/Dir. - Finance, Treasurer, Roger Downs/61/VP - Operations, Infospherix, Wallace Hayes/Consultant, Jeffrey T. Lowe/51/VP - Corporate Communications, Steven M. Wade/52/VP - Information Technology, Infospherix, Yongming Lu/Mgr.

Directors: Richard C. Levin/Dir., CEO, CFO, Pres., Gilbert V. Levin/Chmn., Exec. Officer Science, Douglas T. Brown/Dir., Paul A. Cox/Dir., George C. Creel/Dir., Karen M. Levin/Dir., Robert A. Lodder/Dir., Robert J. Vander Zanden/Dir.

Owners: George C. Creel, Karen M. Levin/9.20%, Richard C. Levin, Insiders/19.30%, Roger A. Downs, Robert A. Lodder, Gilbert V. Levin/8.70%, Steven M. Wade, Douglas T. Brown, Robert J. Vander Zanden, Jeffrey T. Lowe, Paul A. Cox, Robert L. Clayton

Financial Data: Fiscal Year End:12/31   Latest Annual Data: 12/31/2006

Year	Sales	Net Income
2006	$24,838,000	$3,513,000
2005	$23,046,000	-$2,849,000
2004	$22,348,000	-$2,822,000

Curr. Assets:	$13,774,000	**Curr. Liab.:**	$2,909,000	**P/E Ratio:** 16.23
Plant, Equip.:	$3,914,000	**Total Liab.:**	$3,825,000	**Indic. Yr. Divd.:** NA
Total Assets:	$18,376,000	**Net Worth:**	$14,551,000	**Debt/ Equity:** NA

Spindletop Oil & Gas Co

12850 Spurling Rd., Ste. 200, Dallas, TX, 75230; **PH:** 1-972-644-2581; **Fax:** 1-972-661-2701; **http://** www.spindletopoil.com; **Email:** info@spindletopoil.com

General - Incorporation .... TX
Employees 14
Auditor .... Farmer Fuqua & Huff P.C
Stk Agt. .... NA
Counsel .... NA
DUNS No. 06-634-9580

Stock - Price on:12/24/2007 .... $5.5
Stock Exchange .... OTC
Ticker Symbol .... SPND
Outstanding Shares 7,600,000
E.P.S. $0.15
Shareholders .... NA

Business: The group's principal activities are the exploration, development and production of oil and natural gas, the rental of oil field equipment, the gathering and marketing of natural gas. The subsidiaries of the group include prairie pipeline co. And spindletop drilling group. The group owns rental equipment, including natural gas compressors, pumping units, natural gas dehydrators and other pieces of oil field production equipment. The group's products are sold to major oil and gas companies, brokers, pipelines and distributors. The major customers of the group include devon gas services/mitchell marketing co. Shell trading (us) company, lig chemical company and plains marketing, l.p.

Primary SIC and add'l.: 7359 1311

CIK No: 0000867038

Subsidiaries: Prairie Pipeline Co, Spindletop Drilling Company

Officers: Chris G. Mazzini/Chmn., CEO, Pres., Mike Keen/Operations Mgr., Michelle H. Mazzini/46/Dir., VP, Sec., Treasurer, General Counsel, Robert E. Corbin/Controller, Principal Financial Officer, Dick A. Mastin/Petroleum Landman, Glenn E. Sparks/Land Dir., Assoc. General Counsel, Mark Cook/Petroleum Geologist

Directors: Chris G. Mazzini/Chmn., CEO, Pres., Michelle H. Mazzini/46/Dir., VP, Sec., Treasurer, General Counsel, Paul E. Cash/75/Dir.

Owners: Insiders/81.00%, West Coast Asset Management, Inc./5.00%, Chris Mazzini/77.00%, Paul E. Cash/4.00%

Financial Data: Fiscal Year End:12/31   Latest Annual Data: 12/31/2006

Year	Sales	Net Income
2006	$6,174,000	$920,000
2005	$6,395,000	$1,417,000
2004	$4,515,000	$1,266,000

Curr. Assets:	$7,418,000	**Curr. Liab.:**	$2,454,000	**P/E Ratio:** 61.11
Plant, Equip.:	$5,606,000	**Total Liab.:**	$5,349,000	**Indic. Yr. Divd.:** NA
Total Assets:	$13,024,000	**Net Worth:**	$7,675,000	**Debt/ Equity:** 0.1719

Spire Corp

1 Patriots Pk., Bedford, MA, 01730; **PH:** 1-781-275-6000; **Fax:** 1-781-275-7470; **http://** www.spirecorp.com

General - Incorporation .... MA
Employees 113
Auditor .... Vitale, Caturano & Co., Ltd.
Stk Agt...... American Stock Transfer & Trust Co.
Counsel .... Hale & Dorr LLP
DUNS No. 06-513-7978

Stock - Price on:12/24/2007 .... $8.85
Stock Exchange .... NDQ
Ticker Symbol .... SPIR
Outstanding Shares 8,190,000
E.P.S. .... -$0.97
Shareholders .... NA

Business: The group's principal activities are developing, manufacturing and marketing of highly engineered solar electric manufacturing equipment and systems and the provision of biomedical processing services. The group operates through four segments namely: solar equipment, solar systems, biomedical and biophotonics. The group designs and manufactures equipment for the production of terrestrial photovoltaic modules from solar cells. The group also offers value-added services to biomedical customers, which provide surface treatments to enhance the performance of medical products. The group conducts research and development activities for the United States government. On 27-May-2003, the group acquired bandwidth semiconductor, llc.

Primary SIC and add'l.: 3842 3845 3674

CIK No: 0000731657

Subsidiaries: Exelon Corporation

Officers: Mark C. Little/Dir., CEO - Spire Biomedical/$170,029.00, Roger G. Little/Chmn., CEO, Pres./$530,695.00, Rodger W. Lafavre/COO/$170,711.00, Stephen J. Hogan/Exec. VP, GM - Spire Solar, Michael W. Odougherty/Sec., Christian Dufresne/CFO, Treasurer, Richard P. Thomley/Chief Accounting Officer, Corporate Controller

Directors: Mark C. Little/Dir., CEO - Spire Biomedical, Roger G. Little/Chmn., CEO, Pres., David R. Lipinski/Dir., Roger W. Redmond/54/Dir., Udo Henseler/Dir., Guy L. Mayer/Dir., Michael J. Magliochetti/Dir.

Owners: Insiders/29.40%, Rodger W. LaFavre, Roger G. Little/26.80%, Udo Henseler, Guy L. Mayer, David R. Lipinski, Federated Investors, Inc./11.40%, Michael J. Magliochetti, Mark C. Little/1.60%, Leviticus Partners, L.P./5.30%, Roger W. Redmond

Financial Data: Fiscal Year End:12/31   Latest Annual Data: 12/31/2006

Year	Sales	Net Income
2006	$20,125,000	-$8,151,000
2005	$22,422,000	$44,000
2004	$17,278,000	-$4,120,000

Curr. Assets:	$18,349,000	**Curr. Liab.:**	$14,411,000	
Plant, Equip.:	$6,673,000	**Total Liab.:**	$18,221,000	**Indic. Yr. Divd.:** NA
Total Assets:	$27,684,000	**Net Worth:**	$9,463,000	**Debt/ Equity:** NA

Spirent Plc

Spirent House, Crawley Business Quarter, Fleming Way W Sussex, Crawley, RH10 9QL; **PH:** 44-4143551130; **http://** www.spirent.com

General - Incorporation .... UK
Employees .... NA
Auditor .... Ernst & Young LLP
Stk Agt .... Bank of New York
Counsel .... Linklaters
DUNS No. .... NA

Stock - Price on:12/24/2007 .... NA
Stock Exchange .... OTC
Ticker Symbol .... SPMYY
Outstanding Shares .... NA
E.P.S. .... NA
Shareholders .... NA

Business: The group's principal activities are carried out through its three divisions namely communications, network products and systems group. Communications group provides performance analysis and service assurance solutions that enable the deployment of networking technologies such as broadband services, Internet telephony, 3g wireless and Web applications and security testing. Network products business develops and manufactures innovative solutions for fastening, identification, protection and connectivity in electrical and communications networks marketed under the global brand hellerman tyton. Systems group comprises pg drives technology, which develops power control systems for specialist electrical vehicles in the mobility and industrial markets, and an aerospace business that provides ground-based logistics support software systems for the aviation market.

Primary SIC and add'l.: 3670 3679 3620 3643 3610

CIK No: 0001130498

Subsidiaries: Calabasas, California, USA, Eatontown, New Jersey, USA, Honolulu, Hawaii, USA, PG Drives Technology Inc, PG Drives Technology Ltd, QuadTex Systems, Inc., Spirent BV, Spirent Communications (Asia) Limited, Spirent Communications (India) Pvt Limited, Spirent Communications (International) Ltd., Spirent Communications (Scotland) Ltd, Spirent Communications (SW) Ltd, Spirent Communications Inc, Spirent Communications Ltd, Spirent Communications of Ottawa Ltd 20 Subsidiaries included in the Index

Officers: Edward Bramson/Executive Chmn., Eric Hutchinson/Dir., CFO, William Burns/Exec. VP - Communications Group, Pres. - Service Assurance Broadband, Hal Chenhall/MD - PG Drives Technology, Robert Piconi/COO - Communications Group, Pres. - Performance Analysis Broadband, Michael Anscombe/Company Sec., Sharon Genberg/Sr. VP - Human Resources, Charles Simmons/Pres. - Performance Analysis, Wireless, Positioning

Directors: Edward Bramson/Executive Chmn., Tom Maxwell/Non Exec. Dir., Eric Hutchinson/Dir., CFO, Ian Brindle/Non Exec. Dir., Gerard Eastman/Non Exec. Dir., Alex Walker/Non Exec. Dir., Duncan Lewis/Non Exec. Dir.

Financial Data: Fiscal Year End:12/31   Latest Annual Data: 12/31/2005

Year	Sales	Net Income
2005	$853,001,000	$19,273,000
2004	$915,135,000	$47,972,000
2003	$850,834,000	$10,137,000

Curr. Assets:	$384,427,000	**Curr. Liab.:**	$281,351,000	
Plant, Equip.:	$202,022,000	**Total Liab.:**	$597,806,000	**Indic. Yr. Divd.:** NA
Total Assets:	$723,080,000	**Net Worth:**	$125,274,000	**Debt/ Equity:** NA

Spirit Aerosystems Holdings Inc

3801 S Oliver, Wichita, KS, 67210; **PH:** 1-316-526-9000; **Fax:** 1-316-523-8814; **http://** www.spiritaero.com; **Email:** communications@spiritaero.com

General - Incorporation .... DE
Employees 11,845
Auditor .... PricewaterhouseCoopers LLP
Stk Agt .... NA
Counsel .... NA
DUNS No. .... NA

Stock - Price on:12/24/2007 .... $36.6
Stock Exchange .... NYSE
Ticker Symbol .... SPR
Outstanding Shares 139,480,000
E.P.S. $0.78
Shareholders .... NA

Business: The groups principle activities include designing and manufacturing of aerostructures. The group operates through three segments namely, fuselage systems, propulsion systems and wing systems. In the year 2006, the group acquired BAE systems limited. The group operates from the United States. The groups quarterly revenue for September 2007 was 968.00 millions of USD.

Primary SIC and add'l.: 3728

CIK No: 0001364885

Subsidiaries: Spirit AeroSystems (Europe) Limited, Spirit AeroSystems Finance, Inc, Spirit AeroSystems International Holdings, Inc., Spirit AeroSystems, GmbH, Spirit AeroSystems, Inc

Officers: Jeffrey L. Turner/Dir., CEO, Pres., Ron Brunton/COO, Exec. VP, Gloria Flentje/VP, General Counsel, Sec., Sr. VP - Administration, Human Resources, John Lewelling/Sr. VP - Strategy, Information Technology, Rick Schmidt/CFO, Exec. VP, H. D. Walker/Sr. VP - Marketing, Sales, Robert Waner/CTO, Sr. VP, Janet S. Nicolson/51/Sr. VP - Human Resources, Richard Buchanan/57/VP, GM - Fuselage Structures, Systems Business Unit, Michael G. King/52/VP, GM -

Propulsion Structures, Systems Business Unit, Neil McManus/42/MD, VP, Donald R. Carlisle/54/VP, GM - Aerostructures Business Unit, David H. Walker/Sr. VP - Marketing, Sales, Philip D. Anderson/Primary Investor Relations Officer, Daniel R. Davis/Corporate Controller, Principal Accounting Officer

Directors: Jeffrey L. Turner/Dir., CEO, Pres., Seth M. Mersky/Dir., Nigel S. Wright/Dir., Paul Fulchino/Dir., Ike Evans/Dir., Richard Gephardt/Dir., Ronald T. Kadish/Dir., Connie Mack/Dir., Francis Raborn/Dir., Robert Johnson/Dir.

Owners: Onex Partners LP, Onex Spirit Co-Invest LP, Ulrich Schmidt, Richard Gephardt, JGD Management Corp/5.20%, Ronald C. Brunton, Jeffrey L. Turner, Nigel Wright, Onex Corporation, AXA Financial, Inc./10.90%, OAH Wind LLC, Seth Mersky, Janet S. Nicolson, Francis Raborn, Insiders *(16 Owners included in Index)*

Financial Data: *Fiscal Year End:* 12/31 *Latest Annual Data:* 12/31/2006

Year		Sales			Net Income
2006		$3,207,700,000			$16,800,000
Curr. Assets:	$1,420,500,000	**Curr. Liab.:**	$569,700,000	**P/E Ratio:**	73.20
Plant, Equip.:	$773,800,000	**Total Liab.:**	$1,863,200,000	**Indic. Yr. Divd.:**	NA
Total Assets:	$2,722,200,000	**Net Worth:**	$859,000,000	**Debt/ Equity:**	0.6310

Spirit Finance Corp

14631 N Scottsdale Rd., Ste. 200, Scottsdale, AZ, 85254; *PH:* 1-480-606-0820; *http://* www.spiritfinance.com

General - Incorporation	MD	**Stock** - Price on: 12/24/2007	$14.52
Employees	41	Stock Exchange	NA
Auditor	Ernst& Young LLP	Ticker Symbol	NA
Stk Agt	American Stock Transfer & Trust Co.	Outstanding Shares	114,090,000
Counsel	NA	E.P.S.	$0.51
DUNS No.	NA	Shareholders	NA

Business: The groups principle activities include operating and acquiring single tenant, real estate properties. In the year 2006, the group acquired 398 single tenant commercial real estate properties. The group operates from the United States.

Primary SIC and add'l.: 6798

CIK No: 0001277406

Subsidiaries: Retail Endeavors Group VII, Ltd., Spirit Finance Acquisitions, LLC, Spirit Limited Holdings, LLC, Spirit Management Company, Spirit Master Funding II, LLC, Spirit Master Funding III, LLC, Spirit Master Funding, LLC, Spirit Pocono Corporation, Spirit Property Holdings, LLC, Spirit SK Acquisition, LLC, Spirit SPE Canton, LLC, Spirit SPE Columbia, LLC, Spirit SPE Covina, LLC, Spirit SPE General Holdings II, LLC, Spirit SPE General Holdings, LLC 46 Subsidiaries included in the Index

Officers: Christopher H. Volk/Co - Founder, CEO, Pres., Christopher K. Burbach/VP - Underwriting, Catherine Long/Sr. VP, CFO, Gregg A. Seibert/Sr. VP - Underwriting, Jeffrey M. Fleischer/Sr. VP - Acquisitions, Julie N. Dimond/VP - Tax, Michael T. Bennett/Sr. VP - Operations, Chief Compliance Officer, Sec., Andrew S. Begal/VP - Acquisitions, Catherine L. Stevenson/Principal Accounting Officer, Dan J. Rice/VP - Acquisitions, Dennis P. Pepperd/VP - Information Systems, Sean D. Hufford/VP - Acquisitions, Joni G. Barrett/VP - Real Estate Closings, April Ronchetti Little/Acquisitions

Directors: Christopher H. Volk/Co - Founder, CEO, Pres., Morton H. Fleischer/Co - Founder, Chmn., Willie R. Barnes/76/Dir., Linda J. Blessing/57/Dir., Dennis E. Mitchem/76/Dir., James R. Parish/61/Dir., Kenneth B. Roath/72/Dir., Casey J. Sylla/64/Dir., Paul Oreffice/80/Dir., Shelby Yastrow/72/Dir.

Owners: Redford Holdco, LLC/9.50%, Michael T. Bennett, The Vanguard Group, Inc./5.50%, Catherine Long, Gregg A. Seibert, Jeffrey M. Fleischer, Cohen & Steers Capital Management, Inc./7.40%, Davis Selected Advisers, L.P./5.60%, Dennis E. Mitchem, Insiders/4.00%, Shelby Yastrow, Willie R. Barnes, Paul F. Oreffice, Christopher H. Volk/1.60%, Jim Parish *(19 Owners included in Index)*

Financial Data: *Fiscal Year End:* 12/31 *Latest Annual Data:* 12/31/2006

Year		Sales			Net Income
2006		$188,556,000			$52,360,000
2005		$84,501,000			$27,819,000
2004		$26,228,000			$8,972,000
Curr. Assets:	$52,317,000	**Curr. Liab.:**	$63,191,000	**P/E Ratio:**	24.61
Plant, Equip.:	$2,667,127,000	**Total Liab.:**	$1,862,565,000	**Indic. Yr. Divd.:**	NA
Total Assets:	$2,856,590,000	**Net Worth:**	$994,025,000	**Debt/ Equity:**	1.8925

Splinex Technologies Inc

500 W Cypress Creek Rd., Ste. 100, Fort Lauderdale, FL, 33309; *PH:* 1-954-556-4020; *Fax:* 1-954-556-4031; *http://* www.splinex.com; *Email:* info@splinex.com

General - Incorporation	DE	**Stock** - Price on: 12/24/2007	$0.06
Employees	2	Stock Exchange	OTC
Auditor	Daszkal Bolton LLP	Ticker Symbol	SPLX
Stk Agt	American Stock Transfer & Trust Co.	Outstanding Shares	100,760,000
Counsel	NA	E.P.S.	NA
DUNS No.	NA	Shareholders	NA

Business: The groups principal activities include developing, licensing and servicing software that enables the generating, manipulating, viewing and imaging based searching of complex, multi dimensional mathematical objects and information. The group operates from the United States.

Primary SIC and add'l.: 7372

CIK No: 0001293330

Subsidiaries: ANTAO Ltd., Ener1, Inc.

Officers: Gerard A. Herlihy/CFO, Pres.

Financial Data: *Fiscal Year End:* 03/31 *Latest Annual Data:* 03/31/2006

Year		Sales			Net Income
2006		$2,000			-$2,263,000
2005		$0			-$3,296,000
Curr. Assets:	$49,000	**Curr. Liab.:**	$4,498,000		
Plant, Equip.:	$7,000	**Total Liab.:**	$4,498,000	**Indic. Yr. Divd.:**	NA
Total Assets:	$86,000	**Net Worth:**	-$4,412,000	**Debt/ Equity:**	NA

Splinternet Holdings Inc

535 Connecticut Ave., Norwalk, CT, 06854; *PH:* 1-203-354-9164; *http://* www.splinter.net

General - Incorporation	DE	**Stock** - Price on: 12/24/2007	$1.48
Employees	1	Stock Exchange	OTC
Auditor	Goldstein Golub Kessler LLP	Ticker Symbol	SLNH
Stk Agt	Registrar & Transfer Co	Outstanding Shares	53,500,000
Counsel	NA	E.P.S.	-$0.02
DUNS No.	NA	Shareholders	NA

Business: The groups principle activities include developing of Voice over Internet Protocol technology and services, which enable the customer to make phone calls utilizing the Internet as an alternative to the traditional Public Switched Telephone Network. The group operates from the United States.

Primary SIC and add'l.: 6719

CIK No: 0001364561

Subsidiaries: Splinternet Communications, Inc.

Officers: James C. Ackerly/Chmn., Pres., Sec., Treasurer, CEO, Edmund L. Resor/Dir., VP, John T. Grippo/52/CFO, Scott McNulty/Chief Marketing Officer, Jeanine Oburchay/Primary Investor Relations Officer

Directors: James C. Ackerly/Chmn., Pres., Sec., Treasurer, CEO, Edmund L. Resor/Dir., VP, Thomas M. Flohr/Dir.

Owners: James C. Ackerly/43.70%, Edmund L. Resor/14.30%, Mary M. Ackerly/7.10%, Insiders/66.10%, Steven Cloyes/5.00%, Thomas M. Flohr/8.10%, Richard Rankin/12.90%

Financial Data: *Fiscal Year End:* 12/31 *Latest Annual Data:* 12/31/2006

Year		Sales			Net Income
2006		$73,000			-$609,000
Curr. Assets:	$2,375,000	**Curr. Liab.:**	$54,000		
Plant, Equip.:	$17,000	**Total Liab.:**	$54,000	**Indic. Yr. Divd.:**	NA
Total Assets:	$2,392,000	**Net Worth:**	$2,338,000	**Debt/ Equity:**	NA

Spongetech Delivery Systems Inc

350 5th Ave. Ste. 2204, New York, NY, 10118; *PH:* 1-212-594-4175; *Fax:* 1-212-594-4172; *http://* www.spongetech.com; *Email:* info@spongetech.com

General - Incorporation	DE	**Stock** - Price on: 12/24/2007	$0.14
Employees	NA	Stock Exchange	OTC
Auditor	Drakeford & Drakeford, LLC	Ticker Symbol	SPNG
Stk Agt	Olde Monmouth Stk Trnsfer Co. Inc.	Outstanding Shares	37,300,000
Counsel	NA	E.P.S.	NA
DUNS No.	NA	Shareholders	NA

Business: The groups principal activities include designing, producing, marketing and distributing cleaning products for vehicular use. The group operates from the United States.

Primary SIC and add'l.: 2841

CIK No: 0001201251

Officers: Michael Metter/56/Dir., CEO, Pres., Steven Moskowitz/44/Dir., Sec., Treasurer, CFO

Directors: Michael Metter/56/Dir., CEO, Pres., Steven Moskowitz/44/Dir., Sec., Treasurer, CFO, Frank Lazauskas/48/Dir.

Owners: The Rubin Family Irrevocable Stock Trust/15.75%, Steven Moskowitz/13.09%, Insiders/7.90%, Frank Lazaukas/11.90%, RM Enterprises International, Inc./1.94%, Michael Metter/15.61%

Sport Chalet Inc

1 Sport Chalet Dr., La Caada, CA, 91011; *PH:* 1-818-949-5300; *Fax:* 1-818-949-5301; *http://* www.sportchalet.com

General - Incorporation	DE	**Stock** - Price on: 12/24/2007	$10.37
Employees	NA	Stock Exchange	NDQ
Auditor	Moss Adams LLP	Ticker Symbol	SPCHA
Stk Agt	American Stock Transfer & Trust Co.	Outstanding Shares	NA
Counsel	NA	E.P.S.	NA
DUNS No.	02-834-0883	Shareholders	NA

Business: The group's principal activity is to operate specialty sporting goods superstores in southern California and Nevada. The group operates 31 stores that sells traditional sporting goods merchandise like footwear, apparel and other general athletic products and nontraditional merchandise like downhill skiing, mountaineering and scuba products. In addition, the group's stores offer custom golf club fitting and repair, ski/snowboard rental and repair, full dive training and certification programs, scuba charters and other services. The group operates a retail e-commerce store through gsi commerce inc at www.sportchalet.com.

Primary SIC and add'l.: 5941

CIK No: 0000892907

Officers: Craig L. Levra/Chmn., CEO, Pres./$670,491.00, Dennis D. Trausch/59/Exec. VP - Growth, Development/$230,999.00, Howard K. Kaminsky/50/CFO, Exec. VP - Finance/$257,473.00, Tim A. Anderson/48/VP - Retail Operations/$189,102.00, Theodore F. Jackson/52/VP - Information Systems/$176,305.00

Directors: Craig L. Levra/Chmn., CEO, Pres., Al D. McCready/Dir., Norbert Olberz/Dir., Kenneth Olsen/Dir., Frederick H. Schneider/Dir., John R. Attwood/Dir., Eric S. Olberz/Dir., Donald J. Howard/Dir.

Owners: Kenneth Olsen, Eric S. Olberz, Wedbush, Inc./8.20%, Insiders/68.00%, Norbert Olberz/62.30%, Al D. McCready, Dimensional Fund Advisors L.P./5.40%, Theodore F. Jackson, Wedbush, Inc./8.70%, Eric S. Olberz, Al D. McCready, Frederick H. Schneider, Tim A. Anderson, John R. Attwood, Craig L. Levra/2.90% *(29 Owners included in Index)*

Financial Data: *Fiscal Year End:* 03/31 *Latest Annual Data:* 4/1/2007

Year		Sales			Net Income
2007		$388,209,000			$7,099,000
2006		$343,204,000			-$87,000
2005		$309,090,000			$6,171,000
Curr. Assets:	$107,257,000	**Curr. Liab.:**	$61,764,000		
Plant, Equip.:	$59,487,000	**Total Liab.:**	$84,823,000	**Indic. Yr. Divd.:**	NA
Total Assets:	$171,249,000	**Net Worth:**	$86,426,000	**Debt/ Equity:**	NA

Sport Haley Inc

4600 E 48th Ave., Denver, CO, 80216; *PH:* 1-303-320-8800; *Fax:* 1-303-320-8822; *http://* www.sporthaley.com; *Email:* info@sporthaley.com

General - Incorporation	CO	*Stock* - Price on:12/24/2007	$4.17
Employees	67	Stock Exchange	NDQ
Auditor	Gordon, Hughes & Banks, LLP	Ticker Symbol	SPOR
Stk Agt	Computershare Trust Co	Outstanding Shares	2,280,000
Counsel	Karsh & Fulton	E.P.S.	-$0.62
DUNS No.	15-523-0477	Shareholders	NA

Business: The group's principle activities are to design and market fashion golf apparel for men and women. The products include shirts, shorts, pants, pullovers/vests, outerwear, tops, jackets and sweaters. The customers of the group include colleges, universities and corporates. The group markets its golf apparel under the SPORTS HALEY(R) and Ben Hogan(R) labels.

Primary SIC and add'l.: 2339 2329

CIK No: 0000892653

Subsidiaries: B&L Sportswear, Inc, Reserve Apparel Group LLC

Owners: Ronald J. Norick/10.71%, Dimensional Fund Advisors Inc./9.20%, James H. Everest/9.86%, Daniel Zeff, Zeff Holding Co., LLC,/18.20%, MicroCapital, LLC, Ian P. Ellis and MicroCapital Fund, LP/11.09%, Hillson Partners Limited Partnership/9.56%, Donald W. Jewell/2.14%, Tilson Growth Fund, LP, Tilson Capital Partners, LLC/6.25%, Mark J. Stevenson/3.18%, Insiders/24.48%, Patrick W. Hurley/2.14%, Catherine B. Blair/2.14%

*Financial Data: Fiscal Year End:*06/30 *Latest Annual Data:* 06/30/2007

Year	Sales	Net Income
2007	$18,893,000	-$1,301,000
2006	$20,962,000	-$415,000
2005	$22,041,000	-$3,281,000

Curr. Assets:	$17,411,000	*Curr. Liab.:*	$2,956,000		
Plant, Equip.:	$613,000	*Total Liab.:*	$2,990,000	*Indic. Yr. Divd.:*	NA
Total Assets:	$18,027,000	*Net Worth:*	$15,015,000	*Debt/ Equity:*	NA

Sport Supply Group Inc

Formerly: Collegiate Pacific Inc
1901 Diplomat Dr., Farmers Branch, Dallas, TX, 75234; *PH:* 1-972-484-9484; *http://* www.colpac.com

General - Incorporation	DE	*Stock* - Price on:12/24/2007	$9.04
Employees	863	Stock Exchange	AMEX
Auditor	Grant Thornton LLP	Ticker Symbol	BOO
Stk Agt	Continental Stock Transfer & Trust Co	Outstanding Shares	10,230,000
Counsel	NA	E.P.S.	$0.31
DUNS No.	NA	Shareholders	NA

Business: The groups principle activities include producing and marketing sporting goods. The group operates from the United States.

Primary SIC and add'l.: 5961

CIK No: 0000828747

Subsidiaries: CMS of Central Florida Inc., Dixie Sporting Goods Co. Inc., Kesslers Team Sports Inc., Salkeld & Sons Inc., Sport Supply Group Inc., Tomark Sports Inc.

Officers: Adam L. Blumenfeld/38/Chmn., CEO, Terrence M. Babilla/46/Pres., Tevis Martin/52/Exec. VP - US Operations, Kurt Hagan/40/Exec. VP - Sales, Marketing, John Pitts/43/CFO

Directors: Adam L. Blumenfeld/38/Chmn., CEO, Jeff Davidowitz/52/Dir., William H. Watkins/66/Dir., Robert W. Hampton/61/Dir., Richard Ellman/37/Dir.

Owners: Double Black Diamond Offshore LDC/12.30%, Robert W. Hampton, Insiders/5.90%, Michael J. Blumenfeld, William H. Watkins, Adam Blumenfeld/2.90%, HSO Limited Partnership/14.80%, Tevis Martin/1.00%, Jeff Davidowitz/1.30%, Charles Bronfman Trust/15.00%, William R. Estill, Wellington Management Company, LLP/11.40%

*Financial Data: Fiscal Year End:*06/30 *Latest Annual Data:* 6/30/2006

Year	Sales	Net Income
2006	$224,238,000	$1,896,000
2005	$106,339,000	$3,601,000
2004	$39,562,000	$1,884,000

Curr. Assets:	$78,699,000	*Curr. Liab.:*	$23,508,000	*P/E Ratio:*	29.16
Plant, Equip.:	$10,087,000	*Total Liab.:*	$89,051,000	*Indic. Yr. Divd.:*	$0.100
Total Assets:	$144,435,000	*Net Worth:*	$47,234,000	*Debt/ Equity:*	1.6132

Sports Arenas Inc

7415 Carroll Rd., Ste. C, San Diego, CA, 92121; *PH:* 1-858-587-1060

General - Incorporation	DE	*Stock* - Price on:12/24/2007	$0.0175
Employees	NA	Stock Exchange	NA
Auditor	Peterson & Co. LLP	Ticker Symbol	NA
Stk Agt	U.S. Stock Transfer Corp	Outstanding Shares	NA
Counsel	NA	E.P.S.	NA
DUNS No.	02-792-9389	Shareholders	NA

Business: The group's principal activity is the manufacture of graphite golf club shafts. The group operates principally in two business segments: commercial real estate rental and golf club shaft manufacturing. The golf club shaft division manufactures golf shafts that are sold to custom golf shops. The group also performs a minor amount of services in property management and real estate brokerage related to commercial leasing. The group disposed its bowling and real estate development segments in 2003.

Primary SIC and add'l.: 7999 6531 7933 3949

CIK No: 0000093003

Subsidiaries: Cabrillo Lanes, Inc., Sports Arenas Properties, Inc., UCVNV, Inc.

*Financial Data: Fiscal Year End:*06/30 *Latest Annual Data:* 6/30/2004

Year	Sales	Net Income
2004	$2,821,000	-$2,434,000
2003	$4,044,000	$19,159,000
2002	$5,079,000	-$2,179,000

Curr. Assets:	$1,095,000	*Curr. Liab.:*	$1,517,000		
Plant, Equip.:	$830,000	*Total Liab.:*	$6,742,000	*Indic. Yr. Divd.:*	NA
Total Assets:	$7,129,000	*Net Worth:*	$372,000	*Debt/ Equity:*	NA

Sports Club Co Inc

11100 Santa Monica Blvd., Ste. 300, Los Angeles, CA, 90025; *PH:* 1-310-479-5200; *Fax:* 1-310-479-8350; *http://* www.thesportscluba.com

General - Incorporation	DE	*Stock* - Price on:12/24/2007	$1.5
Employees	NA	Stock Exchange	OTC
Auditor	KPMG LLP	Ticker Symbol	SCYL
Stk Agt	American Stock Transfer & Trust Co.	Outstanding Shares	19,980,000
Counsel	Resch Polster Alpert & Berger	E.P.S.	-$0.2
DUNS No.	87-807-2123	Shareholders	NA

Business: The group's principal activities are to own and operate sports and fitness clubs. The group offers fitness and recreation options and amenities. The facilities offered by the group include spas, restaurants, fitness centers, swimming pools and basketball courts. The other facilities offered include fully equipped gyms with fitness equipment, basketball, volleyball, squash and tennis, group exercise studios including weight training, cardio-vascular equipment, flexibility centers and functional performance areas. The group currently owns and operates four clubs in the United States of America.

Primary SIC and add'l.: 7991 7997 5813

CIK No: 0000924373

Subsidiaries: El Segundo-TDC, Ltd., HFA Services, Inc., Irvine Sports Club, Inc., LA/Irvine Sports Clubs, Ltd., NY Sports Club, Inc., Pontius Realty, Inc., SCC California, Inc., SCC Development Company, SCC Nevada, Inc., SCC Realty Company, SCC Sports Club, Inc., Sepulveda Realty and Development Co., Inc., SF Sports Club, Inc., Sports Club, Inc. of California, SportsMed Company, Inc. 20 Subsidiaries included in the Index

*Financial Data: Fiscal Year End:*12/31 *Latest Annual Data:* 12/31/2005

Year	Sales	Net Income
2005	$56,205,000	-$22,249,000
2004	$43,672,000	-$20,757,000
2003	$133,371,000	-$18,374,000

Curr. Assets:	$141,807,000	*Curr. Liab.:*	$201,018,000		
Plant, Equip.:	$60,743,000	*Total Liab.:*	$228,519,000	*Indic. Yr. Divd.:*	NA
Total Assets:	$212,562,000	*Net Worth:*	-$32,082,000	*Debt/ Equity:*	NA

Sportsman's Guide Inc

411 Farwell Ave. So, St Paul, MN, 55075; *PH:* 1-612-451-3030; *http://* www.sportsmansguide.com

General - Incorporation	MN	*Stock* - Price on:12/24/2007	$25.55
Employees	NA	Stock Exchange	NA
Auditor	Grant Thornton LLP	Ticker Symbol	NA
Stk Agt	Corporate Stock Transfer, Inc.	Outstanding Shares	NA
Counsel	Chernesky, Heyman & Kress	E.P.S.	NA
DUNS No.	04-082-5176	Shareholders	NA

Business: The group's principal activity is to market value priced outdoor and general merchandise with an emphasis on outdoor clothing, equipment and footwear. The group markets its merchandise through mail and specialty catalogs and through a network of e-commerce websites. The catalogs of the group are advertised as the 'fun-to-read' catalog and the Web site is advertised as the 'fun-to-browse' Web site. The group's Web sites include bargainoutfitters.com and sportsmansguide.com and operates in the United States. The products of the group include clothing and accessories, footwear, hunting and shooting accessories, camping and outdoor recreation, optics, electronics, personal accessories, furniture, novelty and collectibles and other. The customers of the group include hunters, shooters, campers, hikers and outdoorsmen. Service marks include 'the sportsman's guide', 'bargain outfitters', the fund-to-read' catalog and 'the fun-to-browse' Web site.

Primary SIC and add'l.: 7375 5661 5961 5531 5941 5719

CIK No: 0000791450

Subsidiaries: The Golf Warehouse, Inc., The Sportsmans Guide Outlet, Inc.

SportsNuts Inc

Towers At S Towne No. 2, Ste 550, 10421 S 400 W, Salt Lake City, UT, 84095; *PH:* 1-800-816-2500; *http://* www.sportsnuts.com; *Email:* customerservice@sportsnuts.com

General - Incorporation	DE	*Stock* - Price on:12/24/2007	$0.0048
Employees	3	Stock Exchange	OTC
Auditor	Bouwhuis, Morrill & Co LLC	Ticker Symbol	SPCI
Stk Agt	Colonial Stock Transfer Co Inc	Outstanding Shares	121,670,000
Counsel	NA	E.P.S.	-$0.001
DUNS No.	60-282-0680	Shareholders	NA

Business: The group's principle activity is to organize and manage a wide variety of sports events, providing online registration and merchandise sales, event sponsorship, event coordination, and targeted promotion using technology and strategic media. It operates in three segments: online services, sports event management and information technology consulting. The online services segment provides Internet team and league management for amateur sports organizations and online registrations for sporting events. The sports event management segment creates, promotes and manages sporting events. The information technology consulting segment provides services related to computer hardware, software and websites. The group quarterly revenue for September 2007 was 0.01millions of USD.

Primary SIC and add'l.: 7375

CIK No: 0001024920

Subsidiaries: Networks, Inc, Synerteck

Officers: John Thomas/33/CEO, General Counsel, Mary Foster/Office Mgr. - Salt Lake City, Clayton Barlow/Dir. - Information Technology, Chene Gardner/41/Financial Controller, Walt Pera/Dir. - Hardware Sales, Todd Drummond/Dir. - Business Development, Bryan Green/Dir. - Events, Kenneth Denos/37/CFO

Owners: Insiders, Kenneth Denos, Prestbury Investment Holdings Limited, Nigel Wray, Gardner Management, Inc. Profit Sharing Plan and Trust, Nicholas Leslau, Moore, Clayton & Co., Inc., Todd Shell

*Financial Data: Fiscal Year End:*12/31 *Latest Annual Data:* 03/31/2007

Year	Sales	Net Income
2007	NA	NA
2006	NA	NA
2005	$639,000	$321,000

Curr. Assets:	$63,000	*Curr. Liab.:*	$2,666,000		
Plant, Equip.:	$1,000	*Total Liab.:*	$2,666,000	*Indic. Yr. Divd.:*	NA
Total Assets:	$64,000	*Net Worth:*	-$2,601,000	*Debt/ Equity:*	NA

SportsQuest Inc

Formerly: Air Brook Airport Express Inc
115 W Passaic St., Rochelle Park, NJ, 07662; *PH:* 1-201-843-6100; *http://* www.airbrook.com

General - Incorporation.............................. DE
Employees ....NA
Auditor ....Robert G. Jeffrey
Stk Agt............. Continental Stock Transfer & Trust Co
Counsel ....NA
DUNS No. ....NA

Stock - Price on:12/24/2007 ....$0.16
Stock Exchange...OTC
Ticker Symbol..SPQS
Outstanding Shares 2,280,000
E.P.S. $0.26
Shareholders...NA

Business: The groups principle activity is to provide transportation for airlines. The groups services include Vans, Mini-buses, and Buses. The group operates from the United States.

Primary SIC and add'l.: 4111

CIK No: 0000803097

Subsidiaries: A.B. Park & Fly, Inc.

Officers: Donald M. Petroski/69/Dir., CFO, Pres., Jeffrey M. Petroski/44/Sec.

Directors: Donald M. Petroski/69/Dir., CFO, Pres.

Owners: Rick Altmann, Insiders/89.97%, Thomas R. Kidd/89.96%

Financial Data: *Fiscal Year End:*10/31 *Latest Annual Data:* 10/31/2006

Year	Sales	Net Income
2006	$69,000	$50,000
2005	$59,000	$49,000
2004	$62,000	$49,000

Curr. Assets:	$0	*Curr. Liab.:*	$356,000	*P/E Ratio:*	0.62
Plant, Equip.:	NA	*Total Liab.:*	$356,000	*Indic. Yr. Divd.:*	NA
Total Assets:	$0	*Net Worth:*	-$356,000	*Debt/ Equity:*	NA

Sprout Development Inc

21 Country Hills Gardens Nw, Calgary, AL, T3K 5G1;

General - Incorporation.............................. AB
Employees ....NA
Auditor ....Bateman & Co., Inc., P.C.
Stk Agt............Interwest Transfer Company, Inc.
Counsel ....NA
DUNS No. ....NA

Stock - Price on:12/24/2007 ....$2.4
Stock Exchange...NA
Ticker Symbol...NA
Outstanding Shares ....NA
E.P.S. ....NA
Shareholders...NA

Business: The groups principal activity is establishing the Company, its business plan, and conducting an informal market survey that was primarily based on Internet searches. The group operates from the United States.

Primary SIC and add'l.: 7372

CIK No: 0001302401

Officers: R. W. Walchuk/52/Dir., Founder, CEO, Pres., Tassos Golnas/Technology Assessment, Development, Darryl Cozac/41/Dir., CFO, Pres., Jim Balsara/35/Sec., Treasurer, James Korovilas/Strategic Planning, Rania Todoulou/International Business Development, Marketing Strategy

Directors: R. W. Walchuk/52/Dir., Founder, CEO, Pres., Darryl Cozac/41/Dir., CFO, Pres., David Little/58/Dir.

Owners: Darryl Cozac/77.70%, Jim Balsara, Insiders/77.70%

SPSS Inc

233 S Wacker Dr., 11th Fl., Chicago, IL, 60606; *PH:* 1-312-651-3000; *http://* www.spss.com;
Email: sales@spss.com

General - Incorporation.............................. DE
Employees 1,193
Auditor ....Grant Thornton LLP
Stk Agt..... Computershare Investor Services LLC
Counsel ....Ross & Hardies
DUNS No. 03-088-0488

Stock - Price on:12/24/2007 ....$42.92
Stock Exchange...NDQ
Ticker Symbol...SPSS
Outstanding Shares 18,360,000
E.P.S. $1.26
Shareholders...NA

Business: The group's principle activity is to provide technology that transforms data into insight through the use of predictive analytics and other data mining techniques. The group's solutions and products enable organizations to improve decision-making by learning from the past, understanding the present, as well as anticipating future problems and opportunities. Commercial firms use this technology to better target their marketing and sales programs. The group's quarterly revenue for September 2007 was 72.28 millions of USD.

Primary SIC and add'l.: 6794 8733 7371 7372 8732 7379

CIK No: 0000869570

Subsidiaries: Data Distilleries Gmbh, Data Distilleries United Kingdom Ltd, Integral Solutions Limited, ISL Decision Systems, Inc. ., Lexiquest Benelux S.A. ., Lexiquest Limited., Lexiquest S.A. ., Lexiquest, Inc. , NetGenesis Corp. ., NetGenesis Limited, Quantime Limited, Showcase Benelux NV/SA, ShowCase Corporation, Showcase France sarl, Showcase International, Inc. . 39 Subsidiaries included in the Index

Officers: Jack Noonan/Dir., CEO, Pres./$3,098,191.00, Raymond Panza/Exec. VP - Corporate Operations, CFO, Sec./$2,411,786.00, Douglas P. Dow/50/Sr. VP - Corporate Development/$835,579.00, John Shap/48/Sr. VP - Worldwide Sales/$1,169,025.00, Jonathan Otterstatter/47/CTO, Exec. VP/$1,870,172.00, Marc D. Nelson/52/VP, Corporate Controller, Principal Accounting Officer

Directors: Jack Noonan/Dir., CEO, Pres., Norman Nie/Chmn., Co - Founder, Charles R. Whitchurch/Dir., Michael Blair/Dir., Merritt Lutz/Dir., William Binch/Dir., Michael E. Lavin/Dir.

Owners: Michael E. Lavin, Kenneth Holec, Michael D. Blair, Insiders/7.99%, Norman and Carol Nie Foundation, Inc./2.56%, Raymond H. Panza, William Binch, Barclays Global Investors, NA/6.92%, Brown Capital Management, Inc./7.37%, Douglas P. Dow, Jonathan Otterstatter/1.20%, Daruma Asset Management, Inc./7.39%, Merritt Lutz, T. Rowe Price Associates, Inc./10.44%, John Shap (17 Owners included in Index)

Financial Data: *Fiscal Year End:*12/31 *Latest Annual Data:* 12/31/2006

Year	Sales	Net Income
2006	$261,532,000	$15,140,000
2005	$236,063,000	$16,092,000
2004	$224,074,000	$5,543,000

Curr. Assets:	$206,530,000	*Curr. Liab.:*	$114,431,000	*P/E Ratio:*	37.98
Plant, Equip.:	$17,708,000	*Total Liab.:*	$115,971,000	*Indic. Yr. Divd.:*	NA
Total Assets:	$332,494,000	*Net Worth:*	$216,523,000	*Debt/ Equity:*	0.8413

SPX Corp

13515 Ballantyne Corporate Pl, Charlotte, NC, 28277; *PH:* 1-704-752-4478; *http://* www.spx.com;
Email: investor@spx.com

General - Incorporation .... DE
Employees 14,300
Auditor ....Deloitte & Touche LLP
Stk Agt..... Computershare Investor Services LLC
Counsel ....Gardner, Carton & Douglas
DUNS No. 00-602-4129

Stock - Price on:12/24/2007 ....$88.35
Stock Exchange..NYSE
Ticker Symbol...SPW
Outstanding Shares 56,920,000
E.P.S. $4.73
Shareholders...NA

Business: The group's principle activity is to provide technical products, industrial products and services, flow technology, cooling technologies and services and service solutions. The group operates through four segments include flow technology, test and measurement, thermal equipment and services, and industrial products and services. The group's products include networking and switching products, fire detection and building life-safety products, TV and radio broadcast antennas and towers, life science products, transformers, cooling towers and air filtration products. The group also provides specialty service tools, diagnostic systems, service equipment and technical information services. The groups servicing areas include chemical processing, pharmaceutical, infrastructure and power generation. The group operates from United States.

Primary SIC and add'l.: 3429 3443 3599 3663 3444 3593 3679

CIK No: 0000088205

Subsidiaries: 997958 Ontario Inc., Administraciones Directas Interactive Especializadas, S.C., AIA Commercial, S.A., Airflow Construction Limited, AMCA International Canada Corporation, AMPROBE Europe GmbH, Anglo-American Direct Tea Trading Company Limited (The), Arrendadora Korco, S.A. de C.V., Atex Filter Nederland BV, Atex Filter Verwaltungsgesellschaft mbH, Atex-Filter GmbH & Co. OHG, Attack Engineering Limited, Automotive Diagnostics U.K. Limited, Balcke Duerr Austria GmbH, Balcke-Duerr Italiana, S.r.l. 270 Subsidiaries included in the Index

Officers: Christopher J. Kearney/Chmn., CEO, Pres./$8,145,652.00, Don Canterna/Segment Pres. - Flow Technology/$2,085,797.00, Robert B. Foreman/Exec. VP - Human Resources, Asia Pacific/$4,243,314.00, Dave Kowalski/Segment Pres. - Test, Measurement/$1,938,242.00, Patrick J. O'Leary/CFO, Exec. VP, Kevin L. Lilly/Sr. VP, Sec., General Counsel, Michael A. Reilly/VP, Corporate Controller, Chief Accounting Officer, Jim Peters/VP - Operations, Sharon Jenkins/49/VP, Chief Marketing Officer, an Officer

Directors: Christopher J. Kearney/Chmn., CEO, Pres., Charles E. Johnson/Chmn., Sarah R. Coffin/Dir., Michael J. Mancuso/Dir., Emerson U. Fullwood/Dir., Kermit J. Campbell/Dir., David P. Williams/Dir., Michael J. Fitzpatrick/Dir., Albert A. Koch/Dir.

Owners: Sarah R. Coffin, David A. Kowalski, FMR Corp./13.30%, Insiders/5.30%, David P. Williams, Robert B. Foreman, Hotchkis and Wiley Capital Management, LLC/10.70%, Charles E. Johnson, Thomas J. Riordan, Michael J. Mancuso, Don L. Canterna, AXA Financial, Inc./14.80%, Kermit J. Campbell, Patrick J. O'Leary/2.50%, Christopher J. Kearney (17 Owners included in Index)

Financial Data: *Fiscal Year End:*12/31 *Latest Annual Data:* 12/31/2006

Year	Sales	Net Income
2006	$4,313,300,000	$170,700,000
2005	$4,292,200,000	$1,090,000,000
2004	$4,372,000,000	-$17,100,000

Curr. Assets:	$2,458,500,000	*Curr. Liab.:*	$1,723,400,000	*P/E Ratio:*	39.27
Plant, Equip.:	$374,600,000	*Total Liab.:*	$3,327,700,000	*Indic. Yr. Divd.:*	$1.000
Total Assets:	$5,437,100,000	*Net Worth:*	$2,109,400,000	*Debt/ Equity:*	0.3523

SR Telecom Inc

8150 Trans-Canada Hwy, Montreal, QC, H4S 1M5; *PH:* 1-514-335-1210;
http:// www.srtelecom.com; *Email:* communications@srtelecom.com

General - Incorporation ....Canada
Employees ....NA
Auditor ....Deloitte & Touche LLP
Stk Agt.........Computershare Trust Co of Canada
Counsel ....NA
DUNS No. ....NA

Stock - Price on:12/24/2007 ....$0.14
Stock Exchange...OTC
Ticker Symbol..SRXAF
Outstanding Shares ....NA
E.P.S. ....NA
Shareholders...NA

Business: The groups principle activities include designing, producing and selling fixed wireless access products. The groups products include symmetry, SR500 and SR500ip. The group operates from Canada.

Primary SIC and add'l.: 4812

CIK No: 0001223165

Subsidiaries: Communicacion y Telefonia Rural S.A. (CTR)

Officers: Serge Fortin/CEO, Pres., Investor Relations Officer Information, Chad Pralle/VP - Business Development, Marc Girard/Sr. VP, CFO, Garry Forbes/Sr. VP - Sales, Marketing, Anna Di Giorgio/VP - Corporate Communications, Luc Dugas/VP - Operations, Maurice Gregoire/VP - Customer Solutions, Interim, Serge Legris/VP - Marketing, Chris Gervais/Sr. VP - Research & Development and Customer Solutions, Donna Hughes/VP - Human Resources, Chaz Immendorf/Sr. VP - Innovation, Michael J. Morris/VP - Contracts, Legal

Directors: Lionel P. Hurtubise/Chmn., Louis A. Tanguay/Dir., Paul J. Griswold/Dir., Patrick J. Lavelle/Dir.

Owners: Guardian Capital LP/8.00%, DDJ Capital Management, LLC/35.30%, Morgan Stanley & Co/12.40%, Catalyst Fund General Partner I Inc/10.00%, Greywolf Capital Management LP/17.40%

Financial Data: *Fiscal Year End:*12/31 *Latest Annual Data:* 12/31/2004

Year	Sales	Net Income
2004	$102,904,000	-$70,398,000
2003	$98,814,000	-$33,767,000

Curr. Assets:	$63,603,000	*Curr. Liab.:*	$62,482,000		
Plant, Equip.:	$34,029,000	*Total Liab.:*	$126,275,000	*Indic. Yr. Divd.:*	NA
Total Assets:	$105,086,000	*Net Worth:*	-$21,188,000	*Debt/ Equity:*	NA

SRA International Inc

4300 Fair Lakes Ct, Fairfax, VA, 22033; **PH:** 1-703-803-1500; **http://** www.sra.com;
Email: investor@sra.com

General - Incorporation	DE	**Stock**- Price on:12/24/2007	$25.11
Employees	4,975	Stock Exchange	NYSE
Auditor	Deloitte & Touche LLP	Ticker Symbol	SRX
Stk Agt	American Stock Transfer & Trust Co.	Outstanding Shares	56,970,000
Counsel	NA	E.P.S	$1.14
DUNS No.	NA	Shareholders	NA

Business: The group's principal activity is to provide information technology services and solutions to the U.S. Federal government organizations. The services provided include strategic consulting, systems designing, development, integration and outsourcing and operations management. The group's activities are carried out through three segments:the consulting and systems integration business segment provides high-end consulting services and information technology solutions for federal government clients. The emerging technologies segment performed advanced technology research and development and managed the commercial software products and services. During fiscal 2003, the group acquired adroit systems inc and in fiscal 2004, orion scientific systems.

Primary SIC and add'l.: 7389

CIK No: 0000906192

Subsidiaries: Galaxy Scientific Corp., Research and Applications Corporation, Spectrum Solutions Group, Inc., SRA Technical Services Center, Inc., SRA Ventures, LLC, Systems Research and Applications Corporation, The Orion Center for Counterterrorism, Counterintelligence, and Law Enforcement, Touchstone Consulting Group, Inc

Officers: Stanton D. Sloane/Dir., CEO, Pres./$483,219.00, Michael L. Yocom/Dir. - Integrated Solutions, Charles D. Brooks/VP - Government Affairs, Mark D. Connel/Executive Dir. - Contracts, Procurement, Tony Summerlin/MD - Consulting, Sra's Touchstone Consulting Group, Stephen M. Tolbert/Dir. - Financial Oversight Business Programs, Peter B. Trick/Dir. - Environmental, Organizational Services, Craig P. Weston/Deputy Dir. - SRA Command, Control, Communications, Computers, Intelligence, Karl R. Gumtow/VP, Dir. - Intelligence, Space, David F. Keffer/VP, Dir. - Investor Relations, John M. Luongo/VP, Dir. - Capture Strategy, Gregory A. Roman/Dir. - Remote Sensing Programs, Jennifer E. Smith/Deputy Dir. - Marketing, Sales, Martha N. Johnson/Dir. - Civilian Agencies, James H. Jones/VP - Department, Veterans Affairs *(74 Officers included in Index)*

Directors: Stanton D. Sloane/Dir., CEO, Pres., Ernst Volgenau/Chmn., Renato A. Dipentima/Dir., Anne M. Donohue/VP, Chief Legal Officer, Dir. - Contracts, Procurement, John W. Barter/Dir., Jennifer E. Smith/Deputy Dir. - Marketing, Sales, Miles R. Gilburne/Dir., Larry R. Ellis/62/Dir., Michael K. Klein/Dir., David H. Langstaff/Dir., William K. Brehm/Dir., Edward E. Legasey/Dir., Exec. VP, COO, Steven A. Denning/Dir., Delbert C. Staley/Dir., Gail R. Wilensky/Dir.

Owners: Munder Capital Management/5.40%, Ernst Volgenau, Eminence Capital, LLC/9.40%, David H. Langstaff, Barry S. Landew/1.80%, Stanton D. Sloane, Gail R. Wilensky, FMR Corp./14.10%, Neuberger Berman, LLC/5.30%, William K. Brehm, Delbert C. Staley, Wasatch Advisors, Inc./5.50%, Insiders/4.70%, Stephen C. Hughes, Renato A. DiPentima/1.00% *(22 Owners included in Index)*

Financial Data: Fiscal Year End:06/30 **Latest Annual Data:** 06/30/2007

Year	Sales	Net Income
2007	$1,268,872,000	$63,430,000
2006	$1,179,267,000	$62,520,000
2005	$881,770,000	$57,723,000

Curr. Assets:	$477,779,000	Curr. Liab.:	$178,212,000		
Plant, Equip.:	$37,462,000	Total Liab.:	$188,677,000	Indic. Yr. Divd.:	NA
Total Assets:	$721,974,000	Net Worth:	$533,297,000	Debt/ Equity:	NA

SRI Surgical Express Inc

12425 Race Track Rd., Tampa, FL, 33626; **PH:** 1-813-891-9550; **Fax:** 1-813-818-9076;
http:// www.surgicalexpress.com; **Email:** investorrelations@srisurgical.com

General - Incorporation	FL	**Stock**- Price on:12/24/2007	$5.17
Employees	808	Stock Exchange	NDQ
Auditor	Grant Thornton LLP	Ticker Symbol	STRC
Stk Agt	Wachovia Bank N.A	Outstanding Shares	6,460,000
Counsel	Hill, Ward & Henderson	E.P.S	-$0.28
DUNS No.	55-651-6185	Shareholders	NA

Business: The group's principal activity is to provide a comprehensive surgical procedure-based daily delivery service to hospitals and surgery centers. The group's reusable surgical products include gowns, towels, drapes and basins and its daily delivery and retrieval of these products for each customer. The group introduced new service, surgical express, which uses daily delivery and retrieval service as a foundation to provide customers an expanded program of products and services.

Primary SIC and add'l.: 7299 7389

CIK No: 0001014041

Officers: Wallace D. Ruiz/Sr. VP, CFO, Sec./$317,856.00, Jack A. Hamilton/Sr. VP - Process Engineering, Quality Assurance, Jon D. McGuire/Sr. VP - Strategic Sourcing

Directors: Charles W. Federico/Chmn., Charles T. Orsatti/Dir., Wayne R. Peterson/Dir., John N. Simmons/Dir., James T. Boosales/Dir., James M. Emanuel/Dir.

Owners: John Simmons, Lee R. Kemberling/9.10%, James M. Emanuel, Christopher S. Carlton, F&C Management, Ltd./3.40%, James T. Boosales/12.40%, Standard Textile Co., Inc./5.40%, Charles T. Orsatti, T. Rowe Price Associates, Inc./8.50%, Wayne R. Peterson/13.00%, Insiders/29.10%, Wallace D. Ruiz, Heartland Advisors, Inc./13.10%

Financial Data: Fiscal Year End:12/31 **Latest Annual Data:** 12/31/2006

Year	Sales	Net Income
2006	$93,831,000	-$1,953,000
2005	$91,734,000	$393,000
2004	$91,310,000	-$4,998,000

Curr. Assets:	$21,029,000	Curr. Liab.:	$13,686,000		
Plant, Equip.:	$32,371,000	Total Liab.:	$27,636,000	Indic. Yr. Divd.:	NA
Total Assets:	$74,354,000	Net Worth:	$46,718,000	Debt/ Equity:	0.3790

SRKP 5 Inc

210 S Federal Hwy., Ste. 205, Deerfield Beach, FL, 33441; **PH:** 1-310-203-2902

General - Incorporation	DE	**Stock**- Price on:12/24/2007	NA
Employees	NA	Stock Exchange	NA
Auditor	Aj. Robbins, P.C	Ticker Symbol	NA
Stk Agt	NA	Outstanding Shares	NA
Counsel	NA	E.P.S	NA
DUNS No.	NA	Shareholders	NA

Business: The group's principal activity is to obtain initial financing, to seek the acquisition of, or merger with an existing company and pursue a business combination. As a result, the group has not conducted negotiations or entered into a letter of intent concerning any target business.

Primary SIC and add'l.: 6770

CIK No: 0001335103

Officers: Richard A. Rappaport/48/Dir., Pres., Principal Executive Officer, Anthony C. Pintsopoulos/52/Dir., CFO, Sec.

Directors: Richard A. Rappaport/48/Dir., Pres., Principal Executive Officer, Anthony C. Pintsopoulos/52/Dir., CFO, Sec.

Owners: Glenn Krinsky/5.00%, Debbie Schwartzberg/38.50%, Anthony C. Pintsopoulos/9.00%, Insiders/47.50%, Tom Poletti/9.00%, Richard Rappaport/38.50%

SRKP 6 Inc

2300 Corporate Blvd. Nw, Ste. 123, Boca Raton, FL, 33431; **PH:** 1-561-995-7313

General - Incorporation	DE	**Stock**- Price on:12/24/2007	NA
Employees	NA	Stock Exchange	NA
Auditor	Aj. Robbins, P.C	Ticker Symbol	NA
Stk Agt	NA	Outstanding Shares	NA
Counsel	NA	E.P.S	NA
DUNS No.	NA	Shareholders	NA

Business: The group's principle activity is to engage in organizational efforts and obtaining initial financing. The Company was formed as a vehicle to pursue a business combination and has made no efforts to identify a possible business combination. As a result, the Company has not conducted negotiations or entered into a letter of intent concerning any target business. The business purpose of the Company is to seek the acquisition of, or merger with, an existing company. The group operates from United States.

Primary SIC and add'l.: 6770

CIK No: 0001335104

Officers: Richard A. Rappaport/48/Dir., Pres., Anthony C. Pintsopoulos/52/Dir., CFO, Sec.

Directors: Richard A. Rappaport/48/Dir., Pres., Anthony C. Pintsopoulos/52/Dir., CFO, Sec.

Owners: Daniel N. Weiss/0.90%, James E. Skinner/11.90%, Jerry M. Anchin/5.80%, David H. Fater/3.30%, Insiders/25.80%, Edward M. Wiesmeier/3.90%

SRKP 8 Inc

No. 2, Jing You Rd., Kunming National Economy &technology Developin, 650217;
PH: 86-871-728-2628

General - Incorporation	DE	**Stock**- Price on:12/24/2007	NA
Employees	NA	Stock Exchange	NA
Auditor	Hansen, Barnett & Maxwell, P.c	Ticker Symbol	NA
Stk Agt	NA	Outstanding Shares	NA
Counsel	NA	E.P.S	NA
DUNS No.	NA	Shareholders	NA

Business: The group's principal activities include seeking the acquisition of, or merger with, an existing company. Main activities include obtaining initial financing, pursuing a business combination. The group has not conducted negotiations or entered into a letter of intent concerning any target business.

Primary SIC and add'l.: 6770

CIK No: 0001335106

Officers: Gui Hua Lan/65/Chmn., CEO, Feng Lan/35/Dir., Pres., Lei Lan/33/Dir., Executive Dir. - Sales, Qiong Hua Gao/41/CFO, Peng Chen/33/Chief Technological Officer, Zheng Yi Wang/62/Dir., Executive Dir. - Exports, Corp. Sec.

Directors: Feng Lan/35/Dir., Pres., Lei Lan/33/Dir., Executive Dir. - Sales, Zheng Yi Wang/62/Dir., Executive Dir. - Exports, Corp. Sec.

Owners: Lans Intl Medicine Investment Co., Limited, Feng Lan, Zheng Yi Wang, Peng Chen, Gui Hua Lan, Insiders

SRS Labs Inc

2909 Daimier St., Santa Ana, CA, 92705; **PH:** 1-949-442-1070; **http://** www.srslabs.com;
Email: ir@srslabs.com

General - Incorporation	DE	**Stock**- Price on:12/24/2007	$10.49
Employees	39	Stock Exchange	NDQ
Auditor	Squar, Peterson, LLP	Ticker Symbol	SRSL
Stk Agt	Geraldine Zarbo American Stk T & T Co	Outstanding Shares	16,150,000
Counsel	John Della - Grotta Paul, Hastings	E.P.S	$0.35
DUNS No.	87-266-7464	Shareholders	NA

Business: The group's principal activities are to develop and provide audio and voice technology solutions for the consumer electronics, home theater, computer, game, Internet and telecommunication market. The group operates in five segments: the licensing segment develops and licenses audio and voice technology to software providers and semiconductor manufactures. The proprietary audio and speaker segment develops and sells consumer products to proprietary audio and speaker technologies. Internet and broadcast segment develops and license software and hardware audio for Internet and broadcast markets. Semiconductor segment develops technology solutions in the form of analog and digital signal processor. Component distribution segment distributes semiconductor components, subassemblies and finished goods. The group operates in the United States, Asia-Pacific and Europe.

Primary SIC and add'l.: 3661 4899 3674 6794

CIK No: 0001016470

Subsidiaries: SRSWOWcast.com, inc

Officers: Thomas C.K. Yuen/Chmn., CEO/$466,781.00, Michael J. Franzi/VP - Sales, Licensing/$466,812.00, Sarah Yang/VP - Software Engineering/$414,563.00, Alan D. Kraemer/CTO/$425,028.00, Ulrich Gottschling/CFO/$438,236.00

Directors: Thomas C.K. Yuen/Chmn., CEO, David R. Dukes/Dir., Winston E. Hickman/Dir., Carol L. Miltner/Dir., Sam Yau/Dir.

Owners: Thomas C.K. Yuen, Sarah Yang, Insiders, Janet M. Biski, Thomas C.K. Yuen and Misako Yuen, Sandler Capital Management; Andrew Sandler, Alan D. Kraemer, Kern Capital Management, LLC

Financial Data: Fiscal Year End:12/31   Latest Annual Data: 12/31/2006

Year	Sales	Net Income
2006	$18,548,000	$4,708,000
2005	$23,228,000	-$1,424,000
2004	$21,602,000	$1,579,000

Curr. Assets:	$37,001,000	Curr. Liab.:	$2,305,000	P/E Ratio:	26.23
Plant, Equip.:	$390,000	Total Liab.:	$2,305,000	Indic. Yr. Divd.:	NA
Total Assets:	$45,049,000	Net Worth:	$42,744,000	Debt/ Equity:	NA

SS&C Technologies Inc

80 Lamberton Rd., Windsor, CT, 06095; *PH:* 1-860-298-4500; *http://* www.ssctech.com; *Email:* solution@sscinc.com

General - Incorporation	DE	Stock - Price on:12/24/2007	NA
Employees	NA	Stock Exchange	NDQ
Auditor	PricewaterhouseCoopers LLP	Ticker Symbol	SSNC
Stk Agt	NA	Outstanding Shares	NA
Counsel	Hale & Dorr LLP	E.P.S.	NA
DUNS No.	NA	Shareholders	NA

Business: The group's principal activity is to provide client server-based financial software solutions and related consulting services, designed to improve the efficiency and effectiveness of investment management, actuarial and analytical functions across a broad range of financial institutions. The group's family of software products support trading, accounting, reporting and analysis requirements of a broad range of users within financial organizations, including senior executives, portfolio managers, actuaries, analysts, portfolio accountants and traders. The products are classified under portfolio management, investment accounting, trade order management, asset/liability management, dynamic financial analysis, loan management, real estate equity management and ss&c direct (sm). On 20-Jan-2004, the group acquired investment advisory network, llc, on 18-Feb-2004, assets of neovision hypersystems inc & on 12-Apr-2004, omr systems international ltd & omr systems corp.

Primary SIC and add'l.: 7389 7372

CIK No: 0001011661

Subsidiaries: 1651943 Ontario Inc., EisnerFast LLC, HC Investments Ltd., HedgeWare, Inc., OMR Systems Corporation, OMR Systems International Limited, OMR Systems S.A.R.L., OMR Systems United Kingdom, Quantra Software Corporation, SAVID International Inc., Shepro Braun Systems, Inc., SS&C (Bahamas) Ltd., SS&C Fund Services (B.V.I.) Limited, SS&C Fund Services N.V., SS&C Pacific, Inc. 24 Subsidiaries included in the Index

Officers: William C. Stone/Chmn., CEO, Ward McGraw/Sr. VP, Colleen Nelsen/Sr. VP, GM - Financial Institutions, James R. Colvin/Sr. VP, GM, Normand A. Boulanger/COO, Pres., Thomas McMackin/Sr. VP, GM, John R. Sharpe/CIO, Sr. VP, Patrick J. Pedonti/Sr. VP, CFO, Stephen V.R. Whitman/Sr. VP, General Counsel, Richard Shalowitz/Sr. VP, GM, Steve H. Kremidas/Chief Development Officer, Sr. VP, Suresh Thekkenmar/Sr. VP - Professional Services, Alex Marasco/Sr. VP - Sscnet, SVC

Directors: William C. Stone/Chmn., CEO, Claudius E. /46/Dir., Allan M. Holt/55/Dir., William A. Etherington/66/Dir., Todd R. Newnam/37/Dir.

Owners: William A. Etherington, Normand A. Boulanger, Stephen V.R. Whitman, Insiders, TCG Holdings, L.L.C., Patrick J. Pedonti, William C. Stone

Financial Data: Fiscal Year End:12/31   Latest Annual Data: 12/31/2006

Year	Sales	Net Income
2006	$205,469,000	$1,075,000
2004	$95,888,000	$19,010,000
2003	$65,531,000	$11,796,000

Curr. Assets:	$51,236,000	Curr. Liab.:	$52,548,000		
Plant, Equip.:	$10,019,000	Total Liab.:	$589,389,000	Indic. Yr. Divd.:	NA
Total Assets:	$1,152,521,000	Net Worth:	$563,132,000	Debt/ Equity:	0.8146

St Joe Co

245 Riverside Ave., Ste. 500, Jacksonville, FL, 32202; *PH:* 1-904-301-4200; *Fax:* 1-904-301-4201; *http://* www.joe.com

General - Incorporation	FL	Stock - Price on:12/24/2007	$48
Employees	938	Stock Exchange	NYSE
Auditor	KPMG LLP	Ticker Symbol	JOE
Stk Agt	American Stock Transfer & Trust Co.	Outstanding Shares	74,360,000
Counsel	NA	E.P.S.	$0.99
DUNS No.	00-405-9614	Shareholders	NA

Business: The group's principle activities are to provide a broad range of residential and commercial real estate services. The group operates through four business segments. Community development segment develops large-scale, mixed- use communities on land. Commercial real estate development and services segment develops and sells real estate for commercial purposes. Land sales segment markets parcels included in the group's vast holdings of timberlands in northwest Florida. The forestry segment focuses on the management and harvesting of our extensive timberland holdings. The group's quarterly revenue for Sep '07 was 79.10 millions of USD.

Primary SIC and add'l.: 0811 4011 6552 0831

CIK No: 0000745308

Subsidiaries: 1133 D.c., LLC, 280 Interstate North, LLC, 5660 Nnd, LLC, Apalachicola Northern Railroad Company, Artisan Park, LLC, Arvida Housing L.p., Inc., Arvida Mid-atlantic Homes, Inc., C Ridge One, LLC, Crooked Creek Real Estate Company, Crooked Creek Utility Company, Deer Point I & Ii, LLC, Deerfield Commons I, LLC, Deerfield Park, LLC, Eagle Point, LLC, Georgia Timber, LLC 76 Subsidiaries included in the Index

Officers: Peter S. Rummell/62/Chmn., CEO, Pres./$4,195,469.00, Britton Wm. Greene/COO/$1,493,801.00, Christine M. Marx/General Counsel, Corp. Sec., Michael N. Regan/60/Sr. VP - Finance, Planning/$914,905.00, Christopher T. Corr/Chief Strategy Officer/$845,264.00, Michael Daly/VP - Investor Relations, Jerry Ray/Sr. VP - Corporate Communications, Molly Walker/Web Mgr. - Marketing, William McCalmont/CFO

Directors: Peter S. Rummell/62/Chmn., CEO, Pres., Harry H. Frampton/63/Dir., John S. Lord/61/Dir., Thomas A. Fanning/51/Dir., Delores M. Kesler/67/Dir., Adam W. Herbert/64/Dir., Hugh M. Durden/65/Dir., William H. Walton/56/Dir., Michael L. Ainslie/64/Dir., Walter L. Revell/73/Dir.

Owners: Janus Capital Management, LLC/7.00%, William H. Walton, Hugh M. Durden/2.50%, Peter S. Rummell/1.80%, Britton Wm. Greene, Walter L. Revell, Adam W. Herbert, Insiders/4.70%, Thomas A. Fanning, John S. Lord/2.50%, Michael L. Ainslie, Delores M. Kesler, Hotchkis and Wiley Capital Management, LLC/10.50%, Marsico Capital Management, LLC/10.30%, Harry H. Frampton (18 Owners included in Index)

Financial Data: Fiscal Year End:12/31   Latest Annual Data: 12/31/2006

Year	Sales	Net Income
2006	$748,192,000	$51,020,000
2005	$938,192,000	$126,658,000
2004	$951,503,000	$90,100,000

Curr. Assets:	$88,803,000	Curr. Liab.:	$250,611,000	P/E Ratio:	48.48
Plant, Equip.:	$1,258,155,000	Total Liab.:	$1,099,315,000	Indic. Yr. Divd.:	$0.640
Total Assets:	$1,560,395,000	Net Worth:	$461,080,000	Debt/ Equity:	1.2742

St John Knits International Inc

2722 Michelson Dr., Irvine, CA, 92612; *PH:* 1-949-863-1171; *http://* www.stjohnknits.com

General - Incorporation	DE	Stock - Price on:12/24/2007	$29
Employees	NA	Stock Exchange	OTC
Auditor	Deloitte & Touche LLP	Ticker Symbol	SJKI
Stk Agt	NA	Outstanding Shares	NA
Counsel	NA	E.P.S.	NA
DUNS No.	NA	Shareholders	NA

Business: The group's principal activities are to design, manufacture and market women's clothing and accessories. The knitwear product line consists of a collection of lifestyle clothing for women's business, evening and casual needs. The group manufactures its products primarily to order and distributes them on a highly selective basis through a group of upscale retailers as well as through company-owned stores. The products are distributed primarily through a select group of specialty retailers and 34 boutiques and 13 outlet stores. The group owns and utilizes several trademarks including st. John (R), st. John by marie gray(R) and st. John sport (r).

Primary SIC and add'l.: 5137 5999 2389 2399 2361

CIK No: 0001080280

Subsidiaries: St. John

Financial Data: Fiscal Year End:10/31   Latest Annual Data: 10/31/2004

Year	Sales	Net Income
2004	$395,603,000	$13,448,000
2003	$370,143,000	$14,882,000
2002	$362,234,000	$24,305,000

Curr. Assets:	$133,428,000	Curr. Liab.:	$47,391,000		
Plant, Equip.:	$83,762,000	Total Liab.:	$311,639,000	Indic. Yr. Divd.:	NA
Total Assets:	$235,907,000	Net Worth:	-$129,790,000	Debt/ Equity:	NA

St Joseph Capital Corp

3820 Edison Lakes Pk.way, Mishawaka, IN, 46545; *PH:* 1-574-273-9700; *http://* www.sjcb.com

General - Incorporation	DE	Stock - Price on:12/24/2007	$25.55
Employees	79	Stock Exchange	NDQ
Auditor	Plante & Moran, PLLC	Ticker Symbol	SJOE
Stk Agt	Computershare Investor Services LLC	Outstanding Shares	NA
Counsel	NA	E.P.S.	NA
DUNS No.	80-497-3048	Shareholders	NA

Business: The group's principal activity is to provide commercial banking services to individuals and local businesses located in northern Indiana communities and certain Michigan communities. The lending and deposit services of the group include checking accounts, money market, savings, time deposits and consumer, commercial and mortgage loans. The other services offered by the group include credit cards, cashiers checks, traveler's checks, deposits and assets management and automated teller access. The group's subsidiary includes st. Joseph capital bank.

Primary SIC and add'l.: 6712 6022

CIK No: 0001015856

Subsidiaries: Riverfront Partners LLC, St. Joseph Capital Bank, St. Joseph Capital Holdings, Inc, St. Joseph Capital Trust I, St. Joseph Capital Trust II

St Joseph Inc

4870 S Lewis, Ste 250, Tulsa, OK, 74105; *PH:* 1-918-742-1888; *http://* www.stjosephinc.com; *Email:* sji@stjosephinc.com

General - Incorporation	CO	Stock - Price on:12/24/2007	$0.7
Employees	15	Stock Exchange	OTC
Auditor	Cordovano & Honeck LLP	Ticker Symbol	STJO
Stk Agt	Schroeder & Schreiner	Outstanding Shares	6,050,000
Counsel	NA	E.P.S.	NA
DUNS No.	NA	Shareholders	NA

Business: The groups principle activities include recruiting and placement of professional technical staff. The group provides specialist in programming, networking, systems integration, database design, and help desk support. The group provides computer training, online assessments, and certification in various IT skill sets. The group operates from United States.

Primary SIC and add'l.: NA

CIK No: 0001177135

Subsidiaries: StafMed Global, Inc, StafTek Services, Inc

Officers: Gerald McIlhargey/60/Dir., CEO, Pres./$36,300.00, Kenneth L. Johnson/48/Dir., CFO, Sec., Treasurer/$18,150.00

Directors: Gerald McIlhargey/60/Dir., CEO, Pres., Donal Kent Ford/52/Dir., Kenneth L. Johnson/48/Dir., CFO, Sec., Treasurer, Bruce E. Schreiner/52/Dir., David Goler/59/Member - Advisory Board, John Hershenberg/45/Member - Advisory Board, Ted Key/30/Member - Advisory Board, John K. Lucas/57/Member - Advisory Board, Maureen O'Brien/59/Dir., Brian R. Smith/42/Member - Advisory Board

Owners: Phyllis L. Bell/11.14%, David William Dean Core/18.60%, Maureen OBrien/1.23%, Desert Projects, Inc./76.92%, Kenneth L. Johnson/2.46%, Bruce Schreiner/2.42%, Gerald McIlhargey/3.25%, Insiders/10.08%, Wildwood Partners/23.08%, Wildwood Partners/2.79%, Phyllis L. Bell/85.45%, Donal Ford/1.23%

Curr. Assets:	$247,000	Curr. Liab.:	$590,000		
Plant, Equip.:	$3,000	Total Liab.:	$590,000	Indic. Yr. Divd.:	NA
Total Assets:	$510,000	Net Worth:	-$80,000	Debt/ Equity:	NA

St Jude Medical Inc

One Lillehei Plz., St Paul, MN, 55117; *PH:* 1-800-444-4069; *http://* www.sjm.com

General - Incorporation	MN	Stock - Price on:12/24/2007	$43.59
Employees	11,000	Stock Exchange	NYSE
Auditor	Ernst & Young LLP	Ticker Symbol	STJ
Stk Agt	EquiServe Trust Co N.A	Outstanding Shares	338,320,000
Counsel	NA	E.P.S.	$1.52
DUNS No.	08-023-2168	Shareholders	NA

Business: The groups principle activities include developing, manufacturing and distributing cardiovascular medical devices for the global cardiac rhythm management, cardiac surgery, cardiology and atrial fibrillation therapy areas, and implantable neuromodulation devices. The groups products include tachycardia implantable cardioverter defibrillator and bradycardia pacemaker systems. The group operates from United States.

Primary SIC and add'l.: 3841 3845

CIK No: 0000203077

Subsidiaries: Advanced Neuromodulation Systems, Advanced Neuromodulation Systems Australia Pty Limited, Advanced Neuromodulation Systems France S.A.S, Advanced Neuromodulation Systems, Inc, ANS Germany GmbH, Beijing, China representative office, Beijing, Shanghai and Guangzhou representative offices, Bio-Med Sales, Inc., Brussels, Belgium branch, Endocardial Solutions NV/SA, Endocardial Solutions, Inc, Epicor Medical, Inc, Epicor Medical, Inc., Frank Merger Corporation, Hi-Tronics Designs, Inc 48 Subsidiaries included in the Index

Officers: Daniel J. Starks/Chmn., CEO, Pres./$5,791,647.00, William J. McGarry/VP, General Counsel, Company Sec., Paul Bae/VP - Human Resources, Mark D. Carlson/Chief Medical Officer, Sr. VP - Clinical Affairs, Cardiac Rhythm Management Division, Denis M. Gestin/Pres. - SJM Europe, Angela D. Craig/VP - Corporate Relations, Christopher G. Chavez/Pres. - Neuromodulation Division, Pamela S. Krop/VP, General Counsel, Company Sec., Joseph H. McCullough/Pres. - St. Jude Medical International Division/$2,031,802.00, Michael J. Coyle/Pres. - Cardiac Rhythm Management Division/$2,309,305.00, Jane J. Song/Pres. - Atrial Fibrillation Division, Michael T. Rousseau/Pres. - US Division/$2,140,670.00, Eric S. Fain/Pres. - Cardiac Rhythm Management Division, John C. Heinmiller/CFO, Exec. VP/$2,667,444.00, Thomas R. Northenscold/VP - Administration *(17 Officers included in Index)*

Directors: Daniel J. Starks/Chmn., CEO, Pres., Stuart M. Essig/Dir., Stefan K. Widensohler/Dir., Michael A. Rocca/Dir., Wendy L. Yarno/Dir., David A. Thompson/Dir., Richard R. Devenuti/Dir., Thomas H. Garrett/Dir., John W. Brown/Dir.

Owners: Joseph P. McCullough, Wellington Management Company, LLP/5.40%, Stefan K. Widensohler, Wendy L. Yarno, Richard R. Devenuti, Michael T. Rousseau, Daniel J. Starks/2.60%, Capital Research and Management Company/6.50%, Insiders/4.10%, Stuart M. Essig, John C. Heinmiller, Michael J. Coyle, Thomas H. Garrett, John W. Brown, Goldman Sachs Asset Management, L.P./5.50% *(19 Owners included in Index)*

Financial Data: *Fiscal Year End:*12/31 *Latest Annual Data:* 12/30/2006

Year		Sales		Net Income
2006		$3,302,447,000		$548,251,000
2005		$2,915,280,000		$393,490,000
2004		$2,294,173,000		$409,934,000
Curr. Assets:	$1,941,141,000	Curr. Liab.:	$1,534,382,000	P/E Ratio: 28.68
Plant, Equip.:	$438,416,000	Total Liab.:	$1,961,795,000	Indic. Yr. Divd.: NA
Total Assets:	$4,844,840,000	Net Worth:	$2,883,045,000	Debt/ Equity: 0.4400

St Lawrence Seaway Corp

200 Connecticut Ave, 5th Fl., Norwalk, CT, 06854; *PH:* 1-203-853-8700

General - Incorporation	IN	Stock - Price on:12/24/2007	$2.4
Employees	NA	Stock Exchange	OTC
Auditor	Mahoney Sabol & Co LLP	Ticker Symbol	STLS
Stk Agt	Continental Stock Transfer & Trust Co	Outstanding Shares	NA
Counsel	Nutter McClennen & Fish	E.P.S.	-$1.53
DUNS No.	04-509-4489	Shareholders	NA

Business: The group's principle activity is to invest in drug development programs and evaluate alternatives to its former business. It is evaluating operating companies for acquisition, merger or investment and commencement of a new business. Prior to 1998, the main business was farming, timber, harvesting, leasing of the property to farmers and other traditional agricultural activities. The group operates from United States.

Primary SIC and add'l.: 9999

CIK No: 0000086264

Officers: Jack C. Brown/88/Dir., Sec., Daniel L. Nir/47/Dir., Pres., Treasurer, Edward B. Grier/49/Dir., VP

Directors: Joel M. Greenblatt/50/Chmn., Jack C. Brown/88/Dir., Sec., Daniel L. Nir/47/Dir., Pres., Treasurer, Edward B. Grier/49/Dir., VP

Owners: Insiders/48.60%, Daniel L. Nir/10.40%, Bernard Zimmerman & Company, Inc./43.20%, Joel M. Greenblatt/17.70%, Ronald Alan Zlatniski/8.10%

Financial Data: *Fiscal Year End:*03/31 *Latest Annual Data:* 03/31/2007

Year		Sales		Net Income
2007		$6,000		-$96,000
2006		$4,000		-$727,000
2005		$2,000		-$71,000
Curr. Assets:	$123,000	Curr. Liab.:	$52,000	
Plant, Equip.:	NA	Total Liab.:	$52,000	Indic. Yr. Divd.: NA
Total Assets:	$213,000	Net Worth:	$161,000	Debt/ Equity: NA

St Mary Land & Exploration Co

1776 Lincoln St., Ste. 700, Denver, CO, 80203; *PH:* 1-303-861-8140; *Fax:* 1-303-861-0934; *http://* www.stmaryland.com; *Email:* information@stmaryland.com

General - Incorporation	DE	Stock - Price on:12/24/2007	$39
Employees	359	Stock Exchange	NYSE
Auditor	Deloitte & Touche LLP	Ticker Symbol	SM
Stk Agt	Computershare Trust Co	Outstanding Shares	62,780,000
Counsel	NA	E.P.S.	$3.12
DUNS No.	07-647-8155	Shareholders	NA

Business: The group's principal activities are to explore, develop, acquire and produce natural gas and crude oil. The group has operations in mid-continent region, the arklatex region, the gulf coast region, the williston basin in North Dakota and Montana and the permian basin in west Texas and New Mexico. The group's operations are conducted entirely in the continental United States.

Primary SIC and add'l.: 1311 1382 4932

CIK No: 0000893538

Subsidiaries: Box Church Gas Gathering LLC., Four Winds Marketing LLC., Nance Petroleum Corporation, SMEC Texas LLC., SMT Texas LLC., St. Mary Energy Company., Trinity River Services LLC.

Officers: Mark A. Hellerstein/Chmn., CEO/$4,060,316.00, Garry A. Wilkening/VP - Administration, Paul M. Veatch/Sr. VP, Regional Mgr., Linda A. Ditsworth/Assist. VP - Land, Assistant Sec., Jerry R. Schuyler/52/Sr. VP, Regional Mgr., David W. Honeyfield/VP, CFO, Treasurer, Sec./$373,810.00, Larry W. Bickle/Houston, Texas MD Haddington Ventures LLC, Mark T. Solomon/Controller, John M. Seidl/Chief Program Officer - Aspen, Colorado, Milam Randolph Pharo/VP - Land, Legal, Assist. Sec./$1,107,803.00, David J. Whitcomb/Assist. VP, Dir. - Marketing, William D. Hart/56/VP, GM - Arklatex, Michael F. Roach/Assist. VP, Dir. - Taxation, Robert L. Nance/Sr. VP/$1,068,687.00, Javan D. Ottoson/49/COO, Exec. VP

Directors: Mark A. Hellerstein/Chmn., CEO, William D. Sullivan/Dir., Thomas E. Congdon/Dir., Barbara M. Baumann/Dir., William J. Gardiner/Dir., Julio M. Quintana/Dir., Anthony J. Best/58/Dir.

Owners: Insiders/3.00%, William D. Sullivan, Thomas E. Congdon/0.20%, Milam Randolph Pharo/0.10%, Douglas W. York, Neuberger Berman LLC/6.20%, William J. Gardiner/0.10%, Anthony J. Best, John M. Seidl, Larry W. Bickle/0.20%, Kevin E. Willson, Barbara M. Baumann/0.10%, David W. Honeyfield, Harris Associates L.P./5.30%, Julio M. Quintana *(17 Owners included in Index)*

Financial Data: *Fiscal Year End:*12/31 *Latest Annual Data:* 12/31/2006

Year		Sales		Net Income
2006		$787,701,000		$190,015,000
2005		$739,590,000		$151,936,000
2004		$483,398,000		$92,479,000
Curr. Assets:	$226,940,000	Curr. Liab.:	$204,070,000	P/E Ratio: 12.54
Plant, Equip.:	$1,638,464,000	Total Liab.:	$1,155,723,000	Indic. Yr. Divd.: $0.100
Total Assets:	$1,899,097,000	Net Worth:	$743,374,000	Debt/ Equity: 0.6462

ST Online Corp

Ste. 300, 840-6th Ave. S.w., Calgary, AL, T2P 3E5; *PH:* 1-403-360-5375; *http://* www.simpletennis.com

General - Incorporation	NV	Stock - Price on:12/24/2007	$1.1
Employees	NA	Stock Exchange	OTC
Auditor	Manning Elliott LLP	Ticker Symbol	PRPL
Stk Agt	Pacific Stock Transfer Co.	Outstanding Shares	NA
Counsel	NA	E.P.S.	NA
DUNS No.	NA	Shareholders	NA

Business: The groups principle activity is in the operations which are limited to developing website. The group operate a website www.simpletennis.com that offers downloadable tennis lessons, ebooks and offer other tennis related products to individual retail customers in the future. The group operates form the United States.

Primary SIC and add'l.: 1311

CIK No: 0001310982

Officers: David Stadnyk/Dir., CEO, Pres., Principal Financial Officer, Principal Accounting Officer, Oxana Avdasseva/23/Dir., Sec.

Directors: David Stadnyk/Dir., CEO, Pres., Principal Financial Officer, Principal Accounting Officer, Oxana Avdasseva/23/Dir., Sec.

Owners: Scott Pedersen/29.01%, Elena Avdasseva/48.35%

St Paul Travelers Cos Inc

385 Washington St. , St. Paul, MN, 55102; *PH:* 1-651-310-7911; *http://* www.stpaultravelers.com

General - Incorporation	MN	Stock - Price on:12/24/2007	NA
Employees	31,900	Stock Exchange	NA
Auditor	KPMG LLP	Ticker Symbol	NA
Stk Agt	Wells Fargo Bank Minnesota N.A	Outstanding Shares	NA
Counsel	NA	E.P.S.	NA
DUNS No.	00-696-3540	Shareholders	NA

Business: The group's principal activities are the provision of commercial property-liability and non life reinsurance products and services worldwide. The group operates through seven business segments: specialty commercial, commercial lines, surety and construction, international and lloyd's, health care, reinsurance and other. The other global specialty operations of the group include traditional insurance financial and risk management services. On 01-Apr-2004, the group acquired travelers property casualty corp.

Primary SIC and add'l.: 6282 6331 9999

CIK No: 0000086312

Subsidiaries: 350 Market Street, Inc., AE Development Group, Inc., AE Properties, Inc., Afianzadora Insurgentes, S.A. De C.V., American Equity Insurance Company, American Equity Specialty Insurance Company, Aprilgrange Limited, Arch Street North LLC, Athena Assurance Company, Atlantic Insurance Company, Auto Hartford Investments LLC, BAP Investor Pine, Inc., Bayhill Associates, Bayhill Restaurant II Associates, Camperdown Corporation 147 Subsidiaries included in the Index

Officers: Jay S. Fishman/Chmn., CEO, Pres./$16,077,140.00, William H. Heyman/Vice Chmn., Chief Investment Officer/$6,915,167.00, Alan D. Schnitzer/Vice Chmn., Chief Legal Officer, Jay S. Benet/Vice Chmn., CFO/$5,563,464.00, Joseph P. Lacher/Exec. VP - Personal Insurance, Select Accounting, Bruce Backberg/Sr. VP, Corp. Sec., Andy F. Bessette/Exec. VP, Chief Administrative Officer, Maria Olivo/Exec. VP - Investor Relations, Corporate Communications, Samuel Liss/Exec. VP - Strategic Development, Exec. VP - Financial, Professional, International

Insurance/$6,063,329.00, Brian W. MacLean/COO, Exec. VP/$6,559,573.00, Kenneth F. Spence/Exec. VP, General Counsel, John Clifford/Exec. VP - Human Resources, John J. Albano/Exec. VP - Business Insurance, Doreen Spadoria/Exec. VP - Claim Services, Kathleen Preston/Exec. VP - Enterprise Development *(16 Officers included in Index)*

Directors: Jay S. Fishman/Chmn., CEO, Pres., William H. Heyman/Vice Chmn., Chief Investment Officer, Charles Clarke/Vice Chmn., Irwin R. Ettinger/Vice Chmn., Jay S. Benet/Vice Chmn., CFO, Alan D. Schnitzer/Vice Chmn., Chief Legal Officer, Cleve L. Killingsworth/Dir., Robert I. Lipp/Dir., Janet M. Dolan/Dir., Thomas R. Hodgson/Dir., Blythe J. McGarvie/Dir., Lawrence G. Graev/Dir., Glen D. Nelson/Dir., John H. Dasburg/Dir., Laurie J. Thomsen/Dir. *(18 Directors included in Index)*

Owners: Barclays Global Investors, NA, K. M. Duberstein, T. R. Hodgson, L. B. Disharoon, J. S. Fishman, B. J. McGarvie, J. M. Dolan, L. G. Graev, L. J. Thomsen, R. I. Lipp, Dodge & Cox, J. H. Dasburg, J. S. Benet, W. H. Heyman, B. W. MacLean *(20 Owners included in Index)*

St. Bernard Software Inc

15015 Ave. of Science, San Diego, CA, 92128; *PH:* 1-858-676-2277; *Fax:* 1-858-676-5055; *http://* www.stbernard.com; *Email:* info@stbernard.com

General - Incorporation	CA	Stock - Price on:12/24/2007	$1.08
Employees	169	Stock Exchange	OTC
Auditor	Mayer Hoffman Mccann, P.C	Ticker Symbol	SBSW
Stk Agt	American Stock Transfer & Trust Co.	Outstanding Shares	14,810,000
Counsel	NA	E.P.S.	-$0.59
DUNS No.	NA	Shareholders	NA

Business: The groups principle activity is a dedicated and optimized network appliance that enables organizations to enforce their acceptable internet use policies by providing multi protocol web filtering and access control. In October 2006, the group acquired AgaveOne, Inc. and In July 2006, the group merged with Sand Hill IT. The group operates from the United States, the United Kingdom and Australia.

Primary SIC and add'l.: 7372
CIK No: 0001288496
Subsidiaries: St. Bernard Merger Subsidiary, St. Bernard Software Australia PTY. Limited, St. Bernard Software U.K. Ltd.
Officers: Vince Rossi/Dir., CEO, Pres., Al Riedler/CFO, Steve Yin/VP - Sales, Andrew Lochart/VP - Marketing, Product Management, Steve Saxton-Getty/GM - On, Demand Services
Directors: Vince Rossi/Dir., CEO, Pres., Humphrey P. Polanen/Dir., Scott R. Broomfield/Dir., Bart A.M. Van Hedel/Dir., Mel S. Lavitt/Dir., Louis E. Ryan/Dir.
Owners: Steve Yin, Scott Broomfield/1.89%, Alfred Riedler, Mel Lavitt/1.10%, John Jones/9.14%, William J. Del Biaggio/5.26%, Humphrey Polanen/4.13%, Insiders/39.29%, Bart Van Hedel/17.41%, Louis Ryan

Financial Data: *Fiscal Year End:*12/31 *Latest Annual Data:* 12/31/2006

Year	Sales	Net Income
2006	$22,558,000	-$8,023,000
2005	NA	-$1,545,000
2004	NA	-$50,000

Curr. Assets:	$10,020,000	Curr. Liab.:	$18,622,000		
Plant, Equip.:	$1,726,000	Total Liab.:	$24,606,000	Indic. Yr. Divd.:	NA
Total Assets:	$23,393,000	Net Worth:	-$1,213,000	Debt/ Equity:	NA

Staar Surgical Co

1911 Walker Ave., Monrovia, CA, 91016; *PH:* 1-626-303-7902; *Fax:* 1-626-359-8402; *http://* www.staar.com; *Email:* info@staar.com

General - Incorporation	DE	Stock - Price on:12/24/2007	NA
Employees	284	Stock Exchange	NDQ
Auditor	BDO Seidman LLP	Ticker Symbol	STAA
Stk Agt	American Stock Transfer & Trust Co.	Outstanding Shares	29,310,000
Counsel	NA	E.P.S.	-$0.63
DUNS No.	05-475-1110	Shareholders	NA

Business: The group's principal activities are to develop, produce and market intraocular lenses and other products for minimally invasive ophthalmic surgery. The products include intraocular lenses and other products for minimally invasive surgery, the sonic wave phacoemulsification system, implantable contact lenses tm, toric intraocular lens and the aquaflow(TM) collagen glaucoma drainage device. The group sells its products worldwide to ophthalmologists, surgical centers, hospitals, managed care providers, health maintenance organizations and group purchasing organizations. It also sells other instruments, devices and equipment manufactured or supplied from other manufacturers. The group operates mainly in the United States and Germany.

Primary SIC and add'l.: 3842 3851 3841
CIK No: 0000718937
Subsidiaries: Canon Sales Co., Inc., STAAR Surgical AG
Officers: David Bailey/Dir., CEO, Pres./$753,285.00, Nick Curtis/Sr. VP - Sales, Marketing/$439,366.00, Paul Hambrick/VP - Operations, Rob Lally/VP - Quality Assurance, Regulatory Affairs, Charles S. Kaufman/VP, General Counsel, Sec., Deborah Andrews/CFO, VP/$424,793.00, Jennifer Beugelmans/Investors Contact, Douglas Sherk/Investors Contact, Craig Felberg/VP - Research, Development, Clinical Affairs, Robin Hughes/VP - Marketing
Directors: David Bailey/Dir., CEO, Pres., David L. Schlotterbeck/Dir., David Morrison/Dir., Donald Duffy/Dir., Don M. Bailey/Dir., Barry Caldwell/Dir.
Owners: David Bailey/4.10%, Thomas Paul, David Schlotterbeck, Insiders/6.60%, Nick Curtis, Deborah Andrews, Winslow Management Company LLP/6.20%, Broadwood Partners, L.P./9.70%, David Morrison, Heartland Advisors, Inc/12.00%, Donald Duffy, James E. Flynn/5.90%, Don Bailey

Financial Data: *Fiscal Year End:*12/30 *Latest Annual Data:* 12/29/2006

Year	Sales	Net Income
2006	$56,282,000	-$15,044,000
2005	$51,303,000	-$11,175,000
2004	$51,685,000	-$11,332,000

Curr. Assets:	$32,582,000	Curr. Liab.:	$13,479,000		
Plant, Equip.:	$6,163,000	Total Liab.:	$14,133,000	Indic. Yr. Divd.:	NA
Total Assets:	$51,973,000	Net Worth:	$37,840,000	Debt/ Equity:	NA

Stage Stores Inc

10201 Main St., Houston, TX, 77025; *PH:* 1-713-667-5601; *http://* www.stagestoresinc.com; *Email:* customercomments@stagestores.com

General - Incorporation	NV	Stock - Price on:12/24/2007	$20.95
Employees	14,608	Stock Exchange	NYSE
Auditor	Deloitte & Touche LLP	Ticker Symbol	SSI
Stk Agt	Mellon Investor Services LLC	Outstanding Shares	43,100,000
Counsel	NA	E.P.S.	$1.39
DUNS No.	80-814-5536	Shareholders	NA

Business: The group's principal activity is to operate family apparel stores. The group operates under the names bealls, palais royal and stage offering branded fashion apparel and accessories, cosmetic and footwear for women, men and children. The group operates through 550 stores located in 31 states. The group has developed a franchise focused on small markets offering brand name merchandise with customer service in convenient locations. On February 27, 2006, the group acquired privately held B.C. Moore & Sons, Incorporated ("B.C. Moore"). The group operates mainly in the United States.

Primary SIC and add'l.: 5651
CIK No: 0000006885
Subsidiaries: Specialty Retailers (TX) LP, Specialty Retailers, Inc., SRI General Partner LLC, SRI Limited Partner LLC
Officers: James Scarborough/Chmn., CEO/$3,117,833.00, Gough Grubbs/Sr. VP - Logistics, Distribution, Cynthia Murray/Exec. VP, Chief Merchandising Officer - Stage Division/$1,153,418.00, Mel Ward/Sr. VP - Real Estate, Ernest Cruse/Exec. VP - Store Operations, Stage Division, Ron Lucas/Exec. VP - Human Resources, Jeff Kish/CIO, Exec. VP, Richard Stasyszen/Sr. VP - Finance, Controller, Joanne Swartz/Exec. VP - Advertising, Sales Promotion, Bob Aronson/VP - Investor Relations, Michael McCreery/Dir., CFO, Exec. VP, Sec./$1,115,058.00, Dennis Abramczyk/Exec. VP, COO - Peebles Division/$1,020,420.00, Russell Lundy/Sr. VP - Store Operations, Peebles Division, Andrew Hall/COO, Pres./$1,388,142.00
Directors: James Scarborough/Chmn., CEO, William Montgoris/Dir., Sharon Mosse/Dir., John Mentzer/Dir., Alan Barocas/Dir., Margaret Monaco/Dir., Scott Davido/Dir., Michael Glazer/Dir., Michael McCreery/Dir., CFO, Exec. VP, Sec.
Owners: William J. Montgoris, Paradigm Capital Management, Inc./6.60%, Michael L. Glazer, Scott J. Davido, Andrew T. Hall, Insiders/5.90%, Margaret T. Monaco, Wellington Management Company, LLP/5.60%, Dimensional Fund Advisors LP/7.00%, John T. Mentzer, Michael E. McCreery, Dennis E. Abramczyk, James R. Scarborough/3.60%

Financial Data: *Fiscal Year End:*01/28 *Latest Annual Data:* 2/3/2007

Year	Sales	Net Income
2007	$1,550,180,000	$55,302,000
2006	$1,344,100,000	$55,887,000
2005	$1,243,851,000	$51,388,000

Curr. Assets:	$414,372,000	Curr. Liab.:	$160,704,000		
Plant, Equip.:	$278,839,000	Total Liab.:	$253,578,000	Indic. Yr. Divd.:	$0.200
Total Assets:	$824,986,000	Net Worth:	$571,408,000	Debt/ Equity:	0.0289

StakTek Holdings Inc

8900 Shoal Creek Blvd, Ste 125, Austin, TX, 78757; *PH:* 1-512-454-9531; *http://* www.staktek.com; *Email:* info@staktek.com

General - Incorporation	DE	Stock - Price on:12/24/2007	$4.1
Employees	504	Stock Exchange	NDQ
Auditor	Ernst & Young LLP	Ticker Symbol	STAK
Stk Agt	Computershare Investor Services LLC	Outstanding Shares	47,510,000
Counsel	NA	E.P.S.	NA
DUNS No.	NA	Shareholders	NA

Business: The group provides of memory stacking solutions for systems and applications such as servers, workstations, high-end computing platforms and networking equipment. The products are distributed directly to large original equipment manufacturers, such as cisco systems, dell, hewlett-packard, IBM, intel and sun microsystems. The groups major semiconductor, memory module and contract manufacturing customers include celestica, infineon, kingston, micron and smart modular. Celestica and smart modular are supply-chain partners of IBM and hewlett-packard. On 21-Aug-2003, the group acquired staktek corporation, which is the predecessor company.

Primary SIC and add'l.: 7379
CIK No: 0000866830
Subsidiaries: merger Staktek Corporation
Officers: Wayne R. Lieberman/Dir., CEO, Pres./$783,673.00, Damian Cook/VP, GM - Business Operations, Stephanie A. Lucie/Sr. VP, General Counsel, Corp. Sec./$398,198.00, Kirk W. Patterson/Sr. VP, CFO/$419,699.00, Robert Fan/VP, GM - Corporate Strategic Business Development, John R. Meehan/Exec. VP, Joe C. Meehan/Exec. VP, David M. Tremblay/VP - Worldwide Sales, Joseph Villani/VP - Engineering
Directors: Wayne R. Lieberman/Dir., CEO, Pres., Joseph C. Aragona/Chmn., Clark W. Jernigan/Dir., Harvey B. Cash/Dir., Kevin P. Hegarty/Dir., Travis A. White/Dir., Joseph Marengi/Dir.
Owners: Clark W. Jernigan, Kevin P. Hegarty, James W. Cady, Stephanie A. Lucie, Insiders, Edward E. Olkkola, Travis A. White, Kirk W. Patterson, Wayne R. Lieberman, Harvey B. Cash, Austin Ventures, Joseph C. Aragona

Financial Data: *Fiscal Year End:*12/31 *Latest Annual Data:* 03/31/2007

Year	Sales	Net Income
2007	NA	NA
2006	NA	NA
2005	$52,526,000	-$7,477,000

Curr. Assets:	$89,362,000	Curr. Liab.:	$4,832,000		
Plant, Equip.:	$6,766,000	Total Liab.:	$5,163,000	Indic. Yr. Divd.:	NA
Total Assets:	$135,191,000	Net Worth:	$130,028,000	Debt/ Equity:	0.0005

Stallion Group (The)

4800 I-5 N, Ste. 210, Jackson, MS, 39211; *PH:* 1-604-760-6468; *http://* www.thestalliongroup.com; *Email:* IR@thestalliongroup.com

General - Incorporation	NV
Employees	NA
Auditor	Cordovano and Honeck, LLP
Stk Agt.	Pacific Stock Transfer Company
Counsel	NA
DUNS No.	NA

Stock - Price on:12/24/2007	$0.83
Stock Exchange	OTC
Ticker Symbol	SLGR
Outstanding Shares	NA
E.P.S.	NA
Shareholders	NA

Business: The groups principal activity is in exploration stage company engaged in the search for gold and related minerals. The group operates from the United States.

Primary SIC and add'l.: 1040

CIK No: 0001285894

Officers: Christopher Paton-Gay/Chmn., CEO, William K. Griffin/CEO, Pres., John Andrew Griffin/VP - Exploration, Bob Boyett/Drilling Mgr. - Joint Operations, Marion Smith/Legal Counsel - Joint Lands, Kulwant Sandher/Dir., CFO/$13,333.00, Raymond Lewand/Sr. Geologist, Pittman S. Calhoun/Chief Geophysist

Directors: Christopher Paton-Gay/Chmn., CEO, Kulwant Sandher/Dir., CFO

Owners: Gerald W. Williams/44.30%, Kulwant Sandher/2.39%, Caverly Management Inc./6.84%, Christopher Paton-Gay/2.07%

Stamford Industrial Group Inc

Formerly: NetPerceptions
One Landmark Sq., 22nd Fl., Stamford, CT, 06901; **PH:** 1-203-428-2040;
http:// www.netperceptions.com

General - Incorporation	DE
Employees	245
Auditor	Mcgladrey & Pullen, LLP
Stk Agt.	Wells Fargo Shareowner Services
Counsel	NA
DUNS No.	NA

Stock - Price on:12/24/2007	$2.64
Stock Exchange	OTC
Ticker Symbol	NETP
Outstanding Shares	41,280,000
E.P.S.	-$0.28
Shareholders	NA

Business: The group's principle activities are to develop and market software solutions that integrate and analyze information about customers, products and promotional activity and convert this data into actionable sales and marketing intelligence. These solutions enable companies to establish, maintain and continually improve customer interactions across, both, traditional and modern customer communication channels. Product solutions include personalization manager, distribution analyst, advertising advisor and retail analyst. The group's customers are 3m, brylane, great universal stores, half.com, jcpenney, j & l industrial supply and musician's friend. The group's quarterly revenue for September 2007 was 28.20 millions of USD.

Primary SIC and add'l.: 7372 7371 7373 7379

CIK No: 0001078203

Subsidiaries: Knowledge Discovery One, Inc.

Officers: Albert W. Weggeman/44/CEO, Pres./$2,406,746.00, Jonathan Labarre/38/CFO, Sec., Treasurer/$710,666.00, Paul Vesey/52/Pres., GM - Concord Steel/$571,710.00

Directors: Warren B. Kanders/Chmn., David A. Jones/Dir., Nicholas Sokolow/Dir.

Owners: Susan Luckfield, Nigel P. Ekern/1.00%, Paul Vesey, CRC Acquisition Co., LLC/8.50%, Nicholas Sokolow/1.40%, David A. Jones, Insiders/32.80%, Austin W. Marxe/3.30%, Albert W. Weggeman, Warren B. Kanders/29.80%, Gianmaria C. Delzanno, White Rock Capital Management, L.P./10.30%

Financial Data: Fiscal Year End: 12/31 **Latest Annual Data:** 03/31/2007

Year	Sales	Net Income
2007	$27,904,000	$752,000
2006	$24,058,000	-$29,000
2005	$118,000	$207,000

Curr. Assets:	-$2,959,000	Curr. Liab.:	NA		
Plant, Equip.:	NA	Total Liab.:	NA	Indic. Yr. Divd.:	NA
Total Assets:	-$2,959,000	Net Worth:	NA	Debt/ Equity:	1.4736

Stamps.com Inc

12959 Coral Tree Pl, Los Angeles, CA, 90066; **PH:** 1-310-482-5800; **http://** www.stamps.com;
Email: enterprise_inquiries@stamps.com

General - Incorporation	DE
Employees	165
Auditor	Ernst & Young LLP
Stk Agt.	U.S. Stock Transfer Corp
Counsel	Wilson Sonsini Goodrich & Rosati
DUNS No.	NA

Stock - Price on:12/24/2007	$14.01
Stock Exchange	NDQ
Ticker Symbol	STMP
Outstanding Shares	21,920,000
E.P.S.	$0.69
Shareholders	NA

Business: The group's principle activity is to provide Internet mailing services. The company offers a secure Internet mailing solution that lets customers print postage using their existing PC, printer and Internet connection without having to go to the post office. It is approved by the U.S. Postal service to offer a software-only solution for PC postage customers. The company markets its PC postage service via Web partner channels, retail partner channels and direct mail among others. Currently, the company partners with auctionwatch, compusa, earthlink, hp, microsoft, ncr, office depot and the U.S. Postal service. The customers of the company include, home businesses, small businesses, corporations, shippers and individuals. The group operates from United States.

Primary SIC and add'l.: 7389

CIK No: 0001082923

Officers: Ken McBride/Dir., CEO, Pres./$541,067.00, Seth Weisberg/VP, General Counsel, Sec., Michael Biswas/VP - Information Technology, James A. Harper/37/VP - Finance, Chief Accounting Officer, Corporate Controller/$529,443.00, Kyle Huebner/CFO/$332,733.00, James M. Bortnak/VP - Sales, Marketing/$322,070.00, Jp Leon/VP - Postal Affairs, Technology, Mike Boswell/VP - Postal Affairs, John Clem/VP - Product, Service Operations/$515,217.00

Directors: Ken McBride/Dir., CEO, Pres., Mohan P. Ananda/Dir., Kevin Douglas/Dir., Bradford G. Jones/Dir., Lloyd I. Miller/Dir.

Owners: Kevin Douglas/7.86%, Barclays Global Investors/5.59%, Passport Capital, LLC/8.53%, Bradford G. Jones, Jamie Harper, Insiders/20.64%, Fidelity Management & Research Company/10.65%, James Bortnak, Mohan Ananda/3.18%, John Clem, Kyle Huebner, Ken McBride/1.76%, Waddell & Reed Investment Management Co./6.31%, Munder Capital Mangement/World Asset Mang/5.92%, Lloyd Miller/6.17%

Financial Data: Fiscal Year End: 12/31 **Latest Annual Data:** 12/31/2006

Year	Sales	Net Income
2006	$84,586,000	$16,462,000
2005	$61,911,000	$10,429,000
2004	$38,112,000	-$4,733,000

Curr. Assets:	$38,739,000	Curr. Liab.:	$11,015,000	P/E Ratio:	20.30
Plant, Equip.:	$5,084,000	Total Liab.:	$11,015,000	Indic. Yr. Divd.:	NA
Total Assets:	$121,550,000	Net Worth:	$110,535,000	Debt/ Equity:	NA

Stanadyne Corp

92 Deerfield Rd. , Windsor, CT, 06095; **PH:** 1-860-525-0821; **http://** www.stanadyne.com;
Email: stanadyne@stanadyne.com

General - Incorporation	DE
Employees	NA
Auditor	Deloitte & Touche LLP
Stk Agt	NA
Counsel	NA
DUNS No.	NA

Stock - Price on:12/24/2007	NA
Stock Exchange	NA
Ticker Symbol	NA
Outstanding Shares	NA
E.P.S.	NA
Shareholders	NA

Business: The group's principle activities include designing and manufacturing highly engineered, precision manufactured engine components, including fuel injection equipment for diesel engines and hydraulic lash compensating devices for gasoline engines. The group operates from United States.

Primary SIC and add'l.: 3714

CIK No: 0001053439

Subsidiaries: Precision Engine Products Corp, Precision Engine Products LTDA, Stanadyne Amalgamations Private Limited, Stanadyne, SpA, a S.p.A.

Officers: David M. Jones/60/Dir., CEO, Pres., Stephen S. Langin/49/VP, CFO, Sec., William W. Kelly/56/CTO, Sr. VP, Jean S. McCarthy/60/VP - Human Resources, John J. Lyons/50/Executive Dir. - Operations, Joseph M. Vorih/40/VP - International, Shawn F. Sullivan/50/VP - Fluid Management Technologies

Directors: David M. Jones/60/Dir., CEO, Pres., James D. Wiggins/60/Chmn., Gordon H. Woodward/39/Dir., Seth H. Hollander/31/Dir., Samuel P. Frieder/43/Dir., Christopher Lacovara/43/Dir., James A. Wier/64/Dir.

Owners: James D. Wiggins/1.60%, Shawn F. Sullivan, Stephen S. Langin, Co-Investment Partners, L.P./18.90%, William K. Kelly/1.10%, William D. Gurley/1.00%, Kohlberg Funds/56.60%, Jean S. McCarthy, David M. Jones/1.60%, Insiders/6.10%, James A. Wier

Stancorp Financial Group Inc

1100 S W Sixth Ave., Portland, OR, 97204; **PH:** 1-971-321-6127; **http://** www.stancorpfinancial.com

General - Incorporation	OR
Employees	3,280
Auditor	Deloitte & Touche LLP
Stk Agt	Mellon Investor Services LLC
Counsel	NA
DUNS No.	NA

Stock - Price on:12/24/2007	$52.89
Stock Exchange	NYSE
Ticker Symbol	SFG
Outstanding Shares	53,410,000
E.P.S.	$4.39
Shareholders	NA

Business: The group's principle activities are underwriting of group and individual disability, life and annuity products and dental insurance. The group's subsidiaries provide complementary financial and management services. The operations of the group are divided into three segments: employee benefits insurance, retirement plans and individual insurance. The employee benefit insurance markets accidental death and dismemberment and dental insurance. The retirement plans segment offers full service and other pension plan products and services to private and public employers. The individual insurance segment markets disability insurance and annuities to individuals. The group's quarterly revenue for Sep '07 was 683.30 millions of USD.

Primary SIC and add'l.: 6311 6321

CIK No: 0001079577

Subsidiaries: StanCorp Equities, Inc, StanCorp Investment Advisers, Inc., StanCorp Mortgage Investors, LLC, Standard Insurance Company, The Standard Life Insurance Company

Officers: Eric E. Parsons/Chmn., CEO, Pres./$3,821,201.00, Cindy J. McPike/CFO, Sr. VP/$1,223,354.00, Michael T. Winslow/Sr. VP, General Counsel/$1,009,894.00, Kim W. Ledbetter/Sr. VP - Asset Management Group/$1,607,523.00, Greg J. Ness/Sr. VP - Insurance Services Group/$1,735,562.00, David O'Brien/Sr. VP - Information Technology Standard Insurance Company, William W. Pfeiffer/Sr. VP - Human Resources Standard Insurance Company, Robert M. Erickson/Assist. VP, Controller, Jeffrey J. Hallin/Second VP Investor Relations, Financial Planning, Holley Y. Franklin/Second VP, Corp. Sec., Assist. Counsel

Directors: Eric E. Parsons/Chmn., CEO, Pres., Wanda G. Henton/Dir., Virginia L. Anderson/Dir., Michael G. Thorne/Dir., Peter O. Kohler/Dir., Frederick W. Buckman/Dir., John E. Chapoton/Dir., Ronald E. Timpe/Dir., Jerome J. Meyer/Dir., Stanley R. Fallis/Dir., Ralph R. Peterson/Dir., Kay E. Stepp/Dir.

Owners: Kim W. Ledbetter, Jerome J. Meyer, Michael G. Thorne, Frederick W. Buckman, Gregory J. Ness, Peter O. Kohler, Eric E. Parsons, John E. Chapoton, Wanda G. Henton, Michael T. Winslow, Insiders/2.80%, Virginia L. Anderson, Stanley R. Fallis, Ronald E. Timpe, Ralph R. Peterson (18 Owners included in Index)

Financial Data: Fiscal Year End: 12/31 **Latest Annual Data:** 12/31/2006

Year	Sales	Net Income
2006	$2,492,900,000	$203,800,000
2005	$2,337,200,000	$211,100,000
2004	$2,149,700,000	$199,400,000

Curr. Assets:	$1,068,800,000	Curr. Liab.:	$2,400,000	P/E Ratio:	12.84
Plant, Equip.:	$84,600,000	Total Liab.:	$12,174,100,000	Indic. Yr. Divd.:	$0.720
Total Assets:	$13,638,600,000	Net Worth:	$1,464,500,000	Debt/ Equity:	0.1782

Standard Energy Corp

447 Bearcat Dr., Sallake, UT, 84115; **PH:** 1-801-364-9000

General - Incorporation	UT
Employees	2
Auditor	HJ & Assoc. LLC
Stk Agt	American Stock Transfer & Trust Co.
Counsel	NA
DUNS No.	09-881-4312

Stock - Price on:12/24/2007	$0.055
Stock Exchange	OTC
Ticker Symbol	STDE
Outstanding Shares	187,540,000
E.P.S.	-$0.001
Shareholders	NA

Business: The group's principal activity is to acquire unproven oil and gas leaseholds and resell the same to third parties. The group has acquired federal oil and gas leaseholds through the bureau of land management's leasing program. It also obtains leases through purchases in competitive bidding programs offered by various state agencies, principally the states of Utah and Wyoming. The group operates through its three segments: oil and gas information services, oil and gas leasehold interests and oil and gas leases royalties. The group provides a variety of geologic lease evaluation services through its wholly owned subsidiary, petroleum investment company. The group has operations in the United States of America.

Primary SIC and add'l.: 9999 1389 6792

CIK No: 0000205921

Subsidiaries: Petroleum Investment Company

Owners: Insiders/72.00%, Pamela K. Nelson/7.00%, Michael M. Cannon, Dean W. Rowell/65.00%

Financial Data: *Fiscal Year End:*03/31 *Latest Annual Data:* 03/31/2007

Year	Sales	Net Income
2007	$68,000	-$100,000
2006	$98,000	-$25,000
2005	$76,000	-$57,000

Curr. Assets:	$224,000	Curr. Liab.:	$127,000		
Plant, Equip.:	$61,000	Total Liab.:	$128,000	Indic. Yr. Divd.:	NA
Total Assets:	$375,000	Net Worth:	$247,000	Debt/ Equity:	NA

Standard Mgmt Corp

10689 N Pennsylvania St., Indianapolis, IN, 46280; *PH:* 1-317-574-6200; *Fax:* 1-317-574-6227; *http://* www.smancorp.com; *Email:* hr@sman.com

General		Stock	
Incorporation	IN	Price on:12/24/2007	$0.13
Employees	48	Stock Exchange	OTC
Auditor	BDO Seidman, LLP	Ticker Symbol	SMAN
Stk Agt	Mellon Investor Services LLC	Outstanding Shares	38,020,000
Counsel	NA	E.P.S	-$0.406
DUNS No.	61-030-8256	Shareholders	NA

Business: The group's principal activities are to develop, market, administer annuity and life insurance products and distribute pharmacy goods and services. The products are distributed through its subsidiaries: standard life insurance company of Indiana, dixie national life insurance company, savers marketing corporation and u s health services corporation. The products include deferred annuities, equity-indexed annuities, single premium immediate annuities and traditional, universal and interest-sensitive life insurance policies. The group's products are sold primarily in the United States.

Primary SIC and add'l.: 6311

CIK No: 0000853971

Subsidiaries: Apothecary Solutions Corporation, HomeDoc Corporation ., HomeMed Channel, Inc., Long Term Rx, Inc, PCA, LLC, Precision Healthcare, Inc., Premier Life (Bermuda) Limited ., Rainier Home Health Care Pharmacy, Inc., Standard Development LLC, Standard Management Financial Corporation ., Standard Management LLCCapital Trust ., Standard Marketing Corporation ., U.S. Health Services Corporation

Officers: Ronald D. Hunter/Chmn., CEO, Pres./$667,232.00, Martial Knieser/Exec. VP - Corporate Development/$351,996.00, Mark B.L. Long/Exec. VP - National Operations/$251,874.00, Daniel K. Calvert/Exec. VP, Chief Accounting Officer/$23,269.00, Brett A. Flora/Dir. - Information Technology

Directors: Ronald D. Hunter/Chmn., CEO, Pres., James H. Steane/Dir., Dan B. French/Dir., Sam Schmidt/43/Dir., Dennis F. King/61/Dir.

Owners: Sam Schmidt/46.40%, Ronald D. Hunter/10.05%, Martial R. Knieser/6.80%, Stephen M. Coons, Dainforth B. French, James H. Steane, Mark B.L. Long/2.45%, Insiders/53.37%

Financial Data: *Fiscal Year End:*12/31 *Latest Annual Data:* 12/31/2006

Year	Sales	Net Income
2006	$9,029,000	-$19,421,000
2005	$28,922,000	-$54,264,000
2004	$118,291,000	-$10,868,000

Curr. Assets:	$3,802,000	Curr. Liab.:	$9,598,000		
Plant, Equip.:	$8,968,000	Total Liab.:	$33,564,000	Indic. Yr. Divd.:	NA
Total Assets:	$18,493,000	Net Worth:	-$15,071,000	Debt/ Equity:	6.6438

Standard Microsystems Corp

80 Arkay Dr., Hauppauge, NY, 11788; *PH:* 1-631-435-6000; *http://* www.smsc.com

General		Stock	
Incorporation	DE	Price on:12/24/2007	$32.86
Employees	856	Stock Exchange	NDQ
Auditor	PricewaterhouseCoopers LLP	Ticker Symbol	SMSC
Stk Agt	American Stock Transfer & Trust Co.	Outstanding Shares	22,870,000
Counsel	Cleary Gottlieb Steen & Hamilton	E.P.S	$0.92
DUNS No.	18-501-0972	Shareholders	NA

Business: The group's principal activity is to design, develop and market semiconductor integrated circuits for the personal computer peripheral and embedded system markets. The group's products provide solutions in advanced input/output (i/o) technology, environmental monitoring and control, usb (universal serial bus) connectivity, networking and embedded control systems. Advanced i/o circuits contain individual functions and i/o controllers delivered in a single package. The group also serves the usb connectivity market with connectivity products, which provide solutions using both usb 1.1 and usb 2.0 technologies. Embedded networking products are designed to serve machine-to-machine communication applications, such as set-top boxes, home gateway products, printers and wireless communication interfaces. The group has operations in North America, Taiwan, Europe and Japan.

Primary SIC and add'l.: 3674 3577

CIK No: 0000093384

Subsidiaries: OASIS SiliconSystems AG, SiliconSystems Multimedia Engineering Gmbh, SMSC Analog Technology Center, Inc., SMSC Europe GmbH, SMSC North America, Inc., SMSC Sweden AB, Standard Microsystems Corporation, Standard Microsystems K.K.

Officers: Steven J. Bilodeau/Chmn., CEO, Pres./$3,039,918.00, Peter S. Byrnes/VP/$749,059.00, Robert E. Hollingsworth/Sr. VP, Walter Siegel/VP, General Counsel/$741,554.00, David S. Smith/Sr. VP, CFO/$1,152,545.00, Mitchell A. Statham/VP/$738,656.00, Yasuo Suzuki/Pres. - Smsc Japan, Joseph Durko/VP, Controller, Chief Accounting Officer/$487,683.00, Johnson Tan/VP/$763,644.00, Christian Thiel/VP, George W. Houseweart/Sr. VP, Aaron L. Fisher/Sr. VP - Products, Technology, Douglas Smith/CTO, VP

Directors: Steven J. Bilodeau/Chmn., CEO, Pres., Timothy P. Craig/Dir., Peter F. Dicks/Corp. Dir., Andrew M. Caggia/Dir., Ivan T. Frisch/Dir., James A. Donahue/Dir.

Owners: Peter F. Dicks, Steven J. Bilodeau, Johnson Tan, Barclays Global Investors, NA/4.95%, James A. Donahue, Peter S. Byrnes, Clear Bridge Advisors/8.26%, Timothy P. Craig, Joseph Durko, Mitchell Statham, Andrew M. Caggia, Dimensional FundAdvisors, Inc./5.52%, David S. Smith, Insiders/2.35%, Ivan T. Frisch *(16 Owners included in Index)*

Financial Data: *Fiscal Year End:*02/28 *Latest Annual Data:* 2/28/2007

Year	Sales	Net Income
2007	$370,594,000	$27,015,000
2006	$319,118,000	$12,030,000
2005	$208,815,000	$1,602,000

Curr. Assets:	$279,621,000	Curr. Liab.:	$67,395,000	P/E Ratio:	35.72
Plant, Equip.:	$58,020,000	Total Liab.:	$94,345,000	Indic. Yr. Divd.:	NA
Total Assets:	$486,287,000	Net Worth:	$391,942,000	Debt/ Equity:	0.0089

Standard Motor Products Inc

37 18 Nern Blvd, Long Island City, NY, 11101; *PH:* 1-718-392-0200; *http://* www.smpcorp.com

General		Stock	
Incorporation	NY	Price on:12/24/2007	$14.66
Employees	4,000	Stock Exchange	NYSE
Auditor	Grant Thornton LLP	Ticker Symbol	SMP
Stk Agt	Bank of America	Outstanding Shares	18,880,000
Counsel	NA	E.P.S	$0.56
DUNS No.	00-131-5266	Shareholders	NA

Business: The group's principal activity is to manufacture and distribute replaced parts of motor vehicles. The group operates in two divisions: the engine management and the temperature control. The engine management division consists primarily of ignition and emission parts, on-board computers, ignition wires, battery cables and fuel system parts. The temperature control division consists primarily of air conditioning compressors, other air conditioning parts and heater parts. The group's customers include carquest and napa auto parts, advance auto parts, autozone and o'reilly automotive. On 03-Feb-2004, the group acquired dana corporation's Canadian engine management business.

Primary SIC and add'l.: 3694 3714 5013

CIK No: 0000093389

Subsidiaries: Eaglemotive Corporation, Four Seasons Europe S.A.R.L., Four Seasons Italy S.R.L., Industrial & Automotive Associates, Inc., Mardevco Credit Corp. (2), Motortronics, Inc., S. De R.L. De C. V. , SMP Motor Products Limited, SMP Real Estate LLC, Standard Motor Products (Hong Kong) Limited, Standard Motor Products de Mexico, Standard Motor Products Holdings Limited, Stanric, Inc. (1)

Officers: Robert Kimbro/53/VP - Distribution Sales, Ray Nicholas/44/VP - Information Technology, Eric Sills/39/VP - Engine Management Division, Thomas S. Tesoro/53/VP - Human Resources

Directors: Roger M. Widmann/68/Dir.

Owners: Robert M . Gerrity, Susan F . Davis/5.00%, GAMCO Investors, Inc/10.90%, Roger M . Widmann, Carmine J . Broccole, Richard S . Ward, Lawrence I . Sills/5.70%, Insiders/17.80%, Arthur D . Davis/6.30%, William H . Turner, Dimensional Fund Advisors Inc/8.40%, Frederick D . Sturdivant, Arthur S . Sills/8.70%, Dale Burks, John P . Gethin *(19 Owners included in Index)*

Financial Data: *Fiscal Year End:*12/31 *Latest Annual Data:* 12/31/2006

Year	Sales	Net Income
2006	$812,024,000	$9,411,000
2005	$830,413,000	-$3,545,000
2004	$824,283,000	-$14,380,000

Curr. Assets:	$461,838,000	Curr. Liab.:	$278,525,000	P/E Ratio:	26.18
Plant, Equip.:	$80,091,000	Total Liab.:	$449,393,000	Indic. Yr. Divd.:	$0.360
Total Assets:	$640,092,000	Net Worth:	$190,699,000	Debt/ Equity:	0.5046

Standard Pacific Corp

15326 Alton Pkwy, Irvine, CA, 92618; *PH:* 1-949-789-1600; *http://* www.standardpacifichomes.com

General		Stock	
Incorporation	DE	Price on:12/24/2007	$18.65
Employees	2,580	Stock Exchange	NYSE
Auditor	Ernst & Young LLP	Ticker Symbol	SPF
Stk Agt	Mellon Investor Services LLC	Outstanding Shares	64,740,000
Counsel	NA	E.P.S	-$6.57
DUNS No.	00-838-8373	Shareholders	NA

Business: The group's principle activity is to construct homes within wide range of prices and sizes. The group also provides mortgage financing and title services to homebuyers. The group operates from United States.

Primary SIC and add'l.: 1521 6162 6159

CIK No: 0000878560

Subsidiaries: CH Construction, Inc., CH Florida, Inc., Family Lending Services, Inc., Hilltop Residential, Ltd., HSP Arizona, Inc., HSP Tucson, Inc., HWB Construction, Inc., HWB Investments, Inc., LB/L-Duc II Franceschi, LLC, LMD El Dorado 134, LLC, LMD Rocklin 89, LLC, OLP Forty Development, LLC, Pala Village Investments, Inc., Residential Acquisition GP, LLC, S.P.S. Affiliates, Inc. 74 Subsidiaries included in the Index

Officers: Stephen J. Scarborough/Chmn., CEO, Pres. - Standard Pacific Corp/$8,445,189.00, Keith D. Wood/Pres. - Raleigh, North Carolina, Edward T. McKibbin/Pres. - Southern California, Orange County, Michael J. White/Mgr. - Southern California, Inland North, Thomas C. Burrill/Pres. - Northern California, East Bay, Michael J. Lilly/Pres. - Sarasota, Florida, Craig Campbell/Pres. - Tucson, Arizona, Andrew H. Parnes/CFO, Exec. VP - Finance/$2,647,266.00, Steven G. Delva/Pres. - Northern California, South Bay, Bruce F. Dickson/Pres. - Southeast Region/$2,571,230.00, Jari L. Kartozian/Sr. VP, Michael C. Cortney/60/Dir., Pres./$5,555,096.00, August Belmont/Pres. - Southern California, Inland Empire, David Pelletz/Pres. - Tampa Bay, Florida, John P. Moroney/Pres. - Phoenix, Arizona *(32 Officers included in Index)*

Directors: Stephen J. Scarborough/Chmn., CEO, Pres. - Standard Pacific Corp, Douglas C. Jacobs/Dir., James L. Doti/Dir., Patt F. Schiewitz/Dir., Larry D. McNabb/Dir., Jeffrey V. Peterson/Dir., Ronald R. Foell/Dir., Michael C. Cortney/60/Dir., Pres., Bruce A. Choate/Dir., Wayne J. Merck/Dir.

Owners: Insiders/6.72%, Michael C. Cortney/1.36%, Ronald R. Foell, Legg Mason Capital Management, Inc./9.18%, Scott D. Stowell, Bruce F. Dickson, Earnest Partners, LLC/9.38%, Douglas C. Jacobs, Andrew H. Parnes, Wayne J. Merck, Tremblant Capital Group/5.43%, The Goldman Sachs Group, Inc./6.21%, James L. Doti, Patt F. Schiewitz, Stephen J. Scarborough/3.03% *(19 Owners included in Index)*

Financial Data: *Fiscal Year End:*12/31 *Latest Annual Data:* 12/31/2006

Year		Sales		Net Income	
2006		$3,963,987,000		$123,693,000	
2005		$4,011,361,000		$440,984,000	
2004		$3,354,454,000		$315,817,000	
Curr. Assets:	$3,581,813,000	**Curr. Liab.:**	$447,251,000		
Plant, Equip.:	NA	**Total Liab.:**	$2,738,571,000	**Indic. Yr. Divd.:**	$0.160
Total Assets:	$4,502,941,000	**Net Worth:**	$1,764,370,000	**Debt/ Equity:**	1.1993

Standard Parking Corp

900 N Michigan Ave., Ste. 1600, Chicago, IL, 60611; ***PH:*** 1-312-274-2000; ***http://*** www.standardparking.com

General - Incorporation	DE	**Stock**- Price on:12/24/2007	$33.14
Employees	6,800	Stock Exchange	NDQ
Auditor	Ernst & Young LLP	Ticker Symbol	STAN
Stk Agt	Wells Fargo Shareowner Services	Outstanding Shares	9,530,000
Counsel	NA	E.P.S	$3.61
DUNS No.	NA	Shareholders	NA

Business: The group's principal activity is to provide parking facilities management services in urban markets and at airports. It provides on-site management services at multi-level and surface parking facilities for all major markets of the parking industry. The group operates its clients' parking properties through two types of arrangements: management contracts and leases. As of Mar 31, 2004, it operated 84% of its locations under management contracts and 16% under leases. The group manages parking facilities in over 275 cities across 42 states and the district of columbia in the United States and three provinces in Canada. It became publicly held on 27-May-2004.

Primary SIC and add'l.: 7510

CIK No: 0001059262

Officers: James A. Wilhelm/Dir., CEO, Pres./$952,727.00, Michael E. Swartz/Sr. VP, John Ricchiuto/Exec. VP - Operations, Daniel R. Meyer/Sr. VP, Michael K. Wolf/Exec. VP, Chief Administrative Officer, Assoc. General Counsel/$549,816.00, Thomas L. Hagerman/Exec. VP - Operations, Edward E. Simmons/Exec. VP - Operations, Robert N. Sacks/Exec. VP, General Counsel, Sec., Steven A. Warshauer/Exec. VP - Operations/$501,471.00, Marc G. Baumann/CFO, Exec. VP/$590,116.00

Directors: James A. Wilhelm/Dir., CEO, Pres., Myron C. Warshauer/Vice Chmn. Emeritus, John V. Holten/Chmn., Robert S. Roath/Dir., Gunnar E. Klintberg/Dir., Leif F. Onarheim/Dir., Karen M. Garrison/Dir., Charles L. Biggs/Dir., Petter A. Ostberg/Dir.

Owners: Petter A. stberg, Gunnar E. Klintberg, Charles L. Biggs, Michael K. Wolf, Karen M. Garrison, Insiders, Marc G. Baumann, Steven A. Warshauer, John V. Holten, Leif F. Onarheim, John V. Holten and The JVH Descendants' 2007 Trust, Pequot Capital Management Inc., Robert S. Roath, James A. Wilhelm

Financial Data: ***Fiscal Year End:***12/31 ***Latest Annual Data:*** 12/31/2006

Year		Sales		Net Income	
2006		$605,945,000		$35,751,000	
2005		$586,654,000		$14,719,000	
2004		$563,635,000		$10,421,000	
Curr. Assets:	$58,572,000	**Curr. Liab.:**	$65,020,000	**P/E Ratio:**	9.34
Plant, Equip.:	$16,902,000	**Total Liab.:**	$171,275,000	**Indic. Yr. Divd.:**	NA
Total Assets:	$212,528,000	**Net Worth:**	$41,253,000	**Debt/ Equity:**	1.9112

Standard Register Co

600 Albany St., Dayton, OH, 45408; ***PH:*** 1-937-221-1000; ***Fax:*** 1-937-221-1855; ***http://*** www.standardregister.com

General - Incorporation	OH	**Stock**- Price on:12/24/2007	$11.8
Employees	3,760	Stock Exchange	NYSE
Auditor	Battelle & Battelle LLP	Ticker Symbol	SR
Stk Agt	Bank of New York	Outstanding Shares	28,690,000
Counsel	Kathryn A. Lamme	E.P.S	-$0.36
DUNS No.	00-427-7893	Shareholders	NA

Business: The group's principal activity is to design, manufacture and sell business forms. It operates through three business segments: document and label solutions provides custom printed documents, integrated systems, business supplies, equipment services, and distribution services that help its customers manage their business information and transact with their customers and suppliers. Fulfillment services provide information and marketing materials that are customized to each of their customers. Products are monthly billing statements, customized marketing brochures and information kits, or one-to-one marketing communications. Insystems provides of e-business solutions for financial services that enable companies to improve processes and organize, manage and distribute information in both paper and digital infrastructures.

Primary SIC and add'l.: 7372 2759 2761 3579 7371

CIK No: 0000093456

Subsidiaries: Stellent AB, Stellent Asia Pty. Limited, Stellent B.V., Stellent Canada Ltd, Stellent Chicago Sales, Inc, Stellent Chicago, Inc, Stellent Colorado Springs, Inc, Stellent GmbH, Stellent Holding B.V. Company, Stellent Information Systems Company Limited, Stellent Japan K.K, Stellent Limited, Stellent S.A.R.L, Stellent Sales, Inc, Stellent, S.A. De C.V.

Officers: Dennis L. Rediker/Dir., CEO, Pres./$1,349,091.00, Donna L. Beladi/58/VP, Chief Strategy Officer, Craig J. Brown/CFO, Sr. VP, Treasurer/$656,535.00, Kathryn A. Lamme/Sr. VP, General Counsel, Sec./$750,571.00, Joe Morgan/CTO, VP, GM - On Demand Solutions, Tom Furey/Chief Supply Chain Officer, VP, GM - Document, Label Solutions/$360,730.00, Robert J. Cestelli/VP - Investor Relations, Joseph P. Morgan/48/CTO, VP/$479,249.00, Brad Cates/VP - Sales, Marketing, Lesley Sprigg/Dir. - Corporate Communications, Ball Rick/Dir. - Procurement, Cole Tracy/VP - Client Care, Klenke L. Joseph/VP, GM - POD Services, Jeffrey M. Strasser/VP, GM - Pathforward

Directors: Dennis L. Rediker/Dir., CEO, Pres., David F. Clarke/Chmn., John Q. Sherman/Dir., John J. Schiff/Dir., Roy W. Begley/Dir., Ann Scavullo/Dir., Sherrill W. Hudson/Dir.

Owners: Roy W. Begley, The Fifth Third Bank ,/10.61%, Mary C. Nushawg/4.05%, Mary C. Nushawg, The Fifth Third Bank/1.80%, James L. Sherman, The Fifth Third Bank ,, The Fifth Third Bank ,, The Fifth Third Bank ,/10.71%, Roy W. Begley/23.97%, Patricia L. Begley, James L. Sherman/4.32%, Patricia L. Begley/3.99%

Financial Data: ***Fiscal Year End:***01/01 ***Latest Annual Data:*** 12/31/2006

Year	Sales	Net Income
2006	$894,904,000	-$11,661,000
2005	$890,249,000	-$30,218,000

Curr. Assets:	$217,770,000	**Curr. Liab.:**	$101,314,000		
Plant, Equip.:	$119,339,000	**Total Liab.:**	$333,912,000	**Indic. Yr. Divd.:**	$0.920
Total Assets:	$452,079,000	**Net Worth:**	$118,167,000	**Debt/ Equity:**	0.3471

Standex International Corp

6 Manor Pkwy, Salem, NH, 03079; ***PH:*** 1-603-893-9701; ***http://*** www.standex.com

General - Incorporation	DE	**Stock**- Price on:12/24/2007	$29.67
Employees	5,200	Stock Exchange	NYSE
Auditor	Deloitte & Touche LLP	Ticker Symbol	SXI
Stk Agt	Computershare Trust Co	Outstanding Shares	12,430,000
Counsel	Hale & Dorr LLP	E.P.S	$1.21
DUNS No.	00-103-2002	Shareholders	NA

Business: The group's principal activity is to manufacture and market equipment used in industries and by consumers in the United States and Europe. The group's activities are divided into three segments: industrial segment, food service and consumer products. The industrial segment provides original equipment to manufacturers. It produces specialized components that make the products more appealing, useful and competitive. The food service segment develops systems for the preparation, storage and presentation of food for the way it is marketed. The consumer products segment conducts markets publishing, direct marketing and home construction products. On 17-Dec-2003, the group acquired nor-lake incorporated.

Primary SIC and add'l.: 3569 2796 3579 3585 2761 2721 3589

CIK No: 0000310354

Subsidiaries: ATC-Frost Magnetics, Inc., Custom Hoists, Inc., Nor-Lake, Incorporated, Roehlen Industries Pty. Limited, S. I. de Mexico S.A. de C.V., Snappy Air Distribution Products, Inc., Standex Air Distribution Products, Inc., Standex Electronics (U.K.) Limited, Standex Electronics, Inc., Standex Engraving LLC, Standex Financial Corp., Standex Holdings Limited, Standex International GmbH, Standex International Limited, SXI Limited

Officers: Roger L. Fix/Dir., CEO, Pres./$1,595,188.00, Christian Storch/Dir., VP, CFO, Treasurer/$662,188.00, Deborah A. Rosen/Dir., VP, Chief Legal Officer, Sec./$507,799.00, Timothy S. O'Neil/Treasurer, Chief Accounting Officer, John Abbott/Group VP - Food Service Group/$306,348.00

Directors: Roger L. Fix/Dir., CEO, Pres., Thomas L. King/Vice Chmn., Edward J. Trainor/Chmn., Daniel B. Hogan/Dir., Deborah A. Rosen/Dir., VP, Chief Legal Officer, Sec., Walter F. Greeley/Dir., Christian Storch/Dir., VP, CFO, Treasurer, Gerald H. Fickenscher/Dir., Charles H. Cannon/Dir., Thomas E. Chorman/Dir., William R. Fenoglio/Dir.

Owners: Thomas E. Chorman, Gerald H. Fickenscher, Charles F. Cannon, Roger L. Fix/1.00%, Christian Storch, Walter F. Greeley, Duane L. Stockburger, Thomas L. King, Royce & Associates LLC/6.05%, Nicholas H. Muller, Insiders/2.50%, Fidelity Management Trust Company/4.67%, Daniel B. Hogan, Edward J. Trainor, Deborah A. Rosen *(18 Owners included in Index)*

Financial Data: ***Fiscal Year End:***06/30 ***Latest Annual Data:*** 6/30/2006

Year		Sales		Net Income	
2006		$589,938,000		$23,143,000	
2005		$666,240,000		$23,643,000	
2004		$577,450,000		$10,605,000	
Curr. Assets:	$243,049,000	**Curr. Liab.:**	$115,810,000	**P/E Ratio:**	14.69
Plant, Equip.:	$97,072,000	**Total Liab.:**	$278,378,000	**Indic. Yr. Divd.:**	$0.840
Total Assets:	$478,673,000	**Net Worth:**	$200,295,000	**Debt/ Equity:**	0.7652

Stanley Furniture Co Inc

1641 Fairystone Pk. Hwy., Stanleytown, VA, 24168; ***PH:*** 1-276-627-2000; ***Fax:*** 1-276-629-5114; ***http://*** www.stanleyfurniture.com; ***Email:*** investor@stanleyfurniture.com

General - Incorporation	DE	**Stock**- Price on:12/24/2007	$21.49
Employees	2,200	Stock Exchange	NDQ
Auditor	PricewaterhouseCoopers LLP	Ticker Symbol	STLY
Stk Agt	Continental Stock Transfer & Trust Co	Outstanding Shares	10,590,000
Counsel	McGuire-Woods	E.P.S	$1.13
DUNS No.	09-743-0417	Shareholders	NA

Business: The group's principle activity is to design and manufacture residential wood furniture. The group's product lines include dining room, bedroom, youth bedroom (young America(r)), home entertainment, accent tables and home office furniture. These products cover design categories such as European traditional, contemporary or transitional, American traditional and country or casual designs. The group distributes its products through approximately 60 independent sales representatives to independent furniture retailers, department stores and regional furniture chains. Customers include breuners home furnishings, furnitureland south, jordan's, Nebraska furniture mart, raymour & flanigan, robb & stucky and rooms to go kids.The group's quarterly revenue for Sep '07 was 73.18 millions of USD.

Primary SIC and add'l.: 2511

CIK No: 0000797465

Subsidiaries: Stellent AB, Stellent Asia Pty. Limited, Stellent B.V., Stellent Canada Ltd, Stellent Chicago Sales, Inc, Stellent Chicago, Inc, Stellent Holding B.V. Company

Officers: Jeffrey R. Scheffer/52/Chmn., CEO, Pres./$468,926.00, Douglas I. Payne/Contact/$320,693.00, Glenn R. Prillaman/36/Sr. VP - Marketing, Sales/$205,996.00, Ricky D. Lovorn/51/Sr. VP - Manufacturing/$259,568.00, Dennis K. Taggart/50/VP - Human Resources/$164,108.00

Directors: Jeffrey R. Scheffer/52/Chmn., CEO, Pres., Thomas L. Millner/54/Dir., Michael P. Haley/57/Dir., Albert L. Prillaman/62/Dir., Robert G. Culp/61/Dir., Scott T. McIlhenny/60/Dir.

Owners: Ricky D. Lovorn, T. Rowe Price Associates, Inc./14.80%, Douglas I. Payne/2.10%, Thomas L. Millner, Michael P. Haley, Robert G. Culp, Glenn R. Prillaman/1.20%, FMR Corp./12.30%, Royce& Associates, LLC/14.10%, Third Avenue Management LLC/10.90%, Insiders/8.40%, Philip D. Haney, Wellington Management Company, LLP/8.50%, Muhlenkamp& Company, Inc./7.90%, Albert L. Prillaman/2.60% *(18 Owners included in Index)*

Financial Data: ***Fiscal Year End:***12/31 ***Latest Annual Data:*** 12/31/2006

Year		Sales		Net Income	
2006		$307,547,000		$16,781,000	
2005		$333,646,000		$23,231,000	
2004		$305,815,000		$20,789,000	
Curr. Assets:	$103,906,000	**Curr. Liab.:**	$31,870,000	**P/E Ratio:**	19.02
Plant, Equip.:	$49,159,000	**Total Liab.:**	$53,031,000	**Indic. Yr. Divd.:**	$0.400
Total Assets:	$162,678,000	**Net Worth:**	$109,647,000	**Debt/ Equity:**	0.0553

Stanley Inc

3101 Wilson Blvd., Ste. 700, Arlington, VA, 22201; *PH:* 1-703-684-1125; *Fax:* 1-703-683-0039; *http://* www.stanleyassociates.com; *Email:* businessintel@stanleyassociates.com

General - Incorporation	DE	**Stock**- Price on:12/24/2007	$19.06
Employees	2,700	Stock Exchange	NYSE
Auditor	Deloitte & Touche LLP	Ticker Symbol	SXE
Stk Agt	Computershare Investor Services LLC	Outstanding Shares	22,090,000
Counsel	NA	E.P.S.	NA
DUNS No.	NA	Shareholders	NA

Business: The groups principle activity is to provide information technology services and solutions. In the year 2006, the group acquired Morgan Research Corporation. The group operates from the United States. The group's quarterly revenue for September 2007 was 150.24 millions of USD.

Primary SIC and add'l.: 7371 7373 7389 8748 7376 7379 5045 8742 8999

CIK No: 0001360555

Subsidiaries: Fuentez Systems Concepts, Inc., Morgan Research Corporation, Stanley Associates, Inc.

Officers: Phil Nolan/Chmn., CEO, Pres., George Wilson/Dir., Exec. VP, Greg Denkler/Sr. VP, Chris Torti/Sr. VP, Mike Zaramba/Sr. VP, Mike Flint/VP, Tom Fradette/VP, Bill Karlson/Dir., Sr. VP, Mike Kaszubinski/VP, Al Killen/VP, John Robbins/VP, Ralph Sebacher/VP, Chris Smith/VP, Bill Gerhart/VP, Scott Hill/VP *(31 Officers included in Index)*

Directors: Phil Nolan/Chmn., CEO, Pres., George Wilson/Dir., Exec. VP, Bill Karlson/Dir., Sr. VP, Lawrence A. Gallagher/Dir., James C. Hughes/Dir., Richard L. Kelly/Dir., Charles S. Ream/Dir., John P. Riceman/Dir., Jimmy D. Ross/Dir., William E. Karlson/48/Sr. VP - Outsourcing Solutions Division, Dir.

Owners: Christopher J. Torti/2.03%, Jimmy D. Ross, James C. Hughes, Gregory M. Denkler/2.43%, Brian J. Clark, George H. Wilson/3.98%, United States Trust Company/28.17%, The PNC Financial Service Group,Inc/5.95%, John P. Riceman, Insiders/30.96%, Charles S. Ream, William E. Karlson/6.67%, Philip O. Nolan/10.75%, Lawrence A. Gallagher/3.47%

Curr. Assets:	$124,396,000	**Curr. Liab.:**	$63,477,000	**P/E Ratio:**	24.61
Plant, Equip.:	$11,736,000	**Total Liab.:**	$103,823,000	**Indic. Yr. Divd.:**	NA
Total Assets:	$237,975,000	**Net Worth:**	$134,152,000	**Debt/ Equity:**	NA

Stanley Works

1000 Stanley Dr., New Britain, CT, 06053; *PH:* 1-860-225-5111; *Fax:* 1-860-827-3895; *http://* www.stanleyworks.com

General - Incorporation	CT	**Stock**- Price on:12/24/2007	$60.3
Employees	17,600	Stock Exchange	NYSE
Auditor	Ernst & Young LLP	Ticker Symbol	SWK
Stk Agt	Computershare Investor Services LLC	Outstanding Shares	83,380,000
Counsel	NA	E.P.S.	$3.82
DUNS No.	00-115-2461	Shareholders	NA

Business: The group's principle activities include producing and selling tools, hardware and security products. The groups consumer products include hand tools, consumer mechanic tools and storage units, hardware and home decor. The group manufactures Industrial tools include mac tools, proto mechanic tools, pneumatic tools, storage systems, specialty tools, assembly technologies, hydraulic tools and measuring tools. The groups products sold under the brand names include Stanley(R), Powerlock(R), Fatmax(R), Labounty(R), Mac(R), Proto(R), Jensen(R), Goldblatt(R) and Best(R). The group operates from United States.

Primary SIC and add'l.: 3442 3544 3429 3423 3545 3542 3541

CIK No: 0000093556

Subsidiaries: 3495981 Canada Inc., 6181708 Canada Inc., African Time Systems Corporation (Proprietary) Limited, Alfia Limited, Amano Blick International (Europe) Ltd., Armetsa, S.A. de C.V., BAI, Inc., Beijing Bostitch Fastening Systems Co., Ltd., Best Access Systems Co. / Les Systemes D'Access Best Cie, Bimontysa, S.A. de C.V., Blick Dormants Limited, Blick France S.A.R.L., Blick International Systems Limited, Blick Ireland Limited, Blick Software Systems Limited 132 Subsidiaries included in the Index

Officers: John F. Lundgren/Chmn., CEO/$6,163,714.00, Mark J. Mathieu/VP - Human Resources, Bruce H. Beatt/VP, General Counsel, Sec., Bert W. Davis/CIO, VP, James M. Loree/CFO, Exec. VP - Finance/$3,196,704.00, Donald R. McIlnay/Sr. VP/$1,351,620.00, Justin C. Boswell/VP, Pres. - Stanley Security Solutions, Jeff H. Chen/Pres. - Stanley Asia, Jeff D. Ansell/VP, Pres. - Stanley Consumer Tools Group, Thierry Paternot/Pres. - Stanley Tools, Europe/$2,558,545.00, Hubert W. Davis/CIO, VP/$1,277,297.00, Donald Allan/VP, Corporate Controller, Gerry Gould/VP - Investor Relations

Directors: John F. Lundgren/Chmn., CEO, John G. Breen/Dir., Stillman B. Brown/Dir., Kathryn D. Wriston/Dir., Lawrence A. Zimmerman/Dir., Eileen S. Kraus/Dir., Virgis W. Colbert/Dir., Emmanuel A. Kampouris/Dir.

Owners: John F. Lundgren, Hubert W. Davis, Kathryn D. Wriston, Stillman B. Brown, Emmanuel A. Kampouris, Lawrence A. Zimmerman, Thierry Paternot, Virgis W. Colbert, John G. Breen, Donald R. McIlnay, Eileen S. Kraus, James M. Loree, FMR Corp./7.79%, Insiders/1.67%, Allianz Global Investors Managed Accounts LLC/6.23% *(16 Owners included in Index)*

Financial Data: *Fiscal Year End:*12/31   *Latest Annual Data:* 12/30/2006

Year	Sales	Net Income
2006	NA	NA
2005	NA	NA

Curr. Assets:	$1,825,600,000	**Curr. Liab.:**	$875,300,000	**P/E Ratio:**	15.79
Plant, Equip.:	$467,100,000	**Total Liab.:**	$2,100,200,000	**Indic. Yr. Divd.:**	$1.240
Total Assets:	$3,545,100,000	**Net Worth:**	$1,444,900,000	**Debt/ Equity:**	0.7720

Stantec Inc

10160-112 St., Edmonton, AB, T5K 2L6; *PH:* 1-780-917-7000; *http://* www.stantec.com

General - Incorporation	Canada	**Stock**- Price on:12/24/2007	$34.3701
Employees	5,990	Stock Exchange	NYSE
Auditor	Ernst & Young LLP	Ticker Symbol	SXC
Stk Agt	Computershare Trust Co	Outstanding Shares	45,530,000
Counsel	NA	E.P.S.	$1.45
DUNS No.	NA	Shareholders	NA

Business: The groups principle activity is to provide professional design and consulting services in planning, engineering, architecture, surveying, economics, and project management. the groups practicing areas include buildings engineering, energy and resources, environmental infrastructure, environmental management, facilities planning and operations, infrastructure management and pavement engineering, manufacturing, planning and landscape architecture, and program and project management. The group operates from North America.

Primary SIC and add'l.: 8711

CIK No: 0001131383

Subsidiaries: 0714993 B.c. Ltd, 0715004 B.c. Ltd, 0715007 B.c. Ltd., 1208023 Alberta ULC, 3053837 Nova Scotia Company, 3102452 Nova Scotia Company, 455499 B.c. Ltd., 659243 B.c. Ltd., Amerex International, Inc., APAI Architecture Inc., Architectura Inc., CPV Architects & Engineers Ltd., Dunlop Murphy Hilgers Architects Inc., GKO Power Engineering Ltd., International Insurance Group Inc. 44 Subsidiaries included in the Index

Officers: Anthony P. Franceschini/Dir., CEO, Pres., Simon Stelfox/Mgr. - Investor Relations, Sherry /Financial Services, Jennifer /Marketing, Garry /Transportation

Directors: Anthony P. Franceschini/Dir., CEO, Pres., Ronald P. Triffo/Chmn., Aram H. Keith/Vice Chmn., Ivor M. Ruste/Dir., Robert R. Mesel/Dir., William D. Grace/Dir., Susan E. Hartman/Dir., Robert J. Bradshaw/Dir.

Financial Data: *Fiscal Year End:*12/31   *Latest Annual Data:* 12/31/2006

Year	Sales	Net Income
2006	$607,472,000	$51,642,000
2005	$450,066,000	$34,854,000

Curr. Assets:	$225,540,000	**Curr. Liab.:**	$133,608,000	**P/E Ratio:**	41.85
Plant, Equip.:	$55,784,000	**Total Liab.:**	$188,423,000	**Indic. Yr. Divd.:**	NA
Total Assets:	$541,012,000	**Net Worth:**	$352,589,000	**Debt/ Equity:**	NA

Staples Inc

500 Staples Dr., Framingham, MA, 01702; *PH:* 1-508-253-5000; *http://* www.staples.com; *Email:* support@orders.staples.com

General - Incorporation	DE	**Stock**- Price on:12/24/2007	$24.94
Employees	39,437	Stock Exchange	NDQ
Auditor	Ernst & Young LLP	Ticker Symbol	SPLS
Stk Agt	Mellon Investor Services LLC	Outstanding Shares	715,230,000
Counsel	NA	E.P.S.	$1.36
DUNS No.	15-106-4821	Shareholders	NA

Business: The group's principle activity is to provide office products. The groups products include staples, quill and other branded products. The group operates from United States.

Primary SIC and add'l.: 5999 5943 7375 5734 5712

CIK No: 0000791519

Subsidiaries: 3053840 Nova Scotia Company, 3053841 Nova Scotia Company, 3094494 Nova Scotia Company, Agawam Mill, LP, Bernard Belgium SA, Bernard France SAS, Bernard Supplies Limited, Business Office Supply B.V., Cherokee Mill, LP, Clip & Paper B.V., Coppell Mill, LP, Damster Kantooristallaties B.V., Fareham Developments (One) Limited, Fareham Developments (Two) Limited, Filatures du Vert Touquet S.a.r.l. 94 Subsidiaries included in the Index

Officers: Ronald L. Sargent/Chmn., CEO/$13,711,040.00, John J. Mahoney/Vice Chmn., CFO/$7,482,099.00, Joseph G. Doody/Pres. - North American Delivery/$3,435,753.00, Kristin A. Campbell/Sr. VP, General Counsel, Sec., Demos Parneros/Pres. - US Retail/$3,172,866.00, Michael Miles/COO, Pres./$5,149,326.00, Jack A. Vanwoerkom/Exec. VP, General Counsel, Sec., Christine T. Komola/Sr. VP, Corporate Controller

Directors: Ronald L. Sargent/Chmn., CEO, John J. Mahoney/Vice Chmn., CFO, Martin Trust/Dir., Arthur M. Blank/Dir., Basil L. Anderson/Dir., Brenda C. Barnes/Dir., Mary Elizabeth Burton/Dir., Gary L. Crittenden/Dir., Rowland T. Moriarty/Dir., Robert C. Nakasone/Dir., Paul F. Walsh/Dir., Vijay Vishwanath/Dir.

Owners: Mary Elizabeth Burton, Joseph G. Doody, Basil L. Anderson, Ronald L. Sargent, Rowland T. Moriarty, Demos Parneros, Gary L. Crittenden, Brenda C. Barnes, Martin Trust, Insiders/1.73%, Michael A. Miles, John J. Mahoney, FMR Corp./10.18%, Arthur M. Blank, Paul F. Walsh *(16 Owners included in Index)*

Financial Data: *Fiscal Year End:*01/28   *Latest Annual Data:* 2/3/2007

Year	Sales	Net Income
2007	$18,160,789,000	$973,677,000
2006	$16,078,852,000	$834,409,000
2005	$14,448,378,000	$708,388,000

Curr. Assets:	$4,431,363,000	**Curr. Liab.:**	$2,788,383,000	**P/E Ratio:**	18.34
Plant, Equip.:	$1,974,121,000	**Total Liab.:**	$3,366,491,000	**Indic. Yr. Divd.:**	$0.290
Total Assets:	$8,397,265,000	**Net Worth:**	$5,021,665,000	**Debt/ Equity:**	0.1276

Star Buffet Inc

1312 N Scottsdale Rd., Scottsdale, AZ, 85257; *PH:* 1-602-425-0397

General - Incorporation	DE	**Stock**- Price on:12/24/2007	$8.5
Employees	1,700	Stock Exchange	NDQ
Auditor	Mayer Hoffman Mccann, P.C	Ticker Symbol	STRZ
Stk Agt	Mellon Investor Services LLC	Outstanding Shares	3,170,000
Counsel	NA	E.P.S.	-$0.18
DUNS No.	03-537-6276	Shareholders	NA

Business: The group's principal activity is to offer wide variety of fresh, high quality food through chain of restaurants. It owns and operates 16 franchised hometown buffet restaurants, 12 buddyfreddys restaurants, 10 jb's restaurants, seven jj north's country buffet restaurants, one north's star buffet restaurant, two holiday house restaurants, two Mexican-themed restaurants operated under the casa bonita name and one jj north's family restaurant. The restaurants are located in nine western states, Oklahoma and Florida.

Primary SIC and add'l.: 5812

CIK No: 0001043156

Subsidiaries: Buffets, Inc., HTB Restaurants, Inc, Northstar Buffet, Inc, Star Buffet Management, Inc, Summit Family Restaurants, Inc

Owners: Todd S. Brown, Thomas G. Schadt/1.10%, Insiders/54.60%, Robert E. Wheaton/48.10%, Craig B. Wheaton/1.20%, Thomas M.B. Smith/4.80%, Phillip Johnson, Paul D. Sonkin/12.50%

Financial Data: *Fiscal Year End:*01/30   *Latest Annual Data:* 1/29/2007

Year	Sales	Net Income
2007	$58,648,000	$716,000
2006	$56,305,000	$1,797,000
2005	$64,856,000	-$172,000

Curr. Assets:	$1,873,000	**Curr. Liab.:**	$6,169,000	**P/E Ratio:**	53.13
Plant, Equip.:	$25,644,000	**Total Liab.:**	$15,105,000	**Indic. Yr. Divd.:**	$0.600
Total Assets:	$34,880,000	**Net Worth:**	$19,775,000	**Debt/ Equity:**	NA

Star Energy Corp

317 Madison Ave., 21st Fl., New York, NY, 10017; ***PH:*** 1-212-500-5006; ***Fax:*** 1-212-986-7691; ***http://*** www.starenergycorp.com; ***Email:*** info@starenergycorp.com

General - Incorporation	NV	**Stock**- Price on:12/24/2007	NA
Employees	NA	Stock Exchange	OTC
Auditor	Jones Simkins, P.C.	Ticker Symbol	SERGE
Stk Agt	Interwest Transfer Company, Inc.	Outstanding Shares	NA
Counsel	David Lubin & Associates, PLLC	E.P.S	NA
DUNS No.	NA	Shareholders	NA

Business: The groups principal activities include producing oil and natural gas involved in the exploring, developing, production and selling gas derived from properties. The group operates from the United States.

Primary SIC and add'l.: 1311

CIK No: 0001104671

Officers: Patrick Kealy/CEO, Pres., Howard Margulis/Advisor, Elena Furman/Pres., Michael Kravchenko/Sr. VP, CFO, Leonid Blyakher/VP

Directors: Bryson Farrill/Chmn., Marcus Segal/Dir., Clarke Keough/Dir., Richard T. McDermott/Dir.

Owners: Insiders/1.50%, Bryson F. Farrill, Patrick J. Kealy, Marcus Segal

Star Gas Partners LP

Clearwater House, 2187 Atlantic St., Stamford, CT, 06902; ***PH:*** 1-203-328-7310; ***http://*** www.star-gas.com

General - Incorporation	DE	**Stock**- Price on:12/24/2007	$4.41
Employees	2,610	Stock Exchange	NYSE
Auditor	KPMG LLP	Ticker Symbol	NA
Stk Agt	LaSalle Bank N.A	Outstanding Shares	75,770,000
Counsel	NA	E.P.S	$0.50
DUNS No.	NA	Shareholders	NA

Business: The groups principal activities include installing, maintaining, repairing, distributing heating and air conditioning equipments. The group operates from the United States. The groups total assets in the year 2006 were $355,117 (thousands).

Primary SIC and add'l.: 5983

CIK No: 0001002590

Subsidiaries: A.P. Woodson Company, Columbia Petroleum Transportation, LLC, Marex Corporation, Maxwhale Corp., Meenan Holdings of New York, Inc., Meenan Oil Co., Inc., Meenan Oil Co., L.P., Ortep of Pennsylvania, Inc., Petro Holdings, Inc., Petro Plumbing Corporation, Petro, Inc., Petroleum Heat and Power Co., Inc., RegionOil Plumbing, Heating and Cooling Co., Inc., Richland Partners, LLC, Star Gas Finance Company 17 Subsidiaries included in the Index

Officers: Daniel P. Donovan/61/Dir., COO, Pres., Richard F. Ambury/51/CFO, Richard G. Oakley/48/VP, Controller, Steven J. Goldman/48/Sr. VP - Operations

Directors: Paul A. Vermylen/61/Chmn., Joseph P. Cavanaugh/71/Dir., Daniel P. Donovan/61/Dir., COO, Pres., Henry D. Babcock/68/Dir., Scott C. Baxter/47/Dir., Bryan H. Lawrence/66/Dir., Sheldon B. Lubar/79/Dir., William P. Nicoletti/63/Dir.

Owners: Richard F. Ambury, MacKay Shields, LLC/11.27%, William P. Nicoletti, Kestrel/100.00%, Kestrel/16.90%, Henry D. Babcock, Insiders/16.98%, Insiders/100.00%, Bandera Partners LLC/5.63%

Financial Data: **Fiscal Year End:**09/30 **Latest Annual Data:** 9/30/2006

Year	Sales	Net Income
2006	$1,296,512,000	-$54,263,000
2005	$1,259,478,000	-$25,928,000
2004	$1,453,937,000	-$5,863,000

Curr. Assets:	$295,880,000	**Curr. Liab.:**	$208,578,000		
Plant, Equip.:	$43,387,000	**Total Liab.:**	$407,883,000	**Indic. Yr. Divd.:**	NA
Total Assets:	$581,208,000	**Net Worth:**	$173,325,000	**Debt/ Equity:**	NA

Star Scientific Inc

801 Liberty Way, Chester, VA, 23836; ***PH:*** 1-800-486-0681; ***http://*** www.starscientific.com

General - Incorporation	DE	**Stock**- Price on:12/24/2007	$0.92
Employees	117	Stock Exchange	NDQ
Auditor	Aidman, Piser & Co. P.A	Ticker Symbol	STSI
Stk Agt	Wells Fargo Shareowner Services	Outstanding Shares	79,290,000
Counsel	NA	E.P.S	-$0.46
DUNS No.	11-426-4724	Shareholders	NA

Business: The group's principal activity is to develop proprietary scientific technology for the curing of starcured (TM) tobacco so as to reduce the formation of carcinogenic toxins present in tobacco and tobacco smoke. The group sells, markets and develops less toxic and harmful tobacco products and discount cigarettes with activated charcoal filters. The group's research and development activities include reducing the various health hazards associated with the use of smoked and smokeless tobacco products. The group's operating segments are discount cigarettes and smokeless tobacco products and leaf tobacco.

Primary SIC and add'l.: 5194 3851 3845 2111 8731

CIK No: 0000776008

Subsidiaries: Star Tobacco, Inc.

Officers: Jonnie R. Williams/51/Dir., CEO, Paul L. Perito/70/Chmn., COO, Pres., Paul H. Lamb/73/Pres. - Star Tobacco, Inc, Sheldon Bogaz/41/VP - Trade Operations, Robert E. Pokusa/56/General Counsel, David M. Dean/47/VP - Sales, Marketing, Sara Troy MacHir/VP - Communications, Investor Relations, Park A. Dodd/55/CFO

Directors: Jonnie R. Williams/51/Dir., CEO, Paul L. Perito/70/Chmn., COO, Pres., Ambassador Gerald P. Carmen/76/Dir., Christopher C. Chapman/54/Dir., Marc D. Oken/60/Dir., Leo S. Tonkin/69/Dir., David C. Vorhoff/51/Dir., Alan Weichselbaum/Dir., Neil L. Chayet/Dir.

Owners: Insiders/24.30%, David M. Dean, Sheldon L. Bogaz, Jonnie R. Williams/20.50%, Christopher C. Chapman, Paul L. Perito/3.40%, Joseph L. Schwarz/7.20%, Marc D. Oken, Park A. Dodd, Leo S. Tonkin, Neil Chayet, Kathleen M. ODonnell as Trustee for Irrevocable Trust #1 FBO/9.30%, Robert E. Pokusa

Financial Data: **Fiscal Year End:**12/31 **Latest Annual Data:** 12/31/2006

Year	Sales	Net Income
2006	$37,746,000	-$12,285,000
2005	$46,436,000	-$25,062,000
2004	$66,657,000	-$16,576,000

Curr. Assets:	$11,200,000	**Curr. Liab.:**	$7,054,000		
Plant, Equip.:	$10,066,000	**Total Liab.:**	$22,029,000	**Indic. Yr. Divd.:**	NA
Total Assets:	$60,938,000	**Net Worth:**	$38,909,000	**Debt/ Equity:**	1.1826

Starbucks Corp

2401 Utah Ave. S, Seattle, WA, 98134; ***PH:*** 1-206-447-1575; ***http://*** www.starbucks.com

General - Incorporation	WA	**Stock**- Price on:12/24/2007	$27.59
Employees	145,800	Stock Exchange	NDQ
Auditor	Deloitte & Touche LLP	Ticker Symbol	SBUX
Stk Agt	Mellon Investor Services LLC	Outstanding Shares	740,780,000
Counsel	NA	E.P.S	$0.81
DUNS No.	15-536-6107	Shareholders	NA

Business: The group's principle activity is to purchase, roast and market whole bean coffees. The group also markets rich-brewed coffees, Italian-style espresso beverages, cold blended beverages, a variety of pastries and confections, coffee-related accessories and equipment, a selection of premium teas and a line of compact discs. These products are marketed through retail stores. It also markets coffee and tea products through other channels of distribution. The group produces and markets bottled frappuccino(R) and starbucks doubleshottm coffee drinks and a line of premium ice creams. At 29-Sep-2002, the group had 3,496 stores operating in the United States, Canadian provinces, the United Kingdom, Australia and Thailand. The group's quarterly revenue for Sep '07 was 2,440.93 millions of USD.

Primary SIC and add'l.: 5411 5499 5441

CIK No: 0000829224

Subsidiaries: Chengdu Starbucks Coffee Company Limited, Coffee Concepts, Coffee Concepts Coffee Concepts (Shenzhen) Ltd., Coffee Concepts(Guangdong) Ltd., Emerald City C.V., Olympic Casualty Insurance Company, Qingdao American Starbucks Coffee Company Limited, Rain City C.V., SBI Nevada, Inc., SCI Europe I, Inc., SCI Europe II, Inc., SCI Investment, Inc., SCI Ventures, S.L., Seattle Coffee Company, Seattle's Best Coffee LLC 44 Subsidiaries included in the Index

Officers: James L. Donald/Dir., CEO, Pres., James C. Alling/Pres. - Starbucks Coffee International, Buck Hendrix/Sr. VP, Pres. - Latin America, Sandra E. Taylor/Sr. VP - Corporate Social Responsibility, Michelle Gass/Sr. VP - Category Management, Margaret Giuntini/Sr. VP - North America Partner Resources, Julio Gutierrez/Sr. VP, Pres. - Latin America, Willard Hay/Sr. VP - Coffee, Global Procurement, Charles Jemley/Sr. VP - Finance, Starbucks Coffee International, Cosimo Laporta/Sr. VP - Western Division, Barbara Lemarrec/Sr. VP - Operations, Starbucks Coffee International, David A. Pace/Exec. VP - Partner Resources, Troy Alstead/Sr. VP - Finance, Cliff Burrows/Pres. - Europe, Middle East, Africa, Bryan Crynes/CIO, Sr. VP *(46 Officers included in Index)*

Directors: James L. Donald/Dir., CEO, Pres., Howard Schultz/Chmn., Founder, William Bradley/Dir., Olden Lee/Dir., James Shennan/Dir., Barbara Bass/Dir., Javier Teruel/Dir., Howard Behar/Dir., Mellody Hobson/Dir., Myron Ullman/Dir., Craig Weatherup/Dir.

Owners: David A. Pace, Barbara Bass, Howard P. Behar, Javier G. Teruel, Sands Capital Management, LLC/5.60%, Insiders/5.30%, Mellody Hobson, James L. Donald, Craig E. Weatherup, William W. Bradley, James G. Shennan, Howard Schultz/4.10%, Olden Lee, Michael Casey, Martin Coles *(17 Owners included in Index)*

Financial Data: **Fiscal Year End:**10/02 **Latest Annual Data:** 10/1/2006

Year	Sales	Net Income
2006	$7,786,942,000	$564,259,000
2005	$6,369,300,000	$494,467,000
2004	$5,294,247,000	$390,559,000

Curr. Assets:	$1,350,895,000	**Curr. Liab.:**	$746,259,000	**P/E Ratio:**	34.06
Plant, Equip.:	$1,551,416,000	**Total Liab.:**	$916,330,000	**Indic. Yr. Divd.:**	NA
Total Assets:	$3,390,548,000	**Net Worth:**	$2,474,218,000	**Debt/ Equity:**	0.0007

Starcore International Ventures Ltd

580 Hornby St., Ste. 600, Vancouver, BC, V6C 3B6; ***PH:*** 1-604-602-4935; ***http://*** www.starcore.com

General - Incorporation	Canada	**Stock**- Price on:12/24/2007	$0.66
Employees	NA	Stock Exchange	NA
Auditor	MacKay LLP	Ticker Symbol	NA
Stk Agt	Computershare Investor Services LLC	Outstanding Shares	NA
Counsel	NA	E.P.S	NA
DUNS No.	NA	Shareholders	NA

Business: The group's principle activities include acquiring and exploring of mineral properties throughout North America. The company is studying the 80:20 joint ventures with Goldcorp Inc., flagship property Cerro Dolores El Transito Deposit, and to re-invest in exploration and development of other areas at Cerro Dolores. Previous work includes mineralization over vertical and strike dimensions of 600 and 4000 meters respectively. Cerro Dolores has a possibility of developing a reserves of 3-5 million tones range of grading stones, some 11 oz/t silver and a combined 8% lead-zinc. The company is in the process of acquiring a 100% interest in the Black Silver Property located in southern Arizona. The recent surface sampling has identified a mineralized zone, which appears to be approximately 50 feet thick and averages 5.2 oz/ton silver. The group operates from United States.

Primary SIC and add'l.: 1400

CIK No: 0001301713

Officers: Robert Eadie/Dir., Pres., Gary Arca/Dir., CFO, Arturo Prestamo Elizondo/Country Mgr.

Directors: Robert Eadie/Dir., Pres., Gary Hawthorn/Dir., Gary Arca/Dir., CFO, Carlos Galvan Pastoriza/Dir., Cory Kent/Dir., Ken Sumanik/Dir., Hugh McPherson/Dir., Federico Villasenor/Dir., Charles A. Jeannes/Dir.

Starfield Resources Inc

420-625 Howe St., Vancouver, BC, V6C 2T6 ; ***PH:*** 1-604-608-0400; ***http://*** www.starfieldres.com; ***Email:*** corporate@starfieldres.com

General - Incorporation............ AB
Employees............ NA
Auditor............ Loewen, Stronach & Co
Stk Agt..... Computershare Investor Services LLC
Counsel............ NA
DUNS No............ NA

Stock- Price on:12/24/2007............ $1.13
Stock Exchange............ OTC
Ticker Symbol............ SRFDF
Outstanding Shares............ NA
E.P.S............ NA
Shareholders............ NA

Business: The group's principle activity is to explore natural resource properties. The group operates from United States.

Primary SIC and add'l.: 1499

CIK No: 0001074795

Officers: Andre J. Douchane/CEO, Pres., Greg Van Staveren/CFO, Michael G. Moran/Dir. - Engineering

Directors: Robert Maddigan/Dir., Henry Giegerich/Dir., Ross Glanville/Dir., Norman M. Betts/Dir., Stuart H. Bottomley/Dir., Shirley Mears/Dir., Ulrich E. Rath/Dir.

Owners: David R. Lewis, Glen J. Indra/1.20%, Henry Giegerich, Robert Maddigan, Stuart H. Bottomley, Glen C. MacDonald, Norman Betts, Ross Glanville

Financial Data: ***Fiscal Year End:***02/28 ***Latest Annual Data:*** 02/28/2007

Year	Sales	Net Income
2007	NA	-$18,507,000
2006	NA	-$12,843,000
2005	NA	-$9,549,000

Curr. Assets:	$771,000	**Curr. Liab.:**	$1,095,000		
Plant, Equip.:	$11,000	**Total Liab.:**	$1,095,000	**Indic. Yr. Divd.:**	NA
Total Assets:	$783,000	**Net Worth:**	-$313,000	**Debt/ Equity:**	NA

Stargold Mines Inc

Formerly: Sockeye Seafood Group Inc
1840 Gateway Dr., Ste. 200, San Mateo, CA, 94404; ***PH:*** 1-650-378-1214;
http:// www.sockeyeseafood.com

General - Incorporation............ NV
Employees............ 2
Auditor............ Sf Partnership, LLP
Stk Agt............ Holladay Stock Transfer, Inc.
Counsel............ NA
DUNS No............ NA

Stock- Price on:12/24/2007............ $0.7795
Stock Exchange............ OTC
Ticker Symbol............ SGDM
Outstanding Shares............ 81,110,000
E.P.S............ $0.00
Shareholders............ NA

Business: The group's principle activity is to engage in the business of procuring seafood products directly from Pacific Northwest First Nations organizations, and marketing them to North American and International wholesalers, distributors, and retailers. The group currently developing our business operations using the proceeds we raised in our initial offering. The group operates from United States.

Primary SIC and add'l.: 6770

CIK No: 0001301557

Officers: Marcus Segal/36/Dir., CEO, CFO, Pres.

Directors: Marcus Segal/36/Dir., CEO, CFO, Pres.

Owners: David F.Knapfel/25.00%, Sheldon Goldberg/25.00%

Financial Data: ***Fiscal Year End:***12/31 ***Latest Annual Data:*** 12/31/2006

Year	Sales	Net Income
2006	$4,000	-$51,000
2005	$17,000	-$6,000

Curr. Assets:	$8,000	**Curr. Liab.:**	$26,000		
Plant, Equip.:	NA	**Total Liab.:**	$26,000	**Indic. Yr. Divd.:**	NA
Total Assets:	$1,008,000	**Net Worth:**	$982,000	**Debt/ Equity:**	NA

Starinvest Group Inc

115 E 57th St., 11th Fl., New York, NY, 10168; ***PH:*** 1-212-514-6600; ***Fax:*** 1-432-618-9923;
http:// www.starinvestgroup.com; ***Email:*** info@starinvestgroup.com

General - Incorporation............ NV
Employees............ 2
Auditor............ Larry O'donnell, CPA, P.C
Stk Agt............ Manhattan Transfer Registrar Co
Counsel............ NA
DUNS No............ 03-875-4420

Stock- Price on:12/24/2007............ $0.027
Stock Exchange............ OTC
Ticker Symbol............ STIV
Outstanding Shares............ 47,590,000
E.P.S............ -$0.02
Shareholders............ NA

Business: The group's principal activity is to provide investment to small and mid-sized companies in the education and communication sectors.the group is focusing on the markets of central Asia, eastern Europe and Africa.the group also provides significant managerial assistance to developing companies.the group has declared a distribution of shares of e education network, inc to shareholders of record.the group has no fixed policy as to any particular industry or business in which it may invest or as to the type of securities or assets it may acquire.the board of directors uses four basic guidelines for its investments, these are cost method, appraisal method, private market method and public market method.the groups major competitors are business development companies, venture capital firms, new product development companies, marketing companies and diversified manufacturers. On 15-Jan-2004, the group acquired agi partners limited.

Primary SIC and add'l.: 4812 4899 4813

CIK No: 0000810270

Officers: Robert H. Cole/Chmn., CEO, Glenn Matthews/Exec. VP, COO - China Rep

Directors: Robert H. Cole/Chmn., CEO, Stephen J. Cole-Hatchard/Dir., Ron Signore/Dir., Roger Moreau/Dir., Cristiano Germinario/Dir.

Owners: Steve Cole-Hatchard, Robert H. Cole, Scarborough Ltd., Allen Notowitz, Gregg Gaylord, Insiders, Henry Fortier, Marc Finkelstein, David L. Cohen, Aqua Alta Ltd., Beaufort Ltd., 3111 Broadway Realty CRT

Financial Data: ***Fiscal Year End:***12/31 ***Latest Annual Data:*** 03/31/2007

Year	Sales	Net Income
2007	NA	NA
2006	$87,000	-$1,023,000
2005	$42,000	-$627,000

Curr. Assets:	$117,000	**Curr. Liab.:**	$305,000		
Plant, Equip.:	NA	**Total Liab.:**	$1,400,000	**Indic. Yr. Divd.:**	NA
Total Assets:	$1,735,000	**Net Worth:**	$335,000	**Debt/ Equity:**	3.1940

Starmed Group Inc

2029 Century Pk. E, Los Angeles, CA, 90067; ***PH:*** 1-310-226-2555; ***Fax:*** 1-310-551-2724;
http:// www.starmedgroup.com; ***Email:*** info@starmedgroup.com

General - Incorporation............ NV
Employees............ 4
Auditor............ Mendoza Berger & Company, LLP
Stk Agt............ Nevada Agency & Trust Co.
Counsel............ NA
DUNS No............ NA

Stock- Price on:12/24/2007............ $0.15
Stock Exchange............ OTC
Ticker Symbol............ SMED
Outstanding Shares............ 32,400,000
E.P.S............ -$0.08
Shareholders............ NA

Business: The groups principle activities include developing a network of StarMed Wellness Centers that will offer preventative, traditional medical and alternative treatments and marketing a line of over the counter, alternative medicinal products. The group operates from the United States.

Primary SIC and add'l.: 5999

CIK No: 0001135263

Subsidiaries: Sierra Medicinals, Inc., Vet Medicinals, Inc.

Officers: Herman H. Rappaport/Chmn., CEO, Pres., Acting CFO, Steven L. Rosenblatt/62/Dir., Exec. VP, Elleesa Wilson/Controller, Shelley Hess/Dir. - Esthetics, Martha Snook/Consultant, Bob Schneiderman/Dir. - Product Development, Joel Feinstein/62/Dir., VP, Avner Manzoor-Mandel/61/Dir., VP, Hector Rodriguez/64/VP, Dir.

Directors: Herman H. Rappaport/Chmn., CEO, Pres., Acting CFO, Steven L. Rosenblatt/62/Dir., Exec. VP, Joel Feinstein/62/Dir., VP, Avner Manzoor-Mandel/61/Dir., VP, Seymour Levine/Dir., Hector Rodriguez/64/VP, Dir.

Owners: Herman Rappaport/27.70%, Seymour Levine, Avner Mangoors Mandell, Steven Rosenblatt/11.70%, Hector Rodriquez, Joel Feinstein

Financial Data: ***Fiscal Year End:***12/31 ***Latest Annual Data:*** 12/31/2006

Year	Sales	Net Income
2006	$18,000	-$2,751,000
2005	$48,000	-$806,000
2004	$1,847,000	-$100,000

Curr. Assets:	$75,000	**Curr. Liab.:**	$71,000		
Plant, Equip.:	$19,000	**Total Liab.:**	$71,000	**Indic. Yr. Divd.:**	NA
Total Assets:	$101,000	**Net Worth:**	$31,000	**Debt/ Equity:**	NA

Startech Environmental Corp

88 Old Danbury Rd., Ste 203, Wilton, CT, 06897; ***PH:*** 1-202-762-2499; ***http://*** www.startech.net;
Email: starmail@startech.net

General - Incorporation............ CO
Employees............ 16
Auditor............ Marcum & Kliegman LLP
Stk Agt............ Corporate Stock Transfer, Inc.
Counsel............ Foreht Last Landau Miller & Katz
DUNS No............ NA

Stock- Price on:12/24/2007............ $2.29
Stock Exchange............ OTC
Ticker Symbol............ STHK
Outstanding Shares............ 23,050,000
E.P.S............ -$0.21
Shareholders............ NA

Business: The group's principal activities are to develop, produce and market low cost waste minimization, resource recovery and pollution prevention systems that convert waste into valuable commodities. The recycling system is called the plasma waste converter. The recycling system provides benefits such as treatment and disposal of hazardous toxic waste at reduced costs, converts wastes into products for use or sale and is available in small and large capacities and in stationary and mobile configurations.

Primary SIC and add'l.: 4953

CIK No: 0000875762

Subsidiaries: Argentina S.A., CAM Chile Ltda., Compaa Elctrica Cono Sur S.A., Edegel, Elctricas Reunidas de Zaragoza, Endesa Chile, Endesa Chiles, Endesa Costanera e Hidroelctrica El Choln S.A., IMV, Ingendesa Ltda., Synapsis

Officers: Joseph F. Longo/75/Chmn., CEO, Pres., Ralph N. Dechiaro/59/VP - Business Development, Karl N. Hale/43/VP - Engineering, Peter J. Scanlon/CFO, VP, Stephen J. Landa/VP - Sales, Marketing

Directors: Joseph F. Longo/75/Chmn., CEO, Pres., Scott L. Barnard/65/Dir., Joseph A. Equale/62/Dir., John J. Fitzpatrick/69/Dir., Chase P. Withrow/64/Dir.

Owners: Stephen J. Landa, John J. Fitzpatrick, Francisco J. Rivera Fernandez, Cornell Capital Partners LP, Northshore Asset Management, LLC, Paradigm Group L.P., Insiders, Joseph A. Equale, Chase P. Withro, FB US Investments, Scott L. Barnard, Peter J. Scanlon, Ralph N. Dechiaro, Connecticut Banking Commissioner John P. Burke, Arthur J. Steinberg *(16 Owners included in Index)*

Financial Data: ***Fiscal Year End:***10/31 ***Latest Annual Data:*** 10/31/2006

Year	Sales	Net Income
2006	$949,000	-$6,620,000
2005	$290,000	-$3,679,000
2004	$1,709,000	-$2,646,000

Curr. Assets:	$3,007,000	**Curr. Liab.:**	$3,668,000		
Plant, Equip.:	$2,064,000	**Total Liab.:**	$3,668,000	**Indic. Yr. Divd.:**	NA
Total Assets:	$5,174,000	**Net Worth:**	$1,506,000	**Debt/ Equity:**	NA

StarTek Inc

44 Cook St., Ste. 400, Denver, CO, 80206; ***PH:*** 1-303-262-4500; ***http://*** www.startek.com

General - Incorporation............ DE
Employees............ 8,300
Auditor............ Ernst & Young LLP
Stk Agt............ NY Drop-SS Bank & Trust Co
Counsel............ NA
DUNS No............ 83-696-3983

Stock- Price on:12/24/2007............ $10.35
Stock Exchange............ NYSE
Ticker Symbol............ SRT
Outstanding Shares............ 14,730,000
E.P.S............ -$0.06
Shareholders............ NA

Business: The group's principal activities are to provide business process and supply chain management services. Business process management services provides provisioning management, wireless telephone number porting, receivables management, wireless telephone activations and high-end technical support and customer care services. Supply chain management services provide packaging, fulfillment, marketing support and logistics services. The group's customers are in the operations of telecommunications, software industries, computer hardware, consumer products, cable, Internet, entertainment and e-commerce industries. The group provides services from 18 operational facilities and operates in the United States, the United Kingdom and Canada.

Primary SIC and add'l.: 6719 7373 7389 8742

CIK No: 0001031029

Subsidiaries: Stellent AB, Stellent Asia Pty. Limited, Stellent B.V., Stellent Canada Ltd, Stellent Chicago Sales, Inc, Stellent Chicago, Inc, Stellent Colorado Springs, Inc, Stellent Holding B.V. Company

Officers: Larry Jones/54/Dir., CEO, Pres., David Durham/CFO, Treasurer, Patrick Hayes/COO/$289,259.00, Michael Griffith/Sr. VP - Sales/$471,030.00, Michael Clayton/General Counsel, Sec., Mary Beth Beth Loesch/Sr. VP - Business Development, Susan Morse/Sr. VP - Human Resources

Directors: Larry Jones/54/Dir., CEO, Pres., Ed Zschau/Chmn., Albert C. Yates/Dir., Kay Norton/Dir.

Owners: Steven Boyer, Insiders, Rodd E. Granger, T. Rowe Price Associates, Inc./8.80%, Kay Norton, Steven D. Butler, Patrick M. Hayes, Laurence A. Jones, Emmet A. Stephenson/22.50%, Michael Griffith, Bank of America Corporation/5.80%, Barclays Global Investors, N.A./8.30%, Albert C. Yates, Ed Zschau

Financial Data: ***Fiscal Year End:***12/31 ***Latest Annual Data:*** 12/31/2006

Year	Sales	Net Income
2006	$237,612,000	$5,764,000
2005	$216,371,000	$12,860,000
2004	$258,120,000	$20,976,000

Curr. Assets:	$90,024,000	***Curr. Liab.:***	$24,330,000		
Plant, Equip.:	$60,101,000	***Total Liab.:***	$37,353,000	***Indic. Yr. Divd.:***	$1.000
Total Assets:	$155,735,000	***Net Worth:***	$118,382,000	***Debt/ Equity:***	0.0770

Starwood Hotels & Resorts Worldwide Inc

1111 Wchester Ave., White Plains, NY, 10604; ***PH:*** 1-914-640-8100; ***http://*** www.starwoodhotels.com

General - Incorporation	MD	***Stock***- Price on:12/24/2007	$70.15
Employees	145,000	Stock Exchange	NYSE
Auditor	Ernst & Young LLP	Ticker Symbol	HOT
Stk Agt	American Stock Transfer & Trust Co.	Outstanding Shares	215,100,000
Counsel	NA	E.P.S	$2.77
DUNS No.	NA	Shareholders	NA

Business: The group's principle activity is to provide restaurant services. The group operates from North America, Europe, Africa, Middle East, and Latin America.

Primary SIC and add'l.: 6531 7011 6798

CIK No: 0000048595

Subsidiaries: CIGA S.p.A., Sheraton Holding Corporation, Sheraton International, Inc., Sheraton Overseas Management Corporation, SLC Operating Limited Partnership, SLT Realty Limited Partnership, Starwood Hotels & Resorts, Starwood Hotels & Resorts Holdings, Inc., Starwood Hotels & Resorts Worldwide, Inc., The Sheraton Corporation

Officers: Frits Van Paasschen/CEO, Kenneth S. Siegel/Chief Administrative Officer, General Counsel, Ross A. Klein/Pres. - Starwood Luxury Brands Group, Aloft Hotels, Vasant M. Prabhu/CFO, Exec. VP, Sue A. Brush/Sr. VP - Westin Hotels, Resorts, Osvaldo V. Librizzi/Pres. - Latin America, Roeland Vos/Pres. - Europe, Africa, Middle East Division, Hoyt H. Harper/Sr. VP - Brand Management, Sheraton Hotels, Resorts, Matt Ouimet/Pres. - Hotel Group, Raymond L. Gellein/Pres. - Global Development Group, Miguel Ko/Pres. - Asia, Pacific Division, Geoffrey A. Ballotti/Pres. - North America Division, Alan Schnaid/Sr. VP, Corporate Controller, Eva Ziegler/Sr. VP - Le Meridien Hotels, Resorts, Lynne Dougherty/Sr. VP - Owner Relations, Franchise *(16 Officers included in Index)*

Directors: Bruce W. Duncan/57/Chmn., Trustee, Charlene Barshefsky/55/Dir., Lizanne Galbreath/48/Dir., Trustee, Stephen R. Quazzo/46/Dir., Trustee, Thomas O. Ryder/61/Dir., Trustee, Adam Aron/52/Dir., Jean-Marc Chapus/46/Dir., Trustee, Kneeland C. Youngblood/50/Dir., Trustee, Eric Hippeau/54/Dir., Trustee

Financial Data: ***Fiscal Year End:***12/31 ***Latest Annual Data:*** 12/31/2006

Year	Sales	Net Income
2006	$5,979,000,000	$1,043,000,000
2005	$5,977,000,000	$422,000,000
2004	$5,368,000,000	$395,000,000

Curr. Assets:	$1,810,000,000	***Curr. Liab.:***	$2,461,000,000	***P/E Ratio:***	13.39
Plant, Equip.:	$3,833,000,000	***Total Liab.:***	$6,272,000,000	***Indic. Yr. Divd.:***	$0.900
Total Assets:	$9,280,000,000	***Net Worth:***	$3,008,000,000	***Debt/ Equity:***	NA

State Auto Financial Corp

518 E Brd St., Columbus, OH, 43215; ***PH:*** 1-614-464-5000; ***http://*** www.stfc.com

General - Incorporation	OH	***Stock***- Price on:12/24/2007	$31.34
Employees	2,060	Stock Exchange	NDQ
Auditor	Ernst & Young LLP	Ticker Symbol	STFC
Stk Agt	National City Bank	Outstanding Shares	41,110,000
Counsel	Baker & Hostetler	E.P.S	$2.94
DUNS No.	00-486-8287	Shareholders	NA

Business: The group's principal activities are to provide property and casualty insurance. The group operates through the following subsidiaries: state auto property and casualty insurance co, milbank insurance co, farmers casualty insurance co and state auto insurance co. The group's line of business includes personal and commercial auto, homeowners, commercial multi-peril, workers' compensation, general liability and fire insurance. Other service includes insurance premium finance services and investment management services to certain policyholders. The group's insurance products are marketed primarily in the central and eastern part of the United States excluding New York, New Jersey and the new England states.

Primary SIC and add'l.: 6331 7389 6719

CIK No: 0000874977

Subsidiaries: 518 Property Management and Leasing LLC, Farmers Casualty Insurance Company, Milbank Insurance Company, State Auto Insurance Company of Ohio, State Auto National Insurance Company, State Auto Property and Casualty Insurance Company, Stateco Financial Services Inc., Strategic Insurance Software Inc.

Officers: Richard L. Miley/CEO, Pres. - Broadstreet Capital Partners/$480,438.00, Jean Reynolds/VP, Dir. - Marketing, State Auto Insurance Companies, Lori M. Siegworth/VP, Dir. - Strategy, Organization Effectiveness, State Auto Insurance Companies, Larry D. Williams/VP, Dir. - Middle Marketing Operations, State Auto Insurance Companies Inc, Mark A. Blackburn/COO, Exec. VP, James A. Yano/VP, Sec., General Counsel - State Auto Insurance Companies Inc, Cathy B. Miley/VP, Dir. - Branch, Regional Operations, State Auto Insurance Companies, Terrence L. Bowshier/VP, Dir. - Investor Relations, State Auto Insurance Companies, Steven P. Hazelbaker/VP, Dir. - Branch, Regional Operations, State Auto Insurance Companies, Cynthia A. Powell/VP, Chief Accounting Officer, Treasurer - State Auto Insurance Companies/$462,975.00, Terrence P. Higerd/VP, Dir. - Information Technology Infrastructure Services, State Auto Insurance Companies, Doug Allen/VP, Dir. - Information Technology, State Auto Insurance Companies, Steven E. English/CFO, VP - State Auto Insurance Companies/$402,271.00, James E. Duemey/VP, Investment Officer - State Auto Insurance Companies, Noreen W. Johnson/VP, Dir. - Administration, State Auto Insurance Companies *(21 Officers included in Index)*

Directors: Thomas E. Markert/Dir., Alison Coolbrith/Dir. - State Automobile Mutual Insurance Company, Kenan L. Schultheis/Dir. - State Automobile Mutual Insurance Company, Edwin J. Simcox/Dir. - State Automobile Mutual Insurance Company, Robert E. Baker/61/Dir., Robert P. Restrepo/Dir., Richard K. Smith/Dir., David J. D'Antoni/Dir., Paul S. Williams/Dir., Elaine S. Roberts/Dir., Alexander B. Trevor/Dir., David R. Meuse/Dir., Dennis R. Blank/Dir. - State Automobile Mutual Insurance Company, Michael F. Dodd/Dir. - State Automobile Mutual Insurance Company, Paul J. Otte/Dir. - State Automobile Mutual Insurance Company *(19 Directors included in Index)*

Owners: Richard K. Smith, Richard L. Miley, Steven E. English, Cynthia A. Powell, Mark A. Blackburn, David J. DAntoni, David R. Meuse, Steven R. Hazelbaker, Paul S. Williams, Robert P. Restrepo, John R. Lowther

Financial Data: ***Fiscal Year End:***12/31 ***Latest Annual Data:*** 12/31/2006

Year	Sales	Net Income
2006	$1,117,400,000	$120,400,000
2005	$1,139,500,000	$125,900,000
2004	$1,092,400,000	$110,000,000

Curr. Assets:	$110,800,000	***Curr. Liab.:***	$681,700,000	***P/E Ratio:***	10.04
Plant, Equip.:	$12,400,000	***Total Liab.:***	$1,420,900,000	***Indic. Yr. Divd.:***	$0.600
Total Assets:	$2,255,100,000	***Net Worth:***	$834,200,000	***Debt/ Equity:***	0.1375

State Bancorp Inc New York

699 Hillside Ave., New Hyde Park, NY, 11040; ***PH:*** 1-516-437-1000; ***Fax:*** 1-516-437-1032; ***http://*** www.statebankofli.com; ***Email:*** info@statebankofli.com

General - Incorporation	NY	***Stock***- Price on:12/24/2007	$17.68
Employees	371	Stock Exchange	NDQ
Auditor	Crowe Chizek & Co. LLC	Ticker Symbol	STBC
Stk Agt	Wells Fargo Shareholder Services	Outstanding Shares	13,740,000
Counsel	Lamb & Barnosky	E.P.S	$0.68
DUNS No.	01-002-6466	Shareholders	NA

Business: The group's principal activity is to provide general banking services to residents and businesses located in nassau, suffolk and queens counties. The group operates through its subsidiary, state bank of long island. The group accepts checking, savings, time, money market and ira accounts. The group provides credit services including commercial and residential mortgages, home equity lines of credit, letters of credit and auto loans. The other services include merchant credit card services, access to annuity products and mutual funds and a consumer debit card with membership in a national ATM network. The group currently has thirteen ATMs of its fifteen branch locations.

Primary SIC and add'l.: 6022 6712

CIK No: 0000723458

Subsidiaries: New Hyde Park Leasing Corporation, SB Financial Services Corp., SB ORE Corp, SB Portfolio Management Corp, State Bancorp Capital Trust I, State Bancorp Capital Trust II, State Bank of Long Island, Studebaker-Worthington Leasing Corp.

Officers: Thomas M. O'Brien/Dir., CEO, Pres., Daniel T. Rowe/Pres., Vice Chmn./$481,435.00, Frederick C. Braun/Sr. Lending Officer, Exec. VP/$418,041.00, Brian K. Finneran/CFO, Exec. VP/$400,538.00, Patricia M. Schaubeck/General Counsel, Janice Clark/Corp. Sec.

Directors: Thomas M. O'Brien/Dir., CEO, Pres., Thomas F. Goldrick/Chmn., Daniel T. Rowe/Pres., Vice Chmn., John F. Picciano/Dir., Jeffrey S. Wilks/Dir., Richard W. Merzbacher/Dir., Suzanne H. Rueck/Dir., Joseph F. Munson/Dir., Arthur Dulik/Dir., Gerard J. McKeon/Dir., Thomas E. Christman/Dir., Andrew J. Simons/Dir., Thomas K. Liaw/Dir., Nicos Katsoulis/Dir., John J. Lafalce/Dir.

Owners: Arthur Dulik, Andrew J. Simons, Richard W. Merzbacher/1.48%, Gerard J. McKeon, Joseph F. Munson, Brian K. Finneran, PL Capital Group/5.33%, Thomas F. Goldrick/1.96%, John F. Picciano, Insiders/9.54%, Thomas K. Liaw, Jeffrey S. Wilks, Suzanne H. Rueck, Thomas M. OBrien, Frederick C. Braun *(18 Owners included in Index)*

Financial Data: ***Fiscal Year End:***12/31 ***Latest Annual Data:*** 12/31/2006

Year	Sales	Net Income
2006	$112,250,000	$11,494,000
2005	$89,231,000	-$36,548,000
2004	$77,088,000	$13,376,000

Curr. Assets:	$216,630,000	***Curr. Liab.:***	$1,653,905,000	***P/E Ratio:***	20.56
Plant, Equip.:	$6,043,000	***Total Liab.:***	$1,684,582,000	***Indic. Yr. Divd.:***	$0.600
Total Assets:	$1,788,722,000	***Net Worth:***	$104,141,000	***Debt/ Equity:***	NA

State National Bancshares Inc

4500 Mercantile Plz. Dr., Ste. 30, Fort Worth, TX, 76137; ***PH:*** 1-817-547-1150; ***http://*** www.statenationalbank.com

General - Incorporation	TX	***Stock***- Price on:12/24/2007	NA
Employees	NA	Stock Exchange	NA
Auditor	Deloitte & Touche, LLP	Ticker Symbol	NA
Stk Agt	Registrar & Transfer Co	Outstanding Shares	NA
Counsel	Eduardo Arbizu	E.P.S	NA
DUNS No.	NA	Shareholders	NA

Business: The group operates through its subsidiaries whose principle activity is to provide financial products and services. The products of the group include commercial loan, real estate loans and construction loan. In October 6, 2005 the group acquired Heritage Financial Corporation. The group operates from the United States. The assets of the group for the year 2006 were $1,662,877 (thousands).

Primary SIC and add'l.: 6712 6021

CIK No: 0001332626

Subsidiaries: State National Bancshares of Delaware, Inc., State National Bank, State National Capital Trust I, State National Properties, LLC, State National Statutory Trust I, State National Statutory Trust II, TWOENC, Inc.

Owners: Mark G. Merlo, Alan L. Lackey, Don E. Cosby, Insiders/11.98%, Franklin Templeton/15.63%, Ben Stribling, Larry G. Autrey, Rick Calhoon/1.77%, James A. Cardwell/1.75%, Gil H. Moutray, Castle Creek Funds/15.55%, Tom C. Nichols/4.27%, James F. Volk/1.10%, Gary J. Fletcher, Edwin L. Schulz

State Street Corp

One Lincoln St., Boston, MA, 02111; ***PH:*** 1-617-786-3000; ***http://*** www.stateSt..com;
Email: publicrelations@stateSt..com

General - Incorporation	MA	**Stock**- Price on:12/24/2007	$70.15
Employees	21,700	Stock Exchange	NYSE
Auditor	Ernst & Young LLP	Ticker Symbol	STT
Stk Agt	Computershare Ltd.	Outstanding Shares	336,380,000
Counsel	NA	E.P.S	$3.76
DUNS No.	06-215-6427	Shareholders	NA

Business: The groups principle activity is to provide financial services to institutional investors. The groups services include investment management, and research and trading. The group operates from United States.

Primary SIC and add'l.: 7389 6021 6712 6282

CIK No: 0000093751

Subsidiaries: International Financial Data Services, Limited Partnership (50% Owned), International Fund Services (ireland) Limited, Investment Management Services, Inc., Princeton Financial Systems, Inc., Ssb Realty, LLC, Ssga Funds Management, Inc., State Street Australia Limited, State Street Bank And Trust Company, State Street Bank And Trust Company Of California, N.a., State Street Bank And Trust Company Of New Hampshire, State Street Bank And Trust Company, N.a., State Street Bank Europe, Limited, State Street Bank Gmbh, State Street Bank Luxembourg, S.a., State Street Banque, S.a. 40 Subsidiaries included in the Index

Officers: Ronald E. Logue/Chmn., CEO/$26,757,510.00, Joseph C. Antonellis/Vice Chmn. - Investment Servicing North America, Investment Mgr. Outsourcing - Global Securities Services, Global Information Technology/$6,334,483.00, Gary E. Enos/Exec. VP, Maureen P. Corcoran/Exec. VP, Sean P. Flannery/Exec. VP, Alan D. Greene/Exec. VP, Timothy J. Caverly/Exec. VP, Stefan M. Gavell/Exec. VP, Madge M. Meyer/Exec. VP, Charles F. Hindmarsh/Exec. VP, George A. Russell/Exec. VP, Drew J. Breakspear/Exec. VP, General Auditor, Joseph W. Chow/Exec. VP - Risk, Corporate Administration, Robert Kaplan/Exec. VP, Stanley W. Shelton/Exec. VP - State Street Global Markets *(49 Officers included in Index)*

Directors: Ronald E. Logue/Chmn., CEO, Joseph L. Hooley/Vice Chmn., William W. Hunt/Vice Chmn., Richard P. Sergel/Dir., Nader F. Darehshori/70/Dir., Tenley E. Albright/Dir., Diana Chapman Walsh/Dir., Peter Coym/Dir., Amelia C. Fawcett/Dir., Maureen J. Miskovic/Dir., Kennett F. Burnes/Dir., David P. Gruber/Dir., Arthur L. Goldstein/Dir., Robert E. Weissman/66/Dir., Linda A. Hill/Dir. *(18 Directors included in Index)*

Owners: Peter Coym, Arthur L. Goldstein, Ronald E. Logue, Robert E. Weissman, Kennett F. Burnes, Tenley E. Albright, Joseph C. Antonellis, Joseph L. Hooley, Amelia C. Fawcett, FMR Corp./6.60%, Edward J. Resch, Ronald L. Skates, Gregory L. Summe, Linda A. Hill, Diana Chapman Walsh *(23 Owners included in Index)*

Financial Data: ***Fiscal Year End:***12/31 ***Latest Annual Data:*** 12/31/2006

Year	***Sales***	***Net Income***
2006	$9,525,000,000	$1,106,000,000
2005	$7,497,000,000	$838,000,000
2004	$5,861,000,000	$798,000,000

Curr. Assets:	$23,067,000,000	***Curr. Liab.:***	$92,918,000,000	***P/E Ratio:***	18.66
Plant, Equip.:	$1,560,000,000	***Total Liab.:***	$100,101,000,000	***Indic. Yr. Divd.:***	$0.880
Total Assets:	$107,353,000,000	***Net Worth:***	$7,252,000,000	***Debt/ Equity:***	0.3499

Stater Bros Holdings Inc

301S. Tippecanoe Ave., San Barnadino, CA, 92408; ***PH:*** 1-909-783-5000; ***http://*** www.staterbros.com

General - Incorporation	DE	**Stock**- Price on:12/24/2007	NA
Employees	NA	Stock Exchange	NA
Auditor	Ernst & young LLP	Ticker Symbol	NA
Stk Agt	NA	Outstanding Shares	NA
Counsel	NA	E.P.S	NA
DUNS No.	05-498-6104	Shareholders	NA

Business: The groups principle activity is to operate supermarkets. The group provides grocery, health and general merchandise products. The group operates from United States.

Primary SIC and add'l.: 5411

CIK No: 0000882829

Subsidiaries: Santee Dairies, Inc., Super Rx, Inc.

Officers: Jack H. Brown/Chmn., CEO, Jim Lee/COO, Pres., Mark Seay/Community Relations Representative

Directors: Jack H. Brown/Chmn., CEO

Owners: Jack H. Brown/100.00%, Insiders/100.00%

Station Casinos Inc

2411 W Sahara Ave., Las Vegas, NV, 89102; ***PH:*** 1-702-797-7040; ***http://*** www.stationcasinos.com

General - Incorporation	NV	**Stock**- Price on:12/24/2007	$87.75
Employees	14,600	Stock Exchange	NA
Auditor	Ernst & Young LLP	Ticker Symbol	NA
Stk Agt	Deloitte & Touche LLP	Outstanding Shares	NA
Counsel	Milbank, Tweed Hadley & McCoy	E.P.S	$1.43
DUNS No.	08-111-5479	Shareholders	NA

Business: The group's principal activities are to operate casino properties and provide slot route management services. The group operates eight major hotel/casino properties and two smaller casino properties in las vegas, Nevada. It also operates gaming and entertainment complexes in st. Charles and Kansas city, Missouri.

Primary SIC and add'l.: 7021 5812 7011 7999

CIK No: 0000898660

Subsidiaries: Aliante Holding, LLC, Aliante Station, LLC:, Boulder Station,Inc., Carey Station Holdings, LLC, Centerline Holdings, LLC, Charleston Station, LLC, d.b.a The Greens, d.b.a. Barleys Casino& Brewing Company, Durango Station,Inc., Fiesta Palms, LLC, Fiesta Station Holdings, LLC, Fiesta Station,Inc., Front Street Station, LLC, Gold Rush Station, LLC, Green Valley Ranch Gaming, LLC 36 Subsidiaries included in the Index

Officers: Frank J. Fertitta/Chmn., CEO, Lorenzo J. Fertitta/Vice Chmn., Pres., Scott M. Nielson/Exec. VP, Chief Development Officer, William W. Warner/COO, Exec. VP, Glenn C. Christenson/CFO, Richard J. Haskins/Exec. VP, General Counsel, Thomas M. Friel/Exec. VP, Chief Accounting Officer, Treasurer

Directors: Frank J. Fertitta/Chmn., CEO, Lorenzo J. Fertitta/Vice Chmn., Pres., Robert E. Lewis/Dir., James E. Nave/Dir., Lowell H. Lebermann/Dir., Lee S. Isgur/Dir.

Owners: Frank J. Fertitta/9.90%, Glenn C. Christenson/1.00%, Janus Capital Management LLC/7.20%, Lowell H. Lebermann, Robert E. Lewis, Scott M. Nielson/1.20%, Lorenzo J. Fertitta/9.90%, Richard J. Haskins, Highfields Capital Management LP/9.00%, Marsico Capital Management/10.30%, Insiders/23.20%, William W. Warner/1.00%, Lee S. Isgur, Blake L. Sartini/6.80%, James E. Nave *(16 Owners included in Index)*

Financial Data: ***Fiscal Year End:***12/31 ***Latest Annual Data:*** 12/31/2006

Year	***Sales***	***Net Income***
2006	$1,339,024,000	$110,212,000
2005	$1,108,833,000	$161,886,000
2004	$986,742,000	$66,350,000

Curr. Assets:	$201,551,000	***Curr. Liab.:***	$251,906,000	***P/E Ratio:***	61.36
Plant, Equip.:	$2,800,847,000	***Total Liab.:***	$3,903,554,000	***Indic. Yr. Divd.:***	NA
Total Assets:	$3,716,696,000	***Net Worth:***	-$186,858,000	***Debt/ Equity:***	NA

Statmon Technologies Corp

3000 Lakeside Dr., Ste. 300S, Bannockburn, CA, 60015; ***PH:*** 1-847-604-5366;
http:// www.statmon.com; ***Email:*** info@statmon.com

General - Incorporation	NV	**Stock**- Price on:12/24/2007	$1.6
Employees	12	Stock Exchange	OTC
Auditor	Marcum & Kliegman LLP	Ticker Symbol	STCA
Stk Agt	Interstate Transfer Company	Outstanding Shares	14,890,000
Counsel	Martin E. Jacobs	E.P.S	NA
DUNS No.	NA	Shareholders	NA

Business: The groups principle activity is a proprietary software development and integration technology products solution provider. Corporate, institutional and governmental customers to manage and control their network operations use the groups proprietary flagship software application Axess and supporting integration products. The group operates from the United States.

Primary SIC and add'l.: 7371

CIK No: 0000319008

Subsidiaries: STATMON - EBI SOLUTIONS, LLC, STC SOFTWARE CORP.

Officers: Geoffrey P. Talbot/Co - Founder, Chmn., CEO, Peter J. Upfold/Co - Founder, CTO, Vice Chmn., Kevin Harris/COO, Nigel Brownett/Exec. VP - Development, Ken Dillard/Exec. VP - Broadcast Sales - Marketing

Directors: Geoffrey P. Talbot/Co - Founder, Chmn., CEO, Peter J. Upfold/Co - Founder, CTO, Vice Chmn., Robert B. Fields/Dir., Len Silverman/Dir.

Owners: Insiders/36.43%, Peter J. Upfold/18.25%, Geoffrey P. Talbot/11.33%, Kevin R. Harris/3.32%, Robert B. Fields/1.39%, Dean Delis/24.97%, Thieme Consulting, Inc/13.06%, Martin E. Jacobs/6.52%, Leonard Silverman/2.15%

Curr. Assets:	$439,000	***Curr. Liab.:***	$6,119,000		
Plant, Equip.:	$41,000	***Total Liab.:***	$6,119,000	***Indic. Yr. Divd.:***	NA
Total Assets:	$874,000	***Net Worth:***	-$5,245,000	***Debt/ Equity:***	NA

Statoil

Forusbeen 50, Stavanger, N-4035; ***PH:*** 47-519-90000; ***http://*** www.statoil.com

General - Incorporation	Norway	**Stock**- Price on:12/24/2007	$29.64
Employees	25,435	Stock Exchange	NYSE
Auditor	Ernst & Young LLP	Ticker Symbol	NA
Stk Agt	Bank of New York	Outstanding Shares	2,140,000,000
Counsel	NA	E.P.S	$3.58
DUNS No.	NA	Shareholders	NA

Business: The groups principle activities include exploration, production, transportation, refining and marketing of petroleum and petroleum-derived products. The group operates through the following divisions: refining, marketing, trading and supply of oil, shipping and maritime technology and natural gas business development; exploration, development and production of oil and gas and marketing and supply of natural gas. The group operates from United States.

Primary SIC and add'l.: 4925 5541 2911 1311 1382 2992

CIK No: 0001140625

Subsidiaries: AS Eesti Statoil, Latvija Statoil SIA, Mongstad Refining DA, Mongstad Terminal DA, Offlect Invest AS, SDS Holding AS, Statholding AS, Statoil AB, Statoil Angola AS, Statoil Angola Block 15 AS, Statoil Angola Block 17 AS, Statoil Apsheron AS, Statoil Asia Pacific Pte. Ltd, Statoil Azerbaijan Alov AS, Statoil Azerbaijan AS 48 Subsidiaries included in the Index

Officers: Helge Lund/45/CEO, Pres., Jens R. Jenssen/54/Exec. VP - Human Resources, Rune Bjornson/49/Exec. VP - Natural Gas, Eldar Satre/52/CFO, Exec. VP, Inger Ostensjo/53/Member - Corporate Assembly, Anne Synnove Hebnes/35/Employee Representative, Einar Arne Iversen/45/Employee Representative, Arvid Faraas/45/Employee Representative, Reidar Gjaerum/47/Exec. VP - Communication, Nina Udnes Tronstad/49/Exec. VP - Health, Safety, The Environment, Jon Arnt Jacobsen/50/Exec. VP - Manufacturing, Marketing, Margareth Ovrum/49/Exec. VP - Technology, Projects, Erlend Grimstad/40/Member - Corporate Assembly, Kjell Bjorndalen/61/Member - Corporate Assembly, Greger Mannsverk/47/Member - Corporate Assembly *(21 Officers included in Index)*

Directors: Jannik Lindbak/68/Chmn., Kaci Kullman Five/56/Dep. Chmn., Knut Am/64/Dir., Ingrid Wiik/63/Dir., Marit Arnstad/45/Dir., Lill-Heidi Bakkerud/44/Dir., Finn A. Hvistendahl/66/Dir., Morten Svaan/51/Dir., Claus Clausen/53/Dir., Grace Reksten Skaugen/54/Dir.

Owners: Helge Lund, Kaci Kullmann Five, Eldar Stre, Margareth vrum, Nina Udnes Tronstad, Peter Mellbye, Jon Arnt Jacobsen, Morten Svaan, Finn A. Hvistendahl, Rune Bjrnson, Jens R. Jenssen, Ingrid Wiik, Claus Clausen, Lill-Heidi Bakkerud, Reidar Gjrum *(18 Owners included in Index)*

Financial Data: ***Fiscal Year End:***12/31 ***Latest Annual Data:*** 12/31/2006

Year	Sales	Net Income
2006	$68,281,660,000	$6,522,769,000
2005	$58,011,455,000	$4,532,675,000
2004	$50,648,457,000	$4,121,106,000

Curr. Assets:	$12,379,209,000	Curr. Liab.:	$12,495,644,000		
Plant, Equip.:	$33,661,921,000	Total Liab.:	$31,034,344,000	Indic. Yr. Divd.:	$0.570
Total Assets:	$50,664,161,000	Net Worth:	$19,629,817,000	Debt/ Equity:	NA

STATS ChipPAC Ltd

47400 Kato Rd., Fremont, CA, 94538; PH: 1-510-979-8000; Fax: 1-510-979-8001;
http:// www.statschippac.com

General - Incorporation	Singapore	Stock - Price on:12/24/2007	NA
Employees	NA	Stock Exchange	OTC
Auditor	PricewaterhouseCoopers LLP	Ticker Symbol	SCIPF
Stk Agt.	NA	Outstanding Shares	NA
Counsel	NA	E.P.S.	NA
DUNS No.	NA	Shareholders	NA

Business: The group's principal activities are the provision of full range semiconductor test and assembly services to fabless companies, vertically integrated device manufacturers (IDMS) and foundries. Test services offers a wafer probe and final testing on many different platforms such as mixed-signal testing of network routers, switches and interface cards; broadband products such as cable set-top boxes and wireless telecommunications products - cellular phones, base stations and bluetooth (TM) devices; and computer components and audio devices. Assembly services offers packaging solutions and full backend turnkey services plus a complete package design, electrical and thermal simulation, measurement and design of lead frames and substrates. The group has operations in Singapore, the United States of America, Japan, Germany and the United Kingdom.

Primary SIC and add'l.: 8711 8734 7379

CIK No: 0001101873

Subsidiaries: ChipPAC International Company Limited, ChipPAC Liquidity Management Hungary Limited Liability Company, ChipPAC Luxembourg S.a.R.L., STATS ChipPAC (Barbados) Ltd., STATS ChipPAC (BVI) Limited, STATS ChipPAC Korea Ltd., STATS ChipPAC Malaysia Sdn. Bhd., STATS ChipPAC Semiconductor Shanghai Co., Ltd., STATS ChipPAC Taiwan Co., Ltd., STATS ChipPAC Test Services (Shanghai) Co., Ltd., STATS ChipPAC Test Services, Inc., STATS ChipPAC, Inc., STATS Holdings Limited, TATS ChipPAC Shanghai Co., Ltd., Winstek Semiconductor Corporation

Officers: Tan Lay Koon/Dir., CEO, Pres., Richard Weng/Chmn. - Stats Chippac Taiwan Semiconductor Corporation, Mark Kelly/GM - Stats Chippac Test Services, SCU, Wong Chee Wai/MD, Pres. - Stats Chippac Singapore, SCS, Sohn Byeong-Kyuck/MD, Pres. - Stats Chippac Korea, SCK, Ng Tiong Gee/45/Sr. VP - Human Resources, CIO, Janet Taylor/Sr. VP, General Counsel, Lee Yik Choong/MD, Pres. - Stats Chippac China, SCC, Lew Hon Sang/MD, Pres. - Stats Chippac Malaysia, SCM, Tham Kah Locke/VP - Corporate Finance, Han Byung Joon/CTO, Exec. VP, Lisa Lavin/Mgr. - Marketing Communications, Michael G. Potter/41/Sr. VP, CFO, Scott J. Jewler/42/Chief Strategy Officer, Exec. VP, Tiong Ng Gee/CIO, Sr. VP - Human Resources (17 Officers included in Index)

Directors: Tan Lay Koon/Dir., CEO, Pres., Charles R. Wofford/Chmn., Douglas R. Norby/Dir., Richard J. Agnich/64/Dir., Peter Seah Lim Huat/Dir., Jimmy Phoon/Dir., Teng Cheong Kwee/Dir., Tokumasa Yasui/Dir., Robert W. Conn/65/Dir., Park Chong Sup/60/Dir., Lim Ming Seong/60/Dir., Steven H. Hamblin/59/Dir.

Owners: Temasek Holdings/35.35%, FMR Corp/11.92%

Steak N Shake Co

36 S Pennsylvania St., Ste. 500, Indianapolis, IN, 46204; PH: 1-317-633-4100; Fax: 1-317-633-4105; http:// www.steaknshake.com

General - Incorporation	IN	Stock - Price on:12/24/2007	$15.11
Employees	7,667	Stock Exchange	NYSE
Auditor	Deloitte & Touche LLP	Ticker Symbol	SNS
Stk Agt.	Computershare Investor Services LLC	Outstanding Shares	28,450,000
Counsel	NA	E.P.S.	$0.42
DUNS No.	00-692-8105	Shareholders	NA

Business: The group's principal activity is to own, operate and franchise restaurants. The restaurants offer full-service dining with counter and dining room seating, as well as drive-thru and carryout service. The group's food is freshly prepared, cooked-to-order in view of the customer and served promptly on China with flatware and glassware. The group has 57 franchised restaurants, located in 19 midwestern and southeastern states. At 17-Dec-2003, the group had 353 company-operated restaurants. It has federally registered trade marks and service marks such as steak n shake(R), takhomasak(R), famous for steakburgers, faxasak(R), in sight it must be right(R), steak n shake - its a meal(R), the original steakburger(R), wing and circle(r). The group has franchise operations in Georgia, Illinois, Indiana, Kentucky, Mississippi, Missouri, North Carolina and Tennessee states.

Primary SIC and add'l.: 5812 6794

CIK No: 0000093859

Subsidiaries: Stellent AB, Stellent Asia Pty. Limited, Stellent B.V., Stellent Canada Ltd, Stellent Chicago Sales, Inc, Stellent Chicago, Inc, Stellent Holding B.V. Company

Officers: Alan B. Gilman/Chmn., Interim CEO, Jeffrey A. Blade/Exec. VP, CFO, Chief Administrative Officer, Omar Janjua/Exec. VP - Operations, Steven C. Schiller/Sr. VP, Chief Marketing Officer, Bradley Manns/VP - Franchising, David C. Milne/VP, General Counsel, Corp. Sec., Duane E. Geiger/VP, Controller, Gary T. Reinwald/Exec. VP - Development, Kenneth L. Faulkner/VP - Operations, Thomas Murrill/Sr. VP - Human Resources, Scott A. Deibert/VP - Supply Chain, Lynn Elson/VP - Operations Support, Michael J. Vance/VP - Strategic Planning, CIO, Douglas D. Willard/VP - Consumer Insight, Innovation

Directors: Alan B. Gilman/Chmn., Interim CEO, Geoffrey Ballotti/Dir., Fred J. Risk/Dir., Edward W. Wilhelm/Dir., Charles E. Lanham/Dir., Steven M. Schmidt/Dir., James Williamson/Dir., Wayne L. Kelley/Dir., Ruth J. Person/Dir., John W. Ryan/Dir.

Owners: John W. Ryan, Wayne L. Kelley/1.70%, Alan B. Gilman, James Williamson, MSD Capital, L.P./9.80%, Jeffrey Blade, Charles E. Lanham, Edward Wilhelm, Peter M. Dunn, Gary T. Reinwald, Fred J. Risk, Insiders/7.10%, Neuberger Berman, Inc./6.00%, Ruth J. Person/1.40%, Steven M. Schmidt

Financial Data: Fiscal Year End:09/28   Latest Annual Data: 9/27/2006

Year	Sales	Net Income
2006	$638,822,000	$28,001,000
2005	$606,912,000	$30,222,000
2004	$553,692,000	$27,591,000

Curr. Assets:	$45,400,000	Curr. Liab.:	$58,604,000	P/E Ratio:	23.98
Plant, Equip.:	$385,258,000	Total Liab.:	$216,921,000	Indic. Yr. Divd.:	NA
Total Assets:	$435,853,000	Net Worth:	$218,932,000	Debt/ Equity:	0.5312

Steakhouse Partners Inc

10200 Willow Creek Rd. , San Diego, CA, 92131; PH: 1-858-689-2333;
http:// www.paragonsteak.com

General - Incorporation	DE	Stock - Price on:12/24/2007	NA
Employees	1,300	Stock Exchange	OTC
Auditor	Mayer Hoffman Mccann, P.C	Ticker Symbol	STKP
Stk Agt	Corporate Stock Transfer, Inc.	Outstanding Shares	NA
Counsel	NA	E.P.S.	-$0.8
DUNS No.	94-581-2105	Shareholders	NA

Business: The group's principal activity is to own and operate steakhouse restaurants in the United States. The group's restaurants specialize in complete steak and prime rib meals and also offer fresh fish and other lunch and dinner dishes. The group operates under the brand names of hungry hunter's, hunter's steakhouse, mountain jack's and carvers. The group's menu also includes seafood, pasta, chicken, appetizers and desserts. The group filed for chapter 11 proceedings on 15-Feb-2002 and emerged from such proceedings on 31-Dec-2003. As of 30-Mar-2004, the group operates 25 full-service steakhouse restaurants located in eight states.

Primary SIC and add'l.: 5812 5813

CIK No: 0001017156

Subsidiaries: Paragon of Michigan, Inc., Paragon of Nevada, Inc., Paragon of Wisconsin, Inc., Paragon Steakhouse Restaurants, Inc

Owners: Insiders/10.10%, Thomas A. Edler/0.70%, Joseph L. Wulkowicz/1.40%, GRI Fund, LP/8.10%, Steven B. Sands/15.20%, Susan Schulze-Claasen/1.40%, Edgar Tod Lindner/0.70%, David Rich/5.40%, Stone A. Douglass/6.20%, Eye of the Round, LLC/13.30%, Pablo Garcia Fernandez/6.00%, George Rich/11.50%

Financial Data: Fiscal Year End:12/28   Latest Annual Data: 12/31/2006

Year	Sales	Net Income
2006	$50,168,000	-$1,770,000
2005	$52,001,000	-$455,000
2004	$55,071,000	-$635,000

Curr. Assets:	$2,036,000	Curr. Liab.:	$13,921,000		
Plant, Equip.:	$9,487,000	Total Liab.:	$23,548,000	Indic. Yr. Divd.:	NA
Total Assets:	$29,405,000	Net Worth:	$5,857,000	Debt/ Equity:	NA

StealthGas Inc

331, Kifisias Ave., Kifisia, 14561; PH: 30-2106250001; http:// www.irwebpage.com;
Email: nbornozis@capitallink.com

General - Incorporation	Marshall Islands	Stock - Price on:12/24/2007	$17.95
Employees	520	Stock Exchange	NDQ
Auditor	Deloitte, Sofianos & Cambanis S.A	Ticker Symbol	GASS
Stk Agt	American Stock Transfer & Trust Co.	Outstanding Shares	NA
Counsel	NA	E.P.S.	$1.32
DUNS No.	NA	Shareholders	NA

Business: The groups principle activity is to provide international sea borne transportation services. Customers served by the group include LPG producers and users. Specific customers of the group include Petredec, Dow Chemical, Finaval, Petrobras and Shell. The group operates from the United States. The group's quarterly revenue for September 2007 was 23.24 millions of USD.

Primary SIC and add'l.: 4412

CIK No: 0001328919

Subsidiaries: Access Consultants Co., Alexis Shipholding S.A., Aracruz Trading Ltd., Atlas Investments S.A., Aubine Services Ltd., Balcan Profit Limited, Balkan Holding Inc., Baroness Holdings Inc., Cedric Finance Inc., Celidon Investments Inc., Continent Gas Inc., Delora Trading Company, Drew International Inc., East Propane Inc., Empire Spirit Ltd. 52 Subsidiaries included in the Index

Officers: Harry N. Vafias/Dir., CEO, Pres., Andrew J. Simmons/CFO

Directors: Harry N. Vafias/Dir., CEO, Pres., Michael G. Jolliffe/Chmn., Thanassis J. Martinos/Dir., Markos Drakos/48/Dir.

Owners: Insiders/29.60%, Zesiger Capital Group LLC/4.40%, Flawless Management Inc./27.80%, Wellington Management Company, LLP/6.40%, Thanassis J. Martinos/1.90%, Harry N. Vafias/27.80%

Financial Data: Fiscal Year End:12/31   Latest Annual Data: 12/31/2006

Year	Sales	Net Income
2006	$73,259,000	$18,493,000
2005	$36,645,000	$14,536,000

Curr. Assets:	$17,892,000	Curr. Liab.:	$28,629,000	P/E Ratio:	9.62
Plant, Equip.:	$301,434,000	Total Liab.:	$155,803,000	Indic. Yr. Divd.:	$0.750
Total Assets:	$319,605,000	Net Worth:	$163,802,000	Debt/ Equity:	NA

Steamship Co Torm A/S

Tuborg Havnevej 18, Hellerup; PH: 45-39179200; http:// www.torm.dk; Email: mail@torm.dk

General - Incorporation	Denmark	Stock - Price on:12/24/2007	$36.99
Employees	339	Stock Exchange	NDQ
Auditor	Deloitte Statsautoriseret	Ticker Symbol	NA
Stk Agt	NA	Outstanding Shares	69,240,000
Counsel	NA	E.P.S.	NA
DUNS No.	NA	Shareholders	NA

Business: The group's principal activity is shipping of clean oil products, such as gasoline, jet fuel, naphtha and diesel oil. In addition, the group's bulk carrier division focuses on the panamax and handysize bulk carrier sectors, carrying various bulk commodities, principally grain, coal and iron ore. Operations are largely conducted through pooling arrangements with major ship owners, leaving the commercial management of the majority of these pools to the group. The group also operates a liner division, and an offshore supply division. The group is responsible for the operation of approximately 90 vessels.

Primary SIC and add'l.: 4731 4412

CIK No: 0001168351

Subsidiaries: Torm Singapore (Pte) Ltd.

Officers: Klaus Kjaerulff/CEO, Pres., Esben Poulsson/CEO, Pres. - Torm Singapore Pte Ltd, Jesper Bo Hansen/VP - Shipowning, S, P Division, Mogens Fynbo/Exec. VP - Technical Division, Per Winther Christensen/VP - Safety - Quality, Bo Ellenton Jensen/VP - Information Technology - Support Functions, Helle Lehmann/VP - Claims, Insurance, Ivan Hill Petersen/VP - Bulk, Mikael Skov/COO, Anders Engholm/Exec. VP - Tankers, Michael Agerholm/VP - Technical, Quality Coordination, Jens Bjergmose/Sr. VP - Human Resources, Claus U. Jensen/Fleet Mgr. - Technical Division, Thomas Andersen/VP - Investor Relations, Communication, Maiken Odegaard/VP - Operations, Strategic Coordination *(23 Officers included in Index)*

Directors: Niels Erik Nielsen/Chmn., Margrethe Bligaard/39/Dir., Christian Frigast/Dir., Ditlev Engel/44/Dir., Lennart Arrias/Dir., Peder Mouridsen/58/Dir., Gabriel Panayotides/Dir., Nicos Zouvelos/Dir.

Owners: Menfield Navigation Company Limited/20.00%, Beltest Shipping Company Ltd./32.20%, A/S Dampskibsselskabet TORM's Underst0ttelsesfond, Denmark/6.30%

Financial Data: Fiscal Year End:12/31   Latest Annual Data: 12/31/2006

Year	Sales	Net Income
2006	$455,394,000	$238,112,000
2005	$586,975,000	$299,363,000
2004	$476,182,000	$418,375,000

Curr. Assets:	$120,905,000	Curr. Liab.:	$106,321,000		
Plant, Equip.:	$1,140,357,000	Total Liab.:	$817,573,000	Indic. Yr. Divd.:	NA
Total Assets:	$2,089,019,000	Net Worth:	$1,271,446,000	Debt/ Equity:	NA

Steel Dynamics Inc

6714 Pointe Inverness Way, Ste 200, Fort Wayne, IN, 46804; *PH:* 1-260-459-3553; *http://* www.steeldynamics.com

General - Incorporation	IN	Stock - Price on:12/24/2007	$43.79
Employees	3,490	Stock Exchange	NDQ
Auditor	Ernst & Young LLP	Ticker Symbol	STLD
Stk Agt	Computershare Trust CO.	Outstanding Shares	94,490,000
Counsel	NA	E.P.S.	$4.01
DUNS No.	80-820-2725	Shareholders	NA

Business: The group's principle activity is steel manufacturing. The group produces steel primarily from steel scrap using electric arc melting furnaces, continuous casting and automated rolling mills. The group owns and operates three steelmaking mini-mills. The group produces a broad range of hot rolled, cold rolled and coated steel products. The group has two reportable segments: steel operations and steel scrap substitute operations. The steel operations segment includes flat roll division, structural and rail division, and bar division. Steel scrap substitute operations include the revenues and expenses associated with the company's wholly owned subsidiary iron dynamics. The group's products are used in the automotive, construction and commercial industries. The group's quarterly revenue for Sep '07 was 1,156.59 millions of USD.

Primary SIC and add'l.: 3312

CIK No: 0001022671

Subsidiaries: Dynamic Aviation, LLC(Indiana), New Millennium Building Systems, LLC(Indiana), Paragon Steel Enterprises, LLC(Indiana), RS Acquisition Corporation (Indiana), SDI Investment Company (Delaware), Steel Dynamics Sales North America,Inc. (Indiana), Steel Holdings,Inc. (Indiana), STLD Holdings,Inc. (Indiana)

Officers: Keith E. Busse/Chmn., CEO, Pres./$3,364,560.00, Bert Hollman/VP, John W. Nolan/VP, GM - Structural, Rail Division, Richard Teets/Dir., Exec. VP/$1,831,314.00, Bill Sarver/Controller - Roanoke Bar Division, Jim Wroble/Sales, Marketing Mgr. - Structural, Rail Division, Bill Kautz/Controller - Structural, Rail Division, Barry Schneider/VP, GM - Engineered Bar Products Division, Bill Brown/Sales Mgr. - Engineered Bar Products Division, Danny Rifkin/Exec. VP, Leon Waninger/Controller, Glenn Pushis/VP, GM - Flat Roll Division, Gary Heasley/Exec. VP - Strategic Planning - Business Development/$1,368,690.00, Mark D. Millett/Dir., Exec. VP - Rolled Steels, Ferrous Resources/$1,969,578.00, Fredrick A. Warner/Mgr. - Investor Relations *(28 Officers included in Index)*

Directors: Keith E. Busse/Chmn., CEO, Pres., Richard Teets/Dir., Exec. VP, Mark D. Millett/Dir., Exec. VP - Rolled Steels, Ferrous Resources, Joseph D. Ruffolo/Dir., Jurgen Kolb/Dir., Richard J. Freeland/Dir., James C. Marcuccilli/Dir., John C. Bates/Dir., Frank D. Byrne/Dir., Paul B. Edgerley/Dir.

Owners: Mark D. Millett/1.30%, Jrgen Kolb, John C. Bates/2.60%, Frank D. Byrne, Joe T. Crawford, Mellon Financial Corporation/5.10%, Richard P. Teets/2.20%, Barclays Global Investors, NA/8.50%, James C. Marcuccilli, Gary E. Heasley, LSV Asset Management/5.70%, Joseph D. Ruffolo, Paul B. Edgerley, Goldman Sachs Asset Management, L.P./5.70%, Keith E. Busse/1.00% *(17 Owners included in Index)*

Financial Data: Fiscal Year End:12/31   Latest Annual Data: 3/31/2007

Year	Sales	Net Income
2007	NA	NA
2006	NA	NA
2005	$2,184,866,000	$221,785,000

Curr. Assets:	$1,036,197,000	Curr. Liab.:	$399,490,000		
Plant, Equip.:	$1,136,703,000	Total Liab.:	$1,014,485,000	Indic. Yr. Divd.:	$0.400
Total Assets:	$2,247,017,000	Net Worth:	$1,231,108,000	Debt/ Equity:	0.2919

Steel Technologies Inc

15415 Shelbyville Rd. , Louisville, KY, 40253; *PH:* 1-502-245-2110; *http://* www.steeltechnologies.com

General - Incorporation	KY	Stock - Price on:12/24/2007	NA
Employees	NA	Stock Exchange	NA
Auditor	PricewaterhouseCoopers LLP	Ticker Symbol	NA
Stk Agt	National City Bank	Outstanding Shares	NA
Counsel	Stites & Harbison PLLC	E.P.S.	NA
DUNS No.	05-682-6910	Shareholders	NA

Business: The group's principal activity is the processing of flat rolled steel to specified close tolerances in response to orders from industrial customers who require steel of precise thickness, width, temper, finish and shape for customers' manufacturing purposes. The processed steel distribution facilities are located in Indiana, Kentucky, Maryland, Michigan, Missouri, North Carolina, Ohio and South Carolina in the United States and four facilities in Mexico. The group's principal processed products include cold-rolled strip and sheet, cold-rolled one-pass strip, high carbon and alloy strip and sheet, hot-rolled strip and sheet, high strength low alloy strip and sheet, hot-rolled pickle and oil and coated strip and sheet, pickling of hot-rolled black coils, blanking and cut-to-length processing of coil steel and fabrication and welding of steel sheets and plates. On 07-Mar-2003, the group acquired certain assets from Cold Metal Products, Inc.

Primary SIC and add'l.: 3316

CIK No: 0000771790

Subsidiaries: Custom Steel, Inc., Ferrolux Metals Co., LCC, Mi-Tech Steel, Inc., Steel Technologies Co., Steel Technologies Corp., Steel Technologies de, Steel Technologies Ohio, Inc., Steel Technologies, LLC

Officers: Bradford T. Ray/Chmn., CEO, Brad A. Goranson/Sr. VP - Sales, Richard P. Furber/VP - Manufacturing, Strip Products, Mark Calcutt/VP - Sales, Southeastern Region, Patrick M. Carroll/VP - Sales, Central Region, Roger D. Shannon/CFO, Treasurer, John M. Baumann/General Counsel, Sec., Douglas R. Bernd/VP - Outside Processing, Michael J. Carroll/Dir., COO, Pres., Carlos A. Von Rossum Garza/VP, Lee F. Watkins/VP - Operations, Joseph P. Robinson/VP - Sales, Mid, South Region, Thomas E. Mottier/VP - Sales, Midwest Region, Curtis L. Chase/VP - Purchasing, Patrick M. Flanagan/VP - Human Resources *(17 Officers included in Index)*

Directors: Bradford T. Ray/Chmn., CEO, Michael J. Carroll/Dir., COO, Pres.

Owners: Royce & Associates, LLC/10.71%, William E. Hellmann, Dimensional Fund Advisors Inc./8.46%, Brad A. Goranson, Insiders/12.39%, Roger D. Shannon, Bradford T. Ray/3.88%, Mark G. Essig, Stuart N. Ray/2.58%, John M. Baumann, Doug A. Bawel, Jimmy Dan Conner, Michael J. Carroll, Andrew J. Payton, Merwin J. Ray/4.07%

Steelcase Inc

901 44th St., Grand Rapids, MI, 49508; *PH:* 1-616-247-2710; *http://* www.steelcase.com

General - Incorporation	MI	Stock - Price on:12/24/2007	$20.25
Employees	13,000	Stock Exchange	NYSE
Auditor	BDO Seidman LLP	Ticker Symbol	SCS
Stk Agt	Computershare Trust Co	Outstanding Shares	146,650,000
Counsel	NA	E.P.S.	$0.82
DUNS No.	00-601-6547	Shareholders	NA

Business: The groups principle activity is to provide office furniture. The groups furniture includes panel-based and freestanding furniture systems, storage, seating, tables, textiles and surface materials, desks and suites, and worktools. The groups services include interior architecture and lighting services. The group operates from United States.

Primary SIC and add'l.: 2522 6159 2511

CIK No: 0001050825

Subsidiaries: AF Steelcase S.A., Design Tex Group Inc., Office Details Inc., Steelcase Canada Ltd, Steelcase Financial Services Inc., Steelcase S.A., Steelcase Werndl AG

Officers: Michael I. Love/CEO, Pres. - Steelcase Design Partnership/$1,553,653.00, James P. Hackett/Dir., CEO, Pres./$5,012,808.00, Robert C. Pew/Non - Exec. Chmn., David C. Sylvester/CFO, VP/$719,907.00, James P. Keane/Pres. - Steelcase Group/$2,035,832.00, Mark T. Greiner/Sr. VP - Workspace Futures, Mark A. Baker/Sr. VP, Global Operations Mgr./$1,704,270.00, Frank H. Merlotti/Pres. - Steelcase North America/$2,088,636.00, James G. Mitchell/Pres. - Steelcase International, Nancy W. Hickey/Sr. VP, Chief Administrative Officer, Sec., Jon D. Botsford/Sr. VP, Sec., Chief Legal Officer

Directors: James P. Hackett/Dir., CEO, Pres., Robert C. Pew/Non - Exec. Chmn., David W. Joos/Dir., Michael J. Jandernoa/Dir., Peter M. Wege/Dir., Earl D. Holton/Dir., William P. Crawford/Dir., Kate Pew Wolters/Dir., Elizabeth Valk Long/Dir., Craig P. Welch/Dir., Cathy D. Ross/50/Dir.

Owners: Elizabeth Valk Long, Insiders/37.80%, James P. Hackett/1.00%, Earl D. Holton, Michael J. Jandernoa, Peter M. Wege, David W. Joos, Mark A. Baker, William P. Crawford/16.80%, Insiders/3.10%, Robert C. Pew/5.90%, William P. Crawford, Kate Pew Wolters, Kate Pew Wolters/7.10%, Robert C. Pew *(23 Owners included in Index)*

Financial Data: Fiscal Year End:02/24   Latest Annual Data: 2/23/2007

Year	Sales	Net Income
2007	$3,097,400,000	$106,900,000
2006	$2,868,900,000	$48,900,000
2005	$2,613,800,000	$12,700,000

Curr. Assets:	$1,057,300,000	Curr. Liab.:	$609,500,000	P/E Ratio:	24.70
Plant, Equip.:	$606,000,000	Total Liab.:	$1,168,000,000	Indic. Yr. Divd.:	$0.600
Total Assets:	$2,364,600,000	Net Worth:	$1,196,600,000	Debt/ Equity:	0.2019

Steelcloud Inc

14040 Pk. Ctr. Rd., Ste. 210, Herndon, VA, 20171; *PH:* 1-703-674-5500; *Fax:* 1-703-674-5506; *http://* www.steelcloud.com; *Email:* IR@steelcloud.com

General - Incorporation	VA	Stock - Price on:12/24/2007	$1.34
Employees	69	Stock Exchange	NDQ
Auditor	Grant Thornton LLP	Ticker Symbol	SCLD
Stk Agt	Continental Stock Transfer & Trust Co	Outstanding Shares	14,280,000
Counsel	NA	E.P.S.	-$0.202
DUNS No.	NA	Shareholders	NA

Business: The group's principal activity is to design and develop original equipment manufacturer server appliances for software and technology companies. The products of the group include network appliances, infrastructure server products and consulting services. The infrastructure server products include specialized custom servers, which are configured with single, dual or quad intel pentium iii, iv or xeon processors. The group provides its products and services to departments, agencies and offices of the federal government and selected businesses. The group conducts its business under the trademarks of steelcloud, steelcloud company, dunn computer corporation, international data products and idp. In Sept 2003, it disposed Puerto Rico industrial manufacturing operations acquisition corporation. On 17-Feb-2004 the group acquired asgard holding llc.

Primary SIC and add'l.: 7373 3571

CIK No: 0001058027

Subsidiaries: International Data Products Corp., Puerto Rico Industrial Manufacturing Operations Acquisition Corporation, STMS Corporation

Officers: Clifton W. Sink/50/Dir., CEO, Pres., Kevin Murphy/CFO, VP - Finance, Administration, Robert Richmond/60/COO

Directors: Clifton W. Sink/50/Dir., CEO, Pres., E. A. Burkhalter/Chmn., Benjamin Krieger/Dir., Jay M. Kaplowitz/Dir., James Bruno/Dir., Ashok Kaveeshwar/Dir.

Owners: James Bruno, Clifton W. Sink, Robert Richmond, Jay M. Kaplowitz, Benjamin Krieger, VADM E.A. Burkhalter, Kevin M. Murphy/1.88%, Insiders/5.54%

Financial Data: Fiscal Year End:10/31   Latest Annual Data: 10/31/2006

Year	Sales	Net Income
2006	$24,216,000	-$10,040,000
2005	$36,475,000	-$130,000
2004	$28,169,000	-$2,524,000

Curr. Assets:	$9,064,000	Curr. Liab.:	$3,994,000	
Plant, Equip.:	$1,482,000	Total Liab.:	$4,391,000	Indic. Yr. Divd.: NA
Total Assets:	$10,603,000	Net Worth:	$6,212,000	Debt/ Equity: 0.0041

Stein Mart Inc

1200 Riverpl Blvd, Jacksonville, FL, 32207; PH: 1-904-346-1500; http:// www.steinmart.com

General - Incorporation .... FL	Stock- Price on:12/24/2007 ....$12.79
Employees...14,500	Stock Exchange..NDQ
Auditor ....PricewaterhouseCoopers LLP	Ticker Symbol...SMRT
Stk Agt..................Mellon Investor Services LLC	Outstanding Shares 43,230,000
Counsel...Mitchell W. Legler	E.P.S..$0.67
DUNS No. 00-704-1346	Shareholders..NA

Business: The group's principal activity is to merchandise apparels for men, women and children. The group also provides accessories, gifts, linens, shoes and fragrances, servicing and presenting traditional department and specialty stores. Accessories consist of fashion-oriented, brand name, designer and private label jewelry. Women's and men's apparel include sportswear, suits, sportcoats, slacks, dress furnishings and various assortments. Gifts and linens departments consist of fashion-oriented gifts for the home and a wide range of table, bath and bed linens. The shoe department is a leased department operated in individual stores by one of two shoe retailers. At 01-Feb-2003, the group operated a chain of 265 retail stores in 29 states.

Primary SIC and add'l.: 5651 5719 5661

CIK No: 0000884940

Owners: Jay Stein/37.00%, Richard L. Sisisky, Michael D. Ray/0.20%, Martin E. Stein, James G. Delfs/0.10%, James H. Winston/0.10%, Linda McFarland Farthing, Insiders/38.80%, Hunt D. Hawkins, William A. Moll/0.10%, Michael D. Fisher/1.00%, T. Rowe Price Associates, Inc./8.30%, Mitchell W. Legler/0.10%, John H. Williams, EARNEST Partners, LLC/11.30% (17 Owners included in Index)

Financial Data: Fiscal Year End:01/28　Latest Annual Data: 2/3/2007

Year	Sales	Net Income
2007	$1,501,296,000	$37,176,000
2006	$1,481,615,000	$50,884,000
2005	$1,459,607,000	$37,973,000

Curr. Assets:	$344,033,000	Curr. Liab.:	$169,248,000	P/E Ratio: 14.87
Plant, Equip.:	$113,254,000	Total Liab.:	$192,179,000	Indic. Yr. Divd.: $0.250
Total Assets:	$480,351,000	Net Worth:	$288,172,000	Debt/ Equity: NA

Steiner Leisure Ltd

770 S Dixie Hwy., 2nd Fl., Coral Gables, FL, 33146; PH: 1-305-358-9002; Fax: 1-305-358-9954; http:// www.steinerleisure.com; Email: jang@str.co.uk

General - Incorporation .... Bahamas	Stock- Price on:12/24/2007 ....$47.5
Employees...4,343	Stock Exchange..NDQ
Auditor ....Ernst & Young LLP	Ticker Symbol..STNR
Stk Agt...NA	Outstanding Shares 17,070,000
Counsel.....................Kelley, Drye & Warren	E.P.S..$2.68
DUNS No. ....NA	Shareholders..NA

Business: The group's principal activity is to provide spa services. The group also develops and markets beauty products, which are sold at its facilities and at third party retail outlets. It owns and operates three post-secondary schools comprised of a total of seven campuses located in Florida, Virginia, Maryland and Pennsylvania. The group offers degrees in massage therapy and skin care. These schools train and qualify spa professionals for health and beauty positions within the group or other industry entities. The group markets its services and products to cruise passengers and at luxury resort and day spas primarily in the United States, the Caribbean, the pacific, Asia and Mexico. As on 26-Feb-2004, the group served 109 cruise ships representing 17 cruise lines, and operated 63 resort spas and two day spas.

Primary SIC and add'l.: 8222 7991

CIK No: 0001018946

Subsidiaries: Cosmetics Limited, Elemis Limited, FCNH, Inc., Florida Luxury Spa Group, Inc., Mandara (Cruise I) LLC, Mandara (Cruise II) LLC, Mandara PSLV, LLC, Mandara Spa (Hawaii) LLC, Mandara Spa Asia Limited, Mandara Spa LLC, Mid-Atlantic Massage Therapy, Inc., Owned by Steiner Spa Limitez, Steiner Beauty Products, Inc., Steiner Education Group, Inc., Steiner Management Services LLC 21 Subsidiaries included in the Index

Officers: James L. Howard/59/Executive Officer, Jeffrey Matthews/51/Executive Officer

Owners: FMR Corp/10.09%, Robert C. Boehm, Michle Steiner Warshaw, Steven J. Preston, Insiders/10.41%, Charles D. Finkelstein, David S. Harris, Leonard Fluxman/1.41%, Wellington Management Company, LLP/8.66%, Glenn Fusfield, Stephen Lazarus, Cynthia R. Cohen, Clive E. Warshaw/7.97%, Franklin Resources, Inc./6.43%, Sean C. Harrington

Financial Data: Fiscal Year End:12/31　Latest Annual Data: 12/31/2006

Year	Sales	Net Income
2006	$470,142,000	$46,145,000
2005	$397,218,000	$41,168,000
2004	$341,491,000	$35,978,000

Curr. Assets:	$112,104,000	Curr. Liab.:	$68,216,000	P/E Ratio: 17.72
Plant, Equip.:	$62,486,000	Total Liab.:	$74,144,000	Indic. Yr. Divd.: NA
Total Assets:	$257,770,000	Net Worth:	$183,626,000	Debt/ Equity: NA

Steinway Musical Instruments Inc

800 S St., Ste 425, Waltham, MA, 02453; PH: 1-219-522-1675; http:// www.steinway.com; Email: info@steinway.com

General - Incorporation .... DE	Stock- Price on:12/24/2007 ....$35.44
Employees...2,363	Stock Exchange..NYSE
Auditor ....Deloitte & Touche LLP	Ticker Symbol..LVB
Stk Agt..............Continental Stock Transfer & Trust Co	Outstanding Shares 8,500,000
Counsel..... Millbank, Tweed, Hadley & McCloy	E.P.S..$1.01
DUNS No. 08-873-5048	Shareholders..NA

Business: The group's principal activities are to design, manufacture and market musical instruments. It operates through its wholly-owned subsidiaries: the steinway piano company inc and conn-selmer inc. The group operates through two segments namely pianos and band and orchestral instruments. The piano division concentrates on the high-end grand piano market, handcrafting steinway pianos in New York and Germany. The products include brasswind, woodwind, percussion and stringed instruments and related accessories with the brand names bach, c. G. Conn, king and ludwig. The band and orchestral division designs and manufactures musical instruments at manufacturing facilities located in Indiana, Ohio, North Carolina, Illinois and Arizona. The group markets its products in the United States, Germany, Japan, the United Kingdom, Switzerland and France.

Primary SIC and add'l.: 3931

CIK No: 0000911583

Subsidiaries: Boston Piano Company, Boston Piano GmbH, Conn-Selmer, Inc, G. Leblanc SNC, Kluge Klaviaturen GmbH, Kluge Klawiatury, Sp.z.o.o. Wilkow, Noblet, LLC, Normandie, LLC, S & B Retail, Inc, Steinway & Sons, Steinway & Sons Japan, Ltd, Steinway Asia, LLC, Steinway Haus Munchen GmbH, Steinway Musical Instruments, Inc, Steinway Piano (Shanghai) Co., Ltd 19 Subsidiaries included in the Index

Officers: Dana D. Messina/46/Dir., CEO/$447,660.00, Bruce A. Stevens/65/Dir., Pres. - Steinway/$686,760.00, Thomas Kurrer/59/MD - Steinway, Germany/$566,000.00, Dennis M. Hanson/54/Sr. Exec. VP/$502,760.00, John M. Stoner/55/Dir., Pres. - Conn, Selmer/$440,052.00, Julie A. Theriault/Dir. - Corporate Planning Communications

Directors: Dana D. Messina/46/Dir., CEO, Kyle R. Kirkland/46/Chmn., Rudolph Kluiber/48/Dir., Peter McMillan/50/Dir., Clinton A. Allen/64/Dir., Bruce A. Stevens/65/Dir., Pres. - Steinway, John M. Stoner/55/Dir., Pres. - Conn, Selmer

Owners: Insiders/8.60%, Dana D. Messina/52.50%, Thomas Kurrer, Dennis M. Hanson, Bruce A. Stevens/1.10%, John M. Stoner, David M. Silfen/6.80%, Peter McMillan, Dimensional Fund Advisors LP/8.40%, American International Group, Inc/5.10%, Royce& Associates, LLC/5.80%, Kyle R. Kirkland/1.30%, Wells Fargo Bank, N.A/5.70%, Dana D. Messina/3.40%, Kyle R. Kirkland/47.50% (20 Owners included in Index)

Financial Data: Fiscal Year End:12/31　Latest Annual Data: 12/31/2006

Year	Sales	Net Income
2006	$384,620,000	-$668,000
2005	$387,143,000	$13,792,000
2004	$375,034,000	$15,867,000

Curr. Assets:	$282,678,000	Curr. Liab.:	$66,048,000	P/E Ratio: 45.44
Plant, Equip.:	$95,598,000	Total Liab.:	$289,174,000	Indic. Yr. Divd.: NA
Total Assets:	$447,175,000	Net Worth:	$158,001,000	Debt/ Equity: 1.3700

Stelax Industries Ltd

3939 Belt Line Rd., Ste. 440, Addison, TX, 75001; PH: 1-972-233-6041; Fax: 1-214-987-3955; http:// www.stelax.com; Email: usa@stelax.com

General - Incorporation .... BC	Stock- Price on:12/24/2007 ....$0.048
Employees...NA	Stock Exchange...OTC
Auditor ....Killman, Murrell & Co. P.C	Ticker Symbol..STAX
Stk Agt ....Signature Stock Transfer, Inc.	Outstanding Shares 49,630,000
Counsel..NA	E.P.S...NA
DUNS No. 83-981-4555	Shareholders..NA

Business: The group's principal activity is to produce a variety of solid stainless steel products utilizing traditional stainless production techniques. The group produces two separate product lines through its aberneath facility: nuovinox(tm), a stainless steel cladded product with a carbon steel core, and steel abrasive shot pellets which are used as an abrasive cleaner and polisher in steel manufacturing. The properties of the stainless steel cladding enable nuovinox to be used for many applications which require an upgrading of carbon steel or a substitute for stainless steel, in particular where corrosion resistance, hygiene and aesthetics are determining factors. The group holds approximately 70 worldwide patents for nuovinox.

Primary SIC and add'l.: 6719 3312

CIK No: 0000847541

Subsidiaries: Stelax Limited, Stelax USA, Inc., Zfax, Inc.

Officers: Harmon Hardy/Chmn., CEO

Directors: Harmon Hardy/Chmn., CEO

Owners: Harmon S. Hardy/24.90%, Insiders/24.90%

Financial Data: Fiscal Year End:03/31　Latest Annual Data: 3/31/2006

Year	Sales	Net Income
2006	NA	-$409,000
2005	NA	-$432,000
2004	NA	-$502,000

Curr. Assets:	$0	Curr. Liab.:	$6,352,000	
Plant, Equip.:	NA	Total Liab.:	$6,352,000	Indic. Yr. Divd.: NA
Total Assets:	$0	Net Worth:	-$6,352,000	Debt/ Equity: NA

Stellar Pharmaceuticals Inc

Formerly: Stellar International Inc
544 Egerton St., London, ON, N5W 3Z8; PH: 1-519-434-1540

General - Incorporation .... ON	Stock- Price on:12/24/2007 ....$0.6
Employees...NA	Stock Exchange...OTC
Auditor ....Mintz & Partners LLP	Ticker Symbol...SLXCF
Stk Agt ....Equity Transfer Services Inc	Outstanding Shares ....NA
Counsel..NA	E.P.S...NA
DUNS No. ....NA	Shareholders..NA

Business: The groups principle activities include development and marketing of polysaccharide-based therapeutic products used in the treatment of osteoarthritis and certain types of cystitis. The groups products include NeoVisc(R), Uracyst(R) and bladderChek(R). The group operates from United States.

Primary SIC and add'l.: NA

CIK No: 0001159019

Officers: Peter Riehl/Dir., CEO, Pres., Arnold Tenney/Chmn., Investor Relations Officer, David Butts/Dir. - Commercial Operations, Including Business Development, Darrin Statchuk/Quality Mgr., Janice Clarke/Dir. - Administration, CFO, Paul MacPherson/Dir. - Operations, Peter Brownrigg/Dir. - Sales, Marketing

Directors: Peter Riehl/Dir., CEO, Pres., Arnold Tenney/Chmn., Investor Relations Officer, Robert H. Kayser/Dir., John J. Kime/Dir., David A. Rosenkrantz/50/Dir., John M. Gregory/Dir.

Owners: John J. Kime/0.80%, David A. Rosenkrantz/2.70%, Peter Riehl/15.10%, Robert H. Kayser/0.20%, SJ Strategic Investments LLC/22.10%, Arnold Tenney/4.20%, Insiders/23.10%, Janice Clarke/0.50%

Financial Data: Fiscal Year End:12/31 Latest Annual Data: 12/31/2006

Year	Sales	Net Income
2006	$3,757,000	$1,077,000
2005	$1,666,000	-$1,189,000
2004	$1,521,000	-$1,117,000

Curr. Assets:	$3,471,000	**Curr. Liab.:**	$311,000		
Plant, Equip.:	$733,000	**Total Liab.:**	$311,000	**Indic. Yr. Divd.:**	NA
Total Assets:	$4,246,000	**Net Worth:**	$3,935,000	**Debt/ Equity:**	NA

Stellar Resources Ltd

Level 7 Exchange Tower, 530 Little Collins St., Melbourne, NV, 03000; **PH:** 1-613-9909-7618; **http://** www.stellarresources.com.au; **Email:** SRZinfo@stellarresources.com.au

General - Incorporation	NV	**Stock** - Price on:12/24/2007	$0.12
Employees	NA	Stock Exchange	OTC
Auditor	Dale Matheson Carr-Hilton LaBonte LLP	Ticker Symbol	SRRL
Stk Agt	NA	Outstanding Shares	NA
Counsel	NA	E.P.S.	NA
DUNS No.	NA	Shareholders	NA

Business: The groups principal activity is an exploration stage company engaged in the acquisition, exploration and development of mineral properties. The group operates from the United States.

Primary SIC and add'l.: 1081

CIK No: 0001217027

Officers: Thomas J. Burrowes/Exec. Chmn., Christopher G. Anderson/Exec. Dir., David J. Isles/Exec. Dir., Melvyn J.S. Drummond/Company Sec., Bryan D. Cumming/Solicitor

Directors: Thomas J. Burrowes/Exec. Chmn., Christopher G. Anderson/Exec. Dir., David J. Isles/Exec. Dir., Barrie E. Laws/Non Exec. Dir.

Owners: Kathy Whyte/20.95%, Insiders/23.48%, Michael Rezac/2.53%

Financial Data: Fiscal Year End:07/31 Latest Annual Data: 07/31/2006

Year	Sales	Net Income
2006	NA	-$62,000
2005	NA	-$35,000

Curr. Assets:	$0	**Curr. Liab.:**	$186,000		
Plant, Equip.:	NA	**Total Liab.:**	$186,000	**Indic. Yr. Divd.:**	NA
Total Assets:	$0	**Net Worth:**	-$186,000	**Debt/ Equity:**	NA

Stem Cell Innovations Inc

Formerly: Interferon Sciences Inc
1812 Front St., Scotch Plains, NJ, 07076; **PH:** 1-908-663-2150

General - Incorporation	DE	**Stock** - Price on:12/24/2007	$0.026
Employees	19	Stock Exchange	NA
Auditor	Eisner LLP	Ticker Symbol	NA
Stk Agt	Computershare Investor Services LLC	Outstanding Shares	1,080,000,000
Counsel	NA	E.P.S.	-$0.011
DUNS No.	09-929-0389	Shareholders	NA

Business: The group's principal activity is to study, manufacture and market pharmaceutical products based on multispecies, natural source alpha interferon. The main product of the group is alferon n injection(R) used in the treatment of refractory or recurring external genital warts. The group's alferon n injection(R) product has been approved by the United States food and drug administration for the treatment of genital warts. The group has also developed alferon n gel and alferon ldo(r). Alferon n gel is a topical, natural alpha interferon, which has potential use in the treatment of cervical dysphasia, intravaginal warts, mucocutaneous and genital herpes. Alferon ldo is a oral liquid natural alpha interferon which has potential use in the treatment of HIV-infected patients.

Primary SIC and add'l.: 2834 8731 3840

CIK No: 0000351532

Subsidiaries: Amphioxus Cell Technologies, Inc., Interferon Sciences Development Corporation, Stem Cell Innovations, BV

Owners: John Macomber, Benjamin J. Jesselson/9.60%, David Perryman/5.30%, Lucio Noto, Margie Chassman/17.30%, Insiders/20.20%, Norman Sussman/1.70%, James H. Kelly/10.50%, Margery Germain/6.70%, Mark Germain/7.90%

Financial Data: Fiscal Year End:12/31 Latest Annual Data: 12/31/2006

Year	Sales	Net Income
2006	$87,000	-$14,330,000
2005	$57,000	-$847,000
2004	$64,000	$1,737,000

Curr. Assets:	$1,215,000	**Curr. Liab.:**	$1,531,000		
Plant, Equip.:	$791,000	**Total Liab.:**	$8,932,000	**Indic. Yr. Divd.:**	NA
Total Assets:	$8,837,000	**Net Worth:**	-$95,000	**Debt/ Equity:**	NA

StemCells Inc

3155 Porter Dr., Palo Alto, CA, 94304; **PH:** 1-650-475-3100; **http://** www.stemcellsinc.com

General - Incorporation	DE	**Stock** - Price on:12/24/2007	$2.48
Employees	46	Stock Exchange	NDQ
Auditor	Grant Thornton LLP	Ticker Symbol	STEM
Stk Agt	Computershare Investor Services LLC	Outstanding Shares	80,040,000
Counsel	Ropes & Gray LLP	E.P.S.	-$0.29
DUNS No.	60-529-1285	Shareholders	NA

Business: The group's principle activity is the research and development of therapies that would use stem and progenitor cells to treat and possibly cure, human diseases and injuries. These therapies are developed to treat and cure neurodegenerative diseases, demyelinating disorders, spinal cord injuries, stroke, hepatitis, chronic liver failure, and diabetes. It derives revenues mainly from collaborative agreements and grants received. The group's quarterly revenue for Sep '07 was 0.01 millions of USD.

Primary SIC and add'l.: 8731

CIK No: 0000883975

Subsidiaries: StemCells California, Inc.

Officers: Martin McGlynn/Dir., CEO, Pres. - Stemcells, Inc/$1,158,549.00, Rodney Young/CFO, VP - Finance, Administration/$777,885.00, Ann Tsukamoto/COO/$488,850.00, Nobuko Uchida/VP - Stem Cell Biology, Elizabeth Leininger/VP - Regulatory Affairs, Quality Assurance, Stephen Huhn/VP, Head - Neural Program, Maria Millan/VP, Head - Liver Program, Ken Stratton/General Counsel

Directors: Martin McGlynn/Dir., CEO, Pres. - Stemcells, Inc, John J. Schwartz/Chmn., Fred Gage/Founder, Member - Scientific Advisory Board, David J. Anderson/Founder, Member - Scientific Advisory Board, Irving L. Weissman/Dir., Roger Perlmutter/Dir., Ricardo Levy/Dir., Eric H. Bjerkholt/Dir., Desmond Oconnell/Dir.

Owners: Eric H. Bjerkholt, Insiders/4.60%, Roger M. Perlmutter, Rodney K.B. Young, Irving Weissman/2.20%, John J. Schwartz, Ann Tsukamoto, Martin McGlynn/1.00%, Desmond OConnell, Ricardo Levy

Financial Data: Fiscal Year End:12/31 Latest Annual Data: 12/31/2006

Year	Sales	Net Income
2006	$93,000	-$18,948,000
2005	$206,000	-$11,738,000
2004	$141,000	-$15,330,000

Curr. Assets:	$57,530,000	**Curr. Liab.:**	$4,150,000		
Plant, Equip.:	$3,596,000	**Total Liab.:**	$12,480,000	**Indic. Yr. Divd.:**	NA
Total Assets:	$66,857,000	**Net Worth:**	$54,376,000	**Debt/ Equity:**	0.0226

STEN Corp

Formerly: Sterion Inc
10275 Wayzata Blvd. S, Ste. 310, Minnetonka, MN, 55305; **PH:** 1-952-545-2776; **http://** www.stencorporation.com

General - Incorporation	MN	**Stock** - Price on:12/24/2007	$3.88
Employees	46	Stock Exchange	NDQ
Auditor	Virchow, Krause & Co. LLP	Ticker Symbol	NA
Stk Agt	American Stock Transfer & Trust Co.	Outstanding Shares	1,990,000
Counsel	Lindquist & Vennum PLLP	E.P.S.	-$1.11
DUNS No.	09-978-2369	Shareholders	NA

Business: The group's principal activities are to develop, manufacture and market medical and surgical devices. The products manufactured and sold by the group are grouped into five product categories namely disposable operating room products, instrument sterilization container products, surgical instrument protection and identification products, surgical tape products and wound drainage systems.

Primary SIC and add'l.: 3841

CIK No: 0000350557

Subsidiaries: Stellent AB, Stellent Asia Pty. Limited, Stellent B.V.

Officers: Kenneth W. Brimmer/52/Chmn., CEO, Mark Buckrey/CFO

Directors: Kenneth W. Brimmer/52/Chmn., CEO, Gary Copperud/49/Dir., Gervaise Wilhelm/64/Dir., Jeffrey A. Zinnecker/51/Dir., Allan D. Anderson/54/Dir.

Owners: Lyle Berman, Gary A. Dachis, Kenneth W. Brimmer, CMM Properties, LLC, Gervaise Wilhelm, Allan D. Anderson, Jeffrey A. Zinnecker, Gary Copperud, Insiders

Financial Data: Fiscal Year End:09/30 Latest Annual Data: 10/1/2006

Year	Sales	Net Income
2006	$8,879,000	-$608,000
2005	$8,358,000	$327,000
2004	$12,141,000	$198,000

Curr. Assets:	$5,013,000	**Curr. Liab.:**	$1,213,000		
Plant, Equip.:	$3,730,000	**Total Liab.:**	$3,893,000	**Indic. Yr. Divd.:**	NA
Total Assets:	$10,420,000	**Net Worth:**	$6,527,000	**Debt/ Equity:**	NA

Stena AB

Masthuggskajen, Gothenburg, 405 19; **PH:** 46-318-55000; **http://** media.stenaline.com

General - Incorporation	Sweden	**Stock** - Price on:12/24/2007	$27.93
Employees	3	Stock Exchange	NA
Auditor	Thord Elmersson	Ticker Symbol	NA
Stk Agt	Medallion Program	Outstanding Shares	15,500,000
Counsel	NA	E.P.S.	$1.06
DUNS No.	35-393-8665	Shareholders	NA

Business: The group's principle activities are to provide shipping, offshore drilling, real estate and finance. The operations also include service and contracting business in oil and gas industry, operation of ferries, tankers and offshore units, ship management training, marine equipment, real estate and financial operations.

Primary SIC and add'l.: 4482 1382 6531 4731

CIK No: 0001003517

Subsidiaries: AB PEGUN, Ab Stena Finans, DRA KVARN I STOCKHOLM AB, Aframax I Ltd, Aframax Ii Ltd, Akrofy Investment Bv, AVAC INC, Backa 110 Kb, Blomsteraffren Vxthuset I Lockryd Ab, Blomsterlandet Arendal Ab, Blomsterlandet I Alingss Ab, Blomsterlandet I Gteborg Ab, Blomsterlandet I Halmstad Ab, Blomsterlandet I Jnkping Ab, Blomsterlandet I Linkping Ab 265 Subsidiaries included in the Index

Officers: Staffan Hultgren/47/Chief Controller

Owners: Madeleine Olsson Eriksson/24.50%, Stefan Sten Olsson Holding Ltd/24.50%, Dan Sten Olsson/51.00%

Financial Data: Fiscal Year End:12/31 Latest Annual Data: 12/31/2006

Year	Sales	Net Income
2006	$69,435,000	$21,464,000
2005	$55,455,000	$21,913,000
2004	$61,246,000	$20,351,000

Curr. Assets:	$17,397,000	**Curr. Liab.:**	$3,289,000		
Plant, Equip.:	$344,973,000	**Total Liab.:**	$232,789,000	**Indic. Yr. Divd.:**	$2.360
Total Assets:	$363,409,000	**Net Worth:**	$130,620,000	**Debt/ Equity:**	1.8267

Stepan Co

22 W Frontage Rd., Northfield, IL, 60093; **PH:** 1-847-446-7500; **Fax:** 1-847-501-2443; **http://** www.stepan.com

General - Incorporation	DE	Stock- Price on:12/24/2007	$31.46
Employees	1,528	Stock Exchange	NYSE
Auditor	Deloitte & Touche LLP	Ticker Symbol	SCL
Stk Agt	Computershare Investor Services LLC	Outstanding Shares	9,250,000
Counsel	Mayer, Brown, Rowe & Maw	E.P.S	$1.09
DUNS No.	00-513-0182	Shareholders	NA

Business: The group's principal activity is to produce and sell specialty and intermediate chemicals to other manufacturers for use in a variety of end products. The group has three reportable segments: surfactants, polymers and specialty products. Surfactants are the key ingredients in consumer and industrial cleaning compounds. These products are used by manufacturers of detergents, shampoos, lotions, toothpaste and cosmetics who depend on surfactants to achieve the foaming and cleaning qualities required for the products. Other applications include lubricating ingredients and emulsifiers for agricultural products, plastics and composites. Polymers segment supplies phthalic anhydride, a commodity chemical intermediate that is used in polyester alkyd resins and plasticizers. Specialty products include flavors, emulsifiers and solubilizers used in food and pharmaceutical industries.

Primary SIC and add'l.: 2843 2841

CIK No: 0000094049

Subsidiaries: Nanjing Stepan Jinling Chemical Limited Liability Company, Stepan Canada, Inc., Stepan Colombiana de Quimicos, Stepan Deutschland GmbH, Stepan Europe S.A., Stepan Mexico, S.A. de C.V., Stepan Quimica Ltda., Stepan UK Limited

Officers: Quinn F. Stepan/Dir., CEO, Pres./$538,921.00, Kathleen M. Owens/Assist. General Counsel, Assist. Sec., Robert J. Wood/VP, GM - Polymers/$386,339.00, Frank Pacholec/VP - Research, Development, James E. Hurlbutt/VP - Finance/$316,035.00, John V. Venegoni/VP, GM - Surfactants/$424,064.00, James S. Pall/VP - Business Development, Tony Martin/VP - Europe, Edward H. Buening/VP - Surfactant Sales, Matthew I. Levinson/VP - Global Process Developmen, Edmund A. Perreault/VP - Purchasing, Richard H. Wehman/VP - Strategic Purchasing, Robert S. Mangold/VP - North American Plant Operations, Anthony J. Zoglio/VP - Supply Chain, Greg Servatius/VP - Human Resources *(16 Officers included in Index)*

Directors: Quinn F. Stepan/Dir., CEO, Pres., Quinn F. Stepan/Chmn., Gregory E. Lawton/Dir., Robert G. Potter/Dir., Edward J. Wehmer/Dir., Thomas F. Grojean/Dir., Robert D. Cadieux/Dir.

Owners: John Stepan/13.40%, Thomas F. Grojean, Mary Louise Wehman/15.60%, James E. Hurlbutt/4.70%, Quinn F. Stepan/7.90%, Insiders/32.90%, Paul H. Stepan/29.70%, Charlotte Stepan Shea/6.10%, Quinn F. Stepan/20.60%, Robert D. Cadieux, Edward J. Wehmer, Paul H. Stepan/5.10%, Gregory E. Lawton, Robert G. Potter, Robert J. Wood *(18 Owners included in Index)*

Financial Data: ***Fiscal Year End:***12/31 ***Latest Annual Data:*** 12/31/2006

Year	Sales	Net Income
2006	$1,172,583,000	$6,670,000
2005	$1,078,377,000	$13,159,000
2004	$935,816,000	$10,324,000

Curr. Assets:	$268,469,000	Curr. Liab.:	$180,495,000	P/E Ratio:	28.86
Plant, Equip.:	$225,604,000	Total Liab.:	$365,269,000	Indic. Yr. Divd.:	$0.820
Total Assets:	$546,055,000	Net Worth:	$180,786,000	Debt/ Equity:	0.6758

Stephan Co

1850 W McNab Rd., Fort Lauderdale, FL, 33309; *PH:* 1-954-971-0600; *Fax:* 1-954-971-2633; *http://* www.thestephanco.com; *Email:* information@thestephanco.com

General - Incorporation	FL	Stock- Price on:12/24/2007	$3.81
Employees	102	Stock Exchange	AMEX
Auditor	Goldstein Lewin & Co	Ticker Symbol	TSC
Stk Agt	NA	Outstanding Shares	4,390,000
Counsel	Kirkpatrick & Lockhart	E.P.S	-$0.818
DUNS No.	00-413-5539	Shareholders	NA

Business: The group's principal activity is to manufacture, sale and distribute hair and personal care products at wholesale and retail levels. The products are marketed under the brand name Stephan. The group is comprised of The Stephan Co. and its nine wholly-owned operating subsidiaries, Foxy Products, Inc., Old 97 Company, Williamsport Barber and Beauty Corp., Stephan & Co., Scientific Research Products, Inc. of Delaware, Sorbie Distributing Corporation, Stephan Distributing, Inc., Morris Flamingo-Stephan, Inc. and American Manicure, Inc. In 2005, the group acquired American Manicure Co.

Primary SIC and add'l.: 2844 5999

CIK No: 0000094056

Subsidiaries: American Manicure, Inc., Foxy Products, Inc, Morris Flamingo-Stephan, Inc., Old 97 Company, Scientific Research Products, Inc, Sorbie Distributing Corporation, Stephan & Co., Stephan Distributing, Inc, Williamsport Barber and Beauty Corp.

Owners: William M. Gross, David M. Knott, et al./8.70%, Frank F. Ferola/21.40%, Richard Barone/8.20%, Elliot Ross, Insiders/38.30%, Merlin Partners, L.P., et al./7.90%, Richard L. Scott/11.10%, Shouky Shaheen/7.92%, Yorktown Avenue Capital, et al./16.70%, Curtis Carlson

Financial Data: ***Fiscal Year End:***12/31 ***Latest Annual Data:*** 12/31/2006

Year	Sales	Net Income
2006	$21,836,000	-$3,602,000
2005	$22,262,000	-$172,000
2004	$23,951,000	-$2,176,000

Curr. Assets:	$15,019,000	Curr. Liab.:	$3,325,000		
Plant, Equip.:	$1,574,000	Total Liab.:	$4,435,000	Indic. Yr. Divd.:	$0.080
Total Assets:	$26,766,000	Net Worth:	$22,331,000	Debt/ Equity:	NA

Stereo Vision Entertainment Inc

15452 Cabrieto Rd., Ste. 204, Van Nuys, CA, 91406; *PH:* 1-818-909-7911; *http://* www.stereovision.com; *Email:* info@stereovision.com

General - Incorporation	NV	Stock- Price on:12/24/2007	NA
Employees	NA	Stock Exchange	OTC
Auditor	Robison, Hill & Co	Ticker Symbol	SVSN
Stk Agt	Holladay Stock Transfer, Inc.	Outstanding Shares	NA
Counsel	NA	E.P.S	NA
DUNS No.	NA	Shareholders	NA

Business: The group's principle activity is to evolve into a vertically integrated, diversified global media entertainment company. The company anticipates generating revenues from several sources, including, production of and exhibition of new and existing feature films and providing integrated solutions to help organizations broadcast audio, video, animation and music over the Internet as well as expanding into other areas of the entertainment industry.

Primary SIC and add'l.: 7922 7819

CIK No: 0001099814

Officers: Jack Honour/Founder, CEO, Doug Schwartz/Chmn., Chief Production Officer, Christopher Dieterich/General Counsel, Donald Moore/Litigation, Legal, David Markman/Contact - Legal, Entertainment, Theodore Botts/CFO, Daniel L. Symmes/Contact - Company, Management Credits, Herky Williams/Dir., Sec., Treasurer, Brent Davies/Audit, Accounting

Directors: Jack Honour/Founder, CEO, Doug Schwartz/Chmn., Chief Production Officer, John C. Bodziak/Dir., Herky Williams/Dir., Sec., Treasurer

Owners: Herky Williams/2.67%, Douglas Schwartz, John C. Bodziak, John Honour/28.90%, Insiders/42.42%, Theodore Botts/9.39%

Curr. Assets:	NA	Curr. Liab.:	$1,397,000		
Plant, Equip.:	NA	Total Liab.:	$1,397,000	Indic. Yr. Divd.:	NA
Total Assets:	$12,000	Net Worth:	-$1,385,000	Debt/ Equity:	NA

Stereotaxis Inc

4320 Forest Pk. Ave., Ste. 100, St Louis, MO, 63108; *PH:* 1-314-615-6940; *http://* www.stereotaxis.com

General - Incorporation	DE	Stock- Price on:12/24/2007	$12.23
Employees	180	Stock Exchange	NDQ
Auditor	Ernst & Young LLP	Ticker Symbol	STXS
Stk Agt	Bank of New York	Outstanding Shares	36,840,000
Counsel	NA	E.P.S	-$1.23
DUNS No.	NA	Shareholders	NA

Business: The group's principle activities include manufacturing and marketing advanced cardiology instrument control system for use in the cath lab that revolutionizes the treatment of coronary artery disease and arrhythmias by enabling important new therapeutic solutions and enhancing the efficiency and efficacy of existing interventional procedures. The company's systems and disposable devices are developed and marketed in the United States and Europe. The group operates from United States.

Primary SIC and add'l.: 3845

CIK No: 0001289340

Officers: Bevil J. Hogg/Dir., CEO, Pres., Melissa Walker/Sr. VP - Regulatory - Quality, Compliance, James M. Stolze/CFO, VP, Michael P. Kaminski/COO, Pres., Doug Bruce/Sr. VP - Research, Development, Ruchir Sehra/Chief Medical Officer, VP - Clinical Affairs

Directors: Bevil J. Hogg/Dir., CEO, Pres., Fred A. Middleton/Chmn., William M. Kelley/Dir., Abhijeet J. Lele/Dir., Gregory R. Johnson/Dir., Christopher Alafi/Dir., Abhi Acharya/Dir., Ralph G. Dacey/Dir., Member - Advisory Board, Bruce Wilkoff/Member - Advisory Board, Patrick Serruys/Member - Advisory Board, Rodrick Meese/Member - Advisory Board, Martin Leon/Member - Advisory Board, George Vetrovec/Member - Advisory Board, John Lasala/Member - Advisory Board, Matthew Howard/Member - Advisory Board *(32 Directors included in Index)*

Owners: Ruchir Sehra, Abhijeet Lele/5.70%, Douglas M. Bruce, Abhi Acharya, David W. Benfer, Next Century Growth Investors, LLC/6.00%, James M. Stolze, Michael P. Kaminski, Federated Kaufmann Fund/6.20%, Insiders/27.90%, Bevil J. Hogg/2.00%, Ralph G. Dacey, Gilder, Gagnon, Howe & Co. LLC/9.70%, TimesSquare Capital Management, LLC/5.60%, William C. Mills *(26 Owners included in Index)*

Financial Data: ***Fiscal Year End:***12/31 ***Latest Annual Data:*** 12/31/2006

Year	Sales	Net Income
2006	$27,192,000	-$45,720,000
2005	$15,026,000	-$43,558,000
2004	$18,817,000	-$27,257,000

Curr. Assets:	$63,294,000	Curr. Liab.:	$22,911,000		
Plant, Equip.:	$4,130,000	Total Liab.:	$24,502,000	Indic. Yr. Divd.:	NA
Total Assets:	$69,291,000	Net Worth:	$44,789,000	Debt/ Equity:	0.0039

Stericycle Inc

28161 N Keith Dr., Lake Forest, IL, 60045; *PH:* 1-847-367-5910; *http://* www.stericycle.com; *Email:* investor@stericycle.com

General - Incorporation	DE	Stock- Price on:12/24/2007	$44.95
Employees	5,035	Stock Exchange	NDQ
Auditor	Ernst & Young LLP	Ticker Symbol	SRCL
Stk Agt	LaSalle Bank N.A	Outstanding Shares	87,670,000
Counsel	Johnson & Colmar	E.P.S	$1.31
DUNS No.	36-359-6297	Shareholders	NA

Business: The group's principal activity is to manage medical waste. The group offers medical waste management services; Bio Systems(R) sharps management services, Steri-Safe(R) OSHA and HIPPA compliance programs, products for infection control treatment and Direct Return(R) pharmaceutical returns. The customers of the group include pharmacies, distributors and manufacturers of pharmaceutical products. In 2005 the group acquired Sanford Motors, Iowa Medical Waste Reduction Center, Automated Health Technologies, L.L. Horizons, Bio-Med Tech, Envirotech, Bio Clean, Medical Systems and Med Trac. The group operates through 45 treatment/collection centers and 105 additional transfer/collection sites throughout the United Kingdom, Ireland, Mexico, Canada, Brazil, Argentina, South Africa, Australia and Japan.

Primary SIC and add'l.: 4953

CIK No: 0000861878

Subsidiaries: 3CI Complete Compliance Corporation, American Medical Disposal, Inc, BFI Medical Waste, Inc, Biowaste Management Corp., Bridgeview, Inc, East Coast Medical Waste, Inc, Enviromed, Inc, Environmental Health Systems, Inc, Five Star Waste, Inc, Ionization Research Co.,Inc, Iowa Medical Waste Reduction Center, Inc, Med-Tech Environmental (MA), Inc, Med-Tech Environmental, Inc, Medam B.A. S.R.L., Medam S.A. de C.V 41 Subsidiaries included in the Index

Officers: Mark C. Miller/52/Dir., CEO, Pres./$1,629,672.00, Michael J. Collins/Pres. - Return Management Services, Richard L. Foss/Exec. VP - Corporate Development/$663,637.00, Frank J.M Ten Brink/Exec. VP, CFO, Chief Administrative Officer/$839,910.00, Shan S. Sacranie/Exec. VP - International/$604,508.00, Richard T. Kogler/COO, Exec. VP/$837,742.00

Directors: Mark C. Miller/52/Dir., CEO, Pres., Jack W. Schuler/67/Chmn., Jonathan T. Lord/53/Dir., Thomas R. Reusche/52/Dir., Rod F. Dammeyer/67/Dir., John Patience/60/Dir., Peter Vardy/77/Dir., William K. Hall/63/Dir.

Owners: David L. Mack/0.20%, Matthew H. Fleeger/4.40%, Steve Evans/0.50%, Steven R. Block/0.20%, Lonnie P. Cole, James M. Treat/0.60%, Tate Investments/14.90%, Winship B. Moody/3.20%, Alan Larosee/0.80%, Ajit S. Brar/3.40%, Insiders/13.60%, Mark Altenau/8.10%

Financial Data: ***Fiscal Year End:***12/31 ***Latest Annual Data:*** 12/31/2006

Year	Sales	Net Income
2006	$789,637,000	$105,270,000
2005	$609,457,000	$67,154,000
2004	$516,228,000	$78,178,000

Curr. Assets:	$218,602,000	Curr. Liab.:	$142,031,000	P/E Ratio:	34.31
Plant, Equip.:	$156,953,000	Total Liab.:	$702,825,000	Indic. Yr. Divd.:	NA
Total Assets:	$1,327,906,000	Net Worth:	$625,081,000	Debt/ Equity:	0.7307

Steris Corp

5960 Heisley Rd. , Mentor, OH, 44060; *PH:* 1-440-354-2600; *http://* www.steris.com

General - Incorporation	OH	**Stock**- Price on:12/24/2007	$30.77
Employees	5,100	Stock Exchange	NYSE
Auditor	Ernst & Young LLP	Ticker Symbol	STE
Stk Agt	National City Bank	Outstanding Shares	65,170,000
Counsel	Thompson Hine & Flory	E.P.S.	$1.23
DUNS No.	17-736-0039	Shareholders	NA

Business: The group's principal activities are to develop, manufacture and market infection prevention, contamination prevention, microbial reduction, and medical, surgical and therapy support systems, services and technologies. The group provides infection prevention material processing systems and specialty chemical products, including those used for cleaning, decontaminating, disinfecting, sterilizing, drying and aerating medical and surgical instruments, devices and hard surfaces. The group serves healthcare, scientific, research and industrial customers. The group has operations in the United States, Germany, Finland, Canada, Sweden and Australia. In 2005, the group acquired FHSurgical, Cosmed Group, Inc., and Albert Browne Limited

Primary SIC and add'l.: 3842 3841

CIK No: 0000815065

Subsidiaries: Albert Browne International Limited, Albert Browne Limited, American Sterilizer Company, Browne Health Care Limited, CLBV Limited, Ecomed, Inc., Family Practitioner Supplies Limited, Global Risk Insurance Company, Hamo UK Limited, Hamo USA Inc., Hausted, Inc., HSTD LLC, HTD Holding Corp., Isomedix Corporation, Isomedix Inc. 55 Subsidiaries included in the Index

Officers: Les C. Vinney/CEO, Pres./$2,794,318.00, Walter M. Rosebrough/Dir., CEO, Pres., Charles L. Immel/Group Pres. - Healthcare, Sohi Mohsen/Dir. - Acquisition, Derivative Securities From Company, Richey B. Joseph/Dir. - Sale, Securities, Brlas Laurie/CFO, Sr. VP - Disposition, Equity Securities, Morten C. Nielsen/VP, Group Pres. - Life Sciences, Acquisition, Derivative Securities, David L. Crandall/VP, Group Pres. - AIC - Acquisition, Derivative Securities, Peter A. Burke/CTO, Sr. VP/$845,382.00, Robert E. Moss/Group Pres. - Steris Isomedix Services/$673,558.00, Patricia K. Fish/VP - Human Resources, Disposition, Equity Securities to The Company, Timothy L. Chapman/Sr. VP - Business Strategy, William L. Aamoth/VP, Corporate Treasurer, Michael J. Tokich/VP, Corporate Controller/$379,796.00, Mark D. McGinley/Sr. VP - Gen Counsel, Sec. *(18 Officers included in Index)*

Directors: John P. Wareham/Chmn., Mohsen M. Sohi/Dir., Cynthia L. Feldmann/Dir., Stephen R. Hardis/Dir., Jacqueline Kosecoff/Dir., Raymond A. Lancaster/Dir., Kevin M. McMullen/Dir., Joseph B. Richey/Dir., Loyal W. Wilson/Dir., Michael B. Wood/Dir.

Owners: Eminence Capital, LLC/6.96%, Les C. Vinney, Gerard J. Reis, John P. Wareham, Kevin M. McMullen, Michael J. Tokich, Raymond A. Lancaster, J.B. Richey, Peter A. Burke, Jacqueline B. Kosecoff, Robert E. Moss, Cynthia L. Feldmann, Loyal W. Wilson, Insiders, Mohsen M. Sohi *(19 Owners included in Index)*

Financial Data: *Fiscal Year End:*03/31   *Latest Annual Data:* 03/31/2007

Year	Sales	Net Income
2007	$1,197,407,000	$82,155,000
2006	$1,160,285,000	$70,289,000
2005	$1,119,745,000	$85,980,000

Curr. Assets:	$484,720,000	Curr. Liab.:	$217,399,000	P/E Ratio:	25.02
Plant, Equip.:	$388,899,000	Total Liab.:	$434,878,000	Indic. Yr. Divd.:	$0.200
Total Assets:	$1,209,170,000	Net Worth:	$774,292,000	Debt/ Equity:	0.1301

Sterling Bancorp

650 Fifth Ave., New York, NY, 10019; *PH:* 1-212-757-3300; *http://* www.sterlingbancorp.com

General - Incorporation	NY	**Stock**- Price on:12/24/2007	$16.1
Employees	535	Stock Exchange	NYSE
Auditor	KPMG LLP	Ticker Symbol	STL
Stk Agt	Mellon Investor Services LLC	Outstanding Shares	18,660,000
Counsel	Sullivan & Cromwell	E.P.S.	$0.36
DUNS No.	04-318-5123	Shareholders	NA

Business: The group's principal activity is to provide full range of banking services to businesses and individuals. The services offered include checking, savings and money market accounts, certificates of deposit, business loans, personal and installment loans, visa/mastercard, safe deposit and night depository facilities. Loan facilities provided include short-term revolving credit arrangements, term loans, letters of credit, accounts receivable management services, asset-based financing, equipment financing, real estate and mortgage loans, leasing and lock box services. The group offers financial services to its customers and correspondents in the world's major financial centers through its international division and international banking facility.

Primary SIC and add'l.: 6153 6712 6021 8741

CIK No: 0000093451

Subsidiaries: SBC Abstract Company, LLC, Sterling Bancorp Trust I, Sterling Banking Corporation, Sterling Factors Corporation, Sterling Financial Services Company, Inc., Sterling Holding Company of Virginia, Inc., Sterling National Asia Limited, Hong Kong, Sterling National Bank, Sterling National Mortgage Company, Inc., Sterling National Servicing, Inc., Sterling Real Estate Abstract Holding Company, Inc., Sterling Real Estate Holding Company, Inc., Sterling Trade Services, Inc.

Officers: Louis J. Cappelli/Chmn., CEO/$2,805,961.00, John La Lota/Pres. - Sterling Factors Corporation, Sterling Capital Funding, John W. Tietjen/Exec. VP, Treasurer, CFO/$467,314.00, John C. Millman/Pres./$1,294,577.00, Michael Bizenov/Pres. - Sterling National Mortgage Company, Inc, Jennifer Updike/MD - Sterling Holding Company, Virginia, Robert Schnitzer/Dir. - Business Development, Asset Based Lending, Pres. - Sterling National Asia Limited, Hong Kong, Michael J. Scheller/Sr. VP - Trade Finance, Jeffrey Fliegel/Sr. VP - Middle Marketing Banking, Howard M. Applebaum/49/Sr. VP/$388,729.00, Elizabeth Forgione/VP, Branch Mgr. - Jamaica Office, Queens, Anna Roina/Certified Treasury Professional, VP - Cash Management Services, Salvatore Costa/First VP, Branch Mgr. - Park Avenue Office, Manhattan, Michael Madeo/VP, Branch Mgr. - Grand Central Plaza, Manhattan, Steve Hebert/First VP - Private, Professional Banking Group, Manhattan *(29 Officers included in Index)*

Directors: Louis J. Cappelli/Chmn., CEO, Eugene T. Rossides/Dir., Joseph M. Adamko/Dir., Walter Feldesman/Dir., Henry J. Humphreys/Dir.

Owners: Robert W. Lazar/0.01%, Eugene T. Rossides/0.21%, Henry J. Humphreys/0.29%, Robert Abrams/0.38%, John W. Tietjen/0.92%, John C. Millman/3.22%, Allan F. Hershfield/0.29%, Fernando Ferrer/0.13%, Insiders/13.02%, Eliot Robinson/0.32%, Walter Feldesman/0.29%, Joseph M. Adamko/0.30%, Louis J. Cappelli/6.87%, Howard M. Applebaum/0.45%

Financial Data: *Fiscal Year End:*12/31   *Latest Annual Data:* 12/31/2006

Year	Sales	Net Income
2006	$150,688,000	$10,760,000
2005	$147,597,000	$24,027,000
2004	$132,517,000	$24,604,000

Curr. Assets:	$77,263,000	Curr. Liab.:	$1,707,584,000	P/E Ratio:	44.72
Plant, Equip.:	$13,566,000	Total Liab.:	$1,753,694,000	Indic. Yr. Divd.:	$0.760
Total Assets:	$1,885,957,000	Net Worth:	$132,263,000	Debt/ Equity:	0.3441

Sterling Bancshares Inc

15000 Nwest Frwy, Ste. 308, Houston, TX, 77040; *PH:* 1-713-466-8300; *http://* www.banksterling.com

General - Incorporation	TX	**Stock**- Price on:12/24/2007	$11.61
Employees	1,074	Stock Exchange	NDQ
Auditor	Deloitte & Touche LLP	Ticker Symbol	SBIB
Stk Agt	American Stock Transfer & Trust Co.	Outstanding Shares	74,410,000
Counsel	Andrews & Kurch LLP	E.P.S.	$0.69
DUNS No.	04-867-9013	Shareholders	NA

Business: The group's principal activities are to provide financial products and services to small and mid-sized businesses through full service banking offices. It provides commercial and consumer banking services, including demand, savings and time deposits, commercial, real estate and consumer loans, merchant credit card services, letters of credit and cash and asset management services. The group operates through 37 banking offices in the greater metropolitan areas of Houston, Dallas and San Antonio, Texas. On 31-Oct-2003, the group acquired South Texas Capital Group Inc.

Primary SIC and add'l.: 6021 6712

CIK No: 0000891098

Subsidiaries: CMCR Holding Company, Sterling Bancorporation, Inc, Sterling Bancshares Capital Trust II, Sterling Bancshares Capital Trust III, Sterling Bancshares Statutory Trust One, Sterling Bank

Officers: Danny L. Buck/52/Regional CEO - Bank, San Antonio Region, Downey J. Bridgwater/Chmn., CEO, Pres./$1,374,131.00, Lynn S. Prude/51/Interim Regional CEO - Bank, Dallas Region, Bob S. Smith/53/Regional CEO - Bank, West Houston Region, Travis Jaggers/59/Regional CEO - Bank, Southeast Houston Region, Deborah A. Dinsmore/48/Exec. VP, Dir. - Operations, John A. Rossitto/63/Exec. VP, Chief Retail Banking Officer/$477,014.00, Christopher D. Reid/34/VP, Dir. - Investment Relations, Stephen C. Raffaele/42/Exec. VP, Chief Investment Officer/$360,120.00, James W. Goolsby/48/Exec. VP, General Counsel, Sec., Graham B. Painter/60/Exec. VP, Dir. - Corporate Communications, Zach L. Wasson/54/CFO, Exec. VP/$72,035.00, Wanda S. Dalton/58/Chief Human Resources Officer, Exec. VP, Sonny B. Lyles/62/Exec. VP, Chief Risk Officer, Chief Credit Officer/$424,998.00, Allen D. Brown/56/Exec. VP - Specialized Banking, Investments *(16 Officers included in Index)*

Directors: Downey J. Bridgwater/Chmn., CEO, Pres., Dan C. Tutcher/59/Dir., David L. Hatcher/65/Dir., Bruce R. Laboon/66/Dir., Edward G. Powell/71/Dir., Max W. Wells/74/Dir., Edward R. Bardgett/65/Dir., Roland X. Rodriguez/55/Dir., Bernard A. Harris/51/Dir., Anat Bird/56/Dir., Glenn H. Johnson/67/Dir., Bruce J. Harper/73/Dir., George Beatty/69/Dir., Raimundo E. Riojas/67/Dir.

Owners: Anat Bird, John Rossitto, Roland X. Rodriguez, Downey J. Bridgwater, Max W. Wells, Wallis C. McMath, Raimundo E. Riojas, James D. Calaway, Bernard A. Harris, George Beatty, Edward G. Powell, Zach L. Wasson, Insiders/2.17%, Barclays Global Investments/7.90%, Glenn H. Johnson *(22 Owners included in Index)*

Financial Data: *Fiscal Year End:*12/31   *Latest Annual Data:* 12/31/2006

Year	Sales	Net Income
2006	$286,608,000	$45,840,000
2005	$231,562,000	$36,222,000
2004	$197,498,000	$24,963,000

Curr. Assets:	$153,665,000	Curr. Liab.:	$3,605,180,000	P/E Ratio:	16.83
Plant, Equip.:	$24,940,000	Total Liab.:	$3,708,274,000	Indic. Yr. Divd.:	$0.210
Total Assets:	$4,117,559,000	Net Worth:	$409,285,000	Debt/ Equity:	0.2900

Sterling Chemicals Inc New

333 Clay St., Ste. 3600, Houston, TX, 77002; *PH:* 1-713-650-3700; *Fax:* 1-713-654-9551; *http://* www.sterlingchemicals.com

General - Incorporation	DE	**Stock**- Price on:12/24/2007	$22
Employees	274	Stock Exchange	OTC
Auditor	Deloitte & Touche LLP	Ticker Symbol	SCHI
Stk Agt	Wells Fargo Shareowner Services	Outstanding Shares	2,830,000
Counsel	NA	E.P.S.	-$35.76
DUNS No.	NA	Shareholders	NA

Business: The groups principle activities include producing selected petrochemicals used to manufacture array of consumer goods and industrial products. The products of the group include acetic acid, styrene and plasticizers. The group operates from the United States.

Primary SIC and add'l.: 2865 2869 2821

CIK No: 0001014669

Subsidiaries: Sterling Chemicals Energy, Inc

Officers: Richard K. Crump/62/Dir., CEO, Pres./$761,042.00, Cindy Kibikas/Contact, Walt Treybig/51/Sr. VP - Manufacturing/$440,271.00, Stanley J. Land/VP - Commercial Management, Kenneth M. Hale/45/Sr. VP, General Counsel, Sec./$307,441.00, John R. Beaver/46/CFO, Sr. VP - Finance, Bruce E. Moore/Treasurer, Paul C. Rostek/52/Sr. VP - Commercial/$380,895.00

Directors: Richard K. Crump/62/Dir., CEO, Pres., Steven L. Gidumal/50/Dir., John W. Gildea/64/Dir., Byron J. Haney/47/Dir., Peter Ting Kai Wu/70/Dir., Philip M. Sivin/36/Dir., Karl W. Schwarzfeld/31/Dir.

Owners: Kenneth M. Hale, Steven L. Gidumal, Paul C. Rostek, Insiders, Merrill Lynch, Pierce, Fenner & Smith, Incorporated, Resurgence Asset Management, L.L.C., Martin D. Sass, Richard K. Crump, Mariner Investment Group, Inc., Karl W. Schwarzfeld, Steven L. Gidumal, Northeast Investors Trust, Resurgence Asset Management International, L.L.C., Byron J. Haney, Philip M. Sivin *(26 Owners included in Index)*

Financial Data: *Fiscal Year End:*12/31 *Latest Annual Data:* 12/31/2006

Year	Sales	Net Income
2006	$667,544,000	-$105,659,000
2005	$641,886,000	-$29,568,000
2004	$851,662,000	-$62,644,000

Curr. Assets:	$152,336,000	**Curr. Liab.:**	$62,212,000		
Plant, Equip.:	$83,833,000	**Total Liab.:**	$212,082,000	**Indic. Yr. Divd.:**	NA
Total Assets:	$245,823,000	**Net Worth:**	-$22,766,000	**Debt/ Equity:**	NA

Sterling Construction Co Inc

20810 Fernbush Ln., Houston, TX, 77073; *PH:* 1-281-821-9091; *Fax:* 1-281-821-2995; *http://* www.sterlingconstructionco.com

General - Incorporation ... DE
Employees ... 1,025
Auditor ... Grant Thornton LLP
Stk Agt ... Computershare Investor Services LLC
Counsel ... NA
DUNS No. ... 92-648-7711

Stock- Price on:12/24/2007 ... $22.39
Stock Exchange ... NDQ
Ticker Symbol ... STRL
Outstanding Shares ... 10,960,000
E.P.S ... $1.09
Shareholders ... NA

Business: The group's principal activity is the construction of underground sanitary sewers, water mains, storm sewers and paving and wholesale distribution of automotive accessories and non-food pet supplies. The group distributes functional, decorative car and truck accessories, automobile care products, chemicals, automobile repair and maintenance items. The customers are general merchandise retail chains, automotive specialty stores, supermarket chains, hardware stores, variety and drug stores and other automotive accessory distributors. The operations of the company are located in northeastern United States. The group provides integrated waste management services through its subsidiary, oakhurst technology, inc.

Primary SIC and add'l.: 5013 6719 5199 1623 3524

CIK No: 0000874238

Subsidiaries: Steel City Products, LLC., Sterling Houston Holdings, Inc

Officers: Patrick T. Manning/Chmn., CEO/$702,833.00, Joseph P. Harper/Dir., COO, Pres./$658,333.00, Karen A. Stempinski/VP, Controller, Chief Accounting Officer, Roger M. Barzun/Sr. VP, General Counsel, Brian Manning/VP - Business Development, James H. Allen/CFO, Sr. VP

Directors: Patrick T. Manning/Chmn., CEO, David R.A. Steadman/Dir., Robert W. Frickel/Dir., Joseph P. Harper/Dir., COO, Pres., Maarten D. Hemsley/Dir., Christopher H.B. Mills/Dir., John D. Abernathy/Dir., Milton L. Scott/Dir., Donald P. Fusilli/Dir.

Owners: Milton L. Scott, Joseph P. Harper/6.55%, Dreman Value Management, LLC/8.54%, North Atlantic Value LLP/6.23%, North Atlantic Smaller Companies/6.23%, David R. A. Steadman, Insiders/18.59%, Robert W. Frickel, John D. Abernathy, Maarten D. Hemsley/2.89%, Christopher H. B. Mills/6.39%, Patrick T. Manning/1.65%, Deutsche Bank AG/5.93%

Financial Data: *Fiscal Year End:*12/31 *Latest Annual Data:* 12/31/2006

Year	Sales	Net Income
2006	$249,348,000	$13,320,000
2005	$219,439,000	$11,100,000
2004	$154,178,000	$5,653,000

Curr. Assets:	$107,408,000	**Curr. Liab.:**	$44,534,000	**P/E Ratio:**	20.17
Plant, Equip.:	$46,617,000	**Total Liab.:**	$76,781,000	**Indic. Yr. Divd.:**	NA
Total Assets:	$167,772,000	**Net Worth:**	$90,991,000	**Debt/ Equity:**	0.2194

Sterling Financial Corp/PA

101 N Pointe Blvd., Lancaster, PA, 17601; *PH:* 1-717-581-6030; *http://* www.sterlingfi.com

General - Incorporation ... PA
Employees ... 1,100
Auditor ... Ernst & Young LLP
Stk Agt ... Mellon Investor Services LLC
Counsel ... NA
DUNS No. ... 18-390-9126

Stock- Price on:12/24/2007 ... $10.16
Stock Exchange ... NDQ
Ticker Symbol ... SLFI
Outstanding Shares ... 29,730,000
E.P.S ... $1.24
Shareholders ... NA

Business: The group's principal activities are to provide a wide range of banking and financial services to individuals and businesses, including commercial and retail banking, leasing, wealth management and insurance. The group operates through 52 branch-banking offices in south central Pennsylvania and northern Maryland. The group offers commercial, financial, agricultural, real estate and consumer loans. The deposits accepted by the group include demand, savings and time. The subsidiaries of the group include bank of lancaster county, n.a., bank of hanover and trust company, first national bank of northeast, town and country, inc. And sterling financial trust company. In 2003, the group acquired Church Capital management llc and bainbridge securities, inc. On 28-May-2004, the group acquired stoudtadvisors.

Primary SIC and add'l.: 6021 6712

CIK No: 0000811671

Subsidiaries: Bainbridge Securities, Inc., Bank of Hanover and Trust Company, Bank of Lancaster County, N.A., Church Capital Management LLC, Corporate Healthcare Strategies, LLC, Delaware Sterling Bank & Trust Company, EFI Holdings, Inc., Equipment Finance LLC, First National Bank of North East, HOVB Investment Company, Lancaster Insurance Group, LLC, Pennbanks Insurance Company SPC, Pennsylvania State Bank, Sterling Community Development Corporation, LLC, Sterling Financial Statutory Trust I 22 Subsidiaries included in the Index

Officers: Roger J. Moyer/Dir., CEO, Pres./$537,147.00, Jean Svoboda/VP, General Counsel, Sec., Bradley J. Scovill/Sr. Exec. VP, Chief Revenue Officer/$325,088.00, Thomas J. Sposito/Sr. VP, Chief Banking Officer/$265,503.00, Kathleen D. Phillips/Sr. VP, Group Executive CIO, Kathleen A. Prime/Sr. VP - Group Executive, Chief People Officer, Tito L. Lima/CFO, Treasurer/$241,089.00, Chad M. Clabaugh/Sr. VP - Personal Services/$213,461.00, Dennis E. Ginder/Sr. VP - Business Services

Directors: Roger J. Moyer/Dir., CEO, Pres., Garth W. Sprecher/Vice Chmn., Glenn R. Walz/Chmn., William E. Miller/Dir., Terrence L. Hormel/Dir., John E. Stefan/Dir., David E. Hosler/Dir., Howard E. Groff/Dir., Richard H. Albright/Dir., Joan R. Henderson/Dir., Michael A. Carenzo/Dir., Anthony D. Chivinski/Dir.

Owners: Chad M. Clabaugh, Glenn R. Walz, Howard E. Groff/6.72%, Anthony D. Chivinski, William E. Miller, Tito L. Lima, Richard H. Albright, John E. Stefan/1.74%, David E. Hosler, Howard E. Groff, Michael A. Carenzo, Insiders/4.50%, Thomas J. Sposito, Scovill J. Bradley, Joan R. Henderson *(18 Owners included in Index)*

Financial Data: *Fiscal Year End:*12/31 *Latest Annual Data:* 12/31/2006

Year	Sales	Net Income
2006	$274,696,000	$36,452,000
2005	$240,046,000	$39,267,000
2004	$196,978,000	$33,329,000

Curr. Assets:	$170,926,000	**Curr. Liab.:**	$2,705,077,000	**P/E Ratio:**	8.19
Plant, Equip.:	$138,148,000	**Total Liab.:**	$2,949,250,000	**Indic. Yr. Divd.:**	$0.600
Total Assets:	$3,279,835,000	**Net Worth:**	$330,585,000	**Debt/ Equity:**	NA

Sterling Financial Corp/WA

111 N Wall St., Spokane, WA, 99201; *PH:* 1-509-458-3711; *Fax:* 1-509-358-6161; *http://* www.sterlingsavingsbank.net

General - Incorporation ... WA
Employees ... 2,405
Auditor ... BDO Seidman LLP
Stk Agt ... American Stock Transfer & Trust Co.
Counsel ... Witherspoon Kelley Davenport Toole
DUNS No. ... 79-637-4155

Stock- Price on:12/24/2007 ... $30.38
Stock Exchange ... NDQ
Ticker Symbol ... STSA
Outstanding Shares ... NA
E.P.S ... $2.09
Shareholders ... NA

Business: The group's principal activity is to provide banking services by accepting deposits and originating loans. It also markets tax-deferred annuities, mutual funds and other financial products. The group serves through 86 retail branches located mainly in rural and suburban areas in Oregon, Washington, Idaho and Montana. The subsidiaries of the group provides full-service banking services, including attracting deposits insured by the federal deposit insurance corporation and originating consumer, business banking, residential and commercial real estate and residential construction loans. On 28-Feb-2003, the group acquired Empire Federal Bancorp Inc and Klamath First Bancorp Inc in 2004.

Primary SIC and add'l.: 6036 6712

CIK No: 0000891106

Subsidiaries: Action Mortgage Company, Evergreen Environmental Development Corporation, Evergreen First Service Corporation, Fidelity Service Corporation, Harbor Financial Services, Inc. (a subsidiary of Evergreen First Service Corporation), Intervest-mortgage Investment Company, Klamath First Capital Trust I, Klamath First Capital Trust II, Pacific Cascades Financial, Inc., Peter W. Wong Associates, Inc., Source Capital Corporation, Source Capital Leasing Corporation , Sterling Capital Statutory Trust V, Sterling Capital Trust II, Sterling Capital Trust III 20 Subsidiaries included in the Index

Officers: Harold B. Gilkey/Chmn., CEO/$3,227,619.00, Heidi B. Stanley/Vice Chmn., COO - Sterling Savings Bank/$999,464.00, John M. Harlow/Pres. - Intervest, Mortgage Investment Company/$1,191,783.00, Stephen L. Page/Exec. VP, Chief Credit Officer - Sterlings Savings Bank, James L. Kirschbaum/Pres. - Action Mortgage Company, Jeffery D. Schlenker/Pres. - Harbor Financial Services, Inc, Daniel G. Byrne/CFO, Exec. VP/$857,322.00, David A. Brukardt/Exec. VP, Mgr. - Corporate Administrative, Sterling Savings Bank, Thomas W. Colosimo/CFO, Sr. VP - Sterling Savings Bank, Nancy R. McDaniel/Exec. VP, Portfolio Mgr. - Sterling Savings Bank, Ezra A. Eckhardt/Exec. VP, Chief Adminstrative Officer - Sterling Savings Bank, Andrew J. Schultheis/Sec., Donn C. Costa/Sr. VP - Mortgage Division, Golf Savings Bank/$565,636.00, Robert G. Butterfield/VP, Controller, Principal Accounting Officer

Directors: Harold B. Gilkey/Chmn., CEO, Heidi B. Stanley/Vice Chmn., COO - Sterling Savings Bank, Rodney W. Barnett/Dir., William W. Zuppe/Dir., Donald N. Bauhofer/Dir., William L. Eisenhart/Dir., Robert D. Larrabee/Dir., James P. Fugate/Dir., Donald J. Lukes/Dir., Michael F. Reuling/Dir., James B. Keegan/Dir.

Owners: Harold B. Gilkey/1.24%, Insiders/6.25%, Earnest Partners, LLC/7.86%, Private Capital Management, L.P./7.85%, Rodney W. Barnett, Donald N. Bauhofer, James P. Fugate, William L. Eisenhart, Michael F. Reuling, William W. Zuppe, Donn C. Costa, John M. Harlow, Donald J. Lukes, Barclays Global Investors/7.07%, Heidi B. Stanley *(17 Owners included in Index)*

Financial Data: *Fiscal Year End:*12/31 *Latest Annual Data:* 12/31/2006

Year	Sales	Net Income
2006	$621,074,000	$73,946,000
2005	$447,882,000	$61,219,000
2004	$368,080,000	$56,305,000

Curr. Assets:	$235,234,000	**Curr. Liab.:**	$8,802,662,000	**P/E Ratio:**	14.47
Plant, Equip.:	$97,848,000	**Total Liab.:**	$9,045,236,000	**Indic. Yr. Divd.:**	$0.380
Total Assets:	$9,828,652,000	**Net Worth:**	$783,416,000	**Debt/ Equity:**	0.2264

Sterling Gold Corp

200 S Main St., Ste. I, Pocatello, ID, 83204; *PH:* 1-208-232-5603

General - Incorporation ... NV
Employees ... NA
Auditor ... Morgan & Company
Stk Agt ... Pacific Stock Transfer Company
Counsel ... NA
DUNS No. ... NA

Stock- Price on:12/24/2007 ... $0.59
Stock Exchange ... OTC
Ticker Symbol ... SGCO
Outstanding Shares ... 6,010,000
E.P.S ... NA
Shareholders ... NA

Business: The groups principal activity is to engage in the acquisition and exploration of mining properties. The group operates from the United States.

Primary SIC and add'l.: 1040

CIK No: 0001280821

Officers: Allen Collins/53/Dir., Pres., Principal Exec. Officer, Sec., Treasurer, Principal Accounting Officer, Principal Financial Officer

Directors: Allen Collins/53/Dir., Pres., Principal Exec. Officer, Sec., Treasurer, Principal Accounting Officer, Principal Financial Officer, Robert M. Baker/54/Dir.

Owners: Papadimas Gerogios/5.50%, Insiders/20.35%, Lawrence Tamera/5.49%, EMEA Trade Ltd./10.07%, Kostouros Ioannis/5.50%, Papadimas Athanasios/5.50%, Johnannson Arni/5.49%, Bank Sal Oppenheim/5.49%, Allen Collins/20.35%, Golden Pig Realty Corp./5.49%, Dugdale Richard/5.49%

Sterling Group Ventures Inc

789 Pender St. W , Ste. 900, Vancouver, BC, V6C 1H2; *PH:* 1-604-893-8891; *http://* www.sterlinggroupventures.com; *Email:* info@sterlinggroupventures.com

General - Incorporation	NV	**Stock**- Price on:12/24/2007	$0.1
Employees	NA	Stock Exchange	OTC
Auditor	Amisano Hanson	Ticker Symbol	SGGV
Stk Agt	Pacific Stock Transfer Company	Outstanding Shares	NA
Counsel	NA	E.P.S	NA
DUNS No.	NA	Shareholders	NA

Business: The groups principal activity is to engage in the business of exploration and development of a mineral property. The group operates from the United States.

Primary SIC and add'l.: 1479

CIK No: 0001175416

Subsidiaries: Huyana Ventures Limited, Makaelo Limited, Micro Express Holdings Inc, Micro Express Ltd

Officers: Raoul N. Tsakok/Chmn., CEO, Richard Shao/Dir., Pres., Kathy Wang/Sec.

Directors: Raoul N. Tsakok/Chmn., CEO, Richard Shao/Dir., Pres., Gerald Runolfson/Dir., Robert G. Smiley/Dir.

Owners: Raoul Tsakok/36.30%, Richard Shao/11.00%, Gerald Runolfson/4.10%

Financial Data: *Fiscal Year End:*05/31 *Latest Annual Data:* 05/31/2007

Year	Sales	Net Income
2007	NA	-$864,000
2006	NA	NA

Curr. Assets:	$315,000	**Curr. Liab.:**	$272,000	**P/E Ratio:**	6.07
Plant, Equip.:	$3,000	**Total Liab.:**	$272,000	**Indic. Yr. Divd.:**	NA
Total Assets:	$318,000	**Net Worth:**	$45,000	**Debt/ Equity:**	NA

Sterling Mining Company

2201 Government Way, Ste. E, Coeur Dalene, ID, 83814; *PH:* 1-208-666-4070; *http://* www.sterlingmining.com

General - Incorporation	ID	**Stock**- Price on:12/24/2007	$3.42
Employees	49	Stock Exchange	OTC
Auditor	Williams & Webster, P.S.	Ticker Symbol	SRLM
Stk Agt	Columbia Stock Transfer Co	Outstanding Shares	23,500,000
Counsel	NA	E.P.S	-$0.4
DUNS No.	NA	Shareholders	NA

Business: The groups principle activities include locating, purchasing or leasing mining claims in key positions throughout the Silver Valley. The group operates through two business segments namely exploration and mining in the United Sates and Mexico. In the year 2006 the group acquired Chester Mining Company. The group operates from the United States and Mexico. The group's quarterly revenue for Sep '07 was 0.29 millions of USD.

Primary SIC and add'l.: 1000

CIK No: 0001346685

Subsidiaries: North American Silver, Limited, Sterling Mining de Mexico, S.A. de C.V.

Officers: Raymond K. De Motte/Chmn., CEO, Pres., Kevin Shiell/Dir., Exec. VP, James N. Meek/CFO, VP, Michael McLean/Mine Mgr., Jeffrey Moe/Chief Geologist, Monique Hayes/Marketing Mgr., Cathy Hume/Contact - Investor Relations, Julia Clark/Contact - Investor Relations, Michael L. Mooney/Corp. Sec., Treasurer

Directors: Raymond K. De Motte/Chmn., CEO, Pres., Kevin Shiell/Dir., Exec. VP, Dave Waisman/Dir., Carol Stephan/Dir., Roger Van Voorhees/Dir., Kenny J. Berscht/Dir.

Owners: Michael L. Mooney, David J. Waisman, GoldmanSachsCanada,Inc/6.60%, James N. Meek, Kevin G. Shiell, Insiders/7.50%, RBCDominionSecurities,Inc/6.90%, Carol Stephen, W. D. Goodfellow/14.90%, Raymond K. DeMotte, Roger A. VanVoorhees/6.70%

Financial Data: *Fiscal Year End:*12/31 *Latest Annual Data:* 12/31/2006

Year	Sales	Net Income
2006	$888,000	-$5,230,000

Curr. Assets:	$4,691,000	**Curr. Liab.:**	$5,862,000		
Plant, Equip.:	$11,648,000	**Total Liab.:**	$6,381,000	**Indic. Yr. Divd.:**	NA
Total Assets:	$20,920,000	**Net Worth:**	$14,539,000	**Debt/ Equity:**	0.0357

Steven Madden Ltd

52-16 Barnett Ave., Long Island City, NY, 11104; *PH:* 1-718-446-1800; *http://* www.stevemadden.com; *Email:* custsvcesm@stevemadden.com

General - Incorporation	DE	**Stock**- Price on:12/24/2007	$32.64
Employees	480	Stock Exchange	NDQ
Auditor	Eisner LLP	Ticker Symbol	SHOO
Stk Agt	American Stock Transfer & Trust Co.	Outstanding Shares	20,490,000
Counsel	Cadwalader, Wickersham & Taft LLP	E.P.S	$1.88
DUNS No.	78-585-1056	Shareholders	NA

Business: The group's principal activities are to design, market and sell footwear brands for women, men and children. It distributes its footwear products through its retail stores, its e-commerce Web sites, catalogs and department and specialty stores located in the United States and Canada. As of 30-Jun-2004, it operated 83 retail stores. The group's products are sold under brand names including steve madden(R), david aaron(R), l.e.i.(R), stevies(R) and steve madden mens brand. The customers of the group include bloomingdale's, bon marche, burdines, macy's, rich's, famous barr, filene's, foley's, hecht's, lord and taylor, robinsons may, journeys, limited too, mandees, victoria's secret and fingerhut.

Primary SIC and add'l.: 5139 3143 3149 3144 5661

CIK No: 0000913241

Subsidiaries: Adesso-Madden, Inc., Daniel M. Friedman & Associates, Inc., Diva Acquisition Corp, Diva International, Inc., Madden Direct, Inc., Shoe Biz, Inc, Steven Madden Retail, Inc., Stevies, Inc., Unionbay Mens Footwear, Inc.

Officers: Jamieson A. Karson/Chmn., CEO/$2,061,385.00, Amelia Newton Varela/Exec. VP - Wholesale Sales/$1,941,766.00, Andrew Shames/Pres. - Madden Mens Division, Joseph Masella/Pres. - Candies Division, Robert Schmertz/Pres. - Steve Madden Womens Wholesale Division, Brand Mgr./$1,550,719.00, Awadhesh Sinha/COO/$1,861,548.00, Arvind Dharia/CFO/$1,297,893.00, Gerald Mongeluzo/Pres. - Adesso, Madden, Inc, Jeffrey Silverman/Pres. - Steven Madden, Ltd

Directors: Jamieson A. Karson/Chmn., CEO, Peter Migliorini/Dir., Harold D. Kahn/Dir., Walter Yetnikoff/Dir., Marc S. Cooper/Dir., John L. Madden/Dir., Thomas H. Schwartz/Dir., Jeffrey Birnbaum/Dir., Richard P. Randall/70/Dir.

Owners: Jamieson A. Karson, John Madden, Jeffrey Birnbaum, Amelia Newton Varela, Robert Schmertz, Harold D. Kahn, Peter Migliorini, Richard P. Randall, Steven Madden/10.72%, Marc S. Cooper, Thomas H. Schwartz, Arvind Dharia/1.09%, BOCAP Corp./5.94%, Walter Yetnikoff, Insiders/3.54%

Financial Data: *Fiscal Year End:*12/31 *Latest Annual Data:* 12/31/2006

Year	Sales	Net Income
2006	$475,163,000	$46,250,000
2005	$375,786,000	$19,200,000
2004	$338,144,000	$12,275,000

Curr. Assets:	$188,043,000	**Curr. Liab.:**	$36,332,000	**P/E Ratio:**	16.82
Plant, Equip.:	$23,375,000	**Total Liab.:**	$39,468,000	**Indic. Yr. Divd.:**	NA
Total Assets:	$251,392,000	**Net Worth:**	$211,924,000	**Debt/ Equity:**	NA

Stewardship Financial Corp

630 Godwin Ave., Midland Park, NJ, 07432; *PH:* 1-201-444-7100; *http://* www.snl.com

General - Incorporation	NJ	**Stock**- Price on:12/24/2007	NA
Employees	100	Stock Exchange	NDQ
Auditor	KPMG LLP	Ticker Symbol	SSFN
Stk Agt	National City Bank	Outstanding Shares	NA
Counsel	NA	E.P.S	$0.94
DUNS No.	NA	Shareholders	NA

Business: The group's principal activity is to provide banking services. The services provided include acceptance of deposits and lending activities. Deposit products of the group include personal and business checking accounts and time deposits, money market accounts and regular savings accounts. Lending products include commercial, consumer, mortgage, home equity and personal loans. The group's area of service primarily consists of the bergen and passaic county, New Jersey market, although the group makes loans throughout New Jersey. It operates its main office in midland park, New Jersey and seven branch offices in hawthorne, ridgewood, waldwick, wayne and pequannock, New Jersey.

Primary SIC and add'l.: 6712 6022

CIK No: 0001023860

Subsidiaries: Stewardship Realty, LLC

Officers: Paul Van Ostenbridge/Dir., CEO, Pres./$344,648.00, Julie E. Holland/Sr. VP, Treasurer/$138,803.00, Timothy G. Madden/Sr. VP/$174,650.00, Mary Beth Beth Steiginga/Investor Relations Contact

Directors: Paul Van Ostenbridge/Dir., CEO, Pres., William C. Hanse/Chmn., Abraham Van Wingerden/Vice Chmn., Margo L. Lane/Dir., Howard R. Yeaton /Dir., William J. Vander Eems/Dir., Michael A. Westra/Dir., Robert J. Turner/Dir., John L. Steen/Dir., Harold Dyer/Dir., Arie Leegwater/Dir.

Owners: John L. Steen/2.09%, Robert J. Turner/2.64%, Arie Leegwater/1.09%, Abe Van Wingerden/4.57%, Howard R. Yeaton, William J. VanderEems/3.92%, Michael Westra, Julie E. Holland, William C. Hanse/2.41%, Paul Van Ostenbridge/1.46%, Insiders/25.52%, Harold Dyer, Margo Lane, Timothy G. Madden, William Almroth/5.10%

Financial Data: *Fiscal Year End:*12/31 *Latest Annual Data:* 12/31/2006

Year	Sales	Net Income
2006	$34,624,000	$4,753,000
2005	$28,140,000	$4,480,000
2004	$23,881,000	$3,848,000

Curr. Assets:	$18,609,000	**Curr. Liab.:**	$447,334,000		
Plant, Equip.:	$7,098,000	**Total Liab.:**	$482,443,000	**Indic. Yr. Divd.:**	$0.360
Total Assets:	$519,749,000	**Net Worth:**	$37,306,000	**Debt/ Equity:**	NA

Stewart & Stevenson Services Inc

2707 N Loop W, Houston, TX, 77008; *PH:* 1-713-868-7700; *http://* www.ssss.com

General - Incorporation	TX	**Stock**- Price on:12/24/2007	$85.4
Employees	8,150	Stock Exchange	NA
Auditor	Ernst & Young LLP	Ticker Symbol	NA
Stk Agt	Bank of New York	Outstanding Shares	35,580,000
Counsel	NA	E.P.S	$3.46
DUNS No.	00-793-2783	Shareholders	NA

Business: The group's principal activity is custom fabrication of engine driven products. The group operates through five business segments. The power products segment sells and rents industrial equipment, components, replacement parts, accessories and other materials. The distributed energy solutions segment provides reciprocating diesel and natural gas engine generator set packaging. The tactical vehicle systems segment assembles and provides sustaining design engineering and service. The engineered products segment manufactures equipment for the well stimulation industries. The airline segment manufactures internal combustion and electric airline ground support equipment.

Primary SIC and add'l.: 3621 3533 5012 7699

CIK No: 0000094328

Subsidiaries: C. Jim Stewart & Stevenson, Inc., Extended Reach Logistics, Inc., IPSC Co., Inc., S&S Trust, Sierra Detroit Diesel Allison, Inc., Stewart & Stevenson (U.K.) Limited, Stewart & Stevenson De Las Americas, Inc., Stewart & Stevenson FMTV International, Inc., Stewart & Stevenson Power, Inc., Stewart & Stevenson Tactical Vehicle Systems, LP, Stewart & Stevenson Transportation, Inc., Stewart & Stevenson Truck Holdings, Inc., Stewart & Stevenson TVS UK Ltd, Stewart & Stevenson TVS, Inc., Stewart & Stevenson TVSIsrael, Ltd. 18 Subsidiaries included in the Index

Financial Data: *Fiscal Year End:*01/31 *Latest Annual Data:* 12/31/2006

Year	Sales	Net Income
2006	$2,360,884,000	$134,562,000
2005	$1,636,930,000	$132,510,000
2004	$979,683,000	$80,539,000

Curr. Assets:	$772,473,000	**Curr. Liab.:**	$867,147,000	**P/E Ratio:**	24.68
Plant, Equip.:	$179,676,000	**Total Liab.:**	$1,467,425,000	**Indic. Yr. Divd.:**	NA
Total Assets:	$2,318,111,000	**Net Worth:**	$850,686,000	**Debt/ Equity:**	0.6151

Stewart Enterprises Inc

110 Veterans Memorial Blvd, Metairie, LA, 70005; *PH:* 1-504-837-5880; *http://* www.stewartenterprises.com; *Email:* klocantr@stei.com

General - Incorporation LA
Employees 5,400
Auditor PricewaterhouseCoopers LLP
Stk Agt Registrar & Transfer Co.
Counsel Jones Walker
DUNS No. 05-501-6943

Stock- Price on:12/24/2007 $8.24
Stock Exchange NDQ
Ticker Symbol STEI
Outstanding Shares 106,020,000
E.P.S. $0.39
Shareholders NA

Business: The group's primary activity is to provide funeral and cemetery products and services in the death care industry in the United States. The group operates through 11 segments consisting of a corporate trust management segment and a funeral and cemetery segment for each of five geographic areas namely, Central, Western, Eastern, Southern - Florida and France.

Primary SIC and add'l.: 7261

CIK No: 0000878522

Subsidiaries: A.P. Boza Funeral Home, Inc., Abbey Plan of Texas, Inc., Acme Mausoleum Corporation, All Faiths Memorial Park, Inc., All Souls Mortuary, Inc., Amling/Schroeder Funeral Service, Inc., Arlington Memorial Park Cemetery and Funeral Home, Inc., Ashes to Ashes, Inc., Assumption Mortuary, Inc., Baldwin-Fairchild Funeral Homes, Inc., Barstow Funeral Homes, Inc., Bartlett-Burdette-Cox Funeral Home, Inc., Bay Area Crematory, Inc., Belew Funeral Home, Inc., Benjamin Franklin P.M., Inc. 229 Subsidiaries included in the Index

Officers: Thomas J. Crawford/Dir., CEO, Pres., Randall L. Stricklin/Sr. VP, Pres. - Corporate Development, Lisa T. Winningkoff/40/VP, Sr. Administrative Officer, Lewis J. Derbes/36/VP, Sec., Treasurer, Thomas M. Kitchen/Dir., Pres. - Corporate Division, CFO/$1,338,775.00, Lawrence B. Hawkins/Exec. VP, Brent F. Heffron/Exec. VP, Pres. - Eastern Division/$866,278.00, Kenneth G. Stephens/Sr. VP, Pres. - Western Division/$903,838.00, Angela M. Lacour/35/VP, Corporate Controller, Chief Accounting Officer

Directors: Thomas J. Crawford/Dir., CEO, Pres., Frank B. Stewart/Chmn. Emeritus, John P. Laborde/Chmn., Alden J. McDonald/Dir., Thomas M. Kitchen/Dir., Pres. - Corporate Division, CFO, James W. McFarland/Dir., John C. McNamara/Dir., Ronald H. Patron/Dir., Michael O. Read/Dir., Ashton J. Ryan/Dir.

Owners: Kenneth G. Stephens, Insiders/100.00%, John P. Laborde, Insiders/7.70%, Michael O. Read, Ashton J. Ryan, Dimensional Fund Advisors, Inc./9.00%, James W. McFarland, Thomas M. Kitchen, Westfield Capital Management/5.50%, Frank B. Stewart/7.10%, John C. McNamara, Brent F. Heffron, Frank B. Stewart/100.00%, Ronald H. Patron *(17 Owners included in Index)*

Financial Data: *Fiscal Year End:*10/31 *Latest Annual Data:* 10/31/2007

Year	Sales	Net Income
2007	$522,817,000	$39,813,000
2006	$517,660,000	$37,593,000
2005	$494,799,000	-$143,326,000

Curr. Assets:	$183,459,000	**Curr. Liab.:**	$92,083,000	**P/E Ratio:**	20.10
Plant, Equip.:	$680,718,000	**Total Liab.:**	$2,015,656,000	**Indic. Yr. Divd.:**	$0.100
Total Assets:	$2,438,974,000	**Net Worth:**	$423,318,000	**Debt/ Equity:**	0.7652

Stewart Information Services Corp

1980 Post Oak Blvd., Houston, TX, 77056; ***PH:*** 1-713-625-8100; ***http://*** www.stewart.com; ***Email:*** customerservice@stewart.com

General - Incorporation DE
Employees 9,900
Auditor KPMG LLP
Stk Agt Mellon Investor Services LLC
Counsel NA
DUNS No. 05-363-0323

Stock- Price on:12/24/2007 $39.575
Stock Exchange NYSE
Ticker Symbol STC
Outstanding Shares 18,260,000
E.P.S. $1.65
Shareholders NA

Business: The groups principle activity is to provide real estate information and transaction management services. The group also provides title insurance and related services. The group operates from United States.

Primary SIC and add'l.: 7389 6361

CIK No: 0000094344

Subsidiaries: 5280 Title Services, LLC, Aaction Title Agency, Inc., Abstract and Title Company, Abstract Title, Acceptance Title, AccountableTitle Services, LLC, Accredited Title, Inc., Ace Title Agency, LLC, Advance Homestead Title, Inc., Advance Title Company, Advanced Land Title of Lexington, LLC, Advanced Title Holding Company, LLC, Advanced Title, LLC, Advantage Title LLC, Affiliated Escrow, Inc. 412 Subsidiaries included in the Index

Officers: Malcolm S. Morris/Chmn., Co - CEO/$773,053.00, Don O'Neill/Group Pres., Region Mgr. - Real Estate Information, Stewart Title Company, Chmn., CEO - Stewart Lender Services, Tom Sagehorn/Exec. VP, Region GM - Stewart Title Guaranty Company, Group Pres. - Stewart Title Company, CEO, Pres. - National Land Title Insurance Co, Stewart Morris/Dir., Co - CEO, Pres./$756,300.00, Patrick Vaden/CEO - Stewart Transaction Solutions, Alison R. Evers/Sr. VP, Corporate Controller, Principal Accounting Officer, Lou Ann Ysaquirre/Assist. VP, Rand Zimmerman/Exec. VP, Region F Mgr. - Stewart Title Guaranty Company, Group Pres. - Stewart Title Company, John F. Welling/COO, Pres. - Stewart Title Insurance Company, VP, North Atlantic Division Mgr. - Stewart Title Guaranty Company, Matthew W. Morris/Sr. Exec. VP - Stewart Title Guaranty Company, Sr. Exec. VP - Stewart Title Company, Pres. - Stewart Professional Solutions/$292,515.00, Stewart Morris/Advisory Dir., Frank Keating/Advisory Dir., Ted C. Jones/Dir. - Investor Relations, Allan Wasserman/Exec. VP, Region E Mgr. - Stewart Title Guaranty Company, Group Pres. - Stewart Title Company, Scott McBee/Contact - Claims Department *(30 Officers included in Index)*

Directors: Malcolm S. Morris/Chmn., Co - CEO, Stewart Morris/Dir., Co - CEO, Pres., Laurie Moore-Moore/Dir., Paul W. Hobby/Dir., Edward Douglas Hodo/Dir., Robert L. Clarke/Dir., Max Crisp/Dir., CFO, Exec. VP, Sec., Treasurer, Nita Hanks/Dir., Sr. VP, Dir. - Employee Services, Stewart Title Guaranty Company, Arthur W. Porter/Dir.

Owners: Nita B. Hanks, Malcolm S. Morris, Paul W. Hobby, Stewart Morris/50.00%, Barclays Global/5.40%, Artisan Partners Limited Partnership/16.60%, Robert L. Clarke, Wachovia Corporation/9.50%, Arthur W. Porter, Insiders/2.30%, Max Crisp, Dimensional Fund Advisors Inc./8.40%, Laurie C. Moore, Stewart Morris/1.10%, Goldman Sachs Asset Management, L.P./5.60% *(18 Owners included in Index)*

Financial Data: *Fiscal Year End:*12/31 *Latest Annual Data:* 12/31/2006

Year	Sales	Net Income
2006	$2,471,481,000	$43,252,000
2005	$2,430,627,000	$88,765,000
2004	$2,182,859,000	$82,518,000

Curr. Assets:	$408,315,000	**Curr. Liab.:**	$130,589,000	**P/E Ratio:**	23.98
Plant, Equip.:	$102,983,000	**Total Liab.:**	$655,945,000	**Indic. Yr. Divd.:**	$0.750
Total Assets:	$1,458,207,000	**Net Worth:**	$802,262,000	**Debt/ Equity:**	0.1365

Stifel Financial Corp

501 N Broadway, St. Louis, MO, 63102; ***PH:*** 1-314-342-2000; ***http://*** www.stifel.com

General - Incorporation DE
Employees 2,809
Auditor Deloitte & Touche LLP
Stk Agt UMB Bank, N.A.
Counsel NA
DUNS No. 10-656-5955

Stock- Price on:12/24/2007 $59.83
Stock Exchange NYSE
Ticker Symbol SF
Outstanding Shares 14,950,000
E.P.S. $1.51
Shareholders NA

Business: The group's principle activity is to provide brokerage, trading, investment banking, investment advisory and related financial services to customers throughout the United States from 112 locations. The group operates through these segments: private client group provide securities brokerage services, including the sale of equities, mutual funds, fixed income products, and insurance, to their private clients. Equity capital markets includes corporate finance management and participation in underwriting, mergers and acquisitions, institutional sales, trading, research, and market making. The fixed income capital markets segment includes public finance, institutional sales and competitive underwriting and trading. Other includes investment advisory fees and clearing income. The group's quarterly revenue for Sep '07 was 190.84 millions of USD.

Primary SIC and add'l.: 6211

CIK No: 0000720672

Subsidiaries: Alliance Realty Corp., Century Securities Associates, Inc, CSA Insurance Agency, Incorporated, Hanifen, Imhoff Inc., S-N Capital Corp., Stifel Asset Management Corp, Stifel CAPCO II, LLC, Stifel CAPCO, LLC, Stifel Nicolaus Insurance Agency of Missouri, Stifel Nicolaus Limited, Stifel Venture Corp., Stifel, Nicolaus & Company, Incorporated

Officers: Ronald J. Kruszewski/Chmn., CEO, Pres./$3,251,081.00, Richard J. Himelfarb/Dir., Sr. VP, Dir., Exec. VP, Dir. - Investment Banking, Stifel, Nicolaus, Company, Incorporated/$3,197,464.00, Thomas P. Mulroy/Dir., Sr. VP, Exec. VP - Stifel, Nicolaus, Company, Incorporated/$3,209,072.00, Joseph A. Sullivan/Dir., Sr. VP, Dir., Exec. VP, Dir. - Fixed Income Capital Markets, Stifel, Nicolaus, Company, Incorporated/$2,675,106.00, James M. Zemlyak/Dir., Sr. VP, Treasurer/$1,417,660.00, David M. Minnick/Dir., Sr. VP, General Counsel, Keith E. Getter/Dir. - Stifel, Nicolaus, Company, Incorporated, Hugo J. Warns/Dir. - Stifel, Nicolaus, Company, Incorporated, Scott B. McCuaig/Dir., Sr. VP; Dir., Pres., Co - COO - Stifel - Nicolaus, Company, Inc/$1,427,777.00, Thomas R. Kendrick/Dir. - Stifel, Nicolaus, Company, Incorporated, Steven H. Bell/Dir. - Stifel, Nicolaus, Company, Incorporated, Walter F. Imhoff/MD, Dir. - Stifel, Nicolaus, Company, Incorporated, Michael F. Imhoff/Dir. - Stifel, Nicolaus, Company, Incorporated, Joseph J. Schlafly/Dir. - Stifel, Nicolaus, Company, Incorporated, David D. Sliney/Dir., Sr. VP, Dir., Sr. VP, Dir. - Strategic Planning, Technology, Operations, Stifel, Nicolaus, Company, Inc *(16 Officers included in Index)*

Directors: Ronald J. Kruszewski/Chmn., CEO, Pres., Robert J. Baer/Dir., David D. Sliney/Dir., Sr. VP, Dir., Sr. VP, Dir. - Strategic Planning, Technology, Operations, Stifel, Nicolaus, Company, Inc, Marcia J. Kellams/Dir., Corp. Sec., John P. Dubinsky/Dir., Richard J. Himelfarb/Dir., Sr. VP, Dir., Exec. VP, Dir. - Investment Banking, Stifel, Nicolaus, Company, Incorporated, Thomas P. Mulroy/Dir., Sr. VP, Exec. VP - Stifel, Nicolaus, Company, Incorporated, Joseph A. Sullivan/Dir., Sr. VP, Dir., Exec. VP, Dir. - Fixed Income Capital Markets, Stifel, Nicolaus, Company, Incorporated, Charles A. Dill/Dir., Frederick O. Hanser/Dir., Scott B. McCuaig/Dir., Sr. VP; Dir., Pres., Co - COO - Stifel - Nicolaus, Company, Inc, Bruce A. Beda/Dir., Walter F. Imhoff/MD, Dir. - Stifel, Nicolaus, Company, Incorporated, Richard F. Ford/Dir., James M. Oates/Dir. *(18 Directors included in Index)*

Owners: David D. Sliney, Richard J. Himelfarb, John P. Dubinsky, Scott B. McCuaig/2.14%, Robert J. Baer, Bruce A. Beda, James M. Oates, Ronald J. Kruszewski/4.35%, Thomas P. Mulroy, Fredrick O. Hanser, Charles A. Dill, Richard F. Ford, Robert E. Lefton, Joseph A. Sullivan, Insiders/12.24% *(17 Owners included in Index)*

Financial Data: *Fiscal Year End:*12/31 *Latest Annual Data:* 12/31/2006

Year	Sales	Net Income
2006	$471,388,000	$15,431,000
2005	$270,010,000	$19,644,000
2004	$251,189,000	$23,148,000

Curr. Assets:	$585,634,000	**Curr. Liab.:**	$766,130,000	**P/E Ratio:**	39.62
Plant, Equip.:	$14,353,000	**Total Liab.:**	$864,509,000	**Indic. Yr. Divd.:**	NA
Total Assets:	$1,084,774,000	**Net Worth:**	$220,265,000	**Debt/ Equity:**	NA

Stillwater Mining Co

1321 Discovery Dr., Billings, MT, 59102; ***PH:*** 1-406-373-8700; ***Fax:*** 1-406-373-8701; ***http://*** www.stillwatermining.com

General - Incorporation DE
Employees 1,719
Auditor KPMG LLP
Stk Agt Computershare Trust Co
Counsel NA
DUNS No. 10-657-2233

Stock- Price on:12/24/2007 $11.43
Stock Exchange NYSE
Ticker Symbol SWC
Outstanding Shares 91,690,000
E.P.S. -$0.13
Shareholders NA

Business: The group's principal activities are to develop, extract, process and refine palladium, platinum and associated metals from a geological formation in southern Montana known as the j-m reef. The j-m reef is a significant source of platinum group metals (pgms) inside the United States. Associated by-product metals of pgms include minor amounts of rhodium, gold, silver, nickel and copper. The group conducts its mining, smelting, refining and exploring activities at columbus and Montana. Pgms are rare precious metals with unique physical properties that are used in diverse industrial applications and in the jewelry industry. It is used in the automotive industry for the production of catalysts that reduce harmful automobile emissions. Palladium is used in the production of electronic components for personal computers and other devices, as well as in dental applications.

Primary SIC and add'l.: 1099

CIK No: 0000931948

Officers: Francis R. McAllister/64/Chmn., CEO/$3,158,825.00, Gregory A. Wing/57/CFO/$684,961.00, Stephen A. Lang/51/COO, Exec. VP/$1,150,044.00, Terrell I. Ackerman/53/VP - Planning, Process Operations/$575,455.00, John R. Stark/54/VP - Human Resources, Sec., Corporate Counsel/$947,171.00

Directors: Francis R. McAllister/64/Chmn., CEO, Joseph P. Mazurek/58/Dir., Sheryl K. Pressler/56/Dir., Craig L. Fuller/56/Dir., Donald W. Riegle/69/Dir., Steven S. Lucas/41/Dir., Todd D. Schafer/45/Dir., Patrick M. James/62/Dir., Jack E. Thompson/Dir.

Owners: Stephen A. Land, Joseph P. Mazurek, Patrick James, Steven S. Lucas, Todd Schafer, MMC Norilsk Nickel/54.40%, Francis R. Mcallister, Gregory Wing, Sheryl K. Pressler, Donald Smith & Co., Inc./5.70%, John Stark, Craig L. Fuller, Insiders, Donald Riegle

Financial Data: *Fiscal Year End:*12/31 *Latest Annual Data:* 12/31/2006

Year	Sales	Net Income
2006	$613,148,000	$7,929,000
2005	$507,462,000	-$13,874,000
2004	$447,527,000	$29,838,000

Curr. Assets:	$284,339,000	**Curr. Liab.:**	$85,590,000		
Plant, Equip.:	$460,328,000	**Total Liab.:**	$243,467,000	**Indic. Yr. Divd.:**	NA
Total Assets:	$756,023,000	**Net Worth:**	$512,556,000	**Debt/ Equity:**	0.2534

Stinger Systems Inc

2701 N Rocky Point Dr., Tampa, FL, 33607; ***PH:*** 1-813-281-1061; ***Fax:*** 1-813-288-9148; ***http://*** www.stingersystems.com; ***Email:*** investors@stingersystems.com

General - Incorporation .... NV
Employees .... NA
Auditor .... Killman, Murrell & Company, P.C.
Stk Agt .... Colonial Stock Transfer Co Inc
Counsel .... NA
DUNS No. .... NA

Stock- Price on:12/24/2007 .... $1.43
Stock Exchange .... OTC
Ticker Symbol .... STIY
Outstanding Shares 16,470,000
E.P.S .... -$0.46
Shareholders .... NA

Business: The group principle activities include producing and marketing less lethal electronic restraint products to law enforcement, correctional facilities, professional security and military sectors. Products of the group include the Ultron II(R) handheld contact stun gun, the Ice-Shield electronic immobilization riot shield, and the Bandit / REACT system, an electronic immobilizing restraint The group operates from the United States.

Primary SIC and add'l.: 3489

CIK No: 0001306944

Subsidiaries: Electronic Defense Technology, LLC,

Officers: Robert F. Gruder/Chmn., CEO, David J. Meador/CFO, Corp. Sec.

Directors: Robert F. Gruder/Chmn., CEO, Yates T. Exley/Vice Chmn., Michael Racaniello/Dir., Andrew P. Helene/Dir.

Owners: Andrew Helene, David J. Meador/1.50%, Insiders/56.30%, Yates T. Exley/28.60%, Robert F. Gruder/26.90%, Bonanza Master Fund Ltd./7.90%, Michael Racaniello, Cannell Capital LLC/16.30%

Financial Data: ***Fiscal Year End:***12/31 ***Latest Annual Data:*** 12/31/2006

Year	Sales	Net Income
2006	$454,000	-$6,306,000
2005	$470,000	-$10,086,000

Curr. Assets:	$502,000	**Curr. Liab.:**	$2,417,000		
Plant, Equip.:	$303,000	**Total Liab.:**	$2,417,000	**Indic. Yr. Divd.:**	NA
Total Assets:	$3,156,000	**Net Worth:**	$739,000	**Debt/ Equity:**	NA

STMicroelectronics

1310 Electronics Dr., Carrollton, TX, 75006; ***PH:*** 1-972-466-6000; ***Fax:*** 1-972-466-8387; ***http://*** www.st.com

General - Incorporation .... Netherlands
Employees 51,770
Auditor .... PricewaterhouseCoopers LLP
Stk Agt .... Bank of New York
Counsel .... NA
DUNS No. 76-826-5407

Stock- Price on:12/24/2007 .... $19.37
Stock Exchange .... NYSE
Ticker Symbol .... STM
Outstanding Shares 897,420,000
E.P.S .... -$0.24
Shareholders .... NA

Business: The group's principal activities are designing, developing, manufacturing and marketing of broad range of semiconductor integrated circuits and discrete devices. The products of the group include microprocessors, micro controllers, semi-custom devices, converters and complete power supplies, motor control modules and battery chargers the group's products are used in high growth applications in the computer, telecommunications, consumer, industrial and automotive sectors. The group is a supplier of analog ics, mixed signal ics, dedicated telecommunications ics, dedicated analog automotive ics and eprom memories. The group has operations in Europe, the United States of America and Asia.

Primary SIC and add'l.: 6799 8731 3699 3674 5065 3694 3629

CIK No: 0000932787

Subsidiaries: Accent S.r.l., Co.ri.m.me., DORA S.p.a., Electronic Holding S.A., INCARD SA, INCARD Sales and Marketing SA, Inmos Limited, Proton World Americas Inc, Proton World International N.V., Shanghai Blue Media Co. Ltd, Shenzhen STS Microelectronics Co. Ltd, ST Incard S.r.l., STMicroelecrtonics Limited, STMicroelectronics (Beijing) R&D Co. Ltd, STMicroelectronics (Canada), Inc. 49 Subsidiaries included in the Index

Officers: Carlo Bozotti/56/CEO, Pres., Jeffrey See/63/Corporate VP - Packaging, Test Manufacturing GM Stmicroelectronics, Patrice Chastagner/61/Corporate VP - Human Resources, Gian Luca Bertino/48/Corporate VP, GM - Computer Peripherals Group Stmicroelectronics, Richard Stockdill/Technical Press Consultant Coordinator, Carol Brown/Technical Press Consultant, Americas Region, Michael Markowitz/Dir. - Americas Region Media Relations, Kristine Wiseman/Press Mgr. - Americas Region, Janice Fenton/Technical Press Consultant, Brazil, Alfred Eiblmayr/Sr. Press Office Mgr. - Central Europe, Alexander Jurman/Press Officer - Finland, Robert Krysiak/54/Corporate VP - GM - Greater China Region Stmicroelectronics, Carlo Ferro/47/Exec. VP, CFO Stmicroelectronics, Jean-Claude Marquet/66/Corporate VP, Alain Dutheil/63/COO *(44 Officers included in Index)*

Directors: Bruno Steve/Vice Chmn. - Supervisory Board, Gerald Arbola/Chmn., Pasquale Pistorio/45/Honorary Chmn., Douglas Dunn/63/Member - Supervisory Board, Robert M. White/69/Member - Supervisory Board, Tom De Waard/Member - Supervisory Board, Matteo Del Fante/Member - Supervisory Board, Antonino Turicchi/42/Member - Supervisory Board, Didier Lombard/Member - Supervisory Board, Raymond Bingham/Member - Supervisory Board, Doug Dunn/Member - Supervisory Board, Didier Lamouche/Member - Supervisory Board, Alessandro Ovi/Member - Supervisory Board

Owners: Public/60.80%, STMicroelectronics Holding II B.V./27.50%, Treasury shares/1.40%, Brandes Investment Partners/10.20%

Financial Data: ***Fiscal Year End:***12/31 ***Latest Annual Data:*** 12/31/2006

Year	Sales	Net Income
2006	$9,854,000,000	$782,000,000
2005	$8,882,000,000	$266,000,000
2004	$8,760,000,000	$601,000,000

Curr. Assets:	$6,586,000,000	**Curr. Liab.:**	$1,963,000,000		
Plant, Equip.:	$6,426,000,000	**Total Liab.:**	$4,451,000,000	**Indic. Yr. Divd.:**	$0.260
Total Assets:	$14,198,000,000	**Net Worth:**	$9,747,000,000	**Debt/ Equity:**	NA

StockerYale Inc

32 Hampshire Rd. , Salem, NH, 03079; ***PH:*** 1-603-893-8778; ***http://*** www.stkr.com; ***Email:*** info@stockeryale.com

General - Incorporation .... MA
Employees 190
Auditor .... Deloitte & Touche, LLP
Stk Agt .... Computershare Investor Services LLC
Counsel .... Goodwin, Procter & Hoar
DUNS No. 00-101-9413

Stock- Price on:12/24/2007 .... $1.4
Stock Exchange .... NDQ
Ticker Symbol .... STKR
Outstanding Shares 35,310,000
E.P.S .... NA
Shareholders .... NA

Business: The group's principle activities are to design and manufacture structured light lasers, light emitting diodes, (leds), fiber optic and fluorescent illumination technologies. The group operates in two segments, namely illumination and optical components. Illumination products include structured light lasers, specialized fiber optic, fluorescent and led products for the machine vision, industrial inspection and defense and security industries. The optical components segment includes communication and sub-component and specialty optical fiber for the telecommunications, aerospace, utility and medical markets. The group's products are sold to customers primarily in North America, Europe and the Pacific Rim. Illumination products are sold through distributors whereas the optical components are sold directly to OEM customers by the group's sales organization. The group's quarterly revenue for Sep '07 ws 7.92 millions of USD.

Primary SIC and add'l.: 3812 3829 3229 3641 3827 3357

CIK No: 0000094538

Subsidiaries: StockerYale (IRL), Ltd., StockerYale Canada, Inc.

Officers: Lawrence W. Blodgett/Chmn., CEO, Pres., Mark W. Blodgett/Chmn., CEO, Pres./$506,390.00, Marianne Molleur/Sr. VP, CFO/$196,189.00, Luc Many/Sr. VP - Operations/$217,472.00, Paul Jortberg/Sr. VP - Sales, Marketing, Optical Components

Directors: Lawrence W. Blodgett/Chmn., CEO, Pres., Mark W. Blodgett/Chmn., CEO, Pres., Raymond J. Oglethorpe/Dir., Steven E. Karol/Dir., Dietmar Klenner/Co - Founder, Dir., Mark Zupan/Dir., Patrick J. Zilvitis/Dir., Ben Levitan/Dir., Bob Drummond/Dir., Robert J. Drummond/64/Dir.

Owners: Mark Zupan, Scott A. Fine/8.10%, Ben Levitan, Johanna Pope/6.80%, Insiders/13.10%, Peter J. Richards/8.10%, Luc Many/1.10%, Raymond J. Oglethorpe, The Eureka Interactive Fund Limited/13.60%, Lewis Asset Management, Corp./5.70%, Dietmar Klenner, Mark W. Blodgett/10.70%, Steven E. Karol, Robert J. Drummond, Marianne Molleur *(18 Owners included in Index)*

Financial Data: ***Fiscal Year End:***12/31 ***Latest Annual Data:*** 12/31/2006

Year	Sales	Net Income
2006	$19,350,000	-$5,162,000
2005	$16,203,000	-$11,891,000
2004	$17,653,000	-$12,686,000

Curr. Assets:	$9,832,000	**Curr. Liab.:**	$8,541,000		
Plant, Equip.:	$11,255,000	**Total Liab.:**	$22,789,000	**Indic. Yr. Divd.:**	NA
Total Assets:	$34,979,000	**Net Worth:**	$12,190,000	**Debt/ Equity:**	0.9413

Stockgroup Information Systems Inc

2 Penn Plz., Ste. 1500, New York, NY, 10121; ***PH:*** 1-212-292-5035; ***Fax:*** 1-212-292-5043; ***http://*** www.stockgroup.com; ***Email:*** ir@stockgroup.com

General - Incorporation .... CO
Employees .... NA
Auditor .... Ernst & Young LLP
Stk Agt .... StockTrans, Inc.
Counsel .... Devlin Jensen
DUNS No. .... NA

Stock- Price on:12/24/2007 .... $1.1
Stock Exchange .... OTC
Ticker Symbol .... SWEB
Outstanding Shares .... NA
E.P.S .... NA
Shareholders .... NA

Business: The group's principle activity is to provide financial software solutions, tools and services to media, corporate and financial services companies. The group uses technologies that enable clients to provide financial data streams and news combined with fundamental, technical, productivity, and disclosure tools to their customers, shareholders, and employees. The group provides Internet communications products for publicly traded companies and an online research center for the investment community through its financial Website. It also provides online financial news and information services. the group's quarterly revenue for September 2007 was 3.48 millions of USD.

Primary SIC and add'l.: 7375 6719

CIK No: 0001054097

Subsidiaries: 579818 B.c. Ltd., Stockgroup Australia Pty Ltd., Stockgroup Media Inc., Stockgroup Systems Ltd., Stockgroup.com (Bahamas) Ltd., Stockscores Analytics Corp.

Officers: Marcus A. New/Founder, CEO, Pres./$194,884.00, Darin Diehl/Publisher, Executive Editor, Bruce Nunn/VP - Marketing/$100,345.00, Susan Lovell/CFO/$116,049.00, Lothar Fabian/VP - Credential Direct Brokerage

Directors: Marcus A. New/Founder, CEO, Pres., Leslie A. Landes/Chmn., Patrick Spain/Dir., Lee Deboer/Dir., David Caddey/Dir., Stephen R. Zacharias/Dir., Thomas Baker/Dir.

Owners: Insiders/17.70%, Elizabeth De Marse, Susan Lovell, Michael Donnelly, Leslie Landes, Thomas Baker, Bruce Nunn, Marcus A. New/12.30%, Stephen Zacharias/1.10%, David Caddey/1.50%, Patrick Spain, Louis deBoer

Financial Data: ***Fiscal Year End:***12/31 ***Latest Annual Data:*** 12/31/2006

Year	Sales	Net Income
2006	$7,766,000	-$791,000
2005	$6,100,000	-$59,000
2004	$4,823,000	$16,000

Curr. Assets:	$3,013,000	**Curr. Liab.:**	$2,015,000		
Plant, Equip.:	$447,000	**Total Liab.:**	$2,177,000	**Indic. Yr. Divd.:**	NA
Total Assets:	$3,460,000	**Net Worth:**	$1,284,000	**Debt/ Equity:**	0.0755

Stolt Offshore

Dolphin House, Windmill Rd., Sunbury-on-thames, TW16 7HT; ; ***http://*** www.acergy-group.com

General - Incorporation .... Luxembourg
Employees 7,000
Auditor .... Deloitte & Touche LLP
Stk Agt .... Registrar & Transfer Co
Counsel .... NA
DUNS No. 26-030-8192

Stock- Price on:12/24/2007 .... $22.06
Stock Exchange .... NDQ
Ticker Symbol .... NA
Outstanding Shares 194,950,000
E.P.S .... NA
Shareholders .... NA

Business: The group's principal activities are those of offshore contractors, providing services to subsea oil and gas operations from exploration to decommissioning. These services include the design, supply and installation of all the subsea architecture, from the subsea wellheads to fixed or floating process platforms. The group operates in more than 60 countries and has regional offices in the UK, France, the USA, Norway, Singapore and Brazil.

Primary SIC and add'l.: 1381 1629 5084 1389

CIK No: 0000898685

Subsidiaries: Acergy Norway AS, Acergy Services SA, Acergy Shipping Ltd, Acergy Treasury Ltd., Acergy West Africa SASU, Class 3 Shipping Limited

Officers: Tom Ehret/Dir., CEO, Bruno Chabas/COO, Caroline Langlais/Contact - Human Resources, Julian Thomson/Investor Relations Officer, Oeyvind Mikaelsen/45/VP - Acergy Northern Europe, Canada, Johan Rasmussen/Corporate VP, General Counsel, Jean-Luc Laloe/Corporate VP - Strategic Planning, Allen Leatt/CTO, Keith Tipson/Corporate VP - Human Resources, Philippe Lamoure/Regional VP - South America, Jeff Champion/Regional VP - Asia, Middle East, Tony Duncan/Regional VP - North America, Mexico, Oyvind Mikaelsen/Regional VP - Northern Europe, Canada, Brian Leith/VP - Marine Assets, Stuart Jackson/CFO *(30 Officers included in Index)*

Directors: Tom Ehret/Dir., CEO, Mark Woolveridge/Chmn., James B. Hurlock/Dep. Chmn., George H. Doremus/Dir., Frithjof J. Skouveroe/Dir., Trond Westlie/Dir., Peter Mason/Dir.

Owners: Stuart Jackson, James B. Hurlock, Folketrygdfondet/7.69%, Tom Ehret, State Street Bank/8.14%, GE Asset Management/9.80%, Artisan Partners, LP/9.70%, Mark Woolveridge, DWS Investment GmBH/9.90%, FMR Corporation/10.36%, Frithjof J. Skouvere

Financial Data: *Fiscal Year End:*11/30 *Latest Annual Data:* 11/30/2006

Year	Sales	Net Income
2006	$2,124,200,000	$236,700,000
2005	$1,483,300,000	$139,500,000
2004	$1,241,900,000	$5,100,000

Curr. Assets:	$1,403,600,000	**Curr. Liab.:**	$919,500,000		
Plant, Equip.:	$645,600,000	**Total Liab.:**	$1,490,800,000	**Indic. Yr. Divd.:**	NA
Total Assets:	$2,209,200,000	**Net Worth:**	$699,700,000	**Debt/ Equity:**	NA

Stolt-Nielsen SA

C/o Stolt Nielsen Limited, Aldwych House 71-91 Aldwych, London, WC2B 4HN; ***PH:*** 203-625-9400; ***http://*** www.stoltnielsen.com

General - Incorporation	Luxembourg	**Stock**- Price on:12/24/2007	NA
Employees	5,025	Stock Exchange	OTC
Auditor	Deloitte & Touche LLP	Ticker Symbol	SNSAY
Stk Agt	DnB NOR Bank ASA	Outstanding Shares	NA
Counsel	NA	E.P.S	NA
DUNS No.	34-629-0943	Shareholders	NA

Business: The group operates through the following divisions: transportation services (worldwide transportation, storage and distribution of bulk liquid chemicals, edible oils, acids and other specialty liquids through SNTG); sub sea services (sub sea engineering, flexible and rigid flow line lay, sub sea construction, inspection, maintenance and repair services to its customers in the offshore oil and gas industry through SCS); seafood business (production, processing and marketing of high quality seafood products, including Atlantic Salmon, Turbot, Halibut, Sturgeon and Caviar through SSF) .

Primary SIC and add'l.: 5146 1389 4491 2091 2092

CIK No: 0000831980

Subsidiaries: Stolt Sea Farm Investments B.V., Stolt-Nielsen Holdings B.V., Stolt-Nielsen Investments N.V., Stolt-Nielsen Transportation Group B.V., Stolt-Nielsen Transportation Group Inc., Stolt-Nielsen Transportation Group Ltd.

Officers: Niels G. Stolt-Nielsen/Dir., CEO, Otto H. Fritzner/CEO - Stolt, Nielsen Transportation Group Ltd, John Wakely/Exec. VP, Jan Chr. Engelhardtsen/CFO, Pablo Garcia/Pres. - Stolt Sea Farm

Directors: Niels G. Stolt-Nielsen/Dir., CEO, Roelof Hendriks/Dir., Christopher J. Wright/Dir., James B. Hurlock/Dir., Christer Olsson/Dir., Jacob Stolt-Nielsen/Dir., Hakan Larsson/Dir.

Owners: Causeway Capital Management LLC/9.30%, Fiducia Ltd/47.70%

Stone Energy Corp

625 E Kaliste Saloom Rd. , Lafayette, LA, 70508; ***PH:*** 1-318-237-0410; ***http://*** www.stoneenergy.com

General - Incorporation	DE	**Stock**- Price on:12/24/2007	$34.9
Employees	240	Stock Exchange	NYSE
Auditor	Ernst & Young LLP	Ticker Symbol	SGY
Stk Agt	Mellon Investor Services LLC	Outstanding Shares	28,030,000
Counsel	NA	E.P.S	-$6.6
DUNS No.	80-666-6459	Shareholders	NA

Business: The group's principal activity is to acquire, explore, develop and operate oil and gas properties. The operations of the group are carried on in the shallow waters and onshore regions of the gulf coast basin in addition to the rocky mountains area. As of Mar 1, 2004, its property portfolio consisted of 60 active properties and 28 primary term leases in the gulf coast basin and 33 active properties in the rocky mountains. Major customers of the group include conoco, inc, duke energy trading and marketing llc and reliant services, inc.

Primary SIC and add'l.: 1311

CIK No: 0000904080

Subsidiaries: Stone Energy, LLC

Officers: David H. Welch/Dir., CEO, Pres./$2,519,254.00, Kent J. Pierret/Sr. VP, Treasurer, Chief Accounting Officer, Richard L. Smith/VP - Exploration Business Development, E. J. Louviere/Sr. VP - Land, Andrew L. Gates/VP, Sec., General Counsel, Kenneth H. Beer/CFO, Sr. VP/$1,081,859.00, Florence M. Ziegler/VP - Human Resources, Jerome F. Wenzel/VP - Production, Drilling

Directors: David H. Welch/Dir., CEO, Pres., James H. Stone/Chmn., Robert A. Bernhard/Dir., Richard A. Pattarozzi/Dir., B. J. Duplantis/Dir., George R. Christmas/68/Dir., Raymond B. Gary/Dir., David R. Voelker/Dir., John P. Laborde/85/Dir., Kay G. Priestly/Dir.

Owners: Robert A. Bernhard, Raymond B. Gary, Dimensional Fund Advisors, Inc./6.40%, Insiders/8.90%, John P. Laborde, Craig L. Glassinger, Kay G. Priestly, Kenneth H. Beer, James H. Stone/5.00%, Michael E. Madden, David R. Voelker, David H. Welch, George R. Christmas, B. J. Duplantis, Donald Smith & Co., Inc./5.70% *(17 Owners included in Index)*

Financial Data: *Fiscal Year End:*12/31 *Latest Annual Data:* 12/31/2006

Year	Sales	Net Income
2006	$688,988,000	-$254,222,000
2005	$636,240,000	$136,764,000
2004	$544,201,000	$134,903,000

Curr. Assets:	$312,673,000	**Curr. Liab.:**	$310,828,000		
Plant, Equip.:	$1,798,538,000	**Total Liab.:**	$1,416,831,000	**Indic. Yr. Divd.:**	NA
Total Assets:	$2,128,471,000	**Net Worth:**	$711,640,000	**Debt/ Equity:**	1.0860

Stonegate Bank FL

1430 N Federal Hwy, Fort Lauderdale, FL, 33304; ***PH:*** 1-954-315-5500; ***Fax:*** 1-954-315-5519; ***http://*** www.stonegatebank.com; ***Email:*** customerservice@stonegatebank.com

General - Incorporation		**Stock**- Price on:12/24/2007	$15.85
Employees	NA	Stock Exchange	OTC
Auditor	NA	Ticker Symbol	SGBK
Stk Agt	NA	Outstanding Shares	3,780,000
Counsel	NA	E.P.S	NA
DUNS No.	NA	Shareholders	NA

Business: The groups principal activities include providing banking and financial services. Services of the group include checking accounts, savings accounts, certificates of deposit, installment loans, real estate mortgage loans, commercial loans, traveler's checks, safe deposit boxes, night depository and automated teller services. The group operates from the United States.

Primary SIC and add'l.: 6022

CIK No:

Officers: David Seleski/Dir., CEO, Pres., Jeff Nudelman/Dir. - Management Consultant, Steve Cameron/COO, Exec. VP, Steve Sanzone/Exec. VP, Sr. Loan Officer, Sharon Jones/VP, Controller, Joseph Bamond/Exec. VP, Kris Barnhart/Exec. VP, Steve Putnam/Exec. VP

Directors: David Seleski/Dir., CEO, Pres., Robin Rodriguez/Chmn., Jeff Holding/Dir., Jeff Nudelman/Dir. - Management Consultant, Alan Robbins/Dir., Gary Rotella/Dir., Robert Souaid/Dir., Glenn Straub/Dir., John L. Tomlinson/Dir.

StoneMor Partners LP

155 Rittenhouse Cir., Bristol, PA, 19007; ***PH:*** 1-215-826-2800; ***http://*** www.stonemor.com; ***Email:*** ContactUs@stonemor.com

General - Incorporation	DE	**Stock**- Price on:12/24/2007	$25.43
Employees	1,581	Stock Exchange	NDQ
Auditor	Deloitte & Touche LLP	Ticker Symbol	STON
Stk Agt	American Stock Transfer & Trust Co.	Outstanding Shares	9,040,000
Counsel	NA	E.P.S	$0.43
DUNS No.	NA	Shareholders	NA

Business: The groups principle activity is to provide cemetery products and services. The products of the group include burial lots, caskets, cremation niches, mausoleum crypts and burial vaults. The groups services include grave markers and grave marker bases, memorials and installation of caskets. The group operates from the United States. The group's quarterly revenue for September 2007 was 35.38 millions of USD.

Primary SIC and add'l.: 7261

CIK No: 0001286131

Subsidiaries: Alleghany Memorial Park LLC, Alleghany Memorial Park Subsidiary, Inc., Altavista Memorial Park LLC, Altavista Memorial Park Subsidiary, Inc., Arlington Development Company, Augusta Memorial Park Perpetual Care Company, Bedford County Memorial Park LLC, Bedford County Memorial Park Subsidiary LLC, Beth Israel Cemetery Association of Woodbridge, New Jersey, Bethel Cemetery Association, Birchlawn Burial Park LLC, Birchlawn Burial Park Subsidiary, Inc., Blue Ridge Memorial Gardens LLC, Blue Ridge Memorial Gardens Subsidiary LLC, Butler County Memorial Park LLC 175 Subsidiaries included in the Index

Officers: Lawrence Miller/Chmn., CEO, Pres., William R. Shane/61/Dir., CFO, Exec. VP, Michael L. Stache/56/COO, Sr. VP, Robert Stache/59/Sr. VP - Sales, Paul Waimberg/50/VP - Finance

Directors: Lawrence Miller/Chmn., CEO, Pres., William R. Shane/61/Dir., CFO, Exec. VP, Allen R. Freedman/67/Dir., Peter K. Grunebaum/74/Dir., Robert B. Hellman/48/Dir., Martin R. Lautman/61/Dir., Fenton R. Talbott/66/Dir., Jeffrey A. Zawadsky/37/Dir., Howard L. Carver/63/Dir.

Owners: Robert B. Hellman, Peter Grunebaum, CFSI LLC, Neuberger Berman, LLC/10.70%, Howard L. Carver, Jeffrey A. Zawadsky, George McCown, Allen R. Freedman, Insiders/2.00%, McCown De Leeuw& Co. IV, L.P., Fenton R. Talbot, David De Leeuw, MDC Management Company IV, LLC, Martin R. Lautman/1.10%

Financial Data: *Fiscal Year End:*12/31 *Latest Annual Data:* 12/31/2006

Year	Sales	Net Income
2006	$115,113,000	$3,040,000
2005	$99,725,000	$4,090,000
2004	$89,258,000	-$3,838,000

Curr. Assets:	$38,216,000	**Curr. Liab.:**	$13,094,000	**P/E Ratio:**	46.24
Plant, Equip.:	$200,741,000	**Total Liab.:**	$525,737,000	**Indic. Yr. Divd.:**	$2.060
Total Assets:	$627,024,000	**Net Worth:**	$101,287,000	**Debt/ Equity:**	1.0817

Stonepath Group Inc

Two Penn Ctr Plz., Ste 605, Philadlephia, PA, 19102; ***PH:*** 1-206-336-5400; ***http://*** www.stonepath.com; ***Email:*** hq@stonepath.com

General - Incorporation	DE	**Stock**- Price on:12/24/2007	NA
Employees	1,111	Stock Exchange	OTC
Auditor	Grant Thornton LLP	Ticker Symbol	SGRZ
Stk Agt	StockTrans, Inc.	Outstanding Shares	NA
Counsel	Buchanan Ingersoll Professional Corp	E.P.S	-$0.62
DUNS No.	NA	Shareholders	NA

Business: The group's principal activity is to provide third-party logistics services, offering a full range of time-definite transportation and distribution solutions. The services provided by the group include movement of raw materials, supplies, components and finished goods for customers. These services are offered through domestic air and ground freight forwarding business. In addition to time-definite transportation services, it also provides a broad range of value added supply chain management services including warehousing, order fulfillment and inventory management. It services a customer base of manufacturers, distributors and national retail chains through a network of offices in 21 major metropolitan areas in North America and Puerto Rico and an extensive network of over 200 independent carriers. On 10-Feb-2004, it acquired shaanxi sunshine cargo services int'l co ltd.

Primary SIC and add'l.: 4214 7389 7375

CIK No: 0001093546

Subsidiaries: Global Container Line, Inc., Stonepath Holdings Limited, Stonepath Logistics Government Services, Inc.

Officers: Bob Arovas/CEO

Directors: Dennis Pelino/Chmn., Aloysius T. Lawn/Dir., John Springer/Dir., David R. Jones/Dir., Douglass J. Coates/Dir., Slobodan Andjic/Dir., Martin Muller-Romheld/Dir., James M. Carter/Dir., Rob McCord/Dir.

Financial Data: Fiscal Year End:12/31 Latest Annual Data: 12/31/2005

Year	Sales	Net Income
2005	$410,255,000	-$9,738,000
2004	$84,722,000	-$13,043,000
2003	$61,979,000	-$786,000

Curr. Assets:	$76,749,000	Curr. Liab.:	$80,002,000		
Plant, Equip.:	$6,856,000	Total Liab.:	$96,978,000	Indic. Yr. Divd.:	NA
Total Assets:	$135,282,000	Net Worth:	$36,500,000	Debt/ Equity:	NA

Stoneridge Inc

9400 E Market St., Warren, OH, 44484; *PH:* 1-248-489-9300; *http://* www.stoneridge.com; *Email:* corporate@stoneridge.com

General - Incorporation	OH	Stock- Price on:12/24/2007	$12.2
Employees	6,000	Stock Exchange	NYSE
Auditor	Ernst & Young LLP	Ticker Symbol	SRI
Stk Agt	National City Bank	Outstanding Shares	24,310,000
Counsel	NA	E.P.S.	$0.50
DUNS No.	60-628-0873	Shareholders	NA

Business: The group's principal activities are to design and manufacture highly engineered electrical and electronic components, modules and systems for the automotive, medium and heavy-duty truck and agricultural vehicle markets. The products comprise of vehicle electrical power and distribution systems, electronic and electrical switch products, electronic instrumentation and information display products, actuator and sensor products. The power and distribution systems regulate and direct the operation of the entire electrical system within a vehicle. The electronic and electromechanical switch products are used to activate headlights and other accessories. The electronic instrumentation and information display products display information such as speed, pressure and other messages related to vehicle performance. The actuator and sensor products enable users to deploy power functions and measure pressure and speed levels.

Primary SIC and add'l.: 3714 3679

CIK No: 0001043337

Subsidiaries: Alphabet de Mexico de Monclova SA de CV, Alphabet de Mexico SA de CV, Minda Instruments Ltd., PST Indstria Eletrnica da Amaznia Ltda., Stoneridge Asia Pacific Electronics (Suzhou) Co. Ltd., Stoneridge Control Devices, Inc., Stoneridge Electronics AB, Stoneridge Electronics AS, Stoneridge Electronics Ltd., Stoneridge Electronics Srl, Stoneridge Electronics, Inc., Stoneridge International Financial Services Company, Stoneridge Pollak Ltd., TED de Mexico SA de CV

Officers: John C. Corey/Dir., CEO, Pres./$1,899,931.00, Andrew M. Oakes/49/VP, GM - China Operations, Edward F. Mosel/59/VP, Pres. - Control Devices/$609,777.00, Avery S. Cohen/Dir., Sec., Mark J. Tervalon/VP, Pres. - Vehicle Management, Power Distribution/$450,159.00, George E. Strickler/CFO, Exec. VP/$521,015.00, Thomas A. Beaver/VP - Global Sales, Systems Engineering/$476,416.00

Directors: John C. Corey/Dir., CEO, Pres., William M. Lasky/Chmn., Richard E. Cheney/Dir., Douglas C. Jacobs/Dir., Avery S. Cohen/Dir., Sec., Earl L. Linehan/Dir., Sheldon J. Epstein/Dir., Jeffrey P. Draime/Dir., D. M. Draime/41/Dir., Kim Korth/Dir.

Owners: John C. Corey/1.20%, C. M. Draime/23.80%, Avery S. Cohen, Wellington Management Group/7.30%, Douglas C. Jacobs, George E. Strickler, Mark J. Tervalon, Earl L. Linehan/1.30%, Richard E. Cheney, Jeffrey P. Draime/12.80%, Dimensional Fund Advisors, Inc./8.30%, Insiders/18.60%, William M. Lasky, Edward F. Mosel, Sheldon J. Epstein *(17 Owners included in Index)*

Financial Data: Fiscal Year End:12/31 Latest Annual Data: 12/31/2006

Year	Sales	Net Income
2006	$708,699,000	$14,513,000
2005	$671,584,000	$933,000
2004	$681,795,000	-$92,503,000

Curr. Assets:	$254,032,000	Curr. Liab.:	$118,117,000	P/E Ratio:	21.40
Plant, Equip.:	$114,586,000	Total Liab.:	$323,185,000	Indic. Yr. Divd.:	NA
Total Assets:	$501,807,000	Net Worth:	$178,622,000	Debt/ Equity:	1.0788

Stora Enso Oyj

231 1st Ave. N, Wisconsin Rapids, WI, 54495; *PH:* 1-715-422-3111; *Fax:* 1-715-422-3469; *http://* www.storaenso.com

General - Incorporation		Stock- Price on:12/24/2007	$19.03
Employees	43,887	Stock Exchange	NYSE
Auditor	NA	Ticker Symbol	SEO
Stk Agt	NA	Outstanding Shares	788,600,000
Counsel	NA	E.P.S.	$0.34
DUNS No.	NA	Shareholders	NA

Business: The groups principle activities include manufacturing and selling paper products. The group operates through four segments namely, publication paper, fine paper, packaging boards and forest products. The group acquire Holzwerke Wimmer Gmbh in the year 2006 and Lamco GmbH in the year 2005. The group operates from the United States, Europe, Asia Pacific and Australia.

Primary SIC and add'l.: 2611 2675 2411 2631 2672 2421 0811 2621 2676

CIK No: 0001120557

Subsidiaries: AB Siefvert& Fornander, Alluma SA, Altpapier Verw Wattenschied GmbH, As Oy Helsingin Oravatalo, AS Papyrus, AS Stora Enso Mets, As. Oy Hanhirinne, As. Oy Petronrinne, Bcke Emballage AB, Berghuizer Papierfabriek N.V., Carl Emil AS, Carl Emil Bergen AS, Cartiberia SA, Cefortia AB, Chai Narai Co Ltd 323 Subsidiaries included in the Index

Officers: Jouko Karvinen/CEO, CEO - Stora Enso, Veli-Jussi Potka/Exec. VP - Industrial Packaging, Aulis Ansaharju/Exec. VP - Fine Paper, Country Mgr. Finland, Mats Nordlander/Exec. VP - Consumer Board, Merchants, Marketing Services, Juha Vanhainen/Exec. VP - Newsprint, John Gillen/Pres., Regional Mgr. - North America, Markku Pentikainen/Exec. VP - Asia Pacific, China, Russia, New Business Creation, Peter Nordquist/VP - Funding, Financial Services, Eeva Starck/VP - Corporate Publishing, Eija Pitkanen/Sustainability Communications, CSR, Stora Enso Oyj, Gary Parafinczuk/Exec. VP - Corporate Human Resources, Business Excellence, Hannu Alalauri/Exec. VP - Magazine Paper, Jan Moritz/VP - Human Resources, Sweden, Eberhard Potempa/Sr. VP, Scott Lipinski/Sr. VP - Human Resources, North America *(31 Officers included in Index)*

Directors: Claes Dahlback/Chmn., Llkka Niemi/Dir., Birgitta Kantola/Dir., Jan Sjoqvist/Dir., Gunnar Brock/Dir., Lee A. Chaden/Dir., Matti Vuoria/Dir., Dominique Heriard Dubreuil/Dir., Marcus Wallenberg/Dir.

Owners: Finnish State, Social Insurance Institution of Finland, Finnish State, Varma Mutual Pension Insurance Company, Insiders, Insiders, Varma Mutual Pension Insurance Company, Knut and Alice Wallenberg Foundation, Social Insurance Institution of Finland

Financial Data: Fiscal Year End:12/31 Latest Annual Data: 12/31/2006

Year	Sales	Net Income
2006	$19,753,404,000	$841,691,000
2005	$15,799,067,000	-$192,939,000
2004	$17,175,886,000	$503,464,000

Curr. Assets:	$6,727,457,000	Curr. Liab.:	$4,486,511,000		
Plant, Equip.:	$12,405,011,000	Total Liab.:	$12,651,379,000	Indic. Yr. Divd.:	$0.440
Total Assets:	$22,422,127,000	Net Worth:	$9,770,748,000	Debt/ Equity:	NA

Storm Cat Energy Corp

1125 17th St., Ste.2310, Denver, CO, 80202; *PH:* 1-303-991-5070; *Fax:* 1-303-991-5075; *http://* www.stormcatenergy.com; *Email:* info@stormcatenergy.com

General - Incorporation	BC	Stock- Price on:12/24/2007	$1.15
Employees	27	Stock Exchange	AMEX
Auditor	Housser & Tupper, LLP	Ticker Symbol	SCU
Stk Agt	Pacific Corporate Trust Co	Outstanding Shares	80,940,000
Counsel	NA	E.P.S.	-$0.093
DUNS No.	NA	Shareholders	NA

Business: The groups principle activity is to develop and explore oil and natural gas. In the year 2006, the group acquired six state tracts. The group operates from the United States and Canada. The groups quarterly revenue for September 2007 was 4.18 millions of USD.

Primary SIC and add'l.: 1311

CIK No: 0001178818

Subsidiaries: Storm Cat Energy (Alaska) LLC, Storm Cat Energy (Powder River) LLC, Storm Cat Energy (USA) Corporation, Storm Cat Energy Mongol Co. Ltd., Storm Cat Energy USA Operating Corporation, Triple Crown Gathering Corporation

Officers: Joseph M. Brooker/Dir., CEO, Lisa Reeves/Staff, Geologist, Rob Garrison/Mgr. - Canadian, International Land, Kurt Bair/Sr. Petroleum Engineer, William I. Kent/Dir. - Investor Relations, Mike Jaeger/Mgr. - Environmental, Regulatory, Paul Wiesner/CFO/$484,046.00, Keith J. Knapstad/COO, Pres./$480,738.00, Donald Martin/50/VP - Canadian, International Operations/$489,905.00, Matt Humphreys/Mgr. - Business Development, Barbara Zimmerman/Dir. - Land

Directors: Joseph M. Brooker/Dir., CEO, Jon Whitney/Dir., David Wight/Dir., Michael OByrne/Dir., Robert Penner/Dir., Mike Wozniak/Dir., Robert J. Clark/Dir.

Owners: William Herbert Hunt Trust Estate/5.01%, Insiders/4.04%, GLG North American Opportunity Fund/9.45%, Keith Knapstad, Touradji Capital Management/7.65%, UBS AG Canada Branch/5.01%, Michael Wozniak, Robert J. Clark, Trapeze Capital Corp./31.01%, Paul Wiesner, David Wight, Joseph M. Brooker, Jon Whitney, Robert Penner, Michael OByrne

Financial Data: Fiscal Year End:12/31 Latest Annual Data: 12/31/2006

Year	Sales	Net Income
2006	$9,444,000	-$6,861,000
2005	$4,627,000	-$8,368,000
2004	$108,000	-$958,000

Curr. Assets:	$13,467,000	Curr. Liab.:	$29,061,000		
Plant, Equip.:	$97,204,000	Total Liab.:	$50,282,000	Indic. Yr. Divd.:	NA
Total Assets:	$111,964,000	Net Worth:	$61,682,000	Debt/ Equity:	1.1998

Strata Oil & Gas Inc

Formerly: Stratabase Inc
918 16th Ave. Nw, Ste. 408, Calgary, AB, T2M 0K3; ; *http://* www.stratabase.com

General - Incorporation	Canada	Stock- Price on:12/24/2007	$1.42
Employees	NA	Stock Exchange	OTC
Auditor	BDO Dunwoody LLP	Ticker Symbol	SOIGF
Stk Agt	Holladay Stock Transfer, Inc.	Outstanding Shares	NA
Counsel	David Lubin and Associates	E.P.S.	NA
DUNS No.	NA	Shareholders	NA

Business: The group's principle activities are to develop open-source customer relationship management software for general distribution and sell hardware solutions to enterprises. The crm software allows enterprises to conduct relationship management through the use of the sales force automation and email marketing automation software modules. These solutions allow enterprises to manage sales relationships and contacts, automate forecasting and the sales opportunity pipeline, conduct mass customized communications and manage large scale custom marketing campaigns. The company also provides hardware solutions to the customers.

Primary SIC and add'l.: 7372

CIK No: 0001227282

Officers: Manny Dhinsa/35/Chmn., CEO, Pres., Sec., Treasurer, Scott Praill/42/Dir., CFO

Directors: Manny Dhinsa/35/Chmn., CEO, Pres., Sec., Treasurer, Pratt Barndollar/48/Dir., Charlie Perity/53/Dir., Scott Praill/42/Dir., CFO, Pol Brisset/32/Dir., Duncan Budge/57/Dir.

Owners: Insiders, Manny Dhinsa, Scott Praill, Pol Brisset

Financial Data: Fiscal Year End:12/31 Latest Annual Data: 12/31/2005

Year	Sales	Net Income
2005	NA	-$2,085,000
2004	NA	-$695,000
2003	$5,000	-$1,027,000

Curr. Assets:	$3,861,000	Curr. Liab.:	$164,000		
Plant, Equip.:	NA	Total Liab.:	$164,000	Indic. Yr. Divd.:	NA
Total Assets:	$6,648,000	Net Worth:	$6,484,000	Debt/ Equity:	NA

Stratagene Corp

11011 N Torrey Pines Rd., La Jolla, CA, 92037; *PH:* 1-858-373-6300; *http://* www.stratagene.com

General - Incorporation	DE	Stock - Price on:12/24/2007	NA
Employees	459	Stock Exchange	NA
Auditor	Fenwick & West LLP	Ticker Symbol	NA
Stk Agt	Continental Stock Transfer & Trust Co	Outstanding Shares	NA
Counsel	NA	E.P.S.	NA
DUNS No.	17-186-9332	Shareholders	NA

Business: The group's principal activities are to manufacture, develop and market biological and instrumentation products to improve the speed and accuracy of life sciences research. The group distributes its products to researchers at academic and government institutions and pharmaceutical, biotechnology and industrial companies, in the U.S. And internationally. The products are used for gene transfer, gene and protein expression, gene cloning, protein and gene functional analysis, nucleic acid and protein purification and analysis, microarrays, dna replication and nucleic acid quantification. It has offices in the Netherlands and Japan. The group acquired hycor biomedical inc on 03-Jun-2004, and biocrest holdings llc on 02-Jun-2004.

Primary SIC and add'l.: 2833 2835 2836

CIK No: 0001108674

Subsidiaries: BioCrest Corporation, BioCrest Limited, LLC, BioCrest Logistics, BV, BioCrest Management, LLC, BioCrest Manufacturing, L.P., BioCrest Sales, L.P., BioCrest, BV, Hycor Biomedical GmbH, Hycor Biomedical Inc., Hycor Biomedical Ltd., Iobion Informatics (Canada) Ltd., Stratagene California, Stratagene Japan KK

Officers: Joseph A. Sorge/Chmn., CEO, Nelson F. Thune/Sr. VP - Operations, John R. Pouk/Sr. VP - Global Sales - International Operations, Steve R. Martin/CFO, VP

Directors: Joseph A. Sorge/Chmn., CEO, Peter Ellman/Dir., Robert C. Manion/Dir., Carlton J. Eibl/Dir., John C. Reed/Dir.

Owners: John C. Reed, Peter Ellman, John R. Pouk, Insiders/57.80%, Steve R. Martin, Carlton J. Eibl, Joseph A. Sorge/56.20%, Wellington Management Company/7.10%, Nelson F. Thune, Robert C. Manion

Stratasys Inc

7665 Commerce Way, Eden Prairie, MN, 55344; **PH:** 1-952-937-3000; *http://* www.stratasys.com; **Email:** support@stratasys.com

General - Incorporation	DE	Stock - Price on:12/24/2007	$48.75
Employees	340	Stock Exchange	NDQ
Auditor	KPMG LLP	Ticker Symbol	SSYS
Stk Agt	Continental Stock Transfer & Trust Co	Outstanding Shares	10,310,000
Counsel	Best & Flanagen LLP	E.P.S.	$0.64
DUNS No.	61-346-5806	Shareholders	NA

Business: The group's principal activities are to develop, manufacture and sell a family of rapid prototyping devices. These devices include a line of three dimensional printing devices which create physical models from computerized designs. The products of the group are categorized into three groups: modeling equipment, modeling material and operating software. These products are sold to the customers throughout the United States, Europe, Asia and other countries.

Primary SIC and add'l.: 7372 3577

CIK No: 0000915735

Subsidiaries: Stratasys Gmbh, Technimold, S.R.L.

Officers: Scott S. Crump/Chmn., CEO, Pres., Treasurer/$477,859.00, Robert F. Gallagher/CFO/$214,808.00, Thomas W. Stenoien/COO/$330,752.00, Paul Blake/VP - Research, Development, Jonathan Lee Cobb/VP, GM Dimension, Woodrow J. Frost/VP - FDM Sales, Marketing, Customer Service, Paul G. Grette/VP - Process Improvement, Kurt Hinrichsen/VP - Operations, Shane Glenn/Dir. - Investor Relations, Larry Doerr/VP - Operations, Joe Hiemenz/Public Relations Mgr., Jerry McLeod/Sr. Sales Exec.

Directors: Scott S. Crump/Chmn., CEO, Pres., Treasurer, Ralph E. Crump/Dir., Edward J. Fierko/Dir., Clifford H. Schwieter/Dir., Arnold J. Wasserman/Dir., Gregory L. Wilson/Dir.

Owners: Thomas W. Stenoien, Edward J. Fierko/1.12%, Robert F. Gallagher, Scott S. Crump/3.96%, Arnold J. Wasserman, Clifford H. Schwieter, Mairs and Power, Inc./5.70%, Merrill Lynch & Co./5.97%, Ralph E. Crump/4.14%, Burgundy Asset Management Ltd./6.10%, Insiders/12.16%, Lord, Abbett & Co. LLC/14.27%, William Blair & Company, L.L.C./6.82%, Gregory L. Wilson

Financial Data: Fiscal Year End:12/31 Latest Annual Data: 12/31/2006

Year	Sales			Net Income
2006	$103,809,000			$11,164,000
2005	$82,844,000			$10,603,000
2004	$70,329,000			$9,129,000
Curr. Assets:	$75,524,000	Curr. Liab.:	$20,212,000	P/E Ratio: 39.31
Plant, Equip.:	$20,413,000	Total Liab.:	$20,212,000	Indic. Yr. Divd.: NA
Total Assets:	$118,004,000	Net Worth:	$97,792,000	Debt/ Equity: NA

Strategic Acquisitions Inc

10 W St., Ste. 28-c, New York, NY, 10004; **PH:** 1-212-750-3355

General - Incorporation	NV	Stock - Price on:12/24/2007	$0.35
Employees	NA	Stock Exchange	OTC
Auditor	Comiskey & Company	Ticker Symbol	STQN
Stk Agt	American Stock Transfer & Trust Co.	Outstanding Shares	NA
Counsel	NA	E.P.S.	$0.00
DUNS No.	NA	Shareholders	NA

Business: The groups principal activity is to seek, investigate, and, if warranted, acquire a business, and to pursue other related activities intended to enhance shareholder value. The group operates from the United States.

Primary SIC and add'l.: 6770

CIK No: 0000847942

Officers: John P. O'Shea/51/Dir., Pres., Principal Financial Officer, Marika Xirouhakis/27/Dir., Sec., Treasurer

Directors: John P. O'Shea/51/Dir., Pres., Principal Financial Officer, Marika Xirouhakis/27/Dir., Sec., Treasurer

Owners: Insiders/58.10%, John P. OShea/57.23%, Marika Xirouhakis, Deborah A. Salerno/28.16%

Financial Data: Fiscal Year End:12/31 Latest Annual Data: 12/31/2006

Year	Sales	Net Income
2006	NA	-$6,000
2005	NA	-$11,000
2004	NA	-$5,000

Curr. Assets:	$80,000	Curr. Liab.:	$1,000		
Plant, Equip.:	NA	Total Liab.:	$1,000	Indic. Yr. Divd.:	NA
Total Assets:	$80,000	Net Worth:	$80,000	Debt/ Equity:	NA

Strategic Defense Alliance Corp

Formerly: Lounsberry Holdings I Inc

12020 Sunrise Valley Dr., Ste. 100, Reston, CT, 20191; **PH:** 1-703-476 2250

General - Incorporation	DE	Stock - Price on:12/24/2007	NA
Employees	NA	Stock Exchange	NA
Auditor	Michael Pollack, CPA	Ticker Symbol	NA
Stk Agt	1st Global Stock Transfer, LLC	Outstanding Shares	NA
Counsel	NA	E.P.S.	NA
DUNS No.	NA	Shareholders	NA

Business: The group's principal activity is to is to seek the acquisition of, or merger with, an existing company. The company is engaged in organizational efforts and obtaining initial financing. The company was formed as a vehicle to pursue a business combination and has made no efforts to identify a possible business combination. As a result, the company has not conducted negotiations or entered into a letter of intent concerning any target business.

Primary SIC and add'l.: 6770

CIK No: 0001328791

Subsidiaries: Computer Networks and Software, Inc

Strategic Diagnostics Inc

111 Pencader Dr., Newark, DE, 19702; **PH:** 1-302-456-6789; *http://* www.sdix.com; **Email:** europe@sdix.com

General - Incorporation	DE	Stock - Price on:12/24/2007	$4.59
Employees	150	Stock Exchange	NDQ
Auditor	KPMG LLP	Ticker Symbol	SDIX
Stk Agt	NY Drop-SS Bank & Trust Co	Outstanding Shares	20,290,000
Counsel	Pepper Hamilton LLP	E.P.S.	$0.06
DUNS No.	19-602-0689	Shareholders	NA

Business: The group's principal activities are to develop, manufacture and market immunoassay and bioluminescence-based test kits for detection of a wide variety of substances in the food safety and water quality markets and also provides antibody and immunoreagent research, development andproduction services to medical diagnostic and pharmaceutical companies, as well as research institutions. The group's test kits include chemicals used to treat drinking water, proprietary chemicals used in industries, environmental contaminants, pesticides, genetically engineered traits and diseases in crops. The group provides developing and marketing test kits and strip tests, fully integrated monoclonal antibody development and manufacturing services to pharmaceutical and medical diagnostic companies through its subsidiary. The group markets its products through a network of over 50 distributors in Canada, Mexico, Latin America, Europe and Asia.

Primary SIC and add'l.: 3821 2834

CIK No: 0000911649

Subsidiaries: AZUR Environmental Limited, SDI Europe Limited

Officers: Matthew H. Knight/Dir., CEO, Pres./$501,775.00, James W. Stave/VP - Research, Development/$211,679.00, Stanley Fronczkowski/CFO, VP - Finance, Corp. Sec.

Directors: Matthew H. Knight/Dir., CEO, Pres., Grover C. Wrenn/Chmn., Richard J. Defieux/Dir., Herbert Lotman/Dir., Morton Collins/Dir., Clifford L. Spiro/Dir., Stephen L. Waechter/Dir.

Owners: Richard M. Rumble, Matthew H. Knight/2.00%, Stanley A. Fronczkowski, T. Rowe Price Associates, Inc/5.40%, Clifford L. Spiro, Stephen L. Waechter, Timothy S. Ramey, BC Advisors .LLC,/10.20%, Insiders/17.50%, Grover C. Wrenn/3.00%, Richard J. Defieux, James W. Stave/1.30%, Anthony J. Simonetta, Herbert Lotman/7.40%, Matthew J. Cody/5.60% (16 Owners included in Index)

Financial Data: Fiscal Year End:12/31 Latest Annual Data: 12/31/2006

Year	Sales		Net Income
2006	$25,522,000		$684,000
2005	$24,845,000		$584,000
2004	$23,705,000		$1,379,000
Curr. Assets:	$19,071,000	Curr. Liab.: $2,340,000	P/E Ratio: 57.38
Plant, Equip.:	$4,058,000	Total Liab.: $2,691,000	Indic. Yr. Divd.: NA
Total Assets:	$37,953,000	Net Worth: $35,262,000	Debt/ Equity: 0.0105

Strategic Distribution Inc

1414 Radcliffe St., Ste. 300, Bristol, PA, 19007; **PH:** 1-215-633-1900; *http://* www.sdi.com

General - Incorporation	DE	Stock - Price on:12/24/2007	NA
Employees	358	Stock Exchange	NA
Auditor	Willkie Farr & Gallagher LLP	Ticker Symbol	NA
Stk Agt	Continental Stock Transfer & Trust Co	Outstanding Shares	NA
Counsel	Willkie Farr & Gallagher LLP	E.P.S.	NA
DUNS No.	04-962-4117	Shareholders	NA

Business: The group's principal activities are to provide maintenance, repair and operating (mro) supply procurement, handling and data management solutions to industrial and institutional customers, primarily through its in-plant store(R) program. It provides services that reduce the costs and inefficiencies in the procurement and management of industrial supplies. The products include abrasives, adhesives, coatings, lubricants and compounds, electical supplies, fasteners, fire protection equipment and clothing, hoses, pipe fittings and valves, hvac and plumbing equipment, janitorial supplies, material handing products, measuring instruments, power transmission equipment, replacement parts, respiratory products, safety products, welding materials and general industrial supplies. The group provides its services in the United States and Mexico.

Primary SIC and add'l.: 8741 7379 5085

CIK No: 0000073822

Subsidiaries: American Technical Services Group,Inc., Coulson Technologies,Inc., FastenMaster Corporation,Inc., National Technical Services Group,Inc., SDI,Inc., Strategic Distribution (Canada) Company, Strategic Distribution (EA) Holdings,Inc., Strategic Distribution Canada Holdings,Inc., Strategic Distribution Marketing De Mexico, S. A. De C. V., Strategic Distribution Services De Mexico, S. A. De C. V., Strategic Supply,Inc., Wholly-Owned Foreign Subsidiaries:

Officers: Missy Decker/VP - Business Development, Cris Ferregur/VP, General Dir.

Owners: William R. Berkley/1.22%, Mitchell I. Quain, Insiders/31.34%, Dimensional Fund Advisors Inc./7.00%, Robert D. Neary, Catherine James Paglia/2.05%, Joshua A. Polan, William R. Berkley/22.41%, Steel Partners II, L.P./9.78%, EagleRock Capital Management, LLC/8.90%, Ronald C. Whitaker, Royce & Associates, LLC/5.90%, Donald C. Woodring, Nader Tavakoli/9.53%, Jack H. Nusbaum *(16 Owners included in Index)*

Strategic Energy Fund

130 King St. W , Ste. 2850, Toronto, ON, M5X 1A4; *PH:* 1-416-364-8788; *http://* www.sentryselect.com; *Email:* info@sentryselect.com

General - Incorporation	Canada	Stock - Price on:12/24/2007	NA
Employees	NA	Stock Exchange	NA
Auditor	Deloitte & Touche LLP	Ticker Symbol	NA
Stk Agt	Computershare Trust Co	Outstanding Shares	NA
Counsel	NA	E.P.S.	NA
DUNS No.	NA	Shareholders	NA

Business: The group's principle activity is to invest in real estate properties. Trust established on February 14, 2002 under the laws of the province of Ontario pursuant to the Trust Agreement. The group operates from United States.

Primary SIC and add'l.: 6726

CIK No: 0001295104

Strategic Hotels & Resorts Inc

200 W Madison St., Ste. 1700, Chicago, IL, 60606; *PH:* 1-312-658-5000; *Fax:* 1-312-658-5799; *http://* www.strategichotels.com; *Email:* info@strategichotels.com

General - Incorporation	MD	Stock - Price on:12/24/2007	$22.85
Employees	54	Stock Exchange	NYSE
Auditor	Deloitte & Touche LLP	Ticker Symbol	BEE
Stk Agt	LaSalle Bank N.A	Outstanding Shares	74,350,000
Counsel	NA	E.P.S.	$1.15
DUNS No.	NA	Shareholders	NA

Business: The groups principle activity is to operate luxury hotels. The group operates from the United States.The group's quarterly revenue for September 2007 was 242.25 millions of USD.

Primary SIC and add'l.: 7011 6798

CIK No: 0001057436

Subsidiaries: Aventine Hotel, LLC, Banian Finance S.a.r.l., Bohus Verwaltung, BV, BRE/Grosvenor Shareholder S.a.r.l., CIMS Limited Partnership, CTU Holdings S.a.r.l., DTRS Burbank, LLC, DTRS Columbus Drive II, LLC, DTRS Columbus Drive, L.L.C., DTRS Half Moon Bay, LLC, DTRS Intercontinental Chicago, LLC, DTRS Intercontinental Miami, LLC, DTRS Laguna, LLC, DTRS LaJolla, LLC, DTRS Lake Buena Vista, LLC 149 Subsidiaries included in the Index

Officers: Laurence S. Geller/Dir., CEO, Pres./$3,220,416.00, James E. Mead/Exec. VP, CFO, Treasurer/$1,036,630.00, Richard J. Moreau/Exec. VP - Asset Management/$1,156,529.00, Jayson C. Cyr/Sr. VP, Controller/$403,126.00, Paula C. Maggio/Sr. VP, Sec., General Counsel/$367,651.00, John Gray/Sr. VP - Capital Projects

Directors: Laurence S. Geller/Dir., CEO, Pres., William A. Prezant/Chmn., Robert P. Bowen/Dir., Michael W. Brennan/Dir., Edward Coppola/Dir., John C. Deterding/Dir., James A. Jeffs/Dir., David M.C. Michels/Dir., Kenneth Fisher/Dir.

Owners: James E. Mead, JPMorgan Chase & Co./5.20%, T. Rowe Price Associates, Inc./6.00%, ING Clarion Real Estate Securities, L.P./7.50%, Michael W. Brennan, David M.C. Michels, Morgan Stanley/14.40%, Cohen& Steers, Inc./13.50%, Robert P. Bowen, Paula C. Maggio, ING Groep N.V./9.80%, William A. Prezant, Insiders, Laurence S. Geller, Security Capital Research & Management Incorporated/10.80% *(17 Owners included in Index)*

Financial Data: *Fiscal Year End:*12/31 *Latest Annual Data:* 12/31/2006

Year		Sales		Net Income
2006		$719,373,000		$120,129,000
2005		$492,745,000		$30,260,000
2004		$490,710,000		$13,333,000
Curr. Assets:	$230,144,000	Curr. Liab.:	$204,468,000	P/E Ratio: 19.87
Plant, Equip.:	$2,375,129,000	Total Liab.:	$1,914,991,000	Indic. Yr. Divd.: $0.960
Total Assets:	$3,255,709,000	Net Worth:	$1,317,290,000	Debt/ Equity: 1.2340

Strategic Internet

1090 W Georgia St., Ste. 250, Vancouver, BC, V6E 3V7; *PH:* 1-604-684-8662; *http://* www.siiincorporated.com

General - Incorporation	DE	Stock - Price on:12/24/2007	$0.19
Employees	NA	Stock Exchange	OTC
Auditor	Amisano Hanson	Ticker Symbol	SIII
Stk Agt	United Stock Transfer, Inc.,	Outstanding Shares	NA
Counsel	NA	E.P.S.	NA
DUNS No.	NA	Shareholders	NA

Business: The groups principal activity is to develop The Dream Island Resort project in Manama, Bahrain. The Dream Island Resort project will be an integrated resort, entertainment, hotel and real estate facility to be built on a 41 acre man made island off the north eastern coast of Manama, Bahrain.

Primary SIC and add'l.: 7372

CIK No: 0000053320

Subsidiaries: 3851630 Canada Inc., Strategic Internet Investment Canada Inc

Officers: Ralph Shearing/Dir., CEO, Pres.

Directors: Ralph Shearing/Dir., CEO, Pres., Abbas Salih/Chmn.

Owners: Abbas Salih/40.00%, Cede & Co./31.00%

Financial Data: *Fiscal Year End:*12/31 *Latest Annual Data:* 12/31/2006

Year		Sales		Net Income
2006		NA		-$402,000
2005		NA		-$517,000
2004		NA		-$517,000
Curr. Assets:	$11,000	Curr. Liab.:	$472,000	
Plant, Equip.:	NA	Total Liab.:	$472,000	Indic. Yr. Divd.: NA
Total Assets:	$11,000	Net Worth:	-$461,000	Debt/ Equity: NA

Strategic Rare Earth Metals Inc

2642 Collins Ave., Ste. 305, Miami, FL, 33140; *PH:* 1-305-534-1684

General - Incorporation	NV	Stock - Price on:12/24/2007	NA
Employees	NA	Stock Exchange	OTC
Auditor	Rotenberg & Co., LLP	Ticker Symbol	SREH
Stk Agt	First American Stock Transfer, Inc.	Outstanding Shares	NA
Counsel	NA	E.P.S.	-$0.287
DUNS No.	NA	Shareholders	NA

Business: The groups principle activity is to conduct granite mining and processing operations. The group operates from the United States and China.

Primary SIC and add'l.: 1423 6799 1499

CIK No: 0000007059

Officers: Paul Eagland/CEO

Financial Data: *Fiscal Year End:*12/31 *Latest Annual Data:* 12/31/2005

Year		Sales		Net Income
2005		$521,000		-$1,530,000
2004		$2,388,000		$343,000
2003		$2,000		-$237,000
Curr. Assets:	$1,051,000	Curr. Liab.:	$1,682,000	
Plant, Equip.:	$4,613,000	Total Liab.:	$3,246,000	Indic. Yr. Divd.: NA
Total Assets:	$8,887,000	Net Worth:	$5,640,000	Debt/ Equity: NA

Strategy International Insurance Group Inc

200 Yorkland Blvd., Ste. 710, Toronto, ON, A6 M2J5C1; *PH:* 1-281-255-6256

General - Incorporation	TX	Stock - Price on:12/24/2007	NA
Employees	NA	Stock Exchange	OTC
Auditor	RMSB & Guttilla P.C	Ticker Symbol	SGYI
Stk Agt	Interwest Transfer Company, Inc.	Outstanding Shares	NA
Counsel	NA	E.P.S.	$1.27
DUNS No.	NA	Shareholders	NA

Business: The group operates through its subsidiaries whose principle activity is to provide insurance and reinsurance services. The group focusing on structured risk, credit risk and credit enhancement services. The group operates from London and Toronto.

Primary SIC and add'l.: NA

CIK No: 0001249869

Subsidiaries: Frank Ney and Kavrav Ltd., Province of Ontario, Strategy Holding Company Limited, Strategy Real Estate Investments, Strategy Resort Financing, Inc., Strategy Senior Life Settlements, Ltd.

Financial Data: *Fiscal Year End:*04/30 *Latest Annual Data:* 04/30/2005

Year		Sales		Net Income
2005		$5,582,000		-$14,959,000
2004		$5,000		-$34,000
Curr. Assets:	$11,386,000	Curr. Liab.:	$12,348,000	
Plant, Equip.:	$85,000	Total Liab.:	$35,348,000	Indic. Yr. Divd.: NA
Total Assets:	$75,027,000	Net Worth:	-$755,000	Debt/ Equity: NA

Stratex Networks Inc

170 Rose Orchard Way, San Jose, CA, 95134; *PH:* 1-408-943-0777; *http://* www.stratexnet.com

General - Incorporation	DE	Stock - Price on:12/24/2007	NA
Employees	453	Stock Exchange	NA
Auditor	Deloitte & Touche LLP	Ticker Symbol	NA
Stk Agt	Mellon Investor Services LLC	Outstanding Shares	NA
Counsel	Morrison & Foerster LLP	E.P.S.	NA
DUNS No.	11-329-9986	Shareholders	NA

Business: The group's principal activity is to design, manufacture and market advanced wireless solutions for worldwide telephone network interconnection and broadband wireless access. The digital wireless systems carry high-speed data and voice across a full spectrum of frequencies and capacities. The operations are carried under two segments: the wireless solutions product segment designs, develops, manufactures and markets digital microwave systems for digital transmission. The services segment undertakes installation, repair and network design, path surveys, integration and other services. The group has customers in Mexico, Colombia, Argentina, Brazil, the United Kingdom, France, Poland, Germany, Greece, South Africa, the united arab emirates, India, Singapore, the People's Republic of China and Malaysia. During oct 2003, the group acquired plessey broadband wireless, a division of tellumat (pty) ltd.

Primary SIC and add'l.: 3663 3669

CIK No: 0000812703

Subsidiaries: DMC Stratex Networks (Africa)(Proprietary) Limited, Midrand, South Africa, Name/Location, Stratex Networks (India) Private Limited, New Delhi, India, Stratex Networks (NZ)Limited, Wellington, New Zealand, Stratex Networks (Philippines), Inc., Makati City, Philippines, Stratex Networks (S)Pte. Ltd., Singapore, Stratex Networks (Thailand) Ltd., Bangkok, Thailand, Stratex Networks (UK)Limited, Lanarkshire, Scotland, Stratex Networks Mexico, S.A. de C.V., Mexico D.F., Mexico, Stratex Networks Polska Spolka z.o.o., Warsaw, Poland

Officers: Guy M. Campbell/Dir., CEO, Pres., Shaun McFall/VP - Marketing, Steve Gilmore/VP - Human Resources, Meena Elliott/Assoc. General Counsel, Assist. Sec., Carol A. Goudey/Corporate Treasurer, Assist. Sec., Juan B. Otero/General Counsel, Sec., Paul A. Kennard/CTO, VP - International Sales, Robert W. Kamenski/Corporate Controller, Principal Accounting Officer, Sally A. Dudash/CFO, John Koenig/VP - Product Line Management, Heinz Stumpe/VP - Global Operations

Directors: Guy M. Campbell/Dir., CEO, Pres., Charles D. Kissner/Chmn., William A. Hasler/Dir., Edward F. Thompson/70/Dir., Clifford H. Higgerson/Dir., Eric C. Evans/Dir., Howard L. Lance/Dir., Mohsen Sohi/Dir., James C. Stoffel/Dir.

Stratford American Corp

2400 E Arizona Biltmore Cir., Building 2, Ste. 1270, Phoenix, AZ, 85016; *PH:* 1-602-956-7809

General - Incorporation	AZ	Stock- Price on:12/24/2007	NA
Employees	NA	Stock Exchange	NA
Auditor	KPMG LLP	Ticker Symbol	NA
Stk Agt	Valley National Bank of Arizona	Outstanding Shares	NA
Counsel	NA	E.P.S.	NA
DUNS No.	14-457-2989	Shareholders	NA

Business: The group's principal activity is to own and lease real estate property and natural gas exploration and development. It has royalty interests in oil and gas properties that are primarily located in Oklahoma and Texas. The oil and gas is marketed to various oil refiners and natural gas purchasers. The group owns a nominal interest in four oil and gas wells located in Arkansas and Oklahoma.

Primary SIC and add'l.: 6519

CIK No: 0000836435

Subsidiaries: SA Oil and Gas Corporation, Stratford American Energy Corporation

Strathmore Resources (US) Ltd

No.810 - 1708 Dolphin Ave., Kelowna, BC, V1Y 9S4; **PH:** 1-250-868-8445

General - Incorporation	Canada	Stock- Price on:12/24/2007	$19.23
Employees	51,770	Stock Exchange	NA
Auditor	NA	Ticker Symbol	NA
Stk Agt	Mellon Trust Co	Outstanding Shares	897,420,000
Counsel	NA	E.P.S.	$0.78
DUNS No.	NA	Shareholders	NA

Business: The group's principle activities include acquiring and evaluating mineral resource properties The Canadian based exploration company has a total of twenty properties located in the Unites States, Canada, and Peru and continuing to acquire attractive uranium exploration and development properties. It has become the largest holder of exploration lands in Canada's Athabasca basin, the world's largest uranium producing region. The company seeks to finance the exploration and development through equity financing, by way of joint venture. the company has acquired a 100 percent interest in Ram Claims located in the Churchrock Mining District and has also acquired a 100 percent interest (99% net) in the Roco Honda deposit. The competitors are Southern Cross Resources Inc., UES Corporation, Cameco Corporation, Can Alaska Ventures Ltd, Northern Continental resources Inc., International Uranium Corp, Hornby Bay Exploration Ltd., La. The group operates from United States.

Primary SIC and add'l.: 1000

CIK No: 0001309787

Financial Data: Fiscal Year End:12/31   Latest Annual Data: 12/31/2006

Year	Sales	Net Income
2006	$9,854,000,000	$782,000,000
2005	$8,882,000,000	$266,000,000
2004	$8,760,000,000	$601,000,000

Curr. Assets:	$6,586,000,000	Curr. Liab.:	$1,963,000,000	P/E Ratio:	41.85
Plant, Equip.:	$6,426,000,000	Total Liab.:	$4,399,000,000	Indic. Yr. Divd.:	$0.260
Total Assets:	$14,198,000,000	Net Worth:	$9,747,000,000	Debt/ Equity:	NA

Stratos International Inc

7444 W Wilson Ave., Chicago, IL, 60656; **PH:** 1-708-867-9600; **http://** www.stratoslightwave.com

General - Incorporation	DE	Stock- Price on:12/24/2007	$7.94
Employees	524	Stock Exchange	NA
Auditor	BDO Seidman LLP	Ticker Symbol	NA
Stk Agt	Mellon Investor Services LLC	Outstanding Shares	14,500,000
Counsel	NA	E.P.S.	$0.09
DUNS No.	15-759-9247	Shareholders	NA

Business: The group's principal activities are to develop, manufacture and sell optical subsystems and components for high data rate networking, data storage and telecommunication applications. The optical subsystems consist of a broad range of optical transceivers and multi-channel optical links. The group's optical component products include optical interconnect products, wdm modules, fiber packaging services and related accessories. These subsystems are designed for use in storage, data networking, metro and wide area telecom networks, military and government applications, and other industrial markets and applications. On 06-Nov-2003, the group acquired sterling holding company.

Primary SIC and add'l.: 3674

CIK No: 0001111721

Subsidiaries: Semflex, Inc., Sterling Holding Company, Stratos Lightwave Florida, Inc., Stratos Lightwave LLC, Stratos Limited, Trompeter Electronics, Inc.

Officers: Phillip A. Harris/Dir., CEO, Pres., Barry Hollingsworth/VP - Finance, CFO, Richard Durrant/Exec. VP, Joe D. Norwood/Exec. VP, John A. Hanssen/VP - Information Technology, CIO, Dale Reed/Sr. VP - Sales - Marketing, Karl Kovack/Content Editor, Jason Davidson/Regional Mgr. - Alabama, Florida, Georgia, Martin Charles/Western Regional Sales Mgr. - California, Colorado, Marc Motazedi/Eastern Regional Sales Mgr. - Connecticut, Dist, California, Delaware, Iowa

Directors: Phillip A. Harris/Dir., CEO, Pres., Reginald Barrett/Chmn., Newell V. Starks/Vice Chmn., Kenne P. Bristol/Dir., David Y. Howe/Dir., Charles Daniel Nelsen/Dir., Edward J. Oconnell/Dir., Brian J. Stark/Dir.

Financial Data: Fiscal Year End:04/30   Latest Annual Data: 4/30/2006

Year	Sales	Net Income
2006	$79,582,000	-$2,831,000
2005	$80,454,000	-$15,307,000
2004	$50,823,000	-$27,085,000

Curr. Assets:	$62,257,000	Curr. Liab.:	$10,968,000	P/E Ratio:	88.22
Plant, Equip.:	$19,301,000	Total Liab.:	$10,968,000	Indic. Yr. Divd.:	NA
Total Assets:	$99,154,000	Net Worth:	$86,207,000	Debt/ Equity:	NA

Stratos Renewables Corp

Formerly: New Design Cabinets Inc

3313 N 83rd Pl, Scottsdale, AZ, 85251; **PH:** 1-480-990-8330; **http://** www.newdesigncabinets.com

General - Incorporation	NV	Stock- Price on:12/24/2007	NA
Employees	NA	Stock Exchange	NA
Auditor	Bagell, Levine & Company, LLC	Ticker Symbol	NA
Stk Agt	Holladay Stock Transfer, Inc.	Outstanding Shares	NA
Counsel	NA	E.P.S.	NA
DUNS No.	NA	Shareholders	NA

Business: The groups principal activities include designing, manufacturing and installing custom cabinetry and wine racks. The group operates from the United States.

Primary SIC and add'l.: 2511

CIK No: 0001321517

Officers: Kenneth P. Laurent/74/Dir., CEO, Pres., Principal Financial Officer

Directors: Kenneth P. Laurent/74/Dir., CEO, Pres., Principal Financial Officer

Owners: Insiders/97.47%, Kenneth P. Laurent/97.47%

Strattec Security Corp

3333 W Good Hope Rd. , Milwaukee, WI, 53209; **PH:** 1-414-247-3333; **http://** www.strattec.com; **Email:** info@strattec.com

General - Incorporation	WI	Stock- Price on:12/24/2007	$48.22
Employees	1,900	Stock Exchange	NDQ
Auditor	Grant Thornton LLP	Ticker Symbol	STRT
Stk Agt	Wells Fargo Bank, N.A.	Outstanding Shares	3,540,000
Counsel	NA	E.P.S.	$2.79
DUNS No.	87-916-8029	Shareholders	NA

Business: The group's principal activity is to design, develop, manufacture and market mechanical and electro-mechanical locks and related access-control products. The principal products of the group are locks and keys for cars and trucks. A typical automobile contains a set of three to four locks: a ignition lock, a glove box lock, left front door lock and a deck lid lock. Some vehicles have additional locks for folding rear seat latches, spare tire locks and burglar alarm locks. Additional products include zinc die-cast and magnesium steering column lock housings. The group is expanding the automotive security/access control product offerings to include hood latches, trunk or liftgate latches, door latches, door handles, and vehicle access modules that contain some or all of these components. The customers of the group include general motors corporation, ford motor company and daimler chrysler corporation. The group has operations in the United States, Canada and Mexico.

Primary SIC and add'l.: 3429

CIK No: 0000933034

Officers: Harold M. Stratton/Chmn., CEO, Pres./$866,177.00, Milan R. Bundalo/VP - Materials, Kathryn E. Scherbarth/VP - Milwaukee Operations, Dennis A. Kazmierski/VP - Marketing, Sales/$294,633.00, Donald J. Harrod/VP - Engineering, Product Development/$293,935.00, Patrick J. Hansen/Sr. VP, CFO, Treasurer, Sec./$293,842.00, Rolando J. Guillot/VP - Mexican Operations/$253,954.00, Vera Latus/Contact - Aftermarket

Directors: Harold M. Stratton/Chmn., CEO, Pres., Michael J. Koss/Dir., Frank J. Krejci/Dir., Robert Feitler/Dir., David R. Zimmer/Dir.

Owners: Donald J. Harrod, Dennis Kazmierski, Harold M. Stratton/2.30%, T. Rowe Price Associates, Inc./15.80%, Insiders/3.80%, FMR Corp./14.10%, Vanguard Horizon Funds/6.20%, Royce & Associates/5.00%, Michael J. Koss, Robert Feitler, Rolando J. Guillot, Frank J. Krejci, PRIMECAP Management Company/11.30%, Patrick J. Hansen

Financial Data: Fiscal Year End:07/03   Latest Annual Data: 7/2/2006

Year	Sales	Net Income
2006	$181,197,000	$12,477,000
2005	$190,314,000	$15,038,000
2004	$195,646,000	$17,282,000

Curr. Assets:	$104,687,000	Curr. Liab.:	$30,068,000	P/E Ratio:	20.97
Plant, Equip.:	$29,592,000	Total Liab.:	$46,339,000	Indic. Yr. Divd.:	$0.600
Total Assets:	$138,090,000	Net Worth:	$91,751,000	Debt/ Equity:	NA

Stratum Holdings Inc

Formerly: Tradestar Services Inc

Three Riverway, Ste. 1500, Houston, TX, 77056; **PH:** 1-713-479-7000

General - Incorporation	NV	Stock- Price on:12/24/2007	NA
Employees	NA	Stock Exchange	OTC
Auditor	PMB Helin Donovan, LLP	Ticker Symbol	STTH
Stk Agt	NA	Outstanding Shares	NA
Counsel	NA	E.P.S.	-$0.02
DUNS No.	NA	Shareholders	NA

Business: The groups principle activities include developing, owning, and operating employment service centers in specific regional areas specializing in the placement of skilled construction labor. The group provides both skilled commercial craftsmen and general unskilled labor to the construction markets. The group operates through four segments namely petroleum engineering, construction staffing, petroleum exploring and oil and gas sales. In March 2007, the group acquired Decca Consulting, Ltd. The group operates from the United States.

Primary SIC and add'l.: 7361

CIK No: 0001277998

Subsidiaries: CYMRI, L.L.C., Petroleum Engineers, Inc., Tradestar Construction Services, Inc.

Officers: Richard A. Piske/Dir., CEO, Pres., Hughes D. Watler/CFO, Kenneth L. Thomas/Sr. VP - Finance, Barry Ahearn/Pres. - Decca Consulting LTD, David Hunter/VP

Directors: Richard A. Piske/Dir., CEO, Pres., Frederick A. Huttner/Chmn., Larry M. Wright/Dir., Robert G. Wonish/Dir., Michael W. Hopkins/Dir., Jesse R. Marion/Dir., Douglas Parker/Dir., David B. Russell/Dir.

Owners: Larry M. Wright/8.50%, Clarence J. Downs/13.10%, Jesse R. Marion, Michael W. Hopkins/15.80%, Douglas Parker, Richard A. Piske, Franklin M. Cantrell/10.20%, Guy D. Knoller, Kenneth L. Thomas/1.60%, Robert G. Wonish/14.70%, Frederick A. Huttner/13.40%, Insiders/54.50%

Financial Data: Fiscal Year End:12/31   Latest Annual Data: 12/31/2006

Year	Sales	Net Income
2006	$34,251,000	-$233,000
2005	$8,071,000	-$541,000

Curr. Assets:	$9,419,000	Curr. Liab.:	$11,306,000		
Plant, Equip.:	$13,510,000	Total Liab.:	$25,262,000	Indic. Yr. Divd.:	NA
Total Assets:	$33,144,000	Net Worth:	$7,881,000	Debt/ Equity:	1.1051

Stratus Properties Inc

98 San Jacinto Blvd, Ste 220, Austin, TX, 78701; **PH:** 1-512-478-5788; **http://** www.stratusprop.com; **Email:** investors@stratusproperties.com

General - Incorporation	DE
Employees	31
Auditor	PricewaterhouseCoopers LLP
Stk Agt	Mellon Investor Services LLC
Counsel	NA
DUNS No.	88-418-7212

Stock - Price on:12/24/2007	$34.16
Stock Exchange	NDQ
Ticker Symbol	STRS
Outstanding Shares	7,570,000
E.P.S.	$0.50
Shareholders	NA

Business: The group's principal activity is to acquire, develop, manage and sell commercial and residential real estate properties in austin, Texas. The group owns 2,034 acres of undeveloped residential, multi-family and commercial property and 43 developed real estate within the barton creek community, 282 acres of undeveloped residential, multi-family and commercial property within the lantana project and 1,000 acres of undeveloped residential, commercial and multi-family property within the circle c ranch community. The group also owns three completed office buildings within the lantana project.

Primary SIC and add'l.: 6552

CIK No: 0000885508

Subsidiaries: Oly Stratus Barton Creek I Joint Venture, Stratus Properties Operating Co., L.P., STRS Plano, L.P.

Officers: William H. Armstrong/Chmn., CEO, Pres./$1,659,128.00, Kenneth N. Jones/General Counsel, John E. Baker/CFO, Sr. VP/$1,074,012.00, Stephen A. Hay/Engineering, Construction, Belinda D. Wells/Advertising, Public Relations, Peter Gardere/Contact - Commercial Leasing, Matt Green/Contact - Commercial Leasing

Directors: William H. Armstrong/Chmn., CEO, Pres., Bruce G. Garrison/62/Dir., James C. Leslie/51/Dir., Michael D. Madden/59/Dir.

Owners: John E. Baker/1.30%, Carl E. Berg/18.70%, Bruce G. Garrison/1.50%, Robert L. Gipson/16.20%, Michael D. Madden, High Rise Capital Advisors, L.L.C./7.60%, James C. Leslie, Insiders/7.60%, William H. Armstrong/3.70%

Financial Data: *Fiscal Year End:*12/31   *Latest Annual Data:* 12/31/2006

Year	Sales	Net Income
2006	$64,007,000	$40,288,000
2005	$35,194,000	$8,474,000
2004	$20,890,000	$672,000

Curr. Assets:	$7,733,000	Curr. Liab.:	$12,589,000	P/E Ratio:	49.51
Plant, Equip.:	$179,912,000	Total Liab.:	$70,004,000	Indic. Yr. Divd.:	NA
Total Assets:	$203,950,000	Net Worth:	$133,946,000	Debt/ Equity:	0.4105

Stratus Services Group Inc

149 Ave. at the Common, Ste. 4, Shrewsbury, NJ, 07702; *PH:* 1-732-866-0300; *http://* www.stratusservices.com; *Email:* info@stratusservices.com

General - Incorporation	DE
Employees	57
Auditor	Pinnacle Investment Partners, LLP
Stk Agt	American Stock Transfer & Trust Co.
Counsel	NA
DUNS No.	NA

Stock - Price on:12/24/2007	$0.0087
Stock Exchange	OTC
Ticker Symbol	SSVG
Outstanding Shares	67,570,000
E.P.S.	-$0.001
Shareholders	NA

Business: The group's principle activities are to provide outsourced labor and operational resources on a long-term contractual basis. It is divided into two service lines: staffing services and information technology services. The staffing services division provides temporary workers for short-term needs, extended-term temporary employees, permanent, permanent placements, payroll processing, on-site supervising and permanent source consulting. The information technology services division provides a customized staffing program designed to reduce labor and management costs and increase workforce efficiency. Stratus technology services ('sts') provides information technology ('it') staffing solutions to fortune 100, middle market and emerging companies. Sts markets its services to client companies seeking staff for project staffing, system maintenance, upgrades, conversions, installations and relocations. The group's quarterly revenue for Jun '07 was 2.08 millions of USD.

Primary SIC and add'l.: 7363 8711

CIK No: 0001044391

Owners: Insiders/100.00%, Pinnacle Investment Partners, LLP/9.99%, Insiders/22.70%, Joseph J. Raymond/100.00%, Michael A. Maltzman/5.30%, Jamie Raymond/4.60%, Joseph J. Raymond/10.50%, Norman Goldstein/3.40%

Financial Data: *Fiscal Year End:*09/30   *Latest Annual Data:* 9/30/2006

Year	Sales	Net Income
2006	$5,131,000	$1,442,000
2005	$112,446,000	-$369,000
2004	$110,499,000	-$1,086,000

Curr. Assets:	$1,863,000	Curr. Liab.:	$9,202,000		
Plant, Equip.:	$146,000	Total Liab.:	$10,070,000	Indic. Yr. Divd.:	NA
Total Assets:	$2,015,000	Net Worth:	-$8,055,000	Debt/ Equity:	NA

Strayer Education Inc

1100 Wilson Blvd, Ste 2500, Arlington, VA, 22209; *PH:* 1-703-247-2500; *http://* www.strayereducation.com

General - Incorporation	MD
Employees	1,097
Auditor	PricewaterhouseCoopers LLP
Stk Agt	American Stock Transfer & Trust Co.
Counsel	NA
DUNS No.	06-939-0466

Stock - Price on:12/24/2007	$121.71
Stock Exchange	NDQ
Ticker Symbol	STRA
Outstanding Shares	14,530,000
E.P.S.	$4.04
Shareholders	NA

Business: The group's principal activity is to provide post-secondary education services to working adults. The group offers undergraduate and graduate degree programs in business administration, accounting and information technology through traditional classroom courses and the Internet. The group operates through its subsidiaries, strayer university, inc and education loan processing, inc. It conducts its programs at 23 campuses in the districts of Maryland, Virginia, North Carolina, Tennessee and Washington, d.c. The group also assists students by offering loans or by financing their educational programs.

Primary SIC and add'l.: 6719 8221

CIK No: 0001013934

Subsidiaries: Education Loan Processing, Inc, Strayer University, Inc, Strayer University, Inc.

Officers: Robert S. Silberman/Chmn., CEO/$6,309,295.00, Lysa A. Hlavinka/Sr. VP - Administration/$774,673.00, Daniel W. Jackson/33/VP - Operations, Strayer University Officers, Sonya G. Udler/VP - Corporate Communications, Karl McDonnell/COO, Pres./$531,145.00, Joel O. Nwagbaraocha/Interim Strayer University Pres. - Provost, Chief Academic Officer, Strayer University Officers, Randi S. Reich/Sr. VP - Academic Administration, Strayer University Officers, Patricia Ardoline-Pellicci/42/VP - Operations, Strayer University Officers, Gregory Ferenbach/48/Sr. VP, General Counsel/$487,045.00, Mark C. Brown/Sr. VP, CFO/$763,544.00, James F. McCoy/VP - Operations, Strayer University Officers, Kevin P. O'Reagan/CTO, VP, Reginald Rainey/40/VP - Operations, Strayer University Officers, Christopher T. Slack/Controller

Directors: Robert S. Silberman/Chmn., CEO, David J. Wargo/Dir., Gary Gensler/Dir., Todd A. Milano/Dir., Robert R. Grusky/Dir., William E. Brock/Dir., Charlotte F. Beason/Dir., David A. Coulter/Dir., Robert L. Johnson/Dir., Thomas G. Waite/Dir.

Owners: Maverick Capital, Ltd./6.20%, David J. Wargo, Lysa A. Hlavinka, Gary Gensler, William E. Brock, Robert S. Silberman/2.30%, Robert R. Grusky, Todd A. Milano, AXA Financial, Inc./6.50%, Baron Capital Group, Inc./9.80%, Morgan Stanley/6.50%, Gregory Ferenbach, Wasatch Advisors, Inc./5.60%, Mark C. Brown, Robert L. Johnson *(20 Owners included in Index)*

Financial Data: *Fiscal Year End:*12/31   *Latest Annual Data:* 12/31/2006

Year	Sales	Net Income
2006	$263,648,000	$52,307,000
2005	$220,507,000	$48,065,000
2004	$183,194,000	$41,240,000

Curr. Assets:	$213,832,000	Curr. Liab.:	$91,628,000	P/E Ratio:	30.13
Plant, Equip.:	$52,748,000	Total Liab.:	$99,317,000	Indic. Yr. Divd.:	$1.250
Total Assets:	$270,844,000	Net Worth:	$171,527,000	Debt/ Equity:	NA

Stream Communications Netwrk & Media Inc

1400-400 Burrard St., Vancouver, BC, V6C 3G2; *PH:* 1-604-669-2826; *Fax:* 1-604-669-2836; *http://* www.streamcn.com; *Email:* investor@streamnc.com

General - Incorporation	BC
Employees	NA
Auditor	MacKay LLP
Stk Agt	Computershare Investor Services LLC
Counsel	NA
DUNS No.	NA

Stock - Price on:12/24/2007	$0.18
Stock Exchange	OTC
Ticker Symbol	SCNWF
Outstanding Shares	NA
E.P.S.	NA
Shareholders	NA

Business: The groups principle activity is to provide cable television, broadband internet and telephony services. The group operates from Poland.

Primary SIC and add'l.: 9999

CIK No: 0001125670

Subsidiaries: Stream Communications Sp. z o.o

Officers: Jan Rynkiewicz/Dir., CEO, Pres., Iwona Kozak/Exec. Dir. - Corporate, Adam Ilczuk/Pres. - Stream Communications Sp Z oo, Stream Poland, Barbara Cano/Breakstone Group, Jens Chr. Christensen/CFO, Maura Gedid/Investor Relations Contact

Directors: Jan Rynkiewicz/Dir., CEO, Pres., Robert J. Wussler/Chmn., Iwona Kozak/Exec. Dir. - Corporate, Przemyslaw Aussenberg/Dir., George H. Bathurst/55/Non Exec. Dir.

Owners: CDS & Co/27.88%, Jan Rynkiewicz/17.32%

Financial Data: *Fiscal Year End:*12/31   *Latest Annual Data:* 12/31/2006

Year	Sales	Net Income
2006	$5,554,000	-$3,814,000
2005	$4,999,000	-$4,986,000
2004	$3,666,000	-$5,451,000

Curr. Assets:	$1,150,000	Curr. Liab.:	$2,684,000		
Plant, Equip.:	$10,076,000	Total Liab.:	$8,026,000	Indic. Yr. Divd.:	NA
Total Assets:	$12,547,000	Net Worth:	$4,521,000	Debt/ Equity:	NA

Streicher Mobile Fueling Inc

200 W Cypress Creek Rd., Ste. 400, Fort Lauderdale, FL, 33309; *PH:* 1-954-308-4200; *http://* www.mobilefueling.com

General - Incorporation	FL
Employees	326
Auditor	Grant Thornton LLP
Stk Agt	American Stock Transfer & Trust Co.
Counsel	Greenberg, Traurig, Hoffman, Lipoff
DUNS No.	11-413-9074

Stock - Price on:12/24/2007	$1.58
Stock Exchange	NDQ
Ticker Symbol	FUEL
Outstanding Shares	13,270,000
E.P.S.	-$0.736
Shareholders	NA

Business: The group's principal activity is to provide mobile fueling and fuel management out-sourced services. The group presently operates over 100 custom mobile fueling trucks from 13 service locations in California, Florida, Georgia, Tennessee and Texas. The group's customers include governmental agencies, utilities, major trucking lines, hauling and delivery services and national courier services. The group currently distributes diesel, gasoline and alternative fuels to approximately 700 customers.

Primary SIC and add'l.: 5172

CIK No: 0001024452

Subsidiaries: H & W Petroleum Company, Inc., SMF Services, Inc., Streicher Realty, Inc.

Officers: Richard E. Gathright/54/Chmn., CEO, Pres., Paul C. Vinger/38/Sr. VP - Fleet Operations, Corporate Planning, Gary G. Williams/52/Sr. VP - Commercial Operations, Michael S. Shore/52/CFO, Sr. VP, Sec., Treasurer, Wayne E.W. Wetzel/59/Sr. VP - Lubricants, Robert W. Beard/54/Sr. VP - Marketing, Sales, Investor Relations Officer, Timothy E. Shaw/46/Sr. VP - Information Services, Administration, CIO, L. Patricia Messenbaugh/44/VP - Finance, Accounting, Chief Accounting Officer

Directors: Richard E. Gathright/54/Chmn., CEO, Pres., Larry S. Mulkey/63/Dir., Wendell R. Beard/78/Dir., Steven R. Golderg/55/Dir., Rodney C. Oconnor/71/Dir., Robert S. Picow/51/Dir., Nat Moore/56/Dir.

Owners: Wayne E. Wetzel, Wendell R. Beard, Michael S. Shore, Joshua Tree Capital Partners/6.22%, Paul C. Vinger, Gary G. Williams, Robert W. Beard, Triage Capital Management LP/3.51%, Steven R. Goldberg, Timothy E. Shaw, Periscope Partners, Larry S. Mulkey, Fred C. Applegate Trust/5.10%, Leon Frenkel/6.49%, Rodney C. OConnor/7.83% *(18 Owners included in Index)*

Financial Data: *Fiscal Year End:*06/30   *Latest Annual Data:* 06/30/2007

Year	Sales	Net Income
2007	$229,769,000	-$6,589,000
2006	$249,541,000	-$4,878,000
2005	$135,166,000	-$1,460,000

Curr. Assets:	$32,182,000	Curr. Liab.:	$30,884,000		
Plant, Equip.:	$11,739,000	Total Liab.:	$42,574,000	Indic. Yr. Divd.:	NA
Total Assets:	$48,114,000	Net Worth:	$5,540,000	Debt/ Equity:	1.5465

Stride Rite Corp

191 Spring St., Lexington, MA, 02420; PH: 1-617-824-6000; http:// www.striderite.com

General - Incorporation	MA	Stock - Price on:12/24/2007	$20.2
Employees	3,100	Stock Exchange	NYSE
Auditor	PricewaterhouseCoopers LLP	Ticker Symbol	SRR
Stk Agt	EquiServe Trust Co N.A	Outstanding Shares	36,540,000
Counsel	NA	E.P.S.	$0.92
DUNS No.	05-598-7135	Shareholders	NA

Business: The group's principal activities are to design and market athletic and casual footwear for children and adults. The products include children's footwear, primarily for consumers between the ages of six months and ten years, dress and recreational shoes, boots, sandals and sneakers, in traditional and contemporary styles. The products are sold in a variety of retail formats including department stores, independent shoe stores, value retailers and specialty stores. An aggregate of 8 stores is currently operating in Costa Rica, Guatemala, haiti, Honduras and kuwait. It also operates in Canada. At 28-Nov-2003, the group operated 173 stride rite children's shoe stores, 59 manufacturers' outlet stores and 5 keds retail stores.

Primary SIC and add'l.: 5661 3149 5641

CIK No: 0000094887

Subsidiaries: Hyde, Inc., Saucony Asia Pacific Limited, Saucony Canada, Inc. (95% ownership), Saucony Deutschland Vertriebs GmbH, Saucony Factory Outlet Stores of Florida, Inc., Saucony Sports, B.V., Saucony UK, Inc., Saucony, Inc., Sperry Top-Sider, Inc., SR Holdings Inc., SR/Ecom, Inc., SRCG/Ecom, SRL, Inc., SRR, Inc., Stride Rite Canada Limited 23 Subsidiaries included in the Index

Officers: David M. Chamberlain/64/Chmn., CEO, Charles W. Redepenning/51/General Counsel, Sec., Richard T. Thornton/55/COO, Pres., Yusef Akyuz/57/CIO, Sr. VP, Frank A. Caruso/54/CFO, Janet M. Depiero/46/Sr. VP - Human Resources, Gordon W. Johnson/53/Treasurer

Directors: David M. Chamberlain/64/Chmn., CEO, Shira D. Goodman/47/Dir., Myles J. Slosberg/71/Dir., Christine M. Cournoyer/Dir., James F. Orr/64/Dir., Frank R. Mori/67/Dir., Lance F. Isham/64/Dir., Edward L. Larsen/63/Dir., Mark J. Cocozza/Dir.

Owners: Richard T. Thornton, Richard Woodworth, Dimensional Fund Advisors Inc./8.40%, Myles J. Slosberg, James F. Orr, David M. Chamberlain/2.87%, Christine M. Cournoyer, Barclays Global Investors, NA/5.54%, Royce& Associates, LLC/9.53%, Lance F. Isham, Frank R. Mori, Shawn R. Neville, Insiders/10.26%, Shira D. Goodman, Pamela J. Salkovitz (17 Owners included in Index)

Financial Data: Fiscal Year End:12/02 Latest Annual Data: 12/1/2006

Year		Sales	Net Income
2006		$706,755,000	$34,290,000
2005		$588,164,000	$24,567,000
2004		$558,324,000	$25,654,000
Curr. Assets:	$255,179,000	Curr. Liab.: $57,739,000	P/E Ratio: 21.96
Plant, Equip.:	$54,246,000	Total Liab.: $74,434,000	Indic. Yr. Divd.: $0.280
Total Assets:	$321,296,000	Net Worth: $246,862,000	Debt/ Equity: 0.3198

StrikeForce Technologies Inc

1090 King George's Post Rd., Ste. 108, Edison, NJ, 08837; PH: 1-732-661-9641; Fax: 1-866-787-4542; http:// www.sftnj.com; Email: info@sftnj.com

General - Incorporation	NJ	Stock - Price on:12/24/2007	$0.015
Employees	11	Stock Exchange	OTC
Auditor	Li & Co., P.C	Ticker Symbol	SKFT
Stk Agt	Worldwide Stock Transfer LLC	Outstanding Shares	39,030,000
Counsel	NA	E.P.S.	-$0.084
DUNS No.	NA	Shareholders	NA

Business: The groups principle activity is reseller of computer hardware, software products, and telecommunications equipment and services. The group markets its products under the tradenames ProtectID(TM) and WebSecure(TM). The group operates from the United States.

Primary SIC and add'l.: 7372

CIK No: 0001285543

Officers: Mark L. Kay/Dir., CEO, Robert Denn/Chmn., Pres., Ram Pemmaraju/Dir., CTO, George Waller/Dir., Exec. VP, Head - Marketing, Mark Corrao/Dir., CFO

Directors: Mark L. Kay/Dir., CEO, Robert Denn/Chmn., Pres., Ram Pemmaraju/Dir., CTO, George Waller/Dir., Exec. VP, Head - Marketing, Mark Corrao/Dir., CFO

Owners: Insiders/38.18%, George Waller, NetLabs.com, Inc./23.98%, Mark Corrao/4.78%, Ramarao Pemmaraju/11.90%, NetLabs.com, Inc., Robert Denn/11.75%, Mark L. Kay/7.76%, Robert Denn, George Waller/4.16%, Insiders, Mark L. Kay, Ramarao Pemmaraju, Mark Corrao

Financial Data: Fiscal Year End:12/31 Latest Annual Data: 12/31/2006

Year	Sales	Net Income
2006	$338,000	-$3,154,000
2005	$31,000	-$5,175,000
Curr. Assets:	$352,000	Curr. Liab.: $2,942,000	
Plant, Equip.:	$27,000	Total Liab.: $5,414,000	Indic. Yr. Divd.: NA
Total Assets:	$2,122,000	Net Worth: -$3,291,000	Debt/ Equity: NA

Stronghold Technologies Inc

16801 Addison Rd., Ste. 310, Addison, TX, 75001; PH: 1-214-866-0606; http:// www.strongholdtech.com

General - Incorporation	NV	Stock - Price on:12/24/2007	NA
Employees	NA	Stock Exchange	NA
Auditor	Anslow & Jaclin LLP	Ticker Symbol	NA
Stk Agt	Continental Stock Transfer & Trust Co	Outstanding Shares	NA
Counsel	Hale & Dorr LLP	E.P.S.	-$0.109
DUNS No.	NA	Shareholders	NA

Business: The group's principle activity is the development of wireless and Internet based systems for auto dealers in the United States. Its products include dealeradvance sales solution(tm) which provides customer history, contact information, personal calendar and instructions on follow-up tasks directly to the handheld mobile unit.

Primary SIC and add'l.: 3829

CIK No: 0001133598

Officers: Steven E. Humphries/55/Dir., CEO, Pres., Christopher J. Carey/Chmn., CEO, Pres.

Directors: Steven E. Humphries/55/Dir., CEO, Pres., Christopher J. Carey/Chmn., CEO, Pres.

Owners: Christopher J. Carey/50.87%, Stanford Venture Capital Holdings/20.54%

Financial Data: Fiscal Year End:12/31 Latest Annual Data: 12/31/2006

Year		Sales	Net Income
2006		$479,000	-$4,444,000
2005		$944,000	-$3,632,000
2004		$2,490,000	-$3,090,000
Curr. Assets:	$234,000	Curr. Liab.:	$8,132,000		
Plant, Equip.:	$3,000	Total Liab.:	$12,551,000	Indic. Yr. Divd.:	NA
Total Assets:	$247,000	Net Worth:	-$12,304,000	Debt/ Equity:	NA

Stryker Corp

2825 Airview Blvd., Kalamazoo, MI, 49002; PH: 1-269-385-2600; Fax: 1-269-385-1062; http:// www.strykercorp.com

General - Incorporation	MI	Stock - Price on:12/24/2007	$66.47
Employees	18,806	Stock Exchange	NYSE
Auditor	Ernst & Young LLP	Ticker Symbol	SYK
Stk Agt	EquiServe Trust Co N.A	Outstanding Shares	409,080,000
Counsel	Winston & Strawn	E.P.S.	$2.24
DUNS No.	00-537-3089	Shareholders	NA

Business: The group's principle activities include developing, manufacturing and marketing surgical and medical technology products. The group operates in two segments namely orthopaedic implants and medsurg equipment. The group also provides physical, occupational and speech therapy services, The group operates from United States, Europe, Japan and other foreign countries.

Primary SIC and add'l.: 3845 3842

CIK No: 0000310764

Subsidiaries: 3090720 Nova Scotia Limited, Alcott Indemnity Company, B.V. Favro, Benoist Girard SAS, Colorado Biomedical, Inc., Diagnostic Treatment Rehabilitation Clinic Limited, Diocom B.V., eTrauma.com Corp., Fourth Generation, Inc., Howmedica International S. de R.L., Howmedica Leibinger Inc., Howmedica Osteonics Corp., Image Guided Technologies, Inc., LifeSigns Management, Inc., Mid Atlantic Outpatient Rehab Network, LLC 92 Subsidiaries included in the Index

Officers: Stephen P. MacMillan/Dir., CEO, Pres./$6,051,568.00, Eric Lum/VP - Tax, Michael W. Rude/VP - Human Resources, James R. Lawson/Exec. VP, Thomas R. Winkel/VP - Administration, Sec., Edward B. Lipes/Exec. VP, James E. Kemler/VP, Group Pres. - Biotech, Spine, Osteosynthesis, Development/$1,992,980.00, Curtis E. Hall/VP, General Counsel, Dean H. Bergy/CFO, VP/$1,509,142.00, Patrick J. Anderson/VP - Corporate Affairs, Bryant S. Zanko/VP - Business Development, James B. Praeger/Controller, Stephen Si Johnson/VP, Group Pres. - Medsurg/$2,385,376.00, David J. Simpson/Exec. VP, Elizabeth A. Staub/VP - Regulatory Affairs, Quality Assurance (18 Officers included in Index)

Directors: Stephen P. MacMillan/Dir., CEO, Pres., John W. Brown/Chmn., Louise L. Francesconi/Dir., Howard E. Cox/Dir., Jerome H. Grossman/Dir., Ronda E. Stryker/Dir., William U. Parfet/Dir., Donald M. Engelman/Dir.

Owners: Stephen P. MacMillan, James E. Kemler, Advisory Committee for the Stryker Trusts/23.34%, William U. Parfet, Dean H. Bergy, John W. Brown/4.92%, Howard E. Cox, Luciano Cattani, Jerome H. Grossman, Ronda E. Stryker/20.53%, Insiders/26.47%, Stephen Si Johnson, Donald M. Engelman

Financial Data: Fiscal Year End:12/31 Latest Annual Data: 12/31/2006

Year		Sales	Net Income
2006		$5,405,600,000	$777,700,000
2005		$4,871,500,000	$675,200,000
2004		$4,262,300,000	$465,700,000
Curr. Assets:	$3,534,300,000	Curr. Liab.:	$1,351,500,000	P/E Ratio:	29.67
Plant, Equip.:	$951,700,000	Total Liab.:	$1,682,800,000	Indic. Yr. Divd.:	$0.220
Total Assets:	$5,873,800,000	Net Worth:	$4,191,000,000	Debt/ Equity:	NA

Student Loan Corp

750 Washington Blvd., Stamford, CT, 06901; PH: 1-203-975-6320; Fax: 1-203-975-6299; http:// www.studentloan.com

General - Incorporation	DE	Stock - Price on:12/24/2007	$208.12
Employees	571	Stock Exchange	NYSE
Auditor	KPMG LLP	Ticker Symbol	STU
Stk Agt	Citibank Stockholder Services	Outstanding Shares	20,000,000
Counsel	NA	E.P.S.	$10.03
DUNS No.	80-340-8582	Shareholders	NA

Business: The group's principle activity is to provide student loans. The company provides subsidized federal stafford loans, unsubsidized federal stafford loans, federal parent loans to undergraduate students (plus) and federal consolidation loans. In addition, the company offers supplemental loans for students (sls loans). The company also owns a portfolio of health education assistance loans (heal loans), composed of guaranteed student loans for borrowers in designated health professions under a federally insured loan program. These programs are administered by the U.S. Department of health and human services. The group operates from United States.

Primary SIC and add'l.: 6111 6141

CIK No: 0000893955

Subsidiaries: American International Group., Citigroup Inc., Educational Loan Center, Inc., Royal & SunAlliance Insurance Group PLC.

Officers: Michael Reardon/Chmn., CEO, Pres./$1,196,807.00, Daniel P. McHugh/CFO/$517,621.00, Christine Y. Homer/VP, Sec., General Counsel/$360,533.00, John P. McGinn/Chief Risk Officer/$418,250.00, Kurt Schneiber/VP, Executive Dir. - Sales/$752,570.00, Patricia A. Morris/VP, Chief Credit Officer, Raja A. Dakkuri/Controller, Chief Accounting Officer

Directors: Michael Reardon/Chmn., CEO, Pres., Bill Beckmann/Dir., Gina Doynow/Dir., Evelyn E. Handler/Dir., Glenda B. Glover/Dir., Carl E. Levinson/Dir., John Affleck-Graves/Dir., Rodman L. Drake/Dir., Richard Garside/Dir., Loretta Moseman/Dir.

Owners: Insiders, John Affleck Graves, Bill Beckmann, Rodman L. Drake
Financial Data: *Fiscal Year End:* 12/31   *Latest Annual Data:* 12/31/2006

Year	Sales	Net Income
2006	$1,869,254,000	$286,812,000
2005	$1,456,670,000	$308,960,000
2004	$980,665,000	$284,956,000

Curr. Assets:	$1,120,913,000	**Curr. Liab.:**	$11,583,597,000	**P/E Ratio:**	16.43
Plant, Equip.:	$42,423,000	**Total Liab.:**	$21,083,302,000	**Indic. Yr. Divd.:**	$5.720
Total Assets:	$22,636,603,000	**Net Worth:**	$1,553,301,000	**Debt/ Equity:**	7.7641

Sturgis Bancorp Inc MI

113-125 E Chicago Rd., Sturgis, MI, 49091; *PH:* 1-616-651-9345; *http://* www.sturgisbank.com

General - Incorporation	MI	Stock - Price on: 12/24/2007	$14.09
Employees	NA	Stock Exchange	OTC
Auditor	NA	Ticker Symbol	STBI
Stk Agt..... Computershare Investor Services LLC		Outstanding Shares	2,380,000
Counsel	NA	E.P.S.	$1.38
DUNS No.	NA	Shareholders	NA

Business: The group operates through its subsidiary whose principal activities include banking and financial states. Services of the group include commercial, retail, and savings banking, including time, savings, money market and demand deposits; commercial, industrial, agricultural, real estate, consumer installment and credit card lending. The group operates from the United States.

Primary SIC and add'l.: 6712 6022 6036
CIK No: 0001166362
Officers: Eric L. Eishen/Pres., CEO - Sturgis Bank, Trust
Financial Data: *Fiscal Year End:* 12/31   *Latest Annual Data:* 12/31/2003

Year	Sales	Net Income
2003	$20,996,000	$2,605,000
2002	$22,803,000	$2,790,000
2001	$24,421,000	$2,788,000

Curr. Assets:	$27,426,000	**Curr. Liab.:**	$200,599,000		
Plant, Equip.:	$7,238,000	**Total Liab.:**	$258,180,000	**Indic. Yr. Divd.:**	$0.480
Total Assets:	$287,338,000	**Net Worth:**	$29,158,000	**Debt/ Equity:**	NA

Sturm Ruger & Co Inc

Lacey Pl., Southport, CT, 06890; *PH:* 1-203-259-7843; *Fax:* 1-203-256-3367; *http://* www.ruger-firearms.com

General - Incorporation	DE	Stock - Price on: 12/24/2007	$14.78
Employees	1,100	Stock Exchange	NYSE
Auditor	McGladrey & Pullen LLP	Ticker Symbol	RGR
Stk Agt..... Computershare Investor Services LLC		Outstanding Shares	22,640,000
Counsel	NA	E.P.S	$0.48
DUNS No.	00-116-2569	Shareholders	NA

Business: The group's principal activities are to design, manufacture and sale firearms and precision investment castings. The group operates through two segments: firearms and investment castings. The firearms division manufactures and sells rifles, shotguns, pistols and revolvers to independent wholesale distributors. The investment casting segment manufactures and sells titanium and ferrous investment castings to a wide variety of markets including sporting goods, commercial and military use. Sportsmen, hunters, law enforcement and other governmental organizations, and gun collectors use the products offered by the group. The group sells its firearms under the trademark ruger. Acusport corporation, davidson's supply company and jerry's sport center are the major customers of the group.

Primary SIC and add'l.: 3324 3484
CIK No: 0000095029
Subsidiaries: larger corporations
Officers: Michael O. Fifer/50/Dir., CEO/$264,106.00, Stephen L. Sanetti/Vice Chmn., COO, Pres., General Counsel/$473,332.00, Leslie M. Gasper/Corp. Sec./$160,754.00, Thomas A. Dineen/CFO, VP, Treasurer/$225,179.00, Robert R. Stutler/VP - Operations The Companys Prescott, Arizona Firearms, Foundry Divisions/$356,242.00, Christopher J. Killoy/VP - Sales, Marketing, Thomas P. Sullivan/VP - Newport Operations, Steven M. Maynard/Dir., VP
Directors: Michael O. Fifer/50/Dir., CEO, Stephen L. Sanetti/Vice Chmn., COO, Pres., General Counsel, James E. Service/Chmn., Michael C. Jacobi/Dir., Stephen T. Merkel/Dir., Ronald C. Whitaker/Dir., John M. Kingsley/Dir., John A. Cosentino/Dir., Richard T. Cunniff/Dir., Steven M. Maynard/Dir., VP
Owners: Michael O. Fifer, Stephen L. Sanetti/1.02%, Ronald C. Whitaker, Insiders/2.88%, Leslie M. Gasper, Richard T. Cunniff, Thomas A. Dineen, Stephen T. Merkel, Royce & Associates, LLC/6.20%, John M. Kingsley, Michael C. Jacobi, Robert R. Stutler, James E. Service, John A. Cosentino
Financial Data: *Fiscal Year End:* 12/31   *Latest Annual Data:* 12/31/2006

Year	Sales	Net Income
2006	$167,620,000	$1,104,000
2005	$154,722,000	$864,000
2004	$145,624,000	$4,823,000

Curr. Assets:	$81,785,000	**Curr. Liab.:**	$21,263,000	**P/E Ratio:**	30.79
Plant, Equip.:	$22,961,000	**Total Liab.:**	$29,740,000	**Indic. Yr. Divd.:**	NA
Total Assets:	$117,066,000	**Net Worth:**	$87,326,000	**Debt/ Equity:**	NA

Sub Surface Waste Mgmt of De Inc

6451 El Camino Real, Ste.C, Carlsbad, CA, 92009; *PH:* 1-760-918-1860; *Fax:* 1-760-918-1855; *http://* www.subsurfacewastemanagement.com

General - Incorporation	DE	Stock - Price on: 12/24/2007	$0.023
Employees	4	Stock Exchange	OTC
Auditor ... Russell Bedford Stefanou Mirchandani		Ticker Symbol	SSWM
Stk Agt.	Fidelity Transfer Co	Outstanding Shares	131,850,000
Counsel	NA	E.P.S.	-$0.028
DUNS No.	15-096-0235	Shareholders	NA

Business: The group's principal activities are to develop, manufacture and market engineered remediation solutions for clean up of toxic waste releases to soil and groundwater and the bio-recycling of spent activated carbon filtration media. The treatments may be made directly to the contaminated soil or groundwater using wells and subsurface injection and extraction points. The group also provides comprehensive civil and environmental engineering project management services including specialists to design, permit, build and operate environmental waste clean-up treatment systems. The group operates entirely in the domestic market.

Primary SIC and add'l.: 4953
CIK No: 0000789887
Subsidiaries: U.S. Microbics, Inc., USM Capital Group, Inc., Waste Management, West Coast Fermentation Center Inc.
Officers: Bruce Beattie/54/Chmn., CEO, Pres., Behzad Mirzayi/51/Dir., COO, VP, Conrad Nagel/66/Dir., CFO, Robert C. Brehm/59/Dir., Pres.
Directors: Bruce Beattie/54/Chmn., CEO, Pres., Bill Hopkins/74/Dir., Behzad Mirzayi/51/Dir., COO, VP, Conrad Nagel/66/Dir., CFO, Robert C. Brehm/59/Dir., Pres.
Owners: Darwin Ting and Kuei Mei Ting TRS FBO Ting Family Trust UA, Mery C. Robinson, Insiders, Behzad Mirzayi, Mark Holmstedt, Thomas Westhoff, Michael Jordan, Robert C. Brehm, U.S. Microbics, Inc., John D. Garber, Conrad Nagel, Bill Hopkins, Bruce S. Beattie
Financial Data: *Fiscal Year End:* 09/30   *Latest Annual Data:* 9/30/2006

Year	Sales	Net Income
2006	$508,000	-$2,499,000
2005	$1,095,000	-$1,628,000
2004	$234,000	-$3,317,000

Curr. Assets:	$817,000	**Curr. Liab.:**	$1,055,000		
Plant, Equip.:	$100,000	**Total Liab.:**	$1,055,000	**Indic. Yr. Divd.:**	NA
Total Assets:	$925,000	**Net Worth:**	-$130,000	**Debt/ Equity:**	NA

Sub-Urban Brands Inc

8723 Bellanca Ave, Bldg. A, Los Angeles, CA, 90045; *PH:* 1-310-670-0132; *http://* www.suburbanbrandsinc.com

General - Incorporation	NV	Stock - Price on: 12/24/2007	$0.07
Employees	NA	Stock Exchange	OTC
Auditor	PMB Helin Donovan, LLP	Ticker Symbol	SUUB
Stk Agt.	Holladay Stock Transfer, Inc.	Outstanding Shares	53,200,000
Counsel	NA	E.P.S.	-$0.13
DUNS No.	NA	Shareholders	NA

Business: The groups principle activity is to provide consulting services for new business plan. The group also obtaining capital through sales of common stock, establishing a website at http://www.itsherday.com and exhibited at a wedding expo. The group operates from United States.

Primary SIC and add'l.: 7389
CIK No: 0001265700
Officers: Joseph Shortal/44/Chmn., CEO, Mark Jacobs/38/Sec., Treasurer, VP - Marketing, Jack Mott/53/Dir., CFO, COO
Directors: Joseph Shortal/44/Chmn., CEO, Jack Mott/53/Dir., CFO, COO, Kenard Gibbs/43/Dir., David Howitt/39/Dir.
Owners: Vision Capital/23.32%, David Howitt/0.60%, Joe Shortal/12.86%, Donald Wilson Trust/15.01%, Mark Jacobs/2.98%, Kenard Gibbs/0.60%, Trilogy Capital/6.86%, Insiders/25.82%, Jack Mott/10.92%, John Stamatis/8.18%, James Blondell/11.72%
Financial Data: *Fiscal Year End:* 12/31   *Latest Annual Data:* 12/31/2006

Year	Sales	Net Income
2006	$136,000	-$5,530,000
2005	$3,000	-$9,000

Curr. Assets:	$139,000	**Curr. Liab.:**	$4,323,000		
Plant, Equip.:	$23,000	**Total Liab.:**	$4,323,000	**Indic. Yr. Divd.:**	NA
Total Assets:	$190,000	**Net Worth:**	-$4,133,000	**Debt/ Equity:**	NA

Subei Business Development Inc

420 Madison Ave., Ste. 801, New York, NY, 10017; *PH:* 1-212-572-6236

General - Incorporation	DE	Stock - Price on: 12/24/2007	NA
Employees	NA	Stock Exchange	NA
Auditor	NA	Ticker Symbol	NA
Stk Agt	NA	Outstanding Shares	NA
Counsel	NA	E.P.S.	NA
DUNS No.	NA	Shareholders	NA

Business: The groups principle activity is to engage in any lawful corporate undertaking, including selected mergers and acquisitions. The group operates from United States.

Primary SIC and add'l.: 9995
CIK No: 0001309052

Subjex Corp

3245 Hennepin Ave. S, Ste 1, Minneapolis, MN, 55408; *PH:* 1-800-820-0888; *http://* www.subjex.com; *Email:* info@subjex.com

General - Incorporation	MN	Stock - Price on: 12/24/2007	$0.155
Employees	3	Stock Exchange	OTC
Auditor	Carver Moquist & O'connor LLC	Ticker Symbol	SBJX
Stk Agt	Affiliated Stock Transfer Co.	Outstanding Shares	69,070,000
Counsel	NA	E.P.S.	-$0.016
DUNS No.	NA	Shareholders	NA

Business: The group's principal activities are to provide intelligent communications solutions for the Internet and intranet environments. The company has developed an artificial intelligence-based next generation dialogue communication platform called subjex exchange. The subjex exchange dialogue engine is a software application that is licensable to business and industry. For Web-connected organizations, the company offers tools and solutions to support Website operations with fully automated, online customer service, knowledge management and marketing. The company's solutions allow clients to improve online sales, service and communication with their customers, transforming a Web site into an automated full-service destination for customer, employee and partner communication.

Primary SIC and add'l.: 7372
CIK No: 0001107699
Officers: Andrew D. Hyder/Founde, Chmn., CEO, Acting CFO, Pres., Brian K. Ahern/Contact, Paul Peterson/Contact - CSR Inquiries

Directors: Andrew D. Hyder/Founde, Chmn., CEO, Acting CFO, Pres., Sharon Rae Hyder/Dir.

Owners: Andrew D. Hyder/5.50%, Insiders/1.70%

Financial Data: *Fiscal Year End:*12/31 *Latest Annual Data:* 12/31/2006

Year	Sales	Net Income
2006	$115,000	-$431,000
2005	$73,000	-$468,000
2004	$38,000	-$335,000

Curr. Assets:	$105,000	Curr. Liab.:	$274,000		
Plant, Equip.:	$14,000	Total Liab.:	$274,000	Indic. Yr. Divd.:	NA
Total Assets:	$127,000	Net Worth:	-$147,000	Debt/ Equity:	NA

Suburban Propane Partners LP

One Suburban Plz., 240 Rte. 10 W, Whippany, NJ, 07981; *PH:* 1-973-503-9252; *http://* www.suburbanpropane.com

General - Incorporation .... DE
Employees 3,441
Auditor .... PricewaterhouseCoopers LLP
Stk Agt .... Computershare Trust Co
Counsel .... NA
DUNS No. .... NA

Stock - Price on:12/24/2007 .... NA
Stock Exchange .... NYSE
Ticker Symbol .... SPH
Outstanding Shares 32,670,000
E.P.S. .... NA
Shareholders .... NA

Business: The groups principle activities include marketing and distributing propane, fuel oil, refined fuels, natural gas and electricity. The group operates through five segments namely, propane, fuel oil and refined fuels, natural gas, and electricity. The group operates from the United States.

Primary SIC and add'l.: 4924 1711 4932 4931 5983 5984

CIK No: 0001005210

Subsidiaries: AGWAY ENERGY SERVICES, LLC, GAS CONNECTION, INC., PLATEAU, INC., SUBURBAN @ HOME HOLDINGS, INC., SUBURBAN @ HOME, INC., SUBURBAN ALBANY PROPERTY, LLC, SUBURBAN BUTLER MONROE STREET PROPERTY, LLC, SUBURBAN CANTON BUCK STREET PROPERTY, LLC, SUBURBAN CANTON ROUTE 11 PROPERTY, LLC, SUBURBAN CHAMBERSBURG FIFTH AVENUE PROPERTY, LLC, SUBURBAN COLONIE PROPERTY LLC, SUBURBAN ELLENBURG DEPOT PROPERTY, LLC, SUBURBAN ENERGY FINANCE CORP., SUBURBAN FRANCHISING, INC., SUBURBAN GETTYSBURG PROPERTY, LLC 45 Subsidiaries included in the Index

Officers: Mark A. Alexander/CEO, Board Supervisor, Harold R. Logan/Chmn., Non - Management Supervisor, John Hoyt Stookey/Supervisor - Non Management Board, Dudley C. Mecum/Supervisor - Non Management Board, Michael J. Dunn/Board Supervisor, Pres., Michael M. Keating/VP - Human Resources, Administration, Mark Anton/VP - Business Development, Douglas T. Brinkworth/VP - Product Supply, Paul Abel/VP, General Counsel, Sec., Davin A. D'Ambrosio/VP, Treasurer, Michael A. Stivala/CFO, Chief Accounting Officer, William E. Anderson/VP - Northeast Area, Steven C. Boyd/VP - Operations, Mark Wienberg/VP - Operational Planning, Analysis, Michael A. Kuglin/Controller *(17 Officers included in Index)*

Directors: Mark A. Alexander/CEO, Board Supervisor, Harold R. Logan/Chmn., Non - Management Supervisor, Michael J. Dunn/Board Supervisor, Pres.

Owners: Jeffrey S. Jolly, Mark A. Alexander/4.00%, Harold R. Logan, John Hoyt Stookey, Steven C. Boyd, Insiders/6.10%, Dudley C. Mecum, Michael M. Keating, Michael J. Dunn, Robert M. Plante

Curr. Assets:	$276,807,000	Curr. Liab.:	$198,438,000	P/E Ratio:	19.87
Plant, Equip.:	$389,477,000	Total Liab.:	$862,152,000	Indic. Yr. Divd.:	NA
Total Assets:	$997,164,000	Net Worth:	$135,012,000	Debt/ Equity:	NA

Suez

16, Rue De La Ville Levque, Cedex 08, Paris, 75383; *PH:* 33-1400666410; *http://* www.suez.fr

General - Incorporation .... France
Employees 186,198
Auditor .... Ernst & Young & Deloitte & Assoc.
Stk Agt .... NA
Counsel .... NA
DUNS No. .... NA

Stock - Price on:12/24/2007 .... $54.46
Stock Exchange .... NA
Ticker Symbol .... NA
Outstanding Shares 1,280,000,000
E.P.S. $3.81
Shareholders .... NA

Business: The group's principal activities are: energy (through tractebel and elyo, electricity production and distribution, gas transmission and distribution, operation and maintenance, municipal heating and cooling systems, cogeneration, waste-to-energy); water (through lyonnaise des eaux, degremont, water management and treatment, water treatment process engineering); waste services (through sita and tractebel, collection, sorting, recycling, bio-recycling, waste-to-energy production and storage of household and industrial waste); communications (through lyonnaise cable, tps, m6 and coficem-sagem. Terrestrial television broadcasting, digital satellite broadcasting, digital television, Internet access and telephone by cable).

Primary SIC and add'l.: 4212 4924 5074 4941 4833 4939 1629

CIK No: 0001158533

Subsidiaries: ACEA Electrabel group, AGBAR, Aguas Andinas, Aguas Argentinas, Al Ezzel Power Company, Alp Energia Italia, AXIMA AG, BAYMINA, CASTELNOU, COLBUN (b), Compagnie Nationale Du Rhone (cnr), Companhia Energeticameridional, CPCU, DEGREMONT, DISTRIGAS 69 Subsidiaries included in the Index

Officers: Gerard Mestrallet/59/Chmn., CEO, Gerard Lamarche/CFO, Sr. Exec. VP - Finance, Dirk Beeuwsaert/Exec. VP, In Charge of Suez Energy International, Jim Olecki/Investor Relations Officer, Arnaud Erbin/Sr. VP - Financial Communications, Eleonore De Larboust/Mgr. - Investors Relations, Jean-Pierre Hansen/COO, Sr. Exec. VP - In Charge - Suez Energy Europe, Yousra Martel/Coordinator - Investors Relations, Jerome Tolot/Exec. VP, In Charge of Suez Energy Services, Valerie Bernis/Exec. VP, In Charge of Communications, Sustainable Development, Emmanuel Van Innis/Exec. VP, In Charge - Group Human Resources, Yves De Gaulle/General Sec., Alain Chaigneau/Exec. VP, In Charge of Business Strategy, Murielle Suire/Assist. - Investors Relations

Directors: Gerard Mestrallet/59/Chmn., CEO, Albert Frere/82/Vice Chmn., Edmond Alphandery/65/Dir., Lord Simon/68/Dir., Richard Goblet D'Alviella/60/Dir., Gerhard Cromme/65/Dir., Rene Carron/66/Dir., Jean-Jacques Salane/57/Dir., Paul Desmarais/54/Dir., Jacques Lagarde/70/Dir., Etienne Davignon/76/Dir., Thierry De Rudder/59/Dir., Anne Lauvergeon/49/Dir., Jean Peyrelevade/69/Dir., Simon /69/Dir.

Owners: Areva/2.20%, Caixa Group/1.10%, CNP Assurances Group/1.60%, Groupe Bruxelles Lambert/8.00%, CDC Group/2.80%, Sofina/1.20%, Crdit Agricole Group/3.40%, Employee shareholders/3.10%, Public/76.30%, Treasury stock/0.30%

Financial Data: *Fiscal Year End:*12/31 *Latest Annual Data:* 12/31/2006

Year	Sales	Net Income
2006	$59,689,179,000	$3,542,365,000
2005	$50,273,990,000	$2,081,583,000
2004	$55,584,837,000	$1,573,017,000

Curr. Assets:	$34,125,926,000	Curr. Liab.:	$32,899,896,000		
Plant, Equip.:	$30,179,946,000	Total Liab.:	$65,236,155,000	Indic. Yr. Divd.:	NA
Total Assets:	$99,527,647,000	Net Worth:	$31,270,513,000	Debt/ Equity:	NA

Suffolk Bancorp

PO Box 9000, Riverhead, NY, 11901; *PH:* 1-637-227-5667; *http://* www.scnb.com; *Email:* invest@suffolkbancorp.com

General - Incorporation .... NY
Employees 343
Auditor .... Grant Thornton LLP
Stk Agt ..... American Stock Transfer & Trust Co.
Counsel .... NA
DUNS No. 00-699-3794

Stock - Price on:12/24/2007 .... $32.34
Stock Exchange .... NDQ
Ticker Symbol .... SUBK
Outstanding Shares 10,050,000
E.P.S. .... NA
Shareholders .... NA

Business: The group's principal activities are to provide domestic, retail and commercial banking services and trust services. The group, through its subsidiary, the suffolk county national bank, provides a wide range of commercial banking services throughout New York state. The suffolk county national bank operates 26 full-service offices and has 24 automatic teller machines.

Primary SIC and add'l.: 6712 6022

CIK No: 0000754673

Subsidiaries: Suffolk County National Bank

Officers: Thomas S. Kohlmann/Chmn., CEO, Pres./$675,518.00, Rose Marie Hodges/Assist. Mgr., Sarah Almeraz/Branch Mgr., Kevin Podlas/Assist. Mgr., Danielle Harris/Assist. Mgr., Dave Barczak/Branch Mgr., Sharon Hildreth/Assist. Mgr., Mark Harrigan/Branch Mgr., Tara Sperduto/Branch Mgr., Susan Nagy/Assist. Mgr., Steve Deluca/Branch Mgr., Wendy Stapon/Branch Mgr., Susan Hughes/Branch Mgr., Laci Cooper/Assist. Mgr., Pat Bolomey/Branch Mgr. *(59 Officers included in Index)*

Directors: Thomas S. Kohlmann/Chmn., CEO, Pres., Terrence X. Meyer/Dir., Joseph A. Gaviola/Dir., Susan V.B. O'Shea/Dir., Edgar F. Goodale/Dir., David A. Kandell/Dir., James E. Danowski/Dir., Joseph A. Deerkoski/Dir.

Owners: Joseph A. Gaviola/0.05%, Private Capital Management/9.77%, David A. Kandell/0.12%, Terence X. Meyer/0.11%, Augustus C. Weaver/0.22%, Thomas S. Kohlmann/0.51%, Edgar F. Goodale/0.55%, James E. Danowski/0.11%, Joseph A. Deerkoski/0.56%, Susan V.B. OShea/0.11%, Gordon J. Huszagh, Frank D. Filipo/0.08%, Robert C. Dick/0.17%, Insiders/2.82%

Financial Data: *Fiscal Year End:*12/31 *Latest Annual Data:* 06/30/2007

Year	Sales	Net Income
2007	$24,922,000	$5,332,000
2006	$24,812,000	$5,597,000
2005	$85,839,000	$22,102,000

Curr. Assets:	$51,185,000	Curr. Liab.:	$1,264,836,000	P/E Ratio:	14.70
Plant, Equip.:	$22,471,000	Total Liab.:	$1,284,083,000	Indic. Yr. Divd.:	NA
Total Assets:	$1,392,649,000	Net Worth:	$108,566,000	Debt/ Equity:	NA

SuffolkFirst Bank

100 Bosley Ave., Suffolk, VA, 23434; *PH:* 1-757-934-8200; *http://* www.suffolkfirstbanks.com

General - Incorporation ....
Employees .... NA
Auditor .... NA
Stk Agt .... Registrar & Transfer Co
Counsel .... NA
DUNS No. .... NA

Stock - Price on:12/24/2007 .... $9.5
Stock Exchange .... NDQ
Ticker Symbol .... SUFB
Outstanding Shares 2,270,000
E.P.S. .... NA
Shareholders .... NA

Business: The groups principal activity is to provide financial services. The groups services include night depository, notary service, safe deposit boxes, stop payments, travelers cheques, United States savings bonds, and wire transfers. The products of the group include debit card, ATM and saving accounts. The group operates from the United States.

Primary SIC and add'l.: 6022

CIK No:

Officers: Darrell G. Swanigan/Dir., CEO, Pres., James R.A. Stanley/Exec. VP, Chief Credit Officer, Robert E. Clary/CFO, Frank J. Taylor/VP, Consumer Loan Officer, Donna McKinney/Customer Accounting Representative, Tiffany Brayshaw/Customer Accounting Representative, Sarah Howell/Customer Accounting Representative, Jim Moodie/Courier, Cheryl T. Carter/Customer Accounting Representative, Mary Means/Accounting Assist., Suzanne C. Galbreath/Branch Mgr., Donna Howell/Customer Accounting Representative, Sarah Gardner/Customer Accounting Representative, Missouri Cooper/Customer Accounting Representative, Catherine A. Robertson/Proof, Transit *(43 Officers included in Index)*

Directors: Darrell G. Swanigan/Dir., CEO, Pres., Larry L. Felton/Chmn., James E. Turner/Vice Chmn., Peter C. Jackson/Dir., Sec., Jonie N. Mansfield/Dir., Clinton L. Varner/Dir., Jack W. Webb/Dir., Clay K. White/Dir., Robert M. Moore/Dir.

Sulphco Inc

5310 Kietzke Ln., Ste.101, Reno, NV, 89431; *PH:* 1-775-829-1310; *Fax:* 1-775-829-1351; *http://* www.sulphco.com; *Email:* info@sulphco.com

General - Incorporation .... NV
Employees 22
Auditor .... Mcdonald Carano Wilson LLP
Stk Agt .... Mark Bailey & Co. Ltd
Counsel .... NA
DUNS No. .... NA

Stock - Price on:12/24/2007 .... $3.69
Stock Exchange .... AMEX
Ticker Symbol .... SUF
Outstanding Shares 76,360,000
E.P.S. .... -$0.5
Shareholders .... NA

Business: The group's principal activities are to develop and license proprietary technology for the reduction of the sulfur content of crude oils and petroleum fuel. The proprietary closed-loop sulfur polishing units will be scaled to treat large or small volumes of petroleum product. The market for the company's product will be the producers of crude oils and refined products. It markets the technology domestically and internationally to petroleum refiners, crude oil producers, fuel distributors and other strategic partners.

Primary SIC and add'l.: 8731 6794

CIK No: 0001096560

Subsidiaries: Patterson Group

Officers: Larry Ryan/Dir., CEO, Brian Savino/Pres., Stanley W. Farmer/CFO, VP, Tim Clemensen/Investor Relations Contact

Directors: Larry Ryan/Dir., CEO, Robert Henri Van Massdijk/Chmn., Hannes Farnleitner/Dir., Edward Urquhart/Dir., Michael T. Heffner/Dir., Larry Schafran/Dir., Edward G. Rosenblum/Dir.

Owners: Michael T. Heffner/0.17%, Insiders/1.30%, Rudolf W. Gunnerman/37.03%, Hannes Farnleitner, Richard L. Masica/0.18%, Lawrence G. Schafran/0.25%, Edward E. Urquhart/0.18%, Robert Henri Charles van Maasdijk, Blizzard Capital Ltd./7.86%

Financial Data: Fiscal Year End:12/31   **Latest Annual Data:** 12/31/2006

Year	Sales	Net Income
2006	NA	-$39,116,000
2005	NA	-$9,428,000
2004	NA	-$4,146,000

Curr. Assets:	$6,579,000	**Curr. Liab.:**	$10,217,000		
Plant, Equip.:	$207,000	**Total Liab.:**	$10,217,000	**Indic. Yr. Divd.:**	NA
Total Assets:	$7,294,000	**Net Worth:**	-$2,923,000	**Debt/ Equity:**	NA

Summer Infant Inc

Formerly: KBL Healthcare Acquisition Corp II

1275 Pk. E Dr., Woonsocket, RI, 02895; **PH:** 1-401-334-9966; **http://** www.kblhealthcare.com

General - Incorporation	DE	**Stock**- Price on:12/24/2007	NA
Employees	NA	Stock Exchange	OTC
Auditor	Goldstein Golub Kessler LLP	Ticker Symbol	KBLH
Stk Agt	Continental Stock Transfer & Trust Co	Outstanding Shares	NA
Counsel	NA	E.P.S.	$2.32
DUNS No.	NA	Shareholders	NA

Business: The groups principal activity is to operate healthcare industry. The group operates from the United States.

Primary SIC and add'l.: 6770

CIK No: 0001314772

Subsidiaries: Summer Infant USA, Inc

Officers: Marlene R. Krauss/62/Dir., CEO, Sec., Zachary C. Berk/60/Chmn., Pres., Michael D. Kaswan/40/Dir., COO, Eli W. Berk/VP

Directors: Marlene R. Krauss/62/Dir., CEO, Sec., Zachary C. Berk/60/Chmn., Pres., Michael D. Kaswan/40/Dir., COO, Steven B. Epstein/Member - Advisory Board, Dennis C. Fill/Member - Advisory Board, Regina E. Herzlinger/Member - Advisory Board, John C. Kane/Member - Advisory Board, Ethan D. Leder/Member - Advisory Board, Ginger M. More/Member - Advisory Board, Wayne K. Nelson/Member - Advisory Board, Eric A. Rose/Member - Advisory Board, William A. Scott/Member - Advisory Board, Daniel L. Vasella/Member - Advisory Board, Myron L. Weisfeldt/Member - Advisory Board, Joseph A. Williamson/Member - Advisory Board

Owners: Zachary Berk/13.40%, Fir Tree, Inc./7.70%, Remy W. Trafelet/6.90%, Insiders/16.90%, Azimuth Opportunity, Ltd/5.10%, Michael Kaswan/3.60%, Jeffrey Feinberg/9.20%, Marlene Krauss/13.40%

Financial Data: Fiscal Year End:12/31   **Latest Annual Data:** 12/31/2006

Year	Sales	Net Income
2006	$1,452,000	$672,000
2005	$896,000	$309,000

Curr. Assets:	$52,137,000	**Curr. Liab.:**	$1,666,000		
Plant, Equip.:	$5,000	**Total Liab.:**	$11,495,000	**Indic. Yr. Divd.:**	NA
Total Assets:	$53,108,000	**Net Worth:**	$41,614,000	**Debt/ Equity:**	NA

Summit Bancshares Inc

1300 Summit Ave., Fort Worth, TX, 76102; **PH:** 1-817-336-8383; **https://** www.summitbank-online.com; **Email:** sbinfo@summitbank.net

General - Incorporation	TX	**Stock**- Price on:12/24/2007	$53.22
Employees	3,652	Stock Exchange	OTC
Auditor	Stovall, Grandey & Whatley LLP	Ticker Symbol	SMAL
Stk Agt	Bank of New York	Outstanding Shares	60,010,000
Counsel	NA	E.P.S.	$3.39
DUNS No.	13-103-7053	Shareholders	NA

Business: The group's principle activity is to provide general, commercial and mortgage banking services. It offers a wide range of loans and accepts demand, savings and other time deposits. The group also offers investment brokerage services, money transfers, ATM facilities and safe deposit facilities. It also provides advice and services to the bank and coordinates financial accounting controls and reports, internal audit programs, regulatory compliance, financial planning and employee benefit programs.

Primary SIC and add'l.: 6712 6021

CIK No: 0000745344

Subsidiaries: SIA Insurance Agency, Inc., Summit Bancshares, Inc. Statutory Trust I, Summit Bank, N.A., Summit Delaware Financial Corporation

Financial Data: Fiscal Year End:12/31   **Latest Annual Data:** 12/31/2006

Year	Sales	Net Income
2006	$924,707,000	$193,591,000
2005	$740,206,000	$165,423,000
2004	$622,031,000	$141,325,000

Curr. Assets:	$1,711,969,000	**Curr. Liab.:**	$11,418,670,000	**P/E Ratio:**	15.70
Plant, Equip.:	$219,533,000	**Total Liab.:**	$11,847,306,000	**Indic. Yr. Divd.:**	$1.600
Total Assets:	$13,224,189,000	**Net Worth:**	$1,376,883,000	**Debt/ Equity:**	0.2983

Summit Bank Co

4360 Chamblee-dunwoody Rd. , Atlanta, GA, 30341; **PH:** 1-770-454-0400; **http://** www.summitbk.com

General - Incorporation	GA	**Stock**- Price on:12/24/2007	NA
Employees	127	Stock Exchange	NA
Auditor	KPMG LLP	Ticker Symbol	NA
Stk Agt	Suntrust Bank	Outstanding Shares	NA
Counsel	NA	E.P.S.	NA
DUNS No.	18-576-1897	Shareholders	NA

Business: The group's principal activity is to provide a full range of banking services to individual and corporate customers. The group serves individuals, professionals, small to medium-sized businesses, ethnic communities and foreign corporations. The group accepts checking accounts, now accounts, savings accounts and other time deposits of various types. The loans provided by the group include a full range of short to medium-term commercial and personal loans. The group also provides other domestic services which include 24-hour multi-lingual telephone banking, Internet banking, cash management services, investment sweep accounts, safe deposit boxes, travelers checks, direct deposit of payroll and social security checks, as well as automatic drafts for various accounts.

Primary SIC and add'l.: 6021 6712

CIK No: 0000820067

Subsidiaries: SBGA California Investments, Inc., SBGA Investments, Inc., The Summit National Bank

Summit Environmental Corp Inc

133 E Tyler St., Longview, TX, 75601; **PH:** 1-800-522-7841; **http://** www.summitenvironmental.com

General - Incorporation	TX	**Stock**- Price on:12/24/2007	NA
Employees	NA	Stock Exchange	OTC
Auditor	Philip Vogel & Co. P.C	Ticker Symbol	SEVTE
Stk Agt	Securities Transfer Corp	Outstanding Shares	NA
Counsel	NA	E.P.S.	NA
DUNS No.	NA	Shareholders	NA

Business: The group's principal activity is to manufacture and market non-toxic chemical cleaners and fire suppression materials. The marketing efforts include television and radio promotions, videotapes and personal demonstration. The group's products are generally biodegradable and non-toxic that are environmentally safe. The group's principal products are firepower 911(TM) and flameout(r). The group is affiliated with moonlighting distribution corporation. This corporation develops and markets health and well being products designed to improve the quality of an individual's life and also markets other products.

Primary SIC and add'l.: 2844 2899

CIK No: 0001057807

Officers: Doug Cox/57/Chmn., CEO, Paula B. Parker/VP, Sec., Don J. Jordon/59/Dir., CFO, Pres.

Directors: Doug Cox/57/Chmn., CEO, Wilton Dennis Stripling/64/Dir., Dennis W. Stripling/Dir., Don J. Jordon/59/Dir., CFO, Pres., Mohsen Amiran/Dir., Thomas J. Kenan/Dir., Dean Haws/Dir., James J. Roach/Dir.

Owners: Insiders/45.20%, Don J. Jordan/9.20%, Paula Parker/7.10%, Wilton Dennis Stripling/4.30%, Doug Cox/19.80%, Keith B. Parker/7.10%, Dean Haws/2.60%, Mohsen Amiran/5.20%, James J. Roach, Thomas J. Kenan

Summit Financial Group Inc

300 N Main St., Moorefield, WV, 26836; **PH:** 1-304-538-1000; **http://** www.summitfgi.com; **Email:** cs@yoursummit.com

General - Incorporation	WV	**Stock**- Price on:12/24/2007	$19.85
Employees	224	Stock Exchange	NDQ
Auditor	Arnett & Foster PLLC	Ticker Symbol	SMMF
Stk Agt	Registrar and Transfer Co	Outstanding Shares	7,080,000
Counsel	NA	E.P.S.	$1.10
DUNS No.	04-856-6582	Shareholders	NA

Business: The group's principal activity is to provide commercial and retail banking services primarily in the eastern panhandle and south central regions of west Virginia and the northwestern region of Virginia. The group accepts demand deposit, savings accounts, now accounts and time deposits. It offers commercial loans, real estate construction loans real estate mortgage loans and consumer loans. The other services of the group are merchant credit card services and letters of credit and cash management services. It provides these services through its three subsidiaries. At 01-Mar-04, it acquired sager insurance agency.

Primary SIC and add'l.: 6712 6022

CIK No: 0000811808

Subsidiaries: SFG Capital Trust I, SFG Capital Trust II, SFG Capital Trust III, Shenandoah Valley National Bank, Summit Community Bank, Inc., Summit Insurance Services, LLC

Officers: Charles H. Maddy/Dir., CEO, Pres./$491,932.00, Ronald F. Miller/Dir., CEO, Pres. - Summit Community Bank/$383,054.00, Patrick N. Frye/Dir., Sr. VP, Chief Credit Officer/$231,130.00, Teresa D. Sherman/Investor Relations Officer, Julie R. Cook/VP, Chief Accounting Officer, Douglas T. Mitchell/Sr. VP, Chief Banking Officer, Scott C. Jennings/COO, Sr. VP, Robert S. Tissue/CFO, Sr. VP/$211,726.00

Directors: Charles H. Maddy/Dir., CEO, Pres., Ronald F. Miller/Dir., CEO, Pres. - Summit Community Bank, Oscar M. Bean/Chmn., George R. Ours/Vice Chmn., Dewey F. Bensenhaver/Dir., John W. Crites/Dir., James Paul Geary/Dir., Phoebe Fisher Heishman/Dir., Gerald W. Huffman/Dir., Duke A. McDaniel/Dir., Charles S. Piccirillo/Dir., Frank A. Baer/Dir., Thomas J. Hawse/Dir., Gary L. Hinkle/Dir., Patrick N. Frye/Dir., Sr. VP, Chief Credit Officer (16 Directors included in Index)

Owners: Sidney M. Bresler, Kletzkin & Ochsman, PLLC, Charles W. Calomiris/5.85%, Jeffrey M. Gitelman/2.81%, Jenifer Calomiris/6.12%, Paul J. Cinquegrana/1.73%, Jeffrey W. Ochsman, George W. Calomiris/6.41%, The Ochsman Children Trust/7.90%, Katherine Calomiris Tompros/6.13%, Robert I. Schattner/14.21%, Edward C. Allen, David E. Ritter, Carroll E. Amos/1.46%, Insiders/14.33% (16 Owners included in Index)

Financial Data: Fiscal Year End:12/31   **Latest Annual Data:** 12/31/2006

Year	Sales	Net Income
2006	$84,578,000	$8,267,000
2005	$87,884,000	$11,242,000
2004	$73,018,000	$10,608,000

Curr. Assets:	$19,171,000	**Curr. Liab.:**	$949,116,000		
Plant, Equip.:	$22,487,000	**Total Liab.:**	$1,156,767,000	**Indic. Yr. Divd.:**	NA
Total Assets:	$1,235,519,000	**Net Worth:**	$78,752,000	**Debt/ Equity:**	2.4333

Summit Financial Services Group Inc

980 N Federal Hwy Ste. 310, Boca Raton, FL, 33432; **PH:** 1-561-338-2600; **Fax:** 1-561-338-2820; **http://** www.summitbrokerage.com; **Email:** info@summitbrokerage.com

General - Incorporation .... FL
Employees 56
Auditor .... Moore Stephens Lovelace, P.A.
Stk Agt .... Florida Atlantic Stock Transfer, Inc.
Counsel .... NA
DUNS No. .... NA

Stock- Price on:12/24/2007 .... $0.4
Stock Exchange .... OTC
Ticker Symbol .... SFNS
Outstanding Shares 28,210,000
E.P.S. $0.02
Shareholders .... NA

Business: The groups principle activity is to provide commercial and retail banking services. The groups services include community banking services, including demand, savings and time deposits, commercial, real estate and consumer loans; letters of credit, and cash management services. The group operates from United States.

Primary SIC and add'l.: NA

CIK No: 0001261436

Subsidiaries: SBS Insurance Agency of Florida, Inc., SBS Insurance Agency of Georgia, Inc., SBS Insurance Agency of Louisiana, Inc., SBS Insurance Agency of North Carolina, Inc., SBS Insurance Agency of Pennsylvania, Inc., SBS of California Insurance Agency, Inc., SBSI Insurance Agency of Texas, Inc., Summit Brokerage Services, Inc., Summit Financial Group, Inc., Summit Holding Group, Inc.

Owners: Steven C. Jacobs/4.50%, Sanford B. Cohen, Antares Capital Fund III Limited Partnership/14.20%, William L. Harvey, The Equity Group Inc. Profit Sharing Plan& Trust/5.70%, Paul D. DeStefanis/1.40%, Marshall T. Leeds/35.60%, Insiders/39.70%, Richard Parker/11.90%

Financial Data: *Fiscal Year End:*12/31 *Latest Annual Data:* 12/31/2006

Year	Sales	Net Income
2006	$29,365,000	$619,000
2005	$22,146,000	-$260,000
2004	$17,918,000	$181,000

Curr. Assets:	$5,350,000	**Curr. Liab.:**	$2,949,000		
Plant, Equip.:	$105,000	**Total Liab.:**	$2,949,000	**Indic. Yr. Divd.:**	NA
Total Assets:	$6,659,000	**Net Worth:**	$3,710,000	**Debt/ Equity:**	NA

Summit Global Logistics Inc

Formerly: Aerobic Creations Inc
201 - 15225 Thrift Ave., White Rock, BC, V4B 2K9; *PH:* 1-604-576-2327

General - Incorporation .... NV
Employees .... NA
Auditor .... Friedman LLP
Stk Agt .... Continental Stock T & T Co.
Counsel .... NA
DUNS No. .... NA

Stock- Price on:12/24/2007 .... NA
Stock Exchange .... NA
Ticker Symbol .... NA
Outstanding Shares .... NA
E.P.S. .... -$4.28
Shareholders .... NA

Business: The group's principle activity is to produce, distribute and market aerobics workout DVDs for personal and professional use. The group intends to operate with two distinct areas of focus, production of aerobics workout DVDs and the distribution and sales of those aerobics workout DVDs. The production of the aerobics workout DVDs will use currently available technologies and will follow proven video to DVD production protocols. Various aerobics movements and routines will be recorded, digitally stored and categorized - forming the Aerobics Movements Library (AML). The movements and routines will then be reformatted and digitally assembled into complete aerobics workouts, at which point they will be burned onto DVD's for sale and distribution. The group intends to offer several different aerobics workout DVDs. These are placed into two different categories, Mass Appeal DVDs (MADs) and Personalized DVDs (PDs).

Primary SIC and add'l.: 7822

CIK No: 0001311953

Officers: Robert A. Agresti/47/Dir., CEO, Pres., William Knight,/Sr. VP/$361,000.00, Paul Shahbazian/CFO/$316,000.00, Christopher Dombalis/Sr. VP/$361,000.00, Raymer McQuiston/45/Dir., Sec., Peter Klaver/56/Sr. VP

Directors: Robert A. Agresti/47/Dir., CEO, Pres., Wesley K. Clark/62/Chmn., Paul Windfield/51/Dir., Raymer McQuiston/45/Dir., Sec., Gregory Desaye/55/Dir., Terence MacAvery/58/Dir., William J. Coogan/53/Dir.

Owners: Peter Klaver, Bay Harbor Group, Gregory DeSaye, Michael DeSaye, CAMOFI Master LDC, JMG Capital LLC, KRG Group, William J. Coogan, Han Huy Ling, William Knight, Radcliffe SPC, Ltd. on the behalf of Class A Segregated Portfolio, Christopher Dombalis, Paul Shahbazian, Credit Suisse Securities, Paul Windfield *(30 Owners included in Index)*

Financial Data: *Fiscal Year End:*12/31 *Latest Annual Data:* 12/31/2006

Year	Sales	Net Income
2006	$39,438,000	-$836,000
2005	NA	-$19,000

Curr. Assets:	$46,692,000	**Curr. Liab.:**	$25,982,000		
Plant, Equip.:	$10,373,000	**Total Liab.:**	$162,623,000	**Indic. Yr. Divd.:**	NA
Total Assets:	$207,293,000	**Net Worth:**	$44,670,000	**Debt/ Equity:**	NA

Summit State Bank

500 Bicentennial Way, Santa Rosa, CA, 95403; *PH:* 1-707-568-6100; *Fax:* 1-707-568-7090; *http://* www.summitstatebank.com

General - Incorporation ....
Employees .... NA
Auditor .... NA
Stk Agt .... NA
Counsel .... NA
DUNS No. .... NA

Stock- Price on:12/24/2007 .... $10.88
Stock Exchange .... NDQ
Ticker Symbol .... SSBI
Outstanding Shares 4,840,000
E.P.S. .... NA
Shareholders .... NA

Business: The groups principal activity is to provide banking and financial services. The groups services include merchant bankcard, official checks, direct deposit and wire transfers. The products of the group include debit cards, ATM and Travelers Cheques. The group operates from the United States.

Primary SIC and add'l.: 6035

CIK No:

Officers: John C. Lewis/Chmn., CEO, Terrance M. Davis/Dir., COO, Pres., Diane Berthinier/Sr. VP, Branch Administrator, Tom Duryea/Sr. VP - CCO, Dennis Kelley/Sr. VP, CFO, Linda Bertauche/Sr. VP - Compliance, Risk Management, Wayne Hoffer/VP - Commercial Lending, Jackie Peterson/Regional VP - Petaluma Regional Office, Judy Reynolds/AVP, Branch Mgr., Gail Baker/AVP, Branch Mgr. - Montgomery Village Branch, D. Marlowe/AVP, Branch Mgr. - Rohnert Park Branch, Candy Yandell/AVP, Branch Mgr. - Windsor Branch, Sheila Cargill/VP - Loan Operations, Nancy Farber/Corp. Sec., Patty Hoagland/Dir. - Information Services

Directors: John C. Lewis/Chmn., CEO, Terrance M. Davis/Dir., COO, Pres., John F. Demeo/Dir., Michael J. Donovan/Dir., Richard A. Dorr/Dir., Todd Fry/Dir., George I. Hamamoto/Dir., Allan J. Hemphill/Dir., Jeanne D. Hubbard/Dir., Ron Metcalfe/Dir., Marshall T. Reynolds/Dir., Robert B. St. Clair/Dir., Eugene W. Traverso/Dir.

Sumtotal Systems Inc

1808 N Shoreline Blvd., Mountain View, CA, 94043; *PH:* 1-650-934-9500; *http://* www.sumtotalsystems.com

General - Incorporation .... DE
Employees 761
Auditor .... BDO Seidman LLP
Stk Agt .... Mellon Investor Services LLC
Counsel .... NA
DUNS No. .... NA

Stock- Price on:12/24/2007 .... $7.5
Stock Exchange .... NDQ
Ticker Symbol .... SUMT
Outstanding Shares 27,170,000
E.P.S. .... -$0.36
Shareholders .... NA

Business: The group's principle activity is to develop, market, distribute and support an integrated suite of enterprise learning software products. It is an integrated suite of eight business performance management applications delivering end-to-end capabilities that improve employee proficiency and organizational productivity. The suite consists of the following applications: total learning management system, total learning content management system, total virtual classroom service, totaldashboard, totalperformance, totalaccess, totalinformation and totalcollaboration. On 18-Mar-2004, click2learn inc acquired docent inc and formed sumtotal systems.

Primary SIC and add'l.: NA

CIK No: 0001269132

Subsidiaries: Pathlore Limited, Pathlore Software Limited, Pathlore Software Pty., Ltd., SumTotal Systems ANZ Pty. Ltd., SumTotal Systems Canada, Ltd., SumTotal Systems France SAS, SumTotal Systems GmbH, SumTotal Systems India Private Limited, SumTotal Systems Japan, SumTotal Systems Limited, SumTotal Systems Netherlands BV, SumTotal Systems U.K. Ltd.

Officers: Don Fowler/Dir., CEO, David Crussell/45/COO, Neil J. Laird/CFO, Sudheer Koneru/MD - India, Srinivasan Chandrasekar/Sr. VP - Products, Sanjay P. Dholakia/Sr. VP - Corporate, Business Development, Erika Rottenberg/Sr. VP, General Counsel, Sec., Harnish Kanani/Sr. VP - Professional Services, Training, Gary Millrood/VP, GM - OEM, Channel Development, Jon Ciampi/VP - Marketing, Product Management, Rick Mongeau/VP - Sales North America, Jack Kramer/VP - Intercontinental Sales, Pam Drew/VP - Human Resources, Talent Management

Directors: Don Fowler/Dir., CEO, Jack Acosta/Chmn., Sally Narodick/Dir., Ali Kutay/Dir., John Cone/Dir., Vijay Vashee/Dir., Kevin Oakes/44/Dir., Stephen Thomas/53/Dir.

Owners: Austin W. Marxe and David M. Greenhouse/Special Situation Funds/8.00%, John Con, Sanjay Dholakia, Insiders/6.40%, David Crussell/1.20%, Kevin Oakes, Stephen Thomas, Ali Kutay, Neil Gagnon/8.50%, Jack Acosta, Erika Rottenberg, Sally Narodick, Vijay Vashee, Donald Fowler/1.10%, Rick D, Leggott / Arbor Capital Management LLC/7.60% *(17 Owners included in Index)*

Financial Data: *Fiscal Year End:*12/31 *Latest Annual Data:* 12/31/2006

Year	Sales	Net Income
2006	$105,988,000	-$11,954,000
2005	$74,970,000	-$11,116,000
2004	$55,204,000	-$16,032,000

Curr. Assets:	$48,136,000	**Curr. Liab.:**	$54,076,000		
Plant, Equip.:	$5,945,000	**Total Liab.:**	$65,838,000	**Indic. Yr. Divd.:**	NA
Total Assets:	$145,063,000	**Net Worth:**	$79,225,000	**Debt/ Equity:**	0.1173

Sun Bancorp Inc

226 Landis Ave., Vineland, NJ, 08360; *PH:* 1-856-691-7700; *http://* www.sunnb.com

General - Incorporation .... NJ
Employees 702
Auditor .... Deloitte & Touche LLP
Stk Agt .... Computershare Investor Services LLC
Counsel .... NA
DUNS No. 15-092-3894

Stock- Price on:12/24/2007 .... $17.3
Stock Exchange .... NDQ
Ticker Symbol .... SNBC
Outstanding Shares 21,680,000
E.P.S. $0.84
Shareholders .... NA

Business: The group's principal activities are to provide consumer and business banking services through 5 regional banking groups and 78 community banking centers in southern and central New Jersey. The group offers lending, depository and financial services to its customers and marketplace. The lending services to businesses include commercial and industrial loans and commercial real estate loans. The commercial deposit services include checking accounts and cash management products such as electronic banking, sweep accounts, lockbox services, Internet banking, PC banking and controlled disbursement services. The lending services to consumers include residential mortgage loans, home equity loans and installment loans. The consumer services include checking accounts, savings accounts, money market deposits, and certificates of deposit and individual retirement accounts. The group offers mutual funds, securities brokerage, annuities and investment advisory services.

Primary SIC and add'l.: 6712 6021

CIK No: 0001017793

Subsidiaries: 2020 Properties, LLC, CBNJ Capital Trust I, Med-Vine, Inc., Sun Capital Trust III, Sun Capital Trust IV, Sun Capital Trust V, Sun Capital Trust VI, Sun Capital Trust VII, Sun Financial Services, LLC, Sun Home Loans, Inc., Sun National Bank

Officers: Sidney R. Brown/Vice Chmn., Acting Pres., Acting CEO, Sec., Treasurer/$233,972.00, Bart A. Speziali/Sr. Lending Officer, Exec. VP, Dan A. Chila/Exec. VP - Cashier, CFO/$311,124.00, Christine Irving/Assist. VP, Mgr. - Communications, Christine Massaro/Assist. VP, Marketing Mgr., Charles Avery/VP, Construction Lending Officer, Midge Huber/Construction Loan Administrator, Bruce A. Dansbury/COO, Exec. VP/$288,466.00, Edward Malandro/Sr. VP - Retail Banking, Thomas J. Townsend/Exec. VP - Operations, Risk Management, Information Technology

Directors: Sidney R. Brown/Vice Chmn., Acting Pres., Acting CEO, Sec., Treasurer, Bernard A. Brown/Chmn., John A. Fallone/Dir., Anne E. Koons/Dir., Jeffrey S. Brown/Dir., Ike Brown/Dir., Anat Bird/Dir., Douglas J. Heun/Dir., Peter Galetto/Dir., Charles Kaempffer/Dir., Eli Kramer/Dir., Alfonse M. Mattia/Dir., George A. Pruitt/Dir., Anthony Russo/Dir., Edward H. Salmon/Dir.

Owners: Insiders/36.63%, Bernard A. Brown/20.92%, Jeffrey L. Gendell/8.21%, Private Capital Management/7.68%, Dimensional Fund Advisors LP/7.78%

Financial Data: *Fiscal Year End:*12/31 *Latest Annual Data:* 06/30/2007

Year	Sales	Net Income
2007	NA	NA
2006	$204,047,000	$17,274,000
2005	$171,520,000	$19,521,000

Curr. Assets:	$187,519,000	**Curr. Liab.:**	$2,823,297,000	**P/E Ratio:**	20.60
Plant, Equip.:	$42,892,000	**Total Liab.:**	$2,983,336,000	**Indic. Yr. Divd.:**	NA
Total Assets:	$3,325,563,000	**Net Worth:**	$342,227,000	**Debt/ Equity:**	0.3214

Sun Communities Inc

The American Ctr., 27777 Franklin Rd., Ste. 200, Southfield, MI, 48034; *PH:* 1-248-208-2500; *http://* www.suncommunities.com

General - Incorporation	MD	**Stock**- Price on:12/24/2007	$29.58
Employees	643	Stock Exchange	NYSE
Auditor	Grant Thornton LLP	Ticker Symbol	SUI
Stk Agt	Computershare Trust Co	Outstanding Shares	18,280,000
Counsel	NA	E.P.S	-$1.4
DUNS No.	NA	Shareholders	NA

Business: The groups principle activities include owning, operating, developing, manufacturing and financing to the housing communities. The group operates through two segments namely, real property operations, and home sales and home rentals. The group operates from the Midwestern and southeastern United States. The group's quarterly revenue for September 2007 was 56.76 millions of USD.

Primary SIC and add'l.: 6798 5271

CIK No: 0000912593

Subsidiaries: Apple Orchard L.L.C, Arizona Finance L.L.C, Aspen-Alpine Project, LLC,, Aspen-Brentwood Project, LLC,, Aspen-Byron Project, LLC,, Aspen-Country Project, LLC,, Aspen-Ft. Collins Limited Partnership,, Aspen-Grand Project, LLC,, Aspen-Holland Estates, LLC,, Aspen-Town & Country Associates II, LLC,, Bright Insurance Agency, Inc, Comal Farms Manager LLC,, CP Comal Farms Limited Partnership,, CP Creekside LLC,, CP Woodlake Limited Partnership, 154 Subsidiaries included in the Index

Officers: Gary A. Shiffman/Chmn., CEO, Pres./$1,854,788.00, Jeffrey P. Jorissen/Exec. VP, Treasurer, CFO, Sec./$1,162,833.00, Brian W. Fannon/COO, Exec. VP/$885,908.00, Jonathan M. Colman/Exec. VP/$352,849.00

Directors: Gary A. Shiffman/Chmn., CEO, Pres., Paul D. Lapides/Dir., Clunet R. Lewis/Dir., Ronald L. Piasecki/Dir., Ted J. Simon/Dir., Arthur A. Weiss/Dir., Robert H. Naftaly/Dir., Stephanie W. Bergeron/Dir.

Owners: Brian W. Fannon, Arthur A. Weiss/4.40%, Barclays Global Fund Advisors/5.90%, Ronald L. Piasecki, Ted J. Simon, Gary A. Shiffman/10.90%, Jonathan M. Colman, Insiders/17.60%, Cohen & Steers Capital Management, Inc./14.00%, Wesley Capital Management, LLC/7.00%, Clunet R. Lewis, Jeffrey P. Jorissen/1.30%, Paul D. Lapides, Robert H. Naftaly, The Vanguard Group, Inc./5.30% *(16 Owners included in Index)*

Financial Data: **Fiscal Year End:**12/31 **Latest Annual Data:** 12/31/2006

Year	Sales	Net Income
2006	$226,894,000	-$24,968,000
2005	$211,554,000	-$5,452,000
2004	$200,853,000	-$40,468,000

Curr. Assets:	$44,590,000	**Curr. Liab.:**	NA	**P/E Ratio:**	19.87
Plant, Equip.:	$1,173,731,000	**Total Liab.:**	$1,210,542,000	**Indic. Yr. Divd.:**	$2.520
Total Assets:	$1,289,739,000	**Net Worth:**	$79,197,000	**Debt/ Equity:**	NA

Sun Healthcare Group Inc

18831 Von Karman, Ste. 400, Irvine, CA, 92612; *PH:* 1-505-468-2341; *http://* www.sunh.com; *Email:* investor.relations@sunh.com

General - Incorporation	DE	**Stock**- Price on:12/24/2007	$14.26
Employees	19,350	Stock Exchange	NDQ
Auditor	Ernst & Young LLP	Ticker Symbol	SUNH
Stk Agt	American Stock Transfer & Trust Co.	Outstanding Shares	42,930,000
Counsel	NA	E.P.S	$0.86
DUNS No.	NA	Shareholders	NA

Business: The groups principle activity is to provide healthcare services. The groups services include Medicaid and Medicare. The groups operates through three segments namely inpatient, rehabilitation therapy and medical staffing. In the year 2005, the group acquired Peak Medical Corporation and ProCare One Nurses, LLC. The group operates from California, Tennessee, Ohio, Maryland and Wyoming. The group's quarterly revenue for September 2007 was 439.57 millions of USD.

Primary SIC and add'l.: 8741 7361 8082 5122 8361 7363 8331 8099 8051 8052 8059

CIK No: 0000904978

Subsidiaries: Americare Health Services Corp., CareerStaff Services Corporation, CareerStaff Unlimited, Inc., Great Falls Health Care Company, L.L.C., HTA of New York, Inc., Masthead Corporation, Pacific Health Care, Inc., Peak Medical Ancillary Services, Inc., Peak Medical Assisted Living, Inc., Peak Medical Colorado No. 2, Inc., Peak Medical Colorado No. 3, Inc., Peak Medical Corporation, Peak Medical Farmington, Inc., Peak Medical FHAPT, Inc., Peak Medical Forest Hills, Inc. 103 Subsidiaries included in the Index

Officers: Richard K. Matros/Chmn., CEO/$2,260,444.00, Bryan L. Shaul/CFO, Exec. VP/$1,153,193.00, Michael Newman/Exec. VP, General Counsel/$641,633.00, Chauncey J. Hunker/Sr. VP, Chief Risk Officer, Corporate Compliance Officer/$638,155.00, Heidi J. Fisher/Sr. VP - Human Resources, William Mathies/Operations Management/$1,214,421.00, Richard Peranton/Operations Management, Michael Montevideo/VP, Treasurer

Directors: Richard K. Matros/Chmn., CEO, Gregory S. Anderson/Dir., Tony M. Astorga/Dir., Christian K. Bement/Dir., Michael Foster/Dir., Barbara B. Kennelly/Dir., Steven M. Looney/Dir., Milton J. Walters/Dir.

Owners: Christian K. Bement, William A. Mathies, FMR Corp./5.60%, Barbara B. Kennelly, Tony M. Astorga, Milton J. Walters, Bryan L. Shaul, Michael Newman, Insiders/13.00%, Michael J. Foster/11.00%, Steven M. Looney, RFE Investment Partners V, L.P./11.00%, Richard K. Matros/1.10%, Chauncey J. Hunker, Gregory S. Anderson

Financial Data: **Fiscal Year End:**12/31 **Latest Annual Data:** 12/31/2006

Year	Sales	Net Income
2006	$1,045,637,000	$27,118,000
2005	$882,109,000	$24,761,000
2004	$820,072,000	-$18,627,000

Curr. Assets:	$299,274,000	**Curr. Liab.:**	$203,029,000	**P/E Ratio:**	16.58
Plant, Equip.:	$217,544,000	**Total Liab.:**	$477,290,000	**Indic. Yr. Divd.:**	NA
Total Assets:	$621,423,000	**Net Worth:**	$144,133,000	**Debt/ Equity:**	0.9624

Sun Hydraulics Corp

1500 W University Pkwy, Sarasota, FL, 34243; *PH:* 1-941-362-1200; *http://* www.sunhydraulics.com; *Email:* suninfo@sunhydraulics.com

General - Incorporation	FL	**Stock**- Price on:12/24/2007	$45.96
Employees	809	Stock Exchange	NDQ
Auditor	Grant Thornton LLP	Ticker Symbol	SNHY
Stk Agt	Computershare Investor Services LLC	Outstanding Shares	10,930,000
Counsel	Shumaker, Loop & Kendrick	E.P.S	NA
DUNS No.	05-259-9727	Shareholders	NA

Business: The group's principal activity is to design, manufacture and sell screw-in hydraulic cartridge valves and manifolds which control force, speed and motion in fluid power systems. Fluid power comprises of valves and manifolds that control the flow of fluids employed to move and position materials, control machines, vehicles and equipment. The group manufactures screw-in cartridge valves for load control, pressure control and flow control, logic and directional control. The group has fluid power system facilities in the United States, the United Kingdom, Germany, Korea and China. The group sells its products through independent distributors.

Primary SIC and add'l.: 3492 3490

CIK No: 0001024795

Subsidiaries: Sun Hydraulics, Sun Hydraulics Korea Corporation, Sun Hydraulics Limited, Sun Hydraulics Systems (Shanghai) Co., Ltd., Sun Hydraulics, SARL, Sun Hydraulik GmbH Sun Ltd., un Hydraulik Holdings Limited., WhiteOak Controls, Inc.

Officers: Allen J. Carlson/Dir., CEO, Pres./$453,416.00, Jeffrey Cooper/Officer - Engineering/$214,320.00, Peter G. Robson/GM - Sun Hydraulics Limited/$234,185.00, Gregory C. Yadley/Corp. Sec., Tricia L. Fulton/CFO/$145,571.00, Tim Twitty/Officer - Operations

Directors: Allen J. Carlson/Dir., CEO, Pres., Robert E. Koski/Chmn. Emeritus, Founder, Clyde G. Nixon/Chmn., David N. Wormley/Dir., John S. Kahler/Dir., Christine L. Koski/Dir., Hirokatsu Sakamoto/Dir., Marc Bertoneche/Dir., Ferdinand E. Megerlin/Dir., Philippe Lemaitre/58/Dir.

Owners: Allen J. Carlson, Beverly Koski, Koski Family Limited Partnership, Royce& Associates, LLC, Jeffrey Cooper, Christine L. Koski, Insiders, Robert C. Koski, Ferdinand E. Megerlin, Hirokatsu Sakamoto, Thomas L. Koski, Tricia L. Fulton, Marc Bertoneche, David N. Wormley, Tim A. Twitty *(17 Owners included in Index)*

Financial Data: **Fiscal Year End:**12/31 **Latest Annual Data:** 12/30/2006

Year	Sales	Net Income
2006	$142,282,000	$16,223,000
2005	$116,757,000	$12,808,000
2004	$94,503,000	$7,830,000

Curr. Assets:	$26,557,000	**Curr. Liab.:**	$10,166,000		
Plant, Equip.:	$45,181,000	**Total Liab.:**	$17,121,000	**Indic. Yr. Divd.:**	$0.240
Total Assets:	$73,561,000	**Net Worth:**	$56,440,000	**Debt/ Equity:**	0.0063

Sun Life Assurance Company of Canada US

1 Sun Life Executive Pk., Wellesley Hills, MA, 02481; *PH:* 1-781-237-6030; *Fax:* 1-800-786-5433; *http://* www.sunlife.com

General - Incorporation	DE	**Stock**- Price on:12/24/2007	$46.92
Employees	14,264	Stock Exchange	NA
Auditor	Deloitte & Touche LLP	Ticker Symbol	NA
Stk Agt	Mellon Trust Co	Outstanding Shares	572,000,000
Counsel	NA	E.P.S	$3.52
DUNS No.	17-358-8393	Shareholders	NA

Business: The group's principal activities are carried out through three segments: wealth management, individual protection and group protection. The wealth management segment markets and administers individual and group variable annuity products, individual and group fixed annuity products, which include market value adjusted annuities and other retirement benefit products. The individual protection segment markets and administers a variety of life insurance products sold to individuals and corporate owners of life insurance. The group protection segment markets and administers group life and long-term disability insurance to small and mid-size employers in the state of New York. The group is a wholly owned subsidiary of sun life of Canada (us) holdings inc.

Primary SIC and add'l.: 6311 6321

CIK No: 0000745544

Subsidiaries: Slc - U.s. Ops Holdings, Sun Life Financial Corp., Sun Life Financial Inc.

Officers: Mary Fay/Dir., Sr. VP, GM - Annuities, Scott M. Davis/Dir., Sr. VP, General Counsel, Robert C. Salipante/Dir., Pres., Ronald H. Friesen/Dir., Sr. VP, CFO, Treasurer, Michael K. Moran/VP, Chief Accounting Officer, Controller

Directors: Ronald W. Osborne/Chmn., Mary Fay/Dir., Sr. VP, GM - Annuities, Krystyna T. Hoeg/Dir., Bertin F. Nadeau/Dir., James C. Baillie/Dir., George W. Carmany/Dir., David W. Kerr/Dir., Vickery W. Stoughton/Dir., John H. Clappison/Dir., David A. Ganong/Dir., Germaine Gibara/Dir., Idalene F. Kesner/Dir., Mitchell M. Merin/Dir., Richard P. McKenney/Dir., Scott M. Davis/Dir., Sr. VP, General Counsel *(19 Directors included in Index)*

Financial Data: **Fiscal Year End:**12/31 **Latest Annual Data:** 12/31/2006

Year	Sales	Net Income
2006	$14,782,489,000	$1,339,494,000
2005	$14,515,644,000	$1,577,004,000
2004	$18,057,364,000	$1,233,826,000

Curr. Assets:	$7,577,023,000	**Curr. Liab.:**	$110,918,006,000		
Plant, Equip.:	$3,435,832,000	**Total Liab.:**	$157,288,872,000	**Indic. Yr. Divd.:**	$1.180
Total Assets:	$173,240,951,000	**Net Worth:**	$15,884,289,000	**Debt/ Equity:**	NA

Sun Life Financial Inc

1 Sun Life Executive Pk., Wellesley Hills, MA, 02481; *PH:* 1-781-237-6030; *http://* www.sunlife.com; *Email:* investor.relations@sunlife.com

General - Incorporation	Canada	**Stock**- Price on:12/24/2007	$47.16
Employees	14,264	Stock Exchange	NYSE
Auditor	Deloitte & Touche LLP	Ticker Symbol	SLF
Stk Agt	Mellon Trust Co (United States)	Outstanding Shares	572,000,000
Counsel	NA	E.P.S	$3.85
DUNS No.	NA	Shareholders	NA

Business: The group's principle activities are to provide savings, retirement and pension products and life and health insurance to individuals and groups through the operations in Canada, the United States, the United Kingdom and Asia. The group also operates mutual fund, investment management banking and trust businesses, primarily in Canada, the United States and Asia.

Primary SIC and add'l.: 6311 6331 6719 6321

CIK No: 0001097362

Subsidiaries: SLF Inc, SLF Inc. U.K, Sun Life Assurance

Officers: Donald A. Stewart/Dir., CEO, Janet C. Fuller/CEO - SUN Life Financial UK, Andrew Cheung/CEO - Sun Life Everbright Life Insurance Company Limited, SUN Life Financial Asia, Robert J. Manning/CEO, Pres., Chief Investment Officer - Massachusetts Financial Services Company, MFS, Douglas W. Mahaffy/Chmn., CEO - Mclean Budden Limited, Henry Joseph M. Herrera/Pres., CEO - Sun Life, Canada, Philippines, Inc, SUN Life Financial Asia, Domenic Provenzale/VP - Wealth Management, SUN Life Financial Asia, Janet V. Whitehouse/Sr. VP - Human Resources Andpublic Relations, SUN Life Financial US, Ken Stearns/VP - Agency Development, SUN Life Financial Asia, Barry S. Halpern/Pres., Dir. - PT Sun Life Financial, Indonesia, SUN Life Financial Asia, John R. Wright/Exec. VP - Operations, SUN Life Financial US, James M.A. Anderson/Exec. VP, Chief Investment Officer, Michel R. Leduc/VP - Public, Corporate Affairs, Claude A. Accum/Pres. - Sun Life Retirement Services, US, Inc, SUN Life Financial Canada, Scott M. Davis/Sr. VP, General Counsel - SUN Life Financial US *(78 Officers included in Index)*

Directors: Douglas W. Mahaffy/Chmn., CEO - Mclean Budden Limited, Donald A. Stewart/Dir., CEO, David W. Davies/Chmn. - SUN Life Financial UK, Robert C. Pozen/Chmn. - Massachusetts Financial Services Company, MFS, Ronald W. Osborne/Chmn., Vickery W. Stoughton/Dir., Mitchell M. Merin/Corp. Dir., David W. Kerr/Dir., George W. Carmany/Dir., Germaine Gibara/Dir., James C. Baillie/Dir., Krystyna T. Hoeg/Dir., David A. Ganong/Dir., Bertin F. Nadeau/Dir., Idalene F. Kesner/Dir.

Financial Data: **Fiscal Year End:**12/31 **Latest Annual Data:** 12/31/2006

Year	Sales	Net Income
2006	$14,782,489,000	$1,339,494,000
2005	$14,515,644,000	$1,577,004,000
2004	$18,057,364,000	$1,233,826,000

Curr. Assets:	$7,577,023,000	**Curr. Liab.:**	$110,918,006,000		
Plant, Equip.:	$3,435,832,000	**Total Liab.:**	$157,356,662,000	**Indic. Yr. Divd.:**	$1.380
Total Assets:	$173,240,951,000	**Net Worth:**	$15,884,289,000	**Debt/ Equity:**	NA

Sun Life Insurance and Annuity Company of New York

150 King St. W Sun Life, Ste. 1900, Toronto, ON, M5H 1J9; ***PH:*** 1-416-9799966; ***http://*** www.sunlife.com

General - Incorporation	NY	**Stock**- Price on:12/24/2007	NA
Employees	NA	Stock Exchange	NA
Auditor	Deloitte & Touche LLP	Ticker Symbol	NA
Stk Agt	Mellon Trust Co	Outstanding Shares	NA
Counsel	NA	E.P.S.	NA
DUNS No.	15-650-5653	Shareholders	NA

Business: The group's principle activity is to provide financial products and services such as fixed and variable annuity contracts, group life insurance stop loss, variable universal life and group disability insurance contracts. Insurance agents sell these contracts, some of who are registered representatives of national and regional stock brokerage firms and brokers. The company is a wholly-owned subsidiary of sun life assurance company of Canada (U.S.). The group operates from United States.

Primary SIC and add'l.: 6321 6311

CIK No: 0000779955

Subsidiaries: Keyport Benefit Life Insurance Company, Sun Life Assurance Company of Canada

Officers: Scott M. Davis/Dir., Sr. VP, General Counsel, Mary M. Fay/Dir., Sr. VP, GM - Annuities, Ronald H. Friesen/Dir., Sr. VP, CFO, Treasurer, Keith Gubbay/Dir., Sr. VP, Chief Actuary, Michael E. Shunney/Dir., Sr. VP, GM - Group Insurance, Michele G. Van Leer/Dir., Sr. VP, GM - Individual Insurance, Robert C. Salipante/Dir., Pres., Principal Executive Officer, Michael K. Moran/VP, Chief Accounting Officer, Controller

Directors: Peter R. O'Flinn/Dir., Scott M. Davis/Dir., Sr. VP, General Counsel, Keith Gubbay/Dir., Sr. VP, Chief Actuary, Michael E. Shunney/Dir., Sr. VP, GM - Group Insurance, Michele G. Van Leer/Dir., Sr. VP, GM - Individual Insurance, Donald B. Henderson/Dir., David K. Stevenson/Dir., Mary M. Fay/Dir., Sr. VP, GM - Annuities, Thomas A. Bogart/Dir., Leila Heckman/Dir., Barbara K. Shattuck/Dir., Robert C. Salipante/Dir., Pres., Principal Executive Officer, Ronald H. Friesen/Dir., Sr. VP, CFO, Treasurer

Sun Media Corp

333 King St. E., Toronto, ON, M5H 2S8; ***PH:*** 1-416-947-2222; ***http://*** www.sunmedia.ca

General - Incorporation	Canada	**Stock**- Price on:12/24/2007	NA
Employees	104	Stock Exchange	OTC
Auditor	KPMG LLP	Ticker Symbol	NXMR
Stk Agt	Mellon Trust Co	Outstanding Shares	NA
Counsel	NA	E.P.S.	NA
DUNS No.	25-214-8689	Shareholders	NA

Business: The group's principle activity is to publishe daily and weekly newspapers in Canada and Florida. The group operates from United States.

Primary SIC and add'l.: 2711

CIK No: 0001036648

Subsidiaries: Bowes Publishers Limited, Groupe de Presse Dynamique /Dynamic, Le Courrier du Sud (1998) inc., Sun Media (Toronto) Corporation, Sun TV Company, Vancouver 24 Hours Partnership

Officers: Ed Huculak/58/Publisher, CEO - Winnipeg Sun, Kin-Man Lee/44/Exec. VP - Publisher, CEO - Toronto Sun, Pierre Francoeur/55/Dir., CEO, Pres., Guy Huntingford/51/Publisher, CEO - Calgary Sun, Gordon Norrie/49/Publisher, CEO - Edmonton Sun, Susan Muszak/55/Publisher, CEO - London Free Press, Rick Gibbons/54/Publisher, CEO - Ottawa Sun, Louis Morin/50/VP, Michel Slight/52/Exec. VP - Finance, Robert Attala/52/Sr. VP - Advertising Sales, Roger Martel/59/VP - Internal Audit, Andre Maynard/50/VP, Bernard Pageau/55/Assist. Corp. Sec., Lyne Robitaille/45/Publisher, Pres. - Le Journal de Montreal, Christopher R. Krygiel/49/VP - Human Resources *(25 Officers included in Index)*

Directors: Pierre Francoeur/55/Dir., CEO, Pres., Serge Gouin/64/Chmn., Pierre Karl Peladeau/46/Dir., Jean L. Couture/61/Dir., Andre Delisle/61/Dir., Michel A. Lavigne/57/Dir.

Curr. Assets:	$97,000	**Curr. Liab.:**	$209,000		
Plant, Equip.:	$23,000	**Total Liab.:**	$314,000	**Indic. Yr. Divd.:**	NA
Total Assets:	$172,000	**Net Worth:**	-$141,000	**Debt/ Equity:**	NA

Sun Microsystems Inc

4150 Network Cir., Santa Clara, CA, 95054; ***PH:*** 1-650-960-1300; ***http://*** www.sun.com

General - Incorporation	DE	**Stock**- Price on:12/24/2007	$5.05
Employees	38,000	Stock Exchange	NDQ
Auditor	Ernst & Young LLP	Ticker Symbol	JAVA
Stk Agt	EquiServe Trust Co N.A	Outstanding Shares	3,570,000,000
Counsel	NA	E.P.S.	$0.13
DUNS No.	NA	Shareholders	NA

Business: The groups principle activity is to provide products services and support solutions for building and maintaining network computing environments. The groups products line include software,desktop system and servers. The group operates from United States, Europe, Middle East, and Africa.

Primary SIC and add'l.: 7372 7373 7379 3571

CIK No: 0000709519

Subsidiaries: IntranetSolutions International Limited, Optika Asia Inc., Optika Imaging Systems Europe LTD, Optika Imaging Systems GmbH, Optika Imaging Systems LTD, Optika Information Systems, Ltda, Optika Technologies Inc, Stellent AB, Stellent Asia Pty. Limited, Stellent B.V., Stellent Canada Ltd, Stellent Chicago Sales, Inc, Stellent Chicago, Inc, Stellent Colorado Springs, Inc, Stellent GmbH 27 Subsidiaries included in the Index

Officers: Jonathan I. Schwartz/Dir., CEO, Pres./$14,114,150.00, Amber Rensen/CEO, Crawford W. Beveridge/62/Exec. VP, Chmn. - EMEA, Apac, The Americas, Mike Dillon/Sr. VP, General Counsel, Exec. VP - Sun Legal Department, Peter Ewens/VP - Sun's Original Equipment Manufacturer, OEM Group, Damien Eastwood/VP - Legal, Gregory M. Papadopoulos/Exec. VP - Research, Development, CTO/$2,709,764.00, Bret C. Schaefer/VP - Shareholder Value Finance Sun Microsystems Inc, Michael A. Dillon/Exec. VP, General Counsel, Sec., Glynn Foster/Opensolaris Governing Dir., John Gage/Chief Researcher,Dir. - Science Office, James Gosling/VP - Sun Fellow, Rick Hetherington/CTO - Microelectronics, Kim Jones/VP - Global Education, Government, Healthcare, Darrell Jordan-Smith/VP - Global Communications, Media Industry Practice *(103 Officers included in Index)*

Directors: Jonathan I. Schwartz/Dir., CEO, Pres., Scott G. McNealy/Chmn., James L. Barksdale/Dir., Stephen M. Bennett/Dir., Robert J. Finocchio/Dir., Patricia E. Mitchell/Dir., Kenneth M. Oshman/Dir., Peter L.S. Currie/Dir., Michael E. Marks/Dir., Anthony P. Ridder/Dir.

Owners: Scott G. McNealy/2.10%, Kenneth M. Oshman, Patricia E. Mitchell, Anthony P. Ridder, James L. Barksdale, David W. Yen, Donald C. Grantham, Jonathan I. Schwartz, AXA Financial, Inc./7.20%, Gregory M. Papadopoulos, FMR Corporation/6.00%, Stephen M. Bennett, Robert J. Finocchio, Peter L.S. Currie, Michael E. Lehman *(17 Owners included in Index)*

Financial Data: **Fiscal Year End:**06/30 **Latest Annual Data:** 6/30/2006

Year	Sales	Net Income
2006	$13,068,000,000	-$864,000,000
2005	$11,070,000,000	-$107,000,000
2004	$11,185,000,000	-$388,000,000

Curr. Assets:	$8,273,000,000	**Curr. Liab.:**	$6,165,000,000	**P/E Ratio:**	38.85
Plant, Equip.:	$1,812,000,000	**Total Liab.:**	$8,738,000,000	**Indic. Yr. Divd.:**	NA
Total Assets:	$15,082,000,000	**Net Worth:**	$6,344,000,000	**Debt/ Equity:**	0.1842

Sun Motor International

Formerly: Wyoming Oil & Minerals Inc
5525 Erindale Dr., Ste. 201, Colorado Springs, CO, 80918; ***PH:*** 1-719-260-8509; ***http://*** www.sunmotor.com.hk

General - Incorporation	WY	**Stock**- Price on:12/24/2007	NA
Employees	NA	Stock Exchange	NA
Auditor	PKF	Ticker Symbol	NA
Stk Agt	NA	Outstanding Shares	NA
Counsel	NA	E.P.S.	NA
DUNS No.	00-303-8965	Shareholders	NA

Business: The group's principle activity is to supply energy. On Apr 2004, the group sold the assets of blue star acid services inc. As of 30-Jun-2003, the group's subsidiary nfe was distributed to shareholders in a spin off. The group is currently investigating opportunities, both within and outside the oil and gas industry, to make acquisitions. The group operates from United States.

Primary SIC and add'l.: 1311 9999

CIK No: 0000108729

Subsidiaries: Bestip Development International Limited

Officers: Kenny Lo/CFO, Shi Kin Bon/VP

Owners: Shi Kai Biu/72.70%, SAOF NO.3 Limited/5.80%, Insiders/72.70%

Sun Motor International Inc

Block B, G/F, Prince, Industrial Bldg., 106 King Fuk St., San Po Kong, Kowloon; ***PH:*** 852-23216108; ***Fax:*** 852-23514668; ***http://*** www.sunmotor.com.hk; ***Email:*** info@sunmotor.com.hk

General - Incorporation	WY	**Stock**- Price on:12/24/2007	$0.51
Employees	NA	Stock Exchange	OTC
Auditor	PKF Witt Mares, PLC	Ticker Symbol	SNMO
Stk Agt	NA	Outstanding Shares	NA
Counsel	NA	E.P.S.	NA
DUNS No.	NA	Shareholders	NA

Business: The groups principle activities include designing, manufacturing and supplying of micro motors to the global market with range of applications in automotive parts, power tools, home appliances, business equipment, medical equipment, personal care products and consumer electronics. The group operates from the United States. The group's quarterly revenue for Jun '07 is 11.01 million USD.

Primary SIC and add'l.: 3621 3568

CIK No: 0000108729

Subsidiaries: Bestip Development International Limited, Billion Top Developments Limited, Classic Choice Investments Limited, Dragon Hero International Limited, Fuvanka Industries Limited, Hysan International Investment Limited, Sun Micro Motor Technology Limited, Sun Motor Auto Parts Company Limited, Sun Motor Holding Company Limited, Sun Motor Industrial Co Limited, Sun Motor Manufactory Limited, Sun Motor OEM Co Limited, Sun Motor Precision Products Limited

Officers: Simon Kai Biu Shi/Chmn., CEO, Pres., Ho Koon Lun/COO, Chang Yung Ying/VP - Sales, Marketing, Jacky Kin Bon Shi/VP, Teruo Ito/VP - Research, Development, Bernard Lenormand/VP - Research, Development, Europe, Hiroshi Tokoro/VP - Quality Assurance, Kenny Lo/CFO

Directors: Simon Kai Biu Shi/Chmn., CEO, Pres., Jeffrey Kai Bon Shi/Dir.

Owners: Shi Kai Biu/72.70%, SAOF NO.3 Limited/5.80%, Insiders/72.70%

Financial Data: Fiscal Year End:03/31 Latest Annual Data: 3/31/2006

Year	Sales	Net Income
2006	$50,843,000	$3,082,000
2005	NA	-$371,000
2004	$1,587,000	-$618,000

Curr. Assets:	$292,000	Curr. Liab.:	$430,000		
Plant, Equip.:	$783,000	Total Liab.:	$492,000	Indic. Yr. Divd.:	NA
Total Assets:	$1,076,000	Net Worth:	$584,000	Debt/ Equity:	0.1515

Sun River Energy Inc

10200 W 44th Ave., Ste. 210 E, Wheat Ridge, CO, 80033; **PH:** 1-303-940-2090; http:// www.sunriverenergy.com

General - Incorporation	CO	Stock - Price on:12/24/2007	$2.25
Employees	NA	Stock Exchange	OTC
Auditor	Jaspers + Hall, PC	Ticker Symbol	SNRV
Stk Agt	NA	Outstanding Shares	12,550,000
Counsel	NA	E.P.S.	NA
DUNS No.	NA	Shareholders	NA

Business: The groups principal activities include developing a website designing, which would respond to an Internet user's computer speed and link the user to a tier of the website. The group operates from the United States.

Primary SIC and add'l.: 9995

CIK No: 0001066551

Officers: Redginald T. Green/53/Dir., Sec., Wesley F. Whiting/75/Dir., Pres., Steve Naremore/Contact - Investor Relations

Directors: Wesley F. Whiting/75/Dir., Pres., Thomas Anderson/41/Dir., Stephen W. Weathers/45/Dir., David Surgnier/58/Dir.

Owners: Michael A. Littman/5.30%, Thomas Anderson, LCP Investments, LLC/14.80%, Stephen W. Weathers, Wesley F. Whiting, David Surgnier, Insiders/1.80%, New Mexico Energy LLC/49.00%, Nova Leasing, LLC/7.90%, Redginald T. Green

Sunair Services Corp

Formerly: Sunair Electronics Inc
595 S Federal Hwy., Ste. 500, Boca Raton, FL, 33432; **PH:** 1-561-208-7400; http:// www.sunairhf.com

General - Incorporation	FL	Stock - Price on:12/24/2007	$3.49
Employees	604	Stock Exchange	AMEX
Auditor	Berenfeld Spritzer Shechter & Sheer	Ticker Symbol	SNR
Stk Agt	American Stock Transfer & Trust Co.	Outstanding Shares	NA
Counsel	NA	E.P.S.	-$0.34
DUNS No.	00-413-5604	Shareholders	NA

Business: The group's principal activities are to design, manufacture and market high frequency single sideband communications equipment. These equipments are used in for long range voice and data communications in fixed station, airborne, mobile and marine strategic applications. The products of the group include high frequency transceivers, high frequency receivers, automatic antenna couplers, linear power amplifiers, computer remote control systems, digital modems, frequency management systems and high frequency airborne transceivers. The group also custom designs systems incorporating various combinations of products into equipment racks and control consoles that interfaces with workstations, power sources, message switching devices, cryptographic equipment and software of other manufacturers. The products are sold through system engineering companies, worldwide commercial and business airframe manufacturers or to the government of United States.

Primary SIC and add'l.: 3663 3669

CIK No: 0000095366

Subsidiaries: Middleton Pest Control, Inc., Percipia Inc., Percipia Networks, Inc., Sunair International Sales Corp., Sunair Southeast Pest Holdings, Inc., Telephone Communications, The Lawn and Pest Control Services

Officers: John J. Hayes/55/CEO, Pres., Edward M. Carriero/52/Interim CFO

Directors: Mario B. Ferrari/30/Vice Chmn., Richard C. Rochon/50/Chmn., Charles P. Steinmetz/68/Dir., Joseph Burke/50/Dir., Joseph S. Dimartino/64/Dir., Arnold Heggestad/64/Dir., Steven P. Oppenheim/61/Dir.

Owners: James E. Laurent, John J. Hayes, Gregory A. Clendenin, Michael D. Herman, Joseph S. DiMartino, Coconut Palm Capital Investors II, Ltd., Synnott B. Durham, Edward M. Carriero, Joseph Burke, Charles P. Steinmetz, Steven P. Oppenheim, Arnold Heggestad, Dru A. Schmitt, Michael Brauser, SunTrust Banks, Inc. (18 Owners included in Index)

Financial Data: Fiscal Year End:09/30 Latest Annual Data: 9/30/2006

Year	Sales	Net Income
2006	$55,445,000	-$5,780,000
2005	$31,452,000	$596,000
2004	$9,885,000	$1,130,000

Curr. Assets:	$10,848,000	Curr. Liab.:	$8,989,000		
Plant, Equip.:	$2,538,000	Total Liab.:	$23,844,000	Indic. Yr. Divd.:	NA
Total Assets:	$83,913,000	Net Worth:	$60,068,000	Debt/ Equity:	0.2501

SunCoast Bank

8592 Potter Pk. Dr., Ste. 200, Sarasota, FL, 34238; **PH:** 1-941-923-0500; http:// www.suncoastnationalbank.com

General - Incorporation	FL	Stock - Price on:12/24/2007	NA
Employees	NA	Stock Exchange	NA
Auditor	Hacker, Johnson & Smith P.A, P.C	Ticker Symbol	NA
Stk Agt	Computershare Investor Services LLC	Outstanding Shares	NA
Counsel	NA	E.P.S.	NA
DUNS No.	NA	Shareholders	NA

Business: The group's principal activity is to provide commercial and consumer banking services. The services are provided through its subsidiary suncoast national bank. The services offered by the group include demand deposits, money market deposits, now accounts, time deposits, safe deposit services and credit cards. The services also includes cash management, direct deposits, notary services, money orders, night depository, travelers' checks, cashier's checks, domestic collections, savings bonds, bank drafts, automated teller services, drive-in tellers and banking by mail. In addition, the group makes secured and unsecured commercial and real estate loans and issues stand-by letters of credit. The group offers its services to businesses and individuals through two banking offices located in sarasota county, Florida.

Primary SIC and add'l.: 6712 6022

CIK No: 0001072695

Subsidiaries: Cadence Bank, Florida state-chartered Bank

Suncom Wireless Holdings Inc

Formerly: Triton Pcs Holdings Inc
1100 Cassatt Rd., Berwyn, PA, 19312; **PH:** 1-610-651-5900; http:// www.tritonpcs.com

General - Incorporation	DE	Stock - Price on:12/24/2007	NA
Employees	1,959	Stock Exchange	NYSE
Auditor	PricewaterhouseCoopers LLP	Ticker Symbol	NA
Stk Agt	Computershare Investor Services LLC	Outstanding Shares	NA
Counsel	Triton Network Newco	E.P.S.	-$9.989
DUNS No.	NA	Shareholders	NA

Business: The group's principle activity is to provide wireless communication services. The group provides personal communication services, personal communications handsets and accessories. The group charges fee to other wireless telecommunications companies for their customer's use of the group's networks facilities. It provides services and products to retail customers, businesses, institutions and government. The group's distribution channels include a network of company-owned retail stores, independent agent retailers, a direct sales force for corporate accounts and online sales. It operates solely in the southeastern United States.

Primary SIC and add'l.: 4812

CIK No: 0001091973

Subsidiaries: Affiliate License Co., LLC, AWS License Newco, LLC, AWS Network Newco, LLC, SunCom Wireless Affiliate Company, LLC, SunCom Wireless International LLC, SunCom Wireless Investment Co., LLC, SunCom Wireless Management Company, Inc., SunCom Wireless Operating Company, LLC, SunCom Wireless Puerto Rico Operating Co., LLC, SunCom Wireless, Inc., Triton Network Newco, LLC, Triton PCS Equipment Company LLC, Triton PCS Finance Company, Inc., Triton PCS Holdings Company, LLC, Triton PCS Investment Company, LLC 17 Subsidiaries included in the Index

Officers: Michael E. Kalogris/Chmn., CEO, Laura M. Shaw-Porter/Sr. VP - Human Resources, William A. Robinson/Exec. VP - Operations, Eric Haskell/CFO, Exec. VP, Harry Roessner/VP, Controller

Directors: Michael E. Kalogris/Chmn., CEO, Scott I. Anderson/Dir., Jerry V. Elliott/Dir., Edward Evans/Dir., Niles K. Chura/Dir., Pat Daugherty/Dir., Gustavo A. Prilick/Dir., Karim Samii/Dir., Joe Thornton/Dir., James Volk/Dir.

Owners: Jerry V. Elliot, Michael E. Kalogris, Pardus Capital Management, L.P., James Dondero, Insiders, Capital Research and Management Company, Deutsche Telekom AG, William A. Robinson, Laura M. Shaw-Porter, Scott Anderson, James J. Volk, DiMaio Ahmad Capital LLC, Eric Haskell, Patrick H. Daugherty, Karim Samii (20 Owners included in Index)

Financial Data: Fiscal Year End:12/31 Latest Annual Data: 12/31/2006

Year	Sales	Net Income
2006	$852,879,000	-$337,378,000
2005	$826,158,000	-$496,808,000
2004	$818,200,000	$682,527,000

Curr. Assets:	$375,310,000	Curr. Liab.:	$188,483,000		
Plant, Equip.:	$480,880,000	Total Liab.:	$2,071,751,000	Indic. Yr. Divd.:	NA
Total Assets:	$1,654,859,000	Net Worth:	-$416,892,000	Debt/ Equity:	NA

Suncor Energy Inc

Suncor Energy Inc, 112 - 4 Ave. S.W, Calgary, AB, T2P 2V5; **PH:** 1-403-269-8100; http:// www.suncor.com

General - Incorporation	Canada	Stock - Price on:12/24/2007	$92.24
Employees	5,766	Stock Exchange	NYSE
Auditor	PricewaterhouseCoopers LLP	Ticker Symbol	SU
Stk Agt	Computershare Trust Co of Canada	Outstanding Shares	460,220,000
Counsel	NA	E.P.S.	$4.50
DUNS No.	24-998-1788	Shareholders	NA

Business: The group's principle activities are exploring, acquiring, producing and marketing crude oil and natural gas. The company operates in three segments: oil sands, natural gas and sunoco. The oil sands segment produces and markets light sweet and light sour crude oil, diesel fuel and various and custom blends. The natural gas segment explores, acquires, develops, produces transports and markets natural gas and crude oil. The sunoco segment refines crude oil and transports and markets finished petroleum and petrochemical products. The group owns mines in the athabasca region of alberta, natural gas facilities in calgary and refining facilities near toronto. Outside Canada, the products are sold in the United States and Europe. The group's quarterly revenue for September 2007 was 4,666.00 millions of USD.

Primary SIC and add'l.: 1311 5172 2911 4924

CIK No: 0000311337

Subsidiaries: Colorado Refining Company, Suncor Energy (Natural Gas) America Inc, Suncor Energy (U.S.A.) Inc, Suncor Energy Marketing Inc., Suncor Energy Oil Sands Limited Partnership., Suncor Energy Products Inc

Officers: Richard L. George/Dir., CEO, Pres., Bart W. Demosky/VP, Treasurer, Kenneth J. Alley/Sr. VP, CFO, Mike Ashar/Exec. VP - Refining, Marketing, USA, Kirk Bailey/Exec. VP - Oil Sands, Gordon Lambert/VP - Sustainable Development, Gail Clayton/Contact - Investor Relations, Thomas L. Ryley/Exec. VP - Refining, Marketing, Canada, Jay Thornton/Sr. VP - Business

Integration, Steven W. Williams/COO, Janice B. Odegaard/VP, Assoc. General Counsel, Corp. Sec., Kevin D. Nabholz/Exec. VP - Major Projects, Sue Lee/Sr. VP - Human Resources, Communications, Terrence J. Hopwood/Sr. VP, General Counsel, David W. Byler/Exec. VP - Refining, Marketing, USA, Natural Gas, Renewable Energy

Directors: Richard L. George/Dir., CEO, Pres., John Ferguson/Dir., Mike O'Brien/Dir., Eira Thomas/Dir., Brian Canfield/Dir., Mel E. Benson/Dir., John Huff/Dir., Bryan Davies/Dir., Brian Felesky/Dir., Ann M. McCaig/Dir., Douglas W. Ford/Dir.

Financial Data: Fiscal Year End:12/31   **Latest Annual Data:** 12/31/2006

Year	Sales	Net Income
2006	$13,582,865,000	$2,536,544,000
2005	$9,511,788,000	$1,093,092,000
2004	$7,158,016,000	$949,033,000

Curr. Assets:	$1,975,346,000	**Curr. Liab.:**	$1,851,780,000	**P/E Ratio:**	20.50
Plant, Equip.:	$13,891,781,000	**Total Liab.:**	$8,570,703,000	**Indic. Yr. Divd.:**	$0.370
Total Assets:	$16,138,287,000	**Net Worth:**	$7,567,584,000	**Debt/ Equity:**	NA

SUNDAY Communications Ltd

13/f Warwick House Taikoo Pl 979 King's Rd. , Quarry Bay, Hong Kong; **PH:** 852-21138118; *http://* www.sunday.com

General - Incorporation .... Cayman Islands	**Stock**- Price on:12/24/2007 ....NA
Employees..NA	Stock Exchange..NA
Auditor ....PricewaterhouseCoopers LLP	Ticker Symbol..NA
Stk Agt...................ButterfieldFund Services Ltd	Outstanding Shares ....NA
Counsel...NA	E.P.S..NA
DUNS No. ....NA	Shareholders...NA

Business: The group's principal activities are the provision of mobile, international telecommunications, data and Internet services. Other activities of the group are the sale of mobile phones and accessories and provision of investment holding. Mobile services acctd for 91% of 2002 revs; sale of mobile phones & accessories, 9% and international telecommunications, nom.

Primary SIC and add'l.: 4813 7375 4899 7377 4822

CIK No: 0001106952

Subsidiaries: Mandarin Communications Limited, Sunday 3g (hong Kong) Limited, Sunday 3g Holdings (hong Kong) Corporation, SUNDAY Communications Services (Shenzhen) Limited, SUNDAY Holdings (China) Corporation, SUNDAY Holdings (Hong Kong) Corporation, Sunday Ip Holdings Corporation, Sunday Ip Limited

Sunesis Pharmaceuticals Inc

341 Oyster Point Blvd., South San Francisco, CA, 94080; **PH:** 1-650-266-3500; *http://* www.sunesis.com; **Email:** info@sunesis.com

General - Incorporation .... DE	**Stock** - Price on:12/24/2007 ....$4.15
Employees..138	Stock Exchange.......................................NDQ
Auditor .... Ernst & Young LLP	Ticker Symbol.. SNSS
Stk Agt...... American Stock Transfer & Trust Co.	Outstanding Shares 29,480,000
Counsel...NA	E.P.S...-$1.13
DUNS No. ....NA	Shareholders...NA

Business: The groups principle activities include discovering, developing and commercializing novel, small molecule therapeutics. The group products sold under the trade name Sunesis and Tethering(R). The group operates from the United States. The group's quarterly revenue for September 2007 was 1.83 millions of USD.

Primary SIC and add'l.: 2834

CIK No: 0001061027

Subsidiaries: Sunesis Europe Limited

Officers: Daniel N. Swisher/Dir., CEO, Pres./$819,390.00, James W. Young/Executive Chmn./$389,926.00, Eric H. Bjerkholt/Sr. VP, CFO/$528,071.00, Daniel C. Adelman/Sr. VP, Chief Medical Officer/$521,361.00, Robert S. McDowell/VP - Research, William L. Schary/VP - Regulatory Affairs, Quality Assurance, Jennifer Troia/VP, Valerie L. Pierce/Sr. VP, General Counsel

Directors: Daniel N. Swisher/Dir., CEO, Pres., James W. Young/Executive Chmn., James A. Wells/Co - Founder, Dir., David C. Stump/Dir., Jonathan Leff/Dir., Homer L. Pearce/Dir., Anthony B. Evnin/Dir., Stephen P.A. Fodor/Dir., Matthew Fust/Dir., Steven D. Goldby/Dir.

Owners: Baker/Tisch Investments, L.P., Baker Bros. Investments, L.P., Baker Bros. Investments II, L.P., Baker Biotech Fund I, L.P./1.50%, 14159, L.P., Baker Brothers Life Sciences, L.P./3.00%

Financial Data: Fiscal Year End:12/31   **Latest Annual Data:** 12/31/2006

Year	Sales	Net Income
2006	$13,709,000	-$31,237,000
2005	$16,522,000	-$27,499,000
2004	$10,305,000	-$20,530,000

Curr. Assets:	$64,187,000	**Curr. Liab.:**	$8,909,000		
Plant, Equip.:	$4,729,000	**Total Liab.:**	$12,473,000	**Indic. Yr. Divd.:**	NA
Total Assets:	$69,276,000	**Net Worth:**	$56,804,000	**Debt/ Equity:**	0.0202

SunGard Availability

680 E Swedesford Rd., Wayne, PA, 19087; **PH:** 1-484-582-2000; *http://* www.sungard.com

General - Incorporation .... DE	**Stock**- Price on:12/24/2007 ....NA
Employees..NA	Stock Exchange..NA
Auditor..NA	Ticker Symbol..NA
Stk Agt..NA	Outstanding Shares ....NA
Counsel...NA	E.P.S..NA
DUNS No. ....NA	Shareholders...NA

Business: The group's principle activity is to provide software and processing solutions. The group operates through three segments namely financial systems, higher education and public sector systems, and availability services. The group servicing areas include serves higher education institutions, state and local governments, and not-for-profit organizations. The group operates from United States.

Primary SIC and add'l.: 7374

CIK No: 0001312161

Officers: Jim Ashton/Division CEO - Financial Systems, Ted Gaasche/Group CEO - Availability Services, Gil Santos/CEO - Public Sector, Brian Madocks/CEO - Higher Education, Harold C. Finders/Division CEO - Financial Systems, Cristobal I. Conde/CEO, Pres., Ronald M. Lang/CEO - Enterprise Solutions, Eric Berg/Group CEO - Availability Services, Kathleen Asser Weslock/Sr. VP -

Human Resources, Chief Human Resources Officer, Michael K. Muratore/Exec. VP, Brian Robins/Sr. VP, Chief Marketing Officer, Michael J. Ruane/CFO, Sr. VP - Finance, Treasurer, Victoria E. Silbey/VP - Legal, General Counsel, Richard C. Tarbox/Sr. VP - Corporate Development, Eric Erickson/VP, Treasurer

Directors: Till M. Guldimann/Vice Chmn.

Sungold International Holdings Corp

300-940 The E Mall, Toronto, ON, M9B 6J7; **PH:** 1-604-669-9580; *http://* www.sungoldintl.com; **Email:** cdemonte@aol.com

General - Incorporation ....Canada	**Stock**- Price on:12/24/2007 ....$0.13
Employees..5	Stock Exchange.......................................OTC
Auditor .... Loewen, Stronach & Co	Ticker Symbol.. SGIHF
Stk Agt .... Computershare Investor Services LLC	Outstanding Shares 133,000,000
Counsel...NA	E.P.S...-$0.01
DUNS No. ....NA	Shareholders...NA

Business: The group's principal activity is to develop and operate entertainment facilities and online virtual horse racing. The group is considered to be in a development stage company.

Primary SIC and add'l.: 7999

CIK No: 0001073674

Subsidiaries: Horsepower Broadcasting Network (HBN) International Ltd., Racing Unified Network (RUN) Inc, SafeSpending Inc.

Officers: Keith T. Blackwell/CEO, CFO, Treasurer, Tony Currie/Pres., Nicholas Desante/VP - Operations, Richard Henley/GM - Commercial Advertising, Les Rankin/Dir. - Horsepower Broadcasting Network

Directors: Donald R. Harris/Chmn., Art Cowie/Vice Chmn., Dennis Hedtke/Dir., Larry Simpson/Dir., Murray Marshall/Dir. - Horsepower Broadcasting Network International Ltd

Owners: Larry Simpson, Dennis Hedtke, Art Cowie, Donald R. Harris

Financial Data: Fiscal Year End:08/31   **Latest Annual Data:** 8/31/2006

Year	Sales	Net Income
2006	NA	-$1,459,000
2005	NA	-$1,167,000
2004	NA	-$967,000

Curr. Assets:	$17,000	**Curr. Liab.:**	$592,000		
Plant, Equip.:	$437,000	**Total Liab.:**	$598,000	**Indic. Yr. Divd.:**	NA
Total Assets:	$453,000	**Net Worth:**	-$145,000	**Debt/ Equity:**	NA

Sunlink Health Systems Inc

900 Cir. 75 Pkwy, Ste 1120, Atlanta, GA, 30339; **PH:** 1-770-933-7000; *http://* www.sunlinkhealth.com; **Email:** sunlink@sunlinkhealth.com

General - Incorporation .... OH	**Stock**- Price on:12/24/2007 ....$6.6
Employees..1,203	Stock Exchange......................................AMEX
Auditor .... Cherry, Bekaert & Holland LLP	Ticker Symbol.. SSY
Stk Agt .... Wachovia Bank N.A	Outstanding Shares 7,510,000
Counsel.........................James J.Mulligan	E.P.S...$0.16
DUNS No. 00-424-3127	Shareholders...NA

Business: The group's principal activities is to provide healthcare services in community hospitals. The group operates through six community hospitals in four states. The group discontinued u.k. Housewares and child safety products segment in 2002. 06-Oct-2003, the group acquired healthmont inc.

Primary SIC and add'l.: 8099

CIK No: 0000096793

Subsidiaries: Bradley International Holdings Limited, Clanton Hospital LLC, Dexter Hospital LLC, HealthMont LLC, HealthMont of Georgia Inc., HealthMont of Missouri, LLC, HomeTown Health LLC, Klippan GmbH, Klippan S.A.R.L., KRUG International (UK) Limited, KRUG Properties Inc., Optima Healthcare Corporation, Pickens Health Care Association, Inc., Southeastern Healthcare Alliance, Inc., Southern Health Corporation of Dahlonega, Inc. 21 Subsidiaries included in the Index

Officers: Robert M. Thornton/58/Chmn., CEO/$345,669.00, Mark J. Stockslager/CFO, Principal Accounting Officer, Corporate Controller/$125,631.00, Jerome D. Orth/VP - Technical, Compliance Services/$165,422.00, Harry R. Alvis/COO/$254,669.00

Directors: Robert M. Thornton/58/Chmn., CEO, Karen B. Brenner/54/Dir., Gene E. Burleson/65/Dir., Steven J. Baileys/53/Dir., Howard E. Turner/64/Dir., Michael C. Ford/67/Dir., Michael W. Hall/57/Dir., James J. Mulligan/83/Dir. Emeritus

Owners: Jerome D. Orth, Robert M. Thornton/6.81%, Steven J. Baileys/7.85%, Gene E. Burleson/1.12%, Mark J. Stockslager/1.36%, Karen B. Brenner/3.18%, Michael W. Hall, Insiders/44.64%, Christopher H. B. Mills/17.06%, Harry R. Alvis/1.66%, Howard E. Turner/3.20%, Berggruen Holdings North America Ltd./6.42%, Michael C. Ford, Jack M. Spurr

Financial Data: Fiscal Year End:06/30   **Latest Annual Data:** 6/30/2006

Year	Sales	Net Income
2006	$135,576,000	$3,909,000
2005	$128,732,000	$4,540,000
2004	$112,436,000	$13,425,000

Curr. Assets:	$27,909,000	**Curr. Liab.:**	$22,295,000	**P/E Ratio:**	28.70
Plant, Equip.:	$41,155,000	**Total Liab.:**	$39,951,000	**Indic. Yr. Divd.:**	NA
Total Assets:	$74,303,000	**Net Worth:**	$34,352,000	**Debt/ Equity:**	0.2217

Sunoco Inc

1735 Market St., Ste. LL, Philadelphia, PA, 19103; **PH:** 1-215-977-3000; *http://* www.sunocoinc.com; **Email:** customerfirst@sunocoinc.com

General - Incorporation ....PA	**Stock**- Price on:12/24/2007 ....$84.51
Employees..14,000	Stock Exchange......................................NYSE
Auditor .... Ernst & Young LLP	Ticker Symbol..NA
Stk Agt ....Computershare Trust Co	Outstanding Shares 121,450,000
Counsel...NA	E.P.S...$8.44
DUNS No. 00-134-4985	Shareholders...NA

Business: The group's principle activities include manufacturing and marketing of petroleum and petrochemical products. The group's products include fuels, lubricants and petrochemicals. The group's services include retail and wholesale marketing, and home heating fuels and comfort services. The group operates from United States.

Primary SIC and add'l.: 2992 1311 2899 1321 5541 1222 2911

CIK No: 0000095304

Subsidiaries: Aristech Chemical Corporation, Aristech Investment Corporation, Atlantic Petroleum (Out) LLC, Atlantic Petroleum Corporation, Atlantic Petroleum Delaware Corporation, Atlantic Pipeline (Out) L.P., Atlantic R&M (Out) L.P., Atlantic Refining& Marketing Corp., BBQ, Inc., Beneco Leasing Two, Inc., Cambria Coke Company, Carrier Systems Motor Freight, Inc., Dominion Coal Corporation, Elk River Minerals Corporation, Epsilon Products Company, LLC 112 Subsidiaries included in the Index

Officers: John G. Drosdick/Chmn., CEO, Pres./$22,957,010.00, Michael J. Hennigan/Sr. VP - Supply, Trading, Sales, Transportation, Thomas W. Hofmann/CFO, Sr. VP/$5,304,306.00, Vincent J. Kelley/Sr. VP - Refining, Joel H. Maness/57/Exec. VP - Refining, Supply/$5,404,682.00, Marie A. Natoli/General Auditor, Robert W. Owens/Sr. VP - Marketing/$3,304,459.00, Charles K. Valutas/Sr. VP, Chief Administrative Officer/$4,123,332.00, Michael H.R. Dingus/Sr. VP/$4,097,278.00, Terence P. Delaney/VP - Investor Relations, Planning, Joseph P. Krott/Controller, Michael S. Kuritzkes/Sr. VP, General Counsel, Rolf D. Naku/Sr. VP - Human Resources, Public Affairs, Ann C. Mule/Chief Governance Officer, Assist. General Counsel, Corp. Sec., Paul A. Mulholland/Treasurer *(16 Officers included in Index)*

Directors: John G. Drosdick/Chmn., CEO, Pres., Robert J. Darnall/Dir., John P. Jones/Dir., Anderson R. Pew/Dir., James G. Kaiser/Dir., Jackson G. Ratcliffe/Dir., John W. Rowe/Dir., John K. Wulff/Dir., Ursula O. Fairbairn/Dir., Thomas P. Gerrity/Dir., Rosemarie B. Greco/Dir.

Owners: M.H.R. Dingus, U. O. Fairbairn, J. G. Kaiser, Insiders/0.01%, J. H. Maness, R. B. Greco, B. G. Fischer, T. P. Gerrity, J. P. Jones, J. K. Wulff, G. J. Ratcliffe, R. J. Darnall, State Street Bank and Trust Company/6.20%, R. A. Pew, J. W. Rowe *(19 Owners included in Index)*

Financial Data: ***Fiscal Year End:***12/31 ***Latest Annual Data:*** 12/31/2006

Year	Sales	Net Income
2006	$38,715,000,000	$979,000,000
2005	$33,777,000,000	$974,000,000
2004	$25,508,000,000	$605,000,000

Curr. Assets:	$4,015,000,000	***Curr. Liab.:***	$4,755,000,000	***P/E Ratio:***	8.99
Plant, Equip.:	$6,365,000,000	***Total Liab.:***	$8,907,000,000	***Indic. Yr. Divd.:***	$1.100
Total Assets:	$10,982,000,000	***Net Worth:***	$2,075,000,000	***Debt/ Equity:***	0.8114

Sunoco Logistics Partners LP

1735 Market St., Ste. LL, Philadelphia, PA, 19103; ***PH:*** 1-215-977-6298; ***http://*** www.sunocologistics.com; ***Email:*** IR@sunocologistics.com

General - Incorporation	DE	***Stock***- Price on:12/24/2007	$57.24
Employees	NA	Stock Exchange	NYSE
Auditor	Ernst& Young LLP	Ticker Symbol	SXL
Stk Agt	American Stock Transfer & Trust Co.	Outstanding Shares	28,590,000
Counsel	NA	E.P.S	$3.23
DUNS No.	NA	Shareholders	NA

Business: The groups principle activities include acquiring, marketing and operating pipeline, terminalling and crude oil properties. The group operates through three segments namely, eastern pipeline system, terminal facilities and western pipeline system. The group's quarterly revenue for September 2007 was 1944.60 millions of USD.

Primary SIC and add'l.: 4922 4923 4925 4613 4612

CIK No: 0001161154

Subsidiaries: Sun Pipe Line Company of Delaware LLC, Sunoco Logistics Partners GP LLC, Sunoco Logistics Partners L.P., Sunoco Logistics Partners Operations GP LLC, Sunoco Logistics Partners Operations L.P., Sunoco Partners Lease Acquisition& Marketing LLC, Sunoco Partners LLC, Sunoco Partners Marketing& Terminals L.P., Sunoco Pipeline Acquisition LLC, Sunoco Pipeline L.P.

Officers: Deborah M. Fretz/Dir., CEO, Pres., Paul S. Broker/47/VP - Western Operations, Bruce D. Davis/VP, General Counsel, Sec., David A. Justin/VP - Eastern Operations, Business Lines Contact, Christopher W. Keene/VP - Business Development, Daniel D. Lewis/Controller, Paul A. Mulholland/Treasurer, Gerald Davis/Contact - Media, Steve Broker/Business Lines Contact, Neal E. Murphy/CFO, VP

Directors: Deborah M. Fretz/Dir., CEO, Pres., John G. Drosdick/Chmn., Cynthia A. Archer/Dir., Wilson L. Berry/Dir., Stephen L. Cropper/Dir., Michael H.R. Dingus/Dir., Gary W. Edwards/Dir., Bruce G. Fischer/52/Dir., Thomas W. Hofmann/Dir.

Owners: Stephen L. Cropper, Thomas W. Hofmann, Michael H.R. Dingus, Deborah M. Fretz, Sunoco Partners LLC/42.30%, David A. Justin, Bruce D. Davis, Cynthia A. Archer, John G. Drosdick, Insiders, Bruce G. Fischer

Financial Data: ***Fiscal Year End:***12/31 ***Latest Annual Data:*** 12/31/2006

Year	Sales	Net Income
2006	$5,854,550,000	$90,341,000
2005	$4,496,907,000	$61,709,000
2004	$3,465,217,000	$57,031,000

Curr. Assets:	$962,584,000	***Curr. Liab.:***	$980,207,000	***P/E Ratio:***	19.87
Plant, Equip.:	$1,006,668,000	***Total Liab.:***	$1,499,166,000	***Indic. Yr. Divd.:***	$3.400
Total Assets:	$2,082,077,000	***Net Worth:***	$582,911,000	***Debt/ Equity:***	0.8438

SunOpta Inc

2838 Bovaird Dr. W, Brampton, ON, L7A 0H2; ***PH:*** 1-905-455-1990; ***http://*** www.staketech.com; ***Email:*** susan.wickenkamp@sunopta.com

General - Incorporation	Canada	***Stock***- Price on:12/24/2007	$10.81
Employees	1,731	Stock Exchange	NDQ
Auditor	PricewaterhouseCoopers LLP	Ticker Symbol	STKL
Stk Agt	Equity Transfer Services Inc	Outstanding Shares	63,030,000
Counsel	NA	E.P.S	$0.29
DUNS No.	NA	Shareholders	NA

Business: The group's principle activities are carried out through three divisions: natural food product sourcing, processing and packaging; processing, distribution and recycling of environmentally responsible aggregate and engineering and marketing of a clean pulping system using patented steam explosion technology. The sunrich food group produces organic and food ingredients with specialization in soy milk and other soy and natural food products. The environmental industrial group processes, sells and distributes abrasives and industrial materials and recycles inorganic materials. The staketech steam explosion group operates a division for developing and commercializing a proprietary steam explosion technology for processing of biomass into high value products. The group's operations are carried out in the United States and Canada. The group's quarterly revenue for September 2007 was 205.67 millions of USD.

Primary SIC and add'l.: 5169 2075 4953 4952

CIK No: 0000351834

Subsidiaries: 3060385 Nova Scotia Company, Cleughs Frozen Foods, Inc., Drive Organics Corp., Opta Minerals Inc., Organic Ingredients Inc., Pacific Fruit Processors, Inc., SunOpta Aseptic, Inc., SunOpta Financing Inc., SunOpta Food Group LLC, SunOpta Holdings Inc., SunOpta Ingredients, Inc., SunOpta LP, Sunrich LLC

Officers: Jeremy N. Kendall/Chmn., CEO, Joseph J. Stern/Pres. - Organic Ingredients, Exec. VP - Sunopta Fruit Group, Arthur J. McEvily/Pres. - Sunopta Ingredients Group, Benjamin Chhiba/VP, General Counsel - Sunopta Inc, Allan G. Routh/Dir., Pres. - Sunopta Grains, Foods Group, Stephen B. Easterbrook/Pres. - Sunopta Canadian Food Distribution Group, David J. Kruse/COO, Pres., John H. Dietrich/CFO, VP, Murray J. Burke/VP, GM - Sunopta Bioprocess Group, Sergio A. Varela/Pres. - Sunopta Fruit Group, Susan Wiekenkamp/Information Officer, Steven R. Bromley/COO, Pres. - Sunopta Inc, Roger G. Eacock/VP - Supply Chain, Frank G. Syer/VP - Human Resources, Organization

Directors: Jeremy N. Kendall/Chmn., CEO, James K. Rifenbergh/Dir., Cyril A. Ing/Dir., Katrina L. Houde/Dir., Joseph Riz/Dir., Allan G. Routh/Dir., Pres. - Sunopta Grains, Foods Group, Robert Fetherstonhaugh/Dir., Stephen R. Bronfman/Dir., Steven Townsend/Dir.

Owners: John Dietrich/0.16%, Robert Fetherstonhaugh/0.06%, Steven Bromley/0.41%, Jeremy Kendall/0.83%, James Rifenbergh/0.39%, Katrina Houde/0.07%, Allan Routh/0.92%, Arthur McEvily/0.09%, Stephen Bronfman/7.89%, Steven Townsend/0.02%, Insiders/11.04%, Joseph Riz/0.10%, Cyril A. Ing/0.11%

Financial Data: ***Fiscal Year End:***12/31 ***Latest Annual Data:*** 12/31/2006

Year	Sales	Net Income
2006	$598,026,000	$10,959,000
2005	$426,101,000	$13,558,000
2004	$306,251,000	$11,016,000

Curr. Assets:	$213,071,000	***Curr. Liab.:***	$132,640,000	***P/E Ratio:***	54.05
Plant, Equip.:	$87,487,000	***Total Liab.:***	$228,027,000	***Indic. Yr. Divd.:***	NA
Total Assets:	$404,730,000	***Net Worth:***	$176,703,000	***Debt/ Equity:***	NA

SunPower Corp

3939 N 1st St., San Jose, CA, 95134; ***PH:*** 1-408-240-5500; ***http://*** www.sunpowercorp.com; ***Email:*** information@sunpowercorp.com

General - Incorporation	DE	***Stock***- Price on:12/24/2007	$63.05
Employees	1,759	Stock Exchange	NDQ
Auditor	PricewaterhouseCoopers LLP	Ticker Symbol	SPWR
Stk Agt	Computershare Investor Services LLC	Outstanding Shares	75,170,000
Counsel	NA	E.P.S	$0.23
DUNS No.	NA	Shareholders	NA

Business: The groups principle activities include designing, developing, manufacturing and marketing solar electric power products. The groups services include energy management systems, building retro commissioning and heating, ventilation and air conditioning upgrades. The products of the group include Solar Cells, Solar Panels and Inverters. The group products sold under the trade names PowerGuard(R), PowerTilt(TM) and SunTile(R). In January 10, 2007, the group acquired PowerLight Corporation. Specific customers of the group include William Lyon Homes, Standard Pacific Homes, Castle and Cook, Inc., Christopherson Homes, Inc. and Community Dynamics, Inc. The group operates from the United States, Germany, Asia and other.

Primary SIC and add'l.: 3663 4911 3674 4911 3663 3674

CIK No: 0000867773

Subsidiaries: SunPower Corporation (Switzerland) Ltd., SunPower Manufacturing Philippines, Ltd., SunPower North America, Inc., SunPower Technology, Ltd.

Officers: Thomas H. Werner/Dir., CEO/$906,029.00, Thomas Dinwoodie/CEO - Powerlight, Howard Wenger/VP - Global Business Units, Bruce Ledesma/General Counsel, Emmanuel T. Hernandez/CFO/$1,107,063.00, P. M. Pai/COO/$508,288.00, Richard Swanson/Pres., CTO, Co - Founder/$429,542.00

Directors: Thomas H. Werner/Dir., CEO, T. J. Rodgers/Chmn., Steve W. Albrecht/Dir., Betsy S. Atkins/Dir., Pat Wood/Dir., Richard Swanson/Pres., CTO, Co - Founder

Owners: Thomas H. Werner/2.50%, Thomas L. Dinwoodie/9.10%, T. J. Rodgers, BlackRock, Inc./9.30%, Steve W. Albrecht, PM Pai, Insiders/14.00%, Pat Wood, Insiders, Janus Capital Management LLC/10.80%, Cypress Semiconductor Corp., Richard Swanson, Betsy S. Atkins, Fidelity Management& Research Company/6.00%, Baron Capital Group, Inc./9.70% *(18 Owners included in Index)*

Financial Data: ***Fiscal Year End:***12/31 ***Latest Annual Data:*** 12/31/2006

Year	Sales	Net Income
2006	$236,510,000	$26,516,000
2005	$78,736,000	-$15,843,000

Curr. Assets:	$288,601,000	***Curr. Liab.:***	$60,332,000		
Plant, Equip.:	$202,428,000	***Total Liab.:***	$88,065,000	***Indic. Yr. Divd.:***	NA
Total Assets:	$576,836,000	***Net Worth:***	$488,771,000	***Debt/ Equity:***	0.3144

Sunrise Real Estate Group Inc

Formerly: Sunrise Real Estate Development Grp Inc
Ste. 701, No. 333, Zhaojiabang Rd., Shanghai, 200032; ***PH:*** 8621-64220505; ***http://*** www.sunrise.sh

General - Incorporation	TX	***Stock***- Price on:12/24/2007	$1.95
Employees	NA	Stock Exchange	OTC
Auditor	BDO McCabe Lo Ltd	Ticker Symbol	SRRE
Stk Agt	Securities Transfer Corp	Outstanding Shares	NA
Counsel	NA	E.P.S	-$0.17
DUNS No.	NA	Shareholders	NA

Business: The groups principle activity is to seek business opportunity to acquire or merge in real estate development. The group operates from United States.

Primary SIC and add'l.: 9999

CIK No: 0001083490

Subsidiaries: Beijing Xin Ji Yang Real Estate Agency Co., Ltd., Lin Ray Yang Enterprise, Ltd., Shanghai Shang Yang Real Estate Consultation Co., Limited, Shanghai Xin Ji Real Estate Consultation Co., Ltd., Sunrise Real Estate Development Group, Inc., Suzhou Gao Feng Hui Property Management Co., Ltd., Suzhou Xin Ji Yang Real Estate Agency Co., Ltd.

Officers: Lin Chi Jung/Chmn., CEO/$390,015.00, Lin Chao Chin/Sr. VP/$390,015.00, Art Honanyan/CFO/$71,606.00, Pan Yu(ren)/MD - Subsidiaries/$242,882.00

Directors: Lin Chi Jung/Chmn., CEO, Chen Ren/58/Dir., Xiao L. Gang/Dir., Fu Xuan-Jie/59/Dir., Zhang Xi/Dir., Lin Hsin Hung/Dir., Li Xiao-Gang/Dir.

Owners: Insiders/39.50%, Lin Hsin-Hung/1.41%, Chi-Jung Lin/38.08%

Financial Data: *Fiscal Year End:*12/31 *Latest Annual Data:* 12/31/2006

Year	Sales	Net Income
2006	$16,417,000	$3,658,000
2005	NA	NA
2004	$7,724,000	$64,000

Curr. Assets:	$8,411,000	**Curr. Liab.:**	$7,281,000		
Plant, Equip.:	$2,492,000	**Total Liab.:**	$11,453,000	**Indic. Yr. Divd.:**	NA
Total Assets:	$21,916,000	**Net Worth:**	$10,087,000	**Debt/ Equity:**	0.4369

Sunrise Senior Living Inc

7902 W Pk. Dr., Mclean, VA, 22102; *PH:* 1-703-273-7500; *http://* www.sunrise-al.com; *Email:* careers@sunriseseniorliving.com

General - Incorporation	DE	**Stock**- Price on:12/24/2007	$41.94
Employees	22,366	Stock Exchange	NYSE
Auditor	Ernst & Young LLP	Ticker Symbol	SRZ
Stk Agt	American Stock Transfer & Trust Co.	Outstanding Shares	50,330,000
Counsel	NA	E.P.S	$1.67
DUNS No.	92-616-2173	Shareholders	NA

Business: The Group's principal activity is to operate senior living facilities in the United States. The group operates through seven segments namely, at home assisted living, independent living, assisted living, alzheimer's care, nursing & rehabilitative care, hospice care, and short-term stays. In May 2005,the group acquired Greystone. At year ended 2005, the group operated 97 communities in the United States, 11 communities in Canada, five communities in the United Kingdom and two communities in Germany.

Primary SIC and add'l.: 8361 8741

CIK No: 0001011064

Subsidiaries: Cedar Parke SL, LLC, Clayton Road Assisted Living, LLC, Dignity Home Care, Inc., Forum NGH, Inc., Greystone Communities, Inc., Greystone Development Company II LP, Greystone Development Company, LLC, Karrington Acquisition, Inc., Karrington Health, Inc., Karrington of Albuquerque Ltd., Karrington of Colorado Springs Ltd., Karrington of Englewood Ltd., Karrington of Findlay Ltd., Karrington of Finneytown Ltd., Karrington of Kenwood Ltd. 91 Subsidiaries included in the Index

Officers: Paul J. Klaassen/Founder, Chmn., CEO, Thomas B. Newell/Pres., Teresa M. Klaassen/Dir., Founder, Chief Cultural Officer, Exec. VP, Sec., Tiffany L. Tomasso/COO, John F. Gaul/General Counsel, Carl Adams/Sr. VP, Treasurer

Directors: Paul J. Klaassen/Founder, Chmn., CEO, Michael B. Lanahan/Chmn. - Greystone Division, William G. Little/Dir., Thomas J. Donohue/Dir., Douglas J. Holladay/58/Dir., Teresa M. Klaassen/Dir., Founder, Chief Cultural Officer, Exec. VP, Sec., Ronald V. Aprahamian/58/Dir., Craig R. Callen/Dir., Lynn Krominga/Dir., Stephen D. Harlan/Dir.

Financial Data: *Fiscal Year End:*12/31 *Latest Annual Data:* 12/31/2005

Year	Sales	Net Income
2005	$1,819,479,000	$79,742,000
2004	$1,461,924,000	$50,687,000
2003	$1,188,301,000	$62,178,000

Curr. Assets:	$416,772,000	**Curr. Liab.:**	$341,909,000	**P/E Ratio:**	25.11
Plant, Equip.:	$458,546,000	**Total Liab.:**	$695,599,000	**Indic. Yr. Divd.:**	NA
Total Assets:	$1,328,276,000	**Net Worth:**	$632,677,000	**Debt/ Equity:**	NA

Sunrise Telecom Inc

302 Enzo Dr., San Jose, CA, 95138; *PH:* 1-408-363-8000; *Fax:* 1-408-363-8313; *http://* www.sunrisetelecom.com; *Email:* info@sunrisetelec.com

General - Incorporation	DE	**Stock**- Price on:12/24/2007	$2.92
Employees	NA	Stock Exchange	OTC
Auditor	KPMG LLP	Ticker Symbol	SRTI
Stk Agt	Computershare Trust Co	Outstanding Shares	NA
Counsel	Orrick, Herrington & Sutcliffe LLP	E.P.S	NA
DUNS No.	NA	Shareholders	NA

Business: The group's principal activities are to manufacture and market service verification equipment. This equipment enables the service providers to verify newly installed services and diagnose problems relating to telecommunications, cable broadband and Internet networks. The group's products offer test broadband services includes wireline access services (including DSL), fiber optics, cable broadband networks and signaling networks. These products are to maximize technicians' effectiveness in network simulations for equipment manufacturers to test their products. The trademarks of the group are sunrise telecom, sunset and sunlite. The group's customers include telecommunications service providers, cable network operators, network infrastructure suppliers and installers, technicians and engineers in North America, Latin America, Europe, Africa, the Middle East and the Asia/pacific region. During the year 2003, the group acquired substantial assets of gie gmbh.

Primary SIC and add'l.: 3825 3829

CIK No: 0000907152

Subsidiaries: Sunrise Telecom Broadband Corp., Sunrise Telecom Broadband, Inc., Sunrise Telecom Pro.Tel Division S.r.l., Taiwan Sunrise Telecom Company Limited

Officers: Scott Clough/Regional Sales Dir. - New York, Allan Mowat/Sunrise Telecom Sales Representative - New York, Jim Manikowski/Sunrise Telecom Sales Representative - Mississippi, James Kyle/Sunrise Telecom Sales Representative - Indiana, Jeff Miller/Sunrise Telecom Sales Representative - Nebraska, Perry Romano/VP - Sales, Eastern Region, Edd Lemoine/Sunrise Telecom Sales Representative - Connecticut, Carl Goldschmidt/Sunrise Telecom Sales Representative - Delaware, Scott Wolfe/Sunrise Telecom Regional Mgr. - Florida, Tony Bracci/Sunrise Telecom Sales Representative - Florida, Jim Knutson/Sunrise Telecom Sales Representative - Wyoming, Bob Bartnett/Sunrise Telecom Sales Representative - South Dakota, Dan Wolfe/Sunrise Telecom Regional Mgr. - Alabama, Rick Schippers/Sunrise Telecom Regional Mgr. - Alaska, Greg Murphy/Sunrise Telecom Sales Representative - Alaska *(38 Officers included in Index)*

Owners: Paul A. Marshall/23.00%, Kirk O. Williams, Robert C. Pfeiffer/12.00%, Paul Ker-Chin Chang/25.00%, Patrick Peng-Koon Ang, Henry P. Huff, Robert G. Heintz, Richard D. Kent, Insiders/62.00%, Jennifer J. Walt

Financial Data: *Fiscal Year End:*12/31 *Latest Annual Data:* 12/31/2004

Year	Sales	Net Income
2004	$61,669,000	-$7,695,000
2003	$54,949,000	-$3,870,000
2002	$54,333,000	-$4,999,000

Curr. Assets:	$63,855,000	**Curr. Liab.:**	$13,289,000		
Plant, Equip.:	$27,176,000	**Total Liab.:**	$14,302,000	**Indic. Yr. Divd.:**	NA
Total Assets:	$109,492,000	**Net Worth:**	$95,190,000	**Debt/ Equity:**	0.0084

Sunset Brands Inc

10990 Wilshire Blvd., Ste. 1220, Los Angeles, CA, 90024; *PH:* 1-310-478-4600

General - Incorporation	NV	**Stock**- Price on:12/24/2007	NA
Employees	NA	Stock Exchange	OTC
Auditor	Hansen, Barnett & Maxwell P.C.	Ticker Symbol	SSBN
Stk Agt	Continental Stock T & T Co.	Outstanding Shares	NA
Counsel	NA	E.P.S	-$0.764
DUNS No.	NA	Shareholders	NA

Business: The groups principle activity is a producer of nutritious food products in selected market segments.The group markets its products under the tradenames include Uncle Sam (R) Cereal, Farina(R), Erewho (R), New Morning(TM) and Skinners Raisin Bran(R). In November 2005, the group acquired US Mills. The group operates from the United States.

Primary SIC and add'l.: 2043

CIK No: 0001137149

Subsidiaries: Low Carb Creations, Inc, U.S. Mills, Inc.

Financial Data: *Fiscal Year End:*12/31 *Latest Annual Data:* 12/31/2005

Year	Sales	Net Income
2005	$2,186,000	-$14,941,000
2004	$2,227,000	-$3,621,000
2003	NA	-$18,000

Curr. Assets:	$116,000	**Curr. Liab.:**	$4,359,000		
Plant, Equip.:	$3,000	**Total Liab.:**	$4,362,000	**Indic. Yr. Divd.:**	NA
Total Assets:	$19,596,000	**Net Worth:**	$32,402,000	**Debt/ Equity:**	NA

Sunstone Hotel Investors Inc

903 Calle Amanecer, San Clemente, CA, 92673; *PH:* 1-949-369-4000; *http://* www.sunstonehotels.com; *Email:* InvestorRelations@sunstonehotels.com

General - Incorporation	MD	**Stock**- Price on:12/24/2007	$28.79
Employees	68	Stock Exchange	NYSE
Auditor	Ernst & Young LLP	Ticker Symbol	SHO
Stk Agt	American Stock Transfer & Trust Co.	Outstanding Shares	62,450,000
Counsel	NA	E.P.S	$1.45
DUNS No.	NA	Shareholders	NA

Business: The groups principle activities include operating and owning luxury, upper upscale and upscale hotels. The groups hotels brand names include Marriott, Hilton, Hyatt, Fairmont and Starwood. In the year 2006, the group acquired Dulbletree Guest Suites Hotel. The group operates from the United States.

Primary SIC and add'l.: 6798 7011

CIK No: 0001295810

Subsidiaries: Sunstone Hotel Partnership, LLC, Sunstone Hotel TRS Lessee, Inc.

Officers: Robert A. Alter/Executive Chmn., CEO/$2,698,417.00, Steven R. Goldman/Dir., CEO, Habib Enayetullah/Sr. VP - Development/$854,260.00, Christopher Lal/VP, General Counsel, Olivier Kolpin/VP - Tax, Thomas K. Naughton/Sr. VP - Acquisitions, Ken Cruse/CFO, Jon D. Kline/41/Pres./$1,540,757.00, Gary A. Stougaard/53/Exec. VP, Chief Investment Officer/$1,364,522.00, Marc A. Hoffman/Sr. VP - Asset Management, William M. Wagner/Chief Accounting Officer, Sr. VP, Lindsay N. Monge/VP, Treasurer, Bryan Giglia/VP - Corporate Finance, Hunter Oliver/VP - Acquisitions, Randy Hulce/VP - Asset Management

Directors: Robert A. Alter/Executive Chmn., CEO, Steven R. Goldman/Dir., CEO, Lewis N. Wolff/Co - Chmn., Jamie Z. Behar/Dir., Anthony W. Dona/Dir., Keith P. Russell/Dir., Thomas A. Lewis/Dir., Keith M. Locker/Dir.

Owners: AXA Financial, Inc. and affiliated companies/7.20%, Anthony W. Dona, Keith M. Locker, J.P. Morgan Chase & Co/5.70%, Thomas A. Lewis, Capital Research and Management Company/6.40%, The Vanguard Group, Inc./6.00%, Security Capital Research & Management Incorporated and Security Pacific Capital Preferred Growth I/100.00%, Keith P. Russell, Barclays Global Investors, N.A./6.60%, Kenneth E. Cruse, Jon D. Kline, Insiders/1.70%, Steven R. Goldman, Lewis N. Wolff *(19 Owners included in Index)*

Financial Data: *Fiscal Year End:*12/31 *Latest Annual Data:* 12/31/2006

Year	Sales	Net Income
2006	$903,056,000	$53,237,000
2005	$651,068,000	$30,205,000
2004	$502,664,000	-$36,100,000

Curr. Assets:	$147,871,000	**Curr. Liab.:**	$140,268,000	**P/E Ratio:**	84.68
Plant, Equip.:	$2,493,917,000	**Total Liab.:**	$1,623,294,000	**Indic. Yr. Divd.:**	$1.400
Total Assets:	$2,760,373,000	**Net Worth:**	$1,037,783,000	**Debt/ Equity:**	1.7525

Suntech Power Holdings Co Ltd

188 The Embarcadero, Ste. 800, San Francisco, CA, 94105; *PH:* 1-415-882-9922; *Fax:* 1-415-882-9923; *http://* www.suntech-power.com

General - Incorporation	Cayman Islands	**Stock**- Price on:12/24/2007	$33.2566
Employees	NA	Stock Exchange	NYSE
Auditor	Deloitte Touche Tohmatsu CPA Ltd	Ticker Symbol	STP
Stk Agt	Bank of New York	Outstanding Shares	150,490,000
Counsel	NA	E.P.S	NA
DUNS No.	NA	Shareholders	NA

Business: The groups principle activities include designing, developing, manufacturing and marketing PV cells and modules. In the year 2005, the group acquired Jiangsu Huariyuan Electronics Technology Co., Ltd. The group operates from the United State, China, Germany and Spain. The group's quarterly revenue of september 2007 was 386.65 millions of USD.

Primary SIC and add'l.: 3629 3692 3674

CIK No: 0001342803

Subsidiaries: Eucken Capital Limited, Jiangsu Huariyuan Electronics Technology Co. Ltd, Luoyang Suntech Power Co., Ltd, Power Solar System Co., Ltd, Power Solar System Pty. Ltd., Quighai suntech Nima Solar Power Co., Ltd, Wuxi Shangneng Photovoltaic Science System Co. Ltd, Wuxi Suntech Power Co., Ltd.,

Officers: Zhengrong Shi/Chmn., CEO, Jingjia Ji/Dir. - Sr. Research Scientist, Amy Yi Zhang/Dir., CFO, Graham Artes/COO, Stuart Wenham/CTO, Guangchun Zhang/Deputy Research Dir. - Research, Development, Yichuan Wang/Dir., Mgr. - PV Cell Research, Development, Roger Efird/Pres. - America, Jerry Stokes/Pres. - Suntechs European Region, Steven Chan/Chief Strategy Officer, Boxun Zhang/Financial Controller - in Accounting Department, Zhi Hao/Investment Controller, Cindy Shao/Investor Relations Officer, Roger Ye/Sales Dir., Wu Hongyan/Marketing Dir.

Directors: Zhengrong Shi/Chmn., CEO, Chengyu Fu/Dir., Jingjia Ji/Dir. - Sr. Research Scientist, Zhi Zhong Qiu/Dir., Julian Ralph Worley/Dir., Songyi Zhang/Dir., Amy Yi Zhang/Dir., CFO, Yichuan Wang/Dir., Mgr. - PV Cell Research, Development

Owners: Goldman, Sachs & Co/7.10%, Goldman Sachs Group, Inc/7.10%, Zhengrong Shi/38.60%, D&M Technologies Limited/38.30%, FMR Corp/11.20%, Janus Capital Management LLC/5.30%

Financial Data: *Fiscal Year End:* 12/31   *Latest Annual Data:* 12/31/2006

Year	Sales		Net Income
2006	$598,870,000		$106,002,000
2005	$226,000,000		$30,628,000
2004	$85,288,000		$19,757,000
Curr. Assets:	$716,408,000	**Curr. Liab.:** $356,823,000	**P/E Ratio:** 84.68
Plant, Equip.:	$113,750,000	**Total Liab.:** $445,492,000	**Indic. Yr. Divd.:** NA
Total Assets:	$1,097,955,000	**Net Worth:** $652,463,000	**Debt/ Equity:** NA

Suntron Corp

2401 W Grandview, Phoenix, AZ, 85023; *PH:* 1-602-789-6600; *http://* www.suntroncorp.com; *Email:* ir@suntroncorp.com

General - Incorporation	DE	**Stock** - Price on: 12/24/2007	$1.18
Employees	1,240	Stock Exchange	NA
Auditor	KPMG LLP	Ticker Symbol	NA
Stk Agt	Computershare Trust Co	Outstanding Shares	27,590,000
Counsel	NA	E.P.S.	-$0.45
DUNS No.	NA	Shareholders	NA

Business: The group's principal activity is to provide manufacturing services and solutions to support the entire life cycle of complex products in the semiconductor capital equipment, aerospace and defense, medical and industrial markets. The group's manufacturing services includes printed circuit card assembly and testing, electronic interconnect assemblies, subassemblies, sheet metal fabrication and powder paint, plastic injection molding, and full systems integration, after-Market repair and warranty services and engineering and design services. In addition, the group also provides to its customer product development and design and test engineering services. The major customers of the group are honeywell international, inc. And applied materials, inc. On 30-May-2003, the group acquired trilogic systems, llc.

Primary SIC and add'l.: 3672 6719 8711

CIK No: 0001160513

Subsidiaries: CathiO LLC, Current Electronics, Inc., EFTC Operating Corp., KTEC Operating Corp., RM Electronics Inc., RodniC LLC, Suntron Corporation, Suntron de Mexico S. De R.L. de C. V., Suntron GCO, L.P., Suntron-Iowa, Inc., Suntron-Kansas, Inc.

Officers: Hargopal Singh/Dir., CEO, Pres., Jim Doran/Chief Accounting Officer, Sec., Treasurer, James Doran/CFO, Sec., Glenn Hunter/VP - Human Resources, Corporate Services, Suresh Chohan/VP - Materials, Mike Churchill/VP - Operations, NEE, NEX, NED, SWE, SWO, James Cogan/VP - Operations, NMO, NWO, Corporate Contracts, Tom Sabol/Dir., CFO, Brian Throneberry/VP - Sales, Marketing

Directors: Hargopal Singh/Dir., CEO, Pres., Ivor J. Evans/Chmn., Scott D. Rued/Dir., Marc Scholvinck/Dir., William Urkiel/Dir., Doug McCormick/Dir., Allen S. Braswell/Dir., Tom Sabol/Dir., CFO, Jim Forese/Dir., Kurt D. Grindstaff/Dir.

Owners: Marc T. Schlvinck, Hargopal Singh, Scott D. Rued, Douglas P. McCormick, William S. Urkiel, James A. Doran, Allen S. Braswell, Insiders, Kurt D. Grindstaff, Thayer-Blum Funding III, L.L.C., Ivor J. Evans, James J. Forese, Thomas B. Sabol

Financial Data: *Fiscal Year End:* 12/31   *Latest Annual Data:* 12/31/2006

Year	Sales		Net Income
2006	$320,786,000		-$11,879,000
2005	$328,730,000		-$11,342,000
2004	$475,388,000		-$4,457,000
Curr. Assets:	$98,026,000	**Curr. Liab.:** $60,253,000	
Plant, Equip.:	$5,184,000	**Total Liab.:** $73,361,000	**Indic. Yr. Divd.:** NA
Total Assets:	$116,913,000	**Net Worth:** $43,552,000	**Debt/ Equity:** 0.2810

Suntrust Banks Inc

919 E Main St., Richmond, VA, 23219; *PH:* 1-804-782-7107; *http://* www.suntrust.com

General - Incorporation	GA	**Stock** - Price on: 12/24/2007	$88.54
Employees	33,599	Stock Exchange	NYSE
Auditor	PricewaterhouseCoopers LLP	Ticker Symbol	STI
Stk Agt	Computershare Acquires SunTrust	Outstanding Shares	356,620,000
Counsel	NA	E.P.S.	$6.19
DUNS No.	14-443-7795	Shareholders	NA

Business: The groups principle activity is to provide financial services. The groups services include mortgage banking, insurance, asset management, brokerage and capital market services. The group operates from United States.

Primary SIC and add'l.: 6799 6021 6282 6712

CIK No: 0000750556

Subsidiaries: 2002 Cdc Manager, LLC, 2003 Cdc Manager, LLC, 2004 Cdc Manager, LLC, 2005 Cdc Manager, LLC, 98-02 Cdc Manager, LLC, Abundance, LLC, Admiral Pointe Management, LLC, Admiral Pointe, L.P., AMA Holdings, Inc., AMA/Lighthouse, Inc., Arrington Place, L.P., Artcraft Afton Gardens, L.P., Artcraft James Crossing, L.P., Asset Management Advisors Eagle, LLC, Asset Management Advisors Atlanta, LLC 366 Subsidiaries included in the Index

Officers: Sterling Edmunds/CEO, Pres. - Suntrust Mortgage, Inc, James M. Wells/Dir., CEO, Pres./$5,684,621.00, Phillip L. Humann/62/Exec. Chmn./$7,565,439.00, William H. Rogers/Corporate Exec. VP/$1,704,071.00, Dennis M. Patterson/Corporate Sales Administration, Craig J. Kelly/Chief Marketing Exec., Mimi Breeden/Dir. - Human Resources, Mike McCoy/Contact - Media, Barry Koling/Contact - Media, Thomas E. Freeman/Chief Risk Officer, Raymond D. Fortin/General Counsel, Corp. Sec., Thomas E. Panther/39/Sr. VP, Controller, Chief Accounting Officer, Timothy E. Sullivan/CIO, David F. Dierker/Chief Administrative Officer, Mark A. Chancy/CFO/$1,556,851.00 *(17 Officers included in Index)*

Directors: James M. Wells/Dir., CEO, Pres., William R. Reed/Vice Chmn., Phillip L. Humann/62/Exec. Chmn., Jeffrey C. Crowe/Dir., Blake P. Garrett/Dir., Patricia C. Frist/Dir., Thomas C. Farnsworth/Dir., Phail Wynn/Dir., Hicks J. Lanier/Dir., Robert M. Beall/Dir., Gilmer G. Minor/Dir., Hyatt J. Brown/Dir., Larry L. Prince/Dir., Alston D. Correll/Dir., Frank S. Royal/Dir. *(19 Directors included in Index)*

Owners: Hyatt J. Brown, William H. Rogers, Neville E. Isdell, Karen Hastie Williams, Hicks J. Lanier, Phail Wynn, Jeffrey C. Crowe, Robert M. Beall, Alston D. Correll, David H. Hughes, Gilmer G. Minor, Blake P. Garrett, James M. Wells, Phillip L. Humann, Frank S. Royal *(23 Owners included in Index)*

Financial Data: *Fiscal Year End:* 12/31   *Latest Annual Data:* 12/31/2006

Year	Sales		Net Income
2006	$13,310,869,000		$2,117,471,000
2005	$10,893,508,000		$1,987,239,000
2004	$7,864,519,000		$1,572,901,000
Curr. Assets:	$8,101,252,000	**Curr. Liab.:** $137,918,160,000	**P/E Ratio:** 14.30
Plant, Equip.:	$1,977,412,000	**Total Liab.:** $164,348,003,000	**Indic. Yr. Divd.:** $2.920
Total Assets:	$182,161,609,000	**Net Worth:** $17,813,606,000	**Debt/ Equity:** 1.5073

SunVesta Inc

Formerly: Openlimit Inc

Zugerstrasse 76 B, Baar, CH 6341; *PH:* 41-41-560-1023; *http://* www.openlimit.com

General - Incorporation	FL	**Stock** - Price on: 12/24/2007	$0.038
Employees	NA	Stock Exchange	OTC
Auditor	Staley, Okada & Partners	Ticker Symbol	SVSA
Stk Agt	Standard Registrar & Transfer Co Inc.	Outstanding Shares	NA
Counsel	NA	E.P.S.	NA
DUNS No.	NA	Shareholders	NA

Business: The groups principle activities include developing, marketing and selling electronic signature and encryption software products. The groups products include OPENLiMiT(r) Products, OPENLiMiT(R) Reader 2.1 and OPENLiMiT(R) CC Sign. The group operates from United States.

Primary SIC and add'l.: NA

CIK No: 0001060409

Subsidiaries: OPENLiMiT Access Marketing AG, OpenLimit AG:

Officers: Heinrich Dattler/Chmn., CEO, Frank Jeschka/CTO, Marc J. Gurov/Dir., CFO, Armin Lukeit/MD - Openlimit Signcubes Gmbh, Thomas Hugi/Dir., COO, Reinhard Stuber/Dir., Sr. VP - Business Development

Directors: Heinrich Dattler/Chmn., CEO, Marc J. Gurov/Dir., CFO, Eduard Egloff/Dir., Thomas Hugi/Dir., COO, Reinhard Stuber/Dir., Sr. VP - Business Development, Urs Heinrich Winzenried/Dir., Rene C. Jaggi/Dir.

Owners: Henry Dattler/14.40%, Insiders/14.40%

Financial Data: *Fiscal Year End:* 12/31   *Latest Annual Data:* 12/31/2006

Year	Sales		Net Income
2006	NA		$6,000
2005	NA		-$3,185,000
2004	$830,000		-$4,416,000
Curr. Assets:	$1,000	**Curr. Liab.:** $20,000	
Plant, Equip.:	NA	**Total Liab.:** $20,000	**Indic. Yr. Divd.:** NA
Total Assets:	$1,000	**Net Worth:** -$19,000	**Debt/ Equity:** NA

Sunwest Bank CA

17542 17th St. Ste. 200, Tustin, CA, 92780; *PH:* 1-714-730-4441; *http://* www.sunwestbank.com

General - Incorporation		**Stock** - Price on: 12/24/2007	$2850
Employees	70	Stock Exchange	OTC
Auditor	NA	Ticker Symbol	SWBC
Stk Agt	American Stock Transfer & Trust Co.	Outstanding Shares	NA
Counsel	NA	E.P.S.	$118.30
DUNS No.	NA	Shareholders	NA

Business: The groups principal activities include custom banking and financial solutions designed to help your business forward. The groups financing options to convenient treasury services, entrepreneurs with the tools to grow their business. The group operates from the United States.

Primary SIC and add'l.: 6022

CIK No:

Officers: Glenn Gray/Dir., CEO, Pres., Francisca Rivera/VP, Branch Mgr. - Newport Beach, Brian Constable/Exec. VP, Chief Commercial Banking Officer, Jason Raefski/CFO, Exec. VP, Milton Flores/Chief Accounting Officer, Sr. VP, Jim Bradley/Sr. VP, Sr. Relationship Mgr. - Commercial Banking, Ken Smith/Sr. VP, Regional Mgr. - Commercial Banking, Benjamin Frank/VP, Relationship Mgr. - Commercial Banking, John Treiber/VP, Relationship Mgr. - Commercial Banking, Lisa Sacquety/VP, Relationship Mgr. - Commercial Banking, Matt Roberson/Sr. VP, Relationship Mgr. - Commercial Banking, Debra Kupp/VP, Cash Management Sales Officer - Commercial Banking, Leah Beal/Sr. VP, Division Mgr. - California, Arizona, Nevada, Sheila Adams/VP, Relationship Mgr. - Northern California, Nevada, Joni Delacqua/VP, Relationship Mgr. - Sunwest Financial, Arizona *(19 Officers included in Index)*

Directors: Glenn Gray/Dir., CEO, Pres., Eric D. Hovde/Dir., Irving R. Beimler/Dir., Tara O. Balfour/Dir., Michael A. Cohen/Dir., Karen D. Conlon/Dir., Cassandra M. Hoag/Dir., Glen R. Mozingo/Dir., Russ Wertz/Dir., Ron Howarth/Dir.

Financial Data: *Fiscal Year End:* NA   *Latest Annual Data:* 12/31/2002

Year	Sales		Net Income
2002	$17,472,000		$2,202,000
2001	$17,328,000		$2,228,000
2000	$17,380,000		$1,387,000
Curr. Assets:	$17,277,000	**Curr. Liab.:** $243,063,000	**P/E Ratio:** 24.09
Plant, Equip.:	$1,282,000	**Total Liab.:** $244,836,000	**Indic. Yr. Divd.:** NA
Total Assets:	$273,591,000	**Net Worth:** $28,755,000	**Debt/ Equity:** NA

Sunwin International Neutraceuticals Inc

6 Youpeng Rd. , Qufu, Shandong, 273100; *PH:* 86-5374424999; *Fax:* 86-5374413350; *http://* www.sunwin.biz; *Email:* info@sunwin.biz

General - Incorporation	NV	*Stock*- Price on:12/24/2007	$0.64
Employees	NA	Stock Exchange	OTC
Auditor	Sherb & Co. LLP	Ticker Symbol	SUWN
Stk Agt	Colonial Stock Transfer Co Inc	Outstanding Shares	NA
Counsel	NA	E.P.S.	NA
DUNS No.	NA	Shareholders	NA

Business: The groups principle activity is to provide stevioside, a natural sweetener, as well as veterinary products and herbs used in traditional Chinese medicine. The groups products line includes stevioside, a natural sweetener. The group operates from United States.

Primary SIC and add'l.: NA

CIK No: 0000806592

Subsidiaries: Qufu Natural Green Engineering Company, Limited, Sunwin (Canada) Pharmaceutical LTD, Sunwin California, Inc, Sunwin Stevia International Corp, Sunwin Tech Group, Inc

Officers: Dongdong Lin/Dir., CEO, Sec., Laiwang Zhang/Chmn., Pres., Fanjun Wu/CFO

Directors: Dongdong Lin/Dir., CEO, Sec., Laiwang Zhang/Chmn., Pres., Chengxiang Yan/Dir.

Owners: Laiwang Zhang/14.40%, Dongdong Lin/5.70%, Fanjun Wu/2.00%, Insiders/22.10%

Financial Data: Fiscal Year End:04/30   Latest Annual Data: 4/30/2006

Year	Sales	Net Income
2006	$15,490,000	$2,430,000
2005	$12,114,000	$829,000
2004	$10,888,000	$465,000

Curr. Assets:	$10,789,000	*Curr. Liab.:*	$1,881,000		
Plant, Equip.:	$5,376,000	*Total Liab.:*	$2,015,000	*Indic. Yr. Divd.:*	NA
Total Assets:	$16,165,000	*Net Worth:*	$14,150,000	*Debt/ Equity:*	NA

Supcor Inc

Rm. 3106, Bldg. B, No. 39 E 3rd Ring Middle Rd., Chaoyang District, Beijing, 100022; *PH:* 86-10-58693011

General - Incorporation	DE	*Stock*- Price on:12/24/2007	NA
Employees	NA	Stock Exchange	NA
Auditor Child, Van Wagoner & Bradshaw, PLLC		Ticker Symbol	NA
Stk Agt	NA	Outstanding Shares	NA
Counsel	NA	E.P.S.	NA
DUNS No.	NA	Shareholders	NA

Business: The groups principle activity is to provide oil & energy exploration services. The group operates from United States.

Primary SIC and add'l.: 6770

CIK No: 0001300734

Subsidiaries: Tenet Jove., Tian Bai, Tian Yi Hua Tai, Tianjin

Owners: Guocong Zhou/12.65%, Shuangpeng Tian/12.65%, Guiqing Liu/5.84%, Min Zhao/19.47%, Yuying Zhang/29.20%, Li Shi/8.76%, Insiders/50.61%, Weixing Yin/8.76%

Super Deal.com Inc

100 Village Sq. Crossing, Ste 202, Palm Beach Gardens, FL, 33410; *PH:* 1-561-207-6395; *http://* www.ecomecom.net

General - Incorporation	FL	*Stock*- Price on:12/24/2007	NA
Employees	NA	Stock Exchange	NA
Auditor	Wieseneck, Andres & Co P.A	Ticker Symbol	NA
Stk Agt	Florida Atlantic Stock Transfer, Inc.	Outstanding Shares	NA
Counsel	NA	E.P.S.	NA
DUNS No.	NA	Shareholders	NA

Business: The groups principle activity is to provide marketing services for authentic hand-signed sports. The group operates from United States.

Primary SIC and add'l.: 9995

CIK No: 0001321507

Subsidiaries: eCom eCom.com, Inc.

Officers: Barney A. Richmond/56/Chmn., Pres., Sec., Richard C. Turner/48/Dir., Treasurer, CFO

Directors: Barney A. Richmond/56/Chmn., Pres., Sec., Richard C. Turner/48/Dir., Treasurer, CFO

Owners: Insiders/19.50%, Barney A. Richmond/18.00%, Richard C. Turner/1.50%, United States Financial Group/8.30%, American Capital Holdings/34.30%

Superclick Inc

10222 St. Michel, Ste. 300, Montreal, QC, H1H-5H1; *PH:* 1-866-271-0333; *Fax:* 1-514-847-9122; *http://* www.superclick.com

General - Incorporation	WA	*Stock*- Price on:12/24/2007	$0.2
Employees	NA	Stock Exchange	OTC
Auditor	Bedinger & Company	Ticker Symbol	SPCK
Stk Agt	American Stock Transfer & Trust Co.	Outstanding Shares	NA
Counsel	NA	E.P.S.	NA
DUNS No.	NA	Shareholders	NA

Business: The groups principal activities include providing IP based data management solutions via its Internet management system supported by a 24x7 customer support center to the hospitality market. The group operates from the United States and Canada.

Primary SIC and add'l.: 4822

CIK No: 0001104891

Officers: Sandro Natale/CEO, Pres., Jean Perrotti/CFO

Directors: Todd M. Pitcher/Chmn., George Vesnaver/Dir., Paul Gulyas/Dir., Chirag Patel/Dir.

Owners: George Vesnaver, Sandro Natale/18.83%, Chirag Patel/2.19%, Todd M. Pitcher/1.13%, Jean Perrotti/7.30%, Insiders/31.31%, Paul Gulyas

---

Financial Data: Fiscal Year End:10/31   Latest Annual Data: 10/31/2006

Year	Sales	Net Income
2006	$3,946,000	-$2,400,000
2005	$3,206,000	-$4,284,000
2004	$2,553,000	-$979,000

Curr. Assets:	$1,556,000	*Curr. Liab.:*	$4,412,000		
Plant, Equip.:	$251,000	*Total Liab.:*	$4,438,000	*Indic. Yr. Divd.:*	NA
Total Assets:	$1,807,000	*Net Worth:*	-$2,631,000	*Debt/ Equity:*	NA

SuperCom Inc

PO Box 2094, Ra; *PH:* 972-977-50800; *http://* www.supercomgroup.com

General - Incorporation	Israel	*Stock*- Price on:12/24/2007	NA
Employees	NA	Stock Exchange	NDQ
Auditor	Bdo Mccabe Lo Ltd.	Ticker Symbol	VUNC
Stk Agt	American Stock Transfer & Trust Co.	Outstanding Shares	NA
Counsel	NA	E.P.S.	$0.65
DUNS No.	NA	Shareholders	NA

Business: The group's principle activities include designing, developing and marketing advanced smart card technologies and products for the governmental and commercial secured identification markets. The group operates from United States.

Primary SIC and add'l.: 3674

CIK No: 0001291855

Subsidiaries: InkSure Technologies, Inc., Pure RF Inc, SuperCom Asia Pacific Ltd., SuperCom Slovakia

Officers: Eyal Tuchman/CEO, Moshe Wolfson/Exec. VP - Sales NA, Joel Konicek/COO, Lior Maza/CFO, Ron Peer/Sr. Exec. VP - Marketing, Technology, Business Development, Jim Perutkca/CTO

Directors: Eli Rozen/Chmn., Avi Landman/Dir., Michal Brikman/Dir., Ilan Horesh/Dir., Jaime Shulman/Dir., James R. Woolsey/Member - Advisory Board, Neil C. Livingstone/Member - Advisory Board, Oliver Revell/Member - Advisory Board

Owners: Avi Landman/10.32%, Special Situations Cayman Fund, L.P./31.51%, Special Situations Fund III, L.P./31.51%, Jacob Hassan/9.94%, Investor through convertible bond/13.12%, Eli Rozen/15.45%, Special Situations Fund III, Q.P./31.51%

Financial Data: Fiscal Year End:12/31   Latest Annual Data: 12/31/2005

Year	Sales	Net Income
2005	$8,462,000	-$3,951,000
2004	$7,344,000	-$1,872,000

Curr. Assets:	$17,992,000	*Curr. Liab.:*	$5,452,000		
Plant, Equip.:	$160,000	*Total Liab.:*	$8,097,000	*Indic. Yr. Divd.:*	NA
Total Assets:	$23,098,000	*Net Worth:*	$15,001,000	*Debt/ Equity:*	NA

Superconductor Technologies Inc

460 Ward Dr., Santa Barbara, CA, 93111; *PH:* 1-805-690-4500; *http://* www.suptech.com; *Email:* info@suptech.com

General - Incorporation	DE	*Stock*- Price on:12/24/2007	$1.6403
Employees	115	Stock Exchange	NDQ
Auditor	PricewaterhouseCoopers LLP	Ticker Symbol	SCON
Stk Agt	Registrar & Transfer Co	Outstanding Shares	12,480,000
Counsel	Guth Christopher	E.P.S.	-$0.69
DUNS No.	18-476-4447	Shareholders	NA

Business: The group's principal activity is to develop, manufacture and market high performance products to service providers, systems integrators and original equipment manufacturers in the wireless telecommunications industry. The products are collectively known as superlink solutions which maximize the performance of wireless networks by improving the quality of uplink signals from subscriber terminals to network base stations and of downlink signals from network base stations to subscriber terminals. Superlink solutions consist of three unique product families: superlink rx solutions, superlink tx solutions and superplex solutions. These solutions increase the minutes of use to the subscribers as they experience better call quality, fewer dropped calls and higher speed data transmissions and allow service providers to benefit from lower capital. The group's manufacturing facility is located in santa barbara, California.

Primary SIC and add'l.: 3669 3674 8731

CIK No: 0000895665

Subsidiaries: Conductus, Inc., STI Investments Limited, Superconductor Investments (Mauritius) Limited

Officers: Jeff Quiram/Dir., CEO, Pres./$477,600.00, Robert B. Hammond/CTO, Sr. VP/$257,902.00, Michael Field/VP - Business, Legal Affairs, Terry A. White/VP - Worldwide Sales, Customer Service, Robert L. Johnson/Sr. VP - Operations/$241,059.00, Adam Shelton/VP - Product Management, Marketing/$318,569.00, Cathy Mattison/Investor Relation Officer

Directors: Jeff Quiram/Dir., CEO, Pres., John D. Lockton/Chmn., Dennis Horowitz/Dir., Lynn J. Davis/Dir., Martin A. Kaplan/Dir., David Vellequette/Dir.

Owners: Dennis J. Horowitz, Robert L. Johnson, Kopp Investment Advisors, LLC/10.00%, John D. Lockton, Robert B. Hammond, Jeffrey A. Quiram/1.00%, Lynn J. Davis, Adam Shelton, Martin A. Kaplan, Insiders/3.00%

Financial Data: Fiscal Year End:12/31   Latest Annual Data: 12/31/2006

Year	Sales	Net Income
2006	$21,078,000	-$29,624,000
2005	$24,209,000	-$14,213,000
2004	$23,004,000	-$31,217,000

Curr. Assets:	$13,507,000	*Curr. Liab.:*	$3,349,000		
Plant, Equip.:	$5,770,000	*Total Liab.:*	$3,953,000	*Indic. Yr. Divd.:*	NA
Total Assets:	$21,904,000	*Net Worth:*	$17,951,000	*Debt/ Equity:*	NA

Supergen Inc

4140 Dublin Blvd, Ste 200, Dublin, CA, 94568; *PH:* 1-925-560-0100; *http://* www.supergen.com; *Email:* careers@supergen.com

General - Incorporation DE
Employees 89
Auditor Ernst & Young LLP
Stk Agt Mellon Investor Services LLC
Counsel Wilson Sonsini Goodrich & Rosati
DUNS No. 55-711-7751

Stock- Price on:12/24/2007 $5.72
Stock Exchange NDQ
Ticker Symbol SUPG
Outstanding Shares 57,390,000
E.P.S $0.03
Shareholders NA

Business: The group's principal activity is to develop and commercialize therapies for solid tumors, hematological malignancies and blood disorders. The group's products include Orathecintm (Rubitecan) capsules, Dacogentm (Decitabine) injection and Nipent(R) (Pentostatin for injection). The other products include generic anti-cancer products used for the treatment of solid tumors and acute leukemias. Non-pharmaceutical product includes surface safe, a two-step disposable towelette cleaning system used to decontaminate work surfaces where chemotherapeutic preparation is conducted. Formulation products are used for solid tumors, neoplastic meningitis and bone marrow transplant. The products are marketed mainly to cancer hospitals, clinics, private practice oncology clinics, oncology distributors and drug wholesalers in the United States.

Primary SIC and add'l.: 2834

CIK No: 0000919722

Subsidiaries: EuroGen Pharmaceuticals Ltd., Sparta Pharmaceuticals, Inc.

Officers: James S. Manuso/Chmn., CEO, Pres./$2,755,349.00, Michael Molkentin/CFO, Corp. Sec./$600,956.00, Joi Ninomoto/VP - Medical Research, Communications, Michael McCullar/VP - Drug Discovery Operations, Timothy L. Enns/Sr. VP - Corporate Communications, Business Development, Sanjeev Redkar/VP - Manufacturing, Pre, Clinical Development, Mark Lewis/MD - Eurogen, Gregory Berk/Chief Medical Officer, David J. Bearss/VP, Chief Scientist, Member - Scientific Advisory Board, Mary M. Vegh/Mgr. - Investor Relations

Directors: James S. Manuso/Chmn., CEO, Pres., Allan R. Goldberg/Dir., Chmn. - Scientific Advisory Board, Michael Young/Dir., Thomas V. Girardi/Dir., Walter J. Lack/Dir., Charles J. Casamento/Dir., David J. Bearss/VP, Chief Scientist, Member - Scientific Advisory Board, Roger D. Kornberg/Member - Scientific Advisory Board, Daniel Von Hoff/Member - Scientific Advisory Board, Robert A. Weinberg/Member - Scientific Advisory Board

Owners: MGI PHARMA,Inc./7.00%, State of Wisconsin Investment Board/9.20%, Michael D. Young, James S.J. Manuso/3.10%, Insiders/5.70%, Walter J. Lack, Audrey F. Jakubowski, Michael Molkenti, Thomas V. Girardi, James E. Flynn and related Deerfield Capital, L.P. and affiliates/5.10%, Edward L. Jacobs, Charles J. Casamento, Allan R. Goldberg

Financial Data: *Fiscal Year End:*12/31 *Latest Annual Data:* 12/31/2006

Year	Sales	Net Income
2006	$38,083,000	-$16,487,000
2005	$30,169,000	-$14,482,000
2004	$31,993,000	-$46,860,000

Curr. Assets:	$71,688,000	**Curr. Liab.:**	$21,276,000		
Plant, Equip.:	$3,752,000	**Total Liab.:**	$22,214,000	**Indic. Yr. Divd.:**	NA
Total Assets:	$88,046,000	**Net Worth:**	$65,832,000	**Debt/ Equity:**	NA

Superior Bancorp

Formerly: Banc Corp
17 N 20th St., Birmingham, AL, 35203; ***PH:*** 1-205-326-2265; ***http://*** www.superiorbank.com

General - Incorporation DE
Employees 711
Auditor Carr, Riggs & Ingram, LLC
Stk Agt Computershare Investor Services LLC
Counsel NA
DUNS No. NA

Stock- Price on:12/24/2007 $10.26
Stock Exchange NDQ
Ticker Symbol NA
Outstanding Shares 34,660,000
E.P.S $0.22
Shareholders NA

Business: The group's principal activity is to provide a wide range of banking and related services to individuals and corporate customers across Alabama and the panhandle of Florida. The services provided by the group include commercial, automobile, consumer, residential mortgage and real estate construction loans and a variety of deposit programs to individuals and businesses. Deposits include personal checking, savings, money market and now accounts, business checking and savings accounts, investment sweep accounts and credit line sweep accounts. It also offers individual retirement accounts and investment services, safe deposit and night depository facilities, traveler's checks, money orders and cashier's checks. The group operates through 26 banking offices in Alabama and Florida.

Primary SIC and add'l.: 6712 6035

CIK No: 0001065298

Subsidiaries: Morris Avenue Management Group, Inc., SFS, LLC, Superior Bank, TBC Capital Statutory Trust II, TBC Capital Statutory Trust III, TBC Real Estate Investment Company, Inc., TBC Realty Holdings Corporation, TBNC Financial Management, Inc.

Officers: Stanley C. Bailey/Chmn., CEO/$628,185.00, Defuniak A. Fox/Dir., Pres. - Marketing, George Hall/Chief Banking Officer, David R. Hiden/CIO, Duane K. Bickings/Chief Credit Officer, Rick D. Gardner/Dir., COO, Sec./$395,762.00, James C. Gossett/45/Chief Accounting Officer/$175,833.00, William Caughran/General Counsel/$179,359.00, Marvin C. Scott/Pres./$501,977.00

Directors: Stanley C. Bailey/Chmn., CEO, Barry Morton/Dir., Defuniak A. Fox/Dir., Pres. - Marketing, Earl K. Durden/Dir., James M. Link/Dir., Robert R. Parrish/Dir., James A. Taylor/Dir., James C. White/Dir., Dewey D. Mitchell/51/Dir., Thomas E. Jernigan/Dir., James Mailon Kent/Dir., Rick D. Gardner/Dir., COO, Sec., Michael E. Stephens/Dir., Roger D. Barker/Dir.

Owners: C. Marvin Scott/1.45%, Barry Morton, Michael E. Stephens, Earl K. Durden/1.83%, James C. Gossett, Glynn C. Debter, Thomas E. Jernigan, William H. Caughran, Dewey D. Mitchell, Robert R. Parrish, Insiders/11.15%, Stanley C. Bailey/2.75%, Rick D. Gardner/1.19%, James M. Link, James Mailon Kent/1.22% *(18 Owners included in Index)*

Financial Data: *Fiscal Year End:*12/31 *Latest Annual Data:* 12/31/2006

Year	Sales	Net Income
2006	$120,588,000	$4,997,000
2005	$93,250,000	-$5,786,000
2004	$77,500,000	$1,187,000

Curr. Assets:	$100,349,000	**Curr. Liab.:**	$2,111,554,000	**P/E Ratio:**	44.61
Plant, Equip.:	$94,626,000	**Total Liab.:**	$2,164,903,000	**Indic. Yr. Divd.:**	NA
Total Assets:	$2,440,990,000	**Net Worth:**	$276,087,000	**Debt/ Equity:**	0.1925

Superior Energy Services Inc

1105 Peters Rd. , Harvey, LA, 70058; ***PH:*** 1-504-362-4321; ***http://*** www.superiorenergy.com

General - Incorporation DE
Employees 4,300
Auditor KPMG LLP
Stk Agt Bank One, Michigan
Counsel Jones Walker Waechter Poitevent Et Al
DUNS No. 93-363-2952

Stock- Price on:12/24/2007 $40.7
Stock Exchange NYSE
Ticker Symbol SPN
Outstanding Shares 80,700,000
E.P.S $3.30
Shareholders NA

Business: The group's principal activities are to provide oilfield services and equipment to oil and gas companies. The group offers well intervention, marine, environmental, field management, and wireline services. Products of the group include housing accessories, living quarters, drilling tools, pressure control equipment, and computer-based data acquisition and monitoring products. The rental tools segment manufactures, sells and rents specialized equipment for use in oil and gas well drilling. In October 2006 the company acquired Houston-based Warrior Energy Services Corp. The group mainly operates in the Gulf of Mexico and has rental tool operations in Venezula, Trinidad, Canada and United Kingdom.

Primary SIC and add'l.: 7359 1389 6719 1381 3533

CIK No: 0000886835

Subsidiaries: 1105 Peters Road, LLC, Ace Rental Tools, LLC, Blowout Tools, Inc., Concentric Pipe and Tool Rentals, LLC, Connection Technology, LLC, CSI Technologies, LLC, Drilling Logistics, LLC, F & F Wireline Services, LLC, Fastorq, LLC, H.B Rentals, L.C., International Snubbing Services, LLC, J.R.B. Consultants, Inc., Non-Magnetic Rental Tools, LLC, Oil Stop, LLC, Premier Oilfield Rentals Limited 42 Subsidiaries included in the Index

Officers: Terence E. Hall/Chmn., CEO - Superior Energy Services, Inc/$2,219,973.00, Kenneth L. Blanchard/COO, Pres./$1,227,756.00, James M. Funk/Dir. - Oil, Gas Consultant, Robert S. Taylor/CFO/$819,885.00

Directors: Terence E. Hall/Chmn., CEO - Superior Energy Services, Inc, Enoch Dawkins/Dir., Harold J. Bouillion/Dir., Justin L. Sullivan/Dir., James M. Funk/Dir. - Oil, Gas Consultant, Ernest E. Howard/Dir., Richard A. Pattarozzi/Dir.

Owners: Patrick A. Bernard, Insiders/3.70%, Ernest E. Howard, Justin L. Sullivan, James M. Funk, Terence E. Hall/1.40%, Enoch L. Dawkins, FMR Corp./8.60%, Kenneth L. Blanchard, Danny R. Young, Richard A. Pattarozzi, Robert S. Taylor, Harold J. Bouillion

Financial Data: *Fiscal Year End:*12/31 *Latest Annual Data:* 12/31/2006

Year	Sales	Net Income
2006	$1,093,821,000	$188,241,000
2005	$735,334,000	$67,859,000
2004	$564,339,000	$35,852,000

Curr. Assets:	$419,787,000	**Curr. Liab.:**	$243,095,000	**P/E Ratio:**	15.07
Plant, Equip.:	$804,228,000	**Total Liab.:**	$1,163,790,000	**Indic. Yr. Divd.:**	NA
Total Assets:	$1,874,478,000	**Net Worth:**	$710,688,000	**Debt/ Equity:**	0.9166

Superior Essex Inc

150 Interstate N Pkwy., Atlanta, GA, 30339; ***PH:*** 1-770-657-6000; ***http://*** www.superioressex.com; ***Email:*** investor_relations@superioressex.com

General - Incorporation DE
Employees 4,100
Auditor Deloitte & Touche LLP
Stk Agt American Stock Transfer & Trust Co.
Counsel NA
DUNS No. NA

Stock- Price on:12/24/2007 $36.7
Stock Exchange NDQ
Ticker Symbol SPSX
Outstanding Shares 20,420,000
E.P.S $2.69
Shareholders NA

Business: The groups principle activity is to manufacture wire and cable manufacturers. The products of the group include LAN copper twisted pair, LAN coaxial cable and voice grade twisted copper pair. The groups operates through four segments namely communications cable, North American magnet wire and distribution, European magnet wire and distribution and copper rod. Customers served by the group include telephone companies, cable television and CATV. In October21, 2005, the group acquired Nexans magnet wire operations. The group operates from the United States. The group's quarterly revenue for September 2007 was 781.41 millions of USD.

Primary SIC and add'l.: 3357 3629 3677

CIK No: 0001271193

Subsidiaries: Essex Group Mexico Inc., Essex Group, Inc., Essex International Inc., Essex Nexans Europe S.A.S., Essex Nexans L&K GmbH, Essex Nexans S.A.S., Essex Nexans U.K., SE Holdings, C.V., Superior Essex Communications LP, Superior Essex Holding Corp.

Officers: Stephen M. Carter/Dir., CEO, Pres./$4,329,821.00, David S. Aldridge/CFO, Exec. VP, Treasurer/$2,039,082.00, Debbie Baker-Oliver/Sr. VP - Corporate Administrative Services, Barbara L. Blackford/Exec. VP, General Counsel, Sec./$990,426.00, Tracye C. Gilleland/Sr. VP - Finance, Corporate Controller, Patrick H. Jack/Pres. - Essex Asia Pacific, Exec. VP - Superior Essex Inc/$1,829,243.00, Justin F. Deedy/Exec. VP/$1,814,935.00, David J. Reed/Exec. VP

Directors: Stephen M. Carter/Dir., CEO, Pres., Monte R. Haymon/Chmn., Andrew P. Hines/Dir., Thomas H. Johnson/Dir., Perry J. Lewis/Dir., Stephanie W. Bergeron/Dir., Denys Gounot/Dir., James F. Guthrie/Dir., Joseph M. O'Donnell/Dir.

Owners: Thomas H. Johnson, Stephen M. Carter/1.26%, Denys Gounot, Patrick H. Jack, Justin F. Deedy, Goldman Sachs Asset Management, LP/8.89%, Monte R. Haymon, Barbara L. Blackford, James F. Guthrie, David S. Aldridge, FMR Corp/8.58%, Perry J. Lewis, Insiders/3.76%, Carlo J. Cannell/5.03%, Marathon Asset Management LLP/16.48% *(16 Owners included in Index)*

Financial Data: *Fiscal Year End:*12/31 *Latest Annual Data:* 12/31/2006

Year	Sales	Net Income
2006	$2,938,153,000	$57,349,000
2005	$1,794,966,000	$31,912,000
2004	$1,424,641,000	$10,488,000

Curr. Assets:	$725,325,000	**Curr. Liab.:**	$287,094,000	**P/E Ratio:**	13.64
Plant, Equip.:	$258,480,000	**Total Liab.:**	$667,831,000	**Indic. Yr. Divd.:**	NA
Total Assets:	$1,026,819,000	**Net Worth:**	$358,988,000	**Debt/ Equity:**	0.7991

Superior Galleries Inc

9478 W Olympic Blvd, Beverly Hills, CA, 90212; ***PH:*** 1-310-203-9855; ***http://*** www.superiorgalleries.com; ***Email:*** info@sgbh.com

General - Incorporation DE
Employees NA
Auditor Haskell & White LLP
Stk Agt Cede & Co
Counsel NA
DUNS No. NA

Stock- Price on:12/24/2007 NA
Stock Exchange NA
Ticker Symbol NA
Outstanding Shares NA
E.P.S NA
Shareholders NA

Business: The group's principle activity is the sale of rare coins, jewelry, fine art and collectibles. The group sells these items on retail, wholesale and auction basis. The retail and wholesale operations are conducted in every state of the United States and several foreign countries. The group's services are marketed nationwide through broadcasting and print media and independent sales agents, as well as on the Internet through third party websites such as ebay and yahoo.

Primary SIC and add'l.: 5699 5999

CIK No: 0001091539

Subsidiaries: DGSE Merger Corp., Superior Galleries Beverly Hills, Inc.

Officers: Paul Inho Song/VP - Auctions, Paul Biberkraut/Dir., Sec., Exec. VP, CFO, Mike Bonham/Rare Coin Portfolio's, Auction Consignments, Larry Abbott/COO, Exec. VP, Dirk Schader/Numismatics, Jason Garnett/Dir. - Auction Operations, Bryan Abbott/Sr. Buyer, Auction Advisor, Paul Simonetti/VP - Numismatics, James Jones/Dir. - Cataloging

Directors: Paul Biberkraut/Dir., Sec., Exec. VP, CFO, Tony Friscia/Dir., Lee Ittner/Dir., David Rector/Dir.

Superior Industries International Inc

7800 Woodley Ave., Van Nuys, CA, 91406; *PH:* 1-818-784-4973; *http://* www.superiorindustries.com

General - Incorporation	CA	**Stock**- Price on:12/24/2007	$21.99
Employees	5,700	Stock Exchange	NYSE
Auditor	PricewaterhouseCoopers LLP	Ticker Symbol	SUP
Stk Agt	Daniel L. Levine	Outstanding Shares	26,610,000
Counsel	Irell & Manella	E.P.S.	-$0.29
DUNS No.	05-080-9177	Shareholders	NA

Business: The group's principal activities are to design and manufacture motor vehicle parts and accessories for sale to original equipment manufacturers. The principal products of the group are passenger car and light truck aluminum road wheels. The products of the group are sold for factory installation as optional or standard equipment on selected vehicle models, to ford, general motors, daimlerchrysler, audi, bmw, isuzu, jaguar, land rover, mazda, mg rover, mitsubishi, nissan, subaru, toyota and volkswagen. The group is also building its position in the market for aluminum suspension and related underbody components to compliment its OEM aluminum wheel business. The group operates in the United States, Mexico and hungary.

Primary SIC and add'l.: 3493 5013 3714

CIK No: 0000095552

Subsidiaries: 50% Owned Joint Venture, Industries Universales Unidas de Mexico, S.A., Suoftec Light Metal Products B.V., Suoftec Light Metal Products Production & Distribution Ltd (50% owned), Superior Automotive Components LLC, Superior Engineered Technologies, Inc., Superior Industries Asia, Limited, Superior Industries de Mexico, S.A. de C.V., Superior Industries International Michigan LLC, Superior Industries International Arkansas, Inc., Superior Industries International California, Inc., Superior Industries International Kansas, Inc., Superior Industries International Michigan, Inc., Superior Industries International Tennessee, LLC, Superior Industries International Distribution Corporation 17 Subsidiaries included in the Index

Officers: Steven J. Borick/Chmn., CEO, Pres./$2,504,586.00, Kola Phillips/54/VP - Quality, Continuous Improvement, William B. Kelley/VP - Operational Planning, Scheduling, Jeffrey R. Ornstein/Dir., VP, Principal Financial Officer/$360,227.00, Robert H. Bouskill/Sr. VP - Manufacturing Technology, Emil J. Fanelli/Acting CFO, VP, Corporate Controller/$254,710.00, Philip W. Colburn/Dir., Business Consultant, Parveen Kakar/VP - Program Development, Robert Bracy/Sr. VP - Project Management, James M. Ferguson/58/Sr. VP - Global Sales, Marketing VP - OEM Marketing Group/$400,926.00, Robert A. Earnest/VP, General Counsel, Corp. Sec., Cameron Toyne/VP - Purchasing, Stephen H. Gamble/VP, Treasurer, Ross Perian/CIO, Eddie Rodriguez/VP - Human Resources *(18 Officers included in Index)*

Directors: Steven J. Borick/Chmn., CEO, Pres., Louis L. Borick/Founder, Chmn., Sheldon I. Ausman/Dir., Philip W. Colburn/Dir., Business Consultant, Jeffrey R. Ornstein/Dir., VP, Principal Financial Officer, Michael J. Joyce/Dir., Bond V. Evans/Dir., Margaret S. Dano/Dir., Francisco S. Uranga/Dir.

Owners: Third Avenue Management LLC/21.14%, Dimensional Fund Advisors, Inc./8.28%, Louis L. Borick/12.85%, Michael J. Joyce, Bond V. Evans, Sheldon I. Ausman, James M. Ferguson, Insiders/18.25%, Met Investors Series Trust/6.98%, Michael J. O'Rourke, Juanita A. Borick/5.29%, Donald Smith & Co., Inc./10.00%, Philip W. Colburn, Barclays Global Investors, NA./6.62%, Jeffrey R. Ornstein *(18 Owners included in Index)*

Financial Data: *Fiscal Year End:*12/31 **Latest Annual Data:** 12/31/2006

Year	Sales	Net Income
2006	$789,862,000	-$9,321,000
2005	$844,884,000	-$5,836,000
2004	$901,755,000	$44,655,000

Curr. Assets:	$346,593,000	**Curr. Liab.:**	$113,110,000		
Plant, Equip.:	$310,414,000	**Total Liab.:**	$151,825,000	**Indic. Yr. Divd.:**	$0.640
Total Assets:	$712,013,000	**Net Worth:**	$560,188,000	**Debt/ Equity:**	NA

Superior Oil & Gas Company

14910 NW 36 St., Yukon, OK, 73099; *PH:* 1-405-350-0404; *Fax:* 1-405-350-0539; *http://* www.superioroilandgas.com; *Email:* info@superioroilandgas.com

General - Incorporation	NV	**Stock**- Price on:12/24/2007	$0.14
Employees	2	Stock Exchange	OTC
Auditor	Sutton Robinson Freeman & Co., P.C.	Ticker Symbol	SIOR
Stk Agt	Nevada Agency & Trust Company	Outstanding Shares	22,450,000
Counsel	NA	E.P.S.	-$0.03
DUNS No.	NA	Shareholders	NA

Business: The groups principle activity is to seek, investigate, and, if warranted, acquire producing and non producing oil and gas properties and to explore, drill and develop properties. In May 2006, the group acquired 28 natural gas wells located in the Cherokee Basin near Southeast Kansas. The group's revenue for Sep '07 was 0.01 millions of USD.

Primary SIC and add'l.: 1382

CIK No: 0001216774

Officers: Daniel H. Lloyd/63/Chmn., CEO, CFO, Gayla McCoy/54/Sec., Treasurer

Directors: Daniel H. Lloyd/63/Chmn., CEO, CFO, Bill Sparks/78/Dir., W. R. Lott/54/Dir.

Owners: W. R. Lott/6.90%, Daniel H. Lloyd/13.00%, Gayla McCoy/12.90%, Thomas Becker/14.20%, Bill Sparks/2.20%, Insiders/49.20%

Financial Data: *Fiscal Year End:*12/31 **Latest Annual Data:** 12/31/2006

Year	Sales	Net Income
2006	NA	-$666,000
2005	$10,000	-$142,000
2004	NA	-$922,000

Curr. Assets:	$358,000	**Curr. Liab.:**	$1,248,000		
Plant, Equip.:	$1,499,000	**Total Liab.:**	$2,010,000	**Indic. Yr. Divd.:**	NA
Total Assets:	$1,856,000	**Net Worth:**	-$153,000	**Debt/ Equity:**	NA

Superior Uniform Group Inc

10055 Seminole Blvd, Seminole, FL, 33772; *PH:* 1-727-397-9611; *http://* www.superioruniformgroup.com; *Email:* info@superioruniformgroup.com

General - Incorporation	FL	**Stock**- Price on:12/24/2007	$12.65
Employees	696	Stock Exchange	AMEX
Auditor	Grant Thornton LLP	Ticker Symbol	SGC
Stk Agt	Wachovia Bank N.A	Outstanding Shares	6,640,000
Counsel	Shumaker Loop & Kendrick LLP	E.P.S.	$0.27
DUNS No.	00-203-6507	Shareholders	NA

Business: The group's principal activities are to manufactures and markets apparel and accessories for medical, health, industrial, leisure and other safety markets. The products of the group are sold to medical and health fields as well as for the industrial, commercial, leisure and public safety markets. Its principal products are: the uniform and service apparel for personnel in hospitals, health facility centers, hotels, commercial and residential buildings, food service centers, banks, airlines and public and private safety organizations. The miscellaneous products include room masks, boots, sheets and industrial laundry bags, corporate and resort embroidered sportswear. On 27-Feb 2004, the group acquired univogue inc.

Primary SIC and add'l.: 2389

CIK No: 0000095574

Subsidiaries: Fashion Seal Corporation

Officers: Michael Benstock/52/Dir., CEO/$388,027.00, Joan Petronella/Investor Contact, Alan D. Schwartz/57/Dir., Pres./$378,335.00, Peter Benstock/46/Dir., Exec. VP/$311,649.00, Andrew D. Demott/44/Sr. VP, CFO, Treasurer/$243,429.00, Richard T. Dawson/62/VP, General Counsel, Sec.

Directors: Michael Benstock/52/Dir., CEO, Gerald M. Benstock/77/Chmn., Alan D. Schwartz/57/Dir., Pres., Peter Benstock/46/Dir., Exec. VP, Manuel Gaetan/70/Dir., Robin M. Hensley/51/Dir., Sidney Kirschner/73/Dir., Paul V. Mellini/55/Dir., Arthur Wiener/70/Dir.

Owners: Insiders/37.00%, PAUL MELLINI/0.10%, ALAN D. SCHWARTZ/3.20%, MOCHELLE A. STETTNER/9.40%, DIMENSIONAL FUND ADVISORS, LP/8.00%, ARTHUR WIENER/0.10%, ANDREW D. DEMOTT/1.10%, Gerald M. Benstock/25.00%, Peter Benstock/3.00%, ROBIN HENSLEY/0.20%, FRANKLIN ADVISORY SERVICES, LLC/6.90%, RICHARD T. DAWSON/0.40%, MANUEL GAETAN, Michael Benstock/3.30%, SIDNEY KIRSCHNER/0.30%

Financial Data: *Fiscal Year End:*12/31 **Latest Annual Data:** 12/31/2006

Year	Sales	Net Income
2006	$127,696,000	$2,197,000
2005	$133,312,000	$1,244,000
2004	$143,567,000	$5,379,000

Curr. Assets:	$65,673,000	**Curr. Liab.:**	$9,262,000	**P/E Ratio:**	46.85
Plant, Equip.:	$15,394,000	**Total Liab.:**	$13,057,000	**Indic. Yr. Divd.:**	$0.540
Total Assets:	$85,159,000	**Net Worth:**	$72,102,000	**Debt/ Equity:**	0.0253

Superior Well Services Inc

121 Airport Professional Building, Indiana, PA, 15701; *PH:* 1-724-465-8904; *http://* www.superiorwells.com

General - Incorporation	DE	**Stock**- Price on:12/24/2007	$25.5421
Employees	1,068	Stock Exchange	NDQ
Auditor	Ernst & Young, LLP	Ticker Symbol	SWSI
Stk Agt	American Stock Transfer & Trust Co.	Outstanding Shares	23,470,000
Counsel	NA	E.P.S.	$1.69
DUNS No.	NA	Shareholders	NA

Business: The groups principle activity is to provide well site solutions. The groups services include technical pumping and down hole surveying. Customer served by the group is oil and natural gas Company. Specific customers of the group include Atlas America, Inc, Cheasapeake Energy Corp, CDX Gas, LLC, Geomet Operating Company and CNX Gas Company, LLC. The group operates from Texas, New Mexico, Ohio, Oklahoma, Utah, Louisiana, Michigan, Arkansas and Colorado. The group's quarterly revenue for September 2007 was 94.32 millions of USD.

Primary SIC and add'l.: 1382 1389

CIK No: 0001323715

Subsidiaries: Bradford Resources, Ltd, Superior GP, L.L.C., Superior Well Services, Ltd

Officers: David E. Wallace/Chmn., CEO, Jacob B. Linaberger/Pres., Thomas W. Stoelk/CFO, VP, Rhys R. Reese/Exec. VP, COO, Sec., Fred E. Kistner/VP, Controller

Directors: David E. Wallace/Chmn., CEO, David E. Snyder/Dir., Mark A. Snyder/Dir., Charles C. Neal/Dir., John A. Staley/Dir., Anthony J. Mendicino/Dir., Edward J. Dipaolo/Dir.

Owners: Insiders/33.20%, Jacob B. Linaberger/5.30%, Rhys R. Reese/5.30%, Insiders/33.20%, Dennis C. Snyder/13.80%, Anthony J. Mendicino, Charles C. Neal, C. H. Snyder/6.20%, Snyder Associated Companies, Inc./5.70%, Thomas C. Snyder/10.20%, David E. Snyder/12.30%, Edward J. DiPaolo, John A. Staley, David E. Wallace/5.30%, Fred E. Kistner *(18 Owners included in Index)*

Financial Data: *Fiscal Year End:*12/31 **Latest Annual Data:** 12/31/2006

Year	Sales	Net Income
2006	$244,626,000	$31,923,000
2005	$131,733,000	$9,467,000
2004	$76,041,000	$9,797,000

Curr. Assets:	$112,443,000	**Curr. Liab.:**	$28,400,000	**P/E Ratio:**	15.11
Plant, Equip.:	$141,424,000	**Total Liab.:**	$45,130,000	**Indic. Yr. Divd.:**	NA
Total Assets:	$259,034,000	**Net Worth:**	$213,904,000	**Debt/ Equity:**	0.0069

Supertel Hospitality Inc

309 N 5th St., Norfolk, NE, 68702; *PH:* 1-402-371-2520; *Fax:* 1-402-371-4229; *http://* www.supertelinc.com

General - Incorporation....VA
Employees....14
Auditor....KPMG LLP
Stk Agt....American Stock Transfer & Trust Co.
Counsel....NA
DUNS No.....NA

Stock- Price on:12/24/2007....$8.03
Stock Exchange....NDQ
Ticker Symbol....SPPR
Outstanding Shares....19,960,000
E.P.S....$0.20
Shareholders....NA

Business: The groups principle activity is to owning equity interests in hotel properties. The group operates from the United States. The group's quarterly revenue for September 2007 was 34.09 millions of USD.

Primary SIC and add'l.: 6798 7011

CIK No: 0000929545

Subsidiaries: E&P Financing Limited Partnership, E&P Reit Trust, Solomons Beacon Inn Limited Partnership, Solomons GP, LLC (SGLLC), SPPR Hotels, LLC, SPPR South Bend, LLC, SPPR Holdings, Inc., SPPR TRS Subsidiary, LLC, Supertel Hospitality Management, Inc., Supertel Hospitality REIT Trust, Supertel Limited Partnership (SLP), TRS Leasing, Inc., TRS Subsidiary, LLC

Officers: Paul J. Schulte/Chmn., CEO, Pres./$327,700.00, Donavon A. Heimes/CFO, Treasurer, Sec./$224,663.00, David L. Walter/VP - Reporting, Compliance, Assist. Treasurer, Corrine L. Scarpello/VP - Accounting, Finance, Assist. Sec., Steve Gilbert/Sr. VP - Cap, Ex

Directors: Paul J. Schulte/Chmn., CEO, Pres., George R. Whittemore/Dir., Steve Borgmann/Dir., Jeffrey M. Zwerdling/Dir., Loren Steele/Dir., Joseph Caggiano/Dir., Allen L. Dayton/Dir., Patrick J. Jung/Dir.

Owners: George R. Whittemore, Clarus Capital Group Management LP/5.80%, Paul J. Schulte/1.50%, Allen L. Dayton/4.70%, Joseph Caggiano, Donavon A. Heimes, Mark H. Tallman/6.70%, George R. Whittemore/1.10%, Jeffrey M. Zwerdling/1.20%, Jeffrey M. Zwerdling, Steve H. Borgmann/4.30%, Loren Steele, Insiders/15.70%, Paul J. Schulte/4.90%, Patrick J. Jung *(16 Owners included in Index)*

Financial Data: **Fiscal Year End:**12/31 **Latest Annual Data:** 12/31/2006

Year	Sales	Net Income
2006	$77,134,000	$3,721,000
2005	$60,695,000	$2,778,000
2004	$57,809,000	$1,977,000

Curr. Assets:	$6,768,000	**Curr. Liab.:**	$8,905,000	**P/E Ratio:**	40.15
Plant, Equip.:	$190,732,000	**Total Liab.:**	$103,783,000	**Indic. Yr. Divd.:**	$0.460
Total Assets:	$202,148,000	**Net Worth:**	$94,837,000	**Debt/ Equity:**	1.2014

Supertex Inc

1235 Bordeaux Dr., Sunnyvale, CA, 94089; ***PH:*** 1-408-744-0100; ***http://*** www.supertex.com

General - Incorporation....CA
Employees....401
Auditor....PricewaterhouseCoopers LLP
Stk Agt....PricewaterhouseCoopers LLP
Counsel....Pillsbury Madison & Sutro
DUNS No.....01-093-8538

Stock- Price on:12/24/2007....$32.07
Stock Exchange....NDQ
Ticker Symbol....SUPX
Outstanding Shares....13,790,000
E.P.S....$1.39
Shareholders....NA

Business: The group's principle activity is to design, develop, manufacture and market integrated circuits to telecommunications, instrumentation and electronic industries. The group uses state-of-the-art high voltage dmos, hvcmos and hvbicmos analog and mixed signal technologies to produce semiconductor products. These semiconductor products act as an interface between the low-voltage computer logic signal and the high voltage requirements. Microtek inc is the major customer of the group. The group markets through direct sales personnel, independent sales representatives and distributors in the United States and abroad. The group provides wafer foundry services for the manufacture of integrated circuits for customers using customer-owned designs and mask toolings. The semiconductor products of the group are sold in North America, Europe and the Pacific Rim. The group's quarterly revenue for Sep '07 was 22.03 millions of USD.

Primary SIC and add'l.: 3674 5065

CIK No: 0000730000

Subsidiaries: Supertex Limited

Officers: Henery C. Pao/70/Dir., CEO, Pres./$464,187.00, Benedict C.K. Choy/62/Dir., Sr. VP, Sec. - Technology Development, Supertex, Inc/$421,156.00, Dilip Kapur/59/VP - Standard Products, William P. Ingram/61/VP - Wafer Fab Operations, Michael Lee/54/VP - IC Design/$428,259.00, Franklin Gonzalez/57/VP - Process Technology, William Petersen/55/VP - Worldwide Sales, Ahmed Massod/47/VP - Marketing/$372,614.00, Michael Tsang/49/VP - Standard Products, Phillip A. Kagel/CFO, VP - Finance/$319,210.00

Directors: Henery C. Pao/70/Dir., CEO, Pres., Benedict C.K. Choy/62/Dir., Sr. VP, Sec. - Technology Development, Supertex, Inc, Milton Feng/Dir., Elliott Schlam/Dir., Mark W. Loveless/Dir.

Owners: Benedict C.K. Choy/1.35%, Insiders/9.01%, FMR Corp/15.06%, Michael Tsang, Elliott Schlam, Columbia Wanger Asset Management LP/10.68%, Michael Lee, Phillip A. Kagel, Dilip Kapur, Henry C. Pao/6.90%, William Ingram, Push, Inc./5.82%, Ahmed Masood, Mark W. Loveless, Frank Gonzalez

Financial Data: **Fiscal Year End:**04/01 **Latest Annual Data:** 3/31/2007

Year	Sales	Net Income
2007	$98,020,000	$21,427,000
2006	$80,098,000	$15,877,000
2005	$56,558,000	$6,459,000

Curr. Assets:	$116,178,000	**Curr. Liab.:**	$19,282,000	**P/E Ratio:**	21.38
Plant, Equip.:	$7,992,000	**Total Liab.:**	$19,282,000	**Indic. Yr. Divd.:**	NA
Total Assets:	$126,377,000	**Net Worth:**	$107,095,000	**Debt/ Equity:**	NA

Supervalu Inc

11840 Valley View Rd. , Eden Prairie, MN, 55344; ***PH:*** 1-952-294-6900; ***http://*** www.supervalu.com; ***Email:*** sv.inquire@supervalu.com

General - Incorporation....DE
Employees....191,400
Auditor....KPMG LLP
Stk Agt....Wells Fargo Shareowner Services
Counsel....NA
DUNS No.....06-044-8602

Stock- Price on:12/24/2007....$47.02
Stock Exchange....NYSE
Ticker Symbol....SVU
Outstanding Shares....210,100,000
E.P.S....$2.50
Shareholders....NA

Business: The group's principle activity is to operate grocery retail stores. The group operates through two business segments namely retail food and supply chain services. The group operates from United States.

Primary SIC and add'l.: 5411 6794 5141 6331 5331

CIK No: 0000095521

Subsidiaries: Advantage Logistics - Southeast, Inc., Advantage Logistics PA LLC, Advantage Logistics Southwest, Inc., Advantage Logistics USA East LLC, Advantage Logistics USA West LLC, Advantage Logistics USA, Inc., Arden Hills 2003 LLC, Blaine North 1996 LLC, Bloomington 1998 LLC, Burnsville 1998 LLC, Butsons Enterprises of Massachusetts, Inc., Butsons Enterprises of Vermont, Inc., Butsons Enterprises, Inc., Cambridge 2006 LLC, Champlin 2005 LLC 109 Subsidiaries included in the Index

Officers: Jeffrey Noddle/Chmn., CEO/$11,896,090.00, David Boehnen/Exec. VP/$2,162,779.00, David Pylipow/Exec. VP - Human Resources, Michael L. Jackson/COO, Pres./$2,987,377.00, Kevin Tripp/Exec. VP, Pres. - Retail Midwest, Pete Van Helden/Exec. VP, Pres. - Retail West, Duncan MacNaughton/Exec. VP - Merchandising, Marketing, Burt M. Fealing/Corp. Sec., Pamela Knous/CFO, Exec. VP/$2,191,136.00, Janel Haugarth/COO, Exec. VP, Pres. - Supply Chain Services

Directors: Jeffrey Noddle/Chmn., CEO, Wayne Sales/Dir., Lawrence A. Del Santo/Dir., Philip L. Francis/Dir., Susan E. Engel/Dir., Ronald E. Daly/Dir., Irwin Cohen/Dir., Gary Ames/Dir., Kathi Seifert/Dir., Charles M. Lillis/Dir., Steven S. Rogers/Dir., Marissa T. Peterson/Dir., Garnett L. Keith/Dir., Edwin C. Gage/Dir.

Owners: Insiders/2.50%, Irwin Cohen, David L. Boehnen, Susan E. Engel, Lawrence A. Del Santo, Wayne C. Sales, Steven S. Rogers, Jeffrey Noddle, Edwin C. Gage, Charles M. Lillis, Pamela K. Knous, Philip L. Francis, Michael L. Jackson, Gary A. Ames, Ronald E. Daly *(19 Owners included in Index)*

Financial Data: **Fiscal Year End:**02/25 **Latest Annual Data:** 2/24/2007

Year	Sales	Net Income
2007	$37,406,000,000	$452,000,000
2006	$19,863,599,000	$206,169,000
2005	$19,543,240,000	$385,823,000

Curr. Assets:	$2,126,500,000	**Curr. Liab.:**	$1,631,591,000	**P/E Ratio:**	20.27
Plant, Equip.:	$2,201,005,000	**Total Liab.:**	$3,767,781,000	**Indic. Yr. Divd.:**	$0.680
Total Assets:	$6,278,342,000	**Net Worth:**	$2,510,561,000	**Debt/ Equity:**	1.7323

Supportsoft Inc

1900 Seaport Blvd, Redwood, CA, 94063; ***PH:*** 1-650—556-9440; ***Fax:*** 1-650-556-1195; ***http://*** www.supportsoft.com; ***Email:*** insidesalesteam@supportsoft.com

General - Incorporation....DE
Employees....278
Auditor....Ernst & Young LLP
Stk Agt....Computershare Investor Services LLC
Counsel....Pillsbury, Winthrop
DUNS No.....NA

Stock- Price on:12/24/2007....$5.31
Stock Exchange....NDQ
Ticker Symbol....SPRT
Outstanding Shares....45,500,000
E.P.S....-$0.35
Shareholders....NA

Business: The group's principle activity is to provide service and support automation software. The software solutions are designed to help corporations automate, manage and personalize the service and support they provide to their employees and customers. It helps to streamline the service and support process by solving and managing problems associated with the use of various types of computing endpoints. The group sells to corporate enterprises, broadband service providers, support outsourcers, and computing and device manufacturers. The group's quarterly revenue for Sep '07 was 11.32 millions of USD.

Primary SIC and add'l.: 7372 6794 7379

CIK No: 0001104855

Officers: Joshua Pickus/Dir., CEO, Pres./$1,108,496.00, Cadir B. Lee/CTO/$347,573.00, Ken Owyang/CFO/$496,756.00, Michael Sayer/Sr. VP - Worldwide Sales/$408,365.00, Anthony Rodio/Sr. VP, Chief Marketing Officer, David Temlak/Sr. VP - Customer Service, Mark Williams/VP - Customer Support, Richard Mandeberg/Sr. VP - Consumer Business Development, Anurag Gupta/Contact - Asia Pacific, Colin Pittham/Contact - EMEA, Robert Barnum/Sr. VP - Global Services/$217,044.00, Mike Harrison/Contact - United Kingdom, Patterson Howard/Contact - Eastern Europe, CIS, Middle East, Africa, Dave Kimball/Contact - Americas, Tom MacEachern/Contact - Canada *(21 Officers included in Index)*

Directors: Joshua Pickus/Dir., CEO, Pres., Kevin C. Eichler/Chmn., James Thanos/Dir., Shawn Farshchi/Dir., Jim Stephens/Dir., Martin J. O'Malley/Dir.

Owners: Kevin C. Eichler, Insiders/9.30%, Ken Owyang, Chris M. Grejtak, Cadir Lee/2.00%, Shawn Farshchi, Capital Research and Management Company/8.30%, Joshua Pickus/1.00%, Martin OMalley, Dimensional Fund Advisors LP/5.00%, Jim Stephens, Michael Sayer, Royce & Associates, LLC/6.60%, James Thanos, Radha R. Basu/4.70%

Financial Data: **Fiscal Year End:**12/31 **Latest Annual Data:** 12/31/2006

Year	Sales	Net Income
2006	$45,028,000	-$8,235,000
2005	$61,931,000	$4,425,000
2004	$60,617,000	$10,154,000

Curr. Assets:	$137,929,000	**Curr. Liab.:**	$19,691,000		
Plant, Equip.:	$937,000	**Total Liab.:**	$20,102,000	**Indic. Yr. Divd.:**	NA
Total Assets:	$152,605,000	**Net Worth:**	$132,503,000	**Debt/ Equity:**	NA

Supreme Industries Inc

2581 E Kercher Rd. , Goshen, IN, 46528; ***PH:*** 1-574-642-4729; ***http://*** www.supermeind.com; ***Email:*** info@supremecorp.com

General - Incorporation....DE
Employees....2,400
Auditor....Crowe Chizek & Co. LLC
Stk Agt....American Stock Transfer & Trust Co.
Counsel....Law, Snakard & Gambill
DUNS No.....07-139-1007

Stock- Price on:12/24/2007....$6.88
Stock Exchange....AMEX
Ticker Symbol....STS
Outstanding Shares....12,790,000
E.P.S....NA
Shareholders....NA

Business: The group's principal activity is to manufacture and market truck bodies, shuttle buses and related equipment. It operates in specialized vehicles and vertically integrated fiberglass products. Specialized vehicle industry consists of companies that manufacture and distribute specialized truck bodies and shuttle buses. Depending on the product, it is either built directly on a truck chassis or built separately and installed at a later date. The truck chassis that consists of an engine, frame with wheels and cabs. The group's truck body products include cut-away and dry freight van bodies, refrigerated units, shuttle buses, stake bodies and other specialized trucks. On 27-Dec-2003, the group had 18 manufacturing, distribution and supply facilities in goshen, Indiana, griffin, Georgia, cleburne, Texas, moreno valley, California, jonestown, Pennsylvania, woodburn and Oregon.

Primary SIC and add'l.: 3713

CIK No: 0000350846

Subsidiaries: SC Tower Structural Laminating,inc, Supreme Corporation, Supreme Corporation of Texas, Supreme Indiana Management,Inc., Supreme Indiana Operations,Inc., Supreme Insurance Company,Inc., Supreme Mid-Atlantic Corporation, Supreme Northwest, LLC Tex, Supreme Properties East,Inc., Supreme Properties North,Inc., Supreme Properties South,Inc., Supreme Properties West,Inc., Supreme Properties West,Inc., a, Supreme SCT Operating Co., LLC, Supreme SCT Operations, L.P. 19 Subsidiaries included in the Index .

Officers: Herbert M. Gardner/68/Chmn., CEO/$262,684.00, Robert W. Wilson/63/Dir., COO, Pres./$463,112.00, William J. Barrett/69/Dir., Exec. VP - Long, Range, Strategic Planning, Assist. Treasurer, Sec./$256,758.00, Jeffery D. Mowery/46/Treasurer, CFO, Assist. Sec. - Supreme Industries, Inc/$167,149.00, Matthew J. Dennis/Supreme Investor Relations

Directors: Herbert M. Gardner/68/Chmn., CEO, Robert W. Wilson/63/Dir., COO, Pres., William J. Barrett/69/Dir., Exec. VP - Long, Range, Strategic Planning, Assist. Treasurer, Sec., Arthur M. Borden/88/Dir., Robert J. Campbell/77/Dir., Thomas Cantwell/81/Dir., Omer G. Kropf/67/Dir., Mark C. Neilson/50/Dir., Edward L. Flynn/74/Dir., William C. Hurtt/63/Dir.

Owners: Omer G. Kropf, Insiders, Arthur M. Borden, Robert J. Campbell, Insiders, Jeffery D. Mowery, William C. Hurtt, William J. Barrett, Herbert M. Gardner, Thomas Cantwell, Wilen Management Company, Inc., William J. Barrett, Mark C. Neilson, Herbert M. Gardner, Robert J. Campbell *(17 Owners included in Index)*

Financial Data: *Fiscal Year End:*12/31 *Latest Annual Data:* 12/30/2006

Year		Sales			Net Income
2006		$340,747,000			$4,595,000
2005		$342,059,000			$8,341,000
2004		$307,962,000			$4,748,000
Curr. Assets:	$88,610,000	**Curr. Liab.:**	$27,820,000		
Plant, Equip.:	$47,458,000	**Total Liab.:**	$62,186,000	**Indic. Yr. Divd.:**	$0.380
Total Assets:	$137,352,000	**Net Worth:**	$75,165,000	**Debt/ Equity:**	0.4868

Surewest Communications

PO Box 969, Roseville, CA, 95661; ***PH:*** 1-916-786-1407; ***http://*** www.surewest.com; ***Email:*** investor@surewest.com

General - Incorporation	CA	**Stock**- Price on:12/24/2007	$28.4
Employees	864	Stock Exchange	NDQ
Auditor	Ernst & Young LLP	Ticker Symbol	SURW
Stk Agt	Continental Stock Transfer & Trust Co	Outstanding Shares	14,470,000
Counsel	NA	E.P.S	$4.44
DUNS No.	NA	Shareholders	NA

Business: The group's principal activity is to provide telecommunications, digital video and other facilities-based communication services. The group operates through three segments: telecom, broadband and wireless segment. The telecom segment primarily provides local, network access and long distance services, directory advertising services, Internet services, digital cable, the sale of non-regulated products and services. The broadband segment provides services to residential, business and carrier customers. The services includes high-speed and dial-up Internet service, digital video, local and network access toll telephone and managed services. The wireless segment provides personal communications services and the sale of related communications equipment.

Primary SIC and add'l.: 4813 6719

CIK No: 0000943117

Subsidiaries: SureWest Broadband, SureWest Custom Data Services, SureWest Directories, SureWest Internet, SureWest Long Distance, SureWest Telephone, SureWest TeleVideo, SureWest TeleVideo of Roseville, SureWest Wireless

Officers: Steve C. Oldham/Dir., CEO, Pres./$503,510.00, Laurel R. Dismukes/Assist. Corp. Sec., Dir. - Benefits, Thomas P. Villa/VP - Customer Operations, Peter C. Drozdoff/VP - Marketing, Scott K. Barber/VP - Network Operations/$328,471.00, Darla J. Yetter/Corp. Sec., Assist. to The Pres., Philip A. Grybas/Sr. VP, CFO/$389,987.00, Bill M. Demuth/CTO, Sr. VP/$484,617.00, Martin T. McCue/Assist. Corp. Sec. - Counsel, Fred A. Arcuri/COO, Sr. VP/$590,703.00, Scott L. Sommers/VP, Treasurer, Reid Cox/Exec. Dir. - Investor Relations

Directors: Steve C. Oldham/Dir., CEO, Pres., Kirk C. Doyle/Chmn., John R. Roberts/Dir., Timothy D. Taron/Dir., Roger J. Valine/Dir., Guy R. Gibson/Dir., Bob D. Kittredge/Dir.

Owners: Philip A. Grybas, Scott K. Barber, Timothy D. Taron, Guy R. Gibson, Bill M. DeMuth, Roger J. Valine, Insiders/3.40%, Kirk C. Doyle, John R. Roberts, Steven C. Oldham, Robert D. Kittredge, Dimensional FundAdvisors LP/7.40%, Vanguard Fiduciary Trust Company/5.30%, Fred A. Arcuri

Financial Data: *Fiscal Year End:*12/31 *Latest Annual Data:* 12/31/2006

Year		Sales			Net Income
2006		$222,745,000			$5,738,000
2005		$218,588,000			$6,378,000
2004		$211,763,000			-$1,128,000
Curr. Assets:	$52,063,000	**Curr. Liab.:**	$45,553,000	**P/E Ratio:**	6.31
Plant, Equip.:	$376,421,000	**Total Liab.:**	$219,974,000	**Indic. Yr. Divd.:**	$1.000
Total Assets:	$445,750,000	**Net Worth:**	$225,776,000	**Debt/ Equity:**	0.4296

Surfect Holdings Inc

12000-G Candelaria NE, Albuquerque, NM, 87112; ***PH:*** 1-505-294-6354; ***Fax:*** 1-505-294-6311; ***http://*** www.surfect.com; ***Email:*** meichhorn@surfect.com

General - Incorporation	NV	**Stock**- Price on:12/24/2007	$0.82
Employees	12	Stock Exchange	OTC
Auditor	Redw, LLC	Ticker Symbol	SUFH
Stk Agt	Empire Stock Transfer Inc.	Outstanding Shares	14,310,000
Counsel	NA	E.P.S	-$0.34
DUNS No.	NA	Shareholders	NA

Business: The groups principle activities include developing automated electroplating tools for the semiconductor assembly industry. The groups tools are designed to deposit conductive metals on wafers through a proprietary electroplating process. The group operates through four segments namely flip chip wafer bumping, wafer scale csp packaging, high density laminate flip chip substrates andsolar cell plating and thru-wafer via interconnections. for Sep 2006, the group merged with wholly owned subsidiary Surfect Technologies. The group operates from the United States.

Primary SIC and add'l.: 3559

CIK No: 0001356505

Subsidiaries: Surfect Technologies, Inc.

Officers: Steven Anderson/Dir., CEO, Pres., Mark W. Eichhorn/Corporate VP - Sales, Marketing, Yixiang Xie/49/CTO, Miles A. Prim/50/COO, Steve Cho/CTO, Tony Maffia/CFO, Patrick Tang/VP, GM - Asia Region

Directors: Steven Anderson/Dir., CEO, Pres., Laurence P. Wagner/47/Dir., Chad Brownstein/34/Dir., Jonah Schnel/34/Dir.

Owners: Steven Anderson, Yixiang Xie, Laurence Wagner, ITU Ventures, Insiders, Chad Brownstein, Jonah Schnel, Thomas P. Griego

Financial Data: *Fiscal Year End:*12/31 *Latest Annual Data:* 12/31/2006

Year		Sales			Net Income
2006		$221,000			-$2,950,000
Curr. Assets:	$2,474,000	**Curr. Liab.:**	$587,000		
Plant, Equip.:	$221,000	**Total Liab.:**	$592,000	**Indic. Yr. Divd.:**	NA
Total Assets:	$2,845,000	**Net Worth:**	$2,253,000	**Debt/ Equity:**	0.0039

Surge Global Energy Inc

12220 El Camino Real, Ste. 410, San Diego, CA, 92130; ***PH:*** 1-858-704-5010; ***Fax:*** 1-858-704-5011; ***http://*** www.surgeglobalenergy.com; ***Email:*** info@surgeglobalenergy.com

General - Incorporation	DE	**Stock**- Price on:12/24/2007	$0.36
Employees	4	Stock Exchange	OTC
Auditor	Russell Bedford Stefanou Mirchandani	Ticker Symbol	SRGG
Stk Agt	American Stock Transfer & Trust Co.	Outstanding Shares	28,970,000
Counsel	NA	E.P.S	-$0.5
DUNS No.	NA	Shareholders	NA

Business: The group's principal activity is the retail distribution and marketing of tobacco, cigars, pipes and related smoking accessories. Prior to 2003, the group was marketing pipes, cigars, tobaccos and related accessories directly to consumers through its full color catalog. The group discontinued marketing of tobacco, cigars, pipes and related smoking accessories in 2003. The group intends to acquire oil and gas project.

Primary SIC and add'l.: 5993

CIK No: 0001053648

Subsidiaries: Signet Energy, Inc

Officers: David Perez/Chmn., CEO/$3,670,563.00, William Greene/CFO/$221,444.00, Dennis Doucette/Corporate Counsel, Luce Forward/Corporate Counsel, Sheila Rockwell/Controller

Directors: David Perez/Chmn., CEO, Richard Collato/64/Dir., Robert Fields/70/Dir., Thomas Page/75/Dir., John Stiska/66/Dir.

Owners: Frederick C. Berndt/8.34%, Richard Collato/1.92%, David Perez/14.60%, Ken Druck/1.36%, Jamie E. Schloss/7.94%, Thomas A. Page/1.02%, John Stiska/1.03%, Insiders/19.20%, Robert Fields, Mark C. Fritz/17.96%, Chet Idziszek/6.30%, William Greene

Financial Data: *Fiscal Year End:*12/31 *Latest Annual Data:* 12/31/2006

Year		Sales			Net Income
2006		NA			-$15,926,000
2005		NA			-$8,731,000
2004		NA			-$3,047,000
Curr. Assets:	$1,553,000	**Curr. Liab.:**	$604,000		
Plant, Equip.:	$17,000	**Total Liab.:**	$2,913,000	**Indic. Yr. Divd.:**	NA
Total Assets:	$6,301,000	**Net Worth:**	$3,388,000	**Debt/ Equity:**	NA

Surgilight Inc

2100 N Alafaya Trl., Ste 600, Orlando, FL, 32826; ***PH:*** 1-407-482-4555; ***Fax:*** 1-407-482-0505; ***http://*** www.surgilight.com; ***Email:*** surgilightsales@aol.com

General - Incorporation	FL	**Stock**- Price on:12/24/2007	NA
Employees	3	Stock Exchange	OTC
Auditor	Richard L. Brown & Co P.A	Ticker Symbol	SRGL
Stk Agt	Signature Stock Transfer, Inc.	Outstanding Shares	NA
Counsel	NA	E.P.S	-$0.02
DUNS No.	NA	Shareholders	NA

Business: The group's principal activities are to develop, manufacture and sell ophthalmic lasers and related products primarily for the use in photoefractive keratectomy and laser in-situkeratomileusis procedures. The group's optivision product is sold for laser presbyopia reversal for clinical trials and other ophthalmic applications including incision, excision and vaporization of eye tissue. The products of the group are used in various medical and industrial applications.

Primary SIC and add'l.: 8093 3827 8042

CIK No: 0001070289

Subsidiaries: American Medical Laser Services, Inc., Plantation Laser Eye Center

Officers: Timothy J. Shea/COO, Pres., Sec., Ming Yi Hwang/Dir. - Research, Development, Mark Murphy/48/CFO, Treasurer

Directors: Louis P. Valente/Vice Chmn., Edward Tobin/Dir., Craig Collins/61/Dir., Ming-Yi Hwang/51/Dir., Nicholas Pliam/Dir.

Owners: Insiders/22.50%, J. T. Lin/15.00%, Ming-yi Hwang, Edward Tobin/18.20%, GEM Global Yield Fund, Ltd./22.90%, Knobbe, Martens, Olson & Bear LLP/11.70%, Louis P. Valente, PLS Liquidating LLC/5.70%, Timothy J. Shea/1.30%, Craig Collins, GEM SurgiLight Investors, LLC/18.20%, Mark Murphy

Financial Data: *Fiscal Year End:*12/31 *Latest Annual Data:* 12/31/2006

Year		Sales			Net Income
2006		$25,000			-$1,388,000
2005		$2,039,000			$316,000
2004		$2,207,000			-$1,051,000
Curr. Assets:	$681,000	**Curr. Liab.:**	$5,375,000		
Plant, Equip.:	$4,099,000	**Total Liab.:**	$5,375,000	**Indic. Yr. Divd.:**	NA
Total Assets:	$4,886,000	**Net Worth:**	-$489,000	**Debt/ Equity:**	NA

SurModics

9924 W 74th St., Eden Prairie, MN, 55344; ***PH:*** 1-952-829-2700; ***Fax:*** 1-952-829-2743; ***http://*** www.surmodics.com; ***Email:*** info@surmodics.com

General - Incorporation	MN	**Stock**- Price on:12/24/2007	$37.26
Employees	146	Stock Exchange	NDQ
Auditor	Deloitte & Touche LLP	Ticker Symbol	SRDX
Stk Agt	American Stock Transfer & Trust CO.	Outstanding Shares	17,960,000
Counsel	Fredrikson & Byron	E.P.S	$0.18
DUNS No.	09-841-4659	Shareholders	NA

Business: The group's principle activity is to develop, manufacture and market surface modification solutions for the medical device industry. The company operates in three business segments: licensing, manufacturing and research and development. The licensing segment includes all license fees and royalty revenue generated from the transfer of the company's coating technology. The manufacturing segment includes revenues from the sale of chemical reagents, stabilization products and dna slides. Some of the stabilizer products include surmodics, stabilcoat, stabilguard and stabilzyme. The research and development segment includes revenue from development projects for commercial customers and research revenue received from government grants. The major customers of the company include cordis corporation, medtronic inc, amersham plc and abbot laboratories. The group's quarterly revenue for Sep '07 was millions of USD.

Primary SIC and add'l.: 2843 3841 8731

CIK No: 0000924717

Officers: Bruce J. Barclay/Dir., CEO, Pres., Paul A. Lopez/VP - Surmodics, Pres. - Surmodics' Ophthalmology Division, Douglas P. Astry/GM - Vitro Technologies, Lise W. Duran/VP, GM - Regenerative Technologies, Loren R. Miller/VP, Controller, Aron B. Anderson/VP, Chief Scientific Officer, Charles W. Olson/VP, GM - Hydrophilic Technologies, VP - Sales, Steven J. Keough/Sr. VP, GM - Orthopedics, Chief Intellectual Property Counsel, Philip D. Ankeny/Sr. VP, CFO, Peter L. Ginsberg/VP - Business Development, Strategic Planning, Brian L. Robey/VP, GM - Drug Delivery, Michael J. Shoup/VP - Quality, Regulatory, Clinical Affairs, Jan M. Webster/VP - Human Resources, Arthur J. Tipton/VP - Surmodics, Pres. - Brookwood Pharmaceuticals

Directors: Bruce J. Barclay/Dir., CEO, Pres., Kendrick B. Melrose/Chmn., Gerald B. Fischer/Dir., Kenneth H. Keller/Dir., John A. Meslow/Dir., John W. Benson/Dir., Dale R. Olseth/Dir., David A. Koch/Dir., Jose H. Bedoya/Dir.

Owners: Mairs & Power, Inc./5.70%, Jos H. Bedoya, Kendrick B. Melrose/1.60%, Gerald B. Fischer, Steven J. Keough, Bruce J. Barclay, John A. Meslow, John W. Benson, William Blair Capital Management LLC/8.40%, Insiders/17.20%, Paul A. Lopez, Kenneth H. Keller, Dale R. Olseth/7.70%, Philip D. Ankeny, David A. Koch/5.30% *(17 Owners included in Index)*

Financial Data: *Fiscal Year End:*09/30 *Latest Annual Data:* 9/30/2006

Year	Sales	Net Income
2006	$69,884,000	$20,334,000
2005	$62,381,000	-$8,246,000
2004	$49,738,000	$7,436,000

Curr. Assets:	$76,096,000	**Curr. Liab.:**	$8,989,000	**P/E Ratio:**	29.11
Plant, Equip.:	$11,686,000	**Total Liab.:**	$12,199,000	**Indic. Yr. Divd.:**	NA
Total Assets:	$157,402,000	**Net Worth:**	$145,203,000	**Debt/ Equity:**	NA

Surrey Bank & Trust

145 N Renfro St., Mount Airy, NC, 27030; *PH:* 1-336-783-3900; *Fax:* 1-336-789-3687; *http://* www.surreybank.com; *Email:* surreybank@surreybank.com

General - Incorporation	NC	**Stock**- Price on:12/24/2007	$13.07
Employees	59	Stock Exchange	OTC
Auditor	Elliott Davis, PLLC	Ticker Symbol	SRYB
Stk Agt	First Citizens Bank & Trust Co	Outstanding Shares	3,110,000
Counsel	NA	E.P.S	NA
DUNS No.	NA	Shareholders	NA

Business: The group's principle activity is to provide banking services to individuals and small to medium sized in northern surry county. The services offered include checking and savings accounts; commercial, installment, mortgage and personal loans; safe deposit boxes and other associated services. The group also offers insurance and investment products and sales and finance services through its subsidiaries, surry investment services inc and friendly finance llc.

Primary SIC and add'l.: 6141 6022

CIK No: 0001229146

Officers: Edward C. Ashby/Dir., CEO, Pres., Peter A. Pequeno/Sr. VP, CLO, Brenda J. Harding/Sr. VP, Sec., COO, Mark H. Towe/Sr. VP, CFO, John Moore/Contact, Pedro A. Pequeno/40/Sr. VP, Assist. Sec.

Directors: Edward C. Ashby/Dir., CEO, Pres., Hylton Wright/Chmn., Robert H. Moody/Vice Chmn., William A. Johnson/Dir., Elizabeth J. Lovill/Dir., Gene Rees/Dir., Tom G. Webb/Dir., Buddy E. Williams/Dir.

Owners: Hylton Wright, Edward C. Ashby, Elizabeth Johnson Lovill, Elizabeth Johnson Lovill, Pedro A. Pequeno, Tom G. Webb, Eugene F. Rees, William A. Johnson, Hylton Wright, William A. Johnson, Tom G. Webb, Robert H. Moody, Buddy E. Williams, Insiders, Robert H. Moody *(20 Owners included in Index)*

Financial Data: *Fiscal Year End:*12/31 *Latest Annual Data:* 12/31/2006

Year	Sales	Net Income
2006	$15,498,000	$2,651,000
2005	$12,732,000	$2,201,000
2004	$10,744,000	$1,829,000

Curr. Assets:	$18,858,000	**Curr. Liab.:**	$152,236,000		
Plant, Equip.:	$4,521,000	**Total Liab.:**	$167,082,000	**Indic. Yr. Divd.:**	NA
Total Assets:	$187,110,000	**Net Worth:**	$20,027,000	**Debt/ Equity:**	0.6584

Susquehanna Bancshares Inc

26 N Cedar St., Lititz, PA, 17543; *PH:* 1-717-626-4721; *http://* www.susquehanna.net; *Email:* communications@susquehanna.net

General - Incorporation	PA	**Stock**- Price on:12/24/2007	$23.18
Employees	2,259	Stock Exchange	NDQ
Auditor	PricewaterhouseCoopers LLP	Ticker Symbol	SUSQ
Stk Agt	American Stock Transfer & Trust Co.	Outstanding Shares	52,140,000
Counsel	NA	E.P.S	$1.38
DUNS No.	10-166-5891	Shareholders	NA

Business: The group's principal activities is to provide a wide range of retail and commercial banking and financial services. Retail banking services include checking, savings and club accounts, check cards,debit cards, money market accounts, certificates of deposit individual retirement accounts, home equity lines of credit, residential mortgage loans, home improvement loans, student loans, automobile loans, personal loans and Internet banking services. Commercial banking services include business checking accounts, cash management services, money market accounts, land acquisition and development loans, commercial loans, floor plan, equipment and working capital lines of credit, small business loans and Internet banking services. Financial services include commercial and personal property and casualty insurance, risk management programs, traditional trust and custodial, investment advisory, asset management and brokerage and comprehensive consumer vehicle financing service.

Primary SIC and add'l.: 6021 6712

CIK No: 0000700863

Subsidiaries: Susquehanna Bank, Susquehanna Bank PA, Susquehanna Patriot Bank

Officers: William J. Reuter/Chmn., CEO, Pres./$1,050,837.00, Bernard A. Francis/Sr. VP - Group Executive/$668,052.00, Gregory A. Duncan/COO, Exec. VP/$429,433.00, Rodney A. Lefever/CTO, Sr. VP, Edward Balderston/Exec. VP, Chief Administrative Officer - Code, Ethics Officer, Michael M. Quick/Exec. VP - Group Executive/$427,718.00, Lisa M. Cavage/Sr. VP, Sec. - Counsel, Peter J. Sahd/Sr. VP - Group Executive, Joseph R. Lizza/Sr. VP - Group Executive, James G. Pierne/Exec. VP - Group Executive, Edward J. Wydock/Sr. VP, Chief Risk Officer, Drew K. Hostetter/CFO, Exec. VP/$404,213.00

Directors: William J. Reuter/Chmn., CEO, Pres., William B. Zimmerman/Dir., Roger V. Wiest/Dir., Henry H. Gibbel/Dir., Guy W. Miller/Dir., James G. Apple/Dir., Michael A. Morello/Dir., Zev M. Rose/Dir., Susan E. Piersol/Dir., Donald L. Hoffman/Dir., Wayne E. Alter/Dir., Russell J. Kunkel/Dir., Bruce A. Hepburn/Dir., John M. Denlinger/Dir.

Owners: Max T. Hall, Drew K. Hostetter, Roger V. Wiest, Wayne E. Alter, Guy W. Miller, Michael M. Quick, Donald L. Hoffman, James G. Apple, Bernard A. Francis, Russell J. Kunkel, Bruce A. Hepburn, Dimensional Fund Advisors LP/6.54%, Barclays Global Investors, NA/6.34%, John M. Denlinger, William B. Zimmerman *(23 Owners included in Index)*

Financial Data: *Fiscal Year End:*12/31 *Latest Annual Data:* 12/31/2006

Year	Sales	Net Income
2006	$600,053,000	$83,638,000
2005	$512,098,000	$79,563,000
2004	$436,349,000	$70,180,000

Curr. Assets:	$330,358,000	**Curr. Liab.:**	$6,863,041,000	**P/E Ratio:**	13.88
Plant, Equip.:	$107,849,000	**Total Liab.:**	$7,288,848,000	**Indic. Yr. Divd.:**	$1.040
Total Assets:	$8,225,134,000	**Net Worth:**	$936,286,000	**Debt/ Equity:**	NA

Susquehanna Media Co

14 Piedmont Ctr., Ste. 1400, Atlanta, GA, 30305; *PH:* 1-404-949-0700; *Fax:* 1-404-949-0740; *http://* www.susquehannamedia.com

General - Incorporation	DE	**Stock**- Price on:12/24/2007	$9.48
Employees	3,400	Stock Exchange	NA
Auditor	KPMG LLP	Ticker Symbol	NA
Stk Agt	NA	Outstanding Shares	43,150,000
Counsel	NA	E.P.S	-$1.01
DUNS No.	NA	Shareholders	NA

Business: The group's principal activities are to provide radio broadcasting, cable television services, Internet services and other communications-related services. The group operates in three segments namely radio, cable and Internet and other. Radio broadcasting segment focuses on acquiring, operating and developing radio stations in the United States. Cable television segment served 105,600 video subscribers as of 31-Dec-2003. Internet and other services segment provides Internet and data networking services to residential and business customers. The group provides its Internet products and services under the trade name 'blazenet'. At 31-Dec-2003, the group owned and operated 19 FM and 8 AM stations. It also own 6 stations operated by third parties. The group serves markets in san francisco, Dallas, houston and atlanta cincinnati, indianapolis, Kansas city, york and Pennsylvania. On 9-Mar-2004 the group acquired carmel.

Primary SIC and add'l.: 7379 4841 4832

CIK No: 0001088146

Subsidiaries: KNBR, Inc., Susquehanna Data Services, Inc., Susquehanna Fiber Systems, Inc., Susquehanna Pfaltzgraff Co., Susquehanna Radio Corp., Susquehanna Technologies, TelCove, Inc.

Financial Data: *Fiscal Year End:*12/31 *Latest Annual Data:* 12/31/2006

Year	Sales	Net Income
2006	$334,321,000	-$44,588,000
2005	$327,756,000	-$213,367,000
2004	$320,132,000	$30,369,000

Curr. Assets:	$62,882,000	**Curr. Liab.:**	$38,326,000		
Plant, Equip.:	$71,474,000	**Total Liab.:**	$996,140,000	**Indic. Yr. Divd.:**	NA
Total Assets:	$1,333,147,000	**Net Worth:**	$337,007,000	**Debt/ Equity:**	2.1852

Susser Holdings Corp

4433 Baldwin Blvd., Corpus Christi, TX, 78408; *PH:* 1-361-884-2463; *http://* www.susser.com; *Email:* info@susser.com

General - Incorporation	DE	**Stock**- Price on:12/24/2007	$16.28
Employees	2,567	Stock Exchange	NDQ
Auditor	Deloitte & Touche, LLP	Ticker Symbol	SUSS
Stk Agt	Computershare Trust Co	Outstanding Shares	16,830,000
Counsel	NA	E.P.S	-$0.18
DUNS No.	NA	Shareholders	NA

Business: The groups principle activities include retailing and distributing motor fuel. The groups services include merchandise, foodservice, motor fuel and other. The groups operates through two segments namely retail and wholesale. In December 21, 2005, the group merged with Stripes Acquisition LLC. The group operates from the United States. The group's quarterly revenue for September 2007 was 674.02 millions of USD.

Primary SIC and add'l.: 5983 5541 5499

CIK No: 0001361709

Officers: Sam L. Susser/Dir., CEO, Pres., Robert Martin/Dir. - Maintenance, Rene Esquivel/Dir. - Internal Audit, Craig Scotton/Dir. - Petroleum Marketing, Mike Cruz/Dir. - Financial Systems, Roger D. Smith/COO, Pres. - Retail, E. V. Bonner/Exec. VP, General Counsel, Rocky B. Dewbre/COO, Pres. - Wholesale, Mary E. Sullivan/CFO, Exec. VP, Treasurer, Ray Brysch/Dir. - Loss Prevention, Ron Coben/Chief Marketing Officer, Exec. VP, Michael Van Gemert/VP - Information Technology, Richard Sebastian/Sr. VP - Retail Operations, Otis Peaks/VP - Human Resources, Sandra Brimhall/VP - Information Technology *(24 Officers included in Index)*

Directors: Sam L. Susser/Dir., CEO, Pres., Bruce W. Krysiak/Non - Exec. Chmn., David P. Engel/Dir., William F. Dawson/Dir., Armand S. Shapiro/Dir., Sam J. Susser/67/Dir., Jerry E. Thompson/Dir.

Owners: Roger D. Smith, Jerry E. Thompson, Insiders, Bruce W. Krysiak, Sam L. Susser, Ronald D. Coben, Wellspring Capital Partners III, L.P. and affiliates, FMR Corp., E. V. Bonner, Armand S. Shapiro, Mary E. Sullivan, William F. Dawson, Lord Abbett& Co. LLC, Sam J. Susser, Rocky B. Dewbre

Financial Data: *Fiscal Year End:*12/31 *Latest Annual Data:* 12/31/2006

Year	Sales	Net Income
2006	$2,265,159,000	-$3,746,000

Curr. Assets:	$116,720,000	Curr. Liab.:	$105,549,000		
Plant, Equip.:	$232,454,000	Total Liab.:	$261,157,000	Indic. Yr. Divd.:	NA
Total Assets:	$422,327,000	Net Worth:	$161,170,000	Debt/ Equity:	0.7526

Sussex Bancorp

399 Rte 23, Franklin, NJ, 07416; *PH:* 1-973-827-2914; *http://* www.sussexbank.com

General - Incorporation	NJ	Stock - Price on:12/24/2007	$14.4
Employees	110	Stock Exchange	NDQ
Auditor	Beard Miller Co. LLP	Ticker Symbol	SBBX
Stk Agt	American Stock Transfer & Trust Co.	Outstanding Shares	3,170,000
Counsel	NA	E.P.S.	$0.70
DUNS No.	03-684-9321	Shareholders	NA

Business: The group's principal activity is to provide traditional banking services to customers, through its subsidiary, sussex bank. The group conducts a traditional commercial banking business and provides services including personal and business checking accounts and time deposits, money market accounts and regular savings accounts. The group provides commercial, consumer, mortgage, home equity and personal loans. In addition, it also provides general insurance services in both commercial and personal lines of insurance. The group operates through its main office located in franklin and seven branch offices in vernon, montague, sparta, wantage, newton, augusta and andover, New Jersey. On 02-Jan-2003, the group acquired certain assets of garrera insurance agency.

Primary SIC and add'l.: 6022 6712

CIK No: 0001028954

Subsidiaries: Federal Reserve Bank

Officers: Donald L. Kovach/Chmn., CEO/$379,474.00, James Ciaravolo/Sr. VP - Facilities, Security Officer - Sussex Bank, Candace Leatham/Dir. - Sussexbank/$114,848.00, Elizabeth Martin/Sr. VP - Operations, Information Technology, Sussexbank, Tammy Case/Exec. VP - Loan Administration, Sussexbank, Maureen Martin/Sr. VP - Retail Banking, Sussexbank

Directors: Donald L. Kovach/Chmn., CEO, Edward J. Leppert/Vice Chmn., George B. Harper/Dir. - Sussexbank, Timothy Marvil/Dir. - Sussexbank, Patrick E. Brady/Dir., Mark J. Hontz/Dir., Katherine H. Caristia/Dir. - Sussexbank, Richard Branca/Dir., Irvin Ackerson/Dir., Richard D. Scott/Dir., Terry H. Thompson/Dir., Anthony S. Abbate/Dir.

Owners: Mark J. Hontz/0.18%, Wellington Management Company, LLP/9.93%, Edward J. Leppert/0.60%, Donald L. Kovach/4.38%, Patrick Brady/0.07%, Terry Thompson/1.52%, Irvin Ackerson/1.17%, Insiders/11.65%, Richard Branca/0.09%, Richard Scott/1.87%

Financial Data: *Fiscal Year End:*12/31 *Latest Annual Data:* 12/31/2006

Year	Sales		Net Income
2006	$25,242,000		$2,464,000
2005	$20,420,000		$2,399,000
2004	$16,338,000		$1,591,000
Curr. Assets:	$24,175,000	Curr. Liab.:	$298,299,000	P/E Ratio:	20.57
Plant, Equip.:	$7,794,000	Total Liab.:	$321,705,000	Indic. Yr. Divd.:	0.280
Total Assets:	$356,297,000	Net Worth:	$34,592,000	Debt/ Equity:	0.7206

Sutor Technology Group Ltd

Formerly: Bronze Marketing Inc
No 8, Huaye Rd., Dongbang Industrial Pk., Changshu, 215534; *PH:* 86-512-52686688

General - Incorporation	NV	Stock - Price on:12/24/2007	NA
Employees	NA	Stock Exchange	OTC
Auditor	Hansen, Barnett & Maxwell, P.c.	Ticker Symbol	SUOT
Stk Agt	NA	Outstanding Shares	NA
Counsel	NA	E.P.S.	NA
DUNS No.	NA	Shareholders	NA

Business: The groups principal activity is to provide inventory financing to facilitate the marketing and sale of bronze sculptures and other art. The group operates from the United States.

Primary SIC and add'l.: 3310

CIK No: 0001041177

Subsidiaries: Changshu Huaye Steel Strip Co., Ltd., Dongbang Sewage Treatment Co., Ltd., Jiangsu Cold-Rolled Technology Co., Ltd., Sutor Steel Technology Co., Ltd.

Officers: Xun Zhang/36/CTO

Owners: Insiders/85.20%, Lifang Chen/85.20%

Financial Data: *Fiscal Year End:*12/31 *Latest Annual Data:* 06/30/2007

Year	Sales		Net Income
2007	$303,439,000		$20,520,000
2006	NA		-$11,000
2005	NA		-$8,000
Curr. Assets:	$8,000	Curr. Liab.:	$1,000		
Plant, Equip.:	NA	Total Liab.:	$1,000	Indic. Yr. Divd.:	NA
Total Assets:	$8,000	Net Worth:	$6,000	Debt/ Equity:	NA

Sutron Corp

21300 Ridgetop Cir., Sterling, VA, 20166; *PH:* 1-703-406-2800; *http://* www.sutron.com;
Email: sales@sutron.com

General - Incorporation	VA	Stock - Price on:12/24/2007	$8.5
Employees	89	Stock Exchange	NDQ
Auditor	Thompson, Greenspon & Co., P.C	Ticker Symbol	STRN
Stk Agt	OTC Corporate Transfer Service Co	Outstanding Shares	4,510,000
Counsel	Tate & Bywater	E.P.S.	$0.59
DUNS No.	02-031-2294	Shareholders	NA

Business: The group's principal activities are to design and manufacture environmental monitoring and control systems, which is used by the government agencies and industry. It provides real-time data collection, telemetry and technical expertise to monitor, control, manage and forecast activities in areas of hydrology, meteorology and water management. The products of the group include sensors, data collection platforms and remote terminal units with telemetry capability and system and application software. The group provides services in the integration and installation of turnkey real-time data collection systems, data management software and in the maintenance and repair of field site sensors and data collection platforms. The group's customers include federal, state and foreign government agencies, universities, the department of defense and hydropower companies.

Primary SIC and add'l.: 7373 3823

CIK No: 0000728331

Subsidiaries: Sutron HydroMet Systems Private Limited .

Officers: Raul S. McQuivey/Chmn., CEO, COO, Pres./$212,566.00, Daniel W. Farrell/Dir., VP/$184,796.00, Sidney C. Hooper/CFO/$183,372.00, Thomas N. Keefer/VP - Software Services/$121,150.00, Cecilia Oh/Dir. - Operations, ISO Management Representative, Ashish Raval/VP, Paul Delisi/Mgr. - Customer Service, Wade Loseman/Mgr. - Southeastern States Sales, Weston Winegar/Mgr. - Sales, Southwestern States, Teddy Soto/Mgr. - Sales, Florida, Latin America, Mike Thomas/Contact - Hydrological Services, Tom Keefer/VP - Special Projects, Naresh Goel/Mgr. - Sutron Country, Dave Johnstone/Contact - Australia, NEW Zealand, Martin Green/Sales, Marketing, Europe, Africa *(23 Officers included in Index)*

Directors: Raul S. McQuivey/Chmn., CEO, COO, Pres., Daniel W. Farrell/Dir., VP, Robert F. Roberts/Dir., Andrew D. Lipman/Dir., Thomas R. Porter/58/Dir.

Owners: Thomas N. Keefer/7.80%, Robert F. Roberts, Raul S. McQuivey/19.30%, Andrew D. Lipman, Kenneth W. Whitt/10.70%, Sidney C. Hooper/4.10%, Daniel W. Farrell/4.90%, Thomas R. Porter, Insiders/37.20%

Financial Data: *Fiscal Year End:*12/31 *Latest Annual Data:* 12/31/2006

Year	Sales		Net Income
2006	$19,407,000		$2,450,000
2005	$15,434,000		$1,470,000
2004	$16,679,000		$1,902,000
Curr. Assets:	$12,779,000	Curr. Liab.:	$3,274,000	P/E Ratio:	19.32
Plant, Equip.:	$620,000	Total Liab.:	$3,441,000	Indic. Yr. Divd.:	NA
Total Assets:	$13,450,000	Net Worth:	$10,009,000	Debt/ Equity:	NA

SVB Financial Group

Formerly: Silicon Valley Bancshares
3003 Tasman Dr, Santa Monica, CA, 95054; *PH:* 1-408-654-7400; *http://* www.sivb.com

General - Incorporation	DE	Stock - Price on:12/24/2007	$53.33
Employees	1,140	Stock Exchange	NDQ
Auditor	KPMG LLP	Ticker Symbol	NA
Stk Agt	Wells Fargo Bank, N.A.	Outstanding Shares	34,280,000
Counsel	NA	E.P.S.	$2.82
DUNS No.	10-277-7836	Shareholders	NA

Business: The group's principal activity is to provide banking and financial services through its five segments: commercial banking, merchant banking, investment banking, private banking, and other business services. Commercial banking provides lending, cash management, trade, foreign exchange, export trade finance, investment and advisory, mutual funds, fixed income securities and investment reporting and monitoring services. Merchant banking makes private equity and venture capital fund investments, international alliances and manages two limited partnerships. Investment banking provides merger and acquisition, private placements and corporate partnering services. Private banking provides a wide array of loan, personal asset management, mortgage services, trust and estate planning tailored for high-net-worth individuals. The other business services unit provides Web-based business services and professional services. The group operates through its 26 regional offices.

Primary SIC and add'l.: 6022 6712

CIK No: 0000719739

Subsidiaries: Gold Hill Venture Lending 03, L.P., Gold Hill Venture Lending Partners 03, LLC, Real Estate Investment Trust, Silicon Valley Bancshares Cayman Islands, Silicon Valley BancVentures, L.P., Silicon Valley BancVentures,Inc., Silicon Valley Bank, SVB Alliant, SVB Alliant Europe, Ltd., SVB Asset Management, SVB Business Partners (Shanghai) Co. Ltd., SVB Capital II, SVB Europe Advisors Limited, SVB Global Financial,Inc., SVB India Advisors, Private Limited 24 Subsidiaries included in the Index

Officers: David T. Ketsdever/42/CEO - SVB Alliant, Harry W. Kellogg/Vice Chmn. - Silicon Valley Bank, Chmn. - SVB Capital, Pres. - Private Client Services/$1,157,392.00, John Jenkins-Stark/57/CFO/$1,368,726.00, Mary Dent/General Counsel, Sec., David C. Webb/CIO, Lynda Ward Pierce/45/Head - Human Resources, Mark MacLennan/Pres. - SVB Capital, Marc J. Verissimo/52/Chief Strategy Officer/$1,271,837.00, Gregory W. Becker/COO/$1,298,587.00

Directors: Harry W. Kellogg/Vice Chmn. - Silicon Valley Bank, Chmn. - SVB Capital, Pres. - Private Client Services, Alex W. Hart/Chmn., C. R. Porter/Dir., Kyung H. Yoon/Dir., Felda G. Hardymon/Dir., Eric A. Benhamou/Dir., Roger F. Dunbar/Dir., Kenneth P. Wilcox/Dir., Michaela K. Rodeno/Dir., David M. Clapper/Dir., Joel P. Friedman/Dir., Larry W. Sonsini/Dir., Richard C. Kramlich/Dir.

Owners: Joel P. Friedman, Kenneth P. Wilcox, Eric A. Benhamou, James R. Porter, Michaela K. Rodeno, Felda G. Hardymon, David M. Clapper, Alex W. Hart, Richard C. Kramlich, Greg Becker, Marc J. Verissimo, John F. Jenkins-Stark, Harry W. Kellogg, Insiders/3.06%, Roger F. Dunbar

Financial Data: *Fiscal Year End:*12/31 *Latest Annual Data:* 12/31/2006

Year	Sales		Net Income
2006	$528,845,000		$89,385,000
2005	$433,954,000		$92,537,000
2004	$348,642,000		$63,866,000
Curr. Assets:	$651,551,000	Curr. Liab.:	$4,741,162,000	P/E Ratio:	20.83
Plant, Equip.:	$37,306,000	Total Liab.:	$5,286,923,000	Indic. Yr. Divd.:	NA
Total Assets:	$6,081,452,000	Net Worth:	$628,514,000	Debt/ Equity:	NA

Swank Inc

656 Joseph Warner Blvd., Taunton, MA, 02780; *PH:* 1-212-867-2600; *http://* www.swankinc.com;
Email: info@swankinc.com

General - Incorporation	DE	Stock - Price on:12/24/2007	$9.4
Employees	260	Stock Exchange	OTC
Auditor	BDO Seidman LLP	Ticker Symbol	SNKI
Stk Agt	American Stock Transfer & Trust Co.	Outstanding Shares	6,070,000
Counsel	Parker Chapin Flattau & Klimpl	E.P.S.	$2.26
DUNS No.	00-120-2340	Shareholders	NA

Business: The group's principal activity is to manufacture, sell and distribute men's accessories. Men's leather accessories, principally belts, wallets and other small leather goods including billfolds, key cases, card holders and suspenders are distributed under the names 'geoffrey beene', 'pierre cardin', 'claiborne', 'john henry', 'kenneth cole', 'tommy hilfiger', 'guess?', 'swank' and 'colours by alexander julian'. Men's jewelry consists of cuff links, tie klips, chains and tacs, bracelets, neck chains, vest chains, collar pins, key rings and money clips. The group also manufactures and distributes men's leather accessories for customers' private labels. The group operats in the United States and abroad also. The groups main customers are (a) federated department stores ("Federated), Inc., (B) Tjx Companies, Inc. ("tjx"), (C) May Department Stores Company ("may") And (D) Target Corporation ("target").

Primary SIC and add'l.: 3911 3172 3961

CIK No: 0000095779

Officers: John Tulin/Chmn., CEO/$741,128.00, James E. Tulin/57/Dir., Sr. VP - Merchandising/$425,384.00, Jerold R. Kassner/Exec. VP, Treasurer, Sec., CFO/$329,275.00, Paul Duckett/Sr. VP - Distribution, Eric P. Luft/Dir., Pres./$570,497.00, Melvin Goldfeder/Sr. VP - Special Markets/$462,638.00, Arthur Gately/VP - Administration, William Rubin/Sr. VP - Regional Sales, Jerry Kassner/Sr. VP, Investor Relations Officer

Directors: John Tulin/Chmn., CEO, James E. Tulin/57/Dir., Sr. VP - Merchandising, Eric P. Luft/Dir., Pres., Raymond Vise/Dir., John J. Macht/Dir.

Owners: Insiders, Melvin Goldfeder, Jerold R. Kassner, The New Swank, Inc., John Tulin, James Tulin, Raymond Vise, Slater Capital Management, L.L.C., Eric P. Luft, John J. Macht

Financial Data: Fiscal Year End:12/31   Latest Annual Data: 12/31/2006

Year	Sales	Net Income
2006	$119,059,000	$13,989,000
2005	$97,914,000	$3,614,000
2004	$93,287,000	$1,571,000

Curr. Assets:	$38,069,000	Curr. Liab.:	$17,231,000	P/E Ratio:	4.16
Plant, Equip.:	$397,000	Total Liab.:	$23,563,000	Indic. Yr. Divd.:	NA
Total Assets:	$45,129,000	Net Worth:	$21,566,000	Debt/ Equity:	0.2975

Swap & Shop.net Corp

1016 Clemons St., Ste. 302, Jupiter, FL, 33477; **PH:** 1-561-745-6789

General - Incorporation	FL	Stock - Price on:12/24/2007	NA
Employees	NA	Stock Exchange	NA
Auditor	Wieseneck, Andres & Co P.A	Ticker Symbol	NA
Stk Agt	Florida Atlantic Stock Transfer, Inc.	Outstanding Shares	NA
Counsel	NA	E.P.S.	NA
DUNS No.	NA	Shareholders	NA

Business: The group's principle activity is to provide critical intelligence for the business, investor, and legal communities. The group operates from United States.

Primary SIC and add'l.: 9995

CIK No: 0001321510

Subsidiaries: eCom eCom.com, Inc

Officers: Barney A. Richmond/56/Chmn., CEO, Pres., Sec., Richard C. Turner/48/Dir., CFO, Treasurer

Directors: Barney A. Richmond/56/Chmn., CEO, Pres., Sec., Richard C. Turner/48/Dir., CFO, Treasurer

Owners: Richard C. Turner/1.50%, United States Financial Group, Inc./10.90%, American Capital Holdings, Inc./33.20%, Barney A. Richmond/17.50%, Insiders/19.00%

Swedish Export Credit Corp

Vastra Tradgardsgatan 11 B, Stockholm; **PH:** 46-86138300; **http://** www.sek.se; **Email:** info@sek.se

General - Incorporation	Sweden	Stock - Price on:12/24/2007	NA
Employees	NA	Stock Exchange	NA
Auditor	KPMG Bohlins AB	Ticker Symbol	NA
Stk Agt	NA	Outstanding Shares	NA
Counsel	NA	E.P.S.	NA
DUNS No.	NA	Shareholders	NA

Business: The groups principle activity is to provide financial support for exports of swedish goods and services. The group operates from United States.

Primary SIC and add'l.: 6159

CIK No: 0000352960

Subsidiaries: AB SEK Securities, Ab Sektionen, SEK Financial Advisors AB, SEK Financial Services AB

Officers: Peter Livijn/CEO - SEK Financial Advisors AB, Jane Lundgren Ericsson/43/CEO, Pres. - AB SEK Securities, Sirpa Rusanen/44/Dir. - Human Resources, Nicholas Anderson/Sr. VP - SEK Advisory Services, Project Finance, Anders Lund/Sr. Mgr. - SEK Advisory Services, Project Finance, Klas Lindgren/Sr. Mgr., Lars Nybom/Sr. Mgr., Per Akerlind/Dir., CFO, Mans Hoglund/57/Dir. - Corporate, Structured Finance, Eva Ohlsson/Sr. Mgr., Carl Engelberth/Head - Structured Finance, Jan Brickner/Sr. Mgr., Peter Yngwe/51/Pres., Sven-Olof Soderlund/56/Dir. - Strategic Analysis, Planning, Per Molinder/Portfolio Mgr., Portfolio Mgr. (43 Officers included in Index)

Directors: Christina Liffner/58/Dep. Chmn., Ulf Berg/57/Chmn., Karin Apelman/47/Dir., Helena Levander/51/Dir., Risto Silander/51/Dir., Markku Hamalainen/Dir. - SEK in Finland, Richard Laftman/Dir. - SEK Financial Advisors AB, Sten Westerberg/Dir., Pirkko Juntti/63/Dir., Bo Netz/46/Dir., Harald Sandberg/58/Dir.

Owners: Kingdom of Sweden/35.35%, Kingdom of Sweden/64.65%

Sweet Success Enterprises Inc

1250 Ne Loop 410 Ste. 630, San Antonio, TX, 78209; **PH:** 1-210-824-2496; **http://** www.sweetsuccess.com; **Email:** info@sweetsuccess.com

General - Incorporation	NV	Stock - Price on:12/24/2007	$0.44
Employees	11	Stock Exchange	OTC
Auditor	PMB Helin Donovan, LLP	Ticker Symbol	SWTS
Stk Agt	Corporate Stock Transfer, Inc.	Outstanding Shares	17,490,000
Counsel	NA	E.P.S.	-$0.46
DUNS No.	NA	Shareholders	NA

Business: The group's principal activities include manufacturing of ready-to-drink diet meal replacement beverages or a food supplement. The products mainline products include: Sweet Success Complete Fuel(TM) dairy based health shake. It contains ingredients like Aktivated Barley(TM) for endurance, ground flax to provide omega-3 fatty acids for heart health, and guarana for a natural energy boost. The group is developing an expanded line of nutritious juice and non-dairy rice-protein based beverages. San Antonio-based Sweet Success Enterprises Inc. acquired the Sweet Success brand in 2002, including all formulas, copyrights, trademarks, records and research. Markets include Las Vegas, Nevada and select cities in Texas.

Primary SIC and add'l.: 2023

CIK No: 0001338067

Officers: William J. Gallagher/Chmn., CEO, Glenn R. Williamson/Dir., COO, Pres., Mike Launer/VP - Sales, Marketing, Chandrasekhara R. Mallangi/Chief Food Scientist

Directors: William J. Gallagher/Chmn., CEO, Graydon D. Webb/Dir., Glenn R. Williamson/Dir., COO, Pres., Robert I. Lippincott/Dir., Theodore M. Heesch/Dir., James Haworth/Dir., Alicia Smith Kriese/Dir., Robert D. Straus/Dir.

Owners: Alicia Smith Kriese/1.60%, Robert D. Straus/2.10%, William J. Gallagher/18.00%, 3CD Consulting LLC/6.30%, James Haworth/3.80%, Mark Burnett Productions/6.40%, Graydon Webb/1.00%, Insiders/30.00%, Glenn Williamson/6.10%, Theodore M. Heesch/0.30%, Robert Lippincott/0.80%

Financial Data: Fiscal Year End:12/31   Latest Annual Data: 12/31/2006

Year	Sales	Net Income
2006	$105,000	-$6,990,000
2005	$4,000	-$3,854,000

Curr. Assets:	$1,166,000	Curr. Liab.:	$9,619,000		
Plant, Equip.:	$48,000	Total Liab.:	$9,619,000	Indic. Yr. Divd.:	NA
Total Assets:	$2,142,000	Net Worth:	-$7,477,000	Debt/ Equity:	NA

Swift Energy Co

16825 Nchase Dr., Ste. 400, Houston, TX, 77060; **PH:** 1-281-874-2700; **Fax:** 1-281-874-2726; **http://** www.swiftenergy.com; **Email:** info@swiftenergy.com

General - Incorporation	TX	Stock - Price on:12/24/2007	$44.5
Employees	345	Stock Exchange	NYSE
Auditor	Ernst & Young LLP	Ticker Symbol	SFY
Stk Agt	American Stock Transfer & Trust Co.	Outstanding Shares	29,900,000
Counsel	Jenkens & Gilchrist	E.P.S.	$4.49
DUNS No.	02-147-1529	Shareholders	NA

Business: The group's principal activities are to develop, explore, acquire and operate oil and gas properties with special emphasis on onshore oil and natural gas reserves. At 31-Dec- 2003, the group operated 504 wells representing 95% of proven reserves. The group's main focus is on the development and exploration in four domestic core areas and in New Zealand. Gas production is sold in the spot market on a monthly basis and oil productions are sold at prevailing market prices.

Primary SIC and add'l.: 1311 1381

CIK No: 0000351817

Subsidiaries: Southern Petroleum (NZ)Exploration Limited, Swift Energy International, Inc., Swift Energy New Zealand Limited, Swift Energy Operating, LLC

Officers: Terry E. Swift/Chmn., CEO/$2,822,509.00, Karen Bryant/Chief Governance Officer, Sec., General Counsel Corporate, Joseph A. D'Amico/COO, Exec. VP/$1,053,104.00, Alton D. Heckaman/CFO, Exec. VP/$1,335,999.00, Adrian D. Shelley/Treasurer, Assist. Secretory, James P. Mitchell/Sr. VP - Commercial Transactions, Land, Thomas E. Schmidt/VP - Operating Compliance, External Relations, Bruce H. Vincent/Dir., Pres./$2,143,465.00, James M. Kitterman/Sr. VP - Operations/$812,170.00, Edward A. Duncan/VP - Exploration, Development, Tara L. Seaman/VP - Reserves, Evaluations, David W. Wesson/Controller, Laurent A. Baillargeon/Chief General Counsel, Robert J. Banks/VP - International Operations, Strategic Ventures, David P. Coatney/VP - Production Operations

Directors: Terry E. Swift/Chmn., CEO, Greg Matiuk/Dir., Douglas J. Lanier/Dir., Bruce H. Vincent/Dir., Pres., Clyde W. Smith/Dir., Henry C. Montgomery/Dir., Raymond E. Galvin/Dir., Deanna L. Cannon/Dir., Charles J. Swindells/Dir., Raymond O. Loen/Dir., Virgil N. Swift/Dir. Emeritus

Owners: Insiders/3.00%, Dimensional Fund Advisors LP/6.30%, Joseph A. DAmico, Henry C. Montgomery, Raymond E. Galvin, Mellon Financial Corporation/5.50%, Alton D. Heckaman, Clyde W. Smith, Bruce H. Vincent, Deanna L. Cannon, Barclays/5.90%, Charles J. Swindells, Terry E. Swift, Greg Matiuk, James M. Kitterman (18 Owners included in Index)

Financial Data: Fiscal Year End:12/31   Latest Annual Data: 12/31/2006

Year	Sales	Net Income
2006	$615,441,000	$161,565,000
2005	$423,226,000	$115,778,000
2004	$310,277,000	$68,451,000

Curr. Assets:	$92,573,000	Curr. Liab.:	$145,975,000	P/E Ratio:	8.83
Plant, Equip.:	$1,483,312,000	Total Liab.:	$787,765,000	Indic. Yr. Divd.:	NA
Total Assets:	$1,585,682,000	Net Worth:	$797,917,000	Debt/ Equity:	NA

Swift Transportation Co Inc

2200 S 75th Ave., Phoenix, AZ, 85043; **PH:** 1-602-269-9700; **http://** www.swifttrans.com

General - Incorporation	NV	Stock - Price on:12/24/2007	NA
Employees	21,900	Stock Exchange	NDQ
Auditor	KPMG LLP	Ticker Symbol	SWFT
Stk Agt	Mellon Investor Services LLC	Outstanding Shares	NA
Counsel	Snell & Wilmer	E.P.S.	NA
DUNS No.	80-872-0296	Shareholders	NA

Business: The groups principle activity is to provide truckload carrier services for large shippers, transporting goods including paper products, nonperishable foods, building materials, and retail and discount store merchandise. The groups fleet includes refrigerated, flatbed and other specialized trailers. The group operates from United States.

Primary SIC and add'l.: 4731 4789

CIK No: 0000863557

Subsidiaries: Common Market Distributing Co. Inc., Common Market Equipment Co. Inc., Cooper Motor Lines Inc., M.S. Carriers Inc., M.S. Carriers Logistics de Mexico S.A. de C.V., M.S. Carriers Warehousing & Distribution Inc., Mohave Transportation Captive Insurance Company, Sparks Finance Co. Inc., Swift Intermodal Ltd., Swift International S.A. de C.V., Swift Leasing Co. Inc., Swift Logistics Co. Inc., Swift Receivables Corporation, Swift Transportation Co. Inc., Swift Transportation Co. of Virginia Inc. 19 Subsidiaries included in the Index

Officers: Jerry Moyes/Chmn., CEO, Pres., Robert W. Cunningham/CEO, Pres., Richard Stocking/Exec. VP - Central Region, Glynis A. Bryan/CFO, Exec. VP, Ginnie Henkels/Primary Investor Relations Officer, Michele Calbi/VP - Procurement, Shop Operations, Mike Ruchensky/CIO, VP, Connie Hills/Sales VP - North West, David Bowers/Sales VP - Mid West, Barbara J. Kennedy/Exec. VP - Human Resources, Safety, Recruiting, Driver Services, Tim Harrington/Sales VP - Memphis, Bryan R. Schumaker/VP, Corporate Controller, Ramey Peru/Dir., CFO, Exec. VP, Earl Scudder/Dir., Chief Administrative Officer, Mark A. Martin/Exec. VP - Eastern Region (17 Officers included in Index)

Directors: Jerry Moyes/Chmn., CEO, Pres., Jock Patton/Chmn., Karl Eller/Dir., Alphonse E. Frei/Dir., David Goldman/Dir., Paul M. Mecray/Dir., Karen E. Rasmussen/Dir., Ramey Peru/Dir., CFO, Exec. VP, Earl Scudder/Dir., Chief Administrative Officer, Jeff Shumway/Dir.

Owners: Jerry Moyes/27.01%, Goldman Sachs Asset Management/5.14%, Robert W. Cunningham, Insiders/28.21%, Alphonse E. Frei, Samuel C. Cowley, Paul M. Mecray, Jeffrey Riley, Jock Patton, Mark A. Martin, Glynis Bryan, Moyes Childrens Limited Partnership/11.97%, Richard Stocking, Karl Eller, Karen E. Rasmussen *(17 Owners included in Index)*

Swiss Medica Inc

375 Britannia Rd. E , Unit B, Mississauga, ON, L4Z 3E2; ***PH:*** 1-905-501-0553; ***Fax:*** 1-905-501-1433; ***http://*** www.swissmedica.com; ***Email:*** info@swissmedica.com

General - Incorporation	DE	**Stock** - Price on:12/24/2007	$0.005
Employees	NA	Stock Exchange	OTC
Auditor	Russell Bedford Stefanou Mirchandani	Ticker Symbol	SWME
Stk Agt	Atlas Stock Transfer Corp	Outstanding Shares	NA
Counsel	NA	E.P.S.	NA
DUNS No.	NA	Shareholders	NA

Business: The groups principle activities include distributing and marketing patented, all natural, clinically tested consumer healthcare products designed to reduce chronic ailments such as pain. The group operates from the United States. The group's quarterly revenue for Jun '07 was 0.09 millions of USD.

Primary SIC and add'l.: 2834

CIK No: 0000318245

Subsidiaries: Anti-Depression BioHealth Solutions, Inc.

Officers: Raghu Kilambi/Co - Founder, CEO, Grant Johnson/Business Development, Anne Dundon/VP - Canadian Sales, Chris Broadhurst/Advisor, Allan N. Fields/Advisor, Gordon D. Ko/Advisor

Directors: Raghu Kilambi/Co - Founder, CEO, Bryson Farrill/Chmn., Sam Halim/Dir., Ronald Springer/Dir.

Owners: Ronald Springer, Insiders, Grant Johnson, Raghunath Kilambi, Bryson Farrill, Raghunath Kilambi, Sam Halim, Insiders

Swisscom

Alte Tiefenaustrasse 6, 3048 Worblaufen, Bern; ; ***http://*** www.swisscom.com

General - Incorporation	Switzerland	**Stock** - Price on:12/24/2007	$34.25
Employees	17,068	Stock Exchange	OTC
Auditor	KPMG	Ticker Symbol	SCMWY
Stk Agt	Bank of New York	Outstanding Shares	518,020,000
Counsel	NA	E.P.S.	$2.45
DUNS No.	48-773-1671	Shareholders	NA

Business: The group's principal activity is the provision of telecommunication services in Switzerland. The activities are carried out through the following divisions. Fixnet division comprises of national and international fixed line voice telecommunications for residential customers and access charges from business customers. Debitel provides mobile communications services in Germany. Mobile division provides mobile telephony, data and wholesale network utilisation charges. Enterprise solutions provides national and international telephony traffic, leased lines, telehousing, hosting and communications solutions. Corporate division covers headquarters and real estate companies.

Primary SIC and add'l.: 3661 4813 7375 4822 4812 4899

CIK No: 0001069336

Subsidiaries: Telecom FL AG

Officers: Jurg Rotheli/45/CEO - Swisscom Participations, Carsten Schloter/45/CEO, Eros Fregonas/44/CEO - Swisscom Information Technology Services, Patrice Haldemann/55/Acting Head - Network, Informatics, Christian Neuhaus/Press Spokesperson, Sepp Frey/Regional Press Spokesperson, Gunter Pfeiffer/50/Head - Group Human Resources, Louis Schmid/Deputy Head - Investor Relations, Sepp Huber/Head - Media Relations, Carsten Roetz/Deputy Head - Media Relations, Mario Rossi/48/CFO - Swisscom AG, Hugo Gerber/53/Dir. - Employee Representative, Daniel Ritz/42/Head - Group Strategy, Business Development, Ueli Dietiker/55/Head - Group Finance, Controlling, Michel Gobet/54/Dir. - Employee Representative *(21 Officers included in Index)*

Directors: Anton Scherrer/66/Chmn., Michel Gobet/54/Dir. - Employee Representative, Hugo Gerber/53/Dir. - Employee Representative, Fides P. Baldesberger/54/Dir., Othmar Vock/64/Dir., Catherine Muhlemann/42/Dir., Martin Vogeli/39/Dir., Sec., Felix Rosenberg/66/Dir., Torsten G. Kreindl/44/Dir., Richard Roy/52/Dir.

Owners: Swiss Confederation/54.80%

Financial Data: *Fiscal Year End:*12/31 *Latest Annual Data:* 12/31/2006

Year		Sales			Net Income
2006		$8,163,155,000			$1,303,775,000
2005		$7,595,918,000			$1,770,506,000
2004		$9,063,511,000			$1,867,681,000
Curr. Assets:	$2,917,698,000	**Curr. Liab.:**	$3,432,972,000		
Plant, Equip.:	$4,754,798,000	**Total Liab.:**	$9,157,601,000	**Indic. Yr. Divd.:**	NA
Total Assets:	$11,957,967,000	**Net Worth:**	$2,800,367,000	**Debt/ Equity:**	NA

SWMX Inc

One Bridge St., Irvington, NY, 10533; ***PH:*** 1-914-406-8400; ***Fax:*** 1-914-478-8330; ***http://*** ir.swmx.com

General - Incorporation	DE	**Stock** - Price on:12/24/2007	$0.14
Employees	64	Stock Exchange	OTC
Auditor	Amper, Politzner & Mattia P.c	Ticker Symbol	SWMX
Stk Agt	Continental Stock Transfer & Trust	Outstanding Shares	205,930,000
Counsel	NA	E.P.S.	-$0.049
DUNS No.	NA	Shareholders	NA

Business: The groups principle activities include operating an electronic open marketplace for the purchase and sale of radio and television advertising media time. In the year 2006, the group merged with SoftWave Media Exchange, Inc. The group operates from the United States, Mexico and Europe. The group's quarterly revenue for Sep '07 was 0.32 millions of USD.

Primary SIC and add'l.: 7389

CIK No: 0001333693

Subsidiaries: SoftWave Media Exchange, Inc.,

Officers: Josh Wexler/CEO, Co - Founder, Dir., Stavros` Aloizos/CTO, Co - Founder, Dir., Chief Architect, Michael Caprio/Exec. VP, Co - Founder, Bill Figenshu/COO, James Caci/CFO

Directors: Josh Wexler/CEO, Co - Founder, Dir., Gary Lee/Chmn., Rick Boyko/Dir., Bruce L. Lev/Dir., Jerry Shereshewsky/Dir., Stavros` Aloizos/CTO, Co - Founder, Dir., Chief Architect, Michael Caprio/Exec. VP, Co - Founder

Owners: Joshua Wexler/16.70%, Jerry Shereshewsky, Gary Lee, Bruce L . Lev, Rick Boyko, Michael Caprio/10.40%, Insiders/44.50%, Charles Omphalius/8.30%, John I. Keay/10.50%, James Caci, Stavros Aloizos/17.10%, Bill Figenshu

Financial Data: *Fiscal Year End:*12/31 *Latest Annual Data:* 12/31/2006

Year		Sales			Net Income
2006		$2,546,000			-$8,956,000
Curr. Assets:	$6,243,000	**Curr. Liab.:**	$6,706,000		
Plant, Equip.:	$3,153,000	**Total Liab.:**	$7,337,000	**Indic. Yr. Divd.:**	NA
Total Assets:	$9,548,000	**Net Worth:**	$2,211,000	**Debt/ Equity:**	NA

SWS Group Inc

1201 Elm St., Ste. 3500, Dallas, TX, 75270; ***PH:*** 1-214-859-1800; ***http://*** www.swsgroupinc.com; ***Email:*** info@swst.com

General - Incorporation	DE	**Stock** - Price on:12/24/2007	$21.97
Employees	889	Stock Exchange	NYSE
Auditor	PricewaterhouseCoopers LLP	Ticker Symbol	SWS
Stk Agt	Computershare Trust Co	Outstanding Shares	27,590,000
Counsel	NA	E.P.S.	$1.33
DUNS No.	05-866-8138	Shareholders	NA

Business: The group's principle activity is to provide investment and related financial services to individuals, institutional investors, broker/dealers, corporations, governmental entities and financial intermediaries. The group operates through three divisions: brokerage, asset management and banking. Brokerage group provides clearing services to over 225 correspondent broker/dealers and over 400 independent contract brokers. Asset management group offers asset management services through sws capital corporation, which administers the local government investment cooperative fund. Banking group offers full-service traditional banking and Internet banking through its subsidiaries. The group also provides Internet services, network design and engineering and disaster recovery services. The westwood holdings group, inc. The group's quarterly revenue for Sep '07 was 112.54 millions of USD.

Primary SIC and add'l.: 6162 6211 6719

CIK No: 0000878520

Subsidiaries: FSB Development, LLC, Southwest Financial Insurance Agency, Inc., Southwest Insurance Agency of Alabama, Inc., Southwest Insurance Agency, Inc., Southwest Investment Advisors, Inc., Southwest Securities, FSB, Southwest Securities, Inc., Sws A, LLC, SWS B, SWS Banc Holdings, Inc., SWS Capital Corporation, SWS Financial Services, Inc.

Officers: Donald W. Hultgren/Dir., CEO, Richard Litton/Officer, William D. Felder/Officer, Kenneth R. Hanks/Exec. VP, CFO, Treasurer, Stacy M. Hodges/Officer, James H. Ross/Exec. VP, Jim Zimcosky/Human Resources, Corporate Communications, Theresa Sheffler/Investor Information Packets, James R. Bowman/Investor Relations Contact, Loura Leventhal/Officer, Allen R. Tubb/Officer, Paul D. Vinton/Officer, Norman W. Thompson/Officer, Dick Driscoll/Officer

Directors: Don A. Buchholz/Chmn., Frederick R. Meyer/Dir., Larry A. Jobe/Dir., Jon L. Mosle/Dir., Brodie L. Cobb/Dir., Jan R. Le Croy/Dir., Mike Moses/Dir., Ron W. Haddok/Dir., Jan J. Collmar/Dir., I. D. Flores/65/Dir.

Owners: Jon L. Mosle, Don A. Buchholz, Richard H. Litton, Mike Moses, Insiders/7.72%, Cobb Partners/3.51%, Larry A. Jobe, Brodie L. Cobb/3.55%, James H. Ross, Donald W. Hultgren, William D. Felder, Jan R. LeCroy, Frederick R. Meyer, Kenneth R. Hanks

Financial Data: *Fiscal Year End:*06/24 *Latest Annual Data:* 6/30/2006

Year		Sales			Net Income
2006		$391,618,000			$41,408,000
2005		$345,452,000			$31,332,000
2004		$273,349,000			$2,710,000
Curr. Assets:	$3,300,067,000	**Curr. Liab.:**	$917,260,000	**P/E Ratio:**	16.52
Plant, Equip.:	NA	**Total Liab.:**	$4,367,738,000	**Indic. Yr. Divd.:**	$0.320
Total Assets:	$4,657,851,000	**Net Worth:**	$289,472,000	**Debt/ Equity:**	NA

Sybase Inc

One Sybase Dr., Dublin, CA, 94568; ***PH:*** 1-925-236-5100; ***http://*** www.sybase.com

General - Incorporation	DE	**Stock** - Price on:12/24/2007	$22.98
Employees	4,067	Stock Exchange	NYSE
Auditor	Ernst & Young LLP	Ticker Symbol	SY
Stk Agt	American Stock Transfer & Trust Co.	Outstanding Shares	91,320,000
Counsel	NA	E.P.S.	$1.00
DUNS No.	13-156-3215	Shareholders	NA

Business: The group's principal activities are to provide software products and professional consulting services. In 2003, the group's business was organized into one principal products group, the infrastructure platform group and two majority-owned subsidiaries, ianywhere solutions inc and financial fusion inc. The group delivers the unwired enterprise through data management and mobile infrastructure, integration and application development solutions. The software products help enterprises, integrate, manage and deliver applications, content and data. This enables organizations to attain maximum value from their data assets by getting the right information to the right people at the right time. Sybase supports some of the world's most critical data, especially in vertical markets including financial services, government, telecommunications, healthcare and defense. The group has operations in us, Europe and Asia-Pacific. On 30-Apr-2004, the group acquired xcellenet inc.

Primary SIC and add'l.: 7372 7371 7379

CIK No: 0000768262

Subsidiaries: Advanced Systems Limited, AvantGo Europe Limited, Christie Partners Holdings C. V., Counterpoint Systems Foundry, Inc., Extended Systems Benelux B.V., Extended Systems Bristol Limited, Extended Systems Canda, Inc., Extended Systems France S.a.r.l., Extended Systems GmbH, Extended Systems Holdings Limited, Extended Systems Limited, Extended Systems of Idaho, Incorporated, Extended Systems U.S. Virgin Islands, Extended Systems, Incorporated, Financial Fusion, Inc. 72 Subsidiaries included in the Index

Officers: John S. Chen/Chmn., CEO, Pres./$9,211,337.00, Nita C. White-Ivy/VP - Worldwide Human Resources, Terry Stepien/Pres. - Ianywhere Solutions, Inc, Pieter A. Van Der Vorst/Sr. VP, CFO/$1,261,931.00, Marty J. Beard/Pres. - Sybase 365/$1,166,915.00, Raj Nathan/Sr. VP, Chief Marketing Officer - Worldwide Marketing Operations/$1,196,470.00, Jeff G. Ross/VP, Corporate Controller, Dan R. Carl/VP, General Counsel, Sec., Steve Capelli/Pres. - Worldwide Field Operations/$1,145,893.00, Billy Ho/Sr. VP - Product, Technology Operations

Directors: John S. Chen/Chmn., CEO, Pres., Alan B. Salisbury/Dir., Richard C. Alberding/Dir., Jack E. Sum/Dir., Linda K. Yates/Dir., Cecilia Claudio/Dir., William L. Krause/Dir., Robert P. Wayman/Dir., Mike Daniels/Dir.

Owners: Marty Beard, Raj Nathan, William L. Krause, Richard C. Alberding, Steve Capelli, Alan B. Salisbury, Linda K. Yates, Pieter A. Van der Vorst, Cecilia Claudio, Jack E. Sum, John S. Chen/3.40%, Insiders/5.80%, Lord, Abbett & Co., LLC/9.55%, Barclays Global Investors, N.A./6.97%, Robert P. Wayman

Financial Data: Fiscal Year End:12/31   Latest Annual Data: 12/31/2006

Year	Sales	Net Income
2006	$876,163,000	$95,064,000
2005	$818,695,000	$85,583,000
2004	$788,536,000	$67,950,000

Curr. Assets:	$871,561,000	Curr. Liab.:	$416,418,000	P/E Ratio:	22.98
Plant, Equip.:	$66,458,000	Total Liab.:	$944,419,000	Indic. Yr. Divd.:	NA
Total Assets:	$1,787,550,000	Net Worth:	$843,131,000	Debt/ Equity:	0.5455

Sybron Dental Specialties Inc

1717 W Collins Ave., Orange, CA, 92867; *PH:* 1-714-516-7400; *http://* www.sybrondental.com

General - Incorporation	DE	**Stock** - Price on:12/24/2007	NA
Employees	NA	Stock Exchange	NA
Auditor	KPMG LLP	Ticker Symbol	NA
Stk Agt	EquiServe Trust Co N.A	Outstanding Shares	NA
Counsel	NA	E.P.S.	NA
DUNS No.	NA	Shareholders	NA

Business: The group's principal activity is to manufacture and market consumable dental products in the medical and dental markets. The group operates in two segments: professional dental and orthodontics. The products of the professional dental segment include light cured composite filling materials, bonding agents, amalgam alloy filling materials and dental burs. The orthodontics segment includes orthodontic appliances such as brackets, bands, buccal tubes, wires and elastomeric products. The group sells its products in the United States and abroad under brand names kerr, ormco, pinnacle, kerrhawe, aoatm, and sybronendotm.

Primary SIC and add'l.: 3843 2834

CIK No: 0001121302

Subsidiaries: 000 Spofa Dental, 1218122 Ontario Inc., Allesee Orthodontic Appliances, Inc., Analytic Endodontics U.K. Limited, Attachments International, Inc., GP eta s.r.o., Hawe Neos Holding AG, Innodent (Aust.) Pty. Ltd., Innova Corp., Innova LifeSciences Corporation, Innova U.K. Limited, Kerr (Europe) A.G., Kerr Australia Pty. Limited, Kerr Corporation, Kerr GmbH 44 Subsidiaries included in the Index

Sycamore Networks Inc

220 Mill Rd. , Chelmsford, MA, 01824; *PH:* 1-978-250-2900; *http://* www.sycamorenet.com

General - Incorporation	DE	**Stock** - Price on:12/24/2007	$4.1
Employees	276	Stock Exchange	NDQ
Auditor	PricewaterhouseCoopers LLP	Ticker Symbol	SCMR
Stk Agt	Computershare Investor Services LLC	Outstanding Shares	278,820,000
Counsel	Testa, Hurwitz & Thibeault	E.P.S.	-$0.04
DUNS No.	NA	Shareholders	NA

Business: The group's principal activity is to develop and market software based-intelligent optical networking products. These products enable network service providers to quickly and cost-effectively provide bandwidth and create new high- speed data services. The group's products are designed to allow telecommunications service providers to improve the flexibility and scalability of their networks. The group's current and prospective customers include incumbent local exchange carriers, interexchange carriers (ixcs), international incumbent operators, international competitive carriers, Internet service providers (isps), non-traditional telecommunications service providers and other corporate and government organizations. The group operates primarily in the United States, England , France and Japan.

Primary SIC and add'l.: 7372 7379 7373

CIK No: 0001092367

Subsidiaries: Sirocco Systems, Inc., Sycamore Networks Americas Inc., Sycamore Networks Asia Inc., Sycamore Networks de Mexico, S.A., Sycamore Networks Europe Inc., Sycamore Networks International BV, Sycamore Networks Japan K.K., Sycamore Securities Corporation

Officers: Daniel E. Smith/Dir., CEO, Pres., Kevin J. Oye/VP - Systems, Technology, John E. Dowling/VP - Operations, Richard J. Gaynor/CFO, VP - Finance, Administration, John Scully/VP - Worldwide Sales, Support, Alan R. Cormier/57/General Counsel

Directors: Daniel E. Smith/Dir., CEO, Pres., Gururaj Deshpande/Co - Founder, Chmn., Paul W. Chisholm/Dir., Paul J. Ferri/Dir., John W. Gerdelman/Dir., Robert E. Donahue/Dir.

Owners: John B. Scully, Gururaj Deshpande/16.20%, Araldo Menegon, Paul W. Chisholm, Paul J. Ferri, Daniel E. Smith/15.30%, Craig R. Benson, Kevin J. Oye, The Gururaj Deshpande Grantor Retained Annuity Trust/6.40%, John W. Gerdelman, Richard J. Gaynor, Alan R. Cormier, Platyko Partners, L.P./7.70%, Robert E. Donahue, Insiders/35.00% (16 Owners included in Index)

Financial Data: Fiscal Year End:07/31   Latest Annual Data: 07/31/2006

Year	Sales	Net Income
2006	$87,395,000	$19,388,000
2005	$65,434,000	-$23,789,000
2004	$44,547,000	-$44,842,000

Curr. Assets:	$972,180,000	Curr. Liab.:	$40,934,000	P/E Ratio:	45.56
Plant, Equip.:	$8,437,000	Total Liab.:	$42,518,000	Indic. Yr. Divd.:	NA
Total Assets:	$982,063,000	Net Worth:	$939,545,000	Debt/ Equity:	NA

Sydys Corp

2741 HASTINGS St., Ste. 209, Vancouver, BC, V5K 1Z8; *PH:* 1-604-251-1206; *http://* www.sydys.com

General - Incorporation	NV	**Stock** - Price on:12/24/2007	NA
Employees	NA	Stock Exchange	OTC
Auditor	L J Soldinger Associates, LLC	Ticker Symbol	SYYC
Stk Agt	Holladay Stock Transfer, Inc.	Outstanding Shares	NA
Counsel	NA	E.P.S.	NA
DUNS No.	NA	Shareholders	NA

Business: The groups principal activities include identifying and acquiring a suitable operating company and have evaluating potential acquisition targets and engaged in general discussions and due diligence activities regarding the acquisition of an operating company. The group operates from the United States.

Primary SIC and add'l.: 7310

CIK No: 0001309141

Owners: Darren Breitkreuz/1.10%, Kenneth J. Koock/35.90%, Insiders/37.00%

Curr. Assets:	$205,000	Curr. Liab.:	$115,000		
Plant, Equip.:	NA	Total Liab.:	$115,000	Indic. Yr. Divd.:	NA
Total Assets:	$205,000	Net Worth:	$90,000	Debt/ Equity:	NA

Sykes Enterprises Inc

400 N Ashley Dr., Ste. 2800, Tampa, FL, 33602; *PH:* 1-813-274-1000; *Fax:* 1-813-273-0148; *http://* www.sykes.com

General - Incorporation	FL	**Stock** - Price on:12/24/2007	$18.7
Employees	26,210	Stock Exchange	NDQ
Auditor	Deloitte & Touche LLP	Ticker Symbol	SYKE
Stk Agt	SunTrust Bank	Outstanding Shares	40,560,000
Counsel	Foley & Lardner LLP	E.P.S.	$0.95
DUNS No.	04-175-9564	Shareholders	NA

Business: The group's principle activities are to offer customer management solutions and services to companies within the technology, communications and financial service markets. It operates in two segments: business services and business solutions. Business services provide customer care outsourcing with emphasis on technical support and customer service. These services are delivered through multiple communications channels encompassing phone, e-mail, Web and chat. The business solutions provide consultative professional services in e-commerce and customer relationship management with a focus on business strategy, project management, business processes redesign, knowledge management, and education training and Web development. The group markets its products with the help of client referrals, personal sales calls, advertising in industry publications, direct mailing to targeted customers. The group's quarterly revenue for Sep '07 was 176.12 millions of USD.

Primary SIC and add'l.: 7375 7389 7379

CIK No: 0001010612

Subsidiaries: 248 Pall Mall (London) Inc., Clinidata Incorporated, Kelly, Luttmer & Associates Limited, LINK Network Limited, McQueen Europe Limited, McQueen International B.V., McQueen International Incorporated, McQueen International Limited, SEI International Services S.a.r.l., Shanghai Pintian Information Technology Service Co., Ltd., Sykes (Bermuda) Holdings Limited, Sykes (Shanghai) Co. Ltd, Sykes Asia Inc., Sykes Canada Corporation, Sykes Central America Ltda 41 Subsidiaries included in the Index

Officers: Charles E. Sykes/Dir., CEO, Pres./$1,531,356.00, David L. Pearson/CIO, Sr. VP/$490,339.00, James T. Holder/Sr. VP, General Counsel, Corp. Sec., Daniel L. Hernandez/Sr. VP - Global Strategy, Jenna R. Nelson/Group Executive, Sr. VP - Human Resources, James C. Hobby/Sr. VP - Global Operations/$641,531.00, David P. Reule/Pres. - Sykes Realty, Incorporated, Michael W. Kipphut/Group Executive, Sr. VP, CFO/$947,159.00, Lawrence Zingale/Sr. VP - Global Sales, Client Management/$717,014.00, Subhaash Kumar/Sr. Dir. - Investor Relations

Directors: Charles E. Sykes/Dir., CEO, Pres., Paul L. Whiting/Chmn., James K. Murray/Dir., Mark Bozek/Dir., William J. Meurer/Dir., James S. MacLeod/Dir., Iain A. MacDonald/Dir., Parks H. Helms/Dir., Michael P. Delong/Dir., Linda McClintock-Greco/Dir., Furman P. Bodenheimer/Dir.

Owners: Michael DeLong, David L. Pearson, Parks H. Helms, James C. Hobby, William J. Meurer, James K. Murray, Iain Macdonald, Michael W. Kipphut, Furman P. Bodenheimer, Charles E. Sykes, Insiders/2.60%, Linda McClintock-Greco, Lawrence R. Zingale, Mark C. Bozek, James S. MacLeod (16 Owners included in Index)

Financial Data: Fiscal Year End:12/31   Latest Annual Data: 12/31/2006

Year	Sales	Net Income
2006	$574,223,000	$42,323,000
2005	$494,918,000	$23,408,000
2004	$466,713,000	$10,814,000

Curr. Assets:	$288,771,000	Curr. Liab.:	$104,875,000	P/E Ratio:	17.64
Plant, Equip.:	$66,205,000	Total Liab.:	$124,100,000	Indic. Yr. Divd.:	NA
Total Assets:	$415,573,000	Net Worth:	$291,473,000	Debt/ Equity:	NA

Symantec Corp

20330 Stevens Creek Blvd., Cupertino, CA, 95014; *PH:* 1-408-517-8000; *http://* www.symantec.com

General - Incorporation	DE	**Stock** - Price on:12/24/2007	$19.69
Employees	16,000	Stock Exchange	NDQ
Auditor	KPMG LLP	Ticker Symbol	SYMC
Stk Agt	Computershare Trust Co	Outstanding Shares	901,020,000
Counsel	Fenwick & West LLP	E.P.S.	$0.41
DUNS No.	06-469-6941	Shareholders	NA

Business: The group's principle activity is to provide content and network security software and appliance solutions to enterprises, individuals and service providers. Consumer product delivers security and problem-solving products to individual users, home, offices and small businesses. Enterprise security provides Internet security technology, global response and services used for information security needs. Enterprise administration offers products for use in information technology departments. The group operates from United States.

Primary SIC and add'l.: 7372

CIK No: 0000849399

Subsidiaries: Axent (emea) Limited, BindView Development Corporation, DataCenter Technologies N.V., Delrina Corporation, Ejasent, Inc., Invio Software, Inc., Jareva Technologies, Inc., Kvault Software Ltd., Precise Software Solutions, Inc., Sygate Technologies LLC, Symantec (Australia) Pty Ltd., Symantec (Canada) Corp., Symantec (Japan), Inc., Symantec Australia Holding Pty. Ltd., Symantec Cyprus Ltd. 40 Subsidiaries included in the Index

Officers: John W. Thompson/Chmn., CEO/$4,781,715.00, Bernard Kwok/Sr. VP - Asia Pacific, Japan Geography, Jeremy Burton/Group Pres. - Enterprise Security, Data Management, Mark Bregman/CTO, Exec. VP, Janice Chaffin/Group Pres. - Consumer Business Unit/$2,923,033.00, Greg Hughes/Group Pres. - Global Services, Steve Messick/Sr. VP - Americas Geography, Art Wong/Sr.

VP - Symantec Security Response, Managed Services, Art Courville/Exec. VP, General Counsel, Sec., Enrique T. Salem/Group Pres. - Worldwide Sales, Marketing, Kristof Hagerman/44/Group Pres. - Data Center Management/$3,732,519.00, John Brigden/Sr. VP - Europe, Middle East, Africa Geography, Rebecca Ranninger/Chief Human Resources Officer, Exec. VP, Thomas Kendra/Group Pres. - Security, Data Management Group/$4,205,095.00, James Socas/Sr. VP - Corporate Development *(24 Officers included in Index)*

Directors: John W. Thompson/Chmn., CEO, Michael Brown/Dir., William Coleman/Dir., David Mahoney/Dir., Robert S. Miller/Dir., George Reyes/Dir., David Roux/Dir., Daniel H. Schulman/Dir., Paul Unruh/Dir., Frank E. Dangeard/Dir.

Owners: George Reyes, David L. Mahoney, Insiders/1.70%, Janice Chaffin, William T. Coleman, James A. Beer, Robert S. Miller, Paul V. Unruh, Thomas W. Kendra, Kristof Hagerman, John W. Thompson/1.10%, Frank E. Dangeard, David J. Roux, Daniel H. Schulman, UBS/5.80% *(16 Owners included in Index)*

Financial Data: *Fiscal Year End:*03/31 *Latest Annual Data:* 3/31/2007

Year	Sales	Net Income
2007	$5,199,366,000	$404,380,000
2006	$4,143,392,000	$156,852,000
2005	$2,582,849,000	$536,159,000

Curr. Assets:	$4,071,047,000	**Curr. Liab.:**	$3,318,089,000		
Plant, Equip.:	$1,092,240,000	**Total Liab.:**	$6,149,357,000	**Indic. Yr. Divd.:**	NA
Total Assets:	$17,750,870,000	**Net Worth:**	$11,601,513,000	**Debt/ Equity:**	0.1828

Symbion Inc

40 Burton Hills Blvd., Ste. 500, Nashville, TN, 37215; *PH:* 1-615-234-5900; *http://* www.symbion.com

General - Incorporation	DE	**Stock**- Price on:12/24/2007	$21.86
Employees	1,600	Stock Exchange	OTC
Auditor	Ernst & Young LLP	Ticker Symbol	SBII
Stk Agt	SunTrust Bank	Outstanding Shares	21,720,000
Counsel	NA	E.P.S	$0.84
DUNS No.	NA	Shareholders	NA

Business: The group's prinicipal activity is to operate surgery and diagnostic centers. Surgery centers provide non-emergency surgical procedures across many specialties. In addition to surgery centers, the group also operates a diagnostic center and manages three physician networks. The group owns and operates 36 surgery centers and manages 8 additional surgery centers.

Primary SIC and add'l.: 8062 8071

CIK No: 0001091312

Subsidiaries: Ambulatory Resource Centres Investment Company, Inc., Ambulatory Resource Centres of Florida, Inc., Ambulatory Resource Centres of Massachusetts, Inc., Ambulatory Resource Centres of Texas, Inc., Ambulatory Resource Centres of Washington, Inc., Ambulatory Resource Centres of Wilmington, Inc., Ambulatory Surgery Center of Cool Springs, LLC, Ambulatory Surgery Center of Worcester, LLC, ARC Development Corporation, ARC Dry Creek, Inc., ARC Financial Services Corporation, ARC Kentucky, LLC, ARC New Hartford, Inc., ARC of Bellingham, L.P., ARC of Georgia, LLC 136 Subsidiaries included in the Index

Officers: Richard E. Francis/Chmn., CEO/$1,502,371.00, Dale R. Kennedy/VP - Management Services, Symbion/$443,140.00, Teresa F. Sparks/Corporate Controller, Sue Ann Hardin/VP - Human Resources, Kenneth C. Mitchell/CFO/$568,213.00, Gregg A. Stanley/Pres. - Symbions National Group, Anthony W. Taparo/Group VP, Clifford G. Adlerz/Dir., COO, Pres./$1,069,518.00

Directors: Richard E. Francis/Chmn., CEO, Clifford G. Adlerz/Dir., COO, Pres.

Financial Data: *Fiscal Year End:*12/31 *Latest Annual Data:* 12/31/2006

Year	Sales	Net Income
2006	$301,534,000	$18,793,000
2005	$265,744,000	$19,055,000
2004	$216,325,000	$13,552,000

Curr. Assets:	$86,905,000	**Curr. Liab.:**	$30,262,000	**P/E Ratio:**	26.02
Plant, Equip.:	$82,365,000	**Total Liab.:**	$185,759,000	**Indic. Yr. Divd.:**	NA
Total Assets:	$503,806,000	**Net Worth:**	$285,279,000	**Debt/ Equity:**	0.4467

Symbollon Pharmaceuticals Inc

37 Loring Dr., Framingham, MA, 01702; *PH:* 1-508-620-7676; *http://* www.symbollon.com

General - Incorporation	DE	**Stock**- Price on:12/24/2007	$0.9
Employees	3	Stock Exchange	OTC
Auditor	Vitale, Caturano & Co. Ltd	Ticker Symbol	SYMBA
Stk Agt	American Stock Transfer & Trust Co.	Outstanding Shares	12,590,000
Counsel	NA	E.P.S	-$0.359
DUNS No.	78-787-6770	Shareholders	NA

Business: The group's principle activity is to develop proprietary iodine-based pharmaceutical agents and antimicrobials. Currently in the development stage, the company concentrates on the development of a proposed product application for the treatment for fibrocystic breast disease. The company has developed a proprietary iodine technology that maximizes the therapeutic index of iodine. The oral dosage form of the technology, called iogen (TM), generates molecular iodine in situ in the stomach of the patient. The company has also co-developed a bovine teat sanitizer, marketed as iodozyme(R), with west agro inc of Kansas city. The principal market for iodozyme is dairy farms. On 28-May-2004, the company acquired certain assets of mimetix inc.

Primary SIC and add'l.: 2834

CIK No: 0000912086

Officers: Paul C. Desjourdy/Dir., CEO, CFO, Pres., General Counsel, Treasurer/$907,267.00, Jack H. Kessler/Chmn., Chief Scientific Officer, Sec./$627,188.00

Directors: Paul C. Desjourdy/Dir., CEO, CFO, Pres., General Counsel, Treasurer, Jack H. Kessler/Chmn., Chief Scientific Officer, Sec., James C. Richards/Dir., Eugene Lieberstein/Dir., Richard F. Maradie/Dir.

Owners: Insiders/15.90%, Jack H. Kessler/7.00%, Richard F. Maradie, Eugene Lieberstein, Paul C. Desjourdy/6.90%, Anthony J. Cantone/14.70%, James C. Richards/1.80%, Richard M. Lilly/5.00%

Financial Data: *Fiscal Year End:*12/31 *Latest Annual Data:* 12/31/2006

Year	Sales	Net Income
2006	$40,000	-$3,047,000
2005	$450,000	-$646,000
2004	$160,000	-$2,647,000

Curr. Assets:	$2,562,000	**Curr. Liab.:**	$302,000		
Plant, Equip.:	$9,000	**Total Liab.:**	$302,000	**Indic. Yr. Divd.:**	NA
Total Assets:	$2,876,000	**Net Worth:**	$2,574,000	**Debt/ Equity:**	NA

Symmetricom Inc

2300 Orchard Pkwy, San Jose, CA, 95131; *PH:* 1-408-428-7907; *http://* www.telecom.com; *Email:* customer_relations@symmetricom.com

General - Incorporation	DE	**Stock**- Price on:12/24/2007	$8.82
Employees	865	Stock Exchange	NDQ
Auditor	Deloitte & Touche LLP	Ticker Symbol	SYMM
Stk Agt	American Stock Transfer & Trust Co.	Outstanding Shares	46,420,000
Counsel	Pillsbury Winthrop LLP	E.P.S	$0.05
DUNS No.	00-824-8593	Shareholders	NA

Business: The group's principal activity is to design, manufacture and market solutions for the telecommunication industry. The products and services include network synchronization systems and timing elements. These products optimize bandwidth utilization and quality of service of wireline, wireless and broadband communications networks enabling customers to increase the efficiency of their networks in today's evolving communications environment. The group also supplies consumer and business broadband access solutions to global network service providers. The major customers of the group are verizon and acterna worldwide. On 04-Oct-2002, the group acquired truetime, inc and on 29-Oct-2002, datum inc. In Jun 2003, the group discontinued the operation of the trusted time division which was acquired as part of the acquisition of datum inc.

Primary SIC and add'l.: 3663 7389 3661

CIK No: 0000082628

Subsidiaries: Manufacturing Solutions Puerto Rico, Inc., SymmCom Beijing Ltd., Symmetricom Global Services, Inc., Symmetricom GmbH, Symmetricom Hong Kong, Ltd., Symmetricom Puerto Rico Ltd., Symmetricom, Ltd.

Officers: Thomas W. Steipp/Dir., CEO, Pres., William Slater/Exec. VP - Finance, Administration, CFO, Dale Pelletier/Exec. VP - Global Manufacturing Operations, Bruce Bromage/Exec. VP, GM - Timing, Test, Measurement Division, Nancy Shemwell/Exec. VP - Global Sales, Services, David Cox/Exec. VP, GM - QoE Assurance Division, Bill Minor/VP - Global Human Resources

Directors: Thomas W. Steipp/Dir., CEO, Pres., Robert T. Clarkson/Chmn., Elizabeth A. Fetter/Dir., Robert J. Stanzione/Dir., Robert Neumeister/Dir., Richard W. Oliver/Dir., Al Boschulte/Dir., Richard N. Snyder/Dir., Jim Chiddix/Dir.

Owners: Richard W. Oliver, ICM Asset Management, Inc. and James M. Simmons/9.45%, Robert T. Clarkson, David Cox, Insiders/5.09%, Robert J. Stanzione, Nancy J. Shemwell, Thomas W. Steipp/2.64%, Dimensional Fund Advisors Inc./6.21%, Bruce Bromage, Alfred Boschulte, Richard N. Snyder, William Slater, Elizabeth A. Fetter, Robert M. Neumeister *(16 Owners included in Index)*

Financial Data: *Fiscal Year End:*06/30 *Latest Annual Data:* 6/30/2006

Year	Sales	Net Income
2006	$188,211,000	$819,000
2005	$189,147,000	$17,916,000
2004	$172,847,000	-$2,237,000

Curr. Assets:	$262,861,000	**Curr. Liab.:**	$41,618,000	**P/E Ratio:**	67.85
Plant, Equip.:	$26,553,000	**Total Liab.:**	$167,857,000	**Indic. Yr. Divd.:**	NA
Total Assets:	$392,418,000	**Net Worth:**	$224,561,000	**Debt/ Equity:**	0.5346

Symmetry Medical Inc

220 W Market St., Warsaw, IN, 46580; *PH:* 1-574-268-2252; *http://* www.symmetrymedical.com

General - Incorporation	DE	**Stock**- Price on:12/24/2007	$14.88
Employees	1,795	Stock Exchange	NYSE
Auditor	Ernst& Young LLP	Ticker Symbol	SMA
Stk Agt	Computershare Ltd.	Outstanding Shares	35,290,000
Counsel	NA	E.P.S	$0.46
DUNS No.	NA	Shareholders	NA

Business: The groups principle activity is to provide implants and related instruments to orthopedic device manufacturers. In the year 2006, the group acquired Riley Medical, Inc. The group operates from the United States, the United Kingdom, Ireland and other foreign countries.

Primary SIC and add'l.: 3728 3845 3842 3841

CIK No: 0001292055

Subsidiaries: Arthur Robinson & Sons (Willenhall) Limited, Jet Engineering, Inc., Medicast Limited, Mettis (UK) Limited, Mettis Group Inc., Othy Limited, Poly-Vac France S.A.R.L., Poly-Vac S.A., Symmetry Medical International Inc., Symmetry Medical USA Inc., Thornton Precision Components Limited, Ultrexx, Inc.

Officers: Brian S. Moore/Dir., CEO, Pres./$558,411.00, Fred L. Hite/Sr. VP, CFO/$303,031.00, Andrew Miclot/52/Sr. VP - Marketing, Sales, Business Development, Investor Relations Officer/$288,055.00, Darin D. Martin/Sr. VP - Quality Assurance, Regulatory Affairs/$195,636.00, Richard J. Senior/44/Sr. VP, GM - Europe/$323,974.00, Michael W. Curtis/Sr. VP, GM - Medical Products, USA/$233,964.00, Nick Laudico/VP - Investor Relations

Directors: Brian S. Moore/Dir., CEO, Pres., Frank Turner/Chmn., James S. Burns/Dir., Francis T. Nusspickel/Dir., Stephen B. Oresman/Dir.

Owners: Richard J. Senior, Darin D. Martin, Insiders/1.20%, Frank Turner, Stephen B. Oresman, James S. Burns, Andrew J. Miclot, Fred L. Hite, Brian S. Moore, Michael W. Curtis, Francis T. Nusspickel

Financial Data: *Fiscal Year End:*12/30 *Latest Annual Data:* 12/30/2006

Year	Sales	Net Income
2006	$253,569,000	$24,149,000
2005	$263,766,000	$31,800,000

Curr. Assets:	$102,246,000	**Curr. Liab.:**	$38,469,000	**P/E Ratio:**	84.68
Plant, Equip.:	$93,106,000	**Total Liab.:**	$84,390,000	**Indic. Yr. Divd.:**	NA
Total Assets:	$337,645,000	**Net Worth:**	$253,255,000	**Debt/ Equity:**	NA

SYMS Corp

1 Syms Way, Secaucus, NJ, 07094; *PH:* 1-201-902-9600; *http://* www.syms.com; *Email:* customerservice@syms.com

General - Incorporation	NJ	**Stock**- Price on:12/24/2007	$20.37
Employees	981	Stock Exchange	NYSE
Auditor	BDO Seidman LLP	Ticker Symbol	SYM
Stk Agt	American Stock Transfer & Trust Co.	Outstanding Shares	14,700,000
Counsel	Robinson, Silverman, Pearce Et Al	E.P.S	$0.30
DUNS No.	01-226-7324	Shareholders	NA

Business: The group's principal activity is to operate a chain of retail clothing and apparel stores. The stores provide a range of off-price, quality and in-season merchandise consisting of tailored clothing, haberdashery, suits and shoes for men, women and children. The trademarks are syms, an educated consumer is our best customer (R), names you must know(R) and the more you know about clothing, the better it is for syms (r). The group operates a chain of 40 retail stores located throughout the northeastern and middle Atlantic regions and in the midwest, southeast and southwest.

Primary SIC and add'l.: 5621 5641 5948 5661 5611

CIK No: 0000724742

Subsidiaries: SYL, LLC

Officers: Marcy Syms/57/Dir., CEO, Pres./$641,327.00, Antone F. Moreira/71/Dir., VP, CFO, Assist. Sec./$174,347.00, Elyse Marks/54/VP - Information Services, John Tyzbir/53/VP - Human Resources, Allen Brailsford/63/Exec. VP - Operations/$154,088.00, Myra Butensky/48/VP, Divisional Merchandise Mgr. Men's Tailored Clothing, James Donato/51/VP - Operations, Moggy Mann/57/VP - Ladies, Karen Day/49/VP - Childrens, Robert Terpstra/46/VP - Mens Haberdashery

Directors: Marcy Syms/57/Dir., CEO, Pres., Sy Syms/Chmn., Antone F. Moreira/71/Dir., VP, CFO, Assist. Sec., Amber M. Brookman/Dir., Henry M. Chidgey/Dir., Bernard H. Tenenbaum/Dir.

Owners: Insiders, Franklin Advisory Services, LLC, Sy Syms, Allen Brailsford, Marcy Syms, Dimensional Fund Advisors, Inc, Amber M. Brookman, Barington Companies Equity Partners, L.P

Financial Data: *Fiscal Year End:*03/01 *Latest Annual Data:* 3/3/2007

Year	Sales	Net Income
2007	$281,178,000	$9,548,000
2006	$280,389,000	$3,436,000
2005	$283,567,000	$2,177,000

Curr. Assets:	$103,373,000	**Curr. Liab.:**	$35,942,000	**P/E Ratio:**	31.39
Plant, Equip.:	$104,323,000	**Total Liab.:**	$37,490,000	**Indic. Yr. Divd.:**	NA
Total Assets:	$239,559,000	**Net Worth:**	$202,069,000	**Debt/ Equity:**	NA

Symyx Technologies Inc

3100 Central Express Way, Santa Clara, CA, 95051; *PH:* 1-408-764-2000; *http://* www.symyx.com; *Email:* ir@symyx.com

General - Incorporation	DE	**Stock**- Price on:12/24/2007	$11.36
Employees	380	Stock Exchange	NDQ
Auditor	Ernst & Young LLP	Ticker Symbol	SMMX
Stk Agt	Wells Fargo Bank Minnesota N.A	Outstanding Shares	33,230,000
Counsel	Wilson Sonsini Goodrich & Rosati	E.P.S	$0.80
DUNS No.	NA	Shareholders	NA

Business: The group's principal activities are to research, develop, manufacture and market products, through the application of combinatorial technologies in the area of materials science. The group is involved in research collaborations with large chemical, life science and electronic companies and undertakes licensing of proprietary materials. Through a combination of powerful miniaturization, automation and parallel processing technologies, the group's scientists are able to generate numerous materials at a time and screen these materials rapidly and automatically for desired properties. The group applies proprietary technologies, instruments, software and methods to cost-effectively accelerate and fundamentally change materials discovery.

Primary SIC and add'l.: 8731

CIK No: 0001095330

Subsidiaries: Symyx Discovery Tools,Inc., Symyx Renaissance Software,Inc., Symyx Technologies (France) SARL, Symyx Technologies (Germany) GmbH., Symyx Technologies (UK) Ltd., Symyx Technologies International,Inc., Symyx Technologies, AG.

Officers: Isy Goldwasser/CEO/$1,396,975.00, Henry W. Weinberg/Chief Scientific Officer, Exec. VP/$1,573,975.00, Paul J. Nowak/53/COO, Exec. VP/$1,308,025.00, Jeryl L. Hilleman/50/Exec. VP/$1,179,325.00, Rex S. Jackson/CFO, Exec. VP, Gerard Abraham/Pres. - Symyx Tools, Richard Boehner/Exec. VP - Chemicals, Energy, Timothy Campbell/Pres. - Symyx Software

Directors: Steven Goldby/Chmn., Samuel D. Colella/68/Dir., Thomas R. Baruch/Dir., Kenneth J. Nussbacher/Dir., Ed F. Gambrell/Dir., Anthony R. Muller/Dir., Mario M. Rosati/Dir., David C. Hill/Dir., Bruce Pasternack/Dir.

Owners: T. Rowe Price Associates, Inc/13.30%, Kenneth J. Nussbacher, Mazama Capital Management, Inc/14.40%, Insiders/9.70%, Steven D. Goldby/2.40%, Edwin F. Gambrell, Isy Goldwasser/2.20%, Thomas R. Baruch, Baron Capital Group, Inc/6.90%, Mario M. Rosati, Paul J. Nowak, Anthony R. Muller, Jeryl L. Hilleman/2.10%, Samuel D. Colella, Henry W. Weinberg/2.50%

Financial Data: *Fiscal Year End:*12/31 *Latest Annual Data:* 12/31/2006

Year	Sales	Net Income
2006	$124,900,000	$8,284,000
2005	$108,137,000	$12,002,000
2004	$83,185,000	$12,882,000

Curr. Assets:	$177,019,000	**Curr. Liab.:**	$30,839,000	**P/E Ratio:**	66.82
Plant, Equip.:	$31,222,000	**Total Liab.:**	$31,630,000	**Indic. Yr. Divd.:**	NA
Total Assets:	$260,006,000	**Net Worth:**	$228,376,000	**Debt/ Equity:**	NA

Synagro Technologies Inc

1800 Bering, Ste 1000, Houston, TX, 77057; *PH:* 1-713-369-1700; *http://* www.synagro.com

General - Incorporation	DE	**Stock**- Price on:12/24/2007	NA
Employees	982	Stock Exchange	NA
Auditor	PricewaterhouseCoopers LLP	Ticker Symbol	NA
Stk Agt	I'Continental Reg & Trnsfer Agency	Outstanding Shares	NA
Counsel	NA	E.P.S	NA
DUNS No.	80-205-3256	Shareholders	NA

Business: The group's principal activity is the management of biosolids through beneficial reuse programs. It provides wastewater residuals management services to municipal and industrial customers. The group offers services that focus on the beneficial reuse of organic non-hazardous residuals resulting from the wastewater treatment process. It provides its customers with complete, vertically-integrated services and capabilities, including facility operations, facility cleanout services and regulatory compliance. The services also include dewatering, collection and transportation, composting, drying and pelletization, product marketing, incineration, alkaline stabilization and land application. On 07-May-2003, the group acquired aspen resources inc.

Primary SIC and add'l.: 4953

CIK No: 0000895565

Subsidiaries: Earthwise Organics LLC, Environmental Protection & Improvement Company LLC, Grand Rapids Biosolids Processing Company LLC, Jabb Ii LLC, NETCO Waterbury, New Haven Residuals, New York Organic Fertilizer Company, Organi Gro LLC, PhiladelphiBiosolids Services LLC, Providence Soils LLC, Sacramento Project Finance Inc., Soaring VistProperties LLC, South Kern Industrial Center LLC, ST Interco Inc., Synagro Baltimore LLC 31 Subsidiaries included in the Index

Officers: Robert C. Boucher/CEO, Pres., Alvin L. Thomas/Exec. VP, General Counsel, Paul J. Withrow/Sr. Exec. VP, CFO

Directors: Roger J. Klatt/Dir., Nolan Lehmann/Dir.

Owners: PowerShares ExchangeTraded Fund Trust/9.90%, Insiders/3.30%, Alvin L. Thomas, Ross M. Patten, Paul J. Withrow, Thomas M. Urban, James B. Mattly, Dimensional Fund Advisors LP/5.40%, Gene A. Meredith, Alfred Tyler, Neuberger Berman Inc./8.70%, T. Rowe Price Associates, Inc./9.10%, Roger J. Klatt, Thornburg Investment Management, Inc./8.30%, Nolan Lehmann *(17 Owners included in Index)*

Synalloy Corp

PO Box 5627, Spartanburg, SC, 29304; *PH:* 1-864-585-3605; *http://* www.synalloy.com; *Email:* invrel@synalloy.com

General - Incorporation	DE	**Stock**- Price on:12/24/2007	$43.94
Employees	437	Stock Exchange	NDQ
Auditor	Dixon Hughes PLLC	Ticker Symbol	SYNL
Stk Agt	American Stock Transfer & Trust Co.	Outstanding Shares	6,200,000
Counsel	Haynsworth, Sinkler & Boyd	E.P.S	$1.93
DUNS No.	00-334-9065	Shareholders	NA

Business: The group's principal activity is to manufacture welded pipes and chemicals. The group operates through three segments: metals, colors and speciality chemicals. The metals segment are operated through bristol metals and whiting metals, both of which are wholly owned subsidiaries. The chemicals segment consists of blackman uhler chemical company, which is a division of the group and manufacturers chemicals lp and organic pigments corporation. The metals segment manufactures welded stainless steel pipe and other products like piping systems, fittings, tanks, pressure vessels and other components. The chemical segment manufactures chemicals and maintains permitted waste treatment system. The colors segment manufactures dyes, pigments and auxiliaries for the textile industry and specialty chemicals for other industries. On 22-Jul-2003 the group acquired certain assets of rite industries inc.

Primary SIC and add'l.: 3498 2865 2816 3312 2869

CIK No: 0000095953

Subsidiaries: Bristol Metals, Inc, Manufacturers Soap and Chemicals Company, Metchem, Inc., Organic-Pigments Corporation

Officers: Ronald H. Braam/Dir., CEO, Pres./$597,015.00, Gregory M. Bowie/VP - Finance/$283,800.00, Cheryl C. Carter/Corp. Sec./$119,200.00

Directors: Ronald H. Braam/Dir., CEO, Pres., James G. Lane/Chmn., Sibyl N. Fishburn/Dir., Craig Bram/Dir., Murray H. Wright/Dir., Carroll D. Vinson/Dir.

Owners: Gregory M. Bowie, Ronald H. Braam/1.10%, Craig C. Bram, James G. Lane/5.82%, Insiders/15.34%, Carroll D. Vinson, Royce & Associates LLC/9.49%, Cheryl C. Carter, Murray H. Wright/3.88%, Michael D. Boling/1.04%, Sibyl N. Fishburn/1.26%, Dimensional Fund Advisors, Inc./5.30%

Financial Data: *Fiscal Year End:*12/31 *Latest Annual Data:* 12/30/2006

Year	Sales	Net Income
2006	$152,047,000	$7,608,000
2005	$128,927,000	$5,096,000

Curr. Assets:	$47,994,000	**Curr. Liab.:**	$19,330,000	**P/E Ratio:**	26.31
Plant, Equip.:	$18,698,000	**Total Liab.:**	$31,686,000	**Indic. Yr. Divd.:**	NA
Total Assets:	$70,982,000	**Net Worth:**	$39,296,000	**Debt/ Equity:**	NA

Synaptics Inc

3120 Scott Blvd., Ste. 130, Santa Clara, CA, 95054; *PH:* 1-408-454-5100; *Fax:* 1-408-454-5200; *http://* www.synaptics.com; *Email:* info@synaptics.com

General - Incorporation	DE	**Stock**- Price on:12/24/2007	$35.29
Employees	254	Stock Exchange	NDQ
Auditor	KPMG LLP	Ticker Symbol	SYNA
Stk Agt	American Stock Transfer & Trust Co.	Outstanding Shares	25,660,000
Counsel	Greenberg Traurig Askew Et Al	E.P.S	$0.74
DUNS No.	NA	Shareholders	NA

Business: The group's principal activity is to develop and supply custom-designed touch pads and user interface solutions for notebook computers. Touchpad(tm) is a small, touch-sensitive pad that senses the position of a person's finger on its surface to provide screen navigation, cursor movement, and a platform for interactive input. Touchstyk , enables computer manufacturers to offer end users the choice of a touch pad, a pointing stick, or a combination of both interface devices. Quickstroke provides a fast, easy, and accurate way to input Chinese characters. Clearpad touch screen solution is a thin sensor that can be placed over any surface, including display devices, such as liquid crystal displays, or lcds. Spiral is a thin inductive pen-sensing system. On 26-Jun-2003, the group acquired nsm technology ltd.

Primary SIC and add'l.: 3577 7372 7379

CIK No: 0000817720

Subsidiaries: Synaptics (UK) Limited, Synaptics Holding GmbH, Synaptics Hong Kong Limited, Synaptics International, Inc., Synaptics LLC

Officers: Francis F. Lee/Dir., CEO, Pres./$3,057,154.00, Shawn P. Day/CTO/$615,518.00, David McKinnon/VP - Onetouch Products, William T. Stacy/VP - Platform Development, Russell J. Knittel/CFO, Exec. VP, Sec.,Treasurer/$1,044,441.00, Thomas J. Tiernan/Exec. VP, GM/$1,321,699.00, James B. Harrington/VP - Global Human Resources/$932,875.00, Wen-Shone Shiau/VP - Synaptics Taiwan, Joe Virginia/VP - Marketing, Handheld Business, Mark Vena/VP - Notebook Business, Kin Cheung/VP - Product Development, Ruth Lutes/VP - Customer Care, Quality, Doug Kahn/VP - Supply Chain Management, Alex Wong/VP - World Wide Operations

Directors: Francis F. Lee/Dir., CEO, Pres., Federico Faggin/Chmn., Keith B. Geeslin/Dir., Richard L. Sanquini/Dir., Ronald W. Van Dell/Dir., Jeffrey D. Buchanan/Dir., Nelson C. Chan/Dir.

Owners: Keith B. Geeslin, Russell J. Knittel, T. Rowe Price Associates, Inc./5.70%, Thomas J. Tiernan, Jeffrey D. Buchanan, Richard L. Sanquini, James B. Harrington, Federico Faggin/3.90%, Insiders/8.60%, Shawn P. Day, Francis F. Lee/3.30%, Waddell & Reed Financial, Inc./5.80%, Ronald Van W. Dell, FMR Corp./9.70%, Nelson C. Chan

Financial Data: *Fiscal Year End:*06/25 *Latest Annual Data:* 6/30/2006

Year	Sales	Net Income
2006	$184,557,000	$13,701,000
2005	$208,139,000	$37,985,000
2004	$133,276,000	$12,992,000

Curr. Assets:	$292,627,000	**Curr. Liab.:**	$34,839,000	**P/E Ratio:**	37.54
Plant, Equip.:	$16,038,000	**Total Liab.:**	$164,379,000	**Indic. Yr. Divd.:**	NA
Total Assets:	$331,421,000	**Net Worth:**	$167,042,000	**Debt/ Equity:**	0.6292

Synbiotics Corp

12200 NW Ambassadar Dr., Ste. 101, Kansas City, MO, 64163; *PH:* 1-800-228-4305; *Fax:* 1-816-464-3521; *http://* www.synbiotics.com

General - Incorporation	CA	**Stock**- Price on:12/24/2007	$0.11
Employees	NA	Stock Exchange	OTC
Auditor	Levitz, Zacks & Ciceric	Ticker Symbol	SYNB
Stk Agt	Mellon Investor Services LLC	Outstanding Shares	NA
Counsel	Brobeck, Phleger & Harrison	E.P.S.	NA
DUNS No.	04-128-3219	Shareholders	NA

Business: The group's principal activity is to provide rapid diagnostic and laboratory diagnostic products for the animal health care industry. The group develops and manufactures specialty products, which are marketed to veterinarians and purebred dog enthusiasts. The group's principal markets are veterinarians and veterinary clinical laboratories. The products are sold in the United States, Canada, Europe and Asia and to a limited extent in Latin America. The group's manufacturing facilities and offices are located in California, New York, France, Pennsylvania and Missouri.

Primary SIC and add'l.: 2836 3841 2835

CIK No: 0000719483

Subsidiaries: Synbiotics Europe SAS

Officers: Paul R. Hays/CEO, Pres., Kent B. Luther/VP - Sales, Marketing, Clifford J. Frank/VP - Strategic Projects, Keith A. Butler/CFO, VP, Mark Mellencamp/VP - Research, Development

Financial Data: *Fiscal Year End:*12/31 *Latest Annual Data:* 12/31/2004

Year	Sales	Net Income
2004	$19,219,000	-$647,000
2002	$21,671,000	-$14,401,000
2001	$27,521,000	$431,000

Curr. Assets:	$10,998,000	**Curr. Liab.:**	$6,055,000		
Plant, Equip.:	$979,000	**Total Liab.:**	$11,203,000	**Indic. Yr. Divd.:**	NA
Total Assets:	$15,522,000	**Net Worth:**	$4,319,000	**Debt/ Equity:**	NA

Synchronoss Technologies Inc

750 Rte. 202 S, Ste. 600, Bridgewater, NJ, 08807; *PH:* 1-866-620-3940; *http://* www.synchronoss.com; *Email:* info@synchronoss.com

General - Incorporation	DE	**Stock**- Price on:12/24/2007	$28.42
Employees	170	Stock Exchange	NDQ
Auditor	Ernst & Young LLP	Ticker Symbol	SNCR
Stk Agt	American Stock Transfer & Trust Co.	Outstanding Shares	32,320,000
Counsel	NA	E.P.S.	$0.39
DUNS No.	NA	Shareholders	NA

Business: The groups principle activity is to provide on demand multi channel transaction management solutions. The group products sold under the trade names PerformancePartner(R) and ActivationNow(R). Specific customers of the group include Cingular Wireless, Vonage Holdings, Cablevision Systems Corporation, Level 3 Communications, SunRocket, Covad and Verizon Business Solutions. The group operates from the United States. The group's quarterly revenue for September 2007 was 34.48 millions of USD.

Primary SIC and add'l.: 7371 7379 7372 7389

CIK No: 0001131554

Officers: Stephen G. Waldis/Founder, Chmn., CEO, Pres./$1,131,387.00, Lawrence R. Irving/CFO, Treasurer/$741,729.00, Bob Garcia/COO, Chris Putnam/Exec. VP - Sales/$958,400.00, Omar Tellez/Exec. VP - Marketing/$724,282.00, Ronald Prague/VP, General Counsel, Andrew Cox/CIO, Robert Garcia/Exec. VP - Product Management, Service Delivery/$1,502,859.00

Directors: Stephen G. Waldis/Founder, Chmn., CEO, Pres., William J. Cadogan/Dir., Charles E. Hoffman/Dir., Thomas J. Hopkins/Dir., James M. McCormick/Dir., Donnie M. Moore/Dir.

Owners: Robert Garcia, Stephen G. Waldis/7.10%, Scott Yaphe/9.30%, William J. Cadogan, Christopher Putnam, Fred Alger Management, Inc./6.00%, Vertek Corporation/6.20%, Insiders/33.80%, Omar Tellez, Charlie E. Hoffman, Institutional Venture Partners XI, L.P./5.30%, Thomas J. Hopkins, Lawrence R. Irving, James M. McCormick/15.10%, ABS Ventures/9.40%

Financial Data: *Fiscal Year End:*12/31 *Latest Annual Data:* 12/31/2006

Year	Sales	Net Income
2006	$72,406,000	$10,142,000
2005	$54,218,000	$12,429,000
2004	$27,191,000	-$7,000

Curr. Assets:	$96,567,000	**Curr. Liab.:**	$9,652,000		
Plant, Equip.:	$5,262,000	**Total Liab.:**	$9,652,000	**Indic. Yr. Divd.:**	NA
Total Assets:	$104,925,000	**Net Worth:**	$95,273,000	**Debt/ Equity:**	NA

Syndication Inc

1250 24th St., Nw Ste. 300, Washington, DC, 20037; *PH:* 1-202-467-2788

General - Incorporation		**Stock**- Price on:12/24/2007	$0.0009
Employees	NA	Stock Exchange	OTC
Auditor	NA	Ticker Symbol	SYDI
Stk Agt	Pacific Stock Transfer Company	Outstanding Shares	266,850,000
Counsel	NA	E.P.S.	-$0.014
DUNS No.	NA	Shareholders	NA

Business: The groups principle activity is to provide recruiting services. The groups service area includes the research and development, engineering, marketing, sales, information technology and manufacturing industries. The group operates from United States.

Primary SIC and add'l.: 6726 6799

CIK No:

Financial Data: *Fiscal Year End:*NA *Latest Annual Data:* 12/31/2006

Year	Sales	Net Income
2006	NA	-$1,398,000
2005	$66,000	-$2,334,000
2004	NA	-$2,274,000

Curr. Assets:	$206,000	**Curr. Liab.:**	$3,544,000		
Plant, Equip.:	NA	**Total Liab.:**	$3,872,000	**Indic. Yr. Divd.:**	NA
Total Assets:	$323,000	**Net Worth:**	-$3,549,000	**Debt/ Equity:**	NA

Synergx Systems Inc

209 Lafayette Dr., Syosset, NY, 11791; *PH:* 1-516-433-4700; *http://* www.synergxsystems.com; *Email:* info@synergxsystems.com

General - Incorporation	DE	**Stock**- Price on:12/24/2007	$2.212
Employees	92	Stock Exchange	NDQ
Auditor	Marcum & Kliegman LLP	Ticker Symbol	SYNX
Stk Agt	American Stock Transfer & Trust Co.	Outstanding Shares	5,210,000
Counsel	Dolgenos, Newman & Cronin	E.P.S.	-$0.12
DUNS No.	60-249-4338	Shareholders	NA

Business: The group's principal activities are to design, manufacture, market and service a variety of data communication products and systems. These products are applied in the fire alarm, life safety, transit, security and communications industry. The group also engineers, markets and sells systems and products manufactured by other parties. The group's proprietary product line features the comtrak 1720 and 2000 life safety systems and the teltrak communications system. The group's subsidiary, general sound (Texas) company, distributes, services, installs and designs a variety of sound, fire alarm, intercom and security systems primarily to electrical contractors. Firetector, casey systems and comtrak are the trademarks of the group.

Primary SIC and add'l.: 4899 3669

CIK No: 0000823130

Subsidiaries: Casey Systems Inc., Comco Technologies Inc., FT Clearing Inc., General Sound (Texas), Systems Service Technology Corp.

Officers: Daniel S. Tamkin/Chmn., CEO, General Counsel, John A. Poserina/Dir., CFO, Sec., Treasurer

Directors: Daniel S. Tamkin/Chmn., CEO, General Counsel, Mitchell Sanders/Dir., John A. Poserina/Dir., CFO, Sec., Treasurer, Gary Oreman/Dir., Harris Epstein/Dir., Ian J. Dalrymple/Dir., Mark Litwin/Dir., Peter Barotz/79/Dir., Orhan Sadik-Khan/78/Dir.

Owners: Insiders/5.94%, Harris Epstein, Ian J. Dalrymple, Heartland Advisors Inc./8.93%, John A. Poserina, Daniel S. Tamkin/4.69%, Mark I. Litwin, Firecom, Inc./25.97%

Financial Data: *Fiscal Year End:*09/30 *Latest Annual Data:* 9/30/2006

Year	Sales	Net Income
2006	$15,825,000	-$745,000
2005	$20,787,000	$130,000
2004	$21,790,000	$420,000

Curr. Assets:	$9,143,000	**Curr. Liab.:**	$3,006,000		
Plant, Equip.:	$776,000	**Total Liab.:**	$4,025,000	**Indic. Yr. Divd.:**	NA
Total Assets:	$10,130,000	**Net Worth:**	$6,105,000	**Debt/ Equity:**	0.0132

Synergy Brands Inc

40 Underhill Blvd, Syosset, NY, 11791; *PH:* 1-516-714-8200; *http://* www.synergybrands.com; *Email:* contactus@synergybrands.com

General - Incorporation	DE	**Stock**- Price on:12/24/2007	$0.89
Employees	40	Stock Exchange	NDQ
Auditor	Holtz Rubenstein Reminick LLP	Ticker Symbol	SYBR
Stk Agt	Holtz Rubenstein Reminick LLP	Outstanding Shares	8,370,000
Counsel	NA	E.P.S.	-$0.19
DUNS No.	36-380-6084	Shareholders	NA

Business: The group's principal activity is to develop and operate Internet platform operations and Internet-based businesses designed to sell products, including health and beauty aids and premium handmade cigars, directly to consumers (b2c) and to businesses (b2b). The group's Internet subsidiaries include beautybuys.com: an online b2c beauty department store. The group has developed dealbynet.com as an Internet domain further developed independently as the group's supply chain integration model for its b2b platform being developed in the health and beauty as well as grocery businesses. Netcigar.com is a leading online retailer of premium cigars and other related luxury items. Phs is the group's fulfillment platform for its business to business Internet operations.

Primary SIC and add'l.: 5122 5141 5149 5146 5194 7231 7375

CIK No: 0000870228

Subsidiaries: BeautyBuys.com, Cigar Kingdom Corporation, Dealbynet.com Inc., Gran Reserve Corporation, Net Cigar.Com Inc., PHS Group Inc., Premium Cigar Wrappers Inc, SYBR.Com Inc., The Ranley Group Inc.

Officers: Mair Faibish/Chmn., CEO/$254,434.00, Randall J. Perry/Dir., Corporate Counsel

Directors: Mair Faibish/Chmn., CEO, Frank Bellis/Dir., Lloyd I. Miller/Dir., Joel Sebastian/Dir., Randall J. Perry/Dir., Corporate Counsel, Bill Rancic/Dir.

Owners: Mair Faibish/3.50%, Insiders/34.95%, Bill Rancic/1.17%, Frank A. Bellis, Lloyd I. Miller/30.11%, Mair Faibish/100.00%, Insiders/100.00%

Financial Data: *Fiscal Year End:*12/31 *Latest Annual Data:* 12/31/2006

Year	Sales	Net Income
2006	$71,760,000	-$2,675,000
2005	$64,137,000	-$2,561,000
2004	$56,705,000	-$1,976,000

Curr. Assets:	$16,696,000	**Curr. Liab.:**	$7,410,000		
Plant, Equip.:	$253,000	**Total Liab.:**	$15,208,000	**Indic. Yr. Divd.:**	NA
Total Assets:	$20,868,000	**Net Worth:**	$5,660,000	**Debt/ Equity:**	1.3757

Synergy Financial Group Inc

310 N Ave E, Cranford, NJ, 07016; *PH:* 1-800-693-3838; *http://* www.synergyonthenet.com

General - Incorporation	NJ	**Stock**- Price on:12/24/2007	$13.59
Employees	119	Stock Exchange	NA
Auditor	Grant Thornton LLP	Ticker Symbol	NA
Stk Agt	Registrar & Transfer Co	Outstanding Shares	11,380,000
Counsel	NA	E.P.S	$0.36
DUNS No.	NA	Shareholders	NA

Business: The group's principal activity is to accept deposits and lending funds. The services provided by the group include accepting retail deposits from the general public and borrow money from the federal home loan bank of New York. The group's lending products include commercial loans, consumer real estate, one-to-four family residential mortgage, multi-family and non-residential loans, home equity loans, consumer products including auto and personal loans.The group's head office is located in Cranford, New Jersey, and has branches in Middlesex, Monmouth, Morris and Union counties, New Jersey. The primary market area of the group is Essex, Middlesex, Monmouth, Morris, Somerset and Union counties, New Jersey.

Primary SIC and add'l.: 6035 6712

CIK No: 0001263766

Subsidiaries: Synergy Bank, Synergy Capital Investments, Inc., Synergy Financial Services, Inc., Synergy Investment Corporation

Officers: John S. Fiore/50/Dir., CEO, Pres./$1,068,846.00, Kevin M. McCloskey/VP, COO/$493,832.00, Kevin A. Wenthen/53/Sr. VP, Chief Administrative Officer, Sec./$452,961.00, Richard A. Abrahamian/48/Sr. VP, CFO/$336,741.00

Directors: John S. Fiore/50/Dir., CEO, Pres., David H. Gibbons/37/Chmn., Nancy A. Davis/68/Dir., Kenneth S. Kasper/53/Dir., Paul T. Lacorte/55/Dir., George Putvinski/59/Dir., Albert N. Stender/62/Dir., Daniel M. Eliades/41/Dir., Daniel P. Spiegel/44/Dir.

Owners: John S. Fiore/3.30%, Kenneth S. Kasper, Financial Edge Fund, L.P./9.50%, George Putvinski, Paul T. LaCorte, Synergy Financial Group, Inc. Employee Stock/8.50%, Insiders/10.50%, Richard A. Abrahamian, Albert N. Stender, Kevin M. McCloskey/2.60%, Kevin A. Wenthen/1.30%, Daniel M. Eliades, Daniel P. Spiegel, David H. Gibbons, Nancy A. Davis

Financial Data: *Fiscal Year End:*12/31 *Latest Annual Data:* 12/31/2006

Year	Sales	Net Income
2006	$59,098,000	$4,095,000
2005	$50,448,000	$4,493,000
2004	$39,684,000	$4,203,000

Curr. Assets:	$13,979,000	*Curr. Liab.:*	$646,467,000	*P/E Ratio:*	37.75
Plant, Equip.:	$20,106,000	*Total Liab.:*	$887,826,000	*Indic. Yr. Divd.:*	$0.240
Total Assets:	$986,326,000	*Net Worth:*	$98,500,000	*Debt/ Equity:*	1.8411

Syneron Medical Ltd

Industrial Zone, Yokneam Illit, 20692; *PH:* 972-732442200; *Fax:* 972-732442202; *http://* www.syneron.com; *Email:* info@syneron.com

General - Incorporation	Israel	**Stock**- Price on:12/24/2007	$25.27
Employees	146	Stock Exchange	NDQ
Auditor	Kost Forer Gabbay & Kasierer	Ticker Symbol	ELOS
Stk Agt	American Stock Transfer & Trust Co.	Outstanding Shares	27,590,000
Counsel	NA	E.P.S	$1.42
DUNS No.	NA	Shareholders	NA

Business: The groups principle activities include designing, developing and marketing aesthetic medical products based on its electro-optical synergy technology. The group operates from United States.

Primary SIC and add'l.: NA

CIK No: 0001291361

Subsidiaries: Syneron Canada Corp, Syneron GmbH, Syneron Inc., Syneron Medical (HK) Ltd

Officers: Doron Gerstel/CEO, Michael Kreindel/Dir., CTO, Fabian Tenenbaum/CFO, Donald Lee Fagen/Pres. - Syneron North America, Amit Meridor/Exec. VP - Business Development - International Sales, Mark Tager/Chief Marketing Officer, Eran Tamir/COO, Boris Vaynberg/VP - Research & Development

Directors: Shimon Eckhouse/Chmn., Michael Kreindel/Dir., CTO, Dan Suesskind/Dir., Marshall Butler/Dir., Michael Anghel/Dir., Yaffa Krindel/Dir.

Owners: Michael Kreindel/5.99%, Shimon Eckhouse/9.59%, Insiders/15.45%

Financial Data: *Fiscal Year End:*12/31 *Latest Annual Data:* 12/31/2006

Year	Sales	Net Income
2006	$116,976,000	$39,654,000
2005	$87,406,000	$41,063,000
2004	$57,918,000	$27,340,000

Curr. Assets:	$152,981,000	*Curr. Liab.:*	$25,722,000	*P/E Ratio:*	17.80
Plant, Equip.:	$1,513,000	*Total Liab.:*	$30,844,000	*Indic. Yr. Divd.:*	NA
Total Assets:	$225,241,000	*Net Worth:*	$194,397,000	*Debt/ Equity:*	NA

Syngenta

2200 Concord Pike, Wilmington, DE, 19803; *PH:* 1-302-425-2000; *Fax:* 1-302-425-2001; *http://* www.syngenta.com

General - Incorporation	Switzerland	**Stock**- Price on:12/24/2007	$38.15
Employees	19,500	Stock Exchange	NYSE
Auditor	Ernst & Young AG	Ticker Symbol	NA
Stk Agt	Bank of New York	Outstanding Shares	485,970,000
Counsel	NA	E.P.S	$1.81
DUNS No.	NA	Shareholders	NA

Business: The group's principal activities are to discover, develop, manufacture and market agricultural products designed to improve crop yields and food quality. The group operates through crop protection segment and seeds segment. Crop protection segment manufactures, distributes and sells herbicides, insecticides and fungicides. The crop protection products improve quality by controlling weeds, diseases and insects. The seed segment sells seeds for growing corn, sugar beet, oilseeds, vegetables and flowers. The group has operations in Europe, Africa and the Middle East. The crop protection and seeds industries offer products that provide essential support to modern agriculture.

Primary SIC and add'l.: 0181 5191 2879

CIK No: 0001123661

Officers: Michael Pragnell/61/CEO, Executive Dir., John Atkin/54/COO - Crop Protection, Christoph Mader/48/Head - Legal, Taxes, Company Sec., Michael Mack/47/COO - Seeds, David Lawrence/58/Head - Research, Development, Domenico Scala/43/CFO, David Jones/59/Head - Global Operations, Human Resources, Robert Berendes/42/Head - Business Development, Mark Peacock/46/Head - Global Operations

Directors: Michael Pragnell/61/CEO, Executive Dir., Martin Taylor/55/Chmn., Rupert Gasser/69/Vice Chmn., Jacques Vincent/61/Non Exec. Dir., Jurg Witmer/59/Non Exec. Dir., Peter Thompson/Dir., Peter Doyle/Non Exec. Dir., Pierre Landolt/60/Non Exec. Dir., Felix Weber/57/Non Exec. Dir., Rolf Watter/Non Exec. Dir., Peggy Bruzelius/58/Non Exec. Dir.

Financial Data: *Fiscal Year End:*12/31 *Latest Annual Data:* 12/31/2006

Year	Sales	Net Income
2006	$8,046,000,000	$504,000,000
2005	$8,104,000,000	$626,000,000
2004	$7,269,000,000	$352,000,000

Curr. Assets:	$5,546,000,000	*Curr. Liab.:*	$2,968,000,000	*P/E Ratio:*	17.80
Plant, Equip.:	$2,007,000,000	*Total Liab.:*	$6,865,000,000	*Indic. Yr. Divd.:*	$0.580
Total Assets:	$11,911,000,000	*Net Worth:*	$5,046,000,000	*Debt/ Equity:*	NA

Syniverse Holdings Inc

8125 Highwoods Palm Way, Tampa, FL, 33647; *PH:* 1-813-637-5000; *Fax:* 1-813-637-5881; *http://* www.syniverse.com

General - Incorporation	DE	**Stock**- Price on:12/24/2007	$12.63
Employees	932	Stock Exchange	NYSE
Auditor	Ernst& Young LLP	Ticker Symbol	SVR
Stk Agt	American Stock Transfer & Trust Co.	Outstanding Shares	68,080,000
Counsel	NA	E.P.S	$1.43
DUNS No.	NA	Shareholders	NA

Business: The groups principle activity is to provide technology services. The groups services includes seamless voice, roaming, short message services, multimedia messaging services, caller id, number portability and wireless video services. In the year 2006, the group acquired Perfect Profits International. The group operates from the United States and other foreign countries.

Primary SIC and add'l.: 4899 4899 7375 4813 7389 4813 7375 7389

CIK No: 0001169264

Subsidiaries: Perfect Profit International Limited, Syniverse Brience, LLC, Syniverse Holdings Limited, Syniverse Technologies Limited, Syniverse Technologies, BV, Syniverse Technologies, Inc.

Officers: Tony G. Holcombe/Dir., CEO, Pres., Eugene Bergen Henegouwen/Exec. VP, MD - Europe, Middle East, Africa, Raymond Cheung/Exec. VP, Robert Garcia/Sec., General Counsel, Leigh M. Hennen/Chief Human Resources Officer, Paul Wilcock/CTO, Jim Huseby/VP - Investor Relations, Yiu Wah Cheung/Exec. VP - Asia Pacific, David W. Hitchcock/CFO, Exec. VP, Wayne G. Nelson/VP, Controller, Michael J. O'Brien/VP - Marketing, Nancy J. White/56/Exec. VP, Chief Marketing Officer, Paul Corrao/VP - Network Operations, Janet Roberts/VP - Corp Comm, Prgm Mgmt, Don Wilkins/VP - Systems Development, Supp

Directors: Tony G. Holcombe/Dir., CEO, Pres., Robert J. Marino/Chmn., Odie C. Donald/Dir., David A. Donnini/Dir., John C. Hofmann/Dir., Jason Few/Dir., Timothy Samples/Dir., Raymond L. Lawless/Dir., James B. Lipham/Dir., Jack Pearlstein/Dir., Collin E. Roche/Dir.

Owners: Insiders, James B. Lipham, Collin E. Roche, David A. Donnini, Raymond L. Lawless, GTCR Fund VII L.P., Timothy A. Samples, John C. Hofmann, GTCR Capital Partners, L.P., GTCR Co-Invest L.P., Jack Pearlstein, GTCR Fund VII/A, L.P., Wellington Management Company, LLP., Snowlake Investment Pte. Ltd., Eugene Bergen Henegouwen *(19 Owners included in Index)*

Financial Data: *Fiscal Year End:*12/31 *Latest Annual Data:* 12/31/2006

Year	Sales	Net Income
2006	$337,019,000	$89,724,000
2005	$341,791,000	$9,804,000
2004	$332,403,000	$15,063,000

Curr. Assets:	$106,004,000	*Curr. Liab.:*	$56,793,000	*P/E Ratio:*	9.09
Plant, Equip.:	$42,880,000	*Total Liab.:*	$369,353,000	*Indic. Yr. Divd.:*	NA
Total Assets:	$784,147,000	*Net Worth:*	$414,794,000	*Debt/ Equity:*	NA

SYNNEX Corp

44201 Nobel Dr., Fremont, CA, 94538; *PH:* 1-510-656-3333; *http://* www.synnex.com; *Email:* ir@synnex.com

General - Incorporation	DE	**Stock**- Price on:12/24/2007	$21.36
Employees	2,647	Stock Exchange	NYSE
Auditor	PricewaterhouseCoopers LLP	Ticker Symbol	SNX
Stk Agt	Computershare Trust Co	Outstanding Shares	31,090,000
Counsel	NA	E.P.S	$1.79
DUNS No.	NA	Shareholders	NA

Business: The group's principle activity is to provide business process services. The group also provides computer systems, peripherals, system components, software and networking products. The group operates from United States.

Primary SIC and add'l.: 7372 3577 5045 5065

CIK No: 0001177394

Subsidiaries: Daisytek Inc, EMJ, MCJ Company Limited, SYNNEX Canada Limited, Synnex K.k

Officers: Robert Huang/Dir., CEO, Pres./$7,269,609.00, Jim Estill/CEO - Synnex Canada Limited/$672,285.00, Dennis Polk/COO/$1,173,966.00, Steve Jow/Sr. VP - Commercial Sales, Tim Rush/Sr. VP - Operations, Thomas Alsborg/CFO, Christopher Caldwell/Sr. VP - Global Business Development, Pradip Madan/Sr. VP - Corporate Strategy, Development, Robert Stegner/Sr. VP - Marketing, North America, Stephen Ichinaga/Sr. VP, GM - Systems Integration Division, Michael R. Thomson/Sr. VP - Partner Advocacy, Peter Larocque/Pres. - US Distribution/$1,362,619.00, Michael P. Van Gieson/Sr. VP - Product Marketing, Charlotte Chou/Sr. VP - Manufacturing Operations, David Dennis/Sr. VP - Product Marketing *(18 Officers included in Index)*

Directors: Robert Huang/Dir., CEO, Pres., Matthew Miau/Chmn., Duane Zitzner/Dir., Fred Breidenbach/Dir., Dwight Steffenson/Dir., James Van Horne/Dir., David Rynne/Dir., Greg Quesnel/Dir.

Owners: Dimensional Fund Advisors LP/7.10%, Matthew Miau/4.50%, Jim Estill, Barclays Global Investors/10.90%, Fred Breidenbach, Dwight Steffensen, Peter Larocque, Gregory Quesnel, FMR Corp./10.70%, David Rynne, Dennis Polk, James Van Horne, John Paget, MiTAC International Corporation/46.70%, Robert Huang/5.70% *(16 Owners included in Index)*

Financial Data: *Fiscal Year End:*11/30 *Latest Annual Data:* 2/28/2007

Year	Sales		Net Income
2007	NA		NA
2006	NA		$241,000
2005	$5,640,769,000		$52,825,000

Curr. Assets:	$1,138,037,000	**Curr. Liab.:**	$721,172,000	**P/E Ratio:**	12.64
Plant, Equip.:	$36,698,000	**Total Liab.:**	$871,188,000	**Indic. Yr. Divd.:**	NA
Total Assets:	$1,382,734,000	**Net Worth:**	$511,546,000	**Debt/ Equity:**	0.0792

Synopsys Inc

700 E Middlefield Rd. , Mountain View, CA, 94043; ***PH:*** 1-650-962-5000;
http:// www.synopsys.com; ***Email:*** invest-info@synopsys.com

General - Incorporation .... DE
Employees 5,130
Auditor .... KPMG LLP
Stk Agt..... Computershare Investor Services LLC
Counsel .... NA
DUNS No. 16-149-9579

Stock- Price on:12/24/2007 .... $26.56
Stock Exchange .... NDQ
Ticker Symbol .... SNPS
Outstanding Shares 143,360,000
E.P.S $0.56
Shareholders .... NA

Business: The group's principal activity is to supply electronic design automation (eda) software to the global electronics industry. The products are used by designers of integrated circuits (ics), including system-on-a-chip ics and the electronic products that use such ics to automate significant portions of their chip design process. The group operates in a single segment and is organized into four primary groups which include implementation, verification, solutions and new ventures. It offers a full range of professional services to help customers, improve their internal design methodologies and design services ranging from specialized assistance to turnkey design. In 2003, the group acquired numerical technologies inc, innologic systems and certain assets of qualis inc and accelerant networks inc, certain test related assets of iroc technologies s a and technology assets of analog design automation inc in feb 2004.

Primary SIC and add'l.: 3825 7373

CIK No: 0000883241

Subsidiaries: Accelerant Networks, Inc., Angel HiTech Limited, Avant! China Holdings, Ltd., Avant! Corporation GmbH, Avant! Corporation Limited, Avant! Europe Manufacturing Ltd., Avant! Global Technologies Ltd., Avant! International Distribution Ltd., Avant! Korea Co., Ltd., Avant! LLC, Avant! Microelectronics (Shanghai) Company Limited, Avant! Software (Israel) Ltd., Avant! Taiwan Holdings, Ltd., Avant! UK Ltd., Avant! Worldwide Holdings, Ltd. 55 Subsidiaries included in the Index

Officers: Aart J. De Geus/Chmn., CEO, Brian Beattie/CFO, Brian Cabrera/VP, General Counsel, Sec., Antun Domic/Sr. VP, GM - Implementation Group, John Chilton/Sr. VP - Marketing, Strategic Development, Manoj Gandhi/Sr. VP, GM - Verification Group, Chi-Foon Chan/58/Dir., COO, Pres., Deirdre Hanford/Sr. VP - Global Technical Services, Jan Collinson/Sr. VP - Human Resources, Facilities, Wolfgang Fichtner/Sr. VP, GM - Silicon Engineering Group, Joachim Kunkel/VP, GM - Solutions Group, Paul Lo/Sr. VP, GM - Analog, Mixed Signal Group, Joe Logan/Sr. VP - Worldwide Sales

Directors: Aart J. De Geus/Chmn., CEO, Steven C. Walske/Dir., Steven K. Shevick/Dir., Deborah A. Coleman/Dir., Alfred J. Castino/Dir., John G. Schwarz/Dir., Sasson Somekh/Dir., Bruce R. Chizen/Dir., Chi-Foon Chan/58/Dir., COO, Pres., Roy Vallee/Dir.

Owners: Steven C. Walske, Bruce R. Chizen, Sasson Somekh, Chi-Foon Chan/1.36%, Joseph Logan, Insiders/5.25%, Deborah A. Coleman, Antun Domic, Entities associated with Goldman Sachs Asset Management, L.P./12.34%, Roy Vallee, Aart J. deGeus/2.17%, Entities associated with J.& W. Seligman& Co. Incorporated/7.00%, Deirdre Hanford

Financial Data: ***Fiscal Year End:***10/31 ***Latest Annual Data:*** 10/31/2006

Year	Sales		Net Income
2006	$1,095,560,000		$24,742,000
2005	$991,931,000		-$15,478,000
2004	$1,092,104,000		$74,337,000

Curr. Assets:	$894,490,000	**Curr. Liab.:**	$871,096,000	**P/E Ratio:**	47.43
Plant, Equip.:	$140,660,000	**Total Liab.:**	$994,655,000	**Indic. Yr. Divd.:**	NA
Total Assets:	$2,157,822,000	**Net Worth:**	$1,163,167,000	**Debt/ Equity:**	NA

Synovics Pharmaceuticals Inc

2575 E Camelback Rd., Ste. 450, Phoenix, AZ, 85016; ***PH:*** 1-602-508-0112; ***Fax:*** 1-602-508-0115;
http:// www.bionutrics.com

General - Incorporation .... NV
Employees .... NA
Auditor .... Miller Ellin & Company, LLP
Stk Agt........ Pacific Stock Transfer Company
Counsel .... NA
DUNS No. .... NA

Stock- Price on:12/24/2007 .... $1
Stock Exchange .... OTC
Ticker Symbol .... SYVC
Outstanding Shares 27,540,000
E.P.S .... -$0.69
Shareholders .... NA

Business: The groups principle activities include developing oral controlled release drug formulations utilizing proprietary licensed drug formulations and delivery technologies. In May 2006, the group acquired Kirk Pharmaceuticals, LLC. The group operates from the United States. The group's quarterly revenue for Jul '07 was 6.88 millions of USD.

Primary SIC and add'l.: 2834

CIK No: 0001030839

Subsidiaries: Andapharm LLC, Andapharm, Inc., Bionutrics Health Products, Inc., Cosmedics, Inc., InCon International Ltd., Kirk Pharmaceuticals, Inc., Kirk Pharmaceuticals, LLC, LipoGenics, Inc., Nutrition Technology Corporation, Synovics Laboratories, Inc.

Owners: Insiders/19.71%, Nalin Rathod/8.15%, Maneesh Pharmaceuticals/5.76%, Ronald H. Lane/15.13%, William M. McCormick/3.10%, Richard M. Feldheim/1.56%, Nirmal Mulye/40.93%

Financial Data: ***Fiscal Year End:***10/31 ***Latest Annual Data:*** 10/31/2006

Year	Sales		Net Income
2006	$10,516,000		-$8,571,000
2005	$8,000		-$2,911,000
2004	$99,000		-$1,124,000

Curr. Assets:	$7,730,000	**Curr. Liab.:**	$13,090,000		
Plant, Equip.:	$1,642,000	**Total Liab.:**	$25,779,000	**Indic. Yr. Divd.:**	NA
Total Assets:	$38,883,000	**Net Worth:**	$13,103,000	**Debt/ Equity:**	NA

Synovis Life Technologies Inc

2575 University Ave. W., St Paul, MN, 55114; ***PH:*** 1-651-796-7300; ***http://*** www.synovislife.com

General - Incorporation .... MN
Employees 390
Auditor .... Deloitte & Touche LLP
Stk Agt ..... American Stock Transfer & Trust Co.
Counsel .... Winthrop & Weinstine
DUNS No. 13-924-5856

Stock- Price on:12/24/2007 .... $14.57
Stock Exchange .... NDQ
Ticker Symbol .... SYNO
Outstanding Shares 12,240,000
E.P.S $0.05
Shareholders .... NA

Business: The group's principal activities are to develop, design, manufacture and market products for the surgical and interventional treatment of disease. The group operates through two segments, the surgical device business and the interventional business. The surgical device business develops, manufactures and markets implantable biomaterial products, devices for microsurgery and surgical tools that reduce risks of critical surgeries, leading to better patient outcomes and lower costs. The interventional business manufactures fixation helices, conductor coils, stylets and other machined components used for cardiac rhythm management, neurostimulation and vascular procedures. It also provides product development engineering and rapid prototyping services. The group operates in the United States, Europe, Asia and pacific region.

Primary SIC and add'l.: 3841 3842 3845

CIK No: 0000780127

Subsidiaries: Bio-Vascular B.V., Breda, BVI - (Barbados), Inc., Micro Companies Alliance, Inc., Synovis Interventional Solutions, Inc.

Officers: Richard W. Kramp/Dir., CEO, Pres., Brett A. Reynolds/VP - Finance, CFO, Corp. Sec., Mary L. Frick/VP - Regulatory Affairs, Quality Assurance, Clinical Affairs, Michael K. Campbell/Pres. - Micro Companies Alliance, David Buche/VP, COO - Synovis Surgical Innovations, Nicholas B. Oray/VP - Research, Development

Directors: Richard W. Kramp/Dir., CEO, Pres., Timothy M. Scanlan/Chmn., Karen Gilles Larson/Dir., Mark F. Palma/Dir., William G. Kobi/63/Dir., Richard W. Perkins/Dir., Sven A. Wehrwein/56/Dir.

Owners: Mark F. Palma, Dimensional Fund Advisors, Inc./5.10%, Sven A. Wehrwein, Timothy M. Scanlan, Richard W. Kramp, Karen Gilles Larson/1.50%, The TCW Group, Inc./15.40%, B. Nicholas Oray, Richard W. Perkins/1.50%, William G. Kobi, Perkins Capital Management, Inc./1.70%, David A. Buche, Mary L. Frick, Insiders/6.80%

Financial Data: ***Fiscal Year End:***10/31 ***Latest Annual Data:*** 10/31/2006

Year	Sales		Net Income
2006	$55,835,000		-$1,481,000
2005	$60,256,000		$883,000
2004	$55,044,000		$1,278,000

Curr. Assets:	$65,068,000	**Curr. Liab.:**	$5,625,000	**P/E Ratio:**	291.40
Plant, Equip.:	$12,228,000	**Total Liab.:**	$5,625,000	**Indic. Yr. Divd.:**	NA
Total Assets:	$85,550,000	**Net Worth:**	$79,925,000	**Debt/ Equity:**	NA

Synovus Financial Corp

PO Box 120, Columbus, GA, 31901; ***PH:*** 1-706-649-2311; ***Fax:*** 1-706-641-6555;
http:// www.synovus.com; ***Email:*** snvir@synovus.com

General - Incorporation .... GA
Employees 13,178
Auditor .... KPMG LLP
Stk Agt .... Mellon Investor Services LLC
Counsel .... NA
DUNS No. 07-586-4314

Stock- Price on:12/24/2007 .... $32.05
Stock Exchange .... NYSE
Ticker Symbol .... SNV
Outstanding Shares 326,980,000
E.P.S $1.88
Shareholders .... NA

Business: The group's principle activity is to provide financial services. The groups financial services include banking, financial management, insurance, mortgage and leasing services. The groups commercial banking services include commercial, financial, agricultural and real estate loans. The groups retail banking services include accepting customary time & demand deposits. The groups other services include safe deposit services, automated banking services, automated fund transfers. Transaction processing provides electronic payment processing services including consumer, debit, commercial, retail and stored value card processing and related services. The group operates from United States.

Primary SIC and add'l.: 6712 6022

CIK No: 0000018349

Subsidiaries: 100 FCBIM Corp., 100 FAL Mortgage Investment Corporation, Athena Service Corporation, Athens First Bank & Trust Company, Bank of Coweta, Bank of North Georgia, Bank of Pensacola, BOP Investment Company, Inc., BOP Mortgage Investment Corporation, BOP Properties, Inc., CB&T 11th Street Loft Company, LLC, CB&T Bank of East Alabama, CB&T Bank of Middle Georgia, CB&T Housing Fund Investor, LLC, CB&T Special Limited Partner, LLC 108 Subsidiaries included in the Index

Officers: Richard E. Anthony/Chmn., CEO/$4,044,095.00, F. C. Greer/Vice Chmn. - CB, T Bank, Middle Georgia, Fort Valley, Georgia, Elizabeth R. James/Vice Chmn., Chief People Officer/$1,697,035.00, Calvin Smyre/Exec. VP - Corporate Affairs, Jeffery Barton Singleton/Pres. - Synovus Securities, Scott B. McGlaun/CIO, William H. Roach/Pres. - Synovus Investment Advisors, Liliana McDaniel/Chief Accounting Officer, Leila S. Carr/Exec. VP, Chief Retail Officer, Sanders G. Griffith/Sr. Exec. VP, General Counsel, Sec./$1,753,739.00, Andrew R. Klepchick/Exec. VP, Thomas J. Prescott/CFO, Exec. VP/$1,628,734.00, Fred L. Green/Dir., COO, Pres./$1,587,395.00, Mark G. Holladay/Exec. VP, Chief Credit Officer, Paul M. Todd/Exec. VP *(18 Officers included in Index)*

Directors: Richard E. Anthony/Chmn., CEO, Elizabeth R. James/Vice Chmn., Chief People Officer, Lynn H. Page/Vice Chmn., Neal J. Purcell/Dir., Elizabeth C. Ogie/Dir., John T. Oliver/Dir., John L. Moulton/Dir., Nathaniel V. Hansford/Dir., John P. Illges/Dir., Robert V. Royall/Dir., Melvin T. Stith/Dir., Philip W. Tomlinson/Dir., William B. Turner/Dir., George C. Woodruff/Dir., James H. Blanchard/Dir. *(31 Directors included in Index)*

Owners: Daniel P. Amos, Frank W. Brumley, Neal J. Purcell, Sanders G. Griffith, Richard E. Anthony, Michael T. Goodrich, Lynn H. Page, Elizabeth C. Ogie/1.00%, Elizabeth R. James, Frederick L. Green, Alfred W. Jones, James D. Yancey/1.00%, Gardiner W. Garrard, Mason H. Lampton, Melvin T. Stith *(22 Owners included in Index)*

Financial Data: ***Fiscal Year End:***12/31 ***Latest Annual Data:*** 12/31/2006

Year	Sales		Net Income
2006	$4,152,170,000		$616,917,000
2005	$3,414,704,000		$516,446,000
2004	$2,680,031,000		$437,033,000

Curr. Assets:	$1,272,321,000	**Curr. Liab.:**	$25,867,256,000	**P/E Ratio:**	16.69
Plant, Equip.:	$752,738,000	**Total Liab.:**	$28,146,123,000	**Indic. Yr. Divd.:**	$0.820
Total Assets:	$31,854,773,000	**Net Worth:**	$3,708,650,000	**Debt/ Equity:**	NA

Synplicity Inc

600 W California Ave., Sunnyvale, CA, 94086; *PH:* 1-405-215-6000; *http://* www.synplicity.com; *Email:* info@synplicity.com

General - Incorporation	CA	**Stock** - Price on:12/24/2007	$6.87
Employees	287	Stock Exchange	NDQ
Auditor	Ernst & Young LLP	Ticker Symbol	SYNP
Stk Agt	Computershare Investor Services LLC	Outstanding Shares	26,780,000
Counsel	Wilson Sonsini Goodrich & Rosati	E.P.S	$0.16
DUNS No.	NA	Shareholders	NA

Business: The group's principal activity is to provide software products that enable the design and verification of large and complex semiconductors. These products are used in networking and communications, computer and peripheral, consumer, military and aerospace and other electronics systems. The product performs essential steps in the process of designing and verifying semiconductors that are tailored to field programmable gate arrays (fpgas) and application specific integrated circuits (asics). Fpga provides equipment manufacturers with the ability to create and modify semiconductor. Asic provides higher performance, lower power consumption and lower unit cost. The group markets its products in the United States, North America, Europe, Japan and other parts of Asia.

Primary SIC and add'l.: 7379 7372

CIK No: 0001027362

Subsidiaries: SYNP AB, Synplicity Arastirma Gelistirme Limited Sirketi, Synplicity Deutschland GmbH, Synplicity Europe Ltd., Synplicity France SARL, Synplicity International, Inc, Synplicity International, Inc., Synplicity Israel Ltd., Synplicity Japan KK, Synplicity Software India Pvt. Ltd

Officers: Gary Meyers/Dir., CEO, Pres./$477,977.00, Alisa Yaffa/Co - Founder, Chmn., VP - Intellectual Property, Joe Gianelli/VP - Business Development, Strategic Alliances, Jim Lovas/VP - Worldwide Sales/$675,788.00, John J. Hanlon/Sr. VP, CFO/$330,941.00, Andrew Haines/Sr. VP - Marketing/$304,235.00, Andrew Dauman/Sr. VP - Worldwide Engineering, Ken McElvain/Co - Founder, CTO, VP, Dir./$276,549.00, Jim Robinson/VP - Corporate Applications, Lars-Eric Lundgren/GM - Synplicity Hardware Platforms Group

Directors: Gary Meyers/Dir., CEO, Pres., Alisa Yaffa/Co - Founder, Chmn., VP - Intellectual Property, Prabhu Goel/Dir., Thomas Weatherford/Dir., Dennis Segers/Dir., Ken McElvain/Co - Founder, CTO, VP, Dir., Paul Weiskopf/Dir.

Owners: Prabhu Goel/4.70%, James Lovas, Alisa Yaffa/37.10%, Gary Meyers/2.20%, Insiders/44.90%, Kenneth S. McElvain/37.10%, Buckingham Capital Management Incorporated/6.70%, Brown Advisory Holdings Incorporated/4.30%, John J. Hanlon, Andrew Haines

Financial Data: *Fiscal Year End:*12/31 *Latest Annual Data:* 12/31/2006

Year	Sales	Net Income
2006	$62,543,000	$3,175,000
2005	$61,935,000	$6,554,000
2004	$56,954,000	$2,214,000

Curr. Assets:	$77,949,000	**Curr. Liab.:**	$25,694,000	**P/E Ratio:**	42.94
Plant, Equip.:	$2,390,000	**Total Liab.:**	$25,694,000	**Indic. Yr. Divd.:**	NA
Total Assets:	$83,809,000	**Net Worth:**	$58,115,000	**Debt/ Equity:**	NA

Syntec Biofuel Inc

388 Drake St., Ste. 206, Vancouver, BC, V6B 6A8; *PH:* 1-604-648-2092; *Fax:* 1-604-648-2091; *http://* www.syntecbiofuel.com; *Email:* info@syntecbiofuel.com

General - Incorporation	WA	**Stock** - Price on:12/24/2007	$0.05
Employees	NA	Stock Exchange	OTC
Auditor	Dale Matheson Carr-hilton Labonte LLP	Ticker Symbol	SYBF
Stk Agt	NA	Outstanding Shares	NA
Counsel	NA	E.P.S	NA
DUNS No.	NA	Shareholders	NA

Business: The groups principle activities include vitamins, homeopathic supplements and pre-packaged vacuum packed raw foods, in meal sized portions, for domesticated household animals i.e. dogs and cats, via the Internet and commissioned sales agents. The group operates from the United States.

Primary SIC and add'l.: 5149

CIK No: 0001123425

Officers: George Kosanovich/CEO, Timothy Meterko/Pres., CTO, Caili Su/Sr. Scientist, Janet Cheng/CFO, Nancy Ross/VP - Management

Directors: Michael Jackson/Chmn.

Owners: Ryerson Corporation A.V.V./50.29%, Cary Martin, Insiders, National Financial Services LLC/8.86%

Financial Data: *Fiscal Year End:*12/31 *Latest Annual Data:* 12/31/2006

Year	Sales	Net Income
2006	NA	-$191,000
2005	NA	-$51,000

Curr. Assets:	$15,000	**Curr. Liab.:**	$187,000		
Plant, Equip.:	$2,000	**Total Liab.:**	$187,000	**Indic. Yr. Divd.:**	NA
Total Assets:	$18,000	**Net Worth:**	-$169,000	**Debt/ Equity:**	NA

Syntel Inc

525 E Big BeAve.r Rd. , Third Fl., Troy, MI, 48083; *PH:* 1-248-619-2800; *http://* www.syntelinc.com; *Email:* info@syntelinc.com

General - Incorporation	MI	**Stock** - Price on:12/24/2007	$33.54
Employees	8,364	Stock Exchange	NDQ
Auditor	Crowe Chizek & Co. LLC	Ticker Symbol	SYNT
Stk Agt	Computershare Investor Services LLC	Outstanding Shares	41,140,000
Counsel	Crowe Chizek & Company LLC	E.P.S	$1.37
DUNS No.	10-844-4944	Shareholders	NA

Business: The group's principal activity is to provide information technology services such as programming, systems integration, outsourcing and overall project management. The group provides services to customers in the financial, healthcare, transportation, information/communication industries and government entities. The group operates through three segments, applications outsourcing, e-business and teamsourcing. Application outsourcing provides higher-value applications management services for ongoing management and maintenance of customer's business applications. E-business provides development and implementation services for a number of emerging and rapidly growing high technology applications, including Web development, crm, oracle and sap. Teamsourcing provides professional information technology consulting services directly to customers on a staff augmentation basis.

Primary SIC and add'l.: 8742 7372 7379 7371

CIK No: 0001040426

Subsidiaries: Mauritius Limited, Private Limited, SkillBay LLC, Syntel (Australia) Pty Limited, Syntel (Hong Kong) Ltd., Syntel (Mauritius) Ltd., Syntel (Singapore) PTE. LTD., Syntel Canada Inc., Syntel Consulting Inc., Syntel Delaware LLC, Syntel Deutschland GmbH, Syntel Europe Limited, Syntel Global Private Limited, Syntel International Private Limited, Syntel Limited 20 Subsidiaries included in the Index

Officers: Bharat Desai/55/Chmn., CEO, Co - Founder/$362,535.00, Keshav Murugesh/COO, Pres./$820,100.00, Daniel Moore/Chief Administrative Officer, General Counsel, Jonathan James/VP - Global Marketing, Investor Relations, Neerja Sethi/53/Dir., VP, Co - Founder, Srikanth Karra/VP - Global Human Resources, Rakesh Khanna/Pres. - Business Unit, Banking, Finance, Arvind Godbole/CFO, Chief Information Security Officer/$104,543.00, Anil Jain/Business Unit Head, Sr. VP - Insurance Vertical, Nitin Rakesh/VP, Head - B, FS BPO Operations, T. N. Shekar/VP, Head - Healthcare BPO Practice, Murlidhar Reddy/VP - Operations, Healthcare Vertical, Ram Singampalli/VP - Operations, Diversified Vertical, Sanjay Bhagat/Assist. Mgr. - Finance, Sathya Narayanaswamy/Head - Business Unit Telecom *(17 Officers included in Index)*

Directors: Bharat Desai/55/Chmn., CEO, Co - Founder, Paritosh K. Choksi/55/Dir., Vasant Raval/68/Dir., Neerja Sethi/53/Dir., VP, Co - Founder, Paul Donovan/61/Dir., Prashant Ranade/55/Dir.

Owners: Bharat Desai, Lakshmanan Chidambaram, Parashar Ranade, Neerja Sethi, Neerja Sethi, Revathy Ashok, Keshav Murugesh, George R. Mrkonic, Insiders, Paul R. Donovan, R. S. Ramdas, James C. Swayzee, Arvind Godbole, Paritosh K. Choksi, Vasant Raval

Financial Data: *Fiscal Year End:*12/31 *Latest Annual Data:* 12/31/2006

Year	Sales	Net Income
2006	$270,229,000	$50,916,000
2005	$226,189,000	$30,321,000
2004	$186,573,000	$40,974,000

Curr. Assets:	$153,510,000	**Curr. Liab.:**	$47,947,000	**P/E Ratio:**	24.48
Plant, Equip.:	$38,314,000	**Total Liab.:**	$47,947,000	**Indic. Yr. Divd.:**	$0.240
Total Assets:	$197,689,000	**Net Worth:**	$149,742,000	**Debt/ Equity:**	NA

Synthenol Inc

Formerly: Legalplay Entertainment Inc

388 Drake St., Ste. 206, Vancouver, BC, V6B 6A8; *PH:* 1-604-648-2090; *http://* www.poker.com

General - Incorporation	FL	**Stock** - Price on:12/24/2007	NA
Employees	NA	Stock Exchange	NA
Auditor	Dale Matheson Carr-hilton Labonte LLP	Ticker Symbol	NA
Stk Agt	Interwest Transfer Company, Inc.	Outstanding Shares	NA
Counsel	NA	E.P.S	NA
DUNS No.	NA	Shareholders	NA

Business: The group's principal activity is to provide licensing and marketing services for Internet gaming companies. Currently, the group is in development stage. The group operates under three subsidiaries casino marketing sa, 564448 bc ltd and skill poker.com. Casino marketing sa provides technical management for company's licensees, 564448 bc ltd provides administrative management services to parent company and skill poker.com is currently developing skill poker system. In 2003, the group discontinued casino marketing sa.

Primary SIC and add'l.: 7372 7375

CIK No: 0001102432

Subsidiaries: Blue Diamond International Inc, Casino Marketing S.A, Skill Poker.com Inc

Officers: Cecil Morris/76/Dir., Pres., Sec.

Directors: Cecil Morris/76/Dir., Pres., Sec., John Page/78/Dir.

Owners: Montilla Capital/6.84%, Eurocapital Holdings A.V.V./8.21%, Iris International Holdings Limited/12.30%, Cecil Morris/1.78%, PokerSoft Corporation A.V.V./8.20%, John Page/0.68%, CEDE & Co./52.59%

Financial Data: *Fiscal Year End:*12/31 *Latest Annual Data:* 12/31/2006

Year	Sales	Net Income
2006	NA	-$37,000
2005	NA	-$54,000
2004	NA	-$795,000

Curr. Assets:	$13,000	**Curr. Liab.:**	$226,000		
Plant, Equip.:	NA	**Total Liab.:**	$226,000	**Indic. Yr. Divd.:**	NA
Total Assets:	$13,000	**Net Worth:**	-$213,000	**Debt/ Equity:**	NA

Synthetech Inc

1290 Industrial Way, Albany, OR, 97321; *PH:* 1-541-967-6575; *http://* www.synthetech.com

General - Incorporation	OR	**Stock** - Price on:12/24/2007	NA
Employees	50	Stock Exchange	OTC
Auditor	KPMG LLP	Ticker Symbol	NZYM
Stk Agt	Computershare Trust Co	Outstanding Shares	NA
Counsel	Perkins Coie LLP	E.P.S	NA
DUNS No.	05-534-0319	Shareholders	NA

Business: The group's principle activity is to produce chemically modified, naturally occurring and synthetic amino acids referred to as peptide building blocks (pbbs). The group's products support the development and manufacture of therapeutic peptides and peptidomimetic small molecule drugs at every stage of a customer's clinical development pipeline. The group also manufactures products for use in cosmeceuticals, a cosmetic product that makes no therapeutic claims. The products are used predominately by pharmaceutical companies to make a wide range of peptide-based drugs under development or on the market for the treatment of aids, cancer, cardiovascular and other diseases. The group has international sales in Europe, Japan and other. The group's quarterly revenue for Sep '07 was 2.98 millions of USD.

Primary SIC and add'l.: 2869 3826

CIK No: 0000749290

Officers: Daniel T. Fagan/55/Chmn., CEO/$151,112.00, Gregory R. Hahn/52/COO, Pres./$216,251.00, Brett Reynolds/35/Dir. - Sales, Marketing, Gary A. Weber/49/VP - Finance, CFO, Sec./$135,131.00, Joel D. Melka/52/VP - Operations/$132,930.00, Joseph Murphy/60/Dir. - Business Development/$126,247.00, Michael C. Standen/46/Technical Dir.

Directors: Daniel T. Fagan/55/Chmn., CEO, Hans Noetzli/66/Dir., Paul C. Ahrens/55/Dir., Charles B. Williams/60/Dir., Howard L. Farkas/83/Dir., Donald E. Kuhla/64/Dir.

Owners: Insiders/19.10%, M. Sreenivasan/4.50%, Joel D. Melka/1.30%, Howard L. Farkas, Gary A. Weber/1.80%, Daniel T. Fagan, Paul C. Ahrens/6.30%, Hans Noetzli, Charles B. Williams/2.10%, Joseph Murphy, Gregory R. Hahn, Donald E. Kuhla

Curr. Assets:	$7,586,000	Curr. Liab.:	$2,001,000		
Plant, Equip.:	$3,746,000	Total Liab.:	$2,001,000	Indic. Yr. Divd.:	NA
Total Assets:	$11,332,000	Net Worth:	$9,331,000	Debt/ Equity:	NA

Synthetic Blood International Inc

3189 Airway Ave. Ste. C, Costa Mesa, CA, 92626; **PH:** 1-800-809-6054; **Fax:** 1-714-427-6361; **http://** www.sybd.com

General - Incorporation	NJ	Stock - Price on:12/24/2007	$0.139
Employees	6	Stock Exchange	OTC
Auditor	Haskell and White LLP	Ticker Symbol	SYBD
Stk Agt	Interwest Transfer Company, Inc.	Outstanding Shares	139,370,000
Counsel	NA	E.P.S.	NA
DUNS No.	NA	Shareholders	NA

Business: The groups principal activity is developing biotechnology products. The group markets its products under the tradenames include Oxycyte(TM) and Fluorovent(TM). The group received approval of investigational new drug application for Oxycyte filed with the U.S. Food and Drug Administration. The group operates from the United States.

Primary SIC and add'l.: 8731

CIK No: 0000034956

Officers: Robert Nicora/68/Dir., CEO, Pres., David Johnson/61/Dir., CFO, Richard Kiral/VP - Product Development, Dir., Douglas Kornbrust/Consultant - Preclinical Toxicology, Pharmacolog, Anthony Fox/Consulting Clinical Pharmacologist, Jody Cain/Investor Relations Officer, Brandi Floberg/Investor Relations Officer

Directors: Robert Nicora/68/Dir., CEO, Pres., David Johnson/61/Dir., CFO, Richard Kiral/VP - Product Development, Dir., Jonathan J. Spees/54/Dir.

Owners: Aventis Invest/15.30%, Richard Kiral/0.62%, David Johnson/0.14%, Insiders/2.50%, Robert W. Nicora/1.34%, Jonathan Spees/0.37%, Till Gontersweiler/7.80%

Syntony Group Inc

1035 Pk. Ave., Ste. 7b, New York, NY, 10028; **PH:** 1-646-827-9362

General - Incorporation	UT	Stock - Price on:12/24/2007	$3
Employees	NA	Stock Exchange	OTC
Auditor	Raich Ende Malter & Co. LLP	Ticker Symbol	ACAQ
Stk Agt	NA	Outstanding Shares	1,370,000
Counsel	NA	E.P.S.	-$0.14
DUNS No.	NA	Shareholders	NA

Business: The group's principle activity is to engage in all facets of the business comprising the oil and gas industry. The group operates from United States.

Primary SIC and add'l.: 9995

CIK No: 0001286690

Subsidiaries: Syntony, Syntony Acquisition Corp

Officers: Alain U. Vetterli/Dir., CEO, CFO, Pres., Treasurer, Sec.

Directors: Alain U. Vetterli/Dir., CEO, CFO, Pres., Treasurer, Sec., Ian Ilsley/Dir.

Owners: Tendall FZCO/96.50%, Ian Ilsley, Robert Lawrence Banner, Alain U. Vetterli

Financial Data: Fiscal Year End:12/31 Latest Annual Data: 12/31/2006

Year	Sales	Net Income
2006	NA	-$169,000
2005	NA	-$21,000
2004	NA	-$24,000

Curr. Assets:	NA	Curr. Liab.:	$1,075,000		
Plant, Equip.:	NA	Total Liab.:	$1,075,000	Indic. Yr. Divd.:	NA
Total Assets:	$938,000	Net Worth:	-$138,000	Debt/ Equity:	NA

Syntroleum Corp

4322 S 49th W Ave., Tulsa, OK, 74107; **PH:** 1-918-592-7900; **http://** www.syntroleum.com; **Email:** investor@syntroleum.com

General - Incorporation	DE	Stock - Price on:12/24/2007	$2.82
Employees	62	Stock Exchange	NDQ
Auditor	Grant Thornton LLP	Ticker Symbol	SYNM
Stk Agt	American Stock Transfer & Trust Co.	Outstanding Shares	58,020,000
Counsel	NA	E.P.S.	-$0.37
DUNS No.	18-922-2334	Shareholders	NA

Business: The group's principal activities are to develop and license proprietary process for converting natural gas to synthetic liquid hydrocarbon known as gas-to-liquids or gtl technology. The group sells licenses to use the gtl technology, the syntroleum process for the production of fuels. The syntroleum process produces synthetic liquid hydrocarbons, also known as synthetic crude oil, that are substantially free of contaminants normally found in conventional products made from crude oil. These synthetic liquid hydrocarbons can be further processed into other liquid fuels through conventional refining processes. These products include diesel, kerosene, gasoline, and naptha and specialty products such as synthetic lubricants, process oils, high melting point waxes, liquid normal paraffins, drilling fluids, and chemical feedstocks. On 21-Jul-2003, the group discontinued its houston project.

Primary SIC and add'l.: 6552 2911

CIK No: 0001029023

Subsidiaries: Carousel Apartment Homes, Inc. (a Georgia Corporation), Ringneck Resources, LLC, Scout Development Corporation (a Missouri Corporation), Syntroleum Australia Credit Corporation, Syntroleum Australia Licensing Corporation, Syntroleum Australia, Ltd., Syntroleum Bolivia Holdings LLC, Syntroleum Cameroon, Ltd., Syntroleum Gas Development, LLC, Syntroleum Gas Processing, LLC, Syntroleum Gas Resources Corporation, Syntroleum International Corporation, Syntroleum International Holdings Company, Syntroleum International Holdings, Ltd., Syntroleum Nigeria Limited 19 Subsidiaries included in the Index

Officers: John B. Holmes/Dir., CEO, Kenneth L. Agee/Chmn., Chief Research Officer/$640,463.00, Gary Gamino/VP - Investor - Media Relations, Karen L. Gallagher/Sr. VP, Principal Financial Officer, Richard L. Edmonson/Sr. VP, General Counsel, Corp. Sec./$452,299.00, Edward G. Roth/Dir., COO, Pres./$1,493,082.00, Greg G. Jenkins/CFO, Exec. VP - Business Development/$1,785,268.00, Ronald E. Stinebaugh/Sr. VP - Finance, Acquisitions

Directors: John B. Holmes/Dir., CEO, Kenneth L. Agee/Chmn., Chief Research Officer, Ziad Ghandour/Dir., Frank M. Bumstead/Dir., Edward G. Roth/Dir., COO, Pres., Robert Rosene/Dir., Gary Roth/51/Dir., Alvin Albe/Dir., Anthony P. Jacobs/Dir., James R. Seward/Dir.

Owners: Richard L. Edmonson, Frank M. Bumstead, Ziad Ghandour/2.00%, John B. Holmes/2.00%, Greg G. Jenkins/1.00%, James R. Seward/1.00%, Legg Mason Opportunity Trust/10.00%, Alvin R. Albe, Anthony P. Jacobs/1.00%, Kenneth L. Agee/7.30%, Robert B. Rosene, Robert A. Day/8.50%, Insiders/15.00%, Edward G. Roth/1.00%, Peak Investments, LLC/13.00%

Financial Data: Fiscal Year End:12/31 Latest Annual Data: 12/31/2006

Year	Sales	Net Income
2006	$3,789,000	-$54,625,000
2005	$7,908,000	-$41,394,000
2004	$6,606,000	-$42,550,000

Curr. Assets:	$37,472,000	Curr. Liab.:	$8,273,000		
Plant, Equip.:	$4,956,000	Total Liab.:	$57,789,000	Indic. Yr. Divd.:	NA
Total Assets:	$43,937,000	Net Worth:	-$14,558,000	Debt/ Equity:	0.6457

Synutra International Inc

Formerly: Vorsatech Ventures Inc

2275 Research Blvd. Ste. 500, Rockville, MD, 20850; **PH:** 1-301-840-3888

General - Incorporation	DE	Stock - Price on:12/24/2007	NA
Employees	1,890	Stock Exchange	NA
Auditor	Rotenberg & Co. LLP	Ticker Symbol	NA
Stk Agt	Signature Stock Transfer, Inc.	Outstanding Shares	NA
Counsel	NA	E.P.S.	$0.43
DUNS No.	NA	Shareholders	NA

Business: The group's principle activities include production, distribution and sales of infant formulas based on dairy products. The groups extensive sales network covers 24 provinces, 227 cities and more than 800 counties throughout China. The group's products can be purchased in over 11,800 retail stores within China.

Primary SIC and add'l.: 9995

CIK No: 0001293593

Subsidiaries: Illinois corporation (Synutra Illinois), Synutra International, Inc.

Owners: Liang Zhang/80.84%, Insiders/80.84%, Warburg Pincus LLC/7.41%

Financial Data: Fiscal Year End:03/31 Latest Annual Data: 03/31/2006

Year	Sales	Net Income
2006	$132,692,000	$11,035,000
2005	NA	-$20,000

Curr. Assets:	$72,151,000	Curr. Liab.:	$80,432,000		
Plant, Equip.:	$51,472,000	Total Liab.:	$84,570,000	Indic. Yr. Divd.:	NA
Total Assets:	$127,271,000	Net Worth:	$42,701,000	Debt/ Equity:	NA

Synvista Therapeutics Inc

Formerly: Alteon Inc

221 W Grand Ave., Montvale, NJ, 07645; **PH:** 1-201-934-5000; **http://** www.alteonpharma.com

General - Incorporation	DE	Stock - Price on:12/24/2007	$0.06
Employees	7	Stock Exchange	AMEX
Auditor	J. H. Cohn LLP	Ticker Symbol	SYI
Stk Agt	American Stock Transfer & Trust Co.	Outstanding Shares	129,320,000
Counsel	Mintz, Levin, Glovsky & Popeo PC	E.P.S.	-$6.22
DUNS No.	18-696-1439	Shareholders	NA

Business: The group's principle activities include discovering and developing pharmaceutical products for the treatment of diabetes and cardiovascular aging. These products are developed as a result of a research on a pathological process, the advanced glycosylation end-product pathway. This process causes or contributes to many medical disorders, including cardiovascular, kidney and eye diseases. The product alt-711 inhibits, measures and reverses damage to cells, tissues and organs caused by it. Another product, alt-744 is being clinically evaluated in skin aging for cosmetic applications. Pimagedine is a lead compound employed by the company. It has been licensed to yamanouchi pharmaceutical co, ltd for commercial distribution in Japan, South Korea, Taiwan and the People's Republic of China. The company has also entered into an exclusive licensing arrangement with roche diagnostics gmbh for development of drug therapies and diagnostics utilizing its scientific platforms. The group operates from United States.

Primary SIC and add'l.: 8731 2834

CIK No: 0000878903

Subsidiaries: W. P. Stewart & Co., Ltd

Officers: Noah Berkowitz/Dir., CEO, Pres./$297,558.00, Malcolm W. MacNab/VP - Clinical Development/$334,206.00, Carl M. Mendel/VP - Clinical Development, Chief Medical Officer, Jacob Victor/Executive Dir. - Product Development, Clinical Diagnostics

Directors: Noah Berkowitz/Dir., CEO, Pres., Thomas A. Moore/Dir., Mary C. Tanner/Dir., Wayne Yetter/Dir., John F. Bedard/Dir.

Owners: Marilyn G. Breslow, Noah C. Berkowitz Family Trust/5.00%, Insiders/15.00%, Genentech, Inc./11.00%, Noah Berkowitz/7.00%, Mary C. Tanner/6.00%, Malcolm MacNab/1.00%, Wayne P. Yetter/1.00%, Thomas A. Moore

Financial Data: Fiscal Year End:12/31 Latest Annual Data: 12/31/2006

Year	Sales	Net Income
2006	$62,000	-$17,680,000
2005	$458,000	-$12,614,000
2004	$334,000	-$13,959,000

Curr. Assets:	$1,793,000	Curr. Liab.:	$1,063,000		
Plant, Equip.:	$11,000	Total Liab.:	$1,063,000	Indic. Yr. Divd.:	NA
Total Assets:	$2,305,000	Net Worth:	$1,243,000	Debt/ Equity:	NA

Sypris Solutions Inc

101 Bullitt Ln., Ste 450, Louisville, KY, 40222; **PH:** 1-502-329-2000; **http://** www.sypris.com; **Email:** ir@sypris.com

General - Incorporation	DE	Stock - Price on:12/24/2007	$8.1
Employees	2,639	Stock Exchange	NDQ
Auditor	Ernst & Young LLP	Ticker Symbol	SYPR
Stk Agt	LaSalle Bank N.A	Outstanding Shares	18,900,000
Counsel	Wyatt, Tarrant & Combs	E.P.S.	-$0.05
DUNS No.	55-549-1489	Shareholders	NA

Business: The group's principal activities are to provide diversified technology-based outsourced services and specialty products. The group has contracts with corporations and government agencies in the markets for aerospace and defense electronics, truck components and users of test and measurement equipment. Electronics group is primarily engaged in the sale of electronics manufacturing and technical services to customers in the aerospace and defense electronics market, as well as from customers who require test and measurement services. Industrial group is primarily engaged in the sale of industrial manufacturing services to customers in the truck components and assemblies market. The group also designs and builds secure communications equipment and write encryption software. The group's major customers include arvinmeritor, dana, honeywell, raytheon and visteon.

Primary SIC and add'l.: 3823 3462 3679

CIK No: 0000864240

Subsidiaries: Sypris Data Systems, Inc., Sypris Electronics, LLC, Sypris Technologies Kenton, Inc., Sypris Technologies Marion, LLC, Sypris Technologies Mexican Holdings, LLC, Sypris Technologies Mexico, S. de R.L. de C.V., Sypris Technologies Toluca, S.A. de C.V., Sypris Technologies, Inc., Sypris Test & Measurement, Inc.

Officers: Jeffrey T. Gill/Dir., CEO, Pres./$652,657.00, T. S. Hatton/41/CFO, VP/$617,914.00, Anthony C. Allen/VP, Treasurer, Assist. Sec., John R. McGeeney/General Counsel, Sec., Kathy Smith Boyd/VP - Sypris Solutions, Pres. - Sypris Test, Measurement, Richard L. Davis/Sr. VP/$349,012.00, Darrell G. Robertson/VP - Sypris Solutions, Pres. - Sypris Data Systems, Scott T. Hatton/41/CFO, VP, Jeffrey T. Reibel/Controller, Sergio L.M. De Carvalho/VP - Sypris Solutions, Pres. - Sypris Technologies

Directors: Jeffrey T. Gill/Dir., CEO, Pres., Robert E. Gill/Chmn., Sidney R. Petersen/Dir., Scott R. Gill/Dir., William G. Ferko/Dir., Robert Sroka/Dir., John F. Brinkley/Dir., William L. Healey/Dir.

Owners: William G. Ferko, Kennedy Capital Management, Wellington Management Company, LLP, Robert B. Sanders, Insiders, John F. Brinkley, Jeffrey T. Gill, Scott R. Gill, Robert Sroka, Sidney R. Petersen, Robert E. Gill, Gill Family Capital Management, Inc., Richard L. Davis, Virginia G. Gill, John M. Kramer (19 Owners included in Index)

Financial Data: Fiscal Year End:12/31 Latest Annual Data: 12/31/2006

Year	Sales		Net Income
2006	$497,664,000		-$1,362,000
2005	$522,766,000		$5,321,000
2004	$425,402,000		$7,407,000
Curr. Assets:	$201,438,000	**Curr. Liab.:** $100,721,000	
Plant, Equip.:	$155,341,000	**Total Liab.:** $169,147,000	**Indic. Yr. Divd.:** $0.120
Total Assets:	$379,033,000	**Net Worth:** $209,886,000	**Debt/ Equity:** 0.2634

Syringa Bancorp

999 W Main St. Ste. 100, Boise, ID, 83702; *PH:* 1-208-336-6865; *http://* www.syringabank.com; *Email:* smills@syringabank.com

General - Incorporation		**Stock**- Price on:12/24/2007	$13
Employees	NA	Stock Exchange	OTC
Auditor	NA	Ticker Symbol	SGBP
Stk Agt	Registrar & Transfer Co	Outstanding Shares	NA
Counsel	NA	E.P.S.	NA
DUNS No.	NA	Shareholders	NA

Business: The groups principal activities include providing banking and financial services. Services of the group include checking accounts, savings accounts, certificates of deposit, installment loans, real estate mortgage loans, commercial loans, traveler's checks, safe deposit boxes, night depository and automated teller services. The group operates from the United States.

Primary SIC and add'l.: 6712

CIK No:

Officers: Jerry F. Aldape/CEO, Pres., Lou Ratto/Sr. VP, District Mgr., Andy Warren/VP, Branch Mgr., Rick Fried/VP, Middleton Branch Mgr., Brian Manship/VP, Regional Branch Operations Mgr., Fred Drzayich/VP, Business Development Officer, Jim Cobbs/VP, Business Relationship Mgr., Teresa Hommel/VP, Loan Servicing Mgr., Dave Lumley/VP, Commercial Loan Officer, Debbie Pemberton/VP, Sr. Bank Operations Mgr., Ellen Heath/Sr. VP, Construction Loan Mgr., Cindy Parks/VP, Real Estate Lending Officer, Brian Heim/VP, Controller, Dee G. Carter/VP, Real Estate Lending Mgr., Wally Lee/VP, Business Relationship Mgr. (31 Officers included in Index)

Directors: Hilario J. Arguinchona/Chmn., Skip Anderson/Chmn. - Advisory Board, Ron A. Coulter/Member - Advisory Board, Stacy King Powers/Member - Advisory Board, Rod Carr/Member - Advisory Board, Scott J. Chandler/Dir., Don H. Deters/Dir., Harvey L. Neef/Dir., Timothy D. Viehweg/Dir., Cheryl A. Larabee/Dir., Lew H. Andrews/Dir., Thomas B. Chandler/Dir., Terry L. Hayden/Dir., Bruce C. Parker/Dir., Charles Wilson/Dir. (20 Directors included in Index)

SYS Technologies

5050 Murphy Canyon Rd., Ste. 200, San Diego, CA, 92123; *PH:* 1-858-715-5500; *Fax:* 1-858-715-5510; *http://* www.syys.com

General - Incorporation	CA	**Stock** - Price on:12/24/2007	$1.98
Employees	404	Stock Exchange	AMEX
Auditor	Grant Thornton, LLP	Ticker Symbol	NA
Stk Agt	Mellon Investor Services LLC	Outstanding Shares	18,900,000
Counsel	NA	E.P.S.	-$0.06
DUNS No.	04-850-5366	Shareholders	NA

Business: The group's principle activities are to provide engineering, management and technical services. The services offered are in the fields of systems planning, management and analysis, system engineering, naval architecture, marine engineering and related support services. Its services include operations analysis, design development, computer system analysis, office automation, information management systems and related support services and hardware integration and fabrication. The group provides support services to agencies of the United States government and private industry as a primary contractor and as sub contractors. Majority of its revenue are from contracts with the United States government, principally agencies of the department of defense. The group's quarterly revenue for Sep '07 was 20.51 millions of USD.

Primary SIC and add'l.: 8742 7373

CIK No: 0000096057

Subsidiaries: Polexis, Inc., Shadow I, Inc.

Officers: Clifton L. Cooke/Dir., CEO, Pres., Robert A. Babbush/Sr. VP - Corporate Administration, Assist. Corp. Sec., Ben Goodwin/Pres. - Public Safety, Security, Industrial Systems Group, Sr. VP - Sales, Marketing, Kenneth D. Regan/Pres. - Defense Solutions Group, Michael W. Fink/51/Sec., Sr. VP, Edward M. Lake/CFO, Exec. VP, Phil Carrai/Pres. - Network Security, Management Group

Directors: Clifton L. Cooke/Dir., CEO, Pres., Alfred M. Gray/80/Chmn., Charles E. Vandeveer/Dir., John R. Hicks/Dir., Gail K. Naughton/Dir., Thomas A. Page/Dir., Philip P. Trahanas/37/Dir.

Owners: David A. Derby/0.80%, John R. Hicks/2.00%, Charles E. Vandeveer/1.40%, AST Capital Trust/6.40%, Philip P. Trahanas/8.50%, Clifton L. Cooke/7.70%, Alfred M. Gray/0.30%, Kenneth D. Regan/0.80%, Insiders/25.90%, Ben Goodwin/1.10%, Gail K. Naughton/0.20%, Thomas A. Page/1.60%, Michael W. Fink/1.10%, Edward M. Lake/1.40%

Financial Data: Fiscal Year End:06/30 Latest Annual Data: 6/30/2007

Year	Sales		Net Income
2007	$75,798,000		-$1,693,000
2006	$55,861,000		-$1,743,000
2005	$45,769,000		$1,407,000
Curr. Assets:	$20,568,000	**Curr. Liab.:** $12,377,000	
Plant, Equip.:	$1,951,000	**Total Liab.:** $17,304,000	**Indic. Yr. Divd.:** NA
Total Assets:	$52,383,000	**Net Worth:** $35,079,000	**Debt/ Equity:** 0.1067

Sysco Corp

1390 EnclAve. Pkwy., Houston, TX, 77077; *PH:* 1-281-584-1390; *http://* www.sysco.com

General - Incorporation	DE	**Stock**- Price on:12/24/2007	$33.77
Employees	49,600	Stock Exchange	NYSE
Auditor	Ernst & Young LLP	Ticker Symbol	SYY
Stk Agt	American Stock Transfer & Trust Co.	Outstanding Shares	617,960,000
Counsel	Arnall Golden Gregory	E.P.S.	$1.66
DUNS No.	05-109-9661	Shareholders	NA

Business: The group's principle activity is to distribute food and related products to foodservice or food-prepared-away-from-home industry. Customers served by the group include restaurants, healthcare and educational facilities, lodging establishments and various foodservice customers. During the fiscal year ended June 30, 2007, the group acquired Bunn Capitol. The group operates from United States and Europe.

Primary SIC and add'l.: 5144 5148 5142 5147 5113 5149 5143

CIK No: 0000096021

Subsidiaries: A-One-A Produce & Dairy Puerto Rico, LLC, A-One-A Produce & Provisions, Inc., A.M. Briggs, Inc., American Produce & Vegetable Company, Banner Beef & Seafood Co., Inc., Baugh Midwest Cooperative, Inc., Baugh Northeast Co-Op, Inc., Baugh Southeast Cooperative, Inc., Baugh Southwest Cooperative, Inc., Baugh Supply Chain Cooperative, Inc., Baugh Western Cooperative, Inc., Buckhead Beef Company, Carnival Fruit Company, Inc., Contract Administrative Services, Inc., DiPaolo/Sysco Food Services, Inc. 183 Subsidiaries included in the Index

Officers: Richard J. Schnieders/Chmn., CEO/$14,351,230.00, Cameron L. Blakely/Group Pres. - Strategic Management Office, Thomas P. Randt/Assist. VP - Employee Relations, Kirk G. Drummond/Sr. VP - Finance, Treasurer, Craig G. Watson/VP - Quality Assurance, Agricultural Sustainability, Susan K. Billiot/VP - Human Resources, Mark Wisnoski/VP - Employee Benefits, Brian M. Sturgeon/VP, Larry J. Accardi/Exec. VP - Sales/$6,171,502.00, Gary W. Cullen/VP - Distribution Services, Albert L. Gaylor/VP - Industry Relations, Diversity, Kenneth F. Spitler/COO, Pres./$6,505,846.00, Christopher J. Shepardson/VP - Merchandising, Sourcing, Robert E. Howell/VP - Sourcing, Supply Chain, William B. Day/Sr. VP - Supply Chain (57 Officers included in Index)

Directors: Richard J. Schnieders/Chmn., CEO, Judith B. Craven/Dir., Jackie M. Ward/Dir., Manny A. Fernandez/Dir., Joseph A. Hafner/Dir., Richard G. Tilghman/Dir., John M. Cassaday/Dir., Nancy S. Newcomb/Dir., Jonathan Golden/Dir., Richard G. Merrill/Dir., Phyllis S. Sewell/Dir.

Owners: Jackie M. Ward, Richard J. Schnieders, Nancy S. Newcomb, John M. Cassaday, Insiders, Joseph A. Hafner, Phyllis S. Sewell, Judith B. Craven, Kenneth F. Spitler, Richard G. Merrill, Larry G. Pulliam, Larry J. Accardi, Manuel A. Fernandez, John K. Stubblefield, Richard G. Tilghman (16 Owners included in Index)

Financial Data: Fiscal Year End:07/02 Latest Annual Data: 7/1/2006

Year	Sales		Net Income
2006	$32,628,438,000		$855,325,000
2005	$30,281,914,000		$961,457,000
2004	$29,335,403,000		$907,214,000
Curr. Assets:	$3,851,411,000	**Curr. Liab.:** $3,126,634,000	**P/E Ratio:** 22.22
Plant, Equip.:	$2,166,809,000	**Total Liab.:** $5,283,126,000	**Indic. Yr. Divd.:** $0.880
Total Assets:	$7,847,632,000	**Net Worth:** $2,564,506,000	**Debt/ Equity:** 0.4896

System Energy Resources Inc

Echelon One, 1340 Echelon Pkwy., Jackson, MS, 39213; *PH:* 1-603-368-5000

General - Incorporation	AR	**Stock**- Price on:12/24/2007	NA
Employees	NA	Stock Exchange	NA
Auditor	Deloitte & Touche LLP	Ticker Symbol	NA
Stk Agt	Registrar & Transfer Co	Outstanding Shares	NA
Counsel	Parker, McCay & Criscuolo	E.P.S.	NA
DUNS No.	08-555-7056	Shareholders	NA

Business: The group's principle activity is to supply energy. The company transmits and distributes electricity to retailers. It also provides domestic utility operations, power marketing and trading, global power development and domestic non-utility nuclear operations. It operates primarily in the states of Arkansas, gulf states, Louisiana, Mississippi and new orleans. The group operates from United States.

Primary SIC and add'l.: 4911

CIK No: 0000202584

Subsidiaries: Arkansas Power & Light Company, Bom Jardim Energetica LTDA, Damhead Finance (Netherlands Antilles) N.V., Damhead Finance LDC, EK Holding III, LLC, EKLP, LLC, EN Services II, EN Services L.P., EN Services, L.P., Entergy Arkansas, Inc., Entergy Asset Management, Inc, Entergy Asset Management, Inc., Entergy Commerce, Inc., Entergy Corporation, Entergy Enterprises, Inc. 141 Subsidiaries included in the Index

Systemax Inc

11 Harbor Pk. Dr., Port Washington, NY, 11050; *PH:* 1-516-608-7000; *http://* www.systemax.com

General - Incorporation	DE	**Stock**- Price on:12/24/2007	$1.26
Employees	2,961	Stock Exchange	NYSE
Auditor	Deloitte & Touche LLP	Ticker Symbol	SYX
Stk Agt	American Stock Transfer & Trust Co.	Outstanding Shares	35,980,000
Counsel	NA	E.P.S.	$1.45
DUNS No.	88-447-5039	Shareholders	NA

Business: The groups principle activity is to market brand names and private label products including personal desktop and notebook computers, computer related products and industrial products. The groups products are sold under the brand names Systemax(TM), Tiger(R) and Ultra(TM). The group operates through three business segments namely technology products, industrial products and hosted software. The group operates from United States.

Primary SIC and add'l.: 5044 5045 5084

CIK No: 0000945114

Subsidiaries: Dabus Dataproducktor AB, Dartek Corporation, Global Computer Products BV, Global Computer Supplies Inc., Global Equipment Company Inc., H C S Global SA, Misco Germany Inc., Misco Iberia Computer Supplies S.A., Misco Italy Computer Supplies S.P.A., Nexel Industries Inc., Profit Center Software Inc., Systemax Europe Ltd., Systemax Manufacturing Inc., Tiger Direct Inc.

Officers: Richard Leeds/48/Chmn., CEO/$1,047,795.00, Curt S. Rush/General Counsel, Sec.

Directors: Richard Leeds/48/Chmn., CEO, Bruce Leeds/52/Vice Chmn., Robert Leeds/52/Vice Chmn., Gilbert Fiorentino/48/Dir., Robert D. Rosenthal/59/Dir., Stacy S. Dick/51/Dir., Ann R. Leven/67/Dir.

Owners: Bruce Leeds/21.90%, Robert D. Rosenthal, Insiders/66.20%, Stacy S. Dick, Robert Leeds/21.90%, Richard Leeds/27.30%, Gilbert Fiorentino/2.20%, Ann R. Leven, Steven M. Goldschein, Dimensional Fund Advisors Inc./5.50%

Financial Data: Fiscal Year End: 12/31 **Latest Annual Data:** 12/31/2006

Year	Sales	Net Income
2006	$2,345,165,000	$45,147,000
2005	$2,115,518,000	$11,441,000
2004	$1,928,147,000	$10,188,000

Curr. Assets:	$519,361,000	Curr. Liab.:	$289,962,000	P/E Ratio:	1.13
Plant, Equip.:	$48,586,000	Total Liab.:	$294,671,000	Indic. Yr. Divd.:	NA
Total Assets:	$584,161,000	Net Worth:	$289,490,000	Debt/Equity:	0.0012

Systems Management Solutions Inc

4703 Shavano Oak Ste. 104, San Antonio, TX, 78249; **PH:** 1-210-541-9100; http:// www.smsholdings.net/contact.htm

General - Incorporation	NV	Stock - Price on:12/24/2007	$0.18
Employees	3	Stock Exchange	OTC
Auditor	Malone & Bailey, PC	Ticker Symbol	SSMG
Stk Agt	Signature Stock Transfer, Inc.	Outstanding Shares	20,690,000
Counsel	NA	E.P.S.	-$0.07
DUNS No.	NA	Shareholders	NA

Business: The groups principle activities include providing business services, software and solutions primarily to the small and mid sized business sector and through groups subsidiary SMSE, provides biodiesel to distributors. The group operates through two segments namely software sales, programming, and data capturing and storage and renewable energies. In the year April 2005, the group acquired SMS Envirofuels, Inc. The group operates from the United States.

Primary SIC and add'l.: 8742

CIK No: 0001116198

Subsidiaries: SMSN Merger Sub, Inc

Officers: Jim Karlak/Dir., CEO, Pres., Morris Kunofsky/56/CFO, Jenelle Stehle/43/Sec., Treasurer

Directors: Jim Karlak/Dir., CEO, Pres., Clifford A. Hagler/55/Dir., Bruce Culver/54/Dir., Jesse Whittenton/53/Dir.

Owners: American Continental Management Inc., United Managers Group, Inc./72.15%, Bruce Culver, Insiders

Financial Data: Fiscal Year End: 12/31 **Latest Annual Data:** 12/31/2006

Year	Sales	Net Income
2006	$3,621,000	-$1,442,000
2005	$2,464,000	-$3,033,000
2004	$69,000	-$1,306,000

Curr. Assets:	$124,000	Curr. Liab.:	$6,227,000		
Plant, Equip.:	$582,000	Total Liab.:	$6,519,000	Indic. Yr. Divd.:	NA
Total Assets:	$961,000	Net Worth:	-$5,558,000	Debt/Equity:	NA

Systems Xcellence Inc

2441 Warrenville Rd., Ste. 610, Lisle, IL, 60532; **PH:** 1-630-577-3100; http:// www.sxc.com

General - Incorporation	Canada	Stock - Price on:12/24/2007	$27.58
Employees	426	Stock Exchange	NA
Auditor	NA	Ticker Symbol	NA
Stk Agt	Mellon Trust Co	Outstanding Shares	20,590,000
Counsel	NA	E.P.S.	$0.57
DUNS No.	NA	Shareholders	NA

Business: The groups principal activity is to provide healthcare transaction processing services and information technology solutions. The group products sold under the trade names InformedRx(TM) and RxEXPRESS(R). The groups services include online claims processing, pharmacy data warehousing, rebate management, Web portal deployment, and drug dispensing. The group operates from the United States.

Primary SIC and add'l.: 7371

CIK No: 0001363851

Subsidiaries: 1131836 Ontario inc, Health Business Systems, InC, InformedRx,Inc, SXC Health Solutions,Inc

Officers: Gordon S. Glenn/Chmn., CEO, Mark A. Thierer/Dir., COO, Pres., Jeffrey Park/Sr. VP - Finance, CFO, Mike Bennof/Exec. VP - Healthcare Information Technology, John Romza/Exec. VP - Research, Development, CTO, Mike Meyer/Sr. VP - Sales, Marketing, Michael Zaslav/Sr. VP - Provider Development

Directors: Gordon S. Glenn/Chmn., CEO, Mark A. Thierer/Dir., COO, Pres., Terrence C. Burke/Dir., William J. Davis/Dir., Philip R. Reddon/Dir., Steven D. Cosler/Dir., Anthony R. Masso/Dir., Curtis J. Thorne/Dir.

Financial Data: Fiscal Year End: 12/31 **Latest Annual Data:** 12/31/2006

Year	Sales	Net Income
2006	$80,922,995,000	$13,646,185,000

Curr. Assets:	$91,877,000	Curr. Liab.:	$16,268,000		
Plant, Equip.:	$10,114,000	Total Liab.:	$19,734,000	Indic. Yr. Divd.:	NA
Total Assets:	$131,224,000	Net Worth:	$111,490,000	Debt/Equity:	NA

Sysview Technology Inc

Formerly: Syscan Imaging Inc
1772 Technology Dr., San Jose, CA, 95110; **PH:** 1-408-436-9888; http:// www.syscaninc.com

General - Incorporation	DE	Stock - Price on:12/24/2007	$0.76
Employees	26	Stock Exchange	OTC
Auditor	Clancy & Co. PLLC	Ticker Symbol	SYVT
Stk Agt	Interwest Transfer Company, Inc.	Outstanding Shares	NA
Counsel	NA	E.P.S.	-$0.28
DUNS No.	NA	Shareholders	NA

Business: The group's principal activity is to develop and manufacture a new generation of cis (cmos-complimentary metal oxide silicon) imaging sensor devices. Its patented cis and mobile imaging scanner technology provides very high quality images but at extremely low power consumption, allowing it to manufacture very compact scanners in a form ideally suited for the mobile computer user who needs to scan and or fax documents while away from their office. The group acquired syscan inc on 02-Apr-2004.

Primary SIC and add'l.: 7375 5045

CIK No: 0001096857

Subsidiaries: Nano Acquisition Corp, Syscan, Inc., Sysview Technology, Inc

Officers: Darwin Hu/Chmn., CEO, Pres., David P. Clark/Sr. VP - Investment, Business Development, William Hawkins/Sec., COO, Interim CFO, George Mihalakis/CTO, Hank Lee/VP - Operations, Strategic Display Business, Gihong Kim/VP - Nano, Lcos Technology, Charles Koo/VP - CNT Process Technology, John Shih/VP - Materials, Business Development, Peter Seltzberg/Investor Relations Contact

Directors: Darwin Hu/Chmn., CEO, Pres.

Owners: Darwin Hu/7.20%, David Clark/4.40%, Insiders/15.10%, Lawrence Liang, Syscan Imaging Limited/75.10%, William Hawkins/5.00%

Financial Data: Fiscal Year End: 12/31 **Latest Annual Data:** 12/31/2006

Year	Sales	Net Income
2006	$12,469,000	-$5,199,000
2005	$7,848,000	-$1,493,000
2004	$6,058,000	-$180,000

Curr. Assets:	$4,861,000	Curr. Liab.:	$2,821,000		
Plant, Equip.:	$108,000	Total Liab.:	$4,159,000	Indic. Yr. Divd.:	NA
Total Assets:	$5,129,000	Net Worth:	$970,000	Debt/Equity:	NA

T 3 Energy Services Inc

13111 Nwest Fwy., Ste. 500, Houston, TX, 77040; **PH:** 1-713-996-4110; http:// www.t3energyservices.com

General - Incorporation	DE	Stock - Price on:12/24/2007	$31.24
Employees	573	Stock Exchange	NDQ
Auditor	Ernst & Young LLP	Ticker Symbol	TTES
Stk Agt	Mellon Investor Services LLC	Outstanding Shares	10,770,000
Counsel	NA	E.P.S.	$1.86
DUNS No.	61-677-2042	Shareholders	NA

Business: The group's principal activity is to manufacture, remanufacture and distribute oilfield products and services to the oil and gas industry. It operates through three segments: pressure control, products and distribution. The pressure control division manufactures, remanufactures and repairs high pressure, severe service products including valves, chokes, actuators, blow out preventers, manifolds and wellhead equipment. The products segment remanufactures and repairs pumps, electric motors and generators, fabricates equipment and components, provides specialty machining for repair, remanufactures natural gas and diesel engines and applies custom coating to customers' products used in the oil and gas industry. The distribution segment is engaged in the specialty distribution of pipes, valves, stud bolts, gaskets and other ancillary products to the upstream and downstream oil and gas industry, offshore fabrication companies and shipyards.

Primary SIC and add'l.: 3443 3492 3429

CIK No: 0000879884

Subsidiaries: A&B Bolt & Supply, Inc., ARC Disposition, Inc., Cor-Val Holdings, Inc., Cor-Val LP, Inc., Cor-Val, L.P., Landreth Metal Forming, Inc., Manifold Valve Services, Inc., O&M Equipment Holdings, Inc., O&M Equipment LP, Inc., O&M Equipment, L.P., OF Acquisition, L.P., Philform, Inc., Pipeline Valve Specialty, Inc., Preferred Industries Holdings, Inc., Preferred Industries LP, Inc. 42 Subsidiaries included in the Index

Officers: Keith Klopfenstein/Contact - Operations/$266,150.00, Michael Rai Anderson/Contact - Quality, EH, S, Gary Shaeper/Contact - Engineering, Michael T. Mino/Contact - Finance/$301,550.00, Pete Skertich/Contact - Human Resources, Adam Barrilleaux/Contact - Information Technology, Richard Safier/Contact - Legal, Deborah Fifer/Contact - Marketing, James McMullan/Contact - Sales

Owners: James M. Tidwell, Insiders/3.90%, Michael T. Mino, Keith A. Klopfenstein, Stephen A. Snider, Joseph R. Edwards, Gus D. Halas/2.70%, Michael W. Press, Carlo J. Cannell/9.30%, First Reserve Fund VIII, L.P./44.20%

Financial Data: Fiscal Year End: 12/31 **Latest Annual Data:** 12/31/2006

Year	Sales	Net Income
2006	$163,145,000	$18,092,000
2005	$103,218,000	$4,513,000
2004	$110,293,000	$1,519,000

Curr. Assets:	$64,033,000	Curr. Liab.:	$28,995,000	P/E Ratio:	17.95
Plant, Equip.:	$24,639,000	Total Liab.:	$32,483,000	Indic. Yr. Divd.:	NA
Total Assets:	$162,643,000	Net Worth:	$130,160,000	Debt/Equity:	NA

T Bancshares Inc

Formerly: First Metroplex Capital Inc
16000 Dallas Pk.way, Ste. 125, Dallas Texas, TX, 75248; **PH:** 1-972-720-9000; https:// www.tbank.com

General - Incorporation	TX	Stock - Price on:12/24/2007	$13.5
Employees	25	Stock Exchange	NA
Auditor	Weaver and Tidwell, LLP	Ticker Symbol	NA
Stk Agt	American Stock Transfer & Trust Co.	Outstanding Shares	1,690,000
Counsel	NA	E.P.S.	$0.64
DUNS No.	NA	Shareholders	NA

Business: The group operates through its subsidiary whose principle activity is to provide banking services. Services of the group include consumer and commercial loans, demand deposits, regular savings accounts, money market accounts, certificates of deposit, individual retirement accounts, credit and debit cards, automatic transfers, travelers checks, domestic and foreign wire transfers, cashiers checks and personalized checks. Customers served by the group include business departments, residential, commercial contractors and consumers. The group operates from the United States.

Primary SIC and add'l.: 6712

CIK No: 0001272754

Subsidiaries: T Bank, N.A.

Owners: James D. Rose/0.27%, Steven M. Jones/1.41%, David Carstens/0.78%, Anthony Pusateri/0.78%, Eric Langford/2.04%, Security Financial Life Insurance Company/5.49%, Charles M. Mapes/0.78%, Insiders/20.21%, Thomas McDougal/0.08%, Patrick Adams/3.25%, Mark Foglietta/1.05%, Ron Denheyer/0.78%, Gordon R. Youngblood/0.78%, Stanley Allred/0.78%, Frankie Basso/1.74% (20 Owners included in Index)

Financial Data: Fiscal Year End:12/31 Latest Annual Data: 12/31/2006

Year	Sales	Net Income
2006	$8,109,000	$12,000
2005	$1,783,000	-$1,581,000
2004	$93,000	-$1,322,000

Curr. Assets:	$37,766,000	Curr. Liab.:	$117,134,000	P/E Ratio:	1350.00
Plant, Equip.:	$1,754,000	Total Liab.:	$117,313,000	Indic. Yr. Divd.:	NA
Total Assets:	$130,391,000	Net Worth:	$13,078,000	Debt/ Equity:	NA

T H Lehman & Co Inc

1155 Dairy Ashford Rd., Ste. 650, Houston, TX, 77079; **PH:** 1-281-870-1197

General - Incorporation	DE	Stock- Price on:12/24/2007	NA
Employees	NA	Stock Exchange	OTC
Auditor	Jeffrey S. Gilbert, CPA	Ticker Symbol	THLM
Stk Agt	North American Transfer Co	Outstanding Shares	6,950,000
Counsel	NA	E.P.S.	$0.17
DUNS No.	10-328-6548	Shareholders	NA

Business: The group's principal activity is to provide medical business management services including billing and collection through its wholly owned subsidiaries. The group finances and collects accounts receivable generated by medical practitioners through their provision of diagnostic services and patient treatment. The group through its subsidiary provides non-medical general and administrative services to medical practitioners. The services provided are accounting, marketing, management, non-medical staffing, facilities and billing and collection of receivables. The company is winding down its business by feb 2005.

Primary SIC and add'l.: 7322

CIK No: 0000721647

Owners: Insiders/77.54%, Dibo Attar, Monahan Corporation, N.V./45.11%, Raffaele Attar, Russell Molina/6.89%, Burton, N.V./4.04%, Beech Glen, Inc./8.58%, New Horizons Investments Fund N.V./8.76%

Financial Data: Fiscal Year End:03/31 Latest Annual Data: 3/31/2007

Year	Sales	Net Income
2007	$1,387,000	$1,261,000
2006	$37,000	-$189,000
2005	$29,000	-$649,000

Curr. Assets:	$1,041,000	Curr. Liab.:	$404,000		
Plant, Equip.:	NA	Total Liab.:	$404,000	Indic. Yr. Divd.:	NA
Total Assets:	$1,284,000	Net Worth:	$881,000	Debt/ Equity:	NA

T J T Inc

843 N Washington Ave., Emmett, ID, 83617; **PH:** 1-208-365-5321; **http://** www.tjt-inc.com

General - Incorporation	WA	Stock- Price on:12/24/2007	$1.15
Employees	93	Stock Exchange	OTC
Auditor	Moss Adams LLP, Eide Bailly LLP	Ticker Symbol	AXLE
Stk Agt	Corporate Stock Transfer, Inc.	Outstanding Shares	4,510,000
Counsel	Moffatt, Thomas Et Al	E.P.S.	$0.11
DUNS No.	NA	Shareholders	NA

Business: The group's principal activities are in two business segments: axels & tire reconditioning and housing accessories. Axels & tire reconditioning provides reconditioned axles and tires to manufactured housing factories. The group buys used axles and tires, they are dismantled at the company's recycling facilities and tires are graded and repaired. The axles and tires are then sold to manufactured housing factories. Housing accessories provides skirting, siding, and other aftermarket accessories to manufactured housing dealers and contractors. It provides skirting, siding and housing accessories such as vinyl skirting, piers and other ancillary products to manufactured housing dealers and set-up contractors.

Primary SIC and add'l.: 7539 5033

CIK No: 0001002577

Officers: Terrence J. Sheldon/Chmn., CEO, Pres., Cristy Tuggle/Sale, Service - TJT, Inc, Colorado, Gary Crafton/Sale, Service - TJT, Incoregon, Vicki Hines/Sale, Service - TJT, Inc Idaho, Gail Simpson/Sale, Service - TJT, Inc California, Craig Jones/Sale, Service - TJT, Inc Washington, Fred Amen/Sale, Service - TJT, Inc Colorado

Directors: Terrence J. Sheldon/Chmn., CEO, Pres.

Financial Data: Fiscal Year End:09/30 Latest Annual Data: 9/30/2004

Year	Sales	Net Income
2004	$19,701,000	$397,000
2003	$19,728,000	$132,000
2002	$20,386,000	-$887,000

Curr. Assets:	$5,346,000	Curr. Liab.:	$1,196,000	P/E Ratio:	8.21
Plant, Equip.:	$728,000	Total Liab.:	$1,253,000	Indic. Yr. Divd.:	NA
Total Assets:	$7,703,000	Net Worth:	$6,450,000	Debt/ Equity:	NA

T-Bay Holdings Inc

18th Fl. Yongsheng Bldg., Xhongshang Xi Rd., Xuhui, Shanghai; **PH:** 86-021-51539900

General - Incorporation		Stock- Price on:12/24/2007	$3.95
Employees	150	Stock Exchange	OTC
Auditor	NA	Ticker Symbol	TBYH
Stk Agt	OTC Stock Transfer, Inc.	Outstanding Shares	30,090,000
Counsel	NA	E.P.S.	$0.35
DUNS No.	NA	Shareholders	NA

Business: The groups principal activities include manufacturing and selling whole mobile handsets to providing design services and mobile phone components. The group operates from the United States.

Primary SIC and add'l.: 1081

CIK No:

Subsidiaries: Shanghai Sunplus Communication Technology Co., Ltd

Owners: Li Meilian/53.01%, Insiders/61.65%, Li Xiaofeng/8.64%

Financial Data: Fiscal Year End:NA Latest Annual Data: 12/31/2004

Year	Sales	Net Income
2004	NA	-$27,000
1999	NA	-$96,000

Curr. Assets:	NA	Curr. Liab.:	$53,000	P/E Ratio:	11.29
Plant, Equip.:	NA	Total Liab.:	$53,000	Indic. Yr. Divd.:	NA
Total Assets:	NA	Net Worth:	-$53,000	Debt/ Equity:	NA

T. Rowe Price Group Inc

100 E Pratt St., Baltimore, MD, 21202; **PH:** 1-410-345-2000; **http://** www.troweprice.com; **Email:** information@trowepriceglobal.com

General - Incorporation		Stock- Price on:12/24/2007	$53
Employees	4,605	Stock Exchange	NDQ
Auditor	NA	Ticker Symbol	TROW
Stk Agt	Wells Fargo Shareowner Services	Outstanding Shares	265,620,000
Counsel	NA	E.P.S.	$2.25
DUNS No.	NA	Shareholders	NA

Business: The groups principle activities include designing, discovering and developing a new class of drugs. The group products sold under the trade names NNR Therapeutics(TM), Targacept(R), Inversine(R), Pentad(TM) and TRIDMAC(TM). The group operates from the United States. The group's quarterly revenue for September 2007 was 572.20 millions of USD.

Primary SIC and add'l.: 6211 6282 6722 6289

CIK No: 0001214556

Officers: Sarah Cadden/Contact - Media, Steve Norwitz/Contact - Media, Brian Lewbart/Contact - Media, Robert Benjamin/Contact - Media

Financial Data: Fiscal Year End:NA Latest Annual Data: 12/31/2006

Year	Sales	Net Income
2006	$1,819,300,000	$529,600,000
2005	$1,512,164,000	$430,929,000
2004	$1,280,349,000	$337,260,000

Curr. Assets:	$996,500,000	Curr. Liab.:	$338,400,000		
Plant, Equip.:	$264,900,000	Total Liab.:	$338,400,000	Indic. Yr. Divd.:	$0.680
Total Assets:	$2,765,300,000	Net Worth:	$2,426,900,000	Debt/ Equity:	NA

Table Trac Inc

15612 Hwy 7 No. 250, Minnetonka, MN, 55345; **PH:** 1-952-548-8877; **http://** www.tabletrac.com; **Email:** ttsales@tabletrac.com

General - Incorporation	NV	Stock- Price on:12/24/2007	$1.7
Employees	4	Stock Exchange	OTC
Auditor	Carver Moquist & O'connor LLC	Ticker Symbol	TBTC
Stk Agt	NA	Outstanding Shares	4,000,000
Counsel	NA	E.P.S.	$0.06
DUNS No.	NA	Shareholders	NA

Business: The group's principle activities include developing and commercializing proprietary information and management system that automates and monitors the operations of casino table games. The trademark of the product is table trac. The company continues to develop in the field of hardware, firmware and software to enhance the product and to provide product functionality. The general intent of the company is a system to acquire, evaluate, and provide immediate access to a new level of detailed table games management and player tracking information. The company has also developed related systems for casino management including promotion administration and delivery systems, self-service customer kiosks, marketing analysis, vault operations module for chip banks. The company has contracts with five casinos in Minnesota and Wisconsin. The group operates from United States.

Primary SIC and add'l.: 7372

CIK No: 0001090396

Officers: Chad B. Hoehne/45/Chmn., Pres., CEO, Principal Financial Officer, Robert R. Siqveland/63/Sec.

Directors: Chad B. Hoehne/45/Chmn., Pres., CEO, Principal Financial Officer, Thomas Oliveri/45/Dir.

Owners: Thomas Oliveri/0.38%, Insiders/32.10%, Chad and Sally Hoehne/28.28%, Robert Siqveland/3.44%

Financial Data: Fiscal Year End:12/31 Latest Annual Data: 12/31/2006

Year	Sales	Net Income
2006	$859,000	$259,000
2005	$1,185,000	$303,000
2004	$595,000	$104,000

Curr. Assets:	$642,000	Curr. Liab.:	$207,000	P/E Ratio:	28.33
Plant, Equip.:	NA	Total Liab.:	$207,000	Indic. Yr. Divd.:	NA
Total Assets:	$841,000	Net Worth:	$634,000	Debt/ Equity:	NA

Tactical Air Defense Services Inc

5501 Airport Dr., Denison, TX, 75020; **PH:** 1-903-786-5300; **http://** www.tads-usa.com

General - Incorporation NV
Employees NA
Auditor Marcum & Kliegman, LLP
Stk Agt Transfer Online, Inc.
Counsel NA
DUNS No. NA

Stock- Price on:12/24/2007 NA
Stock Exchange OTC
Ticker Symbol TADF
Outstanding Shares NA
E.P.S NA
Shareholders NA

Business: The groups principal activities include seeking potential operating businesses and business opportunities with the intent to acquire or merge with another business. The group operates from the United States.

Primary SIC and add'l.: 3728

CIK No: 0001077915

Subsidiaries: Aerogroup, Inc

Officers: Alexis C. Korybut/CEO, Pres.

Owners: Fred Daniels, Victor Miller/9.40%, Derick Sinclair, Mark Daniels/51.14%, John Riley Farley

Financial Data: *Fiscal Year End:*12/31 *Latest Annual Data:* 12/31/2006

Year	Sales	Net Income
2006	NA	-$29,990,000
2005	NA	-$23,000
2004	NA	-$5,000

Curr. Assets:	$136,000	**Curr. Liab.:**	$4,757,000		
Plant, Equip.:	$7,129,000	**Total Liab.:**	$4,827,000	**Indic. Yr. Divd.:**	NA
Total Assets:	$7,265,000	**Net Worth:**	$2,438,000	**Debt/ Equity:**	NA

TAG Oil Ltd

1050 Burrard St., Ste. 1407, Vancouver, BC, V6L 2N2; *PH:* 1-403-770-1934; *http://* www.tagoil.com; *Email:* info@tagoil.com

General - Incorporation YT
Employees NA
Auditor De Visser Gray
Stk Agt Computershare Investor Services LLC
Counsel Lang Michener
DUNS No. 24-979-9701

Stock- Price on:12/24/2007 $0.175
Stock Exchange OTC
Ticker Symbol TAGOF
Outstanding Shares NA
E.P.S NA
Shareholders NA

Business: The group's principle activities include exploring and extracting oil and natural gas throughout its properties in Canada, Australia, and New Zealand. The group operates from United States.

Primary SIC and add'l.: 1311

CIK No: 0000912785

Subsidiaries: Cheal Petroleum Limited, Pep 38757 Limited, Pep 38758 Limited, TAG Oil (Canterbury) Limited, TAG Oil (NZ) Limited

Officers: Garth Johnson/Dir., CEO, CFO, Corp. Sec., Drew Cadenhead/Business, Technical Consultant, Mark Webster/Exploration Mgr., Ricardo Bertolotti/Chief Geophysicist, David McCall/Engineering Mgr.

Directors: Garth Johnson/Dir., CEO, CFO, Corp. Sec., David Bennett/Dir., Dan Brown/Dir., Giuseppe Perone/Dir.

Owners: Wellington Management Company, LLP/11.17%, South Pacific Lease Operations Limited/5.46%, Alex Guidi/5.05%, RAB Energy Fund Limited/7.88%

Financial Data: *Fiscal Year End:*03/31 *Latest Annual Data:* 03/31/2007

Year	Sales	Net Income
2007	$813,000	-$16,062,000
2006	NA	-$1,221,000
2005	NA	-$998,000

Curr. Assets:	$17,198,000	**Curr. Liab.:**	$1,910,000		
Plant, Equip.:	$6,866,000	**Total Liab.:**	$1,910,000	**Indic. Yr. Divd.:**	NA
Total Assets:	$26,672,000	**Net Worth:**	$24,761,000	**Debt/ Equity:**	NA

Tagalder Global Investment Inc

Formerly: Golden Media Inc
8th Fl., No., 211 Johnston Rd., Wanchai; *PH:* 852-283-66202; *http://* golden-media.com

General - Incorporation DE
Employees NA
Auditor Child, Van Wagoner & Bradshaw, PLLC
Stk Agt NA
Counsel NA
DUNS No. NA

Stock- Price on:12/24/2007 NA
Stock Exchange NA
Ticker Symbol NA
Outstanding Shares NA
E.P.S NA
Shareholders NA

Business: The group's principal activity is to seek, investigate, and, if warranted, acquire one or more properties or businesses, and to pursue other related activities intended to enhance shareholder value. The acquisition of a business opportunity may be made by purchase, merger, exchange of stock, or otherwise, and may encompass assets or a business entity, such as a corporation, joint venture, or partnership. The company has very limited capital, and it is unlikely that the company will be able to take advantage of more than one such business opportunity. The company intends to seek opportunities demonstrating thepotential of long-term growth as opposed to short-term earnings.

Primary SIC and add'l.: 9995

CIK No: 0001307690

Officers: Chun Ka Tsun/Dir., CEO, CFO

Directors: Chun Ka Tsun/Dir., CEO, CFO

Owners: Insiders/48.60%, Chun Ka Tsun/48.60%

Taitron Components Inc

28040 W Harrison Pkwy., Valencia, CA, 91355; *PH:* 1-661-257-6060; *http://* www.taitroncomponents.com

General - Incorporation CA
Employees 31
Auditor Haskell & White LLP
Stk Agt American Stock Transfer & Trust Co.
Counsel NA
DUNS No. 60-886-7073

Stock- Price on:12/24/2007 $2.79
Stock Exchange NDQ
Ticker Symbol TAIT
Outstanding Shares 5,540,000
E.P.S -$0.15
Shareholders NA

Business: The group's principal activity is to distribute a wide variety of transistors, diodes and other discrete semiconductors, optoelectronic devices and passive components to other electronic distributors, original equipment manufacturers and contract electronic manufacturers. Discrete semiconductors are basic electronic building blocks. The group offers optoelectronic devices such as LED's, infrared sensors and opto couplers, along with passive devices, such as resistors, capacitors and inductors that are electronic components manufactured with non-semiconductor materials. The group purchases components from over 50 different suppliers, including everlight electronics co ltd, fairchild semiconductor corporation, general semiconductor inc, samsung electro-mechanics co and vishay Americas inc.

Primary SIC and add'l.: 5065

CIK No: 0000942126

Subsidiaries: Country of Ownership Incorporation

Officers: Stewart Wang/Co - Founder, Dir., CEO, Pres./$223,100.00, David Vanderhorst/Corp. Sec./$116,100.00

Directors: Stewart Wang/Co - Founder, Dir., CEO, Pres., Tzu S. Ku/Founder, Chmn., Richard Chiang/Dir., Craig Miller/Dir., Felix M. Sung/Dir.

Owners: Richard Chiang/1.17%, FMR Corporation/8.42%, Stewart Wang/20.99%, Insiders/43.79%, Tzu Sheng Ku/14.59%, Craig Miller, Felix Sung/1.04%, David Vanderhorst, Insiders/100.00%, Stewart Wang/100.00%

Financial Data: *Fiscal Year End:*12/31 *Latest Annual Data:* 12/31/2006

Year	Sales	Net Income
2006	$9,559,000	-$29,000
2005	$8,400,000	-$205,000
2004	$9,352,000	-$248,000

Curr. Assets:	$19,772,000	**Curr. Liab.:**	$1,689,000		
Plant, Equip.:	$4,396,000	**Total Liab.:**	$2,198,000	**Indic. Yr. Divd.:**	$0.100
Total Assets:	$25,494,000	**Net Worth:**	$23,296,000	**Debt/ Equity:**	0.0218

Taiwan Semiconductor Mfg Co Ltd

2585 Junction Ave., San Jose, CA, 95134; *PH:* 1-408-382-8000; *Fax:* 1-408-382-8008; *http://* www.tsmc.com.tw

General - Incorporation China
Employees 22,246
Auditor Deloitte & Touche LLP
Stk Agt China Trust Commercial Bank
Counsel NA
DUNS No. 65-612-2470

Stock- Price on:12/24/2007 $10.76
Stock Exchange NYSE
Ticker Symbol TSM
Outstanding Shares 5,160,000,000
E.P.S $0.61
Shareholders NA

Business: The group's principal activities are the manufacturing, selling, packaging, testing and designing of integrated circuits, mask and other semiconductor devices. The group's operations are carried out in Taiwan, North America, Europe, Japan and mainland China.

Primary SIC and add'l.: 3674 3825

CIK No: 0001046179

Subsidiaries: WaferTech LLC

Officers: Rick Tsai/Dir., CEO, Pres., James C. Ho/Supervisor, Deputy Executive Sec. - Development Fund, Michael E. Porter/Independent Supervisor, Steve Tso/Sr. VP, CIO - Information Technology, Materials Management, Risk Management, C. C. Wei/Sr. VP - Operations I, Richard Thurston/VP, General Counsel, P. H. Chang/VP - Human Resources, Wei-Jen Lo/VP - Research, Development, Jason C.S. Chen/VP - Corporate Development, Mark Liu/Sr. VP - Operations II, Lora Ho/VP, CFO - Spokesperson, M. C. Tzeng/VP - Operations, Kenneth Kin/Sr. VP - Worldwide Sales, Service, Charles Byers/Dir. - Brand Management, Tsmc NA, Dan Holden/Public Relations Mgr. - Tsmc NA *(29 Officers included in Index)*

Directors: Rick Tsai/Dir., CEO, Pres., F. C. Tseng/Vice Chmn., Morris Chang/Chmn., Stan Shih/Dir., Peter Leahy Bonfield/Dir., Chintay Shih/Dir., Lester Carl Thurow/Dir., Carleton S. Fiorina/Dir.

Owners: C. C. Wei, J. C. Lobbezoo/16.21%, Stan Shih/0.01%, Kenneth Kin/0.02%, Rick Tsai/0.11%, Jason Chen, Fu-Chieh Hsu, Morris Chang/0.45%, Mark Liu/0.04%, M. C. Tzeng, Richard Thurston/0.01%, Lora Ho/0.02%, W. J. Lo, Chintay Shih/6.31%, Steve Tso/0.05% *(18 Owners included in Index)*

Financial Data: *Fiscal Year End:*12/31 *Latest Annual Data:* 12/31/2006

Year	Sales	Net Income
2006	$9,739,400,000	$2,936,800,000
2005	$8,103,579,000	$2,292,716,000
2004	$8,050,754,000	$2,386,731,000

Curr. Assets:	$7,987,600,000	**Curr. Liab.:**	$1,437,900,000	**P/E Ratio:**	17.80
Plant, Equip.:	$7,732,400,000	**Total Liab.:**	$2,439,500,000	**Indic. Yr. Divd.:**	$0.360
Total Assets:	$18,775,900,000	**Net Worth:**	$16,336,400,000	**Debt/ Equity:**	NA

Take Two Interactive Software Inc

622 Brdway, New York, NY, 10012; *PH:* 1-646-536-2842; *http://* www.take2games.com; *Email:* usa@take2support.com

General - Incorporation DE
Employees 2,020
Auditor PricewaterhouseCoopers LLP
Stk Agt American Stock Transfer & Trust Co.
Counsel Blank Rome Tenzer Greenblatt
DUNS No. 82-968-1063

Stock- Price on:12/24/2007 $20.76
Stock Exchange NDQ
Ticker Symbol TTWO
Outstanding Shares 73,590,000
E.P.S -$1.93
Shareholders NA

Business: The group's principal activities are to develop, publish and distribute interactive software games worldwide. The software operates on personal computers and video game consoles manufactured by sony, microsoft and nintendo. The major customers of the group are wal-Mart, gamestop, best buy, circuit city, toys 'r' electronics boutique blockbuster dixons karstadt and us. The operations of the group are carried out in the United States, United Kingdom, France, Germany, Canada, Norway, Sweden, Denmark, Italy, Australia, Austria and New Zealand. In 2003, the group acquired frog city, inc and angel studios inc. In 2004, the group acquired tdk mediactive, inc. On 08-Apr-2004, it acquired mobius entertainment ltd.

Primary SIC and add'l.: 7379 5045 7372

CIK No: 0000946581

Subsidiaries: 2K Games, Inc., 2K Sports, Inc., Alternative Reality Technology, Inc., Angel Studios, Inc., Barking Dog Studios Ltd., Cat Daddy LLC, DMA Design Holdings Ltd, Firaxis Games, Inc., Freedom Force Properties LLC, Frog City Software, Inc., Gathering of Developers, Inc., Global Star Software, Inc., Indie Built, Inc., Inventory Management Systems, Inc., Irrational Games Australia Pty. Ltd. 53 Subsidiaries included in the Index

Officers: Ben Feder/Dir., CEO, Paul Eibeler/52/Dir., CEO, Seth Krauss/Exec. VP, General Counsel, Lainie Goldstein/CFO, Jim Ankner/Dir. - Corporate Communications, Samuel A. Judd/50/Sr. VP - Planning

Directors: Ben Feder/Dir., CEO, Paul Eibeler/52/Dir., CEO, Strauss Zelnick/Chmn., J. Moses/Dir., Michael Dornemann/Dir., Michael Sheresky/Dir., Robert A. Bowman/Dir., Todd Emmel/Dir., Robert Flug/60/Dir., Mark Lewis/58/Dir., Grover C. Brown/Dir., Oliver R. Grace/53/Dir., John F. Levy/Dir.

Financial Data: ***Fiscal Year End:***10/31 ***Latest Annual Data:*** 10/31/2007

Year	Sales	Net Income
2007	$981,791,000	-$138,406,000
2006	$1,037,840,000	-$184,889,000
2005	$1,202,595,000	$37,475,000

Curr. Assets:	$498,523,000	**Curr. Liab.:**	$312,161,000		
Plant, Equip.:	$44,986,000	**Total Liab.:**	$359,989,000	**Indic. Yr. Divd.:**	NA
Total Assets:	$831,143,000	**Net Worth:**	$471,154,000	**Debt/ Equity:**	NA

TAL International Group Inc

100 Manhattanville Rd., Purchase, NJ, 10577; ***PH:*** 1-914-251-9000; ***Fax:*** 1-914-697-2549; ***http://*** www.talinternational.com; ***Email:*** careers@talinternational.com

General - Incorporation	DE	***Stock***- Price on:12/24/2007	$30.36
Employees	189	Stock Exchange	NYSE
Auditor	Ernst& Young LLP	Ticker Symbol	TAL
Stk Agt	EquiServe Trust Co N.A	Outstanding Shares	33,260,000
Counsel	NA	E.P.S.	$1.51
DUNS No.	NA	Shareholders	NA

Business: The groups principle activity is to transport raw materials, components parts and finished goods. The group operates from the United States, Asia, Europe and other International.

Primary SIC and add'l.: 3799

CIK No: 0001331745

Subsidiaries: Greybox Logistics Services Inc., Greybox Services Ltd., ICS Terminals (UK) Limited, Intermodal Equipment Inc., Spacewise Inc., TAL Advantage I LLC, TAL do Brasil Investimento de Capital Propio Ltda., TAL International Container (HK) Limited, TAL International Container Corporation, TAL International Container Limited, TAL International Container NV, TAL International Container Pty. Limited, TAL International Container SRL, TAL International Structured Inc., Trans Ocean Container Corporation 16 Subsidiaries included in the Index

Officers: Brian M. Sondey/40/Dir., CEO, Pres., Chand Khan/55/CFO, VP, Frederico Baptista/VP - Asia Pacific, John Burns/47/VP - Corporate Development, Adrian Dunner/43/VP - Marketing, Sales, Marc Pearlin/Sec.

Directors: Brian M. Sondey/40/Dir., CEO, Pres., Malcolm P. Baker/Dir., Bruce R. Berkowitz/49/Dir., Richard A. Caputo/42/Dir., Brian J. Higgins/32/Dir., John W. Jordan/60/Dir., Frederic H. Lindeberg/67/Dir., David W. Zalaznick/53/Dir., Douglas J. Zych/35/Dir.

Owners: John Burns, Frederic H. Lindeberg, Seacon Holdings Limited./3.66%, Frederico Baptista, Chand Khan, Brian M. Sondey/2.66%, Insiders/11.93%, Adrian Dunner, Bruce R. Berkowitz/8.32%

Financial Data: ***Fiscal Year End:***12/31 ***Latest Annual Data:*** 12/31/2006

Year	Sales	Net Income
2006	$303,448,000	$42,133,000
2005	$318,515,000	$9,672,000

Curr. Assets:	$97,485,000	**Curr. Liab.:**	$1,056,913,000	**P/E Ratio:**	9.09
Plant, Equip.:	$1,104,146,000	**Total Liab.:**	$1,056,913,000	**Indic. Yr. Divd.:**	$1.500
Total Assets:	$1,455,663,000	**Net Worth:**	$398,750,000	**Debt/ Equity:**	NA

Talbots Inc

One Talbots Dr., Hingham, MA, 02043; ***PH:*** 1-781-749-7600; ***http://*** www.talbots.com; ***Email:*** investor.relations@talbots.com

General - Incorporation	DE	***Stock***- Price on:12/24/2007	$22.25
Employees	6,267	Stock Exchange	NYSE
Auditor	Deloitte & Touche LLP	Ticker Symbol	TLB
Stk Agt	EquiServe Trust Co N.A	Outstanding Shares	54,430,000
Counsel	NA	E.P.S.	-$0.33
DUNS No.	01-939-7892	Shareholders	NA

Business: The group's principal activity is to market and mail catalogs of women's and children's classic apparel, accessories and shoes. The group offers a distinctive collection of sportswear, casual wear, dresses, coats, sweaters, accessories and shoes. The group also provides an assortment of classic clothing and accessories for infants, toddlers, boys and girls and key basic and fashion items including complementary assortment of accessories and shoes. As of 31-Jul-2004, the group operated 1,003 stores in 47 states. The online shopping is provided through the Web site www.talbots.com. The catalogs and Website provide customers with a broader selection of merchandise, sizes and colors than its stores.

Primary SIC and add'l.: 5632 5961

CIK No: 0000912263

Subsidiaries: Talbots Classics Finance Company, Talbots Classics National Bank, The Classics Chicago, Inc.

Officers: Trudy F. Sullivan/Dir., CEO, Pres., Randy Richardson/Sr. VP - Information Services, John Fiske/Sr. VP - Human Resources, Bruce Lee Prescott/Sr. VP - Direct Marketing, Talbots Brand, Customer Service, Edward L. Larsen/Sr. VP - Finance, CFO, Treasurer/$1,316,834.00, Isao Tsuruta/Dir., Exec. VP, Richard T. O'Connell/Exec. VP - Legal, Real Estate, Sec., Michele M. Mandell/Exec. VP - Stores, Talbots Brand/$1,950,276.00, Philip H. Kowalczyk/COO/$1,921,570.00, Andrea M. McKenna/Sr. VP - Marketing, Catalog Development, Talbots Brand, Paul V. Kastner/Sr. VP - International, Talbots Brand, Strategic Planning, Assist. Treasurer, Assist. Sec.

Directors: Trudy F. Sullivan/Dir., CEO, Pres., Arnold B. Zetcher/Chmn., Isao Tsuruta/Dir., Exec. VP, Susan M. Swain/Dir., Tom Kajita/53/Dir., Motoya Okada/Dir., John W. Gleeson/Dir., Gary M. Pfeiffer/56/Dir., Yoshihiro Sano/Dir.

Owners: S. M. Swain, T. Kajita, A. B. Zetcher, E. L. Larsen, H. B. Bosworth, Insiders, P. H. Kowalczyk, J. W. Gleeson, M. M. Mandell, I. Tsuruta, AEON (U.S.A.), Inc./55.40%, Y. Sano, M. Okada, G. M. Pfeiffer, Van Der Berg Management/5.90%

Financial Data: ***Fiscal Year End:***01/28 ***Latest Annual Data:*** 2/3/2007

Year	Sales	Net Income
2007	$2,231,033,000	$31,576,000
2006	$1,808,606,000	$93,151,000
2005	$1,697,843,000	$95,366,000

Curr. Assets:	$692,409,000	**Curr. Liab.:**	$429,800,000	**P/E Ratio:**	123.61
Plant, Equip.:	$533,216,000	**Total Liab.:**	$1,105,377,000	**Indic. Yr. Divd.:**	$0.520
Total Assets:	$1,748,688,000	**Net Worth:**	$643,311,000	**Debt/ Equity:**	0.5735

Taleo Corp

575 Market St. , 8th Fl., San Francisco, CA, 94105; ***PH:*** 1-925-452-3000; ***http://*** www.taleo.com; ***Email:*** info@taleo.com

General - Incorporation	DE	***Stock***- Price on:12/24/2007	$21.49
Employees	585	Stock Exchange	NDQ
Auditor	Deloitte & Touche LLP	Ticker Symbol	TLEO
Stk Agt	Computershare Trust Co	Outstanding Shares	23,950,000
Counsel	NA	E.P.S.	$0.07
DUNS No.	NA	Shareholders	NA

Business: The groups principle activity is to provide support, education and consulting services. The groups solutions include Taleo Enterprise Edition, Taleo Business Edition and Taleo Hourly Express. The group's specific customers include Aramark, Areva, Auckland District Health Board, Booz Allen Hamilton, CDW Corporation, Children's Healthcare, Cornell University, DeticaDFI, Direct Energy, Dow Benelux and Dow Chemical. The group operates from United States.

Primary SIC and add'l.: 7372

CIK No: 0001134203

Subsidiaries: 9090-5415 Quebec Inc., Recruitforce.com, Inc., Recruitsoft (Asia Pacific) Pte. Ltd., Taleo (Australia) Pty. Limited, Taleo (Canada) Inc., Taleo (Europe) B.V., Taleo (France) SAS, Taleo (UK)Limited

Officers: Michael Gregoire/Dir., CEO, Pres./$1,897,863.00, Katy Murray/CFO, Exec. VP/$297,791.00, Bradford Benson/Exec. VP - Products, Technology, CTO/$612,778.00, Jeff Carr/Exec. VP - Global Alliances, Americas Sales/$728,906.00, Guy Gauvin/Exec. VP - Global Services/$345,806.00, Debbie Shotwell/Group VP - Human Resources, Talent, Neil Hudspith/Sr. VP - International Operations, Jason Blessing/Group VP, GM - SMB, Michael Boese/Group VP - Corporate Business Development, Al Campa/Group VP, Chief Marketing Officer, Paul Pronsati/Group VP - Operations

Directors: Michael Gregoire/Dir., CEO, Pres., Eric Herr/Chmn., Jeffrey Schwartz/Dir., Patrick Gross/Dir., Howard Gwin/Dir., Louis Tetu/Co - Founder, Gary Bloom/Dir., Greg Santora/Dir., Doug Castor/Member - Advisory Board, Christine Deputy/Member - Advisory Board, Christian Foerg/Member - Advisory Board, Belinda Grant-Anderson/Member - Advisory Board, Helen O'Loughlin/Member - Advisory Board, Scott Read/Member - Advisory Board, Gary S. Emerick/Member - Advisory Board *(17 Directors included in Index)*

Financial Data: ***Fiscal Year End:***12/31 ***Latest Annual Data:*** 06/30/2007

Year	Sales	Net Income
2007	$30,954,000	-$1,753,000
2006	$97,043,000	-$2,628,000
2005	$78,410,000	-$2,495,000

Curr. Assets:	$95,511,000	**Curr. Liab.:**	$37,716,000		
Plant, Equip.:	$12,928,000	**Total Liab.:**	$39,990,000	**Indic. Yr. Divd.:**	NA
Total Assets:	$117,420,000	**Net Worth:**	$77,430,000	**Debt/ Equity:**	NA

Talisman Energy Inc

888 - 3rd St. SW, Ste. 3400, Calgary, AB, T2P 5C5; ***PH:*** 1-403-237-1234; ***http://*** www.talisman-energy.com; ***Email:*** tlm@talisman-energy.com

General - Incorporation	Canada	***Stock***- Price on:12/24/2007	$21.04
Employees	2,388	Stock Exchange	NYSE
Auditor	Ernst& Young LLP	Ticker Symbol	TLM
Stk Agt	Computershare Trust Co	Outstanding Shares	1,050,000,000
Counsel	NA	E.P.S.	$1.90
DUNS No.	NA	Shareholders	NA

Business: The groups principal activity is to operates oil and gas properties. The group operates from the Canada.

Primary SIC and add'l.: 1311 1321

CIK No: 0000201283

Subsidiaries: Fortuna Energy Inc, Petromet Resources Limited, Talisman (Corridor) Ltd, Talisman Energy (UK) Limited, Talisman Energy Norge AS, Talisman Malaysia Limited, Talisman North Sea Limited

Officers: James W. Buckee/CEO, Pres., Paul Blakeley/Exec. VP - International Operations, East, Phil Dolan/VP - Finance, CFO, Ronald J. Eckhardt/Exec. VP - North American Operations, T.nigel D. Hares/Exec. VP - International Operations, West, Robert M. Redgate/Exec. VP - Corporate Services, Jacqueline M. Sheppard/Exec. VP - Corporate, Legal, Corp. Sec., John Hart/Exec. VP - Exploration, Tamiko C. Ohta/Assist. Corp. Sec., Christine D. Lee/Assist. Corp. Sec., Leslie A. Lawson/Assist., Corp. Sec.

Directors: James W. Buckee/CEO, Pres., Douglas D. Baldwin/Chmn., William R.P. Dalton/Dir., Kevin S. Dunne/Dir., Lawrence G. Tapp/Dir., Stella M. Thompson/Dir., Robert G. Welty/Dir.

Financial Data: ***Fiscal Year End:***12/31 ***Latest Annual Data:*** 12/31/2006

Year	Sales	Net Income
2006	$6,816,746,000	$1,647,552,000
2005	$6,904,326,000	$1,283,568,000
2004	$4,446,257,000	$576,228,000

Curr. Assets:	$1,780,558,000	**Curr. Liab.:**	$2,733,049,000	**P/E Ratio:**	9.09
Plant, Equip.:	$15,382,301,000	**Total Liab.:**	$12,177,297,000	**Indic. Yr. Divd.:**	$0.160
Total Assets:	$18,644,797,000	**Net Worth:**	$6,467,500,000	**Debt/ Equity:**	NA

Talon International Inc

Formerly: Tag It Pacific Inc
21900 Burbank Blvd., Ste. 270, Woodland Hills, CA, 91367; **PH:** 1-818-444-4100;
http:// www.tag-it.com

General - Incorporation	DE	**Stock**- Price on:12/24/2007	$1.01
Employees	135	Stock Exchange	AMEX
Auditor ... Singer Lewak Greenbaum & Goldstein		Ticker Symbol	TAG
Stk Agt...... American Stock Transfer & Trust Co.		Outstanding Shares	18,540,000
Counsel	Stubbs Alderson & Markiles	E.P.S.	$0.01
DUNS No.	78-227-3197	Shareholders	NA

Business: The group's principal activity is to distribute a full range of trim items to manufacturers of fashion apparel and licensed consumer products, specialty retailers and mass merchandisers. The group customers manufacturers of fashion apparel such as tarrant apparel group and azteca production international, abercrombie & fitch, express, the limited, lerner and miller's outpost. The group also develops and sells apparel components that utilize the patented pro-fit technology, including a stretch waistband. The customers are located primarily in Mexico, Hong Kong and the Dominican Republic.

Primary SIC and add'l.: 3965
CIK No: 0001047881
Subsidiaries: A.G.S. Stationary, Inc, Tag-It Pacific (HK) Ltd, Tag-It Pacific Limited, Tag-It, Inc, Tagit de Mexico, S.A. de C.V, Talon International, Inc
Owners: Lonnie D. Schnell/1.30%, Mark Dyne/6.70%, Susan White, William Sweedler, The Pinnacle Fund, L.P./5.60%, Joseph M. Miller, Jonathan Burstein/3.70%, Wouter van Biene/1.00%, Insiders/22.70%, Colin Dyne/5.80%, Raymond Musci, Todd Kay/5.40%, Brent Cohen, Stephen P. Forte/4.50%

Financial Data: *Fiscal Year End:*12/31 **Latest Annual Data:** 12/31/2006

Year	Sales	Net Income
2006	$48,825,000	$309,000
2005	$47,331,000	-$29,538,000
2004	$55,109,000	-$17,609,000
Curr. Assets: $12,570,000	**Curr. Liab.:** $22,471,000	**P/E Ratio:** 101.00
Plant, Equip.: $6,450,000	**Total Liab.:** $24,007,000	**Indic. Yr. Divd.:** NA
Total Assets: $25,693,000	**Net Worth:** $1,686,000	**Debt/ Equity:** 1.9243

TALX Corp

11432 Lackland Rd., St. Louis, St. Louis, MO, 63146; **PH:** 1-314-214-7000; *http://* www.talx.com

General - Incorporation	MO	**Stock**- Price on:12/24/2007	NA
Employees	1,751	Stock Exchange	NA
Auditor	KPMG LLP	Ticker Symbol	NA
Stk Agt	Mellon Investor Services LLC	Outstanding Shares	NA
Counsel	Bryan Cave LLP	E.P.S	NA
DUNS No.	05-920-8835	Shareholders	NA

Business: The group's principle activities are to provide automated employment and income verification and unemployment cost management services. The services enable mortgage lenders, pre-employment screening companies, employers and other authorized users to obtain employee human resources and payroll information. The group also provides outsourced employee self-service applications. These services enable mortgage lenders, pre-employment screening companies, employers and other authorized users to obtain employee human resources and payroll information. The group operates in the domestic market. On 01-Apr-2004 it acquired sheakley-uniservice, inc. And its wholly owned subsidiary, sheakley interactive services, llc.

Primary SIC and add'l.: 7372 9999 8748 7375
CIK No: 0000917524
Subsidiaries: Johnson & Associates, LLC, Jon-Jay Associates, Inc., Management Insight Incentives, LLC, Net Profit, Inc., Performance Assessment Network, Inc., TALX Employer Services, LLC, TALX FasTime Services, Inc., TALX Limited, TALX Tax Credits and Incentives, LLC, TALX Tax Incentive Services, LLC, Talx Ucm Services, Inc., TBT Enterprises, Incorporated, UI Advantage, Inc., Unemployment Services, LLC
Officers: William Canfield/Chmn., CEO, Pres., Michael E. Smith/Sr. VP - Marketing Development, Keith L. Graves/Sr. VP, CFO, Edward Chaffin/Pres. - UC Express, Stacey Simpson/Pres. - Work Number, Mike Smith/VP - Marketing Development, Frank Gottschall/VP - Human Resources
Directors: William Canfield/Chmn., CEO, Pres., Richard Ford/Dir., Tony G. Holcombe/Dir., Eugene M. Toombs/Dir., Craig Labarge/Dir., Steve M. Yoakum/Dir.

TAM S.A.

Av. Jurandir, 856 Jd. Aeroporto, Sao Paulo, Rio de Janeiro; **PH:** 55-01155828811;
http:// www.tam.com.br; **Email:** invest@tam.com

General - Incorporation	Federative Republic of Brazil	**Stock**- Price on:12/24/2007	$33.6
Employees	13,159	Stock Exchange	NYSE
Auditor	NA	Ticker Symbol	TAM
Stk Agt	JP Morgan Chase Bank, N.A.	Outstanding Shares	150,560,000
Counsel	NA	E.P.S	$0.60
DUNS No.	NA	Shareholders	NA

Business: The groups principle activity is to provide air transportation. The group operates from the Brazil. The group's quarterly revenue for September 2007 was 2058.41 millions of USD.

Primary SIC and add'l.: 4512 4725
CIK No: 0001353691
Subsidiaries: Fidelidade Viagens e Turismo Ltda., TAM Linhas Aereas S.A., Transportes Aereos del Mercosur S.A
Officers: Marco Antonio Bologna/Dir., CEO, Libano Miranda Barroso/CFO, Dir. - Investor Relations, Alberto Fajerman/Operations Officer, Jose Wagner Ferreira/Dir. - Commercial, Marketing, Ruy Antonio Mendes Amparo/Dir. - Technical Operations, David Barioni Neto/Dir. - Operating, Paulo Cezar Castello Branco/Dir. - Planning, Guilherme Cavalieri/Dir. - Knowledge, People Management
Directors: Marco Antonio Bologna/Dir., CEO, Mauricio Rolim Amaro/Vice Chmn., Maria Claudia Oliveira Amaro Demenato/Chmn., Luiz Antonio Correa Nunes Viana Oliveira/Dir., Noemy Almeida Oliveira Amaro/Dir., Waldemar Verdi Junior/Dir., Adalberto De Moraes Schettert/Dir., Roger Ian Wright/Dir., Pedro Pullen Parente/Dir.

Owners: Aerosystem S.A. Empreendimentos e Participaes/2.12%, Waldemar Verdi, Agropecuria Nova Fronteira Ltda., Aerosystem S.A. Empreendimentos e Participaes/2.53%, Adalberto de Moraes Schettert, Luiz Antnio Corra Nunes Viana Oliveira, TAM Empreendimentos e Participaes S.A./22.44%, Maria Cludia Oliveira Amaro Demenato, Insiders/75.44%, Roger Ian Wright, Noemy Almeida Oliveira Amaro, Mauricio Rolim Amaro, TAM Empreendimentos e Participaes S.A./97.31%, Pedro Pullen Parente

Financial Data: *Fiscal Year End:*12/31 **Latest Annual Data:** 12/31/2006

Year	Sales	Net Income
2006	$3,436,867,000	$379,227,000
2005	$5,633,580,000	$426,525,000
2004	$4,520,371,000	$430,037,000
Curr. Assets: $1,806,428,000	**Curr. Liab.:** $1,108,219,000	**P/E Ratio:** 9.09
Plant, Equip.: $1,590,177,000	**Total Liab.:** $2,872,248,000	**Indic. Yr. Divd.:** $0.430
Total Assets: $3,590,555,000	**Net Worth:** $718,307,000	**Debt/ Equity:** NA

TAMM Oil & Gas Corp

Formerly: Hola Communications Inc
103-3065 Beyer Blvd., San Diego, CA, 92154; **PH:** 1-604-614-8711

General - Incorporation	NV	**Stock**- Price on:12/24/2007	NA
Employees	NA	Stock Exchange	OTC
Auditor	Squar, Peterson, LLP	Ticker Symbol	TAMO
Stk Agt	Nevada Agency & Trust Co.	Outstanding Shares	NA
Counsel	NA	E.P.S	NA
DUNS No.	NA	Shareholders	NA

Business: The groups principal activity is to provide wireless broadband Internet services. The group operates from the United States and Mexico.

Primary SIC and add'l.: 4812
CIK No: 0001374845
Officers: Sean Dickenson/34/Dir., Pres., Sec., Treasurer
Directors: Sean Dickenson/34/Dir., Pres., Sec., Treasurer
Owners: Insiders/63.30%, Sean Dickenson/63.30%

Curr. Assets: $4,000	**Curr. Liab.:** $6,000	
Plant, Equip.: $35,000	**Total Liab.:** $6,000	**Indic. Yr. Divd.:** NA
Total Assets: $39,000	**Net Worth:** $33,000	**Debt/ Equity:** NA

Tampa Electric Co

TECO Plz., 702 N. Franklin St., Tampa, FL, 33602; **PH:** 1-813-228-1111;
http:// www.tampaelectric.com; **Email:** lpduda@tecoenergy.com

General - Incorporation	FL	**Stock**- Price on:12/24/2007	$17.05
Employees	5,200	Stock Exchange	NA
Auditor	PricewaterhouseCoopers LLP	Ticker Symbol	NA
Stk Agt	Computershare Investor Services LLC	Outstanding Shares	209,620,000
Counsel	NA	E.P.S	$1.32
DUNS No.	00-692-4286	Shareholders	NA

Business: The group's principal activities are to generate, purchase, transmit, distribute and sell electric energy and natural gas. The group is a public utility operating in the state of Florida. The group operates through its two divisions: electric and gas. Tampa electric division generates, transmits and distributes electric energy. Peoples gas system division purchases, distributes and markets natural gas. Tampa electric has franchise agreements with 13 incorporated municipalities within its retail service area the group caters to residential, commercial, industrial and customers for electric power generation and natural gas in the state of Florida.

Primary SIC and add'l.: 4911 4923
CIK No: 0000096271
Subsidiaries: Bear Branch Coal Company, Clintwood Elkhorn Mining Company, Gatliff Coal Company, McAdams Holding, LLC, Perry County Coal Corporation, Pike-Letcher Land Company, Premier Elkhorn Coal Company, Rich Mountain Coal Company, San Jose Power Holding Company, LTD, TECO Barge Line, Inc, TECO Bulk Terminal, LLC, TECO Coal Corporation, TECO Diversified, Inc, TECO EnergySource, Inc., TECO Guatemala Holdings, LLC 32 Subsidiaries included in the Index
Officers: Thomas L. Hernandez/VP - Energy Supply Tampa Electric, Charles R. Black/Pres., Deirdre A. Brown/VP - Customer Service, Regulatory Affairs Teco Energy, William T. Whale/VP - Energy Delivery Tampa Electric

Financial Data: *Fiscal Year End:*12/31 **Latest Annual Data:** 12/31/2006

Year	Sales	Net Income
2006	$3,448,100,000	$246,300,000
2005	$3,010,100,000	$274,500,000
2004	$2,669,100,000	-$552,000,000
Curr. Assets: $1,285,700,000	**Curr. Liab.:** $1,350,400,000	**P/E Ratio:** 12.92
Plant, Equip.: $4,766,900,000	**Total Liab.:** $5,632,800,000	**Indic. Yr. Divd.:** $0.780
Total Assets: $7,361,800,000	**Net Worth:** $1,729,000,000	**Debt/ Equity:** 1.8151

Tandy Brands Accessories Inc

690 E Lamar Blvd, Ste 200, Arlington, TX, 76011; **PH:** 1-817-548-0090;
http:// investors.globalcrossing.com

General - Incorporation	DE	**Stock**- Price on:12/24/2007	$12.5
Employees	1,160	Stock Exchange	NDQ
Auditor	Ernst & Young LLP	Ticker Symbol	TBAC
Stk Agt	Computershare	Outstanding Shares	6,900,000
Counsel	Winstead Sechrest & Minick	E.P.S	$0.56
DUNS No.	61-327-4133	Shareholders	NA

Business: The group's principal activities are to design, manufacture and market fine leather goods and fashion accessories for men, women and children. The product line includes belts, wallets, handbags, socks, scarves, gloves, hats, hair accessories, suspenders, cold weather accessories and sporting goods accessories. The products are sold to a variety of retail outlets, including national chain stores, discount stores, major department stores, specialty stores, catalog retailers, grocery stores, drug stores and the retail exchange operations of the United States military. The brand names are dockers, levi's, jones New York, perry ellis, rolfs, haggar, woolrich, jordache, Indian motorcycle, bugle boy, canterbury, prince gardner, princess gardner, amity, don loper, accessory design group, tex tan and tiger.

Primary SIC and add'l.: 2387 3172 3171 2389

CIK No: 0000869487

Subsidiaries: Accessory Design Group, Inc., Amity/Rolfs, Inc., H.A. Sheldon Canada, Ltd., Stagg Industries, Inc., Superior Merchandise Company, Tandy Brands Accessories Handbags, Inc., TBAC Mass Merchant Quality Control, Inc., TBAC Acquisition, Inc., TBAC Torel, Inc., TBAC General Management Company, TBAC Investment Trust, TBAC Investments, Inc., TBAC Management Company, L.P., TBAC-Prince Gardner, Inc.

Officers: J. S.B. Jenkins/63/Dir., CEO, Pres., Mark J. Flaherty/45/CFO, David Lawhon/VP - Operations

Directors: J. S.B. Jenkins/63/Dir., CEO, Pres., James F. Gaertner/63/Chmn., Grady W. Rosier/58/Dir., George C. Lake/54/Dir., Colombe M. Nicholas/61/Dir., Gene Stallings/71/Dir., Roger R. Hemminghaus/70/Dir.

Owners: George C. Lake, Colombe M. Nicholas, James F. Gaertner, Morris D. Mitchell, Insiders/15.45%, Franklin Resources, Inc./7.84%, J. S.B. Jenkins/11.54%, Roger R. Hemminghaus, David Lawhon, Tandy Brands Accessories, Inc./7.05%, Dimensional FundAdvisors LP/6.56%, Advisory Research, Inc./10.02%, Jane A. Batts, Mark J. Flaherty, Gene Stallings *(16 Owners included in Index)*

Financial Data: *Fiscal Year End:* 06/30 *Latest Annual Data:* 6/30/2006

Year	Sales	Net Income
2006	$227,323,000	-$3,462,000
2005	$221,232,000	$3,987,000
2004	$215,420,000	$7,037,000

Curr. Assets:	$102,850,000	Curr. Liab.:	$16,320,000	P/E Ratio: 22.32
Plant, Equip.:	$12,430,000	Total Liab.:	$34,105,000	Indic. Yr. Divd.: $0.160
Total Assets:	$138,944,000	Net Worth:	$104,839,000	Debt/ Equity: NA

Tandy Leather Factory Inc

Formerly: Leather Factory Inc

3847 E Loop 820 S, Fort Worth, TX, 76119; *PH:* 1-817-496-4414; *http://* www.leatherfactory.com

General - Incorporation	DE	Stock - Price on:12/24/2007	$7.05
Employees	310	Stock Exchange	AMEX
Auditor	Weaver & Tidwell LLP	Ticker Symbol	TLF
Stk Agt	Securities Transfer Corp	Outstanding Shares	10,910,000
Counsel	NA	E.P.S.	$0.30
DUNS No.	03-993-7917	Shareholders	NA

Business: The group's principal activity is the wholesale and retail distribution of leather and related products. The operations are carried through three segments: leather factory, tandy leather co and roberts, cushman & co. Leather factory segment sells on wholesale, leather and leathercraft-related products in the United States and Canada. Tandy leather co segment consists of retail sale throughout the unites states. The products include leather, leatherworking tools, buckles and adornments for belts, leather dyes and finishes, saddle and tack hardware, kits etc. The group also manufactures leather lacing and kits. Roberts cushman & co segment designs, manufactures hat trims and markets ribbons, buckle sets, name pins, feathers to hat manufactures and distributors. On 31-Dec-2003, the group had 30 leather factory stores and 26 tandy leather stores.

Primary SIC and add'l.: 3149 5999 3199

CIK No: 0000909724

Subsidiaries: Hi-Line Leather & Manufacturing Company, Leather Factory ,Inc., Leather Factory of Canada Ltd., Leather Factory of Nevada Investments, Inc., Leather Factory, LP, a Texas limited, Roberts, Cushman & Company, Inc., Tandy Leather Company Investments, Inc, Tandy Leather Company, Inc, Tandy Leather Company, LP, Tandycrafts, Inc

Officers: Wray Thompson/73/Chmn., CEO/$176,242.00, Shannon L. Greene/39/Dir., CFO, Treasurer/$208,515.00, Brian Walker/Mgr. - Littleton, Colorado, Bruce Kabel/Mgr. - East Hartford, Connecticut, Chris Howard/Mgr. - Union City, California, Ron Ruck/Mgr. - Van Nuys, California, Mark Barnes/Mgr. - Reno, Nevada, Ruben Saiz/Mgr. - Albuquerque, New Mexico, Larry Bartels/Mgr. - Springfield, Missouri, Darlene Earles/Mgr. - St. Louis, Missouri, Kermit Creek/Mgr. - Billings, Montana, Jerry Kritenbrink/Mgr. - Omaha, Nebraska, Dee Easterbrook/Mgr. - Las Vegas, Nevada, Meridith McBean/Mgr. - Colorado Springs, Colorado, Violeta Ochoa/Mgr. - Westminster, Colorado *(105 Officers included in Index)*

Directors: Wray Thompson/73/Chmn., CEO, Shannon L. Greene/39/Dir., CFO, Treasurer, Ronald C. Morgan/57/Dir., COO, Pres., Edward L. Martin/Dir., Joseph R. Mannes/46/Dir., Michael A. Nery/32/Dir., Field T. Lange/Dir.

Owners: Tandy Leather Factory, Inc./8.51%, Wellington Management Company, LLP/12.18%, Joseph R. Mannes, Ron & Robin Morgan/16.27%, Field T. Lange, David M . Greenhouse/7.33%, Nery Capital Partners, L.P./9.09%, Wray Thompson/2.00%, Austin W. Marxe/7.33%, Shannon L. Greene/1.51%, Insiders/29.14%

Financial Data: *Fiscal Year End:* 12/31 *Latest Annual Data:* 12/31/2006

Year	Sales	Net Income
2006	$55,199,000	$4,777,000
2005	$50,720,000	$3,714,000
2004	$46,146,000	$2,654,000

Curr. Assets:	$27,864,000	Curr. Liab.:	$5,372,000	
Plant, Equip.:	$2,129,000	Total Liab.:	$5,594,000	Indic. Yr. Divd.: NA
Total Assets:	$31,917,000	Net Worth:	$26,323,000	Debt/ Equity: NA

Tanger Factory Outlet Centers Inc

3200 Nline Ave., Ste. 360, Greensboro, NC, 27408; *PH:* 1-336-292-3010; *Fax:* 1-336-852-2096; *http://* www.tangeroutlet.com; *Email:* tangermail@tangeroutlet.com

General - Incorporation	NC	Stock - Price on:12/24/2007	$39.26
Employees	200	Stock Exchange	NYSE
Auditor	PricewaterhouseCoopers LLP	Ticker Symbol	SKT
Stk Agt	Computershare Trust Co	Outstanding Shares	31,280,000
Counsel	NA	E.P.S.	$0.64
DUNS No.	NA	Shareholders	NA

Business: The groups principle activities include acquiring, developing, managing and operating factory outlet centers. The group operates from the Unites States. The group's quarterly revenue for September 2007 was 58.39 millions of USD.

Primary SIC and add'l.: 6798

CIK No: 0000899715

Subsidiaries: COROC Holdings, LLC, COROC/Hilton Head I L.L.C., COROC/Hilton Head II L.L.C., COROC/Lakes Region L.L.C., COROC/Lincoln City L.L.C., COROC/Myrtle Beach L.L.C., COROC/Park City L.L.C., COROC/Rehoboth I L.L.C., COROC/Rehoboth II L.L.C., COROC/Rehoboth III L.L.C., COROC/Riviera L.L.C., COROC/Tilton L.L.C., COROC/Tuscola L.L.C., COROC/Westbrook I L.L.C., COROC/Westbrook II L.L.C. 28 Subsidiaries included in the Index

Officers: Stanley K. Tanger/Founder, Chmn., CEO/$2,672,474.00, Steven B. Tanger/Dir., COO, Pres./$1,972,753.00, Frank C. Marchisello/CFO, Exec. VP/$929,750.00, Joseph H. Nehmen/Sr. VP - Operations/$324,094.00, Virginia R. Summerell/VP, Treasurer, Assist. Sec., Carrie A. Warren/Sr. VP - Marketing, Kevin D. Dillon/Sr. VP - Construction, Development, James F. Williams/Sr. VP, Controller, Lisa J. Morrison/Sr. VP - Leasing/$313,513.00

Directors: Stanley K. Tanger/Founder, Chmn., CEO, Steven B. Tanger/Dir., COO, Pres., Jack Africk/Dir., William G. Benton/Dir., Thomas E. Robinson/Dir., Allan L. Schuman/Dir.

Owners: Steven B. Tanger, Allan L. Schuman, The Vanguard Group, Inc./7.10%, Joe Nehmen, Frank C. Marchisello, Jack Africk, Deutsche Bank AG/7.30%, William G. Benton, Stanley K. Tanger/2.70%, Insiders/4.30%, FMR Corp/11.10%, Thomas E. Robinson, Cohen & Steers Inc./7.00%, Lisa J. Morrison

Financial Data: *Fiscal Year End:* 12/31 *Latest Annual Data:* 12/31/2006

Year	Sales	Net Income
2006	$211,711,000	$37,309,000
2005	$202,799,000	$5,089,000
2004	$194,553,000	$7,046,000

Curr. Assets:	$8,453,000	Curr. Liab.:	$48,598,000	P/E Ratio: 9.09
Plant, Equip.:	$941,475,000	Total Liab.:	$727,177,000	Indic. Yr. Divd.: $1.440
Total Assets:	$1,040,877,000	Net Worth:	$274,676,000	Debt/ Equity: NA

Tank Sports Inc

10925 Schmidt Rd., El Monte, CA, 91733; *PH:* 1-626-350-4039; *http://* www.tank-sports.com

General - Incorporation	CA	Stock - Price on:12/24/2007	$0.5
Employees	NA	Stock Exchange	OTC
Auditor	Kabani & Company, Inc.	Ticker Symbol	TNSP
Stk Agt	American Stock Transfer & Trust Co.	Outstanding Shares	32,900,000
Counsel	NA	E.P.S.	-$0.03
DUNS No.	NA	Shareholders	NA

Business: The groups principle activities include marketing, selling and distributing recreational and transportation motorcycles, all terrain vehicles, dirt bikes, scooters and Go Karts. The group operates from the United States and China.

Primary SIC and add'l.: 5571

CIK No: 0001345059

Officers: Jing Jing Long/54/Dir., Pres., Treasurer, Principal Financial Officer, Principal Financial Officer, Jim Ji/26/Dir., Sec.

Directors: Jiangyong Ji/51/Chmn., Jing Jing Long/54/Dir., Pres., Treasurer, Principal Financial Officer, Principal Financial Officer, Jim Ji/26/Dir., Sec.

Owners: Insiders/81.20%, Jing Long/49.23%, Jiangyong Ji/32.97%

Financial Data: *Fiscal Year End:* 02/28 *Latest Annual Data:* 02/28/2007

Year	Sales	Net Income
2007	$9,588,000	-$249,000
2006	$7,539,000	-$207,000

Curr. Assets:	$6,080,000	Curr. Liab.:	$6,946,000	
Plant, Equip.:	$510,000	Total Liab.:	$8,709,000	Indic. Yr. Divd.: NA
Total Assets:	$8,257,000	Net Worth:	-$452,000	Debt/ Equity: NA

Tankless Systems Worldwide Inc

7650 E Evans Rd., Ste. C, Scottsdale, AZ, 85260; *PH:* 1-480-993-2300; *http://* www.tankless.com

General - Incorporation	NV	Stock - Price on:12/24/2007	$0.175
Employees	6	Stock Exchange	NA
Auditor	Moore & Assoc. Chartered	Ticker Symbol	NA
Stk Agt	First American Stock Transfer, Inc.	Outstanding Shares	NA
Counsel	NA	E.P.S.	NA
DUNS No.	NA	Shareholders	NA

Business: The group's principal activities are to design, develop, manufacture and market several models of an electronic, tankless water heater. The unit is a microprocessor controlled electric water heater contained in a compact unit, eliminating the space demands of conventional water heaters. The unit saves energy, space, and water and is suitable to all areas of the U.S. And worldwide. On 07-Nov-2003, the group acquired envirotech systems worldwide inc.

Primary SIC and add'l.: 3639

CIK No: 0001095751

Subsidiaries: Envirotech Systems Worldwide, Inc, Ion Tankless, Inc., Valeo Industries, Inc.

Officers: Ronald O. Abernathy/63/CEO, Pres., Treasurer, Chief Accounting Officer, Gregg C. Johnson/43/Exec. VP, Sec., David Kreitzer/Pres.

Directors: Ronald O. Abernathy/63/CEO, Pres., Treasurer, Chief Accounting Officer, Mark D. Chester/46/Chmn., Wesley G. Sprunk/71/Dir., William S. Papazian/Dir., Barry M. Goldwater/69/Dir., Thadeus F. Marek/66/Dir., Perry D. Logan/79/Dir.

Owners: Gregg C. Johnson/4.06%, Mark D. Chester/2.50%, Digital Crossing, LLC/6.23%, Ted F. Marek/1.71%, Insiders/16.39%, William S. Papazian/0.42%, Barry M. Goldwater, Sundance Financial Corp./6.24%, Wesley G. Sprunk/1.03%, Ronald O. Abernathy/0.23%, Perry D. Logan/6.12%

Tanzanian Royalty Exploration Corp

93 Benton Hill Rd., Sharon, CT, 06069; *PH:* 1-860-364-1830; *Fax:* 1-860-364-0673; *http://* www.tanzanianroyaltyexploration.com; *Email:* investors@tanrange.com

General - Incorporation	Canada	Stock - Price on:12/24/2007	$4.829
Employees	NA	Stock Exchange	AMEX
Auditor	KPMG LLP	Ticker Symbol	TRE
Stk Agt	Computershare Trust Co of Canada	Outstanding Shares	86,510,000
Counsel	Macleod Dixon LLP	E.P.S.	-$0.05
DUNS No.	NA	Shareholders	NA

Business: The group's principal activity is to engage in the acquisition of interests in and the exploration of natural resource properties. The comapny's principal operations are located in Tanzania. The group is in development stage.

Primary SIC and add'l.: 1040

CIK No: 0001173643

Subsidiaries: Dia Consult Limited, Itetemia Mining Company Limited, Kabahelele Mining Company Limited, Lunguya Mining Company Ltd., Tancan Mining Company Limited (Tancan), Tanzania American International Development Corporation 2000 Limited

Officers: Jim Sinclair/Chmn., CEO, John Deane/Dir., Pres., Regina Kuo-Lee/CFO

Directors: Jim Sinclair/Chmn., CEO, Norman Betts/Dir., John Deane/Dir., Pres., Marek Kreczmer/Dir., Victoria Luis/Dir., Anton Esterhuizen/Dir., William M. Harvey/Dir., Ulrich Rath/Dir., Rosalind Morrow/Dir.

Owners: Victoria Luis, Regina Kuo-Lee, Ulrich E. Rath, Jonathan G. Deane, Marek J. Kreczmer, Rosalind Morrow, Norman Betts, Anton Esterhuizen, Helen Hansen, William Harvey, Florian Ngunangwa, James E. Sinclair/3.40%

Financial Data: *Fiscal Year End:*08/31 *Latest Annual Data:* 8/31/2006

Year	Sales	Net Income
2006	NA	-$5,129,000
2005	NA	-$3,031,000

Curr. Assets:	$3,098,000	*Curr. Liab.:*	$536,000		
Plant, Equip.:	$6,976,000	*Total Liab.:*	$646,000	*Indic. Yr. Divd.:*	NA
Total Assets:	$7,587,000	*Net Worth:*	$6,941,000	*Debt/ Equity:*	NA

Tao Minerals Ltd

Oficina 501 Edificio Colmena, Carrerra 43A N01 A SUR 29, Medellin, Antioquia; *PH:* 57-3057260602; *http://* www.taomining.com

General - Incorporation	NV	Stock - Price on:12/24/2007	$48.45
Employees	NA	Stock Exchange	OTC
Auditor	De Leon & Company, P.A.	Ticker Symbol	TAOL
Stk Agt	Empire Stock Transfer Inc.	Outstanding Shares	NA
Counsel	NA	E.P.S.	NA
DUNS No.	NA	Shareholders	NA

Business: The groups principal activity is engaged in no significant operations other than organizational activities, acquiring and staking properties, preparing the registrations of securities and planning of exploration. The group operates from the United States.

Primary SIC and add'l.: 1000

CIK No: 0001320338

Officers: James A. Sikora/Dir., CEO, Pres., Julio De Leon/Dir., CFO

Directors: James A. Sikora/Dir., CEO, Pres., Julio De Leon/Dir., CFO, Duncan James Bain/Dir., Walter Terrence. Plummer/Dir.

Owners: Julio De Leon/1.44%, Duncan Bain, Insiders/12.03%, Walter Plummer, Don Axent/33.97%, James Sikora/8.68%

Financial Data: *Fiscal Year End:*01/31 *Latest Annual Data:* 01/31/2007

Year	Sales	Net Income
2007	NA	-$400,000
2006	NA	-$49,000

Curr. Assets:	$61,000	*Curr. Liab.:*	$812,000		
Plant, Equip.:	NA	*Total Liab.:*	$812,000	*Indic. Yr. Divd.:*	$0.570
Total Assets:	$414,000	*Net Worth:*	-$398,000	*Debt/ Equity:*	NA

Tapestry Pharmaceuticals Inc

4840 Pearl E Cir., Ste 300w, Boulder, CO, 80301; *PH:* 1-303-516-8500; *http://* www.tapestrypharma.com; *Email:* info@tapestrypharma.com

General - Incorporation	DE	Stock - Price on:12/24/2007	$1.8
Employees	32	Stock Exchange	NDQ
Auditor	Grant Thornton, LLP	Ticker Symbol	TPPH
Stk Agt	American Stock Transfer & Trust Co.	Outstanding Shares	16,370,000
Counsel	NA	E.P.S.	-$1.29
DUNS No.	NA	Shareholders	NA

Business: The group's principal activities were the production, sale and licensing of complex natural product pharmaceuticals. The group produced and sold paclitaxel, a naturally occurring chemotherapeutic anti-cancer agent found in certain species of yew, or taxus, trees. It also developed other anti-cancer agents and licenses novel genomic technologies for applications in human therapeutics and diagnostics and agrobiotechnology. The group primarily used its gene editing technology to develop the agents that specifically and precisely edit genes. The products were sold under the trade names anzatax (TM), biotaxtm and napro paclitaxel and are used for injection to treat breast, ovarian and non-small cell lung cancers. The group sold the analytical services group and discontinued and disposed generic injectable paclitaxel business in 2003 and currently conducts only research and development.

Primary SIC and add'l.: 8731 2834 2836

CIK No: 0000891504

Subsidiaries: Faulding Pharmaceutical Co., NaPro BioTherapeutics, Inc.

Officers: Leonard P. Shaykin/Chmn., CEO/$1,812,913.00, Kai P. Larson/VP, General Counsel/$611,342.00, Matthew J. Majoros/Controller, Lawrence Helson/VP - Bio Research, Gordon Link/CFO, Sr. VP/$784,659.00, Gilles H. Tapolsky/VP - Product Development, James D. McChesney/CSO, Natural Products Chemistry, Martin Batt/COO, Sr. VP/$732,910.00, David L. Emerson/VP - Cancer Pharma, Donald H. Picker/Pres., Sandra Silberman/CMO

Directors: Leonard P. Shaykin/Chmn., CEO, Paul A. Bunn/Chmn. - Scientific Advisory Board, Gail S. Eckhardt/Member - Scientific Advisory Board, Stephen K. Carter/Dir., Robert E. Pollack/Member - Scientific Advisory Board, Elliot Maza/Dir., Arthur Hull. Hayes/Dir., Richard N. Perle/Dir., Susan Band Horwitz/Member - Scientific Advisory Board, Eric K. Rowinsky/Member - Scientific Advisory Board, Daniel D. Von Hoff/Member - Scientific Advisory Board, George M. Gould/Dir.

Owners: Patricia A. Pilia, Biotechnology Value Fund, L.P./10.00%, George M. Gould, Stephen K. Carter, Gordon H. Link, Leonard P. Shaykin/1.30%, Insiders/3.60%, Capital Ventures International/10.00%, Xmark JV Investment Partners, LLC/5.80%, Special Situations Fund III, L.P./30.30%, Baker Brothers Life Science Capital LLC/12.20%, Arthur H. Hayes, Elliot M. Maza, Tang Capital Partners, LP/13.10%, Kai P. Larson *(19 Owners included in Index)*

Financial Data: *Fiscal Year End:*12/28 *Latest Annual Data:* 12/27/2006

Year	Sales	Net Income
2006	NA	-$16,652,000
2005	NA	-$17,538,000
2004	NA	-$24,174,000

Curr. Assets:	$31,741,000	*Curr. Liab.:*	$8,268,000		
Plant, Equip.:	$676,000	*Total Liab.:*	$11,513,000	*Indic. Yr. Divd.:*	NA
Total Assets:	$39,293,000	*Net Worth:*	$27,780,000	*Debt/ Equity:*	0.0045

Tapimmune Inc

Formerly: GeneMax Corp

1681 Chestnut St., Ste. 400, Vancouver, BC, V6J 4M6; *PH:* 1-604-331-0400; *http://* www.genemax.com

General - Incorporation	NV	Stock - Price on:12/24/2007	$0.13
Employees	NA	Stock Exchange	OTC
Auditor	Dale Matheson Carr-Hilton Labonte	Ticker Symbol	TPIM
Stk Agt	Computershare Trust Co. of Canada	Outstanding Shares	NA
Counsel	NA	E.P.S.	NA
DUNS No.	NA	Shareholders	NA

Business: The group's principal activity is to develop immunotherapeutics to treat and eradicate cancer and therapies for infectious diseases, autoimmune disorders and transplant tissue rejection. The group's technologies are based on an understanding of the function of a protein 'pump' within cells that is essential in the processing of tumor antigens, known as tap. The group currently has none of its product candidates on the market and is focusing on the development and testing of its product candidates. The group has operations in Canada and United States.

Primary SIC and add'l.: 8731

CIK No: 0001094038

Subsidiaries: British Columbia corporation

Officers: Denis Corin/CEO, Pres./CAD8,819.00, Wilfred A. Jefferies/Principle Scientist, Terry Pearson/Scientific Advisor, Patrick A. McGowan/Sec., Treasurer, CFO, Principal Accounting Officer/CAD34,781.00

Directors: Alan P. Lindsay/Chmn., Glynn Wilson/Dir.

Owners: Denis Corin, Wilfred A. Jefferies/9.70%, Newport Capital Corp./3.40%, Alan P. Lindsay, Insiders/9.90%

Financial Data: *Fiscal Year End:*12/31 *Latest Annual Data:* 12/31/2006

Year	Sales	Net Income
2006	NA	-$1,304,000
2005	$4,000	-$986,000
2004	NA	-$2,683,000

Curr. Assets:	$154,000	*Curr. Liab.:*	$3,154,000		
Plant, Equip.:	$0	*Total Liab.:*	$3,154,000	*Indic. Yr. Divd.:*	NA
Total Assets:	$154,000	*Net Worth:*	-$3,000,000	*Debt/ Equity:*	NA

Targacept Inc

200 E First St., Ste. 300, Winston-salem, NC, 27101; *PH:* 1-336-480-2100; *http://* www.targacept.com

General - Incorporation	DE	Stock - Price on:12/24/2007	$9.45
Employees	88	Stock Exchange	NDQ
Auditor	Ernst & Young, LLP	Ticker Symbol	TRGT
Stk Agt	American Stock Transfer & Trust Co.	Outstanding Shares	19,140,000
Counsel	NA	E.P.S.	-$0.19
DUNS No.	NA	Shareholders	NA

Business: The groups principal activity is to provide investment management services. The group operates from the United States.

Primary SIC and add'l.: 2834 2834

CIK No: 0001124105

Officers: Donald J. Debethizy/Dir., CEO, Pres./$806,787.00, Merouane Bencherif/VP - Preclinical Research/$389,836.00, Jeffrey P. Brennan/VP - Business, Commercial Development/$421,340.00, William S. Caldwell/VP - Drug Discovery, Development, Geoffrey C. Dunbar/VP - Clinical Development, Regulatory Affairs/$483,393.00, Alan A. Musso/CFO, VP, Treasurer/$427,694.00, Peter A. Zorn/VP - Legal Affairs, General Counsel, Sec., Mauri K. Hodges/Sr. Dir. - Finance, Controller, Karen A. Hicks/Sr. Dir. - Human Resources

Directors: Donald J. Debethizy/Dir., CEO, Pres., Mark Skaletsky/Chmn., James M. Barrett/Dir., Charles A. Blixt/Dir., Steven G. Burrill/Dir., Alan W. Dunton/Dir., Errol B. De Souza/Dir., John P. Richard/Dir., Ralph Snyderman/Dir.

Owners: Jeffrey P. Brennan, Steven G. Burrill/4.10%, Insiders/37.40%, Entities affiliated with Nomura Phase4 Ventures Limited/11.20%, Donald J. deBethizy/2.50%, Steven M. Barrett/17.10%, Entities affiliated with BVF Partners L.P./5.70%, Alan A. Musso, Entities affiliated with New Enterprise Associates 10, Limited Partnership/17.10%, John P. Richard, Wellington Management Company, LLP/5.20%, Entities affiliated with EuclidSR Partners, L.P./9.90%, Errol B. DeSouza, Mark Skaletsky, Merouane Bencherif *(18 Owners included in Index)*

Financial Data: *Fiscal Year End:*NA *Latest Annual Data:* 12/31/2006

Year	Sales	Net Income
2006	$27,538,000	$2,097,000
2005	$1,180,000	-$28,992,000
2004	$3,738,000	-$24,025,000

Curr. Assets:	$78,853,000	*Curr. Liab.:*	$8,950,000		
Plant, Equip.:	$2,040,000	*Total Liab.:*	$16,370,000	*Indic. Yr. Divd.:*	NA
Total Assets:	$81,368,000	*Net Worth:*	$64,999,000	*Debt/ Equity:*	0.0108

Target Corp

1000 Nicollet Mall, Minneapolis, MN, 55403; *PH:* 1-612-370-6948; *http://* www.targetcorp.com; *Email:* investorrelations@target.com

General - Incorporation	MN	Stock - Price on:12/24/2007	$63.98
Employees	352,000	Stock Exchange	NYSE
Auditor	Ernst & Young LLP	Ticker Symbol	TGT
Stk Agt	Mellon Investor Services LLC	Outstanding Shares	851,490,000
Counsel	NA	E.P.S.	$3.334
DUNS No.	00-696-1700	Shareholders	NA

Business: The group's principle activity is to operate large-format general merchandise discount stores. The group also operates an online business named Target.com. The group operates from United States.

Primary SIC and add'l.: 5311

CIK No: 0000027419

Subsidiaries: AMC Dominican Republic, S.A., AMC El Salvador, S.A., AMC Guatemala Sociedad Anonima, AMC Honduras, S.A., AMC Nicaragua, S.A., AMC(s) Pte., Ltd., Amcrest Corporation, Amcrest France Sarl, Associated Merchandising Corporation, Associated Merchandising Corporation GmBH, Associated Merchandising Korea Corporation, Dayton Credit Company, Dayton Development Company, Eighth Street Development Company, Highbridge Company 38 Subsidiaries included in the Index

Officers: Robert J. Ulrich/Chmn., CEO, Jodeen A. Kozlak/Sr. VP - Human Resources, Gregory J. Duppler/Sr. VP - Merchandising, Mitchell L. Stover/Sr. VP - Distribution, Bryan Berg/Sr. VP - Region I, Richard N. Maguire/Sr. VP - Merchandise Planning, Janet M. Schalk/Sr. VP - Technology Services, CIO, Stacia J. Anderson/Pres. - Target Sourcing Service, Michael R. Francis/Exec. VP - Marketing/$5,135,240.00, Patricia Adams/Sr. VP - Merchandising, Terrence J. Scully/Pres. - Target Financial Services, Jane P. Windmeier/Sr. VP - Finance, Susan D. Kahn/VP - Communications, Nathan K. Garvis/VP - Government Affairs, Timothy R. Baer/Exec. VP, General Counsel, Corp. Sec. *(30 Officers included in Index)*

Directors: Robert J. Ulrich/Chmn., CEO, Roxanne S. Austin/Dir., Calvin Darden/Dir., James A. Johnson/Dir., Derica W. Rice/Dir., Richard M. Kovacevich/Dir., George W. Tamke/Dir., Anne M. Mulcahy/Dir., Mary E. Minnick/Dir., Stephen W. Sanger/Dir., Solomon D. Trujillo/Dir., Mary N. Dillon/Dir.

Owners: Douglas A. Scovanner, Robert J. Ulrich, George W. Tamke, Roxanne S. Austin, Richard M. Kovacevich, Stephen W. Sanger, Calvin Darden, Gregg W. Steinhafel, John D. Griffith, Anne M. Mulcahy, Insiders, Warren R. Staley, State Street Bank and Trust Company/8.30%, Mary E. Minnick, Capital Research and Management Company/16.60% *(18 Owners included in Index)*

Financial Data: ***Fiscal Year End:***01/28 ***Latest Annual Data:*** 2/3/2007

Year	Sales	Net Income
2007	$59,490,000,000	$2,787,000,000
2006	$52,620,000,000	$2,408,000,000
2005	$46,839,000,000	$3,198,000,000

Curr. Assets:	$14,706,000,000	***Curr. Liab.:***	$11,117,000,000	***P/E Ratio:***	19.19
Plant, Equip.:	$21,431,000,000	***Total Liab.:***	$21,716,000,000	***Indic. Yr. Divd.:***	$0.560
Total Assets:	$37,349,000,000	***Net Worth:***	$15,633,000,000	***Debt/ Equity:***	0.6461

Target Logistics Inc

500 Harborview Dr., 3rd Fl., Baltimore, MD, 21230; ***PH:*** 1-410-332-1598; ***http://*** www.targetlogistics.com

General - Incorporation	DE	***Stock***- Price on:12/24/2007	$1.84
Employees	256	Stock Exchange	NA
Auditor	Stonefield Josephson, Inc	Ticker Symbol	NA
Stk Agt	American Stock Transfer & Trust Co.	Outstanding Shares	18,080,000
Counsel	Neuberger, Quinn, Gielen Et Al	E.P.S.	$0.086
DUNS No.	94-310-3259	Shareholders	NA

Business: The group's principal activity is to provide freight forwarding services and logistics services, through its wholly owned subsidiary, target logistic services, inc. The group has a network of offices in 36 cities throughout the United States. The freight forwarding services involve arranging for the transport of customers freight from the shippers' location to the designated recipients, including the preparation of shipping documents and providing of handling, packing and containerization services. The group also assembles bulk cargo and arranges for insurance. The group has international freight forwarding operations in China and Philippines. The principal customers of the group include manufacturers and distributors of computers and other electronic and high-technology equipment, computer software and wearing apparel.

Primary SIC and add'l.: 4731 6719

CIK No: 0001009480

Officers: Chris Coppersmith/CEO, Pres., Philip J. Dubato/52/VP, CFO, Sec., Treasurer, Sue Beattie/VP, Denis Dillon/VP - Operations, George Frey/VP - Sales, Marketing, S. K. Leong/VP - Business Development, Ron Frady/Controller, Pat Kirwan/Dir. - Business Systems, Bob McGhee/Dir. - International Operations, Bruce Slawinski/Dir. - Information Systems, Peter Burke/VP - Fashion Services, Craig Meador/Dir. - Canada, Italy Business Development, Marc Widelitz/Dir. - Domestic Operations

Directors: Stuart Hettleman/58/Dir., Stephen J. Clearman/57/Dir., Michael Barsa/63/Dir., Brian K. Coventry/43/Dir., David E. Swirnow/50/Dir.

Owners: Stephen J. Clearman, David E. Swirnow, Michael Barsa, Christopher A. Coppersmith, Stuart Hettleman

Financial Data: ***Fiscal Year End:***06/30 ***Latest Annual Data:*** 6/30/2006

Year	Sales	Net Income
2006	$160,369,000	$2,706,000
2005	$138,392,000	$1,561,000
2004	$126,089,000	$540,000

Curr. Assets:	$29,798,000	***Curr. Liab.:***	$23,015,000	***P/E Ratio:***	20.44
Plant, Equip.:	$2,300,000	***Total Liab.:***	$23,570,000	***Indic. Yr. Divd.:***	NA
Total Assets:	$45,251,000	***Net Worth:***	$21,681,000	***Debt/ Equity:***	0.0099

Targeted Genetics Corp

1100 Olive Way, Ste 100, Seattle, WA, 98101; ***PH:*** 1-206-623-7612; ***http://*** www.targen.com

General - Incorporation	WA	***Stock***- Price on:12/24/2007	$2.89
Employees	70	Stock Exchange	NDQ
Auditor	Ernst & Young LLP	Ticker Symbol	TGEN
Stk Agt	Mellon Investor Services LLC	Outstanding Shares	13,110,000
Counsel	Perkins Coie LLP	E.P.S.	-$0.891
DUNS No.	78-437-9745	Shareholders	NA

Business: The group's principal activities are to develop gene therapy and cell therapy products and technologies for the treatment of acquired and inherited diseases. The gene therapy products are designed to treat diseases by regulating cellular function at a genetic level. The cell therapy involves transplanting living cells into a patient to treat diseases, either in place of, or in combination with, other pharmaceuticals. Currently, the group has ongoing preclinical product development activities in the areas of cystic fibrosis, hemophilia a, arthritis, cancer, lysosomal storage disorders, cardiovascular diseases and aids prophylaxis. The product candidates under clinical development program include tgaavc-f for treatment of cystic fibrosis and tgddc-e1a for treatment of cancer.

Primary SIC and add'l.: 2836 2835 8731

CIK No: 0000921114

Subsidiaries: Genovo, Inc., TGCF Manufacturing, Inc.

Officers: Stewart H. Parker/Dir., CEO, Pres./$520,180.00, Barrie J. Carter/Chief Scientific Officer, Exec. VP/$350,665.00, David J. Poston/VP - Finance, CFO, Treasurer/$259,415.00, Pervin Anklesaria/VP - Therapeutic Development, Richard W. Peluso/VP - Process Development, Susan B.G. Robinson/VP - Business Development, Stacie D. Byars/Dir. - Communications

Directors: Stewart H. Parker/Dir., CEO, Pres., Jeremy Curnock Cook/Chmn., Nelson L. Levy/Dir., Roger L. Hawley/Dir., Jack L. Bowman/Dir., Joseph M. Davie/Dir., Michael Perry/Dir.

Owners: Elan International Services, Ltd./5.90%, Michael S. Perry, Stewart H. Parker, Insiders/1.90%, Joseph M. Davie, Special Situations/24.50%, Jack L. Bowman, David J. Poston, OrbiMed Advisors LLC and affiliates/12.50%, Jeremy L. Curnock Cook, Roger L. Hawley, Barrie J. Carter, Nelson L. Levy, Biogen Idec Inc./11.00%

Financial Data: ***Fiscal Year End:***12/31 ***Latest Annual Data:*** 12/31/2006

Year	Sales	Net Income
2006	$9,864,000	-$33,990,000
2005	$6,874,000	-$19,198,000
2004	$9,652,000	-$14,257,000

Curr. Assets:	$8,235,000	***Curr. Liab.:***	$5,188,000		
Plant, Equip.:	$1,100,000	***Total Liab.:***	$12,100,000	***Indic. Yr. Divd.:***	NA
Total Assets:	$17,467,000	***Net Worth:***	$5,367,000	***Debt/ Equity:***	0.0578

Taro Pharmaceutical Industries Ltd

Italy House, Euro Pk., Yakum, 60972; ***PH:*** 972-99711800; ***http://*** www.taro.com; ***Email:*** ir@taro.com

General - Incorporation	Israel	***Stock***- Price on:12/24/2007	$10.6
Employees	NA	Stock Exchange	OTC
Auditor	Kost Forer Gabbay & Kasierer	Ticker Symbol	TARO
Stk Agt	American Stock Transfer & Trust Co.	Outstanding Shares	NA
Counsel	Weil, Gotshal & Manges LLP	E.P.S.	NA
DUNS No.	60-007-2078	Shareholders	NA

Business: The groups principle activities include manufacturing, marketing and distribution of prescription and over-the-counter pharmaceutical products, such as dermatological and gynecologic creams, ointments, tablets, capsules and lotion products. The group operates from United States.

Primary SIC and add'l.: 2834

CIK No: 0000906338

Subsidiaries: Taro Pharmaceuticals Europe B.V., Taro Pharmaceuticals Inc., Taro Pharmaceuticals Ireland Ltd., Taro Pharmaceuticals North America, Inc., Taro Pharmaceuticals U.S.A., Inc., Taro Research Institute Ltd., Thames Pharmacal Company, Inc.

Officers: Tzvi Tal/57/VP - Information Technology, Israel, Tal Levitt/Dir., Sr. VP - Corporate Affairs, Treasurer, Daniel Saks/Primary Investor Relations Officer, VP - Corporate Affairs, Samuel Rubinstein/68/Sr. VP, GM, Avraham Yacobi/61/Sr. VP - Research, Development, Zahava Rafalowicz/60/Group VP - Sales, Marketing, Deputy GM - Israel, Mariana Bacalu/57/VP - Quality Affairs, Rebecca Roof/52/Interim Chief Administrative, Restructuring Officer, Ron Kolker/53/Group VP, Corporate Controller, Interim CFO, Ram Zajicek/44/Group VP, Haifa Site Mgr., Yohanan Dichter/60/VP - Pharmacist in Charge, Sr. Quality Mgr., Roman Kaplan/61/VP - Technical Operations, Pharmaceuticals, Hagai Reingold/42/VP - API Division, Inbal Rothman/36/VP - Human Resources, Community Affairs, Israel, Noam Shamir/45/VP - Supply Chain, Industrial Engineer *(16 Officers included in Index)*

Directors: Barrie Levitt/Chmn., Daniel Moros/Vice Chmn., Heather Douglas/Dir., Myron Strober/Dir., Haim Fainaro/Dir., Micha Friedman/Dir., Ben Zion Hod/Dir., Eric Johnsten/Dir., Gad Keren/Dir., Tal Levitt/Dir., Sr. VP - Corporate Affairs, Treasurer

Owners: Taro Development Corporation/7.90%, Brandes Investment Partners, Inc./10.00%, Franklin Resources, Inc. and related entities/9.90%

Tarpon Industries Inc

2420 Wills St., Marysville, MI, 48040; ***PH:*** 1-810-364-7421; ***Fax:*** 1-810-364-5610; ***http://*** www.tarponind.com

General - Incorporation	MI	***Stock***- Price on:12/24/2007	$0.52
Employees	232	Stock Exchange	OTC
Auditor	Grant Thornton LLP	Ticker Symbol	NA
Stk Agt	NA	Outstanding Shares	5,850,000
Counsel	NA	E.P.S.	-$1.89
DUNS No.	NA	Shareholders	NA

Business: The group operates through its subsidiaries whose principle activities include manufacturing and selling structural, mechanical steel tubing and engineered steel storage rack systems. The group products include selective rack, pushback racks, cantilever rack, archival storage system, order picking systems. The group marketed its products under the trade name SpaceRak(R). Customers of the group include equipment manufacturer automotive, boating, industrial equipment, construction, agricultural, steel service center, leisure and recreational markets. The group operates through two segments namely Steelbank and EWCO. The group operates from the United States and Canada. The group's quarterly revenue for September 2007 was 8.73 millions of USD.

Primary SIC and add'l.: 3469 3479 3444 3471 3441 3494 3317 3498

CIK No: 0001303565

Subsidiaries: Eugene Welding Co., FM, Inc., JS&T Acquisition Company, MTM Acquisition Company, Steelbank Tubular, Inc.

Officers: James W. Bradshaw/Chmn., CEO, Patrick J. Hook/COO, Pres.

Directors: James W. Bradshaw/Chmn., CEO, Michael A. Ard/Dir., Tracy Shellabarger/Dir., Gerald Stein/Dir.

Owners: Tracy L. Shellabarger, Insiders/2.40%, Gary D. Lewis/7.40%, Michael A. Ard, Patrick Hook, Gerald Stein, James W. Bradshaw

Financial Data: ***Fiscal Year End:***12/31 ***Latest Annual Data:*** 12/31/2006

Year	Sales	Net Income
2006	$75,331,000	-$9,993,000
2005	$60,851,000	-$7,309,000
2004	$37,622,000	-$1,995,000

Curr. Assets:	$17,585,000	***Curr. Liab.:***	$27,433,000		
Plant, Equip.:	$5,146,000	***Total Liab.:***	$27,544,000	***Indic. Yr. Divd.:***	NA
Total Assets:	$24,116,000	***Net Worth:***	-$3,427,000	***Debt/ Equity:***	NA

Tarragon Corp

423W55th st. 12th fl., Ste 200, New York, NY, 10019; ***PH:*** 1-212-949-5000; ***http://*** www.tarragoncorp.com

General - Incorporation	NV	**Stock** - Price on:12/24/2007	$9.73
Employees	602	Stock Exchange	NDQ
Auditor	Grant Thornton LLP	Ticker Symbol	TARR
Stk Agt	American Stock Transfer & Trust Co.	Outstanding Shares	28,690,000
Counsel	NA	E.P.S	-$13.85
DUNS No.	NA	Shareholders	NA

Business: The group's principal activity is to own, develop and build homes. It operates through two business segments: homebuilding division and investment division. Homebuilding division develops, renovates, builds and markets homes in high-density, in-fill locations and in master planned communities and develops and sells lots in single-family subdivisions. Investment division owns, acquires and operates residential and commercial rental properties, including almost 5,000 garden apartment homes. At 31-Dec-2003, the group had 18 residential communities with 2,257 homes or home sites under development in four states and had interests in 14,345 rental apartment units.

Primary SIC and add'l.: 6531

CIK No: 0001038217

Subsidiaries: 100 East Las Olas, Ltd., 1100 Adams Street Urban Renewal, LLC, 1118 Adams Street Urban Renewal, LLC, 1200 Grand Street Urban Renewal, LLC, 1300 Grand Street Urban Renewal, LLC, 5600 Collins Avenue, LLC, 5600 Gp, Inc., 900 Monroe Development LLC, Acadian Place Apartments, LLC, Acadian Place Holdings, LLC, Accord Properties Associates, LLC, Adams Street Development, LLC, Alexandria Pointe, LC, Alta Marina, LLC, AltaMar Development, LLC 259 Subsidiaries included in the Index

Officers: William S. Friedman/Dir., CEO, Investor Relations Officer, Robert C. Rohdie/Dir., CEO, Pres. - Tarragon Development, Eileen A. Swenson/Pres. - Tarragon Management, Inc, Richard Schaffer/MD, William J. Rosato/Sr. VP - Tarragon Development Corporation, Ron Leichtner/VP - Tarragon Corporation, Todd Martin Schefler/Exec. VP - Development, Charles Rubenstein/Exec. VP, Chief Real Estate Counsel, Todd C. Minor/Exec. VP, Treasurer, Robert P. Rothenberg/Dir., COO, Pres. - Tarragon Development, Saul Spitz/Exec. VP - Acquisitions, Kathryn Mansfield/Exec. VP, Sec., General Counsel, Erin Davis Pickens/CFO, Exec. VP, Jaime Hellman/VP - Tarragon South Development Corporation, William M. Thompson/Exec. VP - Operations *(16 Officers included in Index)*

Directors: William S. Friedman/Dir., CEO, Investor Relations Officer, Robert C. Rohdie/Dir., CEO, Pres. - Tarragon Development, Martha E. Stark/47/Dir., Robert P. Rothenberg/Dir., COO, Pres. - Tarragon Development, Richard S. Frary/Dir., Lawrence G. Schafran/Dir., Carl B. Weisbrod/Dir., Willie K. Davis/Dir., Lance Liebman/Dir., Raymond V.J. Schrag/Dir.

Owners: Martha E. Stark, Richard S. Frary, Raymond V.J. Schrag/1.00%, Lance Liebman, Erin D. Pickens, Todd C. Minor, Robert C. Rohdie/3.90%, Insiders/51.60%, Lawrence G. Schafran, Charles D. Rubenstein, Willie K. Davis, William S. Friedman/43.20%, Carl B. Weisbrod, Kathryn Mansfield, Robert P. Rothenberg/3.90% *(19 Owners included in Index)*

Financial Data: ***Fiscal Year End:*** 12/31 ***Latest Annual Data:*** 12/31/2006

Year	Sales	Net Income
2006	$544,884,000	$11,153,000
2005	$596,207,000	$88,498,000
2004	$310,956,000	$44,708,000

Curr. Assets:	$116,121,000	**Curr. Liab.:**	$142,513,000		
Plant, Equip.:	$1,796,631,000	**Total Liab.:**	$1,743,247,000	**Indic. Yr. Divd.:**	NA
Total Assets:	$2,022,761,000	**Net Worth:**	$279,514,000	**Debt/ Equity:**	5.4639

Tarrant Apparel Group

3151 E Washington Blvd, Los Angeles, CA, 90023; ***PH:*** 1-213-780-8250; ***http://*** www.tags.com

General - Incorporation	CA	**Stock** - Price on:12/24/2007	$1.2399
Employees	286	Stock Exchange	NDQ
Auditor	Singer Lewak Greenbaum & Goldstein	Ticker Symbol	TAGS
Stk Agt	Computershare Trust Co	Outstanding Shares	30,540,000
Counsel	Manatt, Phelps & Phillips LLP	E.P.S	$0.10
DUNS No.	19-447-4995	Shareholders	NA

Business: The group's principal activities are to design, manufacture and sell casual apparel. The group serves specialty retail, mass merchandise department store chains and international brands located primarily in the United States. The products of the group are manufactured in a variety of woven and knit fabrications. The products are jeans wear, casual pants, t-shirts, shorts, blouses, shirts and other tops, dresses, leggings and jackets. The customers include k-Mart, kohl's, mervyns, sears, abercrombie, fitch, northern reflection, tropical sports wear, j.c. Penney, express, a division of the limited, as well as lerner New York and wal-Mart.

Primary SIC and add'l.: 2325 2331 2339

CIK No: 0000944948

Subsidiaries: Fashion Resource (TCL), Inc., Jane Doe Hong Kong Ltd., Jane Doe International, LLC., Marble Limited., NO! Jeans, Inc., PBCR, Inc., Pbg7, LLC., Private Brands, Inc., Rocky Apparel, LLC, TAG Fin, S.A. de C.V, Tag Mex, Inc, Tag Mex, LLC., Tarrant Company Limited, Tarrant Luxembourg, Sarl, Tarrant Mexico, S. de R.L. de C.V 17 Subsidiaries included in the Index

Officers: Gerard Guez/52/Chmn., Interim CEO/$52,000.00, David N. Burke/58/CFO

Directors: Gerard Guez/52/Chmn., Interim CEO, Todd Kay/51/Vice Chmn., Joseph Mizrachi/62/Dir., Simon Mani/56/Dir.

Owners: Guggenheim Capital, LLC/10.30%, Charles Ghailian/1.00%, Insiders/52.40%, Henry Chu, Corazon Reyes, Joseph Mizrachi, Mitchell Simbal, Simon Mani, Todd Kay/14.90%, Stephane Farouze, Milton Koffman, Barry Aved/2.00%, David N. Burke, Gerard Guez/38.50%, GMM Capital LLC./5.20%

Financial Data: ***Fiscal Year End:*** 12/31 ***Latest Annual Data:*** 12/31/2006

Year	Sales	Net Income
2006	$232,402,000	-$22,221,000
2005	$214,648,000	$993,000
2004	$155,453,000	-$104,677,000

Curr. Assets:	$72,143,000	**Curr. Liab.:**	$81,937,000		
Plant, Equip.:	$1,414,000	**Total Liab.:**	$93,210,000	**Indic. Yr. Divd.:**	NA
Total Assets:	$111,132,000	**Net Worth:**	$17,922,000	**Debt/ Equity:**	0.7107

Taseko Mines Ltd

800 W Pender St., Ste. 1020, Vancouver, BC, V6C 2V6; ***PH:*** 1-604-684-6365; ***Fax:*** 1-604-684-8092; ***http://*** www.tasekomines.com; ***Email:*** info@hdgold.com

General - Incorporation	BC	**Stock** - Price on:12/24/2007	$3.76
Employees	264	Stock Exchange	AMEX
Auditor	KPMG LLP	Ticker Symbol	TGB
Stk Agt	Computershare Trust Co of Canada	Outstanding Shares	128,660,000
Counsel	NA	E.P.S	$0.37
DUNS No.	25-385-2107	Shareholders	NA

Business: The group's principal activity is to explore gold-copper property in the prosperity gold-copper property. The group also operates the gibraltar copper mine. The group carries on business in the province of british columbia, Canada.

Primary SIC and add'l.: 1041 1021

CIK No: 0000878518

Subsidiaries: Cuisson Lakes Mines Ltd, Gibraltar Mines Ltd

Officers: Russell E. Hallbauer/Dir., CEO, Pres., Jeffrey R. Mason/Dir., Sec., CFO, John McManus/VP - Operation, Brian Bergot/Investor Relations Contact, Lang Michener/Attorney, Barrister, Solicitor

Directors: Russell E. Hallbauer/Dir., CEO, Pres., Ronald Thiessen/Chmn., David J. Copeland/Dir., Scott D. Cousens/Dir., Jeffrey R. Mason/Dir., Sec., CFO, William Armstrong/Dir., Barry T. Coughlan/Dir., David Elliott/Dir., Wayne Kirk/Dir.

Owners: Robert A. Dickinson/0.25%, David Elliott/0.05%, Scott D. Cousens/0.53%, Wayne Kirk/0.04%, Barry Coughlan/0.08%, Ronald W. Thiessen/1.22%, Insiders/3.11%, David J. Copeland/0.77%, Russell E. Hallbauer/0.16%, Jeffrey R. Mason/0.01%, John W. McManus/0.01%

Financial Data: ***Fiscal Year End:*** 09/30 ***Latest Annual Data:*** 09/30/2006

Year	Sales	Net Income
2006	$145,370,000	$30,064,000
2005	$74,861,000	$20,813,000
2004	NA	-$51,292,000

Curr. Assets:	$49,868,000	**Curr. Liab.:**	$44,438,000		
Plant, Equip.:	$30,777,000	**Total Liab.:**	$142,700,000	**Indic. Yr. Divd.:**	NA
Total Assets:	$167,694,000	**Net Worth:**	$24,993,000	**Debt/ Equity:**	NA

Taser International Inc

17800 N 85th St., Scottsdale, AZ, 85260; ***PH:*** 1-480-905-2000; ***http://*** www.taser.com; ***Email:*** TASER@TASER.com

General - Incorporation	DE	**Stock** - Price on:12/24/2007	$12.42
Employees	240	Stock Exchange	NDQ
Auditor	Deloitte & Touche LLP	Ticker Symbol	TASR
Stk Agt	U.S. Stock Transfer Corp	Outstanding Shares	62,080,000
Counsel	Tonkon Torp LLP	E.P.S	$0.20
DUNS No.	NA	Shareholders	NA

Business: The group's principle activities include developing, assembling and marketing less-lethal, conducted energy weapons primarily for use in the law enforcement and corrections market. The company's principal products are the advanced taser and air taser. The advanced taser is sold with an integrated laser sight and a built-in memory option to record the time and date of up to 585 firings. The advanced taser has a comparable or lower injury rate than other less-lethal weapons with no adverse after-effects. The air taser product consists of cartridge electrified probes, an optional laser sight and a number of holstering accessories. These products are sold to the private security, military and consumer markets. The group operates from United States.

Primary SIC and add'l.: 3482

CIK No: 0001069183

Officers: Patrick W. Smith/Dir., CEO, Co - Founder, Marcy Rigoni/Primary Investor Relations Officer, Rick Guilbault/Dir. - Training, Steve Ward/VP - Marketing, International Sales, Kathy Hanrahan/Pres., Daniel M. Behrendt/CFO/$392,909.00, John F. Szakach/VP - Quality Assurance, Max Nerheim/VP - Research, Development, Kathleen C. Hanrahan/COO/$265,155.00, Stephen D. Tuttle/VP - Communications, Douglas E. Klint/VP, General Counsel, Stacie Sundberg/VP - US Sales, Raymond G. Rivera/CIO

Directors: Patrick W. Smith/Dir., CEO, Co - Founder, Thomas P. Smith/Chmn., Co - Founder, John S. Caldwell/Dir., Michael Garnreiter/Dir., Bruce R. Culver/Dir., Judy Martz/Dir., Matthew R. McBrady/Dir., Mark W. Kroll/Dir., Richard H. Carmona/58/Dir.

Owners: Matthew R. McBrady, Daniel M. Behrendt, Bruce R. Culver/2.60%, Patrick W. Smith/4.60%, Insiders/11.80%, Michael Garnreiter, Thomas P. Smith/2.90%, John S. Caldwell, Judy Martz, Kathleen C. Hanrahan, Mark W. Kroll

Financial Data: ***Fiscal Year End:*** 12/31 ***Latest Annual Data:*** 12/31/2006

Year	Sales	Net Income
2006	$67,718,000	-$4,088,000
2005	$47,694,000	$1,063,000
2004	$67,640,000	$18,882,000

Curr. Assets:	$56,116,000	**Curr. Liab.:**	$18,303,000		
Plant, Equip.:	$20,843,000	**Total Liab.:**	$20,509,000	**Indic. Yr. Divd.:**	NA
Total Assets:	$119,838,000	**Net Worth:**	$99,329,000	**Debt/ Equity:**	0.0001

Tasker Products Corp

Formerly: Tasker Capital Corp

39 Old Ridgebury Rd., Danbury, CT, 06810; ***PH:*** 1-203-730-4350; ***http://*** www.taskerproducts.com

General - Incorporation	NV	**Stock** - Price on:12/24/2007	$0.229
Employees	33	Stock Exchange	OTC
Auditor	Rothstein, Kass & Co, P.C	Ticker Symbol	TKER
Stk Agt	Pacific Corporate Trust Co	Outstanding Shares	108,670,000
Counsel	NA	E.P.S	-$0.605
DUNS No.	NA	Shareholders	NA

Business: The group's principal activities are to sell, develop, market and distribute consumer deodorant breath products, animal deodorant breath products and soft drink products. The group is a development stage company. Prior to 2002, the group was engaged in exploring, acquiring and developing mineral properties through its wholly owned subsidiary. During 2001, the group allowed the option on its mineral property to lapse and began to investigate other business opportunities.

Primary SIC and add'l.: 5999 1081

CIK No: 0001084557

Subsidiaries: Coast to Coast Laboratories Corp, Tanuta Ventures Corp

Officers: Lanny Dacus/Dir., CEO, Pres./$25,878.00, Greg Osborn/Exec. Chmn., Stathis Kouninis/CFO, Treasurer, Sec./$348,006.00

Directors: Lanny Dacus/Dir., CEO, Pres., Greg Osborn/Exec. Chmn., Joseph P. Carfora/Dir., William P. Miller/Dir., Timothy Lane/Dir., Frederick G. Ledlow/Dir., Peter O'Gorman/Dir., Leonid Frenkel/61/Dir.

Owners: Greg Osborn/14.80%, Frederick G. Ledlow, Peter OGorman/1.20%, Stathis Kouninis/1.10%, James Burns/2.50%, Joseph P. Carfora/1.10%, Insiders/24.70%, Timothy M. Lane/1.70%, Lanny Dacus/6.70%, Robert Jenkins, Richard Falcone/2.50%, William P. Miller

Financial Data: *Fiscal Year End:*12/31 *Latest Annual Data:* 12/31/2006

Year	Sales	Net Income
2006	$1,486,000	-$62,943,000
2005	$705,000	-$18,269,000
2004	NA	-$6,072,000

Curr. Assets:	$2,227,000	Curr. Liab.:	$5,708,000		
Plant, Equip.:	$1,311,000	Total Liab.:	$5,738,000	Indic. Yr. Divd.:	NA
Total Assets:	$21,967,000	Net Worth:	$16,229,000	Debt/ Equity:	NA

Tasty Baking Co

2801 Hunting Pk. Ave., Philadelphia, PA, 19129; *PH:* 1-215-221-8500; *Fax:* 1-215-223-3288; *http://* www.tastykake.com

General - Incorporation	PA	Stock - Price on:12/24/2007	$9.7799
Employees	845	Stock Exchange	NDQ
Auditor	PricewaterhouseCoopers LLP	Ticker Symbol	TSTY
Stk Agt	American Stock Transfer & Trust Co.	Outstanding Shares	8,260,000
Counsel	NA	E.P.S.	$0.45
DUNS No.	00-226-6369	Shareholders	NA

Business: The group's principal activity is to manufacture and sell a variety of cakes, pies, cookies, pastries and other similar products under the brand name tastykake(r). The group offers approximately 100 varieties of these products and three varieties of low-fat products in response to the customer preferences. The group's products are available in single packs, family packs or jumbo packs. The group operates two regional bakeries and markets its products under the brands tastykake, classic baked goods, dutch mill, mrs. Bauer's bakery, aunt sweetie's bakery and snack n' fresh.

Primary SIC and add'l.: 2051 2052

CIK No: 0000096412

Subsidiaries: Tasty Baking Oxford, Inc., Tastykake Investment Company, TBC Financial Services, Inc.

Officers: Charles P. Pizzi/Dir., CEO, Pres./$1,128,190.00, David S. Marberger/CFO, Exec. VP/$457,417.00, Robert V. Brown/VP - Sales/$214,621.00, Christopher J. Rahey/VP - Direct Sales/$211,583.00, Autumn R. Bayles/Sr. VP - Strategic Operations, Technology/$278,577.00, Joseph W. Carboy/VP, GM - Hunting Park, Edwin E. Pixler/VP, GM - Oxford, Paul D. Ridder/VP, Controller, Chad Ramsey/Contact - Corporate, David A. Vidovich/VP - Human Resources, Labor Relations, Laurence Weilheimer/Sr. VP, General Counsel, Corp. Sec., Jonathan L. Silvon/Dir. - Marketing, Eugene P. Malinowski/Corporate Treasurer

Directors: Charles P. Pizzi/Dir., CEO, Pres., James E. Ksansnak/Chmn., Mark T. Timbie/Dir., Fred C. Aldridge/74/Dir., Mark G. Conish/Dir., James E. Nevels/Dir., James C. Hellauer/Dir., Ronald J. Kozich/Dir., Judith M. Von Seldeneck/Dir., David J. West/Dir.

Owners: Dimensional Fund Advisors Inc./8.50%, Dalton, Greiner, Hartman, Maher& Co./8.30%, Fred C. Aldridge, Autumn R. Bayles, Mark G. Conish, Insiders/7.90%, Heartland Advisors, Inc./6.20%, James E. Ksansnak, The TCW Group Inc./14.30%, Christopher J. Rahey, Wachovia Bank, N.A./5.20%, Robert V. Brown, David J. West, Ronald J. Kozich, James E. Nevels *(20 Owners included in Index)*

Financial Data: *Fiscal Year End:*12/31 *Latest Annual Data:* 12/30/2006

Year	Sales	Net Income
2006	$167,715,000	$4,196,000
2005	$172,273,000	$1,843,000
2004	$159,061,000	$1,243,000

Curr. Assets:	$29,008,000	Curr. Liab.:	$19,372,000	P/E Ratio:	19.56
Plant, Equip.:	$66,248,000	Total Liab.:	$84,018,000	Indic. Yr. Divd.:	$0.200
Total Assets:	$121,307,000	Net Worth:	$37,289,000	Debt/ Equity:	NA

TAT Technologies Ltd

5304 Lawton Ave., Tulsa, OK, 74107; *PH:* 1-918-445-4300; *Fax:* 1-918-445-2210; *http://* www.tat.co.il; *Email:* sales@limcoairepair.com

General - Incorporation	Israel	Stock - Price on:12/24/2007	$20.9599
Employees	658	Stock Exchange	NDQ
Auditor	Kost Forer Gabbay & Kasierer	Ticker Symbol	TATTF
Stk Agt	Gal Tech Inc	Outstanding Shares	6,260,000
Counsel	NA	E.P.S.	$1.20
DUNS No.	60-001-0425	Shareholders	NA

Business: The groups principle activities include development, manufacture and marketing of a broad range of heat transfer equipment used in mechanical and electronic systems on board aircraft, aluminum honeycomb bonded products and other electronic equipment. The group also designs and markets software for military and civilian systems, manufactures personal computers, graphic controllers and add-on systems. The groups services include remanufacture, overhaul and repair of heat transfer equipment for the aviation industry. The group operates from United States.

Primary SIC and add'l.: 3443 7372

CIK No: 0000808439

Subsidiaries: Limco-Airepair International, Inc., Piedmont Aviation Component Services, LLC

Officers: Shlomo Ostersetzer/Chmn., CEO, Shaul Menachem/61/CEO, Pres. - Limco, Piedmont Inc, Dov Zeelim/68/Vice Chmn., Pres., Yossi Rosenberg/42/VP - Economics, Israel Ofen/VP - Finance, Shraga Katz/VP - Operations, Jacob Danan/VP - Engineering, Marketing, Eran Frenkel/VP - Business Development, Avi Kahana/64/Mgr. - Import, Export Division, Sec., Jonathan Hulaty/Dir. - Marketing, Sales, Jacob Salomon/Dir. - Quality, Information Technology

Directors: Shlomo Ostersetzer/Chmn., CEO, Dov Zeelim/68/Vice Chmn., Pres., Meir Dvir/77/Dir., Yaacov Fish/61/Dir., Ishay Davidi/46/Dir., Gillon Beck/46/Dir., Yechiel Gutman/62/Dir., Michael Shevi/72/Dir., Rami Daniel/42/Dir.

Owners: Insiders/4.68%, Yaacov Fish, TAT Industries Ltd./47.80%, Meir Dvir, Ta-Top/14.60%, Shlomo Ostersetzer/3.81%, Dov Zeelim

Financial Data: *Fiscal Year End:*12/31 *Latest Annual Data:* 12/31/2006

Year	Sales	Net Income
2006	$77,533,000	$6,066,000
2005	$49,193,000	$3,529,000
2004	$33,243,000	$3,739,000

Curr. Assets:	$47,977,000	Curr. Liab.:	$18,234,000	P/E Ratio:	17.80
Plant, Equip.:	$7,235,000	Total Liab.:	$26,517,000	Indic. Yr. Divd.:	NA
Total Assets:	$66,237,000	Net Worth:	$39,720,000	Debt/ Equity:	NA

Tata Motors Ltd

Bombay House, 24, Homi Mody St., 3rd Fl., Nanavati Mahalaya, Mumbai, Maharashtra, 400001; *PH:* 91-22-6665 7219; *Fax:* 91-22-6665 7260; *http://* www.tatamotors.com

General - Incorporation	India	Stock - Price on:12/24/2007	NA
Employees	29,606	Stock Exchange	NYSE
Auditor	Deloitte Haskins & Sells	Ticker Symbol	TTM
Stk Agt	TSR Darashaw Ltd	Outstanding Shares	NA
Counsel	Mr. Naik	E.P.S.	$1.44
DUNS No.	86-218-7622	Shareholders	NA

Business: The groups principle activity is to provide automobile products consisting of all types of commercial and passenger vehicles. The groups products line include passenger car, trucks and buses. The group operates from United States.

Primary SIC and add'l.: 3713

CIK No: 0000926042

Subsidiaries: Concorde Motors (India) Ltd., HV Axles Ltd., HV Transmissions Ltd, Sheba Properties Ltd., TAL Manufacturing Solutions Ltd., Tata AutoComp Systems Ltd. and its 7 subsidiaries, Tata Daewoo Commercial Vehicle Co. Ltd, Tata Motors European Technical Centre plc, Tata Precision Industries Pte. Ltd Singapore and its subsidiary, Tata Technologies Ltd. and its 20 subsidiaries, Telco Construction Equipment Co. Ltd.

Officers: Zackria Sait/VP - Technical Services, Akshaykumar Mankad/Head - Car Plant, P. Y. Gurav/VP - Corporate Finance, Accounting, Taxation, S. J. Tambe/VP - Human Resources, Ravi Kant/Dir., MD, Rajiv Dube/Pres. - Passenger Cars, C. Ramakrishnan/CFO, H. K. Sethna/Company Sec., Debasis Ray/Head - Corporate Communications, R. S. Thakur/VP - Finance, S. Krishnan/VP - Commercial, Pcbu

Directors: Ratan N. Tata/Chmn., S. M. Palia/Dir., Ravi Kant/Dir., MD, N. A. Soonawala/Dir., Nusli N. Wadia/Dir., Jamshed J. Irani/Dir., V. R. Mehta/Dir., R. Gopalakrishnan/Dir., Prakash M. Telang/Dir.

Owners: Tata Industries Limited/2.01%, J.J. Irani, Tata Steel Ltd./8.62%, Life Insurance Corporation of India Ltd./6.10%, R. Gopalakrishnan, Ratan N. Tata, Citibank N.A., as Depositary/10.97%, The New India Assurance Company Limited/1.38%, S. M. Palia, C. Ramakrishnan, HSBC Global Investment Funds/1.82%, V.R. Mehta, P. M. Telang, Tata Sons Limited and subsidiaries/22.05%, DaimlerChrysler AG/6.64% *(16 Owners included in Index)*

Financial Data: *Fiscal Year End:*03/31 *Latest Annual Data:* 03/31/2007

Year	Sales	Net Income
2007	$7,692,000,000	$420,300,000
2006	$5,409,500,000	$337,400,000
2005	$4,548,100,000	$304,000,000

Curr. Assets:	$2,643,500,000	Curr. Liab.:	$2,802,400,000		
Plant, Equip.:	$1,476,800,000	Total Liab.:	$4,168,200,000	Indic. Yr. Divd.:	$0.370
Total Assets:	$6,288,100,000	Net Worth:	$2,119,900,000	Debt/ Equity:	NA

Tatonka Oil and Gas Inc

950 Seventeenth St., Ste. 2300, Denver, CO, 80202; *PH:* 1-303-476-4100; *Fax:* 1-303-476-4101; *http://* www.tatonkaoilandgas.com; *Email:* info@tatonkaong.com

General - Incorporation	CO	Stock - Price on:12/24/2007	NA
Employees	10	Stock Exchange	OTC
Auditor	Utah's/Madsen & Associates, CPAs Inc	Ticker Symbol	TTKA
Stk Agt	National Stock Transfer, Inc.	Outstanding Shares	NA
Counsel	NA	E.P.S.	-$0.08
DUNS No.	NA	Shareholders	NA

Business: The groups principal activity is an independent oil and gas company focused on the exploration and development of unconventional oil and gas resources. The group plan to drill for and extract Methane gas from Coalbeds, known as Coalbed Methane, and to drill for and extract oil from fractured shales. The group operates from the United States and Canada.

Primary SIC and add'l.: 1000

CIK No: 0001220819

Officers: Dirck Tromp/CEO, Pres., Dave Weisgerber/VP - Operations, Paul Stroud/COO, Keith Reeves/VP - Geology, Paul Slevin/CFO

Directors: Brian Hughes/Chmn., Anthony Yeats/Dir., Brent Petterson/46/Dir., Scott J. Zimmerman/Dir.

Owners: Brent Petterson/7.27%, Brian Hughes/27.27%, LMA Hughes LLP/27.27%, Insiders/34.55%

Financial Data: *Fiscal Year End:*10/31 *Latest Annual Data:* 10/31/2006

Year	Sales	Net Income
2006	$23,000	-$54,000
2005	$0	-$24,000

Curr. Assets:	$4,441,000	Curr. Liab.:	$1,388,000		
Plant, Equip.:	$1,977,000	Total Liab.:	$1,388,000	Indic. Yr. Divd.:	NA
Total Assets:	$13,390,000	Net Worth:	$12,002,000	Debt/ Equity:	NA

Taubman Centers Inc

200 E Long Lake Rd., Ste. 300, Bloomfield Hills, MI, 48303; *PH:* 1-248-258-6800; *Fax:* 1-248-258-7596; *http://* www.taubman.com

General - Incorporation	MI	Stock - Price on:12/24/2007	$52.33
Employees	547	Stock Exchange	NYSE
Auditor	KPMG LLP	Ticker Symbol	TCO
Stk Agt	Mellon Investor Services LLC	Outstanding Shares	53,600,000
Counsel	NA	E.P.S.	$0.83
DUNS No.	NA	Shareholders	NA

Business: The groups principle activities include owning, developing, acquiring and operating regional shopping centers. The group operates from the United States.

Primary SIC and add'l.: 6798

CIK No: 0000890319

Subsidiaries: Beverly Associates L.P. 1, Beverly Partners 1, Inc., Biltmore Holdings Associates 1 LLC, Biltmore Holdings Associates 2 LLC, Cherry Creek Holdings LLC, Dolphin Mall Associates LLC, Fairlane Town Center LLC, Great Lakes Crossing, L.L.C., International Plaza Holding Company, LLC, La Cienega Partners Limited Partnership, Lakeside/Novi Land Partnership LLC, LCA Holdings, LLC, MacArthur Holdings, Inc., MacArthur Shopping Center LLC, Mall Financing, Inc. 90 Subsidiaries included in the Index

Officers: Robert S. Taubman/Chmn., CEO, Pres./$3,887,893.00, Lisa A. Payne/Vice Chmn., CFO/$2,557,146.00, Barbara Baker/VP - Investor Relations, William S. Taubman/COO/$2,452,263.00, Morgan Parker/Pres. - Taubman Asia, Esther R. Blum/Sr. VP, Controller, Chief Accounting Officer, Steven J. Kieras/Sr. VP - Development/$1,092,472.00, David T. Weinert/Sr. VP - Leasing/$1,234,822.00, Denise Anton/Sr. VP - Center Operations, Robert R. Reese/Sr. VP, Chief Administrative Officer, Karen MacDonald/Dir. - Communications, Emily Dewolfe/Interactive Marketing Mgr., Steven E. Eder/Sr. VP, Treasurer, Chris B. Heaphy/Sr. VP, General Counsel, Sec.

Directors: Robert S. Taubman/Chmn., CEO, Pres., Lisa A. Payne/Vice Chmn., CFO, William U. Parfet/Dir., Graham T. Allison/Dir., Jerome A. Chazen/Dir., Craig M. Hatkoff/Dir., Peter Karmanos/Dir.

Owners: The Vanguard Group, Inc./4.10%, Graham T. Allison, Alfred A. Taubman/28.30%, Jerome A. Chazen, William U. Parfet, Craig M. Hatkoff, David T. Weinert, Adelante Capital Management, LLC/3.30%, Robert S. Taubman/3.50%, Insiders/4.10%, William S. Taubman/2.40%, Lisa A. Payne, LaSalle Investment Management, Inc./4.80%, Stephen J. Kieras, ING Groep N.V/4.90% (16 Owners included in Index)

Financial Data: Fiscal Year End:12/31 Latest Annual Data: 12/31/2006

Year	Sales	Net Income
2006	$579,284,000	$45,117,000
2005	$473,438,000	$71,735,000
2004	$431,453,000	$12,378,000

Curr. Assets:	$65,376,000	Curr. Liab.:	$267,281,000	P/E Ratio:	9.09
Plant, Equip.:	$2,576,738,000	Total Liab.:	$2,717,980,000	Indic. Yr. Divd.:	$1.660
Total Assets:	$2,826,622,000	Net Worth:	$108,642,000	Debt/ Equity:	NA

Tayco Developments Inc

90 Taylor Dr., North Tonawanda, NY, 14120; **PH:** 1-716-694-0877; **http://** www.taylordevices.com; **Email:** info@tayco.com

General - Incorporation	NY	Stock- Price on:12/24/2007	$3.75
Employees	NA	Stock Exchange	OTC
Auditor	Lumsden & McCormick LLP	Ticker Symbol	TYCO
Stk Agt	Taylor Devices Inc	Outstanding Shares	NA
Counsel	NA	E.P.S.	NA
DUNS No.	NA	Shareholders	NA

Business: The group's principal activity is to provide research, development and licensing services to its affiliate, taylor devices, inc. These services are provided for the manufacture of shock and vibration isolators, energy storage and shock absorption components for vehicles, machinery and equipment. In addition, the group has licensed its affiliate to manufacture and market certain of its patented products that are used in the defense, aerospace and commercial industries.

Primary SIC and add'l.: 8731 6794

CIK No: 0000894952

Officers: Douglas P. Taylor/CEO

Financial Data: Fiscal Year End:06/30 Latest Annual Data: 5/31/2004

Year	Sales	Net Income
2004	$624,000	$94,000
2003	$526,000	$187,000
2002	$622,000	$257,000

Curr. Assets:	$121,000	Curr. Liab.:	$14,000		
Plant, Equip.:	NA	Total Liab.:	$14,000	Indic. Yr. Divd.:	NA
Total Assets:	$3,418,000	Net Worth:	$3,404,000	Debt/ Equity:	NA

Taylor Calvin B Bankshares Inc

24 N Main St., Berlin, MD, 21811; **PH:** 1-410-641-1700; **Fax:** 1-410-641-0543; **http://** www.taylorbank.com; **Email:** taylorbk@dmv.com

General - Incorporation	MD	Stock- Price on:12/24/2007	$38.5
Employees	98	Stock Exchange	OTC
Auditor	Rowles & Company, LLP	Ticker Symbol	TYCB
Stk Agt	American Stock Transfer & Trust Co.	Outstanding Shares	3,140,000
Counsel	NA	E.P.S.	$2.38
DUNS No.	NA	Shareholders	NA

Business: The groups principal activity is engaged in a general commercial and retail banking business. Services of the group include deposit services including checking, NOW, Money Market, and savings accounts, and time deposits including certificates of deposit. The customers of the group include serving individuals, small to medium sized businesses, professional organizations, and governmental units. The group operates from the United States. In the year 2006, the groups total assets were $375,232.

Primary SIC and add'l.: 6022

CIK No: 0001003986

Subsidiaries: Calvin B. Taylor Banking Company

Officers: Raymond M. Thompson/45/Dir., CEO, Pres., William H. Mitchell/58/Dir., VP, Jennifer Hawkins/Treasurer

Directors: Raymond M. Thompson/45/Dir., CEO, Pres., Reese F. Cropper/66/Chmn., William H. Mitchell/58/Dir., VP, James R. Bergey/53/Dir., Todd E. Burbage/35/Dir., Charlotte K. Cathell/57/Dir., John H. Burbage/65/Dir., Joseph E. Moore/65/Dir., Bruce D. Rogers/51/Dir., Gerald T. Mason/60/Dir., Hale Harrison/60/Dir., Michael L. Quillin/68/Dir., Reese F. Cropper/47/Dir.

Owners: Michael L. Quillin/1.03%, John H. Burbage/6.88%, Reese F. Cropper/5.43%, Reese F. Cropper, Raymond M. Thompson, Todd E. Burbage, Joseph E. Moore, Bruce D. Rogers, Kenneth D. Bates, Gerald T. Mason, William H. Mitchell, James R. Bergey, Mary E. Humphreys/6.24%, Charlotte K. Cathell, Jennifer G. Hawkins (17 Owners included in Index)

Financial Data: Fiscal Year End:12/31 Latest Annual Data: 12/31/2006

Year	Sales	Net Income
2006	$22,134,000	$7,400,000
2005	$19,481,000	$6,798,000
2004	$17,002,000	$5,613,000

Curr. Assets:	$49,504,000	Curr. Liab.:	$296,289,000		
Plant, Equip.:	$6,563,000	Total Liab.:	$297,363,000	Indic. Yr. Divd.:	$0.800
Total Assets:	$367,532,000	Net Worth:	$70,170,000	Debt/ Equity:	NA

Taylor Capital Group Inc

350 E Dundee Rd. , Wheeling, IL, 60090; **PH:** 1-847-653-7978; **http://** www.taylorcapitalgroup.com

General - Incorporation	DE	Stock- Price on:12/24/2007	$28.39
Employees	421	Stock Exchange	NDQ
Auditor	KPMG LLP	Ticker Symbol	NA
Stk Agt.	NA	Outstanding Shares	11,130,000
Counsel	Katten, Muchin, Zavis & Rosenman	E.P.S.	$3.91
DUNS No.	NA	Shareholders	NA

Business: The group's principal activity is to provide commercial banking services through its wholly owned subsidiary, cole taylor bank. The group also offers wealth management, community banking and trust products and services. The products and services include secured and un-secured commercial banking loans, checking, savings and money market accounts, time deposits, repurchase agreements, corporate cash management options, Internet balance reporting, automated clearing house products, lock-box processing and controlled disbursement accounts. The group operates 10 bank branches throughout the Chicago metropolitan area.

Primary SIC and add'l.: 6022 6712

CIK No: 0001025536

Subsidiaries: 1965 Milwaukee Ave. Building Corp., Cole Taylor Bank, Cole Taylor Deferred Exchange Corp., Cole Taylor Financial Services, Inc., Cole Taylor Insurance Services, Inc., CT Group, LLC Illinois limited liability company, CT Mortgage Company, Inc., TAYC Capital Trust I Delaware statutory trust, TAYC Capital Trust II Delaware statutory trust, TCGRE, Inc.

Owners: Shepherd G. Pryor, Mark L. Yeager, Louise OSullivan, Richard W. Tinberg, Ronald D. Emanuel, Melvin E. Pearl, Edward T. McGowan, Insiders, John F. Timmer, Ronald L. Bliwas, Taylor Voting Trust, Bank of America Corporation, Jeffrey W. Taylor, Daniel C. Stevens, Bruce W. Taylor (17 Owners included in Index)

Financial Data: Fiscal Year End:12/31 Latest Annual Data: 12/31/2006

Year	Sales	Net Income
2006	$237,265,000	$46,163,000
2005	$199,561,000	$31,771,000
2004	$158,872,000	$22,973,000

Curr. Assets:	$134,920,000	Curr. Liab.:	$2,679,549,000	P/E Ratio:	7.26
Plant, Equip.:	$15,211,000	Total Liab.:	$3,108,475,000	Indic. Yr. Divd.:	$0.400
Total Assets:	$3,379,667,000	Net Worth:	$271,192,000	Debt/ Equity:	1.3027

Taylor Devices Inc

90 Taylor Dr., North Tonawanda, NY, 14120; **PH:** 1-716-694-0800; **http://** www.taylordevices.com

General - Incorporation	NY	Stock- Price on:12/24/2007	$5.86
Employees	86	Stock Exchange	NDQ
Auditor	Lumsden & McCormick LLP	Ticker Symbol	TAYD
Stk Agt.	NA	Outstanding Shares	3,140,000
Counsel	NA	E.P.S.	$0.26
DUNS No.	00-210-5799	Shareholders	NA

Business: The group's principal activity is to design, develop, manufacture and market shock absorption, rate control and energy storage devices for use in various types of machinery, equipment and structures. The group has six major products: seismic dampers, fluidicshoks, crane and industrial buffers, self-adjusting shock absorbers, liquid die springs and vibration dampers. Seismic dampers are designed to ameliorate the effects of earthquake tremors on structures. Fluidicshoks are small, extremely compact shock absorbers for use in defense, aerospace and commercial industry. Crane and industrial buffers are used for industrial application on cranes, ships, railroad cars etc. Self-adjusting shock absorbers are designed for high cycle application primarily in heavy industry. Liquid die springs are used to manufacture of tools and dies. Vibration dampers are used in the aerospace and defense industries. Products are sold to customers in domestic and foreign markets.

Primary SIC and add'l.: 3569

CIK No: 0000096536

Subsidiaries: Tayco Developments, Inc., Tayco Realty Corporation

Officers: Douglas P. Taylor/CEO, Pres., D. Taylor/Chmn., Pres., J. Dragonette/Contact - Technical Literature, Vibration, Shock, Damping, Isolation, C. D. Huang/Contact - Technical Literature, Vibration, Shock, Damping, Isolation, V. Wan/Contact - Technical Literature, Vibration, Shock, Damping, Isolation, Mark V. McDonough/48/CFO, Treasurer/$155,282.00, David Lee/Contact - West Coast Division, T. Tanner/Contact - Technical Literature, Vibration, Shock, Damping, Isolation, B. Breukelman/Contact - Technical Literature, Vibration, Shock, Damping, Isolation, Richard G. Hill/Contact - Technical Literature, Vibration, Shock, Damping, Isolation/$229,994.00, L. Determan/Contact - Technical Literature, Vibration, Shock, Damping, Isolation, A. Gilani/Contact - Technical Literature, M. Gemmill/Contact - Technical Literature, Vibration, Shock, Damping, Isolation, K. Lindorfer/Contact - Technical Literature, Vibration, Shock, Damping, Isolation, Kit Miyamoto/Contact - Technical Literature, Vibration, Shock, Damping, Isolation (52 Officers included in Index)

Directors: D. Taylor/Chmn., Pres., Randall L. Clark/Dir., Reginald B. Newman/70/Dir.

Owners: Randall L. Clark/1.00%, Richard G. Hill/2.30%, Reginald B. Newman, Tayco Developments, Inc./22.20%, Insiders/5.40%, John Burgess/0.20%, Douglas P. Taylor/1.30%

Financial Data: Fiscal Year End:05/31 Latest Annual Data: 5/31/2006

Year	Sales	Net Income
2006	$14,751,000	$486,000
2005	$11,216,000	$202,000
2004	$13,021,000	-$59,000

Curr. Assets:	$12,816,000	Curr. Liab.:	$6,050,000	P/E Ratio:	25.48
Plant, Equip.:	$3,962,000	Total Liab.:	$7,548,000	Indic. Yr. Divd.:	NA
Total Assets:	$17,385,000	Net Worth:	$9,836,000	Debt/ Equity:	0.0171

TB Wood's Corp

440 N Fifth Ave, Chambersburg, PA, 17201; **PH:** 1-717-264-7161; **http://** www.tbwoods.com

General - Incorporation .... DE
Employees 830
Auditor .... Grant Thornton LLP
Stk Agt...... American Stock Transfer & Trust Co.
Counsel .... Dechert, Price & Rhoads
DUNS No. 00-301-7951

Stock- Price on:12/24/2007 .... NA
Stock Exchange .... NA
Ticker Symbol .... NA
Outstanding Shares .... NA
E.P.S .... NA
Shareholders .... NA

Business: The group's principal activity is to design, manufacture and market industrial power transmission products. The group classifies the products into two segments: mechanical business and electronics business. The mechanical business segment includes belted drives, couplings, gear motors and gearboxes. The electronics business segment includes electronic drives and electric drive systems. Products of these segments are sold to distributors, original equipment manufacturers, and end users for manufacturing and commercial applications. The group operates 11 manufacturing facilities in the United States, Mexico, Germany, Italy and India. The group has network of more than 1,000 select independent and multi-branch distributors with over 3,000 locations in North America.

Primary SIC and add'l.: 3699 3568 3566 4911

CIK No: 0001000227

Subsidiaries: Berges electronic GmbH, Industrial Blaju, S.A. de C.V., Plant Engineering Consultants, LLC, T.B. Wood's Canada Ltd, TB Wood's (India) Private Limited, TB Wood's Enterprises, Inc., TB Wood's Incorporated

Officers: Joseph C. Horvath/CFO, Tim Horn/Sales Correspondent, Michelle Hull/Sales Correspondent, Nicole Keefer/Sales Correspondent, Gwen Mooney/Sales Correspondent, Kimberly Miller/Sales Correspondent, Julia Richter/Sales Correspondent, Tammy Shaw/Sales Correspondent, Kris Wile/Inside Sales Order Editor, Tom Palamar/Inside Sales Mgr., Kerry Divelbiss/Sales Correspondent, Anthony J. Metz/41/VP - Human Resources, Lean

Directors: John G. Krediet/57/Chmn.

Owners: Larry McPherson, Steven A. Cohen/7.00%, Michael L. Hurt/1.80%, Insiders/5.50%, Gerald Ferris, Carl R. Christenson/1.70%, Edward L. Novotny, David A. Wall, Capital Research and Management Company/5.00%, Carlo J. Cannell/6.30%

TBC Corp

7111 Fairway Dr., Ste. 201, Palm Beach Gardens, FL, 33418; *PH:* 1-561-227-0955; *http://* www.tbccorp.com

General - Incorporation .... DE
Employees .... NA
Auditor .... PricewaterhouseCoopers LLP
Stk Agt............................ EquiServe Trust Co N.A
Counsel .... Thompson Hine LLP
DUNS No. 04-456-9531

Stock- Price on:12/24/2007 .... NA
Stock Exchange .... NA
Ticker Symbol .... NA
Outstanding Shares .... NA
E.P.S .... NA
Shareholders .... NA

Business: The group's principle activities are to market and distribute tires in the automotive replacement market. The group's wholesale business include sales of the group's proprietary cordovan(R), multi-mile(R), sigma(R) & vanderbilt(R) brand tires. The products of the group are marketed through a network of distributors who operate under written distributor agreements with the group. The group also distributes tires under other brands for automobile, truck, sport utility vehicle, farm, industrial, recreational and other applications. The group's retail business provide full service tire replacement including tire balancing, wheel alignment, extended service programs and warranties. The group also performs maintenance and mechanical services such as brake repairs, suspension system replacement, and oil changes.

Primary SIC and add'l.: 5531 5014

CIK No: 0000718449

Subsidiaries: Big O Tire of Idaho, Inc, Big O Tires, Inc., Carroll's, Inc., Merchant's, Incorporated, NTW Incorporated, TBC Brands, LLC, TBC Capital, LLC, TBC International Inc., TBC Private Brands of Texas LLC, TBC Private Brands, Inc, TBC Retail Enterprises,Inc, Tire Kingdom, Inc.

Officers: Lawrence C. Day/CEO, Pres., Orland M. Wolford/Pres., CEO - Tire Kingdom, Kenneth P. Dick/Pres., CEO - TBC Wholesale Division, John B. Adams/Pres., CEO - Big O Tires, Glenn J. Gravatt/Exec. VP - Purchasing

TBS International Ltd

612 E Grassy Sprain Rd., Yonkers, NY, 10710; *PH:* 1-914-961-1000; *Fax:* 1-914-961-2286; *http://* www.tbsship.com; *Email:* info@tbsship.com

General - Incorporation .... Bermuda
Employees 100
Auditor .... PricewaterhouseCoopers LLP
Stk Agt...... American Stock Transfer & Trust Co.
Counsel .... NA
DUNS No. .... NA

Stock- Price on:12/24/2007 .... $25.3
Stock Exchange .... NDQ
Ticker Symbol .... TBSI
Outstanding Shares 27,730,000
E.P.S $1.62
Shareholders .... NA

Business: The groups principle activity is to provide ocean transportation services. The groups services include Eastbound Liner Service, TBS Pacific Westbound, TBS Ocean Carriers and TBS Middle East Carriers. Specific customers of the group include Dangote Industry Limited, Nippon Yusen Kaisha and Honeywell International Inc. The group operates from Brazil, Japan, Chile, Peru, United Arab Emirates, Venezuela, Korea, China and other. The group's quarterly revenue for September 2007 was 92.40 millions of USD.

Primary SIC and add'l.: 4491 4449 4499 4412

CIK No: 0001065648

Subsidiaries: Albemarle Maritime Corp., Arden Maritime Corp., Argyle Maritime Corp., Asia-America Ocean Carriers Ltd., Avon Maritime Corp., Azalea Shipping & Chartering Inc., Bedford Maritime Corp., Beckman Shipping Corp., Birnam Maritime Corp., Brighton Maritime Corp., Bristol Maritime Corp., Chester Shipping Corp., Columbus Maritime Corp., Compass Chartering Corp., Cortland Navigation Corp. 61 Subsidiaries included in the Index

Officers: Joseph E. Royce/Chmn., CEO, Pres./$780,281.00, Gregg L. McNelis/Dir., Sr. Exec. VP, COO/$650,000.00, Lawrence A. Blatte/Sr. Exec. VP/$650,000.00, Ferdinand V. Lepere/CFO, Exec. VP/$600,514.00, James W. Bayley/Dir., VP, William J. Carr/VP, Treasurer, Nicolas Bornozis/Investor Relations, Media

Directors: Joseph E. Royce/Chmn., CEO, Pres., Gregg L. McNelis/Dir., Sr. Exec. VP, COO, James W. Bayley/Dir., VP, Randee E. Day/Dir., Peter S. Shaerf/Dir., William P. Harrington/Dir., James P. Cahill/Dir., Alexander Smigelski/Dir.

Owners: Lawrence A. Blatte/3.90%, Randee E. Day, Insiders/88.60%, Wachovia Corporation/7.90%, Alkiviades N. Meimaris/2.40%, Ferdinand V. Lepere, Treetops Holdings LLC/4.80%, Gregg L. McNelis/18.00%, Lawrence A. Blatte/1.50%, Insiders/34.50%, James W. Bayley/3.30%, Gregg L. McNelis/4.50%, Joseph E. Royce/25.00%, Treetops Holdings LLC/9.90%, James W. Bayley/5.90% *(18 Owners included in Index)*

Financial Data: **Fiscal Year End:**12/31 **Latest Annual Data:** 12/31/2006

Year	Sales	Net Income
2006	$253,586,000	$39,060,000
2005	$248,031,000	$53,274,000
2004	$208,807,000	$41,907,000

Curr. Assets:	$52,369,000	**Curr. Liab.:**	$56,186,000	**P/E Ratio:**	15.62
Plant, Equip.:	$336,869,000	**Total Liab.:**	$179,487,000	**Indic. Yr. Divd.:**	NA
Total Assets:	$403,091,000	**Net Worth:**	$223,604,000	**Debt/ Equity:**	0.4657

TBX Resources Inc

3030 Lbj Fwy., Ste 1320, LB 47, Dallas, TX, 75234; *PH:* 1-972-243-2610; *http://* www.tbxresources.com; *Email:* info@tbxresources.com

General - Incorporation .... TX
Employees .... NA
Auditor .... Turner, Stone & Co., LLP
Stk Agt .... Securities Transfer Corp
Counsel .... NA
DUNS No. .... NA

Stock- Price on:12/24/2007 .... $2.55
Stock Exchange .... OTC
Ticker Symbol .... TBXC
Outstanding Shares 3,910,000
E.P.S .... -$0.32
Shareholders .... NA

Business: The group's principal activity is to acquire and develop oil and gas properties. The group's mission is to be publicly traded, independent oil and gas and production company which can take full advantage of opportunities resulting from all the major oil companies' divestiture of domestic oil and gas properties. The group own or operate all the portion of 23 wells located in gregg, hopkins, franklin panola and wood counties, Texas. In order to finance future development and exploration activities, the group will sponsor or manage public or private partnerships depending upon the number, sizeand economic feasibility of the generated prospects. The group also acquired several wells and acreages in Oklahoma.

Primary SIC and add'l.: 1382

CIK No: 0001108645

Officers: Tim Burroughs/Founder, CEO, CFO, Pres., Sherri Cerotti/43/Sec., Treasurer, Clifton Kees/Assoc. Geologist, Harold O. Neff/Registered Professional Engineer, Ellis Randolph/Owner, Pres. - Creede Oil, Gas Company, De Wayne Pitt/Owner, Pres. - PAX Energy, Merlin Corporation, Dick Odonnell/VP - Investor Relations

Directors: Tim Burroughs/Founder, CEO, CFO, Pres., Ellis Randolph/Owner, Pres. - Creede Oil, Gas Company, De Wayne Pitt/Owner, Pres. - PAX Energy, Merlin Corporation, Jeffery Reynolds/50/Dir., Sam Warren/65/Dir.

Owners: Tim Burroughs Family Tr/13.13%, Sam Warren/1.31%, Tim Burroughs/9.41%, Insiders/27.13%, Bernard R. ODonnell/3.28%

Financial Data: **Fiscal Year End:**11/30 **Latest Annual Data:** 11/30/2006

Year	Sales	Net Income
2006	$906,000	-$1,129,000
2005	$1,170,000	-$418,000
2004	$1,064,000	-$832,000

Curr. Assets:	$32,000	**Curr. Liab.:**	$398,000		
Plant, Equip.:	$263,000	**Total Liab.:**	$657,000	**Indic. Yr. Divd.:**	NA
Total Assets:	$301,000	**Net Worth:**	-$355,000	**Debt/ Equity:**	NA

TC PipeLines LP

PO Box 799060, Dallas, TX, 75379; *PH:* 1-508-877-7046; *http://* www.tcpipelineslp.com; *Email:* investor_relations@tcpipelineslp.com

General - Incorporation .... DE
Employees .... NA
Auditor .... KPMG LLP
Stk Agt .... Chase Mellon Shareholder Services LLC
Counsel .... NA
DUNS No. .... NA

Stock- Price on:12/24/2007 .... $39.75
Stock Exchange .... NDQ
Ticker Symbol .... TCLP
Outstanding Shares 34,860,000
E.P.S $2.49
Shareholders .... NA

Business: The Group's principle activity is to transport natural gas. Customers served by the group include natural gas producers, marketers, industrial facilities, local distribution companies and electric power generating plants. Specific customers of the group include BP Canada Energy Marketing Corp and Cargill Inc. The group acquired Great Lakes Gas Transmission Limited Partnership in the year 2007 and Northern Border Pipeline Company in the year 2006. The group operates from the United States.

Primary SIC and add'l.: 4922 4922

CIK No: 0001075607

Subsidiaries: Northern Border Pipeline Company, TC GL Intermediate Limited Partnership, TC PipeLines Intermediate Limited Partnership, TC Tuscarora Intermediate Limited Partnership, Tuscarora Gas Transmission Company

Officers: Russell K. Girling/Chmn., CEO, Mark Zimmerman/Pres., Max Feldman/VP, Sean Brett/VP, Treasurer, Ronald L. Cook/VP - Taxation, Amy Leong/Controller, Donald J. Degrandis/Sec., Shela Shapiro/Media Contact

Directors: Russell K. Girling/Chmn., CEO, Steven D. Becker/Dir., Kristine Delkus/Dir., Jack F. Jenkins-Stark/Dir., Greg Lohnes/Dir., David L. Marshall/Dir., Walentin Mirosh/Dir., Ronald J. Turner/Dir.

Owners: TC Pipelines GP, Inc./5.80%, TransCan Northern Ltd./24.90%, David L. Marshall, Jack F. Jenkins-Stark

Financial Data: **Fiscal Year End:**12/31 **Latest Annual Data:** 12/31/2006

Year	Sales	Net Income
2006	$63,400,000	$44,700,000
2005	$53,200,000	$50,200,000
2004	$57,500,000	$55,100,000

Curr. Assets:	$6,500,000	**Curr. Liab.:**	$9,300,000	**P/E Ratio:**	15.96
Plant, Equip.:	$127,000,000	**Total Liab.:**	$473,900,000	**Indic. Yr. Divd.:**	$2.600
Total Assets:	$777,800,000	**Net Worth:**	$303,900,000	**Debt/ Equity:**	0.6395

TC X Calibur Inc

4685 S Highland Dr., Ste. 202, Salt Lake City, UT, 84117; *PH:* 1-801-278-9424; *http://* www.filmopticals.com

General - Incorporation	NV	**Stock**- Price on:12/24/2007	$0.3
Employees	NA	Stock Exchange	OTC
Auditor	Mantyla McReynolds LLC	Ticker Symbol	TCXC
Stk Agt	NA	Outstanding Shares	NA
Counsel	NA	E.P.S	$0.00
DUNS No.	NA	Shareholders	NA

Business: The group's principal activity is to provide a full range of special effects to producers of feature films, documentaries, short films, TV commercials and TV shows. The services offered by the group include digital effects, such as blue and green screen composition, wire removal, scratch and dust removal, and computer animation. The group also supplies computer animation camera services, creative services for credits and special effects for use in commercials, theatrical features, movies of the week and television productions. The group also specializes in 16mm to 35mm blow-ups for theatrical features. The products and services of the group are distributed directly to its clients.

Primary SIC and add'l.: 7819 6719

CIK No: 0000847015

Subsidiaries: Berliner Holdings, Inc, Film Opticals Investments Limited, Film Opticals of Canada Limited

Officers: Travis T. Jenson/35/Dir., Pres., Thomas J. Howells/35/Dir., Sec., Treasurer, Claus Voellmecke/Dir., Pres., Michael S. Smith/Dir., Sec., Treasurer

Directors: Travis T. Jenson/35/Dir., Pres., Harold T. Jenson/38/Dir., Thomas J. Howells/35/Dir., Sec., Treasurer, Claus Voellmecke/Dir., Pres., Michael S. Smith/Dir., Sec., Treasurer

Owners: Thomas J. Howells/13.00%, Jenson Services/29.00%, Duane S. Jenson/8.00%, Travis T. Jenson/25.00%

Financial Data: **Fiscal Year End:**12/31 **Latest Annual Data:** 12/31/2006

Year	Sales	Net Income
2006	NA	-$6,000
2005	NA	-$33,000
2004	NA	$223,000

Curr. Assets:	NA	**Curr. Liab.:**	NA		
Plant, Equip.:	NA	**Total Liab.:**	NA	**Indic. Yr. Divd.:**	NA
Total Assets:	NA	**Net Worth:**	NA	**Debt/ Equity:**	NA

TCF Financial Corp

200 Lake St. E, Wayzata, MN, 55391; ***PH:*** 1-612-661-6500; ***http://*** www.tcfbank.com

General - Incorporation	DE	**Stock**- Price on:12/24/2007	$28.5999
Employees	5,645	Stock Exchange	NYSE
Auditor	KPMG LLP	Ticker Symbol	TCB
Stk Agt	Computershare Trust Co	Outstanding Shares	129,320,000
Counsel	NA	E.P.S	$2.07
DUNS No.	16-196-3707	Shareholders	NA

Business: The group's principal activities are comprised of traditional and supermarket bank branches, campus banking, express teller(R) ATMs, visa(R) debit cards, commercial lending, small business banking, consumer lending, mortgage banking, leasing and equipment finance and investment, brokerage and insurance services. The group's products include commercial, small business, consumer and residential mortgage loans and deposit products, leasing and equipment finance, securities brokerage and investment and insurance services. The group emphasizes the "Totally Free" checking account as its anchor account, which provides opportunities to cross sell other convenience products and services and generate additional fee income. The products of the group such as commercial equipment loans and leases are offered in markets outside areas. At 31-Dec-03, the group had 401 retail banking branches.

Primary SIC and add'l.: 6021 6712

CIK No: 0000814184

Subsidiaries: Golf Course Properties, LLC, Great Lakes Mortgage LLC, Service Corporation II, TCF Agency Insurance Services, Inc., TCF Agency, Inc., TCF Equipment Finance, Inc., TCF Foundation, TCF Illinois Realty Investments, LLC, TCF Insurance Agency, Inc., TCF International Management Services, LLC, TCF International Operations, Inc., TCF Investments Management, Inc., TCF Investments, Inc., TCF Management Corporation, TCF Mortgage Corporation 20 Subsidiaries included in the Index

Officers: Lynn A. Nagorske/CEO/$1,021,895.00

Owners: Peter L. Scherer, Advisory Committee of TCF/5.80%, Lynn A. Nagorske/1.00%, Douglas A. Scovanner, Luella G. Goldberg, Insiders/8.20%, William A. Cooper/3.00%, Thomas A. Cusick, George G. Johnson, JPMorgan Chase & Co./5.20%, Rodney P. Burwell, Barry N. Winslow, William F. Bieber, Ralph Strangis, Neil W. Brown *(18 Owners included in Index)*

Financial Data: **Fiscal Year End:**12/31 **Latest Annual Data:** 12/31/2006

Year	Sales	Net Income
2006	$1,375,602,000	$244,943,000
2005	$1,210,352,000	$265,132,000
2004	$1,113,275,000	$254,993,000

Curr. Assets:	$348,980,000	**Curr. Liab.:**	$10,261,932,000	**P/E Ratio:**	13.65
Plant, Equip.:	$406,087,000	**Total Liab.:**	$13,636,360,000	**Indic. Yr. Divd.:**	NA
Total Assets:	$14,669,734,000	**Net Worth:**	$1,033,374,000	**Debt/ Equity:**	3.3633

TD Banknorth Inc

Formerly: Banknorth Group Inc ME

Two Portland Sq, Portland, ME, 04101; ***PH:*** 1-800-462-3666; ***http://*** www.peoplesheritage.com

General - Incorporation	ME	**Stock**- Price on:12/24/2007	NA
Employees	7,500	Stock Exchange	NA
Auditor	KPMG LLP	Ticker Symbol	NA
Stk Agt	American Stock Transfer & Trust Co.	Outstanding Shares	NA
Counsel	NA	E.P.S	NA
DUNS No.	00-694-9424	Shareholders	NA

Business: The group's principal activities are to accept deposits from the general public and use the deposits to originate loans secured by first mortgage liens on existing single-family residential real estate and existing multi-family residential and commercial real estate, construction loans, commercial business loans and leases and consumer loans. It also provide various mortgage banking services and investment management services. The other services provided by the group include equipment leasing, investment planning, securities brokerage and insurance brokerage activities. The group operates in four segments: community banking, insurance brokerage, investment banking and investment management. The group has 359 banking offices located in Maine, New Hampshire, Massachusetts, Vermont, New York and Connecticut. On 30-Apr-2004 the group acquired foxborough savings bank and ccbt financial companies inc.

Primary SIC and add'l.: 6712 6211 6021 6411

CIK No: 0000829750

Subsidiaries: Bancnorth Investment Planning Group, Inc., Banknorth Capital Trust I, Banknorth Capital Trust II, Banknorth Insurance Group, Banknorth Leasing Corp, Banknorth, NA, Cape Cod Capital Trust 1, Ipswich Statutory Trust I, Northgroup Asset Management Company, Northgroup Captive Insurance, Inc., Northgroup Realty, Inc., Peoples Heritage Capital Trust I

Officers: Robert B. Esau/CEO, Pres., Curt G. Ehler/Sr. VP, Retirement Group Mgr., Molly Dillon/Sr. VP, MD, Alicia A. Donahue/VP, Sr. Financial Consultant, Glenn S. Davis/Sr. VP, Chief Investment Strategist, Dir. - Fixed Income, Alan J. Day/VP, Sr. Portfolio Mgr., Dean D. Deltosta/VP, Business Development Officer, Brenda C. Deschenes/Assist. VP - Financial Advisor II, Andrea K. Francis/Financial Advisor, Lorrie L. Garcia/VP - Wealth Advisor, Laura F. Greene/VP - Regional Tax Advisor, Financial Planner, James W. Gribbons/Exec. VP, MD, Thomas E. Hobin/VP - Wealth Advisor, Tricia J. Hoppe/Tax Advisor, Martha A. Fezzie/VP - Financial Advisor, Trust Officer *(110 Officers included in Index)*

Directors: William J. Ryan/Chmn., Gerry S. Weidema/Dir., Dana S. Levenson/Dir., William E. Bennett/Dir., Edmund W. Clark/Dir., Robert G. Clarke/Dir., Peter G. Vigue/Dir., Bharat B. Masrani/Dir., Brian M. Flynn/Dir., Kevin P. Condron/Dir.

TDC

Noerregade 21, Copenhagen C, 900; ***PH:*** 4566637680; ***http://*** www.tdc.dk

General - Incorporation	Denmark	**Stock**- Price on:12/24/2007	NA
Employees	NA	Stock Exchange	NA
Auditor	PricewaterhouseCoopers LLP	Ticker Symbol	NA
Stk Agt	Bank of New York	Outstanding Shares	NA
Counsel	NA	E.P.S	NA
DUNS No.	30-611-6914	Shareholders	NA

Business: The group's principal activity is to provide domestic and international telephone services. The group operates through the following divisions: tele Denmark: telephony services, data communications, leased lines and broadband and communications solutions; mobile: mobile telephony and mobile Internet services; directories: directory and operator services; cable TV: supply and installation of cable TV and telecommunications services; Internet: provision of isp services, Web hosting and Internet security; services: provision of cost-effective solutions in billing, procurement, logistics, it, accounting, payroll administration, risk management and security.

Primary SIC and add'l.: 4841 4812 7389 4813 7379

CIK No: 0000920602

Subsidiaries: TDC Mobil A/S and Telmore

Officers: Jens Alder/CEO, Pres., Jesper Theill Eriksen/40/Sr. Exec. VP - Corporate Human Resources, Chief - Staff Pres., International Holdings, Eigil Waagstein/60/Sr. VP - Corporate Financial Services, TDC A, S, Pernille Erenbjerg/41/Exec. VP - Corporate Accounting, Tax, TDC A, S, Anne Romer/42/Sr. VP, Chief Internal Auditor - TDC A, S, Henriette Wadum Iversen/Chief Treasury Analyst, Mgr. - Investor Relations, Jakob D De La Cour/Board Sec., Flemming Jacobsen/38/Sr. VP - Group Treasury, TDC A, S, Eva Berneke/39/Sr. Exec. VP, Chief Strategy Officer, Mads Mathias Middelboe/48/Sr. Exec. VP - TDC A - S, Pres. Mobile Nordic, Klaus Pedersen/41/Sr. Ececutive VP - TDC A - S, Pres. Business Nordic, Carsten Dilling/46/Sr. Exec. VP - tdc A - S, Pres. Fixnet Nordic, Dan Kronholm/49/Sr. VP - Supply Nordic, TDC A, S, Heine Stenholt Winther/VP - Billing, TDC A, S, Hans Munk Nielsen/62/Sr. Exec. VP, CFO *(18 Officers included in Index)*

Directors: Vagn Ove Sorensen/49/Vice Chmn., Henning Dyremose/63/Chmn., Jan Bardino/56/Dir., Bo Magnussen/61/Dir., Kurt Bjorklund/39/Dir., Lawrence H. Guffey/40/Dir., Oliver Haarmann/41/Dir., Gustavo Schwed/46/Dir., Richard Charles Wilson/43/Dir., Leif Hartmann/65/Dir., Steen Jacobsen/59/Dir.

TDK Corp

901 Franklin Ave., Garden City, NY, 11530; ***PH:*** 1-516-535-2600; ***Fax:*** 1-516-294-8318; ***http://*** www.tdk.co.jp

General - Incorporation	Japan	**Stock**- Price on:12/24/2007	$93.9
Employees	51,614	Stock Exchange	NYSE
Auditor	KPMG Azsa & Co	Ticker Symbol	TDK
Stk Agt	Citibank Shareholder Services	Outstanding Shares	132,480,000
Counsel	NA	E.P.S	$5.23
DUNS No.	69-055-1346	Shareholders	NA

Business: The group's principal activity is to manufacture recording media, electronic materials and components. The group operates through two segments: electronic materials and components and recording media and systems. Electronic materials and components provide multiplayer ceramic chip capacitors, ferrite cores for coils and transformers, emc components, sensors, ic's for modems and LAN/wan applications and rare-earth magnets. Also includes coils, emc components, transformers, high-frequency components, sensors, gmr heads for hard disk drives, heads for high-capacity floppy disk drives and optical pickups. Recording media systems provide audiotapes, CD-r's, mini discs (mds), dvds and tape-based data storage media for computers. The group operates in Japan, America, Europe, Asia and other parts of the world.

Primary SIC and add'l.: 3679 3695

CIK No: 0000203383

Subsidiaries: Allied Focus Industry Ltd., Densei-Lambda K.K., Headway Technologies, Inc., Lambda Far East Ltd., Lambda Holdings Inc., Media Technology Corporation, SAE Magnetics (H.K.) Ltd., TDK (Thailand) Co., Ltd., TDK Core Co., Ltd., TDK Corporation of America, TDK Dalian Corporation, TDK Electronics Corporation, TDK Electronics Europe GmbH, TDK Europe S.A., TDK Fujitsu Philippines Corporation 26 Subsidiaries included in the Index

Officers: Hajime Sawabe/Chmn., CEO, Seiji Enami/Dir., Sr. VP, Shinichi Araya/Sr. VP, Noboru Hara/Corporate Auditor, Yukio Yanase/Outside Corporate Auditor, Masaaki Miyoshi/Corporate Auditor, Masatoshi Shikanai/Corp. Officer, Kenichiro Fujihara/Corp. Officer, Shinya Yoshihara/Corp. Officer, Kaoru Matsumoto/Corporate Auditor, Takehiro Kamigama/Dir., COO, Pres., Ryoichi Ohno/Outside Corporate Auditor, Shinji Yoko/Dir., Sr. VP, Shiro Nomi/Sr. VP, Jiro Iwasaki/Dir., Exec. VP *(21 Officers included in Index)*

Directors: Hajime Sawabe/Chmn., CEO, Minoru Takahashi/Dir., Sr. VP, Seiji Enami/Dir., Sr. VP, Yasuhiro Hagihara/Dir., Takehiro Kamigama/Dir., COO, Pres., Shinji Yoko/Dir., Sr. VP, Jiro Iwasaki/Dir., Exec. VP

Owners: Shunji Itakura, Insiders, Michinori Katayama, Takehiro Kamigama, Masaaki Miyoshi, Noboru Hara, Takeshi Nomura, Seiji Enami, TDK Employees Shareholding Association/0.35%, Jiro Iwasaki, Yasuhiro Hagihara, Takaya Ishigaki, Shiro Nomi, Hajime Sawabe, Masatoshi Shikanai *(18 Owners included in Index)*

Financial Data: **Fiscal Year End:**03/31 **Latest Annual Data:** 3/31/2006

Year	Sales	Net Income
2006	$6,796,410,000	$376,932,000
2005	$6,148,159,000	$311,215,000
2004	$6,215,679,000	$397,179,000

Curr. Assets:	$4,844,043,000	**Curr. Liab.:**	$1,449,761,000	**P/E Ratio:**	17.80
Plant, Equip.:	$2,082,607,000	**Total Liab.:**	$1,889,607,000	**Indic. Yr. Divd.:**	$0.400
Total Assets:	$7,893,188,000	**Net Worth:**	$6,003,581,000	**Debt/ Equity:**	NA

Team Financial Inc

8 W Peoria, Ste. 200, Paola, KS, 66071; ***PH:*** 1-913-294-9667; ***http://*** www.teamfinancialinc.com

General - Incorporation	KS	**Stock**- Price on:12/24/2007	$15.4
Employees	235	Stock Exchange	NDQ
Auditor	KPMG LLP	Ticker Symbol	NA
Stk Agt	Computershare Trust Co	Outstanding Shares	3,650,000
Counsel	Hartley Nicholson & Hartley P.A	E.P.S	$1.33
DUNS No.	NA	Shareholders	NA

Business: The group's principal activities are to provide community banking and financial services. The lending services include multi-family real estate loans, commercial real estate loans, home equity lines of credit, auto loans, recreational vehicle, commercial loans to businesses, construction lending and agricultural lending. The deposit products provided by the group include checking and now accounts for personal and business accounts, savings accounts, money market accounts, certificate of deposits and individual retirement accounts. The group also provides federal tax depository services, merchant bankcard services, electronic fund transfer, debit and credit cards and telephone banking services. The group operates through 17 locations in the Kansas city metropolitan area, southeastern Kansas, western Missouri, the omaha, Nebraska metropolitan area and in Colorado springs, Colorado.

Primary SIC and add'l.: 6712 6021

CIK No: 0001082484

Subsidiaries: Colorado National Bank, Post Bancorp, Inc., TBNA Holdings, LLC, Tbna Reit, LLC, Team Financial Acquisition Subsidiary, Inc., Team Financial Capital Trust 1, TeamBank, N.A. Asset Corporation, TeamBank, National Association

Officers: Robert J. Weatherbie/Chmn., CEO/$692,916.00, David Alley/CEO, Pres. - Colorado National Bank, Lois Rausch/Corp. Sec., Sandra J. Moll/COO, Exec. VP/$231,091.00, Michael L. Gibson/Dir., Pres. - Corporate Development/$383,502.00, Carolyn S. Jacobs/Dir., Corporate Treasurer, Richard J. Tremblay/CFO/$119,911.00

Directors: Robert J. Weatherbie/Chmn., CEO, Michael L. Gibson/Dir., Pres. - Corporate Development, Keith B. Edquist/Dir., Carolyn S. Jacobs/Dir., Corporate Treasurer, Denis A. Kurtenbach/Dir., Harold G. Sevy/Dir., Gregory D. Sigman/Dir., Kenneth L. Smith/Dir., Jerry Wiesner/Dir.

Owners: Collective Reporting Group/11.20%, Denis A. Kurtenbach, Insiders/16.40%, Carolyn S. Jacobs/3.20%, Keith B. Edquist/2.80%, Connie Hart, Employee Stock Ownership Plan/23.70%, Michael L. Gibson/6.90%, Kenneth L. Smith, Sandra J. Moll/1.10%, Richard J. Tremblay, Gregory D. Sigman, Harold G. Sevy, Robert J. Weatherbie/8.70%

Financial Data: ***Fiscal Year End:***12/31 ***Latest Annual Data:*** 03/31/2007

Year	Sales	Net Income
2007	NA	NA
2006	$52,508,000	$3,985,000
2005	$44,316,000	$3,970,000

Curr. Assets:	$42,708,000	**Curr. Liab.:**	$683,230,000		
Plant, Equip.:	$18,445,000	**Total Liab.:**	$705,911,000	**Indic. Yr. Divd.:**	$0.320
Total Assets:	$756,428,000	**Net Worth:**	$50,517,000	**Debt/ Equity:**	0.4429

Team Inc

PO Box 123, Alvin, TX, 77512; ; ***http://*** www.teamindustrialservices.com

General - Incorporation	TX	**Stock**- Price on:12/24/2007	NA
Employees	2,700	Stock Exchange	AMEX
Auditor	KPMG LLP	Ticker Symbol	TMI
Stk Agt	Registrar & Transfer Co	Outstanding Shares	NA
Counsel	Chamberlain, Hrdlicka, White Et Al	E.P.S	$0.92
DUNS No.	14-811-9779	Shareholders	NA

Business: The group's principle activity is to provide a wide range of industrial repair services. The group also designs, manufactures, sells and rents portable machine tools. Industrial services consist of leak repair, hot tapping, emissions control monitoring, on-site field machining and inspection. Equipment sales and rental segment offers boring bars, pipe beveling tools, key mills, portable flange facers and portable lathes. Leak repair services includes on-stream repairs of leaks in pipes, valves, flanges and other parts of piping system. Hot tapping services include hot tapping and line stop services. Emission control consists of leak detection, fugitive emission identification, monitoring and record emission. The customers of the group include chemical, petrochemical, refining, pulp and paper, power, steel and other industries. The group's quarterly revenue for Sep '07 was 59.15 millions of USD.

Primary SIC and add'l.: 4213 8711 8742

CIK No: 0000318833

Subsidiaries: Global Heat (1988), Inc., Global Heat U.K. Ltd., Team Cooperheat-MQS Canada, Inc., Team Cooperheat-MQS de Venezuela, C.V. de S.A., Team Cooperheat-MQS Trinidad, Ltd., Team Facilities& Services, L.P., Team Industrial Services Asia (PTE) Ltd., Team Industrial Services International, Inc., Team Industrial Services of Canada, ULC, Team Industrial Services Trinidad, Ltd., Team Industrial Services, Inc., Team Investment, Inc., Teaminc. Europe

Officers: Ted W. Owen/56/Sr. VP, CFO, Treasurer/$547,680.00, John P. Kearns/Sr. VP/$487,963.00, Gregory T. Sangalis/52/Sr. VP - Law, Administration, Sec./$526,292.00, David C. Palmore/Sr. VP, Art Victorson/Sr. VP, Pete W. Wallace/Sr. VP

Directors: Louis A. Waters/70/Dir., Jack M. Johnson/70/Dir., Emmett J. Lescroart/57/Dir., Vincent D. Foster/51/Dir., Robert A. Peiser/60/Dir.

Owners: Philip J. Hawk/3.80%, FMR Corp./11.00%, Gregory T. Sangalis, Vincent D. Foster, Insiders/14.10%, Sidney B. Williams/1.50%, Kenneth M. Tholan, Ted W. Owen, Louis A. Waters/3.90%, Jack M. Johnson/1.10%, Emmett J. Lescroart/1.20%, Robert A. Peiser, John P. Kearns

Financial Data: ***Fiscal Year End:***05/31 ***Latest Annual Data:*** 5/31/2006

Year	Sales	Net Income
2006	$259,838,000	$10,636,000
2005	$209,045,000	$4,788,000
2004	$107,669,000	$5,776,000

Curr. Assets:	$84,831,000	**Curr. Liab.:**	$35,612,000		
Plant, Equip.:	$26,448,000	**Total Liab.:**	$76,086,000	**Indic. Yr. Divd.:**	NA
Total Assets:	$139,971,000	**Net Worth:**	$63,885,000	**Debt/ Equity:**	NA

Teamstaff Inc

300 Atrium Dr., South Plainfield, NJ, 08873; ***PH:*** 1-866-352-5304; ***http://*** www.teamstaff.com

General - Incorporation	NJ	**Stock**- Price on:12/24/2007	$0.95
Employees	122	Stock Exchange	NDQ
Auditor	Lazar Levine & Felix LLP	Ticker Symbol	TSTF
Stk Agt	Versus Net	Outstanding Shares	19,240,000
Counsel	Goldstein & Digioia	E.P.S	NA
DUNS No.	06-867-8788	Shareholders	NA

Business: The group's principal activity is to provide employment related services. These services are provided in two segments. The medical staffing segment provides temporary and permanent staffing for medical imaging professionals and nurses with hospitals, clinics and therapy centers. The payroll services segment provides payroll services such as preparation of payroll checks, filing of payroll taxes, government reports, w-2's and remote processing to its clients in the construction industry. The group disposed its professional employer organization segment in fiscal 2003.

Primary SIC and add'l.: 8741 7361

CIK No: 0000785557

Subsidiaries: BrightLane.com, Inc., Digital Insurance Services, Inc., DSI Staff ConnXions Northeast, Inc., DSI Staff ConnXions Southwest, Inc., Employer Support Services, Inc., HR2, Inc., RS Staffing Services, Inc., TeamStaff I, Inc., TeamStaff II, Inc., TeamStaff III, Inc., TeamStaff Insurance Services, Inc., TeamStaff IV, Inc., TeamStaff IX, Inc., TeamStaff Rx, Inc., TeamStaff Solutions, Inc. 18 Subsidiaries included in the Index

Officers: Rick J. Filippelli/Dir., CEO, CFO, Pres., Gregory J. Haygood/CTO, Cheryl Presuto/Controller, Rick Wasserman/Dir. - Financial Management Consultant

Directors: Rick J. Filippelli/Dir., CEO, CFO, Pres., Karl W. Dieckmann/Vice Chmn., Stephen T. Johnson/Chmn., William H. Alderman/Dir., Rick Wasserman/Dir. - Financial Management Consultant, Peter Black/Dir., Martin J. Delaney/Dir.

Owners: Rick J. Filippelli, Wynnefield Capital Management, LLC/9.15%, Bernard J. Korman/11.93%, Insiders/17.17%, Stephen T. Johnson/1.47%, Karl W. Dieckmann, Peter Black, Nationwide Financial Services/11.70%, Hummingbird Microcap Value Fund/3.30%, Wynnefield Capital Inc./5.15%, Hummingbird Value Fund/3.62%, Martin J. Delaney

Financial Data: ***Fiscal Year End:***09/30 ***Latest Annual Data:*** 9/30/2006

Year	Sales	Net Income
2006	$74,968,000	-$13,247,000
2005	$55,804,000	-$2,489,000
2004	$37,288,000	-$4,079,000

Curr. Assets:	$12,886,000	**Curr. Liab.:**	$8,483,000		
Plant, Equip.:	$879,000	**Total Liab.:**	$9,572,000	**Indic. Yr. Divd.:**	NA
Total Assets:	$30,776,000	**Net Worth:**	$21,204,000	**Debt/ Equity:**	0.0108

Tech Data Corp

5350 Tech Data Dr., Clearwater, FL, 33760; ***PH:*** 1-727-539-7429; ***http://*** www.techdata.com

General - Incorporation	FL	**Stock**- Price on:12/24/2007	$37.4
Employees	8,000	Stock Exchange	NDQ
Auditor	Ernst & Young LLP	Ticker Symbol	TECD
Stk Agt	Mellon Investor Services LLC	Outstanding Shares	55,000,000
Counsel	Gray, Harris & Robinson	E.P.S	-$1.82
DUNS No.	08-194-0553	Shareholders	NA

Business: The group's principle activity is to provide IT products. The group operates from United States.

Primary SIC and add'l.: 7375 5045

CIK No: 0000790703

Subsidiaries: 1250895 Ontario Ltd., Azlan European Finance Limited, Azlan GmbH, Azlan Group Limited, Azlan Limited, Azlan Logistics Limited, Azlan Norge A/S, Azlan Overseas Holdings Ltd, Azlan SAS, Azlan Scandinavia AB, Azlan VAD s.r.o., Computer 2000 Distribution Ltd., Computer 2000 Immobilien-und-Beteiligungsverwaltungs Gesellschaft m.b.H., Computer 2000 Portuguesa Lda., Computer 2000 Publishing AB 86 Subsidiaries included in the Index

Officers: Robert M. Dutkowsky/Dir., CEO/$1,488,509.00, William K. Todd/63/Sr. VP - Logistics, Integration Services, Mike Zava/Member - Exec. Board, Gerard Youna/Member - Exec. Board, Tracey Bradshaw/Member - Exec. Board, Katie Dumala/Member - Exec. Board, Nestor Cano/Pres. - Europe/$1,528,937.00, Joseph A. Osbourn/Exec. VP, Worldwide CIO/$976,091.00, David R. Vetter/Sr. VP, General Counsel, Sec., Kenneth Lamneck/Pres. - Americas/$804,389.00, Joe Quaglia/Member - Exec. Board, John Tonnison/Member - Exec. Board, Donna Turgeon/Member - Exec. Board, Rick Reid/Member - Exec. Board, Manfred Steinhardt/Member - Exec. Board *(36 Officers included in Index)*

Directors: Robert M. Dutkowsky/Dir., CEO, Steven A. Raymund/Chmn., Jeffery P. Howells/Dir., CFO, Exec. VP, Charles E. Adair/Dir., Maximilian Ardelt/Dir., Kathy Misunas/Dir., David M. Upton/Dir., John Y. Williams/Dir., Thomas Morgan/Dir.

Owners: Barclays Global Investors, NA./11.60%, Donald Smith& Co., Inc./7.10%, Kenneth T. Lamneck, Vanguard Whitehall Funds/5.20%, Kathy Misunas, Thomas I. Morgan, AXA Assurances I.A.R.D. Mutuelle/12.80%, David M. Upton, Joseph A. Osbourn, Maximilian Ardelt, Goldman Sachs Asset Management/6.80%, Jeffery P. Howells, John Y. Williams, Steven A. Raymund/4.30%, Insiders/6.70% *(18 Owners included in Index)*

Financial Data: ***Fiscal Year End:***01/31 ***Latest Annual Data:*** 1/31/2007

Year	Sales	Net Income
2007	$21,440,445,000	-$96,981,000
2006	$20,482,851,000	$26,586,000
2005	$19,790,333,000	$162,460,000

Curr. Assets:	$4,407,852,000	**Curr. Liab.:**	$2,591,288,000		
Plant, Equip.:	$140,762,000	**Total Liab.:**	$3,001,144,000	**Indic. Yr. Divd.:**	NA
Total Assets:	$4,703,864,000	**Net Worth:**	$1,702,720,000	**Debt/ Equity:**	0.2036

Tech Ops Sevcon Inc

155 Nboro Rd., Southborough, MA, 01772; ***PH:*** 1-508-281-5500; ***Fax:*** 1-508-281-5341; ***http://*** www.techopssevcon.com; ***Email:*** sales.us@sevcon.com

General - Incorporation............................ DE
Employees 159
Auditor .... Vitale, Caturano & Co., Ltd.
Stk Agt...... American Stock Transfer & Trust Co.
Counsel .... Palmer & Dodge LLP
DUNS No. 18-410-3380

Stock - Price on:12/24/2007 ....$9.8
Stock Exchange.......................................AMEX
Ticker Symbol.. TO
Outstanding Shares 3,220,000
E.P.S. $0.40
Shareholders..NA

Business: The group's principal activities are to design, manufacture, market and service solid-state products, which control motor speed and acceleration for battery powered electric vehicles. The products of the group are used primarily for electric fork life trucks, aerial lifts and underground coal-mining equipment. The group also manufactures special metallized film capacitors for electronics applications. These capacitors are used as components in the power electronics, signaling and audio equipment markets. The group operates through subsidiaries located in the United States, the United Kingdom, France and Korea.

Primary SIC and add'l.: 3625

CIK No: 0000825411

Subsidiaries: Industrial Capacitors (Wrexham) Ltd., Sevcon Asia Limited, Sevcon Ltd., Sevcon SA, Sevcon, Inc.

Officers: Matthew Boyle/Dir., CEO, Pres., Paul A. McPartlin/CFO, VP, Matthew C. Dallett/Sec., Counsel, Paul Farquhar/VP, Treasurer, Principal Accounting Officer, Raymond J. Thibault/Assist. Treasurer

Directors: Matthew Boyle/Dir., CEO, Pres., Bernard F. Start/Vice Chmn., David R.A. Steadman/Chmn., Paul B. Rosenberg/Dir., Maarten D. Hemsley/Dir., Marvin G. Schorr/Dir., Paul O. Stump/Dir.

Owners: Paul D. Sonkin/6.50%, Bernard F. Start/7.50%, Matthew Boyle/1.70%, Paul N. Farquhar, Paul A. McPartlin/2.60%, Marvin G. Schorr/11.20%, Wachovia Corporation/7.00%, Mario J. Gabelli/8.70%, Insiders/27.40%

Financial Data: Fiscal Year End:09/30   **Latest Annual Data:** 9/30/2006

Year	Sales	Net Income
2006	$34,630,000	$1,114,000
2005	$31,675,000	$641,000
2004	$29,150,000	$611,000

Curr. Assets:	$13,041,000	**Curr. Liab.:**	$5,673,000	**P/E Ratio:**	22.74
Plant, Equip.:	$3,295,000	**Total Liab.:**	$8,615,000	**Indic. Yr. Divd.:**	$0.120
Total Assets:	$18,652,000	**Net Worth:**	$10,037,000	**Debt/ Equity:**	NA

TechAlt Inc

601 Union St. , Ste. 4500, Seattle, WA, 98101; **PH:** 1-206-838-9736; **Fax:** 1-206-262-9513; **http://** www.techaltinc.com

General - Incorporation............................NV
Employees ....NA
Auditor ....Salberg & Company, P.A.
Stk Agt..NA
Counsel ....NA
DUNS No. ....NA

Stock - Price on:12/24/2007 ....NA
Stock Exchange..OTC
Ticker Symbol..TCLT
Outstanding Shares ....NA
E.P.S $0.031
Shareholders..NA

Business: The groups principle activities include developing technologies for sale and implementation into the homeland security market. The group currently focuses on secure wireless communications toolset. In the year April 2006, the group acquired Cypher Wireless, Inc. The group operates from the United States.

Primary SIC and add'l.: 3669

CIK No: 0001097945

Subsidiaries: Technology Alternatives, Inc.

Financial Data: Fiscal Year End:12/31   **Latest Annual Data:** 12/31/2005

Year	Sales	Net Income
2005	$2,764,000	-$3,755,000
1999	NA	-$25,000

Curr. Assets:	NA	**Curr. Liab.:**	$4,141,000	**P/E Ratio:**	0.15
Plant, Equip.:	$30,000	**Total Liab.:**	$4,141,000	**Indic. Yr. Divd.:**	NA
Total Assets:	$30,000	**Net Worth:**	-$9,293,000	**Debt/ Equity:**	NA

Teche Holding Co

1120 Jefferson Ter. Blvd., New Iberia, LA, 70538; **PH:** 1-337-828-3212; **Fax:** 1-337-365-7130; **http://** www.teche.com

General - Incorporation............................ LA
Employees 215
Auditor ....Dixon Hughes PLLC
Stk Agt..............................Deloitte & Touche LLP
Counsel..............Biggs, Trowbrige, Supple Et Al
DUNS No. 88-468-9514

Stock - Price on:12/24/2007 ....$45.5
Stock Exchange.......................................AMEX
Ticker Symbol..TSH
Outstanding Shares 2,210,000
E.P.S. $2.94
Shareholders..NA

Business: The group's principal activity is to provide financial services to small and medium sized business. The group is a community oriented federal savings bank. The group operates through fourteen branch offices located in st. Mary, iberia, st. Martin, and upper lafourche parishes. The group attracts deposits from general public including now, money market, savings and originates residential, construction, commercial and real estate loans.

Primary SIC and add'l.: 6712 6035

CIK No: 0000934538

Subsidiaries: Teche Federal Bank

Officers: Patrick O. Little/CEO, Pres., J. L. Chauvin/Sr. VP, CFO

Owners: Mary Coon Biggs/1.27%, Robert L. Wolfe, Henry L. Friedman/1.26%, Thomas F. Kramer/1.81%, W. Ross Little/4.69%, Scott T. Sutton/2.14%, Donelson T. Caffery/1.16%, J. L. Chauvin/2.07%, Robert Judice, Patrick O. Little/9.01%, Darryl R. Broussard/0.78%, Ernest Freyou/0.07%, Jeffery L. Gendell/9.13%, First Manhattan Company/6.08%

Financial Data: Fiscal Year End:09/30   **Latest Annual Data:** 9/30/2006

Year	Sales	Net Income
2006	$52,228,000	$7,317,000
2005	$46,913,000	$5,199,000
2004	$40,640,000	$5,926,000

Curr. Assets:	$20,230,000	**Curr. Liab.:**	$619,864,000		
Plant, Equip.:	$20,882,000	**Total Liab.:**	$621,821,000	**Indic. Yr. Divd.:**	$1.320
Total Assets:	$685,750,000	**Net Worth:**	$63,929,000	**Debt/ Equity:**	NA

Techlabs Inc

1820 Ne Jensen Beach Blvd., Ste. 634, Jensen Beach, FL, 34957; **PH:** 1-267-350-9210

General - Incorporation .... FL
Employees ....NA
Auditor ....Baumann, Raymondo & Co. P.A
Stk Agt.............. Florida Atlantic Stock Transfer, Inc.
Counsel ....NA
DUNS No. ....NA

Stock - Price on:12/24/2007 ....NA
Stock Exchange..OTC
Ticker Symbol..TELAE
Outstanding Shares ....NA
E.P.S. ....NA
Shareholders..NA

Business: The group's principle activities are to develop, acquire and operate Internet and fulfillment services of Internet companies and businesses. The group derives revenue from the delivery of advertising impressions through its own or third party Web-sites. The group operates business through its wholly owned subsidiaries, interplanner.com, inc., mystartingpoint.com, inc. And internetchic marketing, inc. Interplanner.com provides free online calendar and personal information management service. Mystartingpoint.com offers a variety of Web searching tools and internetchic marketing provides a business-to-business marketing solution.

Primary SIC and add'l.: 7375 4899 7379

CIK No: 0001082530

Subsidiaries: Florida Fountain of Youth Spas

Officers: Jayme Dorrough/39/Dir., Pres., Sec.

Directors: Jayme Dorrough/39/Dir., Pres., Sec.

Owners: Yucatan Holding Company, Jayme Dorrough, Insiders, Thomas J. Taule, Jayme Dorrough, Insiders, Insiders, Jayme Dorrough, Yucatan Holding Company, Yucatan Holding Company

Techne Corp

614 McKinley Pl NE, Minneapolis, MN, 55413; **PH:** 1-612-379-8854; **http://** www.techne-corp.com; **Email:** techinfo@techne-corp.com

General - Incorporation .... MN
Employees 577
Auditor ....KPMG LLP
Stk Agt...... American Stock Transfer & Trust Co.
Counsel ....Fredrikson & Byron
DUNS No. 19-668-7362

Stock - Price on:12/24/2007 ....$57.07
Stock Exchange...NDQ
Ticker Symbol......................................TECH
Outstanding Shares 39,450,000
E.P.S. $2.07
Shareholders..NA

Business: The group's principal activity is to manufacture, develop and distribute biological products. The group operates through three segments: hematology controls, biotechnology products and r&d systems Europe. Hematology controls are used to check the accuracy of blood analysis instruments. Biotechnology products inclusive of purified proteins (cytokines) and antibodies are used for the purpose of research and assay kits. R&d systems supplies cytokines and cytokine-related reagents to the biotechnology research community. The customers of the group are hospitals, clinical laboratories, research and clinical diagnostic markets. The foreign operations of the group are located in Germany.

Primary SIC and add'l.: 3841 6719 2835 2836

CIK No: 0000842023

Officers: Thomas E. Oland/67/Chmn., CEO, Pres., Treasurer/$277,804.00, Monica Tsang/VP - Research/$356,871.00, Marcel Veronneau/VP - Hematology Operations, Gregory J. Melsen/VP - Finance, CFO

Directors: Thomas E. Oland/67/Chmn., CEO, Pres., Treasurer, Roger C. Lucas/65/Vice Chmn., Howard V. O'Connell/78/Dir., Arthur G. Herbert/82/Dir., Randolph C. Steer/58/Dir., Robert V. Baumgartner/52/Dir., Charles A. Dinarello/65/Dir., Karen A. Holbrook/65/Dir.

Owners: Karen A. Holbrook, Insiders, Charles A. Dinarello, Robert V. Baumgartner, Arthur G. Herbert, Monica Tsang, Thomas E. Oland/3.90%, Randolph C. Steer, Marcel Veronneau, Morgan Stanley Investment/13.10%, Howard V. O'Connell, Roger C. Lucas, Gregory J. Melsen

Financial Data: Fiscal Year End:06/30   **Latest Annual Data:** 6/30/2006

Year	Sales	Net Income
2006	$202,617,000	$73,351,000
2005	$178,652,000	$66,132,000
2004	$161,257,000	$52,928,000

Curr. Assets:	$149,822,000	**Curr. Liab.:**	$17,966,000		
Plant, Equip.:	$88,772,000	**Total Liab.:**	$30,164,000	**Indic. Yr. Divd.:**	NA
Total Assets:	$370,512,000	**Net Worth:**	$340,348,000	**Debt/ Equity:**	NA

Technest Holdings Inc

88 Royal Little Dr., Providence, RI, 02904; **PH:** 1-617-973-5104; **http://** www.technestholdings.com

General - Incorporation .... NV
Employees 181
Auditor .... Wolf & Co., P.c.
Stk Agt..................................Liberty Transfer Co
Counsel ....NA
DUNS No. ....NA

Stock - Price on:12/24/2007 ....$0.5
Stock Exchange..OTC
Ticker Symbol..TCNH
Outstanding Shares 16,880,000
E.P.S. ....-$0.23
Shareholders..NA

Business: The group's principal activity is to invest in development stage companies with promising technology designed for commercial applications. It operated through its subsidiary, technest inc in the United States of America. On 25-Mar-2003, the group sold its subsidiary technest inc. Its objective is to maintain good standing as it explores a corporate and entity growth through merger and or acquisition.

Primary SIC and add'l.: 7375 7389

CIK No: 0001077800

Subsidiaries: Argus Sensors, Inc., E-OIR Technologies, Inc., Genex Technologies

Officers: Joe MacKin/Chmn., CEO, Pres., Gino Pereira/Dir., CFO, Diana Durbin/Sr. VP, Nitin Kotak/VP - Finance - Operations, Stanley Wunderlich/Investor Relations, Kim Hines/Corporate Recruiter

Directors: Joe MacKin/Chmn., CEO, Pres., Gino Pereira/Dir., CFO, David Gust/Dir., Darlene Deptula-Hicks/Dir., Robert Doto/Dir.

Owners: Markland Technologies, Inc/27.14%, Joseph P. Mackin, Southridge Partners LP/28.21%, Insiders/2.55%, Verdi Consulting, Inc./5.23%, David R. Gust, Aberdeen Avenue LLC/7.07%, Darlene M. Deptula-Hicks, Gino M. Pereira/2.23%, Southshore Capital Fund Ltd./4.88%, Robert Doto

Financial Data: Fiscal Year End:06/30   **Latest Annual Data:** 6/30/2006

Year	Sales	Net Income
2006	$81,092,000	$20,253,000
2005	$1,664,000	-$2,729,000
2004	NA	-$113,000

Curr. Assets:	$15,216,000	**Curr. Liab.:**	$18,741,000		
Plant, Equip.:	$772,000	**Total Liab.:**	$24,469,000	**Indic. Yr. Divd.:**	NA
Total Assets:	$41,651,000	**Net Worth:**	$17,183,000	**Debt/ Equity:**	0.1442

Technical Communications Corp

100 Domino Dr., Concord, MA, 01742; *PH:* 1-978-287-5100; *http://* www.tccsecure.com; *Email:* tccinfo@tccsecure.com

General - Incorporation	MA	**Stock** - Price on:12/24/2007	$4.56
Employees	22	Stock Exchange	OTC
Auditor	Vitale, Caturano & Co. Ltd	Ticker Symbol	TCCO
Stk Agt	American Stock Transfer & Trust Co.	Outstanding Shares	1,380,000
Counsel	White, White & Van Etten LLP	E.P.S.	$0.55
DUNS No.	00-141-9266	Shareholders	NA

Business: The group's principal activity is to design, develop, manufacture, distribute and market communications security devices and systems. The group's products include sophisticated electronic devices that enable users to transmit information in an encrypted format and permit receivers to reconstitute the information in a deciphered format. The products are used to protect confidentiality in communication between radios, telephones, facsimile machines and data processing equipment over wires, fiber optic cables, radio waves and microwave and satellite links. The products are marketed to financial institution, foreign and domestic governmental agencies, law enforcement agencies and multinational companies requiring protection of mission-critical information.

Primary SIC and add'l.: 3669

CIK No: 0000096699

Subsidiaries: TCC Investment Corp.

Officers: Carl H. Guild/Chmn., CEO, Pres., Michael P. Malone/CFO, Treasurer, Assist. Sec., David A. White/Sec., Robert T. Lessard/Dir., Consultant, Thomas E. Peoples/Dir., Consultant

Directors: Carl H. Guild/Chmn., CEO, Pres., Mitchell B. Briskin/Dir., Robert T. Lessard/Dir., Consultant, Thomas E. Peoples/Dir., Consultant

Owners: Michael P. Malone/7.40%, Thomas E. Peoples/1.10%, Hummingbird Management, LLC/11.80%, Robert T. Lessard/1.10%, Mitchell B. Briskin/1.00%, Carl H. Guild/22.40%, Insiders/28.60%

Financial Data: *Fiscal Year End:*09/24 *Latest Annual Data:* 9/30/2006

Year	Sales	Net Income
2006	$3,897,000	-$94,000
2005	$3,721,000	-$30,000
2004	$4,876,000	$1,134,000

Curr. Assets:	$3,674,000	**Curr. Liab.:**	$527,000	**P/E Ratio:**	19.00
Plant, Equip.:	$83,000	**Total Liab.:**	$527,000	**Indic. Yr. Divd.:**	NA
Total Assets:	$3,757,000	**Net Worth:**	$3,230,000	**Debt/ Equity:**	NA

Technical Olympic USA Inc

4000 Hollywood Blvd, Ste 500n, Hollywood, FL, 33021; *PH:* 1-954-364-4000; *http://* www.tousa.com; *Email:* investor@tousa.com

General - Incorporation	DE	**Stock** - Price on:12/24/2007	$4.24
Employees	2,123	Stock Exchange	NA
Auditor	Ernst & Young LLP	Ticker Symbol	NA
Stk Agt	EquiServe Trust Co N.A	Outstanding Shares	59,600,000
Counsel	NA	E.P.S.	-$8.76
DUNS No.	11-848-4500	Shareholders	NA

Business: The group's principle activity is to design, build and sell single family homes, town homes and condominiums. The group operates in 14 metropolitan markets located in four major geographic regions: Florida, Texas, the mid-Atlantic and the west. The homes are marketed under the brand names of engle homes, newmark homes, fedrick, harris estate homes, marksman homes, d.s. Ware homes, masonry homes, trophy homes and james company. The homes are sold through commissioned sales personnel and independent real estate brokers. The group also provides mortgage financing and closing services and offer title, homeowners and other insurance products.

Primary SIC and add'l.: 6141 1521

CIK No: 0001046578

Subsidiaries: Alliance Insurance and Information Services, LLC, EH/Transeastern, LLC, Engle Homes Delaware, Inc., Engle Homes Reinsurance Limited, Engle Homes Residential Construction, LLC, Engle/James LLC, HomePartners Title Services, LLC, McKay Landing LLC, Newmark Homes Business Trust, Newmark Homes Purchasing, L.P., Newmark Homes, L.P., Newmark Homes, LLC, Preferred Builders Realty, Inc., Preferred Home Mortgage Company, Prestige Abstract & Title, LLC 58 Subsidiaries included in the Index

Officers: Antonio B. Mon/Executive Vice Chmn., CEO, Pres. - Tousa/$2,465,357.00, Tommy L. McAden/Dir., Exec. VP, Russell Devendorf/VP, Treasurer, Corp. Sec., Eric J. Rome/Exec. VP - Tousa Homes, Inc, Harry Engelstein/Sr. Exec. VP - Tousa's Florida Region/$2,080,540.00, Bill Carmichael/Exec. VP - Tousa's Florida Region, Mark R. Upton/Exec. VP - Tousa's West Region/$2,420,000.00, Michael R. Glass/Pres. - Universal Land Title, Inc, Angie Valdes/Chief Accounting Officer, Paul Berkowitz/Exec. VP, Chief Staff, Stephen M. Wagman/CFO, Exec. VP, Glen A. Tulk/Pres. - Land Division, Jim Proakis/Land Contact, George Yeonas/Dir., Exec. VP - Tousa's Atlantic, Texas Regions, Cora Wiltshire/Exec. VP - Tousa's Capitol Region *(18 Officers included in Index)*

Directors: Antonio B. Mon/Executive Vice Chmn., CEO, Pres. - Tousa, Konstantinos A. Stengos/Chmn., Michael J. Poulos/Dir., Tommy L. McAden/Dir., Exec. VP, George Stengos/Dir., Marianna Stengou/Dir., Karen A. Hoffman/Dir. - Human Resources Operations, Susan B. Parks/Dir., Larry D. Horner/Dir., William A. Hasler/Dir., Bryan J. Whitworth/Dir., Andreas Stengos/Dir.

Owners: John Kraynick, Technical Olympic S.A./66.94%, Andreas Stengos, Marianna Stengou, Antonio B. Mon/4.26%, Bryan J. Whitworth, Harry Engelstein, Michael J. Poulos, William A. Hasler, Konstantinos Stengos, Tommy L. McAden/1.10%, Larry D. Horner, Insiders/7.27%, Susan B. Parks, Randy Kotler *(17 Owners included in Index)*

Financial Data: *Fiscal Year End:*12/31 *Latest Annual Data:* 12/31/2006

Year	Sales	Net Income
2006	$2,637,300,000	-$201,200,000
2005	$2,509,000,000	$218,300,000
2004	$2,135,300,000	$119,600,000

Curr. Assets:	$2,283,400,000	**Curr. Liab.:**	$632,700,000		
Plant, Equip.:	$30,000,000	**Total Liab.:**	$2,067,300,000	**Indic. Yr. Divd.:**	$0.060
Total Assets:	$2,842,200,000	**Net Worth:**	$774,900,000	**Debt/ Equity:**	1.6102

Technical Ventures Inc

3411 McNicoll Ave., Unit 10-12, Toronto, ON, M1V 1Z5; *PH:* 1-416-299-9280; *http://* www.mortile.com; *Email:* mortile@interlog.com

General - Incorporation	NY	**Stock** - Price on:12/24/2007	$0.059
Employees	NA	Stock Exchange	OTC
Auditor	Schwartz Levitsky Feldman LLP	Ticker Symbol	TEVT
Stk Agt	American Stock Transfer & Trust Co.	Outstanding Shares	NA
Counsel	NA	E.P.S.	NA
DUNS No.	NA	Shareholders	NA

Business: The group's principle activity is to develop proprietary thermoplastic compounds, composite compounds which combine plastic with other granulated materials and specialty compounding in which the company compounds and pelletizes proprietary formulations of the customer. The company developed flame retardant, non-toxic plastic compund which minimize the hazards of fire. Thermoplastic hffr's classified as thermoplastic pololefins are based on polyers and co-polymers of ethylene and propylene and have been the focus of much research for the construction and transportation industries of their greater ease of use in fabrication and their ability to be recycled and trimmed into scrap. During the year the company introduced supplying samples of new product morfoam a chemical foaming agent, pigment extender and nucleating agent which reacts with process temperatures to produce a fine cell structure in extrusion molded parts. The group operates from United States.

Primary SIC and add'l.: 3087

CIK No: 0000788340

Financial Data: *Fiscal Year End:*06/30 *Latest Annual Data:* 6/30/2003

Year	Sales	Net Income
2003	$850,000	-$593,000
2002	$1,145,000	$139,000
2001	$1,282,000	-$328,000

Curr. Assets:	$201,000	**Curr. Liab.:**	$1,072,000		
Plant, Equip.:	$313,000	**Total Liab.:**	$1,334,000	**Indic. Yr. Divd.:**	NA
Total Assets:	$530,000	**Net Worth:**	-$804,000	**Debt/ Equity:**	NA

Technip

92973 Paris, La Dfense Cedex, switchboard, 92400; *PH:* 33-147782121; *http://* www.technip-coflexip.com; *Email:* investor-relations@technip.com

General - Incorporation	France	**Stock** - Price on:12/24/2007	$79.68
Employees	21,665	Stock Exchange	OTC
Auditor	Ernst & Young, LLP	Ticker Symbol	TKPPY
Stk Agt	CT Corporation System	Outstanding Shares	103,720,000
Counsel	NA	E.P.S.	NA
DUNS No.	NA	Shareholders	NA

Business: The groups principle activities include engineering and construction services. The group operates from United States.

Primary SIC and add'l.: 1629 2911 4925 2819 8711 8712

CIK No: 0001157654

Subsidiaries: Abay Engineering, Angoflex, Angoflex Ltda, Bechtel Technip Goro LLC, Brasflex Overseas Inc., Brasflex Tubos Flexiveis Ltda, Citex, Clecel, Coflexip Dveloppement, Coflexip Maritime Inc., Coflexip Singapore Pte Ltd., Coflexip Stena Offshore AS, Coflexip Stena Offshore Mauritius Ltd., Coflexip U.K. Ltd., Compagnie Franaise de Ralisation Industrielles 124 Subsidiaries included in the Index

Officers: Thierry Pilenko/Chmn., CEO, Olivier Dubois/CFO, Pres., Anne Decressac/Pres. - Human Resources, Communications, Bernard D. Tullio/COO, Guy Arlette/Pres. - Global Processes, Development

Directors: Daniel Lebegue/Dir., Roger Milgrim/Dir., Olivier Appert/Dir., Pierre Vaillaud/73/Dir., Bruno Weymuller/Dir., Miguel Caparros/64/Dir., Jacques Deyirmendjian/Dir., Rolf-Erik Rolfsen/Dir., Jean-Pierre Lamoure/Dir., Roger Cairns/65/Dir., Pascal Colombani/Dir., Germaine Gibara/Dir., John Oleary/Dir.

Owners: Oppenheimer Funds/5.50%, Insiders/1.65%, Tradewinds NWQ/6.50%, IFP/2.90%

Financial Data: *Fiscal Year End:*12/31 *Latest Annual Data:* 12/31/2006

Year	Sales	Net Income
2006	$9,145,058,000	$296,011,000
2005	$6,407,722,000	$110,978,000
2004	$7,014,380,000	$113,655,000

Curr. Assets:	$6,133,718,000	**Curr. Liab.:**	$6,160,124,000	**P/E Ratio:**	17.80
Plant, Equip.:	$1,082,514,000	**Total Liab.:**	$7,508,678,000	**Indic. Yr. Divd.:**	NA
Total Assets:	$10,924,822,000	**Net Worth:**	$3,416,144,000	**Debt/ Equity:**	NA

Technitrol Inc

1210 Nbrook Dr., Ste 470, Trevose, PA, 19053; *PH:* 1-215-355-2900; *http://* www.technitrol.com

General - Incorporation	PA	**Stock** - Price on:12/24/2007	$27.82
Employees	28,100	Stock Exchange	NYSE
Auditor	KPMG LLP	Ticker Symbol	TNL
Stk Agt	Registrar & Transfer Co	Outstanding Shares	40,790,000
Counsel	Stradley Ronon Stevens & Young LLP	E.P.S.	$1.46
DUNS No.	00-230-0556	Shareholders	NA

Business: The group's principal activities are to produce precision-engineered passive magnetics-based electronic components and electrical contact products and materials. The group operates in two segments: electronic component and electrical contact products. Electronic component segment designs and manufactures customized passive magnetics-based electronic components. The products are used in telecommunications, enterprise networking, automotive, consumer electronics and aerospace industries. The electrical contact products segment manufactures electrical contact products that range from contact materials to completed contact subassemblies. These products are used in appliance, building construction circuitry, electric power and telephone equipment industries.

Primary SIC and add'l.: 3824 3677 3643 3679 3674

CIK No: 0000096763

Subsidiaries: AMI Doduco (DE), LLC, AMI Doduco (France) S. A. S., AMI Doduco (Mexico), S. de R. L. de C. V., AMI Doduco (NC), Inc., AMI Doduco (PR), LLC, AMI Doduco (Tianjin) Electrical Contacts Manufacturing Co. Ltd., AMI Doduco (UK) Ltd., AMI Doduco Components B.V., AMI Doduco Espana, S. L., AMI Doduco GmbH, AMI Doduco Holding GmbH, AMI Doduco Hungary Kft., AMI Doduco Investors (DE), LLC, AMI Doduco Italia Holdings S.r.l., AMI Doduco Italia S.r.l. 53 Subsidiaries included in the Index

Officers: James M. Papada/Chmn., CEO/$1,529,625.00, John L. Kowalski/64/Sr. VP/$736,921.00, David J. Stakun/VP - Corporate Communications, Ann Marie Janus/Sec., Edward J. Prajzner/VP, Corporate Controller, Chief Accounting Officer, Drew A. Moyer/43/CFO, Sr. VP/$754,132.00, Thomas Dale/VP - Human Resources

Directors: James M. Papada/Chmn., CEO, David H. Hofmann/Dir., John E. Burrows/Dir., Edward M. Mazze/Dir., Alan E. Barton/Dir., Jeffrey A. Graves/46/Dir., Mark C. Melliar-Smith/Dir.

Owners: David H. Hofmann, Mark C. Melliar-Smith, Alan E. Barton, Barclays Global Investors, N.A./5.45%, John E. Burrows, Drew A. Moyer, Jeffrey A. Graves, AXA Financial, Inc./5.30%, Edward M. Mazze, Boston Partners Asset Management, LLC/5.03%, John L. Kowalski, Insiders, Royce & Associates, LLC/5.94%, James M. Papada

Financial Data: Fiscal Year End:12/30 Latest Annual Data: 12/29/2006

Year	Sales	Net Income
2006	$954,096,000	$57,203,000
2005	$616,378,000	-$25,464,000
2004	$582,314,000	$6,928,000

Curr. Assets:	$364,002,000	**Curr. Liab.:**	$125,104,000	**P/E Ratio:**	20.31
Plant, Equip.:	$102,176,000	**Total Liab.:**	$161,725,000	**Indic. Yr. Divd.:**	$0.350
Total Assets:	$626,587,000	**Net Worth:**	$464,862,000	**Debt/ Equity:**	0.1013

TechnoConcepts Inc

6060 Sepulveda Blvd., Ste. 202, Van Nuys, CA, 91411; **PH:** 1-818-988-3364; http:// www.technoconcepts.com

General - Incorporation	CO	**Stock**- Price on:12/24/2007	$1.46
Employees	NA	Stock Exchange	OTC
Auditor	Seligson & Giannattasio, LLP	Ticker Symbol	TCPS
Stk Agt	Signature Stock Transfer, Inc.	Outstanding Shares	40,030,000
Counsel	NA	E.P.S.	NA
DUNS No.	NA	Shareholders	NA

Business: The groups principle activities include designing, developing, manufacturing and marketing wireless communications semiconductors, or microchips. The group markets its products under the tradenames include True Software Radio(TM), IntraCore(R) and FriendlyNET(R). In June 2005, the group acquired Asant Technologies Inc. The group operates from the United States and Canada. The group's quarterly revenue for Jun '07 was 0.08 millions of USD.

Primary SIC and add'l.: 3663

CIK No: 0001165758

Subsidiaries: Asante Acquisition Corp, TechnoConcepts (Hong Kong) Ltd., TechnoConcepts, inc

Officers: Antonio E. Turgeon/Chmn., CEO, Oleg Panfilov/Chief Scientific Officer, Michael Handelman/CFO, Eric Pommer/VP, General Counsel, Richard A. Hahn/COO, Chun-Tsung Lee/VP - Engineering, Douglas Craig Morrison/VP - Sales, Marketing, Ronald M. Hickling/CTO, Dir.

Directors: Antonio E. Turgeon/Chmn., CEO, Feng Yuh Juang/Vice Chmn., Michael Ussery/Dir., George Lange/Dir., John Mansfield/Dir., Ronald M. Hickling/CTO, Dir.

Owners: Antonio E. Turgeon/10.07%, John Mansfield, Michael Handelman, Eric Pommer, Feng Yuh Juang/2.53%, Michael Ussery, George Lange, Insiders/14.71%, Richard Hines, Fiber Optic Techno Inc./6.94%

Curr. Assets:	$1,556,000	**Curr. Liab.:**	$9,885,000		
Plant, Equip.:	$980,000	**Total Liab.:**	$10,499,000	**Indic. Yr. Divd.:**	NA
Total Assets:	$2,649,000	**Net Worth:**	-$7,850,000	**Debt/ Equity:**	NA

Technol Fuel Conditioners Inc

12 Christopher Way, Eatontown, NJ, 07724; **PH:** 1-732-542-0111; http:// www.technol.com; **Email:** info@technol.com

General - Incorporation	CO	**Stock**- Price on:12/24/2007	NA
Employees	1,261	Stock Exchange	NA
Auditor	Jewett, Schwartz, & Assoc.	Ticker Symbol	NA
Stk Agt	NA	Outstanding Shares	NA
Counsel	NA	E.P.S	NA
DUNS No.	NA	Shareholders	NA

Business: The group's principal activity is to manufacture, market and distribute unique and technologically superior lubricants, fuel improvers, surfactants and detergents.

Primary SIC and add'l.: 8734

CIK No: 0001109262

Subsidiaries: Allied Syndications

Technology General Corp

12 Cork Hill Rd. , Franklin, NJ, 07416; **PH:** 1-973-827-4143; http:// www.technology-general.com

General - Incorporation	NJ	**Stock**- Price on:12/24/2007	$0.22
Employees	25	Stock Exchange	OTC
Auditor	Donald T. Sienkiewicz	Ticker Symbol	TCGN
Stk Agt	NY Drop-Depository Trust Co.	Outstanding Shares	5,940,000
Counsel	NA	E.P.S.	-$0.02
DUNS No.	10-124-0497	Shareholders	NA

Business: The group's principal activity is to manufacture deep-drawn metal-formed products, ice crushing and shaving equipment and spray coating and industrial mixer systems. The group operates through four divisions: the precision metalform division, the eclipse systems division, the clawson machine division and the aerosystems division. The products manufactured by the group are used primarily in the writing instruments industry, cosmetic industry, chemical and food processing industry and hotel industry. In addition, the group leases space at its corporate office complex to industrial tenants.

Primary SIC and add'l.: 3569 6512 3469 3563

CIK No: 0000768914

Subsidiaries: Transbanc International Investors Corporation

Financial Data: Fiscal Year End:03/31 Latest Annual Data: 3/31/2006

Year	Sales	Net Income
2006	$2,109,000	-$87,000
2005	$2,106,000	-$12,000
2003	$2,324,000	-$109,000

Curr. Assets:	$677,000	**Curr. Liab.:**	$407,000		
Plant, Equip.:	$1,613,000	**Total Liab.:**	$2,229,000	**Indic. Yr. Divd.:**	NA
Total Assets:	$2,342,000	**Net Worth:**	$113,000	**Debt/ Equity:**	15.6814

Technology Research Corp

5250 140th Ave. N, Clearwater, FL, 33760; **PH:** 1-813-535-0572; http:// www.trci.net; **Email:** productinfo@trci.net

General - Incorporation	FL	**Stock**- Price on:12/24/2007	$5.07
Employees	557	Stock Exchange	NDQ
Auditor	KPMG LLP	Ticker Symbol	TRCI
Stk Agt	Registrar and Transfer CO.	Outstanding Shares	5,890,000
Counsel	Bush, Ross, Gardner, Warren & Rudy	E.P.S.	$0.47
DUNS No.	03-526-1049	Shareholders	NA

Business: The group's principal activity is to design, develop, manufacture and market electronic control and measurement devices related to the distribution of electric power. The group also engaged in electrical safety products that prevents electrocution, electrical fires and protects against serious injury from electrical shock. These products are sold to original equipment manufacturers involved in a variety of industries including business machinery and personal care appliances and to governmental entities. Apart from the military, the major customers of the group include xerox corporation, fermont and other xerox suppliers and fermont.

Primary SIC and add'l.: 3825

CIK No: 0000741556

Subsidiaries: Technology Research Corporation, Honduras S.A. de C.V

Owners: Insiders/13.00%, Gerry Chastelet/0.50%, Barry H. Black/0.20%, Raymond B. Wood/1.00%, David F. Walker/0.50%, Owen Farren/0.30%, Edmund F. Murphy/0.50%, Patrick M. Murphy/0.10%, Robert S. Wiggins/3.10%, Donald W. Burton/7.30%

Financial Data: Fiscal Year End:03/31 Latest Annual Data: 3/31/2007

Year	Sales	Net Income
2007	$37,992,000	$1,462,000
2006	$45,620,000	$1,751,000
2005	$39,433,000	$2,013,000

Curr. Assets:	$22,447,000	**Curr. Liab.:**	$6,415,000	**P/E Ratio:**	15.36
Plant, Equip.:	$4,412,000	**Total Liab.:**	$8,554,000	**Indic. Yr. Divd.:**	$0.080
Total Assets:	$28,279,000	**Net Worth:**	$19,725,000	**Debt/ Equity:**	NA

Technology Solutions Co

55 E Monroe St., Ste. 2600, Chicago, IL, 60603; **PH:** 1-312-228-4500; **Fax:** 1-312-228-4501; http:// www.techsol.com; **Email:** info@techsol.com

General - Incorporation	DE	**Stock**- Price on:12/24/2007	$7.19
Employees	150	Stock Exchange	NDQ
Auditor	Grant Thornton LLP	Ticker Symbol	TSCC
Stk Agt	Mellon Investor Services LLC	Outstanding Shares	2,540,000
Counsel	NA	E.P.S.	-$4.61
DUNS No.	18-776-9278	Shareholders	NA

Business: The group's principal activities are to provide systems integration and business consulting services that focus on rapid results for the clients. Its suite of offerings encompasses all phases of technology lifecycle, from strategy, assessment and planning activities to implementation and integration and ending with extended support. The group's core competencies include enterprise resource planning, supply chain management, customer relationship management and change management and training as well as support services and other technical and specialty services. The group also provides solutions for unique industry processes and challenges. The group has worked with 840 clients worldwide including exxon mobil corp, caterpillar inc and pfizer inc. The group has international operations in Europe, Brazil and Canada.

Primary SIC and add'l.: 7371 8748

CIK No: 0000877645

Subsidiaries: Technology Solutions Company de Mexico S.A. de C.V., TSC Canada Corp. f/k/a Zamba Solutions Canada Inc., TSC Colombia, Inc., TSC Europe (U.K.) Ltd, TSC South America, Inc., Zamba Solutions LLC

Officers: Milton G. Silva-Craig/40/Dir., CEO, Pres., Philip J. Downey/56/VP, General Counsel, Corp. Sec., Timothy G. Rogers/CFO, Grant Thornton/Independent Accountant, David Wasson/Sr. VP, Client Officer - Enterprise Application Experts, Sandor Grosz/52/VP, Client Officer - Manufacturing Experts, Yvonne Hyland/Sr. VP, Client Officer - Manufacturing Experts, Christopher A. Cotteleer/Sr. VP - Financial Services Experts, Peter Kushmeider/VP - Financial Services Experts, Byron Niekamp/Sr. VP, Client Officer - Enterprise Application Experts, Michael Randle/VP, Client Dir. - Enterprise Application Experts, Stephen Ardill/VP, Client Dir. - CRM Experts, Jerry D. Alderman/VP - Customer Value Creation, CVC Experts, Craig Aguiar/VP - Solution Architect, Manufacturing Experts *(22 Officers included in Index)*

Directors: Milton G. Silva-Craig/40/Dir., CEO, Pres., Carl F. Dill/Chmn., Raymond P. Caldiero/Dir., Gerald Luterman/Dir., Paula Kruger/Dir., Kathryn A. Dcamp/Dir., Timothy R. Zoph/Dir.

Owners: Lloyd I. Miller/14.40%, Insiders/9.20%, Raymond P. Caldiero, Michael T. Tokarz/5.70%, CCI Consulting, Inc./5.90%, Dimensional Fund Advisors LP/6.00%, Gerald Luterman, State of Wisconsin Investment Board/15.20%, Sandor Grosz, Milton G. Silva-Craig, Philip J. Downey, David B. Benjamin/5.80%, Carl F. Dill, Paula Kruger

Financial Data: Fiscal Year End:12/31 Latest Annual Data: 12/31/2006

Year	Sales	Net Income
2006	$42,622,000	-$8,834,000
2005	$41,495,000	-$17,405,000
2004	$36,525,000	-$8,547,000

Curr. Assets:	$25,140,000	**Curr. Liab.:**	$7,962,000		
Plant, Equip.:	$35,000	**Total Liab.:**	$7,962,000	**Indic. Yr. Divd.:**	NA
Total Assets:	$26,042,000	**Net Worth:**	$18,080,000	**Debt/ Equity:**	NA

Technology Visions Group Inc

17080 Newhope St., Fountain Valley, CA, 92708; **PH:** 1-714-437-9801; http:// www.sutura.us

General - Incorporation	DE	**Stock**- Price on:12/24/2007	$0.0722
Employees	32	Stock Exchange	NA
Auditor	Kabani & Co, Inc	Ticker Symbol	NA
Stk Agt	Continental Stock T & T Co.	Outstanding Shares	265,110,000
Counsel	NA	E.P.S	-$0.04
DUNS No.	86-928-0784	Shareholders	NA

Business: The group's principal activity is the research and development of new and innovative technologies, engineering ideas, methods, and processes that hold the potential to become commercially viable products or processes. The technology portal employs and retains independent engineers, research consultants, research institutes, universities and other consultants as needed to develop and analyze technologies. The group plans to take base technologies, develop these technologies until commercially viable products are possible and license these technologies and any products resulting from the technologies to affiliated or unaffiliated entities. It is focused on commercializing pet (polymer encapsulation technology) and gment for use in the environmental waste cleanup market. The group operates in the United States of America. It is a development stage company.

Primary SIC and add'l.: 6794 3086 8731

CIK No: 0000937814

Subsidiaries: Sutura, Inc.

Officers: David Teckman/51/Dir., CEO, Pres., Anthony Nobles/43/Chmn., Chief Science Officer, Egbert Ratering/59/Dir., Exec. VP, Robert Hill/VP - Operations, Benjamin Brosch/VP - Engineering, Research, Development, Barry Forward/Investor Relations Officer, Richard Bjorkman/58/Dir., CFO, VP - Finance

Directors: David Teckman/51/Dir., CEO, Pres., Anthony Nobles/43/Chmn., Chief Science Officer, Egbert Ratering/59/Dir., Exec. VP, John Crew/73/Dir., Charles Terrell/69/Dir., Richard Bjorkman/58/Dir., CFO, VP - Finance, Richard Moran/57/Dir.

Owners: Teckman David, Insiders, Grootkasteel, B.V., Richard Moran, Go Industries, Inc., Anthony Nobles, Alfred Novak, Synapse Capital Fund, John Crew, Richard Bjorkman, Egbert Ratering, Whitebox, Charles Terrell

Financial Data: ***Fiscal Year End:***12/31 ***Latest Annual Data:*** 12/31/2006

Year	Sales	Net Income
2006	$635,000	-$11,998,000
2005	$239,000	-$12,404,000
2004	NA	-$758,000

Curr. Assets:	$1,799,000	***Curr. Liab.:***	$6,746,000		
Plant, Equip.:	$422,000	***Total Liab.:***	$22,693,000	***Indic. Yr. Divd.:***	NA
Total Assets:	$2,365,000	***Net Worth:***	-$20,328,000	***Debt/ Equity:***	NA

Technoprises Ltd

55 Hamasger St., Tel Aviv, 61571; ; ***http://*** www.technoprises.com

General - Incorporation	Israel	**Stock**- Price on:12/24/2007	$0.0025
Employees	NA	Stock Exchange	OTC
Auditor	Ziv Haft	Ticker Symbol	TNOLF
Stk Agt	American Stock Transfer & Trust Co.	Outstanding Shares	NA
Counsel	NA	E.P.S	NA
DUNS No.	NA	Shareholders	NA

Business: The group operates through its subsidiaries whose principle activities include development, manufacturing and marketing of technologically-advanced training and computer-based simulation systems for the aircraft and related industries. The group operates from United States.

Primary SIC and add'l.: 7373 7372 3663 3699 6719

CIK No: 0000874516

Subsidiaries: Tatneft Europe AG

Financial Data: ***Fiscal Year End:***12/31 ***Latest Annual Data:*** 12/31/2004

Year	Sales	Net Income
2004	$190,000	-$20,411,000
2003	NA	-$385,000
2002	$145,000	-$6,295,000

Curr. Assets:	$381,000	***Curr. Liab.:***	$3,960,000	***P/E Ratio:***	17.80
Plant, Equip.:	$100,000	***Total Liab.:***	$4,035,000	***Indic. Yr. Divd.:***	NA
Total Assets:	$527,000	***Net Worth:***	-$3,958,000	***Debt/ Equity:***	NA

Techprecision Corp

90 Grove St., Ste 204, Ridgefield, CT, 06877; ***PH:*** 1-203-438-3300; ***http://*** www.techprecision.com

General - Incorporation	DE	**Stock**- Price on:12/24/2007	NA
Employees	NA	Stock Exchange	OTC
Auditor	Tabriztchi & Co., CPA, P.C	Ticker Symbol	TPCS
Stk Agt	NA	Outstanding Shares	NA
Counsel	NA	E.P.S	NA
DUNS No.	NA	Shareholders	NA

Business: The group has been engaged in organizational efforts and obtaining initial financing. The group was formed as a vehicle to pursue a business combination and has made no efforts to identify a possible business combination. The group has not conducted negotiations or entered into a letter of intent concerning any target business. The business purpose of the group is to seek the acquisition of, or merger with, an existing company. The group operates from United States.

Primary SIC and add'l.: 6770

CIK No: 0001328792

Subsidiaries: Ranor, Inc

Officers: James G. Reindl/49/Chmn., CEO/$99,615.00, Mary Desmond/CFO/$89,870.00

Directors: James G. Reindl/49/Chmn., CEO, Stanley A. Youtt/Dir., Michael Holly/62/Dir., Larry Steinbrueck/Dir., Louis A. Winoski/Dir.

Owners: Larry Steinbrueck, Martin M. Daube, Louis A. Winoski, Howard Weingrow, Stanley A. Youtt, James G. Reindl, Mary Desmond, Stanoff Corporation, Insiders, Michael Holly, Andrew A. Levy

TechTeam Global Inc

27335 W Eleven Mile Rd., Southfield, MI, 48034; ***PH:*** 1-800-522-4451; ***http://*** www.techteam.com

General - Incorporation	DE	**Stock**- Price on:12/24/2007	$12.8
Employees	2,337	Stock Exchange	NDQ
Auditor	Ernst & Young LLP	Ticker Symbol	TEAM
Stk Agt	Richard Brown	Outstanding Shares	10,450,000
Counsel	Foley & Lardner LLP	E.P.S	$0.39
DUNS No.	02-911-9013	Shareholders	NA

Business: The group's principal activities are to provide information technology and business process outsourcing services. The services are provided to Fortune 1000 companies, multinational companies, product providers and governments. The group also provides it support solutions namely, help desk/call center services, technical staffing, systems integration and training programs. On 31-Dec-2003, the group acquired digital support corporation and techteam a.n.e on 13-May-2004.

Primary SIC and add'l.: 7389 7376

CIK No: 0000805054

Subsidiaries: S.C. TechTeam Global SRL, Sytel, Inc., TechTeam A.N.E. NV, TechTeam Akela SRL, TechTeam Asia Pacific (Private) Ltd., TechTeam Capital Group, LLC, TechTeam Cyntergy, LLC, TechTeam Global AB, TechTeam Global GmbH, TechTeam Global Ltd, TechTeam Global NV/SA

Officers: William C. Brown/Dir., CEO, Pres./$1,302,749.00, Marc J. Lichtman/CFO, VP, Treasurer/$213,149.00, Dennis J. Kelly/Pres. - Techteam Government Solutions/$426,256.00, Larry W. Granger/VP - Business Development, Christoph A. Neut/VP - Sales, Marketing, EMEA/$327,487.00, Michael A. Sosin/VP, General Counsel, Sec., Heidi K. Hagle/VP - Human Resources, Jeffery J. Ruffini/VP - Service Delivery, Tami M. Shultz/VP, Accounting Mgr. - Ford Motor Company, Marc Van Remoortere/VP - Service Delivery, EMEA, Robert W. Gumber/VP - Service Delivery/$275,954.00, Kevin Burke/Sr. VP - Americas, Steve Eydelman/CTO, VP

Directors: William C. Brown/Dir., CEO, Pres., Alok Mohan/Chmn., Kent Heyman/Dir., John P. Jumper/63/Dir., James A. Lynch/Dir., James G. Roche/Dir., Andrew R. Siegel/Dir., Richard R. Widgren/Dir.

Owners: Dennis J. Kelly, Marc J. Lichtman, William C. Brown/1.20%, Costa Brava Partnership III L.P./11.50%, James A. Lynch, Christoph A. Neut, Richard R. Widgren, Robert W. Gumber, Heartland Advisors, Inc./10.20%, Andrew R. Siegel/11.60%, Diker GP, L.L.C./5.20%, Dimensional Fund Advisors, Inc./7.40%, Ramius Capital Group, L.L.C./9.50%

Financial Data: ***Fiscal Year End:***12/31 ***Latest Annual Data:*** 12/31/2006

Year	Sales	Net Income
2006	$167,364,000	$1,834,000
2005	$166,497,000	$5,468,000
2004	$127,988,000	$4,725,000

Curr. Assets:	$76,367,000	***Curr. Liab.:***	$26,196,000	***P/E Ratio:***	32.82
Plant, Equip.:	$9,117,000	***Total Liab.:***	$31,622,000	***Indic. Yr. Divd.:***	NA
Total Assets:	$117,930,000	***Net Worth:***	$86,308,000	***Debt/ Equity:***	NA

Techwell Inc

408 E Plumeria Dr., San Jose, CA, 95134; ***PH:*** 1-408-435-3888; ***http://*** www.techwellinc.com; ***Email:*** sales@techwellinc.com

General - Incorporation	DE	**Stock**- Price on:12/24/2007	$15.1
Employees	96	Stock Exchange	NDQ
Auditor	Deloitte & Touche LLP	Ticker Symbol	TWLL
Stk Agt	Mellon Investor Services LLC	Outstanding Shares	20,770,000
Counsel	NA	E.P.S	NA
DUNS No.	NA	Shareholders	NA

Business: The groups principle activities include designing, marketing and selling mixed signal integrated circuits. The products of the group include video decoders, security surveillance and LCD display. Specific customers of the group include IC Land and Lacewood. The group operates from the United States. The group operates from South Korea, Taiwan, China, Japan and other. The group's quarterly revenue for September 2007 was 15.12 millions of USD.

Primary SIC and add'l.: 3679 3674

CIK No: 0001171529

Subsidiaries: Techwell International, Inc., Techwell Shenzhen Technology, Inc.

Officers: Fumihiro Kozato/Dir., CEO, Pres., Feng Kuo/CTO, Mark Voll/CFO, VP - Finance, Administration, Joe Kamei/VP - Operations, Tom Krause/VP - Business Development, David Nam/VP - Sales, Marketing

Directors: Fumihiro Kozato/Dir., CEO, Pres., Rick Kimball/Dir., Robert Cochran/Dir., C. J. Koomen/Dir., Phillip J. Salsbury/Dir., Justine Lien/Dir.

Owners: FMR Corp./12.70%, Phillip J. Salsbury, Entities affiliated with TCV IV, L.P./19.50%, Justine Lien, Robert D. Cochran, Feng Kuo/3.20%, Mark Voll, J. C. Koomen, Insiders/30.40%, Richard H. Kimball/19.70%, Dongwook Nam, Fumihiro Kozato/6.60%

Financial Data: ***Fiscal Year End:***12/31 ***Latest Annual Data:*** 12/31/2006

Year	Sales	Net Income
2006	$53,712,000	$13,222,000
2005	$36,051,000	$4,541,000
2004	$17,251,000	-$1,742,000

Curr. Assets:	$58,320,000	***Curr. Liab.:***	$6,847,000	***P/E Ratio:***	21.88
Plant, Equip.:	$625,000	***Total Liab.:***	$6,847,000	***Indic. Yr. Divd.:***	NA
Total Assets:	$63,993,000	***Net Worth:***	$57,146,000	***Debt/ Equity:***	NA

Teck Cominco Ltd

501 N Riverpoint Blvd., Ste. 300, Spokane, WA, 99202; ***PH:*** 1-509-747-6111; ***Fax:*** 1-509-459-4400; ***http://*** www.teckcominco.com; ***Email:*** info@teckcominco.com

General - Incorporation	Canada	**Stock**- Price on:12/24/2007	$44.73
Employees	NA	Stock Exchange	NYSE
Auditor	PricewaterhouseCoopers LLP	Ticker Symbol	TCK
Stk Agt	Mellon Trust Co	Outstanding Shares	428,070,000
Counsel	NA	E.P.S	$5.15
DUNS No.	20-574-8163	Shareholders	NA

Business: The group's principle activities are mining, producing and refining gold, copper, zinc, lead, molybdenum, niobium, silver and metallurgical coal.

Primary SIC and add'l.: 1041 1031 3341 1221 1021

CIK No: 0000886986

Subsidiaries: Cominco Mining Partnership, Teck Base Metals Ltd., Teck Cominco Alaska Incorporated, Teck Cominco American Incorporated, Teck Cominco Coal Partnership, Teck Cominco Metals Ltd., Teck Financial Ltd., Teck Gold Limited, Teck Resources Inc., Teck-Hemlo Inc, Teck-Pogo Inc.

Officers: Donald R. Lindsay/Dir., CEO, Pres., John F.H. Thompson/VP - Technology, Howard C. Chu/Concentrate Sales Mgr. - Copper, Gary M. Jones/VP - Business Development, Anthony A. Zoobkoff/Sr. Counsel, Assist. Sec., Ronald A. Millos/Sr. VP - Finance, Chief Finanical Officer, Peter C. Rozee/Sr. VP - Commercial Affairs, Ronald J. Vance/Sr. VP - Corporate Development, Peter Kukielski/COO, Exec. VP, Douglas H. Horswill/Sr. VP - Environment, Corporate Affairs, Fred S. Daley/VP - Exploration, Michael J. Allan/VP - Engineering, Lawrence A. MacKwood/Treasurer, Michel P. Filion/VP - Environment, Health, Safety, James A. Utley/VP - Human Resources *(55 Officers included in Index)*

Directors: Donald R. Lindsay/Dir., CEO, Pres., Robert J. Wright/Dep. Chmn., Norman B. Keevil/70/Chmn., Jalynn Bennett/Dir., Takuro Mochihara/Dir., Lloyd I. Barber/Dir., Takashi Kuriyama/Dir., Norman B. Keevil/Dir., Derek G. Pannell/Dir., Janice G. Rennie/Corp. Dir., Hugh J. Bolton/Dir., Christopher M.T. Thompson/60/Dir., Warren S.R. Seyffert/Dir., Brian J. Aune/Dir., David A. Thompson/Dir. *(16 Directors included in Index)*

Financial Data: *Fiscal Year End:*12/31 *Latest Annual Data:* 12/31/2006

Year	Sales	Net Income
2006	$5,611,116,000	$2,200,168,000
2005	$3,788,070,000	$1,128,270,000
2004	$2,846,268,000	$504,822,000

Curr. Assets:	$5,916,600,000	**Curr. Liab.:**	$1,475,074,000		
Plant, Equip.:	$3,151,801,000	**Total Liab.:**	$4,194,393,000	**Indic. Yr. Divd.:**	$1.000
Total Assets:	$9,767,752,000	**Net Worth:**	$5,573,360,000	**Debt/ Equity:**	NA

TECO Energy Inc

702 N Franklin St., Tampa, FL, 33602; *PH:* 1-813-228-1111; *http://* www.teco.net; *Email:* investorrelations@tecoenergy.com

General - Incorporation	FL	**Stock** - Price on:12/24/2007	$17.05
Employees	5,200	Stock Exchange	NYSE
Auditor	PricewaterhouseCoopers LLP	Ticker Symbol	TE
Stk Agt	Bank of New York	Outstanding Shares	209,620,000
Counsel	NA	E.P.S.	$1.26
DUNS No.	04-829-5869	Shareholders	NA

Business: The groups principle activity is to provide retail electric service. The group operates through two business segments namely Tampa Electric division and Peoples Gas System. The group also purchases, distributes and sells natural gas for residential, commercial, industrial and electric power generation customers. The group operates from United States.

Primary SIC and add'l.: 4931 4911 4923 1222 1311 4932 4424

CIK No: 0000350563

Subsidiaries: Bear Branch Coal Company, Clintwood Elkhorn Mining Company, Gatliff Coal Company, McAdams Holding, LLC, Perry County Coal Corporation, Pike-Letcher Land Company, Premier Elkhorn Coal Company, Rich Mountain Coal Company, San Jose Power Holding Company, LTD, Tampa Electric Company, TECO Barge Line, Inc., TECO Bulk Terminal, LLC, TECO Coal Corporation, TECO Diversified, Inc., TECO EnergySource, Inc. 33 Subsidiaries included in the Index

Officers: Sherrill W. Hudson/Chmn., CEO/$4,132,079.00, William T. Whale/VP - Energy Delivery - Tampa Electric, Henry L. Bell/Administrator - Training, Development, Laura Willis/Coordinator Corporate Compliance, Thomas L. Hernandez/VP - Energy Supply Tampa Electric, J. J. Shackleford/Pres. - Teco Coal, Sheila M. McDevitt/61/Sr. VP, General Counsel, Chief Legal Officer, Burnis Kilpatrick/Corporate Compliance Officer, Karen M. Mincey/VP - Information Technology, CIO, Janet L. Sena/VP - Federal Affairs, Sal Litrico/Pres. - Teco Transport, P. L. Barringer/Chief Accounting Officer, Bruce R. Christmas/VP - Fuels Management, Charles R. Black/Pres. - Tampa Electric/$1,373,691.00, S. W. Callahan/VP - Treasury, Risk Management *(24 Officers included in Index)*

Directors: Sherrill W. Hudson/Chmn., CEO, Paul L. Whiting/64/Dir., Joseph P. Lacher/62/Dir., Thomas J. Touchton/69/Dir., William D. Rockford/62/Dir., Tom L. Rankin/67/Dir., William P. Sovey/74/Dir., Loretta A. Penn/58/Dir., Luis Guinot/72/Dir., Dubose Ausley/70/Dir., James L. Ferman/64/Dir.

Owners: T. Rowe Price Associates, Inc./5.60%, Franklin Resources, Inc./7.80%

Financial Data: *Fiscal Year End:*12/31 *Latest Annual Data:* 12/31/2006

Year	Sales	Net Income
2006	$3,448,100,000	$246,300,000
2005	$3,010,100,000	$274,500,000
2004	$2,669,100,000	-$552,000,000

Curr. Assets:	$1,285,700,000	**Curr. Liab.:**	$1,350,400,000	**P/E Ratio:**	13.53
Plant, Equip.:	$4,766,900,000	**Total Liab.:**	$5,632,800,000	**Indic. Yr. Divd.:**	$0.780
Total Assets:	$7,361,800,000	**Net Worth:**	$1,729,000,000	**Debt/ Equity:**	1.8151

Tectonic Network Inc

6621 Bay Cir., Ste 170, Atlanta, GA, 30071; *PH:* 1-770-354-8988; *http://* www.tectonicnetwork.com; *Email:* info@tectonicnetwork.com

General - Incorporation	DE	**Stock** - Price on:12/24/2007	$0.0135
Employees	168	Stock Exchange	OTC
Auditor	BDO Seidman LLP	Ticker Symbol	TNWKQ
Stk Agt	Wachovia Bank N.A	Outstanding Shares	13,870,000
Counsel	NA	E.P.S.	-$0.081
DUNS No.	NA	Shareholders	NA

Business: The group's principal activity is to develop and market software and services for credit card, debit card and check transaction processing. Processing software for virtually any computing platform include windows, unix and linux, and the other which provides connectivity and communications software for IBM midrange computers that facilitates e-mail and e-commerce communications. The products and services of the group include pccharge, rita, as/400 support for pos-port and javacard. The group's new division is into developing and marketing software solutions for the construction community. On 18-Nov-2003, the group acquired bbn acquisition, inc, on 26-Nov-2003, construction yellow pages llc and on 02-Jan-2004, the group acquired specsource.com, inc.

Primary SIC and add'l.: 7379 7372

CIK No: 0000866492

Financial Data: *Fiscal Year End:*06/30 *Latest Annual Data:* 6/30/2004

Year	Sales	Net Income
2004	$10,586,000	-$5,998,000
2003	$7,861,000	-$3,135,000
2002	$8,421,000	-$4,564,000

Curr. Assets:	$2,063,000	**Curr. Liab.:**	$6,401,000		
Plant, Equip.:	$495,000	**Total Liab.:**	$6,401,000	**Indic. Yr. Divd.:**	NA
Total Assets:	$10,753,000	**Net Worth:**	$4,352,000	**Debt/ Equity:**	0.1408

Tecumseh Products Co

100 E Patterson St., Tecumseh, MI, 49286; *PH:* 1-517-423-8411; *Fax:* 1-517-423-8760; *http://* www.tecumseh.com

General - Incorporation	MI	**Stock**- Price on:12/24/2007	$15.32
Employees	18,500	Stock Exchange	NDQ
Auditor	PricewaterhouseCoopers LLP	Ticker Symbol	TECUA
Stk Agt	EquiServe Trust Co N.A	Outstanding Shares	18,480,000
Counsel	NA	E.P.S.	-$11.18
DUNS No.	00-504-9440	Shareholders	NA

Business: The group's principle activity is to manufacture hermetic compressors for residential and commercial refrigerators, freezers, water coolers and dehumidifiers. The group also manufactures electric motors and components, including alternating current and direct current motors. The group operates from United States.

Primary SIC and add'l.: 3561 3511 5078

CIK No: 0000096831

Subsidiaries: Evergy, Inc., FASCO Asia Pacific Ltd., FASCO Australia Pty. Ltd., FASCO Industries, Inc., FASCO Motors, Ltd, FASCO Motors, Ltd., FASCO Yamabishi Co., Ltd., Little Giant Pump Company, M.P. Pumps, Inc., Manufacturing Data Systems, Inc., Motoco a.s., Motores FASCO de Mexico, Societe Immobiliere de Construction de la Verpilliere, Tecumseh Compressor Company, Tecumseh do Brasil Europe Srl. 26 Subsidiaries included in the Index

Officers: Edwin L. Buker/CEO, Pres., Teresa Hess/Dir. - Investor Relations, James J. Bonsall/55/COO, Pres./$1,760,540.00, Ronald E. Pratt/55/Pres. - Electrical Components Business Unit/$244,275.00, James S. Nicholson/46/CFO, VP, Treasurer/$359,483.00, Michael R. Forman/61/VP - Global Human Resources, Kent B. Herrick/39/Dir., VP - Global Business Development, Daryl P. McDonald/General Counsel, Sec.

Directors: David M. Risley/63/Chmn., Peter M. Banks/70/Dir., Albert A. Koch/65/Dir., Kent B. Herrick/39/Dir., VP - Global Business Development, Kevin E. Sheehan/62/Dir.

Owners: Tricap Partners II L.P., Peter M. Banks, Albert A. Koch, Kent B. Herrick, Franklin Resources, Inc., David M. Risley, Brandes Investment, Aegis Financial, Insiders, Todd W. Herrick/5.90%, Herrick Foundation, Donald Smith & Co., Inc., Insiders, James S. Nicholson, Todd W. Herrick *(16 Owners included in Index)*

Financial Data: *Fiscal Year End:*12/31 *Latest Annual Data:* 12/31/2006

Year	Sales	Net Income
2006	$1,769,100,000	-$80,300,000
2005	$1,847,000,000	-$223,500,000
2004	$1,911,700,000	$10,100,000

Curr. Assets:	$733,400,000	**Curr. Liab.:**	$509,300,000		
Plant, Equip.:	$552,400,000	**Total Liab.:**	$984,300,000	**Indic. Yr. Divd.:**	NA
Total Assets:	$1,782,700,000	**Net Worth:**	$798,400,000	**Debt/ Equity:**	0.2886

Teeka Tan Products Inc

5499 N Federal Hwy., Ste. D, Boca Raton, FL, 33487; *PH:* 1-561-989-3600; *Fax:* 1-561-989-0069; *http://* www.teekatan.com

General - Incorporation	DE	**Stock** - Price on:12/24/2007	$0.022
Employees	2	Stock Exchange	OTC
Auditor	Webb & Company, P. A.	Ticker Symbol	TKAT
Stk Agt	Florida Atlantic Stock Transfer, Inc.	Outstanding Shares	88,510,000
Counsel	NA	E.P.S.	-$0.011
DUNS No.	NA	Shareholders	NA

Business: The groups principle activity is to distribute Teeka Tan(R) suncare products and distributor of the line of Safe Sea Sunscreen with Jellyfish Sting. The group sells these products directly to resorts, hotels and retailers with beach locations. The group operates from the United States.

Primary SIC and add'l.: 2844

CIK No: 0001217021

Subsidiaries: Teeka Tan, Inc.

Officers: Brian S. John/39/Dir., CEO, Pres., Frank V. Benedetto/36/Dir., Treasurer, Sec., Christopher Sheldon/Contact - Sales, Marketing, Richard Miller/40/Dir., VP, COO, Spiro J. Vetas/54/Dir. - Sales

Directors: Brian S. John/39/Dir., CEO, Pres., Richard Miller/40/Dir., VP, COO, Frank V. Benedetto/36/Dir., Treasurer, Sec.

Owners: Frank V. Benedetto/14.20%, Insiders/54.30%, Richard M. Miller/20.10%, Brian S. John/20.10%

Financial Data: *Fiscal Year End:*12/31 *Latest Annual Data:* 12/31/2006

Year	Sales	Net Income
2006	$245,000	-$646,000
2005	$131,000	-$412,000

Curr. Assets:	$166,000	**Curr. Liab.:**	$624,000		
Plant, Equip.:	$25,000	**Total Liab.:**	$624,000	**Indic. Yr. Divd.:**	NA
Total Assets:	$193,000	**Net Worth:**	-$431,000	**Debt/ Equity:**	NA

Teekay Corp

Formerly: Teekay Shipping Corp
Bayside House, Bayside Executive Pk., W Bay St. & Blake Rd., Nassau, AP, 59212; ; *http://* www.teekay.com

General - Incorporation	Marshall Islands	**Stock** - Price on:12/24/2007	$57.98
Employees	5,600	Stock Exchange	NYSE
Auditor	Ernst & Young LLP	Ticker Symbol	NA
Stk Agt	Bank of NY Shareholder Relations Dept	Outstanding Shares	73,600,000
Counsel	NA	E.P.S.	$3.10
DUNS No.	87-502-9860	Shareholders	NA

Business: The group operates through its subsidiaries whose principle activity is to provide international crude oil and petroleum product transportation services, using medium size oil tankers, to major oil companies, major oil traders and government agencies, primarily in the region spanning. The group operates from United States.

Primary SIC and add'l.: 4412 6719

CIK No: 0000911971

Subsidiaries: Navion Offshore Loading As, Navion Shipping Ltd, Norsk Teekay As, Norsk Teekay Holdings Ltd, Single Ship Companies, Single Ship Limited Liability Companies, Teekay Chartering Limited, Teekay Lightering Services LLC, Teekay LNG Partners L.P., Teekay Lng Partners Lp, Teekay Marine Services, Teekay Marine Services As, Teekay Navion Offshore Loading Pte Ltd, Teekay Nordic Holdings Inc, Teekay Norway As 17 Subsidiaries included in the Index

Officers: Bjorn Moller/Dir., CEO, Pres., David Glendinning/Pres. - Teekay Gas Services, Arthur Bensler/Exec. VP, General Counsel, Bruce Chan/Exec. VP - Corporate Resources, Graham Westgarth/Pres. - Teekay Marine Services, Peter Evensen/Chief Strategy Officer, Exec. VP, Paul Wogan/Pres. - Teekay Tanker Services, Vincent Lok/CFO, Exec. VP, Stein Rynning/Sr. VP - Offshore Loading, Kenneth Hvid/Pres. - Teekay Navion Shuttle Tankers, Offshore

Directors: Bjorn Moller/Dir., CEO, Pres., Sean C. Day/Chmn., Thomas Kuo-Yuen Hsu/Dir., Ian D. Blackburne/Dir., Axel Karlshoej/Dir., Eileen A. Mercier/Dir., Rod J. Clark/Dir., Tore I. Sandvold/Dir., Peter S. Janson/Dir.

Owners: FMR Corp/15.40%, Resolute Investments, Inc./44.80%, Iridian Asset Management, LLC/11.00%, Insiders/1.80%

Financial Data: ***Fiscal Year End:***12/31 ***Latest Annual Data:*** 12/31/2006

Year	Sales	Net Income
2006	$2,013,306,000	$262,244,000
2005	$1,954,618,000	$570,900,000
2004	$2,219,238,000	$757,440,000

Curr. Assets:	$747,140,000	**Curr. Liab.:**	$774,069,000		
Plant, Equip.:	$5,308,068,000	**Total Liab.:**	$5,205,254,000	**Indic. Yr. Divd.:**	$1.100
Total Assets:	$7,733,476,000	**Net Worth:**	$2,528,222,000	**Debt/ Equity:**	NA

Teekay Lng Partners LP

909 Fannin St., Ste. 3350, Houston, TX, 77010; ***PH:*** 1-832-366-0004; ***Fax:*** 1-832-366-0046; ***http://*** www.teekaylng.com; ***Email:*** investor.relations@teekaylng.com

General - Incorporation	Marshall Islands	**Stock**- Price on:12/24/2007	$35.5
Employees	408	Stock Exchange	NYSE
Auditor	Ernst& Young LLP	Ticker Symbol	TGP
Stk Agt	Bank of New York	Outstanding Shares	34,970,000
Counsel	NA	E.P.S	-$0.45
DUNS No.	NA	Shareholders	NA

Business: The groups principle activity is to transport crude and oil. The group operates through two segments namely LNG carrier and Suezmax tanker. The group operates from the Canada. The group's quarterly revenue for September 2007 was 63.72 millions of USD.

Primary SIC and add'l.: 4412

CIK No: 0001308106

Subsidiaries: Naviera Teekay Gas II, SL, Naviera Teekay Gas III, SL, Naviera Teekay Gas IV, SL, Naviera Teekay Gas, SL, Single Ship Limited Liability Companies, Teekay Luxembourg Sarl, Teekay Shipping Spain SL

Officers: Peter Evensen/Dir., CEO, CFO, Andres Luna/MD - Teekay Shipping Spain SL, Pedro Solana/Dir. - Finance, Accounting, Teekay Shipping Spain SL, David Glendinning/Pres. - Teekay LNG Projects Ltd, Mark J. Kremin/VP - Teekay LNG Projects Ltd, Roy Spires/VP - Finance, Teekay LNG Projects Ltd, Scott Gayton/Investor Relations Officer, David Drummond/Mgr. - Investor Relations, Kim Barbero/Dir. - Corporate Communications, Branding

Directors: Peter Evensen/Dir., CEO, CFO, Sean C. Day/Chmn., Bjorn Moller/Vice Chmn., Robert E. Boyd/Dir., Ida Jane Hinkley/Dir., Joseph I. Massoud/Dir., George Watson/Dir.

Owners: Teekay Shipping Corporation/43.20%, Neuberger Berman, Inc. and Neuberger Berman, LLC, as a group/10.20%

Financial Data: ***Fiscal Year End:***12/31 ***Latest Annual Data:*** 12/31/2006

Year	Sales	Net Income
2006	$182,773,000	-$9,591,000
2005	$145,459,000	$79,547,000

Curr. Assets:	$99,817,000	**Curr. Liab.:**	$245,512,000	**P/E Ratio:**	9.09
Plant, Equip.:	$1,401,020,000	**Total Liab.:**	$1,812,916,000	**Indic. Yr. Divd.:**	$2.120
Total Assets:	$2,531,413,000	**Net Worth:**	$718,497,000	**Debt/ Equity:**	NA

Tefron Ltd

Pk. Azorim, Derech Em Hamoshavot 94, Petach Tikva, 49527; ***PH:*** 972-49900881; ***http://*** www.tefron.com

General - Incorporation	Israel	**Stock**- Price on:12/24/2007	$9.28
Employees	2,085	Stock Exchange	NYSE
Auditor	Mcgladrey & Pullen, LLP	Ticker Symbol	NA
Stk Agt	American Stock Transfer & Trust Co.	Outstanding Shares	21,190,000
Counsel	Michal Baumwald Oron	E.P.S	$0.35
DUNS No.	60-002-9409	Shareholders	NA

Business: The groups principle activities include designing and manufacturing of boutique-quality everyday seamless intimate apparel, producing garments made of cotton and man-made fibers. The group products are sold under the brand names victoria's secrete, gap, banana republic, target, nike, dkny, dim and schiesser, as well as three other well-known American designer labels. The group operates from United States.

Primary SIC and add'l.: 2389 2342

CIK No: 0001044863

Subsidiaries: AlbaHealth, LLC, El-Masira Textile Company Ltd., Hi-Tex Founded By Tefron Ltd., Macro Clothing Ltd., Tefron Holding Netherland B.V., Tefron USA, Inc

Officers: Yosef Shiran/Dir., CEO, Asaf Alperovitz/CFO, Amit Tal/VP - Marketing, Sales, Kimiko Rotvik/Contact

Directors: Yosef Shiran/Dir., CEO, Eli Admoni/68/External Dir.

Owners: Macpell Industries Ltd./13.46%, Insiders/43.18%, Meir Shamir/21.77%, Ishay Davidi/21.77%, Arie Wolfson/18.04%, Yos Shiran/3.23%, Norfet, Limited Partnership/21.77%

Financial Data: ***Fiscal Year End:***12/31 ***Latest Annual Data:*** 12/31/2006

Year	Sales	Net Income
2006	$188,104,000	$18,380,000
2005	$205,585,000	$3,293,000
2004	$182,819,000	-$6,865,000

Curr. Assets:	$82,763,000	**Curr. Liab.:**	$47,493,000		
Plant, Equip.:	$77,086,000	**Total Liab.:**	$82,426,000	**Indic. Yr. Divd.:**	NA
Total Assets:	$164,656,000	**Net Worth:**	$82,230,000	**Debt/ Equity:**	NA

Tegal Corp

2201 S McDowell Blvd, Petaluma, CA, 94954; ***PH:*** 1-707-763-5600; ***http://*** www.tegal.com

General - Incorporation	DE	**Stock**- Price on:12/24/2007	$5.5
Employees	83	Stock Exchange	NDQ
Auditor	Burr, Pilger & Mayer, LLP	Ticker Symbol	TGAL
Stk Agt	Registrar & Transfer Co	Outstanding Shares	7,110,000
Counsel	Latham & Watkins	E.P.S	-$1.14
DUNS No.	06-656-0970	Shareholders	NA

Business: The group's principal activities are to manufacture, market and provide services to plasma etch systems. These systems are used in the fabrication of integrated circuits, memory and related microelectronics devices, contact-less transaction devices, radio frequency identification devices, smart cards, data storage and micro-level actuators. The group offers several models of its 6,500 series critical etch products configured to address film type and application desired by the customers. The customers of the group include matsushita, sumitomo, ams, motorola, st microelectronics, analog devises, nec, tesla sezam,s.a., toshiba, fuji microdevice, oki, hewlett packard, intel, sony, setech, walsin lihwa corp. The systems of the group are marketed in Japan, Taiwan, Germany, Italy, Austria, China Israel, India, turkey, China, South Korea and Singapore. On 11-Nov-2003, the group acquired simplus systems corporation & on 16-Jun-2004 it acquired first derivative systems inc.

Primary SIC and add'l.: 3559 3679

CIK No: 0000931059

Subsidiaries: Sputtered Films, Incorporated

Owners: Special Situations Funds/26.98%, Bonanza Capital/10.44%, Scott Brown, Duane Wadsworth, Lloyd I. Miller/5.03%, Thomas R. Mika, Edward A. Dohring, Steven Selbrede, Jeffrey M. Krauss, Christine T. Hergenrother, Insiders/2.45%

Financial Data: ***Fiscal Year End:***03/31 ***Latest Annual Data:*** 3/31/2006

Year	Sales	Net Income
2006	$21,757,000	-$8,880,000
2005	$14,888,000	-$15,363,000
2004	$16,528,000	-$12,602,000

Curr. Assets:	$28,022,000	**Curr. Liab.:**	$5,443,000		
Plant, Equip.:	$1,849,000	**Total Liab.:**	$5,451,000	**Indic. Yr. Divd.:**	NA
Total Assets:	$31,491,000	**Net Worth:**	$26,040,000	**Debt/ Equity:**	NA

Tejas Inc

8226 Bee CAve.s Rd., Austin, TX, 78746; ***PH:*** 1-512-306-8222; ***Fax:*** 1-512-306-1348; ***http://*** www.tejassec.com

General - Incorporation	DE	**Stock**- Price on:12/24/2007	$3.3
Employees	67	Stock Exchange	OTC
Auditor	PMB Helin Donovan, LLP	Ticker Symbol	TEJS
Stk Agt	Corporate Stock Transfer, Inc.	Outstanding Shares	4,830,000
Counsel	NA	E.P.S	-$3.73
DUNS No.	NA	Shareholders	NA

Business: The group's principal activities are to offer brokerage and related financial services to institutional and retail customers. The group is a holding company for tejas securities group, inc. The other services provided by the group include, high quality investment research to institutional and retail customers, market-making activities in stocks traded on the Nasdaq national market system and other national exchanges and investment banking services.

Primary SIC and add'l.: 6719 6512 6211

CIK No: 0000869688

Subsidiaries: Capital & Technology Advisors, Inc., Capital Advisors Securities Group, Inc., Tejas Securities Group Holding Company, Tejas Securities Group, Inc., TI Building Partnership, LP., Tsbgp, LLC.

Officers: Mark M. Salter/CEO/$1,401,646.00, Craig Biddle/Dir. - Investor Relations, Corporate Communications, Kurt J. Rechner/Pres., COO, Interim CFO/$941,999.00

Directors: John J. Gorman/Chmn., Michael F. Dura/Vice Chmn., William A. Inglehart/Dir., Charles H. Mayer/Dir., Dennis G. Punches/Dir., Clark N. Wilson/Dir., Barry A. Williamson/Dir.

Owners: Michael F. Dura, IBS Capital Corporation/8.50%, Charles H. Mayer, Mark M. Salter/7.10%, William A. Inglehart/1.00%, John J. Gorman/40.40%, Barry A. Williamson/1.10%, Clark N. Wilson/1.10%, Dennis G. Punches, Insiders/49.70%, Kurt J. Rechner/4.50%

Financial Data: ***Fiscal Year End:***12/31 ***Latest Annual Data:*** 12/31/2006

Year	Sales	Net Income
2006	$18,854,000	-$43,355,000
2005	$30,887,000	-$4,484,000
2004	$48,680,000	$7,281,000

Curr. Assets:	$4,493,000	**Curr. Liab.:**	$8,115,000		
Plant, Equip.:	$6,750,000	**Total Liab.:**	$12,147,000	**Indic. Yr. Divd.:**	NA
Total Assets:	$31,750,000	**Net Worth:**	$19,603,000	**Debt/ Equity:**	0.1928

Tejon Ranch Co

4436 Lebec Rd., Lebec, CA, 93243; ***PH:*** 1-661-248-4231; ***http://*** www.tejon.com

General - Incorporation	DE	**Stock**- Price on:12/24/2007	$46.46
Employees	118	Stock Exchange	NYSE
Auditor	Ernst & Young LLP	Ticker Symbol	TRC
Stk Agt	Mellon Investor Services LLC	Outstanding Shares	16,800,000
Counsel	NA	E.P.S	$0.05
DUNS No.	00-690-4189	Shareholders	NA

Business: The group's principle activity is to develop land and agribusiness to increase the value of real estate and resource holdings. The group operates in two segments: real estate and farming. Real estate consists of land planning and entitlement, real estate development, commercial sales and leasing and income portfolio management. This segment also leases land, microwave repeater locations, radio and cellular transmitter sites, and fiber optic cable routes to tenants. The farming segment operates farms of

permanent crops like wine grapes, almonds, pistachios and walnuts. The group's major customer is pistachio growers incorporated, a purchaser of pistachios. It owns land located in san joaquin valley, tehachapi mountains, antelope valley, kern county, California and los angeles county. The group's quarterly revenue for Sep '07 was 10.96 millions of USD.

Primary SIC and add'l.: 0179 6519

CIK No: 0000096869

Subsidiaries: Laval Agricultural Company, Rsf 6051 LLC, Tejon Development Corporation., Tejon Industrial Corp., Tejon Ranch Feedlot, Inc., Tejon Ranchcorp, White Wolf Corporation.

Officers: Robert A. Stine/61/Dir., CEO, Pres./$4,292,803.00, Allen E. Lyda/VP, CFO, Corporate Treasurer/$1,369,591.00, Teri A. Bjorn/VP, General Counsel, Kathleen J. Perkinson/VP - Community Development, Dennis Atkinson/VP - Agriculture/$637,084.00, Joseph E. Drew/Sr. VP - Real Estate/$1,296,724.00, Eileen Reynolds/VP - Government Affairs, Rebecca Swiggum/Contact - Investor Relations, Barry Zoeller/VP, Dir. - Corporate Communications, Andrew E. Daymude/VP - Planning, Entitlements, Barry G. Hibbard/VP - Commercial - Industrial Marketing, Carla Walker/VP, Controller, Aaron Dickinson/Contact - Equestrian Sports Complex, Debbie Gabel/Contact - Filming, Donald N. Geivet/VP - Ranch Operations *(16 Officers included in Index)*

Directors: Robert A. Stine/61/Dir., CEO, Pres., Kent G. Snyder/Chmn., Barbara Grimm-Marshall/Dir., John L. Goolsby/Dir., George G.C Parker/Dir., Geoffrey L. Stack/Dir., Robert C. Ruocco/Dir., Michael H. Winer/Dir., Norman Metcalfe/Dir.

Owners: Barbara Grimm-Marshall, Third Avenue Management LLC/26.52%, FMR Corp./5.85%, Geoffrey L. Stack, John L. Goolsby, Robert C. Ruocco/3.54%, Michael H. Winer/26.52%, Dennis Mullins, Norman Metcalfe, Insiders/34.22%, Robert A. Stine/2.53%, Wesley Capital Management, LLC/13.30%, Kent G. Snyder, Dennis J. Atkinson, Allen E. Lyda *(17 Owners included in Index)*

Financial Data: ***Fiscal Year End:***12/31 ***Latest Annual Data:*** 12/31/2006

Year		Sales			Net Income
2006		$28,422,000			-$2,729,000
2005		$26,360,000			$1,546,000
2004		$20,912,000			$389,000
Curr. Assets:	$95,960,000	***Curr. Liab.:***	$5,235,000	***P/E Ratio:***	929.20
Plant, Equip.:	$45,657,000	***Total Liab.:***	$10,087,000	***Indic. Yr. Divd.:***	NA
Total Assets:	$159,117,000	***Net Worth:***	$149,030,000	***Debt/ Equity:***	0.0027

Tekelec

5200 Paramount Pkwy., Morrisville, NC, 27560; ***PH:*** 1-888-628-5521; ***http://*** www.tekelec.com; ***Email:*** sales@tekelec.com

General - Incorporation	CA	***Stock***- Price on:12/24/2007	$14.16
Employees	1,409	Stock Exchange	NDQ
Auditor	PricewaterhouseCoopers LLP	Ticker Symbol	TKLC
Stk Agt	U.S. Stock Transfer Corp	Outstanding Shares	69,950,000
Counsel	Bryan Cave LLP	E.P.S	$0.43
DUNS No.	09-944-9076	Shareholders	NA

Business: The group's principal activities are to design, manufacture and market network systems products for telecommunications network. The group operates in three segments: network systems, contact center and next-generation switching. The network system consists of the eagle 5 sas and related products, features and applications based on the eagle platform. Contact center provides planning, management and call routing and control tools for single contact and for complex, multiple site contact center environments. The next-generation switching segment is focused primarily on creating and enhancing next-generation switching solutions for both traditional (tdm-based) and new (packet-based) class 5 and class 4 global applications. The group operates in calabasas, California, Colorado, Georgia, Illinois, New Jersey, North Carolina, Virginia and Texas. On 08-Apr-2004, the group acquired taqua. On 20-Sep-2004, the group acquired vocaldata inc.

Primary SIC and add'l.: 3669

CIK No: 0000790705

Subsidiaries: IEX Corporation, iptelorg GmbH, Santera Systems Inc., Taqua, Inc., Tekelec Argentina SRL, Tekelec Canada Inc., Tekelec do Brasil Ltda., Tekelec France, Tekelec Germany GmbH, Tekelec International Inc., Tekelec Italy srl, Tekelec Limited, Tekelec Malaysia Sdn. Bhd, Tekelec Mexico, S.de R.L. de C.V., Tekelec Singapore Pte. Ltd. 19 Subsidiaries included in the Index

Officers: Frank Plastina/Dir., CEO, Pres., Jean-Claude Asscher/Dir., Chmn. Emeritus, Private Investor, Danny L. Parker/Chief Strategy, Corporate Development Officer, Anne Patton/Dir. - Industry Analyst Relations, Marykay Wells/VP - Information Technology, CIO, David K. Rice/Sr. VP - Operations, Gregory Rush/VP, Corporate Controller, Chief Accounting Officer, William H. Everett/CFO, Exec. VP/$1,096,055.00, Ronald J. Delange/Sr. VP - Global Product Solutions/$771,937.00, Scott J. Weidenfeller/47/Sr. VP - Global Marketing, Jim Chiafery/Dir. - Investor Relations, Joni Brooks/Dir. - Public Relations, Richard E. Mace/53/Exec. VP - Global Business Group Solutions/$976,149.00, Stuart H. Kupinsky/Sr. VP - Corporate Affairs, General Counsel

Directors: Frank Plastina/Dir., CEO, Pres., Mark A. Floyd/52/Chmn., Jean-Claude Asscher/Dir., Chmn. Emeritus, Private Investor, Daniel L. Brenner/Dir., Martin A. Kaplan/Dir., Jerry Elliott/Dir., Carol G. Mills/Dir., Michael P. Ressner/Dir. - Tekelec, Robert V. Adams/Dir.

Owners: Robert V. Adams, Jon F. Rager, Ronald J. deLange, Glenn J. Krevlin/12.90%, Ronald W. Buckly, Insiders/1.80%, Brookside Capital Partners Fund, L.P./8.90%, Daniel L. Brenner, Stirling Trustees Limited/12.70%, Richard E. Mace, Mark A. Floyd, William H. Everett, Martin A. Kaplan, Franco Plastina, Michael P. Ressner

Financial Data: ***Fiscal Year End:***12/31 ***Latest Annual Data:*** 12/31/2006

Year		Sales			Net Income
2006		$553,647,000			$86,056,000
2005		$536,909,000			-$33,741,000
2004		$397,072,000			$36,373,000
Curr. Assets:	$777,794,000	***Curr. Liab.:***	$342,404,000	***P/E Ratio:***	32.93
Plant, Equip.:	$53,273,000	***Total Liab.:***	$475,016,000	***Indic. Yr. Divd.:***	NA
Total Assets:	$969,257,000	***Net Worth:***	$494,241,000	***Debt/ Equity:***	0.2733

Teknik Digital Arts Inc

36889 N Tom Darlington Dr., Carefree, AZ, 85377; ***PH:*** 1-480-443-1488; ***http://*** www.teknikcorp.com

General - Incorporation	NV	***Stock***- Price on:12/24/2007	$0.2
Employees	2	Stock Exchange	OTC
Auditor	Semple, Marchal & Cooper, LLP	Ticker Symbol	TKNK
Stk Agt	NA	Outstanding Shares	14,400,000
Counsel	NA	E.P.S	-$0.18
DUNS No.	NA	Shareholders	NA

Business: The groups principle activities include publishing and distributing physically interactive video game systems for play on personal computers and video game consoles, and instructional and game software for play on mobile telephones. The group operates from the United States.

Primary SIC and add'l.: 5734

CIK No: 0001299648

Subsidiaries: Playentertainment-Teknik, LLC, Teknik Powergrid, LLC

Officers: John R. Ward/Founder, Chmn., CEO, Benjamin Robins/Dir., VP - Business Development, Ray J. Artigue/Sr. VP - Marketing, Craig M. Phelps/Medical, Exercise, Wellness Advisors, Charles B. Corbin/Medical, Exercise, Wellness Advisors

Directors: John R. Ward/Founder, Chmn., CEO, Benjamin Robins/Dir., VP - Business Development

Owners: Cede & Co/5.60%, John R. Ward/39.70%, Insiders/40.70%, CodeFire Acquisition Corp./10.00%, Benjamin Robins/1.10%

Financial Data: ***Fiscal Year End:***09/30 ***Latest Annual Data:*** 9/30/2006

Year		Sales			Net Income
2006		$4,000			-$1,256,000
2005		NA			-$2,167,000
Curr. Assets:	$281,000	***Curr. Liab.:***	$1,317,000		
Plant, Equip.:	$9,000	***Total Liab.:***	$1,672,000	***Indic. Yr. Divd.:***	NA
Total Assets:	$361,000	***Net Worth:***	-$1,348,000	***Debt/ Equity:***	NA

Teknowledge Corp

1800 Embarcadero Rd. , Palo Alto, CA, 94303; ***PH:*** 1-310-578-5350; ***http://*** www.teknowledge.com; ***Email:*** support@teknowledge.com

General - Incorporation	DE	***Stock***- Price on:12/24/2007	$0.84
Employees	19	Stock Exchange	NDQ
Auditor	Burr, Pilger & Mayer LLP	Ticker Symbol	TEKC
Stk Agt	Registrar & Transfer Co	Outstanding Shares	NA
Counsel	NA	E.P.S	NA
DUNS No.	01-311-4806	Shareholders	NA

Business: The group's principal activity is to provide advanced software products and services which, transform business data into customer value. The group provides financial account aggregation software, and is a us government prime contractor for research and development in Internet security, Web-based training, distributed systems and knowledge processing. The group operates five operating units within two reporting segments: commercial and government. The commercial segment includes financial solutions, patent and technology licensing, and the commercial business applications of security systems. The government segment includes the security systems, training systems, distributed systems and knowledge systems.

Primary SIC and add'l.: 7371 7372

CIK No: 0000716214

Subsidiaries: Teknowledge Federal Systems, Inc.

Officers: Neil Jacobstein/Chmn., CEO, Pres., Robert Balzer/CTO, Program Mgr. - Distributed Systems, Kevin White/Dir. - Financial Solutions Integration Services, Allan Terry/Dir. - Associate Systems, Program Mgr. - Knowledge Systems, Benedict O'Mahoney/Dir., VP - Administration, Legal Affairs, Michael Kaplan/VP - Finance, CFO

Directors: Neil Jacobstein/Chmn., CEO, Pres., Larry E. Druffel/Dir., Irwin T. Roth/Dir., Robert T. Marsh/Dir., Benedict O'Mahoney/Dir., VP - Administration, Legal Affairs

Owners: Insiders/16.90%, Benedict OMahoney/2.70%, Neil A. Jacobstein/12.70%, Larry E. Druffel/1.10%, Irwin Roth

Tektronix Inc

14200 SW Karl Braun Dr., Beaverton, OR, 97077; ***PH:*** 1-503-627-7111; ***http://*** www.tek.com; ***Email:*** investor-relations@tektronix.com

General - Incorporation	OR	***Stock***- Price on:12/24/2007	$33.79
Employees	4,359	Stock Exchange	NYSE
Auditor	Deloitte & Touche LLP	Ticker Symbol	TEK
Stk Agt	Mellon Investor Services LLC	Outstanding Shares	78,940,000
Counsel	Stoel Rives LLP	E.P.S	$1.11
DUNS No.	00-902-0231	Shareholders	NA

Business: The group's principal activities are to manufacture, market and service test, measurement and monitoring solutions. Its products and services are used in various industries such as computing, communications, semiconductors, broadcast, education government, military/aerospace, research, automotive and consumer electronics. It enables its customers to design, manufacture, deploy, monitor and service next-generation global communications networks, computing and advanced and pervasive technologies. The products of the group include oscilloscopes, logic analyzers, signal sources, communication test equipment, video test equipment and related components, support services and accessories. The group operates in the United States and other Americas, which include Mexico, Canada and South America; Europe, which includes Russia, the Middle East and Africa; the pacific, including China, India, Korea and Singapore and Japan.

Primary SIC and add'l.: 3663 3825 3829

CIK No: 0000096879

Subsidiaries: Inet Technologies International, Inc., Inet Technologies Netherlands BV, Maxtek Components Corporation, Tayvin 160 Limited, Tektronix (China) Co., Ltd., Tektronix (India) Private Limited, Tektronix AB, Tektronix Analysis Software, Inc., Tektronix Asia, Ltd., Tektronix Berlin GmbH & Co. KG, Tektronix Berlin Verwaltungs GmbH, Tektronix Cambridge Limited, Tektronix Canada Inc., Tektronix Development Company, Tektronix Electronics (China) Co., Ltd. 43 Subsidiaries included in the Index

Officers: Richard H. Wills/Chmn., CEO, Pres./$2,185,746.00, James Dalton/Sr. VP - Corporate Development, General Counsel, Sec./$745,311.00, Sue Kirby/VP - Human Resources, John Major/VP - Worldwide Manufacturing Operations, Gary Grossman/Worldwide Sr. Public Relations Mgr. - Test, Measurement, Video Products, Carol Dematteo/Public Relations Mgr. - Communications Products, Solutions, Tanja Konatar/Contact - Tektronix International Sales, Gonzague Bufquin/Contact - Tektronix SA, Rich McBee/Sr. VP, GM - Communications Business/$837,843.00, Craig Overhage/Sr. VP, GM - Instruments Business/$900,531.00, Colin Slade/Sr. VP, CFO/$933,409.00, Chuck McLaughlin/VP - Finance, Corporate Controller, Paul Oldham/VP, Treasurer, Dir. - Investor Relations, Rob Blaskowsky/CIO, VP, Tom Buzak/VP - Tektronix, Pres., GM - Maxtek *(17 Officers included in Index)*

Directors: Richard H. Wills/Chmn., CEO, Pres., Cyril J. Yansouni/Dir., Gary A. Ames/Dir., David N. Campbell/Dir., Frank C. Gill/Dir., Robin Washington/Dir., Gerry B. Cameron/Dir., Pauline Lo Alker/Dir., Kaj Juul-Pedersen/Dir.

Owners: Robin L. Washington, Cyril J. Yansouni, Colin L. Slade, Kaj Juul-Pedersen, Gary A. Ames, Private Capital Management, L.P./7.70%, Gerry B. Cameron, David N. Campbell, PRIMECAP Management Company/13.81%, James F. Dalton, Richard H. Wills/1.01%, Frank C. Gill, Craig L. Overhage, Richard D. McBee, Insiders/2.75% *(17 Owners included in Index)*

Financial Data: *Fiscal Year End:*05/27 *Latest Annual Data:* 5/27/2006

Year	Sales	Net Income
2006	$1,039,870,000	$92,355,000
2005	$1,034,654,000	$81,596,000
2004	$920,620,000	$116,095,000

Curr. Assets:	$545,030,000	**Curr. Liab.:**	$248,507,000	**P/E Ratio:**	30.44
Plant, Equip.:	$105,310,000	**Total Liab.:**	$460,123,000	**Indic. Yr. Divd.:**	$0.240
Total Assets:	$1,330,703,000	**Net Worth:**	$870,580,000	**Debt/ Equity:**	NA

Tel Instrument Electronics Corp

728 Garden St., Carlstadt, NJ, 07072; ***PH:*** 1-201-933-1600; ***http://*** www.telinst.com

General - Incorporation .... NJ
Employees 52
Auditor .... BDO Seidman LLP
Stk Agt............ Continental Stock Transfer & Trust Co
Counsel .... NA
DUNS No. 00-201-2516

Stock- Price on:12/24/2007 .... $3.73
Stock Exchange .... AMEX
Ticker Symbol .... TIK
Outstanding Shares 2,320,000
E.P.S. .... -$0.41
Shareholders .... NA

Business: The group's principal activities are to design, manufacture and market avionics test equipment for the general and commercial aviation markets and for the government/military aviation markets. The equipment is used to test navigation and communications equipment installed in aircraft. These products are sold either directly or through distributors to its many domestic commercial customers. The general aviation market consists of 1000 repair and maintenance service shops, at private and commercial airports in the United States and commercial aviation consists of 80 domestic and foreign commercial airlines. The group operates in three segments avionics government, avionics commercial and marine systems. On 16-Jan-2004, the group acquired innerspace technology inc.

Primary SIC and add'l.: 3812

CIK No: 0000096885

Officers: Harold K. Fletcher/83/Chmn., CEO, Pres., Robert J. Melnick/74/Dir., VP - Marketing, Management Consultant, Jeffrey C. O'Hara/50/Dir., COO, Pres., VP, Charles R. Palanzo/COO, Joseph P. MacAluso/CFO - Tel, Instrument Electronics Corp, Jack Nemeth/Sales Mgr. - Commercial Equipment, Mia Pindar/Contact - Repair Department, Adel Tawadros/Contact - Repair Department, Dave Shappiro/Contact - Parts Department, Jim Miller/Contact - Technical, Product Customer Support, Training, Anthony Gannon/Contact - Quality Mgr.

Directors: Harold K. Fletcher/83/Chmn., CEO, Pres., George J. Leon/64/Dir., Robert J. Melnick/74/Dir., VP - Marketing, Management Consultant, Jeffrey C. O'Hara/50/Dir., COO, Pres., VP, Robert A. Rice/53/Dir., Robert H. Walker/72/Dir.

Owners: Jeffrey C. O'Hara/6.20%, Insiders/56.80%, Robert A. Rice/3.80%, George J. Leon/14.30%, Robert H. Walker/2.50%, Donald S. Bab/3.60%, Harold K. Fletcher/25.10%, Robert J. Melnick/1.80%

Financial Data: *Fiscal Year End:*03/31 *Latest Annual Data:* 3/31/2006

Year	Sales	Net Income
2006	$11,196,000	-$395,000
2005	$10,511,000	-$29,000
2004	$10,704,000	$363,000

Curr. Assets:	$6,027,000	**Curr. Liab.:**	$1,725,000		
Plant, Equip.:	$775,000	**Total Liab.:**	$1,949,000	**Indic. Yr. Divd.:**	NA
Total Assets:	$7,117,000	**Net Worth:**	$5,168,000	**Debt/ Equity:**	0.0206

Telanetix Inc

6197 Cornerstone Ct E, Ste 108, San Diego, CA, 92121; ***PH:*** 1-858-362-2250; ***Fax:*** 1-858-362-2251; ***http://*** www.telanetix.com; ***Email:*** info@telanetix.com

General - Incorporation .... DE
Employees 9
Auditor .... Burnham & Schumm P.C.
Stk Agt............ Empire Stock Transfer Inc.
Counsel .... NA
DUNS No. .... NA

Stock- Price on:12/24/2007 .... $4.95
Stock Exchange .... OTC
Ticker Symbol .... TNXI
Outstanding Shares 20,090,000
E.P.S. .... -$0.62
Shareholders .... NA

Business: The groups principle activities include selling videoconference products. The groups primary business objectives were to develop channel partner relationships with audio video resellers and systems integrators. In August 2005, the group acquired Telanetix California. The group operates from the United States. The group's quarterly revenue for Sep '07 was 2.26 millions of USD.

Primary SIC and add'l.: 7373

CIK No: 0001277270

Subsidiaries: Telanetix, Inc

Officers: Thomas A. Szabo/Chmn., CEO, Founder, Rick Ono/COO, Rob Arnold/Founder, CTO, Richard M. Ono/48/CFO, COO, Corp. Sec., Todd Barrish/Sr. VP, Moriah Shilton/VP

Directors: Thomas A. Szabo/Chmn., CEO, Founder, Rob Arnold/Founder, CTO

Owners: Aequitas Hybrid Fund, LLC/5.46%, Crescent International Ltd./4.99%, Aequitas Capital Management, Inc./5.46%, Enable Growth Partners LP/4.99%, Aequitas Hybrid Fund QP, LLC/5.46%, Enable Opportunity Partners LP/4.99%, Robert S. Alford/8.10%, Thomas A. Szabo/14.19%, Pierce Diversified Strategy Master Fund LLC, Ena./4.99%, Insiders/17.23%, Richard M. Ono/3.70%, Robert C. Arnold/7.01%

Financial Data: *Fiscal Year End:*12/31 *Latest Annual Data:* 12/31/2006

Year	Sales	Net Income
2006	$1,311,000	-$3,119,000
2004	NA	-$22,000

Curr. Assets:	$3,941,000	**Curr. Liab.:**	$3,822,000		
Plant, Equip.:	$117,000	**Total Liab.:**	$5,767,000	**Indic. Yr. Divd.:**	NA
Total Assets:	$4,280,000	**Net Worth:**	-$1,487,000	**Debt/ Equity:**	NA

Tele Norte Leste Participacoes

Rua Humberto De Campos, 425/8 Andar-Leblon, Rio De Janeiro; ***PH:*** 55-31311315; ***http://*** www.telemar.com.br

General - Incorporation .... Brazil
Employees 7,098
Auditor .... PricewaterhouseCoopers LLP
Stk Agt .... CT Corporation
Counsel .... NA
DUNS No. .... NA

Stock- Price on:12/24/2007 .... $18.83
Stock Exchange .... NYSE
Ticker Symbol .... TNE
Outstanding Shares 382,120,000
E.P.S. $3.08
Shareholders .... NA

Business: The group's principal activities are the exploration of telephone services, leased lines, data transmission, mobile telephone services, teletext and telex transmission and other related services in the following brazilian states: rio de janeiro, minas gerais, espirito santo, bahia, sergipe, alagoas, pernambuco, paraiba, rio grande do norte, ceara, piaui, maranhao, para, amazonas, roraima, and amapa.

Primary SIC and add'l.: 4813 4812 4822 4899

CIK No: 0001066113

Subsidiaries: Companhia AIX de Participacoes S.A., Telemar Internet Ltda., Telemar Norte Leste S.A., Tnl Pcs S.a.

Officers: Luis Eduardo Falco/Dir., CEO

Directors: Luis Eduardo Falco/Dir., CEO, Jose Mauro Mettrau Carneiro Da Cunha/Chmn., Alvaro Avelino Carvalho Dos Santos/Dir., Carlos Francisco Jereissati/Alternate Dir., Otavio Marques De Azevedo/57/Dir., Jose Augusto Da Gama Figueira/Dir., Luciano Siani Pires/38/Dir., Julio Cesar Pinto/Dir., Jose Luis Magalhaes Salazar/Alternate Dir., Paulo Altmayer Goncalves/Dir., Fabio Schvartsman/Dir., Alan Adolfo Fischler/Dir., Marcelo Cunha Ribeiro/Dir., Celso Fernandez Quintella/Dir.

Owners: Fiago Participaes, AG Telecom Participaes, Lexpart Participaes, Telemar Participaes S.A., Alutrens Participaes, Insiders, BNDE, Asseca Participaes, L.F. Tel, Fundao Atlntico de Seguridade Social, Caixa de Previdncia dos Funcionrios do Banco do Brasil-PREVI

Financial Data: *Fiscal Year End:*12/31 *Latest Annual Data:* 12/31/2006

Year	Sales	Net Income
2006	$7,878,458,000	$563,149,000
2005	$7,173,022,000	$381,808,000
2004	$5,945,785,000	$281,121,000

Curr. Assets:	$4,864,369,000	**Curr. Liab.:**	$2,759,945,000		
Plant, Equip.:	$5,473,939,000	**Total Liab.:**	$8,925,980,000	**Indic. Yr. Divd.:**	NA
Total Assets:	$12,774,712,000	**Net Worth:**	$3,848,731,000	**Debt/ Equity:**	NA

Tele2 AB

PO Box 2094, Stockholm; ***PH:*** 46-856200060; ***http://*** www.tele2.com

General - Incorporation .... Sweden
Employees .... NA
Auditor .... Deloitte AB
Stk Agt .... U.S. Stock Transfer Corp
Counsel .... NA
DUNS No. 35-677-4828

Stock- Price on:12/24/2007 .... $16.29
Stock Exchange .... OTC
Ticker Symbol .... TLTZF
Outstanding Shares .... NA
E.P.S. .... NA
Shareholders .... NA

Business: The group's principal activity is to provide fixed and mobile telephone services, data communications services, Internet services and cable TV. The group operates through the following divisions: fixed telephone and Internet service, mobile gsm services; data communications services; cable TV service. The group is active in 22 European countries and has operations in the following market areas: nordic, eastern Europe and Russia, central Europe, southern Europe and luxembourg.

Primary SIC and add'l.: 4813

CIK No: 0001122535

Subsidiaries: 01047 Telecommunication GmbH, 3C Communicacoes a Credito Ltda, 3C Communications A/S, 3C Communications AB, 3C Communications BV, 3C Communications BVBA, 3C Communications Equipment SA, 3C Communications Espana SA, 3C Communications GmbH, 3C Communications International SA, 3C Communications Ltd, 3C Communications Luxembourg SA, 3C Communications OY, 3C Communications SRL Italy, 3C Transac Ltd 141 Subsidiaries included in the Index

Officers: Lars-Johan Jarnheimer/48/CEO, Pres., Karl-Johan Nybell/40/Dir. - Product Implementation, New Markets, Johnny Svedberg/46/Exec. VP, Operations Marketing Area Dir. - Baltic, Russia, Ib Andersen/53/Dir. - Carrier Business, Bo Lindgren/Dir. - Human Resources - Behavioral Scientist, Anders Candell/Dir. - Billing, Information Technology, Johan Hellstrom/Special Assignments, Malin Sparf Rydberg/Information Mgr., Bjorn Lundstrom/43/Technical Dir., Ene Raja/44/Dir. - Customer Service, Niclas Palmstierna/35/Marketing Area Dir. - Nordic, Anders Olsson/39/Exec. VP - Sales, Marketing Market Area Dir. - Central Europe, UK, Benelux, Andrea Filippetti/48/Marketing Area Dir. - Southern Europe, Fredrik Linton/42/Marketing Area Dir. - Services, Dir. - Mergers, Acquisitions, Donna Cordner/52/Exec. VP - Corporate Finance, Treasury *(16 Officers included in Index)*

Directors: Vigo Carlund/62/Chmn., John Shakeshaft/54/Dir., Cristina Stenbeck/31/Dir., Daniel Johannesson/65/Dir., Jan Loeber/65/Dir., Mia Brunell/43/Dir., Mike Parton/54/Dir., Pelle Tornberg/52/Dir., John Hepburn/59/Dir.

Telecom Argentina

Alicia Moreau De Justo 50, 10th Fl., Buenos Aires; ***PH:*** 54-1149683627; ***http://*** www.telecom.com.ar; ***Email:*** inversores@intersrv.telecom.com.ar

General - Incorporation .... AR
Employees 14,542
Auditor .... PricewaterhouseCoopers LLP
Stk Agt .... Bank of New York
Counsel .... NA
DUNS No. .... NA

Stock- Price on:12/24/2007 .... $25.79
Stock Exchange .... NYSE
Ticker Symbol .... TEO
Outstanding Shares 196,880,000
E.P.S. $1.10
Shareholders .... NA

Business: The group's principal activity is the provision of telecommunication services and other services related to telecommunications and telecomputing. Telecommunication services include voice, public telephone, data and broadcast signal transmission, Internet access, cellular, national and international long distance, national telex, video conferencing and directories distribution services. Related services include marketing of equipment, infrastructure and goods and consultancy and security services.

Primary SIC and add'l.: 4812 4899 7389 7375

CIK No: 0000932470

Subsidiaries: Cable Insignia S.A. (1)(2), Micro Sistemas S.A. (2), Neleo S.A. (1), Publicom S.A., Telecom Argentina USA Inc., Telecom Personal S.A.

Officers: Carlos A. Felices/Chmn., CEO, Edmundo S. Poggio/59/Dir. - Strategy, Technology Development, Luis A. Perazo/61/Dir. - Communications, External Affairs, Jose M. Pena Fernandez/57/Dir. - Procurement, Hector Caram/43/Dir. - Internal Audit, Ricardo Luttini/47/Dir. -

Special Evaluations, Guglielmo Noya/46/General Dir. - Telecom Personal, Guillermo P. Gully/64/Dir. - Human Resources, Information Services, Jorge A. Ferrarotti/59/Dir. - Institutional Relationships, Carlos A. Zubiaur/44/Dir. - Legal Matters, Valerio Cavallo/48/CFO, Controller, Marco Emilio Patuano/44/Alternate Dir., Dir. - Fixed, Line Telephony, Juan Jose Schaer/54/Dir. - Human Resources, Services, Guillermo Desimoni/48/Dir. - Information Technology, Gonzalo A. Martinez/54/Dir. - Regulatory Matters *(21 Officers included in Index)*

Directors: Carlos A. Felices/Chmn., CEO, Gerardo Werthein/Vice Chmn., Raul Antonio Miranda/58/Dir., Osvaldo Canova/74/Alternate Dir., Franco Alfredo Livini/80/Alternate Dir., Ruben Osvaldo Mosi/59/Alternate Dir., Julio Pedro Naveyra/66/Dir., Marco Emilio Patuano/44/Alternate Dir., Dir. - Fixed, Line Telephony, Adrian Werthein/56/Alternate Dir., Amadeo R. Vazquez/Dir., Maria Delia Carrera Sala/60/Dir., General Sec., Oscar Carlos Cristianci/66/Dir., Jorge Alberto Firpo/54/Dir., Luis Maria Gomez Iza/70/Alternate Dir., Giorgio Della Seta Ferrari Corbelli Greco/72/Alternate Dir. *(18 Directors included in Index)*

Owners: Mxima AFJP/6.10%, Consolidar AFJP/9.10%, Nacin AFJP/6.80%, Nortel/100.00%, Nortel/8.40%, Fideicomiso Banco de la Ciudad de Buenos Aires/100.00%, Orgenes AFJP/8.50%, Brandes Investment Partners, L.P./10.00%, MET AFJP/8.80%

Financial Data: Fiscal Year End:12/31 Latest Annual Data: 12/31/2006

Year	Sales	Net Income
2006	$2,427,437,000	$186,701,000
2005	$1,884,081,000	$374,971,000
2004	$1,512,680,000	-$263,221,000

Curr. Assets:	$576,749,000	**Curr. Liab.:**	$1,100,947,000			
Plant, Equip.:	$1,880,064,000	**Total Liab.:**	$2,430,048,000	**Indic. Yr. Divd.:**	NA	
Total Assets:	$2,882,765,000	**Net Worth:**	$452,717,000	**Debt/ Equity:**	NA	

Telecom Corp of New Zealand Ltd

Telecom Networks House, 68 Jervois Quay, Wellington; *PH:* 64-800454777; *http://* www.telecom.co.nz; *Email:* enquiry@telecom-media.co.nz

General - Incorporation	New Zealand	**Stock** - Price on:12/24/2007	$28.02
Employees	9,136	Stock Exchange	NYSE
Auditor	KPMG LLP	Ticker Symbol	NZT
Stk Agt	Computershare Investor Services LLC	Outstanding Shares	249,750,000
Counsel	NA	E.P.S.	$1.50
DUNS No.	76-003-5576	Shareholders	NA

Business: The group's principle activity is the provision of telecommunication services including local, national, international and value-added telephone services, cellular and other mobile services, data and Internet services, equipment sales and installation services, leased services and directories. It operates in Australia and New Zealand.

Primary SIC and add'l.: 5065 4813 4812 4822

CIK No: 0000875809

Subsidiaries: AAPT Limited, TCNZ (Bermuda) Limited, Tcnz (uk) Investments Limited, TCNZ (United Kingdom) Securities Limited, TCNZ Australia Investments Pty Limited, TCNZ Australia Pty Limited, TCNZ Equities, TCNZ Finance Limited, TCNZ Financial Services Limited, Teleco Insurance Investments Limited, Teleco Insurance Limited, Telecom Directories Holdings Limited, Telecom Directories Limited, Telecom Enterprises Limited, Telecom Europe 3G APS 30 Subsidiaries included in the Index

Officers: Simon Moutter/COO - Business, Trisha McEwan/GM - Human Resources, Mark Verbiest/Group General Counsel, Mark Ratcliffe/COO - Technology, Enterprises, Marko Bogoievski/CFO, Kevin Kenrick/COO - Consumer, Paul Reynolds/Dir., Chief Executive

Directors: Wayne Boyd/Chmn., Michael Tyler/Dir., Patsy Reddy/Dir., Rod McGeoch/Dir., Paul Reynolds/Dir., Chief Executive, Murray Horn/Dir., Ron Spithill/Dir.

Owners: Marko Bogoievski, Kevin Kenrick, Michael Tyler, Mondrian Investment Partners Limited/5.67%, Brandes Investment Partners LP/6.48%, Theresa Gattung, Commonwealth Banking Group/9.03%, Patsy Reddy, Mark Ratcliffe, Ron Spithill, Rob McLeod, Lazard Asset Management Pacific Co/6.16%, Rod McGeoch, Mark Verbiest, Westpac Banking Corporation/7.31% *(16 Owners included in Index)*

Financial Data: Fiscal Year End:06/30 Latest Annual Data: 6/30/2006

Year	Sales	Net Income
2006	$3,466,903,000	-$36,368,000
2005	$4,030,724,000	$685,902,000
2004	$3,400,160,000	$127,664,000

Curr. Assets:	$2,374,525,000	**Curr. Liab.:**	$1,226,208,000			
Plant, Equip.:	$2,838,787,000	**Total Liab.:**	$3,601,504,000	**Indic. Yr. Divd.:**	$1.300	
Total Assets:	$6,373,968,000	**Net Worth:**	$2,772,464,000	**Debt/ Equity:**	NA	

Telecom Italia SpA

Piazza Degli Affari 2, Milan, 20123; *PH:* 39-0285951; *http://* www.telecomitalia.it; *Email:* investor_relations@telecomitalia.it

General - Incorporation	Italy	**Stock** - Price on:12/24/2007	$2.2604
Employees	NA	Stock Exchange	OTC
Auditor	Reconta Ernst & Young S.P.A	Ticker Symbol	TIAJF
Stk Agt	NA	Outstanding Shares	NA
Counsel	NA	E.P.S.	NA
DUNS No.	NA	Shareholders	NA

Business: The group's principal activities are the provision of: telecommunications networks, fixed and mobile, and related services such as installation of telephone apparatus for commercial and private use; Internet applications and satellite networks. The company is also involved in the it sector manufacturing hardware and offering software solutions to private and business customers. Other activities include real estate management and related services.

Primary SIC and add'l.: NA

CIK No: 0000948642

Subsidiaries: BBNED group, HanseNet Telekommunikation GmbH, Liberty Surf group, Loquendo S.p.A, Matrix S.p.A., Nuova Tin.it S.r.l., Path. Net S.p.A., Telecom Italia Deutschland Holding GmbH, Telecontact Center S.p.A.

Officers: Riccardo Ruggiero/Dir., MD, CEO, Carlo Orazio Buora/Executive Dep. Chmn., Massimiliano Paolucci/45/Co - Dir. External Relations - Area Communication, Francesco Chiappetta/48/Dir., Sec., Head, General Counsel - Corporate, Legal Affairs, Germanio Spreafico/56/Head - Purchasing, Giuseppe Sala/GM, Stefano Pileri/53/GM - Technology, Luca Luciani/41/GM - Domestic Mobile Services, Gustavo Bracco/60/Head - Human Resources,

Organization, Security, Massimo Castelli/GM - Domestic Fixed Services, Mauro Nanni/47/Chief Executive - Top Clients, ICT Services, Guglielmo Bove/Head - Legal Unit, Giorgio Rossi/Contact - Human Resources, Ottorino Passariello/Quality, Feild Services Management, Alessandro Talotta/National Wholesale Servies *(32 Officers included in Index)*

Directors: Riccardo Ruggiero/Dir., MD, CEO, Carlo Orazio Buora/Executive Dep. Chmn., Pasquale Pistorio/Chmn., Francesco Chiappetta/48/Dir., Sec., Head, General Counsel - Corporate, Legal Affairs, Giovanni Consorte/Dir., Enzo Grilli/Dir., John Robert Sotheby Boas/Dir., Francesco Denozza/Dir., Paolo Baratta/69/Dir., Claudio De Conto/45/Dir., Luciano Gobbi/55/Dir., Luigi Roth/Dir., Massimo Moratti/Dir., Luigi Fausti/79/Dir., Carlo A. Puri Negri/Dir. *(30 Directors included in Index)*

Owners: Hopa S.p.A./3.72%, Olimpia S.p.A./17.99%, Assicurazioni Generali S.p.A./4.75%

Telecommunication Systems Inc

275 W St., Annapolis, MD, 21401; *PH:* 1-410-263-7616; *http://* www.telecomsys.com

General - Incorporation	MD	**Stock** - Price on:12/24/2007	$5.3
Employees	591	Stock Exchange	NDQ
Auditor	Ernst & Young LLP	Ticker Symbol	TSYS
Stk Agt	American Stock Transfer & Trust Co.	Outstanding Shares	40,910,000
Counsel	Piper Rudnick LLP	E.P.S.	-$0.21
DUNS No.	NA	Shareholders	NA

Business: The group's principal activities are to provide wireless network application software services and communication engineering services. It conducts its operations through three operating segments: network solutions, service bureau and network software. The network solutions segment designs and installs complex information processing and communication systems for corporate and government enterprise networks. The service bureau segment owns and leases network operation centers that host software for which customers make recurring monthly usage payments. The network software segment designs and develops network software for wireless carriers and enterprises that provides the delivery of secure and personalized content, services and transactions to various wireless devices. On 01-Jan-2004, the group acquired enterprise mobility solutions business of aether systems inc.

Primary SIC and add'l.: 7379 7372 7373

CIK No: 0001111665

Subsidiaries: Aether Systems (UK) Limited, TeleCommunication Systems (Holdings) Limited., TeleCommunication Systems (Maryland) AB, TeleCommunication Systems Benelux BV, TeleCommunication Systems Corp of Maryland, TeleCommunication Systems Iberian, TeleCommunication Systems Limited, TeleCommunication Systems Technology Limited

Officers: Maurice B. Tose/51/Chmn., CEO, Pres./$1,200,083.00, Richard A. Young/COO, Exec. VP/$775,801.00, Tom Brandt/CFO, Sr. VP/$693,812.00, Drew Morin/CTO, Sr. VP/$683,009.00, Tim Lorello/Sr. VP, Chief Marketing Officer, Kevin M. Webb/51/Sr. VP - Global Sales, Alliances/$450,007.00, Dan Allen/Sr. VP - Service Bureau Operations, Weldon H. Latham/Dir., VP, General Counsel, Byron F. Marchant/Dir., Exec. VP, General Counsel, Chief Administrative Officer, Bruce A. White/Sec., Michael Bristol/Sr. VP - Government Solutions Group, Jane Bryant/Contact - Public Relations

Directors: Maurice B. Tose/51/Chmn., CEO, Pres., James M. Bethmann/Vice Chmn., Byron F. Marchant/Dir., Exec. VP, General Counsel, Chief Administrative Officer, Clyde A. Heintzelman/Dir., Richard A. Kozak/Dir., Weldon H. Latham/Dir., VP, General Counsel

Owners: Maurice B. Tos/4.70%, Drew A. Morin/3.10%, Diker GP, LLC/5.00%, Clyde A. Heintzelman, Timothy J. Lorello/1.90%, Thomas M. Brandt/2.30%, Richard A. Kozak, Byron F. Marchant, Insiders/16.80%, Maurice B. Tos/100.00%, Marathon Capital Management, LLC/5.90%, Kevin M. Webb/1.30%, Richard A. Young/3.00%, Insiders/100.00%, James M. Bethmann *(17 Owners included in Index)*

Financial Data: Fiscal Year End:12/31 Latest Annual Data: 12/31/2006

Year	Sales	Net Income
2006	$124,936,000	-$21,695,000
2005	$102,153,000	-$11,467,000
2004	$142,925,000	-$18,548,000

Curr. Assets:	$61,245,000	**Curr. Liab.:**	$35,869,000			
Plant, Equip.:	$12,853,000	**Total Liab.:**	$48,590,000	**Indic. Yr. Divd.:**	$0.560	
Total Assets:	$83,695,000	**Net Worth:**	$35,105,000	**Debt/ Equity:**	NA	

Telecommunications Co of Chile

Avenida Providencia 111, Santiago; *PH:* 56-26912020; *http://* www.ctc.cl

General - Incorporation	Chile	**Stock** - Price on:12/24/2007	NA
Employees	NA	Stock Exchange	NYSE
Auditor	Ernst & Young LTDA.	Ticker Symbol	NA
Stk Agt	Citibank N.A	Outstanding Shares	NA
Counsel	NA	E.P.S.	NA
DUNS No.	98-039-8291	Shareholders	NA

Business: The group's principal activities are the provision of domestic services and local and international long distance telephone services. Additionally, the group sells equipment, provides cable television services, data transmission, value-added services and computer-related services. It also operates a cellular network with domestic coverage.

Primary SIC and add'l.: 4813 4841 4899 1731 4812

CIK No: 0000863614

Subsidiaries: Globus 120 S.A., Telefnica Asistencia y Seguridad S.A., Telefnica Mundo S.A.

Officers: Julio Covarrubias Fernandez/50/VP, CFO, GM - t, Gestiona

Directors: Marco Colodro Hadjes/66/Dir.

Owners: Alfonso Ferrari Herrero, AFP Habitat S.A/6.99%, Citibank, N.A., as depositary/13.29%, Franco Faccilongo Forno, AFP Habitat S.A/6.99%, AFP Provida S.A/5.56%, Telefnica Internacional Chile/44.39%, Marco Colodro Hadjes, Rafael Zamora Sanhueza, Insiders, AFP Provida S.A/6.89%, Insiders, Telefnica Internacional Chile/50.19%

Telecomunicacoes de Sao Paulo S.A.

Rua Martiniano de Carvalho 851, 21st Fl., So Paulo; *PH:* 55-1135497200; *Fax:* 55-1135497202; *http://* www.telesp.com.br; *Email:* ri.telefonicabr@telefonica.com.br

General - Incorporation		**Stock**- Price on:12/24/2007	$32.82
Employees	NA	Stock Exchange	NYSE
Auditor	NA	Ticker Symbol	TSP
Stk Agt	Bank of New York	Outstanding Shares	505,840,000
Counsel	NA	E.P.S	$2.76
DUNS No.	NA	Shareholders	NA

Business: The groups principle activity is to provide fixed-line telecommunications services. The group also provides interconnection services to cellular service providers and other fixed telecommunications companies through the use of its network. The group operates from the Sao Paulo.

Primary SIC and add'l.: 4822 4813 7389 4899

CIK No:

Financial Data: *Fiscal Year End:*NA *Latest Annual Data:* 12/31/2006

Year		Sales			Net Income
2006		$6,866,113,000			$1,373,992,000
2005		$6,184,135,000			$1,133,185,000
2004		$5,009,368,000			$822,084,000
Curr. Assets:	$2,194,007,000	**Curr. Liab.:**	$2,936,052,000	**P/E Ratio:**	9.09
Plant, Equip.:	$5,040,001,000	**Total Liab.:**	$3,533,521,000	**Indic. Yr. Divd.:**	$2.530
Total Assets:	$8,608,562,000	**Net Worth:**	$5,075,041,000	**Debt/ Equity:**	NA

Teleconnect Inc

Formerly: Its Networks Inc

Centro Comercial Camojan Cor.1(a), Plta Camino De Camojan, Urb. Sierra Blanca, Malaga, Marbella, 29603;

General - Incorporation	FL	**Stock**- Price on:12/24/2007	$0.075
Employees	NA	Stock Exchange	NA
Auditor	Murrell, Hall, McIntosh & Co., PLLP	Ticker Symbol	NA
Stk Agt	Florida Atlantic Stock Transfer, Inc.	Outstanding Shares	NA
Counsel	NA	E.P.S	NA
DUNS No.	NA	Shareholders	NA

Business: The group's principal activity is to provide telecommunications services for home and business use in Spain. The services provided by the group include postpaid and prepaid local and long distance calling, prepaid calling cards, wifi (wireless Internet access), wifi project design, installation, commissioning, maintenance and consultancy, e-mail accounts, Internet and Web design services. On 05-Dec-2002, the group acquired teleconnect comunicaciones, s.a.

Primary SIC and add'l.: 4813 4822 7372

CIK No: 0001101688

Subsidiaries: Openvia S. L., Shareworks Espana S. L.

Officers: Gustavo Gomez/Pres., CEO - Teleconnect Inc, Alfonso De Borbon/VP - Corporate Development, Dir. - Sales Teleconnect Comunicaciones SA, Alvaro Lopez/Dir. - Business Development, Operations, Marketing, Barbara Ocana/Human Resources, Legal, Financial, Office Administration, Teleconnect Comunicaciones SA

Owners: Geeris Holding Nederland B.V. and Diepandael BV, Alfonso De Borbon, Leonardus Geeris, Volim Holding B.V., Gustavo A. Gomez

Financial Data: *Fiscal Year End:*09/30 *Latest Annual Data:* 9/30/2006

Year		Sales			Net Income
2006		$4,657,000			-$3,891,000
2005		$4,930,000			-$3,005,000
2004		$6,167,000			-$3,202,000
Curr. Assets:	$813,000	**Curr. Liab.:**	$7,209,000		
Plant, Equip.:	$265,000	**Total Liab.:**	$7,222,000	**Indic. Yr. Divd.:**	NA
Total Assets:	$1,420,000	**Net Worth:**	-$5,802,000	**Debt/ Equity:**	NA

Teledyne Technologies Inc

1049 Camino Dos Rios, Thousand Oaks, CA, 91360; ***PH:*** 1-805-371-4545; ***http://*** www.teledyne.com

General - Incorporation	DE	**Stock**- Price on:12/24/2007	$45.98
Employees	7,700	Stock Exchange	NYSE
Auditor	Ernst & Young LLP	Ticker Symbol	TDY
Stk Agt	Mellon Investor Services LLC	Outstanding Shares	34,960,000
Counsel	NA	E.P.S	$2.41
DUNS No.	NA	Shareholders	NA

Business: The group's principal activities are conducted through four segments. Electronic and communication provides a wide range of specialized electronic systems, instruments, components and services that address niche market applications in commercial aerospace, defence, communications, industrial and medical markets. Systems engineering solutions provides innovative systems engineering, advanced technology, and manufacturing solutions to defence, space, environmental, and homeland security requirements. Aerospace engines and components provide design, development and manufacture of piston engines, turbine engines, electronic engine controls and aviation batteries. Energy systems provides hydrogen gas generators and thermoelectric and fuel cell-based power sources. The group acquired tekmar company on 19-May-2003, spirents aviation information solutions businesses on 27-Jun-2003, Iceman labs inc on 27-Feb-2004 and isco inc on 18-Jun-2004.

Primary SIC and add'l.: 3812 3669

CIK No: 0001094285

Subsidiaries: Aerosance, Inc., Ensembles de Precision S.A. de C.V., Isco GmbH, Isco Holdings, Inc., Reynolds Industries Limited, Teledyne Advanced Pollution Instrumentation, Inc., Teledyne Benthos, Inc., Teledyne Brown Engineering, Inc., Teledyne Brown Idaho, Inc., Teledyne Continental Motors, Inc., Teledyne Controls Simulation Limited, Teledyne Controls Wichita, Inc., Teledyne Cougar, Inc., Teledyne Energy Systems, Inc, Teledyne France 36 Subsidiaries included in the Index

Officers: Robert Mehrabian/Chmn., CEO, Pres./$3,756,336.00, Melanie S. Cibik/VP, Assoc. General Counsel, Assist. Sec., James M. Link/Pres. - Teledyne Brown Engineering/$946,065.00, Bryan L. Lewis/Pres. - Teledyne Continental Motors, Jason Vanwees/VP - Corporate Development, Investor Relations, Ivars R. Blukis/Chief Business Risk Assurance Officer, Robert W. Steenberge/CTO, VP, Aldo Pichelli/COO, Sr. VP - Electronics, Communications Segment/$944,642.00, Robyn E. McGowan/VP - Administration, Human Resources, Assist. Sec., Dale A. Schnittjer/Sr. VP, CFO/$1,750,299.00, Simon M. Lorne/Dir., Chief Legal Officer, John T. Kuelbs/Exec. VP, General Counsel, Sec./$1,460,905.00, Susan L. Main/VP, Controller, Robert L. Schaefer/Assoc. General Counsel, Assist. Sec., General Counsel Electronics - Communications, Roxanne S. Austin/Dir., Pres. - Austin Investment Advisors *(16 Officers included in Index)*

Directors: Robert Mehrabian/Chmn., CEO, Pres., Simon M. Lorne/Dir., Chief Legal Officer, Robert P. Bozzone/Dir. - Allengery Technologies Incorporated, Frank V. Cahouet/Dir., Charles Crocker/Dir., Kenneth C. Dahlberg/Dir., Paul David Miller/Dir., Michael T. Smith/Dir., Wesley W. Von Schack/Dir., Roxanne S. Austin/Dir., Pres. - Austin Investment Advisors

Owners: Dale A. Schnittjer, Wesley W. von Schack, John T. Kuelbs, Roxanne S. Austin, Robert Mehrabian/1.10%, Simon M. Lorne, James M. Link, Frank V. Cahouet, Singleton Group LLC/5.70%, Paul D. Miller, Barclays Global Investors, N.A./6.70%, Insiders/5.60%, Robert P. Bozzone/2.30%, Aldo Pichelli, Kenneth C. Dahlberg *(18 Owners included in Index)*

Financial Data: *Fiscal Year End:*01/01 *Latest Annual Data:* 12/31/2006

Year		Sales			Net Income
2006		$1,433,200,000			$80,300,000
2005		$1,016,600,000			$41,700,000
Curr. Assets:	$446,800,000	**Curr. Liab.:**	$230,400,000	**P/E Ratio:**	19.82
Plant, Equip.:	$164,800,000	**Total Liab.:**	$629,600,000	**Indic. Yr. Divd.:**	NA
Total Assets:	$1,061,400,000	**Net Worth:**	$431,800,000	**Debt/ Equity:**	NA

Teleflex Inc

155 S Limerick Rd., Limerick, PA, 19468; ***PH:*** 1-610-948-5100; ***Fax:*** 1-610-948-0811; ***http://*** www.teleflex.com

General - Incorporation	DE	**Stock**- Price on:12/24/2007	$81.38
Employees	19,800	Stock Exchange	NYSE
Auditor	PricewaterhouseCoopers LLP	Ticker Symbol	TFX
Stk Agt	American Stock Transfer & Trust Co.	Outstanding Shares	39,190,000
Counsel	NA	E.P.S	$5.37
DUNS No.	00-234-8191	Shareholders	NA

Business: The groups principle activities include designing, manufacturing, and distributing specialty engineered products for the commercial, medical and aerospace industries. The groups products include power, vehicle and fluid management systems, disposable medical products, medical devices and specialty devices. The group operates from United States.

Primary SIC and add'l.: 3714 3841 3728

CIK No: 0000096943

Subsidiaries: 4045181 Canada Inc., Access Medical S.A., Advanced Thermodynamics Inc., AeroForge Corporation, Air Cargo Equipment Corporation, Airfoil Technologies International LLC, Airfoil Technologies International-California, Inc, Airfoil Technologies International-Ohio, Inc. (APS), Airfoil Technologies International-UK, Ltd., Airfoil Technologies Singapore PTE LTD, American General Aircraft Holding Co., Inc., Astraflex Limited, Autogas Techniek Holland B.V., Bavaria Cargo Technologie GmbH, Capro de Mexico, S.A. de C.V. 177 Subsidiaries included in the Index

Officers: Jeffrey P. Black/Chmn., CEO/$3,150,031.00, Randall P. Gaboriault/CIO - Strategic Development, Julie McDowell/VP - Corporate Communications, John B. Suddarth/Pres. - Aerospace/$672,651.00, Ernest R. Waaser/Pres. - Medical, Charles E. Williams/Chief Accounting Officer, Corporate Controller, Gregg Winter/VP - Taxes, Martin S. Headley/51/CFO, Exec. VP/$948,224.00, Laurence G. Miller/Sr. VP, General Counsel, Sec., Jeffrey C. Jacobs/Treasurer, Kevin K. Gordon/CFO, Exec. VP, Vince Northfield/Pres. - Commercial/$636,200.00

Directors: Jeffrey P. Black/Chmn., CEO, John J. Sickler/Vice Chmn., Sigismundus W.W. Lubsen/Dir., Donald Beckman/Dir., Judith M. Von Seldeneck/Dir., Patricia C. Barron/Dir., James W. Zug/Dir., Jeffrey A. Graves/Dir., Benson F. Smith/Dir., Harold L. Yoh/Dir., George Babich/Dir., William R. Cook/Dir.

Owners: George Babich, Insiders/2.33%, Harold L. Yoh, Franklin Resources Inc./6.34%, Patricia C. Barron, Vince Northfield, Donald Beckman/3.72%, Martin S. Headley, Barclays Global Investors, NA/5.31%, Judith M. von Seldeneck, John B. Suddarth, James W. Zug, Jeffrey P. Black/1.00%, Benson F. Smith, William R. Cook *(17 Owners included in Index)*

Financial Data: *Fiscal Year End:*12/25 *Latest Annual Data:* 12/31/2006

Year		Sales			Net Income
2006		$2,646,757,000			$139,430,000
2005		$2,514,552,000			$138,817,000
2004		$2,485,378,000			$9,517,000
Curr. Assets:	$1,139,529,000	**Curr. Liab.:**	$470,775,000	**P/E Ratio:**	15.15
Plant, Equip.:	$422,178,000	**Total Liab.:**	$1,169,631,000	**Indic. Yr. Divd.:**	$1.280
Total Assets:	$2,359,052,000	**Net Worth:**	$1,189,421,000	**Debt/ Equity:**	0.4001

Telefonica

Gran Via, 28, planta 3, Madrid, 28013; ***PH:*** 34-915848949; ***http://*** www.telefonica.com

General - Incorporation	Spain	**Stock**- Price on:12/24/2007	$66.68
Employees	227,137	Stock Exchange	NYSE
Auditor	Deloitte, S.L.	Ticker Symbol	TEF
Stk Agt	Citibank N.A	Outstanding Shares	1,610,000,000
Counsel	NA	E.P.S	NA
DUNS No.	56-290-4136	Shareholders	NA

Business: The group's principal activities are the provision and operation of a wide range of telecommunication services on a national and international level. The group operates through the following business lines: telefonica de espana (basic telecommunications in Spain); telefonica servicios moviles (wireless communications businesses); telefonica international (responsible for making and managing investments in the telecommunications industry in America); admira media (media and entertainment); telefonica data (integral data transmission services); terra networks (Internet service provider); atento holding (call-centre business); telefonica publicidad e informacion (directory business).

Primary SIC and add'l.: 4813 4822

CIK No: 0000814052

Subsidiaries: Al-Pi Telecommunicaciones, Cesky Telecom and Telefnica Deutschland., Tele Leste Celular Participaes S.A., Telefnica Group, Telefnica Mviles Espaa, Vodafone PLC, and Retevisin Mvil S.A

Officers: Cesar Alierta Izuel/63/Chmn., CEO, Calixto Rios Perez/63/GM - Internal Audit, Luis Abril Perez/46/Technical General Sec., Ramiro Sanchez De Lerin/53/Sec., Antonio Hornedo Muguiro/Vice Sec., Jose Maria alvarez pallete/44/GM - Telefonica Latinoamerica, Santiago Fernandez Valbuena/50/CFO, GM - Finance, Corporate Development

Directors: Cesar Alierta Izuel/63/Chmn., CEO, Isidro Faine Casas/66/Vice Chmn., Vitalino Manuel Nafria Aznar/58/Vice Chmn., Enrique Aznar Used/67/Dir., Jose Fernando De Almansa Moreno-Barreda/59/Dir., Antonio Viana-Baptista/50/Dir., Alfonso Ferrari Herrero/44/Dir., Gonzalo

Fernandez De Angulo Hinojosa/63/Dir., Pablo alvarez De Tejera Isla/44/Dir., Antonio Lavilla Massanell/54/Dir., Jose Maria Abril/Dir., Julio Lopez Linares/63/Dir., Gregorio Villalabeitia Galarraga/57/Dir., Jose Fernando De Almansa Moreno-Barreda/60/Dir., Jose Maria Lopez alvarez-Pallete/45/Dir. *(19 Directors included in Index)*

Owners: Chase Nominees LTD./9.90%, Banco Bilbao Vizcaya Argentaria, S.A./6.44%, Caja de Ahorros y Pensiones de Barcelona/5.08%

Financial Data: ***Fiscal Year End:***12/31 ***Latest Annual Data:*** 12/31/2006

Year	Sales	Net Income
2006	$71,919,382,000	$8,372,022,000
2005	$46,547,417,000	$4,908,390,000
2004	$42,584,138,000	$3,517,437,000

Curr. Assets:	$23,386,474,000	***Curr. Liab.:***	$34,771,421,000		
Plant, Equip.:	$44,190,441,000	***Total Liab.:***	$120,954,003,000	***Indic. Yr. Divd.:***	$1.980
Total Assets:	$151,817,336,000	***Net Worth:***	$30,863,333,000	***Debt/ Equity:***	NA

Telefnica del Per

Avenida Arequipa 1155, Santa Beatriz, Lima, 1155; ; ***http://*** www.telefonica.com.pe; ***Email:*** accion.telefonica@telefonica.es

General - Incorporation	Peru	***Stock*** - Price on:12/24/2007	NA
Employees	NA	Stock Exchange	NA
Auditor	Deloitte & Touche LLP	Ticker Symbol	NA
Stk Agt	JP Morgan Chase Bank, N.A.	Outstanding Shares	NA
Counsel	NA	E.P.S	NA
DUNS No.	93-426-9564	Shareholders	NA

Business: The group's principle activities are the provision of telecommunication services which include public telephone, cellular phone, paging services of business communications and related services; cable television; telephone directory advertising; courier services; Internet access and other networks related services and operation of public telephone system.

Primary SIC and add'l.: 4841 4215 7311 3661 4812 4813 2741

CIK No: 0001014620

Subsidiaries: Media Networks Per S.A.C., Servicios Editoriales del Per S.A.C, Servicios Globales de Telecomunicaciones S.A.C, Telefnica Empresas Per S.A.A., Telefnica Multimedia S.A.C, Telefnica Servicios Comerciales S.A.C, Telefnica Servicios Digitales S.A.C, Telefnica Servicios Integrados S.A.C, Telefnica Servicios Tcnicos S.A.C, Telefnica Soluciones Globales Holding S.A.C., Transporte Urgente de Mensajera S.A.C

Telefonica Mobile Inc

Goya, 24, Madrid, 28001; ; ***http://*** www.telefonicamoviles.com

General - Incorporation	Spain	***Stock*** - Price on:12/24/2007	NA
Employees	NA	Stock Exchange	NA
Auditor	Ernst & Young, S.l	Ticker Symbol	NA
Stk Agt	NA	Outstanding Shares	NA
Counsel	NA	E.P.S	NA
DUNS No.	NA	Shareholders	NA

Business: The group's principal activity is the provision of mobile telecommunications services, including voice and data communications. The group was incorporated in the wireless telecommunications businesses sector worldwide in Feb 2000. The group is present in Europe, Latin America and north Africa. On Nov 22, 2000 the company became listed through a public offering of its shares on the Spanish and New York stock exchanges.

Primary SIC and add'l.: 4899 7389 6719 4813 4812

CIK No: 0001127866

Subsidiaries: Avista Part. S.L., Brasilcel, N.V., Sudestecel Participaes, S.A., Tagilo Participaes, S.A., TBS Celular Participaes, S.A., Tele Sudeste Celular Participaes,S.A., Telerj Celular, S.A., Telest Celular, S.A., Vivo Brasil Comunicao Ltda

Telefonica of Argentina Inc

Avenida Ingeniero Huergo 723, Buenos Aires; ***PH:*** 54-1143322066; ***http://*** www.telefonica.com.ar

General - Incorporation	AR	***Stock*** - Price on:12/24/2007	$19.7
Employees	8,910	Stock Exchange	NYSE
Auditor	Deloitte & Co. S.R.L.	Ticker Symbol	TAR
Stk Agt	Bank of New York	Outstanding Shares	698,420,000
Counsel	Telinver	E.P.S	$0.10
DUNS No.	97-071-7179	Shareholders	NA

Business: The group's principle activity is the provision of telecommunication services. Other activities include investment and marketing fixed and mobile units.

Primary SIC and add'l.: 7389 8999 4899 4812

CIK No: 0000914242

Subsidiaries: Telefnica DataCorp, Telefnica Mviles, TISA

Officers: Rodolfo Enrique Holzer/43/Dir. - Service Network, Gonzalo Lopez-Barajas/Contact - Spain, Ana Casilda Andres/Contact - Spain, Consuelo Martin/Contact - Spain, Maria Eugenia Perea/Contact - Spain, Antonio Hornedo Muguiro/Vice Sec., Alejandro Pinedo/45/Sec., Jose Luis Aiello Montes/38/Dir. - Wholesale Business Unit, Ricardo Pablo Galli/34/Dir. - Local Quality, Ezequiel Nieto/Head - Investor Relations, John Crosse/Mgr. - Investor Relations, London, Daniel Andrade Gomes/Mgr. - Investor Relations, Brazil, Dolores Garcia/Contact - Spain, Isabel Beltran/Contact - Spain, Angela Azcona/Contact - Spain *(23 Officers included in Index)*

Directors: Vitalino Manuel Nafria Aznar/58/Vice Chmn., Eduardo Fernando Caride/51/Chmn., Isidro Faine Casas/66/Vice Chmn., Jose Maria Alvarez-pallete Lopez/45/Vice Chmn., Jose Fernando De Almansa Moreno-Barreda/59/Dir., David Arculus/62/Dir., Maximino Carpio Garcia/63/Dir., Manuel Echanove Pasquin/43/Alternate Dir., Javier Delgado Martinez/48/Alternate Dir., Gaspar Arino Ortiz/72/Alternate Dir., Juan Jorge Waehner/47/Alternate Dir., Guillermo Harteneck/79/Dir., Jaime Urquijo Chacon/76/Dir., Javier Benjumea Llorente/55/Alternate Dir., Jose Maria Abril Perez/56/Dir. *(31 Directors included in Index)*

Owners: Cointel/62.53%, TIHBV, Cointel/2.30%, TISA/32.25%

Financial Data: ***Fiscal Year End:***12/31 ***Latest Annual Data:*** 12/31/2006

Year	Sales	Net Income
2006	$1,223,021,000	$164,179,000
2005	$1,109,427,000	$511,714,000
2004	$1,029,996,000	$227,878,000

Curr. Assets:	$267,648,000	***Curr. Liab.:***	$613,632,000		
Plant, Equip.:	$1,013,472,000	***Total Liab.:***	$1,406,131,000	***Indic. Yr. Divd.:***	$1.970
Total Assets:	$1,627,430,000	***Net Worth:***	$221,299,000	***Debt/ Equity:***	NA

Telefonos de Mexico SA de CV

Parque Va No. 190, Col. Cuauhtemoc, Mexico, DF, 6599; ***PH:*** 52-5552221212; ***http://*** www.telmex.com.mx

General - Incorporation	United Mexican States	***Stock*** - Price on:12/24/2007	$39.25
Employees	76,395	Stock Exchange	NYSE
Auditor	C.P.C. Fernando Espinosa Lpez	Ticker Symbol	TMX
Stk Agt	Morgan ADR Service Center	Outstanding Shares	993,490,000
Counsel	NA	E.P.S	$2.90
DUNS No.	NA	Shareholders	NA

Business: The groups principle activity is to provide local telephone service. The group operates through six geographic segments. In the year 2006, the group acquired 2Wire. The group operates from the Mexico, Brazil, Chile, Argentina, Colombia and Peru.

Primary SIC and add'l.: 3661 4822 4812 4813 7379 3669 7389 4899

CIK No: 0000866213

Subsidiaries: Alquiladora de Casas, S.A. de C.V., Anuncios en Directorios, S.A. de C.V., Compaa de Telfonos y Bienes Races, S.A. de C.V., Consorcio Red Uno, S.A. de C.V., Controladora de Servicios de, Embratel Participaes S.A., Empresa Brasileira de Telecomunicaes S.A. EMBRATEL, Grupo Telvista S.A. de C.V., Metrored Telecomunicaciones S.R.L., Net Servios de Comunicao S.A., PrimeSys Solues Empresariais S.A., Star One S.A., Techtel-LMDS Comunicaciones Interactivas, S.A., Telecomunicaciones, S.A. de C.V., Telfonos del Noroeste, S.A. de C.V. 23 Subsidiaries included in the Index

Officers: Hector Slim Seade/Dir., CEO, Sergio F. Medina Noriega/Sec., Arturo Elias Ayub/Dir. - Strategic Alliances, Communications, Institutional Relations, Javier Mondragon Alarcon/Regulation, Legal Affairs, Adolfo Cerezo Perez/CFO

Directors: Hector Slim Seade/Dir., CEO, Carlos Slim Domit/Co - Chmn., Jaime Chico Pardo/Chmn., Juan Antonio Perez Simon/67/Vice Chmn., Antonio Cosio Arino/Dir., Angeles Espinosa Iglesias/Dir., Eric D. Boyer/Dir., Laura Diez Barroso De Laviada/Dir., Amparo Espinosa Rugarcia/Dir., Elmer Franco Maclas/Dir., Angel Losada Moreno/Dir., Antonio Del Valle Ruiz/70/Dir., Jose Kuri Harfush/Dir., Fernando Solana Morales/Dir., Eduardo Valdes Acra/Dir. *(33 Directors included in Index)*

Owners: Patrick Slim Domit, Carlos Slim Helu, Carlos Slim Domit, Carlos Slim Helu, Brandes Investment Partners, L.P., Antonio Cosio Ario, AT&T International, Patrick Slim Domit, Marco Antonio Slim Domit, Carlos Slim Domit, Carlos Slim Helu, Patrick Slim Domit, Carso Global Telecom, Carso Global Telecom, Antonio Coso Pando *(20 Owners included in Index)*

Financial Data: ***Fiscal Year End:***12/31 ***Latest Annual Data:*** 12/31/2006

Year	Sales	Net Income
2006	$16,240,568,000	$2,561,632,000
2005	$15,154,174,000	$2,515,517,000
2004	$12,450,536,000	$2,532,648,000

Curr. Assets:	$5,628,913,000	***Curr. Liab.:***	$4,791,234,000	***P/E Ratio:***	9.09
Plant, Equip.:	$15,717,089,000	***Total Liab.:***	$16,332,056,000	***Indic. Yr. Divd.:***	$0.810
Total Assets:	$25,040,047,000	***Net Worth:***	$8,707,991,000	***Debt/ Equity:***	NA

Telekom Austria

Lassallestrasse 9, A-1020 Vienna, Vienna; ***PH:*** 43-59059119000; ***http://*** www.telekom.at; ***Email:*** investor.relations@telekom.at

General - Incorporation	Austria	***Stock*** - Price on:12/24/2007	NA
Employees	15,595	Stock Exchange	OTC
Auditor	KPMG Alpen-Treuhand GmbH	Ticker Symbol	TKAGY
Stk Agt	Bank of New York	Outstanding Shares	NA
Counsel	NA	E.P.S	NA
DUNS No.	NA	Shareholders	NA

Business: The group's principal activities are to provide fixed-line and wireless communication services. The group also offers Internet services. The group re-organised its segments during 2002 and is now operating through two main segments: wire line (which comprises of fixed line services, data communication services and Internet services) and wireless (mobile communication services). Fixed line provides fixed line telephony, carrier services, leased lines, fixed line Internet services and voice telephony. Data communication provides network infrastructure installation, network management, database and information services and e-commerce and electronic data interchange. Internet provides analogue and digital Internet access, portal services, e-commerce and multimedia services. Mobile communication provides mobile telephone and data services.

Primary SIC and add'l.: 3663 4841 4813 5999 4812 4822

CIK No: 0001127051

Officers: Rudolf Fischer/CEO, Vice Chmn. - Telekom Austria Group, Gernot Schieszler/Vice Chmn., CFO, Stephan Koren/Chief Marketing Officer, Waltraud Wultsch/Administration, Katharina Schatz/Investor Relations Officer, Vera Sokulskyj/Investor Relations Officer, Peter Zydek/Head - Investor Relations, Barbara Plobnig/Investor Relations Officer, Stefano Colombo/46/CFO

Directors: Rudolf Fischer/CEO, Vice Chmn. - Telekom Austria Group, Edith Hlawati/Vice Chmn. - Supervisory Board, Gernot Schieszler/Vice Chmn., CFO, Peter Michaelis/Chmn. - Supervisory Board, Boris Nemsic/50/Chmn., Michael Kolek/Member - Supervisory Board, Willhelm Eidenberger/Member - Supervisory Board, Walter Hotz/Member - Supervisory Board, Rainer Wieltsch/Member - Supervisory Board, Franz Kusin/Member - Supervisory Board, Hans Haider/Member - Supervisory Board, Harald Stober/Member - Supervisory Board, Johann Georg Schelling/Member - Supervisory Board, Wolfgang C. Berndt/Member - Supervisory Board, Wilfried Stadler/Member - Supervisory Board *(16 Directors included in Index)*

Financial Data: ***Fiscal Year End:***12/31 ***Latest Annual Data:*** 12/31/2006

Year	Sales	Net Income
2006	$6,362,172,000	$819,605,000
2005	$5,184,463,000	$494,068,000
2004	$5,534,372,000	$310,078,000

Curr. Assets:	$1,531,746,000	***Curr. Liab.:***	$2,188,080,000		
Plant, Equip.:	$4,246,028,000	***Total Liab.:***	$6,253,223,000	***Indic. Yr. Divd.:***	NA
Total Assets:	$9,974,810,000	***Net Worth:***	$3,721,586,000	***Debt/ Equity:***	NA

Telemig Celular Participacoes S.A.

SCN Qd 4, Ed. Centro Empresarial Varig, sala 702-A, Braslia, 70714000; ***PH:*** 55-34295600; ***Fax:*** 55-34295626; ***http://*** www.telemigcelular.com.br

General - Incorporation	Federative Republic of Brazil	**Stock**- Price on:12/24/2007	$50.9
Employees	NA	Stock Exchange	NYSE
Auditor	PricewaterhouseCoopers LLP	Ticker Symbol	NA
Stk Agt	Bank of New York	Outstanding Shares	17,890,000
Counsel	NA	E.P.S	$4.95
DUNS No.	NA	Shareholders	NA

Business: The groups principal activity is to provide telecommunication services. The group operates from the Brazil.

Primary SIC and add'l.: 4813

CIK No: 0001066118

Officers: Oscar Thompson/42/CEO, CFO, Head - Investor Relations, Marcus Roger Meireles Martins Da Costa/50/Chief Human Resources Officer, Jose Arthur Escodro/57/Member - Fiscal Counsel, Jorge Luiz Gouvea Luiz Gouvea/47/Member - Fiscal Counsel, Edmilson Gama Dasilva/45/Member - Fiscal Counsel, Alexsandro De Souza/30/Member - Fiscal Counsel

Directors: Sergio Spinelli Silva/42/Chmn., Alberto Ribeiro Guth/48/Vice Chmn., Kevin Michael Altit/44/Dir., Elemer Andre Suranyi/42/Dir., Jose Luiz Rodrigues/53/Dir., Pedro Paulo Elejalde De Campos/53/Dir., Carlos Alberto Rosa/42/Dir., Danilo De Siqueira Campos/48/Dir., Jose Wilson Da Silva/53/Dir., Wagner Pinheiro De Oliveira/45/Dir.

Owners: Telpart Participaes S.A. Latinvest Holding/53.90%, Utilitivest II Delaware LLC/5.39%, Telpart Participaes S.A. Latinvest Holding/4.27%, Caixa de Previdencia dos Funcionrios do Banco do Brasil/2.64%, Delaware LLC/6.43%, Caixa de Previdencia dos Funcionrios do Banco do Brasil/5.11%

Financial Data: ***Fiscal Year End:***12/31 ***Latest Annual Data:*** 12/31/2006

Year	*Sales*	*Net Income*
2006	$570,529,000	$60,369,000
2005	$508,358,000	$69,041,000
2004	$458,498,000	$56,684,000

Curr. Assets:	$421,126,000	*Curr. Liab.:*	$207,124,000	*P/E Ratio:*	9.09
Plant, Equip.:	$367,982,000	*Total Liab.:*	$784,066,000	*Indic. Yr. Divd.:*	$0.990
Total Assets:	$1,323,581,000	*Net Worth:*	$539,515,000	*Debt/ Equity:*	NA

Telenor ASA

Snaryveien 30, Fornebu, N-1331; ***PH:*** 47-810-77000; ***http://*** www.telenor.com

General - Incorporation	Norway	**Stock**- Price on:12/24/2007	NA
Employees	27,600	Stock Exchange	NDQ
Auditor	Ernst & Young AS	Ticker Symbol	TELN
Stk Agt	Norwegian Account Agent	Outstanding Shares	NA
Counsel	Nordea Bank Norge ASA	E.P.S	NA
DUNS No.	NA	Shareholders	NA

Business: The group's activities are divided into four main business areas: telenor networks: management of infrastructure within telecommunications and data communication (telephony , data, broadband); telenor mobile: mobile services operations within voice, data, Internet, content services and electronic commerce; telenor plus: sales and distribution of the group's communications, entertainment and information services; telenor business solutions: development, sales and implementation of the group's communication and it solutions.

Primary SIC and add'l.: 4899 4813 7372 3669 7374 4833

CIK No: 0001126113

Subsidiaries: DiGi Telecommunications Sdn Bhd, Kyivstar GSM JSC, Pannon GSM RT, Telenor Mobil AS, Telenor Mobil Holding AS, Telenor Mobile Communications AS, Telenor Network Holding, Telenor Telecom Solutions AS

Officers: Jon Fredrik Baksaas/CEO, Pres., Arve Johansen/Sr. Exec. VP, Deputy CEO, Head - Telenor's Asia Operations, Jan Edvard Thygesen/Exec. VP, Head - Telenor's Central, Eastern European Operations, Morten Karlsen Sorby/Exec. VP, Head - Telenor's Nordic Mobile, Fixed Network Operations, Trond O. Westlie/CFO, Exec. VP, Bjorn Magnus Kopperud/Exec. VP, Head - Human Resources, Ragnar H. Korsth/Exec. VP, Head - Global Coordination, Hilde M. Tonne/Exec. VP, Head - Group Communications

Directors: Bjorg Ven/Vice Chmn., Harald Norvik/Chmn., Bjorn Andre Anderssen/Dir., John Giverholt/Dir., Paul Bergqvist/Dir., Harald Stavn/Dir., Liselott Kilaas/Dir., Kjersti Kleven/Dir., Olav Volldal/Dir., May Krosby/Dir.

Telephone and Data Systems Inc

30 N Lasalle St., Ste 4000, Chicago, IL, 60602; ***PH:*** 1-312-630-1900; ***http://*** www.teldta.com; ***Email:*** tdsinfo@teldta.com

General - Incorporation	DE	**Stock**- Price on:12/24/2007	$63.3
Employees	11,500	Stock Exchange	AMEX
Auditor	PricewaterhouseCoopers LLP	Ticker Symbol	TDS
Stk Agt	Computershare Investor Services LLC	Outstanding Shares	NA
Counsel	Sidley, Austin, Brown & Wood	E.P.S	NA
DUNS No.	05-057-5695	Shareholders	NA

Business: The group's principle activity is to provide telecommunication services with wireless telephone and wireline telephone operations. The group operates from United States.

Primary SIC and add'l.: 4813 4812

CIK No: 0001051512

Subsidiaries: Affiliate Fund, Alltel Newco #4 LLC, Amelia Telephone Corporation, Arcadia Telephone Company, Arizona Telephone Company, Arvig Telephone Company, Asotin Telephone Company, Badger Telecom, LLC, Bangor Cellular Telephone, L.p., Barnardsville Telephone Company, Black Earth Telephone Company, LLC, Blue Ridge Telephone Company, Bonduel Telephone Company, LLC, Bridge Water Telephone Company, Burlington, Brighton& Wheatland Telephone Company, LLC 261 Subsidiaries included in the Index

Officers: John E. Rooney/66/CEO, Pres. - United States Cellular Corporation/$5,433,875.00, David A. Wittwer/47/CEO, Pres. - TDS Telecommunications Corporation, Leroy T. Carlson/Dir., CEO, Pres./$5,293,119.00, Kurt Thaus/CIO, Sr. VP, Theodore C. Herbert/VP - Human Resources, Byron A. Wertz/VP - Corporate Development, Peter L. Sereda/VP, Treasurer, Joseph R. Hanley/VP - Technology Planning, Services, Mark A. Steinkrauss/VP - Corporate Relations, James W. Twesme/VP - Corporate Finance, Michael D. Jack/65/Sr. VP, Corporate Controller, Douglas D. Shuma/Sr. VP, Corporate Controller, John M. Toomey/Assist. Treasurer, Timothy J. Kleespies/VP - Finance, Tax, Kenneth R. Meyers/Dir., CFO, Exec. VP *(20 Officers included in Index)*

Directors: Leroy T. Carlson/Dir., CEO, Pres., Walter C.D Carlson/Chmn., James Barr/Dir., George W. Off/Dir., Christopher D. O'Leary/Dir., Herbert S. Wander/Dir., Letitia G.C. Carlson/Dir., Donald C. Nebergall/Dir., Mitchell H. Saranow/Dir., Kenneth R. Meyers/Dir., CFO, Exec. VP, Gregory P. Josefowicz/Dir.

Owners: James Barr, Insiders/5.30%, Martin L. Solomon, LeRoy T. Carlson, Insiders/1.10%, Kenneth R. Meyers, Mitchell H. Saranow, LeRoy T. Carlson, Walter C.D. Carlson, Walter C.D. Carlson, Letitia G. Carlson, LeRoy T. Carlson, Prudence E. Carlson/5.20%, Donald C. Nebergall, John E. Rooney *(20 Owners included in Index)*

Teleplus World Corp

6101 Blue Lagoon Dr., Ste. 450, Miami, FL, 33126; ***PH:*** 1-514-344-0778; ***Fax:*** 1-786-594-3930; ***http://*** www.teleplusworld.com

General - Incorporation	NV	**Stock**- Price on:12/24/2007	$0.03
Employees	50	Stock Exchange	OTC
Auditor	PKF	Ticker Symbol	TLPE
Stk Agt	Transfer Online, Inc.	Outstanding Shares	137,190,000
Counsel	NA	E.P.S	-$0.04
DUNS No.	NA	Shareholders	NA

Business: The groups principle activities include providing wireless and telecom products and services. The groups wholly owned subsidiaries include TelePlus Connect, Corp., a competitive local exchange carrier that provides landline, long distance and Internet services. The group operates through two segments namely wireless services and telecom services. In December 2005, the group acquired Liberty Wireless and In June 2006, the group acquired Maximo Impact, Inc. The group operates from the United States and Canada. The group's quarterly revenue for Sep '07 was 5.70 millions of USD.

Primary SIC and add'l.: 4899

CIK No: 0001133754

Subsidiaries: Teleplus Retail Services, Inc

Officers: Marius Silvasan/Chmn., CEO, Pres., Tom Davis/58/Dir., COO, Carlos I. Cardelle/General Counsel, Irina Abraham/Contact - Accounting Receivable, Payable, Kelly McLaren/Dir., Pres., Cris Neely/Dir., CFO

Directors: Marius Silvasan/Chmn., CEO, Pres., Tom Davis/58/Dir., COO, Michael L. Karpheden/Dir., Hakan Wretsell/Dir., Gordon Chow/Dir., Kelly McLaren/Dir., Pres., Cris Neely/Dir., CFO, Nicholas Shamy/Dir.

Owners: Marius Silvasan/39.40%, Gordon Chow, Nicholas Shamy, Hakan Wretsell, Michael Karpheden, Carlos Cardelle, Insiders/40.20%

Financial Data: ***Fiscal Year End:***12/31 ***Latest Annual Data:*** 12/31/2006

Year	*Sales*	*Net Income*
2006	$24,670,000	-$2,699,000
2005	$8,093,000	-$4,820,000
2004	$12,181,000	-$1,074,000

Curr. Assets:	$3,165,000	*Curr. Liab.:*	$16,947,000		
Plant, Equip.:	$761,000	*Total Liab.:*	$23,062,000	*Indic. Yr. Divd.:*	NA
Total Assets:	$21,471,000	*Net Worth:*	-$1,591,000	*Debt/ Equity:*	NA

Telesis Technology Corp

1611 12TH St. E, UNIT B, Palmetto, FL, 34221; ***PH:*** 1-941-795-7441; ***http://*** www.telesistechnology.com; ***Email:*** ir@telesistechnology.com

General - Incorporation	FL	**Stock**- Price on:12/24/2007	NA
Employees	7	Stock Exchange	OTC
Auditor	E. Randall Gruber, CPA, P.C	Ticker Symbol	ITKH
Stk Agt	NA	Outstanding Shares	NA
Counsel	NA	E.P.S	NA
DUNS No.	NA	Shareholders	NA

Business: The group's principal activity is a global Aerospace & Defense Contractor with sevices such as design, develop tests, manufacture and market a diverse range of sub-component products and systems. Capabilities include maintenance, repair and overhaul of an extensive assortment of aerospace component systems. The company has two fully operational facilities, which have the ability to efficiently and economically process the MRO project requirements. The company headquarters, light assembly and testing facility is located in Florida and the contract manufacturing facility is located in Singapore.

Primary SIC and add'l.: 3674

CIK No: 0001290416

Financial Data: ***Fiscal Year End:***12/31 ***Latest Annual Data:*** 12/31/2005

Year	*Sales*	*Net Income*
2005	$2,608,000	$23,000
2004	$1,545,000	$76,000

Curr. Assets:	$1,251,000	*Curr. Liab.:*	$217,000		
Plant, Equip.:	$409,000	*Total Liab.:*	$279,000	*Indic. Yr. Divd.:*	NA
Total Assets:	$1,685,000	*Net Worth:*	$1,406,000	*Debt/ Equity:*	NA

Telestone Technologies Corp

275 Madison Ave., 6th Fl., New York, NY, 10016; ***PH:*** 1-212-880-3794; ***Fax:*** 1-212-880-4241; ***http://*** www.telestonecorp.com; ***Email:*** info@telestonetech.com

General - Incorporation	DE	**Stock**- Price on:12/24/2007	$6.88
Employees	NA	Stock Exchange	NDQ
Auditor	Moores Rowland Mazars	Ticker Symbol	TSTC
Stk Agt	Corporate Stock Transfer, Inc.	Outstanding Shares	9,600,000
Counsel	NA	E.P.S	$0.49
DUNS No.	NA	Shareholders	NA

Business: The group's principle activity is to provide reorganization operations. On 26-Sep-2003, the company along with its subsidiary, elite agents mortgage services inc filed voluntary petitions for reorganization under chapter 11 of the United States bankruptcy code. The group operates from United States.

Primary SIC and add'l.: 6799

CIK No: 0000817129

Subsidiaries: EliteAgents Leasing Services, Inc.

Officers: Han Daqing/Chmn., CEO/$80,000.00, Lu Hanying/Deputy CEO, Yu Yongjing/45/COO, Wang Jianjun/VP/$40,000.00, Luo Zhengbin/VP/$50,000.00, Zhang Shuijun/VP

Directors: Han Daqing/Chmn., CEO, Lian Rengaung/45/Dir., Cheng Guanghui/64/Dir.

Owners: Insiders/40.12%, Han Daqing/34.15%, Wang Jianjun/3.42%, Luo Zhengbin/2.56%

Financial Data: Fiscal Year End:12/31 Latest Annual Data: 12/31/2006

Year	Sales	Net Income
2006	$21,708,000	$4,614,000
2005	$17,410,000	$3,731,000
2004	$19,935,000	$6,917,000

Curr. Assets:	$40,302,000	Curr. Liab.:	$16,853,000	P/E Ratio:	14.04
Plant, Equip.:	$821,000	Total Liab.:	$16,853,000	Indic. Yr. Divd.:	NA
Total Assets:	$41,123,000	Net Worth:	$24,270,000	Debt/ Equity:	NA

Telesystem International Wireless Inc

1250 Rene-levesque Blvd. W, 38th Fl., Montreal, QC, H3B 4W8; ; http:// www.tiw.ca

General - Incorporation	Canada	Stock- Price on:12/24/2007	$22.29
Employees	NA	Stock Exchange	NA
Auditor	Ernst & Young LLP	Ticker Symbol	NA
Stk Agt	Computershare Trust Co	Outstanding Shares	NA
Counsel	NA	E.P.S	NA
DUNS No.	25-247-3400	Shareholders	NA

Business: The group's principle activiy is to develop, acquire and operate wireless telecommunications networks. The group operates in two segments: cellular service and equipment. Cellular service consists of variable airtime charges and in-bound international connection charges and recurring fixed access charges. Equipment revenue consists of revenues from the sale of handset. The group has cellular operations in romania, czech republic and India.

Primary SIC and add'l.: 1731 4812 3663

CIK No: 0001045632

Subsidiaries: Mobifon S.a., Oskar Mobil A.s.

Officers: Jacques Lacroix/Investors Contact

Teletech Holdings Inc

9197 S Peoria St., Englewood, CO, 80112; PH: 1-303-397-8100; http:// www.teletech.com

General - Incorporation	DE	Stock- Price on:12/24/2007	$32.67
Employees	39,010	Stock Exchange	NDQ
Auditor	Ernst & Young LLP	Ticker Symbol	TTEC
Stk Agt	American Stock Transfer & Trust Co.	Outstanding Shares	70,720,000
Counsel	NA	E.P.S	$0.84
DUNS No.	92-634-8103	Shareholders	NA

Business: The group's principal activity is to provide customer relationship management services and solutions for large domestic, foreign and multinational companies and helps clients to acquire, serve, retain and grow their customers by strategically managing inbound telephone, e-mail and Internet based inquires on their behalf. The international operations of the group are located in Canada, Australia, Argentina, Mexico, New Zealand, Brazil, China, Singapore, the United Kingdom, Asia and Europe.

Primary SIC and add'l.: 7389

CIK No: 0001013880

Subsidiaries: Apoyo Empresarial de Servicios, S. de R.L. de C.V., Carabunga.com. Inc., Comlink, S.A., Customer Solutions Maritius, Enhansiv UK, Global One Colorado, Inc., Global One Insurance Company, Newgen Results Canada, Ltd., Newgen Results Corporation, Percepta Germany GmbH, Percepta Holdings, Inc., Percepta Philippines, Inc., Percepta UK Limited, Percepta, LLC, Percepta, ULC 56 Subsidiaries included in the Index

Officers: Kenneth Tuchman/Chmn., CEO/$410,985.00, Brian Delaney/Exec. VP - Global Service Delivery/$787,462.00, Gregory Hopkins/Exec. VP - Global Accounting/$1,729,391.00, Kamalesh Dwivedi/CIO, Exec. VP/$587,545.00, Alan Schutzman/Exec. VP, General Counsel, Sec., John Troka/Interim CFO/$363,790.00, Mike Jossi/Exec. VP - Human Capital Delivery

Directors: Kenneth Tuchman/Chmn., CEO, James Barlett/Vice Chmn., William A. Linnenbringer/59/Dir., Shrikant Mehta/64/Dir., Shirley Young/72/Dir., Ruth Lipper/56/Dir.

Owners: Greg Hopkins, Kenneth D. Tuchman/42.00%, William A. Linnenbringer, Kamalesh Dwivedi, Brian Delaney, Shirley Young, John R. Troka, James E. Barlett/1.20%, John Simon, Shrikant C. Mehta, Insiders/43.20%, Ruth C. Lipper

Financial Data: Fiscal Year End:12/31 Latest Annual Data: 12/31/2006

Year	Sales	Net Income
2006	$1,211,297,000	$51,842,000
2005	$1,086,673,000	$28,158,000
2004	$1,052,690,000	$24,003,000

Curr. Assets:	$361,144,000	Curr. Liab.:	$182,015,000	P/E Ratio:	38.89
Plant, Equip.:	$156,047,000	Total Liab.:	$295,309,000	Indic. Yr. Divd.:	NA
Total Assets:	$658,716,000	Net Worth:	$363,407,000	Debt/ Equity:	0.1177

Teletouch Communications Inc

5718 Airport Fwy., Ft.worth, TX, 76117; PH: 1-817-654-6225; http:// www.teletouch.com;
Email: information@teletouch.com

General - Incorporation	DE	Stock- Price on:12/24/2007	NA
Employees	293	Stock Exchange	OTC
Auditor	BDO Seidman LLP	Ticker Symbol	TLLE
Stk Agt	Continental Stock Transfer & Trust Co	Outstanding Shares	NA
Counsel	Cozen O'Connor	E.P.S	-$0.04
DUNS No.	07-256-3638	Shareholders	NA

Business: The group's principle activities are to provide paging and messaging, cellular and two-way radio services. Operating in the wireless telecommunications industry, the group offers four categories of paging services: numeric, alphanumeric, tone-only and tone-plus-voice. The operations are conducted through 26 offices located in non-major metropolitan areas such as Alabama, Arkansas, Louisiana, Mississippi, Missouri, Oklahoma, Texas, Tennessee and Florida. The customers include various-sized companies with field sales and service operations, individuals in occupations requiring substantial mobility.

Primary SIC and add'l.: 4812

CIK No: 0000928659

Subsidiaries: Progressive Concepts, Inc., Teletouch Licenses, Inc., TLL Georgia, Inc., Visao Systems, Inc.

Officers: Robert M. McMurrey/Chmn., CEO, George Hechtman/Pres., COO - Progressive Concepts, Inc, Thomas A. Hyde/COO, Pres., Douglas E. Sloan/CFO, Keith Cole/Exec. VP, General Counsel - Progressive Concepts, Inc

Directors: Robert M. McMurrey/Chmn., CEO, Susan Stranahan Ciallella/Dir., Marshall G. Webb/Dir., Henry Y.L. Toh/Dir., Clifford E. McFarland/Dir.

Financial Data: Fiscal Year End:05/31 Latest Annual Data: 5/31/2006

Year	Sales	Net Income
2006	$20,906,000	-$1,174,000
2005	$24,669,000	-$3,452,000
2004	$26,754,000	-$519,000

Curr. Assets:	$3,745,000	Curr. Liab.:	$3,628,000		
Plant, Equip.:	$4,299,000	Total Liab.:	$6,404,000	Indic. Yr. Divd.:	NA
Total Assets:	$8,606,000	Net Worth:	$2,202,000	Debt/ Equity:	NA

Televideo Inc

2342 Harris Way, San Jose, CA, 95131; PH: 1-408-954-8333; http:// www.televideo.com;
Email: ts_support@televideo.com

General - Incorporation	DE	Stock- Price on:12/24/2007	$0.002
Employees	19	Stock Exchange	OTC
Auditor	Burr, Pilger & Mayer LLP	Ticker Symbol	TELVQ
Stk Agt	NA	Outstanding Shares	11,310,000
Counsel	NA	E.P.S	-$0.131
DUNS No.	06-069-8040	Shareholders	NA

Business: The group's principal activities are to design, manufacture and market video display terminal and network computer products. The products of the group include teleclient family, video display terminals, itelepc and auto safety devices. Teleclient products consist of a range of thin-client windows-based terminals. Video display terminals are general-purpose terminals with ascii, ansi and PC term operating modes. Itelepc is an Internet appliance designed for Internet access and specialized business use. The products of the group are sold in the United States, Europe, Asia-Pacific, Africa and Latin America.

Primary SIC and add'l.: 3577 3579 3575

CIK No: 0000353779

Subsidiaries: Global Telemann Systems, Inc

Officers: Philip K. Hwang/Chmn., CEO, Richard I. Kim/VP

Directors: Philip K. Hwang/Chmn., CEO

Financial Data: Fiscal Year End:10/31 Latest Annual Data: 10/31/2004

Year	Sales	Net Income
2004	$9,483,000	-$474,000
2002	$8,204,000	-$2,634,000
2001	$6,936,000	-$6,464,000

Curr. Assets:	$3,442,000	Curr. Liab.:	$5,481,000		
Plant, Equip.:	$4,918,000	Total Liab.:	$14,150,000	Indic. Yr. Divd.:	NA
Total Assets:	$9,125,000	Net Worth:	-$5,025,000	Debt/ Equity:	NA

Telex Communications Inc

12000 Portland Ave. S, Burnsville, MN, 55337; PH: 1-952-884-4051; http:// www.telex.com;
Email: humanresources@telex.com

General - Incorporation	DE	Stock- Price on:12/24/2007	NA
Employees	NA	Stock Exchange	NA
Auditor	Ernst & Young LLP	Ticker Symbol	NA
Stk Agt	NA	Outstanding Shares	NA
Counsel	NA	E.P.S	NA
DUNS No.	06-653-4611	Shareholders	NA

Business: The group's principal activities are to design, manufacture and market sophisticated audio, wireless and multimedia communications equipment to commercial, professional and industrial customers. The group provides communication products designed to meet the specific needs of customers in commercial, professional and industrial markets, and in the retail consumer electronics market. The products are used in airports, theaters, sports arenas, concert halls, cinemas, stadiums, convention centers, television and radio broadcast studios. The major trademarks of the group includes audiocom(R), midas(r),prostar(R) ,klark-teknik(r),classmate(R) & telex(r). The group primarily operates in United States,Germany, the United Kingdom, Japan, Singapore, Hong Kong, Australia, Singapore and France.

Primary SIC and add'l.: 3651

CIK No: 0000857668

Subsidiaries: Audio Consultants (macau) Company Limited, Dongguan Telex Shinwa Technology Limited, Evi Audio (deutschland) Gmbh, Evi Audio (hong Kong) Ltd., Evi Audio France S.a.s, Evi Audio Gmbh, Evi Audio Japan, Ltd, Ex Tc (uk) Limited, Saguaro Electronica, S.a. De C.v., Tecnologia Especializada Edd, S.a. De C. V, Telex Communications (sea) Pte, Ltd, Telex Communications (uk) Ltd, Telex Communications International, Ltd, Telex Communications, Inc, Telex Communications, Ltd.. Ontario 19 Subsidiaries included in the Index

TeliaSonera

2201 Cooperative Way, Ste. 302, Herndon, VA, 20171; PH: 1-703-546-4000; Fax: 1-703-546-4125;
http:// www.teliasonera.com

General - Incorporation	Sweden	Stock- Price on:12/24/2007	$7.35
Employees	NA	Stock Exchange	OTC
Auditor	PricewaterhouseCoopers LLP	Ticker Symbol	TLSNF
Stk Agt	NA	Outstanding Shares	NA
Counsel	NA	E.P.S	NA
DUNS No.	NA	Shareholders	NA

Business: The group's principle activity is that of a telecommunications provider. It provides reliable, innovative and easy-to-use telecommunications services for carrying and packaging of voice, images, data, information, transactions and entertainment in the nordic and baltic countries, Russia and selected eurasian markets. The group also provides wholesale carrier services between selected destinations in Europe and across the Atlantic. The group's operations are carried out through two segments: mobile communication and fixed communication. The mobile communication segment provides mobile services and development of integrated fixed/mobile services. The fixed communication segment includes Internet and data services and equipment sales.

Primary SIC and add'l.: 4899 4812 4822 4813

CIK No: 0001169870

Subsidiaries: AB Lietuvos Telekomas, AS Eesti Telekom, Auria Oy, Fintur Holdings B.V., Latvijas Mobilais Telefons SIA, NetCom AS, Sonera Mobile Networks Oy, Telia Nttjnster Norden AB, TeliaSonera Chess Holding AS, TeliaSonera Finland Oyj, TeliaSonera International Carrier AB, TeliaSonera Mobile Networks AB, TeliaSonera Sverige AB, UAB Omnitel

Officers: Lars Nyberg/CEO, Pres., Kenneth Karlberg/54/Pres. - Business, Anders Bruse/Pres. - Business, Tero Kivisaari/Pres. - Business, Ewa Lagerqvist/Group VP, Head - Group Communications, Mica Wulff Kamm/Alliance Co - Ordinator, Rickard Safstrom/Bid Mgr. - Sales, Carina Kampe/Communications, Public Relations, Magnus Nerell/Offering, Product Development, Kim Ignatius/52/CFO, Exec. VP, Juho Lipsanen/47/Pres. - Teliasonera Finland, Jan Henrik Ahrnell/49/Group VP, General Counsel - Teliasonera, Rune Nyberg/59/Group VP, Head - Group Human Resources

Directors: Tom V. Weymarn/64/Chmn. - Teliasonera, Carl Bennet/57/Vice Chmn., Eva Liljeblom/Dir., Berith Westman/63/Dir., Sven-Christer Nilsson/67/Dir., Elof Isaksson/66/Dir., Caroline Sundewall/50/Dir., Arja Kovin/44/Dir., Maija-Liisa Friman/56/Dir., Conny Karlsson/53/Dir., Lars G. Nordstrom/Dir., Jon Risfelt/47/Dir., Timo Peltola/62/Dir.

Financial Data: Fiscal Year End:12/31   Latest Annual Data: 12/31/2005

Year	Sales	Net Income
2005	$11,018,988,000	$555,468,000
2004	$12,405,262,000	$1,861,160,000
2003	$11,382,893,000	$1,253,948,000

Curr. Assets:	$5,090,222,000	Curr. Liab.:	$3,804,939,000		
Plant, Equip.:	$6,082,246,000	Total Liab.:	$10,750,995,000	Indic. Yr. Divd.:	NA
Total Assets:	$23,761,951,000	Net Worth:	$13,010,956,000	Debt/ Equity:	NA

Telik Inc

3165 Porter Dr., Palo Alto, CA, 94304; **PH:** 1-650-845-7700; **http://** www.telik.com; **Email:** inquiry@telik.com

General - Incorporation	DE	**Stock**- Price on:12/24/2007	$3.32
Employees	118	Stock Exchange	NDQ
Auditor	Ernst & Young LLP	Ticker Symbol	TELK
Stk Agt	EquiServe Trust Co N.A	Outstanding Shares	52,460,000
Counsel	Cooley Godward LLP	E.P.S.	-$1.14
DUNS No.	NA	Shareholders	NA

Business: The group's principal activities are to discover, develop and commercialize small molecule therapeutics. The therapeutic drugs are used for the treatment of cancer, diabetes and inflammatory diseases. The group's development product includes tlk286, tlk199 and tlk19781. Tlk286, is a small molecule tumor-activated cancer drug that is resistant to standard chemotherapy drugs. Tlk199, is a small molecule bone marrow stimulant developed for the treatment of blood disorders associated with low white blood cell levels or neutropenia. Tlk19781 is a proprietary, orally active small molecule insulin receptor activator for the treatment of type 2 diabetes and other conditions related to insulin resistance.

Primary SIC and add'l.: 8731 2834

CIK No: 0001109196

Officers: Michael M. Wick/Chmn., CEO, Pres./$2,461,455.00, Marc L. Steuer/Sr. VP - Business Development/$592,728.00, Cynthia M. Butitta/CFO, COO/$1,319,259.00, Gail L. Brown/Sr. VP, Chief Medical Officer, William P. Kaplan/VP, General Counsel, Corp. Sec./$604,560.00

Directors: Michael M. Wick/Chmn., CEO, Pres., Mary Ann Gray/Dir., Stefan Ryser/Dir., Edward W. Cantrall/Dir., Steven R. Goldring/Dir., Richard B. Newman/Dir., Robert W. Frick/Dir., Herwig Von Morze/Dir.

Owners: Cynthia M. Butitta/1.12%, Herwig von Morz, Mary Ann Gray, Entities affiliated with Icahn Associates Corp./9.91%, Steven R. Goldring, Edward W. Cantrall, Stefan Ryser, Michael M. Wick/3.90%, Richard B. Newman, Marc L. Steuer, Robert W. Frick, William P. Kaplan, Entities affiliated with Delaware Management Holdings/8.28%, Entities affiliated with Eastbourne Capital Management, L.L.C./26.31%, Insiders/6.06% (16 Owners included in Index)

Financial Data: Fiscal Year End:12/31   Latest Annual Data: 12/31/2006

Year	Sales	Net Income
2006	NA	-$79,624,000
2005	$19,000	-$75,542,000
2004	$163,000	-$69,817,000

Curr. Assets:	$137,437,000	Curr. Liab.:	$16,592,000		
Plant, Equip.:	$4,753,000	Total Liab.:	$16,592,000	Indic. Yr. Divd.:	NA
Total Assets:	$149,214,000	Net Worth:	$132,622,000	Debt/ Equity:	NA

Telkom Sa Ltd

Telkom Towers N, 152 Proes St., Pretoria; **PH:** 27-123113566; **http://** www.telkom.co.za

General - Incorporation	South Africa	**Stock**- Price on:12/24/2007	$99.25
Employees	31,458	Stock Exchange	NYSE
Auditor	Deloitte & Touche, Ernst & Young	Ticker Symbol	NA
Stk Agt	Computershare Investor Services LLC	Outstanding Shares	133,210,000
Counsel	NA	E.P.S.	$9.48
DUNS No.	NA	Shareholders	NA

Business: The group's principle activity is the provision of fixed-line voice and data and mobile communications services in South Africa and other African countries. The group's services and products include fixed line telephony, including domestic, prepaid, international, public payphone and carrier services, as well as enhanced services, customer premises equipment sales and directory services; mobile telephony; data communications using fibre connections, including data transmission, data networking and leased lines and related services; and e-commerce, including Internet access service provider, application service provider, hosting, data storage, e-mail and security services.

Primary SIC and add'l.: 4812 4813

CIK No: 0001214299

Subsidiaries: Acajou, Rossal, Rossal No 65 (Pty) Limited, Telkom Directory Services, Telkom purchased Acajou (Pty) Limited

Officers: Reuben September/Exec. Dir., Acting CEO, Steven Hayward/42/Managing Exec., Assist. to CEO,COO, Johan Mare/52/Managing Exec., Information Systems Development, Pierre Marais/48/Managing Exec., Network Infrastructure Provisioning, Theo Hess/Managing Exec., Network Core Operations, Pieter Schreuder/51/Acting Managing Exec. - Wholesale Services, Ravin Maharaj/Media Relations, Charlotte Mokoena/42/Group Exec., Human Resources, Ouma Rasethaba/48/Acting Chief Corporate Affairs, Kaushik Patel/46/CFO, Godfrey Ntoele/48/Chief Sales, Marketing Officer, Nicola White/34/Group Exec., Investor Relations, Deon Fredericks/47/Group Exec., Accounting Services, Ian Timmerman/36/Acting Group Exec. - Specialised Services, Rob Cowley/48/Acting Managing Exec. - Retail Business (25 Officers included in Index)

Directors: Reuben September/Exec. Dir., Acting CEO, Shirley Lue Arnold/Non - Exec. Chmn., Keitumetse Matthews/Non - Exec. Dir., Mark Lamberti/57/Non - Exec. Dir., Tshepo Mahloele/Non - Exec. Dir., Yekani Tenza/Non - Exec. Dir., Victor Lawrence/Non - Exec. Dir., Ekwow Spio-Garbrah/Non - Exec. Dir., Reitumetse Jackie Huntley/Non - Exec. Dir., Sibusiso Luthuli/Non - Exec. Dir., Thabo Mosololi/Non - Exec. Dir., Brahm Du Plessis/47/Non - Exec. Dir.

Owners: Elephant Consortium, Government of the Republic of South Africa, N. E. Mtshotshisa, T. F. Mosololi, Public Investment Corporation

Financial Data: Fiscal Year End:03/31   Latest Annual Data: 3/31/2006

Year	Sales	Net Income
2006	$7,706,421,000	$1,399,828,000
2005	$6,921,822,000	$993,207,000
2004	$4,842,502,000	$669,186,000

Curr. Assets:	$2,039,506,000	Curr. Liab.:	$2,513,057,000		
Plant, Equip.:	$5,971,295,000	Total Liab.:	$4,498,095,000	Indic. Yr. Divd.:	$3.330
Total Assets:	$8,834,229,000	Net Worth:	$4,287,913,000	Debt/ Equity:	NA

Telkonet Inc

902a Commerce Rd. , Annapolis, MD, 21401; **PH:** 1-240-912-1800; **http://** www.telkonet.com

General - Incorporation	UT	**Stock**- Price on:12/24/2007	$1.73
Employees	104	Stock Exchange	AMEX
Auditor	RBS Mirchandani LLP	Ticker Symbol	TKO
Stk Agt	Stock Trans	Outstanding Shares	66,740,000
Counsel	NA	E.P.S.	-$0.53
DUNS No.	NA	Shareholders	NA

Business: The group's principal activity is to design and develop high technology applications for the commercial and industrial markets. The group is in the development stage and seeking to develop, produce and market proprietary equipment enabling the transmission of voice and data over electric utility lines. The solutions provided utilize their patent-pending technology for the transmission of high-speed data, communications and Internet access over the existing electrical wiring in the buildings. The plugplus Internet system of the group is a viable alternative for the challenges of wired and wireless lans. The customers or target markets include office buildings, hotels, schools, shopping malls, commercial buildings, and multi-dwelling units, government facilities, and any other commercial facilities that have a need for Internet access and network connectivity.

Primary SIC and add'l.: 3612 3613

CIK No: 0001094084

Subsidiaries: Interactivewifi.com, LLC, Microwave Satellite Technologies, Inc. (MST), Telkonet Communications, Inc., Tevue, LLC

Officers: Ronald W. Pickett/59/Dir., CEO, Pres., Robert P. Crabb/60/Chief Marketing Office, James F. Landry/51/CTO, Stephen L. Sadle/62/Dir., Sr. VP, Co - Founder, Joe Noel/Investor Relations Officer, Richard J. Leimbach/39/VP - Finance, Dorothy Cleal/58/Exec. VP, Jason L. Tienor/33/COO, Andrew Hellman/Investor Relations Officer

Directors: Ronald W. Pickett/59/Dir., CEO, Pres., Warren V. Musser/80/Chmn., Thomas M. Hall/55/Dir., James L. Peeler/73/Dir., Stephen L. Sadle/62/Dir., Sr. VP, Co - Founder, Thomas C. Lynch/65/Dir., Seth Blumenfeld/Dir., Anthony J. Paoni/Dir.

Owners: Jason Tienor/1.20%, Thomas C. Lynch, Insiders/10.10%, Stephen L. Sadle/5.90%, Frank T. Matarazzo, James Landry, James L. Peeler, Ronald W. Pickett/3.60%, Dorothy Cleal, Seth D. Blumenfeld, Richard J. Leimbach, Anthony Paoni, Warren V. Musser/2.70%, Thomas M. Hall/1.00%

Financial Data: Fiscal Year End:12/31   Latest Annual Data: 12/31/2006

Year	Sales	Net Income
2006	$5,181,000	-$27,437,000
2005	$2,488,000	-$15,778,000
2004	$699,000	-$13,093,000

Curr. Assets:	$3,766,000	Curr. Liab.:	$4,297,000		
Plant, Equip.:	$4,251,000	Total Liab.:	$4,381,000	Indic. Yr. Divd.:	NA
Total Assets:	$12,517,000	Net Worth:	$8,135,000	Debt/ Equity:	NA

Tellabs Inc

One Tellabs Ctr, 1415 W Diehl Rd., Naperville, IL, 60563; **PH:** 1-630-798-8800; **http://** www.tellabs.com

General - Incorporation	DE	**Stock**- Price on:12/24/2007	$10.8
Employees	3,713	Stock Exchange	NDQ
Auditor	Ernst & Young LLP	Ticker Symbol	TLAB
Stk Agt	Computershare Investor Services LLC	Outstanding Shares	437,770,000
Counsel	NA	E.P.S.	$0.32
DUNS No.	07-441-0333	Shareholders	NA

Business: The groups principle activities include designing and marketing equipment to telecommunications service providers. The groups products include Tellabs(R) 1000 Multiservice Access Series, Tellabs(R) 2300 Telephony Distribution System and Tellabs(R) 5590 Element Manager. Customers served by the group include local telephone administrations (post, telephone and telegraph administrations), original equipment manufacturers, cable operators, alternate service providers, Internet service providers, government agencies and system integrators. The group operates from United States.

Primary SIC and add'l.: 3669 3661 3674

CIK No: 0000317771

Subsidiaries: AccessLan India, Advanced Fibre Communications (HK) Limited, Advanced Fibre Communications International GmbH, Advanced Fibre Communications International Limited, Advanced Fibre Communications Mexico S. de R.L. de C.V., Advanced Fibre Communications U.K. Limited, Advanced Fibre Technology Communications (HK) Limited, AFC Foreign Sales Corporation, AFC Harris Multimedia Communications Limited, AFC Harris Multimedia Communications Private Limited, AFC India Private Limited, E. Coherent Communications Systems Ltd., Future Networks, Inc., Hangzhou AFTEK Communication Company, Ltd., Kiinteisto Oy Mestarinkaare 78 Subsidiaries included in the Index

Officers: Krish A. Prabhu/53/Dir., CEO, Pres./$3,343,946.00, James A. Dite/VP, Controller, Principal Accounting Officer, James M. Sheehan/44/Exec. VP, General Counsel, Chief Administrative Officer/$965,901.00, Timothy J. Wiggins/51/CFO, Exec. VP/$1,231,290.00, Daniel P. Kelly/47/Exec. VP - Product Development, Carl A. Dewilde/61/Exec. VP - Global Sales, Strategy/$943,263.00, John M. Brots/47/Exec. VP - Global Operations, Jean K. Holley/48/CIO, Exec. VP

Directors: Krish A. Prabhu/53/Dir., CEO, Pres., Michael J. Birck/70/Chmn., Co - Founder, Stephanie Pace Marshall/62/Dir., Bo Hedfors/64/Dir., William F. Souders/79/Dir., Michael E. Lavin/62/Dir., Frank Ianna/58/Dir., Jan H. Suwinski/66/Dir., Linda Beck/44/Dir., Fred A. Krehbiel/66/Dir.

Owners: William F. Souders, Jan H. Suwinski, Columbia Wanger Asset Management, L.P/7.23%, Krish A. Prabhu, Linda W. Beck, Lord, Abbett& Co. LLC/5.56%, Frank Ianna, Michael J. Birck/8.00%, Fred A. Krehbiel, Stephen M. McCarthy, Timothy J. Wiggins, Bo Hedfors, Carl A. DeWilde, Michael E. Lavin, Insiders/8.60% *(17 Owners included in Index)*

Financial Data: *Fiscal Year End:*12/30 *Latest Annual Data:* 12/29/2006

Year	Sales	Net Income
2006	$2,041,200,000	$194,100,000
2005	$1,883,400,000	$175,800,000
2004	$1,231,800,000	-$29,800,000

Curr. Assets:	$1,819,400,000	**Curr. Liab.:**	$524,200,000	**P/E Ratio:**	33.75
Plant, Equip.:	$328,800,000	**Total Liab.:**	$725,300,000	**Indic. Yr. Divd.:**	NA
Total Assets:	$3,522,500,000	**Net Worth:**	$2,797,200,000	**Debt/ Equity:**	NA

Telos Corp

19886 Ashburn Rd. , Ashburn, VA, 20147; *PH:* 1-703-724-3800; *http://* www.telos.com;
Email: info@telos.com

General - Incorporation	MD	**Stock**- Price on:12/24/2007	NA
Employees	NA	Stock Exchange	OTC
Auditor	Navigant Consulting, Inc.	Ticker Symbol	TLSRP
Stk Agt	Mellon Investor Services LLC	Outstanding Shares	NA
Counsel	NA	E.P.S.	NA
DUNS No.	05-628-0621	Shareholders	NA

Business: The group's principal activity is to deliver enterprise security and integration solutions and services. It operates through two segments: the products group and xacta. The products group delivers solutions that combine information technology products and services to address customer issues and requirements. Its automated message handling system (amhs), is a recognized standard within the department of defense, which enables users to securely access, send, search and profile message traffic. The xacta division develops enterprise risk management software to help organizations proactively monitor the security of their network environments in accordance with internationally recognized industry and security standards. The us defense agencies, the intelligence and the treasury departments form the major customers of the group.

Primary SIC and add'l.: 7373 7372

CIK No: 0000320121

Subsidiaries: Enterworks International, Inc, Telos Delaware, Inc., Ubiquity.com, Inc., Xacta Corporation

Officers: John B. Wood/Chmn., CEO/$416,689.00, Robert J. Marino/Dir., Exec. VP - Special Projects/$296,481.00, Richard P. Tracy/CTO, Sr. VP, Chief Security Officer, Michael P. Flaherty/Exec. VP, General Counsel, Chief Administrative Officer/$362,631.00, Edward L. Williams/COO, Exec. VP/$310,506.00, Warren Jones/VP - Marketing, Michele Nakazawa/Sr. VP, CFO/$192,904.00, Alvin F. Whitehead/59/Sr. VP - Enterprise Messaging Management, Ronald J. Dorman/44/VP - Information Assurance, Mark Griffin/48/VP - Identity Management, David S. Easley/37/Dir. - Finance, Accounting, Ralph M. Buona/VP, GM - Telos Managed Solutions

Directors: John B. Wood/Chmn., CEO, Robert J. Marino/Dir., Exec. VP - Special Projects

Owners: North Atlantic Small Companies Investment Trust PLC/7.94%, Graphite Enterprise Trust LP/10.41%, North Atlantic Small Companies Investment Trust PLC/7.94%, Robert J. Marino, Insiders, Toxford Corporation/72.62%, John B. Wood, Michael P. Flaherty, Toxford Corporation/72.62%, Edward L. Williams, Telos Corporation Shared, David Borland, North Atlantic Small Companies Investment Trust PLC/29.39%, Graphite Enterprise Trust PLC/11.17%, Graphite Enterprise Trust PLC/41.66% *(19 Owners included in Index)*

Financial Data: *Fiscal Year End:*12/31 *Latest Annual Data:* 12/31/2006

Year	Sales	Net Income
2006	$140,873,000	-$29,681,000
2005	$142,595,000	-$14,060,000
2004	$116,705,000	-$2,953,000

Curr. Assets:	$39,658,000	**Curr. Liab.:**	$51,763,000		
Plant, Equip.:	$8,534,000	**Total Liab.:**	$166,219,000	**Indic. Yr. Divd.:**	NA
Total Assets:	$48,460,000	**Net Worth:**	-$126,782,000	**Debt/ Equity:**	NA

Telstra Corp Ltd

242 Exhibition St. Level 41, Melbourne, Victoria, 3000; *PH:* 03-9634 8014; *Fax:* 03-9634 1189; *http://* www.telstra.com

General - Incorporation	Australia	**Stock**- Price on:12/24/2007	NA
Employees	44,452	Stock Exchange	OTC
Auditor	Ernst & Young LLP, Ian Mcphee	Ticker Symbol	TLSYY
Stk Agt	Link Market Services Ltd	Outstanding Shares	NA
Counsel	NA	E.P.S.	NA
DUNS No.	75-805-670	Shareholders	NA

Business: The group's principal activities are carried out through the following business segments: consumer and marketing: provides fixed, wireless and data products and manages the group's brands; country wide: addresses the telecommunication needs of customers outside the mainland state capital cities, in outer metropolitan areas and in tasmania and the northern territory; business and government: provides a range of products and services to small and medium enterprises and government customers; international: manages the group's international investments, particularly its operations in Hong Kong and New Zealand; infrastructure services: services, delivers and maintains the group's fixed, mobile, ip and data networks; wholesale: provides telecommunications services, infrastructure sharing solutions and related services to other carriers, carriage service providers and isps; and technology innovation and products: plans, designs and manages the communication networks.

Primary SIC and add'l.: 7389 4813 4812 4822

CIK No: 0001046126

Officers: Solomon Trujillo/Dir., CEO, Phil Burgess/Group MD - Public Policy, Communications, David Thodey/Group MD - Telstra Enterprise, Government, Andrea Grant/Group MD - Human Resources, Holly Kramer/Group MD - Telstra Product Management, Kate McKenzie/Group MD - Telstra Wholesale, Justin Milne/Group MD - Telstra Bigpond, Geoff Booth/Group MD - Telstra Country Wide, David Moffatt/Group MD - Telstra Consumer Marketing, Channels, Will Irving/Group General Counsel, Ben Spincer/Dir. - Investor Relations, Carmel Mulhern/Company Sec., Rod Bruem/Mgr. - International Media Relation, Greg Winn/COO, William J. Stewart/Group MD - Strategic Marketing *(19 Officers included in Index)*

Directors: Solomon Trujillo/Dir., CEO, Donald G. McGauchie/Chmn., John W. Stocker/Dir., Charles MacEk/Dir., Catherine B. Livingstone/Dir., Peter J. Willcox/Non Exec. Dir., John D. Zeglis/Dir., Geoffrey Cousins/Dir.

Financial Data: *Fiscal Year End:*06/30 *Latest Annual Data:* 06/30/2006

Year	Sales	Net Income
2006	$16,630,948,000	$1,805,537,000
2005	$16,891,254,000	$3,179,064,000
2004	$14,314,751,000	$953,304,000

Curr. Assets:	$3,820,613,000	**Curr. Liab.:**	$5,717,413,000		
Plant, Equip.:	$17,514,369,000	**Total Liab.:**	$17,503,417,000	**Indic. Yr. Divd.:**	NA
Total Assets:	$26,120,788,000	**Net Worth:**	$8,617,370,000	**Debt/ Equity:**	NA

Teltronics Inc

2150 Whitefield Industrial Way, Sarasota, FL, 34243; ; *http://* www.teltronics.com;
Email: irissupport@teltronics.com

General - Incorporation	DE	**Stock**- Price on:12/24/2007	$0.57
Employees	248	Stock Exchange	OTC
Auditor	Kirkland, Russ, Murphy & Tapp P.A	Ticker Symbol	TELT
Stk Agt	Computershare Trust Co	Outstanding Shares	8,650,000
Counsel	Blair & Roach	E.P.S.	-$0.22
DUNS No.	19-820-5619	Shareholders	NA

Business: The group's principle activity is to design, develop, manufacture and market electronic hardware, application software products and engage in contract manufacturing for the telecommunication industry. Through its subsidiary, interactive solutions, inc. ('isi'), the group designs and manufactures small, pentium(R) powered, multimedia computer for the wearable computer industry. The group through its securitas products offers a complete solution to the emergency services agencies of states, counties and municipalities. These products ensure timely and accurate response to 911 calls. The group has international sales in Mexico. The group's quarterly revenue for Sep '07 was 11.71 millions of USD.

Primary SIC and add'l.: 7372 7373 3661

CIK No: 0000097052

Subsidiaries: 36371 Yukon Inc., Teltronics Limited, Teltronics S.a. De C.v., Ttg Acquisition Corp.

Officers: Ewen R. Cameron/CEO, Pres., Robert Lindsay/VP - Engineering, Duncan Anderson/MD - Teltronics Limited, Dominick Catinella/VP - Technical Services, Peter G. Tuckerman/VP - Product Management - Intelligent Systems Management, Kevin Wilson/CTO, Blair O'Keefe/VP - Legal Affairs, Richard Begando/Exec. VP - Sales, Marketing, Russell R. Lee/VP - Finance, CFO, Robert B. Ramey/VP - Manufacturing Operations, Ernesto Chavez/GM - Mexico Operation, Patrick Hutchison/VP - Intelligent Systems Management - Public Safety Systems Group Sales, Candy Mizer/Dir. - Marketing Communications, Norman R. Dobiesz/Dir., Sr. VP - Business Development, John Compton/VP - Latin America

Directors: Norman R. Dobiesz/Dir., Sr. VP - Business Development, Gregory G. Barr/Dir., Richard L. Stevens/Dir., Peter Friedmann/Dir.

Owners: FGC Holdings Ltd./8.35%, Russell R. Lee/1.16%, Ewen R. Cameron/8.62%, Norman R. Dobiesz/100.00%, Tri-Link Technologies, Inc./13.03%, Robert B. Ramey/1.82%, Norman R. Dobiesz/17.68%, Peter G. Tuckerman/95.00%, Gregory G. Barr/2.45%, Insiders/100.00%, Harris Corporation/16.84%, Insiders/35.20%, Richard L. Stevens/2.32%

Financial Data: *Fiscal Year End:*12/31 *Latest Annual Data:* 12/31/2006

Year	Sales	Net Income
2006	$46,863,000	$1,607,000
2005	$46,229,000	-$3,816,000
2004	$46,045,000	$539,000

Curr. Assets:	$15,076,000	**Curr. Liab.:**	$14,278,000		
Plant, Equip.:	$809,000	**Total Liab.:**	$18,144,000	**Indic. Yr. Divd.:**	NA
Total Assets:	$16,692,000	**Net Worth:**	-$1,452,000	**Debt/ Equity:**	NA

Telular Corp

647 N Lakeview Pkway, Vernon Hills, IL, 60061; *PH:* 1-847-465-4500; *http://* www.telular.com

General - Incorporation	DE	**Stock**- Price on:12/24/2007	$4.67
Employees	123	Stock Exchange	NDQ
Auditor	Ernst & Young LLP	Ticker Symbol	WRLS
Stk Agt	Computershare Investor Services	Outstanding Shares	18,240,000
Counsel	NA	E.P.S.	-$0.11
DUNS No.	80-998-8595	Shareholders	NA

Business: The group's principal activity is to design, engineer, manufacture and market telecommunications equipment assemblies and complementary products.the group has worldwide customer base over 130 countries. The technology helps to connect the standard telecommunications equipment, including standard telephones, fax machines, data modems and alarm panels with wireless communication networks in the cellular and pcs frequency bands. The group operates in two business segments, phonecell(R), a line of cellular fixed wireless terminals and phones and telguard(R), a line of wireless security products. Fixed wireless terminals, bridge wireline telecommunication equipment with cellular-type transceivers for use in wireless communication networks. Security products provide wireless backup systems for both commercial and residential alarms systems.

Primary SIC and add'l.: 3669 7382 3661 3663

CIK No: 0000915324

Subsidiaries: Telular - Adcor Security Products, Inc, Telular International, Inc

Officers: Michael J. Boyle/Dir., CEO, Pres., Robert L. Deering/Controller, Treasurer, Chief Accounting Officer, Jeffrey L. Herrmann/Exec. VP, COO, Sec., George S. Brody/Sr. VP, General Mgr. Terminal Segment, Joseph A. Beatty/CFO, Exec. VP, Sec. - Telular

Directors: Michael J. Boyle/Dir., CEO, Pres., John E. Berndt/Chmn., Betsy Bernard/Dir., Brian McCarthy/Dir., Larry J. Ford/Dir., Brian J. Clucas/Dir., Lawrence S. Barker/Dir.

Owners: Brian M. McCarthy, Brian J. Clucas, George S. Brody, Bonanza Master Fund Ltd./9.99%, Michael J. Boyle, Betsy J. Bernard, Walker Smith Capital Management, L.P./5.90%, John E. Berndt, Larry J. Ford, Insiders/2.13%, Lawrence S. Baker, Robert L. Deering

Financial Data: *Fiscal Year End:*09/30 *Latest Annual Data:* 9/30/2006

Year	Sales	Net Income
2006	$93,100,000	-$11,818,000
2005	$52,435,000	-$10,882,000
2004	$75,959,000	-$703,000

Curr. Assets:	$46,586,000	**Curr. Liab.:**	$19,125,000		
Plant, Equip.:	$4,625,000	**Total Liab.:**	$19,125,000	**Indic. Yr. Divd.:**	NA
Total Assets:	$57,937,000	**Net Worth:**	$38,812,000	**Debt/ Equity:**	NA

TELUS Corp

8 - 555 Robson St., Vancouver, BC, V6B 3K9; *PH:* 1-604-432-2151; *Fax:* 1-604-432-9681; *http://* www.telus.com; *Email:* ir@telus.com

General - Incorporation	BC	**Stock**- Price on:12/24/2007	$60.34
Employees	29,819	Stock Exchange	NYSE
Auditor	Deloitte & Touche LLP	Ticker Symbol	TU
Stk Agt	Computershare Trust Co of Canada	Outstanding Shares	334,430,000
Counsel	NA	E.P.S.	$3.27
DUNS No.	NA	Shareholders	NA

Business: The group's principle activities are to provide data, Internet protocol (ip) , voice and wireless communication services in Canada. The group operates in two segments: telus communications: offers local, long distance, data, Internet and other services to businesses and consumers through full-service incumbent local exchange carrier (ilec). This segment also provides data, ip and voice solutions to business customers. Telus mobility: provides national facilities-based wireless service. The group's quarterly revenue for September 2007 was 2,309.90 millions of CAD.

Primary SIC and add'l.: 4899 4812 4822 4813

CIK No: 0000868675

Subsidiaries: 1219723 Alberta ULC, Canada Inc., Tele-mobile Company, TELUS Communications Inc., TELUS Corporation, TELUS Wireless Segment

Officers: Darren Entwistle/Dir., CEO, Pres., Joe M. Natale/Exec. VP, Pres. - Business Solutions, Joseph R. Grech/Exec. VP - Network Planning, Operations, Karen Radford/Exec. VP, Pres. - Telus Partner Solutions, Darrell Rae/Mgr. Investor Relations, Eros Spadotto/Exec. VP - Technology Strategy, Robert Mitchell/Dir. - Investor Relations, John Watson/Exec. VP, Pres. - Consumer Solutions, John Wheeler/VP - Investor Relations, Janet S. Yale/Exec. VP - Corporate Affairs, Robert G. McFarlane/CFO, VP, Judy A. Shuttleworth/Exec. VP - Human Resources, Kevin A. Salvadori/Exec. VP - Business Transformations, CIO

Directors: Darren Entwistle/Dir., CEO, Pres., Brian A. Canfield/Chmn., Micheline Bouchard/Dir., R. H. Auchinleck/Dir., Brian F. MacNeill/Dir., John R. Butler/Dir., Pierre Ducros/Dir., Donald P. Woodley/Dir., Ruston E.T. Goepel/Dir., Ronald P. Triffo/Dir., Charles A. Baillie/Dir., John S. Lacey/Dir.

Financial Data: *Fiscal Year End:* 12/31 *Latest Annual Data:* 12/31/2006

Year	Sales	Net Income
2006	$7,449,166,000	$976,089,000
2005	$6,986,437,000	$567,567,000
2004	$6,294,670,000	$439,063,000

Curr. Assets:	$1,154,059,000	Curr. Liab.:	$3,207,749,000	P/E Ratio:	21.78
Plant, Equip.:	$6,407,004,000	Total Liab.:	$8,726,191,000	Indic. Yr. Divd.:	$1.790
Total Assets:	$15,601,717,000	Net Worth:	$6,875,526,000	Debt/ Equity:	NA

Telvent GIT S.A.

Valgrande, 6, Alcobendas, Madrid, 28108; *PH:* 34-917147000; *http://* www.telvent.com; *Email:* info@telvent.com

General - Incorporation	Kingdom of Spain	**Stock**- Price on:12/24/2007	$26.06
Employees	3,502	Stock Exchange	NDQ
Auditor	NA	Ticker Symbol	TLVT
Stk Agt	American Stock Transfer & Trust Co.	Outstanding Shares	29,250,000
Counsel	NA	E.P.S.	$1.191
DUNS No.	NA	Shareholders	NA

Business: The groups principle activity is to provide information technology services. The groups services include data center management, system management and application management. The products of the group include TiCares and TiWorks. The groups operates through five segments namely energy, traffic, transport, environment and other. The group acquired Beijing Blue Shield in the year 2006 and Almos Systems Pty Ltd in the year 2005. The group operates from Europe, North America, Asia Pacific, Latin America and Middle East and Africa. The group's quarterly revenue for September 2007 was 128.64 millions of USD.

Primary SIC and add'l.: 7371 7389 7378 7375 7377 7373 7374 7379 7376

CIK No: 0001257803

Subsidiaries: Miner & Miner, Consulting Engineers, Inc., Telvent Australia Pty. Ltd. (formerly Almos Systems Pty Ltd.), Telvent Brasil S.A., Telvent Canada Ltd., Telvent Control System (Beijing) Co., Ltd., Telvent Energia y Medio Ambiente, S.A., Telvent Farradyne Inc. (formerly P.B. Farradyne, Inc.), Telvent Housing, S.A., Telvent Interactiva, S.A., Telvent Mexico S.A. de C.V., Telvent Netherlands B.V. (formerly Almos Systems B.V.), Telvent Outsourcing, S.A., Telvent Trafico y Transporte, S.A., Telvent U.S.A. Inc.

Officers: Manuel Sanchez/Chmn., CEO, Jose Ignacio Del Barrio/Exec. VP - Telvent Global Services, Larry Stack/Pres. - Telvent Energy, Adolfo Borrero/Exec. VP - Telvent Public Administration, Ana Plaza/CFO, Head - Investor Relations, Francisco Caceres/CTO, Raul Aguera/Chief Accounting Officer, Gema Montoya/Dir. - Marketing, Communication, Aranzazu Caja/Dir. - Human Resources, Carmen Rodriguez/Internal Auditing, Telvent, Jose M. Flores/Exec. VP - Telvent Transportation, Jose Montoya/Pres. - Telvent Transportation, Ignacio Gonzalez Dominguez/Exec. VP - Telvent Energy, Javier Garoz/Exec. VP - Telvent Environment, Lidia Garcia Paez/Legal Counsel *(16 Officers included in Index)*

Directors: Manuel Sanchez/Chmn., CEO, Jose B. Terceiro/63/Dir., Candido Velazquez-Gaztelu/71/Dir., Bernardo Villazan/48/Dir., Emilio Cassinello/70/Dir., Carlos De Borbon/70/Dir., Miguel Cuenca/58/Dir., Eduard Punset/71/Dir., Javier Salas/59/Dir.

Owners: Adolfo Borrero, Insiders/3.72%, Ignacio Gonzlez, Bernardo Villazn, Jos Montoya, Dave Jardine, Jos Mara Flores, Ana Plaza, Larry Stack, Jos I. Del Barrio, Manuel Snchez/1.14%

Financial Data: *Fiscal Year End:* 12/31 *Latest Annual Data:* 12/31/2006

Year	Sales	Net Income
2006	$665,225,000	$28,833,000
2005	$476,566,000	$17,015,000
2004	$426,472,000	$13,842,000

Curr. Assets:	$551,562,000	Curr. Liab.:	$460,746,000	P/E Ratio:	21.88
Plant, Equip.:	$67,619,000	Total Liab.:	$500,275,000	Indic. Yr. Divd.:	NA
Total Assets:	$733,600,000	Net Worth:	$233,325,000	Debt/ Equity:	NA

Telvue Corp

16000 Horizon Way, Ste 500, Mt Laurel, NJ, 08054; *PH:* 1-856-273-8888; *http://* www.telvue.net; *Email:* info@telvue.com

General - Incorporation	DE	**Stock**- Price on:12/24/2007	$0.1
Employees	27	Stock Exchange	OTC
Auditor	Pressman Ciocca Smith LLP	Ticker Symbol	TEVE
Stk Agt	Continental Stock Transfer & Trust Co	Outstanding Shares	48,360,000
Counsel	NA	E.P.S.	-$0.04
DUNS No.	60-102-4185	Shareholders	NA

Business: The group's principal activities are the provision of automatic number identification services and customized business solutions. The group operates in two segments. The first segment sells automatic number identification and telecommunications services to the cable television industry. The services are used for automated ordering of pay-per-view features and events. They permit cable television companies to process special ordering services without the high-manpower requirements or extensive physical plant and facilities. The other segment, operating under the name of source communications group, provides communication and network integration solutions. The segment sources hardware from a number of well-known equipment, software and communications service suppliers and molds them into customized voice, video and data communications solutions.

Primary SIC and add'l.: 7373 7389 4899

CIK No: 0000839443

Officers: Joseph M. Murphy/Dir., CEO, Pres./$199,751.00, Randy Gilson/47/VP - Technical Services/$125,103.00, John Fell/Sec., Treasurer, Jesse Lerman/35/Exec. VP - Engineering

Directors: Joseph M. Murphy/Dir., CEO, Pres., H. F. Lenfest/77/Chmn., Robert M. Lawrence/Dir., Frank J. Carcione/Dir., Joy Tarter/Dir.

Owners: Robert Lawrence, Randy Gilson/0.80%, Joy Tartar/0.10%, Frank J. Carcione/0.10%, H.F. (Gerry) Lenfest/78.60%, Insiders/81.60%, Joseph M. Murphy/1.00%

Financial Data: *Fiscal Year End:* 12/31 *Latest Annual Data:* 12/31/2006

Year	Sales	Net Income
2006	$2,089,000	-$1,835,000
2005	$2,245,000	-$1,273,000
2004	$3,286,000	-$810,000

Curr. Assets:	$646,000	Curr. Liab.:	$633,000		
Plant, Equip.:	$897,000	Total Liab.:	$3,885,000	Indic. Yr. Divd.:	NA
Total Assets:	$1,952,000	Net Worth:	-$1,933,000	Debt/ Equity:	NA

Telzuit Medical Technologies Inc

5422 Carrier Dr., Ste 306, Orlando, FL, 32819; *PH:* 1-305-692-3732; *http://* www.telzuit.com; *Email:* sales@taylor-madison.com

General - Incorporation	FL	**Stock**- Price on:12/24/2007	$0.1
Employees	11	Stock Exchange	NA
Auditor	Cross, Fern&ez & Riley, LLP	Ticker Symbol	NA
Stk Agt	American Stock Transfer & Trust Co.	Outstanding Shares	38,200,000
Counsel	NA	E.P.S.	-$0.13
DUNS No.	NA	Shareholders	NA

Business: The group's principal activities were to provide online catalog of authentic collectibles and factory-new specialty merchandise. These catalogs were sold at online auction sites such as ebay(sm), amazon(sm), yahoo(sm). In Jan 2002, the group decided to dispose its wholly owned subsidiary taketoauction.com. Currently, the group is in the planning stage of wholesale distribution of fragrances, both proprietary and under license, as well as other skincare products.

Primary SIC and add'l.: 7375

CIK No: 0001093837

Subsidiaries: Immediate Quality Care Clinics, Inc, Taylor Madison Holdings Inc.

Officers: Warren D. Stowell/Dir., CEO, Michael J. Vosch/Dir., Sr. VP - Product Development, Jerry Balter/CFO, Enrique G. Estevez/Company Consultant, Markus G. Muhlhauser/Company Consultant, Carole Sue Feagan/VP - Human Resources, Kathleen A. Fishman/Dir. - Information Technology, Cindy Nolte/Company Consultant

Directors: Warren D. Stowell/Dir., CEO, Jon C. Stemples/Chmn., Christopher Phillips/Dir., Kenneth F. Adams/Dir., Richard J. Bischoff/Dir., Michael J. Vosch/Dir., Sr. VP - Product Development, Ronald D. Berger/Member - Medical Advisory Board, Hugh G. Calkins/Member - Medical Advisory Board, Alan Howard Kadish/Member - Medical Advisory Board, Alfred E. Buxton/Member - Medical Advisory Board, Ronald Krochak/Member - Medical Advisory Board, John Gayden/Member - Medical Advisory Board, Michael E. Cain/Member - Medical Advisory Board

Owners: Richard J. Bischoff, Kenneth F. Adams, Warren D. Stowell/5.80%, Michael Vosch/3.40%, Jerry Balter/2.40%, Jon C. Stemples, Insiders/12.10%

Financial Data: *Fiscal Year End:* 06/30 *Latest Annual Data:* 6/30/2007

Year	Sales	Net Income
2007	$843,000	-$5,580,000
2006	$4,000	-$11,136,000
2005	NA	-$1,494,000

Curr. Assets:	$610,000	Curr. Liab.:	$1,187,000		
Plant, Equip.:	$293,000	Total Liab.:	$13,823,000	Indic. Yr. Divd.:	NA
Total Assets:	$3,692,000	Net Worth:	-$10,130,000	Debt/ Equity:	NA

Tembec Inc

800, Ren-Lvesque Blvd., Ouest - Bureau 1050, Montreal, QC, H3B 1Y8; *PH:* 1-514-870137; *http://* www.tembec.ca

General - Incorporation	Canada	**Stock**- Price on:12/24/2007	NA
Employees	NA	Stock Exchange	NA
Auditor	KPMG LLP	Ticker Symbol	NA
Stk Agt	Nationall Bank Trust Inc	Outstanding Shares	NA
Counsel	NA	E.P.S.	NA
DUNS No.	20-762-9387	Shareholders	NA

Business: The group's principle activity is to produce integrated forest products. The group operates in five segments: pulp, forest products, paper, paperboard and chemical and other. The pulp group has 10 manufacturing units with products divided into 2 major sectors: paper pulps which include softwood kraft pulp, hardwood kraft pulp and high yield pulp and specialty pulps which include specialty cellulose pulp, fluff pulp and dissolving pulp. The forest product segment consists primarily of forest and sawmill operations which produce lumber, building materials and wood chips, the paper segment primarily produces and sells newsprint and coated papers. The paperboard segment manufactures coated bleached board. The chemical and other segment consist primarily of the transformation and sale of resins pulp by-products. The group's quarterly revenue for September 2007 was 592.00 millions of USD.

Primary SIC and add'l.: 2421 2611 2621 2631 0831 2869

CIK No: 0000949011

Subsidiaries: Spruce Falls Inc, Tembec Industries Inc

Officers: James Lopez/Dir., CEO, Pres., Richard Tremblay/Corporate Controller, Jacques Rochon/VP - Information Technology, Stephen J. Norris/Treasurer, Mahendra Patel/VP - Engineering, Purchasing, Services, Yves Ouellet/VP - Administration, Mel Zangwill/Sr. VP, Pres. - Paperboard Group, Dan C. Alexander/Exec. VP, Pres. - Paper Group, Tony Fratianni/VP, General Counsel, Sec., Yvon Pelletier/Exec. VP - Pulp Group, Randy Fournier/Sr. VP - Chemical Group, Paul Dottori/VP - Energy, Environment, Technology, Dennis Rounsville/Exec. VP, Pres. - Forest Products Group, John D. Valley/Exec. VP - Business Development, Corporate Affairs, eric Bergeron/VP - Human Resources *(16 Officers included in Index)*

Directors: James Lopez/Dir., CEO, Pres., Guy G. Dufresne/Chmn., Peter S. Janson/Dir., Emanuele Saputo/Dir., Luc Rossignol/Dir., James E. Brumm/Dir., Andre Berard/Dir., Gilles Chevalier/Dir., Norman M. Betts/Dir.

Tembec Industries Inc

1479 Theatre Rd. , Cranbrook, BC, V1C 7G3; ***PH:*** 1-250-426-4244; ***http://*** www.tembec.com

General - Incorporation	Canada	**Stock**- Price on:12/24/2007	NA
Employees	NA	Stock Exchange	NA
Auditor	KPMG LLP	Ticker Symbol	NA
Stk Agt	Nationall Bank Trust Inc	Outstanding Shares	NA
Counsel	NA	E.P.S	NA
DUNS No.	20-755-0344	Shareholders	NA

Business: The group's principle activities include manufacturing, producing and selling market pulp, wood products and paper to north American and overseas markets. The group operates from United States.

Primary SIC and add'l.: 2421 2611

CIK No: 0000925559

Subsidiaries: Spruce Falls Inc

Officers: James Lopez/Dir., CEO, Pres., Michel J. Dumas/CFO, Exec. VP - Finance, Paul Dottori/Corporate VP, Randy Fournier/Sr. VP - Chemical Group, John Valley/Exec. VP - Business Development - Corporate Affairs, Yves Ouellet/VP - Administration, Dan C. Alexander/Exec. VP, Pres. - Paper Group, Yvon Pelletier/Exec. VP, Pres. - Pulp Group, Mel Zangwill/Sr. VP, Pres. - Paperboard Group, Stephen J. Norris/Treasurer, Eric Bergeron/VP - Human Resources, Richard Tremblay/Corporate Controller, Jacques Rochon/VP - Information Technology, Antonio Fratianni/VP, General Counsel, Sec., Dennis Rounsville/Exec. VP *(16 Officers included in Index)*

Directors: James Lopez/Dir., CEO, Pres., Guy G. Dufresne/Chmn., James E. Brumm/Dir., Luc Rossignol/Dir., Gilles Chevalier/Dir., Norman M. Betts/Dir., Peter S. Janson/Dir., Andre Berard/Dir., Emanuele Saputo/Dir.

Temecula Valley Bancorp Inc

27710 Jefferson Ave., Ste A-100, Temecula, CA, 92590; ***PH:*** 1-909-694-9940; ***http://*** www.temvalbank.com

General - Incorporation	CA	**Stock**- Price on:12/24/2007	$18.89
Employees	299	Stock Exchange	NDQ
Auditor	Crowe Chizek & Co. LLP	Ticker Symbol	TMCV
Stk Agt	U.S. Stock Transfer Corp	Outstanding Shares	10,630,000
Counsel	NA	E.P.S	$1.69
DUNS No.	NA	Shareholders	NA

Business: The group's principal activity is to provide banking services to customers in the temecula valley and san diego county. The group provides personal and business checking accounts and various types of interest-bearing deposit accounts including interest-bearing checking, money market, savings, ira, sep and time certificates of deposits. Loan products include consumer installment (including automobile), construction loans, commercial (including letters of credit), residential real estate (including va, fha and cal vet), second mortgages, home improvement loans and tract construction loans. The deposits are insured by the federal deposit insurance corporation. The group operates five full-service banking offices in California.

Primary SIC and add'l.: 6712 6021

CIK No: 0001172678

Subsidiaries: Temecula Valley Statutory Trust I, Temecula Valley Statutory Trust II, Temecula Valley Statutory Trust III, Temecula Valley Statutory Trust IV

Officers: Dan Stake/Contact - Construction Loans, Linda Thomas/Contact - Escondido Business Banking, Carl J. Sorena/Contact - Temecula Main Office, Jeff Minch/Branch Mgr. - Fallbrook Office, Larry Tidwell/Contact - San Rafael Real Estate Industries Group, Dennis Godfrey/Contact - Escondido Business Banking, Steve Janda/Contact - Corona Real Estate Industries Group, Mark Grassi/Contact - Encinitas Commercial, Construction Division, Chris Spivey/Contact - Irvine, CA, Kay Anderson/Contact - St. Petersburg, FL, Donald A. Pitcher/CFO, Exec. VP, Sec., Joanne R. Matthewson/VP, Mgr., William H. McGaughey/Sr. Exec. VP - Dir. - Finance, SBA, Don C. Johnson/Contact - Texas Dallas, Jason Lorenz/Contact - San Rafael Real Estate Industries Group *(68 Officers included in Index)*

Owners: Thomas M. Shepherd, Neil M. Cleveland/1.50%, William McGaughey, George Cossolias, Robert P. Beck/2.01%, Richard W. Wright/1.84%, Insiders/21.46%, Robert R. Flores, Stephen H. Wacknitz/7.48%, Donald A. Pitcher, Luther J. Mohr/3.31%, Steven W. Aichle/3.00%

Financial Data: ***Fiscal Year End:***12/31 ***Latest Annual Data:*** 12/31/2006

Year	Sales	Net Income
2006	$116,288,000	$16,920,000
2005	$81,969,000	$13,953,000
2004	$62,381,000	$10,578,000

Curr. Assets:	$52,839,000	**Curr. Liab.:**	$1,083,595,000	**P/E Ratio:**	10.92
Plant, Equip.:	$6,747,000	**Total Liab.:**	$1,134,926,000	**Indic. Yr. Divd.:**	$0.040
Total Assets:	$1,238,189,000	**Net Worth:**	$103,263,000	**Debt/ Equity:**	0.3827

Temple Inland Inc

1300 S Mopac Expressway, Austin, TX, 78746; ***PH:*** 1-512-434-5800; ***http://*** www.templeinland.com; ***Email:*** info@templeinland.com

General - Incorporation	DE	**Stock**- Price on:12/24/2007	$62.33
Employees	15,500	Stock Exchange	NYSE
Auditor	Ernst & Young LLP	Ticker Symbol	TIN
Stk Agt	EquiServe Trust Co N.A	Outstanding Shares	105,820,000
Counsel	NA	E.P.S	$2.25
DUNS No.	10-384-4346	Shareholders	NA

Business: The group operates through its subsidiaries whose principle activities include operating and developing real estate properties. The group operates through segments include corrugated packaging, forest products, real estate and financial services. The groups financial services include checking, savings, online banking, deposit services, treasury management and trade services. The group operates from United States.

Primary SIC and add'l.: 2671 6035 2653 2435 6719 2631

CIK No: 0000731939

Subsidiaries: 507789 N.b. Ltd., American Finance Group, Inc., Angelina Free Press, Inc., The, CCA Hospitality, Inc., CCRHD Limited Partnership, CL Realty, LLC, Cls, S.a. De C.v., Crockett Baja, S.A. de C.V., Del-Tin Fiber LLC, Double Horn Water Supply Corporation, Inc., El Morro Corrugated Box Corporation, Gaylord Central National, Inc., Gaylord Chemical Corporation, Gaylord Container de Mexico, S.A. de C.V., Gaylord-USF Gasification 2020, LLC 76 Subsidiaries included in the Index

Officers: Kenneth M. Jastrow/61/Chmn., CEO/$12,373,370.00, Scott Smith/53/CIO, Morris C. Davis/65/General Counsel, Bradley J. Johnston/52/Chief Administrative Officer, Leslie K. ONeal/52/VP, Assist. General Counsel, Sec., Doyle R. Simons/Exec. VP/$2,958,157.00, Dennis J. Vesci/60/Group VP, Troy L. Hester/51/Principal Accounting Officer, Corporate Controller, David W. Turpin/57/Treasurer, Kenneth R. Dubuque/59/Group VP, Patrick J. Maley/46/Exec. VP - Paper/$3,001,822.00, Jack C. Sweeny/61/Group VP/$3,803,727.00, Randall D. Levy/56/CFO/$3,008,983.00, James M. Decosmo/49/Group VP - Real Estate, Bart J. Doney/58/Group VP

Directors: Kenneth M. Jastrow/61/Chmn., CEO, James A. Johnson/64/Dir., Linn E. Draper/66/Dir., James T. Hackett/54/Dir., Larry R. Faulkner/63/Dir., Afsaneh M. Beschloss/52/Dir., Donald M. Carlton/70/Dir., Cassandra C. Carr/63/Dir., Allen W. Reed/61/Dir., Arthur Temple/66/Dir., Larry E. Temple/72/Dir., Jeffrey M. Heller/68/Dir., Richard Smith/62/Dir.

Owners: Kenneth M. Jastrow, Larry E. Temple, James T. Hackett, Cassandra C. Carr, Randall D. Levy, James A. Johnson, Jack C. Sweeny, Arthur Temple, Carl C. Icahn, etal/6.73%, Franklin Mutual Advisers, LLC/9.40%, Doyle R. Simons, Linn E. Draper, Patrick J. Maley, Donald M. Carlton, Larry R. Faulkner *(21 Owners included in Index)*

Financial Data: ***Fiscal Year End:***12/31 ***Latest Annual Data:*** 12/30/2006

Year	Sales	Net Income
2006	$5,558,000,000	$468,000,000
2005	$4,888,000,000	$176,000,000

Curr. Assets:	$1,280,000,000	**Curr. Liab.:**	$16,989,000,000	**P/E Ratio:**	15.98
Plant, Equip.:	$2,646,000,000	**Total Liab.:**	$19,553,000,000	**Indic. Yr. Divd.:**	$1.120
Total Assets:	$21,633,000,000	**Net Worth:**	$2,080,000,000	**Debt/ Equity:**	NA

Tempur Pedic International Inc

1713 Jaggie Fox Way, Lexington, KY, 40511; ***PH:*** 1-800-878-8889; ***http://*** www.tempur.com

General - Incorporation	DE	**Stock**- Price on:12/24/2007	$26.53
Employees	1,300	Stock Exchange	NYSE
Auditor	Ernst & Young LLP	Ticker Symbol	TPX
Stk Agt	Ernest & Young LLP	Outstanding Shares	82,990,000
Counsel	NA	E.P.S	$1.34
DUNS No.	13-753-2797	Shareholders	NA

Business: The group's principal activities are to manufacture, market and distribute visco-elastic foam products including pillows, mattresses and other related products. The group's products are distributed through retail (furniture and specialty stores, as well as department stores internationally), direct (direct response and Internet), healthcare (chiropractors, medical retailers, hospitals and other healthcare channels) and third party distributors channels. The products are sold in 54 countries under the trademark of tempur(R) and tempur-pedic(R) brands. Swedish sleep system(R) and tempur-med(R) are some of the other trademarks of the group. The group operates in the United States, the United Kingdom, Germany, France, Spain, Japan and Asia.

Primary SIC and add'l.: 2515 7389

CIK No: 0001206264

Subsidiaries: Dan-Foam ApS, Dawn Sleep Technologies, Inc., Tempur Benelux B.V., Tempur Danmark A/S, Tempur Deutschland GmbH, Tempur France SARL, Tempur Holding GmbH, Tempur International Limited, Tempur Italia Srl, Tempur Japan Yugen Kaisha, Tempur Norge AS, Tempur Pedic Espana SA, Tempur Production USA, Inc., Tempur Schweiz AG, Tempur Singapore Pte Ltd. 26 Subsidiaries included in the Index

Officers: Thomas H. Bryant/CEO, Pres., Rick Anderson/Exec. VP, Pres., Dale E. Williams/CFO, Exec. VP, Sec., David Montgomery/Exec. VP, Pres. - International Operations, Matt Clift/Exec. VP - Global Operations

Directors: Robert B. Trussell/Vice Chmn., Andrews P. McLane/Chmn., Nancy F. Koehn/Dir., Peter K. Hoffman/Dir., Paul Judge/Dir., Christopher A. Masto/Dir., Francis A. Doyle/Dir.

Owners: David Montgomery, Dale E. Williams, Nancy F. Koehn, Andrews P. McLane/6.00%, Matthew D. Clift, Robert B. Trussell, Thomas H. Bryant, AMVESCAP PLC/14.50%, Peter K. Hoffman, Christopher A. Masto, Sir Paul Judge, Jeffrey S. Barber/5.30%, TA Associates Funds/5.30%, Kayne Anderson Rudnick Investment Management LLC/7.00%, Francis A. Doyle *(16 Owners included in Index)*

Financial Data: ***Fiscal Year End:***12/31 ***Latest Annual Data:*** 12/31/2006

Year	Sales	Net Income
2006	$945,045,000	$112,322,000
2005	$836,732,000	$99,329,000
2004	$684,866,000	$75,007,000

Curr. Assets:	$237,556,000	**Curr. Liab.:**	$131,767,000	**P/E Ratio:**	19.80
Plant, Equip.:	$215,428,000	**Total Liab.:**	$512,318,000	**Indic. Yr. Divd.:**	$0.320
Total Assets:	$725,666,000	**Net Worth:**	$213,348,000	**Debt/ Equity:**	1.6162

Tenaris

46a Ave. John F. Kennedy, 2nd Fl., L-1855; ***PH:*** 352-26 47 89 78; ***Fax:*** 352-26 47 89 79; ***http://*** www.tenaris.com; ***Email:*** investors@tenaris.com

General - Incorporation	Luxembourg	**Stock**- Price on:12/24/2007	$47.75
Employees	21,751	Stock Exchange	NYSE
Auditor	Price Waterhouse & Co. S.R.L.	Ticker Symbol	TS
Stk Agt	Computershare Trust Co	Outstanding Shares	585,740,000
Counsel	NA	E.P.S	$3.40
DUNS No.	NA	Shareholders	NA

Business: The groups principle activity is to manufacture and distribute seamless steel pipe products and associated services. Customers served by the group include the oil, gas and energy industries and their principal products are casing, tubing, line pipe and mechanical and structural pipes. The group products are sold under the brand names siderca, tamsa, dalmine and tenaris global services. The group operates from United States.

Primary SIC and add'l.: 3533 3317 3312 3498

CIK No: 0001190723

Subsidiaries: Algoma Tubes Inc., Confab Industrial S.A. and subsidiaries, Dalmine Energie S.p.A., Dalmine Holding B.V. and subsidiaries, Dalmine S.p.A., Energy Network S.R.L., Exiros S.A., Information Systems and Technologies N.V., Information Systems and Technologies S.A., Inmobiliaria Tamsa S.A. de C.V., Insirger S.A. and subsidiaries, Intermetal Com SRL, Inversiones Berna S.A., Inversiones Lucerna S.A., Invertub S.A. and subsidiaries 74 Subsidiaries included in the Index

Officers: Paolo Rocca/Chmn., CEO, Alejandro Lammertyn/Commercial Dir., Guillermo Noriega/South American Area Mgr., Marco Radnic/Dir. - Human Resources, Giancarlo Miglio/Information Technology Dir., Vincenzo Crapanzano/European Area Mgr., German Cura/North American Area Mgr., Ricardo Soler/CFO, Carlos Pappier/Planning Dir., Tulio Chipoletti/Area Mgr. - Brazil, Emyr Berbare/Dir. - Confab Equipamentos, Claudio Leali/MD - Japanese Operations, Cecilia Bilesio/Dir., Sec., Nigel Worsnop/Dir. - Investor Relations, Sergio De La Maza/Central American Area Mgr. *(20 Officers included in Index)*

Directors: Paolo Rocca/Chmn., CEO, Cecilia Bilesio/Dir., Sec., Roberto Bonatti/Dir., Carlos Franck/Dir., Bruno Marchettini/Dir., Jaime Serra Puche/Dir., Gianfelice Mario Rocca/Dir., Guillermo Vogel/Dir., VP - Finance, Carlos Condorelli/Dir., Amadeo Vazquez Y Vazquez/Dir., Roberto Monti/Dir.

Owners: Guillermo Vogel, Insiders, San Faustn, Carlos Condorelli

Financial Data: *Fiscal Year End:*12/31 *Latest Annual Data:* 12/31/2005

Year		Sales		Net Income	
2005		$6,736,197,000		$1,295,465,000	
2004		$4,136,063,000		$730,339,000	
2003		$3,179,652,000		$203,908,000	
Curr. Assets:	$6,028,832,000	**Curr. Liab.:**	$2,765,504,000		
Plant, Equip.:	$2,939,241,000	**Total Liab.:**	$7,260,913,000	**Indic. Yr. Divd.:**	$0.600
Total Assets:	$12,526,715,000	**Net Worth:**	$5,265,802,000	**Debt/ Equity:**	NA

Tendercare International Inc

675 Industrial Blvd, Delta, CO, 81416; ***PH:*** 1-800-344-6379; ***http://*** www.tushies.com;
Email: sales@tushies.com

General - Incorporation	CO	**Stock**- Price on:12/24/2007	$0.45
Employees	5	Stock Exchange	OTC
Auditor	Wipfli LLP	Ticker Symbol	TCAR
Stk Agt	U.S. Stock Transfer Corp	Outstanding Shares	7,450,000
Counsel	NA	E.P.S	-$0.048
DUNS No.	NA	Shareholders	NA

Business: The group's principal activity is to market, distribute and sell disposable baby diapers and related products. The group distributes the following products under the brand name: tushies (R), tushieswipes and tendercare(R) tendercare plus(R), and mother nature(R) brand disposable diapers. The group's diapers are marketed through independent commissioned brokers and sold through health product stores, through its 800 direct mail number and via Internet.

Primary SIC and add'l.: 2676

CIK No: 0000777513

Officers: Edward Reiss/69/Chmn., Co - CEO, Brenda Schenk/64/Dir., Co - CEO, Pres.

Directors: Edward Reiss/69/Chmn., Co - CEO, Brenda Schenk/64/Dir., Co - CEO, Pres., Craig Silverman/44/Dir.

Owners: Walter Fox/5.70%, Edward Reiss/16.50%, Craig Silverman/1.00%, Insiders/54.90%, Brenda Schenk/37.30%, Jesse Greenfield/8.70%

Financial Data: *Fiscal Year End:*12/31 *Latest Annual Data:* 12/31/2006

Year		Sales		Net Income	
2006		$3,311,000		-$349,000	
2005		$3,094,000		$6,000	
2004		$3,184,000		$17,000	
Curr. Assets:	$586,000	**Curr. Liab.:**	$1,017,000		
Plant, Equip.:	$31,000	**Total Liab.:**	$1,017,000	**Indic. Yr. Divd.:**	NA
Total Assets:	$899,000	**Net Worth:**	-$118,000	**Debt/ Equity:**	NA

Tenet Healthcare Corp

13737 Noel Rd. , Dallas, TX, 75240; ***PH:*** 1-469-893-6321; ***http://*** www.tenethealth.com;
Email: feedback@tenethealth.com

General - Incorporation	NV	**Stock**- Price on:12/24/2007	$6.63
Employees	50,557	Stock Exchange	NYSE
Auditor	KPMG LLP	Ticker Symbol	THC
Stk Agt	Bank of New York	Outstanding Shares	473,020,000
Counsel	E. Peter Urbanowicz	E.P.S	-$0.85
DUNS No.	05-386-6661	Shareholders	NA

Business: The groups principle activity is to provide health care services. The groups services include radiology, respiratory therapy, pharmacies and clinical laboratories, intensive-care units, and physical therapy. The group operates from United States.

Primary SIC and add'l.: 8059 8069 8062

CIK No: 0000070318

Subsidiaries: 11 Physicians, AHM Acquisition Co.,Inc., AHM CGH,Inc., Ahm Gemch,inc., AHM SMC,Inc., Airmed, II,Inc., Alabama Health Services (St. Clair), LLCownership, Alliance for Community Health, LLC, Alvarado Hospital Medical Center,Inc., Ambulatory CareBroward Development Corp., America Home Patient,Inc., American Homepatient of Sanford, LLC, American Medical (Central),Inc., American Medical Home Care,Inc., American Medical International N.V. 476 Subsidiaries included in the Index

Officers: Trevor Fetter/48/Dir., CEO, Pres., Biggs C. Porter/54/CFO, Cathy Kusaka Fraser/Sr. VP - Human Resources, Audrey T. Andrews/41/Chief Compliance Officer, Jennifer Daley/58/Chief Medical Officer, Sr. VP - Clinical Quality, Peter E. Urbanowicz/44/General Counsel, Stephen F. Brown/52/CIO, Exec. VP, Timothy L. Pullen/52/Chief Accounting Officer, Exec. VP, Tom Rice/Investor Relations Officer, Daniel R. Waldmann/Contact - Government Relation, Steven W. Ortquist/44/Sr. VP - Ethics, Compliance, Chief Compliance Officer, Stephen L. Newman/58/COO

Directors: Trevor Fetter/48/Dir., CEO, Pres., Reynold J. Jennings/62/Vice Chmn., James A. Unruh/66/Dir., Floyd D. Loop/71/Dir., Brenda J. Gaines/Dir., Karen M. Garrison/58/Dir., Edward Kangas/63/Dir., Robert J. Kerrey/64/Dir., Richard R. Pettingill/54/Dir., Williams J. McDonald/66/Dir., John Ellis Bush/Dir.

Owners: Robert J. Kerrey, Hotchkis and Wiley Capital Management, LLC/12.80%, Brandes Investment Partners, L.P./13.30%, Insiders, Trevor Fetter, Karen M. Garrison, Timothy E. Pullen, Peter E. Urbanowicz, Franklin Resources, Inc./17.80%, Edward A. Kangas, McDonald J. Williams, Floyd D. Loop, James A. Unruh, Reynold J. Jennings, The TCW Group, Inc./9.90% *(18 Owners included in Index)*

Financial Data: *Fiscal Year End:*12/31 *Latest Annual Data:* 12/31/2006

Year		Sales		Net Income	
2006		$8,701,000,000		-$803,000,000	
2005		$9,614,000,000		-$724,000,000	
2004		$9,919,000,000		-$2,640,000,000	
Curr. Assets:	$3,025,000,000	**Curr. Liab.:**	$1,925,000,000		
Plant, Equip.:	$4,341,000,000	**Total Liab.:**	$8,275,000,000	**Indic. Yr. Divd.:**	NA
Total Assets:	$8,539,000,000	**Net Worth:**	$264,000,000	**Debt/ Equity:**	NA

Tenfold Corp

698 W 10000 S, Ste. 200, South Jordan, UT, 84095; ***PH:*** 1-801-495-1010; ***http://*** www.10fold.com;
Email: sales@tenfold.com

General - Incorporation	DE	**Stock**- Price on:12/24/2007	$0.32
Employees	46	Stock Exchange	OTC
Auditor	Tanner LC	Ticker Symbol	TENF
Stk Agt	EquiServe Trust Co N.A	Outstanding Shares	46,950,000
Counsel	Wilson Sonsini Goodrich & Rosati	E.P.S	-$0.07
DUNS No.	NA	Shareholders	NA

Business: The group's principal activity is to provide universal application tm, a software applications platform that accelerates development and deployment and reduces costs of maintaining complex enterprise applications. The universal application automates most of the things that application programmers typically do. This enables small teams of predominantly non-technical business users to design, build, test, deploy and maintain complex, transaction-intensive applications, with limited demand on scarce it resources. The group also provides basic and advanced applications development training, assistance in building, implementing and maintaining applications and technical support.

Primary SIC and add'l.: 7372 7371

CIK No: 0001051118

Officers: Robert Felton/Chmn., CEO, Pres./$870,086.00, Jeffrey L. Walker/Founder, Dir., CTO, Exec. VP/$683,361.00, Rob Trounce/VP - Consulting, Sally N. White/VP - Business Development, Samer Diab/Sr. VP - Customer Services/$273,628.00, Alexei Chadovich/Sr. VP - Research, Development/$402,618.00, Robert Hughes/CFO, Chief - Staff/$184,935.00, Gay Wyn Quance/VP - Accounting Management

Directors: Robert Felton/Chmn., CEO, Pres., Jeffrey L. Walker/Founder, Dir., CTO, Exec. VP, Ralph Hardy/Dir., Robert E. Parsons/Dir., Stephen H. Coltrin/Dir.

Owners: Gary D. Kennedy/8.30%, Alexei Chadovich/1.40%, Ralph W. Hardy/23.80%, Jeffrey L.& Cassandra M. Walker/33.10%, Nancy M. Harvey/5.90%, First Media TF Holdings, LLC/23.00%, Stephen H. Coltrin/5.30%, Insiders/66.80%, Samer Diab/3.40%, Robert P. Hughes/1.70%, Robert E. Parsons/0.50%, Walker Childrens Trust/8.20%, Jon M. Huntsman/12.30%

Financial Data: *Fiscal Year End:*12/31 *Latest Annual Data:* 12/31/2006

Year		Sales		Net Income	
2006		$4,998,000		-$5,183,000	
2005		$5,710,000		-$5,434,000	
2004		$17,593,000		$3,416,000	
Curr. Assets:	$4,461,000	**Curr. Liab.:**	$2,778,000		
Plant, Equip.:	$141,000	**Total Liab.:**	$2,778,000	**Indic. Yr. Divd.:**	NA
Total Assets:	$4,676,000	**Net Worth:**	$1,898,000	**Debt/ Equity:**	NA

Tengasco Inc

603 Main Ave., Ste 500, Knoxville, TN, 37902; ***PH:*** 1-865-675-1554; ***http://*** www.tengasco.com;
Email: csorensen@tengasco.com

General - Incorporation	TN	**Stock**- Price on:12/24/2007	$0.67
Employees	25	Stock Exchange	AMEX
Auditor	Rodefer Moss & Co. PLLC	Ticker Symbol	TGC
Stk Agt	Mellon Investor Services LLC	Outstanding Shares	59,140,000
Counsel	Robson, Ferber, Frost, Chan & Essner	E.P.S	$0.038
DUNS No.	88-418-9036	Shareholders	NA

Business: The group's principal activities are the exploration, production and transportation of oil and natural gas in Tennessee and Kansas. The group leases oil and gas properties for exploration and development. The group has 22 natural gas producing wells and six oil producing wells in the swan creek field in Tennessee. Its products are supplied to local refining companies, local utilities and private industry end users. The group, through its subsidiary, transmits natural gas through its pipeline to the customers.

Primary SIC and add'l.: 4924 1382 4922

CIK No: 0001001614

Subsidiaries: Tengasco Pipeline Corporation, Tennessee Land and Mineral Corporation

Officers: Jeffrey R. Bailey/50/Dir., CEO, Cary V. Sorensen/59/VP, General Counsel, Corp. Sec., Mark A. Ruth/49/CFO, Gary J. Wagner/Production Mgr., Rod Tremblay/Sr. Geologist, Robert M. Carter/71/Pres. - Tengasco Pipeline Corporation

Directors: Jeffrey R. Bailey/50/Dir., CEO, Peter E. Salas/53/Chmn., John A. Clendening/75/Dir., Carlos P. Salas/36/Dir., Matthew K. Behrent/37/Dir.

Owners: Peter E. Salas/35.70%, Jeffrey R. Bailey/1.10%, Robert M. Carter, Carlos P. Salas, Insiders/37.80%, John A. Clendening, Mark A. Ruth, Cary V. Sorensen

Financial Data: *Fiscal Year End:*12/31 *Latest Annual Data:* 12/31/2006

Year		Sales		Net Income	
2006		$9,002,000		$2,141,000	
2005		$7,173,000		$1,088,000	
2004		$6,109,000		-$1,994,000	
Curr. Assets:	$1,664,000	**Curr. Liab.:**	$792,000	**P/E Ratio:**	33.50
Plant, Equip.:	$26,432,000	**Total Liab.:**	$4,034,000	**Indic. Yr. Divd.:**	NA
Total Assets:	$28,454,000	**Net Worth:**	$24,420,000	**Debt/ Equity:**	0.1118

Tengtu International Corp

236 Ave. Rd. , Toronto, ON, M5R 2J4; *PH:* 1-416-963-3999; *http://* www.tengtu.com

General - Incorporation	DE	**Stock** - Price on:12/24/2007	$0.014
Employees	NA	Stock Exchange	OTC
Auditor	Moore Stephens Ellis Foster Ltd	Ticker Symbol	TNTU
Stk Agt	U.S. Stock Transfer Corp	Outstanding Shares	NA
Counsel	NA	E.P.S.	NA
DUNS No.	NA	Shareholders	NA

Business: The group's principal activity is to develop, source and market software and educational materials including education resource for Microsoft(R) Office software, educational resources based on K-12 curriculum, and teacher training resources. The services offered include software installation and network cabling. The group operates in China and Canada. In September 2003, the group acquired Tengtu United.

Primary SIC and add'l.: 7373 7379 7372

CIK No: 0000847597

Financial Data: *Fiscal Year End:*06/30   *Latest Annual Data:* 6/30/2004

Year	Sales		Net Income
2004	$2,399,000		-$73,016,000
2003	$5,344,000		-$1,862,000
2002	$14,255,000		$1,578,000
Curr. Assets:	$4,151,000	**Curr. Liab.:**	$7,974,000
Plant, Equip.:	$197,000	**Total Liab.:** $8,052,000	**Indic. Yr. Divd.:** NA
Total Assets:	$5,578,000	**Net Worth:** -$2,473,000	**Debt/ Equity:** NA

Tennant Co

701 N Lilac Dr., Minneapolis, MN, 55440; *PH:* 1-763-540-1200; *Fax:* 1-763-540-1437; *http://* www.tennantco.com; *Email:* Info@tennantco.com

General - Incorporation	MN	**Stock** - Price on:12/24/2007	$36.05
Employees	2,653	Stock Exchange	NYSE
Auditor	KPMG LLP	Ticker Symbol	TNC
Stk Agt	Wells Fargo Bank, N.A.	Outstanding Shares	18,830,000
Counsel	NA	E.P.S.	$1.70
DUNS No.	00-624-7126	Shareholders	NA

Business: The group's principle activity is to design, manufacture and market products used in the maintenance of non-residential floors. The group's products include floor maintenance equipment, outdoor cleaning equipment, coatings and related products. The group's products are mainly used to clean factories, office buildings, parking lots and streets, airports, hospitals, schools, warehouses and shopping centers. The group's customers include building service contract cleaners, health care facilities, schools, state and local governments. The group markets and distributes its products through direct sales and a strong network of authorized distributors worldwide. The group operates in North America, Australia, Canada, Japan, Spain, the Netherlands, the United Kingdom, France and Germany. The group's quarterly revenue for Sep '07 was 161.33 millions of USD.

Primary SIC and add'l.: 3589 7349 5169

CIK No: 0000097134

Subsidiaries: Tennant Holding B.V., Tennant Maintenance Systems, Limited, Tennant N.V., Tennant Sales and Service Company

Officers: Chris H. Killingstad/Dir., CEO, Pres./$1,713,824.00, Steven M. Coopersmith/VP - Global Marketing, Thomas J. Dybsky/VP - Administration/$752,946.00, Andrew J. Eckert/VP - North America Sales, Mark J. Fleigle/VP - Research, Development, Heidi M. Hoard/VP, General Counsel, Sec./$578,088.00, Patrick J. O'Neill/Treasurer/$370,362.00, Thomas Paulson/CFO, VP/$554,515.00, Steven K. Weeks/VP - North America Strategic Planning, Don W. Westman/VP - Global Operations, Anthony Lenders/MD, VP - Europe/$666,689.00

Directors: Chris H. Killingstad/Dir., CEO, Pres., Pamela K. Knous/Dir., Jeffrey A. Balagna/Dir., James T. Hale/Dir., David Mathieson/Dir., Edwin L. Russell/Dir., Stephen G. Shank/Dir., Frank L. Sims/Dir., Steven A. Sonnenberg/Dir., William F. Austen/Dir.

Owners: Frank L. Sims, Thomas Paulson, Royce & Associates, LLC/5.40%, Chris H. Killingstad, Anthony Lenders, Wellington Management Company,LLP/5.20%, William F. Austen, Jeffrey A. Balagna, Stephen G. Shank, Steven A. Sonnenberg, Insiders/2.60%, Thomas J. Dybsky, Edwin L. Russell, James T. Hale, Patrick J. ONeill *(19 Owners included in Index)*

Financial Data: *Fiscal Year End:*12/31   *Latest Annual Data:* 12/31/2006

Year	Sales		Net Income
2006	$598,981,000		$29,809,000
2005	$552,908,000		$22,936,000
2004	$507,785,000		$13,380,000
Curr. Assets:	$235,404,000	**Curr. Liab.:**	$94,804,000	**P/E Ratio:** 21.21
Plant, Equip.:	$82,835,000	**Total Liab.:**	$124,586,000	**Indic. Yr. Divd.:** $0.480
Total Assets:	$354,250,000	**Net Worth:**	$229,664,000	**Debt/ Equity:** 0.0072

Tenneco Automotive Inc

500 N Field Dr., Lake Forest, IL, 60045; *PH:* 1-847-482-5000; *http://* www.tenneco-automotive.com

General - Incorporation	DE	**Stock** - Price on:12/24/2007	$32.8
Employees	19,000	Stock Exchange	NYSE
Auditor	Deloitte & Touche LLP	Ticker Symbol	TEN
Stk Agt	Wells Fargo Bank, N.A.	Outstanding Shares	46,290,000
Counsel	NA	E.P.S.	$1.45
DUNS No.	18-144-2526	Shareholders	NA

Business: The group's principle activity is to manufacture automotive emissions control and ride control products and systems. The group's products include ride and emission controls, and elastomeres. The groups products sold under the brand name Monroe(R), Rancho(R) and Fric Rot Ride Control And Walker(R), and Gillet(TM). The groups specific customers include Ford, General Motors, Daimlerchrysler and Volkswagen. The group operates from United States.

Primary SIC and add'l.: 2655 3714

CIK No: 0001024725

Subsidiaries: an unaffiliated individual, and an affiliated party, and each of Proveedora Walker and Tenneco, and each of Proveedora Walker and Tenneco Inc., and each of Walker Europe, Inc., Tenneco Automotive, and each of Wimetal S.A., and unaffiliated parties own the remainder), Armstrong Hydraulics South Africa, Armstrong Properties, Automotive France S.A., Automotive France, S.A., Automovel, Unipessoal, Lda, Autopartes Walker S.A. de C.V., Autopartes Walker, S.A. de C.V., Barasset Corporation 143 Subsidiaries included in the Index

Officers: Gregg Sherrill/Chmn., CEO, William H. Haser/47/CIO, VP, Neal Yanos/Sr. VP, GM - North American Original Equipment Ride Control, Aftermarket/$1,474,328.00, Richard P. Schneider/Sr. VP - Global Administration, John Kunz/VP - Treasurer - Tax, Hari N. Nair/Exec. VP, Pres. - International/$2,026,334.00, Jeff Jarrell/VP - Japan - Korea Global OEM Business, Brent Bauer/Sr. VP, GM, Paul D. Novas/VP, Controller, Josep Fornos/VP, GM - European Original Equipment Ride Control, Kenneth R. Trammell/CFO, Exec. VP/$1,721,565.00, Jeffrey J. Zimmerman/48/VP - Law, Corp. Sec., Paul Schultz/57/Sr. VP - Global Manufacturing, Supply Chain Management, James K. Spangler/VP - Global Communications, Timothy R. Donovan/52/Exec. VP - Strategy, Business Development, General Counsel/$2,225,103.00 *(21 Officers included in Index)*

Directors: Gregg Sherrill/Chmn., CEO, Charles W. Cramb/Dir., David B. Price/Dir., Mitsunobu Takeuchi/Dir., Jane L. Warner/Dir., Frank E. MacHer/Dir., Paul T. Stecko/Dir., Roger B. Porter/Dir.

Owners: Insiders/3.70%, Mitsunobu Takeuchi, Paul T. Stecko, Charles W. Cramb, Neal Yanos, Frank E. Macher, Kenneth R. Trammell, Jane L. Warner, Kathryn M. Eickhoff-Smith, Dennis G. Severance, Gregg Sherrill, Timothy R. Donovan, Hari N. Nair, Roger B. Porter, Jeffrey L. Gendell/6.80% *(17 Owners included in Index)*

Financial Data: *Fiscal Year End:*12/31   *Latest Annual Data:* 12/31/2006

Year	Sales		Net Income
2006	$4,685,000,000		$51,000,000
2005	$4,441,000,000		$58,000,000
2004	$4,213,000,000		$15,000,000
Curr. Assets:	$1,415,000,000	**Curr. Liab.:**	$1,119,000,000	**P/E Ratio:** 32.80
Plant, Equip.:	$1,093,000,000	**Total Liab.:**	$3,048,000,000	**Indic. Yr. Divd.:** NA
Total Assets:	$3,274,000,000	**Net Worth:**	$226,000,000	**Debt/ Equity:** 5.8122

Tennessee Commerce Bank

381 Mallory Sta. Rd., Ste. 207, Franklin, TN, 37067; *PH:* 1-615-599-2274; *Fax:* 1-615-599-2275; *http://* www.tncommercebank.com; *Email:* info@tncommercebank.com

General - Incorporation	TN	**Stock** - Price on:12/24/2007	$25.6
Employees	50	Stock Exchange	NDQ
Auditor	Crowe Chizek & Co. LLC	Ticker Symbol	TNCC
Stk Agt	Registrar & Transfer Co	Outstanding Shares	4,510,000
Counsel	NA	E.P.S.	$1.17
DUNS No.	NA	Shareholders	NA

Business: The groups principle activity is to provide commercial banking, leasing, personal banking and mortgage services. The groups commercial banking services include business checking, business NOW, sweep account, money fund accounts, market watch money fund, business savings and certificated of deposits. The group operates from United States.

Primary SIC and add'l.: 6021

CIK No: 0001323033

Subsidiaries: Tennessee Commerce Bank Statutory Trust I

Officers: Arthur F. Helf/Chmn., CEO, Michael R. Sapp/Pres., Chief Lending Officer, Dir., Lamar H. Cox/Chief Administrative Officer, Dir., George W. Fort/CFO

Directors: Arthur F. Helf/Chmn., CEO, Michael R. Sapp/Pres., Chief Lending Officer, Dir., Lamar H. Cox/Chief Administrative Officer, Dir., Dorris E. Bennett/Dir., Paul W. Dierksen/Dir., Dennis L. Grimaud/Dir., William W. McInnes/Dir., Thomas R. Miller/Dir., Darrel Reifschneider/Dir., Paul A. Thomas/Dir.

Owners: Michael R. Sapp/5.90%, Arthur F. Helf/5.30%, Gilder Gagnon Howe & Co./16.10%

Financial Data: *Fiscal Year End:*12/31   *Latest Annual Data:* 12/31/2006

Year	Sales		Net Income
2006	$43,561,000		$4,749,000
2005	$24,962,000		$3,067,000
Curr. Assets:	$18,113,000	**Curr. Liab.:**	$562,918,000	**P/E Ratio:** 21.88
Plant, Equip.:	$1,633,000	**Total Liab.:**	$572,294,000	**Indic. Yr. Divd.:** NA
Total Assets:	$623,518,000	**Net Worth:**	$51,224,000	**Debt/ Equity:** 0.1541

Tennessee Gas Pipeline Co

El Paso Bldg, 1001 Louisiana St, Houston, TX, 77002; *PH:* 1-713-420-2600; *http://* www.tennesseeadvantage.com

General - Incorporation	DE	**Stock** - Price on:12/24/2007	NA
Employees	NA	Stock Exchange	NA
Auditor	Ernst & Young, LLP	Ticker Symbol	NA
Stk Agt	Computershare Trust Co	Outstanding Shares	NA
Counsel	NA	E.P.S.	NA
DUNS No.	00-193-9164	Shareholders	NA

Business: The group's principal activities are interstate transportation and storage of natural gas. The group operates through two natural gas transmission systems and a storage facility. The group also has non-regulated operations, including intrastate transportation, gathering and processing of natural gas, marketing of natural gas. The multiple pipe line system begins in the natural gas producing regions of Louisiana, including gulf of Mexico, and south Texas and extends to the north east section of the us including New York city and Boston metropolitan areas. The group also has an inter connect at the us Mexico border and has sufficient underground working storage capacity.

Primary SIC and add'l.: 4922 4924 4923

CIK No: 0000097142

Subsidiaries: El Paso Corporation, Sabine River Investors III, LLC

Officers: James C. Yardley/Chmn., Principal Executive Officer, Pres., Ann Nelson/Contact - Nominations, Melva Harris/Contact - Measurement, Patricia De La Rosa/Contact - Nominations, Sharon Kimball/Contact - Credit Requirements, Ted Chavez/Contact - Credit Requirements, Daniel B. Martin/Dir., Sr. VP, Richard Denney/Contact - Marketing, Kourtney Calhoun/Dir. - Transportation Services, Jim Bujnoch/Dir. - Marketing, Business Development, Stuart Neck/Contact - Asset Optimization, Richard Wheatley/Mgr. - Media Relations, John R. Sult/CFO, Sr. VP, Controller, Scott Minear/Contact - Asset Optimization, Adam Harris/Contact - Capacity Release *(21 Officers included in Index)*

Directors: James C. Yardley/Chmn., Principal Executive Officer, Pres., Daniel B. Martin/Dir., Sr. VP

Tennessee Valley Financial Holdings Inc

401 S Illinois Ave., Oak Ridge, TN, 37830; *PH:* 1-865-483-9444; *http://* www.tnbank.net; *Email:* tbaird@tnbank.net

General - Incorporation	TN	**Stock**- Price on:12/24/2007	NA
Employees	NA	Stock Exchange	OTC
Auditor	Pugh & Co, P.C	Ticker Symbol	TVFH
Stk Agt	Illinois Stock Transfer Co	Outstanding Shares	NA
Counsel	NA	E.P.S.	NA
DUNS No.	NA	Shareholders	NA

Business: The groups principle activity is to provide financial services. The groups services include consumer and business customers checking, savings, and money market accounts. The groups loan products include mortgage and home equity, construction and business, and automobile and personal. The group also provides long term, fixed rate, and adjustable rate mortgages, second mortgages, and jumbo loans. The group operates from United States.

Primary SIC and add'l.: NA

CIK No: 0001175158

Subsidiaries: Tennessee Valley Statutory Trust I, TNBANK

Officers: Thomas E. Tuck/58/Dir., CEO, Pres., Mike Moore/Contact - Mortgage Experts, Vana Demarinis/Contact - Mortgage Experts, Linda Natour/Contact - Mortgage Experts, Rick Hudolin/Contact - Mortgage Experts, Penny Cooper/Contact - Mortgage Experts, Jason B. Wilkinson/VP, Kenneth F. Scarbro/CFO, VP

Directors: Thomas E. Tuck/58/Dir., CEO, Pres., Frank J. Jamison/68/Chmn., A. P. Cappiello/Dir., Larry Beeman/Dir., Terry L. Kerbs/Dir., William Robert Witt/67/Dir., Thomas D. Moye/59/Dir.

Owners: Insiders/18.76%, A. P. Cappiello/1.06%, Terry L. Kerbs/2.46%, Larry Beeman/2.11%, Thomas E. Tuck/5.17%, Mark B. Holder, Braxton Sadler/1.26%, Frank J. Jamison/2.98%, Robert W. Witt/1.41%, James Stalsworth, Thomas D. Moye/1.13%

TEPPCO Partners LP

1100 Louisiana St., Houston, TX, 77002; *PH:* 1-713-381-3636; *http://* www.teppco.com

General - Incorporation	DE	**Stock**- Price on:12/24/2007	$44.15
Employees	NA	Stock Exchange	NYSE
Auditor	Deloitte & Touche LLP	Ticker Symbol	TPP
Stk Agt	Mellon Investor Services LLC	Outstanding Shares	89,800,000
Counsel	NA	E.P.S.	$2.72
DUNS No.	NA	Shareholders	NA

Business: The groups principle activity is to transport refined, petrochemical and natural gas products. The group operates through three segments namely, downstream, midstream and upstream. The group operates from the United States. The group's quarterly revenue for September 2007 was 2580.66 millions of USD.

Primary SIC and add'l.: 4612 4613

CIK No: 0000857644

Subsidiaries: Chaparral Pipeline Company, L.P., Dean Pipeline Company, L.P., Lubrication Services, L.P., Panola Pipeline Company, L.P., Quanah Pipeline Company, L.P., TCTM, L.P., TE Products Pipeline Company, Limited Partnership, TEPPCO Colorado, LLC, TEPPCO Crude GP, LLC, TEPPCO Crude Oil, L.P., TEPPCO Crude Pipeline, L.P., TEPPCO GP, Inc., TEPPCO Interests, LLC, TEPPCO Midstream Companies, L.P., TEPPCO NGL Pipelines, LLC 20 Subsidiaries included in the Index

Officers: Jerry E. Thompson/Dir., CEO, Pres., Samuel N. Brown/VP - Commercial Downstream, Michael J. Cockrell/Pres. - Teppco Crude GP, LLC, Sr. VP - Commercial, Upstream, John N. Goodpasture/VP - Corporate Development, Merle D. Bone/Mgr. - Area Supply, South Oklahoma, Leonard W. Mallett/Sr. VP - Operations, Danny Belf/Area Dir., William G. Manias/CFO, VP, Patricia A. Totten/VP, General Counsel, Sec., Blair L. Armstrong/Area Mgr. - Val Verde Gas Gathering, Mike St. John/Area Mgr. - Chaparral NGL Pipeline, Bill Rutherford/VP, GM - LSI, John E. Bales/Mgr. - Operations, Crescent, Oklahoma, Matt E. Buchheit/Sales, Longview, Texas, John R. Gracia/Mgr. - District, Hobbs, New Mexico *(66 Officers included in Index)*

Directors: Jerry E. Thompson/Dir., CEO, Pres., Murray H. Hutchison/Chmn., Michael B. Bracy/Vice Chmn., Richard S. Snell/Dir.

Owners: Duncan Family Interests, Inc./14.90%, Leonard W. Mallet, EPCO Holdings, Inc./14.90%, EPCO, Inc./14.90%, Dan Duncan LLC/3.60%, DFI Holdings LLC/2.80%, John N. Goodpasture, Jerry E. Thompson, Michael J. Cockrell, Michael B. Bracy, William G. Manias, DFI GP Holdings L.P./2.80%, Dan L. Duncan/18.60%, James C. Ruth, Insiders

Financial Data: ***Fiscal Year End:*** 12/31 ***Latest Annual Data:*** 12/31/2006

Year	*Sales*	*Net Income*
2006	$9,607,485,000	$202,051,000
2005	$8,618,488,000	$162,551,000
2004	$5,958,192,000	$142,381,000

Curr. Assets:	$966,710,000	***Curr. Liab.:***	$976,548,000	***P/E Ratio:***	16.29
Plant, Equip.:	$1,642,095,000	***Total Liab.:***	$2,601,762,000	***Indic. Yr. Divd.:***	$2.780
Total Assets:	$3,922,092,000	***Net Worth:***	$1,320,330,000	***Debt/ Equity:***	1.0905

Teradyne Inc

600 RiverPk. Dr., North Reading, MA, 01864; *PH:* 1-978-370-2700; *http://* www.teradyne.com; *Email:* investorrelations@teradyne.com

General - Incorporation	MA	**Stock**- Price on:12/24/2007	$17.44
Employees	3,800	Stock Exchange	NYSE
Auditor	PricewaterhouseCoopers LLP	Ticker Symbol	TER
Stk Agt	Computershare Investor Services LLC	Outstanding Shares	189,720,000
Counsel	NA	E.P.S.	$0.49
DUNS No.	15-592-0507	Shareholders	NA

Business: The group's principal activities are to design, manufacture, market and service test system and related software, backplanes and associated connectors. The group's test systems include systems to test semiconductors, circuit-boards, telephone lines and networks used by equipment manufacturers and telephone operating companies. The group's software test systems are used to test communications networks, computerized telecommunication systems and Web based applications. The group's backplane connection systems are primarily used by the computer, communications and military/aerospace industries for use in data storage systems, telecommunications gear and outers and servers.

Primary SIC and add'l.: 3675 3823

CIK No: 0000097210

Subsidiaries: 1000 Washington, Inc, Aegis Properties Limited, GenRad A.B., GenRad Europe Limited, GenRad Holdings Limited, GenRad S.A., GenRad, Inc., Herco Technology Corp., Mastertech Automotive Ltd., Mitron Europe Limited, Perception Laminates, Inc., Teradyne (Shanghai) Co., Ltd, Teradyne (Sweden) AB, Teradyne Asia Pte., Ltd., Teradyne Assembly Holdings Ltd. 41 Subsidiaries included in the Index

Officers: Michael A. Bradley/Dir., CEO, Pres./$3,002,977.00, James W. Bagley/Exec. Chmn. - Lam Research Corporation, Jeffrey R. Hotchkiss/Pres. - System Test Group/$928,176.00, Eileen Casal/VP, General Counsel, Sec./$792,246.00, Mark E. Jagiela/Pres. - Semiconductor Test Division/$1,098,324.00, Tom Newman/VP - Corporate Relations, Albert Carnesale/Chancellor, University, California, Los Angeles, CA, Dir., Gregory R. Beecher/CFO, VP, Treasurer/$1,262,569.00, Vincent M. O'Reilly/Distinguished Sr. Lecturer, Carroll Graduate School, Management, Boston College, Boston MA, Kyle Klatka/Product Mgr. - Wireless Broadband Test, Brooke Shell/Software Engineer, Damien Tufts/Mgr. - Financial Planning, Analysis, Helen Chen/Applications Engineer, Chris Giovanniello/South Europe Applications Mgr., Ayse Acar/Manufacturing Engineer *(18 Officers included in Index)*

Directors: Michael A. Bradley/Dir., CEO, Pres., James W. Bagley/Exec. Chmn. - Lam Research Corporation, Albert Carnesale/Chancellor, University, California, Los Angeles, CA, Dir., Patricia S. Wolpert/Dir., Paul J. Tufano/Dir., Vincent M. O'Reilly/Distinguished Sr. Lecturer, Carroll Graduate School, Management, Boston College, Boston MA, Edwin J. Gillis/Dir., Roy A. Vallee/Dir.

Owners: Eileen Casal, Vincent M. OReilly, Jeffrey Hotchkiss, Michael A. Bradley, Capital Group International, Inc/8.70%, Patricia S. Wolpert, Gregory R. Beecher, Paul J. Tufano, Insiders/1.20%, FMR Corp/14.90%, James W. Bagley, T. Rowe Price Associates, Inc./9.10%, Roy A. Vallee, Mark E. Jagiela, Albert Carnesale

Financial Data: ***Fiscal Year End:*** 12/31 ***Latest Annual Data:*** 12/31/2006

Year	*Sales*	*Net Income*
2006	$1,376,818,000	$198,757,000
2005	$1,075,232,000	$90,648,000
2004	$1,791,880,000	$165,237,000

Curr. Assets:	$889,410,000	***Curr. Liab.:***	$259,716,000	***P/E Ratio:***	35.59
Plant, Equip.:	$366,349,000	***Total Liab.:***	$359,868,000	***Indic. Yr. Divd.:***	NA
Total Assets:	$1,721,055,000	***Net Worth:***	$1,361,187,000	***Debt/ Equity:***	NA

Teraforce Technology Corp

1240 Campbell Rd., Richardson, TX, 75081; *PH:* 1-469-330-4960

General - Incorporation	DE	**Stock**- Price on:12/24/2007	$0.0007
Employees	NA	Stock Exchange	OTC
Auditor	Grant Thornton LLP	Ticker Symbol	TERA
Stk Agt	American Stock Transfer & Trust Co.	Outstanding Shares	NA
Counsel	NA	E.P.S.	NA
DUNS No.	92-646-2193	Shareholders	NA

Business: The group's principal activities are to design, develops, produces and sells embedded computing platforms and systems. Embedded computing generally refers to the physical integration of computing nodes (microprocessor and memory) into a host system or application. These nodes are often deployed in arrays. Embedded computing platforms and systems are widely applied in a number of industries including communications, medical imaging, seismic processing, industrial control and defense electronics. The products are organized into four broader categories dsp products, powerpc single board computers, embedded sub-systems & wingspantm software suite.

Primary SIC and add'l.: 3678 3669 3661

CIK No: 0000316672

Subsidiaries: 1240 Campbell Corp., DNA Computing Solutions, Inc., Intelect Technologies, Inc.

Financial Data: ***Fiscal Year End:*** 12/31 ***Latest Annual Data:*** 12/31/2004

Year	*Sales*	*Net Income*
2004	$9,385,000	-$2,880,000
2003	$6,207,000	-$8,559,000
2002	$5,036,000	-$4,350,000

Curr. Assets:	$1,523,000	***Curr. Liab.:***	$9,988,000		
Plant, Equip.:	$335,000	***Total Liab.:***	$11,352,000	***Indic. Yr. Divd.:***	NA
Total Assets:	$3,044,000	***Net Worth:***	-$8,308,000	***Debt/ Equity:***	NA

Terax Energy Inc

One Galleria Tower, 13355 Noel Rd., Ste. 1370, Dallas, TX, 75240; *PH:* 1-972-503-0900; *Fax:* 1-972-503-0901; *http://* www.teraxenergy.com; *Email:* Info@teraxenergy.com

General - Incorporation	NV	**Stock**- Price on:12/24/2007	NA
Employees	NA	Stock Exchange	OTC
Auditor	Malone & Bailey, PC	Ticker Symbol	TEXG
Stk Agt	Pacific Stock Transfer Company	Outstanding Shares	NA
Counsel	NA	E.P.S.	NA
DUNS No.	NA	Shareholders	NA

Business: The groups principle activity is an independent oil and gas exploration and development company headquartered in Dallas, Texas. The groups principle properties consist of two blocks of oil and gas leases. In May 2005, the group acquired Erath Energy Inc.

Primary SIC and add'l.: 1311

CIK No: 0001143548

Subsidiaries: Erath Energy Inc

Officers: Linda Contreras/Dir., CEO

Directors: Linda Contreras/Dir., CEO

Owners: Westar Oil, Inc./52.00%

Curr. Assets:	$16,000	***Curr. Liab.:***	NA		
Plant, Equip.:	NA	***Total Liab.:***	NA	***Indic. Yr. Divd.:***	NA
Total Assets:	$16,000	***Net Worth:***	$16,000	***Debt/ Equity:***	NA

Terayon Communication Systems Inc

2450 Walsh Ave., Santa Clara, CA, 95051; *PH:* 1-408-235-5500; *http://* www.terayon.com

General - Incorporation	DE	**Stock**- Price on:12/24/2007	$1.77
Employees	NA	Stock Exchange	OTC
Auditor	Ernst & Young LLP	Ticker Symbol	TERN
Stk Agt	Computershare Trust Co	Outstanding Shares	NA
Counsel	NA	E.P.S.	NA
DUNS No.	87-811-5435	Shareholders	NA

Business: The group's principal activity is to provide broadband services to cable operators. The group operates in two segments: cable broadband access systems and telecom carrier systems. Cable consist of docsis standards based products, s-cdma products, cherrypicker digital video management system, multigate telephony and data access system. These products are marketed to cable operators for

the deployment of data, video and voice services over the existing cable infrastructure. Telecom consist of miniplex DSL multiplexer system, the iptl dslam, mainsail mmap and mainsail iad. These products are marketed to broadband service providers for the deployment of voice and data services over the existing copper wire infrastructure. The group operates in Europe, Japan, Belgium, Hong Kong, the United Kingdom, Canada and Israel.

Primary SIC and add'l.: 3661 3663

CIK No: 0001052303

Subsidiaries: ComBox, Inc., Digital Transmission Equipment, Imedia Corporation, Imedia Semiconductor Corporation, Nippon Terayon Kabushiki Kaisha, Radwiz, Inc., Terayon Canada Ltd., Terayon Cayman Ltd., Terayon Communication Systems Europe, S.A., Terayon Communication Systems Ltd., Terayon Communication Systems SRO, Terayon do Brazil Ltd, Terayon Hong Kong Limited, Terayon International Holdings, Inc., Terayon Korea Ltd. 16 Subsidiaries included in the Index

Owners: Matthew J. Aden, Howard W. Speaks, Insiders/13.40%, Lewis Solomon, Zaki Rakib/11.10%, David M. Woodrow, Shlomo Rakib/11.10%, Jerry D. Chase, Kern Capital Management, LLC/14.90%, Matthew Miller, Mark A. Richman

Financial Data: Fiscal Year End:12/31 **Latest Annual Data:** 12/31/2006

Year	Sales	Net Income
2006	$76,430,000	-$3,831,000
2005	$90,664,000	-$26,951,000
2004	$150,538,000	-$36,531,000

Curr. Assets:	$46,916,000	Curr. Liab.:	$24,064,000		
Plant, Equip.:	$3,309,000	Total Liab.:	$32,148,000	Indic. Yr. Divd.:	NA
Total Assets:	$51,970,000	Net Worth:	$19,822,000	Debt/ Equity:	0.0922

Tercica Inc

2000 Sierra Point Pkwy., Ste.400, Brisbane, CA, 94005; **PH:** 1-650-624-4900; **Fax:** 1-650-243-5111; http:// www.tercica.com; **Email:** hr@tercica.com

General - Incorporation	DE	**Stock**- Price on:12/24/2007	$5.95
Employees	106	Stock Exchange	NDQ
Auditor	Ernst & Young LLP	Ticker Symbol	TRCA
Stk Agt	EquiServe Trust Co N.A	Outstanding Shares	50,160,000
Counsel	NA	E.P.S.	-$1.26
DUNS No.	NA	Shareholders	NA

Business: The group's principal activity is to develop, manufacture and commercialize rhigf-1 for the treatment of short stature, diabetes and other endocrine system disorders. The group's product, recombinant human insulin-like growth factor-1 (rhigf-1), is a hormone with a broad range of activity central to growth and metabolism. It commercializes its products in the United States and Europe. The group is in its development stage.

Primary SIC and add'l.: 2834 8731

CIK No: 0001262175

Officers: John A. Scarlett/Dir., CEO, Pres., Ajay Bansal/CFO, Sr. VP - Finance, Corporate Development, Corporate Communications, Andrew Grethlein/Sr. VP - Pharmaceutical Operations, Stephen N. Rosenfield/Exec. VP - Legal Affairs, General Counsel, Sec., Susan Wong/VP - Finance, Chief Accounting Officer, George Bright/VP, Medical Dir. - Endocrinology, Thorsten V. Stein/Sr. VP, Chief Medical Officer, Ross G. Clark/CTO, Founder, Dir., Chris E. Rivera/Sr. VP - Commercial Operations, Sandra L. Blethen/VP - Medical Affairs, Michael D. Allen/VP - Marketing, William Yates/VP - Human Resources, Information Technology, Richard A. King/COO, Gordon Treadway/VP - Sales, Mike Parker/VP - Quality

Directors: John A. Scarlett/Dir., CEO, Pres., Alex Barkas/Chmn., Dennis Henner/Dir., Ross G. Clark/CTO, Founder, Dir., Karin Eastham/Dir., Mark Leschly/Dir., David L. Mahoney/Dir., Jean-Luc Belingard/59/Dir., Christophe Jean/Dir.

Owners: Entities affiliated with MPM BioVentures III LLC, Karin Eastham, Dennis Henner, AMVESCAP PLC, Thorsten von Stein, Christophe Jean, John A. Scarlett, Alexander Barkas, Stephen N. Rosenfield, Jean-Luc Blingard, Andrew Grethlein, Entities affiliated with Rho Capital Partners, Inc., David L. Mahoney, Insiders, MedImmune, Inc. (20 Owners included in Index)

Financial Data: Fiscal Year End:12/31 **Latest Annual Data:** 06/30/2007

Year	Sales	Net Income
2007	$2,242,000	-$12,807,000
2006	$942,000	-$40,981,000
2005	NA	-$46,233,000

Curr. Assets:	$132,950,000	Curr. Liab.:	$9,769,000		
Plant, Equip.:	$3,861,000	Total Liab.:	$47,756,000	Indic. Yr. Divd.:	NA
Total Assets:	$137,687,000	Net Worth:	$89,931,000	Debt/ Equity:	0.3198

Terex Corp

200 Nyala Farm Rd., Westport, CT, 06880; **PH:** 1-203-222-7170; **Fax:** 1-203-222-7976; http:// www.terex.com; **Email:** info@terex.com

General - Incorporation	DE	**Stock**- Price on:12/24/2007	$82.76
Employees	18,200	Stock Exchange	NYSE
Auditor	PricewaterhouseCoopers LLP	Ticker Symbol	TEX
Stk Agt	American Stock Transfer & Trust Co.	Outstanding Shares	NA
Counsel	NA	E.P.S.	$5.18
DUNS No.	NA	Shareholders	NA

Business: The groups principle activity is to manufacture equipment for the construction, infrastructure, quarrying, mining, shipping, transportation, refining and utility industries. The group operates through five segments namely, work platforms, construction, cranes, materials processing and mining, and roadbuilding. The group operates from the United States.

Primary SIC and add'l.: 3531 3532

CIK No: 0000097216

Subsidiaries: American Truck Company LLC, Amida Industries, Inc., Atlas Terex UK Limited, Atlas Weyhausen Norge A/S, Atlasquip Ltee., B-L Pegson Limited, Benford Limited, Brown Lenox & Co. Limited, Cedarapids, Inc., Cliffmere Limited, CMI Belgium NV, CMI Terex Corporation, Demag Mobile Cranes Gpgyrt Kft., Demag Mobile Cranes Spain, S.A., Drion Constructie B.V.B.A. 163 Subsidiaries included in the Index

Officers: Ronald M. Defeo/Chmn., CEO/$15,480,380.00, Kevin A. Barr/Sr. VP - Human Resources, Jonathan D. Carter/VP, Controller, Chief Accounting Officer, Eric I. Cohen/Sr. VP, General Counsel, Sec./$3,049,175.00, Katia Facchetti/Chief Marketing Officer, Sr. VP, Tim Ford/Pres. - Terex Aerial Work Platforms, Colin Robertson/43/Exec. VP - Operations/$4,808,005.00, Robert R. Wilkerson/57/Pres. - Terex Aerial Work Platforms, Exec. VP, Chief Change Officer, Mike

Bazinet/Dir. - Global Communications, Colin Fox/Sr. VP - Terex Business Systems, Steve Filipov/Pres. - Terex Cranes, Tom Gelston/Dir. - Investor Relations, Financial Planning, Analysis, Brian J. Henry/Sr. VP - Finance, Business Development/$2,899,442.00, Robert G. Isaman/Pres. - Terex Construction, Hyeryun Lee Park/Pres. - Terex Asia (19 Officers included in Index)

Directors: Ronald M. Defeo/Chmn., CEO, Chris G. Andersen/Dir., Paula H.J. Cholmondeley/Dir., Donald Defosset/Dir., William H. Fike/Dir., Donald P. Jacobs/Dir., David A. Sachs/Dir., Oren G. Shaffer/Dir., Helge H. Wehmeier/Dir., J. C. Watts/Dir.

Owners: William H. Fike, Donald P. Jacobs, FMR Corp./7.20%, State Street Bank and Trust Company/5.50%, Paula H. J. Cholmondeley, Brian J. Henry, Insiders/3.10%, Neuberger Berman, Inc./11.20%, Colin Robertson, Don DeFosset, Oren G. Shaffer, David A. Sachs, Eric I. Cohen, Helge H. Wehmeier, Ronald M. DeFeo/1.30% (17 Owners included in Index)

Financial Data: Fiscal Year End:12/31 **Latest Annual Data:** 12/31/2006

Year	Sales	Net Income
2006	$7,647,600,000	$399,900,000
2005	$6,380,400,000	$188,500,000
2004	$5,019,800,000	$324,100,000

Curr. Assets:	$3,432,800,000	Curr. Liab.:	$2,027,200,000	P/E Ratio:	16.29
Plant, Equip.:	$338,500,000	Total Liab.:	$3,034,900,000	Indic. Yr. Divd.:	$1.500
Total Assets:	$4,785,900,000	Net Worth:	$1,751,000,000	Debt/ Equity:	NA

Ternium S.A.

420 Fifth Ave., 18th Fl., New York, NY, 10018; **PH:** 1-212-376-6500; http:// www.ternium.com

General - Incorporation Grand Duchy of Luxembourg		**Stock**- Price on:12/24/2007	$28.67
Employees	18,257	Stock Exchange	NYSE
Auditor	PricewaterhouseCoopers LLP	Ticker Symbol	TX
Stk Agt	NA	Outstanding Shares	200,470,000
Counsel	NA	E.P.S.	$3.79
DUNS No.	NA	Shareholders	NA

Business: The groups principle activity is to provide flat and long steel products. The group operates through two segments namely, flat steel products, long steel products. The group operates from the United States, Mexico, Argetina and Venezuela. The group's quarterly revenue for September 2007 was 2343.35 millions of USD.

Primary SIC and add'l.: 3317 3315 3325 3316 3462

CIK No: 0001342874

Subsidiaries: Acerex S.A. de C.V., Acerex Servicios S.A. de C.V., Alvory S.A., Comesi San Luis S.A.I.C., Compaa Afianzadora de Empresas Siderrgicas S.G.R., Consorcio Minero Benito Juarez Pea Colorada S.A.de C.V., Consorcio Siderurgia Amazonia Ltd., Express Anahuac S.A. de C.V., Fasnet International S.A., Ferropak Comercial S.A. de C.V., Ferropak Servicios S.A. de C.V., Galvacer America Inc., Galvamet America Corp, Galvatubing Inc., Hylsa Latin LLC 37 Subsidiaries included in the Index

Officers: Daniel Novegil/Dir., CEO, Roberto Philipps/CFO, Oscar Montero/Planning, Operations General Dir., Luis Andreozzi/Technical Dir., Miguel Angel Punte/Dir. - Human Resources, Ruben Bocanera/CIO, Raul Darderes/Sec., Sebastian Marti/Dir. - Investor Relations

Directors: Daniel Novegil/Dir., CEO, Paolo Rocca/Chmn., Rinaldo Campos Soares/Vice Chmn., Ubaldo Aguirre/Dir., Roberto Bonatti/Dir., Carlos Condorelli/Dir., Adrian Lajous Vargas/Dir., Bruno Marchettini/Dir., Gianfelice Rocca/Dir., Bertoldo Machado Veiga/Dir., Pedro Pablo Kuczynski/Dir.

Owners: San Faustn, ISL, I.I.I. CI/59.06%, Usiminas/14.25%, Alfredo Indaco, Insiders/0.03%, Daniel Novegil, Roberto Philipps, Tenaris/11.46%, Martn Berardi, Adrin Lajous

Financial Data: Fiscal Year End:12/31 **Latest Annual Data:** 12/31/2006

Year	Sales	Net Income
2006	$6,568,975,000	$841,018,000
2005	$4,447,680,000	$559,305,000
2004	$1,598,925,000	$424,655,000

Curr. Assets:	$2,646,213,000	Curr. Liab.:	$1,407,504,000	P/E Ratio:	16.29
Plant, Equip.:	$4,112,709,000	Total Liab.:	$4,148,280,000	Indic. Yr. Divd.:	$0.500
Total Assets:	$7,583,796,000	Net Worth:	$3,435,516,000	Debt/ Equity:	NA

Terra Energy & Resource Technologies Inc

Formerly: CompuPrint Inc

99 Pk. Ave., 16th Fl., New York, NY, 10016; **PH:** 1-212-286-9197; http:// www.terrainsight.com

General - Incorporation	NC	**Stock**- Price on:12/24/2007	$0.25
Employees	11	Stock Exchange	NA
Auditor	Rosen Seymour Sherb & Co. LLP	Ticker Symbol	NA
Stk Agt	Stock Transfer & Trust Co	Outstanding Shares	56,530,000
Counsel	Dan Brecher	E.P.S.	-$0.09
DUNS No.	NA	Shareholders	NA

Business: The group's principle activity is to seek for new business opportunities in the laser and inkjet printer cartridge industry. Prior to 2003, the company repaired and marketed laser printers and collected empty laser and ink jet cartridges for reuse. On 19-Aug-2003, the company sold all operations and net assets of its laser and inkjet printer cartridge operations. The group operates from United States.

Primary SIC and add'l.: 9999

CIK No: 0001084828

Subsidiaries: New Found Oil Partners, LP, Terra Insight Corporation, Terra Resources, Inc, Tierra Nevada Exploration Partners, LP

Officers: Roman Rozenberg/Dir., CEO - Terra Insight Corporation, Ivan Railyan/Chmn., Pres. - Terra Insight Corporation, Dan Brecher/Dir., MD, Treasurer - Terra Insight Corporation, Dmitry Vilbaum/COO - Terra Insight Corporation, Kenneth Oh/36/Sec., Eric M. Weiss/53/CFO

Directors: Roman Rozenberg/Dir., CEO - Terra Insight Corporation, Ivan Railyan/Chmn., Pres. - Terra Insight Corporation, Dan Brecher/Dir., MD, Treasurer - Terra Insight Corporation

Owners: Enficon Establishment/17.90%, Ivan Railyan/53.80%, Roman Rozenberg/7.40%, Dan Brecher/4.40%, Insiders/65.90%

Financial Data: Fiscal Year End:12/31 **Latest Annual Data:** 12/31/2006

Year	Sales	Net Income
2006	$2,800,000	-$10,914,000
2005	$732,000	-$2,306,000
2004	NA	-$50,000

Curr. Assets:	$1,103,000	Curr. Liab.:	$2,566,000		
Plant, Equip.:	$1,274,000	Total Liab.:	$2,566,000	Indic. Yr. Divd.:	NA
Total Assets:	$2,377,000	Net Worth:	-$189,000	Debt/ Equity:	NA

Terra Firma Technologies Inc

Formerly: Highriver Acquisition Corp
PO Box 42198, Philadelphia, PA, 19101; *PH:* 1-215-359-2163

General - Incorporation	DE	Stock- Price on:12/24/2007	NA
Employees	NA	Stock Exchange	NA
Auditor	Lake & Assoc. CPA's LLC	Ticker Symbol	NA
Stk Agt	NA	Outstanding Shares	NA
Counsel	NA	E.P.S.	NA
DUNS No.	NA	Shareholders	NA

Business: The group is in development stage. The group desires to seek the perceived advantages of a corporation which has a class of securities registered under the Exchange Act. The group operates from United States.

Primary SIC and add'l.: 6770

CIK No: 0001302647

Officers: Brian Kawamura/Dir., CEO, Pres., Thomas W. Schlosser/CFO

Directors: Brian Kawamura/Dir., CEO, Pres.

Owners: William Tay/100.00%, Insiders/100.00%

Terra Industries Inc

600 Fourth St., Sioux City, IA, 51102; *PH:* 1-712-277-1340; *http://* www.terraindustries.com

General - Incorporation	MD	Stock- Price on:12/24/2007	$22.4
Employees	1,238	Stock Exchange	NYSE
Auditor	Deloitte & Touche LLP	Ticker Symbol	TRA
Stk Agt	Computershare Trust Co	Outstanding Shares	92,850,000
Counsel	NA	E.P.S.	$1.38
DUNS No.	00-749-3851	Shareholders	NA

Business: The groups principle activities include producing and marketing nitrogen products for the agricultural and industrial markets. The groups products include anhydrous ammonia, ammonium nitrate and granular urea. The group operates through two business segments namely nitrogen business segment and methanol business segment. The group operates from United States.

Primary SIC and add'l.: 2869 5191 2873

CIK No: 0000722079

Subsidiaries: Beaumont Ammonia Inc., Beaumont Holdings Corporation, BMC Holdings, Inc., Houston Ammonia Terminal, L.P., Inspiration Coal Inc., Inspiration Consolidated Copper Company, Inspiration Development Company, Inspiration Gold Incorporated, Koch Terra LLC, Oklahoma Co2, Point Lisas Nitrogen, Ltd., Port Neal Corporation, Terra (Barbados) SRL, Terra (U.K.) Holdings Inc., Terra Capital Holdings, Inc. 34 Subsidiaries included in the Index

Officers: Michael L. Bennett/54/Dir., CEO, Pres./$1,742,453.00, John W. Huey/61/VP, General Counsel, Corp. Sec., Francis G. Meyer/Exec. VP/$826,630.00, Donna Bauder/Nitrogen Customer Service Rep, John Bergeron/Mgr. - Industrial Sales Accounting, Rod Eden/Mgr. - Accounting, Darlene Elkins-Olson/Nitrogen Customer Service Rep, Fred Freidel/Nitrogen Customer Service Rep, Luanne Giesler/Mgr. - Accounting, Matt Green/Dir. - Agricultural Sales, Dan Heffernan/Mgr. - Industrial Sales Accounting, Warren Holleman/Industrial Nitrogen Sales Mgr., Dottie Johnson/Nitrogen Customer Service Rep, Julie Laughlin/Nitrogen Customer Service Representative Team Leader, Carl McCormack/Mgr. - Accounting *(38 Officers included in Index)*

Directors: Michael L. Bennett/54/Dir., CEO, Pres., Henry R. Slack/Chmn., Martha O. Hesse/65/Dir., James R. Kroner/46/Dir., Dennis McGlone/58/Dir., Peter S. Janson/60/Dir., David E. Fisher/65/Dir., Dod A. Fraser/57/Dir.

Owners: M. O. Hesse, P. S. Janson, F. G. Meyer, The Goldman Sachs Group Inc., Dawson-Herman Capital Management, Inc., Whippoorwill Associates, Incorporated, D. E. Fisher, J. D. Giesler, Anchorage Capital Master Offshore, Ltd., H. R. Slack, D. McGlone, R. S. Sanders, Insiders, D. A. Fraser, Tontine Capital Partners L.P. *(19 Owners included in Index)*

*Financial Data: Fiscal Year End:*12/31   *Latest Annual Data:* 12/31/2006

Year	Sales	Net Income
2006	$1,836,722,000	$4,213,000
2005	$1,939,065,000	$22,087,000
2004	$1,509,110,000	$67,596,000

Curr. Assets:	$620,505,000	Curr. Liab.:	$309,447,000	P/E Ratio:	68.71
Plant, Equip.:	$720,897,000	Total Liab.:	$973,917,000	Indic. Yr. Divd.:	NA
Total Assets:	$1,572,713,000	Net Worth:	$482,996,000	Debt/ Equity:	NA

Terra Nitrogen Company LP

600 Fourth St., Sioux City, IA, 51102; *PH:* 1-712-277-1340; *Fax:* 1-712-277-7383; *http://* www.terranitrogen.com

General - Incorporation	DE	Stock- Price on:12/24/2007	$117.83
Employees	NA	Stock Exchange	NYSE
Auditor	Deloitte & Touche LLP	Ticker Symbol	TNH
Stk Agt	EquiServe Trust Co N.A	Outstanding Shares	18,680,000
Counsel	NA	E.P.S.	$8.24
DUNS No.	NA	Shareholders	NA

Business: The groups principle activities include producing and distributing nitrogen fertilizer products. The groups principle products are ammonia and urea. The group operates from the United States. The group's quarterly revenue for September 2007 was 133.15 millions of USD.

Primary SIC and add'l.: 2873

CIK No: 0000879575

Officers: Michael L. Bennett/54/Chmn., CEO, Pres., Francis G. Meyer/56/Exec. VP, Joseph D. Giesler/50/Sr. VP - Commercial Operations, Daniel D. Greenwell/46/Sr. VP, CFO, John W. Huey/61/VP, General Counsel, Corp. Sec., Richard Sanders/51/VP - Manufacturing, Douglas M. Stone/43/Sr. VP - Sales, Marketing, Joe A. Ewing/VP - Investor Relations, Human Resources, Kim Mathers/Mgr. - Communications, Will Watson/Legal, Corporate Communications Assist.

Directors: Michael L. Bennett/54/Chmn., CEO, Pres., Coleman L. Bailey/57/Dir. - Terra Nitrogen GP Inc, Michael A. Jackson/53/Dir. - Terra Nitrogen GP Inc, Dennis B. Longmire/63/Dir. - Terra Nitrogen GP Inc, Theodore D. Sands/62/Dir. - Terra Nitrogen GP Inc

Owners: Coleman L. Bailey, Joseph D. Giesler, Insiders, Daniel D. Greenwell, Richard S. Sanders, Michael L. Bennett, Francis G. Meyer

*Financial Data: Fiscal Year End:*12/31   *Latest Annual Data:* 12/31/2006

Year	Sales	Net Income
2006	$425,097,000	$46,192,000
2005	$455,522,000	$55,941,000
2004	$419,641,000	$45,871,000

Curr. Assets:	$128,463,000	Curr. Liab.:	$73,668,000	P/E Ratio:	17.99
Plant, Equip.:	$74,096,000	Total Liab.:	$74,142,000	Indic. Yr. Divd.:	$8.400
Total Assets:	$218,214,000	Net Worth:	$144,072,000	Debt/ Equity:	NA

Terra Nostra Resources Corp

Formerly: Terra Nostra Technology Ltd
790 E Colorado Blvd., 9th Fl., Pasadena, CA, 91101; *PH:* 1-626-796-0088; *http://* www.tnr-corp.com

General - Incorporation	NV	Stock- Price on:12/24/2007	$0.91
Employees	NA	Stock Exchange	OTC
Auditor	Rotenberg & Co., LLP	Ticker Symbol	TNRO
Stk Agt	Holladay Stock Transfer, Inc.	Outstanding Shares	49,210,000
Counsel	W. Scott Lawler Esq. Lawler & Asst	E.P.S.	-$0.02
DUNS No.	NA	Shareholders	NA

Business: The group's principal activities are developing, producing and marketing viral and fungal bio-insecticides for north American markets with applications for agricultural and forestry industries. It is also investigating the application of certain of its existing bio-insecticides for application directly to the consumer market in the form of home use pest control. The group is poised to provide effective, efficient and cost-competitive fungal bio-insecticides to global markets.

Primary SIC and add'l.: 1381

CIK No: 0001167370

Subsidiaries: Shandong Quanxin Stainless Steel Co., Shandong Terra-Nostra Jinpeng Metallurgical Co. Ltd.

Officers: James Sun Liu Po/Chmn., CEO, Manna Hung/PRC Chief Administrator, Dir. - Joint Venture Board, Assist. to The Joint Venture, Chmn. - Terra Nostra Resources Corp, Donald Nicholson/Strategic, Compliance Advisor to The Dir. - Terra Nostra Resources Corp, Shi Zhong Liu/GM - Shandong Jinpeng Metallurgical, Don C. Nicholson/Dir., Acting CFO, Pres., George Chua/Dir., COO - Terra Nostra Resource Corp, Robert Ng/VP - PRC Finance - Terra Nostra Resources Corp, Jeff Reynolds/CFO, Feng Yu Wang/CFO - Shandong Jinpeng Metallurgical, Sen Zhang/Vice GM - Shandong Jinpeng Metallurgical, Chang Chun Qu/Deputy GM - Shandong Jinpeng Metallurgical, Nai Biao Zhai/GM - Shandong Quanxin Stainless Steel, Xuen Wen Yuan/Deputy GM - Shandong Quanxin Stainless Steel, Hao Ming Li/Vice GM - Shandong Quanxin Stainless Steel

Directors: James Sun Liu Po/Chmn., CEO, Ke Zhang/Co - Chmn. - Shandong Quanxin Stainless - Shandong Jingpeng Metallurgical, Manna Hung/PRC Chief Administrator, Dir. - Joint Venture Board, Assist. to The Joint Venture, Chmn. - Terra Nostra Resources Corp, Crystal Poe/Dir., Don C. Nicholson/Dir., Acting CFO, Pres., George Chua/Dir., COO - Terra Nostra Resource Corp, Donald G. Burrell/Dir. - Terra Nostra Resources Corp, Felix Chung/Dir.

Owners: Felix Chung/6.08%, Kiat Hiung Lai/16.40%, Charnwood Green Ltd./11.40%, George Chua, Sun Liu James Po/40.32%, Donald C. Nicholson/1.64%, Insiders/39.27%, Crystal Poe, Donald Burrell

*Financial Data: Fiscal Year End:*12/31   *Latest Annual Data:* 5/31/2006

Year	Sales	Net Income
2006	$5,108,000	-$11,596,000
2004	$22,000	-$439,000
2003	$107,000	-$9,392,000

Curr. Assets:	$102,070,000	Curr. Liab.:	$131,466,000		
Plant, Equip.:	$58,604,000	Total Liab.:	$157,632,000	Indic. Yr. Divd.:	NA
Total Assets:	$169,921,000	Net Worth:	$12,289,000	Debt/ Equity:	NA

Terra Systems Inc

7001 S 900 E , Ste. 260, Salt Lake City, UT, 84047; *PH:* 1-801-208-1289; *Fax:* 1-801-208-5714; *http://* www.tsyi.com; *Email:* terrasystems@earthlink.net

General - Incorporation	UT	Stock- Price on:12/24/2007	$0.28
Employees	3	Stock Exchange	OTC
Auditor	Hansen, Barnett & Maxwell P.C.	Ticker Symbol	TSYI
Stk Agt	Atlas Stock Transfer Corp	Outstanding Shares	48,150,000
Counsel	NA	E.P.S.	$1.96
DUNS No.	NA	Shareholders	NA

Business: The groups principal activities include manufacturing, marketing and selling low pressure pneumatic conveyance system. In September 2005, the group acquired Mountain Island Energy, LLC. The group operates from the United States.

Primary SIC and add'l.: 3535

CIK No: 0001027876

Subsidiaries: Mountain Island Energy, LLC

Officers: Clayton D. Timothy/Dir., CEO, George W. Ford/Dir., Pres., Kent L. Harmon/VP - Technical Development, Dir., Mitchell J. Hart/VP, Dir., Tim Gwyther/Consultant, Jay R. Martin/Consultant

Directors: Clayton D. Timothy/Dir., CEO, George W. Ford/Dir., Pres., Kent L. Harmon/VP - Technical Development, Dir., Mitchell J. Hart/VP, Dir., Frederick W. Buckman/Dir., Reynold Roeder/Dir., J. R. Key/Dir.

Owners: Kent L. Harmon/7.70%, Reynold Roeder/10.56%, Clayton Timothy/10.53%, George W. Ford/2.04%, Robert Underwood/5.68%, Insiders/25.75%, Mitchell Hart, CHT Holding Trust/5.87%

*Financial Data: Fiscal Year End:*12/31   *Latest Annual Data:* 12/31/2006

Year	Sales	Net Income
2006	$46,000	-$1,412,000
2005	NA	-$6,487,000
2004	NA	-$612,000

Curr. Assets:	$57,000	Curr. Liab.:	$2,357,000		
Plant, Equip.:	$119,000	Total Liab.:	$2,357,000	Indic. Yr. Divd.:	NA
Total Assets:	$568,000	Net Worth:	-$1,789,000	Debt/ Equity:	NA

Terrace Ventures Inc

810 Peace Portal Dr, Ste. 202, Blaine, WA, 98230; *PH:* 1-360-220-5218

General - Incorporation	NV	**Stock** - Price on:12/24/2007	$0.19
Employees	1	Stock Exchange	OTC
Auditor	Sarna & Co	Ticker Symbol	TVEN
Stk Agt	NA	Outstanding Shares	34,180,000
Counsel	NA	E.P.S.	-$0.04
DUNS No.	NA	Shareholders	NA

Business: The group is an exploration stage company engaged in the acquisition and exploration of mineral properties. The group was incorporated in 2001 and is based in Blaine, Washington. It owns 100% undivided interest in Peach mineral claim property and Osoyoos Mining Divisions. Peach claim property consists of 1 mineral claim with approximately 1,236 acres located in Nicola, Simalkameen, and Osoyoos Mining Divisions located in British Columbia, Canada.

Primary SIC and add'l.: 1400

CIK No: 0000821899

Subsidiaries: Sporg Technology Corp.

Officers: Howard Thomson/62/Dir., CEO, CFO, Pres., Sec., Treasurer

Directors: Howard Thomson/62/Dir., CEO, CFO, Pres., Sec., Treasurer

Owners: Insiders/1.10%, Gordon F. Burley/43.00%, Howard Thomson/1.10%

Financial Data: *Fiscal Year End:*04/30 *Latest Annual Data:* 4/30/2006

Year	Sales	Net Income
2006	NA	-$988,000
2005	NA	-$38,000

Curr. Assets:	$1,000	**Curr. Liab.:**	$95,000		
Plant, Equip.:	NA	**Total Liab.:**	$95,000	**Indic. Yr. Divd.:**	NA
Total Assets:	$1,000	**Net Worth:**	-$94,000	**Debt/ Equity:**	NA

Terremark Worldwide Inc

2601 S Bayshore Dr., 9th Fl., Miami, FL, 33133; *PH:* 1-305-856-3200; *http://* www.terremark.com; *Email:* contact@terremark.com

General - Incorporation	DE	**Stock** - Price on:12/24/2007	NA
Employees	288	Stock Exchange	NDQ
Auditor	PricewaterhouseCoopers LLP , KPMG LLP	Ticker Symbol	TMRK
Stk Agt	American Stock Transfer & Trust Co.	Outstanding Shares	NA
Counsel	NA	E.P.S.	-$0.93
DUNS No.	88-429-0610	Shareholders	NA

Business: The group's principal activity is to provide Internet infrastructure and managed services. The group owns and operates network access point (nap) of the Americas, the fifth tier-1 network access point in the world. Network access points are locations where two or more networks meet to interconnect and exchange Internet traffic (traffic of data, voice, images, video and all forms of digital telecommunications). The nap of the Americas provides premium class space for carriers, Internet service providers, application service providers, content providers, Internet businesses and telecommunications providers.

Primary SIC and add'l.: 6531 4812 4813

CIK No: 0000912890

Subsidiaries: Dedigate, N.V., Global Arete, S.L., NAP de las Americas Madrid, S.A., NAP of the Americas, Inc., a Flori, NAP of the Americas, West Inc., Optical Communications, Inc., Park West Telecommunications Investors, Inc., Spectrum Telecommunications Corp., Technology Center of the Americas,LLC, TECOTA Services Corp., Terremark Asia, Terremark Asia Company, Ltd., Terremark do Brasil Ltda., Terremark Europe, Inc., Terremark Federal Group Inc. 34 Subsidiaries included in the Index

Officers: Manuel D. Medina/Chmn., CEO/$622,116.00, Jamie Dos Santos/CEO, Pres. - Terremark Federal Group/$474,260.00, Marvin Wheeler/COO/$323,618.00, Jose A. Segrera/CFO, Exec. VP/$324,546.00, John Neville/Sr. VP - Sales/$376,312.00, Herman Oggel/Pres. - European Business Unit, Adam Smith/Chief Legal Officer/$272,103.00, Jamie Dos Santos/Pres. - Terremark Federal Group, Agustin Abalo/Pres. - Latin American Business Unit, Barry Field/Sr. VP - US Commercial Sales, Xavier Gonzalez/Primary Investor Relations Officer

Directors: Manuel D. Medina/Chmn., CEO, Joseph R. Wright/Vice Chmn., Guillermo Amore/67/Dir., Antonio S. Fernandez/66/Dir., Arthur L. Money/66/Dir., Marvin S. Rosen/67/Dir., Miguel J. Rosenfeld/56/Dir., Rodolfo A. Ruiz/58/Dir., Timothy Elwes/71/Dir.

Owners: Timothy Elwes, Sun Equity Assets Limited, Marvin Wheeler, Jamie Dos Santos, Jose A. Segrera, Cyrte Investments GP I BV, Marvin S. Rosen, Miguel J. Rosenfeld, Insiders, Guzapa Properties, Inc., John S. Neville, Joseph R. Wright, Promociones Bursatiles, S.A., Antonio S. Fernandez, Palmetto, S.A. (22 Owners included in Index)

Financial Data: *Fiscal Year End:*03/31 *Latest Annual Data:* 3/31/2007

Year	Sales	Net Income
2007	$100,948,000	-$14,952,000
2006	$62,529,000	-$37,149,000
2005	$48,148,000	-$9,859,000

Curr. Assets:	$137,211,000	**Curr. Liab.:**	$35,638,000		
Plant, Equip.:	$137,937,000	**Total Liab.:**	$220,147,000	**Indic. Yr. Divd.:**	NA
Total Assets:	$309,646,000	**Net Worth:**	$89,499,000	**Debt/ Equity:**	NA

Tesco Corp

3993 W Sam Houston Pkwy. N, Ste. 100, Houston, TX, 77043; *PH:* 1-713-359-7000; *Fax:* 1-713-359-7001; *http://* www.tescocorp.com; *Email:* marketing@tescocorp.com

General - Incorporation	Canada	**Stock** - Price on:12/24/2007	$22.29
Employees	1,295	Stock Exchange	NDQ
Auditor	PricewaterhouseCoopers LLP	Ticker Symbol	NA
Stk Agt	Computershare Trust Co of Canada	Outstanding Shares	NA
Counsel	Bennett Jones	E.P.S.	$0.98
DUNS No.	24-983-0985	Shareholders	NA

Business: The group's principle activities are to design, manufacture and service technology-based solutions for the upstream energy industry. The group provides a range of products and services to reduce the cost of drilling and producing oil and gas. During 2001, the completions division was discontinued. The group has two operating divisions: services and products. Services division provides services, including the use of specialized equipment primarily to oil and gas operators. Products division provides the design, manufacture and sale, including after-sales support, of specialized equipment to the oil and gas and mining industry. The group's quarterly revenue for Septembeer 2007 was 113.89 millions of USD.

Primary SIC and add'l.: 1381 3533 3532 3593

CIK No: 0001022705

Subsidiaries: Casing Drilling International Ltd., PT Tesco Indonesia, Servicios Especializados Tesco SACV, Tesco Canada International Inc., Tesco Canada International Inc. (Middle East) FZE, Tesco Corporation (Norway) AS, Tesco Corporation (UK) Limited, Tesco Corporation (US), Tesco Oil Field Services de Mexico S.A. de C.V., Tesco Services Inc., Tesco Singapore Pte. Ltd., Tesco US Holding LP

Officers: Julio M. Quintana/Dir., Pres., CEO - Tesco Corporation/$1,243,050.00, Nigel M. Lakey/Sr. VP - Marketing, Business Development/$435,746.00, Keith Lowley/VP - Manufacturing, Anthony Tripodo/CFO, Exec. VP, Jeff Foster/Sr. VP - Operations, James A. Lank/General Counsel, Corp. Sec., Steven J. Smart/Assoc. General Counsel, Assist. Corp. Sec.

Directors: Julio M. Quintana/Dir., Pres., CEO - Tesco Corporation, Norman W. Robertson/Chmn., Raymond Vance Milligan/Dir., Peter K. Seldin/Dir., Michael W. Sutherlin/Dir., Fred J. Dyment/Dir., Robert M. Tessari/Dir., Gary L. Kott/Dir., Clifton T. Weatherford/Dir.

Owners: O.S.S. Capital Management LP/11.10%, Centennial Energy Partners, L.L.C./17.00%, Royce& Associates, LLC/12.30%, Hoplite Capital Management, LLC/5.40%

Financial Data: *Fiscal Year End:*12/31 *Latest Annual Data:* 12/31/2006

Year	Sales	Net Income
2006	$386,177,000	$30,545,000
2005	$209,878,000	$8,534,000
2004	$148,674,000	-$5,665,000

Tesoro Corp

300 Concord Plz., San Antonio, TX, 78216; *PH:* 1-210-283-2000; *http://* www.tsocorp.com; *Email:* info@amstock.com

General - Incorporation	DE	**Stock** - Price on:12/24/2007	$62.25
Employees	3,950	Stock Exchange	NYSE
Auditor	Deloitte & Touche LLP	Ticker Symbol	TSO
Stk Agt	American Stock Transfer & Trust Co.	Outstanding Shares	136,640,000
Counsel	NA	E.P.S.	$5.49
DUNS No.	00-813-3480	Shareholders	NA

Business: The groups principle activities include refining and marketing of crude oil. The group operates through two segments namely refining and retailing. The group operates from United States.

Primary SIC and add'l.: 2911 1311 4491

CIK No: 0000050104

Subsidiaries: Tesoro Alaska Company, Tesoro Hawaii Corporation, Tesoro Refining and Marketing Company

Officers: Bruce A. Smith/Chmn., CEO, Pres./$15,441,190.00, Eugene W. Burden/Sr. VP - External Affairs, Lynn Westfall/Sr. VP - External Affairs, Chief Economist, Susan A. Lerette/VP - Human Resources, Scott G. Spendlove/VP - Strategy, Long, Term Planning, Scott Phipps/Investor Relations Officer, William J. Finnerty/COO, Exec. VP/$3,730,522.00, Natalie Silva/Contact - Media Center, Phillip Anderson/VP, Treasurer, Arlen Glenewinkel/VP, Controller, Charles S. Parrish/Sr. VP, General Counsel, Sec., Everett Lewis/Exec. VP - Strategy, Asset Management/$2,874,421.00, William J. Haywood/Sr. VP - Refining/$2,074,336.00, Sarah S. Simpson/VP - Corporate Communications, Joseph M. Monroe/53/Sr. VP - Business Development, Logistics (19 Officers included in Index)

Directors: Bruce A. Smith/Chmn., CEO, Pres., Steven H. Grapstein/Dir., Patrick J. Ward/Dir., Donald H. Schmude/Dir., William J. Johnson/Dir., Maurice A. Myers/Dir., Michael E. Wiley/Dir., J. W. Nokes/Dir., John F. Bookout/Dir., Rodney Frank Chase/Dir., Robert W. Goldman/Dir.

Owners: Everett D. Lewis, Bruce A. Smith/4.31%, Donald H. Schmude, Michael E. Wiley, Insiders/6.56%, William J. Finnerty, Rodney F. Chase, John F. Bookout, Gregory A. Wright, Robert W. Goldman, William J. Johnson, William J. Haywood, Patrick J. Ward, Steven H. Grapstein, J.W. Nokes (16 Owners included in Index)

Financial Data: *Fiscal Year End:*12/31 *Latest Annual Data:* 12/31/2006

Year	Sales	Net Income
2006	$18,104,000,000	$801,000,000
2005	$16,581,000,000	$507,000,000
2004	$12,262,200,000	$327,900,000

Curr. Assets:	$2,811,000,000	**Curr. Liab.:**	$1,672,000,000	**P/E Ratio:**	9.91
Plant, Equip.:	$2,687,000,000	**Total Liab.:**	$3,402,000,000	**Indic. Yr. Divd.:**	$0.400
Total Assets:	$5,904,000,000	**Net Worth:**	$2,502,000,000	**Debt/ Equity:**	NA

Tessco Technologies Inc

11126 McCormick Rd., Hunt Valley, MD, 21031; *PH:* 1-410-229-1000; *Fax:* 1-410-527-0005; *http://* www.tessco.com; *Email:* cs@tessco.com

General - Incorporation	DE	**Stock** - Price on:12/24/2007	$19.15
Employees	749	Stock Exchange	NDQ
Auditor	Ernst & Young LLP	Ticker Symbol	TESS
Stk Agt	Mellon Investor Services LLC	Outstanding Shares	5,460,000
Counsel	Ballard Spahr Andrews & Ingersoll LLP	E.P.S.	$0.87
DUNS No.	02-263-4265	Shareholders	NA

Business: The group's principal activity is to provide an integrated product plus supply chain solutions to the professionals that design, build, run, maintain and use wireless voice, data, messaging, location tracking and Internet systems. The products and services of the group are broadly classified as network infrastructure, mobile devices and accessories and installation, test and maintenance products. The group currently serves approximately 9,400 commercial customers and 34,500 consumers per month, including a diversified mix of cellular, pcs and paging carriers, wireless isps, fixed broadband and mobile dispatch operators, infrastructure site owners, contractors and integrators, wireless dealers, value-added resellers, retailers, self-maintained users and consumers.

Primary SIC and add'l.: 5065

CIK No: 0000927355

Subsidiaries: GW Services Solutions,Inc., TESSCO Business Services LLC, TESSCO Communications Incorporated, TESSCO de Mexico S.A. de C.V., TESSCO Financial Corporation, TESSCO Incorporated, TESSCO Integrated Solutions, LP, TESSCO Product Solutions, LLC, TESSCO Service Solutions,Inc., TESSCO Supply Chain Services, LLC, Wireless Solutions Inc.

Officers: Robert B. Barnhill/Founder, Chmn., CEO, Pres./$1,837,788.00, Gerald Garland/Sr. VP/$682,648.00, Douglas A. Rein/Sr. VP/$560,977.00, David Young/Sr. VP, CFO, Corp. Sec./$517,267.00, Saeed Tofighi/Sr. VP/$517,007.00

Directors: Robert B. Barnhill/Founder, Chmn., CEO, Pres., Morton F. Zifferer/Dir., Daniel Okrent/Dir., Benn R. Konsynski/Dir., Jerome C. Eppler/Dir. Emeritus, John D. Beletic/Dir., Dennis J. Shaughnessy/Dir., Jay G. Baitler/Dir.

Owners: Gerald T. Garland, Dennis J. Shaughnessy, Benn R. Konsynski/1.10%, Morton F. Zifferer, Insiders/35.70%, David M. Young, Said Tofighi, Daniel Okrent, Douglas A. Rein, Jerome C. Eppler, Robert B. Barnhill/31.00%, Bjurman, Barry& Associates/7.60%, John D. Beletic, Susan D. Goodman, Discovery Group L.P./7.00%

Financial Data: Fiscal Year End:03/26 **Latest Annual Data:** 4/1/2007

Year	Sales	Net Income
2007	$492,328,000	$7,042,000
2006	$477,329,000	$5,115,000
2005	$513,027,000	$6,067,000

Curr. Assets:	$91,904,000	**Curr. Liab.:**	$58,377,000	**P/E Ratio:**	18.41
Plant, Equip.:	$24,256,000	**Total Liab.:**	$66,531,000	**Indic. Yr. Divd.:**	NA
Total Assets:	$123,683,000	**Net Worth:**	$57,151,000	**Debt/ Equity:**	0.0735

Tessera Technologies Inc

3099 Orchard Dr., San Jose, CA, 95134; **PH:** 1-408-894-0700; *http://* www.tessera.com;
Email: sales@tessera.com

General - Incorporation	DE	**Stock**- Price on:12/24/2007	$42.8
Employees	271	Stock Exchange	NDQ
Auditor	PricewaterhouseCoopers LLP	Ticker Symbol	TSRA
Stk Agt	Computershare Trust Co	Outstanding Shares	47,920,000
Counsel	NA	E.P.S.	$0.94
DUNS No.	78-638-3687	Shareholders	NA

Business: The group's principal activities are to develop semiconductor packaging technology that meets the demand for miniaturization and increased performance of electronic products. It licenses its technology to its customers, enabling them to produce semiconductors that are smaller, faster and incorporate more features. These semiconductors are utilized in a broad range of electronics products including digital cameras, mp3 players, personal computers, personal digital assistants, video game consoles and wireless phones. In addition, by using the group's technology, customers are also able to reduce the time to market and development costs of their semiconductors. Its major customer is Texas instruments. The group operates in United States, Taiwan, Korea, Japan, Europe and other countries.

Primary SIC and add'l.: 7372

CIK No: 0001261694

Subsidiaries: Tessera Cayman, Tessera Global, Limited, Tessera Interconnect Materials, Inc., Tessera International, Inc., Tessera Israel Limited, Tessera Technologies Hungary Holding Limited Liability Company, Tessera, Inc.

Officers: Bruce McWilliams/Chmn., CEO, Pres., David B. Tuckerman/CTO, Sr. VP, Liam Goudge/Sr. VP - Emerging Markets, Technologies, Charles A. Webster/CFO, Exec. VP, Michael Bereziuk/COO, Scot A. Griffin/Sr. VP, General Counsel, Steve Chen/Sr. VP - Business Development, Sales, Thomas H. Blanco/VP - Human Resources, Administration, Moriah Shilton/Investor Relations Contact

Directors: Bruce McWilliams/Chmn., CEO, Pres., John Goodrich/Dir., Al S. Joseph/Dir., Henry R. Nothhaft/Dir., Robert A. Young/Dir., Robert Boehlke/Dir., David C. Nagel/Dir.

Owners: Robert J. Boehlke, Insiders/3.96%, Bruce M. McWilliams/1.35%, Charles A. Webster, Scot A. Griffin, David C. Nagel, Fred Alger Management, Inc/5.30%, John B. Goodrich, Morgan Stanley/9.92%, Liam C. Goudge, Michael Bereziuk, Goldman Sachs Asset Management, L.P./12.79%, Henry R. Nothhaft, Robert A. Young/1.41%, Al S. Joseph (16 Owners included in Index)

Financial Data: Fiscal Year End:12/31 **Latest Annual Data:** 03/31/2007

Year	Sales	Net Income
2007	$46,819,000	$11,094,000
2006	$208,726,000	$61,351,000
2005	$94,700,000	$31,449,000

Curr. Assets:	$220,655,000	**Curr. Liab.:**	$15,433,000	**P/E Ratio:**	33.70
Plant, Equip.:	$24,705,000	**Total Liab.:**	$15,433,000	**Indic. Yr. Divd.:**	NA
Total Assets:	$321,288,000	**Net Worth:**	$305,855,000	**Debt/ Equity:**	NA

Teton Energy Corp

410 17th St., Ste. 1850, Denver, CO, 80202; **PH:** 1-303-565-4600; *http://* www.teton-energy.com

General - Incorporation	DE	**Stock**- Price on:12/24/2007	$5.86
Employees	11	Stock Exchange	AMEX
Auditor	Ehrhardt Keefe Steiner & Hottman P.C	Ticker Symbol	TEC
Stk Agt.	Computershare Investor Services LLC	Outstanding Shares	16,120,000
Counsel	NA	E.P.S.	-$0.77
DUNS No.	79-538-9071	Shareholders	NA

Business: The group's principal activities are oil and gas exploration and production. The group concentrates on operating existing wells, drilling new wells and constructing a pipeline to carry oil. The group's current focus is on the Russian Federation. The business of the group is conducted through its subsidiary, Goltech Petroleum LLC, which in turn operates solely through ownership of a majority interest in Goloil, a Russian joint stock company. Goloil performs all of the group's oil and gas exploration, development, production and marketing activities. The oil produced by the group is sold in Poland, Germany, Belorussia and Russia.

Primary SIC and add'l.: 1382 6719 1381

CIK No: 0001131072

Subsidiaries: Goltech Petroleum, LLC, Teton DJ LLC, Teton Piceance LLC

Officers: Karl F. Arleth/Dir., CEO, Pres./$1,683,224.00, Andrew M. Schultz/VP - Production/$474,706.00, Dominic Bazile/COO, William P. Brand/Controller, Chief Accounting Officer, Bill Brand/Interim CFO - Teton Energy Corporation

Directors: Karl F. Arleth/Dir., CEO, Pres., James J. Woodcock/Chmn., John T. Connor/Dir., Bill I. Pennington/Dir., Tom Conroy/Dir., Robert F. Bailey/Dir.

Owners: John T. Connor/2.43%, Karl F. Arleth/5.72%, William K. White, Insiders/13.07%, Thomas F. Conroy/1.05%, Wellington Management Company, LLP/11.15%, James J. Woodcock/4.20%, Robert Bailey, Richard Bosher

Financial Data: Fiscal Year End:12/31 **Latest Annual Data:** 12/31/2006

Year	Sales		Net Income
2006	$3,529,000		-$5,724,000
2005	$707,000		-$4,032,000
2004	NA		$7,190,000

Curr. Assets:	$6,280,000	**Curr. Liab.:**	$7,399,000		
Plant, Equip.:	$34,772,000	**Total Liab.:**	$7,477,000	**Indic. Yr. Divd.:**	NA
Total Assets:	$41,244,000	**Net Worth:**	$33,767,000	**Debt/ Equity:**	NA

Tetra Tech Inc

3475 E Foothill Blvd, Pasadena, CA, 91107; **PH:** 1-626-351-4664; *http://* www.tetratech.com

General - Incorporation	DE	**Stock**- Price on:12/24/2007	$22.95
Employees	6,800	Stock Exchange	NDQ
Auditor	PricewaterhouseCoopers LLP	Ticker Symbol	TTEK
Stk Agt	U.S. Stock Transfer Corp	Outstanding Shares	58,100,000
Counsel	Riordan & McKinzie	E.P.S.	$0.76
DUNS No.	04-522-4250	Shareholders	NA

Business: The group's principal activity is to provide specialized management consulting and technical services. The group operates through two segments: resource management and infrastructure. Resource management segment provides specialized environmental engineering and consulting services relating to water quality and availability. Infrastructure segment provides engineering services for development, upgrading and replacement of existing infrastructure. The group provides its services to a diverse base of federal, state and local government agencies, and commercial and international clients. The group acquired certain assets and certain related liabilities of foster wheeler environmental corporation and hartman consulting corporation in Mar 2003 and engineering management concepts inc in Jul 2003. On 08-Mar-2004, the group acquired advanced management technology inc.

Primary SIC and add'l.: 8748 8711 8712 4813 8742

CIK No: 0000831641

Subsidiaries: Advanced Management Technology, Inc., Americas Schoolhouse Consulting Services, Inc., Americas Schoolhouse Council, LLC, Ardaman & Associates, Inc., Chen Northern, Inc., Cosentini Associates, Inc., Engineering Management Concepts, Inc., Evergreen Utility Contractors, Inc., FHC, Inc., Foster Wheeler Environmental Corporation (Mass.), Foster Wheeler Environmental Corporation (Ohio), GeoTrans, Inc., Hartman & Associates, Inc., Kansas City Testing Laboratory, Inc., KCM International, Inc. 49 Subsidiaries included in the Index

Officers: Dan L. Batrack/Dir., CEO, COO, Jorge Casado/Investor Relations Officer, Janis B. Salin/VP, General Counsel, Sec., Michael A. Bieber/VP - Corporate Development, Richard A. Lemmon/Sr. VP - Corporate Administration, Steven M. Burdick/VP, Corporate Controller, David W. King/CFO, Exec. VP, Treasurer, Talia Starkey/Contact - Media, Public Relations, Cathy Leslie/Dir., Civil Engineer, Carl V. Anderson/Conservation Engineer, Craig L. Christensen/CIO, VP, Sam W. Box/Pres., Mark A. Walsh/Sr. VP - Marketing Development, William R. Brownlie/Sr. VP - Environmental Engineering, Consulting, Donald I. Rogers/Sr. VP - Remediation, Construction (19 Officers included in Index)

Directors: Dan L. Batrack/Dir., CEO, COO, Li-San Hwang/Chmn. Emeritus, Albert E. Smith/Chmn., Patrick C. Haden/Dir., Hugh M. Grant/Dir., Christopher J. Lewis/Dir., Cathy Leslie/Dir., Civil Engineer, Richard H. Truly/Dir., Kenneth J. Thompson/Dir.

Owners: T. Rowe Price Associates,Inc./5.00%, Dan L. Batrack, Donald I. Rogers, Richard H. Truly, David W. King, Christopher J. Lewis, Capital Research and Management Company/5.50%, Hugh M. Grant, Insiders/1.90%, Tontine Partners, L.P./6.30%, Patrick C. Haden, Sam W. Box, Albert E. Smith, SMALLCAP World Fund,Inc./5.20%, Douglas G. Smith

Financial Data: Fiscal Year End:10/02 **Latest Annual Data:** 10/1/2006

Year	Sales	Net Income
2006	$1,414,704,000	$36,604,000
2005	$1,286,031,000	-$99,469,000
2004	$1,437,556,000	$23,742,000

Curr. Assets:	$452,667,000	**Curr. Liab.:**	$307,838,000	**P/E Ratio:**	30.20
Plant, Equip.:	$41,281,000	**Total Liab.:**	$411,007,000	**Indic. Yr. Divd.:**	NA
Total Assets:	$808,507,000	**Net Worth:**	$397,500,000	**Debt/ Equity:**	0.0884

Tetra Technologies Inc

25025 Interstate 45 N, Ste. 600, The Woodlands, TX, 77380; **PH:** 1-281-367-1983;
http:// www.tetratec.com; **Email:** employment@tetratec.com

General - Incorporation	DE	**Stock**- Price on:12/24/2007	$27.13
Employees	2,536	Stock Exchange	NYSE
Auditor	Ernst & Young LLP	Ticker Symbol	TTI
Stk Agt	Computershare Trust Co	Outstanding Shares	72,610,000
Counsel	NA	E.P.S.	$1.28
DUNS No.	02-444-3327	Shareholders	NA

Business: The group's principal activities are to provide oil and gas service with an integrated calcium chloride and brominated products manufacturing operation that supplies feedstocks to energy markets, as well as other markets. It operates in three divisions: fluids, well abandonment and decommissioning and testing and services. The fluids division manufactures and markets clear brine fluids to the oil and gas industry for use in well drilling, completion and workover operations. The well abandonment & decommissioning division provides services required for the abandonment of depleted oil and gas wells and decommissioning of platforms, pipelines and other associated equipment. The testing and services division provides production testing services to the Texas, Louisiana, Alabama, Mississippi, offshore gulf of Mexico and certain latin American markets. In 2003, the group disposed its subsidiary damp rid inc.

Primary SIC and add'l.: 1389 5169 2819

CIK No: 0000844965

Subsidiaries: Ahmad Albinali & TETRA Arabia Company Ltd. (LLC), Compressco Canada, Inc., Compressco Field Services, Inc., Compressco Testing, LLC, Compressco, Inc., Kemax BV, Maritech Holdings, Inc., Maritech Louisiana, LLC, Maritech Partner, LLC, Maritech Resources, Inc., Maritech Timbalier Bay, LP, Providence Natural Gas, Inc., SeaJay Industries, Inc., T-International Holdings, C.V., T-Production Testing LLC 43 Subsidiaries included in the Index

Officers: Geoffrey M. Hertel/Dir., CEO, Pres./$980,343.00, Bass C. Wallace/General Counsel, Sec., Linden H. Price/VP - Administration, Dennis R. Mathews/Sr. VP, Stuart M. Brightman/COO, Exec. VP/$814,867.00, Joseph M. Abell/Sr. VP, CFO/$427,628.00, Gary C. Hanna/Sr. VP/$529,594.00, Ben C. Chambers/VP - Accounting, Controller, Raymond D. Symens/Sr. VP/$520,812.00, Bruce A. Cobb/VP - Finance, Treasurer, Eileen Price/Mgr. - Investor Relations

Directors: Geoffrey M. Hertel/Dir., CEO, Pres., Ralph S. Cunningham/Chmn., Kenneth E. White/Dir., Hoyt Ammidon/Dir., Paul D. Coombs/Dir., Tom H. Delimitros/Dir., Allen T. McInnes/Dir., Kenneth P. Mitchell/Dir., William D. Sullivan/Dir.

Owners: Joseph M. Abell, Ralph S. Cunningham, Insiders/6.30%, Hoyt Ammidon, Gary C. Hanna, Stuart M. Brightman, Geoffrey M. Hertel/1.30%, Mellon Financial Corporation/5.50%, Allen T. McInnes, Paul D. Coombs/1.50%, T. Rowe Price Associates, Inc./11.20%, Raymond D. Symens, Tom H. Delimitros, Kenneth E. White, Kenneth P. Mitchell

Financial Data: *Fiscal Year End:*12/31 *Latest Annual Data:* 12/31/2006

Year	Sales	Net Income
2006	$784,868,000	$101,878,000
2005	$531,019,000	$38,062,000
2004	$353,186,000	$17,699,000

Curr. Assets:	$408,097,000	**Curr. Liab.:**	$161,758,000	**P/E Ratio:**	21.20
Plant, Equip.:	$508,149,000	**Total Liab.:**	$665,810,000	**Indic. Yr. Divd.:**	NA
Total Assets:	$1,086,190,000	**Net Worth:**	$420,380,000	**Debt/ Equity:**	0.7157

TetriDyn Solutions Inc

1651 Alvin Ricken Dr., Pocatello, ID, 83201; *PH:* 1-208-232-4200; *Fax:* 1-208-232-4236; *http://* tetridyn.com; *Email:* tetridyn@tetridyn.com

General - Incorporation	FL	**Stock**- Price on:12/24/2007	$0.09
Employees	9	Stock Exchange	OTC
Auditor	Webb & Company, P. A.	Ticker Symbol	TDYS
Stk Agt	Interwest Transfer Company, Inc.	Outstanding Shares	20,880,000
Counsel	NA	E.P.S.	-$0.01
DUNS No.	NA	Shareholders	NA

Business: The groups principle activities include providing technology and data integration solutions that increase professional or worker productivity through the use of customized data input screens, wireless technologies. The group operates from the United States.

Primary SIC and add'l.: 7372

CIK No: 0000827099

Subsidiaries: TetriDyn Solutions, Inc.

Officers: Brian S. John/Investor Relations Officer, Antoinette R. Knapp/43/Dir., Sec., Treasurer, CTO, John N. Iasonides/32/COO, Chief Marketing Officer

Directors: Antoinette R. Knapp/43/Dir., Sec., Treasurer, CTO, Orville J. Hendrickson/83/Dir., Larry J. Ybarrondo/70/Dir.

Owners: Sawtooth Meadows, Larry J. Ybarrondo, Antoinette R. Knapp, Orville J. Hendrickson, David W. Hempstead, Insiders

Financial Data: *Fiscal Year End:*12/31 *Latest Annual Data:* 12/31/2006

Year	Sales	Net Income
2006	$772,000	-$721,000

Curr. Assets:	$82,000	**Curr. Liab.:**	$512,000		
Plant, Equip.:	$14,000	**Total Liab.:**	$924,000	**Indic. Yr. Divd.:**	NA
Total Assets:	$96,000	**Net Worth:**	-$828,000	**Debt/ Equity:**	NA

Teva Pharmaceutical Industries Ltd

1090 Horsham Rd., North Wales, PA, 19454; *PH:* 1-215-591-3000; *Fax:* 1-215-591-8600; *http://* www.tevapharm.com

General - Incorporation	Israel	**Stock**- Price on:12/24/2007	$39.6
Employees	26,700	Stock Exchange	NDQ
Auditor	Kesselman & Kesselman	Ticker Symbol	TEVA
Stk Agt	Mellon Investor Services LLC	Outstanding Shares	764,000,000
Counsel	Willkie Farr & Gallagher LLP	E.P.S.	$2.28
DUNS No.	60-002-9649	Shareholders	NA

Business: The group's principal activities are the development, production, marketing and distribution of two types of products: pharmaceuticals - development, manufacturing and selling of medicines in various dosages and forms, disposable of hospital products and equipment for hospital use and veterinary products, and active pharmaceutical ingredients (api) - development, manufacturing and selling of api for the pharmaceutical industry, including the group's pharmaceutical segment.

Primary SIC and add'l.: 2899 2869 2834 2833

CIK No: 0000818686

Subsidiaries: Abic Biological Laboratories Teva Ltd., Abic Ltd., Assia Chemical Industries Ltd., Dorom S.r.l., Genchem Pharma Ltd., Humantrade Kft, Humantrade Pharmaceutical Wholesale Company Limited by Shares, Lemery S.A. de C.V., Medica A.G., Novopharm Limited, Orphahell BV, Pharmachemie Group, Plantex Ltd., Plantex USA, Inc., Prosintex Industrie Chimiche Italiane S.r.l. 38 Subsidiaries included in the Index

Officers: George S. Barrett/CEO, Teva North America Corporate Exec. VP - Global Pharmaceutical Markets, William S. Marth/CEO, Pres. - Teva Pharmaceuticals USA, Inc, Shlomo Yanai/CEO, Pres., Isaac Abravanel/Corporate VP - Human Resources, Itzhak Krinsky/Corporate VP - Business Development, Gerard Van Odijk/Group VP - Europe, Shosh Neumann/VP - Product Portfolio Management, Judith Vardi/VP - Israel Pharmaceutical Sales, Aharon Schwartz/VP - Strategic Business Planning, New Ventures, Yehuda Arad/VP - Safety, Environment, Shmuel Ben-Zvi/VP - Planning, Economics, Information Technology, Rodney Kasan/CTO, VP, Amir Elstein/Exec. VP - Global Resources, David Reisman/VP - Israel Pharmaceutical Operations, Bruria Sofrin/53/Corporate VP - Human Resources *(30 Officers included in Index)*

Directors: Eli Hurvitz/Chmn., Phillip Frost/Vice Chmn., Abraham E. Cohen/Dir., Ruth Cheshin/Dir., Gabriela Shalev/Dir., David Shamir/Dir., Harold Snyder/Dir., Roger Abravanel/Dir., Dan Propper/67/Dir., Roger D. Kornberg/61/Dir., Meir Heth/Dir., Moshe Many/Dir., Michael Sela/Dir., Leora Meridor/Dir., Max Reis/Dir. *(16 Directors included in Index)*

Financial Data: *Fiscal Year End:*12/31 *Latest Annual Data:* 12/31/2006

Year	Sales	Net Income
2006	$8,408,000,000	$546,000,000
2005	$5,250,400,000	$1,072,300,000
2004	$4,798,900,000	$331,800,000

Curr. Assets:	$7,640,000,000	**Curr. Liab.:**	$4,071,000,000		
Plant, Equip.:	$2,193,000,000	**Total Liab.:**	$9,329,000,000	**Indic. Yr. Divd.:**	$0.340
Total Assets:	$20,471,000,000	**Net Worth:**	$11,142,000,000	**Debt/ Equity:**	NA

Texada Ventures Inc

977 Keith Rd., West Vancouver, BC, V7T 1M6; *PH:* 1-604-816-2555

General - Incorporation	NV	**Stock**- Price on:12/24/2007	$0.96
Employees	NA	Stock Exchange	OTC
Auditor	Telford Sadovnick, PLLC	Ticker Symbol	TXDV
Stk Agt	Pacific Stock Transfer Company	Outstanding Shares	NA
Counsel	NA	E.P.S.	NA
DUNS No.	NA	Shareholders	NA

Business: The groups principal activities include evaluating the progress of mining business. The group intends to continue to develop current mining business and seeking other business opportunities. The group operates from the United States.

Primary SIC and add'l.: 1000

CIK No: 0001174907

Officers: John Veltheer/41/Dir., CEO, CFO, Pres., Treasurer, Sec.

Directors: John Veltheer/41/Dir., CEO, CFO, Pres., Treasurer, Sec.

Owners: John Veltheer/49.00%, Insiders/49.00%

Financial Data: *Fiscal Year End:*11/30 *Latest Annual Data:* 11/30/2006

Year	Sales	Net Income
2006	NA	-$86,000

Curr. Assets:	$139,000	**Curr. Liab.:**	$208,000		
Plant, Equip.:	NA	**Total Liab.:**	$208,000	**Indic. Yr. Divd.:**	NA
Total Assets:	$139,000	**Net Worth:**	-$69,000	**Debt/ Equity:**	NA

Texas Capital Bancshares Inc

2100 McKinney Ave., Ste. 900, Dallas, TX, 75201; *PH:* 1-214-932-6600; *http://* www.texascapitalbank.com

General - Incorporation	DE	**Stock**- Price on:12/24/2007	$21.78
Employees	503	Stock Exchange	NDQ
Auditor	Ernst & Young LLP	Ticker Symbol	TCBI
Stk Agt	Computershare Investor Services LLC	Outstanding Shares	26,120,000
Counsel	NA	E.P.S.	$1.21
DUNS No.	NA	Shareholders	NA

Business: The group's principal activity is provide commercial banking services. The loans offered by the group include commercial loans, permanent real estate loans, construction loans, equipment leasing, consumer loans, both secured and unsecured, mortgages and home equity loans. The other services include cash management services, trust and escrow services, letters of credit and business insurance products. The deposit offered by the group include certificates of deposit, interest bearing and non-interest bearing checking accounts with optional features such as visa(R) debit/ ATM cards and overdraft protection, traditional savings accounts, branded visa(R) credit card accounts, including gold-status accounts.

Primary SIC and add'l.: 6022 6712

CIK No: 0001077428

Subsidiaries: Texas Capital Bank, National Association

Officers: Joseph M. Grant/Chmn., CEO/$712,379.00, George F. Jones/Dir., CEO, Pres. - Texas Capital Bank/$620,294.00, Vince Ackerson/Exec. VP, Chief Lending Officer - Dallas Region, Peter Bartholow/Dir., CFO/$590,116.00, John Hudgens/Chief Credit Officer, Jim White/COO, Exec. VP, David Cargill/Exec. VP, Keith Cargill/Pres. - Dallas Region, Chief Lending Officer/$470,948.00, Russell Hartsfield/Exec. VP, Patty Sullivan/Sr. VP - Marketing, Media Relations, Myrna Vance/Dir. - Investor Relations

Directors: Joseph M. Grant/Chmn., CEO, George F. Jones/Dir., CEO, Pres. - Texas Capital Bank, Steven P. Rosenberg/Dir., Larry L. Helm/Dir., James R. Holland/Dir., Leo Corrigan/Dir., John Snyder/Dir., Lee Roy Mitchell/Dir., Ian J. Turpin/Dir., Robert W. Stallings/Dir., Fred B. Hegi/Dir., Peter Bartholow/Dir., CFO, Walter W. McAllister/Dir.

Owners: John C. Snyder/1.20%, Steven P. Rosenberg, Lee Roy Mitchell, Peter B. Bartholow, James R. Holland/1.11%, Transamerica Investment Management, LLC/10.38%, Insiders/10.26%, W. W. McAllister, Ian J. Turpin, Frederick B. Hegi, Robert W. Stallings, C. Keith Cargill, Larry L. Helm, George F. Jones, T. Rowe Price Associates, Inc./8.42% *(17 Owners included in Index)*

Financial Data: *Fiscal Year End:*12/31 *Latest Annual Data:* 12/31/2006

Year	Sales	Net Income
2006	$258,366,000	$28,924,000
2005	$188,344,000	$27,192,000
2004	$124,510,000	$19,560,000

Curr. Assets:	$179,537,000	**Curr. Liab.:**	$3,284,425,000	**P/E Ratio:**	18.15
Plant, Equip.:	$33,818,000	**Total Liab.:**	$3,421,834,000	**Indic. Yr. Divd.:**	NA
Total Assets:	$3,675,349,000	**Net Worth:**	$253,515,000	**Debt/ Equity:**	0.4301

Texas Industries Inc

1341 W Mockingbird Ln., Ste 700w, Dallas, TX, 75247; *PH:* 1-972-647-6700; *http://* www.txi.com; *Email:* tlacaze@txi.com

General - Incorporation	DE	**Stock**- Price on:12/24/2007	$82.69
Employees	2,600	Stock Exchange	NYSE
Auditor	Ernst & Young LLP	Ticker Symbol	TXI
Stk Agt	Mellon Investor Services LLC	Outstanding Shares	27,310,000
Counsel	NA	E.P.S.	$3.32
DUNS No.	04-108-3403	Shareholders	NA

Business: The group's principal activity is to produce and supply construction materials. The group operates through two segments: cement, aggregate and concrete products (cac segment) and structural steel and specialty bar products (steel segment). The cac segment produces and sells cement, stone, gravel, expanded shale, clay aggregate and concrete products. The products of the cac segment are marketed in the United States. The steel segment produces and sells structural steel, piling products, specialty bar products, merchant bar-quality rounds, reinforcing bar and channels. The group's steel products are marketed throughout the United States and to a limited extent in Canada and Mexico.

Primary SIC and add'l.: 3449 3241 3272 3312 3271

CIK No: 0000097472

Subsidiaries: Ambulatory Resource Centres Investment Company, Inc., Ambulatory Resource Centres of Florida, Inc., Ambulatory Resource Centres of Massachusetts, Inc., Ambulatory Resource Centres of Texas, Inc., Ambulatory Resource Centres of Washington, Inc., Ambulatory Resource Centres of Wilmington, Inc., Ambulatory Surgery Center of Cool Springs, LLC, Ambulatory Surgery Center of Worcester, LLC, ARC Development Corporation, ARC Dry Creek, Inc., ARC Financial Services Corporation, ARC Kentucky, LLC, ARC New Hartford, Inc., ARC of Bellingham, L.P., ARC of Georgia, LLC 22 Subsidiaries included in the Index

Officers: Mel G. Brekhus/Dir., CEO, Pres./$7,858,330.00, William J. Durbin/VP - Human Resources/$1,127,259.00, Philip L. Gaynor/VP - Cement Manufacturing, Randall D. Jones/VP - Communications, Government Affairs, Barry M. Bone/VP - Real Estate, Wesley E. Schlenker/Assist. Sec., Leo E. Faciane/VP - Environmental Affairs, Daniel J. McAuliffe/VP - Real Estate Marketing, Kenneth R. Allen/VP, Treasurer, Carl Gentile/VP - Information Services, Tim Bourcier/VP - Operations, Steel, Micheal J. Link/VP, Controller - Cement, Aggregate, Concrete, Fred Anderson/VP, General Counsel, Sec., Tommy A. Valenta/Exec. VP - Steel, Lynn J. Davis/VP - Cement/$872,970.00 *(29 Officers included in Index)*

Directors: Mel G. Brekhus/Dir., CEO, Pres., Robert D. Rogers/Chmn., Ronald G. Steinhart/Dir., Eugenio Clariond Reyes/Dir., Ian Wachtmeister/Dir., Thomas R. Ransdell/Dir., Gordon E. Forward/Dir., Keith W. Hughes/Dir., Henry H. Mauz/Dir., Robert Alpert/Dir., Sam Coats/Dir.

Owners: Richard M. Fowler, Frederick G. Anderson, William J. Durbin, Henry H. Mauz, Keith W. Hughes, NNS Holding/14.90%, Gordon E. Forward, Ronald G. Steinhart, Robert Alpert, Robert D. Rogers/1.10%, Sam Coats, Thomas R. Ransdell, Southeastern Asset Management, Inc./12.00%, Insiders/4.10%, Mel G. Brekhus *(17 Owners included in Index)*

Financial Data: Fiscal Year End:05/31 Latest Annual Data: 5/31/2006

Year	Sales	Net Income
2006	$943,922,000	$8,102,000
2005	$1,951,179,000	$124,523,000
2004	$1,672,503,000	$36,348,000

Curr. Assets:	$403,245,000	Curr. Liab.:	$119,321,000	P/E Ratio:	21.76
Plant, Equip.:	$596,224,000	Total Liab.:	$607,506,000	Indic. Yr. Divd.:	$0.300
Total Assets:	$1,080,570,000	Net Worth:	$473,064,000	Debt/ Equity:	0.5631

Texas Instruments Inc

12500 TI Blvd., Dallas, TX, 75266; **PH:** 1-972-995-2011; **Fax:** 1-972-927-6377; **http://** www.ti.com

General - Incorporation	DE	Stock- Price on:12/24/2007	$36.75
Employees	30,986	Stock Exchange	NYSE
Auditor	Ernst & Young LLP	Ticker Symbol	TXN
Stk Agt	Computershare Investor Services LLC	Outstanding Shares	1,430,000,000
Counsel	NA	E.P.S	$1.67
DUNS No.	00-732-1904	Shareholders	NA

Business: The groups principle activity is to provide a complete portfolio of data converter solutions for precision and high-speed applications. The groups products include amplifiers and liners, data converters and micro controllers. The group operates through two segments namely Semiconductor and education technology. In the year 2007, the group acquired POWERPRECISE Solutions, Inc. The group operates from United States.

Primary SIC and add'l.: 3678 3679 3674 3578 3571

CIK No: 0000097476

Subsidiaries: Auto Circuits, Inc., Benchmarq Microelectronics Corporation of South Korea, Burr-Brown Europe Limited, Burr-Brown International Holding Corporation, Butterfly Communications Inc., Condat Edinburgh Ltd., European Engineering and Technologies S.p.A., Intelligent Instrumentation GmbH, Intelligent Instrumentation S.A.S., Intelligent Instrumentation S.R.L., Intelligent Instrumentation, Inc., Telogy Networks, Inc., Texas Instrumentos Eletronicos do Brasil Limitada, Texas Instruments (Bahamas) Limited, Texas Instruments (Changzhou) Co., Ltd. 63 Subsidiaries included in the Index

Officers: Richard K. Templeton/49/Dir., CEO, Pres./$11,724,070.00, Kevin P. March/CFO, Sr. VP/$3,015,073.00, John Van Scoter/Sr. VP, GM - Dlp Products, Eric Zimits/MD - Granite Ventures, Standish H. O'Grady/Sr. MD - Granite Ventures, Greg Delagi/Sr. VP, GM - Wireless Terminals Business Unit, David Heacock/Sr. VP - High, Volume Analog, Logic, Mark Denissen/VP - Strategic Marketing, Martin Izzard/Dir. - Dsps Research & Development Center, Arthur L. George/Sr. VP - High, Performance Analog, Darla Whitaker/Sr. VP, Dir. - Worldwide Human Resources, Len Rand/MD - Granite Ventures, Brian Panoff/Principal, Granite Ventures, Terri West/Sr. VP, Mgr. - Communications, Investor Relations, Chung-Shing Lee/53/Sr. VP *(25 Officers included in Index)*

Directors: Richard K. Templeton/49/Dir., CEO, Pres., Thomas J. Engibous/55/Chmn., James R. Adams/69/Dir., Gerald W. Fronterhouse/Dir., David L. Boren/67/Dir., Daniel A. Carp/60/Dir., Carrie S. Cox/51/Dir., David R. Goode/67/Dir., Pamela H. Patsley/51/Dir., Christine Todd Whitman/62/Dir., Wayne R. Sanders/61/Dir., Ruth J. Simmons/63/Dir.

Owners: Insiders/1.37%, T. J. Engibous, Barclays entities/5.50%, Capital Research and Management Company/7.60%, K. P. March, R. K. Templeton, G. A. Lowe, G. Delfassy

Financial Data: Fiscal Year End:12/31 Latest Annual Data: 12/31/2006

Year	Sales	Net Income
2006	$14,255,000,000	$4,341,000,000
2005	$13,392,000,000	$2,324,000,000
2004	$12,580,000,000	$1,861,000,000

Curr. Assets:	$7,854,000,000	Curr. Liab.:	$2,078,000,000	P/E Ratio:	22.01
Plant, Equip.:	$3,950,000,000	Total Liab.:	$2,570,000,000	Indic. Yr. Divd.:	$0.320
Total Assets:	$13,930,000,000	Net Worth:	$11,360,000,000	Debt/ Equity:	NA

Texas New Mexico Power Co

4100 International Plz., Fort Worth, TX, 76113; **PH:** 1-817-731-0099; **http://** www.tnpe.com

General - Incorporation	TX	Stock- Price on:12/24/2007	$28.21
Employees	3,294	Stock Exchange	NA
Auditor	Deloitte & Touche LLP	Ticker Symbol	NA
Stk Agt	Mellon Investor Services LLC	Outstanding Shares	76,690,000
Counsel	NA	E.P.S	$1.73
DUNS No.	00-792-9441	Shareholders	NA

Business: The group's principal activities are the generation, purchasing, transmission, distribution and sale of electricity to customers located in 85 municipalities in Texas and New Mexico. The group is a wholly owned subsidiary of tnp enterprises, inc. The operations of the group are conducted in the gulf coast region, the north-central region and the mountain region. As at 31-Dec-2003, the group had 252,255 customers. The group serves residential, commercial and industrial customers.

Primary SIC and add'l.: 4911

CIK No: 0000022767

Subsidiaries: FCP Enterprises Inc, First Choice Power Special Purpose, LP, First Choice Power, LP, Public Service Company of New Mexico, Texas-New Mexico Power Company, TNP Enterprises, Inc

Officers: T. G. Sategna/CEO, Principal Financial Officer, Principal Accounting Officer, W. D. Hobbs/Dir., Principal Executive Officer

Directors: J. E. Sterba/Chmn., W. D. Hobbs/Dir., Principal Executive Officer

Financial Data: Fiscal Year End:12/31 Latest Annual Data: 12/31/2005

Year	Sales	Net Income
2005	$2,076,810,000	$67,227,000
2004	$1,604,792,000	$87,686,000
2003	$1,455,714,000	$95,173,000

Curr. Assets:	$596,297,000	Curr. Liab.:	$723,496,000	P/E Ratio:	16.31
Plant, Equip.:	$2,988,306,000	Total Liab.:	$3,826,721,000	Indic. Yr. Divd.:	$0.920
Total Assets:	$5,124,709,000	Net Worth:	$1,297,988,000	Debt/ Equity:	1.3342

Texas Pacific Land Trust

1700 Pacific Ave, Dallas, TX, 75201; **PH:** 1-214-969-5530

General - Incorporation		Stock- Price on:12/24/2007	$274.5
Employees	8	Stock Exchange	NYSE
Auditor	Lane Gorman Trubitt, LLP	Ticker Symbol	TPL
Stk Agt	Bank of New York	Outstanding Shares	2,120,000
Counsel	NA	E.P.S	$0.96
DUNS No.	NA	Shareholders	NA

Business: The groups principle activity is to invest in oil and gas properties. The group operates from the United States.

Primary SIC and add'l.: 6798

CIK No: 0000097517

Owners: Roy Thomas, John R. Norris, James K. Norwood, Maurice Meyer, Insiders/0.73%

Financial Data: Fiscal Year End:12/31 Latest Annual Data: 12/31/2006

Year	Sales	Net Income
2006	$22,461,000	$11,570,000
2005	$15,408,000	$8,513,000
2004	$29,141,000	$17,413,000

Curr. Assets:	$9,679,000	Curr. Liab.:	$925,000	P/E Ratio:	52.29
Plant, Equip.:	$1,894,000	Total Liab.:	$8,028,000	Indic. Yr. Divd.:	$0.160
Total Assets:	$32,468,000	Net Worth:	$24,439,000	Debt/ Equity:	NA

Texas Regional Bancshares Inc

3900 N 10th St., 11th Fl., Mcallen, TX, 78502; **PH:** 1-956-631-5400; **http://** www.trbsinc.com

General - Incorporation	TX	Stock- Price on:12/24/2007	NA
Employees	NA	Stock Exchange	NA
Auditor	KPMG LLP	Ticker Symbol	NA
Stk Agt	Computershare Investor Services LLC	Outstanding Shares	NA
Counsel	NA	E.P.S	NA
DUNS No.	13-755-7062	Shareholders	NA

Business: The group's principal activities are to provide financial services to businesses, individuals and third party correspondent banks. The group offers checking facilities, certificates of deposit, short-term loans, construction financing, mortgage loans, term loans and other commercial loans to business customers. For individual customers it offers checking accounts, savings accounts, certificates of deposit, individual retirement accounts, consumer loan programs for home repair and for purchases of consumer goods, including automobiles, trucks and boats and mortgage loans. It also provides travelers checks, money orders and safe deposit facilities and trust services. It operates through thirty-four full service banking locations, of which twenty-eight are located in the rio grande valley, one banking location each in bishop, corpus christi, eagle pass, sugar land and two banking locations in houston. On 14-Feb-2003, the group acquired corpus christi bancshares, inc.

Primary SIC and add'l.: 6712 6022

CIK No: 0000787648

Subsidiaries: Hydrox Holdings,Inc., Port Arthur Abstract and Title Company, Riverway Holdings Capital Trust I, Riverway Holdings Capital Trust II, Southeast Texas Insurance Services Holdings, LLC, Southeast Texas Insurance Services, L.P., Southeast Texas Title Company, Texas Regional Delaware,Inc., Texas Regional Statutory Trust I, Texas State Bank, TSB Properties,Inc., TSB Securities,Inc., Valley Mortgage Company,Inc.

Officers: Glen E. Roney/Chmn., CEO, Pres. - Texas Regional Bancshares, Inc, Paul S. Moxley/Sr. Exec. VP, Advisory Dir., R. T. Pigott/CFO, Exec. VP, Janie Moran/Sr. VP, Controller, Assist. Sec., Danny L. Buttery/Advisory Dir.

Directors: Glen E. Roney/Chmn., CEO, Pres. - Texas Regional Bancshares, Inc, Jack H. Mayfield/Dir., Kenneth C. Landrum/Dir., Frank N. Boggus/Dir., Robert G. Farris/Dir., Julie G. Uhlhorn/Dir., Mario Max Yzaguirre/Dir., Paul S. Moxley/Sr. Exec. VP, Advisory Dir., David L. Lane/Dir., Morris Atlas/Dir., Jack Whetsel/Dir.

Texas Roadhouse Inc

6040 Dutchmans Ln., Ste. 400, Louisville, KY, 40205; **PH:** 1-502-426-9984; **http://** ir.texasroadhouse.com; **Email:** investment@texasroadhouse.com

General - Incorporation	DE	Stock- Price on:12/24/2007	$12.96
Employees	1,009	Stock Exchange	NDQ
Auditor	KPMG LLP	Ticker Symbol	TXRH
Stk Agt	Texas Roadhouse's	Outstanding Shares	74,600,000
Counsel	NA	E.P.S	$0.52
DUNS No.	NA	Shareholders	NA

Business: The groups principle activity is to provide restaurant services. The groups services include guest satisfaction, atmosphere and food quality. The products of the group include fish, seafood, chicken and vegetable plates, and an assortment of hamburgers, salads and sandwiches. The group products sold under the trade name Texas Roadhouse(R). The group operates from Texas in the United States.

Primary SIC and add'l.: 5812 5812

CIK No: 0001289460

Subsidiaries: Armadillo, Inc., Aspen Steaks Exchange Subsidiary Inc., Aspen Steaks, Ltd., Longview Roadhouse II, Ltd., Roadhouse Enterprises, Inc., Roadhouse Holdings of Texas, Ltd., Texas Roadhouse Delaware LLC, Texas Roadhouse Development Corporation, Texas Roadhouse Holdings LLC, Texas Roadhouse Louisville I LLC, Texas Roadhouse Management Corp., Texas Roadhouse of Abilene, Ltd., Texas Roadhouse of Amarillo, Ltd., Texas Roadhouse of Austin, Ltd., Texas Roadhouse of Austin-North, Ltd. 63 Subsidiaries included in the Index

Officers: G. J. Hart/Dir., CEO, Pres., Steven L. Ortiz/COO, Scott M. Colosi/CFO, Sheila C. Brown/General Counsel, Sec.

Directors: G. J. Hart/Dir., CEO, Pres., Kent W. Taylor/Chmn., James R. Ramsey/Dir., James R. Zarley/Dir., Martin T. Hart/Dir., Gregory N. Moore/Dir., James F. Parker/Dir.

Owners: Martin T. Hart, Steven L. Ortiz/1.50%, Scott M. Colosi, James R. Zarley, Sheila C. Brown, Kent W. Taylor/19.80%, Insiders/24.00%, James F. Parker, James R. Ramsey, G. J. Hart/1.80%, Gregory N. Moore

Financial Data: *Fiscal Year End:*12/26 *Latest Annual Data:* 12/26/2006

Year	Sales	Net Income
2006	$597,131,000	$34,009,000
2005	$458,784,000	$30,322,000
2004	$363,011,000	$21,701,000

Curr. Assets:	$61,647,000	**Curr. Liab.:**	$73,132,000	**P/E Ratio:**	25.92
Plant, Equip.:	$162,991,000	**Total Liab.:**	$103,452,000	**Indic. Yr. Divd.:**	NA
Total Assets:	$276,663,000	**Net Worth:**	$173,211,000	**Debt/ Equity:**	0.0896

Texas Vanguard Oil Co

9811 Anderson Mill Rd., Ste. 202, Austin, TX, 78750; *PH:* 1-512-331-6781

General - Incorporation	TX	**Stock**- Price on:12/24/2007	$9
Employees		Stock Exchange	OTC
Auditor	Sprouse & Anderson LLP	Ticker Symbol	TVOC
Stk Agt	Computershare Trust Co	Outstanding Shares	1,420,000
Counsel	NA	E.P.S.	$0.95
DUNS No.	09-979-4927	Shareholders	NA

Business: The group's principal activities are to explore, acquire, develop and operate onshore oil and natural gas properties. The group sells all of its production to traditional industry purchasers who have the facilities to transport the oil and gas from the well site. The group's customers include aquila southwest, duke energy/gpm and plains marketing. The group activities are mainly carried out in Texas, Wyoming and New Mexico.

Primary SIC and add'l.: 1311

CIK No: 0000315261

Owners: Insiders/77.81%, Robert L. Patterson/2.13%, William G. Watson/1.98%, Linda R. Watson/73.63%, Teresa Nuckols/0.06%

Financial Data: *Fiscal Year End:*12/31 *Latest Annual Data:* 12/31/2006

Year	Sales	Net Income
2006	$7,210,000	$1,441,000
2005	$6,587,000	$1,024,000
2004	$5,423,000	$854,000

Curr. Assets:	$3,563,000	**Curr. Liab.:**	$683,000	**P/E Ratio:**	9.47
Plant, Equip.:	$3,445,000	**Total Liab.:**	$1,152,000	**Indic. Yr. Divd.:**	NA
Total Assets:	$7,008,000	**Net Worth:**	$5,856,000	**Debt/ Equity:**	NA

TEXCOM Inc

3600 S Gessner, Ste 200, Houston, TX, 77063; *PH:* 1-757-397-0035; *http://* www.texcominc.com; *Email:* info@texcominc.com

General - Incorporation	TX	**Stock**- Price on:12/24/2007	$0.24
Employees	NA	Stock Exchange	OTC
Auditor	NA	Ticker Symbol	TEXC
Stk Agt	Registrar & Transfer Co	Outstanding Shares	37,420,000
Counsel	NA	E.P.S.	NA
DUNS No.	NA	Shareholders	NA

Business: The groups principle activity is to provide information technology services. The groups services include project management, systems engineering and integration, operation and maintenance, and installation and assembly. The group's specific customers include U.S. Dept. of Energy, U.S. Dept. of Treasury, Defense Information Systems Agency, MCI, NationsBank, and First Union Bank. The group operates from United States.

Primary SIC and add'l.: 4581

CIK No: 0001288934

Officers: Clemon H. Wesley/CEO, Pres.

Texhoma Energy Inc

1777 W Hastings St., Ste. 1750, Vancouver, BC, V6J 1K7; *PH:* 1-604-683-2220; *http://* www.texhomaenergy.com; *Email:* info@texhomaenergy.com

General - Incorporation	NV	**Stock**- Price on:12/24/2007	$0.04
Employees		Stock Exchange	OTC
Auditor	Glo Cpas, LLP	Ticker Symbol	TXHE
Stk Agt	Madison Stock Transfer, Inc.	Outstanding Shares	NA
Counsel	NA	E.P.S.	-$0.017
DUNS No.	NA	Shareholders	NA

Business: The group's principal activity is to design, develop and market game products and technologies. The group's core products are cube checkers, doubles chess, doubles checkers and doubles backgammon. The group proposes to be a designer, developer and marketer of a wide range of educational products and technology. It is focused on delivering those unique products across a variety of profitable platforms. The group is in the development stage.

Primary SIC and add'l.: 7372

CIK No: 0001127572

Officers: Daniel Vesco/Dir., CEO, Mike Simmons/Chmn., Pres.

Directors: Daniel Vesco/Dir., CEO, Mike Simmons/Chmn., Pres.

Owners: Insiders, Pagest Services SA, Lucayan Oil and Gas Investments, Ltd., Polaris Holdings, Inc., William M. Simmons, Structured Capital Corporation, Valeska Energy Corp., Capersia Pte. Ltd., Hobart Global Ltd., Nafi Onat

Financial Data: *Fiscal Year End:*09/30 *Latest Annual Data:* 09/30/2005

Year	Sales	Net Income
2005	NA	-$2,832,000
2004	NA	-$3,223,000
2003	$25,000	-$568,000

Curr. Assets:	NA	**Curr. Liab.:**	$172,000		
Plant, Equip.:	NA	**Total Liab.:**	$172,000	**Indic. Yr. Divd.:**	NA
Total Assets:	NA	**Net Worth:**	-$172,000	**Debt/ Equity:**	NA

Texola Energy Corp

206 - 475 Howe St., Vancouver, BC, V6B 2B3; *PH:* 1-604-685-2300; *Fax:* 1-604-488-0239; *http://* www.texolaenergy.com; *Email:* info@texolaenergy.com

General - Incorporation	NV	**Stock**- Price on:12/24/2007	$0.2
Employees	NA	Stock Exchange	OTC
Auditor	Moore & Assoc., Chartered	Ticker Symbol	TXLA
Stk Agt	Empire Stock Transfer Inc.	Outstanding Shares	NA
Counsel	Virgil Hlus Clark Wilson LLP	E.P.S.	NA
DUNS No.	NA	Shareholders	NA

Business: The groups principal activity is an exploration stage company engaged in the acquisition of prospective oil and gas properties. The group operates from the United States and Canada.

CIK No: 0000217209

Subsidiaries: Audiyo, Inc.

Officers: Thornton J. Donaldson/Pres.

Owners: Thornton Donaldson/7.30%, Insiders/7.30%

Financial Data: *Fiscal Year End:*12/31 *Latest Annual Data:* 12/31/2006

Year	Sales	Net Income
2006	NA	-$1,944,000
2005	NA	-$82,000

Curr. Assets:	$384,000	**Curr. Liab.:**	$626,000		
Plant, Equip.:	$2,104,000	**Total Liab.:**	$3,326,000	**Indic. Yr. Divd.:**	NA
Total Assets:	$2,553,000	**Net Worth:**	-$773,000	**Debt/ Equity:**	NA

Textron Inc

40 Westminster St., Providence, RI, 02903; *PH:* 1-401-421- 2800; *http://* www.textron.com; *Email:* pr@textron.com

General - Incorporation	DE	**Stock**- Price on:12/24/2007	$108.83
Employees	40,000	Stock Exchange	NYSE
Auditor	Ernst & Young LLP	Ticker Symbol	TXT
Stk Agt	American Stock Transfer & Trust Co.	Outstanding Shares	124,600,000
Counsel	Mr. Odonnell	E.P.S.	$6.02
DUNS No.	00-133-8979	Shareholders	NA

Business: The group's principle activity is to provide innovative, market-leading solutions. The group operates through four segments namely Bell, Cessna, Industrial and finance. The group operates from United States, Latin America, Mexico, Germany, Asia, Australia, United Kingdom and France.

Primary SIC and add'l.: 3799 3721 6159 3429 3714 3825 7359

CIK No: 0000217346

Subsidiaries: AB Benzlers, Aeronautical Accessories Rhode IslandInc., Aeronautical Accessories,Inc., Aeronautical Rotor Blades,Inc., ARS Two Inc., Australian Aircraft Service Pty Limited, Avco Corporation, Avco Rhode Island Inc., Avdel Cherry Rhode Island Inc., Avdel Cherry Textron Inc., Avdel International B.V., Avdel plc/Avdel plc Inc., Avdel Verbindungselemente GmbH, Bell Aerospace Services Inc., Bell Aircraft Services Company 225 Subsidiaries included in the Index

Officers: Lothar R. Rosenkranz/CEO, Pres. - Kautex, Lewis B. Campbell/Chmn., CEO, Pres./$23,671,030.00, Jack J. Pelton/CEO, Pres. - Cessna Aircraft Company, Lynn D. Kelley/VP - Textron Six Sigma, Frank Tempesta/Pres. - Textron Systems Corporation, Victoria Lutz/Contact - Lycoming Engines, Karen Papa/Contact - Textron Financial, Barclay Olson/Pres. - Industrial Segment, Daniel F. Wilkinson/Pres. - Jacobsen, Gary Cantrell/Sr. VP, Corporate Controller - Textron Inc, Marianne Corr/VP, Deputy General Counsel, John R. Curran/VP - Mergers - Acquisitions, Arnold M. Friedman/VP, Deputy General Counsel, Michael A. Gardner/VP - Internal Audit, Mary F. Lovejoy/VP, Treasurer *(51 Officers included in Index)*

Directors: Lewis B. Campbell/Chmn., CEO, Pres., Lord Powell/Dir., Kathleen M. Bader/Dir., Dain M. Hancock/Dir., Jesse H. Arnelle/Dir., Kerry R. Clark/Dir., Ivor J. Evans/Dir., Lawrence K. Fish/Dir., Joe T. Ford/Dir., Paul E. Gagne/Dir., Thomas B. Wheeler/Dir., James L. Ziemer/Dir.

Owners: James L. Ziemer, Lord Powell of Bayswater KCMG, Kathleen M. Bader, Joe T. Ford, Kerry R. Clark, Ivor J. Evans, Ted R. French, Dain M. Hancock, John D. Butler, Terrence ODonnell, Lawrence K. Fish, Jesse H. Arnelle, Thomas B. Wheeler, Paul E. Gagn, Lewis B. Campbell *(17 Owners included in Index)*

Financial Data: *Fiscal Year End:*12/31 *Latest Annual Data:* 12/30/2006

Year	Sales	Net Income
2006	$11,490,000,000	$601,000,000
2005	$10,043,000,000	$203,000,000

Curr. Assets:	$4,985,000,000	**Curr. Liab.:**	$3,147,000,000	**P/E Ratio:**	18.08
Plant, Equip.:	$1,574,000,000	**Total Liab.:**	$13,223,000,000	**Indic. Yr. Divd.:**	$0.920
Total Assets:	$16,499,000,000	**Net Worth:**	$3,276,000,000	**Debt/ Equity:**	3.2401

Tf Financial Corp

3 Penns Trl., Newtown, PA, 18940; *PH:* 1-215-579-4600; *http://* www.thirdfedbank.com

General - Incorporation	DE	**Stock**- Price on:12/24/2007	$30
Employees	176	Stock Exchange	NDQ
Auditor	Grant Thornton LLP	Ticker Symbol	THRD
Stk Agt	Computershare Investor Services LLC	Outstanding Shares	2,930,000
Counsel	Malizia, Spidi & Fisch	E.P.S.	$1.85
DUNS No.	86-103-9436	Shareholders	NA

Business: The group's principal activities are to offer the financial services through thirteen branch offices in bucks and philadelphia counties, Pennsylvania and in mercer county, New Jersey. The group accepts deposits from the general public and uses such deposits, together with borrowings and other funds mainly to originate or purchase loans secured by first mortgages on owner-occupied, one- to four-family residences. The group also originates commercial real estate and multi-family, construction and consumer loans. The group operates only in domestic market.

Primary SIC and add'l.: 6712 6035

CIK No: 0000921051

Subsidiaries: Penns Trail Development Corporation, Teragon Financial Corporation, TF Investments Corporation, Third Delaware Corporation, Third Federal Bank

Officers: Kent C. Lufkin/Dir., CEO, Pres./$648,953.00, Dennis R. Stewart/CFO, Exec. VP/$426,969.00, Elizabeth Kaspern/Sr. VP - Retail Banking/$167,772.00

Directors: Kent C. Lufkin/Dir., CEO, Pres., Robert N. Dusek/Chmn., Dennis L. McCartney/Dir., John R. Stranford/Dir., Carl F. Gregory/Dir., George A. Olsen/Dir., Albert M. Tantala/Dir.

Owners: Elizabeth A. Kaspern, Jeffrey L. Gendell/6.54%, Kent C. Lufkin/1.54%, Private Capital Management, L. P./6.78%, Insiders/21.69%, Floyd P. Haggar, Third Federal Savings Bank/5.87%, Dennis R. Stewart/1.12%

Financial Data: Fiscal Year End:12/31 **Latest Annual Data:** 12/31/2006

Year	Sales	Net Income
2006	$40,880,000	$5,514,000
2005	$36,693,000	$6,153,000
2004	$33,829,000	$6,567,000

Curr. Assets:	$15,434,000	**Curr. Liab.:**	$582,730,000	**P/E Ratio:**	14.49
Plant, Equip.:	$6,544,000	**Total Liab.:**	$586,964,000	**Indic. Yr. Divd:**	$0.800
Total Assets:	$652,603,000	**Net Worth:**	$65,639,000	**Debt/ Equity:**	NA

TGC Industries Inc

1304 Summit Ave., Ste 2, Plano, TX, 75074; **PH:** 1-972-881-1099; *http://* www.tgcseismic.com; **Email:** info@tgcseismic.com

General - Incorporation	TX	**Stock**- Price on:12/24/2007	$11.8
Employees	481	Stock Exchange	NDQ
Auditor	Lane Gorman Trubitt LLP	Ticker Symbol	TGE
Stk Agt	American Stock Transfer & Trust Co.	Outstanding Shares	16,540,000
Counsel	Law, Snakard & Gambill	E.P.S.	$0.45
DUNS No.	13-957-1194	Shareholders	NA

Business: The group's principle activity is to provide geophysical services. The services are provided through conducting seismic surveys and to a lesser extent through sales of gravity information from the company's data bank to companies engaged in the exploration for oil and gas in the United States. The survey is done using seismic, gravity or magnetic instruments and provides data about the properties of earth, which is then interpreted by various means to obtain useful information for oil and gas companies. The two survey techniques used by the company in acquiring geophysical data are seismic and 3 gravity. Land seismic surveys are the group's principal method of data acquisition and are the most widely used geophysical technique. The group's quarterly revenue for Sep '07 was 24.21 millions of USD.

Primary SIC and add'l.: 8713

CIK No: 0000799165

Subsidiaries: ESI Industries, Inc., Tidelands Geophysical Co., Inc.

Officers: Wayne A. Whitener/56/Dir., CEO, Pres. - Geophysical Division/$367,326.00, Daniel Winn/VP/$153,705.00, Tom Pierce/Marketing Mgr. - Plano, Powell Ytsma/Sales Representative - Houston, Tim Bishop/Contact - Employment Opportunities, Mark Steele/Contact - Employment Opportunities, Rick Gay/Contact - Employment Opportunities, Kenneth W. Uselton/65/Principal Financial, Accounting Officer, Sec., Treasurer/$101,395.00, Jim Craft/Marketing Representative - Oklahoma City, Tyler Mintz/Sales Representative - Denver

Directors: Wayne A. Whitener/56/Dir., CEO, Pres. - Geophysical Division, Allen T. McInnes/70/Dir., William J. Barrett/68/Dir., Herbert M. Gardner/68/Dir., Edward L. Flynn/73/Dir., William C. Hurtt/63/Dir.

Owners: Kenneth W. Uselton, Herbert M. Gardner/3.65%, Daniel G. Winn, Royce & Associates, LLC/5.12%, Allen T. McInnes/5.30%, OTR/5.71%, Insiders/32.61%, William C. Hurtt/4.84%, Wayne A. Whitener, Systematic Financial/6.74%, Edward L. Flynn/7.64%, William J. Barrett/10.24%

Financial Data: Fiscal Year End:12/31 **Latest Annual Data:** 12/31/2006

Year	Sales	Net Income
2006	$67,760,000	$8,111,000
2005	$30,852,000	$6,201,000
2004	$20,084,000	$2,868,000

Curr. Assets:	$18,529,000	**Curr. Liab.:**	$17,350,000		
Plant, Equip.:	$37,649,000	**Total Liab.:**	$21,356,000	**Indic. Yr. Divd:**	NA
Total Assets:	$56,400,000	**Net Worth:**	$35,043,000	**Debt/ Equity:**	NA

Tgfin Holdings Inc

1517 N 260 E, North Logan, UT, 84321; **PH:** 1-435-755-0188; *http://* www.tradingear.com

General - Incorporation	DE	**Stock**- Price on:12/24/2007	$0.05
Employees	1	Stock Exchange	OTC
Auditor	HJ & Assoc. LLC	Ticker Symbol	TGFN
Stk Agt	Computershare Trust Co	Outstanding Shares	22,570,000
Counsel	NA	E.P.S.	-$0.017
DUNS No.	09-694-2479	Shareholders	NA

Business: The group's principal activity is to produce trading software designed for the financial services industry. The software technology is designed to provide stock exchanges and broker dealers in the securities industry the ability to offer to its customers an on-line electronic system for securities trading.

Primary SIC and add'l.: 6719 7372

CIK No: 0000876134

Subsidiaries: TradinGear.Com

Officers: Scott Emerson Lybbert/CEO, CFO, Pres., Emerson S. Lybbert/50/Chmn., Pres., Marni Gaer/41/Dir., Sec.

Directors: Emerson S. Lybbert/50/Chmn., Pres., Marni Gaer/41/Dir., Sec., Aaron Etra/67/Dir.

Owners: Insiders/12.10%, Global Net Financial/5.90%, S. Emerson Lybbert/2.40%, Ronald Comerchero/9.20%, Marni Gaer/9.10%, Norman Fuchs/4.30%, Aaron Etra/0.70%, Samuel Gaer/29.60%, Kim Hemphill/8.70%, Bruce Frank/7.60%

Financial Data: Fiscal Year End:12/31 **Latest Annual Data:** 12/31/2006

Year	Sales	Net Income
2006	NA	-$406,000
2005	NA	-$509,000
2004	NA	-$458,000

Curr. Assets:	$1,158,000	**Curr. Liab.:**	$2,000		
Plant, Equip.:	NA	**Total Liab.:**	$2,000	**Indic. Yr. Divd:**	NA
Total Assets:	$1,159,000	**Net Worth:**	$1,157,000	**Debt/ Equity:**	NA

The Fashion House Holdings Inc

Formerly: TDI Holding Corp
6310 San Vicente Blvd., Ste. 275, Los Angeles, CA, 90048; **PH:** 1-323-939-3031; *http://* www.thefashionhouseinc.com.

General - Incorporation	CO	**Stock**- Price on:12/24/2007	$0.13
Employees	31	Stock Exchange	OTC
Auditor	KMJ Corbin & Co. LLP	Ticker Symbol	FHHI
Stk Agt	Corporate Stock Transfer, Inc.	Outstanding Shares	24,890,000
Counsel	NA	E.P.S.	-$0.673
DUNS No.	15-651-2857	Shareholders	NA

Business: The group's principal activity was to provide user driven e-content publishing and delivery solutions for business and consumer markets. The products and services offered by the group include duplication and distribution of digital content, hosting and storage of content for future duplication and distribution and optional delivery of content over the Internet. The group also develops custom solutions and related CD and Web contents. In addition, the group licenses tangible Web and provides brokerage services including print, package management and large-volume CD replication. Customers of the group consist of business oriented software companies, computer related product manufacturers and data publishing companies.

Primary SIC and add'l.: 7372

CIK No: 0000797329

Subsidiaries: Fashion House, Inc

Officers: John Hanna/Chmn., CEO, Pres., Jennifer Hinkle/Dir. - Public Relations, Marketing, Oscar Valencia/Group Pres. - Sales, Roy Herbst/Accounting Exec., Michael P. McHugh/CFO, VP - Finance, Meldy Rafols/Finance Mgr. - Administration, Operations, Yolanda Talay/Credit, Collection Coordinator, Christopher Wyatt/Dir., VP - International Marketing, Melanie Coxson/Dir. - Production, Alice Gu/Junior Accountant, John Irwin/Blass Bill Blass National Sales Mgr., Jennifer Gumbrecht/Isaac Isaac Mizrahi Sales, J. J. Taylor/Sr. Mgr. - Key Accounting, O Oscar, an Oscar de la Renta Company Sales, Barbara Henry/Accounting Exec., Mimi Bongo/Customer Service - Blass Bill Blass, O Oscar, an Oscar de La Renta Company *(19 Officers included in Index)*

Directors: John Hanna/Chmn., CEO, Pres., Christopher Wyatt/Dir., VP - International Marketing, Joseph J. McCann/67/Dir., Alan F. Broidy/52/Dir.

Owners: American Microcap Investment Fund 1, LLC/10.60%, John Hanna/24.20%, Alan F. Broidy/1.00%, Westrec Capital Partners, LLC/31.50%, Lazarus Investment Partners LLP/7.20%, Christopher Wyatt/24.20%, Insiders/49.40%

Financial Data: Fiscal Year End:12/31 **Latest Annual Data:** 12/31/2006

Year	Sales	Net Income
2006	$9,391,000	-$14,691,000
2005	NA	-$63,000

Curr. Assets:	$1,000	**Curr. Liab.:**	$350,000		
Plant, Equip.:	NA	**Total Liab.:**	$350,000	**Indic. Yr. Divd.:**	NA
Total Assets:	$1,000	**Net Worth:**	-$349,000	**Debt/ Equity:**	NA

The Inventure Group Inc

Formerly: Poore Brothers Inc
5050 N 40th St., Ste. 300, Phoenix, AZ, 85018; **PH:** 1-623-932-6200; **Fax:** 1-602-522-2690; *http://* www.poorebrothers.com; **Email:** info@amstock.com

General - Incorporation	DE	**Stock**- Price on:12/24/2007	NA
Employees	268	Stock Exchange	NDQ
Auditor	Deloitte & Touche LLP	Ticker Symbol	SNAK
Stk Agt	American Stock Transfer & Trust Co.	Outstanding Shares	19,300,000
Counsel	Mariscal Weeks McIntyre & Friedlander	E.P.S.	$0.03
DUNS No.	83-733-0679	Shareholders	NA

Business: The group's principal activities are to produce, market and distribute salty snack food products and potato chips. These products are sold through grocery retailers, mass merchandisers, club stores, convenience stores and vend distributors across the United States. The group manufactures and sells salty snack food including Poore Brothers(R), Bob's Texas Style(R) and Boulder Potato Company(R) brand Batch-Fried Potato Chips, Tato Skins(R) brand potato snacks and Pizzarias(R) brand pizza chips. It also manufactures and sells T.G.I. Friday's(R) brand salted snacks under license from T.G.I. Friday's Inc. and manufactures private label potato chips for grocery chains. It also distributes snack food products that are manufactured by others. The group operates in the United States.

Primary SIC and add'l.: 2096

CIK No: 0000944508

Subsidiaries: BN Foods, Inc., Boulder Natural Foods, Inc., La Cometa Properties, Inc., Poore Brothers Bluffton, LLC, Tejas PB Distributing, Inc.

Officers: Eric J. Kufel/Dir., CEO/$500,928.00, Steven M. Sklar/Sr. VP - Marketing/$294,445.00, Terry E. McDaniel/COO/$312,868.00, Steve Weinberger/CFO/$144,010.00, Ashton Asensio/Dir. - Financial, Operations Consultant, Bryce Edmonson/Dir. - Food Industry Consultant

Directors: Eric J. Kufel/Dir., CEO, Larry R. Polhill/Chmn., Ashton Asensio/Dir. - Financial, Operations Consultant, Mark S. Howells/Dir., Bryce Edmonson/Dir. - Food Industry Consultant

Owners: BC Advisors, LLC, Terry McDaniel, Bradley J. Crandall, Mark S. Howells, Insiders, Heartland Advisors, Inc., Steven Sklar, Brian E. Foster, Stillwater Capital, LLC, Dakota Farms, LLC, Eric J. Kufel, Larry Polhill, SRB Management, L.P., Steven R. Becker, Capital Foods, LLC *(16 Owners included in Index)*

Financial Data: Fiscal Year End:12/30 **Latest Annual Data:** 12/30/2006

Year	Sales	Net Income
2006	$69,819,000	$1,093,000
2005	$75,333,000	$280,000
2004	$68,735,000	$2,135,000

Curr. Assets:	$21,412,000	**Curr. Liab.:**	$7,523,000		
Plant, Equip.:	$10,110,000	**Total Liab.:**	$11,561,000	**Indic. Yr. Divd:**	NA
Total Assets:	$41,804,000	**Net Worth:**	$30,243,000	**Debt/ Equity:**	0.1327

The9 Ltd

No.3 Building, No.690 Bibo Rd, Pu Dong New Area, Shanghai, 201203; **PH:** 86-2151729990; *http://* www.corp.the9.com; **Email:** IR@corp.the9.com

General - Incorporation	Cayman Islands	**Stock**- Price on:12/24/2007	$45.11
Employees	NA	Stock Exchange	NDQ
Auditor	PricewaterhouseCoopers	Ticker Symbol	NDAQ
Stk Agt	NA	Outstanding Shares	24,770,000
Counsel	NA	E.P.S.	$1.70
DUNS No.	NA	Shareholders	NA

Business: The groups principle activity is to operate online game services. The products of the group include WoW, MU, Guild Wars, Mystina Online and SUN. The group operates from the United States and china. The group's quarterly revenue for September 2007 was 315.97 millions of USD.

Primary SIC and add'l.: 7372 7379

CIK No: 0001296774

Subsidiaries: China The9 Interactive (Shanghai) Co., Ltd., China The9 Interactive Limited, GameNow.net (Hong Kong) Ltd., Shanghai Jiucheng Advertisement Co., Ltd., Shanghai The9 Information Technology Co., Ltd., The9 Computer Technology Consulting (Shanghai) Co., Ltd.

Officers: Jun Zhu/Chmn., CEO, Xudong He/VP, Hannah Lee/Sr. VP, CFO, Chris Shen/VP - Marketing, Jun Yao/Sr. VP, Yong Wang/VP, Lingdong Huang/VP, Swun Woo Park/VP, Fumin Lin/VP, Dahlia Wei/Investor Relations Sr. Mgr., Huanxin Jiang/VP

Directors: Jun Zhu/Chmn., CEO, Stephen Law/Dir., Davin Alexander MacKenzie/Dir., Chao Y. Wang/Dir., Ka Keung Yeung/Dir.

Owners: EA International Studio and Publishing Ltd./15.38%, Insiders/20.81%, Jun Zhu/20.50%, Bosma Limited/17.56%

Financial Data: *Fiscal Year End:* 12/31   *Latest Annual Data:* 12/31/2005

Year	Sales	Net Income
2005	$57,623,000	$8,980,000
2004	$4,426,000	$2,958,000
2003	$2,086,000	$5,857,000

Curr. Assets:	$139,298,000	**Curr. Liab.:**	$36,958,000	**P/E Ratio:**	25.92
Plant, Equip.:	$29,153,000	**Total Liab.:**	$36,958,000	**Indic. Yr. Divd.:**	NA
Total Assets:	$208,171,000	**Net Worth:**	$171,212,000	**Debt/ Equity:**	NA

Theater Xtreme Entertainment Group Inc

250 Corporate Blvd. Ste. Ef, Newark, DE, 19702; *PH:* 1-302-455-1334; *Fax:* 1-302-455-1612; *http://* www.theaterxtreme.com; *Email:* info@theaterxtreme.com

General - Incorporation	FL	**Stock**- Price on:12/24/2007	$0.68
Employees	26	Stock Exchange	OTC
Auditor	Morison Cogen LLP	Ticker Symbol	TXEG
Stk Agt	StockTrans, Inc.	Outstanding Shares	19,910,000
Counsel	NA	E.P.S.	-$0.15
DUNS No.	NA	Shareholders	NA

Business: The groups principle activities include designing, selling and installing affordable large screen front projection in home cinema rooms comprised of video and audio home theater components. In February 2005, the group acquired BF Acquisition Group II, Inc. and in February 2005, Theater Xtreme Entertainment Group, Inc. completed its merger with the group. The group operates from the United States.

Primary SIC and add'l.: 5999

CIK No: 0001089775

Officers: Scott R. Oglum/Chmn., CEO, Kenneth D. Warren/Pres., COO - Franchising, James J. Vincenzo/CFO, Justin L. Schakelman/Dir., Corporate VP, Sec. - Marketing, Communications, Training

Directors: Scott R. Oglum/Chmn., CEO, Justin L. Schakelman/Dir., Corporate VP, Sec. - Marketing, Communications, Training, David Hludzinski/Dir., Jim Ludlow/Dir., Gregory H. Silber/Dir.

Owners: Kenneth D. Warren, Gregory H. Silber, Insiders/23.94%, Justin L. Schakelman/2.52%, James J. Vincenzo, David Hludzinski, Linda Oglum/15.02%, The Werwinski Family Limited Partnership/10.45%, James W. Ludlow, Scott R. Oglum/18.26%

Financial Data: *Fiscal Year End:* 09/30   *Latest Annual Data:* 03/31/2007

Year	Sales	Net Income
2007	NA	NA
2006	$4,619,000	-$2,133,000

Curr. Assets:	$1,384,000	**Curr. Liab.:**	$1,683,000		
Plant, Equip.:	$357,000	**Total Liab.:**	$1,730,000	**Indic. Yr. Divd.:**	NA
Total Assets:	$1,762,000	**Net Worth:**	$32,000	**Debt/ Equity:**	NA

Theglobe.com Inc

110 E Broward Blvd, 14th Fl., Fort Lauderdale, FL, 33301; *PH:* 1-954-769-5900; *http://* www.theglobe.com; *Email:* info@tglo.com

General - Incorporation	DE	**Stock**- Price on:12/24/2007	$0.035
Employees	37	Stock Exchange	OTC
Auditor	Rachlin Cohen & Holtz LLP	Ticker Symbol	TGLO
Stk Agt	American Stock Transfer & Trust Co.	Outstanding Shares	172,480,000
Counsel	Fried Frank Harris Shriver & Jacobson	E.P.S.	-$0.067
DUNS No.	94-706-9811	Shareholders	NA

Business: The group's principal activities are selling print advertisements, video games, computer games and related products and providing telephone service through Internet. It operates through two divisions: computer games division and voip telephony services division. The computer games division consists of computer games print magazine and the associated Website computer games online (www.cgonline.com) and the operations of chips & bits inc, its games distribution business. The voip telephony services division is involved in the sale of telecommunications services over the Internet to consumers and other telecommunications service providers. On 28-May-2003, the group acquired direct partner telecom inc.

Primary SIC and add'l.: 7311 4813 7319

CIK No: 0001066684

Subsidiaries: Chips & Bits, Inc, Direct Partner Telecom, Inc., EDP Holdings, Inc. (formerly known as SendTec, Inc.), Strategy Plus, Inc, tglo.com, inc, Tralliance Corporation, US VOIP Corp, VOIP Staffing, Inc.

Officers: Michael S. Egan/Chmn., CEO, Edward A. Cespedes/Dir., CFO, Pres., Treasurer, Robin S. Lebowitz/Dir., VP - Finance, Sec.

Directors: Michael S. Egan/Chmn., CEO, Edward A. Cespedes/Dir., CFO, Pres., Treasurer, Robin S. Lebowitz/Dir., VP - Finance, Sec.

Owners: E&C Capital Partners II, LLLP, Dancing Bear Investments, Inc., Michael S. Egan, E&C Capital Partners, LLLP, Carl Ruderman, Insiders, Edward A. Cespedes, Robin S. Lebowitz

Financial Data: *Fiscal Year End:* 12/31   *Latest Annual Data:* 12/31/2006

Year	Sales	Net Income
2006	$3,482,000	-$16,974,000
2005	$2,395,000	-$11,510,000
2004	$16,041,000	-$24,273,000

Curr. Assets:	$6,473,000	**Curr. Liab.:**	$11,776,000		
Plant, Equip.:	$366,000	**Total Liab.:**	$12,008,000	**Indic. Yr. Divd.:**	NA
Total Assets:	$7,405,000	**Net Worth:**	-$4,603,000	**Debt/ Equity:**	NA

Theragenics Corp

5203 Bristol Industrial Way, Buford, GA, 30518; *PH:* 1-770-271-0233; *http://* www.theragenics.com

General - Incorporation	DE	**Stock**- Price on:12/24/2007	$4.15
Employees	315	Stock Exchange	NYSE
Auditor	Grant Thornton LLP	Ticker Symbol	TGX
Stk Agt	Suntrust Bank Atlanta Georgia	Outstanding Shares	33,260,000
Counsel	Tracy M. Culver	E.P.S.	$0.25
DUNS No.	11-437-9522	Shareholders	NA

Business: The group's principle activities include developing, manufacturing and marketing radiological pharmaceuticals and devices used in the treatment of cancer. The company's product, theraseed, is an implantable radiation device used primarily in the treatment of prostate cancer. The company has developed therasphere, a microscopic glass sphere, which is used for the treatment of liver cancer. It is also involved in the research and development using pd-103 for the treatment of restenosis, macular degeneration and other diseases and programs involving other isotopes and their uses. The company's customers include physicians, hospitals and other healthcare providers. The group operates from United States.

Primary SIC and add'l.: 3842 2834

CIK No: 0000795551

Subsidiaries: CP Medical Corporation

Officers: Christine M. Jacobs/Chmn., CEO, Pres./$890,218.00, John V. Herndon/Dir. - Advisor, to, The, Pres., James R. Eddings/70/Pres. - Galt Medical Corp, Patrick J. Ferguson/Pres. - CP Medical/$330,727.00, Michael R. Obannon/Exec. VP - Organizational Development/$293,971.00, Bruce W. Smith/Exec. VP - Strategy, Business Development Corp. Sec./$422,523.00, Francis J. Tarallo/CFO, Treasurer/$428,033.00, Lisa Rassel/Primary Investor Relations Officer, Dixon Hughes/Contact - Accountants - Atlanta, GA, Michael Lang/Pres. - Galt Medical

Directors: Christine M. Jacobs/Chmn., CEO, Pres., Luther T. Griffith/Dir., Judith E. Starkey/Dir., David C. Moody/Dir., Orwin L. Carter/65/Dir., John V. Herndon/Dir. - Advisor, to, The, Pres., Peter A.A. Saunders/Dir., Otis W. Brawley/Dir.

Owners: Luther T. Griffith, Insiders/10.00%, Conus Partners, Inc./6.50%, John V. Herndon, Dimensional Fund Advisors Inc./8.40%, Otis W. Brawley, Healthinvest Partners AB/5.20%, Patrick J. Ferguson/5.40%, Christine M. Jacobs/1.90%, FMR Corp. Fidelity Management & Research Company/8.90%, Peter A.A. Saunders, Francis J. Tarallo, Michael R. OBannon, Bruce W. Smith/1.00%, Orwin L. Carter

Financial Data: *Fiscal Year End:* 12/31   *Latest Annual Data:* 12/31/2006

Year	Sales	Net Income
2006	$54,096,000	$6,865,000
2005	$44,270,000	-$29,006,000
2004	$33,338,000	-$4,310,000

Curr. Assets:	$62,645,000	**Curr. Liab.:**	$4,381,000	**P/E Ratio:**	16.60
Plant, Equip.:	$30,901,000	**Total Liab.:**	$20,103,000	**Indic. Yr. Divd.:**	NA
Total Assets:	$146,244,000	**Net Worth:**	$126,141,000	**Debt/ Equity:**	0.0587

Theravance Inc

901 Gateway Blvd., South San Francisco, CA, 94080; *PH:* 1-650-808-6000; *http://* www.theravance.com; *Email:* investor.relations@theravance.com

General - Incorporation	DE	**Stock**- Price on:12/24/2007	$0.5
Employees	285	Stock Exchange	NDQ
Auditor	Ernst& Young LLP	Ticker Symbol	THRX
Stk Agt	American Stock Transfer & Trust Co.	Outstanding Shares	60,280,000
Counsel	NA	E.P.S.	-$2.73
DUNS No.	NA	Shareholders	NA

Business: The groups principle activities include discovering, developing and commercializing small molecule medicines. The group operates from the United States. The group's quarterly revenue for September 2007 was 5.67 millions of USD.

Primary SIC and add'l.: 2834

CIK No: 0001080014

Subsidiaries: Advanced Medicine East, Inc., Theravance UK Limited

Officers: Rick E. Winningham/Dir., CEO/$2,323,009.00, Joseph J. Tsiakals/VP - Quality, Sharath S. Hegde/VP, Mathai Mammen/Co - Founder, VP - Molecular, Cellular Biology, Dan Marquess/VP - Medicinal Chemistry, Allison Parker/Dir. - Investor Relations, Leonard M. Blum/Sr. VP, Chief Commercial Officer, Dennis O. Driver/VP - Human Resources, Patrick P.A. Humphrey/Exec. VP - Research/$1,140,236.00, Michael W. Aguiar/CFO, Sr. VP/$1,421,183.00, David L. Brinkley/Sr. VP - Commercial Development, Arthur L. Campbell/Sr. VP - Technical Operations, Michael M. Kitt/Sr. VP - Development/$839,498.00, Bradford J. Shafer/Sr. VP, General Counsel, Sec./$894,836.00, Michael Conner/Sr. Dir. - Safety Assessment, Toxicology (21 Officers included in Index)

Directors: Rick E. Winningham/Dir., CEO, Roy P. Vagelos/Co - Founder, Chmn., Julian C. Baker/Dir., Burton Malkiel/Dir., Jeffrey M. Drazan/Dir., Robert V. Gunderson/Dir., Arnold J. Levine/Dir., Ronn C. Loewenthal/Dir., Eve E. Slater/Dir., William H. Waltrip/Dir., George M. Whitesides/Dir., William D. Young/Dir.

Owners: Julian C. Baker, GlaxoSmithKline plc/15.60%, Roy P. Vagelos/2.80%, Jeffrey M. Drazan/4.60%, Sowood Capital Management L.P./4.70%, Arnold J. Levine, Patrick P.A. Humphrey, William D. Young, Michael W. Aguiar, George M. Whitesides/1.30%, FMR Corp./6.60%, Sierra Ventures VI, L.P./4.50%, Insiders, Bradford J. Shafer, Chesapeake Partners Management Co., Inc./4.40% (21 Owners included in Index)

Financial Data: *Fiscal Year End:* 12/31   *Latest Annual Data:* 12/31/2006

Year	Sales	Net Income
2006	$19,587,000	-$166,044,000
2005	$12,054,000	-$143,164,000
2004	$8,940,000	-$102,654,000

Curr. Assets:	$207,167,000	**Curr. Liab.:**	$59,609,000		
Plant, Equip.:	$15,101,000	**Total Liab.:**	$199,114,000	**Indic. Yr. Divd.:**	NA
Total Assets:	$262,424,000	**Net Worth:**	$63,310,000	**Debt/ Equity:**	NA

TheRetirementSolution.com Inc

556 Kimball Pond Rd., Aiken, SC, 29803; *PH:* 1-714-322-2263; *Fax:* 1-803-641-2010; *http://* www.theretirementsolution.com; *Email:* support@theretirementsolution.com

General - Incorporation	NV	Stock - Price on:12/24/2007	$0.32
Employees	2	Stock Exchange	OTC
Auditor	Rbsm LLP	Ticker Symbol	TRES
Stk Agt	Fidelity Transfer Co	Outstanding Shares	137,640,000
Counsel	NA	E.P.S.	-$0.03
DUNS No.	NA	Shareholders	NA

Business: The groups principal activity is a broadband business communications company. The group operates from the United States.

Primary SIC and add'l.: 7389

CIK No: 0000862651

Officers: Nicholas S. Maturo/60/Chmn., CEO, William Kosoff/66/Dir., CFO, Pres.

Directors: Nicholas S. Maturo/60/Chmn., CEO, William Kosoff/66/Dir., CFO, Pres., Louis Sagar/55/Dir.

Owners: William Kosoff/2.44%, Newsgrade Corporation/44.07%, Nicholas S. Maturo/1.06%, Louis Sagar, Insiders/4.37%

*Financial Data: Fiscal Year End:*12/31   *Latest Annual Data:* 12/31/2005

Year	Sales	Net Income
2005	NA	-$1,000,000
2004	NA	-$122,000
2003	NA	-$160,000

Curr. Assets:	$0	Curr. Liab.:	$628,000	P/E Ratio:	0.75
Plant, Equip.:	NA	Total Liab.:	$628,000	Indic. Yr. Divd.:	NA
Total Assets:	$0	Net Worth:	-$628,000	Debt/ Equity:	NA

Thermadyne Holdings Corp

16052 Swingley Ridge Rd. , Ste 300, St. Louis, MO, 63017; *PH:* 1-636-728-3032; *http://* www.thermadyne.com

General - Incorporation	DE	Stock - Price on:12/24/2007	$11
Employees	2,728	Stock Exchange	OTC
Auditor	Ernst & Young LLP	Ticker Symbol	THMD
Stk Agt	Computershare Ltd.	Outstanding Shares	NA
Counsel	NA	E.P.S.	NA
DUNS No.	18-359-0025	Shareholders	NA

Business: The group's principal activity is the manufacture of cutting and welding products and consumables, including repair parts used in the cutting and welding industry. The group manufactures a broad range of gas and electric arc cutting and welding products. The customers of the group are principally engaged in the aerospace, automotive, construction, metal fabrication, mining, mill and foundry, petroleum and shipbuilding industries. The operations of the group are conducted through three subsidiaries: thermal dynamics corporation, tweco products, inc. And victor equipment company.

Primary SIC and add'l.: 3589 6719 3548 3479 3545

CIK No: 0000850660

Subsidiaries: C&G Systems Holding, Inc., C&G Systems, Inc., Canadian Cylinder Company, Cigweld Pty Ltd., Comet Property Holdings Inc., Comweld (Philippines) Inc., Comweld Malaysia SDN. BHD., Duxtech Pty Ltd., Maxweld & Braze Pty. Ltd., MECO Holding Company, O.c.i.m. S.r.l., Palco Trading Company, Philippine Welding Equipment, Inc., Pro Tip Corporation, PT Comweld Indonesia 46 Subsidiaries included in the Index

Officers: Paul D. Melnuk/Chmn., CEO/$975,192.00, Donna Lee/Contact - Financial Information

Directors: Paul D. Melnuk/Chmn., CEO, James B. Gamache/Dir., Andrew L. Berger/Dir., Bradley G. Pattelli/Dir., Marnie S. Gordon/Dir., Joe J. Adorjan/Dir., John G. Johnson/Dir.

Owners: Insiders/4.30%, Bradley G. Pattelli, Andrew L. Berger, Goldman, Sachs & Co., The Goldman Sachs Group, Inc./8.50%, Terry J. Downes, John Boisvert, Flagg Street Capital LLC and Affiliates/5.50%, Paul D. Melnuk/2.50%, Dennis Klanjscek, Steven A. Schumm, John G. Johnson, Angelo, Gordon & Co., L.P./33.70%, Marnie S. Gordon, Martin Quinn, James B. Gamache *(18 Owners included in Index)*

Thermage Inc

25881 Industrial Blvd, Hayward, CA, 94545; *PH:* 1-510-782-2286; *http://* www.thermage.com; *Email:* info@thermage.com

General - Incorporation	DE	Stock - Price on:12/24/2007	$8.28
Employees	154	Stock Exchange	NDQ
Auditor	Pricewaterhousecoopers LLP	Ticker Symbol	THRM
Stk Agt	NA	Outstanding Shares	23,030,000
Counsel	NA	E.P.S.	-$0.1
DUNS No.	NA	Shareholders	NA

Business: The groups principle activities include designing, developing, manufacturing and marketing medical devices. The products of the group include RF generators, and ThermaTips and other consumables. The group products sold under the trade names Thermage, ThermaCool and ThermaCool TC. Customer served by the group is physician. The group operates from the United States, Asia Pacific, Europe Middle East and Rest of the world. The group's quarterly revenue for September 2007 was 13.87 millions of USD.

Primary SIC and add'l.: 3845

CIK No: 0001171298

Officers: Stephen J. Fanning/Chmn., CEO, Pres., Laureen Debuono/CFO, Bader Bellahsene/VP - Research, Development, Pamela M. Buckman/VP - Clinical - Regulatory Affairs, Clint Carnell/VP - Domestic Sales, Doug W. Heigel/VP - Operations, Sherree L. Lucas/VP - Marketing, Richard J. Meader/VP - Clinical, Regulatory, Quality Affairs, Gary L. Wilson/VP - International Sales

Directors: Stephen J. Fanning/Chmn., CEO, Pres., Robert F. Byrnes/Dir., Samuel D. Colella/Dir., Joseph M. Devivo/Dir., Edward W. Knowlton/Founder, Dir., Gary Shaffer/Dir., Mark M. Sieczkarek/Dir., Harold L. Covert/Dir., Cathy L. McCarthy/Dir., Marti Morfitt/Dir.

Owners: Stephen J. Fanning/1.70%, Entities affiliated with Morgenthaler Venture Partners/12.50%, Kenneth Ludlum, Edward W. Knowlton/4.00%, Essex Woodlands Health Ventures Fund V, L.P./7.30%, Laureen DeBuono/1.20%, Insiders/26.10%, Entities affiliated with Technology Partners/10.70%, Sherree Lucas, Marti Morfitt, Samuel D. Colella/13.00%, Robert F. Byrnes/4.20%, Clint Carnell, Draper Fisher Jurvetson ePlanet Ventures L.P./6.10%, Entities affiliated with Institutional Venture Partners/12.90% *(16 Owners included in Index)*

---

*Financial Data: Fiscal Year End:*12/31   *Latest Annual Data:* 12/31/2006

Year	Sales	Net Income
2006	$54,320,000	-$3,909,000
2005	$40,655,000	-$8,233,000
2004	$50,384,000	$5,033,000

Curr. Assets:	$56,136,000	Curr. Liab.:	$9,983,000		
Plant, Equip.:	$3,638,000	Total Liab.:	$10,754,000	Indic. Yr. Divd.:	NA
Total Assets:	$59,875,000	Net Worth:	$49,121,000	Debt/ Equity:	NA

Thermodynetics Inc

651 Day Hill Rd. , Windsor, CT, 06095; *PH:* 1-203-683-2005; *http://* www.thermodynetics.com; *Email:* information1212@thermodynetics.com

General - Incorporation	DE	Stock - Price on:12/24/2007	$1.81
Employees	87	Stock Exchange	OTC
Auditor	Mahoney Sabol & Co LLP	Ticker Symbol	TDYT
Stk Agt	Continental Stock Transfer & Trust Co	Outstanding Shares	4,030,000
Counsel	Kenneth B. Lerman	E.P.S.	$0.03
DUNS No.	02-381-3124	Shareholders	NA

Business: The group's principle activity is to design, manufacture and market enhanced surface metal tubing and related assemblies for heat transfer and plumbing applications. The products are primarily used in heat pumps, chillers, heat reclaimers and biomedical heat exchangers serving the heating, air conditioning, refrigeration, food processing, beverage, medical equipment, marine, plumbing, construction and aerospace industries. The enhanced tubing is primarily used in applications involving laminar or turbulent flow of fluids for efficient transfer of heat. The products are marketed in the United States, Canada and other foreign countries through its sales department, sales representatives and distributors. Turbotec(R) is the registered trademark of the group. The group's quarterly revenue for Sep '07 was 7.21 millions of USD.

Primary SIC and add'l.: 3432 3499 3443

CIK No: 0000351902

Subsidiaries: National Energy Systems, Inc., TPI Systems, Inc., Turbotec Products Plc, Turbotec Products, Inc., Vulcan Industries, Inc.

Officers: Robert A. Lerman/Dir., CEO, Pres./$362,027.00, John F. Ferraro/Chmn., Sec./$197,295.00

Directors: Robert A. Lerman/Dir., CEO, Pres., John F. Ferraro/Chmn., Sec., Fred Samuelson/Dir., John Hughes/Dir.

Owners: John F. Ferraro/20.30%, Robert A. Lerman/25.60%, Fred H. Samuelson/0.30%, Turbotec Products, Inc./8.20%, Thermodynetics, Inc./1.70%, Insiders/46.50%, John J. Hughes/0.30%

*Financial Data: Fiscal Year End:*03/31   *Latest Annual Data:* 3/31/2007

Year	Sales	Net Income
2007	$23,530,000	$2,494,000
2006	$18,750,000	-$710,000
2005	$24,459,000	-$3,609,000

Curr. Assets:	$7,252,000	Curr. Liab.:	$3,300,000	P/E Ratio:	2.92
Plant, Equip.:	$7,635,000	Total Liab.:	$11,546,000	Indic. Yr. Divd.:	NA
Total Assets:	$16,161,000	Net Worth:	$4,614,000	Debt/ Equity:	NA

Thermoenergy Corp

323 Ctr. St., Ste 1300, Little Rock, AR, 72201; *PH:* 1-501-376-6477; *http://* www.thermoenergy.com; *Email:* ir@thermoenergy.com

General - Incorporation	AR	Stock - Price on:12/24/2007	$1.35
Employees	9	Stock Exchange	OTC
Auditor	Kelly & Co	Ticker Symbol	TMEN
Stk Agt	Registrar & Transfer Co	Outstanding Shares	24,660,000
Counsel	NA	E.P.S.	-$0.24
DUNS No.	19-692-2439	Shareholders	NA

Business: The group's principal activities are to develop and market technologies that solve wastewater problems, enable renewable energy process and enhance biogas production. The chemical process technologies include stors, thermofuel, ammonia recovery process, nitrogen removal process and enhanced biogas production, which address wastewater problems for municipal and broad-based industrial markets. The hardware technology includes dual-shell reactor system. The technologies are licensed from battelle memorial institute and alexander g. Fassbender. The group is also the owner of a patented clean energy technology known as the thermoenergy integrated power system, which converts fossil fuels into electricity without producing air emissions. The group is a development stage company.

Primary SIC and add'l.: 4959

CIK No: 0000884504

Subsidiaries: ThermoEnergy Environmental, LLC, ThermoEnergy Power Systems, LLC

Officers: Dennis C. Cossey/Chmn., CEO, Pres./$420,110.00, Alex G. Fassbender/Exec. VP - Engineering, Research, Development, William McCabe/VP - Energy Marketing

Directors: Dennis C. Cossey/Chmn., CEO, Pres., Martin A. Roenigk/65/Dir.

Owners: Dennis C. Cossey, Alexander G. Fassbender, Martin A. Roenigk, Andrew T. Melton, Robert Trump, Estate of P.L. Montesi, Louis J. Ortmann, Insiders, Dan Cowart, Security Management, Lowell E. Faulkenberry, Paul A. Loeffler, The Focus Fund

*Financial Data: Fiscal Year End:*12/31   *Latest Annual Data:* 12/31/2006

Year	Sales	Net Income
2006	$1,057,000	-$3,693,000
2005	$269,000	-$5,237,000
2004	NA	-$1,925,000

Curr. Assets:	$2,156,000	Curr. Liab.:	$848,000		
Plant, Equip.:	$252,000	Total Liab.:	$1,195,000	Indic. Yr. Divd.:	NA
Total Assets:	$2,409,000	Net Worth:	$1,213,000	Debt/ Equity:	0.3510

Thermogenesis Corp

2711 Citrus Rd. , Rancho Cordova, CA, 95742; *PH:* 1-916-858-5100; *http://* www.thermogenesis.com; *Email:* epoutre@thermogenesis.com

General - Incorporation	DE	**Stock**- Price on:12/24/2007	$2.46
Employees	67	Stock Exchange	NDQ
Auditor	Ernst & Young LLP	Ticker Symbol	KOOL
Stk Agt	Computershare Investor Services LLC	Outstanding Shares	55,310,000
Counsel	Bartel, Eng & Schroder	E.P.S	-$0.1
DUNS No.	17-571-9335	Shareholders	NA

Business: The group's principal activities are to design, manufacture and distribute food and drug administration and blood processing systems and their companion products that enable the manufacturer of cell therapy drugs from donor blood. These systems consist of an automated blood processing device and dedicated sterile single-use disposables that our customers use to manufacture cell therapy and products sourced from single units of blood. These products include hematopoietic stem cells from placental/cord blood for bone marrow rescue transplants and blood derived proteins and wound healing growth factors that provide surgeons with a means of arresting bleeding and/or bonding excised tissue together thereby initiating cellular repair of the excised tissues. The group primarily operates in the United States, with exports to Europe and Asia.

Primary SIC and add'l.: 3841

CIK No: 0000811212

Officers: William R. Osgood/CEO, Dan Segal/VP - Emerging Stem Cell Therapy, Jennifer Gerhart/Contact, Sandra Lacava/Contact, Philip H. Coelho/Dir., Chief Technology Architect, Matt T. Plavan/CFO, John Chapman/VP - Research & Development and Scientific Affairs, David C. Adams/Corp. Sec.

Directors: Hubert E. Huckel/Chmn., Woodrow Myers/Dir., Philip H. Coelho/Dir., Chief Technology Architect, Patrick J. McEnany/Dir.

Owners: Dennis Marr, Woodrow A. Myers, Insiders/3.10%, John Chapman, Patrick McEnany, William R. Osgood, Hubert E. Huckel, Philip H. Coelho/2.10%, Matthew T. Plavan

Financial Data: ***Fiscal Year End:***06/30 ***Latest Annual Data:*** 6/30/2006

Year	Sales	Net Income
2006	$12,048,000	-$6,142,000
2005	$10,177,000	-$8,220,000
2004	$11,646,000	-$4,777,000

Curr. Assets:	$46,026,000	***Curr. Liab.:***	$3,684,000		
Plant, Equip.:	$1,489,000	***Total Liab.:***	$5,631,000	***Indic. Yr. Divd.:***	NA
Total Assets:	$47,603,000	***Net Worth:***	$41,972,000	***Debt/ Equity:***	0.0003

Thestreet.com

14 Wall St., 15th Fl., New York, NY, 10005; ***PH:*** 1-212-321-5000; ***Fax:*** 1-212-321-5015; ***http://*** www.thestreet.com

General - Incorporation	DE	**Stock**- Price on:12/24/2007	$11.08
Employees	181	Stock Exchange	NDQ
Auditor	Marcum & Kliegman LLP	Ticker Symbol	TSCM
Stk Agt	American Stock Transfer & Trust Co.	Outstanding Shares	28,480,000
Counsel	NA	E.P.S	$1.05
DUNS No.	NA	Shareholders	NA

Business: The group's principle activity is to operate through two segments: electronic publishing and securities research and brokerage. Electronic publishing provides investment commentary, analysis and news to both retail and professional customers. This product is distributed to customers through Web sites, email reports and newsletters, syndicated radio programming and conferences. Securities research and brokerage segment provides proprietary equity research and brokerage services to institutional clients, and as a broker-dealer, receives revenue from trading commissions, a standard payment method in the professional markets. The groups electronic publishing segment receives revenue from subscription sales, advertising and sponsorship sales, as well as content syndication and conference attendees. The group's quarterly revenue for Sep '07 was 16.12 millions of USD.

Primary SIC and add'l.: 7375 6282

CIK No: 0001080056

Subsidiaries: Delaware limited liability company, Independent Research Group LLC

Officers: Thomas J. Clarke/Chmn., CEO/$1,364,889.00, Pia Sarkar/Staff Reporter, Ivy Lessner/Staff Reporter, Scott Moritz/Staff Reporter, Brian Cronk/Managing Editor, Life, Money, Ana Dane/Sr. Editor, Life, Money, Annika Mengisen/Staff Reporter, Lifestyle, Danielle Sonnenberg/Staff Reporter, Lifestyle, Allison Bisbey Colter/Personal Finance Editor, Lawrence Carrel/Sr. Writer, Personal Finance, Gregg Greenberg/Staff Reporter, Personal Finance, Christopher Sahl/Staff Reporter, Personal Finance, Kristin Bentz/Managing Editor, Realmoneycom, Gretchen Lembach/Deputy Managing Editor, Realmoneycom, Jason Meyer/Assoc. Editor, Realmoneycom *(78 Officers included in Index)*

Directors: Thomas J. Clarke/Chmn., CEO, Martin Peretz/Dir., William R. Gruver/Dir., Daryl Otte/Dir., Jeffrey A. Sonnenfeld/Dir., James J. Cramer/Co - Founder, Dir., Jeffrey Cunningham/Dir.

Owners: Martin Peretz/12.10%, Insiders/29.70%, Jeffrey A. Sonnenfeld, Thomas J. Clarke/2.80%, Peretz Partners L.L.C./8.70%, Cramer Partners, L.L.C./6.20%, Daryl Otte, Richard Broitman, James J. Cramer/14.00%, Lisa Mogensen, William R. Gruver, Jordan Goldstein, Independence Investments LLC/7.80%, Jeffrey M. Cunningham, James Lonergan

Financial Data: ***Fiscal Year End:***12/31 ***Latest Annual Data:*** 12/31/2006

Year	Sales	Net Income
2006	$50,889,000	$12,868,000
2005	$33,744,000	$246,000
2004	$35,223,000	-$2,189,000

Curr. Assets:	$54,175,000	***Curr. Liab.:***	$20,378,000		
Plant, Equip.:	$3,018,000	***Total Liab.:***	$20,378,000	***Indic. Yr. Divd.:***	$0.100
Total Assets:	$64,570,000	***Net Worth:***	$44,191,000	***Debt/ Equity:***	NA

Think Partnership Inc

15550Lightw Ave.Dr., Ste. 300, Clearwater, FL, 33760; ***PH:*** 1-727-324-0046; ***http://*** www.thinkpartnership.com; ***Email:*** eric@liolios.com

General - Incorporation	NV	**Stock**- Price on:12/24/2007	$2.93
Employees	254	Stock Exchange	AMEX
Auditor	Blackman Kallick Bartelstein, LLP	Ticker Symbol	THK
Stk Agt	Colonial Stock Transfer Co Inc	Outstanding Shares	67,420,000
Counsel	NA	E.P.S	-$0.123
DUNS No.	NA	Shareholders	NA

Business: The group operates through its subsidiaries whose principle activity is to provide marketing and technology solutions to businesses and individuals. The group operates through five segments namely network segment, direct advertising, consumer services and corporate. The group acquired Morex Marketing Group, LLC in January 20, 2006, Litmus Media, Inc in April 5, 2006, Web Diversity Ltd in April 27, 2006, and of iLead Media, Inc in may 23,2006. The group operates from the United States, Canada, Hong Kong and the United Kingdom. The group's quarterly revenue for September 2007 was 18.86 millions of USD.

Primary SIC and add'l.: 7389 7379 7331 8999 7319 4899 7311

CIK No: 0000829323

Subsidiaries: CheckUp Marketing Inc., Cherish Inc., iLead Media LLC, Intipro DatingInc., KowaBunga! Marketing Inc., Litmus Media Inc., MarketSmart Advertising Inc., MarketSmart Interactive Inc., Morex Marketing Group LLC, Ozona Online Network Inc., Personal Plus, Inc, PrimaryAds Inc., Real Estate School Online Inc., Relationship Exchange Holdings Ltd., Relationship Exchange Limited 22 Subsidiaries included in the Index

Officers: Scott P. Mitchell/36/Dir., CEO, Pres., Sec./$1,033,359.00, Jody Brown/38/CFO/$384,750.00, Stan Antonuk/40/COO/$268,962.00, John Linden/29/CTO/$376,141.00, Brady R. Whittingham/38/Sr. VP - Business Development, Vaughn W. Duff/60/General Counsel, Tobias Teeter/VP - Strategic Partnerships, Rachel Honoway/VP - Marketing, Jim Banks/Pres. - Think International, Kate Dennison/VP - Finance

Directors: Scott P. Mitchell/36/Dir., CEO, Pres., Sec., Robert T. Geras/61/Dir., George Mellon/61/Dir., Joshua Metnick/34/Dir., Patrick W. Walsh/42/Dir., Alex M. White/Dir.

Owners: John Linden/1.42%, Scott P. Mitchell/2.62%, Insiders/6.80%, George Mellon, Jody Brown, Magnetar Capital Master Fund, Ltd./5.48%, Patrick W. Walsh, William Blair Small Cap Growth Fund/8.06%, Robert T. Geras/1.64%

Financial Data: ***Fiscal Year End:***12/31 ***Latest Annual Data:*** 12/31/2006

Year	Sales	Net Income
2006	$71,882,000	$565,000
2005	$40,441,000	-$4,000
2004	$17,621,000	$1,774,000

Curr. Assets:	$17,166,000	***Curr. Liab.:***	$11,143,000		
Plant, Equip.:	$4,011,000	***Total Liab.:***	$27,073,000	***Indic. Yr. Divd.:***	NA
Total Assets:	$120,397,000	***Net Worth:***	$89,464,000	***Debt/ Equity:***	NA

ThinkEngine Networks

Formerly: Cognitronics Corp

3 Corporate Dr., Danbury, CT, 06810; ***PH:*** 1-203-830-3400; ***Fax:*** 1-203-830-3405; ***http://*** www.cognitronics.com; ***Email:*** shipping@cognitronics.com

General - Incorporation	NY	**Stock**- Price on:12/24/2007	NA
Employees	63	Stock Exchange	NA
Auditor	Carlin, Charron & Rosen LLP	Ticker Symbol	NA
Stk Agt	Bank of New York	Outstanding Shares	NA
Counsel	Hughes Hubbard & Reed LLP	E.P.S	NA
DUNS No.	05-063-1381	Shareholders	NA

Business: The group's principal activity is to design, manufacture and market voice-processing systems. In the United States, the group designs, manufactures and sells equipment for use in telephone central offices. In Europe, the group distributes equipment for use in customers' premises. The products include network media servers and intelligent announcers, mcias(tm) 16xx, 16xx, mcias 1607/ip, 1623/ip, passive announcers and call processors.

Primary SIC and add'l.: 5046 3661

CIK No: 0000021438

Subsidiaries: American Computer Corp., Dacon Electronics Corp., Reed Printing, Inc., Stamford Crescent Corp., ThinkEngine Networks, Inc.

Officers: Michael G. Mitchell/CEO, Pres./$341,959.00, John E. Steinkrauss/VP, Treasurer, Chieffinancial Officer/$277,766.00, Jack Steinkrauss/VP, Mike Wixon/VP - Product Management, Thinkengine Networks, Amy Tefft/Corp. Sec. - Thinkengine Networks

Directors: Robert C. Fleming/51/Chmn., William A. Merritt/Dir., William J. Stuart/56/Dir., Robert H. Scott/53/Dir., John E. Sweeney/50/Dir.

Owners: Insiders/7.70%, Michael N. Keefe/1.70%, Paul J. Gagne/1.20%, Michael G. Mitchell/3.00%, Kenneth G. Brix, Brian J. Kelley/9.30%, Prism Venture Partners III, LLC/17.20%, William J. Stuart/1.00%, John E. Steinkrauss/1.10%, Robert H. Scott, William A. Merritt/1.30%, John E. Sweeney, Bruce Galloway/8.30%, Garrett Sullivan/1.80%

Curr. Assets:	$5,827,000	***Curr. Liab.:***	$2,534,000		
Plant, Equip.:	$970,000	***Total Liab.:***	$3,498,000	***Indic. Yr. Divd.:***	NA
Total Assets:	$10,646,000	***Net Worth:***	$7,148,000	***Debt/ Equity:***	0.2777

Thinkpath Inc

16 Four Seasons Pl., Ste. 215, Toronto, ON, M9B 6E5; ***PH:*** 1-416-622-5200; ***http://*** www.thinkpath.com; ***Email:*** contactme@thinkpath.com

General - Incorporation	Canada	**Stock**- Price on:12/24/2007	$0.16
Employees	NA	Stock Exchange	OTC
Auditor	Schwartz Levitsky Feldman LLP	Ticker Symbol	THPHF
Stk Agt	Continental Stock Transfer & Trust Co	Outstanding Shares	NA
Counsel	NA	E.P.S	NA
DUNS No.	25-517-3874	Shareholders	NA

Business: The group's principle activity is to provide technological solutions and services in engineering knowledge management, the services also includes designing, drafting, technical publishing, e-learning and staffing. The group also provides technical translation services and training services in the areas of microsoft, cisco software products, proengineer and unigraphics products. The customers include financial services, software and technology companies, Canadian and American governmental entities. The other customers include bank of montreal, bell Canada, goldman sachs, chapters, lucent technologies, cummins engine, general motors, xerox corporation, American express and universal industrial corp. The group's quarterly revenue for September 2007 was 3.67 millions of USD.

Primary SIC and add'l.: 7361 7372 2741 8711 8299

CIK No: 0001070630

Officers: Declan French/Chmn., CEO, Pres., Kelly Hankinson/CFO, Sec., Treasurer, Robert J. Trick/COO

Directors: Declan French/Chmn., CEO, Pres., Patrick Power/46/Dir., Lloyd MacLean/Dir., David M. Barnes/Dir., Judd Bedford/Dir.

Owners: Insiders, Kelly Hankinson, Lloyd MacLean, Patrick Power, Robert Trick, John Kennedy, Laurus Master Fund, Ltd., Financial Media Relations, LLC, David Barnes, Declan A. French

Financial Data: ***Fiscal Year End:***12/31 ***Latest Annual Data:*** 12/31/2006

Year	Sales	Net Income
2006	$13,504,000	-$4,858,000
2005	$13,275,000	-$2,835,000
2004	$12,624,000	-$4,205,000

Curr. Assets:	$2,397,000	Curr. Liab.:	$5,240,000		
Plant, Equip.:	$590,000	Total Liab.:	$6,788,000	Indic. Yr. Divd.:	NA
Total Assets:	$5,649,000	Net Worth:	-$1,139,000	Debt/ Equity:	NA

Third Century Bancorp

80 E Jefferson St., Franklin, IN, 46131; *PH:* 1-317-736-7151; *http://* www.mutualsavingsbank.net

General - Incorporation	IN	Stock - Price on:12/24/2007	$11.85
Employees	43	Stock Exchange	OTC
Auditor	BKD LLP	Ticker Symbol	TDCB
Stk Agt	Registrar & Transfer Co	Outstanding Shares	1,610,000
Counsel	NA	E.P.S.	$0.24
DUNS No.	NA	Shareholders	NA

Business: The group's principal activity is that of a holding company. The group is a savings and loan holding company that accepts deposits from public and lends loans secured by residential real estate. The loans include residential lending, commercial and consumer lending. The group also provides deposit and trust services. The group operates solely in the United States of America. As at 31-Mar-2004, the group had 6 branches.

Primary SIC and add'l.: 6712 6036

CIK No: 0001282847

Subsidiaries: Mutual Financial Services, Inc, Mutual Savings Bank

Officers: Robert D. Heuchan/Dir., CEO, Pres., Debra K. Harlow/CFO

Directors: Robert D. Heuchan/Dir., CEO, Pres., David A. Coffey/Dir., Robert L. Ellett/Dir., Jerry D. Petro/Dir., Robert D. Schafstall/Dir.

Owners: Jerry D. Petro/3.10%, Robert D. Heuchan/4.00%, Debra K. Harlow, Robert D. Schafstall/2.80%, Insiders/16.90%, Wellington Management Company, LLP/6.80%, Advisory Research, Inc./9.40%, Robert L. Ellett/2.90%, David A. Coffey/3.80%, HomeFederal Bank, Trustee/8.00%

Financial Data: Fiscal Year End:12/31   Latest Annual Data: 12/31/2006

Year	Sales	Net Income
2006	$8,758,000	$457,000
2005	$7,703,000	$534,000
2004	$6,939,000	$625,000

Curr. Assets:	$10,135,000	Curr. Liab.:	$113,754,000	P/E Ratio:	49.38
Plant, Equip.:	$4,328,000	Total Liab.:	$114,077,000	Indic. Yr. Divd.:	$0.160
Total Assets:	$133,503,000	Net Worth:	$19,426,000	Debt/ Equity:	NA

Third Wave Technologies Inc

502 S Rosa Rd. , Madison, WI, 53719; *PH:* 1-608-273-8933; *http://* www.twt.com

General - Incorporation	DE	Stock - Price on:12/24/2007	$5.37
Employees	162	Stock Exchange	NDQ
Auditor	Grant Thornton LLP	Ticker Symbol	TWTI
Stk Agt	Computershare Investor Services LLC	Outstanding Shares	42,280,000
Counsel Kennedy Covington Lobdell & Hickman		E.P.S.	-$0.32
DUNS No.	78-894-3918	Shareholders	NA

Business: The group's principle activities are to develop, manufacture and market molecular diagnostics and genetic analysis products. The products are used in the discovery and validation of the genetic basis of disease and the delivery of personalized medicine. Genetic information delivered by the group provides a basis for understanding biological and medical functions in organisms. These products are based on invader(R) technology that has applications in genetics, chromosomal analysis, infectious disease, etc and it has been extended to agriculture/biotechnology also. The group markets and sells products through a combination of direct sales personnel and through collaborative relationships. The group has operations in the United States, Japan and the United Kingdom. The group's quarterly revenue for Sep '07 was 8.16 millions of USD.

Primary SIC and add'l.: 8731 2835

CIK No: 0001120438

Subsidiaries: Third Wave Agbio, Inc., Third Wave-Japan KK

Officers: Kevin Conroy/Dir., CEO, Pres./$1,040,043.00, Cindy Ahn/VP, General Counsel, Maneesh Arora/Sr. VP, CFO/$785,634.00, John Bellano/VP - Sales/$343,367.00, Jorge Garces/VP - Research, Development/$352,518.00, Gregory Hamilton/VP - Finance, Operations, Ivan Trifunovich/Sr. VP/$537,538.00

Directors: Kevin Conroy/Dir., CEO, Pres., David Thompson/Chmn., Gordon Brunner/Dir., Lionel Sterling/Dir., James Connelly/Dir., Kay Napier/Dir., Lawrence Murphy/Dir.

Owners: Lionel Sterling, Lawrence Murphy, Jorge Garces, Insiders/2.90%, Ivan Trifunovich, James Connelly, Kevin T. Conroy, Katherine Napier, David A. Thompson, John Bellano, Maneesh Arora, Gordon F. Brunner, Deerfield Group/11.80%, State of Wisconsin Investment Board/10.50%

Financial Data: Fiscal Year End:12/31   Latest Annual Data: 12/31/2006

Year	Sales	Net Income
2006	$28,027,000	-$18,887,000
2005	$23,906,000	-$22,346,000
2004	$46,493,000	-$1,942,000

Curr. Assets:	$52,932,000	Curr. Liab.:	$13,001,000		
Plant, Equip.:	$4,222,000	Total Liab.:	$33,561,000	Indic. Yr. Divd.:	NA
Total Assets:	$64,234,000	Net Worth:	$30,673,000	Debt/ Equity:	NA

Thomas & Betts Corp

8155 T&b Blvd, Memphis, TN, 38125; *PH:* 1-902-252-5466; *http://* www.tnb.com; *Email:* elec_custserv@tnb.com

General - Incorporation	TN	Stock - Price on:12/24/2007	$57.8
Employees	9,000	Stock Exchange	NYSE
Auditor	KPMG LLP	Ticker Symbol	TNB
Stk Agt	Computershare Ltd.	Outstanding Shares	58,170,000
Counsel	NA	E.P.S.	$2.99
DUNS No.	00-215-4433	Shareholders	NA

Business: The groups principle activities include designing and manufacturing electrical components for the industrial, commercial, communications and utility markets. The groups products include cable ties and accessories, connectors - power and grounding, metal framing and support systems, and wire management systems. In the year 2007 the group acquired The Lamson and Sessions Co. The group operates from United States.

Primary SIC and add'l.: 3644 3357 3441 3444 3643

CIK No: 0000097854

Subsidiaries: Thomas & Betts Caribe Corp., Thomas & Betts Commander LP, Thomas & Betts International, Inc., Thomas & Betts Limited

Officers: Dominic J. Pileggi/Chmn., CEO/$8,208,334.00, Thomas C. Oviatt/VP, Treasurer, J. N. Raines/VP, General Counsel, Sec./$1,470,825.00, David W. Smith/Chief Compliance Officer, Assist. General Counsel, Assist. Sec., Hugh Windsor/Pres. - HVAC, Kenneth W. Fluke/CFO, Sr. VP/$1,882,429.00, Joseph Dicianni/VP - Information Technologies, Michael Kenney/Pres. - Canada, Christopher P. Hartmann/COO, Exec. VP/$1,643,869.00, James R. Wiederholt/Pres. - Steel Structures Division, Stanley P. Locke/VP, Controller, Imad Hajj/Chief Development Officer/$2,052,210.00, Patricia A. Bergeron/VP - Investor, Corporate Relations

Directors: Dominic J. Pileggi/Chmn., CEO, Ronald B. Kalich/Dir., Jeananne K. Hauswald/Dir., David D. Stevens/Dir., Kenneth R. Masterson/Dir., Jean-Paul Richard/Dir., Dean Jernigan/Dir., Ernest H. Drew/Dir., William H. Waltrip/Dir., Kevin L. Roberg/Dir.

Owners: Jeananne K. Hauswald, Vanguard Horizon Funds/6.29%, Insiders/1.40%, Gabelli Investors, etal./11.16%, J. N. Raines, Dean Jernigan, Kenneth R. Masterson, David D. Stevens, Imad Hajj, William H. Waltrip, Ernest H. Drew, Kenneth W. Fluke, Ronald B. Kalich, Christopher P. Hartmann, Jean-Paul Richard *(16 Owners included in Index)*

Financial Data: Fiscal Year End:12/31   Latest Annual Data: 12/31/2006

Year	Sales	Net Income
2006	$1,868,689,000	$175,130,000
2005	$1,695,383,000	$113,408,000
2004	$1,516,292,000	$93,255,000

Curr. Assets:	$868,370,000	Curr. Liab.:	$248,529,000	P/E Ratio:	19.33
Plant, Equip.:	$267,200,000	Total Liab.:	$761,864,000	Indic. Yr. Divd.:	NA
Total Assets:	$1,830,223,000	Net Worth:	$1,068,359,000	Debt/ Equity:	0.3769

Thomas Equipment Inc

1818 N Farwell Ave., Milwaukee, WI, 53202; *PH:* 1-312-224-8812; *http://* www.thomasloaders.com; *Email:* info@thomasloaders.com

General - Incorporation	DE	Stock - Price on:12/24/2007	$0.14
Employees	323	Stock Exchange	OTC
Auditor	Kingery, Crouse & Hohl P.A	Ticker Symbol	THME
Stk Agt	Interwest Transfer Company, Inc.	Outstanding Shares	22,330,000
Counsel	NA	E.P.S.	$0.61
DUNS No.	NA	Shareholders	NA

Business: The group's principal activity is to provide brokerage and originate mortgage loan for commercial and residential purposes. The group also provides conventional, non-conforming and government loan programs. The group operates in the states of Georgia, Florida and atlanta.

Primary SIC and add'l.: 6162

CIK No: 0001122380

Subsidiaries: McCain Foods Limited

Officers: James E. Patty/Interim CEO, Luigi Lobasso/CFO, Joel Arberman/Managing Member - Investor Relations

Directors: David M. Marks/Chmn., Kenneth Shirley/Dir., Mike Woods/Dir.

Financial Data: Fiscal Year End:06/30   Latest Annual Data: 6/30/2005

Year	Sales	Net Income
2005	$60,133,000	-$78,747,000
2003	$2,246,000	-$110,000
2002	$2,213,000	-$91,000

Curr. Assets:	$67,509,000	Curr. Liab.:	$45,282,000	P/E Ratio:	0.23
Plant, Equip.:	$21,504,000	Total Liab.:	$163,176,000	Indic. Yr. Divd.:	NA
Total Assets:	$96,048,000	Net Worth:	-$67,129,000	Debt/ Equity:	NA

Thomas Group Inc

Williams Sq., 5221 N Oconnor Blvd., Ste. 500, Irving, TX, 75039; *PH:* 1-972-869-3400; *http://* www.thomasgroup.com; *Email:* tgi@thomasgroup.com

General - Incorporation	DE	Stock - Price on:12/24/2007	$9.89
Employees	144	Stock Exchange	NDQ
Auditor	Ernst & Young, LLP	Ticker Symbol	TGIS
Stk Agt	Computershare Investor Services LLC	Outstanding Shares	10,940,000
Counsel	Haynes & Boone	E.P.S.	$0.84
DUNS No.	04-976-5068	Shareholders	NA

Business: The group's principle activity is to provide management services designed to improve the competitiveness and profitability of its clients. The group provides professional services focusing on improving operations, competitiveness and financial performance of major corporate clients through process improvement and strategically aligning operations with technology. The group's specific methodology in its core product, known as process value management (pvm) focuses on reducing the time spent on revenue-producing, product development and administrative processes. This results in operational and financial improvements. The group's products are based on three fundamental principles: a metrics-driven process, attaining and sustaining significant results for clients and program implementation by consultants with senior management experience in industry. The clients of the group include many of the Fortune 1000 companies. The group's quarterly revenue for Sep '07 was 13.47 millions of USD.

Primary SIC and add'l.: 8742

CIK No: 0000900017

Subsidiaries: Thomas Group (Schweiz) GMBH, Thomas Group (Schweiz) Results GMBH, Thomas Group Hong Kong, Ltd.

Officers: Jim Taylor/CEO, Pres./$2,504,423.00, David English/CFO, VP/$354,943.00, Tom Zych/Pres. - Government Operations, Kerry Shaughnessy/VP - Human Resources, Thad Wolfe/Pres. - Government, Air Force

Directors: John T. Chain/Chmn., Edward P. Evans/66/Dir., Dorsey R. Gardner/Dir., David B. Mathis/Dir.

Owners: Jimmy C. Houlditch, James T. Taylor/2.50%, John T. Chain/29.70%, David B. Mathis, Insiders/72.00%, Dorsey R. Gardner/3.40%, Edward P. Evans/35.70%, David English, Terry Stinson

Financial Data: Fiscal Year End:12/31 Latest Annual Data: 12/31/2006

Year	Sales	Net Income
2006	$59,478,000	$11,506,000
2005	$43,062,000	$6,752,000
2004	$30,030,000	$1,475,000

Curr. Assets:	$21,487,000	Curr. Liab.:	$4,700,000	P/E Ratio:	10.41
Plant, Equip.:	$616,000	Total Liab.:	$4,803,000	Indic. Yr. Divd.:	$0.400
Total Assets:	$23,466,000	Net Worth:	$18,663,000	Debt/ Equity:	0.0150

Thomas Properties Group Inc

515 S Flower St., Sixth Fl., Los Angeles, CA, 90071; PH: 1-213-613-1900; http:// www.tpgre.com

General - Incorporation	DE	**Stock**- Price on:12/24/2007	$16.47
Employees	127	Stock Exchange	NDQ
Auditor	Deloitte & Touche LLP	Ticker Symbol	TPGI
Stk Agt	Computershare Investor Services LLC	Outstanding Shares	23,740,000
Counsel	NA	E.P.S	-$0.05
DUNS No.	NA	Shareholders	NA

Business: The groups principle activities include acquiring, developing, ownership and managing commercial and mixed use real estate. The group operates from the United States. The group's quarterly revenue for September 2007 was 26.97 millions of USD.

Primary SIC and add'l.: 6512 6552 6519 6531

CIK No: 0001283709

Subsidiaries: 2121 Market Street Associates, LP, 505 Flower Associates, LLC, 515/555 Flower Associates, LLC, 515/555 Flower Junior Mezzanine Associates, LLC, 515/555 Flower Mezzanine Associates, LLC, Commerce Square Partners Philadelphia Plaza, LP, Harris Building Associates, LP, Harris Building General Partners, LLC, New TPG Four Points, LP, Philadelphia PlazaPhase II, LP, Reflections I, LLC, Reflections II, LLC, TCS Gen Par, LLC, TCS Mezzanine GP, LLC, TCS SPE 1, LP 59 Subsidiaries included in the Index

Officers: James A. Thomas/Chmn., CEO, Pres., Thomas S. Ricci/Exec. VP, Randall L. Scott/Dir., Exec. VP, John R. Sischo/Dir., Exec. VP, Diana M. Laing/CFO, Sec., Jerry D. Hackney/VP, Joseph P. McManus/Sr. VP, Robert D. Morgan/VP, Dennis A. Watsabaugh/Sr. VP

Directors: James A. Thomas/Chmn., CEO, Pres., Bruce R. Andrews/Dir., Edward D. Fox/Dir., John Goolsby/Dir., Winston H. Hickox/Dir., Randall L. Scott/Dir., Exec. VP, John R. Sischo/Dir., Exec. VP

Owners: Winston H. Hickox, John L. Goolsby, James A. Thomas, Bruce R. Andrews, Edward D. Fox, Insiders/1.90%

Financial Data: Fiscal Year End:12/31 Latest Annual Data: 12/31/2006

Year	Sales	Net Income
2006	$78,574,000	-$2,049,000
2005	$69,250,000	$644,000
2004	$57,835,000	-$5,587,000

Curr. Assets:	$92,112,000	Curr. Liab.:	$37,374,000		
Plant, Equip.:	$336,154,000	Total Liab.:	$455,830,000	Indic. Yr. Divd.:	$0.240
Total Assets:	$518,080,000	Net Worth:	$62,250,000	Debt/ Equity:	5.5234

Thomas Weisel Partners Group Inc

One Montgomery St., San Francisco, CA, 94104; PH: 1-415-364-2500; http:// www.tweisel.com; Email: TWPInfo@tweisel.com

General - Incorporation	DE	**Stock**- Price on:12/24/2007	$17.26
Employees	590	Stock Exchange	NDQ
Auditor	Deloitte & Touche LLP	Ticker Symbol	TWPG
Stk Agt	Mellon Investor Services LLC	Outstanding Shares	25,740,000
Counsel	NA	E.P.S	$0.72
DUNS No.	NA	Shareholders	NA

Business: The groups principle activity is to provide financial services. The groups services include securities brokerage, investment banking, equity research and asset management. The group operates from the United States. The group's quarterly revenue for September 2007 was 66.40 millions of USD.

Primary SIC and add'l.: 8742 6726 6799 6289 6722 6211

CIK No: 0001340354

Subsidiaries: Q Street Management LLC, Tailwind Associates, LLC, Thomas Weisel Asset Management LLC, Thomas Weisel Capital Management LLC, Thomas Weisel Capital Partners (Dutch) LLC, Thomas Weisel Global Growth Partners LLC, Thomas Weisel Healthcare Venture Associates LLC, Thomas Weisel Healthcare Venture Partners LLC, Thomas Weisel India Opportunity LLC, Thomas Weisel International Private Limited, Thomas Weisel Partners (Mauritius), Thomas Weisel Partners Insurance Services LLC, Thomas Weisel Partners International Limited, Thomas Weisel Partners LLC, Thomas Weisel Venture Associates LLC 19 Subsidiaries included in the Index

Officers: Thomas W. Weisel/Chmn., CEO, David Baylor/Dir., COO, CFO, Stephen Buell/Dir. - Research, Mark Manson/Partner, Paul Slivon/Dir. - Institutional Sales, Mark Fisher/General Counsel, Bill McLeod/Co - Dir. - Investment Banking, Brad Raymond/Co - Dir. - Investment Banking

Directors: Thomas W. Weisel/Chmn., CEO, Matthew R. Barger/Dir., Michael W. Brown/Dir., Kipling B. Hagopian/Dir., Timothy A. Koogle/Dir., Michael G. McCaffery/Dir., Tony Stais/Dir. - Trading

Owners: Anthony V. Stais, Michael W. Brown, David A. Baylor, Michael G. McCaffery, Timothy A. Koogle, Nomura America Investment, Inc./5.10%, Kipling B. Hagopian, Thomas W. Weisel/9.40%, William L. McLeod, Paul C. Slivon/1.70%, Insiders/14.10%, Matthew R. Barger

Financial Data: Fiscal Year End:12/31 Latest Annual Data: 12/31/2006

Year	Sales	Net Income
2006	$287,222,000	$34,921,000
2005	$256,000,000	-$7,058,000

Curr. Assets:	$147,051,000	Curr. Liab.:	$183,636,000	P/E Ratio:	23.97
Plant, Equip.:	$24,189,000	Total Liab.:	$216,135,000	Indic. Yr. Divd.:	NA
Total Assets:	$483,189,000	Net Worth:	$267,054,000	Debt/ Equity:	0.1153

Thomasville Bancshares Inc

301 N Brd. St., Thomasville, GA, 31792; PH: 1-229-226-3300; http:// www.tnbank.com

General - Incorporation	GA	**Stock**- Price on:12/24/2007	$25
Employees	69	Stock Exchange	OTC
Auditor	Francis & Co	Ticker Symbol	THVB
Stk Agt	Computershare Investor Services, LLC	Outstanding Shares	2,960,000
Counsel	NA	E.P.S	$1.48
DUNS No.	17-812-7734	Shareholders	NA

Business: The group's principal activities are to obtain deposits and to provide commercial, consumer and real estate loans to the general public. The group's offers a full range of interest-bearing and non-interest bearing accounts including commercial and retail checking accounts, money market accounts, individual retirement and keogh accounts, regular interest-bearing statement savings accounts and certificates of deposit. The group's lending activities include commercial loans, real estate loans, home equity loans and consumer or installment loans. In addition, the group also provides U.S. Savings bonds, travelers checks, cashiers checks, safe deposit boxes, bank by mail services, direct deposit and automatic teller services. The group operates through nine branches in thomasville and four additional branches in thomas county.

Primary SIC and add'l.: 6022 6712

CIK No: 0000944468

Subsidiaries: Thomasville National Bank, TNB Financial Services Inc.

Officers: Stephen H. Cheney/50/Dir., CEO, Pres., Principal Financial Officer, Principal Accounting Officer/$253,697.00, Charles H. Hodges/43/Exec. VP/$200,284.00, Harold L. Jackson/60/Exec. VP

Directors: Stephen H. Cheney/50/Dir., CEO, Pres., Principal Financial Officer, Principal Accounting Officer, Charles E. Hancock/48/Dir., Diane W. Parker/67/Dir., Richard L. Singletary/48/Dir., Joel W. Barrett/39/Dir., Charles A. Balfour/44/Dir., David A. Cone/43/Dir., Randall L. Moore/48/Dir., Mark J. Parker/46/Dir., Cochran A. Scott/52/Dir.

Owners: Mark J. Parker/2.00%, Richard L. Singletary/5.10%, Charles A. Balfour/1.60%, Charles H. Hodges/3.10%, Cochran A. Scott/2.60%, Charles E. Hancock/2.30%, David A. Cone, Insiders/28.30%, Randall L. Moore/2.20%, Stephen H. Cheney/5.30%, Diane W. Parker/1.60%, Harold L. Jackson/1.00%, Joel W. Barrett/1.90%

Financial Data: Fiscal Year End:12/31 Latest Annual Data: 12/31/2006

Year	Sales	Net Income
2006	$23,299,000	$4,321,000
2005	$18,307,000	$3,549,000
2004	$14,416,000	$2,655,000

Curr. Assets:	$34,048,000	Curr. Liab.:	$261,256,000	P/E Ratio:	17.36
Plant, Equip.:	$5,901,000	Total Liab.:	$273,151,000	Indic. Yr. Divd.:	NA
Total Assets:	$299,260,000	Net Worth:	$26,109,000	Debt/ Equity:	0.4527

Thomson

46, Quai Alphonse Le Gallo, Boulogne-billancourt, 92100; PH: 33-141865723; http:// www.thomson.net

General - Incorporation	France	**Stock**- Price on:12/24/2007	$18.68
Employees	29,628	Stock Exchange	NYSE
Auditor	Barbier Frinault & Autres	Ticker Symbol	TMS
Stk Agt	CACEIS Corporate Trust	Outstanding Shares	261,230,000
Counsel	NA	E.P.S	$0.50
DUNS No.	NA	Shareholders	NA

Business: The groups' principal activities are in technologies, systems, finished products, services and solutions provider with a particular focus on video, to consumers and professionals in the entertainment and media industries. The group is operating through four main segments:the consumer products segment produces and sells retail products such as televisions, video, audio and DVD. The digital media solutions segment provides services to the film and media industry, produces and distributes motion picture films, dvds, cds and video cassettes. The new media services segment develops and commercializes new products and services related to interactive television and associated technologies. The patents and licensing segment manages the licenses and patents of the group and on behalf of third parties.

Primary SIC and add'l.: 7379 3661 3669 6719 3651 6794

CIK No: 0001080259

Subsidiaries: 46 quai Le Gallo 92100 Boulogne Billancourt, ATLINKS Communications Canada, Inc., ATLINKS Hong Kong Ltd., ATLINKS Telecommunication, Atlinks Usa, Inc., Baja Hughes S. de R.L. de C.V., Beijing Thomson Commerce Co. Ltd., Broadcast Television Systems, Broadcast Television Systems Australia Pty Ltd., Broadcast Television Systems Ltd., Canal+ Technologies, Inc., Celstream Technologies Private Ltd., Comercializadora de Productos Electronicos del Norte, S.A. de C.V., Deutsche Thomson Brandt GmbH, Direct Solutions, Inc. 24 Subsidiaries included in the Index

Financial Data: Fiscal Year End:12/31 Latest Annual Data: 12/31/2006

Year	Sales	Net Income
2006	$7,729,036,000	-$262,740,000
2005	$6,740,420,000	-$853,952,000
2004	$10,907,014,000	-$948,258,000

Curr. Assets:	$4,751,760,000	Curr. Liab.:	$4,860,024,000		
Plant, Equip.:	$1,073,404,000	Total Liab.:	$8,836,768,000	Indic. Yr. Divd.:	$0.450
Total Assets:	$10,774,968,000	Net Worth:	$1,938,200,000	Debt/ Equity:	NA

Thomson Corp

Metro Ctr., 1 Station Pl., Stamford, CT, 06902; PH: 1-203-539-8000; Fax: 1-203-539-7734; http:// www.thomson.com; Email: investor.relations@thomson.com

General - Incorporation	ON	**Stock**- Price on:12/24/2007	$41.59
Employees	32,375	Stock Exchange	NYSE
Auditor	PricewaterhouseCoopers LLP	Ticker Symbol	TOC
Stk Agt	Computershare Trust Co. of Canada	Outstanding Shares	641,070,000
Counsel	TLR International	E.P.S	$6.14
DUNS No.	NA	Shareholders	NA

Business: The group's principal activities are carried out through four sectors: thomson legal and regulatory: provides integrated information solutions to legal, tax, accounting, intellectual property, compliance and business professionals. Thomson learning: provides integrated learning products, services and solutions to individuals and businesses. Thomson financial: provides integrated information and workflow solutions to the worldwide financial community. Thomson scientific and healthcare: provides integrated information, services and solutions to researchers and other professionals in the healthcare,

academic, scientific and government market places. The group operates in the United States, Europe, Asia-pacific, Canada & other countries. In 2003, the group acquired techstreet inc, core technology group inc & elite information group. In 2004, it acquired education to go, corporate communications broadcast network (ccbn), biological abstracts inc, biosis & expert ease.

Primary SIC and add'l.: 7375 7375 2731 8299 2741 2721

CIK No: 0001075124

Subsidiaries: The Gale Group Inc., The MEDSTAT Group, Inc., The Thomson Corporation Delaware Inc., The Thomson Corporation PLC, Thi (u.s.) Inc., Thomson Canada Limited, Thomson Finance SA, Thomson Financial Holdings Inc., Thomson Financial Inc., Thomson Financial Limited, Thomson Healthcare Inc., Thomson Holdings B.V., Thomson Holdings Inc., Thomson Holdings S.A., Thomson Information & Solutions Limited 26 Subsidiaries included in the Index

Officers: Sharon Rowlands/Pres., CEO - Thomson Financial, Robert C. Cullen/Pres., CEO - Thomson Healthcare, Mike Boswood/Pres., CEO - International Legal, Regulatory, Roy M. Martin/Pres., CEO - Thomson Tax, Accounting, Peter Warwick/Pres., CEO - North American Legal, Vin Caraher/Pres., CEO - Thomson Scientific, Richard J. Harrington/Dir., CEO, Pres., Ronald H. Schlosser/Pres., CEO - Thomson Learning, Robert B. Bogart/Exec. VP - Human Resources, Robert D. Daleo/Dir., CFO, Exec. VP, David H. Shaffer/Exec. VP, James C. Smith/COO, Exec. VP, Jason Stewart/VP - Media Relations, Michael Goddard/Dir. - Investor Relations, Frank J. Golden/VP - Investor Relations *(19 Officers included in Index)*

Directors: Richard J. Harrington/Dir., CEO, Pres., David Thomson/Chmn., Geoffrey W. Beattie/Dep. Chmn., Ron D. Barbaro/Dir., Robert D. Daleo/Dir., CFO, Exec. VP, Michael Sabia/Dir., Maureen V. Kempston Darkes/Dir., John A. Tory/Dir., Mary Cirillo/Corp. Dir., Steven A. Denning/Dir., Roger L. Martin/Dir., Vance K. Opperman/Dir., John M. Thompson/Dir., Peter J. Thomson/Dir., Richard M. Thomson/Corp. Dir.

Financial Data: Fiscal Year End:12/31   Latest Annual Data: 12/31/2006

Year	Sales	Net Income
2006	$6,641,000,000	$1,143,000,000
2005	$8,703,000,000	$947,000,000
2004	$8,098,000,000	$1,016,000,000

Curr. Assets:	$3,265,000,000	Curr. Liab.:	$3,739,000,000		
Plant, Equip.:	$625,000,000	Total Liab.:	$9,651,000,000	Indic. Yr. Divd.:	$0.980
Total Assets:	$19,378,000,000	Net Worth:	$9,727,000,000	Debt/ Equity:	NA

Thor Industries Inc

419 W Pike St., Jackson Center, OH, 45334; *PH:* 1-937-596-6849; *http://* www.thorindustries.com

General - Incorporation .... DE	**Stock**- Price on:12/24/2007 ....$44.94
Employees...9,363	Stock Exchange...NYSE
Auditor ....Deloitte & Touche LLP	Ticker Symbol...THO
Stk Agt.....Computershare Investor Services LLC	Outstanding Shares 55,710,000
Counsel... NA	E.P.S..$2.55
DUNS No. 03-820-4913	Shareholders...NA

Business: The groups principle activity is to manufacture recreation vehicles and commercial buses. The group operates through three business segments namely towable recreation vehicles, motorized recreation vehicles and buses. The group operates from United States.

Primary SIC and add'l.: 3792 3711 6719 3799 3714 3716

CIK No: 0000730263

Subsidiaries: Airstream, Inc., Champion Bus, Inc., Citair, Inc., Damon Corporation, DS Corp. dba CrossRoads RV, Dutchmen Manufacturing, Inc., ElDorado National California, Inc., ElDorado National Kansas, Inc., Four Winds International, Inc., General Coach America, Inc., Goshen Coach, Inc., Keystone RV Company, Komfort Corp., T.h.o.r. Insurance Company Limited, Thor California, Inc. 16 Subsidiaries included in the Index

Officers: Wade F.B. Thompson/Chmn., CEO, Pres., Peter B. Orthwein/Vice Chmn., Treasurer, Walter L. Bennett/CFO, Exec. VP, Sec.

Directors: Wade F.B. Thompson/Chmn., CEO, Pres., Peter B. Orthwein/Vice Chmn., Treasurer, Neil D. Chrisman/71/Dir., Alan Siegel/Dir., Geoffrey A. Thompson/Dir., Coleman H. Davis/59/Dir., Jan H. Suwinski/67/Dir., William C. Tomson/72/Dir.

Owners: Wade F. B. Thompson/29.40%, William C. Tomson, Royce & Associates, LLC/10.50%, Insiders/36.20%, Alan Siegel, Geoffrey A. Thompson, Coleman H. Davis, Neil D. Chrisman, Richard E. Riegel, Jan H. Suwinski, Ted J. Bartus, Peter B. Orthwein/4.60%, Walter L. Bennett

Financial Data: Fiscal Year End:07/31   Latest Annual Data: 7/31/2007

Year	Sales	Net Income
2007	$2,856,308,000	$134,731,000
2006	$3,066,276,000	$163,405,000
2005	$2,558,351,000	$121,767,000

Curr. Assets:	$705,528,000	Curr. Liab.:	$277,199,000	P/E Ratio:	19.71
Plant, Equip.:	$157,242,000	Total Liab.:	$292,966,000	Indic. Yr. Divd.:	$0.280
Total Assets:	$1,059,297,000	Net Worth:	$766,331,000	Debt/ Equity:	NA

Thoratec Corp

6035 Stoneridge Dr., Pleasanton, CA, 94588; *PH:* 1-925-847-8600; *http://* www.thoratec.com

General - Incorporation .... CA	**Stock**- Price on:12/24/2007 ....$18.98
Employees...925	Stock Exchange...NDQ
Auditor ....Deloitte & Touche LLP	Ticker Symbol...THOR
Stk Agt.....................................Computershare Trust Co	Outstanding Shares 53,200,000
Counsel. Heller Ehrman White & McAuliffe LLP	E.P.S..$0.05
DUNS No. 07-015-6955	Shareholders...NA

Business: The group's principal activity is to manufacture circulatory support products for use by patients with congestive heart failure. The products of the group are used by physicians and hospitals for cardiac assist, vascular and diagnostic applications. It operates in two business segments: cardiovascular and other medical equipment. The cardiovascular segment develops, manufactures and markets proprietary medical devices used for circulatory support and vascular graft applications. The other medical equipment segment develops, manufactures and markets near-patient, whole-blood coagulation testing equipment and related disposables as well as premium quality, single-use skin incision devices. The group has operations in Europe and other countries.

Primary SIC and add'l.: 3845 3841

CIK No: 0000350907

Subsidiaries: International Technidyne Corporation

Officers: Gary F. Burbach/CEO, Pres./$2,441,332.00, Lawrence Cohen/Pres. - International Technidyne Corporation, ITC/$999,451.00, David A. Lehman/Sr. VP, General Counsel/$616,967.00

Owners: FMRCorp/12.82%, Howard E. Chase, George W. Holbrook, Gerhard F. Burbach, Insiders/4.64%, J. Donald Hill/1.75%, J. Daniel Cole, Cynthia L. Lucchese, Neil F. Dimick, David A. Lehman, Lawrence Cohen, Daniel M. Mulvena, William M. Hitchcock, Jeffrey W. Nelson, David V. Smith *(17 Owners included in Index)*

Financial Data: Fiscal Year End:12/31   Latest Annual Data: 12/30/2006

Year	Sales	Net Income
2006	$214,133,000	$3,973,000
2005	$201,712,000	$13,198,000

Curr. Assets:	$300,884,000	Curr. Liab.:	$31,591,000	P/E Ratio:	210.89
Plant, Equip.:	$28,906,000	Total Liab.:	$225,771,000	Indic. Yr. Divd.:	NA
Total Assets:	$573,918,000	Net Worth:	$348,147,000	Debt/ Equity:	NA

Thornburg Mortgage Inc

150 Washington Ave., Ste. 302, Santa Fe, NM, 87501; *PH:* 1-505-989-1900; *Fax:* 1-505-989-8156; *http://* www.thornburgmortgage.com; *Email:* ir@thornburgmortgage.com

General - Incorporation .... MD	**Stock**- Price on:12/24/2007 ....$27.1364
Employees...NA	Stock Exchange...NYSE
Auditor ....KPMG LLP	Ticker Symbol...NA
Stk Agt .... American Stock Transfer & Trust Co.	Outstanding Shares 120,830,000
Counsel..NA	E.P.S..$2.54
DUNS No. ....NA	Shareholders...NA

Business: The groups principal activities include originating, acquiring and retaining investment from residential housing markets. In the year 2006, the group acquired Adfitech. The group operates from the United States. The groups total assets in the year 2006 were $52,705,052 (thousands).

Primary SIC and add'l.: 6798

CIK No: 0000892535

Subsidiaries: Adfitech, Inc., Thornburg Mortgage Capital Resources, LLC, Thornburg Mortgage Depositor, L.L.C., Thornburg Mortgage Hedging Strategies, Inc., Thornburg Mortgage Home Loans, Inc.

Officers: Garrett Thornburg/Chmn., CEO/$882,982.00, Joseph H. Badal/Dir., Sr. Exec. VP, Chief Lending Officer/$402,540.00, Larry A. Goldstone/Dir., COO, Pres./$839,168.00, Clarence G. Simmons/Sr. CFO, Exec. VP/$106,898.00, Deborah J. Burns/Sr. VP - Securitization, Drew Ferguson/Cushman Amberg Communications, Mark Plasters/Exec. VP, Mgr. - National Sales, Caren Shiozake/CIO, Exec. VP, Patrick Feldman/Sr. VP, Assist. Sec., Mike McMinn/Sr. VP - National Broker Sales, Amy Pell/Sr. VP - Finance, Investor Relations Officer, Judy Balch/Sr. VP - Lending Partners, Brian Caesar/Sr. VP - Human Resources, Suzanne OLeary Lopez/Assist. VP - Public Relations, Paul Decoff/Sr. Exec. VP - Lending Operations, Product Development *(21 Officers included in Index)*

Directors: Garrett Thornburg/Chmn., CEO, Joseph H. Badal/Dir., Sr. Exec. VP, Chief Lending Officer, Owen M. Lopez/Dir., Francis I. Mullin/Dir., Stuart C. Sherman/Dir., Larry A. Goldstone/Dir., COO, Pres., Anne-Drue M. Anderson/Dir., David A. Ater/Dir., Eliot R. Cutler/Dir., Michael B. Jeffers/Dir., Ike Kalangis/Dir.

Owners: Garrett Thornburg, Larry A. Goldstone, Anne-Drue M. Anderson, Clarence G. Simmons, Ike Kalangis, Insiders/1.39%, Michael B. Jeffers, Joseph H. Badal, Owen M. Lopez, David A. Ater, Francis I. Mullin, Eliot R. Cutler

Financial Data: Fiscal Year End:12/31   Latest Annual Data: 12/31/2006

Year	Sales	Net Income
2006	$2,525,201,000	$297,697,000
2005	$1,538,068,000	$282,844,000
2004	$935,756,000	$232,564,000

Curr. Assets:	$590,240,000	Curr. Liab.:	$21,062,700,000	P/E Ratio:	10.68
Plant, Equip.:	NA	Total Liab.:	$50,327,980,000	Indic. Yr. Divd.:	$2.720
Total Assets:	$52,705,052,000	Net Worth:	$2,377,072,000	Debt/ Equity:	12.6716

THQ Inc

29903 Agoura Rd. , Ste No. 325, Agoura hills, CA, 91301; *PH:* 1-818-875-0000; *http://* www.thq.com; *Email:* admin@thq.com

General - Incorporation .... DE	**Stock**- Price on:12/24/2007 ....$32.03
Employees..2,000	Stock Exchange...NDQ
Auditor ....Deloitte & Touche LLP	Ticker Symbol...THQI
Stk Agt .... Computershare Investor Services LLC	Outstanding Shares 66,910,000
Counsel............... Sidley, Austin, Brown & Wood	E.P.S..$0.76
DUNS No. 61-572-7450	Shareholders...NA

Business: The group's principal activity is to develop, publish and distribute interactive entertainment software for use in hardware platforms in the home video game market. It currently develops and publishes titles for sony playstation 2, microsoft xbox, nintendo gamecube, nintendo game boy advance, pcs, wireless devices and online. The group's titles span most interactive entertainment software genres, including action, adventure, children's driving, fighting, puzzle, role-playing, simulation, sports and strategy. The original brands include red faction tm, mx 2002 featuring ricky carmichael, summoner tm, new legends and dark summit tm. It licenses intellectual property from world wrestling federation entertainment, nickelodeon, disney, sega, time warner, tetris company, mattel, lucasarts and others. The group has operations in the United States, the United Kingdom, Germany, France, Australia and Korea. On 03-May-2004, the group acquired relic entertainment inc.

Primary SIC and add'l.: 7375 7372

CIK No: 0000865570

Subsidiaries: Blue Tongue Entertainment Pty. Ltd., dba Relic Entertainment, Juice Games Limited, Locomotive Games, Inc., MINICK Holding AG (50% owned), Minick USA Inc. (75% owned), Rainbow Multimedia Group, Inc., T.HQ (Holdings) Limited, Thq (uk) Limited, THQ Asia Pacific Pty. Ltd., THQ Canada Inc., THQ Entertainment GmbH, THQ France S.a r.l., THQ Interactive Entertainment Espana, S.L., THQ International GmbH 27 Subsidiaries included in the Index

Officers: Brian J. Farrell/Chmn., CEO, Pres./$3,365,392.00, Bill Goodmen/Exec. VP - Human Resources, Administration, James M. Kennedy/Exec. VP - Business, Legal Affairs, Corp. Sec., Jack Sorensen/Exec. VP - Worldwide Studios/$1,842,004.00, Edward Zinser/CFO, Exec. VP/$1,937,914.00, Scott Guthrie/43/Sr. VP - North American Sales, Distribution

Directors: Brian J. Farrell/Chmn., CEO, Pres., Brian Dougherty/Dir., Lawrence Burstein/Dir., Henry T. Denero/Dir., Jeffrey Griffiths/Dir., James L. Whims/Dir., Gary Rieschel/Dir.

Owners: James M. Kennedy, Barclays Global Investors UK Holdings Limited/5.21%, Henry T. DeNero, Brian J. Farrell/1.57%, Brian P. Dougherty, Scott Guthrie, FMR Corp./6.16%, William W. Goodmen, Insiders/3.76%, Ian Curran, Lawrence Burstein, James Whims, Jeffrey W. Griffiths, Jack Sorensen, Gary E. Rieschel *(17 Owners included in Index)*

Financial Data: Fiscal Year End:03/31   Latest Annual Data: 3/31/2007

Year	Sales	Net Income
2007	$1,026,856,000	$68,038,000
2006	$806,560,000	$32,106,000
2005	$756,731,000	$62,790,000

Curr. Assets: $759,606,000 **Curr. Liab.:** $197,290,000 **P/E Ratio:** 30.80
Plant, Equip.: $45,095,000 **Total Liab.:** $244,584,000 **Indic. Yr. Divd.:** NA
Total Assets: $1,013,541,000 **Net Worth:** $768,957,000 **Debt/ Equity:** NA

Threshold Pharmaceuticals Inc

1300 Seaport Blvd., 5th Fl., Redwood City, CA, 94063; *PH:* 1-650-474-8200; *http://* www.thresholdpharm.com

General - Incorporation........DE | **Stock**- Price on:12/24/2007........$1.47
Employees........52 | Stock Exchange........NDQ
Auditor........PricewaterhouseCoopers LLP | Ticker Symbol........THLD
Stk Agt........Mellon Investor Services LLC | Outstanding Shares........37,330,000
Counsel........NA | E.P.S........-$1.39
DUNS No........NA | Shareholders........NA

Business: The groups principle activities include discovering and developing drugs. The group products sold under the trade name Metabolic Targeting. The group operates from the United States. The group's quarterly revenue for September 2007 was 0.36 millions of USD.

Primary SIC and add'l.: 7374 8731 8734 2834

CIK No: 0001183765

Subsidiaries: THLD Enterprises (UK)

Officers: Harold E. Selick/Dir., CEO, Michael K. Brawer/Interim Chief Medical Officer, Mark G. Matteucci/Sr. VP - Discovery Research, Kevin R. Kaster/48/Sr. VP - Corporate Development, Cathleen P. Davis/VP - Finance, Controller, John G. Curd/Pres., Chief Medical Officer, Stewart M. Kroll/VP - Biostatistics, Clinical Operations, Joel Fernandes/Sr. Dir. - Finance, Controller

Directors: Harold E. Selick/Dir., CEO, Bruce Cozadd/Dir., William A. Halter/Dir., Wilfred E. Jaeger/Dir., George G.C. Parker/Dir., Michael F. Powell/Dir., Alan B. Colowick/Member - Scientific Advisory Board, Theodore J. Lampidis/Member - Scientific Advisory Board, Marc Lippman/Member - Scientific Advisory Board, Alan P. Venook/Member - Scientific Advisory Board, Richard Wahl/Member - Scientific Advisory Board, David R. Hoffmann/Dir., George F. Tidmarsh/Member - Scientific Advisory Board

Owners: Harold E. Selick/3.20%, Kevin R. Kaster, Felix J. Baker and Julian C. Baker/8.70%, Michael F. Powell/2.40%, Three Arch Partners/6.50%, William A. Halter, David R. Hoffmann, Kevin C. Tang and entities affiliated with Tang Capital Partners/11.60%, Janet I. Swearson, Bruce C. Cozadd, George G.C. Parker, Wilfred E. Jaeger/6.60%, Insiders/13.50%, Perry Corp/9.90%, Cathleen P. Davis *(18 Owners included in Index)*

Financial Data: *Fiscal Year End:*12/31 *Latest Annual Data:* 12/31/2006

Year	Sales	Net Income
2006	$1,461,000	-$55,686,000
2005	$690,000	-$44,408,000
2004	NA	-$23,566,000

Curr. Assets: -$9,952,000 **Curr. Liab.:** NA
Plant, Equip.: NA **Total Liab.:** NA **Indic. Yr. Divd.:** NA
Total Assets: -$9,952,000 **Net Worth:** NA **Debt/ Equity:** 0.0279

Thunder Mountain Gold Inc

3605 E 16th Ave., Spokane, WA, 99223; *PH:* 1-775-738-9826; *http://* www.thundermountaingold.com

General - Incorporation........ID | **Stock**- Price on:12/24/2007........$0.16
Employees........1 | Stock Exchange........OTC
Auditor........Decoria, Maichel & Teague, P.S | Ticker Symbol........THMG
Stk Agt........TranSecurities International, Inc | Outstanding Shares........11,060,000
Counsel........NA | E.P.S........-$0.03
DUNS No........10-809-1182 | Shareholders........NA

Business: The group's principle activities include developing and exploring its property located in thunder mountain mining district in central Idaho. The company, through a joint venture with dewey mining own a total of 50-patented lode-mining claims (735.5 acres total) and 272 unpatented lode claims (5,245 acres total). During 2003, the company conducted minimal exploration for precious minerals. The company's interest ironside platinum group metals (pgm) prospect located in the goodsprings mining district, clark county, Nevada was dropped during 2003. The group operates from United States.

Primary SIC and add'l.: 1044 1041

CIK No: 0000711034

Officers: James E. Collord/Dir., CEO, Pres., Peter G. Parsley/Dir., VP, Mgr. - Exploration, Eric T. Jones/45/Dir., CFO, Sec., Treasurer

Directors: James E. Collord/Dir., CEO, Pres., Peter G. Parsley/Dir., VP, Mgr. - Exploration, Robin McRae/66/Dir., Edward D. Fileds/69/Dir., Eric T. Jones/45/Dir., CFO, Sec., Treasurer

Owners: Insiders/15.40%, Pete Parsley/2.79%, James E. Collord/9.22%, Edward Fields/0.04%, Robin S. McRae/2.44%, Eric Jones/0.06%

Financial Data: *Fiscal Year End:*12/31 *Latest Annual Data:* 12/31/2006

Year	Sales	Net Income
2006	NA	-$172,000
2005	NA	$1,856,000
2004	NA	-$92,000

Curr. Assets: $1,164,000 **Curr. Liab.:** $8,000
Plant, Equip.: $32,000 **Total Liab.:** $8,000 **Indic. Yr. Divd.:** NA
Total Assets: $1,197,000 **Net Worth:** $1,189,000 **Debt/ Equity:** NA

Thunderball Entertainment Inc

800 Nicollet Mall, Ste. 2690, Minneapolis, MN, 55402; *PH:* 1-612-338-8948

General - Incorporation........NV | **Stock**- Price on:12/24/2007........$0.3
Employees........3 | Stock Exchange........NA
Auditor........Virchow, Krause & Co. LLP | Ticker Symbol........NA
Stk Agt........NA | Outstanding Shares........9,450,000
Counsel........NA | E.P.S........NA
DUNS No........NA | Shareholders........NA

Business: The group's principle activity is to develop and distribute products in the redemption game market. The redemption game market allows patrons to play games, receive 'tickets' for playing the games and then redeem the tickets for prizes. The tickets utilized for these games include, gift certificates, phone cards and gas cards. These types of games are usually placed in bars and restaurants. The group operates from United States.

Primary SIC and add'l.: 9995

CIK No: 0001301046

Subsidiaries: Domino Entertainment, Inc.

TIB Financial Corp

599 9th St. N, Naples, FL, 34102; *PH:* 1-239-263-3344; *http://* www.tibbank.com

General - Incorporation........FL | **Stock**- Price on:12/24/2007........$13.35
Employees........337 | Stock Exchange........NDQ
Auditor........Crowe Chizek & Co. LLC | Ticker Symbol........TIBB
Stk Agt......American Stock Transfer & Trust Co. | Outstanding Shares........12,810,000
Counsel........Karl Beckheyer | E.P.S........NA
DUNS No........07-600-5644 | Shareholders........NA

Business: The group's principle activity is to provide commercial banking services through its wholly owned subsidiary, TIB Bank of the Keys. The group operates through the following segments: community banking, merchant bankcard, government guaranteed loans sales and servicing and insurance agency sales. The group attracts deposits from the public and uses such deposits to make real estate, business and consumer loans. It offers deposit services such as NOW, money market checking, demand, savings accounts, certificates of deposit and other time deposits. Its operations are in Monroe, Miami-Dade, Collier and Lee counties of Florida. The group operates through the main office and 14 branch offices located at Key Largo, Homestead, Naples and Bonita Springs, Florida. During 2003, the group discontinued the operations of Keys Insurance Agency, Inc. The group's quarterly revenue for Sep '07 was 0.49 millions of USD.

Primary SIC and add'l.: 6712 6022

CIK No: 0001013796

Subsidiaries: TIB Bank, TIBFL Statutory Trust I, TIBFL Statutory Trust II

Officers: Michael D. Carrigan/CEO, Pres. - TIB Bank/$264,332.00, Edward V. Lett/Dir., CEO, Pres./$900,063.00, Mack R. Wilcox/Dir., CEO, Pres. - Bank, Venice, Robert H. Magnuson/Exec. VP, Residential Mortgage Division Head - TIB Bank, Stephen J. Gilhooly/CFO, Exec. VP, Treasurer/$276,566.00, David P. Johnson/Exec. VP, Treasurer - TIB Bank/$257,922.00, Edward J. Crann/Exec. VP, Chief Administrative Officer - TIB Bank, Vicki Walker/Corp. Sec., Andrew D. Wallace/CIO, Exec. VP - TIB Bank, Alma R. Shuckhart/Sr. Exec. VP, Pres. - Southwest Florida Marketing - TIB Bank/$315,802.00, Millard J. Younkers/Exec. VP/$447,971.00

Directors: Edward V. Lett/Dir., CEO, Pres., Mack R. Wilcox/Dir., CEO, Pres. - Bank, Venice, David F. Voigt/Chmn., The Bank - Venice, Thomas J. Longe/Chmn., Robert J. Deboer/Dir. - Bank, Venice, Joseph P. Dalton/Dir. - Bank, Venice, Paul W. Moseley/Dir. - Bank, Venice, Steven W. MacRis/Dir. - Bank, Venice, Charles E. Johnson/Dir. - Bank, Venice, M. M. Dalton/Dir. - Bank, Venice, Marvin F. Schindler/Dir., Otis T. Wallace/Dir., James H. Brandt/Dir. - Bank, Venice, Paul O. Jones/Dir., John G. Parks/Dir. *(19 Directors included in Index)*

Owners: John G. Parks, Thomas J. Longe, Richard C. Bricker, Insiders/5.30%, Millard J. Younkers, Paul O. Jones, Otis T. Wallace, Kenneth W. Meeks/6.30%, Edward V. Lett/1.50%, Michael D. Carrigan, Alma R. Shuckhart, Stephen J. Gilhooly, Marvin F. Schindler, David P. Johnson

Financial Data: *Fiscal Year End:*12/31 *Latest Annual Data:* 06/30/2007

Year	Sales	Net Income
2007	NA	NA
2006	$91,509,000	$9,247,000
2005	$65,692,000	$11,824,000

Curr. Assets: $97,092,000 **Curr. Liab.:** $1,196,231,000
Plant, Equip.: $34,102,000 **Total Liab.:** $1,233,231,000 **Indic. Yr. Divd.:** $0.250
Total Assets: $1,319,093,000 **Net Worth:** $85,862,000 **Debt/ Equity:** 0.3744

Tibco Software Inc

3303 Hillview Ave., Palo Alto, CA, 94304; *PH:* 1-650-846-1000; *http://* www.tibco.com; *Email:* investor.relations@tibco.com

General - Incorporation........DE | **Stock**- Price on:12/24/2007........$8.75
Employees........1,597 | Stock Exchange........NDQ
Auditor........PricewaterhouseCoopers LLP | Ticker Symbol........TIBX
Stk Agt........Computershare Trust Co | Outstanding Shares........208,490,000
Counsel........Wilson Sonsini Goodrich & Rosati | E.P.S........$0.25
DUNS No........NA | Shareholders........NA

Business: The group's principal activity is to provide business integration and optimization software. The group develops and markets a suite of software products that enables businesses to link internal operations, business partners and customer channels through the real-time distribution of information. The group's trademarks are tibco, tibco software, tibco activeenterprise, tibco rendezvous, tibco smartsockets, tibco businessworks, tibco activeexchange, tibco activeportal and tibco businessfactor. The professional services provided by the group include a wide range of consulting services such as systems planning and design custom development and systems integration. The products are used by telecommunications, manufacturing, energy, financial services and Internet portal sectors. It has operations in the United States, Europe and Pacific Rim. On 13-Jul-2004, the group acquired tibco software inc.

Primary SIC and add'l.: 7372 7371

CIK No: 0001085280

Subsidiaries: 3301 Hillview Holdings Inc., TIBCO BPM

Officers: Vivek Ranadive/Chmn., CEO, Tom Laffey/Exec. VP - Products, Technology, Ram Menon/Exec. VP - Worldwide Marketing, Murat Sonmez/Exec. VP - Global Field Operations, Bill Hughes/Exec. VP, General Counsel, Sec., Christopher Ahlberg/Exec. VP, Pres. Spotfire Division, Bob Stefanski/Exec. VP - Human Resources, Organization Development, William R. Hughes/47/Exec. VP, General Counsel, Sec., Robert P. Stefanski/46/Exec. VP - Organizational Development, Human Resources

Directors: Vivek Ranadive/Chmn., CEO, Eric C.W. Dunn/Dir., Peter Job/Dir., Philip K. Wood/Dir., Bernard Bourigeaud/Dir., Naren Gupta/Dir.

Owners: Peter J. Job, William R. Hughes, Christopher Larsen, Insiders/7.50%, Bernard J. Bourigeaud, Vivek Y. Ranadiv/6.30%, Murat Sonmez, Narendra K. Gupta, Massachusetts Financial Services Company/5.20%, Eric C.W. Dunn, Philip K. Wood, Murray D. Rode

Financial Data: *Fiscal Year End:*11/30 *Latest Annual Data:* 11/30/2006

Year	Sales	Net Income
2006	$517,279,000	$72,864,000
2005	$445,910,000	$72,555,000
2004	$387,220,000	$44,920,000

Curr. Assets:	$724,410,000	**Curr. Liab.:**	$195,410,000	**P/E Ratio:**	30.17
Plant, Equip.:	$113,787,000	**Total Liab.:**	$280,352,000	**Indic. Yr. Divd.:**	NA
Total Assets:	$1,226,359,000	**Net Worth:**	$946,007,000	**Debt/ Equity:**	0.0493

Tidelands Bancshares Inc

875 Lowcountry Blvd., Mount Pleasant, SC, 29464; *PH:* 1-843-388-8433; *https://* www.tidelandsbank.com

General - Incorporation	SC	**Stock**- Price on:12/24/2007	$13.5
Employees	66	Stock Exchange	NDQ
Auditor	Elliott Davis, LLC	Ticker Symbol	TDBK
Stk Agt	Registrar & Transfer Co	Outstanding Shares	4,280,000
Counsel	NA	E.P.S	NA
DUNS No.	NA	Shareholders	NA

Business: The groups principal activity is to provide banking and financial services. The groups services include deposit boxes, travelers checks, direct deposit, United States Savings Bonds, and banking by mail. The products of the group include checking accounts, commercial accounts, savings accounts, Consumer Loans and Commercial Business Loans. The group operates from the United States.The assets of the group for the year 2006 were $336,572,084.

Primary SIC and add'l.: 6712 6021

CIK No: 0001178409

Subsidiaries: Tidelands Bank, Tidelands Statutory Trust

Officers: Robert E. Coffee/Dir., Pres., CEO - Tidelands Bank, John T. Parker/Dir. - Tidelands Bank, Michael W. Burrell/Dir. - Tidelands Bank, Robert H. Mathewes/Exec. VP - Sr. Commercial Lender, Tidelands Bank, Milon C. Smith/Exec. VP, Chief Credit Officer - Tidelands Bank, Thomas H. Lyles/Exec. VP, Chief Administrative Officer - Tidelands Bank, Michael W. Hambrick/Sr. VP, Treasurer - Tidelands Bank, James M. Bedsole/Sr. VP, Chief Risk Officer - Tidelands Bank, Kenneth M. Pickens/Sr. VP - Mid, Coast Executive, Tidelands Bank, Jeffrey A. Cooper/Sr. VP - South, Coast Executive, Tidelands Bank, James A. Kimbell/Sr. VP - North, Coast Executive, Tidelands Bank

Directors: Robert E. Coffee/Dir., Pres., CEO - Tidelands Bank, Barry I. Kalinsky/Chmn., John N. Cagle/Dir., Morris Kalinsky/Dir. - Tidelands Bank, Larry W. Tarleton/Dir. - Tidelands Bank, Alan D. Clemmons/Dir., Richard L. Granger/Dir. - Tidelands Bank, Paul J. Kerwin/Dir. - Tidelands Bank, Tanya D. Robinson/Dir. - Tidelands Bank

Owners: John N. Cagle/1.49%, Alan D. Clemmons/1.19%, Robert H. Mathewes, Paul J. Kerwin/1.18%, Alan W. Jackson, Larry W. Tarleton/0.20%, Michael W. Burrell/0.59%, Robert E. Coffee/2.53%, Service Capital Partners LP/6.33%, John T. Parker, Richard L. Granger/0.72%, Insiders/11.34%, Barry I. Kalinsky/0.48%, Financial Stocks Capital Partners LP/7.02%, Tanya D. Robinson/0.46% *(17 Owners included in Index)*

Financial Data: **Fiscal Year End:**12/31 **Latest Annual Data:** 3/31/2007

Year	Sales	Net Income
2007	$7,206,000	$176,000
2006	$6,271,000	$385,000
2005	$9,707,000	$40,000

Curr. Assets:	$7,334,000	**Curr. Liab.:**	$286,104,000	**P/E Ratio:**	37.50
Plant, Equip.:	$8,785,000	**Total Liab.:**	$294,752,000	**Indic. Yr. Divd.:**	NA
Total Assets:	$336,572,000	**Net Worth:**	$41,820,000	**Debt/ Equity:**	0.1955

Tidelands Oil & Gas Corp

1862 W Bitters Rd., Bldg. 1, San Antonio, TX, 78248; *PH:* 1-210-764-8642; *Fax:* 1-210-764-2930; *http://* www.tidelandsoilandgas.com; *Email:* info@tidelandsoilandgas.com

General - Incorporation	TX	**Stock**- Price on:12/24/2007	$0.15
Employees	14	Stock Exchange	OTC
Auditor	NA	Ticker Symbol	TIDE
Stk Agt	Signature Stock Transfer, Inc.	Outstanding Shares	102,630,000
Counsel	NA	E.P.S	-$0.163
DUNS No.	NA	Shareholders	NA

Business: The groups principle activity is gas and oil sales. The group operates from the United States. The group's quarterly revenue for Sep '07 was 0.39 millions of USD.

Primary SIC and add'l.: 1311 5171 4922 5984 5172 4923

CIK No: 0001088881

Officers: James B. Smith/Dir., CEO, CFO, Pres., Ahmed Karim/Dir., Sec., Robert Dowies/VP, Terry Mitchell/VP - Esperanza Energy LLC, Jason Jones/Pres. - Sonterra Energy Corporation, Julio Bastarrachea/Dir. General - Terranova Energia, S de RL de CV

Directors: James B. Smith/Dir., CEO, CFO, Pres., Ahmed Karim/Dir., Sec., Carl Hessel/Dir.

Financial Data: **Fiscal Year End:**12/31 **Latest Annual Data:** 12/31/2006

Year	Sales	Net Income
2006	$2,223,000	-$11,837,000
2005	$1,861,000	-$7,663,000
2004	$1,884,000	-$6,517,000

Curr. Assets:	$989,000	**Curr. Liab.:**	$4,100,000		
Plant, Equip.:	$12,364,000	**Total Liab.:**	$13,034,000	**Indic. Yr. Divd.:**	NA
Total Assets:	$15,187,000	**Net Worth:**	$2,153,000	**Debt/ Equity:**	1.1627

Tidewater Inc

601 Poydras St., Ste. 1900, New Orleans, LA, 70130; *PH:* 1-504-568-1010; *http://* www.tdw.com

General - Incorporation	DE	**Stock**- Price on:12/24/2007	$69.86
Employees	8,000	Stock Exchange	NYSE
Auditor	Deloitte & Touche LLP	Ticker Symbol	TDW
Stk Agt	Computershare Trust Co	Outstanding Shares	56,280,000
Counsel	NA	E.P.S	$6.34
DUNS No.	00-197-2496	Shareholders	NA

Business: The group's principal activities are to provide equipment and services to the offshore energy industry. The services support all phases of offshore exploration, development and production. The services include towing of and anchor-handling of mobile drilling rigs and equipment, transporting supplies and personnel. The group operates though a fleet of 569 vessels. The principal area of operations are U.S. Gulf of Mexico, the north sea, the Persian Gulf, the capsian sea and areas offshore Australia, Brazil, egypt, India, Indonesia, Malaysia, Mexico, trinidad, venezuela and west Africa.

Primary SIC and add'l.: 4492 4424 4412

CIK No: 0000098222

Subsidiaries: Al Wasl Marine LLC, Antilles Marine Service Limited, Candies Tidewater Joint Venture, LLC, Compania Martima de Magallanes Limitada, Divetide Limited, Equipo Mara, C.A., Equipo Zulia, C.A., Fairway Personnel Services Limited, Four Star Marine, Inc., Gulf Fleet Abu Dhabi, Gulf Fleet Middle East Limited, Gulf Fleet N.V., Gulf Fleet Supply Vessels, LLC, Hilliard Oil& Gas, Inc., Hornbeck Shipping Limited 94 Subsidiaries included in the Index

Officers: Dean E. Taylor/Chmn., CEO, Pres./$5,058,313.00, Joseph M. Bennett/Sr. VP, Principal Accounting Officer, Chief Investor Relations Officer, Keith J. Lousteau/CFO, Exec. VP, Treasurer/$2,062,242.00, Stephen W. Dick/Exec. VP/$1,950,605.00, Bruce D. Lundstrom/Sr. VP, General Counsel, Sec., Reg McNee/Sr. VP, Jeffrey M. Platt/Sr. VP/$1,328,591.00, Craig J. Demarest/VP, William R. Brown/VP, Gerard P. Kehoe/VP, Monty Orr/VP - International Sales, Chris Orth/VP - Domestic Sales, Nancy Morovich/Sr. VP

Directors: Dean E. Taylor/Chmn., CEO, Pres., James C. Day/Dir., William C. O'Malley/Dir., Richard A. Pattarozzi/65/Dir., Jon C. Madonna/Dir., Richard T. Du Moulin/Dir., Wayne J. Leonard/Dir., Jack E. Thompson/Dir., Nicholas J. Sutton/Dir., Jay M. Allison/Dir.

Owners: Cliffe F. Laborde, Richard A. Pattarozzi, Goldman Sachs Asset Management, L.P./7.16%, Richard T. du Moulin, Barclays Global Investors, NA./6.77%, Keith J. Lousteau, Dean E. Taylor, Jon C. Madonna, Insiders/2.33%, William C. OMalley, Jack E. Thompson, Jeffrey M. Platt, Paul W. Murrill, Stephen W. Dick, Arthur R. Carlson *(16 Owners included in Index)*

Financial Data: **Fiscal Year End:**03/31 **Latest Annual Data:** 3/31/2007

Year	Sales	Net Income
2007	$1,125,260,000	$356,646,000
2006	$877,617,000	$235,756,000
2005	$692,150,000	$101,339,000

Curr. Assets:	$731,549,000	**Curr. Liab.:**	$146,680,000	**P/E Ratio:**	10.52
Plant, Equip.:	$1,482,097,000	**Total Liab.:**	$763,288,000	**Indic. Yr. Divd.:**	$0.600
Total Assets:	$2,649,298,000	**Net Worth:**	$1,886,010,000	**Debt/ Equity:**	0.1695

Tiens Biotech Group (USA) Inc

No. 6, Yuanquan Rd. , Wuqing Development Area, New Tech Industrial Pk., Tianjin, 301700; *PH:* 86-22-8213-7915; *Fax:* 86-22-8213-7667; *http://* www.tiens-bio.com; *Email:* info@tiens-bio.com

General - Incorporation	DE	**Stock**- Price on:12/24/2007	$4.1399
Employees	1,342	Stock Exchange	AMEX
Auditor	Moore Stephens Wurth F & T LLP	Ticker Symbol	TBV
Stk Agt	Securities Transfer Corp	Outstanding Shares	71,330,000
Counsel	NA	E.P.S	$0.37
DUNS No.	NA	Shareholders	NA

Business: The groups principle activities include researching, developing, manufacturing and marketing nutrition supplements andpersonal careproducts. The groups products include tianshi garlic tablets and tianshi pine pollen powder capsules. The group operates from United States.

Primary SIC and add'l.: NA

CIK No: 0001168556

Subsidiaries: Tianjin Tianshi Biological Development Co. Ltd.

Officers: Jinyuan Li/Chmn., CEO, Pres., Ping Bai/CEO, Executive Assist.to Pres., Eric Doering/General Counsel, Wenjun Jiao/Dir., CFO, Sec., Yupeng Yan/Dir., Exec. VP

Directors: Jinyuan Li/Chmn., CEO, Pres., Howard R. Balloch/Dir., Gilbert D. Raker/Dir., Socorro Maria Quintero/Dir., Wenjun Jiao/Dir., CFO, Sec., Yupeng Yan/Dir., Exec. VP

Owners: Insiders/94.20%, Jinyuan Li/92.30%, Yupeng Yan, Wenjun Jiao

Financial Data: **Fiscal Year End:**12/31 **Latest Annual Data:** 12/31/2006

Year	Sales	Net Income
2006	$66,790,000	$26,292,000
2005	$68,689,000	$26,878,000
2004	$58,911,000	$27,438,000

Curr. Assets:	$85,054,000	**Curr. Liab.:**	$11,046,000	**P/E Ratio:**	11.31
Plant, Equip.:	$30,511,000	**Total Liab.:**	$29,327,000	**Indic. Yr. Divd.:**	NA
Total Assets:	$148,747,000	**Net Worth:**	$119,420,000	**Debt/ Equity:**	0.0502

Tier Technologies Inc

10780 Pk.ridge Blvd, 4th Fl., Reston, VA, 20191; *PH:* 1-571-382-1000; *http://* www.tier.com; *Email:* resume@tier.com

General - Incorporation	CA	**Stock**- Price on:12/24/2007	NA
Employees	NA	Stock Exchange	NDQ
Auditor	Mcgladrey & Pullen, LLP	Ticker Symbol	NA
Stk Agt	Mellon Investor Services LLC	Outstanding Shares	NA
Counsel	Cooley Godward LLP	E.P.S	-$0.16
DUNS No.	NA	Shareholders	NA

Business: The group's principal activity is to provide information technology consulting, application development and software engineering services to the companies worldwide. The services provided by the group include systems design and integration, transaction processing, business process reengineering and business process outsourcing. The services are provided primarily to the government, healthcare, financial services, insurance and utilities sectors. The group has operations in the United States and the United Kingdom. The group acquired official payments corporation in fiscal 2003 and e-procurement software solution and related assets of publicbuy.net llc and epos corporation in fiscal 2004.

Primary SIC and add'l.: 7372 7371 7379

CIK No: 0001045150

Subsidiaries: ADC Consultants PTY Limited, EPOS Corporation, Official Payments Corporation, Simsion Bowles & Associates, Tier Technologies (Australia) PTY Limited, Tier Technologies (United Kingdom), Inc.

Officers: Ronald L. Rossetti/Chmn., CEO, Pres., Michael A. Lawler/Sr. VP - Electronic Payment Processing, David E. Fountain/CFO, Todd F. Vucovich/Sr. VP - Packaged Software, Systems Integration, Deanne M. Tully/VP, General Counsel, Sec., Steven M. Beckerman/Sr. VP - Government Business Process Outsourcing, Kevin Connell/Sr. VP - Sales, Marketing, Klara Reilly/Contact

Directors: Ronald L. Rossetti/Chmn., CEO, Pres., Bruce Spector/Dir., Charles W. Berger/Dir., Morgan Guenther/Dir., Samuel Cabot/Dir., Michael T. Scott/Dir., John Delucca/Dir., Jim Stone/Dir.

Owners: Wellington Management Company, LLP/6.10%, Michael A. Lawler/1.10%, Dimensional Fund Advisors Inc./9.20%, Heartland Advisors, Inc/11.60%, Morgan P. Guenther, Todd F. Vucovich, Bruce R. Spector, Ronald L. Rossetti/2.20%, Giant Investment, LLC/9.40%, Kennedy Capital Management, Inc./8.60%, Charles W. Berger, Stephen V. Wade, Deanne M. Tully, Steven M. Beckerman, Wells Fargo & Company/11.00% *(20 Owners included in Index)*

Financial Data: *Fiscal Year End:*09/30 *Latest Annual Data:* 9/30/2006

Year	Sales	Net Income
2006	$168,731,000	-$9,451,000
2005	$150,601,000	$1,126,000
2004	$127,777,000	-$1,503,000

Curr. Assets:	$118,825,000	Curr. Liab.:	$28,710,000		
Plant, Equip.:	$3,745,000	Total Liab.:	$28,910,000	Indic. Yr. Divd.:	NA
Total Assets:	$166,424,000	Net Worth:	$137,514,000	Debt/ Equity:	NA

Tierone Corp

1235 N St., Lincoln, NE, 68501; *PH:* 1-402-475-0521; *http://* www.tieronebank.com; *Email:* investorrelations@tieronecorp.com

General - Incorporation	WI	Stock- Price on:12/24/2007	NA
Employees	850	Stock Exchange	NDQ
Auditor	KPMG LLP	Ticker Symbol	TONE
Stk Agt	American Stock Transfer & Trust Co.	Outstanding Shares	18,050,000
Counsel	NA	E.P.S	$1.99
DUNS No.	NA	Shareholders	NA

Business: The group's principal activities are to provide diversified financial services through its fifty-seven branch offices located in Nebraska, southwest Iowa and northern Kansas. It provides a variety of deposit accounts consisting of checking (both interest-bearing and non-interest-bearing), money market, savings, certificate accounts and individual retirement accounts. It originates loans comprising of commercial real estate and land loans, consumer loans, warehouse mortgage lines of credit and construction loans, one- to four-family residential mortgage loans, single-family mortgage loans and multi-family residential mortgage loans and commercial business loans. In addition, the group provides other products and services related to investment and insurance. On 30-Aug-2004, the group acquired united Nebraska financial co.

Primary SIC and add'l.: 6712 6035

CIK No: 0001170605

Subsidiaries: TierOne Bank., TierOne Investments and Insurance Inc., TMS Corporation of the Americas, United Farm & Ranch Management, Inc.

Officers: Gilbert G. Lundstrom/Chmn., CEO/$2,455,241.00, Eugene B. Witkowicz/Exec. VP, CFO, Corp. Sec./$544,687.00, Joyce Person Pocras/Dir., Independent Investor, Gale R. Furnas/Exec. VP, Dir. - Lending, Tierone Bank/$566,942.00, Edward J. Swotek/Sr. VP - Strategic Planning, Investor Relations Officer - Tierone Bank, Paula J. Luther/Sr. VP, Human Resources Officer - Tierone Bank, Charles W. Hoskins/Dir. - Financial Advisor, James A. Laphen/Dir., COO, Pres./$1,397,916.00, Roger R. Ludemann/Exec. VP, Dir. - Retail Banking, Tierone Bank, Larry L. Pfeil/Exec. VP, Dir. - Administration, Tierone Bank/$502,469.00, Craig E. Champion/Sr. VP, Deposit Services Mgr. - Tierone Bank, David L. Hartman/Sr. VP, Dir. - Real Estate Lending, Tierone Bank, Audrey M. Huelsdonk/Sr. VP - Loan Operations, Servicing Mgr. - Tierone Bank, David L. Kellogg/Sr. VP, Controller - Tierone Bank, Monte E. Olson/Sr. VP, Dir. - Marketing, Tierone Bank *(18 Officers included in Index)*

Directors: Gilbert G. Lundstrom/Chmn., CEO, Joyce Person Pocras/Dir., Independent Investor, Charles W. Hoskins/Dir. - Financial Advisor, Campbell R. McConnell/Dir., Ann Lindley Spence/Dir., James A. Laphen/Dir., COO, Pres.

Owners: Insiders/13.06%, Ann Lindley Spence, TierOne Corporation Employee Stock Ownership/9.87%, Gale R. Furnas, James A. Laphen/1.98%, Gilbert G. Lundstrom/4.67%, Private Capital Management, L.P./9.99%, Joyce Person Pocras, Charles W. Hoskins, Eugene B. Witkowicz, Campbell R. McConnell/1.03%, Larry L. Pfeil, Keeley Asset Management Corp./6.39%

Financial Data: *Fiscal Year End:*12/31 *Latest Annual Data:* 12/31/2006

Year	Sales	Net Income
2006	$253,374,000	$41,315,000
2005	$203,935,000	$32,832,000
2004	$148,901,000	$23,865,000

Curr. Assets:	$109,831,000	Curr. Liab.:	$3,050,683,000		
Plant, Equip.:	$39,821,000	Total Liab.:	$3,077,886,000	Indic. Yr. Divd.:	$0.320
Total Assets:	$3,431,169,000	Net Worth:	$353,283,000	Debt/ Equity:	NA

Tiffany & Co

727 Fifth Ave., New York, NY, 10022; *PH:* 1-212-230-5317; *http://* www.tiffany.com

General - Incorporation	DE	Stock- Price on:12/24/2007	$49.02
Employees	8,900	Stock Exchange	NYSE
Auditor	PricewaterhouseCoopers LLP	Ticker Symbol	TIF
Stk Agt	Mellon Investor Services LLC	Outstanding Shares	136,740,000
Counsel	NA	E.P.S	$2.34
DUNS No.	00-121-1473	Shareholders	NA

Business: The groups principle activities include product designing, manufacturing and retailing services. The groups products include jewellery, clocks, trophies, key holders, picture frames and desk accessories. The group operates from United States.

Primary SIC and add'l.: 5999 5094 5961 5944

CIK No: 0000098246

Subsidiaries: Dpfh Co.ltd., Eastpond Holding Inc., Iridesse Inc., L,s. Holding Inc., L.s Holding Inc., L.s. Wholesale Inc., Laurenton Diamonds Inc., Laurenton Diamonds Vietnam Ltd., Lct Insurance Co., Little Switzerland Inc., NHC LLC, Powbridge Portfolio Inc., Rand Precision Cut Diamond (pty) Ltd., Sindat Ltd., T. Risk Holding Inv. 37 Subsidiaries included in the Index

Officers: Michael J. Kowalski/56/Chmn., CEO/$7,036,945.00, James E. Quinn/56/Dir., Pres./$5,208,088.00, Beth O. Canavan/53/Exec. VP/$2,529,636.00, James N. Fernandez/52/CFO, Exec. VP/$3,510,679.00, Victoria Berger-Gross/52/Sr. VP - Human Resources, Patrick B. Dorsey/57/Sr. VP, General Counsel, Sec., Fernanda M. Kellogg/61/Sr. VP - Public Relations, Jon M. King/51/Sr. VP - Merchandising/$2,083,979.00, Caroline D. Naggiar/50/Sr. VP - Marketing, John S. Petterson/49/Sr. VP - Operations, Mark L. Aaron/VP - Investor Relations, Henry Iglesias/VP, Controller, Pamela H. Cloud/38/Sr. VP - Merchandising, Patrick F. McGuiness/42/Sr. VP - Finance

Directors: Michael J. Kowalski/56/Chmn., CEO, Rose Marie Bravo/57/Dir., William R. Chaney/75/Dir., Samuel L. Hayes/64/Dir., Abby F. Kohnstamm/54/Dir., Charles K. Marquis/65/Dir., Thomas J. Presby/68/Dir., James E. Quinn/56/Dir., Pres., William A. Shutzer/61/Dir., Gary E. Costley/64/Dir.

Owners: Thomas J. Presby, Rose Marie Bravo, Samuel L. Hayes, Beth O. Canavan, James N. Fernandez, Insiders/4.80%, Trian Fund Management, L.P./5.50%, William A. Shutzer, Michael J. Kowalski/1.20%, Jon M. King, William R. Chaney, James E. Quinn, Abby F. Kohnstamm, Charles K. Marquis, OppenheimerFunds, Inc./5.11%

Financial Data: *Fiscal Year End:*01/31 *Latest Annual Data:* 1/31/2007

Year	Sales	Net Income
2007	$2,648,321,000	$253,927,000
2006	$2,395,153,000	$254,655,000
2005	$2,204,831,000	$304,299,000

Curr. Assets:	$1,706,644,000	Curr. Liab.:	$452,671,000	P/E Ratio:	26.21
Plant, Equip.:	$932,389,000	Total Liab.:	$1,040,615,000	Indic. Yr. Divd.:	$0.600
Total Assets:	$2,845,510,000	Net Worth:	$1,804,895,000	Debt/ Equity:	0.2251

Tiger Ethanol Intl

6600, Trans-canada, Ste. 519, Pointe-claire, QC, H9R 4S2; *PH:* 1-514-771-3795

General - Incorporation	NV	Stock- Price on:12/24/2007	$3.09
Employees	NA	Stock Exchange	OTC
Auditor	Raymond Chabot Grant Thornton, LLP	Ticker Symbol	TGEI
Stk Agt	Pacific Stock Transfer Company	Outstanding Shares	NA
Counsel	NA	E.P.S	NA
DUNS No.	NA	Shareholders	NA

Business: The groups principal activity is to produce ethanol in the peoples Republic of China. The group operates from China.

Primary SIC and add'l.: 2860

CIK No: 0001307701

Officers: James Pak Chiu Leung/51/Dir., CEO, Pres., Michel St-Pierre/45/CFO, Claude Pellerin/38/Sec.

Directors: James Pak Chiu Leung/51/Dir., CEO, Pres., Arthur Rawl/65/Chmn., Guy Chevrette/46/Dir., Naim Kosaric/80/Dir.

Owners: Arthur Rawl, Capex Investements Limited/9.40%, Gallant Energy International Inc./31.40%, Guy Chevrette/4.20%, Claude Pellerin, Insiders/39.40%, Naim Kosaric, James Pak Chiu Leung/34.50%

Financial Data: *Fiscal Year End:*11/30 *Latest Annual Data:* 11/30/2006

Year	Sales	Net Income
2006	NA	-$512,000
2005	NA	-$59,000

Curr. Assets:	$1,394,000	Curr. Liab.:	$557,000		
Plant, Equip.:	NA	Total Liab.:	$614,000	Indic. Yr. Divd.:	NA
Total Assets:	$1,394,000	Net Worth:	$780,000	Debt/ Equity:	NA

TII Network Technologies Inc

1385 Akron St., Copiague, NY, 11726; *PH:* 1-888-844-4720; *http://* www.tii-industries.com

General - Incorporation	DE	Stock- Price on:12/24/2007	$2.79
Employees	99	Stock Exchange	NDQ
Auditor	KPMG LLP	Ticker Symbol	TIII
Stk Agt	Computershare Investor Services LLC	Outstanding Shares	12,640,000
Counsel	Leonard W. Suroff	E.P.S	$0.14
DUNS No.	04-764-7466	Shareholders	NA

Business: The group's principle activity is to design, produce and market overvoltage surge protection products principally for the telco industry. Overvoltage protectors are required by the national electric safety code to be installed in telephone lines in the subscriber's home or in offices to prevent injury to the users and damage to telecommunication equipment due to lighting and other hazardous electrical occurrences. The products are sold to the customers primarily through direct sales force, a network of distributors and sales representatives. The customers of the group include verizon corporation, tyco electronics corporation, corning cable systems llc and telco sales inc. The products are distributed in the United States, the Caribbean, south and Central America, Canada, the Pacific Rim and Europe. The group's quarterly revenue for Sep '07 was millions of USD.

Primary SIC and add'l.: 3669 3357 3613 3612

CIK No: 0000277928

Subsidiaries: U.S. based corporation, U.S. telephone operating companies

Officers: Kenneth A. Paladino/51/Dir., CEO, Pres./$465,414.00, Nisar A. Chaudhry/VP - Engineering, CTO/$206,159.00, Jennifer E. Katsch/32/VP - Finance, CFO, Sec., Treasurer/$38,004.00, Martin J. Pucher/40/Exec. VP/$440,001.00, Todd Shimirak/Western Region Sales Mgr., Jim Joling/Dir. - Business Development, Thomas R. McDonough/Accounting Executive, Kevin M. Stepp/Eastern Region Sales Mgr.

Directors: Kenneth A. Paladino/51/Dir., CEO, Pres., Charles H. House/Chmn., James R. Grover/Dir., Joseph C. Hogan/Dir., Mark T. Bradshaw/40/Dir., Lawrence M. Fodrowski/59/Dir., Bruce Barksdale/Dir., Dave Garwood/Dir.

Owners: Virginia M. Hall, Mark T. Bradshaw, Joseph C. Hogan/1.30%, Al Frank Asset Management, Inc./6.20%, Alfred J. Roach/9.00%, James R. Grover/1.40%, Bruce C. Barksdale/1.60%, Martin J. Pucher, Dave R. Garwood/2.20%, Nisar A. Chaudhry, David Foley, Lawrence M. Fodrowski, Insiders/12.10%, Charles H. House/1.00%, Timothy J. Roach/7.70% *(16 Owners included in Index)*

Financial Data: *Fiscal Year End:*06/24 *Latest Annual Data:* 12/31/2006

Year	Sales	Net Income
2006	$39,104,000	$2,681,000
2005	$26,796,000	$1,392,000

Curr. Assets:	$17,738,000	Curr. Liab.:	$5,296,000	P/E Ratio:	19.93
Plant, Equip.:	$4,229,000	Total Liab.:	$5,296,000	Indic. Yr. Divd.:	NA
Total Assets:	$22,149,000	Net Worth:	$16,853,000	Debt/ Equity:	NA

Tikcro Technologies Ltd

126 Yigal Allon St., Tel Aviv, 67443; *PH:* 972-3-694-8648; *Fax:* 972-3-694-8684; *http://* www.tikcro.com

General - Incorporation .... Israel
Employees .... NA
Auditor .... Kost Forer Gabbay & Kasierer
Stk Agt..... American Stock Transfer & Trust Co.
Counsel .... NA
DUNS No. .... NA

Stock- Price on:12/24/2007 .... $1.26
Stock Exchange .... OTC
Ticker Symbol .... TIKRF
Outstanding Shares .... NA
E.P.S .... NA
Shareholders .... NA

Business: The groups principle activities include designing, development and marketing of DSL chips used by manufacturers of telecommunications equipment. The group operates from United States.

Primary SIC and add'l.: 3669 4899

CIK No: 0001117095

Officers: Izhak Tamir/Chmn., Principal Executive Officer, Principal Financial Officer, Eric Paneth/Dir., Pres., Jeff Corbin/Investor Relations Officer, Lee Roth/Investor Relations Officer

Directors: Izhak Tamir/Chmn., Principal Executive Officer, Principal Financial Officer, Irit Gal/Dir., Eric Paneth/Dir., Pres., Yiftach Atir/Dir.

Owners: Eric Paneth/13.30%, Steven N. Bronson/14.60%, Eugene Oshinsky/5.90%, Izhak Tamir/13.30%

Financial Data: *Fiscal Year End:*12/31 *Latest Annual Data:* 12/31/2006

Year	Sales	Net Income
2006	NA	$210,000
2005	NA	$4,000
2004	NA	-$211,000

Curr. Assets:	$10,149,000	**Curr. Liab.:**	$182,000	**P/E Ratio:**	11.31
Plant, Equip.:	NA	**Total Liab.:**	$182,000	**Indic. Yr. Divd.:**	NA
Total Assets:	$10,149,000	**Net Worth:**	$9,967,000	**Debt/ Equity:**	NA

Tim Hortons Inc

4150 Tuller Rd., Unit 236, Dublin, OH, 43017; *PH:* 1-614-791-4200; *Fax:* 1-614-791-4235; *http://* www.timhortons.com; *Email:* customer_service@timhortons.com

General - Incorporation .... DE
Employees 500
Auditor .... PricewaterhouseCoopers LLP
Stk Agt..... Computershare Investor Services LLC
Counsel .... NA
DUNS No. .... NA

Stock- Price on:12/24/2007 .... $31.46
Stock Exchange .... NYSE
Ticker Symbol .... THI
Outstanding Shares 189,370,000
E.P.S .... NA
Shareholders .... NA

Business: The groups principle activities include franchising and operating restaurants. The group operates from the United States and Canada. The group's quarterly revenue for September 2007 was 490.54 millions of USD.

Primary SIC and add'l.: 5812

CIK No: 0001345111

Subsidiaries: Barhav Developments Limited, Bayers Centre Plaza Limited, Brigid No. 1 LP, Coffman No. 3 LP, Courtneys Alberta Co. Inc., Tartan No. 2 LP, TD US Finance Co., THD Nevada Inc., The TDL Group Co., The TDL Group Corp., The TDL Group No. 2, The TDL Group Partnership, The TDL Marks Corporation, The THD Group LLC*, The Tims National Advertising Program, Inc. 20 Subsidiaries included in the Index

Officers: Paul D. House/Chmn., CEO, Pres./$4,308,261.00, Cynthia J. Devine/CFO, Exec. VP/$1,243,589.00, David F. Clanachan/Exec. VP - Training, Operations Standards, Research, Development/$1,287,625.00, William A. Moir/Exec. VP - Marketing/$1,364,424.00, Donald B. Schroeder/Exec. VP - Administration/$1,691,962.00, Roland M. Walton/Exec. VP - Operations/$1,273,913.00, Scott Bonikowsky/VP - Investor Relations, Rachel Douglas/Dir. - Public Affairs

Directors: Paul D. House/Chmn., CEO, Pres., Ron Joyce/Co - Founder, Chmn. Emeritus, Michael J. Endres/Dir., Frank Iacobucci/Dir., David P. Lauer/65/Dir., David H. Lees/Dir., Randolph J. Lewis/58/Dir., Wayne C. Sales/Dir., Craig S. Miller/Dir., John Lederer/Dir., Shan M. Atkins/Dir.

Owners: Insiders, Randolph J. Lewis, Craig S. Miller, Frank Iacobucci, Roland M. Walton, Cynthia J. Devine, Wayne C. Sales, David H. Lees, Paul D. House, Michael J. Endres, David F. Clanachan, FMR Corp. and a joint filer/10.50%, AMVESCAP PLC and subsidiaries/5.60%, Donald B. Schroeder, David P. Lauer *(17 Owners included in Index)*

Financial Data: *Fiscal Year End:*12/31 *Latest Annual Data:* 12/31/2006

Year	Sales	Net Income
2006	$1,424,059,000	$222,759,000
2005	$1,338,266,000	$205,051,000

Curr. Assets:	$331,994,000	**Curr. Liab.:**	$236,140,000	**P/E Ratio:**	25.37
Plant, Equip.:	$999,288,000	**Total Liab.:**	$623,481,000	**Indic. Yr. Divd.:**	$0.250
Total Assets:	$1,497,373,000	**Net Worth:**	$873,892,000	**Debt/ Equity:**	NA

Tim Participacoes SA

Formerly: Tele Celular Sul Participacoes
Avenida Das Amricas, 3434-7 Andar, Rio De Janeiro, RJ, 22640-102; ;
http:// www.telecelularsul.com.br

General - Incorporation .... Brazil
Employees 9,500
Auditor .... Ernst & Young LLP
Stk Agt.......... Banco ABNAMRO Real S.A.
Counsel.......... Lara Cristina Ribeiro Piau Marques
DUNS No. .... NA

Stock- Price on:12/24/2007 .... $36.57
Stock Exchange .... NYSE
Ticker Symbol .... TSU
Outstanding Shares 232,970,000
E.P.S $30.00
Shareholders .... NA

Business: The group's principal activities are the management and exploration of private, public and industrial telephone services at both local and regional levels. The group provides services such as line leases, data transmission, cellular mobile telephone services, video text & telex transmission. The group's gsm technology covers 69 cities which represents 49% of its population. It has total 488 gsm stations, 806 radio base stations and 2055884 clients.

Primary SIC and add'l.: 4841 4822 4813 4812 3661

CIK No: 0001066116

Subsidiaries: Maxitel S.A., TIM Celular S.A., TIM Nordeste Telecomunicaces S.A, TIM Sul S.A.

Officers: Francesco Saverio Locati/Dir., COO, Mario Cesar Pereira De Araujo/Dir., CFO, Pres. - IRO ad Interim, Stefano De Angelis/CFO, Investor Relations Officer, Claudio Roberto De Argollo Bastos/Supply Officer, Orlando Lopes/Dir. - Human Resources, Lara Cristina Ribeiro Piau Marques/Legal Dir.

Directors: Giorgio Della Seta Ferrari Corbelli Greco/Chmn., Mario Cesar Pereira De Araujo/Dir., CFO, Pres. - IRO ad Interim, Ana Carla Abrao Costa/Dir., Sheila Periard Henrique/Dir., Josino De Almeida Fonseca/68/Dir., Antonio Carlos Rovai/Dir., Isaac Selim Sutton/Dir., Franco Bertone/Dir., Raffaelo Sevarese/Dir., Francesco Saverio Locati/Dir., COO, Patrizia Alfiero/Dir., Stefano Ciurli/Dir., Mario Girasole/Dir., Mailson Ferreira Da Nobrega/65/Dir.

Financial Data: *Fiscal Year End:*12/31 *Latest Annual Data:* 12/31/2006

Year	Sales	Net Income
2006	$4,766,579,000	-$102,173,000
2005	$1,243,799,000	$149,241,000
2004	$965,327,000	$87,830,000

Curr. Assets:	$2,032,125,000	**Curr. Liab.:**	$1,856,916,000		
Plant, Equip.:	$3,449,288,000	**Total Liab.:**	$2,868,267,000	**Indic. Yr. Divd.:**	$0.990
Total Assets:	$6,692,104,000	**Net Worth:**	$3,823,836,000	**Debt/ Equity:**	NA

Timberland Bancorp Inc

624 Simpson Ave., Hoquiam, WA, 98550; *PH:* 1-360-533-4747; *http://* www.timberlandbank.com; *Email:* customerservice@timberlandbank.com

General - Incorporation .... WA
Employees 236
Auditor .... McGladrey & Pullen LLP
Stk Agt ..... American Stock Transfer & Trust Co.
Counsel.......... Parker,Johnson & Parker Ps
DUNS No. 07-926-6631

Stock- Price on:12/24/2007 .... $18.24
Stock Exchange .... NDQ
Ticker Symbol .... TSBK
Outstanding Shares 7,250,000
E.P.S $1.17
Shareholders .... NA

Business: The group's principal activity is to provide a wide range of banking services which includes saving products and origination of real estate mortgage loans through thirteen branches. It acts as a holding company for timberland bank. It attracts deposits from the general public, and uses those funds, along with other borrowings, to provide primarily real estate loans to borrowers in western Washington, and to invest in investment securities and mortgage-backed securities. The group accepts deposits including money market deposit accounts, checking accounts, regular savings accounts and certificates of deposit. It originates loans secured by one-to-four family residential dwellings, including an emphasis on construction and land development loans, as well as multi-family and commercial real estate loans.

Primary SIC and add'l.: 6035 6712

CIK No: 0001046050

Subsidiaries: Timberland Service Corporation

Officers: Michael R. Sand/Dir., CEO, Pres., Dean J. Brydon/CFO, Sec. - Timberland Bancorp, Inc, Timberland Bank, Kathie M. Bailey/COO, Sr. VP - Timberland Bank, Timberland Bancorp, Inc, John Norawong/Sr. Management, Roger A. Johansen/Exec. VP, Chief Lending Officer - Timberland Bank, Robert A. Drugge/Exec. VP - Business Banking Division, Marci A. Basich/Sr. VP, Treasurer, Denise R. Burke/VP - Timberland Bank, Marketing Dir., Jonathan A. Fischer/VP - Timberland Bank, Compliance Officer, CRA Officer, Privacy Officer, Karin M. Fry/Assist. VP, Savings Officer - Timberland Bank, Patrick K. Horan/Sr. VP - Timberland Bank Business Banking Division, John G. Owens/VP - Timberland Bank, Branch Mgr. - Puyallup, WA, Marianne A. Price/VP - Timberland Bank, Human Resources Mgr., Sandra L. Sterling/VP - Timberland Bank, Data Processing Mgr., Janet L. Deegan/VP - Timberland Bank, Residential Loan Mgr.

Directors: Michael R. Sand/Dir., CEO, Pres., Clarence E. Hamre/Chmn., Andrea Clinton/Dir., James C. Mason/Dir., Jon C. Parker/Dir., Ronald A. Robbel/Dir., David A. Smith/Dir., Harold L. Warren/Dir.

Owners: Roger A. Johansen, Harold L. Warren, Timberland Bank Employee Stock Ownership/13.10%, Clarence E. Hamre/2.30%, Jon C. Parker, Dimensional Fund Advisors LP/8.70%, Michael R. Sand/2.20%, David A. Smith/1.00%, Ronald A. Robbel, John P. Norawong, Andrea M. Clinton, James C. Mason, Dean J. Brydon/1.10%, Insiders/10.20%, Robert A. Drugge

Financial Data: *Fiscal Year End:*09/30 *Latest Annual Data:* 09/30/2007

Year	Sales	Net Income
2007	$47,906,000	$8,163,000
2006	$41,696,000	$8,157,000
2005	$37,009,000	$6,618,000

Curr. Assets:	$25,695,000	**Curr. Liab.:**	$497,722,000		
Plant, Equip.:	$16,745,000	**Total Liab.:**	$497,722,000	**Indic. Yr. Divd.:**	$0.400
Total Assets:	$577,087,000	**Net Worth:**	$79,365,000	**Debt/ Equity:**	0.7033

Timberland Co

200 Domain Dr., Stratham, NH, 03885; *PH:* 1-603-772-9500; *Fax:* 1-603-773-1640; *https://* www.timberland.com; *Email:* investor_relations@timberland.com

General - Incorporation .... DE
Employees 6,300
Auditor .... Deloitte & Touche LLP
Stk Agt .... Computershare Investor Services LLC
Counsel.......... Ropes & Gray LLP
DUNS No. 06-675-4250

Stock- Price on:12/24/2007 .... $26.77
Stock Exchange .... NYSE
Ticker Symbol .... TBL
Outstanding Shares 62,040,000
E.P.S $1.67
Shareholders .... NA

Business: The group's principal activities are to design, engineer, market and distribute premium quality footwear, apparel and accessories products for men, women and children. The group's footwear products include casual, rugged casual, sandals, trek travel, outdoor recreation and boots. The apparel and accessories products include outerwear, sweaters, shirts, pants and shorts knits, tee-shirts, sweatpants and sweatshirts. It also manufactures watches, men's belts, day packs and travel gear, socks and legwear, gloves, sunglasses and ophthalmic frames, hats and caps and men's leather goods. The group sells products internationally through operating divisions in the United Kingdom, Italy, France, Germany, Spain, Japan, Hong Kong, Singapore, Taiwan, Malaysia and South Korea.

Primary SIC and add'l.: 2389 3144 2339 3021 3143 2329

CIK No: 0000814361

Subsidiaries: Component Footwear Dominicana, S.A., Les Vetements & Chaussures Timberland Inc., SmartWool Corporation, The Outdoor Footwear Company, The Recreational Footwear Company, The Recreational Footwear Company (Dominicana), S.A., The Timberland Company (Asia-Pacific) Pte. Ltd., The Timberland Finance Company, Timberland (Gibraltar) Holding Limited, Timberland (UK) Limited, Timberland Asia LLC, Timberland Aviation, Inc., Timberland Canada Co., Timberland Direct Sales, Inc., Timberland Espana, S.L. 40 Subsidiaries included in the Index

Officers: Jeffrey B. Swartz/Dir., CEO, Pres./$5,639,017.00, John Crimmins/CFO, Danette Wineberg/VP, General Counsel, Sec., Michael J. Harrison/Sr. VP, GM - International/$1,445,765.00, Kenneth P. Pucker/COO, Exec. VP/$5,963,603.00, Gary S. Smith/Sr. VP - Supply Chain/$1,205,796.00, Brian P. McKeon/Exec. VP - Finance, Administration/$1,501,255.00

Directors: Jeffrey B. Swartz/Dir., CEO, Pres., Sidney W. Swartz/Chmn., Bill Shore/Dir., Terdema L. Ussery/Dir., Ian W. Diery/Dir., Peter R. Moore/Dir., John A. Fitzsimmons/Dir., Irene M. Esteves/Dir., Edward W. Moneypenny/Dir., Kenneth T. Lombard/Dir., Virginia H. Kent/Dir.

Owners: Edward W. Moneypenny, Jeffrey B. Swartz/2.10%, Royce & Associates, LLC/6.20%, Kenneth T. Lombard, Insiders/8.90%, Gary S. Smith, Peter R. Moore, Jeffrey B. Swartz/3.10%, Harris Associates L.P./8.50%, Judith H. Swartz, MetLife Advisers, LLC/7.40%, FMR Corp./8.20%, Insiders/100.00%, Sidney W. Swartz/70.50%, Brian P. McKeon *(26 Owners included in Index)*

Financial Data: Fiscal Year End:12/31   Latest Annual Data: 12/31/2006

Year	Sales	Net Income
2006	$1,567,619,000	$101,205,000
2005	$1,565,681,000	$164,624,000
2004	$1,500,580,000	$152,693,000

Curr. Assets:	$648,771,000	**Curr. Liab.:**	$285,628,000
Plant, Equip.:	$94,640,000	**Total Liab.:**	$298,692,000	**Indic. Yr. Divd.:** NA
Total Assets:	$860,377,000	**Net Worth:**	$561,685,000	**Debt/ Equity:** NA

Timberline Resources Corp

5909 Far View Dr., Billings, MT, 59105; **PH:** 1-406-860-5525;
http:// www.timberline-resources.com; **Email:** info@timberline-resources.com

General - Incorporation	ID	Stock - Price on:12/24/2007	$4.2
Employees	NA	Stock Exchange	OTC
Auditor	Williams & Webster, P.S	Ticker Symbol	TBLC
Stk Agt	Columbia Stock Transfer Co	Outstanding Shares	20,080,000
Counsel	Thomas E. Boccieri	E.P.S.	-$0.18
DUNS No.	NA	Shareholders	NA

Business: The group's principle activity is to operate mineral exploration properties. Mineral exploration is essentially a research activity that does not produce a product. Successful exploration often results in increased project value that can be realized through the optioning or selling of the claimed site to larger companies. As such, we acquire properties, which we believe have potential to host economic concentrations of minerals, particularly gold, silver and copper. These acquisitions have and may take the form of unpatented mining claims on federal land, or leasing claims, or private property owned by others. The group perform basic geological work to identify specific drill targets on the properties, and then collect subsurface samples by drilling to confirm the presence of mineralization. We may enter into joint venture agreements with other companies to fund further exploration work. The group operates from United States.

Primary SIC and add'l.: 8748
CIK No: 0001288750

Officers: John Swallow/Chmn., CEO, Paul Dircksen/Dir., VP - Exploration, Thomas Gurkowski/66/Sec., Treasurer, Thomas E. Boccieri/Counsel, Michael P. Wilson/53/CFO
Directors: John Swallow/Chmn., CEO, Vance Thornsberry/Dir., Eric Klepfer/Dir., Paul Dircksen/Dir., VP - Exploration, Stephen Goss/Dir., Doug Kettle/Member - Advisory Board, David Deeds/Member - Advisory Board, Cassandra Mulligan/Member - Advisory Board
Owners: Randal Hardy, David Deeds, Paul Dircksen, Insiders, Douglas Kettle, John Swallow, Praetorian Capital Management LLC, Vance Thornsberry, Eric Klepfer

Financial Data: Fiscal Year End:09/30   Latest Annual Data: 9/30/2006

Year	Sales	Net Income
2006	$6,470,000	-$1,966,000
2005	NA	-$523,000

Curr. Assets:	$2,991,000	**Curr. Liab.:**	$3,907,000
Plant, Equip.:	$4,417,000	**Total Liab.:**	$5,131,000	**Indic. Yr. Divd.:** NA
Total Assets:	$10,595,000	**Net Worth:**	$5,464,000	**Debt/ Equity:** 0.1537

Time Lending California Inc

1580 N Batavia St., Ste. 2, Orange, CA, 92867; **PH:** 1-714-288-5901

General - Incorporation	NV	Stock - Price on:12/24/2007	$0.14
Employees	NA	Stock Exchange	OTC
Auditor	Jaspers & Hall, P.C	Ticker Symbol	TIML
Stk Agt	NA	Outstanding Shares	22,820,000
Counsel	NA	E.P.S.	$0.00
DUNS No.	NA	Shareholders	NA

Business: The groups principle activity is to provide real estate and mortgage products and services. The group operates through three divisions include Real estate sales, Mortgages and Direct mail marketing. The group operates from United States.

Primary SIC and add'l.: NA
CIK No: 0001137005

Subsidiaries: Interruption Television, Inc., Tenth Street Inc., Time Financial Services, Inc., Time Management Inc., Time Marketing Associates Inc.
Officers: Michael F. Pope/59/Dir., Pres., Philip C. La Puma/69/Dir., CFO, Sec., Treasurer
Directors: Victoria A. Pope/60/Dir., Michael F. Pope/59/Dir., Pres., Philip C. La Puma/69/Dir., CFO, Sec., Treasurer
Owners: Michael F. Pope/42.60%, Philip C. La Puma/42.60%

Financial Data: Fiscal Year End:06/30   Latest Annual Data: 6/30/2006

Year	Sales	Net Income
2006	$4,728,000	$1,000
2005	$4,479,000	-$88,000
2004	$3,345,000	-$5,000

Curr. Assets:	$533,000	**Curr. Liab.:**	$502,000
Plant, Equip.:	$24,000	**Total Liab.:**	$502,000	**Indic. Yr. Divd.:** NA
Total Assets:	$556,000	**Net Worth:**	$54,000	**Debt/ Equity:** NA

Time Warner Inc

One Time Warner Ctr, New York, NY, 10019; **PH:** 1-212-484-8000; *http://* www.timewarner.com

General - Incorporation	DE	Stock - Price on:12/24/2007	$21.66
Employees	92,700	Stock Exchange	NYSE
Auditor	Ernst & Young LLP	Ticker Symbol	TWX
Stk Agt	Chase Manhattan Bank	Outstanding Shares	3,790,000,000
Counsel	NA	E.P.S.	$1.33
DUNS No.	NA	Shareholders	NA

Business: The group's principle activity is to provide media and entertainment services including interactive services, cable systems, filmed entertainment, television networks and publishing. The group operates from United States.

Primary SIC and add'l.: 4833 7375 4841 2721 3651 7389 7319
CIK No: 0001105705

Subsidiaries: Advertising.com, Inc, America Online, Inc, American Television and Communications Corporation, AMSE France SAS, Aol (uk) Limited., AOL Asia Limited., AOL Canada, Inc, AOL Community, Inc, AOL Deutschland GmbH & Co. KG, AOL Deutschland Service Operations GmbH & Co. KG, AOL Enhanced Services LLC, AOL Europe Operations Limited, AOL Europe Sarl, AOL Europe Services Sarl., AOL France SNC. 160 Subsidiaries included in the Index
Officers: Glenn A. Britt/CEO, Pres. - Time Warner Cable, Bill Nelson/Chmn., CEO - Home Box Office, Robert K. Shaye/Co - Chmn., Co - CEO - New Line Cinema, Michael Lynne/Co - Chmn., Co - CEO - New Line Cinema, Ann S. Moore/Chmn., CEO - Time Inc, Philip I. Kent/Chmn., CEO - Turner Broadcasting System, Barry M. Meyer/Chmn., CEO - Warner Bros Entertainment, Randy Falco/Chmn., CEO - AOL, Richard D. Parsons/Chmn., CEO/$22,479,350.00, Patricia Fili-Krushel/Exec. VP - Administration/$3,879,847.00, Edward I. Adler/Exec. VP - Corporate Communications, Carol A. Melton/Exec. VP - Global Public Policy, Ann Brown/Sr. VP - Creative Strategy, Global Media Group, Wayne H. Pace/CFO, Exec. VP/$8,920,421.00, James E. Burtson/Sr. VP - Investor Relations *(137 Officers included in Index)*
Directors: Bill Nelson/Chmn., CEO - Home Box Office, Robert K. Shaye/Co - Chmn., Co - CEO - New Line Cinema, Michael Lynne/Co - Chmn., Co - CEO - New Line Cinema, Ann S. Moore/Chmn., CEO - Time Inc, Philip I. Kent/Chmn., CEO - Turner Broadcasting System, Barry M. Meyer/Chmn., CEO - Warner Bros Entertainment, Randy Falco/Chmn., CEO - AOL, Richard D. Parsons/Chmn., CEO, Ted Leonsis/Vice Chmn. Emeritus, AOL, Michael A. Miles/Dir., Mathias Dopfner/Dir., Deborah C. Wright/Dir., Jeffrey L. Bewkes/Dir., COO, Pres., James L. Barksdale/Dir., Stephen F. Bollenbach/Dir. *(21 Directors included in Index)*
Owners: AXA Financial, Inc./5.60%, Deborah C. Wright, Paul T. Cappuccio, Stephen F. Bollenbach, Insiders, Liberty Media Corporation/100.00%, Michael A. Miles, Richard D. Parsons, Robert C. Clark, Reuben Mark, Jeffrey L. Bewkes, Francis T. Vincent, Patricia Fili-Krushel, James L. Barksdale, Jessica P. Einhorn *(18 Owners included in Index)*

Financial Data: Fiscal Year End:12/31   Latest Annual Data: 12/31/2006

Year	Sales	Net Income
2006	$44,224,000,000	$6,552,000,000
2005	$43,652,000,000	$2,921,000,000
2004	$42,089,000,000	$3,364,000,000

Curr. Assets:	$10,851,000,000	**Curr. Liab.:**	$12,780,000,000	**P/E Ratio:** 13.97
Plant, Equip.:	$22,169,000,000	**Total Liab.:**	$70,980,000,000	**Indic. Yr. Divd.:** $0.250
Total Assets:	$131,669,000,000	**Net Worth:**	$60,389,000,000	**Debt/ Equity:** NA

Time Warner Telecom Inc

10475 Pk. Meadows Dr., Littleton, CO, 80124; **PH:** 1-303-566-1000; *http://* www.twtelecom.com; **Email:** ir@twtelecom.com

General - Incorporation	DE	Stock - Price on:12/24/2007	$19.9
Employees	2,784	Stock Exchange	NDQ
Auditor	Ernst & Young LLP	Ticker Symbol	TWTC
Stk Agt	Wells Fargo Shareowner Services	Outstanding Shares	144,710,000
Counsel	Shearman & Sterling LLP	E.P.S.	-$0.42
DUNS No.	01-950-6133	Shareholders	NA

Business: The group's principal activity is to provide telecommunication services in selected metropolitan areas in the United States. The services include dedicated Internet access, and local and long distance voice services. The services are provided to telecommunications-intensive businesses, long distance carriers, incumbent local exchange carriers, competitive local exchange carriers, wireless communications companies, Internet service providers, educational institutions, and governmental entities.

Primary SIC and add'l.: 4813
CIK No: 0001057758

Subsidiaries: Time Warner Telecom Holdings Inc
Officers: Larissa L. Herda/Chmn., CEO, Pres./$3,921,352.00, Paul B. Jones/Sr. VP, General Counsel - Regulatory Policy/$1,241,680.00, David J. Rayner/Sr. VP, Steve Hardardt/Sr. VP - Human Resources, Business Administration, Catherine A. Hemmer/Exec. VP - Corporate Operations, Engineering, Technology/$1,269,907.00, John T. Blount/Exec. VP - Field Operations/$2,419,254.00, Robert W. Gaskins/Sr. VP - Corporate Development, Strategy, Michael A. Rouleau/Sr. VP - Business Development, Strategy/$901,636.00, Jill R. Stuart/VP - Accounting, Finance, Chief Accounting Officer/$661,047.00, Julie A. Rich/Sr. VP - Human Resources, Business Administration, Mark A. Peters/CFO, Sr. VP/$1,192,127.00, Mark D. Hernandez/CIO, Sr. VP
Directors: Larissa L. Herda/Chmn., CEO, Pres., Gregory J. Attorri/49/Dir., Spencer B. Hays/63/Dir., Kevin W. Mooney/50/Dir., Roscoe C. Young/57/Dir., Kirby G. Pickle/51/Dir.
Owners: Catherine A. Hemmer, Gregory J. Attorri, T. Rowe Price Associates, Inc./9.30%, Columbia Wanger Asset Management, L.P./6.00%, Kevin W. Mooney, Larissa L. Herda/1.30%, Kirby G. Pickle, Spencer B. Hays, Paul B. Jones, FMR Corp./14.90%, Roscoe C. Young, Michael A. Rouleau, Insiders/1.90%, Jill R. Stuart, John T. Blount *(17 Owners included in Index)*

Financial Data: Fiscal Year End:12/31   Latest Annual Data: 12/31/2006

Year	Sales	Net Income
2006	$812,375,000	-$98,819,000
2005	$708,727,000	-$108,064,000
2004	$653,087,000	-$133,037,000

Curr. Assets:	$414,673,000	**Curr. Liab.:**	$284,506,000
Plant, Equip.:	$1,294,112,000	**Total Liab.:**	$1,700,589,000	**Indic. Yr. Divd.:** NA
Total Assets:	$2,253,237,000	**Net Worth:**	$552,648,000	**Debt/ Equity:** 2.4592

Timeline Inc

1700 Seventh Ave., Ste. 2100, Seattle, WA, 98101; **PH:** 1-206-357-8422; *http://* www.tmln.com

General - Incorporation	WA	Stock - Price on:12/24/2007	$0.55
Employees	1	Stock Exchange	OTC
Auditor	Williams & Webster, P.S	Ticker Symbol	TMLN
Stk Agt	American Stock Transfer & Trust Co.	Outstanding Shares	4,190,000
Counsel	Cairncross & Hempelmann	E.P.S.	-$0.31
DUNS No.	09-903-5529	Shareholders	NA

Business: The group's principal activities are to develop, market and support financial management. The group also offers full suite of budgeting and reporting software, event-based notification, application integration and process automation systems. The software products enable customers to automatically

access and distribute information. The main products of the group are timeline data server and timeline analyst. Timeline data server is a storehouse of financial and management reporting data. Timeline analyst is a database that enables the user to view, create and distribute reports. The other products consists of applications and tools that access and manipulate information. The group operates in the United States and Europe.

Primary SIC and add'l.: 7372 7379 9999

CIK No: 0000909736

Subsidiaries: Why Systems Incorporated, WorkWise Software, Inc.

Officers: Charles R. Osenbaugh/59/Dir., CEO, CFO, Pres., Treasurer/$62,630.00, Paula H. McGee/Sec.

Directors: Charles R. Osenbaugh/59/Dir., CEO, CFO, Pres., Treasurer, Donald K. Babcock/71/Dir., Kent L. Johnson/64/Dir., Terry Harvey/57/Dir.

Owners: Infinium Software, Inc./7.00%, Insiders/24.60%, Kent L. Johnson/1.30%, Donald K. Babcock/3.80%, Charles R. Osenbaugh/14.80%, Terry Harvey/5.30%

Financial Data: Fiscal Year End:03/31 Latest Annual Data: 03/31/2007

Year	Sales	Net Income
2007	NA	-$1,297,000
2006	$801,000	$2,303,000
2005	$3,531,000	-$476,000

Curr. Assets:	$1,225,000	Curr. Liab.:	$71,000	
Plant, Equip.:	$4,000	Total Liab.:	$71,000	Indic. Yr. Divd.: NA
Total Assets:	$2,552,000	Net Worth:	$2,481,000	Debt/ Equity: NA

Timken Co

1835 Dueber Ave. SW, Canton, OH, 44706; **PH:** 1-330-438-3000; **Fax:** 1-330-471-3810; http:// www.timken.com

General - Incorporation	OH	**Stock**- Price on:12/24/2007	$34.85
Employees	25,000	Stock Exchange	NYSE
Auditor	Ernst & Young LLP	Ticker Symbol	TKR
Stk Agt	First Chicago Trust Co Of New York	Outstanding Shares	94,890,000
Counsel	NA	E.P.S.	$2.17
DUNS No.	00-446-5100	Shareholders	NA

Business: The group's principle activity is to manufacture bearings, alloy, steel and related components. The groups products include Kelly Products, AdvanTec Process, Impact Steel, Microtec Steels, Solids, Seamless Steel Tubing, and Oilfield Applications. The groups services include fast track tubing warehouse, sales support and research and development. The groups servicing areas include bearings, automotive transmissions, engine crankshafts and aerospace. The group operates from United States, Europe and other countries.

Primary SIC and add'l.: 3562 3312 3317

CIK No: 0000098362

Subsidiaries: Australian Timken Proprietary, Limited, Bearing Inspection, Inc., British Timken Limited, EDC, Inc., HHC1, Inc., KILT Holdings, Inc., Latrobe Steel Company, MPB Corporation, MPB Export Corporation, Nadella SA, Nihon Timken K.K., OH&R Special Steels Company, Rail Bearing Service Corporation, The Timken Corporation, The Timken Service & Sales Co. 67 Subsidiaries included in the Index

Officers: James W. Griffith/Dir., CEO, Pres./$6,654,267.00, Debra L. Miller/Sr. VP - Communications, Community Affairs, Hans J. Sack/Pres. - Specialty Steel, Michael C. Arnold/Exec. VP, Pres. - Bearings, Power Transmission Group/$2,435,327.00, Scott A. Scherff/Corp. Sec., Assist. General Counsel, Jacqueline A. Dedo/Sr. VP - Innovation, Growth/$1,685,990.00, Salvatore J. Miraglia/Pres. - Steel, William R. Burkhart/Sr. VP, General Counsel, Mark J. Samolczyk/Sr. VP - Corporate Planning, Development, Donald L. Walker/Sr. VP - Human Resources, Organizational Advancement, Jon T. Elsasser/CIO, Sr. VP, Alastair R. Deane/Sr. VP - Technology, Glenn A. Eisenberg/Exec. VP - Finance, Administration/$2,490,795.00, Philip D. Fracassa/Sr. VP - Tax, Treasury, Ted J. Mihaila/Sr. VP, Controller (19 Officers included in Index)

Directors: James W. Griffith/Dir., CEO, Pres., Ward J. Timken/Chmn., John M. Timken/Dir., Jerry J. Jasinowski/Dir., John A. Luke/Dir., Robert W. Mahoney/Dir., John P. Reilly/Dir., Frank C. Sullivan/Dir., Joseph F. Toot/Dir., Phillip R. Cox/Dir., Jacqueline F. Woods/Dir., Joseph W. Ralston/Dir.

Owners: Jacqueline A. Dedo, Ward J. Timken/7.40%, John P. Reilly, Insiders/10.50%, Michael C. Arnold, Frank C. Sullivan, James W. Griffith, Phillip R. Cox, John M. Timken/1.70%, Jerry J. Jasinowski, Ward J. Timken/5.90%, Jacqueline F. Woods, Joseph W. Ralston, Robert W. Mahoney, John A. Luke (17 Owners included in Index)

Financial Data: Fiscal Year End:12/31 Latest Annual Data: 12/31/2006

Year	Sales	Net Income
2006	$4,973,365,000	$222,527,000
2005	$5,168,434,000	$260,281,000
2004	$4,513,671,000	$135,656,000

Curr. Assets:	$1,900,280,000	Curr. Liab.:	$835,569,000	P/E Ratio: 15.56
Plant, Equip.:	$1,601,559,000	Total Liab.:	$2,555,353,000	Indic. Yr. Divd.: $0.680
Total Assets:	$4,031,533,000	Net Worth:	$1,476,180,000	Debt/ Equity: 0.3396

Tirex Corp

PO Box 1000, 1307 Ste-Catherine St., Stratford, CT, 06614; **PH:** 1-203-522-3247; http:// www.tirex-tcs.com; **Email:** info@tirex-tcs.com

General - Incorporation	DE	**Stock**- Price on:12/24/2007	$0.0001
Employees	3	Stock Exchange	OTC
Auditor	Pinkham & Pinkham	Ticker Symbol	TXMC
Stk Agt	Continental Stock Transfer & Trust Co	Outstanding Shares	249,900,000
Counsel	NA	E.P.S.	NA
DUNS No.	80-226-9597	Shareholders	NA

Business: The group's principle activity is to develop and construct a system for the cryogenic disintegration and recycling of scrap tires; and intends to own and operate plants that will manufacture finished rubber products out of recycled rubber crumb. The group operates from United States.

Primary SIC and add'l.: 3559

CIK No: 0000823072

Subsidiaries: Tirex Canada, Tirex Canada R & D Inc

Officers: John L. Threshie/Chmn., CEO, Pres., Louis V. Muro/VP - Engineering, Dir., Mauro Gallo Rosso/Contact Person, Michael D.A Ash/Sec., Treasurer, Chief Financial, Accounting Officer, Lou Muro/VP - Engineering - Research & Development

Directors: John L. Threshie/Chmn., CEO, Pres., Louis V. Muro/VP - Engineering, Dir., Henry Meir/Dir.

Owners: John L. Threshie, Insiders/4.52%, Estate of Louis A. Sanzaro/6.52%, Louis V. Muro/17.00%, John L. Threshie/34.00%, Louis V. Muro/2.39%, Michael Ash/1.19%, Insiders/51.00%, Henry P. Meier/0.13%

Financial Data: Fiscal Year End:06/30 Latest Annual Data: 03/31/2007

Year	Sales	Net Income
2007	NA	-$105,000
2006	NA	-$221,000
2005	NA	-$577,000

Curr. Assets:	$94,000	Curr. Liab.:	$2,771,000	
Plant, Equip.:	$50,000	Total Liab.:	$5,417,000	Indic. Yr. Divd.: NA
Total Assets:	$233,000	Net Worth:	-$5,183,000	Debt/ Equity: NA

Tissera Inc

8 Maskit St., Herzliya, 46733; **PH:** 972-99561151; **Fax:** 972-99561152; http:// www.tissera.com; **Email:** info@tissera.com

General - Incorporation	WA	**Stock**- Price on:12/24/2007	$0.1
Employees	NA	Stock Exchange	OTC
Auditor	Ernst & Young Global-Kost	Ticker Symbol	TSSR
Stk Agt	First American Stock Transfer, Inc.	Outstanding Shares	NA
Counsel	NA	E.P.S.	NA
DUNS No.	NA	Shareholders	NA

Business: The groups principal activities include developing, testing and intending to commercialize solid organ transplantation therapies based on an approach employing organ specific precursor tissues. The group operates from the United States.

Primary SIC and add'l.: 8731

CIK No: 0001122573

Subsidiaries: Tissera Ltd.

Officers: Amos Eiran/Chmn., Acting CEO, Uri Elmaleh/61/VP - Research, Alex Werber/Controller, CFO

Directors: Amos Eiran/Chmn., Acting CEO, Yair Reisner/Chmn. - Scientific Advisory Board, Meir Segev/Dir., Robert G. Pico/Dir., Giuseppe Remuzzi/Member - Scientific Advisory Board, Abraham Shaked/Member - Scientific Advisory Board, Roy York Calne/Member - Scientific Advisory Board, Peretz Shmuel/67/Dir.

Owners: Alpha Capital Anstalt/6.62%, Peretz Shmuel, Uri Elmaleh, Yaron Sagi, Amos Eiran/4.86%, Meir Segev, Alex Werber, Insiders/5.38%, Robert G. Pico, Whalehaven Capital Fund Ltd./5.19%

Financial Data: Fiscal Year End:07/31 Latest Annual Data: 04/30/2007

Year	Sales	Net Income
2007	NA	-$395,000
2006	NA	-$533,000

Curr. Assets:	$1,129,000	Curr. Liab.:	$630,000	
Plant, Equip.:	$13,000	Total Liab.:	$674,000	Indic. Yr. Divd.: NA
Total Assets:	$1,180,000	Net Worth:	$506,000	Debt/ Equity: NA

Titan Global Holdings Inc

Formerly: Ventures-National Inc
1700 Jay Ell Dr., Ste. 200, Richardson, TX, 75081; **PH:** 1-972-470-9100

General - Incorporation	UT	**Stock**- Price on:12/24/2007	$1.1
Employees	176	Stock Exchange	NA
Auditor	KBA Group, LLP	Ticker Symbol	NA
Stk Agt	Continental Stock Transfer & Trust Co	Outstanding Shares	49,130,000
Counsel	NA	E.P.S.	-$0.03
DUNS No.	17-567-6824	Shareholders	NA

Business: The group's principle activity is to manufacture electronic components. The group operates from United States.

Primary SIC and add'l.: 5947

CIK No: 0000770471

Subsidiaries: Oblio Telecom, Inc., Titan PCB East, Titan PCB West

Officers: Kurt Jensen/CEO, Pres. - Oblio Telecom, Inc, Bryan Chance/CEO, Pres., Curtis Okumura/Dir., CEO, Pres. - Titan PCB, Inc, Sammy M. Jibrin/VP - Product Management, Oblio Telecom, Inc, Daniel Guimond/CFO, Controller, Radu Achiriloaie/COO - Oblio Telecom, Inc

Directors: Curtis Okumura/Dir., CEO, Pres. - Titan PCB, Inc, David M. Marks/Chmn., Stephen Saul Kennedy/Dir.

Owners: Crivello Group, LLC, Curtis Okumura, Kurt Jensen, Irrevocable Children's Trust, Insiders, Scott R. Hensell, David M. Marks, Farwell Equity Partners, LLP, Stephen S. Kennedy, Bryan Chance

Financial Data: Fiscal Year End:08/31 Latest Annual Data: 8/31/2006

Year	Sales	Net Income
2006	$109,802,000	-$5,114,000
2005	$22,779,000	-$4,351,000
2004	$16,367,000	-$7,402,000

Curr. Assets:	$19,693,000	Curr. Liab.:	$51,185,000	
Plant, Equip.:	$2,213,000	Total Liab.:	$51,558,000	Indic. Yr. Divd.: NA
Total Assets:	$52,004,000	Net Worth:	-$8,282,000	Debt/ Equity: NA

Titan International Inc

2701 Spruce St., Quincy, IL, 62301; **PH:** 1-856-786-1147; http:// www.titanintl.com

General - Incorporation	IL	**Stock**- Price on:12/24/2007	$32.53
Employees	2,700	Stock Exchange	NYSE
Auditor	PricewaterhouseCoopers LLP	Ticker Symbol	TWI
Stk Agt	Computershare Investor Services LLC	Outstanding Shares	26,940,000
Counsel	NA	E.P.S.	-$0.42
DUNS No.	10-319-8883	Shareholders	NA

Business: The group's principal activity is to manufacture off-highway wheels and tires for agricultural, earthmoving and construction and consumer equipment. The group operates in three segments based on customer markets: agricultural, earthmoving and construction and consumer markets.

Agricultural market consists of rims, wheels and tires manufactured for use on various agricultural and forestry equipment, including tractors, combines, skidders, plows, planters and irrigation equipment. Earthmoving and construction market consists of rims and wheels for earthmoving, mining, military and construction equipment, including skid steers, aerial lifts, cranes, graders and levelers, scrapers, self-propelled shovel loaders, load transporters, haul trucks and backhoe loaders. Consumer market consists of products for all terrain vehicle, turf, golf, and trailer applications. The group's markets include the United States, Europe, France, Germany, Italy and the United Kingdom.

Primary SIC and add'l.: 3011 3714 3312 3462

CIK No: 0000899751

Subsidiaries: Titan Luxembourg S.a.r.l., Titan Tire Corporation, Titan Tire Corporation of Freeport, Titan Tire Corporation of Natchez, Titan Tire Corporation of Texas, Titan Wheel Corporation of Illinois, Titan Wheel Corporation of Virginia

Officers: Maurice M. Taylor/63/Dir., CEO/$1,813,686.00, Ernest J. Rodia/64/COO, Exec. VP/$375,000.00, Kent W. Hackamack/VP - Finance, Treasurer, Corporate Controller/$386,476.00, David Kidd/Mgr. - Metal Powders Product, Charlotte Mietz/Contact - Operations, Vic Fante/Sales Engineer, Cheri T. Holley/60/VP, Sec., General Counsel/$386,476.00

Directors: Maurice M. Taylor/63/Dir., CEO, Richard M. Cashin/Dir., Erwin H. Billig/Dir., Anthony L. Soave/Dir., Albert J. Febbo/68/Dir., Mitchell I. Quain/Dir., Edward J. Campbell/Dir.

Owners: Luxor Capital Group, LP/5.10%, Richard M. Cashin/1.90%, Kent W. Hackamack, Erwin H. Billig, Wellington Management Company, LLP/6.30%, Jana Partners LLC/22.60%, Mitchell I. Quain/1.00%, Insiders/13.90%, Edward J. Campbell, Albert J. Febbo, Maurice M. Taylor/6.40%, Barclays Bank PLC/5.20%, Anthony L. Soave/3.60%, Ernest J. Rodia, Cheyne Capital Management (UK) LLP/5.40%

Financial Data: Fiscal Year End:12/31 **Latest Annual Data:** 12/31/2006

Year	Sales	Net Income
2006	$679,454,000	$5,144,000
2005	$470,133,000	$11,042,000
2004	$510,571,000	$11,107,000

Curr. Assets:	$309,933,000	Curr. Liab.:	$62,924,000		
Plant, Equip.:	$184,616,000	Total Liab.:	$397,949,000	Indic. Yr. Divd.:	$0.020
Total Assets:	$585,126,000	Net Worth:	$187,177,000	Debt/ Equity:	0.7089

Titan Pharmaceuticals Inc

400 Oyster Point Blvd, Ste 505, South San Francisco, CA, 94080; **PH:** 1-415-244-4990; **http://** www.titanpharm.com; **Email:** info@titanpharm.com

General - Incorporation	DE	Stock - Price on:12/24/2007	$2.05
Employees	38	Stock Exchange	AMEX
Auditor	Odenberg, Muranishi & Co. LLP	Ticker Symbol	TTP
Stk Agt	Continental Stock Transfer & Trust Co	Outstanding Shares	44,470,000
Counsel	Loeb & Loeb	E.P.S.	-$0.359
DUNS No.	80-718-2720	Shareholders	NA

Business: The group's principal activity is to develop proprietary therapeutics for the treatment of central nervous system (cns) disorders, cancer and cardiovascular disease. The product development programs of the group focus on large pharmaceutical markets with significant unmet medical needs and commercial potential. The group develops products independently and also in collaboration with companies like novartis pharma ag and schering ag and government sponsored clinical cooperative groups. The trademarks of the group are spheramine (R), pivanex (R), probuphine (R), ceavac (R), triab(R) , trigem(TM) and ccm tm. In Oct 2003, the group acquired developmental therapeutics inc.

Primary SIC and add'l.: 2836 8731

CIK No: 0000910267

Subsidiaries: Developmental Therapeutics, Inc., Ingenex, Inc

Officers: Marc Rubin/Dir., CEO, Pres., Louis R. Bucalo/Executive Chmn./$516,390.00, Sunil Bhonsle/Dir., Exec. VP, COO/$376,184.00, Robert E. Farrell/CFO, Exec. VP/$296,330.00

Directors: Marc Rubin/Dir., CEO, Pres., Louis R. Bucalo/Executive Chmn., Konrad M. Weis/Dir., Hubert Huckel/Dir., Eurelio Cavalier/Dir., Sunil Bhonsle/Dir., Exec. VP, COO, Victor J. Bauer/Dir., Ley S. Smith/Dir., David M. MacFarlane/Dir., Joachin-Friedrich Kapp/Dir.

Owners: Sunil Bhonsle/2.40%, Robert E. Farrell/1.20%, Hubert E. Huckel, Konrad M. Weis, Victor J. Bauer, Insiders/11.60%, Eurelio M. Cavalier, David M. MacFarlane, Louis R. Bucalo/5.30%, Joachim Friedrich Kapp, Ley S. Smith

Financial Data: Fiscal Year End:12/31 **Latest Annual Data:** 12/31/2006

Year	Sales	Net Income
2006	$32,000	-$15,737,000
2005	$89,000	-$22,462,000
2004	$31,000	-$26,004,000

Curr. Assets:	$14,219,000	Curr. Liab.:	$3,394,000		
Plant, Equip.:	$457,000	Total Liab.:	$4,635,000	Indic. Yr. Divd.:	NA
Total Assets:	$15,040,000	Net Worth:	$10,405,000	Debt/ Equity:	NA

Titan Technologies Inc

3206 Candelaria Rd. NE, Albuquerque, NM, 87107; **PH:** 1-505-884-0272; **http://** www.titantechnologiesinc.com; **Email:** titan@nmia.com

General - Incorporation	NM	Stock - Price on:12/24/2007	$0.21
Employees	4	Stock Exchange	OTC
Auditor	Stark Winter Schenkein & Co. LLP	Ticker Symbol	TITT
Stk Agt	Jersey Transfer & Trust Co	Outstanding Shares	45,600,000
Counsel	NA	E.P.S.	-$0.01
DUNS No.	14-648-4365	Shareholders	NA

Business: The group's principle activity is to develop technology for recycling of tires, electronic scrap and certain components of salvaged automobiles. The recycling technology of the company involves shredding the feed waste using conventional equipment and utilizes pyrolysis to recycle tires and other scrap material. Recycling of tires using the technology which results in production of oil similar in quality to fuel oil, scrap steel and carbon black. The pyrolysis is also utilized to recover hydrocarbons, carbon and metals from electronic scrap and automobile fluff. The company has also designed and built a fully operational mobile unit, which is used for research and development on plastics, oil recovery from oil soaked sand, the neutralization of poultry waste and other organic wastes. The group operates from United States.

Primary SIC and add'l.: 6794 7389

CIK No: 0000932144

Officers: Ronald L. Wilder/Dir., CEO, CFO, COO, Pres., Robert S. Simon/62/Sec., Corporate Counsel

Directors: Ronald L. Wilder/Dir., CEO, CFO, COO, Pres., Ronald E. Allred/61/Dir., Dana J. Finley/61/Dir.

Owners: Colonel Walter Long, Ret./5.58%, Insiders/2.27%, Cyrene Inman/5.34%, Ronald L. Wilder, Ronald E. Allred, Robert S. Simon, Dana J. Finley

Financial Data: Fiscal Year End:07/31 **Latest Annual Data:** 7/31/2006

Year	Sales	Net Income
2006	NA	-$428,000
2005	$180,000	-$110,000
2004	NA	-$333,000

Curr. Assets:	$35,000	Curr. Liab.:	$340,000		
Plant, Equip.:	$0	Total Liab.:	$340,000	Indic. Yr. Divd.:	NA
Total Assets:	$61,000	Net Worth:	-$279,000	Debt/ Equity:	NA

Titan Trading Analytics Inc

2nd Floor, 9735 42nd, Avenue, AB, T6E 5P8; **PH:** 1-780-438-1239; **Fax:** 1-780-438-1249; **http://** www.titantrading.com; **Email:** inquiries123@titantrading.com

General - Incorporation	AB	Stock - Price on:12/24/2007	$0.615
Employees	NA	Stock Exchange	OTC
Auditor	Collins Barrow Edmonton LLP	Ticker Symbol	TITAF
Stk Agt	Deloitte & Touche LLP	Outstanding Shares	NA
Counsel	NA	E.P.S.	NA
DUNS No.	NA	Shareholders	NA

Business: The group's principle activities include developing and marketing financial software systems for various futures trading applications, including currencies and stock futures. The group operates from United States.

Primary SIC and add'l.: 7372

CIK No: 0001076639

Subsidiaries: Titan Holdings USA, LLC, Titan Trading Corp, Titan Trading GP Inc, Titan Trading USA, LLC

Officers: Kenneth W. Powell/Dir., CEO, Pres., David Terk/35/CFO - Titan USA, Michael Gossland/Dir., CTO, Sec., Philip Carrozza/Dir. - US Trading Operations, Tony Robinson/Principal, Eric Davidson/Principal, Janet L. Gentry/Principal, Mark J. Van Dyke/Software Architect, Project Coordinator

Directors: Kenneth W. Powell/Dir., CEO, Pres., Michael Gossland/Dir., CTO, Sec., Robert Roddick/63/Dir.

Owners: Michael Gossland/7.09%, Robert F. Roddick/0.64%, Philip S. Carrozza/10.87%, David Terk/0.65%, Insiders/50.00%, Kenneth Powell/23.26%, Harold Elke/7.49%

Financial Data: Fiscal Year End:10/31 **Latest Annual Data:** 10/31/2006

Year	Sales	Net Income
2006	NA	-$3,219,000
2005	NA	-$1,142,000
2004	NA	-$376,000

Curr. Assets:	$351,000	Curr. Liab.:	$444,000	P/E Ratio:	21.78
Plant, Equip.:	$56,000	Total Liab.:	$444,000	Indic. Yr. Divd.:	NA
Total Assets:	$407,000	Net Worth:	-$38,000	Debt/ Equity:	NA

Titanium Group Ltd

3723 HAve.n Ave., Menlo Park, CA, 94025; **PH:** 1-650-368-8128; **http://** www.titanium-tech.com

General - Incorporation British Virgin Islands		Stock - Price on:12/24/2007	$0.24
Employees	NA	Stock Exchange	OTC
Auditor	Zhong Yi (hong Kong) C.P.A. Co. Ltd.	Ticker Symbol	TTNUF
Stk Agt	Computershare Trust Co	Outstanding Shares	NA
Counsel	NA	E.P.S.	NA
DUNS No.	NA	Shareholders	NA

Business: The groups principle activity is a software development company. Services of the group include primarily to biometrics Industry. In June 2005, the group acquired Titanium Technology Limited. Specific customers of the group include Xintec Enterprise (HK) Ltd, Xintec Information Technology (HK) Ltd. and ELM Computer Technologies Ltd. The group operates from the United States and Hong Kong.

Primary SIC and add'l.: 7373

CIK No: 0001338520

Subsidiaries: Titanium Technology Limited, Titanium Technology Shenzhen Co., Ltd

Officers: Jason Ma/CEO - Titanium Technology Limited, Johnny Ng/Chmn. - Titanium Technology Limited, Jing Li/Corporate VP, Pres. - China, Titanium Technology Limited, Humphrey Cheung/CTO, Dir. - Titanium Technology Limited, Billy Tang/COO, Dir. - Titanium Technology Limited, Patrick Lo/CIO - Titanium Technology Limited

Directors: Humphrey Cheung/CTO, Dir. - Titanium Technology Limited

Owners: Johnny Ng, Golden Mass Technologies Ltd., Humphrey Cheung, Jason Ma, Insiders, Billy Tang

Financial Data: Fiscal Year End:12/31 **Latest Annual Data:** 12/31/2006

Year	Sales	Net Income
2006	$2,521,000	-$427,000

Curr. Assets:	$862,000	Curr. Liab.:	$680,000		
Plant, Equip.:	$378,000	Total Liab.:	$680,000	Indic. Yr. Divd.:	NA
Total Assets:	$1,579,000	Net Worth:	$907,000	Debt/ Equity:	NA

Titanium Metals Corp

5430 LBJ Fwy., Ste. 1700, Dallas, TX, 75240; **PH:** 1-972-233-1700; **http://** www.timet.com; **Email:** corporate.denver@timet.com

General - Incorporation	DE	Stock - Price on:12/24/2007	$32.64
Employees	2,380	Stock Exchange	NYSE
Auditor	PricewaterhouseCoopers LLP	Ticker Symbol	TIE
Stk Agt	American Stock Transfer & Trust Co.	Outstanding Shares	161,980,000
Counsel	NA	E.P.S.	$1.74
DUNS No.	04-182-9318	Shareholders	NA

Business: The group's principal activities are to produce titanium sponge, melted products, mill products and industrial fabrications. The titanium sponge is the basic form of titanium metal, which is used in processed titanium products. The mill products of the group consist of titanium billet, bar, rod,

plate, sheet, strip, pipe and pipe fittings. The melted products of the group consists of ingot and slab which is the result of melting sponge and titanium scrap, either alone or with various other alloying elements. The group also markets other products, such as titanium tetrachloride and fabricated titanium assemblies. The production facilities of the group are located in the United States, United Kingdom, France & Italy.

Primary SIC and add'l.: 3356 3339 3369 3463

CIK No: 0001011657

Subsidiaries: Loterios SpA, MZI, LLC, Ti-Pro, LLC, TIMET Capital Trust I, TIMET Castings Corporation, TIMET Colorado Corporation, TIMET Europe Limited, TIMET Finance Management Company, TIMET Germany, GmbH, TIMET Millbury Corporation, TIMET Real Estate Corporation, TIMET Savoie, SA, Timet Uk (export) Limited, Timet Uk Limited, Titanium Hearth Technologies, Inc. 18 Subsidiaries included in the Index

Officers: Steven L. Watson/Vice Chmn., CEO/$653,440.00, Paul J. Zucconi/Dir., Consultant, Robert D. Graham/52/Exec. VP/$254,000.00, Bobby D. Obrien/50/CFO, Exec. VP/$402,300.00, Kelly D. Luttmer/44/VP, Dir. - Tax/$137,200.00, Scott E. Sullivan/39/VP, Controller/$338,921.00, A. Andrew R. Louis/Sec., Charles H. Entrekin/59/COO, Pres., James W. Brown/51/VP - Corporate Finance, Andrew B. Nace/43/VP, General Counsel, John A. St. Wrba/51/VP, Treasurer

Directors: Steven L. Watson/Vice Chmn., CEO, Harold C. Simmons/Chmn., Norman N. Green/Dir., Glenn R. Simmons/Dir., Paul J. Zucconi/Dir., Consultant, Keith R. Coogan/Dir., Thomas P. Stafford/Dir.

Owners: Glenn R. Simmons, Norman N. Green, NL Industries, Inc/1.40%, Insiders/52.10%, Steven L. Watson, Harold C. Simmons/3.20%, Annette C. Simmons/94.50%, Paul J. Zucconi, The Annette Simmons Grandchildrens Trust, Harold Simmons Foundation, Inc., Bruce P. Inglis, Keith R. Coogan, Annette C. Simmons/11.50%, Thomas P. Stafford, The Combined Master Retirement Trust/9.50% *(22 Owners included in Index)*

Financial Data: ***Fiscal Year End:***12/31 ***Latest Annual Data:*** 12/31/2006

Year	Sales	Net Income
2006	$1,183,168,000	$281,277,000
2005	$749,777,000	$155,945,000
2004	$501,828,000	$39,938,000

Curr. Assets:	$757,566,000	***Curr. Liab.:***	$211,131,000	***P/E Ratio:***	18.76
Plant, Equip.:	$329,836,000	***Total Liab.:***	$338,001,000	***Indic. Yr. Divd.:***	$0.080
Total Assets:	$1,216,873,000	***Net Worth:***	$878,872,000	***Debt/ Equity:***	NA

TiVo Inc

2160 Gold St., Alviso, CA, 95002; ***PH:*** 1-408-519-9100; ***http://*** www.tivo.com

General - Incorporation	DE	***Stock***- Price on:12/24/2007	$5.9
Employees	451	Stock Exchange	NDQ
Auditor	KPMG LLP	Ticker Symbol	TIVO
Stk Agt	Wells Fargo Bank, N.A.	Outstanding Shares	97,540,000
Counsel	NA	E.P.S.	-$0.46
DUNS No.	NA	Shareholders	NA

Business: The group's principal activity is to provide technology and services for digital video recorders (dvr's). Its subscription-based television service improves home entertainment by providing consumers with an easy way to record, watch and control television. The tivo service also offers the televisi on industry a platform for advertising, content delivery and audience research. The group's services relies on three key components: the tivo client software platform consists of all operational software required for tivo enabled dvr to deliver the tivo service properly and reliably. The tivo service infrastructure consists of a collection of server-side technologies developed and optimized by tivo to enable the ongoing operations of tivo services. The dvr hardware design provides the design to the contract manufacturer that produces tivo-branded dvr's. The products and services are licensed to and used by sony, philips, thomson multimedia, pioneer, toshiba and hughes.

Primary SIC and add'l.: 4841 7389

CIK No: 0001088825

Subsidiaries: STB Software DVR, LLC, TiVo Brands LLC, TiVo International, Inc., TiVo Intl. II, Inc

Officers: Thomas S. Rogers/Dir., CEO, Pres./$3,567,703.00, Mark A. Roberts/Sr. VP - Consumer Products - Operations/$860,637.00, Jim Barton/Tivo Co - Founder, CTO, Sr. VP/$810,915.00, Steve Sordello/Sr. VP, CFO/$451,454.00, Karen Bressner/Sr. VP - Advertising Sales, Cal Hoagland/Interim CFO, Clent Richardson/Chief Marketing Officer, Nancy Kato/Sr. VP - Human Resources, Matthew Zinn/Sr. VP, General Counsel, Chief Privacy Officer, Jeff Klugman/Sr. VP, GM - Service Provider, Advertising Engineering Division/$714,321.00, Joe Miller/Sr. VP - Consumer Sales, Distribution

Directors: Thomas S. Rogers/Dir., CEO, Pres., Michael Ramsay/58/Chmn., Joseph Uva/Dir., Charles B. Fruit/Dir., Jim Barton/Tivo Co - Founder, CTO, Sr. VP, Randy Komisar/Dir., Mark W. Perry/Dir., Jeff Hinson/Dir., Tom Wolzien/Dir., Geoffrey Y. Yang/Dir., David M. Zaslav/Dir.

Owners: Insiders/9.40%, Thomas Rogers/1.20%, Jeffrey Hinson, James Barton/1.00%, Mark Roberts, FMR Corp./13.60%, Geoffrey Y. Yang/2.60%, Steven Sordello, Mark Perry, Charles Fruit, Michael Ramsay/3.10%, Randy Komisar, Joseph Uva, Jeffrey Klugman, David Zaslav *(16 Owners included in Index)*

Financial Data: ***Fiscal Year End:***01/31 ***Latest Annual Data:*** 1/31/2007

Year	Sales	Net Income
2007	$258,589,000	-$47,754,000
2006	$195,925,000	-$34,398,000
2005	$172,055,000	-$79,842,000

Curr. Assets:	$182,457,000	***Curr. Liab.:***	$138,541,000		
Plant, Equip.:	$11,706,000	***Total Liab.:***	$194,954,000	***Indic. Yr. Divd.:***	NA
Total Assets:	$211,950,000	***Net Worth:***	$16,996,000	***Debt/ Equity:***	NA

Tix Corp

12001 Ventura Pl., Ste. 340, Studio City, CA, 91604; ***PH:*** 1-818-761-1002; ***Fax:*** 1-818-761-1072; ***http://*** www.tixcorp.com

General - Incorporation	DE	***Stock***- Price on:12/24/2007	$6
Employees	50	Stock Exchange	OTC
Auditor	Weinberg & Company, P.A.	Ticker Symbol	TIXC
Stk Agt	Continental Stock Transfer & Trust Co	Outstanding Shares	19,180,000
Counsel	NA	E.P.S.	$0.00
DUNS No.	NA	Shareholders	NA

Business: The groups principle activity is in the sale of tickets for Las Vegas shows at a discount to the original box office price, on the same day of the performance, from ticket booths located on the Las Vegas Strip. In December 2006, the group acquired Stand By Golf Las Vegas. The group's quarterly revenue for Sep '07 was 5.70 millions of USD.

Primary SIC and add'l.: 7999

CIK No: 0000925956

Subsidiaries: Tix4Tonight, LLC

Officers: Mitch Francis/Chmn., CEO, Kim Simon/COO, Matt Natalizio/CFO

Directors: Mitch Francis/Chmn., CEO, Sam Georges/62/Dir.

Owners: Joe Marsh/8.90%, Benjamin Frankel/2.40%, Mitch Francis/33.10%, Insiders/40.70%, Kimberly Simon/3.90%, Rick Kraniak/5.10%, Iqbal Ashraf/15.60%, Norman Feirstein/2.30%, Sam Georges

Financial Data: ***Fiscal Year End:***12/31 ***Latest Annual Data:*** 12/31/2006

Year	Sales	Net Income
2006	$5,388,000	$39,000
2005	$2,695,000	-$1,023,000
2004	$1,557,000	-$1,617,000

Curr. Assets:	$1,983,000	***Curr. Liab.:***	$1,939,000		
Plant, Equip.:	$499,000	***Total Liab.:***	$2,255,000	***Indic. Yr. Divd.:***	NA
Total Assets:	$2,632,000	***Net Worth:***	$378,000	***Debt/ Equity:***	NA

Tj Roasters Inc

4535 W Sahara Ave., Ste. 217, Las Vegas, NV, 89102; ***PH:*** 1-209-952-0535

General - Incorporation	NV	***Stock***- Price on:12/24/2007	NA
Employees	NA	Stock Exchange	NA
Auditor	NA	Ticker Symbol	NA
Stk Agt	NA	Outstanding Shares	NA
Counsel	NA	E.P.S.	NA
DUNS No.	NA	Shareholders	NA

Business: The group conducts a wholesale coffee operation, including blending, packaging, marketing and distributing coffees for sale under private labels as well as its own brands of specialty coffees. Our current sales are primarily to customers located in Mexico.

Primary SIC and add'l.: 6500

CIK No: 0001303421

TJX Companies Inc (The)

770 Cochituate Rd., Framingham, MA, 01701; ***PH:*** 1-508-390-1000; ***Fax:*** 1-508-390-2828; ***http://*** www.tjx.com

General - Incorporation	DE	***Stock***- Price on:12/24/2007	$28.05
Employees	125,000	Stock Exchange	NYSE
Auditor	PricewaterhouseCoopers LLP	Ticker Symbol	TJX
Stk Agt	Bank of New York	Outstanding Shares	454,870,000
Counsel	Ropes & Gray LLP	E.P.S.	$1.44
DUNS No.	00-695-5215	Shareholders	NA

Business: The group's principle activity is to provide off-price apparel and home fashions retailer services. Customers served by the group include off-price chains and middle-to upper-middle income shopper. The group operates from United States.

Primary SIC and add'l.: 5331 5621 5632 5611 5399 5719

CIK No: 0000109198

Subsidiaries: AJW Merchants Inc., AJW Realty of Fall River, Inc., AJW South Bend Merchants, Inc., AJW South Bend Realty Corp., Bob's Conn. Merchants, Inc., Bob's Stores Corp, Cochituate Realty, Inc., Concord Buying Group, Inc., H. G. Conn. Merchants, Inc., H.G. Brownsburg Realty Corp., H.G. Conn. Realty Corp., H.G. Indiana Distributors, Inc., H.G. Merchants, Inc., HomeGoods of Puerto Rico, Inc., HomeGoods, Inc. 73 Subsidiaries included in the Index

Officers: Carol Meyrowitz/54/Dir., CEO, Pres./$7,585,246.00, Arnold Barron/Sr. Exec. VP, Group Pres./$2,988,893.00, Jeffrey G. Naylor/Sr. Exec. VP, Chief Administrative, Business Development Officer/$2,562,049.00, Ann McCauley/Sec., Ernie Herrman/Sr. Exec. VP, Jerome R. Rossi/Sr. Exec. VP, Group Pres., Paul Sweetenham/Sr. Exec. VP, Group Pres. - Europe, Nirmal K. Tripathy/CFO, Exec. VP, Sherry Lang/VP - Investor, Public Relations

Directors: Carol Meyrowitz/54/Dir., CEO, Pres., Donald G. Campbell/Vice Chmn., Bernard Cammarata/68/Chmn., David A. Brandon/55/Dir., Willow B. Shire/60/Dir., Fletcher H. Wiley/65/Dir., Gail Deegan/Dir., Amy B. Lane/55/Dir., John F. O'Brien/65/Dir., Robert F. Shapiro/73/Dir., David T. Ching/55/Dir., Michael F. Hines/52/Dir.

Owners: Ruane, Cunniff & Goldfarb Inc./5.50%, Robert F. Shapiro, Arnold S. Barron, FMR Corp./5.20%, Fletcher H. Wiley, David A. Brandon, Carol Meyrowitz, Bernard Cammarata, John F. OBrien, Capital Research and Management Company/5.40%, Richard G. Lesser, Willow B. Shire, Amy B. Lane, Gail Deegan, Donald G. Campbell *(17 Owners included in Index)*

Financial Data: ***Fiscal Year End:***01/28 ***Latest Annual Data:*** 1/27/2007

Year	Sales	Net Income
2007	$17,404,637,000	$738,039,000
2006	$16,057,935,000	$690,423,000
2005	$14,913,483,000	$664,144,000

Curr. Assets:	$2,905,120,000	***Curr. Liab.:***	$2,204,112,000	***P/E Ratio:***	20.18
Plant, Equip.:	$1,861,127,000	***Total Liab.:***	$3,421,991,000	***Indic. Yr. Divd.:***	$0.360
Total Assets:	$5,075,473,000	***Net Worth:***	$1,653,482,000	***Debt/ Equity:***	0.3528

TLC Vision Corp

5280 Solar Dr., Ste. 100, Mississauga, ON, L4W 5M8; ***PH:*** 1-800-852-1033; ***http://*** www.tlcv.com; ***Email:*** tlc.info@tlcvision.com

General - Incorporation	NB	***Stock***- Price on:12/24/2007	$5.08
Employees	1,100	Stock Exchange	NDQ
Auditor	Ernst & Young LLP	Ticker Symbol	TLCV
Stk Agt	Ernest & Young LLP	Outstanding Shares	69,240,000
Counsel	NA	E.P.S.	$0.03
DUNS No.	25-221-8706	Shareholders	NA

Business: The group's principle activity is to provide laser vision correction services in North America. The group owns and manages eye care centers with a network of eye care doctors. The two segments of the group are refractive and other. The group provides laser vision correction of common refractive disorders such as myopia (nearsightedness), hyperopia (farsightedness) and astigmatism. Laser vision correction is an outpatient procedure which is designed to change the curvature of the cornea to reduce or eliminate a patient's reliance on eyeglasses or contact lenses. It operates in 62 eye care centers in the United States and 6 centers in Canada. the group's quarterly revenue for September 2007 was 70.67 millions of USD.

Primary SIC and add'l.: 8099 3851 3827 8069
CIK No: 0001010610
Subsidiaries: ADA Ambulatory Surgery Center LLC, American Eye Instruments, Inc., California Refractive LLC, Coastal Vision Laser Eye Centers, LLC, Cusa 2002 Investments, LLC, Dakota Dunes, LLC, Del Val ASC, LLC, Delaware Valley Vision Assoc. Group Practice, LLC, Eastern Oregon Regional Surgery Center, LLC, Huntsville Center for Advanced Cataract Surgery LLC, Laser Access of Indiana LLC, Laser Eye Care of California, LLC, Laser Eye Surgery, Inc., Laser Vision Center of Edina LLC, Laser Vision Centers, Inc. 94 Subsidiaries included in the Index
Officers: James C. Wachtman/Dir., CEO/$485,396.00, James J. Hyland/VP - Investor Relations, James B. Tiffany/Executive/$326,447.00, Michael F. McEnaney/Exec. VP, Chief Marketing Officer, Rikki Bradley/Exec. VP - Human Resources, Clinical Services, Quality Assurance, Henry Lynn/Exec. VP - Information Systems, Tlcvision, Steven P. Rasche/CFO/$282,621.00, Brian L. Andrew/General Counsel/$270,076.00
Directors: James C. Wachtman/Dir., CEO, Warren S. Rustand/Chmn., Thomas N. Davidson/Dir., Toby S. Wilt/Dir., Richard L. Lindstrom/Dir., Michael D. Depaolis/Dir., Elias Vamvakas/Dir.
Owners: S. N. Joffe & Joffe Foundation/7.70%, James C. Wachtman, Toby S. Wilt, Steven P. Rasche, Brian L. Andrew, Warren S. Rustand, James B. Tiffany, Sowood Capital/8.10%, Richard L. Lindstrom, William P. Leonard, Thomas N. Davidson, Insiders/6.20%, I.G. Investment/5.00%, Kensico Capital/6.30%, Michael D. DePaolis *(17 Owners included in Index)*
Financial Data: Fiscal Year End:12/31 Latest Annual Data: 12/31/2006

Year	Sales	Net Income
2006	$281,826,000	$11,519,000
2005	$260,025,000	$8,119,000
2004	$242,195,000	$43,708,000

Curr. Assets:	$80,871,000	Curr. Liab.:	$40,856,000	P/E Ratio:	169.33
Plant, Equip.:	$56,888,000	Total Liab.:	$75,003,000	Indic. Yr. Divd.:	NA
Total Assets:	$294,302,000	Net Worth:	$219,299,000	Debt/ Equity:	0.0664

TMS Inc

5811 Trenton Ave., Stillwater, OK, 74074; **PH:** 1-405-707-9060; *http://* www.tms-rep.com

General - Incorporation	OK	Stock- Price on:12/24/2007	NA
Employees	NA	Stock Exchange	NA
Auditor	KPMG LLP	Ticker Symbol	NA
Stk Agt	UMB Bank, N.A.	Outstanding Shares	NA
Counsel	NA	E.P.S	NA
DUNS No.	04-650-4411	Shareholders	NA

Business: The group's principle activities are to develop, design and distribute software tools and applications for document capture, image enhancement, image viewing and forms processing. The company also develops technologies to improve the overall process of scoring standardized tests in the educational marketplace. The company operates in two segments: component product technologies and assessment scoring technologies. The company's primary market include large corporations, original equipment manufacturers, value added resellers, systems integrators, branches of federal government, financial institutions, pharmaceutical companies, law firms, transportation and aerospace companies, private and public utilities and defense agencies. The group operates from United States.
Primary SIC and add'l.: 7372 7375 7379
CIK No: 0000835412
Subsidiaries: Pegasus Imaging Corporation
Officers: Joe Caruso/Sales Engineer - Northeast Ohio, Western Pennsylvania, West Virginia, Leroy Rothenberger/Sales Engineer - Southwest Ohio, Kentucky, Indiana, Michael Brown/Sales Engineer - Michigan

TMSF Holdings Inc

660 S Figueroa St., 9th Fl., Los Angeles, CA, 90017; **PH:** 1-213-234-2494; **Fax:** 1-213-234-2801; *http://* www.tmsfholdings.com

General - Incorporation	DE	Stock- Price on:12/24/2007	NA
Employees	NA	Stock Exchange	OTC
Auditor	Singer Lewak Greenbaum & Goldstein	Ticker Symbol	TMFZ
Stk Agt	Interwest Transfer Company, Inc.	Outstanding Shares	NA
Counsel	NA	E.P.S	NA
DUNS No.	NA	Shareholders	NA

Business: The group operates through its subsidiaries whose principal activities include wholesale division that soliciting business from mortgage brokers and a retail division that markets directly to general public. The group is a mortgage banker that originates, finances, and sells conforming and non conforming mortgage loans secured by single family residences. The group operates from the United States.
Primary SIC and add'l.: 6162
CIK No: 0001100125
Subsidiaries: CPV Limited, Inc., The Mortgage Store Financial, Inc, TMSF REIT, Inc
Officers: Raymond Eshaghian/Chmn., CEO, Pres., Sec., Daniel M. Rood/CFO
Directors: Raymond Eshaghian/Chmn., CEO, Pres., Sec., Wayne H. Snavely/Dir., Aaron M. Yashouafar/Dir., David A. Sklar/Dir.
Owners: Daniel Rood, Raymond Eshaghian/57.80%, Wayne H. Snavely/4.50%, Insiders/74.70%, Solayman Yashouafar/10.80%, Aaron M. Yashouafar/12.30%

Curr. Assets:	$164,368,000	Curr. Liab.:	$147,493,000
Plant, Equip.:	$880,000	Total Liab.:	$147,493,000	Indic. Yr. Divd.:	NA
Total Assets:	$165,779,000	Net Worth:	$18,286,000	Debt/ Equity:	NA

TMT Capital Corp

Formerly: Jane Butel Corp
1890 Kentucky Ave., Winter Park, FL, 32789; **PH:** 1-407-622-5999; *http://* www.janebutel.com

General - Incorporation	FL	Stock- Price on:12/24/2007	NA
Employees	10	Stock Exchange	OTC
Auditor	Jaspers & Hall, P.C	Ticker Symbol	TMTP
Stk Agt	Interwest Transfer Company, Inc.	Outstanding Shares	NA
Counsel	NA	E.P.S	-$0.15
DUNS No.	NA	Shareholders	NA

Business: The groups principle activity is to provide finance services to the beer brewing, real estate, and wireless communications industries. The group operates from United States.
Primary SIC and add'l.: 8748

CIK No: 0001204853
Subsidiaries: Bootie Beer Company
Officers: Charly McCue/48/Sec.
Owners: Charly McCue/0.39%, Bootie Beer Holdings, LLC/5.30%, The Torruella Family Trust, LLC/47.03%, Stephanie Stans Warren/1.56%, Stans Foundation/10.06%, Tyler Stans/1.56%, Steve & Susan E. Stans/7.57%, SICAV Placeuro Compatiment Global US Equities/7.57%, Mercatus & Partners Limited/7.57%
Financial Data: Fiscal Year End:06/30 Latest Annual Data: 12/31/2006

Year	Sales	Net Income
2006	NA	-$6,605,000
2005	$222,000	-$1,454,000

Curr. Assets:	$43,000	Curr. Liab.:	$6,557,000		
Plant, Equip.:	$53,000	Total Liab.:	$13,423,000	Indic. Yr. Divd.:	NA
Total Assets:	$127,000	Net Worth:	-$13,296,000	Debt/ Equity:	NA

TNMP

PO Box 2943, Fort Worth, TX, 76113; **PH:** 1-817-730-0099; *http://* www.tnpe.com

General - Incorporation	TX	Stock- Price on:12/24/2007	NA
Employees	NA	Stock Exchange	NA
Auditor	Deloitte & Touche LLP	Ticker Symbol	NA
Stk Agt	NA	Outstanding Shares	NA
Counsel	NA	E.P.S	NA
DUNS No.	11-335-1803	Shareholders	NA

Business: The group's principle activities include generating, purchasing, transmitting, distributing, and selling of electricity to customers in Texas and New Mexico. The group operates from United States.
Primary SIC and add'l.: 4911
CIK No: 0000741612
Subsidiaries: Facility Works, Inc., First Choice Power GP, LLC, First Choice Power Special Purpose, LP, First Choice Power, LP, First Choice Special Purpose GP, LLC, Texas Generating Company II, LLC, Texas Generating Company, L.P., Texas-New Mexico Power Company, TNP Operating Company
Officers: Allan Burke/Representative Liaison Mgr., Andrea Couch/Representative Liaison Representativeresentative, Pam Coleman/Sr. Billing Analyst, Debbie Fielding/Contact - Critical Care Eligibility, Nancy Harvey/Contact - Critical Care Eligibility, Alton Aars/Coordinator Regional Engineering, North Texas, Rex McDaniel/Coordinator Regional Engineering, South, West Texas, Frank Billman/Metering Supervisor, Evans Spanos/Industrial Accounting Representative, Jeff Buell/Media Contact, Valerie Smith/Media Contact

TNR Technical Inc

279 Douglas Ave., Ste 1112, Altamonte Springs, FL, 32714; **PH:** 1-407-682-4311; *http://* www.tnrtechnical.com; **Email:** wayne@tnrtechnical.com

General - Incorporation	NY	Stock- Price on:12/24/2007	$35
Employees	NA	Stock Exchange	OTC
Auditor	Cross, Fern&ez & Riley, LLP	Ticker Symbol	TNRK
Stk Agt	American Stock Transfer & Trust Co.	Outstanding Shares	NA
Counsel	NA	E.P.S	$2.63
DUNS No.	07-629-7043	Shareholders	NA

Business: The group's principle activities include designing, assembling and marketing primary and secondary batteries to a wide network of industrial markets. the company acts as a distributor of nickle-cadmium, alkaline, lithium and sealed lead-acid batteries manufactured by saft America, power-sonic battery, varta battery, enersys, duracell, renata, gp battery, eveready battery, sanyo energy and other companies. As an authorized distributor, the company purchases cells and assembles them into battery packs for general sale to industrial users and wholesalers. The company also designs and assembles battery packs to customer specifications. The company's batteries are used to supply power for medical instruments, tools, communication equipment and other electronic equipment. The group operates from United States.
Primary SIC and add'l.: 3691 5063
CIK No: 0000723615
Officers: Wayne Thaw/51/Chmn., CEO, Pres., Patrick Hoscoe/45/Dir., VP, Operations Mgr. - Company's West Coast
Directors: Wayne Thaw/51/Chmn., CEO, Pres., Anthony Guadagnino/61/Dir., Larry J. Kaczmarek/46/Dir., Jerrold Lazarus/76/Dir., Mitchell Thaw/52/Dir., Patrick Hoscoe/45/Dir., VP, Operations Mgr. - Company's West Coast
Owners: Hummingbird Value Funds/6.50%, Wayne Thaw/31.90%, Norman L. Thaw/18.50%, Insiders/58.00%, Patrick Hoscoe, Mitchell A. Thaw/7.70%
Financial Data: Fiscal Year End:06/30 Latest Annual Data: 6/30/2007

Year	Sales	Net Income
2007	$9,615,000	$844,000
2006	$9,724,000	$726,000
2005	$7,318,000	$534,000

Curr. Assets:	$5,301,000	Curr. Liab.:	$301,000	P/E Ratio:	12.82
Plant, Equip.:	$141,000	Total Liab.:	$320,000	Indic. Yr. Divd.:	$4.750
Total Assets:	$5,458,000	Net Worth:	$5,138,000	Debt/ Equity:	NA

TNS Inc

11480 Commerce Pk. Dr., Ste. 600, Reston, VA, 20191; **PH:** 1-703-453-8300; *http://* www.tnsi.com; **Email:** investorrelations@tnsi.com

General - Incorporation	DE	Stock- Price on:12/24/2007	$13.8
Employees	622	Stock Exchange	NYSE
Auditor	Ernst & Young LLP	Ticker Symbol	TNS
Stk Agt	American Stock Transfer & Trust CO.	Outstanding Shares	24,210,000
Counsel	NA	E.P.S	-$0.37
DUNS No.	NA	Shareholders	NA

Business: The group's principle activity is to provide data communications services to processors of credit card, debit card and ATM transactions. The group operates through four segments: Point-of-Services Division, Telecom Services Division, Financial Services Division and International Service Division. The group operates in the United States and increasingly to international customers in 27 countries, including Canada and countries in Europe, Latin America and the Asia-Pacific region. The group's quarterly revenue for Sep '07 was 84.54 millions of USD.

Primary SIC and add'l.: 4899 4813

CIK No: 0001268671

Subsidiaries: TNS Transline, LLC, Transaction Network Services, Inc

Officers: Henry H. Graham/57/Dir., CEO, Alan R. Schwartz/Sr. VP, GM - Financial Services Division, Michael Q. Keegan/COO, Dennis L. Randolph/Exec. VP, CFO, Treasurer, Raymond Low/Pres., Edward C. O'Brien/60/Sr. VP, Corporate Controller, Mark G. Cole/Exec. VP - Network Operations, Scott E. Ziegler/Sr. VP, Chief Systems Officer, James T. McLaughlin/Exec. VP, General Counsel, Sec., Kent M. Phillips/Sr. VP - GM - POS Division

Directors: Henry H. Graham/57/Dir., CEO, John V. Sponyoe/69/Non Exec. Chmn., Stephen X. Graham/Dir., John B. Benton/Dir., Jay E. Ricks/Dir.

Owners: Shamrock Group/6.90%, Tennenbaum Group/7.00%, John B. Benton, Alan R. Schwartz, Michael Q. Keegan, Federated Investors Group/6.90%, Henry H. Graham/1.20%, Insiders/2.70%, Elliott Group/6.60%, Raymond Low, Stephen X. Graham, John V. Sponyoe, Jay E. Ricks, Philip C. Timon/14.50%, Artisan Group/6.90% *(16 Owners included in Index)*

Financial Data: Fiscal Year End:12/31 Latest Annual Data: 12/31/2006

Year	Sales	Net Income
2006	$286,160,000	-$9,896,000
2005	$258,940,000	$5,766,000
2004	$249,112,000	$4,984,000

Curr. Assets:	$100,345,000	Curr. Liab.:	$68,516,000		
Plant, Equip.:	$58,376,000	Total Liab.:	$202,412,000	Indic. Yr. Divd.:	NA
Total Assets:	$381,677,000	Net Worth:	$179,265,000	Debt/ Equity:	2.7644

TNT N.V.

Formerly: TPG

41-63 Neptunusstraat, Hoofddorp, 2132 JA; ; *http://* www.tnt.com

General - Incorporation .... Netherlands	Stock - Price on:12/24/2007 .... $41.8
Employees 92,973	Stock Exchange .... NA
Auditor ....PricewaterhouseCoopers Accountants	Ticker Symbol .... NA
Stk Agt .... NA	Outstanding Shares 388,800,000
Counsel .... NA	E.P.S. .... NA
DUNS No. 40-227-0685	Shareholders .... NA

Business: The groups principle activity is to provides business and consumers worldwide with a range of services for their express delivery and mail needs. the group's services include collection, storage, sorting, transport and distribution of a variety of items for its customers within specific timeframes, and related data and document management services. In March 2007, the Company completed the acquisition of Hoau, a transporter of freight and packages in China. The group operates from United States.

Primary SIC and add'l.: 4311 4225 4212 4214 4213

CIK No: 0001062573

Subsidiaries: G3 Worldwide Mail N.V., Royal Mail Investments Limited, Royal TNT Post B.V.

Officers: Peter M. Bakker/47/Dir., CEO, Harry M. Koorstra/57/MD, James McCormac/MD, Roger Corcoran/MD, Rob Van Den Helder/MD, Michael Drake/MD, Eric Jacquemet/45/MD, Donald Pilz/45/MD, Marie-Christine Lombard/50/Dir., MD, Mark Gunton/MD, Pieter Schaffels/Dir. - Media Relations, Daphne Andriesse/Sr. Press Officer, Cyrille Gibot/Sr. Press Officer, Marc Potma/Mgr. - Communications Network, Toby Ellson/Mgr. - Media Relations, Public Relations *(32 Officers included in Index)*

Directors: Peter M. Bakker/47/Dir., CEO, J. H.M Hommen/65/Chmn. - Supervisory Board, J. G. Haars/Dir., Robert R.J.N. Abrahamsen/70/Member - Supervisory Board, Shemaya S. Levy/61/Member - Supervisory Board, R. Dahan/67/Member - Supervisory Board, R. W.H. Stomberg/68/Member - Supervisory Board, Wim Kok/70/Member - Supervisory Board, Giovanna Kampouri Monnas/53/Member - Supervisory Board, Henk C.H. Van Dalen/56/Dir., CFO, R. King/68/Member - Supervisory Board, Marie-Christine Lombard/50/Dir., MD, M. Harris/42/Member - Supervisory Board

TODCO

2000 W Sam Houston Pkwy S, Ste. 800, Houston, TX, 77042; *PH:* 1-713-278-6000; *http://* www.todco.com

General - Incorporation .... DE	Stock - Price on:12/24/2007 .... $49.64
Employees 3,030	Stock Exchange .... NA
Auditor .... Ernst & Young LLP	Ticker Symbol .... NA
Stk Agt .... Bank of New York	Outstanding Shares 57,770,000
Counsel .... NA	E.P.S. $1.48
DUNS No. .... NA	Shareholders .... NA

Business: The group's principle activities are carried out through two segments: international and U.S. Floater contract drilling services and gulf of Mexico shallow and inland water. The international and U.S. Floater contract drilling services segment consists of high-specification floaters, other floaters, non-U.S. Jackups, other mobile offshore and land drilling units, other assets used in support of offshore drilling activities and other offshore support services. The gulf of Mexico shallow and inland water segment consists of jackup and submersible drilling rigs and inland drilling barges and a platform rig located in the U.S. Gulf of Mexico and trinidad, as well as land and lake barge drilling units located in venezuela.

Primary SIC and add'l.: 1381

CIK No: 0001210697

Subsidiaries: Cliffs Drilling (Barbados) Holdings SRL, Cliffs Drilling (Barbados) SRL, Cliffs Drilling Company, Cliffs Drilling Trinidad LLC, Cliffs Drilling Trinidad Offshore Limited, Perforaciones Venrig S.A., Servicios TODCO S. de R.L. de C.V., The Offshore Drilling Company, TODCO Americas Inc., TODCO International Inc., TODCO Management Services Inc. LLC, TODCO Mexico Inc., TODCO Trinidad Ltd.

Officers: Jan Rask/Dir., CEO, Pres., Dale W. Wilhelm/CFO, VP, Mark Skiles/National Accounting Mgr., Dennis J. Lubojacky/Principal Accounting Officer, Controller, Joanne Scott/Customer Service Representative, Keith Frank/Order Detailer, Skip Phillips/General Sales Mgr., Ken Hall/National Fleet Mgr., Jay Sloan/Customer Service Mgr., Edie Baker/Customer Service Representative, Wendy Parsell/Customer Service Representative, Carol King/Customer Service Representative, Juan Camacho/Customer Service Representative Swing Doors

Directors: Jan Rask/Dir., CEO, Pres., Thomas N. Amonett/Chmn., Thomas R. Hix/Dir., Suzanne V. Baer/Dir., Thomas M. Hamilton/Dir., Don R. Cash/Dir., Robert L. Zorich/Dir.

Owners: Don P. Rodney, Steven A. Webster/2.30%, John T. Reynolds/4.90%, Thomas E. Hord, Steven A. Manz, AMVESCAP PLC/5.20%, Insiders/17.70%, Thomas J. Madonna, Thierry Pilenko, Gardner F. Parker, Randall D. Stilley/3.00%, John T. Rynd, Thomas R. Bates/4.90%, Randal R. Reed, James W. Noe

Financial Data: Fiscal Year End:12/31 Latest Annual Data: 12/31/2006

Year	Sales	Net Income
2006	$912,100,000	$183,600,000
2005	$534,200,000	$59,400,000
2004	$351,400,000	-$28,800,000

Curr. Assets:	$427,300,000	Curr. Liab.:	$198,500,000	P/E Ratio:	13.71
Plant, Equip.:	$451,300,000	Total Liab.:	$325,300,000	Indic. Yr. Divd.:	NA
Total Assets:	$889,200,000	Net Worth:	$563,900,000	Debt/ Equity:	0.0257

Todd Shipyards Corp

1801 16th Ave. SW, Seattle, WA, 98134; *PH:* 1-206-786-3353; *http://* www.toddpacific.com

General - Incorporation .... DE	Stock - Price on:12/24/2007 .... $19.9
Employees 900	Stock Exchange .... NYSE
Auditor .... Grant Thornton LLP	Ticker Symbol .... TOD
Stk Agt .... Mellon Investor Services LLC	Outstanding Shares 5,640,000
Counsel .... NA	E.P.S. $0.70
DUNS No. 00-128-8828	Shareholders .... NA

Business: The group's principal activity is to operate shipyard. The operations include shipbuilding, ship overhaul, conversion and repair in the United States. The repair and overhaul operations of the group include minor repair, major overhauls and involve the dry-docking of the vessel under repair. The customers of the group include the United States government, Washington state ferry system and domestic and international commercial customers.

Primary SIC and add'l.: 3731

CIK No: 0000098537

Subsidiaries: Todd Pacific Shipyards Corporation (Todd Pacific).

Officers: Stephen G. Welch/51/Dir., CEO, VP/$321,880.00, Webster King/Dir. - Policy, Procedure, Ron Sykes/Fire Marshal, Michael G. Marsh/Sec., General Counsel/$168,452.00, Berger A. Dodge/39/CFO, Treasurer/$127,364.00, Jim Newman/Weekend Superintendent, Clarence Dias/Security Supervisor

Directors: Stephen G. Welch/51/Dir., CEO, VP, Patrick W.E. Hodgson/67/Chmn., Joseph D. Lehrer/59/Dir., Brent D. Baird/69/Dir., Steven A. Clifford/65/Dir., Paul J. Reason/67/Dir., Philip N. Robinson/71/Dir., William L. Lewis/56/Dir.

Owners: Insiders/7.90%, John D. Weil/8.20%, Joseph D. Lehrer, Stephen G. Welch/4.80%, Dimension Fund Advisors/5.90%, Philip N. Robinson, Patrick W.E. Hodgson/1.40%, Steven A. Clifford, Brent D. Baird

Financial Data: Fiscal Year End:04/02 Latest Annual Data: 4/1/2007

Year	Sales	Net Income
2007	$125,504,000	$3,240,000
2006	$201,926,000	$8,181,000
2005	$134,037,000	$8,993,000

Curr. Assets:	$87,629,000	Curr. Liab.:	$41,434,000	P/E Ratio:	64.19
Plant, Equip.:	$27,333,000	Total Liab.:	$77,644,000	Indic. Yr. Divd.:	$0.600
Total Assets:	$156,451,000	Net Worth:	$78,807,000	Debt/ Equity:	NA

Tofutti Brands Inc

50 Jackson Dr., Cranford, NJ, 07016; *PH:* 1-908-272-2400; *http://* www.tofutti.com;
Email: info@tofutti.com

General - Incorporation .... DE	Stock - Price on:12/24/2007 .... $3.06
Employees 10	Stock Exchange .... AMEX
Auditor .... Amper, Politziner & Mattia P.C	Ticker Symbol .... TOF
Stk Agt ..... American Stock Transfer & Trust Co.	Outstanding Shares 5,650,000
Counsel ...... Snitow Kanfer Holtzer & Millus LLP	E.P.S. $0.08
DUNS No. 04-629-7974	Shareholders .... NA

Business: The group's principle activities include developing, producing and marketing nondiary-frozen desserts and other foods products. The products are non-dairy, soy-based that does not contain butterfat, cholesterol or lactose. In frozen desserts wave cuties with three flavours, jazzy cutie, new version of beeter than cream cheese and sour supreme made without hydrogenated fat and potassium sorbate. During the year the company eliminated candy and nut products, slowing moving frozen desserts items. The products are sold and distributed by food brokers to distributors and on a direct basis to retail chain accounts. The products are sold through forty-two distributors in the national health food market. The company's registered trademark is tofutti(r). The group operates from Australia, Bermuda, Canada, England, Israel, Mexico and Panama.

Primary SIC and add'l.: 2024

CIK No: 0000730349

Owners: Financial & Investment Management Group, Ltd./13.80%, Steven Kass/10.20%, Reuben Rapoport/1.50%, Franklyn Snitow/1.30%, David Mintz/46.50%, Joseph Fischer, Insiders/56.50%, Philip Gotthelf

Financial Data: Fiscal Year End:12/31 Latest Annual Data: 12/30/2006

Year	Sales	Net Income
2006	$19,465,000	$617,000
2005	$18,613,000	$352,000

Curr. Assets:	$6,572,000	Curr. Liab.:	$2,899,000	P/E Ratio:	30.60
Plant, Equip.:	$34,000	Total Liab.:	$2,899,000	Indic. Yr. Divd.:	NA
Total Assets:	$6,622,000	Net Worth:	$3,723,000	Debt/ Equity:	NA

Toledo Edison Co

76 S Main St., Akron, OH, 44308; *PH:* 1-800-736-3402; *http://* www.firstenergycorp.com

General - Incorporation	OH	Stock- Price on:12/24/2007	NA
Employees	NA	Stock Exchange	NA
Auditor	PricewaterhouseCoopers LLP	Ticker Symbol	NA
Stk Agt	NA	Outstanding Shares	NA
Counsel	NA	E.P.S	NA
DUNS No.	00-790-4626	Shareholders	NA

Business: The group's principle activties include generating, purchasing, transmitting, distributing and selling electric energy in northwestern Ohio. The group operates from United States.

Primary SIC and add'l.: 4911

CIK No: 0000352049

Subsidiaries: American Transmission Systems, Inc., Centerior Service Company, FE Acquisition Corp., FELHC, Inc., FirstEnergy Facilities Services Group, LLC, FirstEnergy Foundation, FirstEnergy Nuclear Generation Corp., FirstEnergy Nuclear Operating Company, FirstEnergy Properties Company, FirstEnergy Securities Transfer Company, FirstEnergy Service Company, FirstEnergy Solutions Corp., FirstEnergy Telecom Services, Inc., FirstEnergy Ventures Corp., GPU Capital, Inc. 26 Subsidiaries included in the Index

Officers: A. J. Alexander/56/Dir., CEO, Pres., R. R. Grigg/59/Dir., Exec. VP, COO, R. H. Marsh/57/Dir., Sr. VP, CFO, Leila L. Vespoli/48/Sr. VP, General Counsel, Harvey L. Wagner/55/VP, Controller, C. E. Jones/52/Sr. VP - Energy Delivery, Customer Service, J. M. Murray/61/Pres. - Ohio Operations, J. F. Pearson/53/VP, Treasurer

Directors: A. J. Alexander/56/Dir., CEO, Pres., R. R. Grigg/59/Dir., Exec. VP, COO, R. H. Marsh/57/Dir., Sr. VP, CFO

Toll Brothers Inc

3103 Philmont Ave., Huntingdon Valley, PA, 19006; *PH:* 1-215-938-8000; *http://* www.tollbrothers.com

General - Incorporation	DE	Stock- Price on:12/24/2007	$26.59
Employees	5,542	Stock Exchange	NYSE
Auditor	Ernst & Young LLP	Ticker Symbol	TOL
Stk Agt	American Stock Transfer & Trust Co.	Outstanding Shares	154,880,000
Counsel	Wolf Block Schorr & Solis-Cohen LLP	E.P.S	$0.22
DUNS No.	06-182-8521	Shareholders	NA

Business: The groups principle activities include developing and constructing residential complexes. The group operates from United States.

Primary SIC and add'l.: 1521 1522 6163

CIK No: 0000794170

Subsidiaries: 110-112 Third Ave Realty Corp, Amwell Chase, Brentwood Investments I Inc, Bunker Hill Estates Inc, Chesterbrooke Inc, Connecticut Land Corp, Daylesford Development Corp, Eastern States Engineering Inc, Fairway Valley Inc, First Brandywine Finance Corp, First Brandywine Investment Corp II, First Brandywine Investment Corp III, First Brandywine Investment Corp IV, First Huntingdon Finance Corp, Franklin Farms GP Inc 160 Subsidiaries included in the Index

Officers: Robert I. Toll/Chmn., CEO, Joel H. Rassman/Dir., CFO, Exec. VP, Treasurer, Zvi Barzilay/COO, Pres., Michael I. Snyder/Sec., Joseph R. Sicree/Chief Accounting Officer, Sr. VP

Directors: Robert I. Toll/Chmn., CEO, Joel H. Rassman/Dir., CFO, Exec. VP, Treasurer, Bruce E. Toll/64/Dir., Robert S. Blank/67/Dir., Edward G. Boehne/67/Dir., Richard J. Braemer/66/Dir., Roger S. Hillas/80/Dir., Carl B. Marbach/66/Dir., Stephen A. Novick/67/Dir., Paul E. Shapiro/66/Dir.

Financial Data: *Fiscal Year End:*10/31 *Latest Annual Data:* 10/31/2007

Year	Sales	Net Income
2007	$4,646,979,000	$35,651,000
2006	$6,123,453,000	$687,213,000
2005	$5,793,425,000	$806,110,000

Curr. Assets:	$6,608,902,000	Curr. Liab.:	$1,419,221,000		
Plant, Equip.:	$84,265,000	Total Liab.:	$3,693,082,000	Indic. Yr. Divd.:	NA
Total Assets:	$7,220,316,000	Net Worth:	$3,527,234,000	Debt/ Equity:	NA

Tollgrade Communications Inc

493 Nixon Rd. , Cheswick, PA, 15024; *PH:* 1-412-274-2156; *http://* www.tollgrade.com; *Email:* info@tollgrade.com

General - Incorporation	PA	Stock- Price on:12/24/2007	$10.62
Employees	225	Stock Exchange	NDQ
Auditor	PricewaterhouseCoopers LLP	Ticker Symbol	TLGD
Stk Agt	Mellon Investor Services LLC	Outstanding Shares	13,260,000
Counsel	Reed Smith LLP	E.P.S	$0.27
DUNS No.	18-584-6953	Shareholders	NA

Business: The group's principal activities are to design, engineer, market and support test system, test access and status monitoring products for the telecommunications and cable television industries. The group's telecommunications proprietary test access products enable telephone companies to use their existing line test systems to remotely diagnose problems in plain old telephone service (pots) lines containing both copper and fiber optics.

Primary SIC and add'l.: 8711 3829 4841 4899 3661

CIK No: 0001002531

Officers: Mark B. Peterson/Dir., CEO, Pres./$452,259.00, Daniel P. Barry/Chmn. - Private Investor, Sara M. Antol/General Counsel, Corp. Sec., Joseph G. O'Brien/VP - Human Resources, Jeffrey J. Tatusko/CIO, Gregory L. Quiggle/39/Exec. VP - Marketing/$275,147.00, Samuel C. Knoch/CFO, Treasurer/$230,899.00, Carol M. Franklin/VP - Research, Development/$240,038.00, Matthew J. Rosgone/VP - Operations, Gail M. Walsh/VP - Global Sales/$199,546.00, Sean M. Reilly/Controller, Joseph A. Ferrara/Sr. VP - Sales, Marketing

Directors: Mark B. Peterson/Dir., CEO, Pres., Daniel P. Barry/Chmn. - Private Investor, Richard H. Heibel/Dir., James J. Barnes/Dir., Robert W. Kampmeinert/Dir., David S. Egan/Dir., Brian C. Mullins/Dir.

Owners: Carol M. Franklin, Royce & Associates, LLC/6.41%, David S. Egan, Brown Capital Management, Inc./7.99%, Mark B. Peterson, The Killien Group, Inc./5.18%, Daniel P. Barry, Insiders/5.64%, James J. Barnes, Dimensional Fund Advisors, L.P./7.80%, Gregory L. Quiggle, Samuel C. Knoch, Gail M. Walsh, Richard H. Heibel, Robert W. Kampmeinert *(16 Owners included in Index)*

Financial Data: *Fiscal Year End:*12/31 *Latest Annual Data:* 12/31/2006

Year	Sales	Net Income
2006	$65,394,000	-$1,834,000
2005	$66,319,000	$3,518,000
2004	$62,818,000	$1,345,000

Curr. Assets:	$93,229,000	Curr. Liab.:	$10,043,000		
Plant, Equip.:	$3,301,000	Total Liab.:	$12,908,000	Indic. Yr. Divd.:	NA
Total Assets:	$162,352,000	Net Worth:	$149,444,000	Debt/ Equity:	NA

Tombstone Exploration Corp

Formerly: Pure Capital Inc

250 Blairgowrie Pl., Nanaimo, BC, V9T 4P5; *PH:* 1-250-741-6340

General - Incorporation	Canada	Stock- Price on:12/24/2007	NA
Employees	NA	Stock Exchange	NA
Auditor	Morgan & Co	Ticker Symbol	NA
Stk Agt	Computershare Investor Services LLC	Outstanding Shares	NA
Counsel	NA	E.P.S	NA
DUNS No.	NA	Shareholders	NA

Business: The group's principal activity is to register and re-sell Internet domain names for the .cc Internet domain registration business. The business plan is to market new .cc names, receiving a commission for each sale and to register marketable domain names under the .cc registration domain and re-sell these domain names at marked-up prices. Presently the group is creating and developing a Web-site that incorporates all of the various requirements to register, buy, market, bid and search for domain names.

Primary SIC and add'l.: 7389

CIK No: 0001072772

Subsidiaries: VCL Communications Corp.

Officers: Alan M. Brown/45/Dir., CEO, CFO, Pres., John Escapule/56/Operations Consultant, Dennis Dalton/Chief Geologist

Directors: Alan M. Brown/45/Dir., CEO, CFO, Pres.

Owners: Red Hawk Exploration and Development Inc./0.32%, CEDE & Co./0.08%, Performance Capital Corporation/0.19%, Alan M. Brown/0.08%

Curr. Assets:	$43,000	Curr. Liab.:	$81,000		
Plant, Equip.:	$900,000	Total Liab.:	$81,000	Indic. Yr. Divd.:	NA
Total Assets:	$943,000	Net Worth:	$862,000	Debt/ Equity:	0.3057

Tomkins Plc

E Putney House, 84 Upper Richmond Rd., London, SW15 2ST; *PH:* 44-2088714544; *http://* www.tomkins.co.uk; *Email:* ir@tomkins.co.uk

General - Incorporation	UK	Stock- Price on:12/24/2007	$20.95
Employees	38,299	Stock Exchange	NYSE
Auditor	Deloitte & Touche LLP	Ticker Symbol	TKS
Stk Agt	Lloyds TSB Registrars	Outstanding Shares	213,590,000
Counsel	NA	E.P.S	$1.43
DUNS No.	21-832-6395	Shareholders	NA

Business: The group's principal activities are engineering and manufacturing carried out through three businesses namely industrial and automotive, air systems components and engineered and construction products. Industrial and automotive manufactures a range of systems and components for the industrial and automotive markets selling to original equipment manufacturers and the replacement markets throughout the world. Engineered and construction products manufactures a range of engineered products for a variety of end markets primarily related to the building, construction, truck and trailer and automotive industries. Air systems components manufactures air handling components supplying the heating, ventilation and air conditioning market. During 2003, the group acquired Stackpole Ltd and disposed Gates Formed-Fibre Products Inc, Milliken Valve Company Inc, and 62.4% of Cobra Investments (PTY) Ltd.

Primary SIC and add'l.: 3442 3429 3494 3535 3432 3564 3599

CIK No: 0000838877

Subsidiaries: Air System Components LP, Aquatic Industries Inc, Dearborn Mid-West Conveyor Company, Dexter Axle Company Inc, Dongfeng-Fuji-Thomson Thermostat Co. Ltd, Eifeler Maschinenbau GmbH, Formflo Ltd, Gates (India) Private Ltd, Gates (U.K.) Ltd, Gates Argentina SA, Gates Australia Pty Ltd, Gates Canada Inc, Gates do Brasil Industria e Comercio Ltda, Gates Europe NV, Gates GmbH 56 Subsidiaries included in the Index

Officers: James Nicol/53/Dir., CEO, John Zimmerman/45/Dir. - Finance, Nina Delangle/Dir. - Investor Relations, Corporate Communications, Gareth Harries/Mgr. - Investor Relations, Strategic Analysis

Directors: James Nicol/53/Dir., CEO, David Newlands/60/Non Exec. Chmn., Richard Gillingwater/50/Dir., Struan Robertson/58/Dir., David Richardson/55/Dir., Iain Napier/59/Dir., John McDonough/56/Dir., Leo Quinn/50/Dir.

Owners: J. Nicol, K. Lever, Insiders, J.M. J. Keenan, D.H. Richardson, D.B. Newlands, D. D.S. Robertson, Sir Brian Pitman, R. D. Gillingwater

Financial Data: *Fiscal Year End:*12/31 *Latest Annual Data:* 12/30/2006

Year	Sales	Net Income
2006	$5,418,700,000	$251,700,000
2005	$5,776,000,000	$313,000,000
2004	$5,650,242,000	$475,995,000

Curr. Assets:	$2,223,000,000	Curr. Liab.:	$1,111,400,000	P/E Ratio:	11.31
Plant, Equip.:	$1,466,700,000	Total Liab.:	$2,748,900,000	Indic. Yr. Divd.:	$0.850
Total Assets:	$5,783,300,000	Net Worth:	$3,034,400,000	Debt/ Equity:	NA

Tompkins Financial Corp

Formerly: Tompkins Trustco Inc

PO Box 460 , The Commons, Ithaca, NY, 14851; *PH:* 1-607-273-3210; *http://* www.tompkinstrust.com

General - Incorporation	NY	Stock- Price on:12/24/2007	$40.55
Employees	623	Stock Exchange	AMEX
Auditor	KPMG LLP	Ticker Symbol	TMP
Stk Agt	American Stock Transfer & Trust Co.	Outstanding Shares	9,780,000
Counsel	NA	E.P.S	$2.71
DUNS No.	00-697-7789	Shareholders	NA

Business: The group's principal activities include commercial and retail banking, trust and investment management and insurance services. Commercial banking include accepting deposits and offering loans. Loans offered include real estate, construction, equipment and receivable financing and commercial leasing. Other services include deposit and cash management services, letters of credit, sweep accounts, credit cards, purchasing cards, merchant processing and Internet-based account services. Retail banking include checking and savings accounts, time deposits, brokerage services, personal loans, credit cards, debit cards and safe deposit services. Trust and investment management includes money management services, estate settlement, and financial planning. The group operates 34 banking offices in local market areas throughout New York state. On 01-Nov-2003, the group acquired youngs & linfoot, inc.

Primary SIC and add'l.: 6022 6712

CIK No: 0001005817

Subsidiaries: Castile Funding Corporation, Inc., Mahopac Funding Corporation, Inc., Tompkins Insurance Agencies, Inc., Tompkins Real Estate Holdings, Inc.

Officers: Stephen S. Romaine/Dir., CEO, Pres./$397,937.00, James W. Fulmer/Vice Chmn., Pres./$470,218.00, Robert B. Bantle/Exec. VP, Francis M. Fetsko/CFO, Exec. VP/$358,429.00, David S. Boyce/Exec. VP, Cindy A. Cute/VP - Personnel, Human Resources, Susan C. Lalonde/Assist. VP, Mgr. - Corporate Compliance, Bradley G. James/VP - Regional Information Technology Services, Thomas James Rogers/Exec. VP, Gerald J. Klein/Exec. VP, Randy C. Lovell/VP, Corporate Risk Mgr., Kathleen Rooney/Exec. VP, Linda M. Carlton/Assist. VP, Corp. Sec.

Directors: Stephen S. Romaine/Dir., CEO, Pres., Thomas R. Salm/Vice Chmn., James J. Byrnes/Chmn., James W. Fulmer/Vice Chmn., Pres., Michael H. Spain/Dir., Elizabeth W. Harrison/Dir., Reeder D. Gates/Dir., Hunter R. Rawlings/Dir., Russell K. Achzet/Dir., Patricia A. Johnson/Dir., Michael D. Shay/Dir., Carl E. Haynes/Dir., Craig Yunker/Dir., John E. Alexander/Dir., James R. Hardie/Dir. (16 Directors included in Index)

Owners: James W. Fulmer/1.08%, Francis M. Fetsko, Reeder D. Gates/1.16%, Hunter R. Rawlings, James J. Byrnes, Stephen S. Romaine, Carl D. Haynes, Michael H. Spain/4.36%, John E. Alexander, Russell K. Achzet, Thomas R. Salm, Lawrence A. Updike, James R. Hardie, Insiders/11.58%, Craig Yunker (18 Owners included in Index)

Financial Data: Fiscal Year End:12/31   Latest Annual Data: 12/31/2006

Year	Sales	Net Income
2006	$162,132,000	$27,767,000
2005	$139,016,000	$27,685,000
2004	$122,656,000	$25,615,000

Curr. Assets:	$90,326,000	Curr. Liab.:	$1,900,910,000		
Plant, Equip.:	$43,273,000	Total Liab.:	$2,021,217,000	Indic. Yr. Divd.:	$1.280
Total Assets:	$2,210,837,000	Net Worth:	$189,620,000	Debt/ Equity:	0.2427

Tonga Capital Corp

2600 S Shore Blvd., Ste. 100, League City, TX, 77573; **PH:** 1-281-334-5161; http:// www.momentumbiofuels.com

General - Incorporation	CO	Stock- Price on:12/24/2007	$1.55
Employees	10	Stock Exchange	OTC
Auditor	Malone & Bailey, P.C	Ticker Symbol	MMBF
Stk Agt	Mountain Share Transfer	Outstanding Shares	NA
Counsel	NA	E.P.S.	NA
DUNS No.	NA	Shareholders	NA

Business: The groups principal activity is seeking a business opportunity to acquire. The group operates from the United States.

Primary SIC and add'l.: 7389

CIK No: 0000813718

Officers: Barent W. Cater/CEO, Pres., Charles T. Phillips/65/Chmn., Pres./$140,000.00, Jim O'Neal/COO, Gary S. Johnson/COO/$8,850,000.00, John V. Olsen/Dir., Exec. VP/$3,650,000.00, Stuart Cater/CFO

Directors: Charles T. Phillips/65/Chmn., Pres., Jeffrey Ploen/Dir., John V. Olsen/Dir., Exec. VP, Richard C. Cilento/Dir., Richard A. Robert/Dir., David M. Fick/Dir.

Owners: Shortline Equity Partners, Inc./5.21%, Charles T. Phillips/15.86%, Ultimate Investments Corp./1.40%, Jim Oneal, Barent W. Cater/4.10%, Stuart C. Cater, Elizabeth Evans/4.62%, Momentum Employee and Consultant Trust/10.48%, Donald W. Guggenheim/9.12%, Jackson L. Wilson, Elevation Fund, LLC, Insiders/22.25%, J. Paul Consulting Corp./5.47%, Richard C. Cilento/4.92%, Coastal Safety & Environmental Systems, LLC/14.95% (17 Owners included in Index)

Financial Data: Fiscal Year End:12/31   Latest Annual Data: 12/31/2006

Year	Sales	Net Income
2006	NA	-$1,279,000
2005	NA	$0
2004	NA	-$286,000

Curr. Assets:	$59,000	Curr. Liab.:	$1,794,000		
Plant, Equip.:	$2,577,000	Total Liab.:	$1,794,000	Indic. Yr. Divd.:	NA
Total Assets:	$2,662,000	Net Worth:	$868,000	Debt/ Equity:	NA

Too Inc

8323 Walton Pk.way, New Albany, OH, 43054; **PH:** 1-614-775-3500; http:// www.tooinc.com

General - Incorporation	DE	Stock- Price on:12/24/2007	$42.5
Employees	3,900	Stock Exchange	NYSE
Auditor	Deloitte & Touche LLP	Ticker Symbol	NA
Stk Agt	American Stock Transfer & Trust Co.	Outstanding Shares	30,760,000
Counsel	Porter Wright Morris & Arthur LLP	E.P.S.	$1.80
DUNS No.	NA	Shareholders	NA

Business: The group's principal activity is to design and sell retail branded apparel and lifestyle products for teenage girls. The group operates in two retailing businesses, limited too and mishmash. Limited too sells apparel, underwear, sleepwear, swimwear, footwear, lifestyle and personal care products for young girls aged between seven to fourteen years. Mishmash sells cosmetics, sportswear, intimate apparel and footwear to young women aged between fourteen to nineteen years. The group's products also include accessories, jewelry, room decor furnishings and lifestyle products. It has 553 stores in 46 states. On 28-May-2003, the group announced the discontinuation of its mishmash retail concept in favor of redirecting its resources to the development of a new concept focused on value-priced sportswear and accessories for teen girls, ages 7 to 14.

Primary SIC and add'l.: 5632

CIK No: 0001085482

Subsidiaries: American Factoring, Inc., Floret, LLC, G Too, LLC, Justice Stores, LLC, Limited Too Catalog Production, Inc., Limited Too Creative Design, Inc., Limited Too Direct, LLC, Limited Too Purchasing, Inc., Limited Too Store Planning, Inc., LT Holding, Inc., LT Import Corp., Mish Mash, LLC, Too Brands Investment, LLC, Too Brands, Inc., Too G.C., LLC 18 Subsidiaries included in the Index

Officers: Michael W. Rayden/Chmn., CEO/$5,743,169.00, Scott M. Bracale/Pres. - Marketing Agency/$1,329,019.00, Ronnie Robinson/Sr. VP - Sourcing, Technical Design, Brand Compliance, Sally A. Boyer/Brand Executive, Pres., GM - Justice/$1,409,625.00, John T. Moore/Sr. VP, CIO - Logistics, Gregory J. Henchel/Sr. VP, General Counsel/$461,721.00, Alan J. Hochman/Sr. VP - Real Estate, Store Planning, Elizabeth M. Eveillard/Dir., Independent Consultant, Phillip E. Mallott/Dir., Independent Financial Consultant, Paul C. Carbone/Sr. VP, CFO/$284,151.00, Kenneth T. Stevens/Dir., COO, Pres., Sec., Jill Dean/Executive

Directors: Michael W. Rayden/Chmn., CEO, Fredric M. Roberts/Dir., Nancy J. Kramer/Dir., Kenneth J. Strottman/Dir., David A. Krinsky/Dir., Elizabeth M. Eveillard/Dir., Independent Consultant, Phillip E. Mallott/Dir., Independent Financial Consultant, Kenneth T. Stevens/Dir., COO, Pres., Sec.

Owners: Elizabeth M. Eveillard, Gregory J. Henchel, Kenneth J. Strottman, Nancy J. Kramer, Michael W. Rayden/1.80%, Insiders/2.80%, Wellington Management Company, LLP/6.10%, Sally A. Boyer, Cramer Rosenthal McGlynn, LLC/6.60%, Scott M. Bracale, William E. May, Philip E. Mallott, David A. Krinsky, Fredric M. Roberts

Financial Data: Fiscal Year End:01/28   Latest Annual Data: 2/3/2007

Year	Sales	Net Income
2007	$883,683,000	$64,821,000
2006	$757,936,000	$54,451,000
2005	$675,834,000	$41,589,000

Curr. Assets:	$284,455,000	Curr. Liab.:	$110,462,000	P/E Ratio:	21.14
Plant, Equip.:	$235,516,000	Total Liab.:	$198,351,000	Indic. Yr. Divd.:	NA
Total Assets:	$569,677,000	Net Worth:	$371,326,000	Debt/ Equity:	NA

Tootsie Roll Industries Inc

7401 S Cicero Ave., Chicago, IL, 60629; **PH:** 1-773-838-3400; http:// www.tootsie.com

General - Incorporation	VA	Stock- Price on:12/24/2007	$28.12
Employees	2,200	Stock Exchange	NYSE
Auditor	PricewaterhouseCoopers LLP	Ticker Symbol	TR
Stk Agt	Mellon Investor Services LLC	Outstanding Shares	55,300,000
Counsel	Becker, Ross, Stone Et Al	E.P.S.	$1.00
DUNS No.	00-128-9495	Shareholders	NA

Business: The group's principal activity is to manufacture and market candy products. The group's products are sold under the registered trademarks tootsie roll, tootsie roll pops, child's play, caramel apple pops, charms, blow-pop, blue razz, zip-a-dee-doo-da pops, cella's, mason dots, mason crows, junior mint, charleston chew, sugar daddy, sugar babies, andes and fluffy stuff. The products are distributed through 100 candy and grocery brokers and by the group to 15,000 customers throughout the United States. The customers include wholesale distributors of candy and groceries, supermarkets, variety stores, chain grocers, drug chains, discount chains, cooperative grocery associations, warehouse and membership club stores, vending machine operators and fund raising charitable organizations. The group's operates in the United States, Canada and Mexico.

Primary SIC and add'l.: 2064

CIK No: 0000098677

Subsidiaries: Andes Candies,Inc., Andes Manufacturing LLC, Andes Services LLC, C. C. L. P.,inc., C. G. C. L. P.,inc., C. G. P.,Inc., Cambridge Brands Manufacturing..,Inc., Cambridge Brands Services,Inc., Cambridge Brands,Inc., Candy Realty,Inc., Cella's Confections,Inc., Charms LLC, Concord (GP)Inc., Concord Brands,Ltd, Concord Canada Holdings ULC 42 Subsidiaries included in the Index

Owners: Ellen R. Gordon/22.60%, Insiders/41.60%, Barre A. Seibert, Ellen R. Gordon/46.90%, John W. Newlin, Melvin J. Gordon/3.60%, Leigh R. Weiner/4.40%, Insiders/81.10%, John W. Newlin, Lana Jane Lewis-Brent, Leigh R. Weiner/13.80%, G. Howard Ember, Melvin J. Gordon/7.00%, Richard P. Bergeman

Financial Data: Fiscal Year End:12/31   Latest Annual Data: 12/31/2006

Year	Sales	Net Income
2006	$495,990,000	$65,919,000
2005	$487,739,000	$77,227,000
2004	$420,110,000	$64,174,000

Curr. Assets:	$190,917,000	Curr. Liab.:	$62,211,000	P/E Ratio:	25.56
Plant, Equip.:	$202,898,000	Total Liab.:	$160,958,000	Indic. Yr. Divd.:	$0.320
Total Assets:	$791,639,000	Net Worth:	$630,681,000	Debt/ Equity:	0.0118

Top Image Systems Ltd

591 N Ave., 3 Lakeside Office Pk., Wakefield, MA, 01880; **PH:** 1-781-245-1154; **Fax:** 1-781-245-2999; http:// www.topimagesystems.com; **Email:** contact@TopImageSystems.com

General - Incorporation	Israel	Stock- Price on:12/24/2007	$3.11
Employees	108	Stock Exchange	NDQ
Auditor	Kost Forer Gabbay & Kasierer	Ticker Symbol	TISA
Stk Agt	American Stock Transfer & Trust Co.	Outstanding Shares	8,850,000
Counsel	Ben-Zvi Koren Law Offices	E.P.S.	-$0.38
DUNS No.	60-036-9177	Shareholders	NA

Business: The groups principle activities include development and marketing of variety of form processing, information recognition and data entry systems and technologies. The group operates from United States.

Primary SIC and add'l.: 3577 7373

CIK No: 0001021991

Subsidiaries: TiS America, Inc., TIS Deutschland GmbH, Top Image Systems UK Limited, Top Image Systems, TiS Japan Ltd

Officers: Ido Schechter/CEO, Arie Rand/CFO, Ofir Shalev/VP - Research & Development, CTO, Gideon Shmuel/VP - Sales, Marketing, Oded Leiba/VP - Engineering

Directors: Izhak Nakar/Founder, Chmn., Elie Housman/Dir., Zamir Bar-Zion/External Dir., Yehezkel Yeshurun/Dir., Victor Halpert/Dir., William Landuyt/Dir.

Financial Data: Fiscal Year End:12/31   Latest Annual Data: 12/31/2006

Year	Sales	Net Income
2006	$20,224,000	$801,000
2005	$16,820,000	-$461,000
2004	$11,178,000	-$178,000

Curr. Assets:	$30,554,000	Curr. Liab.:	$3,702,000	P/E Ratio:	11.31
Plant, Equip.:	$588,000	Total Liab.:	$18,915,000	Indic. Yr. Divd.:	NA
Total Assets:	$34,295,000	Net Worth:	$15,380,000	Debt/ Equity:	NA

Top Tankers Inc

1, Vassilissis Sofias Str. & Meg., Alexandrou Str., Maroussi, 15124; *PH:* 30-2108128206; *http://* www.toptankers.com

General - Incorporation......... Marshall Islands
Employees...71
Auditor .... Seward & Kissel LLP
Stk Agt.....Computershare Investor Services LLC
Counsel...NA
DUNS No. ....NA

Stock- Price on:12/24/2007 ....$7.17
Stock Exchange...NDQ
Ticker Symbol...TOPT
Outstanding Shares 32,430,000
E.P.S...$0.47
Shareholders..NA

Business: The group's principal activities are to provide international seaborne transportation services, carrying refined petroleum products and crude oil. The group owns vessels through its wholly owned subsidiaries incorporated in the marshall islands. The group's wholly owned subsidiary top tanker management inc, manages combined fleet and provides services such as managing day-to-day vessel operations, supervising the crewing, supplying, maintaining and drydocking of vessels. It also provides commercial management services by identifying suitable vessel charter opportunities and monitoring the performance of third-party technical management subcontractors. As of Mar 31, 2004, the group owns and operates a fleet of 7 tankers, consisting of 2double-hull handymax tankers, 2 double-hull suezmax tankers and 3 single-hull handysize tankers. During the year 2003, the group acquired rupel shipping company inc, kalidromo shipping company limited & gramos shipping company inc.

Primary SIC and add'l.: 4412

CIK No: 0001296484

Subsidiaries: Agion Oros Shipping Company Limited, Agrafa Shipping Company Limited, Ardas Shipping Company Limited, Falakro Shipping Company Limited, Giona Shipping Company Limited, Gramos Shipping Company Inc., Helidona Shipping Company Limited, Idi Shipping Company Limited, Ilisos Shipping Company Limited, Imitos Shipping Company Limited, Kalidromo Shipping Company Limited, Kifisos Shipping Company Limited, Kisavos Shipping Company Limited, Lefka Shipping Company Limited, Litochoro Shipping Company Limited 35 Subsidiaries included in the Index

Officers: Evangelos J. Pistiolis/Dir., CEO, Pres., George Goumopoulos/CTO - TOP Tanker Management Inc, Stamatios N. Tsantanis/Dir., CFO, Vangelis G. Ikonomou/Dir., Exec. VP, Stavros Emmanuel/COO - TOP Tanker Management Inc, Michael Mason/Investor Relations Officer - New York

Directors: Evangelos J. Pistiolis/Dir., CEO, Pres., Thomas F. Jackson/Chmn., Christopher J. Thomas/Dir., Roy Gibbs/Dir., Stamatios N. Tsantanis/Dir., CFO, Michael G. Docherty/Dir., Vangelis G. Ikonomou/Dir., Exec. VP

Owners: Insiders/5.90%, QVT Financial LP/9.50%, Evangelos Pistiolis/5.30%, Kingdom Holdings Inc./7.30%

Financial Data: Fiscal Year End:12/31 Latest Annual Data: 12/31/2006

Year	Sales	Net Income
2006	$310,043,000	$15,141,000
2005	$244,215,000	$68,684,000
2004	$93,829,000	$32,794,000

Curr. Assets:	$72,799,000	Curr. Liab.:	$40,609,000	P/E Ratio:	15.26
Plant, Equip.:	$338,296,000	Total Liab.:	$324,880,000	Indic. Yr. Divd.:	NA
Total Assets:	$522,735,000	Net Worth:	$197,855,000	Debt/ Equity:	2.4783

Tor Minerals International Inc

722 Burleson St., Corpus Christi, TX, 78402; *PH:* 1-361-883-5591; *http://* www.torminerals.com

General - Incorporation............................ DE
Employees...180
Auditor ....UHY LLP
Stk Agt..................Registrar & Transfer Co
Counsel...NA
DUNS No. 09-957-3172

Stock- Price on:12/24/2007 ....$2.45
Stock Exchange...NDQ
Ticker Symbol...TORM
Outstanding Shares 7,840,000
E.P.S...NA
Shareholders..NA

Business: The group's principal activities are manufacturing and marketing mineral products. These are used as pigments, pigment extenders and flame retardants used in the manufacture of paints, industrial coatings, plastics and solid surface applications. The principal product of the group is hitox, which are used by major international paint and plastics manufacturers. The other products of the group are bartex, pigment extender that is used to increase the efficiency of titanium dioxide pigment and haltex, pigment filler used primarily in plastics and coatings. These products are marketed in the United States and in 60 other countries, including Canada, Mexico, Asia, Australia, Africa and Europe. Major customers of the group are ppg, uponor, dunn edwards and j-m manufacturing co.

Primary SIC and add'l.: 2816 2819

CIK No: 0000842295

Subsidiaries: TOR Minerals Malaysia, Sdn. Bhd., Tp&t (tor Processing & Trade) B.v.

Officers: Olaf Karasch/MD, CEO, Pres./$215,982.00, Ralf Laven/Mgr. - Sales, Marketing, Europe, Mark Schomp/Exec. VP - Sales, Marketing/$163,221.00, Lance Silstorf/Mgr. - Sales, Marketing, North America, Annemarie Tijssen/Customer Service - Europe, Lee Hee Chew/VP - Operations, Asia/$129,852.00, Kuan Kean Kee/Mgr. - Sales, Marketing, Asia, Steve Parker/CFO, Twanee Swanson/Customer Service - North America, David Mossberg/Investor Relations Officer, Elizabeth K. Morgan/67/Sec.

Directors: Bernard A. Paulson/79/Chmn., Thomas W. Pauken/64/Dir., Tan Chin Yong/43/Dir., John J. Buckley/52/Dir., Craig W. Epperson/65/Dir., David A. Hartman/71/Dir., Douglas M. Hartman/40/Dir.

Owners: Olaf Karasch/1.20%, Insiders/2.50%, Tan Chin-Yong, Douglas M. Hartman/7.90%, Thomas W. Pauken/1.30%, Lee Hee Chew/1.10%, Mark J. Schomp/1.90%, Bernard A. Paulson/15.90%, The D and CH Trust/7.90%, Insiders/39.40%, Paulson Ranch, Ltd/15.90%, Richard L. Bowers/3.10%, The Douglas MacDonald Hartman/7.90%, David A. Hartman/7.90%, Thomas W. Pauken/2.50% *(17 Owners included in Index)*

Financial Data: Fiscal Year End:12/31 Latest Annual Data: 12/31/2006

Year	Sales	Net Income
2006	$26,079,000	$93,000
2005	$32,669,000	$483,000
2004	$30,476,000	$1,104,000

Curr. Assets:	$15,993,000	Curr. Liab.:	$6,355,000		
Plant, Equip.:	$20,034,000	Total Liab.:	$13,182,000	Indic. Yr. Divd.:	NA
Total Assets:	$38,011,000	Net Worth:	$24,829,000	Debt/ Equity:	0.2930

Torbay Holdings Inc

PO Box 1117, Long Beach, NY, 11561; *PH:* 1-516-747-5955; *http://* www.trby.com

General - Incorporation .... DE
Employees..2
Auditor .... Weinberg & Co. P.A
Stk Agt........................... StockTrans, Inc.
Counsel...NA
DUNS No. ....NA

Stock- Price on:12/24/2007 ....$0.019
Stock Exchange...OTC
Ticker Symbol...TRBY
Outstanding Shares 152,840,000
E.P.S. ....-$0.003
Shareholders..NA

Business: The group's principle activity is to develop household appliances designed to be attractive to a premium, upscale market. The group operates from United States.

Primary SIC and add'l.: 3632 3639 3631 6719

CIK No: 0001078724

Subsidiaries: Designer Appliances, Inc., Designer Appliances, Ltd.

Officers: Richard K. Lauer/CEO, Pres., Acting CFO

Directors: George Q. Stevens/64/Chmn., Carmine Castellano/74/Dir., Harvey Altholtz/62/Dir.

Owners: Insiders/4.00%, The Black Diamond Fund, LLLP/100.00%, Alexander G. Lane/3.00%, Richard K. Lauer/2.10%, William T. Large/9.20%, George Q. Stevens/2.10%, Financial Alchemy, LLC/6.10%, Nutmeg Group, LLC/26.10%, The Black Diamond Fund, LLLP/18.40%, Thomas A. Marchant/0.80%

Financial Data: Fiscal Year End:12/31 Latest Annual Data: 12/31/2006

Year	Sales	Net Income
2006	$364,000	-$668,000
2005	$343,000	-$555,000
2004	$345,000	-$1,128,000

Curr. Assets:	NA	Curr. Liab.:	NA		
Plant, Equip.:	NA	Total Liab.:	NA	Indic. Yr. Divd.:	NA
Total Assets:	NA	Net Worth:	NA	Debt/ Equity:	NA

Torch Energy Royalty Trust

1221 Lamar, Ste. 1175, Houston, TX, 77010; *PH:* 1-302-651-8775; *http://* www.torchroyalty.com

General - Incorporation .... DE
Employees...NA
Auditor ....T.j. Smith & Co., Inc
Stk Agt.................. Wilmington Trust Company
Counsel...NA
DUNS No. ....NA

Stock- Price on:12/24/2007 ....$8.21
Stock Exchange...NYSE
Ticker Symbol...TRU
Outstanding Shares 8,600,000
E.P.S...NA
Shareholders..NA

Business: The groups principle activity is to invest in oil and gas properties. The group operates from the United States. The groups quarterly revenue for September 2007 was 1.37 millions of USD.

Primary SIC and add'l.: 6792

CIK No: 0000912030

Officers: Bruce L. Bisson/VP, Maria Barber/Contact

Owners: Fairchild Energy Investment Co. LLC/8.88%

Financial Data: Fiscal Year End:12/31 Latest Annual Data: 12/31/2006

Year	Sales	Net Income
2006	$8,312,000	$7,262,000
2005	$6,526,000	$5,601,000
2004	$6,604,000	$5,657,000

Curr. Assets:	NA	Curr. Liab.:	$222,000		
Plant, Equip.:	NA	Total Liab.:	$222,000	Indic. Yr. Divd.:	NA
Total Assets:	$18,386,000	Net Worth:	$18,164,000	Debt/ Equity:	NA

Torchmark Corp

2001 3rd Ave. S, Birmingham, AL, 35233; *PH:* 1-205-325-4200; *http://* www.torchmarkcorp.com

General - Incorporation .... DE
Employees..2,495
Auditor ....Deloitte & Touche LLP
Stk Agt....................................Bank of New York
Counsel....................Baxley, Mcknight & Barclift
DUNS No. 04-563-1009

Stock- Price on:12/24/2007 ....$68.77
Stock Exchange...NYSE
Ticker Symbol...TMK
Outstanding Shares 95,500,000
E.P.S...$5.39
Shareholders..NA

Business: The groups principle activity is to provide insurance services. The group operates through two segments namely insurance, which includes the insurance product lines of life, health and annuities, and investments, which supports the product lines. In January, 2007, Torchmark acquired Direct Marketing and Advertising Distributors, Inc. (DMAD), an advertising and publication company. The group operates from United States.

Primary SIC and add'l.: 6311 6321 6411

CIK No: 0000320335

Subsidiaries: American Income Life Insurance Company, Globe Life And Accident Insurance Company, Liberty National Life Insurance Company, United American Insurance Company, United Investors Life Insurance Company

Officers: Charles F. Hudson/CEO, Pres. - Globe Life/$2,736,020.00, Anthony L. McWhorter/CEO - Liberty National Life, CEO, Pres. - United Investors Life, Mark S. McAndrew/Chmn., CEO/$2,029,891.00, Vern D. Herbel/Exec. VP, Chief Administrative Officer, CEO - United American, Roger Smith/CEO, Pres. - American Income Life, Michael W. Pressley/VP, Chief Investment Officer, Danny H. Almond/VP, Chief Accounting Officer, Michael J. Klyce/VP, Treasurer, Spencer H. Stone/Controller, Frank M. Svoboda/VP, Dir. - Tax, Tony G. Brill/Exec. VP/$1,183,627.00, Joyce L. Lane/VP - Investor Relations, Larry M. Hutchison/Exec. VP, General Counsel/$1,025,768.00, Gary L. Coleman/CFO, Exec. VP/$1,052,733.00, Rosemary J. Montgomery/Exec. VP, Chief Actuary/$1,042,344.00 *(20 Officers included in Index)*

Directors: Mark S. McAndrew/Chmn., CEO, Harold T. McCormick/Dir., Jane M. Buchan/Dir., Charles E. Adair/Dir., David L. Boren/Dir., Joseph L. Lanier/Dir., Lloyd W. Newton/Dir., Lamar C. Smith/Dir., Robert W. Ingram/Dir., Paul J. Zucconi/Dir., Sam R. Perry/Dir.

Owners: Sam R. Perry, Charles E. Adair, Paul J. Zucconi, Charles F. Hudson, Gary L. Coleman, Mark S. McAndrew, Roger C. Smith, Larry M. Hutchison, Andrew W. King, Anthony L. McWhorter, Joseph L. Lanier, Pzena Investment Management, LLC, Lamar C. Smith, Vern D. Herbel, Insiders *(25 Owners included in Index)*

Financial Data: Fiscal Year End:12/31 Latest Annual Data: 12/31/2006

Year	Sales	Net Income
2006	$3,421,178,000	$518,631,000
2005	$3,125,910,000	$495,390,000
2004	$3,071,500,000	$468,600,000

Curr. Assets:	$252,196,000	Curr. Liab.:	$537,503,000	P/E Ratio:	12.76
Plant, Equip.:	NA	Total Liab.:	$11,521,162,000	Indic. Yr. Divd.:	$0.520
Total Assets:	$14,980,355,000	Net Worth:	$3,459,193,000	Debt/ Equity:	0.1760

Toreador Resources Corp

4809 Cole Ave., Ste 108, Dallas, TX, 75205; *PH:* 1-214-559-3933; *http://* www.toreador.net

General - Incorporation	DE	Stock- Price on:12/24/2007	$16
Employees	96	Stock Exchange	NDQ
Auditor	Grant Thornton, LLP	Ticker Symbol	TRGL
Stk Agt..... American Stock Transfer & Trust Co.		Outstanding Shares	19,370,000
Counsel...... Feder, Kaszovitz, Bass & Rhine LLP		E.P.S.	-$3.61
DUNS No.	00-792-8401	Shareholders	NA

Business: The group's principal activities are to explore and produce oil and gas and acquire properties. The group's operations are conducted through the ownership of perpetual mineral and royalty interests. The group holds interests in foreign developed and undeveloped oil and gas properties in the Paris basin, France, the cendere and zeynel fields in turkey and the bonasse field and southwest cedros peninsula license in trinidad, west indies. The group's domestic properties are located in the Texas, Alabama, Mississippi, Louisiana, Arkansas, California, Kansas and Michigan. In Jan 2004, the group sold U.S. Mineral and royalty assets to black stone acquisitions partners i, l.p.

Primary SIC and add'l.: 1311 6792

CIK No: 0000098720

Subsidiaries: Capstone Royalty of Texas, LLC, EnergyNet.com, Inc., ePsolutions, Madison (Turkey), Inc., Madison Oil Company, Madison Oil Company Europe, Madison Oil France, S.A.S., Madison Petroleum, Inc., Toreador Acquisition Corporation., Toreador Energy France SCS, Toreador Exploration & Production Inc., Toreador Exploration Ltd., Toreador Holdings International SRL, Toreador Hungary Ltd., Toreador Resources Corp. USA Sucursaia Bucuresti (Branch Office) 20 Subsidiaries included in the Index

Officers: Nigel J.B. Lovett/61/Dir., CEO, Pres., Shirley Anderson/Corp. Sec., Douglas W. Weir/CFO, Sr. VP/$539,656.00, Michael J. Fitzgerald/57/Exec. VP - Exploration, Production/$636,047.00, Stewart P. Yee/VP - Investor Relations, Charles J. Campise/58/VP - Finance, Accounting, Chief Accounting Officer/$333,782.00, Edward Ramirez/57/Sr. VP - Exploration, Production

Directors: Nigel J.B. Lovett/61/Dir., CEO, Pres., John Mark McLaughlin/75/Chmn., Herbert L. Brewer/79/Dir., Peter L. Falb/69/Dir., H. R. Sanders/73/Dir., Alan D. Bell/61/Dir., David M. Brewer/52/Dir., William I. Lee/81/Dir., Nicholas Rostow/56/Dir., Herbert C. Williamson/58/Dir.

Financial Data: Fiscal Year End:12/31   Latest Annual Data: 12/31/2006

Year	Sales	Net Income
2006	$40,387,000	$2,578,000
2005	$31,117,000	$10,595,000
2004	$21,028,000	$25,019,000

Curr. Assets:	$52,420,000	Curr. Liab.:	$39,572,000		
Plant, Equip.:	$251,015,000	Total Liab.:	$170,053,000	Indic. Yr. Divd.:	NA
Total Assets:	$317,204,000	Net Worth:	$147,151,000	Debt/ Equity:	0.6444

Tornado Gold

8600 Technology Way, Ste 118, Reno, NV, 89521; *PH:* 1-775-852-3770; *http://* www.tornadogold.com; *Email:* info@tornadogold.com

General - Incorporation	NV	Stock- Price on:12/24/2007	$0.29
Employees	1	Stock Exchange	OTC
Auditor	Jonathon P. Reuben CPA	Ticker Symbol	TOGI
Stk Agt	Transfer Online, Inc.	Outstanding Shares	30,110,000
Counsel	Susan M. Wilk	E.P.S.	-$0.05
DUNS No.	NA	Shareholders	NA

Business: The group's principle activity is to invest in mining properties for future development and production. On 19-Mar-2004 the company sold its subsidiary salty's warehouse inc. The group operates from United States.

Primary SIC and add'l.: 1081 5722 5531 7389

CIK No: 0001168895

Subsidiaries: Saltys Warehouse Inc

Officers: Earl W. Abbott/65/Chmn., CEO, Pres., Stanley B. Keith/Dir., VP - Exploration, George Drazenovic/CFO

Directors: Earl W. Abbott/65/Chmn., CEO, Pres., Stanley B. Keith/Dir., VP - Exploration, Carl Pescio/Dir.

Owners: Earl W. Abbott/11.96%, Insiders/22.91%, Stanley Keith/5.98%, Carl Pescio/5.98%

Financial Data: Fiscal Year End:12/31   Latest Annual Data: 12/31/2006

Year	Sales	Net Income
2006	NA	-$1,346,000
2005	NA	-$617,000
2004	NA	-$261,000

Curr. Assets:	$144,000	Curr. Liab.:	$1,255,000		
Plant, Equip.:	$1,000	Total Liab.:	$1,255,000	Indic. Yr. Divd.:	NA
Total Assets:	$1,834,000	Net Worth:	$579,000	Debt/ Equity:	NA

Toro Co

8111 Lyndale Ave. S, Bloomington, MN, 55420; *PH:* 1-952-888-8801; *Fax:* 1-952-887-8258; *http://* www.toro.com; *Email:* info.toro@toro.com

General - Incorporation	DE	Stock- Price on:12/24/2007	$58.12
Employees	5,262	Stock Exchange	NYSE
Auditor	KPMG LLP	Ticker Symbol	TTC
Stk Agt	Wells Fargo Bank, N.A.	Outstanding Shares	39,680,000
Counsel	Hunton & Williams LLP	E.P.S.	$3.40
DUNS No.	00-647-7400	Shareholders	NA

Business: The groups principle activity is to provide turf maintenance equipment and precision irrigation systems. The groups products include snowthrowers, yard tools, lawn and garden tractors, and garden tools. The group operates from United States.

Primary SIC and add'l.: 3523 3524 5083

CIK No: 0000737758

Subsidiaries: Electronic Industrial Controls,Inc., Exmark Manufacturing Company Incorporated, Hayter Limited, Irritrol Systems Europe Productions, S.r.L., Irritrol Systems Europe, S.r.L., MTI Distributing,Inc., Red Iron Insurance, Limited, Toro Australia Group Sales Pty. Ltd, Toro Australia Pty. Limited, Toro Briggs& Stratton LLC, Toro Credit Company, Toro Europe BVBA, Toro Factoring Company Limited, Toro Finance Company, Toro Foreign Sales Corporation 28 Subsidiaries included in the Index

Officers: Michael J. Hoffman/Chmn., CEO, Pres., William E. Brown/VP - Consumer Business, LCB, Toro, Dennis P. Himan/Group VP, Stephen P. Wolfe/CFO, VP - Finance, Philip A. Burkart/VP - Irrigation Businesses, Sandra J. Meurlot/VP - Operations, Michael D. Drazan/CIO, VP - Corporate Services, Lawrence J. McIntyre/VP, Sec., General Counsel, Mark B. Stinson/GM - Exmark Landscape Contractor Business, Rick W. Rodier/GM - Landscape Contractor Business, Timothy P. Dordell/VP, Sec., General Counsel, Peter M. Ramstad/VP - Human Resources, Business Development, Karen M. Meyer/VP - Administration

Directors: Michael J. Hoffman/Chmn., CEO, Pres., Gary Ellis/Dir., Gregg Steinhafel/Dir., Inge Thulin/Dir., Winslow Buxton/Dir., Janet Cooper/Dir., Christopher Twomey/Dir., Ronald Baukol/Dir., Robert Nassau/Dir., Katherine Harless/Dir., Robert Buhrmaster/Dir.

Owners: Katherine J. Harless, Sandra J. Meurlot, T. Rowe Price Associates, Inc./5.67%, Insiders/5.55%, Christopher A. Twomey, Karen M. Meyer, Stephen P. Wolfe/1.08%, Michael J. Hoffman/1.05%, Gregg W. Steinhafel, Mairs and Power,Inc./5.39%, Gary L. Ellis, Winslow H. Buxton, Janet K. Cooper, Ronald O. Baukol, Robert C. Buhrmaster *(17 Owners included in Index)*

Financial Data: Fiscal Year End:10/31   Latest Annual Data: 10/31/2007

Year	Sales	Net Income
2007	$1,876,904,000	$142,436,000
2006	$1,835,991,000	$129,145,000
2005	$1,779,387,000	$114,082,000

Curr. Assets:	$664,928,000	Curr. Liab.:	$341,470,000	P/E Ratio:	18.05
Plant, Equip.:	$170,672,000	Total Liab.:	$580,399,000	Indic. Yr. Divd.:	$0.600
Total Assets:	$950,837,000	Net Worth:	$370,438,000	Debt/ Equity:	0.4937

Toronto-Dominion Bank

31 W 52nd St., New York, NY, 10019; *PH:* 1-212-827-7000; *Fax:* 1-212-827-7248; *http://* www.td.com; *Email:* idir@td.com

General - Incorporation	Canada	Stock- Price on:12/24/2007	$69.22
Employees	51,147	Stock Exchange	NYSE
Auditor	PricewaterhouseCoopers LLP	Ticker Symbol	TD
Stk Agt	Mellon Trust Co	Outstanding Shares	719,900,000
Counsel	Cassels Brock & Blackwell LLP	E.P.S.	$5.54
DUNS No.	20-265-6150	Shareholders	NA

Business: The group's principal activity is to provide a full range of financial products and services to personal customers. Services include telephone banking, Web banking, insurance and access to 2,767 automated banking machines. The group operates through divisions: investment banking provides capital market products and services to corporate, government and institutional clients. Self-directed brokerage provides integrated brokerage, mutual fund banking and other financial products and services to customers through the Web, telephone, wireless technology and 230 branches. Asset management provides investment management services for mutual funds, pension funds, corporations, institutions, endowments, foundations and high net worth individuals.

Primary SIC and add'l.: 6021

CIK No: 0000947263

Subsidiaries: TD Bank Financial Group, TD Waterhouse Group, Inc.

Officers: Edmund W. Clark/60/Dir., CEO, Pres., Joe Moglia/CEO - TD Ameritrade, Fred Tomczyk/Vice Chmn. - Corporate Operations, TD Bank Financial Group, Craig Alexander/VP, Deputy Chief Economist, Don Drummond/Sr. VP, Chief Economist, Mike Pedersen/Group Head - Corporate Operations, TD Bank Financial Group, Ritu Sapra/Economist, Pascal Gauthier/Economist, Dina Cover/Economist, Charmaine Buskas/Sr. Economics Strategist, Millan Mulraine/Economics Strategist, Nicholas Petter/Mgr. - Corporate Communications, Stephen Hewitt/Sr. Mgr. - External Communications, Richard Kelly/Sr. Economist, Beata Caranci/Dir. - Economic Forecasting *(44 Officers included in Index)*

Directors: Edmund W. Clark/60/Dir., CEO, Pres., John M. Thompson/65/Chmn., Frank McKenna/Dep. Chmn. - TD Bank Financial Group, Donna M. Hayes/51/Dir., William E. Bennett/61/Dir., Irene R. Miller/55/Dir., Henry H. Ketcham/58/Dir., Pierre H. Lessard/65/Dir., Helen K. Sinclair/50/Dir., Hugh J. Bolton/69/Dir., Wilbur J. Prezzano/67/Dir., Harold H. MacKay/67/Dir., Brian F. MacNeill/68/Dir., John L. Bragg/67/Dir., Wendy K. Dobson/66/Dir. *(18 Directors included in Index)*

Owners: The Toronto-Dominion Bank

Financial Data: Fiscal Year End:10/31   Latest Annual Data: 10/31/2006

Year	Sales	Net Income
2006	$19,900,075,000	$4,120,641,000
2005	$15,867,117,000	$1,822,614,000
2004	$13,272,311,000	$1,544,113,000

Curr. Assets:	$124,743,540,000	Curr. Liab.:	$285,854,550,000		
Plant, Equip.:	$1,661,463,000	Total Liab.:	$339,230,153,000	Indic. Yr. Divd.:	$2.300
Total Assets:	$357,469,657,000	Net Worth:	$18,239,504,000	Debt/ Equity:	NA

Torotel Inc

13402 S 71 Hwy, Grandview, MO, 64030; *PH:* 1-913-747-6111; *http://* www.torotelprod.com; *Email:* torotel@torotelprod.com

General - Incorporation	MO	Stock- Price on:12/24/2007	$0.35
Employees	65	Stock Exchange	OTC
Auditor	Mayer Hoffman Mccann, P.C	Ticker Symbol	TTLO
Stk Agt	Mellon Investor Services LLC	Outstanding Shares	5,380,000
Counsel	Triton Network Newco	E.P.S.	$0.01
DUNS No.	00-713-8928	Shareholders	NA

Business: The group's principal activities are to design and manufacture precision magnetic components and ballast transformers through its subsidiaries. The group operations are carried out through its two subsidiaries, Torotel Products, Inc and Elecktronika. Torotel Products, Inc designs precision magnetic components, which consist of transformers, inductors, reactors, chokes and toroidal coils. Elecktronika designs, markets and licenses ballast transformers to the airline industry.

Primary SIC and add'l.: 3612 6719 3677

CIK No: 0000098752

Subsidiaries: Electronika, Inc., Electronika-Kansas, Inc., Torotel Products, Inc.

Officers: James H. Serrone/53/Dir., VP - Finance, Sec., CFO

Directors: James H. Serrone/53/Dir., VP - Finance, Sec., CFO, Kirk S. Lambright,/39/Dir.

Owners: Alexandra Z. Caloyeras/14.20%, Basil P. Caloyeras/14.20%, Dale H. Sizemore/4.50%, Richard A. Sizemore/4.50%, Aliki S. Caloyeras/14.20%, Insiders/15.30%, James H. Serrone/1.80%, Benjamin E. Ames/4.50%

Financial Data: Fiscal Year End:04/30 **Latest Annual Data:** 4/30/2006

Year	Sales	Net Income
2006	$5,493,000	$463,000
2005	$4,409,000	-$107,000
2004	$4,020,000	-$1,439,000

Curr. Assets:	$1,583,000	Curr. Liab.:	$1,175,000		
Plant, Equip.:	$1,069,000	Total Liab.:	$1,945,000	Indic. Yr. Divd.:	NA
Total Assets:	$3,355,000	Net Worth:	$1,410,000	Debt/ Equity:	0.6734

Torrent Energy Corp

1 S.W. Columbia St., Ste. 640, Portland, OR, 97258; *PH:* 1-604-639-3118; *http://* www.torrentenergy.com; *Email:* info@torrentenergy.com

General - Incorporation	CO	Stock - Price on:12/24/2007	$1.3
Employees	10	Stock Exchange	OTC
Auditor	Ernst & Young LLP	Ticker Symbol	TREN
Stk Agt	Computershare Trust Co	Outstanding Shares	33,420,000
Counsel	NA	E.P.S.	-$0.28
DUNS No.	NA	Shareholders	NA

Business: The group's principal activity is to acquire and explore natural gas and coalbed methane properties in the United States. The group operates through its subsidiary, methane energy corp. The group has acquired, under leases, approximately 60,000 acres of certain properties in the coos bay area of Oregon. Its current focus is to develop the coos bay basin project in Oregon.

Primary SIC and add'l.: 7375 1311

CIK No: 0000859747

Subsidiaries: Cascadia Energy Corp., Methane Energy Corp

Officers: John D. Carlson/CEO, Pres., Michael D. Fowler/CFO, Corp. Sec., Faron Belseck/Corporate Controller

Directors: William A. Lansing/Chmn., Michael Raleigh/Dir., Thomas J. Deacon/Member - Advisory Board, George L. Hampton/Dir., Curtis Hartzler/Dir.

Owners: Michael Raleigh/0.34%, Insiders/5.63%, William A. Lansing/0.63%, George L. Hampton/2.50%, Curtis Hartzler/0.34%, Michael D. Fowler/0.68%, John D. Carlson/1.32%

Financial Data: Fiscal Year End:03/31 **Latest Annual Data:** 03/31/2007

Year	Sales	Net Income
2007	NA	-$6,360,000
2006	NA	-$4,036,000
2005	NA	-$2,419,000

Curr. Assets:	$3,479,000	Curr. Liab.:	$2,328,000		
Plant, Equip.:	$16,377,000	Total Liab.:	$2,328,000	Indic. Yr. Divd.:	NA
Total Assets:	$19,927,000	Net Worth:	$17,600,000	Debt/ Equity:	NA

Tortoise North American Energy Corp

10801 Mastin St., Ste.222, Shawnee Mission, KS, 66210; *PH:* 1-913-981-1020; *Fax:* 1-913-981-1021; *http://* www.tortoiseadvisors.com; *Email:* pkearney@tortoiseadvisors.com

General - Incorporation		Stock - Price on:12/24/2007	$26.8
Employees	NA	Stock Exchange	NYSE
Auditor	NA	Ticker Symbol	TYN
Stk Agt	Computershare Investor Services LLC	Outstanding Shares	4,610,000
Counsel	NA	E.P.S.	$2.049
DUNS No.	NA	Shareholders	NA

Business: The groups principal activity is to invest in royalty and income trusts. The group operates from the United States.

Primary SIC and add'l.: 1731

CIK No:

Officers: David J. Schulte/CEO, Pres., MD, Terry Matlack/Dir., CFO, Assist. Treasurer, MD, Kenneth P. Malvey/Sr. VP, Treasurer, Zachary A. Hamel/Sr. VP, MD, Diane M. Bono/Chief Compliance Officer, Assist. Sec., Kyle M. Krueger/Other Investment Professional, James Mick/Investment Professional, Abel Mojica/Other Investment Professional, Edward Russell/Investment Professional, Matthew G.P. Sallee/Investment Professional, Robert J. Thummel/Investment Professional, Connie J. Savage/Sec., Brad P. Adams/Assist. Treasurer, Jeff Fulmer/Other Investment Professional, Dave Henriksen/Other Investment Professional *(17 Officers included in Index)*

Directors: David J. Schulte/CEO, Pres., MD, Kevin H. Birzer/Chmn., Terry Matlack/Dir., CFO, Assist. Treasurer, MD, Conrad S. Ciccotello/Dir., John R. Graham/Dir., Charles E. Heath/Dir.

Owners: Terry C. Matlack, Zachary A. Hamel, Kevin H. Birzer, Charles E. Heath, John R. Graham, Insiders, David J. Schulte, Kenneth P. Malvey, Conrad S. Ciccotello

Financial Data: Fiscal Year End:NA **Latest Annual Data:** 11/30/2006

Year	Sales	Net Income
2006	$8,872,000	$5,336,000
2005	$1,544,000	$1,357,000

Curr. Assets:	$683,000	Curr. Liab.:	$7,594,000		
Plant, Equip.:	NA	Total Liab.:	$48,862,000	Indic. Yr. Divd.:	$1.480
Total Assets:	$173,188,000	Net Worth:	$124,326,000	Debt/ Equity:	NA

Tortuga Mexican Imports Inc

10654 82 Ave., Ste. 219, Edmonton, AB, T6E 2A7; *PH:* 1-780-710-9840; *http://* www.shoptortuga.com; *Email:* info@shoptortuga.com

General - Incorporation	NV	Stock - Price on:12/24/2007	NA
Employees	NA	Stock Exchange	OTC
Auditor	LBB & Associates Ltd., LLP	Ticker Symbol	TTGX
Stk Agt	Empire Stock Transfer Inc.	Outstanding Shares	NA
Counsel	NA	E.P.S.	NA
DUNS No.	NA	Shareholders	NA

Business: The groups principle activity is launched our e commerce site on the Internet for the purpose of engaging in the business of selling jewelry and crafts online to the customers. In the year June 2006, the group acquired Tortuga Canada. The group operates from the United States and Canada.

Primary SIC and add'l.: 5944

CIK No: 0001213106

Officers: Vanessa Avila/32/Dir., Pres., Sec., Eduardo Avila/35/Treasurer, Dir.

Directors: Vanessa Avila/32/Dir., Pres., Sec., Eduardo Avila/35/Treasurer, Dir.

Owners: Vanessa Avila/72.00%, Insiders/72.00%

Torvec Inc

Powder Mills Office Pk., 1169 Pittsford-Victor Rd., Ste. 125, Pittsford, NY, 14534; *PH:* 1-585-248-0740; *http://* www.torvec.com; *Email:* info@torvec.com

General - Incorporation	NY	Stock - Price on:12/24/2007	$3.41
Employees	NA	Stock Exchange	OTC
Auditor	Eisner LLP	Ticker Symbol	TOVC
Stk Agt	Continental Stock Transfer & Trust Co	Outstanding Shares	31,340,000
Counsel	NA	E.P.S.	-$0.26
DUNS No.	NA	Shareholders	NA

Business: The groups principal activity is developing six fields of automotive and related technology, each of which having individual commercial potential. The group operates from the United States.

Primary SIC and add'l.: 3711

CIK No: 0001063197

Subsidiaries: Ice Surface Development, Inc., Iso-Torque Corporation, IVT Diesel C, Variable Gear, LLC

Officers: James A. Gleasman/Dir., CEO, Interim CFO, Chief Strategist - Investor Relations, Keith E. Gleasman/Dir., Pres., CTO, Herbert H. Dobbs/Dir., Sec., Andrew Gleasman/Technology Mgr.

Directors: James A. Gleasman/Dir., CEO, Interim CFO, Chief Strategist - Investor Relations, Gary A. Siconolfi/Chmn., David M. Flaum/Dir., Keith E. Gleasman/Dir., Pres., CTO, Daniel R. Bickel/Dir., Herbert H. Dobbs/Dir., Sec., Joseph B. Rizzo/43/Dir.

Owners: Margaret F. Gleasman, Herbert H. Dobbs, Joseph B. Rizzo, Keith E. Gleasman, Gary A. Siconolfi, Daniel R. Bickel, James Y. Gleasman, David M. Flaum

Financial Data: Fiscal Year End:12/31 **Latest Annual Data:** 12/31/2006

Year	Sales	Net Income
2006	NA	-$7,727,000
2005	NA	-$5,445,000
2004	NA	-$9,805,000

Curr. Assets:	$793,000	Curr. Liab.:	$1,950,000		
Plant, Equip.:	$156,000	Total Liab.:	$2,159,000	Indic. Yr. Divd.:	NA
Total Assets:	$1,201,000	Net Worth:	-$958,000	Debt/ Equity:	NA

Total

2 Pl. De La Coupole, Paris La Dfense, Cedex, 92078; ; *http://* www.total.com

General - Incorporation	France	Stock - Price on:12/24/2007	$78.72
Employees	95,070	Stock Exchange	NYSE
Auditor	Ernst & Young, KPMG LLP	Ticker Symbol	NA
Stk Agt	NA	Outstanding Shares	4,520,000,000
Counsel	NA	E.P.S.	$7.63
DUNS No.	NA	Shareholders	NA

Business: The groups principle activity is to explore and produce crude oil and natural gas and the refining and marketing of petroleum products. The group operates through three major divisions namely upstream operations; downstream operations; and chemicals. The group operates from United States.

Primary SIC and add'l.: 6719 1221 2899 2911 1311 1094

CIK No: 0000879764

Subsidiaries: Total Energy Resources, Total Gas & Power Ltd

Officers: Christophe De Margerie/Dir., CEO, Francois Cornelis/Vice Chmn., Pres. - Chemicals, Pierre-Christian Clout/Sr. VP, Chmn. - Hutchinson, Chemicals, Patrick Pouyanne/Sr. VP - Strategy, Business Development and Research & Development, Exploration & Production, Upstream, Ian Howat/VP - Corporate Strategy, Holding, Alain Gremillet/General Sec - Downstream, Refining, Marketing, Francoise Leroy/General Sec. - Chemicals, Andre Tricoire/Exec. Officers - Downstream, Refining, Refining, Marketing, Robert Castaigne/CFO, Yves-Marie Dalibard/VP - Corporate Communications, Holding, Peter Herbel/General Counsel, Philippe Boisseau/Sr. VP - Middle East, Exploration, Production, Upstream, Jean-Marc Jaubert/Sr. VP - Industrial Safety, Bruno Weymuller/Pres. - Strategy, Risk Assessment, Charles Paris De Bollardiere/Treasurer - Chemical Group *(30 Officers included in Index)*

Directors: Christophe De Margerie/Dir., CEO, Thierry Desmarest/Chmn., Francois Cornelis/Vice Chmn., Pres. - Chemicals, Peter Levene/Dir., Michel Pebereau/Dir., Pierre Vaillaud/Dir., Antoine Jeancourt-Galignani/Dir., Serge Tchuruk/Dir., Daniel Bouton/Dir., Bertrand Collomb/Dir., Thierry De Rudder/Dir., Anne Lauvergeon/Dir., Daniel Boeuf/Dir., Paul Desmarais/Dir., Bertrand Jacquillat/Dir. *(16 Directors included in Index)*

Financial Data: Fiscal Year End:12/31 **Latest Annual Data:** 12/31/2006

Year	Sales	Net Income
2006	$175,189,287,000	$15,051,420,000
2005	$145,228,759,000	$13,735,487,000
2004	$167,411,880,000	$9,852,332,000

Curr. Assets:	$56,469,231,000	Curr. Liab.:	$44,259,097,000	P/E Ratio:	15.26
Plant, Equip.:	$62,130,677,000	Total Liab.:	$88,817,901,000	Indic. Yr. Divd.:	$2.330
Total Assets:	$183,726,347,000	Net Worth:	$94,908,445,000	Debt/ Equity:	NA

Total Luxury Group Inc

PO Box 568, Rumson, NJ, 07760; *PH:* 1-212-682-7888; *http://* www.totalluxurygroup.com;
Email: info@totalluxurygroup.com

General - Incorporation	DE	Stock- Price on:12/24/2007	NA
Employees	NA	Stock Exchange	OTC
Auditor	Total Luxury Group Inc.	Ticker Symbol	TLEI
Stk Agt	Equity Transfer Services Inc	Outstanding Shares	NA
Counsel	NA	E.P.S.	-$0.391
DUNS No.	NA	Shareholders	NA

Business: The group's principal activity is to provide interactive software based games of chance and sports wagering facilities. These services are offered online and are accessible world-wide through the Internet. The operations are conducted through two subsidiaries intercapital global fund ltd. And total entertainment Canada, ltd. The customer plays various casino-style games that include slots, blackjack, poker, roulette, red dog, keno, craps, let em ride and mini baccarat or bingo, if the customer is using one of the bingo sites.

Primary SIC and add'l.: 7999 7379 6719

CIK No: 0001098301

Officers: Robert D. Bonnell/Dir., Chief Exec Officer, Robert Lawand/Dir., CFO, Janon A. Costley/Dir., COO

Directors: Robert D. Bonnell/Dir., Chief Exec Officer, Robert Lawand/Dir., CFO, Janon A. Costley/Dir., COO

Financial Data: *Fiscal Year End:*12/31   *Latest Annual Data:* 12/31/2006

Year	Sales	Net Income
2006	$9,000	-$11,458,000
2005	NA	-$26,000
2004	NA	-$16,000

Curr. Assets:	$70,000	Curr. Liab.:	$1,430,000		
Plant, Equip.:	$38,000	Total Liab.:	$1,430,000	Indic. Yr. Divd.:	NA
Total Assets:	$161,000	Net Worth:	-$1,269,000	Debt/ Equity:	NA

Total System Services Inc

1600 First Ave., Columbus, GA, 31901; *PH:* 1-706-649-5220; *http://* www.tsys.com;
Email: news@tsys.com

General - Incorporation	GA	Stock- Price on:12/24/2007	$30.72
Employees	6,644	Stock Exchange	NYSE
Auditor	KPMG LLP	Ticker Symbol	TSS
Stk Agt	Mellon Investor Services LLC	Outstanding Shares	197,400,000
Counsel	NA	E.P.S.	$1.34
DUNS No.	10-199-1222	Shareholders	NA

Business: The group's principal activity is to provide electronic payment processing and related services. It operates under two segments: domestic-based processing services and international-based processing services. The services include card production, statement preparation, electronic commerce services, portfolio management services, account acquisition, credit evaluation, risk management and customer service to clients. In addition, the group provides other services consisting of mail and correspondence processing services, teleservicing and offset printing. The group links buyers and sellers with a comprehensive on-line system of data processing services throughout the United States, Canada, Mexico, Honduras and the Caribbean. On 28-Apr-2003, the group acquired enhancement services corporation. On 03-Aug-2004, the group acquired clarity payment solutions inc.

Primary SIC and add'l.: 7374 7377

CIK No: 0000721683

Subsidiaries: China Unionpay Data Services Company Limited, Columbus Depot Equipment Company, Columbus Productions, Inc., Enhancement Services Corporation, Golden Retriever Systems, LLC, GP Network Corporation, Merlin Solutions LLC, ProCard, Inc., Total System Services de Mexico, S.A. de C.V., TSYS Canada, Inc., TSYS Europe (Netherlands) B.V., TSYS Japan Co., Ltd., TSYS Prepaid, Inc., TSYS Servicios Corporativos, TSYS Servicos De Transacoes Eletronicas Ltda 20 Subsidiaries included in the Index

Officers: Philip W. Tomlinson/Chmn., CEO/$3,692,005.00, Dorenda K. Weaver/Group Executive, Chief Accounting Officer, Troy M. Woods/Dir., COO, Pres./$2,650,611.00, George C. Woodruff/Dir. Emeritus, Dir. - Real Estate Developer, Connie C. Dudley/Exec. VP, Rebecca K. Yarbrough/Dir., Private Investor, Sanders G. Griffith/Sec., James B. Lipham/Sr. Exec. VP, CFO/$1,735,632.00, Colleen W. Kynard/Exec. VP, Gaylon Jowers/Exec. VP - Sales, Strategy, Emerging Markets, William A. Pruett/Sr. Exec. VP/$1,929,539.00, John T. Turner/Dir. - Private Investor, Cyle Mims/Media Relations, External Communications, Shawn Roberts/Investor Relations Officer, Ryland L. Harrelson/Exec. VP *(17 Officers included in Index)*

Directors: Philip W. Tomlinson/Chmn., CEO, Griffin B. Bell/Dir. Emeritus, Gardiner W. Garrard/Dir., Richard Anthony/Dir., James D. Yancey/Dir., George C. Woodruff/Dir. Emeritus, Dir. - Real Estate Developer, Mason H. Lampton/Dir., William B. Turner/Dir. Emeritus, Richard Y. Bradley/Dir., Rebecca K. Yarbrough/Dir., Private Investor, Troy M. Woods/Dir., COO, Pres., James H. Blanchard/Dir., Kriss Cloninger/Dir., Wayne G. Clough/Dir., Sidney E. Harris/Dir. *(26 Directors included in Index)*

Owners: Richard E. Anthony, James H. Blanchard/1.00%, Wayne G. Clough, Lynn H. Page, Rebecca K. Yarbrough, John T. Turner, Alfred W. Jones, Troy M. Woods, Gardiner W. Garrard, Kriss Cloninger, Philip W. Tomlinson, James B. Lipham, Insiders/2.90%, Mason H. Lampton, Richard Y. Bradley *(22 Owners included in Index)*

Financial Data: *Fiscal Year End:*12/31   *Latest Annual Data:* 12/31/2006

Year	Sales	Net Income
2006	$1,787,171,000	$249,163,000
2005	$1,602,931,000	$194,520,000
2004	$1,187,008,000	$150,558,000

Curr. Assets:	$744,716,000	Curr. Liab.:	$295,787,000	P/E Ratio:	23.63
Plant, Equip.:	$271,321,000	Total Liab.:	$416,881,000	Indic. Yr. Divd.:	$0.280
Total Assets:	$1,634,241,000	Net Worth:	$1,217,360,000	Debt/ Equity:	NA

Touchstone Mining Ltd

808 Nelson St., Ste. 2103, Vancouver, BC, V6Z 2H2; *PH:* 1-604-684-7619

General - Incorporation	NV	Stock- Price on:12/24/2007	NA
Employees	NA	Stock Exchange	OTC
Auditor	Child, Van Wagoner & Bradshaw, PLLC	Ticker Symbol	THSM
Stk Agt	Pacific Stock Transfer Company	Outstanding Shares	NA
Counsel	NA	E.P.S.	NA
DUNS No.	NA	Shareholders	NA

Business: The groups principal activity is engaging in the search of mineral deposits or reserves, which are not in either the development or production stage. The group has conducted exploration activities on the Boulder Group property, lode mining claims, in Humboldt County, Nevada.

Primary SIC and add'l.: 1400

CIK No: 0001347858

Owners: Douglas W. Scheving/54.00%, Insiders/54.00%

Touchstone Resources USA Inc

1600 Smith St., Ste. 5100, Houston, TX, 19004; *PH:* 1-713-784-1113; *http://* cygnusoilandgas.com

General - Incorporation	DE	Stock- Price on:12/24/2007	NA
Employees	8	Stock Exchange	NA
Auditor	L J Soldinger Assoc. LLC	Ticker Symbol	NA
Stk Agt	StockTrans, Inc.	Outstanding Shares	NA
Counsel	NA	E.P.S.	-$0.222
DUNS No.	NA	Shareholders	NA

Business: The group is in its development stage seeking to explore, develop and produce oil and natural gas. The group also seeks to acquire oil and gas producing properties located primarily in Texas, Mississippi, Louisiana and other traditional oil producing states in the southern United States and New Zealand. During 2004, the group acquired touchstone Texas, touchstone Louisiana inc, touchstone vicksburg inc, touchstone awakino inc, 75% membership interest in knox gas llc, maverick basin exploration llc and touchstone pierce exploration llc

Primary SIC and add'l.: 1311 1321 1382 1381 4612

CIK No: 0001162721

Subsidiaries: CE Operating, LLC, PF Louisiana, LLC, PHT West Pleito, LLC, Touchstone Louisiana, Inc., Touchstone Mississippi, LLC, Touchstone New Zealand, Inc, Touchstone Oklahoma, LLC, Touchstone Resources USA, Inc., Touchstone Texas Properties, Inc.

Officers: Roger L. Abel/Chmn., CEO, Stephen C. Haynes/CFO, Patrick R. Oenbring/COO, Jerry Walrath/VP - Land, Project Development

Directors: Roger L. Abel/Chmn., CEO, Gerald R. Bennett/Dir.

Owners: Millennium Global High Yield FundLimited/9.50%, Kings Road HoldingsII LLC/22.00%, Insiders/1.30%, Altafin BV/7.30%, Gerald R. Bennett, Michael Marcus/9.30%, Roger L. Abel, SF Capital Partners Ltd./6.90%, Stephen C. Haynes, RHP Master Fund, Ltd./5.10%, Jerry Walrath, Stephen P. Harrington/10.20%, Capital Ventures International/6.90%

Financial Data: *Fiscal Year End:*12/31   *Latest Annual Data:* 12/31/2005

Year	Sales	Net Income
2005	$489,000	-$13,685,000
2004	$201,000	-$15,595,000
2003	NA	-$42,000

Curr. Assets:	$8,681,000	Curr. Liab.:	$10,339,000		
Plant, Equip.:	$7,699,000	Total Liab.:	$11,873,000	Indic. Yr. Divd.:	NA
Total Assets:	$16,465,000	Net Worth:	$4,592,000	Debt/ Equity:	NA

Touchstone Software Corp

1538 Tpke. St., North Andover, MA, 01845; *PH:* 1-978-686-6468;
http:// www.touchstonesoftware.com; *Email:* investor@esupport.com

General - Incorporation	DE	Stock- Price on:12/24/2007	$1.8
Employees	13	Stock Exchange	OTC
Auditor	Sullivan Bille P.C.	Ticker Symbol	TSSW
Stk Agt	American Stock Transfer & Trust Co.	Outstanding Shares	12,120,000
Counsel	Devine Millimet & Branch	E.P.S.	$0.08
DUNS No.	06-818-5081	Shareholders	NA

Business: The group's principal activities are to design, develop and market system management software. The group markets and supports a line of computer problem-solving utility software and supporting products and engineering services which simplify personal computer installation, support and maintenance. The system management software includes basic input and output (bios) software upgrades, personal computer diagnostics for personal computers and embedded systems. The products of group include bios upgrade solutions, checkit portable edition, isa and pci postcards. The group also provides bios engineering and OEM services.

Primary SIC and add'l.: 7372

CIK No: 0000751160

Subsidiaries: eSupport.com, Inc.

Officers: Jason K. Raza/CEO, Pres.

Directors: Pierre A. Narath/Chmn., Ronald M. Maas/Dir.

Owners: Insiders/36.70%, Jason K. Raza/6.20%, Ronald R. Maas/2.20%, Pierre A. Narath/28.30%

Financial Data: *Fiscal Year End:*12/31   *Latest Annual Data:* 12/31/2006

Year	Sales	Net Income
2006	$3,219,000	$724,000
2005	$1,615,000	-$20,000
2004	$1,606,000	-$75,000

Curr. Assets:	$964,000	Curr. Liab.:	$288,000	P/E Ratio:	22.50
Plant, Equip.:	$436,000	Total Liab.:	$392,000	Indic. Yr. Divd.:	NA
Total Assets:	$1,584,000	Net Worth:	$1,192,000	Debt/ Equity:	0.0687

Tournigan Gold Corp

24th Fl., 1111 W Georgia St., Vancouver, BC, V6E 4M3; *PH:* 1-604-683-8320;
http:// www.tournigan.com; *Email:* info@tournigan.com

General - Incorporation	Canada	Stock- Price on:12/24/2007	$3.976
Employees	NA	Stock Exchange	OTC
Auditor	Bedfordcurry Andco.	Ticker Symbol	TVCZF
Stk Agt	Computershare Trust Co	Outstanding Shares	NA
Counsel	Stikeman Elliott LLP	E.P.S.	NA
DUNS No.	NA	Shareholders	NA

Business: The group's principal activity is to provide mineral exploration and development with a focus on European gold projects. The company is focused on developing two advanced gold projects in Europe: Curraghinalt in Northern Ireland and Kremnica in Slovakia. Both wholly owned projects host defined gold resources that can be advanced to production but also encompass exploration potential. In mid-January 2005, drilling programs were underway at Kremnica, with a new resource estimation almost complete and engineering studies in progress at Curraghinalt. In December 2004, the company completed the acquisition of Ulster Minerals Limited, owner of the exploration license covering the Curraghinalt gold project.

Primary SIC and add'l.: 1040

CIK No: 0001271199

Subsidiaries: Dalradian Gold Limited, Kremnica Gold, a.s., Ludovika Holding, s.r.o., Tournigan Resources Ukraine Ltd., Ulster Minerals Limited

Officers: James Walchuck/Dir., CEO, Pres., Mike Mracek/COO, Kent Ausburn/VP - Exploration, Nancy La Couvee/48/Corp. Sec., Hans Retterath/CFO, Joseph Ringwald/VP - Technical Services, Patrick Soares/VP - Investor, Stephen Stine/VP - Corporate Development

Directors: James Walchuck/Dir., CEO, Pres., Ronald Shorr/Dir., Rex McLennan/Dir., Hein Poulus/Dir., Peter Bojtos/Dir., Michael J. Hopley/Dir., David Montgomery/Dir.

Tower Automotive Inc

27175 Haggerty Rd., Novi, MI, 48377; ***PH:*** 1-248-675-6000; ***http://*** www.towerautomotive.com

General		**Stock**	
Incorporation	DE	Price on:12/24/2007	$0.02
Employees	NA	Stock Exchange	NA
Auditor	Deloitte & Touche LLP	Ticker Symbol	NA
Stk Agt.	EquiServe Trust Co N.A	Outstanding Shares	58,640,000
Counsel	Varnum Riddering S & H LLP	E.P.S	-$3.45
DUNS No.	80-895-1248	Shareholders	NA

Business: The groups principle activity is to supply automotive metal structural components and assemblies. The groups products include lower vehicle frames and structures, complex body-in-white assembly and suspension components. Specific customers of the group include BMW, Chrysler and Citroen. The group operates from United States.

Primary SIC and add'l.: 3711 3465 3714

CIK No: 0000925548

Subsidiaries: Algoods USA, Inc., Algoods, Inc., Carron Industries, LLC, Changchun Tower Golden Ring Automotive Products Company, Ltd., CJT Automotive LLC, DTA Development, LLC, FELISSA Grundstrucks Vermietungsgesellschaft mbH, FELISSA Grundstrucks Vermietungsgesellschaft mbH & Co. Objekt Duisburg GmbH, Metalsa S. de R. L., MT Stahl Handelsgesellschaft GmbH, MT Stahl Handelsgesellschaft GmbH & Co KG, MT Stahl Handelsgesellschaft Verwaltung GmbH, Oslamt, S.p.A., R.J. Tower Corporation, Seojin Industrial Co., Ltd. 74 Subsidiaries included in the Index

Officers: Kathleen A. Ligocki/51/Dir., CEO, Pres., Jeffrey L. Kersten/40/Sr. VP, Corporate Controller, Vincent Pairet/45/Pres. - Europe, South America, James A. Mallak/52/CFO, Chief Accounting Officer, Sec., William D. Pumphrey/48/Pres. - North America Operations, Gyula Meleghy/52/Pres. - Asia, Renee E. Franklin/42/Sr. VP - Global Human Resources, Kathy J. Johnston/50/Sr. VP - Strategy, Business Development, Paul Radkoski/48/Sr. VP - Global Purchasing, Joe Kirik/Contact - Media

Directors: Kathleen A. Ligocki/51/Dir., CEO, Pres., S. A. Johnson/67/Chmn., Anthony G. Fernandes/62/Dir., Juergen M. Geissinger/48/Dir., Ali Jenab/45/Dir., Joseph F. Loughrey/58/Dir., James R. Lozelle/62/Dir., Georgia R. Nelson/57/Dir.

Financial Data: *Fiscal Year End:*12/31 *Latest Annual Data:* 12/31/2006

Year	Sales	Net Income
2006	$2,539,443,000	-$202,066,000
2005	$3,283,653,000	-$373,372,000
2004	$3,178,724,000	-$533,905,000

Curr. Assets:	$737,910,000	**Curr. Liab.:**	$699,819,000		
Plant, Equip.:	$1,038,794,000	**Total Liab.:**	$2,778,849,000	**Indic. Yr. Divd.:**	NA
Total Assets:	$2,291,226,000	**Net Worth:**	-$487,623,000	**Debt/ Equity:**	NA

Tower Bancorp Inc

40 Ctr Sq., Greencastle, PA, 17225; ***PH:*** 1-717-597-2137; ***http://*** www.fnbgc.com

General		**Stock**	
Incorporation	PA	Price on:12/24/2007	$43.9
Employees	153	Stock Exchange	OTC
Auditor	Smith Elliott Kearns & Co. LLC	Ticker Symbol	TOBC
Stk Agt.	Registrar & Transfer Co	Outstanding Shares	2,360,000
Counsel	NA	E.P.S	$2.86
DUNS No.	15-650-6461	Shareholders	NA

Business: The group's principal activity is the provision of banking and related services in south central Pennsylvania. The services provided by the group include accepting demand, time and savings deposits and granting loans to individuals, corporations, partnerships, associations, municipalities and other governmental bodies. The group also renders services as a trustee, executor, administrator, guardian, managing agent, custodian, investment advisor and other fiduciary activities. The group's operations are conducted through nine branch offices.

Primary SIC and add'l.: 6712 6021

CIK No: 0000740942

Subsidiaries: The First National Bank of Greencastle

Officers: Jeff B. Shank/52/CEO, Pres./$264,199.00, Donald G. Kunkle/VP, John H. McDowell/Sr. Exec. VP/$181,306.00, Frank Klink/CFO/$121,313.00, John Duffey/Exec. VP/$459,203.00, Margaret Kobel/Sr. VP/$97,393.00

Directors: Robert L. Pensinger/74/Vice Chmn., Kermit G. Hicks/72/Dir., Mark E. Gayman/55/Dir., James H. Craig/74/Dir., Harry D. Johnston/71/Dir., Patricia A. Carbaugh/64/Dir.

Owners: Patricia A. Carbaugh, Kermit G. Hicks/1.46%, Robert L. Pensinger, James H. Craig, Terry L. Randall/2.34%, Mark E. Gayman, Harry D. Johnston, John H. McDowell, Franklin T. Klink, Lois E. Easton, Insiders/9.49%, Jeff B. Shank/1.18%, Frederic M. Frederick

Financial Data: *Fiscal Year End:*12/31 *Latest Annual Data:* 12/31/2006

Year	Sales	Net Income
2006	$33,123,000	$6,132,000
2005	$21,296,000	$5,032,000
2004	$18,462,000	$4,723,000

Curr. Assets:	$22,596,000	**Curr. Liab.:**	$410,829,000	**P/E Ratio:**	15.35
Plant, Equip.:	$11,579,000	**Total Liab.:**	$460,614,000	**Indic. Yr. Divd.:**	$1.040
Total Assets:	$542,167,000	**Net Worth:**	$81,553,000	**Debt/ Equity:**	0.4444

Tower Financial Corp

116 E Berry St., Fort Wayne, IN, 46802; ***PH:*** 1-260-427-7000; ***http://*** www.towerbank.net

General		**Stock**	
Incorporation	IN	Price on:12/24/2007	$15.05
Employees	186	Stock Exchange	NDQ
Auditor	Crowe Chizek & Co. LLC	Ticker Symbol	TOFC
Stk Agt.	Computershare Trust Co	Outstanding Shares	4,080,000
Counsel	Baker & Daniels	E.P.S	-$0.248
DUNS No.	NA	Shareholders	NA

Business: The group's principal activities are to provide various commercial and consumer banking services in allen county, Indiana, the city of fort wayne and huntington county. The operations are conducted through its wholly owned banking subsidiary, tower bank and trust company. The services are mainly offered to small and medium-sized businesses and individual customers. The loans offered by the group include commercial, consumer and residential mortgage loans. It accepts deposits that include checking, savings and money market accounts, certificates of deposit. The group also offers trust and courier services to customers through its investment management and trust services.

Primary SIC and add'l.: 6022 6712

CIK No: 0001072847

Subsidiaries: Tower Bank & Trust Company, Tower Capital Trust 1, Tower Capital Trust 2

Officers: Donald F. Schenkel/Chmn., CEO, Pres./$662,644.00, Amy Thompson/Private Banking Advisor, Michael D. Cahill/COO, Exec. VP, Sec./$279,942.00, Darrell L. Jaggers/Chief Lending Officer, Sr. VP/$226,984.00, Gary D. Shearer/Exec. VP/$220,003.00, Wendell L. Bontrager/Sr. VP, Chief Deposit Officer, Kevin Noll/First VP - Financial Advisor, Tower Investment Services, Doug Stephens/VP - Private Banking Advisor, Timothy L. Frey/VP, Investment Officer, Jo Ellen Gustin/VP, Trust Operations Mgr., Rebecca A. Hillyard/VP, Trust Officer, Bob Nicholas/VP - Financial Advisor, Tower Investment Services, Sharon J. Peters/VP, Trust Officer, Graig Stettner/VP, Investment Officer, Dan Kelker/First VP - Small Business Services *(32 Officers included in Index)*

Directors: Donald F. Schenkel/Chmn., CEO, Pres., Michael S. Gouloff/Dir., Kathryn D. Callen/Dir., William G. Niezer/Dir., Jerome F. Henry/Dir., John V. Tippmann/Dir., Irene A. Walters/Dir., Debra A. Niezer/Dir., R.V. Prasad Mantravadi/Dir., Keith E. Busse/Dir., Joseph D. Ruffolo/Dir.

Owners: Michael S. Gouloff, Donald F. Schenkel/2.14%, Keith E. Busse/1.39%, Debra A. Niezer, Gary D. Shearer, John V. Tippmann/2.05%, Joseph D. Ruffolo, Michael D. Cahill, Irene A. Walters, William G. Niezer, Jerome F. Henry/6.64%, Darrell L. Jaggers, Prasad R.V. Mantravadi, Edwin Fraser/6.12%, Donald R. Willis *(17 Owners included in Index)*

Financial Data: *Fiscal Year End:*12/31 *Latest Annual Data:* 12/31/2006

Year	Sales	Net Income
2006	$46,183,000	$3,688,000
2005	$33,273,000	$3,439,000
2004	$25,239,000	$2,479,000

Curr. Assets:	$32,485,000	**Curr. Liab.:**	$599,687,000	**P/E Ratio:**	28.94
Plant, Equip.:	$5,871,000	**Total Liab.:**	$620,197,000	**Indic. Yr. Divd.:**	$0.180
Total Assets:	$671,155,000	**Net Worth:**	$50,958,000	**Debt/ Equity:**	0.3410

Tower Group Inc

120 Broadway, 31st Fl., New York, NY, 10271; ***PH:*** 1-212-655-2000; ***http://*** www.twrgrp.com; ***Email:*** info@twrgrp.com

General		**Stock**	
Incorporation	DE	Price on:12/24/2007	$32.79
Employees	403	Stock Exchange	NDQ
Auditor	Lambert & Co. LLP	Ticker Symbol	TWGP
Stk Agt.	Bank of New York	Outstanding Shares	23,100,000
Counsel	NA	E.P.S	$2.02
DUNS No.	NA	Shareholders	NA

Business: The groups principle activity is to provide property and casualty insurance products. The products of the group include Commercial multiple-peril, Workers Compensation, Homeowners and Fire and allied lines. The groups operates through three segments namely Insurance, Reinsurance and Insurance Services. The group operates from the United States. The group's quarterly revenue for September 2007 was 112.01 millions of USD.

Primary SIC and add'l.: 6411 6331

CIK No: 0001289592

Subsidiaries: Tower Insurance Company of New York, Tower National Insurance Company, Tower Risk Management Corp.

Officers: Michael H. Lee/Chmn., CEO, Pres., Francis M. Colalucci/Dir., Sr. VP, CFO, Treasurer, Gary S. Maier/Sr. VP, Chief Underwriting Officer, Christian K. Pechmann/Sr. VP - Underwriting Operations, Jerome H. Kaiser/CIO, Sr. VP, Stephen L. Kibblehouse/Sr. VP, General Counsel, Michael Haines/Managing VP, Chief Accounting Officer, Catherine M. Wragg/Managing VP - Human Resources, Sheri Singh/Assist. VP - Operations, Marina Contiero/VP - Reinsurance, Angelica Lopez/VP - Planning, Laurie A. Ranegar/Sr. VP - Operations, Michael Mihalik/VP - Business Information Technology, Ray Lamitola/Business Development Representative, Helen Nigro/Business Development Representative *(44 Officers included in Index)*

Directors: Michael H. Lee/Chmn., CEO, Pres., Francis M. Colalucci/Dir., Sr. VP, CFO, Treasurer, Steven W. Schuster/Dir., Charles A. Bryan/Dir., William W. Fox/Dir., Austin P. Young/Dir.

Owners: Francis M. Colalucci, Michael H. Lee/12.69%, Charles A. Bryan, Gary S. Maier, Steven G. Fauth, William W. Fox, Austin P. Young, Christian K. Pechmann, Steven W. Schuster, Insiders/13.52%

Financial Data: *Fiscal Year End:*12/31 *Latest Annual Data:* 12/31/2006

Year	Sales	Net Income
2006	$299,263,000	$36,764,000
2005	$219,754,000	$20,754,000
2004	$107,690,000	$9,029,000

Curr. Assets:	$391,509,000	**Curr. Liab.:**	$61,786,000	**P/E Ratio:**	16.23
Plant, Equip.:	$20,563,000	**Total Liab.:**	$730,162,000	**Indic. Yr. Divd.:**	$0.100
Total Assets:	$954,082,000	**Net Worth:**	$223,920,000	**Debt/ Equity:**	0.3207

Tower Properties Co

911 Main St., Ste 100, Kansas City, MO, 64105; ***PH:*** 1-816-421-8255; ***http://*** www.towerproperties.com; ***Email:*** propertymanagement@towerproperties.com

General - Incorporation .... MO
Employees 54
Auditor .... KPMG LLP
Stk Agt .... UMB Bank, N.A.
Counsel .... NA
DUNS No. 07-306-9346

Stock - Price on:12/24/2007 .... $350
Stock Exchange .... OTC
Ticker Symbol .... TOWP
Outstanding Shares .... NA
E.P.S. $32.33
Shareholders .... NA

Business: The group's principal activities are to own, develop, lease and manage real property located in johnson county, Kansas, clay, st. Louis and jackson counties, Missouri. At 31-Dec- 2003, the group owns and manages 1,278,800 square feet of office and warehouse space. The real estate includes office buildings, warehouse/office facility held for lease, automobile parking garages, apartments and land held for future sale.

Primary SIC and add'l.: 6531

CIK No: 0000098827

Subsidiaries: Tower Acquisition Corp.

Officers: Buzz Willard/CEO, Pres., Margaret V. Allinder/VP, Controller, Dan Ellerman/VP - Construction, Gibson E. Kerr/VP, Thomas R. Willard/Pres., Margaret V. Schroeder/VP, Controller, Chris Erdley/VP, Dir. - Real Estate Services, Stan Weber/CFO, VP, Michael Schumacher/Sr. Project Mgr., Regina T. Camden/Property Mgr.

Financial Data: Fiscal Year End:12/31   **Latest Annual Data:** 12/31/2004

Year	Sales	Net Income
2004	$24,115,000	-$397,000
2003	$22,676,000	$789,000
2002	$23,927,000	$1,795,000

Curr. Assets:	$606,000	Curr. Liab.:	$2,238,000	P/E Ratio:	10.83
Plant, Equip.:	$104,456,000	Total Liab.:	$80,121,000	Indic. Yr. Divd.:	NA
Total Assets:	$115,892,000	Net Worth:	$35,771,000	Debt/ Equity:	NA

Tower Semiconductor Ltd

2350 Mission College Blvd., Ste. 500, Santa Clara, CA, 95054; **PH:** 1-408-327-8900; **Fax:** 1-408-969-9831; **http://** www.towersemi.com

General - Incorporation .... Israel
Employees 1,238
Auditor .... Brightman Almagor & Co
Stk Agt .... Registrar & Transfer Co
Counsel ...... Ehrenreich Eilenberg & Krause LLP
DUNS No. 60-036-8252

Stock - Price on:12/24/2007 .... $1.5
Stock Exchange .... NDQ
Ticker Symbol .... TSEM
Outstanding Shares 120,880,000
E.P.S. .... -$0.69
Shareholders .... NA

Business: The groups principle activity is to provide manufacturing and related designing services for integrated circuits, or ic's, on silicon wafers in geometries from 1.0 to 0.35 micron, using its advanced technological capabilities. The group operates from United States.

Primary SIC and add'l.: 3674

CIK No: 0000928876

Subsidiaries: Tower Semiconductor USA, Inc.

Officers: Russell Ellwanger/CEO, Rafi Nave/CTO, Fra Drumm/VP, GM - TSU, North America, Ami Herman/VP - Sales, Israel, Europe, Asia, Ephie Koltin/VP, Fab 1 Mgr., Nati Somekh Gilboa/Legal Counsel - Corp. Sec., Dalit Dahan/Dir. - Human Resources, Rafi Mor/VP - Business Development, Shirazi Oren/CFO, VP - Finance, Itzhak Edrei/Sr. VP - Product Lines, VP - Sales, Dudu Vidan/VP, Fab 2 Mgr., Shimon Dahan/VP, Corporate Manufacturing Service Mgr., Oren Shirazi/CFO, VP - Finance

Directors: Dov Moran/52/Chmn., Melvin Keating/61/Dir., Nir Gilad/51/Dir., Miri Katz/57/Dir.

Owners: Bank Hapoalim, SanDisk Corporation, Macronix International Co. Ltd, Israel Corporation Ltd., Alliance Semiconductor Corporation, Bank Leumi

Financial Data: Fiscal Year End:12/31   **Latest Annual Data:** 12/31/2006

Year	Sales	Net Income
2006	$187,438,000	-$167,927,000
2005	$101,991,000	-$203,082,000
2004	$126,055,000	-$137,768,000

Curr. Assets:	$120,437,000	Curr. Liab.:	$84,126,000	P/E Ratio:	15.26
Plant, Equip.:	$531,209,000	Total Liab.:	$674,616,000	Indic. Yr. Divd.:	NA
Total Assets:	$714,132,000	Net Worth:	$39,516,000	Debt/ Equity:	NA

Tower Tech Holdings Inc

101 S 16TH ST., Manitowoc, WI, 54221; **PH:** 1-920-684-5531; **Fax:** 1-920-684-5579; **http://** www.towertechsystems.com; **Email:** info@towertechsystems.com

General - Incorporation .... NV
Employees 92
Auditor .... Carver Moquist & Oconnor, LLC
Stk Agt .... Pacific Stock Transfer Company
Counsel .... NA
DUNS No. .... NA

Stock - Price on:12/24/2007 .... $4
Stock Exchange .... OTC
Ticker Symbol .... TWRT
Outstanding Shares 47,720,000
E.P.S. $0.03
Shareholders .... NA

Business: The groups principle activities include manufacturing fabricated towers for wind turbines that are sold for use in the support of wind turbines. The group operates from the United States.

Primary SIC and add'l.: 3511

CIK No: 0001120370

Subsidiaries: Tower Tech Systems, Inc

Officers: Terence P. Fox/52/Dir., Sec., General Counsel, Raymond L. Brickner/50/Dir., COO, Pres., Randall D. Brumbelow/56/Interim CFO

Directors: Christopher C. Allie/59/Chmn., Daniel P. Wergin/66/Dir., Raymond L. Brickner/50/Dir., COO, Pres.

Owners: Daniel P. Wergin/11.10%, Christopher C. Allie/11.00%, Insiders/44.20%, Terence P. Fox/11.00%, Raymond L. Brickner/11.00%, Jeffrey L. Gendell/26.50%, Randall D. Brumbelow

Financial Data: Fiscal Year End:12/31   **Latest Annual Data:** 12/31/2006

Year	Sales	Net Income
2006	$4,023,000	-$2,734,000
2005	NA	-$8,000
2004	NA	-$7,000

Curr. Assets:	$588,000	Curr. Liab.:	$8,402,000		
Plant, Equip.:	$2,799,000	Total Liab.:	$9,208,000	Indic. Yr. Divd.:	NA
Total Assets:	$3,895,000	Net Worth:	-$5,314,000	Debt/ Equity:	NA

Town Sports International Holdings Inc

888 Seventh Ave., 25th Fl., New York, NY, 10106; **Fax:** 1-212-664-8906; **http://** corporate.mysportsclubs.com

General - Incorporation .... DE
Employees 3,000
Auditor .... PricewaterhouseCoopers LLP
Stk Agt .... Bank of New York
Counsel .... NA
DUNS No. .... NA

Stock - Price on:12/24/2007 .... $19.89
Stock Exchange .... NDQ
Ticker Symbol .... CLUB
Outstanding Shares 26,120,000
E.P.S. $0.53
Shareholders .... NA

Business: The groups principle activities include owning and operating fitness. The group products sold under the trade names New York Sports Clubs, Washington Sports Clubs, Boston Sports Clubs and Philadelphia Sports Clubs. The group operates the United States. The group's quarterly revenue for September 2007 was 118.89 millions of USD.

Primary SIC and add'l.: 7991 7991

CIK No: 0001281774

Subsidiaries: Services, LLC, Town Sports AG, Town Sports International, LLC, TSI 217 Broadway, LLC, TSI Alexandria, LLC, TSI Allston, LLC, TSI Andover, LLC, TSI Ardmore, LLC, TSI Arthro-Fitness, TSI Astoria, LLC, TSI Battery Park, LLC, TSI Bay Ridge 86thStreet, LLC, TSI Bayridge, LLC, TSI Bethesda, LLC, TSI Boylston, LLC 185 Subsidiaries included in the Index

Officers: Alexander A. Alimanestianu/CEO, Pres./$813,132.00, Robert J. Giardina/Dir., COO, Pres./$1,074,943.00, Kelley Bubolo/Boston Sports Clubs, VP - Operations, Matt Daniel/VP - Corporate Operations, Karl Derleth/VP - Facilities, Merrill Richmond/VP - Marketing, Christopher Ruta/Sr. VP - Sales - Operations, Randall C. Stephen/COO/$452,280.00, Ed Trainor/VP - Fitness, Services, Product Development, James Rizzo/Sr. VP - Human Resources, Timothy Keightley/VP - Fitness - Personal Training, Rich Destasio/New York Sports Clubs, VP - Operations, David Kastin/Sr. VP, General Counsel, Sec., Raymond Dewhirst/VP - Development, Real Estate, Daniel Gallagher/VP - Finance (22 Officers included in Index)

Directors: Rice J. Edmonds/Dir., Bruce C. Bruckmann/Dir., Kevin McCall/Dir., Jason M. Fish/Dir., Keith E. Alessi/Dir., Paul N. Arnold/Dir., Robert J. Giardina/Dir., COO, Pres., Thomas J. Galligan/Dir.

Owners: BRS./27.10%, Robert J. Giardina/3.40%, Randall C. Stephen, Jennifer H. Prue, Mark N. Smith/1.80%, Rice J. Edmonds/27.10%, Insiders/37.80%, Paul N. Arnold, Barclays Global Entities/5.00%, Bruce C. Bruckmann/28.10%, Keith E. Alessi, Farallon Entities/20.50%, Alexander A. Alimanestianu/2.90%, Richard G. Pyle/3.00%

Financial Data: Fiscal Year End:12/31   **Latest Annual Data:** 12/31/2006

Year	Sales	Net Income
2006	$433,080,000	$4,647,000
2005	$388,556,000	$1,769,000
2004	$353,031,000	-$3,905,000

Curr. Assets:	$30,030,000	Curr. Liab.:	$88,396,000		
Plant, Equip.:	$281,606,000	Total Liab.:	$441,356,000	Indic. Yr. Divd.:	NA
Total Assets:	$423,527,000	Net Worth:	-$17,829,000	Debt/ Equity:	NA

Towne Bank VA

5716 High St. W, Portsmouth, VA, 23703; **PH:** 1-757-638-7500; **Fax:** 1-757-484-7544; **http://** www.townebankonline.com

General - Incorporation .... OH
Employees 607
Auditor .... NA
Stk Agt .... Registrar & Transfer Co
Counsel .... NA
DUNS No. .... NA

Stock - Price on:12/24/2007 .... $18.17
Stock Exchange .... NDQ
Ticker Symbol .... TOWN
Outstanding Shares 23,990,000
E.P.S. .... NA
Shareholders .... NA

Business: The group operates through its subsidiary whose principal activities include banking and financial states. Services of the group include commercial, retail, and savings banking, including time, savings, money market and demand deposits; commercial, industrial, agricultural, real estate, consumer installment and credit card lending. The group operates from the United States.

Primary SIC and add'l.: 6022

CIK No: 0000887203

Officers: Robert G. Aston/Chmn., CEO, Morgan J. Davis/Dir., Pres., CEO - Towne Financial Services, Ken Wren/Chmn. - Towne Investment Group, William I. Foster/Dir., Pres. - Townebank, Norfolk, Alonzo C. Brandon/Regional Dir. - Norfolk, Ulysses Turner/Regional Dir. - Norfolk, Walter S. Segaloff/Regional Dir. - Peninsula, Charles V. McPhillips/Regional Dir. - Norfolk, Jeffrey G. Miller/Regional Dir. - Norfolk, Keith H. Newby/Regional Dir. - Norfolk, Alan E. Gollihue/Regional Dir. - Portsmouth, William H. Hargrove/Regional Dir. - Portsmouth, James W. Holley/Regional Dir. - Portsmouth, Chris S. Jones/Regional Dir. - Portsmouth, William H. Kline/Regional Dir. - Portsmouth (135 Officers included in Index)

Directors: Robert G. Aston/Chmn., CEO, Morgan J. Davis/Dir., Pres., CEO - Towne Financial Services, Ken Wren/Chmn. - Towne Investment Group, Durbin W. Donahue/Chmn. - Portsmouth, Thomas K. Norment/Chmn. - Williamsburg, John A. Tilhou/Chmn. - Virginia Beach, Thomas C. Broyles/Vice Chmn. - Hampton Roads, Ernest F. Hardee/Vice Chmn., John W. Brown/Chmn. - Chesapeake, Alvin P. Anderson/Dir., Alan S. Witt/Dir., Richard S. Bray/Dir., Paul J. Farrell/Dir., William Ashton Lewis/Dir., Juan M. Montero/Dir. (33 Directors included in Index)

Toyota Motor Corp

9 W 57th St., Ste. 4900, New York, NY, 10019; **PH:** 1-212-223-0303; **Fax:** 1-212-759-7670; **http://** www.toyota.co.jp

General - Incorporation .... Japan
Employees 299,394
Auditor .... PricewaterhouseCoopers LLP
Stk Agt .... Mitsubishi UFJ Trust & Banking Corp
Counsel .... NA
DUNS No. 69-056-4737

Stock - Price on:12/24/2007 .... $124.99
Stock Exchange .... NYSE
Ticker Symbol .... TM
Outstanding Shares 1,600,000,000
E.P.S. $10.35
Shareholders .... NA

Business: The group's principal activities are to manufacture and sell automobiles and provide financial services. The group operates through three segments: automotive, financial services and other. Automotive segment designs, manufactures, assembles and sells passenger cars, recreational and sport-utility vehicles, minivans and trucks and related parts and accessories. Financial services segment provides financing to dealers and their customers for the purchase or lease of toyota vehicles. Other services segment provides intelligent transport systems, information technology-based systems

encompassing car multimedia systems, on-board intelligent systems, advanced transportation systems and transportation infrastructure and logistics systems. The group sells vehicles in 140 countries and other regions. During the year 2004, the group acquired toyota auto body co ltd, kanto auto works ltd, central motor co ltd and pt toyota motor manufacturing Indonesia.

Primary SIC and add'l.: 3714 7514 5010 5511 3711 6141 3713

CIK No: 0001094517

Subsidiaries: Daihatsu Motor Co., Ltd., Daihatsu Motors Co., Ltd., Higashi-Fuji Technical Center, Hino Motors, Ltd., Honsha Plant, Kamigo Plant, Kanto Auto Works, Ltd., Kinu-ura Plant, Motomachi Plant, Myochi Plant, Ooo Toyota Motor, Tahara Plant, Takaoka Plant, Tokyo Financial Services Corporation, Tokyo Toyo-Pet Motor Sales Co., Ltd. 48 Subsidiaries included in the Index

Officers: Tokuichi Uranishi/Dir., Exec. VP, Representative Dir., Yoichi Kaya/74/Corporate Auditor, Kazuo Okamoto/Dir., Exec. VP, Representative Dir., Katsuaki Watanabe/Dir., Pres., Representative Dir., Hiroshi Okuda/Sr. Advisor, Kyoji Sasazu/Dir., Exec. VP, Representative Dir., Koichi Ina/Dir., Sr. MD, Yoshikazu Amano/59/Corporate Auditor, Takeshi Yoshida/Sr. MD, Shinzo Kobuki/Sr. MD, Akira Sasaki/Sr. MD, Hiroshi Kawakami/Sr. MD, Yoichi Morishita/74/Corporate Auditor, Akishige Okada/70/Corporate Auditor, Satoshi Ozawa/Sr. MD *(34 Officers included in Index)*

Directors: Fujio Cho/Chmn., Katsuhiro Nakagawa/Vice Chmn., Shoichiro Toyoda/Honorary Chmn., Mitsuo Kinoshita/Dir., Exec. VP, Representative Dir., Takeshi Uchiyamada/Dir., Exec. VP, Representative Dir., Masatami Takimoto/Dir., Exec. VP, Representative Dir., Akio Toyoda/Dir., Exec. VP, Representative Dir., Kyoji Sasazu/Dir., Exec. VP, Representative Dir., Kazuo Okamoto/Dir., Exec. VP, Representative Dir., Katsuaki Watanabe/Dir., Pres., Representative Dir., Tokuichi Uranishi/Dir., Exec. VP, Representative Dir., Koichi Ina/Dir., Sr. MD, James E. Press/Dir., Sr. MD

Owners: Tokuichi Uranishi, Mamoru Furuhashi, Kazuo Okamoto, Satoshi Ozawa, Akio Toyoda, Koichi Ina, Masaki Nakatsugawa, Masatami Takimoto, Mitsuo Kinoshita, Shoichiro Toyoda, Fujio Cho, Shinzo Kobuki, Hiroshi Okuda, Akira Okabe, Teiji Tachibana *(32 Owners included in Index)*

Financial Data: ***Fiscal Year End:***03/31 ***Latest Annual Data:*** 3/31/2007

Year	Sales	Net Income
2007	$202,864,000,000	$13,927,000,000
2006	$179,083,000,000	$11,681,000,000
2005	$172,749,000,000	$10,907,000,000

Curr. Assets:	$91,387,000,000	***Curr. Liab.:***	$85,373,000,000	***P/E Ratio:***	15.26
Plant, Equip.:	$60,157,000,000	***Total Liab.:***	$154,688,000,000	***Indic. Yr. Divd.:***	$2.230
Total Assets:	$244,587,000,000	***Net Worth:***	$89,899,000,000	***Debt/ Equity:***	NA

Toyota Motor Credit Corp

19001 S Western Ave., Torrance, CA, 90509; ***PH:*** 1-800-334-3331; ***http://*** www.toyotafinancial.com

General - Incorporation	CA	**Stock**- Price on:12/24/2007	$124.7
Employees	299,394	Stock Exchange	NA
Auditor	PricewaterhouseCoopers LLP	Ticker Symbol	NA
Stk Agt.	Chase Manhattan Bank Luxembourg S.A	Outstanding Shares	1,600,000,000
Counsel	NA	E.P.S	$9.66
DUNS No.	12-202-8798	Shareholders	NA

Business: The group's principle activity is to provide retail and wholesale leasing and other financial services to toyota and lexus vehicle authorized dealers and their customers. The group is a wholly owned subsidiary of toyota financial services Americas corporation. The group operates through two segments: financing operations and insurance operations. The financing operations segment includes the retail leasing, retail and wholesales financing and other financial services. The insurance operations segment markets and underwrites claims. The insurance operations segment also provides insurance and contractual coverage related to vehicle service agreements and contractual liability agreements sold by the dealers. The group operates in the United States, Puerto Rico, Mexico and venezuela.

Primary SIC and add'l.: 7359 6411 6159

CIK No: 0000834071

Subsidiaries: Toyota Financial Services Americas Corporation, Toyota Financial Services Corporation, Toyota Motor Corporation, Toyota Motor Insurance Services, Inc.

Officers: George E. Borst/59/Dir., CEO, Pres., Thomas A. Kiel/41/VP, Chief Accounting Officer, Tadashi Nagashino/56/Dir., Exec. VP, Treasurer, John F. Stillo/55/Group VP, CFO, David Pelliccioni/60/Dir., Sr. VP, Sec.

Directors: George E. Borst/59/Dir., CEO, Pres., Tadashi Nagashino/56/Dir., Exec. VP, Treasurer, John F. Stillo/55/Group VP, CFO, Hideto Ozaki/62/Dir., Yukitoshi Funo/61/Dir., Takeshi Suzuki/60/Dir., David Pelliccioni/60/Dir., Sr. VP, Sec., James Lentz/52/Dir.

Financial Data: ***Fiscal Year End:***03/31 ***Latest Annual Data:*** 03/31/2007

Year	Sales	Net Income
2007	$202,864,000,000	$13,927,000,000
2006	$179,083,000,000	$11,681,000,000
2005	$172,749,000,000	$10,907,000,000

Curr. Assets:	$91,387,000,000	***Curr. Liab.:***	$85,373,000,000	***P/E Ratio:***	10.83
Plant, Equip.:	$60,157,000,000	***Total Liab.:***	$149,669,000,000	***Indic. Yr. Divd.:***	NA
Total Assets:	$244,587,000,000	***Net Worth:***	$89,899,000,000	***Debt/ Equity:***	NA

Toys R US Inc

One Geoffrey Way, Wayne, NJ, 07470; ***PH:*** 1-973-617-3500; ***http://*** www.tru.com

General - Incorporation	DE	**Stock**- Price on:12/24/2007	NA
Employees	NA	Stock Exchange	NA
Auditor	Deloitte & Touche LLP	Ticker Symbol	NA
Stk Agt.	Ernest & Young LLP	Outstanding Shares	NA
Counsel	Christopher K. Kay	E.P.S	NA
DUNS No.	00-698-5808	Shareholders	NA

Business: The group's principal activities are to sell toys, children's apparel and baby products. The products include toys, plush, games, bicycles, sporting goods, vhs and DVD movies, electronic and video games, small pools and books. It also provides infant and juvenile furniture and electronics, educational and development products and entertainment computer software for children. The products are also sold through Internet. The trademarks of the group include toys 'r' us(R), babies ' r' us(R), imaginarium (R), and geoffrey(r). At 31-Jan-2004, the group operated 1,501 retail stores worldwide. These consisted of 927 locations comprised of 685 toy stores, 198 specialty baby-juvenile stores and 44 children's clothing stores. The group operates 574 retail stores internationally through licensed and franchised stores.

Primary SIC and add'l.: 5945 5941 5734 5999 5735 5641

CIK No: 0001005414

Subsidiaries: Babies R Us (Australia) Pty Ltd, Babiesrus.com, LLC, Definitive Solutions Company, Inc., G.G. Realty Corp., Ltd., Geoffrey Europe, Inc., Geoffrey Holdings, LLC, Geoffrey International, LLC, Geoffrey School SARL, Geoffrey, Inc., Giraffe Holdings, LLC, Giraffe Intermediate Holdings, LLC, Giraffe Intermediate, LLC, Giraffe Junior Holdings, LLC, Giraffe Junior, LLC, Giraffe Properties, LLC 76 Subsidiaries included in the Index

Officers: Gerald L. Storch/Chmn., CEO, Deborah Derby/Pres. - Babies"r"us, Ron Boire/Exec. VP, Clay Creasey/CFO, Dan Caspersen/Exec. VP - Human Resources, Claire Babrowski/COO, Exec. VP, Rick Ruppert/Exec. VP - Development, Safety, Sourcing

Directors: Gerald L. Storch/Chmn., CEO, Dean Nelson/49/Dir.

Owners: Affiliates of Bain Capital Partners, LLC/32.41%, Gerald L. Storch, Insiders, Vornado Truck LLC/32.41%, Jon Kimmins, Toybox Holdings, LLC/32.41%, Deborah M. Derby, Ronald Boire, Daniel Caspersen

TraceGuard Technologies Inc

330 Madison Ave., 9th Fl., New York, NY, 10017; ***PH:*** 1-646-495-5277; ***Fax:*** 1-646-495-5009; ***http://*** www.traceguard.net; ***Email:*** traceguard@traceguard.com

General - Incorporation	NV	**Stock**- Price on:12/24/2007	$0.9
Employees	27	Stock Exchange	OTC
Auditor	Kesselman & Kesselman	Ticker Symbol	TCGD
Stk Agt.	Nevada Agency & Trust Company	Outstanding Shares	36,180,000
Counsel	NA	E.P.S	-$0.25
DUNS No.	NA	Shareholders	NA

Business: The groups principal activities include designing to deliver explosive trace extraction solutions for the luggage and freight items screened each year. The groups products vary in capability and target market segment, they have a shared objective of speeding up passenger and baggage throughput and deliver savings in manpower by reducing the need for manual inspection of luggage and cargo. The group operates from the United States.

Primary SIC and add'l.: 7371

CIK No: 0001174890

Subsidiaries: TraceGuard Technologies Ltd

Officers: Ehud Ganani/56/Chmn., CEO, Pres./$560,927.00, Gil Perlberg/48/VP - Product Management, Engineering/$229,224.00, David Ben-Yair/37/CFO, Sec./$199,540.00

Directors: Ehud Ganani/56/Chmn., CEO, Pres., Jack Hornstein/61/Dir., David Cohen/47/Dir.

Owners: Fredy Ornath/28.90%, David Ben-Yair, Insiders/31.22%, Jack Hornstein, David Cohen, Ehud Ganani/1.81%, Gil Perlberg

Financial Data: ***Fiscal Year End:***12/31 ***Latest Annual Data:*** 12/31/2006

Year	Sales	Net Income
2006	NA	-$5,967,000
2005	NA	-$13,000

Curr. Assets:	$9,000	***Curr. Liab.:***	$48,000		
Plant, Equip.:	NA	***Total Liab.:***	$48,000	***Indic. Yr. Divd.:***	NA
Total Assets:	$9,000	***Net Worth:***	-$39,000	***Debt/ Equity:***	NA

Track Data Corp

95 Rockwell Pl, Brooklyn, NY, 11217; ***PH:*** 1-212-815-3982; ***http://*** www.tdc.com

General - Incorporation	DE	**Stock**- Price on:12/24/2007	$3.12
Employees	135	Stock Exchange	NDQ
Auditor	Marcum & Kliegman LLP	Ticker Symbol	TRAC
Stk Agt.	American Stock Transfer & Trust Co.	Outstanding Shares	8,390,000
Counsel	NA	E.P.S	-$0.13
DUNS No.	80-666-4421	Shareholders	NA

Business: The group's principal activity is to provide financial market data, fundamental research, charts and analytical services to institutional and individual investors through dedicated telecommunication lines and the Internet. It also provides a proprietary, integrated Internet-based online trading and market data system. The group operates through two segments: Internet-based online trading and ecn services. The group operates through protrack for the professional institutional traders and mytrack and tracktrade for the individual trader. It also operates in track ecn an electronic communications network that enables traders to display and match limit orders for stocks. The group disseminates news and third-party database information from more than 100 sources worldwide.

Primary SIC and add'l.: 7373 7375 7376 7372

CIK No: 0000922811

Subsidiaries: Track Data Securities Corp.

Officers: Martin Kaye/60/Dir., CEO, CFO, Sec., Barry Hertz/57/Chief, Technology Officer, Albert Drillick/61/Dir., Sr. Systems Analyst, Jesper Theill Eriksen/40/Sr. Exec. VP - Corporate Human Resources - Chieff, Staff, TDC A, S, Pres. - International Holdings, Dan Kronholm/49/Sr. VP - Supply Nordic, TDC A, S, Heine Stenholt Winther/37/VP - Billing, TDC A, S, Eva Berneke/39/Sr. Exec. VP, Chief Strategy Officer, Mads Mathias Middelboe/48/Sr. Exec. VP - TDC A - S, Pres. - Mobile Nordic, Klaus Pedersen/41/Sr. Ececutive VP - TDC A - S, Pres. - Business Nordic, Carsten Dilling/46/Sr. Exec. VP - TDC A - S, Pres. - Fixnet Nordic, Jens Hauge/56/Sr. VP - Regulatory Affairs, TDC A, S, Eigil Waagstein/60/Sr. VP - Corporate Financial Services, TDC A, S, Pernille Erenbjerg/41/Exec. VP - Corporate Accounting, Tax, TDC A, S, Anne Romer/42/Sr. VP, Chief Internal Auditor - TDC A, S, Flemming Jacobsen/38/Dir., Sr. VP - Group Treasury, TDC A, S *(22 Officers included in Index)*

Directors: Martin Kaye/60/Dir., CEO, CFO, Sec., Bruce E. Fredrikson/69/Chmn., Vagn Ove Sorensen/49/Vice Chmn., Kurt Bjorklund/39/Dir., Oliver Haarmann/41/Dir., Gustavo Schwed/46/Dir., Leif Hartmann/65/Dir., Steen Jacobsen/59/Dir., Bo Magnussen/61/Dir., Jan Bardino/56/Dir., Philip Ort/58/Dir., Albert Drillick/61/Dir., Sr. Systems Analyst, Abraham Biderman/59/Dir., Stanley Stern/57/Dir., Chief Compliance Officer, Richard Charles Wilson/43/Dir. *(18 Directors included in Index)*

Owners: Abraham Biderman, Philip Ort, Stanley Stern, Barry Hertz/57.10%, Martin Kaye/1.60%, Shaya Sofer, Albert Drillick, Insiders/3.40%, Bruce E. Fredrikson

Financial Data: ***Fiscal Year End:***12/31 ***Latest Annual Data:*** 12/31/2006

Year	Sales	Net Income
2006	$41,986,000	$1,549,000
2005	$36,094,000	-$37,000
2004	$40,093,000	$5,200,000

Curr. Assets:	$21,242,000	***Curr. Liab.:***	$10,030,000	***P/E Ratio:***	39.00
Plant, Equip.:	$1,998,000	***Total Liab.:***	$12,415,000	***Indic. Yr. Divd.:***	NA
Total Assets:	$34,848,000	***Net Worth:***	$22,433,000	***Debt/ Equity:***	0.0470

TrackPower Inc

3565 King Rd., Unit 102, King City, ON, L7B 1A3; *PH:* 1-905-773-1987;
http:// www.trackpower.com

General - Incorporation	WY	Stock- Price on:12/24/2007	NA
Employees	NA	Stock Exchange	OTC
Auditor	Rotenberg & Co., LLP	Ticker Symbol	TPWR
Stk Agt	Corporate Stock Transfer, Inc.	Outstanding Shares	NA
Counsel	NA	E.P.S.	-$0.008
DUNS No.	80-959-4997	Shareholders	NA

Business: The group's principle activity is to acquire racehorses and evaluate other horseracing industry related opportunities. In 2002, the company announced it had entered into an exclusive worldwide distribution agreement with post time technologies, inc, (ptt) under which the company would become the exclusive re-seller of ptt's racevision kiosk product when combined with an ATM solution in racetracks and gaming related facilities. Racevision was a horseracing video replay and archiving service available to customers via a kiosk located within a racetrack or gaming facility. The group operates from United States.

Primary SIC and add'l.: 7948 7999 7389

CIK No: 0000819927

Officers: John G. Simmonds/57/Chmn., CEO, CFO, Pres., Carrie J. Weiler/49/Corp. Sec., Edward M. Tracy/Pres., Gary N. Hokkanen/CFO

Directors: John G. Simmonds/57/Chmn., CEO, CFO, Pres., Michael Connell/34/Dir.

Owners: Insiders/14.10%, John Simmonds/13.10%, Asolare II LLC/11.50%, Carrie Weiler/1.20%

*Financial Data: Fiscal Year End:*02/28 *Latest Annual Data:* 02/28/2007

Year	Sales	Net Income
2007	NA	-$6,620,000
2006	NA	-$1,753,000
2005	NA	-$479,000

Curr. Assets:	$119,000	Curr. Liab.:	$852,000		
Plant, Equip.:	$6,000	Total Liab.:	$1,552,000	Indic. Yr. Divd.:	NA
Total Assets:	$825,000	Net Worth:	-$727,000	Debt/ Equity:	0.2206

Tractor Supply Co

200 Powell Pl., Brentwood, TN, 37027; *PH:* 1-615-366-4600; *http://* www.mytscstore.com

General - Incorporation	DE	Stock- Price on:12/24/2007	$52.81
Employees	5,500	Stock Exchange	NDQ
Auditor	Ernst & Young LLP	Ticker Symbol	TSCO
Stk Agt	EquiServe Trust Co N.A	Outstanding Shares	39,740,000
Counsel	NA	E.P.S.	$2.35
DUNS No.	00-693-2917	Shareholders	NA

Business: The groups principle activity is to operate retail farms and ranch stores. The group supplies the lifestyle needs of recreational farmers and ranchers and those who enjoy the rural lifestyle, including tradesmen and small businesses. The group operates from United States.

Primary SIC and add'l.: 5191 5251 5661 0782 5261 5999 5651

CIK No: 0000916365

Officers: James F. Wright/Chmn., CEO, Pres./$2,854,756.00, Anthony F. Crudele/CFO, Exec. VP, Treasurer/$751,545.00, Stanley L. Ruta/Exec. VP - Store Operations/$1,070,508.00, Gerald W. Brase/54/Sr. VP - Merchandising/$1,026,856.00, George Argodale/VP - Information Technology, Blake A. Fohl/Sr. VP - Marketing, David Lewis/VP, Controller, Clay Teter/VP - Real Estate, Kimberly D. Vella/Sr. VP - Human Resources, Gregory A. Sandfort/Exec. VP, Chief Merchandising Officer

Directors: James F. Wright/Chmn., CEO, Pres., Joseph H. Scarlett/65/Chmn., Edna K. Morris/Dir., Gerard E. Jones/Dir., Sam K. Reed/Dir., Joseph D. Maxwell/69/Dir., Joseph M. Rodgers/Dir., Cynthia T. Jamison/Dir., Jack C. Bingleman/Dir., S. P. Braud/Dir., John Adams/60/Dir., Richard W. Frost/57/Dir., George MacKenzie/Dir.

Owners: Joe M. Rodgers, Gerald W. Brase, Gerard E. Jones, Joseph H. Scarlett/11.90%, Blair & Company, L.L.C./6.20%, Edna K. Morris, S. P. Braud, Sam K. Reed, Jack C. Bingleman, Stanley L. Ruta, Insiders/15.80%, Joseph D. Maxwell/1.00%, James F. Wright/1.60%, Capital Research and Management Company/9.20%, Anthony F. Crudele

*Financial Data: Fiscal Year End:*12/31 *Latest Annual Data:* 12/30/2006

Year	Sales	Net Income
2006	$2,369,612,000	$91,008,000
2005	$2,067,979,000	$85,669,000
2004	$1,738,843,000	$64,069,000

Curr. Assets:	$531,413,000	Curr. Liab.:	$290,681,000	P/E Ratio:	22.47
Plant, Equip.:	$258,475,000	Total Liab.:	$337,097,000	Indic. Yr. Divd.:	NA
Total Assets:	$814,795,000	Net Worth:	$477,698,000	Debt/ Equity:	0.0957

Tradequest International Inc

801 Brickell Ave., 9th Fl., Miami, FL, 33131; *PH:* 1-305-377-2110

General - Incorporation	NV	Stock- Price on:12/24/2007	$0.012
Employees	NA	Stock Exchange	OTC
Auditor	Webb & Co., P.A.	Ticker Symbol	TRDQ
Stk Agt	Corporate Stock Transfer, Inc.	Outstanding Shares	24,800,000
Counsel	NA	E.P.S.	$0.066
DUNS No.	NA	Shareholders	NA

Business: The groups principle activity is Internet based communications service provider. The groups services turnkey Internet protocol (IP) based communication solutions to distributors, which are telecommunications companies, cable providers and integrators that deliver Voice over Internet Protocol. During August 2005, group acquired IP1. The group's revenue for Sep '07 was 0.03 millions of USD.

Primary SIC and add'l.: 4813

CIK No: 0000029322

Subsidiaries: IP1 Network Corporation

Officers: Luis Alvarez/48/Chmn., CEO/$115,750.00, Thomas M. Biggs/33/Dir., Sec., Frank J. Erbiti/46/COO, Pres./$175,000.00

Directors: Luis Alvarez/48/Chmn., CEO, Vincent A. Landis/61/Dir., Thomas M. Biggs/33/Dir., Sec.

Owners: Thomas M. Biggs/4.10%, Frank J. Erbiti/9.40%, Charles S. Arnold/12.10%, Insiders/100.00%, Insiders/36.30%, Vincent A. Landis/6.80%, Luis Alvarez/16.00%, Luis Alvarez/100.00%

*Financial Data: Fiscal Year End:*12/31 *Latest Annual Data:* 12/31/2006

Year	Sales	Net Income
2006	$24,000	$5,764,000
2005	$12,000	-$15,286,000
2004	$14,000	-$124,000

Curr. Assets:	$172,000	Curr. Liab.:	$2,788,000	P/E Ratio:	0.75
Plant, Equip.:	$18,000	Total Liab.:	$2,788,000	Indic. Yr. Divd.:	NA
Total Assets:	$388,000	Net Worth:	-$2,400,000	Debt/ Equity:	NA

Tradeshow Marketing Co Ltd

11359-162Nd St., Surrey, BC, V4N 4P5; *PH:* 1-604-585-8762; *http://* www.tsmc.ca

General - Incorporation	NV	Stock- Price on:12/24/2007	$0.5
Employees	NA	Stock Exchange	OTC
Auditor	Moore & Assoc. Chartered	Ticker Symbol	TSHO
Stk Agt	Holladay Stock Transfer, Inc.	Outstanding Shares	NA
Counsel	NA	E.P.S.	NA
DUNS No.	NA	Shareholders	NA

Business: The group's principle activity is to develop and market proprietary and private label products for the home and office environments. The group is now ramping up a multi-pronged sales approach for introducing and distributing consumer goods in North America and beyond. The company is developing five complementary sales channels through retail, television, trade show demonstration sales, print catalogue and an e-commerce online catalogue to achieve its goals. They have acquired two retail stores in highly trafficked malls in Phoenix, Arizona. The acquisitions mark the beginning of the group's plan to operate ONTV-style stores that feature a unique mix of both new and proven consumer products and popular ONTV items that will be sold nationwide. Their approach is to exclusively sell products that are quality manufactured to its specifications from Asia and around the world.

Primary SIC and add'l.: 8742

CIK No: 0001337340

Officers: Bruce Kirk/64/Dir., CEO, Pres., Marion Huff/52/Dir., COO, Peggie-Ann Kirk/62/Dir., CFO, Pres., Luniel De Beer/CTO, John Kirk/Investor Relations Officer, Thomas Degarmo/Dir. - Creative Services, Megan Helgerson/Dir. - Training, Aksel Firat/Construction, Logistics Coordinator, Tim McCarthy/46/Dir., VP - Franchise Development

Directors: Bruce Kirk/64/Dir., CEO, Pres., Marion Huff/52/Dir., COO, Peggie-Ann Kirk/62/Dir., CFO, Pres., Norm Friend/52/Dir., Hashem Sharifi/55/Dir., Robert Detwiler/37/Dir., Tim McCarthy/46/Dir., VP - Franchise Development

Owners: Robert Detwiler/1.03%, Hashem Sharifi, Timothy McCarthy, Bruce Kirk/49.20%, Peggie-Ann Kirk, Julia Sol/5.00%, Luniel De Beer, Marion Huff, Norm Friend

Curr. Assets:	$196,000	Curr. Liab.:	$123,000		
Plant, Equip.:	$40,000	Total Liab.:	$129,000	Indic. Yr. Divd.:	NA
Total Assets:	$277,000	Net Worth:	$148,000	Debt/ Equity:	NA

Tradestation Group Inc

8050 SW 10th St., Ste 4000, Plantation, FL, 33324; *PH:* 1-954-652-7000;
http:// www.tradestation.com

General - Incorporation	FL	Stock- Price on:12/24/2007	$12.03
Employees	302	Stock Exchange	NDQ
Auditor	Ernst & Young LLP	Ticker Symbol	TRAD
Stk Agt	American Stock Transfer & Trust Co.	Outstanding Shares	44,570,000
Counsel	Bilzin Sumberg Baena Price & Axelrod	E.P.S.	$0.76
DUNS No.	NA	Shareholders	NA

Business: The group's principal activity is to provide Internet-based securities brokerage for institutional, professional and serious, active individual traders. Tradestation securities, inc. and tradestation technologies, inc. Are the two operating subsidiaries of the group. It operates in two segments: brokerage services and software products and services. Brokerage services include direct Internet connections to electronic marketplaces, such as electronic communication networks (ecns) or e-mini exchanges, where buyers and sellers participating on the network are matched. These services are provided through an electronic trading platform, tradestation 7. Tradestation securities, inc provides brokerage services. The group also provides subscription services for tradestation 7 through it's subsidiary, tradestation technologies, inc.

Primary SIC and add'l.: 7372 6211 7375

CIK No: 0001111559

Subsidiaries: TradeStation Europe Limited, TradeStation Securities, Inc., TradeStation Technologies, Inc.

Officers: Janette Perez/VP - Strategic Relations, Marc J. Stone/Dir., VP - Corporate Development, General Counsel, Sec./$395,068.00, Salomon Sredni/Dir., COO, Pres./$893,265.00, David H. Fleischman/CFO, VP - Finance, Treasurer/$405,175.00, Joe Nikolson/Chief Growth Officer - Tradestation Group, Pres. - Tradestation Securities/$402,183.00, Melody Blais/Customer Support, Keith T. Black/45/VP - Product Development, Tradestation Technologies, Mark Glassman/40/Chief Accounting Officer, Corporate Controller

Directors: William R. Cruz/Chmn., Ralph L. Cruz/Chmn., Marc J. Stone/Dir., VP - Corporate Development, General Counsel, Sec., Salomon Sredni/Dir., COO, Pres., Denise Dickins/46/Dir., Michael W. Fipps/65/Dir., Stephen C. Richards/54/Dir., Charles F. Wright/57/Dir.

Owners: FMR Corp./6.20%, Marc J. Stone, Ralph L. Cruz/16.80%, William R. Cruz/17.10%, Stephen C. Richards, Denise Dickins, Joseph Nikolson, David H. Fleischman, Michael W. Fipps, Charles F. Wright, Salomon Sredni/1.40%, Insiders/36.40%

*Financial Data: Fiscal Year End:*12/31 *Latest Annual Data:* 12/31/2006

Year	Sales	Net Income
2006	$128,545,000	$31,019,000
2005	$100,512,000	$21,066,000
2004	$71,840,000	$14,694,000

Curr. Assets:	$603,930,000	Curr. Liab.:	$530,883,000	P/E Ratio:	17.19
Plant, Equip.:	$8,735,000	Total Liab.:	$530,883,000	Indic. Yr. Divd.:	NA
Total Assets:	$649,087,000	Net Worth:	$118,205,000	Debt/ Equity:	NA

Trafalgar Resources Inc

6867 S 700 W, Ste. A, Midvale, UT, 84047; *PH:* 1-801-748-1114

General - Incorporation	UT	Stock - Price on:12/24/2007	NA
Employees	NA	Stock Exchange	OTC
Auditor Child, Van Wagoner & Bradshaw, PLLC		Ticker Symbol	TFLG
Stk Agt.	NA	Outstanding Shares	NA
Counsel	NA	E.P.S.	NA
DUNS No.	NA	Shareholders	NA

Business: The group's activity includes mining and investigating business potential ventures. The group is expecting to acquire an existing business or the acquire assets to establish subsidiary businesses.

Primary SIC and add'l.: 6770

CIK No: 0001310630

Officers: Anthony Brandon Escobar/33/Dir., CEO, Pres., Sean Escobar/27/Dir., VP, Anthony Coletti/37/Dir., Sec., Treasurer, Chief Accounting Officer

Directors: Anthony Brandon Escobar/33/Dir., CEO, Pres., Sean Escobar/27/Dir., VP, Anthony Coletti/37/Dir., Sec., Treasurer, Chief Accounting Officer

Owners: Anthony Coletti, Insiders/95.22%, Anthony Brandon Escobar/94.03%, Sean Escobar

Traffic.com Inc

851 Duportail Rd., Wayne, PA, 19087; **PH:** 1-610-725-9700; *http://* www.traffic.com; **Email:** info@traffic.com

General - Incorporation	DE	Stock - Price on:12/24/2007	NA
Employees	NA	Stock Exchange	NA
Auditor	Ernst & Young LLP	Ticker Symbol	NA
Stk Agt.	NA	Outstanding Shares	NA
Counsel	NA	E.P.S.	NA
DUNS No.	NA	Shareholders	NA

Business: The groups principal activity is to provide real time traffic information. The groups service is Mobile e-mail alerts, Phone alerts and Traffic hotline. Customers served by the group include radio, television and website. Specific customers of the group include Hubbard Broadcasting Inc, Cox Broadcasting, Inc, Greater Media, Inc and Post Newsweek Stations, Inc. The group operates from the United States.

Primary SIC and add'l.: 4899 7375 7375 7379 7379 7310 4899

CIK No: 0001097503

Officers: Robert N. Verratti/CEO, Andrew Maunder/CFO

Owners: David L. Jannetta/4.20%, John H. Josephson, Brian J. Sisko, Samuel A. Plum, Insiders/42.10%, Tom A. Vadnais, Joseph A. Reed, Entities affiliated with TL Ventures/34.90%, Robert N. Verratti/2.30%, Andrew Maunder, George MacKenzie, Christopher M. Rothey, Mark J. DeNino/35.50%

Traffix Inc

One Blue Hill Plz., Pearl River, NY, 10965; **PH:** 1-914-620-1212; *http://* www.traffixinc.com; **Email:** info@traffixinc.com

General - Incorporation	DE	Stock - Price on:12/24/2007	$5.49
Employees	161	Stock Exchange	NDQ
Auditor	Goldstein Golub Kessler LLP	Ticker Symbol	TRFX
Stk Agt.	American Stock Transfer & Trust Co.	Outstanding Shares	14,940,000
Counsel	Feder, Kaszovitz, Bass & Rhine LLP	E.P.S.	$0.15
DUNS No.	83-761-6440	Shareholders	NA

Business: The group's principal activity is to provide consumer targeted direct marketing and customer acquisition services for businesses. The group utilizes its proprietary and affiliate on-line databases for direct marketing activities delivered by the Internet. The operating segments of the group consists of e-commerce, off-line customer acquisition services and lec billed products and services. The e-commerce segment markets third party products and services on Web sites and through e-mail promotions. The off-line customer acquisition services segment operates through off-line direct marketing channels. The lec billed products and services segment represents telecommunication-related products and services marketed by the group directly to consumers who are billed by local exchange was reintroduced during 2003. On 30-Jun-2004, the group acquired assets of sendtraffic.com inc and the traffic group llc.

Primary SIC and add'l.: 8999 7379 4813 7375

CIK No: 0001000297

Subsidiaries: Atlas Sites, Inc., Calling Card Company, Inc., Creative Direct Marketing, Inc., Direct Deposit Promotions, Inc., GroupLotto, Inc., Hot Rocket Marketing, Inc., iMatchup.com, Inc., InfiKnowledge, ULC, Montvale Management, LLC, MultiBuyer, Inc., N.L. Corp., New Lauderdale L.C., Quintel E-Mail, Inc., Quintel Financial Information Services, Inc., Quintel Hair Products, Inc. 26 Subsidiaries included in the Index

Officers: Jeffrey L. Schwartz/Chmn., CEO, Andrew Stollman/Dir., Pres., Sec., Richard Wentworth/COO, Daniel Harvey/CFO

Directors: Jeffrey L. Schwartz/Chmn., CEO, Mark Gutterman/Dir., Andrew Stollman/Dir., Pres., Sec., Robert MacHinist/Dir., Lawrence Burstein/Dir.

Owners: Jeffrey L. Schwartz/13.73%, Daniel Harvey, Insiders/25.20%, Andrew Stollman/8.58%, Lawrence Burstein, Robert Machinist, Dimensional Fund Advisors, L.P./7.18%, Richard Wentworth, Mark Gutterman, Al Frank Asset Management, Inc./5.92%

Financial Data: Fiscal Year End:11/30 **Latest Annual Data:** 11/30/2006

Year	Sales	Net Income
2006	$72,844,000	$1,903,000
2005	$62,857,000	$2,428,000
2004	$37,281,000	$1,014,000

Curr. Assets:	$40,791,000	**Curr. Liab.:**	$9,084,000	**P/E Ratio:** 34.31
Plant, Equip.:	$1,965,000	**Total Liab.:**	$9,397,000	**Indic. Yr. Divd.:** $0.320
Total Assets:	$52,726,000	**Net Worth:**	$43,328,000	**Debt/ Equity:** NA

Trailer Bridge Inc

10405 New Berlin Rd. E, Jacksonville, FL, 32226; **PH:** 1-904-751-7100; *http://* www.trailerbridge.com

General - Incorporation	DE	Stock - Price on:12/24/2007	$12.89
Employees	194	Stock Exchange	NDQ
Auditor	BDO Seidman LLP	Ticker Symbol	TRBR
Stk Agt.	Computershare Investor Services LLC	Outstanding Shares	11,790,000
Counsel	NA	E.P.S.	$0.87
DUNS No.	55-697-8922	Shareholders	NA

Business: The group's principal activities are to offer trucking and marine freight carrier services. These services enable and increase equipment utilization and minimize empty miles. The group operates in the United States and Puerto Rico. As on 31-Dec-2003, the group operated a fleet of 113 tractors, 500 high-cube trailers, 2,796 53' high cube containers and 2,165 53' chassis to transport truckload freight. The group's customers include daimlerchrysler, general motors, k mart, walmart, jc penney, home depot, Georgia pacific, general electric, procter & gamble, whirlpool, sc johnson, walgreen's and toys 'r' us.

Primary SIC and add'l.: 4731

CIK No: 0001039184

Officers: John McCown/Chmn., CEO/$348,608.00, David A. Miskowiec/VP - Sales, Ralph W. Heim/COO, Pres./$319,143.00, William G. Gotimer/Sec., General Counsel/$333,389.00, Edward J. Morley/VP - Marine Operations, Mark A. Tanner/CFO, VP/$214,608.00, Robert Van Dijk/VP - Pricing/$212,654.00, Adam E. Gawrysh/VP - Inland Operations

Directors: John McCown/Chmn., CEO

Owners: Ralph W. Heim/3.20%, Robert Van Dijk/1.30%, Greggory B. Mendenhall/12.60%, Allen L. Stevens, Clara L. McLean/11.30%, Nancy McLean Parker/12.20%, Edward J. Morley/1.30%, Insiders/49.60%, Mark A. Tanner/1.40%, Irena Z. McLean/8.70%, Malcom P. McLean/12.40%, David A. Miskowiec, Rober P. Burke, John D. McCown/13.40%, Adam E. Gawrysh (16 Owners included in Index)

Financial Data: Fiscal Year End:12/31 **Latest Annual Data:** 12/31/2006

Year	Sales	Net Income
2006	$110,250,000	-$18,000
2005	$105,859,000	$7,834,000
2004	$98,775,000	$4,441,000

Curr. Assets:	$29,599,000	**Curr. Liab.:**	$13,755,000	**P/E Ratio:** 14.82
Plant, Equip.:	$79,967,000	**Total Liab.:**	$117,261,000	**Indic. Yr. Divd.:** NA
Total Assets:	$118,204,000	**Net Worth:**	$943,000	**Debt/ Equity:** 43.7082

Tramford International Ltd

Unit 1712-13, Tower 1, Admiralty Ctr., No.18 Harcourt Rd., Hong Kong, Hong Kong; ; *http://* www.chinactdc.com

General - Incorporation British Virgin Islands		Stock - Price on:12/24/2007	NA
Employees	NA	Stock Exchange	NDQ
Auditor	PricewaterhouseCoopers LLP	Ticker Symbol	NA
Stk Agt.	American Stock Transfer & Trust Co.	Outstanding Shares	NA
Counsel	NA	E.P.S.	NA
DUNS No.	NA	Shareholders	NA

Business: The group operates through its subsidiaries whose principle activity is to manufacture and sell mid-range interior ceramic wall tiles; and manufacture and sell standard enameled steel, enameled steel with aprons, manually cast iron and vacuum cast iron bathtubs. The group operates from United States.

Primary SIC and add'l.: 3253 3431 6719

CIK No: 0001027454

Subsidiaries: Anji Science Bio-Product Inc., Beijing BHL Networks Technology Co. Ltd., BHL Networks Technology Co. Ltd., China Natures Technology Inc., Innoessen Bio-technology Inc., Jianou Yingshi Food Technology Ltd, Jing Tai Industrial Investment Co. Ltd., Jingle Technology Co. Ltd., Shenzhen Innoessen Bio-Tech Inc., Zhejiang University (Hangzhou)

Officers: Alan Li/40/Chmn., CEO, Zhenwei Lu/37/Executive Dir., Chief Operating Office, Xu Qian/44/Executive Dir., Kang Li/Dir., Executive Dir., Acting CFO, Company Sec., Brendan Lahiff/Primary Investor Relations Officer, May Li/Primary Investor Relations Officer

Directors: Alan Li/40/Chmn., CEO, Ju Zhang/45/Dir., Yezhong Ni/38/Dir., Weidong Wang/41/Dir., Xinping Shi/49/Dir., Zhenwei Lu/37/Executive Dir., Chief Operating Office, Yu Keung Poon/Dir., Leong Cheong Chang/Dir., Kang Li/Dir., Executive Dir., Acting CFO, Company Sec., Xiaoping Wang/48/Dir.

Owners: Great Legend Internet Technology and Service Co., Ltd./3.59%, Beijing Holdings/14.20%, China Biotech Holdings Limited/24.74%, Insiders/55.26%, Harvest Smart Overseas Limited/7.07%, Eastern Ceremony Group Limited/5.66%

Curr. Assets:	$8,207,000	**Curr. Liab.:**	$1,808,000	
Plant, Equip.:	$90,000	**Total Liab.:**	$1,808,000	**Indic. Yr. Divd.:** NA
Total Assets:	$8,297,000	**Net Worth:**	$6,489,000	**Debt/ Equity:** NA

Trammell Crow Co

2001 Rose Ave., Ste. 3400, Dallas, TX, 75201; **PH:** 1-214-863-3000; *http://* www.trammellcrow.com

General - Incorporation	DE	Stock - Price on:12/24/2007	NA
Employees	6,440	Stock Exchange	NA
Auditor	Ernst & Young LLP	Ticker Symbol	NA
Stk Agt.	Mellon Investor Services LLC	Outstanding Shares	NA
Counsel	Vinson & Elkins LLP	E.P.S.	NA
DUNS No.	19-692-8311	Shareholders	NA

Business: The group's principle activity is to provide diversified commercial real estate services. The group delivers three core services: management services, transaction services and development and project management services. The management services provided to institutional customers include services relating to building operations, tenant relations and building improvement processes and services provided to corporate customers consist primarily of providing occupancy-related services to large corporations. The transaction services include services such as project leasing and investment sales. The development and investment services include financial planning, site acquisition, project closeout and project finance coordination.

Primary SIC and add'l.: 8741 8744 7389 6531

CIK No: 0001022438

Subsidiaries: 1996 Dfw Office, Inc., 3865 Tcmp Venture, LLC, 3865 Wilson, LLC, 777 6th Street LLC, Aew #10 Corporation, Arvada Marketplace East, LLC, Atascocita Commons Associates, Lp, Atlanta Westside Village Partners, LLC, Atwater 12 Lp, Austin Retail Investment, Inc., Baltimore Land Holdings, LLC, Bc Plaza Ii/iii, Ltd., Beaumont Associates, LLC, Bolingbrook Mob, LLC, Bpp-cm, L.p. 30 Subsidiaries included in the Index

Officers: Robert E. Sulentic/Chmn., CEO, John A. Stirek/Pres. - Development, Investment, Western Operations, James R. Groch/Chief Investment Officer, Matthew S. Khourie/Pres. - Development, Investment, Central Operations, Christopher T. Roth/Pres. - Development, Investment, Eastern Operations, Chris Kirk/Sr. MD, Arlin Gaffner/MD

Directors: Robert E. Sulentic/Chmn., CEO

Tranquility Inc

PO Box 110310, Naples, FL, 34108; *PH:* 1-239-598-2300; *http://* www.relaxattranquility.com

General - Incorporation	DE	**Stock**- Price on:12/24/2007	NA
Employees	NA	Stock Exchange	NA
Auditor	Gruber & Co., LLC	Ticker Symbol	NA
Stk Agt	Liberty Transfer Co	Outstanding Shares	NA
Counsel	NA	E.P.S.	NA
DUNS No.	NA	Shareholders	NA

Business: The groups principle activities include designing, developing and marketing scientific based skincare system to stimulate skins own immune system. The group also provide massage services include Raindrop Therapy Massage, Thai Massage, Hot Stone Massage, Signature Tranquility Massage, Herbal Body Wrap and Purify Naturally. The group operates from United States.

Primary SIC and add'l.: 9995

CIK No: 0001111468

Subsidiaries: Mellow Anti-Counterfeit Net System

Officers: Dominick Pope/73/Dir., CEO, CFO, Pres., Treasurer, Jose Acevedo/51/Dir., Sec.

Directors: Dominick Pope/73/Dir., CEO, CFO, Pres., Treasurer, Jose Acevedo/51/Dir., Sec.

Owners: Mid-Continental Securities Corp./26.46%, Equity Investors/29.38%, Insiders/2.15%, Glenn Little/19.59%, Dominick Pope/2.15%

Trans Energy Inc

210 Second St. , St. Marys, WV, 26170; *PH:* 1-304-684-7053; *http://* www.transenergy.com

General - Incorporation	NV	**Stock**- Price on:12/24/2007	NA
Employees	111	Stock Exchange	OTC
Auditor	Malone & Bailey, P.C	Ticker Symbol	TENGE
Stk Agt	NA	Outstanding Shares	NA
Counsel	NA	E.P.S.	NA
DUNS No.	92-883-5537	Shareholders	NA

Business: The group's principal activities are to transport, market and produce natural oil and gas. The group also conducts exploration and development activities. The group owns interest in seven oil and gas wells in west Virginia and owns an interest in seven oil wells in Wyoming that it does not operate. It also owns and operates over 100 miles of three-inch, four-inch and six-inch gas transmission lines located in west Virginia. The customers of the group are various intrastate and interstate pipeline companies and natural gas marketing companies.

Primary SIC and add'l.: 1311 4923

CIK No: 0000919721

Subsidiaries: Arvilla, Inc., Belmont Energy, Inc., Cobham Gas Industries, Inc., Penine Resources, Inc., Prima Oil Company, Inc., Ritchie County Gathering Systems, Inc., Tyler Construction Company, Inc., Tyler Energy, Inc.

Officers: James K. Abcouwer/54/Chmn., CEO, Pres., Lisa A. Corbitt/CFO, William F. Woodburn/65/Dir., COO, Sec., Treasurer, Loren E. Bagley/65/Dir., Exec. VP

Directors: James K. Abcouwer/54/Chmn., CEO, Pres., William F. Woodburn/65/Dir., COO, Sec., Treasurer, Robert L. Richards/62/Dir., Loren E. Bagley/65/Dir., Exec. VP, John G. Corp/47/Dir.

Owners: John G. Corp, Loren E. Bagley/12.60%, Robert L. Richards/2.80%, William F. Woodburn/18.50%, James K. Abcouwer/15.50%

Trans Industries Inc

1780 Opdyke Ct., Auburn Hills, MI, 48326; *PH:* 1-248-364-0400; *http://* www.transindustries.com

General - Incorporation	DE	**Stock**- Price on:12/24/2007	$0.02
Employees	160	Stock Exchange	OTC
Auditor	Plante & Moran, PLLC	Ticker Symbol	TRNIQ
Stk Agt	NA	Outstanding Shares	6,200,000
Counsel	NA	E.P.S.	-$1.77
DUNS No.	04-899-9999	Shareholders	NA

Business: The group's principle activities are to manufacture and supply lighting and information display for mass transit operations. The group products include electronic information display systems, liquid crystal displays, and the dust control products. The group is designed to provide comfort, convenience and safety to passengers and properties in the mass transit market. The products are manufactured & marketed in the United States, Canada, the United Kingdom and to the customers of Europe, Australia and Asia. The group's foreign sales are made on an export basis from domestic offices as well as through certain agents in abroad. The group produced mechanical signage for the mass transit market, but its current efforts are concentrated on electronic systems for the display of information, bus lighting products, and source extraction systems for the environmental market.

Primary SIC and add'l.: 3564 3647

CIK No: 0000099102

Subsidiaries: The Lobb Company, Transign, Inc, Transmatic, Inc, Vultron, Inc.

Financial Data: *Fiscal Year End:*12/31   *Latest Annual Data:* 12/31/2004

Year	Sales	Net Income
2004	$27,760,000	-$3,910,000
2003	$33,721,000	-$3,761,000
2002	$34,567,000	-$1,344,000

Curr. Assets:	$12,062,000	Curr. Liab.:	$11,532,000		
Plant, Equip.:	$3,128,000	Total Liab.:	$13,267,000	Indic. Yr. Divd.:	NA
Total Assets:	$15,729,000	Net Worth:	$2,462,000	Debt/ Equity:	NA

Trans Lux Corp

110 Richards Ave., Norwalk, CT, 06854; *PH:* 1-203-853-4321; *http://* www.trans-lux.com
Email: investor@trans-lux.com

General - Incorporation	DE	**Stock**- Price on:12/24/2007	$6.38
Employees	431	Stock Exchange	AMEX
Auditor	Eisner LLP	Ticker Symbol	TLX
Stk Agt	Continental Stock Transfer & Trust Co	Outstanding Shares	2,310,000
Counsel	Weisman, Celler, Spett & Modlin	E.P.S.	-$1.81
DUNS No.	00-132-8350	Shareholders	NA

Business: The group's principal activities are to manufacture and distribute large-scale real-time electronic information displays for both indoor and outdoor use. The group operates in three segments: indoor display, outdoor display, and entertainment/real estate. The group's products are used in data graphics, video displays for stock and commodity exchanges, financial institutions, sports venues, casinos, convention centers, corporate, government, theatre, retail, airports and other applications. The group owns and operates motion picture theatres. The group operates only in domestic market.

Primary SIC and add'l.: 3669 7312 7812

CIK No: 0000099106

Officers: Thomas Brandt/Exec. VP, Co - CEO/$207,330.00, Michael R. Mulcahy/59/Dir., Pres., Co - CEO/$303,238.00, Angela D. Toppi/CFO, Exec. VP/$174,237.00, Thomas Mahoney/Sr. VP - Sales/$192,560.00, Karl P. Hirschauer/Sr. VP - Engineering, Al L. Miller/Exec. VP, John A. Long/Sr. VP, Matthew Brandt/44/Dir., Exec. VP/$201,943.00

Directors: Michael R. Mulcahy/59/Dir., Pres., Co - CEO, Howard M. Brenner/74/Dir., Matthew Brandt/44/Dir., Exec. VP, Howard S. Modlin/76/Dir., Gene Jankowski/73/Dir., Richard Brandt/80/Dir., Jean Firstenberg/72/Dir., Victor Liss/71/Dir.

Owners: Victor Liss, Jean Firstenberg, Michael R. Mulcahy/1.02%, Thomas Brandt/14.54%, Thomas F. Mahoney, Matthew Brandt/14.54%, Thomas Brandt, Richard Brandt/46.44%, Richard Brandt, Matthew Brandt, Gabelli Funds, LLC./42.35%, Victor Liss/3.39%, Howard M. Brenner, Gene Jankowski, Howard S. Modlin (19 Owners included in Index)

Financial Data: *Fiscal Year End:*12/31   *Latest Annual Data:* 12/31/2006

Year	Sales	Net Income
2006	$53,911,000	-$1,647,000
2005	$54,368,000	-$1,793,000
2004	$3,548,000	$794,000

Curr. Assets:	$20,972,000	Curr. Liab.:	$12,503,000		
Plant, Equip.:	$61,218,000	Total Liab.:	$68,298,000	Indic. Yr. Divd.:	NA
Total Assets:	$88,472,000	Net Worth:	$20,174,000	Debt/ Equity:	2.5546

Trans Max Technologies Inc

7473 Lake Mead Blvd, Las Vegas, NV, 89128; *PH:* 1-702-382-3377; *http://* www.perma-tune.com

General - Incorporation	NV	**Stock**- Price on:12/24/2007	$0.02
Employees	1	Stock Exchange	OTC
Auditor	Bagell, Josephs, Levine & Co. LLC	Ticker Symbol	TMAX
Stk Agt	Pacific Stock Transfer Company	Outstanding Shares	59,450,000
Counsel	NA	E.P.S.	$0.002
DUNS No.	NA	Shareholders	NA

Business: The group's principal activity is to design and manufacture high-energy electronic ignition systems for street vehicles, race cars, boats, scientific and industrial applications, space and aviation applications, as well as clean burning fuel applications. It develops new product lines in order to supply repair and performance parts for a variety of cars, trucks, and boats, as well as developing new ignition technologies that will increase an engines performance while improving fuel economy. The product can be used to ignite liquid fuel rockets, turbine engines, to ignite boilers used in the petrochemical industry, and for commercial automotive applications. As a result of the acquisition of trans max technologies inc on 21-Jul-2003, the group changed its name from perma-tune electronics inc to trans max technologies inc. The group acquired bogner industries inc in 12-Aug-2004 & victor vartovy & co in 31-Aug-2004.

Primary SIC and add'l.: 3694

CIK No: 0001074663

Subsidiaries: Bogner subsidiary

Officers: Linda Decker/CEO, Pres., Lonnie Lenarduzzi/Chief Scientist, CTO

Financial Data: *Fiscal Year End:*12/31   *Latest Annual Data:* 12/31/2005

Year	Sales	Net Income
2005	NA	-$1,620,000
2004	NA	-$7,403,000
2003	$289,000	-$315,000

Curr. Assets:	$0	Curr. Liab.:	$2,419,000	P/E Ratio:	10.00
Plant, Equip.:	$5,000	Total Liab.:	$2,419,000	Indic. Yr. Divd.:	NA
Total Assets:	$307,000	Net Worth:	-$2,112,000	Debt/ Equity:	NA

Trans World Entertainment Corp

38 Corporate Cir., Albany, NY, 12203; *PH:* 1-518-452-1242; *http://* www.twec.com;
Email: corpcomm@twec.com

General - Incorporation	NY	**Stock**- Price on:12/24/2007	$4.98
Employees	4,400	Stock Exchange	NDQ
Auditor	KPMG LLP	Ticker Symbol	TWMC
Stk Agt	Mellon Investor Services LLC	Outstanding Shares	31,080,000
Counsel	Kaye, Scholer LLP	E.P.S.	$0.30
DUNS No.	05-937-1823	Shareholders	NA

Business: The group's principal activity is to operate a chain of retail entertainment stores of compact discs, prerecorded audiocassettes, prerecorded videocassettes, digital versatile discs and related accessories. The group offers a broad selection of music and video titles at competitive prices in convenient and attractive stores. It operates four distinct store concepts, fye (for your entertainment) stores, super fye stores, saturday matinee stores and freestanding stores, designed to take advantage of real estate opportunities and to satisfy varying consumer demands. Music categories include rock, pop, rap, soundtracks, latin, urban and classical. The group stocks and promotes brand name blank audio cassettes, compact discs, audio cassettes and videocassettes, including maintenance and cleaning products, storage cases, portable electronics and headphones. As of 01-Feb-2003, it operated 881 stores in 47 states. The group operates only in the domestic market.

Primary SIC and add'l.: 5735

CIK No: 0000795212

Subsidiaries: Media Logic USA, LLC., Record Town USA, LLC, Record Town, Inc, Trans World Florida, LLC, Trans World New York, LLC

Officers: Robert J. Higgins/Chmn., CEO/$2,810,576.00, Bruce J. Eisenberg/Exec. VP - Real Estate/$513,462.00, James A. Litwak/COO, Pres./$787,267.00, John J. Sullivan/Exec. VP, Treasurer, Sec., CFO/$561,042.00

Directors: Robert J. Higgins/Chmn., CEO, Brett Brewer/Dir.

Owners: Bruce J. Eisenberg, Riley Investment Management, LLC, Michael B. Solow, Martin E. Hanaka, Wells Fargo & Company, Edmond Thomas, Dimensional Fund Advisors Inc., Isaac Kaufman, Robert J. Higgins, Joseph G. Morone, Lloyd I. Miller, John J. Sullivan, James A. Litwak, Mark A. Cohen, Lori Schafer (16 Owners included in Index)

Financial Data: Fiscal Year End:01/28 **Latest Annual Data:** 2/3/2007

Year	Sales		Net Income
2007	$1,471,157,000		$11,669,000
2006	$1,238,486,000		$609,000
2005	$1,365,133,000		$41,841,000
Curr. Assets:	$646,356,000	**Curr. Liab.:** $380,152,000	**P/E Ratio:** 16.60
Plant, Equip.:	$138,252,000	**Total Liab.:** $436,485,000	**Indic. Yr. Divd.:** NA
Total Assets:	$829,690,000	**Net Worth:** $393,205,000	**Debt/ Equity:** 0.0393

Trans-Orient Petroleum Ltd

999 Canada Pl., Ste. 404, World Trade Ctr., Vancouver, BC, V6C 3B5; **PH:** 1-604-682-6496; **http://** www.transorient.com

General - Incorporation	BC	**Stock**- Price on:12/24/2007	$0.75
Employees	NA	Stock Exchange	OTC
Auditor	De Visser Gray	Ticker Symbol	TOPLF
Stk Agt	Computershare Trust Company of Canada	Outstanding Shares	NA
Counsel	Lang Michener Lawrence & Shaw	E.P.S.	NA
DUNS No.	25-408-7307	Shareholders	NA

Business: The group's principle activities include exploring and developing oil and natural gas properties. The group operates from United States.

Primary SIC and add'l.: 6719 1311

CIK No: 0001007023

Subsidiaries: AMG Oil Ltd, DLJ Management Corp

Officers: Peter Loretto/Dir., CEO, Pres., David J. Bennett/Executive Chmn., David Francis/Geological Advisor, Barry MacNeil/Dir., Sec., CFO, Roger Brand/Technical Consultant

Directors: Peter Loretto/Dir., CEO, Pres., David J. Bennett/Executive Chmn., Michael Hart/Dir., Barry MacNeil/Dir., Sec., CFO

Owners: Alex Guidi/13.32%, Lukas H. Lundin/24.10%, Peter Loretto/23.62%

Financial Data: Fiscal Year End:07/31 **Latest Annual Data:** 7/31/2006

Year	Sales		Net Income
2006	NA		$382,000
2005	NA		$1,142,000
Curr. Assets:	$485,000	**Curr. Liab.:** $12,000	
Plant, Equip.:	$84,000	**Total Liab.:** $12,000	**Indic. Yr. Divd.:** NA
Total Assets:	$3,304,000	**Net Worth:** $3,292,000	**Debt/ Equity:** NA

Transact Technologies Inc

1 Hamden Ctr., 2319 Whitney Ave., Ste. 3B, Hamden, CT, 06518; **PH:** 1-203-859-6800; **Fax:** 1-203-949-9048; **http://** www.transact-tech.com; **Email:** Corporate@Transact-tech.com

General - Incorporation	DE	**Stock**- Price on:12/24/2007	$6.53
Employees	172	Stock Exchange	NDQ
Auditor	PricewaterhouseCoopers LLP	Ticker Symbol	TACT
Stk Agt	American Stock Transfer & Trust Co.	Outstanding Shares	9,500,000
Counsel	Shipman & Goodwin	E.P.S.	$0.212
DUNS No.	95-839-2557	Shareholders	NA

Business: The group's principle activity is to design, develop, manufacture and market transaction-based printers under the ithaca(R) and magnetec(R) brand names. In addition the group markets related consumables, spare parts and service. The group's printers are used worldwide to provide transaction records such as receipts, tickets, coupons, register journals and other documents. The group focus on two core markets: point-of-sale and banking and gaming and lottery. The group's products are distributed across the Americas, Europe, the Middle East, Africa, the Caribbean islands and the south pacific. The group has export sales to its foreign customers from the United States. The group's quarterly revenue for Sep '07 was 11.74 millions of USD.

Primary SIC and add'l.: 3555 9999

CIK No: 0001017303

Subsidiaries: TransAct Technologies Ltd.

Officers: Bart C. Shudman/Chmn., CEO, Pres./$840,208.00, Michael S. Kumpf/Exec. VP - Engineering/$314,640.00, Steven A. Demartino/Exec. VP, CFO, Treasurer, Sec./$403,259.00, James B. Stetson/Sr. VP, Business Mgr./$281,015.00, Tracey S. Chernay/Sr. VP - Sales, Marketing, Andrew J. Hoffman/Sr. VP - Operations, David Pasquale/Investor Relations Officer, David Roche/Investor Relations Officer

Directors: Bart C. Shuldman/Chmn., CEO, Pres.

Owners: Graham Y. Tanaka/3.87%, Jon D. Berkley, Michael S. Kumpf, Thomas R. Schwarz/1.01%, Steven A. DeMartino, Insiders/13.09%, James B. Stetson, Bart C. Shuldman/3.09%, Charles A. Dill/2.12%, Bares Capital Management, Inc./5.12%

Financial Data: Fiscal Year End:12/31 **Latest Annual Data:** 12/31/2006

Year	Sales		Net Income
2006	$64,328,000		$3,916,000
2005	$51,091,000		$377,000
2004	$59,847,000		$5,458,000
Curr. Assets:	$25,186,000	**Curr. Liab.:** $8,748,000	
Plant, Equip.:	$5,938,000	**Total Liab.:** $9,416,000	**Indic. Yr. Divd.:** NA
Total Assets:	$33,706,000	**Net Worth:** $24,290,000	**Debt/ Equity:** NA

Transaction Systems Architects Inc

120 Broadway, Ste. 3350, New York, NY, 10271; **PH:** 1-646-348-6700; **http://** www.tsainc.com

General - Incorporation	DE	**Stock**- Price on:12/24/2007	$34.54
Employees	1,960	Stock Exchange	NDQ
Auditor	KPMG LLP	Ticker Symbol	ACIW
Stk Agt	Wells Fargo Shareowner Services	Outstanding Shares	37,160,000
Counsel	NA	E.P.S.	$0.06
DUNS No.	84-748-6990	Shareholders	NA

Business: The group's principal activities are to develop, market, install and support software products and services that facilitate e-payments and e-commerce. The group operates through three segments. Aci worldwide software products carry transactions from the transaction generators to the acquiring institutions. Insession technologies markets and supports a suite of e-infrastructure software products that facilitate communication, data movement, monitoring of systems and business process automation across computing systems and the Internet. Intranet includes products that offer high value payments processing, bulk payments processing, wire room processing, global messaging and continuous link settlement processing. The group markets its products through distribution networks in America, Europe, Middle East, Africa and Asia/pacific.

Primary SIC and add'l.: 7372 7376 7379

CIK No: 0000935036

Subsidiaries: ACI (Brasil) LLC, ACI (India) Inc., ACI Applied Communications (Netherlands) B.V., ACI Soluciones, S.L. (51% ownership), ACI Worldwide (Asia) Pte. Ltd., ACI Worldwide (Brasil) Ltda., ACI Worldwide (Canada) Inc., ACI Worldwide (EMEA) Limited, ACI Worldwide (Germany) GmbH& Co. KG, ACI Worldwide (Hellas) EPE, ACI Worldwide (Italia) S.R.L., ACI Worldwide (Japan) K.K., ACI Worldwide (Malaysia) Inc., ACI Worldwide (Mexico) S.A. de C.V., ACI Worldwide (New Zealand) Limited 51 Subsidiaries included in the Index

Officers: Philip G. Heasley/CEO, Pres., Henry C. Lyons/CFO, Sr. VP, Treasurer, Jeremy Wilmot/Pres. - Asia Pacific Region, Ralph Dangelmaier/Pres. - Americas Channel Service, Tim Thompson/Contact - Sales, Clearwater, Anthony O'Connor/Dir. - Applied Communications, Ireland Limited, Iain Kenny/Dir. - Applied Communications, Ireland Limited, Michele Schwappach/Sr. Technology Mgr., David N. Morem/Chief Administrative Officer, Dennis Byrnes/Sr. VP, General Counsel, Sec., Richard N. Launder/Pres. - Global Operations, Charles H. Linberg/CTO, Mark R. Vipond/COO, Verna Okell/Development Group Mgr., Sharon Adelmann/VP (23 Officers included in Index)

Directors: Rick Steckroth/Dir. - Business Development, John M. Shay/60/Dir.

Owners: David R. Bankhead, BlackRock Advisors, Inc./6.15%, Westfield Capital Management Co. LLC/5.32%, John M. Shay, Mark R. Vipond, Anthony J. Parkinson, John D. Curtis, Waddell and Reed Investment Management Co./8.22%, John E. Stokely, Roger K. Alexander, Philip G. Heasley/1.25%, Harlan F. Seymour, Insiders/3.50%, Jim D. Kever, Richard Launder

Financial Data: Fiscal Year End:09/30 **Latest Annual Data:** 09/30/2006

Year	Sales		Net Income
2006	$347,902,000		$55,365,000
2005	$313,237,000		$43,246,000
2004	$292,784,000		$46,685,000
Curr. Assets:	$225,519,000	**Curr. Liab.:** $157,587,000	**P/E Ratio:** 23.66
Plant, Equip.:	$14,306,000	**Total Liab.:** $266,935,000	**Indic. Yr. Divd.:** NA
Total Assets:	$534,147,000	**Net Worth:** $267,212,000	**Debt/ Equity:** 0.2806

TransAKT Ltd

Formerly: TransAKT Corp

1414 8th St. SW, Ste. 260, Calgary, AB, T2R 1J6; ; **http://** www.transaktcorp.com

General - Incorporation	Canada	**Stock**- Price on:12/24/2007	$0.145
Employees	NA	Stock Exchange	OTC
Auditor	Kabani & Co.,Inc.	Ticker Symbol	TAKDF
Stk Agt	Olympia Trust Co	Outstanding Shares	NA
Counsel	Daniel Horner	E.P.S.	NA
DUNS No.	NA	Shareholders	NA

Business: The groups principle activity is to provide Voice over Internet Protocol hardware and network services for small office-home office and residential users. The group operates from Canada and Taiwan. .

Primary SIC and add'l.: 9999

CIK No: 0001263872

Subsidiaries: TransAKT Holdings Limited, TransAKT USA Corp, Transakt USA Ltd

Officers: James Wu/Chmn., CEO, Pres., J. T. Wang/VP - Asia Operations, Mark Fletcher/Corp. Sec., Dir., Taifen Betsy Day/CFO

Directors: James Wu/Chmn., CEO, Pres., Tseng Ming-Huang/Dir., Mark Fletcher/Corp. Sec., Dir., Cheng Chun-Chih/Dir., Shiau Tzong-Huei/Dir.

Owners: Shiau Tzong-Huei/1.00%, Cheng Chun Chih/5.40%, Pan Yu-Jung/5.90%, Tseng Ming-Huang, Cheng Chun-Chih/4.90%, Hsieh Chi-Hsien/7.50%, James Wu/5.40%, Lin Yu-Hsiung/9.70%, Mark Fletcher, James Wu/6.10%, Taifen Day, Insiders/12.40%

Financial Data: Fiscal Year End:12/31 **Latest Annual Data:** 12/31/2006

Year	Sales		Net Income
2006	$8,385,000		-$237,000
2005	$124,000		-$5,275,000
2004	$280,000		-$2,038,000
Curr. Assets:	$5,460,000	**Curr. Liab.:** $4,270,000	**P/E Ratio:** 15.88
Plant, Equip.:	$70,000	**Total Liab.:** $4,270,000	**Indic. Yr. Divd.:** NA
Total Assets:	$5,540,000	**Net Worth:** $1,269,000	**Debt/ Equity:** NA

TransAlta Corp

110 12th Ave. SW, Calgary, AB, T2P 2M1; **PH:** 1-403-267-7110; **http://** www.transalta.com; **Email:** investor_relations@transalta.com

General - Incorporation	Canada	**Stock**- Price on:12/24/2007	$24.98
Employees	2,687	Stock Exchange	NYSE
Auditor	Ernst & Young LLP	Ticker Symbol	TAC
Stk Agt	Mellon Trust Co	Outstanding Shares	202,700,000
Counsel	NA	E.P.S.	$0.166
DUNS No.	NA	Shareholders	NA

Business: The group's principle activities are to produce electricity, build power projects and market energy in the province of alberta. The group operates in three segments: energy marketing, electric generation and independent power projects. The energy marketing segment is engaged in wholesale trading of electricity and other energy-related commodities. The electric generation segment is engaged in generation of power. The independent power project segment is engaged in building, owning and operating power projects. The group's quarterly revenue for September 2007 was 770 millions of CAD.

Primary SIC and add'l.: 4911

CIK No: 0001144800

Officers: Stephen G. Snyder/Dir., CEO, Pres., Frank W. Hawkins/VP, Treasurer, Jubran R. Whalan/VP - Commodity Trading, Origination, Linda K. Chambers/Exec. VP - Generation Technology, William D.A. Bridge/Exec. VP - Generation Technology, PMM, Derek Goodmanson/VP - Major Maintenance, Daniel Pigeon/VP - Portfolio Strategy, Execution, Mike Williams/Exec. VP - Human Resources, Information Technology, Communications, Brian Burden/CFO, Exec. VP, Thomas M. Rainwater/Exec. VP - Corporate Development, Marketing, Ken S. Stickland/Exec. VP - Legal, SD and EH&S, Mike H. Bartel/VP - Engineering Services, Kelly L. Gunsch/VP - Commercial Operations, Mark B. MacKay/VP - Energy Technology, Parviz Mohamed/VP - Information Technology *(27 Officers included in Index)*

Directors: Stephen G. Snyder/Dir., CEO, Pres., Donna Soble Kaufman/Dir., Kent C. Jespersen/Dir., Timothy W. Faithfull/Dir., Gordon G. Giffin/Dir., Michael M. Kanovsky/Dir., Gordon S. Lackenbauer/Dir., Martha C. Piper/Dir., Luis Vasquez Senties/Dir., William D. Anderson/Dir., Stanley J. Bright/Dir.

Financial Data: Fiscal Year End: 12/31   **Latest Annual Data:** 12/31/2006

Year	Sales	Net Income
2006	$2,399,677,000	$34,667,000
2005	$2,435,433,000	$176,062,000
2004	$2,356,640,000	$134,343,000

Curr. Assets:	$769,716,000	**Curr. Liab.:**	$1,204,000,000		
Plant, Equip.:	$4,420,674,000	**Total Liab.:**	$4,318,131,000	**Indic. Yr. Divd.:**	$1.020
Total Assets:	$6,401,512,000	**Net Worth:**	$2,083,381,000	**Debt/ Equity:**	NA

Transatlantic Holdings Inc

80 Pine St., New York, NY, 10005; **PH:** 1-212-770-2000; **http://** www.transre.com

General - Incorporation	DE	Stock - Price on:12/24/2007	$71.13
Employees	515	Stock Exchange	NYSE
Auditor	PricewaterhouseCoopers LLP	Ticker Symbol	TRH
Stk Agt	American Stock Transfer & Trust Co.	Outstanding Shares	66,070,000
Counsel	Fried Frank Harris Shriver & Jacobson	E.P.S.	$6.85
DUNS No.	00-699-1376	Shareholders	NA

Business: The group's principal activities are to provide reinsurance for a full range of property and casualty products to insurers and reinsurers on a treaty and facultative basis. Treaty reinsurance is a contractual arrangement that provides for the automatic reinsuring of a type or category of risk underwritten by the ceding company. Facultative reinsurance is the reinsurance of individual risks. The principal lines of insurance include general liability, medical malpractice, ocean marine and aviation, accident and health and surety and credit in the casualty lines and fire, homeowners and auto physical damage in the property lines. The group is a holding company, which operates through Transatlantic Reinsurance Company, Trans Re Zurich and Putnam Reinsurance Company. The group has operations in Europe and Asia-Pacific.

Primary SIC and add'l.: 6331 6719

CIK No: 0000862510

Subsidiaries: Putnam Reinsurance Company, TransRe Zurich, Transatlantic PolskaSp. z o.o, Transatlantic Reinsurance Company, TransatlanticRe (Argentina) S.A., TransatlanticRe (Brasil) Ltda

Officers: Robert F. Orlich/Dir., CEO, Pres./$4,122,442.00, Alain Manfre/CEO - Trans Re Zurich, Lorne Zalkowitz/Deputy CEO - Trans Re Zurich, Geoff Peach/Sr. VP - Treaty Underwriting, Dominique Lemonnier/Assist. VP - Treaty Underwriter, Rob Barclay/Regional Assist. VP, Facultative Property Mgr., Dominika Debreza/Treaty Underwriter TRC Paris, Laurent Montador/Treaty Underwriter TRC Paris, Pascal Bonhoure/Facultative Underwriter TRC Paris, Nigel Parker/VP, MD - Technical Lines Division, Howard I. Smith/Assist. VP, Asia Pacific Facultative Mgr., Christine Cheung/Mgr. - Accounting, Graz Perizzolo/Regional Assist. VP - Treaty Operations, Yukie Matsushita/Administration TRC Tokyo, Takae Sato/Administration TRC Tokyo *(82 Officers included in Index)*

Directors: Robert F. Orlich/Dir., CEO, Pres., Martin J. Sullivan/Chmn., James Balog/Dir., Steven J. Bensinger/Dir., Fred C. Bergsten/Dir., Thomas R. Tizzio/Dir., Ian H. Chippendale/Dir., John G. Foos/Dir., Diana K. Mayer/Dir., Richard Press/Dir.

Owners: Steven S. Skalicky/0.26%, John J. Mackowski/0.09%, Fred C. Bergsten, Insiders/2.05%, James Balog/0.08%, Javier E. Vijil/0.23%, Robert F. Orlich/0.78%, Steven J. Bensinger, Thomas R. Tizzio/0.15%, Michael C. Sapnar/0.07%, Martin J. Sullivan, Davis Selected Advisers, LP/22.46%, American International Group, Inc./59.17%, Paul A. Bonny/0.29%

Financial Data: Fiscal Year End: 12/31   **Latest Annual Data:** 12/31/2006

Year	Sales	Net Income
2006	$4,049,496,000	$428,152,000
2005	$3,768,125,000	$37,910,000
2004	$3,990,057,000	$254,584,000

Curr. Assets:	$4,153,637,000	**Curr. Liab.:**	$1,694,841,000	**P/E Ratio:**	10.38
Plant, Equip.:	NA	**Total Liab.:**	$11,310,194,000	**Indic. Yr. Divd.:**	$0.640
Total Assets:	$14,268,464,000	**Net Worth:**	$2,958,270,000	**Debt/ Equity:**	0.7784

Transax International Ltd

5201 Blue Lagoon Dr., 8th Fl., Miami, FL, 33126; **PH:** 1-305-629-3090; **http://** www.transax.com; **Email:** ir@transax.com

General - Incorporation	CO	Stock - Price on:12/24/2007	$0.06
Employees	36	Stock Exchange	OTC
Auditor	Moore Stephens, P.C	Ticker Symbol	TNSX
Stk Agt	Transfer Online, Inc.	Outstanding Shares	32,030,000
Counsel	Diane D. Dalmy	E.P.S.	$0.06
DUNS No.	NA	Shareholders	NA

Business: The groups principle activity is to provide information network solutions, products and services. The groups servicing areas include coding and reimbursement management; abstracting, and record management. The group operates from United States.

Primary SIC and add'l.: 1041 1044

CIK No: 0001097896

Subsidiaries: TDS Telecommunication Data Systems

Officers: Stephen Walters/Dir., CEO, Pres., Adam Wasserman/CFO, Americo M. De Castro/Pres. - TDS, Carlos Fernando Dos Santos Bartholo/CTO, David Sasso/VP - Investor Relations

Directors: Stephen Walters/Dir., CEO, Pres., Laurie Bewes/Dir., David Bouzaid/Dir., Christine Bennett/Member - Advisory Board

Owners: David Sasso, Insiders/36.57%, Stephen Walters/10.64%, Laurie Bewes/3.32%, Carlingford Investments Limited/25.07%, Adam Wasserman

Financial Data: Fiscal Year End: 12/31   **Latest Annual Data:** 12/31/2006

Year	Sales	Net Income
2006	$4,164,000	-$2,011,000
2005	$3,380,000	-$764,000
2004	$1,200,000	-$1,792,000

Curr. Assets:	$693,000	**Curr. Liab.:**	$5,087,000		
Plant, Equip.:	$1,032,000	**Total Liab.:**	$5,591,000	**Indic. Yr. Divd.:**	NA
Total Assets:	$2,063,000	**Net Worth:**	-$3,528,000	**Debt/ Equity:**	NA

Transbotics Corp

3400 Latrobe Dr., Charlotte, NC, 28211; **PH:** 1-704-362-1115; **http://** www.transbotics.com; **Email:** info@transbotics.com

General - Incorporation	DE	Stock - Price on:12/24/2007	$0.6
Employees	44	Stock Exchange	OTC
Auditor	Grant Thornton LLP	Ticker Symbol	TNSB
Stk Agt	First Citizens Bank & Trust Co	Outstanding Shares	4,850,000
Counsel	Shumaker Loop & Kendrick LLP	E.P.S.	$0.09
DUNS No.	06-257-0791	Shareholders	NA

Business: The group's principle activity is to acquire, develop, market and sell hardware, software and engineering services used to control automatic guided vehicles (AGV). AGVs are driverless, computer-controlled vehicles that are programmed to transport materials through designated pickup and delivery routines within a particular facility. The company offers over 20 standard items of equipment and over 10 standard software products with multiple options to its customers. The company markets its products and services to designers of integrated automation systems, original equipment manufacturers and end users primarily within the North American continent. The company's AGV system products and services have been used in a variety of industries including textiles, automotive, entertainment, newspaper publishing and electronics. The group operates from United States.

Primary SIC and add'l.: 3572 7372 8711 3679

CIK No: 0000859621

Officers: Robert T. Plyler/39/Principal Accounting Officer

Directors: Larrimore Wright/74/Dir.

Owners: Curt Kennington/9.70%, C. A. Austin/6.70%, Randall E. Jennings/0.30%, Charles W. Robison/0.50%, Claude Imbleau/12.20%, John H. Robison/22.50%, D. Bruce Wise/0.20%, Larrimore Wright, Tommy Hessler/12.20%, Insiders/45.60%, Anthony Packer/9.70%

Financial Data: Fiscal Year End: 11/30   **Latest Annual Data:** 05/31/2007

Year	Sales	Net Income
2007	NA	NA
2006	$8,469,000	$121,000
2005	$8,432,000	$128,000

Curr. Assets:	$2,430,000	**Curr. Liab.:**	$1,504,000		
Plant, Equip.:	$129,000	**Total Liab.:**	$1,811,000	**Indic. Yr. Divd.:**	NA
Total Assets:	$2,591,000	**Net Worth:**	$780,000	**Debt/ Equity:**	0.7611

TransCanada Corp

TransCanada Tower, 450 - 1st St. SW, Calgary, AB, T2P 5H1; **PH:** 1-403-920-2000; **Fax:** 1-403-920-2200; **http://** www.transcanada.com; **Email:** communications@transcanada.com

General - Incorporation	Canada	Stock - Price on:12/24/2007	$35.05
Employees	2,350	Stock Exchange	NYSE
Auditor	KPMG LLP	Ticker Symbol	TRP
Stk Agt	Computershare Trust Co of Canada	Outstanding Shares	534,720,000
Counsel	NA	E.P.S.	$2.03
DUNS No.	NA	Shareholders	NA

Business: The group's principle activities are transmitting, processing and marketing natural gas in Canada, the rest of North America and the world. The group operates in two business segments: transmission and power. Transmission provides natural gas transmission from western Canada to the rest of Canada and the United States. Power builds, owns and operates electrical power plants and markets and trades electricity. It also provides electricity-managed account services to energy and industrial customers. The group's quarterly revenue for 207 was 2,210.00millions of CAD.

Primary SIC and add'l.: NA

CIK No: 0001232384

Subsidiaries: 701671 Alberta Ltd Alberta, Nova Gas Tranmission Ltd Alberta, TransCanada Energy Ltd Canada., TransCanada Pipeline USA Ltd Nevada, TransCanada PipLine Limited Canada

Officers: Harold N. Kvisle/55/Dir., CEO, Pres., Ronald L. Cook/VP - Taxation, Donald R. Marchand/VP - Finance, Treasurer, Garry E. Lamb/VP - Risk Management, Russell K. Girling/Pres. - Pipelines, Alexander J. Pourbaix/Pres. - Energy, Gregory A. Lohnes/CFO, Exec. VP, Dennis McConaghy/Exec. VP - Pipeline Strategy, Development, Sean McMaster/Exec. VP - Corporate, General Counsel, Sarah E. Raiss/Exec. VP - Corporate Services, Don Wishart/Exec. VP - Operations, Engineering

Directors: Harold N. Kvisle/55/Dir., CEO, Pres., Barry S. Jackson/55/Chmn., Thomas W. Stephens/65/Dir., Kevin E. Benson/61/Dir., Derek H. Burney/68/Dir., Wendy K. Dobson/66/Dir., Linn E. Draper/66/Dir., Paule Gauthier/64/Dir., Kerry L. Hawkins/66/Dir., Paul L. Joskow/60/Dir., John A. MacNaughton/62/Dir., David P. O'Brien/66/Dir., Harry G. Schaefer/Dir., Michael D.G. Stewart/56/Dir.

Financial Data: Fiscal Year End: 12/31   **Latest Annual Data:** 12/31/2006

Year	Sales	Net Income
2006	$5,146,026,000	$925,032,000
2005	$4,575,714,000	$1,033,032,000
2004	$3,902,410,000	$742,288,000

Curr. Assets:	$50,780,000	**Curr. Liab.:**	$37,882,000		
Plant, Equip.:	$273,376,000	**Total Liab.:**	$43,163,000	**Indic. Yr. Divd.:**	$1.170
Total Assets:	$17,400,000	**Net Worth:**	$126,931,000	**Debt/ Equity:**	NA

Transcat Inc

35 Vantage Point Dr., Rochester, NY, 14624; **PH:** 1-585-352-7777; **http://** www.transcat.com

General - Incorporation	OH	Stock - Price on:12/24/2007	$5.65
Employees	238	Stock Exchange	NDQ
Auditor	BDO Seidman LLP	Ticker Symbol	TRNS
Stk Agt	National City Bank	Outstanding Shares	7,010,000
Counsel	Harter, Secrest & Emery	E.P.S.	$0.29
DUNS No.	00-246-4964	Shareholders	NA

Business: The group's principal activity is to distribute professional grade test, measurement, and calibration equipment and provide calibration and repair services. The group operates in two segments: the distribution products segment markets and distributes national and proprietary brand instruments including calibrators, deadweight testers, temperature devices, multimeters, oscilloscopes, pressure pumps, testers, recorders and related accessories. The calibration services segment provides calibration services and repairs for measurement, test and diagnostic instruments. The group sells its products primarily to process, life science, and manufacturing industries. It operates in the United States of America and Canada.

Primary SIC and add'l.: 3823 3829

CIK No: 0000099302

Subsidiaries: metersandinstruments.com, Inc., Transmation (Canada) Inc.

Officers: Charles P. Hadeed/58/Dir., CEO, COO, Pres./$402,199.00, Lexi Terrero/Sr. Dir. - Van Negris, Company, Inc, John Devoldre/VP - Human Resources/$190,657.00, Jennifer Gnage/Contact, Jay F. Woychick/51/VP - Marketing/$235,615.00, John J. Zimmer/50/CFO, VP - Finance/$198,464.00, Andrew M. Weir/57/VP - Field Sales

Directors: Charles P. Hadeed/58/Dir., CEO, COO, Pres., Carl E. Sassano/58/Chmn., Francis R. Bradley/62/Dir., Cornelius J. Murphy/77/Dir., Alan H. Resnick/64/Dir., Richard J. Harrison/63/Dir., Nancy D. Hessler/62/Dir., Robert G. Klimasewski/Dir., Paul D. Moore/57/Dir., Harvey J. Palmer/62/Dir., John T. Smith/60/Dir., Lee E. Garelick/73/Dir.

Owners: John T. Smith, Paul D. Moore, Cornelius J. Murphy, Charles P. Hadeed/1.80%, Jay F. Woychick, John J. Zimmer, Carl E. Sassano/4.30%, Richard J. Harrison, Alan H. Resnick, Francis R. Bradley, Insiders/17.20%, Lee E. Garelick/3.70%, Brown Advisory Holdings Incorporated/32.30%, Harvey J. Palmer/1.10%, Nancy D. Hessler *(17 Owners included in Index)*

Financial Data: Fiscal Year End:03/25 Latest Annual Data: 3/25/2006

Year	Sales	Net Income
2006	$60,471,000	$3,577,000
2005	$55,307,000	$256,000
2004	$53,317,000	$353,000

Curr. Assets:	$13,291,000	**Curr. Liab.:**	$13,074,000	**P/E Ratio:**	18.83
Plant, Equip.:	$2,206,000	**Total Liab.:**	$14,957,000	**Indic. Yr. Divd.:**	NA
Total Assets:	$18,385,000	**Net Worth:**	$3,428,000	**Debt/ Equity:**	NA

Transcend Services Inc

945 E Paces Ferry Rd. , Ste 1475, Atlanta, GA, 30326; **PH:** 1-404-364-8000;
http:// www.transcendservices.com

General - Incorporation	DE	Stock - Price on:12/24/2007	$19.52
Employees	613	Stock Exchange	NDQ
Auditor	Miller Ray, Houser & Stewart LLP	Ticker Symbol	TRCR
Stk Agt	Sue Hampton Computershare	Outstanding Shares	8,160,000
Counsel	Morris Manning & Martin LLP	E.P.S.	$0.45
DUNS No.	61-310-5402	Shareholders	NA

Business: The group's principle activities are to provide health information management services, which include medical transcription services, consulting and reimbursement coding services to hospitals. The group provides medical records transcription services through computer and telephone links from centralized facilities to hospital customers. The group provides medical records, coding and compliance services and state-of-the-art software for the management of patient information. The group through its subsidiary, transcend case management, inc. Provides case management services to insurance carriers, third party benefit administrators and self insured employees. Hospitals, hospital systems, multi-specialty clinics and individual physician practices are the major customers of the group. The group's quarterly revenue for Sep '07 was 10.63 millions of USD.

Primary SIC and add'l.: 7374

CIK No: 0000858452

Subsidiaries: Medical Dictation, Inc.

Officers: Larry G. Gerdes/Chmn., CEO/$302,912.00, Lance Cornell/CFO/$206,057.00, Jeffrey Mckee/Sr. VP - Sales, Marketing/$177,748.00, Susan McGrogan/COO/$162,814.00, Tara Goehring/Dir. - Staffing, Employee Development, Sue Hampton/Transfer Agent

Directors: Larry G. Gerdes/Chmn., CEO, Joseph P. Clayton/58/Dir., James D. Edwards/64/Dir., Walter S. Huff/73/Dir., Charles E. Thoele/72/Dir., Sidney V. Sack/Dir., Joseph G. Bleser/Dir.

Owners: Joseph P. Clayton, James D. Edwards, Larry G. Gerdes/13.55%, Insiders/32.82%, Walter S. Huff/12.13%, Laumar Investors Limited Partnership/6.71%, Charles E. Thoele, Joseph G. Bleser

Financial Data: Fiscal Year End:12/31 Latest Annual Data: 12/31/2006

Year	Sales	Net Income
2006	$32,912,000	$1,457,000
2005	$25,817,000	-$1,192,000
2004	$15,197,000	$277,000

Curr. Assets:	$4,871,000	**Curr. Liab.:**	$3,210,000	**P/E Ratio:**	43.38
Plant, Equip.:	$1,334,000	**Total Liab.:**	$6,313,000	**Indic. Yr. Divd.:**	NA
Total Assets:	$10,620,000	**Net Worth:**	$4,307,000	**Debt/ Equity:**	0.3088

Transcontinental Gas Pipe Line Corp

PO Box 1396, Houston, TX, 77251; **PH:** 1-713-215-2000; **http://** www.tgpl.twc.com

General - Incorporation	DE	Stock - Price on:12/24/2007	$31.64
Employees	4,313	Stock Exchange	NA
Auditor	Ernst & Young LLP	Ticker Symbol	NA
Stk Agt	Computershare Investor Services LLC	Outstanding Shares	598,860,000
Counsel	NA	E.P.S.	NA
DUNS No.	00-793-3021	Shareholders	NA

Business: The group's principle activity is to provide natural gas transmission. The company is a wholly owned subsidiary of williams gas pipeline company and indirectly wholly owned subsidiary of the williams companies, inc. The company owns natural gas pipeline system extending from Texas, Louisiana, Mississippi and the gulf of Mexico through the states of Alabama, Georgia, South Carolina, North Carolina, Virginia, Maryland, Pennsylvania and New Jersey to the New York city metropolitan area. The pipeline system serves customers in Texas and eleven southeast and Atlantic seaboard states including major metropolitan areas in Georgia, North Carolina, New York, New Jersey and Pennsylvania. The customers of the company include public utilities and municipalities, which provides services to residential, commercial, industrial and electric generation end users. The group operates from United States.

Primary SIC and add'l.: 4922

CIK No: 0000099250

Subsidiaries: The Williams Companies, Inc, Williams Gas Pipeline Company, LLC

Officers: Frank J. Ferazzi/Dir., VP, Phillip D. Wright/Dir., Sr. VP, Principal Executive Officer, Richard D. Rodekohr/VP, Treasurer, Principal Financial Officer, Jeffrey P. Heinrichs/Controller

Directors: Steven J. Malcolm/Chmn., Frank J. Ferazzi/Dir., VP, Phillip D. Wright/Dir., Sr. VP, Principal Executive Officer

Financial Data: Fiscal Year End:12/31 Latest Annual Data: 12/31/2006

Year	Sales	Net Income
2006	$11,812,900,000	$308,500,000
2005	$12,583,600,000	$313,600,000
2004	$12,461,300,000	$163,700,000

Curr. Assets:	$6,322,000,000	**Curr. Liab.:**	$4,693,600,000		
Plant, Equip.:	$14,180,700,000	**Total Liab.:**	$18,248,400,000	**Indic. Yr. Divd.:**	$0.400
Total Assets:	$25,402,400,000	**Net Worth:**	$6,073,200,000	**Debt/ Equity:**	1.5785

Transcontinental Realty Investors Inc

1800 Valley View Ln., Ste. 300, Dallas, TX, 75234; **PH:** 1-469-522-4233; **Fax:** 1-469-522-4299; **http://** www.transconrealty-invest.com; **Email:** investor.relations@primeasset.com

General - Incorporation	NV	Stock - Price on:12/24/2007	$15.53
Employees	NA	Stock Exchange	NYSE
Auditor	Farmer, Fuqua & Huff, PC	Ticker Symbol	TCI
Stk Agt	American Stock Transfer & Trust Co.	Outstanding Shares	7,890,000
Counsel	NA	E.P.S.	-$1.63
DUNS No.	NA	Shareholders	NA

Business: The groups principle activities include operating, owning, acquiring and developing real estate properties. The group operates through four segments namely, apartments, commercial properties, hotels and land ownership. The group operates from the United States. The groups quarterly revenue for September 2007 was 38.38 millions of USD.

Primary SIC and add'l.: 6519

CIK No: 0000733590

Subsidiaries: ART One Hickory Corporation, ART Two Hickory, Corporation, Bridgeknight Holdings B.V., Centura-Ewing, Inc., Century Realty, Inc., Continental Baronne, Inc., Continental Common, Continental Common Lease, Inc., Continental Durham Centre, Inc., Continental Indcon Corporation, Continental Mortgage and Equity Investors, Inc., Continental Pines Corporation, Continental Poydras Corp., Continental Promenade Corporation, Continental Signature, Inc. 176 Subsidiaries included in the Index

Officers: Louis J. Corna/Exec. VP - Tax, General Counsel, Sec., Steven A. Abney/CFO, Exec. VP, Robert A. Jakuszewski/45/Dir., VP - Sales, Marketing, Mickey N. Phillips/Mgr., Ryan T. Phillips/Mgr., Reagan K. Vidal/47/Exec. VP, MD - Capital Markets, Alfred Crozier/55/Exec. VP - Residential Construction, Daniel J. Moos/57/COO, Pres.

Directors: Ted P. Stokely/74/Chmn., Sharon Hunt/65/Dir., Robert A. Jakuszewski/45/Dir., VP - Sales, Marketing, Ted R. Munselle/52/Dir., Henry A. Butler/57/Dir.

Owners: Daniel J. Moos, Louis J. Corna, Henry A. Butler, Ted R. Munselle, American Realty Investors, Inc, American Realty Trust, Inc, Robert A. Jakuszewski, EQK Holdings, Inc, Sharon Hunt, Transcontinental Realty Acquisition Corporation, Ted P. Stokley, Insiders, Alfred Crozier, Steven A. Abney, Reagan K. Vidal

Financial Data: Fiscal Year End:12/31 Latest Annual Data: 12/31/2006

Year	Sales	Net Income
2006	$128,064,000	$3,506,000
2005	$105,444,000	$9,069,000
2004	$125,509,000	$23,706,000

Curr. Assets:	$4,803,000	**Curr. Liab.:**	NA	**P/E Ratio:**	24.65
Plant, Equip.:	$1,047,389,000	**Total Liab.:**	$984,238,000	**Indic. Yr. Divd.:**	NA
Total Assets:	$1,250,167,000	**Net Worth:**	$265,929,000	**Debt/ Equity:**	NA

Transdigm Group Inc

1301 E 9th St., Ste.3710, Cleveland, OH, 44114; **PH:** 1-216-706-2960; **http://** www.transdigm.com; **Email:** info@transdigm.com

General - Incorporation	DE	Stock - Price on:12/24/2007	$42.05
Employees	1,400	Stock Exchange	NYSE
Auditor	Ernst & Young, LLP	Ticker Symbol	TDG
Stk Agt	National City Bank	Outstanding Shares	46,810,000
Counsel	NA	E.P.S.	$1.83
DUNS No.	NA	Shareholders	NA

Business: The groups principal activities include designing, producing and supplying engineered aircraft components. In the year 2005, the group acquired Fluid Regulators Corporation. The group acquired from the United States.

Primary SIC and add'l.: 5088 3728 3724

CIK No: 0001260221

Subsidiaries: Adams Rite Aerospace, Inc., Avionic Instruments, Inc., CDA InterCorp, Champion Aerospace Inc., Christie Electric Corp., DAC Realty Corp., Marathon Power Technologies Limited, MarathonNorco Aerospace, Inc., Skurka Aerospace Inc., Sweeney Engineering Corp., ZMP, Inc.

Officers: Nicholas W. Howley/Chmn., CEO, Raymond F. Laubenthal/COO, Pres., Gregory Rufus/CFO, Exec. VP, Sec., Robert S. Henderson/Exec. VP, Pres. - Adelwiggins Group, an Operating Division, Transdigm Inc, Albert J. Rodriguez/Exec. VP - Mergers, Acquisitions, Bernt G. Iversen/Pres. - Champion Aerospace Inc, John F. Leary/Pres. - Adams Rite Aerospace, Inc, Ralph McClelland/Pres. - Marathonnorco Aerospace, Inc., James Riley/Pres. - Aerocontrolex Group, Howard A. Skurka/Pres. - Skurka Aerospace Inc., Bryce Wiedemann/Pres. - Avionic Instruments Inc.

Directors: Nicholas W. Howley/Chmn., CEO, David A. Barr/Dir., Michael Graff/Dir., Sean P. Hennessy/Dir., Kevin Kruse/Dir., Kewsong Lee/Dir., Douglas W. Peacock/Dir., Dudley P. Sheffler/Dir., Merv Dunn/Dir.

Owners: Michael Graff, Kevin Kruse, Raymond F. Laubenthal, Albert J. Rodriguez, Sean P. Hennessy, Warburg Pincus Private Equity VIII, L.P., TD Group Holdings, LLC, Nicholas w. Howley, Dudley Sheffler, Gregory Rufus, David A. Barr, Douglas Peacock, Robert S. Henderson, Kewsong Lee, Insiders

Financial Data: Fiscal Year End:09/30 Latest Annual Data: 9/30/2006

Year	Sales	Net Income
2006	$435,164,000	$25,117,000
2005	$374,253,000	$34,687,000
2004	$300,703,000	$13,622,000

Curr. Assets:	$234,181,000	Curr. Liab.:	$43,439,000	P/E Ratio:	25.48
Plant, Equip.:	$62,851,000	Total Liab.:	$1,053,671,000	Indic. Yr. Divd.:	NA
Total Assets:	$1,416,712,000	Net Worth:	$363,041,000	Debt/ Equity:	3.2944

Transgene

11 Rue De Molsheim, Strasbourg Cedex, Strasbourg, 67082; *PH:* 33-478872000;
http:// www.transgene.fr

General - Incorporation	France	Stock- Price on:12/24/2007	NA
Employees	NA	Stock Exchange	OTC
Auditor	Ernst & Young LLP	Ticker Symbol	TGBXF
Stk Agt	NA	Outstanding Shares	NA
Counsel	NA	E.P.S.	NA
DUNS No.	26-729-4486	Shareholders	NA

Business: The groups principle activities include research and development of gene delivery technologies and gene therapy products for the treatment of acquired and inherited diseases. The group's servicing areas include molecular biology, virology, immunology and protein chemistry. The group operates from United States.

Primary SIC and add'l.: 8731 8071

CIK No: 0001056910

Subsidiaries: Transgene, Inc

Officers: Philippe Archinard/Dir., CEO, Remi Gloeckler/VP - Pharmaceutical Operations, Elisabeth Keppi/Qualified Pharmacist, Philippe Poncet/CFO, Francois Valencony/VP - Corporate Development, Jean-Yves Bonnefoy/VP - Research, Development, Ghislaine Gilleron/General Counsel, Laurence Bertaud/Dir. - Human Resources, Sec. to The Management Board

Directors: Philippe Archinard/Dir., CEO, Michel Dubois/Chmn., Christopher Walker/Member - Scientific Advisory Board, Jean-Claude Weill/Member - Scientific Advisory Board, Dana J. Philpott/Member - Scientific Advisory Board, Monika M. Pietrek/Member - Scientific Advisory Board, Suzy M.E. Scholl/Member - Scientific Advisory Board, Rafick-Pierre Sekaly/Member - Scientific Advisory Board, Jean-Yves Blay/Member - Scientific Advisory Board, Pierre Chambon/Member - Scientific Advisory Board, Pierre Coulie/Member - Scientific Advisory Board, James Di Santo/Member - Scientific Advisory Board, Steven K. Dower/Member - Scientific Advisory Board, Philippe Kourilsky/Member - Scientific Advisory Board, Sjoerd Van Der/Member - Scientific Advisory Board *(22 Directors included in Index)*

Transgenomic Inc

12325 Emmet St., Omaha, NE, 68164; *PH:* 1-402-452-5400; *http://* www.transgenomic.com;
Email: info@transgenomic.com

General - Incorporation	DE	Stock- Price on:12/24/2007	NA
Employees	156	Stock Exchange	OTC
Auditor	Deloitte & Touche LLP	Ticker Symbol	TBIO
Stk Agt	Wells Fargo Bank Minnesota N.A	Outstanding Shares	NA
Counsel	Kutak Rock LLP	E.P.S.	NA
DUNS No.	NA	Shareholders	NA

Business: The group's principal activity is to provide innovative products and services for the synthesis, purification and analysis of nucleic acids. The group operates in two segments: biosystems and nucleic acids. The biosystems segment sells automated instrument systems, associated consumable products and chemical building blocks for nucleic acid synthesis. The segment's main products are the wave system, related bio-consumables and research services. The nucleic acids segment sells products and services based upon group's core competencies, nucleic acid chemistries, separations chemistries and enzymology. This segment's main products are nucleic acid building blocks or phosphoramidites, oligonucleotides, fluorescent markers, dyes and associated reagents and novel chemistry and process development services. The group operates in the United States, Europe, Pacific Rim and other countries.

Primary SIC and add'l.: 3826 2869

CIK No: 0001043961

Subsidiaries: Annovis, Inc., Cruachem, Ltd., Todd Campus, Ltd., Transgenomic Japan, Inc., Transgenomic, Ltd.

Officers: Craig Tuttle/Dir., CEO, Pres./$173,994.00, Debra A. Schneider/CFO/$16,741.00

Directors: Rodney S. Markin/Chmn., Gregory J. Duman/Dir., Jeffrey Sklar/Dir., Gregory T. Sloma/Dir., Frank R. Witney/Dir.

Owners: Michael A. Roth and Brian J. Stark/8.60%, David M. Knott and Dorset Management Corporation/9.90%, LeRoy C. Kopp/17.60%, Steven R. Becker/9.90%, Jeffrey L. Sklar, Gregory T. Sloma, Gregory J. Duman, Insiders/10.90%, Collin J. DSilva/9.90%, LB I Group Inc./9.90%, Michael A. Summers

Curr. Assets:	$15,605,000	Curr. Liab.:	$5,329,000		
Plant, Equip.:	$1,498,000	Total Liab.:	$5,329,000	Indic. Yr. Divd.:	NA
Total Assets:	$21,367,000	Net Worth:	$16,038,000	Debt/ Equity:	NA

TransGlobe Energy Corp

605 - 5th Ave. SW, Ste. 2500, Calgary, AB, T2P 3H5; *PH:* 1-403-264-9888;
http:// www.trans-globe.com; *Email:* contact@trans-globe.com

General - Incorporation	AB	Stock- Price on:12/24/2007	$4.37
Employees	24	Stock Exchange	AMEX
Auditor	Deloitte & Touche LLP	Ticker Symbol	TGA
Stk Agt	Computershare Trust Co of Canada	Outstanding Shares	59,660,000
Counsel	Burnet, Duckworth & Palmer	E.P.S.	$0.30
DUNS No.	20-798-0947	Shareholders	NA

Business: The group's principal activity is to explore, develop and produce oil and gas properties in Canada and the republic of yemen.

Primary SIC and add'l.: 1382 1311

CIK No: 0000736744

Subsidiaries: TG Holdings Yemen Inc, TransGlobe International (Holdings) Inc., TransGlobe Oil and Gas Corporation, TransGlobe Power Development

Officers: Ross G. Clarkson/Dir., CEO, Pres., Edward Bell/VP - Exploration, Lloyd W. Herrick/Dir., VP, COO, David C. Ferguson/VP - Finance, CFO, Sec., James Bambrick/Mgr. - Geophysics, James W. Dowhaniuk/Mgr. - Domestic Exploration, Brad Goldie/Mgr. - Exploration, Egypt, Rob Pankiw/Mgr. - Enginering, Domestic, Glenn B. Taylor/Mgr. - Operations, Domestic, Ned Kljucec/GM - Transglobe Petroleum Egypt Inc, Brett Norris/Mgr. - International Exploitation, Bartek Jankowski/Controller

Directors: Ross G. Clarkson/Dir., CEO, Pres., Robert A. Halpin/Chmn., Geoffrey C. Chase/Dir., Lloyd W. Herrick/Dir., VP, COO, Fred Dyment/Dir., Erwin L. Noyes/Dir.

Owners: Geoffrey C. Chase/0.33%, Robert A. Halpin/1.60%, Edward Bell/0.06%, Erwin L. Noyes/0.53%, David C. Ferguson/0.59%, Lloyd W. Herrick/1.28%, Ross G. Clarkson/3.90%

Financial Data: Fiscal Year End:12/31 *Latest Annual Data:* 12/31/2006

Year	Sales	Net Income
2006	$70,297,000	$26,195,000
2005	$59,040,000	$20,573,000
2004	$31,643,000	$7,229,000

Curr. Assets:	$17,868,000	Curr. Liab.:	$15,678,000		
Plant, Equip.:	$96,608,000	Total Liab.:	$15,678,000	Indic. Yr. Divd.:	NA
Total Assets:	$116,473,000	Net Worth:	$100,795,000	Debt/ Equity:	NA

Transmeridian Exploration Inc

397 N Sam Houston Pkwy E, Ste 300, Houston, TX, 77060; *PH:* 1-289-299-9091;
http:// www.tmei.com

General - Incorporation	DE	Stock- Price on:12/24/2007	$2.02
Employees	219	Stock Exchange	AMEX
Auditor	UHY LLP	Ticker Symbol	TMY
Stk Agt	Bank of New York	Outstanding Shares	103,490,000
Counsel	NA	E.P.S.	-$0.6
DUNS No.	NA	Shareholders	NA

Business: The group's principal activity is to explore, develop and produce oil and gas properties. The group acquires identified and underdeveloped hydrocarbon reserves in the region of the former soviet union known as the confederation of independent states (cis). The group conducts its operations in kazakhstan through a wholly subsidiary caspineft tme. The group, during the year started new venture to develop natural gas properties in south Texas and gulf coast regions of U.S.

Primary SIC and add'l.: 1311 1382

CIK No: 0001132645

Subsidiaries: Bramex Management, Inc., Emba-Trans LLP, JSC Caspi Neft TME, TMEI Operating, Inc., Transmeridian (Kazakhstan), Transmeridian Caspian Petroleum LLP, Transmeridian Exploration Inc.

Officers: Lorrie T. Olivier/Chmn., CEO, Pres./$1,156,121.00, Bruce A. Falkenstein/VP - Exploration, Geology, Earl W. McNiel/CFO, VP/$894,124.00, Alan W. Halsey/VP, COO, Nicolas J. Evanoff/VP, General Counsel, Sec./$723,558.00, Edward G. Brantley/VP, Chief Accounting Officer/$451,600.00

Directors: Lorrie T. Olivier/Chmn., CEO, Pres., Frank J. Haasbeek/Dir., James H. Dorman/Dir., Marvin R. Carter/Dir., Wolfgang Rupf/Dir., Alfred L. Shacklett/Dir.

Owners: James H. Dorman, Frank J. Haasbeek, Edward G. Brantley, Alfred L. Shacklett, Wolfgang Rupf, Insiders/19.70%, Earl W. McNiel/1.00%, Nicolas J. Evanoff, Vicis Capital Master Fund/15.30%, Lorrie T. Oliver/14.20%, Bruce A. Falkenstein/1.60%, Alan W. Halsey, North Sound Capital LLC/18.30%, Marvin R. Carter

Financial Data: Fiscal Year End:12/31 *Latest Annual Data:* 12/31/2006

Year	Sales	Net Income
2006	$24,672,000	-$53,247,000
2005	$8,443,000	-$20,541,000
2004	$3,923,000	-$3,848,000

Curr. Assets:	$23,866,000	Curr. Liab.:	$18,064,000		
Plant, Equip.:	$320,806,000	Total Liab.:	$289,686,000	Indic. Yr. Divd.:	NA
Total Assets:	$356,636,000	Net Worth:	$25,997,000	Debt/ Equity:	14.9908

Transmeta Corp

3990 Freedom Cir., Santa Clara, CA, 95054; *PH:* 1-408-919-6907; *http://* www.transmeta.com;
Email: customersupport@transmeta.com

General - Incorporation	DE	Stock- Price on:12/24/2007	$0.4817
Employees	198	Stock Exchange	NDQ
Auditor	Burr, Pilger & Mayer, LLP	Ticker Symbol	TMTA
Stk Agt	Mellon Investor Services LLC	Outstanding Shares	199,930,000
Counsel	Fenwick & West LLP	E.P.S.	-$5.868
DUNS No.	NA	Shareholders	NA

Business: The group's principal activities are to develop and distribute software-based microprocessors and additional hardware and software technologies for mobile Internet computers. The products are portable computing and communication devices that are compatible with PC software. The products also deliver the performance required to run standard PC and Internet applications and also offer long battery life. Crusoe microprocessors have been developed for lightweight notebook computers and wireless Internet access devices and other Internet appliances. The crusoe microprocessors are suitable for a broad set of existing and emerging end markets where energy efficiency and x86 software compatibility are desirable. The group's customers include sharp, fujitsu, hewlett-packard and uniquest.

Primary SIC and add'l.: 5999

CIK No: 0001001193

Officers: Lester M. Crudele/Dir., CEO, Pres., John O'Hara Horsley/Exec. VP, General Counsel, Sec./$413,196.00, John Heinlein/VP - Business Development, Marketing, Sujan Jain/CFO, Kristine Mozes/Contact - Investor Relations, Financial Media

Directors: Lester M. Crudele/Dir., CEO, Pres., Hugh Barnes/Chmn., Rick Timmins/Dir., Robert Dickinson/Dir., Murray Goldman/Dir., William P. Tai/Dir., Peter T. Thomas/Dir.

Owners: Hugh R. Barnes, Robert V. Dickinson, William P. Tai/1.93%, Ralph J. Harms, Rick Timmins, Lester M. Crudele, Insiders/10.85%, Murray A. Goldman, Peter T. Thomas/5.93%, John OHara Horsley, David R. Ditzel/1.09%, Robert Bismuth

Financial Data: Fiscal Year End:12/31 *Latest Annual Data:* 12/31/2006

Year	Sales	Net Income
2006	$48,550,000	-$23,498,000
2005	$72,731,000	-$6,181,000
2004	$29,444,000	-$106,798,000

Curr. Assets:	$44,589,000	Curr. Liab.:	$11,725,000		
Plant, Equip.:	$758,000	Total Liab.:	$14,046,000	Indic. Yr. Divd.:	NA
Total Assets:	$56,729,000	Net Worth:	$42,683,000	Debt/ Equity:	0.0519

TransMontaigne Inc

1670 Brd.way, Ste. 3100, Denver, CO, 80202; *PH:* 1-303-626-8200; *http://* www.transmontaigne.com

General - Incorporation	DE	**Stock**- Price on:12/24/2007	$15.68
Employees	NA	Stock Exchange	NA
Auditor	KPMG LLP	Ticker Symbol	NA
Stk Agt	Fleet Nat'l Bank	Outstanding Shares	9,570,000
Counsel	NA	E.P.S.	NA
DUNS No.	12-279-3458	Shareholders	NA

Business: The group's principal activity is to provide an integrated supply, distribution, marketing, terminal storage and transportation services of refined petroleum products, fertilizer, chemicals and other commercial liquids. The services of the group are provided to refiners, distributors, marketers and industrial/commercial end-users of refined petroleum products. It operates through two segments: terminals, pipelines and tugs and barges and supply, distribution and marketing. The group owns and operates terminal infrastructure that handles refined petroleum products with transportation connections by pipelines, tankers, barges, rail cars and trucks to their facilities. They purchase refined petroleum products from refineries and deliver them to their terminals and then sell their products to cruise ship operators, commercial and industrial end-users. The group operates in the gulf coast, midwest and east coast regions of the United States.

Primary SIC and add'l.: 4613 5171 5172 6719

CIK No: 0000755199

Subsidiaries: Coastal Fuels Marketing, Inc., Coastal Terminal LLC, Coastal Tug and Barge, Inc., Razorback LLC, TPSI Terminals LLC, TransMontaigne GP LLC, TransMontaigne Operating Company L.P., TransMontaigne Operating GP LLC, TransMontaigne Partners L.P., TransMontaigne Product Services Inc., TransMontaigne Services Inc., TransMontaigne Transport Inc.

Officers: Randall J. Larson/CEO, Pres., CFO, Chief Accounting Officer, Erik B. Carlson/Sr. VP, Corp. Sec., General Counsel, Frederick W. Boutin/Sr. VP, Treasurer, William S. Dickey/Exec. VP, COO, Dir.

Directors: Donald H. Anderson/Chmn., William S. Dickey/Exec. VP, COO, Dir., Jerry R. Masters/Dir., David A. Peters/Dir., Dale D. Shaffer/Dir., Javed Ahmed/Dir., Rex L. Utsler/Dir.

Financial Data: *Fiscal Year End:*06/30 *Latest Annual Data:* 9/30/2006

Year		Sales		Net Income
2006		$10,372,000		$6,619,000
2005		$15,523,000		$7,084,000
2004		$13,278,000		$11,604,000
Curr. Assets:	$2,291,000	*Curr. Liab.:*	$596,000	
Plant, Equip.:	NA	*Total Liab.:*	$596,000	*Indic. Yr. Divd.:* $0.930
Total Assets:	$167,459,000	*Net Worth:*	$166,862,000	*Debt/ Equity:* NA

Transnational Financial Network Inc

401 Taraval St., 2nd Fl., San Francisco, CA, 94116; *PH:* 1-415-242-7800; *http://* www.transnational.com

General - Incorporation	CA	**Stock**- Price on:12/24/2007	$0.32
Employees	95	Stock Exchange	OTC
Auditor	Bedinger & Co	Ticker Symbol	TRFN
Stk Agt	American Stock Transfer & Trust Co.	Outstanding Shares	10,250,000
Counsel	Robert A. Forrester	E.P.S.	-$0.56
DUNS No.	14-710-1109	Shareholders	NA

Business: The group's principal activity is to originate and lend mortgage loans secured by one to four family residential properties in the san francisco bay area, southern California and Arizona. The group provides these mortgage banking services through wholesale and retail divisions. The wholesale division purchases loan applications from mortgage brokers and sells the same to investors for a price higher than the purchase price. The mortgage loans are processed, closed and funded by the group. The retail division processes and completes the mortgage loan applications and prepares and originates necessary mortgage loan documents. The mortgage loan products include mortgage loans that conform to fnma (federal national mortgage association) and non-conforming mortgage loans.

Primary SIC and add'l.: 6162

CIK No: 0001059579

Officers: Joseph Kristul/Chmn., CEO, Maria Kristul/Pres., Mike Lawson/Chief Compliance Officer, Elena Logutova/Exec. VP, Dir. - Secondary Marketing, Leo Hmarny/Dir. - Management Information Systems, Information Technology, Thomas Schott/Sr. VP, CFO, Walter Pajares/Sr. VP - Mortgage Operations

Directors: Joseph Kristul/Chmn., CEO, Robert A. Forrester/64/Dir., Alex Rotzang/64/Dir., Dennis R. Orsi/58/Dir.

Owners: Joseph Kristul/1.50%, Dicken Yung/2.90%, Chris Chen/5.00%, Carlington HK Limited/44.60%, Boaz Yung/1.60%, Insiders/17.40%, Baldwin Yung/6.40%

Financial Data: *Fiscal Year End:*04/30 *Latest Annual Data:* 4/30/2006

Year		Sales		Net Income
2006		$12,582,000		-$1,954,000
2005		$11,283,000		-$3,899,000
2004		$17,789,000		$191,000
Curr. Assets:	$5,141,000	*Curr. Liab.:*	$1,391,000	
Plant, Equip.:	$107,000	*Total Liab.:*	$4,279,000	*Indic. Yr. Divd.:* NA
Total Assets:	$5,906,000	*Net Worth:*	$1,627,000	*Debt/ Equity:* 12.5524

TransNet Corp

45 Columbia Rd. , Somerville, NJ, 08876; *PH:* 1-908-253-0500; *http://* www.transnet.com; *Email:* contact_us@transnet.com

General - Incorporation	DE	**Stock**- Price on:12/24/2007	$1.2
Employees	125	Stock Exchange	OTC
Auditor	Moore Stephens P.C.	Ticker Symbol	TRNT
Stk Agt	Continental Stock Transfer & Trust Co	Outstanding Shares	4,820,000
Counsel	Susan M. Wilk	E.P.S.	-$0.32
DUNS No.	04-750-3537	Shareholders	NA

Business: The group's principal activity is to provide information technology products and technology management services. These products and services enable the enhancement of productivity of the information systems of its customers. The products of the group include microcomputers, workstations, servers, monitors, printers and operating systems software. The group is the authorized dealer for apple, bay networks, compaq, hewlett-packard, IBM, intel, nec and toshiba. The principal markets for the group's products are commercial, governmental and educational customers. The group also sells software to general business applications and specialized business applications such as research, pharmaceuticals, education and integrated packages.

Primary SIC and add'l.: 5045 7379

CIK No: 0000099313

Subsidiaries: Century American Corporation

Owners: Raymond J. Rekuc, Jay A. Smolyn/3.00%, Vincent Cusumano, Insiders/18.00%, Earle Kunzig, Steven J. Wilk/9.00%, John J. Wilk/4.00%, Susan M. Wilk/2.00%

Financial Data: *Fiscal Year End:*06/30 *Latest Annual Data:* 6/30/2006

Year		Sales		Net Income
2006		$35,415,000		-$998,000
2005		$34,041,000		-$1,376,000
2004		$30,600,000		-$1,130,000
Curr. Assets:	$9,179,000	*Curr. Liab.:*	$1,037,000	
Plant, Equip.:	$564,000	*Total Liab.:*	$1,085,000	*Indic. Yr. Divd.:* NA
Total Assets:	$10,022,000	*Net Worth:*	$8,938,000	*Debt/ Equity:* NA

Transocean Inc

4 Greenway Plz., Houston, TX, 77046; *PH:* 1-713-232-7500; *http://* www.deepwater.com

General - Incorporation	Cayman Islands	**Stock**- Price on:12/24/2007	$104.14
Employees	10,700	Stock Exchange	NYSE
Auditor	Ernst & Young LLP	Ticker Symbol	RIG
Stk Agt	Bank of New York	Outstanding Shares	288,150,000
Counsel	NA	E.P.S.	$6.64
DUNS No.	NA	Shareholders	NA

Business: The group's principal activity is to provide offshore and inland marine contract drilling services for oil and gas wells. At 01-Mar-2004, the group owned and operated 96 mobile offshore and barge drilling units. The fleet of the group consists of 32 high-specification semisubmersibles and drillships floaters, 26 other floaters, 26 jackup rigs and 12 other rigs. The fleet of the todco consists of 24 jackup rigs, 30 drilling barges, 9 land rigs, 3 submersible drilling rigs and 4 other drilling rigs. The group provides these drilling rigs, related equipment and work crews to its customers primarily on a dayrate basis to drill offshore wells. In addition, the group also provides management of third party well service activities. In feb-2004, the group completed an ipo of todco, representing 23% of todco's common stock. At 01-Mar-2004, the group held 77% common stock of todco.

Primary SIC and add'l.: 1381

CIK No: 0001083269

Subsidiaries: Agua Profundas Limitada, Arcade Drilling AS, Blegra Asset Management Limited, Blegra Financing Limited, Cariba Ships Corporation N.V., Caspian Sea Ventures International Ltd., Cliffs Drilling do Brasil Servicos de Petroleo S/C Ltda., Deepwater Drilling II LLC, Deepwater Drilling LLC, Falcon Atlantic Ltd., Hellerup Finance International Ltd., International Chandlers, Inc., NRB Drilling Services Limited, Overseas Drilling Ltd., PT Hitek Nusantara Offshore Drilling 130 Subsidiaries included in the Index

Officers: Robert L. Long/Dir., CEO, Pres./$4,469,335.00, Jean P. Cahuzac/COO, Exec. VP/$1,780,221.00, David A. Tonnel/VP, Controller, Steven L. Newman/COO, Exec. VP/$807,268.00, Eric B. Brown/Sr. VP, General Counsel, Corp. Sec./$1,241,498.00, Ricardo H. Rosa/VP - Asia, Pacific Unit, David J. Mullen/Sr. VP - Marketing, Planning, Arnaud A.Y. Bobillier/VP - Europe, Africa Unit, Gregory S. Panagos/VP - Investor Relations, Communications, Guy A. Cantwell/Contact - Communications, Michel Moy/Marketing Contact - North Sea, UK, Norway Division, Terry Bonno/Marketing Contact - North, South America Business Unit, Gilberto Cardarelli/Marketing Contact - South, Central America Division, Joe Swales/Marketing Contact - Worldwide, Bob MacChesney/Marketing Contact - Asia, Pacific Business Unit (24 Officers included in Index)

Directors: Robert L. Long/Dir., CEO, Pres., Michael J. Talbert/Chmn., Michael E. McMahon/Dir., Ian C. Strachan/Dir., Mark A. Hellerstein/Dir., Robert M. Sprague/Dir., Martin B. McNamara/Dir., Roberto L. Monti/Dir., Kristian Siem/Dir., Victor E. Grijalva/Dir., Judy J. Kelly/Dir., Arthur Lindenauer/Dir.

Owners: Jean P. Cahuzac, Kristian Siem, Michael E. McMahon, Ian C. Strachan, Eric B. Brown, Judy J. Kelly, Martin B. McNamara, Robert L. Long, Gregory L. Cauthen, Victor E. Grijalva, Mark A. Hellerstein, Arthur Lindenauer, Robert M. Sprague, Michael J. Talbert, Roberto Monti (17 Owners included in Index)

Financial Data: *Fiscal Year End:*12/31 *Latest Annual Data:* 12/31/2006

Year		Sales		Net Income
2006		$3,882,000,000		$1,385,000,000
2005		$2,891,700,000		$715,600,000
2004		$2,613,900,000		$152,200,000
Curr. Assets:	$1,656,000,000	*Curr. Liab.:*	$1,039,000,000	*P/E Ratio:* 15.68
Plant, Equip.:	$7,326,000,000	*Total Liab.:*	$4,640,000,000	*Indic. Yr. Divd.:* NA
Total Assets:	$11,476,000,000	*Net Worth:*	$6,836,000,000	*Debt/ Equity:* 0.5065

Transport Corp of America Inc

1715 Yankee Doodle Rd., Eagan, MN, 55121; *PH:* 1-651-686-2500; *http://* www.transportamerica.com

General - Incorporation	MN	**Stock**- Price on:12/24/2007	NA
Employees	NA	Stock Exchange	NA
Auditor	KPMG LLP	Ticker Symbol	NA
Stk Agt	Wells Fargo Shareowner Services	Outstanding Shares	NA
Counsel	Robins, Kaplan, Miller & Ciresi LLP	E.P.S.	NA
DUNS No.	01-719-7450	Shareholders	NA

Business: The group's principal activities are to provide truckload carriage, logistics and other transportation services in the United States and parts of Canada. The services offered by the group includes time-definite pickup and delivery to support just-in-time inventory management, specialized equipment, carriage services such as line-haul, multi-stop capability, regional and local operations, temperature controlled trailers, satellite monitored transit and information technology services. The group's major customers include hon company, 3m company, toys-r-us, federal express, ford motor company, and general mills. The principal categories of freight hauled by the group are department store merchandise, grocery, industrial, commercial, paper products and expedited services.

Primary SIC and add'l.: 4213

CIK No: 0000809246

Subsidiaries: FV Leasing Company, TA Logistics, Inc., TCA of Ohio, Inc., Transport International Express, Inc.

Officers: Scott C. Arves/CEO, Pres., Scott D. Hunt/VP - Operations, Craig A. Coyan/Sr. VP - Sales - Marketing, Peggy C. Farra/VP - Driver Recruitment - Safety, Keith R. Klein/COO, Exec. VP, Mark J. Emmen/CFO, VP

Transportadora de Gas del Sur SA TGS

Don Bosco 3672, 6th Fl., Buenos Aires; *PH:* 54-1148659050; *http://* www.tgs.com.ar; *Email:* totgs@tgs.com.ar

General - Incorporation		**Stock**- Price on:12/24/2007	$8.14
Employees	NA	Stock Exchange	NYSE
Auditor	NA	Ticker Symbol	TGS
Stk Agt	Caja de Valores S.A.	Outstanding Shares	158,900,000
Counsel	NA	E.P.S.	$0.42
DUNS No.	NA	Shareholders	NA

Business: The groups principle activity is to transport natural gas. The group operates from the Argentina.

Primary SIC and add'l.: 4922

CIK No:

Officers: Pablo Ferrero/CEO, Gonzalo Castro Olivera/Finance, Investor Relations Officer Mgr., Francisco Vila/Investor Relations Officer, Mario Yaniskowski/Contact - Media Relation, Daniela Viola/Deputy MD

Financial Data: *Fiscal Year End:*NA *Latest Annual Data:* 12/31/2006

Year	Sales	Net Income
2006	$404,333,000	$132,382,000
2005	$330,655,000	$89,169,000
2004	$334,609,000	$51,040,000

Curr. Assets:	$232,345,000	**Curr. Liab.:**	$123,623,000	**P/E Ratio:**	25.48
Plant, Equip.:	$1,376,713,000	**Total Liab.:**	$1,004,539,000	**Indic. Yr. Divd.:**	NA
Total Assets:	$1,636,285,000	**Net Worth:**	$631,747,000	**Debt/ Equity:**	NA

Transtech Industries Inc

200 Centennial Ave., Ste 202, Piscataway, NJ, 08854; *PH:* 1-732-564-3122; *http://* www.hometown.aol.com

General - Incorporation	DE	**Stock**- Price on:12/24/2007	$0.31
Employees	13	Stock Exchange	OTC
Auditor	WithumSmith & Brown, P.C	Ticker Symbol	TRTI
Stk Agt	Continental Stock Transfer & Trust Co	Outstanding Shares	2,980,000
Counsel	NA	E.P.S.	$0.11
DUNS No.	00-257-5082	Shareholders	NA

Business: The group's principal activities are monitoring landfill and closure procedures, managing methane gas recovery operations and generating electricity using methane gas. The group's operations consist of two segments namely, electricity generation and environmental services. The electricity generating facility consists of four generating units each capable of generating approximately 11,000 kwh per day at 85% capacity. Electricity generated is sold pursuant to a contract with a local utility that has two years remaining. The environmental services segment supervises and performs landfill monitoring and closure procedures and manages methane gas operations.

Primary SIC and add'l.: 4931 4953

CIK No: 0000087799

Subsidiaries: ACC Investment Co., Inc., Arrow Realty, Inc., Birchcrest, Inc., Camden Energy Recycling, Inc., Chambers Brook, Inc., Del Valley Farms, Inc., Delsea Realty, Inc., Energy Recycling, Inc., Filcrest Realty, Inc., Genetic Farms, Inc., Harrison Returns, Inc., Kin-Buc, Inc., Kinsley's Landfill, Inc., Mac Sanitary Land Fill, Inc., Methane Energy Recycling, Inc. 21 Subsidiaries included in the Index

Officers: Robert V. Silva/64/Chmn., CEO, Pres., Andrew J. Mayer/52/VP - Finance, CFO

Directors: Robert V. Silva/64/Chmn., CEO, Pres., Arthur C. Holdsworth/59/Dir.

Owners: Nancy M. Ernst/10.80%, Robert V. Silva/2.40%, Insiders/5.00%, Arthur C. Holdsworth, Andrew J. Mayer/1.50%, Gary A. Mahan/10.40%, Roger T. Mahan/12.30%

Financial Data: *Fiscal Year End:*12/31 *Latest Annual Data:* 12/31/2006

Year	Sales	Net Income
2006	$364,000	$630,000
2005	$451,000	$1,972,000
2004	$359,000	$1,333,000

Curr. Assets:	$7,401,000	**Curr. Liab.:**	$1,903,000	**P/E Ratio:**	2.82
Plant, Equip.:	$1,845,000	**Total Liab.:**	$11,262,000	**Indic. Yr. Divd.:**	NA
Total Assets:	$15,931,000	**Net Worth:**	$4,669,000	**Debt/ Equity:**	0.1993

Transwitch Corp

Three Enterprise Dr., Shelton, CT, 06484; *PH:* 1-203-929-8810; *http://* www.transwitch.com

General - Incorporation	DE	**Stock**- Price on:12/24/2007	$1.84
Employees	232	Stock Exchange	NDQ
Auditor	UHY LLP	Ticker Symbol	TXCC
Stk Agt	KPMG LLP	Outstanding Shares	132,230,000
Counsel	Testa, Hurwitz & Thibeault	E.P.S.	-$0.13
DUNS No.	19-795-4761	Shareholders	NA

Business: The group's principal activities are to design, develop, market and support integrated digital and mixed signal semiconductor solutions for the telecommunications and data communications markets. The products of the group include very large-scale integrated (vlsi) semiconductor solutions that are used as components in telecommunications and data communications equipment. The products of the group are also used in telecommunications systems, wide area networks and local area networks equipment, Internet-oriented original equipment manufacturers, communications test and performance measurement equipment. The customers of the group are public network systems suppliers, university and private laboratories. On 18-Aug-2003, it acquired asic design services, inc.

Primary SIC and add'l.: 3674

CIK No: 0000944739

Subsidiaries: ASIC Design Service, Inc., Horizon Semiconductors, Inc., Lehman Silicon Solutions S.A., Opal Acquisition Corporation, Systems On Silicon, Inc., TranSwitch Asia Ltd., TranSwitch Asia PTE Ltd., TranSwitch Europe N.V./S.A., TranSwitch II Corp., TranSwitch III, Inc., TranSwitch India Private Limited, TranSwitch International Corp., TranSwitch S.A., TranSwitch Silicon Valley, Inc., TranSwitch Technologies Canada, Inc. 16 Subsidiaries included in the Index

Officers: Santanu Das/CEO, Pres./$794,590.00, Suresh Sane/Contact - Sales, US, Arkansas, Steve Lam/Contact - Apac Sales, William G. Bartholomay/CTO, Jorge S. Hurtarte/Sr. VP - Asia Sales, Michael MacAri/VP - Engineering, Operations, Pascal Astrie/VP - Europe Sales, Jitender K. Vij/Sr. VP - Systems Engineering, Technology, Hoshang Mulla/VP - Marketing, Maurizio Mansueto/RSM, Ted Chung/VP - Business Development, Interm CFO, Mary A. Lombardo/Sr. Investor Relations, Robert Schwaber/Contact - Sales, Canada, East, US, Alabama, Chuck Sinha/Contact - Sales, Canada, West, US, Alaska, Patricia V. Agudow/VP - Human Resources

Directors: Erik H. Van Der Kaay/67/Dir.

Owners: Albert E. Paladino, Theodore Chung, Alfred F. Boschulte, Herbert Chen/14.52%, Santanu Das/2.66%, Gerald F. Montry, Hagen Hultzsch, James M. Pagos, Michael H. Steinhardt/9.68%, Insiders/3.89%, Erik H. van der Kaay

Financial Data: *Fiscal Year End:*12/31 *Latest Annual Data:* 12/31/2006

Year	Sales	Net Income
2006	$38,920,000	-$10,856,000
2005	$32,900,000	-$23,754,000
2004	$33,687,000	-$44,624,000

Curr. Assets:	$68,236,000	**Curr. Liab.:**	$37,913,000		
Plant, Equip.:	$5,079,000	**Total Liab.:**	$58,602,000	**Indic. Yr. Divd.:**	NA
Total Assets:	$82,656,000	**Net Worth:**	$24,054,000	**Debt/ Equity:**	NA

Travel Hunt Holdings Inc

1314 E Las Olas Blvd, Fort Lauderdale, FL, 33301; *PH:* 1-561-943-4868; *http://* www.travelhunt.com; *Email:* huntforfun@travelhunt.com

General - Incorporation	FL	**Stock**- Price on:12/24/2007	NA
Employees	1	Stock Exchange	OTC
Auditor	Webb & Company, P. A.	Ticker Symbol	TVHT
Stk Agt	Corporate Stock Transfer, Inc.	Outstanding Shares	70,910,000
Counsel	NA	E.P.S.	NA
DUNS No.	NA	Shareholders	NA

Business: The groups principal activity is providing online travel related products and services. The group established a technological Internet component through the development of the TravelHunt.com website. The group operates from the United States.

Primary SIC and add'l.: 4724

CIK No: 0001262159

Subsidiaries: Travel Hunt, Inc.

Officers: Geoffrey Alison/35/CEO, Pres., Treasurer, Sec.

Owners: La Pergola Investments Limited/14.81%, Fountainhead Capital Management Limited/83.90%

Travelers Property Casualty Corp

One Tower Sq., Hartford, CT, 06183; *PH:* 1-860-277-0111; *http://* www.stpaultravelers.com

General - Incorporation	CT	**Stock**- Price on:12/24/2007	NA
Employees	NA	Stock Exchange	NA
Auditor	KPMG LLP	Ticker Symbol	NA
Stk Agt	EquiServe Trust Co N.A	Outstanding Shares	NA
Counsel	NA	E.P.S.	NA
DUNS No.	NA	Shareholders	NA

Business: The group operates through its subsidiaries whose principal activity is to provide commercial and personal property and casualty insurance products and services. The group operated through two segments namely, commercial and personal. The group operates from the United States.

Primary SIC and add'l.: 6331

CIK No: 0000919482

Subsidiaries: AE Development Group, Inc., AE Properties, Inc., American Equity Insurance Company, American Equity Specialty Insurance Company, Arch Street North LLC, Associates Insurance Company, Associates Lloyds Insurance Company, Atlantic Insurance Company, Auto Hartford Investments LLC, BAP Investor Pine, Inc., Bayhill Restaurant II Associates, Charter Oak Services Corporation, Citigroup Alternative Investments European Real Estate Investments I, L.L.C., Citigroup Alternative Investments Limited Real Estate Mezzanine Investments I, LLC, Citigroup Alternative Investments Limited Real Estate Mezzanine Investments II, LLC 120 Subsidiaries included in the Index

Officers: Jay S. Fishman/Chmn., CEO, Alan D. Schnitzer/Vice Chmn., Chief Legal Officer, Jay S. Benet/Vice Chmn., CFO, William H. Heyman/Vice Chmn., Chief Investment Officer, Andy F. Bessette/Exec. VP, Chief Administrative Officer, John J. Albano/Exec. VP - Business Insurance, Joseph P. Lacher/Exec. VP - Personal Insurance, Select Accounting, Brian W. MacLean/COO, Exec. VP, Samuel Liss/Exec. VP - Strategic Development, Exec. VP - Financial, Professional, International Insurance, Maria Olivo/Exec. VP - Investor Relations, Corporate Communications, Kathleen Preston/Exec. VP - Enterprise Development, Doreen Spadorcia/Exec. VP - Claim Services, Kenneth F. Spence/Exec. VP, General Counsel, Bruce Backberg/Sr. VP, Corp. Sec., John Clifford/Sr. VP - Human Resources *(16 Officers included in Index)*

Directors: Jay S. Fishman/Chmn., CEO, Alan D. Schnitzer/Vice Chmn., Chief Legal Officer, Charles Clarke/Vice Chmn., Irwin R. Ettinger/Vice Chmn., Jay S. Benet/Vice Chmn., CFO, William H. Heyman/Vice Chmn., Chief Investment Officer, Glen D. Nelson/Dir., Laurie J. Thomsen/Dir., Lawrence G. Graev/Dir., Thomas R. Hodgson/Dir., Robert I. Lipp/Dir., Blythe J. McGarvie/Dir., John H. Dasburg/Dir., Alan L. Beller/Dir., Patricia L. Higgins/Dir. *(18 Directors included in Index)*

Travelstar Inc

Formerly: Joystar Inc

95 Argonaut St. , 1st Fl., Aliso Viejo, CA, 92656; *PH:* 1-949-837-8101; *http://* www.joystar.com

General - Incorporation	CA	**Stock**- Price on:12/24/2007	$0.75
Employees	30	Stock Exchange	NA
Auditor	Mendoza Berger & Co LLP	Ticker Symbol	NA
Stk Agt	Integrity Stock Transfer, Inc.	Outstanding Shares	48,930,000
Counsel	NA	E.P.S.	-$0.11
DUNS No.	NA	Shareholders	NA

Business: The group's principal activities are to design, manufacture and market energy efficiency and evaporator fan motor controller. The group's product is energy related inventions program (erip). It is an energy saving device that can be easily integrated into existing or new walk-in refrigerator or freezer systems. It regulates the speed of the evaporator fan motors in a cooler or freezer to meet the need of each phase of the refrigeration cycle. It can save the customer 25-50% in refrigeration energy costs. It operates solely in the domestic market. On 12-Jun-2003, the group acquired joystar inc.

Primary SIC and add'l.: 3569

CIK No: 0001085661

Officers: William M. Alverson/43/Chmn., CEO, CFO, Katherine West/Dir. - Executive, VP, Robin Moore/Dir. - Agent Services, Jo Beemer/VP - Agency Operations, Sandra Darcy/COO, Jerry Galant/58/CFO

Directors: William M. Alverson/43/Chmn., CEO, CFO, William W. Fawcett/Dir., Katherine West/Dir. - Executive, VP

Owners: Insiders/32.00%, Katherine T. West/32.00%, Myint J. Kyaw/19.00%, William M. Alverson/32.00%, Sandra DArcy

Financial Data: Fiscal Year End:12/31　**Latest Annual Data:** 12/31/2006

Year	Sales	Net Income
2006	$6,932,000	-$10,649,000
2005	$1,943,000	-$3,885,000
2004	$69,000	-$3,372,000

Curr. Assets:	$4,881,000	Curr. Liab.:	$10,319,000		
Plant, Equip.:	$267,000	Total Liab.:	$10,319,000	Indic. Yr. Divd.:	NA
Total Assets:	$5,217,000	Net Worth:	-$5,102,000	Debt/ Equity:	NA

Travelzoo Inc

590 Madison Ave., 21st Fl., New York, NY, 10022; **PH:** 1-212-521-4200; **http://** www.travelzoo.com

General - Incorporation	DE	Stock- Price on:12/24/2007	$26.7299
Employees	82	Stock Exchange	NDQ
Auditor	KPMG LLP	Ticker Symbol	TZOO
Stk Agt	U.S. Stock Transfer Corp	Outstanding Shares	15,250,000
Counsel	NA	E.P.S.	$1.015
DUNS No.	NA	Shareholders	NA

Business: The group's principal activity is to provide an online advertising medium for the travel industry. Its media properties include the travelzoo Website, www.travelzoo.com, the top 20 e-mail newsletter, the newsflash e-mail alert service and supersearch, a pay-per-click travel search engine. The group provides advertising opportunities for airlines, hotels, cruise lines, vacation packagers and other travel companies. In addition, it also provides Internet users with a free source of information on current offers from travel companies.

Primary SIC and add'l.: 7375

CIK No: 0001133311

Subsidiaries: Travelzoo (Europe) Ltd, Travelzoo.com Canada, Inc.

Officers: Ralph A. Bartel/Chmn., CEO, Pres., Steven M. Ledwith/CTO, Jason Yap/Exec. VP - Japan, India, Australia, Raymond Ng/Exec. VP - Asia, Holger Bartel/Dir., Exec. VP/$347,500.00, Shirley Tafoya/Sr. VP - Sales/$529,010.00, Wayne Lee/CFO/$158,583.00, Christopher Loughlin/Exec. VP - Europe/$456,330.00

Directors: David J. Ehrlich/Dir., Kelly M. Urso/Dir., Donovan Neale-May/Dir., Holger Bartel/Dir., Exec. VP

Owners: Barclays Global Investors, NA/6.02%, Christopher Loughlin, Ralph Bartel/56.37%, Holger Bartel, Kelly M. Urso, Insiders/56.92%, Prudential Financial, Inc./6.34%

Financial Data: Fiscal Year End:12/31　**Latest Annual Data:** 12/31/2006

Year	Sales	Net Income
2006	$69,525,000	$16,803,000
2005	$50,772,000	$7,963,000
2004	$33,679,000	$6,037,000

Curr. Assets:	$43,352,000	Curr. Liab.:	$6,880,000	P/E Ratio:	26.33
Plant, Equip.:	$172,000	Total Liab.:	$6,883,000	Indic. Yr. Divd.:	NA
Total Assets:	$43,700,000	Net Worth:	$36,817,000	Debt/ Equity:	NA

TRB Systems International Inc

1472 Cedarwood Dr., Piscataway, NJ, 08854; **PH:** 1-201-994-4488; **http://** www.trbsystems.com

General - Incorporation	DE	Stock- Price on:12/24/2007	NA
Employees	14	Stock Exchange	OTC
Auditor	Stan J.h. Lee, Cpa	Ticker Symbol	TRBX
Stk Agt	Continental Stock Transfer & Trust Co	Outstanding Shares	NA
Counsel	NA	E.P.S.	-$0.01
DUNS No.	86-703-4258	Shareholders	NA

Business: The group's principal activity is to develop, market and manufacture bicycles, exercycle, electric bicycle and wheelchair. It uses the transbar power system (tps) technology in three main product groups: a select line of bicycles, electric bicycles and two types of ergometers. Tps bicycles are high quality, sophisticated products that closely resemble conventional bicycles. Electric bike of the group includes power+bike, which is an outdoor bike that has the ability to become an electric bike with speed capability of 23mph. The group's bicycles are sold mainly through retail outlets and specialty bike shops and institutional exercise equipment is sold through trade shows, magazines and direct mail. The group's fitness/home trainer allows an individual to exercise their abdominals, hips, quadriceps, hamstrings, and gluteus muscles. All actions are performed in the correct biomechanical positions.

Primary SIC and add'l.: 3949 3751 6719 7389

CIK No: 0001042610

Subsidiaries: Alenax (Tianjing) Bicycle Corp.

Officers: Joon Ki Moon/29/Sec.

Owners: Insiders/12.67%, August Rheem/0.11%, Marn T. Seol/4.23%, Joon K. Moon/0.10%, Motion Plus International/24.27%

Financial Data: Fiscal Year End:06/30　**Latest Annual Data:** 06/30/2007

Year	Sales	Net Income
2007	$317,000	-$277,000

Curr. Assets:	$2,352,000	Curr. Liab.:	$2,793,000		
Plant, Equip.:	$167,000	Total Liab.:	$3,617,000	Indic. Yr. Divd.:	NA
Total Assets:	$3,005,000	Net Worth:	-$612,000	Debt/ Equity:	NA

TRC Companies Inc

5 Waterside Crossing, Windsor, CT, 06095; **PH:** 1-860-298-6385; **http://** www.trcsolutions.com; **Email:** hire_windsor@trcsolutions.com

General - Incorporation	DE	Stock- Price on:12/24/2007	$14.56
Employees	NA	Stock Exchange	NYSE
Auditor	Deloitte & Touche LLP	Ticker Symbol	TRR
Stk Agt	American Stock Transfer & Trust Co.	Outstanding Shares	NA
Counsel	NA	E.P.S.	-$0.334
DUNS No.	05-418-3884	Shareholders	NA

Business: The group's principal activity is to provide technical, financial, risk management and construction services to industry and government customers across the United States. The group also provides engineering, scientific and technical environmental services to customers through a national network of 85 offices. Environmental services provided by the group include pollution control, waste management, auditing and assessment, permitting and compliance, design and engineering and natural and cultural resource management. The customers of the group include aes enterprises, asarco, burlington northern santa fe rr, Connecticut edison, conoco phillips, el paso energy, lockheed martin corporation, duke energy, express pipeline, general electric and general motors.

Primary SIC and add'l.: 8711 8748

CIK No: 0000103096

Subsidiaries: BV Engineering, Co-Energy Group, LLC, Cubix Corporation, E/PRO Engineering and Environmental Consulting LLC, ECON Capital LP, Engineered Automation Systems, Inc., Essex Environmental, Inc., GBF Holdings, LLC, Hunter Associates Texas Ltd., Imbsen & Associates, Lowney Associates, Metuchen Realty Acquisition, LLC, Novak Engineering, Inc., Omni Environmental Corporation, PBWO Holdings, LLC 27 Subsidiaries included in the Index

Officers: Christopher P. Vincze/Chmn., CEO, Michael C. Salmon/Sr. VP, Glenn Harkness/Sr. VP, Martin H. Dodd/Sr. VP, General Counsel, Carl Paschetag/Sr. VP, CFO

Directors: Christopher P. Vincze/Chmn., CEO, Jeffrey J. McNealey/Dir., Stephen Duff/Dir., Sherwood L. Boehlert/Dir., Friedl Bohm/Dir., Edward G. Jepsen/Dir., Edward W. Large/Dir., John M.F. MacDonald/Dir., Thomas F. Casey/Dir., Robert W. Harvey/Dir.

Owners: Peter R. Kellogg/17.48%, Edward W. Large, Dimensional Fund Advisors LP/6.27%, Martin H. Dodd, John M. F. MacDonald, Jeffrey L. Gendell/6.00%, Royce & Associates, LLC./8.68%, John H. Claussen, Friedrich K. M. Bohm, The Clark Estates, Inc./10.60%, Jeffrey J. McNealey, Insiders/6.70%, Carl d. Paschetag, Fletcher International, Ltd./7.01%, Glenn E. Harkness (20 Owners included in Index)

Financial Data: Fiscal Year End:06/30　**Latest Annual Data:** 6/30/2006

Year	Sales	Net Income
2006	$406,321,000	-$23,847,000
2005	$388,406,000	-$7,262,000
2004	$368,834,000	$13,168,000

Curr. Assets:	$189,437,000	Curr. Liab.:	$164,432,000		
Plant, Equip.:	$19,416,000	Total Liab.:	$325,247,000	Indic. Yr. Divd.:	NA
Total Assets:	$485,403,000	Net Worth:	$145,156,000	Debt/ Equity:	NA

Treaty Oak Bancorp Inc TX

101 Westlake Dr., Austin, TX, 78746; **PH:** 1-512-617-3600; **Fax:** 1-512-617-3697; **http://** www.treatyoakbank.com; **Email:** info@treatyoakbank.com

General - Incorporation	TX	Stock- Price on:12/24/2007	$10.95
Employees	29	Stock Exchange	OTC
Auditor	McGladrey & Pullen, LLP	Ticker Symbol	TOAK
Stk Agt	Continental Stock Transfer & Trust Co	Outstanding Shares	2,750,000
Counsel	NA	E.P.S.	NA
DUNS No.	NA	Shareholders	NA

Business: The groups principle activity is to provide banking and financial services to the customers. Services of the group include personal and commercial deposit accounts and loans, as well as finance, consulting, and treasury services. In November 2006, the group acquired Treaty Oak Holdings, Inc. The group operates from the United States.

Primary SIC and add'l.: 6022

CIK No: 0001276130

Subsidiaries: PGI Capital, Inc., PGI Equity Partners, LP, Treaty Oak Bank, Treaty Oak Financial Holdings, Inc.

Officers: Jeffrey L. Nash/Dir., Pres., CEO - Organizers, Carol Thompson/Dir., Organizer, Jim Stone/Dir., Organizer, Marsha Kelliher/Dir., Organizer, Thomas Borders/Dir., Organizer, Chris Lambert/Investor Relations Officer, Coralie S. Pledger/CFO

Directors: Jeffrey L. Nash/Dir., Pres., CEO - Organizers, Charles T. Meeks/Chmn., Darrell K. Royal/Dir., Member - Advisory Board, Hayden D. Watson/Dir., Arthur H. Coleman/Dir., Bill F. Schneider/Dir., Carl J. Stolle/Dir., Carol Thompson/Dir., Organizer, Jim Stone/Dir., Organizer, Elias F. Urbina/Dir., Marsha Kelliher/Dir., Organizer, Marvin L. Schrager/Dir., Thomas Borders/Dir., Organizer, Angelos Angelou/Member - Advisory Board, Marvin Bendele/Member - Advisory Board (42 Directors included in Index)

Owners: Insiders/22.19%, Sheila A. Bostick, Terry W. Hamann/7.44%, Charles T. Meeks/2.02%, Thomas G. Clark, Marvin L. Schrager/1.47%, Bill F. Schneider/4.80%, Jeffrey L. Nash/4.44%, Hayden D. Watson/2.80%, Elias F. Urbina, Coralie S. Pledger, Randall M. Meeks, Carl J. Stolle/5.62%

Tredegar Corp

1100 Boulders Pkwy, Richmond, VA, 23225; **PH:** 1-804-330-1000; **http://** www.tredegar.com; **Email:** invest@tredegar.com

General - Incorporation	VA	Stock- Price on:12/24/2007	$21.89
Employees	3,000	Stock Exchange	NYSE
Auditor	PricewaterhouseCoopers LLP	Ticker Symbol	TG
Stk Agt	National City Bank	Outstanding Shares	39,490,000
Counsel	Hunton & Williams LLP	E.P.S.	$1.04
DUNS No.	10-825-3014	Shareholders	NA

Business: The group's principal activities are carried out through two divisions: film products and aluminum extrusions. It also develops healthcare-related technologies and has direct and indirect interests in venture capital investments. The film product segment manufactures plastic films for disposable personal hygiene products and packaging, medical, industrial and agricultural products. Aluminum extrusions manufactures mill, anodized and painted aluminum extrusions for the building and

construction, distribution, transportation, electrical and consumer durable markets. The group also operates therics inc, a biotechnology company. Their main trademark is theriform. The procter & gamble company is a leading customer of film products. The group operates in Canada, Europe, Latin America and Asia. On 28-Jul-2004, the group acquired shanghai yaheng perforated film material co ltd.

Primary SIC and add'l.: 3089 3354 2821 2833 3081

CIK No: 0000850429

Subsidiaries: AFBS, Inc., Apolo Tool & Die Manufacturing, Inc., AUS Corporation, Bon L Aluminum LLC, Bon L Campo Limited Partnership, Bon L Canada Inc., Bon L Holdings Corporation, Bon L Manufacturing Company, Capital Square Insurance Company, El Campo GP, LLC, Guangzhou Tredegar Film Products Limited, Idlewood Properties, Inc., Molecumetics Institute, Ltd.(1), Molecumetics, Ltd., PROMEA Engineering srl 38 Subsidiaries included in the Index

Officers: John D. Gottwald/Dir., CEO, Pres./$790,680.00, Nancy M. Taylor/Pres. - Tredegar Film Products, Corporate Sr. VP/$586,673.00, Larry J. Scott/VP - Audit/$379,832.00, Andrew D. Edwards/VP, CFO, Treasurer - Tredegar Corporation/$489,617.00, Mcalister C. Marshall/VP, General Counsel, Corp. Sec./$105,855.00

Directors: John D. Gottwald/Dir., CEO, Pres., Norman A. Scher/Vice Chmn., Richard L. Morrill/Chmn., Donald T. Cowles/Dir., William M. Gottwald/Dir., Gregory R. Williams/Dir., Austin Brockenbrough/Dir., Thomas G. Slater/Dir.

Owners: Thomas G. Slater, McAlister C. Marshall, Larry J. Scott, Dimensional Fund Advisors Inc., Norman A. Scher, Austin Brockenbrough, Andrew D. Edwards, Richard L. Morrill, John D. Gottwald, William M. Gottwald, Floyd D. Gottwald, Gregory R. Williams, Donald T. Cowles, Frank Russell Trust Company,, Hildebrandt W. Surgner *(18 Owners included in Index)*

Financial Data: Fiscal Year End:12/31   Latest Annual Data: 12/31/2006

Year	Sales	Net Income
2006	$1,117,969,000	$38,201,000
2005	$956,425,000	$16,229,000
2004	$876,769,000	$29,181,000

Curr. Assets:	$253,250,000	Curr. Liab.:	$112,010,000		
Plant, Equip.:	$325,763,000	Total Liab.:	$265,192,000	Indic. Yr. Divd.:	$0.160
Total Assets:	$781,787,000	Net Worth:	$516,595,000	Debt/ Equity:	0.0783

Tree Top Industries Inc

666 Fifth Ave., Ste. 302, New York, NY, 10103; *PH:* 1-212-554-4111

General - Incorporation	NV	Stock- Price on:12/24/2007	$2.9
Employees		Stock Exchange	OTC
Auditor	Chisholm Bierwolf & Nilson LLC	Ticker Symbol	TTII
Stk Agt	Computershare Trust Co	Outstanding Shares	NA
Counsel	NA	E.P.S.	-$1.47
DUNS No.	NA	Shareholders	NA

Business: The group is attempting to identify and negotiate with a business target for the merger of that entity with and into the group. In certain instances, the target group may wish to become a subsidiary of the group or may wish to contribute assets to the group rather than merger.

Primary SIC and add'l.: 9999

CIK No: 0000356590

Officers: David Reichman/63/Chmn., CEO, CFO, Pres., Frank Benintendo/59/Dir., Sec.

Directors: David Reichman/63/Chmn., CEO, CFO, Pres., Frank Benintendo/59/Dir., Sec., Michael Valle/50/Dir., Don Gilbert/70/Dir.

Owners: Frank Benintendo, David Reichman/96.10%, Michael Valle, Insiders/96.30%, Don Gilbert

Financial Data: Fiscal Year End:12/31   Latest Annual Data: 12/31/2006

Year	Sales	Net Income
2006	$33,000	-$956,000
2005	NA	-$64,000
2004	NA	-$635,000

Curr. Assets:	$31,000	Curr. Liab.:	$652,000		
Plant, Equip.:	NA	Total Liab.:	$652,000	Indic. Yr. Divd.:	NA
Total Assets:	$31,000	Net Worth:	-$622,000	Debt/ Equity:	NA

Treehouse Foods Inc

Two Westbrook Corporate Ctr., Ste. 1070, Westchester, IL, 60154; *PH:* 1-214-303-3400; *http://* www.treehousefoods.com; *Email:* info@treehousefoods.com

General - Incorporation	DE	Stock- Price on:12/24/2007	$27.42
Employees	2,417	Stock Exchange	NYSE
Auditor	Deloitte & Touche LLP	Ticker Symbol	THS
Stk Agt	NA	Outstanding Shares	31,200,000
Counsel	NA	E.P.S.	$1.43
DUNS No.	NA	Shareholders	NA

Business: The group's principle activity is to manufacture food services to the retail grocery and foodservice channels. The products include pickles and related products; non-dairy powdered coffee creamer; and other food products including aseptic sauces, refrigerated salad dressings, and liquid non-dairy creamer. The Company is also the leading retail supplier of private label pickles and private label non-dairy powdered creamer in the United States

Primary SIC and add'l.: 2030

CIK No: 0001320695

Subsidiaries: Bay Valley Foods LLC, TreeHouse THF Equities, LP, TreeHouse THF Partner, Inc

Officers: Sam K. Reed/61/Chmn., CEO/$7,958,140.00, Harry J. Walsh/51/Sr. VP - Operations/$3,447,456.00, Thomas E. O'Neill/52/Sr. VP, General Counsel, Chief Administrative Officer, Corp. Sec./$3,447,456.00, David B. Vermylen/57/COO, Pres./$5,167,193.00, Dennis F. Riordan/50/Sr. VP, CFO/$930,702.00, Alan T. Gambrel/53/Sr. VP - Human Resources, Erik T. Kahler/42/Sr. VP - Corporate Development, Danny J. Coning/60/Sr. VP

Directors: Sam K. Reed/61/Chmn., CEO, Gary D. Smith/65/Dir., George V. Bayly/66/Dir., Gregg L. Engles/51/Dir., Michelle R. Obama/44/Dir., Frank J. O'Connell/65/Dir., Terdema L. Ussery/49/Dir.

Owners: FMR Corp./11.40%, Harry J. Walsh, Barclays Global Investors NA/5.10%, Highfields Capital Ltd./8.30%, Iridian Asset Management LLC/12.60%, Sam K. Reed/1.20%, Gary D. Smith, Terdema L. Ussery, Frank J. OConnell, David B. Vermylen, Insiders/5.60%, Thomas E. ONeill, Gregg L. Engles/2.90%, George V. Bayly, Janus Capital Management LLC/9.70% *(17 Owners included in Index)*

Financial Data: Fiscal Year End:12/31   Latest Annual Data: 12/31/2006

Year	Sales	Net Income
2006	$939,396,000	$44,856,000
2005	$707,731,000	$11,576,000

Curr. Assets:	$284,771,000	Curr. Liab.:	$89,446,000	P/E Ratio:	19.17
Plant, Equip.:	$207,197,000	Total Liab.:	$359,374,000	Indic. Yr. Divd.:	NA
Total Assets:	$935,623,000	Net Worth:	$576,249,000	Debt/ Equity:	0.3244

Trend Micro Inc

10101 N De Anza Blvd, Cupertino, CA, 95014; *PH:* 1-800-228 5651; *http://* www.trendmicro.com

General - Incorporation	Japan	Stock - Price on:12/24/2007	NA
Employees	2,982	Stock Exchange	NA
Auditor	Chuoaoyama PricewaterhouseCoopers	Ticker Symbol	NA
Stk Agt	Mitsubishi UFJ Trust & Banking Corp	Outstanding Shares	NA
Counsel	NA	E.P.S.	NA
DUNS No.	NA	Shareholders	NA

Business: The group's principle activities are the development and sale of anti-virus software for family and company use. The group is also involved in the other related services with Internet server security products and services.

Primary SIC and add'l.: 7372 8999 7379 7373 5045

CIK No: 0001089463

Subsidiaries: Servicentro TMLA S.A.de C.V., Trend Micro (China) Incorporated, Trend Micro (EMEA) Limited, Trend Micro (NZ) Limited, Trend Micro (Singapore) Private Limited, Trend Micro (Thailand) Limited, Trend Micro (UK) Limited, Trend Micro Australia Pty. Ltd., Trend Micro Deutschland Gmbh, Trend Micro do Brasil Ltda., Trend Micro France, Trend Micro Hong Kong Limited, Trend Micro Inc., Trend Micro Incorporated, Trend Micro India Private Limited 19 Subsidiaries included in the Index

Officers: Eva Chen/Co - Founder, CEO, Mahendra Negi/Dir., CFO, COO - Irofficer, Exec. VP, Raimund Genes/CTO Anti - Malware, GM - Trend Micros Incubation Business, Max Cheng/Executive GM - XSP, VLE, Enterprise Business, Lane M. Bess/Pres. - North America Operations, GM - Consumer Products, Services, Oscar Chang/Exec. VP - Global Security Service, Response, Akihiko Omikawa/Sr. VP, Japan Region Mgr., Steve Quane/Executive GM - SMB Business Unit, Gustavo Moroni/VP - Latin America Operations, Jenny Chang/Co - Founder, Sr. Exec. VP, Thomas J. Miller/Global VP, GM - XSP, VLE, Enterprise Business Unit

Directors: Eva Chen/Co - Founder, CEO, Steve Chang/Chmn., Founder, Mahendra Negi/Dir., CFO, COO - Irofficer, Exec. VP, Jenny Chang/Co - Founder, Sr. Exec. VP

Financial Data: Fiscal Year End:12/31   Latest Annual Data: 12/31/2005

Year	Sales	Net Income
2005	$618,897,000	$158,220,000
2004	$602,420,000	$154,125,000
2003	$449,424,000	$86,449,000

Curr. Assets:	$946,229,000	Curr. Liab.:	$391,702,000		
Plant, Equip.:	$20,327,000	Total Liab.:	$432,776,000	Indic. Yr. Divd.:	NA
Total Assets:	$1,126,570,000	Net Worth:	$693,755,000	Debt/ Equity:	NA

Trend Mining Co

401 Front Ave., Ste 1, Coeur D'alene, ID, 83814; *PH:* 1-303-798-7363; *http://* www.trendmining.com; *Email:* thomas.loucks@att.net

General - Incorporation	DE	Stock - Price on:12/24/2007	$0.0735
Employees	1	Stock Exchange	OTC
Auditor	Richey, May & Co., LLP	Ticker Symbol	TRDM
Stk Agt	Columbia Stock Transfer Co	Outstanding Shares	55,970,000
Counsel	NA	E.P.S.	-$0.05
DUNS No.	NA	Shareholders	NA

Business: The group's principal activities are to acquiring, exploring and leasing of mining properties. The group's properties are located in Wyoming, Montana, Nevada, saskatchewan and Canada. The group owns in six platinum group metals mineral exploration properties. Platinum group comprises of platinum, palladium, rhodium, iridium, ruthenium and osmium. Platinum group metals are used in industrial applications, automotive industry for the production of catalysts that reduce automobile emissions and in the jewelry industry. Palladium is also used in the production of electronic components for personal computers, cellular telephones, facsimile machines and other devices, dental applications and jewelry. Platinum used in industrial applications like production of data storage disks, glass, paints, nitric acid, anti-cancer drugs, fiber optic cables, fertilizers, unleaded and high-Octane gasoline and fuel cells.

Primary SIC and add'l.: 1099

CIK No: 0001115954

Subsidiaries: New Trend of Montana Company

Officers: Ishiung J. Wu/CEO, Pres., John P. Ryan/VP, Thomas Loucks/58/Dir., Pres.

Directors: Jeffrey M. Christian/Dir., Thomas Loucks/58/Dir., Pres.

Owners: Ishiung J. Wu/1.50%, John P. Ryan/2.90%, ALPHA CAPITAL AKTIENGESELLSCHAFT/10.00%, Insiders/7.60%, Howard Schraub/19.90%, Longview Entities/9.70%, Thomas Kaplan/33.00%, Thomas Loucks/2.60%, Jeffrey M. Christian

Financial Data: Fiscal Year End:09/30   Latest Annual Data: 9/30/2006

Year	Sales	Net Income
2006	$169,000	-$2,669,000
2005	NA	-$2,181,000
2004	NA	-$993,000

Curr. Assets:	$426,000	Curr. Liab.:	$715,000		
Plant, Equip.:	$11,000	Total Liab.:	$2,212,000	Indic. Yr. Divd.:	NA
Total Assets:	$523,000	Net Worth:	-$1,689,000	Debt/ Equity:	NA

Trend Technology Corp

1166 Alberni St., Ste. 501, Vancouver, BC, V6E 3Z3; *PH:* 1-604-681-9588

General - Incorporation	NV	Stock - Price on:12/24/2007	$0.25
Employees	NA	Stock Exchange	OTC
Auditor	Peterson Sullivan, PLLC	Ticker Symbol	TRET
Stk Agt	NA	Outstanding Shares	NA
Counsel	NA	E.P.S.	NA
DUNS No.	NA	Shareholders	NA

Business: The group's principle activities include exploring and producing minerals. The group operates from United States.

Primary SIC and add'l.: 1000

CIK No: 0001137239

Officers: Leonard MacMillan/59/Dir., CEO, CFO, Pres., Sec., Gerry Diakow/58/VP - Exploration

Directors: Leonard MacMillan/59/Dir., CEO, CFO, Pres., Sec.

Owners: Kevin Bell/7.35%, Ryan Bateman/7.35%, Graham Crabtree/9.80%, Lloyd Blackmore/7.35%, Gerald R. Tuskey/29.40%, Leonard MacMillan/0.05%, Lyn Bell/7.84%, Katrin Braun/7.35%

Financial Data: *Fiscal Year End:* 12/31 *Latest Annual Data:* 03/31/2007

Year	Sales	Net Income
2007	NA	-$38,000

Curr. Assets:	$43,000	*Curr. Liab.:*	$1,000		
Plant, Equip.:	NA	*Total Liab.:*	$1,000	*Indic. Yr. Divd.:*	NA
Total Assets:	$43,000	*Net Worth:*	$42,000	*Debt/ Equity:*	NA

Trestle Holdings Inc

199 Technology Dr., Ste. 105, Irvine, CA, 92618; *PH:* 1-949-673-1907; *http://* www.trestlecorp.com

General - Incorporation	DE	**Stock**- Price on:12/24/2007	$0.065
Employees	17	Stock Exchange	OTC
Auditor	Goldman & Parks LLP	Ticker Symbol	TLHO
Stk Agt	American Stock Transfer & Trust Co.	Outstanding Shares	NA
Counsel	NA	E.P.S.	NA
DUNS No.	NA	Shareholders	NA

Business: The group's principal activity is to develops and sells digital imaging and telemedicine applications linking dispersed users and data primarily in the health care and pharmaceutical markets. The group operates digital imaging products - medmicroa and medscana - provide a digital platform to share, store, and analyze tissue images. The group has discontinued the operations of merchandising division. On may 20, 2003 the group acquired trestle corporation and certain assets of med diversified, inc.

Primary SIC and add'l.: 7829

CIK No: 0000904350

Subsidiaries: Trestle Acquisition Corp.

Officers: Maurizio Vecchione/CEO, Ronald A. Andrews/CEO, Pres., James V. Agnello/Sr. VP, CFO, Kenneth J. Bloom/Chief Medical Dir., David J. Daly/Sr. VP - Commercial Operations, Eric Stoppenhagen/34/Interim Pres., Sec., Jack Zeineh/Chief Science Officer, Barry Hall/CFO, Pres., Anselm Hii/Hematopathologist, Dir. - Consultative Services, Swati Shah/Sr. Hematopathologist, Craig D. Allred/Specialty, Breast Pathology, Ruth L. Katz/Specialty, Cytopathology, Hematocytopathology, Jonathan W. Said/Specialty, Hematopathology, Clive R. Taylor/Specialty, Immunohistochemistry, Lawrence M. Weiss/Specialty, Surgical Pathology, Hematopathology, Immunohistochemistry *(22 Officers included in Index)*

Directors: Richard J. Cote/Chmn. - Scientific Advisory Board, James A. Datin/Chmn., Michael S. Doherty/54/Chmn., Michael S. Hope/65/Dir., Crosby Haffner/35/Dir., Allon Guez/55/Dir., Peter J. Boni/Dir., Frank P. Slattery/Dir., Dennis M. Smith/Dir., Gregory D. Waller/Dir., Jon R. Wampler/Dir., William D. Dallas/52/Dir.

Owners: Gary Freemanp, W Holdings, LLC, David Weinerp, Eric Stoppenhagen, Insiders

Financial Data: *Fiscal Year End:* 12/31 *Latest Annual Data:* 12/31/2006

Year	Sales	Net Income
2006	$1,587,000	-$1,998,000
2005	$4,007,000	-$5,564,000
2004	$4,807,000	-$5,065,000

Curr. Assets:	$916,000	*Curr. Liab.:*	$59,000		
Plant, Equip.:	NA	*Total Liab.:*	$59,000	*Indic. Yr. Divd.:*	$0.120
Total Assets:	$916,000	*Net Worth:*	$857,000	*Debt/ Equity:*	NA

Trex Company Inc

160 Exeter Dr., Winchester, VA, 22603; *PH:* 1-540-678-4070; *http://* www.trex.com

General - Incorporation	DE	**Stock**- Price on:12/24/2007	$18.96
Employees	909	Stock Exchange	NYSE
Auditor	Ernst & Young LLP	Ticker Symbol	TWP
Stk Agt	Mellon Investor Services LLC	Outstanding Shares	15,090,000
Counsel	Hogan & Hartson LLP	E.P.S.	-$3.28
DUNS No.	03-306-1750	Shareholders	NA

Business: The group's principal activity is to manufacture and distribute non-wood decking alternative products. The products of the group are marketed under the brand name Trex(R). Trex Wood-Polymer(R) lumber is a wood/plastic composite that offers an attractive appearance and the workability of wood without wood's on-going maintenance requirements and functional disadvantages. Trex is primarily used for residential and commercial decking and for parks, recreational areas, floating and fixed docks, other marine applications and landscape edging.

Primary SIC and add'l.: 3089 2421

CIK No: 0001069878

Subsidiaries: Trex Wood Polymer Espana, S.L., Winchester Capital, Inc., Winchester SP, Inc.

Officers: Andrew U. Ferrari/Dir., CEO/$772,216.00, Anthony J. Cavanna/Chmn., Interim CFO/$857,331.00, James Mitchell Cox/VP - Sales, Patrick M. Burns/VP - Planning, Business Development, Harold F. Monahan/Exec. VP - Materials, Engineering/$676,381.00, William R. Gupp/VP, General Counsel, Lynn E. MacDonald/Sec., Robert L. Thibodeau/VP - Manufacturing, Colleen T. Combs/VP - Human Resources, Administration, Richard D. McWilliams/VP, Chief Marketing Officer

Directors: Andrew U. Ferrari/Dir., CEO, Anthony J. Cavanna/Chmn., Interim CFO, Patricia B. Robinson/Dir., William H. Martin/Dir., William F. Andrews/Dir., Paul A. Brunner/Dir., Frank H. Merlotti/Dir., Jay M. Gratz/Dir.

Owners: Pzena Investment Management, LLC/12.70%, Insiders/14.80%, Anthony J. Cavanna/8.40%, Patricia B. Robinson, Rutabaga Capital Management/5.50%, Harold F. Monahan, Frank H. Merlotti, William F. Andrews, Wellington Management Company, LLP/6.70%, Robert G. Matheny/7.90%, William H. Martin, Philip J. Pifer, Paul A. Brunner, Paul D. Fletcher, Andrew U. Ferrari/4.40%

Financial Data: *Fiscal Year End:* 12/31 *Latest Annual Data:* 12/31/2006

Year	Sales	Net Income
2006	$336,956,000	$2,343,000
2005	$294,133,000	$2,251,000
2004	$253,628,000	$27,155,000

Curr. Assets:	$143,107,000	*Curr. Liab.:*	$113,548,000		
Plant, Equip.:	$198,525,000	*Total Liab.:*	$182,902,000	*Indic. Yr. Divd.:*	NA
Total Assets:	$352,317,000	*Net Worth:*	$169,415,000	*Debt/ Equity:*	0.3033

Trey Resources Inc

293 Eisenhower Pkwy., Ste. 250, Livingston, NJ, 07039; *PH:* 1-973-758-9555; *Fax:* 1-973-758-9449; *http://* www.treyresources.com; *Email:* mark.meller@swktech.com

General - Incorporation	DE	**Stock**- Price on:12/24/2007	$0.0004
Employees	38	Stock Exchange	OTC
Auditor	Bagell, Josephs, Levine & Co. LLC	Ticker Symbol	TYRIA
Stk Agt	Fidelity Transfer Co	Outstanding Shares	387,770,000
Counsel	NA	E.P.S.	-$0.014
DUNS No.	NA	Shareholders	NA

Business: The groups principle activity is to provide financial accounting software and electronic data interchange (EDI) software, and financial accounting solutions. The group provides software integration and deployment, programming, and training and technical support. The group operates from United States.

Primary SIC and add'l.: NA

CIK No: 0001236275

Subsidiaries: BTSG Acquisition Corp., SWK Technologies, Inc.

Officers: Mark Meller/48/CEO, Pres., Jeffrey D. Roth/CEO, Pres. - SWK Technologies, Lynn Klein Berman/Pres.

Directors: Jerome Mahoney/47/Non - Exec. Chmn., John C. Rudy/62/Dir.

Owners: Insiders, Jerome R. Mahoney, Mark Meller

Financial Data: *Fiscal Year End:* 12/31 *Latest Annual Data:* 12/31/2006

Year	Sales	Net Income
2006	$6,586,000	-$2,322,000
2005	$4,180,000	-$2,409,000
2004	$1,703,000	-$2,391,000

Curr. Assets:	$1,321,000	*Curr. Liab.:*	$5,328,000		
Plant, Equip.:	$265,000	*Total Liab.:*	$6,010,000	*Indic. Yr. Divd.:*	NA
Total Assets:	$2,355,000	*Net Worth:*	-$3,655,000	*Debt/ Equity:*	NA

Tri City National Bank

6400 S 27th St., Oak Creek, WI, 53154; *PH:* 1-414-761-1610; *http://* www.tcnb.com

General - Incorporation	WI	**Stock**- Price on:12/24/2007	$19.5
Employees	289	Stock Exchange	OTC
Auditor	Virchow, Krause & Co. LLP	Ticker Symbol	TRCY
Stk Agt	American Stock Transfer & Trust Co.	Outstanding Shares	8,840,000
Counsel	NA	E.P.S.	$1.13
DUNS No.	03-103-2857	Shareholders	NA

Business: The group's principal activity is the provision of commercial banking services to domestic markets, primarily to individuals and businesses in the metropolitan milwaukee, Wisconsin area. The group provides services through its wholly owned subsidiary, tri city national bank. It provides a full range of consumer and commercial banking services to individuals and businesses. The basic services offered include: demand deposit accounts, money market deposit accounts, now accounts, time deposits, safe deposit services, credit cards, direct deposits, notary services, money orders, night depository, travelers' checks, cashier's checks, savings bonds, secured and unsecured consumer, commercial, installment, real estate and mortgage loans. The group offers automated teller machine cards.

Primary SIC and add'l.: 6712 6022

CIK No: 0000313337

Subsidiaries: Title Service of Southeast Wisconsin, Inc, Tri City Capital Corporation

Officers: Henry Karbiner/67/Chmn., CEO, Pres., Treasurer, Scott D. Gerardin/49/Dir., Sr. VP, General Counsel, Assist. Sec., Robert W. Orth/61/Dir., Sr. VP, Ronald K. Puetz/59/Dir., Exec. VP, Scott A. Wilson/61/Dir., Exec. VP, Sec.

Directors: Henry Karbiner/67/Chmn., CEO, Pres., Treasurer, Christ Krantz/83/Dir., Scott D. Gerardin/49/Dir., Sr. VP, General Counsel, Assist. Sec., William Gravitter/79/Dir., David A. Ulrich/Founder, Frank J. Bauer/81/Dir., William N. Beres/50/Dir., Sanford Fedderly/73/Dir., Brian T. McGarry/57/Dir., Robert W. Orth/61/Dir., Sr. VP, Ronald K. Puetz/59/Dir., Exec. VP, Agatha T. Ulrich/79/Dir., David A. Ulrich/47/Dir., William J. Werry/81/Dir., Scott A. Wilson/61/Dir., Exec. VP, Sec.

Owners: William Gravitter/7.00%, Sanford Fedderly/2.30%, Ulrich Voting Trust/34.00%, Agatha T. Ulrich Marital Trust/22.10%, William N. Beres, Brian T. McGarry/1.80%, Frank J. Bauer, Insiders/44.10%, Scott D. Gerardin, Henry Karbiner/2.40%, Scott A. Wilson, Agatha T. Ulrich/23.40%, Christ Krantz/3.00%, David A. Ulrich/2.60%, Robert W. Orth *(17 Owners included in Index)*

Financial Data: *Fiscal Year End:* 12/31 *Latest Annual Data:* 12/31/2006

Year	Sales	Net Income
2006	$51,344,000	$9,284,000
2005	$45,498,000	$8,949,000
2004	$40,346,000	$8,388,000

Curr. Assets:	$90,636,000	*Curr. Liab.:*	$662,511,000	*P/E Ratio:*	17.26
Plant, Equip.:	$20,172,000	*Total Liab.:*	$665,981,000	*Indic. Yr. Divd.:*	NA
Total Assets:	$770,014,000	*Net Worth:*	$104,033,000	*Debt/ Equity:*	0.0126

Tri County Financial Corp

3035 Leonardtown Rd. , Waldorf, MD, 20601; *PH:* 1-301-645-5601

General - Incorporation	MD	**Stock**- Price on:12/24/2007	$82
Employees	NA	Stock Exchange	OTC
Auditor	Stegman & Co	Ticker Symbol	TYFG
Stk Agt	NA	Outstanding Shares	NA
Counsel	Semmes, Bowen & Semmes	E.P.S.	NA
DUNS No.	06-489-2847	Shareholders	NA

Business: The group's principal activities are to provide full service commercial banking operation throughout southern Maryland through its subsidiary, community bank of tri-county. The group's lending activities include residential and commercial real estate loans, construction loans, loan acquisition and development loans, equipment financing and commercial and consumer demand and installment loans. The deposit services provided by the group are regular savings, money market deposit, demand deposit, ira and sep accounts, christmas club and certificate of deposit. Other services of the group include safe deposit boxes, travelers checks, night depositories, wire transfers, ATMs and telephone banking. The group operates through its main office and seven branches located in waldorf, bryans road, dunkirk, leonardtown, la plata, charlotte hall, and lexington park, Maryland.

Primary SIC and add'l.: 6022 6712

CIK No: 0000855874

Subsidiaries: Community Bank of Tri-County, Community Mortgage Corporation, of Tri-County, Tri-County Capital Trust I, Tri-County Capital Trust II, Tri-County Investment Corporation

Officers: Michael L. Middleton/Dir., CEO, Pres./$577,364.00, Marie C. Brown/65/Dir., COO/$410,997.00, Gregory C. Cockerham/Exec. VP, Chief Lending Officer/$292,903.00, William J. Pasenelli/CFO, Exec. VP/$279,196.00

Directors: Michael L. Middleton/Dir., CEO, Pres., Marie C. Brown/65/Dir., COO, Beaman H. Smith/62/Dir., James R. Shepherd/63/Dir., Herbert N. Redmond/67/Dir., Joseph A. Slater/54/Dir., Louis P. Jenkins/36/Dir., Joseph V. Stone/53/Dir., Philip T. Goldstein/59/Dir.

Owners: Insiders/29.87%, Beaman H. Smith/4.86%, Louis P. Jenkins, Herbert N. Redmond/1.46%, Community Bank of Tri-County Employee Stock Ownership Plan/7.09%, C. Marie Brown/5.55%, Joseph A. Slater, William J. Pasenelli/1.53%, Gregory C. Cockerham/4.02%, Philip T. Goldstein, Michael L. Middleton/12.84%, Joseph V. Stone, James R. Shepherd

Tri Valley Bank

2410 San Ramon Valley Blvd., Ste. 115, San Ramon, CA, 94583; **PH:** 1-925-791-4340; **Fax:** 1-925-837-2569; **http://** www.trivalleybank.com

General - Incorporation		**Stock**- Price on:12/24/2007	$11.5
Employees	NA	Stock Exchange	OTC
Auditor	NA	Ticker Symbol	TRVB
Stk Agt	U.S. Stock Transfer Corp	Outstanding Shares	NA
Counsel	NA	E.P.S.	NA
DUNS No.	NA	Shareholders	NA

Business: The groups principal activities include providing community banking and financial services. Services of the group include checking accounts, savings accounts, certificates of deposit, installment loans, real estate mortgage loans, commercial loans, traveler's checks, safe deposit boxes, night depository and automated teller services.

Primary SIC and add'l.: 6021

CIK No:

Officers: William B. Nethercott/47/Dir., CEO, Pres., Brian D. Kehoe/48/Sr. VP - Commercial Lending, Doreen Rosengarth/VP, Operations Mgr. - Livermore, John D. Rockwell/50/Exec. VP, Chief Credit Officer, Celeste Andrade/Administrative Assist. - SAN Ramon, Ryan Banta/VP - SBA, Commercial Lending, SAN Ramon, Cristine Silva/Sr. Loan Administrative Assist. - Livermore, Patti Velasco/Service Mgr. - Livermore, Toni Copeman/VP - Compliance, SAN Ramon, Margaret Lowell/VP - Construction Lending, SAN Ramon, Maria Mabardy/VP - Private, Professional Lending, SAN Ramon, Monica Phillips/Executive Assist. - Shareholder Relations, SAN Ramon, Maria Catanzaro-Sahines/VP - Commercial Lending, SAN Ramon, Charles Crohare/VP - Business Development, Livermore, Kathryn Hohl/AVP - Commercial Lending, Livermore (23 Officers included in Index)

Directors: William B. Nethercott/47/Dir., CEO, Pres., James C. Snell/68/Chmn., Richard A. Saso/65/Dir., Daljit Hundal/47/Dir., Piardip Joe Johal/41/Dir., David L. Beretta/51/Dir., Roland W. Chow/32/Dir., Robert A. Dimino/62/Dir., William Hogarty/41/Dir.

Tri Valley Corp

5555 Business Pk. S, Ste 200, Bakersfield, CA, 93309; **PH:** 1-661-864-0500; **http://** www.tri-valleycorp.com; **Email:** info@tri-valleycorp.com

General - Incorporation	DE	**Stock**- Price on:12/24/2007	$8.2128
Employees	35	Stock Exchange	AMEX
Auditor	Brown Armstrong Paulden	Ticker Symbol	TIV
Stk Agt	Registrar & Transfer Co	Outstanding Shares	24,610,000
Counsel	NA	E.P.S.	$0.01
DUNS No.	06-668-6130	Shareholders	NA

Business: The group's principal activities are to explore, develop and produce petroleum and precious metal properties. It generates exploration prospects from internal database and screens prospect submittals from other geologists and companies. The group has two wholly owned subsidiaries: tri-valley oil and gas company, which deals with gas production and tri valley power corporation, which is an inactive subsidiary. The group operates in three segments: drilling and development, oil and gas production and precious metals. The group's products are sold in the northern California gas market.

Primary SIC and add'l.: 1081 1382 5172

CIK No: 0000022551

Subsidiaries: Great Valley Production Services, Inc., Select Resources, Inc., Tri-Valley Oil & Gas Company

Officers: Joseph R. Kandle/CEO, Pres. - Tri, Valley Oil, Gas Co/$169,208.00, Lynn F. Blystone/Dir., CEO, Pres./$211,220.00, Paul Hacker/Sr. Geologist, Tri, Valley Engineering, Geology, Ted Pompa/Tri, Valley Administrative Staff, Terry Ray/Tri, Valley Field Superintendent, Darin Holden/Tri, Valley Field Superintendent, Raven Langley/Tri, Valley Administrative Staff, Daneva Cofield/Tri, Valley Administrative Staff, Thomas J. Cunningham/Chief Administrative Officer, VP - Tri, Valley Corporation/$134,758.00, Felicia Todd/Tri, Valley Administrative Staff, Egan J. Gost/Special Projects Mgr., Helen Ordway/Mgr. - Environmental, Safety, Health, Gary Borgna/GM - Great Valley Drilling Company LLC, Michael Cain/GM - Great Valley Production Services, Myron Tiede/Sr. Geologist, Tri, Valley Engineering, Geology (20 Officers included in Index)

Directors: Lynn F. Blystone/Dir., CEO, Pres., Henry Lowenstein/Dir., William H. Marumoto/Dir., Thomas G. Gamble/Dir., Paul W. Bateman/Dir., Edward M. Gabriel/Dir., Milton J. Carlson/Dir., Loren J. Miller/Dir.

Owners: Paul W. Bateman, Loren Miller/1.20%, Insiders/14.90%, William H. Marumoto, Lynn F. Blystone/5.00%, Milton Carlson/1.40%, Henry Lowenstein, Thomas G. Gamble/6.50%

Financial Data: Fiscal Year End:12/31   **Latest Annual Data:** 12/31/2006

Year	Sales	Net Income
2006	$4,937,000	-$941,000
2005	$12,529,000	-$9,730,000
2004	$4,499,000	-$1,171,000

Curr. Assets:	$16,018,000	**Curr. Liab.:**	$9,047,000		
Plant, Equip.:	$12,076,000	**Total Liab.:**	$12,011,000	**Indic. Yr. Divd.:**	NA
Total Assets:	$28,654,000	**Net Worth:**	$16,644,000	**Debt/ Equity:**	NA

Tri-Isthmus Group Inc

149 S Barrington Ave., Ste. 808, Los Angeles, CA, 90049; **PH:** 1-818-887-6659; **http://** www.tig3.com; **Email:** sales_enquiry@vsource.com

General - Incorporation	DE	**Stock**- Price on:12/24/2007	$0.315
Employees	2	Stock Exchange	OTC
Auditor	Mendoza Berger & Co., LLP	Ticker Symbol	TISG
Stk Agt	U.S. Stock Transfer Corp	Outstanding Shares	3,780,000
Counsel	NA	E.P.S.	-$0.43
DUNS No.	NA	Shareholders	NA

Business: The group's principle activities are to provide seamless, customizable and comprehensive business process outsourcing solutions globally. The group's activities are carried out through 5 segments. The warranty solutions segment includes a range of after-sales and customer support functions like telephone, Web and email technical support and field services. The human resource solutions include payroll processing, expense claims processing, and payment solutions. Sales solutions include demand generation and development of market channels. Human capital management solutions focus on business process outsourcing payroll and benefits processing. Vsource foundation solutions comprises of customer relationship management, supply chain management and financial administration. The group operates in Asia-pacific, the United States, Malaysia, Taiwan, Japan, Hong Kong and 21 countries in Europe. The group's quarterly revenue for July 2007 was 0.87 millions of USD.

Primary SIC and add'l.: 7373 7380 7372

CIK No: 0001003226

Subsidiaries: Del Mar Acquisition, Inc., Del Mar GenPar, Inc., Point Loma Acquisition, Inc., Surgical Center Acquisition Holdings, Inc., Surgical Center Management, Inc., Virtual Source, Inc., Vsource (Asia) Ltd, Vsource (Australia) Pty Ltd, Vsource (BVI)Ltd, Vsource (California) Inc., Vsource (CI)Ltd, Vsource (Singapore) Pte Ltd, Vsource (USA)Inc.

Officers: David Hirschhorn/Co - Chmn., Co - CEO, CO - CFO, Todd Parker/Co - Chmn., Co - CEO, Co - CFO, Dennis M. Smith/Dir. - Sr. Consultant

Directors: David Hirschhorn/Co - Chmn., Co - CEO, CO - CFO, Todd Parker/Co - Chmn., Co - CEO, Co - CFO, Dennis M. Smith/Dir. - Sr. Consultant, Rich Sells/Dir., Robert N. Schwartz/Dir., Michael J. Issa/Member - Advisory Board, William Houlihan/Member - Advisory Board, William McGrath/Member - Advisory Board, John Jay Beaghen/Member - Advisory Board, John Vangel/Member - Advisory Board, Bobby I. Majumder/Member - Advisory Board, Steven Spector/Member - Advisory Board, Bill Simon/Member - Advisory Board, Operations, Mark D. Moses/Member - Advisory Board, Operations, Rod Trujillo/Member - Advisory Board, Operations (18 Directors included in Index)

Owners: Eparfin SA/1.93%, Insiders/13.91%, Susan Lacerra & Steven Tingey JT/11.24%, David Hirschhorn/13.49%, Richardson E. Sells/1.40%, Ali R. Moghaddami/100.00%, SMP Investments I, LLC/9.04%, Dennis M. Smith/3.86%, Todd Parker/6.75%, Todd Parker/4.88%, Symphony House Berhad/5.10%, David Hirschhorn/4.52%, Robert N. Schwartz/1.44%, Ron Soderling/59.17%, Dennis M. Smith/4.52% (17 Owners included in Index)

Financial Data: Fiscal Year End:01/31   **Latest Annual Data:** 1/31/2007

Year	Sales	Net Income
2007	$702,000	-$1,580,000
2006	NA	-$2,170,000
2005	$254,000	$15,242,000

Curr. Assets:	$2,469,000	**Curr. Liab.:**	$839,000		
Plant, Equip.:	$1,115,000	**Total Liab.:**	$1,030,000	**Indic. Yr. Divd.:**	NA
Total Assets:	$4,571,000	**Net Worth:**	-$1,603,000	**Debt/ Equity:**	NA

Tri-S Security Corp

Royal Ctr. One, 11675 Great Oaks Way, Ste. 120, Alpharetta, GA, 30022; **PH:** 1-678-808-1540; **Fax:** 1-678-808-1551; **http://** www.trissecurity.com; **Email:** investor@trissecurity.com

General - Incorporation	GA	**Stock**- Price on:12/24/2007	$2.79
Employees	2,400	Stock Exchange	NDQ
Auditor	Houser & Stewart LLP	Ticker Symbol	TRIS
Stk Agt	EquiServe Trust Co N.A	Outstanding Shares	3,500,000
Counsel	NA	E.P.S.	-$1.25
DUNS No.	NA	Shareholders	NA

Business: The groups principle activity is to provide security services. The groups services include uniformed guards, electronic monitoring systems, personnel protection, access control, crowd control and the prevention of sabotage, terrorist and criminal activities. The groups operates through two segments namely cornwall and paragon. Specific customers of the group include the Department of Homeland Security, the Social Security Administration, the Army Corps of Engineers, the United States Coast Guard, ASA, and the Department of Defense. In October 18, 2005, the group acquired Cornwall Group, Inc. The group operates from the United States. The group's quarterly revenue for September 2007 was 23.80 millions of USD.

Primary SIC and add'l.: 7381 7382 8744

CIK No: 0001304901

Subsidiaries: Armor Security, Inc., Forestville Corporation, Guardsource Corp., International Monitoring, Inc., On Guard Security and Investigations, Inc., Paragon Systems, Inc., Protection Technologies Corporation, The Cornwall Group, Inc., Vanguard Security of Broward County, Inc., Vanguard Security, Inc., Virtual Guard Source, Inc.

Officers: Ronald G. Farrell/Chmn., CEO, Pres., Roy P. Langford/Corporate Controller, Leslie Kaciban/Pres. - Paragon Systems, Mark Machi/VP, General Counsel - Paragon Systems, Shyron Beavers/Dir. - Government Markets, John R. Oliver/CFO

Directors: Ronald G. Farrell/Chmn., CEO, Pres., James A. Verbrugge/68/Dir., L. K. Toole/Dir., James M. Logsdon/Dir.

Owners: Robert K. Mills, Ronald G. Farrell/36.80%, Charles Keathley/9.30%, L. K. Toole, James A. Logsdon, James A. Verbrugge, Insiders/37.70%, Kaizen Management, L.P/9.90%

Financial Data: Fiscal Year End:12/31   **Latest Annual Data:** 12/31/2006

Year	Sales	Net Income
2006	$75,725,000	-$3,833,000
2005	$41,985,000	-$2,278,000
2004	$25,425,000	-$627,000

Curr. Assets:	$14,028,000	Curr. Liab.:	$20,998,000		
Plant, Equip.:	$597,000	Total Liab.:	$30,245,000	Indic. Yr. Divd.:	NA
Total Assets:	$37,101,000	Net Worth:	$6,856,000	Debt/ Equity:	1.1964

Triad Guaranty Inc

101 S Stratford Rd. , Winston-salem, NC, 27104; *PH:* 1-336-723-1282;
http:// www.triadguaranty.com

General - Incorporation	DE	Stock- Price on:12/24/2007	$42.99
Employees	250	Stock Exchange	NDQ
Auditor	Ernst & Young LLP	Ticker Symbol	TGIC
Stk Agt	EquiServe Trust Co N.A	Outstanding Shares	NA
Counsel	NA	E.P.S.	$3.80
DUNS No.	60-674-4589	Shareholders	NA

Business: The group's principal activity is to provide private mortgage insurance, also known as mortgage guaranty insurance, to residential mortgage lenders. The service provided by the group helps to protect the lender against loss from defaults on low down payment residential mortgage loans. There are two types of private mortgage insurance coverage, primary and pool. Primary insurance provides mortgage default protection on individual loans and covers unpaid loan principal, delinquent interest and expenses associated with the default and subsequent foreclosure. Pool insurance offers lenders an additional credit enhancement for certain mortgage/backed securities and provides coverage for the full amount of the net loss on each individual loss included in the pool.

Primary SIC and add'l.: 6351 6719

CIK No: 0000911631

Subsidiaries: Triad Guaranty Assurance Corporation, Triad Guaranty Insurance Corporation, Triad Re Insurance Corporation

Officers: Mark K. Tonnesen/Dir., CEO, Pres./$2,707,015.00, Ron D. Kessinger/Sr. Exec. VP, Assist. to The Pres./$600,345.00, Julia H. Turner/Assist. VP, Assistant Sec., Assistant General Counsel, Bruce Van Fleet/Exec. VP - Sales, Marketing, Triad Guaranty Insurance Corporation, Chris Stanfield/Supervisor - Customer Service, Triad Guaranty Insurance Corporation, George Jackson/VP - Information Services, VP, VP - Information Services, Rick Brown/Internal Audit Services Mgr. - Triad Guaranty Insurance Corporation, Diane Hartman/Mgr. - Project Implementation Team, Kaye Sain/VP, Dir. - Underwriting, Triad Guaranty Insurance Corporation, Gwen Goodnight/Assist. VP, Regional Underwriting Mgr. - Dallas, TX, Mike Keyes/Assist. VP, Regional Underwriting Mgr. - Horsham, PA, Georgia Copeland/Assist. VP, Regional Underwriting Mgr. - Houston, TX, Jenny Day/Assist. VP, Regional Underwriting Mgr. - Irvine, CA, David Nichting/Assist. VP, Regional Underwriting Mgr. - Lombard, IL, Greg Williams/Assist. VP, Regional Underwriting Mgr. - Phoenix, AZ (31 Officers included in Index)

Directors: Mark K. Tonnesen/Dir., CEO, Pres., William T. Ratliff/Chmn., Henry G. Williamson/Dir., Glenn T. Austin/Dir., Richard S. Swanson/Dir., David W. Whitehurst/Dir., Michael A.F. Roberts/Dir., Lee H. Durham/Dir., Robert T. David/Dir.

Owners: Stephen J. Haferman, Dimensional FundAdvisors LP/7.80%, Mark K. Tonnesen, Michael A. F. Roberts, Putnam, LLC/6.20%, Richard S. Swanson, Kenneth W. Jones, Lee H. Durham, Kenneth C. Foster, Insiders/6.00%, William T. Ratliff/4.70%, Robert T. David, David W. Whitehurst, Kenneth N. Lard, Collateral Holdings, Ltd./17.30% (18 Owners included in Index)

Financial Data: Fiscal Year End:12/31   Latest Annual Data: 12/31/2006

Year	Sales	Net Income
2006	$239,144,000	$65,635,000
2005	$192,046,000	$56,813,000
2004	$196,970,000	$58,417,000

Curr. Assets:	$44,802,000	Curr. Liab.:	$16,869,000		
Plant, Equip.:	$17,848,000	Total Liab.:	$325,407,000	Indic. Yr. Divd.:	NA
Total Assets:	$895,631,000	Net Worth:	$570,224,000	Debt/ Equity:	0.0587

Triad Hospitals Inc

5800 Tennyson Pk.way, Plano, TX, 75024; *PH:* 1-214-473-7000; *http://* www.triadhospitals.com

General - Incorporation	DE	Stock- Price on:12/24/2007	$53.6
Employees	42,000	Stock Exchange	NA
Auditor	Ernst & Young LLP	Ticker Symbol	NA
Stk Agt	National City Bank of Clevel	Outstanding Shares	89,200,000
Counsel	NA	E.P.S.	$2.05
DUNS No.	NA	Shareholders	NA

Business: The group's principle activity is to provide industrial automation power, control and information solutions. The group operates from United States. The group merged with Community Health Systems, Inc.

Primary SIC and add'l.: 8093 8062 8011

CIK No: 0001074771

Subsidiaries: A Womans Place, LLC, Abilene Hospital, LLC, Abilene Merger, LLC, Affinity Health Systems, LLC, Affinity Hospital, LLC, Affinity Physician Services, LLC, Alaska Physician Services, LLC, Alice Hospital, LLC, Alice Surgeons, LLC, American Health Facilities Development, LLC, Anesthesiology Group of Hattiesburg, LLC, APS Medical, LLC, Arizona ASC Management, Inc., Arizona DH, LLC, Arizona Medco, LLC 367 Subsidiaries included in the Index

Officers: James D. Shelton/Chmn., CEO, Michael J. Parsons/Dir., COO, Exec. VP, Stephen W. Love/CFO, Sr. VP

Directors: James D. Shelton/Chmn., CEO, Michael K. Jhin/Dir., Nancy Ann Deparle/Dir., William J. Hibbitt/Dir., Uwe E. Reinhardt/Dir., Barbara A. Durand/Dir., Michael J. Parsons/Dir., COO, Exec. VP, Gale Sayers/Dir., Donald B. Halverstadt/Dir.

Owners: Barbara A. Durand, Dale V. Kesler, Michael J. Parsons, Nancy-Ann DeParle, Harriet R. Michel, James D. Shelton/1.30%, Insiders/3.80%, William R. Huston, Stephen W. Love, Thomas G. Loeffler, Uwe E. Reinhardt, Gale E. Sayers, Daniel J. Moen, TPG-Axon GP, LLC/8.80%, Waddell & Reed Financial, Inc./6.00% (18 Owners included in Index)

Financial Data: Fiscal Year End:12/31   Latest Annual Data: 12/31/2006

Year	Sales	Net Income
2006	$5,537,900,000	$222,300,000
2005	$4,747,300,000	$226,000,000
2004	$4,450,200,000	$191,000,000

Curr. Assets:	$1,494,400,000	Curr. Liab.:	$601,500,000	P/E Ratio:	26.15
Plant, Equip.:	$2,940,200,000	Total Liab.:	$2,666,600,000	Indic. Yr. Divd.:	NA
Total Assets:	$6,233,800,000	Net Worth:	$3,226,400,000	Debt/ Equity:	0.5110

Triangle Petroleum Corp

521 3 Ave. SW Ste. 1250, Calgary, AB, T2P 3T3; *PH:* 1-403-374-1234; *Fax:* 1-403-262-4472;
http:// www.trianglepetroleum.com; *Email:* info@trianglepetroleum.com

General - Incorporation	NV	Stock- Price on:12/24/2007	$2
Employees	NA	Stock Exchange	OTC
Auditor	Manning Elliott LLP	Ticker Symbol	TPLM
Stk Agt	Continental Stock Transfer & Trust Co	Outstanding Shares	NA
Counsel	Sichenzia Ross Friedman Ference	E.P.S.	NA
DUNS No.	NA	Shareholders	NA

Business: The groups principal activity is exploration company primarily focused on large resource. The group operates from the United States and Canada.

Primary SIC and add'l.: 1382

CIK No: 0001281922

Subsidiaries: Elmworth Energy Corporation, Triangle USA Petroleum Corporation

Officers: Mark G. Gustafson/Dir., CEO, Pres., Troy Wagner/38/COO, VP - Engineering, Andy Prefontaine/Land Mgr., Art Bowman/Geophysicist, Clarence Campbell/VP - Exploration, Greg Caswell/Consultant, Petroleum Engineer, Brad J. Hayes/Consultant - Exploration Geologist, Jason Krueger/Contact - Investor Relations, Shaun Toker/CFO, Brad Affleck/Operations Mgr., Nick Steinsberger/Drilling, Completions Consultant

Directors: Mark G. Gustafson/Dir., CEO, Pres., Ron Hietala/Dir., John D. Carlson/53/Dir., Stephen A. Holditch/Dir., David L. Bradshaw/Dir., Randal J. Matkaluk/Dir.

Owners: Insiders/18.76%, John D. Carlson/4.39%, Mark Gustafson/7.40%, Stephen A. Holditch, Palo Alto Investors, LLC/17.58%, Troy T. Wagner, Aly Musani, Ron W. Hietala/5.86%

Financial Data: Fiscal Year End:01/31   Latest Annual Data: 01/31/2007

Year	Sales	Net Income
2007	$54,000	-$18,339,000
2006	NA	-$8,245,000
2005	NA	-$31,000

Curr. Assets:	$8,662,000	Curr. Liab.:	$8,996,000		
Plant, Equip.:	$21,169,000	Total Liab.:	$24,165,000	Indic. Yr. Divd.:	NA
Total Assets:	$30,747,000	Net Worth:	$6,582,000	Debt/ Equity:	NA

Triarc Cos Inc

280 Pk. Ave., New York, NY, 10017; *PH:* 1-212-451-3000; *Fax:* 1-212-451-3134;
http:// www.triarc.com; *Email:* investor-relations@triarc.com

General - Incorporation	DE	Stock- Price on:12/24/2007	$16.15
Employees	24,372	Stock Exchange	NYSE
Auditor	Deloitte & Touche LLP	Ticker Symbol	TRY
Stk Agt	American Stock Transfer & Trust Co.	Outstanding Shares	92,610,000
Counsel	Paul Weiss Rifkind Et Al	E.P.S.	NA
DUNS No.	00-503-8773	Shareholders	NA

Business: The group's principal activity is the franchising of the arby's quick service restaurants. The group licenses the owners and operators of independent businesses to use the arby's brand name and trademarks in the operation of arby's restaurants. These restaurants are specialized in the roast beef sandwich segment of the quick service restaurant industry. The restaurants also offer an extensive menu of chicken, turkey, ham and submarine sandwiches, side dishes and salads. As of Dec 28, 2003, the group operated 236 domestic arby's restaurants. Of such 236 restaurants, 210 were free-standing units, 13 were located in shopping malls, eight were in food courts and five were in strip center locations. The group owns several trademarks few of them are arbysr, t.j. Cinnamonsr, arby's market freshtm, market freshr and sidekickers'r'. On 22-Jul-2004, the group acquired 64% interest in deerfield & company llc.

Primary SIC and add'l.: 5812

CIK No: 0000030697

Subsidiaries: 1725 Contra Costa Property, Inc., 280 Acquisition, LLC, 280 BT Holdings LLC, 280 Holdings II, Inc., 280 Holdings, LLC, Adams Packing Association, Inc., Arby's Brands, LLC, Arby's Building and Construction Co., Arby's Finance, LLC, Arby's Franchise Trust, Arby's Holdings, LLC, Arby's IP Holder Trust, Arby's Merger Co., Arby's of Canada Inc., Arby's Restaurant Group, Inc. 78 Subsidiaries included in the Index

Officers: Roland C. Smith/CEO, Daniel T. Collins/Sr. VP, Treasurer, Assist. Sec., Francis T. McCarron/Exec. VP/$3,871,715.00, Robert J. Crowe/VP - Taxes, Steven B. Graham/Chief Accounting Officer, Sr. VP, Stephen E. Hare/CFO, Sr. VP, Thomas A. Garrett/COO, Exec. VP, Nils H. Okeson/Sr. VP, Assoc. General Counsel, Sec., Fred H. Schaefer/Sr. VP, Stuart I. Rosen/Sr. VP, General Counsel, Assist. Sec., Greg Essner/46/Sr. VP, Treasurer, Anne A. Tarbell/49/Sr. VP - Corporate Communications, Investor Relations, Brian L. Schorr/49/Exec. VP, General Counsel, Assist. Sec./$3,745,554.00

Directors: Nelson Peltz/Chmn., Peter W. May/Vice Chmn., David E. Schwab/Dir., Hugh L. Carey/Dir., Joseph A. Levato/Dir., Gerald Tsai/Dir., Jack G. Wasserman/Dir., Gregory H. Sachs/42/Dir., Edward P. Garden/Dir., Clive Chajet/Dir., Russell V. Umphenour/Dir., Raymond S. Troubh/Dir.

Owners: Insiders/31.40%, Brian L. Schorr/1.10%, Nelson Peltz, Nelson Peltz/21.80%, Peter W. May/21.50%, Russell V. Umphenour/5.70%, Francis T. McCarron, Cardinal Capital Management, LLC., Gerald Tsai, Brian L. Schorr, Jack G. Wasserman, Francis T. McCarron, Hugh L. Carey, Peter W. May, Joseph A. Levato (33 Owners included in Index)

Tricell Inc

6 Howard Pl, Stoke-on-trent, ST1 4NQ; *PH:* 44-8707532360; *http://* www.tricellinc.com

General - Incorporation	NV	Stock- Price on:12/24/2007	NA
Employees	NA	Stock Exchange	OTC
Auditor	Whitley Penn	Ticker Symbol	TCLL
Stk Agt	Signature Stock Transfer, Inc.	Outstanding Shares	NA
Counsel	NA	E.P.S.	NA
DUNS No.	NA	Shareholders	NA

Business: The group's principal activity is to supply and distribute mobile telephones, telephone accessories and electronic commodities. The group handles wireless products manufactured by technology companies such as nokia, motorola, sony ericsson, kyocera, samsung, siemens, panasonic, nec and toshiba. The customers of the group include wireless network operators, resellers, retailers and wireless equipment manufacturers. The group distributes the commodities in the United Kingdom, Netherlands, Belgium, Hong Kong, France and other countries.

Primary SIC and add'l.: 5065

CIK No: 0001178156

Subsidiaries: Ace Telecom Limited, LA Names, Tricell Distribution, Tricell Global Limited

Officers: James Reed/Dir., CEO, Neil Pursell/Dir., CFO

Directors: James Reed/Dir., CEO, Melyvn Langley/Chmn., Ian Herman/Dir., Neil Pursell/Dir., CFO, Raymond Pirtle/Dir., John Boyd/Dir.

Owners: Neil A. Pursell/16.20%, John Sumnall/16.20%, Andre Salt/7.10%, James E. Reed/16.20%, Neil Proctor/16.20%, Insiders/64.10%

Financial Data: ***Fiscal Year End:***12/31 ***Latest Annual Data:*** 12/31/2005

Year	Sales	Net Income
2005	$662,904,000	$68,000
2004	$13,899,000	-$7,524,000
2003	$99,850,000	$159,000

Curr. Assets:	$53,331,000	***Curr. Liab.:***	$57,236,000		
Plant, Equip.:	$137,000	***Total Liab.:***	$57,236,000	***Indic. Yr. Divd.:***	NA
Total Assets:	$53,598,000	***Net Worth:***	-$3,638,000	***Debt/ Equity:***	NA

Trico Bancshares

63 Constitution Dr., Chico, CA, 95973; ***PH:*** 1-530-898-0300; ***http://*** www.tricountiesbank.com

General - Incorporation	CA	***Stock***- Price on:12/24/2007	$23.16
Employees	702	Stock Exchange	NDQ
Auditor	KPMG LLP	Ticker Symbol	TCBK
Stk Agt	Mellon Investor Services LLC	Outstanding Shares	15,920,000
Counsel	NA	E.P.S	$1.64
DUNS No.	10-755-0733	Shareholders	NA

Business: The group's principal activity is to provide general commercial banking services. Acting as a holding company for the tri counties bank, the group accepts demand, savings and time deposits and provides commercial, real estate and consumer loans. It also offers installment note collection, issues cashier's checks and money orders, sells travelers checks and provides safe deposit boxes and other customary banking services. The group also offers brokerage services through its subsidiary raymond james financial services. It operates 33 traditional branches and 12 in-store branches in eighteen counties of California.

Primary SIC and add'l.: 6022 6712 6159

CIK No: 0000356171

Subsidiaries: Tri Counties Bank, TriCo Capital Trust I, TriCo Capital Trust II

Officers: Richard P. Smith/Dir., CEO, Pres./$968,212.00, Thomas Reddish/CFO, Exec. VP/$441,684.00, Richard O'Sullivan/Exec. VP - Wholesale Banking/$403,199.00, Carroll R. Taresh/Dir., Executive Officer, Rick Hagstrom/Exec. VP - Risk Management/$515,059.00, Rick Miller/Sr. VP, Dir. - Human Resources, Daniel K. Bailey/Exec. VP - Retail Banking, Ray Rios/Sr. VP, Mgr. Information Systems, Craig Carney/Exec. VP, Chief Credit Officer

Directors: Richard P. Smith/Dir., CEO, Pres., Donald E. Murphy/Vice Chmn., William J. Casey/Chmn., Donald J. Amaral/Dir., Alex A. Vereschagin/Dir., John S. Hasbrook/Dir., Steve G. Nettleton/Dir., Craig S. Compton/Dir., Michael W. Koehnen/Dir., Carroll R. Taresh/Dir., Executive Officer

Owners: Michael W. Koehnen, W. R. Hagstrom, Craig S. Compton, John S. A. Hasbrook, Donald E. Murphy/1.22%, Richard O'Sullivan/1.72%, Richard P. Smith/10.53%, Insiders/26.55%, Donald J. Amaral, Alex A. Vereschagin/8.10%, TriCo Bancshares/7.40%, Thomas J. Reddish/1.16%, William J. Casey/11.46%, Andrew Mastorakis, Carroll R. Taresh *(16 Owners included in Index)*

Financial Data: ***Fiscal Year End:***12/31 ***Latest Annual Data:*** 12/31/2006

Year	Sales	Net Income
2006	$146,578,000	$26,830,000
2005	$123,646,000	$23,671,000
2004	$109,726,000	$20,182,000

Curr. Assets:	$111,741,000	***Curr. Liab.:***	$1,644,697,000	***P/E Ratio:***	14.21
Plant, Equip.:	$21,830,000	***Total Liab.:***	$1,750,530,000	***Indic. Yr. Divd.:***	$0.520
Total Assets:	$1,919,966,000	***Net Worth:***	$169,436,000	***Debt/ Equity:***	NA

Trico Marine Services Inc

250 N American Ct, Houma, LA, 70363; ***PH:*** 1-713-780-9926; ***http://*** www.tricomarine.com

General - Incorporation	DE	***Stock***- Price on:12/24/2007	$42.39
Employees	834	Stock Exchange	NDQ
Auditor	PricewaterhouseCoopers LLP	Ticker Symbol	TRMA
Stk Agt	Mellon Investor Services LLC	Outstanding Shares	14,900,000
Counsel	Jones, Walker Et Al	E.P.S	$3.47
DUNS No.	92-728-9405	Shareholders	NA

Business: The group's principal activities are to provide marine support vessels and related services to the oil and gas industry primarily in the U.S. Gulf of Mexico, the north sea and Latin America. The services provided include transportation of drilling materials, supplies and crews to offshore facilities; towing drilling rigs and equipment from one location to another and support for the construction, installation, maintenance and removal of offshore facilities. The group also provides support for deepwater rov (remotely operated vehicle) and well stimulation and maintenance services. The group has a total fleet of 84 vessels, including 48 supply vessels, 13 large capacity platform supply vessels, seven large anchor handling, towing and supply vessels, 11 crew boats and 6 line-handling vessels.

Primary SIC and add'l.: 4499

CIK No: 0000921549

Subsidiaries: Albyn Marine Limited, Coastal Inland Marine Services Ltd., Naviera Mexicana de Servicios, S. de R.L de CV., Servicios de Apoyo Maritimo de Mexico, S. de R.L. de CV., Trico HoldCo LLC, Trico Marine Assets, Inc., Trico Marine International Holdings B.V., Trico Marine International, Inc., Trico Marine International, Ltd., Trico Marine Operators, Inc., Trico Marine Services (Hong Kong) Limited, Trico Servicos Maritimos Ltda., Trico Shipping AS, Trico Supply (UK)Limited, Trico Supply AS

Officers: Trevor Turbidy/Dir., CEO, Pres./$1,565,765.00, Charlie E. Tizzard/VP - Administration, Jan Magne Goksoyr/Global Sales, Marketing, North Sea, Jimmy De Desouza/Global Sales, Marketing, Brazil, Scott Worhington/GM - Mexico, Rishi Varma/VP, General Counsel, Corp. Sec./$449,419.00, Tony May/MD - Scotland, Nick Anderson/MD - West Africa, Gerald Gray/VP - International Operations, Oyvind Saevik/Dir. - Norwegian Operations, Norway, Fernando Martins/GM - Brazil, Tomas Salazar/Global Dir. - Sales, Marketing, Kenneth W. Bourgeois/VP - US, Geoff A. Jones/CFO, VP/$578,398.00, Robert V. O'Connor/Sr. VP - Business Development/$302,430.00 *(19 Officers included in Index)*

Directors: Trevor Turbidy/Dir., CEO, Pres., Joseph S. Compofelice/Chmn., Per Staehr/Dir., Edward C. Hutcheson/Dir., Richard A. Bachmann/Dir., Myles W. Scoggins/Dir., M. W. Scoggins/Dir., Kenneth M. Burke/Dir.

Owners: Richard A. Bachmann, Edward C. Hutcheson, Michael D. Wallace, Robert V. OConnor, Kenneth M. Burke, Rishi A. Varma, Larry Francois, Joseph S. Compofelice, Insiders/3.00%, Geoff Jones, Trevor Turbidy/1.00%, Myles W. Scoggins, Per Staehr

Financial Data: ***Fiscal Year End:***12/31 ***Latest Annual Data:*** 12/31/2006

Year	Sales	Net Income
2006	$248,717,000	$58,724,000
2005	$182,285,000	-$41,261,000
2004	$112,510,000	-$95,952,000

Curr. Assets:	$183,235,000	***Curr. Liab.:***	$32,167,000	***P/E Ratio:***	12.22
Plant, Equip.:	$234,163,000	***Total Liab.:***	$122,984,000	***Indic. Yr. Divd.:***	NA
Total Assets:	$435,322,000	***Net Worth:***	$312,338,000	***Debt/ Equity:***	0.4729

Trident Microsystems Inc

1090 E Arques Ave., Sunnyvale, CA, 94085; ***PH:*** 1-408-991-8800; ***http://*** www.tridentmicro.com; ***Email:*** staffing@tridentmicro.com

General - Incorporation	DE	***Stock***- Price on:12/24/2007	$19.66
Employees	344	Stock Exchange	NDQ
Auditor	PricewaterhouseCoopers LLP	Ticker Symbol	TRID
Stk Agt	Mellon Investor Services LLC	Outstanding Shares	57,100,000
Counsel	NA	E.P.S	$0.47
DUNS No.	18-105-9304	Shareholders	NA

Business: The group's principal activity is to design, develop and market integrated circuits. These integrated circuits are used for videographics, multi-media and digitally processed television products for the desktop and notebook personal computer and consumer television market. The products are sold through a network of original design manufacturers and system integrators. The graphics and video controllers are sold with software drivers, a bios and related system integration support.

Primary SIC and add'l.: 3577 3674 7372

CIK No: 0000859475

Subsidiaries: Trident Microsystems (Far East) Ltd, Trident Technologies, Inc. (TTI)

Officers: Glen M. Antle/Chmn., Acting CEO, Sylvia D. Summers/55/Dir., CEO, David L. Teichmann/General Counsel, VP - Human Resources, Corp. Sec., John Edmunds/Sr. VP, CFO, Jung-Herng Chang/Pres.

Directors: Glen M. Antle/Chmn., Acting CEO, Sylvia D. Summers/55/Dir., CEO, Raymond K. Ostby/Dir., Millard Phelps/80/Dir., Brian R. Bachman/Dir., Hans Geyer/Dir.

Owners: Jung-Herng Chang/1.40%, Chris P. Siu, Raymond K. Ostby, Adage Capital Partners, L.P./5.52%, Millard Phelps, Wellington Management Company, LLP/10.48%, David L. Teichmann, Glen M. Antle, John S. Edmunds, Insiders/2.11%

Financial Data: ***Fiscal Year End:***06/30 ***Latest Annual Data:*** 06/30/2007

Year	Sales	Net Income
2007	$270,795,000	$30,118,000
2006	$171,442,000	$26,176,000
2005	$69,011,000	-$10,534,000

Curr. Assets:	$103,513,000	***Curr. Liab.:***	$25,429,000	***P/E Ratio:***	85.48
Plant, Equip.:	$2,154,000	***Total Liab.:***	$25,429,000	***Indic. Yr. Divd.:***	NA
Total Assets:	$134,884,000	***Net Worth:***	$109,435,000	***Debt/ Equity:***	NA

Trikon Technologies Inc

Ringland Way, Newport, X0 NP18 2TA; ; ***http://*** www.trikontech.com

General - Incorporation	DE	***Stock***- Price on:12/24/2007	NA
Employees	NA	Stock Exchange	NA
Auditor	Deloitte & Touche, LLP	Ticker Symbol	NA
Stk Agt	American Stock Transfer & Trust Co.	Outstanding Shares	NA
Counsel	Wilson Sonsini Goodrich & Rosati	E.P.S	NA
DUNS No.	18-130-8008	Shareholders	NA

Business: The group's principal activities are the designing, manufacturing, marketing and servicing of a broad line of production equipment used in the manufacturing of semiconductor devices. The products are used to manufacture integrated circuits and optical components, such as semiconductor lasers and optical wave-guides. Integrated circuits are used in electronic products, such as telecommunications devices, consumer and industrial electronics and computers. The group supplies equipment for three key processes in the manufacture of semiconductor devices: chemical vapor deposition, physical vapor deposition and plasma etching. The group's has operations in North America, Europe, South Korea and Japan.

Primary SIC and add'l.: 3559

CIK No: 0000868326

Subsidiaries: E.t. Electrotech Research Limited, E.t. Equipments Limited, Trikon Equipments Limited, Trikon Holdings Ltd., Trikon Technologies (israel) Limited, Trikon Technologies B.v, Trikon Technologies Co. Ltd. (korea), Trikon Technologies Gmbh, Trikon Technologies Limited, Trikon Technologies Sarl

Officers: Benoit Lariviere/Technologist, Service Support Web Designer, Bruce Metcalf/Business Development Mgr., Claude Konikow/Dir. - Business Development, Heyvar Pinzon/Customer Service, Logistics, Stewart Spence/Business Development Mgr.

Trimble Navigation Ltd

935 Stewart Dr., Sunnyvale, CA, 94085; ***PH:*** 1-408-481-8000; ***Fax:*** 1-408-481-7781; ***http://*** www.trimble.com

General - Incorporation	CA	***Stock***- Price on:12/24/2007	$31.57
Employees	2,842	Stock Exchange	NDQ
Auditor	Ernst & Young LLP	Ticker Symbol	TRMB
Stk Agt	American Stock Transfer & Trust Co.	Outstanding Shares	119,450,000
Counsel	Wilson Sonsini Goodrich & Rosati	E.P.S	$0.95
DUNS No.	79-487-4412	Shareholders	NA

Business: The group's principal activities are to provide advance positioning product solutions to commercial and government users. It operates in five segments: engineering and construction, field solutions, mobile solutions, component technologies and portfolio technologies. Engineering and construction offers hardware and software product solutions used by survey and construction professionals. Field solutions addresses the two business areas of agriculture and geographical information system (gis). Mobile solutions provides the market for fleet management by providing a bundled solution component technologies provides components for applications that require embedded position or time based on gps technology. Portfolio technologies is an aggregation of operations and products like navigation modules and embedded sensors. The group has operations in the United States, Europe, Middle East Africa and Asia. The group acquired tracernet corporation in 2004.

Primary SIC and add'l.: 3523 7375 3674 3829 3812

CIK No: 0000864749

Subsidiaries: Advanced Public Safety, Inc., Apache Technologies Europe GmbH, Apache Technologies, Inc., Applanix Corporation, Applanix LLC, GeoNav GmbH, Jamestown Manufacturing Corporation, Mensi, Inc., Mensi, KK, Mensi, S.A., MobileTech Solutions, Inc., Pacific Crest Corporation, Spectra Precision Pty Ltd., Spectra Precision Scandinavia AB, SPHM Inc. 47 Subsidiaries included in the Index

Officers: Steven W. Berglund/Dir., CEO, Pres., Michael W. Lesyna/VP - Business Transformation, Bryn A. Fosburgh/VP, GM - Engineering, Construction Division, Ann Ciganer/VP - Strategic Policy, Bruce E. Peetz/VP - Advanced Technology, Systems, Debi Hirshlag/VP - Human Resources, Alan R. Townsend/VP, GM - Field Solutions Division, Mark Harrington/VP - Strategy, Business Development, Joseph F. Denniston/VP - Operations, Rajat Bahri/CFO, Dennis L. Workman/VP, GM - Component Technologies Division, Irwin L. Kwatek/VP, General Counsel, John B. Goodrich/Dir., Sec. - Business Consultant, Rick Beyer/Pres. - Trimble Mobile Solutions, TMS, Julie Shepard/VP - Finance, Chief Accounting Officer

Directors: Steven W. Berglund/Dir., CEO, Pres., Robert S. Cooper/Chmn., William Hart/Dir., Ulf J. Johansson/Dir., Bradford W. Parkinson/Dir., John B. Goodrich/Dir., Sec. - Business Consultant, Nickolas W. Vande Steeg/Dir.

Owners: Janus Capital Management, LLC/6.18%, PRIMECAP Management Company/7.14%, Franklin Resources, Inc./7.07%

Financial Data: Fiscal Year End:12/30   Latest Annual Data: 12/29/2006

Year	Sales		Net Income
2006	$940,150,000		$103,658,000
2005	$774,913,000		$84,855,000
2004	$668,808,000		$67,680,000
Curr. Assets:	$317,467,000	Curr. Liab.:	$128,977,000	P/E Ratio: 33.23
Plant, Equip.:	$30,991,000	Total Liab.:	$181,817,000	Indic. Yr. Divd.: NA
Total Assets:	$653,978,000	Net Worth:	$472,161,000	Debt/ Equity: 0.0006

Trimedia Entertainment Group Inc

101 Charles Dr., Bryn Mawr, PA, 19010; *PH:* 1-215-426-5536; *http://* www.trimediaent.com; *Email:* contact-us@trimediaent.com

General - Incorporation	DE	Stock - Price on:12/24/2007	$0.015
Employees	2	Stock Exchange	OTC
Auditor	Morison Cogen LLP	Ticker Symbol	TMEG
Stk Agt	StockTrans, Inc.	Outstanding Shares	47,710,000
Counsel	NA	E.P.S.	$0.008
DUNS No.	NA	Shareholders	NA

Business: The group's principle activity is to develop, produce and distribute music, motion picture and other filmed entertainment content. The group operates through its subsidiaries ruffnation music inc, metropolitan recording inc, ruffnation films llc and snipes production llc. Ruffnation films produces, distributes and markets feature-length DVD films and movies, taking projects from initial creative development through principal photography, post-production, distribution and ancillary sales. Ruffnation music operates its record division. Metropolitan recording provides support for the in-house recording of its artists.

Primary SIC and add'l.: 7812 7389

CIK No: 0001163680

Subsidiaries: FourPoint Play Productions, LLC, Metropolitan Recording Inc., Ruffnation Films LLC, Ruffnation Music, Inc., Snipes Productions, LLC, TM Film Distribution, Inc., TME Entertainment Film-und Musik-Productions and-Verwertungs-Gessellschaft m.b.H., TriMedia Film Group, Inc.

Officers: Chris Schwartz/Chmn., CEO, Ernest J. Cimadamore/Pres. - Music Group, Richard Murray/Pres. - Film, Television Group

Directors: Chris Schwartz/Chmn., CEO

Owners: Christopher Schwartz/42.63%, Richard Murray/0.48%, Insiders/43.07%

Financial Data: Fiscal Year End:10/31   Latest Annual Data: 10/31/2006

Year	Sales		Net Income
2006	$74,000		-$3,586,000
2005	$6,000		-$7,090,000
2004	$239,000		-$4,778,000
Curr. Assets:	$48,000	Curr. Liab.:	$9,178,000	P/E Ratio: 1.88
Plant, Equip.:	$16,000	Total Liab.:	$10,278,000	Indic. Yr. Divd.: NA
Total Assets:	$64,000	Net Worth:	-$10,214,000	Debt/ Equity: NA

Trimedyne Inc

15091 Bake Pkwy, Irvine, CA, 92619; *PH:* 1-949-951-3800; *http://* www.trimedyne.com; *Email:* info@trimedyne.com

General - Incorporation	NV	Stock - Price on:12/24/2007	$1.03
Employees	58	Stock Exchange	OTC
Auditor	Corbin & Co LLP	Ticker Symbol	TMED
Stk Agt	American Stock Transfer & Trust Co.	Outstanding Shares	17,590,000
Counsel	Heller, Horowitz	E.P.S.	$0.01
DUNS No.	05-700-7239	Shareholders	NA

Business: The group's principal activities are to develop, manufacture and market lasers and disposable fiber optic delivery devices. The group's operations also include the rental and service of lasers and medical equipment to hospitals and surgery centers. The products developed include holmium 'cold' pulsed lasers and disposable and reusable fiber-optic laser energy delivery devices. These products are used in orthopedics, urology, gynecology, ear, nose and throat (ent) surgery, general surgery and other medical specialties. The products are marketed primarily in the United States, Europe, Asia, Latin America and Middle East.

Primary SIC and add'l.: 7352 3842 3845

CIK No: 0000357001

Subsidiaries: Mobile Surgical Technologies, Inc

Officers: Marvin P. Loeb/Chmn., CEO, Brian T. Kenney/VP - Sales, Marketing, Glenn D. Yeik/COO, Pres., Jeffrey S. Rudner/Treasurer

Directors: Marvin P. Loeb/Chmn., CEO

Owners: Richard F. Horowitz, Donald Baker, Brian T. Kenney, Glenn D. Yeik/2.30%, Lewis Asset Management, Inc./6.30%, Bruce J. Haber/5.30%, Marvin P. Loeb/15.20%, Insiders/19.10%

Financial Data: Fiscal Year End:09/30   Latest Annual Data: 9/30/2006

Year	Sales		Net Income
2006	$6,237,000		$97,000
2005	$6,482,000		$186,000
2004	$5,973,000		$1,001,000
Curr. Assets:	$4,324,000	Curr. Liab.:	$868,000	P/E Ratio: 103.00
Plant, Equip.:	$925,000	Total Liab.:	$1,278,000	Indic. Yr. Divd.: NA
Total Assets:	$5,870,000	Net Worth:	$4,592,000	Debt/ Equity: NA

Trimeris Inc

3500 Paramount Pkwy, Morrisville, NC, 27560; *PH:* 1-919-419-6050; *http://* www.trimeris.com

General - Incorporation	DE	Stock - Price on:12/24/2007	$6.94
Employees	64	Stock Exchange	NDQ
Auditor	KPMG LLP	Ticker Symbol	TRMS
Stk Agt	EquiServe Trust Co N.A	Outstanding Shares	22,200,000
Counsel	Wilmer, Cutler & Pickering	E.P.S.	$1.05
DUNS No.	80-476-2532	Shareholders	NA

Business: The group's principle activity is to discover and develop new drugs for the treatment of viral diseases. The core technology platform is based on fusion inhibition aimed at treating disease by preventing viruses from entering host immune cells. Fuzeon is the company's first-generation HIV fusion inhibitor. It is used in combination of other anti-HIV drugs for the treatment of HIV-1 infection in treatment-experienced patients. T-1249 is the second-generation fusion inhibitor. The company is focused on the discovery and development of novel peptides with enhanced resistance profiles to target HIV strains that become resistant to other HIV fusion inhibitors. The group operates from United States.

Primary SIC and add'l.: 8731 2836

CIK No: 0000911326

Officers: Steven D. Skolsky/CEO/$3,079,235.00, Andrew L. Graham/Corp. Sec., Dir. - Finance/$201,990.00, Robert R. Bonczek/General Counsel/$819,096.00, Lawrence E. Hill/COO, Pres., Daniel Ratto/CFO, Carol-Ann Ohmstede/VP - Corporate Alliances, Project Planning

Directors: Jeffrey M. Lipton/Chmn., Dani P. Bolognesi/Dir., Felix J. Baker/Dir., Gary E. Cook/Dir., Richard J. Crout/Dir., Kevin C. Tang/Dir., Julian C. Baker/Dir., Stephen R. Davis/Dir., Barry Quart/Dir.

Owners: Carol Ohmstede, Gary E. Cook, Dani P. Bolognesi/3.54%, Andrew L. Graham, T. Rowe Price Associates, Inc./6.59%, OrbiMed Advisors/6.48%, Insiders/24.97%, Franklin Resources, Inc./5.79%, Felix J. Baker/16.25%, Jeffrey M. Lipton/1.59%, Kevin C. Tang/2.08%, Accipiter Capital Management/6.37%, Healthinvest Partners/7.39%, Barclays Global Investors/5.74%, Richard J. Crout

Financial Data: Fiscal Year End:12/31   Latest Annual Data: 12/31/2006

Year	Sales		Net Income
2006	$36,980,000		$7,384,000
2005	$19,059,000		-$8,106,000
2004	$6,708,000		-$40,088,000
Curr. Assets:	$62,480,000	Curr. Liab.:	$8,907,000	
Plant, Equip.:	$2,160,000	Total Liab.:	$37,131,000	Indic. Yr. Divd.: NA
Total Assets:	$74,903,000	Net Worth:	$37,772,000	Debt/ Equity: NA

Trimol Group Inc

1285 Ave. Of The Americas, 35th Fl., New York, NY, 10019; *PH:* 1-212-554-4394

General - Incorporation	DE	Stock - Price on:12/24/2007	$0.01
Employees	NA	Stock Exchange	OTC
Auditor	Paritz & Co P.A	Ticker Symbol	TMOL
Stk Agt	Interstate Transfer Company	Outstanding Shares	100,470,000
Counsel	NA	E.P.S.	-$0.02
DUNS No.	NA	Shareholders	NA

Business: The group's principal activity is to provide proprietary technology, equipment and consumables used to produce secure essential government identification documents through its subsidiary intercomsoft limited. The group has worldwide license to make, use and sell a mechanically rechargeable metal-air (aluminum) fuel cell solely for use with consumer portable electronic devices. The group supplies all of the equipment, technology, software and materials necessary to produce all national passports, drivers' licenses, vehicle permits, identification cards and other national documents in the republic of moldova. The group operates in a two segment i.e intercomsoft, research and development of the aluminum-air fuel cell technology plus corporate and administrative functions.

Primary SIC and add'l.: 7372 3629 3577

CIK No: 0001011733

Subsidiaries: Intercomsoft Limited

Owners: Aluminum-Power Inc., Jack Braverman, Insiders, P.L.T. International, Inc, Boris Birshtein, Walter J. Perchal

Financial Data: Fiscal Year End:12/31   Latest Annual Data: 12/31/2006

Year	Sales		Net Income
2006	$640,000		-$1,328,000
2005	$8,129,000		$455,000
2004	$4,858,000		$225,000
Curr. Assets:	$13,000	Curr. Liab.:	$1,482,000	
Plant, Equip.:	$61,000	Total Liab.:	$1,482,000	Indic. Yr. Divd.: NA
Total Assets:	$74,000	Net Worth:	-$1,408,000	Debt/ Equity: NA

Trinity 3 Corp

20261 Acacia St., Ste. 200, Newport Beach, CA, 92660; *PH:* 1-949-660-1212; *Fax:* 1-949-660-7111; *http://* www.trinitythreecorp.com; *Email:* info@trinity3corp.com

General - Incorporation	DE	**Stock**- Price on:12/24/2007	NA
Employees	NA	Stock Exchange	OTC
Auditor	Mendoza Berger & Company, LLP	Ticker Symbol	TRYT
Stk Agt	Interwest Transfer Company, Inc.	Outstanding Shares	NA
Counsel	NA	E.P.S	-$0.047
DUNS No.	NA	Shareholders	NA

Business: The groups principle activity is services healthcare and hospital organizations, orthopedic surgeon physician practices, and physical and sports therapy clinics. Products of the group include continuous passive motion equipment, and a wide variety of orthopedic soft goods, including braces and supports for arms, elbows, knees and legs. Patients use continuous Passive Motion equipment during post operative recovery and rehabilitation from knee or shoulder surgery. The group operates from the United States.

Primary SIC and add'l.: 5047

CIK No: 0001090051

Subsidiaries: Caiban Holdings, Inc., Core Management Systems, Inc, Skyline Orthopedics, Inc, Trinity3 Acceptance Corporation

Officers: Steven D. Hargreaves/CFO, Pres.

Owners: Jeffrey S. Willmann, Steven D. Hargreaves, Insiders, Shannon T. Squyres

Financial Data: *Fiscal Year End:*12/31 *Latest Annual Data:* 12/31/2005

Year	Sales	Net Income
2005	$1,152,000	-$262,000
2004	$846,000	-$190,000
2003	$20,000	-$138,000

Curr. Assets:	$535,000	**Curr. Liab.:**	$871,000		
Plant, Equip.:	$159,000	**Total Liab.:**	$1,148,000	**Indic. Yr. Divd.:**	NA
Total Assets:	$698,000	**Net Worth:**	-$450,000	**Debt/ Equity:**	NA

Trinity Bank NA TX

3500 W Vickery Blvd., Fort Worth, TX, 76107; ***PH:*** 1-817-763-9966; ***Fax:*** 1-817-569-7277; ***http://*** www.trinitybk.com; ***Email:*** customerservice@trinitybk.com

General - Incorporation		**Stock**- Price on:12/24/2007	$17.65
Employees	NA	Stock Exchange	OTC
Auditor	NA	Ticker Symbol	TYBT
Stk Agt	NA	Outstanding Shares	NA
Counsel	NA	E.P.S	NA
DUNS No.	NA	Shareholders	NA

Business: The groups principal activities include providing banking and financial services. Services of the group include checking accounts, savings accounts, certificates of deposit, installment loans, real estate mortgage loans, commercial loans, traveler's checks, safe deposit boxes, night depository and automated teller services.

Primary SIC and add'l.: 6036

CIK No:

Officers: Jeffrey M. Harp/Chmn., Pres., Dana B. Shipp/VP, Barney C. Wiley/VP, Renee Hicks/Assist. VP, Richard A. Burt/Exec. VP, Melanie C. Moncrief/Sr. VP - Cashier, Karen M. Kittle/Sr. VP, Donna J. Johnson/VP, Kris Nordyke/Assist. VP

Directors: Jeffrey M. Harp/Chmn., Pres., Jimmy Bilderback/Dir., Linda J. Jackson/Dir., Craig L. Kelly/Dir., Malcolm Street/Dir., Don Weeks/Dir.

Trinity Biotech Plc

1930 Innerbelt Business Ctr. Dr., St. Louis, MO, 63114; ***PH:*** 1-800-325-3424; ***http://*** www.trinitybiotech.com; ***Email:*** info@trinitybiotech.com

General - Incorporation	Ireland	**Stock**- Price on:12/24/2007	$11.31
Employees	826	Stock Exchange	NDQ
Auditor	KPMG	Ticker Symbol	TRIB
Stk Agt	Bank of New York	Outstanding Shares	18,970,000
Counsel	O'donnell, Sweeney	E.P.S	$0.36
DUNS No.	98-829-8840	Shareholders	NA

Business: The group's principal activities are the development, manufacture and marketing of diagnostic test kits used for the clinical laboratory and point-of-care segments of the diagnostic market. The line of test kits are mostly used to detect infectious diseases, sexually transmitted diseases, blood coagulation disorders and autoimmune diseases. The group's products are in areas of enzyme immunoassays, fluorescence assays, rapid assays, western blot, clinical chemistry and haemostasis using the brand names such as Amax, Biopool, Captia, Microtrak, Mardx, Recombigen, Bartels, Serocard, Unigold, Capillus, EZ HDL and EZ LDL. The group operates in 80 countries including Ireland, the United States and Germany.

Primary SIC and add'l.: 2835

CIK No: 0000888721

Subsidiaries: Benen Trading Limited, Biopool AB, Biopool Us Inc, Chronomed Inc., Clark Laboratories Inc, Eastcourt Limited, FHC Corporation, Fitzgerald Industries International, Inc, Mardx Diagnostics Inc, Primus Corporation, Primus International LLC, Primus International LLCH.K. Ltd., Primus Medical (Shanghai) Company Ltd., Trinity Biotech (UK Sales) Limited, Trinity Biotech GmbH 22 Subsidiaries included in the Index

Officers: Ronan O'Caoimh/Chmn., CEO, Co - Founder, Rory Nealon/Dir., CFO, Brendan Farrell/Dir., Pres., Jim Walsh/Dir., Non Exec. Dir.

Directors: Ronan O'Caoimh/Chmn., CEO, Co - Founder, Denis R. Burger/Dir., Brendan Farrell/Dir., Pres., Peter Coyne/Dir., Jim Walsh/Dir., Non Exec. Dir., Rory Nealon/Dir., CFO

Owners: Potenza Investments Inc/71.40%, Peter Coyne/0.20%, Rory Nealon/0.60%, Jim Walsh/2.50%, Insiders/11.40%, Brendan Farrell/2.30%, Ronan OCaoimh/6.00%, Denis R. Burger/0.20%

Financial Data: *Fiscal Year End:*12/31 *Latest Annual Data:* 12/31/2006

Year	Sales	Net Income
2006	$118,674,000	$3,276,000
2005	$98,721,000	$2,582,000
2004	$79,944,000	$4,048,000

Curr. Assets:	$97,376,000	**Curr. Liab.:**	$35,941,000	**P/E Ratio:**	15.26
Plant, Equip.:	$22,255,000	**Total Liab.:**	$81,869,000	**Indic. Yr. Divd.:**	NA
Total Assets:	$249,131,000	**Net Worth:**	$167,262,000	**Debt/ Equity:**	NA

Trinity Industries Inc

2525 Stemmons Fwy., Dallas, TX, 75207; ***PH:*** 1-214-634-4420; ***http://*** www.trin.net

General - Incorporation	DE	**Stock**- Price on:12/24/2007	$45.3
Employees	13,800	Stock Exchange	NYSE
Auditor	Ernst & Young LLP	Ticker Symbol	TRN
Stk Agt	Bank of New York	Outstanding Shares	80,300,000
Counsel	NA	E.P.S	$2.94
DUNS No.	00-732-4254	Shareholders	NA

Business: The groups principle activities include manufacturing and selling railcars and railcar parts, inland barges, concrete and aggregates, highway products, beams and girders used in highway construction, tank containers and structural wind towers. The group operates through five business segments namely Rail Group, Railcar Leasing and Management Services Group, Construction Products Group, Inland Barge Group and the Energy Equipment Group. The group operates from United States.

Primary SIC and add'l.: 3743 3272 3731 7359 3411 9999 3544

CIK No: 0000099780

Subsidiaries: Administradora Especializada, S. de R.L. de C.V, Apromat, S.A. Arad, Asistencia Profesional Corporativa, S.de R.L. de C.V, Astra Vagoane Arad, S.A, DIFCO, Inc, Grupo Tatsa, S. de R.L. de C.V, Icpv, S.a. Arad, International Industrial Indemnity Company, McConway & Torley Anniston, Inc, McConway & Torley Corporation, OFE, S. de R.L. de C.V, Rail Project, s r.o, Reunion General Agency, Inc, Servicios Corporativos Tatsa, S. de R.L. de C.V, Standard Forged Products, Inc 77 Subsidiaries included in the Index

Officers: Timothy R. Wallace/54/Chmn., CEO, Pres./$7,068,879.00, Andrea F. Cowan/45/VP - Human Resources, Shared Services, William A. McWhirter/43/CFO, Sr. VP/$1,741,919.00, Mark W. Stiles/59/Sr. VP, Group Pres./$2,315,266.00, Theis S. Rice/57/VP, Chief Legal Officer, Charles Michel/54/VP, Controller, Chief Accounting Officer, John M. Lee/47/VP - Business Development, Michael G. Fortado/64/VP, Corp. Sec., Stephen D. Menzies/52/Sr. VP, Group Pres./$2,136,490.00, Martin Graham/60/Pres. - Trinity North American Freight Car, Inc/$1,780,939.00, Don Collum/59/VP, Chief Audit Exec., Virginia C. Gray/48/VP - Organizational Development, James E. Perry/36/VP, Treasurer

Directors: Timothy R. Wallace/54/Chmn., CEO, Pres., Ron W. Haddock/Dir., Rhys J. Best/Dir., David W. Biegler/Dir., Clifford J. Grum/Dir., Diana S. Natalicio/Dir., Ronald J. Gafford/Dir., Jess T. Hay/Dir., John L. Adams/Dir., Adrian Lajous/Dir.

Owners: Jess T. Hay, Lord, Abbett& Co. LLC/5.90%, Rhys J. Best, David W. Biegler, First Pacific Advisors, LLC/6.60%, William A. McWhirter, Mark W. Stiles, Franklin Resources, Inc./6.70%, Martin Graham, Jeffrey L. Gendell/12.60%, Stephen D. Menzies, Ronald W. Haddock, John L. Adams, Clifford J. Grum, Insiders/3.60% *(19 Owners included in Index)*

Financial Data: *Fiscal Year End:*12/31 *Latest Annual Data:* 12/31/2006

Year	Sales	Net Income
2006	$3,218,900,000	$230,100,000
2005	$2,902,000,000	$86,300,000
2004	$2,198,100,000	-$9,300,000

Curr. Assets:	$1,092,900,000	**Curr. Liab.:**	$655,800,000	**P/E Ratio:**	15.41
Plant, Equip.:	$1,601,100,000	**Total Liab.:**	$2,022,100,000	**Indic. Yr. Divd.:**	$0.240
Total Assets:	$3,425,600,000	**Net Worth:**	$1,403,500,000	**Debt/ Equity:**	0.8553

Trinsic Inc

Formerly: Z-Tel Technologies Inc
601 S Harbour Island Blvd., Ste. 220, Tampa, FL, 33602; ***PH:*** 1-813-273-6261; ***http://*** www.trinsic.com

General - Incorporation	DE	**Stock**- Price on:12/24/2007	NA
Employees	426	Stock Exchange	OTC
Auditor	PricewaterhouseCoopers LLP	Ticker Symbol	TRINQ
Stk Agt	American Stock Transfer & Trust Co.	Outstanding Shares	NA
Counsel	NA	E.P.S	-$0.83
DUNS No.	NA	Shareholders	NA

Business: The group's principal activity is to provide advanced integrated local and long distance telephone services in combination with Internet based enhanced communication features. Its activities are carried out through two divisions: retails and wholesale services. Retail services are residential and business bundle service lines of business. The services are z-linebusiness(TM) and z-linehome and touch 1 long distance. Z-linehome is a local residential telephone service bundled with long distance telephone service, calling card services, caller identification, call forwarding, three way calling, call waiting and speed calling. Z-linebusiness is a complement service to z-linehome targeted to small businesses typically having four lines or fewer. Touch 1 long distance is a residential long distance call. Wholesale services provide to other companies giving them the ability to offer telephone exchange and enhanced services to their own residential and business customers.

Primary SIC and add'l.: 4813

CIK No: 0001096509

Subsidiaries: DirectCONNECT, Inc., DirecTEL, Inc., Touch 1 Communications, Inc., Trinsic Communications of Virginia, Inc., Trinsic Communications, Inc., Z-Tel Business Networks, Inc., Z-Tel Consumer Services, LLC, Z-Tel Holdings, Inc., Z-Tel Investments, Inc., Z-Tel Network Services, Inc., Z-Tel, Inc.

Officers: Chandra Kidd/Customer Migration Contact - Second Level, Karen Jay/Customer Migration Contact - Second Level

Owners: Lawrence C. Tucker, Paul T. Kohler, Horace J. Davis, Insiders, Andrew W. Krusen, Roy Neel, Richard F. LaRoche, Raymond L. Golden, Brown Brothers Harriman & Co., Michael Slauson, Donald C. Davis, Andrew C. Cowen

Financial Data: *Fiscal Year End:*12/31 *Latest Annual Data:* 12/31/2005

Year	Sales	Net Income
2005	$189,205,000	-$14,427,000
2004	$251,477,000	-$33,613,000
2003	$289,180,000	-$16,127,000

Curr. Assets:	$18,505,000	**Curr. Liab.:**	$48,679,000		
Plant, Equip.:	$19,931,000	**Total Liab.:**	$49,704,000	**Indic. Yr. Divd.:**	NA
Total Assets:	$41,320,000	**Net Worth:**	-$8,384,000	**Debt/ Equity:**	NA

Trintech Group Plc

15851 Dallas Pkwy., Ste. 855, Addison, TX, 75001; ***PH:*** 1-972-701-9802; ***Fax:*** 1-972-701-9337; ***http://*** www.trintech.com; ***Email:*** info@trintech.com

General - Incorporation	Ireland
Employees	306
Auditor	Ernst & Young LLP
Stk Agt	Bank of New York
Counsel	Wilson Sonsini Goodrich & Rosati
DUNS No.	NA

Stock - Price on:12/24/2007	$4.31
Stock Exchange	NDQ
Ticker Symbol	TTPA
Outstanding Shares	15,580,000
E.P.S.	-$0.21
Shareholders	NA

Business: The group's principal activity is the provision of secure payment infrastructure and transaction management solutions globally. The group operates in two market segments. Electronic point-of-sale systems that securely process card-payment transactions in a physical point-of-sale environment and e-payment software products that enable the secure processing, accounting and reconciliation and settlement of on-line car-payment transactions over private and public networks, including Internet. The group also provides related development and professional services, including project management, implementation and training services. The group's customers include banks, card associations, financial transaction processors and merchants in major markets including United States of America, United Kingdom, Europe and South America.

Primary SIC and add'l.: 7379 7372

CIK No: 0001094316

Subsidiaries: Actipay Limited, CW & Associates, Inc, Exceptis Technologies Limited, Trintech GmbH, Trintech Group Finance Limited, Trintech Inc, Trintech Limited (Ireland), Trintech Limited (United Kingdom), Trintech S.A, Trintech Technologies Limited

Officers: Cyril P. McGuire/Chmn., CEO, Paul Byrne/Dir., Pres., John M. Harte/GM, Exec. VP, Donna Martinez/Mgr. - Marketing Communications, Media, David Colf/VP, General Counsel, Joseph Seery/VP - Finance, Ed Gallo/Sr. VP - Healthcare Group, Kevin Connelly/Sr. VP - Financial Services Group, Bob Pritchard/VP - Commercial Group, Tony Bethell/VP - EMEA

Directors: Cyril P. McGuire/Chmn., CEO, Paul Byrne/Dir., Pres., Kevin C. Shea/Non Exec. Dir., Trevor D. Sullivan/Non Exec. Dir., Jim Mountjoy/Non Exec. Dir., Robert M. Wadsworth/Non Exec. Dir.

Owners: Instove Limited/10.30%, Edward Gallo, Robert M. Wadsworth, Trevor D. Sullivan, Insiders/26.90%, Paul Byrne/2.80%, Cyril P. McGuire/20.90%, John Harte/1.00%, Kevin C. Shea/1.00%, David A. Colf, Jim Mountjoy, Joseph Seery

Financial Data: Fiscal Year End:01/31 Latest Annual Data: 1/31/2007

Year	Sales	Net Income
2007	$25,797,000	-$2,167,000
2006	$48,625,000	-$1,541,000
2005	$42,856,000	-$44,819,000

Curr. Assets:	$34,340,000	Curr. Liab.:	$14,776,000	P/E Ratio:	15.26
Plant, Equip.:	$1,567,000	Total Liab.:	$17,290,000	Indic. Yr. Divd.:	NA
Total Assets:	$58,168,000	Net Worth:	$40,878,000	Debt/ Equity:	NA

Trio Tech International

14731 Califa St., Van Nuys, CA, 91411; **PH:** 1-818-787-7000; *http://* www.triotech.com; **Email:** info@berkmanassociates.com

General - Incorporation	CA
Employees	605
Auditor	BDO Raffles
Stk Agt	American Stock Transfer & Trust Co.
Counsel	NA
DUNS No.	04-440-4077

Stock - Price on:12/24/2007	$20.8
Stock Exchange	AMEX
Ticker Symbol	TRT
Outstanding Shares	3,230,000
E.P.S.	$1.02
Shareholders	NA

Business: The group's principal activities are to design, manufacture and market equipment for the manufacturing and testing of semiconductor wafers, devices and other electronic components. The group operates in three business segments namely: manufacturing, testing services and distribution. The manufacturing segment tests the structural integrity of integrated circuits and other products. The testing services segment tests the semiconductor devices and other electronic components to meet the requirements of military, aerospace, industrial and commercial applications. The distribution segment distributes the various products from other manufacturers in Singapore and southeast Asia. The operating facilities are in the United States, Europe and southeast Asia.

Primary SIC and add'l.: 5084 8734 9999 3559

CIK No: 0000732026

Subsidiaries: European Electronic Test Center. Ltd., Express Test Corporation, KTS Incorporated, dba Universal Systems, Prestal Enterprise Sdn. Bhd., Trio-Tech (Shanghai) Co. Ltd., Trio-Tech (Suzhou) Co. Ltd., Trio-Tech Bangkok, Trio-Tech International Pte. Ltd., Trio-Tech Kuala Lumpur, Trio-Tech Malaysia, Trio-Tech Reliability Services, Trio-Tech Thailand, Universal (Far East) Pte. Ltd.

Officers: S. W. Yong/CEO, Pres., Victor Ting/CFO, VP, Richard Lim/VP

Directors: Charles A. Wilson/Chmn.

Owners: Victor H.M. Ting/1.75%, Richard M. Horowitz/5.64%, S.W. Yong/10.20%, Daniel Zeff/6.85%, Charles A. Wilson/6.53%, Insiders/24.12%

Financial Data: Fiscal Year End:06/30 Latest Annual Data: 6/30/2006

Year	Sales	Net Income
2006	$29,099,000	$9,056,000
2005	$25,694,000	$221,000
2004	$19,154,000	$220,000

Curr. Assets:	$21,831,000	Curr. Liab.:	$8,536,000	P/E Ratio:	20.19
Plant, Equip.:	$7,073,000	Total Liab.:	$11,992,000	Indic. Yr. Divd.:	NA
Total Assets:	$29,384,000	Net Worth:	$17,392,000	Debt/ Equity:	NA

Tripath Technologies Inc

2560 Orchard Pkwy., San Jose, CA, 95131; **PH:** 1-408-750-3000; **Fax:** 1-408-750-3001; *http://* www.tripath.com; **Email:** info@tripath.com

General - Incorporation	DE
Employees	NA
Auditor	Stonefield Josephson, Inc.
Stk Agt	Mellon Investor Services LLC
Counsel	Wilson Sonsini Goodrich & Rosati
DUNS No.	NA

Stock - Price on:12/24/2007	NA
Stock Exchange	OTC
Ticker Symbol	TRPH
Outstanding Shares	NA
E.P.S.	-$0.208
Shareholders	NA

Business: The groups principle activities include designing and selling digital amplifiers based on proprietary digital power processing technology. The group currently supplies amplifiers for audio electronics applications, as well as amplifiers for DSL applications. The group operates from the United States, Japan, Singapore, Taiwan, China and Korea.

Primary SIC and add'l.: 3674

CIK No: 0001045739

Subsidiaries: Tripath Technology Japan Ltd.

Owners: Gryphon Master Fund, L.P./10.70%, George Fang, Y. S. Fu, Insiders/21.92%, A. K. Acharya, Jeffrey L. Garon, GSSF Master Fund, L.P./5.59%, Gamma Opportunity Capital Partners, LP/5.59%, Andy Jasuja, Bushido Capital Master Fund, LP/10.70%, Adya S. Tripathi/20.11%, Akifumi Goto, Naresh Sharma

Financial Data: Fiscal Year End:09/30 Latest Annual Data: 9/30/2005

Year	Sales	Net Income
2005	$10,761,000	-$9,972,000
2004	$9,421,000	-$11,572,000
2003	$13,891,000	-$7,215,000

Curr. Assets:	$8,857,000	Curr. Liab.:	$8,505,000		
Plant, Equip.:	$875,000	Total Liab.:	$8,693,000	Indic. Yr. Divd.:	NA
Total Assets:	$9,854,000	Net Worth:	$1,161,000	Debt/ Equity:	NA

Tripos Inc

1699 S Hanley Rd. , St. Louis, MO, 63144; **PH:** 1-800-323-2960; *http://* www.tripos.com

General - Incorporation	UT
Employees	327
Auditor	BDO Seidman LLP
Stk Agt	Mellon Investor Services LLC
Counsel	Blackwell Sanders Peper Martin LLP
DUNS No.	09-966-6216

Stock - Price on:12/24/2007	$0.59
Stock Exchange	NA
Ticker Symbol	NA
Outstanding Shares	10,390,000
E.P.S.	$1.03
Shareholders	NA

Business: The group's principal activities are to deliver chemistry products and services to pharmaceutical, agrochemical and biotechnology industries. The group provides integrated discovery software products, software consulting services and research services. The products are used in the pre-clinical phases of new pharmaceutical development, pre-approval phase of agrochemical product and product discovery phase of chemical research. The pharmaceutical clients include aventis, bayer, bristol-myers squibb, pfizer, and schering ag. The biotechnology clients include biovitrum, chronogen, and critical therapeutics. The group has operations in the United States, Europe, Germany, France and Pacific Rim.

Primary SIC and add'l.: 7371 7372 7379 5045

CIK No: 0000920691

Subsidiaries: Optive Research, Inc., Tripos Discovery Inc., Tripos Discovery Research Ltd., Tripos GmbH, Tripos Realty, LLC, Tripos SARL, Tripos UK Holdings Ltd., Tripos UK Ltd.

Officers: John P. McAlister/Dir., CEO, Pres., Jim Hopkins/Dir., CEO - Tripos Discovery Informat, Mark C. Allen/58/Sr. VP - Discovery Research, John D. Yingling/VP, Chief Accounting Officer, James B. Rubin/Sr. VP - Finance, CFO, Robert D. Clark/VP - Research, Philip Small/VP - High Throughput Chemistry - Tripos Receptor Research, David E. Patterson/Sr. Management, Richard D. Cramer/Sr. VP - Science, Chief Scientific Officer, Gregory B. Smith/CTO, Dieter Schmidt-Base/Sr. VP - Worldwide Sales, Mary P. Woodward/Sr. VP - Strategic Development, Bryan S. Koontz/Sr. VP, GM - Discovery Informatics

Directors: John P. McAlister/Dir., CEO, Pres., Jim Hopkins/Dir., CEO - Tripos Discovery Informat, Ralph S. Lobdell/Chmn., Gary Meredith/Dir., Amish Mehta/Dir., Stewart Carrell/Dir., Alfred Alberts/Dir., Ferid Murad/Dir.

Owners: Huntleigh Advisors, Inc/5.10%, Ralph S. Lobdell/2.20%, Stewart Carrell/1.90%, Alfred Alberts, Midwood Capital Management, LLC/100.00%, Mark C. Allen, Insiders/18.79%, Ferid Murad/1.50%, Gary Meredith, Bryan S. Koontz/2.00%, Dieter Schmidt-Bse, John D. Yingling, John P. McAlister/3.20%, James B. Rubin/1.90%

Financial Data: Fiscal Year End:12/31 Latest Annual Data: 12/31/2006

Year	Sales	Net Income
2006	$27,384,000	-$38,593,000
2005	$55,421,000	-$4,288,000
2004	$64,779,000	$232,000

Curr. Assets:	$18,288,000	Curr. Liab.:	$36,621,000	P/E Ratio:	0.57
Plant, Equip.:	$5,084,000	Total Liab.:	$38,788,000	Indic. Yr. Divd.:	NA
Total Assets:	$33,674,000	Net Worth:	-$9,046,000	Debt/ Equity:	NA

Triquint Semiconductor Inc

2300 NE Brookwood Pkwy, Hillsboro, OR, 97124; **PH:** 1-503-615-9000; *http://* www.tqs.com; **Email:** info-general@tqs.com

General - Incorporation	DE
Employees	1,780
Auditor	KPMG LLP
Stk Agt	Chase Mellon Shareholder Services LLC
Counsel	Wilson Sonsini Goodrich & Rosati
DUNS No.	04-544-4635

Stock - Price on:12/24/2007	$5.145
Stock Exchange	NDQ
Ticker Symbol	TQNT
Outstanding Shares	139,120,000
E.P.S.	$0.109
Shareholders	NA

Business: The group's principal activities are to design, develop, manufacture and market a broad range of components and modules for communications applications. The group's products are incorporated into a variety of communication products, including wireless phones and pagers, base stations for wireless communications, digital microwave communications systems, fiber optic telecommunications equipment, satellite communications systems, data networking products, broadband access systems and aerospace applications. The group acquired the products, technology and some facilities of agere systems inc on 02-Jan-2003.

Primary SIC and add'l.: 3663 4813 3674 3661

CIK No: 0000913885

Subsidiaries: Sawtek Far East, Inc., Sawtek S.R.L., Sawtek Sweden AB, Sawtek, Inc., TFR Technologies, Inc., TriQuint (Shanghai) Trading Company, Ltd., TriQuint Hungary Holding Kft., TriQuint International Holding Co., TriQuint Japan TYK, TriQuint Sales and Design, Inc., TriQuint Semiconductor GmbH, TriQuint Semiconductor Korea, Ltd., TriQuint Semiconductor Texas, LP, TriQuint Technology Holding Co., TriQuint Texas General Holding Company 16 Subsidiaries included in the Index

Officers: Ralph G. Quinsey/Dir., CEO, Pres./$1,188,809.00, Michael J. Sanna/VP - Networks, Azhar Waseem/VP - Florida Operations, Stephanie Welty/52/VP - Finance, Administration, Sec./$443,030.00, Todd Debonis/VP - Worldwide Sales, Customer Service/$728,052.00, Glen A. Riley/VP - Commercial Foundry, Supply Chain Management/$542,885.00, Thomas Cordner/VP - Military, Texas Operations, Brian P. Balut/VP - Networks, Bruce R. Fournier/VP - Business Development, David Pye/VP - Oregon Operations/$458,568.00, Timothy A. Dunn/46/VP - Handsets, Steve Buhaly/CFO, Debbie Burke/VP - Human Resources, Tim Dunn/VP - Handsets

Directors: Ralph G. Quinsey/Dir., CEO, Pres., Steven J. Sharp/Chmn., Willis C. Young/Dir., Charles Scott Gibson/Dir., Walden C. Rhines/Dir., Paul A. Gary/Dir., Nicolas Kauser/Dir.

Owners: Glen Riley, Nicolas Kauser, Paul A. Gary, Ralph G. Quinsey, Mazama Capital Management/5.70%, Dimensional Fund Advisors Inc/7.40%, Todd A. DeBonis, Charles Scott Gibson, Insiders, Stephanie Welty, Barclays Global Investors UK Holdings Ltd/6.40%, David J. Pye, Walden C. Rhines, Willis C. Young, Steven J. Sharp

Financial Data: **Fiscal Year End:** 12/31 **Latest Annual Data:** 12/31/2006

Year	Sales	Net Income
2006	$401,793,000	$21,751,000
2005	$294,787,000	$3,980,000
2004	$347,005,000	-$29,054,000

Curr. Assets:	$537,777,000	**Curr. Liab.:**	$282,227,000	**P/E Ratio:**	34.30
Plant, Equip.:	$200,346,000	**Total Liab.:**	$286,968,000	**Indic. Yr. Divd.:**	NA
Total Assets:	$754,415,000	**Net Worth:**	$467,447,000	**Debt/ Equity:**	NA

TriStone Community Bank

401 Knollwood St., Winston-salem, NC, 27103; ***PH:*** 1-336-794-0811; ***Fax:*** 1-336-794-0815; ***http://*** www.tristonebank.com; ***Email:*** customercare@tristonebank.com

General - Incorporation		**Stock**- Price on:12/24/2007	$11.75
Employees	NA	Stock Exchange	OTC
Auditor	NA	Ticker Symbol	TCMB
Stk Agt	NA	Outstanding Shares	1,500,000
Counsel	NA	E.P.S.	NA
DUNS No.	NA	Shareholders	NA

Business: The groups principal activities include providing community banking and financial services. Services of the group include checking accounts, savings accounts, certificates of deposit, installment loans, real estate mortgage loans, commercial loans, traveler's checks, safe deposit boxes, night depository and automated teller services. The group operates from the United States.

Primary SIC and add'l.: 6022

CIK No:

Officers: Simpson O. Brown/Dir., CEO, Pres., Mark R. Evans/Exec. VP, Chief Lending Officer, Rosemary Howell/VP - Mortgage Services, Donald E. Brown/Certified Sr. Advisor, VP - Financial Services

Directors: Simpson O. Brown/Dir., CEO, Pres., Gordon H.T. Sheeran/Chmn., Ched Neal/Dir., Debi Tornow/Dir., Ron Wellman/Dir., Sandra Boyette/Dir., Gerald Chrisco/Dir., Vernon Foster/Dir., Scott Gerding/Dir., Robert Helms/Dir., Ronald Joyce/Dir., David Meyer/Dir.

Triton Distribution Systems Inc

Formerly: Petramerica Oil Inc
One Harbor Dr., Ste. 300, Sausalito, CA, 94965; ***PH:*** 1-415-339-4600

General - Incorporation	CO	**Stock**- Price on:12/24/2007	$1.7
Employees	45	Stock Exchange	OTC
Auditor	Moore Stephens Wurth F & T LLP	Ticker Symbol	TTDS
Stk Agt	Computershare Trust Co	Outstanding Shares	45,560,000
Counsel	NA	E.P.S.	-$0.17
DUNS No.	NA	Shareholders	NA

Business: The group activities are providing oil and gas activities. The group operates in the Rocky Mountain region of the United States. The group has been primarily involved in raising capital and has not conducted any significant operations. The group intends to evaluate, structure and complete a merger with, or acquire one or a small number of private companies, for forming partnerships or sole proprietorships. The group may seek to acquire a controlling interest in one or more private companies in contemplation of later completing an acquisition.

Primary SIC and add'l.: 1382

CIK No: 0001309541

Subsidiaries: Federal Investment Company Act

Officers: Michael W. Overby/50/CFO

Directors: Khaled El-Marsafy/38/Dir.

Owners: Khaled El-Marsafy/8.30%, Michael L. Underwood/5.00%, West Hampton Special Situations Fund, LLC/9.80%, Insiders/29.00%, Al-Deera Holding Co KSCC/7.70%, The Elevation Fund, LLC/9.80%, Gregory Lykiardopoulos/28.40%

Financial Data: **Fiscal Year End:** 12/31 **Latest Annual Data:** 12/31/2006

Year	Sales	Net Income
2006	NA	-$6,552,000
2005	NA	-$22,000

Curr. Assets:	$2,790,000	**Curr. Liab.:**	$277,000		
Plant, Equip.:	$351,000	**Total Liab.:**	$277,000	**Indic. Yr. Divd.:**	NA
Total Assets:	$3,369,000	**Net Worth:**	$3,092,000	**Debt/ Equity:**	NA

Triumph Group Inc

1550 Liberty Ridge Dr., Ste. 100, Wayne, PA, 19087; ***PH:*** 1-610-975-0420; ***http://*** www.triumphgroup.com; ***Email:*** support@triumphgroup.com

General - Incorporation	DE	**Stock**- Price on:12/24/2007	$67.42
Employees	4,152	Stock Exchange	NYSE
Auditor	Ernst & Young LLP	Ticker Symbol	TGI
Stk Agt	National City Bank	Outstanding Shares	16,640,000
Counsel	NA	E.P.S.	$3.30
DUNS No.	80-763-6451	Shareholders	NA

Business: The group's principal activities are to design, engineer, manufacture, repair, overhaul and distribute aircraft components. The components include mechanical and electromechanical control systems, aircraft and engine accessories, auxiliary power units, avionics and aircraft instruments. The group serves the aerospace industry, including commercial and regional airlines and air cargo carriers, as well as original equipment manufacturers of commercial, regional, business and military aircraft and components. The group also produces and distributes blanked and slitted cold-rolled steel, which can be electrogalvanized or coated. On may-2003, the group acquired all the assets of parker hannifin's united aircraft products division and on 19-Jan-2004, rolls-royce gear systems inc.

Primary SIC and add'l.: 3724 1791

CIK No: 0001021162

Subsidiaries: CBA Acquisition LLC, CBA Marine SAS, Construction Brevetees dAlfortville SAS, HT Parts LLC, Kilroy Steel, Inc., Kilroy Structural Steel Co., Lamar Electro-Air Corp., MGP Holding SAS, Nu-Tech Brands, Inc., The Triumph Group Operations Holdings, Inc., The Triumph Group Operations, Inc., Triumph Actuation Systems Connecticut, LLC, Triumph Actuation Systems Valencia, Inc., Triumph Actuation Systems, LLC, Triumph Aerospace Systems Wichita, Inc. 47 Subsidiaries included in the Index

Officers: Richard C. /Dir., Pres., CEO - Triumph Group, Inc/$2,086,883.00, Jeffry D. Frisby/Group Pres. - Triumph Aerospace Systems Group, John R. Bartholdson/Dir., Sr. VP, Treasurer/$1,363,964.00, Kevin E. Kindig/VP, Controller - Triumph Group, Inc/$367,662.00, John B. Wright/VP, General Counsel, Sec. - Triumph Group, Inc/$460,162.00, Larry J. Resnick/Sr. VP - Operations, Sheila Gin Spagnolo/VP, John M. Brasch/Group Pres. - Triumph Aftermarket Services Group, Lawrence J. Resnick/Sr. VP - Operations, Triumph Group, Inc/$823,360.00, David M. Kornblatt/CFO, Sr. VP, Treasurer, William Bauer/Dir. - Risk Management, Employee Benefits

Directors: Richard C. /Dir., Pres., CEO - Triumph Group, Inc, John R. Bartholdson/Dir., Sr. VP, Treasurer, George Simpson/Dir., William O. Albertini/Dir., Richard C. Gozon/Dir., Claude F. Kronk/Dir., Terry D. Stinson/Dir.

Owners: Private Capital Management, L.L.P./8.10%, George Simpson, Terry D. Stinson, Richard C. Ill/1.90%, John R. Bartholdson, William O. Albertini, Claude F. Kronk, Dimensional Fund Advisors Inc./8.20%, Insiders/4.60%, Richard C. Gozon, John B. Wright, Wellington Management Company, LLP/13.80%, Lawrence J. Resnick, FMR Corporation/7.90%, Kevin E. Kindig

Financial Data: **Fiscal Year End:** 03/31 **Latest Annual Data:** 3/31/2007

Year	Sales	Net Income
2007	$954,735,000	$47,071,000
2006	$760,421,000	$34,515,000
2005	$688,485,000	$11,428,000

Curr. Assets:	$507,569,000	**Curr. Liab.:**	$188,542,000		
Plant, Equip.:	$294,479,000	**Total Liab.:**	$601,795,000	**Indic. Yr. Divd.:**	$0.160
Total Assets:	$1,229,158,000	**Net Worth:**	$627,363,000	**Debt/ Equity:**	0.4948

Trizec Canada Inc

181 Bay St. Ste. 3820, Bce Pl., Toronto, ON, M5J 2T3; ***PH:*** 1-416-682-8600; ***http://*** www.trizeccanada.com

General - Incorporation	Canada	**Stock**- Price on:12/24/2007	NA
Employees	NA	Stock Exchange	NA
Auditor	PricewaterhouseCoopers LLP	Ticker Symbol	NA
Stk Agt	Mellon Trust Co	Outstanding Shares	NA
Counsel	NA	E.P.S.	NA
DUNS No.	NA	Shareholders	NA

Business: The group's principal activity is to provide real estate services. The company is primarily engaged in the U.S. real estate business through its 38% interest in Trizec Properties, Inc., a publicly-traded U.S. Real Estate Investment Trust.The company is a mutual fund corporation, which provides Canadian investors the opportunity to invest indirectly in Trizec Properties.The company has ownership interests in and manages a high-quality portfolio of 50 office properties totaling approximately 37 million square feet concentrated in the metropolitan areas of seven major U.S. cities.

Primary SIC and add'l.: 6500

CIK No: 0001172367

Subsidiaries: Emerald Blue Kft, Trizec Hahn Corporation, Trizec Properties, Inc, TrizecHahn Holdings (Cyprus) Limited

Trizetto Group Inc

567 San Nicolas Dr., Ste. 360, Newport Beach, CA, 92660; ***PH:*** 1-949-719-2200; ***Fax:*** 1-949-219-2197; ***http://*** www.trizetto.com; ***Email:*** salesinfo@trizetto.com

General - Incorporation	DE	**Stock**- Price on:12/24/2007	$19.51
Employees	1,600	Stock Exchange	NDQ
Auditor	Ernst & Young LLP	Ticker Symbol	TZIX
Stk Agt	U.S. Stock Transfer Corp	Outstanding Shares	45,250,000
Counsel	Stradling Yocca Carlson & Rauth	E.P.S.	$0.31
DUNS No.	NA	Shareholders	NA

Business: The group's principal activity is to offer healthcare information technology products and services that can be provided individually or combined to create a comprehensive solution. It provides remotely hosted software applications, third-party packaged, proprietary software and related services. It also develops and supports software products for the healthcare industry. It also offers proprietary enterprise software and outsourced business services which includes software hosting, business process outsourcing, it outsourcing and consulting services. The group provides its products and services to health plans, benefits administrators and physician groups. The group serves 433 customers approximately as of 31-Dec-2003. It markets its software and services to customers primarily in the United States. During 2003, the group discontinued its outsourcing services to certain non-facets(r)payer customers. On 26-Apr-2004, the group acquired diogenes inc.

Primary SIC and add'l.: 7372 7375

CIK No: 0001092458

Subsidiaries: CareKey, Inc., Creative Business Solutions, Inc., Digital Insurance Systems Corporation, Diogenes, Inc., Finserv Health Care Systems, Inc., Health Networks of America, Inc., Healthcare Media Enterprises, Inc., HealthWeb, Inc., Infotrust Company, Margolis Health Enterprises, Inc., Novalis Corporation, Novalis Development & Licensing Corporation, Novalis Development Corporation, Novalis Services Corporation, Options Services Group, Inc. 17 Subsidiaries included in the Index

Officers: Jeff Margolis/Chmn., CEO/$2,092,160.00, Patricia Gorman/CIO, Quality Officer - Corporate Information Services, Philip Tamminga/Exec. VP - Development, Support/$793,438.00, Kathleen Earley/COO, Pres./$1,367,867.00, Tony Bellomo/Exec. VP - Product Management, Jim Sullivan/Sr. VP, General Counsel, Sec., Alan Ross/Sr. VP - Human Capital Management, Mark M. Tomaino/47/Sr. VP - Corporate Development, Bob Barbieri/CFO, Joseph Manheim/Sr. VP - Benefits Administration, Dan Spirek/Sr. VP - Integrated Health Solutions, John G. Jordan/56/Sr. VP - Payer Sales

Directors: Jeff Margolis/Chmn., CEO, Jerry P. Widman/Dir., Thomas B. Johnson/Dir., Paul F. Lefort/Dir., Donald J. Lothrop/Dir., William L. Krause/Dir., Nancy H. Handel/Dir.

Owners: Paul F. LeFort, Anthony Bellomo, Gilder, Gagnon, Howe& Co. LLC/5.84%, Thomas B. Johnson, James C. Malone, Donald J. Lothrop, Kathleen Earley, Philip J. Tamminga, Lois A. Evans, William L. Krause, Jerry P. Widman, AXA Financial, Inc./5.38%, Insiders/9.23%, Wellington Management Company, LLP/11.64%, Jeffrey H. Margolis/4.74%

Financial Data: **Fiscal Year End:** 12/31 **Latest Annual Data:** 12/31/2006

Year	Sales	Net Income
2006	$347,937,000	$15,115,000
2005	$292,219,000	$22,021,000
2004	$274,565,000	$8,458,000

Curr. Assets:	$197,879,000	Curr. Liab.:	$111,770,000	P/E Ratio:	81.29
Plant, Equip.:	$26,777,000	Total Liab.:	$248,693,000	Indic. Yr. Divd.:	NA
Total Assets:	$382,600,000	Net Worth:	$133,907,000	Debt/ Equity:	1.1621

TRM Corp

5208 NE 122nd Ave., Portland, OR, 97230; *PH:* 1-503-257-8766; *http://* www.trm.com; *Email:* info@trm.com

General		Stock	
Incorporation	OR	Price on:12/24/2007	$1.42
Employees	364	Stock Exchange	NDQ
Auditor	PricewaterhouseCoopers LLP	Ticker Symbol	TRMM
Stk Agt	Registrar & Transfer Co	Outstanding Shares	17,140,000
Counsel	Stoel Rives LLP	E.P.S	NA
DUNS No.	04-494-3355	Shareholders	NA

Business: The group's principal activity is to provide convenience services to consumers in retail environments. Convenience services include: self-service cash delivery and account balance inquiry, delivered through automatic teller machines and photocopy services delivered through photocopy centers. The group operates in three segments. Photocopy, ATMs and software development. Photocopy owns and maintains self-service photocopiers in retail establishments. Atm owns and operates ATM machines in retail establishments. The software development business develops software to deliver products and services through ATMs. On 02-Apr-2004, the group acquired inkas financial corp ltd.

Primary SIC and add'l.: 7334 5044 7371

CIK No: 0000749254

Subsidiaries: Access Cash International LLC, FPC France Ltd., Inkas Financial Corp. Ltd., S-3 Corporation, Strategic Software Solutions Limited, TRM (ATM)Limited, TRM (Canada) Corporation, TRM ATM Corporation, TRM Copy Centers (USA)Corporation, TRM Copy Centres (U.K.) Limited, TRM Services Limited

Officers: Jeffrey F. Brotman/44/Chmn., CEO, Pres./$924,251.00, Richard Stern/COO/$96,277.00, Jon S. Pitcher/58/Principal Accounting Officer, John S. White/Dir., Certified Public Accountant, Michael J. Dolan/CFO

Directors: Jeffrey F. Brotman/44/Chmn., CEO, Pres., Alan D. Schreiber/Dir., Harmon S. Spolan/Dir., Nancy Alperin/Dir., Tony C. Banks/Dir., Edward E. Cohen/Dir., John S. White/Dir., Certified Public Accountant

Owners: Danial J. Tierney, Alan D. Schreiber, Kenneth L. Tepper/2.00%, GSO Funds/9.90%, Stark Master Fund/5.00%, Richard B. Stern, Jeffrey F. Brotman/1.20%, Peninsula Capital Management, LP/9.90%, Harmon S. Spolan, Nancy Alperin, Daniel E. OBrien, Lance Laifer/6.50%, Edward E. Cohen/6.40%, Ashley S. Dean, Insiders/8.30%

Financial Data: *Fiscal Year End:*12/31 *Latest Annual Data:* 12/31/2006

Year	Sales	Net Income
2006	$45,485,000	-$120,091,000
2005	$124,682,000	-$8,871,000
2004	$92,642,000	$7,928,000

Curr. Assets:	$196,632,000	Curr. Liab.:	$199,251,000		
Plant, Equip.:	$11,646,000	Total Liab.:	$200,751,000	Indic. Yr. Divd.:	NA
Total Assets:	$226,444,000	Net Worth:	$25,693,000	Debt/ Equity:	NA

Tronox Inc

One Leadership Sq., Ste. 300, 211 N. Robinson Ave., Oklahoma City, OK, 73102; *PH:* 1-405-775-5000; *Fax:* 1-405-775-5155; *http://* www.tronox.com

General		Stock	
Incorporation	DE	Price on:12/24/2007	$14.64
Employees	NA	Stock Exchange	NYSE
Auditor	Ernst & Young LLP	Ticker Symbol	TRX
Stk Agt	Computershare Trust CO.	Outstanding Shares	41,450,000
Counsel	NA	E.P.S	-$1.04
DUNS No.	NA	Shareholders	NA

Business: The groups principle activities include producing and marketing titanium dioxide pigment. The group also produced electrolytic manganese dioxide, sodium chlorate and other specialty chemicals. The groups products marketed under the brand name TRONOX(R). The group operates from the United States and international countries.The group's quarterly revenue of september 2007 was 363.10 millions of USD.

Primary SIC and add'l.: 2816 2899 2819

CIK No: 0001328910

Subsidiaries: Tronox (Luxembourg) Holding S.a.r.l., Tronox (Switzerland) Holding GmbH, Tronox B.V., Tronox Finance B.V., Tronox GmbH, Tronox Holdings, Inc., Tronox International ApS, Tronox LLC, Tronox Luxembourg S.a.r.l., Tronox Pigments (Holland) B.V., Tronox Pigments (Netherlands) B.V., Tronox Pigments (Savannah), Inc., Tronox Pigments GmbH, Tronox Pigments International GmbH, Tronox Pigments Ltd. 19 Subsidiaries included in the Index

Officers: Thomas W. Adams/47/Chmn., CEO, Marty J. Rowland/50/COO, Mary Mikkelson/47/Sr. VP, CFO, Roger G. Addison/57/VP, General Counsel, Sec., Robert Y. Brown/48/VP - Strategic Planning, Development, Patrick S. Corbett/56/VP - Safety, Environmental Affairs, Robert C. Gibney/45/VP - Investor Relations, External Affairs, Kelly A. Green/46/VP - Product, Quality Management, Mark S. Meadors/54/VP - Human Resources, John D. Romano/43/VP - Sales, Gregory E. Thomas/54/VP - Supply Chain, Strategic Sourcing, David J. Klvac/38/VP, Controller, Debbie Schramm/Contact - Media Inquiries

Directors: Thomas W. Adams/47/Chmn., CEO, Peter D. Kinnear/61/Dir., Jerome Adams/62/Dir., Robert D. Agdern/58/Dir., David G. Birney/65/Dir., Bradley C. Richardson/49/Dir.

Owners: Magnetar Financial LLC/4.90%, Peter D. Kinnear, Magnetar Financial LLC/9.10%, Dimensional Fund Advisors LP/8.40%, Shapiro Capital Management LLC/14.10%, Gregory E. Thomas, Insiders/3.40%, Paulson& Co. Inc./10.40%, Insiders, Jerome Adams, Thomas W. Adams, Barclays Global Investors, NA/7.50%, Roger G. Addison, Gregory E. Thomas, U.S. Trust Corporation/14.90% *(26 Owners included in Index)*

Financial Data: *Fiscal Year End:*12/31 *Latest Annual Data:* 12/31/2006

Year	Sales	Net Income
2006	$1,411,600,000	-$200,000
2005	$1,364,000,000	$18,800,000
2004	$1,301,800,000	-$127,600,000

Curr. Assets:	$794,100,000	Curr. Liab.:	$411,900,000	P/E Ratio:	25.48
Plant, Equip.:	$864,600,000	Total Liab.:	$1,386,100,000	Indic. Yr. Divd.:	$0.200
Total Assets:	$1,823,400,000	Net Worth:	$437,300,000	Debt/ Equity:	1.2213

Trubion Pharmaceuticals Inc

2401 4th Ave., Ste. 1050, Seattle, WA, 98121; *PH:* 1-206-838-0500; *http://* www.trubion.com; *Email:* hr@trubion.com

General		Stock	
Incorporation	DE	Price on:12/24/2007	$19.89
Employees	79	Stock Exchange	NDQ
Auditor	Ernst & Young, LLP	Ticker Symbol	TRBN
Stk Agt	U.S. Stock Transfer Corp	Outstanding Shares	17,610,000
Counsel	NA	E.P.S	-$1.37
DUNS No.	NA	Shareholders	NA

Business: The groups principle activity is to provide protein therapeutic product. The group operates from the United States.

Primary SIC and add'l.: 2834

CIK No: 0001298521

Officers: Peter A. Thompson/Co - Founder, Dir., CEO, Pres., Kendall M. Mohler/Co - Founder, Sr. VP - Research, Development, Daniel J. Burge/Sr. VP, Chief Medical Officer, Leander F. Lauffer/Sr. VP - Business Development, Corporate Strategy, Judith Woods/Sr. VP - Legal Affairs, Chief Patent Counsel, Michelle G. Burris/Sr. VP, CFO, Hans Van Houte/Contact - Finance, Administration

Directors: Peter A. Thompson/Co - Founder, Dir., CEO, Pres., Edward A. Clark/Co - Founder, Chmn. - Scientific Advisory Board, Jeffrey Bluestone/Member - Scientific Advisory Board, Tasuko Honjo/Member - Scientific Advisory Board, Thomas Kipps/Member - Scientific Advisory Board, Antonio Lanzavecchia/Member - Scientific Advisory Board, Gerald Nepom/Member - Scientific Advisory Board, Michel Nussenzweig/Member - Scientific Advisory Board, Oliver Press/Member - Scientific Advisory Board, Lee R. Brettman/Dir., Steven Gillis/Dir., Patrick J. Heron/Dir., Anders D. Hove/Dir., David A. Mann/Dir., Samuel R. Saks/Dir. *(16 Directors included in Index)*

Owners: Davidson Kemper Partners, Patrick J. Heron, Lee T. Brettman FACP, Venrock Associates, Maverick Capital, Ltd, Oxford Bioscience Partners, ARCH Venture Partners, Samuel R. Saks, Prospect Venture Partners, Frazier Healthcare Ventures, David Schnell, Anders D. Hove, Michelle G. Burris, Insiders, FMR Corp *(18 Owners included in Index)*

Financial Data: *Fiscal Year End:*NA *Latest Annual Data:* 12/31/2006

Year	Sales	Net Income
2006	$36,530,000	-$3,929,000
2005	$349,000	-$18,927,000
2004	$294,000	-$14,213,000

Curr. Assets:	$110,947,000	Curr. Liab.:	$17,759,000		
Plant, Equip.:	$10,334,000	Total Liab.:	$48,740,000	Indic. Yr. Divd.:	NA
Total Assets:	$121,394,000	Net Worth:	$72,654,000	Debt/ Equity:	NA

Trudy Corp

353 Main Ave., Norwalk, CT, 06851; *PH:* 1-203-846-2274; *http://* www.soundprints.com; *Email:* soundprints@soundprints.com

General		Stock	
Incorporation	DE	Price on:12/24/2007	$0.0022
Employees	24	Stock Exchange	OTC
Auditor	Dworken, Hillman, LaMorte & Sterczala	Ticker Symbol	TRDY
Stk Agt	Computershare Trust Co	Outstanding Shares	612,470,000
Counsel	NA	E.P.S	$0.00
DUNS No.	00-117-9266	Shareholders	NA

Business: The group's principal activity is to publish children's storybooks, audiocassettes and cds. The products are produced by sub-contracting with independent toy factories and printing plants located in Asia. Approximately 86% of the toys are purchased from a vendor in China and 59% of the books are purchased from a us company, which subcontracts production to various printers in Asia. The plush and toy products are done by the group's overseas contractors; the audiocassettes are duplicated locally whereas the cds are duplicated in hong-kong and Singapore. The group's products are sold under the trade names of both sound prints and studio mouse llc (the subsidiary).

Primary SIC and add'l.: 5092 2731 3652

CIK No: 0000815098

Owners: Brad Mead, Insiders/59.80%, Alice B. Burnham/21.10%, Fred M. Filoon/2.40%, William W. Burnham/30.60%, Ashley C. Andersen/5.40%, Patty Sullivan/0.30%

Financial Data: *Fiscal Year End:*03/31 *Latest Annual Data:* 03/31/2007

Year	Sales	Net Income
2007	$6,271,000	-$17,000
2006	$6,457,000	$218,000
2005	$6,345,000	$267,000

Curr. Assets:	$3,189,000	Curr. Liab.:	$3,357,000		
Plant, Equip.:	$22,000	Total Liab.:	$4,965,000	Indic. Yr. Divd.:	NA
Total Assets:	$3,934,000	Net Worth:	-$1,031,000	Debt/ Equity:	0.7463

True Health Inc

15473 E Fwy., Channelview, TX, 77530; *PH:* 1-281-862-2201

General		Stock	
Incorporation	UT	Price on:12/24/2007	NA
Employees	NA	Stock Exchange	NA
Auditor	Malone & Bailey, P.C	Ticker Symbol	NA
Stk Agt	Cottonwood Stock Transfer	Outstanding Shares	NA
Counsel	NA	E.P.S	NA
DUNS No.	NA	Shareholders	NA

Business: The group's principal activity is to provide proprietary branded specialist pressure relieving equipment and medical professionals to the health care industry. The group specializes in providing equipment that helps relieve pressure on sensitive skin, providing prevention and relief of sores and wounds. It offers mattress systems, pumps and lifting equipment that are specifically designed to provide comfort to fragile skin. Dynamic systems of the group automatically inflate and deflate depending upon the patient's weight. Static systems include pressure reducing, foam and gel-based duotron, premier, resteasy bed mattresses and cushions for wheel chairs. It also offers hoists for patient moving and handling, as well as electric, profiling hospital beds. On 27-Jun-2003 the group acquired westmeria healthcare limited.

Primary SIC and add'l.: 7352 2099

CIK No: 0001110607
Subsidiaries: Westmeria Health Care Limited
Officers: Ronald E. Smith/Dir., CEO, Pres., John C. Siedhoff/Dir., CFO, Steven C. Pahls/Sales Mgr., John B. Vanhyfte/VP, David C. Allensworth/Engineering Mgr., Stanley O. Stuckey/Operations Mgr.
Directors: Ronald E. Smith/Dir., CEO, Pres., Robert E. Chamberlain/Chmn., John C. Siedhoff/Dir., CFO, Daniel L. Ritz/Dir.
Owners: Insiders/76.70%, Ronald E. Smith/25.80%, John C. Siedhoff/37.20%, Robert E. Chamberlain/37.20%

True North Energy Corp

1200 Smith St., 16th Fl., Houston, TX, 77002; *PH:* 1-832-295-9639; *Fax:* 1-832-553-7244; *http://* www.tnecorp.com; *Email:* info@tnecorp.com

General - Incorporation	NV	Stock- Price on:12/24/2007	$0.58
Employees	1	Stock Exchange	OTC
Auditor	Williams & Webster, P.S.	Ticker Symbol	TNEN
Stk Agt	Empire Stock Transfer Inc.	Outstanding Shares	64,640,000
Counsel	NA	E.P.S.	-$0.266
DUNS No.	NA	Shareholders	NA

Business: The groups principal activity is engage in the business of providing printing and packaging solutions to entities of all sizes and to specialize in providing templated, quality printing and print materials. In January 2006, the group acquired Alaska Oil and Gas Leases. The group operates from the United States.
Primary SIC and add'l.: 8748
CIK No: 0001292521
Officers: John I. Folnovic/CEO, Max Pozzoni/CFO, Anthony Zelen/Vp - Corporate Communications
Directors: Jeffrey B. Ahbe/Member - Advisory Board, James Gouveia/Member - Advisory Board, George Lindahl/Member - Advisory Board, Neville W. Patterson/Member - Advisory Board, Lanier J. Yeates/Member - Advisory Board
Owners: Massimiliano Pozzoni/28.95%, Insiders/52.26%, John Folnovic/23.31%
Financial Data: Fiscal Year End:04/30 Latest Annual Data: 04/30/2007

Year	Sales	Net Income
2007	NA	-$9,069,000
2006	NA	-$121,000
2005	NA	-$13,000

Curr. Assets:	$833,000	Curr. Liab.:	$500,000		
Plant, Equip.:	$695,000	Total Liab.:	$750,000	Indic. Yr. Divd.:	NA
Total Assets:	$1,542,000	Net Worth:	$792,000	Debt/ Equity:	NA

True Product ID Inc

2600 Ctr. Sq. W, 1500 Market St., Philadelphia, PA, 19102; *PH:* 1-215-496-8102; *Fax:* 1-215-320-1991; *http://* www.tpid.net; *Email:* rbendis@tpid.net

General - Incorporation	DE	Stock- Price on:12/24/2007	$0.09
Employees	6	Stock Exchange	OTC
Auditor	NA	Ticker Symbol	TPDI
Stk Agt	United Stock Transfer, Inc.,	Outstanding Shares	339,620,000
Counsel	NA	E.P.S.	-$0.019
DUNS No.	NA	Shareholders	NA

Business: The groups principal activity is to produce integrators for anti counterfeiting and security surveillance applications and is a provider of integrated tracking devices. The groups customers include solutions for governments, armed forces, and industry, through its own proprietary technology. In the year March 2006, the group acquired Sure Trace Security Corporation. The group operates from the United States.
Primary SIC and add'l.: 7382
CIK No: 0001011550
Officers: William Dunavant/Chmn., CEO, Sergio Luz/Pres., Principal Financial Officer
Directors: William Dunavant/Chmn., CEO
Owners: James MacKay/14.90%, Insiders/17.30%, Sichuan Valencia Trading Limited/22.20%, Michael Antonopolos/0.20%, Richard A. Bendis/6.80%, Li Ning/2.20%
Financial Data: Fiscal Year End:06/30 Latest Annual Data: 6/30/2006

Year	Sales	Net Income
2006	NA	-$1,165,000
2005	$5,111,000	$159,000
2004	$3,935,000	-$500,000

Curr. Assets:	NA	Curr. Liab.:	$539,000		
Plant, Equip.:	NA	Total Liab.:	$1,237,000	Indic. Yr. Divd.:	NA
Total Assets:	$894,000	Net Worth:	-$342,000	Debt/ Equity:	NA

True Religion Apparel Inc

2263 E Vernon Ave., Vernon, CA, 90058; *PH:* 1-323-266-3072; *http://* www.truereligionbrandjeans.com

General - Incorporation	DE	Stock- Price on:12/24/2007	$20.14
Employees	163	Stock Exchange	NDQ
Auditor	Phelps & Phillips, LLP	Ticker Symbol	TRLG
Stk Agt	American Stock Transfer & Trust Co.	Outstanding Shares	23,440,000
Counsel	NA	E.P.S.	$0.94
DUNS No.	NA	Shareholders	NA

Business: The groups principal activities include designing, developing, manufacturing, marketing, distributing and selling denim jeans and other apparel. The products of the group include denim jackets, corduroy jeans and jackets, velvet jeans, fleece jeans and hooded sweatshirts, skirts, shorts, shirts, sweaters and sportswear. The group products sold under the trade name True Religion Brand Jeans. The groups operates through two segments namely wholesale and retail. Specific customers of the group include Jameric, Nordstrom and Neiman Marcus. The group operates from the United States. The net sale of the group for the year 2006 was wholesale accounted for $134,799,348 and retail $4,978,644.
Primary SIC and add'l.: 2311 2321 2844 5137 2325 2331 2339 2337 5136 2329
CIK No: 0001160858

Subsidiaries: Guru Denim, Inc.
Officers: Jeffrey Lubell/Chmn., CEO/$2,603,116.00, Daryl Rosenberg/COO/$222,358.00, Michael Buckley/Pres./$1,004,905.00, Peter Collins/CFO, Rob Whetstone/Contact
Directors: Jeffrey Lubell/Chmn., CEO, Joseph H. Coulombe/Dir., Louis G. Graziadio/Dir., Robert L. Harris/Dir., Mark Maron/Dir.
Owners: Columbia Wanger Asset Management, L.P./12.00%, Charles A. Lesser/2.00%, Insiders/40.00%, Robert L. Harris, Mark S. Maron, Daryl Rosenberg, Michael F. Buckley, Joseph Coulombe, Jeffrey Lubell/36.00%, Kymberly Gold-Lubell/33.00%, G. Louis Graziadio
Financial Data: Fiscal Year End:12/31 Latest Annual Data: 12/31/2006

Year	Sales	Net Income
2006	$139,046,000	$24,435,000
2005	$102,572,000	$19,508,000
2004	$27,667,000	$4,228,000

Curr. Assets:	$74,455,000	Curr. Liab.:	$12,192,000		
Plant, Equip.:	$4,993,000	Total Liab.:	$12,684,000	Indic. Yr. Divd.:	NA
Total Assets:	$80,167,000	Net Worth:	$67,483,000	Debt/ Equity:	NA

Trueyou.com

7 Corporate Pk., Norwalk, CT, 06851; *PH:* 1-203-295-2121; *Fax:* 1-203-295-2102; *http://* www.trueyou.com

General - Incorporation	DE	Stock- Price on:12/24/2007	$0.04
Employees	535	Stock Exchange	OTC
Auditor	Amper, Politziner & Mattia P.c	Ticker Symbol	TUYU
Stk Agt	American Registrar & Transfer Co	Outstanding Shares	16,760,000
Counsel	NA	E.P.S.	-$9.5
DUNS No.	NA	Shareholders	NA

Business: The group were formed to deliver exceptional content via the internet to people worldwide in order to help them achieve their personal and professional goals as rapidly as possible. We strive to deliver training and professional self-help programs to people at a far lower cost, in terms of money and time, than conventional training methods. We generate revenues by selling advertising on our website. We believe that the individuals benefit directly from using the content by fostering their personal and professional development. The group's quarterly revenue for Jun '07 was 3.60 millions of USD.
Primary SIC and add'l.: 7389
CIK No: 0001316924
Owners: Insiders, Richard Rakowski, Kidd & Company, LLC, Andrew Lipman, Philippe Franchet, Affiliates of Pequot Capital Management Inc., FCPR L Capital, Matthew Burris, Seapine Investments, LLC, Jane Terker, Daniel Piette
Financial Data: Fiscal Year End:12/31 Latest Annual Data: 7/1/2006

Year	Sales	Net Income
2006	$33,052,000	-$171,705,000

Curr. Assets:	$5,151,000	Curr. Liab.:	$47,691,000		
Plant, Equip.:	$12,981,000	Total Liab.:	$253,085,000	Indic. Yr. Divd.:	NA
Total Assets:	$43,171,000	Net Worth:	-$209,914,000	Debt/ Equity:	NA

Trump Atlantic City Assoc

1000 Boardwalk At Virginia Ave., Atlantic City, NJ, 08401; *PH:* 1-609-449-6515; *http://* www.fwc.com

General - Incorporation	NJ	Stock- Price on:12/24/2007	NA
Employees	NA	Stock Exchange	NA
Auditor	Ernst & Young LLP	Ticker Symbol	NA
Stk Agt	NA	Outstanding Shares	NA
Counsel	NA	E.P.S.	NA
DUNS No.	80-096-8257	Shareholders	NA

Business: The group's principle activities are to operate trump hotels, casinos and resorts. The group operates through its subsidiaries: trump plaza associates, trump taj mahal associates, trump Atlantic city funding, inc, trump Atlantic city funding ii, inc and trump Atlantic city funding iii, inc. The group provides amenities and services, entertainment and convention facilities to its casino patrons and hotel guests. The other services of the group include entertainment and sporting events and player promotions. The group offers credit facility to certain qualified patrons on a discretionary basis. The group's main source of revenue is from gaming activities.
Primary SIC and add'l.: 7021 5812 7993
CIK No: 0000897729
Subsidiaries: Trump Atlantic City Corporation, Trump Plaza Associates, Trump Taj Mahal Associates, TrumpAtlanticCityFunding,Inc., TrumpAtlanticCityFundingII,Inc., TrumpAtlanticCityFundingIII,Inc.

Trump Hotels & Casino Resorts Inc

1000 Boardwalk At Virginia Ave., Atlantic City, NJ, 08401; *PH:* 1-609-449-6515; *http://* www.trump.com

General - Incorporation	DE	Stock- Price on:12/24/2007	$14.4
Employees	7,300	Stock Exchange	NDQ
Auditor	Ernst & Young LLP	Ticker Symbol	TRMP
Stk Agt	Continental Stock T & T Co.	Outstanding Shares	31,100,000
Counsel	Willkie Farr & Gallagher LLP	E.P.S.	-$0.79
DUNS No.	10-652-9662	Shareholders	NA

Business: The group's principle activity is to owns and manages casino operations, room rentals, food and beverage sales and entertainment revenues. The group has the right to use the trademark "Trump" according to the trademark license agreement. The group operates three casinos in the Atlantic city market and a riverboat casino, trump casino, at buffington harbor.
Primary SIC and add'l.: 7999 5812 7011
CIK No: 0000943320
Subsidiaries: Keystone Redevelopment Partners, LLC, TCI 2 Holdings, LLC, TER Development Co. LLC, TER Keystone Development Co., LLC, TER Management Co., LLC, Trump Entertainment Resorts Development Company, LLC, Trump Entertainment Resorts Funding, Inc., Trump Entertainment Resorts Holdings, L.P., Trump Marina Associates, LLC, Trump Plaza Associates, LLC, Trump Taj Mahal Associates, LLC
Officers: Donald J. Trump/Chmn., Pres.
Directors: Donald J. Trump/Chmn., Pres.

Owners: James J. Florio, Dale R. Black, Insiders/29.80%, James A. Rigot, Insiders/100.00%, Prides Capital Partners, LLC/5.90%, Cezar M. Froelich, Paul B. Keller, Edward H. DAlelio, Donald J. Trump/100.00%, Morton E. Handel, Donald J. Trump/28.80%, Morgan Stanley & Co. Incorporated/17.90%, Wallace B. Askins, Michael A. Kramer *(21 Owners included in Index)*

Financial Data: Fiscal Year End:12/31　Latest Annual Data: 03/31/2007

Year	Sales	Net Income
2007	$234,279,000	-$8,133,000
2006	$244,170,000	-$9,683,000
2005	$992,221,000	$251,856,000

Curr. Assets:	$215,940,000	Curr. Liab.:	$156,732,000		
Plant, Equip.:	$1,535,852,000	Total Liab.:	$1,847,728,000	Indic. Yr. Divd.:	NA
Total Assets:	$2,260,496,000	Net Worth:	$412,768,000	Debt/ Equity:	3.3824

Truserv Corp

8600 W Bryn Mawr Ave, Chicago, IL, 60631; *PH:* 1-773-695-5000; *http://* www.truserv.com

General - Incorporation	DE	Stock - Price on:12/24/2007	NA
Employees	NA	Stock Exchange	NA
Auditor	PricewaterhouseCoopers LLP	Ticker Symbol	NA
Stk Agt	NA	Outstanding Shares	NA
Counsel	NA	E.P.S	NA
DUNS No.	06-440-4742	Shareholders	NA

Business: The group's principal activity is distribution of hardware and related merchandise in the United States and in other 51 countries. The group also manufactures and sells paint and paint applicators. At 31-Dec-2002, the group serves approximately 6,600 retail and distribution outlets. The group sells its products to hardware retailers, industrial distributors and rental retailers. The group operates through two segments namely: hardware and paint manufacturing and distribution. The trademarks of the group include true value(R), grand rental station(R), taylor rental(R), home & garden showplace(R) and induserve supply(r).

Primary SIC and add'l.: 5072 5074 5031 5083 2851 5198

CIK No: 0000025095

Subsidiaries: Advocate Services Corporation, General Paint and Manufacturing Co., Servistar Paint Company, True Value Company HK Limited, TruServ Logistic Company, TruServ Specialty Company, LLC, TruValue.com

Officers: Lyle Heidemann/Dir., CEO, Pres., Don Deegan/VP, Controller, Leslie Weber/CIO, Sr. VP, Dave Shadduck/Sr. VP, CFO, Jon Johnson/VP - Retail Finance, Amy W. Mysel/Sr. VP - Human Resources, Communications, Steven L. Mahurin/Sr. VP, Chief Merchandising Officer, Carol Wentworth/VP - Marketing, Cathy Anderson/Sr. VP, General Counsel, Steve Poplawski/Sr. VP - Logistics, Supply Chain Management, Fred Kirst/VP - Retail, Specialty Business Development, Barbara Wagner/VP, Corporate Treasurer

Directors: Lyle Heidemann/Dir., CEO, Pres., Brian A. Webb/Chmn., Kenneth A. Niefeld/Dir., Michael S. Glode/Dir., Brent A. Burger/Dir., Thomas S. Hanemann/Dir., Charles M. Welch/Dir., Richard E. George/Dir., Cheryl Bachelder/Dir., David Y. Schwartz/Dir., Larry Zigerelli/Dir.

Trustco Bank Corp

5 Sarnowski Dr., Glenville, NY, 12302; *PH:* 1-518-377-3311; *Fax:* 1-518-381-3668; *http://* www.trustcobank.com

General - Incorporation	NY	Stock - Price on:12/24/2007	$9.82
Employees	554	Stock Exchange	NDQ
Auditor	KPMG LLP	Ticker Symbol	TRST
Stk Agt	National City Bank	Outstanding Shares	75,110,000
Counsel	NA	E.P.S	$0.55
DUNS No.	00-699-4396	Shareholders	NA

Business: The group's principal activity is to provide general commercial banking business to individuals, partnerships, corporations, municipalities and government of New York. The group provides commercial, construction, residential mortgage, home equity lines of credit and installment loans. The group also accepts demand, savings, checking accounts, money market accounts and certificates of deposit from customers. The group operates 64 automatic teller machines and 69 banking offices in albany, columbia, dutchess, greene, rensselaer, rockland, saratoga, schenectady, schoharie, warren, Washington and westchester counties of New York state.

Primary SIC and add'l.: 6712 6035

CIK No: 0000357301

Subsidiaries: ORE Subsidiary Corp., Trustco Bank, Trustco Charitable Foundation, Inc., Trustco Realty Corp., Trustco Vermont Investment Company

Officers: Robert J. McCormick/Dir., CEO, Pres./$1,022,281.00, Robert T. Cushing/CFO, Exec. VP/$859,693.00, Scot R. Salvador/Exec. VP - CBO/$607,950.00, Robert M. Leonard/45/Administrative VP, Assist. Sec./$164,104.00, Sharon J. Parvis/57/VP, Assist. Sec./$169,927.00, Thomas M. Poitras/45/VP, Sec.

Directors: Robert J. McCormick/Dir., CEO, Pres., Robert A. McCormick/Chmn., Anthony J. Marinello/Dir., William D. Power/Dir., Joseph A. Lucarelli/Dir., William J. Purdy/Dir., Thomas O. Maggs/Dir.

Owners: Barclays Global Investors, N.A./6.91%

Financial Data: Fiscal Year End:12/31　Latest Annual Data: 12/31/2006

Year	Sales	Net Income
2006	$184,662,000	$45,325,000
2005	$177,821,000	$58,989,000
2004	$170,751,000	$56,540,000

Curr. Assets:	$291,338,000	Curr. Liab.:	$2,921,605,000	P/E Ratio:	16.37
Plant, Equip.:	$24,050,000	Total Liab.:	$2,921,664,000	Indic. Yr. Divd.:	$0.640
Total Assets:	$3,161,187,000	Net Worth:	$239,523,000	Debt/ Equity:	NA

Trustmark Corp

248 E Capitol St., Jackson, MS, 39201; *PH:* 1-601-208-5111; *http://* www.trustmark.com

General - Incorporation	MS	Stock - Price on:12/24/2007	$25.6
Employees	2,707	Stock Exchange	NDQ
Auditor	KPMG LLP	Ticker Symbol	TRMK
Stk Agt	NA	Outstanding Shares	58,130,000
Counsel	NA	E.P.S	$3.09
DUNS No.	07-195-2345	Shareholders	NA

Business: The group's principal activities are retail and commercial banking, indirect and real estate lending, investment services and trust services. It operates through its subsidiaries: trustmark national bank, trustmark financial services, inc and trustmark insurance agency, inc. The services are offered to corporate, institutional and individual customers in Mississippi and Tennessee. The operations are conducted through 144 full service banking offices and an ATM network, which includes 179 ATMs in 163 locations. On 29-Aug- 2003, acquired seven Florida branches of the banc corporation of birmingham, known as emerald coast division.

Primary SIC and add'l.: 6021 6712

CIK No: 0000036146

Subsidiaries: F. S. Corporation, First Building Corporation, Fisher-Brown, Incorporated, Somerville Bank & Trust Company, The Bottrell Insurance Agency, Inc., TRMK Risk Management, Inc., Trustmark Investment Advisors, Inc., Trustmark National Bank, Trustmark Securities, Inc.

Officers: Richard G. Hickson/Chmn., CEO, Pres., Member - Executive/$2,100,689.00, Harris T. Collier/Sec., Melanie A. Morgan/Assist. Sec., Louis E. Greer/Treasurer, Principal Financial Officer

Directors: Richard G. Hickson/Chmn., CEO, Pres., Member - Executive, William C. Deviney/Dir., Kenneth W. Williams/Dir., Kelly J. Allgood/Dir., Reuben V. Anderson/Dir., Gerald C. Garnett/Dir., John M. McCollouch/Dir., Richard H. Puckett/Dir., Michael R. Summerford/Dir., William G. Yates/Dir., Adolphus B. Baker/Dir., Daniel A. Grafton/Dir.

Owners: Harry M. Walker, Gerard R. Host, James M. Outlaw, William G. Yates, Duane A. Dewey, Gerald C. Garnett, Kelly J. Allgood, Richard H. Puckett, Robert M. Hearin Foundation, William C. Deviney, Michael R. Summerford, Insiders/2.30%, William C. Deviney, Daniel A. Grafton, Adolphus B. Baker *(18 Owners included in Index)*

Financial Data: Fiscal Year End:12/31　Latest Annual Data: 12/31/2006

Year	Sales	Net Income
2006	$637,874,000	$119,273,000
2005	$562,448,000	$102,951,000
2004	$493,026,000	$116,709,000

Curr. Assets:	$419,342,000	Curr. Liab.:	$7,717,665,000		
Plant, Equip.:	$134,372,000	Total Liab.:	$7,949,635,000	Indic. Yr. Divd.:	$0.880
Total Assets:	$8,840,970,000	Net Worth:	$891,335,000	Debt/ Equity:	NA

TRW Automotive

12001 Tech Ctr. Dr., Livonia, MI, 48150; *PH:* 1-734-855-2600; *Fax:* 1-734-855-2999; *http://* www.trwauto.com

General - Incorporation	DE	Stock - Price on:12/24/2007	$38.28
Employees	63,800	Stock Exchange	NYSE
Auditor	Ernst & Young LLP	Ticker Symbol	TRW
Stk Agt	National City Bank	Outstanding Shares	98,970,000
Counsel	NA	E.P.S	$0.42
DUNS No.	NA	Shareholders	NA

Business: The groups principle activity is to provide automobiles parts. The group's products include breaking, steering and suspension, and body control systems. The group operates from United States.

Primary SIC and add'l.: 3714 3465

CIK No: 0001267097

Subsidiaries: ABC Sistemas e Modulos Ltda., Austrian Holdco LLC, Autocruise Limited, Autocruise SA, Automotive Holdings (Czech Republic) s.r.o., Automotive Holdings (France) SAS, Automotive Holdings (Korea), Ltd., Automotive Holdings (Poland), Sp. Z.o.o., Automotive Holdings (Spain), S.L., Automotive Holdings (UK), Limited, Brakes India Limited, British Sealed Beams Limited, Bryce Berger Limited, CAV Limited, Celtica De Componentes Del Automovil, S.L. 225 Subsidiaries included in the Index

Officers: John C. Plant/Dir., CEO, Pres./$17,937,210.00, Dave Chew/VP - European Steering Operations, Moises Bucci/Pres. - South America, Ken Kaiser/VP, GM Body Controls North America, Ann Lipanski/VP - Internal Audit, Kai-Uwe Wollenhaupt/VP, GM Engineered Fasteners - Components, Patrick Stobb/Dir. - Investor Relations, Ed Carpenter/VP - Asia Pacific, Joseph Drouin/CIO, VP, Ron Muckley/VP - Braking - Suspension North America, Peter Markowsky/VP, GM Body Controls Europe - Emerging Markets, Thomas Koenig/VP - Health - Safety, Environmental, Theo Benz/VP - Braking - Suspension Europe, Bryce Currie/VP - Quality, Doug Campbell/VP - Engineering Occupant Safety Systems *(40 Officers included in Index)*

Directors: John C. Plant/Dir., CEO, Pres., Neil P. Simpkins/Chmn., Matthew Kabaker/Dir., Jody Miller/Dir., Francois J. Castaing/Dir., Michael J. Losh/Dir., Robert L. Friedman/Dir., James F. Albaugh/Dir., Paul H. O'Neill/Dir.

Owners: Robert L. Friedman, Blackstone, Michael J. Losh, Insiders, Paul H. O'Neil, Peter J. Lake, Peter G. Peterson, Neil P. Simpkins, Stephen A. Schwarzman, Joseph S. Cantie, Jody G. Miller, Francois J. Castaing, Wellington Management, LLP, Steven Lunn, John C. Plant *(16 Owners included in Index)*

Financial Data: Fiscal Year End:12/31　Latest Annual Data: 12/31/2006

Year	Sales	Net Income
2006	$13,144,000,000	$176,000,000
2005	$12,643,000,000	$204,000,000
2004	$12,011,000,000	$29,000,000

Curr. Assets:	$3,676,000,000	Curr. Liab.:	$3,675,000,000		
Plant, Equip.:	$2,714,000,000	Total Liab.:	$8,736,000,000	Indic. Yr. Divd.:	NA
Total Assets:	$11,133,000,000	Net Worth:	$2,397,000,000	Debt/ Equity:	1.3248

TRX Inc

6 W Dr.uid Hills Dr., Atlanta, GA, 30329; *PH:* 1-404-929-6154; *http://* www.trx.com; *Email:* trxmarketing@trx.com

General - Incorporation	GA	Stock - Price on:12/24/2007	$3.05
Employees	636	Stock Exchange	NDQ
Auditor	Mckenna Long & Aldridge LLP	Ticker Symbol	TRXI
Stk Agt	EquiServe Trust Co N.A	Outstanding Shares	18,280,000
Counsel	NA	E.P.S	-$0.14
DUNS No.	NA	Shareholders	NA

Business: The groups principle activities include developing and hosting software applications. The groups services include scalability of solutions, continuity of business, rapid product development, compliance with and adaptability to business rules, and speed to market. The groups product is DATATRAX. Specific customers of the group include American Airlines, Inc., Carlson Wagonlit Travel, Inc., Travel and Transport, Inc and Navigant International, Inc. The group acquired Hi-Mark, LLC in the year 2007 and Travel Analytics, Inc in the year 2006. The group operates from the United States. The group's quarterly revenue for September 2007 was 22.53 millions of USD.

Primary SIC and add'l.: 7389 8999 7375 7374 7379

CIK No: 0001103025

Subsidiaries: Technology Licensing Company, LLC, Travel Technology, LLC, TRX Data Services, Inc., TRX Europe, Ltd., TRX Fulfillment Services, LLC, TRX Germany GmbH, TRX Luxembourg, S..r.l., TRX Technology Services, L.P., TRX UK, Ltd.

Officers: Norwood H. Davis/Dir., CEO, Pres./$1,292,725.00, Victor P. Pynn/COO/$408,586.00, David Cathcart/CFO/$316,486.00, Shane Hammond/Exec. VP, Pres. - Resx Technologies/$317,470.00, Susan Hopley/Exec. VP - Emerging Markets, Kevin G. Austin/45/Exec. VP

Directors: Norwood H. Davis/Dir., CEO, Pres., Johan G. Drechsel/Chmn., John A. Fentener Van Vlissingen/Dir., John F. Davis/Dir., Harry A. Feuerstein/Dir.

Owners: David D. Cathcart, Shane H. Hammond, John F. Davis, Victor P. Pynn, Johan G.Drechsel, Peter J. Grover, Timothy J. Severt, Cortina Asset Management, LLC, Norwood H. Davis, BCD Technology, S.A., John A. Fentener van Vlissingen, Harry A. Feuerstein, Insiders, Michael W.Gunn

Financial Data: Fiscal Year End:12/31   Latest Annual Data: 12/31/2006

Year	Sales	Net Income
2006	$116,340,000	$7,300,000
2005	$118,616,000	-$6,664,000
2004	$113,459,000	-$11,177,000

Curr. Assets:	$49,104,000	Curr. Liab.:	$47,655,000		
Plant, Equip.:	$16,412,000	Total Liab.:	$48,581,000	Indic. Yr. Divd.:	NA
Total Assets:	$89,713,000	Net Worth:	$41,132,000	Debt/ Equity:	NA

Trycera Financial Inc

18023 Sky Pk. Cir Ste. G, Irvine, CA, 92614; **PH:** 1-949-273-4300; **Fax:** 1-949-273-4310; http:// www.trycera.com; **Email:** info@trycera.com

General - Incorporation	NV	Stock - Price on:12/24/2007	$1.01
Employees	10	Stock Exchange	OTC
Auditor	Chisholm, Bierwolf & Nilson, LLC	Ticker Symbol	TRYF
Stk Agt	Interwest Transfer Company, Inc.	Outstanding Shares	7,930,000
Counsel	NA	E.P.S.	-$0.17
DUNS No.	NA	Shareholders	NA

Business: The groups principle activities include developing, deploying and marketing semi custom and customized branded prepaid and stored value card solutions. The group operates through three segments namely open, PIN based semi open and closed loop product offerings. The group operates from the United States.

Primary SIC and add'l.: 7389

CIK No: 0001117045

Officers: Matthew S. Kerper/Dir., CEO, Pres./$126,963.00, Bryan Kenyon/CFO, COO/$107,984.00, Alex McClure/Dir. - Product Development

Directors: Matthew S. Kerper/Dir., CEO, Pres., Alan Knitowski/Chmn., Luan Dang/Dir., Randy Cherkas/Dir., Robert Lang/Dir.

Owners: Eric Bronk/9.40%, Randolph Cherkas/2.70%, Luan Dang/10.50%, Knitowski Family Trust UDT/12.90%, Alan S. Knitowski/15.90%, Robert M. Lang/1.40%, Trymetris Capital Fund I, LLC/5.70%, Matthew S. Kerper/22.40%, Insiders/56.10%, Bryan W. Kenyon/16.00%

Financial Data: Fiscal Year End:12/31   Latest Annual Data: 12/31/2006

Year	Sales	Net Income
2006	$1,095,000	-$1,362,000

Curr. Assets:	$191,000	Curr. Liab.:	$175,000	P/E Ratio:	0.75
Plant, Equip.:	$18,000	Total Liab.:	$175,000	Indic. Yr. Divd.:	NA
Total Assets:	$261,000	Net Worth:	$85,000	Debt/ Equity:	NA

Tsakos Energy Navigation Ltd

367 Syngrou Ave., Faliro Hellas, Athens; **PH:** 30-210940771013; **Fax:** 30-2109407716; http:// www.tenn.gr; **Email:** ten@tenn.gr

General - Incorporation	Bermuda	Stock - Price on:12/24/2007	$68.72
Employees	NA	Stock Exchange	NYSE
Auditor	Ernst & Young LLP	Ticker Symbol	TNP
Stk Agt	Bank of New York	Outstanding Shares	19,040,000
Counsel	NA	E.P.S.	$5.45
DUNS No.	NA	Shareholders	NA

Business: The groups principle activity is to provide marine transportation services. The group operates from United States, China, Greece and India.

Primary SIC and add'l.: 4412

CIK No: 0001166663

Subsidiaries: Activity Excellence S.A., Annapolis Shipping Co. Ltd., Apollo Excellence S.A., Apollo Glory S.A., Apollo Honour S.A., Avra Trading Co. Ltd., Azimuth Shipping Company Ltd., Bosphorus Shipping Co. Ltd., Ergo Glory S.A., Essex Shipping Co. Ltd, Figaro Shipping Company Limited, Fortitude Shipping Co. Ltd., Fortune Faith S.A., Global Triumph S.A., Grevia Marine Co. Ltd. 39 Subsidiaries included in the Index

Officers: Nikolas P. Tsakos/Dir., CEO, Pres., Paul Durham/CFO, Chief Accounting Officer, George V. Saroglou/Dir., COO

Directors: Nikolas P. Tsakos/Dir., CEO, Pres., John D. Stavropoulos/Chmn., Michael G. Jolliffee/Dep. Chmn., Francis T. Nusspickel/Dir., William A. O'Neil/Dir., Torben Janholt/Dir., George V. Saroglou/Dir., COO, Peter Nicholson/Dir., Aristides A.N. Patrinos/60/Dir.

Owners: Kelley Enterprises Inc./11.70%, Nikolas P. Tsakos, Torben Janholt, Sea Consolidation S.A. of Panama/10.00%, Aristides A.N. Patrinos, Redmont Trading Corp./5.90%, Peter C. Nicholson, Insiders, George V. Saroglou, William A. ONeil, John D. Stavropoulos, Marsland Holdings Limited/7.10%, Michael G. Jolliffe, Paul Durham, Francis T. Nusspickel

Financial Data: Fiscal Year End:12/31   Latest Annual Data: 12/31/2006

Year	Sales	Net Income
2006	$427,654,000	$196,404,000
2005	$295,623,000	$161,755,000
2004	$318,278,000	$143,290,000

Curr. Assets:	$222,493,000	Curr. Liab.:	$101,430,000	P/E Ratio:	15.26
Plant, Equip.:	$1,719,889,000	Total Liab.:	$1,214,602,000	Indic. Yr. Divd.:	$1.650
Total Assets:	$1,969,875,000	Net Worth:	$755,273,000	Debt/ Equity:	NA

TSB Financial Corp

1057 Providence Rd., Charlotte, NC, 28207; **PH:** 1-704-331-8686

General - Incorporation	NC	Stock - Price on:12/24/2007	$17
Employees	NA	Stock Exchange	NA
Auditor	Dixon Hughes PLLC	Ticker Symbol	NA
Stk Agt	First-citizens Bank & Trust Co	Outstanding Shares	NA
Counsel	NA	E.P.S.	NA
DUNS No.	NA	Shareholders	NA

Business: The groups principal activity is to provide banking, financial and loan services to the customers. Services of the group include consumer and commercial loans to individuals and small and medium sized businesses for various personal and business purposes, including term and installment loans, equity lines of credit, and overdraft checking credit. The group operates from the United States. In the year 2006, the groups total assets were $186,529 (thousands).

Primary SIC and add'l.: 6035

CIK No: 0001374537

Officers: John B. Stedman/46/Dir., CEO, Pres./$193,703.00, Jan H. Hollar/52/CFO, Exec. VP, Allan R. Schlick/64/Exec. VP, Chief Credit Officer/$125,581.00, Robert C.M. Thomas/50/Exec. VP - City Exec./$150,899.00

Directors: John B. Stedman/46/Dir., CEO, Pres., James H. Barnhardt/63/Chmn., William B. Allen/58/Dir., William B. Barnhardt/56/Dir., Amy Rice Blumenthal/55/Dir., P. W. Davis/68/Dir., Jubal A. Early/47/Dir., Herbert L. Harriss/65/Dir., William States Lee/52/Dir., David J. Zimmerman/46/Dir., Donald J. Sherrill/54/Dir., Marc H. Silverman/69/Dir.

Owners: Herbert L. Harriss, P. W. Davis/1.57%, Allan R. Schlick, Amy Rice Blumenthal/1.12%, William B. Allen/6.68%, Insiders/26.39%, William B. Barnhardt/1.78%, David J. Zimmerman/1.22%, William States Lee, Jubal A. Early, Marc H. Silverman/2.42%, Donald J. Sherrill, John B. Stedman/7.52%, James H. Barnhardt/2.17%, Robert C.M. Thomas/1.40%

Financial Data: Fiscal Year End:12/31   Latest Annual Data: 12/31/2006

Year	Sales	Net Income
2006	$12,699,000	$1,216,000

Curr. Assets:	$9,712,000	Curr. Liab.:	$169,907,000		
Plant, Equip.:	$1,287,000	Total Liab.:	$181,014,000	Indic. Yr. Divd.:	NA
Total Assets:	$195,892,000	Net Worth:	$14,878,000	Debt/ Equity:	0.7171

TSR Inc

400 Oser Ave., Hauppauge, NY, 11788; ; **http:**// www.tsrconsulting.com; **Email:** tsrli@tsrconsulting.com

General - Incorporation	DE	Stock - Price on:12/24/2007	$4
Employees	259	Stock Exchange	NDQ
Auditor	BDO Seidman LLP	Ticker Symbol	TSRI
Stk Agt	Continental Stock Transfer & Trust Co	Outstanding Shares	4,570,000
Counsel	NA	E.P.S.	$0.31
DUNS No.	04-308-1405	Shareholders	NA

Business: The group's principal activity is to provide contract computer programming services to commercial customers and state and local government agencies located in the metropolitan New York area, new England and the mid-Atlantic region. The services provided are in the areas of mainframe and mid-range computer operations, personal computers and client-server support, Internet and e-commerce operations, voice and data communications (local and wide area network) and help desk support. The group provides its clients with technical computer personnel to supplement the in-house information technology capabilities. It provides services through its offices located in New Jersey, long island, New York and Connecticut. The focus of its marketing efforts are on large businesses and institutions with significant it budgets and recurring staffing and software development needs which is conducted through account executives that are responsible for customers in an assigned territory.

Primary SIC and add'l.: 7371

CIK No: 0000098338

Subsidiaries: Logixtech Solutions, LLC, TSR Consulting Services, Inc.

Officers: Joseph F. Hughes/Chmn., CEO, Pres., Treasurer, John G. Sharkey/VP - Finance, Sec.

Directors: Joseph F. Hughes/Chmn., CEO, Pres., Treasurer, Christopher Hughes/Dir., John H. Hochuli/Dir., Raymond A. Roel/Dir., Robert A. Esernio/Dir., James J. Hill/Dir.

Owners: Daniel Zeff/10.00%, Joseph F. Hughes/40.30%

Financial Data: Fiscal Year End:05/31   Latest Annual Data: 5/31/2006

Year	Sales	Net Income
2006	$48,109,000	$1,214,000
2005	$51,445,000	$2,145,000
2004	$51,725,000	$2,124,000

Curr. Assets:	$16,950,000	Curr. Liab.:	$4,582,000	P/E Ratio:	12.90
Plant, Equip.:	$36,000	Total Liab.:	$4,614,000	Indic. Yr. Divd.:	$0.320
Total Assets:	$18,635,000	Net Worth:	$14,021,000	Debt/ Equity:	NA

TTI Team Telecom International Ltd

2 Hudson Pl., 6th Fl., Hoboken, NJ, 07030; **PH:** 1-201-795-3883; **Fax:** 1-201-795-3920; http:// www.tti-telecom.com; **Email:** info@tti-telecom.com

General - Incorporation	Israel	Stock - Price on:12/24/2007	$2.87
Employees	361	Stock Exchange	NDQ
Auditor	Kost Forer Gabbay & Kasierer	Ticker Symbol	TTIL
Stk Agt	American Stock Transfer & Trust Co.	Outstanding Shares	16,000,000
Counsel	NA	E.P.S.	-$0.1
DUNS No.	NA	Shareholders	NA

Business: The groups principle activity is to develop, market and support of advanced, modular, integrated software products and services for operations support systems and network management systems in telecommunications-related industries. The group operates from United States.

Primary SIC and add'l.: 7372 7373

CIK No: 0001026266

Subsidiaries: Axarte Ltd., CDR Technologies, TTI BVI Ltd, TTI Team Software (Malta) Ltd., TTI Telecom (HK) Limited, TTI Telecom Australia PTY. Ltd., TTI Telecom de Costa Rica S.A., TTI Telecom Software Private Limited, TTI-Telecom International B.V., TTI-Telecom International Inc.

Officers: Meir Lipshes/62/Chmn., Acting CEO, Duby Yoely/VP - Marketing, Solution Engineering, Shachar Ebel/CTO, Gerard Halimi/VP - Projects, Tal Sharon/VP - Operations, Israel, Michael Halperin/Exec. VP - Sales, Moshe Moran/Exec. VP - Sales, Marketing, Americas, Asaf Shirazi/VP - Research, Development, Ronen Givon/VP - Business Development, Hagit Ashkenazi/VP - Operations, Americas, Lee Roth/Investor Relations Officer, Marybeth Csaby/Investor Relations Officer, Israel Ofer/CFO, COO

Directors: Meir Lipshes/62/Chmn., Acting CEO, Julie Kunstler/52/Dir., Meir Dvir/77/Dir., Ilan Toker/38/Dir., Doron Zinger/55/Dir., Lior Bregman/49/Dir.

Owners: Lior Bregman/1.30%, Meir Lipshes/2.90%, Shlomo Eisenberg/22.30%, S Squared Technology/6.70%, Neuberger & Berman/21.00%, Insiders, Rima Management, LLC/7.00%

Financial Data: *Fiscal Year End:*12/31 *Latest Annual Data:* 12/31/2006

Year	Sales	Net Income
2006	NA	NA
2005	NA	NA
2004	NA	NA

Curr. Assets:	$42,530,000	**Curr. Liab.:**	$18,068,000	**P/E Ratio:**	15.26
Plant, Equip.:	$3,842,000	**Total Liab.:**	$23,090,000	**Indic. Yr. Divd.:**	NA
Total Assets:	$53,585,000	**Net Worth:**	$30,495,000	**Debt/ Equity:**	NA

TTM Technologies Inc

2630 S Harbor Blvd, Santa Ana, CA, 92704; *PH:* 1-714-241-0303; *http://* www.ttmtechnologies.com

General - Incorporation	DE	**Stock**- Price on:12/24/2007	$12.54
Employees	4,009	Stock Exchange	NDQ
Auditor	KPMG LLP	Ticker Symbol	TTMI
Stk Agt	Mellon Investor Services LLC	Outstanding Shares	42,190,000
Counsel	Karr Tuttle Campbell	E.P.S	NA
DUNS No.	NA	Shareholders	NA

Business: The group's principal activity is to manufacture complex multilayer printed circuit boards used in sophisticated electronic equipment. The group provides time-critical, one-stop manufacturing services for highly complex printed circuit boards. The printed circuit boards serve as the foundation of electronic products such as routers, switches, servers, medical equipment and communications infrastructure equipment. The customers are provided with an integrated manufacturing solution that encompasses all stages of an electronic product's life cycle from prototype through ramp-to-volume and volume production. The customers of the group include original equipment manufacturers and electronic manufacturing services providers that serve rapidly growing segments of the electronics industry including networking, high-end computing and computer peripherals.

Primary SIC and add'l.: 3672

CIK No: 0001116942

Subsidiaries: Power Circuits, Inc., TTM Advanced Circuits, Inc., TTM Technologies International, Inc.

Officers: Kenton K. Alder/Dir., CEO, Pres./$1,165,117.00, Shane S. Whiteside/COO, Exec. VP/$602,058.00, Steven W. Richards/CFO, VP, Sec./$520,060.00, Clay O. Swain/Sr. VP - Marketing/$489,722.00, Jeanette Newman/VP - Human Resources, Daniel L. Felsenthal/51/VP, Corporate Controller/$288,829.00, Douglas L. Soder/Exec. VP, Dale Knecht/VP - Information Technology

Directors: Kenton K. Alder/Dir., CEO, Pres., Robert E. Klatell/Chmn., Thomas T. Edman/Dir., John G. Mayer/Dir., James K. Bass/Dir., Richard P. Beck/Dir.

Owners: Robert E. Klatell, John G. Mayer, Royce & Associates, LLC/10.20%, Steven W. Richards, Daniel L. Felsenthal, Richard P. Beck, Insiders/2.80%, Clay O. Swain, Kenton K. Alder/1.10%, James K. Bass, Shane S. Whiteside, Thomas T. Edman, Putnam Investments/6.50%, Barclays Global Investors, NA/7.20%

Financial Data: *Fiscal Year End:*12/31 *Latest Annual Data:* 12/31/2006

Year	Sales	Net Income
2006	$369,316,000	$35,039,000
2005	$240,209,000	$30,841,000
2004	$240,650,000	$28,330,000

Curr. Assets:	$271,748,000	**Curr. Liab.:**	$144,343,000	**P/E Ratio:**	15.29
Plant, Equip.:	$150,837,000	**Total Liab.:**	$286,383,000	**Indic. Yr. Divd.:**	NA
Total Assets:	$573,698,000	**Net Worth:**	$287,315,000	**Debt/ Equity:**	0.3194

Tucows Inc

96 Mowat Ave., Toronto, ON, M6K 3M1; *PH:* 1-416-535-0123; *Fax:* 1-416-531-5584; *http://* www.tucows.com

General - Incorporation	PA	**Stock**- Price on:12/24/2007	$1.27
Employees	200	Stock Exchange	AMEX
Auditor	KPMG LLP	Ticker Symbol	TCX
Stk Agt	StockTrans, Inc.	Outstanding Shares	74,750,000
Counsel	NA	E.P.S	$0.049
DUNS No.	80-479-8700	Shareholders	NA

Business: The group's principal activity is to provide Internet domain name registration and other online products and services. The group offers its Internet services through a global Internet-based distribution network of resellers. These resellers are a heterogeneous group of companies including Internet service providers, Web hosting providers, telecommunications and cable companies. The group provides electronic publishing tools and services for publishers and other content creators. The group also provides full text document and images from variety of publications such as time, fortune, money and usa today. On 27-Feb-2004, the group acquired blogrolling.com.

Primary SIC and add'l.: 7375

CIK No: 0000909494

Subsidiaries: Infoloans Corp., InfoLoans2 Corp., Infonautics Co., Infoprop, Inc., Tucows (Delaware) Inc., Tucows (UK) Limited, Tucows.com Co.

Officers: Elliot Noss/Dir., CEO, Pres./$330,289.00, Carla Goertz/VP - Human Resources, Michael Cooperman/CFO/$267,974.00, David Woroch/VP - Sales, Marketing/$194,452.00, Ross Rader/Dir. - Research, Innovation, Ken Schafer/VP - Product Management, Marketing

Directors: Elliot Noss/Dir., CEO, Pres., Stanley Stern/48/Chmn., Erez Gissin/44/Dir., Alan Lipton/52/Dir., Lloyd Morrisett/73/Dir., Jeffrey Schwartz/43/Dir., Eugene Fiume/48/Dir., Allen Karp/66/Dir.

Owners: Elliot Noss/3.30%, Allen Karp, Eugene Fiume, Insiders/5.80%, Stanley Stern, Diker GP, LLC/12.60%, Jeffrey Schwartz, David Woroch, Mark Cuban/9.30%, Alain Chesnais, Michael Cooperman/1.30%, Wellington Management Company, LLP/12.80%, Erez Gissin, Judith Fields, Lloyd Morrisett

Financial Data: *Fiscal Year End:*12/31 *Latest Annual Data:* 12/31/2006

Year	Sales	Net Income
2006	$65,029,000	$2,160,000
2005	$48,517,000	$2,773,000
2004	$44,717,000	$5,500,000

Curr. Assets:	$35,809,000	**Curr. Liab.:**	$41,084,000	**P/E Ratio:**	15.88
Plant, Equip.:	$5,648,000	**Total Liab.:**	$66,123,000	**Indic. Yr. Divd.:**	NA
Total Assets:	$84,665,000	**Net Worth:**	$18,543,000	**Debt/ Equity:**	0.3309

Tuesday Morning Corp

6250 LBJ Fwy., Dallas, TX, 75240; *PH:* 1-972-387-3562; *http://* www.tuesdaymorning.com; *Email:* custserv@tuesdaymorning.com

General - Incorporation	DE	**Stock**- Price on:12/24/2007	$13.03
Employees	2,100	Stock Exchange	NDQ
Auditor	Ernst & Young LLP	Ticker Symbol	TUES
Stk Agt	Mellon Investor Services LLC	Outstanding Shares	41,440,000
Counsel	Hallett & Perrin PC	E.P.S	$0.10
DUNS No.	06-637-8175	Shareholders	NA

Business: The group's principal activity is to own and operate retail stores in the United States. The group purchases first quality, brand name merchandise at closeout and sells it at prices 50% to 80% below those generally charged by department stores and catalog retailers. The group's closeout merchandise has included brand name items like waterford crystal, steinbach and hummel collectibles, royal doulton and wedgwood China and giftware, martex bath towels, samsonite luggage, madame alexander dolls, calphalon cookware, krups, kitchenaid and cuisinart appliances and wallace flatware. The group generally sells lamps, rugs, crystal, dinnerware, silver serving pieces, gourmet housewares, bathroom, bedroom and kitchen accessories, linens, luggage, christmas trim, toys, stationery and silk plants. The group has registered the name tuesday morning as a service mark with the United States patent and trademark office. The group operates through 577 stores in 42 states.

Primary SIC and add'l.: 5945 5947 5023 5712 5331

CIK No: 0000878726

Subsidiaries: Days of the Week, Inc., Friday Morning, Inc., Nights of the Week, Inc., TMI Holdings, Inc., Tuesday Morning Partners, Ltd., Tuesday Morning, Inc., a Texas corporation

Officers: Kathleen Mason/Dir., CEO, Pres./$2,183,821.00, Ross Manning/Sr. VP, General Merchandise Mgr./$624,496.00, Michael Marchetti/COO, Exec. VP/$973,318.00, Elizabeth Schroeder/CFO, Exec. VP/$203,492.00, Melinda Page/Sr. VP, General Merchandise Mgr./$356,780.00, Dennis Billings/VP - Distribution, Karen Goodman/VP - Real Estate, Andrew Paris/VP - Store Operations, Jeff Toffer/VP - Store Standards, Veronica Arroyo Perez/VP - Merchandise Planning, Steve Heinmiller/CIO, Sr. VP

Directors: Kathleen Mason/Dir., CEO, Pres., Benjamin Chereskin/Chmn., Henry Frigon/Dir., William Hunckler/Dir., Robin Selati/Dir., Bruce A. Quinnell/Dir.

Owners: Insiders, Elizabeth A. Schroeder, Franklin Resources, Inc., Michael J. Marchetti, FMR Corp., Melinda Page, Benjamin D. Chereskin, Ross E. Manning, Henry F. Frigon, Bruce A. Quinnell, Kathleen Mason, William J. Hunckler, Robin P. Selati, Madison Dearborn Capital Partners II, LP.

Financial Data: *Fiscal Year End:*12/31 *Latest Annual Data:* 06/30/2007

Year	Sales	Net Income
2007	$408,520,000	$3,081,000
2006	$911,107,000	$36,429,000
2005	$931,827,000	$60,959,000

Curr. Assets:	$301,086,000	**Curr. Liab.:**	$139,991,000	**P/E Ratio:**	17.61
Plant, Equip.:	$86,397,000	**Total Liab.:**	$149,257,000	**Indic. Yr. Divd.:**	$0.800
Total Assets:	$393,134,000	**Net Worth:**	$243,877,000	**Debt/ Equity:**	0.2140

Tufco Technologies Inc

4800 Simonton Rd. , Green Bay, WI, 54305; *PH:* 1-920-336-0054; *http://* www.tufco.com

General - Incorporation	DE	**Stock**- Price on:12/24/2007	$8.28
Employees	395	Stock Exchange	NDQ
Auditor	Deloitte & Touche LLP	Ticker Symbol	NA
Stk Agt	StockTrans, Inc.	Outstanding Shares	4,540,000
Counsel	NA	E.P.S	$0.22
DUNS No.	80-354-5649	Shareholders	NA

Business: The group's principal activities are to offer diversified contract manufacturing and specialty printing services. The group also manufactures and distributes business imaging paper products and paint sundry products used in home improvement projects. Contract manufacturing services include custom packaging, coating, cutting, folding, thermal and adhesive laminating, embossed bonding, slitting and rewinding. The group produces printed and unprinted paper products used in architectural and engineering design, high speed data processing markets, point of sale, automatic teller machines and other office equipment under business imaging segment. Under the paint sundry segment, the group manufactures and distributes home improvement products that are sold to paint and hardware distributors, home centers, and retail paint stores.

Primary SIC and add'l.: 2759 2679 3999

CIK No: 0000895329

Subsidiaries: Executive Converting Corporation, Hamco Industries, Inc, Tufco Industries, Inc, Tufco LLC, Tufco Tech, Inc.

Officers: Louis Lecalsey/Dir., CEO, Pres., Michael B. Wheeler/Exec. VP, CFO, COO, Madge Joplin/VP - Business Imaging Sector, Michele M. Cherney/Sr. VP - Sales - Marketing, Contract Manufacturing Sector

Directors: Louis Lecalsey/Dir., CEO, Pres., Robert Simon/Chmn., William J. Malooly/Dir., Samuel J. Bero/Dir., Seymour S. Preston/Dir., Hamilton C. Davison/Dir., Brian Kelly/Dir.

Owners: Barbara M. Henagan, C. Hamilton Davison, Insiders, Michele M. Cherney, Samuel J. Bero, Seymour S. Preston, Michael B. Wheeler, Madge Joplin, Brian Kelly, Robert J. Simon, Louis LeCalsey, Bradford Venture Partners, L.P., Overseas Equity Investors Partners

Financial Data: *Fiscal Year End:*09/30 *Latest Annual Data:* 09/30/2007

Year	Sales	Net Income
2007	$119,708,000	$983,000
2006	$100,284,000	$563,000
2005	$79,781,000	$700,000

Curr. Assets:	$30,382,000	**Curr. Liab.:**	$10,973,000	**P/E Ratio:**	72.63
Plant, Equip.:	$18,941,000	**Total Liab.:**	$20,149,000	**Indic. Yr. Divd.:**	NA
Total Assets:	$56,689,000	**Net Worth:**	$36,540,000	**Debt/ Equity:**	0.2084

Tumbleweed Communications Corp

700 Saginaw Dr., Redwood City, CA, 94063; *PH:* 1-650-216-2000; *http://* www.tumbleweed.com;
Email: info@tumbleweed.com

General - Incorporation	DE	**Stock**- Price on:12/24/2007	$2.64
Employees	362	Stock Exchange	NDQ
Auditor	KPMG LLP	Ticker Symbol	TMWD
Stk Agt..... Computershare Investor Services LLC		Outstanding Shares	51,100,000
Counsel	Skadden, Arps	E.P.S.	-$0.15
DUNS No.	NA	Shareholders	NA

Business: The group's principle activity is to provide secure messaging applications for businesses and government organizations using the Internet. The group enables businesses to share sensitive information via e-mail with customers, business partners and suppliers, transforming e-mail into a tool for enhancing communication and increasing and productivity. The group's products enables businesses to improve their ability to enhance customer service, automate traditional paper and voice-based processes, enable secure collaboration with partners, comply with government and company policies to limit liability, enhance employee productivity and prevent network disruption. The group's secure guardian protection solutions include tumbleweed secure mail, tumbleweed secure archive and tumbleweed secure Web. The group's quarterly revenue for Sep '07 was 14.05 millions of USD.

Primary SIC and add'l.: 7372 7379

CIK No: 0001022509

Subsidiaries: Corvigo, LLC, Interface Systems, Inc., Receipt.com, Inc., TC EMEA Ltd., Tumbleweed Communications EOOD, Tumbleweed Communications GmbH, Tumbleweed Communications Holding GmbH, Tumbleweed Communications Limited (1), Tumbleweed Communications Pte. Ltd., Tumbleweed Communications K.K., Valicert B.V., Valicert Japan K.K.

Officers: James P. Scullion/Chmn., CEO/$4,561,367.00, Joseph Fisher/VP - Product Management, Timothy G. Conley/Sr. VP - Finance, CFO/$494,510.00, Bernard J. Cassidy/Sr. VP, General Counsel, Jim W. Cumella/VP - North American Sales, Taher Elgamal/Dir., CTO/$446,443.00, Nicholas Hulse/Exec. VP - Worldwide Field Operations, Michael Norwood/VP - Global Channel Sales

Directors: James P. Scullion/Chmn., CEO, Christopher H. Greendale/Dir., Kenneth R. Klein/Dir., Standish H. O'Grady/Dir., Jeffrey C. Smith/Dir., Taher Elgamal/Dir., CTO, Deborah D. Rieman/Dir., James A. Heisch/Dir.

Owners: Christopher H. Greendale, Denis M. Brotzel, Empire Capital Partners, L.P./9.90%, Insiders/11.20%, Kenneth R. Klein, Jeffrey C. Smith/3.40%, Columbia Wanger Asset Management, L.P./6.90%, James P. Scullion/2.70%, Deborah D. Rieman, Standish H. OGrady, Diker GP, LLC/8.20%, UBS AG/8.80%, Timothy G. Conley/1.40%, Daniel G. Greenberg, James A. Heisch (17 Owners included in Index)

Financial Data: Fiscal Year End:12/31   Latest Annual Data: 12/31/2006

Year	Sales	Net Income
2006	$61,994,000	-$4,882,000
2005	$50,001,000	-$3,909,000
2004	$43,438,000	-$7,497,000

Curr. Assets:	$44,955,000	**Curr. Liab.:**	$29,430,000		
Plant, Equip.:	$1,820,000	**Total Liab.:**	$34,221,000	**Indic. Yr. Divd.:**	NA
Total Assets:	$96,931,000	**Net Worth:**	$62,710,000	**Debt/ Equity:**	NA

Tumi Resouces Ltd

1090 W Georgia St., Ste. 1305, Vancouver, BC, V6E 3V7; *PH:* 1-604-685-9316;
Fax: 1-604-683-1585; *http://* www.tumiresources.com; *Email:* info@tumiresources.com

General - Incorporation	BC	**Stock**- Price on:12/24/2007	$0.98
Employees	NA	Stock Exchange	OTC
Auditor	D&H Group LLP	Ticker Symbol	TUMIF
Stk Agt	Computershare Trust Co	Outstanding Shares	NA
Counsel	NA	E.P.S.	NA
DUNS No.	NA	Shareholders	NA

Business: The groups principal activity is in the exploration on its mineral properties for gold and silver. The group operates from Canada.

Primary SIC and add'l.: 1400

CIK No: 0001191832

Subsidiaries: COMPANIA MINERA CINCO MINAS S.A. DE C.V., KAY METALS LTD., TM RESOURCES AB, TMXI RESOURCES S.A. DE C.V.

Officers: David A. Henstridge/Dir., CEO, Pres., Mariana Bermudez/Sec., Nick L. Nicolaas/Financial, Marketing Consultant, Vancouver, British Columbia, Canada

Directors: David A. Henstridge/Dir., CEO, Pres., Nick Demare/Dir., Harvey Lim/Dir.

Owners: Nick DeMare/5.27%, David Henstridge/7.48%, Harvey Lim/0.91%, Mariana Bermudez/0.29%

Financial Data: Fiscal Year End:12/31   Latest Annual Data: 12/31/2006

Year	Sales	Net Income
2006	NA	-$1,707,000
2005	NA	-$1,205,000
2004	NA	-$3,076,000

Curr. Assets:	$2,581,000	**Curr. Liab.:**	$102,000		
Plant, Equip.:	$203,000	**Total Liab.:**	$102,000	**Indic. Yr. Divd.:**	NA
Total Assets:	$3,350,000	**Net Worth:**	$3,248,000	**Debt/ Equity:**	NA

Tunex International Inc

556 E 2100 S, Salt Lake City, UT, 84106; *PH:* 1-800-486-8133; *http://* www.tunex.com

General - Incorporation	UT	**Stock**- Price on:12/24/2007	$0.35
Employees	19	Stock Exchange	OTC
Auditor .....Wisan, Smith, Racker & Prescott LLP		Ticker Symbol	TNEX
Stk Agt	NA	Outstanding Shares	NA
Counsel	NA	E.P.S	NA
DUNS No.	06-981-5843	Shareholders	NA

Business: The group's principle activity is to provide diagnostic tests and evaluations of the performance of automotive engines and engine related systems. The company also inspects, services and repairs automobiles through its licensed franchisees and franchisee-owned centers named tunex service centers. These centers specialize in the service and repair of most engine-related systems, by using a proven diagnostic approach and analyzing systems, such as ignition, fuel injection, carburetion, emission, computer controls etc. At 31-Mar-2004, there were 32 such company-owned and franchised centers in operation. The company operates in the states of Arizona, colarado, Idaho, Nevada, Ohio, Utah and the commonwealth of Puerto Rico. The group operates from United States.

Primary SIC and add'l.: 7549 7538

CIK No: 0000806129

Subsidiaries: Tunex, Inc.

Officers: Michael Woo/CEO, James Loo/CFO

Financial Data: Fiscal Year End:03/31   Latest Annual Data: 3/31/2006

Year	Sales	Net Income
2006	$1,359,000	-$375,000
2005	$1,142,000	-$61,000
2004	$1,240,000	$51,000

Curr. Assets:	$546,000	**Curr. Liab.:**	$652,000		
Plant, Equip.:	$244,000	**Total Liab.:**	$682,000	**Indic. Yr. Divd.:**	NA
Total Assets:	$1,056,000	**Net Worth:**	$375,000	**Debt/ Equity:**	NA

Tupperware Brands Corp

Formerly: Tupperware Corp
14901 S Orange Blossom Trl., Orlando, FL, 32837; *PH:* 1-407-826-5050;
http:// order.tupperware.com

General - Incorporation	DE	**Stock**- Price on:12/24/2007	$28.81
Employees	12,300	Stock Exchange	NYSE
Auditor	PricewaterhouseCoopers LLP	Ticker Symbol	TUP
Stk Agt	Wells Fargo Bank, N.A.	Outstanding Shares	61,460,000
Counsel	NA	E.P.S.	$1.75
DUNS No.	94-356-1720	Shareholders	NA

Business: The groups principle activity is to operate retail stores. The groups products include storage and serving solutions for the kitchen and beauty and personal care products. The groups products are sold under the brand names Avroy Shlain, BeautiControl, Fuller, NaturCare, Nutrimetics, Nuvo and Swissgarde brands. The group operates from United States.

Primary SIC and add'l.: 3089 3411 3944 5999 2844 2841

CIK No: 0001008654

Subsidiaries: Academia de Negocios S/C Ltda., Centro de Distribuicao Mineira de Produtos de Plastico Ltda., Centro de Distribuicao RS Ltda., Centro Oeste Distribuidora de Produtos Plasticos Ltda., CH Laboratories Pty Ltd, Corcovado-Plast Distribuidora de Artigos Domesticos Ltda., Cosmetic Manufacturers (Malaysia) Pty. Ltd., Dart de Venezuela, C.A., Dart do Brasil Industria e Comercio Ltda., Dart Far East Sdn. Bhd., Dart Industries (New Zealand) Limited, Dart Industries Hong Kong Limited, Dart Industries Inc., Dart, S.A. de C.V., Dartco Manufacturing Inc. 41 Subsidiaries included in the Index

Officers: E. V. Goings/62/Chmn., CEO/$8,516,915.00, Jane V. Garrard/45/VP - Internal Audit, Michael S. Poteshman/44/CFO, Exec. VP/$852,867.00, Lillian D. Garcia/51/Chief Human Resources Officer, Exec. VP, Robert F. Wagner/47/CTO, VP, Jose R. Timmerman/58/Sr. VP - Worldwide Operations, Timothy A. Kulhanek/43/VP, Controller, Josef Hajek/49/Sr. VP - Tax, Government Relations, Edward R. Davis/45/VP, Treasurer, Rashit Ismail/46/VP - Global Product Marketing, Nick Poucher/46/VP, Controller, Carl Benkovich/51/VP - Internal Audit, Glenn R. Drake/55/Group Pres. - Europe, Africa, The Middle East/$1,021,031.00, Gregory T. Sipla/41/VP - Strategy, Business Development, Morgan C. Hare/60/Exec. VP, Chief Marketing Office (21 Officers included in Index)

Directors: E. V. Goings/62/Chmn., CEO, Anne M. Szostak/Dir., Angel R. Martinez/Dir., Rita Bornstein/Dir., Kriss Cloninger/Dir., Joyce M. Roche/Dir., Catherine A. Bertini/Dir., Clifford J. Grum/Dir., Joe R. Lee/Dir., Bob Marbut/Dir., Robert J. Murray/Dir., David R. Parker/Dir., Patrick J. Spainhour/Dir.

Owners: Lord, Abbett & Co. LLC/10.47%, Capital Research and Management Company/11.80%

Financial Data: Fiscal Year End:12/31   Latest Annual Data: 12/30/2006

Year	Sales	Net Income
2006	$1,743,700,000	$94,200,000
2005	$1,279,300,000	$85,400,000
2004	$1,224,300,000	$86,900,000

Curr. Assets:	$672,700,000	**Curr. Liab.:**	$454,700,000	**P/E Ratio:**	16.46
Plant, Equip.:	$254,500,000	**Total Liab.:**	$1,404,700,000	**Indic. Yr. Divd.:**	$0.880
Total Assets:	$1,740,200,000	**Net Worth:**	$335,500,000	**Debt/ Equity:**	1.5494

Turbine Project Services Inc

270 Nw 3rd Ct., Boca, Raton, FL, 33432; *PH:* 1-561-368-1427

General - Incorporation	FL	**Stock**- Price on:12/24/2007	NA
Employees	NA	Stock Exchange	NA
Auditor	NA	Ticker Symbol	NA
Stk Agt	NA	Outstanding Shares	NA
Counsel	NA	E.P.S.	NA
DUNS No.	NA	Shareholders	NA

Business: The group's principal activity is to provide project management services to various aerospace and defense manufacturers.

Primary SIC and add'l.: 9995

CIK No: 0001267874

Turbine Truck Engines Inc

1301 E Inter Speed Blvd., Deland, FL, 32724; *PH:* 1-386-943-8358; *Fax:* 1-386-943-6232;
http:// www.turbinetruckengines.com

General - Incorporation	DE	**Stock**- Price on:12/24/2007	$0.43
Employees	NA	Stock Exchange	OTC
Auditor	Pender Newkirk & Company LLP	Ticker Symbol	NA
Stk Agt	Florida Atlantic Stock Transfer, Inc.	Outstanding Shares	14,710,000
Counsel	NA	E.P.S.	-$0.15
DUNS No.	NA	Shareholders	NA

Business: The groups principal activities include designing and prototyping 540 hp engine for use in highway trucks. The group operates from the United States.

Primary SIC and add'l.: 3511

CIK No: 0001138978

Officers: Michael H. Rouse/Founder, Chmn., CEO, Robert Scragg/Research, Development Team Member, Zlatko Petrovic/Research, Development Team, Member, James A. Teters/Dir., Pres., Phyllis J. Rouse/Dir., VP, Sec., Treasurer

Directors: Michael H. Rouse/Founder, Chmn., CEO, Magdy Attia/Chmn. - Advisory Board, James A. Teters/Dir., Pres., Phyllis J. Rouse/Dir., VP, Sec., Treasurer

Owners: James A. Teters, Phyllis J. Rouse/1.13%, Insiders/74.64%, Michael Rouse/35.14%, Alpha Engines Corporation/37.61%

Financial Data: Fiscal Year End:12/31 **Latest Annual Data:** 12/31/2006

Year	Sales	Net Income
2006	NA	-$1,465,000
2005	NA	-$1,069,000

Curr. Assets:	$1,000	Curr. Liab.:	$462,000		
Plant, Equip.:	$3,000	Total Liab.:	$464,000	Indic. Yr. Divd.:	NA
Total Assets:	$4,000	Net Worth:	-$460,000	Debt/ Equity:	NA

Turbochef Technologies Inc

Six Concourse Pkwy, Ste 1900, Atlanta, GA, 30328; *PH:* 1-678-987-1700; *http://* www.turbochef.com

General - Incorporation	DE	Stock - Price on:12/24/2007	$14.02
Employees	158	Stock Exchange	NDQ
Auditor	Ernst & Young LLP	Ticker Symbol	OVEN
Stk Agt.	Mellon Investor Services LLC	Outstanding Shares	NA
Counsel	Hallett & Perrin PC	E.P.S.	-$0.92
DUNS No.	78-798-7171	Shareholders	NA

Business: The group's principal activities are to design, develop and market proprietary cooking systems. These technologies provide foodservice operators the flexibility to "Cook-To-Order" a variety of foods items at speed, which are faster than those permitted by conventional commercial ovens. The proprietary systems include turbocom, a centralized cook setting system, which, through the use of a computer modem, can reprogram turbochef ovens installed in various restaurant locations from a single central site. Commercial cooking systems are marketed under the name of turbochef. Turbostage, a food preparation management system, which can be incorporated into a restaurant's existing electronic order processing system, sort the items to be cooked by required cook times, and indicate, on real-time basis, when such food items are to be inserted into turbochef oven. On 24-May-2004, the group acquired enersyst development center llc.

Primary SIC and add'l.: 3589

CIK No: 0000916545

Officers: James K. Price/48/Dir., CEO, Pres., Paul P. Lehr/COO, Al Cochran/CFO, Joe McGrain/Pres. - Residential Division, Steve Beshara/Chief Branding Officer, Dennis J. Stockwell/General Counsel, Maxwell T. Abbott/Chief Strategy Officer, Peter J. Ashcraft/Sr. VP - Global Sales, Business Development

Directors: James K. Price/48/Dir., CEO, Pres., Richard Perlman/60/Chmn., James W. Deyoung/63/Dir., Anthony Jolliffe/68/Dir., Thomas J. Presby/67/Dir., William A. Shutzer/59/Dir., Raymond H. Welsh/75/Dir.

Owners: Richard E. Perlman/8.60%, Steven Shapiro/5.00%, Jack Silver/5.20%, Thomas J. Presby, James K. Price/7.40%, James K. Price/7.10%, Ergates Capital Management, LLC/9.70%, Joseph T. McGrain, Insiders/26.10%, William A. Shutzer/6.40%, Paul P. Lehr, Jeffrey B. Bogatin/5.00%, FMR Corp./14.60%, James A. Cochran/1.10%, James W. DeYoung/1.20% *(17 Owners included in Index)*

Financial Data: Fiscal Year End:12/31 **Latest Annual Data:** 12/31/2005

Year	Sales	Net Income
2005	$52,249,000	-$28,154,000
2004	$70,894,000	$9,679,000
2003	$3,690,000	-$14,349,000

Curr. Assets:	$46,886,000	Curr. Liab.:	$21,209,000		
Plant, Equip.:	$7,944,000	Total Liab.:	$26,070,000	Indic. Yr. Divd.:	NA
Total Assets:	$71,775,000	Net Worth:	$45,705,000	Debt/ Equity:	NA

Turbodyne Technologies Inc

36 E Barnett St., Ventura, CA, 93109; *PH:* 1-805-201-3133; *http://* www.turbodyne.com

General - Incorporation	NV	Stock - Price on:12/24/2007	$0.038
Employees	NA	Stock Exchange	OTC
Auditor	Vasquez & Co. LLP	Ticker Symbol	TRBD
Stk Agt.	Computershare Investor Services LLC	Outstanding Shares	357,460,000
Counsel	NA	E.P.S.	-$0.01
DUNS No.	NA	Shareholders	NA

Business: The groups principle activity is to produce Turbopac(TM) products. The group operates from the United States. The group's revenue for Sep '07 was 0.01 millions of USD.

Primary SIC and add'l.: 3714

CIK No: 0001022097

Subsidiaries: Electronic Boosting Systems, Inc., Turbodyne Germany Ltd., Turbodyne Systems Inc.

Officers: Albert F. Case/Dir., CEO, Pres., Debi Kokinos/VP, CFO, Corp. Sec., Arnold W. Kwong/VP - Product Development, Engineering, Thomas M. Prusinski/VP - Engineering, Al Case/Investor Relations Officer - US, Sven Liebetanz/Investor Relations Officer - European

Directors: Albert F. Case/Dir., CEO, Pres., Jason Meyers/Chmn.

Owners: Aspatuck Holdings Ltd/28.37%, Insiders/30.47%, Debi Kokinos, Albert F. Case/1.06%, Jason Meyers/29.20%

Financial Data: Fiscal Year End:12/31 **Latest Annual Data:** 12/31/2006

Year	Sales	Net Income
2006	$22,000	-$1,480,000
2005	$22,000	$221,000
2004	$22,000	$2,910,000

Curr. Assets:	$15,000	Curr. Liab.:	$7,973,000		
Plant, Equip.:	$1,000	Total Liab.:	$8,292,000	Indic. Yr. Divd.:	NA
Total Assets:	$16,000	Net Worth:	-$8,276,000	Debt/ Equity:	NA

TurboSonic Technologies Inc

239 New Rd., Bldg. B, Ste. 205, Parsippany, NJ, 07054; *PH:* 1-973-244-9544; *Fax:* 1-973-244-9545; *http://* www.turbosonic.com; *Email:* info@turbosonic.com

General - Incorporation	DE	Stock - Price on:12/24/2007	$1.14
Employees	NA	Stock Exchange	OTC
Auditor	Ernst & Young, Mintz & Partners LLP	Ticker Symbol	TSTA
Stk Agt.	American Stock Transfer & Trust Co.	Outstanding Shares	NA
Counsel	Sonnenschein Nath & Rosenthal LLP	E.P.S.	NA
DUNS No.	00-152-2713	Shareholders	NA

Business: The group's principal activities are to design and market integrated pollution control systems and to provide rehabilitation, maintenance and other services. The group's proprietary technology is designed to control a wide variety of air pollution control problems for industries including pulp and paper, wood products, mining, non-ferrous metallurgical, iron and steel, chemical, food and beverage, waste processing, power generation, automotive and cement. The group's operations are carried out through two segments: scrubber and nozzle systems. The wet scrubber systems are used to absorb gaseous pollutants and particulate matter contained in exhaust gas streams, such as smokestacks, and incorporate the use of the group's proprietary air-atomizing nozzle technology. Nozzle systems typically operate in conjunction with products and systems supplied by others.

Primary SIC and add'l.: 3589 3564

CIK No: 0000900393

Subsidiaries: TurboSonic Canada, Inc., TurboSonic Europe Limited, TurboSonic Inc.

Officers: Edward F. Spink/Chmn., CEO, David J. Hobson/VP - Finance - Administration, Robert A. Allan/VP - Engineering, Egbert Q. Van Everdingen/Dir., Pres., Sec., Treasurer, Richard C. Gimpel/VP - Marketing, Sales, Carl Young/CFO

Directors: Edward F. Spink/Chmn., CEO, Egbert Q. Van Everdingen/Dir., Pres., Sec., Treasurer, Julien J. Hradecky/Dir., Richard D. Hurd/Dir., Donald Spink/Founder, Dir., Glen O. Wright/Dir., Andrew T. Meikle/Dir., Ken Kivenko/Dir.

Owners: Julien J. Hradecky/1.40%, Richard C. Gimpel, Andrew T. Meikle, Edward F. Spink/7.00%, Dynamis Advisors, LLC/10.00%, Donald R. Spink/8.10%, Bard Associates, Inc./7.00%, Boston Partners Asset Management LLC/5.00%, Glen O. Wright, Richard H. Hurd, Egbert Q. van Everdingen/2.10%, Insiders/21.20%, Heartland Advisors, Inc./6.10%, Ronald A. Berube, Ken Kivenko *(16 Owners included in Index)*

Financial Data: Fiscal Year End:06/30 **Latest Annual Data:** 06/30/2007

Year	Sales	Net Income
2007	$22,893,000	$1,281,000
2006	$16,047,000	$816,000
2005	$11,096,000	-$227,000

Curr. Assets:	$7,717,000	Curr. Liab.:	$5,440,000		
Plant, Equip.:	$378,000	Total Liab.:	$5,440,000	Indic. Yr. Divd.:	NA
Total Assets:	$8,507,000	Net Worth:	$3,067,000	Debt/ Equity:	NA

Turkcell Iletisim Hizmetleri

Turkcell Plz., Mesrutiyet Caddesi No: 71, Tepebasi, Istanbul, 80050; *PH:* 0212-313 10 00; *http://* www.turkcell.com.tr

General - Incorporation	Turkey	Stock - Price on:12/24/2007	$15.99
Employees	7,476	Stock Exchange	NYSE
Auditor	Pricewaterhousecoopers LLP	Ticker Symbol	TKC
Stk Agt.	Morgan Guaranty Trust Co	Outstanding Shares	880,000,000
Counsel	Paksoy & Co	E.P.S.	$1.41
DUNS No.	NA	Shareholders	NA

Business: The group's principle activities are the provision of mobile services, network services and other related activities. The company operates under a license where by the company pays the turkish treasury a monthly fee equal to 15% of gross revenue. The group's quarterly revenue for Sep '07 was 1,722.77 millions of USD.

Primary SIC and add'l.: 4899 4813

CIK No: 0001071321

Subsidiaries: Astelit LLC, Azercell Telekom B.M., Azeronline Ltd., Azertel, Bilisim Telekomunikasyon Hizmetleri A.S., Closed Joint Stock Company of Digital Cellular Communications, Corbuss Kurumsal Telekom Servis Hizmetleri A.S., East Asian Consortium B.V., Euroasia Telecommunications Holdings B.V., Fintur Holdings B.V., Fintur International B.V., Geocell Ltd., Global Bilgi Pazarlama Danisma ve Cagri Servisi Hizmetleri A.S., Gurtel, Hayat Boyu Egitim ve Iletisim Hizmetleri A.S. 25 Subsidiaries included in the Index

Officers: Sureyya Ciliv/49/CEO, Serkan Okandan/38/CFO, Tulin Karabuk/43/Chief Investment Officer, Selen Kocabas/39/Chief Business Support Officer, Ilter Terzioglu/41/Chief Network Operations, Regulations Officer, Cenk Bayrakdar/39/Chief Servicesl, Product Development Officer, Cenk Serdar/39/Chief Value Added Services Officer, Lale Saral Develioglu/39/Chief Marketing Officer, Levent Burak Demiralp/43/Chief Sales Officer

Directors: Mehmet Emin Karamehmet/Chmn., Tero Erkki Kivisaari/Dir., Erdal A. Durukan/32/Dir., Mehmet Bulent Ergin/Dir., Anders Igel/57/Dir., Oleg Malis/Dir., Alexey Khudyakov/Dir., Colin J. Williams/Dir.

Owners: M.V. Holding A.S./3.82%, Bankrupt Bilka Bilgi Kaynak Ve Iletisim San.ve Tic. A.S./0.01%, Cukurova Holding A.S./4.46%, Turkiye Genel Sigorta A.S./0.07%, Turkcell Holding A.S./51.00%, M.V. Investments N.V./1.25%, Sonera Holding B.V./13.07%, Cukurova Investments N.V./2.93%

Financial Data: Fiscal Year End:12/31 **Latest Annual Data:** 12/31/2006

Year	Sales	Net Income
2006	$4,700,307,000	$1,015,638,000
2005	$4,268,492,000	$910,927,000
2004	$3,200,765,000	$511,821,000

Curr. Assets:	$2,182,118,000	Curr. Liab.:	$1,635,674,000	P/E Ratio:	15.26
Plant, Equip.:	$1,916,991,000	Total Liab.:	$2,063,143,000	Indic. Yr. Divd.:	$0.470
Total Assets:	$5,512,368,000	Net Worth:	$3,449,225,000	Debt/ Equity:	NA

Turnaround Partners Inc

Formerly: Nuwave Technologies Inc
109 N Post Oak Ln., Ste. 422, Houston, TX, 77024; *PH:* 1-713-621-2737; *http://* www.nuwave-tech.com

General - Incorporation	DE	Stock - Price on:12/24/2007	NA
Employees	5	Stock Exchange	NA
Auditor	Thomas Leger & Co. LLP	Ticker Symbol	NA
Stk Agt.	American Stock Transfer & Trust Co.	Outstanding Shares	NA
Counsel	NA	E.P.S.	$0.034
DUNS No.	94-938-4606	Shareholders	NA

Business: The group's principle activities include developing, manufacturing and marketing proprietary video-enhancement technology. The company's three product lines are the nuwave video processor technology, retail products and digital filtering technology. The video processor technology is designed to enhance video output devices with clearer, sharper details and more vibrant colors when viewed on the display screen. The retail products include set-top boxes for use with vcr's, DVD's. The digital filtering technologies are used to remove graininess and digital artifacts. The company markets its products in the United States, European common union, Japan and Korea. The group operates from United States.

Primary SIC and add'l.: 3663

CIK No: 0001009802

Subsidiaries: Lehigh Acquisition Corp

Officers: Timothy J. Connolly/55/Vice Chmn., CEO, Pres., Mark Roy/Sr. Consultant, Ernest L. Guerrera/Pres., Dave Belliveau/Sr. Software Architect, William Chris Mathers/48/CFO

Directors: Timothy J. Connolly/55/Vice Chmn., CEO, Pres., Fred S. Zeidman/61/Chmn.

Owners: Timothy J. Connolly, Michael O. Sutton, Michael Kesselbrenner, Adam Gottbetter, Mary-Ellen Viola, Gerald Holland, Louis Kesselbrenner, Sarah Kesselbrenner, Joanna Saporito, Insiders, Jan Carson Connolly, David Kesselbrenner

Financial Data: Fiscal Year End:12/31 Latest Annual Data: 12/31/2006

Year	Sales	Net Income
2006	$1,178,000	$4,936,000
2005	$592,000	-$4,221,000
2004	NA	-$336,000

Curr. Assets:	$2,068,000	Curr. Liab.:	$4,002,000		
Plant, Equip.:	$70,000	Total Liab.:	$9,417,000	Indic. Yr. Divd.:	NA
Total Assets:	$7,107,000	Net Worth:	-$2,311,000	Debt/ Equity:	NA

Turner Valley Oil & Gas Inc

6160 Genoa Bay Rd. , Duncan, BC, V9L 5Y5; *PH:* 1-250-745-1551; *http://* www.turvagas.com; *Email:* ir@turvagas.com

General - Incorporation	NV	Stock- Price on:12/24/2007	$0.017
Employees	NA	Stock Exchange	OTC
Auditor	Chisholm Bierwolf & Nilson LLC	Ticker Symbol	TVOG
Stk Agt	Madison & Co.	Outstanding Shares	NA
Counsel	NA	E.P.S.	NA
DUNS No.	NA	Shareholders	NA

Business: The group's principal activity is to explore oil and gas. The operations are carried out through its wholly owned subsidiary, TV oil and gas Canada limited, which has, over 9,000 acres of prime exploration lands in the triangle project. The group also operates in partnership with win energy inc. The operations are focused on increasing production by means of continuing acquisitions, development projects and exploration drilling within a joint venture framework. The group changed its business from originally organized to create a series of 16 specialized auto salvage yards.

Primary SIC and add'l.: 5015

CIK No: 0001098343

Subsidiaries: TV Oil and Gas Canada Limited

Officers: Christopher Paton-Gay/Chmn., CEO, Kulwant Sandher/CFO, Pres., Greg Werbowski/Investor Relations Officer

Directors: Christopher Paton-Gay/Chmn., CEO

Owners: Kulwant Sander/2.14%, Christopher Paton-Gay/3.90%, Donald Jackson Wells/0.13%, Joseph Kane/0.13%, Insiders/6.30%

Financial Data: Fiscal Year End:12/31 Latest Annual Data: 03/31/2007

Year	Sales	Net Income
2007	NA	NA
2006	$10,000	-$287,000
2005	$2,000	-$473,000

Curr. Assets:	$9,000	Curr. Liab.:	$427,000		
Plant, Equip.:	$954,000	Total Liab.:	$427,000	Indic. Yr. Divd.:	NA
Total Assets:	$1,567,000	Net Worth:	$1,140,000	Debt/ Equity:	NA

Turnstone Systems Inc

7650 Marathon Dr., Ste. A, Livermore, CA, 94550; *PH:* 1-408-907-1400; *http://* www.turnstone.com

General - Incorporation	DE	Stock- Price on:12/24/2007	$0.011
Employees	NA	Stock Exchange	OTC
Auditor	KPMG LLP	Ticker Symbol	TSTN
Stk Agt	Bank of Boston	Outstanding Shares	NA
Counsel	Wilson Sonsini Goodrich & Rosati	E.P.S.	NA
DUNS No.	NA	Shareholders	NA

Business: The group had adopted a plan of complete liquidation and dissolution on 06-Aug-2003. Formerly it was a provider of hardware and software product.

Primary SIC and add'l.: 7389 3669

CIK No: 0001054131

Subsidiaries: Turnstone Australia Pty. Ltd., Turnstone do Brasil Ltda., Turnstone Holdings LLC, Turnstone Hong Kong Ltd., Turnstone International (UK) Limited, Turnstone Singapore Ltd., Turnstone Systems GmbH, Turnstone Systems International Ltd., Turnstone Systems SARL

Officers: Eric S. Yeaman/37/Dir., CEO, CFO, Albert Y. Liu/35/Dir., General Counsel, Dir. - Human Resources

Directors: Eric S. Yeaman/37/Dir., CEO, CFO, Albert Y. Liu/35/Dir., General Counsel, Dir. - Human Resources

Owners: Eric S. Yeaman, Richard N. Tinsley/8.70%, Benchmark Capital Partners/6.80%, Kingston P. Duffie/8.80%, Albert Y. Liu, Insiders

Financial Data: Fiscal Year End:12/31 Latest Annual Data: 12/31/2002

Year	Sales	Net Income
2002	$3,787,000	-$25,540,000
2001	$13,431,000	-$80,561,000
2000	$149,365,000	$22,362,000

Curr. Assets:	$165,390,000	Curr. Liab.:	$4,203,000		
Plant, Equip.:	$1,495,000	Total Liab.:	$4,878,000	Indic. Yr. Divd.:	NA
Total Assets:	$217,825,000	Net Worth:	$212,947,000	Debt/ Equity:	NA

Tuscany Minerals Ltd

1155 20th St., West Vancouver, BC, V7V 3Z4; *PH:* 1-604-926-4300

General - Incorporation	NV	Stock- Price on:12/24/2007	NA
Employees	NA	Stock Exchange	OTC
Auditor	Morgan & Co	Ticker Symbol	TCAY
Stk Agt	Pacific Stock Transfer Company	Outstanding Shares	NA
Counsel	NA	E.P.S.	NA
DUNS No.	NA	Shareholders	NA

Business: The group's principle activities include acquiring and exploring mineral properties. The company's current plan is to acquire an interest in either a new prospective or existing mineral property or a prospective or producing oil and gas property. The group operates from United States.

Primary SIC and add'l.: 1041

CIK No: 0001128790

Officers: Stephen J. Barley/51/Dir., Pres., Sec., Treasurer, CEO

Directors: Stephen J. Barley/51/Dir., Pres., Sec., Treasurer, CEO

Owners: Insiders/50.40%, Stephen J. Barley/50.40%

Tutogen Medical Inc

13709 Progress Blvd., Alachua, FL, 32615; *PH:* 1-386-462-0402; *http://* www.tutogen.com

General - Incorporation	FL	Stock- Price on:12/24/2007	$9.29
Employees	222	Stock Exchange	AMEX
Auditor	Deloitte & Touche LLP	Ticker Symbol	TTG
Stk Agt	Computershare Investor Services LLC	Outstanding Shares	18,640,000
Counsel	NA	E.P.S.	NA
DUNS No.	16-080-6964	Shareholders	NA

Business: The group's principal activities are to develop, manufacture and market bio-implants and medical devices. The devices are used for tissue and bone repair for neuro, orthopedic, spine, dental and reconstructive and general surgical applications. The core activity of the group is processing human donor tissue using tutoplast(R) process of tissue preservation and viral inactivation. The group distributes products mainly to hospitals and select physicians. The international markets for the group consist mainly of European countries, Germany, France, Italy, Spain and the United Kingdom.

Primary SIC and add'l.: 3842

CIK No: 0000816949

Subsidiaries: Tutogen Medical (United States), Inc, Tutogen Medical GmbH

Owners: Roy D. Crowninshield, Adrian J. R. Smith, Zimmer CEP (formerly Centerpulse) USA Holding Co./27.30%, Guy L. Mayer, Clifton Seliga, Carlton E. Turner, Harold J. Helderman, Udo Henseler, Russell G. Cleveland, Insiders/3.50%, Claude Pering, Millenco, LLC/5.20%, Robert L. Johnston, Neal B. Freeman

Financial Data: Fiscal Year End:09/30 Latest Annual Data: 9/30/2006

Year	Sales	Net Income
2006	$37,947,000	-$589,000
2005	$31,860,000	-$7,017,000
2004	$29,330,000	$1,503,000

Curr. Assets:	$24,250,000	Curr. Liab.:	$16,035,000	P/E Ratio:	211.14
Plant, Equip.:	$12,940,000	Total Liab.:	$23,696,000	Indic. Yr. Divd.:	NA
Total Assets:	$38,917,000	Net Worth:	$15,221,000	Debt/ Equity:	0.1731

Tuxis Corp

11 Hanover Sq., New York, NY, 10005; *PH:* 1-212-785-9300; *Fax:* 1-212-363-1102; *http://* www.tuxis.com

General - Incorporation	MD	Stock- Price on:12/24/2007	NA
Employees	NA	Stock Exchange	NA
Auditor	Tait, Weller & Baker LLP	Ticker Symbol	NA
Stk Agt	American Stock Transfer & Trust Co.	Outstanding Shares	NA
Counsel	NA	E.P.S.	NA
DUNS No.	NA	Shareholders	NA

Business: The group operates through its subsidiary, whose principal activity is real estate business. The group operates from the United States.

Primary SIC and add'l.: 6199

CIK No: 0000736952

Subsidiaries: Tuxis Operations LLC, Tuxis Real Estate Brokerage LLC, Tuxis Real Estate I LLC, Tuxis Real Estate II LLC, Winmark Properties I LLC

TVI Corp

7100 Holladay Tyler Rd. , Glen Dale, MD, 20769; *PH:* 1-301-352-8800; *http://* www.tvicorp.com; *Email:* sales@tvicorp.com

General - Incorporation	MD	Stock- Price on:12/24/2007	$0.59
Employees	280	Stock Exchange	NDQ
Auditor	Stegman & Co	Ticker Symbol	NA
Stk Agt	Securities Transfer Corp	Outstanding Shares	33,230,000
Counsel	NA	E.P.S.	-$0.511
DUNS No.	08-351-0149	Shareholders	NA

Business: The group's principal activity is to design, manufacture and sell rapidly deployable integrated shelter systems. It also designs and manufactures the key accessories used with shelters that are required to make integrated system for decontamination, command control, forensic investigation, disaster assistance, communication centers, patient isolation. In addition to shelters, the group supplies lighting, water heaters, air heaters, power generators, flooring, trailers and air filtration units. On 28-Apr-2004, the group acquired capa manufacturing, llc.

Primary SIC and add'l.: 3812

CIK No: 0000352079

Subsidiaries: CAPA Manufacturing Corp., Safety Tech International, Inc.

Officers: Harley A. Hughes/CEO, Interim Pres., Sean R. Hunt/VP, General Counsel, Sec., Jim Buckley/Investor Relations, George J. Roberts/Sr. VP, CFO, Treasurer, Assist. Sec./$274,127.00, Donald C. Yount/COO, Interim Sr. VP, Jim Gaffney/Regional Sales Mgr. - Upper Midwest, USA, Canada, Gordon Jack/Regional Sales Mgr. - Northwest, USA, Canada, Mark Harris/Regional Sales

Mgr. - Lower Midwest, Manny Diaz/Regional Sales Mgr. - Southeast, Lee Milton/Regional Sales Mgr. - Southwest, Kevin Kairys/Regional Sales Mgr. - Southwest, Randy Deal/Regional Sales Mgr. - South Central, Glen Howard/Regional Sales Mgr. - US, Military Sales, Thomas N. Brown/49/Pres. - Companys Subsidiary

Directors: Harley A. Hughes/CEO, Interim Pres., Mark N. Hammond/Chmn.

Owners: Atlas Master Fund, Ltd./7.20%, Todd L. Parchman, Insiders/8.30%, Donald C. Yount, Royce& Associates, LLC/8.50%, Kern Capital Management, LLC/6.50%, Harley A. Hughes, Schwartz Investment Counsel, Inc./5.00%, Mark N. Hammond/2.10%, Charles L. Sample/1.80%, Thomas N. Brown, Richard V. Priddy/1.90%, Matthew M. OConnell, George J. Roberts

Financial Data: Fiscal Year End:12/31 Latest Annual Data: 12/31/2006

Year	Sales	Net Income
2006	$36,165,000	$1,908,000
2005	$32,836,000	$5,038,000
2004	$37,862,000	$6,442,000

Curr. Assets:	$27,407,000	Curr. Liab.:	$7,680,000		
Plant, Equip.:	$18,428,000	Total Liab.:	$34,093,000	Indic. Yr. Divd.:	NA
Total Assets:	$72,791,000	Net Worth:	$38,698,000	Debt/ Equity:	NA

Tvia Inc

4001 Burton Dr., Santa Clara, CA, 95054; **PH:** 1-408-982-8588; **http://** www.tvia.com; **Email:** ir@tvia.com

General - Incorporation	DE	**Stock**- Price on:12/24/2007	$0.26
Employees	205	Stock Exchange	OTC
Auditor	BDO Seidman LLP	Ticker Symbol	TVIA
Stk Agt	Mellon Investor Services LLC	Outstanding Shares	30,120,000
Counsel	Pillsbury Winthrop LLP	E.P.S.	-$0.52
DUNS No.	NA	Shareholders	NA

Business: The group's principle activity is to design, develop and market display processors for the interactive-television market as well as a family of flexible high-quality display processors. The group offers five product families: the trueview 5700 family, the cyberpro 5600 family, the cyberpro 5202 family, the cyberpro 5300 family and the cyberpro 5000 family. These products generate revenue through broadband set-box market of the emerging interactive display market, primarily for video-on-demand applications. The group markets its products directly to original equipment manufacturers and through a number of distributors. The products are sold to customers in the United States, Europe, Taiwan and Japan.

Primary SIC and add'l.: 3674 7372

CIK No: 0001109279

Subsidiaries: Tvia, Inc.

Officers: Eli Porat/Chmn., CEO, Pres., Diane Bjorkstrom/CFO, David Medin/CTO, VP - Engineering, Keith Yee/CFO

Directors: Eli Porat/Chmn., CEO, Pres., James Bunker/Dir., Du Baichuan/Dir., Tom Oswold/Dir., David Levi/Dir., Celso Azevedo/Dir., Bruce Berkoff/Dir.

Financial Data: Fiscal Year End:03/31 Latest Annual Data: 3/31/2006

Year	Sales	Net Income
2006	$5,600,000	-$9,580,000
2005	$3,281,000	-$7,640,000
2004	$2,309,000	$936,000

Curr. Assets:	$21,406,000	Curr. Liab.:	$6,969,000		
Plant, Equip.:	$928,000	Total Liab.:	$7,180,000	Indic. Yr. Divd.:	NA
Total Assets:	$22,637,000	Net Worth:	$15,457,000	Debt/ Equity:	NA

TWC

545 5th Ave., Ste. 940, New York, NY, 10017; **PH:** 1-212-983-3355; **Fax:** 1-212-983-8129; **http://** www.transwc.com; **Email:** info@transwc.com

General - Incorporation	NV	**Stock**- Price on:12/24/2007	$3.6
Employees	564	Stock Exchange	OTC
Auditor	Rothstein, Kass & Co, P.C	Ticker Symbol	TWOC
Stk Agt	Continental Stock Transfer & Trust Co	Outstanding Shares	7,840,000
Counsel	NA	E.P.S.	$0.40
DUNS No.	87-438-0546	Shareholders	NA

Business: The group's principal activities are to acquire, develop and manage niche casino operations in Europe, which feature gaming tables and mechanized gaming devices, such as slot and video poker machines. The group also develops and manages small to midsize hotels. Presently, the group owns three casinos, which are located in ceska kubice, rozvadov and hate (near znojmo) in the czech republic. The group competes with a number of local and foreign casinos. Presently there are no operations in the United States.

Primary SIC and add'l.: 7993 5812 7011

CIK No: 0000914577

Subsidiaries: 21st Century Resorts a.s., American Chance Casinos a.s., Atlantic Properties, s.r.o., Hollywood Spin s.r.o., LMJ Slots s.r.o., SC98A, s.r.o., Sibylle Hotel GmbH, Trans World Gaming International U.S. Corp., Trans World Hotels, s.r.o.

Officers: Rami S. Ramadan/59/Dir., CEO, CFO, Pres./$452,000.00, Hung Le/Corporate Controller, Sarah Wagner/Dir. - Project Development, Jill Yarussi/Mgr. - Administration, Corporate Communications, Simon Newton/MD - Casino Division, Paul Benkley/Dir. - Development, Pavel Marsik/Regional Controller, Tomas Kment/Dir. - Administration, Roland Stamberger/Dir. - Regional Marketing

Directors: Rami S. Ramadan/59/Dir., CEO, CFO, Pres., Julio E. Heurtematte/72/Dir., Malcolm M.B. Sterrett/65/Dir., Geoffrey B. Baker/58/Dir., Timothy G. Ewing/47/Dir.

Owners: Julio E. Heurtematte, Insiders/41.40%, SC Fundamental Funds Group/6.70%, Rami S. Ramadan/4.70%, Geoffrey B. Baker, Special Situations Funds/23.50%, Malcolm M.B. Sterrett, Wynnefield Small Cap Value Offshore Fund, Ltd./16.00%, Timothy G. Ewing/37.60%

Financial Data: Fiscal Year End:12/31 Latest Annual Data: 12/31/2006

Year	Sales	Net Income
2006	$26,216,000	$2,027,000
2005	$23,249,000	$79,000
2004	$18,938,000	$1,247,000

Curr. Assets:	$4,785,000	Curr. Liab.:	$7,405,000	P/E Ratio:	13.33
Plant, Equip.:	$18,099,000	Total Liab.:	$10,972,000	Indic. Yr. Divd.:	NA
Total Assets:	$31,226,000	Net Worth:	$20,254,000	Debt/ Equity:	0.1304

Twenty Services Inc

20 Cropwell Dr., Ste. 100, Pell City, AL, 35128; **PH:** 1-205-884-7932

General - Incorporation	AL	**Stock**- Price on:12/24/2007	NA
Employees	NA	Stock Exchange	NA
Auditor	Bkr Borland Benefield	Ticker Symbol	NA
Stk Agt	NA	Outstanding Shares	NA
Counsel	NA	E.P.S.	NA
DUNS No.	07-546-4263	Shareholders	NA

Business: The group's principal activity is to provide finance for purchase and sale of real estate. The general finance business includes extending credit to finance various real estate projects, including the purchase of single-family dwellings and commercial real estate, and to finance home improvements and also for business and miscellaneous purposes.

Primary SIC and add'l.: 6159

CIK No: 0000031704

Officers: Jack C. Bridges/80/Exec. VP

Directors: David J. Noble/76/Chmn., A. J. Strickland/66/Vice Chmn.

Owners: A. J. Strickland/3.88%, David J. Noble/52.29%, Insiders/56.18%

Twin Disc Inc

1328 Racine St., Racine, WI, 53403; **PH:** 1-262-638-4000; **Fax:** 1-262-638-4481; **http://** www.twindisc.com

General - Incorporation	WI	**Stock**- Price on:12/24/2007	$73.15
Employees	872	Stock Exchange	NDQ
Auditor	PricewaterhouseCoopers LLP	Ticker Symbol	TWIN
Stk Agt	Mellon Investor Services LLC	Outstanding Shares	5,850,000
Counsel	Von Briesen & Roper	E.P.S.	$1.97
DUNS No.	00-609-0997	Shareholders	NA

Business: The group's principle activity is to design, manufacture and market heavy-duty off-highway power transmission equipment for domestic and foreign customers. The products include marine transmissions and surface drives; power-shift transmissions; power take-offs and reduction gears; industrial clutches; and control systems. The group sells its products to customers primarily in the construction equipment, industrial equipment, government, marine, energy and natural resources and agricultural markets. The group's worldwide sales to both domestic and foreign customers are transacted through a direct sales force and a distributor network. The group operates in the United States, Belgium and other countries. The group's quarterly revenue for Sep '07 was 73.61 millions of USD.

Primary SIC and add'l.: 3568 3569

CIK No: 0000100378

Subsidiaries: Mill-Log Equipment Co., Inc, Twin Disc, Twin Disc (Far East) Ltd

Officers: Michael E. Batten/Chmn., CEO, Pres./$3,477,986.00, Christopher J. Eperjesy/VP - Finance, CFO, Sec./$888,990.00, Dean J. Bratel/VP - Engineering, Jeffrey S. Knutson/Corporate Controller, Henri-Claude Fabry/VP - Global Distribution, John H. Batten/Dir., Exec. VP/$762,596.00, James E. Feiertag/Exec. VP/$861,270.00, Denise L. Wilcox/VP - Human Resources

Directors: Michael E. Batten/Chmn., CEO, Pres., David R. Zimmer/Dir., David L. Swift/Dir., John H. Batten/Dir., Exec. VP, John A. Mellowes/Dir., David B. Rayburn/Dir., Harold M. Stratton/Dir., Malcolm F. Moore/Dir.

Owners: Christopher J. Eperjesy, Insiders/24.20%, Harold M. Stratton, Michael E. Batten/22.60%, John A. Mellowes, James E. Feiertag, John H. Batten, David B. Rayburn, David R. Zimmer, Malcolm F. Moore, David L. Swift, Clarus Capital Group Management LP/5.20%

Financial Data: Fiscal Year End:06/30 Latest Annual Data: 6/30/2006

Year	Sales	Net Income
2006	$243,287,000	$14,453,000
2005	$218,472,000	$6,910,000
2004	$186,089,000	$5,643,000

Curr. Assets:	$151,131,000	Curr. Liab.:	$79,621,000	P/E Ratio:	19.88
Plant, Equip.:	$46,958,000	Total Liab.:	$146,939,000	Indic. Yr. Divd.:	$0.560
Total Assets:	$236,172,000	Net Worth:	$89,233,000	Debt/ Equity:	0.5027

TWL Corp

Formerly: Trinity Learning Corp
4101 International Pk.way, Carrollton, TX, 75007; **PH:** 1-972-309-4000; **http://** www.trinitycompanies.com

General - Incorporation	UT	**Stock**- Price on:12/24/2007	$0.14
Employees	210	Stock Exchange	OTC
Auditor	KBA Group, LLP	Ticker Symbol	TWLO
Stk Agt	Bank of New York	Outstanding Shares	43,980,000
Counsel	NA	E.P.S.	-$0.17
DUNS No.	13-085-9903	Shareholders	NA

Business: The group's principal activity is to provide advanced learning solutions for corporations, organizations and individuals. The group through its subsidiary cbl global corp. Markets a suite of workplace learning guides for mining and related industries. The group operates in the United States and Australia. In 2003, the group acquired competency based learning inc., touchvision inc, river murray training pty ltd and 51% interest in ayrshire trading limited. On Mar 1, 2004, the group acquired vilpas(virtual learning partners as).

Primary SIC and add'l.: 7375 8299 6719

CIK No: 0000101704

Subsidiaries: River Murray Training Proprietary Ltd., TWL Knowledge Corporation, VILPAS Norway.

Officers: Dennis J. Cagan/Chmn., CEO, Pres., David Batstone/Dir. - Professor, Speaker, Consultant, Bill Buchanan/VP - Operations, Lonny Wilder/VP - Government Solutions, Pat Quinn/CFO, Thomas E. Morris/Sr. VP, Chief Marketing Officer, Andrew Lechner/CIO, VP, Lane Rubrecht/Sr. VP - Worldwide Sales, Debbie Clark/VP - Sales, Randy Corbin/Member - EMS Advisory Board

Directors: Dennis J. Cagan/Chmn., CEO, Pres., Douglas D. Cole/Vice Chmn., William D. Jobe/Dir., Jeff Tokar/Member - EMS Advisory Board, Richard G. Thau/Dir., Mary R. Mailloux/Member - EMS Advisory Board, David I. Page/Member - EMS Advisory Board, John

Sinclair/Member - EMS Advisory Board, David Batstone/Dir. - Professor, Speaker, Consultant, Phyllis Farragut/Dir., Laird Q. Cagan/Dir., Debra Cason/Member - EMS Advisory Board, Dir. - Emergency Medicine Education, Amanda J. Cotter/Member - EMS Advisory Board, Alice Dalton/Member - EMS Advisory Board, Art Hsieh/Member - EMS Advisory Board

Owners: Laird Cagan/56.31%, Fredrick Vogel/5.29%, Mary Losty/5.29%, David B. Batstone, Doug Cole, Dennis J. Cagan/3.06%, Phyllis Farragut, Richard G. Thau, Insiders/58.00%, William Jobe, Patrick R. Quinn, Linden Growth Partners//8.82%

Financial Data: ***Fiscal Year End:***06/30 ***Latest Annual Data:*** 6/30/2006

Year	Sales	Net Income
2006	$25,840,000	-$21,780,000
2005	$11,177,000	-$15,615,000
2004	$2,590,000	-$11,462,000

Curr. Assets:	$3,802,000	***Curr. Liab.:***	$17,159,000		
Plant, Equip.:	$5,105,000	***Total Liab.:***	$34,877,000	***Indic. Yr. Divd.:***	NA
Total Assets:	$11,229,000	***Net Worth:***	-$23,648,000	***Debt/ Equity:***	NA

TXCO Resources Inc

Formerly: Exploration Co of Delaware Inc

777 E Sonterra Blvd, Ste. 350, San Antonio, TX, 78258; ***PH:*** 1-210-496-5300; ***http://*** www.txco.com

General - Incorporation	DE	***Stock***- Price on:12/24/2007	$11.68
Employees	77	Stock Exchange	NDQ
Auditor	Akin, Doherty, Klein & Feuge P.C	Ticker Symbol	NA
Stk Agt	American Stock Transfer & Trust Co.	Outstanding Shares	33,710,000
Counsel	NA	E.P.S	$0.12
DUNS No.	NA	Shareholders	NA

Business: The group's principle activities include acquiring, exploring, developing and producing oil and gas properties. The group is developing its core mineral interests in the maverick basin in south Texas. The group's 480,000-acre position in the basin offers multi-play/multi-pay opportunities from numerous oil and gas-producing horizons. It also holds interests in more than 90,000 acres of the williston basin in the western dakotas and eastern Montana. It also operates and directs the drilling of oil and gas wells and participates in non-operated wells. At Jun 2003, the group had proved reserves of 24.7 billion cubic feet of gas equivalent with a reserve mix of 41% crude oil and 59% natural gas. The group operates from United States.

Primary SIC and add'l.: 1382 1311

CIK No: 0000313395

Officers: James E. Sigmon/Chmn., CEO, Pres./$1,260,085.00, James J. Bookout/VP, COO/$269,242.00, Roberto R. Thomae/VP - Capital Markets, Corp. Sec./$252,042.00, Richard A. Sartor/Controller, Robert E. Lee/Land Mgr., Mark P. Stark/VP, Treasurer, CFO/$281,742.00, Frank M. Russell/VP, General Counsel/$233,371.00, Paul Hart/Mgr. - Communications, Gary S. Grinsfelder/VP - Exploration

Directors: James E. Sigmon/Chmn., CEO, Pres., Michael J. Pint/Dir., Robert L. Foree/Dir., Alan L. Edgar/Dir., Dennis B. Fitzpatrick/Dir., Jon Michael Muckleroy/Dir.

Owners: Frank M. Russell, Lazard Asset Management, LLC/6.38%, Insiders/5.28%, Michael J. Muckleroy, Michael J. Pint/0.60%, James J. Bookout/0.17%, Alan L. Edgar/0.87%, James E. Sigmon/1.66%, Robert L. Foree, Roberto R. Thomae/0.38%, Mark P. Stark, Richard A. Sartor/0.08%, Dennis B. Fitzpatrick/0.41%

Financial Data: ***Fiscal Year End:***12/31 ***Latest Annual Data:*** 12/31/2006

Year	Sales	Net Income
2006	$72,418,000	$7,241,000
2005	$67,000,000	$13,741,000
2004	$57,735,000	$2,797,000

Curr. Assets:	$18,369,000	***Curr. Liab.:***	$16,095,000	***P/E Ratio:***	97.33
Plant, Equip.:	$119,574,000	***Total Liab.:***	$20,149,000	***Indic. Yr. Divd.:***	NA
Total Assets:	$143,801,000	***Net Worth:***	$123,652,000	***Debt/ Equity:***	0.1859

TXP Corp

1299 Commerce Dr., Richardson, TX, 75081; ***PH:*** 1-214-575-9300; ***Fax:*** 1-214-575-9314; ***http://*** www.texasprototypes.com; ***Email:*** txp@txpcorporation.com

General - Incorporation	NV	***Stock***- Price on:12/24/2007	$0.39
Employees	82	Stock Exchange	OTC
Auditor	Payne, Smith & Jones, P.c.	Ticker Symbol	TXPO
Stk Agt	NA	Outstanding Shares	112,410,000
Counsel	NA	E.P.S.	-$0.05
DUNS No.	NA	Shareholders	NA

Business: The groups principle activities include providing pre manufacturing services for the global electronics industry. Customers of the group include original equipment manufacturers, original design manufacturers, contract manufacturers and new technology innovators. The group operates from the United States.

Primary SIC and add'l.: 3672 3679 3661 3674

CIK No: 0001171749

Officers: Michael C. Shores/42/Chmn., CEO, Pres., Chris Ryan/CFO, Eric H. Miscoll/VP, Pedro A. Fernandez/Dir. - Engineering Services, Cindy Pearson/Regional Sales Mgr., Robert R. Walden/CIO, Joel Z. Futterman/VP - ONT Development, Masoud Vaziri/VP - Photonics, Thanh Tran/Dir. - SMT Technology, Eric Prince/Dir. - Materials, David Heim/Dir. - Design Manufacturability

Directors: Michael C. Shores/42/Chmn., CEO, Pres., William L. Martin/61/Dir., Theodore Dubbs/46/Dir., Pat Lavecchia/42/Dir., David P. McNeil/40/Dir.

Owners: Richard Smitten/1.05%, Michael Shores/77.40%, Robert Bruce, Insiders/79.30%, Cornell Capital Partners, L.P/9.99%

Financial Data: ***Fiscal Year End:***12/31 ***Latest Annual Data:*** 12/31/2006

Year	Sales	Net Income
2006	$8,228,000	-$4,592,000
2005	NA	-$644,000
2004	NA	-$501,000

Curr. Assets:	$2,223,000	***Curr. Liab.:***	$4,130,000		
Plant, Equip.:	$2,667,000	***Total Liab.:***	$7,861,000	***Indic. Yr. Divd.:***	NA
Total Assets:	$4,903,000	***Net Worth:***	-$2,958,000	***Debt/ Equity:***	NA

TXU Corp

1601 Bryan St., Dallas, TX, 75201; ***PH:*** 1-214-812-4600; ***http://*** www.txu.com

General - Incorporation	TX	***Stock***- Price on:12/24/2007	$67.26
Employees	7,262	Stock Exchange	NA
Auditor	Deloitte & Touche LLP	Ticker Symbol	NA
Stk Agt	American Stock Transfer & Trust Co.	Outstanding Shares	459,150,000
Counsel	NA	E.P.S.	$2.39
DUNS No.	00-792-8344	Shareholders	NA

Business: The group operates through its subsidiary whose principle activity is to provide electricity and related services. The group operates from United States.

Primary SIC and add'l.: 6719 1311 4911 1321

CIK No: 0001023291

Subsidiaries: Basic Resources Inc., Communications License Holdings I, Inc, Ebasco Services of Canada Limited, EDC Four Inc., ENS Holdings I, Inc., ENS Holdings II, Inc., ENS Holdings Limited Partnership, Enserch E&c Holdings, Inc., Enserch E&c, Inc., Enserch Finance (II), Inc., Enserch Finance N.V., Enserch House, Inc., Enserch International Investments Limited, Enserch SACROC, Inc., Fuelco LLC 87 Subsidiaries included in the Index

Officers: Jim Burke/39/Chmn., CEO - TXU Energy, John C. Wilder/Chmn., CEO, Micheal Childers/47/CEO - Luminant Development, Chuck Enze/Chmn., CEO - Luminant Construction, Mike Greene/62/Chmn., CEO - Luminant Power, Mike McCall/50/Chmn., CEO - Luminant Energy, Stanley J. Szlauderbach/Sr. VP, Controller, Principal Accounting Officer, Talivaldis Spalvins/Metallurgy, Technical Publications, Bill Huber/Investor Relations Officer, Craig D. Harrington/Eng, Mechanical, Technical Publications, Clay D. Yates/Mgr. - TXU Generation Services, Jerry D. Kidd/Supervisor, Plasmabond, Instrumentation Services, Tom Kleckner/Contact - Media, Grace Hastings/Supplier, Diversity Coordinator, Carol Riggall/Sec. - Supplier Diversity *(30 Officers included in Index)*

Directors: Jim Burke/39/Chmn., CEO - TXU Energy, John C. Wilder/Chmn., CEO, Mike McCall/50/Chmn., CEO - Luminant Energy, Chuck Enze/Chmn., CEO - Luminant Construction, Tom Baker/62/Vice Chmn., Jack E. Little/Dir., Gerardo I. Lopez/Dir., J. E. Oesterreicher/Dir., Leonard H. Roberts/Dir., Kerney Laday/Dir., Leldon E. Echols/Dir., Gail De E. Planque/Dir., Glenn F. Tilton/Dir., Michael W. Ranger/Dir.

Owners: Insiders, Wellington Management Company, LLP/6.49%, Leonard H. Roberts, Michael W. Ranger, Jack E. Little, David P. Poole, Eric H. Peterson, Gerardo I. Lopez, David A. Campbell, Barclays Global Investors, NA/9.74%, T. L. Baker, Leldon E. Echols, Glenn F. Tilton, M. S. Greene, Kirk R. Oliver *(18 Owners included in Index)*

Financial Data: ***Fiscal Year End:***12/31 ***Latest Annual Data:*** 12/31/2006

Year	Sales	Net Income
2006	$10,856,000,000	$2,552,000,000
2005	$10,437,000,000	$1,722,000,000
2004	$9,308,000,000	$485,000,000

Curr. Assets:	$2,837,000,000	***Curr. Liab.:***	$5,107,000,000	***P/E Ratio:***	28.14
Plant, Equip.:	$18,756,000,000	***Total Liab.:***	$23,782,000,000	***Indic. Yr. Divd.:***	$1.730
Total Assets:	$25,922,000,000	***Net Worth:***	$2,140,000,000	***Debt/ Equity:***	10.8152

Tyco International Ltd

90 Pitts Bay Rd. , The Zurich Ctr., 2nd Fl., Pemroke; ***PH:*** 441-292-8674; ***http://*** www.tycoint.com

General - Incorporation	Bermuda	***Stock***- Price on:12/24/2007	$33.46
Employees	238,200	Stock Exchange	NYSE
Auditor	Deloitte & Touche, LLP	Ticker Symbol	TYC
Stk Agt	Mellon Investor Services LLC	Outstanding Shares	1,980,000,000
Counsel	NA	E.P.S.	-$1.32
DUNS No.	87-563-2788	Shareholders	NA

Business: The group's principal activities are to manufacture engineered products and provide services through four segments: fire and security services, electronics, healthcare and specialty products and engineered products and services. Through its fire and security services, the group provides electronic and fire protection services. The electronics segment supplies passive electronic components and provides undersea fiber optic networks and services. Healthcare and specialty products include medical devices and supplies and polyethylene film and film products. Engineered products and services segment manufactures industrial valves and controls. The group purchased seven businesses within the healthcare, engineered products and services, fire and security and electronics segments in fiscal 2003.

Primary SIC and add'l.: 3679 3823 2671 1731 3669 7382

CIK No: 0000833444

Subsidiaries: A&E GP Holding, Inc., A&E Holding GP, A&E India Pvt Ltd, A&E Products de Honduras S.A., A&E Products do Brasil Ltda., A&E Products Guatemala, S.A., A&E Products Korea Ltd., A&E Products South Africa (Proprietary) Limited, A-G Holding, Inc. I, A.c.n. 069 907 384 Pty Limited, A.E. Silver Limited, A.G. Marvac Limited, A.R.C. Fire Protection Limited, A.V.S. Systems Limited, Abbey Security International Limited. 1890 Subsidiaries included in the Index

Officers: Edward D. Breen/51/Chmn., CEO, Christopher J. Coughlin/55/CFO, Exec. VP, Martina Hund-Mejean/Sr. VP, Treasurer, Laurie A. Siegel/51/Sr. VP - Human Resources, Carol Anthony Davidson/52/Sr. VP, Controller, Chief Accounting Officer, Edward C. Arditte/52/Sr. VP - Investor Relations, John E. Evard/61/Sr. VP, Chief Tax Officer, Patrick Decker/Pres. - Flow Control, Naren K. Gursahaney/Pres. - ADT Worldwide, George R. Oliver/Pres. - Safety Products, Electrical, Metal Products, Judith A. Reinsdorf/Exec. VP, General Counsel, Jim Spicer/Acting Pres. - Simplexgrinnell, VP - Business Operations, Shelley Stewart/Sr. VP - Operational Excellence, Chief Procurement Officer

Directors: Edward D. Breen/51/Chmn., CEO, Dennis C. Blair/60/Dir., Brian Duperreault/Dir., Bruce S. Gordon/61/Dir., Rajiv L. Gupta/62/Dir., John A. Krol/71/Dir., Carl H. McCall/Dir., Brendan R. O'Neill/59/Dir., Sandra S. Wijnberg/Dir., Jerome B. York/69/Dir., William S. Stavropoulos/Dir.

Owners: Rajiv L. Gupta, Jerome B. York, Capital Research and Management Company/9.30%, Davis Selected Advisers LP/6.40%, Brian Duperreault, Sandra S. Wijnberg, Carol Anthony Davidson, Dennis C. Blair, John A. Krol, William S. Stavropoulos, Bruce S. Gordon, Christopher J. Coughlin, John E. Evard, Insiders, Brendan R. O'Neill *(18 Owners included in Index)*

Financial Data: ***Fiscal Year End:***09/30 ***Latest Annual Data:*** 9/29/2006

Year	Sales	Net Income
2006	$40,938,000,000	$3,590,000,000
2005	$39,727,000,000	$3,032,000,000
2004	$40,153,000,000	$2,879,000,000

Curr. Assets:	$18,537,000,000	***Curr. Liab.:***	$11,835,000,000	***P/E Ratio:***	18.18
Plant, Equip.:	$9,238,000,000	***Total Liab.:***	$30,110,000,000	***Indic. Yr. Divd.:***	$0.400
Total Assets:	$62,621,000,000	***Net Worth:***	$32,450,000,000	***Debt/ Equity:***	0.2335

Tyler Resources Inc

No. 500 - 926 - 5th Ave. SW, Calgary, AB, T2P 0N7; *PH:* 1-403-269-6753;
http:// www.tylerresources.com

General - Incorporation		Stock - Price on:12/24/2007	
Incorporation	AB	Stock - Price on:12/24/2007	NA
Employees	NA	Stock Exchange	OTC
Auditor	PricewaterhouseCoopers LLP	Ticker Symbol	TYRRF
Stk Agt	Computershare Trust Co of Canada	Outstanding Shares	NA
Counsel	Graubard Miller	E.P.S.	NA
DUNS No.	NA	Shareholders	NA

Business: The group's principle activities include acquiring and exploring of prospects with anticipated specific mineralizations of copper, silver and gold and diamonds. The group operates from United States.

Primary SIC and add'l.: 1400

CIK No: 0000930164

Subsidiaries: Recursos Tyler S.A. de C.V

Officers: Jean Pierre Jutras/Dir., CEO, Pres., Shane Ebert/41/Dir., VP - Exploration, Jennifer Munro/CFO

Directors: Jean Pierre Jutras/Dir., CEO, Pres., Gregory H. Smith/Dir., Lesley Hayes/Dir., Alan Craven/Dir., Gary Simmerman/Dir.

Owners: Jennifer Munro/0.20%, Shane Ebert/1.20%, Gregory H. Smith/1.80%, Jean Pierre Jutras/2.50%, Theodore Renner/1.60%, Alan Craven/30.00%, Lesley Hayes/0.40%, Barbara ONeill/0.60%

Financial Data: Fiscal Year End:07/31 Latest Annual Data: 7/31/2006

Year	Sales	Net Income
2006	$200,000	-$8,043,000
2005	$61,000	-$4,740,000

Curr. Assets:	$3,220,000	Curr. Liab.:	$838,000		
Plant, Equip.	$60,000	Total Liab.:	$887,000	Indic. Yr. Divd.:	NA
Total Assets:	$3,296,000	Net Worth:	$2,408,000	Debt/ Equity:	NA

Tyler Technologies Inc

5949 Sherry Ln., Ste 1400, Dallas, TX, 75225; *PH:* 1-972-713-3700; *http://* www.tylerworks.com;
Email: info@tylerworks.com

General - Incorporation		Stock - Price on:12/24/2007	
Incorporation	DE	Stock - Price on:12/24/2007	$12.09
Employees	1,530	Stock Exchange	NYSE
Auditor	Ernst & Young LLP	Ticker Symbol	TYL
Stk Agt	EquiServe Trust Co N.A	Outstanding Shares	38,940,000
Counsel	Gardere, Wynne Sewell LLP	E.P.S.	$0.37
DUNS No.	04-108-9293	Shareholders	NA

Business: The group's principle activity is to design, develop and market software products to serve mission-critical back-office functions of local governments. It's software applications are designed primarily for use on hardware supporting unix / nt operating systems. It also provides professional it services to its customers, including software and hardware installation, data conversion, training, product modifications and customer support services to ensure proper product performance and reliability. The group also provide property appraisal outsourcing services for taxing jurisdictions. The group markets its products and services through direct sales and marketing personnel located throughout the United States. The group has customer base of nearly 6,000 local government offices and customers in 50 states of the United States, Canada, Puerto Rico and United Kingdom. The group's quarterly revenue for Sep '07 was 54.93 millions of USD.

Primary SIC and add'l.: 7373 7376 7379 7372 7378

CIK No: 0000860731

Subsidiaries: Swan Transportation Company

Owners: John S. Marr/4.70%, MSD Capital, L.P./10.40%, John M. Yeaman/2.50%, Michael D. Richards, Insiders/9.90%, Noonday Asset Management LP/8.80%, G. Stuart Reeves, Luther King, Dustin R. Womble/1.00%, Brian K. Miller, Donald R. Brattain, H. Lynn Moore

Financial Data: Fiscal Year End:12/31 Latest Annual Data: 06/30/2007

Year	Sales	Net Income
2007	NA	NA
2006	NA	NA
2005	$170,457,000	$8,193,000

Curr. Assets:	$111,674,000	Curr. Liab.:	$85,185,000	P/E Ratio:	34.54
Plant, Equip.:	$7,390,000	Total Liab.:	$94,401,000	Indic. Yr. Divd.:	NA
Total Assets:	$220,276,000	Net Worth:	$125,875,000	Debt/ Equity:	NA

Tyson Foods Inc

2210 W Oaklawn Dr., Springdale, AR, 72762; *PH:* 1-479-290-4000; *http://* www.tyson.com

General - Incorporation		Stock - Price on:12/24/2007	
Incorporation	DE	Stock - Price on:12/24/2007	$22.83
Employees	107,000	Stock Exchange	NYSE
Auditor	Ernst & Young LLP	Ticker Symbol	TSN
Stk Agt	EquiServe Trust Co N.A	Outstanding Shares	356,060,000
Counsel	James B. Blair	E.P.S.	$0.76
DUNS No.	00-690-3702	Shareholders	NA

Business: The group's principle activity is to provide food services. The group's products include Tysonchicken, beaf and pork. The group operates from United States.

Primary SIC and add'l.: 2015 5499 0251 2048 5147

CIK No: 0000100493

Subsidiaries: Avicultores Tecnicos, S. de R.L. de C.V., Carneco Foods, LLC, Carolina Brand Foods, LLC, CBFA Management Corp., Central Industries, Inc., Cobb Breeders B.V., Cobb Caribe S.A., Cobb Denmark A/S, Cobb Espanola S.A., Cobb Europe B.V., Cobb France Eurl, Cobb Poland B.V., Cobb-Istanbul Ana Damizlik Isletmeleri Ve Ticaret A.S., Cobb-Vantress Brazil LTDA, Cobb-Vantress Holding company, Inc. 82 Subsidiaries included in the Index

Officers: Richard L. Bond/60/Dir., CEO, Pres., Dennis Leatherby/Sr. VP - Finance, Treasurer, William W. Lovette/Sr. Group VP - Poultry, Prepared Foods, James Rice/Contact - Tyson International, China, K. C. Lin/Contact - Tyson International, Taiwan, Scott Ko/Contact - Tyson International, Korea, Jeff McNeill/Contact - Tyson International, Japan, Read R. Hudson/VP, Assoc. General Counsel, Sec., Alberto J. Gonzalez-Pita/Exec. VP, General Counsel, Craig Hart/Sr. VP,

Controller, Chief Accounting Officer, Archie Schaffer/Sr. VP - External Relations, Howell P. Carper/Sr. VP - Research, Development, Mike Baker/Sr. VP - International, Cobb, Vantress Operations, James V. Lochner/Sr. Group VP - Fresh Meats, Margin Optimization, Jeff Webster/Sr. VP - Corporate Strategic Development, Renewable Energy *(52 Officers included in Index)*

Directors: Richard L. Bond/60/Dir., CEO, Pres., John Tyson/54/Chmn., Don Tyson/77/Sr. Chmn., Scott T. Ford/45/Dir., Kevin McNamara/52/Dir., Jim Kever/55/Dir., Lloyd V. Hackley/67/Dir., Jo Ann R. Smith/68/Dir., Barbara A. Tyson/58/Dir., Albert C. Zapanta/66/Dir., Leland E. Tollett/70/Dir.

Owners: James V. Lochner, Greg W. Lee, Don Tyson/99.97%, Scott T. Ford, Insiders/99.97%, Jim Kever, Goldman Sachs Group Inc./12.86%, William W. Lovette, Barbara A. Tyson, Jo Ann R. Smith, Lloyd V. Hackley, Don Tyson, Barclays Global Investors UK Holdings Limited/5.03%, Richard L. Bond, Insiders/3.28% *(19 Owners included in Index)*

Financial Data: Fiscal Year End:10/01 Latest Annual Data: 9/30/2006

Year	Sales	Net Income
2006	$25,559,000,000	-$196,000,000
2005	$26,014,000,000	$353,000,000
2004	$26,441,000,000	$403,000,000

Curr. Assets:	$4,187,000,000	Curr. Liab.:	$2,846,000,000	P/E Ratio:	44.76
Plant, Equip.:	$3,945,000,000	Total Liab.:	$6,681,000,000	Indic. Yr. Divd.:	$0.160
Total Assets:	$11,121,000,000	Net Worth:	$4,440,000,000	Debt/ Equity:	0.6019

U-Store-It Trust

50 Public Sq., Ste. 2800, Cleveland, OH, 44130; *PH:* 1-440-234-0700; *Fax:* 1-440-260-2204;
http:// www.snl.com

General - Incorporation		Stock - Price on:12/24/2007	
Incorporation	MD	Stock - Price on:12/24/2007	$17.96
Employees	981	Stock Exchange	NYSE
Auditor	Deloitte & Touche LLP	Ticker Symbol	YSI
Stk Agt	LaSalle Bank N.A	Outstanding Shares	57,410,000
Counsel	NA	E.P.S.	-$0.23
DUNS No.	NA	Shareholders	NA

Business: The groups principle activities include owning, acquiring and developing self-storage facilities. In the year 2006, the group acquired 252 facilities. The group operates from the United States. The groups quarterly revenue for September 2007 was 58.31 millions of USD.

Primary SIC and add'l.: 6798

CIK No: 0001298675

Subsidiaries: Acquiport/Amsdell I Limited Partnership, Acquiport/Amsdell III LLC, Acquiport/Amsdell IV LLC, Acquiport/Amsdell VI LLC, U-Store-It Development LLC, U-Store-It L.P., U-Store-It Mini Warehouse Co., USI II LLC, Yasky LLC, YSI I LLC, YSI II LLC, YSI III LLC, YSI IV LLC, YSI IX GP LLC, YSI IX LP 70 Subsidiaries included in the Index

Officers: Dean Jernigan/62/Trustee, CEO, Pres., Todd C. Amsdell/38/COO, Tedd D. Towsley/52/Interim CFO, Kathleen A. Weigand/49/Exec. VP, General Counsel, Sec., Christopher P. Marr/43/CFO, Treasurer, Stephen R. Nichols/57/Sr. VP - Operations, Timothy M. Martin/37/Chief Accounting Officer, Sr. VP

Directors: Dean Jernigan/62/Trustee, CEO, Pres., William M. Diefenderfer/62/Chmn., John C. Dannemiller/69/Trustee, Barry L. Amsdell/62/Trustee, Thomas A. Commes/65/Trustee, Harold S. Haller/69/Trustee, David J. Larue/46/Trustee

Owners: Dean Jernigan, William M. Diefenderfer, Robert J. Amsdell Family Irrevocable Trust/6.30%, Stephen R. Nichols, David J. LaRue, Insiders/17.70%, Robert J. Amsdell/2.80%, Harold S. Haller, Cohen & Steers Capital Management, Inc./9.00%, Tedd D. Towsley, Todd C. Amsdell/13.30%, Thomas A. Commes, Christopher P. Marr, Loretta Amsdell Family Irrevocable Trust/6.30%, Barry L. Amsdell/1.40% *(18 Owners included in Index)*

Financial Data: Fiscal Year End:12/31 Latest Annual Data: 12/31/2006

Year	Sales	Net Income
2006	$213,112,000	-$8,551,000
2005	$148,121,000	$2,777,000
2004	$91,608,000	-$32,347,000

Curr. Assets:	$34,474,000	Curr. Liab.:	$41,778,000	P/E Ratio:	7.23
Plant, Equip.:	$1,566,815,000	Total Liab.:	$987,846,000	Indic. Yr. Divd.:	$1.160
Total Assets:	$1,615,339,000	Net Worth:	$627,493,000	Debt/ Equity:	NA

U.S. BioDefense Inc

13674 E Valley Blvd, City Of Industry, CA, 91746; *PH:* 1-626-961-8039;
http:// www.usbiodefense.com; *Email:* info@usbiodefense.com

General - Incorporation		Stock - Price on:12/24/2007	
Incorporation	UT	Stock - Price on:12/24/2007	$0.012
Employees	9	Stock Exchange	OTC
Auditor	Gruber & Co., LLC	Ticker Symbol	UBDE
Stk Agt	Atlas Stock Transfer Corp	Outstanding Shares	39,060,000
Counsel	NA	E.P.S.	-$0.012
DUNS No.	NA	Shareholders	NA

Business: The group's principle activity is to develop an on-line shopping mall on the Internet which offers goods and services for sale to consumers over the Internet. The company's six different retail websites also sell toys, electronics, health and beauty, sporting goods, gifts, books, music and videos. The company provides value to both the end-user and to the vendors by providing a range of goods and services in one location. The group operates from United States.

Primary SIC and add'l.: 5961 7375

CIK No: 0001122130

Officers: David Chin/Chmn., CEO, Eddie Cruz/Consultant, Charles Wright/51/Dir., VP

Directors: David Chin/Chmn., CEO, Charles Wright/51/Dir., VP

Owners: David Chin/69.90%, Erin Rahe/7.70%, Insiders/69.90%

Financial Data: Fiscal Year End:11/30 Latest Annual Data: 11/30/2006

Year	Sales	Net Income
2006	$450,000	-$214,000
2005	$159,000	-$46,000
2004	$29,000	-$29,000

Curr. Assets:	$226,000	Curr. Liab.:	$44,000		
Plant, Equip.:	$2,000	Total Liab.:	$44,000	Indic. Yr. Divd.:	NA
Total Assets:	$237,000	Net Worth:	$192,000	Debt/ Equity:	NA

U.S. Can Corp

700 E Butterfield Rd., Ste 250, Lombard, IL, 60148; **PH:** 1-630-678-8000;
http:// www.uscanco.com; **Email:** generalsales@uscanco.com

General - Incorporation	DE	**Stock** - Price on:12/24/2007	NA
Employees	NA	Stock Exchange	OTC
Auditor	Deloitte & Touche LLP	Ticker Symbol	USCKF
Stk Agt	Computershare Trust Co	Outstanding Shares	NA
Counsel	NA	E.P.S.	NA
DUNS No.	10-693-7378	Shareholders	NA

Business: The group's principle activities include manufacturing steel and plastic containers for personal care products and household, automotive, paint and industrial supplies; manufacturing of a broadline of aerosol containers for consumer and household products in the United States and Europe; production of metal and plastic, round and oblong containers for household and industrial paints and additives and other industrial products in the United States; and manufacturing of a wide variety of custom and specialty tins, decorative containers and products. The group operates from United States.

Primary SIC and add'l.: 3411 3356

CIK No: 0000895726

Subsidiaries: U.S.C. Europe N.V., U.S.C. Europe Netherlands B.V., United States Can Company, USC May Verpackungen Holding, Inc.

U.S. Concrete Inc

2925 BriarPk., Ste. 1050, Houston, TX, 77042; **PH:** 1-713-499-6200; **Fax:** 1-713-499-6201;
http:// www.us-concrete.com; **Email:** info@us-concrete.com

General - Incorporation	DE	**Stock** - Price on:12/24/2007	$8.92
Employees	3,185	Stock Exchange	NDQ
Auditor	PricewaterhouseCoopers LLP	Ticker Symbol	RMIX
Stk Agt	Mellon Investor Services LLC	Outstanding Shares	39,080,000
Counsel	Baker & Botts LLP	E.P.S.	-$0.33
DUNS No.	NA	Shareholders	NA

Business: The group's principal activity is to produce and provide ready-mixed concrete and related products and services. The group also manufactures and delivers various precast and concrete masonry products to the construction industry. Its operation consists of formulating, preparing and delivering ready-mixed concrete to the job sites of its customers. It also provides services intended to reduce its customers' overall construction costs by lowering the installed cost of concrete. Its customers include general contractors, developers and home builders whose focus extends beyond the price of ready-mixed concrete to product quality and consistency and reduction of in-place concrete costs. As of 10-Mar-2004, the group had 89 fixed and eight portable ready-mixed concrete plants, eight precast concrete plants, three concrete block plants and one aggregates quarry. In feb 2003, it acquired builders redi-mix, inc.

Primary SIC and add'l.: 3273

CIK No: 0001073429

Subsidiaries: American Concrete Products, Inc., Atlas-Tuck Concrete, Inc., B.W.B., Inc. of Michigan, Beall Concrete Enterprises, Ltd., Beall Industries, Inc., Beall Investment Corporation, Inc., Beall Management, Inc., Builders Redi-Mix, LLC, Central Concrete Corp., Central Concrete Supply Co., Inc., Central Precast Concrete, Inc., Concrete XXXI Acquisition, Inc., Concrete XXXII Acquisition, Inc., Concrete XXXIII Acquisition, Inc., Concrete XXXIV Acquisition, Inc. 33 Subsidiaries included in the Index

Officers: Michael W. Harlan/Dir., CEO, Pres./$789,833.00, Gary J. Konnie/VP - Human Resources, Terry J. Green/Sr. VP - Operations, Raymond C. Turpin/VP - Technical Affairs, Wallace H. Johnson/VP - Sales, Marketing, William T. Albanese/Dir., Regional VP - Northern California/$414,936.00, Cesar G. Monroy/47/Treasurer, Thomas J. Albanese/Exec. VP - Sales/$392,279.00, Robert D. Hardy/CFO, Exec. VP/$467,252.00, Scott R. Evans/Regional VP - South Central Region, Sean M. Gore/VP - Finance, Jeff Davis/Executive Staff, Curt M. Lindeman/VP, General Counsel, Doug McLaughlin/Precast Division VP, Jeffery Spahr/Pres., GM - Michigan Region *(16 Officers included in Index)*

Directors: Michael W. Harlan/Dir., CEO, Pres., Eugene P. Martineau/68/Dir., Murray S. Simpson/Dir., William T. Albanese/Dir., Regional VP - Northern California, Mary P. Ricciardello/Dir., William T. Porter/Dir., Robert S. Walker/Dir., Vincent D. Foster/Dir., John M. Piecuch/Dir.

Owners: Wells Fargo & Company/12.89%, Michael W. Harlan/1.84%, GLG Partners LP/6.22%, Murray S. Simpson, Vincent D. Foster/1.69%, Insiders/18.04%, William T. Porter, The Galleon Group/5.24%, Thomas J. Albanese/3.33%, Barclays Global Investors Japan Limited/7.08%, Mary P. Ricciardello, John M. Piecuch, Eugene P. Martineau/2.83%, Robert S. Walker/4.29%, William T. Albanese/2.40% *(16 Owners included in Index)*

Financial Data: Fiscal Year End:12/31   **Latest Annual Data:** 12/31/2006

Year	Sales	Net Income
2006	$789,522,000	-$8,090,000
2005	$575,655,000	$12,612,000
2004	$500,589,000	-$10,539,000

Curr. Assets:	$171,122,000	**Curr. Liab.:**	$106,435,000		
Plant, Equip.:	$281,021,000	**Total Liab.:**	$447,069,000	**Indic. Yr. Divd.:**	NA
Total Assets:	$716,646,000	**Net Worth:**	$269,577,000	**Debt/ Equity:**	1.1656

U.S. Energy Corp

877 N 8th W, Riverton, WY, 82501; **PH:** 1-307-856-9271; **Fax:** 1-307-857-3050;
http:// www.usey.com; **Email:** ir@usnrg.com

General - Incorporation	WY	**Stock** - Price on:12/24/2007	$5.77
Employees	26	Stock Exchange	NDQ
Auditor	Moss Adams LLP	Ticker Symbol	USEG
Stk Agt	Computershare Trust Co	Outstanding Shares	20,590,000
Counsel	NA	E.P.S.	$0.04
DUNS No.	04-109-7684	Shareholders	NA

Business: The group's principal activity is to operate in two segments: minerals and commercial operations. The group's minerals operations include the acquisition, exploration, holding, sale and/or development of mineral and coalbed methane gas properties, the production of petroleum properties and marketing of minerals and methane gas. Principal mineral interests are in coalbed methane, uranium, gold and molybdenum. The commercial operations include interest in various real and personal properties used in commercial activities. On 14-Aug-2003, the group sold its interest in the ticaboo townsite to the cactus group llc.

Primary SIC and add'l.: 4581 6211 6531

CIK No: 0000101594

Subsidiaries: Crested Corp., Four Nines Gold, Inc., Pinnacle Gas Resources, Inc, Plateau Resources Limited, Sutter Gold Mining Inc., USECC Joint Venture, Yellowstone Fuels Inc.

Officers: Keith G. Larsen/Chmn., CEO/$928,500.00, Harold F. Herron/Dir., Sr. VP/$575,100.00, Mark J. Larsen/Dir., COO, Pres./$575,100.00, Scott R. Lorimer/VP - Finance, CFO, Treasurer, Steven R. Youngbauer/Corp. Sec., General Counsel/$301,800.00, Jerry R. Falkner/Investor Relations Contact, Alan H. Oshiki/Investor Relations Contact

Directors: Keith G. Larsen/Chmn., CEO, Michael Thomas Anderson/Dir., Russel H. Fraser/Dir., Harold F. Herron/Dir., Sr. VP, Mark J. Larsen/Dir., COO, Pres., Allen Winters/Dir.

Owners: Keith G. Larsen/8.10%, Steven R. Youngbauer/0.70%, Insiders/19.00%, Harold F. Herron/6.60%, Michael H. Feinstein/2.30%, Robert Scott Lorimer/5.10%, Russell H. Fraser/2.90%, Allen S. Winters/2.20%, Mike Anderson/2.60%, Mark J. Larsen/2.80%

Financial Data: Fiscal Year End:12/31   **Latest Annual Data:** 12/31/2006

Year	Sales	Net Income
2006	$813,000	$1,052,000
2005	$850,000	$8,842,000
2004	$4,642,000	-$6,249,000

Curr. Assets:	$43,325,000	**Curr. Liab.:**	$11,595,000	**P/E Ratio:**	144.25
Plant, Equip.:	$7,929,000	**Total Liab.:**	$18,924,000	**Indic. Yr. Divd.:**	NA
Total Assets:	$51,901,000	**Net Worth:**	$32,977,000	**Debt/ Equity:**	0.0084

U.S. Energy Systems Inc

545 Madison Ave., 6th Fl., New York, NY, 10022; **PH:** 1-212-588-8901; **Fax:** 1-212-588-1635;
http:// www.usenergysystems.com; **Email:** info@usenergysystems.com

General - Incorporation	DE	**Stock** - Price on:12/24/2007	$2.65
Employees	30	Stock Exchange	OTC
Auditor	Eisner LLP	Ticker Symbol	USEY
Stk Agt	American Stock Transfer & Trust Co.	Outstanding Shares	21,700,000
Counsel	Greenberg Traurig	E.P.S.	-$1.72
DUNS No.	87-925-3383	Shareholders	NA

Business: The group's principal activities are to provide customer-focused energy outsourcing services, including the management, development, operation and ownership of small-to-medium-sized energy facilities. At the end of 2003, the group's operating portfolio comprised of 35 controlled or managed projects in North America totaling the equivalent of 264 megawatts (mw). The customers of the group include large retail energy consumers, such as industrial and commercial concerns and local wholesale energy suppliers. The group owned and financed 34 green energy, district energy and cogeneration projects in North America and Europe with a total of 262mw of thermal and electric generation capacity. The group discontinued use Canada operations and sold geothermal llc in 2003.

Primary SIC and add'l.: 4911 8999

CIK No: 0000351917

Subsidiaries: Lehi Envirosystems, Inc, Plymouth Envirosystems, Inc., U.S. Energy Biogas Corp., U.S. Energy Geothermal, LLC, UK Energy Systems Limited

Officers: Richard J. Augustine/Chief Accounting Officer - US Energy, CEO - US Energy Biogas Corp, Asher E. Fogel/59/Chmn., CEO, Pres., Joseph P. Reynolds/CEO - US Energy Systems, Programme, Dir. - UK Energy Systems, James A. Lobban/COO, Steve Laliberty/Pres. - US Energy Biogas Corp, Adam D. Greene/44/Sr. VP, Sec., James B. Boffardi/Sr. VP - Finance, Analysis

Directors: Asher E. Fogel/59/Chmn., CEO, Pres., Stephen L. Brown/70/Dir., Carl W. Greene/73/Dir., Jacob Feinstein/Dir., Ronny Strauss/Dir., Robert Schneider/Dir.

Owners: Robert Schneider, Jacob Feinstein, Silver Point Capital Management, LLC and affiliates/14.70%, Rita Schneider/8.60%, Asher E. Fogel/2.10%, Lawrence I. Schneider/9.70%, Insiders/3.30%, Ronny Strauss, Adam D. Greene, Mark S. Brody/7.40%, Richard J. Augustine

Financial Data: Fiscal Year End:12/31   **Latest Annual Data:** 12/31/2006

Year	Sales	Net Income
2006	$21,244,000	-$27,574,000
2005	$19,620,000	-$9,466,000
2004	$20,108,000	-$9,244,000

Curr. Assets:	$51,263,000	**Curr. Liab.:**	$52,348,000		
Plant, Equip.:	$139,950,000	**Total Liab.:**	$297,445,000	**Indic. Yr. Divd.:**	NA
Total Assets:	$346,930,000	**Net Worth:**	$31,480,000	**Debt/ Equity:**	4.3368

U.S. Global Investors Inc

7900 Callaghan Rd., San Antonio, TX, 78229; **PH:** 1-210-308-1222; **Fax:** 1-210-308-1223;
http:// www.usfunds.com; **Email:** shsvc@usfunds.com

General - Incorporation	TX	**Stock** - Price on:12/24/2007	$24.25
Employees	77	Stock Exchange	NDQ
Auditor	BDO Seidman LLP	Ticker Symbol	GROW
Stk Agt	United Shareholder Services Inc	Outstanding Shares	15,180,000
Counsel	NA	E.P.S.	NA
DUNS No.	03-835-2399	Shareholders	NA

Business: The group's principal activities are to provide investment advisory services, investment management and transfer agency to U.S. Global investors funds (usgif) and U.S. Global accolade funds (usgaf). The group provides investment advisory services, record keeping services, mailing services, custodial and administrative services and distribution services. The group furnishes an investment program for each of the mutual funds it manages and determines, subject to overall supervision by the boards of trustees of the funds, the funds' investments pursuant to advisory agreements. The group's subsidiary is a transfer agent registered under the securities exchange act of 1934 providing transfer agency, lockbox and printing services to investment company clients. The group provides mail-handling services and brokerage services to various entities through its subsidiaries.

Primary SIC and add'l.: 6289 6799 6282 7331

CIK No: 0000754811

Subsidiaries: A & B Mailers, Inc., U.S. Global Brokerage, Inc., U.S. Global Investors (Bermuda) Ltd., U.S. Global Investors (Guernsey) Limited, United Shareholder Services, Inc., Weblabs, Inc.

Officers: Frank E. Holmes/CEO, Chief Investment Officer, John Derrick/Dir. - Research, Romeo A. Dator/Research Analyst, Bernard Austin/Research Analyst, Xian Liang/Asia Research Analyst, Ralph P. Aldis/Sr. Mining Analyst, Brian K. Hicks/Research Analyst, Evan W. Smith/Co - Portfolio Mgr., Jack Dzierwa/Portfolio Mgr.

Owners: Thomas F. Lydon/0.00%, Frank E. Holmes/1.54%, Insiders/2.53%, Susan B. McGee/0.61%, Roy D. Terracina/0.27%, Catherine A. Rademacher/0.10%, Frank E. Holmes/92.40%, Jerold H. Rubinstein/0.00%

Financial Data: Fiscal Year End:06/30 Latest Annual Data: 6/30/2006

Year	Sales	Net Income
2006	$44,854,000	$10,435,000
2005	$16,981,000	$1,446,000
2004	$12,984,000	$2,167,000

Curr. Assets:	$26,780,000	Curr. Liab.:	$8,504,000		
Plant, Equip.:	$2,123,000	Total Liab.:	$8,504,000	Indic. Yr. Divd.:	$0.120
Total Assets:	$29,047,000	Net Worth:	$20,543,000	Debt/ Equity:	NA

U.S. Gold Corp

2201 Kipling St. , Ste 100, Lakewood, CO, 80215; **PH:** 1-303-238-1438;
http:// www.usgoldmining.com; **Email:** info@goldcorp.com

General - Incorporation............CO	Stock - Price on:12/24/2007 ....NA
Employees 4	Stock Exchange....................AMEX
Auditor ....Stark Winter Schenkein & Co. LLP	Ticker Symbol..........................UXG
Stk Agt..................Equity Transfer Services Inc	Outstanding Shares ....NA
Counsel.............................NA	E.P.S....................................-$0.45
DUNS No. 09-928-2097	Shareholders...........................NA

Business: The group's principal activities are the exploration for, development of and the production and sale of gold and silver, as well as base metals. The group's mining activities include exploration, land acquisition, geological evaluation and feasibility studies of properties, development and construction of mining and processing facilities, mining and processing and the sale of gold and other metals and by-products. The group owns the tonkin springs gold mine property, which is located in eureka county, Nevada. Tonkin springs is an open-pit gold mining and processing project consisting of unpatented mining claims, an integrated milling facility, and support facilities on approximately 23,640 acres of federal land. The group has equity interest in the gold resource corporation and manages the mining activities under a contract with the gold resource corporation. The group conducts its activities in the United States and Mexico.

Primary SIC and add'l.: 1041 8741

CIK No: 0000314203

Subsidiaries: Tonkin Springs Gold Mining Corporation, U.S. Environmental Corporation

Officers: Rob McEwen/Chmn., CEO, Ann Carpenter/Dir., COO, Pres./$180,000.00, William F. Pass/CFO, VP/$125,661.00, Ana Aguirre/Mgr. - Investor Relations

Directors: Rob McEwen/Chmn., CEO, Ann Carpenter/Dir., COO, Pres., Michele L. Ashby/Dir., Leanne M. Baker/Dir., Peter Bojtos/Dir., Declan J. Costelloe/Dir.

Owners: Insiders/22.30%, Peter Bojtos, Michele L. Ashby, NovaGold Resources, Inc./6.10%, Ann S. Carpenter, Declan Costelloe, Leanne M. Baker, William F. Pass, Robert R. McEwen/21.40%

Financial Data: Fiscal Year End:12/31 Latest Annual Data: 12/31/2006

Year	Sales	Net Income
2006	NA	-$72,650,000
2005	NA	-$2,991,000
2004	$39,000	-$794,000

Curr. Assets:	$51,207,000	Curr. Liab.:	$3,404,000		
Plant, Equip.:	$1,520,000	Total Liab.:	$6,915,000	Indic. Yr. Divd.:	NA
Total Assets:	$59,399,000	Net Worth:	$52,485,000	Debt/ Equity:	NA

U.S. Home Systems Inc

405 State Hwy 121 Bypass, Bldg. A, Ste. 250, Lewisville, TX, 75067; **PH:** 1-214-488-6300;
Fax: 1-972-459-4800; **http://** www.ushomesystems.com

General - Incorporation............DE	Stock - Price on:12/24/2007 ....$14.14
Employees 550	Stock Exchange......................NDQ
Auditor ....Grant Thornton LLP	Ticker Symbol........................USHS
Stk Agt................Corporate Stock Transfer, Inc.	Outstanding Shares 8,350,000
Counsel.............D.S. Berenson	E.P.S....................................$0.62
DUNS No. 09-928-0398	Shareholders...........................NA

Business: The group's principle activities are to manufacture, design, market and install custom quality specialty home improvement products and provide consumer financing services to the home improvement and remodeling industry. It operates through two segments: home improvement and consumer financing. The home improvement product lines include replacement and refacing of kitchen cabinet and countertop products utilized in kitchen remodeling, bathroom refacing and related products utilized in bathroom remodeling and replacement windows. The consumer financing product line arranges finance to its customers. The group operates sales and installation centers in 14 major metropolitan areas in the United States. The group's quarterly revenue for September 2007 was 34.25 millions of USD.

Primary SIC and add'l.: 6159 2434

CIK No: 0000844789

Subsidiaries: Facelifters Home Systems, Inc., First Consumer Credit, Inc., U.S. Remodelers, Inc., U.S. Windows Corporation, USA Deck, Inc.

Officers: Murray H. Gross/Chmn., CEO/$836,679.00, Peter T. Bulger/COO, Pres./$687,644.00, Robert A. Defronzo/CFO, Sec., Treasurer/$296,077.00, Steven L. Gross/Exec. VP, Chief Marketing Officer/$486,513.00, Richard B. Goodner/VP - Legal Affairs, General Counsel/$229,139.00

Directors: Murray H. Gross/Chmn., CEO, Kenneth W. Murphy/Dir., Don A. Buchholz/Dir., D. S. Berenson/Dir., Larry A. Jobe/Dir.

Owners: David M. Greenhouse/6.50%, Kenneth W. Murphy, Don A. Buchholz/5.80%, Robert A. DeFronzo, D. S. Berenson, Richard B. Goodner, Murray H. Gross/6.50%, Larry A. Jobe, Peter T. Bulger/2.90%, Midwood Capital Management LLC/9.30%, Steven L. Gross/2.00%, Insiders/18.90%, Austin W. Marxe/6.50%

Financial Data: Fiscal Year End:12/31 Latest Annual Data: 12/31/2006

Year	Sales	Net Income
2006	$127,760,000	$4,219,000
2005	$104,389,000	-$405,000
2004	$88,766,000	-$600,000

Curr. Assets:	$21,829,000	Curr. Liab.:	$8,396,000	P/E Ratio:	22.81
Plant, Equip.:	$5,796,000	Total Liab.:	$12,046,000	Indic. Yr. Divd.:	NA
Total Assets:	$38,933,000	Net Worth:	$26,887,000	Debt/ Equity:	0.1032

U.S. Microbics Inc

6451 El Camino Real, Ste. C, Carlsbad, CA, 92009; **PH:** 1-760-918-1860; **Fax:** 1-760-918-1855;
http:// www.bugsatwork.com

General - Incorporation ....CO	Stock - Price on:12/24/2007 ....$0.0099
Employees 4	Stock Exchange........................OTC
Auditor ... Russell Bedford Stefanou Mirchandani	Ticker Symbol........................BUGS
Stk Agt.................Corporate Stock Transfer, Inc.	Outstanding Shares 436,510,000
Counsel.............................NA	E.P.S...................................-$0.01
DUNS No. ....NA	Shareholders...........................NA

Business: The group's principal activities are to provide proprietary products and services for applications in the global bioremediation, wastewater treatment and regenerative agriculture markets. The group facilitates and develops the deployment of environmental technologies through its two segments: usm solutions and usm capital. Usm solutions consists of five majority owned subsidiaries that use the biological technology to revolutionize environmental cleanup and agricultural growth usm capital assists in the financing and development of the five usm solutions companies and additional equity holdings. It also provides management consulting, administrative services and investor relations services to its clients. The group's products and services include soil, groundwater remediation and carbon reactivation, waste water and odor control, agricultural enhancement and related professional and support services.

Primary SIC and add'l.: 8748 4953 2836 6719 2834

CIK No: 0000774454

Subsidiaries: Bio-Con Microbes, Inc, Sol Tech, Inc, Sub-Surface Waste Management of Delaware, Inc., USM Capital Group, Inc, West Coast Fermentation Center, Inc, XyclonyX

Officers: Robert C. Brehm/Chmn., CEO, Pres., Conrad Nagel/CFO

Directors: Robert C. Brehm/Chmn., CEO, Pres.

Owners: Bezhad Mirzay/0.26%, Robert C. Brehm/6.52%, Mark A. Holmstedt/0.55%, Mery C. Robinson/1.14%, Conrad Nagel/0.94%, Robert Key/0.18%, Bruce Beattie/0.06%, Insiders/9.34%

Financial Data: Fiscal Year End:09/30 Latest Annual Data: 9/30/2006

Year	Sales	Net Income
2006	$514,000	-$3,539,000
2005	$1,199,000	-$2,998,000
2004	$419,000	-$4,041,000

Curr. Assets:	$547,000	Curr. Liab.:	$2,198,000		
Plant, Equip.:	$153,000	Total Liab.:	$2,198,000	Indic. Yr. Divd.:	NA
Total Assets:	$730,000	Net Worth:	-$7,586,000	Debt/ Equity:	NA

U.S. Neurosurgical Inc

1899 Sawyer Ln., Alva, FL, 33920; **PH:** 1-239-872-1272; **http://** www.usneurosurgical.com;
Email: info@usneurosurgical.com

General - Incorporation ....DE	Stock - Price on:12/24/2007 ....$0.05
Employees 4	Stock Exchange........................OTC
Auditor ....Goodman & Co. LLP	Ticker Symbol........................USNU
Stk Agt...... American Stock Transfer & Trust Co.	Outstanding Shares 7,700,000
Counsel.............................NA	E.P.S...................................-$0.04
DUNS No. ....NA	Shareholders...........................NA

Business: The group's principal activity is to own and operate stereotactic radiosurgery centers, utilizing the gamma knife technology. The gamma knife is a radiosurgical device used to treat brain tumors and other malformations of the brain without invasive surgery. The group owns and operates two gamma knife centers in Kansas city and New York. The group's target market is medical centers in major health care catchment areas that have physicians experienced with and dedicated to use gamma knife.

Primary SIC and add'l.: 8099

CIK No: 0001089815

Subsidiaries: U.S. Neurosurgical Physics Inc.

Officers: Alan Gold/63/Chmn., CEO, CFO, Pres., Susan Greenwald/62/VP, Sec., Jim Bazziontti/Pres.

Directors: Alan Gold/63/Chmn., CEO, CFO, Pres., William F. Leimkuhler/56/Dir., Charles H. Merriman/73/Dir.

Owners: Charles H. Merriman/1.70%, Insiders/19.50%, Allen & Company Incorporated/23.40%, Alan Gold/14.50%, Stanley S. Shuman/34.20%, William F. Leimkuhler/1.30%

Financial Data: Fiscal Year End:12/31 Latest Annual Data: 12/31/2006

Year	Sales	Net Income
2006	$2,002,000	-$383,000
2005	$2,108,000	-$285,000
2004	$2,403,000	$123,000

Curr. Assets:	$710,000	Curr. Liab.:	$589,000		
Plant, Equip.:	$2,673,000	Total Liab.:	$2,400,000	Indic. Yr. Divd.:	NA
Total Assets:	$3,496,000	Net Worth:	$1,096,000	Debt/ Equity:	1.4698

U.S. Physical Therapy Inc

1300 W Sam Houston Pkwy. S, Ste. 300, Houston, TX, 77042; **PH:** 1-713-297-7000;
Fax: 1-713-297-7090; **http://** www.usph.com

General - Incorporation ....NV	Stock - Price on:12/24/2007 ....$13.58
Employees 1,210	Stock Exchange......................NDQ
Auditor ....Grant Thornton LLP	Ticker Symbol........................USPH
Stk Agt...........Continental Stock Transfer & Trust Co	Outstanding Shares 11,550,000
Counsel............ Mayor, Day, Caldwell & Keeton	E.P.S...................................$0.59
DUNS No. 62-568-9880	Shareholders...........................NA

Business: The group's principle activity is to operate outpatient physical and occupational therapy clinics, which provide post-operative care and treatment for a variety of orthopedic-related disorders and sports-related injuries. The treatment plan includes the use of modalities and procedures such as ultrasound, electrical stimulation, hot packs, iontophoresis, therapeutic exercise, manual therapy techniques, education on management of daily life skills and home exercise programs.the primary sources of revenue for the group are commercial health insurance, workers compensation insurance, managed care programs, and medicare and personal injury cases. The group's quarterly revenue for Sep '07 was 37.45 millions of USD.

Primary SIC and add'l.: 8093

CIK No: 0000885978

Subsidiaries: Achieve Physical Therapy, Action Physical Therapy Clinic, Ltd., Active Physical Therapy, Active PT and Sports Rehabilitation, Adams County Physical Therapy, Airpark Physical Therapy, Ankeny Physical & Sports Therapy, Aquatic and Orthopedic Rehab, Arrow Physical Therapy, Limited, Ashland Physical Therapy, Audubon Physical Therapy, Bay View Physical Therapy, Ltd., Beaufort Physical Therapy, Bosque River Physical Therapy, Bow Physical Therapy & Spine 188 Subsidiaries included in the Index

Officers: Larry McAfee/CFO/$759,597.00

Owners: Insiders/9.10%, Bruce D. Broussard, Mark J. Brookner, Bernard A. Harris, Marlin W. Johnston, Jerald L. Pullins, Livingston J. Kosberg/2.40%, Christopher J. Reading/1.20%, Albert L. Rosen/1.10%, Glenn D. McDowell, Daniel C. Arnold/1.10%, Lawrance W. McAfee/1.00%, Clayton K. Trier

Financial Data: Fiscal Year End:12/31 Latest Annual Data: 12/31/2006

Year	Sales	Net Income
2006	$135,194,000	$6,296,000
2005	$132,122,000	$8,791,000
2004	$118,308,000	$6,678,000

Curr. Assets:	$35,981,000	Curr. Liab.:	$9,170,000	P/E Ratio:	23.02
Plant, Equip.:	$13,371,000	Total Liab.:	$12,069,000	Indic. Yr. Divd.:	NA
Total Assets:	$71,457,000	Net Worth:	$55,517,000	Debt/ Equity:	0.0143

U.S. Shipping Partners LP

399 Thornall St., 8th Fl., Edison, NJ, 08837; *PH:* 1-732-635-1500; *Fax:* 1-732-635-1918; *http://* www.usslp.com

General - Incorporation	DE	Stock- Price on:12/24/2007	$20.94
Employees	440	Stock Exchange	NYSE
Auditor	PricewaterhouseCoopers LLP	Ticker Symbol	USS
Stk Agt	American Stock Transfer & Trust Co.	Outstanding Shares	18,240,000
Counsel	Fulbright & Jaworski L.L.P.	E.P.S.	$0.28
DUNS No.	NA	Shareholders	NA

Business: The groups principle activity is to transport refined petroleum, petrochemical and commodity chemical products. In the year 2005, the group acquired Sea Venture parcel tanker. The group operates from the United States. The groups quarterly revenue for September 2007 was 45.56 millions of USD.

Primary SIC and add'l.: 4424

CIK No: 0001299716

Subsidiaries: ITB Baltimore LLC, ITB Groton LLC, ITB Jacksonville LLC, ITB Mobile LLC, ITB New York LLC, ITB Philadelphia LLC, U.S. Shipping Finance Corp., U.S. Shipping Operating LLC, USCS ATB LLC, USCS Charleston Chartering LLC, USCS Charleston LLC, USCS Chemical Chartering LLC, USCS Chemical Pioneer Inc, USCS Sea Venture LLC, USS ATB 1 LLC 23 Subsidiaries included in the Index

Officers: Paul B. Gridley/Dir., Chmn. - General Partner, CEO, Joseph P. Gehegan/Dir., Pres., COO - our General Partner, Albert E. Bergeron/CFO, VP, Alan E. Colletti/VP - Operations, Jeffrey M. Miller/VP - Chartering

Directors: Paul B. Gridley/Dir., Chmn. - General Partner, CEO, Joseph P. Gehegan/Dir., Pres., COO - our General Partner, Bryan S. Ganz/Dir., William M. Kearns/Dir., Gerald Luterman/Dir., William J. MacEy/Dir., Douglas L. Newhouse/Dir., Ronald L. Okelley/Dir.

Owners: GPS Partners LLC/5.90%, Fiduciary Asset Management, LLC/12.60%, Ronald OKelley, Alan E. Colletti, Jeffrey M. Miller, Sterling Investment, Bryan Ganz, Paul B. Gridley, Joseph P. Gehegan, Insiders/1.00%, Sterling/US Shipping L.P./1.20%, William M. Kearns, Albert E. Bergeron

Financial Data: Fiscal Year End:12/31 Latest Annual Data: 12/31/2006

Year	Sales	Net Income
2006	$150,133,000	$5,875,000
2005	$131,534,000	$18,079,000
2004	$122,355,000	$1,448,000

Curr. Assets:	$99,398,000	Curr. Liab.:	$35,657,000	P/E Ratio:	25.48
Plant, Equip.:	$349,897,000	Total Liab.:	$438,347,000	Indic. Yr. Divd.:	$1.800
Total Assets:	$605,424,000	Net Worth:	$167,077,000	Debt/ Equity:	2.2764

U.S. Wireless Data Inc

2121 Ave. Of The Stars, Ste. 1650, Los Angeles, CA, 90067; *PH:* 1-310-601-2500; *http://* www.uswirelessdata.com

General - Incorporation	DE	Stock- Price on:12/24/2007	$3.75
Employees	1	Stock Exchange	NA
Auditor	Friedman LLP, Deloitte & Touche	Ticker Symbol	NA
Stk Agt	The Depository Trust Co.	Outstanding Shares	NA
Counsel	Mintz Levin Cohn Ferris Et Al	E.P.S.	-$0.61
DUNS No.	80-941-6043	Shareholders	NA

Business: The group's principle activities are to provide wireless transaction delivery and gateway services to the payments processing industry. The group provides credit card processors, merchant acquirers, banks, automatic teller machine distributors and their respective sales organizations with turnkey wireless and other transaction management services. The revenues of the group are derived from service revenues and product sales. Service revenues are generated from the group's synapse service and revenue from product sales is primarily derived from the sale of synapse adapter and synapse enabler products.

Primary SIC and add'l.: 3663 3578

CIK No: 0000895716

Subsidiaries: StarVox Acquisition

Officers: Thomas E. Rowley/Dir., CEO, Christopher Dunn/CFO, Douglas S. Zorn/Dir., Pres., Sherri L. Bakos/VP - Sales, Richard J. Barry/VP - Marketing, Michael Sharman/VP - Operations

Directors: Thomas E. Rowley/Dir., CEO, Douglas S. Zorn/Dir., Pres.

Owners: Robert S. Ellin, Robert S. Ellin, Insiders, Douglas S. Zorn, Trinad, Jay A. Wolf, Thomas Rowley, Daniel D. Tompkins, Richard J. Barry, David S. Smith, Lyrical Partners, L.P., Insiders, Lyrical Partners, L.P., Barry I. Regenstein, Michael C. Sharman (22 Owners included in Index)

Financial Data: Fiscal Year End:06/30 Latest Annual Data: 6/30/2006

Year	Sales	Net Income
2006	NA	-$1,105,000
2005	NA	-$25,000
2004	NA	$1,185,000

Curr. Assets:	$1,341,000	Curr. Liab.:	$161,000		
Plant, Equip.:	NA	Total Liab.:	$161,000	Indic. Yr. Divd.:	NA
Total Assets:	$4,865,000	Net Worth:	$4,704,000	Debt/ Equity:	NA

U.S.B. Holding Co Inc

100 Dutch Hill Rd., Orangeburg, NY, 10962; *PH:* 1-845-365-4826; *Fax:* 1-845-365-2130; *http://* www.unionstate.com; *Email:* customerservices@unionstate.com

General - Incorporation	DE	Stock- Price on:12/24/2007	$19.75
Employees	367	Stock Exchange	NYSE
Auditor	Deloitte & Touche LLP	Ticker Symbol	UBH
Stk Agt	Mellon Investor Services LLC	Outstanding Shares	21,930,000
Counsel	Satterlee Stephens Burke & Burke LLP	E.P.S.	$1.31
DUNS No.	13-179-6336	Shareholders	NA

Business: The group's principal activity is to provide banking and related financial services. The products and services include checking accounts, now accounts, money market accounts, savings accounts (passbook and statement), certificates of deposit, retirement accounts, commercial, personal, residential, construction, home equity (second mortgage) and condominium mortgage loans, consumer loans, credit cards, safe deposit facilities and other consumer oriented financial services. The group also provides automated teller machines (ATMs) and has a remote (PC) banking service. The group provides these services primarily to customers in rockland and westchester counties, manhattan, New York city, and long island, New York, northern New Jersey and southern Connecticut, as well as orange, putnam and dutchess counties, New York.

Primary SIC and add'l.: 6022 6712

CIK No: 0000707805

Subsidiaries: Ad Con, Inc., Dutch Hill Realty Corp., TPNZ Preferred Funding Corporation, U.S.B. Financial Services, Inc., Union State Bank, Union State Capital Trust I, Union State Statutory Trust II, Union State Statutory Trust IV, USB Delaware Inc., USB Statutory Trust III

Officers: Thomas E. Hales/Chmn., CEO/$3,674,240.00, Raymond J. Crotty/Dir., COO, Pres., Sec./$1,057,187.00, Thomas M. Buonaiuto/CFO, Exec. VP/$340,428.00, Francis X. Sansone/Exec. VP, Chief Credit Officer/$262,509.00, Diane O'Connor/Exec. VP, Sr. Operations Officer, Lawerence D. Stewart/Exec. VP, Chief Lending Officer/$346,357.00

Directors: Thomas E. Hales/Chmn., CEO, Edward T. Lutz/Dir., Raymond J. Crotty/Dir., COO, Pres., Sec., Howard V. Ruderman/Dir., Michael H. Fury/Dir., Kevin J. Plunkett/Dir., Kenneth J. Torsoe/Dir.

Owners: Harald R. Torsoe/6.71%, Howard V. Ruderman/5.87%, U.S.B. Holding Co., Inc./7.80%, Kenneth J. Torsoe/10.33%, Thomas E. Hales/16.17%

Financial Data: Fiscal Year End:12/31 Latest Annual Data: 12/31/2006

Year	Sales	Net Income
2006	$186,164,000	$31,557,000
2005	$166,440,000	$33,192,000
2004	$154,693,000	$28,065,000

Curr. Assets:	$79,754,000	Curr. Liab.:	$2,632,827,000	P/E Ratio:	14.85
Plant, Equip.:	$13,943,000	Total Liab.:	$2,699,685,000	Indic. Yr. Divd.:	$0.600
Total Assets:	$2,923,247,000	Net Worth:	$223,436,000	Debt/ Equity:	0.2713

UAL Corp/DE

PO Box 66100, Chicago, IL, 60666; *PH:* 1-847-700-9838; *http://* www.united.com; *Email:* investorrelations@ual.com

General - Incorporation	DE	Stock- Price on:12/24/2007	$37.61
Employees	55,000	Stock Exchange	NDQ
Auditor	Deloitte & Touche LLP	Ticker Symbol	UAUA
Stk Agt	Computershare Investor Services LLC	Outstanding Shares	115,590,000
Counsel	Kirkland & Ellis LLP	E.P.S.	$2.99
DUNS No.	04-834-2034	Shareholders	NA

Business: The group operates through its subsidiary whose principle activity is to provide commercial air transportation services. The group operates through two segments namely mainline and united express. The group operates from United States.

Primary SIC and add'l.: 4512 4731 6719

CIK No: 0000100517

Subsidiaries: Air Wis Services, Inc., Air Wisconsin, Inc., Ameniti Travell Clubs, Inc., Covia LLC, Domicile Management Services, Inc., Four Star Insurance Company, Ltd., Kion de Mexico, S.A. de C.V., Mileage Plus Holdings, Inc., Mileage Plus Holdings, Inc., Mileage Plus Marketing, Inc., Mileage Plus, Inc., MyPoints.com, Inc., UAL Benefits Management, Inc., UAL Corporation, UAL Loyalty Services, Inc. 20 Subsidiaries included in the Index

Officers: Glenn F. Tilton/Chmn., CEO, Pres./$23,809,560.00, Sara A. Fields/Sr. VP - Office, Chmn. - United Airlines/$8,472,129.00, Sean P. Donohue/Sr. VP - Flight Operations, Onboard Service, United Airlines, Dennis M. Cary/Sr. VP - Marketing, United Airlines, Scott J. Dolan/Sr. VP - Airport Operations, Cargo, United Airlines, Rosemary Moore/Sr. VP - Corporate, Government Affairs, United Airlines, William R. Norman/Sr. VP - United Services, United Airlines, Gregory T. Taylor/Sr. VP - Corporate Planning, Strategy, United Airlines, Charles L. Ahmes/VP - Onboard Service, United Airlines, Kathryn A. Mikells/VP - Investor Relations, United Airlines, Mark F. Schwab/VP - Pacific, United Airlines, Ajay K. Singh/VP - Corporate Real Estate, United Airlines, Frederic F. Brace/CFO, Exec. VP/$10,374,380.00, Peter D. McDonald/COO, Exec. VP/$13,209,030.00, John P. Tague/Exec. VP, Chief Revenue Officer/$10,118,780.00 (43 Officers included in Index)

Directors: Glenn F. Tilton/Chmn., CEO, Pres., David J. Vitale/Dir., Richard J. Almeida/Dir., Mark A. Bathurst/Dir., Mary K. Bush/Dir., Stephen R. Canale/Dir., James W. Farrell/Dir., Walter Isaacson/Dir., Robert D. Krebs/Dir., Robert S. Miller/Dir., James J. O'Connor/Dir., John H. Walker/Dir.

Owners: Glenn F. Tilton, Mark A. Bathurst, Capital Research and Management Company, Robert D. Krebs, U. S. Trust Corporation, United States Trust Company, N.A, Walter Isaacson, James W. Farrell, Frederic F. Brace, Vanguard Windsor Funds, Richard J. Almeida, Wellington Management Company, LLP, International Association of Machinists and Aerospace Workers, Sara Fields, Impala Asset Management LLC, Mary K. Bush (23 Owners included in Index)

Financial Data: Fiscal Year End:12/31 Latest Annual Data: 12/31/2006

Year	Sales	Net Income
2006	$19,340,000,000	$22,876,000,000
2005	$17,379,000,000	-$21,176,000,000
2004	$16,391,000,000	-$1,721,000,000

Curr. Assets:	$6,273,000,000	Curr. Liab.:	$7,945,000,000	P/E Ratio:	19.69
Plant, Equip.:	$11,463,000,000	Total Liab.:	$22,860,000,000	Indic. Yr. Divd.:	NA
Total Assets:	$25,369,000,000	Net Worth:	$2,148,000,000	Debt/ Equity:	4.2464

UAP Holding Corp

7251 W 4th St., Greeley, CO, 80634; *PH:* 1-970-356-4400; *http://* www.uap.com

General - Incorporation............................ DE	Stock - Price on:12/24/2007 ....$30.17
Employees...3,170	Stock Exchange...NDQ
Auditor ....Mckenna & Cuneo, LLP	Ticker Symbol...UAPH
Stk Agt.................Mellon Investor Services LLC	Outstanding Shares 51,480,000
Counsel..NA	E.P.S...$1.82
DUNS No. ....NA	Shareholders..NA

Business: The groups principle activity is to distribute agricultural inputs and professional non crop products. The groups services include comprehensive crop and soil nutritional. The products of the group include chemicals, fertilizer, seed and other. The group products sold under the trade names Signature(R), Bisect(R) ACA(R), Awaken(R) and Nortrace(R). Customers served by the group include farmers, commercial growers and regional dealers. The group operates from United States and Canada. The group's total revenue in the year 2007 was 2854.11 millions of USD.

Primary SIC and add'l.: 5159 2879 5191 2874 2873 2875 5169 0762

CIK No: 0001279529

Subsidiaries: Loveland Industries, Inc., Loveland Products, Inc., Platte Chemical Co., Snake River Chemicals, Inc., Transbas, Inc., UAP Distribution, Inc., UAP Timberland, LLC, United Agri Products Canada Inc., United Agri Products, Inc.

Officers: Kenny L. Cordell/Chmn., CEO, Pres., David W. Bullock/CFO, Exec. VP, David Tretter/Exec. VP - North Divisions, Kevin Howard/Exec. VP - Products, Todd A. Suko/VP, General Counsel, Sec., Jim Benshoof/VP - Information Technology, Kent McDaniel/Exec. VP - Human Resources, Administration, Alan E. Kessock/48/Chief Accounting Officer, Jeff Tarsi/Exec. VP - Strategic Planning, Dean Williams/Exec. VP - South Divisions

Directors: Kenny L. Cordell/Chmn., CEO, Pres., Michael E. Ducey/59/Dir., Carl J. Rickertsen/Dir., Thomas R. Miklich/Dir., William H. Schumann/Dir., Steven Y. Gold/Dir., Scott L. Thompson/Dir., David R. Birk/Dir.

Owners: Insiders/2.90%, Thomas R. Miklich, Neuberger Berman LLC/5.60%, David W. Bullock, Kevin M. Howard, Legg Mason Capital Management, Inc./6.10%, David J. Tretter, Iridian Asset Management LLC/6.60%, Kent J. McDaniel, Capital Research & Management Co/9.20%, Michael E. Ducey, Fidelity Management & Research/11.10%, Wellington Management Co, LLP/5.80%, Steven Y. Gold, Kenneth L. Cordell/1.10% *(18 Owners included in Index)*

Financial Data: *Fiscal Year End:*02/26 *Latest Annual Data:* 2/25/2007

Year	Sales	Net Income
2007	$2,854,108,000	$33,454,000
2006	$2,727,789,000	$66,377,000
2005	$2,506,730,000	$28,812,000

Curr. Assets:	$1,155,188,000	Curr. Liab.:	$898,446,000		
Plant, Equip.:	$89,665,000	Total Liab.:	$1,220,855,000	Indic. Yr. Divd.:	$0.900
Total Assets:	$1,337,342,000	Net Worth:	$116,487,000	Debt/ Equity:	1.0125

uBid.com Holdings Inc

8725 W Higgins Rd., 9th Fl., Chicago, IL, 60631; *PH:* 1-773-272-5000; *Fax:* 1-773-272-4000; *http://* www.ubid.com

General - Incorporation............................ DE	Stock - Price on:12/24/2007 ....$1.81
Employees...78	Stock Exchange...OTC
Auditor ....BDO Seidman, LLP	Ticker Symbol...UBHI
Stk Agt............Pacific Stock Transfer Company	Outstanding Shares 18,200,000
Counsel..NA	E.P.S...-$0.27
DUNS No. ....NA	Shareholders..NA

Business: The groups principle activities include selling computer and consumer electronics on online auction style marketplace. The group operates from the United States.

Primary SIC and add'l.: 7375 5963 7379 7389

CIK No: 0001219097

Subsidiaries: uBid, Inc.

Officers: Jeffrey D. Hoffman/Dir., CEO, Amy Powers/VP - Technology, Timothy E. Takesue/Pres., Miguel Martinez/VP - Finance, Sec.

Directors: Jeffrey D. Hoffman/Dir., CEO, Stuart R. Romenesko/44/Chmn., Steven Sjoblad/Chmn. - Ubidcom Inc, David Baer/Dir., Mary L. Jeffries/Dir., Kenneth J. Roering/Dir., Casey L. Gunnell/Dir., Paul Traub/56/Dir.

Owners: Mary L. Jeffries, Thomas J. Petters/36.72%, Miguel A. Martinez, D.E. Shaw Valence Portfolios, L.L.C./6.07%, Timothy E. Takesue/2.29%, Tudor Investment Corporation/10.04%, Steven Sjoblad, Smithfield Fiduciary LLC/9.38%, Kenneth J. Roering, Alexandra Global Master Fund Ltd./5.17%, Insiders/5.04%, Robert H. Tomlinson/2.29%, XI Asset Management, LLC/6.11%, Petters Group Worldwide, LLC/30.39%

Financial Data: *Fiscal Year End:*12/31 *Latest Annual Data:* 12/31/2006

Year	Sales	Net Income
2006	$66,559,000	-$7,555,000
2005	$84,592,000	-$9,049,000
2004	NA	-$16,000

Curr. Assets:	$22,052,000	Curr. Liab.:	$3,843,000		
Plant, Equip.:	$924,000	Total Liab.:	$3,843,000	Indic. Yr. Divd.:	NA
Total Assets:	$23,578,000	Net Worth:	$19,735,000	Debt/ Equity:	NA

Ubiquitel Inc

One W Elm St., Ste. 400, Conshohocken, PA, 19428; *PH:* 1-610-832-3300; *http://* www.ubiquitelpcs.com

General - Incorporation............................ DE	Stock - Price on:12/24/2007 ....$22
Employees..64,600	Stock Exchange..NA
Auditor ....PricewaterhouseCoopers LLP	Ticker Symbol...NA
Stk Agt.................PricewaterhouseCoopers LLP	Outstanding Shares 2,890,000,000
Counsel...............................Greenberg Traurig	E.P.S...$0.24
DUNS No. ....NA	Shareholders..NA

Business: The group's principal activity is to provide digital wireless personal communications services. The group's products and services are provided under the sprint brand name and include sprint pcs wireless Web, single band and dual band handsets and sprint pcs traveling and roaming services. These products and services are offered in the western and midwestern United States, including California, Nevada, Washington, Idaho, Montana, Wyoming, Utah, Oregon, Arizona, Indiana, Kentucky, Illinois and Tennessee. As of 31-Dec-2003, the group had approximately 327,700 subscribers.

Primary SIC and add'l.: 5999 4812 4899

CIK No: 0001108487

Subsidiaries: UbiquiTel Operating Company

Financial Data: *Fiscal Year End:*12/31 *Latest Annual Data:* 12/31/2006

Year	Sales	Net Income
2006	$41,028,000,000	$1,329,000,000
2005	$34,680,000,000	$1,785,000,000
2004	$27,428,000,000	-$1,012,000,000

Curr. Assets:	$10,304,000,000	Curr. Liab.:	$9,798,000,000	P/E Ratio:	91.67
Plant, Equip.:	$25,868,000,000	Total Liab.:	$44,030,000,000	Indic. Yr. Divd.:	$0.100
Total Assets:	$97,161,000,000	Net Worth:	$53,131,000,000	Debt/ Equity:	0.4145

UBS

1285 Ave. of the Americas, 2nd Fl., New York, NY, 10019; *PH:* 1-212-713-2000; *Fax:* 1-212-713-2099; *http://* www.ubs.com

General - Incorporation ....Switzerland	Stock - Price on:12/24/2007 ....$61.73
Employees..78,140	Stock Exchange...NYSE
Auditor ....Ernst & Young Ltd.	Ticker Symbol..UBS
Stk Agt.................Mellon Investor Services LLC	Outstanding Shares 1,940,000,000
Counsel..NA	E.P.S...$5.19
DUNS No. ....NA	Shareholders..NA

Business: The group's principal activity is the provision of a range of global banking services. The group operates through the following divisions: ubs Switzerland (private and corporate clients and swiss private banking services focusing on consumer banking products, lending for swiss corporations, and portfolio management and trust services for private banking clients); ubs asset management (all group investment management businesses, e.g. Mutual funds, global asset management, institutional asset management) and ubs warburg (investment banking and securities businesses, e.g. Corporate finance, equities, fixed income and treasury products and private equity).

Primary SIC and add'l.: 6211 6021 6282 6099 6289

CIK No: 0001114446

Subsidiaries: Aare-Tessin AG fr Elektrizitt 3, Atel Energia S.r.l. 3, Atel Installationstechnik AG 3, ATR Acquisition LLC, Azienda Energetica Municipale S.p.A., Banco UBS SA, BDL Banco di Lugano (Singapore) Ltd, BDL Banco di Lugano Lugano, Switzerland, Cantrade Private Bank Switzerland (CI) Limited St. Helier, Jersey, Chou Mitsui Private Equity Partners Investment Limited, Crdit Industriel SA, Ehinger & Armand von Ernst AG Zurich, Switzerland, Electricit dEmosson SA, Engadiner Kraftwerke AG, Entrade GmbH 3 154 Subsidiaries included in the Index

Officers: John A. Fraser/Chmn., CEO - Global Asset Management, Mark Branson/CEO - UBS Securities Japan Ltd, Brad Orgill/Chmn., CEO - Australasia, Investment Bank, Jeremy Palmer/CEO - Investment Bank in Europe, Middle East, Africa, EMEA, Marcel Rohner/Group Chmn., CEO, CEO - Investment Bank, Peter A. Wuffli/Group CEO, Pres. - Group Exec. Board, Huw Jenkins/CEO - Investment Bank, Rory Tapner/Chmn., CEO - Asia Pacific, Raoul Weil/Chmn., CEO - Global Wealth Management - Business Banking, Chris Brodie/Business Group Vice Chmn. - Investment Bank, Phil Gramm/Business Group Vice Chmn. - Investment Bank, Thomas K. Escher/Business Group Vice Chmn. - Global Wealth Management, Business Banking, Carlo Grigioni/Business Group Vice Chmn. - Global Wealth Management, Business Banking, Senator Phil Gramm/Vice Chmn. - Investment Bank, Busiiness Group, Robert Gillespie/Vice Chmn. - Global Business Group, Investment Bank *(86 Officers included in Index)*

Directors: John A. Fraser/Chmn., CEO - Global Asset Management, Brad Orgill/Chmn., CEO - Australasia, Investment Bank, Marcel Rohner/Group Chmn., CEO, CEO - Investment Bank, Rory Tapner/Chmn., CEO - Asia Pacific, Raoul Weil/Chmn., CEO - Global Wealth Management - Business Banking, Peter W. Burnett/Exec. Chmn. - Middle East, Investment Bank, Stephan Haeringer/Exec. Vice Chmn., Marcel Ospel/Chmn., Peter Davis/Dir., Sergio Marchionne/Dir., Ernesto Bertarelli/Dir., Gabrielle Kaufmann-Kohler/Dir., Peter Spuhler/Dir., Rolf A. Meyer/Dir., Helmut Panke/Dir. *(18 Directors included in Index)*

Financial Data: *Fiscal Year End:*12/31 *Latest Annual Data:* 12/31/2006

Year	Sales	Net Income
2006	$105,753,425,000	$10,461,375,000
2005	$76,292,152,000	$10,664,846,000
2004	$60,641,727,000	$7,794,230,000

Curr. Assets:	$680,993,668,000	Curr. Liab.:	$510,450,281,000	P/E Ratio:	18.18
Plant, Equip.:	$6,756,818,000	Total Liab.:	$1,925,569,913,000	Indic. Yr. Divd.:	$1.190
Total Assets:	$1,966,337,276,000	Net Worth:	$40,767,363,000	Debt/ Equity:	NA

UC Hub Group Inc

10390 Commerce Ctr Dr., Ste 250, Rancho Cucamonga, CA, 91730; *PH:* 1-888-425-5266; *http://* www.uchub.net

General - Incorporation .... NV	Stock - Price on:12/24/2007 ....$0.021
Employees...1	Stock Exchange...OTC
Auditor ..... Lawrence Scharfman & Co, Cpa P.A.	Ticker Symbol...UCHB
Stk Agt..NA	Outstanding Shares 27,690,000
Counsel..NA	E.P.S...$0.00
DUNS No. ....NA	Shareholders..NA

Business: The group's principal activity is to distribute digital, bundled services and software solutions for small to medium sized cities and affinity groups. The services presently being offered include banking, communications and government management.

Primary SIC and add'l.: 7372

CIK No: 0001072935

Subsidiaries: eSafe, Inc

Officers: Larry Wilcox/Chmn., CEO, CFO, Pres.

Directors: Larry Wilcox/Chmn., CEO, CFO, Pres., John Cheney/Dir., Andy Mercer/Dir., Stephen Herold/Dir., David Dearman/Dir.

Owners: Insiders, Larry Wilcox, Larry Wilcox, Insiders

Financial Data: *Fiscal Year End:*07/31 *Latest Annual Data:* 07/31/2007

Year	Sales	Net Income
2007	NA	-$220,000
2006	$306,000	-$733,000
2005	$2,758,000	-$1,353,000

Curr. Assets:	$1,424,000	Curr. Liab.:	$2,258,000		
Plant, Equip.:	$29,000	Total Liab.:	$2,613,000	Indic. Yr. Divd.:	NA
Total Assets:	$1,452,000	Net Worth:	-$1,160,000	Debt/ Equity:	NA

UCI Medical Affiliates Inc

4416 Forest Dr., Columbia, SC, 29206; **PH:** 1-803-252-3661; **http://** www.doctorscare.com;
Email: info@doctorscare.com

General - Incorporation	DE	**Stock** - Price on:12/24/2007	$3.65
Employees	576	Stock Exchange	OTC
Auditor	Scott McElveen LLP	Ticker Symbol	UCIA
Stk Agt	American Stock Transfer & Trust Co.	Outstanding Shares	9,910,000
Counsel	Nexsen Pruet Jacobs & Pollard	E.P.S.	$0.15
DUNS No.	11-812-8776	Shareholders	NA

Business: The group's principal activities are to provide non-medical management and administrative services for a network of 36 freestanding medical centers located in South Carolina and Tennessee. The medical services provided at the centers include outpatient medical care, routine care of general medicine problems, treatment of injuries, minor surgery, diagnostic tests and occupational and industrial medical services. The services are provided by licensed physicians, nurses and auxiliary support personnel. The services are also provided for members of health maintenance organizations.

Primary SIC and add'l.: 8741 8093

CIK No: 0000737561

Subsidiaries: South Carolina, Inc. (UCI-SC)

Officers: Michael Stout/CEO, Pres., Jerry F. Wells/CFO

Directors: Charles M. Potok/58/Chmn., Timothy L. Vaughn/43/Dir., Thomas G. Faulds/66/Dir., Jean E. Duke/52/Dir., Joseph A. Boyle/53/Dir., John M. Little/56/Dir., Harold H. Adams/60/Dir.

Owners: Thomas G. Faulds, Jean E. Duke, Harold H. Adams, Michael D. Stout/3.90%, Charles M. Potok, Blue Cross Blue Shield of South Carolina/68.42%, Insiders/4.04%

Financial Data: *Fiscal Year End:*09/30 *Latest Annual Data:* 9/30/2006

Year	Sales	Net Income
2006	$63,672,000	$2,710,000
2005	$56,642,000	$7,541,000
2004	$47,474,000	$3,214,000

Curr. Assets:	$14,165,000	**Curr. Liab.:**	$6,800,000	**P/E Ratio:**	13.04
Plant, Equip.:	$8,749,000	**Total Liab.:**	$11,879,000	**Indic. Yr. Divd.:**	NA
Total Assets:	$28,126,000	**Net Worth:**	$16,246,000	**Debt/ Equity:**	NA

UCN Inc

14870 Pony Express Rd. , None, Bluffdale, UT, 84065; **PH:** 1-800-320-3200; **http://** www.ucn.net;
Email: info@ucn.net

General - Incorporation	DE	**Stock** - Price on:12/24/2007	$4.5
Employees	202	Stock Exchange	NDQ
Auditor	Deloitte & Touche LLP	Ticker Symbol	UCNN
Stk Agt	Mellon Investor Services LLC	Outstanding Shares	28,370,000
Counsel	NA	E.P.S.	-$0.26
DUNS No.	NA	Shareholders	NA

Business: The group's principal activity is to provide telecommunication services. The services are sold to small businesses and residential consumers across America. The group offers long distance, toll free, data transmission, and related communication service options and related products, including calling cards, automatic call distribution, interactive voice response, toll free 800/888/877/866 services and other related services. The group has two brands namely united carrier networks (ucn) and buyersonline (bol). United carrier networks caters to business customers, while buyersonline caters to residential consumer.

Primary SIC and add'l.: 7375 4813 7299

CIK No: 0001087934

Subsidiaries: Buyers United - Virginia, Inc., MyACD, Inc.

Officers: Paul Jarman/Dir., CEO/$273,708.00, Kevin L. Childs/Exec. VP, Pres. - Sales, Marketing, Support/$302,923.00, Jim Elliot/Sr. VP - Marketing, Training, Tom Milligan/VP - Incontact Operations, Scott Welch/COO, Exec. VP/$223,516.00, Jon B. Heaps/VP - Western Region Sales, Jan Johnson/VP - Business Development, Brian Moroney/CFO, Exec. VP/$232,086.00, Mike Perry/VP - Network Planning, Telecom Services, Chris Bijou/Sr. VP - Sales, Andrew J. Judkins/VP - Product Management, Dale Kennedy/VP - Sales, Eastern Region, Anita Rockwell/VP - Echo Solutions

Directors: Paul Jarman/Dir., CEO, Theodore Stern/Chmn., Paul F. Koeppe/55/Dir., Steve Barnett/Dir., Blake O. Fisher/61/Dir.

Owners: Insiders/11.60%, Kevin Childs, Select Contrarian Value Partners, LP/7.40%, Scott Welch, Steve Barnett/1.50%, CCM Master Qualified Fund, Ltd./5.60%, Paul Jarman/2.50%, Diker Management, LLC/8.30%, Blake Fisher, Theodore Stern/5.60%, Brian Moroney, Paul Koeppe

Financial Data: *Fiscal Year End:*12/31 *Latest Annual Data:* 12/31/2006

Year	Sales	Net Income
2006	$82,800,000	-$7,775,000
2005	$81,587,000	-$8,147,000
2004	$65,159,000	-$2,113,000

Curr. Assets:	$14,159,000	**Curr. Liab.:**	$12,542,000		
Plant, Equip.:	$4,810,000	**Total Liab.:**	$19,111,000	**Indic. Yr. Divd.:**	NA
Total Assets:	$25,959,000	**Net Worth:**	$6,848,000	**Debt/ Equity:**	0.6408

UDR Inc

Formerly: United Dominion Realty Trust Inc
1745 Shea Ctr. Dr., Ste. 200, Highlands Ranch, CO, 80129; **PH:** 1-804-780-2691;
http:// www.udrt.com

General - Incorporation	MD	**Stock** - Price on:12/24/2007	$27.74
Employees	1,809	Stock Exchange	NYSE
Auditor	Ernst & Young LLP	Ticker Symbol	UDR
Stk Agt	Wells Fargo Bank, N.A.	Outstanding Shares	135,870,000
Counsel	NA	E.P.S.	$0.99
DUNS No.	NA	Shareholders	NA

Business: The groups principle activities include owning, renovating, developing and manages apartment communities. In the year 2006, the group acquired eight communities. The group operates from the United States. The groups quarterly revenue for September 2007 was 183.44 millions of USD.

Primary SIC and add'l.: 6513

CIK No: 0000074208

Subsidiaries: AAC Funding II, Inc., AAC Funding IV LLC, AAC Funding IV, Inc., AAC Funding Partnership II, AAC Funding Partnership III, AAC Seattle I, Inc., AAC Vancouver I, L.P., AAC/FSC Crown Pointe Investors, LLC, AAC/FSC Hilltop Investors, LLC, AAC/FSC Seattle Properties, LLC, Arizona Properties, LLC, Ashwood Commons, L.L.C., ASR Investments Corporation, ASR of Delaware LLC, Bellevue JV LLC 129 Subsidiaries included in the Index

Officers: Thomas W. Toomey/Dir., CEO, Pres./$3,496,143.00, Michael A. Ernst/CFO, Exec. VP/$1,014,367.00, Mark W. Wallis/Sr. Exec. VP/$1,958,169.00, Martha R. Carlin/Exec. VP - Operations/$1,441,235.00, Douglas F. Fee/VP - Asset Quality, Nellcine Ford/VP, Dir. - Associate Services, Terry D. Fulbright/VP, Dir. - Ancillary Services, David F. Houghton/VP - Strategic Sourcing, Corporate Services, Richard A. Giannotti/Exec. VP - Redevelopment, Matthew T. Akin/Sr. VP - Acquisitions, Dispositions, Lester C. Boeckel/59/Sr. VP - Condominiums/$827,060.00, Mark M. Culwell/Sr. VP - Development, Patrick S. Gregory/58/Sr. VP, CIO - Richmond Corporate Headquarters, David L. Messenger/Chief Accounting Officer, Sr. VP, Stacy M. Riffe/Sr. VP, CFO - RE3 *(43 Officers included in Index)*

Directors: Thomas W. Toomey/Dir., CEO, Pres., James D. Klingbeil/Vice Chmn., Robert C. Larson/Chmn., Thomas R. Oliver/Dir., Lynne B. Sagalyn/Dir., Katherine A. Cattanach/Dir., Eric J. Foss/Dir., Robert P. Freeman/Dir., Jon A. Grove/Dir., Mark J. Sandler/Dir., Thomas C. Wajnert/Dir.

Owners: Eric J. Foss, FMR Corp./14.87%, Lynne B. Sagalyn, Jon A. Grove, The Vanguard Group, Inc./6.36%, Robert P. Freeman, James D. Klingbeil/1.09%, Thomas C. Wajnert, Mark J. Sandler, Mark W. Wallis, Barclays Global Investors, N.A./5.32%, Christopher D. Genry, Michael A. Ernst, Martha R. Carlin, Thomas W. Toomey/1.12% *(20 Owners included in Index)*

Financial Data: *Fiscal Year End:*12/31 *Latest Annual Data:* 12/31/2006

Year	Sales	Net Income
2006	$698,058,000	$128,605,000
2005	$701,217,000	$155,166,000
2004	$606,878,000	$97,152,000

Curr. Assets:	$7,745,000	**Curr. Liab.:**	$186,967,000	**P/E Ratio:**	28.02
Plant, Equip.:	$4,579,347,000	**Total Liab.:**	$3,531,787,000	**Indic. Yr. Divd.:**	$1.250
Total Assets:	$4,675,875,000	**Net Worth:**	$1,055,255,000	**Debt/ Equity:**	3.3210

UFP Technologies Inc

172 E Main St., Georgetown, MA, 01833; **PH:** 1-800-372-3172; **http://** www.ufpt.com;
Email: info@ufpt.com

General - Incorporation	DE	**Stock** - Price on:12/24/2007	$5.26
Employees	531	Stock Exchange	NDQ
Auditor	Carlin, Charron & Rosen LLP	Ticker Symbol	UFPT
Stk Agt	American Stock Transfer & Trust Co.	Outstanding Shares	5,260,000
Counsel	Lynch Brewer Hoffman & Fink LLP	E.P.S.	$0.55
DUNS No.	00-104-2100	Shareholders	NA

Business: The group's principal activity is to design and manufacture a broad range of high-performance cushion packaging and specialty foam products. Cushion packaging products are made from polyethylene and polyurethane foams. They are custom designed and fabricated or molded to provide protection for fragile and valuable items. These packaging products are primarily sold to original equipment and component manufacturers in the computer, electronics, telecommunications, industrial, medical and pharmaceutical markets. The specialty products include door panels and other interior automotive components, athletic and industrial safety belts. They also include components for medical diagnostic equipment, nail files and other beauty aids and shock absorbing inserts used in athletic and leisure footwear.

Primary SIC and add'l.: 3089 3086

CIK No: 0000914156

Subsidiaries: Moulded Fibre Technology, Inc. (MFT), UFP Technologies, Inc

Owners: Ellen Shaw/5.60%, Richard LeSavoy/1.70%, Ronald J. Lataille/2.40%, David K. Stevenson, Marc Kozin, Jeffrey R. Bailly/17.20%, Mitchell C. Rock/2.40%, Thomas W. Oberdorf, Michael J. Ross/1.90%, David B. Gould/1.10%, Insiders/31.70%, Daniel J. Shaw/1.10%, Kenneth L. Gestal/2.40%, Richard L. Bailly/4.60%

Financial Data: *Fiscal Year End:*12/31 *Latest Annual Data:* 12/31/2006

Year	Sales	Net Income
2006	$93,749,000	$2,515,000
2005	$83,962,000	$659,000
2004	$68,624,000	$871,000

Curr. Assets:	$20,374,000	**Curr. Liab.:**	$12,138,000	**P/E Ratio:**	10.96
Plant, Equip.:	$10,137,000	**Total Liab.:**	$20,412,000	**Indic. Yr. Divd.:**	NA
Total Assets:	$39,037,000	**Net Worth:**	$18,625,000	**Debt/ Equity:**	0.3366

UGI Corp

460 N Gulph Rd. , King Of Prussia, PA, 19406; **PH:** 1-610-337-1000; **http://** www.shareholder.com

General - Incorporation	PA	**Stock** - Price on:12/24/2007	$27.26
Employees	9,800	Stock Exchange	NYSE
Auditor	PricewaterhouseCoopers LLP	Ticker Symbol	UGI
Stk Agt	Mellon Investor Services LLC	Outstanding Shares	106,240,000
Counsel	NA	E.P.S.	$1.89
DUNS No.	00-791-5069	Shareholders	NA

Business: The group operates through its subsidiaries whose principle activities include distributing and marketing energy products and services. The group provides domestic and international distribution of propane, natural gas, electricity and related services. The group also provides heating, air conditioning, refrigeration and electrical services. The group operates from United States, Austria, the Czech Republic, Slovakia, France and China.

Primary SIC and add'l.: 1321 4932 4931

CIK No: 0000884614

Subsidiaries: Active Propane of Wisconsin, LLC, AGZ Finance , AGZ Holding, AmerE Holdings, Inc., AmeriGas Eagle Finance Corp., AmeriGas Eagle Holdings, Inc., AmeriGas Eagle Parts & Service, Inc., AmeriGas Eagle Propane, Inc., AmeriGas Eagle Propane, L.P., AmeriGas Finance Corp., AmeriGas Partners, L.P., AmeriGas Propane L.P., AmeriGas Propane Parts & Service, Inc., Amerigas Propane, Inc., AmeriGas Technology Group, Inc. 67 Subsidiaries included in the Index

Officers: Lon R. Greenberg/Chmn., CEO, John L. Walsh/52/Dir., COO, Pres., Brenda Blake/Investor Relations Officer, Margaret M. Calabrese/Corp. Sec., Michael J. Cuzzolina/63/VP - Accounting, Financial Control, Chief Risk Officer, Bradley C. Hall/55/VP - New Business Development, Robert H. Knauss/55/VP, General Counsel, Assist. Sec., Robert Krick/Investor Relations Officer, Peter Kelly/51/CFO, VP - Finance

Directors: Lon R. Greenberg/Chmn., CEO, James W. Stratton/71/Dir., Richard C. Gozon/69/Dir., Stephen D. Ban/67/Dir., Marvin O. Schlanger/59/Dir., Anne Pol/60/Dir., Ernest E. Jones/63/Dir., John L. Walsh/52/Dir., COO, Pres., Roger B. Vincent/62/Dir.

Owners: Barclays Global Investors UK/12.86%, Wellington Management Company, LLP/10.35%

Financial Data: Fiscal Year End:09/30   Latest Annual Data: 09/30/2007

Year	Sales	Net Income
2007	$5,476,900,000	$204,300,000
2006	$5,221,000,000	$176,200,000
2005	$4,888,700,000	$187,500,000

Curr. Assets:	$1,040,600,000	Curr. Liab.:	$1,026,600,000	P/E Ratio:	15.49
Plant, Equip.:	$2,214,700,000	Total Liab.:	$3,841,400,000	Indic. Yr. Dvd.:	$0.740
Total Assets:	$5,080,500,000	Net Worth:	$1,099,600,000	Debt/ Equity:	1.5268

UGI Utilities In

100 Kachel Blvd., Ste. 400, Reading, PA, 19612; *PH:* 1-610-796-3400; *http://* www.ugi.com

General - Incorporation	PA	Stock- Price on:12/24/2007	NA
Employees	NA	Stock Exchange	NA
Auditor	PricewaterhouseCoopers LLP	Ticker Symbol	NA
Stk Agt	Mellon Investor Services LLC	Outstanding Shares	NA
Counsel	NA	E.P.S.	NA
DUNS No.	79-937-6595	Shareholders	NA

Business: The group's principal activity is to own and operate natural gas distribution utility and an electric utility. The group is a wholly owned subsidiary of ugi corporation. The natural gas is distributed to 14 eastern and southeastern Pennsylvania counties through its distribution system of gas mains extending 4700 miles. The group purchases gas from gulf coast, mid continent, appalachian and Canadian sources. The electric utility segment supplies electricity to about 61,500 customers in different areas of northeastern Pennsylvania through a system consisting of 2,100 miles of transmission and distribution lines and 14 transmission substations. The group owns and operates hunlock generating station located near kingston, Pennsylvania.

Primary SIC and add'l.: 4932 4924 4911

CIK No: 0000100548

Subsidiaries: UGI Corporation, UGI Utilities, Inc.

Officers: David W. Trego/CEO, Pres.

Directors: Lon R. Greenberg/Chmn., John L. Walsh/Vice Chmn., Stephen D. Ban/Dir.

UIL Holdings Corp

157 Church St., New Haven, CT, 06506; *PH:* 1-203-499-3333; *http://* www.uil.com; *Email:* uil@uinet.com

General - Incorporation	CT	Stock- Price on:12/24/2007	$32.28
Employees	920	Stock Exchange	NYSE
Auditor	PricewaterhouseCoopers LLP	Ticker Symbol	UIL
Stk Agt	American Stock Transfer & Trust Co.	Outstanding Shares	25,150,000
Counsel	Wiggin & Dana LLP	E.P.S.	-$0.24
DUNS No.	NA	Shareholders	NA

Business: The group's principal activities are purchase, transmission, distribution and sale of electricity for residential, commercial and industrial purposes. The group operated under four segments: utility retail, utility wholesale, utility other and non-utility business. The utility business consists of the electric transmission and distribution operations of the united illuminating company (ui), the non-utility businesses includes the operations of xcelecom, inc. (xcelecom), passive investments in united capital investments, inc. (uci) and united bridgeport energy, inc. (ube). The united illuminating company transmits and distributes electricity. Xcelecom provides provides general and specialty electrical, mechanical and voice-data-video design, construction, and related services. The group discontinued the American payment systems, inc operations under its non-utility business segment.

Primary SIC and add'l.: 4911

CIK No: 0001082510

Subsidiaries: Xcelecom

Officers: James P. Torgerson/Dir., CEO, Pres., Michelle Hanson/Investor Relation Officer, Susan E. Allen/VP - Investor Relations, Sec., Treasurer/$422,408.00, Deborah C. Hoffman/VP - Audit Services, Chief Compliance Officer, Richard J. Nicholas/CFO, Exec. VP/$1,013,041.00, Gregory W. Buckis/VP, Controller, Linda Randell/Sr. VP, General Counsel, Corp. Sec., Steven P. Favuzza/VP, Controller

Directors: Nathaniel D. Woodson/Chmn., William F. Murdy/Dir., James A. Thomas/Dir., Patrick F. McFadden/Dir., Daniel J. Miglio/Dir., Arnold L. Chase/Dir., Thelma R. Albright/Dir., John L. Lahey/Dir., Marc C. Breslawsky/Dir., John F. Croweak/Dir., Betsy Henley-Cohn/Dir.

Owners: Anthony J. Vallillo, Richard J. Nicholas, Nathaniel D. Woodson, Susan E. Allen, James A. Thomas, Patrick F. McFadden, RLC Investments LLC, Insiders, DTC Holdings Corporation Foundation, Inc., Marc C. Breslawsky, Cheryl A. Chase, Thelma R. Albright, DTC Family Investments LLC, John L. Lahey, Betsy Henley-Cohn (27 Owners included in Index)

Financial Data: Fiscal Year End:12/31   Latest Annual Data: 12/31/2006

Year	Sales	Net Income
2006	$845,950,000	-$65,164,000
2005	$1,213,096,000	$31,254,000
2004	$1,101,287,000	$86,945,000

Curr. Assets:	$295,430,000	Curr. Liab.:	$229,851,000		
Plant, Equip.:	$647,014,000	Total Liab.:	$1,170,912,000	Indic. Yr. Dvd.:	$1.730
Total Assets:	$1,631,493,000	Net Worth:	$460,581,000	Debt/ Equity:	0.8914

Ulticom Inc

1020 Briggs Rd. , Mt Laurel, NJ, 08054; *PH:* 1-856-787-2760; *http://* www.ulticom.com; *Email:* sales@ulticom.com

General - Incorporation	NJ	Stock- Price on:12/24/2007	NA
Employees	235	Stock Exchange	OTC
Auditor	Deloitte & Touche LLP	Ticker Symbol	ULCM
Stk Agt	American Stock Transfer & Trust Co.	Outstanding Shares	NA
Counsel	Weil, Gotshal & Manges LLP	E.P.S.	$0.46
DUNS No.	NA	Shareholders	NA

Business: The group's principle activities are to designing, developing, and marketing of software for wireline, wireless and Internet communications. The group's signalware product consists of software licenses, interface boards, training and support services. The group products are sold through a direct sales force to network equipment manufacturers, application developers and service providers who include the company's products within their products. The group's products are used by equipment manufacturers, application developers and communication service providers. The group markets products in the United States, Europe and Asia.

Primary SIC and add'l.: 7372

CIK No: 0001103184

Subsidiaries: Ulticom Europe, S.A.S.

Officers: Shawn K. Osborne/Dir., CEO, Pres., Mark Kissman/Sr. VP, CFO

Directors: Shawn K. Osborne/Dir., CEO, Pres., Paul D. Baker/Dir., Michael J. Chill/Dir., Yaacov Koren/Dir., Rex A. McWilliams/Dir., Ron Hiram/Dir., Andre Dahan/Dir., Avi Aronovitz/Dir., Shefali Shah/Dir.

Financial Data: Fiscal Year End:01/31   Latest Annual Data: 01/31/2005

Year	Sales	Net Income
2005	$63,436,000	$15,971,000
2004	$38,378,000	$4,580,000
2003	$29,231,000	-$1,735,000

Curr. Assets:	$262,578,000	Curr. Liab.:	$16,428,000		
Plant, Equip.:	$2,274,000	Total Liab.:	$16,428,000	Indic. Yr. Divd.:	NA
Total Assets:	$271,992,000	Net Worth:	$255,564,000	Debt/ Equity:	NA

Ultimate Security Systems Ltd

18271 W McDurmott, Ste. F, Irvine, CA, 92614; *PH:* 1-44-1792795380; *http://* www.ultimatesecuritysystems.co.uk; *Email:* enquiries@ultimatesecuritysystems.co.uk

General - Incorporation	NV	Stock- Price on:12/24/2007	NA
Employees	NA	Stock Exchange	NA
Auditor	John Kinross-kennedy, C.P.A	Ticker Symbol	NA
Stk Agt	NA	Outstanding Shares	NA
Counsel	NA	E.P.S.	NA
DUNS No.	NA	Shareholders	NA

Business: The group's principal activity is to manufacture Power Lock (TM) security systems and immuno technology. Power Lock (TM) is the only solid-state auto security system that is guaranteed to prevent any vehicle from being hot-wired and driven away. The product attaches permanently to a vehicle's starter motor and cannot be circumvented by cutting and jumping ignition wires, the "hot-wiring" technique used by professional car thieves in the vast majority of stolen vehicle cases nationwide.

Primary SIC and add'l.: 3600

CIK No: 0001047306

Ultimate Software Group Inc

2000 Ultimate Way, Weston, FL, 33326; *PH:* 1-954-331-7000; *Fax:* 1-954-331-7300; *http://* www.usgroup.com; *Email:* ultiproinfo@ultimatesoftware.com

General - Incorporation	DE	Stock- Price on:12/24/2007	$28.86
Employees	623	Stock Exchange	NDQ
Auditor	KPMG LLP	Ticker Symbol	ULTI
Stk Agt	Computershare Trust Co	Outstanding Shares	24,670,000
Counsel	Dewey Ballantine	E.P.S.	$0.43
DUNS No.	62-599-7614	Shareholders	NA

Business: The group's principle activities are to design, market, implement and support technologically advanced cross-industry human resources management and payroll software solutions. The group's main product is ultipro Web, which includes manager self-service, employee self-service, and benefits enrollment. It is integrated with and supported by a back-office client server solution known as ultipro hrms and payroll, that can also be purchased stand-alone. The group's product allows customers to empower their entire workforce - employees, managers and executives, to improve communications and efficiencies. The product offers business intelligence reporting, access to benefits and paycheck history, direct deposit maintenance and human resources management including Internet employee administration, benefits enrollment, recruitment and training features. The group has its operation in the United States of America. The group's quarterly revenue for Sep '07 was 37.82 millions of USD.

Primary SIC and add'l.: 7372 7373 7379

CIK No: 0001016125

Officers: Scott Scherr/Chmn., CEO, Pres./$1,829,623.00, Marc D. Scherr/Vice Chmn., COO/$1,429,651.00, Mitchell K. Dauerman/Exec. VP, CFO, Treasurer/$641,469.00, Daniel Taylor/38/Sr. VP - Talent Management

Directors: Scott Scherr/Chmn., CEO, Pres., Marc D. Scherr/Vice Chmn., COO, Robert A. Yanover/Dir., James A. Fitzpatrick/Dir., Leroy A. Vander Putten/Dir., Rick A. Wilber/Dir., Al Leiter/Dir.

Owners: Rick A. Wilber/1.40%, Marc D. Scherr/2.40%, Insiders/8.30%, Janus Capital Management L.L.C. and Janus Venture Fund/7.70%, Robert A. Yanover/0.90%, Alois T. Leiter/0.60%, Scott Scherr/1.70%, LeRoy A. Vander Putten, Mitchell K. Dauerman/0.70%, James A. FitzPatrick, William Blair& Company, L.L.C./12.20%

Financial Data: Fiscal Year End:12/31   Latest Annual Data: 12/31/2006

Year	Sales	Net Income
2006	$114,811,000	$4,133,000
2005	$88,603,000	$3,425,000
2004	$72,028,000	-$5,024,000

Curr. Assets:	$65,835,000	Curr. Liab.:	$51,665,000	P/E Ratio:	72.15
Plant, Equip.:	$13,480,000	Total Liab.:	$62,508,000	Indic. Yr. Divd.:	NA
Total Assets:	$93,530,000	Net Worth:	$31,022,000	Debt/ Equity:	0.0506

Ultra Clean Holdings Inc

150 Independence Dr., Menlo Park, CA, 94025; *PH:* 1-650-323-4100; *http://* www.uct.com

General - Incorporation	DE	Stock- Price on:12/24/2007	$14.35
Employees	807	Stock Exchange	NDQ
Auditor	Deloitte & Touche LLP	Ticker Symbol	UCTT
Stk Agt	Wells Fargo Shareowner Services	Outstanding Shares	21,200,000
Counsel	NA	E.P.S.	$0.94
DUNS No.	05-599-1053	Shareholders	NA

Business: The group's principal activity is to develop and supply critical subsystems for the semiconductor capital equipment industry. It provides customers with a full range of services such as development, design, prototyping, engineering, manufacturing and testing of gas delivery systems that enable the precise delivery of numerous specialty gases used in a majority of the key steps in the semiconductor manufacturing process. The products of the group control the flow, pressure, sequencing and mixing of specialty gases into and out of the process chambers of semiconductor manufacturing tools. The customer of the group mainly consists of original equipment manufacturers of semiconductor capital equipment such as applied materials, inc., novellus systems, inc. And lam research corporation. It operates solely in the domestic market.

Primary SIC and add'l.: 3674 6719

CIK No: 0001275014

Subsidiaries: Ultra Clean International Holding Company, Ultra Clean Technology (Shanghai) Co., LTD, Ultra Clean Technology Systems and Service, Inc

Officers: Clarence Granger/Chmn., CEO, Bruce Wier/Sr. VP - Engineering, Deborah Hayward/Sr. VP - Sales, Business Management, Jack Sexton/CFO, VP, Sowmya Krishnan/VP - Technology, CTO, Leonard Mezhvinsky/Pres.

Directors: Clarence Granger/Chmn., CEO, David T. Ibnale/Dir., Thomas M. Rohrs/Dir., Brian R. Bachman/Dir., Sue Billat/Dir., Kevin C. Eichler/Dir.

Owners: Clarence L. Granger/3.50%, Thomas M. Rohrs, Deborah Hayward, Sowmya Krishnan, Susan H. Billat, Bear Stearns Asset Management Inc./7.00%, Kevin C. Eichler, Brian R. Bachman, Wellington Management Company, LLP/7.50%, Leonid Mezhvinsky/8.90%, Bruce Wier, Jack Sexton, Dipanjan Deb, Insiders/14.20%, David ibnAle

Financial Data: Fiscal Year End:12/31   Latest Annual Data: 12/31/2006

Year	Sales	Net Income
2006	$337,228,000	$16,310,000
2005	$147,535,000	$2,003,000
2004	$184,204,000	$8,550,000

Curr. Assets:	$121,267,000	Curr. Liab.:	$49,680,000	P/E Ratio:	15.27
Plant, Equip.:	$9,433,000	Total Liab.:	$79,879,000	Indic. Yr. Divd.:	NA
Total Assets:	$187,047,000	Net Worth:	$107,168,000	Debt/ Equity:	0.2385

Ultra Petroleum Corp

363 N Sam Houston Pkwy E, Ste 1200, Houston, TX, 77060; **PH:** 1-281-876-0120;
http:// www.ultrapetroleum.com

General - Incorporation	Canada	**Stock**- Price on:12/24/2007	$56.5
Employees	68	Stock Exchange	NYSE
Auditor	KPMG LLP	Ticker Symbol	UPL
Stk Agt	Computershare Trust Co	Outstanding Shares	151,960,000
Counsel	NA	E.P.S.	$1.35
DUNS No.	24-996-2416	Shareholders	NA

Business: The group's principal activities of the group are exploration, development and operation of oil and gas properties located in the United States and China. The group's quarterly revenue for Seo '07 was 117.22 millions of USD.

Primary SIC and add'l.: 1382 1311

CIK No: 0001022646

Subsidiaries: Sino-American Energy Corporation, Ultra Resources, Inc, UP Energy Corporation

Officers: Michael D. Watford/Chmn., CEO, Pres./$5,046,097.00, Stuart E. Nance/VP - Marketing, Kelly L. Whitley/Mgr. - Investor Relations, Stephen R. Kneller/VP - Exploration Domestic/$727,190.00, Mike Patterson/VP - Exploration International, William R. Picquet/VP - Operations Rocky Mountains/$702,190.00, Marshall D. Smith/CFO/$717,498.00

Directors: Michael D. Watford/Chmn., CEO, Pres., Stephen J. McDaniel/Dir., Charles Helton/Dir., Robert E. Rigney/Dir., Roger A. Brown/Dir.

Owners: Fidelity Management& Research Company/15.00%, William R. Picquet, James C. Roe, Michael D. Watford/4.20%, Robert E. Rigney/1.10%, Insiders/7.70%, Morgan Stanley/10.60%, George M. Patterson, Charles W. Helton/1.00%, Stephen R. Kneller, Marshall D. Smith, Stephen J. McDaniel

Financial Data: Fiscal Year End:12/31   Latest Annual Data: 12/31/2006

Year	Sales	Net Income
2006	$592,668,000	$231,195,000
2005	$516,493,000	$228,300,000
2004	$258,037,000	$109,150,000

Curr. Assets:	$136,571,000	Curr. Liab.:	$177,999,000		
Plant, Equip.:	$1,121,198,000	Total Liab.:	$628,764,000	Indic. Yr. Divd.:	NA
Total Assets:	$1,257,769,000	Net Worth:	$629,005,000	Debt/ Equity:	0.3137

Ultralife Batteries Inc

2000 Technology Pkwy, Newark, NY, 14513; **PH:** 1-315-332-7100; *http://* www.ulbi.com

General - Incorporation	DE	**Stock**- Price on:12/24/2007	$10.24
Employees	1,078	Stock Exchange	NDQ
Auditor	PricewaterhouseCoopers LLP	Ticker Symbol	ULBI
Stk Agt	American Stock Transfer & Trust Co.	Outstanding Shares	15,180,000
Counsel	NA	E.P.S.	$1.65
DUNS No.	62-331-6726	Shareholders	NA

Business: The group's principal activities are to develop, manufacture and market standard and customized primary lithium, lithium ion and lithium polymer rechargeable batteries. The group operates through four segments: primary batteries, rechargeable batteries, technology contracts and corporate. The primary batteries consist of lithium-manganese dioxide (li-mno2) primary batteries including 9-volt, cylindrical, thin cell(R), in addition to magnesium silver-chloride seawater-activated batteries. The rechargeable batteries consist of lithium polymer and lithium ion rechargeable batteries. The technology contracts segment includes identify and develop new applications for its products and to advance its technologies through contracts with both government agencies and third parties. These batteries are used in military, industrial and consumer applications. The group operates in the United States, the United Kingdom and Hong Kong.

Primary SIC and add'l.: 3691 8731

CIK No: 0000875657

Subsidiaries: Ultralife Batteries (UK) Ltd

Officers: John D. Kavazanjian/Dir., CEO, Pres./$620,773.00, William A. Schmitz/COO/$276,789.00, Philip M. Meek/VP - Manufacturing, Patrick R. Hanna/VP - Corporate Business Strategy, Robert W. Fishback/VP - Finance, CFO/$248,082.00, Peter F. Comerford/VP - Administration, General Counsel/$219,734.00, Julius M. Cirin/VP - Corporate Marketing, Technology, Andrew J. Naukam/COO - Mcdowell Research

Directors: John D. Kavazanjian/Dir., CEO, Pres., Ranjit C. Singh/Chmn., Carole L. Anderson/Dir., Paula H.J. Cholmondeley/Dir., Patricia C. Barron/Dir., Anthony J. Cavanna/Dir., Daniel W. Christman/Dir., Bradford T. Whitmore/Dir.

Owners: Nancy C. Naigle, Grace Brothers, Ltd./29.80%, State of Wisconsin Investment Board/9.70%, Insiders/34.60%, Paula H.J. Cholmondeley, FMR Corp./5.50%, Daniel W. Christman, Ranjit C. Singh, Patricia C. Barron, Anthony J. Cavanna, John D. Kavazanjian/1.30%, Carole Lewis Anderson, Bradford T. Whitmore/29.90%, Robert W. Fishback, William A. Schmitz (16 Owners included in Index)

Financial Data: Fiscal Year End:12/31   Latest Annual Data: 12/31/2006

Year	Sales	Net Income
2006	$93,546,000	-$27,488,000
2005	$70,501,000	-$4,345,000
2004	$98,182,000	$22,332,000

Curr. Assets:	$55,880,000	Curr. Liab.:	$37,810,000		
Plant, Equip.:	$19,396,000	Total Liab.:	$58,169,000	Indic. Yr. Divd.:	NA
Total Assets:	$97,758,000	Net Worth:	$39,589,000	Debt/ Equity:	0.4955

Ultrapar Participacoes S.A.

Ave. Brigadeiro Luis Antnio, 1343, 9 Andar, Sao Paulo, Rio de Janeiro; **PH:** 55-1131776695;
http:// www.ultra.com.br

General - Incorporation	Republic of Brazil	**Stock**- Price on:12/24/2007	$32.24
Employees	6,885	Stock Exchange	NYSE
Auditor	NA	Ticker Symbol	UGP
Stk Agt	Bank of New York	Outstanding Shares	81,110,000
Counsel	NA	E.P.S.	$1.06
DUNS No.	NA	Shareholders	NA

Business: The groups principle activities include distributing, producing and marketing of LPG, chemicals and integrated logistics services. The group operates from the Brazil and Mexico.

Primary SIC and add'l.: 4924

CIK No: 0001094972

Subsidiaries: Imaven Imveis e Agropecuria Ltda, Oxiteno S.A., Ultracargo

Officers: Pedro Wongtschowski/62/CEO, Andre Covre/38/CFO, Investor Relations, Joao Benjamin Parolin/50/Officer - Oxiteno, Eduardo De Toledo/44/Officer - Ultracargo

Directors: Paulo Guilherm Aguiar Cunha/68/Chmn., Lucio De Castro Andrade Filho/63/Vice Chmn., Ana Maria Levy Villela Igel/66/Dir., Renato Ochman/48/Dir., Nildemar Secches/60/Dir., Paulo Vieira Belotti/76/Dir., Olavo Egydio Monteiro De Carvalho/66/Dir.

Owners: Olavo Egydio Monteiro de Carvalho, Ultra S.A. Participaes, Ana Maria Levy Villela Igel, Ultra-DI Participaes S.A, Paulo Vieira Belotti, Renato Ochman, Pedro Jorge Filho, Nildemar Secches, Paulo Vieira Belotti, Olavo Egydio Monteiro De Carvalho, Monteiro Aranha S.A./2.00%, Ana Maria Levy Villela Igel, Pedro Wongtschowski, Nildemar Secches, Eduardo de Toledo (29 Owners included in Index)

Financial Data: Fiscal Year End:12/31   Latest Annual Data: 12/31/2006

Year	Sales	Net Income
2006	$2,247,953,000	$131,526,000
2005	$2,016,456,000	$125,486,000
2004	$1,800,773,000	$155,943,000

Curr. Assets:	$871,873,000	Curr. Liab.:	$226,854,000		
Plant, Equip.:	$518,697,000	Total Liab.:	$922,748,000	Indic. Yr. Divd.:	$0.830
Total Assets:	$1,800,951,000	Net Worth:	$878,203,000	Debt/ Equity:	NA

Ultrapetrol (Bahamas) Ltd

PO Box SS-19084, Nassau; ; *http://* www.ultrapetrol.net

General - Incorporation	Bahamas	**Stock**- Price on:12/24/2007	$24.69
Employees	855	Stock Exchange	NDQ
Auditor	Henry Martin Y Asociados SRL	Ticker Symbol	ULTR
Stk Agt	NA	Outstanding Shares	28,350,000
Counsel	NA	E.P.S.	-$0.16
DUNS No.	NA	Shareholders	NA

Business: The groups principle activity is to provide marine transportation services. Specific customers of the group include Archer Daniels Midland, British Gas, Cargill, Chevron, Continental Grain, ENAP, Industrias Oleaginosas and Panocean. In March 2006, the group acquired Ravenscroft Shipping. The group operates from South America, Europe, Asia and other.

Primary SIC and add'l.: 4412

CIK No: 0001062781

Officers: Felipe Ross Menendez/Dir., CEO, Pres., Ricardo Ross Menendez/Dir., Exec. VP, Leonard J. Hoskinson/Dir., CFO, Sec., Alberto G. Deyros/Chief Accountant

Directors: Felipe Ross Menendez/Dir., CEO, Pres., Ricardo Ross Menendez/Dir., Exec. VP, Leonard J. Hoskinson/Dir., CFO, Sec., James F. Martin/Dir., Katherine A. Downs/Dir., Michael C. Hagan/Dir., George Wood/Dir.

Owners: Insiders/20.60%, Inversiones Los Avellanos S.A./19.70%, Solimar Holdings Ltd./34.50%, Hazels (Bahamas) Investments Inc./2.50%

Financial Data: Fiscal Year End:12/31   Latest Annual Data: 12/31/2006

Year	Sales	Net Income
2006	$173,466,000	$10,526,000
2005	$125,361,000	$14,568,000
2004	$95,160,000	$5,139,000

Curr. Assets:	$54,770,000	Curr. Liab.:	$22,771,000		
Plant, Equip.:	$333,191,000	Total Liab.:	$246,950,000	Indic. Yr. Divd.:	NA
Total Assets:	$426,379,000	Net Worth:	$179,429,000	Debt/ Equity:	NA

Ultratech Inc

3050 Zanker Rd. , San Jose, CA, 95134; **PH:** 1-408-321-8835; *http://* www.ultratech.com

General - Incorporation ... DE
Employees ... 332
Auditor ... Ernst & Young LLP
Stk Agt ... Computershare Trust Co
Counsel ... Brobeck, Phleger & Harrison
DUNS No. ... 80-205-1722

Stock- Price on:12/24/2007 ... $13.32
Stock Exchange ... NDQ
Ticker Symbol ... UTEK
Outstanding Shares ... 23,230,000
E.P.S ... -$0.42
Shareholders ... NA

Business: The group's principal activity is to manufacture and market photolithography and laser processing equipment for manufacturers of integrated circuits and nanotechnology components. The group supplies step-and-repeat photolithography systems based on one-to-one imaging technology. Markets for the group's photolithography products include advanced packaging and the manufacture of various nanotechnology components, including thin film head magnetic recording devices, optical networking devices, laser diodes and LED's. The products of the group are sold throughout North America, Europe, Japan and the rest of Asia.

Primary SIC and add'l.: 3559

CIK No: 0000909791

Subsidiaries: Ultratech (Shanghai) Co. Ltd., Ultratech (Singapore) Pte, Ltd., Ultratech CH, Ultratech Corporation, Ultratech International,Inc., Ultratech Kabushiki Kaisha, Ultratech Stepper (Thailand) Co. LTD., Ultratech Stepper East,Inc., Ultratech UK Limited

Officers: Arthur W. Zafiropoulo/Chmn., CEO/$987,965.00, Bruce R. Wright/Sr. VP, Finance CFO, Sec., Treasurer/$392,095.00, Ron Volk/Sr. VP - Operations, Dave Holmes/Sr. VP - Human Resources, Laura Rebouche/VP - Investor Relations - Corporate Communications, Andy Hawryluk/Sr. VP - Engineering, David A. Markle/CTO, Sr. VP

Directors: Arthur W. Zafiropoulo/Chmn., CEO, Joel F. Gemunder/Dir., Nicholas Konidaris/Dir., Vincent F. Sollitto/Dir., Dennis Raney/Dir., Henri Richard/Dir., Rick Timmins/Dir.

Owners: Barclays Global Investors, NA/5.51%, Nicholas Konidaris, Tocqueville Asset Management, LP/9.77%, Arthur W. Zafiropoulo/9.57%, Henri Richard, Bruce R. Wright/2.81%, John E. Denzel/1.62%, Dennis Raney, Insiders/13.13%, Wells Fargo & Company/6.80%, Rick Timmins, Thales Fund Management, LLC/15.17%, Schroder Investment Management of North America Inc./5.98%, David J. Greene and Company, LLC/5.45%, Vincent F. Sollitto *(17 Owners included in Index)*

Financial Data: *Fiscal Year End:*12/31 *Latest Annual Data:* 12/31/2006

Year	Sales	Net Income
2006	$119,633,000	-$8,968,000
2005	$122,366,000	-$2,343,000
2004	$109,892,000	$624,000

Curr. Assets:	$139,313,000	**Curr. Liab.:**	$34,362,000		
Plant, Equip.:	$25,043,000	**Total Liab.:**	$41,942,000	**Indic. Yr. Divd.:**	NA
Total Assets:	$216,050,000	**Net Worth:**	$174,108,000	**Debt/ Equity:**	NA

ULURU Inc

4452 Beltway Dr., Addison, TX, 75001; *PH:* 1-214-905-5145; *Fax:* 1-214-905-5130;
http:// www.uluruinc.com

General - Incorporation ... NV
Employees ... 11
Auditor ... Braverman International, P.C.
Stk Agt ... Continental Stock Transfer & Trust Co
Counsel ... NA
DUNS No. ... NA

Stock- Price on:12/24/2007 ... $5.19
Stock Exchange ... OTC
Ticker Symbol ... ULUR
Outstanding Shares ... 61,830,000
E.P.S ... -$0.33
Shareholders ... NA

Business: The groups principle activity is engage in the development of novel topically applied therapeutics based primarily on the adaptation of existing therapeutic agents using proprietary drug delivery platforms. The group operates from the United States.

Primary SIC and add'l.: 2834

CIK No: 0001168220

Subsidiaries: Uluru Delaware Inc.,

Officers: Kerry P. Gray/Dir., CEO, Pres., Terry Wallberg/CFO, VP, Daniel G. Moro/VP - Development, John V. St. John/VP - Material Science, Eric W. Bowditch/VP - Business Development

Directors: Kerry P. Gray/Dir., CEO, Pres., William W. Crouse/Chmn., Jeffrey B. Davis/Dir., David E. Reese/Dir.

Owners: Oscar S. Schafer & Partners I, LP, Pequot Capital Management, Inc./13.10%, Kerry P. Gray/16.20%, Terrance K. Wallberg, Entities affiliated with Brencourt Advisors LLC/12.90%, JANA Partners LLC/10.00%, OSS Overseas LTD/9.10%, William L. Collins, Oscar S. Schafer & Partners II, LP/7.40%, Entities affiliated with Tudor Investment Corporation/5.10%, Insiders/16.70%, William W. Crouse, Prenox, LLC/7.10%

Financial Data: *Fiscal Year End:*12/31 *Latest Annual Data:* 12/31/2006

Year	Sales	Net Income
2006	$1,534,000	-$11,709,000
2005	NA	-$782,000
2004	$6,000	-$892,000

Curr. Assets:	$17,856,000	**Curr. Liab.:**	$1,382,000		
Plant, Equip.:	$691,000	**Total Liab.:**	$1,382,000	**Indic. Yr. Divd.:**	NA
Total Assets:	$30,667,000	**Net Worth:**	$29,285,000	**Debt/ Equity:**	NA

UMB Financial Corp

1010 Grand Ave., Kansas City, MO, 64106; *PH:* 1-816-860-7000; *https://* www.umb.com;
Email: Investor.Relations@umb.com

General - Incorporation ... MO
Employees ... 3,432
Auditor ... Deloitte & Touche LLP
Stk Agt ... UMB Bank, N.A.
Counsel ... NA
DUNS No. ... 05-544-4384

Stock- Price on:12/24/2007 ... $38.07
Stock Exchange ... NDQ
Ticker Symbol ... UMBF
Outstanding Shares ... 42,070,000
E.P.S ... $1.77
Shareholders ... NA

Business: The group's principal activity is to provide banking services to commercial, retail, government and correspondent bank customers. The other services offered include international banking services, investment and cash management services, data processing services for correspondent banks. It also provides a full range of trust activities for individuals, estates, business corporations, governmental bodies and public authorities. The services of the group are provided in the states of Missouri, Kansas, Colorado, Illinois, Oklahoma, Iowa and Nebraska. The group owns 5 commercial banks, a credit card bank, a reinsurance company, community development corporation, a consulting company and a mutual fund servicing company.

Primary SIC and add'l.: 6712 6021

CIK No: 0000101382

Subsidiaries: Grand Avenue Distribution Services, LLC, Kansas City Financial Corporation, Kansas City Realty Company, Scout Investment Advisors, Inc., UMB Banc Leasing Corp., UMB Bank Arizona, n.a., UMB Bank Colorado, UMB Bank, n.a., UMB Bank& Trust, n.a., UMB Capital Corp., Umb Cdc, Inc., UMB Consulting Services, LLC, UMB Distribution Services, LLC, UMB Financial Corporation, UMB Financial Corporation owns 100% 25 Subsidiaries included in the Index

Officers: Gil Trout/Chmn., CEO - Southwest Missouri Region, Dan K. Gomez/CEO, Pres. - UMB Omaha, Craig L. Anderson/Chmn., CEO - Kansas Region, Mariner J. Kemper/Chmn., CEO/$992,519.00, Peter J. Genovese/Vice Chmn. - UMB Bank na, Eastern Region/$614,411.00, Royce M. Hammons/Chmn., Pres. - Oklahoma Region, Begonya Klumb/Investor Relations Officer, Bradley J. Smith/Exec. VP - Consumer Services, Dennis R. Rilinger/Divisional Exec. VP, General Counsel, Jann Burley/Contact - St. Louis Correspondent Banking Group, Mandie Nelson/Mgr. - Corporate Communication, Douglas F. Page/Exec. VP, Chief Lending Officer, James A. Sangster/Pres. - UMB Bank, na, Ken Kotiza/Pres. - UMB Bank, St. Louis, Terry D'Amore/Exec. VP - Payment, Technology Solutions *(26 Officers included in Index)*

Directors: Mariner J. Kemper/Chmn., CEO, Craig L. Anderson/Chmn., CEO - Kansas Region, Gil Trout/Chmn., CEO - Southwest Missouri Region, Vince J. Ciavardini/Vice Chmn., Royce M. Hammons/Chmn., Pres. - Oklahoma Region, Kevin C. Gallagher/Dir., Terrence P. Dunn/Dir., Joshua L. Sosland/Dir., David R. Bradley/Dir., Richard Harvey/Dir., Thomas J. Wood/Dir., Gregory M. Graves/50/Dir., Theodore M. Armstrong/Dir., Michael J. Chesser/59/Dir., Peter J. Desilva/46/Dir., COO, Pres. *(21 Directors included in Index)*

Owners: Marshall& Ilsley Corporation/5.18%, Thomas D. Sanders, Kris A. Robbins, Crosby R. Kemper/13.75%, David R. Bradley, Vincent J. Ciavardini, Peter J. Genovese, Michael D. Hagedorn, Richard Harvey, Jon Wefald, Mariner J. Kemper/3.77%, Terrence P. Dunn, Joshua L. Sosland, Michael J. Chesser, Paul Uhlmann *(24 Owners included in Index)*

Financial Data: *Fiscal Year End:*12/31 *Latest Annual Data:* 12/31/2006

Year	Sales	Net Income
2006	$624,028,000	$59,767,000
2005	$524,009,000	$56,318,000
2004	$447,263,000	$42,839,000

Curr. Assets:	$1,444,644,000	**Curr. Liab.:**	$8,000,171,000	**P/E Ratio:**	23.36
Plant, Equip.:	$243,216,000	**Total Liab.:**	$8,068,890,000	**Indic. Yr. Divd.:**	$0.600
Total Assets:	$8,917,765,000	**Net Worth:**	$848,875,000	**Debt/ Equity:**	0.0432

Umpqua Holdings Corp

One SW Columbia St., Ste 1200, Portland, OR, 97258; *PH:* 1-503-727-4109;
http:// www.southumpquabank.com

General - Incorporation ... OR
Employees ... 1,530
Auditor ... Moss Adams LLP
Stk Agt ... Mellon Investor Services LLC
Counsel ... NA
DUNS No. ... NA

Stock- Price on:12/24/2007 ... $24.43
Stock Exchange ... NDQ
Ticker Symbol ... UMPQ
Outstanding Shares ... 57,870,000
E.P.S ... $1.48
Shareholders ... NA

Business: The group's principal activities are carried out through three segments: retail banking offers loan and deposit products to its customers who consist of individuals, state and local governmental bodies and small to medium size commercial companies. Mortgage banking originates, sells and services residential mortgage loans. Retail brokerage offers a full range of retail brokerage services and products to its clients who consist primarily of individual investors. The group operates through 57 full-service financial stores and 7 limited service retirement community stores in vancouver, Oregon, eugene, roseburg, grants pass, medford, salem, springfield, albany, ashland, bandon, beaverton, brookings, canyonville and central point. The group acquired humboldt bancorp and its subsidiary humboldt bank in 2004.

Primary SIC and add'l.: 6022 6719

CIK No: 0001077771

Subsidiaries: Bancorp Financial Services, Inc., CIB Capital Trust, HB Capital Trust I, Humboldt Bancorp Statutory Trust I, Humboldt Bancorp Statutory Trust II, Humboldt Bancorp Statutory Trust III, Strand, Atkinson, Williams & York, Inc., Umpqua Bank, Umpqua Holdings Statutory Trust I, Umpqua Statutory Trust II, Umpqua Statutory Trust III, Umpqua Statutory Trust IV, Umpqua Statutory Trust V

Officers: Raymond P. Davis/Dir., CEO, Pres./$2,462,729.00, Ric Carey/Exec. VP - Retail Sales, Service - Umpqua Bank, Oregon, Barbara J. Baker/Exec. VP - Cultural Enhancement, Umpqua Bank, Lani Hayward/Exec. VP - Creative Strategies, Ron Farnsworth/Sr. VP - Treasury, Mark Tarmy/CIO, Exec. VP, Steven L. Philpott/Exec. VP, General Counsel - Umpqua Bank, Steven A. May/Exec. VP - Retail Sales, Service - Umpqua Bank, California, Daniel A. Sullivan/CFO, Exec. VP/$565,194.00, William Fike/Pres. - Umpqua Bank, California Region/$651,461.00, Neal McLaughlin/Sr. VP, Controller, David M. Edson/Pres. - Umpqua Bank Oregon, Washington Region, Brad F. Copeland/Sr. Exec. VP, Chief Credit Officer - Credit Quality, Umpqua Bank

Directors: Raymond P. Davis/Dir., CEO, Pres., Allyn C. Ford/Chmn., Mathew A. Bruno/64/Dir., Diana E. Goldschmidt/60/Dir., Thomas W. Weborg/65/Dir., Stephen M. Gambee/Dir., William A. Lansing/Dir., Scott D. Chambers/Dir., David B. Frohnmayer/Dir., Theodore S. Mason/Dir., Ronald F. Angell/Dir., Dan Giustina/Dir., Lynn K. Herbert/56/Dir., Diane D. Miller/Dir., Bryan Timm/Dir.

Owners: Stephen M. Gambee, Scott D. Chambers, Diane D. Miller, Allyn C. Ford, Daniel A. Sullivan, Lynn K. Herbert/1.00%, Mathew A. Bruno, William A. Lansing, Ronald F. Angell, Bryan L. Timm, Dan Giustina, Raymond P. Davis, David M. Edson, Theodore S. Mason, Diana E. Goldschmidt *(23 Owners included in Index)*

Financial Data: *Fiscal Year End:*12/31 *Latest Annual Data:* 06/30/2007

Year	Sales	Net Income
2007	NA	NA
2006	NA	NA
2005	$330,058,000	$69,735,000

Curr. Assets:	NA	**Curr. Liab.:**	NA	**P/E Ratio:**	16.51
Plant, Equip.:	NA	**Total Liab.:**	NA	**Indic. Yr. Divd.:**	$0.720
Total Assets:	NA	**Net Worth:**	NA	**Debt/ Equity:**	0.1823

Ungava Mines Inc

Formerly: Byron Global Corp
40 University Ave, Ste. 720, Toronto, ON, M5J 1T1; *PH:* 1-416-594-0528

General - Incorporation	ON	Stock - Price on:12/24/2007	$1
Employees	NA	Stock Exchange	NA
Auditor	Larry O'Donnell, CPA, P.C.	Ticker Symbol	NA
Stk Agt	Transfer Agency Inc.	Outstanding Shares	NA
Counsel	NA	E.P.S.	NA
DUNS No.	NA	Shareholders	NA

Business: The groups principle activity is to provide recruiting services. The groups service area includes the research and development, engineering, marketing, sales, information technology and manufacturing industries. The group operates from United States.

Primary SIC and add'l.: 6712

CIK No: 0001041019

Subsidiaries: Intl Resources Inc.

Officers: David L. Hynes/62/Dir., CEO, Pres., Ross McGroarty/69/Chmn., Sec.

Directors: David L. Hynes/62/Dir., CEO, Pres., Ross McGroarty/69/Chmn., Sec., George E. Mara/59/Dir.

Unibanco Holdings

65 E 55th St., 29th Fl., New York, NY, 10022; *PH:* 1-212-207-9422; *Fax:* 1-212-754-4872; *http://* www.unibanco.com.br; *Email:* investor.relations@unibanco.com.br

General - Incorporation	Brazil	Stock - Price on:12/24/2007	$116.81
Employees	29,504	Stock Exchange	NYSE
Auditor	PricewaterhouseCoopers LLP	Ticker Symbol	UBB
Stk Agt	NA	Outstanding Shares	2,800,000,000
Counsel	NA	E.P.S.	$0.65
DUNS No.	90-120-5187	Shareholders	NA

Business: The groups principal activities are those of a commercial bank such as retail banking, wholesale banking, consumer finance and other related activities. The group also has interests within the insurance and wealth management sectors.

Primary SIC and add'l.: 6021

CIK No: 0001038584

Subsidiaries: Administradora E Corretora De Seguros Unibanco Ltda.1, Aig Brasil Companhia De Seguros, Banco Dibens S.a., Banco Fininvest S.a., Banco Investcred Unibanco S.a., Banco Surinvest S.a.2, BANCO NICO S.A., Bandeirantes Processamento De Dados Ltda. 3, BWU COMRCIO E ENTRETENIMENTO LTDA., CIBRASEC COMPANHIA BRASILEIRA DE SECURITIZAO4, CIBRASEC DISTRIBUIDORA DE TTULOS E VALORES MOBILIRIOS5, CNF CONSRCIO NACIONAL LTDA., Companhia Hipotecria Unibanco-rodobens, Conabinu Participaes Ltda.6, CORPORACIN INTERAMERICANA PARA EL FINANCIAMIENTO DEINFRAESTRUCTURA S.A.7 97 Subsidiaries included in the Index

Officers: Pedro Moreira Salles/Vice Chmn., CEO, Rogerio Carvalho Braga/52/Executive Officer, Demosthenes Madureira De Pinho Neto/Dir., VP, Gabriel Jorge Ferreira/73/Dir. - Presidant, Jose Lucas Ferreira De Melo/43/Officer, Marcio De Andrade Schettini/Retail Exec. VP, Romildo Goncalves Valente/42/Officer, Marcelo Da Silva Mitri/43/Officer, Marcia Maria Freitas De Aguiar/42/Officer, Marcos Braga Dainesi/50/Officer, Antonio Carlos Azevedo/40/Officer, Roberto Lamy/50/Executive Officer, Ulio Almeida Gomes/42/Officer, Carlos Henrique Zanvettor/42/Officer, Jose Roberto Haym/49/Executive Officer (*55 Officers included in Index*)

Directors: Pedro Moreira Salles/Vice Chmn., CEO, Pedro Sampaio Malan/Chmn., Joao Dionisio Filgueira Barreto Amoedo/Dir., Francisco Eduardo De Almeida Pinto/Dir., Arminio Fraga Neto/Dir., Joaquim Francisco De Castro Neto/64/Dir., Demosthenes Madureira De Pinho Neto/Dir., VP, Gabriel Jorge Ferreira/73/Dir. - Presidant, Israel Vainboim/Dir., Guy A. Andrade/Dir., Pedro Luiz Bodin De Moraes/Dir., Guilherme Affonso Ferreira/Dir.

Owners: Sul America Group/2.23%, Moreira Salles Group/0.04%, Float/98.20%, Float, Bahema Group/5.12%, Treasury/1.30%, Insiders/0.47%, Moreira Salles Group/92.66%

Financial Data: *Fiscal Year End:*12/31 *Latest Annual Data:* 12/31/2006

Year	Sales		Net Income
2006	$11,341,284,000		$914,824,000
2005	$9,406,092,000		$708,840,000
2004	$6,814,722,000		$440,764,000
Curr. Assets:	$18,365,875,000	Curr. Liab.: $28,260,603,000	P/E Ratio: 18.18
Plant, Equip.:	$751,647,000	Total Liab.: $43,196,944,000	Indic. Yr. Divd.: $2.800
Total Assets:	$48,091,791,000	Net Worth: $4,894,847,000	Debt/ Equity: NA

Unica Corp

Reservoir Pl. N, 170 Tracer Ln., Waltham, MA, 02451; *PH:* 1-781-839-8000; *http://* www.unica.com; *Email:* unica@unica.com

General - Incorporation	DE	Stock - Price on:12/24/2007	$20.06
Employees	3,000	Stock Exchange	NDQ
Auditor	Ernst& Young LLP	Ticker Symbol	UNCA
Stk Agt	American Stock Transfer & Trust Co.	Outstanding Shares	26,120,000
Counsel	NA	E.P.S.	$0.02
DUNS No.	NA	Shareholders	NA

Business: The groups principle activity is to provide enterprise marketing management. The groups services include Professional, Maintenance and Technical Support and On demand and Managed Infrastructure. The products of the group include Affinium ampaign, Plan, Detect, Leads, NetInsight and Model. The group acquired Sane Solutions, LLC in the year 2006 and MarketSoft Software Corporation in the year 2005. The group operates from North America and International. The group's quarterly revenue for September 2007 was 23.04 millions of USD.

Primary SIC and add'l.: 7372

CIK No: 0001138804

Subsidiaries: Sane Solutions, Inc., Software Pte Limited, Unica Corporation Limited, Unica Corporation Software Pte Limited, Unica France SAS, Unica Securities Corporation, Unica Softech Systems India Private Limited, Unica, L.P., Unica, LLC.

Officers: Yuchun Lee/Chmn., CEO, Ralph A. Goldwasser/CFO, Sr. VP, Eric Schnadig/Sr. VP - Worldwide Sales, Carol Meyers/Chief Marketing Officer, Sr. VP, David Sweet/Sr. VP - Corporate Development, Richard Hale/57/VP - Consulting, Rand Schulman/VP, GM - Unicas Internet Marketing Solutions Group, John Hogan/VP - Engineering, Kevin Keane/VP - Business Development, Edmund Ang/VP, MD - Asia Pacific, Jonathan D. Salon/39/VP, General Counsel, Sec., Richard Welch/Sr. VP - Professional Services, Jason Joseph/VP, General Counsel, Corp. Sec.

Directors: Yuchun Lee/Chmn., CEO, Ruby Kennedy/Co - Founder, David Cheung/Co - Founder, Aron J. Ain/Dir., Bruce R. Evans/Dir., Carla Hendra/Dir., Jim Perakis/Dir., Robert P. Schechter/Dir., Bradford D. Woloson/Dir., Michael H. Balmuth/44/Dir., John B. Landry/60/Dir.

Owners: Summit Partners/5.40%, Yuchun Lee/25.90%, Aron J. Ain, Richard Hale, Carol Meyers, James A. Perakis, David Sweet, Michael H. Balmuth, JMI Equity Fund IV, L.P./9.10%, John B. Landry, Eric Schnadig, Bruce R. Evans/5.40%, David Cheung/10.30%, Bradford D. Woloson/9.10%, Insiders/42.70% (*18 Owners included in Index*)

Financial Data: *Fiscal Year End:*09/30 *Latest Annual Data:* 12/31/2006

Year	Sales		Net Income
2006	$433,000,000		$4,647,000
2005	$388,556,000		$1,769,000
2004	$353,031,000		-$3,905,000
Curr. Assets:	$30,030,000	Curr. Liab.: $88,396,000	
Plant, Equip.:	$281,606,000	Total Liab.: $441,356,000	Indic. Yr. Divd.: NA
Total Assets:	$423,527,000	Net Worth: -$17,829,000	Debt/ Equity: NA

Unico American Corp

23251 Mulholland Dr., Woodland Hills, CA, 91364; *PH:* 1-818-599-8800; *http://* www.crusaderinsurance.com

General - Incorporation	NV	Stock - Price on:12/24/2007	$13.02
Employees	121	Stock Exchange	NDQ
Auditor	KPMG LLP	Ticker Symbol	UNAM
Stk Agt	Registrar & Transfer Co	Outstanding Shares	5,600,000
Counsel	NA	E.P.S.	$1.99
DUNS No.	05-009-5124	Shareholders	NA

Business: The group's principal activities are underwriting property, casualty, health and life insurance and related premium financing. The group operates in two segments: insurance company operation and other insurance operations. The insurance company operation segment provides property, casualty, health and life insurance. The other insurance operations segment provides insurance premium financing, claim administration services and membership association services. The insurance operations are carried on through its wholly owned subsidiary crusader insurance company. The operations are carried on in the United States.

Primary SIC and add'l.: 6321 6331 6311 6719

CIK No: 0000100716

Subsidiaries: American Insurance Brokers, Inc, Crusader Insurance Company, Insurance Club, Inc, U.S. Risk Managers, Inc.

Officers: Erwin Cheldin/Chmn., CEO, Pres./$401,919.00, Cary L. Cheldin/Dir., Exec. VP/$656,565.00, John Dinapoli/Claims Management, Crusader Insurance Company, Lester A. Aaron/Dir., CFO, Treasurer/$372,618.00, George C. Gilpatrick/63/Dir., VP, Sec./$322,776.00

Directors: Erwin Cheldin/Chmn., CEO, Pres., David A. Lewis/86/Dir., Cary L. Cheldin/Dir., Exec. VP, Lester A. Aaron/Dir., CFO, Treasurer, George C. Gilpatrick/63/Dir., VP, Sec., Warren D. Orloff/73/Dir., Donald B. Urfrig/66/Dir.

Owners: Dimensional Fund Advisors, Inc./9.10%, Schwartz Investment Counsel, Inc., and Schwartz/9.20%, Erwin Cheldin/41.80%, Cary L. Cheldin/3.70%, Donald B. Urfrig/0.40%, Lester A. Aaron/2.70%, George C. Gilpatrick/1.90%, Insiders/50.50%, David A. Lewis/0.10%, FMR Corp./5.50%

Financial Data: *Fiscal Year End:*12/31 *Latest Annual Data:* 12/31/2006

Year	Sales		Net Income
2006	$54,717,000		$11,794,000
2005	$61,183,000		$6,715,000
2004	$61,903,000		$5,682,000
Curr. Assets:	$36,485,000	Curr. Liab.: $6,900,000	P/E Ratio: 6.54
Plant, Equip.:	$739,000	Total Liab.: $126,931,000	Indic. Yr. Divd.: NA
Total Assets:	$187,802,000	Net Worth: $60,871,000	Debt/ Equity: NA

UNICO Inc AZ

8880 Rio San Diego Dr., 8th Fl., San Diego, CA, 92108; *PH:* 1-619-209-6124; *Fax:* 1-619-209-6125; *http://* www.unicomining.com; *Email:* investors@unicomining.com

General - Incorporation	AZ	Stock - Price on:12/24/2007	$0.0021
Employees	NA	Stock Exchange	OTC
Auditor	HJ Associates & Consultants, LLP	Ticker Symbol	UCOI
Stk Agt	Transfer Online, Inc.	Outstanding Shares	1,910,000,000
Counsel	NA	E.P.S.	-$0.016
DUNS No.	NA	Shareholders	NA

Business: The groups principal activity is exploration drilling and designed to identify near surface deposits, determine potential resources and define limits of mineralization. The group operates from the United States and Canada.

Primary SIC and add'l.: 1000

CIK No: 0001110737

Subsidiaries: Bromide Basin Mining Company, LLC, Deer Trail Mining Company, LLC, Silver Bell Mining Company, Inc

Officers: Mark A. Lopez/CEO, Wayne C. Hartle/Sec., Richard Kennedy/Consulting Geologist, Dean Misantoni/Sr. Geologist, Edgar Blanco/Sr. Metallurgist

Directors: Ray C. Brown/Chmn., Kiyoshi Kasai/Dir.

Owners: Ray Brown, Wayne Ash, Mark A. Lopez/55.00%, Wayne Hartle, Insiders/95.00%, Ray Brown, Insiders, Mark A. Lopez, Wayne Hartle/4.00%

Financial Data: *Fiscal Year End:*02/28 *Latest Annual Data:* 02/28/2007

Year	Sales		Net Income
2007	NA		-$18,333,000
2006	$26,000		-$2,272,000
2005	$0		-$5,730,000
Curr. Assets:	$7,000	Curr. Liab.: $5,302,000	
Plant, Equip.:	$2,310,000	Total Liab.: $5,302,000	Indic. Yr. Divd.: NA
Total Assets:	$2,545,000	Net Worth: -$2,757,000	Debt/ Equity: NA

Unicorp Inc

5075 Wheimer Rd., Ste. 975, Houston, TX, 77056; *PH:* 1-713-402-6700; *Fax:* 1-713-402-6799; *http://* www.unicorpinc.net; *Email:* investors@unicorpinc.net

General - Incorporation NV
Employees NA
Auditor Thomas Leger & Co. LLP
Stk Agt American Stock Transfer & Trust Co.
Counsel NA
DUNS No. NA

Stock- Price on:12/24/2007 $0.35
Stock Exchange OTC
Ticker Symbol UCPI
Outstanding Shares NA
E.P.S -$0.03
Shareholders NA

Business: The groups principle activity is engage in the exploration, acquisition, development, production and sale of natural gas, crude oil and natural gas liquids primarily from conventional reservoirs. The group operates from the United States. The group's quarterly revenue for Sep '07 was 0.81 millions of USD.

Primary SIC and add'l.: 1542

CIK No: 0000354507

Subsidiaries: Affiliated Holdings, Inc, Laissez-Faire Group, Inc, Marcap International, Inc

Officers: Robert P. Munn/CEO, Carl A. Chase/Principal Financial, Accounting Officer, Dir.

Directors: Kevan Casey/Chmn.

Owners: Carl A. Chase, Kevan Casey, Trevor Ling, Tommy Allen, Insiders

Financial Data: **Fiscal Year End:**12/31 **Latest Annual Data:** 03/31/2007

Year	Sales	Net Income
2007	NA	NA
2006	$924,000	-$3,310,000
2005	$242,000	-$2,749,000

Curr. Assets:	$3,029,000	**Curr. Liab.:**	$1,029,000		
Plant, Equip.:	$3,613,000	**Total Liab.:**	$1,098,000	**Indic. Yr. Divd.:**	NA
Total Assets:	$6,668,000	**Net Worth:**	$5,570,000	**Debt/ Equity:**	NA

Unifi Inc

7201 W Friendly Ave., Greensboro, NC, 27410; *PH:* 1-336-294-4410; *Fax:* 1-336-316-5422; *http://* www.unifi-inc.com; *Email:* marketing@unifi.com

General - Incorporation NY
Employees 3,275
Auditor Ernst & Young LLP
Stk Agt American Stock Transfer & Trust Co.
Counsel NA
DUNS No. 05-554-5925

Stock- Price on:12/24/2007 $2.83
Stock Exchange NYSE
Ticker Symbol UFI
Outstanding Shares 60,540,000
E.P.S -$1.98
Shareholders NA

Business: The group's principal activity is to produce and process textile yarns. The group operates through two business segments: polyester and nylon. The polyester segment produces textured, dyed, twisted and beamed yarns. The nylon segment produces textured nylon and covered spandex products. These products are sold to knitters and weavers who produce fabrics for the apparel, automotive and furniture upholstery, home furnishings, hosiery, socks and industrial markets. The primary suppliers of raw materials for the group include dupont, nanya plastics corp and reliance industries ltd. The group has foreign operations in Ireland, England, Brazil and columbia.

Primary SIC and add'l.: 2297 2281 2282

CIK No: 0000100726

Subsidiaries: Charlotte Technology Group, Inc., Glentouch Yarn Company, LLC, Spanco Industries, Inc. (SI), Spanco International, Inc., UNF Industries, Ltd., Unifi Asia Holding, SRL, Unifi Asia, Ltd., Unifi do Brasil, Ltda, Unifi Dyed Yarns, Ltd., Unifi Export Sales, LLC, Unifi GmbH, Unifi Holding 1, BV, Unifi Holding 2, BV, Unifi International Services, Inc., Unifi Kinston, LLC 25 Subsidiaries included in the Index

Officers: George R. Perkins/68/Chmn., CEO, William M. Sams/71/Dir., Pres., Chief Investment Officer, Alfred G. Webster/60/Dir., Exec. VP, Roger R. Berrier/39/VP - Commercial Operations, Charles F. McCoy/44/VP, Sec., General Counsel/$423,878.00, William M. Lowe/55/CFO, VP/$920,764.00, Thomas H. Caudle/56/VP - Global Operations/$484,221.00, William L. Jasper/55/VP - Sales/$430,619.00

Directors: George R. Perkins/68/Chmn., CEO, Chiu Cheng Anthony Loo/56/Dir., William J. Armfield/73/Dir., Kenneth G. Langone/72/Dir., William M. Sams/71/Dir., Pres., Chief Investment Officer, Alfred G. Webster/60/Dir., Exec. VP, Stephen Wener/64/Dir.

Owners: Insiders/24.30%, William M. Sams/4.46%, Alfred G. Webster, William M. Lowe, Benny L. Holder, William L. Jasper, Thomas H. Caudle, William J. Armfield/1.42%, Kenneth G. Langone/3.64%, Charles F. McCoy, Brian R. Parke/2.48%, Dillon Yarn Corporation/9.18%, George R. Perkins/1.55%, Roger R. Berrier, Stephen Wener/9.18% *(16 Owners included in Index)*

Financial Data: **Fiscal Year End:**06/26 **Latest Annual Data:** 6/25/2006

Year	Sales	Net Income
2006	$738,825,000	-$14,366,000
2005	$799,446,000	-$41,225,000
2004	$746,455,000	-$69,793,000

Curr. Assets:	$331,059,000	**Curr. Liab.:**	$130,374,000		
Plant, Equip.:	$355,458,000	**Total Liab.:**	$466,074,000	**Indic. Yr. Divd.:**	NA
Total Assets:	$872,535,000	**Net Worth:**	$401,901,000	**Debt/ Equity:**	0.6584

Unified Western Grocers Inc

5200 Sheila St., Commerce, CA, 90040; *PH:* 1-323-264-5200; *http://* www.uwgrocers.com; *Email:* spoc@uwgrocers.com

General - Incorporation CA
Employees NA
Auditor Deloitte & Touche LLP
Stk Agt NA
Counsel NA
DUNS No. 12-622-6224

Stock- Price on:12/24/2007 NA
Stock Exchange NA
Ticker Symbol NA
Outstanding Shares NA
E.P.S NA
Shareholders NA

Business: The groups principle activity is to operate retail grocery stores. The groups products include meat, dairy goods, fresh produce, general merchandise and specialty items. The groups products are sold under the brand names Cottage Hearth, Golden Creme and Western Family. The group operates from United States.

Primary SIC and add'l.: 5149 5141

CIK No: 0000320431

Subsidiaries: Banner Marketing, Inc., Certified Grocers of California, Ltd., Crown Grocers, Inc., Grocers and Merchants Insurance Service, Inc., Grocers and Merchants Management Company, Grocers Capital Company, Grocers Development Center, Inc., Grocers General Merchandise Company, Grocers Specialty Company, Northwest Process, Inc., Preferred Public Storage Company, R&R Liquidating Corporation, SavMax Foods, Inc., Springfield Insurance Company, Springfield Insurance Company Limited 21 Subsidiaries included in the Index

Officers: Alfred A. Plamann/CEO, Pres., Philip S. Smith/Exec. VP, Chief Marketing, Procurement Officer, Robert M. Ling/Exec. VP, General Counsel, Sec., Richard J. Martin/Exec. VP - Finance, Administration, CFO, Daniel J. Murphy/Sr. VP - Retail Support Services

Directors: Oscar Gonzalez/Dir., John Najjar/51/Dir., Louis A. Amen/78/Dir., John Berberian/56/Dir., Mark Kidd/57/Dir., John D. Lang/54/Dir., Jay T. McCormack/57/Dir., Peter J. ONeal/62/Dir., Michael A. Provenzano/65/Dir., Thomas S. Sayles/57/Dir., Kenneth Ray Tucker/60/Dir., Richard L. Wright/70/Dir., Darioush Khaledi/61/Dir., Douglas A. Nidiffer/58/Dir., Robert E. Stiles/68/Dir.

Owners: Louis A. Amen/2.68%, Robert E. Stiles/2.46%, Mark Kidd/0.93%, John Najjar/0.05%, Robert E. Stiles, John Berberian/1.56%, Kenneth Ray Tucker/0.05%, Kenneth Ray Tucker, Michael A. Provenzano, Darioush Khaledi, Jay T. McCormack, Douglas A. Nidiffer/4.40%, Oscar Gonzalez, John Najjar, Darioush Khaledi/4.53% *(43 Owners included in Index)*

Unifirst Corp

68 Jonspin Rd. , Wilmington, MA, 01887; *PH:* 1-978-658-8888; *http://* www.unifirst.com; *Email:* ufirst@unifirst.com

General - Incorporation MA
Employees 9,800
Auditor Ernst & Young LLP
Stk Agt EquiServe Trust Co N.A
Counsel Goodwin, Procter & Hoar
DUNS No. 01-972-3535

Stock- Price on:12/24/2007 $43.04
Stock Exchange NYSE
Ticker Symbol UNF
Outstanding Shares 19,270,000
E.P.S $2.18
Shareholders NA

Business: The group's principal activities are to design, manufacture, rent, deliver and sell personalized occupational garments, career apparel and image wear programs. The group also manufactures and sells uniforms and protective clothing, industrial wiping products, floor mats and other non-garment items, including first aid cabinet services and other safety supplies. In addition, the group decontaminates and cleans garments, which may have been exposed to radioactive materials. The products include shirts, pants, jackets, coveralls, jump suits, lab coats, smocks and aprons. The customers of the group are automobile centers and dealers, delivery services, food and general merchandise retailers, restaurants, service companies and transportation companies. The group also operates in Canada and Europe. On 02-Sep-2003, the group acquired textilease corporation.

Primary SIC and add'l.: 2326 2337 2392 7218

CIK No: 0000717954

Subsidiaries: Euro Nuclear Services B.V., Euro Nuclear Services Limited, Euro Nuklear Services, GmbH, Interstate Uniform Manufacturing of Puerto Rico, Inc., Pride America Garments, Inc., RC Air LLC, UniFirst Canada Ltd., UniFirst First-Aid Corporation, UniFirst Holdings, L.P., UniFirst S.A. de C.V., Uniform Supply Alliance L.P., Uniformes de San Luis S.A. de C.V., UniTech Services Canada Ltd., UniTech Services Group, Inc., UniTech Services SAS 17 Subsidiaries included in the Index

Officers: Ronald D. Croatti/Chmn., CEO, Pres., Bruce P. Boynton/Sr. VP - Operations, John B. Bartlett/Sr. VP, CFO, David A. Difillippo/Sr. VP - Operations, Cynthia Croatti/Dir., Exec. VP, Treasurer

Directors: Ronald D. Croatti/Chmn., CEO, Pres., Phillip L. Cohen/Dir., Michael Iandoli/Dir., Robert F. Collings/Dir., Donald J. Evans/Dir., Anthony F. Difillippo/Dir., Cynthia Croatti/Dir., Exec. VP, Treasurer

Owners: Robert F. Collings, John B. Bartlett, Insiders/4.80%, Bruce P. Boynton, Cynthia Croatti, David A. DiFillippo, Thomas S. Postek, Michael Iandoli, Ronald D. Croatti/4.40%, Donald J. Evans, Anthony F. DiFillippo, Phillip L. Cohen

Financial Data: **Fiscal Year End:**08/27 **Latest Annual Data:** 8/26/2006

Year	Sales	Net Income
2006	$820,972,000	$39,208,000
2005	$763,842,000	$43,348,000
2004	$719,356,000	$33,578,000

Curr. Assets:	$170,121,000	**Curr. Liab.:**	$113,175,000	**P/E Ratio:**	19.74
Plant, Equip.:	$288,790,000	**Total Liab.:**	$333,073,000	**Indic. Yr. Divd.:**	$0.150
Total Assets:	$700,822,000	**Net Worth:**	$367,749,000	**Debt/ Equity:**	NA

Unify Corp

181 Metro Dr., 3rd Fl, San Jose, CA, 95110; *PH:* 1-916-928-6400; *http://* www.unify.com; *Email:* info@unify.com

General - Incorporation DE
Employees 60
Auditor Grant Thornton LLP
Stk Agt American Stock Transfer & Trust Co.
Counsel Gray, Cary, Ware & Freidenrich
DUNS No. 05-787-0859

Stock- Price on:12/24/2007 $0.53
Stock Exchange OTC
Ticker Symbol UFYC
Outstanding Shares 29,720,000
E.P.S -$0.23
Shareholders NA

Business: The group's principal activity is to provide enterprise software solutions to mid-size and large organizations. The group's software products and services enable businesses to build applications that deliver the right information to the right people at the right time. The software platform gives organizations the ability to connect multiple data sources, quickly build forms-based applications, automate business processes and integrate disparate information to run, manage and optimize their business. The products of the group include unify nxj, unify accell(R), accell/webtm, accell/sqltm, accell/idstm, unify vision(R), dataserver(R) and dataserver(R) els. The group's customers include bmw lease bv, boeing, business console limited, canon, cast & crew entertainment inc, citigroup and contractors warehouse. The group markets its products in the United States, the United Kingdom, France, Australia, Asia-Pacific, Europe, Japan, Latin America, Russia and South Africa.

Primary SIC and add'l.: 7372 7379 7374

CIK No: 0000880562

Subsidiaries: Acuitrek Inc, Unify Corporation Delaware, Inc, Unify Corporation France S.A.

Officers: Todd E. Wille/Dir., CEO, Pres./$279,540.00, Frank Verardi/VP - Americas, Apac, Russia Sales/$189,663.00, Steve Bonham/VP - Finance, Administration, CFO/$198,800.00, Kevin Kane/VP, GM - Composer Solutions, Mark Bygraves/VP, GM - Software Group, MD - EMEA, Duane George/VP - Product Development, CTO, Charles Messman/Investor Relations Contact, Todd Kehrli/Investor Relations Contact, Deb Thornton/Press, Media, Analyst Contact - Americas, Ines Piech/Press, Media, Analyst Contact - Europe, Middle East, Asia Pac, David Drager/Project Lead, Sabertooth Development

Directors: Todd E. Wille/Dir., CEO, Pres., Steve D. Whiteman/Chmn., Tery R. Larrew/Dir., Richard M. Brooks/Dir., Robert J. Majteles/Dir.

Owners: Insiders/6.66%, Frank Verardi/1.13%, Todd E. Wille/3.10%, Tery R. Larrew, Duane George, Richard M. Brooks, Steven D. Whiteman, Steven D. Bonham, Robert J. Majteles, Diker Management LLC/11.47%, Kevin Kane, David Drager, AWM Investment Company, Inc./35.52%, ComVest Capital, LLC/16.16%

Financial Data: Fiscal Year End:04/30 Latest Annual Data: 04/30/2007

Year	Sales	Net Income
2007	$11,187,000	-$2,422,000
2006	$11,249,000	-$628,000
2005	$11,303,000	-$2,364,000

Curr. Assets:	$6,053,000	Curr. Liab.:	$5,377,000		
Plant, Equip.:	$267,000	Total Liab.:	$6,116,000	Indic. Yr. Divd.:	NA
Total Assets:	$8,351,000	Net Worth:	$2,235,000	Debt/ Equity:	NA

Unigene Laboratories Inc

110 Little Falls Rd. , Fairfield, NJ, 07004; *PH:* 1-973-882-0860; *http://* www.unigene.com

General - Incorporation	DE	**Stock**- Price on:12/24/2007	$2.08
Employees	91	Stock Exchange	OTC
Auditor	Grant Thornton LLP	Ticker Symbol	UGNE
Stk Agt	Registrar & Transfer Co	Outstanding Shares	87,730,000
Counsel	Covington & Burling LLP	E.P.S.	-$0.06
DUNS No.	06-108-8118	Shareholders	NA

Business: The group's principal activity is to research, produce and deliver peptides for medical use. The group has developed manufacturing technology for producing peptides cost-effectively. It has also patented oral and nasal delivery technology that has been shown to deliver medically useful amounts of various peptides into the bloodstream. The initial products of the group will be injectable, nasal and oral formulations of calcitonin for the treatment of osteoporosis and other indications. The group has also developed novel drug delivery technology that delivers therapeutic levels of the amidated peptide calcitonin into the bloodstream.

Primary SIC and add'l.: 2834

CIK No: 0000352747

Officers: Warren P. Levy/Dir., Pres., CEO - Unigene Laboratories, Inc/$298,360.00, Jay Levy/Chmn., Treasurer - Unigene Laboratories, Inc, James P. Gilligan/VP - Product Development/$691,992.00, Paul Shields/VP - Manufacturing Operations/$418,721.00, Nozer M. Mehta/VP - Biological Research, Development/$450,869.00, William Steinhauer/VP - Finance/$433,292.00, Ronald S. Levy/Dir., Exec. VP, Sec./$284,409.00, Allen Bloom/Dir., Independent Consultant, Thomas J. August/Dir. - Distinguished Service Professor, Johns Hopkins University School, Medicine, Robert F. Hendrickson/Dir., Independent Consultant, Marvin L. Miller/Dir., Independent Consultant, Bruce Morra/Dir., Independent Consultant

Directors: Warren P. Levy/Dir., Pres., CEO - Unigene Laboratories, Inc, Jay Levy/Chmn., Treasurer - Unigene Laboratories, Inc, Ronald S. Levy/Dir., Exec. VP, Sec., Allen Bloom/Dir., Independent Consultant, Thomas J. August/Dir. - Distinguished Service Professor, Johns Hopkins University School, Medicine, Robert F. Hendrickson/Dir., Independent Consultant, Marvin L. Miller/Dir., Independent Consultant, Peter Slusser/Dir., Bruce Morra/Dir., Independent Consultant

Financial Data: Fiscal Year End:12/31 Latest Annual Data: 12/31/2006

Year	Sales	Net Income
2006	$6,059,000	-$11,784,000
2005	$14,276,000	-$496,000
2004	$8,400,000	-$5,941,000

Curr. Assets:	$10,184,000	Curr. Liab.:	$19,711,000		
Plant, Equip.:	$2,364,000	Total Liab.:	$28,239,000	Indic. Yr. Divd.:	NA
Total Assets:	$14,051,000	Net Worth:	-$14,188,000	Debt/ Equity:	NA

Unilens Vision Inc

1285 W Pender , Ste 700, Vancouver, BC, V6E 4B1; *PH:* 1-604-685-0763; *Fax:* 1-604-688-4078; *http://* www.unilens.com; *Email:* information@unilens.com

General - Incorporation	BC	**Stock**- Price on:12/24/2007	$3.69
Employees	NA	Stock Exchange	OTC
Auditor	Pender Newkirk & Company LLP	Ticker Symbol	UVICF
Stk Agt	Computershare Trust Co	Outstanding Shares	NA
Counsel	NA	E.P.S.	NA
DUNS No.	NA	Shareholders	NA

Business: The groups principle activities include manufacturing, distributing and licensing specialty lens products using proprietary design and manufacturing technology from manufacturing distribution and administrative facility. In the year February 2005, the group acquired SoftCon and Aquaflex brands from CIBA Vision. The group operates from the United States. The group's quarterly revenue for Sep '07 was 1.67 millions of USD.

Primary SIC and add'l.: 6712

CIK No: 0000852564

Subsidiaries: Unilens Contact Lens Laboratory, Inc, Unilens Corp. USA

Officers: Michael J. Pecora/CEO, Pres., Alan Frazer/Dir. - Quality Assurance, David Boyd/Mgr. - Production, Josepha Bruno/Dir. - Quality Control, Kelly Mcknight-Goelz/VP - Sales, Marketing, Denis Rehse/Dir. - Research, Development, William S. Harper/59/Sec., Leonard F. Barker/CFO

Directors: Alfred W. Vitale/Chmn., Elizabeth Harrison/Dir., Nick Bennett/Dir., William D. Baxter/Dir.

Owners: William S. Harper, Nicholas Bennett, Insiders, CDS & Co., Leonard F. Barker, Cede & Co., Michael J. Pecora, William D. Baxter, Kelly McKnight-Goelz, Boston Partners Asset Management, LLC, Alfred W. Vitale, UNINVEST HOLDING AG IN LIQUIDATION

Financial Data: Fiscal Year End:06/30 Latest Annual Data: 06/30/2006

Year	Sales	Net Income
2006	$6,110,000	$1,597,000
2005	$4,972,000	$2,238,000
2004	$4,075,000	$6,077,000

Curr. Assets:	$5,745,000	Curr. Liab.:	$997,000	P/E Ratio:	30.88
Plant, Equip.:	$508,000	Total Liab.:	$997,000	Indic. Yr. Divd.:	NA
Total Assets:	$8,969,000	Net Worth:	$7,972,000	Debt/ Equity:	NA

Unilever

700 Sylvan Ave., Englewood Cliffs, NJ, 07632; *PH:* 1-201-894-4000; *Fax:* 1-201-871-8079; *http://* www.unilever.com

General - Incorporation	Netherlands	**Stock**- Price on:12/24/2007	$29.76
Employees	153,000	Stock Exchange	NYSE
Auditor	PricewaterhouseCoopers LLP	Ticker Symbol	UN
Stk Agt	Computershare Investor Services LLC	Outstanding Shares	2,890,000,000
Counsel	NA	E.P.S.	$2.57
DUNS No.	40-532-2116	Shareholders	NA

Business: The group's principal activity is the supply of consumer goods in foods, household care and personal product categories. The group's activities are carried out through six divisions. The savoury and dressings include soups, bouillons, sauces, snacks, noodles, frozen food and meal solutions and dresses. The spreads and cooking products provides healthier alternatives to traditional oils and fats. The health and beverages include meal replacement drinks, soups and breakfast bars and branded packet tea. The home care and professional cleaning includes products that meet the requirements of consumers to clean and care their homes and clothes. The personal care includes skin and hair care, deodorants and anti-perspirants.

Primary SIC and add'l.: 2024 2051 2022 2038 2844 2841 2026

CIK No: 0000110390

Officers: Alan Johnson/53/Chief Auditor, Vindi Banga/53/Pres. - Foods, Kees Van Der Graaf/58/Pres. - Europe, Harish Manwani/Pres. - Asia Africa, Sandy Ogg/54/Chief Human Resources Officer, Sven Dumoulin/38/Group Sec., James A. Lawrence/55/CFO, Ralph Kugler/Pres. - Home, Personal Care, Pascal Visee/47/Group Treasurer, Stephen Williams/60/Group General Counsel, Chief Legal Officer, John Ripley/Deputy CFO, Manvinder Singh Banga/Pres. - Foods, Jan Van Der Bijl/Sec., Patrick Cescau/60/Group Chief Executive

Directors: Antony Burgmans/61/Chmn. - Unilever NV, PLC, Michael Treschow/65/Chmn., Kees J. Storm/66/Non Exec. Dir., Lord Simon/69/Non Exec. Dir., Byron E. Grote/Non Exec. Dir., Charles E. Golden/Non Exec. Dir., Jean-Cyril Spinetta/64/Non Exec. Dir., Wim Dik/Non Exec. Dir., Baroness Chalker/66/Non Exec. Dir., Jeroen Van Der Veer/61/Non Exec. Dir., Lord Brittan/69/Non Exec. Dir., Genevieve Berger/53/Non Exec. Dir., Narayana N.R. Murthy/Non Exec. Dir., Hixonia Nyasulu/Non Exec. Dir.

Financial Data: Fiscal Year End:12/31 Latest Annual Data: 12/31/2006

Year	Sales	Net Income
2006	$52,339,333,000	$5,433,035,000
2005	$46,987,517,000	$4,707,990,000
2004	$55,075,370,000	$3,664,778,000

Curr. Assets:	$12,544,170,000	Curr. Liab.:	$18,331,045,000	P/E Ratio:	18.18
Plant, Equip.:	$8,286,203,000	Total Liab.:	$34,119,193,000	Indic. Yr. Divd.:	$0.900
Total Assets:	$56,070,500,000	Net Worth:	$21,951,308,000	Debt/ Equity:	NA

Unilever Plc

700 Sylvan Ave., Englewood Cliffs, NJ, 07632; *PH:* 1-201-894-4000; *Fax:* 1-201-871-8257; *http://* www.unilever.com

General - Incorporation	England And Wales	**Stock**- Price on:12/24/2007	$31.27
Employees	153,000	Stock Exchange	NYSE
Auditor	PricewaterhouseCoopers LLP	Ticker Symbol	UL
Stk Agt	Computershare Investor Services LLC	Outstanding Shares	722,640,000
Counsel	NA	E.P.S.	$10.29
DUNS No.	21-030-0901	Shareholders	NA

Business: The group's principal activities are the manufacture and supply of moving consumer goods in foods, household care and personal product categories. Major brands include dove, lipton, bertolli, hellmann's, knorr, birds eye, findus, iglo, breyers, sunsilk, domestos, cif, omo, comfort, lux, ponds, axe, rexona, slim-fast, signal, becel/flora pro.activ, blue band, country crock, doriana, rama, ades, ubf foodsolutions, brilhante, surf, amora, calve, wishbone, skip, snuggle, suave, magnum, cornetto and solero. The group operates in Europe, North America, Africa, Middle East and turkey, Asia-Pacific and Latin America.

Primary SIC and add'l.: 2026 2841 2022 2844 2038 2051 2024

CIK No: 0000217410

Officers: John Ripley/Deputy CFO, Narayana N.R. Murthy/Non Exec. Dir., James A. Lawrence/CFO, Kees Van Der Graaf/Pres. - Europe, Manvinder Singh Banga/Pres. - Foods, Sandy Ogg/Chief Human Resources Officer, Alan Johnson/Chief Auditor, Pascal Visee/Group Treasurer, Patrick Cescau/Group Chief Executive, Vindi Banga/53/Pres. - Foods, Harish Manwani/Pres. - Asia Africa, Jan Van Der Bijl/Joint Sec., Head - Group Taxation, Stephen Williams/Group General Counsel, Chief Legal Officer, Ralph Kugler/Pres. - Home, Personal Care

Directors: Michael Treschow/Chmn., Genevieve Berger/Non Exec. Dir., Wim Dik/Non Exec. Dir., Hixonia Nyasulu/Non Exec. Dir., Lord Simon/Non Exec. Dir., W. Dik/69/Non Exec. Dir., Antony Burgmans/Non Exec. Dir., Lord Brittan/Non Exec. Dir., Jeroen Van Der Veer/Non Exec. Dir., Baroness Chalker/Non Exec. Dir., Byron E. Grote/Non Exec. Dir., Charles E. Golden/Non Exec. Dir., Jean-Cyril Spinetta/64/Non Exec. Dir., Kees J. Storm/Non Exec. Dir.

Financial Data: Fiscal Year End:12/31 Latest Annual Data: 12/31/2006

Year	Sales	Net Income
2006	$52,339,333,000	$6,264,824,000
2005	$46,987,517,000	$3,381,462,000
2004	$55,075,370,000	$3,664,778,000

Curr. Assets:	$12,544,170,000	Curr. Liab.:	$18,331,045,000	P/E Ratio:	18.18
Plant, Equip.:	$8,286,203,000	Total Liab.:	$33,786,477,000	Indic. Yr. Divd.:	$0.990
Total Assets:	$55,737,785,000	Net Worth:	$21,951,308,000	Debt/ Equity:	NA

Union Bankshares Corp

212 N Main St., Bowling Green, VA, 22427; *PH:* 1-804-633-5031; *http://* www.ubsh.com

General - Incorporation	VA	**Stock**- Price on:12/24/2007	$22.88
Employees	646	Stock Exchange	NDQ
Auditor	Yount, Hyde & Barbour, P.C	Ticker Symbol	UBSH
Stk Agt	Registrar & Transfer Co	Outstanding Shares	13,350,000
Counsel	Yount, Hyde & Barbour	E.P.S.	$1.265
DUNS No.	80-762-8656	Shareholders	NA

Business: The group's principal activity is to provide financial services through affiliated independent community banks and financial services companies. The group's subsidiaries includes union bank and trust company, northern neck state bank, rappahannock national bank and bank of williamsburg and its non-bank affiliates are union investment services and mortgage capital investors. Through its banking subsidiaries, the group provides commercial and consumer deposit accounts and loans, credit cards, automated teller machines, Internet banking and many other services to its customers in the United States. On 01-May-2004 the group, acquired guaranty financial corporation.

Primary SIC and add'l.: 6712 6022

CIK No: 0000883948

Subsidiaries: Bank of Williamsburg, Carmel Church Properties, LLC, Mortgage Capital Investors, Inc., Northern Neck State Bank, Rappahannock National Bank, Union Bank and Trust Company, Union Insurance Group, Inc., Union Investment Services, Inc.

Officers: William G. Beale/Dir., CEO, Pres./$491,767.00, Robert J. McDonough/Pres., Chmn. - Prosperity Bank, Trust Company, Daniel I. Hansen/Chmn. - Union Bank, Trust Company, Thomas R. Tucker/Chmn. - Bay Community Bank, Al Meadows/Dir. - Bay Community Bank, Anthony M. Aiken/Dir. - Prosperity Bank, Trust Company, Robert E. Gray/Exec. VP, Dir. - Prosperity Bank, Trust Company, Alison Morrison/Dir. - Bay Community Bank, Mckinley L. Price/Dir. - Bay Community Bank, Scott A. Wise/Dir. - Bay Community Bank, Robert L. Bailey/Pres., Dir. - Bay Community Bank, James V. Debergh/Dir. - Rappahannock National Bank, Mary L. Payne/Dir. - Rappahannock National Bank, Sharon G. Luke/Dir. - Rappahannock National Bank, Samuel D. Snead/Dir. - Rappahannock National Bank *(54 Officers included in Index)*

Directors: William G. Beale/Dir., CEO, Pres., Ronald L. Hicks/Chmn., Tayloe W. Murphy/Vice Chmn., Douglas E. Caton/Dir., Patrick J. McCann/Dir., Hullihen W. Moore/Dir., Hunter R. Morin/Dir., Ronald L. Tillett/Dir., A. D. Whittaker/Dir.

Owners: A. D. Whittaker, Hullihen W. Moore, Hunter R. Morin, Insiders/6.67%, Patrick J. McCann, John C. Neal, Anthony D. Peay, Ronald L. Hicks, William G. Beale, Douglas E. Caton/3.16%, Ronald L. Tillett, Tayloe W. Murphy/1.09%

Financial Data: Fiscal Year End:12/31 *Latest Annual Data:* 12/31/2006

Year	Sales	Net Income
2006	$29,255,000	$6,255,000
2005	$26,312,000	$6,237,000
2004	$23,953,000	$5,835,000
Curr. Assets:	$28,375,000	Curr. Liab.: $323,312,000	P/E Ratio: 12.93
Plant, Equip.:	$6,080,000	Total Liab.: $339,226,000	Indic. Yr. Divd.: $1.120
Total Assets:	$381,149,000	Net Worth: $41,923,000	Debt/ Equity: 0.7227

Union Bankshares Inc

PO Box 667, Morrisville, VT, 05661; *PH:* 1-802-888-6600; *http://* www.unionbankut.com

General - Incorporation	VT	Stock- Price on:12/24/2007	$21.15
Employees	162	Stock Exchange	AMEX
Auditor	UHY LLP	Ticker Symbol	UNB
Stk Agt	Union Bank	Outstanding Shares	4,530,000
Counsel	NA	E.P.S.	$1.265
DUNS No.	00-895-5080	Shareholders	NA

Business: The group's principal activity is to provide services through 12 community banking locations in lamoille counties of Vermont. The group provides financial services to individuals and corporate customers through its branches, ATM's, telebanking and Internet systems in northern Vermont. The group accepts deposits from the general public and uses those funds to originate commercial, real estate, municipal and consumer loans. The group has primarily retail consumers, small businesses, municipal, agriculture, and the tourism industry.

Primary SIC and add'l.: 6022 6712

CIK No: 0000706863

Subsidiaries: Union Bank

Officers: Kenneth D. Gibbons/CEO, Pres./$365,667.00, Joann A. Tallman/Assist., Sec., Melyssa Whitcomb/Consumer Lender, Rodney Milburn/Assist. Branch Mgr., Barbara Olden/VP, Branch Mgr., Craig Provost/Stowe, Assist. VP, Susan Lassiter/VP, Branch Mgr., Millie Nelson/VP, Branch Mgr., Claire Hindes/Assist. VP, Branch Mgr., Stephen Kendall/VP, Karen Carlson Noyes/Assist. VP, Branch Mgr., Ruth P. Schwartz/VP, Mike Curtis/VP - St. Albans, Susan Laferriere/VP, Melissa Greene/Fairfax, Assist. VP *(30 Officers included in Index)*

Owners: Insiders/28.51%, Kenneth D. Gibbons/1.39%, Walter M. Sargent Revocable Trust/8.37%, Susan Hovey Mercia/13.33%, Marsha A. Mongeon/0.03%, Richard C. Marron/0.10%, Steven J. Bourgeois/0.03%, Robert P. Rollins/0.16%, David S. Silverman/0.03%, John H. Steel/0.17%, Cynthia D. Borck/0.16%, Genevieve L. Hovey Trust/9.33%, Richard C. Sargent/13.12%, Franklin G. Hovey/13.33%

Financial Data: Fiscal Year End:12/31 *Latest Annual Data:* 12/31/2006

Year	Sales	Net Income
2006	$29,255,000	$6,255,000
2005	$26,312,000	$6,237,000
2004	$23,953,000	$5,835,000
Curr. Assets:	$28,375,000	Curr. Liab.: $323,312,000	P/E Ratio: 15.90
Plant, Equip.:	$6,080,000	Total Liab.: $339,226,000	Indic. Yr. Divd.: $1.120
Total Assets:	$381,149,000	Net Worth: $41,923,000	Debt/ Equity: NA

Union Carbide Corp

400 W Sam Houston Pkwy S, Houston, TX, 77042; *PH:* 1-713-978-2016; *http://* www.unioncarbide.com

General - Incorporation	NY	Stock- Price on:12/24/2007	$45.44
Employees	42,578	Stock Exchange	NA
Auditor	B. Thomas Florence	Ticker Symbol	NA
Stk Agt	Bank of New York	Outstanding Shares	953,240,000
Counsel	NA	E.P.S.	$3.60
DUNS No.	00-128-9008	Shareholders	NA

Business: The group's principle activity is organized into two business segments: specialties & intermediates (s&i) and basic chemicals & polymers (bc&p). The s&i segment produces a broad range of products, including specialty polyolefins used in wire and cable insulation and jacketing; surfactants for industrial cleaners; catalysts for the manufacture of polymers, etc. The bc&p segment converts various hydrocarbon feedstocks, principally liquefied petroleum gases and naphtha, into the basic building-block chemicals ethylene and propylene, which are in turn converted to polyethylene, polypropylene and ethylene oxide and ethylene glycol. This segment provides ethylene, propylene, ethylene oxide, ethylene glycol and various other derivatives to the s&i segment.

Primary SIC and add'l.: 2865 2821

CIK No: 0000100790

Subsidiaries: The Dow Chemical Company

Officers: John R. Dearborn/Dir., CEO, Pres., Edward W. Rich/VP, Treasurer, CFO, William H. Weideman/VP, Controller

Directors: John R. Dearborn/Dir., CEO, Pres., Enrique Larroucau/Dir., Glenn J. Moran/Dir.

Financial Data: Fiscal Year End:12/31 *Latest Annual Data:* 12/31/2006

Year	Sales	Net Income
2006	$49,124,000,000	$3,724,000,000
2005	$46,307,000,000	$4,515,000,000
2004	$40,161,000,000	$2,797,000,000
Curr. Assets:	$17,209,000,000	Curr. Liab.: $10,601,000,000	P/E Ratio: 12.62
Plant, Equip.:	$13,722,000,000	Total Liab.: $27,151,000,000	Indic. Yr. Divd.: $1.680
Total Assets:	$45,581,000,000	Net Worth: $17,065,000,000	Debt/ Equity: 0.4603

Union Dental Holdings Inc

1700 N University Dr., Coral Springs, FL, 33071; *PH:* 1-954-575-2252; *http://* uniondental.com

General - Incorporation	FL	Stock- Price on:12/24/2007	$0.021
Employees	1	Stock Exchange	OTC
Auditor	Kramer, Weisman & Assoc., LLP	Ticker Symbol	UDHI
Stk Agt	Interwest Transfer Company, Inc.	Outstanding Shares	60,790,000
Counsel	NA	E.P.S.	NA
DUNS No.	NA	Shareholders	NA

Business: The groups principle activity is operating a network of duly licensed dental providers to a network of union members. In May 2005, the group acquired certain assets of Dental Visions, Inc. The group operates from the United States.

Primary SIC and add'l.: 8021

CIK No: 0001138586

Subsidiaries: Direct Dental Services, Inc, National Business Investors, Inc, Union Dental Corp

Officers: George D. Green/50/Chmn., CEO, Pres., Sec.

Directors: George D. Green/50/Chmn., CEO, Pres., Sec.

Owners: Insiders/38.10%, George D. Green/38.10%

Financial Data: Fiscal Year End:12/31 *Latest Annual Data:* 12/31/2006

Year	Sales	Net Income
2006	$2,197,000	-$2,013,000
2005	$2,067,000	-$1,440,000
2004	$1,932,000	$5,000
Curr. Assets:	$432,000	Curr. Liab.: $3,567,000	
Plant, Equip.:	$231,000	Total Liab.: $3,567,000	Indic. Yr. Divd.: NA
Total Assets:	$672,000	Net Worth: -$2,896,000	Debt/ Equity: NA

Union Drilling Inc

4055 International Plz., Ste. 610, Fort Worth, TX, 76109; *PH:* 1-817-735-8793; *http://* www.uniond.com

General - Incorporation	DE	Stock- Price on:12/24/2007	$15.97
Employees	1,515	Stock Exchange	NDQ
Auditor	Ernst & Young LLP	Ticker Symbol	UDRL
Stk Agt	NA	Outstanding Shares	21,850,000
Counsel	NA	E.P.S.	$1.62
DUNS No.	NA	Shareholders	NA

Business: The groups principle activity is to provide land drilling services and equipment. Customers served by the group include natural gas producers. Specific customers of the group include XTO Energy, Fortuna, Consol and Comlumbia. In April 2005, the group acquired Thornton Drilling Company. The group operates from the United States. The group's quarterly revenue for September 2007 was 76.94 millions of USD.

Primary SIC and add'l.: 1381 3533

CIK No: 0001133260

Subsidiaries: Thornton Drilling Company, Union Drilling (Canada) Inc., Union Drilling Texas GP, LLC, Union Drilling Texas, LP

Officers: Christopher D. Strong/CEO, Pres./$1,047,709.00, Dan E. Steigerwald/VP/$632,938.00, A. J. Verdecchia/VP, CFO, Treasurer, Sec., David S. Goldberg/VP, General Counsel, Corp. Sec.

Directors: Thomas H. O'Neill/Chmn., Thomas M. Mercer/Dir., Gregory D. Myers/Dir., Theodore James Glauthier/Dir., Joseph M. McHugh/Dir., Ronald Harrell/Dir., Howard I. Hoffen/Dir.

Owners: Insiders, T. Rowe Price Associates, Inc., Wellington Management. Company, LLP, A. J. Verdecchia, Dan Steigerwald, Gregory D. Myers, Thomas M. Mercer, Christopher D. Strong, Wolf Marine S.A., Union Drilling Company LLC, Luther King Capital Management Corporation, T. J. Glauthier, Howard I. Hoffen, Joseph M. McHugh

Financial Data: Fiscal Year End:12/31 *Latest Annual Data:* 12/31/2006

Year	Sales	Net Income
2006	$256,944,000	$31,852,000
2005	$141,621,000	$5,599,000
2004	$67,832,000	$3,527,000
Curr. Assets:	$59,456,000	Curr. Liab.: $32,443,000	P/E Ratio: 10.86
Plant, Equip.:	$187,084,000	Total Liab.: $89,818,000	Indic. Yr. Divd.: NA
Total Assets:	$257,418,000	Net Worth: $167,600,000	Debt/ Equity: 0.2134

Union Electric Co

1901 Chouteau Ave., Mc 1370, St Louis, MO, 63103; *PH:* 1-314-623-2222; *http://* www.ameren.com

General - Incorporation	MO	Stock- Price on:12/24/2007	$49.9925
Employees	8,988	Stock Exchange	NA
Auditor	PricewaterhouseCoopers LLP	Ticker Symbol	NA
Stk Agt	NA	Outstanding Shares	207,020,000
Counsel	NA	E.P.S.	$3.00
DUNS No.	00-696-8655	Shareholders	NA

Business: The group's principle activity is to provide electric and gas services in Missouri and Illinois. The company is wholly owned subsidiary of ameren corporation. The company generates, transmits, distributes and sells electric energy. The company also purchases, distributes, transports and sells natural gas. The company supplies electric service in territories of Missouri and Illinois having an estimated population of 2,600,000 within an area of approximately 24,500 square miles, including the greater st. Louis area. Retail gas utility service is supplied in 90 Missouri communities and in the city of alton, Illinois and vicinity. The company supplies electric service to about 1.2 million customers and natural gas service to about 130,000 customers.

Primary SIC and add'l.: 4923 4911 4961 4931

CIK No: 0000100826

Subsidiaries: AFS Development Company, LLC, Agricultural Research& Development Corp., Ameren Corporation, Ameren Development Company, Ameren Energy Communications, Inc., Ameren Energy Development Company, Ameren Energy Fuels and Services Company, Ameren Energy Generating Company, Ameren Energy Marketing Company, Ameren Energy Resources Company, Ameren Energy, Inc., Ameren ERC, Inc., Ameren Services Company, AmerenEnergy Medina Valley Cogen (No. 2) LLC, AmerenEnergy Medina Valley Cogen, (No. 4) LLC 72 Subsidiaries included in the Index

Owners: Gary L. Rainwater, Thomas R. Voss, Warner L. Baxter, Steven R. Sullivan, Insiders, Charles D. Naslund, Daniel F. Cole, Richard J. Mark

Financial Data: *Fiscal Year End:* 12/31 *Latest Annual Data:* 12/31/2006

Year	Sales	Net Income
2006	$6,880,000,000	$547,000,000
2005	$6,780,000,000	$606,000,000
2004	$5,160,000,000	$530,000,000

Curr. Assets:	$1,874,000,000	**Curr. Liab.:**	$2,202,000,000	**P/E Ratio:**	16.66
Plant, Equip.:	$14,299,000,000	**Total Liab.:**	$12,766,000,000	**Indic. Yr. Divd.:**	$2.540
Total Assets:	$19,578,000,000	**Net Worth:**	$6,778,000,000	**Debt/ Equity:**	0.8021

Union Light Heat & Power Co

139 E Fourth St., Cincinnati, OH, 45201; *PH:* 1-513-419-5943; *http://* www.duke-energy.com

General - Incorporation	KY	**Stock**- Price on:12/24/2007	NA
Employees	NA	Stock Exchange	NA
Auditor	Deloitte & Touche LLP	Ticker Symbol	NA
Stk Agt	NA	Outstanding Shares	NA
Counsel	NA	E.P.S	NA
DUNS No.	00-694-4672	Shareholders	NA

Business: The group's principle activity is to transmit, distribute and sell electricity and sell and transport natural gas in northern Kentucky. It serves a population of 345 thousand people and includes the cities of covington, florence and newport. The company is a wholly owned subsidiary of cincinnati gas & electric company. The group operates from United States.

Primary SIC and add'l.: 4923 4931

CIK No: 0000100858

Subsidiaries: 1388368 Ontario Inc., 3036243 Nova Scotia Company, ACcess Broadband, LLC, Attiki Denmark ApS, Attiki Gas Supply Company SA, Avon Energy Partners, LLC, Barre Energy Partners, L.P., Biogas Financial Corporation, Biomass New Jersey, LLC, BMC Energy, LLC, Brickyard Energy Partners, LLC, Brookhaven Energy Partners, LLC, Brown County Energy Associates, LLC, Brown County Landfill Gas Associates, L.P., Brownsville Power I, LLC 233 Subsidiaries included in the Index

Union National Financial Corp PA

570 Lausch Ln., Lancaster, PA, 17601; *PH:* 1-717-653-1441; *Fax:* 1-717-492-2212; *http://* www.uncb.com; *Email:* customerservice@uncb.com

General - Incorporation	PA	**Stock**- Price on:12/24/2007	$15
Employees	185	Stock Exchange	OTC
Auditor	Beard Miller Company LLP	Ticker Symbol	UNNF
Stk Agt	Wealth Management Group	Outstanding Shares	2,530,000
Counsel	NA	E.P.S	$0.52
DUNS No.	NA	Shareholders	NA

Business: The group operates through its subsidiaries whose principal activities include providing banking and financial services to the customers. Services of the group include accepts time, demand, and savings deposits and makes secured and unsecured commercial, real estate and consumer loans. The group has nine branch locations within Lancaster County, Pennsylvania, including seven traditional branch locations and two innovative retail offices. The group operates from the United States.

Primary SIC and add'l.: 6712 6021

CIK No: 0000874482

Subsidiaries: Home Team Financial, LLC, TA of Lancaster, LLC, Union National Capital Trust I, Union National Capital Trust II, Union National Community Bank, Union National Insurance Agency, Inc.

Officers: Mark D. Gainer/Chmn., CEO, Pres., Darwin A. Nissley/Dir., Sec., Stephen D. Staman/VP, Michael D. Peduzzi/Treasurer, CFO, Charles R. Starr/Insider Trading Compliance Officer

Directors: Mark D. Gainer/Chmn., CEO, Pres., James R. Godfrey/62/Vice Chmn., Carl R. Hallgren/70/Dir., Barry C. Huber/Dir., Thomas J. McGrath/Dir., Donald Cargas/Dir., Nancy Shaub Colarik/Dir., Kevin D. Dolan/Dir., William M. Nies/Dir., Darwin A. Nissley/Dir., Sec., Lloyd C. Pickell/Dir.

Owners: Donald Cargas, Michael A. Frey/1.15%, William M. Nies, Thomas J. McGrath, Donald Cargas, Insiders/5.95%, Kevin D. Dolan, Mark D. Gainer/1.53%, Barry C. Huber, Darwin A. Nissley, James R. Godfrey, Nancy Shaub Colarik, Donegal Mutual Insurance Company/7.16%, Clement M. Hoober, Charles R. Starr *(17 Owners included in Index)*

Financial Data: *Fiscal Year End:* 12/31 *Latest Annual Data:* 12/31/2006

Year	Sales	Net Income
2006	$38,552,000	$2,444,000
2005	$29,989,000	$3,353,000
2004	$23,733,000	$3,223,000

Curr. Assets:	$15,462,000	**Curr. Liab.:**	$350,619,000	**P/E Ratio:**	28.85
Plant, Equip.:	$9,580,000	**Total Liab.:**	$488,974,000	**Indic. Yr. Divd.:**	$0.240
Total Assets:	$517,597,000	**Net Worth:**	$28,548,000	**Debt/ Equity:**	NA

Union Pacific Corp

1400 Douglas St., Omaha, NE, 68179; *PH:* 1-402-544-5000; *http://* www.up.com

General - Incorporation	UT	**Stock**- Price on:12/24/2007	$119.1
Employees	50,739	Stock Exchange	NYSE
Auditor	Deloitte & Touche LLP	Ticker Symbol	UNP
Stk Agt	Computershare Investor Services LLC	Outstanding Shares	269,450,000
Counsel	NA	E.P.S	$6.83
DUNS No.	04-834-1283	Shareholders	NA

Business: The group operates through its subsidiary whose principle activity is to provide rail transportation services. The group operates from United States.

Primary SIC and add'l.: 4011

CIK No: 0000100885

Subsidiaries: Southern Pacific Rail Corporation, Union Pacific Railroad Company

Officers: James R. Young/Chmn., CEO, Pres./$8,282,037.00, Robert M. Knight/CFO, Exec. VP/$2,407,448.00, Bernard R. Gutschewski/VP - Taxes, Union Pacific Corporation, Mike Payette/Assist. VP - Government Affairs, Illinois, Minnesota, Wisconsin, Beth Ryan/Special Representative, Nebraska, Joe Bateman/VP - Public Affairs - Northern Region, Ron Olson/Dir. - Public Affairs, Oklahoma, Texas, Brenda Mainwaring/Dir. - Public Affairs, Iowa, Nebraska, Tom Zapler/Dir. - Public Affairs, Illinois, Joe Adams/VP - Public Affairs - Southern Region, Royce S. Fisk/Sr. Business Dir. - Food, Refrigerated Sales, Omaha, Lori A. Loschen/Sr. Business Dir. - Food, Refrigerated Marketing, Omaha, Matthew G. Bosch/Business Mgr. - Food, Refrigerated, Roseville, CA, Ryan A. Kolb/Sr. Business Mgr. Food - Refrigerated Products, Fresno, Elizabeth K. Weist/Product Mgr. - Refrigerated Products, Omaha *(213 Officers included in Index)*

Directors: James R. Young/Chmn., CEO, Pres., Thomas F. McLarty/Dir., Michael W. McConnell/Dir., Andrew H. Card/Dir., Erroll B. Davis/Dir., Thomas J. Donohue/Dir., Archie W. Dunham/Dir., Judith Richards Hope/Dir., Charles C. Krulak/Dir., Steven R. Rogel/65/Dir.

Owners: Marsico Capital Management, LLC/5.50%, Dennis J. Duffy, Richard K. Davidson, Insiders/1.40%, Michael J. Hemmer, Thomas J. Donohue, Archie W. Dunham, Andrew H. Card, Erroll B. Davis, Charles C. Krulak, Judith Richards Hope, Dodge & Cox/10.40%, Robert M. Knight, Michael W. McConnell, James R. Young *(17 Owners included in Index)*

Financial Data: *Fiscal Year End:* 12/31 *Latest Annual Data:* 12/31/2006

Year	Sales	Net Income
2006	$15,578,000,000	$1,606,000,000
2005	$13,578,000,000	$1,026,000,000
2004	$12,215,000,000	$604,000,000

Curr. Assets:	$2,411,000,000	**Curr. Liab.:**	$3,539,000,000	**P/E Ratio:**	18.67
Plant, Equip.:	$32,873,000,000	**Total Liab.:**	$21,203,000,000	**Indic. Yr. Divd.:**	$1.760
Total Assets:	$36,515,000,000	**Net Worth:**	$15,312,000,000	**Debt/ Equity:**	0.4268

Union Security Insurance Co

500 Bielenberg Dr., Woodbury, MN, 55125;

General - Incorporation	IA	**Stock**- Price on:12/24/2007	NA
Employees	NA	Stock Exchange	NA
Auditor	PricewaterhouseCoopers LLP	Ticker Symbol	NA
Stk Agt	Mellon Investor Services LLC	Outstanding Shares	NA
Counsel	Pricewaterhousecoopers LLP	E.P.S	NA
DUNS No.	00-696-3615	Shareholders	NA

Business: The group's principle activity is to provide group employee benefits and individual life and annuity insurance in the district of columbia and in all states except New York. It is an indirect wholly owned subsidiary of assurant inc. The products offered by the group include group disability and dental, group medical, group life and annuity and life insurance products. The group markets its products to small businesses and individuals through a national network of independent agents, brokers and financial institutions.

Primary SIC and add'l.: 6321

CIK No: 0000823533

Union Tank Car Co

175 W Jackson Blvd., Chicago, IL, 60604; *PH:* 1-312-372-9500; *http://* www.utlx.com

General - Incorporation	DE	**Stock**- Price on:12/24/2007	NA
Employees	NA	Stock Exchange	NA
Auditor	Deloitte & Touche LLP	Ticker Symbol	NA
Stk Agt	NA	Outstanding Shares	NA
Counsel	NA	E.P.S	NA
DUNS No.	00-516-1112	Shareholders	NA

Business: The group's principal activity is leasing of railway tank cars and other railcars. The group also distributes carbon and stainless steel, aluminum tubular products, chrome and stainless bar, other carbon steel products and aircraft grade tubing, rolled form shapes and other raw materials. Other activities of the group include sulphur processing and storage, manufacturing fasteners, mobile railcar moving vehicles and metal containment vessel heads. The customers of the group are manufacturers and other shippers of chemical products, petroleum products, food products and bulk plastics. The group operates in the United States, Canada, France and Belgium. At 31-Dec-2003, the group's railcar fleet comprised of 65,670 tank cars and 14,978 railway cars of other types.

Primary SIC and add'l.: 4741 3452

CIK No: 0000100923

Subsidiaries: Amarillo Gear Company, Bushwick Metals, Inc., E. S. Investments Inc., Enersul Inc., EXSIF SAS, EXSIF Worldwide, Inc., Future Metals, Inc., M/K Express Company, M/K Express Services Company, Marmon Distribution Services LLC, Marmon Transportation Services LLC, Marmon/Keystone Corporation, McKenzie Valve& Machining Company, Penn Machine Company, Procor Alberta Inc. 27 Subsidiaries included in the Index

Officers: Kenneth P. Fischl/59/Dir., CEO, Pres., Mark J. Garrette/54/VP, Principal Financial Officer, Mike Tessman/Supervisor, Alvin, Texas, Mini Shop 159, Denver Christian/Mgr. - Alvin, Texas, Mini Shop 137, Larry Belk/Supervisor, Alvin, Texas, Mini Shop 137, Bill Hoekstra/Mgr. - Anacortes, Washington, Mobile Unit 129, Calvin J. Stocking/Supervisor, Anacortes, Washington, Mobile Unit 129, Mike Reveal/Mgr. - Augusta, Georgia, Mobile Unit 164, Bryan E. Hagan/Supervisor, Augusta, Georgia, Mobile Unit 164, Glenn Meche/Area Mgr. - Baton Rouge, Louisiana, Office 120, Jason Dalfrey/Supervisor, Baton Rouge, Louisiana, Mobile Unit 122, Randy Huff/Supervisor, Baton Rouge, Bob Driscoll/Contact - Short, Term Leasing, Chicago, Andrea Mazerik/Contact - Updating Mechanical Records, Chicago, Phil Mijal/Contact - Used Equipment Sale, Chicago *(116 Officers included in Index)*

Directors: Kenneth P. Fischl/59/Dir., CEO, Pres., Robert K. Lorch/Dir., VP, Robert W. Webb/69/Dir., General Counsel, Sec., Frank S. Ptak/64/Dir.

Union Trust Company

66 Main St. , Ellsworth, ME, 04605; *PH:* 1-207-667-2504; *http://* www.uniontrust.com

General - Incorporation	ME	**Stock**- Price on:12/24/2007	NA
Employees	165	Stock Exchange	OTC
Auditor	Berry, Dunn, Mcneil & Parker	Ticker Symbol	UNBH
Stk Agt	Registrar and Transfer Co.	Outstanding Shares	NA
Counsel	NA	E.P.S	$3.65
DUNS No.	83-523-1754	Shareholders	NA

Business: The group's principle activity is to provide a variety of financial services to individuals, businesses, municipalities and nonprofit organizations. The operations are conducted through 15 offices stretching from waldoboro to machias. The group is a one bank holding entity, which operates through its subsidiary, union trust company. The loans offered include real estate loans, commercial loans, municipal loans and consumer loans. The other services provided by the group include trust and investment services, investment management, real estate planning, custody and retirement planning and employee benefits services.

Primary SIC and add'l.: 6022 6712

CIK No: 0000745083

Officers: Peter A. Blyberg/Dir., CEO, Pres./$348,629.00, Craig Worcester/VP - Cornerstone Investment Services, Mary Silverman/Branch Mgr. - Bar Harbor, Chris Keefe/Commercial Lender, Bar Harbor, Candace Gray/Branch Mgr. - Belfast, Valerie Shields/Residential Lender, Belfast, Paul Doody/Commercial Lender, Belfast, Dianne Thompson/Branch Mgr. - Blue Hill, Deborah Ehrlenbach/Sr. VP - Internal Audit, Mikey Bannister/VP - Training Offcier, James Callnan/VP - Information Services, Terance G. Fancy/VP, Compliance Officer, Michael J. Marino/VP, Credit Administrator, Bette Pierson/VP - Mortgages, Sandy Salsbury/VP, Human Resources Officer *(45 Officers included in Index)*

Directors: Peter A. Blyberg/Dir., CEO, Pres., Sandra H. Collier/Chmn., Arthur J. Billings/Dir., Blake B. Brown/Dir., Peter A. Clapp/Dir., Samuel G. Cohen/Dir., James L. Markos/Dir., Harry E. Mikkelsen/Dir., Stephen C. Shea/Dir., Robert W. Spear/Dir., Karen Stanley/Dir., Paul Tracy/Dir.

Owners: Stephen C. Shea/2.63%, Arthur J. Billings, Harry E. Mikkelsen, Insiders/4.50%, Sandra H. Collier, Peter A. Blyberg, Robert W. Spear, James L. Markos, Paul L. Tracy, Karen W. Stanley, Estate of Fitz Eugene Dixon, Jr./5.52%, Samuel G. Cohen, Timothy R. Maynard, Rebecca J. Sargent, Peter A. Clapp *(17 Owners included in Index)*

Financial Data: *Fiscal Year End:*12/31 *Latest Annual Data:* 12/31/2006

Year		Sales		Net Income	
2006		$35,780,000		$3,801,000	
2005		$31,263,000		$4,747,000	
2004		$27,845,000		$4,829,000	
Curr. Assets:	$11,900,000	**Curr. Liab.:**	$477,494,000		
Plant, Equip.:	$8,647,000	**Total Liab.:**	$509,382,000	**Indic. Yr. Divd.:**	$1.720
Total Assets:	$550,975,000	**Net Worth:**	$41,593,000	**Debt/ Equity:**	0.6876

UnionBanCal Corp

400 California St., 9th Fl., San Francisco, CA, 94104; *PH:* 1-415-765-2969; *https://* www.uboc.com; *Email:* Investor.Relations@uboc.com

General - Incorporation	DE	**Stock**- Price on:12/24/2007	$60.95
Employees	10,164	Stock Exchange	NYSE
Auditor	Deloitte & Touche LLP	Ticker Symbol	UB
Stk Agt	Computershare Investor Services LLC	Outstanding Shares	138,200,000
Counsel	NA	E.P.S	$4.78
DUNS No.	NA	Shareholders	NA

Business: The groups principle activity is to provide financial services. The group operates through two segments namely, wholesale banking and retail banking. The group operates from the United States.

Primary SIC and add'l.: 6282 6021 6153 6159 6712 6411 6211

CIK No: 0001011659

Subsidiaries: Bankers Commercial Corporation, Business Capital Trust I, Cal First Properties, Inc., California First Advisory Services, California First Capital Management, California First Corporation, HighMark Capital Management, Inc., MCB Statutory Trust I, Mills-Ralston, Inc., SBS Realty Inc., Stanco Properties, Inc., The California-Sansome Corporation, UBOC Community Development Corporation, UBOC Comstock I, UBOC Foundation (Charitable Trust) 29 Subsidiaries included in the Index

Officers: Takashi Morimura/55/CEO, Pres./$598,191.00, Masaaki Tanaka/55/CEO, Pres./$1,921,378.00, John A. Rice/Investor Relations Officer, Bruce H. Cabral/52/Exec. VP, Chief Credit Officer, Paul E. Fearer/64/Exec. VP, Dir. - Human Resources, David I. Matson/63/Vice Chairperson, CFO/$1,872,709.00, Linda F. Betzer/60/Exec. VP - Operations, Customer Services/$1,549,716.00, William Stolte/61/Exec. VP - Independent Risk Monitoring Group, John H. McGuckin/61/Exec. VP, General Counsel, Sec., James Yee/54/CIO, Exec. VP, Philip B. Flynn/50/Vice Chairperson, COO/$3,096,337.00, Masashi Oka/53/Vice Chairperson, Chief Risk Officer, Joann M. Bourne/52/Exec. VP - Commercial Deposits, Treasury Management/$1,626,699.00, John C. Erickson/46/Exec. VP, Deputy Chief Risk Officer, Steven L. Glaser/59/Exec. VP - Retail Banking *(16 Officers included in Index)*

Directors: Norimichi Kanari/61/Chmn., Masashi Oka/53/Vice Chairperson, Chief Risk Officer, Tetsuo Shimura/68/Dir., Philip B. Flynn/50/Vice Chairperson, COO, David R. Andrews/Dir., Dale L. Crandall/Dir., Richard D. Farman/72/Dir., Mohan Gyani/56/Dir., David I. Matson/63/Vice Chairperson, CFO, Nicholas B. Binkley/62/Dir., Murray Dashe/65/Dir., Stanley F. Farrar/64/Dir., Michael J. Gillfillan/60/Dir., Ronald L. Havner/50/Dir., Shigemitsu Miki/73/Dir. *(18 Directors included in Index)*

Owners: David I. Matson, Norimichi Kanari, Dale L. Crandall, Murray H. Dashe, Fernando J. Niebla, Insiders, Philip B. Flynn, David R. Andrews, Aida M. Alvarez, JoAnn M. Bourne, Barclays Global Investors, N.A. and other entities/7.10%, Mary S. Metz, Mohan S. Gyani, Ronald H. Kendrick, The Bank of Tokyo-Mitsubishi UFJ, Ltd. and affiliates/65.40% *(23 Owners included in Index)*

Financial Data: *Fiscal Year End:*12/31 *Latest Annual Data:* 12/31/2006

Year		Sales		Net Income	
2006		$3,559,984,000		$752,996,000	
2005		$3,078,807,000		$862,933,000	
2004		$2,846,292,000		$732,534,000	
Curr. Assets:	$4,375,593,000	**Curr. Liab.:**	$44,732,292,000		
Plant, Equip.:	$495,302,000	**Total Liab.:**	$48,048,175,000	**Indic. Yr. Divd.:**	$2.080
Total Assets:	$52,619,576,000	**Net Worth:**	$4,571,401,000	**Debt/ Equity:**	NA

UniPixel Displays Inc

192 Searidge Ct., Shell Beach, CA, 93449; *PH:* 1-281-825-4500; *http://* www.unipixel.com; *Email:* publicrelations@unipixel.com

General - Incorporation	DE	**Stock**- Price on:12/24/2007	$1.35
Employees	12	Stock Exchange	OTC
Auditor	PMB Helin Donovan, LLP	Ticker Symbol	UNXL
Stk Agt	Securities Transfer Corp	Outstanding Shares	18,190,000
Counsel	Winstead Sechrest & Minick	E.P.S	-$0.57
DUNS No.	NA	Shareholders	NA

Business: The group operates through its subsidiaries whose principle activity is to develop flat-panel color display technology. The groups technology is known as Time Multiplexed Optical Shutter. The groups technology is used in research, development and commercialization of new flat panel displays using TMOS in a variety of applications include mobile phones, digital cameras, notebook computers, televisions and other consumer electronic devices. The group operates from United States.

Primary SIC and add'l.: 3679

CIK No: 0001171012

Subsidiaries: Uni-Pixel Displays, Inc.

Officers: Reed J. Killion/Pres., Principal Executive Officer, Dir., James A. Tassone/44/CFO

Directors: Frank Delape/54/Chmn., Reed J. Killion/Pres., Principal Executive Officer, Dir.

Owners: Reed J. Killion/4.00%, Insiders/17.00%, Frank M. DeLape/10.90%, James A. Tassone/2.10%, Bob Weatherly/8.60%, James Herndon/8.60%

Financial Data: *Fiscal Year End:*12/31 *Latest Annual Data:* 12/31/2006

Year		Sales		Net Income	
2006		$200,000		-$6,486,000	
2005		$20,000		-$4,967,000	
Curr. Assets:	$136,000	**Curr. Liab.:**	$3,522,000		
Plant, Equip.:	$641,000	**Total Liab.:**	$3,531,000	**Indic. Yr. Divd.:**	NA
Total Assets:	$813,000	**Net Worth:**	-$2,719,000	**Debt/ Equity:**	NA

Unisource Energy Corp

One S Church Ave., Ste 100, Tucson, AZ, 85702; *PH:* 1-520-884-3650; *http://* www.unisourceenergy.com

General - Incorporation	AZ	**Stock**- Price on:12/24/2007	$33.77
Employees	1,896	Stock Exchange	NYSE
Auditor	PricewaterhouseCoopers LLP	Ticker Symbol	UNS
Stk Agt	Bank of New York	Outstanding Shares	35,270,000
Counsel	NA	E.P.S	$1.47
DUNS No.	00-302-2014	Shareholders	NA

Business: The group's principal activity is to operate through its wholly owned subsidiaries, tucson electric power company (tep), millennium energy holdings, inc (millennium) and unisource energy development company (ued). Tep is a vertically integrated utility that provides regulated electric service to over 367,000 retail customers in its retail service territory. Millennium invests in unregulated ventures related primarily to the energy business, including a developer of thin-film batteries, a developer of small-scale commercial satellites and a developer and manufacturer of thin-film photo voltaic cells. Ued engages in developing generating resources and other project development activities, including facilitating the expansion of the springerville generating station. On 11-Aug-2003, the group acquired assets of citizens communications company.

Primary SIC and add'l.: 4911

CIK No: 0000941138

Subsidiaries: Advanced Energy Technologies, Inc., Global Solar Energy, Inc., Millennium Energy Holdings, Inc., San Carlos Resources Inc., Tucson Electric Power Company, UniSource Energy Services, Inc., UNS Electric, Inc., UNS Gas, Inc.

Officers: James S. Pignatelli/63/Chmn., CEO, Pres./$2,197,837.00, Raymond S. Heyman/Sr. VP, General Counsel/$731,934.00, Kentton C. Grant/VP - Finance, Rates, David G. Hutchens/VP - Wholesale Energy, Michael J. Deconcini/COO, Sr. VP - Transmission, Distribution/$680,987.00, Steven W. Lynn/VP - Communications, Governmental Relations, Karen G. Kissinger/VP, Controller, Chief Compliance Officer, Kevin P. Larson/Sr. VP, CFO, Treasurer/$711,299.00, Jo Smith/Dir. - Investor Relations, Chris Norman/Financial Analyst, Arie Hoekstra/VP - Generation, Thomas A. McKenna/VP - Engineering, Catherine E. Ries/VP - Human Resources, Herlinda H. Kennedy/Corp. Sec.

Directors: James S. Pignatelli/63/Chmn., CEO, Pres., Robert A. Elliott/51/Dir., Larry W. Bickle/61/Dir., Daniel W.L. Fessler/65/Dir., Elizabeth T. Bilby/67/Dir., Harold W. Burlingame/66/Dir., Lawrence J. Aldrich/54/Dir., Kenneth Handy/68/Dir., Joaquin Ruiz/55/Dir., John L. Carter/72/Dir., Barbara Baumann/51/Dir., Warren Y. Jobe/66/Dir.

Financial Data: *Fiscal Year End:*12/31 *Latest Annual Data:* 12/31/2006

Year		Sales		Net Income	
2006		$1,316,869,000		$67,447,000	
2005		$1,229,535,000		$46,144,000	
2004		$1,168,978,000		$45,919,000	
Curr. Assets:	$455,910,000	**Curr. Liab.:**	$395,920,000		
Plant, Equip.:	$2,325,814,000	**Total Liab.:**	$2,533,260,000	**Indic. Yr. Divd.:**	$0.900
Total Assets:	$3,187,409,000	**Net Worth:**	$654,149,000	**Debt/ Equity:**	2.6176

Unisys Corp

Unisys Way, Blue Bell, PA, 19424; *PH:* 1-585-487-2430; *http://* www.unisys.com

General - Incorporation	DE	**Stock**- Price on:12/24/2007	$8.32
Employees	31,500	Stock Exchange	NYSE
Auditor	Ernst & Young LLP	Ticker Symbol	UIS
Stk Agt	American Stock Transfer & Trust Co.	Outstanding Shares	347,750,000
Counsel	NA	E.P.S	-$0.34
DUNS No.	00-535-8932	Shareholders	NA

Business: The group's principle activity is to provide consulting, systems integration, outsourcing, infrastructure, and server technology services. The groups servicing areas include financial services, public sector, communications, transportation, and commercial industries. The group operates from United States.

Primary SIC and add'l.: 7373 3572 7374

CIK No: 0000746838

Subsidiaries: Intelligent Processing Solutions Limited, Unisys (Schweiz) A.G., Unisys Belgium, Unisys Brasil Ltda., Unisys Deutschland G.m.b.H., Unisys France, Unisys Funding Corporation I, Unisys Insurance Services Ltd., Unisys Italia S.r.l., Unisys Korea Limited, Unisys Limited, Unisys Nederland N.V., Unisys Philippines Limited

Officers: Joseph W. McGrath/Dir., CEO, Pres./$2,570,593.00, Randy J. Hendricks/Sr. VP, Pres. - Global Outsourcing, Infrastructure Services/$1,259,629.00, Joseph Munnelly/VP, Corporate Controller, Janet B. Haugen/CFO, Sr. VP/$1,044,827.00, David Engstrom/Partner, DoD, Intelligence, Federal Systems, Bart Steukers/Managing Partner, Continental Europe, Global Public Sector, Holli I. Ploog/VP - Managing Partner, UK, Middle East, Africa, Ukmea, Global Public Sector, Guillermo Bocanegra/Managing Partner, Latin America Commercial Industry, Arthur Filip/VP - Managing Partner Global Commercial Industries, Brett Cumberland/VP - Solutions Management Global

Transportation, Mike McNamara/VP - Unisys Partner Passenger Services Solutions, Christopher Shawdon/VP - Logistics Solutions Global Transportation, Urs Von Euw/Acting VP - Airport Solutions Global Transportation, Andrew Whittaker/GM - Asia Pacific Global Transportation, Olivier Houri/Pres. - Global Transportation *(53 Officers included in Index)*

Directors: Joseph W. McGrath/Dir., CEO, Pres., J. P. Bolduc/68/Dir., Craig Conway/Dir., Theodore M. Martin/Dir., James J. Duderstadt/Dir., Henry C. Duques/Dir., Matthew J. Espe/Dir., Denise K. Fletcher/Dir., Edwin A. Huston/Dir., Clayton M. Jones/58/Dir., Leslie F. Kenne/Dir., Theodore E. Martin/68/Dir.

Owners: Randy J. Hendricks, Henry C. Duques, MMI Investments, L.P./6.00%, Edwin A. Huston, J. P. Bolduc, Joseph W. McGrath, Matthew J. Espe, Janet B. Haugen, Black Rock, Inc./10.69%, Leslie F. Kenne, Peter Blackmore, Theodore E. Martin, Insiders, James J. Duderstadt, Denise K. Fletcher *(18 Owners included in Index)*

Financial Data: *Fiscal Year End:*12/31   *Latest Annual Data:* 12/31/2006

Year	Sales	Net Income
2006	$5,757,200,000	-$278,700,000
2005	$5,758,700,000	-$1,731,900,000
2004	$5,820,700,000	$38,600,000

Curr. Assets:	$2,238,500,000	*Curr. Liab.:*	$1,931,700,000			
Plant, Equip.:	$341,300,000	*Total Liab.:*	$4,102,100,000	*Indic. Yr. Divd.:*	NA	
Total Assets:	$4,037,900,000	*Net Worth:*	-$64,200,000	*Debt/ Equity:*	NA	

Unit Corp

PO Box 702500, Tulsa, OK, 74170; *PH:* 1-918-493-7700; *http://* www.unitcorp.com

General - Incorporation	DE	Stock- Price on:12/24/2007	$64.84
Employees	2,567	Stock Exchange	NYSE
Auditor	PricewaterhouseCoopers LLP	Ticker Symbol	UNT
Stk Agt	American Stock Transfer & Trust Co.	Outstanding Shares	46,400,000
Counsel	NA	E.P.S.	$6.29
DUNS No.	15-352-3840	Shareholders	NA

Business: The group's principal activities are contract drilling of onshore oil and natural gas wells and the exploration, development, acquisition and production of oil and natural gas properties. The group explores and produces oil and natural gas primarily in the natural gas producing provinces of Oklahoma and Texas areas of the anadarko and arkoma basins, the Texas gulf cost and the rocky mountain regions. The group acquired serdrilco incorporated and its subsidiary and service drilling southwest llc on 08-Dec-2003, petrocorp incorporated on 02-Feb-2004 & sauer drilling company and superior pipe line company llc 02-Aug-2004.

Primary SIC and add'l.: 1381 1311

CIK No: 0000798949

Subsidiaries: Superior Pipeline Company, LLC, Unit Drilling Company, Unit Petroleum Company

Officers: John G. Nikkel/Chmn., CEO, Pres., Mike Fankhouser/VP - Land, Production Administration, Brad Guidry/VP - Exploration Unit Petroleum/$486,091.00, Carl Hansen/VP - East Division, Mark Colclasure/Sr. VP - Operations, Larry D. Pinkston/Dir., Assist. Controller, Treasurer/$962,312.00, Phil Livingston/VP - Exploration Coordinator, John Cromling/Sr. VP - Drilling Operations/$494,875.00, Mark E. Schell/Sec., General Counsel/$540,457.00, David T. Merrill/VP - Finance, CFO, Treasurer/$443,171.00, Frank Young/VP - Central Division

Directors: John G. Nikkel/Chmn., CEO, Pres., William B. Morgan/Dir., Gary R. Christopher/Dir., King P. Kirchner/Co - Founder, Dir., Larry D. Pinkston/Dir., Assist. Controller, Treasurer, Don Cook/Dir., John H. Williams/Dir., Michael J. Adcock/Dir., Robert J. Sullivan/Dir.

Owners: John G. Nikkel, Michael J. Adcock, Don Cook, Bradford J. Guidry, King P. Kirchner, John H. Williams, Larry D. Pinkston, David T. Merrill, Royce & Associates, LLC/11.75%, Neuberger Berman Inc./5.99%, John Cromling, Gary R. Christopher, Barclays Global Investors, N.A./8.74%, Mark E. Schell, William B. Morgan *(16 Owners included in Index)*

Financial Data: *Fiscal Year End:*12/31   *Latest Annual Data:* 12/31/2006

Year	Sales	Net Income
2006	$1,162,385,000	$312,177,000
2005	$885,608,000	$212,442,000
2004	$519,203,000	$90,275,000

Curr. Assets:	$232,940,000	*Curr. Liab.:*	$160,942,000	*P/E Ratio:*	10.31
Plant, Equip.:	$1,552,663,000	*Total Liab.:*	$716,060,000	*Indic. Yr. Divd.:*	NA
Total Assets:	$1,874,096,000	*Net Worth:*	$1,158,036,000	*Debt/ Equity:*	0.1240

United Air Lines Inc

77 W Wacker Dr., Chicago, IL, 60601; *PH:* 1-312-997-8000; *http://* ir.united.com; *Email:* investorrelations@ual.com

General - Incorporation	DE	Stock- Price on:12/24/2007	$39.35
Employees	55,000	Stock Exchange	NDQ
Auditor	Deloitte & Touche LLP	Ticker Symbol	NA
Stk Agt	Computershare Investor Services LLC	Outstanding Shares	115,590,000
Counsel	NA	E.P.S.	NA
DUNS No.	00-693-3030	Shareholders	NA

Business: The group's principle activity is to provide commercial air transportation of persons, property and mail throughout the United States and abroad. The group is a wholly owned subsidiary of united airlines corporation. The group provides service within North America and to international destinations like pacific, Atlantic and Latin America. During 2003, united carried approximately 66 million passengers and flew approximately 104 billion revenue passenger miles. United cargo offers both domestic and international shipping through a variety of services including small package delivery, t.d. Guaranteed(R), first freight, international freight and global sp. United cargo's door-to-door delivery services include united same day for packages under 70 pounds and united same day plus for heavy freight.

Primary SIC and add'l.: 4512

CIK No: 0000101001

Subsidiaries: Covia LLC, Kion de Mexico, S.A. de C.V., Mileage Plus Holdings, Inc., Mileage Plus Holdings, Inc., Mileage Plus Marketing, Inc., Mileage Plus, Inc., UAL Loyalty Services, Inc., UAL Loyalty Services, Inc., United Air Lines, Inc., United Aviation Fuels Corporation, United Cogen, Inc., United Vacations, Inc.

Officers: Glenn F. Tilton/Chmn., CEO, Pres., Sara A. Fields/Sr. VP - Office of the Chmn., Paul R. Lovejoy/Sr. VP, General Counsel, Sec., Rosemary Moore/Sr. VP - Corporate, Government Affairs, Charlie L. Ahmes/VP - Onboard Service, Robert B. Sahadevan/VP - Mileage Plus, Simha Sudarshan/Sr. Mgr. - Investor Relations, Grace M. Puma/Sr. VP - Strategic Sourcing, Chief

Procurement Officer, Todd D. Arkenberg/VP - Employee Experience, Ajay K. Singh/VP - Corporate Real Estate, Frederic F. Brace/Dir., CFO, Exec. VP, Peter D. McDonald/Dir., COO, Exec. VP, Michael F. Dingboom/VP - Finance, United Services, Barbara A. Higgins/VP - Customer Experience, David K. Myrick/VP - Sales, Americas *(44 Officers included in Index)*

Directors: Glenn F. Tilton/Chmn., CEO, Pres., Richard J. Almeida/Dir., Mark A. Bathurst/Dir., Mary K. Bush/Dir., Stephen R. Canale/Dir., James W. Farrell/Dir., Walter Isaacson/Dir., Robert D. Krebs/Dir., Robert S. Miller/Dir., James J. O'Connor/Dir., David J. Vitale/Dir., John H. Walker/Dir., Frederic F. Brace/Dir., CFO, Exec. VP, Peter D. McDonald/Dir., COO, Exec. VP, John P. Tague/Dir., Exec. VP, Chief Revenue Officer

Owners: Frederic F. Brace, Sara Fields, Peter McDonald, John P. Tague, Glenn F. Tilton, Insiders/1.29%

Financial Data: *Fiscal Year End:*12/31   *Latest Annual Data:* 12/31/2006

Year	Sales	Net Income
2006	NA	NA
2005	NA	NA
2004	NA	NA

Curr. Assets:	$6,273,000,000	*Curr. Liab.:*	$7,945,000,000	*P/E Ratio:*	53.18
Plant, Equip.:	$11,463,000,000	*Total Liab.:*	$22,860,000,000	*Indic. Yr. Divd.:*	NA
Total Assets:	$25,369,000,000	*Net Worth:*	$2,148,000,000	*Debt/ Equity:*	4.2464

United America Indemnity Ltd

Formerly: United National Group Ltd
Walker House, 87 Mary St., George Town, Grand Cayman, KY1-9002; *PH:* 1-604-537-5905; *http://* www.uai.ky

General - Incorporation	Cayman Islands	Stock- Price on:12/24/2007	$24.65
Employees	405	Stock Exchange	NDQ
Auditor	PricewaterhouseCoopers LLP	Ticker Symbol	INDM
Stk Agt	StockTrans, Inc.	Outstanding Shares	37,370,000
Counsel	Fox Paine & Company LLC	E.P.S.	$2.79
DUNS No.	NA	Shareholders	NA

Business: The group's principal activity is to provide specialty property and casualty insurance. The group writes specialty insurance products that are designed to meet the specific needs of targeted niche insurance markets. The products that the group writes for these markets include property and casualty insurance for social service agencies, insurance for equine mortality risks and insurance for vacant property risks. The operations are carried on in three segments, e and s segment, specialty admitted and reinsurance. The e and s and specialty admitted segment offers specific specialty insurance, umbrella and excess insurance, property and general liability insurance and non-medical professional liability insurance. Reinsurance segment includes assumed business written in support of a select group of direct writing reinsurers. On 5-09-2003, the group acquired wind river investment corporation.

Primary SIC and add'l.: 6331 6719

CIK No: 0001263813

Subsidiaries: American Insurance Adjustment Agency, Inc., American Insurance Service, Inc., Apex Insurance Agency, Inc., APEX Insurance Services of Illinois, Inc., Delaware Valley Underwriting Agency, Inc., Diamond State Insurance Company, DVUA Massachusetts, Inc., DVUA North Carolina, Inc., DVUA of New Jersey, Inc., DVUA of New York, Inc., DVUA of Ohio, Inc., DVUA Pittsburgh, Inc., DVUA South Carolina, Inc., DVUA Virginia, Inc., DVUA West Virginia, Inc. 49 Subsidiaries included in the Index

Officers: Larry Frakes/Dir., CEO, Pres., Thomas M. McGeehan/VP, Corporate Controller, Kevin L. Tate/Sr. VP, CFO/$701,302.00, Garland Pezzuolo/Sr. VP, Sec., General Counsel

Directors: Larry Frakes/Dir., CEO, Pres., Saul A. Fox/Chmn., Richard L. Duszak/Dir., Stephen A. Cozen/Dir., James R. Kroner/Dir., Justin Reyna/Dir., Michael J. Marchio/Dir.

Owners: Richard S. March, David J. Myers, James R. Kroner, Stephen A. Cozen, Fox Paine & Company/40.70%, Insiders/1.75%, Richard L. Duszak, Hotchkis & Wiley Capital Management/5.70%, Columbia Wanger Asset Management, L.P./8.50%, FMR Corp./6.10%, Larry A. Frakes, Raymond S. McDowell, Kevin L. Tate, Morgan Stanley/7.30%, Justin Reyna *(17 Owners included in Index)*

Financial Data: *Fiscal Year End:*12/31   *Latest Annual Data:* 12/31/2006

Year	Sales	Net Income
2006	$612,437,000	$99,418,000
2005	$561,539,000	$65,593,000
2004	$252,982,000	$37,047,000

Curr. Assets:	$1,389,570,000	*Curr. Liab.:*	$18,411,000	*P/E Ratio:*	8.84
Plant, Equip.:	NA	*Total Liab.:*	$2,221,346,000	*Indic. Yr. Divd.:*	NA
Total Assets:	$2,984,616,000	*Net Worth:*	$763,270,000	*Debt/ Equity:*	0.1945

United American Bank CA

101 S Ellsworth Ave., San Mateo, CA, 94401; *PH:* 1-650-579-1500; *Fax:* 1-650-579-1501; *http://* www.unitedamericanbank.com; *Email:* info@unitedamericanbank.com

General - Incorporation		Stock- Price on:12/24/2007	$17.55
Employees	NA	Stock Exchange	OTC
Auditor	NA	Ticker Symbol	UABK
Stk Agt	U.S. Stock Transfer Corp	Outstanding Shares	NA
Counsel	NA	E.P.S.	NA
DUNS No.	NA	Shareholders	NA

Business: The groups principal activities include providing banking and financial services. Services of the group include checking accounts, savings accounts, certificates of deposit, installment loans, real estate mortgage loans, commercial loans, traveler's checks, safe deposit boxes, night depository and automated teller services. The group operates from the United States.

Primary SIC and add'l.: 6029

CIK No:

Officers: John C. Schrup/Dir., Pres., CEO - Founder, Gerald Brown/Exec. VP, Founder, Angelique Randolph/Sr. VP, Note Dept Mgr., Joseph Simoni/VP, Compliance Officer, Craig Walsh/Sr. VP, Deposit Officer, Glen Nissen/Sr. VP - Mid, Peninsula Regional Mgr., Concepcion Torres/Assist. VP, Client Service Mgr., Chris Nettles/Credit Analyst, William R. Walters/Co - Founder, Exec. VP, Chief Credit Officer, Gerry Brown/Exec. VP, Judi Anderson/VP, Exec Admin Officer, Cathleen M. Colgan/MD, VP, Trust Officer, Pat Torres/Exec. VP - Operations Administration, Steve Dworetzky/Sr. VP - Business Development - Community Relations, Sharon Ingram/VP, Client Service Mgr. *(34 Officers included in Index)*

Directors: John C. Schrup/Dir., Pres., CEO - Founder, Margaret A. Taylor/Chmn., Co - Founder, William W. Hill/Co - Founder, Dir., Carrie Schrup/Co - Founder, Sarah O'rourke Schrup/Co - Founder, Doreen L. Sinclair/Co - Founder, James H. Smith/Co - Founder, Mark Solomon/Co - Founder, Glen Strauss/Co - Founder, Norm I. Book/Dir., Frank A. Baldanzi/Co - Founder, Dir., Wallace A. Krone/Co - Founder, Dir., Floyd Gonella/Co - Founder, William R. Walters/Co - Founder, Exec. VP, Chief Credit Officer, Jay Paul Leupp/Dir. *(60 Directors included in Index)*

United American Corp

3273 E Warm Springs Rd., Las Vegas, NV, 89120; **PH:** 1-514-313-3432;
http:// www.unitedamericancorp.com; **Email:** info@unitedamericancorp.com

General - Incorporation	FL	**Stock**- Price on:12/24/2007	$0.048
Employees	1	Stock Exchange	OTC
Auditor	Schwartz Levitsky Feldman LLP	Ticker Symbol	UAMA
Stk Agt	Interwest Transfer Company, Inc.	Outstanding Shares	51,080,000
Counsel	NA	E.P.S.	$0.00
DUNS No.	NA	Shareholders	NA

Business: The group's principal activity is to seek products or businesses that have potential for profit. The group is in its development stage. The group is in the process of entering the telecommunications business.

Primary SIC and add'l.: 7375
CIK No: 0001096688
Subsidiaries: American United Corporation, Teliphone, Inc.
Officers: Simon Lamarche/53/Dir., CEO, CFO
Directors: Simon Lamarche/53/Dir., CEO, CFO, George Metrakos/36/Dir.
Owners: Insiders, George Metrakos, Benoit Lalibert/52.50%

Financial Data: Fiscal Year End:12/31   **Latest Annual Data:** 12/31/2006

Year	Sales	Net Income
2006	$19,991,000	-$614,000
2005	$4,845,000	-$1,422,000
2004	$583,000	-$539,000

Curr. Assets:	$1,938,000	Curr. Liab.:	$3,126,000		
Plant, Equip.:	$420,000	Total Liab.:	$3,126,000	Indic. Yr. Divd.:	NA
Total Assets:	$2,358,000	Net Worth:	-$767,000	Debt/ Equity:	NA

United American Healthcare Corp

300 River Pl, Ste 4950, Detroit, MI, 48207; **PH:** 1-313-393-4571; *http://* www.uahc.com

General - Incorporation	MI	**Stock**- Price on:12/24/2007	$4.63
Employees	107	Stock Exchange	NDQ
Auditor	UHY LLP	Ticker Symbol	UAHC
Stk Agt	Computershare Investor Services LLC	Outstanding Shares	8,590,000
Counsel	Honigman Miller Schwartz & Cohn	E.P.S.	-$0.16
DUNS No.	15-140-5677	Shareholders	NA

Business: The group's principal activity is healthcare management service, which provides management, marketing, consulting and administrative services to healthcare plans and self-funded employers. The services include feasibility studies for licensure, strategic planning, corporate governance, management consulting, information services, marketing, pre-certification, utilization review programs, individual case management, budgeting, enrollment processing and reconciliation and other administrative services. It also arranges for the financing of health care services and delivery of these services by primary case physicians and specialists, hospitals, pharmacies and other ancillary providers to commercial employer groups and government sponsored populations in Tennessee and Michigan.

Primary SIC and add'l.: 8742 8099
CIK No: 0000867963
Subsidiaries: UAHC Health Plan, Inc., United American of Tennessee, Inc.
Officers: William Brooks/Chmn., CEO, Pres., Stephanie Dowell/CEO - Uahc Health Plan, Emmett S. Moten/Sec. - Subsidiary Operations, Stephen Harris/CFO
Directors: William Brooks/Chmn., CEO, Pres., Tom A. Goss/62/Vice Chmn., Eddie R. Munson/58/Dir., Darrel W. Francis/55/Dir., Richard M. Brown/73/Dir., Ronald E. Hall/65/Dir.
Owners: Robert W. Morey/7.70%, Turnaround Equity Partners, L.P./6.70%, Richard M. Brown/5.30%

Financial Data: Fiscal Year End:06/30   **Latest Annual Data:** 06/30/2007

Year	Sales	Net Income
2007	$18,065,000	-$1,117,000
2006	$18,114,000	$1,373,000
2005	$22,079,000	$5,345,000

Curr. Assets:	$10,983,000	Curr. Liab.:	$3,176,000	P/E Ratio:	57.88
Plant, Equip.:	$142,000	Total Liab.:	$3,176,000	Indic. Yr. Divd.:	NA
Total Assets:	$25,226,000	Net Worth:	$22,050,000	Debt/ Equity:	NA

United Artists Theatre Circuit Inc

7132 Regal Ln., Knoxville, TN, 37918; **PH:** 1-865-922-1123

General - Incorporation	MD	**Stock** - Price on:12/24/2007	NA
Employees	NA	Stock Exchange	NA
Auditor	KPMG LLP	Ticker Symbol	NA
Stk Agt	NA	Outstanding Shares	NA
Counsel	NA	E.P.S.	NA
DUNS No.	07-615-9771	Shareholders	NA

Business: The group's principle activity is to operate theatres. The group derives revenues primarily from admissions and concession sales. The group generates additional revenues from electronic video games located adjacent to the lobbies of certain of the group's theatres, vendor marketing programs, on-screen advertisements, rental of theatres for business meetings and other events generated by regal cinemedia, which is an affiliate of the group. The group operates solely in the domestic market. At 01-Jan-2004, the group operated 935 screens in 120 theatres in 21 states with over 46 million annual attendees.

Primary SIC and add'l.: 7819 3944 7389 7832
CIK No: 0000889570

Subsidiaries: CDP Limited Liability Company, Orix RAM Montgomery Venture General Partnership, R and S Theaters,Inc., Ram/u-kop, LLC, San Francisco Theatres,Inc., Staten Theatre Group, Staten Theatre Group II, Ua Shor LLC, United Artists/Pacific Media Joint Venture, United Stonestown Corporation, Vogue Realty Company
Officers: Michael L. Campbell/Chmn., CEO, Gregory W. Dunn/COO, Pres., Amy E. Miles/Exec. VP, CFO, Treasurer, Peter B. Brandow/Exec. VP, General Counsel, Sec., Donald De Laria/VP - Investor Relations
Directors: Michael L. Campbell/Chmn., CEO, Alex Yemenidjian/Dir., Thomas D. Bell/Dir., Stephen A. Kaplan/Dir., David H. Keyte/Dir., Lee M. Thomas/Dir., Jack Tyrrell/Dir., Nestor R. Weigand/Dir., Charles E. Brymer/Dir.

United Auto Group Inc

2555 Telegraph Rd. , Bloomfield Hills, MI, 48302; **PH:** 1-248-648-2500; *http://* www.unitedauto.com

General - Incorporation	DE	**Stock**- Price on:12/24/2007	$21.04
Employees	15,800	Stock Exchange	NYSE
Auditor	Deloitte & Touche LLP	Ticker Symbol	NA
Stk Agt	EquiServe Trust Co N.A	Outstanding Shares	94,880,000
Counsel	NA	E.P.S.	$1.36
DUNS No.	79-649-1330	Shareholders	NA

Business: The group's principle activity is to provide used motor vehicles and related products and services. The group operates from United States.

Primary SIC and add'l.: 7549 5013 5511 6719
CIK No: 0001019849
Subsidiaries: Alpina GB Limited, Aston Green Limited, Atlantic Auto Funding Corporation, Atlantic Auto Second Funding Corporation, Atlantic Auto Third Funding Corporation, Auto Mall Payroll Services, Inc., Autocare Insurance Agency, Inc., Boostmicro Limited, Brett Morgan Chevrolet-Geo, Inc., Central Ford Center, Inc., CJNS, LLC, Classic Auto Group, Inc., Classic Enterprises, LLC, Classic Imports, Inc., Classic Management Company, Inc. 245 Subsidiaries included in the Index
Officers: Roger S. Penske/71/Chmn., CEO/$1,143,878.00, Paul F. Walters/64/Exec. VP - Human Resources/$371,704.00, Shane M. Spradlin/39/VP, Sec., Anthony R. Pordon/43/Sr. VP, Roger S. Penske/48/Pres., Robert T. OShaughnessy/42/CFO, Exec. VP - Finance/$986,897.00, Calvin C. Sharp/57/Exec. VP - Human Resources, George Brochick/58/Exec. VP - West Operations, Gerard Nieuwenhuys/47/MD - Sytner Group, Whitfield R. Ramonat/45/Exec. VP - Central Operations, Financial Services
Directors: Roger S. Penske/71/Chmn., CEO, Robert H. Kurnick/46/Vice Chmn., Ronald G. Steinhart/67/Dir., Brian H. Thompson/68/Dir., John Barr/60/Dir., Michael R. Eisenson/52/Dir., Hiroshi Ishikawa/45/Dir., William J. Lovejoy/67/Dir., Kimberly J. McWaters/43/Dir., Eustace W. Mita/53/Dir., Lucio A. Noto/69/Dir., Richard J. Peters/60/Dir.
Owners: Robert H. Kurnick, Brian H. Thompson, Richard J. Peters, William J. Lovejoy, Baron Capital Group, Inc., Roger S. Penske, Roger S. Penske, Hiroshi Ishikawa, Insiders, Penske Corporation, Kimberly J. McWaters, Mitsui & Co, Michael R. Eisenson, Dimension Fund Advisors LP, Ronald G. Steinhart *(21 Owners included in Index)*

Financial Data: Fiscal Year End:12/31   **Latest Annual Data:** 12/31/2006

Year	Sales	Net Income
2006	$11,242,313,000	$124,701,000
2005	$10,190,284,000	$118,973,000
2004	$9,384,741,000	$111,687,000

Curr. Assets:	$2,286,689,000	Curr. Liab.:	$1,752,957,000	P/E Ratio:	17.25
Plant, Equip.:	$582,646,000	Total Liab.:	$3,174,149,000	Indic. Yr. Divd.:	$0.360
Total Assets:	$4,469,802,000	Net Worth:	$1,295,653,000	Debt/ Equity:	0.6634

United Bancorp Inc

201 N Columbus St., Lancaster, OH, 43130; **PH:** 1-740-633-0445; *http://* www.unitedbancorp.com

General - Incorporation	OH	**Stock**- Price on:12/24/2007	$10.5
Employees	114	Stock Exchange	NDQ
Auditor	Grant Thornton LLP	Ticker Symbol	UBCP
Stk Agt	American Stock Transfer & Trust Co.	Outstanding Shares	4,600,000
Counsel	NA	E.P.S.	$0.56
DUNS No.	19-647-3698	Shareholders	NA

Business: The group's principal activities are to provide commercial, retail banking and financial services to the general public. It operates through its wholly owned subsidiaries located in northeastern, eastern and southeastern Ohio. The group accepts demand, savings and time deposits and grants commercial, real estate and consumer loans to its customers. It provides services to customers located mainly in athens, belmont, carroll, fairfield, harrison, hocking and tuscarawas counties. At 31-Dec-2003, it operated through 9 branches in Ohio.

Primary SIC and add'l.: 6022 6712
CIK No: 0000731653
Subsidiaries: The Citizens Savings Bank, The Glouster Community Bank
Officers: James W. Everson/Chmn., CEO, Pres./$267,594.00
Directors: James W. Everson/Chmn., CEO, Pres.
Owners: Norman F. Assenza, James A. Lodes, Michael J. Arciello, James W. Everson/3.40%, Terry A. McGhee, Matthew C. Thomas, Insiders/9.40%, United Bancorp, Inc. Employee/7.00%, L. E. Richardson/1.80%, John M. Hoopingarner, Scott A. Everson, Randall M. Greenwood, Richard L. Riesbeck

Financial Data: Fiscal Year End:12/31   **Latest Annual Data:** 12/31/2006

Year	Sales	Net Income
2006	$27,925,000	$2,068,000
2005	$24,575,000	$3,293,000
2004	$22,706,000	$3,233,000

Curr. Assets:	$17,132,000	Curr. Liab.:	$385,073,000	P/E Ratio:	22.83
Plant, Equip.:	$8,055,000	Total Liab.:	$389,073,000	Indic. Yr. Divd.:	$0.520
Total Assets:	$421,653,000	Net Worth:	$32,580,000	Debt/ Equity:	NA

United Bancorp Inc/MI

205 E Chicago Blvd., Tecumseh, MI, 49286; **PH:** 1-517-423-8373; **Fax:** 1-517-423-5041;
http:// www.ubat.com

General - Incorporation ....MI
Employees..202
Auditor ....BKD LLP
Stk Agt...........................Registrar & Transfer Co
Counsel..NA
DUNS No..00-696-0967

Stock- Price on:12/24/2007 ....$22
Stock Exchange...OTC
Ticker Symbol..UBMI
Outstanding Shares 5,230,000
E.P.S..$1.63
Shareholders..NA

Business: The group's principal activities are to provide financial services to individuals, corporations, fiduciaries and other institutions through the subsidiary, united bank & trust. The services of the group include checking, now accounts, savings, time deposit accounts, money market deposit accounts, safe deposit facilities, money transfers and lending loans. The group also provides non-deposit investment products through licensed representatives in the banking offices and sell credit and life insurance products. Loan portfolio consists of real estate loans, secured and unsecured business loans, personal loans, consumer installment loans, credit card and check-credit loans, home equity loans, accounts receivable and inventory financing, equipment lease financing and construction financing. The group conducts its operations through sixteen banking offices and fifteen automated teller machines in lenawee, washtenaw and monroe counties situated in Michigan.

Primary SIC and add'l.: 6712 6035

CIK No: 0000775345

Subsidiaries: United Bank & Trust, United Bank & Trust - Washtenaw

Officers: Robert K. Chapman/Dir., CEO, Pres./$427,215.00, Randal Rabe/CEO, Pres. - United Bank, Trust/$312,785.00, Thomas Gannon/Sr. VP - Human Resources, United Bank, Trust/$160,392.00, John Odenweller/Sr. VP - Technology, Operations, Michelle Sumerix/Assist. VP - Trust Administration, Wealth Management Group, Rodney Clark/VP - Financial Advisor, Wealth Management Group, Jim Winslow/VP - Financial Advisor, Wealth Management Group, Jamie Guise/Sr. VP, Chief Marketing Officer - United Bank, Trust, Joseph Zuchowski/VP - Mortgage Sales, United Bank, Trust, Joe Williams/Exec. VP, Chief Community Banking Officer - United Bank, Trust, Rachel Emery/Community Banking Administration Officer - United Bank, Trust, Tammy Hall/Community Banking Officer - United Bank, Trust, Todd Clark/Pres., Chief Banking Officer United Bank - Trust, Washtenaw/$273,133.00, Tiffaney Gruber/Human Resources Officer - United Bank, Trust, Diane Schuler/Assist. VP - Client Accounting (71 Officers included in Index)

Directors: Robert K. Chapman/Dir., CEO, Pres., David S. Hickman/Chmn., George H. Cress/Dir. Emeritus, Kathryn M. Mohr/45/Dir., James D. Buhr/59/Dir., James C. Lawson/60/Dir., Donald J. Martin/68/Dir., David E. Maxwell/68/Dir., John H. Foss/65/Dir., James G. Haeussler/49/Dir., Robert G. MacOmber/Dir., Joseph D. Butcko/66/Dir.

Owners: David S. Hickman/1.91%, John H. Foss, Insiders/11.38%, Randal J. Rabe, Robert G. Macomber, Robert K. Chapman, James C. Lawson/1.42%, David E. Maxwell/1.64%, Dale L. Chadderdon, James G. Haeussler, Kathryn M. Mohr, Donald J. Martin/2.56%, John A. Odenweller, George H. Cress, Joseph D. Butcko (20 Owners included in Index)

Financial Data: Fiscal Year End:12/31 **Latest Annual Data:** 12/31/2006

Year	Sales	Net Income
2006	$59,231,000	$8,972,000
2005	$50,319,000	$8,324,000
2004	$42,759,000	$7,653,000

Curr. Assets:	$33,081,000	**Curr. Liab.:**	$635,508,000	**P/E Ratio:**	13.50
Plant, Equip.:	$13,215,000	**Total Liab.:**	$676,453,000	**Indic. Yr. Divd.:**	$0.800
Total Assets:	$750,989,000	**Net Worth:**	$74,536,000	**Debt/ Equity:**	0.5662

United BanCorp of Alabama Inc

PO Box 8, Atmore, AL, 36504; **PH:** 1-254-446-6100; **http://** www.ubankal.com

General - Incorporation ....DE
Employees..165
Auditor ....Mauldin & Jenkins LLC
Stk Agt...........................Registrar & Transfer Co
Counsel..NA
DUNS No..10-208-0801

Stock- Price on:12/24/2007 ....$16.85
Stock Exchange...OTC
Ticker Symbol..UBAB
Outstanding Shares 2,240,000
E.P.S..$0.93
Shareholders..NA

Business: The group's principal activity is to provide commercial banking services. The depositary products offered include checking accounts, now accounts, money market deposit accounts, statement savings accounts, repurchase agreements and various other time deposit savings programs. The loans offered include business loans, personal, automobile, home and home improvement loans. The other services offered include securities brokerage services, visa and master card, multi-purpose, nationally recognized credit card and trust services. The group also offers Internet banking, bill pay and online brokerage services. The operations are conducted through nine full service banking offices located in atmore, frisco city, monroeville, flomaton, foley, lillian, bay minette, silverhill and magnolia springs Alabama, a drive up facility in atmore and a loan production office in jay, Florida.

Primary SIC and add'l.: 6022 6712

CIK No: 0000704561

Subsidiaries: United Bancorp Capital Trust I, United Bank, United Insurance Service

Officers: Bob Jones/Pres., CEO - United Bank, Robert R. Jones/CEO, Pres., Dottie Baker/Contact - Frisco City, United Bank, Tina Brooks/Corp. Sec. - United Bank, Wayne Briske/Florida Pres. - United Bank, Elaine Haynie/Lillian Branch Mgr. - United Bank, Rudy Baugh/Administration, United Bank, Phyllis Bell/Monroeville Branch Manage, United Bank, B. J. Maher/Flomaton Branch Mgr. - United Bank, Alton McRee/Agri, Finance Services, United Bank, Barbara Ward/Summerdale Branch Mgr. - United Bank, Bruce Trammell/Collection Recovery, United Bank, Carolyn Crane/Atmore Branch Mgr. - United Bank, Cathy Lowrey/Deposite Operations Mgr. - United Bank, Chris Coaker/Foley Branch Mgr. - United Bank (39 Officers included in Index)

Directors: William J. Justice/Dir., David D. Swift/Dir., Michael R. Andreoli/Dir., Dale M. Ash/Dir., J. W. Trawick/Dir., Walter L. Crim/Dir.

Owners: Walter L. Crim, Insiders/13.29%, Wayne J. Trawick, Leon H. Esneul/4.31%, Dale M. Ash, Michael R. Andreoli, David D. Swift/1.59%, William J. Justice/1.40%, Robert R. Jones/4.09%

Financial Data: Fiscal Year End:12/31 **Latest Annual Data:** 12/31/2006

Year	Sales	Net Income
2006	$28,967,000	$3,135,000
2005	$22,230,000	$2,895,000
2004	$17,398,000	$2,153,000

Curr. Assets:	$54,784,000	**Curr. Liab.:**	$381,123,000	**P/E Ratio:**	14.40
Plant, Equip.:	$11,796,000	**Total Liab.:**	$395,446,000	**Indic. Yr. Divd.:**	NA
Total Assets:	$426,171,000	**Net Worth:**	$30,725,000	**Debt/ Equity:**	NA

United Bancshares Inc/OH

100 S High St., Columbus Grove, OH, 45830; **PH:** 1-419-659-2141; **Fax:** 1-419-659-2069; **http://** www.theubank.com; **Email:** onlinemortgages@theubank.com

General - Incorporation ....OH
Employees..152
Auditor ....Clifton Gunderson LLP
Stk Agt ....Mellon Investor Services LLC
Counsel..NA
DUNS No..NA

Stock- Price on:12/24/2007 ....$15.7
Stock Exchange...NDQ
Ticker Symbol..UBOH
Outstanding Shares 3,530,000
E.P.S..$1.29
Shareholders..NA

Business: The group's principal activities are to provide full banking services to individuals and small to middle market businesses. The deposit products of the group include checking accounts, passbook savings account, money market accounts and time certificates of deposit. The loan products of the group include commercial, consumer, agricultural, residential mortgage loans and home equity loans. The other services provided by the group include automatic teller machines, credit card services, safe deposit box rentals and other personalized banking services. The operations of the group are carried out through its offices in columbus grove, kalida, ottawa and lima.

Primary SIC and add'l.: 6022 6712

CIK No: 0001087456

Subsidiaries: The Union Bank Company, United (OH) Statutory Trust I

Officers: Daniel W. Schutt/Dir., CEO, Pres./$327,940.00, Brian D. Young/Exec. VP, Treasurer, CFO/$156,388.00, Bonita R. Selhorst/Sec.

Directors: Daniel W. Schutt/Dir., CEO, Pres., James N. Reynolds/Chmn., Edward E. Rigel/Dir., David P. Roach/Dir., Steven R. Unverferth/Dir., Robert L. Benroth/Dir., Robert L. Dillhoff/Dir.

Owners: Steven R. Unverferth, Edward H. Rigel, James N. Reynolds/1.75%, Brian D. Young/0.17%, Robert L. Benroth/0.20%, Robert L. Dillhoff/0.63%, Bonita R. Selhorst/0.57%, Daniel W. Schutt/0.20%, David P. Roach/0.49%, Insiders/4.92%

Financial Data: Fiscal Year End:12/31 **Latest Annual Data:** 12/31/2006

Year	Sales	Net Income
2006	$35,951,000	$4,927,000
2005	$32,669,000	$4,622,000
2004	$30,008,000	$3,088,000

Curr. Assets:	$12,310,000	**Curr. Liab.:**	$377,640,000	**P/E Ratio:**	11.89
Plant, Equip.:	$7,088,000	**Total Liab.:**	$504,223,000	**Indic. Yr. Divd.:**	$0.560
Total Assets:	$550,375,000	**Net Worth:**	$46,152,000	**Debt/ Equity:**	NA

United Bancshares Inc/PA

The Graham Bldg, 30 S 15th St, Ste. 1200, Philadelphia, PA, 19102; **PH:** 1-304-424-8800; **http://** www.unitedbankofphiladelphia.com

General - Incorporation ....PA
Employees..162
Auditor ....McGladrey & Pullen LLP
Stk Agt ....NA
Counsel..NA
DUNS No..62-522-8630

Stock- Price on:12/24/2007 ....NA
Stock Exchange..NA
Ticker Symbol...NA
Outstanding Shares ....NA
E.P.S...NA
Shareholders..NA

Business: The group's principal activity is to offer commercial and consumer banking services through its subsidiary, bank of philadelphia. These services include a wide range of deposit products including checking accounts, interest-bearing now accounts, money market accounts, certificates of deposit, savings accounts and individual retirement accounts. The lending products include commercial loans, mortgage loans, student loans, home improvement loans, auto loans, personal loans and home equity loans. In addition, the group offers safe deposit boxes, travelers' checks, money orders, direct deposit of payroll and social security checks, wire transfers, automated teller networks and trust services. The operations are carried through four branches located in philadelphia.

Primary SIC and add'l.: 6712 6022

CIK No: 0000944792

Subsidiaries: United Bank of Philadelphia

Officers: Evelyn F. Smalls/Dir., CEO, Pres., Brenda M. Hudson-Nelson/CFO, Exec. VP, Marionette Y. Wilson/Dir., Assist. Sec., William B. Moore/Dir., Sec., Norman W. Greene/VP, Chief Risk Officer, Terrence Barclift/Sr. VP, Sr. Lending Officer

Directors: Evelyn F. Smalls/Dir., CEO, Pres., Armstead L. Edwards/Chmn., David R. Bright/Dir., Joseph T. Drennan/Dir., Marionette Y. Wilson/Dir., Assist. Sec., Ahsan M. Nasratullah/Dir., Bernard E. Anderson/Dir., Ernest L. Wright/Dir., William B. Moore/Dir., Sec.

Owners: Armstead Edwards/1.24%, William B. Moore, Evelyn F. Smalls, Bernard E. Anderson, Marionette Y. Wilson/2.05%, Ernest L. Wright, Ahsan M. Nasratullah, The Estate of James F. Bodine/5.11%, Brenda M. Hudson-Nelson, Joseph T. Drennan, Philadelphia Municipal Retirement System/8.21%, Greater Philadelphia Urban Affairs Coalition/5.44%, Insiders/4.75%, Wachovia Corporation/5.73%, David R. Bright

United Bankshares Inc

5th and Ave.ry St.s, Parkersburg, WV, 26101; **PH:** 1-304-424-8800; **http://** www.ubsi-wv.com

General - Incorporation ....WV
Employees...1,367
Auditor ....Ernst & Young LLP
Stk Agt ....Mellon Investor Services LLC
Counsel..NA
DUNS No..14-730-7029

Stock- Price on:12/24/2007 ....$32.23
Stock Exchange...NDQ
Ticker Symbol..UBSI
Outstanding Shares 40,730,000
E.P.S..$2.39
Shareholders..NA

Business: The group's principal activity is to provide community and mortgage banking services. It accepts demand deposits, checking accounts, savings deposits, money market accounts, certificates of deposits and time deposits. The group lends commercial loans, construction loans, residential mortgage loans, commercial mortgage loans, residential real estate loans, construction loans and consumer loans. It also provides retirement accounts, safe deposit boxes and other banking products and services. The group's subsidiaries offer credit card services, executors and administrators of estates and performs a variety of investment and security services. At 31-Dec-2003, the group had 52 offices located throughout west Virginia, 36 offices throughout the northern Virginia, Maryland and Washington and 3 in Ohio. On 10-Oct-2003, group acquired sequoia bancshares inc.

Primary SIC and add'l.: 6021 6111 6712 6531

CIK No: 0000729986

Subsidiaries: Century Capital Trust I, George Mason Bankshares, Inc., GMBS Capital Management Co., GMBS Investment Co., LLC, Sequoia Trust I, Sequoia Trust II, UBC Capital Management, Co., UBC Holding Company, Inc., UBC Investment Co., LLC, United Asset Management Corp., United Bank, United Bank, Inc., United Brokerage Services, Inc., United Loan Management Co., United Real Estate Property Services, Inc. 21 Subsidiaries included in the Index

Officers: Richard M. Adams/61/Chmn., CEO/$1,721,273.00, John Neuner/62/Exec. VP, James B. Hayhurst/Exec. VP/$388,993.00, Joe L. Wilson/Exec. VP/$360,798.00, Steven E. Wilson/CFO, Exec. VP, Treasurer/$409,096.00, James J. Consagra/Exec. VP/$817,860.00

Directors: Richard M. Adams/61/Chmn., CEO, William C. Pitt/63/Dir., Robert G. Astorg/64/Dir., Thomas J. Blair/75/Dir., Gaston W. Caperton/68/Dir., Lawrence K. Doll/58/Dir., Theodore J. Georgelas/61/Dir., F. T. Graff/69/Dir., Russell L. Isaacs/75/Dir., John M. McMahon/67/Dir., Paul J. McNamara/59/Dir., Ogden G. Nutting/72/Dir., I. N. Smith/Dir., Mary K. Weddle/58/Dir., Clinton P. Winter/60/Dir.

Owners: Donald L. Unger, Clifton L. Good/1.36%, James C. Youngblood, Frank D. Hill, Walter H. Aikens, Paul R. Yoder/1.65%, Joseph W. Hollis/1.29%, John A. Willingham, Mensel D. Dean, John K. Stephens/1.69%, Meryl G. Kiser, Frederick A. Board, Banc Fund V L.P./9.50%, Thomas M. Boyd, Wayne B. Ruck/2.64% (*17 Owners included in Index*)

Financial Data: Fiscal Year End:12/31 Latest Annual Data: 06/30/2007

Year	Sales	Net Income
2007	NA	NA
2006	$457,491,000	$89,249,000
2005	$397,903,000	$100,409,000

Curr. Assets:	$293,521,000	**Curr. Liab.:**	$5,455,564,000	**P/E Ratio:**	15.06
Plant, Equip.:	$42,342,000	**Total Liab.:**	$6,083,506,000	**Indic. Yr. Divd.:**	$1.160
Total Assets:	$6,717,598,000	**Net Worth:**	$634,092,000	**Debt/ Equity:**	NA

United Breweries Co Inc

Bandera 84, Sixth Fl., Santiago; *PH:* 56-24273000; *http://* www.ccu-sa.com

General - Incorporation...... Republic Of Chile	Stock- Price on:12/24/2007 ....$37.47
Employees 3,706	Stock Exchange..............................NYSE
Auditor ....PricewaterhouseCoopers LLP	Ticker Symbol....................................CU
Stk Agt..NA	Outstanding Shares 63,700,000
Counsel............................Manuel Jose Noguera	E.P.S..$2.028
DUNS No. ....NA	Shareholders.....................................NA

Business: The group's principal activities are the manufacturing, purchasing, marketing, bottling and selling of beers, wines, malt, liquor, carbonated beverages, soft drinks, mineral water, nectars, concentrated juice and byproducts and all types of non-alcoholic beverages. Other activities include provision of financial and investment services, real estate brokerage, acquisition and transfer of securities, shares and debentures, distribution agricultural products such as grapes and operation in the livestock, fruits, forest and farm industries. Brands include cristal, escudo, royal guard, royal light, malta morenita, morenita especial del sur, dorada 6.0, aysen, lemon stones, orange stones, austral, paulaner, budweiser, guinness draught, schneider, schneider fuerte, santa fe, salta, cordoba dorada, rosario, corona, karlovacko, crystal, bilz and pap, kem, show, pepsi, seven up, crush, Canada dry limon soda, watt's, cachantun, porvenir, cabo de hornos, 1865 and late harvest.

Primary SIC and add'l.: 3085 2086 3089 5181 2084 2082

CIK No: 0000888746

Subsidiaries: CCU Argentina, CCU Chile, ECUSA, VSP

Owners: Insiders, Inversiones y Rentas S.A./66.11%

Financial Data: Fiscal Year End:12/31 Latest Annual Data: 12/31/2005

Year	Sales	Net Income
2005	$934,889,000	$94,195,000
2004	$757,149,000	$81,712,000
2003	$652,909,000	$93,856,000

Curr. Assets:	$496,197,000	**Curr. Liab.:**	$284,533,000	**P/E Ratio:**	18.18
Plant, Equip.:	$651,848,000	**Total Liab.:**	$698,468,000	**Indic. Yr. Divd.:**	$0.790
Total Assets:	$1,353,026,000	**Net Worth:**	$654,558,000	**Debt/ Equity:**	NA

United Business Media Plc

Ludgate House, 245 Blackfriars Rd., London, SE1 9UY; *PH:* 44-2079215000; *http://* www.unitedbusinessmedia.com; *Email:* investorrelations@ubmgroup.biz

General - Incorporation..............................UK	Stock- Price on:12/24/2007 ....NA
Employees ....NA	Stock Exchange..................................NA
Auditor ....Ernst & Young LLP	Ticker Symbol...................................NA
Stk Agt..........................Lloyds TSB Registrars	Outstanding Shares ....NA
Counsel...NA	E.P.S...NA
DUNS No. 21-030-1818	Shareholders....................................NA

Business: The group's principal activities are the provision of business information services to the technology, healthcare, media, automotive and financial services industries. The services are provided by market research, news distribution, publishing and events organising businesses. The group operates mainly in the United Kingdom, North America, Europe and Middle East and the pacific.

Primary SIC and add'l.: 2711 7383 2741 2721 4833

CIK No: 0000813811

Subsidiaries: Allison-Fisher International LLC, CMP Asia Ltd, CMP Europe Ltd, CMP Information Ltd, CMP Information, Inc., CMP Media LLC, CMPi Group Ltd (formerly Aprovia (UK) Ltd), CMPMedica Asia Pte Ltd, Eurisko NOPWorld Srl, Expoconsult B.V., Market Measures/Cozint L.P, Mediamark Research, Inc., Medizinische Medien Information GmbH, NOP Research Group Ltd, NOP World Strategic Marketing L.P. 24 Subsidiaries included in the Index

Officers: Gary Hughes/CEO - CMP Information, Alan Glass/Pres., CEO - Commonwealth Business Media, Henry Elkington/42/CEO - Cmpmedica, David Levin/46/Dir., Group CEO, Christiana Sosah/Communications, Investor Relations Assist., Peter Wrankmore/Head - Treasury, Janene Langley/Human Resources Mgr., Neil Mepham/Head - Taxation, Sekyoo Oh/GM - Seoul, Korea, Kate Gerwig/Editor - Custom Publishing, Beatrix Eriksen/Group Dir. - Research, Circulation, Cliggott Publishing Group, Part, CMP Healthcare Media, Based in Darien, Connecticut, Peter Bancroft/Dir. - Communications, Nigel Wilson/51/Dir., CFO, Anne Siddell/Company Sec., Letitia Chow Mei Lai/Dir. - Business Development, Jewellery Group, Hong Kong (*25 Officers included in Index*)

Directors: David Levin/46/Dir., Group CEO, Geoff Unwin/65/Chmn., Christopher Hyman/44/Non Exec. Dir., Adair Turner/52/Non Exec. Dir., Jonathan Newcomb/60/Non Exec. Dir., Nigel Wilson/51/Dir., CFO, John Botts/67/Non Exec. Dir., Karen Thomson/47/Non Exec. Dir., Pradeep Kar/49/Non Exec. Dir., Sandy Leitch/60/Non Exec. Dir., Charles Gregson/61/Dir.

United Capital Corp

9 Pk. Pl., Great Neck, NY, 11021; *PH:* 1-516-466-6464

General - Incorporation ....DE	Stock- Price on:12/24/2007 ....$29.05
Employees 230	Stock Exchange................................AMEX
Auditor ....Goldstein Golub Kessler LLP	Ticker Symbol.....................................AFP
Stk Agt..............Continental Stock Transfer & Trust Co	Outstanding Shares ....NA
Counsel...NA	E.P.S...$2.80
DUNS No. 05-686-4259	Shareholders.....................................NA

Business: The group's principal activities are the manufacture and sale of engineered products and investment and management of real estate. Engineered products are manufactured using knitted wire mesh, to solve the problems of high temperature, noise, vibration, emission control and filtration. Real estate and investment segment is in the business of investing in and managing real estate properties and making of high-yield, short term loans secured by desirable properties. The group also leases shopping center retail outlets, restaurants, hotels and other places to single tenants.

Primary SIC and add'l.: 3312 6531

CIK No: 0000065358

Subsidiaries: AFP Hospitality Corp., AFP Realty Corp., Metex Mfg. Corporation

Owners: A. F. Petrocelli/77.20%, Arnold S. Penner/1.60%, Michael J. Weinbaum/4.00%, Insiders/80.20%, Anthony J. Miceli/3.10%, Michael T. Lamoretti/3.50%, Robert M. Mann/1.20%, Howard M. Lorber/2.80%

Financial Data: Fiscal Year End:12/31 Latest Annual Data: 12/31/2006

Year	Sales	Net Income
2006	$65,368,000	$30,560,000
2005	$60,248,000	$14,596,000
2004	$59,061,000	$37,357,000

Curr. Assets:	$155,587,000	**Curr. Liab.:**	$15,388,000		
Plant, Equip.:	$55,722,000	**Total Liab.:**	$44,127,000	**Indic. Yr. Divd.:**	NA
Total Assets:	$223,600,000	**Net Worth:**	$179,473,000	**Debt/ Equity:**	NA

United China Acquisitions I Corp

3490 Rte. One, Building 16a, Princeton, NJ, 08540; *PH:* 1-609-514-9849

General - Incorporation ....DE	Stock- Price on:12/24/2007 ....NA
Employees ....NA	Stock Exchange..................................NA
Auditor ....Paritz & Co P.A	Ticker Symbol...................................NA
Stk Agt...NA	Outstanding Shares ....NA
Counsel...NA	E.P.S...NA
DUNS No. ....NA	Shareholders....................................NA

Business: The group's principal activity is developing our acquisition plan and raising initial capital. It is a development stage company, whose business plan is to seek, investigate, and if warranted, acquire one or more companies with significant business operations in the People's Republic of China (PRC) and to pursue other related activities intended to enhance shareholder value. The acquisition of a business opportunity may be made by purchase, merger, exchange of stock, or otherwise. The company has very limited capital, and it is unlikely that it will be able to take advantage of more than one such business opportunity.

Primary SIC and add'l.: 6770

CIK No: 0001329268

United Commerce Bancorp

211 S College Ave., Bloomington, IN, 47404; *PH:* 1-812-336-2265; *Fax:* 1-812-336-6682; *http://* www.unitedcommercebank.com

General - Incorporation	Stock- Price on:12/24/2007 ....$15.72
Employees ....NA	Stock Exchange..................................OTC
Auditor ....NA	Ticker Symbol.................................UCBN
Stk Agt...NA	Outstanding Shares ....NA
Counsel...NA	E.P.S...NA
DUNS No. ....NA	Shareholders....................................NA

Business: The groups principal activity is engaged in a general commercial and retail banking business. Services of the group include deposit services including checking, NOW, Money Market, and savings accounts, and time deposits including certificates of deposit. The group operates from the United States.

Primary SIC and add'l.: 6022

CIK No: 0001317815

United Community Banks Inc

PO Box 398, Blairsville, GA, 30514; *PH:* 1-588-807-3041; *http://* www.ucbi.com

General - Incorporation ....GA	Stock- Price on:12/24/2007 ....$26.87
Employees 1,866	Stock Exchange..................................NDQ
Auditor ....Porter Keadle Moore LLP	Ticker Symbol.................................UCBI
Stk Agt.....Computershare Investor Services LLC	Outstanding Shares 43,040,000
Counsel...........................Kilpatrick Stockton	E.P.S...$1.60
DUNS No. 85-849-1574	Shareholders....................................NA

Business: The group's principal activity is to provide a full range of community oriented retail and corporate banking services. The group conducts its operations through its wholly-owned subsidiaries, ucb Georgia and united community bank. The services provided includes checking, savings and time deposit accounts, secured and unsecured loans, wire transfers, trust services, and rental of safe deposit boxes. The group also provides consulting and advisory services for network, Internet banking and Web site development services. The group owns an insurance agency, united community insurance services, inc., formed to hold intellectual property rights such as trademarks and trade names. It operates in 87 locations of Georgia and North Carolina, United States. On 31-Mar-2003, the group acquired first central bancshares inc, on 01-May-2003, first Georgia holding inc & first Georgia bank and on 01-Jun-2004, fairbanco holding company.

Primary SIC and add'l.: 6022 6712

CIK No: 0000857855

Subsidiaries: Better Government Committee of United Community Banks, Inc., Brintech, Inc., Carolina Holdings, Inc., Carolina Investments, Inc., Fairbanco Capital Trust I, Union Holdings, Inc., Union Investments, Inc., United Community Bank, United Community Bank Tennessee, United Community Capital Trust, United Community Capital Trust II, United Community Development Corporation, United Community Insurance Services, Inc., United Community Mortgage Services, Inc., United Community Statutory Trust I

Officers: Jimmy Tallent/55/Dir., CEO, Pres./$1,533,693.00, Rex S. Schuette/CFO, Exec. VP/$778,021.00, Guy W. Freeman/Dir., Exec. VP - Banking/$964,143.00, Thomas C. Gilliland/Dir., Exec. VP, Sec., General Counsel/$605,964.00, Craig Metz/Exec. VP - Marketing, David Shearrow/Exec. VP, Chief Risk Officer

Directors: Jimmy Tallent/55/Dir., CEO, Pres., W. C. Nelson/Vice Chmn., Robert Head/Chmn., Guy W. Freeman/Dir., Exec. VP - Banking, Robert Blalock/Dir., Thomas C. Gilliland/Dir., Exec. VP, Sec., General Counsel, Clarence Mason/Dir., Zell B. Miller/Dir. Emeritus, William Bennett/Dir., Hoyt Holloway/Dir., Charles Hill/Dir., Tim Wallis/Dir., John D. Stephens/Dir.

Owners: Tim Wallis, Clarence W. Mason, Rex S. Schuette, Ray K. Williams, W.C. Nelson/4.26%, Charles E. Hill/1.26%, Insiders/15.70%, Robert Blalock, Thomas C. Gilliland/1.43%, Hoyt O. Holloway, Robert L. Head/4.32%, William A. Bennett, Jimmy C. Tallent/1.69%, Guy W. Freeman

Financial Data: *Fiscal Year End:*12/31 *Latest Annual Data:* 12/31/2006

Year	Sales	Net Income
2006	$494,565,000	$68,815,000
2005	$384,139,000	$56,742,000
2004	$277,711,000	$46,591,000

Curr. Assets:	$229,575,000	**Curr. Liab.:**	$6,371,331,000	**P/E Ratio:**	17.34
Plant, Equip.:	$139,716,000	**Total Liab.:**	$6,484,482,000	**Indic. Yr. Divd.:**	$0.360
Total Assets:	$7,101,249,000	**Net Worth:**	$616,767,000	**Debt/ Equity:**	0.1834

United Community Financial Corp

275 Federal Plz. W, Youngstown, OH, 44503; *PH:* 1-330-742-0500; *http://* www.homesavings.com; *Email:* info@homesavings.com

General		Stock	
Incorporation	OH	Price on:12/24/2007	$10.7
Employees	807	Stock Exchange	NDQ
Auditor	Crowe Chizek & Co. LLC	Ticker Symbol	UCFC
Stk Agt	Registrar & Transfer Co	Outstanding Shares	30,650,000
Counsel	Vorys, Sater, Seymour & Pease	E.P.S	$0.58
DUNS No.	01-970-5800	Shareholders	NA

Business: The group's principal activity is to provide consumer and business banking services in Ohio and western Pennsylvania. The services include origination of mortgage loans on one- to four-family residential real estate, loans secured by nonresidential real estate, commercial loans and consumer loans, including home equity loans, education loans, loans secured by savings accounts, motor vehicles, boats and recreational vehicles and unsecured loans. Deposit services include savings account, checking accounts, certificate of deposits and other non-interest bearing deposits. Investment advisory services include investment brokerage services and a network of integrated financial services. At 31-Dec-2003, the group operated through 35 full-service banking branches and six loan production offices.

Primary SIC and add'l.: 6036 6712

CIK No: 0000707886

Subsidiaries: Butler Wick Corp., The Home Savings and Loan Company of Youngstown, Ohio

Officers: Douglas M. Mckay/Chmn., CEO/$711,137.00, Patrick W. Bevack/61/COO, Pres. - Home Savings/$402,552.00, Bryan Ignazio/Mgr. - Branch Sales, Richard Michaels/Assist. VP, Branch Sales Mgr., Patti Davis/Mgr. - Customer Service, Morgan Stanley/Assist. VP, Branch Sales Mgr., Kathy R. Lake/Assist. VP, Branch Sales Mgr., Jane Hepler/Mgr. - Customer Service, Jessica Gonzalez/Mortgage Loan Specialist, Stacey Wolcott/Mgr. - Customer Service, Tim Linich/Mortgage Loan Specialist, Norman Wise/Mortgage Loan Specialist, Jeff Kolenic/Mortgage Loan Specialist, Stephanie Elick/Mgr. - Branch Sales, Patty Young/Mgr. - Customer Service *(58 Officers included in Index)*

Directors: Douglas M. Mckay/Chmn., CEO, Thomas J. Cavalier/Dir., Clarence R. Smith/Dir., David C. Sweet/Dir., Richard J. Buoncore/Dir., Donald J. Varner/76/Dir., Richard J. Schiraldi/Dir., David G. Lodge/Dir., COO, Pres., Eugenia C. Atkinson/Dir.

Owners: Thomas J. Cavalier, Douglas M. McKay/1.70%, Eugenia C. Atkinson, David C. Sweet, Donald J. Varner, Clarence R. Smith, Patrick A. Kelly/1.50%, David G. Lodge, United Community Financial Corp./12.60%, Richard J. Schiraldi, Dimensional Fund Advisors, Inc/8.50%, Insiders/5.70%, Patrick W. Bevack

Financial Data: *Fiscal Year End:*12/31 *Latest Annual Data:* 12/31/2006

Year	Sales	Net Income
2006	$205,767,000	$24,111,000
2005	$174,334,000	$23,197,000
2004	$149,600,000	$17,865,000

Curr. Assets:	$60,126,000	**Curr. Liab.:**	$2,404,741,000	**P/E Ratio:**	13.90
Plant, Equip.:	$28,434,000	**Total Liab.:**	$2,422,212,000	**Indic. Yr. Divd.:**	$0.380
Total Assets:	$2,703,545,000	**Net Worth:**	$281,333,000	**Debt/ Equity:**	NA

United Energy Corp

600 Meadowlands Pkwy, Secaucus, NJ, 07094; *PH:* 1-208-842-0288; *http://* www.unitedenergycorp.net; *Email:* sales@unitedenergycorp.net

General		Stock	
Incorporation	NV	Price on:12/24/2007	$0.545
Employees	11	Stock Exchange	OTC
Auditor	Imowitz Koenig & Co. LLP	Ticker Symbol	UNRG
Stk Agt	Interstate Transfer Company	Outstanding Shares	31,030,000
Counsel	Seaman & Wehle, Attorneys	E.P.S	-$0.07
DUNS No.	NA	Shareholders	NA

Business: The group's principal activities are to develop, manufacture and market environmentally safe specialty chemical products. The principal products of the group includes kh-30(R) oil well cleaner and related products and uniproof(R) used to produce proofing paper or blue line paper. The group's major customers include the alameda company, uniproof(R) paper distributor, general services administration and defense supply center (combined) for aircraft cleaning products and paint removers, two oil field service companies for the group's kh-30(R) and kx-91(R) oil well cleaning products.

Primary SIC and add'l.: 2672 2869

CIK No: 0001116734

Subsidiaries: Green Globe Industries Inc., Nor Industries Inc.

Officers: Robert Guinta/Investor Relations Contact

Owners: Louis Bernstein, James McKeever, Andrea Pampanini, Brian King/3.90%, Ronald Wilen/13.10%, Jack Silver/10.10%, Joseph J. Grano/7.90%, Martin Rappaport/9.50%, Insiders/25.40%

Financial Data: *Fiscal Year End:*03/31 *Latest Annual Data:* 03/31/2007

Year	Sales	Net Income
2007	$812,000	-$2,273,000
2006	$492,000	-$10,837,000
2005	$1,851,000	-$1,855,000

Curr. Assets:	$3,200,000	**Curr. Liab.:**	$477,000		
Plant, Equip.:	$88,000	**Total Liab.:**	$477,000	**Indic. Yr. Divd.:**	NA
Total Assets:	$3,653,000	**Net Worth:**	$3,176,000	**Debt/ Equity:**	NA

United Financial Banking Cos Inc

8399 Leesburg Pike, Vienna, VA, 22182; *PH:* 1-703-734-0070; *Fax:* 1-703-556-0654; *http://* www.businessbankva.com

General		Stock	
Incorporation	VA	Price on:12/24/2007	$30
Employees	63	Stock Exchange	OTC
Auditor	Goodman & Co. LLP	Ticker Symbol	UFBC
Stk Agt	NA	Outstanding Shares	1,090,000
Counsel	NA	E.P.S	$1.33
DUNS No.	11-621-1228	Shareholders	NA

Business: The group's principal activity is to provide banking services to business and professional customers through its subsidiaries. The services include the usual deposit functions of commercial banks, now accounts and savings accounts business and commercial loans and processing of collections. The group markets its services to professionals and small and medium sized businesses in its service area of northern Virginia and surrounding communities.

Primary SIC and add'l.: 6712 6022

CIK No: 0000714286

Subsidiaries: Business Venture Capital, Inc., The Business Bank, The Business Bank Insurance Agency, Inc., UFBC Capital Trust I, United Facilities LLC, United Title LLC

Officers: Harold C. Rauner/Chmn., CEO, Pres., Member - Advisory Board, Michael P. Mullen/Chmn. - Advisory Board, Robert E. Carpenter/Dir. - Consultant, Sharon A. Stakes/Dir., Exec. VP, Assist. Sec., Laurence Baker/Exec. VP, Lisa M. Porter/CFO, Gail Edmonds/Sr. VP, Marcus Perry/Sr. VP, Robert Barton/Contact - Commercial Loans, Services, Larry Baker/Contact - Commercial Loans, Services, Lori Davis/Contact - Commercial Loans, Services, Elaine Tomaseski/VP - Bankers Insurance, LLC, Brenda Tucker/Contact - Consumer Loans, Services, Mgr. Mclean Office, Tracy Murphy/Contact - Consumer Loans, Services, Mgr. Reston Office, Donna Wilson/Contact - Consumer Loans, Services, Mgr. Vienna Office *(18 Officers included in Index)*

Directors: Harold C. Rauner/Chmn., CEO, Pres., Member - Advisory Board, Manuel V. Fernandez/Vice Chmn., Jeffrey T. Valcourt/Vice Chmn., Charles S. Evans/Dir., Robert W. Pitts/Dir., John R. Motz/Dir., Robert E. Carpenter/Dir. - Consultant, Carl F. Desmarais/Member - Advisory Board, Dean M. Xenos/Member - Advisory Board, Laura Degnon/Member - Advisory Board, Dennis I. Meyer/Dir. - Baker, Mckenzie, Sr. Counsel, Melinda Gaertner/Member - Advisory Board, Casey Veatch/Member - Advisory Board, Sharon A. Stakes/Dir., Exec. VP, Assist. Sec., Charles W. Bray/Member - Advisory Board *(16 Directors included in Index)*

Financial Data: *Fiscal Year End:*12/31 *Latest Annual Data:* 12/31/2005

Year	Sales	Net Income
2005	$11,945,000	$1,365,000
2004	$8,867,000	$1,170,000
2003	$7,236,000	$831,000

Curr. Assets:	$13,455,000	**Curr. Liab.:**	$183,815,000	**P/E Ratio:**	22.56
Plant, Equip.:	$2,568,000	**Total Liab.:**	$190,720,000	**Indic. Yr. Divd.:**	NA
Total Assets:	$205,811,000	**Net Worth:**	$15,090,000	**Debt/ Equity:**	NA

United Financial Corp

120 1st Ave. N, Great Falls, MT, 59403; *PH:* 1-406-727-6106; *http://* www.ufcmontana.com

General		Stock	
Incorporation	MN	Price on:12/24/2007	NA
Employees	126	Stock Exchange	NA
Auditor	McGladrey & Pullen LLP	Ticker Symbol	NA
Stk Agt	NA	Outstanding Shares	NA
Counsel	NA	E.P.S	NA
DUNS No.	63-728-208	Shareholders	NA

Business: The group's principal activities are to provide banking services to individual and corporate customers. Heritage bank and valley bancorp inc. Are the subsidiaries of the group. The loans offered by the group include real estate loans, commercial, agricultural and commercial loans. The deposits accepted by the group include now accounts, money market accounts, regular savings accounts, certificates of deposit and retirement savings plans. The group has operations only in the United States.

Primary SIC and add'l.: 6712 6035

CIK No: 0001011309

Subsidiaries: Heritage Bank, United FinancialMontana Capital Trust I

United Fire & Casualty Co

118 2nd Ave. SE, Cedar Rapids, IA, 52407; *PH:* 1-319-399-5700; *Fax:* 1-319-399-5499; *http://* www.unitedfiregroup.com

General		Stock	
Incorporation	IA	Price on:12/24/2007	$35.58
Employees	645	Stock Exchange	NDQ
Auditor	Ernst & Young LLP	Ticker Symbol	UFCS
Stk Agt	Computershare Investor Services LLC	Outstanding Shares	27,650,000
Counsel	Bradley & Riley P.C	E.P.S	$4.12
DUNS No.	00-530-2724	Shareholders	NA

Business: The group's principal activities are underwriting of property, casualty and life insurance. The group writes both personal and commercial lines of insurance. Personal lines are composed of automobile, homeowners, recreational vehicles, watercraft, dwelling fire and umbrella policies. The majority of commercial insurance consists of business packages, which include property, liability, inland marine, commercial automobile, workers' compensation and umbrella. The group also writes fidelity and surety bonds. The group underwrites and markets single-premium whole life insurance, term life and universal life insurance, annuities, credit life insurance and individual disability income.

Primary SIC and add'l.: 6311 6331

CIK No: 0000101199

Subsidiaries: Addison Insurance Company, American Indemnity Company, American Indemnity Financial Corporation, Lafayette Insurance Company, Texas General Indemnity Company, United Fire & Indemnity Company, United Fire Lloyds, United Life Insurance Company

Officers: Randy A. Ramlo/CEO, Pres., Michael T. Wilkins/Exec. VP, Dianne M. Lyons/CFO, VP, Stanley A. Wiebold/63/VP - Midwest Regional Office, Galen E. Underwood/67/Treasurer, Dave Hellen/Branch Mgr., John R. Cruise/66/VP - Reinsurance, David A. Lange/50/Corp. Sec. - Fidelity, Surety Claims Mgr., Brian S. Berta/43/VP - Great Lakes Regional Office, Neal R. Scharmer/VP, General Counsel, Corp. Sec., John A. Rife/Dir., Pres. - United Life Ins Co, David E. Conner/VP, Chief Claims Officer, Barrie W. Ernst/VP, Chief Investment Officer

Directors: Scott J. McIntyre/Chmn., Frank S. Wilkinson/Dir., John A. Rife/Dir., Pres. - United Life Ins Co, Christopher R. Drahozal/Dir., Jack B. Evans/Dir., Thomas W. Hanley/Dir., Casey D. Mahon/Dir., George D. Milligan/Dir., Mary K. Quass/Dir., Byron G. Riley/Dir., Kyle D. Skogman/Dir.

Owners: George D. Milligan, Randy A. Ramlo/0.04%, Dianne M. Lyons/0.02%, Kent G. Baker, Christopher R. Drahozal/1.50%, Scott McIntyre/18.93%, Kyle D. Skogman, Mary K. Quass, Insiders/20.84%, Jack B. Evans, John A. Rife/0.14%, Barrie W. Ernst/0.07%, Byron G. Riley, Thomas W. Hanley, EARNEST Partners LLC/8.42% *(17 Owners included in Index)*

Financial Data: **Fiscal Year End:**12/31 **Latest Annual Data:** 12/31/2006

Year	Sales	Net Income
2006	$635,600,000	$88,085,000
2005	$619,605,000	$9,044,000
2004	$608,125,000	$78,817,000

Curr. Assets:	$491,055,000	**Curr. Liab.:**	$67,690,000	**P/E Ratio:**	8.39
Plant, Equip.:	$12,663,000	**Total Liab.:**	$2,095,259,000	**Indic. Yr. Divd.:**	$0.600
Total Assets:	$2,776,067,000	**Net Worth:**	$680,808,000	**Debt/ Equity:**	NA

United Fuel & Energy Corp

13431 Beach Ave., Marina Del Rey, CA, 90292; ***PH:*** 1-310-825-2200; ***http://*** www.ufeonline.com

General - Incorporation	NV	**Stock**- Price on:12/24/2007	$1.5
Employees	262	Stock Exchange	OTC
Auditor	Johnson Miller & Co. CPAs Pc	Ticker Symbol	UFEN
Stk Agt	Pacific Stock Transfer Company	Outstanding Shares	14,790,000
Counsel	NA	E.P.S	$0.09
DUNS No.	NA	Shareholders	NA

Business: The group's principal activity is to provide branded consumer products from nationally recognized retailers through the television. The group provides television time, production, and distribution to nationally branded retailers who in turn will provide the branded products and entertainment for the channel.

Primary SIC and add'l.: 5012

CIK No: 0001137031

Subsidiaries: Eddins-Walcher Company, Three D Oil of Kilgore, Inc, United Fuel - Texas

Officers: Charles McArthur/52/Dir., CEO, Pres./$516,375.00, Bobby W. Page/CFO, VP/$342,480.00, Lawrence L. Merworth/VP - Operations/$174,699.00, Michael Blake Foy/VP - Sales, Marketing/$110,478.00, Dexter B. Woodworth/VP - Information Services, Sal Rivera/Contact - United Fuel, Energy Trading, Richard Rodriguez/Contact - United Fuel, Energy Trading

Directors: Charles McArthur/52/Dir., CEO, Pres., Thomas E. Kelly/Chmn., Michael B. Chadwick/55/Dir., E. H. Dewhurst/60/Dir., Jesse B. Tutor/60/Dir.

Owners: Jesse B. Tutor, Falcon Seaboard Investment Company, L.P., Kelcy Warren, Insiders, Penninsula Fund, JVL Global Energy (QP), L.P., Quattro Global Capital, LLC, Bobby W. Page, Tamalpais Asset Management, L.P., Belridge Advisors, Michael S. Chadwick, E. H. Dewhurst, Charles McArthur, Thomas E. Kelly, Michael Blake Foy *(17 Owners included in Index)*

Financial Data: **Fiscal Year End:**12/31 **Latest Annual Data:** 12/31/2006

Year	Sales	Net Income
2006	$335,741,000	$1,987,000
2005	$283,588,000	$879,000
2004	NA	-$127,000

Curr. Assets:	$65,692,000	**Curr. Liab.:**	$22,839,000	**P/E Ratio:**	16.67
Plant, Equip.:	$22,972,000	**Total Liab.:**	$72,480,000	**Indic. Yr. Divd.:**	NA
Total Assets:	$94,175,000	**Net Worth:**	$21,695,000	**Debt/ Equity:**	2.0215

United Guardian Inc

230 Marcus Blvd, Hauppauge, NY, 11788; ***PH:*** 1-631-273-0900; ***http://*** www.u-g.com

General - Incorporation	DE	**Stock**- Price on:12/24/2007	$13.01
Employees	41	Stock Exchange	AMEX
Auditor	Eisner LLP	Ticker Symbol	UG
Stk Agt	Continental Stock Transfer & Trust Co	Outstanding Shares	4,940,000
Counsel.. Wolf Block Schorr & Solis-Cohen LLP		E.P.S	$0.679
DUNS No.	05-059-4555	Shareholders	NA

Business: The group's principal activities are to conduct the research, product development, manufacturing and marketing of cosmetic ingredients, personal and health care products, pharmaceuticals and specialty industrial products. The group also distributes a line of over 3,000 fine organic chemicals, research chemicals, test solutions, indicators, dyes and reagents. The operations are carried out through two subsidiaries: guardian laboratories division and eastern chemical corporation. The products include lubrajel(R), renacidin(R), clorpactin(R) and klensoft(tm). The customers of the group include drug wholesalers, drug stores, surgical supply houses, hospitals, physicians and other manufacturers. The products are sold in the United States, Canada, Europe, Asia, South America and Central America.

Primary SIC and add'l.: 2869 2834 8731 2844 5047 2833

CIK No: 0000101295

Subsidiaries: Eastern Chemical Corporation, Paragon Organic Chemicals, Inc.

Officers: Alfred R. Globus/Chmn., CEO/$145,189.00, Peter A. Hiltunen/VP, Production Mgr., Andrew A. Boccone/Dir., Independent Business Consultant, Robert S. Rubinger/Dir., Exec. VP, Sec., Treasurer, Dir. - Product Development/$160,962.00, Cecile M. Brophy/Treasurer, Controller, Derek Hampson/VP, Kenneth H. Globus/Dir. CFO, Pres., General Counsel/$278,784.00, Joseph J. Vernice/VP - Research, Development Mgr., Dir. - Technical Services, Charles W. Castanza/Dir., Sr. VP, Dir. - Plant Operations/$138,957.00

Directors: Alfred R. Globus/Chmn., CEO, Andrew A. Boccone/Dir., Independent Business Consultant, Robert S. Rubinger/Dir., Exec. VP, Sec., Treasurer, Dir. - Product Development, Arthur M. Dresner/Dir., Kenneth H. Globus/Dir. CFO, Pres., General Counsel, Lawrence F. Maietta/Dir., Christopher W. Nolan/Dir., Henry P. Globus/Dir., Charles W. Castanza/Dir., Sr. VP, Dir. - Plant Operations

Owners: Banque Carnegie Luxembourg S.A./5.40%, Lawrence F. Maietta, Insiders/42.80%, Arthur M. Dresner, Henry P. Globus, Irwin Uran/11.30%, Alfred R. Globus/25.90%, Kenneth H. Globus/16.00%, Robert S. Rubinger, Charles W. Castanza

Financial Data: **Fiscal Year End:**12/31 **Latest Annual Data:** 12/31/2006

Year	Sales	Net Income
2006	$12,196,000	$2,737,000
2005	$12,135,000	$2,617,000
2004	$11,123,000	$2,475,000

Curr. Assets:	$14,947,000	**Curr. Liab.:**	$1,963,000	**P/E Ratio:**	19.16
Plant, Equip.:	$849,000	**Total Liab.:**	$2,718,000	**Indic. Yr. Divd.:**	$0.540
Total Assets:	$15,944,000	**Net Worth:**	$13,226,000	**Debt/ Equity:**	0.0009

United Heritage Corp

2 Caddo St., Cleburne, TX, 76031; ***PH:*** 1-817-643-6811; ***http://*** www.unitedheritagecorp.com; ***Email:*** uhcp@aol.com

General - Incorporation	UT	**Stock**- Price on:12/24/2007	$0.8097
Employees	7	Stock Exchange	NDQ
Auditor	Weaver & Tidwell LLP	Ticker Symbol	UHCP
Stk Agt	Computershare Trust Co	Outstanding Shares	6,450,000
Counsel	MC Development LLC	E.P.S	-$1.36
DUNS No.	05-326-6193	Shareholders	NA

Business: The group's principle activities are to explore and develop oil and gas properties and to distribute meat products. The group operates its businesses through its wholly owned subsidiaries, national heritage sales corporation (national), uhc petroleum corporation (petroleum), uhc petroleum services corporation (services) and uhc New Mexico corporation (New Mexico). The group operates in two segments: oil and gas and meat. New Mexico and services are engaged in activities related to the oil and gas industry. Petroleum holds leases to approximately 10,500 acres of oil and gases interests in south Texas that produce from the val verde basin. New Mexico holds properties in the southeastern New Mexico portion of the permian basin. Services act as the field operator for the oil and gas properties located in Texas. National supplies meat and poultry products to retail food stores.

Primary SIC and add'l.: 1311 2011

CIK No: 0000354567

Subsidiaries: National Heritage Sales Corporation, UHC New Mexico Corporation, UHC Petroleum Corporation, UHC Petroleum Services Corporation

Officers: Scott C. Wilson/56/Dir., CEO, Pres., Kenneth Levy/61/Dir., CFO, Sec.

Directors: Scott C. Wilson/56/Dir., CEO, Pres., Kenneth Levy/61/Dir., CFO, Sec., Thomas Kelly/53/Dir., Raoul J. Baxter/59/Dir., Franz A. Skryanz/70/Dir.

Owners: Thomas Kelly, Scott C. Wilson/7.56%, Lothian Oil Inc./71.01%

Financial Data: **Fiscal Year End:**03/31 **Latest Annual Data:** 03/31/2007

Year	Sales	Net Income
2007	$1,015,000	-$11,435,000
2006	$602,000	-$17,371,000
2005	$538,000	-$813,000

Curr. Assets:	$2,209,000	**Curr. Liab.:**	$3,427,000		
Plant, Equip.:	$5,948,000	**Total Liab.:**	$9,180,000	**Indic. Yr. Divd.:**	NA
Total Assets:	$9,984,000	**Net Worth:**	$804,000	**Debt/ Equity:**	NA

United Industrial Corp

124 Industry Ln., Hunt Valley, MD, 21030; ***PH:*** 1-410-628-8786; ***http://*** www.unitedindustrial.com

General - Incorporation	DE	**Stock**- Price on:12/24/2007	$65.57
Employees	2,316	Stock Exchange	NYSE
Auditor	KPMG LLP	Ticker Symbol	UIC
Stk Agt..... American Stock Transfer & Trust Co.		Outstanding Shares	10,510,000
Counsel	Proskauer Rose LLP	E.P.S	$3.53
DUNS No.	00-152-7852	Shareholders	NA

Business: The group's principal activity is the provision of military electronics and aerospace systems and components under defense contracts. The group operates under two segments, defense and energy systems. The defense products include unmanned aerial vehicles, training and simulation systems, automated aircraft test and maintenance equipment, and combat vehicles and ordnance systems. The energy segments manufactures combustion equipment for biomass and refuse fuels.

Primary SIC and add'l.: 3812 3433

CIK No: 0000101271

Subsidiaries: Aai / Acl Technologies Europe Limited, Aai / Acl Technologies,inc., AAI Australia Pty Ltd., AAI Corporation, AAI Services Corporation, Detroit Stoker Company, ESL Defence (Holding) Ltd., ESL Defence Limited

Officers: Frederick M. Strader/Dir., CEO, Pres./$1,280,655.00, James H. Perry/CFO, VP, Controller/$545,893.00, Jonathan A. Greenberg/VP, General Counsel, Sec., Chief Compliance, Ethics Officer/$558,117.00, Robert J. Peters/VP - Business Development, Training Systems, AAI Corporation, Edward E. Buffington/VP - Test Systems, AAI Corporation, Austin T. Malooly/Assist. Treasurer - AAI Corporation, Paul Lavin/Pres. - AAI Services Corporation, David A. Phillips/VP - Advanced Programs, AAI Corporation, Steven E. Reid/VP - Unmanned Aircraft Systems, AAI Corporation, Francis X. Reinhardt/Assist. Treasurer, Cynthia A. Eaton/Assist. Sec., Kathleen T. Heydt/VP - Internal Audit, Stuart F. Gray/Treasurer/$241,795.00, Susan E. Pendery/Assist., Sec., Gary S. Crampton/VP - Tax *(21 Officers included in Index)*

Directors: Frederick M. Strader/Dir., CEO, Pres., Warren G. Lichtenstein/Chmn., Thomas A. Corcoran/Dir., Glen M. Kassan/Dir., Robert F. Mehmel/Dir., Richard I. Neal/Dir.

Owners: Frederick M. Strader/2.20%, Friess Associates LLC/5.50%, Steel Partners II, L.P./18.40%, Glen M. Kassan, Robert F. Mehmel, John F. Michitsch, James H. Perry/1.00%, Stuart F. Gray, Jonathan A. Greenberg, Thomas A. Corcoran, Insiders/22.40%, Warren G. Lichtenstein/18.70%, Richard I. Neal, Michael A. Boden, Goldman Sachs Asset Management L.P./9.60%

Financial Data: **Fiscal Year End:**12/31 **Latest Annual Data:** 12/31/2006

Year	Sales	Net Income
2006	NA	NA
2005	NA	NA
2004	NA	NA

Curr. Assets:	$207,292,000	**Curr. Liab.:**	$120,592,000	**P/E Ratio:**	18.58
Plant, Equip.:	$47,042,000	**Total Liab.:**	$295,341,000	**Indic. Yr. Divd.:**	$0.400
Total Assets:	$358,640,000	**Net Worth:**	$63,299,000	**Debt/ Equity:**	4.3584

United Medicorp Inc

10210 N Central Exprwy, Ste 400, Dallas, TX, 75231; *PH:* 1-972-926-4950;
http:// www.umcinc.com; *Email:* pseaman@umcinc.com

General - Incorporation	DE	*Stock*- Price on:12/24/2007	$0.05
Employees	41	Stock Exchange	OTC
Auditor	KBA Group LLP	Ticker Symbol	UMCN
Stk Agt..... American Stock Transfer & Trust Co.		Outstanding Shares	30,770,000
Counsel	NA	E.P.S.	-$0.01
DUNS No.	55-550-3473	Shareholders	NA

Business: The group's principal activities are to provide medical insurance claims processing and accounts receivable management services primarily to hospitals, medical clinics and physician practices. The medical claims processing service is designed to provide electronic claims processing, billing and collection service. The group expedites payment of claims from private insurance carriers or government payors such as medicare and medicaid. The other services offered include processing and collection of uncollected backlog claims. The major customers include presbyterian healthcare services of New Mexico, valley baptist medical center, inova health services and brownsville surgical hospital.

Primary SIC and add'l.: 8099 7322

CIK No: 0000831460

Subsidiaries: Hospital Systems, Inc.

Officers: Pete Seaman/Chmn., CEO - United Medicorp, Inc, Nathan Porterfield/Marketing Specialist

Directors: Pete Seaman/Chmn., CEO - United Medicorp, Inc

Financial Data: *Fiscal Year End:*12/31 *Latest Annual Data:* 12/31/2005

Year		Sales		Net Income
2005		$2,794,000		-$102,000
2004		$4,099,000		$338,000
2003		$3,901,000		$288,000
Curr. Assets:	$975,000	*Curr. Liab.:*	$400,000	
Plant, Equip.:	$387,000	*Total Liab.:*	$634,000	*Indic. Yr. Divd.:* NA
Total Assets:	$1,462,000	*Net Worth:*	$827,000	*Debt/ Equity:* 0.2875

United Microelectronics Corp

488 DeGuigne Dr., Sunnyvale, CA, 94085; *PH:* 1-408-523-7800; *Fax:* 1-408-733-8090;
http:// www.umc.com; *Email:* sales@umc.com

General - Incorporation	Taiwan	*Stock*- Price on:12/24/2007	$3.55
Employees	13,265	Stock Exchange	NYSE
Auditor	Diwan, Ernst & Young	Ticker Symbol	UMC
Stk Agt.	Horizon Securities	Outstanding Shares	3,560,000,000
Counsel	Simpson Thacher & Bartlett LLP	E.P.S.	$0.21
DUNS No.	NA	Shareholders	NA

Business: The group's principal activities are design, manufacture and sale of integrated circuits and related electronics and semiconductor products. Other activity includes provision of wafer foundry and investing services. Operations are carried out in Taiwan, the United States of America, Asia, Europe and other countries.

Primary SIC and add'l.: 3577 3674

CIK No: 0001033767

Subsidiaries: Fortune Venture Capital Corp., Hsun Chieh Investment Co., Ltd., Thintek Optronics Corp., TLC Capital Co., Ltd, UMC Capital Corporation, UMC Group, UMC Japan, UMCi Ltd., United Microdisplay Optronics Corp., United Microelectronics (Europe) B.V., United Microelectronics Corp.

Officers: Jackson Hu/Chmn., CEO, Peter Courture/Chief Strategic Officer, Peter Chang/Sr. Consultant, Fu-Tai Liou/Pres., Pres. - QA, RT&A, Tzyy-Jang Tseng/58/Supervisor, Tsing-Yuan Hwang/Supervisor, Frank Wen/Pres., Stan Hung/Sr. VP, Shih-Wei Sun/COO, Chitung Liu/42/CFO, Ta-Sing Wang/35/Supervisor

Directors: Jackson Hu/Chmn., CEO, John Hsuan/Vice Chmn. Emeritus, Jack K.C. Wang/Dir., Mao-Chung Lin/Dir., Paul S.C. Hsu/Dir., Ching-Chang Wen/Dir., Chung-Laung Liu/74/Dir., Chun-Yen Chang/71/Dir.

Owners: Hsun Chieh Investment Co., Ltd./3.20%, Xilinx, Inc., Insiders/6.15%, Silicon Integrated Systems Corp./2.30%

Financial Data: *Fiscal Year End:*12/31 *Latest Annual Data:* 12/31/2006

Year		Sales		Net Income
2006		$3,436,754,000		$668,817,000
2005		$3,058,414,000		-$477,725,000
2004		$4,070,282,000		-$448,546,000
Curr. Assets:	$4,060,864,000	*Curr. Liab.:*	$1,107,818,000	*P/E Ratio:* 18.18
Plant, Equip.:	$4,658,734,000	*Total Liab.:*	$2,510,418,000	*Indic. Yr. Divd.:* $0.190
Total Assets:	$12,457,089,000	*Net Worth:*	$9,946,671,000	*Debt/ Equity:* NA

United Natural Foods Inc

260 Lake Rd., Dayville, CT, 06241; ; *http://* www.unfi.com; *Email:* info@unfi.com

General - Incorporation	DE	*Stock*- Price on:12/24/2007	$27.54
Employees	4,500	Stock Exchange	NDQ
Auditor	KPMG LLP	Ticker Symbol	UNFI
Stk Agt.	Continental Stock Transfer & Trust Co	Outstanding Shares	42,820,000
Counsel	Cameron & Mittleman LLP	E.P.S.	$1.20
DUNS No.	94-355-6183	Shareholders	NA

Business: The groups principle activity is to distribute natural food and related products including nutritional supplements, personal care items and organic produce. In the year 2007, the group acquired Organic Brands LLC. In the year 2007, the group merged with Millbrook Distribution Services, Inc. The group operates from United States.

Primary SIC and add'l.: 5142 5999 5141 5411

CIK No: 0001020859

Subsidiaries: Alberts Organics,Inc., d/b/a Hershey Imports Company,Inc., Natural Retail Group,Inc., Nutrasource,Inc., Rainbow Natural Foods,Inc., Select Nutrition Distributors,Inc., Stow Mills,Inc., United Natural Foods Pennsylvania,Inc., United Natural Foods West,Inc., United Natural Trading,Inc. Co., United Natural Transportation Co., United Northeast LLC

Officers: Michael S. Funk/Dir., CEO, Pres., Thomas A. Dziki/VP - Sustainable Development, Gary Glenn/VP - Information Technology, Daniel V. Atwood/Exec. VP, Chief Marketing Officer, Pres. - United Natural Brands, Richard Antonelli/Dir., COO, Exec. VP, Pres. - Distribution, Michael D. Beaudry/Pres. - Eastern Region, Randle E. Lindberg/Pres. - Western Region, Mark E. Shamber/CFO, VP, Treasurer, Carrie Walker/Corporate Assist. Sec., Denise Friedman/Contact - Customer Inquiries, Leeanne Parker/Contact - Foodservice, Others, Melody Meyer/Contact - Produce Inquiries, National, Jay Bambara/Import Mgr. - International, Vince Thaner/Sr. Buyer, Domestic, Hershey Import Company, Gale Hogan/Contact - New Customer Inquiries *(18 Officers included in Index)*

Directors: Michael S. Funk/Dir., CEO, Pres., Thomas B. Simone/Chmn., Peter Roy/Dir., Gordon D. Barker/Dir., Richard Antonelli/Dir., COO, Exec. VP, Pres. - Distribution, Gail A. Graham/Dir., James P. Heffernan/Dir., Joseph M. Cianciolo/Dir.

Owners: Gordon D. Barker/0.20%, Michael D. Beaudry/0.10%, Randle E. Lindberg, Munder Capital Management/5.70%, Joseph M. Cianciolo/0.10%, Peter Roy, Employee Stock Ownership Trust/6.40%, Daniel V. Atwood/0.70%, Gail A. Graham, Insiders/2.30%, Michael S. Funk/0.30%, Richard Antonelli/0.10%, Mark E. Shamber/0.10%, Thomas B. Simone/0.40%, Gary A. Glenn/0.10% *(18 Owners included in Index)*

Financial Data: *Fiscal Year End:*07/31 *Latest Annual Data:* 07/28/2007

Year		Sales		Net Income
2007		$2,754,280,000		$50,153,000
2006		$2,433,594,000		$43,277,000
2005		$2,059,568,000		$41,572,000
Curr. Assets:	$402,894,000	*Curr. Liab.:*	$283,509,000	*P/E Ratio:* 23.74
Plant, Equip.:	$167,909,000	*Total Liab.:*	$355,739,000	*Indic. Yr. Divd.:* NA
Total Assets:	$651,258,000	*Net Worth:*	$295,519,000	*Debt/ Equity:* 0.1636

United Online Inc

21301 Burbank Blvd, Woodland Hills, CA, 91367; *PH:* 1-818-287-3000; *http://* www.unitedonline.net

General - Incorporation	DE	*Stock*- Price on:12/24/2007	$16.775
Employees	1,006	Stock Exchange	NDQ
Auditor	PricewaterhouseCoopers LLP	Ticker Symbol	UNTD
Stk Agt	U.S. Stock Transfer Corp	Outstanding Shares	66,730,000
Counsel	NA	E.P.S.	$0.70
DUNS No.	NA	Shareholders	NA

Business: The group's principal activity is to provide free and value-priced Internet access and e-mail. Internet access services are currently offered through the group's netzero and juno subsidiaries under their brands. These services are available in more than 6,500 cities across the United States and Canada. The group also offers marketers a variety of online advertising products, including online market research and measurement services. At 30-Jun-2003, the group had 2.5 million subscribers to its pay Internet access services and approximately 5.2 million active users. The group acquired certain assets of bluelight llc in fiscal year 2003.

Primary SIC and add'l.: 7379 7375 7331

CIK No: 0001142701

Subsidiaries: Classmates Online, Inc., Juno Online Services Development Private Limited, Juno Online Services, Inc., NetBrands, Inc., NetZero, Inc., United Online Advertising Network, Inc., United Online Communications, Inc., United Online Web Services, Inc.

Officers: Mark R. Goldston/Chmn., CEO, Pres./$5,746,891.00, Robert Taragan/Exec. VP - Operations, GM - Cybertarget, Frederic A. Randall/Exec. VP, General Counsel, Sec./$2,034,213.00, Charles S. Hilliard/44/Pres./$2,445,585.00, Gerald J. Popek/CTO, Exec. VP/$1,327,093.00, Jeremy Helfand/Exec. VP, Chief Sales Officer, Matt Wisk/Corporate Exec. VP, Chief Marketing Officer/$1,778,848.00, Scott Matulis/VP - Corporate Communications, Paul E. Jordan/Exec. VP, Chief Personnel Officer, Scott H. Ray/CFO, Exec. VP, Erik Randerson/VP - Investor Relations

Directors: Mark R. Goldston/Chmn., CEO, Pres., Robert Berglass/Dir., Ken Coleman/Dir., James T. Armstrong/Dir., Dennis Holt/Dir., Carol A. Scott/Dir., Kenneth L. Coleman/65/Dir.

Owners: Matthew J. Wisk, Robert Berglass, Kenneth L. Coleman, Frederic A. Randall, Entities Affiliated with Barclays/6.90%, James T. Armstrong, Gerald J. Popek, Dennis Holt, Mark R. Goldston/5.10%, Carol A. Scott, Charles S. Hilliard/1.40%, Morgan Stanley/5.80%, Insiders/8.60%, Putnam LLC/5.80%

Financial Data: *Fiscal Year End:*12/31 *Latest Annual Data:* 12/31/2006

Year		Sales		Net Income
2006		$522,654,000		$42,272,000
2005		$525,061,000		$47,127,000
2004		$448,617,000		$117,480,000
Curr. Assets:	$219,719,000	*Curr. Liab.:*	$145,070,000	*P/E Ratio:* 26.42
Plant, Equip.:	$34,296,000	*Total Liab.:*	$156,053,000	*Indic. Yr. Divd.:* $0.800
Total Assets:	$503,019,000	*Net Worth:*	$346,966,000	*Debt/ Equity:* NA

United Panam Financial Corp

18191 Von Karman Ave., Ste. 300, Irvine, CA, 92612; ; *http://* www.upfc.com

General - Incorporation	CA	*Stock*- Price on:12/24/2007	$15.8
Employees	954	Stock Exchange	NDQ
Auditor	Grobstein, Horwath & Co. LLP	Ticker Symbol	UPFC
Stk Agt	U.S. Stock Transfer Corp	Outstanding Shares	15,850,000
Counsel	NA	E.P.S.	$0.71
DUNS No.	01-840-8315	Shareholders	NA

Business: The group's principle activities are to originate and acquire for investment automobile installment sales and insurance premium contracts. The group has three operating segments: auto finance, insurance premium finance and banking. The auto finance segment acquires, holds for investment and services, retail automobile installment sales contracts. The insurance premium finance underwrites and finances automobile and commercial insurance premium. The banking segment operates a federal savings bank and is the principal funding source for the auto and insurance premium finance segments. The group has 70 branches located in California, Florida, Texas, North Carolina, Arizona, Georgia, Washington, Colorado, Maryland, Missouri, Oregon, Utah, Virginia, Kansas, Illinois and others. The group's quarterly revenue for Sep '07 was 2.56 millions of USD.

Primary SIC and add'l.: 6162 6035 6411 6712

CIK No: 0001049231

Subsidiaries: Pan American Service Corporation, UAC Investment Corporation, United Auto Credit Corporation, United PanAm Mortgage Corporation, UPFC Auto Receivables Corp., UPFC Funding Corp., UPFC Sub I, Inc., Worldcash Technologies, Inc.

Owners: Ray C. Thousand, Arash Khazei, Garland W. Koch, Giles H. Bateman, PAFGP, LLC, Insiders, Stacy M. Friederichsen, Ron R. Duncanson, Guillermo Bron, Wasatch Advisors, Inc., Mario Radrigan, Pan American Financial, L.P., Mitchell G. Lynn, Luis Maizel

Financial Data: Fiscal Year End:12/31 Latest Annual Data: 12/31/2006

Year	Sales	Net Income
2006	$197,007,000	$19,069,000
2005	$178,843,000	$26,665,000
2004	$140,286,000	$23,705,000

Curr. Assets:	$105,299,000	Curr. Liab.:	$10,977,000	P/E Ratio:	19.75
Plant, Equip.:	$5,034,000	Total Liab.:	$719,624,000	Indic. Yr. Divd.:	NA
Total Assets:	$879,489,000	Net Worth:	$159,865,000	Debt/ Equity:	4.8935

United Parcel Service Inc

55 Glenlake Pkwy NE, Atlanta, GA, 30328; *PH:* 1-404-828-6000; *http://* www.ups.com

General - Incorporation DE
Employees 428,000
Auditor Deloitte & Touche LLP
Stk Agt Mellon Investor Services LLC
Counsel NA
DUNS No. NA

Stock- Price on:12/24/2007 $72.9
Stock Exchange NYSE
Ticker Symbol UPS
Outstanding Shares 1,060,000,000
E.P.S $3.76
Shareholders NA

Business: The group's principle activity is to provide package delivery, transportation and logistic services. The group's services include supply chain solutions, professional, freight, air cargo and consulting services. The group operates from United States.

Primary SIC and add'l.: 4215 8742 6719 7372 4513

CIK No: 0001090727

Subsidiaries: Overnite Corporation, United Parcel Service Co., United Parcel Service Deutschland Inc., United Parcel Service General Services Co., United Parcel Service of America, Inc., United Parcel Service, Inc., UPICO Corporation, UPS Capital Corporation, UPS International, Inc., UPS Supply Chain Solutions, Inc., UPS Worldwide Forwarding, Inc.

Officers: Michael L. Eskew/Chmn., CEO/$6,165,586.00, Scott D. Davis/Vice Chmn., CFO, Alan Gershenhorn/Pres. - UPS International, Tracy Smith/US Contact - North Central, Megan Tompkins/US Contact - Northeast, East, Becky Cleaveland/US Contact - Pacific, Northwest, West, Robert Bean/US Contact - Pacific, Northwest, West, Orestes Rodriguez/US Contact - Southwest, Steve Arden/US Contact - Southwest, Raymond Ramos/US Contact - Caribbean, Imelda Hill/US Contact - East Central, Robert E. Stoffel/Sr. VP, Kurt Kuehn/Sr. VP - Worldwide Sales, Marketing, John McDevitt/Sr. VP - Global Transportation Services, David Abney/COO - UPS, Pres. - UPS Airlines/$1,284,540.00 *(25 Officers included in Index)*

Directors: Michael L. Eskew/Chmn., CEO, Scott D. Davis/Vice Chmn., CFO, Rudy Markham/Dir., Ann M. Livermore/Dir., James P. Kelly/Dir., Carol Tome/Dir., Michael J. Burns/Dir., Stuart E. Eizenstat/Dir., Victor A. Pelson/Dir., John W. Thompson/Dir., Ben Verwaayen/Dir., Duane Ackerman/Dir.

Owners: James P. Kelly, John J. Beystehner, Stuart E. Eizenstat, Gary E. MacDougal, Carol B. Tome, David P. Abney, Michael L. Eskew, Michael J. Burns, Carol B. Tome, James P. Kelly, Insiders, James F. Winestock, David P. Abney, Victor A. Pelson, Insiders *(25 Owners included in Index)*

Financial Data: Fiscal Year End:12/31 Latest Annual Data: 12/31/2006

Year	Sales	Net Income
2006	$47,547,000,000	$4,202,000,000
2005	$42,581,000,000	$3,870,000,000
2004	$36,582,000,000	$3,333,000,000

Curr. Assets:	$9,377,000,000	Curr. Liab.:	$6,719,000,000	P/E Ratio:	19.08
Plant, Equip.:	$16,779,000,000	Total Liab.:	$17,728,000,000	Indic. Yr. Divd.:	$1.680
Total Assets:	$33,210,000,000	Net Worth:	$15,482,000,000	Debt/ Equity:	0.2023

United Rentals Inc

Five Greenwich Office Pk., Greenwich, CT, 06831; *PH:* 1-203-622-3131; *Fax:* 1-203-622-6080; *http://* www.ur.com

General - Incorporation DE
Employees 12,000
Auditor Ernst & Young LLP
Stk Agt NA
Counsel NA
DUNS No. NA

Stock- Price on:12/24/2007 $33.29
Stock Exchange NYSE
Ticker Symbol URI
Outstanding Shares 81,660,000
E.P.S $2.37
Shareholders NA

Business: The groups principle activity is to provide equipment on rent. The groups equipments include construction equipment, industrial and heavy machinery, aerial work platforms, trench safety equipment and homeowner items. The group operates through two segments namely, rentals, and trench safety, pump and power. In the year 2006, the group acquired Handy Rent-All Center. The group operates from the United States. The groups quarterly revenue for September 2007 was 183.44 millions of USD.

Primary SIC and add'l.: 7359 7353

CIK No: 0001047166

Subsidiaries: Provisto, S. de R.L. de C.V. (United Rentals (Delaware), Inc., United Equipment Rentals Gulf, L.P., United Rentals (Delaware), Inc., United Rentals (North America), Inc., United Rentals Financing Limited Partnership, United Rentals Gulf, Inc., United Rentals of Canada, Inc., United Rentals of Nova Scotia (No. 1), ULC, United Rentals of Nova Scotia (No. 2), ULC, United Rentals Trust I, UNITED RENTALS, INC., United Rentals, S. de R.L. de C.V. (United Rentals (Delaware), Inc., UR Canadian Financing Partnership

Officers: Michael J. Kneeland/CEO, COO, Exec. VP, Martin E. Welch/CFO, Exec. VP, Eric D. Mertz/VP - Internal Audit, Roger E. Schwed/Exec. VP, General Counsel, Leroy J. Dieter/VP - Midwest Region, William F. Locklin/VP - Southwest Region, Bruce W. Lafky/VP - Service, Maintenance, Matthew J. Flannery/VP - Aerial East Region, Paul I. McDonnell/VP - Trench Safety, Pump, Power Region, Ron D. Groff/VP - Northeast Canada Region, Honey S. Harris/VP - Gulf Region, Fred L. Ransom/VP - Northeast Region, Kurtis T. Barker/Exec. VP - Corporate Services, Elise Arsenault/VP - Marketing, Stephen D. Baird/VP - Corporate Security *(34 Officers included in Index)*

Directors: Wayland R. Hicks/Vice Chmn., Bradley S. Jacobs/Chmn., Michael S. Gross/Dir., Leon D. Black/Dir., Jenne K. Britell/Dir., Howard L. Clark/Dir., Singleton B. McAllister/Dir., Brian D. McAuley/Dir., John S. McKinney/Dir., Jason D. Papastavrou/Dir., Mark A. Suwyn/Dir., Gerald Tsai/Dir., Keith L. Wimbush/Dir., Lawrence Wimbush/Dir.

Financial Data: Fiscal Year End:12/31 Latest Annual Data: 12/31/2006

Year	Sales	Net Income
2006	$3,640,000,000	$224,000,000
2005	$3,563,000,000	$187,000,000
2004	$3,094,000,000	-$84,000,000

Curr. Assets:	$1,005,000,000	Curr. Liab.:	$599,000,000		
Plant, Equip.:	$2,920,000,000	Total Liab.:	$3,828,000,000	Indic. Yr. Divd.:	NA
Total Assets:	$5,366,000,000	Net Worth:	$1,538,000,000	Debt/ Equity:	NA

United Retail Group Inc

365 W Passaic St., Rochelle Park, NJ, 07662; *PH:* 1-208-845-0880; *http://* www.unitedretail.com; *Email:* investor_kit@unitedretail.com

General - Incorporation DE
Employees 1,892
Auditor Eisner LLP
Stk Agt Continental Stock Transfer & Trust Co
Counsel NA
DUNS No. 05-452-7635

Stock- Price on:12/24/2007 $12.1
Stock Exchange NA
Ticker Symbol NA
Outstanding Shares 13,870,000
E.P.S $0.76
Shareholders NA

Business: The group's principle activity is to provide the retail sale of large size women's fashion apparel and accessories. This includes casual wear, career wear, specialty items, women's shoes and accessories. The casual wear assortment includes comfortably fitted jeans, slacks, t-shirts, skirts, active wear and sweaters. Casual wear comprises the majority of the group's sales. The career assortment includes slacks, skirts, jackets, soft blouses and dresses. Accessories include earrings, pins, scarves and a selection of gift items. These products are sold under the trademark avenue(R), which is used on storefronts and principal trademarks avenue(R) and cloudwalkers(R), which are used on merchandise labels. The group operates over 546 stores throughout the United States. The group's quarterly revenue for November 2007 was 106.59 millions of USD.

Primary SIC and add'l.: 5961 5661 5621 5632

CIK No: 0000881905

Subsidiaries: Avenue Giftcards, Inc.

Officers: Raphael Benaroya/Chmn., CEO, Pres./$1,286,836.00, George R. Remeta/Vice Chmn., Chief Administrative Officer/$966,144.00, Aaron Fleishaker/Sr. VP - Real Estate, Patricia Ippoliti/Sr. VP - Human Resources, David D. English/VP - Store Construction, Paul D. McFarren/CIO, Sr. VP/$392,190.00, Kenneth P. Carroll/Sr. VP, General Counsel/$515,579.00, Jon Grossman/VP - Financial Planning, Analysis/$240,789.00, Bradley Orloff/VP - Marketing, Gerald Schleiffer/VP - Planning, Distribution, Julie L. Daly/Pres. - Shop@home Operations, Joann Fielder/Sr. VP, Chief Design Officer, Scott Lucas/VP - Western Zone Sales, Kent Frauenberge/VP - Logistics, Patrick McGahan/VP - Sales *(23 Officers included in Index)*

Directors: Raphael Benaroya/Chmn., CEO, Pres., George R. Remeta/Vice Chmn., Chief Administrative Officer

Owners: Raphael Benaroya/17.60%, Insiders/21.90%, Ilan Kaufthal/1.00%, Jon Grossman, Ross B. Glickman, Paul D. McFarren, Michael Goldstein, Joseph A. Alutto, George R. Remeta/1.10%, Richard W. Rubenstein, Joseph Ciechanover, Vincent P. Langone, Kenneth P. Carroll

Financial Data: Fiscal Year End:01/28 Latest Annual Data: 2/3/2007

Year	Sales	Net Income
2007	$462,134,000	$12,602,000
2006	$438,738,000	$28,251,000
2005	$399,250,000	-$10,480,000

Curr. Assets:	$122,834,000	Curr. Liab.:	$60,561,000	P/E Ratio:	15.92
Plant, Equip.:	$62,887,000	Total Liab.:	$86,179,000	Indic. Yr. Divd.:	NA
Total Assets:	$205,572,000	Net Worth:	$119,393,000	Debt/ Equity:	0.0088

United Security Bancshares Inc

131 W Front St., Thomasville, AL, 36784; *PH:* 1-334-636-5424; *http://* www.firstusbank.com

General - Incorporation DE
Employees 136
Auditor Ernst & Young LLP
Stk Agt Wells Fargo Shareowner Services
Counsel Maynard, Cooper & Gale
DUNS No. 00-821-2961

Stock- Price on:12/24/2007 $21.01
Stock Exchange NDQ
Ticker Symbol USBI
Outstanding Shares 12,210,000
E.P.S $0.33
Shareholders NA

Business: The group's principal activities are to provide commercial banking services. The group holds one banking subsidiary through which the operations are conducted. The services provided includes receipt of demand, savings and time deposits, personal and commercial loans, credit card and safe deposit box services and the purchase and sale of government securities. The group operates through 18 banking offices located in thomasville, coffeeville, fulton, gilbertown, grove hill, butler, jackson, brent, centreville, woodstock, bucksville and harpersville, Alabama.

Primary SIC and add'l.: 6712 6022

CIK No: 0000717806

Subsidiaries: Acceptance Loan Company, Inc., First Security Courier Corporation, First United Security Bank, FUSB Reinsurance, Inc.

Officers: Terry R. Phillips/54/Dir., CEO, Pres./$469,470.00, Daniel J. Matheson/50/Sr. VP, Investment Officer, Robert Steen/59/CFO, Exec. VP/$216,825.00, William D. Morgan/59/VP, Sec./$168,091.00, Larry M. Sellers/59/VP, Sec., Treasurer/$259,853.00

Directors: Terry R. Phillips/54/Dir., CEO, Pres., Hardie B. Kimbrough/70/Chmn., Jack W. Meigs/50/Dir., John C. Gordon/50/Dir., William G. Harrison/61/Dir., Linda H. Breedlove/64/Dir., Gerald P. Corgill/66/Dir., Wayne C. Curtis/68/Dir., Bruce N. Wilson/53/Dir., James C. Stanley/71/Dir.

Owners: John C. Gordon/0.03%, Jack W. Meigs, Dan R. Barlow, Gerald P. Corgill/0.03%, Wayne C. Curtis, Hardie B. Kimbrough/0.01%, Ray Sheffield/0.01%, William D. Morgan, Bruce N. Wilson, James C. Stanley, Insiders/0.10%, Linda H. Breedlove, Howard M. Whitted, Larry M. Sellers, R. Terry Phillips *(17 Owners included in Index)*

Financial Data: Fiscal Year End:12/31 Latest Annual Data: 12/31/2006

Year	Sales	Net Income
2006	$64,840,000	$14,245,000
2005	$57,995,000	$13,656,000
2004	$55,066,000	$13,131,000

Curr. Assets:	$34,581,000	Curr. Liab.:	$454,989,000	P/E Ratio:	18.59
Plant, Equip.:	$20,182,000	Total Liab.:	$554,701,000	Indic. Yr. Divd.:	$1.040
Total Assets:	$646,296,000	Net Worth:	$91,596,000	Debt/ Equity:	NA

United Security Bank

2126 Inyo St., Fresno, CA, 93721; *PH:* 1-559-248-4943; *Fax:* 1-559-248-5088;
http:// www.unitedsecuritybank.com; *Email:* info@unitedsecuritybank.com

General - Incorporation	CA	*Stock* - Price on:12/24/2007	$20.74
Employees	136	Stock Exchange	NDQ
Auditor	Moss Adams LLP	Ticker Symbol	NA
Stk Agt	Wells Fargo Shareowner Services	Outstanding Shares	12,210,000
Counsel	NA	E.P.S.	$1.14
DUNS No.	NA	Shareholders	NA

Business: The group's principal activities are to provide commercial banking, mortgage banking and other financial services through its subsidiary united security bank. The bank is a state-chartered commercial bank, which offers a full range of commercial banking services primarily to the business and professional community and individuals. It offers a wide range of deposit instruments including personal and business checking accounts and savings accounts, interest-bearing negotiable order of withdrawal accounts, money market accounts and time certificates of deposit. The lending activities include real estate mortgage, commercial and industrial, real estate construction, agricultural and consumer loans. On 31-Dec-2003, the group operated seven bank branches and one construction lending office in fresno and madera counties. On 23-Apr-2004, the group acquired taft national bank.

Primary SIC and add'l.: 6712 6022

CIK No: 0001137547

Subsidiaries: Community Development Entity (CDE), Real Estate Investment Trust, United Security Bancshares Capital Trust I, United Security Emerging Capital Fund

Officers: Dennis R. Woods/Chmn., CEO, Pres./$1,234,808.00, Ken L. Donahue/Sr. VP, CFO/$341,049.00, Rhodlee A. Braa/Sr. VP, CCO/$339,740.00, Dave L. Eytcheson/COO, Sr. VP/$357,090.00, William F. Scarborough/Sr. VP, CBO/$286,698.00

Directors: Dennis R. Woods/Chmn., CEO, Pres.

Owners: Robert G. Bitter/1.80%, Insiders/27.10%, Stanley J. Cavalla/4.10%, Kenneth L. Donahue/2.30%, Michael T. Woolf, Dennis R. Woods/6.50%, Tom Ellithorpe/1.70%, David L. Eytcheson/1.30%, Gary Hong, William F. Scarborough, John Terzian/1.50%, Audry Thomason/5.80%, Ronnie D. Miller/1.40%, Robert M. Mochizuki, Walter Reinhard/3.70% *(16 Owners included in Index)*

*Financial Data: Fiscal Year End:*12/31 *Latest Annual Data:* 12/31/2006

Year		Sales		Net Income
2006		$56,462,000		$13,360,000
2005		$45,178,000		$11,008,000
2004		$35,714,000		$8,405,000
Curr. Assets:	$55,198,000	*Curr. Liab.:*	$596,808,000	
Plant, Equip.:	$17,221,000	*Total Liab.:*	$612,272,000	*Indic. Yr. Divd.:* $0.500
Total Assets:	$678,314,000	*Net Worth:*	$66,042,000	*Debt/ Equity:* 0.3116

United States Antimony Corp

PO Box 643, 1250 Prospect Creek Rd., Thompson Falls, MT, 59873; *PH:* 1-406-827-3523;
http:// www.usantimony.com; *Email:* contact@usantimony.com

General - Incorporation	MT	*Stock* - Price on:12/24/2007	$0.8
Employees	52	Stock Exchange	OTC
Auditor	Decoria, Maichel & Teague, P.S	Ticker Symbol	UAMY
Stk Agt	Computershare Trust Co	Outstanding Shares	40,910,000
Counsel	NA	E.P.S.	$0.00
DUNS No.	05-026-1833	Shareholders	NA

Business: The group's principal activities are to refine and produce antimony products and zeolite products. The group produces four antimony oxide products, using raw antimony metal obtained from foreign sources. Proprietary furnace technology and hydro metallurgical techniques are used for the production of these oxide products. The antimony products are marketed under the trade name 'Montana brand antimony oxide'. The group operates solely in the domestic market.

Primary SIC and add'l.: 1099

CIK No: 0000101538

Subsidiaries: Antimonio de Mexico SA de Cv, Bear River Zeolite Company

Officers: John C. Lawrence/69/Chmn., CEO, Pres., Sec., Treasurer, Principal Financial, Accounting Officer, Matt Keane/Sales, Customer Service

Directors: John C. Lawrence/69/Chmn., CEO, Pres., Sec., Treasurer, Principal Financial, Accounting Officer, Leo Jackson/64/Dir., Gary A. Babbitt/Dir.

Owners: John C. Lawrence/91.00%, Richard A. Woods/27.00%, Warren A. Evans/27.00%, Robert A. Rice, Reed Family Limited Partnership/12.00%, Edward Robinson/18.00%, Insiders/12.00%, John C. Lawrence/8.00%, The Dugan Family/16.00%, Leo Jackson, Gary Babbitt, Leo Jackson/5.00%

*Financial Data: Fiscal Year End:*12/31 *Latest Annual Data:* 12/31/2006

Year		Sales		Net Income
2006		$4,395,000		-$285,000
2005		$3,564,000		-$576,000
2004		$3,123,000		-$93,000
Curr. Assets:	$602,000	*Curr. Liab.:*	$1,592,000	
Plant, Equip.:	$2,065,000	*Total Liab.:*	$2,269,000	*Indic. Yr. Divd.:* NA
Total Assets:	$2,750,000	*Net Worth:*	$481,000	*Debt/ Equity:* 0.0986

United States Basketball League Inc

46 Quirk Rd., Milford, CT, 06460; *PH:* 1-203-877-9508; *http://* www.usbl.com

General - Incorporation	DE	*Stock* - Price on:12/24/2007	$0.52
Employees	4	Stock Exchange	OTC
Auditor	Michael T. Studer CPA P.C	Ticker Symbol	USBL
Stk Agt	Continental Stock Transfer & Trust Co	Outstanding Shares	3,480,000
Counsel	NA	E.P.S.	-$0.05
DUNS No.	11-616-2041	Shareholders	NA

Business: The group's principle activity is to operate professional summer basketball league through franchises located in the eastern part of the United States. The company sells franchises and manages the league. The company helps college graduates to improve their skills in a professional environment. Players consist of free agents seeking to join a nba team. The group acquired meisenheimer capital real estate holdings in may 2003. The group operates from United States.

Primary SIC and add'l.: 7997 7312 7941

CIK No: 0000764630

Subsidiaries: MCI Capital Real Estate Holdings Inc

Officers: Daniel Meisenheimer/Chmn., Principal Executive Officer, Pres., Richard C. Meisenheimer/Dir., CFO, Lynn Casa/Dir. - Administration, Jacob Gordon/Dir. - Media, Public Relations, Al Mayles/Exec. League Coordinator, Supervisor, Officials, Mark Argenziano/Dir. - Scouting, Jeff Argenziano/Dir. - Player Evaluation, Tom Hughes/Expansion Coordinator, Southeast Region, Terry Layton/Expansion Coordinator, Midwest Region, Dwayne Jacobs/Expansion Agent

Directors: Daniel Meisenheimer/Chmn., Principal Executive Officer, Pres., Richard C. Meisenheimer/Dir., CFO

Owners: Meisenheimer Capital Inc./12.70%, Daniel T. Meisenheimer, Daniel T. Meisenheimer/13.00%, Richard C. Meisenheimer/12.90%, Spectrum Associates, Inc./34.10%, Richard C. Meisenheimer, Insiders/25.90%, Daniel T. Meisenheimer/16.50%, Meisenheimer Capital Inc./60.20%, Daniel T. Meisenheimer/12.60%, Spectrum Associates, Inc./6.70%, Insiders/12.70%

*Financial Data: Fiscal Year End:*02/28 *Latest Annual Data:* 02/28/2007

Year		Sales		Net Income
2007		$414,000		-$145,000
2006		$367,000		-$80,000
2005		$493,000		-$328,000
Curr. Assets:	$29,000	*Curr. Liab.:*	$1,004,000	
Plant, Equip.:	$258,000	*Total Liab.:*	$1,128,000	*Indic. Yr. Divd.:* NA
Total Assets:	$286,000	*Net Worth:*	-$841,000	*Debt/ Equity:* NA

United States Cellular Corp

8410 W Bryn Mawr, Ste. 700, Chicago, IL, 60631; *PH:* 1-773-399-8900; *https://* www.uscc.com

General - Incorporation	DE	*Stock* - Price on:12/24/2007	$90.34
Employees	8,100	Stock Exchange	AMEX
Auditor	PricewaterhouseCoopers LLP	Ticker Symbol	USM
Stk Agt	Computershare Investor Services LLC	Outstanding Shares	87,310,000
Counsel	NA	E.P.S.	$2.43
DUNS No.	NA	Shareholders	NA

Business: The group's principle activity is to provide wireless services. The group services include wireless telephones and installations. The group operates from the United States, Canada and Mexico. The groups quarterly revenue for September 2007 was 1,015.83 millions of USD.

Primary SIC and add'l.: 4812 4899

CIK No: 0000821130

Subsidiaries: ALLTEL NEWCO #4 LLC, BANGOR CELLULAR TELEPHONE, L.P., CALIFORNIA RURAL SERVICE AREA #1, INC., CARROLL WIRELESS, LP, CEDAR RAPIDS CELLULAR TELEPHONE, L.P., CELLVEST, INC., CENTRAL CELLULAR TELEPHONES LTD, CHAMPLAIN CELLULAR, INC, CHARLOTTESVILLE CELLULAR PARTNERSHIP, COMMUNITY CELLULAR TELEPHONE COMPANY, CROWN POINT CELLULAR INC., DAVENPORT CELLULAR TELEPHONE COMPANY, DAVENPORT CELLULAR TELEPHONE COMPANY, INC., DUBUQUE CELLULAR TELEPHONE, L.P., EASTERN NORTH CAROLINA CELLULAR JOINT VENTURE 131 Subsidiaries included in the Index

Officers: John E. Rooney/Dir., CEO, Pres./$5,433,875.00, Katherine Hust/VP - Central Operations, George W. Irving/VP - Business Support Services, Kevin R. Lowell/VP - National Network Operations, Thomas S. Weber/VP - Financial Strategy, Nick B. Wright/VP - West Operations, Mark A. Steinkrauss/Primary Investor Relations Officer, Thomas J. Griffin/VP - Organizational Learning, Chief Teaching Officer, Kevin C. Gallagher/VP, Corp. Sec., Lynn R. Costlow/VP - Customer Service, John C. Gockley/VP - Legal, Regulatory Affairs, Nadine A. Heidrich/VP, Controller, Steven T. Campbell/CFO, Exec. VP - Finance, Treasurer, Jay M. Ellison/COO, Exec. VP/$1,704,046.00, Michael S. Irizarry/CTO, Exec. VP/$1,225,366.00 *(21 Officers included in Index)*

Directors: John E. Rooney/Dir., CEO, Pres., Leroy T. Carlson/Chmn., Kenneth R. Meyers/Dir., Walter C.D. Carlson/Dir., Samuel J. Crowley/Dir., Ronald E. Daly/Dir., Paul-Henri Denuit/Dir., Harry Harczak/Dir.

Owners: Gabelli Funds, LLC/6.20%, Telephone and Data Systems, Inc./100.00%, Telephone and Data Systems, Inc./68.90%, Jeffrey J. Childs, LeRoy T. Carlson, Harry J. Harczak, Ronald E. Daly, Insiders/2.10%, Kenneth R. Meyers, Michael S. Irizarry, John E. Rooney, Jay M. Ellison, Walter C.D. Carlson

*Financial Data: Fiscal Year End:*12/31 *Latest Annual Data:* 12/31/2006

Year		Sales		Net Income
2006		$3,473,155,000		$179,490,000
2005		$3,030,765,000		$154,951,000
2004		$2,808,201,000		$109,516,000
Curr. Assets:	$854,918,000	*Curr. Liab.:*	$856,710,000	*P/E Ratio:* 37.18
Plant, Equip.:	$2,628,848,000	*Total Liab.:*	$2,650,637,000	*Indic. Yr. Divd.:* NA
Total Assets:	$5,680,616,000	*Net Worth:*	$2,993,279,000	*Debt/ Equity:* 0.3261

United States Lime & Minerals Inc

5429 LBJ Fwy., Ste. 230, Dallas, TX, 75240; *PH:* 1-972-991-8400; *Fax:* 1-972-385-1340;
http:// www.uslm.com; *Email:* uslime@uslm.com

General - Incorporation	TX	*Stock* - Price on:12/24/2007	$38.6701
Employees	317	Stock Exchange	NDQ
Auditor	Grant Thornton LLP	Ticker Symbol	USLM
Stk Agt	Computershare Investor Services LLC	Outstanding Shares	6,270,000
Counsel	Morgan, Lewis & Bockius LLP	E.P.S.	$1.67
DUNS No.	00-735-1554	Shareholders	NA

Business: The group's principal activity is to extract limestone from its quarries and processing it for sale as pulverized limestone, quicklime and hydrated lime. The group manufactures lime and limestone products used in the agriculture, construction, municipal sanitation and water treatment, paper and steel industries. The customers include highway, street and parking lot contractors, chemical producers, paper manufacturers, roofing shingle manufacturers, steel producers, glass manufacturers, poultry and cattle feed producers, governmental agencies and electrical utility companies. The group sells majority of the products in the states of Arkansas, Colorado, Kansas, Louisiana, Mississippi, New Mexico, Oklahoma, Tennessee and Texas.

Primary SIC and add'l.: 1422

CIK No: 0000082020

Subsidiaries: ACT Holdings, Inc, Arkansas Lime Company, Colorado Lime Company, Texas Lime Company, U.S. Lime Company, U.S. Lime Company O & G LLC, U.S. Lime Company Shreveport, U.S. Lime Company St. Clair

Officers: Timothy W. Byrne/CEO, Pres./$857,261.00, Jim Longenbach/VP, Plant Mgr., Tracy Gunn/GM, Russell W. Riggs/VP - Production/$216,050.00

Owners: Edward A. Odishaw, Insiders/4.22%, Russell W. Riggs, Antoine M. Doumet, Johnney G. Bowers, Wallace G. Irmscher, Timothy W. Byrne/2.58%, Robert S. Beall/10.84%, Michael M. Owens, Richard W. Cardin, Billy R. Hughes/1.13%, Inberdon Enterprises Ltd./57.69%

Financial Data: *Fiscal Year End:* 12/31 *Latest Annual Data:* 12/31/2006

Year	Sales	Net Income
2006	$118,690,000	$12,701,000
2005	$81,085,000	$7,948,000
2004	$55,679,000	$6,329,000

Curr. Assets:	$22,776,000	**Curr. Liab.:**	$18,739,000	**P/E Ratio:**	21.60
Plant, Equip.:	$129,894,000	**Total Liab.:**	$81,675,000	**Indic. Yr. Divd.:**	NA
Total Assets:	$154,168,000	**Net Worth:**	$72,493,000	**Debt/ Equity:**	0.8873

United States Steel Corp

600 Grant St., Pittsburgh, PA, 15219; *PH:* 1-412-433-1184; *http://* www.ussteel.com; *Email:* investorrelations@uss.com

General - Incorporation	DE	**Stock**- Price on:12/24/2007	$114.06
Employees	44,000	Stock Exchange	NYSE
Auditor	PricewaterhouseCoopers LLP	Ticker Symbol	X
Stk Agt	Wells Fargo Shareowner Services	Outstanding Shares	118,310,000
Counsel	NA	E.P.S	$10.77
DUNS No.	NA	Shareholders	NA

Business: The groups principle activity is to produce integrated steel. The group operates through three segments namely flat-rolled products (flat-rolled), U. S. steel Europe (USSE) and tubular products. In the year 2007, the group acquired Stelco Inc. The group operates from United States.

Primary SIC and add'l.: 3443 3312 8711 3317 1011

CIK No: 0001163302

Subsidiaries: Acero Prime Servicios, S.R.L. de C.V., Acero Prime, S.R.L. de C.V., Adela Investment Company S.A., Betrieber Gesellschaft Norbahn GmbH, Birmingham Southern Railroad Company, Chrome Deposit Corporation, Clairton 1314B Partnership, L.P., Compagnie de Gestion de Mifergui-Nimba, LTEE., Compania de Representaciones Mercantiles, Cubacero, S.A., Cygnus Mines Limited, Delaware USS Corporation, Delray Connecting Railroad, Double Eagle Steel Coating Company, Double G Coatings Company, L.P., Double G Coatings, Inc. 117 Subsidiaries included in the Index

Officers: John P. Surma/Chmn., CEO/$8,639,991.00, Dan D. Sandman/Vice Chmn., Chief Legal, Administrative Officer, General Counsel, Sec./$3,722,232.00, John H. Goodish/COO, Exec. VP/$6,093,251.00, Gretchen R. Haggerty/CFO, Exec. VP/$3,638,861.00, George F. Babcoke/VP - Plant Operations, Christopher J. Navetta/Sr. VP - Procurement, Logistics, Diversified Businesses, Joseph R. Scherrbaum/VP - Sales, Larry G. Schultz/VP, Controller, Thomas W. Sterling/Sr. VP - Administration, Terrence D. Straub/Sr. VP - Public Policy, Governmental Affairs, Stephan K. Todd/VP - Law, Environmental Affairs, Eugene P. Trudell/VP - Business Services, John D. Armstrong/Mgr. - Public Affairs, Anthony R. Bridge/VP - Engineering, Technology, Larry T. Brockway/VP, Treasurer *(24 Officers included in Index)*

Directors: John P. Surma/Chmn., CEO, Dan D. Sandman/Vice Chmn., Chief Legal, Administrative Officer, General Counsel, Sec., Gary J. Cooper/71/Dir., Glenda G. McNeal/47/Dir., Patricia A. Tracey/Dir., Frank J. Lucchino/68/Dir., Robert J. Darnall/69/Dir., John G. Drosdick/64/Dir., Richard A. Gephardt/67/Dir., Charles R. Lee/68/Dir., Seth E. Schofield/68/Dir., Douglas C. Yearley/72/Dir., Jeffrey M. Lipton/65/Dir.

Owners: Jeffrey L. Gendell/5.61%, Richard A. Gephardt, NWQ Investment Management Company, LLC/5.01%, Insiders, Dan D. Sandman, Charles R. Lee, Barclays Global Investors, NA;/6.63%, John G. Drosdick, John P. Surma, John H. Goodish, Seth E. Schofield, Douglas C. Yearley, LLM LLC/7.97%, Gretchen R. Haggerty, Frank J. Lucchino *(19 Owners included in Index)*

Financial Data: *Fiscal Year End:* 12/31 *Latest Annual Data:* 12/31/2006

Year	Sales	Net Income
2006	$15,715,000,000	$1,374,000,000
2005	$14,039,000,000	$910,000,000
2004	$14,108,000,000	$1,091,000,000

Curr. Assets:	$5,196,000,000	**Curr. Liab.:**	$2,702,000,000	**P/E Ratio:**	9.94
Plant, Equip.:	$4,429,000,000	**Total Liab.:**	$6,221,000,000	**Indic. Yr. Divd.:**	$0.800
Total Assets:	$10,586,000,000	**Net Worth:**	$4,365,000,000	**Debt/ Equity:**	0.2018

United Stationers Inc

One N Pkwy. Blvd, Ste 100, Deerfield, IL, 60015; *PH:* 1-847-627-7000; *http://* www.unitedstationers.com; *Email:* investorinfo@ussco.com

General - Incorporation	DE	**Stock**- Price on:12/24/2007	$67.51
Employees	5,700	Stock Exchange	NDQ
Auditor	Ernst & Young LLP	Ticker Symbol	USTR
Stk Agt	National City Bank	Outstanding Shares	27,850,000
Counsel	NA	E.P.S	$3.85
DUNS No.	00-798-1038	Shareholders	NA

Business: The group's principle activity is to distribute computer consumables, office products and furniture, facilities supplies and business machines. The group supply to the dealers, mega-dealers, contract stationers, office products superstores, computer products resellers, office furniture dealers, mass merchandisers, mail order companies, sanitary supply distributors, drug and grocery store chains, and e-commerce merchants. The group operates from United States.

Primary SIC and add'l.: 5085 5045 5044 5021 5112 4731

CIK No: 0000355999

Subsidiaries: AZERTY de MEXICO, S.A. de C.V., Lagasse, Inc. (f/k/a/ Lagasse Bros., Inc.), United Stationers Financial Services, LLC, United Stationers Hong Kong Limited, United Stationers Supply Co., United Stationers Technology Services LLC, United Worldwide Limited, Uss Receivables Company, Ltd.

Officers: Richard W. Gochnauer/Dir., CEO, Pres./$3,469,859.00, Joseph R. Templet/Sr. VP - Trade Development, Jeffrey G. Howard/Sr. VP - National Accounting, Channel Management, Eric A. Blanchard/Sr. VP, General Counsel, Sec./$980,390.00, Kathleen S. Dvorak/Contact/$887,798.00, Patrick T. Collins/Sr. VP - Sales/$903,707.00, David S. Bent/CIO, Sr. VP, Mark J. Hampton/Sr. VP - Marketing, Cody P. Phipps/Pres. - United Stationers Supply/$1,107,778.00, Jim Fahey/Sr. VP - Merchandising, MD, Mary Disclafani/Investor Relations Officer, Stephen A. Schultz/41/Sr. VP, Pres. - Lagasse, Inc, Victoria J. Reich/CFO, Sr. VP, Ronald C. Berg/48/Sr. VP - Inventory Management, Timothy P. Connolly/44/Sr. VP - Operations *(20 Officers included in Index)*

Directors: Richard W. Gochnauer/Dir., CEO, Pres., Frederick B. Hegi/Chmn., Ilene S. Gordon/Dir., Roy W. Haley/Dir., Jean S. Blackwell/Dir., Charles K. Crovitz/Dir., Benson P. Shapiro/Dir., Daniel J. Good/Dir., John J. Zillmer/Dir.

Owners: Patrick T. Collins, Ilene S. Gordon, Barclays Global Investors, NA, and various affiliated entities/8.09%, Charles K. Crovitz, Insiders/5.30%, Cody P. Phipps, Wellington Management Company, LLP/5.83%, John J. Zillmer, Frederick B. Hegi/2.06%, Farallon Partners, L.L.C. and various affiliated entities/9.23%, Eric A. Blanchard, Richard W. Gochnauer/1.44%, Neuberger Berman Inc. and various affiliated entities/8.35%, Roy W. Haley, Kathleen S. Dvorak *(17 Owners included in Index)*

Financial Data: *Fiscal Year End:* 12/31 *Latest Annual Data:* 12/31/2006

Year	Sales	Net Income
2006	$4,546,914,000	$132,213,000
2005	$4,408,546,000	$97,501,000
2004	$3,991,190,000	$89,971,000

Curr. Assets:	$1,106,859,000	**Curr. Liab.:**	$555,303,000	**P/E Ratio:**	14.71
Plant, Equip.:	$188,336,000	**Total Liab.:**	$752,454,000	**Indic. Yr. Divd.:**	NA
Total Assets:	$1,553,394,000	**Net Worth:**	$800,940,000	**Debt/ Equity:**	NA

United Surgical Partners International Inc

15305 Dallas Pk.way, Ste. 1600, Addison, TX, 75001; *PH:* 1-972-713-3500; *http://* www.unitedsurgical.com

General - Incorporation	DE	**Stock**- Price on:12/24/2007	NA
Employees	3,600	Stock Exchange	NA
Auditor	KPMG LLP	Ticker Symbol	NA
Stk Agt	Wachovia Bank N.A	Outstanding Shares	NA
Counsel	Nossaman, Guthner, Knox & Elliott	E.P.S	NA
DUNS No.	NA	Shareholders	NA

Business: The group's principal activities are to own and operate short stay surgical facilities including surgery centers and private surgical hospitals. The group acquires and develops the facilities through the formation of strategic relationships with physicians and health care systems. At 31-Dec-2003, the group operated 74 facilities, consisting of 62 in the United States, nine in Spain, and three in the United Kingdom.

Primary SIC and add'l.: 8062 8742

CIK No: 0001101723

Subsidiaries: 25 East Same Day Surgery, LLC, Adventist Midwest Health/USP Surgery Centers, LLC, Alamo Heights Surgicare, L.P., Arlington Surgicare Partners, Ltd., Aspen Healthcare Holdings, Ltd., Aspen Healthcare, Ltd., Aspen Leasing, Ltd., Austintown Surgery Center, LLC, Bagley Holdings, LLC, Baptist Plaza Surgicare, L.P., Baptist Surgery Center, L.P., Bellaire Outpatient Surgery Center, LLP, Bon Secours Surgery Center at Virginia Beach, LLC, Briarcliff Ambulatory Surgery Center, L.P., Cape Surgery Center, L.P. 295 Subsidiaries included in the Index

Officers: William H. Wilcox/Dir., CEO, Pres., Anthony J. Martin/VP, Corporate Controller, Jonathan R. Bond/Sr. VP - Operations, Mark A. Kopser/CFO, Exec. VP, John J. Wellik/Sr. VP - Accounting, Administration, Sec., Brett P. Brodnax/Exec. VP, Chief Development Officer, James A. Jackson/Sr. VP - Operations, Jason B. Cagle/VP, General Counsel, Monica Cintado-Scokin/Sr. VP - Development, Patricia McCann/MD - Global Healthcare Partners United Kingdom, Mark C. Garvin/Sr. VP - Operations, Luke D. Johnson/Sr. VP - Operations, Pres. - Ortholink Physicians Corporation, Neils P. Vernegaard/COO, Exec. VP, Corey Ridgway/VP - Operations, Desmond Shiels/Pres. - Global Healthcare Partners United Kingdom *(19 Officers included in Index)*

Directors: William H. Wilcox/Dir., CEO, Pres., Donald E. Steen/Chmn., Paul B. Queally/Dir., Jerry P. Widman/Dir., Michael E. Donovan/Dir., Scott D. MacKesy/Dir., Raymond A. Ranelli/Dir., Nancy L. Weaver/Dir., Joel T. Allison/Dir., Boone Powell/Dir., Thomas L. Mills/Dir., John C. Garrett/Dir., James Ken Newman/Dir.

Owners: Insiders, Mark A. Kopser, Donald E. Steen, John J. Wellik, California State Teachers Retirement System, Niels P. Vernegaard, William H. Wilcox, Welsh, Carson, Anderson & Stowe, Mark A. Kopser, CPP Investment Board (USRE II) Inc., Brett P. Brodnax, Silvertech Investment PTE Ltd, Paul B. Queally, Welsh, Carson, Anderson & Stowe, Brett P. Brodnax *(24 Owners included in Index)*

United Technologies Corp

United Technologies Bldg, Hartford, CT, 06101; *PH:* 1-860-728-7000; *http://* www.utc.com; *Email:* corpsec@corphq.utc.com

General - Incorporation	DE	**Stock**- Price on:12/24/2007	$71.57
Employees	214,500	Stock Exchange	NYSE
Auditor	PricewaterhouseCoopers LLP	Ticker Symbol	UTX
Stk Agt	Computershare Investor Services LLC	Outstanding Shares	994,430,000
Counsel	NA	E.P.S	$4.06
DUNS No.	00-134-4142	Shareholders	NA

Business: The group's principle activity is to provide high-technology products and services to building systems and aerospace industries. The group operates from United States.

Primary SIC and add'l.: 3585 3724 3534 3721 7382

CIK No: 0000101829

Subsidiaries: Albatre-Servicos de Consultadoria e Marketing, Sociedade Unipessoal Lda, Anoxina-Servicos de Consultadoria, Sociedade Unipessoal Lda, Australia Holdings Inc., CalPeak Power LLC, Carrier Air Conditioning Pty. Limited, Carrier Commercial Refrigeration, Inc., Carrier Corporation, Carrier Espana, SL, Carrier Europe, Middle East, & Africa S.A.S., Carrier HVACR Investments B.V., Carrier Ltd., Carrier Mexico S.A. de C.V., Carrier Sales and Distribution, LLC, Carrier Singapore (PTE) Limited, Carrier SpA 51 Subsidiaries included in the Index

Officers: George David/Chmn., CEO/$27,174,830.00, Louis Chenevert/Dir., COO, Pres./$7,820,312.00, Nancy T. Lintner/VP - Communications, Geraud Darnis/Pres. - Carrier/$5,179,916.00, Jan Van Dokkum/Pres. - UTC Power, William H. Trachsel/Sr. VP, General Counsel, Thomas I. Rogan/55/VP, Treasurer, Stephen N. Finger/Pres. - Pratt, Whitney, David P. Hess/Pres. - Hamilton Sundstrand, Gregory J. Hayes/Pres. - Accounting, Control/$2,404,911.00, John J. Doucette/CIO, VP, Debra A. Valentine/54/VP, Deputy General Counsel, Sec., Ari Bousbib/Pres. - Otis/$5,932,567.00, William L. Bucknall/Sr. VP - Human Resources, Organization, William M. Brown/Pres. - UTC Fire, Security *(21 Officers included in Index)*

Directors: George David/Chmn., CEO, Louis Chenevert/Dir., COO, Pres., Charles R. Lee/Dir., Jamie S. Gorelick/Dir., John V. Faraci/Dir., Richard Myers/Dir., Christine Todd Whitman/Dir., Harold McGraw/Dir., Patrick H. Swygert/Dir., Andre Villeneuve/Dir., Jean-Pierre Garnier/Dir., Frank P. Popoff/Dir., Richard D. McCormick/Dir., Harold A. Wagner/Dir.

Owners: Richard D. McCormick, James E. Geisler, Harold McGraw, Insiders, Geraud Darnis, Frank P. Popoff, Louis R. Chnevert, George David, Gregory J. Hayes, Jean-Pierre Garnier, Patrick H. Swygert, Jamie S. Gorelick, Andr Villeneuve, Charles R. Lee, H. A. Wagner (*17 Owners included in Index*)

Financial Data: *Fiscal Year End:*12/31 *Latest Annual Data:* 12/31/2006

Year	Sales	Net Income
2006	$47,829,000,000	$3,732,000,000
2005	$42,725,000,000	$3,069,000,000
2004	$37,445,000,000	$2,788,000,000

Curr. Assets:	$18,844,000,000	*Curr. Liab.:*	$15,208,000,000	*P/E Ratio:*	18.64
Plant, Equip.:	$5,725,000,000	*Total Liab.:*	$29,844,000,000	*Indic. Yr. Divd.:*	$1.280
Total Assets	$47,141,000,000	*Net Worth:*	$17,297,000,000	*Debt/ Equity:*	0.3885

United Tennessee Bankshares Inc

170 Brdway, Newport, TN, 37821; *PH:* 1-423-623-6088; *http://* www.cockecounty.org/newfed.html

General - Incorporation	TN	**Stock**- Price on:12/24/2007	$21
Employees	NA	Stock Exchange	OTC
Auditor	Pugh & Co, P.C	Ticker Symbol	UNTN
Stk Agt	Registrar & Transfer Co	Outstanding Shares	1,040,000
Counsel	Myers & Bell	E.P.S.	$1.38
DUNS No.	02-472-3707	Shareholders	NA

Business: The group's principal activities are to provide financial services to individuals and corporate customers. The group operates through its subsidiary newport federal bank. The group's services include, attracting deposits from the public and originating first mortgage loans, commercial real estate loans and consumer loans. The activities of the group are carried out through three offices in newport, Tennessee. The group maintains an investment portfolio, primarily of mortgage backed securities issued by the federal agencies.

Primary SIC and add'l.: 6712 6035

CIK No: 0001045689

Subsidiaries: Newport Federal Bank

Financial Data: *Fiscal Year End:*12/31 *Latest Annual Data:* 12/31/2004

Year	Sales	Net Income
2004	$7,386,000	$1,641,000
2003	$7,487,000	$2,006,000
2002	$7,627,000	$1,762,000

Curr. Assets:	$4,017,000	*Curr. Liab.:*	$102,054,000		
Plant, Equip.:	$1,842,000	*Total Liab.:*	$104,240,000	*Indic. Yr. Divd.:*	NA
Total Assets	$122,659,000	*Net Worth:*	$18,419,000	*Debt/ Equity:*	NA

United Therapeutics Corp

1110 Spring St., Silver Spring, MD, 20910; *PH:* 1-301-608-9292; *http://* www.unither.com

General - Incorporation	DE	**Stock**- Price on:12/24/2007	$64.18
Employees	285	Stock Exchange	NDQ
Auditor	Ernst & Young LLP	Ticker Symbol	UTHR
Stk Agt	Bank of New York	Outstanding Shares	20,780,000
Counsel	NA	E.P.S.	$3.36
DUNS No.	NA	Shareholders	NA

Business: The group's principal activities are to develop and manufacture therapeutic products, which focus on combating cardiovascular, infectious and oncological diseases. The group operates in two segments: pharmaceuticals and telemedicine. The pharmaceutical segment includes all activities associated with the research, development, manufacture and commercialization of pharmaceutical products. The telemedicine segment includes all activities associated with the research, manufacture and delivery of patient monitoring services. The group also focuses on the development of iminosugar compounds for the treatment of hepatitis b and c.

Primary SIC and add'l.: 2834 8051

CIK No: 0001082554

Subsidiaries: Lung Rx Ltd, Lung RxInc., MedicompInc., United Therapeutics Europe Ltd., Unither Biotech Inc., Unither NutriceuticalsInc., Unither PharmaInc., Unither PharmaceuticalsInc., Unither Telmed Ltd., Unither.comInc.

Officers: Martine Rothblatt/Chmn., CEO/$6,238,700.00, Victor J. Dzau/Member - Scientific Advisory Board, Peter C. Gonze/COO - Unither Pharmaceuticals, Inc, Paul A. Mahon/Exec. VP - Strategic Planning, General Counsel/$5,041,700.00, Shola Oyewole/CIO - MSc Technology, Management Information Systems, BSc Electronics, Computer Engineering, CNA, Mcse+internet, Roger Jeffs/Dir., COO, Pres./$6,550,100.00, Dan Balda/COO, Pres. Medicomp - Inc, David Walsh/Exec. VP, COO - Production, Urban Ramstedt/Member - Scientific Advisory Board, John Ferrari/CFO, Treasurer

Directors: Martine Rothblatt/Chmn., CEO, Christopher Patusky/Dir., Ray Kurzweil/Dir., Louis W. Sullivan/Dir., Raymond A. Dwek/66/Dir., Member - Scientific Advisory Board, Roger Jeffs/Dir., COO, Pres., Christopher Causey/Dir., Paul R. Gray/Dir., John Vane/Member - Scientific Advisory Board, Baruch S. Blumberg/Member - Scientific Advisory Board, Robert C. Bourge/Member - Scientific Advisory Board, Magdi Yacoub/Member - Scientific Advisory Board

Owners: Ziff Asset Management, L.P./7.50%, Roger Jeffs/1.30%, GLG Partners LP/7.50%, Insiders/10.60%, Shumway Capital Partners LLC/5.20%, Louis Sullivan, Christopher Causey, Raymond Kurzweil, Paul R. Gray, John Ferrari, Kingdon Capital Management/6.00%, Fred Hadeed, Raymond Dwek, Deutsche Bank AG/5.40%, Morgan Stanley/7.30% (*21 Owners included in Index*)

Financial Data: *Fiscal Year End:*12/31 *Latest Annual Data:* 12/31/2006

Year	Sales	Net Income
2006	$159,632,000	$73,965,000
2005	$115,915,000	$65,016,000
2004	$73,590,000	$15,449,000

Curr. Assets:	$277,374,000	*Curr. Liab.:*	$19,250,000	*P/E Ratio:*	21.54
Plant, Equip.:	$34,681,000	*Total Liab.:*	$273,944,000	*Indic. Yr. Divd.:*	NA
Total Assets	$478,550,000	*Net Worth:*	$204,606,000	*Debt/ Equity:*	1.5399

United Traffic Systems Inc

300 - 1055 W Hastings St., Vancouver, BC, V6E 2E9; *PH:* 1-604-681-8080

General - Incorporation	BC	**Stock**- Price on:12/24/2007	$0.005
Employees	NA	Stock Exchange	NA
Auditor	D&H Group LLP	Ticker Symbol	NA
Stk Agt	Holladay Stock Transfer, Inc.	Outstanding Shares	NA
Counsel	NA	E.P.S.	NA
DUNS No.	NA	Shareholders	NA

Business: The groups principal activity is seeking a gold mine in the peoples republic of China. The group located several potential mines and is presently executing a preliminary due diligence before proceeding with assay studies. The group operates from the China.

Primary SIC and add'l.: 1000

CIK No: 0001212787

Officers: Jai Woo Lee/57/Dir., CEO, Pres., Hye Kyung Kim/52/Dir., Sec.

Directors: Jai Woo Lee/57/Dir., CEO, Pres., Hye Kyung Kim/52/Dir., Sec.

Owners: Insiders/45.76%, Jai Woo Lee/28.29%, CDS & Co./12.16%, Hye Kyung Kim/17.47%

Financial Data: *Fiscal Year End:*12/31 *Latest Annual Data:* 12/31/2005

Year	Sales	Net Income
2005	NA	-$373,000
2004	$5,000	-$1,349,000
2003	NA	-$248,000

Curr. Assets:	NA	*Curr. Liab.:*	NA		
Plant, Equip.:	NA	*Total Liab.:*	NA	*Indic. Yr. Divd.:*	NA
Total Assets	NA	*Net Worth:*	NA	*Debt/ Equity:*	NA

United Utilities Plc

Dawson House, Great Sankey, WA5 3LW; *PH:* 44-1925237000; *http://* www.unitedutilities.com; *Email:* info@uuplc.co.uk

General - Incorporation	UK	**Stock**- Price on:12/24/2007	$30.52
Employees	17,029	Stock Exchange	OTC
Auditor	Deloitte & Touche LLP	Ticker Symbol	UUPLY
Stk Agt	Morgan ADR Service Center	Outstanding Shares	877,500,000
Counsel	NA	E.P.S.	$0.98
DUNS No.	23-776-0277	Shareholders	NA

Business: The group's principle activities are managing and operating electricity distribution, water and wastewater assets; managing infrastructure and business processes for its own and other businesses; and providing voice, basic and advanced communication services to the business customer market. It manages more than 700 treatment works and almost 140,000 kilometers of pipes, sewers and cables.

Primary SIC and add'l.: 4941 3823 4952 4911 8741 4813

CIK No: 0001053775

Subsidiaries: 1st Software Group Limited, 4Delivery Limited, Aqua SA, AS Tallinna Vesi, Campaspe Asset Management Services Pty Limited, Catchment (Moray) Limited, Catchment (Tay) Limited, Catchment Limited, First Revenue Assurance LLC, Macarthur Water Pty Limited, Meter Serve (North East) Limited, Meter Serve (North West) Limited, Onkaparinga Pty Limited, Riverland Water Pty Limited, Sofijska Voda A.D. 39 Subsidiaries included in the Index

Officers: Philip Green/55/Dir., CEO, Tim Weller/45/CFO, Joanne Thompson/Wastewater Scheduler, Tom Fallon/Treasurer, Paul Capell/MD - Business Development, Martin Bradbury/52/CIO, Clive Elphick/51/MD - Asset Management, Regulation, Gaynor Kenyon/Communications Dir., Charlie Cornish/48/Dir., MD - Utility Solutions, Darren Jameson/Head - Investor Relation, Adrian Rowley/Sr. Design Engineer, Jerry Holdsworth/Sr. Design Engineer, Caroline Cornwell/Waste Analyst Scientist, Alison Clarke/41/Dir. - Human Resources

Directors: Philip Green/55/Dir., CEO, Peter Middleton/74/Dep. Chmn., Richard Evans/65/Chmn., Catherine Bell/57/Non Exec. Dir., Charlie Cornish/48/Dir., MD - Utility Solutions, Norman Broadhurst/67/Non Exec. Dir., Paul Heiden/51/Non Exec. Dir., Andrew Pinder/61/Non Exec. Dir., David Jones/66/Non Exec. Dir., Nick Salmon/55/Non Exec. Dir.

Financial Data: *Fiscal Year End:*03/31 *Latest Annual Data:* 3/31/2006

Year	Sales	Net Income
2006	$4,190,482,000	$304,639,000
2005	$4,449,848,000	$471,065,000
2004	$3,761,972,000	$357,935,000

Curr. Assets:	$3,671,674,000	*Curr. Liab.:*	$2,957,486,000	*P/E Ratio:*	18.18
Plant, Equip.:	$14,414,417,000	*Total Liab.:*	$15,076,238,000	*Indic. Yr. Divd.:*	$1.770
Total Assets	$21,885,466,000	*Net Worth:*	$6,806,272,000	*Debt/ Equity:*	NA

Unitedhealth Group Inc

9900 Bren Rd. E, Minnetonka, MN, 55343; *PH:* 1-952-936-1300; *http://* www.unitedhealthgroup.com

General - Incorporation	MN	**Stock**- Price on:12/24/2007	$52.68
Employees	58,000	Stock Exchange	NYSE
Auditor	Deloitte & Touche LLP	Ticker Symbol	UNH
Stk Agt	Wells Fargo Bank Minnesota N.A	Outstanding Shares	1,340,000,000
Counsel	Dorsey & Whitney LLP	E.P.S.	$3.34
DUNS No.	11-287-1561	Shareholders	NA

Business: The group's principle activity is to provide health care coverage and related services to health care purchasers and providers. It also provides specially managed care products and services to employers, employee groups, insurers, health maintenance organization and other providers. The group operates in four segments. Uniprise business serves the employee benefit needs of large organizations. Health care service segment coordinates health and well-being services on behalf of local employers and consumers nationwide, Americans age 50 and older, facilitates health care benefits and services for state medicaid and other government-sponsored health care programs and their beneficiaries. Specialized care service business is focused on highly specialized health care and financial assurance needs. Ingenix business serves multiple health care markets. The group's quarterly revenue for September 2007 was 18,679.00 millions of USD.

Primary SIC and add'l.: 6324 8741 8099

CIK No: 0000731766

Subsidiaries: ACN Group IPA of New York, Inc., ACN Group of California, Inc., ACN Group, Inc., Active Transportation, LLC, Ad-Ventures, Inc., Advana, Inc., AIG United HealthCare LLC, All Savers Insurance Company, Alliance Recovery Services, LLC, American Medical Security Group, Inc., American Medical Security Life Ins. Co., AmeriChoice Alliance, Inc., AmeriChoice Corporation, AmeriChoice Health Services, Inc., AmeriChoice of New Jersey, Inc. 232 Subsidiaries included in the Index

Officers: Stephen J. Hemsley/Dir., CEO, COO, Pres. - Unitedhealth Group/$15,549,030.00, Richard H. Anderson/52/Exec. VP/$4,325,612.00, Jeannine M. Rivet/Exec. VP, Reed V. Tuckson/Exec. VP, Chief - Medical Affairs, Lori Sweere/Exec. VP - Human Capital, Forrest G. Burke/46/Acting General Counsel, Lois E. Quam/46/Exec. VP/$3,812,299.00, William A. Munsell/Exec. VP, John S. Penshorn/Sr. VP - Unitedhealth Group, Mike G. Mikan/CFO, Exec. VP - Unitedhealth Group, Anthony Welters/Exec. VP, David S. Wichmann/Exec. VP, George L. Mikan/CFO, Exec. VP/$3,339,278.00, Thomas L. Strickland/Exec. VP, Chief Legal Officer, Don Nathan/Sr. VP, Chief Communications Officer *(16 Officers included in Index)*

Directors: Stephen J. Hemsley/Dir., CEO, COO, Pres. - Unitedhealth Group, Richard T. Burke/Chmn., Donna E. Shalala/Dir., Gail R. Wilensky/Dir., James A. Johnson/Dir., Mary O. Mundinger/Dir., William C. Ballard/Dir., Douglas W. Leatherdale/Dir., Thomas H. Kean/Dir., Robert L. Ryan/Dir.

Owners: George L. Mikan, Thomas H. Kean, Lois E. Quam, FMR Corp./5.02%, Richard H. Anderson, David J. Lubben, William C. Ballard, Mary O. Mundinger, Douglas W. Leatherdale, Insiders/1.69%, Marsico Capital Management, LLC/7.10%, James A. Johnson, Robert L. Ryan, Richard T. Burke, William W. McGuire/2.37% *(20 Owners included in Index)*

Financial Data: **Fiscal Year End:** 12/31 **Latest Annual Data:** 12/31/2006

Year	Sales	Net Income
2006	$71,542,000,000	$4,159,000,000
2005	$45,365,000,000	$3,300,000,000
2004	$37,218,000,000	$2,587,000,000

Curr. Assets:	$16,044,000,000	**Curr. Liab.:**	$18,497,000,000	**P/E Ratio:**	17.56
Plant, Equip.:	$1,894,000,000	**Total Liab.:**	$27,510,000,000	**Indic. Yr. Divd.:**	$0.030
Total Assets:	$48,320,000,000	**Net Worth:**	$20,810,000,000	**Debt/ Equity:**	NA

Uniti Financial Corp

6301 Beach Blvd. No. 100, Buena Park, CA, 90621; *PH:* 1-714-736-5700; *Fax:* 1-714-736-5708; *http://* www.unitibank.com

General - Incorporation		**Stock**- Price on:12/24/2007	$7.65
Employees	NA	Stock Exchange	OTC
Auditor	NA	Ticker Symbol	UIFC
Stk Agt	U.S. Stock Transfer Corp	Outstanding Shares	NA
Counsel	NA	E.P.S	NA
DUNS No.	NA	Shareholders	NA

Business: The groups principal activities include providing banking and financial services to the businesses and customers. Services of the group include checking accounts, savings accounts, certificates of deposit, installment loans, real estate mortgage loans, commercial loans, traveler's checks, safe deposit boxes, night depository and automated teller services.

Primary SIC and add'l.: 8742

CIK No:

Officers: David H. Choi/Exec. VP, Chief Marketing Officer - Uniti Bank, Hannah Yang/First VP, Branch Mgr. - Buena Park Office, Uniti Bank, Young Hwang/First VP, Branch Mgr. - Los Angeles Office, Uniti Bank, Myung Kim/Regional Administrator amp - Garden Grove Office, Uniti Bank, Tae Yon Chung/VP, Regional Mgr. - Washington DC LPO, Uniti Bank, Kenneth Choi/First VP, Mgr. - Trade Financial Department, Uniti Bank, James Jeong/Sr. VP, Mgr. - SBA Department, Uniti Bank, Gloria Lee/Sr. VP, Chief Credit Administrator - Credit Administration Department, Uniti Bank, Chong Lee/Sr. VP, Operations Administration Mgr. - Operations Administration Department, Uniti Bank, Albert Sang/Exec. VP, COO - Uniti Bank

Directors: Yong Oh/Chmn., Myong Ho Ro/Dir., Michael Sangwoong Hyun/Dir., Yong Sung Kim/Dir., Chul Ho Chang/Dir., Myong Kyun Cynn/Dir., Gene Sukjin Han/Dir., Kiong Su Han/Dir., David D. Won/Dir., Shin Yoo/Dir.

Unitil Corp

6 Liberty Ln. W, Hampton, NH, 03842; *PH:* 1-603-773-6504; *http://* www.unitil.com

General - Incorporation	NH	**Stock**- Price on:12/24/2007	$28.05
Employees	304	Stock Exchange	AMEX
Auditor	Vitale, Caturano & Co. Ltd	Ticker Symbol	UTL
Stk Agt	Computershare Investor Services LLC	Outstanding Shares	5,670,000
Counsel	NA	E.P.S	$1.56
DUNS No.	12-136-1729	Shareholders	NA

Business: The group's principal activity is the retail sale and distribution of electricity in New Hampshire and electric and gas services in Massachusetts through its three retail distribution utility subsidiaries. The group's wholesale electric power subsidiary, unitil power corp, provides all the electric power supply requirements for the two utility subsidiaries, concord electric company and exeter and hampton electric company, for resale at retail. Natural gas is supplied and distributed by fitchburg gas and electric light company, a wholly owned utility subsidiary of the group. The group also provides Internet-based energy brokering, consulting and management related services through its non-utility subsidiary, unitil resources inc, usource inc. And usource llc.

Primary SIC and add'l.: 4939 4922

CIK No: 0000755001

Subsidiaries: Electric Light Company., Fitchburg Gas., Unitil Energy Systems Inc., Unitil Power Corp, Unitil Realty Corp., Unitil Resources Inc., Unitil Service Corp., Usource, Inc

Officers: Robert G. Schoenberger/57/Chmn., CEO, Pres./$1,019,013.00

Directors: Robert G. Schoenberger/57/Chmn., CEO, Pres., Edward F. Godfrey/58/Dir., Robert V. Antonucci/62/Dir., Michael B. Green/58/Dir., Brian M. O'Shaughnessy/65/Dir., Charles H. Tenney/60/Dir., Sarah P. Voll/65/Dir., Albert H. Elfner/63/Dir., David P. Brownell/64/Dir., Eben S. Moulton/61/Dir., Michael J. Dalton/67/Dir.

Owners: Todd R. Black, Mark H. Collin, Brian M. OShaughnessy, Insiders/4.73%, Edward F. Godfrey, Michael J. Dalton, Sarah P. Voll, David P. Brownell, Thomas P. Meissner, Albert H. Elfner, Charles H. Tenney, Michael B. Green, Eben S. Moulton, Robert G. Schoenberger/2.31%, Robert V. Antonucci *(16 Owners included in Index)*

Financial Data: **Fiscal Year End:** 12/31 **Latest Annual Data:** 12/31/2006

Year	Sales	Net Income
2006	$260,861,000	$8,033,000
2005	$232,145,000	$8,553,000
2004	$214,137,000	$8,226,000

Curr. Assets:	$46,697,000	**Curr. Liab.:**	$53,470,000	**P/E Ratio:**	17.98
Plant, Equip.:	$231,808,000	**Total Liab.:**	$383,569,000	**Indic. Yr. Divd.:**	$1.380
Total Assets:	$483,427,000	**Net Worth:**	$98,000,000	**Debt/ Equity:**	2.3013

Unitrin Inc

One E Wacker Dr., Chicago, IL, 60601; *PH:* 1-312-664-4600; *http://* www.unitrin.com

General - Incorporation	DE	**Stock**- Price on:12/24/2007	$48.65
Employees	8,000	Stock Exchange	NYSE
Auditor	Deloitte & Touche LLP	Ticker Symbol	UTR
Stk Agt	Computershare Trust Co	Outstanding Shares	66,330,000
Counsel	NA	E.P.S	$4.20
DUNS No.	61-193-5909	Shareholders	NA

Business: The groups principle activity is to provide financial services including property and casualty insurance, life and health insurance, and consumer finance for individuals, families and small businesses. The group operates through six business segments namely Kemper Auto and Home, Unitrin Specialty, Unitrin Direct, Unitrin Business Insurance, Life and Health Insurance and Consumer Finance. The group operates from United States.

Primary SIC and add'l.: 6321 6311 6159 6799 6331 6324

CIK No: 0000860748

Subsidiaries: B.H. Acquisition Ltd., Bantry Holdings Ltd., Blackrock Holdings Ltd., Brittany Insurance Company Ltd., Castlewood (EU) Holdings Ltd., Castlewood (EU) Ltd., Castlewood (US) Inc., Castlewood Brokers Limited, Castlewood Holdings (US) Inc., Castlewood Holdings Limited, Castlewood Investments, Inc., Castlewood Limited, Compagnie Europeene d'Assurances Industrielles SA, Cranmore (Bermud Ltd., Cranmore (US) Inc. 40 Subsidiaries included in the Index

Officers: Donald G. Southwell/Dir., CEO, Pres./$3,330,003.00, Scott Carter/Pres. - Unitrin Direct, Chicago, Illinois, Ronald E. Greco/VP - Corporate Actuary, Unitrin Services Company, Chicago, Illinois, John M. Boschelli/VP, Treasurer/$510,503.00, John W. Mullen/Pres. - Unitrin Specialty, Dallas, Texas, Scott Renwick/Sr. VP, General Counsel, Sec./$1,252,189.00, Joe Cole/Pres. - Reserve National Insurance Company, Oklahoma City, Oklahoma, David F. Bengston/VP, Edward J. Konar/VP, James J. Collins/Pres. - Career Agency Property Program, St. Louis, Missouri, James A. Schulte/Pres. - Unitrin Kemper Auto, Home, Group Exec., Unitrin Business Insurance, Jacksonville, Florida, Fred H. Reichelt/Pres. - Fireside Bank, Pleasanton, California, Eric J. Draut/Dir., CFO, Exec. VP/$2,405,959.00, Milton E. Slaughter/Pres. - Southern States General Agency, Ruston, Louisiana, Charles L. Wood/Group Exec., Fireside Bank, Reserve National Insurance Company, Chicago, Illinois *(18 Officers included in Index)*

Directors: Donald G. Southwell/Dir., CEO, Pres., Richard C. Vie/Chmn., James E. Annable/Dir., Jerrold V. Jerome/Dir., William E. Johnston/Dir., Eric J. Draut/Dir., CFO, Exec. VP, Donald V. Fites/Dir., Reuben L. Hedlund/Dir., Fayez S. Sarofim/Dir., Wayne Kauth/Dir., Ann E. Ziegler/Dir., Douglas G. Geoga/Dir.

Owners: Douglas G. Geoga, Jerrold V. Jerome, John M. Boschelli, Scott Renwick, William E. Johnston, Donald V. Fites, Fayez S. Sarofim/6.80%, Donald G. Southwell, Wayne Kauth, Barclays Global Investors, NA, Barclays Global Investors, Ltd./7.10%, Eric J. Draut, Ann E. Ziegler, Reuben L. Hedlund, Insiders/11.00%, James E. Annable *(18 Owners included in Index)*

Financial Data: **Fiscal Year End:** 12/31 **Latest Annual Data:** 12/31/2006

Year	Sales	Net Income
2006	$3,075,500,000	$283,100,000
2005	$3,048,100,000	$255,500,000
2004	$3,040,800,000	$240,200,000

Curr. Assets:	$1,353,500,000	**Curr. Liab.:**	$1,835,300,000	**P/E Ratio:**	11.58
Plant, Equip.:	NA	**Total Liab.:**	$7,037,400,000	**Indic. Yr. Divd.:**	$1.820
Total Assets:	$9,321,400,000	**Net Worth:**	$2,284,000,000	**Debt/ Equity:**	0.2177

Unity Bancorp Inc

64 Old Hwy 22, Clinton, NJ, 08809; *PH:* 1-908-730-7630; *http://* www.unitybank.com

General - Incorporation	NJ	**Stock**- Price on:12/24/2007	$11.43
Employees	175	Stock Exchange	NDQ
Auditor	KPMG LLP	Ticker Symbol	UNTY
Stk Agt	Registrar & Transfer Co	Outstanding Shares	6,990,000
Counsel	NA	E.P.S	$0.69
DUNS No.	92-827-5841	Shareholders	NA

Business: The group's principal activity is to provide full-service commercial banking services to a wide range of business and consumer financial services through its main office and twelve branch offices in New Jersey. The group is a one-bank holding company for unity bank. The services provided by the group include acceptance of demand, savings and time deposits, extension of consumer, real estate, small business administration and other commercial credits as well as personal investment advisory services. At 31-Dec-2003, the services are provided through its main offices and thirteen other branches located in clinton, colonial, edison, flemington, highland park, linden, north plainfield, scotch plains, south plainfield, springfield, union, bridgewater and whitehouse in New Jersey.

Primary SIC and add'l.: 6022 6712

CIK No: 0000920427

Subsidiaries: Unity Bank and Unity Statutory Trust I., Unity Financial Services, Inc., Unity Investment Company, Inc

Officers: James A. Hughes/Dir., CEO, Pres., Michael F. Downes/Exec. VP, Chief Lending Officer/$222,171.00, Kelly A. Stashko/CTO, Exec. VP, Alan J. Bedner/CFO, Exec. VP/$161,463.00, John J. Kauchak/COO, Exec. VP/$173,272.00

Directors: James A. Hughes/Dir., CEO, Pres., David D. Dallas/Chmn., Allen Tucker/Vice Chmn., Frank Ali/Dir., Mark Stewart Brody/Dir., Charles S. Loring/Dir., Wayne Courtright/Dir., Robert H. Dallas/Dir., Peter E. Maricondo/Dir., Donna S. Butler/Dir. Emeritus, Peter P. Detommaso/Dir. Emeritus, Samuel Stothoff/Dir. Emeritus

Owners: Frank Ali/0.69%, James A. Hughes/1.43%, Peter E. Maricondo/0.06%, Insiders/36.67%, Charles S. Loring/3.61%, The Banc Funds Company/5.20%, Wayne Courtright/1.08%, Michael F. Downes/1.36%, Allen Tucker/3.76%, David D. Dallas/14.14%, Robert H. Dallas/13.56%, Alan J. Bedner/0.36%, Mark S. Brody/8.37%, Wellington Management Company/5.90%, John J. Kauchak/1.46%

Financial Data: **Fiscal Year End:** 12/31 **Latest Annual Data:** 12/31/2006

Year	Sales	Net Income
2006	$50,815,000	$5,845,000
2005	$42,027,000	$6,210,000
2004	$33,795,000	$5,330,000

Curr. Assets:	$59,712,000	**Curr. Liab.:**	$568,134,000	**P/E Ratio:**	15.04
Plant, Equip.:	$11,821,000	**Total Liab.:**	$647,878,000	**Indic. Yr. Divd.:**	$0.200
Total Assets:	$694,106,000	**Net Worth:**	$46,228,000	**Debt/ Equity:**	1.8765

Unity Holdings Inc

950 Joe Frank Harris Pkwy SE, Cartersville, GA, 30121; *PH:* 1-770-606-0555;
http:// www.unitynationalbank.com

General - Incorporation	GA	Stock- Price on:12/24/2007	NA
Employees	NA	Stock Exchange	NA
Auditor	Mauldin & Jenkins LLC	Ticker Symbol	NA
Stk Agt	Computershare Trust Co	Outstanding Shares	NA
Counsel	NA	E.P.S.	NA
DUNS No.	NA	Shareholders	NA

Business: The group's principal activity is the provision of general commercial banking services in the state of Georgia. A holding company of unity national bank, the group accepts various deposits and provides a range of lending services. Depository services include checking, commercial, now, savings accounts, and other time deposit accounts. The group also offers individual retirement accounts and daily money market accounts. Lending services comprise of real estate, commercial and consumer loans to individuals, small and medium-sized businesses and professional concerns. The primary component of the group's portfolio is loans secured by first or second mortgages on real estate. Other services include cash management, safe deposit boxes, traveler's checks, payroll deposits and credit card services. The principal market area for the group consists of bartow and floyd counties, Georgia, with a secondary market in the counties of cherokee, chattooga, gordon and polk.

Primary SIC and add'l.: 6712 6022

CIK No: 0001054929

Subsidiaries: A National Bank, Unity National Bank

Officers: Michael L. McPherson/Dir., Pres., CEO - Unity National Bank/$278,759.00, Stewart Griggs/Exec. VP - Sr. Lender, Unity National Bank/$201,756.00, Mike Stover/VP - Commercial Lender Rome, Unity National Bank, Hazel Temples/BSA, Security Officer Operations Center - Unity National Bank, Eli D. Mullis/Sr. VP, CFO - Unity National Bank/$137,352.00, Kimberly Abernathy/VP - Human Resources, Unity National Bank, Connie Mitchell-White/VP - Retail Division, Marketing, Unity National Bank, Brandon Adams/Compliance Officer Operations Center - Unity National Bank, Joe Lynch/Collections Officer Cartersville - Henderson Drive, Unity National Bank, Christie McLaughlin/VP - Deposit Operations Operations Center, Unity National Bank, April Scott/Business Development Officer - Unity National Bank, Bryan Shealy/Lending Officer Adairsville - Unity National Bank, Jeremy Smith/Lending Officer Main Office - Unity National Bank, Michael Smith/VP - Commercial Lender Adairsville, Unity National Bank, Jeffrey Starke/Technology Officer Operations Center - Unity National Bank *(22 Officers included in Index)*

Directors: Michael L. McPherson/Dir., Pres., CEO - Unity National Bank, Jerry W. Braden/Chmn. - Unity National Bank, Kenneth R. Bishop/Dir., Stanley A. Taylor/Dir. - Unity National Bank, Donald D. George/Dir. - Unity National Bank, Stephen A. Taylor/Dir. - Unity National Bank, John S. Lewis/Dir., Sam R. McCleskey/Dir. - Unity National Bank, Don B. Temples/Dir.

Owners: Stephen A. Taylor/5.62%, Michael L. McPherson/6.80%, Jerry W. Braden/5.32%, Insiders/39.96%, Stewart W. Griggs/5.05%, Sam R. McCleskey/4.22%, B. Don Temples/4.49%, Eli D. Mullis/0.12%, John S. Lewis/3.95%, Kenneth R. Bishop/3.11%, Donald D. George/4.28%

Unity Wireless Corp

1313 E Maple St. , Ste. No.415, Bellingham, WA, 98225; *PH:* 1-360-685-4287;
Fax: 1-360-685-4222; *http://* www.unitywireless.com

General - Incorporation	DE	Stock- Price on:12/24/2007	$0.115
Employees	NA	Stock Exchange	OTC
Auditor	KPMG LLP	Ticker Symbol	UTYW
Stk Agt	Computershare Trust Co	Outstanding Shares	NA
Counsel	NA	E.P.S.	NA
DUNS No.	NA	Shareholders	NA

Business: The groups principle activities include manufacturing and selling high power amplifiers and related integrated RF front end hardware and software subsystems. The group operates from the United States, China, Israel and Canada. The group's quarterly revenue for Sep '07 was 1.07 millions of USD.

Primary SIC and add'l.: 4812

CIK No: 0001100451

Subsidiaries: 321373 B.C. Ltd., Unity Wireless Systems Corporation

Officers: Ilan Kenig/Dir., CEO, Pres./$261,093.00, Andrew James Chamberlain/Dir., Corp. Sec., Dallas Pretty/38/CFO/$213,048.00, Raffi Antepyan/CTO, GM Canada, Nissim Atias/COO, Pres., Michael Manor/Exec. VP - Sales - Coverage Enhancement Solutions, Rick Byrd/VP - Sales, Original Equipment Manufacturers, Gilad Kiper/Finance Eastern Hemisphere, Eric Tsung/Finance Western Hemisphere

Directors: Ilan Kenig/Dir., CEO, Pres., Ken Maddison/Dir., Victor Halpert/Dir., Andrew James Chamberlain/Dir., Corp. Sec., Doron Nevo/Dir., David Goldschmidt/Dir., Amir Gal-Or/Dir., Ellie Barr/Dir.

Owners: IDB Infinity Venture Capital Group/15.69%, Andrew Chamberlain, SVM Star Venture Capital Group/28.12%, Ilan Kenig/1.82%, Gemini Venture Capital Group/7.73%, Doron Nevo, Valley Venture Capital L.P./12.77%, Ken Maddison, Victor Halpert, William Weidman/13.33%, Dallas Pretty

*Financial Data: Fiscal Year End:*12/31 *Latest Annual Data:* 12/31/2006

Year	Sales		Net Income
2006	$7,344,000		-$14,835,000
2005	$4,906,000		-$5,450,000
2004	$5,021,000		-$3,319,000
Curr. Assets:	$7,347,000	Curr. Liab.:	$15,038,000	P/E Ratio:	30.88
Plant, Equip.:	$1,314,000	Total Liab.:	$20,998,000	Indic. Yr. Divd.:	NA
Total Assets:	$24,761,000	Net Worth:	$3,763,000	Debt/ Equity:	NA

Univec Inc

4810 Seton Dr., Baltimore, MD, 21215; *PH:* 1-410-347-9959; *http://* www.univec.com;
Email: univec@univec.com

General - Incorporation	DE	Stock- Price on:12/24/2007	NA
Employees	4	Stock Exchange	OTC
Auditor	Abrams, Foster, Nole & Williams	Ticker Symbol	UNVC
Stk Agt	Continental Stock Transfer & Trust Co	Outstanding Shares	NA
Counsel	NA	E.P.S.	-$0.01
DUNS No.	82-599-0724	Shareholders	NA

Business: The group's principal activities are to license, manufacture and market auto-disable and safety syringes and portable units for onsite disposal of medical and sharps waste. The group also assists pharmaceutical companies in marketing, fulfillment and tracking drug samples. The products of the group include 1cc auto-disable syringes and sliding sheath syringes. The group markets its ad-syringes and sliding sheath safety syringes to governments of developing countries, private hospitals and health facilities and distributors in the United States. The group also licenses its patents and proprietary manufacturing processes relating to its 1cc ad-syringe and other syringe designs.

Primary SIC and add'l.: 3841

CIK No: 0001029825

Subsidiaries: Physician and Pharmaceutical Services Inc

Officers: David Dalton/59/Dir., CEO, Pres., Raphael Langford/63/COO, Exec. VP, Michael Lesisko/57/Treasurer, Sec., CFO

Directors: David Dalton/59/Dir., CEO, Pres., Robert S. Grass/74/Chmn., William Wooldridge/61/Dir.

Owners: Michael Lesisko/4.10%, Raphael Langford/5.05%, William Wooldridge, Robert S. Grass/1.83%, David Dalton/49.82%, Insiders/58.08%, Emerald Capital Partners LP/9.48%

*Financial Data: Fiscal Year End:*12/31 *Latest Annual Data:* 12/31/2006

Year	Sales		Net Income
2006	$21,000		-$1,183,000
2005	$81,000		-$1,889,000
2004	$328,000		-$4,021,000
Curr. Assets:	$58,000	Curr. Liab.:	$4,954,000		
Plant, Equip.:	$407,000	Total Liab.:	$6,602,000	Indic. Yr. Divd.:	NA
Total Assets:	$506,000	Net Worth:	-$6,095,000	Debt/ Equity:	NA

Univercell Holdings Inc

4775 Collins Ave., Ste. 1604, Miami Beach, FL, 33140; *PH:* 1-786-276-7817

General - Incorporation	FL	Stock- Price on:12/24/2007	$0.0035
Employees	1	Stock Exchange	OTC
Auditor	Chisholm Bierwolf & Nilson LLC	Ticker Symbol	UVCL
Stk Agt	Corporate Stock Transfer, Inc.	Outstanding Shares	199,250,000
Counsel	NA	E.P.S.	-$0.001
DUNS No.	60-920-4599	Shareholders	NA

Business: The group's principal activities are to provide mobile telephone services to U.S. Travelers going overseas. The group also offers wireless phone, fax, data and Internet communication services to business travelers, leisure travelers and students. The services of the group include international cellular phone rentals, global system mobile communication services, prepaid international wireless gsm service, satellite phone rentals and high-speed data card rentals.

Primary SIC and add'l.: 4899

CIK No: 0000894680

Subsidiaries: UniverCell Global Phone rentals

Officers: Sean Y. Fulda/31/Chmn., CEO, CFO, CAO, Pres.

Directors: Sean Y. Fulda/31/Chmn., CEO, CFO, CAO, Pres., David M. Friedman/56/Dir., Michael D. Fulda/Dir.

Owners: Michael D. Fulda/0.10%, David M. Friedman/0.30%, Sean Y. Fulda/50.40%

*Financial Data: Fiscal Year End:*12/31 *Latest Annual Data:* 12/31/2006

Year	Sales		Net Income
2006	NA		-$268,000
2005	NA		$37,000
2004	NA		-$581,000
Curr. Assets:	NA	Curr. Liab.:	$475,000		
Plant, Equip.:	NA	Total Liab.:	$475,000	Indic. Yr. Divd.:	NA
Total Assets:	NA	Net Worth:	-$475,000	Debt/ Equity:	NA

Universal American Financial Corp

Six International Dr., Rye Brook, NY, 10573; *PH:* 1-914-934-5200; *http://* www.uafc.com

General - Incorporation	NY	Stock- Price on:12/24/2007	$20.55
Employees	1,400	Stock Exchange	NYSE
Auditor	Ernst & Young LLP	Ticker Symbol	UAM
Stk Agt	American Stock Transfer & Trust Co.	Outstanding Shares	59,440,000
Counsel	Harnett Lesnick & Ripps P.A	E.P.S.	$1.98
DUNS No.	08-136-8391	Shareholders	NA

Business: The group's principal activities are to sell life and accident and health insurance and annuities through its subsidiaries. The principal insurance products include medicare supplement, long term care, home health care, senior life insurance and fixed annuities. The group operates through three segments: career agency: distributes fixed benefit accident and sickness disability insurance, life insurance, senior health insurance and annuities. Senior market brokerage: distributes medicare supplements, long term care, senior life insurance and annuities. Administrative services: provides policy underwriting and issuance, telephone and face-to-face verification, policyholder services, claims adjudication, case management, care assessment and referral to health care facilities. In 2003, the group acquired ameriplus preferred care inc and pyramid life. In 2004 it acquired, heritage health systems inc.

Primary SIC and add'l.: 6311 6321 6719

CIK No: 0000709878

Subsidiaries: American Exchange Life Insurance Company, American Pioneer Life Insurance Company, American Progressive Life& Health Insurance Company of New York, Ameriplus Preferred Care,Inc., CHCS Services,Inc., Constitution Life Insurance Company, Heritage Health Systems,Inc., Marquette National Life Insurance Company, Peninsular Life Insurance Company, Penncorp Life Insurance Company, Pennsylvania Life Insurance Company, Pyramid Life Insurance Company, SelectCare HealthPlans,Inc., SelectCare of Oklahoma,Inc., SelectCare of Texas, LLC 23 Subsidiaries included in the Index

Officers: Richard A. Barasch/Chmn., CEO/$2,182,294.00, Theodore M. Carpenter/CEO, Pres. - Medicare Advantage Division, Jason J. Israel/COO - Chcs Services, Inc, Lisa M. Spivack/38/Sr. VP, General Counsel, Sec., Robert A. Waegelein/CFO, Exec. VP/$849,706.00, Gary W. Bryant/COO, Exec. VP/$938,499.00, Gary Jacobs/Sr. VP - Corporate Development

Directors: Richard A. Barasch/Chmn., CEO, Linda H. Lamel/Dir., Bradley E. Cooper/Dir., Robert A. Spass/Dir., Mark M. Harmeling/Dir., Eric Leathers/Dir., Bertram Harnett/85/Dir., Patrick J. McLaughlin/Dir., Robert F. Wright/Dir., Barry W. Averill/Dir.

Owners: Insiders/9.20%, Richard A. Barasch/4.60%, Ted Carpenter, Patrick J. McLaughlin, Robert A. Spass, Oz Management, L.L.C/5.50%, Linda H. Lamel, Bertram Harnett, Barry Averill, Gary W. Bryant/1.40%, Eric W. Leathers, Capital Z Partners, Ltd./28.00%, Robert A. Waegelein/1.20%, Perry Corp./9.80%, Jason J. Israel *(18 Owners included in Index)*

Financial Data: **Fiscal Year End:**12/31 **Latest Annual Data:** 12/31/2006

Year	Sales	Net Income
2006	$1,305,064,000	$119,306,000
2005	$931,923,000	$53,876,000
2004	$735,345,000	$63,871,000

Curr. Assets:	$981,306,000	**Curr. Liab.:**	$281,203,000	**P/E Ratio:**	10.59
Plant, Equip.:	NA	**Total Liab.:**	$1,961,133,000	**Indic. Yr. Divd.:**	NA
Total Assets:	$2,585,042,000	**Net Worth:**	$623,909,000	**Debt/ Equity:**	0.7499

Universal Capital Mgmt Inc

2601 Annand Dr. Ste. 16, Wilmington, DE, 19808; *PH:* 1-302-998-8824; *http://* www.unicapman.com

General - Incorporation	DE	**Stock**- Price on:12/24/2007	NA
Employees	NA	Stock Exchange	OTC
Auditor	Morison Cogen LLP	Ticker Symbol	UCMT
Stk Agt	NA	Outstanding Shares	NA
Counsel	NA	E.P.S	-$0.22
DUNS No.	NA	Shareholders	NA

Business: The group's principal activities are providing managerial, strategic and financial expertise to other companies. Industries in which the group invests include consumer products, business services, healthcare services, medical devices, nanotechnology and others. They also invest in equity, equity-related securities, a combination of debt and equity instruments as well as other beneficial ownership interest. These interests may include warrants, options, and convertible or exchangeable securities. The company also provides management recruiting services, assist with the strategic planning process and provide managerial assistance on issues such as personnel, real estate, marketing, capital expenditures and other related matters. They sometimes provide financial reporting services and tax reporting services for our investments as well as cash management treasury, auditing and other services.

Primary SIC and add'l.: 6722

CIK No: 0001308569

Officers: Michael D. Queen/Dir., CEO, Pres./$175,000.00, William R. Colucci/VP, Sec./$125,000.00, Joseph T. Drennan/Dir., CFO, VP/$125,000.00

Directors: Michael D. Queen/Dir., CEO, Pres., Joseph T. Drennan/Dir., CFO, VP, Jeff Muchow/Dir., Steven Pruitt/Dir., Thomas M. Pickard/Dir., Robert W. Ashton/Member - Advisory Board, Monterey, California, Jim Ludlow/Member - Advisory Board, Lehigh Valley, Pennsylvania, Jayshree Moorthy/Member - Advisory Board, Hockessin, Delaware, Stuart T. Saunders/Member - Advisory Board, Philadelphia, Pennsylvania, Stewart Taub/Member - Advisory Board, Hockessin, Delaware

Owners: L&B Partnership/5.52%, Zenith Holdings Inc./5.52%, Thomas M. Pickard, Joseph T. Drennan/7.36%, William R. Colucci/4.60%, McCrae Associates LLC/5.52%, Steven P. Pruitt/1.84%, Insiders/16.55%, David Bovi/9.98%, Jeffrey P. Muchow/1.84%

Financial Data: **Fiscal Year End:**04/30 **Latest Annual Data:** 04/30/2007

Year	Sales	Net Income
2007	$3,237,000	$333,000
2006	$895,000	-$888,000
2004	$245,000	-$6,223,000

Curr. Assets:	$2,342,000	**Curr. Liab.:**	$1,112,000		
Plant, Equip.:	$111,000	**Total Liab.:**	$1,112,000	**Indic. Yr. Divd.:**	NA
Total Assets:	$2,560,000	**Net Worth:**	$1,448,000	**Debt/ Equity:**	NA

Universal Corp

1501 N Hamilton St., Richmond, VA, 23230; *PH:* 1-804-359-9311; *http://* www.universalcorp.com

General - Incorporation	VA	**Stock**- Price on:12/24/2007	$61.72
Employees	25,000	Stock Exchange	NYSE
Auditor	Ernst & Young LLP	Ticker Symbol	UVV
Stk Agt	Wells Fargo Bank, N.A.	Outstanding Shares	27,030,000
Counsel	NA	E.P.S	$3.23
DUNS No.	00-794-1420	Shareholders	NA

Business: The groups principle activities include selecting, buying, shipping, processing, packing, storing and financing of leaf tobacco. The group operates from United States.

Primary SIC and add'l.: 5149 5031 5159

CIK No: 0000102037

Subsidiaries: Astrimex B.V., Barrow, Lane& Ballard, Ltd., Beleggings-en Beheermaatschappij De Amstel B. V., Bergenco Beheer B.V., Blending Services International, Inc., Casa Export, Limited, Casalee-Transtobac (Pvt) Ltd., Continental Tobacco S.A., Corrie MacColl& Son Ltd., Crailo B.V., De Verenigde Timmerfabrieken B. V., Deli Services B.V., Deli Universal, Inc., Deli-HTL Tabak Maatschappij B. V., Deli-Mij Holdings Ltd. 74 Subsidiaries included in the Index

Officers: Allen B. King/61/Chmn., CEO/$2,938,751.00, A. B. King/Chmn., CEO, W. K. Brewer/49/Exec. VP - Universal Leaf/$1,074,640.00, Hartwell H. Roper/CFO, VP/$1,175,008.00, George C. Freeman/Pres./$785,313.00, Robert M. Peebles/Controller, David C. Moore/VP, Chief Administrative Officer/$586,033.00, Karen M.L. Whelan/VP, Treasurer/$696,895.00, William J. Coronado/VP, Preston D. Wigner/General Counsel, Sec.

Directors: Allen B. King/61/Chmn., CEO, A. B. King/Chmn., CEO, Eddie N. Moore/59/Dir., Charles H. Foster/65/Dir., Thomas H. Johnson/57/Dir., Hubert R. Stallard/70/Dir., John B. Adams/62/Dir., Chester A. Crocker/65/Dir., Walter A. Stosch/70/Dir., Jeremiah J. Sheehan/68/Dir., Joseph C. Farrell/71/Dir., Eugene P. Trani/67/Dir.

Owners: AXA/6.20%, Hubert R. Stallard, Keith W. Brewer, Thomas H. Johnson, Walter A. Stosch, NFJ Investment Group L.P./5.60%, Barclays Global Investors, NA/10.20%, Hartwell H. Roper, David C. Moore, John B. Adams, Eugene P. Trani, Chester A. Crocker, Karen M. L. Whelan, Eddie N. Moore, Charles H. Foster *(21 Owners included in Index)*

Financial Data: **Fiscal Year End:**03/31 **Latest Annual Data:** 3/31/2006

Year	Sales	Net Income
2006	$3,511,332,000	$7,940,000
2005	$3,276,057,000	$96,013,000
2004	$2,271,152,000	$99,636,000

Curr. Assets:	$1,545,365,000	**Curr. Liab.:**	$692,974,000	**P/E Ratio:**	32.31
Plant, Equip.:	$360,158,000	**Total Liab.:**	$1,298,089,000	**Indic. Yr. Divd.:**	$1.800
Total Assets:	$2,328,822,000	**Net Worth:**	$1,030,733,000	**Debt/ Equity:**	0.3870

Universal Detection Technology

9595 Wilshire Blvd, Ste 700, Beverly Hills, CA, 90212; *PH:* 1-310-248-3655; *http://* www.udetection.com; *Email:* info@udetection.com

General - Incorporation	CA	**Stock**- Price on:12/24/2007	$0.0017
Employees	5	Stock Exchange	OTC
Auditor	Aj. Robbins, P.C	Ticker Symbol	UDTT
Stk Agt	Meyers Associates LP	Outstanding Shares	426,560,000
Counsel	NA	E.P.S	-$0.025
DUNS No.	06-381-5625	Shareholders	NA

Business: The group's principal activity is the research and development of bio-terrorism detection devices. It has developed a collaborative partnering strategy, which identifies and partners with researchers and developers. The group has entered into a technology affiliates agreement with nasa's jet propulsion laboratory (jpl), to develop technology for its bio-terrorism detection equipment. Currently, the group is devoting its efforts to raise capital and development and marketing of its bio-terrorism detection devices.

Primary SIC and add'l.: 7372 3829

CIK No: 0000763950

Subsidiaries: Dasibi Environmental Corp

Officers: Jacques Tizabi/Chmn., CEO, Nima Montazeri/Finance, Strategic Development, Amir Ettehadieh/Dir. - Research, Development, Ali Moussavi/VP - Global Strategy, Michael Collins/38/Dir., Sec.

Directors: Jacques Tizabi/Chmn., CEO, Louis J. Ignarro/Chmn. - Scientific Advisory Board, Leonard Makowka/Member - Scientific Advisory Board, Matin Emouna/39/Dir., Michael Collins/38/Dir., Sec.

Owners: Insiders/18.81%, Jacques Tizabi/18.81%

Financial Data: **Fiscal Year End:**12/31 **Latest Annual Data:** 12/31/2006

Year	Sales	Net Income
2006	$112,000	-$2,703,000
2005	NA	-$3,535,000
2004	$25,000	-$5,753,000

Curr. Assets:	$118,000	**Curr. Liab.:**	$3,464,000		
Plant, Equip.:	$82,000	**Total Liab.:**	$3,483,000	**Indic. Yr. Divd.:**	NA
Total Assets:	$328,000	**Net Worth:**	-$3,154,000	**Debt/ Equity:**	NA

Universal Display Corp

375 Phillips Blvd, Ewing, NJ, 08618; *PH:* 1-609-671-0980; *http://* www.universaldisplay.com

General - Incorporation	PA	**Stock**- Price on:12/24/2007	$16.45
Employees	62	Stock Exchange	NDQ
Auditor	KPMG LLP	Ticker Symbol	PANL
Stk Agt	American Stock Transfer & Trust Co.	Outstanding Shares	31,950,000
Counsel	Morgan, Lewis & Bockius LLP	E.P.S	-$0.52
DUNS No.	96-326-7893	Shareholders	NA

Business: The group's principal activities is to conduct research, develop and commercialize organic light emitting diode technology for use in flat panel displays and other applications. The products are used in notebook and laptop computers, portable televisions, video cameras, cellular phones, pagers and electronic organizers. The products are also used in digital watches, calculators, electronic games, copiers, facsimile machines and other equipment. These products are also used in military applications, including missile controls, ground support and communications equipment and avionics. The group is performing research along with princeton university and the university of southern California.

Primary SIC and add'l.: 3679 2899 8731

CIK No: 0001005284

Subsidiaries: UDC, Inc

Officers: Sherwin I. Seligsohn/Chmn., CEO/$486,698.00, Steven V. Abramson/Dir., COO, Pres./$809,215.00, Sidney D. Rosenblatt/Dir., CFO, Exec. VP/$813,250.00, Julia J. Brown/Member - Scientific Advisory Board, CTO, VP/$508,404.00, Mike Hack/VP - Strategic Product Development, Member - Scientific Advisory Board, Dean L. Ledger/Exec. VP, Ichiro Nakagawa/Official Representative IN Japan, Sui-Yuan Lynn/Official Representative IN Taiwan, Dir. - Southern Asia Operations

Directors: Sherwin I. Seligsohn/Chmn., CEO, Steven V. Abramson/Dir., COO, Pres., Sidney D. Rosenblatt/Dir., CFO, Exec. VP, Leonard Becker/Dir., Elizabeth H. Gemmill/Dir., Keith C. Hartley/Dir., Larry Lacerte/Dir., Julia J. Brown/Member - Scientific Advisory Board, CTO, VP, Stephen R. Forrest/Member - Scientific Advisory Board, Mark E. Thompson/Member - Scientific Advisory Board, Mike Hack/VP - Strategic Product Development, Member - Scientific Advisory Board, Peter Foller/Member - Scientific Advisory Board

Owners: FMR Corp., Sherwin I. Seligsohn, Leonard Becker, Lawrence Lacerte, Sidney D. Rosenblatt, Edward C. Johnson, Steven G. Winters, C. Keith Hartley, Elizabeth H. Gemmill, Lori S. Rubenstein, Insiders, Sherwin I. Seligsohn, Julia J. Brown, American Biomimetics Corporation, Steven V. Abramson

Financial Data: **Fiscal Year End:**12/31 **Latest Annual Data:** 12/31/2006

Year	Sales	Net Income
2006	$11,921,000	-$15,187,000
2005	$10,148,000	-$15,802,000
2004	$7,007,000	-$15,777,000

Curr. Assets:	$51,805,000	**Curr. Liab.:**	$14,383,000		
Plant, Equip.:	$14,074,000	**Total Liab.:**	$17,949,000	**Indic. Yr. Divd.:**	NA
Total Assets:	$72,332,000	**Net Worth:**	$54,382,000	**Debt/ Equity:**	NA

Universal Electronics Inc

6101 Gateway Dr., Cypress, CA, 90630; *PH:* 1-714-820-1000; *http://* www.ueic.com

General - Incorporation	DE	**Stock**- Price on:12/24/2007	$36.06
Employees	392	Stock Exchange	NDQ
Auditor	Grant Thornton LLP	Ticker Symbol	UEIC
Stk Agt	Computershare Investor Services LLC	Outstanding Shares	14,420,000
Counsel	Richard A. Firehammer Jr. Esq	E.P.S	$1.30
DUNS No.	60-205-2169	Shareholders	NA

Business: The group's principal activity is to develop software, build and market pre-programmed, easy-to-use wireless control devices and chips for home entertainment equipment and the subscription broadcasting market. These products are remote controls, wireless keyboards, gaming control devices, antennas, joysticks and library of codes and proprietary software. These are marketed for home video and audio entertainment equipment through various channels of distribution, including international retail,

private label, original equipment manufacturers and cable and satellite service providers. The group sells its wireless control devices internationally under the one for all(R) brand name. In addition, the group has licensed certain proprietary technology and its one for all brand name to a third party. The group also operates in the Netherlands, the United Kingdom, France and Germany.

Primary SIC and add'l.: 3651 3669

CIK No: 0000101984

Subsidiaries: One For All (UKLtd., One For All Argentina S.R.L., One For All France S.A.S., One For All GmbH, One For All Iberia S.L., SimpleDevices Inc., UEIC, LP, Ultra Control Consumer Electronics GmbH, Universal Electronics B.V., Universal Electronics GP, LLC, Universal Electronics LP, LLC

Officers: Paul D. Arling/Chmn., CEO/$1,340,720.00, Richard A. Firehammer/Sr. VP, General Counsel/$491,657.00, Ken Sweeney/Contact - OEM North America, West, Roy Alge/Contact - OEM North America, East, Wouter Schroer/Sales Mgr. Cedia - Outside North America, Erin Olsson/Contact - Media, Analyst Inquiries Only, Hemco Arentsen/Contact - Media, Analyst Inquiries Only, Europe, Jeroen Zuidhof/Contact - OEM EMEA, Middle East, Jill Trinka/Contact - Subscription Broadcast, Cable, North America, West, Wendell Callaway/Contact - Subscription Broadcast, Cable, North America, Central, Steve Gutman/Contact - Subscription Broadcast, Cable, North America, East, Giselle Borgo/Contact - Subscription Broadcast, Cable, Latin America, Olav Pouw/VP - Oemsales Europe, Paul Miller/Dir. - Sales, OEM Europe, Prasad Linganna/Sales Dir. - India, Middle East *(25 Officers included in Index)*

Directors: Paul D. Arling/Chmn., CEO, Satjiv Chahil/Dir., William Mulligan/Dir., Bruce Henderson/Dir., J. C. Sparkman/Dir., Edward Zinser/50/Dir.

Owners: Paul J. M. Bennett, Insiders/8.06%, Paul D. Arling/4.78%, William C. Mulligan, Richard A. Firehammer, Satjiv S. Chahil, J. C. Sparkman, Bruce A. Henderson, Bryan M. Hackworth, Edward K. Zinser, Lord, Abbett & Co. LLC/10.38%

Financial Data: Fiscal Year End:12/31   Latest Annual Data: 12/31/2006

Year	Sales	Net Income
2006	$235,846,000	$13,520,000
2005	$181,349,000	$9,701,000
2004	$158,380,000	$9,113,000

Curr. Assets:	$150,192,000	Curr. Liab.:	$44,013,000	P/E Ratio:	32.78
Plant, Equip.:	$5,899,000	Total Liab.:	$44,391,000	Indic. Yr. Divd.:	NA
Total Assets:	$178,608,000	Net Worth:	$134,217,000	Debt/ Equity:	NA

Universal Energy Corp

Formerly: Universal Tanning Ventures Inc
30 Skyline Dr., Lake Mary, FL, 32746; PH: 1-800-925-2076

General - Incorporation	DE	Stock - Price on:12/24/2007	NA
Employees	1	Stock Exchange	OTC
Auditor	Tedder, James, Worden & Assoc. P.A	Ticker Symbol	UVSE
Stk Agt	Madison Stock Transfer, Inc.	Outstanding Shares	NA
Counsel	NA	E.P.S.	-$0.28
DUNS No.	NA	Shareholders	NA

Business: The groups principle activities include acquiring and developing crude oil and natural gas properties. The group operates from United States and Canada.

Primary SIC and add'l.: NA

CIK No: 0001207029

Subsidiaries: UT Holdings, Inc.

Officers: Billy R. Raley/51/Dir., CEO/$2,465,000.00, Dyron M. Watford/Chmn., CFO/$2,464,000.00, Kevin Tattersall/Chief Exploration Officer/$661,750.00

Directors: Billy R. Raley/51/Dir., CEO, Dyron M. Watford/Chmn., CFO, Derek J. Gillespie/Member - Advisory Board, Peter Forrest/Member - Advisory Board, Zen Buss/Member - Advisory Board

Owners: Billy Raley/13.50%, Glen Woods/20.10%, Charissa Ioppolo/5.60%, Insiders/24.50%, Kevin Tattersall/0.80%, Dyron M. Watford/10.20%

Financial Data: Fiscal Year End:12/31   Latest Annual Data: 12/31/2006

Year	Sales	Net Income
2006	NA	-$773,000
2005	$141,000	-$72,000
2004	$147,000	-$62,000

Curr. Assets:	$497,000	Curr. Liab.:	$86,000		
Plant, Equip.:	$107,000	Total Liab.:	$86,000	Indic. Yr. Divd.:	NA
Total Assets:	$604,000	Net Worth:	$517,000	Debt/ Equity:	NA

Universal Express Inc

1230 Ave. Of The Americas, Ste 771, 7th Fl. Rockefeller Ctr., New York, NY, 10020; PH: 1-561-367-6177; http:// www.usxp.com; Email: info@usxp.com

General - Incorporation	NV	Stock - Price on:12/24/2007	$0.0005
Employees	37	Stock Exchange	OTC
Auditor	Durland & Co, CPAs P.A	Ticker Symbol	USXP
Stk Agt	North American Transfer Co	Outstanding Shares	21,390,000,000
Counsel	NA	E.P.S.	-$0.002
DUNS No.	15-138-8253	Shareholders	NA

Business: The group's principal activities are to provide services to the private postal and international shipping industries. The principal subsidiaries include universal express capital corp. And universal express logistics, inc. (which includes virtual bellhop, llc, luggage express and worldpost, its international shipping divisions), and private postal center network.com (ppn network) and its division postal business center network.com ("Pbc Network"). Worldpost(tm) sells skynet discounted envelopes and services to the postal stores. Luggage express(tm) enables consumers to have their baggage picked up at their home by a local ppn member store and delivered to their destination. Virtual bellhop(R) carries out door-to-door luggage transportation service. Universal express capital corp is a full service asset based transportation/equipment leasing company. On 01-Dec-2003, the group acquired sub-contracting concepts and on 29-Dec-2003, acquired bags to go inc.

Primary SIC and add'l.: 5399 4513 4731

CIK No: 0000857351

Subsidiaries: Downtown Theatre Ticket Agency, Inc., Packaging Plus Advertising, Inc., Packaging Plus Services, Inc., Private Postal Network.com, Inc., Skyworld International Couriers, Inc.

Officers: Richard A. Altomare/Chmn., CEO

Directors: Richard A. Altomare/Chmn., CEO

Owners: Richard A. Altomare

Financial Data: Fiscal Year End:06/30   Latest Annual Data: 6/30/2006

Year	Sales	Net Income
2006	$1,073,000	-$18,872,000
2005	$931,000	-$9,986,000
2004	$2,775,000	-$9,061,000

Curr. Assets:	$2,912,000	Curr. Liab.:	$1,599,000		
Plant, Equip.:	$207,000	Total Liab.:	$1,599,000	Indic. Yr. Divd.:	NA
Total Assets:	$6,022,000	Net Worth:	$4,423,000	Debt/ Equity:	NA

Universal Fog Inc

300 Pk. Ave., Ste 1700, New York, NY, 10022; PH: 1-212-572-6236; http:// www.unifog.com; Email: info@unifog.com

General - Incorporation	DE	Stock - Price on:12/24/2007	$0.05
Employees	12	Stock Exchange	OTC
Auditor	Turner, Stone & Co. LLP	Ticker Symbol	UFOG
Stk Agt	Interwest Transfer Company, Inc.	Outstanding Shares	40,660,000
Counsel	NA	E.P.S.	$0.00
DUNS No.	NA	Shareholders	NA

Business: The groups principle activity is to provide cooling systems. The groups systems are used for residential, commercial, industrial and agricultural applications. The group's specific customers include Disneyland, Disney World, Gietz Builders, Honeywell, Intel, Lockheed, Marriott and Motorola. The group operates from United States.

Primary SIC and add'l.: 9995

CIK No: 0001309057

Subsidiaries: Edmonds 6, Inc

Officers: Tom A. Bontems/Chmn., CEO

Directors: Tom A. Bontems/Chmn., CEO

Owners: Insiders/60.00%, Thomas Bontems/6.20%, Sun Xin/53.80%

Financial Data: Fiscal Year End:12/31   Latest Annual Data: 12/31/2006

Year	Sales	Net Income
2006	$842,000	-$166,000

Curr. Assets:	$238,000	Curr. Liab.:	$265,000		
Plant, Equip.:	$421,000	Total Liab.:	$265,000	Indic. Yr. Divd.:	NA
Total Assets:	$704,000	Net Worth:	-$637,000	Debt/ Equity:	0.5018

Universal Food & Beverage Compny

3830 Commerce Dr., St. Charles, IL, 60174; PH: 1-203-929-3404; Fax: 1-630-584-8674; http:// www.ufbc-inc.com; Email: cardinalmin@aol.com

General - Incorporation	NV	Stock - Price on:12/24/2007	$0.08
Employees	115	Stock Exchange	OTC
Auditor	BDO Seidman LLP	Ticker Symbol	UFBV
Stk Agt	Interwest Transfer Company, Inc.	Outstanding Shares	37,760,000
Counsel	NA	E.P.S.	-$0.19
DUNS No.	NA	Shareholders	NA

Business: The group's principal activity is to develop methodology to produce potable water from brackish water and from seawater. The group uses solar energy and the production of liquid fuels, hydrogen and electricity from carbon dioxide .the group is a development stage company. It has initiated a restructuring program involving a change of business to seek out and acquire mineral resource properties.

Primary SIC and add'l.: 8748 7389

CIK No: 0001097805

Subsidiaries: Colorado, Nevada

Officers: August J. Liguori/CEO, CFO, Sec.

Financial Data: Fiscal Year End:12/31   Latest Annual Data: 12/31/2005

Year	Sales	Net Income
2005	NA	NA
2004	NA	-$186,000
2003	NA	-$1,097,000

Curr. Assets:	$4,086,000	Curr. Liab.:	$4,611,000		
Plant, Equip.:	$7,713,000	Total Liab.:	$7,395,000	Indic. Yr. Divd.:	NA
Total Assets:	$13,784,000	Net Worth:	$6,389,000	Debt/ Equity:	0.3770

Universal Forest Products Inc

2801 E Beltline NE, Grand Rapids, MI, 49525; PH: 1-616-364-6161; http:// www.ufpi.com; Email: customerservice@ufpi.com

General - Incorporation	MI	Stock - Price on:12/24/2007	$45.92
Employees	9,200	Stock Exchange	NDQ
Auditor	Ernst & Young LLP	Ticker Symbol	UFPI
Stk Agt	American Stock Transfer & Trust Co.	Outstanding Shares	18,970,000
Counsel	Varnum Riddering S & H LLP	E.P.S.	$2.13
DUNS No.	01-710-4670	Shareholders	NA

Business: The groups principle activities include manufacturing and distributing wood and wood-alternative products to retail/dealer, site-built construction, manufactured housing and industrial markets. The groups products include decking and railing, trim and moulding, and fences. The group operates from United States.

Primary SIC and add'l.: 2439 2421 2426 2429

CIK No: 0000912767

Subsidiaries: Advanced Component Systems LLC, Atlantic Building Professionals, LLC, AW Construction, LLC, D&L Framing, LLC, D&R Framing Contractors, LLC, Euro-Pacific Building Materials, Inc., Euro-Pacific International Corp., Indianapolis Real Estate, LLC., Maine Ornamental, LLC., Midwest Framing, LLC, Norpac Construction, LLC., Pinelli Universal Tecate, S. de R.L. de C.V., Pinelli Universal, S. de R.L. de C.V., Shawnlee Construction, LLC, Shepardville Construction, LLC 34 Subsidiaries included in the Index

Officers: Michael B. Glenn/CEO/$2,127,309.00, William G. Currie/Exec. Chmn., Pres./$2,598,756.00, Matthew J. Missad/Exec. VP, Michael R. Cole/CFO/$805,748.00, Robert K. Hill/Pres. - Operations, Universal Forest Products Western Division, Inc/$1,388,272.00, Robert D. Coleman/Exec. VP - Manufacturing, Lynn Afendoulis/Dir. - Corporate Communications, Mark Deremo/Dir. - Marketing Communications, Mike Mordell/Western US, Exec. VP - Purchasing, David

Phelps/Eastern US, Exec. VP - Purchasing, Jennifer Meyer/Marketing Information Mgr., Scott C. Greene/Pres. - Universal Forest Products Eastern Division - Inc/$1,066,062.00, Jeff Espinoza/Contact - Product Information, Eric Miller/Contact - Product Information, Jeff Qualle/Contact - Product Information *(41 Officers included in Index)*

Directors: William G. Currie/Exec. Chmn., Pres., Peter F. Secchia/70/Dir., Louis A. Smith/68/Dir., John W. Garside/68/Dir., Dan M. Dutton/60/Dir., John M. Engler/59/Dir., Gary F. Goode/63/Dir., Mark A. Murray/53/Dir.

Owners: William G. Currie/2.90%, Barclays Global Investors, NA/10.80%, John W. Garside, Mark A. Murray, Michael R. Cole, Peter F. Secchia/4.60%, Gary F. Goode, Dan M. Dutton, T. Rowe Price Associates, Inc./5.40%, Robert K. Hill, Insiders/11.60%, Franklin Resources, Inc./5.20%, Michael B. Glenn/1.10%, John M. Engler, Louis A. Smith *(16 Owners included in Index)*

Financial Data: *Fiscal Year End:*12/31 *Latest Annual Data:* 12/30/2006

Year		Sales		Net Income
2006		$2,664,572,000		$70,125,000
2005		$2,691,522,000		$67,373,000
2004		$2,453,281,000		$48,603,000
Curr. Assets:	$502,178,000	**Curr. Liab.:**	$204,151,000	**P/E Ratio:** 15.31
Plant, Equip.:	$224,333,000	**Total Liab.:**	$445,068,000	**Indic. Yr. Divd.:** $0.120
Total Assets:	$876,920,000	**Net Worth:**	$431,852,000	**Debt/ Equity:** 0.5305

Universal Guardian Holdings Inc

4695 MacArthur Ct., Ste 300, Newport Beach, CA, 92008; *PH:* 1-949-861-8295; *Fax:* 1-949-861-8694; *http://* www.universalguardian.com; *Email:* info@universalguardian.com

General - Incorporation	DE	**Stock**- Price on:12/24/2007	$0.5001
Employees	38	Stock Exchange	OTC
Auditor	Aj. Robbins, P.C	Ticker Symbol	UGHO
Stk Agt	Stalt, Inc.	Outstanding Shares	NA
Counsel	NA	E.P.S.	-$0.273
DUNS No.	NA	Shareholders	NA

Business: The group's principal activities are to provide security products and services to mitigate terrorist and security threats to corporate and government assets worldwide. It offers a broad spectrum of security applications ranging from strategic and tactical security services, business risk solutions, interoperable security systems to non-lethal defense products. These products and services offer protection against terrorist and security threats to military installations, government buildings and critical infrastructure such as transportation networks, embassies, ports, airports and borders and commercial and industrial facilities such as power plants, petroleum refineries and chemical plants. On 13-Feb-2004, the group acquired emerging concepts inc.

Primary SIC and add'l.: 7389

CIK No: 0000859916

Subsidiaries: ISR Systems, Inc., MeiDa Information Technology, Ltd., Secure Risks Asia Pacific, Ltd, Secure Risks Ltd., Secure Risks Pakistan, Ltd., Secure Risks Venezuela, Ltd., Shield Defense Corporation, Shield Defense Europe GmbH, Shield Defense International Ltd., Shield Defense Technologies, Inc. , Strategic Security Solutions International Ltd., The Harbour Group, Inc., Universal Guardian Corporation

Officers: Michael J. Skellern/Chmn., CEO

Directors: Michael J. Skellern/Chmn., CEO, Michael Bozarth/Dir., Mel Brashears/Dir., Colonel John Alexander/Member - Board of Advisor, Roger Cressey/Member - Board of Advisor, Kenneth Merchant/Dir., Richard A. Clarke/Member - Advisory Board, Clifford Roth/Member - Board of Advisor

Financial Data: *Fiscal Year End:*12/31 *Latest Annual Data:* 12/31/2006

Year		Sales		Net Income
2006		$21,841,000		-$8,397,000
2005		$14,174,000		-$6,463,000
2004		$4,116,000		-$2,596,000
Curr. Assets:	$7,462,000	**Curr. Liab.:**	$3,525,000	
Plant, Equip.:	$1,250,000	**Total Liab.:**	$4,621,000	**Indic. Yr. Divd.:** NA
Total Assets:	$16,016,000	**Net Worth:**	$11,395,000	**Debt/ Equity:** 0.2144

Universal Health Realty Income Trust

367 S GULPH Rd., KING OF PRUSSIA, PA, 19406; *PH:* 1-610-265-0688; *http://* www.uhrit.com

General - Incorporation	MD	**Stock**- Price on:12/24/2007	$34.17
Employees	NA	Stock Exchange	NYSE
Auditor	KPMG LLP	Ticker Symbol	UHT
Stk Agt	Computershare Trust Co	Outstanding Shares	11,800,000
Counsel	NA	E.P.S.	$2.994
DUNS No.	NA	Shareholders	NA

Business: The groups principle activity is to invest in healthcare and human service related facilities. The group operates from the United States. The groups quarterly revenue for September 2007 was 6.91 millions of USD.

Primary SIC and add'l.: 6798

CIK No: 0000798783

Subsidiaries: 73 Medical Building, LLC, Cypresswood Investments, L.P, Riverdale Realty, L.L.C., Sheffield Properties, L.L.C.

Officers: Alan B. Miller/Chmn., CEO, Pres./$128,802.00, Charles F. Boyle/VP, Controller, CFO/$33,301.00, Cheryl K. Ramagano/VP, Treasurer, Sec./$33,301.00, Timothy J. Fowler/VP - Acquisitions, Development/$23,580.00, Genevieve P. Owsiany/Controller

Directors: Alan B. Miller/Chmn., CEO, Pres., Elliot J. Sussman/Trustee, James E. Dalton/Trustee, Miles L. Berger/Trustee, Myles H. Tanenbaum/Trustee

Owners: The Vanguard Group, Inc./5.54%, Elliot J. Sussman, Charles F. Boyle, Cheryl K. Ramagano, Miles L. Berger, Universal Health Services, Inc./6.70%, Timothy J. Fowler, James E. Dalton, Myles H. Tanenbaum, Barclays Global Investors, N.A./6.20%, Insiders/1.40%, Alan B. Miller

Financial Data: *Fiscal Year End:*12/31 *Latest Annual Data:* 12/31/2006

Year		Sales		Net Income
2006		$32,509,000		$34,697,000
2005		$33,338,000		$25,423,000
2004		$31,777,000		$23,671,000
Curr. Assets:	$2,637,000	**Curr. Liab.:**	$2,941,000	**P/E Ratio:** 11.06
Plant, Equip.:	$143,363,000	**Total Liab.:**	$29,942,000	**Indic. Yr. Divd.:** $2.300
Total Assets:	$194,139,000	**Net Worth:**	$164,197,000	**Debt/ Equity:** 0.1630

Universal Health Services Inc

367 S Gulph Rd., King Of Prussia, PA, 19406; *PH:* 1-610-768-3300; *http://* www.uhsinc.com

General - Incorporation	DE	**Stock**- Price on:12/24/2007	$61.85
Employees	24,600	Stock Exchange	NYSE
Auditor	KPMG LLP	Ticker Symbol	UHS
Stk Agt	Mellon Investor Services LLC	Outstanding Shares	53,850,000
Counsel	Fulbright & Jaworski LLP	E.P.S.	$3.06
DUNS No.	09-372-5133	Shareholders	NA

Business: The groups principle activity is to operate acute care hospitals, behavioral health centers, surgical hospitals, ambulatory surgery centers and radiation oncology centers. The groups medical services include general surgery, internal medicine, obstetrics, emergency room care, radiology, oncology, diagnostic care, coronary care, and pediatric and behavioral health services. The group operates from United States.

Primary SIC and add'l.: 8063 8062

CIK No: 0000352915

Subsidiaries: Aiken Regional Medical Centers, Inc., Alabama Clinical Schools, Inc., Alicante School Elk Grove, LLC, Alliance PPO, Inc., Ambulatory Surgery Center of Brownsville, L.P., Ambulatory Surgery Center of Temecula Valley, Inc., Ambulatory Surgical Center of Aiken, LLC, American Clinical Schools, Inc., Arbour Elder Services, Inc., Arbour Health Systems Foundation, Inc., Arkansas Surgery Center of Fayetteville, Limited Partnership, ASC of Aiken, Inc., ASC of Brownsville, Inc., ASC of Corona, Inc., ASC of East New Orleans, Inc. 240 Subsidiaries included in the Index

Officers: Alan B. Miller/Chmn., CEO, Pres./$14,483,890.00, Karla Perez/Group Dir. - Valley Health System, Acute Care, Michael S. Nelson/VP, Robert A. Deney/Divisional VP - Behavioral Health, Paul Yakulis/VP, Skip Courtney/VP - Ambulatory Surgery Centers, Marc D. Miller/Dir., Co - Division Head, VP, Larry Harrod/VP, Joe C. Crabtree/Divisional VP - Behavioral Health, John Paul Christen/VP, Richard C. Wright/VP, Car Evans/VP - Business Development, Behavioral Health, Steve G. Filton/CFO, Sr. VP/$1,037,189.00, Cheryl K. Ramagano/VP, Treasurer, Craig L. Nuckles/Regional VP - Behavioral Health *(32 Officers included in Index)*

Directors: Alan B. Miller/Chmn., CEO, Pres., Anthony Pantaleoni/Dir., Leatrice Ducat/Dir., John F. Williams/Dir., Robert A. Meister/Dir., Robert H. Hotz/Dir., John H. Herrell/Dir., Marc D. Miller/Dir., Co - Division Head, VP, Rick Santorum/Dir.

Owners: Robert A. Meister, FMR Corp./5.96%, Alan B. Miller/98.50%, Debra K. Osteen, Robert H. Hotz, Insiders, John F. Williams, Anthony Pantaleoni, Marc D. Miller/15.60%, Wellington Management Company, LLP./13.65%, Kevin J. Gross, Insiders/5.14%, Insiders/99.80%, Alan B. Miller/83.10%, Anthony Pantaleoni *(29 Owners included in Index)*

Financial Data: *Fiscal Year End:*12/31 *Latest Annual Data:* 12/31/2006

Year		Sales		Net Income
2006		$4,191,300,000		$259,458,000
2005		$3,935,480,000		$240,845,000
2004		$3,938,320,000		$169,492,000
Curr. Assets:	$728,506,000	**Curr. Liab.:**	$502,451,000	**P/E Ratio:** 13.36
Plant, Equip.:	$1,685,085,000	**Total Liab.:**	$1,874,578,000	**Indic. Yr. Divd.:** $0.320
Total Assets:	$3,277,042,000	**Net Worth:**	$1,402,464,000	**Debt/ Equity:** NA

Universal Hospital Services Inc

7700 France Ave. S, Ste. 275, Edina, MN, 55435; *PH:* 1-952-893-3200; *http://* www.uhs.com

General - Incorporation	DE	**Stock**- Price on:12/24/2007	NA
Employees	386	Stock Exchange	NA
Auditor	PricewaterhouseCoopers LLP	Ticker Symbol	NA
Stk Agt	U.S. Bank, N.A.	Outstanding Shares	NA
Counsel	NA	E.P.S.	NA
DUNS No.	02-286-9937	Shareholders	NA

Business: The group's principle activity is to provide movable medical equipment through "Pay-Per-Use" equipment management programs to hospitals and various other healthcare providers; and sells disposable medical products used in conjunction with the medical equipment it rents. The group operates from United States.

Primary SIC and add'l.: 7352 5047

CIK No: 0000886171

Officers: Gary D. Blackford/Chmn., CEO, Diana Vance-Bryan/Sr. VP, General Counsel, Kenneth Harvey/VP - Sales, East Region, Robert Zdon/VP - Operations, East Region, David G. Lawson/Sr. VP - Information, Strategic Resources, Susan Ellington/VP - Asset Management Partnership Programs, Services, Jeffrey L. Singer/Exec. VP - Sales, Marketing, Walter T. Chesley/Sr. VP - Human Resources, Development, Darren J. Thieding/VP - Sales Operations, Timothy W. Kuck/COO, Exec. VP, Daren Kneeland/VP - Sales, West, Robert Brooks/VP - Operations, West Region, Phil Zeller/VP - Asset Optimization, Scott Madson/Controller, Chief Accounting Officer, Joseph P. Schiesl/Sr. VP - Sales *(18 Officers included in Index)*

Directors: Gary D. Blackford/Chmn., CEO, Michael N. Cannizzaro/58/Dir., David W. Dupree/55/Dir., Steven G. Segal/47/Dir., Mark J. Tricolli/36/Dir., Brent D. Williams/40/Dir., Edward D. Yun/40/Dir.

Owners: Gary D. Blackford, John D. Howard, Robert Juneja, Jeffrey L. Singer, Timothy W. Kuck, BSMB/UHS Co-Investment Partners, L.P., Rex T. Clevenger, Insiders, BSMB/UHS, L.P.

Universal Insurance Holdings Inc

2875 N.E. 191ST St., Ste 302, Miami, FL, 33180; *PH:* 1-305-792-4200; *http://* www.universalheights.com

General - Incorporation	DE	**Stock**- Price on:12/24/2007	$4.79
Employees	81	Stock Exchange	OTC
Auditor	Blackman Kallick Bartelstein LLP	Ticker Symbol	UVIH
Stk Agt	North American Transfer Co	Outstanding Shares	NA
Counsel	NA	E.P.S.	NA
DUNS No.	62-139-6407	Shareholders	NA

Business: The group's principal activity is to provide property and casualty insurance. The group performs various aspects of insurance underwriting, distribution and claims. The group markets and distributes its products and services, primarily in Florida, through a network of approximately 640 active independent agents.

Primary SIC and add'l.: 6331

CIK No: 0000891166

Subsidiaries: Capital Resources Group, Ltd., Coastal Homeowners Insurance Specialists, Inc., Eproperty and Casualty, Inc., Paul Revere Health Plans, Inc., Pinpoint Adjusting Corporation, Pinpoint Inspection Corporation, Pinpoint Property Appraisal Corporation, Pinpoint Residential Inspection Corporation, Quoters, Inc., Tiger Home Services, Inc., Tigerquote.com Insurance & Financial Services Group, Inc., Tigerquote.com Insurance Agency of Georgia, Inc., Tigerquote.com Insurance Agency of New York, Inc., Tigerquote.com Insurance Services of California, Inc., Tigerquote.com Insurance Services of Michigan, Inc. 42 Subsidiaries included in the Index

Officers: Bradley I. Meier/Dir., CEO, Pres./$1,905,634.00, James M. Lynch/CFO, Exec. VP/$383,832.00, Keri Truitt/North Florida, Universal Property, Casualty Insurance Company, Vanessa Boston/South Florida, Universal Property, Casualty Insurance Company, Sean Downe/Dir., COO, Sr. VP/$1,800,122.00, Eric Meier/VP - Universal Property, Casualty Insurance Company, Clint Gillespie/VP - Underwriting, Universal Property, Casualty Insurance Company, Terry Wentroble/VP - Marketing, Universal Property, Casualty Insurance Company, Daniel Frain/Customer Service Department, Universal Property, Casualty Insurance Company, Nikki Delrey/Southern Florida, Universal Property, Casualty Insurance Company, Norman M. Meier/Dir., Sec.

Directors: Bradley I. Meier/Dir., CEO, Pres., Sean Downe/Dir., COO, Sr. VP, Norman M. Meier/Dir., Sec., Ozzie A. Schindler/Dir., Reed J. Slogoff/Dir., Joel M. Wilentz/Dir.

Owners: Insiders/98.00%, Phyllis R. Meier/18.90%, Norman M. Meier/1.30%, Phyllis R. Meier/20.00%, James M. Lynch, Bradley I. Meier/48.00%, Reed J. Slogoff, Martin Steinberg/17.10%, Sean P. Downes/11.10%, Bradley I. Meier/59.10%, Norman M. Meier/52.00%, Ozzie A. Schindler, Belmer Partners/60.00%, Joel M. Wilentz, Belmer Partners/16.90% *(16 Owners included in Index)*

Universal Porperty Development & Acquisition Corp

14255 US Hwy. 1, Ste. 209, Juno Beach, FL, 33408; *PH:* 1-561-630-2977; *Fax:* 1-561-630-2977; *http://* www.updac.com; *Email:* info@updac.com

General - Incorporation	NV	**Stock**- Price on:12/24/2007	$0.05
Employees	19	Stock Exchange	OTC
Auditor	KBL, LLP	Ticker Symbol	UPDA
Stk Agt	Olde Monmouth Stk Trnsfer Co. Inc.	Outstanding Shares	557,810,000
Counsel	NA	E.P.S.	-$0.248
DUNS No.	NA	Shareholders	NA

Business: The groups principle activities include engaging in the oil and natural gas acquisition, production, development, storage, and distribution and blending industry. The group operates from the United States. The group's quarterly revenue for Sep '07 was 12.27 millions of USD.

Primary SIC and add'l.: 1311

CIK No: 0000923771

Subsidiaries: Ambient Wells Services, Inc, Canyon Creek Oil and Gas, Inc., Catlin Oil & Gas, Inc., Texas Energy Pipeline & Gathering Systems, Inc, Texas Energy, Inc, UPDA Operators, Inc, UPDA Texas Trading, Inc, US Petroleum Depot, Inc, West Oil and Gas, Inc.,

Officers: Kamal Abdallah/Chmn., CEO, Christopher J. McCauley/VP, Sec., Brad Moore/VP - Human Resources, Jack Baker/Contact - Corporate Communications, Joseph M. Angioi/Corporate Finance

Directors: Kamal Abdallah/Chmn., CEO, Steve Barrera/Dir.

Owners: Steven Barrera, Christopher J. McCauley/3.46%, Insiders/17.23%, Kamal Abdallah/13.74%

Financial Data: *Fiscal Year End:*12/31   **Latest Annual Data:** 12/31/2006

Year	Sales	Net Income
2006	$581,000	-$5,450,000
2005	$29,000	-$9,034,000
2004	NA	-$1,761,000

Curr. Assets:	$897,000	**Curr. Liab.:**	$3,288,000	**P/E Ratio:**	28.85
Plant, Equip.:	$5,250,000	**Total Liab.:**	$3,471,000	**Indic. Yr. Divd.:**	NA
Total Assets:	$6,296,000	**Net Worth:**	$2,826,000	**Debt/ Equity:**	NA

Universal Security Instruments Inc

7-A Gwynns Mill Ct, Owings Mills, MD, 21117; *PH:* 1-410-363-3000; *http://* www.universalsecurity.com; *Email:* mail@lambert-edwards.com

General - Incorporation	MD	**Stock**- Price on:12/24/2007	$32.75
Employees	15	Stock Exchange	AMEX
Auditor	Grant Thornton LLP	Ticker Symbol	UUU
Stk Agt	Registrar & Transfer Co	Outstanding Shares	2,430,000
Counsel	Gordon Feinblatt Rothman Et Al	E.P.S.	$1.458
DUNS No.	04-992-0689	Shareholders	NA

Business: The group's principal activity is to design and market security and private label products that consist of smoke alarms and related products. The group sells smoke alarms and other security products to retailers, wholesale distributors, home centers, catalog and mail order companies and to other distributors. The group imports all its products from various suppliers overseas. The group markets smoke alarms under the trade names, usi electric, universal and smoke signal(tm), all of which are manufactured by the Hong Kong joint venture. The group also markets a line of electronically advanced outdoor floodlights under the name lite aide(tm), carbon monoxide alarms, door chimes and ground fault circuit interrupters. The group operates in the United States.

Primary SIC and add'l.: 3661 5063 3669 3695

CIK No: 0000102109

Subsidiaries: USI Electric, Inc

Officers: Harvey Grossblatt/Dir., CEO, Pres./$2,505,293.00, Ronald S. Lazarus/Pres./$1,332,081.00, James B. Huff/CFO, VP, Sec., Treasurer/$172,670.00, Manny Pacheco/Mgr. - Western Division/$155,266.00

Directors: Harvey Grossblatt/Dir., CEO, Pres., Howard Silverman/66/Dir., Cary Luskin/51/Dir.

Owners: Cary Luskin/2.93%, James B. Huff/0.70%, Ronald A. Seff/2.92%, Howard B. Silverman, FMR Corp./10.00%, Harvey B. Grossblatt/5.01%, Insiders/12.17%

Financial Data: *Fiscal Year End:*03/31   **Latest Annual Data:** 03/31/2007

Year	Sales	Net Income
2007	$35,824,000	$5,533,000
2006	$28,894,000	$4,600,000
2005	$23,465,000	$3,418,000

Curr. Assets:	$12,664,000	**Curr. Liab.:**	$2,752,000	**P/E Ratio:**	17.15
Plant, Equip.:	$62,000	**Total Liab.:**	$2,752,000	**Indic. Yr. Divd.:**	NA
Total Assets:	$20,359,000	**Net Worth:**	$17,607,000	**Debt/ Equity:**	NA

Universal Stainless & Alloy Products Inc

600 Mayer St., Bridgeville, PA, 15017; *PH:* 1-412-257-7600; *http://* www.univstainless.com

General - Incorporation	DE	**Stock**- Price on:12/24/2007	$39.33
Employees	527	Stock Exchange	NDQ
Auditor	Schneider Downs & Co., Inc	Ticker Symbol	USAP
Stk Agt	Continental Stock Transfer & Trust Co	Outstanding Shares	6,640,000
Counsel	Kirkpatrick & Lockhart	E.P.S.	$3.62
DUNS No.	86-133-6501	Shareholders	NA

Business: The group's principal activities are to manufacture and market semi-finished and finished steel products. The group operates through five segments: stainless steel, tool steel, high-strength low alloy steel, high-temperature alloy steel and conversion services. Stainless steel is used in the automotive, aerospace and power generation industries. Tool steel is used in the manufacturing of metals, plastics, paper and aluminum extrusions, pharmaceuticals, electronics and optics. Alloy steel is used in the aerospace industry. The customers of the group are rerollers, forgers, service centers and original equipment manufacturers, which primarily include the power generation and aerospace industries.

Primary SIC and add'l.: 3312

CIK No: 0000931584

Subsidiaries: Dunkirk Specialty Steel, LLC, USAP Holdings, Inc.

Officers: Clarence M. McAninch/Chmn., CEO/$577,824.00, Paul A. McGrath/VP - Administration, General Counsel, Sec./$366,803.00, Richard M. Ubinger/VP - Finance, CFO, Treasurer/$358,628.00, Kenneth W. Matz/Pres.

Directors: Clarence M. McAninch/Chmn., CEO, Douglas M. Dunn/Dir., Udi Toledano/Dir.

Owners: Systematic Financial Management, L.P./8.50%, Bear Stearns Asset Management Inc./7.20%, Kennedy Capital Management, Inc./6.70%, Richard M. Ubinger, George F. Keane, Udi Toledano/1.30%, Insiders/5.20%, Tamarack Enterprise Fund/6.50%, FMR Corp./8.70%, Keeley Asset Management Corp./10.40%, Clarence M. McAninch/2.30%, Douglas M. Dunn/1.10%, Paul A. McGrath

Financial Data: *Fiscal Year End:*12/31   **Latest Annual Data:** 12/31/2006

Year	Sales	Net Income
2006	$203,873,000	$20,614,000
2005	$170,022,000	$13,056,000
2004	$120,642,000	$7,131,000

Curr. Assets:	$105,280,000	**Curr. Liab.:**	$24,937,000	**P/E Ratio:**	10.69
Plant, Equip.:	$49,251,000	**Total Liab.:**	$50,567,000	**Indic. Yr. Divd.:**	NA
Total Assets:	$155,115,000	**Net Worth:**	$104,548,000	**Debt/ Equity:**	0.1015

Universal Technical Institute Inc

20410 N 19th Ave., Ste 200, Phoenix, AZ, 85027; *PH:* 1-623-445-9500; *http://* www.uticorp.com; *Email:* FAdept-uticentral@uticorp.com

General - Incorporation	DE	**Stock**- Price on:12/24/2007	$23.34
Employees	2,360	Stock Exchange	NYSE
Auditor	PricewaterhouseCoopers LLP	Ticker Symbol	UTI
Stk Agt	Bank of New York	Outstanding Shares	28,210,000
Counsel	NA	E.P.S.	$0.57
DUNS No.	NA	Shareholders	NA

Business: The group's principal activity is to provide post-secondary education for students seeking careers as professional automotive, diesel, collision repair, motorcycle and marine technicians. The group offers undergraduate degree, diploma and certificate programs at seven campuses across the United States, and manufacturer-sponsored advanced programs at 22 dedicated training centers. The group's undergraduate programs under the brands include universal technical institute (uti), motorcycle mechanics institute and marine mechanics institute (collectively, mmi) and nascar technical institute (nti).

Primary SIC and add'l.: 8222 8211

CIK No: 0001261654

Subsidiaries: Clinton Education Group, Inc., Custom Training Group, Inc., U.T.I. of Illinois, Inc., Universal Technical Institute of Arizona, Inc., Universal Technical Institute of California, Inc., Universal Technical Institute of Massachusetts, Inc., Universal Technical Institute of North Carolina, Inc., Universal Technical Institute of Northern California, Inc., Universal Technical Institute of Pennsylvania, Inc., Universal Technical Institute of Phoenix, Inc., Universal Technical Institute of Texas, Inc., UTI Holdings, Inc.

Officers: Kimberly J. McWaters/Dir., CEO, Pres., Jennifer L. Haslip/43/Sr. VP, CFO, Treasurer, Assist. Sec., Chad Freed/Sr. VP, General Counsel, Sec., Julian E. Gorman/Sr. VP - Customer Solutions, Roger L. Speer/Sr. VP - Custom Training Group, Support Services, Larry H. Wolff/CIO, Sr. VP, Thomas E. Riggs/Sr. VP - Human Resources, Sherrell Smith/Sr. VP - Operations, Rick P. Crain/Sr. VP - Marketing, Tina Miller-Steinke/Contact - Universal Technical Institute, Kristy Nied/Contact - Universal Technical Institute, Erinn Figg/Contact - Universal Technical Institute, Colleen Weldin/Investor Relations Officer, Joseph R. Cutler/49/Sr. VP - Field Admissions, Robert K. Adler/45/VP - Campus Admissions

Directors: Kimberly J. McWaters/Dir., CEO, Pres., John C. White/Chmn., Robert D. Hartman/Dir., Conrad A. Conradq/Dir., Richard A. Caputo/Dir., Kevin P. Knight/Dir., Roger S. Penske/Dir., Linda J. Srere/Dir., Allan D. Gilmour/Dir.

Owners: Royce & Associates, LLC/12.30%, Larry H. Wolff, Insiders/21.00%, Kevin P. Knight, Allan D. Gilmour, Scout Capital Management, L.L.C./5.20%, Wasatch Advisors, Inc./5.20%, A. Richard Caputo, John C. White/9.70%, David K. Miller, Robert D. Hartman/6.20%, Roger S. Pensk, Kimberly J. McWaters/1.70%, Linda J. Srere, Jennifer L. Haslip *(21 Owners included in Index)*

Financial Data: *Fiscal Year End:*09/30   **Latest Annual Data:** 9/30/2006

Year	Sales	Net Income
2006	$347,066,000	$27,386,000
2005	$310,800,000	$35,819,000
2004	$255,149,000	$28,820,000

Curr. Assets:	$70,269,000	**Curr. Liab.:**	$96,278,000	**P/E Ratio:**	29.54
Plant, Equip.:	$117,298,000	**Total Liab.:**	$109,259,000	**Indic. Yr. Divd.:**	NA
Total Assets:	$212,161,000	**Net Worth:**	$102,902,000	**Debt/ Equity:**	NA

Universal Travel Group

1425-C SE 17th St., Ft. Lauderdale, FL, 33316; *PH:* 1-702-498-7365; *Fax:* 1-954-463-2703; *http://* www.universal-travel.com

General - Incorporation....NV
Employees....324
Auditor Morgenstern, Svoboda & Baer CPA's PC
Stk Agt....Madison Stock Transfer, Inc.
Counsel....NA
DUNS No.....NA

Stock- Price on:12/24/2007....$2.47
Stock Exchange....OTC
Ticker Symbol....UTVG
Outstanding Shares....34,930,000
E.P.S....$0.08
Shareholders....NA

Business: The groups principle activity is engaged in China domestic and international airline ticketing services and cargo transportation agency services as well as international lines. The group also owns an aviation network that provides a complete air tickets sales network. The group operates from China. The group's quarterly revenue for Sep '07 was 12.81 millions of USD.

Primary SIC and add'l.: 6770

CIK No: 0001336644

Subsidiaries: Merger Sub of Tam, Inc., Shenzhen Yuzhilu Aviation Service Co

Officers: Jiangping Jiang/46/Chmn., CEO, Xin Zhang/39/Dir., CFO, Jing Xie/26/Dir., Sec., Sue Ann Slater/GM, Brian Howes/VP, Bonnie Baskin/Controller, Nancy Pierzchanowski/Operations

Directors: Jiangping Jiang/46/Chmn., CEO, Xin Zhang/39/Dir., CFO, Jing Xie/26/Dir., Sec.

Owners: Jiangping Jiang/34.50%, Xiao Jun/23.40%, Insiders/34.50%

Financial Data: *Fiscal Year End:*12/31 *Latest Annual Data:* 12/31/2006

Year	Sales	Net Income
2006	$10,014,000	$2,558,000

Curr. Assets:	$7,462,000	**Curr. Liab.:**	$3,655,000	**P/E Ratio:**	30.88
Plant, Equip.:	$52,000	**Total Liab.:**	$3,655,000	**Indic. Yr. Divd.:**	NA
Total Assets:	$7,564,000	**Net Worth:**	$3,909,000	**Debt/ Equity:**	NA

Universal Truckload Services Inc

12755E Nine Mile Rd., Warren, MI, 48090; **PH:** 1-586-920-0100; **http://** www.goutsi.com

General - Incorporation....MI
Employees....644
Auditor....KPMG LLP
Stk Agt....SunTrust Bank
Counsel....NA
DUNS No.....NA

Stock- Price on:12/24/2007....$20.18
Stock Exchange....NDQ
Ticker Symbol....UACL
Outstanding Shares....16,120,000
E.P.S....$1.22
Shareholders....NA

Business: The groups principle activity is to provide transportation services. The groups services include road trucking, rail truck and steamship truck. The group acquired Assure Intermodal, LLC, Djewels, Inc., Noble and Pitts, Inc, TriStar Express N.C., Inc., Mallard Transport, Inc in the year 2006 and Xxtreme Trucking, LLC, Marc Largent, Inc., Diamond Logistics of Houston, Inc in the year 2005. The group operates from the United States and Canada. The group's quarterly revenue for September 2007 was 171.78 millions of USD.

Primary SIC and add'l.: 4231 4731 4213

CIK No: 0001308208

Subsidiaries: CrossRoad Carriers Intermodal, Inc., Economy Transport, Inc., Great American Lines, Inc., Louisiana Transportation, Inc., Mason Dixon Intermodal, Inc., NYP of Michigan, Inc., The Mason & Dixon Lines, Inc., Universal Am-Can, Ltd., UT Rent A Car, Inc., UTS Finance, Inc., UTS Leasing, Inc., UTS Realty, LLC

Officers: Donald B. Cochran/Dir., CEO, Pres., Robert E. Sigler/CFO, VP

Directors: Donald B. Cochran/Dir., CEO, Pres., Matthew T. Moroun/34/Chmn., Manuel J. Moroun/Dir., Joseph J. Casaroll/Dir., Angelo A. Fonzi/Dir., Daniel C. Sullivan/Dir., Richard P. Urban/Dir., Ted B. Wahby/Dir.

Owners: Leo Blumenauer, Matthew T. Moroun/31.30%, Insiders/63.21%, Manuel J. Moroun/30.88%, Donald B. Cochran, Joseph J. Casaroll, Robert E. Sigler

Financial Data: *Fiscal Year End:*12/31 *Latest Annual Data:* 12/31/2006

Year	Sales	Net Income
2006	$641,627,000	$21,009,000
2005	$531,339,000	$17,167,000
2004	$362,016,000	$11,118,000

Curr. Assets:	$111,568,000	**Curr. Liab.:**	$49,717,000	**P/E Ratio:**	16.54
Plant, Equip.:	$51,286,000	**Total Liab.:**	$56,447,000	**Indic. Yr. Divd.:**	NA
Total Assets:	$190,900,000	**Net Worth:**	$134,453,000	**Debt/ Equity:**	0.0066

University Bank

2015 Washtenaw Ave., Ann Arbor, MI, 48104; **PH:** 1-734-741-5858; **Fax:** 1-734-741-5859; **http://** www.university-bank.com; **Email:** information@university-bank.com

General - Incorporation....DE
Employees....81
Auditor....UHY LLP
Stk Agt....Computershare Trust Co
Counsel....NA
DUNS No.....15-204-6777

Stock- Price on:12/24/2007....$1.85
Stock Exchange....NDQ
Ticker Symbol....UNIB
Outstanding Shares....4,250,000
E.P.S....-$0.07
Shareholders....NA

Business: The group's principle activities are to provide customary banking services through its subsidiaries. It offers traditional retail savings products and services to its customers. These include demand deposit and now interest-bearing checking accounts, money market deposit accounts, regular savings accounts and term deposit certificates. The group also provides commercial, real estate, personal, home improvement, automotive, other installment credit card loans, self-directed retirement accounts, free access to 24-hour ATM machines, telephone banking, visa debit cards and gold visa accounts. The other services offered include life insurance, annuity and mutual fund sales and foreign currency exchange.

Primary SIC and add'l.: 6712 6022

CIK No: 0000811211

Subsidiaries: Hoover, LLC, Midwest Loan Services, Inc., University Insurance & Investment Services, Inc., University Islamic Financial Corporation

Officers: Edie Kingsley/CEO - University Insurance, Investment Services, Nicholas Fortson/Dir., CEO/$98,794.00, Stephen Lange Ranzini/Chmn., Pres., Pete Richards/Assist. VP - Deposits, Charles McDowell/Exec. VP - Northern Michigan Foundation, Shawn Shepherd/VP - University Insurance, Investment Services, John Sickler/Exec. VP, Residential Lending/$105,465.00, Julie Price/Exec. VP - Residential Lending, COO - University Islamic Financial, Stewart Brannen/Exec. VP - Asset Management, Corp. Sec., Janet Anderson/Exec. VP - Human Resources, Internal Auditor, Stacy Shepanski/Exec. VP - Deposits, Consumer Lending

Directors: Nicholas Fortson/Dir., CEO, Stephen Lange Ranzini/Chmn., Pres.

Owners: Mildred Lange Ranzini/14.70%, Insiders/64.02%, Orpheus Capital, L.P./44.98%, Paul Lange Ranzini/47.80%, Michael Talley/0.59%, Nicholas Fortson/0.81%, Ranzini Family Trust/45.89%, Charles McDowell/1.52%, Stephen Lange Ranzini/61.70%, Joseph Lange Ranzini/47.53%, Gary Baker/0.59%

Financial Data: *Fiscal Year End:*12/31 *Latest Annual Data:* 12/31/2006

Year	Sales	Net Income
2006	$8,521,000	-$402,000
2005	$9,164,000	$1,989,000
2004	$6,567,000	-$585,000

Curr. Assets:	$27,940,000	**Curr. Liab.:**	$79,015,000		
Plant, Equip.:	$2,985,000	**Total Liab.:**	$82,020,000	**Indic. Yr. Divd.:**	NA
Total Assets:	$87,272,000	**Net Worth:**	$5,251,000	**Debt/ Equity:**	NA

Univest Corp of Pennsylvania

PO Box 64197, Souderton, PA, 18964; **PH:** 1-215-723-5571; **http://** www.univest-corp.com; **Email:** customersupport@univest.net

General - Incorporation....PA
Employees....524
Auditor....KPMG LLP
Stk Agt....StockTrans, Inc.
Counsel....NA
DUNS No.....02-007-6238

Stock- Price on:12/24/2007....$22.47
Stock Exchange....NDQ
Ticker Symbol....UVSP
Outstanding Shares....NA
E.P.S....$1.98
Shareholders....NA

Business: The group's principal activity is to provide domestic commercial and retail banking and trust services to its customers. The group attracts deposits from the general public and invests the same in loans secured by residential properties and consumer loans. It operates through 28 branch offices and 5 off-premise automated teller machines. The other services offered include financial planning, investment management, insurance products and brokerage services. Union national bank, pennview savings bank, univest realty corporation, univest Delaware, inc. And univest reinsurance corporation are the subsidiaries of the group. On 17-May-2003, the group acquired first county bank and on 04-Oct-2003, suburban community bank.

Primary SIC and add'l.: 6021 6091 6712

CIK No: 0000102212

Subsidiaries: Delview, Inc, Univest Capital Trust I, Univest Delaware, Inc, Univest Insurance, Inc., Univest Investments, Inc, Univest National Bank and Trust Co, Univest Realty Corporation, Univest Reinsurance Corporation

Officers: William S. Aichele/Chmn., CEO, Pres./$705,821.00, Leon K. Moyer/Sr. Exec. VP/$485,965.00, Wallace H. Bieler/CFO, Sr. Exec. VP/$523,092.00, Philip C. Jackson/Pres. - Marketing, Montgomery County, Univest National Bank, Trust Co, Kenneth L. Keller/Pres. - Marketing, Bucks County, Univest National Bank, Trust Co, Richard R. Swartley/Exec. VP/$208,509.00, Kenneth H. Hochstetler/Exec. VP/$162,946.00, Duane J. Brobst/Exec. VP, Chief Credit Officer, Diane L. Koehler/Exec. VP, Chief Risk Officer, Richard M. O'Donnell/Exec. VP, Barry L. Stoltzfus/Exec. VP, Hugh W. Connelly/Pres. - Vanguard Leasing, Inc, Subsidiary Ofunivest National Bank, Trust Co, Ronald S. Price/Pres. - Marketing, Chester County, Univest National Bank, Trust Co

Directors: William S. Aichele/Chmn., CEO, Pres., Marvin A. Anders/Dir., Lee R. Delp/Dir., Norman L. Keller/Dir., Ray H. Mininger/Dir., James L. Bergey/Dir., Charles H. Hoeflich/Dir., Thomas K. Leidy/Dir., Merrill S. Moyer/Dir., John U. Young/Dir., William G. Morral/Dir., Margaret K. Zook/Dir., Mark A. Schlosser/Dir., Paul Gregory. Shelly/Dir.

Owners: John U. Young, Wallace H. Bieler, H. Ray Mininger, K. Leon Moyer, Richard R. Swartley, Thomas K. Leidy, William G. Morral, Mark A. Schlosser, Merrill S. Moyer/1.03%, Margaret K. Zook, Kenneth H. Hochstetler, P. Gregory Shelly, Marvin A. Anders, R. Lee Delp, James L. Bergey *(19 Owners included in Index)*

Financial Data: *Fiscal Year End:*12/31 *Latest Annual Data:* 12/31/2006

Year	Sales	Net Income
2006	$130,583,000	$25,377,000
2005	$108,164,000	$24,867,000
2004	$97,392,000	$23,591,000

Curr. Assets:	$100,531,000	**Curr. Liab.:**	$1,636,711,000		
Plant, Equip.:	$21,878,000	**Total Liab.:**	$1,723,497,000	**Indic. Yr. Divd.:**	$0.800
Total Assets:	$1,929,501,000	**Net Worth:**	$185,385,000	**Debt/ Equity:**	NA

Univision Communications Inc

1999 Ave. Of The Stars, Ste 3050, Los Angles, CA, 90067; **PH:** 1-310-556-7665; **http://** www.univision.net; **Email:** publicrelations@univision.net

General - Incorporation....DE
Employees....4,219
Auditor....Ernst & Young LLP
Stk Agt....Bank of New York
Counsel....NA
DUNS No.....80-749-9934

Stock- Price on:12/24/2007....NA
Stock Exchange....NA
Ticker Symbol....NA
Outstanding Shares....NA
E.P.S....NA
Shareholders....NA

Business: The groups principle activity is to operate TV stations providing a variety of news, sports, and entertainment programming. The group also operates broadcast network, TeleFutura, and cable network Galavisin. The group operates from United States.

Primary SIC and add'l.: 2741 4833 7375

CIK No: 0001017008

Subsidiaries: Disa LLC, El Trato Inc., Fonohits Music Publishing, Inc., Fonomusic, Inc., Fonovisa, Inc., Galavision, Inc., HBCi, LLC, HPN Numbers, Inc., KAKW License Partnership, L.P., KCYT-FM License Corp., KDTV License Partnership, G.P., KECS-FM License Corp., KESS-AM License Corp., KESS-TV License Corp., KFTV License Partnership, G.P. 129 Subsidiaries included in the Index

Officers: Jerrold A. Perenchio/77/Chmn., CEO, Joe Uva/Dir., CEO, Robert V. Cahill/76/Vice Chmn., Sec. - Corporation, Douglas C. Kranwinkle/Exec. VP, General Counsel, Andrew W. Hobson/Sr. Exec. VP, Chief Financial, Strategic Officer, Ray Rodriguez/COO, Pres., Peter H. Lori/Chief Accounting Officer, Corporate Controller

Directors: Jerrold A. Perenchio/77/Chmn., CEO, Joe Uva/Dir., CEO, Robert V. Cahill/76/Vice Chmn., Sec. - Corporation, Zaid F. Alsikafi/Dir., David Bonderman/Dir., Richard J. Bressler/Dir., James C. Carlisle/Dir., Adam Chesnoff/Dir., Henry G. Cisneros/Dir., Michael P. Cole/Dir., Kelvin L. Davis/Dir., Albert J. Dobron/Dir., Gloria Estefan/Dir., Mark J. Masiello/Dir., Jonathan M. Nelson/Dir. *(28 Directors included in Index)*

Unum Group

Formerly: UnumProvident Corp
1 Fountain Sq., Chattanooga, TN, 37402; *PH:* 1-423-294-1011; *http://* www.unum.com

General - Incorporation .... DE
Employees.. 11,100
Auditor .... Ernst & Young LLP
Stk Agt.................... Computershare Trust Co
Counsel.. NA
DUNS No. 04-024-9948

Stock- Price on:12/24/2007 .... $26.22
Stock Exchange.. NYSE
Ticker Symbol.. UNM
Outstanding Shares 342,800,000
E.P.S... $1.51
Shareholders.. NA

Business: The groups principle activity is to provide insurance services. The groups services include long-term care, life, and employer and employee-paid insurance. The group operates from United States.

Primary SIC and add'l.: 6321 6371 6311 6719

CIK No: 0000005513

Subsidiaries: BenefitAmerica, Inc., Claims Services International Limited, Colonial Companies, Inc., Colonial Life& Accident Insurance Company, Duncanson& Holt Asia PTE Ltd., Duncanson& Holt Canada Ltd., Duncanson& Holt Europe Ltd., Duncanson& Holt Services, Inc., Duncanson& Holt Syndicate Management, Ltd., Duncanson& Holt Underwriters, Ltd., Duncanson& Holt, Inc., First Unum Life Insurance Company, Genex Consultants, Inc., GENEX Services of Canada, Inc., GENEX Services, Inc. 36 Subsidiaries included in the Index

Officers: Thomas R. Watjen/Dir., CEO, Pres./$4,695,705.00, Randall C. Horn/CEO, Pres. - Colonial Supplemental Insurance, Susan Ring/CEO - Unum UK, Eileen Farrar/Sr. VP - Human Resources, David Fussell/Sr. VP - Investments, Kevin P. McCarthy/Pres. - Unum US/$1,400,659.00, Robert O. Best/COO - Unum US/$1,284,818.00, Robert C. Greving/CFO, Exec. VP, Chief Actuary/$1,031,751.00, Susan N. Roth/VP, Corp. Sec., Assist. General Counsel, Joseph R. Foley/Sr. VP, Chief Marketing Officer, Charles L. Glick/Exec. VP, General Counsel

Directors: Thomas R. Watjen/Dir., CEO, Pres., Jon S. Fossel/Chmn., Gloria C. Larson/Dir., A. S. MacMillan/Dir., Edward J. Muhl/Dir., Michael E. Caulfield/Dir., Michael J. Passarella/Dir., William J. Ryan/Dir., Thomas Kinser/Dir., Pamela H. Godwin/Dir., Ronald E. Goldsberry/Dir.

Owners: Michael J. Passarella, A. S. (Pat) MacMillan, Robert O. Best, Pamela H. Godwin, Thomas Kinser, Edward J. Muh, Thomas R. Watjen, Michael Caulfield, William J. Ryan, Jon S. Fossel, Gloria C. Larson, Hugh O. MacLellan, Joseph M. Zubretsky, Robert C. Greving, Kevin P. McCarthy (17 Owners included in Index)

Financial Data: Fiscal Year End:12/31   Latest Annual Data: 12/31/2006

Year	Sales	Net Income
2006	$10,535,300,000	$411,000,000
2005	$10,437,200,000	$513,600,000
2004	$10,464,900,000	-$253,000,000

Curr. Assets:	$8,339,000,000	*Curr. Liab.:*	$44,400,000		
Plant, Equip.:	$370,100,000	*Total Liab.:*	$45,104,500,000	*Indic. Yr. Divd.:*	NA
Total Assets:	$52,823,300,000	*Net Worth:*	$7,718,800,000	*Debt/ Equity:*	0.3388

Uphonia Inc

1818 N Farwell Ave., Milwaukee, WI, 53202; *PH:* 1-414-727-2688; *http://* www.smartserv.com;
Email: sales@smartserv.com

General - Incorporation .... DE
Employees.. 21
Auditor .... Carlin, Charron & Rosen LLP
Stk Agt..............Continental Stock Transfer & Trust Co
Counsel............ Parker Chapin Flattau & Klimpl
DUNS No. 82-573-3082

Stock- Price on:12/24/2007 .... $0.06
Stock Exchange.. OTC
Ticker Symbol.. UPHN
Outstanding Shares 6,350,000
E.P.S... -$2.56
Shareholders.. NA

Business: The group's principal activities are to provide Web and wireless applications and infrastructure that allows its customers to deliver content and transaction-intensive services. The group has developed applications that integrate and deliver Internet and intranet-based information and also effectuate m-commerce transactions through wired and wireless data networks and devices. The products of the group include content, transaction processing and alert engines, proprietary w2w middlewaretm and a suite of applications. The customers of the group include hutchison telecommunications, sunday communications, Asian wireless carrier and global financial institution.

Primary SIC and add'l.: 7371 7375

CIK No: 0001005698

Subsidiaries: Colorado corporation, KPCCD, Inc, nReach, Inc

Financial Data: Fiscal Year End:12/31   Latest Annual Data: 12/31/2004

Year	Sales	Net Income
2004	$359,000	-$10,580,000
2003	$709,000	-$17,538,000
2002	$196,000	-$8,037,000

Curr. Assets:	$2,334,000	*Curr. Liab.:*	$1,903,000		
Plant, Equip.:	$74,000	*Total Liab.:*	$1,916,000	*Indic. Yr. Divd.:*	NA
Total Assets:	$3,338,000	*Net Worth:*	$1,421,000	*Debt/ Equity:*	NA

UPM-Kymmene Group

Etelesplanadi 2, Helsinki; *PH:* 358-204150658; *Fax:* 358-20415110;
http:// www.upm-kymmene.com; *Email:* info@upm-kymmene.com

General - Incorporation .... Finland
Employees.. 28,704
Auditor .... PricewaterhouseCoopers LLP
Stk Agt.. NA
Counsel.. NA
DUNS No. .... NA

Stock- Price on:12/24/2007 .... $25.34
Stock Exchange.. OTC
Ticker Symbol.. UPMKY
Outstanding Shares 523,260,000
E.P.S... $0.71
Shareholders.. NA

Business: The group's principle activity is to manufacture paper, converting materials and wood products. The group operates through six segments: magazine paper: produces magazines, newspaper supplements, printed advertising material and sales catalogues; news print: manufactures for publishers, printers, telephone directories and mail order catalogues; fine paper: supplies paper to paper merchants, office supplies wholesalers, printers and converters; specialty paper; comprises of face and release papers for self-adhesive labels, white and brown sack and kraft papers and white and tinted envelope papers; converting segment: manufactures self-adhesive labelstock, siliconized papers and industrial wrappings and the wood products segment produces sawn timber and plywood for the building and transport vehicle industries. The group has production plants in 16 countries.

Primary SIC and add'l.: 2671 2621 2421 2611 2435

CIK No: 0001089642

Subsidiaries: Nordland Papier GmbH, UPM-Kymmene Administrations GmbH& Co. KgaA, UPM-Kymmene Beteiligungs GmbH, UPM-Kymmene Investment Inc., UPM-Kymmene Miramichi Inc., UPM-Kymmene Papier GmbH& Co. KG, UPM-Kymmene Vervaltung GmbH

Officers: Jussi Pesonen/48/CEO, Pres., John Sanderson/Contact - Environmental Affair, UK, Ulrich Neumann/Contact - Environmental Affair, Continental Europe, Philippe Riebel/Contact - Environmental Affair, North America, Jyrki Ovaska/50/Pres. - Magazine Papers Division, Sari Horkko/Mgr. - Communications, Media Relations, Aili Piironen/Dir. - Issues Management, Miia Narekorpi/VP - Communications, HRD, Wood Products, Matti J. Lindahl/62/Pres. - Wood Products Division, Pauli Hanninen/60/Exec. VP - Technology, Heikki Pikkarainen/45/Pres. - Labelstock Business, Markku Tynkkynen/56/Exec. VP - Resources, Hartmut Wurster/53/Pres. - Newsprint Division, Riitta Savonlahti/44/Exec. VP - Human Resources, Hans Sohlstrom/44/Exec. VP - Business Development Biofuels, Biochemicals (31 Officers included in Index)

Directors: Jorma B. Ollila/58/Vice Chmn., Berndt Brunow/58/Vice Chmn., Vesa Vainio/66/Chmn., Martti Ahtisaari/71/Dir., Karl Grotenfelt/64/Dir., Veli-Matti Reinikkala/51/Dir., Georg Holzhey/69/Dir., Sampermans B. Francoise/61/Dir., Michael C. Bottenheim/61/Dir., Francoise Sampermans/61/Dir., Wendy E. Lane/57/Dir., Ursula Ranin/55/Dir.

Owners: Gustaf Serlachius, Nominees & registered foreign owners, Elke-Fennia Mutual Pension Fund, Franklin Resources Inc., The Finnish Cultural Foundation, Others, Svenska litteratursllskapet i Finland, Capital Group Companies, Inc., The State Pension Fund, Nominees & registered foreign owners, Insiders, Ilmarinen Mutual Pension Insurance Company, The Kymi 100 Year Foundation, Etera Mutual Pension Insurance Company, Holzhey/Bischoff group (16 Owners included in Index)

Financial Data: Fiscal Year End:12/31   Latest Annual Data: 12/31/2006

Year	Sales	Net Income
2006	$13,537,036,000	$559,807,000
2005	$11,210,346,000	$202,532,000
2004	$13,627,627,000	$783,166,000

Curr. Assets:	$4,111,414,000	*Curr. Liab.:*	$3,181,923,000	*P/E Ratio:*	8.84
Plant, Equip.:	$8,678,332,000	*Total Liab.:*	$9,479,755,000	*Indic. Yr. Divd.:*	$0.850
Total Assets:	$18,946,305,000	*Net Worth:*	$9,442,786,000	*Debt/ Equity:*	NA

UpSnap Inc

134 Jackson St., Ste. 203, Davidson, NC, 28036; *PH:* 1-704-895-4121; *http://* www.upsnap.com;
Email: Info@upsnap.com

General - Incorporation .... NV
Employees.. 9
Auditor .... Bedinger & Company
Stk Agt .... Nevada Agency & Trust Co
Counsel.. NA
DUNS No. .... NA

Stock- Price on:12/24/2007 .... $0.29
Stock Exchange.. OTC
Ticker Symbol.. UPSN
Outstanding Shares 22,170,000
E.P.S... -$0.07
Shareholders.. NA

Business: The groups principle activity is mobile search engine that helps consumers to find merchants and local services instantly. Currently mobile consumers must load up a WAP, or wireless application protocol, to browse websites. In January 2006, the group acquired XSVoice, Inc. The group operates from the United States.

Primary SIC and add'l.: 7374

CIK No: 0001261019

Subsidiaries: UpSNAP USA, Inc (Formerly, Up2004Snap, Inc.)

Officers: Tony Philipp/46/Dir., CEO, Pres., Richard Jones/42/Dir., VP - Content - Distribution, Sec., Paul Schmidt/53/CFO

Directors: Tony Philipp/46/Dir., CEO, Pres., Richard Jones/42/Dir., VP - Content - Distribution, Sec., Richard A. Von Gnechten/45/Dir., Mark McDowell/42/Dir.

Owners: XSVoice, Inc./9.99%, Tony Phillip/17.30%, Insiders/32.50%, Richard Jones/15.23%, Richard A. von Gnechten, Wendell Brown/14.33%

Financial Data: Fiscal Year End:09/30   Latest Annual Data: 03/31/2007

Year	Sales	Net Income
2007	NA	NA
2006	NA	NA
2005	NA	-$100,000

Curr. Assets:	$561,000	*Curr. Liab.:*	$137,000	*P/E Ratio:*	28.85
Plant, Equip.:	$124,000	*Total Liab.:*	$250,000	*Indic. Yr. Divd.:*	NA
Total Assets:	$6,523,000	*Net Worth:*	$6,273,000	*Debt/ Equity:*	NA

Upstream Biosciences Inc

570 7 Ave. W , Ste. 100, Vancouver, BC, V5Z 4S6; *PH:* 1-800-539-0289;
http:// www.upstreambio.com; *Email:* info@upstreambio.com

General - Incorporation .... NV
Employees.. NA
Auditor .... Dale Matheson Carr-Hilton LaBonte LLP
Stk Agt .... Nevada Agency & Trust
Counsel.. NA
DUNS No. .... NA

Stock- Price on:12/24/2007 .... $1
Stock Exchange.. OTC
Ticker Symbol.. UPBS
Outstanding Shares .... NA
E.P.S... NA
Shareholders.. NA

Business: The groups principal activities include developing platforms and related technologies. The group will enable the discovery of marketable diagnostic markers to aid in the disease susceptibility and drug response areas of cancer. The group is currently developing technologies, which will enable us to identify and prioritize potential diagnostic markers. The group operates from Canada.

Primary SIC and add'l.: 8733

CIK No: 0001174891

Officers: Joel Lloyd Bellenson/Co - Founder, Chmn., CEO, Dexster L. Smith/Co - Founder, Dir., Pres., Tim Fernback/CFO, Steve Bajic/35/Dir., Sec., Treasurer, Samantha Haynes/Contact

Directors: Joel Lloyd Bellenson/Co - Founder, Chmn., CEO, Dexster L. Smith/Co - Founder, Dir., Pres., Steve Bajic/35/Dir., Sec., Treasurer, Wyeth Wasserman/Member - Scientific Advisory Board, Artem Cherkasov/Member - Scientific Advisory Board, Brett Casey/Member - Scientific Advisory Board, Robert D. Sindelar/Member - Scientific Advisory Board, Philip Rice/Dir., Dale Pfost/Dir., Edward Kiruluta/Member - Scientific Advisory Board

Owners: Dexster L. Smith/26.80%, Joel L. Bellenson/26.80%, Timothy Fernback/1.50%, Steve Bajic/4.50%, Insiders/59.50%

Financial Data: Fiscal Year End:09/30   Latest Annual Data: 09/30/2006

Year	Sales	Net Income
2006	NA	-$1,602,000
2005	NA	-$16,000

Curr. Assets:	$504,000	***Curr. Liab.:***	$231,000	***P/E Ratio:***	28.85
Plant, Equip.:	$12,000	***Total Liab.:***	$799,000	***Indic. Yr. Divd.:***	NA
Total Assets:	$515,000	***Net Worth:***	-$283,000	***Debt/ Equity:***	NA

UQM Technologies Inc

PO Box 439, Frederick, CO, 80530; ***PH:*** 1-303-278-2002; ***http://*** www.uqm.com; ***Email:*** investor@uqm.com

General - Incorporation	CO	***Stock***- Price on:12/24/2007	$3.96
Employees	53	Stock Exchange	AMEX
Auditor	Grant Thornton LLP	Ticker Symbol	UQM
Stk Agt	Computershare Trust Co	Outstanding Shares	25,320,000
Counsel	Holme Roberts & Owen LLP	E.P.S	-$0.16
DUNS No.	04-540-6626	Shareholders	NA

Business: The group's principal activities are to develop and manufacture energy efficient, power dense, electric motors, generators and power electronic controllers. The group operates in two segments mechanical segment and technology segment. The mechanical segment encompasses manufacture and sale of permanent magnet motors, precision gears and gear assemblies through its wholly owned subsidiary uqm power. The technology segment encompasses the operations of the engineering and product development centre. The major customers of the group include invacare corporation. The group operates solely in the United States. On may 18, 2004, the group completed the sale of electronics manufacturing business.

Primary SIC and add'l.: 3714 8731 3621

CIK No: 0000315449

Subsidiaries: UQM Power Products, Inc.

Officers: William G. Rankin/64/Chmn., CEO, Pres., Donald A. French/Sec., Treasurer, CFO/$421,454.00, Jon Lutz/Dir. - Engineering, Ronald M. Burton/54/VP - Operations/$243,372.00, Ron Burton/VP - Operations

Directors: Ernest H. Drew/71/Dir., Stephen J. Roy/58/Dir., Donald W. Vanlandingham/68/Dir., Lieutenant General/71/Dir.

Owners: William G. Rankin/3.64%, PowerShares Capital Management/5.12%, Donald A. French/2.48%, Ernest H. Drew/1.26%, Stephen J. Roy, Security Management Company, LLC/6.06%, Jerome H. Granrud, Insiders/7.74%, Ronald M. Burton/0.52%, Donald W. Vanlandingham

Financial Data: ***Fiscal Year End:***03/31 ***Latest Annual Data:*** 03/31/2007

Year	***Sales***	***Net Income***
2007	$6,653,000	-$3,431,000
2006	$4,323,000	-$2,785,000
2005	$4,763,000	-$1,869,000

Curr. Assets:	$11,635,000	***Curr. Liab.:***	$1,219,000		
Plant, Equip.:	$2,604,000	***Total Liab.:***	$2,052,000	***Indic. Yr. Divd.:***	NA
Total Assets:	$14,796,000	***Net Worth:***	$12,744,000	***Debt/ Equity:***	NA

Uranerz Energy Corp

1701 E St., Casper, WY, 82605; ***PH:*** 1-307-265-8900; ***Fax:*** 1-307-265-8904; ***http://*** www.uranerz.com; ***Email:*** info@uranerz.com

General - Incorporation	NV	***Stock***- Price on:12/24/2007	$5.75
Employees	5	Stock Exchange	AMEX
Auditor	Manning Elliott LLP	Ticker Symbol	URZ
Stk Agt	Pacific Stock Transfer Company	Outstanding Shares	39,050,000
Counsel	Lang & Micherner, LLP	E.P.S	-$0.353
DUNS No.	NA	Shareholders	NA

Business: The groups principal activity is to develop and explore minerals. In the year 2006, the group acquired Rolling Hills Resources LLC. The group operates from Canada and North America.

Primary SIC and add'l.: 1000

CIK No: 0001162324

Subsidiaries: Mongolian limited liability company, Rolling Hills Resources LLC

Officers: Glenn Catchpole/Dir., CEO, Pres./$635,700.00, George J. Hartman/Dir., COO, Sr. VP/$910,326.00, Benjamin D. Leboe/CFO, Corp. Sec./$236,143.00

Directors: Glenn Catchpole/Dir., CEO, Pres., Dennis Higgs/Chmn., George J. Hartman/Dir., COO, Sr. VP, Gerhard F. Kirchner/Dir., Paul Saxton/Dir., Arnold J. Dyck/Dir., Richard W. Holmes/Dir., Peter W. Bell/Dir.

Owners: Paul Saxton, George Hartman/2.77%, Dennis Higgs/10.56%, Richard Holmes, Insiders/21.60%, Gerhard Kirchner/1.77%, Glenn Catchpole/5.11%, Arnold J. Dyck, Benjamin Leboe, Peter Bell

Financial Data: ***Fiscal Year End:***12/31 ***Latest Annual Data:*** 03/31/2007

Year	***Sales***	***Net Income***
2007	NA	-$8,508,000
2006	NA	-$6,549,000
2005	NA	-$5,002,000

Curr. Assets:	$12,369,000	***Curr. Liab.:***	$379,000	***P/E Ratio:***	37.18
Plant, Equip.:	$123,000	***Total Liab.:***	$379,000	***Indic. Yr. Divd.:***	NA
Total Assets:	$12,492,000	***Net Worth:***	$12,113,000	***Debt/ Equity:***	NA

Uranium Energy Corp

1111 W Hastings St. , Ste. 3, Vancouver, BC, V6E 2J3; ***PH:*** 1-604-682-9775; ***Fax:*** 1-604-682-3591; ***http://*** www.uraniumenergy.com

General - Incorporation	NV	***Stock***- Price on:12/24/2007	$4.15
Employees	6	Stock Exchange	AMEX
Auditor	Ernst & Young, LLP	Ticker Symbol	UEC
Stk Agt	Transfer Online, Inc.	Outstanding Shares	37,610,000
Counsel	NA	E.P.S	-$0.56
DUNS No.	NA	Shareholders	NA

Business: The groups principal activity is natural resource exploration engaged in the exploration and development of properties that may contain uranium minerals. The group operates from the United States.

Primary SIC and add'l.: 8731

CIK No: 0001334933

Officers: Amir Adnani/Dir., CEO, Pres., Harry Anthony/Dir., COO, Randall Reneau/Sr. Consulting Geologist, Pat Obara/Sec., Treasurer, CFO, Clyde Yancey/VP - Exploration, James Douglas Norris/VP - Engineering, Leonard Garcia/Land Tenure Mgr., Brad Moore/Exploration, Land Tenure Specialist, Robert Odell/District Geologist, Wyoming, Larry Minter/Sr. Geologist, Curtis O. Sealy/VP - Production, John Nelson/Sr. Geologic Engineer, Paul Pierce/Mgr. - Mine Development, Robert Underdown/Mgr. - Texas Operations, Joshua Leftwich/Environmental Mgr.

Directors: Amir Adnani/Dir., CEO, Pres., Alan Lindsay/Chmn., Harry Anthony/Dir., COO, Erik Essiger/Dir., Ivan Obolensky/Dir., Vincent Della Volpe/Dir., Craig Holmes/Member - Advisory Board, Jon Indall/Member - Advisory Board, Ed Brezinski/Member - Advisory Board

Owners: Ivan Obolensky, Isaiah Capital Trust/7.27%, Insiders/18.23%, Pat Obara, Westcliff Capital Management, LLC/9.73%, Erik Essiger, Morgan Stanley & Co. fbo Passport Global Master Fund/11.17%, Amir Adnani/5.74%, Harry L. Anthony/3.65%, Alan P. Lindsay/7.66%

Financial Data: ***Fiscal Year End:***12/31 ***Latest Annual Data:*** 12/31/2006

Year	***Sales***	***Net Income***
2006	NA	-$14,818,000
2005	NA	-$1,999,000

Curr. Assets:	$13,993,000	***Curr. Liab.:***	$532,000	***P/E Ratio:***	28.85
Plant, Equip.:	$205,000	***Total Liab.:***	$532,000	***Indic. Yr. Divd.:***	NA
Total Assets:	$14,198,000	***Net Worth:***	$13,666,000	***Debt/ Equity:***	NA

Uranium Power Corp

3rd Floor - Bellevue Ctr., 235 - 15th St., Vancouver, BC, V7T 2X1; ***PH:*** 1-604-921-1810; ***Fax:*** 1-604-921-1898; ***http://*** www.uraniumpowercorp.com; ***Email:*** ir@uraniumpowercorp.com

General - Incorporation	CO	***Stock***- Price on:12/24/2007	$1.015
Employees	NA	Stock Exchange	OTC
Auditor	Pannell Kerr Forster	Ticker Symbol	UPCFF
Stk Agt	Pacific Corporate Trust Co	Outstanding Shares	NA
Counsel	NA	E.P.S	NA
DUNS No.	NA	Shareholders	NA

Business: The group's principal activity is to explore and develop natural gas and crude oil properties in Canada. The group's oil and gas operations are carried out in the ft. Mcmurray area of northern alberta and its uranium interests are in the athabasca basin of northern saskatchewan, Canada.

Primary SIC and add'l.: 1382 1094

CIK No: 0001096791

Subsidiaries: Oilsands Quest, Inc, Township Petroleum Corporation, Western Petrochemicals Corporation

Officers: Christopher H. Hopkins/54/Dir., CEO, Pres., Barry A. Sheahan/CEO, Bev Funston/Dir., Corp. Sec., Gregory L. Adams/VP - Exploration, Erdal Yildirim/71/Exec. VP - Project Development, Chris Healey/Dir., Pres., Karim Hirji/45/CFO, Errin Kimball/39/VP - Exploration

Directors: Christopher H. Hopkins/54/Dir., CEO, Pres., Rahoul Sharan/Chmn., Murray T. Wilson/56/Chmn., Michael Waggett/Dir., Chris Healey/Dir., Pres., Ronald Phillips/42/Dir., Thomas Milne/61/Dir., Gordon Tallman/66/Dir., William Scott Thompson/59/Dir., Bev Funston/Dir., Corp. Sec., Pamela Wallin/55/Dir.

Owners: Christopher H. Hopkins/10.00%, Thomas Milne/1.40%, Ronald Phillips, Pamela Wallin, Insiders/18.00%, Gordon Tallman, Karim Hirji/3.20%, Murray T. Wilson/1.80%, William Scott Thompson/1.40%, Errin Kimball/1.60%

Uranium Resources Inc

405 State Hwy. 121 Bypass, Bldg. A, Ste. 110, Lewisville, TX, 75067; ***PH:*** 1-972-219-3330; ***Fax:*** 1-972-219-3311; ***http://*** www.uraniumresources.com; ***Email:*** info@uraniumresources.com

General - Incorporation	DE	***Stock***- Price on:12/24/2007	$9.8
Employees	73	Stock Exchange	OTC
Auditor	Hein & Assoc. LLP	Ticker Symbol	URRE
Stk Agt	Computershare Trust Co	Outstanding Shares	NA
Counsel	NA	E.P.S	NA
DUNS No.	08-766-2029	Shareholders	NA

Business: The group's principal activities are to acquire, explore, develop and mine uranium properties. The group uses in situ leach mining process to extract uranium. The leach mining process fortifies groundwater with oxidizing agents is pumped into the ore body causing the uranium contained in the ore to dissolve. The resulting solution is pumped to the surface where it is further processed to a dried form of uranium that is shipped to conversion facilities for sale. The in situ leach technique avoids the movement and milling of significant quantities of rock and ore as well as mill tailing waste associated with more traditional mining methods.

Primary SIC and add'l.: 1094

CIK No: 0000839470

Officers: David N. Clark/CEO, Pres./$2,678,546.00, Deborah K. Pawlowski/Investor Contact, James M. Culligan/Investor Contact, Kristin Simons/Media Contact, Richard A. Van Horn/61/COO, Exec. VP/$440,155.00, Thomas H. Ehrlich/48/CFO, VP/$155,749.00, Mark S. Pelizza/55/Environmental Mgr./$415,902.00, William M. McKnight/71/VP - Eploration, Craig S. Bartels/Sr. VP - Technology, New Project Development

Directors: Paul K. Willmott/68/Chmn., Leland O. Erdahl/79/Dir., George R. Ireland/51/Dir., Marvin K. Kaiser/Dir., Terence J. Cryan/Dir.

Owners: Gilder, Gagnon, Howe & Co. LLC/11.40%, Mark S. Pelizza/0.70%, Terence J. Cryan, David N. Clark/0.60%, Richard A. Van Horn/0.90%, Paul K. Willmott/2.50%, Deutsche Asset Management, Inc./10.21%, Rudolf J. Mueller c/o The Winchester Group, Inc./5.30%, George R. Ireland/3.60%, Insiders/9.70%, Zesiger Capital Group, LLC/16.60%, Dreman Value Management LLC/12.53%, Thomas H. Ehrlich/0.90%, Leland O. Erdahl/0.50%

Curr. Assets:	$22,904,000	***Curr. Liab.:***	$4,533,000		
Plant, Equip.:	$18,196,000	***Total Liab.:***	$9,167,000	***Indic. Yr. Divd.:***	NA
Total Assets:	$45,936,000	***Net Worth:***	$36,769,000	***Debt/ Equity:***	NA

Uraniumcore CO

3940-7 Broad St., San Luis Obispo, CA, 93401; ***PH:*** 1-805-541-6652; ***http://*** www.ocgt.com; ***Email:*** info@pcare.com

General - Incorporation: DE | Employees: NA | Auditor: Moore & Assoc. Chartered | Stk Agt: Continental Stock Transfer & Trust Co | Counsel: NA | DUNS No.: 60-171-1070

Stock - Price on:12/24/2007: NA | Stock Exchange: OTC | Ticker Symbol: UCCO | Outstanding Shares: NA | E.P.S.: NA | Shareholders: NA

Business: The group's principal activity is to develop, market and distribute software and diagnostic products for the healthcare industry. It creates, owns, maintains, expands and markets the primecare (TM) patient management system, the codecompliertm, a fitness Web site and cardiointergraph, a medical device used for the early detection of coronary artery disease. The group secures Internet enhanced and targeted components of the primecaretm namely primecareontheweb.com, yourowndoctor.com and yourownhealth.com.

Primary SIC and add'l.: 3845 7375 7372

CIK No: 0000073779

Subsidiaries: Primecare Systems, Inc.

Officers: Robert Lunde/39/Chmn., CEO, Pres., Mark Lotz/38/CFO

Directors: Robert Lunde/39/Chmn., CEO, Pres., Ken Lunde/Dir., Marc Applbaum/36/Dir., Dennis Petke/Dir.

Owners: Bobby Vavithis/95.50%

Financial Data: *Fiscal Year End:*06/30 *Latest Annual Data:* 6/30/2006

Year	Sales	Net Income
2006	NA	-$183,000
2005	$316,000	-$662,000
2004	$299,000	-$684,000

Curr. Assets:	NA	**Curr. Liab.:**	$188,000		
Plant, Equip.:	$50,000	**Total Liab.:**	$233,000	**Indic. Yr. Divd.:**	NA
Total Assets:	$50,000	**Net Worth:**	-$183,000	**Debt/ Equity:**	0.1442

Urban Outfitters Inc

5000 sounth broad steet, Philadelphia, PA, 19112; *PH:* 1-215-454-5500; *http://* www.urbanoutfittersinc.com

General - Incorporation: PA | Employees: 3,864 | Auditor: KPMG LLP | Stk Agt: KPMG LLP | Counsel: Drinker Biddle & Reath LLP | DUNS No.: 05-327-5483

Stock - Price on:12/24/2007: $24.01 | Stock Exchange: NDQ | Ticker Symbol: URBN | Outstanding Shares: 165,680,000 | E.P.S.: $0.74 | Shareholders: NA

Business: The group's principal activity is the operation of general consumer product retail business through retail stores, a catalog and two Web sites. The group is a lifestyle merchandising group that operates specialty retail stores under two distinct brands: urban outfitters and anthropologie, as well as the free people wholesale division. Urban outfitters products include women's and men's fashion apparel, footwear and accessories as well as a mix of apartment wares and gifts. Apartment wares range from rugs, pillows and shower curtains to books, candles and novelties. Anthropologie offer products, which include women's casual apparel and accessories, home furnishings and a diverse array of gifts and decorative items. The free people division designs, develops and markets young women's casual apparel. The group operated 61 stores as of 31-Jan-2004.

Primary SIC and add'l.: 5621 5632 5399 5137

CIK No: 0000912615

Subsidiaries: A California limited liability company, A Canadian corporation, A Delaware C corporation, A Delaware corporation, A Delaware Limited Liability Company, A Delaware single member limited liability company, A Florida corporation, A Pennsylvania C corporation, A Pennsylvania Limited Liability Compa, A Pennsylvania Limited Liability Company, A Pennsylvania Limited Partnership, A Pennsylvania single member limited liability company, A United Kingdom corporation, An Irish corporation, Anthropologie (Delaware), Inc. 39 Subsidiaries included in the Index

Officers: Richard A. Hayne/Chmn., Principal Executive Officer, Pres./$446,777.00, Glen T. Senk/Dir., VP/$635,656.00, Freeman M. Zausner/Chief Administrative Officer, Tedford G. Marlow/Pres. - Urban Retail/$491,881.00, Robert Ross/Controller, John E. Kyees/CFO/$580,262.00

Directors: Richard A. Hayne/Chmn., Principal Executive Officer, Pres., Harry S. Cherken/58/Dir., Joel S. Lawson/60/Dir., Glen T. Senk/Dir., VP, Scott A. Belair/60/Dir., Robert H. Strouse/59/Dir.

Owners: John E. Kyees, FMR Corp./1.90%, Insiders/34.10%, Robert H. Strouse, Scott A. Belair/2.50%, Joel S. Lawson, Maverick Capital, Ltd./5.50%, Tedford G. Marlow, Richard A. Hayne/29.10%, Harry S. Cherken, Glen A. Bodzy, Glen T. Senk/1.30%, Ziff Asset Management L.P./9.00%

Financial Data: *Fiscal Year End:*01/31 *Latest Annual Data:* 1/31/2007

Year	Sales	Net Income
2007	$1,224,717,000	$116,206,000
2006	$1,092,107,000	$130,796,000
2005	$827,750,000	$90,489,000

Curr. Assets:	$366,405,000	**Curr. Liab.:**	$135,318,000	**P/E Ratio:**	30.78
Plant, Equip.:	$445,698,000	**Total Liab.:**	$223,968,000	**Indic. Yr. Divd.:**	NA
Total Assets:	$899,251,000	**Net Worth:**	$675,283,000	**Debt/ Equity:**	NA

Urban Television Network Corp

2707 S Cooper, Ste. 119, Arlington, TX, 76015; *PH:* 1-817-303-7449; *Fax:* 1-817-459-2942; *http://* www.uatvn.com; *Email:* info@uatvn.com

General - Incorporation: NV | Employees: 3 | Auditor: The Hall Group, CPAs | Stk Agt: Computershare Investor Services LLC | Counsel: NA | DUNS No.: NA

Stock - Price on:12/24/2007: NA | Stock Exchange: OTC | Ticker Symbol: URBT | Outstanding Shares: 130,160,000 | E.P.S.: -$0.06 | Shareholders: NA

Business: The groups principle activities include provide free over-the-air programming to television viewing audiences in the communities served by its local affiliate television stations. The group operates from the United States.

Primary SIC and add'l.: 4833 4841

CIK No: 0000806171

Subsidiaries: Urban Television Network Corporation, Waste Conversion Systems of Virginia, Inc.

Officers: Jacob R. Miles/Chmn., CEO, Sandra Pate/Exec. VP - Programming, Randy Moseley/Dir., CFO, Exec. VP, Stanley Woods/Dir., Corp. Sec.

Directors: Jacob R. Miles/Chmn., CEO, Randy Moseley/Dir., CFO, Exec. VP, Marc Pace/Dir., Stanley Woods/Dir., Corp. Sec.

Owners: Marc Pace/1.08%, Randy Moseley/2.40%, Stanley Woods, Insiders/28.60%, Jacob R. Miles/5.14%, R.J.Halden Holdings, Inc./19.43%

Financial Data: *Fiscal Year End:*09/30 *Latest Annual Data:* 09/30/2006

Year	Sales	Net Income
2006	$90,000	-$6,355,000
2005	$298,000	-$2,842,000
2004	$223,000	-$7,526,000

Curr. Assets:	$4,000	**Curr. Liab.:**	$3,183,000	**P/E Ratio:**	28.85
Plant, Equip.:	$40,000	**Total Liab.:**	$3,183,000	**Indic. Yr. Divd.:**	NA
Total Assets:	$82,000	**Net Worth:**	-$3,101,000	**Debt/ Equity:**	NA

Urex Energy Corp

10580 N McCarran Blvd., Bldg. 115-208, Reno, NV, 89503; *PH:* 1-775-721-8883; *http://* www.urexenergy.com; *Email:* info@urexenergy.com

General - Incorporation: NV | Employees: NA | Auditor: Jewett, Schwartz & Associates | Stk Agt: Holladay Stock Transfer, Inc. | Counsel: NA | DUNS No.: NA

Stock - Price on:12/24/2007: $0.235 | Stock Exchange: OTC | Ticker Symbol: URXE | Outstanding Shares: 84,430,000 | E.P.S.: -$0.08 | Shareholders: NA

Business: The groups principal activity is seeking new prospects, it currently only has interests in the properties operations and exploration. The group operates from the United States.

Primary SIC and add'l.: 1000

CIK No: 0001182737

Subsidiaries: United Energy Metals S.A.,

Officers: Richard Bachman/Dir., Pres., Sec., Principal Executive Officer, Principal Financial Officer, Principal Accounting Officer, Oscar Yoshitaka Yokoi/South American Mgr., Dir., Amer Smailbegovic/Mgr. - Central Asia, Europe Initiative, Brad Long/Contact - Investor Relations

Directors: Richard Bachman/Dir., Pres., Sec., Principal Executive Officer, Principal Financial Officer, Principal Accounting Officer, Oscar Yoshitaka Yokoi/South American Mgr., Dir., Brian Cole/Dir.

Owners: Richard Bachman/18.95%, Insiders

Financial Data: *Fiscal Year End:*03/31 *Latest Annual Data:* 3/31/2006

Year	Sales	Net Income
2006	NA	-$155,000
2005	NA	-$36,000

Curr. Assets:	$50,000	**Curr. Liab.:**	$277,000		
Plant, Equip.:	NA	**Total Liab.:**	$277,000	**Indic. Yr. Divd.:**	NA
Total Assets:	$100,000	**Net Worth:**	-$178,000	**Debt/ Equity:**	NA

Urigen Pharmaceuticals Inc

Formerly: Valentis Inc

875 Mahler Rd., Ste. 235, Burlingame, CA, 94010; *PH:* 1-650-259-0239; *http://* www.valentis.com

General - Incorporation: DE | Employees: 8 | Auditor: Ernst & Young LLP | Stk Agt: Computershare Trust Co. | Counsel: Latham & Watkins | DUNS No.: 80-808-3885

Stock - Price on:12/24/2007: NA | Stock Exchange: NA | Ticker Symbol: NA | Outstanding Shares: NA | E.P.S.: NA | Shareholders: NA

Business: The group's principal activities are to develop multiple proprietary gene delivery and gene expression systems and pegylation technologies and apply our preclinical and early clinical development expertise to create novel therapeutics and improved versions of currently marketed biopharmaceuticals. The group focuses on research, preclinical and early stage clinical development of products in several therapeutic areas including cardiovascular disorders, oncology, haematology and immunology. The group has three product platforms for the development of novel therapeutics namely the gene medicine, geneswitch(R) and dna vaccine platforms. The gene medicine platform includes a comprehensive array of proprietary nucleic acid delivery systems. Geneswitch(R) platform controls erythropoietin protein production from an injected gene by orally administered drug. Synthetic vaccine delivery systems provide consistent levels of gene expression and enhance efficiency of plasmid.

Primary SIC and add'l.: 2834 2899 8731 2836

CIK No: 0000932352

Subsidiaries: PolyMASC Pharmaceuticals plc

Officers: William J. Garner/42/Dir., CEO, Pres., Martin E. Shmagin/58/CFO, Terry M. Nida/59/COO, Dennis H. Giesing/Chief Scientific Officer, Amie E. Franklin/42/Mgr. - Clinical, Regulatory, Intellectual Property, Bill Douglass/Media Contact, Rachel Colgate/Media Contact

Directors: William J. Garner/42/Dir., CEO, Pres., Benjamin F. McGraw/59/Chmn., George Lasezkay/55/Dir., Martin E. Shmagin/58/CFO, Tracy Taylor/54/Dir., Lowell C. Parsons/63/Dir., Member - Scientific Advisory Board, Grant S. Mulholland/Member - Scientific Advisory Board, Christian Stief/Member - Scientific Advisory Board

Owners: Insiders/38.00%, Martin E. Shmagin/4.21%, C. Lowell Parsons/2.60%, Terry M. Nida/4.52%, William J. Garner/26.67%

Urologix Inc

14405 21st Ave. N, Minneapolis, MN, 55447; *PH:* 1-763-475-1400; *http://* www.urologix.com; *Email:* customerservice@urologix.com

General - Incorporation: MN | Employees: 99 | Auditor: KPMG LLP | Stk Agt: Wells Fargo Bank Minnesota N.A | Counsel: Lindquist & Vennum PLLP | DUNS No.: 78-573-5796

Stock - Price on:12/24/2007: $2.19 | Stock Exchange: NDQ | Ticker Symbol: ULGX | Outstanding Shares: 14,330,000 | E.P.S.: -$0.92 | Shareholders: NA

Business: The group's principal activities are to develop, manufacture and market medical devices for the treatment of urological disorders. The group offers non-surgical, catheter-based therapies that use a proprietary cooled microwave technology known as cooled thermotherapy for the treatment of benign

prostatic hyperplasia (bph). The cooled thermotherapy can be performed without anesthesia or intravenous sedation and can be performed in a physician's office or an outpatient clinic. The therapy provides a safe and cost-effective solution that is superior to medication without the complications and side effects inherent in surgical procedures. The products of the group are marketed under the names targis (TM) and prostatron (r). The group operates in the United States, Europe and Asia.

Primary SIC and add'l.: 3841

CIK No: 0000882873

Officers: Fred B. Parks/Chmn., CEO, Kristin Vonderharr/Primary Investor Relations Officer, Elissa J. Lindsoe/CFO, Kirsten Doerfert/52/Sr. VP, GM

Directors: Fred B. Parks/Chmn., CEO, Daniel J. Starks/Dir., Guy C. Jackson/Dir., Sidney W. Emery/Dir., Jerry C. Cirino/Dir.

Owners: Insiders/5.60%, Fred B. Parks/4.20%, Elissa J. Lindsoe, BlueLine Partners, L.L.C./8.00%, Sidney W. Emery, Jerry C. Cirino, Daniel J. Starks, Guy C. Jackson

Financial Data: Fiscal Year End:06/30 **Latest Annual Data:** 06/30/2007

Year	Sales	Net Income
2007	$21,317,000	-$13,237,000
2006	$25,885,000	$5,494,000
2005	$25,813,000	$2,837,000

Curr. Assets:	$20,098,000	Curr. Liab.:	$3,172,000	P/E Ratio:	8.76
Plant, Equip.:	$2,897,000	Total Liab.:	$3,918,000	Indic. Yr. Divd.:	NA
Total Assets:	$43,898,000	Net Worth:	$39,980,000	Debt/ Equity:	NA

UroMed Corp

115 E 57th St., Ste. 1118, New York, NY, 10022; **PH:** 1-646-202-9679

General - Incorporation	DE	Stock - Price on:12/24/2007	NA
Employees	NA	Stock Exchange	OTC
Auditor	Michael F. Cronin, CPA	Ticker Symbol	UOMD
Stk Agt	Standard Registrar & Transfer Co Inc.	Outstanding Shares	NA
Counsel	NA	E.P.S.	-$0.36
DUNS No.	NA	Shareholders	NA

Business: The groups principal activity is identifying a prospective target business will not be limited to a particular industry and the group may ultimately acquire a business in any industry Management deems appropriate. The group operates from the United States.

Primary SIC and add'l.: 3841

CIK No: 0000917821

Officers: Ivo Heiden/41/Chmn., CEO, CFO

Directors: Ivo Heiden/41/Chmn., CEO, CFO

Owners: Insiders/17.13%, Michael F. Manion/18.18%, Richard Rubin/17.01%, Ivo Heiden/17.13%, Jay Gottlieb/7.75%

Financial Data: Fiscal Year End:12/31 **Latest Annual Data:** 12/31/2006

Year	Sales	Net Income
2006	NA	-$103,000
2005	NA	-$8,000
2002	NA	$5,043,000

Curr. Assets:	$0	Curr. Liab.:	$20,000		
Plant, Equip.:	NA	Total Liab.:	$20,000	Indic. Yr. Divd.:	NA
Total Assets:	$0	Net Worth:	-$20,000	Debt/ Equity:	NA

Uroplasty Inc

2718 Summer St. NE, Minneapolis, MN, 55413; **PH:** 1-612-378-1180; **http://** www.uroplasty.com; **Email:** info.usa@uroplasty.com

General - Incorporation	MN	Stock - Price on:12/24/2007	$4.31
Employees	51	Stock Exchange	AMEX
Auditor	McGladrey & Pullen LLP	Ticker Symbol	UPI
Stk Agt	StockTrans, Inc.	Outstanding Shares	13,160,000
Counsel	Jeffrey C. Robbins	E.P.S.	-$0.33
DUNS No.	NA	Shareholders	NA

Business: The group's principal activity is to design, develop, manufacture, and market medical products for the treatment of urinary incontinence and vesicoureteral reflux. The group's main product is macroplastique(R) implants, an injectable, soft tissue bulking agent used to treat certain types of stress urinary incontinence ("Sui"). Sui refers to the involuntary loss of urine as a result of activities that increase intra-abdominal pressure. Macroplastique is also used to treat vesicoureteral reflux ("Vur"), a condition occurring mostly in children in which urine flows backward from the bladder into the kidney. In addition, the group's implantable bulking material is also sold for reconstructive and cosmetic plastic surgery applications under the trade name bioplastique(tm). The group's international operations are in the Netherlands, the United Kingdom and Canada. The group markets its products only outside the United States, primarily in Europe.

Primary SIC and add'l.: 2836

CIK No: 0000890846

Subsidiaries: Bioplasty BV, Uroplasty BV, Uroplasty, Ltd

Officers: David B. Kaysen/Dir., CEO, Pres./$721,855.00, Jeffrey C. Robbins/Legal Counsel, Susan Hartjes Holman/Sec., COO, VP - Operations, Regulatory Affairs/$235,560.00, Larry Heinemann/VP - Sales, Marketing/$184,185.00, Mahedi A. Jiwani/CFO, VP, Treasurer/$237,014.00, Arie J. Koole/Controller/$182,526.00, Marc M. Herregraven/VP - Manufacturing

Directors: David B. Kaysen/Dir., CEO, Pres., Patrick R. Maxwell/Chmn., Thomas E. Jamison/Dir., Lee A. Jones/Dir., Sven A. Wehrwein/Dir., James P. Stauner/Dir.

Owners: David B. Kaysen/1.30%, SF Capital Partners Ltd/9.90%, Thomas E. Jamison, Heartland Advisors, Inc./7.20%, Sven A. Wehrwein, James P. Stauner, Lee A. Jones, Insiders/8.50%, Susan Hartjes Holman/3.10%, Perkins Capital Management/5.40%, Larry Heinemann, Arie J. Koole, Patrick R. Maxwell/1.10%, Tapestry Investment Partners, LP/6.60%, Mahedi A. Jiwani (16 Owners included in Index)

Financial Data: Fiscal Year End:03/31 **Latest Annual Data:** 03/31/2007

Year	Sales	Net Income
2007	$8,311,000	-$4,977,000
2006	$6,143,000	-$4,543,000
2005	$6,658,000	-$1,735,000

Curr. Assets:	$4,799,000	Curr. Liab.:	$2,132,000		
Plant, Equip.:	$1,079,000	Total Liab.:	$2,994,000	Indic. Yr. Divd.:	NA
Total Assets:	$6,401,000	Net Worth:	$3,407,000	Debt/ Equity:	0.0670

URS Corp

600 Montgomery St., 26th Fl., San Francisco, CA, 94111; **PH:** 1-415-774-2700; **http://** www.urscorp.com; **Email:** investor_relations@urscorp.com

General - Incorporation	DE	Stock - Price on:12/24/2007	$49.03
Employees	26,000	Stock Exchange	NYSE
Auditor	PricewaterhouseCoopers LLP	Ticker Symbol	URS
Stk Agt	Mellon Investor Services LLC	Outstanding Shares	53,030,000
Counsel	Cooley Godward LLP	E.P.S.	$2.52
DUNS No.	04-327-1568	Shareholders	NA

Business: The group's principle activity is to provide professional planning and design, system engineering and technical assistance, program and construction management, and operations and maintenance services. The group operates through two divisions include URS division and EG&G division. Customers served by the group include chemical, pharmaceutical, manufacturing, forest product, energy, oil, gas, mining, healthcare, water supply, retail and commercial development, telecommunication and utility industries. The group operates from United States and United Kingdom.

Primary SIC and add'l.: 9511 8712 8711

CIK No: 0000102379

Subsidiaries: AACM INTL PTY LTD., Advatech, LLC., Agc Woodward-clyde Pty. Ltd., Aman Environmental Construction, Inc., Banshee Construction Company, Inc., Bricolpar Ltd., Business Risk Strategies Pty. Ltd., Clay Street Properties, Cleveland Wrecking Company, D&m Consulting Engineers, Inc., Dames & Moore Bolivia S.a., Dames & Moore De Mexico S De R.l. De C.v., Dames & Moore Group (ny), Inc., Dames & Moore International Srl Japan/venezuela, Dames & Moore Ltd. 114 Subsidiaries included in the Index

Officers: Martin M. Koffel/Chmn., CEO, Pres./$6,675,849.00, Gary V. Jandegian/55/Pres. - URS Division, VP - Since July 2003/$1,478,694.00, Thomas H. Hicks/57/CFO, VP/$1,581,440.00, Sam Ramraj/Investor Relations Officer, Randall A. Wotring/51/Pres. - EG, G Division, VP/$1,556,081.00, Thomas W. Bishop/61/VP - Strategy, Reed N. Brimhall/54/Chief Accounting Officer/$1,086,358.00, Joseph Masters/51/Sec., Susan B. Kilgannon/49/VP - Communications

Directors: Martin M. Koffel/Chmn., CEO, Pres., William D. Walsh/Dir., Joseph W. Ralston/Dir., Armen Der Marderosian/Dir., Jesse H. Arnelle/Dir., Betsy J. Bernard/Dir., Mickey P. Foret/Dir., William P. Sullivan/Dir., John D. Roach/Dir., Lydia H. Kennard/Dir., Douglas W. Stotlar/Dir.

Owners: John D. Roach, Martin M. Koffel/1.93%, Randall A. Wotring, Insiders/3.29%, Joseph W. Ralston, Armen Der Marderosian, William D. Walsh, Kent P. Ainsworth, William P. Sullivan, Gary V. Jandegian, Mickey P. Foret, Thomas H. Hicks, Jesse H. Arnelle, Reed N. Brimhall, Betsy J. Bernard

Financial Data: Fiscal Year End:12/30 **Latest Annual Data:** 12/29/2006

Year	Sales	Net Income
2006	$4,240,150,000	$113,012,000
2005	$3,917,565,000	$82,475,000
2004	$3,381,963,000	$61,704,000

Curr. Assets:	$1,273,060,000	Curr. Liab.:	$698,621,000	P/E Ratio:	20.69
Plant, Equip.:	$146,470,000	Total Liab.:	$1,124,944,000	Indic. Yr. Divd.:	NA
Total Assets:	$2,469,448,000	Net Worth:	$1,344,504,000	Debt/ Equity:	0.0976

Urstadt Biddle Properties Inc

321 Railroad Ave., Greenwich, CT, 06830; **PH:** 1-203-863-8200; **http://** www.ubproperties.com

General - Incorporation	MD	Stock - Price on:12/24/2007	$17.94
Employees	32	Stock Exchange	NYSE
Auditor	PKF Witt Mares, PLC	Ticker Symbol	UBA
Stk Agt	Bank of New York	Outstanding Shares	26,620,000
Counsel	NA	E.P.S.	$2.48
DUNS No.	NA	Shareholders	NA

Business: The groups principle activities include owning, acquiring and management of commercial real estate. In the year 2006, the group acquired three retail properties. The group operates from the United States. The groups quarterly revenue for September 2007 was 18.37 millions of USD.

Primary SIC and add'l.: 4225 6798

CIK No: 0001029800

Subsidiaries: 323 Railroad Corporation,, Eastchester Mall Associate, L.P., UB Danbury, Inc.,, UB Darien, Inc.,, UB Dockside, LLC, UB Railside, LLC, UB Somers, Inc., UB Stamford, L.P., UB Yorktown, LLC

Officers: Charles J. Urstadt/Chmn., CEO/$325,000.00, Willing L. Biddle/Dir., COO, Pres./$309,167.00, James R. Moore/Exec. VP/$254,167.00, Thomas D. Myers/56/Sr. VP, Co - Counsel, Sec./$191,167.00, Raymond P. Argila/Sr. VP/$186,167.00, Virgil E. Conway/Corp. Dir. - Financial Consultant, Athena Blude/Investor Relations Officer

Directors: Charles J. Urstadt/Chmn., CEO, Robert R. Douglass/Vice Chmn., George J. Vojta/72/Dir., Virgil E. Conway/Corp. Dir. - Financial Consultant, George H.C. Lawrence/Dir., Willing L. Biddle/Dir., COO, Pres., Peter Herrick/80/Dir., Robert J. Mueller/66/Dir., Charles D. Urstadt/Dir.

Owners: Virgil E. Conway, Willing L. Biddle, Robert R. Douglass, Raymond P. Argila, Robert R. Douglass, Charles J. Urstadt, George J. Vojta, Peter Herrick, Virgil E. Conway, Willing L. Biddle/0.90%, George H.C. Lawrence, Charles D. Urstadt, James R. Moore/1.00%, Charles D. Urstadt, Insiders/5.20% (23 Owners included in Index)

Financial Data: Fiscal Year End:10/31 **Latest Annual Data:** 10/31/2006

Year	Sales	Net Income
2006	$73,249,000	$25,032,000
2005	$69,964,000	$30,985,000
2004	$64,916,000	$23,315,000

Curr. Assets:	$19,976,000	Curr. Liab.:	$1,785,000	P/E Ratio:	7.23
Plant, Equip.:	$418,285,000	Total Liab.:	$118,147,000	Indic. Yr. Divd.:	$0.920
Total Assets:	$451,350,000	Net Worth:	$280,456,000	Debt/ Equity:	0.3589

US 1 Industries Inc

336 W US Hwy. 30, Ste. 201, Valparaiso, IN, 46385; **PH:** 1-219-476-1300; **Fax:** 1-219-476-1385; **http://** www.us1industries.com; **Email:** IR@us1industries.com

General - Incorporation	IN	**Stock** - Price on:12/24/2007	$1.51
Employees	81	Stock Exchange	OTC
Auditor	BDO Seidman LLP	Ticker Symbol	USOO
Stk Agt	Bank Boston EquiServe	Outstanding Shares	12,170,000
Counsel	NA	E.P.S	$0.30
DUNS No.	09-944-7302	Shareholders	NA

Business: The group's principal activity is to provide interstate truckload carrier services for general commodities through independent agents and owner-operators to contract and haul freight for their customers in 48 states. The group carries all forms of freight transported by truck, except bulk goods, including specialized trucking services such as containerized, refrigerated and flatbed transportation. The group operates solely in the United States.

Primary SIC and add'l.: 4212 4214 4213

CIK No: 0000351498

Subsidiaries: Antler Transport, Inc., Blue and Grey Brokerage, Inc., Blue and Grey Transport, Inc., Cam Transport, Inc., Carolina National Logistics, Inc., Carolina National Transportation, Inc., Five Star Transport, Inc., Friendly Transport, Inc., Gulf Line Brokerage, Inc., Gulf Line Transportation, Inc., Harbor Bridge Intermodal, Inc., Keystone Lines, Inc., Keystone Logistics, Inc., Patriot Logistics, Inc., TC Services, Inc. 18 Subsidiaries included in the Index

Officers: Michael Kibler/67/Dir., CEO, Pres., Harold Antonson/68/Dir., CFO, Treasurer, Curt Banaszek/Compliance Mgr., Mary McCalmont/Mgr. - Detroit, Enterprise Lucas, Carol Verboski/Mgr. - Canton, Enterprise Lucas, Lori Baughcum/Mgr. - Jonesboro, Five Star Transport, Tim Frye/Mgr. - Charlotte, Five Star Transport, Ross Pantano/Mgr. - Linden, Carolina National Transp, Bert Edwards/Mgr. - Brooklyn, Carolina National Transp, Denise Mundl/Mgr. - Radnor, Carolina National Transp, Paul Jarvis/Mgr. - Charleston, Carolina National Transp, Mike Agate/Mgr. - Portsmouth, Five Star Transport, Clarence Wilson/Mgr. - Rahay, Five Star Transport, James Wood/Mgr. - Merrillville, Enterprise Power Only, Rick Holcomb/Mgr. - Douglasville, Five Star Transport *(133 Officers included in Index)*

Directors: Michael Kibler/67/Dir., CEO, Pres., Harold Antonson/68/Dir., CFO, Treasurer, Brad James/52/Dir., Mgr. - Perrysburg, Seagate Transportation, Lex Venditti/55/Dir., Robert I. Scissors/74/Dir.

Financial Data: *Fiscal Year End:*12/31 *Latest Annual Data:* 12/31/2006

Year		Sales		Net Income
2006		$190,976,000		$3,102,000
2005		$166,648,000		$4,117,000
2004		$143,313,000		$15,000

Curr. Assets:	$30,291,000	**Curr. Liab.:**	$19,878,000	**P/E Ratio:**	6.57
Plant, Equip.:	$433,000	**Total Liab.:**	$21,038,000	**Indic. Yr. Divd.:**	NA
Total Assets:	$32,423,000	**Net Worth:**	$11,385,000	**Debt/ Equity:**	NA

US Airways Group Inc

2345 Crystal Dr., Arlington, VA, 22227; *PH:* 1-703-872-7000; *http://* www.usairways.com; *Email:* investor.relations@usairways.com

General - Incorporation	DE	**Stock** - Price on:12/24/2007	$29.71
Employees	37,000	Stock Exchange	NYSE
Auditor	KPMG LLP	Ticker Symbol	LCC
Stk Agt	Computershare Investor Services LLC	Outstanding Shares	91,420,000
Counsel	NA	E.P.S	$2.81
DUNS No.	06-537-7418	Shareholders	NA

Business: The groups principle activity is to provide air transportation for passengers and cargo. The group operates from Latin America, Europe, Canada and United States.

Primary SIC and add'l.: 4512 4513

CIK No: 0000701345

Subsidiaries: Airways Assurance Limited, America West Airlines, Inc., America West Holdings Corporation, Material Services Company, Piedmont Airlines, Inc., PSA Airlines, Inc., US Airways Express, US Airways, Inc.

Officers: Douglas W. Parker/Chmn., CEO/$5,357,582.00, Andrew Nocella/Sr. VP - Scheduling, Planning Alliances, Scott J. Kirby/Pres./$2,893,535.00, Randy Richards/VP - Cargo, Hal Heule/Sr. VP - Technical Operations, Keith D. Houk/Pres., Larry Lesueur/VP - Culture Integration, Donna Paladini/VP - Customer Service, West, Rick Oehme/VP - Engineering, Quality, Paul Morell/VP - Safety, Regulatory Compliance, Mike Minerva/VP, Deputy General Counsel, Stephen R. Farrow/Pres., Caroline Ray/Corp. Sec., Derek Kerr/CFO, Sr. VP/$1,297,472.00, Brad Beakley/VP - Reservations, Inventory Services *(35 Officers included in Index)*

Directors: Douglas W. Parker/Chmn., CEO, Bruce R. Lakefield/Vice Chmn., Richard Bartlett/Dir., Matthew J. Hart/Dir., Richard C. Kraemer/Dir., Herbert M. Baum/Dir., Edward L. Shapiro/Dir., Steven J. Whisler/Dir., Cheryl G. Krongard/Dir., Denise M. O'Leary/Dir., George M. Philip/Dir.

Owners: Derek J. Kerr, Elise R. Eberwein, Insiders/11.80%, Alan W. Crellin, Jeffrey D. McClelland, Bruce R. Lakefield, Matthew J. Hart, Steven J. Whisler, Cheryl G. Krongard, Richard A. Bartlett/3.20%, Richard C. Kraemer, Herbert M. Baum, Edward L. Shapiro/7.70%, George M. Philip, Douglas W. Parker *(18 Owners included in Index)*

Financial Data: *Fiscal Year End:*12/31 *Latest Annual Data:* 12/31/2004

Year		Sales		Net Income
2004		$7,117,000,000		-$611,000,000
2003		$6,846,000,000		$1,461,000,000
2002		$6,977,000,000		-$1,646,000,000

Curr. Assets:	$1,413,000,000	**Curr. Liab.:**	$2,383,000,000	**P/E Ratio:**	9.09
Plant, Equip.:	$3,370,000,000	**Total Liab.:**	$8,856,000,000	**Indic. Yr. Divd.:**	NA
Total Assets:	$8,422,000,000	**Net Worth:**	-$434,000,000	**Debt/ Equity:**	NA

US Airways Inc

111 W Rio Salado Pkwy., Tempe, AZ, 85281; *PH:* 1-703-872-7000; *http://* www.usairways.com; *Email:* investor.relations@americawest.com

General - Incorporation	DE	**Stock** - Price on:12/24/2007	$29.71
Employees	37,000	Stock Exchange	NYSE
Auditor	KPMG LLP	Ticker Symbol	NA
Stk Agt	Computershare Investor Services LLC	Outstanding Shares	91,420,000
Counsel	NA	E.P.S	NA
DUNS No.	00-691-9229	Shareholders	NA

Business: The group's principal activity is to provide transportation to passengers, property and mail. The group operates in the eastern United States with major connecting hubs at the airports in charlotte, philadelphia and pittsburgh. The group is a wholly owned subsidiary of us airways group inc. The us airways operates 282 jet aircraft and provides regularly scheduled service at 90 airports in the continental United States, Canada, Mexico, France, Germany, Italy, Spain, Ireland, the Netherlands, the United Kingdom and the Caribbean. Certain air carriers have code share arrangements with us airways to operate under the trade name 'us airways express.' as of Dec 2003, the us airways express served 143 airports in the continental United States, Canada and the bahamas and enplaned approximately 13.2 million passengers.

Primary SIC and add'l.: 4512 4513

CIK No: 0000714560

Subsidiaries: America West Airlines, Inc., America West Holdings Corporation, Material Services Company Inc., Piedmont Airlines Inc., PSA Airlines, Inc, US Airways Group

Officers: Douglas W. Parker/Chmn., CEO, Stephen R. Farrow/CEO, Pres. - Piedmont Airlines, Inc, Keith D. Houk/CEO, Pres. - PSA Airlines, Inc, Caroline Ray/Corp. Sec., David Seymour/VP - Operations Control, Planning, Thomas Trenga/VP - Revenue Management, Tom Weir/VP, Treasurer, Anthony V. Mule/Sr. VP - Customer Service, Scott Kirby/Pres., Rick Oehme/VP - Engineering, Quality, Andrew Nocella/Sr. VP - Scheduling, Planning Alliances, Ed Bular/Sr. VP - Flight Operations, Inflight, C. A. Howlett/Sr. VP - Public Affairs, Hal Heule/Sr. VP - Technical Operations, Travis Christ/VP - Sales, Marketing *(39 Officers included in Index)*

Directors: Douglas W. Parker/Chmn., CEO, Bruce R. Lakefield/Vice Chmn., Steven J. Whisler/Dir., Richard Bartlett/Dir., Herbert M. Baum/Dir., Matthew J. Hart/Dir., Richard C. Kraemer/Dir., Cheryl G. Krongard/Dir., Denise M. O'Leary/Dir., George M. Philip/Dir., Edward L. Shapiro/Dir.

Financial Data: *Fiscal Year End:*12/31 *Latest Annual Data:* 06/30/2005

Year		Sales		Net Income
2005		NA		NA
2004		NA		NA
2003		$6,846,000,000		$1,461,000,000

Curr. Assets:	$1,413,000,000	**Curr. Liab.:**	$2,383,000,000	**P/E Ratio:**	9.09
Plant, Equip.:	$3,370,000,000	**Total Liab.:**	$8,856,000,000	**Indic. Yr. Divd.:**	NA
Total Assets:	$8,422,000,000	**Net Worth:**	-$434,000,000	**Debt/ Equity:**	NA

US Dataworks Inc

One Sugar Creek Ctr. Blvd., Fifth Fl., Sugar land, TX, 77475; *PH:* 1-866-337-5477; *Fax:* 1-281-504-8000; *http://* www.usdataworks.com

General - Incorporation	NV	**Stock** - Price on:12/24/2007	$0.64
Employees	35	Stock Exchange	AMEX
Auditor	Ham, Langston & Brezina LLP	Ticker Symbol	UDW
Stk Agt	American Stock Transfer & Trust Co.	Outstanding Shares	37,240,000
Counsel	NA	E.P.S	-$0.107
DUNS No.	NA	Shareholders	NA

Business: The group's principal activity is to provide licensing of financial processing software and asp solutions. The group provides clients with a command centre to control and adjust the performance of their businesses. The group's range of service includes application hosting, transaction processing, software/Web development and creative/production. The group's core products are micrworkstm, returnworkstm, remitworkstm and remitworks-daemon. The group's products include check processing, point-of-purchase transactions and turnkey automated clearing house (ach) payments. The products are designed to provide organizations with an in-house solution that will complement and enhance such organizations' existing technologies, systems and operational workflow. The group serves five of the top 25 banking institutions, four of the top 10 credit card issuers, and two United States government agencies.

Primary SIC and add'l.: 7372 7371 7379

CIK No: 0001049505

Officers: Charles Ramey/64/Chmn., CEO/$400,438.00, John J. Figone/47/Sr. VP - Business Development, General Counsel/$288,500.00, Terry Stepanik/55/Dir., COO, Pres./$359,250.00, Mario Villarreal/36/CTO, Sr. VP

Directors: Charles Ramey/64/Chmn., CEO, Terry Stepanik/55/Dir., COO, Pres., Thomas L. West/68/Dir., John L. Nicholson/70/Dir., Joe Abrell/71/Dir., Hayden Watson/56/Dir.

Financial Data: *Fiscal Year End:*03/31 *Latest Annual Data:* 03/31/2007

Year		Sales		Net Income
2007		$7,070,000		-$3,306,000
2006		$6,975,000		-$818,000
2005		$2,687,000		-$6,459,000

Curr. Assets:	$3,187,000	**Curr. Liab.:**	$1,821,000		
Plant, Equip.:	$472,000	**Total Liab.:**	$2,180,000	**Indic. Yr. Divd.:**	NA
Total Assets:	$17,836,000	**Net Worth:**	$15,655,000	**Debt/ Equity:**	NA

US Energy Initiatives Corp

2701 N Rocky Point , Ste. 325, Tampa, FL, 33607; *PH:* 1-813-287-5787; *Fax:* 1-813-287-1518; *http://* www.usenergyic.com

General - Incorporation	GA	**Stock** - Price on:12/24/2007	$0.088
Employees	NA	Stock Exchange	OTC
Auditor	Brimmer, Burek & Keelan LLP	Ticker Symbol	USEI
Stk Agt	Interwest Transfer Company, Inc.	Outstanding Shares	212,070,000
Counsel	NA	E.P.S	-$0.047
DUNS No.	NA	Shareholders	NA

Business: The groups principle activities include manufacturing and marketing retrofit systems. The conversion of gasoline and diesel engines, stationary or vehicular, to non petroleum based fuels such as compressed natural gas and liquefied natural gas. During 2005, the group acquired DRV Energy. The group operates from the United States. The group's quarterly revenue for Sep '07 is 0.18 millions of USD.

Primary SIC and add'l.: 5211

CIK No: 0001107955

Officers: Mark Clancy/52/Dir., CEO, Roger Toale/Exec. VP, Frank Davis/CTO, Michele Hamilton/39/CFO

Directors: Mark Clancy/52/Dir., CEO, John Stanton/59/Chmn.

Owners: Frank Davis, Insiders/13.67%, Sheri Vanhooser/5.51%, Michele Hamilton, John Stanton/41.70%, Mark Clancy/12.39%

Financial Data: *Fiscal Year End:*12/31 *Latest Annual Data:* 12/31/2006

Year		Sales		Net Income
2006		$1,375,000		-$11,029,000
2005		$652,000		-$8,261,000
2004		$139,000		-$2,972,000

Curr. Assets:	$2,156,000	**Curr. Liab.:**	$4,180,000		
Plant, Equip.:	$555,000	**Total Liab.:**	$4,180,000	**Indic. Yr. Divd.:**	NA
Total Assets:	$3,394,000	**Net Worth:**	-$786,000	**Debt/ Equity:**	NA

US Farms Inc

Formerly: International Sports & Media Group Inc
1635 Rosecrans St., Ste. C, San Diego, CA, 92106; *PH:* 1-858-488-7775

General - Incorporation	NV	**Stock**- Price on:12/24/2007	$0.79
Employees	1	Stock Exchange	NA
Auditor	HJ Assoc. & Consultants LLP	Ticker Symbol	NA
Stk Agt	Holiday Stock Transfer	Outstanding Shares	30,770,000
Counsel	NA	E.P.S	-$0.19
DUNS No.	NA	Shareholders	NA

Business: The group principal activity is production, distribution and marketing of soccer related magazine. The group has published 6 issues of "90:00 Minutes" commencing with the premier issue in Jul 2002, followed by the commencement of monthly publications in Sept 2002. The group presently outsources the production and printing of our magazine to several third parties. Magazine production, including writing, layout and editing, is done by livewire communications and sportsvue, inc. Aa one litho printing does printing, again on a per issue basis, which depends on the number of pages and the number of copies printed. The group holds two trademarks namely san diego flash and 90:00 minutes.

Primary SIC and add'l.: 2721 7999 7941

CIK No: 0001054311

Subsidiaries: Pan American Relations, Inc., Smart SMS Mexico, LLC

Officers: Yan K. Skwara/Chmn., Pres., Darin Pines/Dir., VP - Operations

Directors: Yan K. Skwara/Chmn., Pres., Darin Pines/Dir., VP - Operations, Donald Hejmanowski/Dir.

Owners: Donald Hejmanowski/2.00%, Insiders/17.00%, Yan K. Skwara/13.00%, Darin Pines/2.00%

Financial Data: *Fiscal Year End:*12/31 *Latest Annual Data:* 12/31/2006

Year	Sales	Net Income
2006	$361,000	-$4,472,000
2005	NA	-$1,395,000
2004	$23,000	-$1,901,000

Curr. Assets:	$82,000	**Curr. Liab.:**	$3,012,000		
Plant, Equip.:	$7,000	**Total Liab.:**	$3,012,000	**Indic. Yr. Divd.:**	NA
Total Assets:	$89,000	**Net Worth:**	-$2,923,000	**Debt/ Equity:**	NA

US Geothermal Inc

1509 Tyrell Ln., Ste. B, Boise, ID, 83706; *PH:* 1-208-424-1027; *Fax:* 1-208-424-1030; *http://* www.usgeothermal.com

General - Incorporation	DE	**Stock**- Price on:12/24/2007	$2.05
Employees	6	Stock Exchange	OTC
Auditor	Williams & Webster, P.S.	Ticker Symbol	UGTH
Stk Agt	Pacific Corporate Trust Co	Outstanding Shares	43,760,000
Counsel	NA	E.P.S	-$0.05
DUNS No.	NA	Shareholders	NA

Business: The groups principal activities include producing, selling and distributing electricity. The group operates from the United States.

Primary SIC and add'l.: 4911

CIK No: 0001172136

Subsidiaries: Raft River Energy I, LLC, U.S. Cobalt (Colorado) Inc., U.S. Geothermal (Idaho) Inc, US Geothermal Services, LLC

Officers: Daniel Kunz/Dir., CEO, Pres., Doug Glaspey/Dir., COO, Kerry D. Hawkley/CFO, Sec., Kevin Kitz/VP - Project Development, Bob Cline/VP - Engineering, Christopher Harriman/Pres., Robert Cline/51/VP - Engineering, Geo, Idaho

Directors: Daniel Kunz/Dir., CEO, Pres., John Walker/Chmn., Doug Glaspey/Dir., COO, Paul Larkin/Dir., Leland Mink/Dir.

Owners: Paul A. Larkin/1.84%, Daniel J. Kunz/6.44%, Winslow Green Growth Fund/6.17%, John H. Walker, Daniel J. Kunz/6.68%, Leland R. Mink, S.A.C. Capital Associates LLC/6.86%, Kerry D. Hawkley, Goldman, Sachs & Co/9.60%, SPCP Group LLC/18.97%, Douglas J. Glaspey/3.24%, Wexford Capital, Walker House/6.86%

Financial Data: *Fiscal Year End:*03/31 *Latest Annual Data:* 03/31/2007

Year	Sales	Net Income
2007	NA	-$1,943,000
2006	NA	-$1,523,000
2005	NA	-$1,830,000

Curr. Assets:	$12,305,000	**Curr. Liab.:**	$1,456,000		
Plant, Equip.:	$4,138,000	**Total Liab.:**	$3,990,000	**Indic. Yr. Divd.:**	NA
Total Assets:	$22,673,000	**Net Worth:**	$18,683,000	**Debt/ Equity:**	NA

US Global Nanospace Inc

2533 N Carson St., Ste 5107, Carson City, NV, 89706; *PH:* 1-775-841-3246; *http://* www.usgn.com; *Email:* info@usgn.com

General - Incorporation	DE	**Stock**- Price on:12/24/2007	$0.005
Employees	2	Stock Exchange	OTC
Auditor	Grobstein, Horwath & Co. LLP	Ticker Symbol	USGA
Stk Agt	Madison Stock Transfer, Inc.	Outstanding Shares	218,660,000
Counsel	NA	E.P.S	-$0.021
DUNS No.	NA	Shareholders	NA

Business: The group's principal activity is to identify, develop and commercialize advanced products, the core technologies of which are primarily nanoscience derived. The products include complex polymer materials, polymer nanofiber materials, nanofiber filter materials, biological and chemical decontaminants, blast mitigation materials and nano and micro sound generating devices for breach barriers and non-lethal weapon applications. The group currently focuses its efforts on developing a broad range of defense and law enforcement applications for the materials it creates, including products suitable for homeland security and force protection applications.

Primary SIC and add'l.: 3728

CIK No: 0001001111

Subsidiaries: Caring Products International, Inc, FWCC Merger Corp, US Global Aerospace, Inc

Officers: George W. Bush/Pres. - National Strategy Homeland Security, Delores M. Etter/Deputy Under Sec. - Defense

Financial Data: *Fiscal Year End:*03/31 *Latest Annual Data:* 3/31/2006

Year	Sales	Net Income
2006	$260,000	-$5,446,000
2005	$716,000	-$3,842,000
2004	$140,000	-$7,285,000

Curr. Assets:	$153,000	**Curr. Liab.:**	$3,053,000		
Plant, Equip.:	NA	**Total Liab.:**	$3,119,000	**Indic. Yr. Divd.:**	NA
Total Assets:	$153,000	**Net Worth:**	-$2,965,000	**Debt/ Equity:**	NA

US Helicopter Corp

6 E River Piers, Ste. 216, Downtown Manhattan Heliport, New York, NY, 10004; *PH:* 1-212-248-2002; *http://* www.flyush.com

General - Incorporation		**Stock**- Price on:12/24/2007	$0.7
Employees	47	Stock Exchange	OTC
Auditor	NA	Ticker Symbol	USHP
Stk Agt	NA	Outstanding Shares	35,640,000
Counsel	NA	E.P.S	-$0.44
DUNS No.	NA	Shareholders	NA

Business: The groups principal activities include providing helicopter services. The services of the group will provide regular, scheduled passenger helicopter service between many of the nations larger metropolitan airports and surrounding city based heliports. The group operates from the United States.

Primary SIC and add'l.: 4512

CIK No:

Officers: Jerry Murphy/Dir., CEO, Pres., Donal F. McSullivan/Sr. VP, Chief Marketing Officer, George J. Mehm/Sr. VP, CFO, Treasurer, Terence O. Dennison/COO, Sr. VP, Gabriel Roberts/VP - Finance - Administration

Directors: Jerry Murphy/Dir., CEO, Pres., Dean C. Borgman/Chmn., Colonel Clinton Pagano/Dir., John Capozzi/Dir., Christopher D. Brady/Dir., George A. Fechter/Dir., Edward J. Sherman/Dir., Stephen T. Wills/Dir.

Owners: John G. Murphy/17.45%, Insiders/57.61%, Stephen T. Wills, Samama Global Corporation/8.44%, Cornell Capital Partners, LP/20.67%, Dean C. Borgman/2.79%, George J. Mehm/2.43%, Terence O. Dennsion/1.99%, Edward J. Sherman, Clinton Pagano, Christopher D. Brady/1.01%, Donal McSullivan/9.04%, George A. Fechter, International Financial Advisors, K.S.C./10.34%, John Capozzi/10.44% *(16 Owners included in Index)*

Financial Data: *Fiscal Year End:*NA *Latest Annual Data:* 12/31/2006

Year	Sales	Net Income
2006	$1,417,000	-$9,620,000
2005	NA	-$2,546,000

Curr. Assets:	$3,418,000	**Curr. Liab.:**	$2,657,000		
Plant, Equip.:	$976,000	**Total Liab.:**	$8,997,000	**Indic. Yr. Divd.:**	NA
Total Assets:	$6,917,000	**Net Worth:**	-$2,080,000	**Debt/ Equity:**	NA

US LEC Corp

6801 Morrison Blvd., Charlotte, NC, 28211; *PH:* 1-585-340-2500; *http://* www.uslec.com

General - Incorporation	DE	**Stock**- Price on:12/24/2007	NA
Employees	1,128	Stock Exchange	NDQ
Auditor	Deloitte & Touche LLP	Ticker Symbol	CLEC
Stk Agt	Wachovia Bank N.A	Outstanding Shares	NA
Counsel	Moore & Van Allen	E.P.S	NA
DUNS No.	96-080-9663	Shareholders	NA

Business: The group's principal activity is to provide integrated telecommunication services. The services of the group include local, long distance, data, Internet and enhanced telecommunication services to customers in selected markets in Alabama, Florida, Georgia, Kentucky, Louisiana, Maryland, Mississippi, North Carolina, Pennsylvania, South Carolina, Tennessee, Virginia and Washington dc. The group provides telecommunication services to intensive customers including businesses, universities, financial institutions, professional service firms and practices, hospitals, enhanced service providers, Internet service providers, hotels, automobile dealerships and government agencies. The group also provides local dial-tone services and long distance services for completing intrastate, interstate and international calls to customers and toll-free services, calling cards and typical enhanced services such as voice mail.

Primary SIC and add'l.: 4813

CIK No: 0001054290

Subsidiaries: US LEC Acquisition Co, US LEC Communications Inc, US LEC of Alabama Inc, US LEC of Florida Inc, US LEC of Georgia Inc, US LEC of Maryland Inc, US LEC of New York Inc, US LEC of North Carolina Inc, US LEC of Pennsylvania Inc, US LEC of South Carolina Inc, US LEC of Tennessee Inc, US LEC of Virginia LLC

Officers: Aaron D. Cowell/46/Dir., CEO, Pres., James M. Hvisdas/Exec. VP - Operations, John Leach/Sr. VP - Alternate Channels, Paetec Corp, Sean Pflaging/Sr. VP - Network Services, Paetec Corp, Reginald Scales/Sr. VP - Sales, Paetec Corp, Donna B. Wenk/Sr. VP - Process Management, Paetec Corp, Paul Bolz/Industry VP - Public Sector, Paetec Corp, Rick Cunningham/VP, GM, Tim Whelehan/Dir. - Strategic Markets, Healthcares, Lyle J. Patrick/55/CFO, Exec. VP, Edward J. Butler/COO - Paetec Corp, Robert Moore/CIO, Sr. VP - Paetec Corp, Joseph D. Ambersley/Exec. VP - Strategic Development, Paetec Corp, Timothy J. Bancroft/Exec. VP, Treasurer - Paetec Corp, Chris Bantoft/Exec. VP - Alternate Channels, Paetec Corp *(25 Officers included in Index)*

Directors: Aaron D. Cowell/46/Dir., CEO, Pres., Richard T. Aab/Vice Chmn. - Paetec Corp, Arunas A. Chesonis/Chmn. - Paetec Corp, Michael A. Krupka/42/Dir., Russell H. Frisby/Dir. - Paetec Corp, James A. Kofalt/Dir. - Paetec Corp, Steven L. Schoonover/62/Dir., Michael C. Mac Donald/Dir. - Paetec Corp, William R. McDermott/Dir. - Paetec Corp, Keith M. Wilson/Dir., CFO - Paetec Corp, Mark Zupan/Dir. - Paetec Corp, Tansukh V. Ganatra/Dir. - Paetec Corp, Anthony J. Dinovi/45/Dir., David M. Flaum/55/Dir.

Owners: Michael C. Mac Donald, Keith M. Wilson, Mark Zupan, Richard T. Aab/8.80%, Jeffrey L. Burke, Arunas A. Chesonis/8.00%, Edward J. Butler, Gilder, Gagnon, Howe& Co. LLC/6.80%, Tansukh V. Ganatra/2.30%, Insiders/20.50%, James A. Kofalt, John P. Baron

US Precious Metals Inc

5821 Tanagerside Rd., Lithia, FL, 33547; *PH:* 1-813-425-2144

General - Incorporation	DE	Stock - Price on:12/24/2007	$0.33
Employees	NA	Stock Exchange	OTC
Auditor	Robert G. Jeffrey, CPA	Ticker Symbol	USPR
Stk Agt	Interwest Transfer Company, Inc.	Outstanding Shares	31,910,000
Counsel	NA	E.P.S.	-$0.02
DUNS No.	NA	Shareholders	NA

Business: The group's principal activity is to acquire, explore, and develop mineral properties.

Primary SIC and add'l.: 1000

CIK No: 0001286181

Subsidiaries: American International Ventures, Inc., U.S. Precious Metals de Mexico, S.A. de C.V.

Officers: Peter Toscano/59/Chmn., CEO, Jose Garcia/52/VP, Dir., Jack Wagenti/71/Dir., Sec., Treasurer, James O. Rourke/66/Pres.

Directors: Peter Toscano/59/Chmn., CEO, Jose Garcia/52/VP, Dir., Jack Wagenti/71/Dir., Sec., Treasurer, Walter Salvadore/52/Dir., Robert Astore/71/Dir., Brain G. Russell/78/Dir.

Owners: James ORourke, Peter Toscano/15.26%, Jack Wagenti/17.59%, Brian Russell, Walter Salvadore, Jose Garcia/4.20%, Insiders/37.63%

Financial Data: Fiscal Year End:05/31 Latest Annual Data: 5/31/2006

Year	Sales	Net Income
2006	NA	-$280,000

Curr. Assets:	$924,000	Curr. Liab.:	$14,000		
Plant, Equip.:	$28,000	Total Liab.:	$14,000	Indic. Yr. Divd.:	NA
Total Assets:	$1,016,000	Net Worth:	$1,001,000	Debt/ Equity:	NA

US Realty Income Partners LP

PO Box 58006, Nashville, TN, 37205; PH: 1-615-665-5959

General - Incorporation	DE	Stock - Price on:12/24/2007	NA
Employees	NA	Stock Exchange	NA
Auditor	Rayburn, Bates & Fitzgerald, P.C	Ticker Symbol	NA
Stk Agt	NA	Outstanding Shares	NA
Counsel	NA	E.P.S.	NA
DUNS No.	NA	Shareholders	NA

Business: The group's principal activity is acquiring, operating, holding and ultimately disposing of existing income producing residential and commercial real estate properties.

Primary SIC and add'l.: 6532

CIK No: 0000822819

US Xpress Enterprises Inc

4080 Jenkins Rd., Chattanooga, TN, 37421; PH: 1-423-510-3000; http:// www.usxpress.com

General - Incorporation	NV	Stock - Price on:12/24/2007	$14.01
Employees	10,885	Stock Exchange	NA
Auditor	Ernst & Young LLP	Ticker Symbol	NA
Stk Agt	Boston EquiServe, L.P.	Outstanding Shares	15,160,000
Counsel	NA	E.P.S.	$1.08
DUNS No.	78-562-7555	Shareholders	NA

Business: The group's principle activities are to provide transportation and logistics services through its subsidiaries in the United States, Canada and Mexico. The group's operating segments are truckload operations and transportation services. The truckload operations segment provides over-the-road or long-haul services with lengths of haul in the range of 400 to 3,000 miles; regional services with lengths of haul generally in the range of 200 to 550 miles and dedicated contract carriage services. Transportation services include consolidation and distribution of less-than-truckload shipments; coordination of line-haul transportation to the group's service centers and third-party agent facilities for local delivery; warehousing and distribution services and retail sales of installation supplies. It also includes airport-to-airport transportation services.

Primary SIC and add'l.: 4213 4214

CIK No: 0000923571

Subsidiaries: Cargo Movement Corp, Colton Xpress, LLC, U.S. Xpress Leasing, Inc, U.S. Xpress, Inc, Xpress Air, Inc, Xpress Colorado, Inc, Xpress Company Store, Inc, Xpress Global Systems, Inc, Xpress Holdings, Inc, Xpress Nebraska, Inc, Xpress Receivables, LLC, Xpress Waiting, Inc

Officers: Max L. Fuller/55/Chmn., CEO, Sec./$1,217,728.00, Patrick E. Quinn/61/Chmn., Pres., Treasurer/$1,215,812.00, Ray M. Harlin/58/CFO, Exec. VP - Finance/$767,683.00, Jeffrey S. Wardeberg/45/COO, Exec. VP/$514,124.00, Michael S. Walters/Pres. - Arnold/$482,717.00

Directors: Max L. Fuller/55/Chmn., CEO, Sec., Patrick E. Quinn/61/Chmn., Pres., Treasurer, Robert J. Sudderth/65/Dir., James E. Hall/66/Dir., John W. Murrey/65/Dir.

Owners: Max L. Fuller, Ray M. Harlin, Insiders, James E. Hall, Goldman Sachs Asset Management, L.P., Jeffrey S. Wardeberg, Patrick E. Quinn, Galleon Captains Partners, L.P., Robert J. Sudderth, John W. Murrey

Financial Data: Fiscal Year End:12/31 Latest Annual Data: 12/31/2006

Year	Sales	Net Income
2006	$1,471,764,000	$20,104,000
2005	$1,164,232,000	$9,432,000
2004	$1,105,656,000	$16,426,000

Curr. Assets:	$254,144,000	Curr. Liab.:	$236,986,000	P/E Ratio:	12.97
Plant, Equip.:	$528,997,000	Total Liab.:	$647,289,000	Indic. Yr. Divd.:	NA
Total Assets:	$903,367,000	Net Worth:	$252,499,000	Debt/ Equity:	1.0361

USA Mobility Inc

6677 Richmond Hwy., Alexandria, VA, 22306; PH: 1-866-662-3049

General - Incorporation	DE	Stock - Price on:12/24/2007	$25.68
Employees	1,235	Stock Exchange	NDQ
Auditor	Grant Thornton, LLP	Ticker Symbol	USMO
Stk Agt	EquiServe Trust Co N.A	Outstanding Shares	27,320,000
Counsel	NA	E.P.S.	$1.98
DUNS No.	NA	Shareholders	NA

Business: The groups principle activity is to provide wireless communications solutions. The groups services include paging and messaging. The group products sold under the trade names USA Mobility, Arch and Metrocall. The groups operates through two segments namely domestic operations and international operations. Customers served by the group include healthcare, government, large enterprise and emergency response sectors. The group operates from the United States. The group's quarterly revenue for September 2007 was 105.42 millions of USD.

Primary SIC and add'l.: 4899 4812 7389

CIK No: 0001289945

Subsidiaries: Arch Canada, Inc., Arch Wireless Communications, Inc., Arch Wireless Holdings, Inc., Arch Wireless License Co., LLC, Arch Wireless Operating Company, Inc., Arch Wireless, Inc., GTES LLC, Metrocall Holdings, Inc., Metrocall Ventures, Inc., Metrocall, Inc., MobileMedia Communications, Inc., Paging Network Canadian Holdings, Inc.

Officers: Vincent D. Kelly/Dir., CEO, Pres., Thomas L. Schilling/45/CFO, Peter C. Barnett/51/COO, Scott B. Tollefsen/54/General Counsel, Sec., James H. Boso/59/Exec. VP - Sales, Mark Garzone/48/Exec. VP - Marketing

Directors: Vincent D. Kelly/Dir., CEO, Pres., Royce Yudkoff/Chmn., David Abrams/Dir., James V. Continenza/45/Dir., Nicholas A. Gallopo/Dir., Brian OReilly/Dir., Matthew Oristano/Dir., Samme L. Thompson/Dir.

Owners: James V. Continenza, Samme L. Thompson, Vincent D. Kelly, Insiders/15.50%, David Abrams/15.00%, Abrams Group/15.00%, Nicholas A. Gallopo, Matthew Oristano, Brian OReilly, Scott B. Tollefsen, Royce Yudkoff, Thomas L. Schilling, Peter C. Barnett

Financial Data: Fiscal Year End:12/31 Latest Annual Data: 12/31/2006

Year	Sales	Net Income
2006	$497,694,000	$40,181,000
2005	$618,572,000	$12,907,000
2004	$490,160,000	$12,167,000

Curr. Assets:	$123,564,000	Curr. Liab.:	$82,858,000	P/E Ratio:	16.46
Plant, Equip.:	$91,562,000	Total Liab.:	$112,242,000	Indic. Yr. Divd.:	$3.600
Total Assets:	$588,214,000	Net Worth:	$475,972,000	Debt/ Equity:	0.0011

USA Technologies Inc

100 Deerfield Ln., Ste 140, Malvern, PA, 19355; PH: 1-800-633-0340; http:// www.usatech.com

General - Incorporation	PA	Stock - Price on:12/24/2007	NA
Employees	57	Stock Exchange	NDQ
Auditor	Goldstein Golub Kessler LLP	Ticker Symbol	USAT
Stk Agt	American Stock Transfer & Trust Co.	Outstanding Shares	NA
Counsel	Lurio & Associates PC	E.P.S.	-$2
DUNS No.	80-620-4301	Shareholders	NA

Business: The group's principle activity is to provide and license consumer payment systems through a new e-business solution called e-port (TM). The group has focused on developing e-port (TM) - its cashless payment system. At a basic level, the e-port (TM) integrates with copiers, vending machines or other host equipment and gathers information about sales and operations of the host equipment and also allows consumers to use credit card to make purchases. It also provides automated credit card activated control systems for copying, debit card and personal computer industries. The group had a total installed base of 1,309 control systems and 229 standalone transact control systems. The control system devices consist of card reader, printer, amplifier, circuit board and a microchip in a specially designed housing. The group's quarterly revenue for September 2007 was 3.35 millions of USD.

Primary SIC and add'l.: 7373

CIK No: 0000896429

Subsidiaries: Stitch Networks Corporation

Officers: George R. Jensen/Chmn., CEO, Stephen P. Herbert/Dir., COO, Pres., David M. Demedio/CFO

Directors: George R. Jensen/Chmn., CEO, Stephen P. Herbert/Dir., COO, Pres., William L. Vanalen/Dir., Steven Katz/Dir., Douglas M. Lurio/Dir., Stephen W. McHugh/Dir., Joel Brooks/Dir.

Owners: David M. DeMedio, Insiders/3.26%, Stephen P. Herbert, SAC Capital Advisors LLC/15.20%, Cortina Asset Management LLC/9.11%, Douglas M. Lurio, William L. Van Alen, Wellington Management Company, LLP/8.58%, George R. Jensen/1.67%, Steven Katz

Financial Data: Fiscal Year End:06/30 Latest Annual Data: 06/30/2007

Year	Sales	Net Income
2007	$9,158,000	-$17,782,000
2006	$6,415,000	-$14,847,000
2005	$4,678,000	-$15,499,000

Curr. Assets:	$17,354,000	Curr. Liab.:	$5,892,000		
Plant, Equip.:	$1,877,000	Total Liab.:	$6,407,000	Indic. Yr. Divd.:	NA
Total Assets:	$34,491,000	Net Worth:	$28,084,000	Debt/ Equity:	NA

USA Truck Inc

3200 Industrial Pk. Rd. , Van Buren, AR, 72956; PH: 1-479-471-2500; http:// www.usa-truck.com

General - Incorporation	DE	Stock - Price on:12/24/2007	$15.77
Employees	3,777	Stock Exchange	NDQ
Auditor	Ernst & Young LLP	Ticker Symbol	USAK
Stk Agt	Registrar & Transfer Co	Outstanding Shares	10,790,000
Counsel	NA	E.P.S.	$0.27
DUNS No.	10-365-8381	Shareholders	NA

Business: The group's principal activity is to operate as a truckload motor carrier, which provides transportation of general commodity freight in interstate and foreign commerce. The principal types of freight transported include automotive parts and materials, rubber and plastics, retail stores merchandise, paper products, durable consumer goods, metals, electronics and chemicals. At 31-Dec-2003, the group operates 2,177 conventional sleeper tractors and 4,461 van trailers. The group provides services throughout the continental United States, parts of Canada and Mexico.

Primary SIC and add'l.: 4731

CIK No: 0000883945

Officers: Clifton R. Beckham/Dir., CEO, Pres./$332,763.00, Rodney J. Mills/VP - Safety, General Counsel, Craig S. Shelly/VP - Corporate Strategy, Garry R. Lewis/Sr. VP - Operations/$364,258.00, Michael R. Weindel/VP - Human Resources, Recruiting, Training, Brandon D. Cox/35/Sr. VP - Marketing/$328,843.00, Michael E. Brown/VP - Maintenance, Darron R. Ming/CFO, VP - Finance, Treasurer, Terry V. Biehl/Controller, Burton D. Weis/VP - Customer Service, Chad B. Van Kooten/VP - Sales, Rick A. Davis/VP - Information Services

Directors: Clifton R. Beckham/Dir., CEO, Pres., Robert M. Powell/Chmn., Terry A. Elliott/Dir., James B. Speed/Dir., Joe D. Powers/Dir., William H. Hanna/Dir., Jerry D. Orler/Dir., Richard B. Beauchamp/Dir.

Owners: Garry R. Lewis, William H. Hanna, Joe D. Powers, Brandon D. Cox, Wellington Management Company, LLP/8.90%, Clifton R. Beckham, Dimensional Fund Advisors LP/5.50%, Richard B. Beauchamp, Insiders/26.70%, Jerry D. Orler/2.00%, James B. Speed/12.60%, Robert M. Powell/10.10%, GAM Holding AG/6.10%, Terry A. Elliott

Financial Data: Fiscal Year End:12/31 Latest Annual Data: 12/31/2006

Year	Sales	Net Income
2006	$465,618,000	$12,441,000
2005	$439,703,000	$15,568,000
2004	$363,105,000	$7,432,000

Curr. Assets:	$63,804,000	Curr. Liab.:	$66,588,000	P/E Ratio:	28.16
Plant, Equip.:	$275,507,000	Total Liab.:	$179,936,000	Indic. Yr. Divd.:	NA
Total Assets:	$339,494,000	Net Worth:	$159,558,000	Debt/ Equity:	0.4557

USA Video Interactive Corp

8 Main St., Niantic, CT, 06371; PH: 1-860-434-5535; http:// www.usvo.com; Email: contact@usvo.com

General - Incorporation	WY	**Stock**- Price on:12/24/2007	$0.198
Employees	4	Stock Exchange	OTC
Auditor	Goldstein Golub Kessler LLP	Ticker Symbol	USVO
Stk Agt	Mellon Trust Co	Outstanding Shares	161,100,000
Counsel	NA	E.P.S.	-$0.01
DUNS No.	NA	Shareholders	NA

Business: The group's principal activities are to design, develop and market streaming video and video-on-demand systems, services and source-to-destination digital media delivery solutions to business customers. These solutions allow live or recorded digitized and compressed video to be transmitted through Internet, intranet, satellite or wireless connectivity. The group's systems and delivery solutions include video content production, content encoding, multi-mode content distribution, e-commerce and Internet streaming hardware. The products of the group are mediasentineit82; streamhqt82; encodehqt82; zmailt82, and mediaclixt82. The group operates solely in the domestic market.

Primary SIC and add'l.: 3663 7379 3679

CIK No: 0001107280

Subsidiaries: Old Lyme Productions Inc, USA Video (California) Corp, USA Video Corporation, USA Video Technology Corporation, USVO Inc

Officers: Edwin Molina/Dir., CEO, Pres., Mario Gioco/Controller, Anton J. Drescher/Dir., CFO, Sec., Andrew J. Huffman/Patent Counsel

Directors: Edwin Molina/Dir., CEO, Pres., Anton J. Drescher/Dir., CFO, Sec., Maurice Loverso/Dir., Roland Perkins/Dir.

Owners: Anton J. Drescher/5.42%, Maurice Loverso/0.18%, Edwin Molina/7.53%, Rowland Perkins/0.12%

Financial Data: Fiscal Year End:12/31 Latest Annual Data: 12/31/2006

Year	Sales	Net Income
2006	NA	-$1,249,000
2005	$19,000	-$958,000
2004	$5,000	-$1,404,000

Curr. Assets:	$24,000	Curr. Liab.:	$326,000		
Plant, Equip.:	NA	Total Liab.:	$326,000	Indic. Yr. Divd.:	NA
Total Assets:	$55,000	Net Worth:	-$270,000	Debt/ Equity:	NA

USANA Health Sciences Inc

3838 W Pkwy Blvd, Salt Lake City, UT, 84120; PH: 1-800-954-7100; http:// www.usana.com

General - Incorporation	UT	**Stock**- Price on:12/24/2007	$44.28
Employees	889	Stock Exchange	NDQ
Auditor	Grant Thornton LLP	Ticker Symbol	USNA
Stk Agt	American Stock Transfer & Trust Co.	Outstanding Shares	16,800,000
Counsel	Durham Jones & Pinegar	E.P.S.	$2.57
DUNS No.	80-441-3250	Shareholders	NA

Business: The group's principal activities are to develop, manufacture and distribute science-based nutritional health and skin care products. The group operates in two business segments: direct selling and contract manufacturing. Direct selling segment develops, manufactures and distributes nutritional and personal care products through a network marketing system. Contract manufacturing includes manufacture of premium personal care products and packaging for sense product line. The nutritional products include antioxidants, minerals, vitamins, other nutritional supplements, meal replacement drinks, fiber drinks and food bars. The group's markets include the United States, Canada, Australia, New Zealand, Hong Kong, Japan, Taiwan, South Korea, Singapore, and the United Kingdom. In feb 2004, the group acquired fmg productions, llc (fmg).

Primary SIC and add'l.: 2844 2834

CIK No: 0000896264

Subsidiaries: FMG Productions, Inc., USANA Australia Pty, Ltd., USANA Canada Co., USANA Health Sciences (NZ) Corporation, USANA Health Sciences Korea Ltd., USANA Health Sciences Singapore Pte, Ltd., USANA Health Sciences Tianjin Co. Ltd, USANA Hong Kong Limited, USANA Japan, Inc., USANA Mexico S.A. de C.V., Wasatch Product Development, Inc.

Officers: Myron Wentz/Chmn., CEO, Bradford Richardson/Exec. VP - Asia Pacific/$286,739.00, David Wentz/Pres./$656,537.00, Kevin Guest/Exec. VP - Marketing/$805,541.00, Gil Fuller/Exec. VP - Finance/$288,511.00, Bryan Wentz/VP - Special Projects, Doug Hekking/VP - Finance, Deborah Woo/VP - Greater China, North Asia, Roy Truett/VP - Network Development, Public Relations, Alan Bergstrom/VP - Customer Service, James Bramble/VP, General Counsel, Jim Brown/VP - Operations, Shawn McLelland/VP - Media - Events, Bill Duncan/VP - Australasia, Christine Wood/Member - Scientific Advisory Board Counsel *(35 Officers included in Index)*

Directors: Myron Wentz/Chmn., CEO, Peter W. Rugg/Chmn. - Scientific Advisory Board Counsel, Ronald S. Poelman/Dir., Robert Anciaux/Dir., Jerry G. McClain/Dir.

Owners: Ronald S. Poelman, Bradford Richardson, Fred W. Cooper, Mark H. Wilson, Robert Anciaux, Gilbert A. Fuller, Barclays Global Investors, Kevin Guest, Century Capital Management, LLC, Myron W. Wentz, Jerry G. McClain, Insiders, Lord Abbett& Co., LLC, Gull Holdings, Ltd., Denis E. Waitley *(17 Owners included in Index)*

Financial Data: Fiscal Year End:12/31 Latest Annual Data: 12/30/2006

Year	Sales	Net Income
2006	$374,190,000	$41,266,000
2005	$327,742,000	$38,994,000

Curr. Assets:	$41,830,000	Curr. Liab.:	$26,556,000	P/E Ratio:	18.07
Plant, Equip.:	$23,302,000	Total Liab.:	$27,970,000	Indic. Yr. Divd.:	NA
Total Assets:	$73,708,000	Net Worth:	$45,738,000	Debt/ Equity:	NA

USAS Digital Inc

1016 Clemons St., Ste. 302, Jupiter, FL, 33477; PH: 1-561-745-6789

General - Incorporation	FL	**Stock**- Price on:12/24/2007	NA
Employees	NA	Stock Exchange	NA
Auditor	Wieseneck, Andres & Co P.A	Ticker Symbol	NA
Stk Agt	Florida Atlantic Stk Transfer	Outstanding Shares	NA
Counsel	NA	E.P.S.	NA
DUNS No.	NA	Shareholders	NA

Business: The group's principle activity is to provide retail telephone system and equipments. The group operates from United States.

Primary SIC and add'l.: 9995

CIK No: 0001321508

Subsidiaries: Capital Holdings, Inc., eCom.com, Inc.

Officers: Barney A. Richmond/56/Chmn., CEO, Pres., Sec., Richard C. Turner/48/Dir., CFO, Treasurer

Directors: Barney A. Richmond/56/Chmn., CEO, Pres., Sec., Richard C. Turner/48/Dir., CFO, Treasurer

Owners: Insiders/18.80%, Richard C. Turner/1.40%, Barney A. Richmond/17.40%, American Capital Holdings, Inc./39.60%, United States Financial Group, Inc./6.30%

USCorp

4535 W Sahara Ave., Ste 200, Las Vegas, NV, 89102; PH: 1-702-933-4034; http:// www.uscorpnv.com; Email: info@uscorpnv.com

General - Incorporation	NV	**Stock**- Price on:12/24/2007	$0.089
Employees	NA	Stock Exchange	OTC
Auditor	Geological Support Services, LLC	Ticker Symbol	USCS
Stk Agt	U.S. Stock Transfer Corp	Outstanding Shares	33,860,000
Counsel	NA	E.P.S.	-$0.025
DUNS No.	NA	Shareholders	NA

Business: The group's principal activity is to explore and develop mining properties. The group's mining business operations are conducted through its subsidiary, us metals. The group owns the 141 lode mining claims known as the twin peaks mine near baghdad, Arizona.

Primary SIC and add'l.: 1099

CIK No: 0000873185

Subsidiaries: Southwest Resource Development, Inc

Officers: Robert Dultz/62/Chmn., CEO, Acting CFO, Larry Dietz/Dir., Pres., Sec., Treasurer

Directors: Robert Dultz/62/Chmn., CEO, Acting CFO, Carl W. O'Baugh/Dir., Judith A. Ahrens/64/Dir., Larry Dietz/Dir., Pres., Sec., Treasurer

Owners: Larry Dietz/0.15%, Dultz Family Trust/29.58%, Carl OBaugh/0.15%, Judith Ahrens/0.15%, Robert Dultz/22.47%, Insiders/52.50%

Financial Data: Fiscal Year End:09/30 Latest Annual Data: 9/30/2006

Year	Sales	Net Income
2006	NA	-$838,000
2005	NA	-$628,000
2004	NA	-$964,000

Curr. Assets:	$84,000	Curr. Liab.:	$78,000		
Plant, Equip.:	$8,000	Total Liab.:	$1,057,000	Indic. Yr. Divd.:	NA
Total Assets:	$92,000	Net Worth:	-$1,036,000	Debt/ Equity:	NA

USEC Inc

6903 Rockledge Dr., Bethesda, MD, 20817; PH: 1-301-564-3200; http:// www.usec.com; Email: corpcomm@usec.com

General - Incorporation	DE	**Stock**- Price on:12/24/2007	$21.88
Employees	2,677	Stock Exchange	NYSE
Auditor	PricewaterhouseCoopers LLP	Ticker Symbol	USU
Stk Agt	Computershare Trust Co	Outstanding Shares	87,410,000
Counsel	NA	E.P.S.	$1.27
DUNS No.	04-141-1484	Shareholders	NA

Business: The groups principle activity is to supply low enriched uranium for commercial nuclear power plants. The group operates from United States.

Primary SIC and add'l.: 1481

CIK No: 0001065059

Subsidiaries: NAC Holding Inc, NAC International Inc. , United States Enrichment Corporation, USEC Overseas, Inc., USEC Services Corporation

Officers: John K. Welch/Dir., CEO, Pres./$2,231,634.00, Linda M. Johnson/Mgr. - Corporate Communications, Georgann Lookofsky/Public Affairs Mgr. - United States Enrichment Corporation Facilities, Elizabeth Stuckle/Dir. - Corporate Communications, Russell B. Starkey/VP - Operations, Philip G. Sewell/Sr. VP - American Centrifuge, Russian HEU/$1,879,448.00, John M.A. Donelson/VP - Marketing, Sales, Victor N. Lopiano/VP - American Centrifuge, Robert Van Namen/Sr. VP - Uranium Enrichment/$1,297,283.00, Timothy B. Hansen/44/Sr. VP, General Counsel, Sec./$1,075,417.00, John C. Barpoulis/CFO, Sr. VP, Treasurer/$815,347.00, Jeremy Derryberry/Sr. Assoc., Corporate Communications, Richard Rowland/Dir. - Human Resources, Stephen S. Greene/VP - Finance, Treasurer, Tracy J. Mey/Controller, Chief Accounting Officer *(21 Officers included in Index)*

Directors: John K. Welch/Dir., CEO, Pres., James R. Mellor/Chmn., James D. Woods/Dir., Joseph T. Doyle/Dir., Michael H. Armacost/Dir., Joyce F. Brown/Dir., John R. Hall/Dir., Henson W. Moore/Dir., Joseph F. Paquette/Dir.

Owners: Michael H. Armacost, W. Henson Moore, Insiders/2.00%, John R. Hall, Joseph F. Paquette, Timothy B. Hansen, FMR Corp./10.60%, James D. Woods, Joyce F. Brown, Robert Van Namen, Philip G. Sewell, Joseph T. Doyle, John C. Barpoulis, Dimensional FundAdvisors LP/7.70%, James R. Mellor

Financial Data: **Fiscal Year End:** 12/31 **Latest Annual Data:** 12/31/2006

Year	Sales	Net Income
2006	$1,848,600,000	$106,200,000
2005	$1,559,300,000	$22,300,000
2004	$1,417,200,000	$23,500,000

Curr. Assets:	$1,409,100,000	**Curr. Liab.:**	$425,100,000	**P/E Ratio:**	25.15
Plant, Equip.:	$214,100,000	**Total Liab.:**	$875,400,000	**Indic. Yr. Divd.:**	NA
Total Assets:	$1,861,400,000	**Net Worth:**	$986,000,000	**Debt/ Equity:**	0.1491

USG Corp

125 S Franklin St., Chicago, IL, 60606; **PH:** 1-312-606-4000; **http://** www.usg.com; **Email:** investorrelations@usg.com

General - Incorporation	DE	**Stock** - Price on:12/24/2007	$49.06
Employees	14,700	Stock Exchange	NYSE
Auditor	Deloitte & Touche LLP	Ticker Symbol	USG
Stk Agt	Computershare Investor Services LLC	Outstanding Shares	98,930,000
Counsel	NA	E.P.S	$4.10
DUNS No.	12-128-6777	Shareholders	NA

Business: The group's principle activities include manufacturing and distributing building materials. The group's products are used in new residential, new nonresidential, repair and remodel construction. The group operates through three segments including North American Gypsum, Worldwide Ceilings and Building Products Distribution. The group operates from United States, Canada, and Mexico.

Primary SIC and add'l.: 3275 5039 1743

CIK No: 0000757011

Subsidiaries: Alabaster Assurance Company, Ltd., Alabaster Engineering (Nederland) B.V, B-R Pipeline Company, Beadex Manufacturing LLC, CGC Inc., Exploracion de Yeso, S.A. de C.V, Gypsum Engineering Company., Gypsum Transportation Limited, L&W Supply Corporation, La Mirada Products Co., Inc. ., Red Top Technology (Nederland) B.V., Shenzhen USG Zhongbei Building Materials Co., Ltd., Stocking Specialists, Inc., United States Gypsum Company, USG (Netherlands) B.V. 35 Subsidiaries included in the Index

Officers: William C. Foote/Chmn., CEO/$12,301,110.00, Karen L. Leets/VP, Treasurer, Peter K. Maitland/66/VP - Compensation, Benefits, Administration, Edward M. Bosowski/Exec. VP, Chief Strategy Officer, Pres. - USG International/$2,985,217.00, James S. Metcalf/COO, Pres./$2,483,777.00, Brian J. Cook/Sr. VP - Human Resources, Donald S. Mueller/VP, Chief Innovation Officer, Marcia S. Kaminsky/Sr. VP - Communications, Rick D. Lowes/Sr. VP, Controller, Richard H. Fleming/CFO, Exec. VP/$3,971,676.00, Dominic A. Dannessa/VP, Exec. VP - Manufacturing, Building Systems, Fareed A. Khan/VP, Exec. VP - Sales, Marketing, Building Systems, Ellis A. Regenbogen/Corp. Sec., Assoc. General Counsel, Brendan J. Deely/VP, Stanley L. Ferguson/Exec. VP, General Counsel/$2,972,113.00 *(16 Officers included in Index)*

Directors: William C. Foote/Chmn., CEO, Lawrence M. Crutcher/Dir., Marvin E. Lesser/Dir., David W. Fox/Dir., John B. Schwemm/Dir., Steven F. Leer/Dir., Judith A. Sprieser/Dir., Jose Armario/Dir., James C. Cotting/Dir., Robert L. Barnett/Dir., Keith A. Brown/Dir., Douglas W. Ford/Dir., Valerie B. Jarrett/Dir.

Owners: David E. Shaw/6.10%, Gebr. Knauf Verwaltungsgellschaft KG/9.57%, FMR Corp./7.35%, Berkshire Hathaway Inc./19.00%

Financial Data: **Fiscal Year End:** 12/31 **Latest Annual Data:** 12/31/2006

Year	Sales	Net Income
2006	$5,810,000,000	$288,000,000
2005	$5,139,000,000	-$1,436,000,000
2004	$4,509,000,000	$312,000,000

Curr. Assets:	$2,707,000,000	**Curr. Liab.:**	$1,764,000,000	**P/E Ratio:**	11.97
Plant, Equip.:	$2,210,000,000	**Total Liab.:**	$3,831,000,000	**Indic. Yr. Divd.:**	NA
Total Assets:	$5,365,000,000	**Net Worth:**	$1,534,000,000	**Debt/ Equity:**	0.6103

USI Holdings Corp

555 Pleasantville Rd., Briarcliff Manor, NY, 10510; **PH:** 1-914-749-8500; **http://** www.usi.biz

General - Incorporation	DE	**Stock** - Price on:12/24/2007	$17
Employees	2,826	Stock Exchange	NDQ
Auditor	Deloitte & Touche LLP	Ticker Symbol	USIH
Stk Agt	Mellon Investor Services LLC	Outstanding Shares	NA
Counsel	Cahill Gordon & Reindel LLP	E.P.S	NA
DUNS No.	NA	Shareholders	NA

Business: The group's principle activities are to distribute insurance and financial products and services to small and mid-sized businesses. It also provides employee health and welfare products and related consulting and administration services. The group's segments are insurance brokerage, specialized benefits services and corporate segment. Insurance brokerage offers general and specialty property and casualty insurance and individual and group health, life and disability insurance. Specialized benefits services includes core benefits (health and welfare), benefits enrollment and communication and executive and professional benefits.

Primary SIC and add'l.: 8099 6411

CIK No: 0001102643

Subsidiaries: Acquisition Risk Management Services, Inc., American Insurance Administrators, Inc., ANCO Corporation, Anco Insurance Services of Houston, Inc., ANCO Life & Benefits Services, Inc., ANCO Management Corporation, Association Growth Enterprises, Incorporated, B-R Corp. of North Carolina, B-R Insurance Brokers, Inc., Bechard Insurance Agency, Inc., Benefit Strategies of Maine, Inc., Bertholon Rowland, Inc., Bertholon-Rowland Corp., Bertholon-Rowland, Inc., BMI Insurance Services, Inc. 108 Subsidiaries included in the Index

Officers: Mark Smith/Regional CEO, David L. Eslick/Chmn., CEO, Pres., Jeffrey L. Jones/Regional CEO - USI West Coast Region, James M. Butler/Regional, CEO - USI Insurance Services, Thomas Cassady/Regional CEO, Pres. - - USI Midwest, John D. Collado/Regional, CEO - USI Southwest Region, Dudley F. Fulton/Regional CEO - USI Mid Atlantic Region, Jeff Gullickson/Regional CEO, Pres. - USI Retail, Jeff Haynes/Regional CEO, Douglas W. Kreitzberg/Regional CEO, Gregory J. Morano/Regional CEO, Pres., Philip E. Larson/COO, Ernest J. Newborn/Sr. VP, General Counsel, Sec., Robert S. Schneider/54/CFO, Exec. VP, David A. Hess/VP - Finance, Principal Accounting Officer *(21 Officers included in Index)*

Directors: David L. Eslick/Chmn., CEO, Pres., Robert A. Spass/51/Dir., Robert F. Wright/82/Dir., William L. Atwell/57/Dir., Ronald E. Frieden/64/Dir., Thomas A. Hayes/65/Dir., Ben L. Lytle/60/Dir.

Owners: William L. Atwell, Wasatch Advisors, Inc./6.40%, Ronald E. Frieden, Philip E. Larson, Capital Z Financial Services Fund II, L.P./16.30%, Robert F. Wright, Insiders/20.30%, Ernest J. Newborn, Robert A. Spass/16.90%, Jeffrey L. Jones, Lord, Abbett & Co. LLC/5.80%, MSD Capital, L.P./7.60%, Ben L. Lytle, David L. Eslick/1.30%, Robert S. Schneider *(17 Owners included in Index)*

UST Inc

6 High Ridge Pk., Bldg. A, Stamford, CT, 06905; **PH:** 1-203-661-1100; **http://** www.ustinc.com

General - Incorporation	DE	**Stock** - Price on:12/24/2007	$51.67
Employees	5,008	Stock Exchange	NYSE
Auditor	Ernst & Young LLP	Ticker Symbol	UST
Stk Agt	EquiServe Trust Co N.A	Outstanding Shares	160,170,000
Counsel	Skadden, Meagher & Flom LLP	E.P.S	$3.11
DUNS No.	15-118-0080	Shareholders	NA

Business: The groups principle activities include producing and marketing moist smokeless tobacco products including two marquee brands, Copenhagen and Skoal. The group operates from United States.

Primary SIC and add'l.: 2131 5194 5182 2084

CIK No: 0000811669

Subsidiaries: International Wine & Spirits Ltd., Ste. Michelle Wine Estates Ltd., U.S. Smokeless Tobacco Brands Inc., U.S. Smokeless Tobacco Company, U.S. Smokeless Tobacco Manufacturing Limited Partnership

Officers: Theodor P. Baseler/CEO, Pres. - Ste Michelle Wine Estates, Murray S. Kessler/Dir., CEO, Pres./$3,870,188.00, Richard A. Kohlberger/Sr. VP, General Counsel, Chief Administrative Officer, Corp. Sec./$2,656,073.00, Robert T. D'Alessandro/54/CFO, Sr. VP/$2,157,922.00, Daniel W. Butler/Pres. - US Smokeless Tobacco Company/$1,674,219.00, James D. Patracuolla/VP, Controller, Raymond P. Silcock/CFO, Sr. VP

Directors: Murray S. Kessler/Dir., CEO, Pres., Vincent A. Gierer/Chmn., John D. Barr/Dir., Patrick J. Mannelly/Dir., Peter J. Neff/Dir., Joseph E. Heid/Dir., Patricia Diaz Dennis/Dir., John P. Clancey/Dir., Andrew J. Parsons/Dir., Ronald J. Rossi/Dir.

Owners: Bank of America Corporation/5.29%, Capital Research and Management Company/8.40%, Dreman Value Management LLC/7.57%

Financial Data: **Fiscal Year End:** 12/31 **Latest Annual Data:** 06/30/2007

Year	Sales	Net Income
2007	$491,254,000	$139,971,000
2006	$485,721,000	$137,203,000
2005	$1,851,885,000	$534,268,000

Curr. Assets:	$998,110,000	**Curr. Liab.:**	$300,077,000	**P/E Ratio:**	16.61
Plant, Equip.:	$389,810,000	**Total Liab.:**	$1,374,522,000	**Indic. Yr. Divd.:**	$2.400
Total Assets:	$1,440,348,000	**Net Worth:**	$65,826,000	**Debt/ Equity:**	16.3232

USTMAN Technologies Inc

536 Pacific Ave., San Francisco, CA, 94133; **PH:** 1-415-989-7770

General - Incorporation		**Stock** - Price on:12/24/2007	$0.011
Employees	NA	Stock Exchange	OTC
Auditor	NA	Ticker Symbol	USTX
Stk Agt	U.S. Stock Transfer Corp	Outstanding Shares	NA
Counsel	NA	E.P.S	NA
DUNS No.	NA	Shareholders	NA

Business: The groups principle activity is to provide recruiting services. The groups service area includes the research and development, engineering, marketing, sales, information technology and manufacturing industries. The group operates from United States.

Primary SIC and add'l.: 8742

CIK No:

Owners: Sagaponack Partners, L.P./49.20%, Insiders/50.20%, Marc A. Weisman/50.20%, Sagaponack Partners International, L.P./1.00%, Barry S. Rosenstein/50.20%

Utah Medical Products Inc

7043 S 300 W, Midvale, UT, 84047; **PH:** 1-800-566-1200; **http://** www.utahmed.com

General - Incorporation	UT	**Stock** - Price on:12/24/2007	$29.6801
Employees	204	Stock Exchange	NDQ
Auditor	Jones Simkins P.C.	Ticker Symbol	UTMD
Stk Agt	Registrar & Transfer Co	Outstanding Shares	3,930,000
Counsel	Krause Landa & Maycock	E.P.S	$2.00
DUNS No.	09-465-1270	Shareholders	NA

Business: The group's principal activities are to develop, manufacture and market a broad range of medical and healthcare industry devices. The products include blood pressure and utherine contraction pressure monitoring instruments, an electrosurgery generator and disposable electrodes used in the treatment to remove pre-cancerous cervical disease. The group's products also include labor and delivery/obstetrics products, neonatal intensive care products and a line of disposable infant oxygen-therapy products. The products are used in health care industry, critical care, delivery departments of hospitals, outpatient clinics and physician's offices. The group's products are sold in domestic and international markets.

Primary SIC and add'l.: 3841

CIK No: 0000706698

Subsidiaries: Utah Medical Products Ltd

Officers: Kevin L. Cornwell/61/Dir., CEO, Pres./$523,080.00, Paul O. Richins/47/Dir., VP, Principal Financial Officer - Contact - Investor Relations/$109,113.00

Directors: Kevin L. Cornwell/61/Dir., CEO, Pres., Ernst G. Hoyer/70/Dir., Barbara A. Payne/61/Dir., Paul O. Richins/47/Dir., VP, Principal Financial Officer - Contact - Investor Relations, James H. Beeson/66/Dir.

Owners: Barbara A. Payne/0.80%, Insiders/11.50%, Paul O. Richins/0.70%, Ernst G. Hoyer/1.60%, FMR Corp/13.00%, Kevin L. Cornwell/8.50%, Ashford Capital Management, Inc./10.30%

Financial Data: **Fiscal Year End:** 12/31 **Latest Annual Data:** 12/31/2006

Year	Sales	Net Income
2006	$28,753,000	$8,168,000
2005	$27,692,000	$7,547,000
2004	$26,485,000	$10,220,000

Curr. Assets:	$28,411,000	**Curr. Liab.:**	$3,381,000	**P/E Ratio:**	14.81
Plant, Equip.:	$8,331,000	**Total Liab.:**	$8,072,000	**Indic. Yr. Divd.:**	$0.900
Total Assets:	$44,187,000	**Net Worth:**	$36,115,000	**Debt/ Equity:**	NA

UTEK Corp

2109 E Palm Ave., Tampa, FL, 33605; *PH:* 1-813-754-4330; *Fax:* 1-813-754-2383; *http://* www.utekcorp.com; *Email:* info@utekcorp.com

General - Incorporation DE
Employees 48
Auditor Pender Newkirk & Company LLP
Stk Agt Computershare Trust Co
Counsel Sutherland Asbill & Brennan, LLP
DUNS No. NA

Stock- Price on:12/24/2007 $15.11
Stock Exchange AMEX
Ticker Symbol UTK
Outstanding Shares 9,000,000
E.P.S -$2.36
Shareholders NA

Business: The group's principal activity is to market-driven technology transfer business. The group marketed its products under the trade name U2B (R). The groups services include KnowledgeExpress.com Website, Pharma-Transfer.com Website, TechEx.com Website, Uventures.com Website, UTEK Intellectual Capital Consulting. The group acquired 22nd Street of Ybor City, Inc. in the year 2006, INTRA-DMS, Ltd. on January 29, 2005 and Knowledge Express Data Systems on July 7, 2005. The group operates from Pennsylvania, Israel and the United Kingdom.

Primary SIC and add'l.: 6799 6726

CIK No: 0001098482

Subsidiaries: UTEK Europe, Ltd, UTEKip, Ltd.

Officers: Clifford M. Gross/Chmn., CEO/$424,951.00, Doug Schaedler/COO, Chief Compliance Officer/$382,492.00, Bill Cawley/VP - Business Development, Michael Kayat/Pres. - Utek Intellectual Capital Consulting, Carlo Mejia/Pres. - Utek Information Services, Tali Carmi/Pres. - Utek Israel, Rene J. Trasorras/Mgr. - Due Diligence, Jeffrey D. Bleil/Chief Scientific Officer, Bill Porter/Chief Technology Transfer Officer, Carole Wright/CFO/$189,859.00, Joel Edelson/VP - Technology Licensing, Sam Reiber/Dir., VP, General Counsel/$103,646.00, Mark McBride/VP

Directors: Clifford M. Gross/Chmn., CEO, John D. Emanuel/Chmn. - Utek Europe, Ltd, Francis Maude/Dir., Bruce J. Clark/Member - Scientific Advisory Board, Sam Reiber/Dir., VP, General Counsel, Kwabena Gyimah-Brempong/Dir., Holly Callen Hamilton/Dir., John J. Micek/Dir., Keith A. Witter/Dir., Tom L. Blundell/Member - Scientific Advisory Board, Alain M. Boudet/Member - Scientific Advisory Board, Norman O. Nesheim/Member - Scientific Advisory Board, Caroline Popper/Member - Scientific Advisory Board, Ian Wells/Member - Scientific Advisory Board, Brian B. Schwartz/Member - Scientific Advisory Board *(48 Directors included in Index)*

Owners: Carole R. Wright, Clifford M. Gross/21.80%, Holly Callen Hamilton, Sam Reiber, Kwabena Brempong Gyimah, Arthur Chapnik, John Micek, Francis Maude, Insiders/25.20%, Stuart Brooks, Douglas Schaedler, Keith A. Witter

Financial Data: **Fiscal Year End:**12/31 **Latest Annual Data:** 12/31/2006

Year	Sales	Net Income
2006	$56,953,000	-$4,911,000
2005	$22,744,000	$2,096,000
2004	$8,744,000	$2,260,000

Curr. Assets:	$14,804,000	**Curr. Liab.:**	$596,000	**P/E Ratio:**	37.18
Plant, Equip.:	$595,000	**Total Liab.:**	$2,060,000	**Indic. Yr. Divd.:**	$0.080
Total Assets:	$53,041,000	**Net Worth:**	$50,981,000	**Debt/ Equity:**	NA

UTG Inc

Formerly: United Trust Group Inc
5250 S Sixth St., Springfield, IL, 62703; *PH:* 1-217-241-6300; *http://* www.unitedtrustgroup.com

General - Incorporation IL
Employees 65
Auditor Brown Smith Wallace, LLC
Stk Agt UTG
Counsel NA
DUNS No. 18-122-5533

Stock- Price on:12/24/2007 $7.65
Stock Exchange OTC
Ticker Symbol UTGN
Outstanding Shares 3,860,000
E.P.S $0.35
Shareholders NA

Business: The group's principal activity is to sell individual life insurance products through its subsidiaries. The group's principal market is in the midwestern United States. The group's dominant business is to provide individual life insurance, which includes the servicing of existing insurance business in force, the solicitation of new individual life insurance and the acquisition of other companies in the insurance business.

Primary SIC and add'l.: 6321

CIK No: 0000832480

Subsidiaries: Cumberland Woodlands, LLC, Hampshire Plaza Garage, LLC, Hampshire Plaza, LLC, Harbor Village Partners, LLC, North Plaza of Somerset, Inc., RLF Kennessee, Roosevelt Equity Corporation, Universal Guaranty Life Insurance Company, UTAG, Inc.

Officers: Jesse T. Correll/Chmn., CEO/$79,743.00, Randall L. Attkisson/Dir., COO - UTG, Universal Guaranty Life Insurance Company/$79,743.00, James P. Rousey/Dir., Pres., Pres. - UTG, Universal Guaranty Life Insurance Company/$144,906.00

Directors: Jesse T. Correll/Chmn., CEO, Randall L. Attkisson/Dir., COO - UTG, Universal Guaranty Life Insurance Company, John S. Albin/Dir., Joseph A. Brinck/Dir., Ward F. Correll/Dir., Thomas F. Darden/Dir., William W. Perry/Dir., James P. Rousey/Dir., Pres., Pres. - UTG, Universal Guaranty Life Insurance Company, Howard L. Dayton/Dir., Peter L. Ochs/Dir.

Owners: John S. Albin, First Southern Bancorp, Inc., Jesse T. Correll, Joseph A. Brinck, First Southern Holdings, LLC, Insiders, First Southern Capital Corp., LLC, First Southern Investments, LLC, Theodore C. Miller, Howard L. Dayton, First Southern Funding, LLC, Ward F. Correll, WCorrell, Limited Partnership, Thomas F. Darden, William W. Perry *(16 Owners included in Index)*

Financial Data: **Fiscal Year End:**12/31 **Latest Annual Data:** 12/31/2006

Year	Sales	Net Income
2006	$37,585,000	$3,870,000
2005	$27,471,000	$1,260,000
2004	$25,467,000	-$276,000

Curr. Assets:	$87,552,000	**Curr. Liab.:**	$3,331,000		
Plant, Equip.:	$3,129,000	**Total Liab.:**	$437,705,000	**Indic. Yr. Divd.:**	NA
Total Assets:	$482,732,000	**Net Worth:**	$45,026,000	**Debt/ Equity:**	0.5441

UTi Worldwide Inc

100 Oceangate Blvd., Ste. 1500, Long Beach, CA, 90802; *PH:* 1-562-552-9400; *Fax:* 1-562-552-9401; *http://* www.go2uti.com; *Email:* util_info@go2uti.com

General - Incorporation British Virgin Islands
Employees 19,012
Auditor Deloitte & Touche LLP
Stk Agt Computershare Trust Co
Counsel Paul, Hastings, Janofsky & Walker LLP
DUNS No. NA

Stock- Price on:12/24/2007 $27.32
Stock Exchange NDQ
Ticker Symbol UTIW
Outstanding Shares 99,010,000
E.P.S $1.07
Shareholders NA

Business: The groups principle activity is to operates a supply chain management business providing supply chain logistic services and planning and optimization solutions. The group operates from United States.

Primary SIC and add'l.: 4731

CIK No: 0001124827

Subsidiaries: Active Airline Representatives BV, African Investment Holdings NV, African Investments BV, Air & Sea Union Holdings Ltd., Ambassador Brokerage Limited, CCB Ventures Limited, Chilltrac (Pty) Limited, Co-ordinated Investment Holdings (Pty) Limited, Co-ordinated Investment Holdings (Pty) Ltd., Co-ordinated Materials Handling (Pty) Ltd, Co-ordinated Materials Handling (Pty) Ltd., Commerce Customs Brokers and Freight Forwarders Limited, Commerce International Freight Forwarders Limited, Concentrek, Inc., Corrib Limited 145 Subsidiaries included in the Index

Officers: William T. Gates/VP, CEO - UTi Integrated Logistics, Inc, Leader - Utis Contract Logistics Counsel, Roger I. MacFarlane/Dir., CEO/$1,370,139.00, Walter Mapham/CIO, Sr. VP, Ruediger Klug/53/Pres. - Emena Region Solutions Delivery, Elijah Ray/48/Sr. VP - Customer Solutions - UTi Integrated Logistics, Gavin Rimmer/48/Pres. - Africa, Raajeev Bhatnagar/50/Regional VP - Indian Subcontinent, Thomas Blank/47/Pres. - Client Solutions, Asia Pacific, Michael Dunlop/58/Global Leader UTi - Consumer Electronics, Technology, Holger Eckoldt/60/Global Leader UTi - Pharma, Jochen Freese/39/Exec. VP - Automotive, Vincent Gallagher/56/Sr. VP - Sales, Marketing, Americas Freight Forwarding, John S. Hextall/Exec. VP, COO, Member - UTi Worldwide Management Board/$1,363,377.00, Gene Ochi/Exec. VP, Chief Marketing Officer, Member - The UTi Worldwide Management Board/$1,082,718.00, Lance Damico/Sr. VP, Global General Counsel *(27 Officers included in Index)*

Directors: Roger I. MacFarlane/Dir., CEO, Simon J. Stubbings/Chmn., Matthys J. Wessels/Vice Chmn., Brian D. Belchers/Dir., Allan M. Rosenzweig/Dir., John C. Langley/Dir., Leon J. Level/Dir.

Owners: FMR Corp./6.80%, Union-Transport Holdings Inc./5.40%, T. Rowe Price Associates, Inc./11.40%, Allan M. Rosenzweig, Lawrence Samuels, Matthys J. Wessels/4.00%, Insiders/7.80%, PTR Holdings Inc./9.40%, John Hextall, John C. Langley, Simon J. Stubbings, Gene Ochi, Leon J. Level, Roger I. MacFarlane/2.60%, Brian D. Belchers

Financial Data: **Fiscal Year End:**01/31 **Latest Annual Data:** 1/31/2007

Year	Sales	Net Income
2007	$3,561,365,000	$107,939,000
2006	$2,785,575,000	$55,198,000
2005	$2,259,793,000	$67,529,000

Curr. Assets:	$1,009,664,000	**Curr. Liab.:**	$718,277,000	**P/E Ratio:**	25.53
Plant, Equip.:	$127,990,000	**Total Liab.:**	$1,022,596,000	**Indic. Yr. Divd.:**	NA
Total Assets:	$1,659,870,000	**Net Worth:**	$637,274,000	**Debt/ Equity:**	0.3497

Utix Group Inc

7 New England Executive Pk., Ste. 610, Burlington, MA, 01803; *PH:* 1-782-229-2589; *Fax:* 1-781-229-8886; *http://* www.utix.com; *Email:* info@utix.com

General - Incorporation DE
Employees 25
Auditor Carlin, Charron & Rosen, LLP
Stk Agt Olde Monmouth Stk Trnsfer Co. Inc.
Counsel NA
DUNS No. NA

Stock- Price on:12/24/2007 $0.95
Stock Exchange OTC
Ticker Symbol UTIX
Outstanding Shares 1,760,000
E.P.S -$10.44
Shareholders NA

Business: The groups principle activity is to provide prepaid experience tickets. The group developed a business model and technology that identifies and segments merchants and specific lifestyle experiences on a magnetic strip ticket. The group operates from United States.

Primary SIC and add'l.: 2844

CIK No: 0000842010

Subsidiaries: Corporate Sports Incentives, Inc.

Officers: Anthony G. Roth/43/Dir., CEO, Pres., Steve Apesos/MD, Exec. VP, Cynthia Cronan/Chief Accounting Officer, Mark Pover/CFO, Colin Reid/Exec. VP - Business Development, Dan Merrill/Sr. VP - Operaions, Stephen Pitcher/Dir. - Information Technology, Jim Rowins/Sr. VP - Sales, Scott Dmitrenko/VP - Consumer Sales, Suzanne Devoe/VP - Program Development

Directors: Anthony G. Roth/43/Dir., CEO, Pres., Jonathan Adams/Co - Chmn., Charles A. Lieppe/Co - Chmn., Robert J. Corliss/Dir., Robert Powers/Dir., William F. Fenimore/63/Dir., Bill Fenimore/Dir.

Owners: MicroCapital Fund Ltd., Austin W. Marxe and David M. Greenhouse, Merriman, Curhan, Ford & Co., Mort Goulder, Austin W. Marxe and David M. Greenhouse/75.30%, Crescent International Ltd., Summit Trading Limited, Charles Lieppe, The Crown Advisors, The Crown Advisors/2.80%, Little Wing L.P./3.20%, Crown Investment Partners, LP, Jonathan Adams, John Winfield and The InterGroup Corporation, Robert Corliss *(36 Owners included in Index)*

Financial Data: **Fiscal Year End:**09/30 **Latest Annual Data:** 9/30/2006

Year	Sales	Net Income
2006	$1,444,000	-$9,648,000
2005	$6,901,000	-$9,961,000
2004	$2,265,000	-$3,825,000

Curr. Assets:	$2,387,000	**Curr. Liab.:**	$3,315,000		
Plant, Equip.:	$154,000	**Total Liab.:**	$3,318,000	**Indic. Yr. Divd.:**	NA
Total Assets:	$2,569,000	**Net Worth:**	-$6,105,000	**Debt/ Equity:**	NA

UTStarcom Incorporated

1275 Harbor Bay Pkwy., Alameda, CA, 94502; *PH:* 1-510-864-8800; *Fax:* 1-510-864-8802; *http://* www.utstar.com

General - Incorporation DE
Employees 6,300
Auditor PricewaterhouseCoopers LLP
Stk Agt EquiServe Trust Co N.A
Counsel Wilson Sonsini Goodrich & Rosati
DUNS No. NA

Stock- Price on:12/24/2007 $5.18
Stock Exchange NDQ
Ticker Symbol UTSI
Outstanding Shares 120,840,000
E.P.S -$1.76
Shareholders NA

Business: The group's principal activity is to design, manufacture and market wireline and wireless broadband access and switching equipment. The product lines of the group include mswitch, pas, an-2000 and 3g offerings. Mswitch is a highly scalable, ip-based, multiservice switching architecture that bridges the gap between existing circuit-switched and next-generation packet-switched networks. Personal access services allows service providers to offer premium-quality voice, data, and value-added services over mobile and fixed wireless networks using the specially designed pas handsets. An-2000 provides a broadband-ready access platform. 3g network solution enables the transformation of voice-centric mobile communications to content-rich multimedia services. On 30-Jun-2003 the group acquired rollingstreams systems ltd, on 7-May-2003 assets of xebeo communications, inc and on 23-May-2003 certain assets and liabilities from 3com's commworks division

Primary SIC and add'l.: 3661 3663 3669

CIK No: 0001030471

Subsidiaries: ACD Labs Inc., Hangzhou Starcom CEC Telecom Company Limited, Hangzhou Starcom Telecom Co., Ltd., Universal Communication Technology (Hangzhou) Company Limited., UT Starcom Honduras, S. de R.L., UTStarcom (China), Co., Ltd., UTStarcom (Chongqing) Telecom Co., Ltd., UTStarcom (Thailand) Limited, UTStarcom Argentina S.R.L., UTStarcom Australia Pty Ltd., UTStarcom Canada Company, UTStarcom CDMA Technologies Korea Limited, UTStarcom Chile Soluciones De Redes Limitada, UTStarcom France SARL, UTStarcom GmbH 31 Subsidiaries included in the Index

Officers: Hong Liang Lu/Chmn., CEO, Pres., Francis P. Barton/61/Dir., Exec. VP, CFO, Philip Christopher/Pres. - Utstarcom Personal Communications a Division, Utstarcom, Inc, David King/Sr. VP - International Sales, Marketing, Ari Bose/Sr. VP, CIO - Business Transformation Office, Mark Green/Sr. VP - Human Resources, K. P. Lim/VP, Chief Quality Officer, Jack Mar/Pres. - Cdma, GSM Wireless Group, Moon Song/Pres. - Terminal Business Unit, Jimmy Khoo/Sr. VP - Supply Chain Operations, Susan Marsch/General Counsel, Corp. Sec., Chief Ethics Officer, Steve Shaffer/VP - Global Service, Solutions International, Larry Du/VP - Global Service, Solutions China, Brian Caskey/VP - Global Marketing, Peter Blackmore/COO, Pres.

Directors: Hong Liang Lu/Chmn., CEO, Pres., Thomas J. Toy/Dir., Jeffrey J. Clarke/Dir., Francis P. Barton/61/Dir., Exec. VP, CFO, Allen U. Lenzmeier/Dir., Larry D. Horner/Dir.

Owners: Thomas J. Toy, Ying Wu/3.89%, Larry D. Horner, Entities affiliated with SOFTBANK CORP./12.08%, Miura Global Management, LLC/5.45%, Jeff Clarke, Insiders/4.86%, Renaissance Technologies Corp./8.42%, Allen Lenzmeier, Francis P. Barton, Highbridge Capital Management LLC/5.11%, William Huang, Brandes Investment Partners, L.P./8.17%, Goldman Sachs Asset Management, L.P./10.88%, Barclays Global Investors, N.A./8.02% *(16 Owners included in Index)*

Financial Data: *Fiscal Year End:*12/31 *Latest Annual Data:* 12/31/2006

Year	Sales	Net Income
2006	$2,458,861,000	-$117,345,000
2005	$2,929,343,000	-$487,359,000
2004	$2,703,581,000	$73,415,000

Curr. Assets:	$1,836,608,000	**Curr. Liab.:**	$1,043,064,000		
Plant, Equip.:	$213,155,000	**Total Liab.:**	$1,599,590,000	**Indic. Yr. Divd.:**	NA
Total Assets:	$2,373,950,000	**Net Worth:**	$774,360,000	**Debt/ Equity:**	0.3030

Uwharrie Capital Corp

PO Box 338, 132 N First St., Albemarle, NC, 28001; *PH:* 1-704-983-6181; *http://* www.uwharrie.com; *Email:* hr@uwharrie.com

General - Incorporation NC
Employees 124
Auditor Dixon Hughes PLLC
Stk Agt American Stock Transfer & Trust Co.
Counsel NA
DUNS No. 84-938-1595

Stock- Price on:12/24/2007 NA
Stock Exchange OTC
Ticker Symbol UWHR
Outstanding Shares NA
E.P.S $0.36
Shareholders NA

Business: The group's principal activity is to provide a wide range of commercial banking and personal banking services in the United States. The services include personal and commercial checking and savings accounts, money market accounts, certificates of deposit, individual retirement accounts and related business and individual banking services. The group lends commercial and various consumer loans to individuals including installment loans, mortgage loans, equity lines of credit and overdraft checking credit. The other services provided by the group are insurance products including annuities, life insurance, long-term care, disability insurance and medicare supplements and portfolio management services.

Primary SIC and add'l.: 6022 6712

CIK No: 0000898171

Subsidiaries: Anson Bank& Trust Co., Bank of Stanly, BOS Agency, Inc., Cabarrus Bank& Trust Company, Gateway Mortgage, Inc, Strategic Investment Advisors, Inc., The Strategic Alliance Corporation, Uwharrie Mortgage, Inc., Uwharrie Statutory Trust I

Officers: Roger L. Dick/56/CEO, Pres./$316,298.00, Brendan P. Duffey/59/COO, Exec. VP/$233,208.00, Barbara S. Williams/64/Exec. VP, Controller/$103,503.00, Susan Gibson/Contact - Human Resources

Directors: John P. Murray/66/Dir., Timothy J. Propst/47/Dir., Susan J. Rourke/62/Dir., Donald P. Scarborough/57/Dir., John W. Shealy/57/Dir., Hugh E. Wallace/Dir., Joseph R. Kluttz/69/Dir., James E. Nance/56/Dir., Emmett S. Patterson/70/Dir., Cmichael E. Snyder/67/Dir., Douglas L. Stafford/55/Dir., Emily M. Thomas/61/Dir., Charles F. Geschickter/45/Dir., Joe S. Brooks/58/Dir., Thomas M. Hearne/57/Dir. *(17 Directors included in Index)*

Owners: Jimmy L. Strayhorn, John W. Shealy, Insiders/9.71%, Brendan P. Duffey, James E. Nance, Roger L. Dick/1.53%, Christy D. Stoner/1.66%, Joe S. Brooks, Patricia K. Horton, Douglas L. Stafford, Charles D. Horne, Emily M. Thomas, Franklin B. Lee, Michael E. Snyder, John P. Murray *(27 Owners included in Index)*

Financial Data: *Fiscal Year End:*12/31 *Latest Annual Data:* 12/31/2006

Year	Sales	Net Income
2006	$29,822,000	$2,071,000

Curr. Assets:	$36,535,000	**Curr. Liab.:**	$318,736,000		
Plant, Equip.:	$8,618,000	**Total Liab.:**	$353,628,000	**Indic. Yr. Divd.:**	NA
Total Assets:	$383,261,000	**Net Worth:**	$29,633,000	**Debt/ Equity:**	NA

uWink Inc

16106 Hart St., Van Nuys, CA, 91406; *PH:* 1-818-909-6030; *Fax:* 1-818-909-6070; *http://* www.uwink.com; *Email:* info@uwink.com

General - Incorporation UT
Employees 14
Auditor Kabani & Company, Inc.
Stk Agt Continental Stock Transfer & Trust Co
Counsel NA
DUNS No. NA

Stock- Price on:12/24/2007 $1.32
Stock Exchange OTC
Ticker Symbol UWKI
Outstanding Shares 26,070,000
E.P.S -$0.88
Shareholders NA

Business: The groups principle activities include designing and develop interactive entertainment software and platforms for restaurants, bars, and mobile devices. The group operates from the United States. The group's quarterly revenue for Oct '07 was 0.67 millions of USD.

Primary SIC and add'l.: 7372

CIK No: 0001108699

Subsidiaries: uWink California, Inc.

Officers: Nolan K. Bushnell/64/Chmn., Founder, CEO/$240,689.00, John Kaufman/Dir. - Restaurant Operations, Peter Wilkniss/CFO/$182,000.00, Paul Dumais/44/CTO, Alissa Tappan/VP - Marketing, Public Relations, Dan Lindquist/VP - Operations - Development, Nancy Nino/Contact - Investor Relations

Directors: Nolan K. Bushnell/64/Chmn., Founder, CEO, Bruce P. Kelly/61/Dir., Kevin McLeod/52/Dir., Bradley Rotter/52/Dir.

Owners: Kevin W. McLeod/4.90%, Peter F. Wilkniss/2.10%, John S. Kaufman/1.00%, Nolan K. Bushnell/10.90%, Tallac Corp./5.80%, Bradley N. Rotter/4.30%, Elizabeth J. Heller, Insiders/22.30%

Financial Data: *Fiscal Year End:*12/31 *Latest Annual Data:* 1/2/2007

Year	Sales	Net Income
2007	$450,000	-$10,361,000
2005	$683,000	-$3,240,000
2004	$1,820,000	-$3,769,000

Curr. Assets:	$387,000	**Curr. Liab.:**	$1,635,000		
Plant, Equip.:	$19,000	**Total Liab.:**	$1,830,000	**Indic. Yr. Divd.:**	NA
Total Assets:	$406,000	**Net Worth:**	-$1,424,000	**Debt/ Equity:**	NA

V-GPO Inc

2150 Whitfield Indus Way, Sarasota, FL, 34243; *PH:* 1-941-727-1552; *http://* www.vgpo.com

General - Incorporation
Employees NA
Auditor NA
Stk Agt American Registrar & Transfer Co
Counsel NA
DUNS No. NA

Stock- Price on:12/24/2007 NA
Stock Exchange OTC
Ticker Symbol VGPO
Outstanding Shares NA
E.P.S NA
Shareholders NA

Business: The groups principal activity is engage in the business of owning, operating and/or managing healthcare facilities. The group operates from the United States.

Primary SIC and add'l.: 6799

CIK No:

Subsidiaries: International Healthcare Investments Ltd. (IHI)

Officers: Norman R. Dobiesz/Chmn., CEO

Directors: Norman R. Dobiesz/Chmn., CEO

Financial Data: *Fiscal Year End:*NA *Latest Annual Data:* 12/31/2005

Year	Sales	Net Income
2005	NA	-$2,763,000
2004	$37,000	-$3,128,000
2003	$590,000	-$1,876,000

Curr. Assets:	$1,000	**Curr. Liab.:**	$15,486,000		
Plant, Equip.:	$2,000	**Total Liab.:**	$15,486,000	**Indic. Yr. Divd.:**	NA
Total Assets:	$118,000	**Net Worth:**	-$15,368,000	**Debt/ Equity:**	NA

VAALCO Energy Inc

4600 Post Oak Pl., Ste. 309, Houston, TX, 77027; *PH:* 1-713-623-0801; *http://* www.vaalco.com; *Email:* vaalco@vaalco.com

General - Incorporation DE
Employees 16
Auditor Deloitte & Touche LLP
Stk Agt Registrar And Transfer CO.
Counsel NA
DUNS No. 60-232-8478

Stock- Price on:12/24/2007 $5
Stock Exchange NYSE
Ticker Symbol EGY
Outstanding Shares 59,110,000
E.P.S $0.37
Shareholders NA

Business: The group's principal activities are to acquire, explore, develop and produce crude oil and natural gas. The group owns producing properties and conducts exploration activities as operator of consortium internationally in Philippines and gabon. The group's domestic strategy is to produce existing reserves and not to drill new domestic wells. Domestically, the group has interests in the Texas gulf coast area. In both gabon and the Philippines, the group serves as the operator for groups of companies which own the working interests in the production sharing contracts.

Primary SIC and add'l.: 1311

CIK No: 0000894627

Subsidiaries: Alcorn (Philippines), Inc., Alcorn (Production) Philippines, Inc., Altisima Energy, Inc., VAALCO Energy (USA), Inc., VAALCO Gabon (Etame), Inc., VAALCO International, Inc, VAALCO Production (Gabon), Inc.

Officers: Robert L. Gerry/Chmn., CEO/$579,014.00, Russell W. Scheirman/CFO, Pres., Gayla M. Cutrer/Corp. Sec./$176,045.00

Directors: Robert L. Gerry/Chmn., CEO

Owners: Insiders/6.90%, Luigi P. Caflisch, Gayla M. Cutrer, W. Russell Scheirman, O. Donald Chapoton, William S. Farish, Robert H. Allen, Barclays Global Investors NA/5.97%, Robert L. Gerry/4.70%, Arne R. Nielsen, Columbia Wagner Asset Management L.P./7.20%

Financial Data: *Fiscal Year End:*12/31 *Latest Annual Data:* 12/31/2006

Year	Sales	Net Income
2006	$98,325,000	$40,343,000
2005	$84,935,000	$29,182,000
2004	$56,502,000	$22,938,000

Curr. Assets:	$84,181,000	Curr. Liab.:	$26,686,000	P/E Ratio:	11.11
Plant, Equip.:	$70,507,000	Total Liab.:	$45,678,000	Indic. Yr. Divd.:	NA
Total Assets:	$167,942,000	Net Worth:	$122,264,000	Debt/ Equity:	0.0408

Vail Resorts Inc

137 Benchmark Rd. , C/o Anaconda Tower, Avon, CO, 81620; PH: 1-970-845-2500;
http:// www.vailresorts.com

General - Incorporation	DE	Stock- Price on:12/24/2007	$63.97
Employees	3,100	Stock Exchange	NYSE
Auditor	PricewaterhouseCoopers LLP	Ticker Symbol	MTN
Stk Agt	Wells Fargo Bank Minnesota N.A	Outstanding Shares	39,010,000
Counsel	Cahill Gordon & Reindel LLP	E.P.S.	$1.39
DUNS No.	79-619-2243	Shareholders	NA

Business: The group's principal activity is to operate resorts in North America through its subsidiaries. The operations are carried on under three business segments: mountain, lodging and real estate. The mountain segment owns and operates five ski resort properties that provide a comprehensive resort experience throughout the year to a diverse clientele. The lodging segment owns and manages a collection of luxury hotels, a destination resort at grand teton national park and a series of strategic properties located in proximity to the group's mountain operations. The real estate segment holds, develops, buys and sells real estate in and around the resort communities.

Primary SIC and add'l.: 6531 6719 7011 3949

CIK No: 0000812011

Subsidiaries: Arrabelle at Vail Square, LLC, Avon Partners II Limited Liability Company, Beaver Creek Associates, Inc., Beaver Creek Consultants, Inc., Beaver Creek Food Services, Inc., Boulder/Beaver, LLC, Breckenridge Resort Properties, Inc., Breckenridge Terrace, LLC, Chalets at the Lodge at Vail, LLC(The), Colter Bay Corporation, Complete Telecommunications, Inc., Eagle Park Reservoir Company, FFT Investment Partners, Forest Ridge Holdings, Inc., Gillett Broadcasting, Inc. 73 Subsidiaries included in the Index

Officers: Robert A. Katz/Dir., CEO, Blaise T. Carrig/COO, Sr. VP - Heavenly, Jennifer MacLure/Sr. Mgr. - Advertising, Partnership Marketing, John McD. Garnsey/COO, Sr. VP - Beaver Creek, Mountain Division, Christopher E. Jarnot/Sr. VP - Marketing, Sales, Vail Resorts Management Company, Christina Schleicher/Mgr. - Communications, Beaver Creek Resort, Russ Pecoraro/Communications Dir. - Heavenly Mountain Resort, Jennifer Maclure Robertson/Sr. Marketing Mgr. - Advertising Inquiries, Jeffrey W. Jones/Sr. Exec. VP, CFO, Mark L. Schoppet/VP, Controller - Vail Resorts Management Company, Robert N. Urwiler/Sr. VP, CIO - Vail Resorts Management Company, William A. Jensen/Pres. - Mountain Division, Keith A. Fernandez/Pres., COO - Vail Resorts Development Company, Real Estate Division, Alex Iskenderian/VP - Vail Resorts Development Company, Nanci N. Northway/VP - Internal Audit, Vail Resorts Management Company (28 Officers included in Index)

Directors: Robert A. Katz/Dir., CEO, Joe R. Micheletto/Chmn., John F. Sorte/Dir., Roland A. Hernandez/Dir., Thomas D. Hyde/Dir., Richard D. Kincaid/Dir., William P. Stiritz/Dir., John J. Hannan/Dir.

Owners: John F. Sorte, Ralcorp Holdings, Inc./19.18%, Insiders/1.43%, William A. Jensen, Ronald Baron/12.05%, William P. Stiritz, Jeffrey W. Jones, Marsico Capital Management, LLC/10.49%, Roger D. McCarthy, Robert A. Katz, Roland A. Hernandez, Columbia Wanger Asset Management, L.P./7.43%, Martha D. Rehm, Eagle Asset Management, Inc./5.77%, FMR Corp./5.98% (21 Owners included in Index)

Financial Data: Fiscal Year End:07/31   Latest Annual Data: 7/31/2006

Year	Sales	Net Income
2006	$838,852,000	$45,756,000
2005	$809,987,000	$23,138,000
2004	$721,893,000	$5,959,000

Curr. Assets:	$325,974,000	Curr. Liab.:	$254,194,000	P/E Ratio:	39.01
Plant, Equip.:	$1,110,496,000	Total Liab.:	$1,012,306,000	Indic. Yr. Divd.:	NA
Total Assets:	$1,687,643,000	Net Worth:	$642,777,000	Debt/ Equity:	0.7739

Valassis Communications Inc

19975 Victor Pkwy, Livonia, MI, 48152; PH: 1-734-591-3000; http:// www.valassis.com

General - Incorporation	DE	Stock- Price on:12/24/2007	$17.76
Employees	3,600	Stock Exchange	NYSE
Auditor	Deloitte & Touche LLP	Ticker Symbol	VCI
Stk Agt	National City Bank	Outstanding Shares	47,880,000
Counsel	NA	E.P.S.	$0.93
DUNS No.	60-281-3768	Shareholders	NA

Business: The group's provide a wide range of marketing products and services to a variety of premier manufacturers, direct marketers, retailers and franchisees by providing innovative marketing solutions. The group's principal activity is to produce free-standing inserts for customers in the package goods industry throughout the United States. The group offers the clients specialty print promotion products in customized formats such as die-cuts, posters and calendars, as well as traditional free-standing inserts. The products are marketed through retailers. On 13-Feb-2003, it acquired nch marketing services inc and the remaining interest in prevision marketing.

Primary SIC and add'l.: 9999 2759

CIK No: 0000883293

Subsidiaries: NCH Marketing Services, Inc., PreVision Marketing, LLC, Promotion Watch, Inc., Valassis Manufacturing Company, Valassis of Canada Co., Valassis Sales and Marketing Services, Inc., ValassisRelationshipMarketingSystems,LLC, VCI Fulfillment Group

Officers: Alan F. Schultz/49/Chmn., CEO, Pres./$3,023,774.00, Michell Zarem/Investor Relations Officer, Robert L. Recchia/51/Dir., CFO, Exec. VP, Treasurer/$1,244,769.00, William F. Hogg/61/Dir., Exec. VP - Manufacturing, Client Services/$918,778.00, Barry P. Hoffman/67/Dir., Exec. VP, General Counsel, Sec./$1,232,059.00, Richard P. Herpich/55/Dir., Exec. VP - Sales, Marketing/$1,168,985.00

Directors: Alan F. Schultz/49/Chmn., CEO, Pres., Joseph B. Anderson/65/Dir., Patrick F. Brennan/76/Dir., Marcella A. Sampson/77/Dir., Brian J. Husselbee/56/Dir., Robert L. Recchia/51/Dir., CFO, Exec. VP, Treasurer, William F. Hogg/61/Dir., Exec. VP - Manufacturing, Client Services, Ambassador Faith Whittlesey/69/Dir., Barry P. Hoffman/67/Dir., Exec. VP, General Counsel, Sec., Richard P. Herpich/55/Dir., Exec. VP - Sales, Marketing, Kenneth V. Darish/50/Dir., Walter H. Ku/72/Dir.

Owners: Richard Herpich, Patrick F. Brennan, Barrow, Hanley, Mewhinney& Strauss, Inc./7.03%, Walter H. Ku, Prides Capital Partners, L.L.C./5.40%, Robert L. Recchia, Kenneth V. Darish, AMVESCAP PLC/5.29%, Marcella A. Sampson, Insiders/5.60%, Barclays Global Investors, NA./5.56%, William F. Hogg, Faith Whittlesey, Barry P. Hoffman, Alan F. Schultz/2.10% (19 Owners included in Index)

Financial Data: Fiscal Year End:12/31   Latest Annual Data: 12/31/2006

Year	Sales	Net Income
2006	$1,043,491,000	$51,282,000
2005	$1,131,043,000	$95,396,000
2004	$1,044,069,000	$100,747,000

Curr. Assets:	$542,492,000	Curr. Liab.:	$362,220,000	P/E Ratio:	24.67
Plant, Equip.:	$109,386,000	Total Liab.:	$633,852,000	Indic. Yr. Divd.:	NA
Total Assets:	$801,426,000	Net Worth:	$167,574,000	Debt/ Equity:	7.8850

Valcent Products Inc

789 W Pender St. , Ste. 1010, Vancouver, BC, V6C 1H2; PH: 1-604-606-7977;
Fax: 1-604-606-7980; http:// www.valcent.net; Email: info@valcent.net

General - Incorporation	AO	Stock- Price on:12/24/2007	$0.62
Employees	NA	Stock Exchange	OTC
Auditor	Smythe Ratcliffe LLP	Ticker Symbol	VCTPF
Stk Agt	Pacific Stock Transfer	Outstanding Shares	NA
Counsel	NA	E.P.S.	NA
DUNS No.	NA	Shareholders	NA

Business: The groups principal activities include providing consumer retail products in each of the respective markets for potential product lines. The group operates from Canada.

Primary SIC and add'l.: 5122

CIK No: 0001122081

Subsidiaries: Valcent Management, LLC, Valcent Manufacturing Ltd., Valcent USA Inc.

Officers: Glen M. Kertz/Chmn., CEO, Pres., Perry Martin/Exec. VP, Forrest Ely/COO, Jack Potts/VP - Sales Consumer Products, Tim Brock/Advisor to The Board, Finance, Business Planning, George F. Orr/Dir., CFO, Sec. Treasurer

Directors: Glen M. Kertz/Chmn., CEO, Pres., George F. Orr/Dir., CFO, Sec. Treasurer, Robert Wingo/Dir., Naveen Aggarwal/Dir., George T. Stapleton/Dir.

Owners: Pagic LP, Glen M. Kertz, Agosto Corporation Limited, Pinetree Income Partnership, Robert Wingo, Douglas E. Ford, Naveen Aggarwal, Insiders, Carlton Parfitt, Woodburn Holdings Ltd., West Peak Ventures of Canada Ltd., George F. Orr, Steve McGuire

Financial Data: Fiscal Year End:03/31   Latest Annual Data: 03/31/2007

Year	Sales	Net Income
2007	NA	-$9,468,000
2006	NA	-$3,170,000
2005	NA	-$46,000

Curr. Assets:	$1,990,000	Curr. Liab.:	$5,652,000		
Plant, Equip.:	$302,000	Total Liab.:	$5,821,000	Indic. Yr. Divd.:	NA
Total Assets:	$3,524,000	Net Worth:	-$2,297,000	Debt/ Equity:	NA

VALCOM Inc

920 S Commerce St., Las Vegas, NV, 89106; PH: 1-702-385-9000; Fax: 1-702-382-2802;
http:// www.valcom.tv; Email: info@valcom.tv

General - Incorporation	DE	Stock- Price on:12/24/2007	NA
Employees	4	Stock Exchange	OTC
Auditor	Kabani & Co, Inc	Ticker Symbol	VLCO
Stk Agt	New York 10004 Actx	Outstanding Shares	NA
Counsel	NA	E.P.S.	-$1.84
DUNS No.	15-099-7336	Shareholders	NA

Business: The group's principal activities are to lease sound and production stages and produce films and TV programs. The group operates through three segments: studio rental segment leases eight sound stages in valencia, California and production stages to production companies. Studio equipment and rental segment rents and supplies personnel, cameras and other production equipment to various production companies on a short-term or long-term basis. Film and TV production segment includes television productions for the broadcast networks, cable networks or first-run television syndication.

Primary SIC and add'l.: 7819 7812 7389

CIK No: 0001013453

Subsidiaries: Half Day Video, Inc, ValCom Broadcasting, LLC, ValCom Studios, Inc, Valencia Entertainment International, LLC

Officers: Vincent Vellardita/Chmn., CEO, Pres., Tony Vellardita/Contact - Stage Mgr., Sandy Markham/Office Support, Deedee Anderson/Contact - Information, Egan Elledge/GM, VP - Production, Tracy Sciarrino/Corp. Sec., Roger Palme/Contact - Technical Services

Directors: Vincent Vellardita/Chmn., CEO, Pres., Richard Shintaku/Dir., Frank O'Donnell/Dir.

Owners: Sandy Markham, Insiders/15.85%, Richard Shintaku/4.04%, Vincent Vellardita/11.22%

Financial Data: Fiscal Year End:09/30   Latest Annual Data: 09/30/2006

Year	Sales	Net Income
2006	$3,402,000	-$4,531,000
2005	$930,000	-$1,820,000
2004	$1,953,000	-$5,930,000

Curr. Assets:	$975,000	Curr. Liab.:	$3,696,000		
Plant, Equip.:	$674,000	Total Liab.:	$3,696,000	Indic. Yr. Divd.:	NA
Total Assets:	$2,907,000	Net Worth:	-$789,000	Debt/ Equity:	NA

Valeant Pharmaceuticals International

3300 Hyland Ave., Valeant Plz., Costa Mesa, CA, 92626; PH: 1-714-545-0100;
http:// www.valeant.com

General - Incorporation	DE	Stock- Price on:12/24/2007	$16.95
Employees	3,443	Stock Exchange	NYSE
Auditor	PricewaterhouseCoopers LLP	Ticker Symbol	VRX
Stk Agt	American Stock Transfer & Trust Co.	Outstanding Shares	95,020,000
Counsel	NA	E.P.S.	-$0.09
DUNS No.	04-223-0623	Shareholders	NA

Business: The group's principle activities are to develop, manufacture and distribute a broad range of prescription and non-prescription pharmaceuticals under the icn brand name. These pharmaceutical products treat viral and bacterial infections, diseases of the skin, neuromuscular disorders, cancer, cardiovascular disease, diabetes and psychiatric disorders. The group's research and new product development, which exists primarily in its majority owned subsidiary ribapharm inc., focuses on innovative treatments for dermatology, infectious diseases and cancer. The group operates in two segments. The pharmaceuticals group produces and markets a variety of pharmaceutical products worldwide. Ribapharm derives royalty revenues from sales of certain of its products by a third party under a license agreement. The group's quarterly revenue for September 2007 was 208.62 millions of USD.

Primary SIC and add'l.: 8731 2834

CIK No: 0000930184

Subsidiaries: ICN Dutch Holdings B.V., ICN Polfa Rzeszow, Laboratorios Grossman, S.A., Valeant Development Company Pte Ltd., Valeant Farmaceutica, S.A. de C.V., Valeant Pharmaceuticals North America, Valeant Pharmaceuticals Switzerland GmbH, Valeant Research & Development

Officers: Timothy C. Tyson/Dir., CEO, Pres./$4,973,090.00, Geoffrey M. Glass/CIO, Sr. VP, Martin N. Mercer/Exec. VP - International, Eileen C. Pruette/Exec. VP, General Counsel/$1,371,564.00, Kim D. Lamon/Pres., Chief Scientific Officer/$1,880,806.00, Bary G. Bailey/49/Exec. VP/$2,058,243.00, Wesley P. Wheeler/Pres. - North America Global Product Development/$1,480,492.00, Humberto Fernandez/VP - Clinical Research, Chin-Chung Lin/VP - Drug Development, Susan Hall/VP - Global Regulatory Sciences, Harry Mansbach/Sr. VP - Drug Development, Rich Masterson/Sr. VP - Global Commercial Development, Jeff Misakian/VP - Investor Relations, Christina De Vaca/Sec., Julia A. Amo/Sr. Dir. - Business Operations *(23 Officers included in Index)*

Directors: Timothy C. Tyson/Dir., CEO, Pres., Robert A. Ingram/Chmn., Elaine Ullian/Dir., Richard H. Koppes/Dir., Edward A. Burkhardt/69/Dir., Francis V. Chisari/Member - Scientific Advisory Board, David D. Ho/Member - Scientific Advisory Board, James E. Niedel/Member - Scientific Advisory Board, Roberts A. Smith/Member - Scientific Advisory Board, Norma A. Provencio/Dir., Mason G. Morfit/Dir., Theo Melas-Kyriazi/Dir., Lawrence N. Kugelman/Dir.

Owners: Kim D. Lamon, Timothy C. Tyson/1.80%, ValueAct Capital Management, L.P./14.00%, Charles J. Bramlage, Wesley P. Wheeler, Elaine Ullian, Insiders/4.00%, Lawrence N. Kugelman, Iridian Asset Management LLC/9.50%, Robert A. Ingram, Loomis, Sayles& Co., L.P./8.10%, T. Rowe Price Associates, Inc./13.00%, Edward A. Burkhardt, Franklin Mutual Advisers, LLC/7.60%, Eileen C. Pruette *(20 Owners included in Index)*

Financial Data: **Fiscal Year End:**12/31 **Latest Annual Data:** 12/31/2006

Year	Sales	Net Income
2006	$907,238,000	-$56,565,000
2005	$823,886,000	-$188,142,000
2004	$682,520,000	-$169,797,000

Curr. Assets:	$781,975,000	**Curr. Liab.:**	$252,208,000		
Plant, Equip.:	$94,279,000	**Total Liab.:**	$1,070,184,000	**Indic. Yr. Divd.:**	$0.310
Total Assets:	$1,505,437,000	**Net Worth:**	$435,253,000	**Debt/ Equity:**	1.7879

Valence Technology Inc

12201 Technology Blvd., Ste. 150, Austin, TX, 78727; ***PH:*** 1-512-527-2900; ***http://*** www.valence-tech.com; ***Email:*** support@valence.com

General -		**Stock**-	
Incorporation	DE	Price on:12/24/2007	$1.14
Employees	309	Stock Exchange	NDQ
Auditor	Deloitte & Touche LLP	Ticker Symbol	VLNC
Stk Agt	EquiServe Trust Co N.A	Outstanding Shares	108,160,000
Counsel	NA	E.P.S.	-$0.27
DUNS No.	61-186-2327	Shareholders	NA

Business: The group's principal activities are to develop and acquire battery technologies. The group's saphion(tm) technology, a lithium-ion technology which utilizes a phosphate-based cathode addresses the weaknesses of existing oxide based lithium-ion alternatives offering a solution that is competitive in cost and performance. Saphion technology will offer solutions in the form of safer, environmentally friendly, lower-cost, higher performance energy products and caters a variety of products in markets including consumer electronics, appliances, toys, vehicles, uninterrupted power supply systems and other industrial applications.

Primary SIC and add'l.: 3691 6794

CIK No: 0000885551

Subsidiaries: Valence Energy-tech (suzhou) Co., Ltd., Valence Technology (nevada), Inc, Valence Technology (suzhou) Co., Ltd, Valence Technology B.v, Valence Technology Caymen Islands Inc., Valence Technology International, Inc, Valence Technology N.v.

Officers: Carl E. Berg/Chmn. - Private Investor, Joel Sandahl/VP - Engineering, Product Development/$203,114.00, Thomas F. Mezger/CFO/$281,964.00, Roger Williams/General Counsel/$240,312.00, Emilie Harris/Media Contact

Directors: Carl E. Berg/Chmn. - Private Investor, John Locy/Dir., Vassilis G. Keramidas/Dir., Bert C. Roberts/Dir.

Owners: Carl E. Berg/47.60%, Bert C. Roberts, Vassilis G. Keramidas/0.10%, Richard Hanna, Insiders/56.00%, Thomas F. Mezger/0.10%, Joel Sandahl, 1981 Kara Ann Berg Trust/7.40%, Roger A. Williams/0.30%

Financial Data: **Fiscal Year End:**03/31 **Latest Annual Data:** 3/31/2007

Year	Sales	Net Income
2007	$16,674,000	-$22,251,000
2006	$17,214,000	-$32,724,000
2005	$10,665,000	-$31,430,000

Curr. Assets:	$15,025,000	**Curr. Liab.:**	$7,643,000		
Plant, Equip.:	$3,997,000	**Total Liab.:**	$78,508,000	**Indic. Yr. Divd.:**	NA
Total Assets:	$19,200,000	**Net Worth:**	-$67,918,000	**Debt/ Equity:**	NA

Valentec Systems Inc

Formerly: Acorn Holding Corp

2629 York Ave., Minden, LA, 71055; ***PH:*** 1-318-382-4574

General -		**Stock**-	
Incorporation	DE	Price on:12/24/2007	NA
Employees	128	Stock Exchange	OTC
Auditor	Grant Thornton, LLP	Ticker Symbol	VSYN
Stk Agt	Continental Stock Transfer & Trust Co	Outstanding Shares	
Counsel	NA	E.P.S.	-$0.46
DUNS No.	36-401-4167	Shareholders	NA

Business: The group principal activity is to manufacture monocrystalline silicon wafers used in the microelectronics industry. The silicon wafers are made from silicon crystals and are the basic substrate from which integrated circuits and other semiconductor devices are fabricated. The group's products are used by university research departments and microelectronic manufacturers. The silicon wafers are also best suited for use in electronics devices employed in avionics, telecommunications and computers. On 23-Jun-2003, recticon enterprises inc. Wholly owned subsidiary of the group liquidated its assets.

Primary SIC and add'l.: 3674 6719

CIK No: 0000737243

Subsidiaries: AI Liquidating Corp, Recticon Enterprises, Inc., Valentec Systems, Inc.

Officers: Robert A. Zummo/66/Chmn., CEO, Stephen J. Shows/66/VP - Operations, GM

Directors: Robert A. Zummo/66/Chmn., CEO, Avraham Gilat/58/Dir., Zvi Kreizman/53/Dir., August Cianciolo/Dir., Glenn W. Yarborough/Dir.

Owners: Armament Systems International, Inc., Robert A. Zummo, Global Systems, Inc., Avraham Gilat, Larry Matheson, Zvi Kreizman, Insiders

Financial Data: **Fiscal Year End:**12/31 **Latest Annual Data:** 03/31/2007

Year	Sales	Net Income
2007	NA	NA
2006	NA	NA
2005	$19,016,000	$400,000

Curr. Assets:	$18,064,000	**Curr. Liab.:**	$28,107,000		
Plant, Equip.:	$1,671,000	**Total Liab.:**	$28,215,000	**Indic. Yr. Divd.:**	NA
Total Assets:	$25,951,000	**Net Worth:**	-$2,264,000	**Debt/ Equity:**	NA

Valero Energy Corp

One Valero Way, San Antonio, TX, 78249; ***PH:*** 1-210-345-2000; ***http://*** www.valero.com

General -		**Stock**-	
Incorporation	DE	Price on:12/24/2007	$76.68
Employees	21,836	Stock Exchange	NYSE
Auditor	KPMG LLP	Ticker Symbol	VLO
Stk Agt	Computershare Investor Services LLC	Outstanding Shares	548,990,000
Counsel	NA	E.P.S.	$9.55
DUNS No.	03-984-6027	Shareholders	NA

Business: The group's principle activity is to produce refined products including reformulated gasoline blendstock for oxygenate blending, gasoline, diesel fuel, low-sulfur and ultra-low-sulfur diesel fuel, and oxygenates. The group also produces conventional gasolines, distillates, jet fuel, asphalt, petrochemicals and various refined products. The group operates from United States.

Primary SIC and add'l.: 5541 5171 5983 2911 4922

CIK No: 0001035002

Subsidiaries: 3192474 Canada Inc., 585043 Ontario Limited, Autotronic Systems, Inc., Big Diamond Number 1, Inc., Big Diamond, Inc., Canadian Ultramar Company, Colonnade Vermont Insurance Company, Diamond Omega Company, LLC, Diamond Shamrock Arizona, Inc., Diamond Shamrock Boliviana, Ltd., Diamond Shamrock Refining And Marketing Company, Diamond Shamrock Refining Company, L.p., Diamond Shamrock Stations, Inc., Diamond Unit Investments, LLC, Dsrm National Bank 129 Subsidiaries included in the Index

Officers: William R. Klesse/Chmn., CEO/$9,938,473.00, Steve Gilbert/Assist. Sec. - Disclosure, Compliance Officer, Austin Miller/Mgr. - Asphalt Supply, San Antonio, TX, Gregory C. King/Pres./$5,380,435.00, Mike Ciskowski/CFO, Exec. VP/$3,405,466.00, Rich Marcogliese/COO, Exec. VP/$2,766,486.00, Eugene S. Edwards/Exec. VP - Corporate Development, Strategic Planning/$1,919,748.00, Jay D. Browning/Sr. VP - Corporate Law, Sec., Gary Arthur/Sr. VP - Retail Marketing, Joe Gorder/Exec. VP - Marketing, Supply, Kim Bowers/Sr. VP, General Counsel, Clay Killinger/Sr. VP, Controller, Norm Renfro/Sr. VP - Health, Safety, Environmental, Joseph W. Gorder/50/Exec. VP - Marketing, Supply, Hal Zesch/CIO, Sr. VP *(37 Officers included in Index)*

Directors: William R. Klesse/Chmn., CEO, Jerry D. Choate/Dir., Donald L. Nickles/Dir., Don Nickles/Dir., Susan Kaufman Purcell/Dir., Ruben M. Escobedo/Dir., Bob Marbut/Dir., Robert A. Profusek/Dir., W. E. Bradford/Dir., Ronald K. Calgaard/Dir., Irl F. Engelhardt/Dir., Curt Benefield/Dir. - Asphalt Product, Technical Development, San Antonio, TX, Jim OGara/Dir. - East Coast Asphalt Marketing, Oradell, NJ, William Darnell/Dir. - Northwest Asphalt Marketing, Benicia, CA, Lucian Nawrocki/Dir. - Southwest Asphalt Marketing, Wilmington, CA *(17 Directors included in Index)*

Owners: Gregory C. King, Ruben M. Escobedo, Robert A. Profusek, Eugene S. Edwards, Ronald K. Calgaard, Barclays Global Investors, N.A./6.49%, Susan Kaufman Purcell, Michael S. Ciskowski, Irl F. Engelhardt, Donald L. Nickles, Bob Marbut, William R. Klesse, Insiders, Jerry D. Choate, FMR Corp./11.05% *(17 Owners included in Index)*

Financial Data: **Fiscal Year End:**12/31 **Latest Annual Data:** 12/31/2006

Year	Sales	Net Income
2006	$91,833,000,000	$5,463,000,000
2005	$82,162,000,000	$3,590,000,000
2004	$54,618,600,000	$1,803,800,000

Curr. Assets:	$10,760,000,000	**Curr. Liab.:**	$8,822,000,000		
Plant, Equip.:	$21,098,000,000	**Total Liab.:**	$19,148,000,000	**Indic. Yr. Divd.:**	$0.480
Total Assets:	$37,753,000,000	**Net Worth:**	$18,605,000,000	**Debt/ Equity:**	0.2538

Valero LP

2330 N Loop, 1604 W, Sanantonio, TX, 78248; ***PH:*** 1-210-918-2000; ***http://*** www.valerolp.com

General -		**Stock**-	
Incorporation	DE	Price on:12/24/2007	NA
Employees	NA	Stock Exchange	NYSE
Auditor	KPMG LLP	Ticker Symbol	NA
Stk Agt	NA	Outstanding Shares	NA
Counsel	NA	E.P.S.	$2.98
DUNS No.	NA	Shareholders	NA

Business: The groups principle activities include owning, acquiring and developing natural gas and liquefied petroleum pipeline. The group operates through four segments namely, refined product terminals, refined products pipelines, crude oil pipelines and crude oil storage tanks. In the year 2006, the group acquired Kaneb Pipe Line Operating Partnership, L.P. The group operates from the United States.

Primary SIC and add'l.: 5411

CIK No: 0001110805

Subsidiaries: Bicen Development Corporation N.V., Diamond K Limited, Kaneb Investment, LLC, Kaneb LLC, Kaneb Management Company LLC, Kaneb Management, LLC, Kaneb Pipe Line Company LLC, Kaneb Pipe Line Holding Company, LLC, Kaneb Pipe Line Operating Partnership, L.P., Kaneb Pipe Line Partners, L.P., Kaneb Services LLC, Kaneb Terminals (Eastham) Limited, Kaneb Terminals B.V., Kaneb Terminals Limited, Kaneb, Inc. 46 Subsidiaries included in the Index

Officers: Curt Anastasio/Dir., CEO, Pres., Steven Blank/Sr. VP, CFO, Treasurer, James R. Bluntzer/Sr. VP - Operations, Brad Barron/Sr. VP, General Counsel, Sec., Mary F. Morgan/Sr. VP - Marketing, Business Development, Tom Shoaf/VP, Controller, Sandra Lloyd/Mgr. - Jacksonville, FL, Eddie Nobles/Mgr. - Macon, GA, Jon Stubbs/Mgr. - Montgomery, AL, David Tidmore/Mgr. - Moundville, AL, Greg Schmidt/Dir. - Pipelines, Central East, Central West Regions, Chuck Sivil/Mgr. - Selby, Crockett, Frank Padilla/Mgr. - Sparks, Mike Peterson/General Mgr. - Stockton, Chawn Mendoza/Area Mgr. - Stockton *(59 Officers included in Index)*

Directors: Curt Anastasio/Dir., CEO, Pres., William E. Greehey/71/Chmn., Dan Bates/Dir., Dan Hill/Dir., Stan McLelland/Dir., Rod Patton/Dir.

Owners: Insiders/12.42%, Bradley C. Barron, William E. Greehey/12.13%, Stan McLelland, Steven A. Blank, Rodman D. Patton, James R. Bluntzer, Thomas R. Shoaf, Dan J. Bates, Curtis V. Anastasio, Mary F. Morgan, Dan J. Hill

Financial Data: *Fiscal Year End:* 12/31 *Latest Annual Data:* 12/31/2006

Year	Sales	Net Income
2006	$1,135,674,000	$149,530,000
2005	$659,557,000	$111,073,000
2004	$220,792,000	$78,418,000

Curr. Assets:	$212,998,000	**Curr. Liab.:**	$156,735,000		
Plant, Equip.:	$2,345,135,000	**Total Liab.:**	$1,607,185,000	**Indic. Yr. Divd.:**	$3.940
Total Assets:	$3,482,866,000	**Net Worth:**	$1,875,681,000	**Debt/ Equity:**	NA

Valhi Inc

5430 Lbj Frwy, Ste 1700, Dallas, TX, 75240; *PH:* 1-972-233-1700; *http://* www.valhi.net

General - Incorporation	DE	Stock - Price on:12/24/2007	$16.6
Employees	6,078	Stock Exchange	NYSE
Auditor	PricewaterhouseCoopers LLP	Ticker Symbol	VHI
Stk Agt	Computershare Investor Services LLC	Outstanding Shares	114,160,000
Counsel	NA	E.P.S.	$0.41
DUNS No.	00-696-7822	Shareholders	NA

Business: The group operates through its subsidiaries whose principle activity is to produce and market titanium dioxide pigment, manufactures security products, precision ball bearing slides, ergonomic computer support systems, marine instruments, hardware and accessories for performance boats. The group also processes, treats, stores, and disposes hazardous, toxic, and certain low-level radioactive wastes. The group is divided into three segments namely Chemicals, Component Products, and Waste Management. The group operates from North America, Europe and Asia.

Primary SIC and add'l.: 4953 6719 3562 2816

CIK No: 0000059255

Subsidiaries: Titanium Metals Corporation

Officers: Steven L. Watson/Dir., CEO, Pres./$2,332,089.00, Mark J. Hollingsworth/VP, General Counsel, Assist. Sec., Andrew A. Louis/Sec., Assoc. General Counsel, Kelly D. Luttmer/VP, Tax Dir., Robert D. Graham/VP, Assist. Sec., Eugene K. Anderson/VP, Assist. Treasurer, John A. St. Wrba/VP, Treasurer, Gregory M. Swalwell/VP, Controller/$942,300.00, William J. Lindquist/Sr. VP/$1,683,500.00, Bobby D. O'Brien/CFO, VP/$1,623,300.00

Directors: Steven L. Watson/Dir., CEO, Pres., Harold C. Simmons/Chmn., Glenn R. Simmons/Vice Chmn., Hayden W. McIlroy/Dir., Walter J. Tucker/Dir., Thomas E. Barry/Dir., Norman S. Edelcup/Dir.

Owners: Walter J. Tucker, Harold C. Simmons, William J. Lindquist, Insiders/93.80%, Hayden W. McIlroy, Glenn R. Simmons, Norman S. Edelcup, Harold Simmons Foundation, Inc., Valhi Holding Company/92.10%, Contran Corporation, Bobby D. OBrien, The Combined Master Retirement Trust, Steven L. Watson, The Annette Simmons Grandchildrens Trust, Gregory M. Swalwell *(17 Owners included in Index)*

Financial Data: *Fiscal Year End:* 12/31 *Latest Annual Data:* 12/31/2006

Year	Sales	Net Income
2006	$1,676,242,000	$141,682,000
2005	$1,529,307,000	$81,451,000
2004	$1,364,372,000	$227,933,000

Curr. Assets:	$779,357,000	**Curr. Liab.:**	$253,262,000	**P/E Ratio:**	13.50
Plant, Equip.:	$611,321,000	**Total Liab.:**	$1,937,947,000	**Indic. Yr. Divd.:**	$0.400
Total Assets:	$2,804,726,000	**Net Worth:**	$866,779,000	**Debt/ Equity:**	NA

Validian Corp

30 Metcalfe St., Ste. 600, Ottawa, ON, K1P 5L4; *PH:* 1-613-230-7211; *Fax:* 1-613-230-6055; *http://* www.validian.com; *Email:* sales@validian.com

General - Incorporation	NV	Stock - Price on:12/24/2007	NA
Employees	NA	Stock Exchange	OTC
Auditor	KPMG LLP	Ticker Symbol	VLDI
Stk Agt	Interwest Transfer Company, Inc.	Outstanding Shares	NA
Counsel	NA	E.P.S.	NA
DUNS No.	NA	Shareholders	NA

Business: The group's principal activities are to design, develop and market software products. The products allow customers to develop portable applications that run on different platforms. The applications also facilitate safe and reliable Internet communications. The technology enables corporations, institutions and individuals to develop interactive, distributed applications like electronic commerce networks, with security and ease. The customers include telecommunication, banks, Internet service providers, government agencies, distributors, hotel chains and international retailers.

Primary SIC and add'l.: 7374 7372 7373

CIK No: 0001100644

Subsidiaries: Evolusys S.A., Sochrys Technologies Inc

Officers: Bruce Benn/Chmn., CEO, Pres./$105,847.00, Ron Benn/CFO/$105,847.00, Henrik Olsen/CTO, Steve Brown/VP - Sales

Directors: Bruce Benn/Chmn., CEO, Pres.

Owners: Insiders/9.60%, Bruce Benn/7.70%, Ronald Benn/2.10%, Valdosta Corp./7.40%, Waycross Corp./10.40%, Robert B. Prag/5.60%, Leonid Frenkel/8.30%

Valley Bancorp

1300 S Jones Blvd., Las Vegas, NV, 89146; *PH:* 1-702-821-4100; *http://* www.vbnv.com

General - Incorporation	NV	Stock - Price on:12/24/2007	NA
Employees	NA	Stock Exchange	NA
Auditor	McGladrey & Pullen LLP	Ticker Symbol	NA
Stk Agt	U.S. Stock Transfer Corp	Outstanding Shares	NA
Counsel	NA	E.P.S.	NA
DUNS No.	NA	Shareholders	NA

Business: The groups principle activity is to provide banking and other financial services. The group provides banking services and products including personal checking and savings accounts, electronic banking, and other consumer banking products. The group operates from United States.

Primary SIC and add'l.: NA

CIK No: 0001295334

Subsidiaries: Valley Bank

Valley Bank

36 Church Ave. SW, Roanoke, VA, 24011; *PH:* 1-540-342-2265; *Fax:* 1-540-342-4514; *http://* www.myvalleybank.com

General - Incorporation	VA	Stock - Price on:12/24/2007	$10.99
Employees	115	Stock Exchange	NDQ
Auditor	Elliot Davis LLC	Ticker Symbol	NA
Stk Agt	Registrar & Transfer Co	Outstanding Shares	4,170,000
Counsel	Flipin Densmore Morse Rutherford	E.P.S.	$0.51
DUNS No.	83-621-5921	Shareholders	NA

Business: The group's principal activities are to provide commercial banking services to individuals, professional concerns and small-to-medium sized businesses. The deposit products of the group include checking accounts, now accounts, saving accounts and other time deposits. The lending activities of the group include commercial loans, real estate loans and consumer loans. The other services include safe deposit boxes, cash management services including overnight repurchase agreements, merchant purchase and management programs, traveler's checks and direct deposit of payroll. The operations of the group are conducted through its main office and five branch offices located in roanoke and one branch office in salem.

Primary SIC and add'l.: 6712 6022

CIK No: 0000921590

Subsidiaries: Valley Financial (VA) Statutory Trust I, Valley Financial (VA) Statutory Trust II, Valley Financial Corporation., Valley Wealth Management Services, Inc., VB Investments, LLC

Officers: Ellis L. Gutshal/Dir., CEO, Pres., John W. Starr/Dir. - Cardiologist, Joann M. Lloyd/CIO, Sr. VP, Connie W. Stanley/Sr. VP, Chief Retail Banking Officer, Penny Goodwin/Sr. VP, Chief Strategic Planning Officer, Kimberly B. Snyder/Sr. VP, CFO, John T. McCaleb/Chief Lending Officer, Sr. VP, Betty Mitchell/Branch Mgr. - Downtown Office, Lisa W. Hamm/Assist. VP, Mgr. - Investment Associate, Devi S. Kapinos/Assist. VP, Mgr. - Lewis, Gale Office, Barbara B. Lemon/Dir., Civic Leader, Anna L. Lawson/Anthropologist, Dir., Mary P. Hundley/Sr. VP, Chief Risk Officer, Kathleen Warren/Assist. VP, Branch Mgr. - South Roanoke Office, Dianne E. Wright/VP, Mgr. - Investment Associate, Salem Office *(24 Officers included in Index)*

Directors: Ellis L. Gutshal/Dir., CEO, Pres., George W. Logan/Chmn., Anna L. Lawson/Anthropologist, Dir., Wayne A. Lewis/Dir., William D. Elliot/Dir., Mason Haynesworth/Dir., Edward B. Walker/Dir., Michael E. Warner/Dir., Geoffrey M. Ottaway/Dir., John W. Starr/Dir. - Cardiologist, Maury L. Strauss/Dir., Ward W. Stevens/Dir., Barbara B. Lemon/Dir., Civic Leader, Eddie F. Hearp/Dir., James S. Frantz/Dir. *(17 Directors included in Index)*

Owners: Nicholas F. Taubman/9.79%, The Banc Funds Company, LLC/5.98%, George W. Logan/9.70%

Financial Data: *Fiscal Year End:* 12/31 *Latest Annual Data:* 12/31/2006

Year	Sales	Net Income
2006	$37,132,000	$2,882,000
2005	$26,182,000	$3,392,000
2004	$19,216,000	$2,824,000

Curr. Assets:	$29,453,000	**Curr. Liab.:**	$491,257,000	**P/E Ratio:**	18.32
Plant, Equip.:	$6,873,000	**Total Liab.:**	$558,535,000	**Indic. Yr. Divd.:**	$0.140
Total Assets:	$591,936,000	**Net Worth:**	$33,401,000	**Debt/ Equity:**	1.8991

Valley Commerce Bancorp CA

200 S Ct. St. , Visalia, CA, 93291; *PH:* 1-559-622-9000; *http://* www.bankofvisalia.com

General - Incorporation	CA	Stock - Price on:12/24/2007	$21
Employees	75	Stock Exchange	OTC
Auditor	Perry-Smith LLP	Ticker Symbol	VCBP
Stk Agt	Registrar & Transfer Co	Outstanding Shares	2,330,000
Counsel	NA	E.P.S.	$1.16
DUNS No.	NA	Shareholders	NA

Business: The group operates through its subsidiaries whose principal activities include providing banking and financial services to the customers. Services of the group include deposit customers, and fees from the brokerage of loans. The group operates from the United States. In the year 2006, the groups total assets were $263,664,693.

Primary SIC and add'l.: 6022

CIK No: 0001302244

Subsidiaries: Bank of Visalia, Valley Commerce Trust I

Officers: Donald A. Gilles/Dir., CEO, Pres., Micheal Rivera/AVP, Marketing Dir., Richard Smith/AVP, Technology Dir., Nathan Halls/VP, Credit Specialist, Fred P. Lobue/Dir., Sec., Allan W. Stone/Exec. VP, Chief Credit Officer, Roy O. Estridge/CFO, Exec. VP, Micheal A. Stanley/Sr. VP, Operation Administrator, Karen A. Dressel/Sr. VP - Credit Administration, Leroy E. Trippel/VP, Business Banking Officer, Sharon Andrews/AVP, Operation Administrator, Kirsten Holmes/AVP, Credit Specialist, Scott Iverson/AVP, Business Banking Officer, Carolyn Cross/VP, Human Resources Administrator, John Bergman/VP, Business Banking Officer *(21 Officers included in Index)*

Directors: Donald A. Gilles/Dir., CEO, Pres., Walter A. Dwelle/Chmn., Russell F. Hurley/Vice Chmn., Fred P. Lobue/Dir., Sec., David B. Day/Dir., Thomas A. Gaebe/Dir., Kenneth H. MacKlin/Dir., Philip R. Hammond/Dir., Barry R. Smith/Dir.

Owners: David B. Day/1.98%, Barry R. Smith, Allan W. Stone, Wellington Management Company, LLP/8.27%, Thomas A. Gaebe/1.03%, Fred P. LoBue/2.91%, The Banc Fund Company, LLC/9.73%, Philip R. Hammond/3.41%, Russell F. Hurley/3.14%, Donald A. Gilles/1.73%, Roy O. Estridge, Walter A. Dwelle/3.74%, Insiders/18.84%, Kenneth H. Macklin/1.47%

Financial Data: *Fiscal Year End:*12/31   *Latest Annual Data:* 12/31/2006

Year	Sales	Net Income
2006	$17,798,000	$2,956,000
2005	$13,440,000	$2,163,000
2004	$10,078,000	$1,629,000

Curr. Assets:	$16,443,000	**Curr. Liab.:**	$226,576,000	
Plant, Equip.:	$1,832,000	**Total Liab.:**	$238,217,000	**Indic. Yr. Divd.:** NA
Total Assets:	$263,665,000	**Net Worth:**	$25,448,000	**Debt/ Equity:** NA

Valley Community Bank CA

465 Main St., Pleasanton, CA, 94566; *PH:* 1-925-484-5400; *Fax:* 1-925-484-9073; http:// www.vcb-ca.com

General - Incorporation		Stock- Price on:12/24/2007	$17.75
Employees	NA	Stock Exchange	OTC
Auditor	NA	Ticker Symbol	VCBC
Stk Agt	U.S. Stock Transfer Corp	Outstanding Shares	1,780,000
Counsel	NA	E.P.S	NA
DUNS No.	NA	Shareholders	NA

Business: The groups principal activities include providing banking and financial services to the businesses and customers. Services of the group include checking accounts, savings accounts, certificates of deposit, installment loans, real estate mortgage loans, commercial loans, traveler's checks, safe deposit boxes, night depository, automated teller services and Internet banking.

Primary SIC and add'l.: 6022

CIK No:

Officers: Richard P. Loupe/Dir., CEO, Pres., Greg J. Hickel/Exec. VP, Chief Credit Officer, Becky Holowich/CFO, Exec. VP, Phillip R. Boyce/Dir. - Private Investor, Howard Hoover/Sr. VP - SBA Lending Officer - Santa Cruz Loan Production Office, Randy Ruddach/Sr. VP, Mgr. - San Ramon Office, Brent Chaney/Sr. VP, Mgr. - Pleasanton Office, Rick Peterson/Sr. VP, Mgr. - Livermore Office, John Angelesco/Sr. VP, Mgr. - San Jose Office, Cindy Chase/Sr. VP, Mgr. - Construction Lending Department, Bob McDoulett/VP, Mgr. - SBA Lending Department

Directors: Richard P. Loupe/Dir., CEO, Pres., Phillip R. Boyce/Dir. - Private Investor, Jerome W. Carlson/Dir., Richard Alexander Lewis/Dir., Peter MacDonald/Dir., Dean L. Schenone/Dir., George L. Shore/Dir., Anelli P. Stamm/Dir., William M. Eames/Dir.

Valley Forge Composite Technologies Inc

Formerly: Quetzal Capital I Inc
50 E River Ctr. Blvd., Ste. 820, Covington, KY, 41011; *PH:* 1-859-581-5111

General - Incorporation	FL	Stock - Price on:12/24/2007	NA
Employees	NA	Stock Exchange	NA
Auditor	Sherb & Co. LLP	Ticker Symbol	NA
Stk Agt	Florida Atlantic Stock Transfer, Inc.	Outstanding Shares	NA
Counsel	NA	E.P.S	NA
DUNS No.	NA	Shareholders	NA

Business: The group's principle activity is to our organization and the preparation of the registration statement on Form 10-SB. They are a "shell" company conducting no business operations, other than putting efforts to seek merger partners or acquisition candidates. The group operates from United States.

Primary SIC and add'l.: 9995

CIK No: 0001332412

Officers: Louis J. Brothers/55/Chmn., CEO, Pres., Larry K. Wilhide/59/VP - Engineering, Dir.

Directors: Louis J. Brothers/55/Chmn., CEO, Pres., Randy Broadright/41/Dir.

Owners: Insiders/76.50%, Louis & Roe Brothers, TEN ENT/38.30%, Coast To Coast Equity Group, Inc./6.10%, Larry & Pat Wilhide, TEN ENT/38.30%, Charles J. Scimeca/3.40%, Tony N. Frudakis/3.40%, George Frudakis/3.40%

Valley Forge Scientific Corp

3845 Corporate Ctr. Dr., O'fallon, MO, 63368; *PH:* 1-636-939-5100; http:// www.vlfg.com

General - Incorporation	DE	Stock - Price on:12/24/2007	$3.69
Employees	346	Stock Exchange	NA
Auditor	McGladrey & Pullen LLP	Ticker Symbol	NA
Stk Agt	American Stock Transfer & Trust Co.	Outstanding Shares	NA
Counsel	Schenkman Jannings & Howard	E.P.S	NA
DUNS No.	02-105-6726	Shareholders	NA

Business: The group's principal activity is designing, manufacturing and selling medical devices. Its core business consists of bipolar electrosurgical generators and related instrumentation based on its proprietary dualwave(tm) technology. The technology uses two waveforms to perform bipolar cutting of tissue and bipolar coagulation. It is designed to replace the systems in other surgical tools such as monopolar systems, lasers and conventional scalpels used in soft tissue surgery. The disposable instruments are used with the bipolar electrosurgical generators for hospital and office procedures in the field of neurosurgery, dentistry and plastic surgery. They are manufactured at the group's facilities in philadelphia and marketed worldwide by codman and shurtleff inc and bident international llc. The group also manufactures titanium surgical mesh for repair of the skull and a natural dental preparation for healing and lessening post surgical discomfort.

Primary SIC and add'l.: 3841

CIK No: 0000836429

Subsidiaries: Synergetics Development Company, LLC, Synergetics IP, Inc., Synergetics, Inc.

Officers: Gregg D. Scheller/Chmn., CEO, Pres., Pamela G. Boone/45/Exec. VP, CFO, Treasurer, Sec., Jerry L. Malis/Dir., Exec. VP, Chief Scientific Officer, Kurt W. Gampp/Dir., Exec. VP, COO

Directors: Gregg D. Scheller/Chmn., CEO, Pres., Guy Guarch/Dir., Juanita H. Hinshaw/63/Dir., Jerry L. Malis/Dir., Exec. VP, Chief Scientific Officer, Robert H. Dick/64/Dir., Kurt W. Gampp/Dir., Exec. VP, COO, Larry C. Cardinale/70/Dir.

Owners: Kurt W. Gampp/3.60%, Lawrence C. Cardinale, Pamela G. Boone, Jerry L. Malis/4.60%, JPMorgan Chase & Co./5.60%, Gregg D. Scheller/3.40%, Robert H. Dick, Juanita H. Hinshaw/1.40%, Guy R. Guarch, Insiders/13.60%

Financial Data: *Fiscal Year End:*07/31   *Latest Annual Data:* 7/31/2006

Year	Sales	Net Income
2006	$38,246,000	$3,081,000
2005	$21,792,000	$1,458,000
2004	$4,756,000	$111,000

Curr. Assets:	$3,977,000	**Curr. Liab.:**	$258,000	
Plant, Equip.:	$148,000	**Total Liab.:**	$274,000	**Indic. Yr. Divd.:** NA
Total Assets:	$4,523,000	**Net Worth:**	$4,249,000	**Debt/ Equity:** 0.0644

Valley High Mining Co

3098 S Highland Dr., Ste. 323, Salt Lake, UT, 84106; *PH:* 1-801-467-2021

General - Incorporation	NV	Stock- Price on:12/24/2007	$0.32
Employees	NA	Stock Exchange	OTC
Auditor	Pritchett Siler & Hardy P.C	Ticker Symbol	VHMC
Stk Agt	Atlas Stock Transfer Corp	Outstanding Shares	NA
Counsel	North Beck Joint Venture LLC	E.P.S	NA
DUNS No.	NA	Shareholders	NA

Business: The group is considered as an exploration stage company. The group, formed in 1979, has not actively engaged in any mining or energy-related activities since the mid-1980's when it exhausted the funds it had raised in a public offering it undertook in 1980.

Primary SIC and add'l.: 1400

CIK No: 0001301838

Owners: John Michael Coombs/94.70%, Insiders/94.70%

Financial Data: *Fiscal Year End:*12/31   *Latest Annual Data:* 12/31/2006

Year	Sales	Net Income
2006	NA	-$14,000

Curr. Assets:	$0	**Curr. Liab.:**	$36,000	
Plant, Equip.:	NA	**Total Liab.:**	$36,000	**Indic. Yr. Divd.:** NA
Total Assets:	$0	**Net Worth:**	-$35,000	**Debt/ Equity:** NA

Valley National Bancorp

1455 Valley Rd. , Wayne, NJ, 07470; *PH:* 1-973-305-3380; http:// www.valleynationalbank.com

General - Incorporation	NJ	Stock- Price on:12/24/2007	$23.49
Employees	2,489	Stock Exchange	NYSE
Auditor	Ernst & Young LLP	Ticker Symbol	VLY
Stk Agt	American Stock Transfer & Trust Co.	Outstanding Shares	120,340,000
Counsel	NA	E.P.S	$1.41
DUNS No.	15-428-2792	Shareholders	NA

Business: The group's principal activity is to provide commercial and retail banking services through 129 branch offices in northern New Jersey and manhattan. The services include acceptance of demand, savings and time deposits and extension of consumer, real estate, small business administration and other commercial credits. It also offers personal and corporate trust services, as well as pension and fiduciary services. The group operates through four segments: consumer lending, commercial lending, investment portfolio and corporate and other adjustments. The group operates through valley national bank and vnb capital trust i subsidiaries. On 01-Jan-2003, the group acquired glen rauch securities, inc.

Primary SIC and add'l.: 6021 6712

CIK No: 0000714310

Subsidiaries: 18th & 8th LLC, BNV Realty Incorporated (BNV), Glen Rauch Securities, Inc, Hallmark Capital Management, Inc., Masters Coverage Corp, Merchants New York Commercial Corp., New Century Asset Management, Inc., Shrewsbury State Investment Co., Inc., Valley 747 Acquisition, LLC, Valley Commercial Capital, LLC, Valley National Title Services, Inc., VN Investments, Inc. (VNI), VNB Loan Services, LLC, VNB Mortgage Loans, Inc., VNB Mortgage Services, Inc. 16 Subsidiaries included in the Index

Officers: Gerald H. Lipkin/Chmn., CEO, Pres./$5,382,055.00, Steve Erikson/CEO, Pres. - Hallmark Capital Management's, Jeffrey P. Braff/VP, Dir. - Equity and Fixed Income Trading, Mgr.- Portfolio, Peter S. Hagerman/Pres., Thomas S. Moore/Exec. VP, Chief Investment Officer, Albert L. Engel/Exec. VP, Robert M. Meyer/Exec. VP/$951,945.00, Alan D. Eskow/CFO, Exec. VP/$1,033,851.00, Peter Crocitto/Exec. VP/$996,611.00, Mitchell L. Crandell/VP, Controller, Principal Accounting Officer, James G. Lawrence/Exec. VP/$769,522.00, Robert J. Mulligan/Pres. - Wealth Management, Insurance Services

Directors: Gerald H. Lipkin/Chmn., CEO, Pres., Robert E. McEntee/Dir., Eric P. Edelstein/Dir., Richard S. Miller/Dir., Jack Kay/Dir. Emeritus, Graham O. Jones/Dir., Barnett Rukin/Dir., Pamela R. Bronander/Dir., Mary J. Steele Guilfoile/Dir., Gerald Korde/Dir., Robinson Markel/Dir., Andrew B. Abramson/Dir., Spencer B. Witty/Dir. Emeritus, Michael L. Larusso/Dir., Dale H. Hemmerdinger/Dir. *(16 Directors included in Index)*

Owners: Dale H. Hemmerdinger/0.06%, James G. Lawrence/0.36%, Michael L. LaRusso/0.01%, Graham O. Jones/0.79%, Insiders/6.88%, Gerald H. Lipkin/0.46%, Mary J. Steele Guilfoile/0.26%, Robert M. Meyer/0.25%, Barnett Rukin/0.05%, Andrew B. Abramson/0.18%, Peter Crocitto/0.23%, Alan D. Eskow/0.14%, Walter H. Jones/1.02%, Eric P. Edelstein/0.01%, Gerald Korde/1.46% *(19 Owners included in Index)*

Financial Data: *Fiscal Year End:*12/31   *Latest Annual Data:* 12/31/2006

Year	Sales	Net Income
2006	$784,899,000	$163,691,000
2005	$699,253,000	$163,449,000
2004	$603,254,000	$154,398,000

Curr. Assets:	$496,958,000	**Curr. Liab.:**	$8,960,501,000	**P/E Ratio:** 16.66
Plant, Equip.:	$209,397,000	**Total Liab.:**	$11,445,437,000	**Indic. Yr. Divd.:** $0.840
Total Assets:	$12,395,027,000	**Net Worth:**	$949,590,000	**Debt/ Equity:** 2.6730

Valley National Gases Inc

200 W Beau St., Ste. 200, Washington, PA, 15301; *PH:* 1-517-545-8500; http:// www.vngas.com

General - Incorporation ....PA
Employees...748
Auditor ....PricewaterhouseCoopers LLP
Stk Agt..... American Stock Transfer & Trust Co.
Counsel....................Dorsey & Whitney LLP
DUNS No. 05-219-3125

Stock- Price on:12/24/2007 ....$26.87
Stock Exchange...NA
Ticker Symbol...NA
Outstanding Shares ....NA
E.P.S...NA
Shareholders...NA

Business: The group's principal activity is to pack and distribute cylinder and bulk industrial, medical and specialty gases. The group also provides welding equipment and supplies (including welding machines, wire, fluxes and electrodes and a variety of supporting equipment), propane and fire protection equipment. Gases packaged and distributed by the group include oxygen, nitrogen, hydrogen, argon, helium, acetylene, carbon dioxide, nitrous oxide, specialty gases and propane. The group distributes its products through 71 distribution and retail locations. The group acquired buckeye corporation, mansfield oxygen corp and gas arc, inc in fiscal 2002 and gerber's propane, inc in fiscal 2003.

Primary SIC and add'l.: 7359 4923 5084

CIK No: 0001030715

Owners: William A. Indelicato/1.45%, August E. Maier, Ben Exley, Entities affiliated with Bislett Partners L.P./5.83%, Walter F. Riebenack, Gerald W. Zehala, Gary E. West/72.44%, T. Rowe Price Associates, Inc./8.92%, James P. Hart, Insiders/74.50%

Valmont Industries Inc

PO Box 358, Hwy. 275, Valley, NE, 68064; **PH:** 1-402-963-1000; **http://** www.valmont.com; **Email:** investor_relations@valmont.com

General - Incorporation ....DE
Employees...5,684
Auditor ....Deloitte & Touche LLP
Stk Agt.............................Bank of New York
Counsel..............McGrath North Mullin & Kratz
DUNS No. 00-726-7214

Stock- Price on:12/24/2007 ....$72.4
Stock Exchange...NYSE
Ticker Symbol...VMI
Outstanding Shares 25,730,000
E.P.S...$3.36
Shareholders...NA

Business: The group's principal activities are carried out through four segments: engineered support structures, coatings, irrigation & tubing. Engineered support structures consists of the manufacture of engineered metal structures and components for the lighting and traffic, utility, and wireless communication industries, and for other specialty applications. Coatings segment consists of galvanizing, anodizing and powder coating services. Irrigation segment consists of the manufacture of agricultural irrigation equipment and related parts and services. Tubing segment consists of the manufacture of tubular products for industrial customers. The group acquired newmark international inc on 16-Apr-2004.

Primary SIC and add'l.: 3312 3523 3699 3479 3441

CIK No: 0000102729

Subsidiaries: Best-All Electric, Inc., Cascade Earth Sciences, Ltd., Dreamwise Props 32 (Proprietary) Limited, George Industries, Inc., Golden State Irrigation, Inc., Irri Management Argentina S.A., Lampadaires Feralux, Inc., Masstock Ltd., NeuValco GmbH, Newmark International, Inc., PiRod, Inc., Sermeto Equipement Industriel S.A.S., Societe Morocaine des Pivots Oirrigation Valmont, Teeter Irrigation, Inc., Valley Irrigation South Africa,(PTY) Ltd. 44 Subsidiaries included in the Index

Officers: Mogens C. Bay/Chmn., CEO/$5,630,744.00, Terry J. McClain/Sr. VP, CFO/$1,884,472.00, Robert E. Meaney/Sr. VP, Corp. Sec./$1,361,400.00, Mark C. Jaksich/VP, Controller/$717,129.00, Mark E. Treinen/VP - Corporate Development, Treasurer/$694,322.00, Jeff Laudin/Investor Relation Officer, Randy Fullen/Contact - Steel Sales, Valmont, Newmark, Gary Byrd/Contact - Concrete Sales, Valmont, Newmark, Rick Sampson/Contact - Sales, Valmont, Newmark, Randy Wagner/Contact - Sales, Valmont, Newmark, Roger McCleary/Contact - Sales, Valmont, Newmark, Thomas J. Sutko/VP, GM - North American Lighting, Transportation, Engineered Support Structures Division, Richard S. Cornish/VP - Operations - Coatings Division, Earl Foust/Pres. - Utility Support Structures Division, VP - Steel Business Units - Utility Support Structures Division, Douglas C. Sherman/VP - Marketing Development - Utility Support Structures Division *(34 Officers included in Index)*

Directors: Mogens C. Bay/Chmn., CEO, John E. Jones/Dir., Kaj Den Daas/Dir., Robert B. Daugherty/Dir., Thomas F. Madison/Dir., Stephen R. Lewis/Dir., Walter Scott/Dir., Glen Barton/Dir., Charles D. Peebler/Dir., Kenneth E. Stinson/Dir., Daniel P. Neary/Dir.

Owners: Glen A. Barton, John E. Jones, FMR Corporation/7.20%, Daniel P. Neary, Terry J. McClain, Stephen R. Lewis, Robert E. Meaney, Thomas F. Madison, Insiders/6.70%, Mark E. Treinen, Mogens C. Bay/2.70%, Robert B. Daugherty/27.70%, Kaj den Daas, Mark C. Jaksich, Charles D. Peebler *(17 Owners included in Index)*

Financial Data: Fiscal Year End:12/31   Latest Annual Data: 12/30/2006

Year	Sales		Net Income
2006	$1,281,281,000		$61,544,000
2005	$1,108,100,000		$39,079,000
2004	$1,031,475,000		$26,881,000
Curr. Assets:	$408,312,000	**Curr. Liab.:** $179,151,000	**P/E Ratio:** 24.54
Plant, Equip.:	$194,676,000	**Total Liab.:** $473,367,000	**Indic. Yr. Divd.:** $0.420
Total Assets:	$802,042,000	**Net Worth:** $328,675,000	**Debt/ Equity:** 0.4693

Valpey Fisher Corp

75 S St., Hopkinton, MA, 01748; **PH:** 1-508-435-6831; **http://** www.valpeyfisher.com; **Email:** techsupport@valpeyfisher.com

General - Incorporation ....MD
Employees...53
Auditor ....Grant Thornton LLP
Stk Agt...................Computershare Trust Co
Counsel...NA
DUNS No. 05-374-7267

Stock- Price on:12/24/2007 ....$5.85
Stock Exchange..AMEX
Ticker Symbol...VPF
Outstanding Shares 4,270,000
E.P.S...$0.28
Shareholders...NA

Business: The group's principal activities are to design, produce, import and sell quartz crystals, oscillators, frequency control and ultrasonic transducer devices. The operations are conducted through its subsidiary valpey-fisher corporation. These frequency control include quartz crystals and oscillators which are used as integral components in electronic circuitry to assure precise timing and frequency reference and are used in the field of telecommunication, computer and computer peripheral equipment. The ultrasonic transducer devices are sold to the ndt (nondestructive testing), industrial, research and medical markets. Applications include flaw detection, precision thickness gauging, corrosion inspection, weld inspection and various research applications. In, 2003 the company acquired certain assets of mf electronics corporation

Primary SIC and add'l.: 3826

CIK No: 0000085608

Subsidiaries: Matec International, Inc.

Officers: Michael J. Ferrantino/Dir., CEO, Pres./$559,381.00, Valpey Fisher/Investor Relations Officer

Directors: Michael J. Ferrantino/Dir., CEO, Pres., Ted Valpey/Chmn., Eli Fleisher/Dir., Mario Alosco/Dir., Lawrence Holsborg/Dir., John J. McArdle/Dir., Richard W. Anderson/Dir.

Owners: Ted Valpey/24.50%, Robert W. Valpey/6.80%, Mario Alosco, Mary R. Vaccari/7.30%, Michael J. Kroll/1.70%, Walt Oliwa, Insiders/49.60%, Michael J. Ferrantino/6.60%, Lawrence Holsborg/3.80%, Michael J. Ferrantino, John J. McArdle/8.00%, Richard W. Anderson/3.10%, Eli Fleisher/3.60%

Financial Data: Fiscal Year End:12/31   Latest Annual Data: 12/31/2006

Year	Sales		Net Income
2006	$11,782,000		$669,000
2005	$11,427,000		$245,000
2004	$11,545,000		-$165,000
Curr. Assets:	$12,475,000	**Curr. Liab.:** $2,323,000	**P/E Ratio:** 20.89
Plant, Equip.:	$1,893,000	**Total Liab.:** $2,666,000	**Indic. Yr. Divd.:** NA
Total Assets:	$14,529,000	**Net Worth:** $11,863,000	**Debt/ Equity:** NA

Valspar Corp

1101 3rd St. S, Minneapolis, MN, 55415; **PH:** 1-612-332-7371; **Fax:** 1-612-375-7723; **http://** www.valspar.com; **Email:** info@epscca.com

General - Incorporation ....DE
Employees...9,556
Auditor ....Ernst & Young LLP
Stk Agt ....Mellon Investor Services LLC
Counsel...NA
DUNS No. 05-073-6453

Stock- Price on:12/24/2007 ....$28.58
Stock Exchange...NYSE
Ticker Symbol...VAL
Outstanding Shares 100,270,000
E.P.S...NA
Shareholders...NA

Business: The groups principle activities include manufacturing and distributing coatings and paints. The groups products include specialty polymers, colorants and gelcoats. The group also sells furniture protection plans. In the year 2007 the group acquired Teknos Nova Coil TNC Oy. The group operates from United States.

Primary SIC and add'l.: 2851 3479

CIK No: 0000102741

Subsidiaries: Dongguan Lilly Paint Industries Limited, Engineered Polymer Solutions, Inc., Lilly Industries (Shanghai) Limited, Plasti-Kote Co., Inc., Samuel Cabot Incorporated, The Valspar (Australia) Corporation Pty Limited, The Valspar (France) Corporation, S.A.S., The Valspar (Germany) GmbH, The Valspar (H.K.) Corporation Limited, The Valspar (Malaysia) Corporation Sdn Bhd, The Valspar (Nantes) Corporation, S.A.S., The Valspar (Singapore) Corporation Pte Ltd, The Valspar (South Africa) Corporation (Pty) Ltd., The Valspar (UK) Corporation, Limited, The Valspar (Vernicolor) Corporation AG 24 Subsidiaries included in the Index

Officers: William L. Mansfield/Chmn., CEO, Pres., Donald A. Nolan/Sr. VP, Rolf Engh/Exec. VP, Sec., Steven L. Erdahl/Exec. VP, Gary E. Hendrickson/Sr. VP, Paul C. Reyelts/CFO, Exec. VP, Anthony L. Blaine/Sr. VP - Human Resources, Lori A. Walker/VP, Treasurer, Controller

Directors: William L. Mansfield/Chmn., CEO, Pres., John S. Bode/Dir., Susan S. Boren/Dir., Richard L. White/Dir., Charles W. Gaillard/Dir., Jeffrey H. Curler/Dir., Mae C. Jemison/Dir., Thomas R. McBurney/Dir., Peter McCausland/57/Dir., Gregory R. Palen/Dir., Lawrence Perlman/Dir., Janel S. Haugarth/Dir., Stephen D. Newlin/Dir.

Owners: Lawrence Perlman, William L. Mansfield, Charles W. Gaillard, Gregory R. Palen, Mae C. Jemison, Steven L. Erdahl, John S. Bode, Gary E. Hendrickson, Rolf Engh, Susan S. Boren, Thomas R. McBurney, Richard L. White, Jeffrey H. Curler, Insiders, Peter McCausland *(17 Owners included in Index)*

Financial Data: Fiscal Year End:10/28   Latest Annual Data: 10/27/2006

Year	Sales		Net Income
2006	$2,978,062,000		$175,252,000
2005	$2,713,950,000		$147,618,000
2004	$2,440,692,000		$142,836,000
Curr. Assets:	$802,315,000	**Curr. Liab.:** $718,211,000	
Plant, Equip.:	$428,431,000	**Total Liab.:** $1,633,895,000	**Indic. Yr. Divd.:** $0.520
Total Assets:	$2,634,258,000	**Net Worth:** $1,000,363,000	**Debt/ Equity:** 0.4969

Value Line

220 E 42nd St., New York, NY, 10017; **PH:** 1-212-907-1500; **Fax:** 1-212-818-9747; **http://** www.valueline.com; **Email:** vlcr@valueline.com

General - Incorporation ....NY
Employees...228
Auditor ....Horowitz & Ullmann P.C
Stk Agt ....Mellon Investor Services LLC
Counsel...NA
DUNS No. 10-114-6900

Stock- Price on:12/24/2007 ....$44.01
Stock Exchange..NDQ
Ticker Symbol...VALU
Outstanding Shares 9,980,000
E.P.S...$2.477
Shareholders...NA

Business: The group's principal activities are producing investment related periodical publications and provide investment advisory services. The group's operations are carried out through two business segments: publishing and investment management services. Publishing segment of the group produces periodicals in both print and electronic form. The publications of the group include the Value Line Investment Survey, the Value Line 600, Value Line Select, the Value Line Mutual Fund Survey, the Value Line No-load Fund Advisor, the Value Line Insight, the Value Line Special Situations Service, the Value Line Options Survey and the Value Line Convertibles Survey. Investment management services segment of the group provides advisory services to mutual funds, institutions and individual clients. The group also provides current and historical financial databases in standard computer formats.

Primary SIC and add'l.: 6282 2721 2741

CIK No: 0000717720

Subsidiaries: Compupower Corporation, The Vanderbilt Advertising Agency, Inc., Value Line Distribution Center, Inc, Value Line Publishing, Inc., Value Line Securities, Inc.

Officers: Jean Bernhard Buttner/Chmn., CEO, Pres., Samuel Eisenstadt/Chmn. - Research, David T. Henigson/Dir., VP/$404,513.00, Howard A. Brecher/Dir., VP, Sec., Mitchell E. Appel/CFO, Steven R. Anastasio/Treasurer

Directors: Jean Bernhard Buttner/Chmn., CEO, Pres., David T. Henigson/Dir., VP, Howard A. Brecher/Dir., VP, Sec., Herbert Pardes/Dir., Edward J. Shanahan/Dir., Edgar A. Buttner/Dir., Marion Ruth/Dir., Janet Eakman/48/Dir.

Owners: Mitchell E. Appel, David T. Henigson, Marion Ruth, Jean Bernhard Buttner, Edward J. Shanahan, Arnold Bernhard & Co., Inc./86.50%, Stephen R. Anastasio, Insiders, Howard A. Brecher, Herbert Pardes, Janet Eakman, Edgar A. Buttner

Financial Data: *Fiscal Year End:*04/30   *Latest Annual Data:* 04/30/2007

Year	Sales	Net Income
2007	$83,635,000	$24,607,000
2006	$85,186,000	$23,439,000
2005	$84,478,000	$21,318,000

Curr. Assets:	$111,219,000	*Curr. Liab.:*	$47,396,000	*P/E Ratio:*	17.82
Plant, Equip.:	$5,406,000	*Total Liab.:*	$57,279,000	*Indic. Yr. Divd.:*	$1.200
Total Assets:	$119,214,000	*Net Worth:*	$61,935,000	*Debt/ Equity:*	NA

ValueClick Inc

30699 Russell Ranch Rd., Ste. 250, Westlake Village, CA, 91362; *PH:* 1-805-684-6060; *http://* www.valueclick.com

General - Incorporation	DE	Stock- Price on:12/24/2007	$28.83
Employees	1,072	Stock Exchange	NDQ
Auditor	PricewaterhouseCoopers LLP	Ticker Symbol	VCLK
Stk Agt	Mellon Investor Services LLC	Outstanding Shares	99,820,000
Counsel	Brobeck, Phleger & Harrison	E.P.S.	$0.74
DUNS No.	NA	Shareholders	NA

Business: The group's principal activities are to provide products and services that enable marketers to advertise and sell their products. The group provides software that assists advertising agencies with information management regarding their financial, workflow and offline media buying and planning processes. The customers of the group are advertisers and direct marketers, as well as the agencies that service these groups. The group operates in three segments: media segment provides a comprehensive suite of online media services and tailored programs; affiliate marketing segment offers technology and services that enable advertisers to manage, track and analyze a variety of online marketing programs; technology segment offers technology infrastructure tools and services. On 30-May-2003, the group acquired search 123, on 07-Dec-2003, commission junction, inc, 18-Dec-2003, hi-speed media inc and on 03-Aug-2004 pricerunner ab.

Primary SIC and add'l.: 7319 7379

CIK No: 0001080034

Subsidiaries: Be Free France, Be Free Germany GmbH, Be Free UK, Ltd., Be Free,Inc., ClickAgents,Inc., Commission Junction UK Ltd., Commission Junction,Inc., E-Babylon, Inc., Fastclick, Inc., Hi-Speed Media, Inc., Mediaplex Systems,Inc., Mediaplex,Inc., Pricerunner AB, Pricerunner Ltd., Pricerunner SAS 23 Subsidiaries included in the Index

Officers: Tom A. Vadnais/Dir., CEO/$731,619.00, Scott P. Barlow/VP, General Counsel, Samuel J. Paisley/Chief Administrative Officer/$840,522.00, Peter J. Wolfert/CTO, David A. Yovanno/GM - Display Advertising, John Ardis/VP - Corporate Strategy, Carl J. White/COO - Europe/$571,607.00, Joshua R. Gray/Exec. VP - Strategic Development, Scott G. Piotroski/GM - Lead Generation, John P. Pitstick/CFO

Directors: Tom A. Vadnais/Dir., CEO, James R. Zarley/Chmn., Jeffrey F. Rayport/Dir., David S. Buzby/Dir., Martin T. Hart/Dir., Farshad Fardad/Dir., James A. Crouthamel/Dir., James R. Peters/Dir.

Owners: Samuel J. Paisley, Carl White, Jeffrey F. Rayport, Insiders/1.10%, Fidelity Management & Research Company/11.90%, Scott H. Ray, James R. Zarley, Tom A. Vadnais, Martin T. Hart

Financial Data: *Fiscal Year End:*12/31   *Latest Annual Data:* 12/31/2006

Year	Sales	Net Income
2006	$545,616,000	$62,574,000
2005	$304,007,000	$40,644,000
2004	$169,178,000	$87,887,000

Curr. Assets:	$402,990,000	*Curr. Liab.:*	$87,414,000	*P/E Ratio:*	38.96
Plant, Equip.:	$18,995,000	*Total Liab.:*	$149,557,000	*Indic. Yr. Divd.:*	NA
Total Assets:	$793,266,000	*Net Worth:*	$643,709,000	*Debt/ Equity:*	0.0800

ValueVision Media Inc

6740 Shady Oak Rd. , Eden Prairie, MN, 55344; *PH:* 1-612-947-5200; *http://* www.shopnbc.com

General - Incorporation	MN	Stock- Price on:12/24/2007	$11.3
Employees	984	Stock Exchange	NDQ
Auditor	Deloitte & Touche LLP	Ticker Symbol	VVTV
Stk Agt	Wells Fargo Shareowner Services	Outstanding Shares	37,640,000
Counsel	NA	E.P.S.	-$0.07
DUNS No.	62-114-2579	Shareholders	NA

Business: The group's principle activity is to provide television home shopping, Internet e-commerce, vendor programming sales and fulfillment services and outsourced e-commerce and fulfillment solutions through electronic media. The group's primary electronic media activity is its television home shopping network program. It uses recognized on-air television home shopping personalities to market brand name and proprietary/private label consumer products at competitive prices. The group's television programming is produced at the group's eden prairie, Minnesota facility and is transmitted nationally via satellite to cable system operators, satellite dish owners and low power broadcast television stations.

Primary SIC and add'l.: 5961

CIK No: 0000870826

Subsidiaries: Enhanced Broadcasting Technologies, Inc., FanBuzz Retail, Inc., FanBuzz, Inc., Iosota, Inc., Packer Capital, Inc., ValueVision Direct Marketing Company, Inc., ValueVision Interactive, Inc., ValueVision Media Acquisitions, Inc., ValueVision Retail, Inc., VVI Fulfillment Center, Inc., Vvi Lptv, Inc.

Officers: William Lansing/Dir., CEO, Pres./$2,176,483.00, Frank Elsenbast/Sr. VP, CFO/$429,761.00, Brenda Boehler/Exec. VP - TV, Internet Sales/$898,670.00, Nathan Fagre/Sr. VP, General Counsel/$445,296.00

Directors: William Lansing/Dir., CEO, Pres., Marshall S. Geller/Chmn., George Vandeman/Dir., Douglas Holloway/Dir., Robert J. Korkowski/Dir., John Buck/Dir., Jay Ireland/Dir., Jim Barnett/Dir., Ron Herman/Dir.

Owners: GE Capital Equity Investments, Inc., NBC Universal, Inc., William J. Lansing, Robert J. Korkowski, Janus Capital Management LLC, Capital Research and Management Company, Ronald J. Herman, Jay Ireland, Insiders, Insiders, Bryan Venberg, GE Capital Equity Investments, Inc., Fine Capital Partners, L.P., Douglas V. Holloway, James J. Barnett *(27 Owners included in Index)*

Financial Data: *Fiscal Year End:*02/04   *Latest Annual Data:* 2/3/2007

Year	Sales	Net Income
2007	$767,275,000	-$2,396,000
2006	$691,851,000	-$15,753,000
2005	$649,416,000	-$57,601,000

Curr. Assets:	$246,029,000	*Curr. Liab.:*	$100,820,000	*P/E Ratio:*	12.99
Plant, Equip.:	$46,958,000	*Total Liab.:*	$100,950,000	*Indic. Yr. Divd.:*	NA
Total Assets:	$347,139,000	*Net Worth:*	$202,871,000	*Debt/ Equity:*	NA

Van der Moolen Holdings

Keizergracht 307, Amsterdam; *PH:* 31 20 5356 789; *Fax:* 31 20 5356 788; *http://* www.vandermoolen.com; *Email:* info@nl.vandermoolen.com

General - Incorporation	Netherlands	Stock- Price on:12/24/2007	$5.08
Employees	446	Stock Exchange	OTC
Auditor	PricewaterhouseCoopers Accountants	Ticker Symbol	VDMHY
Stk Agt	Bank of New York	Outstanding Shares	46,680,000
Counsel	NA	E.P.S.	-$2.77
DUNS No.	NA	Shareholders	NA

Business: The group's principal activity is acting as an intermediary on the amsterdam stock exchange , through a number of group companies, and functions as a market maker on the options and financial futures exchanges of amsterdam, london, New York & frankfurt. Van der moolen is one of the major jobbers on the amsterdam stock exchange.

Primary SIC and add'l.: 6211

CIK No: 0001072245

Subsidiaries: Curvalue I B.V., Curvalue II B.V., Curvalue II GmbH, Curvalue III B.V., Curvalue IV B.V., Cybertrading B.V., Van der Moolen Effecten Specialist B.V. Amsterdam, Van der Moolen Effecten Specialist B.V. Cologne Branch, Van der Moolen Equities, Ltd., Van der Moolen Financial Services B.V., Van der Moolen Financial Services S.A.S., Van der Moolen Obligaties B.V., VDM Specialists, LLC

Officers: Richard E. Den Drijver/Chmn., CEO, Casper F. Rondeltap/COO, Michiel Wolfswinkel/CFO

Directors: Richard E. Den Drijver/Chmn., CEO, M. Arentsen/Chmn. - Supervisory Board, Gerard L. Van Den Broek/Member - Supervisory Board, Gerrit H. De Marez Oyens/Member - Supervisory Board

Owners: ABP, Fortis Utrecht N.V, Ducatus N.V., DD Foundation

Financial Data: *Fiscal Year End:*12/31   *Latest Annual Data:* 12/31/2006

Year	Sales	Net Income
2006	$227,752,000	-$83,443,000
2005	$132,890,000	-$3,672,000
2004	$167,412,000	-$12,280,000

Curr. Assets:	$379,851,000	*Curr. Liab.:*	$612,223,000	*P/E Ratio:*	25.53
Plant, Equip.:	$8,054,000	*Total Liab.:*	$778,713,000	*Indic. Yr. Divd.:*	NA
Total Assets:	$1,194,739,000	*Net Worth:*	$398,335,000	*Debt/ Equity:*	NA

Vanda Pharmaceuticals Inc

9605 Medical Ctr. Dr., Ste. 300, Rockville, MD, 20850; *PH:* 1-240-599-4500; *http://* www.vandapharma.com

General - Incorporation	DE	Stock- Price on:12/24/2007	$22.2
Employees	44	Stock Exchange	NDQ
Auditor	PricewaterhouseCoopers LLP	Ticker Symbol	VNDA
Stk Agt	American Stock Transfer & Trust Co.	Outstanding Shares	26,580,000
Counsel	NA	E.P.S.	NA
DUNS No.	NA	Shareholders	NA

Business: The groups principal activities include developing and commercializing clinical stage drug candidates. The group operates from the United States.

Primary SIC and add'l.: 2834

CIK No: 0001347178

Subsidiaries: Vanda Pharmaceuticals Pte. Ltd.

Officers: Mihael H. Polymeropoulos/Dir., CEO, Paolo Baroldi/Chief Medical Officer, Chip Clark/Chief Business Officer, Steven A. Shallcross/CFO, Deepak Phadke/VP - Manufacturing, Gunther Birznieks/Acting Clinical Program Head, Head - Informatics, Marlene Dressman/Clinical Operations Lead, Christian Lavedan/Head - Discovery, Curt Wolfgang/Clinical Program Head, Al Gianchetti/Sr. VP, Chief Commerical Officer

Directors: Mihael H. Polymeropoulos/Dir., CEO, Argeris N. Karabelas/Chmn., Richard W. Dugan/Dir., Brian K. Halak/Dir., Thomas H. Watkins/Dir., David Ramsay/Dir., Howard Pien/Dir.

Owners: James B. Tananbaum, Thomas Copmann, Thomas H. Watkins, Paolo Baroldi, Richard W. Dugan, OppenheimerFunds Inc/14.89%, Davidson Kempner Partners/6.41%, Steven A. Shallcross, William D. Clark, FMR Corp./10.43%, Versant Capital Management LLC/7.91%, Insiders/8.34%, Steven A. Cohen/6.07%, David Ramsay/3.76%, Argeris N. Karabelas/3.76% *(18 Owners included in Index)*

Financial Data: *Fiscal Year End:*12/31   *Latest Annual Data:* 06/30/2007

Year	Sales	Net Income
2007	NA	-$15,985,000
2006	NA	-$63,511,000
2005	NA	-$23,884,000

Curr. Assets:	$33,820,000	*Curr. Liab.:*	$9,106,000		
Plant, Equip.:	$1,860,000	*Total Liab.:*	$9,503,000	*Indic. Yr. Divd.:*	NA
Total Assets:	$36,260,000	*Net Worth:*	$26,757,000	*Debt/ Equity:*	NA

VantageMed Corp

11060 White Rock Rd., Ste. 210, Rancho Cordova, CA, 95670; *PH:* 1-916-638-4744; *http://* www.vantagemed.com

General - Incorporation	DE	Stock- Price on:12/24/2007	NA
Employees	130	Stock Exchange	NA
Auditor	Farber Hass Hurley & Mcewen LLP	Ticker Symbol	NA
Stk Agt	Computershare Trust CO.	Outstanding Shares	NA
Counsel	Gray, Cary, Ware & Freidenrich	E.P.S.	NA
DUNS No.	NA	Shareholders	NA

Business: The group's principle activity is to provide software support products and services for physicians and physician organizations and other healthcare providers. The group derives revenues from three segments: customer support, software and systems and electronic services. The software and systems

sales group sells and licenses practice management software products to physicians and other professionals. The customer support provides software, network and hardware support, training, installation services. The electronic services provides electronic claims processing, electronic statement printing and mailing and electronic remittance advice services.

Primary SIC and add'l.: 7375 7379

CIK No: 0001099531

Officers: Steven Curd/48/Dir., CEO, Liesel Loesch/38/CFO, Mark Cameron/52/COO, Richard Altinger/43/Exec. VP - Marketing, Business Development

Directors: Steven Curd/48/Dir., CEO, David M. Philipp/45/Dir., Steven E. Simpson/48/Dir., David Zabrowski/44/Dir.

Owners: Steven Curd/4.10%, Rick Altinger/2.20%, Trinad Advisors, LLC/5.60%, Steven E. Simpson, Gary Herman/12.40%, Mark Cameron/1.30%, Strategic Turnaround Equity Partners LP/12.20%, Bruce Galloway/15.60%, Liesel Loesch, Austin W. Marxe and David M. Greenhouse/27.60%, S Squared Technology, LLC/14.60%, David Zabrowski, David Philipp/1.30%, Philip D. Ranger, Insiders/9.90%

Varian Inc

3120 Hansen Way, Palo Alto, CA, 94304; ***PH:*** 1-650-213-8000; ***http://*** www.varianinc.com; ***Email:*** custserv@varianinc.com

General - Incorporation	DE	***Stock*** - Price on:12/24/2007	$55.52
Employees	3,700	Stock Exchange	NDQ
Auditor	PricewaterhouseCoopers LLP	Ticker Symbol	VARI
Stk Agt	EquiServe Trust Co N.A	Outstanding Shares	30,660,000
Counsel	NA	E.P.S.	$2.05
DUNS No.	NA	Shareholders	NA

Business: The group's principal activities are to design, develop, manufacture and sell scientific instruments, vacuum technologies and manufacture electronic components on contract basis. The group operates through three segments: scientific instruments business develops, manufactures, sells and services chromatography, optical spectroscopy, mass spectroscopy, dissolution testing and nuclear magnetic resonance equipment. Vacuum technologies provide products and solutions to create, control, measure and test vacuum environments in life science, industrial, research, semiconductor and scientific applications where ultra-clean, high-vacuum environments are needed. Electronics manufacturing business is a contract manufacturer of electronic assemblies and subsystems. During the year 2003, the group acquired dat business of roche diagnostics corporation. On 15-Sep-2004, the group acquired certain assets of digilab llc.

Primary SIC and add'l.: 3679 5065 3826 3563

CIK No: 0001079028

Subsidiaries: JEMSY, Magnex Scientific Limited, Varian (Shanghai) International Trading Co. Ltd., Varian A.G., Varian AB, Varian Argentina, Ltd., Varian Australia Pty. Ltd., Varian Australia, LLC, Varian B.V., Varian Belgium N.V., Varian Canada Inc., Varian Deutschland GmbH, Varian Holdings (Australia) Pty. Limited, Varian Iberica S.L., Varian India Pvt. Ltd. 27 Subsidiaries included in the Index

Officers: Garry W. Rogerson/Dir., CEO, Pres., Sergio Piras/Sr. VP - Vacuum Technologies, A. W. Homan/Sr. VP, General Counsel, Sec., Sean M. Wirtjes/VP, Controller, Edward G. McClammy/Sr. VP, CFO, Treasurer, Martin O'Donoghue/Sr. VP - Scientific Instruments

Directors: Garry W. Rogerson/Dir., CEO, Pres., Allen J. Lauer/Chmn., John G. McDonald/Dir., Wayne R. Moon/Dir., Richard U. De Schutter/Dir., Elizabeth E. Tallett/Dir.

Owners: Allen J. Lauer, Sergio Piras, Harris Associates L.P./5.41%, A. W. Homan, Garry W. Rogerson, Martin ODonoghue, Richard U. De Schutter, Elizabeth E. Tallett, Barclays Global Investors U.K. Holdings Limited/8.48%, John G. McDonald, Insiders/3.10%, G. Edward McClammy, The Goldman Sachs Group, Inc./5.73%, Wayne R. Moon

Financial Data: ***Fiscal Year End:***09/30 ***Latest Annual Data:*** 09/28/2007

Year	Sales	Net Income
2007	$920,598,000	$63,616,000
2006	$834,705,000	$50,069,000
2005	$772,795,000	$125,957,000

Curr. Assets:	$506,032,000	***Curr. Liab.:***	$241,148,000		
Plant, Equip.:	$102,290,000	***Total Liab.:***	$296,473,000	***Indic. Yr. Divd.:***	NA
Total Assets:	$795,995,000	***Net Worth:***	$499,522,000	***Debt/ Equity:***	0.0429

Varian Medical Systems Inc

3100 Hansen Way, Palo Alto, CA, 94304; ***PH:*** 1-650-493-4000; ***http://*** www.varian.com; ***Email:*** ca@varian.com

General - Incorporation	DE	***Stock*** - Price on:12/24/2007	$41.11
Employees	3,900	Stock Exchange	NYSE
Auditor	PricewaterhouseCoopers LLP	Ticker Symbol	VAR
Stk Agt	Computershare Investor Services LLC	Outstanding Shares	127,470,000
Counsel	John W. Kuo	E.P.S.	$1.83
DUNS No.	00-912-0817	Shareholders	NA

Business: The groups principle activity is to manufacture medical devices and software. The groups products include flat panel digital image detectors for filmless X-rays used in medical, dental, veterinary, scientific and industrial applications, linear accelerators, image detectors, image processing software and image detection systems for security and inspection purposes, proton therapy systems for cancer treatment, and scientific instruments used in fundamental and applied physics research. The group operates from United States.

Primary SIC and add'l.: 3844 3845

CIK No: 0000203527

Subsidiaries: Mansfield Insurance Company, PageMill Corporation, Sigma Micro Informatique Conseil, Varian Associates Limited, Varian BioSynergy,Inc., Varian FSC B.V., Varian Medical France S.A.S., Varian Medical Systems Australasia Pty Ltd., Varian Medical Systems Belgium N.V., Varian Medical Systems Brazil Limitada, Varian Medical Systems Canada Holdings,Inc., Varian Medical Systems Canada,Inc., Varian Medical Systems Deutschland G.m.b.H., Varian Medical Systems Finland OY, Varian Medical Systems Gesellschaft m.b.H. 32 Subsidiaries included in the Index

Officers: Timothy E. Guertin/Dir., CEO, Pres., Dow R. Wilson/Exec. VP, Pres. - Oncology Systems, John W. Kuo/Corporate VP, General Counsel, Corp. Sec., Robert H. Kluge/Corporate VP, Pres. - X, Ray Products, Franco N. Palomba/Corporate VP, Treasurer, Elisha W. Finney/CFO, Sr. VP, Courtney Patterson/Web Communications Specialist, Sheila Villadelgado/Public Relations Representative, Walter Frei/VP - European Sales, Marketing Operations, Tai-Yun Chen/Corporate VP, Corporate Controller, Wendy S. Reitherman/VP - Human Resources, Spencer R. Sias/VP - Corporate Communications, Investor Relations, A. J. Thorson/VP - Business Development, George A. Zdasiuk/CTO, Group VP, Dir. - Ginzton Technology Center, Meryl Ginsberg/Public Relations Mgr. - US *(16 Officers included in Index)*

Directors: Timothy E. Guertin/Dir., CEO, Pres., Richard M. Levy/Chmn., John Seely Brown/Dir., David W. Martin/Dir., Susan L. Bostrom/Dir., Steven A. Leibel/Dir., Ruediger Naumann-Etienne/Dir., Mark R. Laret/Dir., Andrew R. Eckert/Dir., Kent J. Thiry/Dir.

Owners: The TCW Group, Inc./8.34%, Kent J. Thiry, Richard M. Levy/1.80%, Mark R. Laret, Susan L. Bostrom, Steven A. Leibel, John Seely Brown, Insiders/4.24%, Sands Capital Management, LLC/8.81%, Robert H. Kluge, Dow R. Wilson, Timothy E. Guertin, Ruediger Naumann-Etienne, Elisha W. Finney, Andrew R. Eckert *(17 Owners included in Index)*

Financial Data: ***Fiscal Year End:***09/30 ***Latest Annual Data:*** 9/29/2006

Year	Sales	Net Income
2006	$1,597,820,000	$245,091,000
2005	$1,382,557,000	$206,576,000
2004	$1,235,523,000	$167,243,000

Curr. Assets:	$1,016,895,000	***Curr. Liab.:***	$543,933,000	***P/E Ratio:***	22.34
Plant, Equip.:	$114,540,000	***Total Liab.:***	$658,375,000	***Indic. Yr. Divd.:***	NA
Total Assets:	$1,317,402,000	***Net Worth:***	$659,027,000	***Debt/ Equity:***	0.0686

Varian Semiconductor Equipment Associates Inc

35 Dory Rd. , Gloucester, MA, 01930; ***PH:*** 1-978-282-2000; ***http://*** www.vsea.com

General - Incorporation	DE	***Stock*** - Price on:12/24/2007	$39.49
Employees	1,588	Stock Exchange	NDQ
Auditor	PricewaterhouseCoopers LLP	Ticker Symbol	VSEA
Stk Agt	Computershare Investor Services LLC	Outstanding Shares	90,000,000
Counsel	Hale & Dorr LLP	E.P.S.	$1.73
DUNS No.	NA	Shareholders	NA

Business: The group's principle activity is to design, manufacture, market and service semiconductor processing equipment used in the fabrication of integrated circuits. The group's ion implantation tools are required to build transistors or switches. Ion implanters are used to implant selected elements, called dopants, into the raw silicon wafers by bombarding them with a precisely controlled beam of electrically charged ions of specific atomic weight and energy. It also provides a range of customer support services designed to improve the productivity of its worldwide customers. The group markets, sells, installs and services ion implantation systems directly to semiconductor industry customers. The group has 6 sales and service offices located in the U.S., 6 in western Europe and 14 in Asia-pacific for a total of 26 worldwide. The group has operations in the United States, France, Germany, the United Kingdom, Korea, Italy, the Netherlands, Austria, Japan and Hong Kong. The group's quarterly revenue for September 2007 was 298.68 millions of USD.

Primary SIC and add'l.: 3699 5084 8731

CIK No: 0001079023

Subsidiaries: 4 Stanley Tucker Drive LLC, Altin Ltd., Varian Japan Holdings Ltd., Varian Korea, Ltd., Varian Precision Instruments Maintenance (Shanghai) Co., Ltd., Varian Semiconductor Equipment Associates (HK) Limited, Varian Semiconductor Equipment Associates (Shanghai), Ltd., Varian Semiconductor Equipment Associates Asia, Ltd., Varian Semiconductor Equipment Associates Austria GesmbH, Varian Semiconductor Equipment Associates China, Ltd., Varian Semiconductor Equipment Associates Europe B.V., Varian Semiconductor Equipment Associates GmbH, Varian Semiconductor Equipment Associates International, Inc., Varian Semiconductor Equipment Associates Italia S.r.l., Varian Semiconductor Equipment Associates Pacific, Inc. 19 Subsidiaries included in the Index

Officers: Gary E. Dickerson/Dir., CEO, Yong-Kil Kim/Exec. VP, GM - Asia Operations, Robert J. Halliday/CFO, Exec. VP, Robert J. Perlmutter/Exec. VP - Implant Business Units

Directors: Gary E. Dickerson/Dir., CEO, Richard A. Aurelio/Chmn., Robert W. Dutton/Dir., Dennis G. Schmal/Dir., Eric Chen/Dir., Elizabeth E. Tallett/Dir., Xun Chen/Dir.

Owners: Xun(Eric) Chen, Robert J. Halliday, Wellington Management Company, LLP/8.60%, Richard A. Aurelio, Dennis G. Schmal, Elizabeth E. Tallett, Stanley K. Yarbro, Insiders/2.00%, Robert W. Dutton, Robert J. Perlmutter, Gary E. Dickerson, Yong-Kil Kim

Financial Data: ***Fiscal Year End:***09/30 ***Latest Annual Data:*** 09/28/2007

Year	Sales	Net Income
2007	$1,054,864,000	$142,207,000
2006	$730,714,000	$94,684,000
2005	$600,521,000	$72,010,000

Curr. Assets:	$788,719,000	***Curr. Liab.:***	$153,681,000	***P/E Ratio:***	24.99
Plant, Equip.:	$58,435,000	***Total Liab.:***	$173,743,000	***Indic. Yr. Divd.:***	NA
Total Assets:	$862,819,000	***Net Worth:***	$689,076,000	***Debt/ Equity:***	0.0040

Varsity Group Inc

1850 M St. NW, Ste 1150, Washington, DC, 20036; ***PH:*** 1-202-667-3400; ***http://*** www.varsity-group.com; ***Email:*** press@varsitygroup.com

General - Incorporation	DE	***Stock*** - Price on:12/24/2007	$0.91
Employees	62	Stock Exchange	NDQ
Auditor	PricewaterhouseCoopers LLP	Ticker Symbol	VSTY
Stk Agt	American Stock Transfer & Trust Co.	Outstanding Shares	18,460,000
Counsel	Shaw Pittman	E.P.S.	-$0.653
DUNS No.	NA	Shareholders	NA

Business: The group's principal activity is to operate as an Internet retailer of new textbooks and educational materials targeting private middle/high schools, small colleges and distance and continuing education markets. Through edupartners program, the group partners directly with educational institutions to outsource traditional brick and mortar bookstore operations and markets its textbooks and learning materials directly to parents and students via the varsitybooks.com Website. The group also provides marketing services for other businesses seeking to reach the college and private middle and high school demographics by marketing to students online through its Website and on college campuses utilizing a nationwide network of student marketing representatives.

Primary SIC and add'l.: 5961

CIK No: 0001069502

Officers: Mark F. Thimmig/Dir., CEO, Pres./$836,134.00, Jim M. Craig/CFO/$196,786.00, Jack M. Benson/CIO, Sr. VP - Business Development/$188,262.00, Marcus N. May/Sr. VP - Sales - Marketing, Operations, Thomas E. Feldman/Sr. VP, GM - Varsity Finance, Jay Fee/VP - Sales, Thomas H. Probert/VP - Lydialearn

Directors: Mark F. Thimmig/Dir., CEO, Pres., Eric J. Kuhn/Chmn., John T. Kernan/Dir., Allen L. Morgan/Dir., William J. Pade/Dir., Robert M. Holster/Dir.

Owners: Eric J. Kuhn/6.10%, Insiders/20.60%, Robert M. Holster/1.20%, Mark F. Thimmig/0.10%, Allen L. Morgan/10.30%, William J. Pade/1.20%, Special Situations Funds III and affiliated funds/5.30%, James M. Craig/0.10%, Mayfield Fund/7.90%, Jack M. Benson/1.70%, Thomas Berlin/5.30%, John T. Kernan/1.70%

Financial Data: Fiscal Year End:12/31 Latest Annual Data: 12/31/2006

Year	Sales	Net Income
2006	$53,906,000	-$28,378,000
2005	$50,069,000	$12,129,000
2004	$37,682,000	$6,881,000

Curr. Assets:	$15,775,000	Curr. Liab.:	$9,299,000		
Plant, Equip.:	$1,156,000	Total Liab.:	$9,456,000	Indic. Yr. Divd.:	NA
Total Assets:	$23,648,000	Net Worth:	$14,192,000	Debt/ Equity:	NA

VASAMED Inc

Formerly: Optical Sensors Inc

7615 Golden Triangle Dr., Ste. C, Technology Pk. V, Minneapolis, MN, 55344; **PH:** 1-952-944-5857

General - Incorporation	DE	**Stock** - Price on:12/24/2007	$1.1
Employees	31	Stock Exchange	NA
Auditor	Virchow, Krause & Co. LLP	Ticker Symbol	NA
Stk Agt	Wells Fargo Shareowner Services	Outstanding Shares	3,860,000
Counsel	Oppenheimer Wolff & Donnelly	E.P.S.	-$1.64
DUNS No.	17-920-8673	Shareholders	NA

Business: The group's principal activity is to develop, manufacture and market fiber optic sensors and instruments. The group's product is capnoprobe which is a handheld device that is slipped under the tongue like a thermometer that measurers the tissue of the mucous membrane in the mouth. The capnoprobe sensor system includes a disposable sensor and a bench top instrument. The optochemically based sensors and its optical platform and software systems can be incorporated into a variety of low-cost, fluid, blood and tissue-contacting measurement systems. These products are used to monitor blood gas for medically unstable patients in critical and intensive care units. The trademarks of the group are capnoprobe(tm) and optical cam(tm).

Primary SIC and add'l.: 3845

CIK No: 0000907658

Officers: Paulita M. Laplante/Dir., CEO, Pres., Daniel J. Bartnik/CTO, Kent Winger/49/VP - Operations

Directors: Paulita M. Laplante/Dir., CEO, Pres., Richard B. Egen/69/Dir., Andrew T. Jay/45/Dir.

Financial Data: Fiscal Year End:12/31 Latest Annual Data: 12/31/2005

Year	Sales	Net Income
2005	$1,386,000	-$4,888,000
2004	$1,069,000	-$6,422,000
2003	$2,124,000	-$2,281,000

Curr. Assets:	$970,000	Curr. Liab.:	$986,000		
Plant, Equip.:	$253,000	Total Liab.:	$1,005,000	Indic. Yr. Divd.:	NA
Total Assets:	$1,600,000	Net Worth:	$595,000	Debt/ Equity:	NA

VASCO Data Security International

1901 S Meyers Rd., Ste. 210, Oakbrook Terrace, IL, 60180; **PH:** 1-630-932-8844; **Fax:** 1-630-932-8852; **http://** www.vasco.com; **Email:** info-usa@vasco.com

General - Incorporation	DE	**Stock** - Price on:12/24/2007	$22.09
Employees	184	Stock Exchange	NDQ
Auditor	KPMG LLP	Ticker Symbol	VDSI
Stk Agt	Illinois Stock Transfer Co	Outstanding Shares	37,010,000
Counsel	Katten Muchin Rosenman LLP	E.P.S.	$0.60
DUNS No.	NA	Shareholders	NA

Business: The group's principle activities are to design, develop, market and support open standards based hardware and software security systems that manage and secure access to information assets. The products enable secure financial transactions made over private enterprise networks and public networks, such as Internet. The group sells majority of its products in European countries with significant sales in the United States and other countries, primarily Australia and Asia/pacific. The group's quarterly revenue for September 2007 was 29.98 millions of USD.

Primary SIC and add'l.: 7373 7379 7371

CIK No: 0001044777

Officers: Kendall T. Hunt/Chmn., CEO/$649,192.00, Jan Valcke/COO, Pres./$898,216.00, Clifford K. Bown/Exec. VP, CFO, Sec. - Http, Secgov, Archives, Edgar, Data, 1044777, 000095013706005386, C04669ddef14ahtm/$515,029.00, Chantal Boudaer/Human Resources Mgr.

Directors: Kendall T. Hunt/Chmn., CEO, John R. Walter/Dir., Michael P. Cullinane/Dir., John N. Fox/Dir., Jean K. Holley/Dir.

Owners: John N. Fox, Oberweis Asset Management, Inc./5.99%, Michael P. Cullinane, Jan Valcke/1.14%, Cliff Bown, John R. Walter, Kendall T. Hunt/26.41%, Jean K. Holley, Insiders/28.37%

Financial Data: Fiscal Year End:12/31 Latest Annual Data: 12/31/2006

Year	Sales	Net Income
2006	$76,062,000	$12,587,000
2005	$54,579,000	$7,701,000
2004	$29,893,000	$3,253,000

Curr. Assets:	$41,320,000	Curr. Liab.:	$19,262,000	P/E Ratio:	51.37
Plant, Equip.:	$1,422,000	Total Liab.:	$20,440,000	Indic. Yr. Divd.:	NA
Total Assets:	$62,646,000	Net Worth:	$42,206,000	Debt/ Equity:	NA

Vascular Solutions Inc

6464 Sycamore Ct. N, Minneapolis, MN, 55369; **PH:** 1-888-240-6001; **http://** www.vascularsolutions.com

General - Incorporation	MN	**Stock** - Price on:12/24/2007	$9.38
Employees	210	Stock Exchange	NDQ
Auditor	Virchow, Krause & Co. LLP	Ticker Symbol	VASC
Stk Agt	Wells Fargo Bank Minnesota N.A	Outstanding Shares	15,370,000
Counsel	Dorsey & Whitney LLP	E.P.S.	-$0.31
DUNS No.	NA	Shareholders	NA

Business: The group's principal activities are to design, manufacture and market devices that allow interventional cardiologists and radiologists to seal percutaneous access sites from blood clots. The group's products are the vascular solutions duett(tm) sealing device and the d-stat(tm) flowable hemostat. The vascular solutions duett enables cardiologists and radiologists to rapidly seal the puncture site after catheterization procedures such as angiography, angioplasty and stenting. The d-stat(tm) flowable hemostat enables interventional physicians to seal less-challenging access sites following the removal of sheaths and tubes used in a variety of procedures, such as hemodialysis, electrophysiology and radial arterial access procedures. The products are marketed in Norway, Italy, Austria, the United Kingdom, Ireland, Denmark, Switzerland, Finland, Sweden, Greece, Belgium, Spain, the Netherlands and Portugal.

Primary SIC and add'l.: 3841

CIK No: 0001030206

Subsidiaries: Vascular Solutions, GmbH

Officers: Howard Root/Dir., CEO/$547,396.00, James Quackenbush/VP - Manufacturing/$267,405.00, James Hennen/CFO/$252,120.00, Deborah Neymark/VP - Regulatory, Clinical, Reimbursement/$290,545.00, Frederick Reuning/VP - Marketing/$223,161.00, Brett Demchuk/VP - Quality

Directors: Howard Root/Dir., CEO, John Erb/Dir., Michael Kopp/Dir., Paul O'Connell/Dir., Robert J. Paulson/Dir., Richard Nigon/Dir., Jorge Saucedo/Dir., Charmaine Sutton/Dir.

Financial Data: Fiscal Year End:12/31 Latest Annual Data: 12/31/2006

Year	Sales	Net Income
2006	$43,310,000	-$1,786,000
2005	$32,786,000	-$561,000
2004	$22,265,000	-$3,508,000

Curr. Assets:	$17,105,000	Curr. Liab.:	$5,633,000		
Plant, Equip.:	$3,669,000	Total Liab.:	$6,500,000	Indic. Yr. Divd.:	NA
Total Assets:	$20,967,000	Net Worth:	$14,467,000	Debt/ Equity:	0.0716

Vaso Active Pharmaceuticals Inc

99 Rosewood Dr., Ste 260, Danvers, MA, 01923; **PH:** 1-978-750-1991; **http://** www.vasoactive.us; **Email:** info@vasoactive.us

General - Incorporation	DE	**Stock** - Price on:12/24/2007	$0.16
Employees	4	Stock Exchange	OTC
Auditor	Stowe & Degon	Ticker Symbol	VAPH
Stk Agt	Computershare Investor Services LLC	Outstanding Shares	10,330,000
Counsel	Shapiro, Haber & Urmy LLP	E.P.S.	-$0.27
DUNS No.	NA	Shareholders	NA

Business: The group's principal activity is to develop, manufacture and market pharmaceutical products. The group focuses on vaso active lipid encapsulated or vale, transdermal delivery technology drugs. Currently, we market athlete's relief and osteon in the United States. The group's products include analgesics, toenail fungal treatment, acne, first aid, hand and body lotion and psoriasis treatment. The group is planning to rebrand the defeet athlete's foot anti-fungal medication product as termin8 and xtinguish.

Primary SIC and add'l.: 2834 8731

CIK No: 0001232400

Subsidiaries: OTC pharmaceutical products

Officers: Joseph Frattaroli/CEO, Pres., CFO, Stephen G. Carter/Dir., VP, Chief Scientific Officer, Laura Stephens/Investor Relations

Directors: Robert E. Anderson/Chmn., Danne Hurd/Dir., Bruce A. Shear/Dir., Brian J. Strasnick/Dir., Ronald Guerriero/Dir., Stephen G. Carter/Dir., VP, Chief Scientific Officer

Owners: Robert E. Anderson, Bruce A. Shear, Joseph Frattaroli, Insiders, BioChemics, Inc./100.00%, D'Anne Hurd, Stephen G. Carter, John Masiz/100.00%, BioChemics, Inc., Brian Strasnick, Ronald Guerriero, John Masiz

Financial Data: Fiscal Year End:12/31 Latest Annual Data: 12/31/2006

Year	Sales	Net Income
2006	$105,000	-$2,841,000
2005	$25,000	-$4,465,000
2004	$13,000	-$4,493,000

Curr. Assets:	$364,000	Curr. Liab.:	$5,078,000		
Plant, Equip.:	$39,000	Total Liab.:	$5,087,000	Indic. Yr. Divd.:	NA
Total Assets:	$403,000	Net Worth:	-$4,684,000	Debt/ Equity:	NA

Vasogen Inc

2505 Meadowvale Blvd., Mississauga, ON, L5N 5S2; **PH:** 1-905-817-2000; **http://** www.vasogen.com; **Email:** investor@vasogen.com

General - Incorporation	Canada	**Stock** - Price on:12/24/2007	$2.54
Employees	172	Stock Exchange	NDQ
Auditor	KPMG LLP	Ticker Symbol	VSGN
Stk Agt	Mellon Trust Co	Outstanding Shares	17,320,000
Counsel	McCarthy Ttrault LLP	E.P.S.	-$1.95
DUNS No.	NA	Shareholders	NA

Business: The group's principal activities are research, development and commercialization of therapeutic platform technology, designed to treat diseases by harnessing the power of the human immune systems. The group had clinical progress in five disease indications: atherosclerosis, congestive heart failure, ischemia/reperfusion injury, autoimmune disease and graft-versus-host disease. The group's lead clinical program, now in late-stage development, is focused on the treatment of peripheral arterial disease.

Primary SIC and add'l.: 8099

CIK No: 0001042018

Officers: David G. Elsley/Dir., CEO, Pres., Susan F. Langlois/VP - Regulatory Affairs, Quality Assurance, Michael Shannon/VP - Medical Affairs, Jacqueline Le Saux/VP - Corporate, Legal Affairs, Bernard Lim/Sr. VP - Operations, Anthony E. Bolton/Chief Scientific Officer, Christopher J. Waddick/COO, Eldon R. Smith/Dir., Sr. VP - Scientific Affairs, Chief Medical Officer, Jay Kleiman/Chief Medical Officer, Head - Cardiovascular Development, Glenn Neumann/Investor Relations Officer, Catherine Bouchard/VP - Human Resources, Anne E. Goodbody/VP - Drug Development, Graham D. Neil/CFO, VP - Finance, John Geddes/VP - Marketing, Business Development, Michael J. Martin/VP - Marketing, Business Development *(16 Officers included in Index)*

Directors: David G. Elsley/Dir., CEO, Pres., Terrance H. Gregg/Chmn., Robert Roberts/Chmn. - Scientific Advisory Board, Calvin R. Stiller/Dir., Stanley H. Appel/Member - Scientific Advisory Board, Valentin Fuster/Member - Scientific Advisory Board, Richard G. Miller/Member - Scientific Advisory Board, Milton Packer/Member - Scientific Advisory Board, Benoit La Salle/Dir., Ronald M. Cresswell/Dir., William R. Grant/Dir., Eldon R. Smith/Dir., Sr. VP - Scientific Affairs, Chief Medical Officer, John C. Villforth/Dir., David Wofsy/Member - Scientific Advisory Board

Owners: RONALD M. CRESSWELL, TERRANCE H. GREGG, ELDON R. SMITH, Catherine M. Bouchard, JACQUELINE H. R. LE SAUX, BENOIT LA SALLE, JOHN C. VILLFORTH, DAVID G. ELSLEY, WILLIAM R. GRANT, CHRISTOPHER J. WADDICK, Anthony E. Bolton, CALVIN R. STILLER, SUSAN F. LANGLOIS

Financial Data: Fiscal Year End: 11/30 Latest Annual Data: 11/30/2006

Year	Sales	Net Income
2006	NA	-$53,726,000
2005	NA	-$79,612,000
2004	NA	-$62,609,000

Curr. Assets:	$35,939,000	**Curr. Liab.:**	$14,983,000		
Plant, Equip.:	$542,000	**Total Liab.:**	$24,952,000	**Indic. Yr. Divd.:**	NA
Total Assets:	$37,053,000	**Net Worth:**	$12,101,000	**Debt/ Equity:**	NA

Vasomedical Inc

180 Linden Ave., Westbury, NY, 11590; *PH:* 1-516-997-4600; *http://* www.vasomedical.com; *Email:* customerservice@vasomedical.com

General - Incorporation	DE	**Stock**- Price on:12/24/2007	NA
Employees	46	Stock Exchange	OTC
Auditor	Miller, Ellin & Co., LLP	Ticker Symbol	VASO
Stk Agt	American Stock Transfer & Trust Co.	Outstanding Shares	65,200,000
Counsel	Beckman, Lieberman & Barandes LLP	E.P.S.	-$0.029
DUNS No.	19-721-0248	Shareholders	NA

Business: The group's principle activity is to design, manufacture, market and support eecp external counterpulsation system. The system is a microprocessor-based medical device for the non-invasive, outpatient treatment of patients with cardiovascular disease. The device is used in cases of angina, carcinogenic shock, acute myocardial infarction and most recently, congestive heart failure (chf). It delivers a retrograde arterial pressure wave to the heart, increasing coronary perfusion and reducing ventricular after load. The therapy serves to increase circulation in areas of the heart with less than adequate blood supply and restores systemic vascular function. The products of the group are sold to treatment providers in the United States through a direct sales force.

Primary SIC and add'l.: 3845 7352

CIK No: 0000839087

Subsidiaries: 180 Linden Avenue Corp., Viromedics, Inc.

Officers: John C.K. Hui/Dir., CEO, Pres., Tricia Efstathiou/CFO, Harold Kaefer/VP - Engineering, Manufacturing, Larry Liebman/VP - Sales

Directors: John C.K. Hui/Dir., CEO, Pres., Abraham E. Cohen/Chmn., Martin Zeiger/Dir., Photios T. Paulson/Dir., Simon Srybnik/Dir., Jun Ma/Dir., Behnam Movaseghi/Dir., Derek Enlander/Dir.

Owners: Jun Ma, Derek Enlander, Martin Zeiger, Abraham E. Cohen, Tricia Efstathiou, Simon Srybnik, Insiders, John C. K. Hui, Behnam Movaseghi, Photios T. Paulson

Financial Data: Fiscal Year End: 05/31 Latest Annual Data: 5/31/2006

Year	Sales	Net Income
2006	$10,943,000	-$10,701,000
2005	$15,096,000	-$5,562,000
2004	$22,207,000	-$3,423,000

Curr. Assets:	$6,037,000	**Curr. Liab.:**	$3,169,000		
Plant, Equip.:	$1,570,000	**Total Liab.:**	$4,746,000	**Indic. Yr. Divd.:**	NA
Total Assets:	$7,912,000	**Net Worth:**	$3,166,000	**Debt/ Equity:**	0.4562

VCA Antech Inc

12401 W Olympic Blvd, Los Angeles, CA, 90064; *PH:* 1-310-584-6500; *http://* www.vcaantech.com; *Email:* ir@vcamail.com

General - Incorporation	DE	**Stock**- Price on:12/24/2007	$37.44
Employees	8,000	Stock Exchange	NDQ
Auditor	KPMG LLP	Ticker Symbol	WOOF
Stk Agt	Computershare Trust CO.	Outstanding Shares	84,050,000
Counsel	Akin, Gump, Strauss, Hauer & Feld LLP	E.P.S.	$1.22
DUNS No.	18-171-1672	Shareholders	NA

Business: The group's principal activity is to operate veterinary diagnostic laboratories and free-standing, full-service animal hospitals in the United States. The group's veterinary diagnostic laboratories provide sophisticated testing and consulting services to the veterinarian physician. The testing and consulting services are used in the detection, diagnosis, evaluation, monitoring, treatment and prevention of diseases and other conditions affecting animals. Animal hospitals offers a full range of general medical and surgical services for companion animals, as well as specialized treatments including advanced diagnostic services, internal medicine, oncology, ophthalmology, dermatology and cardiology. On 01-06-2004 group acquired national petcare centers inc.

Primary SIC and add'l.: 8734 0742

CIK No: 0000817366

Subsidiaries: Albany Veterinary Clinic, Animal Care Center at Mill Run, Inc., Animal Care Centers of America, Inc., Arroyo PetCare Center, Inc., Associates in Pet Care, Inc., Diagnostic Veterinary Service, Inc., East Mill Plain Animal Hospital, Inc., Edgebrook, Inc., Florida Veterinary Laboratories, Inc., Indiana Veterinary Diagnostic Lab, Inc., Lewelling Veterinary Clinic, Inc., National PetCare Centers, Inc., Pets Choice, Inc., Pets Rx, Inc., Preston Park Animal Hospital, Inc. 43 Subsidiaries included in the Index

Officers: Robert L. Antin/Chmn., CEO, Pres., Arthur J. Antin/Co - Founder, Dir., COO, Sr. VP, Sec./$1,053,130.00, Tomas W. Fuller/CFO, VP, Sec./$627,985.00, Neil Tauber/Co - Founder, Sr. VP - Development/$662,207.00, Dawn R. Olsen/Principal Accounting Officer, VP, Controller/$350,785.00

Directors: Robert L. Antin/Chmn., CEO, Pres., John Heil/Dir., John M. Baumer/Dir., John B. Chickering/Dir., Arthur J. Antin/Co - Founder, Dir., COO, Sr. VP, Sec., Frank Reddick/Dir., Neil Tauber/Co - Founder, Sr. VP - Development

Owners: John B. Chickering, John A. Heil, Franklin Resources, Inc./6.00%, Tomas W. Fuller, FMR Corp./5.70%, John M. Baumer, Neil Tauber, Frank Reddick, Robert L. Antin/2.90%, Arthur J. Antin, Select Equity Group, Inc. & Select Offshore Advisors, LLC/5.90%, Baillie Gifford & Co/7.70%, Dawn R. Olsen, Insiders/5.10%

Financial Data: Fiscal Year End: 12/31 Latest Annual Data: 12/31/2006

Year	Sales	Net Income
2006	$983,313,000	$105,529,000
2005	$839,666,000	$67,816,000
2004	$674,089,000	$63,572,000

Curr. Assets:	$152,965,000	**Curr. Liab.:**	$94,801,000		
Plant, Equip.:	$166,033,000	**Total Liab.:**	$541,652,000	**Indic. Yr. Divd.:**	NA
Total Assets:	$971,957,000	**Net Worth:**	$430,305,000	**Debt/ Equity:**	0.8297

VCampus Corp

1850 Centennial Pk. Dr., Ste 200, Reston, VA, 20191; *PH:* 1-703-893-7800; *http://* www2.vcampus.com; *Email:* investor@vcampus.com

General - Incorporation	DE	**Stock**- Price on:12/24/2007	$0.1001
Employees	53	Stock Exchange	OTC
Auditor	Reznick Group P.C	Ticker Symbol	VCMP
Stk Agt	Wachovia Bank N.A	Outstanding Shares	11,260,000
Counsel	NA	E.P.S.	$0.40
DUNS No.	79-907-0057	Shareholders	NA

Business: The group's principal activity is to provide outsourced e-learning solutions. It manages and hosts Internet-based learning environments for corporations, government agencies, institutions of higher education, and associations. The group's services cover a broad range of e-learning programs, from enrollment and payment to course development and delivery, as well as tracking of students' progress and reporting of results. The group charges its customers a low upfront fee to establish a customized virtual campus and then charges them on either a subscription or usage basis for the service on an ongoing basis. The group owns registered trademarks for courseware construction set, pointpage, content matters, v (& design), www.vcampus.com, and vcampus.

Primary SIC and add'l.: 2741 7375 8243

CIK No: 0000943742

Officers: Narasimhan P. Kannan/Founder, Chmn., CEO, Ronald E. Freedman/Sr. VP - Worldwide Sales, Marketing, Laura Friedman/45/VP - Publishing, Christopher L. Nelson/45/CFO, CIO, Sec., Lindsay H. Miller/Sr. VP, GM, James Stanger/Chief Certification Architect, John Birdsong/Co - Founder, CFO, Todd Hopkins/VP - Publishing, Anne Marie Pascoe/VP - Strategic Partnerships

Directors: Narasimhan P. Kannan/Founder, Chmn., CEO, John Birdsong/Co - Founder, CFO, Edson D. Decastro/Dir., Martin E. Maleska/Dir.

Owners: St. Cloud Capital Partners, Sherleigh Associates Profit, Barry K. Fingerhut, Sherleigh Associates Profit/50.00%, Chestnut Ridge Partners, David Holzer, Alpha Capital A.G., Nat P. Kannan, Christopher L. Nelson, Chestnut Ridge Partners, Nat P. Kannan, John Birdsong, Dolphin Offshore Partners, St. Cloud Capital Partners, David Holzer *(25 Owners included in Index)*

Financial Data: Fiscal Year End: 12/31 Latest Annual Data: 12/31/2006

Year	Sales	Net Income
2006	$7,446,000	-$7,625,000
2005	$4,564,000	-$5,866,000
2004	$4,864,000	-$6,579,000

Curr. Assets:	$2,058,000	**Curr. Liab.:**	$3,525,000	**P/E Ratio:**	0.25
Plant, Equip.:	$326,000	**Total Liab.:**	$5,875,000	**Indic. Yr. Divd.:**	NA
Total Assets:	$5,176,000	**Net Worth:**	-$699,000	**Debt/ Equity:**	NA

VCG Holding Corp

390 Union Blvd., Ste. 540, Lakewood, CO, 80228; *PH:* 1-303-934-2424; *http://* www.ptsshowclub.com

General - Incorporation	CO	**Stock**- Price on:12/24/2007	$9.199
Employees	449	Stock Exchange	AMEX
Auditor	Causey Demgen & Moore Inc	Ticker Symbol	PTT
Stk Agt	Transfer Online, Inc.	Outstanding Shares	16,900,000
Counsel	NA	E.P.S.	$0.10
DUNS No.	NA	Shareholders	NA

Business: The group's principal activity is to own and operate nightclubs which provides live adult entertainment, restaurant and beverage services. The group owns and operates three nightclubs located in suburbs of memphis, Tennessee, indianapolis, Indiana and st. Louis, Illinois. On 21-Jul-2004, the group acquired the general partnership interest and a 89.5 percent limited partnership interest of glendale restaurant concepts lp, a Colorado limited partnership.

Primary SIC and add'l.: 5813 5812 7997

CIK No: 0001172852

Subsidiaries: Glenarm Restaurant LLC, Glendale Restaurant Concepts LP., Indy Restaurant Concepts, Inc., International Entertainment Consultants, Inc., Platinum of Illinois, Inc., Tennessee Restaurant Concepts, Inc., VCG Real Estate Holding Corporation, VCG Restaurant Denver, Inc.

Officers: Troy H. Lowrie/Chmn., CEO, Mary E. Bowles-Cook/Sec., Treasurer, Michael L. Ocello/Dir., COO, Pres., Donald W. Prosser/Dir., Chief Financial, Accounting Officer, Brent Lewis/Corporate Contact

Directors: Troy H. Lowrie/Chmn., CEO, Robert J. McGraw/Dir., Rand E. Kruger/Dir., Allan S. Rubin/Dir., Michael L. Ocello/Dir., COO, Pres., Donald W. Prosser/Dir., Chief Financial, Accounting Officer, Edward M. Bearman/43/Dir., Martin A. Grusin/63/Dir.

Owners: Robert J. McGraw, Troy H. Lowrie/29.53%, Mary E. Bowles-Cook, Allan S. Rubin, Rand E. Kruger, Donald W. Prosser, Martin A. Grusin, Edward M. Bearman, Micheal L. Ocello/1.26%, Insiders/32.66%

Financial Data: Fiscal Year End: 12/31 Latest Annual Data: 12/31/2006

Year	Sales	Net Income
2006	$16,115,000	$1,116,000
2005	$16,997,000	$414,000
2004	$12,220,000	-$1,798,000

Curr. Assets:	$1,213,000	**Curr. Liab.:**	NA	**P/E Ratio:**	91.99
Plant, Equip.:	NA	**Total Liab.:**	NA	**Indic. Yr. Divd.:**	NA
Total Assets:	$1,213,000	**Net Worth:**	NA	**Debt/ Equity:**	1.3465

Vector Group Ltd

100 S E Second St., Miami, FL, 33131; *PH:* 1-305-579-8000; *http://* www.vectorgroupltd.com

General - Incorporation DE
Employees 430
Auditor PricewaterhouseCoopers LLP
Stk Agt American Stock Transfer & Trust Co.
Counsel NA
DUNS No. 61-506-0886

Stock- Price on:12/24/2007 $21.65
Stock Exchange NYSE
Ticker Symbol VGR
Outstanding Shares 57,120,000
E.P.S $1.16
Shareholders NA

Business: The group's principal activity is to develop and market conventional and nicotine-free cigarette products. The group operates in three segments: liggett, vector tobacco and real estate. The liggett segment consists of the manufacture and sale of conventional cigarettes, as well as the operations of medallion company inc. The vector tobacco segment includes the development and marketing of the low nicotine and nicotine-free cigarette products, as well as, the development of reduced risk cigarette products. The real estate segment includes the operations of its majority-owned subsidiary, new valley corporation. Customers include candy and tobacco distributors, the military, warehouse club chains, and large grocery, drug and convenience store chains.

Primary SIC and add'l.: 6531 6552 2111 5194 6726 6211 2131

CIK No: 0000059440

Subsidiaries: Liggett Group LLC, Liggett Vector Brands Inc., New Valley LLC, Vector Tobacco Inc., VGR Holding LLC

Officers: Howard M. Lorber/Dir., CEO, Pres./$10,514,300.00, Jean Sharpe/Dir. - Private Investor, Richard J. Lampen/Exec. VP/$1,196,600.00, Bryant Kirkland/CFO, VP, Treasurer/$409,100.00, Marc N. Bell/VP, General Counsel, Sec., Carrie Bloom/Investor Contact

Directors: Howard M. Lorber/Dir., CEO, Pres., Bennett S. Lebow/Chmn., Jeffrey Podell/Dir., Henry Beinstein/Dir., Jean Sharpe/Dir. - Private Investor, Robert Eide/Dir., Ronald J. Bernstein/Dir.

Owners: JefferiesGroup, Inc./5.60%, Richard J. Lampen, Ronald J. Bernstein, High River Limited Partnership/20.30%, Bryant J. Kirkland, Henry C. Beinstein, Joselynn D. Van Siclen, Howard M. Lorber/7.20%, Phillip Frost/6.40%, Bennett S. LeBow/17.10%, Insiders/24.50%, Jean E. Sharpe, Robert J. Eide, Jeffrey S. Podell

Financial Data: *Fiscal Year End:*12/31 *Latest Annual Data:* 12/31/2006

Year	Sales	Net Income
2006	$506,252,000	$42,712,000
2005	$478,427,000	$52,385,000
2004	$498,860,000	$6,728,000

Curr. Assets:	$303,156,000	**Curr. Liab.:**	$168,786,000	**P/E Ratio:**	23.53
Plant, Equip.:	$59,921,000	**Total Liab.:**	$542,485,000	**Indic. Yr. Divd.:**	$1.600
Total Assets:	$637,462,000	**Net Worth:**	$94,977,000	**Debt/ Equity:**	NA

Vectren Corp

PO Box 209, Evansville, IN, 47702; *PH:* 1-812-494-0000; *http://* www.vectren.com

General - Incorporation IN
Employees 3,348
Auditor Deloitte & Touche LLP
Stk Agt National City Bank
Counsel NA
DUNS No. NA

Stock- Price on:12/24/2007 $26.88
Stock Exchange NYSE
Ticker Symbol VVC
Outstanding Shares 76,500,000
E.P.S $1.59
Shareholders NA

Business: The groups principle activity is to deliver gas and electricity. The group operates in three groups namely utility group, a nonutility group, and corporate and other. The group operates from United States. The group operates from United States.

Primary SIC and add'l.: 4911 6719 8999 4924 8744

CIK No: 0001096385

Subsidiaries: Energy Realty, Inc., Energy Systems Group, Inc., Energy Systems Group, LLC, Haddington Energy Partners II, LP, Haddington Energy Partners, LP, Indiana Gas Company, Inc., Pace Carbon Synfuels, LP, ProLiance Energy, LLC, Reliant Services, LLC, Southern Indiana Gas and Electric Company, Inc., Southern Indiana Properties, Inc., Vectren Aero, LLC, Vectren Broadband, Inc., Vectren Capital Corp., Vectren Communications Services, Inc. 29 Subsidiaries included in the Index

Officers: Niel C. Ellerbrook/Chmn., CEO, Pres./$2,393,242.00, Ronald G. Jochum/VP - Vuhi, Power Supply, Steven M. Schein/VP - Investor Relations, Carl L. Chapman/COO, Exec. VP/$1,073,945.00, William S. Doty/Exec. VP - Utility Operations/$666,774.00, Jeffrey W. Whiteside/VP - Corporate Communications, Public Affairs, Ellis Redd/VP - Human Resources, Douglas A. Karl/VP - Vuhi, Marketing, Customer Service, Susan M. Hardwick/VP, Controller, Ronald E. Christian/Exec. VP, General Counsel, Sec., Chief Administrative Officer/$757,335.00, Jerrold L. Ulrey/VP - Vuhi, Regulatory Affairs, Fuels, Robert E. Heidorn/VP - Vuhi, General Counsel, John M. Bohls/Pres. - Vectren Enterprises, Daniel C. Bugher/VP - Information Technology, Douglas Petitt/VP - Government Affairs *(18 Officers included in Index)*

Directors: Niel C. Ellerbrook/Chmn., CEO, Pres., John D. Engelbrecht/Dir., Daniel R. Sadlier/Dir., John M. Dunn/Dir., Robert L. Koch/Dir., Timothy J. McGinley/Dir., Michael L. Smith/Dir., Jean L. Wojtowicz/Dir., Martin C. Jischke/Dir., Richard P. Rechter/Dir., William G. Mays/Dir., Richard W. Shymanski/Dir., Anton H. George/Dir.

Owners: William G. Mays, Jean L. Wojtowicz, Richard P. Rechter, Carl L. Chapman, Timothy J. McGinley, William S. Doty, John M. Dunn, Richard W. Shymanski, Niel C. Ellerbrook, Anton H. George, John D. Engelbrecht, R. Daniel Sadlier, Jerome A. Benkert, Michael L. Smith, Insiders *(18 Owners included in Index)*

Financial Data: *Fiscal Year End:*12/31 *Latest Annual Data:* 12/31/2006

Year	Sales	Net Income
2006	$2,041,600,000	$108,800,000
2005	$2,028,000,000	$136,800,000
2004	$1,689,800,000	$107,900,000

Curr. Assets:	$715,900,000	**Curr. Liab.:**	$961,400,000	**P/E Ratio:**	15.45
Plant, Equip.:	$2,679,900,000	**Total Liab.:**	$2,917,400,000	**Indic. Yr. Divd.:**	$1.260
Total Assets:	$4,091,600,000	**Net Worth:**	$1,174,200,000	**Debt/ Equity:**	0.9882

Veeco Instruments Inc

100 Sunnyside Blvd., Ste. B, Woodbury, NY, 11797; *PH:* 1-516-349-8300; *http://* www.veeco.com

General - Incorporation DE
Employees 1,279
Auditor Ernst & Young LLP
Stk Agt American Stock Transfer & Trust CO.
Counsel Kaye, Scholer LLP
DUNS No. 60-751-8297

Stock- Price on:12/24/2007 $19.05
Stock Exchange NDQ
Ticker Symbol VECO
Outstanding Shares 31,160,000
E.P.S NA
Shareholders NA

Business: The group's principal activities are to manufacture and market a broad line of equipment primarily used by manufacturers in the data storage, semiconductor, compound semiconductor/wireless and hb-led industries. The process equipment products of the group precisely deposit or remove (etch) various materials in the manufacturing of advanced thin film magnetic heads for the data storage industry, semiconductor deposition of mask reticles and compound semiconductor/wireless and led devices. The metrology equipment of the group is used to provide critical surface measurements on semiconductor devices and thin film magnetic heads. The group has operations in the United States, Europe, Japan and Asia-Pacific. On 05-Jun-2003, the group acquired the atomic force microscope probe business of nanodevices incorporated and on 18-Nov-2003, the group purchased advanced imaging inc.

Primary SIC and add'l.: 3823 3829 3559

CIK No: 0000103145

Subsidiaries: Nihon Veeco K.K., Veeco Asia Pte. Ltd., Veeco Compound Semiconductor Inc., Veeco Instruments (Shanghai) Co. Ltd., Veeco Instruments B.V., Veeco Instruments GmbH, Veeco Instruments Limited, Veeco Instruments S.A.S., Veeco Ion Beam Equipment Inc., Veeco Korea Inc., Veeco Metrology, LLC, Veeco Slider Process Equipment Inc., Veeco Taiwan Inc., Veeco Tucson Inc.

Officers: John R. Peeler/Dir., CEO, William A. Tomeo/Exec. VP - Worldwide Sales, Service, Paul Charell/Contact - Sales, Northern Cal, Nevada Territory, Eric Rufe/Contact - Sales, Other, Benjamin Loh/44/Exec. VP - Global Field Operations/$668,786.00, Henry Shii/VP, GM - Japan, Randy Beaubien/Contact - Sales, Rocky Mountain, No West, Jeff Doran/Contact - Sales, Eastern Region, Nick Isder/Contact - Sales, Veeco Compound Semiconductor Inc, Chris Rentz/Contact - Sales, Veeco Compound Semiconductor Inc, Jay Anderson/Contact - Sales, Mid, Atlantic Territory, Chris Getz/Contact - Sales, Midwest Territory, Lance Cizdek/Contact - Sales, Central Territory, Dave Laken/Contact - Sales, Southeast Territory, Gregory A. Robbins/Sr. VP, General Counsel *(51 Officers included in Index)*

Directors: John R. Peeler/Dir., CEO, Edward H. Braun/Chmn., Richard A. D'Amore/Dir., Joel A. Elftmann/Dir., Heinz K. Fridrich/Dir., Douglas A. Kingsley/Dir., Paul R. Low/Dir., Roger D. McDaniel/Dir., Irwin H. Pfister/Dir., Peter J. Simone/Dir.

Owners: Paul R. Low, Richard A. DAmore, Benjamin Loh, Capital Research and Management Company/5.10%, Douglas A. Kingsley, Joel A. Elftmann, Robert P. Oates, Paul E. Colombo/5.20%, Insiders/8.40%, John F. Rein/1.40%, Heinz K. Fridrich, Irwin H. Pfister, Edward H. Braun/4.20%, Peter J. Simone, Roger McDaniel *(17 Owners included in Index)*

Financial Data: *Fiscal Year End:*12/31 *Latest Annual Data:* 12/31/2006

Year	Sales	Net Income
2006	$441,034,000	$14,917,000
2005	$410,190,000	-$897,000
2004	$390,443,000	-$62,555,000

Curr. Assets:	$345,933,000	**Curr. Liab.:**	$97,873,000		
Plant, Equip.:	$73,510,000	**Total Liab.:**	$307,849,000	**Indic. Yr. Divd.:**	NA
Total Assets:	$589,600,000	**Net Worth:**	$281,751,000	**Debt/ Equity:**	0.5216

Velocity Asset Management Inc

1800 Rte. 34 N Building 4, Ste. 404A, Wall, NJ, 07719; *PH:* 1-732-556-9090; *Fax:* 1-732-556-0365; *http://* www.velocitycollect.com; *Email:* support@velocitycollect.com

General - Incorporation DE
Employees 8
Auditor Cowan, Gunteski & Co., P.A.
Stk Agt NA
Counsel NA
DUNS No. NA

Stock- Price on:12/24/2007 $1.75
Stock Exchange AMEX
Ticker Symbol JVI
Outstanding Shares 16,150,000
E.P.S $0.03
Shareholders NA

Business: The groups principle activity is engage in acquiring, managing, collecting and servicing distressed assets, consisting of consumer receivable portfolios, interests in distressed real property and tax lien certificates. The group operates from the United States. The group's quarterly revenue for Sep'07 was 4.09 millions of USD.

Primary SIC and add'l.: 6719

CIK No: 0000813565

Subsidiaries: J. Holder, Inc, SH Sales, Inc, TLOP Acquisition Company, Velocity Investments, LLC, VOM, LLC

Officers: John C. Kleinert/49/Chmn., CEO, Pres./$175,000.00, James J. Mastriani/Sec./$428,750.00, Peter W. Ragan/60/Dir., VP

Directors: John C. Kleinert/49/Chmn., CEO, Pres., Peter W. Ragan/60/Dir., VP, Steven Marcus/48/Dir., Michael Kelly/55/Dir., David Granatell/50/Dir.

Owners: James J. Mastriani/1.20%, David Granatell/6.80%, Michael Kelly/2.10%, Peter W. Ragan/14.30%, John C. Kleinert/56.30%, Insiders/94.90%, Peter W. Ragan/14.30%

Financial Data: *Fiscal Year End:*12/31 *Latest Annual Data:* 12/31/2006

Year	Sales	Net Income
2006	$10,284,000	$1,319,000
2005	$8,102,000	$474,000
2004	$4,356,000	-$2,705,000

Curr. Assets:	$41,042,000	**Curr. Liab.:**	$1,474,000		
Plant, Equip.:	$6,383,000	**Total Liab.:**	$26,861,000	**Indic. Yr. Divd.:**	NA
Total Assets:	$48,434,000	**Net Worth:**	$21,572,000	**Debt/ Equity:**	0.7853

Velocity Express Corp

One Morningside Dr. N, Bldg B Ste. 300, Westport, CT, 06880; *PH:* 1-612-492-2400; *http://* www.velocityexp.com; *Email:* general@velocityexp.com

General - Incorporation DE
Employees 1,155
Auditor Ernst & Young LLP
Stk Agt American Stock Transfer & Trust Co.
Counsel Briggs & Morgan
DUNS No. 80-010-8334

Stock- Price on:12/24/2007 $0.95
Stock Exchange NDQ
Ticker Symbol VEXPD
Outstanding Shares 29,460,000
E.P.S -$2.96
Shareholders NA

Business: The group's principal activity is to provide logistics services to individual consumers and businesses. The operations of the group are carried out primarily in the United States with limited operations in Canada. The customers of the group are comprised of multi-location, blue chip customers with operations in the financial, healthcare, office products, technology and energy sectors. The major trademarks of the group are velocity expresssm and relentless reliabilitysm. In Jan 4, 2002 the group acquired united shipping & technology inc.

Primary SIC and add'l.: 4215 7389

CIK No: 0001002902

Subsidiaries: CD&L Air Freight, Inc., CD&L, Inc., Clayton/National Courier Systems, Inc., Click Messenger Service, Inc., Corporate Express Distribution Services, Inc., KBD Services, Inc., Olympic Courier Systems, Inc., Securities Courier Corporation, Silver Star Express, Inc., USDS Canada LTD, Velocity Express Canada LTD, Velocity Express Leasing, Inc., Velocity Express, Inc., VXP Leasing Mid-West, Inc., VXP Mid-West, Inc.

Officers: Vincent A. Wasik/Chmn., CEO, Kay Perry-Durbin/Exec. VP - Workforce Resources, Edward W. Stone/CFO, Jeff Hendrickson/COO, Pres., Drew Kronick/Exec. VP - Business Development, Supply Chain Solutions, Mark T. Carlesimo/General Counsel, Andrew B. Kronick/45/Exec. VP - Business Development, Supply Chain Solutions, David Bassett-Parkins/CIO

Directors: Vincent A. Wasik/Chmn., CEO, Leslie E. Grodd/Dir., John J. Perkins/Dir., James G. Brown/Dir., Richard A. Kassar/Dir., Alex Paluch/Dir.

Owners: Scorpion, Pequot, Context, Insiders, Selz, Richard Kassar, Silver Oak Capital, LLC, James G. Brown, Linden Capital, LP, Andrew Kronick, Alexander I. Paluch, Longview Funds, TH Lee Putnam Ventures, Third Point, Edward W. Stone *(26 Owners included in Index)*

Financial Data: *Fiscal Year End:*07/02 **Latest Annual Data:** 7/1/2006

Year	Sales	Net Income
2006	$202,430,000	-$16,038,000
2005	$256,662,000	-$49,844,000
2004	$287,918,000	-$47,836,000

Curr. Assets:	$38,022,000	**Curr. Liab.:**	$73,565,000		
Plant, Equip.:	$11,362,000	**Total Liab.:**	$87,200,000	**Indic. Yr. Divd.:**	NA
Total Assets:	$93,676,000	**Net Worth:**	$6,476,000	**Debt/ Equity:**	0.9144

VendingData Corp

1120 N Town Ctr. Dr., Ste 260, Las Vegas, NV, 89144; *PH:* 1-702-733-7195; *http://* www.vendingdata.com

General - Incorporation	NV	**Stock**- Price on:12/24/2007	$4.03
Employees	106	Stock Exchange	NA
Auditor	Piercy, Bowler, Taylor & Kern	Ticker Symbol	NA
Stk Agt	Continental Stock Transfer & Trust Co	Outstanding Shares	33,860,000
Counsel	NA	E.P.S.	-$0.46
DUNS No.	96-897-6829	Shareholders	NA

Business: The group's principal activities are to develop, manufacture and market various concepts and products that are providing security, productivity and profitability for the gaming industry. The group's principal products are random ejection shuffler and the securedrop slot accounting system. The group also offers gaming related products such as table games and playing cards. The group operates domestic regional service centers in berkley, Michigan, and tukwila, Washington, and has service personnel located in New Jersey, Florida, and Mississippi.

Primary SIC and add'l.: 7359 3944

CIK No: 0001004673

Subsidiaries: Technical Casino Services, Ltd.

Officers: Gordon Yuen Tien Yau/Chmn., CEO, Joe Pisano/Exec. Dir., Peter Zee/61/VP - Engineering, Manufacturing/$400,348.00, Walter B. Stowe/59/VP - Legal, Compliance, General Counsel, David Reberger/CFO, Traci Mangini/Investor Relations Officer, Michael M. Friedman/Investor Relations Officer

Directors: Gordon Yuen Tien Yau/Chmn., CEO, Robert L. Miodonski/57/Dir., Joe Pisano/Exec. Dir., Lorna Patajo-Kapunan/56/Dir., Clarence Chung/45/Dir., John W. Crawford/66/Dir., Paul A. Harvey/70/Dir., Vincent L. Divito/48/Dir.

Owners: Martha Vlcek, James E. Crabbe/7.60%, Janus Capital Management LLC/5.60%, Insiders, Robert L. Miodunski, Paul A. Harvey, Peter Zee, Walter B. Stowe, Vincent L. DiVito

Financial Data: *Fiscal Year End:*12/31 **Latest Annual Data:** 12/31/2006

Year	Sales	Net Income
2006	$7,868,000	-$13,735,000
2005	$2,361,000	-$17,567,000
2004	$3,437,000	-$9,538,000

Curr. Assets:	$8,433,000	**Curr. Liab.:**	$8,452,000		
Plant, Equip.:	$3,589,000	**Total Liab.:**	$28,558,000	**Indic. Yr. Divd.:**	NA
Total Assets:	$31,531,000	**Net Worth:**	$2,973,000	**Debt/ Equity:**	0.6495

Venoco Inc

370 17th St., Ste. 3900, Denver, CO, 80202; *PH:* 1-805-745-2100; *http://* www.venocoinc.com

General - Incorporation	DE	**Stock**- Price on:12/24/2007	$20.15
Employees	250	Stock Exchange	NYSE
Auditor	Deloitte & Touche LLP	Ticker Symbol	VQ
Stk Agt	Computershare Trust Co	Outstanding Shares	43,010,000
Counsel	NA	E.P.S.	-$0.25
DUNS No.	NA	Shareholders	NA

Business: The groups principle activities include acquiring, exploring, exploitation and developing oil and natural gas properties. The group operates from the United States. The groups quarterly revenue for September 2007 was 87.00 millions of USD.

Primary SIC and add'l.: 1311 1311

CIK No: 0001313024

Subsidiaries: BMC, Ltd., Ellwood Pipeline, Inc, TexCal Energy (GP) LLC, TexCal Energy (LP) LLC, TexCal Energy North Cal L.P., TexCal Energy South Cal L.P., TexCal Energy South Texas L.P., Whittier Pipeline Corporation

Officers: Timothy Marquez/Chmn., CEO, Ed O'Donnell/Sr. VP, William Schneider/Pres., Mark Depuy/COO, Douglas Griggs/Chief Accounting Officer, Gregory B. Schrage/VP - Asset Development, Terry Sherban/VP - Acquisitions, Roger K. Hamson/VP - Coastal, Terry L. Anderson/General Counsel, Sec., Michael G. Edwards/VP - Investor Relations, Kevin Morrato/VP - Sacramento Basin, Timothy A. Ficker/CFO, Brady McConaty/VP - Texas, Carla J. Wolin/Chief Human Resources Officer

Directors: Timothy Marquez/Chmn., CEO, Joel L. Reed/Dir., Glen C. Warren/Dir., J. C. McFarland/Dir., Timothy J. Brittan/Dir., Eloy Ortega/Dir., Mark Snell/Dir., M. W. Scoggins/Dir., Richard S. Walker/Dir.

Owners: Eloy Ortega, William Schneider/2.00%, Timothy J. Brittan, Insiders/68.80%, Terry Anderson, David Christofferson, Mark Snell, Wellington Management Company, LLP/5.80%, Glen Warren, Mark DePuy, Bernadette Marquez/67.60%, Joel Reed, J. C. MacFarland

Financial Data: *Fiscal Year End:*12/31 **Latest Annual Data:** 12/31/2006

Year	Sales	Net Income
2006	$280,283,000	$23,951,000
2005	$137,953,000	$16,110,000

Curr. Assets:	$86,168,000	**Curr. Liab.:**	$86,922,000		
Plant, Equip.:	$774,253,000	**Total Liab.:**	$702,877,000	**Indic. Yr. Divd.:**	NA
Total Assets:	$893,193,000	**Net Worth:**	$190,316,000	**Debt/ Equity:**	NA

Ventana Medical Systems Inc

1910 Innovation Pk. Dr., Tucson, AZ, 85755; *PH:* 1-800-227-2155; *http://* www.ventanamed.com; *Email:* info@ventanamed.com

General - Incorporation	DE	**Stock**- Price on:12/24/2007	$53.25
Employees	952	Stock Exchange	NDQ
Auditor	Ernst & Young LLP	Ticker Symbol	VMSI
Stk Agt	Wells Fargo Shareowner Services	Outstanding Shares	37,680,000
Counsel	Wilson Sonsini Goodrich & Rosati	E.P.S.	$1.02
DUNS No.	18-404-2521	Shareholders	NA

Business: The group's principal activity is to develop, manufacture and market instruments and consumables that are used to automate diagnostic and drug discovery procedures. The products of the group consist of tissue processors, staining systems and associated reagents. The group's renaissance tissue processor is a batch instrument that processes up to 350 specimens in a single run. The group's immunohistochemistry (ihc) staining systems include techmate 500 batch-processing instrument, nexes ihc staining system and the benchmark system. The in situ hybridization (ish) staining systems marketed by the group includes genii system and the discovery system. The group also offers a full line of consumable ancillary products necessary for processing slides. The group markets its products primarily in the United States, France, Germany, Japan and Australia.

Primary SIC and add'l.: 3821 3841

CIK No: 0000893160

Subsidiaries: Ventana Medical Systems, GmbH, Ventana Medical Systems, Japan K.K., Ventana Medical Systems, Ltd., Ventana Medical Systems, Pty. Ltd., Ventana Medical Systems, S.A.

Officers: Christopher M. Gleeson/CEO, Pres./$817,527.00, Thomas M. Grogan/Chmn. Emeritus, Chief Scientific Officer, Dir. - Medical, Sr. VP - Medical Affairs, Founder, Hany Massarany/Exec. VP - Worldwide Operations/$555,163.00, Philippe Feasson/Dir. - Business, Sales Service Europe MEA, Richard Walker/Dir. - Finance, Legal, Information Technology, Administration Europe, MEA, Kendall B. Hendrick/Sr. VP - Operations, Nicholas Malden/Sr. VP, Sec./$444,032.00, Phil Miller/Sr. VP - Discovery, Mark D. Tucker/Sr. VP, General Counsel/$348,247.00, Lawrence L. Mehren/CFO, Sr. VP, Ashley Goldsmith/Sr. VP - Human Resources, Don Ellis/VP - Regulatory, Bernard Colombo/VP - Europe MEA, GM, Trevor White/Dir. - Marketing, Customer, Technical Support Europe MEA, Olivier Le Lann/Dir. - Human Resources - Facility, Communication, Environment, Europe, MEA *(16 Officers included in Index)*

Directors: Thomas M. Grogan/Chmn. Emeritus, Chief Scientific Officer, Dir. - Medical, Sr. VP - Medical Affairs, Founder, Jack Schuler/Chmn., John Patience/Vice Chmn., Edward M. Giles/Dir., Mark C. Miller/Dir., James R. Weersing/Dir., Rod Dammeyer/Dir., Thomas D. Brown/Dir.

Owners: Thomas Brown, Nicholas Malden, Insiders/21.14%, Timothy Johnson, Artisan Partners LP/6.98%, Hany Massarany, John Patience/5.72%, Mark Miller, James Weersing, Fidelity Investments/13.71%, Rod Dammeyer, Thomas Grogan, Oracle Investment Management, Inc./6.69%, Edward Giles, Mark Tucker *(17 Owners included in Index)*

Financial Data: *Fiscal Year End:*12/31 **Latest Annual Data:** 12/31/2006

Year	Sales	Net Income
2006	$238,223,000	$31,578,000
2005	$199,132,000	$25,488,000
2004	$166,102,000	$21,289,000

Curr. Assets:	$173,966,000	**Curr. Liab.:**	$52,121,000	**P/E Ratio:**	43.29
Plant, Equip.:	$65,405,000	**Total Liab.:**	$54,851,000	**Indic. Yr. Divd.:**	NA
Total Assets:	$268,630,000	**Net Worth:**	$213,779,000	**Debt/ Equity:**	0.0117

Ventas Inc

10350 Ormsby Pk. Pl, Ste 300, Louisville, KY, 40223; *PH:* 1-502-357-9000; *http://* www.ventas.com

General - Incorporation	DE	**Stock**- Price on:12/24/2007	$37.35
Employees	37	Stock Exchange	NYSE
Auditor	Ernst & Young LLP	Ticker Symbol	VTR
Stk Agt	National City Bank	Outstanding Shares	106,350,000
Counsel	Willkie Farr & Gallagher LLP	E.P.S.	$2.49
DUNS No.	13-153-0511	Shareholders	NA

Business: The group's principle activity is to provide finance, owning and leasing healthcare-related and senior housing facilities. On 31-Mar-2004, the portfolio of the group consisted of healthcare related facilities that consisted of 42 hospitals, 199 nursing facilities and 25 senior housing facilities and 11 other healthcare facilities facilities in 39 states. The group has investments relating to 25 healthcare and senior housing facilities located in Ohio and Maryland. The group leases these facilities to healthcare operating companies under leases. The group's quarterly revenue for September 2007 was 226.29 millions of USD.

Primary SIC and add'l.: 6798 7352

CIK No: 0000740260

Subsidiaries: BLC Issuer II, LLC, BLC of California-San Marcos, L.P., BLC of Indiana-OL, L.P., Brookdale Holdings, LLC, Brookdale Living Communities of Arizona-EM, LLC, Brookdale Living Communities of California, LLC, Brookdale Living Communities of California-RC, LLC, Brookdale Living Communities of California-San Marcos, LLC, Brookdale Living Communities of Connecticut, LLC, Brookdale Living Communities of Connecticut-WH, LLC, Brookdale Living Communities of Florida-CL, LLC, Brookdale Living Communities of Illinois-2960, LLC, Brookdale Living Communities of Illinois-HLAL, LLC, Brookdale Living Communities of Illinois-Hoffman Estates, LLC, Brookdale Living Communities of Illinois-HV, LLC 108 Subsidiaries included in the Index

Officers: Debra A. Cafaro/Chmn., CEO, Pres./$4,913,988.00, Raymond J. Lewis/Exec. VP, Chief Investment Officer/$1,811,150.00, Richard T. Riney/Exec. VP, General Counsel, Sec./$1,602,007.00, Richard A. Schweinhart/CFO, Exec. VP/$1,882,242.00, Kristen M. Benson/VP - Securities Counsel, Robert J. Brehl/Chief Accounting Officer, Controller, Vincent M. Cozzi/VP - Acquisitions, Timothy A. Doman/Sr. VP - Asset Management, Brian K. Wood/Sr. VP - Tax, Lisabeth Weiner/Contact - Investor Relations, Financial Media, Renee Tilton/Healthcare Media Relations, Joseph G. Solari/MD - Acquisitions, Christian N. Cummings/35/VP - Asset Management

Directors: Debra A. Cafaro/Chmn., CEO, Pres., Douglas Crocker/Dir., Ronald G. Geary/Dir., Jay M. Gellert/Dir., Sheli Z. Rosenberg/Dir., Thomas C. Theobald/Dir.

Owners: ING Groep N.V./5.68%, T. Richard Riney, Wellington Management Company/4.94%, Richard A. Schweinhart, Insiders/2.03%, Christopher T. Hannon, Sheli Z. Rosenberg, Raymond J. Lewis, Thomas C. Theobald, Cohen & Steers, Inc./9.37%, Jay M. Gellert, AMVESCAP PLC/5.32%

Financial Data: Fiscal Year End:12/31 Latest Annual Data: 12/31/2006

Year	Sales	Net Income
2006	$428,349,000	$131,430,000
2005	$332,988,000	$130,583,000
2004	$236,856,000	$120,900,000

Curr. Assets:	$1,246,000	Curr. Liab.:	$176,283,000	P/E Ratio:	13.88
Plant, Equip.:	$3,048,253,000	Total Liab.:	$2,543,924,000	Indic. Yr. Divd.:	$1.900
Total Assets:	$3,253,800,000	Net Worth:	$709,876,000	Debt/ Equity:	NA

Ventura County BK CA

366 W Esplanade, Oxnard, CA, 93036; *PH:* 1-805-604-7600; *Fax:* 1-805-604-4447; *http://* www.vcbbank.com

General - Incorporation		Stock- Price on:12/24/2007	$11.99
Employees	NA	Stock Exchange	OTC
Auditor	NA	Ticker Symbol	VCBB
Stk Agt	NA	Outstanding Shares	NA
Counsel	NA	E.P.S	NA
DUNS No.	NA	Shareholders	NA

Business: The groups principal activities include providing banking and financial services to the businesses and customers. Services of the group include checking accounts, savings accounts, certificates of deposit, installment loans, real estate mortgage loans, commercial loans, traveler's checks, safe deposit boxes, night depository, automated teller services and Internet banking.

Primary SIC and add'l.: 6021

CIK No:

Officers: Gerald J. Lukiewski/Dir., CEO, Pres., Charles A. Myers/Exec. VP, Chief Credit Officer, Keith Sciarillo/CFO, Exec. VP

Directors: Gerald J. Lukiewski/Dir., CEO, Pres., Robert E. Hogan/Dir., John G. Mogler/Dir., Robert B. Hamilton/Dir. Emeritus, Michael D. Bradbury/Dir., Donald K. Facciano/Dir., David T. Gulbranson/Dir., Randall L. Hays/Dir.

Venture Catalyst Inc

591 Camino De La Reina, Ste. 418, San Diego, CA, 92108; *PH:* 1-619-330-4000; *http://* www.vcat.com

General - Incorporation	UT	Stock- Price on:12/24/2007	NA
Employees	38	Stock Exchange	NA
Auditor	Grant Thornton LLP	Ticker Symbol	NA
Stk Agt	Chase Mellon Shareholder Services LLC	Outstanding Shares	NA
Counsel	Paul, Hastings, Janofsky & Walker LLP	E.P.S	NA
DUNS No.	79-353-6939	Shareholders	NA

Business: The group's principal activity is to provide gaming consulting and infrastructure and technology integration services in the California native American gaming market. The services provided by the group include comprehensive gaming and hospitality consulting services, financial advisory services, public and governmental relations, strategic planning, technology solutions and professional and technical expertise. The group currently has one client, the barona group of captain grade band of mission indians, a federally recognized, sovereign native American tribe. The group has also developed a fully integrated customer relationship management and marketing software product for the gaming and hospitality industry known as mariposa.

Primary SIC and add'l.: 7373 7999

CIK No: 0000318291

Officers: Greg Shay/CEO, Pres., Clifford Lachappa/VP - Native American Business Development, Kelly Jacobs Speer/VP - Marketing, Public Relations, Donne Grable/VP - Gaming Operations, Fritz Opel/Marketing Specialist, Kevin McIntosh/CFO, COO, Rick Rinaldi/Contact

Directors: Don Speer/Chmn.

Venture Financial Group Inc

721 College St. S.e., Lacey, WA, 98509; *PH:* 1-360-459-1100

General - Incorporation	WA	Stock- Price on:12/24/2007	NA
Employees	NA	Stock Exchange	NA
Auditor	Moss Adams LLP	Ticker Symbol	NA
Stk Agt	NA	Outstanding Shares	NA
Counsel	NA	E.P.S	NA
DUNS No.	84-979-9259	Shareholders	NA

Business: The group's principal activity is to provide general banking business, which includes accepting demand, time and savings deposits and lending loans in the United States. The operations are conducted through twenty branches located in thurston, grays harbor, lewis and pierce counties. Other services include a full range of banking services, savings accounts, checking accounts, instalment, mortgage and commercial lending, safety deposit facilities, time deposits and other consumer and business-related financial services, including the sale of non-deposit investment products.

Primary SIC and add'l.: 6022 6712

CIK No: 0000892449

Subsidiaries: First Community Financial Group Capital Trust I, First Community Financial Group Capital Trust II, Venture Bank

Officers: Ken F. Parsons/Chmn., CEO/$576,214.00, Brenda Hoffman/Office Mgr., Sandi Drennon/VP - Investment Advisor Representative, Kurt Lamm/Investment Advisor Representative, Sandra L. Sager/CFO, Exec. VP/$288,763.00, James F. Arneson/Dir., Pres./$405,100.00, Kristen Williams/Investment Advisor Representative, Heather Lafranchi/Sales Assist., Patricia A. Graves/Exec. VP - Retail Banking/$213,273.00, Bruce H. Marley/Exec. VP, Chief Lending Officer/$238,372.00, Leann Zembas/Investor Relations Officer, Catherine J. Mosby/Sr. VP - Human Resources, Joseph P. Beaulieu/Sr. VP - Marketing, Larry Messegee/Financial Center Mgr., AVP

Directors: Ken F. Parsons/Chmn., CEO, James F. Arneson/Dir., Pres., Keith W. Brewe/Dir., Lowell E. Bridges/Dir., Linda Buckner/Dir., Jewell C. Manspeaker/Dir., Patrick L. Martin/Dir., Richard A. Panowicz/Dir., Larry J. Schorno/Dir.

Owners: Insiders/21.70%, Ken F. Parsons/6.60%, Linda E. Buckner, Sandra L. Sager, Patricia A. Graves, Patrick L. Martin/1.50%, James F. Arneson, Lowell E. Bridges, Bruce H. Marley, Keith W. Brewe, Larry J. Schorno, Jewell C. Manspeaker, Richard A. Panowicz/1.60%

Veolia Environnement

14950 Heathrow Forest, Ste. 200, Houston, TX, 77032; *PH:* 1-800-522-4774; *http://* www.veoliaenvironnement.com

General - Incorporation	France	Stock- Price on:12/24/2007	$77.66
Employees	260,088	Stock Exchange	NYSE
Auditor	Barbier Frinault & Autres	Ticker Symbol	VE
Stk Agt	NA	Outstanding Shares	394,180,000
Counsel	NA	E.P.S	$2.90
DUNS No.	NA	Shareholders	NA

Business: The group's principle activities are carried out through the following areas: water: management of distribution systems on behalf of cities or counties; distribution, treatment and filtration of water from local communities and industrial sites, bottled water; hygiene: treatment and recycling of domestic and industrial wastes; water treatment; incineration of volatile organic compounds, cleaning of cities; energy: industrial and other heating systems, industrial services, maintenance of equipment ; transport: public transport, road transport.

Primary SIC and add'l.: 9511 8741 4941 5088 3433 4212 4953

CIK No: 0001160110

Officers: Henri Proglio/Chmn., CEO, Antoine Frerot/Exec. VP, CEO - Veolia Water, Denis Gasquet/Exec. VP, CEO - Veolia Environmental Services, Cyrille De Peloux/Exec. VP, CEO - Veolia Transport, Alain Tchernonog/General Sec., Olivier Barbaroux/Exec. VP, Jerome Contamine/Sr. Exec. VP

Directors: Henri Proglio/Chmn., CEO, Jean-Francois Dehecq/Dir., Serge Michel/Dir., Jean Azema/Dir., Augustin De Romanet De Beaune/Dir., Paolo Scaroni/Dir., Georges Ralli/Dir., Jean-Marc Espalioux/Dir., Baudouin Prot/Dir., Daniel Bouton/Dir., Philippe Kourilsky/Dir., Murray Stuart/Dir., Paul-Louis Girardot/Dir., Louis Schweitzer/Dir.

Owners: Groupe Groupama/5.85%, Public and other investors/66.57%, Insiders/100.00%, Capital Research and Management Company/9.92%, Veolia Environnement/3.67%, Caisse des Dpts et Consignations/10.05%, EDF/3.94%

Financial Data: Fiscal Year End:12/31 Latest Annual Data: 12/31/2006

Year	Sales	Net Income
2006	$37,787,514,000	$966,592,000
2005	$29,900,060,000	$658,171,000
2004	$33,664,251,000	$292,664,000

Curr. Assets:	$19,746,935,000	Curr. Liab.:	$20,404,708,000	P/E Ratio:	25.53
Plant, Equip.:	$10,206,447,000	Total Liab.:	$46,848,601,000	Indic. Yr. Divd.:	$2.450
Total Assets:	$51,043,986,000	Net Worth:	$4,195,385,000	Debt/ Equity:	NA

Veramark Technologies Inc

3750 Monroe Ave., Pittsford, NY, 14534; *PH:* 1-585-381-6000; *http://* www.veramark.com

General - Incorporation	DE	Stock- Price on:12/24/2007	$0.75
Employees	94	Stock Exchange	OTC
Auditor	Rotenberg & Co. LLP	Ticker Symbol	VERA
Stk Agt	American Stock Transfer & Trust Co.	Outstanding Shares	8,860,000
Counsel	NA	E.P.S	-$0.05
DUNS No.	01-916-3161	Shareholders	NA

Business: The group's principal activity is to produce telecommunications management systems. The products are used by private branch exchange (pbx) based voice networks, Internet protocol (ip) based voice networks and data networks. These products are used to track, report and manage telephone usage, equipment location and maintenance activity and telecom fraud. The group's products consist primarily of Web-based software applications that run on personal computers or servers that use microsoft windows operating systems and microsoft sql server database management. Its call accounting systems are sold through manufacturers and resellers of telephone systems including avaya, sbc, scansource/catalyst telecom, vodaone, jenne communications, sprint/north supply, and graybar.

Primary SIC and add'l.: 7372

CIK No: 0000747605

Officers: Ronald C. Lundy/VP - Finance, CFO/$150,831.00

Owners: Insiders/19.30%, Ronald C. Lundy/1.70%, Andrew W. Moylan, John E. Gould/1.20%, Summit Capital Management, LLC/15.50%, Charles A. Constantino, Martin LoBiondo/1.80%, Douglas F. Smith/1.50%, David G. Mazzella/10.50%, Michael R. Holly, William J. Reilly/1.40%, Albert J. Montevecchio/6.70%

Financial Data: Fiscal Year End:12/31 Latest Annual Data: 12/31/2006

Year	Sales	Net Income
2006	$10,361,000	-$488,000
2005	$10,859,000	$382,000
2004	$11,036,000	-$114,000

Curr. Assets:	$3,434,000	Curr. Liab.:	$4,834,000		
Plant, Equip.:	$669,000	Total Liab.:	$9,930,000	Indic. Yr. Divd.:	NA
Total Assets:	$10,933,000	Net Worth:	$1,003,000	Debt/ Equity:	NA

Verasun Energy Corp

100 22nd Ave., Brookings, SD, 57006; *PH:* 1-605-696-7200; *Fax:* 1-605-696-7250; *http://* www.verasun.com

General - Incorporation	SD	Stock- Price on:12/24/2007	$13.08
Employees	195	Stock Exchange	NYSE
Auditor	McGladrey & Pullen LLP	Ticker Symbol	VSE
Stk Agt	Wells Fargo Shareowner Services	Outstanding Shares	76,900,000
Counsel	NA	E.P.S	NA
DUNS No.	NA	Shareholders	NA

Business: The groups principle activities include producing and marketing ethanol products. The group operates from the United States. The groups quarterly revenue for September 2007 was 221.87 millions of USD.

Primary SIC and add'l.: 2865 2869

CIK No: 0001343202

Subsidiaries: VeraSun Aurora Corporation, VeraSun BioDiesel, LLC, VeraSun Charles City, LLC, VeraSun Fort Dodge, LLC, VeraSun Granite City, LLC, VeraSun Hartley, LLC, VeraSun Marketing, LLC, VeraSun Reynolds, LLC, VeraSun Welcome, LLC

Officers: Don Endres/Chmn., CEO, Pres., Danny C. Herron/Sr. VP, CFO, Bill Honnef/Sr. VP - Strategic Initiatives, Keith Bruinsma/VP - Corporate Development, Patty Dickerson/Dir. - Investor Relations, Mark Dickey/VP, Assist. General Counsel, Rick Eggebrecht/VP - Marketing Development,

John M. Schweitzer/Sr. VP, General Counsel, Paul J. Caudill/Sr. VP - Operations, Darin Fedt/VP - Corporate Development, Bryan Meier/VP, Controller, Kurt Swenson/VP - Plant Operations, Melissa Ullerich/Dir. - Marketing, Communications, Paul Kreter/VP - Ethanol Sales, Peter Atkins/VP - Corporate Development *(18 Officers included in Index)*

Directors: Don Endres/Chmn., CEO, Pres., Bruce A. Jamerson/56/Dir., Duane D. Gilliam/Dir., Jack Huggins/Dir., Paul Schock/Dir., Steven T. Kirby/Dir., Mark L. First/43/Dir.

Owners: Donald L. Endres/42.80%, Steven T. Kirby/1.20%, Insiders/48.20%, Jack T. Huggins, Duane D. Gilliam, Eos Funds, 320 Park Ave. New York, NY 10022/6.30%, John M. Schweitzer, Paul A. Schock/1.30%, Bruce A. Jamerson/1.80%, Danny C. Herron, William L. Honnef

Financial Data: Fiscal Year End:NA Latest Annual Data: 3/31/2007

Year	Sales	Net Income
2007	NA	NA
2006	NA	NA

Curr. Assets:	$436,216,000	Curr. Liab.:	$52,149,000		
Plant, Equip.:	$301,720,000	Total Liab.:	$288,066,000	Indic. Yr. Divd.:	NA
Total Assets:	$794,497,000	Net Worth:	$506,431,000	Debt/ Equity:	0.4054

Verdant Technology Corp

Formerly: HeartSTAT Technology Inc
530 Wilshire Blvd., Ste. 304, Santa Monica, CA, 90401; *PH:* 1-310-451-7400;
http:// www.heartstat.com

General - Incorporation	DE	Stock - Price on:12/24/2007	$0.82
Employees	NA	Stock Exchange	OTC
Auditor	Bongiovanni & Assoc. P.A	Ticker Symbol	VTHC
Stk Agt	Corporate Stock Transfer, Inc.	Outstanding Shares	NA
Counsel	NA	E.P.S.	NA
DUNS No.	NA	Shareholders	NA

Business: The group's principle activity is to develop a practical system for monitoring blood flow perfusion and important heart dynamics. It is noninvasive, continuous, and uses a simple comfortable disposable sensor. This addresses key issues of hospital critical care. The group's FDA-cleared CNBP system was recently cost re-engineered to be the first price competitive continuous system for upgrading a market of over a million units. The company recently enhanced this technology to include a single-patient use sensor for an optional CNBP for upgrading users to blood flow perfusion monitoring without the delay of capital budgeting. The company serves the health care industry. The group operates from United States.

Primary SIC and add'l.: 3841

CIK No: 0001298700

Subsidiaries: Alexis BioMedical Technology Fund, Inc

Officers: Ted W. Russell/CEO, CTO, Dir., Sandy J. Eames/VP - Marketing, Richard R. Imbruce/VP - Medical Affairs, Michael Stillabower/Member - Scientific Advisory Board, MD

Directors: Ted W. Russell/CEO, CTO, Dir., David A. Lubarsky/Dir., Patrick A. Maley/Dir., Abraham Noordergraaf/Member - Scientific Advisory Board, Nikolaus Gravenstein/Member - Scientific Advisory Board, Baruch Barry Lieber/Member - Scientific Advisory Board, Daniel Baram/Member - Scientific Advisory Board, Michel Safar/Member - Scientific Advisory Board, Daniel Bluestein/Member - Scientific Advisory Board, William Santamore/Member - Scientific Advisory Board, Michael Stillabower/Member - Scientific Advisory Board, MD, Lennart Fagraeus/Member - Scientific Advisory Board

Veri-Tek International Corp

7402 W 100th Pl., Bridgeview, IL, 60455; *PH:* 1-708-430-7500; *Fax:* 1-708-430-1227;
http:// www.veri-tek.com; *Email:* InvestorRelations@veri-tek.com

General - Incorporation	MI	Stock - Price on:12/24/2007	$7.26
Employees	279	Stock Exchange	AMEX
Auditor	UHY LLP	Ticker Symbol	VCC
Stk Agt	NA	Outstanding Shares	7,860,000
Counsel	NA	E.P.S.	-$0.945
DUNS No.	NA	Shareholders	NA

Business: The groups principle activities include designing, developing and built integrated production line assembly and testing equipment for the automotive and heavy equipment industries. The group marketed its products under the trade names S.M.A.R.T.(TM). The group products include VETAG axle test equipment, virtual balancing equipment, half shaft production testers and engine equipment. Specific customers of the group include Hyolim, KASCO, and Dae Seung, Visteon, and Dana. The group operates from the United States, Korea, Mexico and Brazil. The group's quarterely revenue for September 2007 was 26.60 millions of USD.

Primary SIC and add'l.: 3549 7372 3829 3531 3536 3537

CIK No: 0001302028

Officers: David Langevin/Chmn., CEO, David Gransee/CFO

Directors: David Langevin/Chmn., CEO, Terrence P. McKenna/Dir., Marvin B. Rosenberg/Dir.

Owners: Todd C. Antenucci, Insiders/8.50%, Russell B. Faucett/8.80%, Jeffrey L. Feinberg/33.70%, The Pinnacle Fund, L.P./8.80%, David J. Langevin/8.50%

Financial Data: Fiscal Year End:12/31 Latest Annual Data: 12/31/2006

Year	Sales	Net Income
2006	$45,768,000	-$8,889,000
2005	$7,641,000	-$2,253,000
2004	$7,929,000	-$3,454,000

Curr. Assets:	$36,114,000	Curr. Liab.:	$19,321,000		
Plant, Equip.:	$6,417,000	Total Liab.:	$65,404,000	Indic. Yr. Divd.:	NA
Total Assets:	$83,844,000	Net Worth:	$18,440,000	Debt/ Equity:	1.9581

Veridicom International Inc

21 Water St., 5th Fl., Vancouver, BC, V6B 1A1; *PH:* 1-408-734-7980; *http://* www.veridicom.com;
Email: info@veridicom.com

General - Incorporation	DE	Stock - Price on:12/24/2007	NA
Employees	NA	Stock Exchange	OTC
Auditor	Manning Elliott LLP	Ticker Symbol	VRDIE
Stk Agt	U.S. Stock Transfer Corp	Outstanding Shares	NA
Counsel	NA	E.P.S.	NA
DUNS No.	06-460-9878	Shareholders	NA

Business: The group's principal activity is to provide biometric authentication and identity management solutions. These solutions are built on proprietary and patented hardware products, software solution and algorithms. The group offers the only complete 'out-of-the-box' identity management solution, integrating hardware and core enterprise middleware and application software into one seamless authentication suite. Identity management solutions are used in government, defense, enterprise, industry and matters of homeland security. The group has a portfolio of 33 patents and several international patents for its technology. Several pending patent applications include identification and security using biometric measurements, capacitive fingerprint acquisition sensor, method for combining fingerprint templates, method for imaging fingerprints and concealing latent fingerprints, method for live finger and anti-spoofing techniques.

Primary SIC and add'l.: 7373 7372

CIK No: 0000710217

Subsidiaries: Cavio Corporation, Esstec Inc, Veridicom Inc., Veridicom International (Canada) Inc, Veridicom Pakistan (Private) Limited

Officers: Dan Stryker/52/CEO, Pres., Jeremy Coles/Contact, Tony Jackson/Contact

Owners: Dara Bashir Khan/6.70%, Hamid Baradaran/0.20%, Insiders/7.30%, Shannon McCallum/0.20%, Jermey Coles/0.20%, Bill Cheung/1.30%, Paul Mann/5.50%

Veridien Corp

7600 Bryan Dairy Rd., Ste. F, Largo, FL, 33777; *PH:* 1-727-576-1600; *http://* www.veridien.com

General - Incorporation	DE	Stock - Price on:12/24/2007	$0.038
Employees	4	Stock Exchange	OTC
Auditor	Malone & Bailey, P.C	Ticker Symbol	VRDE
Stk Agt	American Stock Transfer & Trust Co.	Outstanding Shares	257,850,000
Counsel	NA	E.P.S.	-$0.02
DUNS No.	NA	Shareholders	NA

Business: The group's principal activity is to develop, manufacture, distribute and sell disinfectants, antiseptics and sterilants that are non-toxic, environment friendly and which decompose into harmless naturally occurring organic molecules. Virahol(R), a hard surface disinfectant and viragel(R), an antiseptic hand gel sanitizer are the major patented products. The products offered by the group are used by the health care and medical industry and also for consumer and commercial applications.

Primary SIC and add'l.: 2834 2842

CIK No: 0001064011

Subsidiaries: Communications Gear, Inc., Marquit Manufacturing Specialties, Inc., Norpak (U.S.), Inc., Rost Inc., Rost Medical Development, Inc., The SunSwipe Corporation, LLC, Veridien.com Inc.

Officers: Sheldon C. Fenton/Dir., CEO, Pres., Rene A. Gareau/Vice Chmn., Corp. Sec., Russell D. Van Zandt/66/Chmn., CFO, Paul Dunnigan/VP - Marketing Group, Cheryl Ballou/Mgr. - Financial, Shareholder, Howard Bochnek/Dir. - Technology, Regulatory Affairs, Mark Krautler/Customer Service Representative, Kimberly Martyn/Assist. Mgr. - Accounting

Directors: Sheldon C. Fenton/Dir., CEO, Pres., Rene A. Gareau/Vice Chmn., Corp. Sec., Russell D. Van Zandt/66/Chmn., CFO, Kenneth C. Cancellara/Dir., Richard B. Klein/Dir., Alfred A. Ritter/Dir.

Owners: Sheldon C. Fenton, Russell D. Van Zandt, Margreat, Inc., Dunvegan Mortgage Corporation, Mineola Holdings Corporation, Richard Klein, Lexxec Corporation, Sarasota Retail Investments, Inc., Rene A. Gareau, Insiders, Allen Greenspoon

Financial Data: Fiscal Year End:12/31 Latest Annual Data: 12/31/2006

Year	Sales	Net Income
2006	$1,850,000	-$2,815,000
2005	$1,064,000	-$1,976,000
2004	$1,802,000	-$637,000

Curr. Assets:	$1,420,000	Curr. Liab.:	$1,636,000		
Plant, Equip.:	$36,000	Total Liab.:	$1,787,000	Indic. Yr. Divd.:	NA
Total Assets:	$2,780,000	Net Worth:	$994,000	Debt/ Equity:	0.0481

Veridigm Inc

17383 Sunset Blvd., Ste. B-280, Pacific Palisades, CA, 90272; *PH:* 1-310-566-4765; *http://* www.veridigm.com

General - Incorporation	DE	Stock - Price on:12/24/2007	$0.18
Employees	NA	Stock Exchange	OTC
Auditor	Michael F. Albanee, CPA	Ticker Symbol	VRDG
Stk Agt	Manhattan Transfer Registrar Co	Outstanding Shares	68,710,000
Counsel	NA	E.P.S.	$0.009
DUNS No.	NA	Shareholders	NA

Business: The groups principle activity is engaged in the payment processing of transactions for banks and their merchants through its terminals and proprietary system. The group operates from the United States.

Primary SIC and add'l.: 7389

CIK No: 0001082594

Officers: Jeffrey Eng/67/Dir., CEO, Pres., Acting CFO, Alise Mills/Dir., VP - Corporate Communications

Directors: Jeffrey Eng/67/Dir., CEO, Pres., Acting CFO, Alise Mills/Dir., VP - Corporate Communications

Owners: Jeffrey Eng/29.11%

Financial Data: Fiscal Year End:12/31 Latest Annual Data: 12/31/2006

Year	Sales	Net Income
2006	NA	-$22,681,000
2005	NA	-$56,000
2004	NA	-$105,000

Curr. Assets:	$56,000	Curr. Liab.:	$1,707,000		
Plant, Equip.:	$5,000	Total Liab.:	$1,707,000	Indic. Yr. Divd.:	NA
Total Assets:	$61,000	Net Worth:	-$1,645,000	Debt/ Equity:	NA

Verigy Ltd

10100 N Tantau, Cupertino, CA, 95014; *PH:* 1-408-864-2900; *http://* www.verigy.com;
Email: support-americas@verigy.com

General - Incorporation.................. Singapore
Employees 1,500
Auditor ....PricewaterhouseCoopers LLP
Stk Agt.....Computershare Investor Services LLC
Counsel...NA
DUNS No. ....NA

Stock- Price on:12/24/2007 ....$28.93
Stock Exchange...NDQ
Ticker Symbol... VRGY
Outstanding Shares 59,140,000
E.P.S..NA
Shareholders..NA

Business: The groups principle activities include designing, developing, manufacturing and selling test systems and solutions. The products of the group include flash memory, multi-chip packages, 93000 Series platform and high speed memory devices. Specific customer of the group is ChipMos Technologies Ltd. The group operates from the United States, Singapore, Japan and Rest of the World. The group's total revenue in the year 2007 was 761.00 millions of USD.

Primary SIC and add'l.: 3825 3826 3559

CIK No: 0001352341

Subsidiaries: Verigy (Canada) Inc., Verigy (Japan) K.K., Verigy (Korea) Ltd., Verigy (Malaysia) Sdn. Bhd., Verigy (Netherlands) B.V., Verigy (Shanghai) Co. Ltd., Verigy (Singapore) Pte. Ltd., Verigy (US) Development,Inc., Verigy France SAS, Verigy Germany GmbH, Verigy Italia S.r.L., Verigy US,Inc.

Officers: Keith L. Barnes/Chmn., CEO, Pres., Robert J. Nikl/52/CFO, Debbora Ahlgren/VP, Chief Marketing Officer, Gayn Erickson/VP - Memory Test, Kristen Robinson/VP - Human Resources, Pascal Ronde/VP - Sales, Service, Support, Kenneth M. Siegel/VP, General Counsel, Hans-Juergen Wagner/VP - SOC Test, Judy Davies/VP - Investor Relations, Dietmar Holler/50/VP - Order Fulfillment

Directors: Keith L. Barnes/Chmn., CEO, Pres., Adrian T. Dillon/54/Dir., Paul Chan Kwai Wah/Dir., Scott C. Gibson/Dir., Ernest L. Godshalk/Dir., Eric Meurice/Dir., Claudine Simson/Dir., Ed Grady/Dir.

Owners: The Goldman Sachs Group,Inc./5.60%, Iridian Asset Management LLC/5.80%, The TCW Group,Inc./5.40%, Fidelity Management& Research Company/10.60%, Pascal Rond, Insiders, Adrian T. Dillon, Keith L. Barnes, Kenneth M. Siegel, Gayn Erickson

Financial Data: Fiscal Year End:10/31   Latest Annual Data: 10/31/2006

Year	Sales	Net Income
2006	$778,000,000	NA
2005	$456,000,000	-$119,000,000
2004	$607,000,000	-$8,000,000

Curr. Assets:	$551,000,000	**Curr. Liab.:**	$251,000,000		
Plant, Equip.:	$44,000,000	**Total Liab.:**	$285,000,000	**Indic. Yr. Divd.:**	NA
Total Assets:	$674,000,000	**Net Worth:**	$389,000,000	**Debt/ Equity:**	NA

Verilink Corp

11551 E Arapahoe Rd. , Ste. 150, Centennial, CO, 80112; ; *http://* www.verilink.com

General - Incorporation.............................. DE
Employees 180
Auditor ...Ehrhardt Keefe Steiner & Hottman P.C
Stk Agt...... American Stock Transfer & Trust Co.
Counsel........Powell, Goldstein, Frazer & Murphy
DUNS No. 10-290-4406

Stock- Price on:12/24/2007 ....$0.005
Stock Exchange...OTC
Ticker Symbol..VRLKQ
Outstanding Shares 25,190,000
E.P.S. ....-$0.687
Shareholders..NA

Business: The group's principal activities are to develop, manufacture and market integrated access products and customer premise equipment products. It's products offer total solutions for network access and Web-based network monitoring and control-providing multi-service networks with optimum performance for all voice and data applications. These products enable connections at broadband access transmission speeds of t1, digital subscriber line and various optical carrier speeds with access services and protocols. The customers of the group include regional bell operating companies, interexchange carriers, incumbent local exchange carriers, competitive local exchange carriers, international post, telephone and telegraph administrations, wireless service providers and various local, state, and federal government agencies. On 05-Feb-2004, the group acquired xel communications, inc and on 28-Jul-2004, the group acquired larscom incorporated.

Primary SIC and add'l.: 3661

CIK No: 0000774937

Financial Data: Fiscal Year End:07/01   Latest Annual Data: 7/1/2005

Year	Sales	Net Income
2005	$53,292,000	-$37,452,000
2004	$46,183,000	-$26,000
2003	$28,104,000	$1,520,000

Curr. Assets:	$18,280,000	**Curr. Liab.:**	$15,502,000		
Plant, Equip.:	$7,650,000	**Total Liab.:**	$21,764,000	**Indic. Yr. Divd.:**	NA
Total Assets:	$46,138,000	**Net Worth:**	$24,374,000	**Debt/ Equity:**	NA

Verint Systems Inc

330 S Service Rd. , Melville, NY, 11747; *PH:* 1-631-962-9600; *http://* www.verint.com;
Email: info@verint.com

General - Incorporation............................. DE
Employees 1,200
Auditor ....Deloitte & Touche LLP
Stk Agt..... American Stock Transfer & Trust Co.
Counsel...NA
DUNS No. ....NA

Stock- Price on:12/24/2007 ....NA
Stock Exchange...OTC
Ticker Symbol...VRNT
Outstanding Shares ....NA
E.P.S..NA
Shareholders..NA

Business: The group's principal activity is to provide analytic software-based solutions for the security and business intelligence markets. The group offers solutions for generating actionable intelligence for communications interception, networked video and contact centers. Communications interception solutions consist of monitoring and recording of voice and data transmissions to and from a specified target over communications networks in order to obtain intelligence and gather evidence. These solutions are used by law enforcement agencies, government agencies and telecommunications carriers. Networked video solutions consist of surveillance of facilities and operations to ensure the proper level of security. These solutions are used by government agencies and public and private organizations. The group's markets include the United States, Australia, Canada, France, Germany, Hong Kong, India, Israel, Japan, the Netherlands, Singapore and the United Kingdom.

Primary SIC and add'l.: 7372 7375

CIK No: 0001166388

Subsidiaries: RP France SARL, RP Security Limited, SmartVideoSystems GmbH, Syborg Informationsysteme OHG, Verint Systems (India) Private Ltd., Verint Systems (Singapore) Pte. Ltd., Verint Systems B.V., Verint Systems Canada Inc., Verint Systems GmbH, Verint Systems Ltd., Verint Systems SAS, Verint Systems UK Ltd., Verint Technology Inc., Verint Video Solutions AB, Verint Video Solutions BV 19 Subsidiaries included in the Index

Officers: Dan Bodner/Dir., CEO, Pres., David Parcell/MD - EMEA, Corp. Officer, Meir Sperling/Pres. - Apac, Corp. Officer, Elan Moriah/Pres. - Americas, Corp. Officer, Doug Robinson/CFO, Peter Fante/Chief Legal Officer

Directors: Dan Bodner/Dir., CEO, Pres., Victor A. De Marines/Chmn., Kenneth A. Minihan/Dir., Howard Safir/Dir., Andre Dahan/Dir., Avi T. Aronovitz/Dir., Paul D. Baker/Dir., Larry Myers/Dir., Lauren Wright/Dir., Shefali Shah/Dir.

Curr. Assets:	$306,633,000	**Curr. Liab.:**	$110,252,000		
Plant, Equip.:	$17,540,000	**Total Liab.:**	$115,603,000	**Indic. Yr. Divd.:**	NA
Total Assets:	$398,978,000	**Net Worth:**	$283,375,000	**Debt/ Equity:**	NA

VeriSign Inc

487 E Middlefield Rd. , Mountain View, CA, 94043; ; *http://* www.verisign.com;
Email: IR@verisign.com

General - Incorporation .... DE
Employees 4,076
Auditor ....KPMG LLP
Stk Agt.................Mellon Investor Services LLC
Counsel...NA
DUNS No. 88-389-4040

Stock- Price on:12/24/2007 ....$28.94
Stock Exchange...NDQ
Ticker Symbol...VRSN
Outstanding Shares 242,890,000
E.P.S..$0.19
Shareholders..NA

Business: The group's principal activity is to provide digital trust services that enable Web site owners, enterprises and communications service providers, e-commerce service providers and individuals to engage in secure digital commerce and communications. It operates through three segments: the Internet services group which consists of the security services business and the naming and directory services business. The communications services group provides signaling system 7, network services, intelligent data base and directory services, application services, and billing and payment services. The network solutions provides domain name registration and value-added services. The group acquired unc-embratel in oct 2003 and guardant in feb 2004. The group sold its network solutions business segment in 2003.on 26-Feb-2004, the group completed the acquisition of guardent inc and on 11-Mar-2004, completed the acquisition of assets of unimobile.

Primary SIC and add'l.: 7372 7371 7373

CIK No: 0001014473

Subsidiaries: Best4U Media Sarl, Elocom Mobile Entertainment GmbH, Embp 455, LLC, Embp 685, LLC, eNIC Corporation, Garden Acquisition LLC, Global Registration Services Limited, iDefense, Inc., iLove GmbH, JAMBA Service GmbH, Jamba! AG Schweiz, Jamba! B.V., Jamba! GmbH, Jamster International Sarl, LightSurf International, Inc. 61 Subsidiaries included in the Index

Officers: Teruhide Hashimoto/CEO, Pres. - Verisign Japan, William A. Roper/Dir., CEO, Pres., Aristotle N. Balogh/CTO, Head - Global Product Development, Robert J. Korzeniewski/Exec. VP - Corporate Development, Strategy/$1,049,384.00, Mark D. McLaughlin/Exec. VP - Products, Marketing, Customer Care/$1,225,761.00, Grant L. Clark/Sr. VP, Chief Administrative Officer, John M. Donovan/Exec. VP - Global Sales, Consulting Services/$6,479,969.00, Albert E. Clement/CFO, Richard H. Goshorn/Sr. VP, General Counsel, Sec., Anne-Marie Law/Sr. VP - Global Human Resources, Russell S. Lewis/Sr. VP - Strategic Development, Kevin A. Werner/Sr. VP - Corporate Development, Strategy

Directors: William A. Roper/Dir., CEO, Pres., James D. Bidzos/Chmn., Michelle Guthrie/Dir., Gregory L. Reyes/Dir., William L. Chenevich/Dir., Len J. Lauer/Dir., Roger H. Moore/Dir., Louis A. Simpson/Dir., Scott G. Kriens/Dir., John D. Roach/Dir., Edward A. Mueller/Dir.

Owners: William A. Roper, Private Capital Management, L.P./7.81%, T. Rowe Price Associates, Inc./8.07%, Eton Park Capital Management, L.P./6.08%, Robert J. Korzeniewski, William L. Chenevich, James D. Bidzos, John D. Roach, John M. Donovan, Dana L. Evan, Edward A. Mueller, Mark D. McLaughlin, Michelle Guthrie, Albert E. Clement, Roger H. Moore *(18 Owners included in Index)*

Financial Data: Fiscal Year End:12/31   Latest Annual Data: 12/31/2006

Year	Sales	Net Income
2006	$1,575,249,000	$379,015,000
2005	$1,609,494,000	$406,461,000
2004	$1,166,455,000	$186,225,000

Curr. Assets:	$1,332,364,000	**Curr. Liab.:**	$1,359,277,000	**P/E Ratio:**	10.76
Plant, Equip.:	$605,292,000	**Total Liab.:**	$1,597,393,000	**Indic. Yr. Divd.:**	NA
Total Assets:	$3,974,253,000	**Net Worth:**	$2,376,860,000	**Debt/ Equity:**	NA

Veritas DGC Inc

10300 Town Pk., Houston, TX, 77072; *PH:* 1-832-351-8300; *http://* www.veritasdgc.com

General - Incorporation .... DE
Employees 2,800
Auditor ....PricewaterhouseCoopers LLP
Stk Agt.................Mellon Investor Services LLC
Counsel...NA
DUNS No. 04-784-3008

Stock- Price on:12/24/2007 ....NA
Stock Exchange...NA
Ticker Symbol..NA
Outstanding Shares ....NA
E.P.S..NA
Shareholders..NA

Business: The group's principal activities are to provide geophysical services to the oil and gas industry worldwide. The group acquires, processes and interprets geophysical data and produces geophysical surveys that are either 2d or 3D images of the subsurface geology in the survey area. It also produces 4d surveys, which records fluid movement in the reservoir, by repeating specific 3D surveys over time. The geophysical technologies are used to identify new areas where subsurface conditions are favorable for the production of hydrocarbons, determine the size and structure for previously identified oil and gas fields and to optimize development and production of hydrocarbon reserves. The group operates in the United States, Canada, Latin America, Europe and Asia-Pacific countries.

Primary SIC and add'l.: 1382

CIK No: 0000028866

Subsidiaries: Alitheia Resources Inc., Digicon (Nigeria) Ltd., Exploraciones Geofisicas Veritas Geophysical Chile Limitada, Guardian Data Seismic Pty Limited, Hampson Russell GP Inc., Hampson Russell Limited Partnership, Inupiat Geophysical LLC, P.T. Veritas DGC Mega Pratama, Time Seismic Exchange Ltd., Time Seismic Leasing Ltd., Veri-Illuq Geophysical Ltd., Veritas Caspian LLP, Veritas DGC (B) Sdn. Bhd., Veritas DGC (Malaysia) Sdn. Bhd., Veritas DGC (Mexico) S. de R.L. de C.V. 44 Subsidiaries included in the Index

Officers: Thierry Pilenko/Dir., Chmn., CEO, Jaime Perez/Sr. Geoscientist, Speaker, Tianfei Zhu/Sr. Research Geophysicist, Speaker, Helmut Jakubowicz/Contact - External Consortia, Sergio Grion/Research Group Mgr. - Speaker, Dan Hampson/Pres. - Hampson, Russell, Speaker, Neil Hargreaves/Research Advisor, Speaker, Yu Zhang/Research Project Dir. - Speaker, Keith Hawkins/Research Geophysicist, Speaker, Jack Taylor/Sr. Geophysicist, Team Lead, Speaker, Sheng Xu/Sr. Research Geophysicist, Speaker, Steve Bircher/Dir. - Consulting, VHR, Houston, Speaker, Jon Downton/Sr. Research Scientist, Speaker, Uzi Egozi/Geophysical Advisor, Speaker, Philip Fontana/Geophysical Mgr. - Marine Acquisition, Speaker *(25 Officers included in Index)*

Directors: Thierry Pilenko/Dir., Chmn., CEO, Clayton P. Cormier/Dir., James R. Gibbs/Dir., Terence K. Young/Dir., Yoram Shoham/Dir., David F. Work/Dir., Jan Rask/Dir., Loren K. Carroll/Dir.

Verizon Communications Inc

140 W St., New York, NY, 10007; ; *http://* www22.verizon.com

General - Incorporation	DE	Stock- Price on:12/24/2007	$42.89
Employees	242,000	Stock Exchange	NYSE
Auditor	Ernst & Young LLP	Ticker Symbol	VZ
Stk Agt	Ernest & Young LLP	Outstanding Shares	2,900,000,000
Counsel	NA	E.P.S.	$1.88
DUNS No.	10-721-2169	Shareholders	NA

Business: The group's principle activity is to provide wireline and wireless communication services. The group operates from United States.

Primary SIC and add'l.: 4899 7375 2741 7359 4813

CIK No: 0000732712

Subsidiaries: Cellco Partnership, GTE Southwest Incorporated, Verizon California Inc., Verizon Capital Corp., Verizon Delaware Inc., Verizon Florida Inc., Verizon Global Funding Corp., Verizon Information Services Inc., Verizon International Holdings Ltd., Verizon Maryland Inc., Verizon New England Inc., Verizon New Jersey Inc., Verizon New York Inc., Verizon North Inc., Verizon Northwest Inc. 21 Subsidiaries included in the Index

Officers: Lowell C. McAdam/CEO, Exec. VP, Pres. - Verizon Wireless Joint Venture, Ivan G. Seidenberg/61/Chmn., CEO/$21,309.20, Lawrence T. Babbio/Vice Chmn., Pres./$11,758.70, William P. Barr/Exec. VP, General Counsel/$6,815.50, John Adams/Mgr. - Investor Relations, Ronald H. Lataille/Sr. VP - Investor Relations, Catherine T. Webster/Sr. VP, Treasurer, Bianca Nebab/Staff Mgr., Mark Gereb/Specialist, Ray Bendas/Exec. Dir. - Investor Relations, Richard J. Lynch/CTO, Exec. VP, John G. Stratton/Exec. VP, Chief Marketing Officer, Kathleen H. Leidheiser/Sr. VP - Internal Auditing, Robin Lochner/Mgr. - Investor Relations, Jim Peshek/Mgr. - Investor Relations *(63 Officers included in Index)*

Directors: Ivan G. Seidenberg/61/Chmn., CEO, Lawrence T. Babbio/Vice Chmn., Pres., Robert D. Storey/71/Dir., Frances M. Keeth/61/Dir., John W. Snow/68/Dir., Hugh B. Price/66/Dir., Walter V. Shipley/72/Dir., John R. Stafford/70/Dir., James R. Barker/72/Dir., Richard L. Carrion/55/Dir., Robert W. Lane/58/Dir., Sandra O. Moose/66/Dir., Joseph Neubauer/66/Dir., Donald T. Nicolaisen/63/Dir., Thomas H. O'Brien/71/Dir. *(16 Directors included in Index)*

Owners: Frances M. Keeth, Clarence Otis, Thomas H. OBrien, William P. Barr, Dennis F. Strigl, Ivan G. Seidenberg, Robert W. Lane, Barclays Global Investors, NA/5.87%, Lawrence T. Babbio, Walter V. Shipley, Doreen A. Toben, Joseph Neubauer, James R. Barker, Richard L. Carrin, Sandra O. Moose *(20 Owners included in Index)*

Financial Data: Fiscal Year End:12/31   Latest Annual Data: 12/31/2006

Year	Sales	Net Income
2006	$88,144,000,000	$6,197,000,000
2005	$75,112,000,000	$7,397,000,000
2004	$71,283,000,000	$7,831,000,000

Curr. Assets:	$22,538,000,000	Curr. Liab.:	$32,280,000,000	P/E Ratio:	20.62
Plant, Equip.:	$82,356,000,000	Total Liab.:	$140,269,000,000	Indic. Yr. Divd.:	$1.720
Total Assets:	$188,804,000,000	Net Worth:	$48,535,000,000	Debt/ Equity:	NA

Verizon New England Inc

140 W St., New York, NY, 10007; ; *http://* www22.verizon.com

General - Incorporation	NY	Stock- Price on:12/24/2007	$25.08
Employees	NA	Stock Exchange	NA
Auditor	Ernst & Young LLP	Ticker Symbol	NA
Stk Agt	Depository Trust Co	Outstanding Shares	NA
Counsel	NA	E.P.S.	NA
DUNS No.	NA	Shareholders	NA

Business: The groups principal activity is to provide telecommunication services. The group operates from the United States.

Primary SIC and add'l.: 4822 4899 4813 4813 4822 4899

CIK No: 0000071344

Officers: Ivan G. Seidenberg/61/Chmn., CEO, Lowell C. McAdam/Exec. VP, Pres., CEO - Verizon Wireless Joint Venture, Shaygan Kheradpir/CIO, Exec. VP, Marc C. Reed/Exec. VP - Human Resources, John G. Stratton/Exec. VP, Chief Marketing Officer, Dennis F. Strigl/COO, Pres., William P. Barr/Exec. VP, General Counsel, John W. Diercksen/Exec. VP - Strategy, Development, Planning, Thomas J. Tauke/Exec. VP - Public Affairs, Policy, Communications, Doreen A. Toben/CFO, Exec. VP, John F. Killian/Pres. - Verizon Business, Virginia P. Ruesterholz/Pres. - Verizon Telecom, John Adams/Mgr., Don Weber/Mgr. - Shareowner Services Staff, Mark Gereb/Specialist - Shareowner Services Staff *(39 Officers included in Index)*

Directors: Ivan G. Seidenberg/61/Chmn., CEO, Richard L. Carrion/55/Dir., Frances M. Keeth/61/Dir., Robert W. Lane/58/Dir., Sandra O. Moose/66/Dir., Joseph Neubauer/66/Dir., Donald T. Nicolaisen/63/Dir., Thomas H. O'Brien/71/Dir., Clarence Otis/51/Dir., Hugh B. Price/66/Dir., Walter V. Shipley/72/Dir., John W. Snow/68/Dir., John R. Stafford/70/Dir., Robert D. Storey/71/Dir., Ray Bendas/Executive Dir. *(17 Directors included in Index)*

Vermilion Energy Trust

2800, 400 - 4Th Ave. SW, Calgary, AB, T2P 0J4; *PH:* 1-403-269-4884; *http://* www.vermilionenergy.com

General - Incorporation	Canada	Stock- Price on:12/24/2007	NA
Employees	NA	Stock Exchange	NA
Auditor	Deloitte & Touche LLP	Ticker Symbol	NA
Stk Agt	Computershare Trust Co	Outstanding Shares	NA
Counsel	Macleod Dixon LLP	E.P.S.	NA
DUNS No.	NA	Shareholders	NA

Business: The group's principle activity is to explore oil and natural gas. The group's operations in France are focused in two core areas, the Paris Basin approximately 60km east of Paris and the Aquitaine Basin, located 90 km southwest of Bordeaux. The company continues to actively drill in the Paris Basin, adding four wells in 2005 in the Champotran/La Torche field. Average production per well is approximately 180 barrels per day of light sweet crude. The group has drilled over thirty wells in this area since acquiring these assets in 1997 and has plans to drill three to five additional wells here in 2006. The Trust is also completing a new 2-D seismic program over this concession to further delineate the boundaries of this reservoir. Offshore southwest France in the Bay of Biscay, the company has completed a seismic program covering its Aquitaine Maritime exploration concession. The group operates from United States, Netherland, Canada, France and Australia. .

Primary SIC and add'l.: 1311

CIK No: 0001293135

Officers: Lorenzo Donadeo/Dir., CEO, Pres., Charles W. Berard/Dir., Corp. Sec., Curtis Hicks/CFO, Exec. VP, Raj Patel/VP - Marketing, G. R MacDougall/COO, Exec. VP, Daniel Goulet/Director General - Vermilion Representative SA, John Donovan/Exec. VP - Business Development, Keith D. Hartman/VP - Exploitation, Paul L. Beique/Dir. - Investor Relations, Cheryl M. Kinzie/Dir. - Human Resources, Administration, Peter Sider/MD - Vermilion Oil, Gas Netherlands BV, Bruce Lake/MD - Vermilion Oil, Gas, Australia

Directors: Lorenzo Donadeo/Dir., CEO, Pres., Lawrence J. MacDonald/Chmn., William F. Madison/Dir., Kenneth W. Davidson/Dir., Claudio Ghersinich/Dir., Charles W. Berard/Dir., Corp. Sec., Joseph Killi/Dir.

Vermillion Inc

Formerly: Ciphergen Biosystems Inc

6611 Dumbarton Cir., Fremont, CA, 94555; *PH:* 1-510-505-2100; *http://* www.ciphergen.com

General - Incorporation	DE	Stock- Price on:12/24/2007	$1
Employees	36	Stock Exchange	NA
Auditor	PricewaterhouseCoopers LLP	Ticker Symbol	NA
Stk Agt	Wells Fargo Shareowner Services	Outstanding Shares	39,240,000
Counsel	Wilson Sonsini Goodrich & Rosati	E.P.S.	-$0.48
DUNS No.	NA	Shareholders	NA

Business: The group's principal activities are to develop, manufacture and market research systems to study proteins. The group's technology, proteinchip(R) system, enables protein discovery, characterization and assay development. The products include the proteinchip biology system, for protein analysis; proteinchip biomarker system and biomarker patterns (TM) software for advanced protein expression profiling; proteinchip tandem ms interface for advanced identification work using tandem mass spectrometry and automation accessories. The group also produces bioprocessors, spin columns and assorted kits designed for proteomics research. It has a joint venture with sumitomo corporation, ciphergen biosystems kk, to distribute its products in Japan. The products are sold to pharmaceutical and biotechnology companies and government research laboratories.

Primary SIC and add'l.: 7372 3674 3826 8731 8999

CIK No: 0000926617

Subsidiaries: Ciphergen (Beijing) Biosystems Co., Ltd., Ciphergen Biosystems A/S, Ciphergen Biosystems AG, Ciphergen Biosystems EURL, Ciphergen Biosystems GmbH, Ciphergen Biosystems International,Inc., Ciphergen Biosystems KK, Ciphergen Biosystems Ltd., Ciphergen Biosystems S.r.l., Ciphergen Technologies,Inc., IllumeSys Pacific,Inc.

Officers: Gail S. Page/Dir., CEO, Pres., James L. Rathmann/Exec. Chmn., William C. Sullivan/VP - Corporate Operations, Eric Fung/VP, Chief Scientific Officer, Simon C. Shorter/VP - Corporate Business Development, Debra A. Young/CFO, VP, Susan Carruthers/Corporate Investor Relations Officer, Lee Lomas/Sr. Dir. Biology Research - Development, Steve Lundy/Sr. VP - Sales, Marketing

Directors: Gail S. Page/Dir., CEO, Pres., James L. Rathmann/Exec. Chmn., Michael J. Callaghan/Dir., Rajen K. Dalal/Dir., Judy Bruner/Dir., John A. Young/Dir., James S. Burns/Dir., Kenneth J. Conway/Dir.

Owners: James L. Rathmann/7.39%, Insiders/10.63%, Judy Bruner, James S. Burns, Rajen K. Dalal, OppenheimerFunds, Inc./7.46%, Highbridge International LLC/8.58%, Michael J. Callaghan, Eric T. Fung, Phronesis Partners, L.P./15.60%, Gail S. Page/1.36%, Kenneth J. Conway, Falcon Technology Partners, L.P./6.30%, Ironwood Investment Management/6.21%, John A. Young *(17 Owners included in Index)*

Financial Data: Fiscal Year End:12/31   Latest Annual Data: 12/31/2006

Year	Sales	Net Income
2006	$18,215,000	-$22,066,000
2005	$27,246,000	-$35,433,000
2004	$40,181,000	-$19,841,000

Curr. Assets:	$20,040,000	Curr. Liab.:	$7,046,000		
Plant, Equip.:	$2,260,000	Total Liab.:	$32,917,000	Indic. Yr. Divd.:	NA
Total Assets:	$23,016,000	Net Worth:	-$9,901,000	Debt/ Equity:	NA

Vermont Pure Holdings Ltd

1050 Buckingham St., Watertown, CT, 06795; *PH:* 1-802-860-1126; *http://* www.vermontpure.com; *Email:* ir@vermontpure.com

General - Incorporation	DE	Stock- Price on:12/24/2007	$1.93
Employees	323	Stock Exchange	AMEX
Auditor	Deloitte & Touche LLP	Ticker Symbol	VPS
Stk Agt	American Stock Transfer & Trust Co.	Outstanding Shares	21,640,000
Counsel	NA	E.P.S.	-$0.95
DUNS No.	NA	Shareholders	NA

Business: The group's principal activities are to bottle, market and distribute natural spring water. The natural spring water are marketed and distributed under Vermont pure natural spring water(R), crystal rock (R), hidden spring (R), and stoneridge(R) brands. The spring water is obtained from group owned properties in radolph and Vermont. The group also distributes coffee, tea and other hot beverage products and related supplies. The group markets its products in the new England, New York, New Jersey, mid-Atlantic and northern mid-western states and the northern Virginia - Washington, d.c. - baltimore metropolitan area. On 02-Mar-2004, the group sold its assets of retail - gallons segments. The group acquired white ribbon spring water of laconia, nh on 02-Aug-2004 and the assets of evans quality coffee service of new England on15-Sep-2004.

Primary SIC and add'l.: 5149

CIK No: 0001123316

Subsidiaries: Crystal Rock, LLC

Officers: Peter K. Baker/Dir., CEO, Pres., John B. Baker/Dir., Exec. VP, Bruce S. MacDonald/CFO, VP

Directors: Peter K. Baker/Dir., CEO, Pres., Ross S. Rapaport/Chmn., Henry E. Baker/Chmn. Emeritus, John B. Baker/Dir., Exec. VP, Phillip Davidowitz/Dir., Martin A. Dytrych/Dir., John M. Lapides/Dir.

Owners: John B. Baker/12.80%, Ross S. Rapaport, individually and as trustee/18.40%, Bruce S. MacDonald/1.30%, Phillip Davidowitz/5.00%, Peter K. Baker/12.80%, Henry E. Baker/4.80%, Insiders/50.60%

Financial Data: *Fiscal Year End:*10/31 *Latest Annual Data:* 10/31/2006

Year	Sales	Net Income
2006	$62,774,000	-$20,670,000
2005	$59,835,000	$871,000
2004	$52,473,000	$660,000

Curr. Assets:	$12,227,000	*Curr. Liab.:*	$9,709,000		
Plant, Equip.:	$10,719,000	*Total Liab.:*	$49,646,000	*Indic. Yr. Divd.:*	NA
Total Assets:	$81,335,000	*Net Worth:*	$31,689,000	*Debt/ Equity:*	1.0271

Vernalis Plc

Oakdene Ct., 613 Reading Rd., Winnersh, Berkshire, RG41 5UA; *PH:* 44-1189773133; *Fax:* 44-118 989 9300; *http://* www.vernalis.com

General - Incorporation	England And Wales	**Stock**- Price on:12/24/2007	NA
Employees	192	Stock Exchange	OTC
Auditor	PricewaterhouseCoopers LLP	Ticker Symbol	VNLSY
Stk Agt	Capita Registrars	Outstanding Shares	NA
Counsel	NA	E.P.S	NA
DUNS No.	NA	Shareholders	NA

Business: The group's principal activity is the research and development of pharmaceutical products for a range of medical disorders. Its product portfolio comprises drugs targeting a variety of diseases and disorders such as migraines, arterial occlusion, Parkinson's diseases, cancer, obesity, inflammatory and depression. Some of the group's products includes frovatriptan, v10153, v2006, v140, 5-ht2c agonist, meis, a2a antagonists, hsp90 and cb1 antagonists

Primary SIC and add'l.: 8071 8731 2834

CIK No: 0000851616

Subsidiaries: Vernalis Group plc

Officers: Simon Sturge/Dir., CEO, Peter Fellner/Executive Chmn., Anthony Weir/Dir., CFO, John Slater/Dir., General Counsel

Directors: Simon Sturge/Dir., CEO, George Kennedy/Dep. Chmn., Peter Fellner/Executive Chmn., Carol Ferguson/Non Exec. Dir., Anthony Weir/Dir., CFO, Allan Baxter/Non Exec. Dir., John Slater/Dir., General Counsel, Peter Read/Non Exec. Dir., Ian Clark/Non Exec. Dir.

Financial Data: *Fiscal Year End:*12/31 *Latest Annual Data:* 12/31/2005

Year	Sales	Net Income
2005	$24,317,000	-$130,672,000
2004	$29,275,000	-$56,503,000
2003	$8,909,000	-$52,076,000

Curr. Assets:	$104,616,000	*Curr. Liab.:*	$55,616,000		
Plant, Equip.:	$3,085,000	*Total Liab.:*	$115,093,000	*Indic. Yr. Divd.:*	NA
Total Assets:	$239,367,000	*Net Worth:*	$124,273,000	*Debt/ Equity:*	NA

Vernon Bank Corpation NY

5238 W Seneca St., Vernon, NY, 13476; *PH:* 1-315-829-2405; *http://* www.thevernonbank.com

General - Incorporation		**Stock**- Price on:12/24/2007	NA
Employees	NA	Stock Exchange	NA
Auditor	NA	Ticker Symbol	NA
Stk Agt	American Stock Transfer & Trust Co.	Outstanding Shares	NA
Counsel	NA	E.P.S	NA
DUNS No.	NA	Shareholders	NA

Business: The groups principle activity is to provide recruiting services. The groups service area includes the research and development, engineering, marketing, sales, information technology and manufacturing industries. The group operates from United States.

Primary SIC and add'l.: 6021

CIK No:

Officers: Kirk A. Pellerin/CEO, Pres., Arlene R. Terrell/Exec. VP - Human Resources, Security Officer, Chief Operational Officers, Taini Bennett/VP, Compliance Officer - Note Department, Judy Mckee/Assist. VP - Note Department, Gabriella Diehl/VP - Cashier, BSA Officer - Operations Center, Justin F. Stanley/Assist. VP, Customer Loan Officer, Alana Stephens/VP - Information Technology Officer - Operations Center, Steven Woods/Sr. VP - Customer, Commerical, Mortage Loan Officers, Bridget Zuniga/Assist. VP - Operations Center, Jennifer Smith/Internet Banking Administrator - Operations Center

Versadial Inc

Formerly: Carsunlimited com Inc

305 Madison Ave., Ste. 4510, New York, NY, 10165; *PH:* 1-212-986-0886

General - Incorporation	NV	**Stock**- Price on:12/24/2007	NA
Employees	NA	Stock Exchange	OTC
Auditor	Sherb & Co., LLP	Ticker Symbol	VSDL
Stk Agt	Worldwide Stock Transfer LLC	Outstanding Shares	NA
Counsel	NA	E.P.S	-$0.69
DUNS No.	NA	Shareholders	NA

Business: The group's principle activity is to provide information about the automobile industry, new and used car sales. The group is in the development stage. It also provides automotive products such as extended warranty information and anti-theft body part marking. The group also accepts immediate orders for warranty products, provides a free automobile classified section for consumers and dealers and sells ancillary products. The group also offers Internet users a quick and easy way to search for automobile related needs according to their interests via the Internet.

Primary SIC and add'l.: 7375 7389

CIK No: 0001118159

Subsidiaries: Innopump, Inc.

Officers: Geoffrey Donaldson/65/Chmn., Chief Executive, Financial Officer, Karen Nazzareno/Controller, Sec.

Directors: Geoffrey Donaldson/65/Chmn., Chief Executive, Financial Officer, Robin Bartosh/65/Dir., Edward P. Bond/74/Dir., Thomas Coyle/57/Dir., Richard Harriton/73/Dir., Michael W. Hawthorne/41/Dir.

Owners: Gerhard Brugger, Prospero Capital, LLC, Paul Block, Geoffrey Donaldson, Richard Harriton, Michael W. Hawthorne, Edward P. Bond, Matthew Harriton, Insiders, Fursa Master, Robin Bartosh, Karen Nazzareno

Financial Data: *Fiscal Year End:*12/31 *Latest Annual Data:* 06/30/2007

Year	Sales	Net Income
2007	$1,396,000	-$7,942,000
2005	NA	-$147,000
2004	NA	-$72,000

Curr. Assets:	$14,000	*Curr. Liab.:*	$108,000		
Plant, Equip.:	NA	*Total Liab.:*	$142,000	*Indic. Yr. Divd.:*	NA
Total Assets:	$14,000	*Net Worth:*	-$128,000	*Debt/ Equity:*	NA

Versant Corp

Wiesenkamp 22b, Hamburg; *PH:* 510-789-1500; *http://* www.versant.com; *Email:* info@versant.com

General - Incorporation	CA	**Stock**- Price on:12/24/2007	$24.2068
Employees	76	Stock Exchange	NDQ
Auditor	Grant Thornton LLP	Ticker Symbol	VSNT
Stk Agt	NA	Outstanding Shares	3,660,000
Counsel	NA	E.P.S	$2.059
DUNS No.	19-962-3273	Shareholders	NA

Business: The group's principal activity is the provision of object-oriented data management and data integration software for real-time computing infrastructure of enterprises. The group's core products are versant object database management system, highly scalable database management system and client server architecture. The group licenses its products directly to end-users, principally through four types of licenses—development licenses, deployment server licenses, deployment client licenses and project licenses. The group operates in the United States, Germany, the United Kingdom, France, Australia and India. On 31-Aug-2004, the group acquired jdo genie product and fast objects inc.

Primary SIC and add'l.: 7373 7372 7379

CIK No: 0000865917

Subsidiaries: FastObjects,Inc., Mokume Software,Inc., Poet Holdings, Inc, Poet Software Corporation, Versant Gmbh, Versant India, Versant Ltd.

Officers: Jochen Witte/Dir., CEO, Jerry Wong/CFO, VP - Finance, Sec., Thomas Huben/Exec. VP, Robert Greene/VP - Product Strategy, Andreas Renner/Sr. Dir. - Research & Development

Directors: Jochen Witte/Dir., CEO, William Henry Delevati/59/Chmn., Bernhard Woebker/58/Dir., Herbert May/Dir., Uday Bellary/Dir.

Owners: Thomas Huben, Bernhard Woebker, Royce& Associates, LLC/6.80%, Renaissance Technologies Corp./5.20%, Uday Bellary, Jochen Witte/2.10%, Insiders/4.30%, Herbert May, Jerry Wong, William Henry Delevati

Financial Data: *Fiscal Year End:*10/31 *Latest Annual Data:* 10/31/2006

Year	Sales	Net Income
2006	$16,745,000	$4,301,000
2005	$20,509,000	-$14,554,000
2004	$22,875,000	-$11,997,000

Curr. Assets:	$11,898,000	*Curr. Liab.:*	$5,699,000	*P/E Ratio:*	14.67
Plant, Equip.:	$385,000	*Total Liab.:*	$6,469,000	*Indic. Yr. Divd.:*	NA
Total Assets:	$20,261,000	*Net Worth:*	$13,792,000	*Debt/ Equity:*	0.0011

Versar Inc

6850 Versar Ctr, Springfield, VA, 22151; *PH:* 1-703-750-3000; *http://* www.versar.com; *Email:* info@versar.com

General - Incorporation	DE	**Stock**- Price on:12/24/2007	$8.04
Employees	295	Stock Exchange	AMEX
Auditor	Grant Thornton LLP	Ticker Symbol	VSR
Stk Agt	Bank of New York	Outstanding Shares	8,240,000
Counsel	Paul, Hastings, Janofsky & Walker LLP	E.P.S	$0.50
DUNS No.	06-676-4747	Shareholders	NA

Business: The group's principal activities are to provide environmental services, architecture and engineering services and defense systems. Its environmental segment includes pollution prevention, compliance management and the environmental restoration of industrial and commercial facilities, sites and military bases. The architecture and engineering segment includes construction services in support of industrial, commercial and government infrastructure and sustainable energy projects. The defense systems include personal protection equipment and technology development efforts in support of chemical and biological agent detection. The group is a professional service firm that uses innovation and technology to help customers to meet infrastructure needs and enhance competitiveness in global economy.

Primary SIC and add'l.: 8742 8731

CIK No: 0000803647

Subsidiaries: GEOMET

Officers: Theodore M. Prociv/Dir., CEO, Pres., Robert L. Durfee/Dir., Consultant, James V. Hansen/Dir., Consultant, Amir A. Metry/Dir., Consultant, Ronald A. Torgerson/VP, William Johnson/VP, James C. Dobbs/Sr. VP, General Counsel, Lawrence W. Sinnott/Exec. VP, CFO, COO, Paul W. Kendall/Sr. VP - Defense Business Segment, Pres. - Geomet Technologies LLC, Gina L. Foringer/VP - Outsourcing, Paul Stiles/VP, Brenda A. Chube/VP, Assist., Sec., Jerome B. Strauss/Sr. VP - Corporate Development, May K. Tom/VP, Assist. Treasurer, Gary M. Owens/CIO, VP *(22 Officers included in Index)*

Directors: Theodore M. Prociv/Dir., CEO, Pres., Michael Markels/Chmn. Emeritus, Paul J. Hoeper/Chmn., Amir A. Metry/Dir., Consultant, James L. Gallagher/Dir., Fernando V. Galaviz/Dir., Robert L. Durfee/Dir., Consultant, James V. Hansen/Dir., Consultant, Amoretta M. Hoeber/Dir.

Owners: Perritt Capital Management/5.20%, Michael Markels/4.40%, James C. Dobbs/1.10%, Amir A. Metry, James V. Hansen, Paul J. Hoeper, Gina Foringer, Insiders/19.30%, Fernando V. Galaviz, Lawrence W. Sinnott/1.40%, Marathon Capital Management/5.80%, James L. Gallagher, Amoretta M. Hoeber, Theodore M. Prociv/3.20%, Versar Employee/5.40% *(17 Owners included in Index)*

Financial Data: *Fiscal Year End:*07/01 *Latest Annual Data:* 6/30/2006

Year	Sales	Net Income
2006	$34,290,000	$1,347,000
2005	$35,638,000	$202,000
2004	$60,454,000	$1,191,000

Curr. Assets:	$17,034,000	Curr. Liab.:	$9,147,000	P/E Ratio:	16.08
Plant, Equip.:	$1,855,000	Total Liab.:	$10,360,000	Indic. Yr. Divd.:	NA
Total Assets:	$20,912,000	Net Worth:	$10,552,000	Debt/ Equity:	NA

Versatech USA

800 Bellevue Way NE, Ste 400, Bellevue, WA, 98004; *PH:* 1-425-990-5599;
http:// www.vusainc.com; *Email:* info@versatech.com

General - Incorporation	NV	Stock - Price on:12/24/2007	$0.0165
Employees	NA	Stock Exchange	OTC
Auditor	Chisholm Bierwolf & Nilson LLC	Ticker Symbol	VRST
Stk Agt	Interwest Transfer Company, Inc.	Outstanding Shares	NA
Counsel	NA	E.P.S.	$1.57
DUNS No.	NA	Shareholders	NA

Business: The group's principle activity is to market unitropin products. This product is a proprietary label mix of herbs, vitamins and adaptogens that increase the growth of hormone in the human body, which declines as body ages. The unitropin product is manufactured by garden state nutritionals. The company markets its products through its Web site, www.unitropin.com, wholesale distributors and retail outlets. The company has transferred the trademark name of its proprietary product, unitropin (hgh formula plus) from universal to versatech. In feb 2003, the company announced that all previous operations consisting of manufacturing, marketing, and distribution of the company's product hgh unitropin would be discontinued. The company is now seeking out new business opportunities. The group operates from United States.

Primary SIC and add'l.: 2833
CIK No: 0000933954
Subsidiaries: LongerLiving.com, Inc., Universal Network of America, Inc.
Financial Data: *Fiscal Year End:*12/31   *Latest Annual Data:* 09/30/2005

Year	Sales	Net Income
2005	NA	-$36,000
2004	$1,000	-$399,000
2003	$1,000	-$543,000

Curr. Assets:	$0	Curr. Liab.:	$482,000		
Plant, Equip.:	NA	Total Liab.:	$482,000	Indic. Yr. Divd.:	NA
Total Assets:	$0	Net Worth:	-$482,000	Debt/ Equity:	NA

Verso Technologies Inc

400 Galleria Pkwy, Ste 200, Atlanta, GA, 30339; *PH:* 1-678-589-3500; *http://* www.verso.com

General - Incorporation	NV	Stock - Price on:12/24/2007	$0.9098
Employees	300	Stock Exchange	NDQ
Auditor	Grant Thornton LLP	Ticker Symbol	VRSO
Stk Agt	American Stock Transfer & Trust Co.	Outstanding Shares	57,030,000
Counsel	Jaffe, Raitt, Heuer & Weiss	E.P.S.	-$0.449
DUNS No.	13-925-0575	Shareholders	NA

Business: The group's principal activities are the provision of technology and solutions for communications service providers and enterprises seeking to implement application-based telephony service, Internet usage management tools and outsourced customer support services. The group operates in two segments: carrier solutions and enterprise solutions. The carrier solutions includes hardware and software, integration, applications and technical training and support. The enterprise solutions offers application and network design, enterprise application integration, network management, support and maintenance, customer response center services, enterprise management system solutions and application services. The customers of the group include domestic and international long-distance providers, seeking to implement a turn-key, pre-paid solution. On 26-Sep-2003, the group acquired mck communications inc.

Primary SIC and add'l.: 7379 7373
CIK No: 0000797448
Subsidiaries: Eltrax International, Inc., Needham (Delaware) Corp., Provo Prepaid (Delaware) Corp., Telemate.Net Software, Inc., Verso Technologies Canada Inc.
Officers: Steve A. Odom/Chmn., CEO, Mark Dunaway/COO, Pres., Marty Kidder/CFO
Directors: Steve A. Odom/Chmn., CEO, James R. Kanely/Dir., William J. West/Dir., Kenneth E. Greenwald/72/Dir., Gary H. Heck/Dir., Mark Dunaway/COO, Pres., James Verbrugge/Dir., Amy L. Newmark/51/Dir.
Owners: Yves Desmet, William J. West, Martin D. Kidder, Donald J. Slowinski/8.80%, James R. Kanely, E. Kenneth Greenwald/4.80%, Mark H. Dunaway, Sentito Funding, LLC/5.90%, Laurus Master Fund, Ltd./3.60%, Steven A. Odom/1.60%, James A. Verbrugge, Montgomery L. Bannerman, Amy L. Newmark, Enable Growth Partners LP/5.60%, Insiders/3.60% *(18 Owners included in Index)*

Financial Data: *Fiscal Year End:*12/31   *Latest Annual Data:* 12/31/2006

Year	Sales	Net Income
2006	$42,530,000	-$17,776,000
2005	$32,873,000	-$20,060,000
2004	$32,263,000	-$38,787,000

Curr. Assets:	$21,498,000	Curr. Liab.:	$21,536,000		
Plant, Equip.:	$1,807,000	Total Liab.:	$34,170,000	Indic. Yr. Divd.:	NA
Total Assets:	$36,849,000	Net Worth:	$2,679,000	Debt/ Equity:	3.1702

Vertex Pharmaceuticals Inc

130 WAve.rly St., Cambridge, MA, 02139; *PH:* 1-617-444-6100; *Fax:* 1-617-444-6680;
http:// www.vpharm.com

General - Incorporation	MA	Stock - Price on:12/24/2007	$26.86
Employees	945	Stock Exchange	NDQ
Auditor	Ernst & Young, LLP	Ticker Symbol	VRTX
Stk Agt	EquiServe Trust Co N.A	Outstanding Shares	130,990,000
Counsel	Kirkpatrick & Lockhart	E.P.S.	-$2.62
DUNS No.	60-247-8257	Shareholders	NA

Business: The group's principle activity is to discover, develop and commercialize small molecule drugs. These drugs are used in the treatment of viral diseases, cancer, auto immune and inflammatory diseases and neurological disorders. The group has created pipeline using a proprietary approach,

information-driven drug design that integrates advanced biology, chemistry, biophysics and information technologies to make drug discovery process more efficient and productive. The group operates in one segment, pharmaceuticals, and all revenues are from U.S. Operations. The group's quarterly revenue for September 2007 was 41.01 millions of USD.

Primary SIC and add'l.: 2834 8733
CIK No: 0000875320
Subsidiaries: Vertex Holdings, Inc, Vertex Pharmaceuticals (Europe) Ltd., Vertex Pharmaceuticals (San Diego) LLC, Vertex Securities Trust, VSD Sub I LLC, VSD Sub II LLC
Officers: Joshua Boger/Dir., CEO, Pres./$5,922,958.00, Mark Murcko/Chmn. - Scientific Advisory Board, CTO, VP, Richard C. Garrison/Sr. VP - Catalyst, Amit K. Sachdev/Sr. VP - Public Policy, Government Affairs, Peter Mueller/Member - Scientific Advisory Board, Exec. VP - Drug Innovation, Realization, Chief Scientific Officer/$1,982,518.00, Michael Partridge/Dir. - Corporate Communications, Lora Pike/Mgr. - Investor Relations, Zachry Barber/Sr. Media Relations Specialist, Kenneth S. Boger/Sr. VP, General Counsel, John J. Alam/Exec. VP - Medicines Development, Chief Medical Officer/$1,766,306.00, Ian F. Smith/CFO, Exec. VP/$1,914,697.00, Lynne H. Brum/VP - Strategic Communications
Directors: Joshua Boger/Dir., CEO, Pres., Charles A. Sanders/Chmn., Mark Murcko/Chmn. - Scientific Advisory Board, CTO, VP, Elaine S. Ullian/Dir., Matthew W. Emmens/Dir., Stuart J.M. Collinson/Dir., Bruce I. Sachs/Dir., Peter Mueller/Member - Scientific Advisory Board, Exec. VP - Drug Innovation, Realization, Chief Scientific Officer, Eric K. Brandt/Dir., Lewis C. Cantley/Member - Scientific Advisory Board, Stephen C. Harrison/Member - Scientific Advisory Board, Jeremy R. Knowles/Member - Scientific Advisory Board, Robert T. Schooley/Member - Scientific Advisory Board, Roger Tsien/Member - Scientific Advisory Board, Eugene H. Cordes/Dir., Member - Scientific Advisory Board *(18 Directors included in Index)*
Owners: Eve E. Slater, Roger W. Brimblecombe, T. Rowe Price Associates, Inc./5.77%, Elaine S. Ullian, Wellington Management Company, LLP/9.36%, Ian F. Smith, Stuart J. M. Collinson, Charles A. Sanders, Insiders/4.03%, Eugene H. Cordes, Victor A. Hartmann, John J. Alam, Eric K. Brandt, Unicredito Italiano S.p.A./5.29%, FMR Corp./14.39% *(19 Owners included in Index)*

Financial Data: *Fiscal Year End:*12/31   *Latest Annual Data:* 12/31/2006

Year	Sales	Net Income
2006	$216,356,000	-$206,891,000
2005	$160,890,000	-$203,417,000
2004	$102,717,000	-$166,247,000

Curr. Assets:	$771,406,000	Curr. Liab.:	$251,014,000		
Plant, Equip.:	$61,535,000	Total Liab.:	$415,644,000	Indic. Yr. Divd.:	NA
Total Assets:	$921,579,000	Net Worth:	$505,935,000	Debt/ Equity:	0.0395

Vertical Branding Inc

16000 Ventura Blvd., Ste. 301, Encino, CA, 91436; *PH:* 1-818-926-4900; *Fax:* 1-818-926-4885;
http:// www.verticalbranding.com; *Email:* info@verticalbranding.com

General - Incorporation	DE	Stock - Price on:12/24/2007	$0.75
Employees	25	Stock Exchange	OTC
Auditor	Holtz Rubenstein Reminick LLP	Ticker Symbol	VBDG
Stk Agt	NA	Outstanding Shares	22,440,000
Counsel	NA	E.P.S.	$0.02
DUNS No.	NA	Shareholders	NA

Business: The groups principle activities include finding or developing products that meet a real need in the marketplace and that appeal to customer demographic, which is essentially the mass consumer market. The group is focus primarily on the personal care, fitness, beauty and household consumer product categories. The group operates through two segments namely direct to consumer transactional marketing and retail distribution. In August 2006, group acquired Retail Distribution business. The group operates from the United States.

Primary SIC and add'l.: 7389 6719 5961
CIK No: 0001125532
Subsidiaries: Adsouth Marketing, LLC, FRM Court Street, LLC, Medical Financial Corp, Nexus Borough Park, LLC, Nexus Garden City, LLC, Worldwide Excellence, Inc., Yolo Equities Corp
Officers: Nancy Duitch/Founder, Dir., CEO, Alan H. Gerson/Dir., COO, Pres., Victor Brodsky/CFO, John Cammarano/Pres. - Retail Sales, Adsouth Marketing, Cynthia Levin/Online Marketing Mgr., Daryl Holliman/Inventory Control Mgr., Orrin Halper/45/VP - Operations, Corporate Controller, Marian McNear/VP - Direct Marketing, Chris Lipp/VP, Corporate Counsel, Jeff Browning/Sr. Dir. - Product Sourcing, Procurement, Paul McKenna/Dir. - Fulfillment, Customer Care
Directors: Nancy Duitch/Founder, Dir., CEO, Jeffrey Edell/Chmn., Roger Burlage/Dir., Alan H. Gerson/Dir., COO, Pres., Victor Imbimbo/Dir.
Owners: Jeffrey S. Edell, Total Gottbetter, Alan Gerson, Roger Burlage, HSK Funding, Inc., Insiders, Nancy Duitch, Victor Imbimbo, Gottbetter Capital Master, Ltd., Gottbetter Capital Finance, LLC, Victor Brodsky

Financial Data: *Fiscal Year End:*12/31   *Latest Annual Data:* 12/31/2006

Year	Sales	Net Income
2006	$23,109,000	-$2,757,000
2005	$8,099,000	-$2,583,000

Curr. Assets:	$7,926,000	Curr. Liab.:	$7,290,000		
Plant, Equip.:	$4,399,000	Total Liab.:	$14,933,000	Indic. Yr. Divd.:	NA
Total Assets:	$17,737,000	Net Worth:	$2,805,000	Debt/ Equity:	2.5176

Vertical Communications Inc

Formerly: Artisoft Inc
One Memorial Dr., Cambridge, MA, 02142; *PH:* 1-617-354-0600; *http://* www.vertical.com

General - Incorporation	DE	Stock - Price on:12/24/2007	$0.75
Employees	217	Stock Exchange	OTC
Auditor	Vitale, Caturano & Co. Ltd	Ticker Symbol	VRCC
Stk Agt	Computershare Investor Services LLC	Outstanding Shares	52,080,000
Counsel	NA	E.P.S.	-$0.32
DUNS No.	11-280-3523	Shareholders	NA

Business: The group's principal activity is to develop, market and sell computer telephony software application products and associated services. Its primary product line, televantage, is a software-based phone system running on windows 2000/nt and intel communications hardware. televantage offers stand-alone private branch exchange and call management features. The group is an original equipment manufacturer to toshiba corporation, which sells and supports the televantage product as strata cs. The group's products include televantage 5.0, televantage call center module, televantage call center

scoreboard, televantage call classifier, televantage smart dialer and televantage persistent pager. Its target market consists of technology vendors in the crm, call centers, voice over ip, business automation and speech recognition fields. The group maintains distribution relationships in Europe and Latin America. On 29-Sep-2004, the group acquired vertical networks inc.

Primary SIC and add'l.: 7372

CIK No: 0000877931

Subsidiaries: Artisoft FSC, Ltd., Triton Technologies, Inc, Vertical Communications Acquisition Corp., Vertical Communications GmbH

Officers: William Y. Tauscher/Chmn., CEO, Michael P. Downey/Dir. - Executive Consultant, Private Investor, Chris Brookins/Sr. VP - Development, Dick Anderson/Exec. VP, GM, Peter H. Bailey/Sr. VP - Business Development - Product Management, Scott Pickett/CTO, Francis E. Girard/Dir. - Private Investor, Ken Clinebell/CFO

Directors: William Y. Tauscher/Chmn., CEO, Matthew J. Rubins/Dir., Michael P. Downey/Dir. - Executive Consultant, Private Investor, Randy R. Stolworthy/Dir., Francis E. Girard/Dir. - Private Investor, John W. Watkins/Dir., Jong-Dae An/Dir.

Owners: Matthew J. Rubins, M/C Venture Partners, Peter H. Bailey, John W. Watkins, Francis E. Girard, Scott K. Pickett, Michael P. Downey, LG-Nortel Co., Ltd., Kenneth M. Clinebell, Richard N. Anderson, Austin W. Marxe, William Y. Tauscher, Pathfinder Ventures, Randy R. Stolworthy, Insiders

Financial Data: Fiscal Year End:06/30   Latest Annual Data: 6/30/2006

Year		Sales		Net Income
2006		$55,535,000		-$15,999,000
2005		$17,460,000		-$15,531,000
2004		$8,991,000		-$3,154,000
Curr. Assets:	$28,671,000	Curr. Liab.:	$35,105,000	
Plant, Equip.:	$2,201,000	Total Liab.:	$48,600,000	Indic. Yr. Divd.: NA
Total Assets:	$70,079,000	Net Worth:	$17,924,000	Debt/ Equity: 0.3727

Vertical Computer Systems Inc

6336 Wilshire Blvd, Los Angeles, CA, 90048; *PH:* 1-323-658-4211; *http://* www.vcsy.com; *Email:* sales@vcsy.com

General - Incorporation	NV	Stock- Price on:12/24/2007	$0.023
Employees	30	Stock Exchange	OTC
Auditor	Weaver & Tidwell LLP	Ticker Symbol	VCSY
Stk Agt	Olde Monmouth Stk Trnsfer Co. Inc.	Outstanding Shares	997,740,000
Counsel	NA	E.P.S.	-$0.002
DUNS No.	NA	Shareholders	NA

Business: The group's principal activity is to provide administrative software services, Internet core technologies, and derivative software application products through its distribution network. Some of the products of the group are, empath 6.2, a human resources and payroll system, siteflash, responseflash, affiiateflash, universityflash, and newsflash, which are Internet core technologies and underlying Web application software products, the emily xml scripting language and its underlying programs.

Primary SIC and add'l.: 7375

CIK No: 0001099509

Subsidiaries: EnFacet, Inc., Globalfare.com, Inc., Government Internet Systems, Inc., Now Solutions, Inc., Pointmail., Inc., Taladin, Inc., Vertical Internet Solutions, Inc.

Officers: Richard S. Wade/Dir., CEO, Pres., David Braun/CFO - Vcsy, Dorothy Spotts/VP - Services, Support, Carmelina Uggenti/VP - Customer Development, James Salz/Corporate Counsel, Luiz Valdetaro/CTO, Laurent Tetard/Dir. - Operations, William K. Mills/Dir., Sec.

Directors: Richard S. Wade/Dir., CEO, Pres., William K. Mills/Dir., Sec.

Owners: Insiders/11.72%, Richard Wade/11.42%, William K. Mills

Financial Data: Fiscal Year End:12/31   Latest Annual Data: 09/30/2007

Year		Sales		Net Income
2007		$1,575,000		-$228,000
2006		$6,230,000		-$1,729,000
2005		$6,600,000		-$1,507,000
Curr. Assets:	$1,188,000	Curr. Liab.:	$11,496,000	
Plant, Equip.:	$84,000	Total Liab.:	$18,193,000	Indic. Yr. Divd.: NA
Total Assets:	$1,282,000	Net Worth:	-$16,911,000	Debt/ Equity: NA

Vertical Health Solutions Inc

6925 112th Cir. N, Ste 102, Largo, FL, 33773; *PH:* 1-727-547-2654; *http://* www.vetmarket.com

General - Incorporation	FL	Stock- Price on:12/24/2007	$0.15
Employees	6	Stock Exchange	OTC
Auditor	Brimmer, Burek & Keelan LLP	Ticker Symbol	VHSL
Stk Agt	Computershare Investor Services LLC	Outstanding Shares	16,420,000
Counsel	Sichenzia Ross Friedman Ference LLP	E.P.S.	-$0.01
DUNS No.	NA	Shareholders	NA

Business: The group's principle activities include developing, marketing and distributing customized private label supplement and health products. The product consists of canine, feline, equine and numerous other household pets. The products are used to address animal healthcare problems such as arthritis, allergies, hip dysplasia, immune function, muscle development, skin care and general health and well-being. The group operates from United States.

Primary SIC and add'l.: NA

CIK No: 0001163332

Subsidiaries: Labelclick, Inc

Officers: Stephen M. Watters/41/Dir., CEO, CFO/$8,042.00

Directors: Stephen M. Watters/41/Dir., CEO, CFO, Brian T. Nugent/34/Dir., Alfred Lehmkuhl/76/Dir., Patrick Sheppard/60/Dir., Jugal K. Taneja/64/Dir.

Owners: Patrick Sheppard/1.10%, Alfred Lehmkuhl/8.90%, Brian T. Nugent/5.40%, Jugal K. Taneja/22.20%, Stephen M. Watters/31.90%, Insiders/69.50%

Financial Data: Fiscal Year End:12/31   Latest Annual Data: 12/31/2006

Year		Sales		Net Income
2006		$755,000		-$185,000
2005		$4,447,000		-$715,000
2004		$3,284,000		$14,000
Curr. Assets:	$296,000	Curr. Liab.:	$338,000	
Plant, Equip.:	$12,000	Total Liab.:	$405,000	Indic. Yr. Divd.: NA
Total Assets:	$320,000	Net Worth:	-$85,000	Debt/ Equity: NA

Verticalnet Inc

400 Chester Field Pkwy, Malvern, PA, 19355; *PH:* 1-215-328-6100; *http://* www.verticalnet.com; *Email:* info@verticalnet.com

General - Incorporation	PA	Stock- Price on:12/24/2007	$0.47
Employees	88	Stock Exchange	NDQ
Auditor	KPMG LLP	Ticker Symbol	VERT
Stk Agt	American Stock Transfer & Trust Co.	Outstanding Shares	12,410,000
Counsel	Morgan, Lewis & Bockius LLP	E.P.S.	-$6.86
DUNS No.	NA	Shareholders	NA

Business: The group's principal activity is to provide collaborative supply chain solutions that enable organizations to communicate, collaborate and conduct commerce effectively across the extended supply chain. The collaborative supply chain application includes strategic sourcing, collaborative planning and multi-tier order management. The group's solutions are differentiated by its private hub architecture, enabling customers to manage diverse communities of suppliers and buyers in a secure, enterprise controlled environment while providing integrated multi-party data integration and a proven ability to support role-based security. On 30-Jan-2004, the group acquired tigris corp and on 19-Jul-2004, the group acquired b2emarkets.

Primary SIC and add'l.: 7372 7375 7319

CIK No: 0001043946

Subsidiaries: B2e Contract Management, Inc., B2e Sourcing Optimization, Inc., B2eMarkets France S.A.R.L., B2eMarkets UK Ltd., B2eMarkets, B.V., Digital Union LTD, Tigris Consulting UK, Ltd., Vert Tech LLC, Verticalnet Employees I Corp., Verticalnet Employees II Corp., Verticalnet Europe B.V., Verticalnet International LLC, Verticalnet LTD, Verticalnet Ltd. (Israel), Verticalnet Software, Inc.

Officers: Nathanael V. Lentz/Dir., CEO, Pres., John H. McNeill/Sr. VP - Sales, Paddy Lawton/Pres. - Verticalnet Europe, MD - Digital Union, Jim Wetekamp/VP - Solution Strategy, Operations, Christopher G. Kuhn/VP, General Counsel, Sec., Jonathan Cohen/Chief Accounting Officer, Brian Cupp/VP - Product Development

Directors: Nathanael V. Lentz/Dir., CEO, Pres., Gregory G. Schott/Chmn., Darryl E. Wash/Dir., Mark L. Walsh/Dir., Michael J. Hagan/Dir., Vincent J. Milano/Dir.

Owners: Insiders/6.40%, BravoSolution U.S.A., Inc./12.10%, John N. Nickolas, Christopher G. Kuhn, Vincent J. Milano, Darryl E. Wash, Nathanael V. Lentz/0.90%, Mark L. Walsh, Jonathan T. Cohen, Michael J. Hagan/3.90%, Gregory G. Schott

Financial Data: Fiscal Year End:12/31   Latest Annual Data: 12/31/2006

Year		Sales		Net Income
2006		$16,164,000		-$24,472,000
2005		$20,650,000		-$13,720,000
2004		$22,925,000		-$9,720,000
Curr. Assets:	$7,464,000	Curr. Liab.:	$11,624,000	
Plant, Equip.:	$920,000	Total Liab.:	$17,751,000	Indic. Yr. Divd.: NA
Total Assets:	$20,693,000	Net Worth:	$2,942,000	Debt/ Equity: 4.1606

VeruTEK Technologies Inc

Formerly: Streamscape Minerals Inc
455 Granville St., Ste. 500, Vancouver, BC, V6C 1T1; *PH:* 1-604-771-3234; *http://* www.verutek.com

General - Incorporation	NV	Stock- Price on:12/24/2007	NA
Employees	NA	Stock Exchange	OTC
Auditor	Manning Elliott LLP	Ticker Symbol	SSMI
Stk Agt	Empire Stock Transfer Inc.	Outstanding Shares	NA
Counsel	NA	E.P.S.	NA
DUNS No.	NA	Shareholders	NA

Business: The groups principal activity is in exploration involved in the search for mineral deposits. The groups interest is in the property consists of the right to explore for and remove minerals from the property. The group operates from the United States.

Primary SIC and add'l.: 4955

CIK No: 0001346988

Owners: George Hoag, John Collins, Collins Family LP, Hoag Environmental LP, Michael Vagnini, Insiders, Nite Capital, L.P, Peter Perakos

Vestin Realty Mortgage I Inc

8379 W Sunset Rd., Las Vegas, NV, 89113; *PH:* 1-702-227-0965; *http://* www.vestinrealtymortgage1.com

General - Incorporation	MD	Stock- Price on:12/24/2007	$5.8
Employees	NA	Stock Exchange	NDQ
Auditor	Moore Stephens Wurth F & T LLP	Ticker Symbol	VRTA
Stk Agt	Stock Transfer & Trust Co	Outstanding Shares	6,870,000
Counsel	Ira S. Levine	E.P.S.	$0.43
DUNS No.	NA	Shareholders	NA

Business: The groups principal activity is to generate income by investing in real estate loans. The products of the group include commercial, construction, acquisition and development, land, and residential loans. The group operates from Arizona, New York, Texas, Washington and Nevada. The total assets of the group for the year 2006 were $65,332,000.

Primary SIC and add'l.: 6162

CIK No: 0001328300

Officers: Michael V. Shustek/Chmn., CEO, James M. Townsend/38/COO, Michael J. Whiteaker/58/VP - Regulatory Affairs, Daniel B. Stubbs/46/Sr. VP, Maria Rocio Revollo/CFO

Directors: Michael V. Shustek/Chmn., CEO, John W. Alderfer/63/Dir., Robert J. Aalberts/Dir., Fredrick J. Zaffarese Leavitt/Dir., Roland M. Sansone/Dir., John E. Dawson/Dir.

Owners: Insiders/1.81%, Michael V. Shustek/1.47%, Vestin Reality Mortgage II, Inc./5.93%, John E. Dawson, Robert J. Aalberts, James M. Townsend

Financial Data: Fiscal Year End:12/31   Latest Annual Data: 12/31/2006

Year		Sales		Net Income
2006		$4,963,000		$587,000
Curr. Assets:	$2,596,000	Curr. Liab.:	$2,661,000	
Plant, Equip.:	$11,600,000	Total Liab.:	$2,993,000	Indic. Yr. Divd.: $0.560
Total Assets:	$65,332,000	Net Worth:	$62,339,000	Debt/ Equity: NA

Vestin Realty Mortgage II Inc

8379 W Sunset Rd., Las Vegas, NV, 89113; *PH:* 1-702-227-0965; *http://* www.vestinmortgage.com; *Email:* info@vestinmortgage.com

General - Incorporation ... MD
Employees ... 23
Auditor ... Moore Stephens Wurth F & T LLP
Stk Agt ... Stock Transfer & Trust Co
Counsel ... NA
DUNS No. ... NA

Stock - Price on:12/24/2007 ... NA
Stock Exchange ... NDQ
Ticker Symbol ... VRTB
Outstanding Shares ... 38,870,000
E.P.S ... $0.49
Shareholders ... NA

Business: The groups principal activity is to generate income by investing in real estate loans. The group operates from the United States. The assets of the group for the year 2006 were $303,042,000.

Primary SIC and add'l.: 6798

CIK No: 0001327603

Officers: Michael V. Shustek/49/Chmn., CEO, Pres., James M. Townsend/38/COO, Michael J. Whiteaker/58/VP - Regulatory Affairs, Daniel B. Stubbs/46/Sr. VP - Underwriting, Rocio Revollo/46/CFO

Directors: Michael V. Shustek/49/Chmn., CEO, Pres., Robert J. Aalberts/56/Dir., Fredrick J. Zaffarese Leavitt/37/Dir., Roland M. Sansone/52/Dir.

Owners: Comerica Bank/7.00%, Robert J. Aalberts, John Alderfer, Insiders/1.66%, James M. Townsend, Michael V. Shustek, John E. Dawson

Financial Data: *Fiscal Year End:*12/31 *Latest Annual Data:* 12/31/2006

Year	Sales	Net Income
2006	$23,479,000	$15,851,000

Curr. Assets:	$19,831,000	**Curr. Liab.:**	$10,279,000		
Plant, Equip.:	$44,853,000	**Total Liab.:**	$24,556,000	**Indic. Yr. Divd.:**	$0.480
Total Assets:	$303,042,000	**Net Worth:**	$278,486,000	**Debt/ Equity:**	NA

VF Corp

105 Corporate Ctr. Blvd., Greensboro, NC, 27408; *PH:* 1-336-424-6000; *http://* www.vfc.com

General - Incorporation ... PA
Employees ... 45,500
Auditor ... PricewaterhouseCoopers LLP
Stk Agt ... Computershare Trust CO.
Counsel ... NA
DUNS No. ... 00-234-4208

Stock - Price on:12/24/2007 ... $93.38
Stock Exchange ... NYSE
Ticker Symbol ... VFC
Outstanding Shares ... 111,370,000
E.P.S ... $4.62
Shareholders ... NA

Business: The groups principle activities include manufacturing and marketing of branded apparel and related products. The groups products include occupational apparel, knitwear, outdoor apparel and equipment, children's playwear and various apparel. The groups products are sold under the brand names lee, wrangler, rustler, riders and brittania. The group operates from United States, Canada, Europe, China, Brazil, Argentina, Chile, and France. The group operates from United States.

Primary SIC and add'l.: 2325 2253 2329 2340 2326 2322

CIK No: 0000103379

Subsidiaries: Greensport Monte Bianco S.p.A., GS Holding S.r.l., JanSport Apparel Corp., Lee Bell, Inc., Les Dessous Boutique Diffusion S.A., Nautica Apparel, Inc., Nautica Enterprises, Inc., Nautica Furnishings, Inc., Nautica International, Inc., Nautica Jeans Company, Nautica Retail USA, Inc., Norte Indumentaria S.A., Reef Holdings Corporation, Ring Company, South Cone, Inc. 50 Subsidiaries included in the Index

Officers: Mackey J. McDonald/61/Chmn., CEO/$12,437,610.00, Robert K. Shearer/56/CFO, Sr. VP/$3,865,434.00, George N. Derhofer/54/Sr. VP - Global Operations/$3,129,506.00, Stephen F. Dull/49/VP - Strategy, Susan Larson Williams/50/VP - Human Resources, Frank C. Pickard/63/VP, Treasurer, Richard Lipinski/63/VP - Corporate Taxes, Boyd Rogers/59/VP, Pres. - Supply Chain, Eric C. Wiseman/52/Dir., COO, Pres./$4,688,540.00, Michael T. Gannaway/56/VP - Customer Management, Bradley W. Batten/52/VP, Controller, Scott F. Moree/51/VP - Internal Audit, Linda J. Matthews/51/Assist. Treasurer, Franklin L. Terkelsen/43/VP - Mergers, Acquisitions, Candace S. Cummings/60/VP - Administration, General Counsel, Sec./$2,162,731.00 *(23 Officers included in Index)*

Directors: Mackey J. McDonald/61/Chmn., CEO, Juan Ernesto De Bedout/63/Dir., Robert J. Hurst/62/Dir., Edward E. Crutchfield/66/Dir., Ursula O. Fairbairn/65/Dir., Alan W. McCollough/58/Dir., Clarence Otis/52/Dir., Rust M. Sharp/67/Dir., Raymond G. Viault/63/Dir., Daniel R. Hesse/54/Dir., Eric C. Wiseman/52/Dir., COO, Pres., Barbara S. Feigin/70/Dir., George Fellows/65/Dir.

Owners: Daniel R. Hesse, Rust M. Sharp, Ursula O. Fairbairn, Alan W. McCollough, Eric C. Wiseman, Candace S. Cummings, Insiders, Ursula O. Fairbairn, M. Rust Sharp and PNC Bank, N.A.,/8.10%, Robert K. Shearer, Raymond G. Viault, Edward E. Crutchfield, George N. Derhofer, JPMorgan Chase & Co./5.80%, Barbara S. Feigin, George Fellows *(21 Owners included in Index)*

Financial Data: *Fiscal Year End:*12/31 *Latest Annual Data:* 12/30/2006

Year	Sales	Net Income
2006	$6,215,794,000	$533,516,000
2005	$6,502,377,000	$506,702,000

Curr. Assets:	$2,365,376,000	**Curr. Liab.:**	$1,152,143,000	**P/E Ratio:**	20.21
Plant, Equip.:	$564,055,000	**Total Liab.:**	$2,339,532,000	**Indic. Yr. Divd.:**	$2.200
Total Assets:	$5,171,071,000	**Net Worth:**	$2,808,213,000	**Debt/ Equity:**	0.1955

vFinance Inc

3010 N Military Trl., Ste 300, Boca Raton, FL, 33431; *PH:* 1-305-374-0282; *http://* www.vfinance.com; *Email:* info@vfinance.com

General - Incorporation ... DE
Employees ... 98
Auditor ... Sherb & Co. LLP
Stk Agt ... North American Transfer Co
Counsel ... NA
DUNS No. ... NA

Stock - Price on:12/24/2007 ... $0.21
Stock Exchange ... OTC
Ticker Symbol ... VFIN
Outstanding Shares ... 54,680,000
E.P.S ... -$0.045
Shareholders ... NA

Business: The group's principal activity is to provide financial services to its customers through its subsidiaries. It conducts activities as a broker-dealer in 49 states and has offices in New York, New Jersey and Florida. The group operates through three segments: brokerage and trading, investment banking and consulting and other. The brokerage and trading segment buys and sells securities for its customers from other dealers on an agency basis. The investment banking segment provides investing and advisory services, performs market research, valuations and offers other services. The management consulting division provides services to corporations and high net worth individuals for expediting corporate development. The corporate segment provides corporate and management services to the other segments.

Primary SIC and add'l.: 8748 6211 8742

CIK No: 0000890285

Subsidiaries: Union Atlantic, LC, vFinance Advisors, LLC, vFinance Capital, LC, vFinance Executive Services, Inc, vFinance Holdings, Inc, vFinance Investments Holdings, Inc, vFinance Investments, Inc, vFinance Investors, LLC, vFinance Lending Services, Inc

Officers: Leonard Sokolow/51/Chmn., CEO, Jonathan C. Rich/Exec. VP - Investment Banking, Richard Campanella/Pres. - Retail Brokerage, Billy Groeneveld/Dir. - Trading, Wholesale Trading, Marcos Konig/Exec. VP - International, Emerging Marketing, Harry Konig/VP - Trading Technology, Glenn M. Desort/National Sales Mgr., Dir. - Business Development, Alan B. Levin/44/CFO

Directors: Leonard Sokolow/51/Chmn., CEO, Charles R. Modica/Dir.

Owners: Timothy E. Mahoney/12.20%, Insiders/12.10%, Oxir Investment Ltd./5.50%, Sterling Financial Group of Companies, Inc./23.80%, Leonard J. Sokolow/11.40%, Highlands Group Holdings, Inc./4.00%, Alan Levin, Global Partners Securities, Inc./8.40%, Richard Campanella, Level2.com, Inc./8.40%

Financial Data: *Fiscal Year End:*12/31 *Latest Annual Data:* 12/31/2006

Year	Sales	Net Income
2006	$38,595,000	-$2,134,000
2005	$25,826,000	-$1,137,000
2004	$26,329,000	$2,774,000

Curr. Assets:	$6,424,000	**Curr. Liab.:**	$4,618,000		
Plant, Equip.:	$661,000	**Total Liab.:**	$4,744,000	**Indic. Yr. Divd.:**	NA
Total Assets:	$11,643,000	**Net Worth:**	$6,900,000	**Debt/ Equity:**	0.0145

VIA Pharmaceuticals Inc

Formerly: Corautus Genetics Inc

750 Battery St., Ste. 330, San Francisco, CA, 94111; *PH:* 1-415-283-2200; *http://* www.corautus.com

General - Incorporation ... DE
Employees ... NA
Auditor ... Ernst & Young LLP
Stk Agt ... U.S. Stock Transfer Corp
Counsel ... McKenna Long & Aldridge
DUNS No. ... 94-737-5192

Stock - Price on:12/24/2007 ... NA
Stock Exchange ... NA
Ticker Symbol ... NA
Outstanding Shares ... NA
E.P.S ... NA
Shareholders ... NA

Business: The group's principal activities are to develop gene therapy products utilizing adenoviral and lentiviral vector technologies. The products of the group are for the treatment of hemophilia, cancer, HIV, aids and other genetic disorders. The two vector products are clinical trials of product candidate for peripheral vascular disease and other technologies and potential products - maximum-ad, dual-ad and il-3 . The group operates only in domestic market. The group is in the development stage. Genstar therapeutics corporation and vascular genetics inc merged to form corautus genetics inc effective as of 05-Feb-2003.

Primary SIC and add'l.: 2836

CIK No: 0001003929

Subsidiaries: Vascular Genetics Inc.

Officers: Richard E. Otto/Dir., CEO, Pres., Lawrence K. Cohen/55/Dir., CEO, Pres., Yawen Chiang/Chief Scientific Officer, Sr. VP, James G. Stewart/55/Sr. VP, CFO, Sec., Robert T. Atwood/Dir., Exec. VP, Jack W. Callicutt/VP - Finance, Administration, Michael K. Steele/VP - Business Development

Directors: Richard E. Otto/Dir., CEO, Pres., Lawrence K. Cohen/55/Dir., CEO, Pres., Douglass B. Given/56/Chmn., Richard L. Anderson/69/Dir., Lynne B. Parshall/Dir., Mark N.K. Bagnall/51/Dir., Fred B. Craves/63/Dir., David T. Howard/59/Dir., James C. Gilstrap/Dir., Robert T. Atwood/Dir., Exec. VP, Victor W. Schmitt/Dir., Eric N. Falkenberg/Dir., John R. Larson/Dir., Ivor Royston/Dir., Richard F. Nichol/Dir.

Owners: Mark N. K. Bagnall, James E. Flynn/10.30%, Douglass B. Given, Robert T. Atwood, David T. Howard, Richard E. Otto, Adeoye Olukotun, XMark Opportunity Partners, LLC/7.60%, Richard L. Anderson, Boston Scientific Corporation/3.80%, Jack W. Callicutt, Insiders/2.90%, John R. Larson, Mitch Levine/8.40%, James G. Stewart *(17 Owners included in Index)*

ViaCell Inc

245 First St., 15th Fl., Cambridge, MA, 02142; *PH:* 1-617-914-3400; *http://* www.viacellinc.com

General - Incorporation ... DE
Employees ... 254
Auditor ... PricewaterhouseCoopers LLP
Stk Agt ... Computershare, ViaCell's
Counsel ... NA
DUNS No. ... NA

Stock - Price on:12/24/2007 ... $5.51
Stock Exchange ... NA
Ticker Symbol ... NA
Outstanding Shares ... 38,760,000
E.P.S ... -$0.59
Shareholders ... NA

Business: The groups principle activity is to provide reproductive health business. The groups services include collection, testing, processing and storage of umbilical cord blood stem cells. The group products sold under the trade names ViaCell(R) and ViaCord(R). The group operates from the United States, Germany and Singapore.

Primary SIC and add'l.: 2836 8099 2834

CIK No: 0001114529

Subsidiaries: Kourion Therapeutics AG, ViaCell BC Corp., ViaCell Endocrine Science, Inc., ViaCell Neuroscience, Inc., ViaCell Securities Corporation, ViaCell Singapore Pte Ltd., Viacord, Inc.

Officers: Marc D. Beer/Dir., CEO, Pres./$1,183,198.00, Anne Marie Cook/46/General Counsel, Sr. VP - Business, Corporate Development/$445,036.00, Jim Corbett/Pres. - Viacell Reproductive Health/$265,071.00, Stephen G. Dance/56/Sr. VP - Finance/$552,977.00, Mary T. Thistle/48/Sr. VP - Business Development, Viacell Reproductive Health/$452,253.00, Morey Kraus/CTO, John F. Thero/Sr. VP - Finance, CFO

Directors: Vaughn Kailian/Chmn., Barbara Bierer/Dir., Member - Advisory Board, Paul Blake/Dir., Paul Hastings/Dir., Denise Pollard-Knight/Dir., James Sigler/Dir., James Tullis/Dir., Jan Van Heek/Dir., George Daley/Member - Advisory Board, Graham Molineaux/Member - Advisory Board, Bertram H. Lubin/Member - Advisory Board, Leonard I. Zon/Member - Advisory Board

Owners: Mary Thistle, MPM Asset Management LLC/14.20%, Jim Corbett, Jan van Heek, Marc D. Beer/2.30%, Barbara Bierer, Paul Hastings, Vaughn M. Kailian, Stephen G. Dance, James Sigler, Anne Marie Cook, HealthCor Management, L.P./8.60%, Paul Blake, Amgen Inc./7.70%, Insiders/4.00%

Financial Data: *Fiscal Year End:*12/31 *Latest Annual Data:* 12/31/2006

Year	Sales	Net Income
2006	$54,426,000	-$21,047,000
2005	$44,443,000	-$14,677,000
2004	$38,274,000	-$21,097,000

Curr. Assets:	$65,869,000	**Curr. Liab.:**	$17,865,000		
Plant, Equip.:	$8,376,000	**Total Liab.:**	$43,965,000	**Indic. Yr. Divd.:**	NA
Total Assets:	$82,282,000	**Net Worth:**	$38,317,000	**Debt/ Equity:**	0.0006

Viacom Inc

51 W 52nd St., New York, NY, 10019; *PH:* 1-212-258-6000; *http://* www.viacom.com;
Email: investor.relations@viacom.com

General - Incorporation DE
Employees 10,600
Auditor PricewaterhouseCoopers LLP
Stk Agt Bank of New York
Counsel NA
DUNS No. 05-155-0606

Stock- Price on:12/24/2007 $42.77
Stock Exchange NYSE
Ticker Symbol VIA-B
Outstanding Shares 689,130,000
E.P.S. NA
Shareholders NA

Business: The groups principle activity is to provide broad casting services. The group operates through four segments namely television, video, cable networks, infinity and entertainment. The group operates from United States.

Primary SIC and add'l.: 2731 4841 7841 7812 7996 4832 4833

CIK No: 0000813828

Subsidiaries: 1020917 Ontario Inc., 13 Radio Corporation, 14 Hours Productions Inc, 1554994 Ontario Inc., 176309 Canada Inc., 4400 Productions Inc., 559733 British Columbia Ltd., 730806 Alberta Ltd., 90210 Productions, Inc., A-R Acquisition Corp., A.S. Payroll Company, Inc., Aaron Spelling Productions, Inc., Abaco Farms, Limited, Acorn Pipe Line Company, Acorn Properties, Inc. 614 Subsidiaries included in the Index

Officers: Philippe P. Dauman/Dir., CEO, Pres., Brad Grey/Chmn., CEO - Paramount Pictures Corporation, Judy McGrath/Chmn., CEO - MTV Networks, Debra Lee/Chmn., CEO - BET Networks, Dede Lea/Exec. VP - Government Affairs, Joanne Adams Griffith/Exec. VP - Human Resources, Anthony G. Ambrosio/47/Exec. VP - Human Resources, Administration, Jacques Tortoroli/Sr. VP, Corporate Controller, Chief Accounting Officer, Angeline C. Straka/62/Sr. VP, Deputy General Counsel, Sec., Martin Shea/64/Exec. VP - Investor Relations, Thomas E. Dooley/Dir., Chief Administrative Officer, Sr. Exec. VP, Carl D. Folta/Exec. VP - Corporate Communications, Susan C. Gordon/54/Sr. VP, Controller, Chief Accounting Officer/$1,747,190.00, Michael D. Fricklas/Exec. VP, General Counsel, Sec., James Bombassei/Sr. VP - Investor Relations *(22 Officers included in Index)*

Directors: Philippe P. Dauman/Dir., CEO, Pres., Judy McGrath/Chmn., CEO - MTV Networks, Brad Grey/Chmn., CEO - Paramount Pictures Corporation, Debra Lee/Chmn., CEO - BET Networks, Shari Redstone/Vice Chmn., Sumner M. Redstone/Founder, Exec. Chmn., George S. Abrams/Dir., Charles E. Phillips/Dir., Joseph A. Califano/76/Dir., Leslie Moonves/58/Dir., Arnold Kopelson/73/Dir., Doug Morris/69/Dir., David R. Andelman/68/Dir., William Schwartz/Dir., Thomas E. Dooley/Dir., Chief Administrative Officer, Sr. Exec. VP *(25 Directors included in Index)*

Owners: Mario J. Gabelli/7.90%, NAIRI,Inc./National Amusements,Inc./5.50%, David R. Andelman, Leslie Moonves, Frederic V. Salerno, Joseph A. Califano, Frederic V. Salerno, Sumner M. Redstone/5.90%, David R. Andelman, Shari Redstone, Susan C. Gordon, Fredric G. Reynolds, NAIRI,Inc./National Amusements,Inc./76.40%, William S. Cohen, William S. Cohen *(25 Owners included in Index)*

Curr. Assets:	$4,211,100,000	**Curr. Liab.:**	$4,616,800,000		
Plant, Equip.:	$4,990,000,000	**Total Liab.:**	$14,630,500,000	**Indic. Yr. Divd.:**	NA
Total Assets:	$21,796,700,000	**Net Worth:**	$7,166,200,000	**Debt/ Equity:**	NA

Viad Corp

1850 N Central Ave., Ste 800, Phoenix, AZ, 85004; *PH:* 1-602-207-4000; *http://* www.viad.com;
Email: ir@viad.com

General - Incorporation DE
Employees 3,620
Auditor Deloitte & Touche LLP
Stk Agt Wells Fargo Shareowner Services
Counsel Mr. Bohannon
DUNS No. 00-693-0366

Stock- Price on:12/24/2007 $42.51
Stock Exchange NYSE
Ticker Symbol VVI
Outstanding Shares 21,070,000
E.P.S. $1.85
Shareholders NA

Business: The group's principle activities is to provide diversified services that address the needs of trade show organizers and exhibitors as well as travel and recreation services. It operates through three segments: ges: provides convention and tradeshow services which includes freight handling, transportation, installation, dismantling and management services to trade associations and tradeshow management companies and exhibitors. Exhibitgroup: specializes in the large and small scale design, construction, installation and warehousing of convention and tradeshow exhibits and displays mainly for corporate customers. Travel and recreation services: provides a variety of tourism services through brewster transport company limited and glacier park inc. The services offered include world-class attractions, motorcoach services, charter and sightseeing services, hotel operations, inbound package tour operations and travel agencies. The group operates from United States.

Primary SIC and add'l.: 6099 7389

CIK No: 0000884219

Subsidiaries: 859371 Alberta Ltd., Brewster Inc., Brewster Tours Inc., Brewster Transport Company Limited, Clarkson-Conway Inc., David H. Gibson Company, Inc., ESR Exposition Service, Inc., EXG, Inc., ExhibitAcquisition, Inc., Exhibitgroup/Giltspur France S.A.R.L., Expo Accessories, Inc., Expo Display & Design, Inc., Exposervice Standard Inc., GES Exposition Services (Canada) Limited, Ges Exposition Services, Inc. 29 Subsidiaries included in the Index

Officers: Paul B. Dykstra/Dir., CEO, Pres./$2,901,934.00, Kevin M. Rabbitt/CEO, Pres. - GES Exposition Services, Inc/$1,045,361.00, David G. Morrison/CEO, Pres. - Brewster Transport Co Inc, John F. Jastrem/CEO, Pres. - Exhibitgroup, Giltspur, Cindy J. Ognjanov/Pres., GM - Glacier Park, Inc, Suzanne Pearl/VP - Human Resources/$1,235,934.00, Carrie Long/Dir. - Investor Relations, Scott E. Sayre/VP, General Counsel, Sec./$1,922,406.00, Ellen M. Lngersoll/CFO/$1,722,280.00, Michael G. Latta/VP, Controller

Directors: Paul B. Dykstra/Dir., CEO, Pres., Robert H. Bohannon/Chmn., Wayne G. Allcott/Dir., Daniel Boggan/Dir., Isabella Cunningham/Dir., Jess Hay/Dir., Judith K. Hofer/Dir., Robert E. Munzenrider/Dir., Albert M. Teplin/Dir.

Owners: Robert E. Munzenrider, Michael G. Latta, Judith K. Hofer, Robert H. Bohannon/2.20%, John F. Jastrem, Kevin M. Rabbitt, Wayne G. Allcott, Paul B. Dykstra, Scott E. Sayre, Jess Hay, Isabella Cunningham, Daniel Boggan, Ellen M. Ingersoll, Albert M. Teplin, Insiders/4.40% *(17 Owners included in Index)*

Financial Data: **Fiscal Year End:**12/31 **Latest Annual Data:** 12/31/2006

Year	Sales	Net Income
2006	$856,031,000	$63,554,000
2005	$826,254,000	$37,754,000
2004	$785,657,000	-$56,002,000

Curr. Assets:	$287,318,000	**Curr. Liab.:**	$131,684,000	**P/E Ratio:**	16.80
Plant, Equip.:	$135,958,000	**Total Liab.:**	$242,641,000	**Indic. Yr. Divd.:**	$0.160
Total Assets:	$672,564,000	**Net Worth:**	$429,923,000	**Debt/ Equity:**	0.0297

Viasat Inc

6155 El Camino Real, Carlsbad, CA, 92009; *PH:* 1-760-476-2200; *http://* www.viasat.com

General - Incorporation CA
Employees 1,410
Auditor PricewaterhouseCoopers LLP
Stk Agt Computershare Investor Services LLC
Counsel Latham & Watkins
DUNS No. 17-509-6619

Stock- Price on:12/24/2007 $30.93
Stock Exchange NDQ
Ticker Symbol VSAT
Outstanding Shares 30,060,000
E.P.S. $0.98
Shareholders NA

Business: The group's principal activities are to design, produce and market advanced broadband digital satellite communications and wireless networking and signal processing equipment and services. The group's products include advanced multifunction information distribution system or mids product line, the simulation and test equipment which allows the testing of sophisticated airborne radio equipment without expensive flight exercises. The UHF dama satellite communications product consists of modems, terminals and network control systems. The major customer of the group for commercial products and services are satellite network integrators, large communications service providers and corporations requiring complex communications networks. The group operates in North America, Europe, Asia-Pacific and Latin America.

Primary SIC and add'l.: 8731 3669 3663

CIK No: 0000797721

Subsidiaries: Efficient Channel Coding Inc., Immeon Networks LLC, U.S. Monolithics LLC, ViaSat Australia PTY Limited, ViaSat Canada Company, ViaSat China Services Inc., ViaSat Europe Limited, ViaSat Europe S.r.l., ViaSat Foreign Sales Corporation, ViaSat India Pvt. Ltd., ViaSat Worldwide Limited

Officers: Mark D. Dankberg/Chmn., CEO/$1,384,663.00, Ken Gamache/Contact - Global Control, Christopher J. Leber/VP - Vsat Networks, Paul D. Baca/VP - Tactical Networks, Gregory D. Monahan/VP, General Counsel, Sec., Steven R. Hart/CTO/$463,684.00, Richard A. Baldridge/COO, Pres./$965,291.00, Benjamin A. Pontano/Pres. Emeritus - Comsat Labs, Keven K. Lippert/36/VP, General Counsel, Sec., Marc H. Agnew/VP - Broadband Systems, Steve W. Thompson/VP - Information Systems, Jack Tassos/VP, GM - US Monolithics, Ron G. Wangerin/CFO, VP/$568,792.00, John R. Zlogar/VP - Antenna Systems, Bill Jensen/VP - Government Contracts, Strategic Relations *(31 Officers included in Index)*

Directors: Mark D. Dankberg/Chmn., CEO, Robert W. Johnson/Dir., Allen B. Lay/Dir., John P. Stenbit/Dir., Michael B. Targoff/Dir., Harvey P. White/Dir.

Owners: Mark D. Dankberg/6.10%, John P. Stenbit, Michael B. Targoff, Jeffrey M. Nash/1.20%, Ronald G. Wangerin, Keven K. Lippert, Insiders/16.22%, Steven R. Hart/2.80%, Robert W. Johnson/2.10%, Harvey P. White, Franklin Resources, Inc. and affiliates/5.70%, Richard A. Baldridge, Steve Estes, Mark J. Miller/1.30%, Allen B. Lay/1.40%

Financial Data: **Fiscal Year End:**03/31 **Latest Annual Data:** 3/30/2007

Year	Sales	Net Income
2007	$516,566,000	$30,166,000
2006	$433,823,000	$23,515,000
2005	$345,939,000	$19,267,000

Curr. Assets:	$209,792,000	**Curr. Liab.:**	$70,933,000	**P/E Ratio:**	33.62
Plant, Equip.:	$33,278,000	**Total Liab.:**	$74,844,000	**Indic. Yr. Divd.:**	NA
Total Assets:	$301,825,000	**Net Worth:**	$226,283,000	**Debt/ Equity:**	0.0118

VIASPACE Inc

Formerly: Global Wide Publication Ltd
171 N Altadena Dr., Ste. 101, Pasadena, CA, 91107; *PH:* 1-626-768-6310; *http://* www.viaspace.com

General - Incorporation NV
Employees 18
Auditor ... Singer Lewak Greenbaum & Goldstein
Stk Agt Nevada Agency & Trust Company
Counsel NA
DUNS No. NA

Stock- Price on:12/24/2007 $0.285
Stock Exchange OTC
Ticker Symbol VSPC
Outstanding Shares 303,960,000
E.P.S. -$0.04
Shareholders NA

Business: The groups principle activity is to leverage proven space and defense technologies from NASA and the Department of Defense to develop industry leading products and applications that solve complex problems and address critical needs in high-growth industries including clean energy and security. The groups products include Viasensor. The group operates from United States.

Primary SIC and add'l.: NA

CIK No: 0001270200

Subsidiaries: Arroyo Sciences, Inc., Concentric Water Technology LLC, eCARmerce, Inc., Ionfinity LLC, Marco Polo World News Inc., Methanol Fuel Cell Corporation

Officers: Carl Kukkonen/Chmn., CEO, Co - Founder, Amjad J. Abdallat/Dir., Co - Founder, COO, VP - Business Development, Stephen J. Muzi/CFO, Treasurer, Jan Vandersande/Investor Relations Contact, Robert W. Zeiler/61/Executive Dir.

Directors: Carl Kukkonen/Chmn., CEO, Co - Founder, Amjad J. Abdallat/Dir., Co - Founder, COO, VP - Business Development, Bernard P. Randolph/Dir., Angelina Galiteva/Dir., Nobuyuki Denda/Dir., Dwight Duston/Member - Scientific Advisory Board, Rick Calacci/Dir., Robert W. Zeiler/61/Executive Dir.

Owners: Amjad S. Abdallat/13.00%, Insiders/34.40%, Carl Kukkonen/21.10%, SNK Capital Trust/20.10%

Financial Data: **Fiscal Year End:**12/31 **Latest Annual Data:** 12/31/2006

Year	Sales	Net Income
2006	$962,000	-$9,601,000
2005	$432,000	-$2,311,000
2004	$147,000	-$91,000

Curr. Assets:	$13,000	**Curr. Liab.:**	$60,000		
Plant, Equip.:	NA	**Total Liab.:**	$60,000	**Indic. Yr. Divd.:**	NA
Total Assets:	$13,000	**Net Worth:**	-$48,000	**Debt/ Equity:**	0.0430

VIASYS Healthcare Inc

227 Washington St., Ste 200, Conshohocken, PA, 19428; *PH:* 1-610-862-0800;
http:// www.viasyshealthcare.com

General - Incorporation .... DE	**Stock**- Price on:12/24/2007 ....$42.72
Employees...2,365	Stock Exchange..NA
Auditor .... Ernst & Young LLP	Ticker Symbol...NA
Stk Agt...... American Stock Transfer & Trust Co.	Outstanding Shares 33,280,000
Counsel...........Morgan, Lewis & Bockius LLP	E.P.S...NA
DUNS No. ....NA	Shareholders...NA

Business: The group's principal activities are to develop, manufacture, market and service medical devices and products, including respiratory care equipment, neurodiagnostic systems, disposable products and other specialty products and materials. The group operates in four segments: respiratory technologies, critical care, neurocare and medical and surgical products. It markets its products in over 100 countries. The group's customers include hospitals, alternate care sites, clinical laboratories, private physicians and original equipment manufacturers. On 03-Apr-2003, the group disposed its medical data electronics business and on 03-Oct-2003, disposed its thermedics polymer business.

Primary SIC and add'l.: 3845

CIK No: 0001123361

Subsidiaries: Bird Products (Japan), Ltd., Bird Products Corporation, E.M.E. (Electro Medical Equipment) Limited, EME Medical Inc., EME Medical Limited, Erich Jaeger Benelux B.V., Erich Jaeger U.K. Ltd., Intermed Precision Ltd., Micro Medical Ltd., MicroGas Ltd., MicroMedical Deutschland GmbH, MicroPulse Ltd., Nicolet Biomedical Japan Inc., PT Netherlands BV, Pulmonetic Systems Inc. 42 Subsidiaries included in the Index

Officers: Randy H. Thurman/58/Chmn., CEO, Pres./$2,594,209.00, Scott W. Hurley/VP, Corporate Controller, Principal Accounting Officer, Arie Cohen/60/Group Pres. - Respiratory Care/$1,006,583.00, Matthew M. Bennett/Exec. VP - Legal, Business Development, Regulatory, Quality Affairs, Sec., Lori J. Cross/Exec. VP, Group Pres. - Neurocare/$851,378.00, John F. Imperato/Sr. VP - Business Operations, Gregory G. Martin/Group Pres. - Customer Care, Information Technology, Edward Pulwer/COO, Exec. VP/$1,089,360.00, Thomas I. Kuhn/Sr. VP, Group Pres. - Medsystems, Giulio A. Perillo/Sr. VP, Group Pres. - Orthopedics, Martin P. Galvan/Exec. VP, CFO - Information Technology, Dir. - Investor Relations, Principal Financial Officer/$843,137.00, Wesley N. Riemer/VP, Corporate Treasurer

Directors: Randy H. Thurman/58/Chmn., CEO, Pres., Kirk E. Gorman/57/Dir., Thomas W. Hofmann/56/Dir., Rebecca W. Rimel/56/Dir., Fred B. Parks/60/Dir., Sander A. Flaum/71/Dir., Ronald A. Ahrens/68/Dir., Elliot J. Sussman/56/Dir.

Financial Data: Fiscal Year End:12/31 Latest Annual Data: 12/30/2006

Year		Sales	Net Income
2006		$610,416,000	$28,990,000
2005		$509,974,000	-$9,769,000
Curr. Assets:	$271,328,000	**Curr. Liab.:**	$136,999,000
Plant, Equip.:	$51,564,000	**Total Liab.:**	$198,471,000 **Indic. Yr. Divd.:** NA
Total Assets:	$648,587,000	**Net Worth:**	$450,116,000 **Debt/ Equity:** 0.0476

ViaVid Broadcasting Inc

11483 Wellington Crescent, Surrey, BC, V3R 9H1 ; *PH:* 1-604-588-8146; *http://* www.viavid.com

General - Incorporation ....NV	**Stock**- Price on:12/24/2007 ....$0.02
Employees..NA	Stock Exchange..OTC
Auditor .... Telford Sadovnick, PLLC	Ticker Symbol...VVDB
Stk Agt............. Pacific Stock Transfer Company	Outstanding Shares ....NA
Counsel...NA	E.P.S...NA
DUNS No. ....NA	Shareholders...NA

Business: The group's principal activities are to provide Web casting, teleconferencing and transcription services to corporate clients throughout North America. The group's services include audio conferencing and webconferencing. These services are based on proprietary systems that integrate traditional telephony technology with powerful streaming media technology and Web-based tools. The automated, on-demand audio conferencing is ideal for the broadcast of earnings. The conference calls and webconferencing are ideal for the creation and broadcast of interactive, dynamic online corporate presentations. Other service enhancements provided include viacontent and viatracker. Viacontent is designed to manage live audio / video streams and viavision events, such as online presentations. The group operates solely in the domestic market.

Primary SIC and add'l.: 7319 7372 7375 7389

CIK No: 0001079110

Subsidiaries: British Columbia company

Financial Data: Fiscal Year End:03/31 Latest Annual Data: 3/31/2005

Year		Sales	Net Income
2005		$1,023,000	-$86,000
2004		$736,000	-$163,000
2003		$569,000	-$343,000
Curr. Assets:	$326,000	**Curr. Liab.:**	$746,000
Plant, Equip.:	$60,000	**Total Liab.:**	$746,000 **Indic. Yr. Divd.:** NA
Total Assets:	$385,000	**Net Worth:**	-$361,000 **Debt/ Equity:** NA

Vical Inc

10390 Pacific Ctr. Ct., San Diego, CA, 92121; *PH:* 1-858-646-1100; *Fax:* 1-858-646-1150;
http:// www.vical.com; *Email:* hr@vical.com

General - Incorporation .... DE	**Stock**- Price on:12/24/2007 ....$5.54
Employees..147	Stock Exchange...NDQ
Auditor .... Ernst & Young, LLP	Ticker Symbol...VICL
Stk Agt.................Mellon Investor Services LLC	Outstanding Shares 39,190,000
Counsel...................Pillsbury Madison & Sutro	E.P.S...-$0.9
DUNS No. 18-319-2855	Shareholders...NA

Business: The group's principle activity is to develop biopharmaceutical products based on its patented gene delivery technologies for the prevention and treatment of serious or life-threatening diseases. Potential applications of its gene delivery technology include gene therapies for cancer, dna vaccines for infectious diseases or cancer, and dna therapeutic protein delivery. The company has retained all rights to its internally developed cancer product candidates. In addition, it collaborates with major pharmaceutical and biotechnology companies that give access to complementary technologies or greater resources. These strategic partnerships provide mutually beneficial opportunities to expand the company's product pipeline and serve significant unmet medical needs. The group operates from United States.

Primary SIC and add'l.: 8731 2836

CIK No: 0000819050

Officers: Vijay B. Samant/54/Dir., CEO, Pres./$1,169,433.00, Kevin R. Bracken/VP - Manufacturing, Alain P. Rolland/Sr. VP - Product Development/$466,172.00, Robin M. Jackman/Sr. VP - Business Operations, Jill M. Church/VP, CFO, Sec./$472,665.00, Ronald B. Moss/VP - Clinical Development, Marilyn Ferrari/Dir. - Business Development, Alan Engbring/Executive Dir. - Investor Relations, Larry R. Smith/VP - Vaccine Research

Directors: Vijay B. Samant/54/Dir., CEO, Pres., Gordon R. Douglas/72/Chmn., Gary A. Lyons/55/Dir., Robert C. Merton/62/Dir., Thomas C. Caskey/Member - Scientific Advisory Board, Phyllis Gardner/Member - Scientific Advisory Board, Paul A. Offit/Member - Scientific Advisory Board, Eric N. Olson/Member - Scientific Advisory Board, Douglas D. Richman/Member - Scientific Advisory Board, George W. Sledge/Member - Scientific Advisory Board, Robert H. Campbell/69/Dir.

Owners: Capital Research and Management/5.70%, R. Gordon Douglas, Jill M. Church, Insiders/3.18%, Vijay B. Samant/1.86%, Temasek Holdings/12.70%, Robert C. Merton, Federated Investors Inc./7.00%, BlackRock, Inc./5.40%, Alain P. Rolland, Robert H. Campbell, Gary A. Lyons

Financial Data: Fiscal Year End:12/31 Latest Annual Data: 12/31/2006

Year		Sales	Net Income
2006		$14,740,000	-$23,148,000
2005		$12,003,000	-$24,357,000
2004		$14,545,000	-$23,733,000
Curr. Assets:	$105,442,000	**Curr. Liab.:**	$8,153,000
Plant, Equip.:	$13,500,000	**Total Liab.:**	$11,126,000 **Indic. Yr. Divd.:** NA
Total Assets:	$125,249,000	**Net Worth:**	$114,123,000 **Debt/ Equity:** 0.0062

Viceroy Explorations Ltd

Formerly: Consolidated Trillion Resources Ltd
700 W Pender St., Ste. 520, Vancouver, BC, V6C 1G8; *PH:* 1-604-669-4777;
http:// www.viceroyexploration.com

General - Incorporation ....Canada	**Stock**- Price on:12/24/2007 ....NA
Employees..63	Stock Exchange..NA
Auditor ....PricewaterhouseCoopers LLP	Ticker Symbol...NA
Stk Agt ....CIBC Mellon Trust Co.	Outstanding Shares ....NA
Counsel.........Lavery De Billy, Montreal, Quebec	E.P.S...NA
DUNS No. 24-861-4752	Shareholders...NA

Business: The group's principle activity is to provide exploration services for gold, diamonds, copper, nickel, platinum and uranium. The group operates from United States.

Primary SIC and add'l.: 1041

CIK No: 0001012454

Subsidiaries: Minas Argentinas SA, Minas Argentinas(Barbardos)Inc, Minera De Oro(BVI) Inc, Oro Bell Resources Corporation

Vicon Industries Inc

89 Arkay Dr., Hauppauge, NY, 11788; *PH:* 1-516-952-2288; *http://* www.vicon-cctv.com;
Email: glutz@vicon-cctv.com

General - Incorporation ....NY	**Stock**- Price on:12/24/2007 ....$9.6
Employees..208	Stock Exchange..AMEX
Auditor ....BDO Seidman LLP, KPMG LLP	Ticker Symbol..VII
Stk Agt .... Computershare Investor Services LLC	Outstanding Shares ,............................4,760,000
Counsel............... Schoeman, Updike & Kaufman	E.P.S..$1.59
DUNS No. 04-383-7947	Shareholders...NA

Business: The group's principal activities are to design, manufacture, assemble and market a range of video systems and system components. The video system is a private network, which transmits and receives video, audio and data signals as per the operational needs of the user. These components are used for security, surveillance, safety and control purposes. The group's products include fire and burglar alarm systems, access control, video systems and article surveillance. The products are mainly used in office buildings, manufacturing plants, apartment complexes, retail stores, government facilities, transportation operations, prisons, casinos, sports arenas, health care facilities and financial institutions. The products of the group are also sold in Europe, China, Japan, Norway and Hong Kong.

Primary SIC and add'l.: 3663

CIK No: 0000310056

Subsidiaries: TeleSite U.S.A., Inc., Vicon Industries, Limited

Officers: Kenneth M. Darby/Chmn., CEO, Kenneth Rohan/Dir. - Customer Service, John M. Badke/48/CFO, Sr. VP - Finance, Yigal Abiri/58/GM - Vicon Systems Ltd, Greg Lutz/Sales Personal, Malcom Ridge/Mgr. - European Training, Training IN Europe, Middle East, Richard Koharik/Mgr. - A&E Services, Tom Cook/Dir. - East Region Sales, Bret M. McGowan/VP - US Sales, Marketing, Peter A. Horn/53/VP - Operations, Gonzalo L. Coronado/Commercial Mgr. - Spain, Mohammed Masood Ali/Mgr. - Middle East Sales, Tina Desiderato/Sales Personal, Joan L. Wolf/Sec., Yacov A. Pshtissky/56/VP - Technology, Development (37 Officers included in Index)

Directors: Kenneth M. Darby/Chmn., CEO, Gregory W. Robertson/64/Dir., Peter F. Neumann/73/Dir., Clifton H.W. Maloney/70/Dir., Arthur D. Roche/69/Dir.

Owners: Peter F. Neumann, Gregory W. Robertson, Christopher Wall, John M. Badke, Bret McGowan, CBC Co., Ltd./0.11%, Dimensional Fund Advisors/0.06%, Al Frank Asset Management, Inc./0.05%, Arthur D. Roche/0.03%, Clifton H.W. Maloney, Yigal Abiri, Kenneth M. Darby/0.06%, Insiders/0.15%

Financial Data: Fiscal Year End:09/30 Latest Annual Data: 9/30/2006

Year		Sales	Net Income
2006		$56,279,000	-$547,000
2005		$56,056,000	-$2,885,000
2004		$53,533,000	-$2,691,000
Curr. Assets:	$29,490,000	**Curr. Liab.:**	$9,309,000 **P/E Ratio:** 15.00
Plant, Equip.:	$6,229,000	**Total Liab.:**	$11,936,000 **Indic. Yr. Divd.:** NA
Total Assets:	$35,955,000	**Net Worth:**	$24,019,000 **Debt/ Equity:** NA

Vicor Corp

25 Frontage Rd. , Andover, MA, 01810; *PH:* 1-978-470-2900; *http://* www.vicr.com;
Email: vicorexp@vicr.com

General - Incorporation.............................DE
Employees...1,030
Auditor ....Ernst & Young LLP
Stk Agt.........................EquiServe Trust Co N.A
Counsel......................Goodwin, Procter & Hoar
DUNS No. 05-063-5986

Stock- Price on:12/24/2007 ....$12.42
Stock Exchange...NDQ
Ticker Symbol...VICR
Outstanding Shares 41,570,000
E.P.S...-$0.81
Shareholders..NA

Business: The group's principle activities are developing, manufacturing and marketing of modular power components and complete power systems. The products of the group are: modular power converters: designed to be mounted directly on a printed circuit board assembly and soldered, these converters are used in input and output voltage and power ratings; configured products: these products are developed to provide power solutions configured to a customer's specific requirements. The products are used primarily by original equipment manufacturers in the communications, data processing, industrial control, test equipment, medical, and military electronics markets. The group sells its products through a network of 29 independent sales representative organizations in north and South America; internationally, 52 independent distributors are utilized.

Primary SIC and add'l.: 3679

CIK No: 0000751978

Subsidiaries: Aegis Power Systems, Inc, Converpower Corporation, Freedom Power Systems, Inc, Mission Power Systems, Inc, Northwest Power Integration, Inc, Picor Corporation, Vicor B.V, Vicor Development Corporation, Vicor France SARL, Vicor GmbH, Vicor Hong Kong Ltd, Vicor Italy SRL, Vicor Japan Company, Ltd, Vicor U.K. Ltd, VICR Securities Corporation 16 Subsidiaries included in the Index

Officers: Patrizio Vinciarelli/Chmn., CEO, Pres./$316,957.00, Douglas W. Richardson/CIO, VP, Mark A. Glazer/CFO, Treasurer, Sec./$219,149.00, Richard E. Zengilowski/VP - Human Resources/$206,423.00, Barry Kelleher/Dir., Pres. - Vicors Brick Business Unit/$435,230.00, Allen H. Henderson/VP - Vicor Corporation, Pres. - Westcor Division/$217,686.00, Richard J. Nagel/51/VP, Chief Accounting Officer

Directors: Patrizio Vinciarelli/Chmn., CEO, Pres., Estia J. Eichten/Dir., Barry Kelleher/Dir., Pres. - Vicors Brick Business Unit, Samuel Anderson/Dir., David T. Riddiford/Dir., Claudio Tuozzolo/Dir.

Owners: Estia J. Eichten/1.70%, Insiders/35.20%, Mark A. Glazer, Patrizio Vinciarelli/32.60%, Allen H. Henderson, Richard E. Zengilowski, Jay M. Prager, Barry Kelleher, Samuel J. Anderson, Michael M. Ansour, David T. Riddiford, Pequot Capital Management, Inc./8.80%

Financial Data: Fiscal Year End:12/31   Latest Annual Data: 12/31/2006

Year	Sales	Net Income
2006	$192,047,000	-$29,738,000
2005	$179,351,000	$3,916,000
2004	$171,580,000	-$3,723,000

Curr. Assets:	$189,669,000	Curr. Liab.:	$68,779,000		
Plant, Equip.:	$51,573,000	Total Liab.:	$76,761,000	Indic. Yr. Divd.:	$0.300
Total Assets:	$248,107,000	Net Worth:	$171,346,000	Debt/ Equity:	NA

Victoria Industries Inc

551 Fifth Ave., Ste 601, New York, NY, 10017; **PH:** 1-212-973-0063; **http://** www.victoriaind.com

General - Incorporation.............................NV
Employees...4
Auditor ....John A. Braden & Co. P.C
Stk Agt.............Pacific Stock Transfer Company
Counsel..NA
DUNS No. ....NA

Stock- Price on:12/24/2007 ....$1.5
Stock Exchange...OTC
Ticker Symbol...VIINE
Outstanding Shares 10,970,000
E.P.S...$0.01
Shareholders..NA

Business: The group does not have an active operating business at the end of year 2002. On 13-Mar-2002, the group acquired certain property and equipment and a license to certain intellectual property to produce salmon caviar and salmon caviar-related products. In contemplation of the acquisition, the group incorporated a wholly owned subsidiary, golden caviar corp on 15-Feb-2002 to operate the caviar business. The processing and sale of caviar and caviar-related products was the group's primary business from late Mar 2002 until Jun 2002. The group terminated its involvement in the caviar business, returned remaining assets and settled liabilities of the caviar business, became inactive and began the search for new business opportunities.

Primary SIC and add'l.: 800

CIK No: 0001111118

Subsidiaries: Coptent Trading Ltd., Victoria Lumber, Victoria Resources, Inc., Victoria Siberian Wood

Officers: Albert Abdoulline/42/Dir., CEO, CFO, Victor Kislinskii/52/VP, Irina Dementieva/46/CFO - Victoria Lumber, Roman Livson/VP

Directors: Albert Abdoulline/42/Dir., CEO, CFO, Leon Golden/40/Dir.

Owners: Stockwell, Inc./34.40%, Albert Abdoulline/0.90%, Inverness, Inc./36.90%, Victor Kislinskii/6.90%, High Peaks Corporation/8.50%, Insiders/7.80%

Financial Data: Fiscal Year End:12/31   Latest Annual Data: 12/31/2006

Year	Sales	Net Income
2006	$8,412,000	$414,000
2005	$5,353,000	$162,000
2004	$2,165,000	-$92,000

Curr. Assets:	$4,140,000	Curr. Liab.:	$2,659,000	P/E Ratio:	37.50
Plant, Equip.:	$1,000	Total Liab.:	$2,659,000	Indic. Yr. Divd.:	NA
Total Assets:	$4,141,000	Net Worth:	$1,481,000	Debt/ Equity:	NA

Victory Divide Mining Company

211 W Wall St., Midland, TX, 79701; **PH:** 1-432-682-1761

General - Incorporation.............................NV
Employees...NA
Auditor ....S. W. Hatfield, CPA
Stk Agt.............................PacWest Transfer LLC
Counsel..NA
DUNS No. ....NA

Stock- Price on:12/24/2007 ....$0.1
Stock Exchange...OTC
Ticker Symbol...VDVM
Outstanding Shares ....NA
E.P.S...NA
Shareholders..NA

Business: The groups principal activity is to engage in a merger or other business combination transaction with a to be identified company or companies, or other entity or person. The group operates from the United States.

Primary SIC and add'l.: 6770

CIK No: 0001368745

Officers: Glenn A. Little/54/Dir., CEO, CFO, Pres.

Directors: Glenn A. Little/54/Dir., CEO, CFO, Pres.

Owners: Insiders/84.80%, Glenn A. Little/84.80%

Financial Data: Fiscal Year End:12/31   Latest Annual Data: 12/31/2006

Year	Sales	Net Income
2006	NA	-$15,000

Curr. Assets:	$0	Curr. Liab.:	$1,000		
Plant, Equip.:	NA	Total Liab.:	$1,000	Indic. Yr. Divd.:	NA
Total Assets:	$0	Net Worth:	-$1,000	Debt/ Equity:	NA

Victory Energy Corp

220 Airport Rd., Indiana, PA, 15701; **PH:** 1-724-349-6366; **Fax:** 1-724-349-6649; **http://** www.victoryenergycorp.com; **Email:** victory@victoryenergycorp.com

General - Incorporation ....NV
Employees...1
Auditor ....John Kinross-Kennedy
Stk Agt...NA
Counsel..NA
DUNS No. ....NA

Stock- Price on:12/24/2007 ....$0.155
Stock Exchange...OTC
Ticker Symbol..VYEY
Outstanding Shares 16,500,000
E.P.S...-$0.203
Shareholders..NA

Business: The groups principal activity is projects in the oil and gas industry. The group has targeted specific prospects and intends to engage in the drilling for oil and gas. The group operates from the United States.

Primary SIC and add'l.: 3823

CIK No: 0000700764

Subsidiaries: Global Card Services, Inc

Officers: Jon Fullenkamp/Chmn., CEO, Pres., Lynn A. Doverspike/Owner, Pres., Cheryl S. Miller/Sr. Accountant, Renea J. Isenberg/Land Mgr., Chris Baker/Operations Foreman

Directors: Jon Fullenkamp/Chmn., CEO, Pres., Lynn A. Doverspike/Owner, Pres., Charles Laser/Member - Advisory Board, Richard May/Dir., Perry R. Mansell/Dir.

Owners: Perry Mansell, Jon Fullenkamp/42.00%, Rick May

Financial Data: Fiscal Year End:12/31   Latest Annual Data: 12/31/2006

Year	Sales	Net Income
2006	NA	-$1,745,000
2005	$20,000	-$1,324,000
2004	NA	-$1,606,000

Curr. Assets:	NA	Curr. Liab.:	$280,000		
Plant, Equip.:	NA	Total Liab.:	$970,000	Indic. Yr. Divd.:	NA
Total Assets:	$50,000	Net Worth:	-$920,000	Debt/ Equity:17.4800

Video Display Corp

1868 Tucker Industrial Dr., Tucker, GA, 30084; **PH:** 1-770-938-2080; **http://** www.videodisplay.com; **Email:** sales@cathoderaytubes.com

General - Incorporation ....GA
Employees...497
Auditor ....Carr, Riggs & Ingram, LLC
Stk Agt.........................Computershare Trust Co
Counsel..............................Cooper & Gibson
DUNS No. 07-592-9067

Stock- Price on:12/24/2007 ....$7.752
Stock Exchange...NDQ
Ticker Symbol..VIDE
Outstanding Shares 9,580,000
E.P.S...$0.277
Shareholders..NA

Business: The group's principal activities are to design, manufacture and supply display devices and component parts for military, medical, industrial and consumer display applications. The group's product line encompasses both cathode ray tube displays and flat panel displays. The group also acts as a facilitator and wholesale distributor of parts and accessories for original equipment manufacturers of consumer products. The group operates under four display oriented divisions: monitor division, home entertainment cathode ray tubes (crts) division, data display crt division and components division as well as distribution of parts and accessories for consumer products. The group operates in the United States and one subsidiary operation in the United Kingdom.

Primary SIC and add'l.: 5065 3679

CIK No: 0000758743

Subsidiaries: Aydin Displays, Inc., Fox International Ltd., Inc., Lexel Imaging Systems, Inc., Mengel Industries, Inc., Southwest Vacuum Devices, IncX, Teltron Technologies, Inc., Video Display (Europe), Ltd., Z-Axis, Inc.

Owners: Insiders/37.90%, T. D. Clinton/3.70%, Ronald D. Ordway/29.30%, Ernest J. Thibeault/1.10%, Ervin Kuczogi, Peter Frend, Jonathan R. Ordway/22.80%, Carolyn C. Howard/2.90%

Financial Data: Fiscal Year End:02/28   Latest Annual Data: 2/28/2007

Year	Sales	Net Income
2007	$81,939,000	$1,623,000
2006	$83,878,000	$445,000
2005	$82,740,000	$3,722,000

Curr. Assets:	$51,809,000	Curr. Liab.:	$12,821,000	P/E Ratio:	27.99
Plant, Equip.:	$7,920,000	Total Liab.:	$35,546,000	Indic. Yr. Divd.:	NA
Total Assets:	$65,087,000	Net Worth:	$29,541,000	Debt/ Equity:	0.7457

Videolocity International Inc

5532 Lillehammer Ln., Ste. 300, Park City, UT, 84098; **PH:** 1-435-615-8338; **http://** www.videolocity.com

General - Incorporation ....NV
Employees...2
Auditor ....Madsen & Associates, CPA's Inc.
Stk Agt.............Colonial Stock Transfer Co Inc
Counsel..NA
DUNS No. ....NA

Stock- Price on:12/24/2007 ....$0.0055
Stock Exchange...OTC
Ticker Symbol..VCTY
Outstanding Shares 30,640,000
E.P.S...-$0.024
Shareholders..NA

Business: The groups principal activities include developing a digital entertainment system that delivers true video on demand streaming anywhere between 40kbps and 1.5mbps depending on the end user device over ethernet, dsl, or wireless WAN and LAN network architectures. The group operates from the United States.

Primary SIC and add'l.: 4813

CIK No: 0000786771

Officers: Mike York/VP

Owners: Cortney L. Taylor/13.44%, Daniel Osorio/5.24%, WAJ Enterprises LLC/7.95%, Robert E. Holt/24.63%, Kirsten Bringhurst Cysewski/6.86%, Bennie L. Williams/6.53%, Dan Driscoll/5.24%, Insiders/38.56%, Marvin Erickson/14.16%

Financial Data: Fiscal Year End:10/31   Latest Annual Data: 10/31/2006

Year	Sales	Net Income
2006	NA	-$642,000
2005	$114,000	-$4,251,000
2004	$10,000	-$2,158,000

Curr. Assets:	$13,000	**Curr. Liab.:**	$6,452,000		
Plant, Equip.:	$541,000	**Total Liab.:**	$8,383,000	**Indic. Yr. Divd.:**	NA
Total Assets:	$731,000	**Net Worth:**	-$7,657,000	**Debt/ Equity:**	NA

Videsh Sanchar Nigam Ltd

Videsh Sanchar Bhavan, Mahatma Gandhi Rd., Mumbai, Maharashtra, 400001; ;
http:// www.vsnl.com; **Email:** customerservice@vsnl.co.in

General - Incorporation	India	**Stock** - Price on:12/24/2007	$21.95
Employees	2,926	Stock Exchange	NYSE
Auditor	Deloitte Haskins & Sells	Ticker Symbol	VSL
Stk Agt	Unit: Videsh Sanchar Nigam Ltd	Outstanding Shares	143,430,000
Counsel	Messrs Little & Co	E.P.S.	-$0.03
DUNS No.	NA	Shareholders	NA

Business: The groups principle activity is to provide national and international telephone, telex and telegraph services. The groups services include gateway, Internet access system, international private leased channels and transmission of signals for international television broadcasts. The group operates from United States.

Primary SIC and add'l.: 4813 7379 4833 4812 4822 4899

CIK No: 0001116134

Subsidiaries: Direct Internet Limited, Panatone Finvest Limited, Primus Telecommunications India Limited, Tata Power Company Limited, The TGN net assets and entities, VSNL Telecommunications (Bermuda) Ltd.

Officers: Sandeep Mathur/56/Head - Corporate Services, Rajiv Dhar/45/CFO - Vsnl India, Satish G. Ranade/Company Sec., VP - Legal, Srinivasa Addepalli/33/Srvp, Corporate Strategy, R. Nanda/45/Srvp, Human Resources, M. R. Madhusudhan/44/Chief Network Officer, Pankaj Agrawala/52/Government Nominee

Directors: Subodh Bhargava/66/Chmn., Vinod Kumar/Dir., Kishor A. Chaukar/Dir., Srinath Narasimhan/46/Dir., P. V. Kalyana Sundaram/50/Dir., Mukund Govind Rajan/40/Dir., V. R. S. Sampath/51/Dir., Amal Ganguli/67/Dir., S. Ramadorai/Dir., A. K. Srivastava/Dir., Arun Gandhi/Dir., H. P. Mishra/Dir.

Owners: Life Insurance Corporation of India/6.97%, Government of India/26.12%, Panatone Finvest Limited/40.70%, Tata Sons Limited/8.51%

Financial Data: Fiscal Year End:03/31   Latest Annual Data: 03/31/2007

Year	Sales	Net Income
2007	$1,995,000,000	$34,000,000
2006	$1,021,000,000	$14,000,000
2005	$744,000,000	$56,000,000

Curr. Assets:	$721,000,000	**Curr. Liab.:**	$901,000,000		
Plant, Equip.:	$1,249,000,000	**Total Liab.:**	$1,354,000,000	**Indic. Yr. Divd.:**	$0.400
Total Assets:	$2,527,000,000	**Net Worth:**	$1,173,000,000	**Debt/ Equity:**	NA

View Systems Inc

1550 Caton Ctr. Dr. , Ste. E, Baltimore, MD, 21227; **PH:** 1-410-646-3000;
http:// www.viewsystems.com; **Email:** info@viewsystems.com

General - Incorporation	NV	**Stock** - Price on:12/24/2007	$0.08
Employees	15	Stock Exchange	OTC
Auditor	Chisholm Bierwolf & Nilson LLC	Ticker Symbol	VYST
Stk Agt	Standard Registrar & Transfer Co Inc.	Outstanding Shares	97,170,000
Counsel	NA	E.P.S.	-$0.009
DUNS No.	NA	Shareholders	NA

Business: The group's principal activities are to develop, produce and market digital security and surveillance systems and products utilizing video based cameras and microphones. Its products include secureview, viewstorage, plateview, faceview and webview. Its security systems are marketed under the trade name secureview that records video images digitally and permit their viewing remotely over the customer's existing cctv systems together with audio output over ordinary telephone lines. Viewstorage is a programmable vcr replacement device that record video output digitally for use with cctv systems. Plateview is a license plate recognition system that uses optical character recognition technology to provide an additional means of identifying individuals in a surveillance area for commercial or law enforcement. It markets its products principally to commercial users, residential users and enforcement agencies.

Primary SIC and add'l.: 3679 3829 3827 7372

CIK No: 0001075857

Subsidiaries: Eastern Tech Manufacturing Corp., Milestone Technology, Inc., RealView Systems, Inc, Xyros Systems, Inc

Officers: Gunther Than/60/Dir., CEO, Treasurer, CFO, Michael L. Bagnoli/52/Dir., Corp Sec.

Directors: Gunther Than/60/Dir., CEO, Treasurer, CFO, Michael L. Bagnoli/52/Dir., Corp Sec., Martin Maassen/65/Dir.

Owners: Michael L. Bagnoli, Martin Maassen/2.70%, Gunther Than/4.60%, Insiders/100.00%, Insiders/78.60%, Gunther Than/100.00%

Financial Data: Fiscal Year End:12/31   Latest Annual Data: 12/31/2006

Year	Sales	Net Income
2006	$1,250,000	-$1,140,000
2005	$1,172,000	-$2,474,000
2004	$476,000	-$1,291,000

Curr. Assets:	$378,000	**Curr. Liab.:**	$1,339,000		
Plant, Equip.:	$31,000	**Total Liab.:**	$1,429,000	**Indic. Yr. Divd.:**	NA
Total Assets:	$1,746,000	**Net Worth:**	$317,000	**Debt/ Equity:**	0.2839

ViewCast Corp

3701 W Plano Pkwy., Ste. 300, Plano, TX, 75075; **PH:** 1-972-488-7200; **Fax:** 1-972-488-7299;
http:// www.viewcast.com; **Email:** info@viewcast.com

General - Incorporation	DE	**Stock** - Price on:12/24/2007	$0.39
Employees	59	Stock Exchange	OTC
Auditor	KBA Group, LLP	Ticker Symbol	VCST
Stk Agt	Continental Stock Transfer & Trust Co	Outstanding Shares	32,050,000
Counsel	NA	E.P.S.	-$0.02
DUNS No.	87-793-0297	Shareholders	NA

Business: The group's principle activities are to design, develop and market video communication products and services and information technology services and products. Video communication products include video capture cards and codecs, streaming systems and video distribution. Information technology products and services include Internet and intranet, networking, maintenance, consulting and disaster recovery services as well as computer and networking product sales. The trademarks of the group includes osprey(R), viewcast(R), niagara scx(tm), simulstream(tm) and viewpoint vbx(tm). The group's quarterly revenue for September 2007 was 4.09 millions of USD.

Primary SIC and add'l.: 7379 6719 7373

CIK No: 0000921313

Subsidiaries: Delta Computec Inc, Osprey Technologies, Inc, VideoWare, Inc, ViewCast Online Solutions, Inc

Officers: George C. Platt/68/Chmn., CEO/$125,000.00, Laurie Latham/CFO, Sr. VP - Finance - Administration/$176,000.00, Dave Stoner/Pres., COO/$188,000.00, Mark Hershey/VP - Engineering, Gwen Goble/North America Regional Sales Mgr., Steve Bogart/North America Regional Sales Mgr., Mark Phillips/MD - UK, East, West Europe, Africa, Middle East Countries, David Zovod/MD - India, Far East, Asia, Mexico, Central, South America, Jeff Lagrone/Sales Mgr. - North America, Chris McCauley/Dir. - Business Development, Gary J. Klembara/56/Sr. VP - Sales

Directors: George C. Platt/68/Chmn., CEO, Joseph Autem/50/Dir., Sherel D. Horsley/66/Dir., John W. Slocum/67/Dir.

Owners: JOHN W. SLOCUM, LAURIE L. LATHAM, DAVID T. STONER, H. T. Ardinger/52.90%, GARY J. KLEMBARA, SHEREL D. HORSLEY, DONALD ADAMS/3.00%, Insiders/3.00%, DAVID RUGGIERI/3.70%, GEORGE C. PLATT/1.40%, Joseph Autem

Financial Data: Fiscal Year End:12/31   Latest Annual Data: 12/31/2006

Year	Sales	Net Income
2006	$13,981,000	-$1,751,000
2005	$11,559,000	-$3,056,000
2004	$20,527,000	-$2,845,000

Curr. Assets:	$4,955,000	**Curr. Liab.:**	$2,006,000		
Plant, Equip.:	$447,000	**Total Liab.:**	$7,158,000	**Indic. Yr. Divd.:**	NA
Total Assets:	$5,639,000	**Net Worth:**	-$1,519,000	**Debt/ Equity:**	NA

Viewpoint Corp

498 Seventh Ave., Ste 1810, New York, NY, 10018; **PH:** 1-212-201-0800;
http:// www.viewpoint.com; **Email:** info@viewpoint.com

General - Incorporation	DE	**Stock** - Price on:12/24/2007	NA
Employees	126	Stock Exchange	NDQ
Auditor	PricewaterhouseCoopers LLP	Ticker Symbol	VWPT
Stk Agt	Equiserve	Outstanding Shares	NA
Counsel	NA	E.P.S.	-$0.29
DUNS No.	18-123-5250	Shareholders	NA

Business: The group's principal activities are to sell software licenses and provide support services. The group operates through its two segments: license segment and service segment. The license segment sells software licenses to use the viewpoint software platform. The service segment provides creative and support services to customers who generally have purchased or received licenses to use the viewpoint software platform. The group's graphics operating system platform, the viewpoint media player, has been licensed by Fortune 500 companies and others for use in online, offline and embedded applications serving a wide variety of needs, including: business process visualizations, marketing campaigns, rich advertising and product presentations. The group also provides cross media digital solutions for film, broadcast television and games.

Primary SIC and add'l.: 7373 7372

CIK No: 0000919794

Subsidiaries: Canoma Inc., MetaCreations Holding Corp., MetaTools Barbados FSC, Viewpoint Digital, Inc.

Officers: Patrick Vogt/Dir., CEO, Andrew J. Graf/VP, General Counsel, Christopher C. Duignan/Mgr. - Treasury Operations, Controller, CFO, Chief Accounting Officer, Ann Charles/VP - Corporate Marketing, James Dillon/VP - Advertising Sales, Andrew Freeman/VP, GM, Jason Mckay/VP - Unicast, Key Search, Consulting, Tony D'Anna/VP, GM - its Search Products Group, Allie Burns/Public Relation

Directors: Patrick Vogt/Dir., CEO, Don Weatherson/Non Exec. Chmn., Samuel Jones/Dir., Dennis R. Raney/Dir., James J. Spanfeller/Dir.

Owners: Chesapeake Partners Management Co., Inc./8.00%, Diker Management, LLC/8.40%, Samuel H. Jones, The Clark Estates/8.10%, DG FastChannel, Inc./13.20%

Financial Data: Fiscal Year End:12/31   Latest Annual Data: 12/31/2006

Year	Sales	Net Income
2006	$17,177,000	-$19,715,000
2005	$25,296,000	-$10,592,000
2004	$14,532,000	-$9,700,000

Curr. Assets:	$7,847,000	**Curr. Liab.:**	$3,296,000		
Plant, Equip.:	$1,023,000	**Total Liab.:**	$7,992,000	**Indic. Yr. Divd.:**	NA
Total Assets:	$27,687,000	**Net Worth:**	$19,695,000	**Debt/ Equity:**	0.2152

ViewSonic Corp

381 Brea Canyon Rd., Walnut, CA, 91789; **PH:** 1-909-869-7976; **http:**// www.treehousefoods.com;
Email: Salesinfo@viewsonic.com

General - Incorporation	DE	**Stock** - Price on:12/24/2007	NA
Employees	NA	Stock Exchange	NA
Auditor	Deloitte & Touche LLP	Ticker Symbol	NA
Stk Agt	NA	Outstanding Shares	NA
Counsel	NA	E.P.S.	NA
DUNS No.	NA	Shareholders	NA

Business: The groups principle activity is to provide visual display technology products. The groups products include cathode ray tube monitors, liquid crystal displays, projectors, high-definition television technology and mobile products. The groups products are sold under the brand name ViewSonic. The group operates from United States.

Primary SIC and add'l.: 3577

CIK No: 0001068806

Subsidiaries: Delaware corporation

Officers: James Chu/Chmn., CEO, Jan Jensen/MD, Pres. - Viewsonic Europe, Robert J. Ranucci/43/VP, General Counsel, Sec., Matthew W. Milne/Pres. - Viewsonic Americas, James A. Morlan/60/CFO, Heng-Chun Ho/55/Pres. - Global Products, Solutions, Timothy Ashcroft/VP - Human Resources, Viewsonic Corporation, Jeff Volpe/VP - Marketing Viewsonic Americas, Viewsonic Corporation, Brian Igoe/VP - Field Sales Viewsonic Americas, Steve Woo/VP - Sales Operations Americas, Viewsonic Corporation, Ted Sanders/CFO

Directors: James Chu/Chmn., CEO, Matthew E. Massengill/47/Dir., William J. Miller/62/Dir., Bruce L. Stein/53/Dir., Luc H. Vanhal/48/Dir.

Owners: Insiders, James Chu, Matthew W. Milne, Bruce L. Stein, Keypoint Investments, L.P., James A. Morlan, Matthew E. Massengill, Jan Jensen, Luc H. Vanhal, William J. Miller, Heng-Chun Ho

Vignette Corp

1301 S Mopac Expressway, Ste. 100, Austin, TX, 78746; *PH:* 1-512-306-4300; *http://* www.vignette.com; *Email:* usinfo@vignette.com

General - Incorporation	DE	**Stock**- Price on:12/24/2007	$18.85
Employees	670	Stock Exchange	NDQ
Auditor	Grant Thornton, LLP	Ticker Symbol	VIGN
Stk Agt	Mellon Shareholder Services LLC	Outstanding Shares	28,560,000
Counsel	NA	E.P.S	$0.65
DUNS No.	95-793-5919	Shareholders	NA

Business: The group's principle activity is to provide content management applications used by organizations to create and maintain effective online relationships with their customers, employees, business partners and suppliers. The group provides services to help define online business objectives and to develop and deliver integrated content management applications. The group's customer list includes successful organizations in the automotive, entertainment, financial services, government, healthcare, high technology, new media and publishing, retail, telecom and travel industries. The group's quarterly revenue for September 2007 was 43.55 millions of USD.

Primary SIC and add'l.: 7371 7372

CIK No: 0001042185

Subsidiaries: Copper Australia Pty Limited, Epicentric (BVI) Inc., Intraspect France SARL organized under the laws of France., Intraspect Software Inc., Tower Technology Inc., Tower Technology Limited, Tower Technology SARL, Vignette Asia Pte Ltd., Vignette B.V. (formerly known as OnDisplay Benelux B.V.), Vignette Canada Corporation, Vignette de Mexico S. de R.L. de C. V., Vignette Deutschland GmbH, Vignette do Brasil Ltda., Vignette Europe Limited, Vignette Holdings LLC 28 Subsidiaries included in the Index

Officers: Mike Aviles/CEO, Pres./$1,595,128.00, Conleth S. O'Connell/CTO, Leo Brunnick/Sr. VP - Products, Marketing/$388,540.00, Bryce M. Johnson/Sr. VP, General Counsel/$441,223.00, Pat Kelly/CFO/$309,653.00, Alex Shootman/Sr. VP - Worldwide Sales, Services, Somesh Singh/Sr. VP - Research, Development, Technical Operations, Gayle Wiley/Sr. VP - Worldwide Human Resources, Gayle Wiley/41/Sr. VP - Global Human Resources

Directors: Jan H. Lindelow/Chmn., Jeffrey S. Hawn/Dir., Joseph M. Grant/Dir., Michael Lambert/Dir., Henry Denero/Dir., Kathleen Earley/56/Dir.

Owners: Wells Fargo & Company/7.60%, Bryce M. Johnson, Patrick T. Kelly, Jeffrey S. Hawn, Michael D. Lambert, Henry DeNero, Dimensional Fund Advisors LP/8.70%, Jan H. Lindelow, Joseph M. Grant, Leo Brunnick, Kathleen Earley, Gayle Wiley, Michael A. Aviles, Insiders/2.69%

Financial Data: *Fiscal Year End:*12/31 *Latest Annual Data:* 12/31/2006

Year	Sales	Net Income
2006	$197,574,000	$12,319,000
2005	$190,675,000	$20,394,000
2004	$177,927,000	-$52,855,000

Curr. Assets:	$247,317,000	**Curr. Liab.:**	$78,049,000		
Plant, Equip.:	$6,899,000	**Total Liab.:**	$83,365,000	**Indic. Yr. Divd.:**	NA
Total Assets:	$421,152,000	**Net Worth:**	$337,787,000	**Debt/ Equity:**	NA

Viking Capital Group Inc

Two Lincoln Ctr., Ste 300, 5420 LBJ Frwy, Dallas, TX, 75240; *PH:* 1-972-386-9996; *http://* www.vcgi.com; *Email:* viking@vcgi.com

General - Incorporation	UT	**Stock**- Price on:12/24/2007	$0.015
Employees	NA	Stock Exchange	OTC
Auditor	KBA Group LLP	Ticker Symbol	VGCP
Stk Agt	Interwest Transfer Company, Inc.	Outstanding Shares	NA
Counsel	NA	E.P.S	NA
DUNS No.	80-323-9425	Shareholders	NA

Business: The group's principle activity is to acquire businesses having potential optimizing opportunities. The group is a diversified holding company that identifies businesses for acquisition. It looks at the overall business environment with a clear focus on fundamental changes in politics, regulation, technology and world economics. The group operates in four segments: real estate, chemical sales, construction and garment manufacturing. All businesses are located and operated in the People's Republic of China. The real estate segment owns and operates a commercial and residential property. The chemical segment trades and transports chemical products. The construction segment is constructing a highway in the jiangsu province of the People's Republic of China. The garment segment manufactures clothing specifically focusing on export garments.

Primary SIC and add'l.: 2899 6531

CIK No: 0000886093

Subsidiaries: Brentwood Re, Ltd., NIAI Insurance Administrators, Inc., Viking Administrators, Inc., Viking Capital Financial Services, Inc., Viking Capital Ventures, Inc., Viking Insurance Services, Inc., Viking Systems, Inc.

Officers: Steve R. Mills/Chmn., CEO, Roger Kron/Dir., COO, Sr. VP, Kingman Hitz/CFO, VP

Directors: Steve R. Mills/Chmn., CEO, Roger Kron/Dir., COO, Sr. VP, David G. Henry/Dir., Mary M. Pohlmeier/Dir., Robin M. Sandifer/Dir., William T. Brown/Member - Advisory Board, Dan H. Curlee/Member - Advisory Board, Jack Hight/Member - Advisory Board, Charles W. Smith/Member - Advisory Board, Bruce P. Mauldin/Member - Advisory Board, Richard Sandifer/Member - Advisory Board

Financial Data: *Fiscal Year End:*12/31 *Latest Annual Data:* 12/31/2004

Year	Sales	Net Income
2004	NA	-$475,000
2003	$286,000	-$7,370,000
2002	$2,873,000	-$19,499,000

Curr. Assets:	$129,000	**Curr. Liab.:**	$2,592,000		
Plant, Equip.:	$3,000	**Total Liab.:**	$3,292,000	**Indic. Yr. Divd.:**	NA
Total Assets:	$136,000	**Net Worth:**	-$3,156,000	**Debt/ Equity:**	NA

Viking Systems Inc

134 Flanders Rd. , Westborough, MA, 01581; *PH:* 1-508-366-8882; *Fax:* 1-508-366-8858; *http://* www.vikingsystems.com; *Email:* vmt@vikingsystems.com

General - Incorporation	NV	**Stock**- Price on:12/24/2007	$0.22
Employees	36	Stock Exchange	OTC
Auditor	Squar, Peterson, LLP	Ticker Symbol	VKSY
Stk Agt	Fidelity Transfer Co	Outstanding Shares	65,860,000
Counsel	NA	E.P.S	-$0.217
DUNS No.	NA	Shareholders	NA

Business: The groups principle activities include designing, manufacturing and marketing high-performance laparoscopic vision systems. The group provides applications in urology, gynecology, bariatric and general surgery. The group operates from United States.

Primary SIC and add'l.: NA

CIK No: 0001065754

Officers: Donald E. Tucker/Chmn., CEO, Pres., Lonna J. Williams/Sr. VP - Commercial Operations, John Kennedy/Pres. - Vision Systems Group, Joseph A. Warrino/Sec., Gregory M. Decker/CFO, Lynn Granito/Contact - Media Relations, Adam Holdsworth/Contact - Investor Relations, Stephen M. Heniges/Sr. VP - Global Marketing, Clinical Development

Directors: Donald E. Tucker/Chmn., CEO, Pres., Michael J. Manyak/Dir., Daniel F. Crowley/Dir., Nathan J. Harrison/Dir., Brian Miller/Dir.

Owners: John Conaton, Midsummer Investment, LTD, Glengar International, Donald E. Tucker, William C. Bopp, Daniel F. Crowley, Vision Opportunity Master Fund, Ltd., Bushido Capital Master Fund, L.P., John Kennedy, GSSF Master Fund, LP, Lonna Williams, Gryphon Master Fund, LP, Insiders, St. Cloud Capital Partners, Pierce Diversified Strategy Master Fund, LLC *(24 Owners included in Index)*

Financial Data: *Fiscal Year End:*12/31 *Latest Annual Data:* 12/31/2006

Year	Sales	Net Income
2006	$5,617,000	-$8,704,000
2005	$3,835,000	-$7,529,000
2004	$2,847,000	-$1,985,000

Curr. Assets:	$2,520,000	**Curr. Liab.:**	$6,678,000		
Plant, Equip.:	$594,000	**Total Liab.:**	$6,755,000	**Indic. Yr. Divd.:**	NA
Total Assets:	$3,465,000	**Net Worth:**	-$11,682,000	**Debt/ Equity:**	NA

Village Bank & Trust Financial Corp

1231 Alverser Dr., Midlothian, VA, 23113; *PH:* 1-804-897-3900; *http://* www.villagebankva.com

General - Incorporation	VA	**Stock**- Price on:12/24/2007	$17.05
Employees	109	Stock Exchange	NDQ
Auditor	BDO Seidman LLP	Ticker Symbol	VBFC
Stk Agt	American Stock Transfer & Trust Co.	Outstanding Shares	2,560,000
Counsel	NA	E.P.S	$0.589
DUNS No.	NA	Shareholders	NA

Business: The group's principle activity is to provide banking and related financial services. The services provided by the group include checking, savings, certificates of deposit and other depository services. The services also include commercial, real estate and consumer loans. The services are offered to individuals, small to medium sized businesses, entrepreneurs and the professional community. The group operates from United States.

Primary SIC and add'l.: 6022

CIK No: 0001290476

Subsidiaries: Village Bank, Village Bank Mortgage Corporation, Village Financial Services Corporation, Village Insurance Agency, Inc.

Officers: Thomas W. Winfree/Dir., CEO, Pres. - Village Bank, Jerry W. Mabry/CEO, Pres. - Village Bank Mortgage Corporation, Robert D. Murphy/VP - Compliance, Security Officer - Village Bank, Mary A. Szulczewski/VP, Loan Administration Mgr. - Village Bank, Susan Wilhelm/Assist. VP, Business Development Officer - Brandermill Branch, Village Bank, Charissa Lynn Johnson/Assist. VP, Business Development Officer - Clover Hill Branch, Villege Bank, Samuel J. Bennett/Assist. VP, Business Development Officer - Chesterfield Towne Center Branch, Village Bank, Joetta B. Sutphin/VP - Operations, Village Bank, Gardner Fields/Assist. VP, Business Development Officer - Willow Lawn Branch, Village Bank, Rebecca Kline/VP, Area Retail Mgr. - Village Bank, George Pulliam/Assist. VP, Business Development Officer - South Creek Branch, Village Bank, Eric A. Tusing/Assist. VP - Commercial Lending, Village Bank, Kathy J. Naworal/Assist. VP, Credit Policy Officer - Village Bank, Gail F. Hubbard/VP - Commercial Lending, Villege Bank, Joseph F. Markley/VP - Commercial Lending, Village Bank *(33 Officers included in Index)*

Directors: Thomas W. Winfree/Dir., CEO, Pres. - Village Bank, Craig D. Bell/Chmn., Donald J. Balzer/Vice Chmn., Michael L. Toalson/Dir., George R. Whittemore/Dir., R. T. Avery/Dir., William B. Chandler/Dir., Calvert R. Esleeck/Dir., Dean Patrick/Dir.

Owners: Dean T. Patrick/2.03%, Jack M. Robeson/0.82%, Insiders/20.63%, Calvert R. Esleeck/1.13%, William B. Chandler/2.51%, Donald J. Balzer/2.40%, Craig D. Bell/2.67%, George R. Whittemore/1.08%, John S. Clark/6.50%, Thomas W. Winfree/3.66%, Harril C. Whitehurst/1.23%, Dennis J. Falk/0.16%, Michael L. Toalson/0.26%, Raymond E. Sanders/0.98%, R. T. Avery/2.78%

Financial Data: *Fiscal Year End:*12/31 *Latest Annual Data:* 12/31/2006

Year	Sales	Net Income
2006	$21,502,000	$1,399,000
2005	$14,815,000	$1,231,000
2004	$9,435,000	$862,000

Curr. Assets:	$19,499,000	Curr. Liab.:	$257,740,000	P/E Ratio:	28.95
Plant, Equip.:	$11,677,000	Total Liab.:	$265,574,000	Indic. Yr. Divd.:	NA
Total Assets:	$291,218,000	Net Worth:	$25,644,000	Debt/ Equity:	0.2170

Village Super Market Inc

733 Mountain Ave., Springfield, NJ, 07081; *PH:* 1-973-467-2200; *http://* www.shoprite.com

General - Incorporation	NJ	*Stock*- Price on:12/24/2007	$47.16
Employees	1,408	Stock Exchange	NDQ
Auditor	KPMG LLP	Ticker Symbol	VLGEA
Stk Agt	American Stock Transfer & Trust Co.	Outstanding Shares	6,500,000
Counsel	NA	E.P.S	$3.14
DUNS No.	05-351-9450	Shareholders	NA

Business: The group's principal activity is to operate a chain of supermarkets. It operates a chain of 23 supermarkets under the name and trademark of shoprite. The retail food co-operative, wakefern food corporation, owns the name and trademark. The group is a member of this co-operative. Food products retailed include dairy and frozen foods, meats, produces, prepared foods and seafood. Non food items consist of pharmaceuticals, cut flowers, health and beauty aids, greeting cards, videocassette rentals and small appliances. In addition, the supermarkets also include salad bars, bakeries, delicatessen and other specialty departments. The group also operates a liquor store and a drug store. Sixteen of the supermarkets are located in northern New Jersey, six in the southern shore area of New Jersey and one in northeastern Pennsylvania.

Primary SIC and add'l.: 5947 5499 5411 5992 5461 5912 5451

CIK No: 0000103595

Subsidiaries: Village Super Market of NJ, LP New Jersey., Village Super Market of PA, Inc.

Officers: James Sumas/75/Chmn., CEO, COO, Kevin Begley/50/CFO, Treasurer, Perry Sumas/93/Dir., Pres., Robert Sumas/67/Dir., Exec. VP, Sec., William Sumas/61/Dir., Exec. VP, John P. Sumas/59/Dir., Exec. VP

Directors: James Sumas/75/Chmn., CEO, COO, Perry Sumas/93/Dir., Pres., Robert Sumas/67/Dir., Exec. VP, Sec., William Sumas/61/Dir., Exec. VP, John P. Sumas/59/Dir., Exec. VP, John J. McDermott/83/Dir., David C. Judge/47/Dir., Steven Crystal/52/Dir.

Owners: Franklin Resources, Inc./6.70%, Robert Sumas/9.10%, Sumas Family Group/71.20%, Perry Sumas/32.00%, David C. Judge/0.50%, Insiders/12.00%, Norman Crystal/13.30%, John P. Sumas/5.60%, Perry Sumas/5.10%, William Sumas/5.30%, Steven Crystal/1.80%, James Sumas/1.40%, Kevin Begley/0.80%, Sumas Family Group/8.80%, Robert Sumas/1.30% *(23 Owners included in Index)*

*Financial Data: Fiscal Year End:*07/30   *Latest Annual Data:* 7/29/2006

Year		Sales		Net Income
2006		$1,016,817,000		$16,487,000
2005		$983,679,000		$15,542,000
2004		$957,647,000		$13,263,000
Curr. Assets:	$99,783,000	Curr. Liab.:	$67,897,000	P/E Ratio: 15.67
Plant, Equip.:	$101,143,000	Total Liab.:	$111,335,000	Indic. Yr. Divd.: $1.000
Total Assets:	$231,425,000	Net Worth:	$120,091,000	Debt/ Equity: 0.1339

VillageEDOCS

1401 N Tustin Ave., Ste. 230, Santa Ana, CA, 92705; *PH:* 1-714-734-1030; *Fax:* 1-714-734-1040; *http://* www.villageedocs.com; *Email:* info@villageedocs.com

General - Incorporation	CA	*Stock*- Price on:12/24/2007	$0.06
Employees	78	Stock Exchange	OTC
Auditor	Corbin & Co LLP	Ticker Symbol	VEDO
Stk Agt	U.S. Stock Transfer Corp	Outstanding Shares	147,870,000
Counsel	NA	E.P.S	-$0.01
DUNS No.	NA	Shareholders	NA

Business: The group's principle activity is to provide worldwide Internet-based business-to-business fax services in the United States and internationally. The Internet-based fax services enables the end user to send the fax through their Web browsers, e-mail package, directly out of their microsoft windows-based application, enterprise resource planning or customer relationship management system. The company's clients currently include e-commerce providers, application service providers, manufacturing companies, value added resellers, weather reporting services, public relations firms and direct marketing organizations. On 17-02-2004 the company acquired tailored business systems inc. The group operates from United States.

Primary SIC and add'l.: 7376

CIK No: 0001122099

Subsidiaries: MessageVision, Inc, Phoenix Forms, Inc, Tailored Business Systems, Inc.

Officers: Mason K. Conner/Dir., CEO/$210,000.00, Michael A. Richard/CFO/$125,417.00, Jerry T. Kendall/Dir., COO, Pres./$286,667.00, Jay H. Hill/Dir., Exec. VP - Corporate Development/$190,593.00, Joe Torano/Sr. VP - Sales, Marketing

Directors: Mason K. Conner/Dir., CEO, Thomas Zender/Chmn., Jay H. Hill/Dir., Exec. VP - Corporate Development, Jerry T. Kendall/Dir., COO, Pres., Ricardo A. Salas/Dir.

Owners: Insiders/9.20%, Thomas J. Zender, Jerry T. Kendall, James Townsend/6.50%, Joe Torano, Mason K. Conner/3.80%, Alan C. Williams/37.70%, Jay H. Hill/3.50%, Michael Richard, GoSolutions Equity LLC/15.60%, Ricardo A. Salas

*Financial Data: Fiscal Year End:*12/31   *Latest Annual Data:* 12/31/2006

Year		Sales		Net Income
2006		$12,912,000		-$882,000
2005		$8,768,000		-$8,145,000
2004		$6,014,000		-$768,000
Curr. Assets:	$1,890,000	Curr. Liab.:	$5,026,000	
Plant, Equip.:	$474,000	Total Liab.:	$5,206,000	Indic. Yr. Divd.: NA
Total Assets:	$15,155,000	Net Worth:	$9,949,000	Debt/ Equity: NA

Vimicro International Corp

1758 N Shoreline Blvd., Mountain View, CA, 94043; *PH:* 1-650-966-1882; *Fax:* 1-650-966-1885; *http://* www.vimicro.com; *Email:* info@vimicro.com

General - Incorporation	Cayman Islands	*Stock*- Price on:12/24/2007	$6.18
Employees	369	Stock Exchange	NDQ
Auditor	PricewaterhouseCoopers	Ticker Symbol	VIMC
Stk Agt	JP Morgan Chase Bank, N.A.	Outstanding Shares	34,850,000
Counsel	WilmerHale	E.P.S	$0.40
DUNS No.	NA	Shareholders	NA

Business: The groups principle activities include designing, developing and marketing proprietary embedded multimedia signal processing chips and solutions. The groups product lines include PC multimedia processors, mobile multimedia processors, advanced multimedia processors and consumer electronic multimedia processors. The groups processing chips are used in mobile phone handsets with advanced multimedia features including mobile video, graphics, music, ringtones, and karaoke. The group operates from United States.

Primary SIC and add'l.: 3674

CIK No: 0001341088

Subsidiaries: Viewtel Corporation, Vimicro Corporation, Vimicro Electronics International Limited

Officers: Zhonghan Deng/Chmn., CEO, Pres., Ryan Bright/Ryan Bright, Xiaodong Yang/Dir., CTO, Zhaowei Jin/Dir., COO, VP - Sales, Hui Zhang/Dir., VP - Business Development, Xiaosong Zhang/VP - Accounting, Yundong Zhang/VP - Marketing, Jun Zhu/VP - Engineering, Qing Yu/VP - Algorithms, Software, Quincy Tang/45/CFO, VP - Accounting

Directors: Zhonghan Deng/Chmn., CEO, Pres., Victor Yang/Dir., Xiaodong Yang/Dir., CTO, Zhaowei Jin/Dir., COO, VP - Sales, Changyong Chen/Dir., Theodore Van Duzer/Dir., Vince Feng/Dir., Donald L. Lucas/Dir., Hui Zhang/Dir., VP - Business Development, Yingyi Qian/52/Dir.

Owners: Investment entities affiliated with General Atlantic LLC/17.50%, Jun Zhu/0.30%, Theodore Van Duzer/0.10%, Donald L. Lucas/0.50%, Xiaodong Yang/6.40%, Qing (Mike) Yu/0.30%, Zhonghan Deng/10.90%, Zhaowei (Kevin) Jin/2.70%, Yundong (Raymond) Zhang/0.50%, Changyong (Robert) Chen/0.30%, Vince Feng/17.50%, Yingyi Qian/0.10%, Insiders/39.70%, Power Pacific (Mauritius) Limited/8.00%

*Financial Data: Fiscal Year End:*12/31   *Latest Annual Data:* 12/31/2005

Year		Sales		Net Income
2005		$95,277,000		$16,390,000
2004		$50,258,000		-$5,612,000
Curr. Assets:	$139,062,000	Curr. Liab.:	$13,463,000	
Plant, Equip.:	$8,498,000	Total Liab.:	$13,493,000	Indic. Yr. Divd.: NA
Total Assets:	$148,350,000	Net Worth:	$134,857,000	Debt/ Equity: NA

Vimpel-Communications Company

10, 8 Marta St., Moscow, 127083; *PH:* 7-4957250700; *Fax:* 7-4957210017; *http://* www.vimpelcom.com; *Email:* Investor_Relations@VimpelCom.com

General - Incorporation		*Stock*- Price on:12/24/2007	$105.89
Employees	21,303	Stock Exchange	NYSE
Auditor	Ernst & Young (CIS) Ltd.	Ticker Symbol	VIP
Stk Agt	JP Morgan Chase Bank, N.A.	Outstanding Shares	203,570,000
Counsel	Akin Gump Strauss Hauer & Feld LLP	E.P.S	$1.27
DUNS No.	NA	Shareholders	NA

Business: The groups principle activity is to provide wireless telecommunications services. In the year 2006, the group acquired OOO Mobitel and ArmenTel. The group operates from the Russia, Kazakhstan, Ukraine, Tajikistan and Uzbekistan. The group's quarterly revenue for September 2007 was 1,955.94 millions of USD.

Primary SIC and add'l.: 4812

CIK No:

Officers: Alexander V. Izosimov/CEO, Elena A. Shmatova/CFO, Exec. VP, Nikolai N. Pryanishnikov/Exec. VP, General Dir. - Regions, Alexander Boreyko/Dir. - International, Investor Relations, Peter Schmidt/Contact - US Public Relations, Michael Polyviou/Contact - US Public Relations, Michael Guerin/Contact - US Public Relations, Dmitri B. Zimin/Founder, Honorary Pres., Marina V. Novikova/VP - Organizational Development, Human Resources, Vladimir A. Filippov/CIO, VP, Marine D. Babayan/Sr. Specialist - International, Investor Relations, Alla Zaytseva/Sr. Specialist - International, Investor Relations, Vladimir V. Riabokon/Regional Dir., Valery V. Frontov/VP - Licensing, Regulatory Affairs, Dmitry A. Pleskonos/VP, GM - Moscow Region *(21 Officers included in Index)*

Directors: Augie K. Fabela/Co - Founder, Chmn. Emeritus, Dmitri B. Zimin/Founder, Honorary Pres., David J. Haines/Dir., Mikhail M. Fridman/Dir., Arve Johansen/Dir., Oleg A. Malis/Dir., Jo Lunder/Dir., Alexey M. Reznikovich/Dir., Leonid R. Novoselsky/Dir., Fridtjof Rusten/Dir.

Owners: Telenor East Invest AS/29.90%, Eco Telecom Limited/35.20%, Eco Telecom Limited

*Financial Data: Fiscal Year End:*NA   *Latest Annual Data:* 12/31/2006

Year		Sales		Net Income
2006		$4,867,978,000		$811,489,000
2005		$3,211,118,000		$615,131,000
2004		$2,146,629,000		$350,396,000
Curr. Assets:	$1,124,556,000	Curr. Liab.:	$1,611,976,000	P/E Ratio: 9.89
Plant, Equip.:	$4,615,675,000	Total Liab.:	$4,493,636,000	Indic. Yr. Divd.: $0.280
Total Assets:	$8,436,546,000	Net Worth:	$3,942,910,000	Debt/ Equity: NA

Vina Concha Y Toro S.A.

Avenida Nueva Tajamar 481, Torre Norte, Piso 15, Santiago; *PH:* 56-24765200; *Fax:* 56-22036740; *http://* www.conchaytoro.com

General - Incorporation		*Stock*- Price on:12/24/2007	$49.46
Employees	NA	Stock Exchange	NYSE
Auditor	NA	Ticker Symbol	VCO
Stk Agt	Bank of New York	Outstanding Shares	35,960,000
Counsel	NA	E.P.S	$1.66
DUNS No.	NA	Shareholders	NA

Business: The groups principle activity is to produce wine. The group operates from Chile and Argentina. The groups quarterly revenue for September 2007 was 208,476.00 millions of CLP.

Primary SIC and add'l.: 5182 2084

CIK No:

Officers: Eduardo Guilisasti Gana/CEO, Andres Larrain/Agriculture Mgr., Osvaldo Solar Venegas/CFO, Thomas Domeyko Cassel/Corporate Export Mgr. - Northern Zone, Cristian Ceppi Lewin/Southern Zone Export Dir., Jose Antonia Manasevich Gavicagogeascoa/Operation Mgr., Adolfo Hurtado Cerda/GM - Vina Cono SUR, Andres Izquierdo Bacarreza/GM - Trivento Bodegas Y

Vinedos, Cristian Lopez Pascual/GM - Concha Y Toro UK, Carlos Saavendra Echeverria/Engineering, Projects Mgr., Daniel Duran Urizar/Information Technology Mgr., Isabel Guilisasti Gana/Marketing Mgr. - Specific Origin Wines, Giancarlo Bianchetti Gonzalez/Marketing Mgr. - Global Brands, Goetz Von Gersdorff/Technical Dir., Carlos Halaby Riadi/Techinal Mgr. *(18 Officers included in Index)*

Directors: Alfonso Larrain/Chmn., Rafael Guilisasti Gana/Vice Chmn., Mariano Fontecilla De Santiago Concha/82/Dir., Christian Skibsted-hansen Cortes/Dir., Pablo Guilisasti Gana/Dir., Francisco Marin Estevez/Dir., Sergio De La Cuadra Fabres/Dir., Mariano Fontecilla De Santigo Concha/Dir.

Financial Data: *Fiscal Year End:*NA *Latest Annual Data:* 12/31/2006

Year	Sales	Net Income
2006	$302,180,000	$22,556,000
2005	$382,597,000	$39,711,000
2004	$338,773,000	$41,238,000

Curr. Assets:	$237,235,000	**Curr. Liab.:**	$122,515,000		
Plant, Equip.:	$222,610,000	**Total Liab.:**	$230,194,000	**Indic. Yr. Divd.:**	$0.310
Total Assets:	$481,468,000	**Net Worth:**	$251,274,000	**Debt/ Equity:**	NA

Vincera Inc

611 S Congress Ave., Ste 350, Austin, TX, 78704; ***PH:*** 1-512-443-8749; ***http://*** www.vincera.com; ***Email:*** investor@vincera.com

General - Incorporation	DE	**Stock**- Price on:12/24/2007	NA
Employees	NA	Stock Exchange	NA
Auditor	PMB Helin Donovan, LLP	Ticker Symbol	NA
Stk Agt	Atlas Stock Transfer Corp	Outstanding Shares	NA
Counsel	NA	E.P.S	NA
DUNS No.	NA	Shareholders	NA

Business: The group's principal activity is to make and market interactive business intelligence software that helps companies track customer activity so they can respond faster and more efficiently to market trends. Its User Activity Management (UAM) applications are used for lead generation, retention forecasting, account compliance assessment, and access control. Vincera customers include Halliburton, Hoover's (the publisher of this profile), Lincoln Financial Group, and Microsoft. The company took its current form when Smarte Solutions acquired Vincera Software (formerly Elegiant) in 2004; the combined company changed its name to Vincera.

Primary SIC and add'l.: 7372

CIK No: 0001303604

Subsidiaries: Vincera Software, Inc

Officers: Dave Malmstedt/Chmn., CEO, Mark Eshelman/Dir. - Sales Development, Kevin Schick/COO, Brian Mantz/VP, Richard Deighton/Dir. - Engineering

Directors: Dave Malmstedt/Chmn., CEO, Ken Murphy/Dir., Pamela Fusco/Member - Vincera Advisory Board, Robert Sanchez/Member - Vincera Advisory Board, Mike Maples/Member - Vincera Advisory Board, Neil Webber/Member - Vincera Advisory Board

Owners: David R. Malmstedt/4.83%, Insiders/10.54%, Ken Murphy/4.04%, William Kruse/8.71%, Draper Fisher Jurvetson/5.73%, Bala Vishwanath/8.56%, Wayne Parkman, Kevin Schick/1.00%

Vineyard National Bancorp

1260 Corona Pointe Ct., Corona, CA, 92879; ; ***http://*** www.vineyardbank.com

General - Incorporation	CA	**Stock**- Price on:12/24/2007	$24.575
Employees	349	Stock Exchange	NDQ
Auditor	KPMG LLP	Ticker Symbol	VNBC
Stk Agt	U.S. Stock Transfer Corp	Outstanding Shares	10,920,000
Counsel	NA	E.P.S	$1.954
DUNS No.	NA	Shareholders	NA

Business: The group operates through its subsidiaries whose principle activity is to provide lending and depository services. The groups services include branching system, remote item capture and online banking. The products of the group include luxury home construction lending, tract construction, sba lending and lockbox processing. The group operates from Chino, Corona, Covina, Crestline, Diamond Bar, Irvine, Irwindale and Lake Arrowhead. The assets of the group for the year 2006 were $2,257,739 (thousands).

Primary SIC and add'l.: 6022 6712

CIK No: 0000840256

Subsidiaries: Vineyard Bank

Officers: Norman A. Morales/Dir., Pres., CEO - Vineyard Bank/$915,927.00, Donald H. Pelgrim/Exec. VP, Chief Administrative Officer - Vineyard Bank/$271,922.00, Richard S. Hagan/Exec. VP, Chief Credit Officer - Vineyard Bank/$423,008.00, Gordon Fong/Exec. VP, CFO - Vineyard Bank/$446,836.00, Chris J. Walsh/Exec. VP, Chief Banking Officer - Vineyard Bank, Louie Couto/Sr. VP, Chief Risk Officer, Michael Cain/Exec. VP, Chief Lending Officer, Karyn Elkington/Sr. VP, Chief Culture Officer, Terra Newcomer Hagel/Investor Relations Officer

Directors: Norman A. Morales/Dir., Pres., CEO - Vineyard Bank, James G. Lesieur/Chmn., Charles L. Keagle/Vice Chmn., David A. Buxbaum/Dir., Robb Quincey/Dir., Frank S. Alvarez/Dir., Joel H. Ravitz/Dir.

Owners: Frank S. Alvarez/1.72%, Charles L. Keagle/3.22%, Insiders/13.95%, Robb D. Quincey, Norman A. Morales/3.71%, David A. Buxbaum/1.06%, James G. LeSieur, Richard Hagan, Donald Pelgrim, Joel H. Ravitz/2.43%, Jacqueline Calhoun Schaefgen, Gordon Fong

Financial Data: *Fiscal Year End:*12/31 *Latest Annual Data:* 12/31/2006

Year	Sales	Net Income
2006	$163,942,000	$19,745,000
2005	$116,164,000	$18,911,000
2004	$80,513,000	$13,987,000

Curr. Assets:	$46,706,000	**Curr. Liab.:**	$1,954,209,000		
Plant, Equip.:	$20,402,000	**Total Liab.:**	$2,114,679,000	**Indic. Yr. Divd.:**	$0.320
Total Assets:	$2,257,739,000	**Net Worth:**	$143,060,000	**Debt/ Equity:**	NA

Vintage Petroleum Inc

110 W Seventh St. , Tulsa, OK, 74119; ***PH:*** 1-918-592-0101; ***http://*** www.oxy.com

General - Incorporation	OK	**Stock**- Price on:12/24/2007	$57.11
Employees	8,886	Stock Exchange	NA
Auditor	Ernst & Young LLP	Ticker Symbol	NA
Stk Agt	Mellon Investor Services LLC	Outstanding Shares	833,810,000
Counsel	NA	E.P.S	$5.55
DUNS No.	10-726-3907	Shareholders	NA

Business: The group's principal activity is to operate in the exploration and production, gas marketing and gathering and processing segments of the oil and gas industry. The group owns and operates oil and gas producing properties in 9 states, with its domestic proved reserves located principally in four core areas. The core areas of exploration and production operations include the west coast, gulf coast, east Texas and mid-continent areas of the United States. The group owns interests in 2,660 gross productive wells in the United States, 645 gross productive wells in Canada, 1,518 gross productive wells in Argentina and 14 gross productive wells in Bolivia. On 20-Sep-2004, the group acquired rio alto resources international inc.

Primary SIC and add'l.: 4924 1311 4932 5172 4925

CIK No: 0000809428

Subsidiaries: Cadipsa S.A., Petrolera Rio Alto S.A., Vintage Gas, Inc., Vintage Marketing, Inc., Vintage Oil Argentina, Inc., Vintage Petroleum Argentina S.A., Vintage Petroleum Argentina, Ltd., Vintage Petroleum Boliviana, Ltd., Vintage Petroleum Bulgaria, Inc., Vintage Petroleum California, Inc., Vintage Petroleum Canada Holdings, Inc., Vintage Petroleum Canada Investments ULC, Vintage Petroleum Capital Trust I, Vintage Petroleum Ecuador, Inc., Vintage Petroleum International Finance, B.V. 26 Subsidiaries included in the Index

Financial Data: *Fiscal Year End:*12/31 *Latest Annual Data:* 12/31/2006

Year	Sales	Net Income
2006	$18,160,000,000	$4,182,000,000
2005	$16,259,000,000	$5,281,000,000
2004	$11,513,000,000	$2,568,000,000

Curr. Assets:	$6,006,000,000	**Curr. Liab.:**	$4,724,000,000	**P/E Ratio:**	10.29
Plant, Equip.:	$24,316,000,000	**Total Liab.:**	$12,830,000,000	**Indic. Yr. Divd.:**	$0.880
Total Assets:	$32,355,000,000	**Net Worth:**	$19,184,000,000	**Debt/ Equity:**	0.0836

Vion Pharmaceuticals Inc

4 Science Pk., New Haven, CT, 06511; ***PH:*** 1-203-498-4210; ***http://*** www.vionpharm.com; ***Email:*** info@vionpharm.com

General - Incorporation	DE	**Stock**- Price on:12/24/2007	$1.15
Employees	39	Stock Exchange	NDQ
Auditor	Ernst & Young LLP	Ticker Symbol	VION
Stk Agt	American Stock Transfer & Trust Co.	Outstanding Shares	72,850,000
Counsel	Fulbright & Jaworski LLP	E.P.S	-$0.479
DUNS No.	87-816-0902	Shareholders	NA

Business: The group's principle activities include researching, developing and commercializing therapeutics and technologies for the treatment of cancer. The company is a development stage biopharmaceutical company. The product portfolio consists of one drug delivery platform and two distinct small molecule anticancer agents. The company has acquired rights to certain oncology and antiviral related patents and technology. The company has developed small molecular weight, pharmaceutical agents with known mechanisms of activity. The group operates from United States.

Primary SIC and add'l.: 2834 8731

CIK No: 0000944522

Subsidiaries: Vion (uk) Limited

Officers: Alan Kessman/Dir., CEO/$2,959,453.00, Ann Cahill/VP - Clinical Development/$1,248,953.00, Ivan King/VP - Research, Development/$886,037.00, Howard B. Johnson/CFO, Pres./$1,493,200.00, Meghan Fitzgerald/Chief Business Officer/$1,072,634.00, Aileen Ryan/VP - Regulatory Affairs, Karen Schmedlin/VP - Finance, Chief Accounting Officer, James Tanguay/VP - Chemistry, Manufacturing, Control

Directors: Alan Kessman/Dir., CEO, Alan C. Sartorelli/Chmn., Ian Williams/Dir., Gary Willis/Dir., Kevin Rakin/Dir., William R. Miller/Dir., George Bickerstaff/Dir., Stephen K. Carter/Dir.

Owners: George Bickerstaff, Alan C. Sartorelli, Kevin Rakin, Ian D. Williams, Stephen K. Carter, Ivan King/1.10%, Meditor Group Ltd./5.70%, OrbiMed Advisors LLC/10.20%, Insiders/12.10%, William R. Miller, Howard B. Johnson/1.90%, Gary K. Willis, Alan Kessman/4.60%, Ann Lee Cahill/1.10%, QVT Financial LP/5.90% *(16 Owners included in Index)*

Financial Data: *Fiscal Year End:*12/31 *Latest Annual Data:* 12/31/2006

Year	Sales	Net Income
2006	$22,000	-$25,347,000
2005	$23,000	-$18,041,000
2004	$275,000	-$16,055,000

Curr. Assets:	$31,226,000	**Curr. Liab.:**	$6,078,000		
Plant, Equip.:	$605,000	**Total Liab.:**	$6,402,000	**Indic. Yr. Divd.:**	NA
Total Assets:	$31,856,000	**Net Worth:**	$25,454,000	**Debt/ Equity:**	2.4856

VioQuest Pharmaceuticals Inc

7 Deer Pk. Dr., Ste E, Princeton Corporate Pl., Monmouth Junction, NJ, 08852; ***PH:*** 1-908-766-4400; ***http://*** www.chiralquest.com

General - Incorporation	DE	**Stock**- Price on:12/24/2007	$0.46
Employees	50	Stock Exchange	OTC
Auditor	J. H. Cohn LLP	Ticker Symbol	VQPH
Stk Agt	Paramount Biocapital	Outstanding Shares	47,800,000
Counsel	NA	E.P.S	-$0.22
DUNS No.	NA	Shareholders	NA

Business: The group's principal activities are to develop asymmetric products and technology for the life sciences industry. The group has two main lines of products and services - proprietary chiral catalysts and chiral building blocks or client-defined molecules. The products are used in pharmaceuticals, producing fine chemicals other than pharmaceuticals - chiral molecules are used in flavors, fragrances, agrochemicals, animal health, food and feed additives (including vitamins) and nutraceuticals. It also develops and makes client-defined building blocks and drug candidate fragments, mainly in the chiral area, which develops new synthetic routes or optimizes existing ones and produce certain quantities of material for further processing at the clients' needs. The group has license to 13 United States patent applications.

Primary SIC and add'l.: 3841

CIK No: 0000745788

Subsidiaries: Chiral Quest, Inc

Subsidiaries: Chiral Quest, Inc

Officers: Daniel Greenleaf/Dir., CEO, Pres./$1,378,053.00, Brian Lenz/Interim CEO, CFO, Treasurer/$249,141.00, Stephen C. Rocamboli/Non - Exec. Chmn., Sec., Yaping Hong/Sr. VP - Global Process Research, Development/$279,872.00, Michael Cannarsa/GM - Chiral Quest, Edward C. Bradley/Chief Scientific Officer, Lawrence Akinsanmi/VP - Clinical Operations, Regulatory Affairs

Directors: Daniel Greenleaf/Dir., CEO, Pres., Stephen C. Rocamboli/Non - Exec. Chmn., Sec., Francis Giles/Chmn. - Advisory Board, Michael Weiser/Dir., Webster K. Cavenee/Member - Advisory Board, Kenneth F. King/Member - Advisory Board, Vincent Aita/34/Dir., Johnson Y.N. Lau/Dir., Brian Leyland-Jones/Member - Advisory Board, Leonard E. Post/Member - Advisory Board

Owners: Lester Lipschutz/18.70%, Stephen C. Rocamboli/1.70%, Edward C. Bradley, Xumu Zhang/5.90%, Insiders/9.60%, Michael Weiser/3.60%, Brian Lenz, Johnson Y.N. Lau, Vincent M. Aita, Daniel Greenleaf/3.40%, Lindsay A. Rosenwald/6.20%

Financial Data: Fiscal Year End:12/31 Latest Annual Data: 12/31/2006

Year	Sales		Net Income
2006	NA		-$8,271,000
2005	$3,805,000		-$12,835,000
2004	$1,485,000		-$4,024,000

Curr. Assets:	$4,430,000	**Curr. Liab.:**	$2,988,000			
Plant, Equip.:	$43,000	**Total Liab.:**	$2,988,000	**Indic. Yr. Divd.:**	NA	
Total Assets:	$5,828,000	**Net Worth:**	$2,841,000	**Debt/ Equity:**	NA	

Virage Logic Corp

47100 Bayside Pkwy, Fremont, CA, 94538; *PH:* 1-510-360-8000; *http://* www.viragelogic.com; *Email:* recruiting@viragelogic.com

General - Incorporation	DE	Stock - Price on:12/24/2007	$7.4
Employees	410	Stock Exchange	NDQ
Auditor	Burr, Pilger & Mayer, LLP	Ticker Symbol	VIRL
Stk Agt	Mellon Investor Services LLC	Outstanding Shares	23,140,000
Counsel	Jones Day, Palo Alto	E.P.S.	-$0.2
DUNS No.	NA	Shareholders	NA

Business: The group's principal activity is to provide semiconductor intellectual property platforms used in the manufacture of system-on-a-chip (soc) integrated circuits. These circuits power today's Internet and high-speed communications, computer and consumer products, such as cellular and digital phones, pagers, digital cameras, DVD players, switches and modems. The group's customers include fabless semiconductor companies such as altera, amcc, ati technologies, broadcom, pmc-sierra, sandisk, transwitch, and vitesse semiconductor and integrated device manufacturers (idms) such as agere, agilent, ami semiconductor, conexant, IBM, infineon, intel, kawasaki, lsi logic, motorola, nec, philips electronics, sharp, sony, stmicroelectronics and toshiba. The group has operations in the United States, Canada, Japan, Taiwan, Europe, Middle East and Africa .

Primary SIC and add'l.: 3674

CIK No: 0001050776

Subsidiaries: In-Chip Systems, Inc., Virage Logic International, Virage Logic International GmbH, Virage Logic International KK, Virage Logic International Ltd.

Officers: Daniel J. McCranie/Dir., CEO, Pres., Christine Russell/VP - Finance, CFO, Ehsan Rashid/VP - Operations, Alexander Shubat/Dir., VP - Research, Development, CTO, Jim Bailey/VP - Worldwide Sales, Yervant Zorian/VP, Chief Scientist, William J. Palumbo/VP, GM - New Jersey Operations, David Sowards/VP - Non - Volatile Memory Products, Sabina Burns/Sr. Dir. - Corporate Marketing, Colin Harris/VP - Operations, COO, Pete Rodriguez/Chief Marketing Officer, Sherif Sweha/VP - Engineering, Brani Buric/VP - Product Marketing, Strategic Foundry Relationships, Kamalesh Ruparel/VP, GM - Application Specific IP Solutions, Silicon Technology

Directors: Daniel J. McCranie/Dir., CEO, Pres., Adam A. Kablanian/Chmn., Michael L. Hackworth/Dir., Michael Stark/Dir., Alexander Shubat/Dir., VP - Research, Development, CTO, Cathal Phelan/Dir., Robert H. Smith/Dir.

Owners: Daniel J. McCranie, Robert H. Smith, Insiders, Cathal Phelan, Michael L. Hackworth, T. Rowe Price Associates, Inc., Alexander Shubat, Adam A. Kablanian, Artis Capital Management LLC, James J. Ensell, Crosslink Capital, Inc., Fidelity Management& Research Company, James Bailey, Michael Stark

Financial Data: Fiscal Year End:09/30 Latest Annual Data: 09/30/2007

Year	Sales		Net Income
2007	$46,527,000		-$4,605,000
2006	$59,303,000		-$879,000
2005	$53,389,000		-$315,000

Curr. Assets:	$91,739,000	**Curr. Liab.:**	$16,765,000			
Plant, Equip.:	$4,842,000	**Total Liab.:**	$17,457,000	**Indic. Yr. Divd.:**	NA	
Total Assets:	$126,275,000	**Net Worth:**	$108,818,000	**Debt/ Equity:**	NA	

Viragen Inc

865 SW 78th Ave., Ste. 100, Plantation, FL, 33324; *PH:* 1-954-233-8746; *http://* www.viragen.com; *Email:* dcalder@viragen.com

General - Incorporation	DE	Stock - Price on:12/24/2007	$0.0351
Employees	54	Stock Exchange	OTC
Auditor	Ernst & Young LLP	Ticker Symbol	VRAI
Stk Agt	Mellon Investor Services LLC	Outstanding Shares	218,660,000
Counsel	NA	E.P.S.	-$0.409
DUNS No.	10-193-5278	Shareholders	NA

Business: The group's principal activities are to conduct research, development and manufacture immunological products for the treatment of life-threatening diseases. The group produces a natural alpha interferon product named multiferon(R) from human white blood cells, also known as leukocytes. Natural interferon stimulates and modulates the human immune system. The group also manufactures medical therapies that stops the growth of various viruses including those associated with diseases such as hepatitis, multiple sclerosis, HIV/aids and some forms of cancer. The group operates in Sweden, Scotland and Germany.

Primary SIC and add'l.: 2836 8731

CIK No: 0000353482

Subsidiaries: Viragen (Scotland) Ltd., Viragen International, Inc., Viragen Technology, Inc., Viragen U.S.A., Inc., ViraGenics, Inc., ViraNative AB

Officers: Charles A. Rice/Dir., CEO, Pres., William H. Stimson/Dir. - Viragen International, Inc, Dennis W. Healey/CFO - Viragen International, Inc, Karen Jervis/VP, MD - VSL, Patrick Yeramian/Consulting Medical Dir., orjan Norberg/MD - Viranative AB, Douglas W. Calder/Dir. - Communications

Directors: Charles A. Rice/Dir., CEO, Pres., Carl N. Singer/Chmn., Richard C. Stafford/Dir., Randolph A. Pohlman/Dir., Robert C. Salisbury/Dir., Charles J. Simons/Dir., Nancy A. Speck/Dir.

Owners: Insiders, Nancy A. Speck, Carl N. Singer, Randolph A. Pohlman, Nicholas M. Burke, Richard C. Stafford, Robert C. Salisbury, Charles J. Simons, Charles A. Rice, Dennis W. Healey

Financial Data: Fiscal Year End:06/30 Latest Annual Data: 6/30/2006

Year	Sales		Net Income
2006	$391,000		-$18,215,000
2005	$279,000		-$26,208,000
2004	$266,000		-$18,177,000

Curr. Assets:	$3,523,000	**Curr. Liab.:**	$3,294,000			
Plant, Equip.:	$4,811,000	**Total Liab.:**	$15,588,000	**Indic. Yr. Divd.:**	NA	
Total Assets:	$13,974,000	**Net Worth:**	-$1,614,000	**Debt/ Equity:**	6.5854	

Viragen International Inc

865 SW 78th Ave., Ste. 100, Plantation, FL, 33324; *PH:* 1-954-233-8377; *http://* www.viragen.com

General - Incorporation	DE	Stock - Price on:12/24/2007	$0.03
Employees	46	Stock Exchange	OTC
Auditor	Ernst & Young LLP	Ticker Symbol	VRGE
Stk Agt	Mellon Investor Services LLC	Outstanding Shares	77,670,000
Counsel	NA	E.P.S.	-$0.19
DUNS No.	10-193-5278	Shareholders	NA

Business: The group's principal activities are to research, develop, manufacture and market a natural human alpha interferon product indicated for treatment of a broad range of viral and malignant diseases. The group produces a natural human alpha interferon product under the tradename of multiferontmfrom human white blood cells, also known as leukocytes. Natural interferon-alpha is one of the body's most important natural defense mechanisms to foreign substances like viruses, but it also stimulates and modulates the human immune system. In addition, interferon inhibits the growth of various viruses including those associated with diseases like hepatitis, some types of cancer, multiple sclerosis, and severe acute respiratory syndrome (sars). The group is a majority owned subsidiary of viragen, inc.

Primary SIC and add'l.: 2834 8731

CIK No: 0000785081

Subsidiaries: Viragen (Scotland) Ltd., ViraNative AB

Officers: Charles A. Rice/Dir., CEO, Pres., orjan Norberg/MD - Viranative AB, Dennis W. Healey/Dir., CFO, Patrick Yeramian/Consulting Medical Dir.

Directors: Charles A. Rice/Dir., CEO, Pres., Carl N. Singer/Chmn., Dennis W. Healey/Dir., CFO, William H. Stimson/Dir.

Owners: William H. Stimson, Insiders, Carl N. Singer, Dennis W. Healey, Nicholas M. Burke, Viragen, Inc./77.00%

Financial Data: Fiscal Year End:06/30 Latest Annual Data: 6/30/2006

Year	Sales		Net Income
2006	$391,000		-$8,516,000
2005	$279,000		-$15,644,000
2004	$266,000		-$7,076,000

Curr. Assets:	$2,549,000	**Curr. Liab.:**	$1,207,000			
Plant, Equip.:	$4,731,000	**Total Liab.:**	$28,920,000	**Indic. Yr. Divd.:**	NA	
Total Assets:	$12,719,000	**Net Worth:**	-$16,200,000	**Debt/ Equity:**	NA	

Viral Genetics Inc

1321 Mountain View Cir., Azusa, CA, 91702; *PH:* 1-323-682-2172; *http://* www.viralgenetics.com; *Email:* info@viralgenetics.com

General - Incorporation	DE	Stock - Price on:12/24/2007	$0.039
Employees	7	Stock Exchange	OTC
Auditor	Killman, Murrell & Co. P.C	Ticker Symbol	VRAL
Stk Agt	Registrar & Transfer Co	Outstanding Shares	127,970,000
Counsel	NA	E.P.S.	-$0.041
DUNS No.	NA	Shareholders	NA

Business: The group's principal activities are to discover, develop and commercialize novel therapeutic and diagnostic systems for the treatment of viral diseases. The group's core technology revolves around a biologically active linear protein, thymus nuclear protein (tnp). The group's main focus has been the development of a treatment to stop the progression of the human immunodeficiency virus (HIV), which is the causative agent in aids.

Primary SIC and add'l.: 8731 2834

CIK No: 0001091326

Subsidiaries: Viral Genetics (Beijing) Ltd., Viral Genetics South Africa (Proprietary) Ltd., Viral Genetics, Inc.

Officers: Haig Keledjian/Chmn., CEO, CFO Pres., Sec., Monica Ord/Sr. VP - Corporate Development, Communications, Michael Capizzano/VP - Finance, Business, Corporate Development, Andre Bagdasarian/VP - Quality Assurance

Directors: Haig Keledjian/Chmn., CEO, CFO Pres., Sec., Hampar Karageozian/Dir., Arthur Keledjian/Dir., Eric Rosenberg/Member - Scientific Advisory Board, Arthur Ammann/Dir., Elizabeth Hoffman/Dir., Todd M. Allen/Member - Scientific Advisory Board, Marcus Altfeld/Member - Scientific Advisory Board, Dan H. Barouch/Member - Scientific Advisory Board, Marie Davidian/Member - Scientific Advisory Board

Financial Data: Fiscal Year End:12/31 Latest Annual Data: 12/31/2006

Year	Sales		Net Income
2006	NA		-$12,609,000
2005	NA		-$5,033,000
2004	NA		-$6,944,000

Curr. Assets:	NA	**Curr. Liab.:**	$5,846,000			
Plant, Equip.:	$980,000	**Total Liab.:**	$8,347,000	**Indic. Yr. Divd.:**	NA	
Total Assets:	$1,023,000	**Net Worth:**	-$7,324,000	**Debt/ Equity:**	NA	

Virco Mfg Corp

2027 Harpers Way, Torrance, CA, 90501; *PH:* 1-310-533-0474; *http://* www.virco.com

General - Incorporation.............................. DE
Employees 1,250
Auditor .... Ernst & Young LLP
Stk Agt............... Mellon Investor Services LLC
Counsel............... Gibson, Dunn & Crutcher LLP
DUNS No. 00-828-9530

Stock- Price on:12/24/2007 ....NA
Stock Exchange...NA
Ticker Symbol..NA
Outstanding Shares ....NA
E.P.S...NA
Shareholders...NA

Business: The group's principal activities are to design, produce and distribute furniture for a diverse family of customers. The products includes tables, chairs and storage equipment for offices, convention centers, auditoriums, places of worship, hotels and related settings. The group offers the broadest line of furniture for the K-12 market of any company in the United States. It provides products for pre-school markets and has recently developed products that are targeted for college, university and corporate learning center environments. The group has an array of support services, including product delivery, installation and repair and computer-assisted layout planning. Major customers include educational institutions, convention centers and arenas, hospitality service providers, government facilities and places of worship.

Primary SIC and add'l.: 2522 2521 2531

CIK No: 0000751365

Subsidiaries: Virco Inc., Virco Mgmt. Corporation

Owners: Donald A. Patrick, Donald S. Friesz, Robert A. Virtue/2.22%, Nancy Virtue-Cutshall/6.14%, Wedbush Inc/11.54%, Insiders/9.29%, Private Capital Manageent, L.P./7.89%, Douglas A. Virtue/4.10%, Lori L. Swafford, Albert J. Moyer, Robert E. Dose, Robert K. Montgomery, Larry O. Wonder, Glen D. Parish, James R. Wilburn (16 Owners included in Index)

ViRexx Medical Corp

8223 Roper Rd. NW, Edmonton, AB, T6E 6S4; **PH:** 1-780-433-4411; **http://** www.virexx.com; **Email:** investor@virexx.com

General - Incorporation......................Canada
Employees 25
Auditor ....PricewaterhouseCoopers LLP
Stk Agt.......................................Mellon Trust Co
Counsel...NA
DUNS No. ....NA

Stock- Price on:12/24/2007 ....$0.84
Stock Exchange...AMEX
Ticker Symbol..REX
Outstanding Shares 72,760,000
E.P.S.. -$0.23
Shareholders..NA

Business: The group's principal activity is to develop novel therapeutic products for the treatment of cancer and chronic viral infections. The company's most advanced clinical programs include drug candidates for the treatment of ovarian cancer, chronic Hepatitis B & C and solid tumors. The lead product from the AIT platform is OvaRex MAb, a therapy for late-stage ovarian cancer. OvaRex MAb is currently the subject of a pivotal Phase III clinical trial at more than 60 sites in the United States.

Primary SIC and add'l.: 2833

CIK No: 0001275011

Subsidiaries: AltaRex Medical Corp, Unither Pharmaceuticals, Inc

Officers: Lorne D. Tyrrell/65/Dir., CEO, Chief Scientific Officer, Darrell Elliott/Chmn., Interim CEO, Rajan George/VP - Research, Development, Michael W. Stewart/51/Sr. VP - Operations, Scott Langille/51/CFO, Macaraig Canton/50/COO, Pres., Andrew Stevens/VP - Clinical, Regulatory, Irwin Griffith/VP - Drug Development, Infectious Diseases, Richard Ascione/Member - Scientific Advisory Board, Interim Chief Scientific Officer, Bruce D. Hirsche/60/Corp. Sec.

Directors: Lorne D. Tyrrell/65/Dir., CEO, Chief Scientific Officer, Darrell Elliott/Chmn., Interim CEO, Peter Smetek/Dir., Thomas E. Brown/48/Dir., Jean Claude Gonneau/58/Dir., Douglas Gilpin/Dir., Bruce D. Brydon/61/Dir., Jacques R. Lapointe/Dir., Michael Marcus/Dir., Yves Cohen/Dir., Richard Ascione/Member - Scientific Advisory Board, Interim Chief Scientific Officer, Timothy M. Block/Member - Scientific Advisory Board, Christopher M. Walker/Member - Scientific Advisory Board, Lorne A. Babiuk/Member - Scientific Advisory Board

Owners: Jacques R. LaPointe/0.24%, Macaraig Canton/0.01%, Thomas E. Brown/1.25%, Lorne D. Tyrrell/2.28%, Michael W. Stewart/0.04%, Rajan George/0.09%, Jean Claude Gonneau/0.03%

Financial Data: Fiscal Year End:12/31 Latest Annual Data: 12/31/2006

Year	Sales	Net Income
2006	NA	-$9,177,000
2005	NA	-$7,259,000

Curr. Assets:	$9,529,000	Curr. Liab.:	$1,371,000		
Plant, Equip.:	$408,000	Total Liab.:	$5,964,000	Indic. Yr. Divd.:	NA
Total Assets:	$33,423,000	Net Worth:	$27,458,000	Debt/ Equity:	NA

Virgin Media Inc

Formerly: Telewest Global Inc
The Atlantic Bldg., 950 F. St. N.w, Washington, DC, 20004; **PH:** 1-202-756-3300; **http://** www.telewest.co.uk

General - Incorporation............................. DE
Employees 8,896
Auditor ....KPMG Audit Plc
Stk Agt..Bank of New York
Counsel...NA
DUNS No. ....NA

Stock- Price on:12/24/2007 ....$25.55
Stock Exchange...NA
Ticker Symbol..NA
Outstanding Shares ....NA
E.P.S...NA
Shareholders...NA

Business: The group's principle activities are the provision of cable television, telephony and Internet services to the consumer and business markets in the United Kingdom. The group also supplies entertainment content, interactive and transactional services to the UK pay-TV broadcasting market. .

Primary SIC and add'l.: NA

CIK No: 0001270400

Subsidiaries: Action Stations (2000) Limited, Action Stations (Lakeside) Limited, Avon Cable Investments Limited, Avon Cable Joint Venture, Avon Cable Limited Partnership, Barnsley Cable Communications Limited, Birmingham Cable Corporation Limited, Birmingham Cable Finance Limited, Birmingham Cable Limited, Blue Yonder Workwise Limited, Bradford Cable Communications Limited, Bravo TV Limited, Cable Adnet Limited, Cable Camden Limited, Cable Communications (Telecom) Limited 207 Subsidiaries included in the Index

Officers: Stephen A. Burch/58/Dir., CEO, Pres., Malcolm Wall/51/CEO - Content Division, Robert C. Gale/48/VP, Controller, Neil A. Berkett/52/COO, Bryan H. Hall/45/General Counsel, Company Sec., Jacques D. Kerrest/61/CFO

Directors: Stephen A. Burch/58/Dir., CEO, Pres., Edwin M. Banks/45/Dir., George R. Zoffinger/60/Dir., James F. Mooney/53/Dir., David Elstein/63/Dir., Charles K. Gallagher/42/Dir., William R. Huff/58/Dir., Gordon D. McCallum/48/Dir., Jeffrey D. Benjamin/46/Dir.

Owners: David K. Elstein, Edwin M. Banks, William J. Connors, Malcolm R. Wall, Virgin Entertainment Investment Holdings Limited/10.50%, Simon P. Duffy, Stephen A. Burch, Bryan H. Hall, Jacques D. Kerrest, Neil A. Berkett, Charles K. Gallagher, France Telecom/5.40%, James F. Mooney, William R. Huff/5.80%, W. R. Huff Asset Management Co., L.L.C./5.80% (22 Owners included in Index)

Virginia Commerce Bank

5350 Lee Hwy., Arlington, VA, 22207; **PH:** 1-703-534-0700; **Fax:** 1-703-534-1782; **http://** www.virginiacommercebank.com; **Email:** bankinfo@vcbonline.com

General - Incorporation .... VA
Employees 275
Auditor ....Yount, Hyde & Barbour, P.C
Stk Agt.....................Registrar and Transfer CO.
Counsel...NA
DUNS No. ....NA

Stock- Price on:12/24/2007 ....$17.08
Stock Exchange...NDQ
Ticker Symbol..VCBI
Outstanding Shares 23,900,000
E.P.S...$1.07
Shareholders...NA

Business: The group's principal activity is to provide general commercial banking business through its subsidiary, Virginia commerce bank. The group is a one-bank holding company, which offers services through 12 banking offices located in arlington county, northern Virginia and surrounding areas. The services of the group include full range of deposit accounts, merchant bankcard services, electronic funds transfer services, lines of credit, term and commercial real estate loans. Other services provided by the group are issuance of cashier's checks and money orders, selling of traveler's checks, providing safe deposit boxes and other customary banking services. The customer base includes small to medium-sized businesses, associations, retailers and industrial businesses, professionals and business executives and consumers.

Primary SIC and add'l.: 6022 6712

CIK No: 0001099305

Officers: Peter A. Converse/Dir., CEO/$699,640.00, Michael G. Anzilotti/Dir., Pres./$231,654.00, Steven A. Reeder/Exec. VP - Retail Banking/$191,723.00, William K. Beauchesne/CFO, Exec. VP/$264,506.00, Richard B. Anderson/Exec. VP, Chief Lending Officer/$354,509.00, Patricia M. Ostrander/Exec. VP - Human Resources, John P. Perseo/Exec. VP - Operations, Technology, Lynda S. Cornell/Assist., Pres.

Directors: Peter A. Converse/Dir., CEO, Arthur L. Walters/Vice Chmn., Douglas W. Fisher/Chmn., David M. Guernsey/Vice Chmn., Norris E. Mitchell/Dir., Leonard Adler/Dir., Michael G. Anzilotti/Dir., Pres., Robert H. L'Hommedieu/Dir.

Owners: Insiders/31.42%, Douglas W. Fisher/2.69%, Leonard Adler/2.65%, Peter A. Converse/3.94%, Richard B. Anderson/0.79%, David M. Guernsey/1.08%, Steven Reeder/0.05%, Norris E. Mitchell/4.14%, William K. Beauchesne/0.47%, Robert H. LHommedieu/3.44%, Arthur L. Walters/13.04%, Michael G. Anzilotti/0.19%

Financial Data: Fiscal Year End:12/31 Latest Annual Data: 12/31/2006

Year	Sales	Net Income
2006	$132,615,000	$24,508,000
2005	$93,154,000	$19,667,000
2004	$63,757,000	$14,229,000

Curr. Assets:	$45,383,000	Curr. Liab.:	$1,760,735,000	P/E Ratio:	16.91
Plant, Equip.:	$9,273,000	Total Liab.:	$1,809,231,000	Indic. Yr. Divd.:	NA
Total Assets:	$1,949,082,000	Net Worth:	$139,851,000	Debt/ Equity:	NA

Virginia Electric & Power Co

120 Tredegar St., Richmond, VA, 23219; **PH:** 1-804-819-2000; **Fax:** 1-804-819-2233; **http://** www.dom.com

General - Incorporation .... VA
Employees 17,500
Auditor ....Deloitte & Touche LLP
Stk Agt...NA
Counsel...NA
DUNS No. 00-794-1446

Stock- Price on:12/24/2007 ....$83.835
Stock Exchange...NYSE
Ticker Symbol..NA
Outstanding Shares 350,320,000
E.P.S...$3.69
Shareholders...NA

Business: The group's principle activity is to generate, transmit and distribute power for sale in Virginia and northeastern North Carolina. The three primary operating segments of the company are generation, energy and delivery. The generation manages the company's electric generating facilities and power purchase contracts. The energy manages the company's electric transmission and energy trading, hedging and arbitrage activities. The delivery manages the company's electric distribution and transmission systems, serving approximately 2 million customers, about 6,000 miles of electric transmission lines and customer service operations. The company sells electricity to approximately 2.1 million retail customers, including governmental agencies, and to wholesale customers such as rural electric cooperatives, municipalities, power marketers and other utilities. The company is a wholly owned subsidiary of dominion resources, inc. The group operates from United States.

Primary SIC and add'l.: 4911 4922

CIK No: 0000103682

Subsidiaries: Dominion Generation Corporation, Virginia Electric and Power Company, Virginia Power Capital Trust II, Virginia Power Fuel Corporation, Virginia Power Nuclear Services Company, Virginia Power Services Energy Corp., Inc., Virginia Power Services, LLC, VP Property, Inc.

Owners: David A. Christian, Jay L. Johnson, Mark F. McGettrick, Thomas N. Chewning, Thomas F. Farrell, Insiders

Financial Data: Fiscal Year End:12/31 Latest Annual Data: 12/31/2006

Year	Sales	Net Income
2006	$16,482,000,000	$1,380,000,000
2005	$18,041,000,000	$1,033,000,000
2004	$13,972,000,000	$1,249,000,000

Curr. Assets:	$8,098,000,000	Curr. Liab.:	$11,229,000,000	P/E Ratio:	22.72
Plant, Equip.:	$29,382,000,000	Total Liab.:	$36,076,000,000	Indic. Yr. Divd.:	$2.840
Total Assets:	$49,269,000,000	Net Worth:	$13,170,000,000	Debt/ Equity:	1.1047

Virginia Financial Group Inc

102 S Main St., Culpeper, VA, 22701; **PH:** 1-540-885-1232; **http://** www.vcfc.com

General - Incorporation VA
Employees 580
Auditor Grant Thornton, LLP
Stk Agt Registrar & Transfer Co
Counsel NA
DUNS No. NA

Stock- Price on:12/24/2007 $21.99
Stock Exchange NDQ
Ticker Symbol VFGI
Outstanding Shares 10,790,000
E.P.S. $1.63
Shareholders NA

Business: The group's principal activities are to provide commercial banking and trust activities. The group is a bank holding company, which provides services through 37 retail offices in central and southwest Virginia. The services offered include consumer and commercial demand and time deposit accounts, mortgage, commercial and consumer loans. The group also provides a network of automated transaction locations, phone banking and a transactional Internet banking product.

Primary SIC and add'l.: 6022 6712

CIK No: 0001036070

Subsidiaries: Planters Bank & Trust Company of Virginia, Planters Insurance Agency, Inc, Second Bank & Trust, Second Service Company, VFG Limited Liability Trust, Virginia Commonwealth Trust Company, Virginia Heartland Bank, Virginia Heartland Service Corporation

Officers: O. R. Barham/57/Dir., CEO, Pres./$544,726.00, James T. Huerth/CEO, Pres. - Planters Bank, Trust Company/$230,587.00, Lori A. Scott/Dir. - Treasury Management, Litz H. Van Dyke/43/COO, Exec. VP/$282,789.00, Tara Y. Harrison/Dir. - Internal Audit, Jeffrey W. Farrar/47/CFO, Exec. VP/$277,540.00, Lisa H. Cannell/Dir. - Human Resources, John E. Meyer/Dir. - Information Technology, Linda L. Caldwell/Dir. - Marketing, Joseph Sciortino/Dir. - Regulatory Management, Richard L. Saunders/Chief Credit Officer/$178,474.00, Patrick Snell/Controller, Kelly Hyson/Dir. - Loan Operations, Risk Management, Fred D. Bowers/71/Dir., Sec.

Directors: O. R. Barham/57/Dir., CEO, Pres., Taylor E. Gore/68/Chmn., Wayne H. Parrish/63/Vice Chmn., Page E. Butler/59/Dir., Christopher M. Hallberg/57/Dir., Martin F. Lightsey/64/Dir., Thomas F. Williams/68/Dir., William P. Moore/65/Dir., Lee S. Baker/56/Dir., Fred D. Bowers/71/Dir., Sec., Gregory L. Fisher/57/Dir., Jan S. Hoover/50/Dir.

Owners: Thomas F. Williams, Page E. Butler, Litz H. Van Dyke, James T. Huerth, Jan S. Hoover, Martin F. Lightsey, Christopher M. Hallberg, P. William Moore, Lee S. Baker, Gregory L. Fisher, Richard L. Saunders, Taylor E. Gore, Insiders/2.70%, O.R. Barham, Jeffrey W. Farrar *(17 Owners included in Index)*

Financial Data: *Fiscal Year End:*12/31 *Latest Annual Data:* 12/31/2006

Year	Sales	Net Income
2006	$111,308,000	$19,497,000
2005	$96,210,000	$18,216,000
2004	$84,966,000	$15,203,000

Curr. Assets:	$65,832,000	**Curr. Liab.:**	$1,387,555,000		
Plant, Equip.:	$35,853,000	**Total Liab.:**	$1,475,337,000	**Indic. Yr. Divd.:**	$0.640
Total Assets:	$1,625,989,000	**Net Worth:**	$150,652,000	**Debt/ Equity:**	0.1376

Virginia Mines Inc

Formerly: Virginia Gold Mines Inc
116, St-Pierre, Ste. 200, Quebec, QC, G1K 4A7; ***PH:*** 1-418-694-9832; ***Fax:*** 1-418-694-9120; ***http://*** www.virginia.qc.ca; ***Email:*** mines@virginia.qc.ca

General - Incorporation Canada
Employees NA
Auditor PricewaterhouseCoopers LLP
Stk Agt Mellon Trust Co
Counsel NA
DUNS No. NA

Stock- Price on:12/24/2007 NA
Stock Exchange NA
Ticker Symbol NA
Outstanding Shares NA
E.P.S NA
Shareholders NA

Business: The group's principle activities include acquiring, developing and exploring mineral properties. The group operates from United States.

Primary SIC and add'l.: 1041

CIK No: 0001020011

Subsidiaries: Virginia Mines Inc

Officers: Andre Gaumond/Dir., CEO, Pres., Vital Pearson/Sr. Research Geologist, Jean-Francois Ouellette/Chief Consultant - Geologist, Amelie Laliberte/Investor Relations, Paul Archer/VP - Exploration, Acquisitions, Gaetan Mercier/CFO, Noella Lessard/Management Sec., Mathieu Savard/Project Geologist, Jerome Lavoie/Project Geologist, Louis Grenier/Project Geologist, David Dechamplain/Chief Technician

Directors: Andre Gaumond/Dir., CEO, Pres., Andre Lemire/Chmn., Claude St-Jacques/Dir., Edmond Legault/Dir., Mario Jacob/Dir.

Virginia National Bank

222 E Main St. , Charlottesville, VA, 22902; ***PH:*** 1-434-817-8503; ***Fax:*** 1-434-817-8624; ***http://*** www.vnbpeople.com; ***Email:*** downtown@vnbpeople.com

General - Incorporation
Employees 92
Auditor NA
Stk Agt American Stock Transfer & Trust Co.
Counsel NA
DUNS No. NA

Stock- Price on:12/24/2007 $37.75
Stock Exchange OTC
Ticker Symbol VABK
Outstanding Shares 2,150,000
E.P.S. $1.07
Shareholders NA

Business: The groups principal activities include providing banking and financial services to the businesses and customers. Services of the group include checking accounts, savings accounts, certificates of deposit, installment loans, real estate mortgage loans, commercial loans, traveler's checks, safe deposit boxes, night depository, automated teller services and Internet banking.

Primary SIC and add'l.: 6021

CIK No:

Officers: Glenn W. Rust/Dir., CEO, Pres., Virginia Robinson/Managing Officer - Arvonia, Jennifer Matheny/Skills Development Coordinator, Operations, Julie Houchens/Contact - VNBtrust, Nancy Jorge/Contact - VNBtrust, Sean Miller/Contact - VNBtrust, Kristin Mitchell/Contact - VNBtrust, Tim Mullen/Contact - VNBtrust, Paula Newcomb/Contact - VNBtrust, Rosie Hunt/Loan Assist., April Harris/Dir. - Marketing, Jenny Droney/Assist. to The Pres. - Charlottesville, Downtown, Mary MacIlwaine/Special Projects, Computers 4 Kids Liason, Charlottesville, Downtown, Joseph D. Miller/Sr. Lending Officer, Hill Ewald/Contact - VNBtrust *(25 Officers included in Index)*

Directors: Glenn W. Rust/Dir., CEO, Pres., Mark T. Giles/Chmn., Hunter E. Craig/Vice Chmn., Steven W. Blaine/Dir., H. K. Benham/Dir., William D. Dittmar/Dir., Janet L. Dorman/Dir., Albert D. Ernest/Dir., Claire W. Gargalli/Dir., Susan King Payne/Dir., Richard Bell/Dir. - Winchester Regional, John S. Campbell/Dir. - Winchester Regional, James E. Haden/Dir., David G. Kalergis/Dir., Neal F. Kassell/Dir. *(24 Directors included in Index)*

Financial Data: *Fiscal Year End:*NA *Latest Annual Data:* 12/31/2002

Year	Sales	Net Income
2002	$9,428,000	$770,000
2001	$8,818,000	$743,000
2000	$7,568,000	$119,000

Curr. Assets:	$20,293,000	**Curr. Liab.:**	$150,290,000		
Plant, Equip.:	$4,140,000	**Total Liab.:**	$150,290,000	**Indic. Yr. Divd.:**	NA
Total Assets:	$170,609,000	**Net Worth:**	$20,319,000	**Debt/ Equity:**	NA

VirnetX Holding Corp

Formerly: Pasw Inc
9453 Alcosta Blvd., San Ramon, CA, 94583; ***PH:*** 1-925-828-0934

General - Incorporation CA
Employees 1
Auditor Farber Hass Hurley & Mcewen, LLP
Stk Agt American Securities T & T Inc.
Counsel Gary A. Agron
DUNS No. NA

Stock- Price on:12/24/2007 $1.35
Stock Exchange OTC
Ticker Symbol PASW
Outstanding Shares 5,000,000
E.P.S. $0.00
Shareholders NA

Business: The group's principle activity is to develop and license Internet, Web related software and software development tools. The operations are conducted principally from the offices in northern California. The group also maintains sales offices in Japan and Asia.

Primary SIC and add'l.: 7379 7372

CIK No: 0001082324

Subsidiaries: Alera Systems Inc, Network Research Corp. Japan, Ltd, Pacific Acquisition Corporation, PASW Europe Limited

Owners: Christopher A. Marlett/6.70%, William E. Sliney, Blue Screen LLC/5.70%, Robert M. Levande/6.70%, Edmund C. Munger/1.40%, Kendall Larsen/26.70%, Michael F. Angelo, Insiders/28.10%, San Gabriel Fund, LLC/5.10%, Gregory H. Bailey/7.30%

Financial Data: *Fiscal Year End:*12/31 *Latest Annual Data:* 12/31/2006

Year	Sales	Net Income
2006	$191,000	$60,000
2005	$213,000	$121,000
2004	$200,000	$65,000

Curr. Assets:	$320,000	**Curr. Liab.:**	$52,000		
Plant, Equip.:	$2,000	**Total Liab.:**	$52,000	**Indic. Yr. Divd.:**	NA
Total Assets:	$322,000	**Net Worth:**	$270,000	**Debt/ Equity:**	NA

ViroPharma Incorporated

397 Eagleview Blvd, Exton, PA, 19341; ***PH:*** 1-610-458-7300; ***http://*** www.viropharma.com

General - Incorporation DE
Employees 67
Auditor KPMG LLP
Stk Agt StockTrans, Inc.
Counsel NA
DUNS No. 92-890-2857

Stock- Price on:12/24/2007 $13.87
Stock Exchange NDQ
Ticker Symbol VPHM
Outstanding Shares 69,790,000
E.P.S. $1.22
Shareholders NA

Business: The group's principal activity is to discover and develop antiviral medicines. The group is a development stage company. The group currently focuses on product discovery and development activities on a number of ribonucleic acid (rna) virus diseases affecting children and adults, including viral respiratory infection (vri), respiratory syncytial virus (rsv) disease and hepatitis c. The group also develops antiviral medicines for the diseases caused by deoxyribonucleic acid (dna).

Primary SIC and add'l.: 8731 2834

CIK No: 0000946840

Subsidiaries: VCO Incorporated, VPDE Incorporated

Officers: Michel De Rosen/54/Chmn., CEO, Pres./$1,278,066.00, Vincent J. Milano/VP, CFO, COO/$927,986.00, Colin Broom/VP, Chief Scientific Officer/$825,306.00, Thomas F. Doyle/VP, General Counsel, Sec./$807,581.00, Joshua M. Tarnoff/VP, Chief Commercial Officer/$474,038.00, Daniel Soland/VP, Chief Commercial Officer/$482,587.00

Directors: Michel De Rosen/54/Chmn., CEO, Pres., William D. Claypool/54/Dir., Paul A. Brooke/62/Dir., Michael R. Dougherty/47/Dir., Robert J. Glaser/53/Dir., John R. Leone/59/Dir., Howard H. Pien/Dir., Frank Baldino/Dir.

Owners: Royce& Associates, LLC/5.60%, Thomas F. Doyle, Michel de Rosen/1.60%, Vincent J. Milano, Michael R. Dougherty, Joshua Tarnoff, Barclays Global Investors/5.50%, William D. Claypool, Julian and Felix Baker/11.70%, Robert J. Glaser, Colin Broom, Insiders/3.50%, Paul A. Brooke, Howard Pien, John R. Leone

Financial Data: *Fiscal Year End:*12/31 *Latest Annual Data:* 12/31/2006

Year	Sales	Net Income
2006	$167,181,000	$66,666,000
2005	$132,417,000	$113,705,000
2004	$22,389,000	-$19,534,000

Curr. Assets:	$284,238,000	**Curr. Liab.:**	$17,795,000	**P/E Ratio:**	10.75
Plant, Equip.:	$2,828,000	**Total Liab.:**	$17,795,000	**Indic. Yr. Divd.:**	NA
Total Assets:	$429,694,000	**Net Worth:**	$411,899,000	**Debt/ Equity:**	0.6057

Viropro Inc

8515 Pl. Devonshire, Ste. 207, Montreal, QC, H4P 2K1; ***PH:*** 1-514-731-8776; ***Fax:*** 1-514-739-7000; ***http://*** www.viropro.com; ***Email:*** info@viropro.com

General - Incorporation NV
Employees 4
Auditor De Joya Griffith & Company LLC
Stk Agt Jersey Transfer & Trust Co
Counsel NA
DUNS No. NA

Stock- Price on:12/24/2007 $0.185
Stock Exchange OTC
Ticker Symbol VPRO
Outstanding Shares 34,430,000
E.P.S. -$0.18
Shareholders NA

Business: The groups principle activities include retailing and wholesaling sales of gourmet and coffees. The groups food concepts are a roaster, packer and seller of roasted coffees and produced over 70 flavored coffees. The group operates from the United States and Canada.

Primary SIC and add'l.: 5141

CIK No: 0000703901

Subsidiaries: Palm Beach Gourmet Coffee, Inc, Savon Coffee, Inc., Viropro Canada Inc., Viropro Pharma Inc, Viropro, International Inc

Officers: Jean-Marie Dupuy/Dir., CEO, Pres., Prosper Azoulay/VP - Operations, Dir., Gino Di Iorio/CFO, Patrick Daoust/Dir. - Therapeutic Proteins Division, Patrick Benoist/Project Dir., Andre Bedard/Consultant - Business Development, International Partnerships

Directors: Jean-Marie Dupuy/Dir., CEO, Pres., Emilio Binavince/Dir., Prosper Azoulay/VP - Operations, Dir., Claude Griscelli/Dir., Peter Tijssen/Member - Scientific Advisory Board, Jean-Louis Boitieux/Member - Scientific Advisory Board

Owners: Immuno-Japan Inc./12.30%, Jean-Marie Dupuy/5.10%, Trivor Group/8.70%, Prosper Azoulay/1.80%, Claude Boulanger/6.20%, Insiders/6.90%

Financial Data: Fiscal Year End:11/30 Latest Annual Data: 11/30/2006

Year	Sales	Net Income
2006	NA	-$4,435,000
2005	NA	-$2,514,000
2004	NA	-$1,160,000

Curr. Assets:	$536,000	Curr. Liab.:	$511,000		
Plant, Equip.:	$17,000	Total Liab.:	$1,058,000	Indic. Yr. Divd.:	NA
Total Assets:	$1,563,000	Net Worth:	$504,000	Debt/ Equity:	NA

Virtra Systems Inc

2500 City, W Blvd., Ste. 300, Houston, TX, 77042; *PH:* 1-832-242-1100; *http://* www.virtrasystems.com; *Email:* tmilks@virtra.com

General - Incorporation	TX	Stock- Price on:12/24/2007	$0.032
Employees	16	Stock Exchange	OTC
Auditor	James B. Mcelravy, Cpa, P.c	Ticker Symbol	VTSI
Stk Agt.	Continental Stock Transfer & Trust Co	Outstanding Shares	102,260,000
Counsel	NA	E.P.S.	-$0.017
DUNS No.	NA	Shareholders	NA

Business: The group's principle activity is to design interactive entertainment system. The company develops, manufactures and operates technically advanced personal and non-personal computer based products that include virtual reality entertainment products. The customers of the company include gaming centers, social bars and entertainment amusement markets. The company solely is in the United States. During 2003 the company discontinued theme park operations. The group operates from United States.

Primary SIC and add'l.: 7373 7993 7997 7379

CIK No: 0001085243

Subsidiaries: Tri-Union Development Corporation

Officers: Perry V. Dalby/64/Chmn., CEO, Member - Advisory Board, David J. Rogers/54/CFO, Matt Burlend/33/VP - Production, Sr. Engineer, Tom Milks/Authorized Agent, Michael Kitchen/31/VP - Training, Simulation Sales, Bob Ferris/34/Dir., Pres., Steven M. Haag/49/VP - Investor Relations

Directors: Perry V. Dalby/64/Chmn., CEO, Member - Advisory Board, Bob Ferris/34/Dir., Pres., Frank Stanley/Dir., Thomas Cloud/44/Dir.

Owners: Perry V. Dalby/4.00%, Kelly L. Jones/7.10%, Andrew L. Wells/5.60%, Insiders/11.50%, Bob Ferris/7.90%

Financial Data: Fiscal Year End:12/31 Latest Annual Data: 12/31/2006

Year	Sales	Net Income
2006	$1,888,000	-$1,474,000
2005	$977,000	-$1,995,000
2004	$1,328,000	$1,566,000

Curr. Assets:	$498,000	Curr. Liab.:	$4,602,000		
Plant, Equip.:	$141,000	Total Liab.:	$4,602,000	Indic. Yr. Divd.:	NA
Total Assets:	$727,000	Net Worth:	-$3,876,000	Debt/ Equity:	NA

Virtual Media Holdings Inc

40218 Wellsline Rd., Abbotsford, BC, V3G 2K7; *PH:* 1-604-852-1806; *http://* www.virtualmediaholdings.com; *Email:* info@novakcapital.com

General - Incorporation	BC	Stock- Price on:12/24/2007	$0.023
Employees	NA	Stock Exchange	OTC
Auditor	Williams & Webster, P.S	Ticker Symbol	VMHIF
Stk Agt.	Pacific Stock Transfer Company	Outstanding Shares	NA
Counsel	NA	E.P.S.	NA
DUNS No.	NA	Shareholders	NA

Business: The groups principal activity is to process of transforming into a technology and marketing firm, The group using a proprietary marketplace platform to link buyers and sellers together, receiving commissions on a per transaction basis as opposed to a mail order company that sold, warehoused and handled ever increasing amounts of rapidly depreciating inventory. The group operates from the United States and Canada.

Primary SIC and add'l.: 7822

CIK No: 0001160164

Officers: Steven Gaspar/56/Dir., Pres., Principal Executive Officer, Treasurer - Principal, Financial Officer, Christopher Gaspar/23/Dir., VP - Operations

Directors: Steven Gaspar/56/Dir., Pres., Principal Executive Officer, Treasurer - Principal, Financial Officer, Christopher Gaspar/23/Dir., VP - Operations

Financial Data: Fiscal Year End:06/30 Latest Annual Data: 06/30/2005

Year	Sales	Net Income
2005	$3,600,000	-$250,000

Curr. Assets:	$526,000	Curr. Liab.:	$488,000		
Plant, Equip.:	$23,000	Total Liab.:	$488,000	Indic. Yr. Divd.:	NA
Total Assets:	$597,000	Net Worth:	$109,000	Debt/ Equity:	NA

VirtualScopics Inc

350 Linden Oaks, Rochester, NY, 14625; *PH:* 1-585-249-6231; *http://* www.virtualscopics.com; *Email:* info@virtualscopics.com

General - Incorporation	DE	Stock- Price on:12/24/2007	$1.33
Employees	48	Stock Exchange	NDQ
Auditor	Marcum & Kliegman LLP	Ticker Symbol	VSCP
Stk Agt.	Continental Stock Transfer & Trust Co	Outstanding Shares	22,980,000
Counsel	NA	E.P.S.	-$0.17
DUNS No.	NA	Shareholders	NA

Business: The groups principle activity is to develop drug and medical device. In November 4, 2005, the group acquired VirtualScopics, LLC. Specific customers of the group include Pfizer, Inc, GlaxoSmithKline and Merck, Inc. The group operates from the United States.

Primary SIC and add'l.: 3821 3841 3841 7372 3821 7372

CIK No: 0001307752

Subsidiaries: VirtualScopics, LLC

Officers: Jeff Markin/Dir., CEO, Pres., Saara Totterman/Chief Medical Officer, Co - Founder, Molly Henderson/CFO, VP - Finance, Jose Tamez-Pena/CTO, Co - Founder, Edward Ashton/Chief Scientific Officer, Rosemary J. Shull/Dir. - Business Development, Jonathan Riek/VP - Government Solutions, Toni Handzel/Dir. - Quality Assurance, Regulatory Affairs, Lisa Bamford/Dir. - Operations, Patricia Gonzalez/Service Planning Mgr., Colin Rhodes/Dir. - Software Development, Tim Ryan/Investor Relation

Directors: Jeff Markin/Dir., CEO, Pres., Robert Klimasewski/Chmn., Sidney Knafel/Dir., Warren Bagatelle/69/Dir., Colby Chandler/Dir., Terence A. Walts/Dir., Charles Phelps/Dir., Saara Totterman/Chief Medical Officer, Co - Founder, Norman N. Mintz/Dir.

Owners: Jeffrey Markin, Insiders/11.00%, Molly Henderson/1.50%, Terence Walts, Pfizer Inc./6.70%, GE Healthcare/5.30%, Robert Klimasewski/1.50%, University of Rochester/19.80%, Sidney Knafel/3.00%, Kevin J. Parker/5.00%, Jose Tamez-Pena/8.70%, Loeb Investors Company/19.30%, Saara Totterman/5.20%

Financial Data: Fiscal Year End:12/31 Latest Annual Data: 12/31/2006

Year	Sales	Net Income
2006	$4,740,000	-$3,704,000
2005	$68,000	-$67,000

Curr. Assets:	$3,000	Curr. Liab.:	$63,000		
Plant, Equip.:	$29,000	Total Liab.:	$63,000	Indic. Yr. Divd.:	NA
Total Assets:	$32,000	Net Worth:	-$31,000	Debt/ Equity:	NA

ViryaNet Ltd

2 Willow St., Southborough, MA, 01745; *PH:* 1-508-490-8600; *Fax:* 1-508-490-8666; *http://* www.viryanet.com

General - Incorporation	Israel	Stock- Price on:12/24/2007	NA
Employees	120	Stock Exchange	OTC
Auditor	Kost Forer Gabbay & Kasierer	Ticker Symbol	VRYAF
Stk Agt.	American Stock Transfer & Trust Co.	Outstanding Shares	NA
Counsel	Meitar, Liquornik, Geva & Co	E.P.S.	NA
DUNS No.	NA	Shareholders	NA

Business: The group's principle activities are the development, marketing and support of wireless workforce management solutions for field service communities. These solutions enable field service organisations to schedule and dispatch field service personnel efficiently; capture and record logistics and labour activity; and monitor, report, and measure this activity meeting an organisation's installation, preventative maintenance, and break-fix obligations. The company's wireless workforce management solution supports wireless devices over standard wireless networks. The company derives its revenues from licenses of software products and from related services, which include implementation, consulting, customer customization and integration, post-contract customer support and training. The group's quarterly revenue for Sep '07 was 3.09 millions of USD.

Primary SIC and add'l.: 7373 7379

CIK No: 0001119744

Subsidiaries: e-Wise Solutions of Australia, iMedeon, Inc., Utility Partners, ViryaNet, Inc

Officers: Memy Ish-Shalom/CEO, Pres., Al Gabrielli/CFO, VP - Finance, Administration, Clint Fuller/VP - Sales, Debra M. Brucato/VP - Professional Services, Jack McAvoy/VP - Marketing, Corporate Communications, Jim Robidoux/VP - Customer Care, Nir Diskin/VP - Engineering, Jeff Oskin/COO

Directors: Samuel Hacohen/Founder, Chmn. - Viryanet, Manuel Sanchez Ortega/Dir., Lior Bregman/Dir., Ronit Lerner/Dir., Vladimir Morgenstern/Co - Founder, Dir., Arie Ovadia/Dir.

Owners: Telvent Investments, S.L./13.40%, The Clal Group/7.60%, C.E. Unterberg, Towbin Capital Partners I, LLC/5.70%, LibertyView Special Opportunities Fund, LP/23.80%, Insiders/25.30%, Jerusalem High-tech Founders, Ltd/5.10%

Financial Data: Fiscal Year End:12/31 Latest Annual Data: 12/31/2005

Year	Sales	Net Income
2005	$14,207,000	-$6,058,000
2004	$11,920,000	-$4,155,000
2003	$11,959,000	-$1,654,000

Curr. Assets:	$2,719,000	Curr. Liab.:	NA		
Plant, Equip.:	NA	Total Liab.:	NA	Indic. Yr. Divd.:	NA
Total Assets:	$2,719,000	Net Worth:	NA	Debt/ Equity:	NA

Viscount Systems Inc

4585 Tillicum St., Burnaby, BC, V5J 5K9; *PH:* 1-604-327-9446; *Fax:* 1-604-327-3859; *http://* www.viscount.com; *Email:* investors@viscount.com

General - Incorporation	NV	Stock- Price on:12/24/2007	$0.43
Employees	NA	Stock Exchange	OTC
Auditor	Davidson & Company LLP	Ticker Symbol	VSYS
Stk Agt.	Pacific Stock Transfer Company	Outstanding Shares	NA
Counsel	NA	E.P.S.	NA
DUNS No.	NA	Shareholders	NA

Business: The groups principle activities include designing, manufacturing and servicing access control and security products, including intercom and door access control systems and emergency communications systems. The group operates from the United States and Canada.

Primary SIC and add'l.: 7382 3669 8744 3829

CIK No: 0001158387

Subsidiaries: Viscount Communication and Control Systems Inc

Officers: Stephen Pineau/Dir., CEO, Pres., Sec./$103,000.00, Les Fong/Accounting, Account Receivables, Michelle Nicholls/Customer Support, George Devries/Technical Support Staff, Ian Dawson/Mesh Technical Support

Directors: Greg Shen/Chmn.

Owners: Les Fong, Greg D.C. Shen/24.64%, Steven Leach/7.77%, Ching Yu Wang/7.21%, Stephen Pineau/15.99%, Hsiao-Ying Pai/8.46%, Insiders/35.03%, Cho Kun Ko/7.87%

Financial Data: Fiscal Year End:12/31 Latest Annual Data: 12/31/2006

Year	Sales	Net Income
2006	$3,915,000	-$372,000
2005	$4,302,000	$0
2004	$3,646,000	-$331,000

Curr. Assets:	$1,563,000	Curr. Liab.:	$1,143,000		
Plant, Equip.:	$77,000	Total Liab.:	$1,143,000	Indic. Yr. Divd.:	NA
Total Assets:	$1,790,000	Net Worth:	$648,000	Debt/ Equity:	NA

Viseon Inc

8445 Freeport Pkwy, Ste 245, Irving, TX, 75063; **PH:** 1-972-220-1500; **http://** www.viseon.com; **Email:** technical@viseon.com

General - Incorporation	NV	**Stock**- Price on:12/24/2007	NA
Employees	17	Stock Exchange	OTC
Auditor	Virchow, Krause & Co. LLP	Ticker Symbol	VSNI
Stk Agt	Wells Fargo Shareholder Services	Outstanding Shares	NA
Counsel	NA	E.P.S.	-$0.156
DUNS No.	87-633-0945	Shareholders	NA

Business: The group's principal activity is to sell desktop and consumer video communications products. The group's product, visifone, is a low-cost broadband videophone. It is a self-contained system that does not require a PC or any external equipment. The visifone operates on any broadband connection and home or office network including high-speed Internet connections via DSL or cable modem. The visifone is h.323 compliant and it is compatible with most corporate video conferencing systems. The visifone can be used by corporations and consumers.

Primary SIC and add'l.: 3661 3669

CIK No: 0000936130

Subsidiaries: RSI Systems, Ltd, Viseon PVT, Inc, VMN, LLC

Officers: John C. Harris/CEO, Pres., Brian R. Day/CFO

Financial Data: Fiscal Year End:06/30 Latest Annual Data: 06/30/2006

Year	Sales	Net Income
2006	$7,000	-$6,633,000
2005	$240,000	-$7,943,000
2004	$286,000	-$3,628,000

Curr. Assets:	$1,975,000	Curr. Liab.:	$1,065,000		
Plant, Equip.:	$123,000	Total Liab.:	$1,065,000	Indic. Yr. Divd.:	NA
Total Assets:	$2,098,000	Net Worth:	$1,033,000	Debt/ Equity:	NA

Vishay Intertechnology Inc

63 Lincoln Hwy, Malvern, PA, 19355; **PH:** 1-610-644-1300; **http://** www.vishay.com

General - Incorporation	DE	**Stock**- Price on:12/24/2007	$17.48
Employees	27,000	Stock Exchange	NYSE
Auditor	Ernst & Young LLP	Ticker Symbol	VSH
Stk Agt	American Stock Transfer & Trust Co.	Outstanding Shares	184,900,000
Counsel	NA	E.P.S.	$0.78
DUNS No.	00-232-7484	Shareholders	NA

Business: The groups principle activity is to manufacture discrete semiconductors and passive components. The groups products include attenuators, inductors, oscillators, transformers and transistors, RF. In the year 2007, the group acquired Power Control Systems business. The group operates from United States.

Primary SIC and add'l.: 3676 3679 3675

CIK No: 0000103730

Subsidiaries: AB Givareteknik, Alpha Electronics Corporation of America, Angstrohm Holdings Inc., Angstrohm Precision Inc., ATC Corp., BCcomponents BVBA, BCcomponents China Ltd, BCcomponents Estate NV, BCcomponents Hong Kong Ltd., BCcomponents Singapore Pte Ltd., BCcomponents South Europe SRL, BCcomponents Taiwan Limited, Billion Way Industrial Limited, Bradford Electronics, Inc., Components Dale de Mexico S.A. de C.V. 172 Subsidiaries included in the Index

Officers: Gerald Paul/Dir., CEO, Pres./$3,194,419.00, Felix Zandman/Chmn., Founder, CTO, Chief Business Development Officer/$4,180,600.00, Peter G. Henrici/Sr. VP - Investor Relations, Ziv Shoshani/Dir., COO/$524,016.00, Thomas C. Wertheimer/Dir. - Accounting Consultant, Ruta Zandman/Dir. - Public Relations Assoc., Richard N. Grubb/CFO, Exec. VP, Treasurer/$2,080,683.00, William M. Clancy/Sr. VP, Corp. Sec., Steven Klausner/VP, Assist. Treasurer, Andrew Post/Mgr. - Global Communications, Brenda R. Tate/Corporate Investor Relations

Directors: Gerald Paul/Dir., CEO, Pres., Felix Zandman/Chmn., Founder, CTO, Chief Business Development Officer, Marc Zandman/Dir., Zvi Grinfas/Dir., Eliyahu Hurvitz/Dir., Abraham Ludomirski/Dir., Ziv Shoshani/Dir., COO, Mark I. Solomon/Dir., Thomas C. Wertheimer/Dir. - Accounting Consultant, Ruta Zandman/Dir. - Public Relations Assoc., Wayne M. Rogers/Dir.

Owners: Richard N. Grubb, Abraham Ludomirski, Insiders, Insiders, Wayne M. Rogers, Marc Zandman, Ruta Zandman, Felix Zandman, Thomas C. Wertheimer, AXA Financial, Inc./7.10%, Eliyahu Hurvitz, Mark I. Solomon, Gerald Paul, FMR Corp./7.40%, Ziv Shoshani (19 Owners included in Index)

Financial Data: Fiscal Year End:12/31 Latest Annual Data: 12/31/2006

Year	Sales	Net Income
2006	$2,581,477,000	$139,736,000
2005	$2,297,484,000	$62,274,000
2004	$2,413,576,000	$44,696,000

Curr. Assets:	$1,727,247,000	Curr. Liab.:	$534,414,000	P/E Ratio:	22.41
Plant, Equip.:	$1,124,365,000	Total Liab.:	$1,611,083,000	Indic. Yr. Divd.:	NA
Total Assets:	$4,691,896,000	Net Worth:	$3,080,813,000	Debt/ Equity:	0.1933

Visicu Inc

217 E Redwood St., Ste. 1900, Baltimore, MD, 21202; **PH:** 1-410-276-1960; **http://** www.visicu.com

---

General - Incorporation	DE	**Stock**- Price on:12/24/2007	$9.67
Employees	104	Stock Exchange	NDQ
Auditor	Ernst& Young LLP	Ticker Symbol	EICU
Stk Agt	American Stock Transfer & Trust Co.	Outstanding Shares	32,670,000
Counsel	NA	E.P.S.	$0.22
DUNS No.	NA	Shareholders	NA

Business: The groups principle activity is to provide healthcare information technology and clinical solutions. The groups services include improved patient outcomes, reduced hospital costs, ecaremanager patient care and best practice tools and increased hospital revenue potential. Customer served by the group is multi hospital systems. Specific customers of the group include Sutter Health System, Sentara Healthcare and Advocate Health Care. The group operates from the United States. The group's quarterly revenue for September 2007 was 10.05 millions of USD.

Primary SIC and add'l.: 7372 7379 7389

CIK No: 0001166463

Officers: Frank T. Sample/Chmn., CEO, Brian Rosenfeld/Co - Founder, Exec. VP, Chief Medical Officer, Michael J. Breslow/Co - Founder, Exec. VP - Clinical Research - Development, Vincent E. Estrada/Sr. VP, CFO, Kathy Herold/VP - Human Resources, Gary Sindler/VP - Finance, Administration, Randy Holl/VP - Engineering, Martin Doerfler/VP - Clinical Operations, Nannette Spurrier/VP - Quality, Client Services, Robert Pepper/VP - Marketing, Connie D'Argenio/VP - Sales

Directors: Frank T. Sample/Chmn., CEO, Brian Rosenfeld/Co - Founder, Exec. VP, Chief Medical Officer, Michael J. Breslow/Co - Founder, Exec. VP - Clinical Research - Development, Stuart H. Altman/70/Dir., Michael G. Bronfein/Dir., John K. Clarke/54/Dir., Frances M. Keenan/53/Dir., James A. Oakey/Dir., Thomas G. McKinley/56/Dir., Ralph C. Sabin/56/Dir., Van R. Johnson/63/Dir.

Owners: Insiders, Partech U.S. Partners IV LLC, Stuart H. Altman, John K. Clarke, James A. Oakey, Pacific Venture Group, Thomas G. McKinley, Sterling Venture Partners, L.P., Brian A. Rosenfeld, Michael J. Breslow, HealthCor Management, L.P., Michael G. Bronfein, Vincent E. Estrada, Joseph Healey, Cardinal Health Partners, L.P. (19 Owners included in Index)

Financial Data: Fiscal Year End:12/31 Latest Annual Data: 12/31/2006

Year	Sales	Net Income
2006	$30,245,000	$6,022,000
2005	$18,352,000	$10,067,000
2004	$5,514,000	-$4,127,000

Curr. Assets:	$141,301,000	Curr. Liab.:	$33,142,000	P/E Ratio:	38.68
Plant, Equip.:	$1,631,000	Total Liab.:	$52,684,000	Indic. Yr. Divd.:	NA
Total Assets:	$157,012,000	Net Worth:	$104,328,000	Debt/ Equity:	NA

Vision Bancshares Inc

2201 W 1st St., Gulf Shores, AL, 36542; **PH:** 1-251-967-4212; **http://** www.visionbanc.com

General - Incorporation	AL	**Stock**- Price on:12/24/2007	NA
Employees	174	Stock Exchange	NA
Auditor	Mauldin & Jenkins LLC	Ticker Symbol	NA
Stk Agt	NA	Outstanding Shares	NA
Counsel	NA	E.P.S.	NA
DUNS No.	NA	Shareholders	NA

Business: The group's principal activities are to provide general retail and commercial banking services to customers in baldwin county, Alabama. The services are provided through five branch offices in baldwin county, Alabama. The group operates under a state bank charter and provides full banking services.

Primary SIC and add'l.: 6035 6712

CIK No: 0001095861

Subsidiaries: Vision Bancshares Financial Group, Inc., Vision Bancshares Trust I, Vision Bank

Officers: Daniel J. Sizemore/Chmn., CEO, John W. Kozak/CFO

Directors: Daniel J. Sizemore/Chmn., CEO

Vision Global Solutions Inc

338 St-Antoine E, Montreal, QC, H2Y 1A3; **PH:** 1-514-848-1166; **Fax:** 1-514-848-0895; **http://** www.visionca.com

General - Incorporation	NV	**Stock**- Price on:12/24/2007	$0.024
Employees	NA	Stock Exchange	OTC
Auditor	Jewett, Schwartz, & Assoc.	Ticker Symbol	VIGS
Stk Agt	Mellon Trust Co	Outstanding Shares	NA
Counsel	NA	E.P.S.	$0.00
DUNS No.	NA	Shareholders	NA

Business: The group's principle activities include developing and marketing accounting and management software that allows companies to apply activitry based management, a common sense systematic method of planing, controlling and improving labor and overhead expenses, to their businesses-management models. The group operates from United States.

Primary SIC and add'l.: 7372

CIK No: 0001135657

Officers: John Kinney/49/Chmn., CEO, Pres., Chief Accounting Officer

Directors: John Kinney/49/Chmn., CEO, Pres., Chief Accounting Officer

Owners: Jean-Paul Ouellette, Insiders/64.30%

Financial Data: Fiscal Year End:03/31 Latest Annual Data: 03/31/2007

Year	Sales	Net Income
2007	NA	$973,000
2006	$1,309,000	-$407,000
2005	$1,775,000	-$3,622,000

Curr. Assets:	$295,000	Curr. Liab.:	$1,073,000		
Plant, Equip.:	$27,000	Total Liab.:	$1,125,000	Indic. Yr. Divd.:	NA
Total Assets:	$323,000	Net Worth:	-$1,252,000	Debt/ Equity:	NA

Vision-Sciences Inc

9 Strathmore Rd., Natick, MA, 01760; **PH:** 1-508-650-9971; **Fax:** 1-508-650-9976; **http://** www.visionsciences.com; **Email:** info@visionsciences.com

General - Incorporation	DE
Employees	89
Auditor	BDO Seidman LLP
Stk Agt	American Stock Transfer & Trust Co.
Counsel	Proskauer Rose LLP
DUNS No.	78-002-4725

Stock - Price on:12/24/2007	$1.48
Stock Exchange	NDQ
Ticker Symbol	VSCI
Outstanding Shares	35,170,000
E.P.S.	$0.55
Shareholders	NA

Business: The group's principal activity is to design, develop, manufacture and market products for endoscopy. The group operates in the medical and industrial segments. The medical segment designs, manufactures and sells ent endosheaths and endoscopes. The endosheath products are primarily manufactured for nasopharyngo-laryngoscopes, sigmoidoscopes and bronchoscopes. The industrial segment manufactures and markets flexible borescopes. These are used for inspection and quality-control functions in industrial applications such as the inspection of aircraft engines and nuclear power plants. The customers of the group include ent doctors, gastroenterologists, colon and rectal surgeons, pulmonologists and primary care physicians in hospitals, medical clinics and physicians' offices.

Primary SIC and add'l.: 3827 3845

CIK No: 0000894237

Officers: Ron Hadani/CEO, Pres., Jitendra Patel/52/VP - Sales, Marketing, Industrial Segment, Mark S. Landman/52/VP - Operations, Medical Segment, Yoav M. Cohen/CFO, VP and Corporate Sec., Carlos Babini/Exec. VP, Chief Sales, Marketing Officer, David Hanuka/VP - Research, Development

Directors: Lewis C. Pell/62/Chmn., Katsumi Oneda/67/Dir., Warren L. Bielke/Dir., John J. Wallace/Dir., David W. Anderson/Dir., Kenneth W. Anstey/62/Dir.

Owners: Katsumi Oneda/20.90%, Kenneth W. Anstey, Mark S. Landman, Insiders/47.00%, David W. Anderson, James A. Tracy, John J. Wallace, Jitendra Patel, Ron Hadani/4.30%, Lewis C. Pell/20.60%, Warren Bielke

Financial Data: Fiscal Year End:03/31   Latest Annual Data: 03/31/2007

Year	Sales	Net Income
2007	$9,487,000	$20,112,000
2006	$11,150,000	-$4,036,000
2005	$10,326,000	-$2,505,000

Curr. Assets:	$10,351,000	Curr. Liab.:	$2,009,000		
Plant, Equip.:	$1,092,000	Total Liab.:	$2,013,000	Indic. Yr. Divd.:	NA
Total Assets:	$11,511,000	Net Worth:	$9,498,000	Debt/ Equity:	NA

VisionGateway Inc

12707 High Bluff Dr., Ste. 200, San Diego, CA, 92130; *PH:* 1-858-794-1416; *Fax:* 1-858-794-1450; *http://* www.visiongateway.net; *Email:* info@visiongateway.net

General - Incorporation	NV
Employees	8
Auditor	Gruber & Co., LLC
Stk Agt	Atlas Stock Transfer Corp
Counsel	NA
DUNS No.	NA

Stock - Price on:12/24/2007	$0.72
Stock Exchange	NA
Ticker Symbol	NA
Outstanding Shares	43,130,000
E.P.S.	NA
Shareholders	NA

Business: The groups principal activities include designing to be embedded onto cable modems and wireless routers. The group operates from the United States.

Primary SIC and add'l.: 7371

CIK No: 0001112902

Subsidiaries: Software Innovisions Pty Ltd, visionGATEWAY Pty Ltd

Officers: Michael F. Emerson/Dir., CEO, VP, Sec., Martin G. Wotton/Dir., Pres., Executive Chmn.

Directors: Michael F. Emerson/Dir., CEO, VP, Sec., Martin G. Wotton/Dir., Pres., Executive Chmn., Andrew B. Wotton/Non Exec. Dir., Trevor Tappenden/Non Exec. Dir.

Owners: Aspen Capital Partners/45.60%, Trevor Tappenden, Andrew Brett Wotton/47.80%, Michael Emerson/4.40%, Insiders/52.30%

Visiphor Corp

725N. 15th St. NW, Ste. 805, Washington, DC, 20005; *PH:* 1-604-412-9892; *http://* www.visiphor.com; *Email:* info@visiphor.com

General - Incorporation	Canada
Employees	NA
Auditor	KPMG LLP
Stk Agt	Mellon Trust Co
Counsel	NA
DUNS No.	NA

Stock - Price on:12/24/2007	$0.067
Stock Exchange	OTC
Ticker Symbol	VISRF
Outstanding Shares	NA
E.P.S.	NA
Shareholders	NA

Business: The groups principle activities include developing and marketing robust software technologies and professional. Products of the group include a standards based data integration toolkit, known as the Briyante Integration. The group operates through two segments namely development and sale of software applications and solutions, and the provision of business integration consulting services. In November 2005, the group acquired Sunaptic Solutions Inc. The group operates from Canada. The group's quarterly revenue for Sep '07 was 1.12 millions of USD.

Primary SIC and add'l.: 7372

CIK No: 0001088393

Subsidiaries: Sunaptic Solutions Incorporated, Sunaptic Solutions International, Inc., Visiphor (U.S.) Corporation

Officers: Roy Trivett/Dir., CEO, Pres., Al Kassam/Dir., VP - Support Services, VP - Sales - Marketing, Sunil Amin/CFO, Steve Hart/Dir. - Engineering, Bob Long/VP - Sales, Marketing

Directors: Roy Trivett/Dir., CEO, Pres., Oliver Revell/Chmn., Al Kassam/Dir., VP - Support Services, VP - Sales - Marketing, Clyde Farnsworth/Dir., Keith Kretschmer/Dir., Michael C. Volker/Dir., Wanda Dorosz/Dir.

Owners: Wanda Dorosz, Roy Davidson Trivett/10.50%, Al Kassam/1.67%, Oliver Revell/3.24%, Clyde Farnsworth/1.34%, Sunil Amin, Keith Kretschmer/3.15%, Michael C. Volker, Insiders/20.37%, Fidelity Canadian Growth Fund/6.64%, Norman Inkster

Financial Data: Fiscal Year End:12/31   Latest Annual Data: 12/31/2006

Year	Sales	Net Income
2006	$5,478,000	-$5,731,000
2005	$2,857,000	-$5,690,000
2004	$858,000	-$4,561,000

Curr. Assets:	$1,101,000	Curr. Liab.:	$2,738,000		
Plant, Equip.:	$356,000	Total Liab.:	$3,874,000	Indic. Yr. Divd.:	NA
Total Assets:	$3,363,000	Net Worth:	-$511,000	Debt/ Equity:	NA

Viskase Companies Inc

8205 S Cass Ave., Ste. 115, Darien, IL, 60561; *PH:* 1-630-874-0700; *http://* www.viskase.com; *Email:* info@viskase.com

General - Incorporation	DE
Employees	1,582
Auditor	Grant Thornton LLP
Stk Agt	Wells Fargo Shareholder Services
Counsel	NA
DUNS No.	05-385-5177

Stock - Price on:12/24/2007	$1.2
Stock Exchange	OTC
Ticker Symbol	VKSC
Outstanding Shares	29,460,000
E.P.S.	$0.03
Shareholders	NA

Business: The group's principal activities are manufacturing of food packaging products like cellulosic casings, heat shrinkable plastic bags and specialty films used in packaging of processed meat and meat products. Cellulosic casings are used in the production of processed meat and poultry products such as hot dogs, salami and other products. Products include nojax cellulosic casings for small diameter processed meat products and precision and zephyr for large diameter casings. The group's principal competitors in cellulosic casings are devro plc located in Scotland. The products are marketed through its own subsidiaries in France, Germany, Italy, Poland, Brazil and Canada. The group has four international manufacturing units in beauvais and thaon, France; guarulhos, Brazil and caronno, Italy.

Primary SIC and add'l.: 3089 3081 2671

CIK No: 0000033073

Subsidiaries: Viskase Brasil Embalagens Ltda., Viskase Canada Inc., Viskase del Norte, S.A. de C.V., Viskase Europe Limited, Viskase Films, Inc., Viskase GMBH, Viskase Holdings Limited, Viskase International Limited, Viskase Limited, Viskase Polska SP.ZO.O, Viskase S.A.S., Viskase S.p.A., WSC Corp.

Officers: Robert L. Weisman/59/CEO, Pres., Volker Steinkamp/Contact - Sales, Germany, Anna Szymanska/Contact - Sales, Europe, Anne Salles/Contact - Sales, France, Laura Ciapparelli/Contact - Sales, Italy, Newton Martins/Contact - Sales, South America, Tom Danko/Contact - Sales, North America, Mike Duvall/Contact - Sales, North America, Gonzalo Valdez/Contact - Sales, Central America, Mark Woessner/Contact - Sales, Asia Pacific, Charles J. Pullin/VP, CFO, Sec., Treasurer, Henry Palacci/VP, COO, Maurice J. Ryan/VP - Sales, North America, John O. Cunningham/VP - Human Resources, Jean-Luc Tillon/Pres. - Viskase SAS *(16 Officers included in Index)*

Directors: Peter K. Shea/57/Dir., Sunghwan Cho/34/Dir., Mayuran Sriskandarajah/28/Dir.

Owners: Insiders/1.70%, Robert L. Weisman/1.10%, Grace Brothers Ltd./6.50%, Carl C. Icahn/67.00%, Henry Palacci, Gordon S. Donovan, Maurice J. Ryan, Bernard Lemoine, Northeast Investors Trust/7.10%

Financial Data: Fiscal Year End:12/31   Latest Annual Data: 12/31/2006

Year	Sales	Net Income
2006	$210,391,000	$1,609,000
2005	$203,769,000	-$2,157,000
2004	$207,106,000	$25,317,000

Curr. Assets:	$99,539,000	Curr. Liab.:	$46,178,000	P/E Ratio:	40.00
Plant, Equip.:	$97,939,000	Total Liab.:	$199,573,000	Indic. Yr. Divd.:	NA
Total Assets:	$203,755,000	Net Worth:	$4,182,000	Debt/ Equity:	NA

Vista Continental Corp

6600 W Charleston Blvd, Ste 118, Las Vegas, NV, 89146; *PH:* 1-702-228-2077; *http://* www.vistacontinental.com

General - Incorporation	NV
Employees	NA
Auditor	Franklin Griffith & Assoc.
Stk Agt	Signature Stock Transfer, Inc.
Counsel	NA
DUNS No.	NA

Stock - Price on:12/24/2007	$0.01
Stock Exchange	OTC
Ticker Symbol	VICC
Outstanding Shares	NA
E.P.S.	NA
Shareholders	NA

Business: The group's principal activities are exploration of gold, zirconium and rare earth. The group's principal asset being ownership of 19 mining concessions in Peru. The group changed its fiscal year from Dec 31 to Sept 30, effective in 2002. The group is in development stage.

Primary SIC and add'l.: 7389

CIK No: 0000018886

Subsidiaries: Miranda Mining I (Guyana), Inc, Quillabamba Mining, S.A.C, VCC Nevada

Financial Data: Fiscal Year End:09/30   Latest Annual Data: 9/30/2004

Year	Sales	Net Income
2004	NA	-$1,108,000
2003	NA	-$2,602,000
2002	NA	-$13,458,000

Curr. Assets:	$24,000	Curr. Liab.:	$1,030,000		
Plant, Equip.:	$206,000	Total Liab.:	$6,316,000	Indic. Yr. Divd.:	NA
Total Assets:	$1,820,000	Net Worth:	-$4,497,000	Debt/ Equity:	NA

Vista Gold Corp

7961 Shaffer Pkwy, Ste 5, Littletown, CO, 80127; *PH:* 1-720-981-1185; *http://* www.vistagold.com

General - Incorporation	YT
Employees	10
Auditor	PricewaterhouseCoopers LLP
Stk Agt	PricewaterhouseCoopers LLP
Counsel	Ladner Downs
DUNS No.	20-864-4534

Stock - Price on:12/24/2007	$4.5506
Stock Exchange	AMEX
Ticker Symbol	VGZ
Outstanding Shares	32,030,000
E.P.S.	-$0.2
Shareholders	NA

Business: The group's principal activities are to explore, acquire and develop mineral properties in north and South America. The group's principal product is gold bullion, which is a commodity produced primarily in South Africa, the United States, Canada, Australia and Latin America. Vista gold owns a 25% equity interest in zamora, a Canadian mineral exploration company with interest in mineral concessions in southern Ecuador.

Primary SIC and add'l.: 1041 1044

CIK No: 0000783324

Subsidiaries: Compania Exploradora Vistex S.A.(5), Compania Inversora Vista S.A.(4), Granges Inc.(1), Hycroft Lewis Mine, Inc.(3), Hycroft Resources & Development, Inc.(2), Idaho Gold Resources LLC(2), Minera Nueva Vista S.A.(5), Minera Paredones Amarillos S.A. de C.V.(1), PT Masmindo Dwi(8), Salu Siwa Pty. Ltd.(7), Victory Exploration Inc., Victory Gold Inc., Vista Australia Pty. Ltd.(9), Vista Gold (Antigua) Corp.(1), Vista Gold (Barbados) Corp.(1) 19 Subsidiaries included in the Index

Officers: Michael B. Richings/Dir., CEO, Pres./$246,071.00, Howard M. Harlan/VP - Business Development/$143,708.00, Gregory G. Marlier/CFO/$173,417.00, Robert V. Perry/VP - Exploration, Fredrick H. Earnest/Sr. VP - Project Development/$308,386.00

Directors: Michael B. Richings/Dir., CEO, Pres., Durand W. Eppler/Dir., Robert A. Quartermain/Dir., John M. Clark/Dir., Thomas C. Ogryzlo/Dir.

Owners: HOWARD M. HARLAN, DURAND W. EPPLER, ROBERT A. QUARTERMAIN, FREDERICK H. EARNEST, JOHN M. CLARK, Insiders/0.02%, MICHAEL B. RICHINGS, GREGORY G. MARLIER, THOMAS C. OGRYZLO

Financial Data: Fiscal Year End:12/31 Latest Annual Data: 12/31/2006

Year	Sales	Net Income
2006	NA	-$4,171,000
2005	NA	-$4,584,000
2004	NA	-$4,924,000

Curr. Assets:	$50,643,000	Curr. Liab.:	$893,000		
Plant, Equip.:	$32,879,000	Total Liab.:	$5,604,000	Indic. Yr. Divd.:	NA
Total Assets:	$92,731,000	Net Worth:	$87,127,000	Debt/ Equity:	0.0002

VistaCare Inc

4800 N Scottsdale Rd., Ste. 5000, Scottsdale, AZ, 85251; *PH:* 1-480-648-4545; *http://* www.vistacare.com

General - Incorporation	DE	Stock- Price on:12/24/2007	$10.49
Employees	2,319	Stock Exchange	NDQ
Auditor	Ernst & Young LLP	Ticker Symbol	VSTA
Stk Agt	Ernest & Young LLP	Outstanding Shares	16,770,000
Counsel	NA	E.P.S.	-$1
DUNS No.	NA	Shareholders	NA

Business: The group's principal activity is to provide medical care services. The group provides a full range of hospice services tailored to the individual needs of patients and their families. The services offered include pain and symptom management, emotional and spiritual support, radiation therapy, chemotherapy and infusion therapy, diagnostic testing. The other services include inpatient and respite care, physician visits, nursing care, personal care by home health aides, spiritual counseling, dietary counseling, physical, occupational and speech therapy, medical equipment and supplies and medications. The services are provided at the patient's home or other residence of choice. The group currently operates two inpatient facilities, a 12-bed, stand-alone facility in cincinnati, Ohio and a 8-bed hospital-based facility in albuquerque, New Mexico.

Primary SIC and add'l.: 8099 8082 8059

CIK No: 0000787030

Subsidiaries: Odyssey Healthcare Inc, SouthernCare Hospice, Inc.

Officers: Richard R. Slager/Chmn., CEO, Pres., Carol MacLean/Executive Dir. - Phoenix, AZ, John Crisci/Chief People Officer, Roseanne Berry/Chief Compliance Officer, Kris Jamsa/Exec. VP - Education, Technology, Monica Braver/Admissions Coordinator, Athens, GA, Linda Gaetani/Executive Dir. - Denver, CO, Kerry Wilson/Executive Dir. - Terre Haute, IN, Danielle Krause/Admissions Coordinator, Tucson, AZ, Jennifer Hale/Executive Dir. - Athens, GA, Helen Powell/Executive Dir. - Columbus, GA, Tamika Nicholson/Admissions Coordinator, Columbus, GA, Sheila Williams/Executive Dir. - Douglasville, GA, Dianna Vermeulen/Executive Dir. - Macon, GA, Philip Tisdale/Executive Dir. - Newnan, GA *(105 Officers included in Index)*

Directors: Richard R. Slager/Chmn., CEO, Pres., Jack A. Henry/Dir., Geneva B. Johnson/Dir., Jon Donnell/Dir., James C. Crews/Dir., Gary Logsdon/Exec. Dir. - Clovis, NM, Brian Tyler/Dir., Perry G. Fine/Dir., Pete A. Klisares/Dir.

Owners: John Crisci, Philip Timon/19.40%, David W. Elliot, Stephen Lewis, Jack A. Henry, Jon M. Donnell, Pete A. Klisares, Perry Corp./12.80%, Todd R. Cot, FMR Corp./7.60%, The Bank of New York Company, Inc./5.00%, Ronald F. Watson, Insiders/7.80%, Perry G. Fine, ICM Asset Management, Inc./10.10% *(21 Owners included in Index)*

Financial Data: Fiscal Year End:09/30 Latest Annual Data: 9/30/2006

Year	Sales	Net Income
2006	$235,993,000	-$11,651,000
2005	$225,432,000	-$2,257,000
2004	$150,436,000	-$4,232,000

Curr. Assets:	$84,021,000	Curr. Liab.:	$40,556,000		
Plant, Equip.:	$6,409,000	Total Liab.:	$41,700,000	Indic. Yr. Divd.:	NA
Total Assets:	$119,792,000	Net Worth:	$78,092,000	Debt/ Equity:	NA

VistaPrint Ltd

100 Hayden Ave., Lexington, MA, 02421; *PH:* 1-781-890-8434; *Fax:* 1-781-676-0601; *http://* www.vistaprint.com

General - Incorporation	Bermuda	Stock- Price on:12/24/2007	$37.99
Employees	695	Stock Exchange	NDQ
Auditor	Ernst& Young LLP	Ticker Symbol	VPRT
Stk Agt	Computershare Trust Co	Outstanding Shares	43,140,000
Counsel	NA	E.P.S.	$0.58
DUNS No.	NA	Shareholders	NA

Business: The groups principle activity is to supply graphic design services and printed products. The products of the group include business cards, newsletters, note cards, magnets, rubber stamps and brochures. The group products sold under the trade name VistaPrint. The group operates from the United States and other. The group's total revenue in the year 2007 was 255.93 millions of USD.

Primary SIC and add'l.: 2759 4812 4899

CIK No: 0001262976

Subsidiaries: VistaPrint B.V., VistaPrint North American Services Corp.

Officers: Robert Keane/Chmn., CEO, Pres./$1,309,561.00, Wendy Cebula/COO, Exec. VP/$720,675.00, Anne Drapeau/Exec. VP, Chief People Officer/$910,812.00, Harpreet Grewal/CFO, Exec. VP/$1,317,931.00, Janet Holian/Exec. VP, Chief Marketing Officer/$797,854.00, Manya Chait/Public Relations Contact/$233,750.00, John Pellegrino/Public Relations Contact, Angela White/Investor Relations

Directors: Robert Keane/Chmn., CEO, Pres., Louis Page/Dir., George Overholser/Dir., Richard Riley/Dir., Daniel Ciporin/Dir., John Gavin/Dir.

Owners: Richard Riley, John J. Gavin, Wendy Cebula, Insiders/9.00%, Entities affiliated with AXA Financial, Inc./7.90%, Robert S. Keane/7.20%, Entities affiliated with Janus Capital Management LLC/10.00%, Daniel Ciporin, Janet Holian, Harpreet Grewal, George Overholser, Entities affiliated with FMR Corp./9.70%, Anne Drapeau, Louis Page

Financial Data: Fiscal Year End:06/30 Latest Annual Data: 6/30/2006

Year	Sales	Net Income
2006	$152,149,000	$19,235,000
2005	$90,885,000	-$16,219,000
2004	$58,784,000	$3,440,000

Curr. Assets:	$114,563,000	Curr. Liab.:	$24,362,000	P/E Ratio:	65.50
Plant, Equip.:	$50,311,000	Total Liab.:	$47,408,000	Indic. Yr. Divd.:	NA
Total Assets:	$171,392,000	Net Worth:	$123,984,000	Debt/ Equity:	0.1385

Visteon Corp

One Village Ctr Dr., Van Buren Township, MI, 48111; *PH:* 1-877-367-6092; *http://* www.visteon.com

General - Incorporation	DE	Stock- Price on:12/24/2007	$8.08
Employees	45,000	Stock Exchange	NYSE
Auditor	PricewaterhouseCoopers LLP	Ticker Symbol	VC
Stk Agt	Bank of New York	Outstanding Shares	129,640,000
Counsel	NA	E.P.S.	-$2.85
DUNS No.	NA	Shareholders	NA

Business: The groups principle activity is to provide automotive systems, modules and components. The group operates through two segments namely automotive and glass operations. Customers served by the group include Ford, General Motors, Toyota, Daimlerchrysler, Honda, Volkswagen, and Renault. The group operates from United States.

Primary SIC and add'l.: 3714 3585 3211

CIK No: 0001111335

Subsidiaries: Aeropuerto Sistemas Automotrices S.de R.L de C.V., Altec Electronica Chihuahua, S.A. de C.V., and Commerce AS, Atlantic Automotive Components, LLC, Autovidrio S.A. de C.V., Brasil Holdings Ltda., Cadiz Electronica, S.A., Carplastic S.A. de C.V., Climate Systems India Limited, Climate Systems Mexicana, S.A. de C.V., Coclisa S.A. de C.V., Duck Yang Industry Co., Ltd., Grupo Visteon, S.de R.L. de C.V., Halla Climate Control (Dalian) Co., Ltd., Halla Climate Control (Portugal) Ar Condicionado, LDA 78 Subsidiaries included in the Index

Officers: Michael F. Johnston/Chmn., CEO, Heidi A. Sepanik/Dir., Sec., Donald J. Stebbins/COO, Pres., William G. Quigley/Sr. VP, Corporate Controller, Chief Accounting Officer, Joel Coque/55/VP - Interiors Product Group, Derek Fiebig/Dir. - Investor Relations, John Donofrio/Sr. VP, General Counsel/$2,043,448.00, Joy Greenway/47/VP - Climate Product Group, Steve Meszaros/44/VP - Electronics Product Group, John F. Kill/58/Sr. VP, Pres. - North America Customer Group, Global Advanced Product Development, James F. Palmer/58/CFO, Exec. VP/$4,672,692.00, Robert C. Pallash/56/Sr. VP, Pres. - Asia Customer Group, Jonathan K. Maples/50/VP - Global Purchasing, Visteon Services, Kimberley Crews Goode/VP - Corporate Communications, Dorothy L. Stephenson/Sr. VP - Human Resources *(19 Officers included in Index)*

Directors: Michael F. Johnston/Chmn., CEO, Heidi A. Sepanik/Dir., Sec., William H. Gray/Dir., Patricia L. Higgins/Dir., Karl J. Krapek/Dir., Charles L. Schaffer/Dir., Richard J. Taggart/Dir., Kenneth B. Woodrow/Dir., James D. Thornton/Dir.

Owners: Schneider Capital Management Corporation/5.53%, Donald J. Stebbins, FMR Corp./5.47%, James F. Palmer, William H. Gray, Heinz Pfannschmidt, Donald Smith & Co., Inc./9.94%, Brandes Investment Partners, L.P./8.10%, Robert H. Marcin, Kenneth B. Woodrow, Pardus Capital Management L.P./17.40%, John Donofrio, Michael F. Johnston/1.10%, James D. Thornton, Insiders/2.50%

Financial Data: Fiscal Year End:12/31 Latest Annual Data: 12/31/2006

Year	Sales	Net Income
2006	$11,418,000,000	-$163,000,000
2005	$16,976,000,000	-$270,000,000
2004	$18,657,000,000	-$1,536,000,000

Curr. Assets:	$3,565,000,000	Curr. Liab.:	$2,568,000,000		
Plant, Equip.:	$3,034,000,000	Total Liab.:	$7,126,000,000	Indic. Yr. Divd.:	NA
Total Assets:	$6,938,000,000	Net Worth:	-$188,000,000	Debt/ Equity:	NA

Vistula Communications Services Inc

40 Portman Sq., 4Th Fl., London, W1H 6LT; *PH:* 212-317-8900; *http://* www.vistula.com; *Email:* info@vistula.com

General - Incorporation	DE	Stock- Price on:12/24/2007	$0.07
Employees	19	Stock Exchange	OTC
Auditor	PKF	Ticker Symbol	VSTLE
Stk Agt	Continental Stock Transfer & Trust Co	Outstanding Shares	66,960,000
Counsel	NA	E.P.S.	-$0.31
DUNS No.	NA	Shareholders	NA

Business: The group's primary activity is providing packaged services like IP telephony, wholesale voice, and cardlink services to the Telecommunications industry . V-Cube, the company's IP telephony solution is a highly scalable VoIP engine that serves an unlimited number of clients. It is a software-only platform using open standards and modular architecture, and features real-time user and call control through an operator console with multi-tiered administrative access, inbuilt Multi-domain handling, IVR, Call Center and Video calling. The company also works in partnership with telecommunications companies worldwide to deliver voice traffic on simple trade terms and via direct correspondent relationships. The features include: Switched international minutes; Carrier-grade quality and quantity; VoIP interconnect and/or TDM interconnect and switching; Multiple Tier 1 and Tier 2 carrier interconnects; 24/7 customer services and network management; In-country intelligent network services (INS) including pre- and post-paid calling card platforms; Competitive pricing and flexible contract options. The company's Cardlink software system handles Electronic Top Up (ETU) for "pay-as-you-go" usage. The company' s products are sold throughout the world. The company was incorporated on 22/09/2003 under the laws of the State of Delaware under the name VCS, Inc. VCS changed its name to Vistula Communications Services, Inc. on 04/03/2004.

Primary SIC and add'l.: 4813

CIK No: 0001288518

Subsidiaries: Cardlink Services Limited, Vistula Limited, Vistula USA, Inc

Officers: Rupert Galliers-Pratt/Founder, Executive Chmn., CEO, Interim CFO, Adam Bishop/48/Pres. - Vistula Limited, Jared P. Taylor/34/CFO, Treasurer, Sec., Ian Cope/COO, Tim Clemensen/SrVP, Nicholas Topham/COO - Vistula LTD, Jeremy Strong/CTO - Vistula, LTD, Richard Parkes/CTO - Goodman Blue LTD, Eunice Oneill/Dir. - Operations

Directors: Rupert Galliers-Pratt/Founder, Executive Chmn., CEO, Interim CFO, Jack Early/53/Dir., Anthony M. Warrender/57/Dir., Marcus J. Payne/Non Exec. Dir., Luca Tenuta/Non Exec. Dir.

Owners: Little Wing, L.P./10.75%, Executive Management Services Limited/8.97%, Marcus J. Payne/1.06%, Ian Cope, Keith J. Markley/1.15%, NetYantra, Inc./21.73%, Rupert Galliers-Pratt/15.29%, Adam Bishop/2.05%, Insiders/19.20%, Jack Early, Anthony Warrender

Financial Data: Fiscal Year End:12/31   Latest Annual Data: 12/31/2006

Year	Sales	Net Income
2006	$1,092,000	-$19,530,000
2005	$840,000	-$12,182,000

Curr. Assets:	$777,000	Curr. Liab.:	$5,459,000		
Plant, Equip.:	$445,000	Total Liab.:	$11,290,000	Indic. Yr. Divd.:	NA
Total Assets:	$27,202,000	Net Worth:	$15,913,000	Debt/ Equity:	NA

Visual Bible International Inc

5100 Town Ctr Cir., Ste 330, Boca Raton, FL, 33486; PH: 1-416-216-8512;
http:// www.visualbible.com

General - Incorporation	ON	Stock - Price on:12/24/2007	$0.008
Employees	NA	Stock Exchange	OTC
Auditor	Samuel Klein & Co	Ticker Symbol	VBIB
Stk Agt	Olde Monmouth Stk Trnsfer Co. Inc.	Outstanding Shares	NA
Counsel	NA	E.P.S.	NA
DUNS No.	NA	Shareholders	NA

Business: The group's principal activity is to operate as a faith-based media company that has secured exclusive visual and digital rights to popular versions of the bible. The group uses all forms of media to inspire the lives of present and future generations by carrying god's word to everyone regardless of the religious affiliation, culture or geographic location. It has produced and released the word-for-word books of matthew and acts and is currently engaged in a production of a word-for-word film adaptation of the gospel of john. The group has license agreements to produce, distribute, market and sell, in visual format, the new international version of the bible, all intellectual property and proprietary information, accounts receivable, video, film and music inventory associated with the production of the gospel of matthew and the book of acts.

Primary SIC and add'l.: 7812 7822 7819

CIK No: 0001073876

Officers: Luc Perron/Contact Person

Financial Data: Fiscal Year End:12/31   Latest Annual Data: 12/31/2002

Year	Sales	Net Income
2002	$773,000	-$1,138,000
2001	$1,324,000	-$22,333,000
2000	$3,073,000	-$13,443,000

Curr. Assets:	$1,629,000	Curr. Liab.:	$5,988,000		
Plant, Equip.:	$2,019,000	Total Liab.:	$6,738,000	Indic. Yr. Divd.:	NA
Total Assets:	$3,948,000	Net Worth:	-$2,790,000	Debt/ Equity:	NA

Visual Networks Inc

2092 Gaither Rd. , Ste. 220-i, Rockville, MD, 20850; ; http:// www.visualnetworks.com

General - Incorporation	DE	Stock - Price on:12/24/2007	$8.25
Employees	1,594	Stock Exchange	NA
Auditor	Grant Thornton LLP	Ticker Symbol	NA
Stk Agt	EquiServe Trust Co N.A	Outstanding Shares	154,250,000
Counsel	Piper Marbury Rudnick & Wolfe LLP	E.P.S.	$0.69
DUNS No.	84-207-9865	Shareholders	NA

Business: The group's principal activity is to design, manufacture, market and support performance management systems for communications networks. The group manufactures and sells hardware devices that embody these software agents as well as perform other network infrastructure functions. The products include visual uptime, visual ip insight, visual Internet benchmark, visual trinity and ewatcher and celltracer. These products provide network performance measurement and analysis. The products are marketed to enterprises and service providers. The major customers of the group are at&t, bellsouth, earthlink, equant, prodigy, sbc, sprint, verizon and worldcom.

Primary SIC and add'l.: 7379 3577 7373 7372

CIK No: 0001000495

Subsidiaries: Avesta Technologies Canada, Inc., Avesta Technologies Pte. Ltd., Avesta Technologies, LLC, Inverse Network Technology, Net2Net, LLC, Visual Networks International Operations, Inc., Visual Networks Investments, Inc., Visual Networks Ltd., Visual Networks Operations, Inc., Visual Networks Technologies, Inc., Visual Networks Texas Operations, Inc., Visual Networks, Italia Srl

Officers: Steven Hindman/Sr. VP - North American Channel Sales, Wayne Fuller/Exec. VP - Operations, Robin Marks/Sr. VP - North American Channel Sales, Mark Skurla/Exec. VP - Worldwide Sales, Jeff Lime/Pres. - Visual Networks

Owners: Donald E. Clarke/1.30%, William H. Washecka, Edward H. Kennedy, FMR Corp./6.70%, Kopp Investment Advisors, LLC/11.50%, Wayne R. Fuller/1.50%, William J. Smith, Edward L. Glotzbach, Austin W. Marxe/33.70%, Insiders/11.20%, Mark Skurla, Lawrence S. Barker/4.10%, Peter J. Minihane/1.80%

Financial Data: Fiscal Year End:12/31   Latest Annual Data: 12/31/2006

Year	Sales	Net Income
2006	$395,261,000	$145,216,000
2005	$325,059,000	$312,345,000
2004	$266,719,000	-$22,997,000

Curr. Assets:	$769,195,000	Curr. Liab.:	$185,070,000	P/E Ratio:	11.96
Plant, Equip.:	$47,743,000	Total Liab.:	$333,650,000	Indic. Yr. Divd.:	NA
Total Assets:	$1,303,416,000	Net Worth:	$969,766,000	Debt/ Equity:	0.1069

Visual Sciences Inc

Formerly: WebSideStory Inc
10182 Telesis Ct. 6th Fl, Ste. 20 5, San Diego, CA, 92121; PH: 1-858-546-0040;
http:// www.websidestory.com

General - Incorporation	DE	Stock - Price on:12/24/2007	NA
Employees	214	Stock Exchange	NA
Auditor	PricewaterhouseCoopers LLP	Ticker Symbol	NA
Stk Agt	U.S. Stock Transfer Corp	Outstanding Shares	NA
Counsel	Brobeck, Phleger & Harrison	E.P.S.	NA
DUNS No.	NA	Shareholders	NA

Business: The groups principle activity is to provide subscription, hosting and support; license; professional services. The group operates from United States.

Primary SIC and add'l.: NA

CIK No: 0001091158

Subsidiaries: HitBox, Inc., Visual Sciences, LLC, WebSideStory Callcenter and Service B.V., WebSideStory Holding B.V., WebSideStory SAS, WebSideStory Search and Content Solutions, Inc., WebSideStory UK Limited

Officers: James W. MacIntyre/CEO/$698,237.00, Chris Reid/Sr. VP - Sales, David Rosenthal/Sr. VP - Development, Daniel Guilloux/Sr. VP - EMEA, Brian Sullivan/Sr. VP, GM - Search, Content Solutions, Aaron Bird/Sr. VP - Services, East, Ray Rauch/Sr. VP - Services, West, Robert Chatham/Sr. VP - Education, Sheryl Roland/Sr. VP - Administration, Claire Long/CFO/$507,243.00, Dru Greenhalgh/Sr. VP, General Counsel

Directors: William H. Harris/Chmn., Kurt R. Jaggers/Dir., Douglas S. Lindroth/Dir., Charles J. Fitzgerald/Dir., Jeffrey W. Lunsford/Dir., James S. Mahan/Dir., Anil Arora/Dir., James R. Glynn/Dir.

Curr. Assets:	$45,624,000	Curr. Liab.:	$50,984,000		
Plant, Equip.:	$6,562,000	Total Liab.:	$51,815,000	Indic. Yr. Divd.:	NA
Total Assets:	$137,568,000	Net Worth:	$85,753,000	Debt/ Equity:	0.0003

Visualant Inc

500 Union St., Ste. 406, Seattle, WA, 98101; PH: 1-206-903-1351; Fax: 1-206-903-1352;
http:// www.visualant.net; Email: info@visualant.net

General - Incorporation	NV	Stock - Price on:12/24/2007	$0.18
Employees	1	Stock Exchange	OTC
Auditor	Madsen & Associates, CPA's Inc.	Ticker Symbol	VSUL
Stk Agt	Nevada Agency & Trust Company	Outstanding Shares	16,650,000
Counsel	NA	E.P.S.	-$0.09
DUNS No.	NA	Shareholders	NA

Business: The groups principal activities include developing color technology providing 3D spectral based pattern file creation and matching. The group operates from the United States.

Primary SIC and add'l.: 3829

CIK No: 0001074828

Officers: Bradley E. Sparks/Dir., CEO, Pres.

Directors: Bradley E. Sparks/Dir., CEO, Pres., Ronald Erickson/Chmn., Masahiro Kawahata/Dir., Jon Pepper/Dir.

Owners: Ronald P. Erickson/3.60%, Insiders/7.40%, Masahiro Kawahata/1.27%, Ralph Brier/1.90%, Jerry Goldberg, William E. Gordon, Jon Pepper

Financial Data: Fiscal Year End:09/30   Latest Annual Data: 9/30/2006

Year	Sales	Net Income
2006	NA	-$1,032,000

Curr. Assets:	$7,000	Curr. Liab.:	$480,000		
Plant, Equip.:	NA	Total Liab.:	$480,000	Indic. Yr. Divd.:	NA
Total Assets:	$7,000	Net Worth:	-$473,000	Debt/ Equity:	NA

VisualMED Clinical Solutions Corp

1035 Laurier W, Ste. 200, Montreal, QC, H2V2L1; PH: 1-514-274-1115; Fax: 1-514-274-8364;
http:// www.visualmedsolutions.com; Email: info@visualmedsolutions.com

General - Incorporation	NV	Stock - Price on:12/24/2007	$0.6
Employees	NA	Stock Exchange	OTC
Auditor	Manning Elliott LLP	Ticker Symbol	VMCS
Stk Agt	Olde Monmouth Stk Trnsfer Co. Inc.	Outstanding Shares	NA
Counsel	NA	E.P.S.	NA
DUNS No.	NA	Shareholders	NA

Business: The groups principle activity is to sale of its suite of clinical software modules. The group operates from the United States, Canada and Europe. The group's quarterly revenue for Sep '07 was 0.06 millions of USD.

Primary SIC and add'l.: 7373

CIK No: 0001102942

Subsidiaries: VisualMed Clinical Systems Marketing Inc

Officers: Gerard Dab/60/Chmn., CEO, Sec., Arthur Gelston/59/Dir., Pres., Chief Science Officer, Barry Scharf/63/COO, VP - Client Services, Larry Kurlender/62/CFO, Treasurer, Principal Accounting Officer, Jayne H. Kirby/50/VP - Finance, Michel Maksud/50/VP - Technology

Directors: Gerard Dab/60/Chmn., CEO, Sec., Arthur Gelston/59/Dir., Pres., Chief Science Officer, Philippe Panzini/43/Dir., Louis J. Lombardo/64/Dir., Chris Marcolefas/41/Dir.

Owners: Barry Scharf, Jayne H. Kirby, Visual Healthcare Corp./32.00%, Michel Maksud, Larry Kurlender

Financial Data: Fiscal Year End:06/30   Latest Annual Data: 06/30/2007

Year	Sales	Net Income
2007	$356,000	-$14,693,000
2006	$309,000	-$7,079,000
2005	NA	-$6,301,000

Curr. Assets:	$323,000	Curr. Liab.:	$398,000		
Plant, Equip.:	$70,000	Total Liab.:	$401,000	Indic. Yr. Divd.:	NA
Total Assets:	$393,000	Net Worth:	-$8,000	Debt/ Equity:	NA

Vita Food Products Inc

2222 W Lake St., Chicago, IL, 60612; PH: 1-312-738-4500; http:// www.vitafoodproducts.com

General - Incorporation	NV	Stock - Price on:12/24/2007	$1.7
Employees	178	Stock Exchange	OTC
Auditor	BDO Seidman LLP	Ticker Symbol	VFPI
Stk Agt	American Stock Transfer & Trust Co.	Outstanding Shares	4,930,000
Counsel	Much Shelist Freed Denenberg Et Al	E.P.S.	-$0.456
DUNS No.	01-357-9164	Shareholders	NA

Business: The group's principal activity is to process and sell various complementary specialty food products. The group operates in two business segments: vita and vita speciality product. Vita processes and sells various herring and cured and smoked salmon products throughout the United States. Vita specialty foods combines the products of Virginia honey and halifax and manufactures and distributes honey, salad dressings, sauces, marinades, jams and jellies and gift baskets. The group's products are sold under the vita and Virginia brand name. Its customers are supermarkets, wholesale clubs and gourmet shops.

Primary SIC and add'l.: 2033 2099 2091

CIK No: 0001024342

Subsidiaries: Vita Specialty Foods, Inc

Officers: Clifford K. Bolen/50/Pres., Chief Executive Offficer/$254,319.00, Antony R. Nelson/CFO

Directors: Stephen D. Rubin/Chmn., Scott Levitt/53/Dir., Glenn Morris/56/Dir., Steven A. Rothstein/56/Dir., John C. Seramur/65/Dir., David S. Lipson/64/Dir., Edward P. Dolanski/Dir., Robert C. Douglas/Dir., Howard Bedford/Dir.

Owners: J.B.F. Enterprises/5.60%, Insiders/56.10%, Clark L. Feldman/9.30%, James Rubin/3.80%, Glenn Morris/4.30%, Howard Bedford/15.10%, Clifford K. Bolen/5.10%, Terry W. Hess, Scott Levitt, David Gorenstein/5.90%, Stephen D. Rubin/31.00%, John C. Seramur/9.50%, Steven A. Rothstein

Financial Data: *Fiscal Year End:*12/31 *Latest Annual Data:* 12/31/2006

Year	Sales	Net Income
2006	$50,954,000	-$2,391,000
2005	$46,856,000	-$889,000
2004	$48,756,000	-$2,717,000

Curr. Assets:	$15,491,000	**Curr. Liab.:**	$9,294,000		
Plant, Equip.:	$5,743,000	**Total Liab.:**	$23,667,000	**Indic. Yr. Divd.:**	NA
Total Assets:	$27,534,000	**Net Worth:**	$3,866,000	**Debt/ Equity:**	3.1103

Vital Images Inc

3300 Fernbrook Ln. N, No. 200, Plymouth, MN, 55447; *PH:* 1-952-487-9500; *http://* www.vitalimages.com

General - Incorporation	MN	**Stock**- Price on:12/24/2007	$26.44
Employees	283	Stock Exchange	NDQ
Auditor	PricewaterhouseCoopers LLP	Ticker Symbol	VTAL
Stk Agt	American Stock Transfer & Trust Co.	Outstanding Shares	17,070,000
Counsel	Winthrop & Weinstine	E.P.S	$0.31
DUNS No.	16-006-1651	Shareholders	NA

Business: The group's principal activity is to develop and market 3D medical imaging software for disease screening, clinical diagnosis and therapy planning. The group's software applies proprietary computer graphics and image processing technologies to a wide variety of data supplied by computed tomography (ct) scanners and magnetic resonance (mr) imaging devices. The products of the group are vitrea 2, vscore, ct brain perfusion, automated vessal measurements, ct colonography and dicom conformance. The products are marketed to healthcare providers and to manufacturers of diagnostic imaging systems in the United States and internationally through distribution channels. On 19-Feb-2004, the group acquired hinnovation, inc.

Primary SIC and add'l.: 7372 7379 7378

CIK No: 0000912888

Subsidiaries: HInnovation (Beijing) Science and Technology Inc., HInnovation Acquisition Inc.

Officers: Jay D. Miller/Dir., CEO, Pres./$806,943.00, Steven P. Canakes/Exec. VP - Global Sales/$428,817.00, Jeremy A. Abbs/VP - Quality, Customer Satisfaction, Stephen S. Andersen/VP - Europe, Michael H. Carrel/CFO, COO, Treasurer, Sec./$943,466.00, Philip I. Smith/Exec. VP - Corporate Development/$712,949.00, Susan A. Wood/Exec. VP - Marketing, Clinical Development/$752,106.00

Directors: Jay D. Miller/Dir., CEO, Pres., Douglas M. Pihl/Chmn., Michael W. Vannier/Dir., Sven A. Wehrwein/Dir., James B. Hickey/Dir., Greg J. Peet/Dir., Richard W. Perkins/Dir.

Owners: Gregory J. Peet, James B. Hickey, Steven P. Canakes, Richard W. Perkins, Jay D. Miller/2.03%, Susan A. Wood, Waddell & Reed Financial, Inc./7.80%, Philip I. Smith, Kairos Partners III Limited Partnership/6.76%, FMR Corp./7.33%, Douglas M. Pihl, Insiders/6.48%, Sven A. Wehrwein, Michael H. Carrel, Michael W. Vannier

Financial Data: *Fiscal Year End:*12/31 *Latest Annual Data:* 12/31/2006

Year	Sales	Net Income
2006	$70,512,000	$6,583,000
2005	$51,717,000	$5,801,000
2004	$36,122,000	$296,000

Curr. Assets:	$188,381,000	**Curr. Liab.:**	$26,179,000	**P/E Ratio:**	71.46
Plant, Equip.:	$9,242,000	**Total Liab.:**	$28,828,000	**Indic. Yr. Divd.:**	NA
Total Assets:	$219,730,000	**Net Worth:**	$190,902,000	**Debt/ Equity:**	NA

Vital Living Inc

1289 Clint Moore Rd. , Boca Raton, FL, 33487; *PH:* 1-602-952-9909; *Fax:* 1-602-952-6907; *http://* www.vitalliving.com

General - Incorporation	NV	**Stock**- Price on:12/24/2007	$0.01
Employees	3	Stock Exchange	OTC
Auditor	Epstein Weber & Conover, PLC	Ticker Symbol	VTLV
Stk Agt	Continental Stock Transfer & Trust Co	Outstanding Shares	164,560,000
Counsel	NA	E.P.S	-$0.009
DUNS No.	NA	Shareholders	NA

Business: The group's principal activity is to design, develop science-based nutritional supplements through mainstream physicians. The group is developing and testing nutritional supplements in collaboration with medical experts based on the scientific evidence. The group currently markets a line of impact (nutritional products that will have a positive impact on the general health and well being of a consumer) nutritional products, through a proprietary chain of distribution to the targeted market of consumers aged 40 and above. The group merged with vcm technology limited on 16-Aug-2001. In 2003, the group acquired christopher's herbs line, enhanced nutriceuticals and doctors for nutrition.

Primary SIC and add'l.: 5912

CIK No: 0001145700

Subsidiaries: Doctors For Nutrition, Inc., E-Nutraceuticals, Inc., MAF Bionutritionals, LLC, Natures System, Inc., Wellness Watchers Systems LLC, X-Fat, Inc.

Officers: Stuart A. Benson/Dir., CEO, Pres., Sec., Stephen S. Chen/Strategic Advisor, Gregg A. Linn/45/Dir., CFO, COO, Moharir/Strategic Advisor

Directors: Stuart A. Benson/Dir., CEO, Pres., Sec., Gregg A. Linn/45/Dir., CFO, COO, Michael Cardamone/Dir.

Owners: Michael Cardamone, Insiders/15.50%, Stuart A. Benson/15.30%

Financial Data: *Fiscal Year End:*12/31 *Latest Annual Data:* 12/31/2006

Year	Sales	Net Income
2006	$4,941,000	-$82,000
2005	$4,858,000	-$21,537,000
2004	$4,161,000	-$28,172,000

Curr. Assets:	$1,098,000	**Curr. Liab.:**	$1,399,000		
Plant, Equip.:	$17,000	**Total Liab.:**	$5,355,000	**Indic. Yr. Divd.:**	NA
Total Assets:	$5,551,000	**Net Worth:**	$196,000	**Debt/ Equity:**	NA

Vital Signs Inc

20 Campus Rd. , Totowa, NJ, 07512; *PH:* 1-973-790-1330; *http://* www.vital-signs.com; *Email:* investorrelations@vital-signs.com

General - Incorporation	NJ	**Stock**- Price on:12/24/2007	$58.13
Employees	1,163	Stock Exchange	NDQ
Auditor	Goldstein Golub Kessler LLP	Ticker Symbol	VITL
Stk Agt	American Stock Transfer & Trust Co.	Outstanding Shares	13,230,000
Counsel	Lowenstein Sandler PC	E.P.S	$2.41
DUNS No.	01-094-5178	Shareholders	NA

Business: The group's principal activity is to design, manufacture and market single-patient use products for the anesthesia, respiratory, critical care, sleep therapy and emergency markets. The anesthetic products include face masks, breathing circuits, infusable (disposable pressure infusor), paxpress, general anesthesia systems, temperature probes, vital view and many other products. The respiratory and critical care products include manual resuscitator, blood pressure cuffs, heated humidification systems, heat and moisture exchangers and other related products. On Oct 30, 2003, the group sold its vital pharma subsidiary to pro-clinical, inc. The group sells its products in the United States, Europe, Asia and other foreign markets.

Primary SIC and add'l.: 7389 5122 3841

CIK No: 0000865846

Subsidiaries: Actar Airforce, Inc., Breas Medical AB, Marquest Medical Products, Inc., Sleep Services of America, Inc., StelexThe Validation Group, Inc., Thomas Medical Products, Inc., Vital Path, Inc., Vital Pharma, Inc., Vital Signs California, Inc., Vital Signs Export, Inc., Vital Signs Limited, Vital Signs MN, Inc.

Officers: Terence D. Wall/Chmn., CEO, Pres., Benn Vennesland/VP - Manufacturing Operations, Douglas Wall/Investor Relations Officer, Anthony Martino/VP - Quality, Regulatory, Jay Sturm/General Counsel, VP - Human Resources, Barry Wicker/Dir., Exec. VP, COO, John R. Easom/Exec. VP - Global Business Development, Planning, Alex J. Chanin/CIO, Mark Jefferson/VP - Sales, Marketing, Alan Furler/VP - Research & Development, George A. Schapiro/Dir. - Consultant

Directors: Terence D. Wall/Chmn., CEO, Pres., George A. Schapiro/Dir. - Consultant, David H. MacCallum/Dir., Barry Wicker/Dir., Exec. VP, COO, Howard W. Donnelly/Dir., Richard L. Robbins/Dir.

Owners: Alex Chanin, J.P. Morgan Trust Company/9.70%, Richard L. Robbins, John Brown/11.90%, George A. Schapiro, Terry D. Wall/16.60%, Anthony P. Martino, David H. MacCallum, Howard W. Donnelly, Insiders/19.10%, William Craig, Barry C. Wicker/2.00%

Financial Data: *Fiscal Year End:*09/30 *Latest Annual Data:* 9/30/2006

Year	Sales	Net Income
2006	$204,058,000	$30,117,000
2005	$194,037,000	$26,389,000
2004	$183,991,000	$22,053,000

Curr. Assets:	$185,146,000	**Curr. Liab.:**	$15,355,000		
Plant, Equip.:	$33,129,000	**Total Liab.:**	$15,355,000	**Indic. Yr. Divd.:**	$0.400
Total Assets:	$305,854,000	**Net Worth:**	$285,813,000	**Debt/ Equity:**	NA

Vitavea Inc

349 - 6540 E Hastings St., Burnaby, BC, V5B 4Z5; *PH:* 1-360-483-8248; *http://* www.vitavea.de

General - Incorporation	NV	**Stock**- Price on:12/24/2007	NA
Employees	NA	Stock Exchange	OTC
Auditor	Manning Elliott LLP	Ticker Symbol	VVEA
Stk Agt	NA	Outstanding Shares	NA
Counsel	NA	E.P.S	NA
DUNS No.	NA	Shareholders	NA

Business: The groups principal activities include producing, marketing and selling openoffice computer software on CD ROM. The group produced CD-ROMs of openoffice software and marketed and sold the discs via the Internet, through website at www.gacompsi.com. The group operates from the United States.

Primary SIC and add'l.: 2834

CIK No: 0001324207

Officers: Roger Liere/38/Dir., CEO, Pres., Hans Buedding/68/Member - Supervisory Board - Vitavea AG, Ralf U. Victor/58/Member - Supervisory Board - Vitavea AG, Birka Marckhoff/41/Member - Supervisory Board - Vitavea AG, John Boschert/38/Dir., CFO, Treasurer, Sec.

Directors: Roger Liere/38/Dir., CEO, Pres., John Boschert/38/Dir., CFO, Treasurer, Sec.

Owners: WKB Beiligungsgesellschaft mbH/65.60%

Curr. Assets:	$34,000	**Curr. Liab.:**	$104,000		
Plant, Equip.:	NA	**Total Liab.:**	$104,000	**Indic. Yr. Divd.:**	NA
Total Assets:	$1,836,000	**Net Worth:**	$1,731,000	**Debt/ Equity:**	NA

Vitesse Semiconductor Corp

741 Calle Plano, Camarillo, CA, 93012; *PH:* 1-805-388-3700; *http://* www.vitesse.com; *Email:* invest@vitesse.com

General - Incorporation	DE	**Stock**- Price on:12/24/2007	$1.18
Employees	720	Stock Exchange	OTC
Auditor	KPMG LLP	Ticker Symbol	VTSS
Stk Agt	Computershare Investor Services LLC	Outstanding Shares	221,430,000
Counsel	Richard A. Boehmer, Esq.	E.P.S	-$0.57
DUNS No.	17-356-6738	Shareholders	NA

Business: The group's principal activities are to design, develop, manufacture and market high-performance integrated circuits and optical modules. The group's products are supplied to the systems manufacturers in the communications and storage industries. The products offered by the group include multiplexers, demultiplexers, framers, network processors, switch fabrics, clock and data generation, laser drivers and amplifiers. In fiscal 2003, the group acquired apt technologies inc and multi link technology corporation and in fiscal 2004, it acquired cicada semiconductor corporation.

Primary SIC and add'l.: 3674

CIK No: 0000880446

Subsidiaries: Multilink Technology Corporation Israel Ltd., Multilink Technology GmbH, Vitesse International Holdings, SRL, Vitesse International, Inc., Vitesse Manufacturing & Development Corporation, Vitesse Semiconductor Canada Corporation, Vitesse Semiconductor Corporation A/S, Vitesse Semiconductor GmbH & Co. KG, Vitesse Semiconductor Japan Corporation, Vitesse Semiconductor S.r.l., Vitesse Semiconductor Sales Corporation

Officers: Christopher Gardner/Dir., CEO, Paul Matranga/VP - Operations, Sabra Bennett/VP - Human Resources, Tony Conoscenti/VP, GM - Network Division, Tim Hornback/VP, GM - Storage Division, Paul Browne/VP, GM - Ethernet Division, Roy Carew/VP - Quality, Rich Yonker/CFO, Michael Green/VP, General Counsel, Corp. Sec., Richard A. Boehmer/Legal Counsel

Directors: Christopher Gardner/Dir., CEO, Edward Rogas/Chmn., Vincent Chan/Dir., Willow B. Shire/Dir., Steve P. Hanson/Dir.

Financial Data: ***Fiscal Year End:*** 09/30 ***Latest Annual Data:*** 9/30/2005

Year	Sales	Net Income
2005	$190,778,000	-$126,879,000
2004	$218,775,000	-$33,065,000
2003	$156,371,000	-$167,189,000

Curr. Assets:	$105,054,000	**Curr. Liab.:**	$51,102,000		
Plant, Equip.:	$58,074,000	**Total Liab.:**	$156,037,000	**Indic. Yr. Divd.:**	NA
Total Assets:	$411,336,000	**Net Worth:**	$254,527,000	**Debt/ Equity:**	NA

Vitran Corp Inc

185 The W Mall, Ste. 701, Toronto, ON, M9C 5L5; ***PH:*** 1-416-596-7664; ***Fax:*** 1-317-543-1228; ***http://*** www.vitran.com; ***Email:*** vtnc@jcir.com

General		***Stock***	
Incorporation	Canada	Price on:12/24/2007	$22.8
Employees	4,929	Stock Exchange	NDQ
Auditor	KPMG LLP	Ticker Symbol	VTNC
Stk Agt	Computershare Trust Co	Outstanding Shares	13,460,000
Counsel	O'melveny & Myers	E.P.S	$1.25
DUNS No.	24-708-9295	Shareholders	NA

Business: The group's principle activities are to provide freight services and distribution solutions to a wide variety of companies and industries. The group operates in three segments: less-than-truckload, logistics and truckload. Less-than-truckload services are provided throughout Canada and the United States utilizing its own infrastructure and exclusive partners. Logistics provides special distribution solutions that range from inventory consolidation to responsibility for the complete distribution function as well as highway and rail brokerage. Truckload services include premium same-day and next-day truckload services in the United States midwest. The group's quarterly revenue for Sepptembere 2007 was 171.93 millions of USD.

Primary SIC and add'l.: 3715 4731

CIK No: 0000946823

Subsidiaries: Vitran Express West Inc.

Officers: Richard E. Gaetz/Dir., CEO, Pres., Sean P. Washchuk/VP - Finance, CFO/$502,339.00, Anthony Trichilo/Pres. - Vitran Express Canada Inc, Dave Kimack/Pres. - Vitran Express Inc, Steve Cook/Pres. - Frontier Transport Inc, Mike Glodziak/Pres. Canadian - US Logistics, Mark Kosovec/Pres. - Pjax Inc

Directors: Richard E. Gaetz/Dir., CEO, Pres., Richard D. McGraw/Chmn., William S. Deluce/Dir., Georges L. Hebert/Dir., John R. Gossling/Dir., Anthony F. Griffiths/Dir.

Owners: Richard D. McGraw, T. Rowe Price Associates, Inc./8.00%, Richard E. Gaetz/2.00%, Wasatch Advisors/10.00%, Insiders/3.00%, Anthony F. Griffiths, Wellington Management/13.00%, Cramer Rosenthal McGlynn/7.00%

Financial Data: ***Fiscal Year End:*** 12/31 ***Latest Annual Data:*** 12/31/2006

Year	Sales	Net Income
2006	$514,059,000	$19,399,000
2005	$428,192,000	$17,938,000
2004	$374,595,000	$14,943,000

Curr. Assets:	$80,021,000	**Curr. Liab.:**	$84,915,000		
Plant, Equip.:	$145,129,000	**Total Liab.:**	$185,037,000	**Indic. Yr. Divd.:**	NA
Total Assets:	$358,334,000	**Net Worth:**	$173,297,000	**Debt/ Equity:**	0.5225

Vitria Technology Inc

945 Stewart Dr, Sunnyvale, CA, 94086; ***PH:*** 1-408-212-2700; ***http://*** www.vitria.com

General		***Stock***	
Incorporation	DE	Price on:12/24/2007	NA
Employees	247	Stock Exchange	NA
Auditor	BDO Seidman LLP	Ticker Symbol	NA
Stk Agt	EquiServe Trust Co N.A	Outstanding Shares	NA
Counsel	Cooley Godward LLP	E.P.S	NA
DUNS No.	NA	Shareholders	NA

Business: The group's principal activity is to develop and deliver software products and services. The products of the group are used to manage complex interactions between computer systems internally, as well as externally with business partners, suppliers and customers. The group's flagship product, businessware is a software platform designed to enable incompatible computer systems to exchange information automatically and in real time, without human intervention. The group also provides pre-built solutions for solving common recurring integration problems by managing collaborative processes within and across enterprises. The customers for the group's products include telecommunications, healthcare, manufacturing, energy, financial services and insurance industries.

Primary SIC and add'l.: 7372 7373 8733 7371

CIK No: 0001050808

Officers: Jomei Chang/CEO, Dale Skeen/Chmn., CTO, John Ounjian/Exec. VP - Healthcare Solutions, John Parillo/Sr. VP - Worldwide Sales, Elizabeth Xu/Sr. VP - Product Development, Bob Meindl/Sr. VP - Worldwide Sales, Mark Roth/VP - Corporate Marketing

Directors: Dale Skeen/Chmn., CTO

Owners: Chang Family Trust, Michael W. Taylor, Trustee/6.60%, Harry G. Van Wickle, John N. Ounjian, Alberto J. Ypez, Michael D. Perry, Elizabeth L. Xu, Dennis P. Wolf, Insiders/34.40%, Dale M. Skeen/31.10%, JoMei Chang/30.90%, Deephaven Capital Management LLC/15.60%, Eric S. Boduch, John N. Parillo, Allen Chin

Vitro

Ave. Ricardo Margin Zozaya 400, Col. Valle Del Campestre, San Pedro Garza Garca, Nuevo Len, 66265; ***PH:*** 52-83291200; ***http://*** www.vitro.com

General		***Stock***	
Incorporation	Mexico	Price on:12/24/2007	$7.85
Employees	NA	Stock Exchange	NYSE
Auditor	Deloitte Touche Tohmatsu	Ticker Symbol	VTO
Stk Agt	Bank of New York	Outstanding Shares	NA
Counsel	Francisco Romero R.	E.P.S	-$0.1
DUNS No.	81-076-8945	Shareholders	NA

Business: The group's principal activities are carried out through three segments: glass containers: manufactures and markets/distributes glasses for the following industries: beer, food, wine and licorice, pharmaceutical and cosmetic. It also manufactures and distributes sodium carbonate, sodium bicarbonate, calcic chloride and salt, fiberglass for laboratories, aluminum cans and packages, precision components as well as machinery and molds for the glass industry. Flat glass: manufactures, processes and distributes flat glass to the construction and automotive industries. Glassware: manufactures and markets/distributes glasswares, covers and other domestic decorative products, food containers and jars for coffee. It also manufactures plastic disposable thermo fold wares. Its products are exported to the United States, Canada, Europe and South America.

Primary SIC and add'l.: 3221 3295 3639 3211 3229

CIK No: 0000880582

Subsidiaries: Comercializadora Alcali, S.A. de C.V., Compania Vidriera, S.A. de C.V., Cristales Automotrices, S.A. de C.V., Distribuidora Nacional de Vidrio, S.A. de C.V., Empresas Comegua, S.A., Fabricacion de Maquinas, S.A. de C.V., Industria del Alcali, S.A. de C.V., Vidriera Guadalajara, S.A. de C.V., Vidriera Los Reyes, S.A. de C.V., Vidriera Mexico, S.A. de C.V., Vidriera Monterrey, S.A. de C.V., Vidriera Queretaro, S.A. de C.V., Vidriera Toluca, S.A. de C.V., Vidrio Lux, S.A., Vidrio Plano de Mexico, S.A. de C.V. 25 Subsidiaries included in the Index

Officers: Federico Sada Gonzalez/Dir., CEO, Pres. - Vitro, SA de CV, Adrian Sada Gonzalez/Chmn., Pres., David Gonzalez Morales/Glass Containers Pres., Leticia Vargas/Investor Relations Officer, Enrique Osorio Lopez/Exec. VP - Finance, Carlos Munoz Olea/Dir. - Private Investor, Adrian Sada Trevino/Pres., Eduardo Brittingham/Dir. - General Excecutive, Claudio Del Valle Cabello/VP - Administrative, Alejandro F. Sanchez Mujica/Exec. VP, General Counsel Sec., Hugo Lara/Mgr. - Sales, GM, Adrian Meouchi/Investor Relations Officer

Directors: Federico Sada Gonzalez/Dir., CEO, Pres. - Vitro, SA de CV, Adrian Sada Gonzalez/Chmn., Pres., Gustavo M. Munoz/Dir., Joaquin Vargas Guajardo/Dir., Jaime Serra Puche/Dir., Andres Yarte Cantu/Dir., Carlos Represas/Dir., Alejandro Garza Laguera/Dir., Ricardo Martin Bringas/Dir., Carlos Bremer Gutierrez/Dir., Julio Escamez Ferreiro/Dir., Manuel Guemez De La Vega/Dir., Tomas Gonzalez Sada/Dir.

Owners: Carlos Munoz Olea/1.14%, Federico Sada Gonzalez/6.78%, Adrian Sada Trevino/8.14%, Adrian Sada Gonzalez/6.98%

Financial Data: ***Fiscal Year End:*** 12/31 ***Latest Annual Data:*** 12/31/2006

Year	Sales	Net Income
2006	$2,294,758,000	-$6,589,000
2005	$2,271,000,000	$31,000,000
2004	$2,178,365,000	-$19,824,000

Curr. Assets:	$734,883,000	**Curr. Liab.:**	$413,053,000		
Plant, Equip.:	$1,338,454,000	**Total Liab.:**	$1,823,427,000	**Indic. Yr. Divd.:**	$0.100
Total Assets:	$2,334,198,000	**Net Worth:**	$510,771,000	**Debt/ Equity:**	NA

Vitro Diagnostics Inc

12635 E Montview Blvd, Ste 218, Aurora, CO, 80010; ***PH:*** 1-720-859-4120; ***http://*** www.vitrodiag.com

General		***Stock***	
Incorporation	NV	Price on:12/24/2007	$0.08
Employees	1	Stock Exchange	OTC
Auditor	Miller & Mccollom	Ticker Symbol	VODG
Stk Agt	Securities Transfer Corp	Outstanding Shares	12,450,000
Counsel	NA	E.P.S	-$0.04
DUNS No.	15-020-1085	Shareholders	NA

Business: The group's principal activity is the research and development of products and technologies for use in the manufacture of human therapeutic products to treat specific diseases. The products are envisioned to treat infertility, consisting of injectible purified urofollitropin. They include vitropin (TM) , vitropin-c (TM) and vitroject (TM). The group is also developing technologies and applications including treatment of alzheimer's disease, diabetes and other degenerative disorders.

Primary SIC and add'l.: 2836

CIK No: 0000793171

Owners: Erik Van Horn/0.03%, The James R. Musick Trust/0.12%, Lloyd Hansen/0.09%, Insiders/0.37%, James R. Musick/0.35%, Roger D. Hurst/0.09%

Financial Data: ***Fiscal Year End:*** 10/31 ***Latest Annual Data:*** 10/31/2006

Year	Sales	Net Income
2006	$2,000	-$536,000
2005	$18,000	-$425,000
2004	$1,000	-$187,000

Curr. Assets:	$5,000	**Curr. Liab.:**	$1,021,000		
Plant, Equip.:	$1,000	**Total Liab.:**	$1,040,000	**Indic. Yr. Divd.:**	NA
Total Assets:	$40,000	**Net Worth:**	-$1,001,000	**Debt/ Equity:**	NA

Vivendi

Formerly: Vivendi Universal

42 Ave. De Friedland, Paris, 75380; ; ***http://*** www.vivendiuniversal.com

General		***Stock***	
Incorporation	France	Price on:12/24/2007	NA
Employees	NA	Stock Exchange	NA
Auditor	Barbier Frinault & Autres	Ticker Symbol	NA
Stk Agt	NA	Outstanding Shares	NA
Counsel	Gotshal & Manges	E.P.S	NA
DUNS No.	NA	Shareholders	NA

Business: The group's principal activities are grouped into the following areas: communications: telecommunications, Internet, audiovisual activities, publishing and multimedia; construction and property. The company is also involved in themed entertainment in world famous theme parks such as universal studios hollywood and Florida.

Primary SIC and add'l.: 4952 7829 4841 7313 8999 4941 4833

CIK No: 0001127055

Subsidiaries: Blizzard Entertainment, Inc., Canal+ SA, CanalSatellite SA, Centenary Holding BV, Centenary Music Holdings Ltd., Cyfra+, Elektrim Telekomunikacja, Groupe Canal+ SA, Maroc Telecom SA, Mauritel, Media Overseas, MultiThmatiques, NBC Universal, Inc., Neuf Telecom SA, PolyGram Holding, Inc. 28 Subsidiaries included in the Index

Officers: Jean-Bernard Levy/52/Chmn. - Management Board, CEO, Abdeslam Ahizoune/Members - Management Board, Jean-Francois Dubos/62/Exec. VP, General Counsel, Sec. - The Supervisory - Management Boards, Bertrand Meheut/56/Members - Management Board, Jacques Espinasse/64/Member - Management Board, Regis Turrini/49/Exec. VP - Mergers, Acquisitions, Frank Esser/49/Members - Management Board, Doug Morris/69/Members - Management Board, Rene Penisson/66/Sr. Exec. VP - Human Resources, Robert De Metz/Sr. Exec. VP - Strategy, Development, Philippe Capron/CFO, Simon Gillham/52/Exec. VP - Communications

Directors: Jean-Bernard Levy/52/Chmn. - Management Board, CEO, Jean-Rene Fourtou/69/Chmn. - Supervisory Board, Henri Lachman/70/Vice Chmn. - Member - Supervisory Board, Jean-Francois Dubos/62/Exec. VP, General Counsel, Sec. - The Supervisory - Management Boards, Claude Bebear/73/Member - Supervisory Board, Gerard Bremond/71/Member - Supervisory Board, Fernando Falco Y Fernandez De Cordova/69/Member - Supervisory Board, Gabriel Hawawini/71/Member - Supervisory Board, Patrick Kron/55/Member - Supervisory Board, Andrzej Olechovski/Member - Supervisory Board, Pierre Rodocanachi/Member - Supervisory Board, Karel Van Miert/66/Member - Supervisory Board, Mehdi Dazi/42/Member - Supervisory Board, Sarah Frank/62/Member - Supervisory Board

Viventia Biotech Inc

5060 Spectrum Way, Ste. 405, Mississauga, ON, L4W 5N6; *PH:* 1-416-291277; *http://* www.viventia.com; *Email:* dloparco@viventia.com

General - Incorporation	ON	Stock - Price on:12/24/2007	NA
Employees	NA	Stock Exchange	NA
Auditor	Ernst & young LLP	Ticker Symbol	NA
Stk Agt	Computershare Trust Co	Outstanding Shares	NA
Counsel	NA	E.P.S.	NA
DUNS No.	NA	Shareholders	NA

Business: The group is engaged biopharmaceutical activities advancing a new generation of monoclonal antibody therapeutics designed to offer safer, more beneficial therapies for cancer patients. The company's Hybridomics, ImmunoMine, and UnLock platforms enable them to rapidly discover novel cancer drug targets and validate the potential of its monoclonal antibodies to deliver potent payloads directly to cancer cells. The group's fully integrated technology platform is based upon the isolation of human monoclonal antibodies from cancer patients and their subsequent development as Armed Antibodies, delivering cancer-killing payloads directly to cancer cells. The group's lead product candidate is Proxinium and several other product candidates are in pre-clinical development. Proxinium, a targeted therapeutic consisting of a proprietary antibody fragment conjugated with a cancer-killing payload. Proxinium targets a cell surface protein found on most head and neck cancers and has been designed to deliver a therapeutically potent anti-cancer payload directly to tumors, avoiding healthy, normal tissue. In February, 2005, the company announced that its lead drug candidate, Proxinium, has been granted orphan drug designation from the U.S. Food and Drug Administration (FDA) for the treatment of advanced, recurrent head and neck cancer. The Canadian group's corporate head office recently relocated to Mississauga, Ontario and the GMP Manufacturing, research development and operations campus is located in Winnipeg, Canada.

Primary SIC and add'l.: 8731

CIK No: 0001316606

Officers: Nick Glover/CEO, Pres., Michael Byrne/CFO, Glen MacDonald/Chief Scientific Officer, VP - Operations, Robyn Bramwell/Mgr. - Human Resources, Wendy Cuthbert/VP - Clinical Operations, Mark M. Kowalski/VP - Medical, Global Regulatory Affairs, Domenic Loparco/Contact

Vivid Learning Systems Inc

5728 Bedford St., Pasco, WA, 99301; *PH:* 1-509-545-1800; *Fax:* 1-509-542-8869; *http://* www.learnatvivid.com; *Email:* customersupport@learnatvivid.com

General - Incorporation	DE	Stock - Price on:12/24/2007	$0.3
Employees	28	Stock Exchange	OTC
Auditor	Williams & Webster, P.S.	Ticker Symbol	VVDL
Stk Agt	Continental Stock Transfer & Trust Co	Outstanding Shares	13,370,000
Counsel	NA	E.P.S.	NA
DUNS No.	NA	Shareholders	NA

Business: The groups principle activities include producing, marketing, and delivering web based compliance training programs designed to help companies meet mandated state and federal regulations. The group operates through two segments namely training subscriptions, and custom products and services. In the year 2007, the group acquired the Engineering & Technical Services business. The group operates from the United States.

Primary SIC and add'l.: 7371

CIK No: 0001290689

Subsidiaries: Vivid Learning Systems, Inc.

Officers: Sandra I. Muller/CEO, Matthew J. Hammer/42/COO, Conrad Suhadolnik/COO, Rabindra Nanda/Chief Marketing Officer, Robert Blodgett/CFO

Directors: Robert L. Ferguson/Chmn., Christopher L. Britton/59/Vice Chmn., William N. Lampson/Dir., Andrew A. Thoresen/Dir., Robert J. Turner/Dir., Diehl R. Rettig/Dir.

Owners: Christopher L. Britton, William N. Lampson, Robert M. Blodgett, Sandra Muller, Robert L. Ferguson, Andrew Thoresen, Insiders/1.20%, Matthew Hammer

Vivo Participacoes S.A.

Av. Roque Petroni Jr. no.1464, 6th Fl. Part, B Bldg., Sao Paulo, Rio de Janeiro, 4707000; *PH:* 55-04583110; *http://* www.vivo.com.br

General - Incorporation	Brazil	Stock - Price on:12/24/2007	$4.88
Employees	NA	Stock Exchange	NYSE
Auditor	Deloitte & Touche LLP	Ticker Symbol	VIV
Stk Agt	Banco ABNAMRO Real S.A.	Outstanding Shares	1,440,000,000
Counsel	NA	E.P.S.	$0.30
DUNS No.	NA	Shareholders	NA

Business: The groups principle activity is to provide cellular telecommunications services. The group operates through three segments namely, Telesp Celular, Global Telecom and TCO. The group operates from the Sao Paulo and Brazil. The groups quarterly revenue for September 2007 was 3,248.46 millions of BRL.

Primary SIC and add'l.: 4813

CIK No: 0001071337

Subsidiaries: Celular CRT S.A., Global Telecom S.A., Tele Centro Oeste Celular Participaes, Telebahia Celular S.A., Telergipe Celular, Telerj Celular S.A., Telesp Celular S.A., Telest Celular S.A.

Officers: Roberto Oliveira De Lima/CEO, Pres., Ernesto Gardelliano/Exec. VP - Finance, Planning, Control, Investor Relations Officer, Rui Manuel De Medeiros D'Espiney Patricio/Councilor, Shakhaf Wine/Councilor, Joao Pedro Amadeu Baptista/VP, Antonio Goncalves De Oliveira/Councilor, Felix Pablo Ivorra Cano/Councilor, Luiz Kaufmann/Councilor, Paulo Cesar Pereira Teixeira/Exec. VP - Operations, Javier Rodriguez Garcia/VP - Networks, Sergio Assenco Tavares Dos Santos/VP - Regulatory Matters, Eduardo Aspesi/Exec. VP - Marketing, Innovation

Directors: Luis Miguel Gilperez Lopez/Chmn., Henri Philippe Reichstul/Dir., Ignacio Aller Malo/Dir.

Owners: Insiders, Portelcom Partic. S.A./12.80%, Avista Partic. Ltda/1.80%, Tagilo Partic. Ltda/2.30%, Sudestecel Partic Ltda/0.10%, Tagilo Partic. Ltda/2.50%, TBS Celular Partic Ltda/13.10%, TBS Celular Partic Ltda/0.10%, Avista Partic. Ltda/5.10%, Sudestecel Partic Ltda/16.80%, Brasilcel/39.70%, Portelcom Partic. S.A., Brasilcel/42.50%

Financial Data: Fiscal Year End:12/31   Latest Annual Data: 12/31/2006

Year	Sales	Net Income
2006	$5,128,225,000	-$215,938,000
2005	$3,210,429,000	-$256,367,000
2004	$2,763,163,000	-$188,468,000

Curr. Assets:	$2,659,832,000	Curr. Liab.:	$2,672,710,000		
Plant, Equip.:	$3,026,854,000	Total Liab.:	$4,299,968,000	Indic. Yr. Divd.:	$0.010
Total Assets:	$8,579,241,000	Net Worth:	$4,279,273,000	Debt/ Equity:	NA

Vivo Participacoes SA

Formerly: Telesp Celular Participacoes
Av. Roque Petroni Jr., No.1464, 6th Fl. Part, B Bldg., Sao Paulo, SP, 04707-000;

General - Incorporation	Brazil	Stock - Price on:12/24/2007	NA
Employees	NA	Stock Exchange	NA
Auditor	Deloitte Touche Tohmatsu	Ticker Symbol	NA
Stk Agt	NA	Outstanding Shares	NA
Counsel	Machado, Meyer, Sendacz Et Al	E.P.S.	NA
DUNS No.	NA	Shareholders	NA

Business: The group's principal activity is the management and exploration of public, private and industrial telephone services. The group also provides data transmission services, leased lines, cellular mobile telephone services, telex transmission and other related activities.

Primary SIC and add'l.: 4899 3661 4812 4813 4822

CIK No: 0001071337

Subsidiaries: Celular CRT S.A, Global Telecom S.A., Tele Centro Oeste Celular Participaes, Telebahia Celular S.A., Telergipe Celular, Telerj Celular S.A., Telesp Celular S.A., Telest Celular S.A.

Owners: Sudestecel Partic Ltda/0.10%, TBS Celular Partic Ltda/13.10%, Portelcom Partic. S.A./12.80%, Avista Partic. Ltda/1.80%, TBS Celular Partic Ltda/0.10%, Avista Partic. Ltda/5.10%, Sudestecel Partic Ltda/16.80%, Insiders, Portelcom Partic. S.A., Brasilcel/42.50%, Brasilcel/39.70%, Tagilo Partic. Ltda/2.30%, Tagilo Partic. Ltda/2.50%, Insiders

VIVUS Inc

1172 Castro St., Mountain View, CA, 94040; *PH:* 1-650-934-5200; *http://* www.vivus.com; *Email:* ir@vivus.com

General - Incorporation	DE	Stock - Price on:12/24/2007	$5.01
Employees	114	Stock Exchange	NDQ
Auditor	Odenberg, Muranishi & Co. LLP	Ticker Symbol	VVUS
Stk Agt	Computershare Investor Services LLC	Outstanding Shares	58,360,000
Counsel	Wilson Sonsini Goodrich & Rosati	E.P.S.	-$0.24
DUNS No.	78-277-2263	Shareholders	NA

Business: The group's principal activity is to develop innovative products to improve quality of life disorders in men and women, with a focus on sexual dysfunction. The group develops and markets muse (medicated urethral system for erection) and actis, two innovations used for the treatment of men with erectile dysfunction (impotence). Currently, the group focuses on the development of the following products: alista, for the treatment of female sexual arousal disorder; ta-1790, for the treatment of male erectile dysfunction; and vi-0162 and vi-0134, for the treatment of premature ejaculation. The group markets and distributes its products in domestic and international markets.

Primary SIC and add'l.: 2834 2835

CIK No: 0000881524

Subsidiaries: Vivus Bv Limited, VIVUS International Limited, VIVUS Ireland Limited, VIVUS Real Estate LLC, Vivus Uk Limited

Officers: Leland F. Wilson/Dir., CEO, Pres./$1,136,397.00, Virgil A. Place/Founder, Dir., Chief Scientific Officer, Timothy E. Morris/VP - Finance, CFO/$536,161.00, John Dietrich/VP - Research, Development, Peter Y. Tam/Sr. VP - Product, Corporate Development/$539,865.00, Guy P. Marsh/VP - US Operations, GM/$412,582.00, Wesley W. Day/VP - Clinical Development/$490,206.00, Changjin Wang/VP - Business Development, Lee B. Perry/Principal Accounting Officer

Directors: Leland F. Wilson/Dir., CEO, Pres., Mark B. Logan/Chmn., Mario M. Rosati/Dir., Linda M. Dairiki Shortliffe/Dir., Graham Strachan/Dir., Virgil A. Place/Founder, Dir., Chief Scientific Officer

Owners: Chilton Investment Co LLC/7.70%, Virgil A. Place/1.30%, Caxton Associates LLC/7.30%, Mark B. Logan, Wesley W. Day, Insiders/6.60%, Graham Strachan, Linda M. Dairiki Shortliffe, Mario M. Rosati, Timothy E. Morris, Royce & Associates LLC/7.60%, Peter Y. Tam, OrbiMed Advisors LLC/7.50%, Guy P. Marsh, Leland F. Wilson/2.80%

Financial Data: Fiscal Year End:12/31   Latest Annual Data: 12/31/2006

Year	Sales	Net Income
2006	$17,245,000	-$21,624,000
2005	$14,654,000	-$24,484,000
2004	$19,601,000	-$21,583,000

Curr. Assets:	$68,965,000	Curr. Liab.:	$11,401,000		
Plant, Equip.:	$8,549,000	Total Liab.:	$25,074,000	Indic. Yr. Divd.:	NA
Total Assets:	$78,214,000	Net Worth:	$53,140,000	Debt/ Equity:	0.1056

VNUS Medical Technologies Inc

5799 Fontanoso Way, San Jose, CA, 95138; *PH:* 1-408-473-1100; *http://* www.vnus.com; *Email:* info@vnus.com

General - Incorporation............................ DE	Stock - Price on:12/24/2007 ....$14.08
Employees...232	Stock Exchange..NDQ
Auditor ....PricewaterhouseCoopers LLP	Ticker Symbol..VNUS
Stk Agt.....................U.S. Stock Transfer Corp	Outstanding Shares 15,200,000
Counsel.........................Latham & Watkins LLP	E.P.S..-$0.55
DUNS No. ....NA	Shareholders...NA

Business: The groups principle activity is to provide medical devices. The products of the group include Catheters and devices, RF Generators and other. The group products sold under the trade names VNUS(R), Closure(R) and VNUS Closure(R). The group operates from the United States, Europe and other. The group's quarterly revenue for September 2007 was 17.50 millions of USD.

Primary SIC and add'l.: 5047 3841 3845 3821 3842

CIK No: 0001040666

Subsidiaries: VNUS Medical Technologies GmbH, VNUS Medical Technologies UK Ltd.

Officers: Brian E. Farley/Dir., CEO, Pres./$742,687.00, Timothy A. Marcotte/51/CFO, VP - Finance, Administration/$424,587.00, Lian X. Cunningham/Medical Dir., VP - Clinical Research, Education, Charlene Friedman/50/VP, General Counsel, Sec./$458,701.00, Dennis Rosenberg/53/VP - Marketing, International Sales/$427,227.00, Mohan F. Sancheti/VP - Manufacturing, William A. Franklin/VP - Quality Assurance, Regulatory Affairs, Mark S. Saxton/VP - US Sales

Directors: Brian E. Farley/Dir., CEO, Pres., James W. Fitzsimmons/Chmn., Michael J. Coyle/Dir., Kathleen D. Laporte/Dir., Lori M. Robson/Dir., Gregory T. Schiffman/Dir., Edward W. Unkart/Dir.

Owners: Michael J. Coyle, James W. Fitzsimmons, Lori M. Robson, Entities affiliated with Credit Suisse First Boston/16.90%, Gregory T. Schiffman, Insiders/23.40%, Edward W. Unkart, Kathleen D. LaPorte/17.20%, Wasatch Advisors, Inc/10.10%, Charlene A. Friedman, Dennis Rosenberg, Scott H. Cramer, Entities affiliated with Banque Carnegie Luxembourg S.A./6.80%, Hambrecht& Quist Capital Management LLC/6.00%, Timothy A. Marcotte *(16 Owners included in Index)*

Financial Data: Fiscal Year End:12/31   Latest Annual Data: 12/31/2006

Year	Sales		Net Income
2006	$51,681,000		-$7,259,000
2005	$49,170,000		$5,350,000
2004	$38,166,000		$2,866,000
Curr. Assets:	$80,086,000	Curr. Liab.:	$9,227,000	P/E Ratio: 65.50
Plant, Equip.:	$4,651,000	Total Liab.:	$10,771,000	Indic. Yr. Divd.: NA
Total Assets:	$85,519,000	Net Worth:	$74,748,000	Debt/ Equity: NA

Vocalscape Networks Inc

170 E Post Rd., Ste. 206, White Plains, NY, 10601; *PH:* 1-914-448-7600; *http://* www.vocalscape.com; *Email:* sales@vocalscape.com

General - Incorporation............................NV	Stock - Price on:12/24/2007 ....$0.014
Employees ....NA	Stock Exchange..OTC
Auditor ....Salberg & Company, P.A.	Ticker Symbol..VOSC
Stk Agt............. Pacific Stock Transfer Company	Outstanding Shares 74,600,000
Counsel...NA	E.P.S...-$0.049
DUNS No. ....NA	Shareholders...NA

Business: The groups principle activities include communications provider that provides voice over Internet protocol solutions. The group operates from the United States.

Primary SIC and add'l.: 3714 7372

CIK No: 0001083721

Subsidiaries: Vocalscape Operating Subsidiary, Inc

Officers: Robert W. Koch/41/Chmn., CEO, Head - Business Development, Ron McIntyre/59/Dir., Pres., Sec., Chav Paskov/CTO, Michael Jung/Chief Architect, Anthony Caridi/VP, Robert Koch/Dir., Sr. Consultant

Directors: Robert W. Koch/41/Chmn., CEO, Head - Business Development, Ron McIntyre/59/Dir., Pres., Sec., David Otto/Dir., Lawrence Hartman/Dir., Robert Koch/Dir., Sr. Consultant

Owners: Insiders/47.49%, Insiders/100.00%, Lawrence Hartman/6.19%, Anthony Caridi/10.12%, Robert C. Koch/100.00%, Robert W. Koch/19.86%, Robert Koch/3.09%, Ron McIntyre/7.02%, David M. Otto/1.21%

Financial Data: Fiscal Year End:12/31   Latest Annual Data: 12/31/2006

Year	Sales		Net Income
2006	$209,000		-$7,684,000
2005	$122,000		-$1,890,000
2004	NA		-$2,680,000
Curr. Assets:	$15,000	Curr. Liab.:	$4,058,000	
Plant, Equip.:	$25,000	Total Liab.:	$4,071,000	Indic. Yr. Divd.: NA
Total Assets:	$42,000	Net Worth:	-$4,029,000	Debt/ Equity: NA

VocalTec Communications Ltd

60 Medinat Hayehudim St., Herzlia, Pituach, 46140; *PH:* 972-99703888; *Fax:* 972-99558175; *http://* www.vocaltec.com; *Email:* info@vocaltec.com

General - Incorporation..........................Israel	Stock - Price on:12/24/2007 ....$2.59
Employees 88	Stock Exchange..NDQ
Auditor ....Kost Forer Gabbay & Kasierer	Ticker Symbol..VOCL
Stk Agt......American Stock Transfer & Trust Co.	Outstanding Shares ....NA
Counsel................Meitar, Liquornik, Geva & Co	E.P.S..-$1.15
DUNS No. 51-452-2440	Shareholders...NA

Business: The groups principle activities include development, marketing and support of software which enables voice and audio communications over the Internet. The group operates from United States.

Primary SIC and add'l.: 7372

CIK No: 0001005699

Subsidiaries: Tdsoft BV, Tdsoft Communications Inc., Tdsoft Ltd, VocalTec Communications Deutschland GmbH, VocalTec Communications Hong-Kong Limited, VocalTec Communications, Inc.

Officers: Joseph Albagli/Dir., CEO, Pres., Rami Amit/CTO, Eli Gendler/CFO, Arye Shaham/Exec. VP - Research, Development, Edu Meytal/VP - Sales, Yair Golan/VP - Marketing, Business Development, Jeff Corbin/Investors Relations Officer, Lee Roth/Investors Relations Officer, Michal Adler/Human Resources Mgr.

Directors: Joseph Albagli/Dir., CEO, Pres., Ilan Rosen/Chmn., Michal Even-Chen/Dir., Joseph Atsmon/Dir., Yoseph Dauber/Dir., Robert M. Wadsworth/Dir., Lior Bregman/Dir.

Owners: Various entities affiliated with Excellence Nessuah/5.56%, Cisco Systems International BV/22.69%, The Israeli Aircraft Industries Workers' Provident Fund/5.56%, HarbourVest International Private Equity Partners III - Direct Fund L.P./16.32%, Various entities affiliated with LibertyView Capital ./13.01%, Provident Funds of the First International Bank of Israel Ltd./5.46%, Insiders/5.59%, Various entities affiliated with Apex/8.24%

Financial Data: Fiscal Year End:12/31   Latest Annual Data: 12/31/2006

Year	Sales		Net Income
2006	$7,280,000		-$7,012,000
2005	$4,593,000		-$6,630,000
2004	$5,452,000		-$13,094,000
Curr. Assets:	$12,516,000	Curr. Liab.:	$4,320,000	
Plant, Equip.:	$888,000	Total Liab.:	$6,049,000	Indic. Yr. Divd.: NA
Total Assets:	$24,587,000	Net Worth:	$18,538,000	Debt/ Equity: NA

Vocus Inc

4296 Forbes Blvd., Lanham, MD, 20706; *PH:* 1-301-459-2590; *Fax:* 1-080-045-5572; *http://* www.vocus.com; *Email:* info@vocus.com

General - Incorporation .... DE	Stock - Price on:12/24/2007 ....$26.96
Employees..317	Stock Exchange..NDQ
Auditor ....Ernst& Young LLP	Ticker Symbol..VOCS
Stk Agt.....................Wachovia Bank N.A	Outstanding Shares 17,330,000
Counsel..NA	E.P.S..$0.05
DUNS No. ....NA	Shareholders...NA

Business: The groups principle activity is to provide software services. The groups product is on demand public relations management. Customers served by the group include financial and insurance, technology, healthcare and pharmaceuticals and retail and consumer products and government agencies. The group operates from the United States. The group's quarterly revenue for September 2007 was 15.07 millions of USD.

Primary SIC and add'l.: 7372

CIK No: 0001329919

Subsidiaries: PAT LLC, Vocus Acquisition LLC, Vocus Europe Limited, Vocus GS Holdings, LLC, Vocus International Holdings LLC, Vocus NM LLC, Vocus PRW Holdings LLC

Officers: Richard Rudman/Co - Founder, Chmn., CEO, Pres., William Donnelly/Sr. VP - Corporate Development, Andrew Muir/MD - Vocus International, Matt Siegal/VP - Business Development, Darren Stewart/VP - Client Services, Stephen Vintz/CFO, William Wagner/Chief Marketing Officer, Norman Weissberg/VP - North American Sales, Bob Lentz/CTO, Co - Founder, Christine Nyirjesy Bragale/Member - Customer Advisory Counsel, Kevin Gould/Member - Customer Advisory Counsel, Donna Hedge/Member - Customer Advisory Counsel, Marianne Holland/Member - Customer Advisory Counsel, Todd Hultquist/Member - Customer Advisory Counsel, Urs Klarer/Member - Customer Advisory Counsel *(23 Officers included in Index)*

Directors: Richard Rudman/Co - Founder, Chmn., CEO, Pres., Richard P. Moore/Dir., Bob Lentz/CTO, Co - Founder, Michael Bronfein/Dir., Kevin J. Burns/Dir., Gary Golding/Dir., Ronald W. Kaiser/Dir.

Owners: Michael Bronfein/1.50%, Stephen Vintz, Norman Weissberg, Arbor Capital Management, LLC/7.20%, Gary Golding/2.20%, Richard Moore, Lazard Alternative Investments LLC./5.40%, Ronald Kaiser, Richard Rudman/5.90%, Robert Lentz/4.20%, Insiders/20.00%, Kevin Burns/5.50%

Financial Data: Fiscal Year End:12/31   Latest Annual Data: 12/31/2006

Year	Sales		Net Income
2006	$40,328,000		$442,000
2005	$28,062,000		-$5,064,000
2004	$20,393,000		-$2,601,000
Curr. Assets:	$41,148,000	Curr. Liab.:	$32,627,000	P/E Ratio: 674.00
Plant, Equip.:	$4,359,000	Total Liab.:	$33,763,000	Indic. Yr. Divd.: NA
Total Assets:	$74,770,000	Net Worth:	$40,974,000	Debt/ Equity: 0.0081

Vodafone Group Plc

Vodafone House, The Connection, Newbury, Berkshire, RG14 2FN; *PH:* 44-016333251; *http://* www.vodafone.com

General - Incorporation .... UK	Stock - Price on:12/24/2007 ....$31.82
Employees...66,000	Stock Exchange...NYSE
Auditor ....Deloitte & Touche LLP	Ticker Symbol..VOD
Stk Agt.....Computershare Investor Services LLC	Outstanding Shares 5,280,000,000
Counsel..NA	E.P.S..NA
DUNS No. 28-993-6783	Shareholders...NA

Business: The group's principal activity is the provision of mobile telecommunications services, including voice and data communications. The group's mobile subsidiaries operate under the brand name vodafone, j-phone vodafone, and verizon wireless. The group operates in such geographical areas as the United Kingdom, Ireland, northern Europe, southern Europe, the Americas Asia-Pacific, Middle East and Africa. During the fiscal 2003 the group acquired societe francaise du radiotelephone and cegetel sas.

Primary SIC and add'l.: 4813 5065 4812

CIK No: 0000839923

Subsidiaries: Arcor AG & Co. KG, Vodafone Albania Sh.A., Vodafone Americas Inc., Vodafone Czech Republic a.s., Vodafone D2 GmbH, Vodafone Egypt Telecommunications S.A.E., Vodafone Espana S.A., Vodafone Europe B.V., Vodafone Group Services Limited, Vodafone Holding GmbH, Vodafone Holdings Europe S.L., Vodafone Hungary Mobile Telecommunications Limited, Vodafone International Holdings B.V., Vodafone Investments Luxembourg S.a.r.l., Vodafone Ireland Limited 25 Subsidiaries included in the Index

Officers: Vittorio Colao/Dir., CEO - Europe, Deputy Group CEO, Arun Sarin/53/Dir., CEO, Charles Butterworth/CEO - Ireland, Gyorgy Beck/CEO - Hungary, Pietro Guindani/CEO - Italy, Fritz Joussen/CEO - Germany, Guy Laurence/CEO - Netherlands, Inaki Berroeta/CEO - Malta, Russell Stanners/CEO - New Zealand, Antonio Carrapatoso/CEO - Portugal, Liliana Solomon/CEO - Romania, Francisco Raman/CEO - Spain, Attila Vitai/CEO - Turkey, Nick Read/CEO - UK, Thomas Papaspyrou/CEO - Albania *(39 Officers included in Index)*

Directors: Vittorio Colao/Dir., CEO - Europe, Deputy Group CEO, Arun Sarin/53/Dir., CEO, John Bond/Chmn., John Buchanan/Dep. Chmn., Andy Halford/Dir., CFO, Luc Vandevelde/57/Dir., Philip Yea/Dir., Lord Broers/Dir., Michael Boskin/Dir., Anne Lauvergeon/Dir., Anthony Watson/Dir., Jurgen Schrempp/Dir., Simon Murray/Dir., Nick Land/Dir., Alan Jebson/Dir.

Owners: Jrgen Schrempp, Anne Lauvergeon, Anthony Watson, John Bond, John Buchanan, Alan Jebson, Lord Broers, Andy Halford, Arun Sarin, Luc Vandevelde, Michael Boskin, Nick Land, Philip Yea

Financial Data: *Fiscal Year End:* 03/31   *Latest Annual Data:* 03/31/2007

Year	Sales	Net Income
2007	$49,919,000,000	-$8,514,000,000
2006	$41,319,000,000	-$23,081,000,000
2005	$78,017,959,000	-$25,896,378,000

Curr. Assets:	$13,100,000,000	**Curr. Liab.:**	$26,980,000,000		
Plant, Equip.:	$42,182,000,000	**Total Liab.:**	$124,847,000,000	**Indic. Yr. Divd.:**	$1.740
Total Assets:	$276,138,000,000	**Net Worth:**	$151,291,000,000	**Debt/ Equity:**	NA

Vodavi Technology Inc

4717 E Hilton Ave., Ste. 400, Phoenix, AZ, 85034; *PH:* 1-480-443-6000; *http://* www.vodavi.com

General - Incorporation	DE	**Stock**- Price on:12/24/2007	NA
Employees	NA	Stock Exchange	NA
Auditor	Mayer Hoffman Mccann, P.C	Ticker Symbol	NA
Stk Agt	Ms Howell & Co	Outstanding Shares	NA
Counsel	Greenberg Traurig	E.P.S.	NA
DUNS No.	87-286-7155	Shareholders	NA

Business: The group's principal activities are to design, develop, market and support telecommunication solutions and computer-telephony products for business applications. The products are broadly classified into three categories: telephony products, voice processing products and computer-telephony products. Telephony products include digital and analog key telephone systems and commercial grade telephones. Voice processing products include automated attendant, automatic call distribution, voice mail and facsimile, and unified messaging systems. Computer-telephony products include windows-based application products (PC telephones and attendant consoles), local area network to pbx connection packages, ip gateways, and Internet messaging systems.

Primary SIC and add'l.: 4813

CIK No: 0000949491

Subsidiaries: Vodavi Communications Systems, Inc., Vodavi Direct, Inc

Officers: Gregory K. Roeper/CEO, Pres., Charles De Tranaltes/VP - Product Development, Marc F. Niknam/VP - Engineering, Manufacturing, Technical Support, David A. Husband/CFO, Rich Gralto/VP - Sales

Voice Mobility International Inc

100-4190 Lougheed Hwy., Burnaby, BC, V5C 6A8; *PH:* 1-604-482-0000; *Fax:* 1-604-482-1169; *http://* www.voicemobility.com; *Email:* info@voicemobility.com

General - Incorporation	NV	**Stock**- Price on:12/24/2007	$0.27
Employees	NA	Stock Exchange	OTC
Auditor	Ernst & Young LLP	Ticker Symbol	VMII
Stk Agt	Computershare Trust Co	Outstanding Shares	NA
Counsel	Clark, Wilson	E.P.S.	NA
DUNS No.	NA	Shareholders	NA

Business: The group's principal activities are to design, develop, sell and market unified voice messaging software. It operates through its wholly owned operating subsidiaries, voice mobility inc. And voice mobility (us) inc. Its primary market is the tier i and tier ii service providers including wireless service providers, competitive local exchange providers, Internet service providers, cable operators and smaller incumbent local exchange carriers. The group's unified communications products allow subscribers to use a single electronic mailbox to store and retrieve voicemail, faxes and e-mail from many types of devices, including wire-line and wireless phones, e-mail or Web browsers. Their geographic markets include North America, Europe and Asia.

Primary SIC and add'l.: 7372 6719

CIK No: 0001094816

Subsidiaries: Voice Mobility Inc

Officers: Randy Buchamer/Dir., CEO, Pres./$330,254.00, David Raffa/Dir., Corporate Counsel, Phil Kelsey/Dir. - Software Development, Harry Chan/Controller, Rob Collins/Dir. - Marketing, Todd Johnson/Dir. - Channel Support

Directors: Randy Buchamer/Dir., CEO, Pres., Gary R. Donahee/Chmn., Morgan P.W. Sturdy/Dir., David Raffa/Dir., Corporate Counsel, Robert E. Neal/Dir., Gerald Butters/Dir., Sherman Henderson/Dir., Bill Laird/Dir., Ken Miller/Dir.

Owners: Randy Buchamer/3.10%, Donald A. Calder, William H. Laird/6.70%, Insiders/6.00%, William E. Krebs/6.30%, Gary Donahee, Robert Neal, Morgan Sturdy/1.00%, David Raffa

Financial Data: *Fiscal Year End:* 12/31   *Latest Annual Data:* 12/31/2006

Year	Sales	Net Income
2006	$94,000	-$3,304,000
2005	$34,000	-$3,031,000
2004	$13,000	-$4,236,000

Curr. Assets:	$3,249,000	**Curr. Liab.:**	$789,000		
Plant, Equip.:	$22,000	**Total Liab.:**	$10,427,000	**Indic. Yr. Divd.:**	NA
Total Assets:	$3,899,000	**Net Worth:**	-$6,528,000	**Debt/ Equity:**	NA

VoIP Inc

151 S Wymore Rd., Ste. 3000, Altamonte Springs, FL, 32714; *PH:* 1-407-389-3232; *Fax:* 1-407-389-3233; *http://* www.voipincorporated.com; *Email:* info@voipincorporated.com

General - Incorporation	TX	**Stock**- Price on:12/24/2007	$0.091
Employees	53	Stock Exchange	OTC
Auditor	Berkovits, Lago & Co LLP	Ticker Symbol	VOIC
Stk Agt	American Stock Transfer & Trust Co.	Outstanding Shares	143,760,000
Counsel	NA	E.P.S.	NA
DUNS No.	NA	Shareholders	NA

Business: The groups principle activity is to provide long-distance and local telephone services through its voice over Internet protocol (VoIP) network. The group's customers include CLECs, IXCs, Internet service providers (ISPs), cable operators and VoIP service providers. The group operates from United States.

Primary SIC and add'l.: NA

CIK No: 0001100954

Subsidiaries: Caerus Billing and Mediation, Inc., Caerus Networks, Inc., Caerus, Inc., Communications Group of Florida, Inc., DTNet Technology, eGlobalphone, Inc, Technologies, VCS Technologies, Inc. d/b/a DT Net, VoiceOne Communications, LLC, VoIP Acquisition Co., VoIP Americas, Inc., VoIP Solutions, Inc., Volo Communications of Arizona, Inc., Volo Communications of California, Inc., Volo Communications of Colorado, Inc. 40 Subsidiaries included in the Index

Officers: Anthony Cataldo/56/Chmn., CEO/$113,083.00, Shawn M. Lewis/CTO/$1,394,821.00, Robert Staats/Chief Accounting Officer, Corporate Controller/$271,289.00

Directors: Gary Post/59/Dir., Stuart Kosh/51/Dir., Nicholas A. Iannuzzi/41/Dir.

Owners: Insiders/13.30%, Shawn Lewis/7.00%, WQN, Inc./23.10%, Stuart Kosh/3.00%, Nicholas A. Iannuzzi, Gary Post/3.50%, Robert Staats

Financial Data: *Fiscal Year End:* 12/31   *Latest Annual Data:* 12/31/2006

Year	Sales	Net Income
2006	$14,677,000	-$41,197,000
2005	$15,507,000	-$28,313,000
2004	$1,828,000	-$5,862,000

Curr. Assets:	$1,277,000	**Curr. Liab.:**	$37,658,000		
Plant, Equip.:	$6,860,000	**Total Liab.:**	$37,881,000	**Indic. Yr. Divd.:**	NA
Total Assets:	$40,925,000	**Net Worth:**	$3,045,000	**Debt/ Equity:**	NA

VOIS Inc

Formerly: Medstrong International Corp

255 Ne 6th Ave., Delray Beach, FL, 33483; *PH:* 1-561-274-4894

General - Incorporation	DE	**Stock**- Price on:12/24/2007	NA
Employees	NA	Stock Exchange	NA
Auditor	Raich Ende Malter & Co. LLP	Ticker Symbol	NA
Stk Agt	American Stock Transfer & Trust Co.	Outstanding Shares	NA
Counsel	NA	E.P.S.	NA
DUNS No.	NA	Shareholders	NA

Business: The group's principle activity is to develop a comprehensive database to store and transfer patient medical records in a secure environment. The company also develops the software to transfer the information over the Internet allowing for data retrieval and modification. The business is designed to provide the consumer member with the ability to input, in a secure database, the member's medical information and to have access to such information on a day-to-day basis or in an emergency from anywhere that has Internet access. The company is in its development stage. The group operates from United States.

Primary SIC and add'l.: 7375

CIK No: 0001136711

Officers: Stephen J. Bartkiw/45/Dir., CEO, Pres., Mark J. Minkin/59/Dir., Sr. VP - Marketing, Sec., Herbert Tabin/40/Dir., Sr. VP - Corporate Development, Marc A. Saitta/46/CFO

Directors: Stephen J. Bartkiw/45/Dir., CEO, Pres., Gary J. Schultheis/42/Chmn.

Owners: Herbert Tabin/22.03%, Gary Schultheis/22.64%, Stephen J. Bartkiw/22.64%, Robert M. Cohen/0.18%, Mark J. Minkin/22.88%, Insiders/90.20%

Financial Data: *Fiscal Year End:* 12/31   *Latest Annual Data:* 12/31/2006

Year	Sales	Net Income
2006	NA	-$225,000
2005	$0	-$259,000
2004	$2,000	$2,000

Curr. Assets:	$311,000	**Curr. Liab.:**	$1,014,000		
Plant, Equip.:	NA	**Total Liab.:**	$1,014,000	**Indic. Yr. Divd.:**	NA
Total Assets:	$311,000	**Net Worth:**	-$703,000	**Debt/ Equity:**	NA

Volcano Corp

2870 Kilgore Rd., Rancho Cordova, CA, 95670; *PH:* 1-800-228-4728; *http://* www.volcanocorp.com; *Email:* info@volcanocorp.com

General - Incorporation	DE	**Stock**- Price on:12/24/2007	$20
Employees	505	Stock Exchange	NDQ
Auditor	Ernst & Young, LLP	Ticker Symbol	VOLC
Stk Agt	American Stock Transfer & Trust Co.	Outstanding Shares	38,350,000
Counsel	NA	E.P.S.	-$0.02
DUNS No.	NA	Shareholders	NA

Business: The groups principle activities include designing, developing, manufacturing and commercializing intravascular ultrasound and functional measurement product. The products of the group include Consoles and Catheters. The group products sold under the trade names Volcano (R), Eagle Eye (R), Visions (R), Revolution(R), ComboWire (R), SmartMap(R) and ComboMap (R). The group operates from the United States, Japan, Europe, the Middle East and Africa, and Rest of world. The group's quarterly revenue for September 2007 was 31.47 millions of USD.

Primary SIC and add'l.: 3841

CIK No: 0001354217

Subsidiaries: Volcano Europe, S.A./N.V., Volcano Japan Co., Ltd.

Officers: Scott Huennekens/Dir., CEO, Pres., John T. Dahldorf/CFO, Sec., Vincent J. Burgess/Exec. VP - New Business Initiatives, Marketing, John F. Sheridan/Exec. VP - Operations, Geoffrey D. Vince/Clinical Affairs and Advanced Research & Development, Michel E. Lussier/Pres. - Volcano Europe, Clinical, Scientific Affairs, Pauliina M. Margolis/VP - Scientific Affairs, Medical Dir., Junichi Osawa/Pres., MD - Volcano Japan, George Quinoy/VP - Global Sales, Connie L. Garrett/VP - Global Human Resources, Paul J. Zalesky/VP - Research, Development

Directors: Scott Huennekens/Dir., CEO, Pres., Olav B. Bergheim/Chmn., James C. Blair/Dir., Lesley H. Howe/Dir., Ronald A. Matricaria/Dir., Connie R. Curran/Dir., Kieran T. Gallahue/Dir., John Onopchenko/Dir.

Owners: John T. Dahldorf, Robert J. Adelman/6.20%, Entities affiliated with Domain Partners V, L.P./21.50%, James C. Blair/21.50%, Jorge J. Quinoy, Capital Research and Management Company/8.00%, Vincent J. Burgess, Olav B. Bergheim/1.50%, Insiders/41.80%, Scott R. Huennekens/3.00%, John F. Sheridan, Carlos A. Ferrer/8.10%, Entities affiliated with OrbiMed Advisors, LLC/6.20%, FFC Partners II, L.P./8.10%, Waddell & Reed Financial, Inc./5.10% (18 Owners included in Index)

Financial Data: Fiscal Year End:12/31 Latest Annual Data: 12/31/2006

Year	Sales	Net Income
2006	$103,048,000	-$8,603,000
2005	$91,900,000	-$15,261,000
2004	$61,098,000	-$16,191,000

Curr. Assets:	$132,731,000	Curr. Liab.:	$23,823,000		
Plant, Equip.:	$9,333,000	Total Liab.:	$25,543,000	Indic. Yr. Divd.:	NA
Total Assets:	$154,725,000	Net Worth:	$129,182,000	Debt/ Equity:	0.0003

Volcom Inc

1740 Monrovia Ave., Costa Mesa, CA, 92627; *PH:* 1-949-646-2175; *http://* www.volcom.com

General - Incorporation	DE	Stock- Price on:12/24/2007	$47.43
Employees	259	Stock Exchange	NDQ
Auditor	Deloitte & Touche LLP	Ticker Symbol	VLCM
Stk Agt	U.S. Stock Transfer Corp	Outstanding Shares	24,330,000
Counsel	Latham & Watkins LLP	E.P.S	$1.23
DUNS No.	NA	Shareholders	NA

Business: The groups principle activities include designing, marketing and distributing young mens and young womens clothing, accessories and related products. The products of the group include T-Shirts and Fleece, Tops and Jackets, Bottoms, Denim, and Outerwear. The group products sold under the trade names Volcom and Volcom Stone. In October 25, 2005, the group acquired Welcom Distribution SARL. The group operates from the United States, Canada, Asia Pacific and other. The group's quarterly revenue for September 2007 was 91.05 millions of USD.

Primary SIC and add'l.: 7929 2329 5091 2339 2369 3949 2353 5941 7822 2389 3151 7812 5699 5621 5611

CIK No: 0001324570

Subsidiaries: Volcom Entertainment, Inc., Volcom International SARL, Volcom SAS, Welcom Distribution SARL

Officers: Richard Woolcott/Dir., CEO, Pres./$657,400.00, Douglas Collier/CFO, Sec./$525,900.00, Jason Steris/COO/$525,900.00, Tom Ruiz/VP - Sales/$589,792.00, Troy Eckert/VP - Marketing/$338,340.00, David Stankunas/Primary Investor Relations Contact, Hoby S. Darling/VP - Strategic Development, General Counsel

Directors: Richard Woolcott/Dir., CEO, Pres., Rene Woolcott/Chmn., Douglas Ingram/Dir., Anthony Palma/Dir., Joseph Tyson/Dir., Carl Womack/Dir., Kevin Wulff/Dir.

Owners: Joseph B. Tyson, Douglas P. Collier/1.60%, Tom D. Ruiz, Ren R. Woolcott/10.90%, Anthony M. Palma, Kevin G. Wulff, Insiders/29.40%, Richard R. Woolcott/15.50%, Carl W. Womack, Kwock Family Trust/10.60%, Troy C. Eckert, Douglas S. Ingram, Jason W. Steris

Financial Data: Fiscal Year End:12/31 Latest Annual Data: 12/31/2006

Year	Sales	Net Income
2006	$205,258,000	$28,753,000
2005	$159,951,000	$29,337,000
2004	$113,175,000	$24,593,000

Curr. Assets:	$136,510,000	Curr. Liab.:	$15,441,000	P/E Ratio:	38.56
Plant, Equip.:	$11,527,000	Total Liab.:	$15,751,000	Indic. Yr. Divd.:	NA
Total Assets:	$149,748,000	Net Worth:	$133,997,000	Debt/ Equity:	0.0007

Volt Information Sciences Inc

560 Lexington Ave., New York, NY, 10022; *PH:* 1-212-704-2400; *http://* www.volt.com

General - Incorporation	NY	Stock- Price on:12/24/2007	$20.08
Employees	5,000	Stock Exchange	NYSE
Auditor	Ernst & Young LLP	Ticker Symbol	VOL
Stk Agt	Registrar & Transfer Co	Outstanding Shares	23,180,000
Counsel	Howard Weinreich	E.P.S	$1.71
DUNS No.	00-132-6479	Shareholders	NA

Business: The group's principle activities are to operate the two businesses that provides staffing services and telecommunications and information solutions. These two businesses operate through four operating segments: staffing services, telephone directory, telecommunication services and computer systems. Staffing services segment provides a broad range of employee staffing services. Telecommunications and information solutions business provides telephone directory, telecommunication services and computer systems. Telephone directory segment publishes independent telephone directories, directory production, database management and other services. Telecommunication services segment provides services related to telecommunication. Computer systems segment provides directory assistance outsourcing services to wireline and wireless telecommunications companies. The group's quarterly revenue for October 2007 was 625.62 millions of USD.

Primary SIC and add'l.: 7371 7361 7375 1731 2741 7363

CIK No: 0000103872

Subsidiaries: 14011 So. Normandie Ave. Realty Corp., 500 South Douglas Realty Corp., Computing Group Limited, DataNational of Georgia, Inc., DataNational, Inc., Fidelity National Credit Services Ltd., Gatton Volt Computastaff Limited, Gatton Volt Consulting Group Limited, India Private Limited, Information Management Associates, Inc., Maintech, Incorporated Delaware, Nuco I, Ltd., Nuco II, Ltd., PCureSys, Ltd., ProcureStaff Canada, Ltd. 74 Subsidiaries included in the Index

Officers: Steven A. Shaw/48/Dir., CEO, COO, Pres., Daniel G. Hallihan/59/VP - Accounting Operations, Howard B. Weinreich/65/General Counsel, Louise Ross/59/Assist. VP - Human Resources, Thomas Daley/53/Sr. VP, Jack Egan/58/Sr. Pres., Ludwig M. Guarino/56/Sr. VP, Ronald Kochman/48/VP

Directors: Steven A. Shaw/48/Dir., CEO, COO, Pres., Mark N. Kaplan/78/Dir., William H. Turner/68/Dir., Theresa A. Havell/Dir., William Shaw/Founder, Jerome Shaw/Founder, Lloyd Frank/82/Dir., Bruce G. Goodman/59/Dir., Deborah Shaw/52/Dir.

Owners: William H. Turner, Barclays Global Investors, NA, Jack Egan, Bruce G. Goodman, Jerome Shaw, Deborah Shaw, Dimensional Fund Advisors Inc., Insiders, Howard B. Weinreich, Lloyd Frank, Linda Shaw, Theresa A. Havell, Estate of William Shaw, Thomas Daley, Goldman Sachs Asset Management, L.P. *(17 Owners included in Index)*

Financial Data: Fiscal Year End:10/30 Latest Annual Data: 10/29/2006

Year	Sales	Net Income
2006	$2,338,453,000	$30,650,000
2005	$2,177,619,000	$17,040,000
2004	$1,924,777,000	$33,716,000

Curr. Assets:	$558,317,000	Curr. Liab.:	$349,661,000	P/E Ratio:	16.19
Plant, Equip.:	$85,038,000	Total Liab.:	$413,519,000	Indic. Yr. Divd.:	NA
Total Assets:	$690,036,000	Net Worth:	$276,517,000	Debt/ Equity:	0.0376

Volterra Semiconductor Corp

3839 Spinnaker Ct, Fremont, CA, 94538; *PH:* 1-510-743-1200; *http://* www.volterra.com; *Email:* sales@volterra.com

General - Incorporation	DE	Stock- Price on:12/24/2007	$14
Employees	151	Stock Exchange	NDQ
Auditor	KPMG LLP	Ticker Symbol	VLTR
Stk Agt	Registrar & Transfer Co	Outstanding Shares	24,480,000
Counsel	Cooley Godward LLP	E.P.S	$0.07
DUNS No.	NA	Shareholders	NA

Business: The group's principal activities are to design, develop and market analog and mixed-signal power management semiconductors for the computing, storage, networking and consumer markets. The products of the group are integrated voltage regulator semiconductors and scalable voltage regulator semiconductor chipsets that transform, regulate, deliver and monitor the power consumed by digital semiconductors. The group sells its products to original equipment manufacturers, original design manufacturers, contract equipment manufacturers and power supply manufacturers. The power management solutions are incorporated into products from system designers including accton technology, ambit microsystems, ciena, cisco systems, emc, ericsson, gemtek, global sun technology, hewlett-packard, hitachi, IBM and nec.

Primary SIC and add'l.: 3679 3674

CIK No: 0001050550

Officers: Jeffrey Staszak/Dir., CEO, Pres./$713,744.00, Marco Zuniga/VP - IC Technology, Process Development, Craig Teuscher/VP - Sales, Applications Engineering/$434,064.00, Daniel Wark/52/VP - Operations, William Numann/VP - Marketing/$443,004.00, David Lidsky/VP - Design Engineering/$456,055.00, Anthony Stratakos/VP - Advanced Research, Development, CTO, Dir., Greg Hildebrand/37/VP - Finance, Treasurer, Sec./$454,556.00, Hamza Yilmaz/Sr. VP - Product Development, Engineering, Manufacturing Operations, Mike Burns/VP, CFO, Treasurer, Sec., Achilleas Veziris/VP - Quality, Reliability

Directors: Jeffrey Staszak/Dir., CEO, Pres., Christopher Paisley/Chmn., Anthony Stratakos/VP - Advanced Research, Development, CTO, Dir., Mel Friedman/Dir., Edward Ross/Dir., Alan King/Dir., Edward Winn/Dir.

Owners: Anthony Stratakos/4.50%, William Blair& Company, LLC/12.10%, Jeffrey Staszak/3.50%, Alan King/3.60%, Entities affiliated with Waddell& Reed Investment Management Company/9.10%, FMR Corp./13.00%, Mel Friedman, Greg Hildebrand/2.10%, Insiders/19.40%, Craig Teuscher/2.50%, Arbor Capital Management LLC/4.80%, Edward Ross, David Lidsky/2.60%, Schroder Investment Management North America, Inc./6.70%, Dan Wark *(16 Owners included in Index)*

Financial Data: Fiscal Year End:12/31 Latest Annual Data: 12/31/2006

Year	Sales	Net Income
2006	$74,588,000	$6,913,000
2005	$53,867,000	$5,406,000
2004	$43,935,000	$5,109,000

Curr. Assets:	$79,135,000	Curr. Liab.:	$11,887,000	P/E Ratio:	116.67
Plant, Equip.:	$4,514,000	Total Liab.:	$11,887,000	Indic. Yr. Divd.:	NA
Total Assets:	$83,703,000	Net Worth:	$71,816,000	Debt/ Equity:	NA

Vonage Holdings Corp

23 Main St., Holmdel, NJ, 07733; *PH:* 1-732-528-2600; *Fax:* 1-732-834-0189; *http://* www.vonage.com; *Email:* info@vonage.com

General - Incorporation	DE	Stock- Price on:12/24/2007	$3.07
Employees	1,790	Stock Exchange	NYSE
Auditor	BDO Seidman, LLP	Ticker Symbol	VG
Stk Agt	American Stock Transfer & Trust Co.	Outstanding Shares	NA
Counsel	NA	E.P.S	-$2.48
DUNS No.	NA	Shareholders	NA

Business: The groups principle activity is to provide broadband telephone services. The group operates from the United States. The groups quarterly revenue for September 2007 was 210.53 millions of USD.

Primary SIC and add'l.: 4899 4813

CIK No: 0001272830

Subsidiaries: Vonage America Inc, Vonage Canada Corp, Vonage Limited, Vonage Marketing Inc, Vonage Network Inc

Officers: Jeffrey A. Citron/Chmn., Chief Strategist, Interim CEO, John S. Rego/Exec. VP, CFO, Treasurer, Louis A. Mamakos/CTO, Exec. VP, Sharon A. O'Leary/Exec. VP, Chief Legal Officer, Sec., Kerry Ritz/MD - Vonage UK, Jamie Haenggi/Chief Marketing Officer

Directors: Jeffrey A. Citron/Chmn., Chief Strategist, Interim CEO, Peter Barris/Dir., Morton David/Dir., Sanford J. Miller/Dir., Thomas J. Ridge/Dir., John J. Roberts/Dir., Harry Weller/38/Dir., Michael Krupka/Dir.

Owners: Sharon A. OLeary, Insiders, Jeffrey A. Citron, New Enterprise Associates, John S. Rego, Sanford J. Miller, Michael Snyder, Peter Barris, Louis A. Mamakos, John J. Roberts, Meritech Capital Partners, Morton David, Harry Weller, Par Investment Partners, L.P, 3i *(18 Owners included in Index)*

Financial Data: Fiscal Year End:12/31 Latest Annual Data: 03/31/2007

Year	Sales	Net Income
2007	NA	NA
2006	$607,397,000	-$338,573,000
2005	$269,196,000	-$261,334,000

Curr. Assets:	$569,772,000	Curr. Liab.:	$259,928,000		
Plant, Equip.:	$131,842,000	Total Liab.:	$574,323,000	Indic. Yr. Divd.:	NA
Total Assets:	$757,524,000	Net Worth:	$183,201,000	Debt/ Equity:	NA

Voorhees Acquisition Corp

100 Garden City Plz., Ste. 500, Garden City, NY, 11530; *PH:* 1-516-663-0509

General - Incorporation	DE	Stock- Price on:12/24/2007	NA
Employees	NA	Stock Exchange	NA
Auditor	NA	Ticker Symbol	NA
Stk Agt	NA	Outstanding Shares	NA
Counsel	NA	E.P.S	NA
DUNS No.	NA	Shareholders	NA

Business: The group's principle activity is to sourcing new business and managing key transactions, opportunities and strategic relationships. The group operates from United States.

Primary SIC and add'l.: 6770

CIK No: 0001293323

Vornado Realty Trust

888 Seventh Ave., New York, NY, 10019; *PH:* 1-212-894-7000; *http://* www.vno.com

General - Incorporation .... MD	*Stock* - Price on:12/24/2007 .... $116.55
Employees 3,477	Stock Exchange .... NYSE
Auditor .... Deloitte & Touche LLP	Ticker Symbol .... VNO
Stk Agt ...... American Stock Transfer & Trust Co.	Outstanding Shares 151,860,000
Counsel .... NA	E.P.S $3.42
DUNS No. .... NA	Shareholders .... NA

Business: The groups principle activities include owning and operating office, retail and showroom properties. In the year 2006, the group acquired four properties. The group operates from the United States. The groups quarterly revenue for September 2007 was 853.04 millions of USD.

Primary SIC and add'l.: 6798

CIK No: 0000899689

Subsidiaries: 14th Street Acquisition II, L.L.C., 14th Street Acquisition, L.L.C., 150 East 58th Street, L.L.C., 1740 Broadway Associates, L.P., 175 Lexington, L.L.C., 20 Broad Company, L.L.C., 20 Broad Lender, L.L.C., 201 East 66th Street, L.L.C., 29 West 57th Street Owner L.L.C., 31 West 57th Street Owner L.L.C., 330 Madison Company, L.L.C., 350 North Orleans, L.L.C., 40 East 14 Realty Associates General Partnership, 40 East 14 Realty Associates, L.L.C., 40 Fulton Street, L.L.C. 689 Subsidiaries included in the Index

Officers: Steven Roth/Chmn., CEO/$4,556,304.00, Michael D. Fascitelli/Trustee, Pres./$4,311,369.00, Michelle Felman/Exec. VP - Acquisitions, Joseph MacNow/CFO, Exec. VP - Finance, Administration/$2,304,645.00, David R. Greenbaum/Pres. - New York Office Division/$2,306,889.00, Sandeep Mathrani/Exec. VP - Retail Real Estate Division/$3,774,750.00, Christopher Kennedy/Pres. - Merchandise Mart Division, Mitchell N. Schear/Pres. - Charles E Smith Commercial Realty Division, Wendy Silverstein/Exec. VP - Capital Markets, Alan J. Rice/Sec.

Directors: Steven Roth/Chmn., CEO, Michael D. Fascitelli/Trustee, Pres., Robert H. Smith/Trustee, Russel B. Wight/Trustee, Richard R. West/Trustee, Anthony W. Deering/Trustee, Ronald Targan/Trustee, David Mandelbaum/Trustee, Michael Lynne/66/Trustee, Robert P. Kogod/75/Trustee, Candace K. Beinecke/Trustee

Owners: Russell B. Wight/4.81%, David R. Greenbaum, Michael Lynne, Interstate Properties/4.74%, Cohen & Steers Capital Management, Inc./4.70%, Sandeep Mathrani, Steven Roth/8.26%, Ronald G. Targan, Michael D. Fascitelli/2.52%, David Mandelbaum/6.42%, Robert H. Smith/1.02%, Robert P. Kogod/1.21%, Richard R. West, Anthony W. Deering, Joseph Macnow (17 Owners included in Index)

Financial Data: *Fiscal Year End:*12/31 *Latest Annual Data:* 12/31/2006

Year	Sales	Net Income
2006	$2,712,095,000	$560,140,000
2005	$2,547,628,000	$539,604,000
2004	$1,707,262,000	$592,917,000
Curr. Assets:	$3,061,755,000	*Curr. Liab.:*	$592,932,000
Plant, Equip.:	$11,584,810,000	*Total Liab.:*	$10,675,307,000	*Indic. Yr. Divd.:*	$3.400
Total Assets:	$17,954,281,000	*Net Worth:*	$6,150,770,000	*Debt/ Equity:*	NA

Votorantim Pulp & Paper Inc

Alameda Santos, 1357, 6th Fl., So Paulo; *PH:* 55-1132694000; *http://* www.vcp.com.br

General - Incorporation .... Brazil	*Stock* - Price on:12/24/2007 .... $23.32
Employees 3,498	Stock Exchange .... NYSE
Auditor .... PricewaterhouseCoopers LLP	Ticker Symbol .... VCP
Stk Agt .... Bank of New York	Outstanding Shares 204,120,000
Counsel .... NA	E.P.S $5.18
DUNS No. .... NA	Shareholders .... NA

Business: The group's principal activities are the production, manufacturing, distribution, marketing and export of pulp, cellulose, short fiber, special and writing paper, cardboard and other related products. The group also has activities in forestry management and exploration.

Primary SIC and add'l.: NA

CIK No: 0001110649

Officers: Jose Luciano Duarte Penido/Dir., CEO, Pres., Antonio Sergio Pinzan De Almeida/Pulp Business Officer, Valdir Roque/CFO - Investor Relations, Luiz Carlos Ganzerli/59/Human Resources, Organizational Development Officer, Francisco Fernandes Campose Valerio/Technical, Growth Officer, Jose Maria De Arruda Mendes Filho/Forest Operations Officer, Sergio Marnio Gandra Vaz/63/Paper Business Officer, Marcelo Strufaldi Castelli/COO, Carlos Roberto Paiva Manteiro/Engineering Officer

Directors: Jose Luciano Duarte Penido/Dir., CEO, Pres., Jose Roberto Ermirio De Moras/Chmn., Fabio Ermirio De Moraes/46/Vice Chmn., Carlos Ermirio De Moras/Dir., Clovis Ermirio De Mscripilliti/Dir.

Owners: Votorantim Participaes S.A./88.95%, BNDES Participaes S.A./7.67%, Insiders, Nova HPI Participaes Ltda./11.05%, Votorantim Participaes S.A.

Financial Data: *Fiscal Year End:*12/31 *Latest Annual Data:* 12/31/2006

Year	Sales	Net Income
2006	$1,317,000,000	$372,000,000
2005	$1,130,000,000	$264,000,000
2004	$1,010,000,000	$303,000,000
Curr. Assets:	$1,347,000,000	*Curr. Liab.:*	$780,000,000
Plant, Equip.:	$1,945,000,000	*Total Liab.:*	$2,129,000,000	*Indic. Yr. Divd.:*	NA
Total Assets:	$4,404,000,000	*Net Worth:*	$2,275,000,000	*Debt/ Equity:*	NA

Voxware Inc

168 Franklin Corner Rd. , Lawrenceville, NJ, 08648; *PH:* 1-609-514-4100; *http://* www.voxware.com; *Email:* investor@voxware.com

General - Incorporation .... DE	*Stock* - Price on:12/24/2007 .... $5.83
Employees 89	Stock Exchange .... NDQ
Auditor .... BDO Seidman LLP	Ticker Symbol .... VOXW
Stk Agt .... Registrar & Transfer Co	Outstanding Shares 6,320,000
Counsel .... Morgan, Lewis & Bockius LLP	E.P.S .... -$0.03
DUNS No. 94-756-3250	Shareholders .... NA

Business: The group's principle activities are to design, develop, market and sell voice-based solutions and speech compression technology for the logistics, distribution, package handling and mail sorting industries. The primary products of the group include voicelogistics(tm), stationary voice-based devices and accessories that complement main products. Voicelogistics is a voice-based solution set of software, hardware, and professional services used for various mobile industrial and warehouse applications that enable workers to perform, through speech interface, typical logistics tasks. Stationary voice-based devices are used for warehouse receiving and package sorting applications. Accessories include microphones, headsets and computer hardware.

Primary SIC and add'l.: 7378 7372

CIK No: 0000933454

Subsidiaries: Verbex Acquisition Corporation, Voxware n.v

Officers: Thomas J. Drury/Dir., CEO, Pres., Yildiray Albayrak/VP - Product Development, Client Hardware, Paul Commons/CFO, Stephen Gerrard/VP, GM - International Operations, Elif Kizilkaya Eracar/VP - Delivery Services, North America, Charles Rafferty/VP - Global Partnerships, David Vetter/CTO, Scott J. Yetter/Pres., Krishna Venkatasamy/VP - Product Development

Directors: Thomas J. Drury/Dir., CEO, Pres., Joseph A. Allegra/Chmn., James L. Alexandre/Dir., Donald R. Caldwell/Dir., Michael Janis/Dir., David B. Levi/Dir., Robert Olanoff/52/Dir., Don Cohen/53/Dir.

Owners: Scott J. Yetter, Insiders, Cross Atlantic Technology Fund II, L.P., Edison Venture Fund V, L.P., Joseph A. Allegra, Scorpion Nominees Limited, Michael Janis, Krishna Venkatasamy, Kenneth W. Riley, David Vetter, Stephen J. Gerrard, Robert Olanoff, Charles K. Rafferty, James L. Alexandre, Donald R. Caldwell

Financial Data: *Fiscal Year End:*06/30 *Latest Annual Data:* 06/30/2007

Year	Sales	Net Income
2007	$15,420,000	-$1,936,000
2006	$15,478,000	-$6,763,000
2005	$17,502,000	-$760,000
Curr. Assets:	$10,071,000	*Curr. Liab.:*	$6,066,000
Plant, Equip.:	$388,000	*Total Liab.:*	$6,319,000	*Indic. Yr. Divd.:*	NA
Total Assets:	$10,646,000	*Net Worth:*	$4,327,000	*Debt/ Equity:*	0.4362

Voyager Entertainment International Inc

4483 W Reno Ave., Las Vegas, NV, 89118; *PH:* 1-702-221-8070; *http://* www.voyager-ent.com

General - Incorporation .... NV	*Stock* - Price on:12/24/2007 .... $0.1
Employees 3	Stock Exchange .... OTC
Auditor .... De Joya Griffith & Co., LLC	Ticker Symbol .... VEII
Stk Agt .... Nevada Agency & Trust Company	Outstanding Shares 114,840,000
Counsel .... NA	E.P.S .... -$0.02
DUNS No. .... NA	Shareholders .... NA

Business: The group's principal plan is to build multiple observation wheels, for which the available locations are being evaluated. The evaluation is done both at the north and south ends of the las vegas strip as well as other off-strip locations in las vegas. "Voyager" is an observation wheel, intended to be designed as a visual icon and experience overlooking the "Las Vegas Strip". With 30 vehicles called orbiters, the vertical revolving vehicle will overlook the las vegas strip as it revolves higher than a 60-story building at 600 (+/-) feet. This project will be located the rio all-suite hotel and casino in las vegas.

Primary SIC and add'l.: 8071

CIK No: 0001028394

Subsidiaries: Dakota Subsidiary Corp., Nevada corporation, Voyager Entertainment Holdings Inc., Voyager Ventures, Inc.

Officers: Richard L. Hannigan/Dir., CEO, Pres., Mimi Hannigan/Dir., Sec., Treasure, Tracy Jones/Dir., COO, Michael Schaunessay/CFO, Sig Ragich/Dir. - Public Relation, Communication, Myong Hannigan/59/Dir., Sec., Treasurer

Directors: Richard L. Hannigan/Dir., CEO, Pres., Mimi Hannigan/Dir., Sec., Treasure, Tracy Jones/Dir., COO, Myong Hannigan/59/Dir., Sec., Treasurer

Owners: Insiders/36.20%, Don and Nancy Tyner/6.40%, Myong Hannigan/21.00%, Gregg Giuffria/8.70%, Tracy Jones/5.80%, Richard Hannigan/30.40%, Dan Jill Fugal/100.00%

Financial Data: *Fiscal Year End:*12/31 *Latest Annual Data:* 12/31/2006

Year	Sales	Net Income
2006	NA	-$1,887,000
2005	NA	-$1,737,000
2004	NA	-$2,456,000
Curr. Assets:	$110,000	*Curr. Liab.:*	$4,401,000
Plant, Equip.:	$16,000	*Total Liab.:*	$4,401,000	*Indic. Yr. Divd.:*	NA
Total Assets:	$626,000	*Net Worth:*	-$3,775,000	*Debt/ Equity:*	NA

Voyager Petroleum Inc

123 E Ogden Ave., Ste. 102A, Hinsdale, IL, 60521; *PH:* 1-630-325-7130; *Fax:* 1-630-325-7140; *http://* www.voyagerpetroleum.com

General - Incorporation .... NV	*Stock* - Price on:12/24/2007 .... $0.128
Employees 4	Stock Exchange .... OTC
Auditor .... Mendoza Berger & Company, LLP	Ticker Symbol .... VYGO
Stk Agt .... Integrity Stock Transfer, Inc.	Outstanding Shares 85,520,000
Counsel .... NA	E.P.S .... -$0.053
DUNS No. .... NA	Shareholders .... NA

Business: The groups principle activity is creating a corporate vehicle to locate and acquire an operating business entity which management believed was a suitable acquisition candidate. The group operates from the United States. The group's quarterly revenue for Sep '07 was 0.38 millions of USD.

Primary SIC and add'l.: 1382

CIK No: 0001140300

Subsidiaries: Silicon Film Technologies, Inc.*

Officers: Jefferson G. Stanley/36/Dir., CEO, CFO, Sebastien Dufort/39/Dir., Pres., Cathy A. Persin/50/VP, Corp. Sec., Anthony D. Altavilla/Pres. - Investor Relations, Jelena Popovic/Contact - Investor Relations

Owners: Insiders/12.57%, Cathy A. Persin/2.78%, Jefferson G. Stanley/3.63%, Sebastien C. DuFort/6.46%

Financial Data: *Fiscal Year End:*12/31   *Latest Annual Data:* 12/31/2006

Year	Sales	Net Income
2006	$20,000	-$1,549,000
2005	NA	-$3,358,000

Curr. Assets:	$557,000	Curr. Liab.:	$1,981,000		
Plant, Equip.:	NA	Total Liab.:	$2,836,000	Indic. Yr. Divd.:	NA
Total Assets:	$1,212,000	Net Worth:	-$1,624,000	Debt/ Equity:	NA

Voyant International Corp

Formerly: Zeros & Ones Inc
530 Lytton Ave., 2nd Fl., Palo Alto, CA, 94301; *PH:* 1-310-393-9992; *http://* www.zerosones.com

General - Incorporation	NV	Stock- Price on:12/24/2007	$0.8
Employees	NA	Stock Exchange	OTC
Auditor	Chang G. Park, Cpa	Ticker Symbol	ZROS
Stk Agt	U.S. Stock Transfer Corp	Outstanding Shares	NA
Counsel	NA	E.P.S.	NA
DUNS No.	NA	Shareholders	NA

Business: The groups principal activities include identifying and developing different media based technologies, media assets, and strategic partnerships, and bringing those together to deliver next generation commercial and consumer solutions. In 2006, the group acquired Rocketstream Holding Corporation. The group operates from the United States.

Primary SIC and add'l.: 7378

CIK No: 0000845807

Subsidiaries: Rocketstream Holding Corporation, RocketStream, Inc., Zeros & Ones Technologies, Inc.

Officers: Dana Waldman/Dir., CEO, Mark Laisure/Exec. Chmn., Scott Fairbairn/Dir., CTO, Steffen D. Koehler/Chief Marketing Officer, Herschel W. Stiles/Chief Development Officer, David R. Wells/CFO

Directors: Dana Waldman/Dir., CEO, Mark Laisure/Exec. Chmn., Scott Fairbairn/Dir., CTO, Volker Anhaeusser/59/Dir.

Owners: Mark M. Laisure/33.30%, Dana R. Waldman/33.30%, Dana R. Waldman/10.90%, Herschel W. Stiles, Mark M. Laisure/10.20%, Steffen D. Koehler, Scott Fairbairn/11.70%, Insiders/34.00%, Insiders/100.00%, David R. Wells/1.90%, Scott Fairbairn/33.30%

VPGI Corp

PO Box 802808, Dallas, TX, 75380; *PH:* 1-972-733-6858; *http://* www.uniview.net;
Email: info@vpgi.com

General - Incorporation	TX	Stock- Price on:12/24/2007	$0.6
Employees	1	Stock Exchange	OTC
Auditor	CF & Co. LLP	Ticker Symbol	VPGC
Stk Agt	American Stock Transfer & Trust Co.	Outstanding Shares	9,710,000
Counsel	NA	E.P.S.	-$0.14
DUNS No.	NA	Shareholders	NA

Business: The group's principle activity is to provide digital media solutions. The digital media device delivers video, audio and gaming features through the Internet to a television set. The products and services of the group are marketed to hospitality, utility, banking and telecommunication companies. The group's operations were carried out through two segments prior to Dec 2002. The product sales segment consists of set-top boxes, network equipment, computer cabling, computer telephony integration (cti) and personal computer equipment and peripherals. The consulting and support services segment consists of services for the implementation of e-business solutions, software support maintenance and network development and support.

Primary SIC and add'l.: 7379 3651

CIK No: 0000755229

Subsidiaries: Curtis Mathes Corporation, uniView Asia Limited, uniView Softgen Corporation, uniView Technologies Products, Venture Pacific Group, Inc. (VPG)

Officers: Joseph R. Rozelle/35/Chmn., CEO, CFO, Pres.

Directors: Joseph R. Rozelle/35/Chmn., CEO, CFO, Pres.

Owners: Hei Shing Lam/6.50%, Trident Growth Fund, LP/90.80%, Joseph R. Rozelle/0.50%, Insiders/0.50%

Financial Data: *Fiscal Year End:*06/30   *Latest Annual Data:* 6/30/2006

Year	Sales	Net Income
2006	NA	-$501,000
2005	$12,000	-$717,000
2004	NA	-$20,000

Curr. Assets:	$32,000	Curr. Liab.:	$1,131,000		
Plant, Equip.:	NA	Total Liab.:	$1,131,000	Indic. Yr. Divd.:	NA
Total Assets:	$88,000	Net Worth:	-$1,044,000	Debt/ Equity:	NA

VSB Bancorp Inc

4142 Hylan Blvd., Staten Island, NY, 10308; *PH:* 1-718-979-1100; *http://* www.victorystatebank.com

General - Incorporation	NY	Stock- Price on:12/24/2007	NA
Employees	51	Stock Exchange	NDQ
Auditor	Crowe Chizek & Co. LLC	Ticker Symbol	VSBN
Stk Agt	NA	Outstanding Shares	NA
Counsel	NA	E.P.S.	$1.20
DUNS No.	NA	Shareholders	NA

Business: The group's principal activities are the provision of banking services. The services of the group include acceptance of deposits, provision of loans, financing rehabilitation, treasury and investment management services to consumers and industries. The group operates solely in the domestic market. On 30-May-2003, the group acquired victory state bank.

Primary SIC and add'l.: 6021 6712

CIK No: 0001225874

Subsidiaries: Victory State Bank, VSB Capital Trust I

Officers: Merton Corn/Pres., CEO - Victory State Bank/$241,061.00, Raffaele M. Branca/Exec. VP, CFO - Victory State Bank/$244,532.00, Richard Boyle/Sr. VP - CLO, Victory State Bank, Elizabeth Scarano/COO, Sr. VP - Victory State Bank, Anna Williams/VP, Compliance Officer - Victory State Bank, Joseph Madory/VP - Business Development, Victory State Bank, Rosemarie Caiazzo/VP - Human Resources, Victory State Bank

Owners: Raffaele M. Branca/4.76%, Joan Nerlino Caddell/3.15%, Bruno Savo/0.86%, Chaim Farkas/2.16%, Merton Corn/9.30%, Joseph J. LiBassi/7.89%, Insiders/32.83%, Robert S. Cutrona/2.25%, Carlos Perez/3.91%, Alfred C. Johnsen/0.46%

Financial Data: *Fiscal Year End:*12/31   *Latest Annual Data:* 12/31/2006

Year	Sales	Net Income
2006	$15,015,000	$2,546,000
2005	$13,402,000	$2,567,000
2004	$11,576,000	$2,275,000

Curr. Assets:	$26,338,000	Curr. Liab.:	$189,388,000		
Plant, Equip.:	$3,697,000	Total Liab.:	$194,543,000	Indic. Yr. Divd.:	$0.060
Total Assets:	$211,885,000	Net Worth:	$17,341,000	Debt/ Equity:	NA

VSE Corp

2550 Huntington Ave., Alexandria, VA, 22303; *PH:* 1-703-960-4600; *http://* www.vsecorp.com;
Email: info@vsecorp.com

General - Incorporation	DE	Stock- Price on:12/24/2007	$76.259
Employees	857	Stock Exchange	NDQ
Auditor	Ernst & Young LLP	Ticker Symbol	VSEC
Stk Agt	Registrar & Transfer Co	Outstanding Shares	2,430,000
Counsel	NA	E.P.S.	$2.43
DUNS No.	04-999-7380	Shareholders	NA

Business: The group's principle activity is to provide engineering, technical management services on a contract basis. The services provided by the group include resources used in program planning; systems integration support; configuration management; computer-aided drafting and design; design and engineering, including prototype development; ship reactivation and transfer support; logistics management and others. Depending on solicitation requirements and other factors, the group offers its professional and technical services and products contract arrangements and business units, which are responsive to customer requirements. The group's customers include non-government organizations and commercial entities. All of the group's revenues are derived from contract services performed for the government.

Primary SIC and add'l.: 8742 8711 7374

CIK No: 0000102752

Subsidiaries: Energetics Incorporated, VSE Services International, Inc.

Officers: Donald M. Ervine/Chmn., CEO, COO, Pres./$724,377.00, James E. Reed/Pres. - Energetics, Incorporated, James M. Knowlton/Exec. VP, Pres. - International Group/$447,052.00, Craig S. Weber/Exec. VP, CAO, Corp. Sec./$380,155.00, Thomas R. Loftus/Sr. VP, CFO/$391,220.00, Thomas G. Dacus/Sr. VP, Pres. - Federal Group/$430,854.00, James W. Lexo/Exec. VP, Michael E. Hamerly/Executie VP, Mgr. - Fleet Maintenance Division, Leonard Goldstein/Dir. - New Business, Product Development, Lori Marraceno/Dir. - Business Development Support Center, Elizabeth M. Price/Dir. - Human Resources, David W. Chivers/CIO, James S. Fallon/Dir. - Contracts, Procurement, Eugene H. Hosier/Dir. - Facilities Management, Robert W. Rouzer/Dir. - Quality Systems Management *(16 Officers included in Index)*

Directors: Donald M. Ervine/Chmn., CEO, COO, Pres., J. F. Lafond/Dir., C. M. Kendall/Dir., C. S. Koonce/Dir., D. M. Osnos/Dir., J. D. Ross/Dir., B. K. Wachtel/Dir.

Owners: Clifford M. Kendall/1.20%, Insiders/35.40%, Michael E. Hamerly, David M. Osnos, Thomas G. Dacus, Thomas R. Loftus/1.30%, Jimmy D. Ross, Steven T. Newby/8.70%, Craig S. Weber/2.40%, James F. Lafond, Bonnie K. Wachtel/1.20%, Donald M. Ervine/3.40%, James M. Knowlton/2.10%, Calvin S. Koonce/23.30%, VSE Corporation Employee/9.90% *(16 Owners included in Index)*

Financial Data: *Fiscal Year End:*12/31   *Latest Annual Data:* 12/31/2006

Year	Sales	Net Income
2006	$363,734,000	$7,789,000
2005	$280,139,000	$6,169,000
2004	$216,011,000	$3,444,000

Curr. Assets:	$83,602,000	Curr. Liab.:	$57,956,000	P/E Ratio:	20.49
Plant, Equip.:	$8,409,000	Total Liab.:	$60,299,000	Indic. Yr. Divd.:	$0.160
Total Assets:	$98,535,000	Net Worth:	$38,236,000	Debt/ Equity:	NA

VTEX Energy Inc

8303 Swest Fwy., Ste. 950, Houston, TX, 77074; *PH:* 1-713-773-3284; *http://* www.vtexenergy.com

General - Incorporation	NV	Stock- Price on:12/24/2007	$0.11
Employees	4	Stock Exchange	OTC
Auditor	Pannell Kerr Forster Of Texas, P.C	Ticker Symbol	VXEN
Stk Agt	Pannell Kerr Forster Of Texas	Outstanding Shares	15,500,000
Counsel	NA	E.P.S.	-$0.47
DUNS No.	NA	Shareholders	NA

Business: The group's principal activities are to explore, produce, acquire and develop oil and gas properties in the United States. The group was formed for the purpose of completing a reverse merger with sunburst.

Primary SIC and add'l.: 1381

CIK No: 0001036265

Subsidiaries: Vector Energy Corporation, Vector Exploration, Inc.

Officers: Marshall Smith/Chmn., CEO, Thomas R. Kaetzer/Operations Consultant, Stephen F. Noser/Dir., COO, Pres., Randal B. McDonald/Dir., Sr. VP, CFO

Directors: Marshall Smith/Chmn., CEO, Stephen F. Noser/Dir., COO, Pres., Randal B. McDonald/Dir., Sr. VP, CFO

Financial Data: *Fiscal Year End:*04/30   *Latest Annual Data:* 4/30/2006

Year	Sales	Net Income
2006	$642,000	-$7,447,000
2005	$1,009,000	-$3,960,000
2004	$1,367,000	-$1,771,000

Curr. Assets:	$1,124,000	Curr. Liab.:	$9,703,000		
Plant, Equip.:	$15,323,000	Total Liab.:	$13,295,000	Indic. Yr. Divd.:	NA
Total Assets:	$17,962,000	Net Worth:	$4,667,000	Debt/ Equity:	0.6173

VuBotics Inc

235 Peachtree St. Ne , Ste. 1725, Atlanta, GA, 30303; *PH:* 1-404-474-2576;
http:// www.vubotics.com; *Email:* IR@vubotics.com

General - Incorporation	NV	Stock - Price on:12/24/2007	$0.175
Employees	1	Stock Exchange	OTC
Auditor	E. Philip Bailey CPA PC	Ticker Symbol	VBTC
Stk Agt	Pacific Stock Transfer Company	Outstanding Shares	52,270,000
Counsel	NA	E.P.S.	-$0.06
DUNS No.	NA	Shareholders	NA

Business: The groups principle activity is researching and building the groups intellectual asset portfolio. The group is also identifying and pursuing markets for the groups products and applications as well as managing various pilot deployments that ultimately define the final attributes of the solution for each market. The group operates from the United States.

Primary SIC and add'l.: 7371

CIK No: 0001100981

Subsidiaries: Annapolis Valley Ventures, Inc, Christopher Partners, Inc., QuantumReader, Inc, Truscom Inc, X-VU, LLC

Officers: John Ellingson/COO, Pres., Dave Rollo/Chief Marketing, Sales Officer, Tom Ridenour/CFO

Directors: Philip Lundquist/Chmn., Ronan Harris/Dir., Robert T. Eramian/63/Dir.

Owners: Ronan A. Harris/1.18%, Robert T. Eramian, Insiders/16.82%, Philip E. Lundquist/14.90%, Potomac Capital Management Inc/10.96%

*Financial Data: Fiscal Year End:*12/31   *Latest Annual Data:* 12/31/2006

Year	Sales	Net Income
2006	$37,000	-$2,653,000
2005	$3,000	-$2,038,000
2004	$6,000	-$741,000

Curr. Assets:	$515,000	Curr. Liab.:	$1,767,000		
Plant, Equip.:	$29,000	Total Liab.:	$2,469,000	Indic. Yr. Divd.:	NA
Total Assets:	$544,000	Net Worth:	-$1,926,000	Debt/ Equity:	NA

Vyrex Corp

2159 Ave.nida De La Playa, La Jolla, CA, 92037; *PH:* 1-858-454-4446; *http://* www.vyrex.com

General - Incorporation	DE	Stock - Price on:12/24/2007	$1.1
Employees	NA	Stock Exchange	OTC
Auditor	Berenfeld, Spritzer, Shechter & Sheer	Ticker Symbol	VYXC
Stk Agt	Mellon Shareholder Services LLC	Outstanding Shares	1,020,000
Counsel	NA	E.P.S.	-$0.12
DUNS No.	18-698-9059	Shareholders	NA

Business: The group's principal activities are to research and develop pharmaceuticals and nutraceuticals for treatment of diseases and conditions associated with aging. The group's research has been focused on targeted antioxidant therapeutics for respiratory, neurological and cardiovascular diseases and the development of nutraceuticals for the dietary support of certain age-related conditions. The nutraceuticals aim at providing benefits through nutritious foods. The group owns registered trademarks for 'panvir', 'vantox' and the logo 'vyrex'.

Primary SIC and add'l.: 8731

CIK No: 0000933972

Officers: Dale D. Garlow/CEO, Pres., Sheldon S. Hendler/Chmn., Founder, Dir. - Scientific, Medical Affair

Directors: Sheldon S. Hendler/Chmn., Founder, Dir. - Scientific, Medical Affair, Michael L. Eagle/Dir., Richard G. Mckee/Dir., Tom K. Larson/Dir.

Owners: Richard G. McKee/3.50%, Tom K. Larson, Dale G. Garlow/7.10%, Sheldon S. Hendler/16.10%, Insiders/27.60%

*Financial Data: Fiscal Year End:*12/31   *Latest Annual Data:* 12/31/2006

Year	Sales	Net Income
2006	$43,000	-$93,000
2005	$98,000	-$69,000
2004	$90,000	-$38,000

Curr. Assets:	$9,000	Curr. Liab.:	$428,000		
Plant, Equip.:	NA	Total Liab.:	$428,000	Indic. Yr. Divd.:	NA
Total Assets:	$9,000	Net Worth:	-$419,000	Debt/ Equity:	NA

Vyta Corp

Formerly: Nanopierce Technologies Inc
370 Seventeenth St., Ste. 3640, Denver, CO, 80202; *PH:* 1-303-592-1010;
http:// www.nanopierce.com

General - Incorporation	NV	Stock - Price on:12/24/2007	$0.47
Employees	2	Stock Exchange	OTC
Auditor	Gelfond Hochstadt Pangburn P.C	Ticker Symbol	VYTC
Stk Agt	Corporate Stock Transfer, Inc.	Outstanding Shares	26,050,000
Counsel	NA	E.P.S.	-$0.15
DUNS No.	04-401-6496	Shareholders	NA

Business: The group's principal activity is to design, develop and license the proprietary connection technology, nanopierce connection system for microelectronics applications. The group is focused on providing the electronics industry with possible solutions to the connectivity problems, through know-how and also through products and services provided either by the group or its subsidiaries. The group operates in the United States and Germany through the three subsidiaries: nanopierce card technologies, gmbh, Germany; nanopierce connection systems, inc., usa; exypnotech, gmbh, Germany. Nanopierce card is responsible for the marketing of the company's technology, services and products on an international basis. Nanopierce connection does research and development activities, including the development of various applications of the ncs on both flexible and rigid substrates. Exypnotech produces inlay components used in the manufacturing of smart labels.

Primary SIC and add'l.: 8731 6794

CIK No: 0000827161

Officers: Paul H. Metzinger/69/Dir., CEO, Pres.

Directors: Paul H. Metzinger/69/Dir., CEO, Pres., Herbert J. Neuhaus/47/Dir., John Hoback/69/Dir., Robert F. Shaw/69/Dir.

Owners: The Paul H. Metzinger Trust/3.18%, The Cheri L. Metzinger Trust/3.18%, Herbert J. Neuhaus/0.86%, Kristi J. Kampmann, Insiders/5.51%, Robert E. Shaw/0.73%, Arizcan Properties, Ltd./41.00%, John Hoback/0.73%

*Financial Data: Fiscal Year End:*06/30   *Latest Annual Data:* 06/30/2006

Year	Sales	Net Income
2006	NA	-$2,408,000
2005	NA	-$998,000
2004	$34,000	-$1,558,000

Curr. Assets:	$647,000	Curr. Liab.:	$186,000		
Plant, Equip.:	$11,000	Total Liab.:	$186,000	Indic. Yr. Divd.:	NA
Total Assets:	$2,672,000	Net Worth:	$2,486,000	Debt/ Equity:	NA

Vyteris Holdings (Nevada) Inc

Formerly: Treasure Mountain Holdings Inc
13-01 Pollitt Dr., Fair Lawn, NJ, 07410; *PH:* 1-201-703-2299; *http://* www.vyteris.com

General - Incorporation	NV	Stock - Price on:12/24/2007	$2.48
Employees	51	Stock Exchange	OTC
Auditor	Ernst & Young LLP	Ticker Symbol	VYHN
Stk Agt	Western States Trnsfer & Reg Inc	Outstanding Shares	79,250,000
Counsel	NA	E.P.S.	-$0.7
DUNS No.	NA	Shareholders	NA

Business: The group's principle activities include designing, manufacturing and selling swizzle sticks for stirring coffee. The product is named 'java stir'. The base color of the java stir is coffee brown or black and consists of a sculptured coffee bean attached to a thin acrylic stick made of abs plastic. The java stir is made from a temperature resistant abs plastic by a process called plastic injection molding. The process involves pushing liquid plastic into a mold under pressure. The mold has cooling channels that cool the mold so it will release the parts. Custom molding is available upon request. The java stir can be custom imprinted on the paddle part, an area approximately 1/2 inch by 1/2 inch, with a company's logo and/or message pursuant to customer specifications. Company logo imprinted on the plastic circular diameter (paddle) of the stir stick combined with a gold or silver foil finish for a sharp, noticeable finish. The group operates from United States.

Primary SIC and add'l.: 3089

CIK No: 0001139950

Subsidiaries: Vyteris Holdings, Inc

Officers: Timothy J. McIntyre/52/CEO, Pres., Dir. - Vyteris Inc/$532,192.00, Ashutosh Sharma/Exec. VP - Vyteris Inc/$227,517.00, Anthony J. Cherichella/CFO, Principal Accounting Officer - Vyteris Inc, Cormac H. Lyons/VP - Development, Vyteris Inc, George M. Baskinger/VP - Quality Assurance - Regulatory Affairs, Vyteris Inc, Michael P. Reidy/VP - Research, Joseph N. Himy/VP - Finance

Directors: Timothy J. McIntyre/52/CEO, Pres., Dir. - Vyteris Inc, Donald Farley/Chmn. - Vyteris Inc, David Digiacinto/Dir. - Vyteris Inc, Russell Owen Potts/Dir. - Vyteris Inc, Gregory B. Lawless/Dir. - Vyteris Inc

Owners: Donald Farley/1.20%, BTR Global Opportunity Trading Ltd/11.30%, Russell O. Potts, Insiders/1.20%, RIG Funds./17.20%, Donald Farley, Kevin Kimberlin/98.80%, Timothy McIntyre, Qubit Holdings LLC/12.80%, Gregory B. Lawless, Insiders/1.10%, Ashutosh Sharma, David DiGiacinto, BTR Global Growth Trading Ltd/11.30%, Kevin Kimberlin/32.60%

*Financial Data: Fiscal Year End:*12/31   *Latest Annual Data:* 12/31/2006

Year	Sales	Net Income
2006	$2,464,000	-$20,251,000
2005	$2,209,000	-$25,261,000
2004	$242,000	-$22,567,000

Curr. Assets:	$2,666,000	Curr. Liab.:	$20,174,000		
Plant, Equip.:	$936,000	Total Liab.:	$25,977,000	Indic. Yr. Divd.:	NA
Total Assets:	$4,259,000	Net Worth:	-$30,568,000	Debt/ Equity:	NA

Vyyo Inc

6625 The Corners Pkwy., Ste. 100, Norcross, GA, 30092; *PH:* 1-678-282-8000;
Fax: 1-770-447-2405; *http://* www.vyyo.com

General - Incorporation	DE	Stock - Price on:12/24/2007	$7.03
Employees	139	Stock Exchange	NDQ
Auditor	Kesselman & Kesselman	Ticker Symbol	VYYO
Stk Agt	Computershare Investor Services LLC	Outstanding Shares	18,480,000
Counsel	Brobeck, Phleger & Harrison	E.P.S.	-$1.7
DUNS No.	NA	Shareholders	NA

Business: The group's principal activities are to design and market broadband wireless access systems to telecommunications service providers. The group supplies broadband wireless access systems used by telecommunications service providers to deliver wireless, high-speed data connections to business and residential subscribers. The group operates mainly in North America, China and Israel. The group also explores alternatives relating to the license, purchase or acquisition of other products, technology, assets or businesses. Its customers include system integrators that deploy our systems as part of their end-to-end network solutions to service providers. The group discontinued its software product segment during the year.

Primary SIC and add'l.: 7373 3669

CIK No: 0001104730

Subsidiaries: Vyyo Asia, Inc., Vyyo Brasil Ltda., Vyyo Hong Kong Inc., Vyyo Ltd., Xtend Networks Inc., Xtend Networks Ltd.

Officers: Wayne H. Davis/CEO, Robert Mills/CFO, Jacob Kruk/GM - Vyyo Israel Ltd, Tee Harton/VP - Marketing, Cable Solutions, Jeff Gardner/VP - Sales, Cable Solutions, Brent Levetan/VP - Business Development, Cable Solutions, Zeev Orbach/CTO - Cable Solutions, Raul Assia/VP - Research, Development, Cable Solutions, Arik Levi/CFO/$535,925.00, Walter Ungerer/VP - Corporate Communications, Investor Relations/$307,140.00, Avner Kol/COO/$621,689.00, Tashia L. Rivard/General Counsel, Corp. Sec./$377,189.00, Gabi Magnezi/VP - Operations, Cable Solutions, Al Johnson/Sr. VP, GM - Ultraband Products, Cable Solutions, Steve Santamaria/Sr. VP, GM - Business Services, Cable Solutions (16 Officers included in Index)

Directors: Davidi Gilo/Chmn., Jim Chiddix/Vice Chmn., Alan L. Zimmerman/Dir., Avraham Fischer/Dir., Samuel L. Kaplan/Dir., Ronn Benatoff/Dir., Lewis S. Broad/Dir., Neill H. Brownstein/Dir., Maggie Bellville/Dir., Benita Fitzgerald Mosley/Dir., Richard Bilotti/Dir.

Owners: Insiders/33.82%, Ronn Benatoff, Avraham Fischer, The Goldman Sachs GroupInc./23.62%, Arik Levi, Neill H. Brownstein, Gilder, Gagnon, Howe&Co.LLC/12.00%, Amir Hochbaum, James A. Chiddix, Tashia L. Rivard, John P. Griffin, Alan L. Zimmerman, Avner Kol, Walter Ungerer, Davidi Gilo/28.83% (20 Owners included in Index)

Financial Data: *Fiscal Year End:* 12/31 *Latest Annual Data:* 12/31/2006

Year	Sales	Net Income
2006	$8,000,000	-$29,426,000
2005	$2,367,000	-$38,692,000
2004	$6,094,000	-$21,093,000

Curr. Assets:	$23,231,000	**Curr. Liab.:**	$13,391,000		
Plant, Equip.:	$1,676,000	**Total Liab.:**	$35,762,000	**Indic. Yr. Divd.:**	NA
Total Assets:	$32,149,000	**Net Worth:**	-$3,613,000	**Debt/ Equity:**	NA

W Holding Co Inc

19 W McKinley St., Mayagez, PR, 00681; *PH:* 1-787-834-8000; *Fax:* 1-787-834-8164; *http://* www.wholding.com; *Email:* Westernbank@wbpr.com

General		**Stock**	
Incorporation	Commonwealth Of Puerto Rico	Price on:12/24/2007	$5.2401
Employees	1,363	Stock Exchange	NYSE
Auditor	Deloitte & Touche LLP	Ticker Symbol	WHI
Stk Agt	Bank of New York	Outstanding Shares	164,900,000
Counsel	Biaggi & Biaggi Law Office	E.P.S	$0.34
DUNS No.	NA	Shareholders	NA

Business: The group's principal activity is to provide a wide range of financial services including banking and trust services. The group operates through four divisions: westernbank international, which offers commercial banking and related services outside of Puerto Rico. Westernbank trust division offers a full array of trust services. Westernbank business credit division specializing in commercial business loans secured principally by accounts receivable, inventory and equipment. Expresso of westernbank division specializing in consumer loans. The group operates through 51 full service branch offices located throughout Puerto Rico and a fully functional banking site on the Internet.

Primary SIC and add'l.: 6712 6022

CIK No: 0001084887

Subsidiaries: SRG Net, Inc, Westernbank Puerto Rico, Westernbank World Plaza, Inc

Officers: Frank C. Stipes/52/Chmn., CEO/$407,850.00, Freddy Maldonado/57/Dir., Pres., Chief Investment Officer, Juan C. Frontera/41/Dir., Sec., Alfredo Archilla/51/COO, Norberto Rivera/45/VP, Corporate Controller, Chief Accounting Officer/$385,124.00, William Vidal/54/VP - Commercial Credit, Chief Lending Officer, Northeastern Region/$588,776.00, Vixson Frank Baez/Corporate Communications, Investor Relations

Directors: Frank C. Stipes/52/Chmn., CEO, Freddy Maldonado/57/Dir., Pres., Chief Investment Officer, Hector L. Del Rio/55/Dir., Juan C. Frontera/41/Dir., Sec., Pedro R. Dominguez/63/Dir., Cornelius Tamboer/64/Dir.

Owners: FMR Corp./9.63%, Juan C. Frontera, Ileana Garca Ramrez de Arellano/8.67%, Freddy Maldonado/1.65%, Cesar A. Ruiz, Cornelius Tamboer/3.57%, Pedro R. Domnguez, Insiders/30.84%, Norberto Rivera, Thomas W. Smith/5.21%, Frank C. Stipes/7.12%, Hctor L. Del Ro, William Vidal, Fredeswinda G. Frontera/7.47%

Financial Data: *Fiscal Year End:* 12/31 *Latest Annual Data:* 12/31/2006

Year	Sales	Net Income
2006	$1,038,464,000	$100,531,000
2005	$831,149,000	$163,086,000
2004	$622,616,000	$171,865,000

Curr. Assets:	$1,198,020,000	**Curr. Liab.:**	$15,880,971,000	**P/E Ratio:**	15.41
Plant, Equip.:	$130,565,000	**Total Liab.:**	$15,926,801,000	**Indic. Yr. Divd.:**	$0.190
Total Assets:	$17,154,688,000	**Net Worth:**	$1,227,887,000	**Debt/ Equity:**	0.0555

W&T Offshore Inc

9 Greenway Plz., Ste. 300, Houston, TX, 77046; *PH:* 1-713-626-8525; *Fax:* 1-713-626-8527; *http://* www.wtoffshore.com; *Email:* investorrelations@wtoffshore.com

General		**Stock**	
Incorporation	TX	Price on:12/24/2007	$29.71
Employees	251	Stock Exchange	NYSE
Auditor	Ernst & Young LLP	Ticker Symbol	WTI
Stk Agt	Computershare Investor Services LLC	Outstanding Shares	76,220,000
Counsel	NA	E.P.S	$2.15
DUNS No.	NA	Shareholders	NA

Business: The groups principle activities include acquiring, exploitation, exploring and producing oil and natural gas properties. The group operates from the United States. The groups quarterly revenue for September 2007 was 255.19 millions of USD.

Primary SIC and add'l.: 1311

CIK No: 0001288403

Subsidiaries: Gulf of Mexico Oil and Gas Properties LLC, N.O. Properties LLC, Offshore Energy I LLC, Offshore Energy II LLC, Offshore Energy III LLC, Offshore Shelf LLC, W&T Energy VI, LLC, W&T Energy VII, LLC, White Shoal Pipeline Corporation

Officers: Tracy W. Krohn/Chmn., CEO, Pres., Jerome F. Freel/94/Founder, Chmn. Emeritus, Sec., Amy M. Brumfield/VP - Corporate Administration, John D. Gibbons/54/CFO, Sr. VP, Karen S. Acree/VP, Controller, Kenneth F. Fagan/VP - Acquisitions, William Flores/VP - Deep Water Operation, Thomas F. Getten/General Counsel, Todd E. Grabois/VP, Treasurer, Daniel P. Huffman/VP - Exploitation, Manuel Mondragon/VP - Finance, Gregory E. Percival/VP - Information Technology, Allen W. Tate/VP - Marketing, Midstream, Jamie Vazquez/VP - Land, William F. Voss/VP - Shelf Operations *(20 Officers included in Index)*

Directors: Tracy W. Krohn/Chmn., CEO, Pres., Jerome F. Freel/94/Founder, Chmn. Emeritus, Sec., Robert I. Israel/Dir., Stuart B. Katz/Dir., Virginia Boulet/Dir., James L. Luikart/Dir., James S. Nelson/Dir.

Owners: FMR Corp./10.00%, William W. Talafuse, J. F. Freel/9.30%, Joseph P. Slattery, Tracy W. Krohn/53.80%, James L. Luikart, Virginia Boulet, Jeffery M. Durrant, Reid W. Lea, Insiders/63.70%, Stuart B. Katz, James S. Nelson

Financial Data: *Fiscal Year End:* 12/31 *Latest Annual Data:* 12/31/2006

Year	Sales	Net Income
2006	$800,466,000	$199,104,000
2005	$585,136,000	$189,023,000
2004	$508,715,000	$149,482,000

Curr. Assets:	$328,693,000	**Curr. Liab.:**	$644,076,000	**P/E Ratio:**	13.82
Plant, Equip.:	$2,265,786,000	**Total Liab.:**	$1,566,768,000	**Indic. Yr. Divd.:**	$0.120
Total Assets:	$2,609,685,000	**Net Worth:**	$1,042,917,000	**Debt/ Equity:**	0.4564

W-H Energy Services

2000 W Sam Houston Pky, S, Ste. 500, Houston, TX, 77042; *PH:* 1-713-974-9071; *Fax:* 1-713-974-7029; *http://* www.whes.com; *Email:* info@whes.com

General		**Stock**	
Incorporation	TX	Price on:12/24/2007	$64.57
Employees	2,959	Stock Exchange	NYSE
Auditor	Grant Thornton LLP	Ticker Symbol	WHQ
Stk Agt	Computershare Trust Co	Outstanding Shares	30,420,000
Counsel	Vinson & Elkins LLP	E.P.S	$4.56
DUNS No.	NA	Shareholders	NA

Business: The group's principal activities are to provide products and services used for drilling, completion and production of oil and natural gas wells. The operations are carried out in three segments: drilling, completion and maintenance and safety related products and services. Drilling segment provides products and services used for drilling of oil and natural gas wells. Completion segment provides products like wireline logging and perforating, polymers and specialty chemicals and tubing. Maintenance segment provides products and services for refinery and petrochemical plant applications and for oil and natural gas companies. The operations are focused in the gulf of Mexico, the north sea, the Mediterranean Sea, the Persian Gulf and Brazil and onshore in the United States, Canada, Brazil and Europe.the group acquired continental directional corp, dutch inc, and hydracoil inc in 2003.

Primary SIC and add'l.: 1389 7389 3823 3829 2821 1381 7359

CIK No: 0001051034

Subsidiaries: Agri-Empresa Transportation, Inc., Agri-Empresa, Inc., Boyd's Bit Service, Inc., Boyd's Holdings, LLC, Boyd's Rental Tools S. de R.L. de C.V., Boyd's Rental Tools Servicios S. de R.L. de C.V., Coil Tubing Services, LLC, Drill Motor Services, Inc., Dutch, Inc., Dyna Drill Technologies, Inc., Dyna-Drill Technologies Canada LP, Dyna-Drill Technologies Canada Ltd., E.M. Hobbs, L.P., Grinding and Sizing Company, Inc., Integrity Industries, Inc. 35 Subsidiaries included in the Index

Officers: Kenneth T. White/Chmn., CEO, Pres./$1,912,799.00, Ernesto Bautista/CFO, VP/$786,363.00, John R. Brock/Dir., Independent Consultant, Milton L. Scott/Dir. - Consultant, Jeffrey L. Tepera/VP, COO/$1,190,199.00, William J. Thomas/VP/$1,151,029.00, Glen J. Ritter/VP/$1,064,067.00, Stuart Ford/VP - Intellectual Property Counsel, Catherine N. Crabtree/Sec.

Directors: Kenneth T. White/Chmn., CEO, Pres., Christopher Mills/Dir., John R. Brock/Dir., Independent Consultant, Milton L. Scott/Dir. - Consultant, Robert H. Whilden/Dir., James D. Lightner/Dir.

Owners: William J. Thomas, Stuart J. Ford, Kenneth T. White/2.40%, T. Rowe Price Associates, Inc/11.90%, FMR Corp./10.10%, Robert H. Whilden, Ernesto Bautista, James D. Lightner, John R. Brock, Jeffrey L. Tepera, Glen J. Ritter, Christopher Mills, Insiders/4.60%, Milton L. Scott

Financial Data: *Fiscal Year End:* 12/31 *Latest Annual Data:* 12/31/2006

Year	Sales	Net Income
2006	$894,754,000	$115,003,000
2005	$634,361,000	$48,953,000
2004	$462,428,000	$17,923,000

Curr. Assets:	$342,980,000	**Curr. Liab.:**	$124,886,000	**P/E Ratio:**	15.56
Plant, Equip.:	$343,496,000	**Total Liab.:**	$332,516,000	**Indic. Yr. Divd.:**	NA
Total Assets:	$825,274,000	**Net Worth:**	$492,758,000	**Debt/ Equity:**	0.2816

W. P. Carey & Co LLC

50 Rockefeller Plz., 2nd Fl., New York, NY, 10020; *PH:* 1-212-492-1100; *http://* www.wpcarey.com

General		**Stock**	
Incorporation	DE	Price on:12/24/2007	$30.48
Employees	122	Stock Exchange	NYSE
Auditor	PricewaterhouseCoopers LLP	Ticker Symbol	WPC
Stk Agt	Mellon Investor Services LLC	Outstanding Shares	38,490,000
Counsel	Reed Smith LLP	E.P.S	$3.02
DUNS No.	NA	Shareholders	NA

Business: The group's principal activity is to acquire and own commercial properties leased to companies on a triple net basis. The group also provides acquisition services, research investment analysis, asset management and capital funding services. As at 31-Dec-2003, the group's portfolio consisted of 171 properties totaling more than 18.4 million square feet. The group operates in the United States and Europe. On 24-Mar-2003, the group acquired polar plastics inc.

Primary SIC and add'l.: 7011 7359 6531

CIK No: 0001025378

Subsidiaries: 308 Route 38 Inc, 308 Route 38 LLC, Alpena Franchise Corp., Alpena License Corp., Azo Driver(de) LLC, Azo Mechanic (de)llc, Azo Navigator (de)llc, Azo Valet (de)llc, Azo-a L.p., Azo-b L.p., Azo-c L.p., Azo-d L.p., Bill Cd LLC, BONE (DE)LLC, Bone Manager, Inc. 60 Subsidiaries included in the Index

Officers: Gordon F. Dugan/Dir., CEO, Pres./$1,773,173.00, Jeffrey S. Lefleur/Executive Dir., Thomas Ridings/Executive Dir., Chief Accounting Officer, Leonard Law/CIO, VP, Jennifer L. Walsh/Assist. Treasurer, David Ford/Pres. - Carey Financial, Kathleen Barthmaier/VP - North America, Fort W. Parker/Second VP - North America, Janusz Hooker/First VP - Asia, Matthew Liu/MD - Asia, David G. Termine/First VP - Finance, Accounting, Sheena R. Laughlin/VP - Human Resources, Anne Coolidge Taylor/MD, Thomas E. Zacharias/MD, COO/$1,363,325.00, John D. Miller/Chief Investment Officer *(37 Officers included in Index)*

Directors: Gordon F. Dugan/Dir., CEO, Pres., Wm Polk Carey/Chmn., Eberhard Faber/Dir., Charles E. Parente/Dir., Karsten Von Koller/Dir., Lawrence R. Klein/Dir., Nathaniel S. Coolidge/Dir., Francis J. Carey/Dir., Douglas E. Barzelay/Executive Dir., General Counsel, George E. Stoddard/Dir., Benjamin H. Griswold/Dir., Robert E. Mittelstaedt/Dir., Jeffrey S. Lefleur/Executive Dir., Charles C. Townsend/Dir. Emeritus, Reginald Winssinger/Dir. *(17 Directors included in Index)*

Owners: Reginald Winssinger, Benjamin H. Griswold, Francis J. Carey/1.31%, Thomas E. Zacharias, Nathaniel S. Coolidge, Edward V. LaPuma, Karsten von Koller, Insiders/35.74%, Charles E. Parente, Gordon F. DuGan/1.68%, Lawrence R. Klein, George E. Stoddard, Mark J. DeCesaris, Wm. Polk Carey/31.40%, Eberhard Faber

Financial Data: *Fiscal Year End:* 12/31 *Latest Annual Data:* 12/31/2006

Year	Sales	Net Income
2006	$273,258,000	$86,303,000
2005	$174,117,000	$48,604,000
2004	$227,774,000	$65,841,000

Curr. Assets:	$110,992,000	**Curr. Liab.:**	$80,250,000	**P/E Ratio:**	10.66
Plant, Equip.:	$575,379,000	**Total Liab.:**	$461,025,000	**Indic. Yr. Divd.:**	$1.910
Total Assets:	$1,093,010,000	**Net Worth:**	$631,985,000	**Debt/ Equity:**	0.4409

W. R. Berkley Corp

475 Steamboat Rd. , Greenwich, CT, 06830; *PH:* 1-203-629-3000; *http://* www.wrbc.com

General - Incorporation	DE	*Stock*- Price on:12/24/2007	$32.14
Employees	5,429	Stock Exchange	NYSE
Auditor	KPMG LLP	Ticker Symbol	BER
Stk Agt	Wells Fargo Bank, N.A.	Outstanding Shares	194,120,000
Counsel	Willkie Farr & Gallagher LLP	E.P.S	$3.78
DUNS No	05-608-5533	Shareholders	NA

Business: The group operates through its subsidiaries whose principle activity is to provide property casualty insurance services. The group operates through segments include Regional Property Casualty Insurance, Reinsurance, Specialty Insurance, Alternative Markets and International. The group operates from United States, Argentina and Philippines.

Primary SIC and add'l.: 6331 6321 6411

CIK No: 0000011544

Subsidiaries: Admiral Insurance Company, Berkley Insurance Company, Berkley Regional Insurance Company, Nautilus Insurance Company

Officers: William R. Berkley/Chmn., CEO/$23,748,340.00, Philip S. Welt/VP - Sr. Counsel, Fred C. Madsen/Sr. VP - Reinsurance Operations, Robert D. Stone/Sr. VP - Alternative Markets Operations, Ira S. Lederman/Sr. VP, General Counsel, Sec./$1,783,329.00, Clement P. Patafio/VP, Corporate Controller, Robert W. Berkley/Dir., Exec. VP/$3,995,264.00, Peter L. Kamford/Sr. VP - Admitted Specialty Lines, Robert C. Hewitt/Sr. VP - Excess, Surplus Lines, Paul J. Hancock/Sr. VP, Chief Corporate Actuary, Kevin H. Ebers/VP - Financial Risk Management, Karen A. Horvath/VP - External Financial Communications, Joan E. Kapfer/VP, Edward F. Linekin/VP - Investments, James W. McCleary/Sr. VP - Underwriting *(25 Officers included in Index)*

Directors: William R. Berkley/Chmn., CEO, Rodney A. Hawes/Dir., Mark L. Shapiro/Dir., George G. Daly/Dir., Robert W. Berkley/Dir., Exec. VP, Phillip J. Ablove/Dir., Ronald E. Blaylock/Dir., Mark E. Brockbank/Dir., Mary C. Farrell/Dir., Jack H. Nusbaum/Dir.

Owners: George G. Daly, James G. Shiel, Mark E. Brockbank, Ronald E. Blaylock, FMR Corp/9.90%, Eugene G. Ballard, Robert W. Berkley, Insiders/16.30%, Jack H. Nusbaum, Mary C. Farrell, Mark L. Shapiro, Rodney A. Hawes, Philip J. Ablove, Ira S. Lederman, William R. Berkley/14.60%

*Financial Data: Fiscal Year End:*12/31   *Latest Annual Data:* 12/31/2006

Year		Sales		Net Income
2006		$5,394,831,000		$699,518,000
2005		$4,996,839,000		$544,892,000
2004		$4,512,235,000		$438,105,000
Curr. Assets:	$4,049,832,000	*Curr. Liab.:*	$319,502,000	*P/E Ratio:* 8.93
Plant, Equip.:	$183,249,000	*Total Liab.:*	$12,321,330,000	*Indic. Yr. Divd.:* $0.200
Total Assets:	$15,656,489,000	*Net Worth:*	$3,335,159,000	*Debt/ Equity:* NA

W. R. Grace & Co

7500 Grace Dr., Columbia, MD, 21044; *PH:* 1-201-329-8660; *http://* www.grace.com

General - Incorporation	DE	*Stock*- Price on:12/24/2007	$25.34
Employees	6,500	Stock Exchange	NYSE
Auditor	PricewaterhouseCoopers LLP	Ticker Symbol	GRA
Stk Agt	Mellon Investor Services LLC	Outstanding Shares	70,080,000
Counsel	NA	E.P.S	$0.66
DUNS No	61-296-7141	Shareholders	NA

Business: The groups principle activity is to provide specialty chemicals and materials. The groups products include catalysts and chemical additives, hydroprocessing catalysts, and silica-based and silica-alumina-based engineered materials. The group operates from United States.

Primary SIC and add'l.: 2819 5039

CIK No: 0001045309

Subsidiaries: A-1 Bit & Tool Co., Inc., A.A. Consultancy & Cleaning Company Limited, Advanced Refining Technologies GmbH, Advanced Refining Technologies K.K., Advanced Refining Technologies LLC, Alewife Boston Ltd., Alewife Land Corporation, Alltech Applied Science B.V., Alltech Applied Science Labs (HK) Limited, Alltech Associates (Australia) Pty. Ltd., Alltech Associates Applied Science Limited, Alltech Associates, Inc., Alltech France S.A.R.L., Alltech Grom GmbH, Alltech Italia S.R.L. 160 Subsidiaries included in the Index

Officers: Fred E. Festa/CEO, Pres., Alfred E. Festa/48/Dir., CEO, Pres., Andrew D. Bonham/VP, J. P. Forehand/VP - Operations, W. B. McGowan/Sr. VP, Michael N. Piergrossi/VP - Human Resources, Robert M. Tarola/CFO, Sr. VP, Mark A. Shelnitz/VP, General Counsel, Sec., Brian W. McGowan/Sr. VP - Administration, Gregory E. Poling/VP, Richard C. Brown/48/VP, William M. Corcoran/VP - Public, Regulatory Affairs

Directors: Alfred E. Festa/48/Dir., CEO, Pres., Paul J. Norris/Non - Exec. Chmn., John J. Murphy/Dir., Thomas A. Vanderslice/Dir., Christopher J. Steffen/Dir., Marye Anne Fox/Dir., John F. Akers/Dir., Furlong H. Baldwin/Dir., Ronald C. Cambre/Dir., Mark Tomkins/Dir.

*Financial Data: Fiscal Year End:*12/31   *Latest Annual Data:* 12/31/2006

Year		Sales		Net Income
2006		$2,826,500,000		$18,300,000
2005		$2,569,500,000		$67,300,000
2004		$2,259,900,000		-$402,300,000
Curr. Assets:	$1,368,800,000	*Curr. Liab.:*	$448,600,000	*P/E Ratio:* 76.79
Plant, Equip.:	$664,500,000	*Total Liab.:*	$4,187,200,000	*Indic. Yr. Divd.:* NA
Total Assets:	$3,637,400,000	*Net Worth:*	-$549,800,000	*Debt/ Equity:* NA

W.W. Grainger Inc

100 Grainger Pkwy., Lake Forest, IL, 60045; *PH:* 1-847-535-1000; *http://* www.grainger.com

General - Incorporation	IL	*Stock*- Price on:12/24/2007	$91.03
Employees	14,708	Stock Exchange	NYSE
Auditor	Ernst & Young, LLP	Ticker Symbol	GWW
Stk Agt	Computershare Investor Services LLC	Outstanding Shares	83,560,000
Counsel	Lord, Bissell & Brook	E.P.S	$4.79
DUNS No	00-510-3494	Shareholders	NA

Business: The group's principle activity is to provide facilities maintenance and other related products to businesses and institutions. The group's services include liighting,safety and storage equipment and installation. The group operates from United States.

Primary SIC and add'l.: 5063 5087 7389

CIK No: 0000277135

Subsidiaries: Acklands - Grainger Inc., AW Direct, Inc., Dayton Electric Manufacturing Co, Grainger Caribe, Inc., Grainger China LLC, Grainger Global Holdings, Inc., Grainger Global Trading (Shanghai) Company Limited, Grainger International, Inc, Grainger Services International Inc., Grainger, S.A. de C.V., Lab Safety Supply, Inc., LSS Acquisition Co., MRO Korea Co., Ltd., ProQuest Brands, Inc, SC Grainger Co., Ltd. 18 Subsidiaries included in the Index

Officers: Richard L. Keyser/Chmn., CEO/$6,595,071.00, Troy Vellinga/VP - Customer Service Support, Chris Smith/Distribution Center Optimization Mgr., William D. Chapman/Dir. - Investor Relations, Nancy A. Hobor/VP - Communications, Investor Relations, Judy Andringa/VP, Controller, Vince Lima/VP - Supply Chain Services, Darren Taylor/Dir. - Supply Chain Systems, James T. Ryan/Dir., COO, Pres./$2,615,929.00, Ogden P. Loux/65/CFO, Sr. VP - Finance/$1,750,382.00, John L. Howard/50/Sr. VP, General Counsel/$1,287,164.00, Y. C. Chen/Sr. VP - Supply Chain Management/$1,376,700.00, L. M. Trusdell/Corp. Sec., Laura Brown/VP - Marketing, Robert Finn/Dir. - Direct Marketing *(40 Officers included in Index)*

Directors: Richard L. Keyser/Chmn., CEO, Stuart L. Levenick/Dir., Ann V. Hailey/Dir., William K. Hall/Dir., Wilbur H. Gantz/Dir., James D. Slavik/Dir., John W. McCarter/Dir., Brian P. Anderson/Dir., Michael J. Roberts/Dir., Gary L. Rogers/Dir., Harold B. Smith/Dir., Neil S. Novich/Dir., James T. Ryan/Dir., COO, Pres.

Owners: Wilbur H. Gantz, Gary L. Rogers, John W. McCarter, John L. Howard, Ogden P. Loux, Brian P. Anderson, Massachusetts Financial Services Company/5.30%, Richard L. Keyser/1.20%, Y. C. Chen, William K. Hall, James D. Slavik/5.20%, Insiders/16.60%, David W. Grainger/9.50%, Stuart L. Levenick, Ann V. Hailey *(19 Owners included in Index)*

*Financial Data: Fiscal Year End:*12/31   *Latest Annual Data:* 12/31/2006

Year		Sales		Net Income
2006		$5,883,654,000		$383,399,000
2005		$5,526,636,000		$346,324,000
2004		$5,049,785,000		$286,923,000
Curr. Assets:	$1,862,086,000	*Curr. Liab.:*	$706,323,000	*P/E Ratio:* 20.32
Plant, Equip.:	$792,935,000	*Total Liab.:*	$868,473,000	*Indic. Yr. Divd.:* $1.400
Total Assets:	$3,046,088,000	*Net Worth:*	$2,177,615,000	*Debt/ Equity:* 0.0022

Wabash National Corp

1000 Sagamore Pkwy S, Lafayette, IN, 47905; *PH:* 1-765-771-5300; *http://* www.wabashnational.com; *Email:* sales@wabashnational.com

General - Incorporation	DE	*Stock*- Price on:12/24/2007	$14.82
Employees	4,100	Stock Exchange	NYSE
Auditor	Ernst & Young LLP	Ticker Symbol	WNC
Stk Agt	LaSalle Bank NA	Outstanding Shares	31,720,000
Counsel	NA	E.P.S	$0.22
DUNS No	12-158-1698	Shareholders	NA

Business: The group's principal activity is to design, manufacture and market standard and customized truck trailers and intermodal equipment. The group operates in two segments namely, manufacturing and retail and distribution. The manufacturing segment produces and sells trailers to customers directly or through independent dealers under the trademarks, wabash(R), fruehauf(R) and roadrailer(r). The retail and distribution segment sells, leases and finances new and used trailers along with aftermarket parts and services through its retail branch network. The group's market consists of truckload common carriers, leasing companies, ltl common carriers, private fleet carriers, package carriers and domestic and international intermodal carriers including railroads. The major customers of the group are schneider national, inc & j.b. Hunt transportation services, inc.

Primary SIC and add'l.: 7359 5013 3715

CIK No: 0000879526

Subsidiaries: Cloud Oak Flooring Company, Inc, Continental Transit Corporation, FTSI Canada, Ltd., FTSI Distribution Company, L.P., National Trailer Funding LLC, RoadRailer Mercosul, Ltda, RoadRailer Technology Development Company, Ltd., Wabash Financing LLC, Wabash National GmbH, Wabash National L.P., Wabash National Lease Receivables, L.P., Wabash National Services L.P., Wabash National Trailer Centers, Inc, Wabash Receivables, LLC, WNC Cloud Merger Sub, Inc 16 Subsidiaries included in the Index

Officers: Richard J. Giromini/Dir., CEO, Pres./$740,545.00, Robert J. Smith/CFO, Sr. VP/$460,555.00, Rodney P. Ehrlich/CTO, Sr. VP/$433,402.00, Timothy J. Monahan/Sr. VP - Human Resources, Bruce N. Ewald/Sr. VP - Sales, Marketing/$565,335.00, Cynthia J. Kretz/VP, General Counsel, Corp. Sec., Joseph M. Zachman/Sr. VP - Manufacturing

Directors: Richard J. Giromini/Dir., CEO, Pres., William P. Greubel/Chmn., James D. Kelly/Dir., Scott K. Sorensen/Dir., Martin C. Jischke/Dir., Stephanie K. Kushner/Dir., David C. Burdakin/Dir., Larry J. Magee/Dir., Ronald L. Stewart/Dir.

Owners: Richard J. Giromini, J.D. Kelly, Artisan Partners Limited Partnership/9.40%, Martin C. Jischke, Unicredito Italiano S.P.A./7.17%, Rodney P. Ehrlich, William P. Greubel/1.34%, Robert J. Smith, Stephanie K. Kushner, Barclays Global Investors, N.A. and affiliates/5.36%, Tontine Capital Management, L.L.C. and affiliates/12.80%, Larry J. Magee, Ronald L. Stewart, BlackRock, Inc. and affiliates/5.95%, Goldman Sachs Asset Management, L.P./11.37% *(20 Owners included in Index)*

*Financial Data: Fiscal Year End:*12/31   *Latest Annual Data:* 12/31/2006

Year		Sales		Net Income
2006		$1,312,180,000		$9,420,000
2005		$1,213,711,000		$111,087,000
2004		$1,041,096,000		$58,405,000
Curr. Assets:	$304,218,000	*Curr. Liab.:*	$149,338,000	*P/E Ratio:* 67.36
Plant, Equip.:	$130,627,000	*Total Liab.:*	$278,528,000	*Indic. Yr. Divd.:* $0.180
Total Assets:	$556,483,000	*Net Worth:*	$277,955,000	*Debt/ Equity:* 0.4676

Waccamaw Bankshares Inc

110 N J.k. Powell Blvd, Whiteville, NC, 28472; *PH:* 1-910-641-0044; *http://* www.waccamawbank.com; *Email:* waccamaw@waccamawbank.com

General - Incorporation	NC	*Stock*- Price on:12/24/2007	$14.5
Employees	101	Stock Exchange	NDQ
Auditor	Elliott Davis, PLLC	Ticker Symbol	WBNK
Stk Agt	First Citizens Bank & Trust Co	Outstanding Shares	4,850,000
Counsel	Gaeta & Eveson P.A	E.P.S	$0.78
DUNS No	NA	Shareholders	NA

Business: The group's principal activities are to provide comprehensive individual and corporate banking services to customers in columbus county, North Carolina and surrounding areas through three banking offices and brunswick county through two banking offices. The group operates through its subsidiary, waccamaw bank and sidus financial, llc . The deposits include demand and time deposits as well as commercial, installment, mortgage and other consumer lending services that are traditionally available from community banks.

Primary SIC and add'l.: 6022

CIK No: 0001144686

Subsidiaries: Federal Reserve Board, North Carolina Commissioner of Banks.

Officers: James G. Graham/CEO, Pres./$309,860.00, Kim T. Hutchens/Sr. VP, Chief Administrative Officer - Waccamaw Bank/$100,604.00, Michelle Brown/Assist. VP, Branch Mgr., Robert Bell/Mortgage Banker, Waccamaw Bank, Richard C. Norris/Sr. VP, Chief Credit Officer - Waccamaw Bank/$124,169.00, Freda H. Gore/COO, Sr. VP - Waccamaw Bank/$124,863.00, David A. Godwin/Sr. VP, CFO/$131,129.00, Geoffrey Hopkins/VP - Area Executive, Waccamaw Bank, Ned Hughes/VP - City Executive, Waccamaw Bank, Gayle N. Watson/Assist. VP, Branch Mgr. - Waccamaw Bank, Mark L. Madden/Assist. VP, Branch Mgr. - Waccamaw Bank, Dianne McRainey/VP - Area Executive, Southern Brunswick County, Waccamaw Bank, Vernon Parker/VP, Branch Mgr. - Waccamaw Bank, Kim Neisler/VP, Waccamaw Mortgage Services Mgr. - Waccamaw Bank, Jonathan Krieps/VP - Area Executive, Waccamaw Bank *(38 Officers included in Index)*

Directors: Alan W. Thompson/Chmn., James E. Hill/Dir., Maudie M. Davis/Dir., Autry E. Dawsey/Dir. Emeritus, Brian Campbell/Dir., Dewey L. Hill/Dir., Crawford Monroe Enzor/Dir., M. B. Biggs/Dir., Dale Ward/Dir., Michael K. Jones/Dir., Lucian P. Stephens/Dir., Densil J. Worthington/Dir.

Owners: Richard C. Norris, Crawford Monroe Enzor/1.70%, Maudie M. Davis, Brian D. Campbell, James G. Graham/4.30%, James E. Hill/1.31%, David A. Godwin, Kim T. Hutchens, Insiders/20.84%, Autry E . Dawsey/4.27%, Alan W. Thompson/2.17%, M. B. Biggs, Densil J. Worthington/2.81%, Dale R. Ward/2.23%, Freda H. Gore

Financial Data: *Fiscal Year End:*12/31 *Latest Annual Data:* 12/31/2006

Year	Sales	Net Income
2006	$27,962,000	$3,652,000
2005	$20,498,000	$3,035,000
2004	$13,896,000	$2,414,000

Curr. Assets:	$12,572,000	**Curr. Liab.:**	$334,174,000	**P/E Ratio:**	18.59
Plant, Equip.:	$6,672,000	**Total Liab.:**	$367,879,000	**Indic. Yr. Divd.:**	NA
Total Assets:	$399,581,000	**Net Worth:**	$31,703,000	**Debt/ Equity:**	0.9694

Wachovia Corp

One Wachovia Ctr, Charlotte, NC, 28288; *PH:* 1-704-374-6565; *http://* www.wachovia.com

General - Incorporation	NC	**Stock**- Price on:12/24/2007	$53.12
Employees	108,238	Stock Exchange	NYSE
Auditor	KPMG LLP	Ticker Symbol	WB
Stk Agt	Wachovia Shareholder Services	Outstanding Shares	1,910,000,000
Counsel	NA	E.P.S	$4.79
DUNS No.	00-699-6094	Shareholders	NA

Business: The group's principle activity is to provide a wide range of commercial and retail banking, and trust services. The group's services include online, lending, investing, insurance, asset and risk management, benefits and retirement, international banking, and cash management and deposit services. In October 2007, the group acquired A.G. Edwards, Inc. The group operates from United States.

Primary SIC and add'l.: 6021 6211 6159 6712

CIK No: 0000036995

Subsidiaries: 1005 Corp., 1020 Leavenworth Street Lessee Limited Liability Company, 1024 Dodge Street Limited Partnership, 110 Monastery Associates, Limited Partnership, 1118 Adams Street Urban Renewal, LLC, 1368 Euclid Street L.P., 1368 Euclid Street Tenant L.P., 150 Miami Associates Tenant, LLC, 1515-1517 St. Johns Place, L.p., 1700 Associates, 2-4 Potter Place Urban Renewal, L.P., 343 South Dearborn II, LLC, 349-59 Lenox LLC, 3716 Third Avenue LLC, 425 South Tryon Street, LLC 1248 Subsidiaries included in the Index

Officers: Kennedy G. Thompson/58/Chmn., CEO, Pres./$23,846,280.00, Benjamin P. Jenkins/64/Vice Chmn., Pres. - General Bank/$10,594,210.00, David M. Carroll/51/Head - Capital Management Group/$6,237,839.00, Shannon W. McFayden/48/Head - Human Resources, Corporate Relations, Stanhope A. Kelly/51/Pres. - Wealth Management, Mark C. Treanor/62/General Counsel, Thomas J. Wurtz/46/CFO/$3,126,515.00, Donald Truslow/50/Chief Risk Officer, Stephen E. Cummings/53/Head - Corporate, Investment Banking/$8,689,070.00, Reginald E. Davis/46/Eastern Banking Group Exec., Gerald A. Enos/49/Head - Operations, Technology, Daniel J. Ludeman/52/Pres., Cecelia S. Sutton/50/Head - Retail Bank, Benjamin F. Williams/46/Head - Global Capital Markets, Investment, Ranjana B. Clark/Sr. Exec. VP, Chief Marketing Officer *(16 Officers included in Index)*

Directors: Kennedy G. Thompson/58/Chmn., CEO, Pres., Benjamin P. Jenkins/64/Vice Chmn., Pres. - General Bank, Dona Davis Young/54/Dir., Lanty L. Smith/66/Dir., William H. Goodwin/68/Dir., Van L. Richey/58/Dir., John T. Casteen/65/Dir., John C. Whitaker/71/Dir., Robert J. Brown/Dir., Peter C. Browning/67/Dir., Robert A. Ingram/66/Dir., Donald M. James/59/Dir., Mackey J. McDonald/62/Dir., Joseph Neubauer/67/Dir., Ernest S. Rady/71/Dir. *(21 Directors included in Index)*

Financial Data: *Fiscal Year End:*12/31 *Latest Annual Data:* 06/30/2007

Year	Sales	Net Income
2007	$14,595,000,000	$2,341,000,000
2006	$46,810,000,000	$7,791,000,000
2005	$35,908,000,000	$6,643,000,000

Curr. Assets:	$94,763,000,000	**Curr. Liab.:**	$465,683,000,000		
Plant, Equip.:	$6,141,000,000	**Total Liab.:**	$634,304,000,000	**Indic. Yr. Divd.:**	$2.240
Total Assets:	$707,121,000,000	**Net Worth:**	$69,716,000,000	**Debt/ Equity:**	2.0395

Wacoal Holdings Corp

Formerly: Wacoal Corp
29, Nakajima-cho, Kisshoin, Minami-ku, Kyoto;

General - Incorporation	Japan	**Stock**- Price on:12/24/2007	$62.1901
Employees	NA	Stock Exchange	NDQ
Auditor	Wacoal Holdings Corp	Ticker Symbol	WACLY
Stk Agt	Mitsubishi UFJ Trust & Banking Corp	Outstanding Shares	NA
Counsel	NA	E.P.S	NA
DUNS No.	69-055-7673	Shareholders	NA

Business: The group's principal activities are to manufacture and market women's intimate apparel. The products include foundation garments-primarily brassieres and girdles and lingerie-mainly slips, bra-slips and women's briefs, nightwear, children's underwear, outerwear and sportswear, hosiery and other textile products. The brands of the group include wacoal, dki and dkny. The other operations of the group include housing and restaurant businesses, cultural and service-related operations and the construction of interiors for commercial premises. The operations of the group are in Japan, Asia, Europe and North America.

Primary SIC and add'l.: 2342 2369 2251 2341 2339

CIK No: 0000104040

Subsidiaries: Dalian Wacoal Co., Ltd., Fukuoka Wacoal Sewing Corp., Guangdong Wacoal Inc., Hokuriku Wacoal Sewing Corp., Kyushu Wacoal Manufacturing Corp., Miyazaki Wacoal Sewing Corp., Nanasai Co., Ltd., Niigata Wacoal Sewing Corp., Philippine Wacoal Corp., Studio Five Corp., Tokai Wacoal Sewing Corp., Torica Inc., Vietnam Wacoal Corp., Wacoal (Shanghai) Human Science R&D Co., Ltd., Wacoal (UK)LTD. 26 Subsidiaries included in the Index

Officers: Yoshikata Tsukamoto/60/Dir., CEO, Exec. VP, Pres., Mamoru Ozaki/73/Dir., Advisor, Shoichi Suezawa/61/CFO, Sr. MD, Tatsuya Kondo/61/Dir., GM - Direct Marketing Operation Division, Supervisor Wellness Department, Managing Corp. Officer, Tadashi Yamamoto/56/Dir., GM - Personnel, Administration Department, Hajime Kotake/59/Standing Corporate Auditor, Yutaka Hasegawa/69/Corporate Auditor, Yoko Takemura/56/Corporate Auditor, Ikuo Otani/GM - Corporate Planning, Hideo Kawanaka/66/Sr. MD, Kimiaki Shiraishi/58/Standing Corporate Auditor, Tomoharu Kuda/62/Corporate Auditor

Directors: Yoshikata Tsukamoto/60/Dir., CEO, Exec. VP, Pres., Tatsuya Kondo/61/Dir., GM - Direct Marketing Operation Division, Supervisor Wellness Department, Managing Corp. Officer, Mamoru Ozaki/73/Dir., Advisor, Kazuo Inamori/76/Dir., Tadashi Yamamoto/56/Dir., GM - Personnel, Administration Department

Owners: Tradewinds Global Investors, LLC/14.48%, Yuzo Ito, Yoshikata Tsukamoto, Tadashi Yamamoto, Kimiaki Shiraishi, Hajime Kotake, Mitsubishi UFJ Financial Group, Inc. and its joint holders/8.95%, Tatsuya Kondo, Shoichi Suezawa, Yoko Takemura

Financial Data: *Fiscal Year End:*03/31 *Latest Annual Data:* 03/31/2007

Year	Sales	Net Income
2007	$1,415,532,000	$76,803,000
2006	$1,397,021,000	$24,013,000
2005	$1,501,287,000	$63,328,000

Curr. Assets:	$942,569,000	**Curr. Liab.:**	$302,392,000	**P/E Ratio:**	15.41
Plant, Equip.:	$455,405,000	**Total Liab.:**	$475,154,000	**Indic. Yr. Divd.:**	NA
Total Assets:	$2,062,445,000	**Net Worth:**	$1,587,291,000	**Debt/ Equity:**	NA

Waddell & Reed Inc

6300 Lamar Ave., Overland Park, KS, 66202; *PH:* 1-913-236-2000; *Fax:* 1-913-236-2017; *http://* www.waddell.com

General - Incorporation	DE	**Stock**- Price on:12/24/2007	$26.52
Employees	1,606	Stock Exchange	NYSE
Auditor	KPMG LLP	Ticker Symbol	WDR
Stk Agt	Computershare Investor Services LLC	Outstanding Shares	83,920,000
Counsel	NA	E.P.S	$1.46
DUNS No.	80-632-0438	Shareholders	NA

Business: The group's principal activities are to provide investment management, investment product underwriting and distribution. The group's other services include shareholder services administration to the waddell & reed advisors funds, the w&r mutual funds, the w&r target funds inc and managed institutional and separate accounts. The group's subsidiary waddell & reed, inc. Is a national distributor and underwriter for shares of mutual funds and the distributor of variable and other insurance products issued by nationwide life insurance company. It is a registered investment advisor that provides investment management and advisory services to the mutual funds, institutions and other private clients. It manages investments for trusts, high net worth families and individuals, hospitals, schools, labor unions, endowments and foundations.

Primary SIC and add'l.: 6719 6211

CIK No: 0001052100

Subsidiaries: Advisory Services Corporation, Austin, Calvert & Flavin, Inc., Fiduciary Trust Company of New Hampshire, Ivy Funds Distributor, Inc., Ivy Investment Management Company, Ivy Services, Inc., LEC Insurance Agency, Inc., Legend Advisory Corporation, Legend Equities Corporation, Legend Group Holdings, LLC, The Legend Group, Inc., Unicon Agency, Inc., Unicon Insurance Agency of Massachusetts, Inc., W & R Insurance Agency of Alabama, Inc., W & R Insurance Agency of Arkansas, Inc. 27 Subsidiaries included in the Index

Officers: Henry J. Herrmann/Dir., CEO/$5,029,927.00, John E. Sundeen/Sr. VP, Chief Administrative Officer - Investments, Michael L. Avery/Sr. VP, Chief Investment Officer/$1,551,789.00, Nicole McIntosh/Dir. - Investor Relations, Daniel P. Connealy/Sr. VP, CFO/$972,726.00, Thomas W. Butch/Sr. VP, Chief Marketing Officer/$1,549,765.00, Michael D. Strohm/COO, Sr. VP, Daniel C. Schulte/Sr. VP, General Counsel/$1,359,094.00, Roger Hoadley/Dir. - Corporate Communications

Directors: Henry J. Herrmann/Dir., CEO, Alan W. Kosloff/Chmn., William L. Rogers/Dir., Jerry W. Walton/Dir., Dennis E. Logue/Dir., Ronald C. Reimer/Dir., James M. Raines/Dir.

Owners: Ronald C. Reimer, Dennis E. Logue, Mark A. Schieber, Thomas W. Butch, Insiders/3.60%, Brent K. Bloss, Alan W. Kosloff, Daniel P. Connealy, Michael L. Avery, Daniel C. Schulte, John E. Sundeen, James M. Raines, Jerry W. Walton, William L. Rogers, Michael D. Strohm

Financial Data: *Fiscal Year End:*12/31 *Latest Annual Data:* 12/31/2006

Year	Sales	Net Income
2006	$718,655,000	$46,112,000
2005	$622,080,000	$60,121,000
2004	$504,077,000	$102,165,000

Curr. Assets:	$352,003,000	**Curr. Liab.:**	$189,551,000	**P/E Ratio:**	19.64
Plant, Equip.:	$50,875,000	**Total Liab.:**	$418,014,000	**Indic. Yr. Divd.:**	$0.680
Total Assets:	$662,714,000	**Net Worth:**	$244,700,000	**Debt/ Equity:**	0.8741

Wainwright Bank & Trust Company

63 Franklin St., Boston, MA, 02110; *PH:* 1-617-478-4000; *http://* www.wainwrightbank.com

General - Incorporation		**Stock**- Price on:12/24/2007	$13.1599
Employees	158	Stock Exchange	NDQ
Auditor	NA	Ticker Symbol	WAIN
Stk Agt	American Stock Transfer & Trust Co.	Outstanding Shares	7,610,000
Counsel	NA	E.P.S	NA
DUNS No.	NA	Shareholders	NA

Business: The Group's principal activity is to provide financial services. The groups services include checking account, saving account, debit card and online banking. The products of the group include consumer, construction and commercial loan. The group operates from the United States.

Primary SIC and add'l.: 6022

CIK No:

Officers: Jan A. Miller/Pres.

Directors: Robert A. Glassman/Co - Chmn., John M. Plukas/Co - Chmn., Brenda L. Cole/Dir., Charles F. Desmond/Dir., James B. Hyman/Dir., Frank J. Keohane/Dir., James A. Pitts/Dir., John E. Reed/Dir., Elliott D. Sclar/Dir., Ranne P. Warner/Dir.

Wake Forest Bancshares Inc

302 S Brooks St., Wake Forest, NC, 27587; *PH:* 1-919-556-5146; *http://* www.wakeforestfederal.com

General - Incorporation	US	Stock- Price on:12/24/2007	$22
Employees	9	Stock Exchange	OTC
Auditor	Dixon Hughes PLLC	Ticker Symbol	WAKE
Stk Agt	Mellon Investor Services LLC	Outstanding Shares	1,160,000
Counsel	Thacher Proffitt & Wood LLP	E.P.S.	$1.45
DUNS No.	NA	Shareholders	NA

Business: The group's principal activities are to attract retail deposits from the general public and invest those deposits, together with other sources of funds in loans. The lending activities of the group include one-to four-family first mortgage loans, construction loans, multi-family residential loans, commercial real estate loans, land loans and loans secured by savings account. It also offers a variety of deposits consisting of regular passbook savings accounts, now accounts, checking accounts, money market deposit accounts, iras and certificates of deposits.

Primary SIC and add'l.: 6712 6035

CIK No: 0001085175

Subsidiaries: Wake Forest Bancorp, M.H.C

Officers: Robert C. White/Dir., CEO, Pres., Wanda R. Keith/Assist. VP, Controller, Compliance Officer, Billy B. Faulkner/VP, Sec., Treasurer, Susan S. Carter/VP, Sr. Residential Loan Officer

Directors: Robert C. White/Dir., CEO, Pres., Howard L. Brown/Chmn., R. W. Wilkinson/Vice Chmn., John D. Lyon/Dir., Harold R. Washington/Dir., Leelan A. Woodlief/Dir., Paul K. Brixhoff/Dir., Rodney M. Privette/Dir., Anna O. Sumerlin/Dir., William S. Wooten/Dir.

Owners: R. W. Wilkinso, Insiders/6.77%, Rodney M. Privette/0.11%, Anna O. Sumerlin/0.81%, Billy B. Faulkner/0.16%, Howard L. Brown/0.71%, William S. Wooten/0.13%, Harold R. Washington/0.39%, John D. Lyon/2.41%, Leelan A. Woodlief/0.54%, Robert C. White/0.66%, Wake Forest Bancorp, M.H.C./54.70%

Financial Data: Fiscal Year End:09/30   Latest Annual Data: 09/30/2006

Year	Sales	Net Income
2006	$7,282,000	$1,656,000
2005	$5,846,000	$1,321,000
2004	$4,946,000	$1,089,000

Curr. Assets:	$24,049,000	Curr. Liab.:	$84,919,000	P/E Ratio:	14.77
Plant, Equip.:	$1,406,000	Total Liab.:	$85,472,000	Indic. Yr. Divd.:	$0.760
Total Assets:	$104,279,000	Net Worth:	$18,806,000	Debt/ Equity:	NA

Wako Logistics Group Inc

200 Howard Ave. Ste. 232, Des Plaines, IL, 60018; *PH:* 1-847-294-1600; *http://* www.wakogroup.com

General - Incorporation	DE	Stock- Price on:12/24/2007	$1.35
Employees	257	Stock Exchange	OTC
Auditor	Moores, Rowland Mazars	Ticker Symbol	WKOL
Stk Agt	Olde Monmouth Stk Trnsfer Co. Inc.	Outstanding Shares	25,390,000
Counsel	NA	E.P.S.	$0.03
DUNS No.	NA	Shareholders	NA

Business: The groups principle activities include providing supply chain logistics services, including warehousing, freight forwarding, customs brokerage and VAS, such as scanning, pick and pack and ground transportation. The group operates through three segments namely airfreight operations, seafreight operations and customs brokerage services. In April 2005, the group acquired Kay O'Neill and In December 2006, the group acquired MSA and its wholly owned subsidiary, Sea Systems, Inc. The group operates from the United States, the United Kingdom, Australia and China.

Primary SIC and add'l.: 4731

CIK No: 0001283236

Subsidiaries: Asean Cargo Services Pty Limited**, Asean Logistics, Inc, Mares-Shreve & Associates, Inc., Sea Systems Ocean Line, Inc., Wako Air Express (HK) Co. Ltd., Wako Express (China) Co. Ltd, Wako Express (HK) Co. Ltd., WLG (Australia) Pty Ltd., WLG (UK) Holdings Limited, WLG (UK) Limited, WLG (USA) LLC

Officers: Christopher Wood/Dir., CEO, Paul John William Pomroy/CEO - Australia, Anthony Leung/CEO - Hong Kong, China, Remo Picchietti/CEO - WLG USA, Exec. VP, Peter John Gialouris/48/CFO - Asean, Kelvin Tang/35/Sec., Nicholas Hilton/43/Mgr. - Asean's Operations, Bill Ip/VP - Central, Northern China, Antony Wilshaw/VP - Operations, UK, Gordon Dean/VP - Bus Development, UK, Mark Fearnley/Operations Mgr., Phillip Forsyth/COO, David Koontz/CFO, Robert Wong/Sr. VP - Hong Kong, South China, Raymond Chan/VP - Hong Kong, South China (17 Officers included in Index)

Directors: Christopher Wood/Dir., CEO

Owners: Chris Wood/79.20%, Paul Pomroy/4.20%, Chris Wood/100.00%, Insiders/84.70%

Financial Data: Fiscal Year End:12/31   Latest Annual Data: 12/31/2006

Year	Sales	Net Income
2006	$100,307,000	$553,000
2005	$52,723,000	$592,000
2004	$16,584,000	$276,000

Curr. Assets:	$17,773,000	Curr. Liab.:	$16,403,000	P/E Ratio:	13.41
Plant, Equip.:	$927,000	Total Liab.:	$17,269,000	Indic. Yr. Divd.:	NA
Total Assets:	$27,087,000	Net Worth:	$9,818,000	Debt/ Equity:	NA

Wal-Mart Stores Inc

702 SW 8th St., Bentonville, AR, 72716; *PH:* 1-479-273-4941; *Fax:* 1-479-277-1830; *http://* www.walmartstores.com

General - Incorporation	DE	Stock- Price on:12/24/2007	$48.689
Employees	1,900,000	Stock Exchange	NYSE
Auditor	Ernst & Young LLP	Ticker Symbol	WMT
Stk Agt	Ernst & Young LLP	Outstanding Shares	4,110,000,000
Counsel	NA	E.P.S.	$3.06
DUNS No.	05-195-7769	Shareholders	NA

Business: The group's principle activity is to provide retail stores. The group operates in three segments including Wal-Mart Stores, Sam's Club and international segment. The group operates from United States.

Primary SIC and add'l.: 5311 5141 5411 5399

CIK No: 0000104169

Subsidiaries: ASDA Group Limited, Wal-Mart Property Company, Wal-Mart Real Estate Business Trust, Wal-Mart Stores East, LP

Officers: Eduardo Castro-Wright/CEO, Exec. VP, Pres. - Wal, Mart Stores Division/$6,201,713.00, Craig R. Herkert/CEO, Exec. VP, Pres. - Americas, International Division, Lee H. Scott/Dir., CEO, Pres./$29,672,530.00, Douglas C. McMillon/CEO, Exec. VP, Pres. - Sam's Club, John B. Menzer/Vice Chmn., Chief Administrative Officer/$12,745,740.00, Michael T. Duke/Vice Chmn. - International Division/$10,634,400.00, Johnnie C. Dobbs/Exec. VP - Logistics, Supply Chain, Leslie Dach/Exec. VP - Corporate Affairs, Government Relations, Linda M. Dillman/Exec. VP - Risk Management, Benefits, Sustainability, Thomas A. Mars/Exec. VP, General Counsel, Susan M. Chambers/Exec. VP - People Division, Patricia A. Curran/Exec. VP - Store Operations, Wal, Mart Stores Division, US, Steven P. Whaley/Sr. VP, Controller, Charles M. Holley/Exec. VP - Finance, Treasurer, Thomas D. Hyde/Exec. VP, Corp. Sec. (23 Officers included in Index)

Directors: Lee H. Scott/Dir., CEO, Pres., Robson S. Walton/Chmn., Jim C. Walton/Dir., Aida Alvarez/Dir., James W. Breyer/Dir., Christopher J. Williams/Dir., Linda S. Wolf/Dir., Roger C. Corbett/Dir., Allen I. Questrom/Dir., Roland A. Hernandez/Dir., Jack C. Shewmaker/Dir., Michele M. Burns/Dir., James Cash/Dir., Douglas N. Daft/Dir., David D. Glass/Dir.

Owners: Michael T. Duke, Estate of John T. Walton, Lee H. Scott, Aida M. Alvarez, Roger C. Corbett, Jack C. Shewmaker, Alice L. Walton, John B. Menzer, Roland A. Hernandez, James I. Cash, David D. Glass, James W. Breyer, Thomas M. Schoewe, Robson S. Walton, Eduardo Castro-Wright (22 Owners included in Index)

Financial Data: Fiscal Year End:01/31   Latest Annual Data: 1/31/2007

Year	Sales	Net Income
2007	$348,650,000,000	$11,284,000,000
2006	$315,654,000,000	$11,231,000,000
2005	$287,989,000,000	$10,267,000,000

Curr. Assets:	$46,588,000,000	Curr. Liab.:	$51,754,000,000	P/E Ratio:	16.12
Plant, Equip.:	$88,440,000,000	Total Liab.:	$89,620,000,000	Indic. Yr. Divd.:	$0.880
Total Assets:	$151,193,000,000	Net Worth:	$61,573,000,000	Debt/ Equity:	0.5527

Walgreen Co

200 Wilmot Rd. , Deerfield, IL, 60015; *PH:* 1-847-940-2500; *http://* www.walgreens.com

General - Incorporation	IL	Stock- Price on:12/24/2007	$43.8273
Employees	142,200	Stock Exchange	NYSE
Auditor	Deloitte & Touche LLP	Ticker Symbol	WAG
Stk Agt	Computershare Investor Services LLC	Outstanding Shares	997,440,000
Counsel	NA	E.P.S.	$2.06
DUNS No.	00-896-5063	Shareholders	NA

Business: The group's principle activity is to operate retail drugstore chains that sell prescription and non-prescription drugs. The group's products include general merchandise with beauty and personal care, household items, candy, photofinishing, greeting cards, seasonal items and convenience foods. The group operates from United States.

Primary SIC and add'l.: 5921 5912 5399 5999

CIK No: 0000104207

Subsidiaries: Bond Drug Company of Illinois, LLC, Bowen Development Company, Grenada Advertising Agency, Inc., Happy Harrys Inc., Medmark, Inc., Schrafts, A Walgreens Specialty Pharmacy, LLC, SeniorMed LLC, Walgreen Arizona Drug Co., Walgreen Eastern Co., Inc., Walgreen Hastings Co., Walgreen Louisiana Co., Inc., Walgreen Mercantile Corp., Walgreen National Corporation, Walgreen of Puerto Rico, Inc., Walgreen of San Patricio, Inc. 22 Subsidiaries included in the Index

Officers: Jeffrey A. Rein/Chmn., CEO, John W. Gleeson/Sr. VP - Corporate Strategy, Treasurer, Corporate VP, Treasurer, William A. Shiel/Sr. VP - Facilities Development, Mark A. Wagner/Exec. VP - Store Operations, George J. Riedl/Exec. VP - Marketing, William M. Handal/Sr. VP - Store Operations, Trent E. Taylor/CIO, Exec. VP, Kevin P. Walgreen/Sr. VP - Store Operations, Chester G. Young/63/General Auditor, Dana I. Green/Sr. VP, General Counsel, Corp. Sec., William M. Rudolphsen/CFO, Sr. VP, Barry L. Markl/Sr. VP - Store Operations, Bruce R. Bryant/Sr. VP - Store Operations, Mia M. Scholz/42/VP, Controller, Randolph J. Lewis/Sr. VP - Distribution, Logistics (24 Officers included in Index)

Directors: Jeffrey A. Rein/Chmn., CEO, William C. Foote/Dir., James J. Howard/Dir., Alan G. McNally/63/Dir., Cordell Reed/70/Dir., David Y. Schwartz/67/Dir., James A. Skinner/64/Dir., Marilou M. Von Ferstel/70/Dir., C. R. Walgreen/73/Dir., Nancy M. Schlichting/54/Dir., Alejandro Silva/61/Dir.

Owners: David Y. Schwartz, David W. Bernauer, Jeffrey A. Rein, Alan G. McNally, George J. Riedl, Alejandro Silva, James A. Skinner, Capital Research and Management Company/10.30%, William M. Rudolphsen, James J. Howard, William C. Foote, Cordell Reed, Charles R. Walgreen, Insiders/0.62%, Trent E. Taylor (17 Owners included in Index)

Financial Data: Fiscal Year End:08/31   Latest Annual Data: 8/31/2006

Year	Sales	Net Income
2006	$47,409,000,000	$1,750,600,000
2005	$42,201,600,000	$1,559,500,000
2004	$37,508,200,000	$1,349,800,000

Curr. Assets:	$9,705,400,000	Curr. Liab.:	$5,755,300,000	P/E Ratio:	21.48
Plant, Equip.:	$6,948,900,000	Total Liab.:	$7,015,300,000	Indic. Yr. Divd.:	$0.380
Total Assets:	$17,131,100,000	Net Worth:	$10,115,800,000	Debt/ Equity:	NA

Walker Financial Corp

990 Stewart Ave., Ste. 650, Garden City, NY, 11530; *PH:* 1-516-746-4141; *http://* www.walkerfinancialcorp.com

General - Incorporation DE | **Stock**- Price on:12/24/2007 NA
Employees 7 | Stock Exchange OTC
Auditor ... Russell Bedford Stefanou Mirchandani | Ticker Symbol WLKF
Stk Agt...... American Stock Transfer & Trust Co. | Outstanding Shares NA
Counsel NA | E.P.S -$0.116
DUNS No. 05-405-9555 | Shareholders NA

Business: The group's principal activities are to provide financial services operating in the death care business and process films and sells photographic portraits. The group also maintains a portrait studio. The group operates its film processing through its subsidiary kelly color laboratories, inc., which processes photographs for professional photographers, principally through mail orders. The group markets its photography services to photographers throughout the United States.

Primary SIC and add'l.: 7261 7221

CIK No: 0000104224

Subsidiaries: American DataSource, Inc., National Preplanning, Inc.

Owners: Mitchell S. Segal/63.70%, Peter Walker/1.30%, Insiders/64.10%

Financial Data: *Fiscal Year End:*12/31 *Latest Annual Data:* 12/31/2006

Year	Sales	Net Income
2006	$531,000	-$2,116,000
2005	$328,000	-$3,296,000
2004	$241,000	-$1,924,000

Curr. Assets:	$121,000	**Curr. Liab.:**	$2,780,000		
Plant, Equip.:	$19,000	**Total Liab.:**	$3,158,000	**Indic. Yr. Divd.:**	NA
Total Assets:	$347,000	**Net Worth:**	-$2,811,000	**Debt/ Equity:**	NA

Walt Disney Co

500 S Buena Vista St., Burbank, CA, 91521; ***PH:*** 1-818-560-1000; ***Fax:*** 1-818-560-1930; ***http://*** www.disney.go.com

General - Incorporation DE | **Stock**- Price on:12/24/2007 $34.73
Employees 133,000 | Stock Exchange NYSE
Auditor PricewaterhouseCoopers LLP | Ticker Symbol DIS
Stk Agt Disney Shareholder Services | Outstanding Shares 1,980,000,000
Counsel NA | E.P.S $2.25
DUNS No. 93-266-0376 | Shareholders NA

Business: The group's principle activity is to provide information and entertainment services. The group is divided into four major business segments namely Studio Entertainment, Parks and Resorts, Consumer Products, and Media Networks. The group operates from United States and Europe.

Primary SIC and add'l.: 4841 7812 7996 5947 4833 7011 7379

CIK No: 0001001039

Subsidiaries: ABC Cable Networks Group, ABC Family Worldwide, Inc., ABC, Inc., American Broadcasting Companies, Inc., Buena Vista International, Inc., Buena Vista Television, Disney Enterprises, Inc., Disney Magic Company Limited, Disney Vacation Development, Inc., ESPN Product Services, ESPN, Inc., Euro Disney Associes S.C.A., Euro Disney S.C.A., Hong Kong International Theme Parks, Limited, International Family Entertainment, Inc. 23 Subsidiaries included in the Index

Officers: Robert A. Iger/56/Dir., CEO, Pres., George W. Bodenheimer/Co - Chmn. - Disney Media Networks, Richard Cook/Chmn. - Walt Disney Studios, Andrew P. Mooney/Chmn. - Disney Consumer Products, Jay Rasulo/Chmn. - Walt Disney Parks, Resorts, Anne Sweeney/Co - Chmn. Disney Media Networks, Pres. - Disney, ABC Television Group, Steve Wadsworth/Pres. - Walt Disney Internet Group, Zenia Mucha/Exec. VP - Corporate Communications, Walter C. Liss/Pres. - ABC Owned Television Stations, Wesley Coleman/Chief Human Resources Officer, Exec. VP, Ronald L. Iden/Sr. VP - Security, Kevin Mayer/Exec. VP - Corporate Strategy, Business Development, Technology Group, Christine M. McCarthy/Exec. VP - Corporate Finance, Real Estate, Treasurer, Andy Bird/Pres. - Walt Disney International, Thomas O. Staggs/CFO, Sr. Exec. VP *(18 Officers included in Index)*

Directors: Robert A. Iger/56/Dir., CEO, Pres., John E. Pepper/69/Chmn., Orin C. Smith/65/Dir., Monica C. Lozano/51/Dir., Robert W. Matschullat/60/Dir., Steve Jobs/53/Dir., Fred H. Langhammer/64/Dir., Aylwin B. Lewis/53/Dir., Susan Arnold/Dir., John E. Bryson/64/Dir., John S. Chen/52/Dir., Judith L. Estrin/53/Dir.

Owners: Alan N. Braverman, Steven P. Jobs/0.07%, Monica C. Lozano, Kevin A. Mayer, Christine M. McCarthy, Robert W. Matschullat, John S. Chen, Robert A. Iger, Leo J. O'Donovan, John E. Mandel, Judith L. Estrin, Fred H. Langhammer, Thomas O. Staggs, John E. Bryson, Aylwin B. Lewis *(16 Owners included in Index)*

Financial Data: *Fiscal Year End:*10/01 *Latest Annual Data:* 09/29/2007

Year	Sales	Net Income
2007	$35,510,000,000	$4,687,000,000
2006	$34,285,000,000	$3,374,000,000
2005	$31,944,000,000	$2,533,000,000

Curr. Assets:	$9,562,000,000	**Curr. Liab.:**	$10,210,000,000		
Plant, Equip.:	$17,167,000,000	**Total Liab.:**	$26,835,000,000	**Indic. Yr. Divd.:**	$0.310
Total Assets:	$59,998,000,000	**Net Worth:**	$31,820,000,000	**Debt/ Equity:**	0.3241

Walter Industries Inc

4211 W Boy Scout Blvd., Tampa, FL, 33607; ***PH:*** 1-813-871-4811; ***http://*** www.walterind.com; ***Email:*** corporatecommunications@walterind.com

General - Incorporation DE | **Stock**- Price on:12/24/2007 $30.7
Employees 2,800 | Stock Exchange NYSE
Auditor PricewaterhouseCoopers LLP | Ticker Symbol WLT
Stk Agt Bank of New York | Outstanding Shares 52,060,000
Counsel NA | E.P.S NA
DUNS No. 18-340-2874 | Shareholders NA

Business: The groups principle activities include producing and exporting metallurgical coal for the steel industry. The group also produces steam coal, coal bed, methane gas, furnace and foundry coke, and other related products. The group also operates a mortgage financing and affordable homebuilding business. The group operates from United States.

Primary SIC and add'l.: 1221 1521 3321 1311

CIK No: 0000837173

Subsidiaries: Anvil 1, LLC, Anvil 2, LLC, Anvil International, LLC, Anvil International, LP, AnvilStar, LLC, Best Insurors, Inc., Black Warrior Methane Corp., Black Warrior Transmission Corp., Blue Creek Coal Sales, Inc., Cardem Insurance Co., Ltd., Coast to Coast Advertising, Inc., Crestline Homes, Inc., Dixie Building Supplies, Inc., Dream Homes USA, Inc., Dream Homes, Inc. 69 Subsidiaries included in the Index

Officers: Victor P. Patrick/Vice Chmn., General Counsel, Sec./$1,542,273.00, William F. Ohrt/Exec. VP/$1,323,556.00, Mark H. Tubb/VP - Investor Relations, Strategic Planning, Mike Monahan/Dir. - Corporate Communications, Larry E. Williams/Sr. VP - Human Resources, Joseph J. Troy/CFO, Exec. VP/$1,525,870.00, Charles E. Cauthen/Pres. - Walter Mortgage Company/$1,261,092.00, Miles C. Dearden/Sr. VP, Treasurer, Cynthia B. Eisch/Assist. Controller, Tax Dir., Catherine C. Bona/VP, Corp. Sec., Ronald L. Loida/VP - Internal Audit, Ronald E. McCaslin/Pres. - Jim Walter Homes, Inc, Kimberly A. Perez/CFO, Exec. VP - Walter Mortgage Company, Billy R. Philbeck/VP - Risk Management, Lisa A. Honnold/Sr. VP, Controller

Directors: Michael T. Tokarz/Chmn., Victor P. Patrick/Vice Chmn., General Counsel, Sec., Patrick A. Kriegshauser/Dir., James Willis Walter/Founder, Mark J. O'Brien/Dir., Joseph B. Leonard/64/Dir., Jerry W. Kolb/Dir., A. J. Wagner/Dir., George R. Richmond/Dir., Bernard G. Rethore/Dir., Howard L. Clark/Dir.

Owners: Patrick A. Kriegshauser, Joseph J. Troy, Harris Associates L.P./6.00%, Bernard G. Rethore, George R. Richmond, JP Morgan Chase & Co./8.00%, Mark J. OBrien, William F. Ohrt, Jerry W. Kolb, Gregory E. Hyland, Michael T. Tokarz, Victor P. Patrick, Charles E. Cauthen, Howard L. Clark, Insiders/1.56% *(16 Owners included in Index)*

Financial Data: *Fiscal Year End:*12/31 *Latest Annual Data:* 12/31/2006

Year	Sales	Net Income
2006	$1,309,856,000	$198,369,000
2005	$2,054,140,000	$7,046,000
2004	$1,461,722,000	$49,917,000

Curr. Assets:	$2,224,769,000	**Curr. Liab.:**	$176,311,000	**P/E Ratio:**	8.25
Plant, Equip.:	$311,189,000	**Total Liab.:**	$2,682,207,000	**Indic. Yr. Divd.:**	$0.200
Total Assets:	$2,684,115,000	**Net Worth:**	$1,908,000	**Debt/ Equity:**	4.0357

Wannigan Ventures Inc

1172 Manito Dr. Nw, Fox Island, WA, 98333; ***PH:*** 1-253-549-4336

General - Incorporation NV | **Stock**- Price on:12/24/2007 NA
Employees NA | Stock Exchange NA
Auditor Child, Van Wagoner & Bradshaw, PLLC | Ticker Symbol NA
Stk Agt Stalt Inc | Outstanding Shares NA
Counsel NA | E.P.S NA
DUNS No. NA | Shareholders NA

Business: The groups principle activity is to acquisition opportunities, investigate, and if such investigation warrants, acquire an interest in one or more business opportunities presented to it by persons or firms desiring the perceived advantages of a publicly held corporation. The group involves in acquiring or merging with a corporation which does not need substantial additional cash but which desires to establish a public trading market for its common stock. The group also purchase assets and establish wholly owned subsidiaries in various businesses or purchase existing businesses as subsidiaries. The group operates from United States.

Primary SIC and add'l.: 9995

CIK No: 0001269879

Officers: Kevin Murphy/60/Chmn., CEO, Pres., Steven Pickett/CFO, Treasurer, Kenneth Liebscher/Sec.

Directors: Kevin Murphy/60/Chmn., CEO, Pres.

Owners: Wannigan Capital Corp./100.00%

Warnaco Group Inc

501 7th Ave., New York, NY, 10018; ***PH:*** 1-212-287-8000; ***Fax:*** 1-212-287-8297; ***http://*** www.warnaco.com; ***Email:*** contactus@warnaco.com

General - Incorporation DE | **Stock**- Price on:12/24/2007 $36.89
Employees 10,287 | Stock Exchange NDQ
Auditor Deloitte & Touche LLP | Ticker Symbol WRNC
Stk Agt Wells Fargo Corporate Trust | Outstanding Shares 46,300,000
Counsel NA | E.P.S $1.83
DUNS No. 00-116-3856 | Shareholders NA

Business: The groups principle activity is to operate retail stores. The groups products include intimate apparel, sportswear and swimwear. The groups products are sold under the brand names Warner's, Olga, Calvin Klein, Speedo, Chaps, Nautica, Catalina, Anne Cole and Lejaby. The group operates from United States.

Primary SIC and add'l.: 2321 5651 5621 9999 2341

CIK No: 0000801351

Subsidiaries: 184 Benton Street Inc., 4278941 Canada Inc., A.B.S. Clothing Collection, Inc., A.E.S. Advanced Euro Service S.r.l., Authentic Fitness de Mexico, S.A. de C.V., Authentic Fitness On-line Inc., C.F. Hathaway Company, C.K. Jeanswear Europe S.p.A., Calvin Klein France SnC, Calvin Klein Jeanswear Company, Calvin Klein Jeanswear Korea Limited, CCC Acquisition Corp., Centro de Corte de Tetla S.A. de C.V., CK Jeanswear Asia Limited, CK Jeanswear Australia Pty Ltd. 87 Subsidiaries included in the Index

Officers: Joseph R. Gromek/Dir., CEO, Pres./$4,310,108.00, Jay A. Galluzzo/Sr. VP - Corporate Development, General Counsel, Sec., Helen McCluskey/Pres. - Warnaco Intimate Apparel/$2,295,854.00, Dwight Meyer/Pres. - Global Sourcing, Distribution, Logistics, Lawrence Rutkowski/CFO, Exec. VP/$1,869,148.00, Frank Tworecke/Pres. - Warnaco Sportswear Group/$2,240,897.00, Stanley P. Silverstein/Exec. VP - International Strategy, Business Development/$1,852,146.00, Elizabeth Wood/Sr. VP - Human Resources

Directors: Joseph R. Gromek/Dir., CEO, Pres., Charles R. Perrin/Non - Exec. Chmn., David A. Bell/Dir., Robert A. Bowman/Dir., Richard Karl Goeltz/Dir., Sheila A. Hopkins/Dir., Nancy A. Reardon/Dir., Donald L. Seeley/Dir., Cheryl Nido Turpin/Dir.

Owners: Frank Tworecke, Insiders/5.20%, David A. Bell, Helen McCluskey, Dimensional Fund Advisors LP/6.60%, Charles R. Perrin, Robert A. Bowman, Glenhill Advisors LLC/6.30%, Snyder Capital Management, L.P./5.80%, Sheila A. Hopkins, Richard Karl Goeltz, Joseph R. Gromek/2.20%, Hotchkis and Wiley Capital Management, LLC/5.90%, Lawrence R. Rutkowski, Stanley P. Silverstein *(18 Owners included in Index)*

Financial Data: *Fiscal Year End:*12/31 *Latest Annual Data:* 12/30/2006

Year	Sales	Net Income
2006	$1,827,486,000	$50,750,000
2005	$1,501,087,000	$49,492,000

Curr. Assets:	$747,968,000	Curr. Liab.:	$253,204,000	P/E Ratio:	20.16
Plant, Equip.:	$116,995,000	Total Liab.:	$590,564,000	Indic. Yr. Divd.:	NA
Total Assets:	$1,220,051,000	Net Worth:	$629,487,000	Debt/ Equity:	0.4542

Warner Chilcott Plc

100 Enterprise Dr., Rockaway, NJ, 07866; PH: 1-973-442-3200; Fax: 1-973-442-3283;
http:// www.warnerchilcott.com

General - Incorporation .... Ireland	Stock- Price on:12/24/2007 ....$17.35
Employees...985	Stock Exchange...NDQ
Auditor ....PricewaterhouseCoopers LLP	Ticker Symbol...WCRX
Stk Agt...... American Stock Transfer & Trust Co.	Outstanding Shares 250,570,000
Counsel ....NA	E.P.S ....-$0.5
DUNS No. ....NA	Shareholders..NA

Business: The group's principal activities are the development, manufacture and distribution of branded prescription pharmaceutical products. The group also provides services to both pharmaceutical and biotechnology companies by designing, manufacturing and compiling patient packs for use un clinical trials, which are then distributed from its facilities in craigavon and Pennsylvania. It also manufactures and supplies intravenous and other sterile solutions, primarily for human use. The group's principal markets are in the United States, the United Kingdom and the republic of Ireland.
Primary SIC and add'l.: 8071 2834
CIK No: 0001113445
Subsidiaries: Galen (Chemicals) Limited, Galen Limited, Warner Chilcott Inc
Officers: Roger M. Boissonneault/Dir., CEO, Pres., Alvin Howard/Sr. VP - Regulatory Affairs, Paul Herendeen/CFO, Exec. VP, Carlton W. Reichel/Pres. - Pharmaceuticals, Izumi Hara/Sr. VP, General Counsel, Corp. Sec., Herman Ellman/Sr. VP - Clinical Development, Leland H. Cross/Sr. VP - Technical Operations, Anthony D. Bruno/Exec. VP - Corporate Development, Warner Chilcott/Contact - Medical Affairs
Directors: Roger M. Boissonneault/Dir., CEO, Pres., Steven Rattner/Dir., Steve Pagliuca/Dir., John A. King/Dir., John P. Connaughton/Dir., David F. Burgstahler/Dir., Stephen P. Murray/Dir., Todd M. Abbrecht/Dir., James G. Andress/Dir., James H. Bloem/Dir.
Financial Data: Fiscal Year End:09/30 Latest Annual Data: 12/31/2006

Year	Sales	Net Income
2006	$754,457,000	-$153,510,000
2005	$515,253,000	-$556,646,000

Curr. Assets:	$295,805,000	Curr. Liab.:	$170,985,000		
Plant, Equip.:	$46,035,000	Total Liab.:	$1,834,313,000	Indic. Yr. Divd.:	NA
Total Assets:	$3,162,545,000	Net Worth:	$1,328,232,000	Debt/ Equity:	1.1160

Warner Music Group Corp

75 Rockefeller Plz., New York, NY, 10019; PH: 1-212-275-2000; http:// www.wmg.com;
Email: Investor.Relations@wmg.com

General - Incorporation .... DE	Stock- Price on:12/24/2007 ....$15.85
Employees...4,000	Stock Exchange...NYSE
Auditor .... Ernst & Young LLP	Ticker Symbol...WMG
Stk Agt...... American Stock Transfer & Trust Co.	Outstanding Shares 149,510,000
Counsel ....NA	E.P.S ....-$0.14
DUNS No. ....NA	Shareholders..NA

Business: The groups principle activities include discovering and developing music and music artist. The group operates through two segments namely, recorded music and music publishing. The group operates from the United States. The groups quarterly revenue for September 2007 was 869.00 millions of USD.
Primary SIC and add'l.: 8999 3652
CIK No: 0001319161
Subsidiaries: A.P. Schmidt Company, Alternative Distribution Alliance, Asylum Records LLC (f/k/a WEA Urban LLC), Atlantic Productions LLC, Atlantic Recording Corporation, Atlantic/143 L.L.C., Atlantic/MR II INC., Atlantic/MR Ventures Inc., BB Investments LLC, Berna Music, Inc., Big Beat Records Inc., Big Tree Recording Corporation, Bute Sound LLC, Cafe Americana Inc., Chappell And Intersong Music Group (Germany) Inc. 120 Subsidiaries included in the Index
Officers: Edgar Bronfman/Chmn., CEO, Lyor Cohen/Chmn., CEO - US Recorded Music Warner Music Group, David H. Johnson/CEO - Warner, Chappell Music, Patrick Vien/Chmn., CEO - Warner Music International, Will Tanous/Sr. VP - Corporate Communications, Paul M. Robinson/50/Exec. VP, General Counsel, Caroline Stockdale/Exec. VP - Global Human Resources, Michael D. Fleisher/CFO, Exec. VP, Alejandro Zubillaga/Exec. VP - Digital Strategy, Business Development
Directors: Edgar Bronfman/Chmn., CEO, Len Blavatnik/Dir., Seth W. Lawry/Dir., Shelby W. Bonnie/Dir., Thomas H. Lee/Dir., Richard Bressler/Dir., Ian Loring/Dir., John P. Connaughton/Dir., Jonathan M. Nelson/Dir., Phyllis E. Grann/Dir., Mark Nunnelly/Dir., Michele J. Hooper/Dir., Scott M. Sperling/Dir., Scott L. Jaeckel/Dir.
Owners: Thomas H. Lee Funds/37.70%, Edgar Bronfman/2.20%, Lyor Cohen/1.10%, Bain Capital Funds/16.10%, Michael D. Fleisher, Music Capital Partners, L.P./9.50%, Richard J. Bressler, Phyllis E. Grann, Shelby W. Bonnie, David H. Johnson, Providence Equity Partners Inc./8.60%, Michele J. Hooper, Alex Zubillaga, Insiders/4.10%
Financial Data: Fiscal Year End:09/30 Latest Annual Data: 09/30/2006

Year	Sales	Net Income
2006	$3,516,000,000	$60,000,000
2005	$3,502,000,000	-$169,000,000

Curr. Assets:	$1,300,000,000	Curr. Liab.:	$1,799,000,000	P/E Ratio:	13.82
Plant, Equip.:	$146,000,000	Total Liab.:	$4,462,000,000	Indic. Yr. Divd.:	$0.520
Total Assets:	$4,520,000,000	Net Worth:	$58,000,000	Debt/ Equity:	NA

Warning Mgmt Services Inc

9440 Santa Monica Blvd, Ste. 400, Beverly Hills, CA, 90210; PH: 1-310-860-9969;
Fax: 1-310-860-9978; http:// www.wellmaninc.com

General - Incorporation .... NY	Stock- Price on:12/24/2007 ....$0.0002
Employees...NA	Stock Exchange...OTC
Auditor .... Berg & Co. LLP	Ticker Symbol...WNMI
Stk Agt..............Continental Stock Transfer & Trust Co	Outstanding Shares ....NA
Counsel ....NA	E.P.S ....NA
DUNS No. ....NA	Shareholders..NA

Business: The group's principal activity is to provide models for commercial and fashion purposes. The group provides both male and female models to advertising media using print, still photography, video and television commercials. It also supplies models for fashion engagements, such as fashion shows and runway walks. The clients of the group includes macy's, nordstorm's, mervyns, robinsons-May, gap, banana republic, bon marche, eddie bauer, j. Crew and talbot's. On 09-Sep-2004, the group acquired employment systems inc.
Primary SIC and add'l.: 7363
CIK No: 0001052706
Subsidiaries: ESI, ESI and Dalrada Financial Corporation (Dalrada), Famous Fixins, Inc, FFNY, Fixins Holding Company, Inc, Fixins Holding Company, Inc., FIXN, Quik Pix, Inc, WAMM
Financial Data: Fiscal Year End:12/31 Latest Annual Data: 12/31/2004

Year	Sales	Net Income
2004	$5,159,000	-$4,656,000
2003	$1,746,000	-$1,601,000
2002	$2,324,000	-$536,000

Curr. Assets:	$1,883,000	Curr. Liab.:	$8,874,000		
Plant, Equip.:	$71,000	Total Liab.:	$8,881,000	Indic. Yr. Divd.:	NA
Total Assets:	$2,304,000	Net Worth:	-$6,577,000	Debt/ Equity:	NA

WARP 9, Inc

50 Castilian Dr., Ste. A, Santa Barbara, CA, 93117; PH: 1-805-964-3313; Fax: 1-805-964-6968;
http:// www.roamingmessenger.com; Email: info@roamingmessenger.com

General - Incorporation .... NV	Stock- Price on:12/24/2007 ....$0.018
Employees...15	Stock Exchange...OTC
Auditor .... Hj Assoc. & Consultants, LLP	Ticker Symbol...WNYN
Stk Agt ....Mountain Share Transfer	Outstanding Shares 227,910,000
Counsel ....Pillsbury Winthrop LLP	E.P.S ....-$0.005
DUNS No. 12-141-2266	Shareholders..NA

Business: The group's principal activity is to provide solution for real-time communication over wired and wireless devices. The group's delivers the information for homeland security, emergency response, military and enterprise applications. Solutions consist of messaging technology such as e-mail, text messaging, voicemail, and roaming messenger packages time-critical information into "Smart Courier" messages. These messages automatically roam throughout the wired and wireless worlds - from mobile devices to desktop pcs to central servers - tracking down people and obtaining responses in real-time. The group offers network appliances configured to meet the various mobile communication demands of users and organizations.
Primary SIC and add'l.: 8741
CIK No: 0000743758
Owners: Kin Ng, Insiders/6.35%, Harinder Dhillon/4.93%, Jonathan Lei/35.46%, Louie Ucciferri/1.43%
Financial Data: Fiscal Year End:06/30 Latest Annual Data: 6/30/2006

Year	Sales	Net Income
2006	$1,758,000	-$2,164,000
2005	$1,184,000	-$2,479,000
2004	$954,000	-$1,036,000

Curr. Assets:	$572,000	Curr. Liab.:	$1,420,000		
Plant, Equip.:	$247,000	Total Liab.:	$2,361,000	Indic. Yr. Divd.:	NA
Total Assets:	$1,102,000	Net Worth:	-$1,259,000	Debt/ Equity:	NA

Warrantech Corp

2220 Hwy. 121, Ste. 100, Bedford, TX, 76021; PH: 1-800-544-9510; http:// www.warrantech.com

General - Incorporation .... NV	Stock- Price on:12/24/2007 ....NA
Employees...349	Stock Exchange...NA
Auditor ....Raich Ende Malter & Co. LLP	Ticker Symbol..NA
Stk Agt ..... American Stock Transfer & Trust Co.	Outstanding Shares ....NA
Counsel .... Tannenbaum, Helpern	E.P.S ....NA
DUNS No. 11-601-3392	Shareholders..NA

Business: The group's principal activity is to provide service contracts and extended warranties on automotive and consumer products. The group operates through four segments: automotive, consumer products, international and other. Automotive segment markets and administers extended warranties on automobiles, light trucks, recreational vehicles and automotive components. Consumer product segment markets and administers service contracts and extended warranties on household appliances, consumer electronics, computers and peripherals, and major mechanical systems within homes. These products are sold by franchised and independent automobile dealers, retail stores and financial institutions. International segment markets and administers service contracts and extended warranties on a same range of products in central and south American, Puerto Rico and the Caribbean.
Primary SIC and add'l.: 7389
CIK No: 0000735571
Subsidiaries: Warrantech Direct, Inc., WT Acquisition Corp
Officers: Joel San Antonio/49/CEO, Pres. - Warrantech Home Services, Tom Fontanetta/49/Sr. VP - Systems Development, Christopher Ford/54/Pres. - Warrantech Automotive, Inc, Randall San Antonio/48/Pres. - Warrantech Direct, Inc, Laurence Tutt/37/Sr. VP - Information Technology, Telecommunications, Richard Gavino/55/CFO, Exec. VP, Jeanine M. Folz/37/Sr. VP - Insurance Services, Assist. Corp. Sec., James F. Morganteen/52/Sr. VP, General Counsel, Sean Hicks/Pres. - Warrantech Consumer Product Services

Warren Resources Inc

489 Fifth Ave., New York, NY, 10017; PH: 1-212-697-9660; http:// www.warrenresources.com;
Email: info@warrenresourcesinc.com

General - Incorporation .... MD	Stock- Price on:12/24/2007 ....$12.3
Employees...57	Stock Exchange...NDQ
Auditor .... Grant Thornton LLP	Ticker Symbol...WRES
Stk Agt ..... American Stock Transfer & Trust Co.	Outstanding Shares 54,180,000
Counsel ....NA	E.P.S $0.04
DUNS No. ....NA	Shareholders..NA

Business: The group's principal activities are to acquire, explore and develop domestic onshore natural gas and oil reserves. It owns natural gas and oil interests in approximately 428,103 gross acres. The group operates through four major segments: turnkey contracts, oil and gas marketing, oil and gas

operations and well services. The group drills oil and natural gas wells for company-sponsored drilling partnerships and retains an interest in each well. It also markets natural gas for affiliated partnerships. Its properties are located in New Mexico, Texas, Wyoming, Montana, North Dakota, Oklahoma, Michigan and California. The group operates solely in the domestic market.

Primary SIC and add'l.: 1382 1381

CIK No: 0000892986

Subsidiaries: Warren E&P

Officers: Norman F. Swanton/Chmn., CEO, Pres./$887,609.00, Stewart P. Skelly/Assist. Controller, Lloyd G. Davies/Dir., Exec. VP/$347,904.00, David E. Fleming/Sr. VP, General Counsel/$338,875.00, Ellis G. Vickers/Sr. VP - Land Management, Regulatory Affairs, Kenneth A. Gobble/COO, Pres./$322,013.00, Timothy A. Larkin/CFO, Exec. VP/$458,918.00

Directors: Norman F. Swanton/Chmn., CEO, Pres., Leonard A. Dececchis/Dir., Michael R. Quinlan/Dir., Thomas G. Noonan/Dir., Chet Borgida/Dir., Lloyd G. Davies/Dir., Exec. VP, Anthony L. Coelho/Dir., Dominick D'Alleva/Dir., Espy P. Price/Dir., James M. McConnell/Dir.

Owners: Timothy A. Larkin, Jennison Associates, LLC/6.00%, Kenneth Gobble, Anthony L. Coelho, Lloyd G. Davies, Dominick DAlleva, Daruma Management/5.00%, Michael R. Quinlan, David E. Fleming, Insiders/7.60%, Neuberger Berman Inc./11.40%, Stewart P. Skelly, Thomas G. Noonan, Capital Research& Management Co./7.20%, Chet Borgida (18 Owners included in Index)

Financial Data: Fiscal Year End:12/31   Latest Annual Data: 12/31/2006

Year	Sales	Net Income
2006	$41,103,000	$1,039,000
2005	$39,947,000	-$5,172,000
2004	$26,435,000	-$9,960,000

Curr. Assets:	$52,438,000	Curr. Liab.:	$22,962,000	P/E Ratio:	410.00
Plant, Equip.:	$262,251,000	Total Liab.:	$31,975,000	Indic. Yr. Divd.:	NA
Total Assets:	$323,859,000	Net Worth:	$291,884,000	Debt/ Equity:	0.0760

Warrior Energy Services Corp

Formerly: Black Warrior Wireline Corp

100 Rosecrest Ln., Columbus, MS, 39701; **PH:** 1-662-329-1047

General - Incorporation	DE	**Stock**- Price on:12/24/2007	NA
Employees	480	Stock Exchange	NA
Auditor	Grant Thornton LLP	Ticker Symbol	NA
Stk Agt	Computershare Trust Co	Outstanding Shares	NA
Counsel	Perkins Coie LLP	E.P.S.	NA
DUNS No.	11-264-8845	Shareholders	NA

Business: The group's principal activity is to provide various services to oil and gas operators. It operates through two business segments: wireline services and directional drilling services. The wireless services segment consists of two business units that perform various procedures to evaluate downhole conditions at different stages of the process of drilling and completing oil and gas wells. The directional drilling segment performs procedures to enter an oil producing zone horizontally, using specialized drilling equipment, and expand the area of interface of hydrocarbons which enhances recoverability of oil. This segment is also involved in oil and gas well surveying activities. The principal markets include all major oil and gas producing regions of the United States.

Primary SIC and add'l.: 1389 1381 7359

CIK No: 0000839871

Warwick Valley Telephone Co

47 Main St., Warwick, NY, 10990; **PH:** 1-845-986-8080; **Fax:** 1-845-986-6699; *http://* www.wvtc.com

General - Incorporation	NY	**Stock**- Price on:12/24/2007	$12.9
Employees	82	Stock Exchange	NDQ
Auditor	Withumsmith+brown, P.C	Ticker Symbol	WWVY
Stk Agt	American Stock Transfer & Trust Co.	Outstanding Shares	5,350,000
Counsel	NA	E.P.S.	$0.78
DUNS No.	00-892-3609	Shareholders	NA

Business: The group's principal activity is to provide communication services. The group operates in two segments: telephone and online. The telephone segment offers local, network access, long distance and cellular telephone service to customers in the towns of warwick, goshen and wallkill and the townships of vernon and west milford. This segment also provides access services to interexchange carriers and sells and leases telecommunications equipment. The online segment provides high speed and dial up Internet services, help desk operations, and video over vdsl. Warwick online, the Internet and data subsidiary, offers ultralink DSL Internet connection, dial-up Internet service and digital TV. The group's customers include end users of local service, toll service, Internet access, video over vdsl and interexchange carriers.

Primary SIC and add'l.: 5999 4813

CIK No: 0000104777

Subsidiaries: Warwick Valley Long Distance, Inc.

Officers: Duane Albro/CEO, Pres., Zigmund C. Nowicki/Sec., Kenneth H. Volz/CFO, Exec. VP, Chris Vecchiarelli/Sr. VP - Marketing, Sales, Nicholas Pascaretti/Sr. VP - Operations, Zig Nowicki/VP - Human Resources, Information Technology, Joyce Stoeberl/VP - External Relations, Corp. Sec.

Directors: Wisner H. Buckbee/71/Chmn., Douglas J. Mello/65/Dir., Philip S. Demarest/71/Dir., Herbert Gareiss/62/Dir., Kelly C. Bloss/44/Dir., Robert J. Devalentino/65/Dir., Joseph J. Morrow/68/Dir., Jeffrey D. Alario/46/Dir., Thomas H. Gray/58/Dir.

Owners: Insiders/1.76%, Julia S. Barry/6.75%, Philip S. Demarest, Wisner H. Buckbee, Julia S. Barry/2.86%, Wisner H. Buckbee, Herbert Gareiss, Philip S. Demarest, Robert J. DeValentino, Joseph J. Morrow, Herbert Gareiss, Insiders/1.70%

Financial Data: Fiscal Year End:12/31   Latest Annual Data: 12/31/2006

Year	Sales	Net Income
2006	$25,236,000	$3,997,000
2005	$27,342,000	$5,170,000
2004	$27,678,000	$8,928,000

Curr. Assets:	$18,559,000	Curr. Liab.:	$7,766,000	P/E Ratio:	16.54
Plant, Equip.:	$37,087,000	Total Liab.:	$27,677,000	Indic. Yr. Divd.:	$0.800
Total Assets:	$60,449,000	Net Worth:	$32,772,000	Debt/ Equity:	0.3234

Washington Banking Co

450 SW Bayshore Dr., Oak Harbor, WA, 98277; **PH:** 1-360-679-3121; **Fax:** 1-360-675-7282; *http://* www.wibank.com

General - Incorporation	WA	**Stock**- Price on:12/24/2007	$15.52
Employees	324	Stock Exchange	NDQ
Auditor	Moss Adams LLP	Ticker Symbol	WBCO
Stk Agt	Computer share & Trust Co.	Outstanding Shares	9,490,000
Counsel	Davis Wright Tremaine	E.P.S.	$0.983
DUNS No.	02-368-4678	Shareholders	NA

Business: The group's principal activities are to provide a full range of commercial banking services to small and medium sized businesses, professionals and other individuals. The group operates through its subsidiary, whidbey island bank, 17 branch offices and one loan production office. These are located in island, skagit and whatcom counties in northwestern Washington. The group provides a loan funding source for brokers of mortgage loans through four offices in Washington and Oregon. The group also offers non-deposit investment products for sale through its subsidiary. During 2004, the group discontinued Washington funding group, inc.

Primary SIC and add'l.: 6712 6022

CIK No: 0001058690

Subsidiaries: Washington Banking Capital Trust I, Whidbey Island Bank

Officers: Michal D. Cann/59/Dir., CEO, Pres./$333,547.00, Richard A. Shields/47/CFO, Sr. VP/$201,532.00, John L. Wagner/64/COO, Exec. VP/$265,947.00, Joseph W. Niemer/55/Chief Credit Officer, Exec. VP/$235,760.00, Shelly L. Angus/Investor Relations Officer

Directors: Michal D. Cann/59/Dir., CEO, Pres., Anthony B. Pickering/59/Chmn., Karl C. Krieg/70/Dir., Robert B. Olson/71/Dir., Jay T. Lien/63/Dir., Edward J. Wallgren/68/Dir., Dennis A. Wintch/Dir.

Owners: Robert B. Olson/1.20%, John L. Wagner, Insiders/10.60%, Dennis A. Wintch, Marlen L. Knutson/1.50%, Edward J. Wallgren/1.90%, Joseph W. Niemer, Karl C. Krieg/1.90%, Michal D. Cann/1.80%, Frontier Financial Corporation/8.30%, Richard A. Shields, Jay T. Lien/1.20%, Anthony B. Pickering

Financial Data: Fiscal Year End:12/31   Latest Annual Data: 12/31/2006

Year	Sales	Net Income
2006	$62,435,000	$9,491,000
2005	$53,139,000	$9,468,000
2004	$45,180,000	$6,176,000

Curr. Assets:	$19,745,000	Curr. Liab.:	$703,767,000	P/E Ratio:	16.17
Plant, Equip.:	$23,372,000	Total Liab.:	$728,152,000	Indic. Yr. Divd.:	$0.240
Total Assets:	$794,545,000	Net Worth:	$66,393,000	Debt/ Equity:	0.2181

Washington Federal Inc

425 Pike St., Seattle, WA, 98101; **PH:** 1-206-624-7930; *http://* www.washingtonfederal.com

General - Incorporation	WA	**Stock**- Price on:12/24/2007	$24.38
Employees	765	Stock Exchange	NDQ
Auditor	Deloitte & Touche LLP	Ticker Symbol	WFSL
Stk Agt	American Stock Transfer & Trust Co.	Outstanding Shares	87,330,000
Counsel	Elias, Matz, Tierman & Herrick	E.P.S.	$1.54
DUNS No.	07-663-3460	Shareholders	NA

Business: The group's principal activity is to provide a wide range of financial services through its one hundred and eleven branch offices locations. It conducts its operations through a federally insured savings and loan association subsidiary, Washington federal savings and loan association. It accepts deposits from the general public and invests these funds in loans secured by first mortgage liens on commercial property and multi-family dwellings. The group also originates other types of loans for its portfolio and invests in the United States government and agency obligations. In addition, it provides real estate development and insurance brokerage services. The group's branch offices are located in Washington, Oregon, Idaho, Arizona, Utah, Nevada and Texas. On 31-Aug-2003, the group acquired united savings and loan bank.

Primary SIC and add'l.: 6712 6035

CIK No: 0000936528

Subsidiaries: First Insurance Agency, Inc., Statewide Mortgage Services, Inc., Washington Federal Savings, Washington Services, Inc.

Officers: Roy M. Whitehead/Chmn., CEO, Pres., Brent Beardall/CFO, Cathy Cooper/Investor Relations Contact

Directors: Roy M. Whitehead/Chmn., CEO, Pres., Barbara L. Smith/59/Dir.

Owners: Barbara L. Smith, Jack B. Jacobson/0.10%, Barclays Global Investors./5.80%, Derek L. Chinn/0.26%, Dennis H. Halvorson, Insiders/1.02%, Edwin C. Hedlund/0.16%, Linda S. Brower/0.06%, Roy M. Whitehead/0.24%, John F. Clearman/0.02%, Charles R. Richmond/0.06%, Thomas F. Kenney/0.01%, Anna C. Johnson/0.01%, Thomas J. Kelley/0.01%, Brent J. Beardall/0.06%

Financial Data: Fiscal Year End:09/30   Latest Annual Data: 09/30/2007

Year	Sales	Net Income
2007	$633,923,000	$135,017,000
2006	$545,947,000	$143,102,000
2005	$474,038,000	$145,889,000

Curr. Assets:	$88,026,000	Curr. Liab.:	$6,906,795,000	P/E Ratio:	15.73
Plant, Equip.:	$66,062,000	Total Liab.:	$7,806,300,000	Indic. Yr. Divd.:	$0.820
Total Assets:	$9,069,020,000	Net Worth:	$1,262,720,000	Debt/ Equity:	0.6179

Washington Group International Inc

PO Box 73, Boise, ID, 83729; **PH:** 1-208-386-5000; *http://* www.wgint.com; **Email:** corporate.staffing@wgint.com

General - Incorporation	DE	**Stock**- Price on:12/24/2007	NA
Employees	23,900	Stock Exchange	NA
Auditor	Deloitte & Touche LLP	Ticker Symbol	NA
Stk Agt	Wells Fargo Bank, N.A.	Outstanding Shares	NA
Counsel	NA	E.P.S.	$1.86
DUNS No.	00-790-0517	Shareholders	NA

Business: The groups principle activities include providing design, engineering, construction, construction management, facilities and operations management, environmental remediation and mining services. The group operates through six business segments namely power, infrastructure, mining, industrial/process, defense, and energy and environment. The group operates from United States.

Primary SIC and add'l.: 8711 1629 4925 1611 1623 9999 1622

CIK No: 0000906469

Subsidiaries: 21st Century Rail Corporation, Badger Energy Inc., Badger Middle East,Inc., Badger-SMAS Ltd., Broadway Insurance Company, Ltd., Catalytic Servicios C.A., CH2M-WG Idaho, LLC, Constructora MK de Mexico, S.A. de C.V., Cosa-United C.A., Dulles Transit Partners, LLC, Ebasco International Corporation, Energy Overseas International Inc., FD/MK Limited Liability Company, GIBSIN Engineers, Ltd, Global Energy Services LLC 121 Subsidiaries included in the Index

Officers: Stephen G. Hanks/Dir., CEO, Pres./$5,899,746.00, Doug Hamrick/Project GM - Umatilla Chemical Agent Disposal Facility, Defense Project, Bob Love/Project GM - Defense Project, David P. Reber/Project GM - Pine Bluff Chemical Agent Disposal, Defense Project, Joe Herrity/Corporate Security Dir., Charles D. Pryor/Dir. - ES, H Middle Eastern Operations, Adina Daniela Georgescu/Mgr. - QA, Safety Washington E, C Romania, Jim Little/Pres. - Energy, Environment Business Unit, Curt Watson/Contact - Oil, Gas, Chemicals, Mark Costello/Contact - Business Development, Industrial, Process, Jeanette Bennion/Contact - Corporate Compliance, Jerry Holloway/Contact - Corporate Communications, John Roberts/Contact - Community Relations, Iz Cakrane/Contact - Labor Relations, Rich Parry/Contact - Legal *(58 Officers included in Index)*

Directors: Stephen G. Hanks/Dir., CEO, Pres., Dennis R. Washington/Chmn., Gail E. Hamilton/Dir., Nancy Zbierajewski/Dir., Jerome Swift/Dir., Dennis Wellen/Dir., Scott Wilson/Dir., Dawn Yantek/Dir., William H. Mallender/Dir., Matthew Reece/Dir., Treasurer, Frank S. Finlayson/Dir., Tony Fountain/Dir., Sheila R. Gilbert/Dir., Laurie Hollick/Dir., James McCallum/Dir. *(23 Directors included in Index)*

Owners: FMR Corp./5.57%, Michael P. Monaco, Stephen M. Johnson, David H. Batchelder, Gail E. Hamilton, Dennis R. Washington/11.10%, William H. Mallender, Dennis K. Williams, Cordell Reed, Michael R. DAppolonia, John R. Alm, Scott C. Greer, Greenlight Capital, L.L.C./10.04%, Thomas H. Zarges, Stephen G. Hanks *(19 Owners included in Index)*

Financial Data: ***Fiscal Year End:***12/30 ***Latest Annual Data:*** 12/29/2006

Year	Sales	Net Income
2006	$3,398,082,000	$80,846,000
2005	$3,188,454,000	$58,366,000
2004	$2,915,382,000	$51,137,000

Curr. Assets:	$949,272,000	**Curr. Liab.:**	$621,864,000		
Plant, Equip.:	$69,213,000	**Total Liab.:**	$807,365,000	**Indic. Yr. Divd.:**	NA
Total Assets:	$1,588,206,000	**Net Worth:**	$732,921,000	**Debt/ Equity:**	NA

Washington Mutual Inc

1301 Second Ave., Seattle, WA, 98101; ***PH:*** 1-626-961-0562; ***http://*** www.wamu.com

General - Incorporation	WA	**Stock**- Price on:12/24/2007	$43.03
Employees	49,824	Stock Exchange	NDQ
Auditor	Deloitte & Touche LLP	Ticker Symbol	NA
Stk Agt	Mellon Investor Services LLC	Outstanding Shares	882,410,000
Counsel	NA	E.P.S	$3.66
DUNS No.	00-794-3350	Shareholders	NA

Business: The group's principle activity is to provide financial services for consumers and small businesses. The group also provides checking and savings, credit cards, business loans, online business banking. The group operates from United States.

Primary SIC and add'l.: 6712 6036 9999 6035 6141 6211

CIK No: 0000933136

Subsidiaries: New American Capital, Inc., Washington Mutual Bank, Washington Mutual Bank, FA

Officers: Kerry K. Killinger/Chmn., CEO/$14,245,860.00, Thomas W. Casey/CFO, Exec. VP/$4,565,581.00, Stephen J. Rotella/COO, Pres./$8,452,994.00, David C. Schneider/Pres. - Home Loans, Todd H. Baker/Exec. VP - Corporate Strategy, Development, Anthony F. Vuoto/Pres. - Wamu Card Services, Alan Magleby/Sr. VP - Investor Relations, Glen Simecek/Contact - Fixed Income, John F. Woods/43/Sr. VP, Controller, Alfred R. Brooks/Pres. - Commercial Group, Daryl D. David/Exec. VP - Human Resources, Debora D. Horvath/CIO, Exec. VP, Fay L. Chapman/Sr. Exec. VP, Chief Legal Officer, Ronald J. Cathcart/Exec. VP, Chief Enterprise Risk Officer, James B. Corcoran/Pres. - Retail Banking/$3,300,500.00

Directors: Kerry K. Killinger/Chmn., CEO, Mary E. Pugh/Dir., Orin C. Smith/Dir., James H. Stever/Dir., Margaret Osmer McQuade/Dir., Stephen E. Frank/Dir., Michael K. Murphy/Dir., Phillip D. Matthews/Dir., Anne V. Farrell/Dir., William G. Reed/Dir., Thomas C. Leppert/Dir., Charles M. Lillis/Dir., Regina T. Montoya/Dir.

Owners: Thomas W. Casey, Margaret Osmer McQuade, Stephen E. Frank, Michael K. Murphy, Stephen J. Rotella, Charles M. Lillis, Insiders, James B. Corcoran, Mary E. Pugh, Regina T. Montoya, William G. Reed, Phillip D. Matthews, Anne V. Farrell, James H. Stever, Joseph Saunders *(18 Owners included in Index)*

Financial Data: ***Fiscal Year End:***12/31 ***Latest Annual Data:*** 12/31/2006

Year	Sales	Net Income
2006	$26,454,000,000	$3,558,000,000
2005	$21,667,000,000	$3,432,000,000
2004	$18,960,000,000	$2,878,000,000

Curr. Assets:	$22,632,000,000	**Curr. Liab.:**	$274,984,000,000	**P/E Ratio:**	11.76
Plant, Equip.:	$3,522,000,000	**Total Liab.:**	$316,871,000,000	**Indic. Yr. Divd.:**	$2.240
Total Assets:	$346,288,000,000	**Net Worth:**	$26,969,000,000	**Debt/ Equity:**	1.6042

Washington Post Co

1150 15th St. NW, Washington, DC, 20071; ***PH:*** 1-202-334-6000; ***Fax:*** 1-202-334-4536; ***http://*** www.washpostco.com; ***Email:*** twpcoreply@washpost.com

General - Incorporation	DE	**Stock**- Price on:12/24/2007	$773.5
Employees	17,100	Stock Exchange	NYSE
Auditor	PricewaterhouseCoopers LLP	Ticker Symbol	WPO
Stk Agt	Computershare Trust Co	Outstanding Shares	9,530,000
Counsel	NA	E.P.S	$31.46
DUNS No.	00-324-5768	Shareholders	NA

Business: The group operates through its subsidiaries whose principle activity is to provide educational services. The group provides services include educational and career services, newspaper and magazine publishing, television broadcasting, cable television systems and electronic information services. The group operates from United States.

Primary SIC and add'l.: 9411 2711 4841 7375 4833 2721

CIK No: 0000104889

Subsidiaries: Accountancy & Business College (Ireland) Limited, Accountancy & Business College (Software) Limited, Accountancy & Business College Holdings Limited, Accountancy & Financial Publishing Limited, Accountancy & Management Training Limited, Accountancy Tuition Centre (Eastern) Limited, Accountancy Tutors Limited, American Educational Resources, Inc., Andon Colleges, Inc., Andover College, APMI Group Pte. Ltd., Asia Pacific Management Institute Limited, Asia Pacific Management Institute Pte. Ltd., Asia Pacific School of Business Pte. Ltd., AT Foulks Lynch Limited 137 Subsidiaries included in the Index

Officers: Donald E. Graham/Chmn., CEO/$865,708.00, Jonathan Grayer/Chmn., CEO - Kaplan, Inc, Alan Frank/CEO, Pres. - Post, Newsweek Stations, Thomas O. Might/CEO, Pres. - Cable One, Caroline H. Little/CEO - Publisher, Washingtonpost, Newsweek Interactive, Greg Titus/CEO, Founder - Courseadvisor, Charles A. Lyons/CEO - Gazette, The Herald, Richard M. Smith/CEO - Editorial, Business Operations, Newsweek, Boisfeuillet Jones/Publisher, CEO, Anna Joyce/Dir. - Promotions, Special Projects, The Gazette, Ruben Rodriguez/Public Relations Mgr. - Washington Post, Melissa Mack/Sr. VP - Marketing, Communications, Kaplan, Inc, Tim Ruder/VP - Marketing, Washingtonpostnewsweek Interactive, Jeanine Katona/Dir. - Human Resources, Post, Newsweek Stations, Melany Stroupe/Public Relations Mgr. - Cable One *(65 Officers included in Index)*

Directors: Donald E. Graham/Chmn., CEO, Jonathan Grayer/Chmn., CEO - Kaplan, Inc, George J. Gillespie/Dir., John L. Dotson/Dir., George W. Wilson/Dir., Warren E. Buffett/Dir., Christopher C. Davis/Dir., Barry Diller/Dir., Melinda French Gates/Dir., Ronald L. Olson/Dir., Richard D. Simmons/Dir., Alice M. Rivlin/Dir., Thomas S. Gayner/Dir., Lee C. Bollinger/Dir.

Owners: Christopher C. Davis, George J. Gillespie, Stephen M. Graham, Daniel L. Mosley/6.20%, William W. Graham, Insiders/37.00%, Donald E. Graham, Richard D. Simmons, Melinda F. Gates, Warren E. Buffett/18.10%, Insiders, John L. Dotson, Elizabeth G. Weymouth, Donald E. Graham/36.60%, Thomas S. Gayner *(22 Owners included in Index)*

Financial Data: ***Fiscal Year End:***01/01 ***Latest Annual Data:*** 12/31/2006

Year	Sales	Net Income
2006	$3,904,927,000	$324,459,000
2005	$3,300,104,000	$332,732,000

Curr. Assets:	$934,825,000	**Curr. Liab.:**	$803,200,000	**P/E Ratio:**	24.59
Plant, Equip.:	$1,218,309,000	**Total Liab.:**	$2,209,738,000	**Indic. Yr. Divd.:**	$8.200
Total Assets:	$5,381,372,000	**Net Worth:**	$3,159,514,000	**Debt/ Equity:**	0.1261

Washington Real Estate Investment Trust

6110 Executive Blvd., Rockville, MD, 20852; ***PH:*** 1-301-984-9400; ***Fax:*** 1-301-984-9610; ***http://*** www.writ.com; ***Email:*** info@writ.com

General - Incorporation	MD	**Stock**- Price on:12/24/2007	$35
Employees	282	Stock Exchange	NYSE
Auditor	Ernst & Young LLP	Ticker Symbol	WRE
Stk Agt	Computershare Trust Co	Outstanding Shares	45,050,000
Counsel	NA	E.P.S	$0.87
DUNS No.	NA	Shareholders	NA

Business: The groups principle activities include owning and operating income-producing properties. The group operates through five segments namely, general-purpose office buildings, medical office buildings, retail centers, multifamily properties, and industrial/flex properties. In the year 2006, the group acquired fourgeneral-purpose office buildings, eight medical office buildings, three retail centers and seven industrial properties. The group operates from the United States. The groups quarterly revenue for September 2007 was 66.03 millions of USD.

Primary SIC and add'l.: 6798

CIK No: 0000104894

Subsidiaries: Dalton Ventures L.L.C, Dulles Station L.L.C, Frederick Crossing Associates L.C, Frederick Crossing Retail Associates L.C, L.L.C. and WRIT 8505 L.L.C., Plumtree Partners L.L.C., SGMB L.P., SGPC L.L.C., Shady Grove Medical Village II L.L.C., SME Rock L.L.C., SME Rock Manager Inc., SYN-Rock L.L.C., WRIT 15005 SG L.L.C., WRIT Beltway 50 Limited Partnership L.L.L.P, WRIT Dulles Holdings, L.L.C 24 Subsidiaries included in the Index

Officers: George F. McKenzie/CEO, Pres./$1,076,883.00, Laura M. Franklin/Exec. VP - Accounting, Administration, Corp. Sec./$732,608.00, Sara L. Grootwassink/CFO, Exec. VP/$734,840.00, David A. Dinardo/MD - Leasing, James B. Cederdahl/MD - Property Management, Thomas L. Regnell/Sr. VP - Acquisitions, Michael Paukstitus/Sr. VP - Real Estate

Directors: Edmund B. Cronin/Chmn. - Board of Trustee, John P. McDaniel/Trustee, David M. Osnos/Trustee, Susan J. Williams/Trustee, John M. Derrick/Trustee, Charles T. Nason/Trustee, Edward S. Civera/Trustee, Thomas E. Russell/Trustee

Owners: Edmund B. Cronin, George F. McKenzie/0.41%, John M. Derrick, Charles T. Nason/0.05%, Edward S. Civera, Insiders/1.77%, Laura M. Franklin/0.18%, John P. McDaniel/0.03%, Thomas Edgie Russell, T. Rowe Price Associates, Inc./7.76%, Susan J. Williams/0.04%, Vanguard Group, Inc./5.73%, David M. Osnos/0.05%, Sara L. Grootwassink/0.11%

Financial Data: ***Fiscal Year End:***12/31 ***Latest Annual Data:*** 12/31/2006

Year	Sales	Net Income
2006	$219,662,000	$38,661,000
2005	$190,046,000	$77,638,000
2004	$172,394,000	$45,564,000

Curr. Assets:	$45,504,000	**Curr. Liab.:**	$45,291,000		
Plant, Equip.:	$1,426,454,000	**Total Liab.:**	$1,089,334,000	**Indic. Yr. Divd.:**	NA
Total Assets:	$1,531,265,000	**Net Worth:**	$441,931,000	**Debt/ Equity:**	2.7576

Washington Trust Bancorp Inc

23 Brd St., Westerly, RI, 02891; ***PH:*** 1-401-348-1200; ***http://*** www.washtrust.com

General - Incorporation	RI	**Stock**- Price on:12/24/2007	$25.74
Employees	419	Stock Exchange	NDQ
Auditor	KPMG LLP	Ticker Symbol	WASH
Stk Agt	American Stock Transfer & Trust Co.	Outstanding Shares	13,360,000
Counsel	Goodwin, Procter & Hoar	E.P.S	$1.77
DUNS No.	01-977-1468	Shareholders	NA

Business: The group's principal activities are to provide banking and other financial services through its subsidiaries. The group accepts commercial and consumer demand deposits, savings, money market deposits and certificate of deposits. The services offered include residential mortgage loans, commercial loans, construction loans, consumer installment loans, home equity lines of credit. The other services

offered include merchant credit card services, automated teller machines, telephone banking services, retirement accounts, cash management services, Internet banking, trust and investment management services. The operations are conducted through 16 banking offices located in Rhode Island and Connecticut counties.

Primary SIC and add'l.: 6712 6022

CIK No: 0000737468

Subsidiaries: The Washington Trust Company of Westerly, Weston Securities Corporation, WT Capital Trust I, WT Capital Trust II

Officers: John C. Warren/Chmn., CEO, Galan G. Daukas/Exec. VP - Wealth Management, John F. Treanor/Dir., COO, Pres., David V. Devault/CFO, Exec. VP, Sec., Treasurer

Directors: John C. Warren/Chmn., CEO, Larry J. Hirsch/Dir., James P. Sullivan/Dir., Neil H. Thorp/Dir., Douglas H. Randall/Dir., Kathleen McKeough/Dir., Patrick J. Shanahan/Dir., Gary P. Bennett/Dir., Mary E. Kennard/Dir., Barry G. Hittner/Dir., Steven J. Crandall/Dir., John F. Treanor/Dir., COO, Pres., Joyce O. Resnikoff/71/Dir., Victor J. Orsinger/Dir., Katherine W. Hoxsie/Dir. (16 Directors included in Index)

Owners: Insiders/7.29%, Katherine W. Hoxsie/1.04%, Mary E. Kennard, Edward M. Mazze, Kathleen E. McKeough/0.01%, Joyce O. Resnikoff/0.08%, Larry J. Hirsch, Douglas H. Randall, Victor J. Orsinger, Patrick J. Shanahan, Steven J. Crandall/0.10%, James P. Sullivan, Gary P. Bennett/0.13%, Neil H. Thorp/0.33%, David V. Devault/0.65% (21 Owners included in Index)

Financial Data: Fiscal Year End: 12/31   **Latest Annual Data:** 12/31/2006

Year	Sales	Net Income
2006	$173,317,000	$25,031,000
2005	$146,639,000	$23,024,000
2004	$123,758,000	$20,829,000

Curr. Assets:	$83,177,000	**Curr. Liab.:**	$2,188,744,000	**P/E Ratio:**	14.07
Plant, Equip.:	$24,307,000	**Total Liab.:**	$2,226,109,000	**Indic. Yr. Divd.:**	$0.800
Total Assets:	$2,399,165,000	**Net Worth:**	$173,056,000	**Debt/ Equity:**	NA

Washtenaw Group Inc

3767 Ranchero Dr., Ann Arbor, MI, 48108; *PH:* 1-734-662-9733; *http://* www.washtenawmortgage.com; *Email:* info@washtenawmortgage.com

General - Incorporation	MI	**Stock**- Price on:12/24/2007	$0.2
Employees	NA	Stock Exchange	AMEX
Auditor	Crowe Chizek & Co. LLC	Ticker Symbol	TWH
Stk Agt	American Stock Transfer & Trust Co.	Outstanding Shares	NA
Counsel	NA	E.P.S.	NA
DUNS No.	NA	Shareholders	NA

Business: The group's principal activity is to acquire, sell and service mortgage loans. It originates or acquires loans through the wholesale, correspondent and retail loan production of its mortgage banking operations. It originates residential mortgages through a network of nearly 1,500 brokers in 41 states and sells loans and mortgage servicing rights in the secondary market. The group's mortgage banking offices are located in ann arbor, Michigan and pleasant hill, California.

Primary SIC and add'l.: 6719 6162

CIK No: 0001263282

Subsidiaries: mortgage banking, Pelican Financial, Inc., Washtenaw Mortgage Company

Waste Connections Inc

35 Iron Point Cir., Ste 200, Folsom, CA, 95630; *PH:* 1-916-608-8200; *http://* www.wcnx.org; *Email:* receptionist@wcnx.org

General - Incorporation	DE	**Stock**- Price on:12/24/2007	$30.63
Employees	4,310	Stock Exchange	NYSE
Auditor	PricewaterhouseCoopers LLP	Ticker Symbol	WCN
Stk Agt	Bank of America	Outstanding Shares	NA
Counsel	Shartsis, Friese & Ginsburg	E.P.S.	$1.38
DUNS No.	NA	Shareholders	NA

Business: The group's principal activity is to provide solid waste collection, transfer, disposal and recycling services in secondary markets primarily in the western United States. The group owns and operates 101 collection operations, 33 transfer stations and 23 recycling facilities. The group's services are provided under governmental certificates, exclusive franchise agreements, exclusive municipal contracts, residential subscriptions and contracts. As of 31-Dec 2003, the group served more than one million commercial, industrial and residential customers in 23 states: Alabama, California, Colorado, Georgia, Illinois, Iowa, Kansas, Kentucky, Minnesota, Mississippi, Montana, Nebraska, New Mexico, Ohio, Oklahoma, Oregon, South Dakota, Tennessee, Texas, Utah, Washington and Wyoming.

Primary SIC and add'l.: 4953

CIK No: 0001057058

Subsidiaries: Amador Services, LLC, American Disposal Company, Inc., American Sanitary Service, Inc., Arrow Sanitary Service, Inc., Bituminous Resources, Inc., Butler County Landfill, Inc., Camino Real Environmental Center, Inc., Cold Canyon Landfill, Inc., Columbia Resource Co., Lp, Community Refuse Disposal, Inc., Contractors Waste Services, Inc., Corral De Piedra Land Company, Curry Transfer And Recycling, Inc., Denver Regional Landfill, Inc., Dm Disposal Co., Inc. 94 Subsidiaries included in the Index

Officers: Ronald J. Mittelstaedt/Chmn., CEO/$645,808.00, Eric O. Hansen/CIO, VP, Worthing F. Jackman/CFO, Exec. VP/$347,291.00, David G. Eddie/VP, Corporate Controller, Steven F. Bouck/Pres./$445,445.00, James M. Little/VP - Engineering, Robert D. Evans/Exec. VP, General Counsel, Sec./$389,617.00, Kenneth O. Rose/Sr. VP - Administration, Jerri L. Hunt/VP - Human Resources, Darrell W. Chambliss/COO, Exec. VP/$379,351.00, David M. Hall/Sr. VP - Sales, Marketing, Ed Quinnan/Business Development Mgr., Greg Popovich/Business Development Mgr., John Hafner/Business Development Mgr.

Directors: Ronald J. Mittelstaedt/Chmn., CEO, Gene Dupreau/Dir., Michael W. Harlan/Dir., William J. Razzouk/Dir., Robert H. Davis/Dir., Edward E. Guillet/Dir., Eugene V. Dupreau/Dir.

Owners: Steven F. Bouck/1.50%, Eugene V. Dupreau/0.40%, William J. Razzouk, Columbia Wanger Asset Management, L.P./5.05%, Robert H. Davis, Ronald J. Mittelstaedt/1.53%, Robert D. Evans/0.79%, Darrell W. Chambliss/0.46%, Insiders/6.64%, Edward E. NedGuillet, Michael W. Harlan, Worthing F. Jackman/0.46%, T. Rowe Price Associates, Inc./9.56%

Financial Data: Fiscal Year End: 12/31   **Latest Annual Data:** 12/31/2006

Year	Sales	Net Income
2006	$824,354,000	$77,423,000
2005	$721,899,000	$83,943,000
2004	$629,363,000	$72,271,000

Curr. Assets:	$160,233,000	**Curr. Liab.:**	$149,865,000	**P/E Ratio:**	23.93
Plant, Equip.:	$736,428,000	**Total Liab.:**	$1,037,409,000	**Indic. Yr. Divd.:**	NA
Total Assets:	$1,773,891,000	**Net Worth:**	$736,482,000	**Debt/ Equity:**	0.8330

Waste Industries USA Inc

3301 Benson Dr., Ste 601, Raleigh, NC, 27609; *PH:* 1-919-325-4000; *http://* www.waste-ind.com

General - Incorporation	NC	**Stock**- Price on:12/24/2007	$32.85
Employees	1,600	Stock Exchange	NDQ
Auditor	Deloitte & Touche LLP	Ticker Symbol	WWIN
Stk Agt	American Stock Transfer & Trust Co.	Outstanding Shares	14,060,000
Counsel	NA	E.P.S.	$1.47
DUNS No.	NA	Shareholders	NA

Business: The group's principal activity is to render integrated solid waste services. The services rendered by the group include waste collection, transfer, disposal and recycling services. The group serves commercial, residential and industrial customers. The operations are conducted through 40 collection centers, 26 transfer stations, approximately 100 county convenience drop-off centers, eight recycling facilities and ten landfills. During 2003, it acquired patriot waste systems, kleen way sanitation, all American waste management inc and waste watchers llc. It operates primarily in North Carolina, South Carolina, Virginia, Tennessee, Mississippi, Georgia and Florida. On 03-May-2004, the group acquired county garbage inc. During Mar 2004 the group acquired American disposal, l&m sanitation and m&m sanitation.

Primary SIC and add'l.: 4953 4959

CIK No: 0001125845

Subsidiaries: Black Bear Disposal, LLC, Douglasville Transfer, LLC, Duplin County Disposal, LLC, ECO Services, LLC, ETC of Georgia, LLC, Laurens County Landfill, LLC, Old Kings Road Solid Waste, LLC, Red Rock Disposal, LLC, Reliable Trash Service, LLC, S & S Enterprises of Mississippi, LLC, Safeguard Landfill Management, LLC, Sampson County Disposal, LLC, Shamrock Environmental Services, LLC, TransWaste Services, LLC, Van Buren County Landfill, LLC 25 Subsidiaries included in the Index

Officers: Jim W. Perry/Dir., CEO, Pres./$870,140.00, Lonnie C. Poole/Chmn., VP - Corporate Development/$565,685.00, Thomas A. Winstead/VP - East Division, Franklin E. Lorick/VP - Central Division, Harrell J. Auten/VP - Sales, Marketing/$328,423.00, Harry M. Habets/VP, COO/$515,906.00, Jerry W. Johnson/VP - Landfill Division, Michael T. Ingle/VP - South Division, Steve D. Grissom/CFO, VP/$350,402.00, Michael J. Durham/VP - Administration, Support Services/$227,866.00, Scott Keeter/Corporate Accounting Mgr.

Directors: Jim W. Perry/Dir., CEO, Pres., Lonnie C. Poole/Chmn., VP - Corporate Development, James A. Walker/Dir., Paul F. Hardiman/Dir., Glenn E. Futrell/Dir.

Owners: Paul F. Hardiman, Michael J. Durham, Bear Stearns Asset Management Inc./7.43%, Scott J. Poole/17.73%, James A. Walker, Stephen D. Grissom, Insiders/63.76%, Lonnie C. Poole/32.32%, Dimensional Fund Advisors Inc ./5.35%, Glenn E. Futrell, Barclays Global Fund Advisors/5.15%, Harrell J. Auten, Harry M. Habets, Lonnie C. Poole/21.08%, Jim W. Perry/9.79%

Financial Data: Fiscal Year End: 12/31   **Latest Annual Data:** 12/31/2006

Year	Sales	Net Income
2006	$327,545,000	$19,281,000
2005	$310,629,000	$12,189,000
2004	$291,725,000	$11,797,000

Curr. Assets:	$43,077,000	**Curr. Liab.:**	$43,186,000	**P/E Ratio:**	21.61
Plant, Equip.:	$218,039,000	**Total Liab.:**	$224,408,000	**Indic. Yr. Divd.:**	$0.480
Total Assets:	$370,279,000	**Net Worth:**	$145,871,000	**Debt/ Equity:**	0.9402

Waste Management Inc

1001 Fannin St., Ste 4000, Houston, TX, 77002; *PH:* 1-713-512-6200; *http://* www.wm.com

General - Incorporation	DE	**Stock**- Price on:12/24/2007	$39.43
Employees	48,000	Stock Exchange	NYSE
Auditor	Ernst & Young LLP	Ticker Symbol	WMI
Stk Agt	Mellon Investor Services LLC	Outstanding Shares	517,430,000
Counsel	NA	E.P.S.	$2.08
DUNS No.	19-467-2085	Shareholders	NA

Business: The groups principle activity is to provide integrated waste services. The groups services include collection, transfer, recycling and resource recovery and disposal of hazardous waste. The group operates from United States.

Primary SIC and add'l.: 4953

CIK No: 0000823768

Subsidiaries: 1019726 Alberta Ltd., 1329409 Ontario Inc., 3368084 Canada Inc., 635952 Ontario Inc., Advanced Environmental Technical Services, LLC, Akron Regional Landfill, Inc., Alabama Waste Disposal Solutions, LLC, Alliance Sanitary Landfill, Inc., Alpharetta Transfer Station, LLC, American Landfill, Inc., American RRT Fiber Supply, L.P., Anderson Landfill, Inc., Antelope Valley Recycling and Disposal Facility, Inc., Apollo Waste Industries, LLC, Apollo Waste Services of Georgia, LLC 470 Subsidiaries included in the Index

Officers: David P. Steiner/Dir., CEO/$5,601,287.00, Greg A. Robertson/54/VP, Chief Accounting Officer, Lawrence O'Donnell/COO, Pres./$3,338,643.00, Lynn M. Caddell/CIO, Sr. VP, Cherie C. Rice/VP - Finance, Treasurer, David A. Aardsma/Sr. VP - Sales, Marketing, Patrick J. Derueda/Pres. - Waste Management Recycle America, Barry H. Caldwell/Sr. VP - Government Affairs, Corporate Communications, Jeff Harris/Sr. VP - Midwest Group, Mark A. Weidman/Pres. - Wheelabrator Technologies Inc, Brett Frazier/Sr. VP - Eastern Group, Jay Romans/Sr. VP - People, Michael J. Romans/57/Sr. VP - People, Duane C. Woods/Sr. VP - Western Group/$1,527,232.00, David R. Hopkins/64/Sr. VP - Southern Group (19 Officers included in Index)

Directors: David P. Steiner/Dir., CEO, John C. Pope/Non - Exec. Chmn., Robert W. Reum/Dir., Thomas H. Weidemeyer/Dir., Pastora San Juan Cafferty/Dir., Frank M. Clark/Dir., Pat W. Gross/Dir., Thomas I. Morgan/Dir., Steven G. Rothmeier/Dir.

Owners: Robert W. Reum, David P. Steiner, James E. Trevathan, Robert P. Damico, Barclays Global Investors, NA/5.61%, Robert G. Simpson, Insiders, Lawrence ODonnell, Steven G. Rothmeier, Patrick W. Gross, Thomas H. Weidemeyer, Duane C. Woods, Pastora San Juan Cafferty, John C. Pope, Frank M. Clark (16 Owners included in Index)

Financial Data: Fiscal Year End: 12/31   **Latest Annual Data:** 12/31/2006

Year	Sales	Net Income
2006	$13,363,000,000	$1,149,000,000
2005	$13,074,000,000	$1,182,000,000
2004	$12,516,000,000	$939,000,000

Curr. Assets:	$3,182,000,000	**Curr. Liab.:**	$3,268,000,000	**P/E Ratio:**	18.78
Plant, Equip.:	$11,179,000,000	**Total Liab.:**	$14,378,000,000	**Indic. Yr. Divd.:**	$0.960
Total Assets:	$20,600,000,000	**Net Worth:**	$6,222,000,000	**Debt/ Equity:**	1.2913

Waste Services Inc

1122 International Blvd., Ste. 601, Burlington, ON, L7L 6Z8; *PH:* 1-905-319-1237;
Fax: 1-905-319-9050; *http://* www.wasteservicesinc.com

General - Incorporation .... DE
Employees 2,160
Auditor .... BDO Seidman, LLP
Stk Agt...... American Stock Transfer & Trust Co.
Counsel .... NA
DUNS No. .... NA

Stock- Price on:12/24/2007 .... $11.5
Stock Exchange .... NDQ
Ticker Symbol .... WSII
Outstanding Shares 45,970,000
E.P.S .... -$0.76
Shareholders .... NA

Business: The groups principle activities include collecting, transferring, disposal and recycling services for non hazardous solid waste. In the year 2006, the group acquired Sun Country Materials, LLC, and Liberty Waste, LLC. The group operates from the United States and Canada. The group's quarterly revenue for September 2007 was 130.60 millions of USD.

Primary SIC and add'l.: 4212 4953

CIK No: 0001065736

Subsidiaries: 6045341 Canada Inc., Cactus Waste Systems, LLC, Capital Environmental Holdings Company, Fort Bend Regional Landfill LP, Jacksonville Florida Landfill, Inc., Jones Road Landfill and Recycling Ltd., Liberty Waste, LLC, Omni Waste of Osceola County LLC, Pro Disposal, Inc., Ram-Pak Compaction Systems Ltd., Ruffino Hills Transfer Station LP, Sanford Recycling and Transfer, Inc., Sun Country Materials, LLC, Taft Recycling, Inc., Waste Services (CA)Inc. 21 Subsidiaries included in the Index

Officers: David Sutherland-Yoest/Chmn., CEO/$1,328,934.00

Directors: David Sutherland-Yoest/Chmn., CEO, Gary W. Degroote/Dir., Michael B. Lazar/Dir., George E. Matelich/Dir., Lucien Remillard/Dir., Jack E. Short/Dir., Wallace L. Timmeny/Dir., Michael J. Verrochi/Dir., Charles E. McCarthy/Dir.

Owners: George E. Matelich, Wallace L. Timmeny, Ivan R. Cairns, Insiders/21.60%, Michael J. Verrochi, Charles E. McCarthy/12.70%, Jack E. Short, Gary W. DeGroote/1.70%, Westbury (Bermuda) Ltd./25.90%, Kelso& Company, L.P./10.90%, David Sutherland-Yoest/3.90%, Prides Capital Partners, L.L.C./12.70%, Brian A. Goebel, Lucien Rmillard/2.20%, Edwin D. Johnson *(16 Owners included in Index)*

Financial Data: **Fiscal Year End:**12/31 **Latest Annual Data:** 12/31/2006

Year	Sales	Net Income
2006	$396,123,000	-$48,531,000
2005	$382,446,000	-$50,290,000
2004	$310,785,000	-$48,154,000

Curr. Assets:	$71,119,000	**Curr. Liab.:**	$86,358,000		
Plant, Equip.:	$382,656,000	**Total Liab.:**	$525,706,000	**Indic. Yr. Divd.:**	NA
Total Assets:	$865,063,000	**Net Worth:**	$339,357,000	**Debt/ Equity:**	1.2766

Waste Technology Corp

5400 Rio Grande Ave, Jacksonville, FL, 32205; *PH:* 1-800-231-9286

General - Incorporation .... DE
Employees 65
Auditor .... KPMG LLP
Stk Agt...... American Stock Transfer & Trust Co.
Counsel .... NA
DUNS No. 14-462-5936

Stock- Price on:12/24/2007 .... $0.76
Stock Exchange .... OTC
Ticker Symbol .... WTEK
Outstanding Shares 4,930,000
E.P.S $0.06
Shareholders .... NA

Business: The group's principle activity is to manufacture and sell balers, which are machines used to compress and compact various waste materials. The group manufactures approximately fifty different types of balers for use with corrugated, paper, municipal waste, textiles, scrap metal and other products. Balers utilize mechanical, hydraulic, and electrical mechanisms to compress a variety of materials into bales for easier and low cost handling, shipping, disposal, storage, and/or bulk sales for recycling. Balers offered by the group include general purpose horizontal and vertical balers; specialty balers, such as those used for low level radioactive waste, fifty-five gallon drums, aluminum cans and rubber and textile waste; and accessory equipment such as conveyors, rufflers, bale tying machines, and plastic bottle piercers. The principal international markets served by the group, include Canada, China, United Kingdom, India, Korea, Japan, Russia and Brazil. The group's quarterly revenue for July 2007 was 3.37 millions of USD.

Primary SIC and add'l.: 3569 6719

CIK No: 0000781902

Subsidiaries: International Baler Corporation

Officers: William E. Nielsen/60/Dir., CEO, Pres., David B. Wilhelmy/53/Dir., VP - Sales - Marketing, Sec.

Directors: William E. Nielsen/60/Dir., CEO, Pres., Larita R. Boren/71/Dir., Leland E. Boren/84/Dir., Robert Roth/82/Dir., David B. Wilhelmy/53/Dir., VP - Sales - Marketing, Sec., Ronald L. McDaniel/68/Dir.

Owners: Robert Roth/2.20%, Alexander C. Toppan/8.60%, Insiders/60.00%, William E. Nielsen/8.60%, LaRita R. Boren/51.80%, Leland E. Boren/4.50%

Financial Data: **Fiscal Year End:**10/31 **Latest Annual Data:** 10/31/2006

Year	Sales	Net Income
2006	$8,146,000	$407,000
2005	$7,359,000	$104,000
2004	$6,581,000	$186,000

Curr. Assets:	$2,881,000	**Curr. Liab.:**	$1,623,000	**P/E Ratio:**	12.67
Plant, Equip.:	$740,000	**Total Liab.:**	$1,898,000	**Indic. Yr. Divd.:**	NA
Total Assets:	$3,703,000	**Net Worth:**	$1,805,000	**Debt/ Equity:**	NA

Wataire International Inc

21550 Oxnard St., Ste. 300, Warner Ctr., Woodland Hills, CA, 91367; *PH:* 1-310-728-6306;
Fax: 1-310-362-8720; *http://* www.wataireinternational.com; *Email:* info@wataireinternational.com

General - Incorporation .... WA
Employees .... NA
Auditor .... Amisano Hanson
Stk Agt .... NA
Counsel .... NA
DUNS No. .... NA

Stock- Price on:12/24/2007 .... $0.34
Stock Exchange .... OTC
Ticker Symbol .... WTAR
Outstanding Shares 60,720,000
E.P.S .... NA
Shareholders .... NA

Business: The groups principle activities include marketing and distributing the PetsCell technology and the "PetsMobility" brand products and services. The group operates from the United States.

Primary SIC and add'l.: 5063

CIK No: 0001127007

Subsidiaries: Aqua Technologies Inc., Petmo Inc.

Officers: Robert Rosner/Chmn., CEO, Richard Jordan/Dir., CFO, Terry Nylander/Dir., COO, Pres., Don Neumann/VP - Consumer Marketing

Directors: Robert Rosner/Chmn., CEO, Richard Jordan/Dir., CFO, Terry Nylander/Dir., COO, Pres., James Marsden/Member - Advisory Board, Brian Baker/Member - Advisory Board

Owners: Phil Fraser/7.10%, Wataire Industries Inc./18.20%, Nand Shankar, Robert Rosner/14.23%

WatchGuard Technologies Inc

505 Fifth Ave. S Ste. 500, Seattle, WA, 98104; *PH:* 1-206-521-8340; *http://* www.watchguard.com

General - Incorporation .... DE
Employees .... NA
Auditor .... Ernst & Young LLP
Stk Agt .... Mellon Investor Services LLC
Counsel......... Orrick, Herrington & Sutcliffe LLP
DUNS No. .... NA

Stock- Price on:12/24/2007 .... NA
Stock Exchange .... NA
Ticker Symbol .... NA
Outstanding Shares .... NA
E.P.S .... NA
Shareholders .... NA

Business: The group's principal activity is to provide Internet security solutions designed to protect enterprises, that use the Internet for e-commerce and secure communications. The group provides pro-active Internet security solutions, which protects against known and future threats in a smart, dynamic and simple way. The market of the group includes small and medium-sized enterprises (smes) and large Internet-distributed enterprises (ides) with high-speed connections supporting virtual private networks (vpns) between the corporate headquarters and geographically dispersed branch offices. Internet security solutions are sold indirectly to end-users through distributors and resellers with customers located in over 125 countries and also to a number of service providers that implement our managed security solution.

Primary SIC and add'l.: 7379 7372

CIK No: 0001062019

Subsidiaries: RapidStream, Inc., WatchGuard Technologies Australia PTY, Ltd., WatchGuard Technologies France, WatchGuard Technologies Germany GmbH, WatchGuard Technologies Japan, K.K., WatchGuard Technologies Limited

Officers: Joe Wang/CEO, Eric Aarrestad/VP - Marketing, Bob Chamberlain/CFO, Matt Deichman/Pres. - Business Development, Bill Foreman/VP - Customer Support, Services, Terry Haas/VP - International Sales, Thom Linden/VP - Engineering, Shari McLaren/VP - Service Subscriptions, Bill Smith/VP - Sales The Americas

Directors: Ashutosh Agrawal/Dir., Benjamin Ball/Dir., Alex Slusky/Dir.

Watchit Media Inc

Formerly: Cotelligent Inc
655 Montgomery St., Ste. 1000, San Francisco, CA, 94111; *PH:* 1-415-477-9900

General - Incorporation .... DE
Employees 30
Auditor .... Rowbotham & Co. LLP
Stk Agt .... Computershare Investor Services LLC
Counsel.............. Morgan, Lewis & Bockius LLP
DUNS No. 92-982-8176

Stock- Price on:12/24/2007 .... $0.04
Stock Exchange .... NA
Ticker Symbol .... NA
Outstanding Shares 42,710,000
E.P.S .... -$0.095
Shareholders .... NA

Business: The group's principle activity is to provide software consulting services to businesses with complex information technology operations. The group also provides maintenance, support and contract services on software products it licenses. As part of its complete solutions, the group offers strategic it consulting services, enterprise resource planning and implementation/integration services, custom application development, sales and field force automation solutions and mobile middleware products. The group also provides hardware and software products, application hosting and vertical solution provider services, remote support services, help desk and education services.

Primary SIC and add'l.: 7371 7379 7376 7373

CIK No: 0001004963

Subsidiaries: Cotelligent USA, Inc., Recency Media USA, Inc., Recency Media, Inc., Watchit Media USA, Inc.

Owners: John C. Dong, Cliff Melby/5.63%, Terry R. Leiweke, Loren W. Willman/2.56%, James R. Lavelle/8.36%, Paul D. Frankel, Colt Melby/8.44%, Insiders/9.53%, Debra J. Richardson, Stiassni Capital Partners, LP/11.25%, Tony C. Vickers

Financial Data: **Fiscal Year End:**12/31 **Latest Annual Data:** 12/31/2005

Year	Sales	Net Income
2005	$1,844,000	-$1,060,000
2004	$862,000	-$4,205,000
2003	$9,936,000	-$12,350,000

Curr. Assets:	$456,000	**Curr. Liab.:**	$2,195,000		
Plant, Equip.:	$177,000	**Total Liab.:**	$2,195,000	**Indic. Yr. Divd.:**	NA
Total Assets:	$4,150,000	**Net Worth:**	$1,955,000	**Debt/ Equity:**	NA

WatchIt Technologies Inc

Formerly: Evans Systems Inc
1 Town Sq. Blvd., Ste. 347, Asheville, NC, 28803; *PH:* 1-828-681-8105

General - Incorporation .... TX
Employees 13
Auditor .... Stephenson & Trlicek, P.C
Stk Agt .... Continental Stock Transfer & Trust Co
Counsel .... NA
DUNS No. 04-821-4522

Stock- Price on:12/24/2007 .... NA
Stock Exchange .... NA
Ticker Symbol .... NA
Outstanding Shares .... NA
E.P.S .... -$0.011
Shareholders .... NA

Business: The group's principal activity is to distribute motor fuels and lubricants to branded retail accounts and commercial industrial users. The group operates through two segments: petroleum marketing sells motor fuels to the public through retail outlets. The gasoline retail outlets consist of group-supplied

equipment such as pumps, lights, canopies and underground storage tanks. It also supplies lubricants to commercial and industrial customers. Environmental remediation services provides environmental assessment and remediation services for the petroleum distribution industry in the southeast Texas. On 18-Nov-2003, the group discontinued its convenience store segment operations.

Primary SIC and add'l.: 4959 5541 5171 9999

CIK No: 0000904901

Subsidiaries: Diamond Mini Mart, Inc., Distributor Information Systems Corporation, Edco Environmental Systems, Inc., Edco, Inc., Evans Oil Company, Inc., In & Out Mini Mart, Inc., Way Energy Systems, Inc.

Officers: Fredrick W. Wicks/61/Chmn., CEO, CFO, Pres., Brian D. Riley/57/Dir., Sec., Treasurer, Ian J. Riley/25/Dir., CTO

Directors: Fredrick W. Wicks/61/Chmn., CEO, CFO, Pres.

Owners: Frank Moody/1.00%, Joshua Ian Riley/0.08%, Frederick Wicks/0.07%, Insiders/1.00%, Brian Riley/0.08%

Financial Data: *Fiscal Year End:*09/30 *Latest Annual Data:* 9/30/2006

Year	Sales	Net Income
2006	NA	-$438,000
2005	$1,019,000	-$868,000
2004	$1,920,000	-$332,000

Curr. Assets:	$188,000	**Curr. Liab.:**	$1,394,000		
Plant, Equip.:	NA	**Total Liab.:**	$1,619,000	**Indic. Yr. Divd.:**	NA
Total Assets:	$188,000	**Net Worth:**	-$1,431,000	**Debt/ Equity:**	NA

Waterbank of America (USA) Inc

Formerly: Autostrada Motors Inc

235 W 500 S, Salt Lake City, UT, 84101; *PH:* 1-801-524-9500; *http://* www.autostradamotors.com

General - Incorporation	UT	**Stock**- Price on:12/24/2007	NA
Employees	NA	Stock Exchange	NA
Auditor	Mantyla McReynolds LLC	Ticker Symbol	NA
Stk Agt	Interwest Transfer Company, Inc.	Outstanding Shares	NA
Counsel	NA	E.P.S	NA
DUNS No.	NA	Shareholders	NA

Business: The groups principle activity is to operate an automobile dealership which participated in the wholesale and retail used car markets. The group operates from United States.

Primary SIC and add'l.: 5010

CIK No: 0001286923

Financial Data: *Fiscal Year End:*12/31 *Latest Annual Data:* 12/31/2005

Year	Sales	Net Income
2005	$4,779,000	-$6,000

Curr. Assets:	$674,000	**Curr. Liab.:**	$548,000		
Plant, Equip.:	$67,000	**Total Liab.:**	$675,000	**Indic. Yr. Divd.:**	NA
Total Assets:	$765,000	**Net Worth:**	$90,000	**Debt/ Equity:**	NA

WaterChef Inc

1007 Glen Cove Ave., Ste. 1, Glen Head, NY, 11545; *PH:* 1-631-577-7915; *Fax:* 1-860-227-2487; *http://* www.waterchef.net; *Email:* conway@waterchef.net

General - Incorporation	DE	**Stock**- Price on:12/24/2007	$0.12
Employees	2	Stock Exchange	OTC
Auditor	Marcum & Kliegman LLP	Ticker Symbol	WTER
Stk Agt	Computershare Trust Co	Outstanding Shares	184,800,000
Counsel	NA	E.P.S	-$0.01
DUNS No.	80-376-7029	Shareholders	NA

Business: The group's principal activities are to design, manufacture and market water dispensers and water purification equipment. It is concentrating on the development, manufacturing and marketing of their patented line of "Puresafe" water purification systems. The puresafe water station is a self-contained, six stage water purification center, constructed with weather resistant fiberglass, aluminum and is equipped with internal and external lighting.the market for the pure safe is substantial and is both world-wide and domestic. Major parts of Africa, the Middle East, southeast Asia, the Indian sub-continent, latin and South America, the Caribbean, eastern Europe, Florida, Georgia, and other regions in the United States is in need of adequate supplies of pure water.

Primary SIC and add'l.: 3589

CIK No: 0000764839

Officers: David Conway/66/Chmn., CEO, CFO, Pres., Doug Davis/Engineering, Richard G. Ayotte/VP - Sales, Marketing

Directors: David Conway/66/Chmn., CEO, CFO, Pres., Ronald Hart/Chmn. - Scientific Advisory Board, Mohamed M. Salem/Member - Scientific Advisory Board, Lord John Gilbert/Member - Scientific Advisory Board, John J. Clarke/65/Dir., Richard Wilson/Member - Scientific Advisory Board, Mostafa K. Tolba/Member - Scientific Advisory Board, Marshall Sterman/76/Dir.

Owners: Peter Hoffman/7.20%, Jerome Anne Asher/9.50%, Insiders/13.70%, John A. Borger/10.80%, Robert Kaszovitz/23.00%, Avi Elizier/6.60%, Marshall S. Sterman, Olshan Grundman Frome/11.50%, Shirley M. Wan/6.50%, C Trade Inc/21.60%, Robert D. Asher/9.50%, John J. Clarke, David A. Conway/12.60%

Financial Data: *Fiscal Year End:*12/31 *Latest Annual Data:* 12/31/2006

Year	Sales	Net Income
2006	$115,000	-$2,073,000
2005	$260,000	-$1,168,000
2004	$56,000	-$3,758,000

Curr. Assets:	$119,000	**Curr. Liab.:**	$3,242,000		
Plant, Equip.:	NA	**Total Liab.:**	$3,768,000	**Indic. Yr. Divd.:**	NA
Total Assets:	$142,000	**Net Worth:**	-$3,626,000	**Debt/ Equity:**	NA

Waterford Wedgwood Plc

Waterford Wedgwood plc, Barlaston, Stoke-on-Trent, ST12 9ES; *PH:* 44-1782204141; *Fax:* 44-1782204501; *http://* www.waterfordwedgewood.com; *Email:* marni.shapiro@waterfordwedgwood.com

General - Incorporation	Ireland	**Stock**- Price on:12/24/2007	NA
Employees	NA	Stock Exchange	NA
Auditor	PricewaterhouseCoopers LLP	Ticker Symbol	NA
Stk Agt	Bank of New York	Outstanding Shares	NA
Counsel	NA	E.P.S	NA
DUNS No.	21-101-8205	Shareholders	NA

Business: The group's principle activities are the manufacture and market of extensive range of crystal objects, stemware, gifts for distribution, lightingware, cookware and premium ceramics. The group's four international brands are waterford crystal, wedgwood, rosenthal and all-clad. Waterford crystals comprises the manufacture, distribution and retailing of high quality crystal products including giftware, stemware and lightingware. Wedgwood comprises the manufacture distribution and retailing of high quality bone China giftware and tableware. Rosenthal manufactures premium ceramics based in Germany. All-clad manufactures high quality cookware based in Pennsylvania. Its products marketed primarily in the United States.

Primary SIC and add'l.: 5023 3269 3229

CIK No: 0000793586

Subsidiaries: Ashling Corporation, Cashs Mail Order Limited, Development Limited, Dungarvan Crystal Limited, Josiah Wedgwood & Sons (Exports) Limited, Josiah Wedgwood & Sons Limited, Josiah Wedgwood (Malaysia) Sdn. Bhd, Manufacturing Limited, P. T. Doulton, Rosenthal AG, Royal Doulton (U.K.) Limited, Royal Doulton Australia Pty. Limited, Royal Doulton Canada Limited, Royal Doulton Hong Kong Limited, Royal Doulton Japan KK 39 Subsidiaries included in the Index

Officers: Peter B. Cameron/61/Dir., CEO, Patrick J. Dowling/Dir., CFO, Company Sec., Barry Dixon/Investor Contact

Directors: Peter B. Cameron/61/Dir., CEO, Anthony O'Reilly/72/Chmn., Peter John Goulandris/60/Dir., Ottmar C. Kusel/56/Dir., Patrick J. Molloy/70/Dir., Lady O'Reilly/57/Dir., John Foley/56/Group Dir., Lord Wedgwood/56/Dir., Patrick J. Dowling/Dir., CFO, Company Sec., Kevin C. McGoran/73/Dir., Redmond P. O'Donogue/65/Dir., David W. Sculley/62/Dir., Alan F. Wedgwood/71/Dir., Anthony Jones/Dir.

Waters Corp

34 Maple St., Milford, MA, 01757; *PH:* 1-508-478-2000; *http://* www.waters.com

General - Incorporation	DE	**Stock**- Price on:12/24/2007	$60.41
Employees	4,700	Stock Exchange	NYSE
Auditor	PricewaterhouseCoopers LLP	Ticker Symbol	WAT
Stk Agt	Bank of New York	Outstanding Shares	100,900,000
Counsel	NA	E.P.S	$2.43
DUNS No.	86-770-4355	Shareholders	NA

Business: The group's principal activities are to design, manufacture and distribute high performance liquid chromatography and mass spectrometry instrument systems and associated service and support products, including chromatography columns and other consumable products. The group also develops and supplies software based products which interface with the group's instruments and are typically purchased by customers as part of the instrument system. The products of the group are used by pharmaceutical, life science, biochemical, industrial, academic and government customers working in research and development, quality assurance and other laboratory applications. In 2003, the group acquired creon lab control ag, worldwide rheology business of rheometrics, remaining 30% of korean distributor businesses. It acquired nugenesis technologies corporation during Feb 2004.

Primary SIC and add'l.: 3826 6719

CIK No: 0001000697

Subsidiaries: Esbee Wire Pvt. Ltd., Grand Duchy Finance SARL, Longpure, Manchester International Limited, Mass Analyser Prod Ltd., Micromass B.V., Micromass Holdings Ltd., Micromass International Ltd., Micromass Investments Ltd., Micromass Ltd., Micromass UK Ltd., Microsep Proprietary Ltd, Milford Finance BV, Milford International Limited, MM European Holdings LLP 63 Subsidiaries included in the Index

Officers: Douglas A. Berthiaume/59/Chmn., CEO, Pres. - Waters Corporation, John Ornell/VP - Finance, Administration, CFO, William Miller/62/Dir. , Independent Investor, Consultant, Arthur G. Caputo/Exec. VP, Pres. - Waters Division, Elizabeth Rae/VP - Human Resources, Mark Beaudouin/VP, General Counsel, Lydia S. Groce/Contracting Officer, Gene Cassis/VP - Investor Relations, Brian J. Murphy/Contact - Corporate Communications

Directors: Douglas A. Berthiaume/59/Chmn., CEO, Pres. - Waters Corporation, Joshua Bekenstein/49/Dir., Michael J. Berendt/59/Dir., Edward Conard/51/Dir., Laurie H. Glimcher/54/Dir., Christopher A. Kuebler/54/Dir., William Miller/62/Dir. , Independent Investor, Consultant, Joann A. Reed/52/Dir., Thomas P. Salice/48/Dir.

Owners: Joshua Bekenstein, Thomas P. Salice, John Ornell, Insiders/5.36%, Michael J. Berendt, Edward Conard, Laurie H. Glimcher, Elizabeth Rae, Christopher A. Kuebler, Arthur G. Caputo/1.07%, UBS Global Asset Management (Americas), Inc./7.08%, Mark T. Beaudouin, William J. Miller, JoAnn A. Reed, Aim Capital Management, Inc./5.62% *(17 Owners included in Index)*

Financial Data: *Fiscal Year End:*12/31 *Latest Annual Data:* 12/31/2006

Year	Sales	Net Income
2006	$1,280,229,000	$222,200,000
2005	$1,158,236,000	$201,975,000
2004	$1,104,536,000	$224,053,000

Curr. Assets:	$999,680,000	**Curr. Liab.:**	$685,834,000		
Plant, Equip.:	$149,262,000	**Total Liab.:**	$1,254,930,000	**Indic. Yr. Divd.:**	NA
Total Assets:	$1,617,313,000	**Net Worth:**	$362,383,000	**Debt/ Equity:**	1.3340

Watsco Inc

2665 S Bayshore Dr., Ste 901, Coconut Grove, FL, 33133; *PH:* 1-305-858-0828; *http://* www.watsco.com; *Email:* info@watsco.com

General - Incorporation	FL	**Stock**- Price on:12/24/2007	$59
Employees	3,300	Stock Exchange	NYSE
Auditor	Grant Thornton, LLP	Ticker Symbol	WSO
Stk Agt	American Stock Transfer & Trust Co.	Outstanding Shares	28,020,000
Counsel	NA	E.P.S	$2.67
DUNS No.	00-412-3576	Shareholders	NA

Business: The groups principle activity is to distribute air conditioning, heating, and refrigeration equipment and related parts and supplies. The groups products include condensing units, compressors, evaporators, valves, refrigerant, walk-in coolers and ice machines. In the year 2007 the group acquired ACR Group, Inc. The group operates from United States.

Primary SIC and add'l.: 5078 7361 5075

CIK No: 0000105016

Subsidiaries: Air Systems Distributors LLC, Atlantic Service& Supply LLC, Baker Distributing Company LLC, Comfort Products Distributing LLC, Comfort Supply, Inc., Dunhill Personnel Systems of New Jersey, Inc., Dunhill Staffing Systems, Inc., Dunhill Temporary Systems, Inc., East Coast Metal Distributors LLC, Gemaire Distributors LLC, Heat Incorporated LLC, Heating& Cooling Supply LLC, Homans Associates LLC, Three States Supply Company LLC, Tradewinds Distributing Company LLC 17 Subsidiaries included in the Index

Officers: Albert H. Nahmad/Chmn., CEO, Pres./$6,265,411.00, Barry S. Logan/Sr. VP, Sec./$768,200.00, Ana M. Menendez/CFO, VP - Finance/$193,864.00, Carole J. Poindexter/52/Pres. - Baker Distributing Company, LLC/$743,245.00, Stephen R. Combs/64/Pres. - Gemaire Distributors, LLC/$707,528.00

Directors: Albert H. Nahmad/Chmn., CEO, Pres., Cesar L. Alvarez/Dir., Bob Dickinson/63/Dir., Fred Joseph/Dir., Victor Lopez/Dir., Paul F. Manley/Dir., Bob L. Moss/Dir., George P. Sape/Dir., Sherwood Weiser/Dir., Gary L. Tapella/Dir., Robert L. Berner/Dir., Denise Dickins/Dir., Frederick H. Joseph/Dir.

Owners: Barclays Global Investors, NA/5.10%, Basswood Capital Management, LLC/5.50%, Albert H. Nahmad, Stephen R. Combs, Barry S. Logan, George P. Sape, Bob L. Moss, Paul F. Manley, Columbia Wanger Asset Management, L.P./12.00%, Carole J. Poindexter, Gary L. Tapella, Denise Dickins, Paul F. Manley, Barry S. Logan/1.00%, Victor M. Lopez *(24 Owners included in Index)*

Financial Data: *Fiscal Year End:*12/31 *Latest Annual Data:* 12/31/2006

Year	Sales	Net Income
2006	$1,800,759,000	$82,364,000
2005	$1,682,724,000	$70,019,000
2004	$1,315,024,000	$48,105,000

Curr. Assets:	$517,808,000	***Curr. Liab.:***	$156,191,000	***P/E Ratio:***	22.10
Plant, Equip.:	$21,476,000	***Total Liab.:***	$194,985,000	***Indic. Yr. Divd.:***	$1.320
Total Assets:	$711,371,000	***Net Worth:***	$516,386,000	***Debt/ Equity:***	0.0582

Watson Pharmaceuticals Inc

311 Bonnie Cir., Corona, CA, 92880; ***PH:*** 1-951-493-5300; ***http://*** www.watsonpharm.com

General - Incorporation	NV	***Stock***- Price on:12/24/2007	$32.59
Employees	5,830	Stock Exchange	NYSE
Auditor	PricewaterhouseCoopers LLP	Ticker Symbol	WPI
Stk Agt	American Stock Transfer & Trust Co.	Outstanding Shares	NA
Counsel	NA	E.P.S	-$3.75
DUNS No.	10-693-1488	Shareholders	NA

Business: The groups principle activity is developing, manufacturing, marketing and distributing brand and generic pharmaceutical products. The groups products include Oxytrol(R), Trelstar(R) and Ferrlecit(R). The group operates from United States.

Primary SIC and add'l.: 2834 8731

CIK No: 0000884629

Subsidiaries: Nicobrand Limited, The Rugby Group, Inc., Watson Laboratories Caribe, Inc., Watson Laboratories, Inc, Watson Laboratories, Inc., Watson Laboratories, Inc.Arizona, Watson Pharma, Inc., Watson Pharmaceuticals (Asia) Ltd., WP Holdings AB

Officers: Paul M. Bisaro/Dir., CEO, Pres., Albert Paonessa/COO, Exec. VP - Anda, Inc, Watson's Distribution Subsidiary, Thomas R. Giordano/CIO, Sr. VP, David C. Hsia/Sr. VP - Scientific Affairs, Gordon Munro/Sr. VP - Quality Assurance, Charles D. Ebert/Sr. VP - Research, Development/$642,375.00, Edward F. Heimers/Exec. VP, Pres. - Brand Division/$656,041.00, Susan Skara/Sr. VP - Human Resources, David A. Buchen/Sr. VP, General Counsel, Sec./$765,204.00, Thomas R. Russillo/Exec. VP, Pres. - US Generics Division, Todd R. Joyce/VP, Corporate Controller, Treasurer/$435,025.00

Directors: Paul M. Bisaro/Dir., CEO, Pres., Allen Chao/Chmn., Fred G. Weiss/Dir., Andrew L. Turner/Dir., Michael J. Fedida/Dir., Jack Michelson/73/Dir., Ronald R. Taylor/Dir., Michel J. Feldman/Dir., Albert F. Hummel/Dir., Catherine M. Klema/Dir.

Owners: Fred G. Weiss, Edward Heimers, Ronald R. Taylor, Andrew L. Turner, Michel J. Feldman, Jack Michelson, Michael J. Fedida, Catherine M. Klema, Todd R. Joyce, Charles D. Ebert, Insiders/8.40%, David A. Buchen, Allen Chao/5.10%, The TCW Group./10.30%, Franklin Resources,Inc./5.70% *(16 Owners included in Index)*

Financial Data: *Fiscal Year End:*12/31 *Latest Annual Data:* 12/31/2006

Year	Sales	Net Income
2006	$1,979,244,000	-$445,005,000
2005	$1,646,203,000	$138,233,000
2004	$1,640,551,000	$151,333,000

Curr. Assets:	$1,261,676,000	***Curr. Liab.:***	$689,929,000		
Plant, Equip.:	$697,415,000	***Total Liab.:***	$2,080,189,000	***Indic. Yr. Divd.:***	NA
Total Assets:	$3,760,577,000	***Net Worth:***	$1,680,388,000	***Debt/ Equity:***	0.6267

Watson Wyatt Worldwide Inc

Formerly: Watson Wyatt & Co Holdings

901 N Glebe Rd., Arlington, VA, 22203; ***PH:*** 1-703-258-8000; ***http://*** www.watsonwyatt.com

General - Incorporation	DE	***Stock***- Price on:12/24/2007	$50.66
Employees	6,235	Stock Exchange	NYSE
Auditor	Deloitte & Touche, LLP	Ticker Symbol	WW
Stk Agt	American Stock Transfer & Trust Co.	Outstanding Shares	42,760,000
Counsel	NA	E.P.S	$2.81
DUNS No.	NA	Shareholders	NA

Business: The group's principal activity is to design, develop and implement hr strategies and programs. The group operates through five segments namely benefits group, technology solutions group, human capital group, international and other. The benefit group deals with retirement plans including pension, 401(k) plan, health care, global compensation and actuarial services. The technology solutions group offers Web-based applications for health and welfare, call center strategy, design and tools, online compensation and benefits statements. The human capital group deals with compensation plans, strategies to align workforce performance with business objectives and performance management. The international consists of operations outside North America including the Asia-pacific and Latin America. The other segment includes communication and data services. The group's clients include emerging growth companies, public institutions and nonprofit organizations.

Primary SIC and add'l.: 6411 9441 8742 8748

CIK No: 0001103126

Subsidiaries: Consulting Holdings Limited, Corredores de Seguros Watson Wyatt Limitada, P.T. Watson Wyatt Indonesia, P.T. Watson Wyatt Purbajaga, Pcl (1991) Limited, PCL Limited, RWS Trustee Limited, The Wyatt Company (UK) Limited, The Wyatt Company Holdings Limited, Watson Wyatt & Company, Watson Wyatt (Ireland) Limited, Watson Wyatt (Malaysia) Sdn. Bhd., Watson Wyatt (Thailand) Ltd., Watson Wyatt (UK) Acquisitions 1 Limited, Watson Wyatt (UK) Acquisitions 2 Limited 80 Subsidiaries included in the Index

Officers: John J. Haley/Chmn., CEO, Pres., Carl D. Mautz/CFO, VP, Peter Mills/VP, Regional Mgr. - Latin America, David M.E. Dow/VP, Global Practice Dir. - Technology, Administration Solutions, Kevin L. Meehan/Regional Mgr. - North America, Robert J. Mckee/Global Dir. - Marketing, Chandrasekhar Ramamurthy/Dir., VP, Regional Mgr. - Europe, Chuly Lee/VP, Regional Mgr. - Asia, Pacific, Roger C. Urwin/Dir., VP, Global Practice Dir., Jeffrey J. Held/VP, Global Information Officer, Walter W. Bardenwerper/VP, General Counsel, Sec., Paul E. Platten/VP, Global Practice Dir. - Human Capital Group, Gene H. Wickes/Dir., VP, Global Dir. - Benefits Practice, Philip G.H. Brook/VP, Global Practice Dir. - Insurance, Financial Services

Directors: John J. Haley/Chmn., CEO, Pres., Michael R. McCullough/Dir., John C. Wright/Dir., John J. Gabarro/Dir., Linda D. Rabbitt/Dir., Chandrasekhar Ramamurthy/Dir., VP, Regional Mgr. - Europe, Roger C. Urwin/Dir., VP, Global Practice Dir., Gene H. Wickes/Dir., VP, Global Dir. - Benefits Practice, Brendan R. O'Neill/Dir., Gilbert T. Ray/Dir.

Financial Data: *Fiscal Year End:*06/30 *Latest Annual Data:* 6/30/2007

Year	Sales	Net Income
2007	$1,486,523,000	$116,275,000
2006	$1,271,811,000	$87,191,000
2005	$737,421,000	$52,162,000

Curr. Assets:	$493,647,000	***Curr. Liab.:***	$296,335,000	***P/E Ratio:***	21.02
Plant, Equip.:	$147,738,000	***Total Liab.:***	$591,598,000	***Indic. Yr. Divd.:***	$0.300
Total Assets:	$1,240,359,000	***Net Worth:***	$648,761,000	***Debt/ Equity:***	NA

Watts Water Technologies Inc

815 Chestnut St., North Andover, MA, 01845; ***PH:*** 1-978-688-1811; ***http://*** www.watts.com

General - Incorporation	DE	***Stock***- Price on:12/24/2007	$38.44
Employees	8,300	Stock Exchange	NYSE
Auditor	KPMG LLP	Ticker Symbol	WTS
Stk Agt	Computershare Investor Services LLC	Outstanding Shares	38,650,000
Counsel	Goodwin, Procter & Hoar	E.P.S	$2.24
DUNS No.	15-216-3093	Shareholders	NA

Business: The group's principal activity is to design, manufacture and market extensive line of valves for the plumbing, heating and water quality markets. The products manufactured are temperature and pressure safety relief valves, water pressure regulators, backflow preventers, thermostatic mixing valves, ball valves, automatic control valves, water distribution manifolds, zone valves, thermostatic radiator valves, check valves and valves for water service primarily in residential & commercial environments. This products includes metal and plastic water supply/drainage products including stop valves, tubular brass products, faucets, drains, sink strainers, compression & flare fittings, plastic tubing & braided metal hose connectors for residential construction and home repair & remodeling. The group acquired Flowmatic Systems Inc, Taizhou Shida Plumbing Manufacturing Co Ltd, McCoy Enterprises Inc & Team Precision Pipe Work Ltd in 2004.

Primary SIC and add'l.: 3491 3492

CIK No: 0000795403

Subsidiaries: Anderson-Barrows Benelux BV, Anderson-Barrows Metals Corporation, Core Industries Inc. (d.b.a. FEBCO, Mueller Steam Specialty & POLYJET Valves), Dormont Manufacturing Company, Electro Controls Ltd., Flowmatic Systems, Inc., Giuliani Anello S.r.l., HF Scientific, Inc., Hosta Investments Ltd., Hunter Innovations, Inc., Orion Enterprises, Inc., Philabel BV, Stern Rubinetti S.r.l., TEAM Precision Pipework, Ltd., Tianjin Tanggu Watts Valve Co., Ltd. 52 Subsidiaries included in the Index

Officers: Patrick S. O'Keefe/Dir., CEO, Pres./$3,076,020.00, William C. McCartney/CFO, Treasurer/$1,035,700.00, Paul A. Lacourciere/Corporate VP - Manufacturing/$664,035.00, Gregory J. Michaud/Exec. VP - Human Resources, Ernest E. Elliott/Exec. VP - Marketing, Lester J. Taufen/General Counsel, VP - Legal Affairs, Sec., Douglas T. White/Group VP, Dennis J. Cawte/Group MD - Europe/$735,090.00

Directors: Patrick S. O'Keefe/Dir., CEO, Pres., Gordon W. Moran/Non - Exec. Chmn., John K. McGillicuddy/Dir., Kenneth J. McAvoy/Dir., Timothy P. Horne/Dir., Ralph E. Jackson/Dir., Daniel J. Murphy/Dir., Robert L. Ayers/Dir.

Owners: Deborah Horne/3.70%, Dennis J. Cawte, Timothy P. Horne, Robert L. Ayers, William C. McCartney, Patrick S. OKeefe, Daniel W. Horne, Daniel J. Murphy, Gabelli Funds, LLC, William D. Martino, Kenneth J. McAvoy, John K. McGillicuddy, John K. McGillicuddy, Patrick S. OKeefe, Paul A. Lacourciere *(34 Owners included in Index)*

Financial Data: *Fiscal Year End:*12/31 *Latest Annual Data:* 12/31/2006

Year	Sales	Net Income
2006	$1,230,777,000	$73,736,000
2005	$924,346,000	$54,599,000
2004	$824,558,000	$46,820,000

Curr. Assets:	$952,382,000	***Curr. Liab.:***	$299,358,000	***P/E Ratio:***	17.16
Plant, Equip.:	$206,160,000	***Total Liab.:***	$834,297,000	***Indic. Yr. Divd.:***	$0.400
Total Assets:	$1,660,850,000	***Net Worth:***	$826,553,000	***Debt/ Equity:***	0.5343

Wausau Paper Corp

Formerly: Wausau Mosinee Paper Corp

100 Paper Pl., Mosinee, WI, 54455; ***PH:*** 1-715-693-4470; ***Fax:*** 1-715-692-2082; ***http://*** www.wausaumosinee.com

General - Incorporation	WI	***Stock***- Price on:12/24/2007	$13.75
Employees	3,000	Stock Exchange	NYSE
Auditor	Deloitte & Touche LLP	Ticker Symbol	WPP
Stk Agt	Continental Stock Transfer & Trust Co	Outstanding Shares	50,750,000
Counsel	NA	E.P.S	$0.67
DUNS No.	00-613-5792	Shareholders	NA

Business: The group's principal activity is to manufacture, convert and sell paper and paper products. The group operates in three segments: printing and writing, specialty paper and towel and tissue. Printing and writing segment manufactures, converts and markets a broad line of printing and writing grades and owns facilities that produce laminated roll wrap and packaging products. Specialty paper segment produces a wide variety of technical specialty papers for a broad range of food, medical and industrial

applications. Towel and tissue segment manufactures a complete line of towel and tissue products, which are marketed along with soap and dispensing system products for the industrial and commercial markets. The products offered include washroom roll towels, windshield folded towels, industrial wipes, tissue products and other premium towel and tissue products.

Primary SIC and add'l.: 2671 2621 2652

CIK No: 0000105076

Subsidiaries: Bay West Paper Corporation, he Middletown Hydraulic Company, Mosinee Holdings, Inc, Mosinee Paper Corporation, Mosinee Timberland Company, LLC, Rhinelander Paper Company, Inc, The Sorg Paper Company, Wausau Paper of Minnesota, LLC, Wausau Papers of New Hampshire, Inc, Wausau Papers Otis Mill Inc, Wausau Timberland Company, LLC, Wausau-Mosinee International, Inc

Owners: Pete R. Chiericozzi, Thomas J. Howatt/1.20%, Wilmington Trust Company/11.10%, Dennis J. Kuester, San W. Orr/3.80%, David B. Smith/4.00%, Dimensional Fund Advisors Inc./8.40%, Stuart R. Carlson, NWQ Investment Management Company, LLC/12.50%, Wells Fargo & Company/5.60%, Insiders/12.00%, Michael M. Knetter, Scott P. Doescher, Andrew N. Baur, Gary W. Freels/2.00% *(16 Owners included in Index)*

Financial Data: *Fiscal Year End:*12/31 *Latest Annual Data:* 12/31/2006

Year	Sales	Net Income
2006	$1,188,178,000	$17,619,000
2005	$1,097,093,000	-$19,465,000
2004	$1,040,717,000	$20,393,000

Curr. Assets:	$294,247,000	**Curr. Liab.:**	$155,182,000	**P/E Ratio:**	20.52
Plant, Equip.:	$468,372,000	**Total Liab.:**	$525,040,000	**Indic. Yr. Divd.:**	$0.340
Total Assets:	$799,114,000	**Net Worth:**	$274,074,000	**Debt/ Equity:**	0.5721

Wauwatosa Holdings Inc

11200 W Plank Ct., Wauwatosa, WI, 53226; *PH:* 1-414-918-0700; *http://* www.wsbonline.com

General - Incorporation	WI	**Stock**- Price on:12/24/2007	$16.46
Employees	248	Stock Exchange	NDQ
Auditor	KPMG LLP	Ticker Symbol	WAUW
Stk Agt	Registrar & Transfer Co	Outstanding Shares	32,430,000
Counsel	NA	E.P.S	$0.12
DUNS No.	NA	Shareholders	NA

Business: The groups principle activity is to provide financial services. The products of the group include consumer, commercial and construction loan. The group operates from the United States.

Primary SIC and add'l.: 6712 6035 6712 6035

CIK No: 0001329517

Subsidiaries: Main Street Real Estate Holdings, LLC, Waterstone Mortgage Corporation, Wauwatosa Investments, Inc, Wauwatosa Savings Bank

Officers: Douglas S. Gordon/CEO, Pres./$514,951.00, Barbara J. Coutley/Sr. VP, Sec./$239,453.00, Richard C. Larson/Sr. VP, CFO/$374,255.00, Judith M. Wagner/Assist. VP, Assistant Controller, Mark Gerke/Controller, Michael T. Jones/VP - Facilities, Security, Delinquent Loans Department Head - Wauwatosa Savings Bank, Jodi L. Johnson/Assist. VP, Assistant Compliance Officer, Holly L. Flemming/Assist. VP, Employee Benefits Department Head, Robert J. Schroeder/VP, Residential Lending Head, Mark J. Bahr/VP - Commercial Real Estate Head - Wauwatosa Savings Bank, William F. Bruss/General Counsel/$297,467.00, Kenneth A. Snyder/VP, Sr. Commercial Loan Officer, Dave C. Hoerig/VP, Sr. Delinquent Loans Officer, Bryan J. Olen/Assist. VP, Facilities Head, Todd M. Cruciani/VP - Consumer Lending Head - Wauwatosa Savings Bank *(22 Officers included in Index)*

Directors: Patrick S. Lawton/Chmn., Thomas E. Dalum/Dir., Michael L. Hansen/Dir., Stephen J. Schmidt/Dir.

Owners: Douglas S. Gordon, Barbara J. Coutley, Insiders/5.45%, William F. Bruss, Michael L. Hansen, Thomas E. Dalum, Lamplighter Financial, MHC/69.81%, Richard C. Larson, Patrick S. Lawton, Stephen J. Schmidt, Rebecca M. Arndt

Financial Data: *Fiscal Year End:*12/31 *Latest Annual Data:* 12/31/2006

Year	Sales	Net Income
2006	$98,249,000	$8,053,000
2005	$44,308,000	$2,713,000

Curr. Assets:	$73,807,000	**Curr. Liab.:**	$1,077,442,000	**P/E Ratio:**	71.57
Plant, Equip.:	$32,625,000	**Total Liab.:**	$1,407,198,000	**Indic. Yr. Divd.:**	NA
Total Assets:	$1,648,470,000	**Net Worth:**	$241,272,000	**Debt/ Equity:**	1.3514

Wave Systems Corp

480 Pleasant St., Lee, MA, 01238; *PH:* 1-413-243-1600; *http://* www.wavesys.com

General - Incorporation	DE	**Stock**- Price on:12/24/2007	$2.02
Employees	96	Stock Exchange	NDQ
Auditor	KPMG LLP	Ticker Symbol	WAVX
Stk Agt	American Stock Transfer & Trust Co.	Outstanding Shares	42,250,000
Counsel	Bingham, Dana & Gould LLP	E.P.S	-$0.46
DUNS No.	62-262-9921	Shareholders	NA

Business: The group's principal activities are to develop, produce and market hardware and software based digital security products for the Internet and e-commerce. The group's products allow authentication, authorization and other security processes to be implemented in hardware at the PC or other platform level, creating a much more secure computing environment. The group is a development stage company.

Primary SIC and add'l.: 7379 7372 3577

CIK No: 0000919013

Subsidiaries: Saflink Corporation

Officers: Steven K. Sprague/Dir., CEO, Pres./$710,671.00, Gerard T. Feeney/CFO/$496,317.00, Lark Allen/Exec. VP - Business Development, Brian Berger/Exec. VP - Sales, Marketing, Len Veil/CTO, Bruno Leconte/VP - European Operations

Directors: Steven K. Sprague/Dir., CEO, Pres., John E. Bagalay/Chmn., Nolan Bushnell/Dir., George Gilder/Dir., John E. McConnaughy/Dir.

Owners: John E. Bagalay, Insiders/3.80%, Steven Sprague/2.10%, Gerard T. Feeney/1.10%, Nolan Bushnell, George Gilder, John E. McConnaughy

Financial Data: *Fiscal Year End:*12/31 *Latest Annual Data:* 12/31/2006

Year	Sales	Net Income
2006	$3,116,000	-$18,785,000
2005	$1,018,000	-$17,562,000
2004	$209,000	-$14,498,000

Curr. Assets:	$8,809,000	**Curr. Liab.:**	$3,439,000		
Plant, Equip.:	$420,000	**Total Liab.:**	$3,439,000	**Indic. Yr. Divd.:**	NA
Total Assets:	$9,360,000	**Net Worth:**	$5,920,000	**Debt/ Equity:**	NA

Wavecom

430 Davis Dr., Ste. 300, Research Triangle Park, NC, 27709; *PH:* 1-919-237-4000; *Fax:* 1-919-237-4140; *http://* www.wavecom.com; *Email:* info@wavecom.com

General - Incorporation	France	**Stock**- Price on:12/24/2007	$35.69
Employees	384	Stock Exchange	NDQ
Auditor	Ernst & Young LLP	Ticker Symbol	WVCM
Stk Agt	NA	Outstanding Shares	15,430,000
Counsel	Sullivan & Cromwell	E.P.S	$1.22
DUNS No.	NA	Shareholders	NA

Business: The group's principal activities are the development, marketing and distribution of a line of digital wireless standard modules. These modules are known as wismo modules and are used in mobile phones and other wireless systems based on the global system for mobile communications standards (gsm) . The group also develops and distributes modems made under the gsm standard. The group's subsidiaries are located in the usa, Hong Kong, South Korea and Germany.

Primary SIC and add'l.: 6794 3661 4812

CIK No: 0001085763

Subsidiaries: Wavecom Asia Pacific Limited, Wavecom Deutschland GMBH, Wavecom Inc., Wavecom Korea Co. Ltd., Wavecom Northern Europe Ltd.

Officers: Aram Hekimian/Dir., Deputy CEO, Ronald D. Black/Dir., CEO, Didier Dutronc/Group VP, Head - Asia, Pacific Region, MD, Philippe Guillemette/Group VP - Marketing, CTO, Luc Degaudenzi/45/Group VP - Research, Development, Lucie Larguier/Contact - Ogilvy Public Relations, Colin Chew/Mgr. - Marketing Communications, Apac Region, Hugues Waldburger/46/Dir. - Performances, Validation, Ghislaine Gasparetto/Contact - Ogilvy Public Relations, Etienne Menut/Group VP - Human Resources, Chantal Bourgeat/CFO, Group VP - Finance - Administration, Pierre Piver/Chief - Staff, Integration, Pres., Pierre Teyssier/Group VP - Operation, Frank Souguir/Sales Dir. - EMEA Region, Claire Oliver/Group Dir. - Quality *(22 Officers included in Index)*

Directors: Ronald D. Black/Dir., CEO, Aram Hekimian/Dir., Deputy CEO, Michel Alard/Chmn., Stephen Imbler/Dir., Jean-Francois Heitz/Dir., Anthony Maher/Dir., Bernard Gilly/Dir.

Owners: Michel Alard/11.00%, Aram Hekimian/13.20%

Financial Data: *Fiscal Year End:*12/31 *Latest Annual Data:* 12/31/2006

Year	Sales	Net Income
2006	$249,217,000	$6,209,000
2005	$153,062,000	$10,297,000
2004	$206,780,000	-$107,456,000

Curr. Assets:	$122,916,000	**Curr. Liab.:**	$66,435,000		
Plant, Equip.:	NA	**Total Liab.:**	$89,144,000	**Indic. Yr. Divd.:**	NA
Total Assets:	$183,755,000	**Net Worth:**	$94,611,000	**Debt/ Equity:**	NA

Wavelit Inc

Formerly: Infotec Business Systems Inc

No.150 - 1152 Mainland St., Vancouver, BC, V6B 4X2; *PH:* 1-604-484-4966; *http://* www.infotecbsi.com

General - Incorporation	NV	**Stock**- Price on:12/24/2007	NA
Employees	NA	Stock Exchange	OTC
Auditor	Mendoza Berger & Company, LLP	Ticker Symbol	IFTCE
Stk Agt	Interwest Transfer Company, Inc.	Outstanding Shares	NA
Counsel	NA	E.P.S	NA
DUNS No.	NA	Shareholders	NA

Business: The groups principle activity is to provide studio services. Services of the group include video editing and encoding, studio rental, casting, directing, and video and audio production, and remote site video. The group operates from the United States.

Primary SIC and add'l.: 4813

CIK No: 0001164012

Subsidiaries: Eventec Inc., Galaxy Networks Inc., Infotec Business Strategies, Inc.

Officers: Arthur Griffiths/CEO, Kent Vaesen/Pres., Sec., Treasurer, Dir., CEO - Principal Finance, Accounting Officer, Ed Clunn/CTO, Lorne Milne/VP, Art Bacon/Mgr. - Los Angeles Operations, Stanley W. McKiernan/Corporate Counsel, Trevor Clunn/Information Technology Mgr., Hayley Wright/Studio Support, Carol Shaw/42/Sec., Treasurer

Directors: Kent Vaesen/Pres., Sec., Treasurer, Dir., CEO - Principal Finance, Accounting Officer

Owners: Robert Danvers/5.57%, Insiders/37.64%, Arthur Griffiths/12.35%, Bram Solloway/4.25%, Edward Clunn/21.96%, Carol Shaw/3.33%

Wayne Savings Bancshares Inc

151 N Market St., Wooster, OH, 44691; *PH:* 1-330-264-5767; *http://* www.waynesavings.com; *Email:* waynesavings@sssnet.com

General - Incorporation	DE	**Stock**- Price on:12/24/2007	$13.47
Employees	102	Stock Exchange	NDQ
Auditor	Grant Thornton LLP	Ticker Symbol	WAYN
Stk Agt	Registrar & Transfer Co	Outstanding Shares	3,190,000
Counsel	Elias, Matz, Tierman & Herrick	E.P.S	$0.67
DUNS No.	94-005-1790	Shareholders	NA

Business: The group's principal activity is to accept deposits from the general public and apply those funds to originate loans. The group accepts deposits such as now, passbook, certificate of deposits and provides one- to four-family residential, real estate loans, multi-family residential and non-residential real estate loans. The group also originates consumer loans and to a lesser extent, construction loans. It invests in mortgage-backed securities and currently maintains a significant portion of its assets in liquid investments, such as United States government securities, federal funds and deposits in other financial institutions. The primary lending and deposit gathering area of the group includes wayne, holmes, ashland and medina counties in Ohio where it operates nine full-service offices. On 02-Jun-2004, the group acquired stebbins bancshares inc.

Primary SIC and add'l.: 6035 6712

CIK No: 0001036030

Subsidiaries: Wayne Savings Community Bank.

Officers: Phillip E. Becker/Dir., CEO, Pres./$202,565.00

Directors: Phillip E. Becker/Dir., CEO, Pres., Russell L. Harpster/Chmn., James C. Morgan/Dir., Frederick J. Krum/Dir., Terry A. Gardner/Dir., Daniel R. Buehler/Dir., Kenneth R. Lehman/Dir.

Owners: Frederick J. Krum, Stewart Fitz H. Gibbon, James C. Morgan/1.10%, Daniel R. Buehler, Insiders/7.20%, Wayne Savings Employee Stock Ownership Plan Trust/7.60%, Terry A. Gardner/1.60%, Russell L. Harpster/2.30%, Kenneth R. Lehman/1.60%, Bryan K. Fehr

Financial Data: Fiscal Year End:03/31   Latest Annual Data: 03/31/2007

Year	Sales	Net Income
2007	$24,076,000	$2,161,000
2006	$21,465,000	$1,640,000
2005	$19,316,000	$381,000

Curr. Assets:	$16,148,000	Curr. Liab.:	$348,359,000	P/E Ratio:	20.10
Plant, Equip.:	$8,713,000	Total Liab.:	$368,163,000	Indic. Yr. Divd.:	$0.480
Total Assets:	$403,679,000	Net Worth:	$35,516,000	Debt/ Equity:	NA

Wayside Technology Group Inc

Formerly: Programmer's Paradise Inc

1157 Shrewsbury Ave, Shrewsbury, NJ, 07702; **PH:** 1-732-389-8950; **http://** www.pparadise.com

General - Incorporation	DE	Stock - Price on:12/24/2007	$16.18
Employees	97	Stock Exchange	NDQ
Auditor	Amper, Politziner & Mattia P.C	Ticker Symbol	WSTG
Stk Agt	American Stock Transfer & Trust Co.	Outstanding Shares	4,670,000
Counsel	Frederick J. Klink	E.P.S.	$0.82
DUNS No.	04-853-0240	Shareholders	NA

Business: The group's principal activity is to market technical software and hardware for microcomputers, servers and networks in the United States and Canada. The group offers technical and general business application software, PC hardware and components from publishers and manufacturers. It markets its products through catalogs, direct mail programs, advertisements in trade magazines, as well as through Internet and e-mail promotion under the trademarks programmer's paradise, the 'island man' cartoon character logo and lifeboat. The group distributes products to dealers and resellers through its wholly-owned subsidiary, lifeboat distribution inc.

Primary SIC and add'l.: 5734

CIK No: 0000945983

Subsidiaries: Lifeboat Distribution Inc, Lifeboat Distribution, Inc

Officers: Simon F. Nynens/36/Chmn., CEO, Pres./$722,860.00, Vito Legrottaglie/VP - MIS/$248,803.00, Jeffrey Largiader/VP - Sales, Marketing/$252,093.00, Dan Jamieson/VP, GM - Lifeboat/$290,653.00, Kevin T. Scull/VP, Chief Accounting Officer/$178,983.00, Freddie Rivera/Dir. - Sales

Directors: Simon F. Nynens/36/Chmn., CEO, Pres., William H. Willett/71/Dir., Duffield F. Meyercord/61/Dir., Edwin H. Morgens/66/Founder, Dir., Allan D. Weingarten/70/Dir., Mark T. Boyer/50/Dir.

Owners: ROI Master Fund, Ltd./5.70%, Simon F. Nynens/6.70%, Dan Jamieson/1.20%, Mark T. Boyer/8.50%, William H. Willett/1.00%, Duffield F. Meyercord/1.70%, Edwin Morgens/4.40%, Vito Legrottaglie/1.00%, Steven J. Emerson/5.60%, Insiders/25.10%, Kevin Scull, Jeffrey Largiader/1.90%, Allan D. Weingarten

Financial Data: Fiscal Year End:12/31   Latest Annual Data: 12/31/2006

Year	Sales	Net Income
2006	$182,319,000	$3,268,000
2005	$137,655,000	$2,653,000
2004	$103,582,000	$6,322,000

Curr. Assets:	$52,413,000	Curr. Liab.:	$35,942,000	P/E Ratio:	19.49
Plant, Equip.:	$488,000	Total Liab.:	$35,983,000	Indic. Yr. Divd.:	$0.600
Total Assets:	$57,281,000	Net Worth:	$21,298,000	Debt/ Equity:	NA

Wca Waste Corp

One Riverway, Ste 1400, Houston, TX, 77056; **PH:** 1-713-292-2400; **http://** www.wcawaste.com; **Email:** contact@wcamerica.com

General - Incorporation	DE	Stock - Price on:12/24/2007	NA
Employees	800	Stock Exchange	NDQ
Auditor	KPMG LLP	Ticker Symbol	WCAA
Stk Agt	Continental Stock Transfer & Trust Co	Outstanding Shares	NA
Counsel	NA	E.P.S.	NA
DUNS No.	NA	Shareholders	NA

Business: The group's principal activities are to provide integrated nonhazardous solid waste collection, transfer, and disposal services. The group serves approximately 87,000 commercial, industrial and residential customers in Alabama, Arkansas, Kansas, Missouri, South Carolina, Texas and Tennessee. It owns fifteen collection operations, eight transfer stations, six municipal solid waste landfills and seven construction and demolition debris landfills. On 18-Aug-2004, the group acquired small collection company, on 07-Sep-2004, the group acquired blount recycling llc, on 08-Sep-2004, power waste and on 20-Sep-2004, translift inc.

Primary SIC and add'l.: 4953

CIK No: 0001282398

Subsidiaries: Eagle Ridge Landfill, LLC, Material Reclamation, LLC, Material Recovery, LLC, Texas Environmental Waste Services, LLC, Transit Waste, LLC, Translift, Inc., Waste Corporation of Arkansas, Inc., Waste Corporation of Kansas, Inc., Waste Corporation of Missouri, Inc, Waste Corporation of Tennessee, Inc., Waste Corporation of Texas, L.P., WCA Capital, Inc., WCA Holdings Corporation, WCA Management Company, L.P., WCA Management General, Inc. 25 Subsidiaries included in the Index

Officers: Tom J. Fatjo/Chmn., CEO/$570,361.00, Jerome M. Kruszka/Dir., COO, Pres./$972,528.00, Charles A. Casalinova/CFO/$671,820.00

Directors: Tom J. Fatjo/Chmn., CEO, Richard E. Bean/Dir., Ballard O. Castleman/Dir., Jerome M. Kruszka/Dir., COO, Pres., Roger A. Ramsey/Dir., Antony P. Ressler/Dir., Jeffrey S. Serota/Dir., Preston Moore/Dir., John V. Singleton/Dir.

Owners: Esping Marital Deduction Trust No. 2, Julie E. Blanton, Ballard O. Castleman, Roger A. Ramsey, Preston Moore, Charles A. Casalinova, Jerome M. Kruszka, Tom J. Fatjo, River Road Asset Management, LLC, Richard E. Bean, Jennifer E. Kirtland, Ares Corporate Opportunities Fund II, L.P./100.00%, William P. Esping, Tom J. Fatjo, Ares Corporate Opportunities Fund II, L.P. (20 Owners included in Index)

Curr. Assets:	$78,641,000	Curr. Liab.:	$24,031,000		
Plant, Equip.:	$207,441,000	Total Liab.:	$203,470,000	Indic. Yr. Divd.:	NA
Total Assets:	$371,249,000	Net Worth:	$167,779,000	Debt/ Equity:	NA

WCI Communities Inc

24301 Walden Ctr Dr., Bonita Springs, FL, 34134; **PH:** 1-239-498-8605; **http://** www.wcicommunities.com

General - Incorporation	DE	Stock - Price on:12/24/2007	$18.91
Employees	3,200	Stock Exchange	NYSE
Auditor	Ernst & Young LLP	Ticker Symbol	WCI
Stk Agt	Computershare Investor Services LLC	Outstanding Shares	42,010,000
Counsel	NA	E.P.S.	-$4.37
DUNS No.	NA	Shareholders	NA

Business: The group's principle activities are to design, construct and operate leisure-oriented, amenity-rich master-planned communities. It designs, sells and builds single- and multi-family homes serving move-up, pre-retirement and retirement home buyers. The group also designs, sells and builds luxury residential towers targeting affluent, leisure-oriented home purchasers.

Primary SIC and add'l.: 6519 7999 6552 1531

CIK No: 0001137778

Subsidiaries: Bay Colony of Naples, Inc., Bay Colony Realty Associates, Inc., Bay Colony-Gateway, Inc., Carpentry Management Associates, LLC, Communities Amenities, Inc., Communities Finance Company, LLC, Communities Home Builders, Inc., Community Specialized Services, Inc., Coral Ridge Communities, Inc., Coral Ridge Properties, Inc., Coral Ridge Realty Sales, Inc., Coral Ridge Realty, Inc., Dix Hills Home& Land Company, LLC, East Fishkill Development LLC, Fair Oaks Parkway, LLC 139 Subsidiaries included in the Index

Officers: Jerry L. Starkey/CEO, Pres., Scott A. Perry/Chief Accounting Officer, Albert F. Moscato/Sr. VP - Business Development, Steven Zenker/VP - Investor Relations, Vivien N. Hastings/Sr. VP, General Counsel, David L. Fry/COO - Traditional Homebuilding, Real Estate Services, Sr. VP, Paul D. Appolonia/Sr. VP - Human Resources, Christopher J. Hanlon/COO - Tower Homebuilding, Sr. VP, Michael R. Curtin/Sr. VP - Marketing, Sales, James P. Dietz/CFO, Exec. VP, Albert H. Small/Pres. - Mid, Atlantic Division

Directors: Carl Icahn/Chmn., Stewart Turley/Dir., Thomas F. McWilliams/Dir., Kathleen M. Shanahan/Dir., Keith Meister/Dir., David Schechter/Dir., Craig W. Thomas/Dir., Nick Graziano/Dir., Jonathan R. MacEy/Dir., James F. McDonald/Dir., Charles E. Cobb/Dir., Don E. Ackerman/Dir., Hilliard M. Eure/Dir., Philip F. Handy/Dir., Lawrence L. Landry/Dir.

Owners: Michael L. Ashner, High River/3.05%, Icahn Partners/6.91%, Icahn Master/4.56%, Jonathan R. Macey

Financial Data: Fiscal Year End:12/31   Latest Annual Data: 12/31/2006

Year	Sales	Net Income
2006	$2,053,698,000	$9,014,000
2005	$2,601,810,000	$186,150,000
2004	$1,805,617,000	$120,203,000

Curr. Assets:	$83,911,000	Curr. Liab.:	$710,693,000		
Plant, Equip.:	$2,230,513,000	Total Liab.:	$2,844,460,000	Indic. Yr. Divd.:	NA
Total Assets:	$3,831,859,000	Net Worth:	$987,399,000	Debt/ Equity:	NA

WD-40 Company

1061 Cudahy Pl., San Diego, CA, 92110; **PH:** 1-619-275-1400; **Fax:** 1-619-275-5823; **http://** www.wd40.com

General - Incorporation	DE	Stock - Price on:12/24/2007	$32.81
Employees	244	Stock Exchange	NDQ
Auditor	PricewaterhouseCoopers LLP	Ticker Symbol	WDFC
Stk Agt	Computershare Investor Services LLC	Outstanding Shares	17,590,000
Counsel	Gordon & Rees	E.P.S.	$1.83
DUNS No.	00-823-2449	Shareholders	NA

Business: The group's principal activities are to manufacture and sell multi-purpose lubricants, heavy-duty hand cleaners and household products. The group's products are sold to retail chain stores, hardware stores, automotive parts outlets and industrial distributors and suppliers. The group has three product categories: multi-purpose lubricants, heavy-duty hand cleaners and household products. The products are sold under the brand names wd-40, 3-in-one oil, lava, solvol, 2000 flushes, x-14, spot shot and carpet fresh. The products are marketed to north, central and South America, Asia, Australia and the Pacific Rim, Europe, the Middle East and Africa.

Primary SIC and add'l.: 2992 2844

CIK No: 0000105132

Subsidiaries: Global Household Brands, Heartland Corporation, HPD Holdings Corp., HPD Laboratories, Inc., HPD Properties, LLC, Shanghai Wu Di Trading Company Limited, WD-40 Company (Australia) Pty. Limited, WD-40 Company Limited, WD-40 Holdings Limited, WD-40 Manufacturing Company, WD-40 Products (Canada) Ltd.

Officers: Garry O. Ridge/Dir., CEO, Pres., Geoffrey J. Holdsworth/MD - Asia Pacific, Graham P. Milner/Exec. VP - Global Development, Chief Branding Officer, Michael J. Irwin/CFO, Exec. VP, William B. Noble/MD - Europe, Middle East, Africa, Michael L. Freeman/Division Pres. - Americas

Directors: Garry O. Ridge/Dir., CEO, Pres., Neal E. Schmale/Chmn., Peter D. Bewley/Dir., John C. Adams/Dir., Richard A. Collato/Dir., Mario L. Crivello/Dir., Linda A. Lang/Dir., Gary L. Luick/Dir., Giles H. Bateman/Dir., Kenneth E. Olson/Dir.

Owners: Neal E. Schmale, Michael J. Irwin, Garry O. Ridge, Peter D. Bewley, Richard A. Collato, Insiders/8.30%, Michael L. Freeman, Kenneth E. Olson, Mario L. Crivello/5.30%, Graham P. Milner, William B. Noble, Linda A. Lang, Giles H. Bateman, John C. Adams

Financial Data: Fiscal Year End:08/31   Latest Annual Data: 8/31/2006

Year	Sales	Net Income
2006	$286,916,000	$28,112,000
2005	$263,227,000	$27,798,000
2004	$242,467,000	$25,643,000

Curr. Assets:	$115,540,000	Curr. Liab.:	$43,667,000	P/E Ratio:	19.77
Plant, Equip.:	$8,940,000	Total Liab.:	$112,744,000	Indic. Yr. Divd.:	$1.000
Total Assets:	$268,475,000	Net Worth:	$155,731,000	Debt/ Equity:	0.2569

Wealth Minerals Ltd

1177 W Hastings St., Ste. 1901, Vancouver, BC, V6E 2K3; **PH:** 1-604-331-0096; **http://** www.wealthminerals.com; **Email:** info@wealthminerals.com

General - Incorporation	BC
Employees	NA
Auditor	STS Partners LLP
Stk Agt	Computershare Investor Services LLC
Counsel	Gowling Lafleur Henderson LLP
DUNS No.	NA

Stock - Price on:12/24/2007	$3.75
Stock Exchange	OTC
Ticker Symbol	WMLLF
Outstanding Shares	NA
E.P.S.	NA
Shareholders	NA

Business: The groups principal activity is engaged in the acquisition and exploration of mineral properties. The group operates from the United States.

Primary SIC and add'l.: 1041 1094

CIK No: 0001077640

Subsidiaries: Triband Resource US Inc

Officers: Hendrik Van Alphen/Dir., CEO, Pres., Jim Dawson/Consultant, John Mericle/Legal Counsel - Washington State, Glenn Shand/Contact - Investor Relations, Michael W. Kinley/CFO, Scott Heffernan/Chief Geologist, Lawrence W. Talbot/VP, General Counsel, Marla K. Ritchie/Corp. Sec.

Directors: Hendrik Van Alphen/Dir., CEO, Pres., Maurice F. Strong/Dir., Jeffrey A. Pontius/Dir., Jerry Pogue/Dir., Michael Bartlett/Dir., Paul Matysek/Dir.

Owners: Maurice F. Strong/1.17%, Michael Bartlett, Lawrence Talbot, Jeff Pontius, Henk Van Alphen/4.08%, Michael Kinley, Marla Ritchie, Insiders/7.00%

Financial Data: Fiscal Year End: 11/30   *Latest Annual Data:* 11/30/2006

Year	Sales	Net Income
2006	NA	-$5,956,000
2005	NA	-$2,717,000
2004	NA	-$1,374,000

Curr. Assets:	$1,786,000	Curr. Liab.:	$258,000		
Plant, Equip.:	$2,218,000	Total Liab.:	$395,000	Indic. Yr. Divd.:	NA
Total Assets:	$4,011,000	Net Worth:	$3,616,000	Debt/ Equity:	NA

Wealthcraft Systems Inc

Formerly: Parque La Qunita Estates

Unit A, 9/f On Hing Bldg., No. 1 On Hing Terrace, Central Hong Kong; *PH:* 852-358-68234

General - Incorporation	NV
Employees	48
Auditor	Kyle L. Tingle, Cpa LLC
Stk Agt	Pacific Stock Transfer Company
Counsel	NA
DUNS No.	NA

Stock - Price on:12/24/2007	$5.85
Stock Exchange	OTC
Ticker Symbol	WCSY
Outstanding Shares	NA
E.P.S.	NA
Shareholders	NA

Business: The group's principle activity is to setting up subsidiaries, general partnerships and limited partnerships, which would be a developer and builder of affordable single-family houses and condominiums in Southern California. The group operates from United States.

Primary SIC and add'l.: 6552

CIK No: 0001119821

Officers: Kelly Jay Michael Tallas/37/Chmn., CEO, Pres., Curtis Hulleman/36/Dir., CIO, Xiao Zhen Li/33/CFO

Directors: Kelly Jay Michael Tallas/37/Chmn., CEO, Pres., Curtis Hulleman/36/Dir., CIO

Owners: Insiders/58.59%, Curtis Hulleman/22.10%, Kelly Jay Michael Tallas/36.49%, James Neil Aitken/6.83%

Financial Data: Fiscal Year End: 12/31   *Latest Annual Data:* 12/31/2006

Year	Sales	Net Income
2006	$744,000	-$380,000

Curr. Assets:	$1,049,000	Curr. Liab.:	$472,000		
Plant, Equip.:	$95,000	Total Liab.:	$857,000	Indic. Yr. Divd.:	NA
Total Assets:	$1,342,000	Net Worth:	$485,000	Debt/ Equity:	1.4728

Weatherford International Ltd

515 Post Oak Blvd, Ste 600, Houston, TX, 77027; *PH:* 1-713-693-4000; *http://* www.weatherford.com; *Email:* investor.relations@weatherford.com

General - Incorporation	Bermuda
Employees	33,000
Auditor	Ernst & Young LLP
Stk Agt	American Stock Transfer & Trust Co.
Counsel	NA
DUNS No.	06-215-7284

Stock - Price on:12/24/2007	$55.93
Stock Exchange	NYSE
Ticker Symbol	WFT
Outstanding Shares	337,300,000
E.P.S.	$2.73
Shareholders	NA

Business: The group's principle activities are to provide equipment and services to the oil and gas exploration and production industry. The group operates in two segments: drilling services and production systems. Drilling services segment provides a wide range of oilfield products and services, including drilling services and equipment, well installation services and cementing products and equipment. Production systems segment designs, manufactures, sells and services a complete line of artificial lift equipment, including progressing cavity pumps, reciprocating rod lift systems, gas lift systems, electrical submersible pumps, product optimization services and automation and monitoring of wellhead production. The group operates in 100 countries, with 500 service and sales locations.

Primary SIC and add'l.: 3533 1381 1389

CIK No: 0001170565

Subsidiaries: 1186443 Alberta Ltd., 315613 Alberta Ltd., 708621 Alberta Ltd., 721260 Alberta Ltd., A-1 Bit & Tool Co., B.V., Advantage R&D, Inc., Aim Oil Tools, Inc., Air Drilling Services Bolivia S.R.L., Air Drilling Services Colombia Limited, Air Drilling Services de Venezuela, C.A., Algerian Oilfield Services S.p.A., Alpine Oil Services (Cyprus) Ltd., Alpine Oil Services Inc., Alpine Oil Services International Ltd., Ampscot Overseas Petroleum Equipment Co., LLC 328 Subsidiaries included in the Index

Officers: Bernard J. Duroc-Danner/Chmn., CEO, Pres., Wolfgang Puennel/VP - Europe, West Africa, Tabetha Stirrett/Canadian Regional Recruitment Mgr., Tham Wai Hou/Expanable Sand Screen, ESS Project Coordinator, Andrew P. Becnel/40/CFO, Steffen Hansen/Coordinator, Drilling, With, Casing, Solid Expandable Systems, Andy Dodds/Applications Engineer - Expandable Technology Unit, Delaney Olstad/Project Engineer, Brad Bogisch/Open, Hole Operations Mgr., Kyle Chapman/Regional Product, Service Line Mgr. - Latin America, Maura Troiana/Project Coordinator, Marwan Roushdy/Sr. Technical Sales Engineer

Directors: Bernard J. Duroc-Danner/Chmn., CEO, Pres., William E. MacAulay/Dir., Robert A. Rayne/Dir., Robert B. Millard/Dir., Nicholas F. Brady/Dir., David J. Butters/Dir., Sheldon B. Lubar/Dir., Robert K. Moses/Dir.

Owners: Jon R. Nicholson, FMR Corp./6.20%, Wellington Management Company, LLP/5.60%, William E. Macaulay, ClearBridge Advisors, LLC/10.90%, Robert A. Rayne, Insiders/2.80%, Andrew P. Becnel, Stuart E. Ferguson, Lee E. Colley, Lisa W. Rodriguez, Nicholas F. Brady, David J. Butters, John R. King, Sheldon B. Lubar *(19 Owners included in Index)*

Financial Data: Fiscal Year End: 12/31   *Latest Annual Data:* 12/31/2006

Year	Sales	Net Income
2006	$6,578,928,000	$896,369,000
2005	$4,333,227,000	$467,420,000
2004	$3,131,774,000	$330,146,000

Curr. Assets:	$3,359,997,000	Curr. Liab.:	$2,043,145,000	P/E Ratio:	20.19
Plant, Equip.:	$3,003,648,000	Total Liab.:	$3,964,449,000	Indic. Yr. Divd.:	NA
Total Assets:	$10,139,248,000	Net Worth:	$6,174,799,000	Debt/ Equity:	0.2469

Web.com Inc

Formerly: Interland Inc

303 Peachtree Ctr. Ave., Ste. 500, Atlanta, GA, 30303; *PH:* 1-404-720-8301; *http://* www.web.com

General - Incorporation	MN
Employees	259
Auditor	Alderton & Markiles, LLP
Stk Agt	Wells Fargo Shareowner Services
Counsel	NA
DUNS No.	NA

Stock - Price on:12/24/2007	$5.16
Stock Exchange	NDQ
Ticker Symbol	WWWW
Outstanding Shares	NA
E.P.S.	-$1.37
Shareholders	NA

Business: The groups principle activity is to provide websites and web services. The groups services include website design and publishing, hosting, eMail, domain registration, online marketing tools and merchant services. The group acquired WebSource Media, LLC in the year 2006 and Web Internet, LLC in the year 2005. The group operates from the United States and other.

Primary SIC and add'l.: 5734

CIK No: 0000854460

Subsidiaries: CommuniTech.Net, Inc., HostPro, Inc., Interland Government Contracting, Inc., MEI California, Inc., Micron Electronics (H.K.) Limited, Micron Electronics Asia-Pacific Holdings, Inc., Micron Electronics Asia-Pacific Operations, Inc., Micron Electronics Asia-Pacific Trading, Ltd., Micron Electronics International, Inc., Micron Electronics Overseas Trading, Inc., Perfect Privacy, LLC, Trellix Corporation, Wazoo Web, Inc., WDC Holdco, Inc., Web Astro GP, Inc. 17 Subsidiaries included in the Index

Officers: David L. Brown/CEO, Vikas Rijsinghani/CTO, Sr. VP, Jeffrey M. Stibel/Pres., Gonzalo Troncoso/CFO, Exec. VP, Kevin Carney/CFO, Roseann Duran/Chief Marketing Officer, Todd Walrath/Exec. VP

Directors: Seymour Holtzman/Chmn., John B. Balousek/Dir., John Patrick Crecine/Dir., Efrem Gerszberg/Dir., Alex Kazerani/Dir., Robert T. Slezak/Dir.

Owners: John Patrick Crecine, PAR Investment Partners, L.P./11.90%, Robert T. Slezak, Seymour Holtzman/ S.H. Holdings, Inc./5.60%, Gonzalo Troncoso/1.00%, Judy Hackett, Jeffrey M. Stibel/12.20%, Kinderhook Partners, L.P./7.00%, Robert Lee, Dimensional Fund Advisors LP./7.40%, Alex A. Kazerani, Efrem Gerszberg, Insiders/20.80%, John B. Balousek

Financial Data: Fiscal Year End: 08/31   *Latest Annual Data:* 12/31/2006

Year	Sales	Net Income
2006	$49,140,000	-$13,724,000
2005	$88,608,000	-$19,889,000
2004	$102,745,000	-$104,663,000

Curr. Assets:	$17,203,000	Curr. Liab.:	$15,067,000	P/E Ratio:	71.57
Plant, Equip.:	$4,128,000	Total Liab.:	$17,472,000	Indic. Yr. Divd.:	NA
Total Assets:	$38,428,000	Net Worth:	$20,956,000	Debt/ Equity:	NA

Web2 Corp

Formerly: 110 Media Group Inc

42 W 38th St., 2nd Fl., New York, NY, 10018; *PH:* 1-631-385-0007; *http://* www.110mediagroup.com

General - Incorporation	DE
Employees	24
Auditor	Marcum & Kliegman LLP
Stk Agt	Computershare Investor Services LLC
Counsel	NA
DUNS No.	NA

Stock - Price on:12/24/2007	$0.36
Stock Exchange	OTC
Ticker Symbol	WBTOE
Outstanding Shares	27,620,000
E.P.S.	-$0.16
Shareholders	NA

Business: The group's principle activity is to develop its technology, market its Website to potential advertisers and building consumer awareness of its Website and services. The group's Website askjade.com is a specialty search engine for the adult entertainment industry. The group intends to distribute its video library of adult content through both the wholesale and retail channels. On 05-Dec-2003, the group acquired jade entertainment group inc.

Primary SIC and add'l.: 7375

CIK No: 0000824104

Subsidiaries: Global Portals Online, Inc.

Officers: William Mobley/Chmn., CEO, Co - Founder, Andre Forde/Dir., Pres., Co - Founder, Darren Cioffi/CFO, Carlos Dunmoodie/VP - Operations, Randy Krull/Dir. - Technology Development

Directors: William Mobley/Chmn., CEO, Co - Founder, Andre Forde/Dir., Pres., Co - Founder, Aaron Stein/54/Dir., William Eric Siedel/44/Dir.

Owners: Eric William John Seidel, William A. Mobley/21.05%, Andre L. Forde/3.97%, Nextelligence, Inc./11.54%, Insiders/25.56%, Gary D. Lipson/5.93%, Aaron Stein, Michele Mobley/9.51%, Darren Cioffi/0.14%

Financial Data: Fiscal Year End: 12/31   *Latest Annual Data:* 12/31/2006

Year	Sales	Net Income
2006	$527,000	-$2,618,000
2005	$275,000	-$587,000
2004	$30,000	-$2,144,000

Curr. Assets:	$222,000	Curr. Liab.:	$4,721,000		
Plant, Equip.:	$419,000	Total Liab.:	$4,721,000	Indic. Yr. Divd.:	NA
Total Assets:	$649,000	Net Worth:	-$4,072,000	Debt/ Equity:	NA

Webb Interactive Services Inc

1899 Wynkoop, Ste 600, Denver, CO, 80202; *PH:* 1-303-296-9200; *http://* www.webb.net

General - Incorporation	CO	**Stock**- Price on:12/24/2007	$0.11
Employees	NA	Stock Exchange	OTC
Auditor	Ehrhardt Keefe Steiner & Hottman P.C	Ticker Symbol	WEBB
Stk Agt	Computershare Trust Co	Outstanding Shares	26,310,000
Counsel	Gray Plant Mooty Mooty & Bennett	E.P.S	-$0.008
DUNS No.	88-349-0492	Shareholders	NA

Business: The group's principal activity is to develop and market instant messaging software for telecommunications carriers, service providers and enterprises. The group operates through two business segments: jabber and webb. The jabber segment provides commercial grade IM solutions, comprised of servers, clients and server modules and also offers professional services to commercial enterprises, Internet service providers, portal companies and other service companies. The webb segment consists of corporate activities such as accounting, administration, public reporting and financing activities. The customers include Buena Vista Internet Group, Bellsouth and France Telecom and subsidiaries. The group has operations in the United States, Europe and Pacific Rim.

Primary SIC and add'l.: 7373 6719 5045 7372

CIK No: 0001011901

Subsidiaries: Jabber, Inc, Nerd Tech

Officers: Paul Guerin/CEO, Rick Emery/VP - Business Development, Harry B. Heisler/GM - Jabber Government, Joe Hildebrand/CTO, Stuart Lucko/CFO, VP - Operations, Dave Uhlir/VP - Products, Services

Financial Data: *Fiscal Year End:*12/31 *Latest Annual Data:* 12/31/2005

Year	Sales	Net Income
2005	NA	-$678,000
2004	NA	-$1,917,000
2003	$647,000	-$2,188,000

Curr. Assets:	$35,000	**Curr. Liab.:**	$31,000		
Plant, Equip.:	NA	**Total Liab.:**	$31,000	**Indic. Yr. Divd.:**	NA
Total Assets:	$35,000	**Net Worth:**	$4,000	**Debt/ Equity:**	NA

Webfinancial Corp

590 Madison Ave., 32nd Fl., New York, NY, 10022; ***PH:*** 1-212-813-1500;
http:// www.webfinancialcorp.com

General - Incorporation	DE	**Stock**- Price on:12/24/2007	$13.9
Employees	10	Stock Exchange	OTC
Auditor	Grant Thornton LLP	Ticker Symbol	WEFN
Stk Agt	Wachovia Bank N.A	Outstanding Shares	2,180,000
Counsel	NA	E.P.S	$3.99
DUNS No.	17-195-0025	Shareholders	NA

Business: The group's principal activity is to operate in niche banking markets. The group provides commercial and consumer specialty financial services which include credit card processing, private label student lending, accounts receivable factoring, elective medical treatment lending, automobile financing via the Internet, structured settlement lending, payday advance lending and business and industry lending guaranteed by federal government. The deposits accepted include non-interest bearing demand, now accounts and certificate of deposit.

Primary SIC and add'l.: 6159 6719

CIK No: 0000085149

Subsidiaries: Praxis Investment Advisors, Inc., Web Film Finance, Inc., WebBank, WebFinancial Holding Corporation, WebFinancial Government Lending, Inc.

Officers: James R. Henderson/48/Dir., COO, CEO, Pres.

Directors: James R. Henderson/48/Dir., COO, CEO, Pres., Jack L. Howard/45/Chmn., Joseph L. Mullen/60/Dir., Mark E. Schwarz/46/Dir., Howard Mileaf/69/Dir.

Financial Data: *Fiscal Year End:*12/31 *Latest Annual Data:* 12/31/2005

Year	Sales	Net Income
2005	$1,571,000	-$1,378,000
2004	$4,821,000	-$930,000
2003	$5,813,000	$2,109,000

Curr. Assets:	$8,639,000	**Curr. Liab.:**	$1,001,000	**P/E Ratio:**	3.48
Plant, Equip.:	$16,000	**Total Liab.:**	$2,492,000	**Indic. Yr. Divd.:**	NA
Total Assets:	$24,368,000	**Net Worth:**	$21,876,000	**Debt/ Equity:**	NA

WebMD Health Corp

111 8th Ave., 7th Fl., New York, NY, 10011; ***PH:*** 1-212-624-3700; ***http://*** www.wbmd.com

General - Incorporation	DE	**Stock**- Price on:12/24/2007	$47.6
Employees	1,025	Stock Exchange	NDQ
Auditor	Ernst& Young LLP	Ticker Symbol	WBMD
Stk Agt	American Stock Transfer & Trust Co.	Outstanding Shares	57,060,000
Counsel	NA	E.P.S	$0.14
DUNS No.	NA	Shareholders	NA

Business: The groups principle activity is to provide health information services. The group products sold under the trade names WebMD(R), WebMD Health(R), Medscape(R), CME Circle(R) and The Little Blue Book(TM). The groups operates through two segments namely online services, and publishing and other services. Customers served by the group include pharmaceutical, biotechnology, medical device and consumer products companies. In the year 2006, the group acquired Subimo, LLC, Medsite, Inc., Summex Corporation, and eMedicine, Inc. The group operates from the United States. The group's quarterly revenue for September 2007 was 87.20 millions of USD.

Primary SIC and add'l.: 7379 8999 8299

CIK No: 0001326583

Subsidiaries: BabyData.com, Inc., Boca Subsidiary Corp., Conceptis, Inc., Crescendo Medical Education LLC, Demand Management, Inc., eMedicine.Com, Inc., Endeavor Technologies, Inc., Health Decisions International, LLC, Health Decisions, Inc., Healtheon/WebMD Cable Corporation, Healtheon/WebMD Internet Corporation, HealthShare Technology, Inc., HW Japan, Inc., MDhub, LLC, MedicineNet, Inc. 34 Subsidiaries included in the Index

Officers: Wayne T. Gattinella/Dir., CEO, Pres./$2,585,752.00, Anthony Vuolo/Dir., COO/$2,563,385.00, Nan-Kirsten Forte/Dir., Exec. VP - Consumer Services/$1,345,822.00, Steven Zatz/Exec. VP - Professional Services Webmd Health, Craig Froude/Exec. VP, Douglas W. Wamsley/Exec. VP, General Counsel, Sec. - Webmd Health, Mark J. Adler/Dir. - Webmd Health, Neil F. Dimick/Dir. - Webmd Health, Jerome C. Keller/Dir. - Webmd Health, James V. Manning/Dir. - Webmd Health, Abdool Rahim Moossa/Dir. - Webmd Health, Mark D. Funston/Dir., Exec. VP, CFO

Directors: Wayne T. Gattinella/Dir., CEO, Pres., Martin J. Wygod/Chmn., Nan-Kirsten Forte/Dir., Exec. VP - Consumer Services, Anthony Vuolo/Dir., COO, Stanley S. Trotman/Dir., Mark D. Funston/Dir., Exec. VP, CFO

Owners: Anthony Vuolo, FMR Corp./1.70%, Insiders/2.30%, Nan-Kirsten Forte, Stanley S. Trotman, Mark J. Adler, Abdool Rahim Moossa, Neil F. Dimick, James V. Manning, Martin J. Wygod, HLTH Corporation/84.20%, Wayne T. Gattinella, Jerome C. Keller

Financial Data: *Fiscal Year End:*12/31 *Latest Annual Data:* 12/31/2006

Year	Sales	Net Income
2006	$253,881,000	$2,536,000
2005	$168,938,000	$7,745,000
2004	$134,148,000	$6,461,000

Curr. Assets:	$294,971,000	**Curr. Liab.:**	$110,577,000	**P/E Ratio:**	71.57
Plant, Equip.:	$44,709,000	**Total Liab.:**	$123,856,000	**Indic. Yr. Divd.:**	NA
Total Assets:	$619,965,000	**Net Worth:**	$496,109,000	**Debt/ Equity:**	NA

webMethods Inc

3877 Fairfax Ridge Rd. - S Tower, Fairfax, VA, 22030; ***PH:*** 1-703-460-2500;
http:// www.webmethods.com

General - Incorporation	DE	**Stock**- Price on:12/24/2007	NA
Employees	826	Stock Exchange	NA
Auditor	PricewaterhouseCoopers LLP	Ticker Symbol	NA
Stk Agt	American Stock Transfer & Trust Co.	Outstanding Shares	NA
Counsel	Shaw Pittman	E.P.S	NA
DUNS No.	NA	Shareholders	NA

Business: The group's principal activities are to provide software products and services for end-to-end integration solutions. The webmethods integration platform enables the customers to implement a single integration solution that allows them to not only integrate their internal systems but also those of their customers, vendors and business partners. The platform also allows customers to integrate cross-enterprise information resources and business processes. The group's solutions also include webmethods workflow, webmethods mainframe and webmethods manager. The customers of the group include companies in manufacturing, process industries, financial services, telecommunications, government and consumer goods manufacturing. The group markets its software products and services in Americas, Europe and Asia-Pacific. During the year, the group acquired the mind electric inc, the dante group and certain assets of datachannel portal.

Primary SIC and add'l.: 7372 7378 7373

CIK No: 0001035096

Subsidiaries: Door Acquisition, Inc., Intelliframe Corporation, The Dante Group, Inc., The Mind Electric, Inc., webMethods Australia Pty Ltd., webMethods BV, webMethods Canada Corporation, webMethods Development Center India Private Limited, webMethods France Sarl, webMethods Germany GmbH, webMethods Hong Kong Ltd., webMethods K.K., webMethods Korea Co., Ltd., webMethods Malaysia Sdn Bhd, webMethods Singapore Pte Ltd. 19 Subsidiaries included in the Index

Websense Inc

10240 Sorrento Valley Rd. , San Diego, CA, 92121; ***PH:*** 1-858-320-8000; ***http://*** www.websense.com

General - Incorporation	DE	**Stock**- Price on:12/24/2007	$21.54
Employees	728	Stock Exchange	NDQ
Auditor	Ernst & Young LLP	Ticker Symbol	WBSN
Stk Agt	U.S. Stock Transfer Corp	Outstanding Shares	44,970,000
Counsel	Cooley Godward LLP	E.P.S	$0.49
DUNS No.	NA	Shareholders	NA

Business: The group's principle activity is to provide employee Internet management (eim) products that enable businesses to analyze, report and manage how their employees use computing resources at work, including Internet access. These solutions supports an organization's efforts to improve employee productivity, conserve network bandwidth and mitigate potential legal liability. The products and services are sold through indirect sales channels in Europe, Africa, Asia/pacific and Latin America. At present the group operates in the United States, the United Kingdom and Japan.

Primary SIC and add'l.: 7372

CIK No: 0001098277

Subsidiaries: Websense (Australia) Pty Limited, Websense Brasil Gerenciamento e Segurana de Internet Ltda., Websense Deutschland GmbH, Websense France S.A.R.L., Websense Holdings International Limited, Websense International Limited, Websense Italia S.r.l., Websense Japan KK, Websense UK Limited

Officers: Gene Hodges/55/Dir., CEO/$4,377,882.00, Jim Haskin/CIO, Michael Newman/Sr. VP, General Counsel/$623,661.00, Susan Brown/VP - Human Resources, John McCormack/Sr. VP - Product Development, Ramon J. Peypoch/VP - Business Development, David Roberts/Sr. VP - Americas, Mike Bouchard/VP - Finance, Accounting, Douglas C. Wride/Pres./$1,422,055.00, Dan Hubbard/VP - Security Research, Dudley Mendenhall/Sr. VP, CFO, Leo J. Cole/VP - Marketing/$744,622.00, Kate Patterson/VP - Investor Relations, Becky Wheeler/Mgr. - Investor Relations, Geoff Haggart/Sr. VP - EMEA, Apac *(16 Officers included in Index)*

Directors: Gene Hodges/55/Dir., CEO, John B. Carrington/63/Chmn., Bruce T. Coleman/68/Dir., John F. Schaefer/64/Dir., Mark S. St. Clare/60/Dir., Gary E. Sutton/64/Dir., Peter C. Waller/52/Dir.

Owners: Gary E. Sutton, Osterweis Capital Management, Inc./6.86%, Barclays Global Investors, NA/8.44%, Insiders/2.65%, Mark St.Clare, T. Rowe Price Associates, Inc./9.68%, Peter C. Waller, Putnam Investment Management, LLC/5.23%, Bruce T. Coleman, Perkins, Wolf, McDonnell & Company, LLC/5.46%, John F. Schaefer

Financial Data: *Fiscal Year End:*12/31 *Latest Annual Data:* 12/31/2006

Year	Sales	Net Income
2006	$178,814,000	$32,093,000
2005	$148,636,000	$38,768,000
2004	$111,859,000	$26,176,000

Curr. Assets:	$401,767,000	**Curr. Liab.:**	$171,728,000	**P/E Ratio:**	43.96
Plant, Equip.:	$5,793,000	**Total Liab.:**	$243,532,000	**Indic. Yr. Divd.:**	NA
Total Assets:	$424,257,000	**Net Worth:**	$180,725,000	**Debt/ Equity:**	NA

Website Pros Inc

12735 Gran Bay Pk.way W, Building 200, Jacksonville, FL, 32258; ***PH:*** 1-904-680-6600;
http:// www.websitepros.com

General - Incorporation.............................DE
Employees..637
Auditor ....Ernst & Young LLP
Stk Agt.......................ComputerShare Trust Co.
Counsel..NA
DUNS No. ....NA

Stock- Price on:12/24/2007 ....$9.93
Stock Exchange...NDQ
Ticker Symbol...WSPI
Outstanding Shares 17,390,000
E.P.S..$0.33
Shareholders...NA

Business: The groups principle activity is to provide web services. The products of the group include eWorks! XL and SmartClicks. The groups services include hosting and technical support, modifications and redesign service, and online web tools. In the year 2006, the group acquired Renex, Inc, 1ShoppingCart.com Canada Corp. and 1ShoppingCart.com Corp. The group operates from the United States and Europe. The group's quarterly revenue for September 2007 was 17.82 millions of USD.

Primary SIC and add'l.: 7372 7379 8748 7371 7374

CIK No: 0001095291

Subsidiaries: Leads.com, Inc., Website Pros Canada Inc

Officers: David Brown/Dir., CEO, Pres./$458,722.00, Kevin Carney/CFO, VP - Finance/$302,478.00, Lisa Anteau/Sr. VP - Web Services, Darin Brannan/40/Sr. VP - Business, Corporate Development/$210,621.00, Roseann Duran/Chief Marketing Officer/$174,392.00, Tobias Dengel/Sr. VP - Business Development, Steve Raubenstine/VP - Netobjects Fusion Group, Todd Walrath/Pres. - Online Marketing, Lead Generation Services, Joel Williamson/VP - Operations, Tim Maudlin/Dir., Managing General Partner, Medical Innovation Partners, Jeffrey M. Stibel/Dir., Pres., Gonzalo Troncoso/Pres. - Web Services, Vikas Rijsinghani/CTO, Matthew P. McClure/In House Counsel

Directors: David Brown/Dir., CEO, Pres., Hugh M. Durden/Chmn. - Board of Trustee, Alfred I Dupont Testamentary Trust, Deven Parekh/Dir., Tim Maudlin/Dir., Managing General Partner, Medical Innovation Partners, Harry G. Durity/61/Dir., Julius Genachowski/Dir., Alex Kazerani/Dir., Robert S. McCoy/Dir.

Owners: Insiders/18.59%, George J. Still/7.39%, Roseann Duran, Parties Affiliated with Artis Capital Management, Inc./5.00%, Harry G. Durity, Hugh Durden, Darin Brannan/1.30%, Parties Affiliated with Norwest Venture Partners/7.20%, Robert McCoy, Timothy Maudlin/1.10%, Parties Affiliated with Supernova Management, LLC/5.45%, Edward Hechter/1.49%, Deven Parekh, David L. Brown/7.34%, Kevin Carney/1.48% (17 Owners included in Index)

Financial Data: Fiscal Year End:12/31 Latest Annual Data: 12/31/2006

Year	Sales	Net Income
2006	$52,041,000	$8,597,000
2005	$37,770,000	$827,000
2004	$23,402,000	$924,000

Curr. Assets:	$48,559,000	Curr. Liab.:	$9,025,000	
Plant, Equip.:	$2,337,000	Total Liab.:	$9,404,000	Indic. Yr. Divd.: NA
Total Assets:	$93,360,000	Net Worth:	$83,956,000	Debt/ Equity: 0.0018

Webster Financial Corp

Webster Plz., WFD730, Waterbury, CT, 06702; **PH:** 1-203-753-2921; **http://** www.websterbank.com; **Email:** service@websterbank.com

General - Incorporation............................DE
Employees...3,204
Auditor ....KPMG LLP
Stk Agt......American Stock Transfer & Trust Co.
Counsel..NA
DUNS No. 11-837-3620

Stock- Price on:12/24/2007 ....$42.88
Stock Exchange...NYSE
Ticker Symbol..WBS
Outstanding Shares 56,520,000
E.P.S..$2.11
Shareholders...NA

Business: The group's principal activities are to provide financial services and businesses through 119 banking offices in the United States. The group operates in four segments. The retail banking segment services include insurance, consumer lending, residential real estate loan origination and secondary marketing activities. The commercial banking segment includes commercial and industrial, business deposits, and cash management activities. The trust and investment services segment provides trust activities. The treasury segment includes repurchase agreements and other borrowings. On 14-May-2004, the group acquired firstfed America bancorp inc.

Primary SIC and add'l.: 6035 6712

CIK No: 0000801337

Subsidiaries: Capital Trust II, Eastern Wisconsin Bancshares, Eastern Wisconsin Bancshares Capital Trust I, Firstfed Insurance Agency, LLC, Fleming, Perry & Cox, Inc., Peoples Bancshares Capital Trust, Webster Bank, N.A., Webster Capital Trust I, Webster Capital Trust II, Webster Capital Trust III, Webster Capital Trust IV, Webster Capital Trust V, Webster Capital Trust VI, Webster Insurance, Inc., Webster Statutory Trust I

Officers: James C. Smith/Chmn., CEO, John J. Queirolo/Pres., CEO - Webster Insurance, Mitchell D. Weiss/Pres., CEO - Center Capital Corporation, Brenda Farrell/Assist. VP - Public Affairs, Webster Financial Corporation, Donald A. Cyr/Exec. VP, Sr. Operational Risk Officer - Webster Bank, NA, Terrence K. Mangan/Sr. VP - Investor Relations, Clark Finley/VP - Public Affairs, Webster Financial Corporation, Joseph J. Savage/Exec. VP - Commercial Banking, Scott M. McBrair/Exec. VP - Retail Banking/$1,272,996.00, Michelle M. Crecca/Exec. VP - Consumer Lending, Webster Bank, NA, Warren K. Mino/Pres. - Webster Business Credit Corporation, Jeffrey N. Brown/Exec. VP, Chief Administrative Officer, William T. Bromage/COO, Pres., Gerald P. Plush/Sr. Exec. VP, CFO, Harriet Munrett Wolfe/Exec. VP, General Counsel, Sec. (18 Officers included in Index)

Directors: James C. Smith/Chmn., CEO, George T. Carpenter/Dir., Robert F. Stoico/67/Dir., John J. Crawford/Dir., Michael C. Jacobi/Dir., Karen R. Osar/Dir., Robert A. Finkenzeller/Dir., Laurence C. Morse/Dir., William T. Bromage/COO, Pres., Roger A. Gelfenbien/Dir., Joel S. Becker/Dir.

Owners: William J. Healy, Gerald P. Plush, John J. Crawford, Michael C. Jacobi, Robert A. Finkenzeller, Joel S. Becker, Karen R. Osar, Laurence C. Morse, Insiders/4.09%, Joseph J. Savage, Robert F. Stoico, James C. Smith/2.26%, Wellington Management Company, LLP/9.30%, George T. Carpenter, William T. Bromage (17 Owners included in Index)

Financial Data: Fiscal Year End:12/31 Latest Annual Data: 12/31/2006

Year	Sales	Net Income
2006	$1,239,801,000	$133,790,000
2005	$1,092,732,000	$185,855,000
2004	$951,815,000	$153,833,000

Curr. Assets:	$582,943,000	Curr. Liab.:	$14,581,820,000	P/E Ratio: 20.32
Plant, Equip.:	$195,909,000	Total Liab.:	$15,220,608,000	Indic. Yr. Divd.: $1.200
Total Assets:	$17,097,471,000	Net Worth:	$1,876,863,000	Debt/ Equity: 0.3270

Webzen Inc

Daelim Acrotel Bldg 6th Floor, 467-6 Dogok-Dong, Kangnam-ku, Seoul; **PH:** 82-234981600; **Fax:** 82-220572568; **http://** www.webzen.co.kr; **Email:** pr@webzen.co.kr

General - Incorporation ....Korea
Employees..933
Auditor ....Samil PricewaterhouseCoopers
Stk Agt..Hana Bank
Counsel..NA
DUNS No. ....NA

Stock- Price on:12/24/2007 ....$4.27
Stock Exchange...NDQ
Ticker Symbol..WZEN
Outstanding Shares ....NA
E.P.S...NA
Shareholders...NA

Business: The groups principle activities include manufacturing and selling of online game mu, 3D engines, software programs and other related products. The group operates from United States.

Primary SIC and add'l.: NA

CIK No: 0001266467

Subsidiaries: 9Webzen Information Technology (Shanghai) Co., Ltd., Webzen America Inc., Webzen China, Co., Ltd, Webzen Taiwan, Inc

Officers: Namju Kim/36/Dir., CEO, Pres., Won-Seon Kim/49/Dir., CFO, Kil-Saup Song/32/Dir., CTO

Directors: Namju Kim/36/Dir., CEO, Pres., Sang-Woo Park/43/Dir., Yong-Ku Kim/37/Dir., Moon-Kyu Kim/52/Dir., Won-Seon Kim/49/Dir., CFO, Kil-Saup Song/32/Dir., CTO

Owners: Won-Seon Kim, Kil-Saup Song/5.10%, Insiders/12.40%, Nam-Ju Kim/6.70%, Delta Partners LLC/6.10%

Financial Data: Fiscal Year End:12/31 Latest Annual Data: 12/31/2005

Year	Sales	Net Income
2005	$31,333,000	-$18,618,000
2004	$52,406,000	$14,598,000
2003	$47,766,000	$30,212,000

Curr. Assets:	$112,429,000	Curr. Liab.:	$9,512,000	
Plant, Equip.:	$19,549,000	Total Liab.:	$18,688,000	Indic. Yr. Divd.: NA
Total Assets:	$156,624,000	Net Worth:	$137,936,000	Debt/ Equity: NA

Wegener Corp

11350 Technology Cir., Duluth, GA, 30097; **PH:** 1-770-814-4000; **http://** www.wegener.com; **Email:** info@wegener.com

General - Incorporation ....DE
Employees...92
Auditor ....BDO Seidman LLP
Stk Agt................................Securities Transfer Corp
Counsel..NA
DUNS No. 09-330-3485

Stock- Price on:12/24/2007 ....$1.01
Stock Exchange...NDQ
Ticker Symbol..WGNR
Outstanding Shares 12,650,000
E.P.S...-$0.06
Shareholders...NA

Business: The group's principal activities are to design, manufacture and distribute communications transmission and receiving equipment primarily for the broadcast and data communication markets. The group provides digital solutions for video, audio and broadcast data networks which includes broadcast television, cable television, radio network, distance education, business music, satellite paging and financial information distribution. The group through its subsidiary, makes transmission and receiving equipment primarily for the broadcast and data communication markets. These include digital compression equipment that increases satellite channel capacity, cue and control products that enable cable networks to insert local commercials, devices that feed data to news and weather services and equipment that transmits music to business.

Primary SIC and add'l.: 4813 4899

CIK No: 0000715073

Subsidiaries: Wegener Communications, Inc.

Officers: Robert A. Placek/Chmn., CEO, Ned L. Mountain/Dir., COO, Pres., Troy C. Woodbury/Dir., CFO, Melanie Charles/Marketing Communications Coordinator, Elias J. Livaditis/CTO

Directors: Robert A. Placek/Chmn., CEO, Ned L. Mountain/Dir., COO, Pres., Phylis A. Eagle-Oldson/Dir., Thomas G. Elliot/Dir., Jeffrey J. Haas/Dir., Stephen Lococo/Dir., Joe K. Parks/Dir., David W. Wright/Dir.

Owners: David W. Wright/7.90%, Phylis A. Eagle-Oldson, Stephen J. Lococo/8.20%, David E. Chymiak/8.80%, Henry Partners, L.P./7.90%, Ned L. Mountain, Footprints Asset Management& Research, Inc./8.20%, C. Troy Woodbury/1.90%, Jeffrey J. Haas, Thomas G. Elliot, Insiders/42.00%, Robert A. Placek/15.60%

Financial Data: Fiscal Year End:09/02 Latest Annual Data: 9/1/2006

Year	Sales	Net Income
2006	$20,388,000	-$2,883,000
2005	$21,902,000	-$5,671,000
2004	$18,104,000	-$2,108,000

Curr. Assets:	$10,323,000	Curr. Liab.:	$3,973,000	
Plant, Equip.:	$2,700,000	Total Liab.:	$3,973,000	Indic. Yr. Divd.: NA
Total Assets:	$17,496,000	Net Worth:	$13,523,000	Debt/ Equity: NA

Weight Watchers International Inc

175 Crossways Pk. W, Woodbury, NY, 11797; **PH:** 1-516-390-1400; **http://** www.weightwatchers.com; **Email:** customerservice@weightwatchers.com

General - Incorporation ....VA
Employees..47,000
Auditor ....PricewaterhouseCoopers LLP
Stk Agt....................EquiServe Trust Co N.A
Counsel..NA
DUNS No. 04-765-7473

Stock- Price on:12/24/2007 ....$51.69
Stock Exchange...NYSE
Ticker Symbol..WTW
Outstanding Shares 78,690,000
E.P.S..$2.29
Shareholders...NA

Business: The group's principal activity is to provide weight loss products and services. The programs of the group helps people lose weight and maintain their weight loss, improve their health, enhance their lifestyles and build self-confidence. It offers weight loss and control programs through the operation of classroom type meetings to the general public. The group also sells proprietary products such as snack bars, books, CD-roms and point calculators. The group markets its products and services to the general public located in United States, Canada, Mexico, United Kingdom, continental Europe, Australia, New Zealand, South Africa and Brazil. During the year, the group acquired certian assets of ww group inc and weight watchers of Dallas inc.

Primary SIC and add'l.: 2721 7299

CIK No: 0000105319

Subsidiaries: 58 Ww Food Corp, Bltc Pty Limited, Centro De Cuidado Del Peso, S. De R.l. De C.v., Fortuity Pty Ltd, Great Day Holdings Limited, Gutbusters Pty Ltd, Il Salvalinea, S.r.l., Lltc Pty Limited, Millhill Enterprises Pty Ltd, Servicios Operativos Cp, E. De R.l. De C.v., W.w. Camps And Spas, Inc., W.w. Inventory Service Corp., W.w. Weight Reduction Services, Inc., W.w.i. European Services, Ltd., W/w Twentyfirst Corporation 51 Subsidiaries included in the Index

Officers: David Kirchhoff/Dir., CEO, Pres./$1,532,578.00, Ann M. Sardini/CFO/$1,281,484.00, Thilo Semmelbauer/COO/$788,520.00

Directors: Raymond Debbane/Chmn., Philippe Amouyal/Dir., John F. Bard/Dir., Marsha J. Evans/Dir., Jonas M. Fajgenbaum/Dir., Sacha Lainovic/Dir., Sam K. Reed/Dir., Christopher J. Sobecki/Dir.

Owners: Ann M. Sardini, Sam K. Reed, Linda Huett, Insiders/1.10%, FMR Corp./10.50%, Marsha Johnson Evans, Philippe Amouyal, Artal Group S.A./55.00%, Delaware Management Business Trust/11.20%, Jeffrey A. Fiarman, John F. Bard, Christopher J. Sobecki, Sacha Lainovic, Thilo Semmelbauer, Jonas M. Fajgenbaum *(17 Owners included in Index)*

Financial Data: Fiscal Year End:12/31   Latest Annual Data: 12/30/2006

Year	Sales	Net Income
2006	$1,233,325,000	$209,825,000
2005	$1,151,251,000	$174,402,000

Curr. Assets:	$127,710,000	**Curr. Liab.:**	$165,888,000	**P/E Ratio:**	22.57
Plant, Equip.:	$20,775,000	**Total Liab.:**	$916,142,000	**Indic. Yr. Divd.:**	$0.700
Total Assets:	$835,491,000	**Net Worth:**	-$80,651,000	**Debt/ Equity:**	NA

Weingarten Realty Investors

2600 Citadel Plz. Dr., Ste. 300, Houston, TX, 77008; *PH:* 1-713-866-6000; *Fax:* 1-713-866-6049; *http://* www.weingarten.com; *Email:* ir@weingarten.com

General - Incorporation	TX	**Stock** - Price on:12/24/2007	$41.64
Employees	457	Stock Exchange	NYSE
Auditor	Deloitte & Touche LLP	Ticker Symbol	WRI
Stk Agt	Mellon Investor Services LLC	Outstanding Shares	86,440,000
Counsel	NA	E.P.S.	$3.27
DUNS No.	NA	Shareholders	NA

Business: The groups principle activities include owning and developing shopping centers and other commercial real estate. The group operates through two segments namely, shopping center and industrial. In the year 2006, the group acquired 17 shopping centers. The group operates from the United States.

Primary SIC and add'l.: 6798

CIK No: 0000828916

Subsidiaries: 6485 Crescent Drive LP, AN/WRI DEVCO #1, Ltd., AN/WRI Partnership, Ltd., Best in the West Holdings, LLC, Brookwood Square Holdings, LLC, Chino Hills Holdings, LLC, Crowfarn Drive LP, Eastex Venture, El Camino Holdings LLC, Falls Pointe Holdings, LLC, Fenton Market Place Venture, Flamingo Pines Holdings, LLC, Heritage HT #1, LLC, High House Holdings LLC, Hollywood Hills Holdings, LLC 220 Subsidiaries included in the Index

Officers: Andrew M. Alexander/CEO, Pres./$2,350,666.00, Johnny L. Hendrix/Exec. VP - Asset Management/$746,274.00, William M. Crook/VP, Assoc. General Counsel, Marc A. Kasner/VP, Assoc. General Counsel, Stephen C. Richter/CFO, Exec. VP/$857,355.00, Candace M. Dufour/Sr. VP, Dir. - Acquisitions, Sec., Robert Smith/Sr. VP, Dir. - New Development, Alan Ferguson/VP, Regional Dir. - Leasing, Jeff Harrision/VP, Regional Dir. - Leasing, Alan R. Kofoed/VP - Construction, Mitch Rippe/VP, Regional Dir. - Acquisitions, George Weatherall/VP, Regional Dir. - New Development, Gary Greenberg/Sr. VP - Capital Markets, Jeffrey A. Tucker/Sr. VP, General Counsel, Timothy M. Frakes/VP, Regional Dir. - New Development, Acquisitions *(39 Officers included in Index)*

Directors: Stanford Alexander/Chmn., Martin Debrovner/Vice Chmn.

Owners: James W. Crownover, Johnny Hendrix, Robert J. Cruikshank, Martin Debrovner, Stephen A. Lasher, Insiders/11.50%, Marc J. Shapiro, Stanford Alexander/6.60%, The Vanguard Group, Inc. 23-1945930/5.00%, Stephen C. Richter, Andrew M. Alexander/1.90%, Barclays Global Investors Japan Limited/5.60%, Douglas W. Schnitzer/1.70%, Melvin A. Dow/1.30%

Financial Data: Fiscal Year End:12/31   Latest Annual Data: 12/31/2006

Year	Sales	Net Income
2006	$561,380,000	$305,010,000
2005	$544,045,000	$219,653,000
2004	$502,291,000	$141,381,000

Curr. Assets:	$244,362,000	**Curr. Liab.:**	$132,821,000	**P/E Ratio:**	12.73
Plant, Equip.:	$3,738,883,000	**Total Liab.:**	$3,162,079,000	**Indic. Yr. Divd.:**	$1.980
Total Assets:	$4,375,540,000	**Net Worth:**	$1,125,781,000	**Debt/ Equity:**	2.1576

Weis Markets Inc

PO Box 471, Sunbury, PA, 17801; *PH:* 1-570-286-4571; *http://* www.weismarkets.com; *Email:* feedback@weismarkets.com

General - Incorporation	PA	**Stock** - Price on:12/24/2007	$42
Employees	18,000	Stock Exchange	NYSE
Auditor	Grant Thornton, LLP	Ticker Symbol	WMK
Stk Agt	American Registrar & Transfer Co	Outstanding Shares	26,990,000
Counsel	NA	E.P.S.	$2.12
DUNS No.	00-791-7420	Shareholders	NA

Business: The groups principle activity is to operate retail stores. The groups products include groceries, dairy products, frozen foods, meats, seafood, prepared foods, fuel and general merchandise items, including health and beauty care, and household products. The group operates from United States.

Primary SIC and add'l.: 5421 5431 5912 5411 5999

CIK No: 0000105418

Subsidiaries: Albany Public Markets, Inc., Dutch Valley Food Company, Inc., King's Supermarkets, Inc., Martin's Farm Market, Inc., Shamrock Wholesale Distributors, Inc., SuperPetz, LLC, Weis Transportation, Inc., WMK Financing, Inc.

Officers: Norman S. Rich/Dir., CEO, Pres./$669,472.00, Jonathan H. Weis/Vice Chmn., Sec./$376,131.00, Williams R. Mills/Dir., CFO, Sr. VP, Treasurer/$366,176.00, Edward W. Rakoskie/VP - Operations/$293,750.00

Directors: Norman S. Rich/Dir., CEO, Pres., Robert F. Weis/Chmn., Jonathan H. Weis/Vice Chmn., Sec., Williams R. Mills/Dir., CFO, Sr. VP, Treasurer, Richard E. Shulman/Dir., Michael M. Apfelbaum/Dir., Steven C. Smith/Dir., Matthew Nimetz/Dir.

Owners: Insiders/47.50%, EKTJ Management LLC/5.20%, Matthew Nimetz, Norman S. Rich, William R. Mills, Robert F. Weis/46.80%, Ellen W. P. Wasserman/6.50%, Steven C. Smith, Jonathan H. Weis, Richard E. Shulman, Michael M. Apfelbaum

Financial Data: Fiscal Year End:12/31   Latest Annual Data: 12/30/2006

Year	Sales	Net Income
2006	$2,244,512,000	$56,010,000
2005	$2,222,598,000	$63,421,000
2004	$2,097,712,000	$57,191,000

Curr. Assets:	$320,703,000	**Curr. Liab.:**	$157,034,000	**P/E Ratio:**	19.81
Plant, Equip.:	$446,517,000	**Total Liab.:**	$184,630,000	**Indic. Yr. Divd.:**	$1.160
Total Assets:	$788,487,000	**Net Worth:**	$603,857,000	**Debt/ Equity:**	NA

WellCare Health Plans Inc

8725 Henderson Rd. , Renaissance One, Tampa, FL, 33634; *PH:* 1-813-290-6200; *http://* www.wellcare.com

General - Incorporation	DE	**Stock** - Price on:12/24/2007	$90.26
Employees	3,000	Stock Exchange	NYSE
Auditor	Deloitte & Touche LLP	Ticker Symbol	WCG
Stk Agt	NA	Outstanding Shares	41,360,000
Counsel	NA	E.P.S.	$3.59
DUNS No.	NA	Shareholders	NA

Business: The group provides managed care services to government sponsored healthcare programs. The group has two reportable segments: medicaid provides healthcare services to recipients that are eligible for state supported programs including medicaid and children's health programs. Medicare provides healthcare services to recipients who are eligible for the federally supported medicare program. The corporate and other segment includes revenue and claims associated with commercial members, investment and other income. The group acquired harmony health systems inc in Jun 2004. The group operates in the United States of America. The group's quarterly revenue for September 2007 was 1,339.76 millions of USD.

Primary SIC and add'l.: 6324

CIK No: 0001279363

Subsidiaries: Comprehensive Health Management of Florida, L.C., Comprehensive Health Management, Inc, Comprehensive Logistics, LLC, Comprehensive Reinsurance, Ltd, Harmony Behavioral Health, Inc, Harmony Health Management, Inc., Harmony Health Plan of Illinois, Inc., Harmony Health Systems, Inc., HealthEase of Florida, Inc, The WellCare Management Group, Inc, WCG Health Management, Inc., WellCare of Connecticut, Inc., WellCare of Florida, Inc., WellCare of Georgia, Inc., WellCare of Louisiana, Inc 18 Subsidiaries included in the Index

Officers: Todd S. Farha/Chmn., CEO, Pres., Rupesh Shah/Sr. VP - Marketing Expansion, Paul L. Behrens/CFO, Sr. VP, Imtiaz Sattaur/45/Pres. - Florida, Thaddeus Bereday/Sr. VP, General Counsel, Randall D. Zomermaand/Sr. VP, Jeffrey Potter/VP - Corporate Development, Michael W. Cotton/COO - Georgia, Gretchen Demartini/VP - Human Resources, Keith Kudla/Pres. - Illinois Operations, Adam Miller/COO - PDP, Pffs, Larry Mitchum/VP - Louisiana, Dan Parietti/Pres. - New York, John L. Sirera/Sr. VP - Pharmacy, Anil Kottoor/CIO, Sr. VP *(20 Officers included in Index)*

Directors: Todd S. Farha/Chmn., CEO, Pres., Neal Moszkowski/Dir., Robert D. Graham/Dir., Ruben Jose King-Shaw/Dir., Regina E. Herzlinger/Dir., Jane Swift/43/Dir., Alif A. Hourani/Dir., Christian P. Michalik/Dir., Kevin F. Hickey/Dir.

Owners: Barclays Global Investors/7.50%, Regina Herzlinger, Neal Moszkowski, Thaddeus Bereday, Alif Hourani, Christian Michalik, Ruben King-Shaw, Paul Behrens, Todd Farha/2.60%, Jane Swift, Waddell & Reed, Inc./5.20%, Insiders/4.90%, State Street Bank and Trust Company/5.40%, Kevin Hickey, Ace Hodgin *(16 Owners included in Index)*

Financial Data: Fiscal Year End:12/31   Latest Annual Data: 12/31/2006

Year	Sales	Net Income
2006	$3,762,926,000	$139,187,000
2005	$1,879,539,000	$51,928,000
2004	$1,395,203,000	$49,250,000

Curr. Assets:	$1,338,414,000	**Curr. Liab.:**	$904,107,000	**P/E Ratio:**	25.14
Plant, Equip.:	$62,005,000	**Total Liab.:**	$1,100,910,000	**Indic. Yr. Divd.:**	NA
Total Assets:	$1,663,965,000	**Net Worth:**	$563,055,000	**Debt/ Equity:**	0.2543

Wellco Enterprises Inc

150 Wwood Cir., Waynesville, NC, 28786; *PH:* 1-828-456-3545; *http://* www.wellco.com

General - Incorporation	NC	**Stock** - Price on:12/24/2007	NA
Employees	719	Stock Exchange	NA
Auditor	Dixon Hughes PLLC	Ticker Symbol	NA
Stk Agt	Mellon Shareholder Services LLC	Outstanding Shares	NA
Counsel	Richard A. Wood Jr., Wood & Bissette	E.P.S.	NA
DUNS No.	00-316-5685	Shareholders	NA

Business: The group's principal activities are to manufacture and sell military and other rugged footwear. It builds specialized footwear manufacturing equipment and provides technical assistance and other services to licensees for the manufacture of footwear. The products of the group include all-leather boot, hot weather boot and desert boot, manufactured using the government specified direct molded sole process. The group provides technology, assistance and related services for manufacturing military and commercial footwear to customers in the United States and abroad. The group's major international customers are in Latin America, Canada, Asia/pacific and Mexico. The group acquired bags to go & cruise staff inc in fiscal 2004

Primary SIC and add'l.: 3149 6794 3559

CIK No: 0000105532

Owners: Fred K. Webb, Rolf Kaufman, John D. Lovelace, Claude S. Abernethy, Katherine J. Emerson, Tammy Francis, Neil Streeter, Sarah E. Lovelace, Estate of James T. Emerson, Insiders, Evan Kent Auberry

Wellman Inc

1041 521 Corporate Ctr. Dr., Fort Mill, SC, 29715; *PH:* 1-803-835-2000; *http://* www.wellmaninc.com

General - Incorporation............................. DE
Employees...1,500
Auditor .... Ernst & Young LLP
Stk Agt................................ Wachovia Bank N.A
Counsel..NA
DUNS No. 00-102-1690

Stock- Price on:12/24/2007 ....$3.18
Stock Exchange...NA
Ticker Symbol..NA
Outstanding Shares 32,860,000
E.P.S..-$4.22
Shareholders...NA

Business: The group's principal activities are to manufacture and market packaging resins and polyester products. The products include fortrel brand polyester textile fibers, polyester fibers made from recycled raw materials and permaclear pet (polyethylene terephtalate). The group operates in two segments namely fibers and recycled products group (frpg) and packaging products group (ppg). Frpg manufactures chemical-based polyester staple fibers and polyester partially oriented yarn for the textile industry and for industrial products. Ppg manufactures solid-stated and amorphous pet resins used in the manufacture of soft drink bottles, food and beverage packaging. The group's products are marketed in the United States and Europe.

Primary SIC and add'l.: 2824 2821

CIK No: 0000812708

Subsidiaries: ALG, Inc., Carpet Recycling of Georgia, Inc., CKB, Co., DRS Holdings NV, Fiber Industries, Inc., Fibres Finance BV, FIISB, Inc., Finwell, Inc., GuardWell Insurance Company, JCT, Ltd., Josdav, Inc., KRP, Ltd., MED Resins, Inc., Middlewich Limited, MJR Recycling BV 38 Subsidiaries included in the Index

Officers: Thomas M. Duff/Chmn., CEO/$1,161,087.00, John Hobson/VP - Fibers Division, Keith Phillips/53/CFO, VP/$582,516.00, Michael E. Dewsbury/VP - PET Resins/$559,138.00, Michael Bermish/Investor Relations Officer, Mark J. Ruday/VP, Chief Accounting Officer, Controller, Principal Accounting Officer/$345,970.00, Joseph Tucker/Sr. VP - Raw Material Procurement, Strategic Development/$500,547.00, David R. Styka/VP, Controller, Chief Accounting Officer, Barry Taylor/VP - Human Resources, Safety, Health, Environmental, Judith Langan/Communications Dir.

Directors: Thomas M. Duff/Chmn., CEO, James B. Baker/62/Dir., Richard F. Heitmiller/79/Dir., Kevin Kruse/38/Dir., David J. McKittrick/62/Dir., James E. Rogers/62/Dir., Roger A. Vandenberg/61/Dir.

Owners: Warburg Pincus Private Equity VIII, L.P/34.90%, Insiders/6.70%, David J. McKittrick, Keith R. Phillips/1.00%, Dimensional FundAdvisors LP/8.00%, James B. Baker, Roger A. Vandenberg, Michael E. Dewsbury, Donald Smith& Co., Inc./9.90%, Citigroup Inc./5.70%, Richard F. Heitmiller, Mark J. Ruday, James E. Rogers, Joseph C. Tucker, The Bessemer Group, Incorporated/5.90% *(17 Owners included in Index)*

Financial Data: Fiscal Year End:12/31 Latest Annual Data: 12/31/2006

Year	Sales	Net Income
2006	$1,332,000,000	-$112,400,000
2005	$1,376,900,000	-$30,000,000
2004	$1,305,000,000	-$38,800,000

Curr. Assets:	$369,900,000	**Curr. Liab.:**	$145,000,000		
Plant, Equip.:	$589,400,000	**Total Liab.:**	$786,200,000	**Indic. Yr. Divd.:**	$0.080
Total Assets:	$993,300,000	**Net Worth:**	$207,100,000	**Debt/ Equity:**	3.2084

WellPoint Inc

120 Monument Cir., Indianapolis, IN, 46204; **PH:** 1-317-532-6000; *http://* www.wellpoint.com

General - Incorporation............................. IN
Employees...42,000
Auditor .... Ernst & Young LLP
Stk Agt.......... American Registrar & Transfer Co
Counsel..NA
DUNS No. ....NA

Stock- Price on:12/24/2007 ....$80.34
Stock Exchange...NYSE
Ticker Symbol..WLP
Outstanding Shares 613,650,000
E.P.S..$4.99
Shareholders...NA

Business: The group's principle activity is to provide products and services to control health of communities, collaborating with community leaders and non-profit organizations to provide resources and information. In August 2007, WellPoint acquired American Imaging Management. The group operates from United States.

Primary SIC and add'l.: 6321 6719

CIK No: 0001156039

Subsidiaries: AdminaStar Federal, Inc., Affiliated Healthcare, Inc., Affiliated Provider Systems, Inc., AHI Healthcare Corporation, American Managing Company, Anthem Blue Cross Blue Shield Partnership Plan, Inc., Anthem East, LLC, Anthem Financial, Inc., Anthem Health Plans of Kentucky, Inc., Anthem Health Plans of Maine, Inc., Anthem Health Plans of New Hampshire, Inc., Anthem Health Plans of Virginia, Inc., Anthem Health Plans, Inc., Anthem Holding Corp., Anthem Insurance Companies, Inc. 137 Subsidiaries included in the Index

Officers: Dijuana Lewis/CEO, Pres. - Comprehensive Health Solutions, Ken Goulet/CEO, Pres. - Wellpoint Commercial Business Unit, Joan E. Herman/CEO, Pres. - Consumer Business Unit, Mark L. Boxer/CEO, Pres. - Operations - Technology, Government Services Business Unit, Angela F. Braly/Dir., CEO, Pres., John S. Watts/CEO, Pres. - Commercial, Consumer Business, Wayne S. Deveydt/CFO, Exec. VP, David C. Colby/54/CFO, Exec. VP, Alice F. Rosenblatt/Exec. VP - Integration Planning, Implementation, Chief Actuary, Randy L. Brown/Chief Human Resources Officer, Exec. VP, Marjorie W. Dorr/Chief Strategy Officer, Exec. VP, Randall J. Lewis/Exec. VP - Internal Audit, Chief Compliance Officer, Samuel R. Nussbaum/Exec. VP - Clinical Health Policy, Chief Medical Officer, Jamie S. Miller/Chief Accounting Officer, Sr. VP, Nancy Purcell/Sec. *(17 Officers included in Index)*

Directors: Angela F. Braly/Dir., CEO, Pres., Larry C. Glasscock/Chmn., John E. Zuccotti/Dir., Lenox D. Baker/Dir., Susan B. Bayh/Dir., Sheila P. Burke/Dir., William H.T. Bush/Dir., Julie A. Hill/Dir., Warren Y. Jobe/Dir., Victor S. Liss/Dir., William G. Mays/Dir., Ramiro G. Peru/Dir., Jane G. Pisano/Dir., Donald W. Riegle/Dir., William J. Ryan/Dir. *(17 Directors included in Index)*

Owners: Susan B. Bayh, Victor S. Liss, William J. Ryan, Alice F. Rosenblatt, Lenox D. Baker, William H.T. Bush, John S. Watts, Insiders/1.10%, Sheila P. Burke, Jackie M. Ward, Capital Research/6.20%, George A. Schaefer, John E. Zuccotti, AXA Financial, Inc./8.90%, William G. Mays *(25 Owners included in Index)*

Financial Data: Fiscal Year End:12/31 Latest Annual Data: 12/31/2006

Year	Sales	Net Income
2006	$56,953,000,000	$3,094,900,000
2005	$45,136,000,000	$2,463,800,000
2004	$20,815,100,000	$960,100,000

Curr. Assets:	$11,806,700,000	**Curr. Liab.:**	$15,323,400,000	**P/E Ratio:**	16.10
Plant, Equip.:	$988,600,000	**Total Liab.:**	$27,184,000,000	**Indic. Yr. Divd.:**	NA
Total Assets:	$51,759,800,000	**Net Worth:**	$24,575,800,000	**Debt/ Equity:**	0.2619

Wells Fargo & Co

420 Montgomery St., San Francisco, CA, 94163; **PH:** 1-866-878-5865; *http://* www.wellsfargo.com

General - Incorporation .... DE
Employees...158,000
Auditor .... KPMG LLP
Stk Agt.......... Wells Fargo Shareowner Services
Counsel..NA
DUNS No. 00-696-2435

Stock- Price on:12/24/2007 ....$35.63
Stock Exchange...NYSE
Ticker Symbol..WFC
Outstanding Shares 3,340,000,000
E.P.S..$2.61
Shareholders...NA

Business: The group's principle activity is to provide banking, insurance, investments, mortgage and consumer financial services. The group also provides retail, commercial and corporate banking services through banking stores. In October 2007, the group was merged with Greater Bay Bancorp. The group operates from United States.

Primary SIC and add'l.: 6021 6712

CIK No: 0000072971

Subsidiaries: 1st Capital Mortgage, LLC, Academy Financial Services, LLC, ACO Brokerage Holdings Corporation, Acordia Brokerage Services, Ltd., Acordia IP Group, Inc., Acordia Management Services Ltd., Acordia Mountain West, Inc., Acordia National, Inc., Acordia Northeast, Inc., Acordia Northwest, Inc., Acordia of Alaska, Inc., Acordia of California Insurance Services, Inc., Acordia of Illinois, Inc., Acordia of Indiana, Inc., Acordia of Indiana, LLC 615 Subsidiaries included in the Index

Officers: John G. Stumpf/Dir., CEO, Pres./$11,755,470.00, Patricia R. Callahan/Exec. VP - Compliance, Risk Management, Avid Modjtabai/46/Exec. VP - Human Resources, Julie M. White/Exec. VP, Dir. - Human Resources, Howard I. Atkins/CFO, Sr. Exec. VP/$5,289,283.00, Laurel A. Holschuh/Sec., Carrie L. Tolstedt/Sr. Exec. VP - Community Banking/$4,654,973.00, Michael J. Loughlin/Exec. VP, Chief Credit Officer, Richard D. Levy/Exec. VP, Controller, Mark C. Oman/Sr. Exec. VP/$6,350,997.00, David A. Hoyt/Group Exec. VP - Wholesale Banking/$6,485,187.00, James M. Strother/Exec. VP, General Counsel

Directors: John G. Stumpf/Dir., CEO, Pres., Richard M. Kovacevich/Chmn., Susan E. Engel/Dir., Philip J. Quigley/Dir., Richard D. McCormick/Dir., Robert L. Joss/Dir., Cynthia H. Milligan/Dir., Susan G. Swenson/Dir., Stephen W. Sanger/Dir., Judith M. Runstad/Dir., Donald B. Rice/Dir., Enrique Hernandez/Dir., Lloyd H. Dean/Dir., Nicholas G. Moore/Dir., John S. Chen/Dir. *(16 Directors included in Index)*

Owners: Michael W. Wright, Richard M. Kovacevich, David A. Hoyt, Judith M. Runstad, John S. Chen, Nicholas G. Moore, Insiders, Robert L. Joss, Cynthia H. Milligan, Philip J. Quigley, Susan G. Swenson, Lloyd H. Dean, Donald B. Rice, John G. Stumpf, Susan E. Engel *(21 Owners included in Index)*

Financial Data: Fiscal Year End:12/31 Latest Annual Data: 12/31/2006

Year	Sales	Net Income
2006	$47,998,000,000	$8,482,000,000
2005	$40,527,000,000	$7,671,000,000
2004	$33,891,000,000	$7,014,000,000

Curr. Assets:	$36,908,000,000	**Curr. Liab.:**	$348,975,000,000	**P/E Ratio:**	13.97
Plant, Equip.:	$8,212,000,000	**Total Liab.:**	$436,120,000,000	**Indic. Yr. Divd.:**	$1.240
Total Assets:	$481,996,000,000	**Net Worth:**	$45,876,000,000	**Debt/ Equity:**	1.9578

Wells Financial Corp

53 First St., S.w., Wells, MN, 56097; **PH:** 1-507-553-3151

General - Incorporation .... MN
Employees...NA
Auditor .... McGladrey & Pullen LLP
Stk Agt.................... Registrar and Transfer agent
Counsel..NA
DUNS No. ....NA

Stock- Price on:12/24/2007 ....$28.83
Stock Exchange...OTC
Ticker Symbol..WEFP
Outstanding Shares ....NA
E.P.S..$2.08
Shareholders...NA

Business: The groups principal activity is to provide financial services to the customers. The group operates from the United States.

Primary SIC and add'l.: 6712 6035

CIK No: 0000934739

Financial Data: Fiscal Year End:12/31 Latest Annual Data: 09/30/2004

Year	Sales	Net Income
2004	NA	NA
2003	$19,264,000	$3,540,000
2002	$19,822,000	$3,340,000

Curr. Assets:	$26,727,000	**Curr. Liab.:**	$169,896,000	**P/E Ratio:**	13.41
Plant, Equip.:	$3,585,000	**Total Liab.:**	$195,937,000	**Indic. Yr. Divd.:**	$1.040
Total Assets:	$223,805,000	**Net Worth:**	$27,868,000	**Debt/ Equity:**	1.1631

Wells Gardner Electronics Corp

9500 W 55th St., Ste. A, Mccook, IL, 60525; **PH:** 1-708-290-2100; *http://* www.wgec.com

General - Incorporation IL
Employees...92
Auditor .... Blackman Kallick Bartelstein LLP
Stk Agt.................................. LaSalle Bank N.A
Counsel.. Pedersen & Houpt
DUNS No. 00-510-6042

Stock- Price on:12/24/2007 ....$3.01
Stock Exchange...AMEX
Ticker Symbol..WGA
Outstanding Shares 9,830,000
E.P.S..$0.11
Shareholders...NA

Business: The group's principal activities are to distribute, design, manufacture, assemble, service and market electronic components like video color monitors and liquid crystal displays, gaming supplies and components and the bonding of touch sensors to video monitors offering full line of video monitors, with cathode ray tube with horizontal scan frequencies. The group's production activities consists primarily of wiring printed circuit boards, assembling finished units, aligning, testing and optically bonding touch sensors.

Primary SIC and add'l.: 3944 3679 3999

CIK No: 0000105608

Officers: Tony Spier/Chmn., CEO, Anthony Spier/Dir., CEO, Pres./$427,317.00, Dan O'Brien/System Administrator, Mark Kessler/Quality, Compliance Mgr. - Quality Assurance, Bob Lube/VP - Engineering, Renee Zimmerman/Corporate Controller, Laurisa Reptowski/Dir. - US Operations, Kathy Hoppe/CIO, Bob Urban/Traffic, Inventory Control Mgr. - Shipping, Larry

Mahl/MD - Strategic Sourcing, Purchasing, Maria Rojas/Customer Service - Repairs, Specialist, RMA Coordinator, Bi, Lingual Spanish, John McGuire/Sr. Buyer, Purchasing, Jeff Gardner/Sales Administrator - Sales, Aleksandra Wojt/Staff Accountant - Accounting, Kathryn Bernards/Sr. Accounts Payable Administrator, Accounting *(28 Officers included in Index)*

Directors: Tony Spier/Chmn., CEO, Anthony Spier/Dir., CEO, Pres., Frank R. Martin/Dir., Marshall L. Burman/Dir., Merle H. Banta/Dir.

Owners: Insiders/5.57%, Frank R. Martin/0.68%, Merle Banta/0.09%, James F. Brace/0.45%, Marshall L. Burman/0.61%, Anthony S. Spier/3.74%

Financial Data: *Fiscal Year End:* 12/31   *Latest Annual Data:* 12/31/2006

Year	Sales	Net Income
2006	$64,748,000	$343,000
2005	$60,774,000	-$2,996,000
2004	$51,535,000	$1,068,000

Curr. Assets:	$26,609,000	*Curr. Liab.:*	$7,746,000	*P/E Ratio:* 27.36
Plant, Equip.:	$873,000	*Total Liab.:*	$16,980,000	*Indic. Yr. Divd.:* NA
Total Assets:	$30,187,000	*Net Worth:*	$13,207,000	*Debt/ Equity:* 0.5807

Wellstar International Inc

6911 Pilliod Rd. , Holland, OH, 43528; *PH:* 1-419-865-0069; *Fax:* 1-419-867-0829; *http://* www.wellstar.us

General - Incorporation	NV	**Stock**- Price on:12/24/2007	$0.013
Employees	NA	Stock Exchange	OTC
Auditor	Simontacchi & Company, LLP	Ticker Symbol	WLSI
Stk Agt	Pacific Stock Transfer Company	Outstanding Shares	105,600,000
Counsel	NA	E.P.S.	-$0.031
DUNS No.	NA	Shareholders	NA

Business: The groups principle activity is in the clinical research that proves disease is a 10 to 20 year progression prior to the development of symptoms and ultimately tumor growth in the form of cancer. In the year 2005, the group acquired Micro Health Systems and In the year July, 2005 Trillennium Medical Imaging, Inc. The group operates from the United States.

Primary SIC and add'l.: 3844

CIK No: 0001346248

Subsidiaries: Trillennium Medical Imaging, Inc.

Officers: John Antonio/Dir., CEO, Pres., Ken McCoppen/Dir., Sr. VP, Leonard Makowka/Speial Adviser to Dir., Howard Bielski/CFO

Directors: John Antonio/Dir., CEO, Pres., McKinley Boston/Dir., Ken McCoppen/Dir., Sr. VP, Michael Y.H. Shen/Dir.

Owners: Insiders/23.60%, McKinley Boston, Cede & Co./35.80%, John A. Antonio/9.30%, Howard Bielski/2.40%, Ken McCoppen/8.40%, Michael Shen/3.20%, Andrew M. Thompson/46.70%

Financial Data: *Fiscal Year End:* 07/31   *Latest Annual Data:* 07/31/2006

Year	Sales	Net Income
2006	$21,000	-$4,781,000

Curr. Assets:	$265,000	*Curr. Liab.:*	$1,414,000	*P/E Ratio:* 13.41
Plant, Equip.:	$538,000	*Total Liab.:*	$5,958,000	*Indic. Yr. Divd.:* NA
Total Assets:	$1,553,000	*Net Worth:*	-$4,405,000	*Debt/ Equity:* NA

Wellstone Filters Inc

300 Market St., Ste. 130-13, Chapel Hill, NC, 27516; *PH:* 1-919-370-4408

General - Incorporation	DE	**Stock**- Price on:12/24/2007	$0.13
Employees	NA	Stock Exchange	OTC
Auditor	De Joya Griffith & Company LLC	Ticker Symbol	WFLT
Stk Agt	Computershare Trust Co	Outstanding Shares	NA
Counsel	NA	E.P.S.	NA
DUNS No.	NA	Shareholders	NA

Business: The groups principal activity is to dependent on the domestic tobacco business. The group operates from the United States.

Primary SIC and add'l.: 5194

CIK No: 0001092802

Subsidiaries: Wellstone LLC, Wellstone Filters, Inc

Officers: Learned Jeremiah Hand/49/Dir., CEO, Acting CFO, Samuel Veasey/CFO

Directors: Learned Jeremiah Hand/49/Dir., CEO, Acting CFO

Owners: Anthony Cerami/11.50%, Insiders/66.30%, Learned Jeremiah Hand/66.30%

Welwind Energy International Corp

Formerly: Vitasti Inc

10-20172 113b Ave., Maple Ridge, BC, V2X 0Y9; *PH:* 1-604-460-8487; *http://* www.vitasti.com

General - Incorporation	DE	**Stock**- Price on:12/24/2007	NA
Employees	NA	Stock Exchange	NA
Auditor	Manning Elliott LLP	Ticker Symbol	NA
Stk Agt	Interwest Transfer Company, Inc.	Outstanding Shares	NA
Counsel	Fidelity Transfer Services Ltd.	E.P.S.	NA
DUNS No.	NA	Shareholders	NA

Business: The group's activity is to specialize in the marketing, rental and distribution of golf merchandise. The group was designing Web sites and operating and maintaining a computer Internet Web site for companies associated with the forest and wood product industries. Due to continued losses and limited financing options in the industry, the same was discontinued. In fiscal 2003, the group acquired golflogix systems Canada inc (golflogix).

Primary SIC and add'l.: 7389 7359

CIK No: 0001052671

Subsidiaries: Golflogix Systems Canada Inc.

Officers: Tammy-Lynn McNabb/Chairwomen, CEO, CFO, Pres., Sec., Kenny Chow/Production Consultants, Jeanne Chow/Production Consultants

Directors: Tammy-Lynn McNabb/Chairwomen, CEO, CFO, Pres., Sec., Patrick Higgins/Dir., David Wing Yiu Cho/Dir., Shannon Dedelley/Dir., Chong-Jian Zhao/49/Dir., Feng Junyi/46/Dir.

Owners: Tammy-Lynn McNabb/8.18%, Shannon de Delley/3.55%, Feng Junyi/21.32%, Larry McNabb/7.00%, Chong-Jian Zhao/2.80%, Luo Yizi/8.52%, David Wing Yiu Cho/1.42%

Financial Data: *Fiscal Year End:* 12/31   *Latest Annual Data:* 12/31/2006

Year	Sales	Net Income
2006	$116,000	-$2,140,000
2005	$260,000	-$2,391,000
2004	$733,000	-$2,153,000

Curr. Assets:	$1,759,000	*Curr. Liab.:*	$666,000	
Plant, Equip.:	$185,000	*Total Liab.:*	$666,000	*Indic. Yr. Divd.:* NA
Total Assets:	$3,415,000	*Net Worth:*	$2,749,000	*Debt/ Equity:* NA

Wendy's International Inc

PO Box 256, Dublin, OH, 43017; *PH:* 1-614-764-3100; *http://* www.wendys.com; *Email:* investor_relations@wendys.com

General - Incorporation	OH	**Stock**- Price on:12/24/2007	$73.91
Employees	10,000	Stock Exchange	NYSE
Auditor	PricewaterhouseCoopers LLP	Ticker Symbol	WEN
Stk Agt	American Stock Transfer & Trust Co.	Outstanding Shares	NA
Counsel	Vorys, Sater, Seymour & Pease	E.P.S.	$0.81
DUNS No.	05-285-6671	Shareholders	NA

Business: The groups principle activity is to operate restaurants. The groups products include hot stuffed baked potatoes, Chicken Temptations(R) and fish, and Frosty(TM) and beverages. The group operates from United States.

Primary SIC and add'l.: 6794 5812

CIK No: 0000105668

Subsidiaries: 2053306 Ontario Limited, Baja Fresh Marketing Development Fund, Inc., Baja Fresh Westlake Village, Inc., Barhav Developments Limited, Bayers Centre Plaza Limited, Bdj 71112, LLC, Boulangerie Chez Tim Inc., Brigid No. 1 LP, Cafe Express, LLC, Coffman No. 3 LP, Courtneys Alberta Co. Inc., Delavest, Inc., Domark Investments, Inc., Findel Corp., Fresh Enterprises, Inc. 56 Subsidiaries included in the Index

Officers: Kerrii B. Anderson/Dir., CEO, Pres./$4,174,313.00, Leon M. McCorkle/Exec. VP, General Counsel, Sec./$1,349,934.00, Jeffrey M. Cava/Exec. VP - Human Resources, Administration, Bakery/$1,302,631.00, Jonathan F. Catherwood/Exec. VP - Mergers, Acquisitions, Treasurer/$1,278,203.00, Tom Spero/Sr. VP - Operations, North Region, Ian B. Rowden/Exec. VP, Chief Marketing Officer, Joseph J. Fitzsimmons/CFO, Exec. VP, John D. Barker/Sr. VP - Corporate Affairs, Investor Relations, Brendan P. Foley/Sr. VP, General Controller, Assist. Sec./$486,587.00, Robert M. Whittington/CIO, Sr. VP, David J. Near/COO, Edward K. Choe/Exec. VP - Restaurant Services, Tad G. Wampfler/Sr. VP - Supply Chain Management, Bob Bertini/Dir. - Consumer Communications, Kimberly Messner/Mgr. - Investor Relations *(21 Officers included in Index)*

Directors: Kerrii B. Anderson/Dir., CEO, Pres., James V. Pickett/Chmn., William E. Kirwan/Dir., James F. Millar/Dir., Ann B. Crane/Dir., Janet Hill/Dir., Thomas F. Keller/Dir., David P. Lauer/Dir., Jerry W. Levin/Dir., Randolph J. Lewis/Dir., Stuart I. Oran/Dir., Peter H. Rothschild/Dir., John R. Thompson/Dir.

Owners: John M. Deane, Ann B. Crane, Thomas F. Keller, Jeffrey M. Cava, William E. Kirwan, Highfields Capital Management LP/7.10%, John R. Thompson, Jonathan F. Catherwood, Leon M. McCorkle, James V. Pickett, Janet Hill, James F. Millar, John T. Schuessler, Brendan P. Foley, Randolph J. Lewis *(20 Owners included in Index)*

Financial Data: *Fiscal Year End:* 01/01   *Latest Annual Data:* 12/31/2006

Year	Sales	Net Income
2006	$2,453,298,000	$94,312,000
2005	$3,635,438,000	$52,035,000

Curr. Assets:	$656,732,000	*Curr. Liab.:*	$394,666,000	
Plant, Equip.:	$1,226,328,000	*Total Liab.:*	$1,048,670,000	*Indic. Yr. Divd.:* $0.500
Total Assets:	$2,060,347,000	*Net Worth:*	$1,011,677,000	*Debt/ Equity:* NA

Werner Enterprises Inc

14507 Frontier Rd. , Omaha, NE, 68138; *PH:* 1-402-895-6640; *http://* www.werner.com

General - Incorporation	NE	**Stock**- Price on:12/24/2007	$19.59
Employees	11,198	Stock Exchange	NDQ
Auditor	KPMG LLP	Ticker Symbol	WERN
Stk Agt	Wells Fargo Bank Minnesota N.A	Outstanding Shares	73,590,000
Counsel	NA	E.P.S.	$1.13
DUNS No.	02-208-6565	Shareholders	NA

Business: The groups principle activity is to provide transportation and logistics services. The groups transportation services include transportation services that includes medium-to-long-haul, regional and local van capacity, temperature-controlled, flatbed, dedicated and expedited. The group also provides freight services including retail store merchandise, consumer products, manufactured products and grocery products. The group operates from United States.

Primary SIC and add'l.: 4212 4231 4213

CIK No: 0000793074

Subsidiaries: Drivers Management Holding, Inc., Drivers Management, LLC, Fleet Truck Sales, Inc., Frontier Clinic, Inc., Gra-Gar, LLC, Professional Truck Drivers School,Inc, Werner Aire, Inc., Werner Cycle Works, Inc., Werner de Mexico, S. de R.L. de C.V, Werner Enterprises Canada Corporation, Werner Leasing de Mexico, S. de R.L. de C.V, Werner Leasing, Inc., Werner Management, Inc., Werner Transportation, Inc.

Officers: Gregory L. Werner/48/Dir., CEO, Pres./$807,093.00, Daniel H. Cushman/53/Sr. Exec. VP, Chief Marketing Officer/$582,133.00, Jim S. Schelble/46/Exec. VP - Sales, Marketing, Robert E. Synowicki/48/CIO, Exec. VP, Richard S. Reiser/60/Exec. VP, General Counsel, James L. Johnson/Sr. VP, Controller, Corp. Sec., John J. Steele/49/CFO, Exec. VP, Treasurer/$304,507.00, Marty H. Nordlund/45/Sr. Exec. VP - Specialized Services, Derek J. Leathers/Sr. Exec. VP - Value Added Services, International

Directors: Gregory L. Werner/48/Dir., CEO, Pres., Clarence L. Werner/70/Chmn., Gary L. Werner/49/Vice Chmn., Duane K. Sather/62/Dir., Patrick J. Jung/59/Dir., Kenneth M. Bird/59/Dir., Michael L. Steinbach/52/Dir., Gerald H. Timmerman/67/Dir.

Owners: Gary L. Werner/2.70%, Duane K. Sather, Insiders/39.10%, Kenneth M. Bird, Clarence L. Werner/31.30%, Lord, Abbett & Co. LLC/6.70%, Daniel H. Cushman, Gregory L. Werner/5.30%, Dimensional Fund Advisors LP/6.50%, Gerald H. Timmerman, Patrick J. Jung, John J. Steele

Financial Data: *Fiscal Year End:* 12/31   *Latest Annual Data:* 12/31/2006

Year	Sales	Net Income
2006	$2,080,555,000	$98,643,000
2005	$1,971,847,000	$98,534,000
2004	$1,678,043,000	$87,310,000

Curr. Assets:	$361,041,000	**Curr. Liab.:**	$190,910,000	**P/E Ratio:**	17.34
Plant, Equip.:	$1,096,340,000	**Total Liab.:**	$607,822,000	**Indic. Yr. Divd.:**	$0.200
Total Assets:	$1,478,173,000	**Net Worth:**	$870,351,000	**Debt/ Equity:**	0.0937

Werner Holding Co Pa Inc

93 Werner Rd., Greenville, PA, 16125; *PH:* 1-888-523-3370; *http://* www.wernerladder.com

General - Incorporation	PA	**Stock**- Price on:12/24/2007	NA
Employees	NA	Stock Exchange	NA
Auditor	PricewaterhouseCoopers LLP	Ticker Symbol	NA
Stk Agt	NA	Outstanding Shares	NA
Counsel	NA	E.P.S	NA
DUNS No.	NA	Shareholders	NA

Business: The group's principal activities are to manufacture and market climbing products and aluminum extruded products. The group operates under two segments namely climbing products and extruded products. Climbing product segment produces fiberglass, aluminum, and wood climbing products and accessories under the brand name keller. The group's products include single and twin stepladders, extension, straight, and multipurpose ladders, attic ladders, stages, planks, work platforms and scaffolds and assorted ladder. Extruded products segment sells aluminum extrusions to customers in the automotive, electronics, architectural and construction industries. During Dec 2003, the group announced that it had entered into a long term strategic alliance with lowe's companies, inc. The group operates at greenville, Pennsylvania, franklin park, Illinois, anniston, Alabama, merced, juarez, California and Mexico, serve both the products.

Primary SIC and add'l.: 3354 3499 2499

CIK No: 0001056112

Subsidiaries: Pennsylvania corporation, Werner Holding Co. (DE), Inc

WesBanco Bank Inc

1 Bank Plz., Wheeling, WV, 26003; *PH:* 1-304-234-9000; *Fax:* 1-304-234-9298; *http://* www.wesbanco.com

General - Incorporation	WV	**Stock**- Price on:12/24/2007	$30.15
Employees	1,168	Stock Exchange	NDQ
Auditor	Ernst & Young LLP	Ticker Symbol	WSBC
Stk Agt	Computershare Investor Services LLC	Outstanding Shares	20,900,000
Counsel	NA	E.P.S	$2.17
DUNS No.	00-794-5512	Shareholders	NA

Business: The group's principal activities are to provide financial services. The services include retail banking, corporate banking, personal and corporate trust services, brokerage, mortgage banking and insurance. The group operates in two reportable segments: community banking and trust and investment services. Community banking segment offers services traditionally offered by full-service commercial banks, including commercial demand, individual demand and time deposit accounts as well as commercial, mortgage and individual installment loans. The trust and investment services segment offers trust services as well as various alternative investment products including mutual funds and annuities. As on 31-Dec-2003, the group has 72 offices in west Virginia, central and eastern Ohio. On 31-Aug-2004, the group acquired western Ohio financial corporation and cornerstone bank.

Primary SIC and add'l.: 6712 6021

CIK No: 0000203596

Subsidiaries: Hometown Finance Company, WesBanco Asset Management, Inc., WesBanco Bank, Inc., WesBanco Insurance Services, Inc., WesBanco Properties, Inc., WesBanco Securities, Inc., WesBanco Services, Inc., WesBanco, Inc

Officers: Paul M. Limbert/Dir., CEO, Pres./$601,624.00, Peter W. Jaworski/Exec. VP, Chief Credit Officer, Jerome B. Schmitt/Exec. VP - Investment, Trusts/$345,376.00, Dennis G. Powell/COO, Exec. VP/$372,970.00, Brent E. Richmond/Exec. VP - Treasury, Robert H. Young/CFO, Exec. VP/$347,203.00, Kristine N. Molnar/Exec. VP - Lending/$237,256.00, John W. Moore/Exec. VP - Human Resources, William E. Nichie/Registered Representative VP - Life Division, Marlene Farcin/Bookkeeper, Rhonda Deavers/Supervising Personal Lines CSR, Robin V. Roberts/Regional Personal Lines Mgr., Rebecca Shuttlesworth/Personal Lines CSR, Nancy James/Personal Lines CSR, Terry Brown/Personal Lines CSR *(24 Officers included in Index)*

Directors: Paul M. Limbert/Dir., CEO, Pres., James C. Gardill/Chmn., Robert M. D'Alessandri/Dir., Henry L. Schulhoff/Dir., John W. Fisher/Dir., Ernest S. Fragale/Dir., Vaughn L. Kiger/Dir., Christopher V. Criss/Dir., Peterson R. Chalfant/Dir., James D. Entress/Dir., Robert E. Kirkbride/Dir., James E. Altmeyer/Dir., Joan C. Stamp/Dir., Jay T. McCamic/Dir., Abigail M. Feinknopf/Dir. *(19 Directors included in Index)*

Owners: Eric F. Nelson, Henry L. Schulhoff, Wesbanco Trust and Investment Services/8.50%, Abigail M. Feinknopf, Dimensional Fund Advisors, LP/7.56%, Kristine N. Molnar, Christopher V. Criss, Peterson R. Chalfant, Vaughn L. Kiger, Insiders/5.57%, Reed J. Tanner, Jay T. McCamic

Financial Data: *Fiscal Year End:*12/31 *Latest Annual Data:* 12/31/2006

Year	Sales	Net Income
2006	$275,475,000	$39,035,000
2005	$263,878,000	$42,757,000
2004	$204,977,000	$38,182,000

Curr. Assets:	$115,785,000	**Curr. Liab.:**	$3,567,189,000	**P/E Ratio:**	13.89
Plant, Equip.:	$67,404,000	**Total Liab.:**	$3,681,268,000	**Indic. Yr. Divd.:**	$1.100
Total Assets:	$4,098,143,000	**Net Worth:**	$416,875,000	**Debt/ Equity:**	0.2139

Wesco Financial Corp

301 E Colorado B, Ste 300, Pasadena, CA, 91101; *PH:* 1-818-449-2345; *http://* www.wescofinancial.com

General - Incorporation	CA	**Stock**- Price on:12/24/2007	$403.5
Employees	2,400	Stock Exchange	AMEX
Auditor	Deloitte & Touche LLP	Ticker Symbol	WSC
Stk Agt	Mellon Investor Services LLC	Outstanding Shares	7,120,000
Counsel	Hahn & Hahn	E.P.S	NA
DUNS No.	00-691-0616	Shareholders	NA

Business: The group's principal activities are classified into three segments: insurance, furniture rental and industrial. The insurance segment engages in the property and casualty insurance and reinsurance business. The furniture rental segment is conducted through cort business services corporation. The industrial segment includes precision steel warehouse, inc. The group is also engaged in several relatively insignificant activities not identified with the three business segments including investment activity unrelated to the insurance segment, ms property's real estate activities and parent company activities.

Primary SIC and add'l.: 6331 7359 5051 6512

CIK No: 0000105729

Subsidiaries: Charlotte Service Center, CORT Business Services Corporation, Kansas Bankers Surety Company, MS Property Company, Precision Brand Products, Precision Steel Warehouse, Inc., Wesco Holdings Midwest, Inc., Wesco-Financial Insurance Company

Officers: Charles T. Munger/Chmn., CEO, Pres., Jeffrey L. Jacobson/60/CFO, VP/$228,000.00, Christopher M. Greco/30/Treasurer/$120,000.00, Margery A. Patrick/Sec.

Directors: Charles T. Munger/Chmn., CEO, Pres., Robert E. Denham/Dir., Robert T. Flaherty/Dir., Carolyn H. Carlburg/Dir., Peter D. Kaufman/53/Dir., Elizabeth Caspers Peters/82/Dir.

Owners: Elizabeth Caspers Peters/1.00%, Robert E. Sahm, Robert E. Denham, Peter D. Kaufman, Insiders/1.10%, Blue Chip Stamps/80.10%

Curr. Assets:	$1,317,737,000	**Curr. Liab.:**	$403,657,000	**P/E Ratio:**	13.89
Plant, Equip.:	$182,846,000	**Total Liab.:**	$569,967,000	**Indic. Yr. Divd.:**	NA
Total Assets:	$2,970,305,000	**Net Worth:**	$2,400,338,000	**Debt/ Equity:**	NA

WESCO International Inc

225 W Sta. Sq. Dr., Ste. 700, Pittsburgh, PA, 15219; *PH:* 1-412-454-2200; *http://* www.wescodist.com

General - Incorporation	DE	**Stock**- Price on:12/24/2007	$63.7
Employees	7,100	Stock Exchange	NYSE
Auditor	PricewaterhouseCoopers LLP	Ticker Symbol	WCC
Stk Agt	Mellon Investor Services LLC	Outstanding Shares	45,600,000
Counsel	NA	E.P.S	$4.37
DUNS No.	88-405-1616	Shareholders	NA

Business: The group's principle activity is to provide electrical construction products, electrical and industrial maintenance, repair and operating services. The groups electrical products include fuses, terminals, connectors, boxes, fittings, tools, lugs, and tape. Industrial products include cutting and other tools, abrasives, filters and safety equipment. Power distribution products include circuit breakers, transformers, switchboards, panelboards and busway. The groups servicing areas include industrial companies, contractors of industrial, commercial and residential projects, utility companies and commercial, institutional and governmental customers. The group operates from United States, Canada, Puerto Rico, Mexico and Singapore.

Primary SIC and add'l.: 6719 5063

CIK No: 0000929008

Subsidiaries: Carlton-Bates Company, CDW Holdco, LLC, WDC Holding, Inc., WESCO Distribution Canada Co., WESCO Distribution Canada LP, WESCO Distribution, Inc., WESCO Equity Corporation, WESCO Finance Corporation, WESCO Receivables Corporation

Officers: Roy W. Haley/59/Chmn., CEO, Ronald P. Van/VP - Operations, John J. Engel/COO, Sr. VP, William M. Goodwin/VP - Operations, Robert B. Rosenbaum/VP - Operations, Daniel A. Brailer/VP, Treasurer - Legal, Investor Relations, Stephen A. Van Oss/CFO, Sr. VP, Administrative Officer, Donald H. Thimjon/VP - Operations, Steve Riordan/VP - Operations, Robert J. Powell/VP - Human Resources, William E. Cenk/VP - Operations, Marcy Smorey-Giger/Corporate Counsel, Sec.

Directors: Roy W. Haley/59/Chmn., CEO, Sandra Beach Lin/48/Dir., William J. Vareschi/63/Dir., Robert J. Tarr/62/Dir., George L. Miles/64/Dir., Steven A. Raymund/51/Dir., James L. Singleton/50/Dir., Lynn M. Utter/44/Dir., Kenneth L. Way/66/Dir.

Owners: Kenneth L. Way, Insiders/5.10%, Robert J. Tarr, William M. Goodwin, Glenview Capital/5.80%, Steven A. Raymund, Stephen A. Van Oss, Sandra Beach Lin, Roy W. Haley/3.10%, William J. Vareschi, James L. Singleton, Putnam, LLC/5.40%, John J. Engel, FMR Corporation/7.26%, Barclays Global Investors, NA/11.95% *(16 Owners included in Index)*

Financial Data: *Fiscal Year End:*12/31 *Latest Annual Data:* 12/31/2006

Year	Sales	Net Income
2006	$5,320,603,000	$217,320,000
2005	$4,421,103,000	$103,526,000
2004	$3,741,253,000	$64,932,000

Curr. Assets:	$1,618,012,000	**Curr. Liab.:**	$1,153,672,000	**P/E Ratio:**	14.58
Plant, Equip.:	$107,016,000	**Total Liab.:**	$2,060,756,000	**Indic. Yr. Divd.:**	NA
Total Assets:	$2,823,983,000	**Net Worth:**	$763,227,000	**Debt/ Equity:**	1.2471

Wescorp Energy Inc

8711 50 Ave., Edmonton, AB, T6B 1E7; *PH:* 1-780-482-4200; *http://* www.wescorpenergy.com; *Email:* info@wescorpenergy.com

General - Incorporation	DE	**Stock**- Price on:12/24/2007	$0.47
Employees	20	Stock Exchange	OTC
Auditor	Williams & Webster, P.S	Ticker Symbol	WSCE
Stk Agt	Interwest Transfer Company, Inc.	Outstanding Shares	52,720,000
Counsel	NA	E.P.S	-$0.15
DUNS No.	NA	Shareholders	NA

Business: The group's principal activity is to acquire those companies, which provide oil and gas technologies and information services to the petroleum industry. The group invests primarily in companies or products where early stage product development has been completed. It contributes its business expertise to assist in the further development of the target company's business and operations. During 2003, the group sold its shares of cobratech industries inc and sentry telecom systems inc and changed its business focus. On 31-Mar-2004, the group acquired flowstar technologies inc and flowray inc.

Primary SIC and add'l.: 7382 3669

CIK No: 0001069489

Subsidiaries: Alberta Ltd, Flowstar, Flowstar Technologies Inc, Quadra

Officers: Douglas E. Biles/Dir., CEO, Pres., Scott Shemwell/COO, John Anderson/Dir., Sec., Treasurer, Terry Mereniuk/Dir., CFO, Dave Lemoine/VP - Sales, Marketing

Directors: Stephen C. Cowper/Chmn., John Anderson/Dir., Sec., Treasurer, Terry Mereniuk/Dir., CFO, Alfred Comeau/Dir., Robert M. Nicolay/Dir., Mark P. Norris/Dir.

Owners: Robert Nicolay/0.09%, Doug Biles/5.24%, Mark Norris/0.36%, Scott Shemwell/4.03%, Alfred Comeau/2.26%, Dave LeMoine/1.58%, John Anderson/2.73%, Steve Cowper/1.03%, Insiders/17.90%, Terry Mereniuk/1.95%

Financial Data: *Fiscal Year End:*12/31 *Latest Annual Data:* 12/31/2006

Year	Sales	Net Income
2006	$3,184,000	-$4,372,000
2005	$2,324,000	-$4,553,000
2004	$1,229,000	-$3,977,000

Curr. Assets:	$2,922,000	**Curr. Liab.:**	$5,225,000		
Plant, Equip.:	$138,000	**Total Liab.:**	$5,301,000	**Indic. Yr. Divd.:**	NA
Total Assets:	$8,483,000	**Net Worth:**	$3,181,000	**Debt/ Equity:**	0.0482

West BanCorp Inc

1601 22nd St., West Des Moines, IA, 50266; ***PH:*** 1-515-222-2300; ***http://*** www.westbankiowa.com; ***Email:*** info@westbankiowa.com

General - Incorporation .... IA
Employees .... NA
Auditor .... McGladrey & Pullen LLP
Stk Agt .... Illinois Stock Transfer Co
Counsel .... Ahlers & Cooney
DUNS No. .... NA

Stock- Price on:12/24/2007 .... $15.29
Stock Exchange .... NDQ
Ticker Symbol .... WTBA
Outstanding Shares 17,540,000
E.P.S $1.12
Shareholders .... NA

Business: The group's principal activities are to provide loans and deposits through eight branches in the des moines metropolitan area. The loans provided include commercial, real estate, business operating loans, lines of credit, equipment loans, vehicle loans, personal loans, home improvement loans, conventional and secondary market mortgage loan origination. The services include demand, savings and time deposits, merchant credit card processing, safe deposit boxes, automated teller machine access, trust services and correspondent bank services. On 18-Jul-2003, the group acquired hawkeye state bank and on 01-Oct-2003, certain assets of vmf capital llc.

Primary SIC and add'l.: 6022 6712

CIK No: 0001166928

Subsidiaries: Investors Management Group, Ltd., WB Capital Management Inc., West Bancorporation Capital Trust I, West Bank

Officers: Thomas E. Stanberry/Chmn., CEO, Pres./$558,762.00, Scott Dean Eltjes/CEO - WB Capital Management Inc/$215,489.00, Sharen K. Surber/Exec. VP - West Bank, Jeffrey David Lorenzen/Pres. - WB Capital Management Inc/$354,819.00, Alice A. Jensen/Corp. Sec., Jill Hansen/Executive Dir. - West Bancorporation Foundation, Inc, Brad L. Winterbottom/51/Exec. VP/$322,242.00, Douglas R. Gulling/CFO, Exec. VP/$270,770.00

Directors: Thomas E. Stanberry/Chmn., CEO, Pres., Frank W. Berlin/Dir., Steven G. Chapman/56/Dir., Michael A. Coppola/Dir., Orville E. Crowley/Dir., George D. Milligan/Dir., Robert G. Pulver/Dir., Jack G. Wahlig/Dir., Connie Wimer/Dir., Wendy Lee Carlson/Dir.

Owners: Michael A. Coppola, Steven G. Chapman, Columbia Wanger Asset Management, L.P./6.25%, The Jay Newlin Trust/5.94%, George D. Milligan, Douglas R. Gulling, Connie Wimer, Robert G. Pulver, Orville E. Crowley, Frank W. Berlin, Jeffrey D. Lorenzen, Thomas E. Stanberry, Scott D. Eltjes, Brad L. Winterbottom, Insiders/2.28%

Financial Data: ***Fiscal Year End:***12/31 ***Latest Annual Data:*** 12/31/2006

Year	Sales	Net Income
2006	$95,778,000	$19,407,000
2005	$74,992,000	$20,075,000
2004	$60,305,000	$18,614,000

Curr. Assets:	$44,265,000	**Curr. Liab.:**	$1,048,705,000	**P/E Ratio:**	13.90
Plant, Equip.:	$5,375,000	**Total Liab.:**	$1,154,724,000	**Indic. Yr. Divd.:**	$0.640
Total Assets:	$1,268,536,000	**Net Worth:**	$113,812,000	**Debt/ Equity:**	1.1594

West Coast Bancorp

5335 SW Meadows Rd. , Ste 201, Lake Oswego, OR, 97035; ***PH:*** 1-503-684-0884; ***http://*** www.wcb.com; ***Email:*** humanresources@wcb.com

General - Incorporation .... OR
Employees 830
Auditor .... Deloitte & Touche LLP
Stk Agt .... Wells Fargo Shareowner Services
Counsel .... Graham & Dunn
DUNS No. 05-769-0315

Stock- Price on:12/24/2007 .... $30.24
Stock Exchange .... NDQ
Ticker Symbol .... WCBO
Outstanding Shares 15,690,000
E.P.S $1.99
Shareholders .... NA

Business: The group's principal activity is to provide comprehensive banking services to individuals, professionals and small to medium-sized businesses. The group operates forty-one full-service and three limited-service branches in thirty-three cities and towns of western Oregon and western Washington. The group offers lines of credit, home equity loans, mortgages, credit cards and other types of loans to its consumer banking customers. The business banking customers are offered with tailored deposit plans, packaged checking, Internet-based cash management and a full array of investment services. The investment services are provided both online and in the form of CD-ROM reporting. The group also provides trust services and acts as fiduciary of estates and conservatorships.

Primary SIC and add'l.: 6022 6712

CIK No: 0000717059

Subsidiaries: Totten Inc., West Coast Bank, West Coast Statutory Trusts I-IV, West Coast Trust Company, Inc.

Officers: Robert D. Sznewajs/Dir., CEO, Pres./$1,299,851.00, Sandy Micoq/Pres. - West Coast Trust, Anders Giltvedt/CFO, Exec. VP/$445,355.00, Dave Hansen/Regional Pres. - Portland, Vancouver Region, Cynthia J. Sparacio/Exec. VP, Dir. - Human Resources, Hadley S. Robbins/Exec. VP, Chief Credit Officer, Xandra T. McKeown/Exec. VP - Commercial Banking/$374,543.00, Dick Rasmussen/Exec. VP, General Counsel, Sec., Richard R. Rasmussen/Exec. VP, General Counsel, Sec., James D. Bygland/CIO, Exec. VP/$246,847.00, Tim Dowling/Regional Pres. - Puget Sound Region, Ken Jundt/Regional Pres. - Coast, Willamette Region, Nancy Verville/Investor Relations Contact, Dave Simons/Sr. VP, Residential Lending Mgr., Kristie Nockleby/Sr. VP - Sales, Marketing Mgr. *(16 Officers included in Index)*

Directors: Robert D. Sznewajs/Dir., CEO, Pres., Lloyd D. Ankeny/Chmn., Steven N. Spence/Dir., David J. Truitt/Dir., J. F. Ouderkirk/Dir., Steven J. Oliva/Dir., Michael Bragg/Dir., Duane C. McDougall/Dir., Nancy A. Wilgenbusch/Dir.

Owners: Michael J. Bragg, Insiders/6.07%, Barclays Global Investors, N.A./6.25%, David Prysock, Xandra McKeown, J. F. Ouderkirk, Duane C. McDougall, Steven N. Spence, Nancy Wilgenbusch, Anders Giltvedt, Robert D. Sznewajs/2.51%, Lloyd D. Ankeny, David J. Truitt, Columbia Wanger Asset/8.69%, Steven J. Oliva *(16 Owners included in Index)*

Financial Data: ***Fiscal Year End:***12/31 ***Latest Annual Data:*** 12/31/2006

Year	Sales	Net Income
2006	$179,580,000	$29,260,000
2005	$138,122,000	$23,840,000
2004	$115,471,000	$22,008,000

Curr. Assets:	$94,875,000	**Curr. Liab.:**	$2,136,770,000	**P/E Ratio:**	15.83
Plant, Equip.:	$32,087,000	**Total Liab.:**	$2,264,490,000	**Indic. Yr. Divd.:**	$0.540
Total Assets:	$2,465,372,000	**Net Worth:**	$200,882,000	**Debt/ Equity:**	NA

West Corp

11808 Miracle Hills Dr., Omaha, NE, 68154; ***PH:*** 1-402-571-7700; ***http://*** www.west.com

General - Incorporation .... DE
Employees .... NA
Auditor .... Deloitte & Touche LLP
Stk Agt .... EquiServe Trust Co N.A
Counsel .... Erickson & Sederstrom
DUNS No. 96-412-5445

Stock- Price on:12/24/2007 .... NA
Stock Exchange .... NA
Ticker Symbol .... NA
Outstanding Shares .... NA
E.P.S .... NA
Shareholders .... NA

Business: The group's principal activity is to provide outsourced communication services and worldwide conferencing services. It enables its clients to outsource a wide range of communication services as well as providing audio, video and Web conferencing services. The group provides services to its clients through two segments, communication services and conferencing services. Communication services operates in the customer relationship management ("Crm") industry. Conferencing services include an integrated suite of audio, video and Web conferencing services. Its automated voice and data processing centers are located in the United States, jamaica, India and Canada. The group acquired worldwide asset management, llc and national asset management enterprises inc on 01-Aug-2004.

Primary SIC and add'l.: 4899 7389

CIK No: 0001024657

Subsidiaries: Asset Direct Mortgage, LLC, Attention Funding Corporation, Attention Funding Trust, BuyDebtCo, LLC, Centracall Limited, CGA Corporation Gerencial de Activos, S. de R.L. de C.V., Cobranza Express de Mexico, S. de R.L. de C.V., Conferencecall Services India Private Limited, InterCall Asia Pacific Holdings Pty. Ltd., InterCall Australia Pty. Ltd., InterCall Conferencing Services, Ltd., InterCall Hong Kong Limited, InterCall Japan KK, InterCall New Zealand Limited, InterCall Singapore Pte. Ltd. 43 Subsidiaries included in the Index

Officers: Thomas B. Barker/CEO, Dir., Nancee Berger/Chife Operating Officer, Pres., Mark V. Lavin/Pres. - West Telemarketing Corporation, Michael E. Mazour/Pres. - West Asset Management, Inc, Scott J. Etzler/Pres. - Intercall, Inc, Michael M. Sturgeon/Exec. VP - Sales, Marketing, Skip Hanson/Chief Administrative Officer, Exec. VP - Corporate Services, Paul M. Mendlik/Exec. VP, CFO, Treasurer, Steve Stangl/Pres. - West Communication Services, George Heinrichs/Pres. - Intrado, Inc, John Sanley/Pres. - West Business Services Corporation, Pam Mortenson/Exec. VP - West Interactive Corporation, Rob Johnson/Exec. VP - Strategic Business Development, Michael S. /Product Mgr., Jon R. Hanson/41/Exec. VP - Administrative Services, Chief Administrative Officer *(17 Officers included in Index)*

Directors: Thomas B. Barker/CEO, Dir., Anthony J. Dinovi/45/Dir., Soren L. Oberg/37/Dir., Joshua L. Steiner/42/Dir., Jeff T. Swenson/32/Dir.

Owners: Mary E. West/12.80%, Quadrangle Group Funds/11.60%, Nancee R. Berger, Thomas B. Barker/1.80%, Thomas B. Barker/3.50%, Insiders/3.60%, Quadrangle Group Funds/12.80%, Gary L. West/11.60%, ThomasH. Lee Funds/61.40%, Nancee R. Berger/1.30%, J. Scott Etzler, Insiders/9.50%, Gary L. West/12.80%, Mary E. West/11.60%, Steven M. Stangl *(20 Owners included in Index)*

West Marine Inc

500 Westridge Dr., Watsonville, CA, 95076; ; ***http://*** www.westmarine.com; ***Email:*** customercare@westmarine.com

General - Incorporation .... DE
Employees 2,231
Auditor .... Deloitte & Touche LLP
Stk Agt .... EquiServe Trust Co N.A
Counsel .... Dow, Lohnes & Albertson
DUNS No. 06-913-4179

Stock- Price on:12/24/2007 .... $13.85
Stock Exchange .... NDQ
Ticker Symbol .... WMAR
Outstanding Shares 21,740,000
E.P.S $0.09
Shareholders .... NA

Business: The group's principal activities are the retail distribution of recreational and commercial boating supplies and apparels. It markets the products through three divisions: stores, wholesale (port supply) and catalog as well as through its Website. The catalog and Internet channels provide approximately fifty thousand products that are exchangeable at the retail stores. The port supply division provides the wholesale distribution of marine equipment, serving boat manufacturers, marine services, commercial vessel operators and government agencies. The group operates 345 retail stores in 38 states, Puerto Rico and Canada and sells its products under the brand names 'west marine' and 'e&b marine'.

Primary SIC and add'l.: 5130 6719 5091 5961

CIK No: 0000912833

Subsidiaries: W Marine Management Company, Inc, West Marine Canada Corp, West Marine IHC I, Inc, West Marine LBC, Inc, West Marine Products, Inc, West Marine Puerto Rico, Inc

Officers: Peter Harris/Dir., CEO, Pres./$823,827.00, Pat Murphy/Sr. VP - Distribution, Logistics, Larry Smith/Sr. VP - Planning, Replenishment, Bruce Edwards/Exec. VP - Stores, Port Supply/$412,385.00, Ron Japinga/Exec. VP - Marketing, Merchandising, Ashlee Aldridge/Sr. VP, CIO - Information Technology, Scott Bauhofer/Sr. VP - Direct Sales, Faith Bosna/Store Mgr., Carlos Prieto/Direct Sales Lead, Nora Salcedo/Category Mgr. Assist., Brooks Brunde/Store Mgr., Khin Khin Slone/Sr. Income Tax Analyst, Peter Van Handel/52/Chief Accounting Officer, VP/$201,734.00, Tom Moran/Sr. VP, CFO - Finance

Directors: Peter Harris/Dir., CEO, Pres., Randy Repass/Chmn., Geoff Eisenberg/Dir., David McComas/Dir., Bill Westerfield/Dir., Daniel Sweeney/Dir., Alice Richter/Dir., Peter Roy/Dir., William U. Westerfield/76/Dir.

Owners: Bruce Edwards, Daniel J. Sweeney, Thomas R. Moran, Peter L. Harris/1.70%, Insiders/35.40%, Randolph K. Repass/29.80%, Geoffrey A. Eisenberg/2.20%, David McComas, Peter Van Handel, Thales Fund Management, L.L.C./12.10%, Alice M. Richter, Dimensional Fund Advisors, LP./8.10%, William U. Westerfield, Franklin Resources, Inc/20.70%, Diane Greene *(17 Owners included in Index)*

Financial Data: ***Fiscal Year End:***12/31 ***Latest Annual Data:*** 12/30/2006

Year	Sales	Net Income
2006	$716,604,000	-$7,099,000
2005	$692,264,000	-$2,179,000

Curr. Assets:	$361,155,000	**Curr. Liab.:**	$81,460,000		
Plant, Equip.:	$82,787,000	**Total Liab.:**	$208,029,000	**Indic. Yr. Divd.:**	NA
Total Assets:	$504,649,000	**Net Worth:**	$296,620,000	**Debt/ Equity:**	0.3640

West Milton Bcp PA

940 High St., West Milton, PA, 17886; *PH:* 1-570-568-6851; *Fax:* 1-570-568-6501;
http:// www.westmiltonstatebank.com; *Email:* info@westmiltonstatebank.com

General - Incorporation.................................	*Stock*- Price on:12/24/2007 ....$48.6
Employees...NA	Stock Exchange...OTC
Auditor..NA	Ticker Symbol......................................WMBC
Stk Agt.......................Registrar & Transfer Co	Outstanding Shares ....NA
Counsel...NA	E.P.S..NA
DUNS No. ....NA	Shareholders..NA

Business: The groups principal activity is to provide you with the answers to your financial needs in a friendly and efficient way to earn your trust and business. Services of the group include checking accounts, savings accounts, certificates of deposit, and installment loans, real estate mortgage loans and telephone banking. The group operates from the United States.

Primary SIC and add'l.: 6022

CIK No:

Officers: Donald A. Byerly/Chmn., CEO, Pres., Ronald E. Baker/VP - Commercial Lender, Belinda M. Diefenbach/VP - Administrative Associate, Dennis E. Keefer/VP, Sr. Agricultural Lending Officer, Mifflinburg Community Office Mgr., David G. Myers/VP - Compliance, Loan Review Officer, Auditor, Jill D. Shambach/Assist. VP, Trust Officer - Investment Representative, Club Representative, Mifflinburg Office, Trisha K. Shearer/VP, Dir. - Marketing, Human Resources, Club Coordinator, Club Representative, West Milton Office, Rodney H. Smith/CFO, VP, William O. Smith/VP - Small Business Lender, Gregory S. Valentine/VP, Credit Administration Division Mgr., William H. Weber/VP, Operations Division Mgr., Paula Snyder/Branch Mgr. - West Milton, Bob Reitz/Branch Mgr. - Lewisburg, Keith Downey/Branch Mgr. - Watsontown, John Aucker/Branch Mgr. - Beaver Springs *(20 Officers included in Index)*

Directors: Donald A. Byerly/Chmn., CEO, Pres., Christian C. Trate/Dir., Robert M. Brubaker/Dir., William F. Kear/Dir., Ray B. Bowersox/Dir., Peter L. Matson/Dir.

*Financial Data: Fiscal Year End:*NA *Latest Annual Data:* 12/31/2002

Year	Sales	Net Income
2002	$11,875,000	$2,053,000
2001	$11,520,000	$1,854,000
2000	$11,027,000	$1,024,000

Curr. Assets:	$8,180,000	*Curr. Liab.:*	$179,982,000
Plant, Equip.:	$3,050,000	*Total Liab.:*	$189,859,000 *Indic. Yr. Divd.:* NA
Total Assets:	$206,975,000	*Net Worth:*	$17,116,000 *Debt/ Equity:* 0.4698

West Pharmaceutical Services Inc

101 Gordon Dr., Lionville, PA, 19341; *PH:* 1-610-594-2900; *http://* www.westpharma.com

General - Incorporation...........................PA	*Stock*- Price on:12/24/2007 ....$48.15
Employees..6,323	Stock Exchange......................................NYSE
Auditor.....................PricewaterhouseCoopers LLP	Ticker Symbol..WST
Stk Agt..... American Stock Transfer & Trust Co.	Outstanding Shares 32,990,000
Counsel...Dechert LLP	E.P.S...$2.36
DUNS No. 00-233-0983	Shareholders..NA

Business: The group's principal activity is to apply value-added technologies to the process of bringing new drug therapies and healthcare products to global markets. The group operates in two segments: pharmaceutical systems segment, which designs, manufactures and sells stoppers, closures, medical device components and provides contract laboratory services for testing injectable drug packaging. The drug delivery systems segment identifies and develops drug delivery systems for biopharmaceutical and other drugs to improve their therapeutic performance and/or their method of administration. The drug delivery system also provides clinical research for phase I, II and III studies and clinical and marketing research services mostly for consumer products organizations.

Primary SIC and add'l.: 3466 3089 3069 3841

CIK No: 0000105770

Subsidiaries: (MFG) Tech Group Puerto Rico,Inc., Charter Laboratories,Inc., Citation Plastics Co., Medimop Israel, Medimop Projects North Israel, Medimop USA LLC, Paco Laboratories,Inc., Pharma-Gummi Beograd, Plasmec PLC, Senetics,Inc., Tech Group de Mexico SRL de CV, Tech Group Grand Rapids,Inc., Tech Group Ireland, Tech Group North America,Inc., Tech Group,Inc. 50 Subsidiaries included in the Index

Officers: Donald E. Morel/49/Chmn., CEO, Pres., Joseph E. Abbott/VP, Corporate Controller, Richard D. Luzzi/VP - Human Resources, Robert J. Keating/Pres. - Europe, Asia Pacific, Pharmaceutical Systems Division, Steven A. Ellers/COO, Pres., John R. Gailey/VP, General Counsel, Sec./$771,326.00, Donald A. McMillan/Pres. - North America Pharmaceutical Systems Division, William J. Federici/CFO, VP, Michael A. Anderson/VP, Treasurer, Robert S. Hargesheimer/Pres. - Tech Group

Directors: Donald E. Morel/49/Chmn., CEO, Pres., Geoffrey F. Worden/67/Dir., Masamichi Sudo/Honorary Dir., Paula A. Johnson/47/Dir., John P. Neafsey/67/Dir., Anthony Welters/52/Dir., Patrick J. Zenner/60/Dir., John H. Weiland/52/Dir., Robert C. Young/67/Dir., Jenne K. Britell/64/Dir., Robert L. Johnson/65/Dir.

Owners: Insiders/5.90%, L. Robert Johnson, William H. Longfield, Geoffrey F. Worden, John P. Neafsey, Patrick J. Zenner, Steven A. Ellers/1.10%, Anthony Welters, Franklin Advisory Services/11.10%, Donald E. Morel/2.20%, Robert C. Young, William J. Federici, John R. Gailey, Robert J. Keating

*Financial Data: Fiscal Year End:*12/31 *Latest Annual Data:* 12/31/2006

Year	Sales	Net Income
2006	$913,300,000	$67,100,000
2005	$699,700,000	$45,600,000
2004	$541,600,000	$19,400,000

Curr. Assets:	$281,700,000	*Curr. Liab.:*	$156,900,000 *P/E Ratio:* 20.40
Plant, Equip.:	$384,700,000	*Total Liab.:*	$503,700,000 *Indic. Yr. Divd.:* $0.520
Total Assets:	$918,200,000	*Net Worth:*	$414,500,000 *Debt/ Equity:* 0.8195

West Suburban Bancorp Inc

711 S Meyers Rd. , Lombard, IL, 60148; *PH:* 1-630-652-2000; *http://* www.westsuburbanbank.com

General - Incorporation IL	*Stock*- Price on:12/24/2007 ....NA
Employees...NA	Stock Exchange...NA
Auditor .... Crowe Chizek & Co. LLC	Ticker Symbol...NA
Stk Agt.......................................West Suburban Bank	Outstanding Shares ....NA
Counsel.....Barack Ferrazzano Kirschbaum Et Al	E.P.S..NA
DUNS No. 00-174-4945	Shareholders..NA

Business: The group's principal activities are to provide financial services to individuals and small and medium size businesses. The group's consumer and commercial products and services include insurance, travel agency, safe deposit boxes and extended banking hours. The group has 33 full service branches and 4 limited service branches throughout the western suburbs of Chicago. The group is a bank holding company for west suburban bank, lombard, Illinois. The bank has 60 automated teller machines. Other services provided by the group include, investment products and visa card through west suburban bank card services.

Primary SIC and add'l.: 6712 6021

CIK No: 0000805080

Subsidiaries: Melrose Holdings, Inc., West Suburban Bank, West Suburban Insurance Services, Inc., West Suburban Management, LLC, West Suburban Realty, LLC

Owners: Insiders/32.44%, Peggy P. LoCicero/1.81%, Keith W. Acker/6.24%, Craig R. Acker/5.39%, Michael P. Brosnahan/0.42%, Charles P. Howard/0.71%, David S. Bell/0.22%, Kevin J. Acker/4.07%, Duane G. Debs/0.32%

Westaff Inc

298 N Wiget Ln., Walnut Creek, CA, 94598; *PH:* 1-925-930-5300; *http://* www.westaff.com

General - Incorporation ....DE	*Stock*- Price on:12/24/2007 ....$4.9
Employees..809	Stock Exchange......................................NDQ
Auditor ....Deloitte & Touche LLP	Ticker Symbol.......................................WSTF
Stk Agt..........................Deloitte & Touche LLP	Outstanding Shares 16,610,000
Counsel......................Morrison & Foerster LLP	E.P.S...$0.21
DUNS No. 00-923-6274	Shareholders..NA

Business: The group's principal activity is to provide staffing services. It places personnel in clerical, light industrial and light technical positions through an international network of offices. Personnel fill positions that include word processing, data entry, reception, customer service and telemarketing, warehouse labor, manufacturing and assembly. As of 01-Nov-2003, the company operated through a network of 270 offices in 45 states and five foreign countries. The group currently operates in the United Kingdom, Australia, New Zealand, Norway, Denmark and Mexico in addition to the United States.

Primary SIC and add'l.: 7361

CIK No: 0000931911

Subsidiaries: Mediaworld International, Westaff (Australia) Pty Ltd, Westaff (Singapore) Pte Ltd, Westaff (U.K.) Limited, Westaff (USA), Inc., Westaff NZ Limited, Westaff Support, Inc., Western Staff Services (UK) Limited

Officers: Michael T. Willis/Chmn., CEO, Pres., Jeffrey A. Elias/Sr. VP - Corporate Services, Heather Heverly/Westaff Staffing Associate, Straub Clinic, Nigel J. Haworth/MD - Australia, New Zealand, John P. Sanders/43/Sr. VP, CFO, Treasurer, Eric Person/VP - Information Services, Kristi Kennedy/Sr. VP - Field Operations, Dawn Jaffray/Sr. VP, Peter E. Person/35/VP - Information Systems, David Mogford/MD - United Kingdom, Jack Graser/Human Resources Mgr. - Meridian Medical Technologies, Kathy Chersy/Employee Relations Assist. - Sunnen Products Company, Jamie Ryan/VP - Legal, Corp. Sec.

Directors: Michael T. Willis/Chmn., CEO, Pres., Janet M. Brady/Dir., John R. Black/Dir., John G. Ball/Dir., Jack D. Samuelson/Dir., Gerald E. Wedren/Dir., Michael R. Phillips/Dir., Walter W. MacAuley/Dir., Ronald D. Stevens/64/Dir.

Owners: Richard Sugerman, Janet M. Brady, Jack D. Samuelson, David P. Wilson, DelStaff LLC, Michael R. Phillips, Dimensional Fund Advisors, Inc., Patricia M. Newman, Osmium Partners, LLC, Michael T. Willis, John R. Black, Ronald D. Stevens, Insiders, John P. Sanders

*Financial Data: Fiscal Year End:*11/02 *Latest Annual Data:* 10/28/2006

Year	Sales	Net Income
2006	$614,950,000	$3,119,000
2005	$612,861,000	$21,126,000
2004	$601,476,000	$3,473,000

Curr. Assets:	$98,245,000	*Curr. Liab.:*	$64,731,000 *P/E Ratio:* 23.33
Plant, Equip.:	$10,184,000	*Total Liab.:*	$82,561,000 *Indic. Yr. Divd.:* NA
Total Assets:	$122,408,000	*Net Worth:*	$39,847,000 *Debt/ Equity:* 0.0097

Westaim Corp

144 - 4th Ave. SW, Calgary, AB, T2P 3N4; *PH:* 1-403-237-7272; *http://* www.westaim.com; *Email:* info@westaim.com

General - Incorporation ....AB	*Stock*- Price on:12/24/2007 ....$0.575
Employees..470	Stock Exchange...OTC
Auditor ....Deloitte & Touche LLP	Ticker Symbol......................................WEDX
Stk Agt.........Computershare Trust Co of Canada	Outstanding Shares 94,020,000
Counsel...NA	E.P.S...-$0.35
DUNS No. ....NA	Shareholders..NA

Business: The group operates in five segments: westaim coating solutions, coinage, nucryst pharmaceutical, ifire technology and other. Westaim coating solutions develops, manufactures and markets coating products for various ethylene, aerospace, electronics and other industrial markets. Coinage products manufactures coin blanks. Nucryst pharmaceuticals markets products based on nanotechnology sciences. Ifire technology develops flat-panel TV modules. The group's quarterly revenue for September 2007 was 7.84 millions of USD.

Primary SIC and add'l.: 3999 2899 2834 3679

CIK No: 0001108828

Subsidiaries: iFire Technology Corp, NUCRYST Pharmaceuticals Corp, NUCRYST Pharmaceuticals Inc, The Westaim Corporation, Viridian Inc.

Officers: Barry M. Heck/Dir., CEO, Pres., Thomas E. Gardner/Chmn., CEO, Pres. - Nucryst Pharmaceuticals Corp, Nicolas W. Khoury/Pres. - Ifire Technology Ltd, Anthony B. Johnston/Sr. VP, G. A. Fitch/CFO, Sr. VP, Brian D. Heck/VP, General Counsel, Corp. Sec.

Directors: Barry M. Heck/Dir., CEO, Pres., Ian W. Delaney/Chmn., Neil Carragher/Dir., Roger G.H. Downer/Dir., Frank W. King/Dir., Daniel P. Owen/Dir., Guy J. Turcotte/Dir., Bruce V. Walter/Dir.

*Financial Data: Fiscal Year End:*12/31 *Latest Annual Data:* 12/31/2006

Year	Sales	Net Income
2006	$23,676,000	-$42,913,000
2005	$24,504,000	$9,588,000
2004	$26,770,000	-$22,391,000

Curr. Assets:	$68,868,000	Curr. Liab.:	$13,555,000
Plant, Equip.:	$54,882,000	Total Liab.:	$19,356,000	Indic. Yr. Divd.: NA
Total Assets:	$126,432,000	Net Worth:	$96,113,000	Debt/ Equity: NA

Westamerica Bancorp.

1108 Fifth Ave., San Rafael, CA, 94901; *PH:* 1-415-257-8000; *http://* www.westamerica.com

General - Incorporation ....CA	**Stock**- Price on:12/24/2007 ....$45.53
Employees...890	Stock Exchange..NDQ
Auditor ....KPMG LLP	Ticker Symbol...WABC
Stk Agt.....Computershare Investor Services LLC	Outstanding Shares 30,050,000
Counsel...NA	E.P.S..$3.07
DUNS No. ....NA	Shareholders...NA

Business: The groups principal activity is to provide banking services. The products of the group include Debit card, ATM, and consumer and commercial loan. In March 1, 2005, the group acquired Redwood Empire Bancorp. The group operates from the United States. The assets of the group for the year 2006 were $4,769,335 (thousands).

Primary SIC and add'l.: 6021 6712

CIK No: 0000311094

Subsidiaries: Community Banker Services Corporation, The Money Outlet, Inc., Westamerica Bank, Westamerica Commercial Credit, Inc., Westamerica Mortgage Company, Weststar Mortgage Corporation

Officers: David L. Payne/Chmn., CEO, Pres./$1,971,940.00, Jennifer J. Finger/Sr. VP, Treasurer/$505,013.00, James Schneck/VP, General Auditor, Robert A. Thorson/Sr. VP, CFO/$442,818.00, Dennis R. Hansen/Sr. VP - Operations, Systems Division Mgr. - Westamerica Bank/$348,161.00, Frank Zbacnik/Sr. VP - Credit Administration - Westamerica Bank/$423,746.00

Directors: David L. Payne/Chmn., CEO, Pres., Etta Allen/Dir., Louis E. Bartolini/Dir., Joseph E. Bowler/Dir., Arthur C. Latno/Dir., Patrick D. Lynch/Dir., Catherine Cope MacMillan/Dir., Ronald A. Nelson/Dir., Edward B. Sylvester/Dir.

Owners: Jennifer J. Finger/0.50%, T. Rowe Price Associates, Inc./9.90%, Robert A. Thorson/0.30%, David L. Payne/7.70%, Ronald A. Nelson/0.20%, Joseph E. Bowler, Barclays Global Investors, N.A./5.01%, Arthur C. Latno, Insiders/9.47%, Edward B. Sylvester/0.30%, Patrick D. Lynch, Etta Allen, Frank R. Zbacnik/0.20%, Catherine Cope MacMillan, Neuberger Berman, Inc./5.19% *(17 Owners included in Index)*

Financial Data: *Fiscal Year End:*12/31 *Latest Annual Data:* 12/31/2006

Year	Sales	Net Income
2006	$301,862,000	$98,806,000
2005	$302,240,000	$107,441,000
2004	$262,135,000	$95,218,000

Curr. Assets:	$297,838,000	Curr. Liab.:	$4,248,711,000	P/E Ratio: 14.83
Plant, Equip.:	$30,835,000	Total Liab.:	$4,345,100,000	Indic. Yr. Divd.: $1.360
Total Assets:	$4,769,335,000	Net Worth:	$424,235,000	Debt/ Equity: 0.0878

Westar Energy Inc

Westar Energy, Topeka, KS, 66675; *PH:* 1-316-383-8600; *Fax:* 1-316-261-6615; *http://* www.wr.com; *Email:* corpcom@wr.com

General - Incorporation ....KS	**Stock**- Price on:12/24/2007 ....$24.76
Employees..2,223	Stock Exchange.......................................NYSE
Auditor ....Deloitte & Touche LLP	Ticker Symbol..WR
Stk Agt..............................Westar Energy Inc	Outstanding Shares 88,850,000
Counsel...NA	E.P.S..$1.86
DUNS No. 00-694-3781	Shareholders...NA

Business: The groups principle activity is to provide electric generation, transmission and distribution services. The group operates from United States.

Primary SIC and add'l.: 4911 4931 4923

CIK No: 0000054507

Subsidiaries: Kansas Gas and Electric Company, WR Receivables Corporation

Officers: James S. Haines/61/Dir., CEO/$1,067,478.00, William B. Moore/Dir., CEO, Pres./$617,948.00, Doug Sterbenz/COO, Exec. VP/$739,441.00, Ken Johnson/VP - Generation, James Ludwig/Exec. VP - Public Affairs, Consumer Services, Larry Irick/VP, General Counsel, Corp. Sec./$591,280.00, Peggy S. Loyd/VP - Customer Care, Leroy P. Wages/VP, Controller, Mark A. Ruelle/CFO, Exec. VP/$379,776.00, Jeff Beasley/VP - Corporate Compliance, Internal Audit, Michael Lennen/VP - Regulatory Affairs, Bruce Burns/Dir. - Investor Relations, Caroline A. Williams/VP - Distribution Power Delivery, Greg A. Greenwood/VP - Generation Construction, Kelly B. Harrison/VP - Transmission Operations, Environmental Services *(17 Officers included in Index)*

Directors: James S. Haines/61/Dir., CEO, William B. Moore/Dir., CEO, Pres., Charles Q. Chandler/Chmn., Arthur Krause/Dir., Sandra A.J. Lawrence/Dir., Anthony Isaac/Dir., Mollie Hale Carter/Dir., Michael Morrissey/Dir., R. A. Edwards/Dir., John C. Nettels/Dir., Jerry B. Farley/Dir.

Owners: Larry D. Irick, Michael F. Morrissey, JPMorgan Chase& Co./6.20%, William B. Moore, Jerry B. Farley, Insiders/1.20%, Barclays Global Investors/5.29%, Arthur B. Krause, Sandra A.J. Lawrence, Mollie H. Carter, Douglas R. Sterbenz, Charles Q. Chandler, John C. Nettels, Anthony B. Isaac, James S. Haines *(18 Owners included in Index)*

Financial Data: *Fiscal Year End:*12/31 *Latest Annual Data:* 12/31/2006

Year	Sales	Net Income
2006	$1,605,743,000	$165,309,000
2005	$1,583,278,000	$135,610,000
2004	$1,464,489,000	$178,870,000

Curr. Assets:	$536,720,000	Curr. Liab.:	$663,176,000	P/E Ratio: 13.03
Plant, Equip.:	$4,071,607,000	Total Liab.:	$3,894,280,000	Indic. Yr. Divd.: $1.080
Total Assets:	$5,455,175,000	Net Worth:	$1,560,895,000	Debt/ Equity: 0.9885

Westborough Financial Services Inc

100 E Main St. , Westborough, MA, 01581; *PH:* 1-508-366-4111

General - Incorporation ....MA	**Stock**- Price on:12/24/2007 ....$34.91
Employees...64	Stock Exchange..NA
Auditor ....Wolf & Co. P.C	Ticker Symbol...NA
Stk Agt ....Registrar & Transfer Co	Outstanding Shares 1,610,000
Counsel............Thacher Proffitt & Wood LLP.	E.P.S. ....-$0.58
DUNS No. ....NA	Shareholders...NA

Business: The group's principle activity is to provide savings and loan products, mortgage banking and other related financial services. The group operates from United States.

Primary SIC and add'l.: 6712 6036

CIK No: 0001087843

Subsidiaries: Eli Whitney Security Corporation, One Hundredth Security Corporation, The Hundredth Corporation, The Westborough Bank

Owners: Nancy M. Carlson, Westborough Bancorp, MHC/63.89%, Charlotte C. Spinn, Paul F. McGrath, Robert A. Klugman, David E. Carlstrom, James E. Tashjian, John L. Casagrande, Edward S. Bilzeria, Insiders/6.01%, Nelson P. Ball, Joseph F. MacDonou/1.40%, Jeffrey B. Leland, Phyllis A. Stone, Benjamin H. Colone *(16 Owners included in Index)*

Financial Data: *Fiscal Year End:*09/30 *Latest Annual Data:* 9/30/2006

Year	Sales	Net Income
2006	$15,292,000	-$42,000
2005	$13,627,000	$898,000
2004	$12,659,000	$1,191,000

Curr. Assets:	$9,685,000	Curr. Liab.:	$214,704,000	
Plant, Equip.:	$6,560,000	Total Liab.:	$272,584,000	Indic. Yr. Divd.: $0.240
Total Assets:	$300,967,000	Net Worth:	$28,383,000	Debt/ Equity: 1.9429

Westbridge Research Group

1150 Josha Way, Vista, CA, 92081; *PH:* 1-760-599-8855; *http://* www.westbridge.com; *Email:* wrg@westbridge.com

General - Incorporation ....CA	**Stock**- Price on:12/24/2007 ....NA
Employees...NA	Stock Exchange..NA
Auditor ....PKF	Ticker Symbol...NA
Stk Agt ....NA	Outstanding Shares ....NA
Counsel...NA	E.P.S. ....NA
DUNS No. 10-667-2215	Shareholders...NA

Business: The group's principal activity is to develop, manufacture and market environmentally compatible products for the agriculture industry. Its products include proprietary formulations based primarily on the use of microbial fermentations and plant extracts. The products of the group also include plant growth regulators like soil triggrr and foliar triggrr and specialty micronutrient fertilizers like foliar sunburst and soil sunburst. The group's environmental products include h4-502 and sewage treatment (st-12), which are organic products formulated to control ammonia, alcohol and hydrogen sulfide odors. The group operates in the United States.

Primary SIC and add'l.: 2874 2899

CIK No: 0000750150

Subsidiaries: Westbridge Agricultural Products

Officers: Christine Koenemann/Pres., Principal Executive Officer, Principal Financial Officer, Lawrence Parker/Dir. - Research, Development, Javier Lopez/Production Mgr., Nancy Tami/Quality Control Mgr., Lanette Dudley/Mgr. - Accounting, Shaun Lough/Product Sales Representative - Western Pacific Northwest, Craig Yearous/Product Sales Representative - Eastern Pacific Northwest, Vicky Segall/Contact- Customer Service

Owners: Mark Cole, Kenneth P. Miles/5.70%, Insiders/6.70%, Christine Koenemann/4.70%, Albert L. Good/8.70%, William Fruehling/2.00%

WestCoast Golf Experiences Inc

333 E 1st St., Ste. 309, Vancouver, BC, V7L 4W9; *PH:* 1-604-988-1083; *http://* www.westcoastgolfexperiences.com

General - Incorporation ....NV	**Stock**- Price on:12/24/2007 ....NA
Employees...NA	Stock Exchange...OTC
Auditor ....Dale Matheson Carr-Hilton LaBonte LLP	Ticker Symbol...WCGE
Stk Agt ....Holladay Stock Transfer, Inc.	Outstanding Shares ....NA
Counsel...NA	E.P.S. ....NA
DUNS No. ....NA	Shareholders...NA

Business: The groups principal activity is hire the website designer to expand groups website at www.westcoastgolfexperiences.com as well as provide search engine optimization for groups website domain. The group operates from the United States.

Primary SIC and add'l.: 7990

CIK No: 0001328670

Officers: Roger Arnet/40/Dir., CEO, CFO, Pres., Sec., Treasurer, Tyler Halls/32/VP - Golf Operations

Directors: Roger Arnet/40/Dir., CEO, CFO, Pres., Sec., Treasurer

Owners: Roger Arnet/67.00%, Insiders/67.00%

Westell Technologies Inc

750 N Commons Dr., Aurora, IL, 60504; *PH:* 1-630-898-2500; *http://* www.westell.com; *Email:* businessdevelopment@westell.com

General - Incorporation ....DE	**Stock**- Price on:12/24/2007 ....$2.67
Employees...898	Stock Exchange..NDQ
Auditor ....Ernst & Young LLP	Ticker Symbol...WSTL
Stk Agt ....LaSalle Bank N.A	Outstanding Shares 71,310,000
Counsel....................McDermott Will & Emery	E.P.S. ....NA
DUNS No. 85-917-1134	Shareholders...NA

Business: The group's principle activities are to design, manufacture, market and service digital and analog products used by telephone companies and other telecommunication service providers. The group comprises of two segments equipment sales and teleconference services. Equipment sales designs, manufacturers and markets digital and analog products to deliver broadband services over existing copper telephone wires. Teleconference service provides audio, video and Web conferencing services to both

business and individuals. The group also provides broadband and digital subscriber line (DSL) technology solutions that allow the transport of high-speed data over the local loop. In addition, the group provides DSL products and solutions for Internet service providers. The group's product lines include customer networking equipment, carrier transport and multiplexer.

Primary SIC and add'l.: 4822 6719 3661

CIK No: 0001002135

Officers: Timothy J. Reedy/46/CEO - Conference Plus, Inc, Thomas E. Mader/59/CEO/$168,313.00, Mark Skurla/VP - Sales, Customer Service, Robert C. Penny/Dir., MD - PF Management, Nicholas C. Hindman/57/CFO/$638,171.00, William J. Noll/66/Sr. VP - Engineering, CTO/$646,621.00, John C. Clark/60/Sr. VP - Operations/$606,381.00

Directors: Paul A. Dwyer/Dir., Bernard F. Sergesketter/Dir., Melvin Simon/Dir., Roger L. Plummer/66/Dir., John W. Seazholtz/71/Dir., Eileen A. Kamerick/49/Dir.

Owners: Insiders/7.10%, Robert C. Penny, John W. Seazholtz, Robert C. Penny, John C. Clark, William J. Noll, Melvin J. Simon/1.00%, Paul A. Dwyer, Eileen A. Kamerick, Nicholas C. Hindman, Thomas E. Mader, Timothy J. Reedy, Van E. Cullens/2.30%, Roger L. Plummer, Insiders *(17 Owners included in Index)*

Financial Data: Fiscal Year End:03/31   Latest Annual Data: 03/31/2007

Year	Sales	Net Income
2007	$260,090,000	$8,694,000
2006	$283,171,000	$12,847,000
2005	$270,263,000	$39,694,000

Curr. Assets:	$124,585,000	**Curr. Liab.:**	$36,154,000	**P/E Ratio:**	38.14
Plant, Equip.:	$12,329,000	**Total Liab.:**	$36,961,000	**Indic. Yr. Divd.:**	NA
Total Assets:	$207,350,000	**Net Worth:**	$167,339,000	**Debt/ Equity:**	NA

Western Alliance Bancorp.

2700 W Sahara Ave., Las Vegas, NV, 89102; **PH:** 1-702-248-4200;
http:// www.westernalliancebancorp.com

General - Incorporation	NV	**Stock** - Price on:12/24/2007	$30.35
Employees	785	Stock Exchange	NYSE
Auditor	McGladrey & Pullen, LLP	Ticker Symbol	WAL
Stk Agt	American Stock Transfer & Trust Co.	Outstanding Shares	30,410,000
Counsel	NA	E.P.S.	$1.29
DUNS No.	NA	Shareholders	NA

Business: The groups principal activity is to provide banking and related services. The group operates from the United States.

Primary SIC and add'l.: 6712 6712 6022 6022

CIK No: 0001212545

Subsidiaries: Alliance Bank of Arizona, Alta Alliance Bank, Bank of Nevada, BW Real Estate, Inc., Miller/Russell & Associates, Inc., Premier Trust, Inc., Torrey Pines Bank

Officers: Robert G. Sarver/Chmn., CEO, Pres./$1,118,931.00, Dale Gibbons/CFO, Exec. VP/$449,543.00, Duane Froeschle/Exec. VP, Chief Credit Officer/$317,295.00, Gary Cady/Exec. VP - California Administration, Mark Dreschler/Pres. - Premier Trust, Nevada, Merrill S. Wall/Exec. VP, Chief Administrative Officer/$551,300.00, Linda N. Mahan/Exec. VP - Operations, James Lundy/Exec. VP - Arizona Administration/$422,629.00, Dennis H. Miller/Pres. - Miller, Russell, Associates

Directors: Robert G. Sarver/Chmn., CEO, Pres., Bruce Beach/Dir., Steven J. Hilton/Dir., Cary Mack/Dir., Arthur Marshall/Dir., Nafees M. Nagy/Dir., Donald D. Snyder/Dir., William S. Boyd/Dir., Marianne Boyd Johnson/Dir., George J. Maloof/Dir., Todd Marsha/Dir., James E. Nave/Dir., Larry L. Woodrum/Dir., John Peter Sande/Dir., Kenneth A. Vecchione/Dir.

Owners: William S. Boyd/2.81%, Paul Baker/1.14%, James Nave/1.90%, Donald D. Snyder, James Lundy, Bruce Beach, Robert G. Sarver/12.69%, Todd Marshall/2.47%, Cary Mack, Merrill Wall, Duane Froeschle, Larry L. Woodrum, Marianne Boyd Johnson/15.10%, Insiders/43.52%, Steven J. Hilton *(22 Owners included in Index)*

Financial Data: Fiscal Year End:12/31   Latest Annual Data: 12/31/2006

Year	Sales	Net Income
2006	$250,955,000	$39,889,000
2005	$147,048,000	$28,065,000
2004	$99,581,000	$20,057,000

Curr. Assets:	$282,305,000	**Curr. Liab.:**	$3,601,157,000	**P/E Ratio:**	12.73
Plant, Equip.:	$99,859,000	**Total Liab.:**	$3,761,025,000	**Indic. Yr. Divd.:**	NA
Total Assets:	$4,169,604,000	**Net Worth:**	$408,579,000	**Debt/ Equity:**	NA

Western Commercl BK

21550 Oxnard St. , Ste. 100, Woodland Hills, California, 91367; **Fax:** 1-818-449-7700;
http:// www.westerncommercialbank.com

General - Incorporation		**Stock** - Price on:12/24/2007	$13.75
Employees	NA	Stock Exchange	OTC
Auditor	NA	Ticker Symbol	WCBH
Stk Agt	Registrar & Transfer Co	Outstanding Shares	NA
Counsel	NA	E.P.S	NA
DUNS No.	NA	Shareholders	NA

Business: The groups principle activity is to provide recruiting services. The groups service area includes the research and development, engineering, marketing, sales, information technology and manufacturing industries. The group operates from United States.

Primary SIC and add'l.: 6712

CIK No:

Officers: Carl Raggio/Dir., CEO, Pres., Kathleen Bryan/Exec. VP, Chief Credit Officer, Tommy H. Woo/CFO, Exec. VP, Rick Levenson/Marketing Maker

Directors: Carl Raggio/Dir., CEO, Pres.

Western Digital Corp

20511 Lake Forest Dr., Lake Forest, CA, 92630; **PH:** 1-949-932-5000; *http://* www.wdc.com

General - Incorporation	DE	**Stock** - Price on:12/24/2007	$19.06
Employees	24,750	Stock Exchange	NYSE
Auditor	KPMG LLP	Ticker Symbol	WDC
Stk Agt	American Stock Transfer & Trust Co.	Outstanding Shares	221,900,000
Counsel	NA	E.P.S.	$2.35
DUNS No.	05-198-3567	Shareholders	NA

Business: The group's principle activities include designing, developing, manufacturing and marketing hard drives technology. The group's products include Wd Caviar and Wd Protege(TM) hard drive products. The hard drive products are used in desktop personal computers, servers, network attached storage devices, video game consoles, digital video recording devices and satellite set-top boxes. The group sells its products to computer manufacturers, distributors, resellers, systems integrators and retailers. The group's computer customers include Dell, Fujitsu, Gateway, Hewlett-Packard, Microsoft, Nec and Trigem. The group operates from United States, Malaysia, Thailand, Europe and Asia.

Primary SIC and add'l.: 3674 3572

CIK No: 0000106040

Subsidiaries: Keen Personal Media, Inc., Keen Personal Technologies, Inc., Pacifica Insurance Corporation, Read-Rite (Malaysia) Sdn. Bhd., Read-Rite International, Read-Rite Philippines, Inc., RS Patent Holding Corporation, Western Digital (Deutschland) GmbH, Western Digital (France) SARL, Western Digital (Fremont), Inc., Western Digital (I.S.) Limited, Western Digital (Malaysia) Sdn. Bhd., Western Digital (S.E. Asia) Pte Ltd., Western Digital (Thailand) Company Limited, Western Digital (UK) Limited 25 Subsidiaries included in the Index

Officers: John F. Coyne/58/CEO/$7,651,246.00, Matthew E. Massengill/Dir., CEO, Pres./$4,221,417.00, Raymond M. Bukaty/Sr. VP, General Counsel, Sec./$2,107,770.00, Hossein Moghadam/CTO, Sr. VP/$2,297,658.00, Joseph R. Carrillo/VP, Corporate Controller, Principal Accounting Officer, Timothy M. Leyden/CFO, Exec. VP/$226,987.00, Stephen D. Milligan/45/CFO, Sr. VP

Directors: Matthew E. Massengill/Dir., CEO, Pres., Thomas E. Pardun/Chmn., Roger H. Moore/Dir., William L. Kimsey/Dir., Michael D. Lambert/Dir., Peter D. Behrendt/Dir., Kathleen A. Cote/Dir., Henry T. Denero/Dir., Arif Shakeel/Dir.

Owners: Henry T. DeNero, William L. Kimsey, Kathleen A. Cote, Hossein M. Moghadam, Insiders/1.10%, Thomas E. Pardun, Raymond M. Bukaty, Roger H. Moore, John F. Coyne, LSV Asset Management/5.14%, Matthew E. Massengill, Stephen D. Milligan, Peter D. Behrendt, Barclays Global Investors, NA., and certain affiliates/10.30%, Michael D. Lambert *(16 Owners included in Index)*

Financial Data: Fiscal Year End:07/01   Latest Annual Data: 6/30/2006

Year	Sales	Net Income
2006	$4,341,300,000	$394,600,000
2005	$3,638,800,000	$198,400,000
2004	$3,046,700,000	$151,300,000

Curr. Assets:	$857,300,000	**Curr. Liab.:**	$586,900,000	**P/E Ratio:**	7.36
Plant, Equip.:	$274,700,000	**Total Liab.:**	$671,600,000	**Indic. Yr. Divd.:**	NA
Total Assets:	$1,159,200,000	**Net Worth:**	$487,600,000	**Debt/ Equity:**	0.0084

Western Goldfields Inc

PO Box 110, 2 Bloor St. W, Ste. 2102, Toronto, ON, M4W 3E2; **PH:** 1-416-324-6005;
http:// www.westerngoldfields.com; **Email:** info@westerngoldfields.com

General - Incorporation	ID	**Stock** - Price on:12/24/2007	$2.35
Employees	NA	Stock Exchange	AMEX
Auditor	HJ & Assoc. LLC	Ticker Symbol	WGW
Stk Agt	Computershare Trust Co	Outstanding Shares	NA
Counsel	NA	E.P.S.	NA
DUNS No.	NA	Shareholders	NA

Business: The groups principle activities include exploring and producing precious metals. The group operates from United States.

Primary SIC and add'l.: NA

CIK No: 0001208038

Subsidiaries: Calumet Mining Company, Western Goldfields (Canada) Inc., Western Mesquite Mines, Inc.

Officers: Raymond W. Threlkeld/Dir., CEO, Pres., Ray Threlkeld/CEO, Pres., Julie Taylor Pantziris/Dir. - Investor Relations, Graham Desson/60/Controller, Sec., Brian W. Penny/CFO, Paul G. Semple/VP - Projects, Wesley C. Hanson/VP - Mine Development

Directors: Raymond W. Threlkeld/Dir., CEO, Pres., Randall Oliphant/Chmn., Gerald Ruth/Dir., Vahan Kololian/Dir., Martyn Konig/Dir.

Owners: Gerald Ruth/1.71%, Graham Desson/0.30%, Insiders/11.68%, Randall Oliphant/5.14%, Ray Threlkeld/1.18%, Hospah Coal Company/5.40%, Investec Bank (UK) Limited/8.23%, RAB Special Situations/5.35%, Vahan Kololian/1.55%, Wesley Hanson/0.15%, Brian Penny/1.03%, Paul Semple/0.41%, Martyn Konig/0.89%

Financial Data: Fiscal Year End:12/31   Latest Annual Data: 12/31/2006

Year	Sales	Net Income
2006	$7,859,000	-$11,583,000
2005	$9,024,000	-$3,340,000
2004	$9,795,000	-$4,419,000

Curr. Assets:	$7,079,000	**Curr. Liab.:**	$2,530,000		
Plant, Equip.:	$7,209,000	**Total Liab.:**	$7,335,000	**Indic. Yr. Divd.:**	NA
Total Assets:	$22,214,000	**Net Worth:**	$14,879,000	**Debt/ Equity:**	NA

Western Massachusetts Electric Co

PO Box 2010, West Springfield, MA, 01090; **PH:** 1-413-785-5871; *http://* www.wmeco.com;
Email: WMECOWebMaster@nu.com

General - Incorporation	MA	**Stock** - Price on:12/24/2007	$28.7
Employees	5,869	Stock Exchange	NDQ
Auditor	Deloitte & Touche LLP	Ticker Symbol	NUCO
Stk Agt	NA	Outstanding Shares	154,550,000
Counsel	NA	E.P.S.	NA
DUNS No.	00-695-6551	Shareholders	NA

Business: The group's principle activities are to generate, transmit and distribute electric services. The group operates, maintains transmission and distribution of franchised retail electric service in New Hampshire and western Massachusetts. The group is generating revenue from wholesale and retail sales in the domestic market. The group is a wholly owned subsidiary of northeast utilities.

Primary SIC and add'l.: 4911

CIK No: 0000106170

Subsidiaries: CL&P Funding LLC, CL&P Receivables Corporation, E. S. Boulos Company, Holyoke Power and Electric Company, Holyoke Water Power Company, Mode 1 Communications, Inc., North Atlantic Energy Corporation, North Atlantic Energy Service Corporation, Northeast Generation Company, Northeast Generation Services Company, Northeast Nuclear Energy Company, Northeast Utilities (a Massachusetts business trust), Northeast Utilities Service Company, NU Enterprises, Inc., PSNH Funding LLC 29 Subsidiaries included in the Index

Officers: Leon J. Olivier/59/Dir., CEO, Gregory B. Butler/50/Sr. VP, General Counsel, Rodney O. Powell/Dir., COO, Pres., David R. McHale/47/CFO, Sr. VP, Frank Vancini/Mgr. - Operations Support, Chuck Dooley/Mgr. - Construction, Maintenance, Ted Pleasant/Mgr. - System Operations, Shirley M. Payne/56/VP - Accounting, Controller, Stan Doe/Mgr. - System Planning, Richard Oswald/Mgr. - Conservation, Load Management, Bliss A. Young/Dir. - Operations, Michael T. Smith/Dir. - Operations Support, Engineering Compliance, Linda Sullivan/Mgr. - Operations Planning, Performance Analysis, Denise Vogel/Mgr. - Customer Operations, East Springfield, Doug Clarke/Mgr. - Customer Operations, Hadley, Greenfield *(16 Officers included in Index)*

Directors: Leon J. Olivier/59/Dir., CEO, Charles W. Shivery/62/Chmn., Rodney O. Powell/Dir., COO, Pres.

Financial Data: *Fiscal Year End:*12/31   *Latest Annual Data:* 12/31/2006

Year	Sales	Net Income
2006	$1,481,843,000	$346,993,000
2005	$7,397,390,000	-$253,488,000
2004	$6,686,699,000	$122,147,000

Curr. Assets:	$1,731,051,000	**Curr. Liab.:**	$1,363,835,000		
Plant, Equip.:	$6,242,186,000	**Total Liab.:**	$8,388,857,000	**Indic. Yr. Divd.:**	$0.800
Total Assets:	$11,303,236,000	**Net Worth:**	$2,798,179,000	**Debt/ Equity:**	1.5860

Western Power & Equipment Corp

6407B N.E., 117th Ave., Vancouver, WA, 98662; *PH:* 1-360-253-2346; *Fax:* 1-360-253-4830; *http://* www.wpec.com

General - Incorporation	DE	**Stock**- Price on:12/24/2007	$0.2
Employees	243	Stock Exchange	OTC
Auditor	Marcum & Kliegman LLP	Ticker Symbol	WPEC
Stk Agt	Corporate Stock Transfer, Inc.	Outstanding Shares	11,230,000
Counsel	NA	E.P.S.	-$1.32
DUNS No.	79-661-2430	Shareholders	NA

Business: The group's principal activities are to market, rent and service light medium-sized and heavy construction, agricultural, industrial equipment and related products. The products sold, rented and serviced by the group include backhoes, excavators, crawler dozers, skid steer loaders, forklifts, compactors, log loaders, trenchers, street sweepers, sewer vacuums and mobile highway signs. The equipment distributed by the group is furnished to contractors, governmental agencies and other customers, primarily for use in the construction of residential and commercial buildings, roads, levees, dams, underground power projects, forestry projects, municipal construction and other projects. On 15-Sep-2004, the group acquired Arizona pacific materials llc.

Primary SIC and add'l.: 1629 7699

CIK No: 0000939729

Subsidiaries: Arizona Pacific Materials, LLC, an Arizona Limited Liability Company, Western Power & Equipment Corp., an Oregon corporation

Officers: Dean C. McLain/55/Chmn., CEO, Pres., Mark J. Wright/CFO, VP - Finance, Treasurer, Sec.

Directors: Dean C. McLain/55/Chmn., CEO, Pres., Mark J. Wright/CFO, VP - Finance, Treasurer, Sec., Michael Metter/56/Dir., Steven Moskowitz/44/Dir., James Fisher/72/Dir.

Owners: Mark J. Wright/1.80%, Steven Moskowitz/1.30%, Potomac Capital Management, LLC/6.10%, Michel Metter/1.30%, JSC, LLC/5.00%, CPW Stock Trust/7.40%, The Rubin Family Irrevocable Stock/27.10%, Robert M. Rubin/6.30%, James Fisher/0.90%, Dean C. McLain/16.70%, SLM Stock Trust/7.40%, Costa Brava Partnership/7.80%, Insiders/22.00%

Financial Data: *Fiscal Year End:*07/31   *Latest Annual Data:* 07/31/2007

Year	Sales	Net Income
2007	$96,824,000	-$12,781,000
2006	$123,007,000	-$3,967,000
2005	$117,222,000	$2,490,000

Curr. Assets:	$53,443,000	**Curr. Liab.:**	$42,868,000		
Plant, Equip.:	$8,653,000	**Total Liab.:**	$59,479,000	**Indic. Yr. Divd.:**	NA
Total Assets:	$64,603,000	**Net Worth:**	$5,124,000	**Debt/ Equity:**	NA

Western Refining Inc

6500 Trowbridge Dr.', El Paso, TX, 79905; *PH:* 1-915-775-3300; *Fax:* 1-915-881-0002; *http://* www.westernrefining.com

General - Incorporation	DE	**Stock**- Price on:12/24/2007	$55
Employees	416	Stock Exchange	NYSE
Auditor	Ernst & Young LLP	Ticker Symbol	WNR
Stk Agt	American Stock Transfer & Trust Co.	Outstanding Shares	68,210,000
Counsel	NA	E.P.S.	$4.67
DUNS No.	NA	Shareholders	NA

Business: The groups principal activities include producing and marketing refined crude oil and its products. The groups specific customers are Chevron, Phoenix Fuel and PMI. The group operates from the United States.

Primary SIC and add'l.: 2911

CIK No: 0001339048

Subsidiaries: Ascarte Group, LLC, Western Refining Company, L.P., Western Refining GP, LLC, Western Refining LP, LLC

Officers: Paul L. Foster/Chmn., CEO, Pres., Jeff A. Stevens/Dir., Exec. VP, Mark J. Smith/Exec. VP - Refining, Scott D. Weaver/Dir., Chief Administrative Officer, Assist. Sec. - Investor, Gary R. Dalke/CFO, Lowry Barfield/Sr. VP - Legal, General Counsel, Sec., Mark Cox/Dir. - Investor Relations, Sr. VP, Treasurer

Directors: Paul L. Foster/Chmn., CEO, Pres., Jeff A. Stevens/Dir., Exec. VP, Scott D. Weaver/Dir., Chief Administrative Officer, Assist. Sec. - Investor, Carin M. Barth/Dir., Frederick L. Francis/Dir., Brian J. Hogan/Dir., William D. Sanders/Dir., Ralph A. Schmidt/Dir.

Owners: Insiders, Carin M. Barth, FMR Corp., Scott D. Weaver, Paul L. Foster, Ralph A. Schmidt, Mark J. Smith, Brian J. Hogan, William D. Sanders, Frederick L. Francis, Gary R. Dalke, WRC Refining Company, Jeff A. Stevens, RHC Holdings, L.P., Lowry Barfield

Financial Data: *Fiscal Year End:*12/31   *Latest Annual Data:* 12/31/2006

Year	Sales	Net Income
2006	$4,199,474,000	$204,780,000
2005	NA	-$33,000

Curr. Assets:	$620,693,000	**Curr. Liab.:**	$343,985,000	**P/E Ratio:**	12.73
Plant, Equip.:	$255,877,000	**Total Liab.:**	$386,922,000	**Indic. Yr. Divd.:**	$0.240
Total Assets:	$908,523,000	**Net Worth:**	$521,601,000	**Debt/ Equity:**	NA

Western Reserve Bank

4015 Medina Rd. , Ste 100, Medina, OH, 44256; *PH:* 1-330-764-1049; *http://* www.westernreservebank.com

General - Incorporation	OH	**Stock**- Price on:12/24/2007	NA
Employees	28	Stock Exchange	OTC
Auditor	Crowe Chizek & Co. LLC	Ticker Symbol	WRBO
Stk Agt	NA	Outstanding Shares	NA
Counsel	NA	E.P.S.	NA
DUNS No.	NA	Shareholders	NA

Business: The group's principal activities are to lend loans and accept deposit in medina county, Ohio. The deposit services include non-interest bearing and interest-bearing checking accounts, savings and money market accounts, time certificates of deposit and individual retirement accounts. The lending activities include commercial loans to businesses, consumer loans to individuals for household, family and other personal expenditures and real estate loans including first mortgage loans, home equity loans and construction loans. It also offers other services which include credit, debit and ATM cards with access to regional and national automated teller networks, a courier service for business deposits, cash management services, safe deposit boxes, cashiers checks, traveler's checks and an ATM. The group operates through a full-service and two satellite offices in retirement communities in medina.

Primary SIC and add'l.: 6022 6712

CIK No: 0001051473

Officers: Edward McKeon/CEO, Pres., Travis Christoffer/VP - Lending, Credit, Ed McGannon/VP - Lending, Credit, Carole Moore/Administrative Assist. - Lending, Credit, Sandi Best/Retail Banking Officer - Brecksville, Lisa Schroeder/Retail Banking Officer - Brecksville, Sharon Repine/Accounting Assist. - Accounting, Operations, Marcia Harmon/Interim Assist. Controller - Accounting, Operations, Brian K. Harr/Sr. VP - Lending, Lending, Credit, Mike Gorman/Lending, Credit, Brecksville Regional Pres., Sue Gibson/Loan Administrator - Lending, Credit, Kate Zenczak/Lending, Credit, Linda Moscalink/Lending, Credit, Robin Bement/Loan Administration Officer - Lending, Credit, Hope Krueger/AVP - Lending, Credit *(38 Officers included in Index)*

Directors: P. M. Jones/Chmn., Bijay Jayaswal/Dir., Glenn Smith/Dir., Ray Laribee/Dir., Richard C. Lynham/Dir., Michael Rose/Dir., Roland Bauer/Dir., Rory O'Neil/Dir., Hal R. Nichols/Dir., Thomas Tubbs/Dir., Victoria Burns/Member - Brecksville Advisory Board, Mike Torchia/Member - Brecksville Advisory Board

Owners: Rory H. ONeil/4.67%, James P. McCready/5.53%, Michael R. Rose/2.70%, Thomas A. Tubbs/3.24%, Roland H. Bauer/6.01%, Hal R. Nichols/2.59%, Brian K. Harr/1.25%, Cynthia A. Mahl/1.39%, Bijay K. Jayaswal/1.76%, Ray E. Laribee/2.47%, Glenn M. Smith/4.71%, Richard C. Lynham/1.62%, Insiders/31.29%, Edward J. McKeon/7.27%, P.M. Jones/2.04%

Curr. Assets:	$21,426,000	**Curr. Liab.:**	$131,184,000		
Plant, Equip.:	$1,503,000	**Total Liab.:**	$131,184,000	**Indic. Yr. Divd.:**	NA
Total Assets:	$144,115,000	**Net Worth:**	$12,931,000	**Debt/ Equity:**	NA

Western Sierra Bancorp

4080 Plz. Goldorado Cir., Cameron Park, CA, 95682; *PH:* 1-530-677-5600; *http://* www.umpquaholdingscorp.com

General - Incorporation	CA	**Stock**- Price on:12/24/2007	$24.38
Employees	1,530	Stock Exchange	NA
Auditor	Perry-Smith LLP	Ticker Symbol	NA
Stk Agt	Lillick & Charles LLP	Outstanding Shares	57,870,000
Counsel	NA	E.P.S.	NA
DUNS No.	NA	Shareholders	NA

Business: The group's principal activity is to offer a broad range of services to individuals and businesses in its primary service areas. The group provides a full line of consumer services and also offers specialized services, such as courier services to small businesses, middle market companies and professional firms. The group offers personal and business checking, savings accounts, money market accounts, ira accounts, time certificates of deposit and direct deposit of social security, pension and payroll checks, computer cash management and Internet banking. In addition, it also provides commercial, construction, accounts receivable, inventory, automobile, home improvement, real estate, sba, leasehold improvement, installment and credit card loans. On 11-Jul-2003, the group acquired central sierra bank and on 12-Dec-2003, it acquired auburn community bank.

Primary SIC and add'l.: 6712 6021

CIK No: 0001072688

Subsidiaries: Auburn Community Bank, Central California Bank, Lake Community Bank, Sentinel Associates, Inc., Western Sierra National Bank

Financial Data: *Fiscal Year End:*12/31   *Latest Annual Data:* 12/31/2006

Year	Sales	Net Income
2006	$459,559,000	$84,447,000
2005	$330,058,000	$69,735,000
2004	$239,431,000	$47,166,000

Curr. Assets:	$372,287,000	**Curr. Liab.:**	$5,888,279,000		
Plant, Equip.:	$101,830,000	**Total Liab.:**	$6,188,025,000	**Indic. Yr. Divd.:**	$0.720
Total Assets:	$7,344,236,000	**Net Worth:**	$1,156,211,000	**Debt/ Equity:**	0.1823

Western Sizzlin Corp

PO Box 12167, Roanoke, VA, 24023; *PH:* 1-540-345-3195; *Fax:* 1-800-247-8325; *http://* www.western-sizzlin.com

General - Incorporation	DE	**Stock**- Price on:12/24/2007	$15.23
Employees	290	Stock Exchange	OTC
Auditor	Grant Thornton LLP	Ticker Symbol	WSZL
Stk Agt	First National Bank of Omaha	Outstanding Shares	1,790,000
Counsel	NA	E.P.S.	$0.33
DUNS No.	NA	Shareholders	NA

Business: The group's principal activity is to franchise and operate restaurants. The group operates and/or franchises the austins steaks & saloon, western sizzlin, western sizzlin wood grill, great American steak & buffet, quincy steakhouses and market street buffet and bakery concepts. The group operates and franchises a total of 159 restaurants located in 21 states, including 7 company-owned and 152 franchise restaurants as of Jun 30, 2004. The group's restaurants are currently located in the states of Alabama, Arizona, Arkansas, Colorado, Florida, Georgia, Illinois, Kansas, Kentucky, Louisiana, Maryland, Mississippi, Missouri, Nebraska, New Mexico, North Carolina, Ohio, Oklahoma, Pennsylvania, South Carolina, Tennessee, Texas, Virginia and west Virginia.

Primary SIC and add'l.: 5812 5813

CIK No: 0000930686

Subsidiaries: Austins 72nd, Inc., Austins Albuquerque East, Inc., Austins Albuquerque, Inc., Austins Lincoln, Inc., Austins New Mexico, Inc., Austins Old Market, Inc., Austins Omaha, Inc., Austins Scottsdale, Inc., Missouri Development Company, The WesterN SizzliN Stores of Little Rock, Inc., The WesterN SizzliN Stores of Louisiana, Inc., The WesterN SizzliN Stores, Inc., WesterN SizzliN Stores of Virginia, Inc.

Officers: Sardar Biglari/30/Chmn., CEO, James C. Verney/55/Pres./$272,000.00, Robyn B. Mabe/46/VP, CFO, Sec., Treasurer/$131,000.00

Directors: Sardar Biglari/30/Chmn., CEO, Philip L. Cooley/64/Vice Chmn., Jonathan Dash/29/Dir., Titus W. Greene/70/Dir., Kenneth R. Cooper/63/Dir.

Owners: Sardar Biglari/34.30%, Titus W. Greene/1.10%, Philip L. Cooley, Kenneth R. Cooper, Robyn B. Mabe, Jonathan Dash/27.20%, James C. Verney/1.50%

Financial Data: ***Fiscal Year End:***12/31 ***Latest Annual Data:*** 12/31/2006

Year	Sales	Net Income
2006	$17,404,000	$274,000
2005	$19,372,000	$681,000
2004	$21,708,000	$566,000

Curr. Assets:	$4,510,000	***Curr. Liab.:***	$1,273,000	***P/E Ratio:***	46.15
Plant, Equip.:	$2,270,000	***Total Liab.:***	$2,422,000	***Indic. Yr. Divd.:***	NA
Total Assets:	$19,820,000	***Net Worth:***	$17,398,000	***Debt/ Equity:***	0.0373

Western Standard Energy Corp

Formerly: Lusora Healthcare Systems Inc

Sheraton St., London, W1K 3AJ; ***PH:*** 44-207-479-4800; ***http://*** www.lusora.com

General - Incorporation	NV	***Stock***- Price on:12/24/2007	$0.45
Employees	NA	Stock Exchange	NA
Auditor	Dale Matheson Carr-Hilton LaBonte LLP	Ticker Symbol	NA
Stk Agt	Nevada Agency & Trust Company	Outstanding Shares	57,280,000
Counsel	NA	E.P.S	NA
DUNS No.	NA	Shareholders	NA

Business: The groups principal activities include developing and deploying wireless smart sensors for security, monitoring and home healthcare applications. The group operates from the United States.

Primary SIC and add'l.: 1382

CIK No: 0001343254

Officers: Dan Bauer/CEO, Pres., Julian Lee/CFO

Directors: Dan Bauer/CEO, Pres.

Owners: Insiders/35.74%, Joseph Bauer/3.22%, Dan Bauer/1.70%, Julian Lee/3.22%, Dan Bauer/30.82%

Western Union Company (The)

12500 E Belford Ave., Englewood, CO, 80112; ***PH:*** 1-720-332-1000; ***Fax:*** 1-720-332-4753; ***https://*** wumt.westernunion.com

General - Incorporation	DE	***Stock***- Price on:12/24/2007	$21.98
Employees	5,900	Stock Exchange	NYSE
Auditor	Ernst & Young LLP	Ticker Symbol	WU
Stk Agt	Western Union money	Outstanding Shares	772,660,000
Counsel	NA	E.P.S	$1.07
DUNS No.	NA	Shareholders	NA

Business: The groups principle activity is to transfer money. The groups services marketed under the brand name The Western Union(R). The group operates through two segments namely, consumer-to-consumer money transfer services and consumer-to-business payment services. In the year 2006, the group acquired Servicio Electrnico de Pago S.A. The group operates from the United States. The groups quarterly revenue for September 2007 was 1,257.20 millions of USD.

Primary SIC and add'l.: 7374 7389 7379 4822 6099

CIK No: 0001365135

Subsidiaries: American Rapid Corporation, Dyoser Investments SL, E Commerce Group Products Inc., E Commerce Group, Inc., E-Pago Fcil SA, FDI Merchant Services Holding CV, Finanzadirecto.com, Inc., First Data (Hellas) International Holdings SA, First Data DSOS Holding (Bermuda) Limited, First Data DSOS Management (Bermuda) Limited, First Data POS Deutschland GbR, First Financial Management Corporation, FirstDataCashCardAcquisitionPartnership, FirstDataDSOS(Bermuda)HoldingFinanceLimited, FirstDataDSOSHolding(Bermuda)Ltd.&Co.OEG 90 Subsidiaries included in the Index

Officers: Christina A. Gold/Dir., CEO, Pres./$4,913.90, Royal Cole/Exec. VP, GM - Payment Services, Hikmet Ersek/Exec. VP, MD - Europe, Middle East, Africa, South Asia/$1,194.90, Robin Heller/Exec. VP - Operations, Information Technology, Ian Marsh/Exec. VP, MD - Asia Pacific Region, Anne McCarthy/Exec. VP - Corporate Affairs, Scott T. Scheirman/CFO, Exec. VP/$1,008.50, Grover Wray/Exec. VP - Human Resources, Dan Diaz/Corporate Communications, US, Canada, Amintore T.X. Schenkel/Chief Accounting Officer, Sr. VP, Controller, Gail Galuppo/Chief Marketing Officer, Exec. VP, David Schlapbach/Exec. VP, General Counsel, Sec., Liz Alicea-Velez/Exec. VP - Latin America, Caribbean, Sherry Johnson/Corporate Communications, Christopher Fischer/Sr. Counsel, Emeasa *(29 Officers included in Index)*

Directors: Christina A. Gold/Dir., CEO, Pres., Jack M. Greenberg/Non - Exec. Chmn., Dinyar S. Devitre/Dir., Hikmet Ersek/Exec. VP, MD - Europe, Middle East, Africa, South Asia, Ian Marsh/Exec. VP, MD - Asia Pacific Region, Betsy D. Holden/Dir., Alan J. Lacy/Dir., Linda Fayne Levinson/Dir., Roberto G. Mendoza/Dir., Michael A. Miles/Dir., Dennis Stevenson/Dir.

Owners: Linda Fayne Levinson, Guy A. Battista, Scott T. Scheirman, Alan J. Lacy, Insiders, Christina A. Gold, William D. Thomas, FMR Corp/6.90%, Betsy D. Holden, Wellington Management Company, LLP/5.40%, David G. Barnes, Dinyar S. Devitre, Jack M. Greenberg, Michael A. Miles, Dennis Stevenson *(17 Owners included in Index)*

Financial Data: ***Fiscal Year End:***12/31 ***Latest Annual Data:*** 12/31/2006

Year	Sales	Net Income
2006	$4,470,200,000	$914,000,000
2005	$3,987,900,000	$927,400,000
2004	$3,547,600,000	$751,600,000

Curr. Assets:	$1,576,200,000	***Curr. Liab.:***	$554,800,000	***P/E Ratio:***	19.63
Plant, Equip.:	$176,100,000	***Total Liab.:***	$5,635,900,000	***Indic. Yr. Divd.:***	$0.040
Total Assets:	$5,321,100,000	***Net Worth:***	-$314,800,000	***Debt/ Equity:***	NA

Westfield Financial Inc

PO Box 1626, Westfield, MA, 01086; ***PH:*** 1-413-568-1911; ***http://*** www.westfieldbank.com

General - Incorporation	MA	***Stock***- Price on:12/24/2007	$10.14
Employees	136	Stock Exchange	NDQ
Auditor	Wolf & Co., P.c.	Ticker Symbol	WFD
Stk Agt	Registrar & Transfer Co	Outstanding Shares	31,930,000
Counsel	NA	E.P.S	$0.65
DUNS No.	NA	Shareholders	NA

Business: The group's principal activities are to provide banking products and services to businesses and individuals. The deposit products include regular savings deposits, interest-bearing demand accounts, noninterest-bearing demand accounts, money market accounts and time deposits. The loan portfolio includes residential real estate loans, home equity loans, commercial real estate loans, commercial and industrial loans and consumer loans. The activities are carried out through 10 banking offices in agawam, east longmeadow, holyoke, southwick, springfield, west springfield and westfield, Massachusetts.

Primary SIC and add'l.: 6712 6035

CIK No: 0001157647

Subsidiaries: Real Estate Investments, Inc, Westfield Bank

Officers: Donald A. Williams/Chmn., CEO/$1,021,560.00, Michael J. Janosco/CFO, Investor Relations Officer/$440,451.00, James C. Hagan/COO, Pres./$323,416.00

Directors: Donald A. Williams/Chmn., CEO, Victor J. Carra/Dir., David C. Colton/Dir., Robert T. Crowley/Dir., Harry C. Lane/Dir., William H. McClure/Dir., Mary C. O'Neil/Dir., Richard C. Placek/Dir., Paul R. Pohl/Dir., Charles E. Sullivan/Dir., Thomas C. Sullivan/Dir.

Owners: Donald A. Williams/2.20%, Alan J. Miles, Victor J. Carra, David C. Colton, Charles E. Sullivan, Employee Stock Option Plan Trust of Westfield Financial, Inc./6.30%, Mary C. O'Neil, James C. Hagan, Thomas C. Sullivan, Paul R. Pohl, Rebecca A. Kozaczka, Insiders/12.00%, William H. McClure, Richard C. Placek, Harry C. Lane *(17 Owners included in Index)*

Financial Data: ***Fiscal Year End:***12/31 ***Latest Annual Data:*** 12/31/2006

Year	Sales	Net Income
2006	$45,508,000	$4,654,000
2005	$40,678,000	$6,219,000
2004	$38,324,000	$6,323,000

Curr. Assets:	$159,010,000	***Curr. Liab.:***	$700,385,000	***P/E Ratio:***	17.79
Plant, Equip.:	$12,247,000	***Total Liab.:***	$707,421,000	***Indic. Yr. Divd.:***	$0.200
Total Assets:	$996,829,000	***Net Worth:***	$289,408,000	***Debt/ Equity:***	NA

Westinghouse Air Brake Technologies Corp

1001 Air Brake Ave., Wilmerding, PA, 15148; ***PH:*** 1-412-825-1000; ***http://*** www.wabtec.com

General - Incorporation	DE	***Stock***- Price on:12/24/2007	$37.96
Employees	5,317	Stock Exchange	NYSE
Auditor	Ernst & Young LLP	Ticker Symbol	WAB
Stk Agt	LaSalle Bank Shareholder Services	Outstanding Shares	48,700,000
Counsel	Reed Smith LLP	E.P.S	$1.98
DUNS No.	61-292-6675	Shareholders	NA

Business: The group's principal activities are to manufacture and provide technology-based equipment and services for locomotives, railway freight cars and passenger transit vehicles. The products of the group include electronic controls and monitors, air brakes, traction motors, cooling equipment, turbochargers, low-horsepower locomotives, couplers, door controls, draft gears and brake shoes. The group operates through two divisions: the freight group and the transit group. The freight group manufactures products and provides services geared to the production and operation of freight cars and locomotives including braking control equipment, engines, traction motors, on-board electronic systems and train coupler equipment. The transit group provides products for passenger transit vehicles especially subways, rail and buses that include braking and monitoring systems, climate control and door equipment.

Primary SIC and add'l.: 3743 9900 3559

CIK No: 0000943452

Subsidiaries: Alinco, Allied Friction Products Australia Pty Ltd., Cobra Europe S.A.S., CoFren S.r.l., CosRail GmbH, Evand Pty Ltd., F.I.P. Pty Ltd., FrenTec S.A.S., Intermodal Trailer Express, Inc., Jinwu Control Systems Co. Ltd., MotivePower, Inc., Pioneer Friction Limited, Railroad Friction Products Corporation, RFPC Holding Corporation, Vapor Europe S.r.l. 30 Subsidiaries included in the Index

Officers: Albert J. Neupaver/56/Dir., CEO, Pres./$3,595,059.00, Robert S. Andress/VP, GM - Vapor Bus International, Luigi Camellini/MD - Vapor Europe, Karl-Heinz Colmer/MD - Becorit Gmbh, Michael E. Ring/GM - Cardwell Westinghouse, Jason T. Connell/VP - Marketing Freight Group, Brian L. Cunkelman/VP, GM - Wabtec Global Services, Tapas Das Gupta/MD - PFL Ltd, Barry L. Anderson/VP, GM Schaefer Equipment, Chris Katakouzinos/GM - FIP, James C. Hoffner/VP, GM - Wabtec Passenger Transit, Ronald L. Witt/VP, GM - Wabtec International , John D. Meehan/MD - Wabtec Rail, Mark R. Cox/VP - Corporate Development, Gerald M. Rowe/Pres. - Vapor Stone Rail Systems *(34 Officers included in Index)*

Directors: Albert J. Neupaver/56/Dir., CEO, Pres., William E. Kassling/Chmn., Emilio A. Fernandez/Vice Chmn., Michael W.D. Howell/Dir., Gary C. Valade/Dir., Robert J. Brooks/Dir., Lee B. Foster/Dir., James V. Napier/Dir., Brian P. Hehir/Dir., Nickolas W. Vande Steeg/Dir.

Owners: Emilio A. Fernandez/1.30%, Gary C. Valade, Lee B. Foster, Albert J. Neupaver, Barry L. Pennypacker, Insiders/7.20%, Alvaro Garcia-Tunon, William E. Kassling/3.50%, Michael W.D. Howell, Robert J. Brooks, Anthony J. Carpani, Timothy J. Logan, James V. Napier

Financial Data: ***Fiscal Year End:***12/31 ***Latest Annual Data:*** 12/31/2006

Year	Sales	Net Income
2006	$1,087,620,000	$84,804,000
2005	$1,034,024,000	$55,776,000
2004	$822,018,000	$32,445,000

Curr. Assets:	$547,191,000	***Curr. Liab.:***	$243,791,000	***P/E Ratio:***	19.17
Plant, Equip.:	$178,309,000	***Total Liab.:***	$502,953,000	***Indic. Yr. Divd.:***	$0.040
Total Assets:	$972,842,000	***Net Worth:***	$469,889,000	***Debt/ Equity:***	0.3000

Westlake Chemical Corp

2801 Post Oak Blvd., Ste. 600, Houston, TX, 77056; *PH:* 1-713-960-9111;
http:// www.westlakechemical.com

General - Incorporation	DE	Stock - Price on:12/24/2007	$27.94
Employees	2,056	Stock Exchange	NYSE
Auditor	PricewaterhouseCoopers LLP	Ticker Symbol	WLK
Stk Agt	American Stock Transfer & Trust Co.	Outstanding Shares	65,470,000
Counsel	NA	E.P.S.	$2.50
DUNS No.	NA	Shareholders	NA

Business: The group's principle activities include manufacturing and marketing basic chemicals, vinyls, polymers and fabricated products. The group operates through two business segments namely olefins and vinyls. The group operates from United States.

Primary SIC and add'l.: 2869 5162 2899

CIK No: 0001262823

Subsidiaries: Geismar Holdings, Inc., GVGP, Inc., North American Bristol Corporation, North American Pipe Corporation, Van Buren Pipe Corporation, Westech Building Products Limited, Westech Building Products, Inc., Westech Profiles Limited, Westlake Chemical Holdings, Inc., Westlake Chemical Investments, Inc., Westlake Chemical Manufacturing, Inc., Westlake Chemical Products, Inc., Westlake Development Corporation, Westlake International Corporation, Westlake International Investments Corporation 30 Subsidiaries included in the Index

Officers: Albert Chao/Dir., CEO, Pres., Jeffrey L. Taylor/VP - Polyethylene, George J. Mangieri/VP, Chief Accounting Officer, Stephen Wallace/VP, General Counsel, Sec., Warren W. Wilder/Sr. VP - Olefins, Wayne D. Morse/Sr. VP - Vinyls, Steven M. Bender/CFO, VP, Treasurer, David R. Hansen/Sr. VP - Administration, Donald M. Condon/Sr. VP - Corporate Planning, Business Development

Directors: Albert Chao/Dir., CEO, Pres., James Chao/Chmn., Gilbert R. Whitaker/76/Dir., Dorothy C. Jenkins/Dir., Robert T. Blakely/Dir., William E. Barnett/Dir., Max L. Lukens/Dir.

Owners: James Chao, Insiders, Albert Chao, TTWF LP/70.27%, Dorothy C. Jenkins, Wayne D. Morse, Stephen Wallace, Barclays Global Investors, NA/13.00%, Gilbert R. Whitaker, Max L. Lukens, David R. Hansen, William E. Barnett, Robert T. Blakely

Financial Data: *Fiscal Year End:* 12/31   *Latest Annual Data:* 12/31/2006

Year	Sales	Net Income
2006	$2,484,366,000	$194,559,000
2005	$2,441,105,000	$226,817,000
2004	$1,985,353,000	$120,722,000

Curr. Assets:	$849,787,000	Curr. Liab.:	$321,912,000	P/E Ratio:	11.18
Plant, Equip.:	$1,076,903,000	Total Liab.:	$908,557,000	Indic. Yr. Divd.:	$0.160
Total Assets:	$2,082,098,000	Net Worth:	$1,173,541,000	Debt/ Equity:	0.2357

Westland Development Co Inc

401 Coors Blvd. NW, Albuquerque, NM, 87121; *PH:* 1-505-832-9600; *http://* www.westlandnm.com

General - Incorporation	NM	Stock - Price on:12/24/2007	NA
Employees	NA	Stock Exchange	NA
Auditor	Grant Thornton LLP	Ticker Symbol	NA
Stk Agt	NA	Outstanding Shares	NA
Counsel	NA	E.P.S.	NA
DUNS No.	07-577-3259	Shareholders	NA

Business: The group's principle activities are to develop, market and lease its real estate holdings, most of which are located near albuquerque, New Mexico. Revenue consist primarily of proceeds from land sales and governmental condemnations and rentals from developed properties, such as single-tenant retail stores and office space. Land sales are primarily to commercial developers and others in the albuquerque area and certain governmental agencies.

Primary SIC and add'l.: 6552 6512 6519

CIK No: 0000106423

Subsidiaries: SCC Acquisitions, Inc.

Officers: Barbara Page/CEO, Pres., CFO, Sosimo Padilla/Chmn., Exec. VP, Joe Chavez/70/Sec., Treasurer, Linda Blair/VP, Brent Lesley/VP - Marketing, Fred Ambrogi/VP - in Development Division, Leroy J. Chavez/VP - Development

Directors: Sosimo Padilla/Chmn., Exec. VP, Joe Chavez/70/Sec., Treasurer

Westmoreland Coal Co

2 N Cascade Ave., 14th Fl., Colorado Springs, CO, 80903; *PH:* 1-719-442-2600;
Fax: 1-719-448-5824; *http://* www.westmoreland.com

General - Incorporation	DE	Stock - Price on:12/24/2007	$26.76
Employees	1,176	Stock Exchange	AMEX
Auditor	KPMG LLP	Ticker Symbol	WLB
Stk Agt.	Computershare Trust Co	Outstanding Shares	9,070,000
Counsel	NA	E.P.S.	-$1.67
DUNS No.	00-791-4930	Shareholders	NA

Business: The group's principal activity is to produce and market coal from coal surface mines in Montana, North Dakota and Texas. It owns five mines: absaloka mine, rosebud mine, jewett mine, beulah mine and savage mine. The group also owns interests in cogeneration and other non-regulated independent power plants. The group's major customers include Texas genco and the owners of colstrip units 3&4, which includes avista corporation, northwestern corporation, pacificorp, portland general electric company, ppl Montana llc and puget sound energy inc.

Primary SIC and add'l.: 1220 4930 1241 1222

CIK No: 0000106455

Subsidiaries: Basin Resources, Inc., Cleancoal Terminal Co., Criterion Coal Co., Dakota Westmoreland Corporation, Deane Processing Co., Eastern Coal and Coke Co., Horizon Coal Services, Inc., Kentucky Criterion Coal Company, North Central Energy Company, Pine Branch Mining Inc., Texas Westmoreland Coal Co., WEI - Fort Lupton, Inc., WEI - Rensselaer, Inc., WEI - Roanoke Valley, Inc., Western Energy Company 28 Subsidiaries included in the Index

Officers: Mark K. Seglem/VP - Strategic Planning, Administration, Colorado Springs, CO, Mary Stoik Dymond/VP - Human Resources, Risk Management, Colorado Springs, CO, Kevin A. Paprzycki/Controller - Colorado Springs, CO, Morris W. Kegley/General Counsel, Assist. Sec. - Colorado Springs, CO, Thomas G. Durham/VP - Planning, Engineering, Colorado Springs, CO, John

V. O'Laughlin/VP - Coal Operations, Colstrip, TX/$341,165.00, Ronald H. Beck/VP - Finance, Treasurer - Colorado Springs, CO, Todd A. Myers/VP - Coal Sales, Colorado Springs, CO, Diane S. Jones/VP - Corporate Relations, Sec. - Colorado Springs, CO, Douglas P. Kathol/VP - Development, Colorado Springs, CO, David J. Blair/CFO - Colorado Springs, CO/$411,166.00

Directors: Keith E. Alessi/Dir., Robert E. Killen/Dir., William M. Stern/Dir., Thomas J. Coffey/Dir., Richard M. Klingaman/Dir.

Owners: Richard M. Klingaman, Insiders/7.80%, David J. Blair, William M. Stern, Christopher K. Seglem/4.50%, Robert W. Holzwarth, Jeffrey L. Gendell/17.00%, Keith E. Alessi, Donald A. Tortorice, Roger D. Wiegley, Thomas W. Ostrander/1.20%, Thomas J. Coffey, John V. OLaughlin, Robert E. Killen/2.60%, Wellington Management/6.10% *(17 Owners included in Index)*

Financial Data: *Fiscal Year End:* 12/31   *Latest Annual Data:* 12/31/2006

Year	Sales	Net Income
2006	$441,386,000	-$7,593,000
2005	$373,744,000	-$5,934,000
2004	$333,032,000	$4,460,000

Curr. Assets:	$128,020,000	Curr. Liab.:	$195,382,000		
Plant, Equip.:	$431,452,000	Total Liab.:	$882,065,000	Indic. Yr. Divd.:	NA
Total Assets:	$761,382,000	Net Worth:	-$126,185,000	Debt/ Equity:	NA

Westpac Banking Corp

575 5th Ave., 39th Fl., New York, NY, 10017; *PH:* 1-212-551-1800; *Fax:* 1-212-551-1999;
http:// www.westpac.com.au

General - Incorporation	Australia	Stock- Price on:12/24/2007	$108.66
Employees	27,224	Stock Exchange	NYSE
Auditor	PricewaterhouseCoopers LLP	Ticker Symbol	WBK
Stk Agt	Link Market Services Ltd	Outstanding Shares	370,200,000
Counsel	Allen Allen & Hemsley	E.P.S.	$8.16
DUNS No.	75-101-6502	Shareholders	NA

Business: The group's principal activities are carried out through five segments: business and consumer banking: consists of the combined results of consumer distribution, business and regional banking distribution and consumer and business products; New Zealand retail: provides solutions for companies, institutions and governments; institutional banking: provides services to middle-Market business banking customers in Australia and New Zealand; wealth management: provides investment, retirement planning and insurance services to retail and wholesale customers; and other: includes the results of business and technology services and solutions, group treasury, pacific banking and head office functions. It operates in Australia, New Zealand, pacific islands, Asia, Americas and Europe.

Primary SIC and add'l.: 6411 6021

CIK No: 0000719245

Subsidiaries: Westpac Funds Management Limited, Westpac New Zealand Limited, Westpac Securities NZ Limited

Officers: David Morgan/61/Dir., CEO, Rob Coombe/44/CEO - BT Financial Group, Phil Coffey/49/CFO, Mike Pratt/54/Group Exec., Consumer Financial Services, Richard Willcock/49/Group Sec., General Counsel, David Lording/Head - Media Relations, Ilana Atlas/52/Group Exec., People, Performance, Philip Chronican/51/Group Exec., Westpac Institutional Bank, Andrew Carriline/48/Chief Risk Officer, Brad Cooper/Group Exec., Westpac New Zealand Limited, Jane Counsel/Sr. Mgr. - Media Relations, Peter Hanlon/53/Group Exec., Business Financial Services, Diane Sias/50/Group Exec., Business, Technology Solutions, Services, Andrew Bowden/Head - Investor Relations, Hugh Devine/Sr. Mgr. - Investor Relations *(16 Officers included in Index)*

Directors: David Morgan/61/Dir., CEO, Ted Evans/65/Chmn., Peter Wilson/65/Dir., David Crawford/62/Dir., Gordon Cairns/56/Dir., Carolyn Hewson/51/Dir., Elizabeth Bryan/61/Dir.

Owners: Suncorp Custodian Services Pty Ltd/0.20%, J P Morgan Nominees Australia Limited/11.81%, Australian Reward Investment Alliance/0.60%, RBC Global Services Australia Nominees Pty Limited/3.17%, Queensland Investment Corporation/1.11%, Citicorp Nominees Pty Limited/6.60%, Insiders/58.82%, Cogent Nominees Pty Limited/2.51%, UBS Nominees Pty Ltd/0.53%, ANZ Nominees Limited/3.02%, Invia Custodian Pty Limited/0.36%, Tasman Asset Management Ltd/0.36%, Bond Street Custodians Limited/0.49%, AMP Life Limited/1.13%, National Nominees Limited/9.86% *(21 Owners included in Index)*

Financial Data: *Fiscal Year End:* 09/30   *Latest Annual Data:* 9/30/2006

Year	Sales	Net Income
2006	$16,180,169,000	$2,192,605,000
2005	$14,197,082,000	$2,138,724,000
2004	$11,607,859,000	$1,986,970,000

Curr. Assets:	$22,213,554,000	Curr. Liab.:	$179,262,241,000		
Plant, Equip.:	$680,514,000	Total Liab.:	$311,207,408,000	Indic. Yr. Divd.:	$5.190
Total Assets:	$326,150,296,000	Net Worth:	$14,942,888,000	Debt/ Equity:	NA

Westside Energy Corp

3131 Turtle Creek Blvd., Ste. 1300, Dallas, TX, 75219; *PH:* 1-214-522-8990; *Fax:* 1-469-916-1401;
http:// www.westsideenergy.com

General - Incorporation	NV	Stock- Price on:12/24/2007	NA
Employees	7	Stock Exchange	AMEX
Auditor	Malone & Bailey, PC	Ticker Symbol	WHT
Stk Agt	Registrar & Transfer Co	Outstanding Shares	NA
Counsel	NA	E.P.S.	-$0.7
DUNS No.	NA	Shareholders	NA

Business: The groups principle activities include developing and exploring oil and natural gas. In the year 2006, the group acquired EBS Oil and Gas Partners Production Company, L.P. and EBS Oil and Gas Partners Operating Company, L.P. The groups quarterly revenue for September 2007 was 1.65 millions of USD. The group operates from the United States and Canada.

Primary SIC and add'l.: 1311

CIK No: 0001024109

Subsidiaries: Westside Energy GP, L.L.C.,, Westside Energy Operating Company, LP, Westside Energy Production Company, LP

Officers: Douglas G. Manner/CEO/$962,500.00, Rebecca Liles/Production Mgr. - Regulatory Supervisor, Jill Vann/Accounting, Sean J. Austin/CFO, VP/$154,500.00, Amy Baker/Office Mgr., Allen Goodling/Land, Legal, Brian Gross/Operations Mgr.

Directors: Douglas G. Manner/CEO, Keith D. Spickelmier/Chmn., Craig S. Glick/Dir., Herbert C. Williamson/Dir., John T. Raymond/Dir.

Owners: Herbert C. Williamson, Wellington Management Company, LLP/11.20%, Sean J. Austin, Keith D. Spickelmier/12.10%, Douglas G. Manner/2.00%, Insiders/14.90%, Westside Resources, L.P./10.90%, John T. Raymond, Jimmy D. Wright/10.90%, Craig S. Glick

Financial Data: Fiscal Year End:12/31 Latest Annual Data: 03/31/2007

Year	Sales		Net Income
2007	NA		NA
2006	$3,915,000		-$13,912,000
2005	$596,000		-$1,939,000
Curr. Assets:	$10,939,000	**Curr. Liab.:**	$11,169,000	
Plant, Equip.:	$23,299,000	**Total Liab.:**	$18,931,000	**Indic. Yr. Divd.:** NA
Total Assets:	$34,504,000	**Net Worth:**	$15,573,000	**Debt/ Equity:** NA

Westsphere Asset Corp Inc

8711 - 50th Ave., Edmonton, AB, T6E 5H4; **PH:** 1-780-482-4200; **http://** www.wescorpenergy.com

General - Incorporation	CO	**Stock**- Price on:12/24/2007	$0.55
Employees	NA	Stock Exchange	OTC
Auditor	Miller & McCollom	Ticker Symbol	WSHE
Stk Agt	Holladay Stock Transfer, Inc.	Outstanding Shares	NA
Counsel	NA	E.P.S.	NA
DUNS No.	NA	Shareholders	NA

Business: The group's principal activities are to provide non-conventional banking services. The group is a holding company and operates through its wholly owned subsidiaries: vencash capital corporation, westsphere financial group ltd, kan-can resorts ltd and e-debit international inc. The group also provides financial services and packages to its subsidiaries. The group's activities are carried out in Canada.

Primary SIC and add'l.: 6719 5046 6282 7389 7359

CIK No: 0001129120

Subsidiaries: Management of Camrose Convention Inn, Inc, Management of Westsphere Development Corporation, Management of Westsphere Entertainment Corporation, Westsphere Systems Inc

Officers: Douglas N. Mac Donald/Dir., CEO, Pres., Kim S. Law/Dir., VP - Finance, CFO, Robert L. Robins/Dir., VP, Sonja J. Dreyer/VP - Administration, Executive Assist., Dir.

Directors: Douglas N. Mac Donald/Dir., CEO, Pres., Bernd Reuscher/Dir., Kim S. Law/Dir., VP - Finance, CFO, Robert L. Robins/Dir., VP, Roy Queen/Dir., Jack Thomson/Dir.

Owners: Sonja Dreyer/5.02%, Jack Thomson/1.32%, Patricia L. Mac Donald/17.23%, Robert L. Robins/9.18%, Kim Law/1.06%, Insiders/54.96%, Sonja Dreyer/1.94%, Bernd Reuscher/18.13%, Jack Thomson/0.50%, Robert L. Robins/2.55%, Roy L. Queen/9.36%, Insiders/37.47%, Patricia L. Mac Donald/20.60%, Roy L. Queen/0.51%, Kim Law/5.03% (17 Owners included in Index)

Financial Data: Fiscal Year End:12/31 Latest Annual Data: 12/31/2006

Year	Sales		Net Income
2006	$4,662,000		$140,000
2005	$4,525,000		$23,000
2004	$3,240,000		-$569,000
Curr. Assets:	$1,003,000	**Curr. Liab.:**	$699,000	
Plant, Equip.:	$277,000	**Total Liab.:**	$937,000	**Indic. Yr. Divd.:** NA
Total Assets:	$1,304,000	**Net Worth:**	$367,000	**Debt/ Equity:** 0.9414

Weststar Financial Services Corp

79 Woodfin Pl, Asheville, NC, 28801; **PH:** 1-828-232-2902; **http://** www.bankofasheville.com

General - Incorporation	NC	**Stock**- Price on:12/24/2007	$13
Employees	48	Stock Exchange	OTC
Auditor	Dixon Hughes PLLC	Ticker Symbol	WFSC
Stk Agt	Registrar & Transfer Co	Outstanding Shares	2,110,000
Counsel	NA	E.P.S.	$0.95
DUNS No.	NA	Shareholders	NA

Business: The group's principal activity is to provide consumer and commercial banking services. The operations of the group are conducted through its wholly owned subsidiary, the bank of asheville. The group's market area consists of asheville, buncombe county, North Carolina and surrounding areas. The group provides consumer and commercial loans to small businesses and professionals.

Primary SIC and add'l.: 6712 6022

CIK No: 0001106181

Subsidiaries: Bank of Asheville Mortgage Company, LLC, The Bank of Asheville, Weststar Financial Services Corporation I

Officers: Gordon G. Greenwood/Dir., CEO, Pres./$207,694.00, Sandra J. White/Assist. VP, Executive Assistant, Judy Price/Sr. VP - Marketing, Training Officer, Kathy E. Fox/VP, Controller, Linda G. Deaton/Assist. VP, Main Office Branch Mgr., Commercial Lending Officer, Diane C. Robinson/Assist. VP, Reynolds Branch Mgr., Commercial Lending Officer, Raynia J. White/Assist. VP - Commercial, Consumer Lender, William F. Schreck/Assist. VP, Candler Branch Mgr., Commercial Lending Officer, Juanita Hendricks/VP - Credit Administration, William W. Nesbit/VP, Branch Administrator, Commercial Lending Officer, Mary Alice Mobley/VP, Training Mgr., Security Officer, John R. Hamrick/Sr. VP, Sr. Credit Officer/$113,660.00, Terry A. Ballard/Assist. VP, Network Administrator, Randall C. Hall/Exec. VP, Sec., Chief Financial Chief Financial/$147,561.00, Eric Morris/Assist. VP, Leicester Highway Branch Mgr., Commercial Lending Officer

Directors: Gordon G. Greenwood/Dir., CEO, Pres., Stephen L. Pignatiello/Vice Chmn., David N. Wilcox/Chmn., Darryl J. Hart/Dir., Laura A. Webb/Dir., Patricia P. Grimes/55/Dir., Carol L. King/62/Dir., Edward W. Anderson/Dir., David M. Cogburn/Dir., Steven D. Cogburn/Dir.

Owners: Stephen L. Pignatiello/2.12%, Steven D. Cogburn/0.36%, Darryl J. Hart/1.67%, Edward W. Anderson/4.42%, Laura A. Webb/1.42%, David N. Wilcox/2.05%, Patricia P. Grimes/0.09%, Carol L. King/2.15%, David M. Cogburn/2.61%, Insiders/21.65%, Gordon G. Greenwood/4.46%, Randall C. Hall/2.46%

Financial Data: Fiscal Year End:12/31 Latest Annual Data: 12/31/2006

Year	Sales		Net Income
2006	$12,783,000		$2,063,000
2005	$9,250,000		$1,079,000
2004	$7,627,000		$658,000
Curr. Assets:	$5,950,000	**Curr. Liab.:**	$135,675,000	**P/E Ratio:** 13.27
Plant, Equip.:	$3,111,000	**Total Liab.:**	$144,672,000	**Indic. Yr. Divd.:** NA
Total Assets:	$157,644,000	**Net Worth:**	$12,973,000	**Debt/ Equity:** NA

Westwood Holdings Group Inc

200 Crescent Ct, Ste 1200, Dallas, TX, 75201; **PH:** 1-214-756-6900; **http://** www.westwoodgroup.com; **Email:** info@westwoodgroup.com

General - Incorporation	DE	**Stock**- Price on:12/24/2007	$30.49
Employees	48	Stock Exchange	NYSE
Auditor	Deloitte & Touche LLP	Ticker Symbol	WHG
Stk Agt	American Stock Transfer & Trust CO.	Outstanding Shares	6,640,000
Counsel	Locke Liddell & Sapp LLP	E.P.S.	$0.87
DUNS No.	NA	Shareholders	NA

Business: The group's principal activity is to provide investment advisory and trust services. The group operates through two segments management and trust. The management segment provides investment advisory services to corporate pension funds, public retirement plans, endowments and foundations, mutual funds and clients of trust. The trust segment provides services to institutions and high net worth individual trust and custodial services and participation in common trust funds that it sponsors.

Primary SIC and add'l.: 7389 6282

CIK No: 0001165002

Subsidiaries: Chicago Pizza Northwest Inc., Chicago Pizza& Brewery LP

Officers: Brian O. Casey/Dir., CEO, Pres./$1,515,809.00, Susan M. Byrne/Chmn., Chief Investment Officer/$2,649,627.00, William R. Hardcastle/VP, CFO, Investor Relations Officer

Directors: Brian O. Casey/Dir., CEO, Pres., Susan M. Byrne/Chmn., Chief Investment Officer, Tom C. Davis/Dir., Jon L. Mosle/Dir., Frederick R. Meyer/Dir., Richard M. Frank/Dir., Raymond E. Wooldridge/Dir., Robert D. McTeer/Dir., Geoffrey R. Norman/Dir.

Owners: Frederick R. Meyer, Dalton, Greiner, Hartman, Maher & Co./5.00%, Tom C. Davis, William R. Hardcastle, Richard M. Frank, Joyce A. Schaer/1.30%, GAMCO Investors, Inc./19.00%, Insiders/25.40%, Brian O. Casey/5.30%, Jon L. Mosle, Raymond E. Wooldridge/1.20%, Third Avenue Management LLC/16.30%, Susan M. Byrne/15.10%

Financial Data: Fiscal Year End:12/31 Latest Annual Data: 12/31/2006

Year	Sales		Net Income
2006	$27,364,000		$4,508,000
2005	$21,940,000		$3,636,000
2004	$19,980,000		$3,686,000
Curr. Assets:	$24,953,000	**Curr. Liab.:**	$5,274,000	**P/E Ratio:** 37.18
Plant, Equip.:	$1,253,000	**Total Liab.:**	$5,987,000	**Indic. Yr. Divd.:** $1.000
Total Assets:	$28,722,000	**Net Worth:**	$22,735,000	**Debt/ Equity:** NA

Westwood One Inc

40 W 57th St., 5th Fl., New York, NY, 10019; **PH:** 1-212-642-2063; **http://** www.westwoodone.com

General - Incorporation	DE	**Stock**- Price on:12/24/2007	$7.26
Employees	1,290	Stock Exchange	NYSE
Auditor	PricewaterhouseCoopers LLP	Ticker Symbol	WON
Stk Agt	EquiServe Trust Co N.A	Outstanding Shares	87,410,000
Counsel	NA	E.P.S.	-$5.5
DUNS No.	11-311-4219	Shareholders	NA

Business: The group's principal activity is to provide information services and programming to radio and television stations. The group broadcasts traffic reporting services, national news, sports, talk, music, weather and other information programs. The group has 10,300 commercial radio stations in the United States. The programs covered by the group include concerts, personality intensive talk shows, music, countdown shows, interview programs and broadcasts major sporting events (the national football league, notre dame football, basketball, national hockey league and the olympics). Smartroute operations of the group collects, organizes and distributes a database of advanced traveller information through various electronic media and telecommunications to automobiles, homes and offices. The group's information services develops non-broadcast traffic information.

Primary SIC and add'l.: 7922 4832

CIK No: 0000771950

Subsidiaries: Metro Networks Communications, Inc., Metro Networks Services, Inc., Metro Networks, Inc., SmartRoute Systems, Inc., Westwood National Radio Corporation, Westwood One Properties, Inc., Westwood One Radio Networks, Inc., Westwood One Radio, Inc., Westwood One Stations-NYC, Inc.

Officers: Peter Kosann/CEO, Pres., Benjamin Kayne/Dir. - Interactive, Patrick Parnham/VP - Technical Services, Gary Yusko/CFO, David Hillman/Chief Administrative Officer, Exec. VP - Business Affairs, General Counsel, Sec., Sherry Rothenberg/VP - Marketing, Communications, Chris Greene/Sr. VP - Affiliate Sales, Gary Krantz/Chief Digital Media Officer, Andrew Zaref/Contact - Finance, Paul Bronstein/VP - Research, Carolyn Jones/VP - Human Resources, Luis Rodriguez/VP - Information Technology, David Halberstam/Exec. VP, GM Westwood One Sports, Howard Deneroff/VP - Executive Producer, Sports, James Starace/VP - Affiliate Information, Compliance (23 Officers included in Index)

Directors: Norman J. Pattiz/Chmn., Gerald Greenberg/Dir., Joel Hollander/Dir., Joseph B. Smith/Dir., David L. Dennis/Dir., Albert Carnesale/Dir., Grant F. Little/Dir., Walter Berger/Dir., Melvin H. Ming/Dir.

Owners: Insiders/1.00%, Peter Kosann, Melvin H. Ming, Paul Gregrey, Andrew Zaref, David L. Dennis, Norman J. Pattiz, Joseph B. Smith, David Hillman, Gerald Greenberg, Gary J. Yusko, Insiders/0.02%, Norman J. Pattiz/1.00%, Grant F. Little, Albert Carnesale

Financial Data: Fiscal Year End:12/31 Latest Annual Data: 12/31/2006

Year	Sales		Net Income
2006	$493,995,000		-$469,453,000
2005	$557,830,000		$84,683,000
2004	$562,246,000		$95,490,000
Curr. Assets:	$149,222,000	**Curr. Liab.:**	$119,909,000	
Plant, Equip.:	$37,353,000	**Total Liab.:**	$493,770,000	**Indic. Yr. Divd.:** $0.080
Total Assets:	$696,701,000	**Net Worth:**	$202,931,000	**Debt/ Equity:** 1.7083

Wet Seal Inc

26972 Burbank, Foothill Ranch, CA, 92610; **PH:** 1-949-699-3900; **Fax:** 1-949-699-4825; **http://** www.wetseal.com; **Email:** orders@wetseal.com

General - Incorporation DE
Employees 1,930
Auditor Deloitte & Touche LLP
Stk Agt Financo SecuritiesLLC, Financo Inc
Counsel NA
DUNS No. 02-806-1257

Stock- Price on:12/24/2007 $6.1
Stock Exchange NDQ
Ticker Symbol WTSLA
Outstanding Shares 95,450,000
E.P.S $0.10
Shareholders NA

Business: The group's principal activities are to retail fashionable and contemporary apparel and accessory items designed for female consumers with a young, active lifestyle. As of 13-Mar-2003, the group operated 608 retail stores in 46 states, Puerto Rico and Washington D.C. Of the 608 stores, 452 were wet seal locations, 26 were contempo casuals locations, 100 were arden b. Locations and 31 were zutopia locations. Wet seal and contempo casual stores are merchandised similarly and target the same fashion-conscious junior customer by providing a balance of moderately priced fashionable brand name and company-developed apparel and accessories. Arden b. Stores cater to the fashionable, sophisticated and contemporary customer. Arden b. Stores offer a collection of fashion separates and accessories for all facets of the customer's lifestyle. On 06-Jan-2004 the group discontinued operations of zutopia division

Primary SIC and add'l.: 5632 5651 5699 5611

CIK No: 0000863456

Subsidiaries: Wet Seal Catalog, Inc., Wet Seal GC, Inc., Wet Seal Retail

Officers: Joel N. Waller/68/Chmn., CEO, Pres./$2,083,158.00, Etienne White/VP - Marketing, John J. Luttrell/CFO, Exec. VP/$996,164.00, Gary White/COO/$933,707.00, Greg Gemette/Pres. - Arden B Merchandise/$715,868.00, Dyan Jozwick/Chief Merchandise Officer/$579,855.00, Pamela Oconnor/Sr. VP - Human Resources, Steve Benrubi/VP, Corporate Controller, Valerie Hutcheson/VP - Real Estate, Jon Kubo/CIO, VP, Charles Torok/VP - Logistics

Directors: Joel N. Waller/68/Chmn., CEO, Pres., Jonathan Duskin/40/Dir., Sidney M. Horn/57/Dir., Harold D. Kahn/62/Dir., Kenneth M. Reiss/65/Dir., Alan Siegel/73/Dir., Michael Zimmerman/37/Dir.

Owners: Alan Siegel, Wells Fargo& Company/6.50%, Gregory S. Gemette, Michael Zimmerman/7.30%, Henry D. Winterstern, Riverview Group, LLC/5.60%, FMR Corp./10.00%, Jonathan Duskin, Gary White, Harold D. Kahn, Insiders/12.30%, Sidney M. Horn, Kenneth M. Reiss, John J. Luttrell, Joel N. Waller/2.10% *(20 Owners included in Index)*

Financial Data: *Fiscal Year End:*01/28 *Latest Annual Data:* 2/3/2007

Year	Sales	Net Income
2007	$564,324,000	-$12,838,000
2006	$500,807,000	-$29,362,000
2005	$435,582,000	-$198,301,000

Curr. Assets:	$151,940,000	**Curr. Liab.:**	$61,986,000	**P/E Ratio:**	61.00
Plant, Equip.:	$50,525,000	**Total Liab.:**	$91,370,000	**Indic. Yr. Divd.:**	NA
Total Assets:	$208,167,000	**Net Worth:**	$116,797,000	**Debt/ Equity:**	0.0234

Weyco Group Inc

333 W Estabrook Blvd, Glendale, WI, 53212; *PH:* 1-414-908-1880; *http://* www.weycogroup.com; *Email:* investor.relations@weycogroup.com

General - Incorporation WI
Employees 412
Auditor Deloitte & Touche LLP
Stk Agt American Stock Transfer & Trust Co.
Counsel NA
DUNS No. 00-607-7069

Stock- Price on:12/24/2007 $25.64
Stock Exchange NDQ
Ticker Symbol WEYS
Outstanding Shares 11,610,000
E.P.S $1.87
Shareholders NA

Business: The group's principal activities are to manufacture, purchase and distribute men's footwear. The principal brands of shoes sold are nunn bush, nunn bush nxxt, brass boot, stacy adams and sao by stacy adams. The business has two divisions - wholesale and retail. In the wholesale division, shoes are marketed nationwide through more than 10,000 shoe, clothing and department stores. In the retail division, there are currently 30 company-operated stores in the United States and three in Europe.

Primary SIC and add'l.: 5661 3143 5139

CIK No: 0000106532

Subsidiaries: Florsheim Shoes Europe S.r.l., Weyco France SARL, Weyco Investments, Inc., Weyco Merger, Inc., Weyco Retail Corp.

Officers: Thomas W. Florsheim/Chmn., CEO/$1,344,395.00, John W. Florsheim/Dir., COO, Pres., Assist. Sec./$856,544.00, John F. Wittkowske/Sr. VP, CFO, Sec./$457,226.00, Peter S. Grossman/Sr. VP, Pres. - Nunn Bush Brand, Retail Division/$1,117,896.00, Judy Anderson/VP - Finance, Treasurer, Steele Davidoff/VP - Licensing, Matthew J. Engerman/VP - Sales, Nunn Bush Brand, Brian Flannery/VP, Pres. Stacy Adams Brand, Beverly Goldberg/VP - Sales, Florsheim Brand, James G. Kehoe/VP - Distribution, David McGinnis/VP, Pres. Florsheim Brand, Kevin Schiff/VP - Sales, Stacy Adams Brand, George Sotiros/VP - Information Technology, Tim Then/VP - Retail Division, Allison Woss/VP - Purchasing

Directors: Thomas W. Florsheim/Chmn., CEO, John W. Florsheim/Dir., COO, Pres., Assist. Sec., Leonard J. Goldstein/Dir., Frederick P. Stratton/Dir., Cory L. Nettles/Dir., Robert Feitler/Dir., Thomas W. Florsheim/77/Dir., Tina Chang/Dir.

Owners: Robert Feitler/5.22%, Cory L. Nettles/0.04%, John W. Florsheim/6.16%, John F. Wittkowske/3.01%, John W. Florsheim/1.19%, Peter S. Grossman/0.63%, Thomas W. Florsheim/1.22%, Insiders/30.34%, Robert Feitler/1.08%, Frederick P. Stratton/1.14%, Peter S. Grossman/0.87%, Thomas W. Florsheim/12.47%, Insiders/80.77%, Leonard J. Goldstein/0.18%, Frederick P. Stratton/2.09%

Financial Data: *Fiscal Year End:*12/31 *Latest Annual Data:* 12/31/2006

Year	Sales	Net Income
2006	$221,047,000	$21,856,000
2005	$209,469,000	$19,401,000
2004	$223,013,000	$20,278,000

Curr. Assets:	$101,222,000	**Curr. Liab.:**	$32,914,000	**P/E Ratio:**	13.71
Plant, Equip.:	$28,446,000	**Total Liab.:**	$41,450,000	**Indic. Yr. Divd.:**	$0.440
Total Assets:	$189,623,000	**Net Worth:**	$148,172,000	**Debt/ Equity:**	NA

Weyerhaeuser Co

33663 Weyerhaeuser Way S, Federal Way, WA, 98003; *PH:* 1-253-924-2345; *Fax:* 1-253-924-2685; *http://* www.weyerhaeuser.com

General - Incorporation WA
Employees 49,887
Auditor KPMG LLP
Stk Agt Mellon Investor Services LLC
Counsel NA
DUNS No. 05-975-8979

Stock- Price on:12/24/2007 $81.57
Stock Exchange NYSE
Ticker Symbol WY
Outstanding Shares 217,630,000
E.P.S $6.46
Shareholders NA

Business: The groups principle activity is to provide food products. The groups products line include wood and building materials,ppaper news print and cellulose fibers. The group operates from United States.

Primary SIC and add'l.: 6162 2421 0811 2621 6798 6552

CIK No: 0000106535

Subsidiaries: 317298 Saskatchewan Ltd., American Cemwood Corporation, Aracruz Produtos de Madeira S.A., Camarin Limited, CCA Timbers (Vic) Pty Ltd., Columbia& Cowlitz Railway Company, DeQueen& Eastern Railroad Company, Fisher Lumber Company, Forest License A49782 Holdings Ltd., Golden Triangle Railroad, Green Triangle Forest Products Limited, Gryphon Asset Management, Inc., Gryphon Investments of Nevada, Inc., Hanaki Pty Ltd., Jasmine Forests, LLC 97 Subsidiaries included in the Index

Officers: Steven R. Rogel/Chmn., CEO, Pres./$4,067,874.00, Daniel S. Fulton/CEO, Pres. - Weyerhaeuser Real Estate Company/$3,199,354.00, Patricia M. Bedient/CFO, Exec. VP, Richard E. Hanson/COO, Exec. VP/$1,844,304.00, James R. Keller/Sr. VP, Craig D. Neeser/Sr. VP - Canada, Industrial Wood Products, International Business Groups, Edward P. Rogel/Sr. VP - Human Resources, Richard J. Taggart/65/CFO, Exec. VP/$1,628,104.00, Ernesta Ballard/Sr. VP - Corporate Affairs, James M. Branson/Sr. VP - Timberlands, Theodore W. Cozine/VP - Acquisitions, Divestments, Timberlands, Carl Bohm/VP - Containerboard Sales, Logistics, Containerboard Packaging, Recycling, James C. Myers/VP - Supply, Containerboard Packaging, Recycling, John Yerke/VP - Containerboard Manufacturing, Containerboard Packaging, Recycling, Catherine I. Slater/VP - Veneer Technologies, Wood Products *(62 Officers included in Index)*

Directors: Steven R. Rogel/Chmn., CEO, Pres., Charles R. Williamson/58/Dir., Debra A. Cafaro/Dir., John I. Kieckhefer/61/Dir., Arnold G. Langbo/69/Dir., Martha R. Ingram/70/Dir., Debra H. Hansen/50/Dir., Richard F. Haskayne/70/Dir., Donald F. Mazankowski/68/Dir., Nicole W. Piasecki/41/Dir., Richard H. Sinkfield/65/Dir., Michael D. Steuert/59/Dir., James N. Sullivan/70/Dir., Kim Williams/52/Dir.

Owners: Capital Research and Management Company/14.80%, Franklin Mutual Advisors, LLC/6.70%

Financial Data: *Fiscal Year End:*12/25 *Latest Annual Data:* 12/31/2006

Year	Sales	Net Income
2006	$21,896,000,000	$453,000,000
2005	$22,629,000,000	$733,000,000
2004	$22,665,000,000	$1,283,000,000

Curr. Assets:	$4,285,000,000	**Curr. Liab.:**	$3,129,000,000	**P/E Ratio:**	12.63
Plant, Equip.:	$16,912,000,000	**Total Liab.:**	$17,777,000,000	**Indic. Yr. Divd.:**	$2.400
Total Assets:	$26,862,000,000	**Net Worth:**	$9,085,000,000	**Debt/ Equity:**	1.0052

WGL Holdings Inc

101 Constitution Ave. NW, Washington, DC, 20080; *PH:* 1-703-750-2000; *http://* www.wglholdings.com; *Email:* info@wglholdings.com

General - Incorporation VA
Employees 1,818
Auditor Deloitte & Touche LLP
Stk Agt Bank of New York
Counsel NA
DUNS No. NA

Stock- Price on:12/24/2007 $33.47
Stock Exchange NYSE
Ticker Symbol WGL
Outstanding Shares 49,220,000
E.P.S $2.19
Shareholders NA

Business: The groups principle activity is to deliver energy. The groups operates from United States.

Primary SIC and add'l.: 6141 1711 4922 1389 4924

CIK No: 0001103601

Subsidiaries: American Combustion Industries, Inc., Crab Run Gas Company, Hampshire Gas Company, Washington Gas Credit Corporation, Washington Gas Energy Services, Inc., Washington Gas Energy Systems, Inc., Washington Gas Light Company, Washington Gas Resources Corp., WG Maritime Plaza I, Inc., WGL Holdings, Inc.

Officers: James H. Degraffenreidt/Chmn., CEO, Terry D. McCallister/COO, Pres., Elizabeth M. Arnold/VP - Strategy, Beverly J. Burke/VP, General Counsel, Vincent L. Ammann/CFO, VP, Gautam Chandra/VP - Business Process Outsourcing, Non - Utility Operations, Shelley C. Jennings/Treasurer, Mark P. O'Flynn/Controller, Douglas V. Pope/Sec., Corporate Governance Officer

Directors: James H. Degraffenreidt/Chmn., CEO, Debra L. Lee/Dir., James F. Lafond/Dir., Karen Hastie Williams/Dir., Michael D. Barnes/Dir., Melvyn J. Estrin/Dir., George P. Clancy/Dir., James W. Dyke/Dir.

Owners: Melvyn J. Estrin, Barclays Global Investors NA/5.50%, James W. Dyke, American Century Investment Management, Inc./9.60%, James H. DeGraffenreidt, Karen Hastie Williams, Frederic M. Kline, Adrian P. Chapman, Michael D. Barnes, Thomas F. Bonner, Terry D. McCallister, George P. Clancy, Beverly J. Burke, James F. Lafond, Debra L. Lee *(16 Owners included in Index)*

Financial Data: *Fiscal Year End:*09/30 *Latest Annual Data:* 09/30/2007

Year	Sales	Net Income
2007	$2,646,008,000	$107,900,000
2006	$2,637,883,000	$87,578,000
2005	$1,355,234,000	$104,813,000

Curr. Assets:	$562,022,000	**Curr. Liab.:**	$560,842,000	**P/E Ratio:**	17.34
Plant, Equip.:	$2,067,895,000	**Total Liab.:**	$1,841,426,000	**Indic. Yr. Divd.:**	$1.370
Total Assets:	$2,791,406,000	**Net Worth:**	$949,980,000	**Debt/ Equity:**	NA

WGNB Corp

PO Box 280, Carrollton, GA, 30112; *PH:* 1-770-832-3557; *http://* www.wgnb.com

General - Incorporation GA
Employees 182
Auditor Porter Keadle Moore LLP
Stk Agt WGNB Corp
Counsel NA
DUNS No. NA

Stock- Price on:12/24/2007 $27.99
Stock Exchange NDQ
Ticker Symbol WGNB
Outstanding Shares 5,000,000
E.P.S $1.69
Shareholders NA

Business: The group's principal activity is the provision of commercial banking services to individuals and medium-sized businesses. The deposit services offered by the group include checking accounts, now accounts, savings accounts and other time deposits of various types, ranging from money market accounts to longer-term certificates of deposit. The group operates a total of seven branches and six additional 24-hour ATM sites, located in carroll and douglas counties in Georgia. In addition, the group operates two other branches in the city of carrollton, two branches in villa rica and one branch in bowdon, Georgia.

Primary SIC and add'l.: 6021 6712

CIK No: 0001115568

Subsidiaries: West Georgia National Bank

Officers: H. B. Lipham/Dir., CEO - Bank, Corporation/$459,887.00, Randall F. Eaves/Dir., Pres. - Bank, Corporation, Galen W. Hobbs/Exec. VP, Sr. Commercial Loan Officer - Bank/$255,174.00, Robert M. Gordy/Exec. VP, Chief Credit Officer - Bank/$194,377.00, Janice C. Fraser/Sr. VP, William R. Whitaker/Sr. VP/$231,543.00, Steven J. Haack/Sec., Treasurer - Corporation, Exec. VP, CFO - Bank/$385,171.00, Dan M. Butler/CIO, Exec. VP - Bank, Mary M. Covington/Dir., Exec. VP - Bank, Corporation

Directors: H. B. Lipham/Dir., CEO - Bank, Corporation, Thomas W. Green/Chmn., L. G. Joyner/Dir., Thomas T. Richards/Dir., Charles M. Willis/Dir., Thomas E. Reeve/Dir., Wanda W. Calhoun/Dir., Oscar W. Roberts/Dir., Richard A. Duncan/Dir., David R. Perry/Dir., Frank T. Thomasson/Dir., Grady Woodfin Cole/Dir., Thomas J. Vance/Dir., Richard L. Plunkett/Dir., Randall F. Eaves/Dir., Pres. - Bank, Corporation *(18 Directors included in Index)*

Owners: Steven J. Haack, W. T. Green/1.55%, Robert M. Gordy, Grady Woodfin Cole/1.04%, Louise Tyus Roberts Jewell/8.05%, Leighton L. Alston/1.24%, Richard L. Plunkett, H. B. Lipham, Thomas J. Vance, Mary M. Covington/2.06%, Donald C. Rhodes/1.68%, Wanda Calhoun, William R. Whitaker, Insiders/23.44%, Thomas T. Richards/4.72% *(19 Owners included in Index)*

Financial Data: *Fiscal Year End:* 12/31 *Latest Annual Data:* 12/31/2006

Year	Sales	Net Income
2006	$48,497,000	$8,327,000
2005	$38,554,000	$7,067,000
2004	$30,905,000	$6,064,000

Curr. Assets:	$17,006,000	**Curr. Liab.:**	$520,170,000	**P/E Ratio:**	16.56
Plant, Equip.:	$8,990,000	**Total Liab.:**	$522,832,000	**Indic. Yr. Divd.:**	$0.810
Total Assets:	$575,329,000	**Net Worth:**	$52,496,000	**Debt/ Equity:**	NA

Wheeling Island Gaming Inc

1 S Stone St., Wheeling, WV, 26003; ***PH:*** 1-877-946-4373; ***http://*** www.wheelingdowns.com; ***Email:*** wi-info@dncinc.com

General - Incorporation	DE	**Stock** - Price on:12/24/2007	NA
Employees	NA	Stock Exchange	NA
Auditor	Ernst & Young, LLP	Ticker Symbol	NA
Stk Agt	NA	Outstanding Shares	NA
Counsel	Proskauer Rose	E.P.S	NA
DUNS No.	NA	Shareholders	NA

Business: The group's principle activity is to operate wheeling downs racetrak and gaming center, and gaming and entertainment complex located in wheeling, west Virginia. The group operates from United States.

Primary SIC and add'l.: 7948 7993

CIK No: 0001166041

Subsidiaries: WDRA Food Service, Inc., Wheeling Land Development Corp

Officers: Ernest J. Butler/Owner, Greyhound Racer's Spotlight, Kim Florence/Mgr. - Communications, Phillip B. Simons/45/VP - Finance

Owners: Delaware North Companies Gaming & Entertainment, Inc./100.00%

Wheeling Pittsburgh Corp

1134 Market St., Wheeling, WV, 26003; ***PH:*** 1-304-234-2460; ***http://*** www.wpsc.com

General - Incorporation	DE	**Stock** - Price on:12/24/2007	$19.5
Employees	3,133	Stock Exchange	NA
Auditor	PricewaterhouseCoopers LLP	Ticker Symbol	NA
Stk Agt	Computershare Investor Services LLC	Outstanding Shares	15,330,000
Counsel	NA	E.P.S	-$6.76
DUNS No.	00-138-1409	Shareholders	NA

Business: The groups principle activity is to produce carbon flat rolled products for the construction, container, appliance, steel service center and automotive industries. The groups products include various sheet products including hot rolled, cold rolled, hot dipped galvanized, electro-galvanized, black plate and electrolytic tinplate. The group operates from United States.

Primary SIC and add'l.: 3316

CIK No: 0000941738

Subsidiaries: Mountain State Carbon, LLC, Wheeling-Pittsburgh Steel Corporation, WP Steel Venture Corporation

Officers: James P. Bouchard/Chmn., CEO, Craig T. Bouchard/Vice Chmn., Pres., Paul J. Mooney/56/Dir., Exec. VP, Chief Financial Offiicer, Michael P. Diclemente/VP, Treasurer - WPC, Wpsc, Dennis Halpin/Dir. - Investor Relations, David A. Luptak/50/Exec. VP, Sec., General Counsel - WPC, Wpsc, Vincent D. Assetta/43/VP, Controller - WPC, Wpsc

Directors: Craig T. Bouchard/Vice Chmn., Pres., Albert G. Adkins/Dir., Clark Burrus/Dir., James V. Koch/Dir., Joseph Peduzzi/Dir., Frederick C. Fetterolf/Dir., George Munoz/Dir., James A. Todd/Dir., Paul J. Mooney/56/Dir., Exec. VP, Chief Financial Offiicer, Lynn R. Williams/83/Dir., James L. Bowen/72/Dir.

Owners: George Munoz, James P. Bouchard, Paul J. Mooney, Lynn R. Williams, Frederick C. Fetterolf, Vincent D. Assetta, Wheeling-Pittsburgh Steel Corporation Retiree Benefits Plan Trust/11.57%, Craig T. Bouchard, Jeffery L. Gendell/12.83%, James L. Bowen, Albert G. Adkins, Wellington Management Company, LLP/13.62%, Deutsche Bank AG/5.44%, James G. Bradley, FMR Corp./5.48% *(21 Owners included in Index)*

Financial Data: *Fiscal Year End:* 12/31 *Latest Annual Data:* 12/31/2006

Year	Sales	Net Income
2006	$1,770,765,000	$6,481,000
2005	$1,560,513,000	-$33,834,000
2004	$1,405,794,000	$62,467,000

Curr. Assets:	$400,487,000	**Curr. Liab.:**	$327,548,000		
Plant, Equip.:	$626,210,000	**Total Liab.:**	$730,062,000	**Indic. Yr. Divd.:**	NA
Total Assets:	$1,122,545,000	**Net Worth:**	$286,193,000	**Debt/ Equity:**	0.8908

Wherify Wireless Inc

2000 Bridge Pkwy., Ste. 201, Redwood Shores, CA, 94404; ***PH:*** 1-650-554-3000; ***Fax:*** 1-650-555-2888; ***http://*** www.wherifywireless.com; ***Email:*** info@wherify.com

General - Incorporation	DE	**Stock** - Price on:12/24/2007	$0.17
Employees	31	Stock Exchange	OTC
Auditor	Malone & Bailey, P.C	Ticker Symbol	WFYW
Stk Agt	American Stock Transfer & Trust Co.	Outstanding Shares	73,370,000
Counsel	NA	E.P.S	-$0.33
DUNS No.	NA	Shareholders	NA

Business: The group's principal activity is to provide facial composite software to police and government agencies in North America. The faces(tm) 4.0 technology allows the easy creation and re-creation of billions of human faces through an exhaustive database of facial features. The faces software creates composite pictures with remarkable ease and speed, and automatically converts the composite into unique biometric alphanumerical codes or bac ids. This technology helps law enforcement to identify and capture criminals quickly and efficiently.

Primary SIC and add'l.: 7372

CIK No: 0001051902

Subsidiaries: IQ Biometrix California, Inc, JVWeb, Inc, Wherify California, Inc, Wherify Wireless, Inc.

Officers: Vincent D. Sheeran/CEO, Pres., Jacqueline Nevilles/CFO, Matthew J. Neher/VP - Business Development, International, Robert Jacobsen/CIO, Evita P. Twerdahl/VP - Product Management, Deborah Ferrari/VP - Professional Services

Directors: Timothy J. Neher/Chmn., Daniel McKelvey/Dir., Douglas W. Hajjar/Dir., Wade Fenn/Dir., Neil Morris/Dir.

Owners: GPS Associates, LLC./48.90%, Douglas Hajjar/5.70%, Timothy J. Neher/13.60%, Vincent Sheeran/1.00%, Daniel McKelvey, Insiders/7.40%, Wade Fenn, Cornell Capital Partners, LP/4.99%

Financial Data: *Fiscal Year End:* 06/30 *Latest Annual Data:* 6/30/2006

Year	Sales	Net Income
2006	$155,000	-$81,345,000
2005	$301,000	-$8,303,000
2004	$270,000	-$8,391,000

Curr. Assets:	$2,296,000	**Curr. Liab.:**	$15,118,000		
Plant, Equip.:	$641,000	**Total Liab.:**	$15,118,000	**Indic. Yr. Divd.:**	NA
Total Assets:	$3,723,000	**Net Worth:**	-$11,394,000	**Debt/ Equity:**	NA

Whirlpool Corp

2000 N M-63, Benton Harbor, MI, 49022; ***PH:*** 1-269-923-5000; ***http://*** www.whirlpool.com

General - Incorporation	DE	**Stock** - Price on:12/24/2007	$116.74
Employees	73,000	Stock Exchange	NYSE
Auditor	Ernst & Young LLP	Ticker Symbol	WHR
Stk Agt	EquiServe Trust Co N.A	Outstanding Shares	78,920,000
Counsel	NA	E.P.S	$6.30
DUNS No.	18-317-4739	Shareholders	NA

Business: The groups principle activities include manufacturing and marketing home appliances. The groups product line includes laundry appliances, refrigerators and freezers, cooking appliances, dishwashers, room air-conditioning equipment, and mixers. The group operates from United States.

Primary SIC and add'l.: 3639 3632 3631 3633

CIK No: 0000106640

Subsidiaries: Brasmotor S.A., Empresa Brasileira de Compressores S.A. ., Multibras S.A. Eletrodomesticos, Whirlpool Canada LP, Whirlpool do Brasil Ltda., Whirlpool Europe B.V., Whirlpool Manufacturing Corporation, Whirlpool Mexico, S.A. de C.V., Whirlpool Patents Company, Whirlpool Properties, Inc.

Officers: Jeff M. Fettig/Chmn., CEO/$8,250,614.00, Jeff D. Noel/Pres., Chmn. - Whirlpool Foundation, Marc Bitzer/Pres. - Whirlpool Europe, Larry Venturelli/VP - Investor Relation, Robert T. Kenagy/Assoc. General Counsel, Corp. Sec., Mark E. Brown/Sr. VP - Global Strategic Sourcing, Frank J. Luongo/Sec., Treasurer - Whirlpool Foundation, Robert Laforest/Trustees, Whirlpool Foundation, Assist. Sec. - Whirlpool Corporation, Timothy W. Yaggi/Exec. VP - Marketing Operations, Daniel F. Hopp/Sr. VP - Corporate Affairs, General Counsel, Barbara A. Hall/Exec. Dir. - Whirlpool Foundation, Pamela Silcox/Administrative Coordinator, Whirlpool Foundation, Michael A. Todman/Dir., Pres. - Whirlpool North America/$3,000,478.00, Mark K. Hu/Exec. VP - Whirlpool Asia, Paulo F.M.O. Periquito/Pres. - Whirlpool International/$7,980,842.00 *(19 Officers included in Index)*

Directors: Jeff M. Fettig/Chmn., CEO, David L. Swift/Dir., Pres. - Whirlpool North America, Herman Cain/Dir., Allan D. Gilmour/73/Dir., Alan Holaday/Trustee - Whirlpool Foundation, Michael A. Todman/Dir., Pres. - Whirlpool North America, Gary T. Dicamillo/Dir., David A. Binkley/Trustee, Sr. VP - Global Human Resources, Michael D. White/Dir., Miles L. Marsh/Dir., Paul G. Stern/Dir., Janice D. Stoney/Dir., Robert Laforest/Trustees, Whirlpool Foundation, Assist. Sec. - Whirlpool Corporation, Tim Reynolds/Trustee - Whirlpool Foundation, Barbara A. Hall/Exec. Dir. - Whirlpool Foundation *(19 Directors included in Index)*

Owners: Roy W. Templin, Allan D. Gilmour, FMR Corp./14.97%, Paulo F. M. Periquito, Herman Cain, Miles L. Marsh, Marsh & McLennan Companies, Inc./5.50%, Janice D. Stoney, Gary T. DiCamillo, Jeff M. Fettig, Kathleen J. Hempel, Michael A. Todman, Paul G. Stern, Pzena Investment Management, LLC/11.45%, Arnold G. Langbo *(22 Owners included in Index)*

Financial Data: *Fiscal Year End:* 12/31 *Latest Annual Data:* 12/31/2006

Year	Sales	Net Income
2006	$18,080,000,000	$433,000,000
2005	$14,317,000,000	$422,000,000
2004	$13,220,000,000	$406,000,000

Curr. Assets:	$6,476,000,000	**Curr. Liab.:**	$6,002,000,000	**P/E Ratio:**	18.53
Plant, Equip.:	$3,157,000,000	**Total Liab.:**	$10,595,000,000	**Indic. Yr. Divd.:**	$1.720
Total Assets:	$13,878,000,000	**Net Worth:**	$3,283,000,000	**Debt/ Equity:**	0.4859

Whispering Oaks International Inc

7080 River Rd. , Ste. 215, Richmond, BC, A1 V6X 1X5; ***PH:*** 1-604-207-9150

General - Incorporation	TX	**Stock** - Price on:12/24/2007	NA
Employees	NA	Stock Exchange	NA
Auditor	Manning Elliott LLP	Ticker Symbol	NA
Stk Agt	Securities Transfer Corp	Outstanding Shares	NA
Counsel	NA	E.P.S	NA
DUNS No.	NA	Shareholders	NA

Business: The group's principle activities include developing, producing, marketing and licensing cancer diagnostic kits. The group acquired and sell thoroughbred race horses for profit. The group operates from United States.

Primary SIC and add'l.: 2835

CIK No: 0001092562

Officers: Ricardo Moro/55/Dir., CEO, Pres., Gerald Wittenberg/56/Dir., Principal Financial Officer, Sec., Treasurer

Directors: Ricardo Moro/55/Dir., CEO, Pres., Gerald Wittenberg/56/Dir., Principal Financial Officer, Sec., Treasurer, Phil Gold/71/Dir.

Owners: Phil Gold, Gerald Wittenberg/11.15%, Insiders/16.89%, Ricardo Moro/5.37%

White Electronic Designs Corp

3601 E University Dr., Phoenix, AZ, 85034; *PH:* 1-602-437-1520; *http://* www.whiteedc.com; *Email:* info@wedc.com

General - Incorporation ... ID	***Stock***- Price on:12/24/2007 ... $5.9
Employees ... 424	Stock Exchange ... NDQ
Auditor ... Grant Thornton, LLP	Ticker Symbol ... WEDC
Stk Agt ... American Stock Transfer & Trust Co.	Outstanding Shares ... 23,560,000
Counsel ... Snell & Wilmer	E.P.S ... $0.20
DUNS No. ... 00-506-9315	Shareholders ... NA

Business: The group's principal activities are to design and manufacture high-density microelectronic memory products, advanced matrix liquid crystal displays, interface products and electromechanical components and packages. The group operates through two segments: microelectronic and display. The microelectronic segment manufactures high-density semiconductor memory and microprocessor products for use in telecommunications, data communications and military aerospace markets. The display segment manufactures liquid crystal displays and electromechanical components for customers in the aviation industry. These consist of rotating devices, gear heads, mechanical counters and dial drives. The products are sold principally to aircraft instrument manufacturers as information displays in aerospace. The group has operations in the United States, Europe and Asia.

Primary SIC and add'l.: 3674 3679

CIK No: 0000013606

Subsidiaries: Bowmar/A.L.I., Inc., Electronic Designs, Inc., Graymor Coatings, Incorporated (2), IDS Acquisition Corporation (1), Interface Data Systems, Inc., Panelview, Incorporated

Officers: Hamid R. Shokrgozar/47/Chmn., CEO, Pres., Jim Kritcher/Dir. - Corporate Information Technology, Dan Doyle/VP - Business Development, Display Systems, Jeff Eidinger/VP - Supply Chain Management Microelectronics, Bj Heggli/VP - Engineering - Microelectronics, Bev Cameron/VP - Operations - Microelectronics, Roger A. Derse/CFO, VP, Dan Wyss/Plant Mgr. - Electromechanical Products, Karen Kock/VP - Corporate Human Resources, Jeff Osmun/VP - Corporate Sales, Marketing, David Slobodin/VP, GM - Display Systems, Eric Tzeng/Dir. - International Operations, Dante V. Tarantine/VP - Sales, Marketing

Directors: Hamid R. Shokrgozar/47/Chmn., CEO, Pres.

Owners: Paul D. Quadros, Roger Derse, Edward A. White/3.16%, Jack A. Henry, Dimensional Fund Advisors Inc./5.72%, Thomas J. Toy, Hamid R. Shokrgozar/4.02%, Thomas M. Reahard, Royce & Associates, LLC/8.06%, Byram Capital Management LLC/6.80%, Dante V. Tarantine, Insiders/9.46%

Financial Data: ***Fiscal Year End:***10/03 ***Latest Annual Data:*** 9/30/2006

Year		Sales		Net Income	
2006		$108,928,000		$6,013,000	
2005		$117,031,000		-$3,535,000	
2004		$108,962,000		$4,807,000	
Curr. Assets:	$107,009,000	***Curr. Liab.:***	$17,433,000	***P/E Ratio:***	29.50
Plant, Equip.:	$13,367,000	***Total Liab.:***	$20,328,000	***Indic. Yr. Divd.:***	NA
Total Assets:	$130,508,000	***Net Worth:***	$110,180,000	***Debt/ Equity:***	NA

White Knight Resources Inc

165 S Unio, Ste. 565, Lakewood, CO, 80228; *PH:* 1-303-238-1438; *http://* www.whiteknightres.com

General - Incorporation ... BC	***Stock***- Price on:12/24/2007 ... $1.425
Employees ... NA	Stock Exchange ... NA
Auditor ... Davidson & Co LLP	Ticker Symbol ... NA
Stk Agt ... Montreal Trust Co of Can (Vancouver)	Outstanding Shares ... NA
Counsel ... NA	E.P.S ... NA
DUNS No. ... NA	Shareholders ... NA

Business: The group's principle activity is to explore mineral operations. The Canadian-based company is set to explore its properties for economic and legal viability. The group explores for multi-million ounce, Carlin type gold deposits in Nevada. The company owns sixteen properties, fourteen of which are located within the prolific Cortez Trend. The recent discoveries of the company totals 9.0 million ounces of gold at Cortez Hills and Pediment. Ongoing drilling at Cortez Hills continues to expand the deposit. The announced gold resource on the Cortez Joint Venture property totals 36.0 million ounces of gold. The company projects include Benmark, Celt, Cottonwood, Fye Canyon, Gold Bar Horst, Gold Pick, Goldstone, Hunter, Indian Ranch, Mc Clusky Pass, New Pass, Pat Canyon, Slaven Canyon, South Cabin Creek, Squaw Creek, and Tonkin Summit. The group operates from United States.

Primary SIC and add'l.: 1000

CIK No: 0001298093

Subsidiaries: CUN Minerals, Inc, Quito Gold Corporation, White Knight Gold (U.S.) Inc

Owners: Robert McEwen/16.10%, Gordon P. Leask/6.20%

White Mountain Titanium Corp

2150 - 1188 W Georgia St., Vancouver, BC, V6E 4A2; *PH:* 1-604-408-2333; *Fax:* 1-604-669-4776; *http://* www.wmtcorp.com; *Email:* info@wmtcorp.com

General - Incorporation ...	***Stock***- Price on:12/24/2007 ... $0.6
Employees ... NA	Stock Exchange ... OTC
Auditor ...	Ticker Symbol ... WMTM
Stk Agt ... Interwest Transfer Company, Inc.	Outstanding Shares ... NA
Counsel ... NA	E.P.S ... NA
DUNS No. ... NA	Shareholders ... NA

Business: The groups principal activity is currently has no ongoing operations and is considered an exploration stage company. The group operates from the United States.

Primary SIC and add'l.: 1000

CIK No:

Subsidiaries: Compaa Minera Rutile Resources Limitada, White Mountain Titanium Corporation

Officers: Michael P. Kurtanjek/Dir., CEO, Pres., Natasha Tschischow/Consulting Chief Geologist, David Rochester/Marketing Consultant, Derek Fray/Titanium Technologies Consultant, Chuck Jenkins/CFO, Howard M. Crosby/Dir., Sr. VP - Investor Relation, Cesar Lopez/Dir. - Chilean Legal Counsel, Terese Gieselman/Corp. Sec.

Directors: Michael P. Kurtanjek/Dir., CEO, Pres., Brian Flower/Chmn., Howard M. Crosby/Dir., Sr. VP - Investor Relation, Cesar Lopez/Dir. - Chilean Legal Counsel

Owners: Cesar Lopez/6.10%, Rubicon Master Fund/44.80%, Insiders/23.40%, Michael P. Kurtanjek/5.30%, Phelps Dodge Corporation/7.40%, Charles E. Jenkins, John P. Ryan/5.60%, Brian Flower/2.70%, Howard M. Crosby/5.20%, Stephanie Ashton/18.40%

Financial Data: ***Fiscal Year End:***NA ***Latest Annual Data:*** 12/31/2006

Year		Sales		Net Income	
2006		NA		-$2,185,000	
Curr. Assets:	$2,112,000	***Curr. Liab.:***	$110,000		
Plant, Equip.:	$57,000	***Total Liab.:***	$110,000	***Indic. Yr. Divd.:***	NA
Total Assets:	$2,169,000	***Net Worth:***	$2,059,000	***Debt/ Equity:***	NA

White Mountains Insurance Group Ltd

80 S Main St., Hanover, NH, 03755; *PH:* 1-603 640-2200; *http://* www.whitemountains.com; *Email:* info@whitemountains.com

General - Incorporation ... Bermuda	***Stock***- Price on:12/24/2007 ... $598.25
Employees ... 5,292	Stock Exchange ... NYSE
Auditor ... PricewaterhouseCoopers LLP	Ticker Symbol ... WTM
Stk Agt ... Computershare Trust Co	Outstanding Shares ... 10,830,000
Counsel ... NA	E.P.S ... $60.75
DUNS No. ... 10-340-1915	Shareholders ... NA

Business: The group's principal activities are to provide property and casualty insurance and reinsurance through its subsidiaries and affiliates. It operates through three segments: onebeacon, reinsurance and other operations. The onebeacon insurance group llc family of companies are U.S. Based property and casualty insurance writers. Reinsurance operations are conducted primarily through folksamerica holding company inc. Folksamerica is a multi-line broker-Market reinsurer, which provides reinsurance to insurers of property and casualty and accident and health risks. Other operations consist of the international American group, esurance and its intermediate holding companies. On 31-Mar-2004, it acquired Atlantic specialty insurance company and on 16-Apr-2004, it acquired sirius insurance group and its subsidiaries.

Primary SIC and add'l.: 6331

CIK No: 0000776867

Subsidiaries: Esurance , Inc., Esurance Holdings Inc., Esurance Insurance Company, Folksamerica Holding Company, Inc., Folksamerica Reinsurance Company, Fund American Companies, Inc., Fund American Enterprises Holdings, Inc., Fund American Financial Services, Inc., Fund American Holdings Ab, Fund American Reinsurance Company, Ltd., Homeland Insurance Company Of New York, Onebeacon America Insurance Company, Onebeacon Insurance Company, Onebeacon Insurance Group LLC, Pennsylvania General Insurance Company 37 Subsidiaries included in the Index

Officers: Raymond Barrette/Chmn., CEO

Directors: Raymond Barrette/Chmn., CEO, Howard L. Clark/Dir., Bruce R. Berkowitz/Dir., John D. Gillespie/Dir., Yves Brouillette/Dir., Morgan W. Davis/Dir., Lowndes A. Smith/Dir., Edith E. Holiday/Dir., Robert P. Cochran/Dir., Michael A. Frinquelli/Dir., George J. Gillespie/Dir., Allan L. Waters/Dir.

Owners: John D. Gillespie, Neuberger Berman LLC/7.40%, Steven E. Fass, Raymond Barrette/7.20%, Edith E. Holiday, Morgan W. Davis, Insiders, Robert P. Cochran, David T. Foy, Bruce R. Berkowitz, Howard L. Clark, Charles B. Chokel, Robert R. Lusardi, Berkshire Hathaway Inc./15.90%, Michael A. Frinquelli *(21 Owners included in Index)*

Financial Data: ***Fiscal Year End:***12/31 ***Latest Annual Data:*** 12/31/2006

Year		Sales		Net Income	
2006		$4,794,200,000		$673,200,000	
2005		$4,631,900,000		$290,100,000	
2004		$4,553,000,000		$418,700,000	
Curr. Assets:	$6,689,000,000	***Curr. Liab.:***	$1,140,200,000	***P/E Ratio:***	9.85
Plant, Equip.:	NA	***Total Liab.:***	$14,726,100,000	***Indic. Yr. Divd.:***	$8.000
Total Assets:	$19,443,700,000	***Net Worth:***	$4,455,300,000	***Debt/ Equity:***	0.2605

Whitehall Jewellers Inc

155 N Wacker Dr, Ste. 500, Chicago, IL, 60606; *PH:* 1-312-782-6800; *http://* www.whitehalljewellers.com

General - Incorporation ... DE	***Stock***- Price on:12/24/2007 ... NA
Employees ... NA	Stock Exchange ... NA
Auditor ... PricewaterhouseCoopers LLP	Ticker Symbol ... NA
Stk Agt ... EquiServe Trust Co N.A	Outstanding Shares ... NA
Counsel ... Sidley, Austin, Brown & Wood	E.P.S ... NA
DUNS No. ... 00-798-0212	Shareholders ... NA

Business: The group's principal activity is to operate specialty retail jewelry stores. It offers an in-depth selection in diamond, gold, precious and semi-precious jewelry. The group's customers include middle to upper-middle income women over 25 years of age. At 30-Apr-2004, the group operated 385 mall-based stores in 38 states under the brand names whitehall co. Jewelers, lundstrom jewelers and marks bros. Jewelers. It also provides jewelry repair services and jewelry service plans. The group's store offers approximately 2,700 individual items, including approximately 1,450 core jewelry items. It markets the products through in-store and point-of-sale marketing and direct mail campaigns.

Primary SIC and add'l.: 5944

CIK No: 0000868984

Subsidiaries: WH Inc. of Illinois, Whitehalljewellers.com, LLC

Whitemark Homes Inc

650 S Central Ave., Ste 1000, Oviedo, FL, 32765; *PH:* 1-407-366-9668; *http://* www.whitemarkhomes.com; *Email:* billrigsby@whitemarkhomes.com

General - Incorporation..............................CO
Employees...5
Auditor .....Tedder, James, Worden & Assoc. P.A
Stk Agt...............Whitemark Homes (Karen Lee)
Counsel...NA
DUNS No. 02-192-7033

Stock- Price on:12/24/2007 ....$0.13
Stock Exchange...OTC
Ticker Symbol...WTMK
Outstanding Shares 21,330,000
E.P.S...-$0.02
Shareholders..NA

Business: The group's principal activity is to purchase and develop land and the construction and sale of single-family conventional homes, primarily targeting first time buyers in the orlando, Florida area. It offers homes in a price range from $100,000 to over $350,000 and is involved in all aspects of the business, including land acquisition, site planning, preparation and improvement of land, as well as design, construction and marketing of planned developments. In 2003, 91 homes/lots were delivered in 7 communities.

Primary SIC and add'l.: 1531

CIK No: 0000042284

Subsidiaries: Home Funding, Inc., Homes of Florida, Inc.:, Sheeler Hills, Ltd., Whitemark at Corner Lake, LLC, Whitemark at Fox Glen, Ltd.neral, Whitemark at Glenbrook, LLC, Whitemark at Little Creek, LLC, Whitemark Homes of Florida, Inc., a Florida corporation

Owners: Larry White/62.43%, Insiders/1.69%, William Rigsby/1.38%, Scott D. Clark/31.00%

*Financial Data: Fiscal Year End:*12/31 *Latest Annual Data:* 12/31/2006

Year	Sales	Net Income
2006	$17,746,000	$1,061,000
2005	$30,042,000	$4,822,000
2004	$36,907,000	-$45,000
Curr. Assets: $2,697,000	*Curr. Liab.:* $1,685,000	*P/E Ratio:* 2.60
Plant, Equip.: $1,011,000	*Total Liab.:* $2,952,000	*Indic. Yr. Divd.:* $0.070
Total Assets: $3,969,000	*Net Worth:* $1,017,000	*Debt/ Equity:* NA

Whiting Petroleum Corp

1700 Brdway, Ste 2300, Denver, CO, 80290; *PH:* 1-303-837-1661; *http://* www.whiting.com; *Email:* ir@whiting.com

General - Incorporation............................DE
Employees...359
Auditor ....Deloitte & Touche LLP
Stk Agt.............................Computershare Trust Co
Counsel...NA
DUNS No. ....NA

Stock- Price on:12/24/2007 ....NA
Stock Exchange...NYSE
Ticker Symbol...WLL
Outstanding Shares 37,050,000
E.P.S...$3.64
Shareholders..NA

Business: The group's principal activity is to acquire, explore and produce natural gas and crude oil. The group operates primarily in the gulf coast/permian basin, rocky mountains, Michigan and mid-continent regions of the United States. On 20-Jul-2004, the group acquired equity oil company.

Primary SIC and add'l.: 1311

CIK No: 0001255474

Subsidiaries: Equity Oil Company, Whiting Oil and Gas Corporation, Whiting Programs, Inc.

Officers: James J. Volker/61/Chmn., CEO, Pres./$1,993,157.00, Mark R. Williams/VP - Exploration, Development/$955,462.00, James T. Brown/Sr. VP/$917,473.00, Patricia J. Miller/VP - Human Resources, David M. Seery/VP - Land, Michael J. Stevens/CFO, VP/$874,526.00, Bruce R. Deboer/VP, General Counsel, Corp. Sec., Douglas J. Lang/VP - Reservoir Engineering, Acquisitions/$861,327.00, Sherwin D. Artus/70/Dir., Sr. VP, Brent P. Jensen/38/Controller, Treasurer, Chief Accounting Officer, Rick A. Ross/VP - Operations, Denver, Gale Keithline/VP - Information Technology, John Kelso/Dir. - Investor Relations

Directors: James J. Volker/61/Chmn., CEO, Pres., Palmer L. Moe/64/Dir., Graydon D. Hubbard/74/Dir., Kenneth R. Whiting/80/Dir., Sherwin D. Artus/70/Dir., Sr. VP

Owners: Third Avenue Management LLC/5.50%, Thomas L. Aller, Graydon D. Hubbard, Michael J. Stevens, Palmer L. Moe, Mark R. Williams, Wellington Management Company, LLP/13.60%, Thomas P. Briggs, Barclays Global Fund Advisors/5.00%, Neuberger Berman, Inc./13.90%, Kenneth R. Whiting, James T. Brown, T. Rowe Price Associates, Inc./5.40%, Insiders/0.90%, Douglas J. Lang *(17 Owners included in Index)*

*Financial Data: Fiscal Year End:*12/31 *Latest Annual Data:* 12/31/2006

Year	Sales	Net Income
2006	$786,328,000	$156,364,000
2005	$540,448,000	$121,922,000
2004	$287,015,000	$70,046,000
Curr. Assets: $121,712,000	*Curr. Liab.:* $143,042,000	
Plant, Equip.: $2,432,661,000	*Total Liab.:* $1,398,733,000	*Indic. Yr. Divd.:* NA
Total Assets: $2,585,403,000	*Net Worth:* $1,186,670,000	*Debt/ Equity:* 0.8912

Whitney Holding Corp

228 St. Charles Ave., New Orleans, LA, 70130; *PH:* 1-504-586-7570; *http://* www.whitneybank.com

General - Incorporation............................LA
Employees..2,484
Auditor ....PricewaterhouseCoopers LLP
Stk Agt.....American Stock Transfer & Trust Co.
Counsel...NA
DUNS No. 08-345-1708

Stock- Price on:12/24/2007 ....$30.29
Stock Exchange...NDQ
Ticker Symbol...WTNY
Outstanding Shares 67,550,000
E.P.S...$2.18
Shareholders..NA

Business: The group's principal activities are to provide commercial and retail banking and trust and investment management services to retirement benefit plans and limited investment brokerage services. The group, through its principal subsidiary whitney national bank, offers community banking services to business and individuals in the five state gulf coast region, stretching from houston, Texas across southern Louisiana and the coastal region of Mississippi to central and south Alabama and into the panhandle of Florida. On 20-Aug-2004, the group acquired madison bancshares, inc.

Primary SIC and add'l.: 6021 6712

CIK No: 0000106926

Subsidiaries: Destin Bancshares, Inc., Madison BancShares, Inc, Southern Coastal Insurance Agency, Inc, Southern Coastal Insurance Agency, Inc., Whitney Holding Corporation, Whitney Securities, LLC

Officers: William L. Marks/Chmn., CEO/$4,871,680.00, Duayne F. Richard/Sr. VP, City Pres. - Lafayette, Sharon Lee/Sr. VP - Western Region Retail Banking, Biff L. Motley/Sr. VP - Retail Banking, Marketing, Omer C. Davis/Sr. VP - Western Region Commercial Banking, Kenneth L. Martinez/Sr. VP - New Orleans Corporate Banking, Eugene C. Crane/Pres. - Central Alabama Region, Milford Blum/Sr. VP - Western Regional Executive, Robert C. Baird/Exec. VP - Louisiana Banking/$1,373,682.00, Luis C. Garza/Sr. VP - International Banking, John C. Hope/Exec. VP - Gulf Coast Banking/$1,400,008.00, Rodney D. Chard/Exec. VP - Operations, Technology, Gary L. Lorio/Sr. VP - New Orleans Corporate Banking, Thomas L. Callicutt/CFO, Exec. VP/$992,547.00, John E. Smith/Sr. VP, Pres. - St. Tammany Parish *(37 Officers included in Index)*

Directors: William L. Marks/Chmn., CEO, King R. Milling/Vice Chmn., John G. Phillips/Dir., James E. Kock/Dir., Michael L. Lomax/Dir., Alfred S. Lippman/Dir., Angus R. Cooper/Dir., William A. Hines/Dir., Dean E. Taylor/Dir., Eric J. Nickelsen/Dir., Richard B. Crowell/Dir., Kathryn M. Sullivan/Dir., Joel B. Bullard/Dir., Thomas D. Westfeldt/Dir.

Owners: Angus R. Cooper, Michael L. Lomax, Kathryn M. Sullivan, Alfred S. Lippman, James M. Cain, Eric J. Nickelsen, Thomas D. Westfeldt, Richard B. Crowell, James E. Kock, Robert C. Baird, Barclays Global Investors, N.A./6.78%, William L. Marks/1.18%, John C. Hope, William A. Hines, Joel B. Bullard *(20 Owners included in Index)*

*Financial Data: Fiscal Year End:*12/31 *Latest Annual Data:* 12/31/2006

Year	Sales	Net Income
2006	$701,162,000	$144,645,000
2005	$550,320,000	$102,349,000
2004	$443,295,000	$97,137,000
Curr. Assets: $680,374,000	*Curr. Liab.:* $9,072,918,000	*P/E Ratio:* 13.89
Plant, Equip.: $175,109,000	*Total Liab.:* $9,072,918,000	*Indic. Yr. Divd.:* $1.160
Total Assets: $10,185,880,000	*Net Worth:* $1,112,962,000	*Debt/ Equity:* 0.1410

Whitney Information Network Inc

1612 E. Cape Coral Pkwy, Cape Coral, FL, 33904; *PH:* 1-239-542-0643; *http://* www.wincorporate.com

General - Incorporation............................CO
Employees...370
Auditor ...Ehrhardt Keefe Steiner & Hottman P.C
Stk Agt.................Corporate Stock Transfer, Inc.
Counsel...NA
DUNS No. ....NA

Stock- Price on:12/24/2007 ....NA
Stock Exchange...OTC
Ticker Symbol...RUSS
Outstanding Shares ....NA
E.P.S...-$0.5
Shareholders..NA

Business: The group's principal activity is to provide financial education and training services through seminars, workshops and publications. The educational and training services are concentrated in the area of financial management and real estate investment. The group markets its services and products primarily through periodic publications, telemarketing, television and radio. The group also develops and markets educational resource materials which are prepared to support course offerings and for sale to the general public. The courses are provided in the United States, Canada and the United Kingdom. The group acquired equity corp holdings inc and whitney leadership group inc in jul 2003, speaktec inc in oct 2003 and success development inc in nov 2003.

Primary SIC and add'l.: 7372 8299

CIK No: 0001095276

Subsidiaries: American Home Buyers Alliance,Inc., Coral Aviation (Owned by AHBA), Edutrades, Inc., MRS Equity Corp, Wealth Intelligence Academy, Whitney (Australia) PTY Limited, Whitney Canada,Inc., Whitney Consulting Services,Inc., Whitney Development, Limited, Whitney Education Espana, S.L., Whitney Education Group,Inc., Whitney International (Singapore) PTE, Ltd, Whitney International Limited, Whitney Leadership Group, Whitney U.K. Limited

Officers: Russell A. Whitney/Chmn., Founder, CEO, Ronald S. Simon/Dir., COO, Co - Pres., Sec., Alfred R. Novas/CFO, Co - Pres., John F. Kane/Exec. VP - Real Estate Education Division, Marie B. Code/40/General Counsel

Directors: Russell A. Whitney/Chmn., Founder, CEO, Ronald S. Simon/Dir., COO, Co - Pres., Sec., Frederick A. Cardin/Dir.

Owners: Alfred R. Novas, Frederick A. Cardin, Ronald S. Simon/3.60%, Marie B. Code, John F. Kane/2.60%, Chester P. Schwartz, Springhouse Capital, LP/8.80%, Russell A. Whitney/44.60%, Heartland Value Fund/5.50%, Prides Capital Fund I, LP/14.10%, Insiders/51.80%

*Financial Data: Fiscal Year End:*12/31 *Latest Annual Data:* 12/31/2006

Year	Sales	Net Income
2006	$224,654,000	$1,755,000
2005	$163,107,000	$3,850,000
2004	$139,859,000	-$29,896,000
Curr. Assets: $66,850,000	*Curr. Liab.:* $136,287,000	
Plant, Equip.: $11,757,000	*Total Liab.:* $140,182,000	*Indic. Yr. Divd.:* $1.370
Total Assets: $95,120,000	*Net Worth:* -$45,062,000	*Debt/ Equity:* NA

Whittier Energy Corp

333 Clay St., Ste. 700, Houston, TX, 77002; *PH:* 1-713-850-1880; *http://* www.whittierenergy.com

General - Incorporation ....NV
Employees..NA
Auditor ....Grant Thornton LLP
Stk Agt..NA
Counsel...NA
DUNS No. ....NA

Stock- Price on:12/24/2007 ....NA
Stock Exchange...NA
Ticker Symbol...NA
Outstanding Shares ....NA
E.P.S...NA
Shareholders..NA

Business: The groups principle activities include acquiring, exploring and developing oil and gas properties. The group operates from the United States.

Primary SIC and add'l.: 1382

CIK No: 0001108520

Subsidiaries: Olympic Resources (Arizona) Ltd., RIMCO Production Company, Inc., Vaquero Gas Company, Whittier Energy Company, Whittier Operating, Inc

Officers: Richard B. Nash/Corp. Sec.

Owners: Dallas Parker, Whittier Holdings,Inc./9.10%, Man Financial Limited/5.10%, Whittier Trust Company/6.70%, Bryce W. Rhodes/2.70%, Arlo G. Sorensen/15.50%, Friedman, Billings, Ramsey& Co.,Inc./5.80%, David A. Dahl, Friedman, Billings, Ramsey Group.,Inc./7.70%, Whittier Ventures LLC/15.10%, Charles Oliver Buckner, Insiders/21.10%, Daniel H. Silverman/1.20%, Geoffrey M. Stone, Wellington Management Company, LLP/6.10% *(17 Owners included in Index)*

Who's Your Daddy Inc

3131 Camino Del Rio N, San Diego, CA, 92108; *PH:* 1-619-284-4807; *http://* www.whosyourdaddyinc.com; *Email:* info@whosyourdaddyinc.com

General - Incorporation	NV	**Stock**- Price on:12/24/2007	$0.79
Employees	10	Stock Exchange	OTC
Auditor	Baum & Company, P.A.	Ticker Symbol	WYDIE
Stk Agt	Holladay Stock Transfer, Inc.	Outstanding Shares	28,380,000
Counsel	NA	E.P.S.	-$0.3
DUNS No.	NA	Shareholders	NA

Business: The groups principle activities include extension of branding, previously consisting of licensing trademarks, is entry into the sale of beverages. The group markets its product under the tradename include King of Energy(TM). The group operates from the United States. The group's quarterly revenue for Sep '07 was 0.54 millions of USD.

Primary SIC and add'l.: 2087

CIK No: 0001164964

Officers: Edon Moyal/26/Chmn., CEO, Dan Fleyshman/26/Dir., Pres., Reuven I. Rubinson/54/CFO

Directors: Edon Moyal/26/Chmn., CEO, Dan Fleyshman/26/Dir., Pres., Derek Jones/69/Dir., Wayne Anderson/42/Dir.

Owners: Edon Moyal/4.49%, Around The Clock Partners LP/5.64%, Reuven I. Rubinson, Dan Fleyshman/4.49%, Insiders/9.70%, Derek Jones

Financial Data: *Fiscal Year End:*12/31 *Latest Annual Data:* 12/31/2006

Year	Sales	Net Income
2006	$1,189,000	-$5,648,000
2005	$77,000	-$4,251,000
2004	NA	-$1,190,000

Curr. Assets:	$410,000	**Curr. Liab.:**	$4,242,000		
Plant, Equip.:	$47,000	**Total Liab.:**	$6,322,000	**Indic. Yr. Divd.:**	NA
Total Assets:	$597,000	**Net Worth:**	-$5,725,000	**Debt/ Equity:**	NA

Whole Foods Market Inc

601 N Lamar Blvd, Ste 300, Austin, TX, 78703; *PH:* 1-512-477-4455; *http://* www.wholefoods.com

General - Incorporation	TX	**Stock**- Price on:12/24/2007	$38.95
Employees	36,200	Stock Exchange	NDQ
Auditor	Ernst & Young LLP	Ticker Symbol	WFMI
Stk Agt	Securities Transfer Corp	Outstanding Shares	141,370,000
Counsel	NA	E.P.S.	$1.32
DUNS No.	18-056-5319	Shareholders	NA

Business: The group's principle activities include owning and operating natural and organic foods supermarket. The groups selling product line includes seafood, grocery, meat, poultry, bakery, prepared foods and catering, floral, pet products and household products. The group operates from United States and United Kingdom.

Primary SIC and add'l.: 5411 5963 5499 5461

CIK No: 0000865436

Subsidiaries: Allegro Coffee Company, Fresh& Wild Holding Limited, Fresh& Wild Limited, Freshlands Holdings Limited, Freshlands Limited, Mrs.Goochs Natural Food Markets, Inc., Natures Heartland, Inc., The Sourdough, A European Bakery, Inc., WFM Beverage Corp., WFM Beverage Holding Company, WFM Cobb Property Investments, LLC, WFM Gift Card, Inc., WFM IP Investments, Inc., WFM IP Management, Inc., WFM Private Label Management, Inc. 36 Subsidiaries included in the Index

Officers: John P. MacKey/53/Chmn., CEO, Co - Founder/$1,346,976.00, Jim Speirs/National VP - Procurement, Non Perishables, Scott Allshouse/Pres. - South Region, Ken Meyer/Pres. - Mid, Atlantic Region, David Lannon/Pres. - North Atlantic Region, Glenda Chamberlain/CFO, Exec. VP/$1,462,332.00, A. C. Gallo/Co - COO, Pres./$1,397,661.00, Mike Clifford/CIO, VP, Michael Besancon/Pres. - Southern Pacific Region, Patrick Bradley/Pres. - Midwest Region, Ron Megahan/Pres. - Pacific Northwest Region, Scott Simons/Regional Contact - Media, Southwest, Includes Texas, Louisiana, Fred Shank/Regional Contact - Media, United Kingdom, Kate Klotz/Regional Contact - Media, Midwest, Includes Illinois, Indiana, Michigan, Missouri, Wisconsin, Ontario, Canada, Missy Cohan/Regional Contact - Media, Northern California, Includes Northern Nevada *(43 Officers included in Index)*

Directors: John P. MacKey/53/Chmn., CEO, Co - Founder, Linda A. Mason/53/Dir., Morris J. Siegel/57/Dir., Garbrielle E. Greene/46/Dir., Ralph Z. Sorenson/73/Dir., Haas Hassan/59/Dir., David W. Dupree/53/Dir., John B. Elstrott/58/Dir.

Financial Data: *Fiscal Year End:*09/25 *Latest Annual Data:* 9/24/2006

Year	Sales	Net Income
2006	$5,607,376,000	$203,828,000
2005	$4,701,289,000	$136,351,000
2004	$3,864,950,000	$132,657,000

Curr. Assets:	$485,572,000	**Curr. Liab.:**	$334,950,000	**P/E Ratio:**	29.51
Plant, Equip.:	$904,825,000	**Total Liab.:**	$579,061,000	**Indic. Yr. Divd.:**	$0.720
Total Assets:	$1,547,716,000	**Net Worth:**	$968,655,000	**Debt/ Equity:**	0.0019

Wi-Tron Inc

Formerly: Amplidyne Inc

59 Lagrange St., Raritan, NJ, 08869; *PH:* 1-908-253-6870

General - Incorporation	DE	**Stock**- Price on:12/24/2007	$0.02
Employees	14	Stock Exchange	OTC
Auditor	Kahn Boyd Levychin LLP	Ticker Symbol	WTRO
Stk Agt	American Stock Transfer & Trust Co.	Outstanding Shares	NA
Counsel	NA	E.P.S.	-$0.028
DUNS No.	61-193-4613	Shareholders	NA

Business: The group's principle activities include designing, manufacturing and marketing ultra linear power amplifiers and related subsystems to the wireless, local loop and satellite uplink telecommunications market. These power amplifiers are a key component in cellular base stations. They increase the power of radio frequency and microwave signals with low distortion, enabling the user to significantly increase the quality and quantity of calls processed by new and existing cellular base stations. The wireless communications products consist of solid-state, radio frequency and microwave, single and multi carrier power amplifiers that support a broad range of analog and digital transmission protocols including code division multiple access (cdma) and time division multiple access (tdma). The customers include wireless communications manufacturers (OEMs) and communications system operators. The group operates from United States.

Primary SIC and add'l.: 3663

CIK No: 0001016151

Officers: John C. Lee/Chmn., CEO, Joe Nordgaard/Business Development Consultant, Tarlochan Bains/58/Dir., COO, Dave Bains/VP - Product Development, Craig H. Bird/Dir., Corp. Sec., Chief Governance Officer

Directors: John C. Lee/Chmn., CEO, Mikio Tajima/Dir., Jessica Hye Lee/Dir., Tarlochan Bains/58/Dir., COO

Owners: Tarlochan Bains/1.20%, Harris Freedman/5.00%, John Chase Lee/28.70%, Craig H. Bird/14.40%, Insiders/41.70%, Devendar S. Bains/4.30%

Financial Data: *Fiscal Year End:*12/31 *Latest Annual Data:* 12/31/2006

Year	Sales	Net Income
2006	$154,000	-$1,891,000
2005	$471,000	-$1,319,000
2004	$744,000	-$769,000

Curr. Assets:	$120,000	**Curr. Liab.:**	$975,000		
Plant, Equip.:	$14,000	**Total Liab.:**	$975,000	**Indic. Yr. Divd.:**	NA
Total Assets:	$139,000	**Net Worth:**	-$836,000	**Debt/ Equity:**	NA

WidePoint Corp

One Lincoln Ctr., 18W140 Butterfield Rd., Ste. 1100, Oakbrook Terrace, IL, 60181; *PH:* 1-630-629-0003; *Fax:* 1-630-629-7559; *http://* www.widepoint.com

General - Incorporation	DE	**Stock**- Price on:12/24/2007	$0.8612
Employees	55	Stock Exchange	AMEX
Auditor	Epstein, Weber & Conover, PLC	Ticker Symbol	WYY
Stk Agt	American Stock Transfer & Trust Co.	Outstanding Shares	52,530,000
Counsel	Foley & Lardner	E.P.S.	$0.001
DUNS No.	NA	Shareholders	NA

Business: The groups principle activates include providing systems engineering, information technology services and information assurance. The groups services include E-Authentication Federation credential services, federal compliant Public Key Infrastructure managed services, and GSA Access Certificates for Electronic Services The group operates through two segments namely consulting services and PKI credentialing and managed services. Specific customers of the group include United States Treasury, Administrative Office of U.S. Courts, United States Department of Agriculture and United States Maritime Administration. The group operates from the United States. The group's quarterly revenue for September 2007 was 4.00 millions of USD.

Primary SIC and add'l.: 7371 8748 7379 7373 7389

CIK No: 0001034760

Subsidiaries: Chesapeake Government Technologies, Inc., Operational Research Consultants, Inc., WidePoint Il, Inc., WidePoint NBIL, Inc.

Officers: Steven L. Komar/Chmn., CEO/$47,200.00, Frank Hawkins/CEO - Hawk Associates, Inc, James T. McCubbin/Dir., CFO, VP, Sec., Treasurer/$125,000.00, Mark Mirabile/COO, VP/$125,000.00, Daniel Turissini/Pres./$225,000.00

Directors: Steven L. Komar/Chmn., CEO, James T. McCubbin/Dir., CFO, VP, Sec., Treasurer, James M. Ritter/Dir., Morton S. Taubman/Dir., Ron Oxley/Dir.

Owners: Insiders/18.00%, Mark Mirabile/5.10%, Capital Group International, Inc.and Capital Guardian Trust Company/9.10%, Ronald Oxley, James McCubbin/5.00%, James Ritter, Steve Komar/5.10%, Daniel Turissini/2.50%, Morton Taubman, Goldman, Sachs & Co./5.10%

Financial Data: *Fiscal Year End:*12/31 *Latest Annual Data:* 12/31/2006

Year	Sales	Net Income
2006	$17,953,000	-$435,000
2005	$13,263,000	-$7,445,000
2004	$5,542,000	-$4,281,000

Curr. Assets:	$9,459,000	**Curr. Liab.:**	$5,764,000		
Plant, Equip.:	$205,000	**Total Liab.:**	$5,832,000	**Indic. Yr. Divd.:**	NA
Total Assets:	$13,604,000	**Net Worth:**	$7,772,000	**Debt/ Equity:**	0.0087

Wilber Corp

245 Main St., Oneonta, NY, 13820; *PH:* 1-607-432-1700; *Fax:* 1-607-433-4161; *http://* www.wilberbank.com

General - Incorporation	NY	**Stock**- Price on:12/24/2007	$9.35
Employees	255	Stock Exchange	AMEX
Auditor	KPMG LLP	Ticker Symbol	GIW
Stk Agt	NA	Outstanding Shares	10,570,000
Counsel	NA	E.P.S.	NA
DUNS No.	NA	Shareholders	NA

Business: The group's principal activities are to offers a full range of commercial and consumer financial products including business, municipal, mortgage and consumer loans, deposits, trust and investment services and insurance through the bank and the bank's subsidiaries. The group operates through 19 full service branch banking offices located in otsego, Delaware, schoharie, ulster, and broome counties, New York, an ATM network and electronic/Internet banking services.

Primary SIC and add'l.: 6022 6712

CIK No: 0000709942

Subsidiaries: Mang-Wilber, LLC, Western Catskill Realty, LLC, Wilber REIT, Inc.

Owners: Joseph E. Sutaris, Olon T. Archer, Alfred S. Whittet, Joseph P. Mirabito, Wilber National Bank/7.70%, Thomas J. Davis, Brian R. Wright/32.49%, Douglas C. Gulotty, Insiders/36.33%, David F. Wilber/2.55%, Mary C. Albrecht, The AE & AT Farone Foundation, Inc./7.65%, Geoffrey A. Smith, James L. Seward

Financial Data: *Fiscal Year End:*12/31 *Latest Annual Data:* 12/31/2006

Year	Sales	Net Income
2006	$49,310,000	$7,152,000
2005	$45,820,000	$7,744,000
2004	$42,799,000	$8,618,000

Curr. Assets:	$27,484,000	**Curr. Liab.:**	$647,503,000	**P/E Ratio:**	13.96
Plant, Equip.:	$5,686,000	**Total Liab.:**	$698,649,000	**Indic. Yr. Divd.:**	$0.380
Total Assets:	$761,981,000	**Net Worth:**	$63,332,000	**Debt/ Equity:**	NA

Willamette Community Bank

333 Lyon St. S, Albany, OR, 97321; *PH:* 1-541-926-9000; *http://* www.wcbalbany.com

General - Incorporation
Employees NA
Auditor NA
Stk Agt NA
Counsel NA
DUNS No. NA

Stock- Price on:12/24/2007 $11.1
Stock Exchange OTC
Ticker Symbol WMCB
Outstanding Shares NA
E.P.S NA
Shareholders NA

Business: The groups principal activity is to provide banking services. Services of the group include savings accounts, Consumer Installment Loans, home loans and agriculture loans. The group operates from the United States.

Primary SIC and add'l.: 6022

CIK No:

Officers: Laurie A. Flynn/Sr. VP

Willamette Valley Vineyards Inc

8800 Enchanted Way S E, Turner, OR, 97392; *PH:* 1-503-588-9463; *http://* www.wvv.com; *Email:* tastingroom@wvv.com

General - Incorporation OR
Employees 96
Auditor Moss Adams LLP
Stk Agt Computershare Trust Co
Counsel NA
DUNS No. 36-105-7607

Stock- Price on:12/24/2007 $6.908
Stock Exchange NDQ
Ticker Symbol WVVI
Outstanding Shares 4,810,000
E.P.S $0.23
Shareholders NA

Business: The group's principal activity is to manufacture and market premium, super premium and ultra premium varieties of wines. It owns and operates vineyards and a winery located in the state of Oregon. The group owns 146 acres of vineyard land, fifty acres of planted vineyards- 42 acres producing and 8 acres in development at the turner site. It markets a variety of wine in 750-ml bottles, which is distributed under willamette valley vineyards, made in Oregon cellars, tualatin estate vineyards and griffin creek label. The names of the some of the products are pinot noir, chardonnay, riesling and Oregon blossom late harvest gewurztraminer, pinot blanc, etc. The group markets the wines directly and indirectly to local restaurants and retail outlets as well as through its shareholders, mailing lists, distributors and wine brokers.

Primary SIC and add'l.: 2084

CIK No: 0000838875

Officers: James W. Bernau/Chmn., CEO, Pres., Founder/$219,115.00, James L. Ellis/Dir., VP - Corporate, Dir. - Human Resources, Sec., Sean M. Cary/34/Principal Accounting Officer, Controller, Jon Mason/Retail Mgr.

Directors: James W. Bernau/Chmn., CEO, Pres., Founder, James L. Ellis/Dir., VP - Corporate, Dir. - Human Resources, Sec., Stan G. Turel/Dir., Delna L. Jones/Dir., Thomas M. Brian/Dir., Lisa M. Matich/Dir., Betty M. O'Brien/Dir.

Owners: Insiders/20.70%, Thomas M. Brian, Delna L. Jones, James W. Bernau/15.70%, Betty M. O'Brien, Lisa M. Matich, Stan G. Turel, James L. Ellis/1.70%

Financial Data: *Fiscal Year End:*12/31 *Latest Annual Data:* 12/31/2006

Year	Sales	Net Income
2006	$14,916,000	$1,292,000
2005	$13,668,000	$1,157,000
2004	$9,387,000	$464,000

Curr. Assets:	$10,189,000	**Curr. Liab.:**	$2,377,000	**P/E Ratio:**	30.03
Plant, Equip.:	$3,986,000	**Total Liab.:**	$4,458,000	**Indic. Yr. Divd.:**	NA
Total Assets:	$15,798,000	**Net Worth:**	$11,340,000	**Debt/ Equity:**	0.1011

Willbros Group Inc

4400 Post Oak Pkwy., Ste. 1000, Houston, TX, 77027; *PH:* 1-713-403-8000; *Fax:* 1-713-403-8066; *http://* www.willbros.com

General - Incorporation Panama
Employees 4,156
Auditor GLO CPAs LLP
Stk Agt Mellon Investor Services LLC
Counsel NA
DUNS No. 85-367-5270

Stock- Price on:12/24/2007 $30.38
Stock Exchange NYSE
Ticker Symbol WG
Outstanding Shares 26,040,000
E.P.S -$3.55
Shareholders NA

Business: The group's principal activity is to provide construction, engineering and specialty services to the oil, gas and power industries. Construction segment build and replace cross-country offshore pipelines, oil and gas production facilities, pump stations, flow stations, gas compressor stations and gas processing facilities. Engineering segment provide project management and procurement services to the oil, gas and power industries. Specialty segment provide a wide range of support and ancillary services related to the construction repair and rehabilitation of pipelines. The group operates in Africa, Asia, Australia, the Middle East, South America, Canada and the United States.

Primary SIC and add'l.: 1623 8741 1622 8711

CIK No: 0000895450

Subsidiaries: 814965 Alberta Ltd., Construcciones Acuticas Mundiales, S.A., Constructora CAMSA, C.A., Constructora Laboral Mexicana Universal, S. de R.L. de C.V., Constructora Willbros de Mxico, S. de R.L. de C.V., Constructora Willbros Tenica Mexicana Universal,S. de R.L. de C.V, Contratistas Transandinos, S.A. d/b/a/ COTRA, Cruzamientos Direccionales Orizzon, S.A. de C.V., ESCA Equipment Service C.A., Harwat Financial Services Corporation, N.V., International Pipeline Equipment, Inc., Inversiones CAMSA, C.A., Kompaniya Willbros ZAO, Monastere Inc., Musketeer Oil B.V. 76 Subsidiaries included in the Index

Officers: Randy Harl/Dir., CEO, Bradley W. Sitton/VP, Corbin L. Porter/Information Technology Project Mgr., John K. Allcorn/Sr. VP/$620,569.00, Van Welch/Sr. VP, CFO/$415,578.00, Jay T. Dalton/Sr. VP, General Counsel/$672,579.00, Ronald A. Lefaive/Corporate Controller, Lonnie R. Hamilton/Operations Management, Alan G. Owens/VP, COO, Latif A. Razek/GM, Norman Sabourin/Corp. Dir. - Health, Safety, Environment, Gay S. Mayeux/VP - Finance, Richard Russler/Administration Mgr., James R. Beasley/VP, Kevin L. Cater/Project Mgr. *(19 Officers included in Index)*

Directors: Randy Harl/Dir., CEO, Michael J. Bayer/Dir., Gerald J. Maier/Dir., Robert L. Sluder/58/Dir., Fred S. Isaacs/Dir., John T. McNabb/Dir., James B. Taylor/Dir., Miller S. Williams/Dir.

Owners: Fred S. Isaacs, Gerald J. Maier, ICM Asset Management, Inc./5.50%, Berggruen Holdings North America Ltd./5.50%, SAB Capital Partners, L.P./5.90%, Robert R. Harl, John T. Dalton, Third Avenue Management LLC/6.40%, Michael J. Bayer, Miller S. Williams, Clay R. Etheridge, Neuberger Berman Inc./5.50%, John T. McNabb, Van A. Welch, John K. Allcorn *(23 Owners included in Index)*

Financial Data: *Fiscal Year End:*12/31 *Latest Annual Data:* 12/31/2006

Year	Sales	Net Income
2006	$543,259,000	-$105,437,000
2005	$706,522,000	-$38,780,000
2004	$483,318,000	-$20,815,000

Curr. Assets:	$499,334,000	**Curr. Liab.:**	$328,509,000		
Plant, Equip.:	$65,347,000	**Total Liab.:**	$490,323,000	**Indic. Yr. Divd.:**	NA
Total Assets:	$588,254,000	**Net Worth:**	$97,931,000	**Debt/ Equity:**	1.9222

Willdan Group Inc

2401 E Katella Ave., Ste. 300, Anaheim, CA, 92806; *PH:* 1-714-940-6300; *Fax:* 1-714-940-4920; *http://* www.willdangroup.com

General - Incorporation DE
Employees 584
Auditor KPMG LLP
Stk Agt U.S. Stock Transfer Corp
Counsel Snell & Wilmer L.L.P.
DUNS No. NA

Stock- Price on:12/24/2007 $9.9
Stock Exchange NDQ
Ticker Symbol WLDN
Outstanding Shares 7,150,000
E.P.S $1.00
Shareholders NA

Business: The groups principle activity is to provide outsourced services. The groups operates through three segments namely engineering, public finance, and homeland security. Customers served by the group include civil engineering and financial and economic consulting. The group operates from the United States.

Primary SIC and add'l.: 8748 8741 7389 8748 781 8712 7389 8742 8713 8713 8712 8711 8742 781 8741 8711

CIK No: 0001370450

Subsidiaries: American Homeland Solutions, Arroyo Geotechnical, MuniFinancial, Public Agency Resources, Willdan

Officers: Frank G. Tripepi/59/Pres., CEO - Munifinancial, Ross Khiabani/57/Pres., CEO - Arroyo Geotechnical, Kenneth L. Bayless/60/Pres., CEO - American Homeland Solutions, Thomas D. Brisbin/Dir., CEO, David L. Hunt/Pres., CEO - Willdan, Marc Tipermas/Pres. - National Programs, Kimberly Gant/CFO, Jean Blythe/VP - Human Resources, Moira Conlon/Exec. VP, Mallory McCamant/COO, Del Conrad/VP - Financial Reporting, Compliance, James A. Jordan/VP - Information Technology, Roy L. Gill/VP, Controller, Sec.

Directors: Thomas D. Brisbin/Dir., CEO, Win Westfall/Chmn., Tracy W. Lenocker/Dir., Linda L. Heil/Dir., Keith W. Renken/Dir., Chell Smith/Dir., John M. Toups/82/Dir.

Owners: Mallory McCamant, Royce& Associates, LLC/5.60%, JLF Asset Management, L.L.C/6.30%, Keith W. Renken, Tracy W. Lenocker/2.80%, Linda L. Heil/12.80%, Insiders/16.10%, Win Westfall, Chell Smith, Jeffrey L. Feinberg/6.30%, Richard Kopecky/4.70%

Financial Data: *Fiscal Year End:*12/31 *Latest Annual Data:* 12/29/2006

Year	Sales	Net Income
2006	$78,339,000	$6,289,000
2005	$67,263,000	-$646,000
2004	$58,263,000	$3,772,000

Curr. Assets:	$18,039,000	**Curr. Liab.:**	$10,844,000	**P/E Ratio:**	14.83
Plant, Equip.:	$2,027,000	**Total Liab.:**	$11,746,000	**Indic. Yr. Divd.:**	NA
Total Assets:	$23,223,000	**Net Worth:**	$11,477,000	**Debt/ Equity:**	NA

William Lyon Homes

4490 Von Karman Ave., Newport Beach, CA, 92660; *PH:* 1-949-833-3600; *http://* www.lyonhomes.com

General - Incorporation DE
Employees NA
Auditor Ernst & Young LLP
Stk Agt Mellon Investor Services LLC
Counsel Irell & Manella
DUNS No. NA

Stock- Price on:12/24/2007 $175
Stock Exchange OTC
Ticker Symbol WLSM
Outstanding Shares NA
E.P.S NA
Shareholders NA

Business: The group's principle activities are to design, construct and market single family detached and attached homes. The group conducts its homebuilding operations through five geographic divisions: southern California, san diego, northern California, Arizona and Nevada. As of 31-Dec-2003,the group owned approximately 6,174 lots. The group marketes homes through 42 sales locations in both its wholly-owned projects and projects being developed in unconsolidated joint ventures.

Primary SIC and add'l.: 1521

CIK No: 0001095996

Subsidiaries: 242 Cerro Plata, LLC, 4S Lot 12, LLC, 4S Lots 2 & 8, LLC, 4S Ranch Planning Area 38, LLC, Bayport Mortgage, L.P., Brentwood Legends, L.P., California Equity Funding, Inc., California Pacific Mortgage, L.P., Cerro Plata Associates, LLC, Chino Reserve 89, LLC, Circle G at the Church Farm North Joint Venture, LLC, Covenant Hills P-30A, LLC, Covenant Hills P30B, LLC, Duxford Escrow, Inc., Duxford Financial, Inc. 63 Subsidiaries included in the Index

Officers: William H. Lyon/Dir., Chmn., CEO, Chief Administrative Officer, Exec. VP, Dean C. Stewart/VP - Operations, Larry I. Smith/Sr. VP, Inland Empire Region Pres., Mary J. Connelly/Sr. VP, Region Pres. - Nevada, Thomas J. Mitchell/Sr. VP, Region Pres. - Southern California Coastal, Douglas K. Ammerman/Dir., Independent Consultant, Colin Severn/Mgr. - Hiring, Todd White/Mgr. - Hiring, Thomas W. Hickcox/Sr. VP, Region Pres. - Arizona, Michael D. Grubbs/CFO, Sr. VP, Treasurer, Mark A. Carver/Pres. - William Lyon Financial Services, Douglass W. Harris/Sr. VP, Corporate Controller, Corp. Sec., Douglas F. Bauer/Dir., COO, Pres., Cynthia E. Hardgrave/VP - Tax, Internal Audit, Richard E. Frankel/Dir., Independent Consultant *(17 Officers included in Index)*

Directors: William H. Lyon/Dir., Chmn., CEO, Chief Administrative Officer, Exec. VP, Richard E. Frankel/Dir., Independent Consultant, Douglas F. Bauer/Dir., COO, Pres., Alex Meruelo/Dir., Wade H. Cable/Dir., Gary H. Hunt/Dir., Lawrence M. Higby/Dir., Arthur B. Laffer/Dir., Douglas K. Ammerman/Dir., Independent Consultant

Owners: William Lyon/66.40%, The William Harwell Lyon 1987 Trust/28.20%, Insiders/66.40%, The William Harwell Lyon Separate Property Trust/5.40%

William Wrigley CL-B

The Wrigley Building, 410 North Michigan Ave., Chicago, IL, 60611; ; *http://* investor.wrigley.com

General - Incorporation	DE	**Stock**- Price on:12/24/2007	$55.49
Employees	NA	Stock Exchange	OTC
Auditor	Ernst & Young LLP	Ticker Symbol	WWYWB
Stk Agt	Computershare Trust Co	Outstanding Shares	NA
Counsel	NA	E.P.S	NA
DUNS No.	NA	Shareholders	NA

Business: The groups principal activities include manufacturing and marketing chewing gum and other confectionery products. The group markets its products under the tradenames include Juicy Fruit(R) and Spearmint(R). In January 2007, the group acquired A. Korkunov, a privately held premium chocolate company in Russia. The group operates from the United States.

Primary SIC and add'l.: 2060

CIK No: 0000108601

Subsidiaries: Cafosa Gum, S.A., Dulces de las Americas, S. de R.L. de C.V., Four-Ten Corporation, Green Arrow Development Corporation, Joyco India Private Limited (India), L. A. Dreyfus Company, Northwestern Flavors, LLC., OOO Wrigley, P.T. Wrigley Indonesia, Regico, S.L., Techninter, S.A., The Wrigley Company (E.A.) Ltd., The Wrigley Company (H.K.) Limited, The Wrigley Company (Malaysia) Sdn. Bhd., The Wrigley Company (N.Z.) Limited 61 Subsidiaries included in the Index

Officers: William D. Perez/60/CEO, Pres., Michael Wong/Group VP, MD - Asia, Pacific, Tawfik Sharkasi/VP - Research, Development, Gum, Confections, Samson Suen/VP, MD - China, John Adams/VP - Worldwide Manufacturing, Surinder Kumar/Sr. VP, Chief Innovation Officer, Denis Schrey/VP, MD - North, Central Europe, Ralph P. Scozzafava/49/VP - Worldwide Commercial Operations, Vincent C. Bonica/VP - Worldwide Gum Base Operations, Reuben Gamoran/Sr. VP, CFO, Peter Hempstead/Sr. VP - Worldwide Strategy, New Business, Susan Henderson/VP - Corporate Communications, Donagh Herlihy/VP - Supply Chain Strategy, Planning, CIO, Howard Malovany/Sr. VP, Sec., General Counsel, Shaun Mara/VP, Controller *(22 Officers included in Index)*

Directors: William Wrigley/Chmn., Thomas A. Knowlton/Dir., Steven B. Sample/Dir., Alex Shumate/Dir., John F. Bard/Dir., Howard B. Bernick/Dir., Melinda R. Rich/Dir., John Rau/Dir., Richard K. Smucker/59/Dir.

Owners: ClearBridge Advisors, LLC/5.42%, William J. Hagenah/4.61%, William Wrigley/4.46%, William J. Hagenah/20.09%, Capital Research and Mgmt. Co/10.32%, William Wrigley/40.77%

Williams Coal Seam Gas Royalty Trust

901 Main St., Ste. 1700, Dallas, TX, 75202; ***Fax:*** 1-214-209-2431;
http:// www.wtu-williamscoalseamgastrust.com; ***Email:*** trustee@wtu-williamscoalseamgastrust.com

General - Incorporation	DE	**Stock**- Price on:12/24/2007	$10.65
Employees	NA	Stock Exchange	NYSE
Auditor	Ernst& Young LLP	Ticker Symbol	WTU
Stk Agt	Mellon Investor Services LLC	Outstanding Shares	9,700,000
Counsel	Thompson & Knight, LLC	E.P.S	$0.98
DUNS No.	NA	Shareholders	NA

Business: The groups principal activities include maintaining, sustaining production from the natural gas properties. The group operates from the United States.

Primary SIC and add'l.: 6792

CIK No: 0000895007

Officers: Ron E. Hooper/Sr. VP, Administrator

Owners: The Williams Companies, Inc./8.14%

Financial Data: ***Fiscal Year End:***12/31 ***Latest Annual Data:*** 12/31/2006

Year	Sales	Net Income
2006	$13,997,000	$13,032,000
2005	$14,526,000	$13,566,000
2004	$15,386,000	$14,641,000

Curr. Assets:	$62,000	**Curr. Liab.:**	$56,000	**P/E Ratio:**	10.65
Plant, Equip.:	NA	**Total Liab.:**	$56,000	**Indic. Yr. Divd.:**	$0.780
Total Assets:	$8,373,000	**Net Worth:**	$8,316,000	**Debt/ Equity:**	NA

Williams Controls Inc

14100 SW 72nd Ave., Portland, OR, 97224; ***PH:*** 1-503-684-8600; ***http://*** www.wmco.com;
Email: info@wmco.com

General - Incorporation	DE	**Stock**- Price on:12/24/2007	$16.81
Employees	236	Stock Exchange	NDQ
Auditor	Moss Adams LLP	Ticker Symbol	WMCO
Stk Agt	Computershare Investor Services LLC	Outstanding Shares	7,480,000
Counsel	Friedlob Sanderson Raskin Paulson	E.P.S	$1.20
DUNS No.	19-846-0511	Shareholders	NA

Business: The group's principal activities are to manufacture, design and develop vehicle components. The vehicle component segment manufactures, assembles, packages and distributes truck and auto accessories for heavy vehicles. The group also manufactures and sells pneumatic and hydraulic controls used in trucks, utility and off-highway equipment, transit busses and underground mining machines. The group's product lines consisted of electronic throttle control systems for the heavy truck, light truck, passenger car, transit bus and off-highway markets. On sep 30th, 2003 the group sold its passenger car and light truck electronic throttle controls product lines to its competitor, teleflex, incorporated. The group markets its product in the United States, Canada, Mexico, Sweden, Europe, South America and Australia.

Primary SIC and add'l.: 3674 3714 3594 3069

CIK No: 0000854860

Subsidiaries: Agrotec Williams, Inc., Aptek Williams, Inc., Hardee Williams, Inc., NESC Williams, Inc., Premier Plastic Technologies, Inc., ProActive Acquisition Corporation, Techwood Williams, Inc., Waccamaw Wheel Williams, Inc., Williams (Suzhou) Controls Co. Ltd., Williams Controls Europe GmbH, Williams Controls Industries, Inc., Williams Technologies, Inc., Williams World Trade, Inc., WMCO-Geo, Inc.

Officers: Patrick Cavanagh/Dir., CEO, Pres., John Herrick/Chief Engineer, Lily Casias/Executive Assist., Scott Thiel/Engineering Mgr., Michael Welter/Quality Mgr., Trent Smith/Dir. - Human Resources, Gary Hafner/VP - Global Manufacturing, Dennis Bunday/CFO, Exec. VP, Mark S. Koenen/VP - Sales, Marketing

Directors: Patrick Cavanagh/Dir., CEO, Pres., Eugene R. Goodson/Chmn., Douglas E. Hailey/Dir., Peter E. Salas/Dir., Donn Viola/Dir., Carlos Salas/Dir.

Owners: Carlos P. Salas/9.52%, Dolphin Offshore Partners, L.P./14.90%, Eugene R. Goodson/1.20%, Dolphin Direct Equity Partners LP/9.50%, Sajid Parvez, Dennis E. Bunday/2.09%, Gary A. Hafner, Mark E. Brady/5.70%, Insiders/31.10%, Bernard J. Holtgreive/5.70%, Patrick W. Cavanagh/2.86%, Donn J. Viola, Robert J. Suttman/5.70%, William E. Hazel/5.70%, Peter E. Salas/24.35% *(20 Owners included in Index)*

Financial Data: ***Fiscal Year End:***09/30 ***Latest Annual Data:*** 9/30/2006

Year	Sales	Net Income
2006	$74,634,000	$9,549,000
2005	$67,416,000	$7,495,000
2004	$58,050,000	-$4,058,000

Curr. Assets:	$24,037,000	**Curr. Liab.:**	$17,697,000	**P/E Ratio:**	14.01
Plant, Equip.:	$8,457,000	**Total Liab.:**	$27,487,000	**Indic. Yr. Divd.:**	NA
Total Assets:	$35,749,000	**Net Worth:**	$8,262,000	**Debt/ Equity:**	0.2718

Williams Cos Inc

One Williams Ctr, Tulsa, OK, 74172; ***PH:*** 1-918-573-2000; ***http://*** www.twc.com

General - Incorporation	DE	**Stock**- Price on:12/24/2007	$31.64
Employees	4,313	Stock Exchange	NYSE
Auditor	Ernst & Young LLP	Ticker Symbol	WMB
Stk Agt	Computershare Investor Services LLC	Outstanding Shares	598,860,000
Counsel	NA	E.P.S	$1.33
DUNS No.	00-718-7305	Shareholders	NA

Business: The groups principle activities include producing, gathering and transporting natural gas. The group operates from United States.

Primary SIC and add'l.: 4923 2911 1321 4619 4925

CIK No: 0000107263

Subsidiaries: Accroserv Srl, Accroven Srl, Alliance Canada Marketing L.P., Alliance Canada Marketing LTD, Apco Argentina, Inc., Apco Argentina, S.A., Apco Properties Ltd., Arctic Fox Assets, LLC, Aspen Products Pipeline LLC, Aux Sable Canada LP, Aux Sable Canada Ltd., Aux Sable Liquid Products Inc., Aux Sable Liquid Products LP, Bargath Inc., Barrett Fuels Corporation 254 Subsidiaries included in the Index

Officers: Steven J. Malcolm/57/Chmn., CEO, Pres./$10,343,900.00, Michael P. Johnson/Sr. VP, Chief Administrative Officer/$2,380,729.00, Ralph A. Hill/Pres. - Exploration, Production/$2,288,653.00, James J. Bender/Sr. VP, General Counsel, Donald R. Chappel/56/CFO, Sr. VP, William E. Hobbs/48/Sr. VP - Power, Don R. Chappel/CFO, Sr. VP/$3,203,782.00, Bill Hobbs/Pres. - Power, Brian K. Shore/Attorney, Kelly Swan/Contact - Media, Michele Swaner/Contact - Media Relations, Chris Stockton/Contact - Media, Carin Andre/Contact - Media Relations, Sara Delgado/Contact - Media Relations, Ted T. Timmermans/Principal Accounting Officer, Controller *(17 Officers included in Index)*

Directors: Steven J. Malcolm/57/Chmn., CEO, Pres., William E. Green/71/Dir., Joseph H. Williams/74/Honorary Dir., Janice D. Stoney/67/Dir., Charles M. Lillis/66/Dir., William R. Granberry/65/Dir., Irl Engelhardt/61/Dir., William G. Lowrie/64/Dir., Kathleen Cooper/63/Dir., Juanita H. Hinshaw/63/Dir., William R. Howell/72/Dir., George A. Lorch/66/Dir., Frank T. MacInnis/61/Dir., John H. Williams/89/Dir.

Owners: Michael P. Johnson, Janice D. Stoney, William R. Granberry, Steven J. Malcolm, W. R. Howell, Charles M. Lillis, Insiders/1.06%, William E. Green, Irl F. Engelhardt, Frank T. MacInnis, Donald R. Chappel, Ralph A. Hill, Juanita H. Hinshaw, George A. Lorch, Phillip D. Wright *(17 Owners included in Index)*

Financial Data: ***Fiscal Year End:***12/31 ***Latest Annual Data:*** 12/31/2006

Year	Sales	Net Income
2006	$11,812,900,000	$308,500,000
2005	$12,583,600,000	$313,600,000
2004	$12,461,300,000	$163,700,000

Curr. Assets:	$6,322,000,000	**Curr. Liab.:**	$4,693,600,000	**P/E Ratio:**	23.79
Plant, Equip.:	$14,180,700,000	**Total Liab.:**	$19,329,200,000	**Indic. Yr. Divd.:**	$0.400
Total Assets:	$25,402,400,000	**Net Worth:**	$6,073,200,000	**Debt/ Equity:**	1.5785

Williams Industries Inc

8624 J.D. Reading Dr., Manassas, VA, 20109; ***PH:*** 1-703-335-7800; ***Fax:*** 1-703-335-7852;
http:// www.wmsi.com; ***Email:*** mpastor@wmsi.com

General - Incorporation	VA	**Stock**- Price on:12/24/2007	NA
Employees	277	Stock Exchange	OTC
Auditor	McGladrey & Pullen LLP	Ticker Symbol	WMSI
Stk Agt	Wachovia Bank N.A	Outstanding Shares	NA
Counsel	NA	E.P.S	NA
DUNS No.	00-325-8183	Shareholders	NA

Business: The group's principal activity is to operate in the commercial, industrial, institutional and infrastructure construction markets in the United States. The group operates through two segments: construction and manufacturing. The group's construction segment includes the erection and installation of steel, precast and pre-stressed concrete and miscellaneous metals as well as rigging and rents cranes and trucks to outside customers. Manufacturing segment provides fabrication of steel plate girders and light structural metal products.

Primary SIC and add'l.: 9999 7359 6411 1796 3441 1791

CIK No: 0000107294

Subsidiaries: Insurance Risk Management Group, Inc., Piedmont Metal Products, Inc., S.I.P. Inc. of Delaware, WII Realty Management, Inc., Williams Bridge Company, Williams Equipment Corporation, Williams Steel Erection Company, Inc.

Officers: Frank E. Williams/49/Chmn., CEO, CFO, Pres., Marianne Pastor/Investor Relations Officer

Directors: Frank E. Williams/49/Chmn., CEO, CFO, Pres., Frank E. Williams/74/Dir., Stephen N. Ashman/60/Dir., William J. Sim/63/Dir., John A. Yerrick/68/Dir.

Owners: Insiders/57.40%, Frank E. Williams/34.40%, Frank E. Williams/50.90%, Stephen N. Ashman/0.86%, William J. Sim/0.63%, John A. Yerrick/0.21%

Financial Data: ***Fiscal Year End:***07/31 ***Latest Annual Data:*** 7/31/2006

Year	Sales	Net Income
2006	$42,118,000	$93,000
2005	$48,572,000	-$11,374,000
2004	$53,884,000	-$780,000

Curr. Assets:	$21,247,000	Curr. Liab.:	$17,348,000		
Plant, Equip.:	$8,668,000	Total Liab.:	$24,954,000	Indic. Yr. Divd.:	NA
Total Assets:	$30,118,000	Net Worth:	$4,987,000	Debt/ Equity:	1.0674

Williams Partners LP

One Williams Ctr., Tulsa, OK, 74172; *PH:* 1-918-573-2000; *http://* www.williamslp.com

General - Incorporation	DE	Stock- Price on:12/24/2007	$47.63
Employees	NA	Stock Exchange	NYSE
Auditor	Ernst & Young LLP	Ticker Symbol	WPZ
Stk Agt	Computershare Trust Co	Outstanding Shares	39,360,000
Counsel	NA	E.P.S	$2.04
DUNS No.	NA	Shareholders	NA

Business: The groups principle activities include gathering, transporting, processing and treating natural gas and fractionating and storing NGLs. The group operates through three segments namely, gathering and processing-Gulf, gathering and processing-West and NGL services. The group operates from the United States and Gulf. The groups quarterly revenue for September 2007 was 149.58 millions of USD.

Primary SIC and add'l.: 1311 4922

CIK No: 0001324518

Subsidiaries: Carbonate Trend Pipeline LLC, Discovery Gas Transmission LLC, Discovery Producer Services LLC, Mid-Continent Fractionation and Storage LLC, Williams Four Corners LLC, Williams Partners Finance Corporation, Williams Partners Operating LLC

Officers: Steven J. Malcolm/Chmn., CEO, Sharna Reingold/Investor Relations Officer, Alan S. Armstrong/Dir., COO, Donald R. Chappel/Dir., CFO, James J. Bender/General Counsel, Ted T. Timmermans/Chief Accounting Officer, Controller

Directors: Steven J. Malcolm/Chmn., CEO, Alan S. Armstrong/Dir., COO, Donald R. Chappel/Dir., CFO, Phillp D. Wright/52/Dir., Bill Z. Parker/59/Dir., Alice M. Peterson/54/Dir., Thomas C. Knudson/61/Dir., Rod Sailor/49/Dir., Michael H. Krimbill/54/Dir.

Owners: Prudential Financial, Inc./10.90%, MAPCO Inc./1.80%, Williams Energy, L.L.C./1.80%, Insiders, Tortoise Capital Advisors L.L.C./1.00%, Donald R. Chappel, Phillip D. Wright, Alan S. Armstrong, Steven J. Malcolm, Bill Z. Parker, GPS Income Fund LTD, Jennison Utility Fund/2.80%, Thomas C. Knudson, Williams Discovery Pipeline LLC, Williams Partners Holdings LLC/1.70% *(22 Owners included in Index)*

Financial Data: Fiscal Year End:12/31 Latest Annual Data: 12/31/2006

Year	Sales		Net Income
2006	$563,410,000		$146,868,000
2005	$51,769,000		$4,831,000
Curr. Assets:	$103,325,000	Curr. Liab.:	$40,033,000	P/E Ratio:	29.58
Plant, Equip.:	$647,578,000	Total Liab.:	$797,746,000	Indic. Yr. Divd.:	$2.200
Total Assets:	$933,148,000	Net Worth:	$135,402,000	Debt/ Equity:	5.5390

Williams Scotsman Inc

8211 Town Ctr Dr., Baltimore, MD, 21236; *PH:* 1-410-931-6000; *http://* www.willscot.com; *Email:* InvestorRelations2@willscot.com

General - Incorporation	MD	Stock- Price on:12/24/2007	NA
Employees	7,700	Stock Exchange	NA
Auditor	Ernst & Young LLP	Ticker Symbol	NA
Stk Agt	Registrar & Transfer Co	Outstanding Shares	NA
Counsel	NA	E.P.S	NA
DUNS No.	00-310-0542	Shareholders	NA

Business: The group's principle activity is to lease mobile office and storage units in the United States and Canada. The group provides relocatable space solutions to 24,000 customers in 450 industries. Leasing operations account for a majority of the group's revenues. Used mobile office units are sold by the group from its lease fleet in the ordinary course of its business. The group also sells new mobile office units and provides delivery, installation and other ancillary products and services.

Primary SIC and add'l.: 7359 5271

CIK No: 0000869231

Subsidiaries: Evergreen Mobile Company, Space Master International, Inc, Truck and Trailer Sales, Inc, Williams Scotsman Europe, S.L, Williams Scotsman of Canada, Inc, Willscot Equipment LLC

Officers: Gerard Holthaus/Chmn., CEO, Raymond Onofrio/VP - Field Operations, Dean T. Fisher/VP - Operations, Daniel R. Stuart/CIO, VP - Information Technology, Rich Shuttie/VP - Finance, Treasurer, Bob Singer/CFO, Michele Cunningham/VP - Marketing, Business Development, Joe Donegan/Exec. VP - Field Operations, William C. Lebuhn/Chief Administrative Officer, John Ross/VP, General Counsel

Directors: Gerard Holthaus/Chmn., CEO, Steven B. Gruber/Dir., James N. Alexander/Dir., Michael F. Finley/Dir., James A. Flick/Dir., Stephen A. Van Oss/Dir., Alan D. Wilson/Dir., James L. Singleton/Dir.

Williams Scotsman International Inc

8211 Town Ctr Dr., Baltimore, MD, 21236; *PH:* 1-800-752-1500; *http://* www.willscot.com; *Email:* InvestorRelations2@willscot.com

General - Incorporation	DE	Stock- Price on:12/24/2007	$23.02
Employees	1,947	Stock Exchange	NA
Auditor	Ernst & Young LLP	Ticker Symbol	NA
Stk Agt	Registrar & Transfer Co	Outstanding Shares	43,460,000
Counsel	NA	E.P.S	$1.20
DUNS No.	00-310-0542	Shareholders	NA

Business: The group's principal activities are to rent, lease and market mobile office units and provide delivery, installation and other ancillary products and services. The group's fleet provides cost-effective relocatable space solutions to over 24,000 customers in 450 industries including construction, education, healthcare and retail. At 31-Dec-2003, the group leased 91,000 units through 80 branch offices in the United States and Canada.

Primary SIC and add'l.: 7389 6719 7359 6519

CIK No: 0000923144

Subsidiaries: American Homes Internacional, S.A. de C.V., Evergreen Mobile Company, Space Master International, Inc., Truck & Trailer Sales, Inc., Williams Scotsman Europe, S.L., and, Williams Scotsman Mexico S. de R.L. de C.V., Williams Scotsman of Canada, Inc., Williams Scotsman, Inc., Willscot Equipment, LLC, WS Servicios de Mexico, S. de R.L. de C.V.

Officers: Gerry Holthaus/Chmn., CEO, Joe Donegan/Exec. VP - Field Operations/$853,766.00, Bob Singer/CFO/$955,392.00, Stephen A. Van Oss/53/Sr. VP, Chief Financial, Administrative Officer, Michele Cunningham/VP - Marketing, Business Development, Daniel R. Stuart/VP - Information Technology, CIO, John Ross/VP, General Counsel/$218,433.00, Dean T. Fisher/VP - Operations, Raymond Onofrio/VP - Field Operations, Bill Lebuhn/Chief Administrative Officer/$570,183.00, Rich Shuttie/VP - Finance, Treasurer, Tom R. Svare/Sr. Sales Representative - Bakersfield Branch, Paula Meany/Administrative Mgr. - Sacramento Branch, Melanie Champniss/Sr. Contracts Administrator - Corporate

Directors: Gerry Holthaus/Chmn., CEO, James L. Singleton/Dir., Gerard E. Holthaus/Dir., Alan D. Wilson/Dir., James N. Alexander/48/Dir., Michael F. Finley/Dir., James A. Flick/Dir., Steven B. Gruber/Dir.

Owners: Michael F. Finley, Lord, Abbett & Co. LLC/5.91%, Cypress Merchant Banking Partners L.P./12.99%, Ristretto Group S.a.r.l./27.32%, James A. Flick, James N. Alexander, Insiders/2.66%, John B. Ross, William C. LeBuhn, Stephen A. Van Oss, Odyssey Investment Partners Fund, LP/5.42%, Alan D. Wilson, Robert C. Singer, TimesSquare Capital Management, LLC/5.18%, Steven B. Gruber *(20 Owners included in Index)*

Financial Data: Fiscal Year End:12/31 Latest Annual Data: 12/31/2006

Year	Sales		Net Income
2006	$680,800,000		$49,116,000
2005	$592,458,000		-$10,324,000
2004	$497,925,000		-$3,411,000
Curr. Assets:	$180,019,000	Curr. Liab.:	$147,716,000	P/E Ratio:	19.18
Plant, Equip.:	$1,159,461,000	Total Liab.:	$1,219,778,000	Indic. Yr. Divd.:	NA
Total Assets:	$1,587,919,000	Net Worth:	$368,141,000	Debt/ Equity:	2.4332

Williams-Sonoma Inc

3250 Van Ness Ave., San Francisco, CA, 94109; *PH:* 1-415-421-7900; *Fax:* 1-415-616-8359; *http://* www.williams-sonoma.com

General - Incorporation	CA	Stock- Price on:12/24/2007	$33.11
Employees	8,000	Stock Exchange	NYSE
Auditor	Deloitte & Touche LLP	Ticker Symbol	WSM
Stk Agt	Wells Fargo Shareowner Services	Outstanding Shares	110,630,000
Counsel	NA	E.P.S	$1.77
DUNS No.	02-926-3563	Shareholders	NA

Business: The groups principle activity is to operates home furnishing retail stores. The groups products are sold under the brand names Williams-Sonoma, Pottery Barn, Pottery Barn Kids, West Elm and Williams-Sonoma Home. The group operates from United States.

Primary SIC and add'l.: 5399 5961 5719

CIK No: 0000719955

Subsidiaries: Hold Everything, Inc., Pottery Barn Kids, Inc., Pottery Barn Teen, Inc., Pottery Barn, Inc., West Elm, Inc., Williams-Sonoma Canada, Inc., Williams-Sonoma Direct, Inc., Williams-Sonoma Gift Management, Inc., Williams-Sonoma Home, Inc., Williams-Sonoma Publishing, Inc., Williams-Sonoma Retail Services, Inc., Williams-Sonoma Stores, Inc., Williams-Sonoma Stores, LLC

Officers: Howard W. Lester/Chmn., CEO/$1,629,385.00, Laura J. Alber/Pres./$2,653,949.00, David M. Demattei/51/Group Pres./$2,924,012.00, Seth R. Jaffe/51/Sr. VP, General Counsel, Sec., Patrick J. Connolly/Exec. VP, Chief Marketing Officer/$1,168,940.00, Sharon L. McCollam/CFO, COO, Exec. VP/$2,594,394.00, Dean Miller/45/Exec. VP, Chief Supply Chain Officer

Directors: Howard W. Lester/Chmn., CEO, Charles E. Williams/Founder, Dir. Emeritus, Sanjiv Ahuja/Dir, Adrian D.P. Bellamy/66/Dir., Adrian T. Dillon/54/Dir., Michael R. Lynch/56/Dir., Richard T. Robertson/62/Dir., David B. Zenoff/70/Dir., James A. McMahan/85/Dir. Emeritus, Anthony A. Greener/67/Dir.

Owners: Howard W. Lester/7.33%, David B. Zenoff, Laura J. Alber, Goldman Sachs Asset Management, L.P./7.93%, Capital Research and Management Company/14.13%, Richard T. Robertson, Insiders/10.75%, Adrian T. Dillon, Patrick J. Connolly/1.47%, David M. DeMattei, Sharon L. McCollam, Adrian D.P. Bellamy, James A. McMahan/10.06%, FMR Corp./11.38%

Financial Data: Fiscal Year End:01/29 Latest Annual Data: 1/28/2007

Year	Sales		Net Income
2007	$3,727,513,000		$208,868,000
2006	$3,538,947,000		$214,866,000
2005	$3,136,931,000		$191,234,000
Curr. Assets:	$873,765,000	Curr. Liab.:	$522,157,000	P/E Ratio:	18.71
Plant, Equip.:	$852,412,000	Total Liab.:	$787,883,000	Indic. Yr. Divd.:	$0.460
Total Assets:	$1,745,545,000	Net Worth:	$957,662,000	Debt/ Equity:	0.0576

Willis Group Holdings Ltd

7 Hanover Sqr., New York, NY, 10004; *PH:* 1-212-837-0880; *Fax:* 1-212-344-2780; *http://* www.willis.com

General - Incorporation	Bermuda	Stock- Price on:12/24/2007	$45.65
Employees	13,000	Stock Exchange	NYSE
Auditor	Deloitte & Touche LLP	Ticker Symbol	WSH
Stk Agt	Bank of New York	Outstanding Shares	141,910,000
Counsel	NA	E.P.S	NA
DUNS No.	NA	Shareholders	NA

Business: The group's principal activity is to provide management consultancy and insurance brokerage services. It provides specialized risk management advisory and other services on a global basis to clients in various industries including the construction, aerospace, marine and energy industries. Services provided by the group include developing and delivering professional insurance, reinsurance, risk management financial and human resource consulting. In 2003, the group acquired ital re s.p.a, cogdill bonding and insurance services inc, t.c.t. Insurance services inc, business of river city agency, willis iberia correduria de seguros y reaseguros s.a, and co, gras savoye, willis a/s, kirecon a/s and vision insurance group.

Primary SIC and add'l.: 6411 6719

CIK No: 0001140536

Subsidiaries: Acn095454247 Pty Ltd (in Liquidation), Arbuthnot Insurance Services Limited, Ascot Technologies Limited, Asesor Auto 911, C.A., Asifina S.A., Asmarin Verwaltungs AG, Associated Insurance Services Limited, Associated International Insurance (Bermuda) Limited, Baccala & Shoop Insurance Services, Bloodstock & General Insurance Services Limited, Bolgey Holding S.A., C Wuppesahl Finanzversicherungsmakler GmbH, C.A. Prima, C.H. Jeffries (Holdings) Limited, C.H. Jeffries (Insurance Brokers) Limited 296 Subsidiaries included in the Index

Officers: Joseph J. Plumeri/64/Chmn., CEO/$4,678,753.00, Kerry K. Calaiaro/Contact, Donald J. Bailey/Member - Partners Group, Mary Caiazzo/Member - Partners Group, Adam Ciongoli/Member - Partners Group, Valerie Di Maria/Member - Partners Group, Susan Sztuka/Member - Partners Group, Joseph J. Trotti/Member - Partners Group, Christopher M. London/Member - Partners Group, Grahame J. Millwater/Member - Partners Group/$1,763,042.00, David B. Margrett/Member - Partners Group, Patrick Regan/Member - Partners Group/$1,160,544.00, Jeanette Scampas/Member - Partners Group, Sarah J. Turvill/Member - Partners Group, Gregory A. Arms/Member

Directors: Joseph J. Plumeri/64/Chmn., CEO, William C. Bartholomay/Dir., Allan C. Gribben/Dir., Patrick Lucas/Dir. - Willis Group Limited, Gordon M. Bethune/65/Dir., William W. Bradley/64/Dir., Joseph A. Califano/76/Dir., Anna C. Catalano/47/Dir., Eric G. Friberg/64/Dir., Roy Gardner/61/Dir., Jeremy Hanley/61/Dir., Wendy E. Lane/56/Dir., James F. McCann/56/Dir., Douglas B. Roberts/59/Dir.

Owners: Douglas B. Roberts, Anna C. Catalano, Jeanette Scampas, Grahame J. Millwater, James F. McCann, Perry Golkin, Roy Gardner, Allan C. A. Gribben, Wendy E. Lane, Stephen G. Maycock, FMR Corp/10.23%, Insiders/2.84%, Eric G. Friberg, Jeremy Hanley, Gordon M. Bethune *(28 Owners included in Index)*

Financial Data: ***Fiscal Year End:***12/31 ***Latest Annual Data:*** 06/30/2007

Year	Sales	Net Income
2007	NA	NA
2006	NA	NA
2005	$2,267,000,000	$300,000,000

Curr. Assets:	$10,874,000,000	***Curr. Liab.:***	$10,116,000,000	***P/E Ratio:***	14.97
Plant, Equip.:	$167,000,000	***Total Liab.:***	$11,924,000,000	***Indic. Yr. Divd.:***	$1.000
Total Assets:	$13,378,000,000	***Net Worth:***	$1,454,000,000	***Debt/ Equity:***	1.0462

Willis Lease Finance Corp

2320 Marinship Way, Ste 300, Sausalito, CA, 94965; ***PH:*** 1-415-250-5100; ***http://*** www.wlfc.com; ***Email:*** tmacaleavey@willislease.com

General - Incorporation	DE	***Stock***- Price on:12/24/2007	$11.1
Employees	53	Stock Exchange	NDQ
Auditor	KPMG LLP	Ticker Symbol	WLFC
Stk Agt	KPMG LLP	Outstanding Shares	8,130,000
Counsel	Gibson, Dunn & Crutcher LLP	E.P.S	$0.073
DUNS No.	08-335-3037	Shareholders	NA

Business: The group's principle activity is to provide aviation services that focus on leasing aftermarket commercial aircraft engines and other aircraft-related equipment. The company provides this service to passenger airlines, air cargo carriers and maintenance and repair organizations. As of 31-Dec-2003, the company had a total lease portfolio of 50 lessees in 25 countries and the company's total lease portfolio consisted of 119 engines, six aircraft and four spare parts packages with an aggregate net book value of $505 million. The leasing business focuses on popular stage iii commercial jet aircraft engines manufactured by cfm international, general electric, pratt & whitney, rolls royce and international aero engines. The group operates from United States.

Primary SIC and add'l.: 7359

CIK No: 0001018164

Subsidiaries: T-11 Inc., WEST Engine Funding (Ireland) Limited, WEST Engine Funding LLC, Willis Engine Funding LLC, WLFC (Ireland) Limited, Wlfc-ac1, Inc.

Officers: Charles F. Willis/Chmn., CEO, Pres./$1,240,527.00, Donald A. Nunemaker/Exec. VP, GM - Leasing/$555,592.00, Thomas E. MacAleavey/55/Sr. VP - Sales, Marketing/$584,392.00, Thomas C. Nord/Sr. VP, General Counsel/$363,804.00, Judith M. Webber/Sr. VP - Technical Services, Lee G. Beaumont/COO, Exec. VP/$368,338.00, Bradley S. Forsyth/Sr. VP, CFO

Directors: Charles F. Willis/Chmn., CEO, Pres., Gerard Laviec/Dir., William W. Coon/Dir., Hans Jorg Hunziker/Dir., Robert T. Morris/Dir.

Owners: Thomas E. MacAleavey, Hans J. Hunziker, Donald A. Nunemaker/4.94%, Dimensional Fund Advisors Inc./6.39%, Robert M. Warwick, Grard Laviec, Wells Fargo& Company/17.13%, Thomas C. Nord, Charles F. Willis/39.82%, Insiders/43.35%, JAM Partners LP/7.52%

Financial Data: ***Fiscal Year End:***12/31 ***Latest Annual Data:*** 06/30/2007

Year	Sales	Net Income
2007	NA	NA
2006	NA	NA
2005	$70,546,000	$4,177,000

Curr. Assets:	$73,146,000	***Curr. Liab.:***	$14,755,000	***P/E Ratio:***	152.06
Plant, Equip.:	$627,197,000	***Total Liab.:***	$590,783,000	***Indic. Yr. Divd.:***	NA
Total Assets:	$737,864,000	***Net Worth:***	$147,081,000	***Debt/ Equity:***	2.8396

Willow Financial Bancorp Inc

170 S Warner Rd., Ste. 300, Wayne, PA, 19087; ***PH:*** 1-610-995-1700; ***http://*** www.ffbonline.com

General - Incorporation	PA	***Stock***- Price on:12/24/2007	$12.59
Employees	312	Stock Exchange	NDQ
Auditor	KPMG LLP	Ticker Symbol	WFBC
Stk Agt	Registrar & Transfer Co	Outstanding Shares	17,420,000
Counsel	NA	E.P.S	$0.65
DUNS No.	NA	Shareholders	NA

Business: The groups principal activity is to provide banking services. The products of the group include mortgage loans, consumer loans and commercial business loans. The group operates from the United States.

Primary SIC and add'l.: 6712 6035

CIK No: 0001163428

Subsidiaries: Willow Financial Bank

Officers: Donna M. Coughey/57/Dir., CEO, Pres., Ammon J. Baus/59/Chief Credit Officer, Richard G. Bertolet/Middle Marketing Lending Mgr., Joseph T. Crowley/46/CFO, Sr. VP, Corp. Sec., Neil Kalani/33/Chief Accounting Officer, Matthew D. Kelly/44/Chief Wealth Management Officer, Thomas J. Saunders/47/Exec. Commercial Sales Mgr.

Directors: Donna M. Coughey/57/Dir., CEO, Pres., Rosemary C. Loring/56/Chmn., Robert J. McCormack/47/Dir., Madeleine Wing-Adler/67/Dir., William W. Langan/67/Dir., John J. Cunningham/66/Dir., Gerard F. Griesser/59/Dir., Charles F. Kremp/65/Dir., Emory S. Todd/66/Dir., Brent A. OBrien/70/Dir., Samuel H. Ramsey/65/Dir., William B. Weihenmayer/61/Dir., James E. McErlane/65/Dir.

Owners: William W. Langan, Donna M. Coughey, James E. McErlane/2.90%, Insiders/11.60%, Richard G. Bertolet, Joseph T. Crowley, Madeleine Wing Adler, Private Capital Management, L.P./5.60%, John J. Cunningham, Emory S. Todd, Willow Grove Bank 401/6.70%, Ammon J. Baus, Samuel H. Ramsey, Charles F. Kremp, Rosemary C. Loring *(23 Owners included in Index)*

Financial Data: ***Fiscal Year End:***06/30 ***Latest Annual Data:*** 6/30/2006

Year	Sales	Net Income
2006	$90,096,000	$11,076,000
2005	$53,156,000	$6,726,000
2004	$44,615,000	$6,111,000

Curr. Assets:	$43,866,000	***Curr. Liab.:***	$1,323,312,000	***P/E Ratio:***	19.37
Plant, Equip.:	$10,115,000	***Total Liab.:***	$1,373,662,000	***Indic. Yr. Divd.:***	$0.460
Total Assets:	$1,576,735,000	***Net Worth:***	$203,073,000	***Debt/ Equity:***	0.1226

Willow Grove Bancorp Inc

Welsh And Norristown Rds, Maple Glen, PA, 19002; ***PH:*** 1-215-643-5696; ***http://*** www.willowgrovebank.com; ***Email:*** wgbops@willowgrovebank.com

General - Incorporation	PA	***Stock***- Price on:12/24/2007	NA
Employees	NA	Stock Exchange	NA
Auditor	KPMG LLP	Ticker Symbol	NA
Stk Agt	Registrar & Transfer Co	Outstanding Shares	NA
Counsel	Duffy, North Et Al	E.P.S	$0.61
DUNS No.	NA	Shareholders	NA

Business: The group's principal activity is provide commercial and retail banking products and services. The group offers home equity loans, construction, commercial real estate and multi-family residential loans and commercial business loans. The deposits include savings accounts, money market accounts, certificates of deposits and other non-interest-bearing deposits. The group operates through 14 branches in philadelphia, bucks and montgomery counties.

Primary SIC and add'l.: 6035 6712

CIK No: 0001163428

Subsidiaries: PCIS, Willow Financial Bank

Officers: Joyce Magyar/Community Outreach Coordinator, Donna M. Coughey/58/Dir., Pres., Chief Executive, Joseph T. Crowley/46/CFO, Treasurer, Corp. Sec., Neil Kalani/33/Chief Accounting Officer, Thomas J. Saunders/47/Executive Commercial Sales Mgr., Ammon J. Baus/59/Chief Credit Officer, Richard G. Bertolet/Middle Marketing Lending Mgr., Matthew D. Kelly/44/Chief Wealth Management Officer, Colin N. Maropis/56/Contact - Construction Financing

Directors: Rosemary C. Loring/58/Chmn., Gerard F. Griesser/59/Dir., Emory S. Todd/66/Dir., John J. Cunningham/66/Dir., James E. McErlane/65/Dir., Robert J. McCormack/47/Dir., Madeleine Wing-Adler/67/Dir., Brent A. Obrien/70/Dir., Samuel H. Ramsey/65/Dir., William W. Langan/67/Dir., Charles F. Kremp/65/Dir., William B. Weihenmayer/61/Dir., Donna M. Coughey/58/Dir., Pres., Chief Executive

Owners: Robert J. McCormack, Richard G. Bertolet, John J. Cunningham, Rosemary C. Loring, Private Capital Management, L.P./5.60%, Frederick A. Marcell/1.80%, Donna M. Coughey, A. Brent OBrien, Insiders/11.60%, Dimensional Fund Advisors LP/7.20%, Willow Grove Bank 401/6.70%, Joseph T. Crowley, Gerard F. Griesser, Emory S. Todd, Charles F. Kremp *(23 Owners included in Index)*

Financial Data: ***Fiscal Year End:***06/30 ***Latest Annual Data:*** 06/30/2006

Year	Sales	Net Income
2006	$90,096,000	$11,076,000
2005	$53,156,000	$6,726,000
2004	$44,615,000	$6,111,000

Curr. Assets:	$43,866,000	***Curr. Liab.:***	$1,323,312,000		
Plant, Equip.:	$10,115,000	***Total Liab.:***	$1,373,662,000	***Indic. Yr. Divd.:***	$0.460
Total Assets:	$1,576,735,000	***Net Worth:***	$203,073,000	***Debt/ Equity:***	0.1226

Wilmington Trust Corp

1100 N Market St., Wilmington, DE, 19890; ***PH:*** 1-302-651-1000; ***http://*** www.wilmingtontrust.com; ***Email:*** info@wilmingtontrust.com

General - Incorporation	DE	***Stock***- Price on:12/24/2007	$41.84
Employees	2,562	Stock Exchange	NYSE
Auditor	KPMG LLP	Ticker Symbol	WL
Stk Agt	Wells Fargo Bank, N.A.	Outstanding Shares	68,720,000
Counsel	NA	E.P.S	$2.07
DUNS No.	00-691-9161	Shareholders	NA

Business: The group's principal activities are to provide banking services. The group operates in 4 segments: regional banking, wealth advisory services, corporate client services and affiliate money managers. The regional banking segment includes lending, deposit taking and branch banking in banking markets of Delaware, southeastern Pennsylvania, and Maryland's eastern shore. The wealth advisory services segment includes financial planning, asset management, investment counseling, trust services, estate settlement, private banking, tax preparation, mutual fund services, broker-dealer services, and insurance services. The corporate client services business provides specialty trust services for national and multinational institutions. The affiliate money managers segment provides fixed-income and equity investing services and investment portfolio management services. As on 31-Dec-2003, the group has 43 operating branches.

Primary SIC and add'l.: 6712 6021

CIK No: 0000872821

Subsidiaries: 100 West Tenth Street Corporation, Bedell SPV Management (Jersey) Limited, Brandywine Finance Corporation, Brandywine Insurance Agency, Crompton Realty Corporation, Drew VIII, Ltd., Grant Tani Barash & Altman, LLC, Grant, Tani, Barash & Altman Management, Inc., GTBA Holdings, Inc., Rodney Square Investors, L.P., Rodney Square Management Corporation, Siobain VI, Ltd., Special Services (Delaware), Inc., SPV Advisors Limited, SPV Management Limited 37 Subsidiaries included in the Index

Officers: Ted Cecala/Chmn., CEO/$2,547,396.00, Robert V.A. Harra/COO, Pres./$1,444,473.00, Kevyn N. Rakowski/Sr. VP, Controller

Directors: Ted Cecala/Chmn., CEO, Donald E. Foley/Dir.

Owners: R. P. Wood, C. S. Burger, R. L. Mears, Insiders/6.37%, D. R. Gibson, T. T. Cecala/1.29%, T. L. du Pont, W. J. Farrell, C. S. Crompton, D. P. Roselle, S. D. Whiting, G. Krug, R. V.A. Harra, R. K. Elliott, S. J. Mobley *(18 Owners included in Index)*

Financial Data: Fiscal Year End:12/31 Latest Annual Data: 12/31/2006

Year	Sales	Net Income
2006	$1,020,900,000	$143,800,000
2005	$829,900,000	$173,000,000
2004	$676,200,000	$141,900,000

Curr. Assets:	$392,600,000	Curr. Liab.:	$9,563,100,000	P/E Ratio:	20.21
Plant, Equip.:	$150,300,000	Total Liab.:	$10,097,700,000	Indic. Yr. Divd.:	$1.340
Total Assets:	$11,157,000,000	Net Worth:	$1,059,300,000	Debt/ Equity:	0.3566

Wilshire Bancorp Inc

3200 Wilshire Blvd., 14th Fl., Los Angeles, CA, 90010; *PH:* 1-213-368-7700; *Fax:* 1-818-775-1000; *http://* www.wilshirebank.com

General - Incorporation	CA	**Stock**- Price on:12/24/2007	$12.17
Employees	325	Stock Exchange	NDQ
Auditor	Deloitte & Touche LLP	Ticker Symbol	WIBC
Stk Agt	U.S. Stock Transfer Corp	Outstanding Shares	29,370,000
Counsel	Fried, Bird & Crumpacker	E.P.S	$1.02
DUNS No.	NA	Shareholders	NA

Business: The groups principle activity is to provide financial products and services. The groups services include ATM machines and Internet banking. The products of the group include commercial, consumer and real estate loans, and issuance and collection of letters of credit. In May 2006, the group acquired Liberty Bank of New York. The groups operates through three segments namely banking operations, trade finance services, and small business administration lending services. The group operates from the Southern California, Texas and the greater New York City in the United States. The group's quarterly net income for September 2007 was 6.64 millions of USD.

Primary SIC and add'l.: 6712 6022

CIK No: 0001285224

Subsidiaries: Wilshire State Bank, Wilshire Statutory Trust I, Wilshire Statutory Trust II, Wilshire Statutory Trust III

Officers: Soo Bong Min/Dir., Pres., CEO - Wilshire State Bank, Joanne W. Kim/Exec. VP, Chief Lending Officer - Wilshire State Bank, Brian E. Cho/Exec. VP, CFO, Corp. Sec. - Wilshire State Bank, Sung Soo Han/Exec. VP, SBA Mgr. - Wilshire State Bank, Fred F. Mautner/Dir. - Wilshire State Bank

Directors: Soo Bong Min/Dir., Pres., CEO - Wilshire State Bank, Steven S. Koh/Chmn., Mel Elliot/Dir. - Wilshire State Bank, Kyu-Hyun Kim/Dir., Richard Y. Lim/Dir. - Wilshire State Bank, Harry Siafaris/Dir. - Wilshire State Bank, Donald D. Byun/Dir. - Wilshire State Bank, Larry D. Greenfield/Dir., Gapsu Kim/Dir. - Wilshire State Bank, Young Hi Pak/Dir. - Wilshire State Bank

Owners: Kyu-Hyun Kim/1.87%, Steven Koh/19.19%, Larry Greenfield/3.50%, Donald Byun/0.61%, Soo Bong Min/1.82%, Richard Y. Lim/1.90%, Insiders/40.39%, Joanne Kim/0.25%, Sung Soo Han/0.22%, Mel Elliott/2.59%, Gapsu Kim/0.87%, Harry Siafaris/1.34%, Brian E. Cho/0.28%, Fred F. Mautner/4.08%, FMR Corp./5.06% *(16 Owners included in Index)*

Financial Data: Fiscal Year End:12/31 Latest Annual Data: 12/31/2006

Year	Sales	Net Income
2006	$167,800,000	$33,942,000
2005	$117,766,000	$27,760,000
2004	$80,795,000	$19,458,000

Curr. Assets:	$217,680,000	Curr. Liab.:	$1,786,364,000		
Plant, Equip.:	$10,603,000	Total Liab.:	$1,858,849,000	Indic. Yr. Divd.:	$0.200
Total Assets:	$2,008,484,000	Net Worth:	$149,635,000	Debt/ Equity:	0.3915

Wilshire Enterprises Inc

One Gateway Ctr., Ste. 1030, Newark, NJ, 07102; *PH:* 1-201-420-2796; *Fax:* 1-201-420-6012; *http://* www.wilshireenterprisesinc.com

General - Incorporation	DE	**Stock**- Price on:12/24/2007	$5.58
Employees	8	Stock Exchange	AMEX
Auditor	J.H. Cohn, LLP	Ticker Symbol	WOC
Stk Agt	Continental Stock Transfer & Trust Co	Outstanding Shares	7,920,000
Counsel	Sullivan & Cromwell	E.P.S	-$0.07
DUNS No.	00-691-6134	Shareholders	NA

Business: The group's principal activity is to conduct real estate operations in Arizona, Florida, Georgia, New Jersey and Texas. The group's properties consist of apartment complexes as well as commercial and retail properties. The group had interests in crude oil and natural gas exploration. Crude oil and natural gas are sold to oil refineries and natural gas pipeline companies. The group also has a portfolio of equity securities. In Jun 2003, the group decided to discontinue its oil and gas operations.

Primary SIC and add'l.: 6531 1311

CIK No: 0000107454

Subsidiaries: 1022778 Alberta Ltd., 1204552 Alberta ULC, 350 Pleasant Valley Corp., Alpine Village Apartments, LLC, Alpine Village Holding, Inc., Belair Drive, LLC, Biltmore Club Apartments, LLC, Biltmore Club Holding, Inc., Britalta Venezolano, Ltd., Calgary, Alberta, Canada, Galsworthy Arms Apartments, LLC, Galsworthy Arms Holding, Inc., Global Equities Management Corp., Newark, NJ, Rockland Resources 24 Subsidiaries included in the Index

Officers: Wilzig S. Izak/Chmn., CEO, Frank Elenio/Sr. VP, CFO, Richard Fracaro/Sr. VP, Asset Mgr.

Directors: Wilzig S. Izak/Chmn., CEO, Martin Willschick/Dir., Sam Halpern/Member - Realty Advisory Board, Milton Donnenberg/Dir., Miles Berger/Dir., Ernest W. Wachtel/Dir., Eric J. Schmertz/Dir.

Owners: Martin W. Willschick, Ernest Wachtel/1.90%, Dimensional Fund Advisors, Inc./6.10%, Phillip Goldstein/14.90%, Donald Brenner/5.20%, Miles Berger, Wilzig S. Izak/2.80%, Estate of Siggi B. Wilzig/21.10%, Eric J. Schmertz, Milton Donnenberg

Financial Data: Fiscal Year End:12/31 Latest Annual Data: 12/31/2006

Year	Sales	Net Income
2006	$8,834,000	$2,285,000
2005	$4,624,000	$6,891,000
2004	$9,706,000	$2,638,000

Curr. Assets:	$18,228,000	Curr. Liab.:	$3,188,000		
Plant, Equip.:	$28,687,000	Total Liab.:	$32,992,000	Indic. Yr. Divd.:	NA
Total Assets:	$46,915,000	Net Worth:	$13,923,000	Debt/ Equity:	2.0385

Wilson Bank & Trust

623 W Main St., Lebanon, TN, 37087; *PH:* 1-615-444-2265; *http://* www.wilsonbank.com; *Email:* ebanking@wilsonbank.com

General - Incorporation	TN	**Stock**- Price on:12/24/2007	NA
Employees	NA	Stock Exchange	OTC
Auditor	Madsen & Assoc. CPAs, Inc	Ticker Symbol	NA
Stk Agt	NA	Outstanding Shares	NA
Counsel	NA	E.P.S	NA
DUNS No.	16-093-5029	Shareholders	NA

Business: The group's principal activity is to provide commercial banking services to its customers. The operations are conducted through eight full service-banking offices located in wilson county, trousdale county and western davidson county. The group operates through its subsidiary wilson bank and trust. It offers a wide range of banking services, including checking, savings and money market deposit accounts, certificates of deposit and loans for consumer, commercial and real estate purposes. The other services offered to its customers are custodial, trust and discount brokerage services.

Primary SIC and add'l.: 6022 6712

CIK No: 0000885275

Subsidiaries: Wilson Bank and Trust

Officers: Randall Clemons/Chmn., CEO, Elmer H. Richerson/Dir., Pres., Angela Forrest/Assist. Deposit Operations Mgr. - Main Office, John Foster/AVP, Gladeville Assist. Office Mgr. Gladeville, Kay Davis/Consumer Loan Officer - Mt. Juliet, Darlene Dickens/Personal Banker Officer - Mt. Juliet, Dale Dies/VP, Hartsville Assist. Office Mgr. Hartsville, Ken Dill/VP, Commercial Loan Officer Main Office, Mark Dubarry/VP, Technology Dir. Main Office, Lois Duke/Personal Banker Officer - Smithville, Bernie Christian/VP, Leeville Office Mgr. Leeville - 109, Chad Colwell/VP, Loan Officer Smithville, Phillip Cripps/AVP, Loan Officer Smithville, Tammy Crook/Customer Service Banker Officer - Smithville, Janice Durnberger/AVP - Highway70, Mt. Juliet Office Mgr. Mt. Juliet *(126 Officers included in Index)*

Directors: Randall Clemons/Chmn., CEO, Jimmy Comer/Dir., Jerry Franklin/Dir., Marshall Griffith/Dir., Elmer H. Richerson/Dir., Pres., Charles Bell/Dir., Jack Bell/Dir., Mackey Bentley/Dir., Harold Patton/Dir., James Anthony Patton/Dir., John R. Trice/Dir., Bob Vanhooser/Dir., John Freeman/Dir.

Owners: Harold R. Patton/0.80%, Randall J. Clemons/1.48%, Mackey Bentley/0.76%, Larry Squires/0.05%, Jerry L. Franklin/1.40%, Robert T. VanHooser/0.34%, Lisa Pominski, John C. McDearman, Insiders/13.77%, Charles Bell/2.00%, John R. Trice/1.88%, John D. Goodman/0.04%, Jack W. Bell/1.49%, Marshall Griffith/0.38%, James Anthony Patton/0.64% *(19 Owners included in Index)*

Wilson Greatbatch Technologies Inc

9645 Wehrle Dr., Clarence, NY, 14031; *PH:* 1-716-759-5600; *http://* www.greatbatch.com

General - Incorporation	DE	**Stock**- Price on:12/24/2007	$32.01
Employees	1,835	Stock Exchange	NYSE
Auditor	Deloitte & Touche LLP	Ticker Symbol	NA
Stk Agt	Greatbatch and Hodgson Russ LLP	Outstanding Shares	22,330,000
Counsel	Hodgson Russ	E.P.S	$0.55
DUNS No.	17-874-4632	Shareholders	NA

Business: The group's principal activities are to develop and manufacture batteries, capacitors, feedthroughs, enclosures and other components used in implantable medical devices. The group operates in two segments: medical technology and commercial power sources. The medical technology segment designs and manufactures batteries, capacitors, filtered feedthroughs, engineered components and enclosures used in implantable medical devices. The commercial power sources division designs and manufactures high performance batteries and battery packs for use in oil and gas exploration, oceanographic equipment and aerospace. The group's customers include Guidant, St. Jude Medical, Medtronic, Biotronik, Cyberonics and Ela/Sorin. During Mar-2004, the group acquired Nanogram Devices Corporation.

Primary SIC and add'l.: 3692

CIK No: 0001114483

Subsidiaries: Battery Engineering, Inc., Greatbatch LLC, Greatbatch Ltd., Greatbatch Technologias de Mexico, S. de C.V., Greatbatch Technologies Advanced Research Laboratories, Inc., Greatbatch-Globe Tool, Inc., Greatbatch-Hittman, Inc., Greatbatch-Sierra, Inc., WGL Intermediate Holdings, Inc.

Officers: Thomas J. Hook/Dir., CEO, Pres./$1,598,693.00, Thomas J. Mazza/Sr. VP, CFO/$680,400.00, Timothy G. McEvoy/VP, General Counsel, Sec., Tony Borowicz/Treasurer & Dir. - Investor Relations, Barbara M. Davis/VP - Human Resources, Mauricio Arellano/Sr. VP - Medical Solutions Group/$597,377.00, Susan M. Bratton/Sr. VP - Commercial Power Group/$643,579.00, Susan Campbell/Sr. VP - Medical Power Group/$603,552.00

Directors: Thomas J. Hook/Dir., CEO, Pres., Edward F. Voboril/Chmn., Pamela G. Bailey/Dir., Peter H. Soderberg/Dir., Thomas S. Summer/Dir., John P. Wareham/Dir., Bill R. Sanford/Dir., Joseph A. Miller/Dir., William B. Summers/Dir., Kevin C. Melia/Dir.

Owners: T. Rowe Price Associates, Inc./6.30%, John P. Wareham, Mauricio Arellano, Dimensional Fund Advisors LP/7.40%, Thomas J. Hook, Insiders/4.90%, Larry T. DeAngelo, Thomas J. Mazza, Bill R. Sanford, FMR Corp./10.80%, SMALLCAP World Fund, Inc./9.40%, Susan H. Campbell, Edward F. Voboril/2.30%, Joseph A. Miller, William B. Summers *(21 Owners included in Index)*

Financial Data: Fiscal Year End:12/31 Latest Annual Data: 12/29/2006

Year	Sales	Net Income
2006	$271,142,000	$16,126,000
2005	$241,097,000	$10,107,000
2004	$200,119,000	$16,257,000

Curr. Assets:	$196,003,000	Curr. Liab.:	$44,045,000	P/E Ratio:	36.38
Plant, Equip.:	$97,705,000	Total Liab.:	$244,306,000	Indic. Yr. Divd.:	NA
Total Assets:	$512,911,000	Net Worth:	$268,605,000	Debt/ Equity:	0.7613

Wilson Holdings Inc

378 N Main, No. 124, Layton, UT, 84041; *PH:* 1-512-732-0932; *Fax:* 1-925-962-0336; *http://* www.wilsonholdings.net/corp-board-wilson.html; *Email:* ronatcole@comcast.net

General - Incorporation	NV	**Stock**- Price on:12/24/2007	$3.25
Employees	11	Stock Exchange	OTC
Auditor	PMB Helin Donovan, LLP	Ticker Symbol	WSHD
Stk Agt	Standard Registrar & Transfer Co Inc.	Outstanding Shares	NA
Counsel	NA	E.P.S	-$0.67
DUNS No.	NA	Shareholders	NA

Business: The group's principle activity is to assemble, sell, service and upgrade computers. The company operates thirteen retail storefront under the name computer masters. The company directly markets its sales and services through the Internet via its Web sites, colecomputer.net and okcmasters.com, along with direct to customer mail order. These Web sites have complete e-commerce capabilities for retail, government and wholesale buyers, including a shopping cart with a secure credit card payment system. The components and upgrade parts are purchased from a number of suppliers for further assembly or resale activities of complete component systems or for further upgrade. Trade name of the company is 'computer masters'. The company's management ceased doing business as a retail computer sales operation. Accordingly, all activities have been treated as discontinued operations. Agreements are currently being negotiated to determine the future operation. The group's total revenue for year 2007 was 4.44 millions of USD.

Primary SIC and add'l.: 5734 7378 5045

CIK No: 0000828189

Subsidiaries: Wilson Family Communities, Inc.

Officers: Clark N. Wilson/Chmn., CEO, Pres., David Goodrum/Dir. - Land Development, Mark Gram/Sr. VP - Marketing, Mark Dotzour/Dir., Advisor, Cindy Dietz/Dir. - Sales, Arun Khurana/CFO, VP, Clay Thornton/Dir. - Construction Operations, Donald Turner/52/VP - Finance, Accounting

Directors: Clark N. Wilson/Chmn., CEO, Pres., Jay Gouline/Dir., Sidney Christopher Ney/Dir., Barry A. Williamson/Dir., Victor Ayad/Dir., Mark Dotzour/Dir., Advisor

Owners: Grandview LLC, Clark N. Wilson, Barry A. Williamson, Arun Khurana, Sidney Christopher Ney, Insiders, Tejas Securities Group, Inc, LC Capital Master Fund, David Goodrum, Jay Gouline

Financial Data: ***Fiscal Year End:***12/31 ***Latest Annual Data:*** 12/31/2005

Year	Sales	Net Income
2005	$255,000	-$1,714,000
2004	NA	-$178,000

Curr. Assets:	$4,865,000	***Curr. Liab.:***	$2,663,000	***P/E Ratio:***	41.10
Plant, Equip.:	$30,854,000	***Total Liab.:***	$36,599,000	***Indic. Yr. Divd.:***	NA
Total Assets:	$37,373,000	***Net Worth:***	$775,000	***Debt/ Equity:***	NA

Wilsons The Leather Experts Inc

7401 Boone Ave. N, St Louis Pk., Brooklyn Park, MN, 55428; ***PH:*** 1-612-394-4000; ***http://*** www.wilsonsleather.com; ***Email:*** customercare@wilsonsleather.com

General - Incorporation	MN	**Stock**- Price on:12/24/2007	$1.71
Employees	3,461	Stock Exchange	NDQ
Auditor	KPMG LLP	Ticker Symbol	WLSN
Stk Agt	Wells Fargo Shareowner Services	Outstanding Shares	39,230,000
Counsel	Faegre & Benson LLP	E.P.S	-$1.22
DUNS No.	02-793-0395	Shareholders	NA

Business: The group's principal activity is the retail distribution of quality leather outerwear, accessories and apparel. As on 01-Nov-2003, the group operated 607 stores located in 45 states, the district of columbia, guam, Puerto Rico and Canada. The group operates 473 mall stores, 114 outlet stores and 20 airport locations under the wilsons leather concept. The products offered by the wilsons leather stores include gloves, handbags, wallets, briefcases, computer cases, planners, CD cases and belts. In 2002, the group liquidated all stores operated by el portal and bentley's.

Primary SIC and add'l.: 5611 5651 5621 5699 5632

CIK No: 0001016607

Subsidiaries: Bermans The Leather Experts Inc., Chicago OHare Leather Concessions Joint Venture, Florida Luggage Corp., River Hills Wilsons, Inc., Rosedale Wilsons, Inc., USA Wilsons Leather Holdings Inc. Qingdao RO, Wilsons Center, Inc., Wilsons International Inc., Wilsons Leather Direct Inc., Wilsons Leather Holdings Inc., Wilsons Leather of Airports Inc., Wilsons Leather of Alabama Inc., Wilsons Leather of Arkansas Inc., Wilsons Leather of Canada Ltd., Wilsons Leather of Connecticut Inc. 42 Subsidiaries included in the Index

Officers: Michael M. Searles/CEO, Philip S. Garon/Corp. Sec., David L. Rogers/Private Investor, Retail Consultant, Stacy A. Kruse/CFO, Treasurer, Adam M. Boucher/46/VP - Store Sales, Real Estate, Karl Karst/Sr. Transportation Analyst, Chris Carlson/Mgr. - Global Logistics, Customs Compliance, Michael Tripp/VP - Global Logistics, Customs Compliance, William S. Hutchison/34/Chief Merchandising, Sourcing Officer, Jeffrey M. Loeb/52/CIO

Directors: Michael T. Sweeney/Chmn., Gail A. Cottle/Dir., Mark G. Schoeppner/Dir., Michael J. McCoy/Dir., Peter V. Handal/Dir., Bradley K. Johnson/Dir., David L. Rogers/Private Investor, Retail Consultant, William F. Farley/Dir., Ted R. Weschler/Dir., Michael T. Cowhig/Dir., Darren L. Acheson/Dir.

Owners: Betty A. Goff, Bradley K. Johnson, Insiders, Sun Capital Securities, Megan L. Featherston, Peter V. Handal, Marathon Fund Limited Partnership V, Peninsula Investment Partners, L.P., David L. Rogers, Michael J. McCoy, Michael M. Searles, Ted R. Weschler, Richard Liu, William F. Farley, Quaker Capital Management Corporation *(19 Owners included in Index)*

Financial Data: ***Fiscal Year End:***02/01 ***Latest Annual Data:*** 2/3/2007

Year	Sales	Net Income
2007	$321,262,000	-$33,095,000
2006	$397,986,000	$12,212,000
2005	$441,071,000	-$23,583,000

Curr. Assets:	$105,205,000	***Curr. Liab.:***	$30,012,000		
Plant, Equip.:	$38,890,000	***Total Liab.:***	$66,844,000	***Indic. Yr. Divd.:***	NA
Total Assets:	$145,345,000	***Net Worth:***	$78,501,000	***Debt/ Equity:***	0.3472

Wilton Bank CT

47 Old Ridgefield Rd. , Wilton, CT, 06897; ***PH:*** 1-203-762-2265; ***http://*** www.thewiltonbank.com

General - Incorporation		**Stock**- Price on:12/24/2007	$69
Employees	NA	Stock Exchange	OTC
Auditor	NA	Ticker Symbol	WIBW
Stk Agt	Registrar & Transfer Co	Outstanding Shares	NA
Counsel	NA	E.P.S	NA
DUNS No.	NA	Shareholders	NA

Business: The groups principal activities include providing banking and financial services to the businesses and customers. Services of the group include checking accounts, savings accounts, certificates of deposit, installment loans, real estate mortgage loans, commercial loans, traveler's checks, safe deposit boxes, night depository, automated teller services and contributing to retirement plan.

Primary SIC and add'l.: 6029

CIK No:

Wimm-Bill-Dann Foods OJSC

16 Yauzsky Blvd, Moscow, 109028; ***PH:*** 7-4951055805; ***Fax:*** 7-4951055800; ***http://*** www.wbd.com; ***Email:*** ir@wbd.ru

General - Incorporation	Russia	**Stock**- Price on:12/24/2007	$83.06
Employees	20,000	Stock Exchange	NYSE
Auditor	Ernst & Young LLC	Ticker Symbol	WBD
Stk Agt	Bank of New York	Outstanding Shares	44,000,000
Counsel	NA	E.P.S	$3.06
DUNS No.	NA	Shareholders	NA

Business: The group's principle activities are the dairy and juice production. The company manufactures around 300 varieties of dairy products and over 170 types of juice and drinks. The company owns 14 manufacturing facilities in 10 locations in Russia and the commonwealth of independent states, as well as distribution centres in 26 cities in Russia and abroad. The company also distributes its products in Canada, Germany, Israel. The company's shares are listed in the nyse. The group's quarterly revenue for Sep '07 was 610.53 millions of USD.

Primary SIC and add'l.: 2033 2023 2026

CIK No: 0001166718

Subsidiaries: Annino Dairy Plant, Atamanskoe Farm, Baltic Milk (former Roska), Bishkek Dairy Plant, Buryn Powder Milk Plant, Dari Valdai, Essentuki Mineral Water Plant at CMW (Caucasian Mineral Waters), Experimental Baby Food Plant, Foods Production CJSC, Fruit Rivers, Fruktola, Geyser, Grande-V, Gulkevichy Dairy Plant, Healing Spring Water Plant 67 Subsidiaries included in the Index

Officers: Tony Denis Maher/CEO, Dmitry A. Anisimov/CFO, Dir. - Management, Vera V. Eliseeva/Head - Human Resources, Member - Management Board, Marina G. Kagan/Head - Public Affairs, Member - Management Board, Gennady K. Krainov/Head - Asset Protection Department, Member - Management Board, Oleg E. Kuzmin/Head - Dairy Business Unit, Member - Management Board, Silviu Popovici/Head - Beverages Business Unit, Member - Management Board, Grant Winterton/Head - Marketing, Innovation, Member - Management Board, Gary Sobel/Head - Baby Food Business Unit

Directors: David M. Iakobachvili/Chmn., Earnest Linwood Tipton/Dir., Gavril A. Yushvaev/Dir., Vladimir N. Sherbak/69/Dir., Evgeny G. Yasin/Dir., Alexander S. Orlov/Dir., Victor A. Tutelyan/66/Dir., Guy De Selliers/Dir., Michael A. O'Neill/Dir., Sergei A. Plastinin/Dir., Mikhail V. Dubinin/Dir., Dmitry A. Anisimov/CFO, Dir. - Management, Jacques Vincent/Dir., Igor V. Kostikov/Dir.

Owners: Mikhail I. Vishnyakov/1.00%, I.M. Arteks Holdings Limited, Mikhail V. Dubinin/4.92%, Gavril A. Yushvaev/19.45%, Sergei A. Plastinin/8.58%, David Iakobachvili/10.14%, Insiders/100.00%, Alexander S. Orlov/3.02%, Viktor E. Evdokimov

Financial Data: ***Fiscal Year End:***12/31 ***Latest Annual Data:*** 12/31/2006

Year	Sales	Net Income
2006	$1,762,127,000	$95,384,000
2005	$1,399,289,000	$30,266,000
2004	$1,189,291,000	$22,974,000

Curr. Assets:	$420,746,000	***Curr. Liab.:***	$330,336,000	***P/E Ratio:***	14.97
Plant, Equip.:	$606,728,000	***Total Liab.:***	$678,442,000	***Indic. Yr. Divd.:***	NA
Total Assets:	$1,175,936,000	***Net Worth:***	$497,494,000	***Debt/ Equity:***	NA

Win Win Gaming Inc

2980 S Rainbow Blvd, Ste 200, Las Vegas, NV, 89146; ***PH:*** 1-702-212-4530; ***http://*** www.winwininc.com; ***Email:*** info@winwininc.com

General - Incorporation	DE	**Stock**- Price on:12/24/2007	NA
Employees	NA	Stock Exchange	OTC
Auditor	Asher & Co Ltd	Ticker Symbol	WNWN
Stk Agt	Integrity Stock Transfer, Inc.	Outstanding Shares	NA
Counsel	NA	E.P.S	-$0.24
DUNS No.	80-820-9092	Shareholders	NA

Business: The group's principal activities are to develop, operate and market lotteries, land-based casinos and Internet lottery and gaming sites. It offers a complete 'turn-key' service providing funding, equipment, training, management and marketing, for lottery and gaming operations. The group specializes in creating lottery and casino games to assist countries, primarily for the purpose of financing national projects, humanitarian causes and special relief fund-raising.

Primary SIC and add'l.: 7999 7993

CIK No: 0000897545

Subsidiaries: Pixiem Inc - Korean, Pixiem, Inc., Win Win Acquisition Corp., Win Win Consulting (Shanghai) Co. Limited, Win Win Holding Limited, Win Win Wireless, LLC, Win Win, Inc

Officers: Patrick Rogers/Chmn., Founder, CEO, Pres., Greg Dewitt/CTO, Peter Pang/Dir., Pres. - China Operations, Exec. VP, Monica Soares/Sr. VP, Co - Founder

Directors: Patrick Rogers/Chmn., Founder, CEO, Pres., Lodwrick Cook/Chmn. - Advisory Board, Emil R. Bedard/Member - Advisory Board, Marshall Geller/Member - Advisory Board, Howard Goldberg/Member - Advisory Board, Dwight Call/Dir., John Gronvall/Dir., Peter Pang/Dir., Pres. - China Operations, Exec. VP, Sigmund Rogich/Member - Advisory Board, Richard Shintaku/Member - Advisory Board, Arthur Petrie/Dir.

Financial Data: ***Fiscal Year End:***12/31 ***Latest Annual Data:*** 12/31/2005

Year	Sales	Net Income
2005	$197,000	-$9,809,000
2004	$14,000	-$7,029,000
2003	$7,000	-$3,016,000

Curr. Assets:	$745,000	***Curr. Liab.:***	$2,999,000		
Plant, Equip.:	$1,287,000	***Total Liab.:***	$3,609,000	***Indic. Yr. Divd.:***	NA
Total Assets:	$3,816,000	***Net Worth:***	$207,000	***Debt/ Equity:***	NA

Wind Energy America Inc

Formerly: Dotronix Inc
12100 Singletree Ln., Ste. 100, Eden Prairie, MN, 55344; *PH:* 1-952-746-1234;
http:// www.dotronix.com

General - Incorporation	MN	**Stock** - Price on:12/24/2007	NA
Employees	2	Stock Exchange	NA
Auditor Child, Van Wagoner & Bradshaw, PLLC		Ticker Symbol	NA
Stk Agt. Wells Fargo Shareowner Services		Outstanding Shares	NA
Counsel	Dorsey & Whitney LLP	E.P.S.	NA
DUNS No.	01-394-6124	Shareholders	NA

Business: The group's principal activities are to design, manufacture and market cathode ray tube (crt) displays. The crt based products and crt replacement products include plasma panels, digital light projectors (dlp), liquid crystal displays (LCD) and light emitting diode displays (led). The group is also developing a systems approach to product development and marketing to provide all products and services, including display devices, for an integrated electronic display system. It supports several types of crt based monitors to end use markets, including medical diagnostic equipment manufactures and transportation hub operators such as airports and train stations. The group is developing marketing relationships with software companies.

Primary SIC and add'l.: 3679
CIK No: 0000351809
Subsidiaries: Grand Realty Group Inc., PuraMed BioScience Inc.
Officers: Robert O. Knutson/71/Dir., CEO, CFO
Directors: Robert O. Knutson/71/Dir., CEO, CFO, Robert A. Williams/Chmn.
Owners: Robert O. Knutson/1.55%, Robert A. Willams/4.54%, Terry L. Myhre/5.46%, Insiders/6.09%

Financial Data: Fiscal Year End:06/30 Latest Annual Data: 6/30/2007

Year	Sales	Net Income
2007	NA	-$2,067,000
2006	$65,000	-$93,000
2005	$642,000	-$928,000

Curr. Assets:	$145,000	Curr. Liab.:	$0		
Plant, Equip.:	NA	Total Liab.:	NA	Indic. Yr. Divd.:	NA
Total Assets:	$2,560,000	Net Worth:	$2,559,000	Debt/ Equity:	NA

Wind River Systems Inc

500 Wind River Way, Alameda, CA, 94501; *PH:* 1-510-748-4100; *http://* www.windriver.com;
Email: inquiries@windriver.com

General - Incorporation	DE	**Stock** - Price on:12/24/2007	$11.24
Employees	1,272	Stock Exchange	NDQ
Auditor	PricewaterhouseCoopers LLP	Ticker Symbol	WIND
Stk Agt. American Stock Transfer & Trust Co.		Outstanding Shares	85,680,000
Counsel	Cooley Godward LLP	E.P.S.	NA
DUNS No.	10-297-5448	Shareholders	NA

Business: The group's principal activities are to provide software solutions and development tools for embedded systems. Embedded system consists of a microprocessor and related software used to monitor or assist the operation of electronic devices, equipment and machinery. Embedded systems are used in diverse products such as digital imaging products, auto braking systems, Internet routers, jet fighter control panels and factory automation devices. The group's products enable customers to enhance product performance, standardize designs across projects and reduce research and development costs and shorten product development cycles. The group's products are sold to customers in aerospace, automotive, digital imaging, industrial measurement and networking markets. The group has operations in the United States, Canada, Europe, Japan and Asia-Pacific.

Primary SIC and add'l.: 7379 7372
CIK No: 0000833829
Subsidiaries: Integrated Systems ISINC (Israel) Ltd., Interpeak AB, a Swedish corporation, Interpeak Holding AB, a Swedish corporation, Interpeak, Inc., a Delaware corporation, Wind River AB, a Swedish corporation., Wind River AG, a Swiss corporation., Wind River GmbH, a German corporation., Wind River Holding AB, a Swedish corporation., Wind River International Limited, a Canadian corporation., Wind River K.K., a Japanese corporation., Wind River Nova Scotia Company, a Canadian corporation., Wind River S.A.R.L., a French corporation., Wind River S.r.l., an Italian corporation., Wind River Sales Co., Inc., a California corporation., Wind River Services, Inc., a Delaware corporation. 18 Subsidiaries included in the Index
Officers: Ken Klein/Chmn., CEO, Pres./$6,392,964.00, John Bruggeman/Chief Marketing Officer/$954,875.00, Jeff Loehr/VP - Human Resources, Scot Morrison/VP - Engineering/$909,495.00, De Anna Mekwunye/Sr. Analyst, Investor Relations, Stock Administration, Ian Halifax/Sr. VP - Finance, Administration CFO, Sec., Barry Mainz/COO, Damian Artt/VP - Worldwide Sales, Services, Vincent Rerolle/VP - Corporate Development, Strategy, Jane E. Bone/42/Chief Accounting Officer
Directors: Ken Klein/Chmn., CEO, Pres., Narendra K. Gupta/Vice Chmn., Standish H. O'Grady/Dir., Harvey C. Jones/Dir., Jerry L. Fiddler/Founder, Dir., John C. Bolger/Dir., William B. Elmore/Dir., Grant M. Inman/Dir.
Owners: Michael W. Zellner, Narendra K. Gupta/5.70%, Scot K. Morrison, Mazama Capital Management, Inc./17.80%, Harvey C. Jones, William B. Elmore/1.90%, John J. Bruggeman, John C. Bolger, Grant M. Inman, Insiders/19.00%, Robert L. Wheaton, Kenneth R. Klein/3.20%, Jerry L. Fiddler/5.40%, T. Rowe Price Associates, Inc./8.10%, Standish H. OGrady

Financial Data: Fiscal Year End:01/31 Latest Annual Data: 1/31/2007

Year	Sales	Net Income
2007	$285,298,000	$573,000
2006	$266,323,000	$29,295,000
2005	$235,400,000	$8,165,000

Curr. Assets:	$202,277,000	Curr. Liab.:	$156,653,000		
Plant, Equip.:	$74,997,000	Total Liab.:	$174,431,000	Indic. Yr. Divd.:	NA
Total Assets:	$498,565,000	Net Worth:	$324,134,000	Debt/ Equity:	NA

Windsortech Inc

400 Royal Palm Way, Palm Beach, FL, 33480; *PH:* 1-561-835-9747; *http://* www.qsgi.com

General - Incorporation	DE	**Stock** - Price on:12/24/2007	$1.72
Employees	NA	Stock Exchange	OTC
Auditor	Rubin Brown LLP	Ticker Symbol	WSRT
Stk Agt. American Stock Transfer & Trust Co.		Outstanding Shares	NA
Counsel	NA	E.P.S.	NA
DUNS No.	NA	Shareholders	NA

Business: The group's principal activities are to purchase and sell computer eqpmt and related products and provide complete equipment asset mangmt services. It purchases excess, used and off-lease computer eqpmt and related products from a variety of sources including Fortune 1000 companies and leasing and finance companies and these are remarketed to brokers, exporters, wholesalers, retailers, schools and individuals. It also disassembles them and separate and sell the components as parts and recycle the components, which are unsold, such as metal covers, plastics and other components. It offers computers of the brand intel pentium class or equivalent products mfrd by IBM, dell, compaq, apple, sony, fujitsu, hewlett-packard, gateway, toshiba and other major mfrs. It also provides computer asset mangmt and recovery services to leasing companies and major corporations. On 28-May-2004, the group acqd qualtech intl corp and its affiliate, qualtech services group inc.

Primary SIC and add'l.: 5045
CIK No: 0000027960
Officers: Marc Sherman/Chmn., CEO, Seth A. Grossman/Dir., COO, Pres., Edward L. Cummings/Dir., CFO, Joel Owens/Exec. VP, Dir. - International Operations, Andy Kerr/Contact - Data Center Maintenance, Hardware Divisions, Mark Jacobson/Dir. - Sales, Data Center Maintenance, Hardware Divisions, Chris Schoeller/VP - Data Security, Compliance Sales
Directors: Marc Sherman/Chmn., CEO, Edward L. Cummings/Dir., CFO, John F. Cunningham/Dir., Geoff Smith/Dir., Robert W. Vanhellemont/Dir., R. Keith Elliot/Dir., Keith R. Elliott/66/Dir.
Owners: Edward L. Cummings/8.10%, Pike Capital Partners, LP/17.80%, David A. Harris, Keith R. Elliott/1.20%, Joel L. Owens, John F. Cunningham, Robert W. VanHellemont, Seth A. Grossman/7.40%, Marc Sherman/13.00%, Circle T Partners, LP/9.40%, Geoffrey A. Smith, Insiders/32.10%

Windstream Corp

4001 Rodney Parham Rd., Little Rock, AR, 72212; ; *http://* www.windstream.com;
Email: Investor.Relations@windstream.com

General - Incorporation	DE	**Stock** - Price on:12/24/2007	$15.01
Employees	8,017	Stock Exchange	NYSE
Auditor	PricewaterhouseCoopers LLP	Ticker Symbol	WIN
Stk Agt. Computershare Investor Services LLC		Outstanding Shares	477,230,000
Counsel	NA	E.P.S.	$0.95
DUNS No.	NA	Shareholders	NA

Business: The groups principle activity is to provide telecommunication services. The group operates from the United States.

Primary SIC and add'l.: 4841 3661 7389 4899 3661 3669 4841 3669 7389 4813 4899 4813
CIK No: 0001282266
Subsidiaries: DCS Holding Co., ECS Holding Co., Georgia Windstream, Inc., KCS Holding Co., Kerrville Cellular Holdings, LLC, Kerrville Cellular Management, LLC, Kerrville Cellular, LP, Kerrville Communications Corporation, Kerrville Communications Enterprises, LLC, Kerrville Communications Management, LLC, Kerrville Mobile Holdings, Inc., Kerrville Wireless Holdings Limited Partnership, Oklahoma Windstream, Inc., SCD Sharing Partnership, LP, SCE Sharing Partnership, LP 72 Subsidiaries included in the Index
Officers: Jeffery R. Gardner/48/CEO, Pres., Dir. - Windstream Communication/$3,794,352.00, Keith D. Paglusch/COO/$817,648.00, Brent Whittington/CFO, Exec. VP - Windstream Communication/$696,636.00, John Fletcher/Exec. VP, General Counsel - Windstream Communication/$627,565.00, Rob Clancy/Sr. VP, Treasurer - Windstream Communication, Susan Bradley/Sr. VP - Human Resources, Windstream Communication, Anthony W. Thomas/36/Controller, William G. Raney/COO, Sr. VP - Valor/$1,814,826.00, Mike Rhoda/Sr. VP - Governmental Affairs, Windstream Communication, Ric Crane/Sr. VP, Chief Marketing Officer - Windstream Communication, Cindy Nash/Sr. VP - Customer Service, Windstream Communication, Frank Schueneman/Sr. VP - Network Services, Windstream Communication, Tony Thomas/Controller - Windstream Communication, Don Wilborne/Sr. VP - Business Sales, Support, Windstream Communication, Grant Raney/Southwest Region Pres. - Windstream Communication *(17 Officers included in Index)*
Directors: Jeffery R. Gardner/48/CEO, Pres., Dir. - Windstream Communication, Francis X. Frantz/54/Chmn. - Windstream Communication, Frank E. Reed/73/Dir. - Windstream Communication, Jeffrey T. Hinson/53/Dir. - Windstream Communication, Judy K. Jones/64/Dir. - Windstream Communication, Dennis E. Foster/67/Dir. - Windstream Communication, William A. Montgomery/59/Dir. - Windstream Communication, Windstream Communication, Samuel E. Beall/57/Dir. - Windstream Communication
Owners: Dennis E. Foster, William A. Montgomery, Jeffrey T. Hinson, Brent Whittington, Frank E. Reed, Keith D. Paglusch, Insiders, Francis X. Frantz, Samuel E. Beall, Morgan Stanley/7.20%, Jeffery R. Gardner, Judy K. Jones, John P. Fletcher

Financial Data: Fiscal Year End:12/31 Latest Annual Data: 12/31/2006

Year	Sales	Net Income
2006	$3,033,300,000	$545,300,000
2005	$505,894,000	$35,347,000
2004	$507,310,000	-$27,755,000

Curr. Assets:	$876,700,000	Curr. Liab.:	$684,600,000	P/E Ratio:	29.58
Plant, Equip.:	$3,939,800,000	Total Liab.:	$7,560,900,000	Indic. Yr. Divd.:	$1.000
Total Assets:	$8,030,700,000	Net Worth:	$469,800,000	Debt/ Equity:	NA

Windswept Environmental Group Inc

100 Sweeneydale Ave., Bay Shore, NY, 11706; *PH:* 1-631-289-5500;
http:// www.tradewindsenvironmental.com

General - Incorporation	DE	**Stock** - Price on:12/24/2007	$0.205
Employees	71	Stock Exchange	OTC
Auditor	Holtz Rubenstein Reminick LLP	Ticker Symbol	WEGI
Stk Agt. OTC Corporate Transfer Service Co		Outstanding Shares	37,440,000
Counsel	NA	E.P.S.	-$0.611
DUNS No.	79-179-4431	Shareholders	NA

Business: The group's principal activities are to provide a full range of emergency response, remediation and disaster restoration services to a broad range of customers. The group provides services through its wholly owned subsidiary, trade-winds environmental restoration, inc and north Atlantic

laboratories, inc. The group provides environmental services in areas of wetlands restoration, wildlife and natural resources rehabilitation, hazardous materials remediation, testing, toxicology, training, technical advisory and site renovation. The other services of the group include demolition renovation and other general construction services. The group operates mainly in the northeastern United States.

Primary SIC and add'l.: 8999

CIK No: 0000814915

Subsidiaries: North Atlantic Laboratories, Trade-Winds Environmental Restoration Inc.

Officers: Michael O'Reilly/Chmn., CEO, Pres., Arthur J. Wasserspring/66/CFO

Directors: Michael O'Reilly/Chmn., CEO, Pres., Anthony P. Towell/77/Dir., Kevin J. Phillips/60/Dir.

Owners: Kevin Phillips/50.00%, Laurus Master Fund, Ltd./9.90%, Anthony P. Towell/1.20%, Gary Molnar/1.50%, Kevin Phillips/2.10%, Insiders/50.00%, Gary Molnar/50.00%, Insiders/54.60%, Michael OReilly/51.40%

Financial Data: *Fiscal Year End:*06/28 *Latest Annual Data:* 6/30/2006

Year	Sales	Net Income
2006	$32,644,000	-$20,517,000
2005	$20,640,000	$53,000
2004	$19,167,000	-$3,535,000

Curr. Assets:	$12,334,000	Curr. Liab.:	$32,555,000		
Plant, Equip.:	$2,920,000	Total Liab.:	$33,243,000	Indic. Yr. Divd.:	NA
Total Assets:	$17,794,000	Net Worth:	-$16,749,000	Debt/ Equity:	2.5228

Winland Electronics Inc

1950 Excel Dr., Mankato, MN, 56001; *PH:* 1-507-625-7231; *http://* www.winland.com; *Email:* info@winland.com

General		Stock	
Incorporation	MN	Price on:12/24/2007	$3.2
Employees	138	Stock Exchange	AMEX
Auditor	McGladrey & Pullen LLP	Ticker Symbol	WEX
Stk Agt	Wells Fargo Shareholder Services	Outstanding Shares	3,600,000
Counsel	Fredrikson & Byron	E.P.S.	-$0.09
DUNS No.	08-237-8290	Shareholders	NA

Business: The group's principle activities include designing and manufacturing custom electronic controls and assemblies. The products of the company is distributed in two categories: electronic manufacturing services and proprietary products and services. The electronic manufacturing services, designs and manufactures circuit board assemblies and higher level products. The services provided include product concept studies, product design, printed circuit board design, higher level assembly, box build and legal support. The proprietary products include microprocessor and mechanically controlled sensors and alarms that monitor and detect environmental changes, such as changes in temperature or humidity, water leakage and power failures. The group operates from the United States.

Primary SIC and add'l.: 3625 3699 3829 4225 8711

CIK No: 0000749935

Officers: Lorin E. Krueger/Dir., CEO, Pres./$233,614.00, Terry E. Treanor/VP, Jennifer A. Thompson/49/CFO, Dale A. Nordquist/Sr. VP - Sales, Marketing/$233,335.00, Greg Burneske/VP - Engineering/$151,718.00, Glenn A. Kermes/CFO, Cameron Donahue/Investor Relations Contact

Directors: Lorin E. Krueger/Dir., CEO, Pres., Thomas J. De Petra/Chmn., Richard T. Speckmann/Dir., James L. Reissner/Dir.

Owners: Insiders/10.60%, Lorin E. Krueger/6.40%, Dale A. Nordquist, James L. Reissner, Gregory W. Burneske, Richard T. Speckmann, Thomas J. de Petra, FMR Corp./9.90%

Financial Data: *Fiscal Year End:*12/31 *Latest Annual Data:* 12/31/2006

Year	Sales	Net Income
2006	$37,945,000	$1,038,000
2005	$29,106,000	$2,049,000
2004	$24,199,000	$1,090,000

Curr. Assets:	$13,085,000	Curr. Liab.:	$6,377,000		
Plant, Equip.:	$5,779,000	Total Liab.:	$8,484,000	Indic. Yr. Divd.:	NA
Total Assets:	$18,867,000	Net Worth:	$10,383,000	Debt/ Equity:	0.1643

Winmark Corp

4200 Dahlberg Dr., Ste. 100, Minneapolis, MN, 55422; *PH:* 1-612-520-8500; *http://* www.winmarkcorporation.com; *Email:* winmark.information@winmarkcorporation.com

General		Stock	
Incorporation	MN	Price on:12/24/2007	$18.74
Employees	104	Stock Exchange	NDQ
Auditor	KPMG LLP	Ticker Symbol	WINA
Stk Agt	Wells Fargo Shareowner Services	Outstanding Shares	5,470,000
Counsel	NA	E.P.S.	$0.50
DUNS No.	62-143-4703	Shareholders	NA

Business: The group's principle activity is to franchise retail brands that buy, sell, trade and consign merchandise. The four retail brands are play it again sports(R), once upon a child(R), music go round(R) and plato's closet(r). Play it again sports stores(R) sell, buy, trade and consign used and new sporting goods, equipments and accessories for athletic activities. Once upon a child stores(R) sell and buy used and new children's clothing, toys, furniture, equipment and accessories. Music go round(R) stores sell, buy, trade and consign used and new musical instruments, speakers, amplifiers, music-related electronics and related accessories. Plato's closet(R) stores sell and buy used and new clothing and accessories geared toward the teenage and young adult market. At 27-Dec-2003, the company owned 813 stores in the United States and Canada. The group operates from United States.

Primary SIC and add'l.: 6794 7319 5736 5399 5945 5641 5712

CIK No: 0000908315

Subsidiaries: Winmark Capital Corporation, Wirth Business Credit, Inc.

Officers: John L. Morgan/Chmn., CEO/$307,167.00, Steven A. Murphy/Pres. - Franchising/$341,462.00, Catherine P. Heaven/General Counsel, Steven C. Zola/Pres. - Winmark Capital Corporation/$361,070.00, Leah A. Goff/VP - Human Resources, Brett D. Heffes/CFO, Treasurer/$512,025.00, Merry Beth Beth Hovey/VP - Marketing

Directors: John L. Morgan/Chmn., CEO, Kirk A. MacKenzie/Vice Chmn., Jenele C. Grassle/Dir., Mark L. Wilson/Dir., William D. Dunlap/Dir. - Petters Media Group, Paul C. Reyelts/Dir., Dean B. Phillips/Dir.

Owners: Ronald G. Olson/18.10%, Sheldon T. Fleck/11.90%, Paul C. Reyelts, Jenele C. Grassle, Dean B. Phillips, Mark T. Hooley/1.60%, Farnum Street Partners, L.P./6.40%, Jeffrey K. Dahlberg/9.80%, Steven C. Zola, William D. Dunlap, Kirk A. MacKenzie/3.10%, Mark L. Wilson, John L. Morgan/24.60%, Insiders/32.60%, Steven A. Murphy *(17 Owners included in Index)*

Financial Data: *Fiscal Year End:*12/31 *Latest Annual Data:* 12/30/2006

Year	Sales	Net Income
2006	$27,371,000	$3,421,000
2005	$26,593,000	$2,100,000
2004	$27,202,000	$4,082,000

Curr. Assets:	$8,531,000	Curr. Liab.:	$3,737,000	P/E Ratio:	37.48
Plant, Equip.:	$449,000	Total Liab.:	$4,262,000	Indic. Yr. Divd.:	NA
Total Assets:	$26,549,000	Net Worth:	$22,287,000	Debt/ Equity:	0.9996

Winmax Trading Group Inc

48 Wall St., 11th Fl., New York, NY, 10005; *PH:* 1-212-918-4513; *http://* www.winmaxtradinggroup.com; *Email:* calgary@winmaxtradinggroup.com

General		Stock	
Incorporation	FL	Price on:12/24/2007	NA
Employees	6	Stock Exchange	OTC
Auditor	Rosen Seymour Shapss Martin & Co. LLP	Ticker Symbol	WNMX
Stk Agt	Transfer Online, Inc.	Outstanding Shares	NA
Counsel	NA	E.P.S.	NA
DUNS No.	NA	Shareholders	NA

Business: The group's principal activities are to design, develop and construct Web sites and provide Internet solutions. It also acquires precious and semi-precious gemstone raw materials and minerals from properties in which they have an interest, and from the third party miners and to thereafter arrange for the finishing. The group markets such gemstone materials and jewellry through their Web site. The Internet solutions of the group include Web services, new media services and Internet broadcast services. Web services include designing with functional programming and structured information for quick and intuitive access. New media services provide interactive media such as CD roms, dvds and flash technology. Internet broadcast services include video streaming technology that includes live, remote live and archived broadcast programming over the Internet with video and editing using an editing program.

Primary SIC and add'l.: 7379 1499 7373

CIK No: 0001035517

Subsidiaries: bnettv Inc., bnettv.com, Inc., The Gemstore Group Inc., The Gemstore of New York , Inc., The Gemstore, Inc., The Gemstore.com, Inc., Winmax media, Inc.

Curr. Assets:	$67,000	Curr. Liab.:	$1,042,000		
Plant, Equip.:	$54,000	Total Liab.:	$3,045,000	Indic. Yr. Divd.:	NA
Total Assets:	$150,000	Net Worth:	-$2,895,000	Debt/ Equity:	NA

Winn-Dixie Stores Inc

5050 Edgewood Ct., Jacksonville, FL, 32254; *PH:* 1-904-783-5000; *Fax:* 1-866-946-6349; *http://* www.winndixie.com

General		Stock	
Incorporation	FL	Price on:12/24/2007	NA
Employees	NA	Stock Exchange	NDQ
Auditor	KPMG LLP	Ticker Symbol	WINN
Stk Agt	American Stock Transfer & Trust Co.	Outstanding Shares	NA
Counsel	NA	E.P.S.	$4.56
DUNS No.	00-692-1902	Shareholders	NA

Business: The groups principle activity is to operate a chain of retail food and drug stores. The groups products include groceries, meats, seafood, produce, deli, bakery, and floral. The group operates from United States.

Primary SIC and add'l.: 5411

CIK No: 0000107681

Subsidiaries: Astor Products, Inc., Bahamas Supermarkets Limited, Crackin Good, Inc., Deep South Products, Inc., Dixie Packers, Inc., Dixie Spirits, Inc., Dixie Stores, Inc., Economy Wholesale Distributors, Inc., Superior Food Company, Table Supply Food Stores, Inc., The City Meat Markets Limited, W-D (Bahamas) Limited, WIN General Insurance, Inc., Winn-Dixie Logistics, Inc., Winn-Dixie Montgomery, Inc. 18 Subsidiaries included in the Index

Officers: Peter L. Lynch/Chmn., CEO, Pres./$6,544,862.00, Bennett L. Nussbaum/61/CFO, Sr. VP/$1,456,405.00, Michael D. Byrum/56/VP, Corporate Controller, Chief Accounting Officer, Charles M. Weston/60/Group VP - Information Technology, Thomas P. Robbins/64/Sr. VP - Merchandising/$781,659.00, Mark A. Sellers/54/Group VP - Operations, Larry B. Appel/Sr. VP, General Counsel, Sec./$1,186,042.00, Anthony Austin/Sr. VP - Human Resources, Chris Scott/Group VP - Logistics, Distribution, Charlie Weston/Group VP - Information Technology, Daniel Portnoy/51/Sr. VP, Chief - Merchandising, Marketing Officer, Sheila C. Reinken/47/VP - Finance, Treasurer, Frank O. Eckstein/61/Sr. VP - Retail Operations/$804,335.00, David F. Henry/58/Sr. VP - Marketing, Phillip E. Pichulo/59/Group VP - Development *(16 Officers included in Index)*

Directors: Peter L. Lynch/Chmn., CEO, Pres., Evelyn Follit/Dir., Charles Garcia/Dir., Jeff Girard/Dir., Yvonne Jackson/Dir., Gregory Josefowicz/Dir., Terry Peets/Dir., Richard Rivera/Dir., James Olson/Dir.

Owners: James P. Olson, Insiders, Advisory Research, Inc./7.26%, Orbis Investment Management Limited/5.04%, Jeffrey C. Girard, Unicredito Italiano, S.p.A./5.03%, FMR Corp./12.74%, Bennett L. Nussbaum

Financial Data: *Fiscal Year End:*06/29 *Latest Annual Data:* 6/28/2006

Year	Sales	Net Income
2006	$7,193,853,000	-$361,301,000
2005	$9,921,319,000	-$832,602,000
2004	$10,632,850,000	-$100,404,000

Curr. Assets:	$1,207,961,000	Curr. Liab.:	$398,450,000		
Plant, Equip.:	$663,087,000	Total Liab.:	$1,928,012,000	Indic. Yr. Divd.:	NA
Total Assets:	$1,987,306,000	Net Worth:	$59,294,000	Debt/ Equity:	NA

Winnebago Industries Inc

605 W Crystal Lake Rd., Forest City, IA, 50436; *PH:* 1-641-585-3535; *http://* www.winnebagoind.com

General		Stock	
Incorporation	IA	Price on:12/24/2007	$29.5
Employees	3,150	Stock Exchange	NYSE
Auditor	Deloitte & Touche LLP	Ticker Symbol	WGO
Stk Agt	Wells Fargo Shareowner Services	Outstanding Shares	31,590,000
Counsel	NA	E.P.S.	$1.41
DUNS No.	00-530-0751	Shareholders	NA

Business: The group's principle activities are to manufacture motor homes and self-contained recreation vehicles used primarily in leisure travel and outdoor recreation activities. The other products include extruded aluminum, commercial vehicles and component products for other manufacturers and

floor plan unit financing. The group sells vehicles through dealer organizations primarily under the winnebago, itasca, rialta and ultimate brand names. The motor homes consist of class a, class b and class c models. The non-recreation vehicle activities consist of original equipment manufacturer sales, commercial vehicles and other products.

Primary SIC and add'l.: 3716 6153 3711

CIK No: 0000107687

Subsidiaries: Winnebago Acceptance Corporation, Winnebago Industries, Inc, Winnebago R.V., Inc

Officers: Bruce D. Hertzke/57/Chmn., CEO, Robert J. Olson/57/Pres., Raymond M. Beebe/66/VP, General Counsel, Sec., Robert L. Gossett/57/VP - Administration, Roger W. Martin/48/VP - Sales, Marketing, Sarah N. Nielsen/35/CFO, VP, William J. O'Leary/59/VP - Product Development, Brian J. Hrubes/57/Controller, Randy J. Potts/49/VP - Manufacturing, Donald L. Heidemann/36/Treasurer

Directors: Bruce D. Hertzke/57/Chmn., CEO, Irvin E. Aal/Dir., Jerry N. Currie/Dir., Joseph W. England/Dir., Lawrence A. Erickson/Dir., John V. Hanson/Dir., John E. Herlitz/Dir., Gerald C. Kitch/Dir.

Owners: FMR Corp./11.90%, Fenimore Asset Management, Inc./6.20%, EARNEST Partners, LLC/8.50%, Vanguard Whitehall Funds/6.30%, Royce & Associates, LLC/11.60%, Barrow, Hanley, Mewhinney & Strauss, Inc./7.70%

Financial Data: Fiscal Year End: 08/27 **Latest Annual Data:** 8/26/2006

Year	Sales	Net Income
2006	$864,403,000	$44,744,000
2005	$991,975,000	$65,073,000
2004	$1,114,154,000	$70,641,000

Curr. Assets:	$270,069,000	Curr. Liab.:	$105,278,000	P/E Ratio:	25.88
Plant, Equip.:	$63,995,000	Total Liab.:	$192,681,000	Indic. Yr. Divd.:	$0.480
Total Assets:	$394,556,000	Net Worth:	$201,875,000	Debt/ Equity:	NA

Winner Medical Group Inc

Winner Industrial Pk., Bulong Rd., Shenzhen City, Longhua, 518109; **PH:** 86-75528138888; **Fax:** 86-075528134588; **http://** www.winnermedical.com; **Email:** info@winnermedical.com

General - Incorporation	NV	Stock - Price on:12/24/2007	$2.3
Employees	NA	Stock Exchange	OTC
Auditor	BDO McCabe Lo Ltd.	Ticker Symbol	WMDG
Stk Agt	Nevada Agency & Trust Company	Outstanding Shares	NA
Counsel	Thelen Reid Brown R & S LLP	E.P.S.	NA
DUNS No.	NA	Shareholders	NA

Business: The groups principle activity is engage in the manufacture of medical dressings and medical disposables. The group operates through two segments namely medical nonwoven fabric market and the self adhesive and elastic bandages market. In December 2005, the group acquired Winner Group Limited. The group operates from the United States. The group's quarterly revenue for Sep '07 was 21.51 millions of USD.

Primary SIC and add'l.: 3842

CIK No: 0000808011

Subsidiaries: Shanghai Winner Medical Apparatus Co., Ltd., Winner Group Limited, Winner Industries (Shenzhen) Co., Ltd., Winner Medical & Textile Ltd. Chongyang, Winner Medical & Textile Ltd. Jiayu, Winner Medical & Textile Ltd. Jingmen, Winner Medical & Textile Ltd. Tianmen, Winner Medical & Textile Ltd. Yichang, Winner Medical & Textile Ltd. Zhuhai, Winner Medical & Textile Ltd., Xishui, Winner Medical (Huanggang) Co., Ltd., Winner Medical International Trading Co., Ltd.

Officers: Jianquan Li/Chmn., CEO, Pres., Xiuyuan Fang/Dir., CFO, Treasurer, VP, Hongwei Jia/VP - Quality Inspection, Jiagan Chen/VP - Project Management, Nianfu Huo/Sr. VP, Yuanni Chen/Sec., Mgr. - Investor Relations, Kathy Price/Investor Relations, Junli Liu/Area Sales Mgr. - Japanese Marketing, Lizzie Zhao/Export Mgr. - Purcotton, Sheling Yang/Contact - Export Mgr. European Marketing, Julie Jiang/Export Mgr. - Purcotton, Suwen Tan/Export Dir.

Directors: Jianquan Li/Chmn., CEO, Pres., Xiuyuan Fang/Dir., CFO, Treasurer, VP, Larry Goldman/Dir., Richard B. Goodner/Dir., Horngjon Shieh/Dir., Yuanni Chen/Sec., Mgr. - Investor Relations

Financial Data: Fiscal Year End: 09/30 **Latest Annual Data:** 09/30/2006

Year	Sales	Net Income
2006	$63,873,000	$5,829,000
2005	NA	-$11,000
2004	NA	-$1,000

Curr. Assets:	$29,833,000	Curr. Liab.:	$14,735,000		
Plant, Equip.:	$35,801,000	Total Liab.:	$14,889,000	Indic. Yr. Divd.:	NA
Total Assets:	$67,154,000	Net Worth:	$52,265,000	Debt/ Equity:	NA

Winning Edge International Inc

Formerly: Gwin Inc
5092 S Jones Blvd, Las Vegas, NV, 89118; **PH:** 1-978-689-2080; **http://** www.winningedge.com

General - Incorporation	DE	Stock - Price on:12/24/2007	NA
Employees	17	Stock Exchange	OTC
Auditor	Moore Stephens, P.C	Ticker Symbol	WTCG
Stk Agt	Bank One Trust Co., N.A.,	Outstanding Shares	NA
Counsel	NA	E.P.S.	$0.36
DUNS No.	13-972-0825	Shareholders	NA

Business: The group's principle activity is to provide sports handicapping information and analysis to sports bettors through direct marketing channels such as television, radio, Internet and print media. The group provides professional handicapping advice on professional (nfl) and college (ncaa) football, professional (nba) and college basketball and professional baseball (mlb) with plans to expand in Europe and Asia covering soccer, cricket, and rugby. The group generates revenue from television show and other advertising by having sports fans and bettors call.

Primary SIC and add'l.: 7999

CIK No: 0000924396

Subsidiaries: Global SportsEDGE, Inc.

Officers: Wayne Allyn Root/47/Chmn., CEO, Ron Meyer/Coach, Chip Chirimbes/Professional Sports Handicapper

Directors: Wayne Allyn Root/47/Chmn., CEO

Owners: Douglas R. Miller/3.70%, Robert L. Seale, Roger L. Harrison, Roger Aspey-Kent, Wayne Allyn Root/8.10%, Insiders/12.40%

Financial Data: Fiscal Year End: 07/31 **Latest Annual Data:** 07/31/2006

Year	Sales	Net Income
2006	$5,601,000	-$1,205,000
2005	$5,503,000	-$1,801,000
2004	$6,081,000	-$1,903,000

Curr. Assets:	$642,000	Curr. Liab.:	$1,775,000		
Plant, Equip.:	$40,000	Total Liab.:	$1,888,000	Indic. Yr. Divd.:	NA
Total Assets:	$832,000	Net Worth:	-$1,056,000	Debt/ Equity:	NA

Winsonic Digital Media Group Ltd

260 Peachtree St., Ste 2200, Atlanta, GA, 30303; **PH:** 1-770-858-0039; **http://** www.winsonic.net

General - Incorporation	NV	Stock - Price on:12/24/2007	$0.51
Employees	NA	Stock Exchange	OTC
Auditor	De Joya Griffith & Co., LLC	Ticker Symbol	WDMG
Stk Agt	Pacific Stock Transfer Company	Outstanding Shares	49,580,000
Counsel	NA	E.P.S.	NA
DUNS No.	NA	Shareholders	NA

Business: The group's principal activity is to provide full spectrum media advertising, media management, communications technologies and related services to the entertainment industry. The group is a development stage company. The group's software and network establishes a new standard for media distribution of digital information via the Internet, ATM, sdi, digital cable, and satellite. The network enables users to view, interact, and listen to all types of audio, on-line video and digital TV in a full screen format. The group's proprietary technology netdvd stream sharet facilitates the digitization of content and enhances the performance of existing hardware and software in the media, technology and telecommunications sectors. It has a built- in Web server that enables the end user to stream share real media, windows media and apple quick time files from desktop to desktop.

Primary SIC and add'l.: 7372 7375

CIK No: 0001120411

Subsidiaries: Winsonic Digital Cable Systems Network, Ltd

Owners: Jon J. Jannotta/12.40%, Jeffrey Burke/3.80%, Thomas Mensah, Joseph Morris/2.10%, Winston Johnson/26.30%, Insiders/44.90%

Financial Data: Fiscal Year End: 12/31 **Latest Annual Data:** 12/31/2006

Year	Sales	Net Income
2006	$759,000	-$8,244,000
2005	NA	-$4,106,000
2004	$25,000	-$5,791,000

Curr. Assets:	$16,000	Curr. Liab.:	$6,530,000		
Plant, Equip.:	$641,000	Total Liab.:	$6,530,000	Indic. Yr. Divd.:	NA
Total Assets:	$658,000	Net Worth:	-$5,872,000	Debt/ Equity:	NA

Winsted Holdings Inc

One Northfield Plz., Ste 3000, Northfield, IL , 60093; **PH:** 1-847-441-1822; **http://** www.appletreecapital.com; **Email:** info@appletreecapital.com

General - Incorporation	FL	Stock - Price on:12/24/2007	$0.0001
Employees	3	Stock Exchange	OTC
Auditor	RBS Mirchandani LLP	Ticker Symbol	WNSH
Stk Agt	Interwest Transfer Company, Inc.	Outstanding Shares	1,670,000,000
Counsel	NA	E.P.S.	-$0.052
DUNS No.	NA	Shareholders	NA

Business: The group's principle activities are to specialize in the consultation, design, implementation and support of voice, data, Internet and wireless applications to small and mid-sized enterprises. The group provides its services over third party networks enabling to offer a comprehensive suite of services without the capital burden of building a communication network. The group services are sold regionally and are limited to the southwestern United States. The group currently has three sales and marketing offices, located in palm desert, California, denver, Colorado and scottsdale, Arizona. On 30-Apr-2004 the group entered into an asset purchase agreement with the site doctors.

Primary SIC and add'l.: 7375 7373

CIK No: 0001132686

Subsidiaries: GaeaCare Syndicate Partners, Inc., Medspa Solutions, Inc

Officers: Mark Ellis/41/Chmn., CEO, CFO, Pres.

Directors: Mark Ellis/41/Chmn., CEO, CFO, Pres., Brian Brittain/46/Dir., John Ryan/48/Dir.

Financial Data: Fiscal Year End: 12/31 **Latest Annual Data:** 12/31/2005

Year	Sales	Net Income
2005	$300,000	-$3,538,000
2004	$24,000	-$62,591,000
2003	NA	-$3,309,000

Curr. Assets:	$45,000	Curr. Liab.:	$665,000		
Plant, Equip.:	$48,000	Total Liab.:	$665,000	Indic. Yr. Divd.:	NA
Total Assets:	$140,000	Net Worth:	-$526,000	Debt/ Equity:	NA

Winston Hotels Inc

2626 Glenwood Ave., Raleigh, NC, 27608; **PH:** 1-919-510-6019; **http://** www.winstonhotels.com

General - Incorporation	NC	Stock - Price on:12/24/2007	$14.89
Employees	26	Stock Exchange	NA
Auditor	PricewaterhouseCoopers LLP	Ticker Symbol	NA
Stk Agt	Branch Banking & Trust Co	Outstanding Shares	29,410,000
Counsel	Wyrick Robbins Yates & Ponton LLP	E.P.S.	NA
DUNS No.	NA	Shareholders	NA

Business: The groups principle activities include operating, owning and financing of hotel properties. The group operates through two segments namely, hotel ownership and hotel financing. The group operates from the United States.

Primary SIC and add'l.: 7011

CIK No: 0000920605

Subsidiaries: 131 East Redwood (Landlord), LLC, 131 East Redwood (Tenant), LLC, Barclay Holding, Inc., Barclay Hospitality Services, Inc., Barclay Redwood Inc., Barclay Redwood Manager Inc., Chapel Hill Hotel Associates, LLC, Chapel Hill Lessee, LLC, Des Moines Springhill Lessee Project Company, LLC, Evanston Hotel Associates, LLC, Gateway Hotel Associates, LLC, Gateway Hotel Lessee, LLC, Houston Lessee Project Company, LLC, Jacksonville Hotel Associates, LLC, Jacksonville Hotel Lessee, LLC 52 Subsidiaries included in the Index

Officers: Robert W. Winston/Dir., CEO, Joseph V. Green/CFO, Pres., Kenneth R. Crockett/Exec. VP, Chief Development Officer, Brent V. West/VP, Chief Accounting Officer, Patti Bell/Assist. VP - Investor Relations - Administration, James P. Frey/VP

Directors: Robert W. Winston/Dir., CEO, Charles M. Winston/Chmn., Thomas F. Darden/Dir., Richard L. Daugherty/Dir., Edwin B. Borden/Dir., David C. Sullivan/Dir.

Owners: Joseph V. Green, Edwin B. Borden, James P. Frey, Thomas F. Darden, Robert W. Winston/6.50%, Richard L. Daugherty, Charles M. Winston/2.40%, Brent V. West, Barclays Global Investors, NA/6.60%, Kenneth R. Crockett, Insiders/10.40%, Wells Fargo & Company/6.50%, David C. Sullivan

Financial Data: Fiscal Year End:12/31 Latest Annual Data: 12/31/2006

Year	Sales	Net Income
2006	$175,392,000	$32,399,000
2005	$151,030,000	$5,253,000
2004	$138,442,000	$16,883,000

Curr. Assets:	$10,545,000	Curr. Liab.:	$27,892,000	P/E Ratio:	29.58
Plant, Equip.:	$439,316,000	Total Liab.:	$267,436,000	Indic. Yr. Divd.:	NA
Total Assets:	$540,209,000	Net Worth:	$258,969,000	Debt/ Equity:	NA

Wintech Digital System Technology Corp

18 Technology Dr., Ste 159, Irvine, CA, 92618; *PH:* 1-949-450-1014; *Fax:* 1-949-203-2235; *http://* www.wintechdigital.com; *Email:* info@wintechdigital.com

General - Incorporation	NV	Stock - Price on:12/24/2007	$0.1
Employees	NA	Stock Exchange	OTC
Auditor	Moores Rowland Mazars	Ticker Symbol	WDSP
Stk Agt	Nevada Agency & Trust Company	Outstanding Shares	NA
Counsel	NA	E.P.S.	NA
DUNS No.	NA	Shareholders	NA

Business: The group's principal activity is to develop and market digital signal processing related products to electrical engineers and universities. Digital signal processing (dsp) technology is widely used in the fields of networking, telecommunication, and digital appliances. The group has developed a series of dsp development tools, including dsp hardware modules, dsp emulators and dsp experiment development systems. These development tools are marketed to electrical engineers. The group also provides training and consulting services to these engineers to help them to use the tools to develop end user. The group markets its products in the United States, Japan, Brazil, Greece, Israel, England, russian and slovenia.

Primary SIC and add'l.: 3669

CIK No: 0001113226

Subsidiaries: Wintech Digital Systems (Beijing), Ltd, Wintech Xing-ye Technology Development Company Limited

Owners: Yonghong Dong/47.91%, Kun Tang/5.73%, Changjiang Deng, Mingrong Li/2.04%, Mingjuan Tan/4.79%, Xiaoming Chen/5.82%

Financial Data: Fiscal Year End:06/30 Latest Annual Data: 6/30/2006

Year	Sales	Net Income
2006	$1,503,000	$87,000
2005	$1,249,000	-$96,000
2004	$1,040,000	-$175,000

Curr. Assets:	$1,375,000	Curr. Liab.:	$1,297,000		
Plant, Equip.:	$138,000	Total Liab.:	$1,297,000	Indic. Yr. Divd.:	NA
Total Assets:	$1,513,000	Net Worth:	$216,000	Debt/ Equity:	NA

Wintrust Financial Corp

727 N Bank Ln., Lake Forest, IL, 60045; *PH:* 1-847-615-4096; *Fax:* 1-847-615-4091; *http://* www.wintrust.com; *Email:* investor_info@wintrust.com

General - Incorporation	IL	Stock - Price on:12/24/2007	$45.87
Employees	1,897	Stock Exchange	NDQ
Auditor	Ernst & Young LLP	Ticker Symbol	WTFC
Stk Agt	Illinois Stock Transfer Co	Outstanding Shares	24,150,000
Counsel	NA	E.P.S.	$2.16
DUNS No.	NA	Shareholders	NA

Business: The groups principal activity is to provide community oriented, personal and commercial banking services. The groups services include home equity, home mortgage, consumer, real estate and commercial loans, safe deposit facilities, ATMs, internet banking. The products of the group include demand, NOW, money market, savings and time deposit accounts. In March 31, 2005 the group acquired First Northwest Bancorp, Inc. The group operates from the United States.

Primary SIC and add'l.: 6021 6022 6712 6162 6159

CIK No: 0001015328

Subsidiaries: 245 Waukegan Road Limited Partnership, Advantage National Bank, Barrington Bank & Trust Company, N.A., Beverly Bank & Trust Company, N.A., Crabtree Capital Corporation, Crystal Lake Bank & Trust Company, N.A., First Insurance Funding Corporation, First Northwest Capital Trust I, Guardian Real Estate Services, Inc., Hinsdale Bank & Trust Company, Lake Forest Bank & Trust Company, Libertyville Bank & Trust Company, North Shore Community Bank & Trust Company, Northbrook Bank & Trust Company, Northview Capital Trust I 36 Subsidiaries included in the Index

Officers: Edward J. Wehmer/Dir., CEO, Pres./$2,431,024.00, David A. Dykstra/Sr. Excecutive VP, COO/$1,819,977.00, James H. Bishop/Exec. VP, Lloyd M. Bowden/Exec. VP - Technology, John S. Fleshood/Exec. VP - Risk Management, Randolph M. Hibben/Exec. VP/$615,465.00, Robert F. Key/Exec. VP - Marketing, Richard B. Murphy/Exec. VP, Chief Credit Officer/$561,315.00, David L. Stoehr/CFO, Exec. VP/$363,168.00, Thomas P. Zidar/Exec. VP - Wealth Management

Directors: Edward J. Wehmer/Dir., CEO, Pres., John S. Lillard/Chmn., Bert A. Getz/Dir., James B. McCarthy/Dir., Albin F. Moschner/Dir., Allan E. Bulley/Dir., Peter D. Crist/Dir., Bruce K. Crowther/Dir., Joseph F. Damico/Dir., Ingrid S. Stafford/Dir., Thomas J. Neis/Dir., Hollis W. Rademacher/Dir., Christopher J. Reyes/Dir., John J. Schornack/Dir.

Owners: Insiders/7.24%, Transamerica Investment Management, LLC/7.60%, Christopher J. Reyes, Joseph F. Damico, John S. Lillard, David A. Dykstra, Bruce K. Crowther, Allan E. Bulley, Ingrid S. Stafford, Richard B. Murphy, James B. McCarthy, Randolph M. Hibben, Bert A. Getz, FMR Corp./9.99%, Thomas J. Neis *(21 Owners included in Index)*

Financial Data: Fiscal Year End:12/31 Latest Annual Data: 12/31/2006

Year	Sales	Net Income
2006	$649,177,000	$66,493,000
2005	$500,593,000	$67,016,000
2004	$347,198,000	$51,334,000

Curr. Assets:	$531,804,000	Curr. Liab.:	$8,298,856,000	P/E Ratio:	19.27
Plant, Equip.:	$311,041,000	Total Liab.:	$8,798,506,000	Indic. Yr. Divd.:	$0.320
Total Assets:	$9,571,852,000	Net Worth:	$773,346,000	Debt/ Equity:	1.2696

Wipro Ltd

1300 Crittenden Ln., 2nd Fl., Mountain View, CA, 94043; *PH:* 1-650-316-3555; *Fax:* 1-650-316-3468; *http://* www.wipro.com; *Email:* info@wipro.com

General - Incorporation	Karnataka	Stock - Price on:12/24/2007	$15.85
Employees	50,350	Stock Exchange	NYSE
Auditor	KPMG	Ticker Symbol	WIT
Stk Agt	Karvy Computershare Private Ltd	Outstanding Shares	1,460,000,000
Counsel	NA	E.P.S.	$0.55
DUNS No.	NA	Shareholders	NA

Business: The group's principal activities are to provide information technology services. Information technology comprises software service and systems, consumer care, lighting, and healthcare technology services. The group also manufactures toilet soaps, toiletries, bulbs, florescent tubes, lighting accessories and hydrogenated cooking fat.

Primary SIC and add'l.: 3648 5122 7373 3229 3572 7375 2841

CIK No: 0001123799

Subsidiaries: BVPENTE Beteiligungsverwaltung GmbH, Cygnus Negri Investments Pvt. Ltd., Enthink Inc. (1), including Wipro, MPACT Technology Services Pvt. Ltd., mPower Software Services Inc., mPower Software Services India Pvt Ltd., New Logic Technologies AG, New Logic Technologies Inc., New Logic Technologies SA, New Logic Technologies SARL, Santoor and Wipro Babysoft, Spectramind Inc., WeP Peripherals Limited, Wipro Chandrika Limited 27 Subsidiaries included in the Index

Officers: T. K. Kurien/CEO, Suresh C. Senapaty/Corporate Exec. VP - Finance, Aniruddha Ganguly/Assoc. COO - Wipro BPO, Srijit Rajappan/VP, Business Unit Head - Product Engineering Solutions Wipro BPO, Anurag Behar/Corporate Executive Counsel Corporate VP - Mission Quality, Corporate Brand, Innovation MD - Wipro Infrastructure Engineering Limited, Vineet Agarwal/Corporate Executive Counsel, Pres. - Wipro Consumer, Lighting Group, A. L. Rao/COO, B. C. Prabhakar/Dir., Sr. Counsel, Sudip Banerjee/Pres. - Enterprise Solutions, Suresh Vaswani/Pres. - Global Information Technology Service Lines, Wipro Technologies, Pres. - Wipro Infotech, Girish S. Paranjpe/Pres. - Finance Solutions, Ranjan Acharya/Corporate Executive Counsel, Ramesh Emani/Pres. - Product Engineering Solutions, Pratik Kumar/Corporate VP - Human Resources, Nagendra P. Bandaru/VP - Global Business Wipro BPO *(21 Officers included in Index)*

Directors: Azim H. Premji/Chmn., Bill Owens/Dir., Jagdish N. Sheth/Dir., Ashok S. Ganguly/Dir., P. M. Sinha/Dir., Narayanan Vaghul/Dir., B. C. Prabhakar/Dir., Sr. Counsel

Owners: Hasham Traders, Zash Traders, Azim H. Premji, Prazim Traders

Financial Data: Fiscal Year End:03/31 Latest Annual Data: 03/31/2007

Year	Sales	Net Income
2007	$3,436,921,000	$670,887,000
2006	$2,387,405,000	$456,074,000
2005	$1,862,972,000	$362,570,000

Curr. Assets:	$2,313,055,000	Curr. Liab.:	$984,900,000	P/E Ratio:	31.70
Plant, Equip.:	$610,453,000	Total Liab.:	$1,026,170,000	Indic. Yr. Divd.:	$0.120
Total Assets:	$3,359,935,000	Net Worth:	$2,333,765,000	Debt/ Equity:	NA

Wireless Age Commnications Inc

6200 Tomken Rd., Mississauga, ON, L5T 1X7; *PH:* 1-905-696-2850; *Fax:* 1-905-696-2851; *http://* www.thewirelessage.com

General - Incorporation	NV	Stock - Price on:12/24/2007	$0.14
Employees	NA	Stock Exchange	OTC
Auditor	Mintz & Partners LLP	Ticker Symbol	WLSA
Stk Agt	Nevada Agency & Trust Company	Outstanding Shares	NA
Counsel	NA	E.P.S.	NA
DUNS No.	NA	Shareholders	NA

Business: The groups principle activity is primarily focus on provision of wireless telecommunications systems products and service solutions to wholesalers, distributors and retailers. The group operates through two segments namely retail and commercial. In March 2005, the group acquired mmwave Technologies Inc. and during September 2005 Infinity Capital Corporation. The group operates from Canada.

Primary SIC and add'l.: 4813

CIK No: 0001130131

Subsidiaries: 1588102 Ontario Inc., DB Sim Holdings Ltd., Knowlton Pass Electronics Inc, Marlon Distributors Ltd., Mmwave Technologies Inc., Prime Battery Products Limited, Prime Wireless Corporation, Wireless Age Communications Ltd., Wireless Source Distribution Ltd.

Officers: John G. Simmonds/Chmn., CEO, Allen G. Cowie/CMA Pres., Gary Hokkanen/CFO, Carrie J. Weiler/Corp. Sec.

Directors: John G. Simmonds/Chmn., CEO, Brad Poulos/Dir., Brian Usher-Jones/Dir., Stephen Dulmage/Dir.

Owners: Bradley J. Poulos/6.80%, Brian Usher-Jones/2.70%, Segal, Talarico, Habib, Molot LLP/8.30%, Insiders/10.10%, Gary Hokkanen

Financial Data: Fiscal Year End:10/31 Latest Annual Data: 12/31/2006

Year	Sales	Net Income
2006	$33,593,000	-$9,927,000
2005	$24,226,000	-$4,640,000
2004	$15,209,000	-$2,043,000

Curr. Assets:	$6,296,000	Curr. Liab.:	$9,892,000	P/E Ratio:	13.41
Plant, Equip.:	$1,239,000	Total Liab.:	$10,379,000	Indic. Yr. Divd.:	NA
Total Assets:	$8,208,000	Net Worth:	-$2,171,000	Debt/ Equity:	NA

Wireless Ronin Technologies Inc

14700 Martin Dr., Minneapolis, MN, 55344; *PH:* 1-952-564-3500; *Fax:* 1-952-974-7887; *http://* www.wirelessronin.com; *Email:* info@wirelessronin.com

inneapolis, MN, 55344; *PH:* 1-952-564-3500; *Fax:* 1-952-974-7887; *http://* www.wirelessronin.com; *Email:* info@wirelessronin.com

General - Incorporation	MN	**Stock** - Price on:12/24/2007	$7.97
Employees	36	Stock Exchange	NDQ
Auditor	Krause & Co.,LLP	Ticker Symbol	RNIN
Stk Agt	NA	Outstanding Shares	13,510,000
Counsel	NA	E.P.S	-$4.2
DUNS No.	NA	Shareholders	NA

Business: The groups principal activity is to provide dynamic digital signage solutions. The products of the group include master controller, site controller, network builder, zone builder and touch screen kiosks. The group products sold under the trade names WIRELESS RONIN(R) and RONIN CAST(R). Specific customers of the group include Sealy Corporation, Canterbury Park, Coca-Cola, GetServd.com, Las Vegas Convention and Visitors Authority. The group operates from the United States. The total sale of the group for the year 2006 was $3,145,389.

Primary SIC and add'l.: 7373

CIK No: 0001356093

Subsidiaries: Wireless Ronin (Europe) Limited

Officers: Jeffrey C. Mack/Chmn., CEO, Pres., John A. Witham/CFO, Exec. VP, Scott W. Koller/Exec. VP - Sales, Marketing, Christopher F. Ebbert/CTO, Exec. VP, Stephen E. Jacobs/59/Exec. VP, Sec., Brian S. Anderson/VP, Corporate Controller, James R. Arble/VP - Operations, Alan D. Buterbaugh/Sr. VP - Business Development, Robert W. Whent/Pres. - WRT Canada

Directors: Jeffrey C. Mack/Chmn., CEO, Pres., Gregory T. Barnum/Dir., Thomas J. Moudry/Dir., William F. Schnell/Dir., Carl B. Walking Eagle/Dir., Brett A. Shockley/Dir.

Owners: Barry W. Butzow/4.10%, Gregory T. Barnum, John A. Witham, Insiders/6.40%, Scott W. Koller, Spirit Lake Tribe/2.40%, William F. Schnell, Symmetry Peak Management, L.L.C./7.50%, Perkins Capital Management, Inc./8.00%, Carl B. Walking Eagle/2.50%, Brian S. Anderson, Thomas J. Moudry, Heartland Advisors, Inc./5.00%, Brett A. Shockley, Christopher F. Ebbert *(17 Owners included in Index)*

Financial Data: *Fiscal Year End:*12/31 *Latest Annual Data:* 12/31/2006

Year		Sales			Net Income
2006		$3,145,000			-$14,788,000
2005		$710,000			-$4,790,000
2004		$1,074,000			-$3,339,000
Curr. Assets:	$17,000,000	**Curr. Liab.:**	$1,653,000		
Plant, Equip.:	$524,000	**Total Liab.:**	$1,808,000	**Indic. Yr. Divd.:**	NA
Total Assets:	$17,546,000	**Net Worth:**	$15,738,000	**Debt/ Equity:**	0.0098

Wireless Telecom Group Inc

E 64 Midland Ave., Paramus, NJ, 07652; *PH:* 1-973-386-9696; *http://* www.wirelesstelecomgroup.com; *Email:* investor@wtt.bz

General - Incorporation	NJ	**Stock** - Price on:12/24/2007	$2.96
Employees	233	Stock Exchange	AMEX
Auditor	PKF	Ticker Symbol	WTT
Stk Agt	American Stock Transfer & Trust Co.	Outstanding Shares	25,850,000
Counsel	Morrison, Cohen, Singer & Weinstein	E.P.S	$0.15
DUNS No.	12-227-6959	Shareholders	NA

Business: The group's principal activities are to develop, manufacture, market electronic noise sources and electronic testing and measuring instruments. Noise source products are used as a method of testing to determine if communications systems are capable of receiving the information being transmitted. The noise source products can test satellite communication receivers for video, telephone and data communications. The group also produces electronic testing and measuring instruments including power meters, voltmeters, capacitance meters, audio and modulation meters and vxi products. The group's products are used to test terrestrial and satellite communications, radar, telemetry and personal communication products. The group's customers include commercial users, governments and multi-national companies. The group exports its products mainly to Asia and Europe.

Primary SIC and add'l.: 3825

CIK No: 0000878828

Subsidiaries: Boonton Electronics Corporation

Officers: James Johnson/CEO, Vice Chmn., Lawrence D. Henderson/Sr. VP - Global Customer Operations, Officer, Paul Genova/CFO, Pres./$295,110.00, Robert Censullo/Sec.

Directors: James Johnson/CEO, Vice Chmn., Savio Tung/Chmn., Hazem Ben-Gacem/Dir., Michael Manza/Dir., Henry L. Bachman/Dir., Joseph Garrity/Dir., Andrew Scelba/Dir., John Wilchek/Dir., Rick MacE/Dir., Adrian Nemcek/Dir.

Owners: Insiders, Michael Manza, Paul Genova, Damany Holding Gmbh, Andrew Scelba, John Wilchek, Savio W. Tung, Henry Bachman, Cayman Islands, BWI, James M., Hazem Ben-Gacem, FMR Corp., Investcorp Technology Ventures, L.P.

Financial Data: *Fiscal Year End:*12/31 *Latest Annual Data:* 12/31/2006

Year		Sales			Net Income
2006		$53,763,000			$3,524,000
2005		$38,771,000			$3,544,000
2004		$22,105,000			$2,331,000
Curr. Assets:	$36,061,000	**Curr. Liab.:**	$14,115,000	**P/E Ratio:**	19.73
Plant, Equip.:	$6,487,000	**Total Liab.:**	$26,433,000	**Indic. Yr. Divd.:**	NA
Total Assets:	$83,329,000	**Net Worth:**	$56,896,000	**Debt/ Equity:**	0.0872

Wireless Xcessories Group Inc

1840 County Line Rd., Ste. 301, Huntingdon Valley, PA, 19006; *PH:* 1-702-212-4530; *Fax:* 1-702-212-4553; *http://* www.wirexgroup.com; *Email:* msmith@wirexgroup.com

General - Incorporation	DE	**Stock** - Price on:12/24/2007	$3.43
Employees	85	Stock Exchange	AMEX
Auditor	Bagell, Josephs, Levine & Co. LLC	Ticker Symbol	XWG
Stk Agt	Bagell Josephs & Co LLC	Outstanding Shares	4,420,000
Counsel	NA	E.P.S	$0.217
DUNS No.	88-467-3005	Shareholders	NA

Business: The group's principle activity is to design and distribute a range of accessories for cellular phones throughout the United States and Canada. It currently offers over 2,000 wireless accessories that include rechargeable batteries, personal and vehicle handsfree kits, portable and vehicle antennas, in-car and travel chargers, plain and colored carrying cases, fashionable accessory faceplates and colored housings. The group markets and sells its products to dealers, distributors, communication carriers, mass merchandisers and retail customers through its in-house sales force and directly from its Website, www.wirexgroup.com. It also creates customized e-commerce websites for its dealers and produces 3 product line catalogs that are circulated nationally and internationally. The group's quarterly revenue for September 2007 was 5.02 millions of USD.

Primary SIC and add'l.: 5063

CIK No: 0001005504

Officers: Stephen Rade/70/Chmn., CEO, Pres., Kathleen Gerland/Human Resources Mgr., Dan Kenderdine/Warehouse Mgr., Christine Mayo/Credit Mgr., Accounting Mgr., Dawn Kenderdine/VP, Ronald E. Badke/CFO, Sec., Operations Mgr., Susan Rade/VP, Bill Earnest/Quality Control Mgr.

Directors: Stephen Rade/70/Chmn., CEO, Pres., Christopher F. McConnell/54/Dir., Bradley T. MacDonald/60/Dir., Allan S. Kalish/82/Dir., Christopher C. Cole/52/Dir.

Owners: Christopher F.McConnell/1.10%, Christopher C. Cole/1.60%, Dawn Kenderdine/1.10%, Stephen Rade/17.30%, Ronald E. Badke, Bradley T. MacDonald, Insiders/23.00%, Allan Kalish/1.20%

Financial Data: *Fiscal Year End:*12/31 *Latest Annual Data:* 12/31/2006

Year		Sales			Net Income
2006		$22,869,000			$1,190,000
2005		$22,059,000			$2,033,000
2004		$15,307,000			$1,008,000
Curr. Assets:	$7,224,000	**Curr. Liab.:**	$955,000		
Plant, Equip.:	$340,000	**Total Liab.:**	$955,000	**Indic. Yr. Divd.:**	NA
Total Assets:	$8,029,000	**Net Worth:**	$7,075,000	**Debt/ Equity:**	NA

Wisconsin Electric Power Co

231 W Michigan St. , Milwaukee, WI, 53201; *PH:* 1-414-221-2345; *http://* www.wisenergy.com

General - Incorporation	WI	**Stock** - Price on:12/24/2007	$100
Employees	NA	Stock Exchange	OTC
Auditor	Deloitte & Touche LLP	Ticker Symbol	WELPM
Stk Agt	NA	Outstanding Shares	NA
Counsel	NA	E.P.S	NA
DUNS No.	00-794-7385	Shareholders	NA

Business: The group's principal activities are to provide electric, gas and steam utilities. It is a wholly owned subsidiary of Wisconsin energy corporation. The group's electric operations involve the generation, transmission, distribution and selling of electric energy. The gas operations involve purchasing, distributing and selling natural gas to retail customers and transport customer-owned gas in four distinct service areas. The steam operations generate, distribute and sells steam supplied by its valley and milwaukee county power plants.

Primary SIC and add'l.: 4911 4924 4961

CIK No: 0000107815

Subsidiaries: American Transmission Company LLC, ATC Management Inc., Blue Sky Wind Farm, LLC, Bostco LLC, Green Field Wind Farm, LLC, Lake Breeze Wind Farm, LLC

Owners: Thomas J. Fischer, Gale E. Klappa, John F. Ahearne, Insiders, John F. Bergstrom, Frederick D. Kuester, Ulice Payne, James C. Fleming, Allen L. Leverett, Curt S. Culver, Frederick P. Stratton, Larry Salustro, Patricia W. Chadwick, Robert A. Cornog, Barbara L. Bowles

Financial Data: *Fiscal Year End:*12/31 *Latest Annual Data:* 12/31/2006

Year		Sales			Net Income
2006		$3,116,700,000			$276,800,000
2005		$2,938,000,000			$284,800,000
2004		$2,616,600,000			$249,900,000
Curr. Assets:	$928,400,000	**Curr. Liab.:**	$1,160,600,000		
Plant, Equip.:	$5,291,000,000	**Total Liab.:**	$5,698,800,000	**Indic. Yr. Divd.:**	NA
Total Assets:	$8,257,800,000	**Net Worth:**	$2,559,000,000	**Debt/ Equity:**	0.7188

Wisconsin Energy Corp

231 W Michigan St., Milwaukee, WI, 53201; *PH:* 1-414-221-2345; *http://* www.wisconsinenergy.com

General - Incorporation	WI	**Stock** - Price on:12/24/2007	$44.54
Employees	5,303	Stock Exchange	NYSE
Auditor	Deloitte & Touche LLP	Ticker Symbol	WEC
Stk Agt	Bank of New York	Outstanding Shares	116,950,000
Counsel	NA	E.P.S	$1.49
DUNS No.	15-730-5780	Shareholders	NA

Business: The group operates through its subsidiaries whose principle activity is to provide energy and natural gas services. The group operates from United States, Australia, Canada, China, United Kingdom, Germany, Italy, Mexico, New Zealand and other countries.

Primary SIC and add'l.: 4924 4931 4911 3594

CIK No: 0000783325

Subsidiaries: American Transmission Company LLC, ATC Management Inc., Blue Sky Wind Farm, LLC, Bostco LLC, CenterPoint WISPARK Land Company LLC, CET Two, LLC, Edison Sault Electric Company, Elm Road Generating Station Supercritical, LLC, Elm Road Services, LLC, GlassPack, LLC, Green Field Wind Farm, LLC, Guardian Pipeline, LLC, Lake Breeze Wind Farm, LLC, Minergy Corp., Minergy Neenah, LLC 24 Subsidiaries included in the Index

Officers: Gale E. Klappa/Chmn., CEO, Pres./$7,928,611.00, Stephen P. Dickson/VP, Controller, Frederick D. Kuester/Exec. VP/$3,650,296.00, Allen L. Leverett/CFO, Exec. VP/$2,788,926.00, Larry Salustro/60/Exec. VP/$2,978,915.00, Kristine Rappe/Sr. VP, Chief Administrative Officer, Darnell Demasters/VP - Federal Policy, Anne K. Klisurich/VP, Corp. Sec., Kristine M. Krause/VP - Environmental, Walter J. Kunicki/VP, Jeffrey P. West/VP, Treasurer, Richard J. White/VP - Corporate Communications, Arthur A. Zintek/VP, Keith H. Ecke/Assist. Corp. Sec., Charles Cole/Member - Foundation Board, Sr. VP - Distribution Operations *(25 Officers included in Index)*

Directors: Gale E. Klappa/Chmn., CEO, Pres., George E. Wardeberg/Dir., Rick Kuester/Member - Foundation Board, Exec. VP, Charles Cole/Member - Foundation Board, Sr. VP - Distribution Operations, John F. Bergstrom/Dir., John F. Ahearne/Dir., Barbara L. Bowles/Dir., Patricia W. Chadwick/Dir., Robert A. Cornog/Dir., Curt S. Culver/Dir., Thomas J. Fischer/Dir., Ulice Payne/Dir., Frederick P. Stratton/Dir.

Owners: Gale E. Klappa, John F. Bergstrom, Robert A. Cornog, Larry Salustro, Curt S. Culver, Pzena Investment Management, LLC/7.19%, Allen L. Leverett, Frederick D. Kuester, John F. Ahearne, Thomas J. Fischer, Insiders, FMR Corp./6.94%, James C. Fleming, Frederick P. Stratton, Ulice Payne *(18 Owners included in Index)*

Financial Data: *Fiscal Year End:*12/31 *Latest Annual Data:* 12/31/2006

Year	Sales	Net Income
2006	$3,996,400,000	$316,400,000
2005	$3,815,500,000	$308,700,000
2004	$3,431,100,000	$306,400,000

Curr. Assets:	$1,228,000,000	Curr. Liab.:	$1,888,000,000	P/E Ratio:	29.89
Plant, Equip.:	$7,052,500,000	Total Liab.:	$8,241,200,000	Indic. Yr. Divd.:	$1.000
Total Assets:	$11,130,200,000	Net Worth:	$2,889,000,000	Debt/ Equity:	1.0381

Wisconsin Power & Light Co

4902 N Biltmore Ln., Madison, WI, 53718; *PH:* 1-608-458-3311; *Fax:* 1-608-458-4824; *http://* www.alliantenergy.com

General - Incorporation	WI	Stock - Price on:12/24/2007	$39.53
Employees	5,151	Stock Exchange	AMEX
Auditor	Deloitte & Touche LLP	Ticker Symbol	NA
Stk Agt	Wells Fargo Shareowner Services	Outstanding Shares	113,740,000
Counsel	NA	E.P.S.	$3.32
DUNS No.	00-794-6452	Shareholders	NA

Business: The group's principle activities include generating, distributing and selling electric energy; the purchase, distribution, transportation and sale of natural gas and the provision of water services. The company is a wholly owned subsidiary of cincinnati gas & electric company. The group operates from United States.

Primary SIC and add'l.: 4941 4931 4932

CIK No: 0000107832

Subsidiaries: Alliant Energy Holdings do Brasil Limitada, Alliant Energy International, Inc., Alliant Energy Resources, Inc., Interstate Power and Light Company, Wisconsin Power and Light Company, WPL Transco LLC

Officers: William D. Harvey/Chmn., CEO, Pres./$5,040,415.00, Eliot G. Protsch/54/Sr. Exec. VP, CFO/$2,472,666.00, Barbara J. Swan/Pres./$1,604,177.00, Thomas L. Aller/58/Sr. VP - Energy Delivery/$1,091,767.00, Peggy Howard Moore/57/VP - Finance Effective, Patricia L. Kampling/48/VP, Treasurer Effective

Directors: William D. Harvey/Chmn., CEO, Pres., Ann K. Newhall/57/Dir., Dean C. Oestreich/56/Dir., Carol P. Sanders/41/Dir., Michael L. Bennett/54/Dir., Singleton B. McAllister/56/Dir., David A. Perdue/58/Dir., Judith D. Pyle/65/Dir., Darryl B. Hazel/60/Dir., James A. Leach/66/Dir.

Owners: David A. Perdue, Ann K. Newhall, Erroll B. Davis, Carol P. Sanders, Judith D. Pyle, Insiders, William D. Harvey, Darryl B. Hazel, John E. Kratchmer, Dean C. Oestreich, Eliot G. Protsch, Thomas L. Aller, Barbara J. Swan, Singleton B. McAllister, Barclays Global Investors, N. A./10.44% *(17 Owners included in Index)*

*Financial Data: Fiscal Year End:*12/31 *Latest Annual Data:* 12/31/2006

Year	Sales	Net Income
2006	$3,359,400,000	$315,700,000
2005	$3,279,600,000	-$7,700,000
2004	$2,958,700,000	$145,500,000

Curr. Assets:	$1,173,800,000	Curr. Liab.:	$1,102,100,000	P/E Ratio:	11.91
Plant, Equip.:	$4,944,900,000	Total Liab.:	$4,184,100,000	Indic. Yr. Divd.:	$1.270
Total Assets:	$7,084,100,000	Net Worth:	$2,895,100,000	Debt/ Equity:	0.5054

Wisconsin Public Service Corp

700 N Adams St., Green Bay, WI, 54307; *PH:* 1-920-433-4901; *http://* www.wisconsinpublicservice.com

General - Incorporation	WI	Stock - Price on:12/24/2007	$93.5
Employees	NA	Stock Exchange	OTC
Auditor	Deloitte & Touche LLP	Ticker Symbol	WIPSO
Stk Agt	American Stock Transfer & Trust Co.	Outstanding Shares	NA
Counsel	NA	E.P.S.	NA
DUNS No.	00-794-7435	Shareholders	NA

Business: The group's principle activities include transmitting and distributing electric energy and gas. The group operates from United States.

Primary SIC and add'l.: 4923 4931

CIK No: 0000107833

Subsidiaries: 3096210 Nova Scotia Company, Advantage Energy, Inc., American Transmission Company LLC, ATC Management Inc., Badger Energy Services, LLC, Boralex WPS Energy, Inc., Boralex WPS Power Limited Partnership, Combined Locks Energy Center, LLC, ECO Coal Pelletization #12 LLC, Guardian Pipeline LLC, Guardian Pipeline, LLC, Michigan Gas Utilities Corporation, Mid-American Power, LLC, Minnesota Energy Resources Corporation, PDI Stoneman, Inc. 41 Subsidiaries included in the Index

Officers: Larry L. Weyers/62/Chmn., CEO, Pres., David W. Harpole/52/VP - Energy Supply, Projects, Thomas P. Meinz/61/Dir., Exec. VP - Public Affairs, Charles A. Schrock/54/Pres., COO - Generation, Joseph P. O'Leary/53/Sr. VP, CFO, Bradley A. Johnson/53/VP, Treasurer, Barth J. Wolf/50/Sec., Mgr. - Legal Services, Diane L. Ford/54/VP, Controller, Chief Accounting Officer, Bernard J. Treml/58/Sr. VP - Human Resources, Lawrence T. Borgard/46/Pres., COO - Energy Delivery

Directors: Larry L. Weyers/62/Chmn., CEO, Pres., Thomas P. Meinz/61/Dir., Exec. VP - Public Affairs, Thomas A. Nardi/Dir., Desiree G. Rogers/Dir., Phillip M. Mikulsky/Dir.

Owners: Insiders/0.03%, Thomas P. Meinz, Insiders/0.03%, Charles A. Schrock, Lawrence T. Borgard

Wisedriver Com Inc

1691 Michigan Ave., Ste. 425, Miami Beach, FL, 33139; *PH:* 1-305-538-7840; *http://* www.wisedriver.com

General - Incorporation	DE	Stock - Price on:12/24/2007	NA
Employees	NA	Stock Exchange	NA
Auditor	Seligson & Giannattasio LLP	Ticker Symbol	NA
Stk Agt	Corporate Stock Transfer, Inc.	Outstanding Shares	NA
Counsel	NA	E.P.S.	NA
DUNS No.	NA	Shareholders	NA

Business: The group's principal activity is to provide automobile drivers with comprehensive information and services related to driving and automobile ownership. The group is a development stage company.the Web site of the group educates users on how to avoid traffic violations, and in instances where a ticket has been issued, to inform the user about techniques for contesting the alleged infractions.

Primary SIC and add'l.: 7375

CIK No: 0001142729

Subsidiaries: WiseDriver, LLC

Witness Systems Inc

300 Colonial Ctr Pkwy, Roswell, GA, 30076; *PH:* 1-770-754-1900; *http://* www.witness.com; *Email:* info@witness.com

General - Incorporation	DE	Stock - Price on:12/24/2007	NA
Employees	619	Stock Exchange	NA
Auditor	KPMG LLP	Ticker Symbol	NA
Stk Agt	Suntrust Bank	Outstanding Shares	NA
Counsel	Morris, Manning & Martin	E.P.S.	NA
DUNS No.	NA	Shareholders	NA

Business: The group's principal activities are to provide customer interaction recording, performance analysis and electronic learning management software. The software enables the companies to enhance customer relationships across multiple communications media. The group's equality software enables customer contact centers to record and evaluate complete customer interactions through multiple media such as telephone, e-mail and the Internet. The customers of the group include banking and finance, general business, insurance, outsourcing, technology, travel, hospitality and utility industries. As of 31-Dec-2003, the group licensed its software to 1,198 customers at 2,341 sites. The group operates in the United States, Australia, Brazil, Canada, Germany, Japan, Mexico and the United Kingdom. On 26-Feb-2003, the group acquired eyretel plc.

Primary SIC and add'l.: 6794 7378 7372

CIK No: 0001097338

Subsidiaries: Blue Pumpkin Software Gmbh, Blue Pumpkin Software Israel Ltd, Blue Pumpkin Software UK limited, Blue Pumpkin Software, LLC, Witness Systems (Malaysia) SDN. BHD., Witness Systems (Singapore) PTE Limited, Witness Systems Canada,Inc., Witness Systems Deutschland GmbH, Witness Systems HK Limited, Witness Systems Limited, Witness Systems Pty Limited, Witness Systems Services, S.A. de C.V., Witness Systems Software (India) Private Limited, Witness Systems Software Hardware E Servico Do BrasilLtda, Witness Systems, K.K 18 Subsidiaries included in the Index

Officers: Nicholas Discombe/45/Dir., CEO, Pres./$2,004,289.00, Loren Wimpfheimer/43/Sr. VP - Corporate Development, Darryl Demos/47/GM - Witness Enterprise Solutions Group, Bruce Richards/53/General Counsel, Kathleen Miller/43/Sr. VP - Global Finance, Accounting, Ed Murray/53/Sr. VP - Engineering, Philip Dawes/51/Sr. VP - Global Operations/$580,859.00, Nancy Treaster/46/Sr. VP - Global Corporate Marketing, William Evans/60/CFO, Exec. VP/$1,261,011.00, John Bourne/51/Sr. VP - Global Channels, Alliances, Bill Robinson/42/Sr. VP - Global Sales/$673,352.00

Directors: Nicholas Discombe/45/Dir., CEO, Pres., Dan J. Lautenbach/62/Chmn., Peter Sinisgalli/52/Dir., Thomas J. Crotty/50/Dir., Tom Bishop/54/Dir., Joel G. Katz/44/Dir.

Owners: William Evans/1.20%, Tom Bishop, Phil Dawes, Pendragon Capital LLP/5.20%, Dan J. Lautenbach, David Gould/3.70%, Joel G. Katz, Artisan Partners Limited Partnership/5.50%, Peter Sinisgalli, Nick Discombe, Bill Robinson, Roxbury Capital Management, LLC/5.40%, Rainier Investment Management Inc./4.80%, Insiders/6.40%, Thomas J. Crotty

Wits Basin Precious Minerals Inc

800 Nicollet Mall, Ste 2690, Minneapolis, MN, 55402; *PH:* 1-612-349-5277; *http://* www.witsbasin.com

General - Incorporation	MN	Stock - Price on:12/24/2007	$0.96
Employees	10	Stock Exchange	OTC
Auditor	Carver Moquist & Oconnor, LLC	Ticker Symbol	WITM
Stk Agt	American Stock Transfer & Trust Co.	Outstanding Shares	104,250,000
Counsel	Kry Boyle Freedman & Sawyer	E.P.S.	-$0.1
DUNS No.	NA	Shareholders	NA

Business: The group's principal activities are to explore precious minerals. It holds interests in two mineral exploration projects in South Africa and Canada. On 06-Feb-2004, the group acquired brazmin ltda. The group sold substantially all of the assets of the accounting software business in 2003.

Primary SIC and add'l.: 7372 1041

CIK No: 0000912875

Subsidiaries: Active Hawk Minerals LLC, AIQ, Inc, Champion Business Systems, Inc, FMS Marketing, Inc, Gregory Gold Producers, Inc, Red Wing Business Systems, Inc, Wits-South America, Ltd.

Officers: Stephen D. King/Dir., CEO, Pres./$309,246.00, Mark D. Dacko/Dir., CFO/$130,000.00, Clyde L. Smith/Pres., William B. Green/Pres. - Asia Operations Subsidiary

Directors: Stephen D. King/Dir., CEO, Pres., Vance H. White/Chmn., Norman Lowenthal/Dir., Mark D. Dacko/Dir., CFO

Owners: Mark D. Dacko, Stephen D. King/2.50%, H. Vance White/4.70%, Hawk Precious Minerals Inc./3.30%, Clyde L. Smith, Insiders/9.00%, Thomas Brazil/7.60%, Andrew Green/9.00%, Norman D. Lowenthal, Pacific Dawn Capital/6.60%

*Financial Data: Fiscal Year End:*12/31 *Latest Annual Data:* 12/31/2006

Year	Sales	Net Income
2006	NA	-$8,891,000
2005	NA	-$5,731,000
2004	NA	-$6,336,000

Curr. Assets:	$171,000	Curr. Liab.:	$212,000		
Plant, Equip.:	$80,000	Total Liab.:	$212,000	Indic. Yr. Divd.:	NA
Total Assets:	$251,000	Net Worth:	$40,000	Debt/ Equity:	NA

Wizzard Software Corp Colorado

5001 Baum Blvd., Pittsburgh, PA, 15213; *PH:* 1-412-621-0902; *Fax:* 1-412-621-2625; *http://* www.wizzardsoftware.com; *Email:* support@wizzardsoftware.com

General		Stock	
Incorporation	CO	Price on:12/24/2007	$2.63
Employees	25	Stock Exchange	OTC
Auditor	Gregory & Assoc. LLC	Ticker Symbol	WIZD
Stk Agt	Interwest Transfer Company, Inc.	Outstanding Shares	41,620,000
Counsel	NA	E.P.S.	-$0.16
DUNS No.	NA	Shareholders	NA

Business: The group's principal activities are to develop, market and service custom and packaged computer software products. The group is also engaged in the research of speech technology software products designed to allow various forms of personal computers to understand human spoken language (speech recognition) and perform actions or turn the spoken language into readable, searchable and archived text. Speak out-loud (text to speech) in a manner which allows humans to hear text being spoken out loud by the computer. The group provides business solutions that incorporate software programming tools, speech technology engines, custom solution project management, developer and end user support and programming services to the medical, law enforcement, military/government, insurance, kiosk, financial and media software markets. The group operates in the United States. On 23-Apr-2004, the group acquired medivoxrx technologies, inc.

Primary SIC and add'l.: 7372

CIK No: 0001074909

Officers: Chris Spencer/Chmn., CEO, Pres., Bruce Phifer/GM - Technology, Services Division, John Busshaus/Dir., CFO, Armen Geronian/Dir., CTO, Assist. Sec., Eugene J. Franz/GM - Solutions, Channels, Marc Lord/Strategic Member - Advisory Board, Gordon Berry/Dir. - Business Development

Directors: Chris Spencer/Chmn., CEO, Pres., Armen Geronian/Dir., CTO, Assist. Sec., John Busshaus/Dir., CFO, David Mansueto/Dir.

Owners: Christopher J. Spencer/7.20%, John Busshaus, Voice Recognition Investment, L.P./8.90%, Armen Geronian/6.90%, Gordon Berry/1.30%, Insiders/18.00%, David Mansueto/2.40%

Financial Data: *Fiscal Year End:*12/31 *Latest Annual Data:* 03/31/2007

Year	Sales	Net Income
2007	NA	NA
2006	NA	NA
2005	$1,694,000	-$5,967,000

Curr. Assets:	$3,165,000	**Curr. Liab.:**	$880,000		
Plant, Equip.:	$184,000	**Total Liab.:**	$962,000	**Indic. Yr. Divd.:**	NA
Total Assets:	$4,298,000	**Net Worth:**	$3,337,000	**Debt/ Equity:**	0.0037

WJ Communications Inc

401 River Oaks Pkwy., San Jose, CA, 95134; *PH:* 1-408-577-6200; *Fax:* 1-408-577-6621; *http://* www.wj.com; *Email:* sales@wj.com

General		Stock	
Incorporation	CA	Price on:12/24/2007	$1.59
Employees	221	Stock Exchange	NDQ
Auditor	Deloitte & Touche LLP	Ticker Symbol	WJCI
Stk Agt	Mellon Investor Services LLC	Outstanding Shares	68,630,000
Counsel	NA	E.P.S.	-$0.13
DUNS No.	00-912-1534	Shareholders	NA

Business: The group's principle activities are to design, develop and market high-performance radio frequency (rf) semiconductor products for wireless communications, broadband cable, rf identification and defense and homeland security markets. The group operates three segments, namely, semiconductor products, fiber optic products and wireless products. The products comprise of advanced rf semiconductors, integrated assemblies and highly functional components. The group sells its products through direct sales, distributors and manufacturer sales representatives. The customers of the group include andrew corporation, ericsson, harris corporation, lucent technologies inc, nokia networks, nortel networks and samsung electronics.

Primary SIC and add'l.: 3674 3669

CIK No: 0000105006

Subsidiaries: WJ Newco, LLC

Officers: Bruce W. Diamond/Dir., CEO, Pres./$1,349,069.00, Morteza Saidi/VP - Engineering/$472,637.00, Haresh P. Patel/Sr. VP - Sales, Marketing/$446,450.00, Rainer N. Growitz/VP - Finance/$236,775.00, Gregory R. Miller/CFO/$408,860.00, Mark S. Knoch/VP - Operations/$571,309.00

Directors: Bruce W. Diamond/Dir., CEO, Pres., Dexter W. Paine/Chmn., Patrice Daniels/Dir., Liane Pelletier/Dir., Bob Whelton/Dir., Angelos J. Dassios/Dir., Catherine P. Lego/Dir., Jack Levin/Dir.

Owners: Fox Paine Capital, LLC, Dexter W. Paine, Haresh Patel, Rainer N. Growitz, Angelos J. Dassios, Mark Knoch, Insiders, Kopp Investment Advisors, LLC, Michael E. Holmstrom, Catherine P. Lego, Jack G. Levin, Partrice M. Daniels, Bruce W. Diamond, Robert Whelton, Liane J. Pelletier *(19 Owners included in Index)*

Financial Data: *Fiscal Year End:*12/31 *Latest Annual Data:* 12/31/2006

Year	Sales	Net Income
2006	$48,779,000	-$8,404,000
2005	$31,597,000	-$20,988,000
2004	$32,336,000	-$9,081,000

Curr. Assets:	$38,026,000	**Curr. Liab.:**	$15,057,000		
Plant, Equip.:	$7,232,000	**Total Liab.:**	$27,643,000	**Indic. Yr. Divd.:**	NA
Total Assets:	$53,233,000	**Net Worth:**	$25,590,000	**Debt/ Equity:**	0.0242

Wm Wrigley Jr Co

410 N Michigan Ave., Chicago, IL, 60611; *PH:* 1-312-644-2121; *http://* www.wrigley.com

General		Stock	
Incorporation	DE	Price on:12/24/2007	$56.34
Employees	15,800	Stock Exchange	NYSE
Auditor	Ernst & Young LLP	Ticker Symbol	WWY
Stk Agt	Computershare Trust Co	Outstanding Shares	272,920,000
Counsel	NA	E.P.S.	$2.12
DUNS No.	00-132-6198	Shareholders	NA

Business: The group's principle activities include manufacturing and marketing chewing gum and other confectionery products. The group products are sold under the brand names include Wrigley's Spearmint, Doublemint, Juicy Fruit, Big Red, Winterfresh, Freedent, Orbit, Extra, Arrowmint, Cool Crunch, Dulce 16, Excel, Juicy Fruit, Airwaves, Icewhite, Hubba Bubba, Big Boy and Big G. The group operates from Australia, Canada, England, France, India, Kenya, China, Philippines, Poland, Taiwan, Russia and Germany.

Primary SIC and add'l.: 2064 2087 2899 2067

CIK No: 0000108601

Subsidiaries: Cafosa Gum, S.A., Dulces de las Americas, S. de R.L. de C.V., Four-Ten Corporation, Green Arrow Development Corporation, Joyco India Private Limited (India), L. A. Dreyfus Company, Northwestern Flavors, LLC., OOO Wrigley, Regico, S.L., Techninter, S.A., The Wrigley Company (E.A.) Ltd., The Wrigley Company (H.K.) Limited, The Wrigley Company (Malaysia) Sdn. Bhd., The Wrigley Company (N.Z.) Limited, The Wrigley Company (P.N.G) Ltd. 57 Subsidiaries included in the Index

Officers: William D. Perez/Dir., CEO, Pres./$1,035,445.00, William Wrigley/Chmn., Pres./$8,680,528.00, Ralph P. Scozzafava/VP - Worldwide Commercial Operations, Dushan Petrovich/Sr. VP, Chief Administrative Officer/$2,566,415.00, Jon Orving/VP - Nordic, Stefan Pfander/VP - International, MD - Europe, Donald E. Balster/VP - Worldwide Manufacturing, Igor Saveliev/MD, Group VP - East, South Europe, Donagh Herlihy/VP - Supply Chain Strategy, Planning, CIO, Martin Schlatter/VP, Chief Marketing Officer, Michael F. Wong/Group VP, MD - Asia, Pacific, Samson Suen/MD, VP - China, Kelly McGrail/Sr. Dir. - Corporate Relations, Alan J. Schneider/VP, Treasurer, Howard Malovany/VP, Sec., General Counsel *(32 Officers included in Index)*

Directors: William D. Perez/Dir., CEO, Pres., William Wrigley/Chmn., Pres., Melinda R. Rich/Dir., Howard B. Bernick/55/Dir., John Rau/59/Dir., Richard K. Smucker/Dir., Steven B. Sample/67/Dir., Alex Shumate/57/Dir., John F. Bard/66/Dir., Thomas A. Knowlton/Dir.

Owners: William Wrigley/4.46%, Peter R. Hempstead, Capital Research and Mgmt. Co./10.32%, Alex Shumate, Steven B. Sample, John Rau, Reuben Gamoran, Insiders, William Wrigley/40.77%, Insiders, Richard K. Smucker, Howard B. Bernick, Alex Shumate, Dushan Petrovich, Richard K. Smucker *(31 Owners included in Index)*

Financial Data: *Fiscal Year End:*12/31 *Latest Annual Data:* 12/31/2006

Year	Sales	Net Income
2006	$4,686,011,000	$529,377,000
2005	$4,159,306,000	$517,252,000
2004	$3,648,592,000	$492,954,000

Curr. Assets:	$1,481,227,000	**Curr. Liab.:**	$1,027,129,000	**P/E Ratio:**	26.58
Plant, Equip.:	$1,422,516,000	**Total Liab.:**	$2,273,506,000	**Indic. Yr. Divd.:**	$1.160
Total Assets:	$4,661,598,000	**Net Worth:**	$2,388,092,000	**Debt/ Equity:**	0.4226

WMS Industries Inc

800 S Npoint Blvd, Waukegan, IL, 60085; *PH:* 1-847-785-3000; *http://* www.wms.com

General		Stock	
Incorporation	DE	Price on:12/24/2007	$27.82
Employees	1,320	Stock Exchange	NYSE
Auditor	Ernst & Young LLP	Ticker Symbol	WMS
Stk Agt	Bank of New York	Outstanding Shares	49,510,000
Counsel	Shack Siegel Katz & Flaherty P.C.	E.P.S.	$0.91
DUNS No.	01-029-7695	Shareholders	NA

Business: The group's principal activity is to design, manufacture and market innovative video and mechanical reel spinning gaming machines and video lottery terminals. The gaming machines incorporate secondary bonus rounds, advanced graphics, digital sound and engaging game themes, some of which include popular songs and recognized trademarks. In addition to gaming machines, the group sells replacement parts and game theme conversions of its gaming machines. It sells and leases its products in Spain, South Africa, Australia and Canada apart from the United States. The trademarks of the group include money grab, puzzle pays, classic TV game show.

Primary SIC and add'l.: 3999

CIK No: 0000350077

Subsidiaries: Lenc-Smith Inc., Williams Electronics Games, Inc., WMS Finance Inc., WMS Gaming (Canada) Ltd., WMS Gaming (UK) Limited, WMS Gaming Africa (Pty) Ltd., WMS Gaming Australia PTY Ltd., WMS Gaming Inc., WMS Gaming International, S.L., WMS Gaming Slovakia, s.r.o., WMS International (Netherlands) Inc.

Officers: Brian R. Gamache/48/Dir., CEO, Pres., Stuart Gribble/Contact - Southern Asia, Orrin J. Edidin/46/COO, Exec. VP, Scott D. Schweinfurth/53/Exec. VP, CFO, Treasurer, John P. McNicholas/Chief Accounting Officer, Executive Dir. - Finance, Adrienne Upah/Marketing Coordinator

Directors: Brian R. Gamache/48/Dir., CEO, Pres., Louis J. Nicastro/Chmn., Ira S. Sheinfeld/Dir., William C. Bartholomay/Dir. Emeritus, Harold H. Bach/Dir., Harvey Reich/Dir., Neil D. Nicastro/Dir., David M. Satz/Dir. Emeritus, William E. McKenna/Dir. Emeritus, Norman J. Menell/Dir. Emeritus, Edward W. Rabin/Dir., William J. Vareschi/Dir., Robert J. Bahash/Dir.

Owners: Harvey Reich, Harold H. Bach, Kathleen J. McJohn, Insiders, Neil D. Nicastro, Robert J. Bahash, Edward W. Rabin, Brian R. Gamache, T. Rowe Price Associates, Inc./7.80%, FMR Corp./9.80%, Sumner M. Redstone and National Amusements, Inc./9.20%, Turner Investment Partners, Inc./6.70%, Orrin J. Edidin, Scott D. Schweinfurth, Louis J. Nicastro *(19 Owners included in Index)*

Financial Data: *Fiscal Year End:*06/30 *Latest Annual Data:* 6/30/2006

Year	Sales	Net Income
2006	$451,200,000	$33,300,000
2005	$388,400,000	$21,200,000
2004	$230,200,000	-$900,000

Curr. Assets:	$308,200,000	**Curr. Liab.:**	$74,000,000	**P/E Ratio:**	32.35
Plant, Equip.:	$134,700,000	**Total Liab.:**	$200,800,000	**Indic. Yr. Divd.:**	NA
Total Assets:	$526,400,000	**Net Worth:**	$325,600,000	**Debt/ Equity:**	0.2833

WNS (Holdings) Ltd

420 Lexington Ave., Ste.2515, New York, NY, 10170; *PH:* 1-212-599-6960; *Fax:* 1-212-599-6962; *http://* www.wnsgs.com; *Email:* info@wnsgs.com

General		Stock	
Incorporation	Channel Islands	Price on:12/24/2007	$29.03
Employees	NA	Stock Exchange	NYSE
Auditor	NA	Ticker Symbol	WNS
Stk Agt	Deutsche Bank Trust Co America	Outstanding Shares	41,840,000
Counsel	NA	E.P.S.	$0.65
DUNS No.	NA	Shareholders	NA

Business: The groups principle activity is to provide offshore business process outsourcing services. The group operates from the Europe and North America. The groups quarterly revenue for September 2007 was 115.58 millions of USD.

Primary SIC and add'l.: 8732 7379 8748 7389 4731

CIK No: 0001356570

Subsidiaries: NTrance Customer Services Pvt. Ltd, Town & Country Assistance Ltd, Trinity Business Process Mgt. Ltd, WNS (Mauritius) Ltd., WNS Customer Solutions(Pvt.) Ltd, WNS Global Services (P) Ltd,, WNS Global Services (Pvt.) Ltd., WNS Global Services (UK)Ltd., WNS North America Inc.

Officers: Neeraj Bhargava/Co - Founder, Group CEO, Bernard Donoghue/CEO - WNS Assistance, WNS Global Services, Anish Nanavaty/CEO - WNS Knowledge Services, WNS Global Services, Arjun Singh/CEO - WNS Bfsi Business Unit, WNS Global Services, Anthony Greener/Dierector, WNS Global Services Limited, Jeremy Young/Dir. - WNS Global Services Limited, Richard Bernays/Dir. - WNS Global Services Limited, Zubin Dubash/Group CFO - WNS Global Services, Anup Gupta/Group COO, J. J. Selvadurai/MD - Europe, Jay Venkateswaran/Sr. VP - Investor Relations, WNS Global, Holdings Limited, Vikas Gupta/General Counsel - WNS Global, Holdings Limited, Eric B. Herr/Dir. - WNS Global Services Limited, Deepak S. Parekh/Dir. - WNS Global Services Limited

Directors: Neeraj Bhargava/Co - Founder, Group CEO, Ramesh N. Shah/Chmn., Guy Sochovsky/32/Dir., Alan Stephen Dunning/50/Co - Founder

Owners: FMR Corp./9.86%, Tiger Global Management, L.L.C./5.36%, Warburg Pincus/51.00%

Financial Data: *Fiscal Year End:*03/31 *Latest Annual Data:* 3/31/2006

Year	Sales	Net Income
2006	$202,809,000	$18,329,000
2005	$162,173,000	-$5,776,000

Curr. Assets:	$57,395,000	Curr. Liab.:	$53,463,000	P/E Ratio:	29.58
Plant, Equip.:	$30,623,000	Total Liab.:	$56,639,000	Indic. Yr. Divd.:	NA
Total Assets:	$134,803,000	Net Worth:	$78,164,000	Debt/ Equity:	NA

Woize International Ltd

1 Kingsway, London, WC2B 6XD; *PH:* 44-12071016560; *http://* www.woize.com

General - Incorporation	NV	Stock- Price on:12/24/2007	$0.17
Employees	NA	Stock Exchange	OTC
Auditor	Whitley Penn LLP	Ticker Symbol	WOIZ
Stk Agt	Standard Registrar & Transfer Co Inc.	Outstanding Shares	NA
Counsel	NA	E.P.S	NA
DUNS No.	NA	Shareholders	NA

Business: The groups principle activity is to develop and refine a digital telephony service based upon voice over Internet protocol for PC to PC and PC to phone communications. The group operates from the United States and Canada.

Primary SIC and add'l.: 3669

CIK No: 0001219584

Subsidiaries: Woize, Ltd.

Officers: Anders Halldin/Dir., CEO, Co - Founder, Daniel Savino/Chmn., Investor Relations Officer - North America, Martin Thorp/CFO, Tim Clemensen/Investor Relations Officer

Directors: Anders Halldin/Dir., CEO, Co - Founder, Daniel Savino/Chmn., Investor Relations Officer - North America

Owners: St Jamess Square Nominee Limited/43.64%, Insiders/46.06%, Daniel Savino/2.42%

Financial Data: *Fiscal Year End:*03/31 *Latest Annual Data:* 03/31/2007

Year	Sales	Net Income
2007	$131,000	-$2,439,000
2006	$205,000	-$647,000
2005	NA	-$26,000

Curr. Assets:	$736,000	Curr. Liab.:	$764,000		
Plant, Equip.:	$62,000	Total Liab.:	$2,075,000	Indic. Yr. Divd.:	NA
Total Assets:	$1,751,000	Net Worth:	-$323,000	Debt/ Equity:	NA

Wolseley Plc

11860 Mostellar Rd., Cincinnati, OH, 45241; *PH:* 1-513-771-9000; *Fax:* 1-513-771-9003; *http://* www.wolseley.com; *Email:* information@wolseley.com

General - Incorporation	UK	Stock- Price on:12/24/2007	$25.14
Employees	65,223	Stock Exchange	NYSE
Auditor	PricewaterhouseCoopers LLP	Ticker Symbol	WOS
Stk Agt	Lloyds TSB Registrars	Outstanding Shares	317,500,000
Counsel	NA	E.P.S	NA
DUNS No.	NA	Shareholders	NA

Business: The group's principal activities are the distribution of plumbing and bathroom materials, central heating equipment and pipes, valves and fittings within Europe, the usa and Canada. The group's three business segments are European distribution, north American plumbing and heating distribution and us building materials distribution. European distribution supplies plumbing, heating and drainage equipment to the professional trade. North American plumbing and heating distribution distributes plumbing, heating and piping, valves and fitting products to professional contractors and industry in the usa. USA building materials distribution supplies lumber and building materials as well as added services to the house builder and professional contractor. During the year, the group acquired pinault bois et materiaux.

Primary SIC and add'l.: 5031 3494 5074

CIK No: 0001139313

Subsidiaries: Brooks Group Limited (Ireland), Brosette SA (France), Centratec N.V. (Belgium), Comptoir des Fer et Mtaux SA (Luxembourg), Electro-Oil International AS (Denmark), Ferguson Enterprises, Inc (US), Heatmerchants Limited (Ireland), Manzardo SpA (Italy), Pb & M Sa (france), Stock Building Supply Holdings, Inc (US), Wasco Holding BV (Netherlands), Wolseley (Schweiz) AG (Switzerland), Wolseley Austria AG (Austria), Wolseley Canada Inc (Canada), Wolseley Czech Republic spol. s r.o. 18 Subsidiaries included in the Index

Officers: Claude A S Hornsby/51/Dir., CEO, Frank W. Roach/56/Dir., CEO - North America, Robert H. Marchbank/47/Dir., CEO - Europe, Steen Weirsoe/CEO, Pres. - Nordic, Philippe Gardies/MD - France, Keith Jones/MD, Nigel Sibley/MD Wolseley UK - Ireland, Fiona MacAllan/Corporate Communications, Kate Miller/Brunswick Group, Sarah McGill/PA to Head - Investor Relations, John English/VP - Investor Relations, North America, Stephen P. Webster/54/Dir., CFO, Guy Stainer/Group Dir. - Investor Relations, Fiona Butchart/Investor Relations Analyst, Adrian Barden/Chief Business Development Officer *(17 Officers included in Index)*

Directors: Claude A S Hornsby/51/Dir., CEO, Frank W. Roach/56/Dir., CEO - North America, Robert H. Marchbank/47/Dir., CEO - Europe, John W. Whybrow/60/Chmn., Andrew J. Duff/48/Non Exec. Dir., Nigel M. Stein/51/Non Exec. Dir., Stephen P. Webster/54/Dir., CFO, Gareth Davis/57/Non Exec. Dir., James I K Murray/61/Non Exec. Dir.

Owners: James I. K. Murray, Nigel M. Stein, Frank W. Roach, Claude A.S. Hornsby, Robert H. Marchbank, Fenton N. Hord, Gareth Davis, Adrian Barden, John W. Whybrow, Stephen P. Webster, Mark J. White, Robert M. Walker, Andrew J. Duff

Financial Data: *Fiscal Year End:*07/31 *Latest Annual Data:* 7/31/2006

Year	Sales	Net Income
2006	$26,384,849,000	$950,436,000
2005	$19,794,414,000	$780,685,000
2004	$18,447,321,000	$735,663,000

Curr. Assets:	$9,966,533,000	Curr. Liab.:	$5,581,482,000	P/E Ratio:	31.70
Plant, Equip.:	$2,145,004,000	Total Liab.:	$10,359,753,000	Indic. Yr. Divd.:	NA
Total Assets:	$15,706,421,000	Net Worth:	$5,346,668,000	Debt/ Equity:	NA

Wolverine Tube Inc

200 Clinton Ave. W, Ste. 1000, Huntsville, AL, 35801; *PH:* 1-256-890-0460; *http://* www.wlv.com

General - Incorporation	DE	Stock- Price on:12/24/2007	NA
Employees	3,087	Stock Exchange	OTC
Auditor	KPMG LLP	Ticker Symbol	WLVT
Stk Agt	Wachovia Bank N.A	Outstanding Shares	NA
Counsel	Skadden, Meagher & Flom LLP	E.P.S	-$5.7
DUNS No.	60-236-2303	Shareholders	NA

Business: The group's principal activities are to manufacture and distribute copper and copper alloy tubular products, fabricated and metal joining products and rod and bar products. The group's products consist of copper and copper alloy tube, steel and aluminum tube products, subassemblies, brazing alloys, fluxes and lead-free solder. The group focuses on custom-engineered, high value-added tubular and fabricated products. The group supplies its products to commercial and residential air conditioning, refrigeration equipment manufacturers, appliance manufacturers, automotive manufacturers and industrial equipment manufacturers. It also supplies its products to utilities and other power generating companies, refining and chemical processing companies and plumbing wholesalers. The group operates in the United States, Canada and other foreign countries.

Primary SIC and add'l.: 3366 3351

CIK No: 0000821407

Subsidiaries: 3072452 Nova Scotia Company, 3072453 Nova Scotia Company, 3072996 Nova Scotia Company, Small Tube Manufacturing, LLC, TF Investor, Inc., Tube Forming Holdings, Inc., Tube Forming, LP, WLV Mexico, S. de R.L. de C.V., WLVN de Latinoamerica, S. de R.L. de C.V., Wolverine China Investments, LLC, Wolverine Europe (EURL), Wolverine Europe Holdings, B.V., Wolverine Finance Company, LLC, Wolverine Joining Technologies Canada, Inc., Wolverine Joining Technologies, LLC 22 Subsidiaries included in the Index

Officers: Dennis J. Horowitz/Dir., CEO, Pres., James E. Deason/Dir., Exec. VP, CFO, Sec./$685,875.00, Johann R. Manning/VP - Human Resources, General Counsel/$1,076,623.00, Garry K. Johnson/Sr. VP - Sales/$487,125.00, Keith I. Weil/Sr. VP - Tubing Products/$543,869.00, Massoud Neshan/Sr. VP - Technology, Thomas A. Morton/VP - Material Handling, Procurement, Allan Williamson/Corporate Controller, John Van Gerwen/VP - Operations/$288,038.00

Directors: Dennis J. Horowitz/Dir., CEO, Pres., Steven S. Elbaum/59/Non Exec. Chmn., Brett Young/32/Dir., David M. Gilchrist/58/Dir., William C. Griffiths/Dir., Mitchell K. Posner/58/Dir., Alan Kestenbaum/46/Dir., James E. Deason/Dir., Exec. VP, CFO, Sec., Chris A. Davis/Dir., Barnes W. Hauptfuhrer/Dir., John L. Duncan/Dir., Jan K. Ver Hagen/Dir., Thomas P. Evans/Dir., Gail O. Neuman/Dir.

Owners: FMR Corporation, Alan Kestenbaum, Alan Kestenbaum, Johann R. Manning, Steven S. Elbaum, Steven S. Elbaum, Plainfield Special Situations Master Fund Limited, Dimensional Fund Advisors, Inc., David M. Gilchrist, The Alpine Group, Inc., The Alpine Group, Inc., Keith I. Weil, William C. Griffiths, Insiders, Garry K. Johnson *(21 Owners included in Index)*

Financial Data: *Fiscal Year End:*12/31 *Latest Annual Data:* 12/31/2006

Year	Sales	Net Income
2006	$1,403,042,000	-$79,224,000
2005	$873,505,000	-$38,616,000
2004	$797,875,000	$382,000

Curr. Assets:	$220,622,000	Curr. Liab.:	$70,017,000		
Plant, Equip.:	$144,394,000	Total Liab.:	$366,154,000	Indic. Yr. Divd.:	NA
Total Assets:	$455,330,000	Net Worth:	$89,176,000	Debt/ Equity:	2.5348

Wolverine World Wide Inc

9341 Ctland Dr., Rockford, MI, 49351; *PH:* 1-616-866-5500; *http://* www.wolverineworldwide.com; *Email:* communications@wwwinc.com

General - Incorporation	DE	Stock- Price on:12/24/2007	$27.82
Employees	4,532	Stock Exchange	NYSE
Auditor	Ernst & Young LLP	Ticker Symbol	WWW
Stk Agt	National City Bank	Outstanding Shares	54,460,000
Counsel	James D. Zwiers	E.P.S	$1.63
DUNS No.	00-601-5069	Shareholders	NA

Business: The group's principal activities are to design, manufacture and market a line of quality comfortable casual shoes, rugged outdoor footwear, work footwear, constructed slippers and moccasins. It markets branded casual, work, outdoor sport and uniform footwear. It also operates a retail division that promotes the brands. The group's portfolio of owned and licensed brands includes: bates uniform footwear, cat footwear, coleman footwear, harley-davidson footwear, hush puppies, hytest footwear, merrell performance footwear, stanley footgear and wolverine boots and shoes. The group operates in Europe, Canada, Asia, Central America, South America, Middle East and Russia. In 2003, the group acquired sebago inc.

Primary SIC and add'l.: 3149 3144 3111 3143

CIK No: 0000110471

Subsidiaries: Brooks France, S.A., BSI Shoes, Inc., Dominican Wolverine Shoe Company Limited, Hush Puppies & Family, Hush Puppies (U.K.) Ltd., Hush Puppies Factory Direct, Hush Puppies Retail, Inc., Hy-Test, Inc., Little Red Shoe House, Merrell (Europe) Limited, Merrell Europe B.V., Sebago Dominican Limited, Sebago International Limited, Sebago Realty, LLC, Sebago USA, LLC 36 Subsidiaries included in the Index

Officers: Nicholas P. Ottenwess/45/VP - Finance, Corporate Controller/$572,138.00, James D. Zwiers/Pres. - Wolverines Hush Puppies US Division/$496,021.00, Stephen L. Gulis/50/Exec. VP, CFO, Treasurer/$1,451,937.00, Blake W. Krueger/54/Dir., COO, Pres./$2,112,418.00, Christi Cowdin/Dir. - Investor Relations, Communications, Cheryl L. Johnson/46/VP - Human Resources/$334,571.00, Kenneth A. Grady/51/General Counsel, Sec.

Directors: Alberto L. Grimoldi/66/Chmn., David P. Mehney/68/Dir., Blake W. Krueger/54/Dir., COO, Pres., David T. Kollat/69/Dir., Brenda J. Lauderback/57/Dir., Shirley D. Peterson/66/Dir., Phillip D. Matthews/69/Dir., Paul D. Schrage/73/Dir., Michael A. Volkema/52/Dir., Timothy J. Odonovan/62/Dir., Jeffrey M. Boromisa/53/Dir.

Owners: Nicholas P. Ottenwess, FMR Corp./6.20%, Jeffrey M. Boromisa, Stephen L. Gulis, Timothy J. ODonovan/2.10%, Brenda J. Lauderback, Blake W. Krueger, Phillip D. Matthews, Cheryl L. Johnson, Barclays Global Investors, NA/5.10%, Shirley D. Peterson, David P. Mehney, Alberto L. Grimoldi, David T. Kollat, Franklin Resources, Inc./6.30% *(19 Owners included in Index)*

Financial Data: *Fiscal Year End:*12/31 *Latest Annual Data:* 12/30/2006

Year	Sales	Net Income
2006	$1,141,887,000	$83,647,000
2005	$1,060,999,000	$74,467,000

Curr. Assets:	$420,748,000	**Curr. Liab.:**	$104,037,000	**P/E Ratio:**	17.95
Plant, Equip.:	$93,202,000	**Total Liab.:**	$164,259,000	**Indic. Yr. Divd.:**	$0.360
Total Assets:	$626,580,000	**Net Worth:**	$462,321,000	**Debt/ Equity:**	0.0217

Wonder Auto Technology Inc

8300 Greensboro Dr., Mc Lean, VA, 22102; ***PH:*** 1-703-918-4926; ***http://*** www.wonderautotech.com

General - Incorporation	NV	**Stock**- Price on:12/24/2007	$7.2
Employees	NA	Stock Exchange	NDQ
Auditor	PKF	Ticker Symbol	WATG
Stk Agt	Securities Transfer Corp	Outstanding Shares	NA
Counsel	Thelen ReidBrown Raysman	E.P.S	NA
DUNS No.	NA	Shareholders	NA

Business: The group operates through its subsidiary whose principle activities include manufacturing automotive electrical parts, specifically, starters and alternators. The groups business is focused on designing, developing, manufacturing and selling automotive electrical parts. The group operates through three segments namely original equipment manufacturer market, replacement market and export market. Specific customers of the group include Beijing Hyundai Motor Company and Shenyang Aerospace Mitsubishi Motors Engine Manufacturing Co. Ltd. The group operates from China. The group's quarterly revenue for Sep '07 was 27.29 millions of USD.

Primary SIC and add'l.: 3714

CIK No: 0001162862

Subsidiaries: Jin Zhou Halla Electrical Equipment Co., Ltd, JinZhou Dong Woo Precision Co., Ltd., Man Do Auto Technology Co. Ltd., Wonder Auto Limited

Officers: Qingjie Zhao/Chmn., CEO, Pres., Yuncong Ma/COO, Seuk Jun Kim/VP - Research, Development, Yuguo Zhao/VP - Sales, Marketing, Yongdong Liu/VP - Production, Meirong Yuan/Dir., CFO, Jim Groh/US Representative

Directors: Qingjie Zhao/Chmn., CEO, Pres., Meirong Yuan/Dir., CFO, Larry Goldman/Dir., David Murphy/Dir., Lei Jiang/52/Dir.

Owners: Empower Century Limited, Insiders, Xiangdong Gao, Choice Inspire Limited, Pinnacle China Fund, L.P, Qingjie Zhao

Financial Data: *Fiscal Year End:*12/31 *Latest Annual Data:* 12/31/2006

Year	Sales	Net Income
2006	$72,150,000	$8,224,000
2005	NA	-$55,000

Curr. Assets:	$56,127,000	**Curr. Liab.:**	$37,194,000		
Plant, Equip.:	$13,946,000	**Total Liab.:**	$37,194,000	**Indic. Yr. Divd.:**	NA
Total Assets:	$78,000,000	**Net Worth:**	$38,227,000	**Debt/ Equity:**	NA

Woodhead Industries Inc

Three Pkwy N, Ste. 550, Deerfield, IL, 60015; ***PH:*** 1-847-236-9300; ***http://*** www.woodhead.com

General - Incorporation	DE	**Stock**- Price on:12/24/2007	$30.5
Employees	32,400	Stock Exchange	NA
Auditor	Ernst & Young LLP	Ticker Symbol	NA
Stk Agt	Computershare Investor Services LLC	Outstanding Shares	184,460,000
Counsel	NA	E.P.S	$1.30
DUNS No.	00-519-5433	Shareholders	NA

Business: The group's principal activity is to develop, manufacture and market electronic and industrial communications products. The group operates through two segments: communications and connectivity products segment (connectivity segment) and electrical safety products segment (electrical segment). The connectivity segment provides single, worldwide source for industrial communications and connectivity solutions through the brands sst(tm), brad harrison(R), mpm(tm), rj-lnxx(R), applicom(R) and netalert(tm) . Electrical segment manufactures highly customized products to support enhanced safety and productivity on the factory floor. The group's products are sold to stocking distributors, original equipment manufacturers (OEM) and system integrators. The group has operations in the United States, Italy, Canada, Mexico, France and other countries.

Primary SIC and add'l.: 3648 3678 3641 3629

CIK No: 0000108215

Subsidiaries: Advanced Interconnect, Inc., Aero-Motive (U.K.) Limited, Aero-Motive Company, Central Rubber Company, Daniel Woodhead Company, Deerfield Partners C.V., DW Holding, LLC, Euroview Services S.A., I.M.A. S.r.l., Micromedia S.A., mPm Limited, mPm S.r.l., WH One, LLC, WH Two, LLC, Woodhead Asia Pte. Ltd. 26 Subsidiaries included in the Index

Officers: Chow Kok Poon/Controller - Asia, Pacific, Terry Carolin/Regional Sales Mgr. - Iowa, Kurt Krutsch/Business Development Mgr. - Automation Products, Iowa, Bill Herndon/Business Development Mgr. - Automation Products, Louisiana, Steve Bodzsar/Regional Sales Mgr. - Michigan, John Wallis/Regional Sales Mgr. - Western Region, Michel Morin/Regional Sales Mgr. - Eastern Region, Jim Kuzemko/Regional Sales Mgr. - Central Region, Ontario, Jim Wood/Business Development Manger, Automation Products, Chuck Frederking/Regional Sales Mgr. - Arizona, Jamie Gallant/Business Development Mgr. - Automation Products, Arizona, Tom Norris/Regional Sales Mgr. - Connecticut, Mark Shimmons/Regional Sales Mgr. - Florida, Mark Schuerman/Business Development Mgr. - Automation Products, Michigan, Steve Mann/Regional Sales Mgr. - Texas *(17 Officers included in Index)*

Financial Data: *Fiscal Year End:*10/01 *Latest Annual Data:* 6/30/2006

Year	Sales	Net Income
2006	$2,861,289,000	$236,091,000
2005	$2,548,652,000	$154,434,000
2004	$2,246,715,000	$175,950,000

Curr. Assets:	$1,548,233,000	**Curr. Liab.:**	$594,812,000	**P/E Ratio:**	23.46
Plant, Equip.:	$1,025,852,000	**Total Liab.:**	$691,669,000	**Indic. Yr. Divd.:**	$0.450
Total Assets:	$2,974,420,000	**Net Worth:**	$2,281,869,000	**Debt/ Equity:**	0.0535

Woodlands Financial Services Inc

25211 Grogans Mill Rd. , Ste. 300, Woodlands, TX, 77380;

General - Incorporation		**Stock**- Price on:12/24/2007	$45.5
Employees	NA	Stock Exchange	OTC
Auditor	NA	Ticker Symbol	WDFN
Stk Agt	Registrar and Transfer agent	Outstanding Shares	NA
Counsel	NA	E.P.S	NA
DUNS No.	NA	Shareholders	NA

Business: The groups principle activity is to provide recruiting services. The groups service area includes the research and development, engineering, marketing, sales, information technology and manufacturing industries. The group operates from United States.

Primary SIC and add'l.: 6141

CIK No: 0000915832

Woodstock Financial Group Inc

Formerly: Raike Financial Group Inc

275 Pk.way 575, Ste. 100, Woodstock, GA, 30188; ***PH:*** 1-770-516-6996; ***http://*** www.raikefinancial.com

General - Incorporation	GA	**Stock**- Price on:12/24/2007	NA
Employees	NA	Stock Exchange	OTC
Auditor	Porter Keadle Moore LLP	Ticker Symbol	WSFL
Stk Agt	NA	Outstanding Shares	NA
Counsel	NA	E.P.S	NA
DUNS No.	NA	Shareholders	NA

Business: The group's principle activity is to provide securities brokerage and investment banking services. The company provides money management services to individual and institutional investors. Through independent representatives, it also provides planning and consulting services in a variety of financial services areas such as financial planning, tax planning, benefits consulting and other financial structures. The company through its Internet site allows electronic delivery of documents and information. The group operates from United States.

Primary SIC and add'l.: 6726 6282 6211

CIK No: 0001095373

Officers: William J. Raike/Founder, CEO, Pres./$559,973.00, Jason Champion/Dir. - Business Development, Christopher Casdia/38/Dir., COO, Melissa Whitley/Dir., Treasurer, CFO, Danielle Tuck/Registration Department, Kelly Hansard/Operations Department, Accounting Inquiries, Marcy Hitt/Trading Department, Rachel Gaumer/Mutual Fund Department, Valerie Perkowski/Insurance, Annuity Products, Dennis Taylor/Compliance Department, Valorie Duckworth/VP - Business Development, Carolyn Preavett/Operations Department, Accounting Inquiries

Directors: William J. Raike/Founder, CEO, Pres., Geoffrey T. Chalmers/72/Dir., Christopher Casdia/38/Dir., COO, Melissa Whitley/Dir., Treasurer, CFO, Morris L. Brunson/68/Dir., William D. Bertsche/63/Dir.

Owners: Insiders/83.25%, William J. Raike/83.02%

Woodward Governor Co

1000 E Drake Rd., Fort Collins, CO, 80525; ***PH:*** 1-970-482-5811; ***Fax:*** 1-970-498-3058; ***http://*** www.woodward.com

General - Incorporation	DE	**Stock**- Price on:12/24/2007	$55.96
Employees	3,700	Stock Exchange	NDQ
Auditor	PricewaterhouseCoopers LLP	Ticker Symbol	WGOV
Stk Agt	American Stock Transfer & Trust Co.	Outstanding Shares	34,300,000
Counsel	Chapman & Cutler	E.P.S	$2.79
DUNS No.	00-506-9380	Shareholders	NA

Business: The group's principal activities are to design, manufacture and service energy control systems and components for aircraft and industrial engines, turbines and other power equipment. The group operates in two segments: industrial controls and aircraft engine systems. Industrial controls segment provides energy control systems and components mainly to original equipment manufacturers of industrial engines, turbines and other power equipment. Aircraft engine systems segment provides energy control systems and components mainly to original equipment manufacturers of aircraft engines. General electric company is one of the major customers of the group. The group acquired synchro-start products, inc and barber-colman dyna products, a division of invensys building systems, inc in fiscal 2003. In jun 2004, the group acquired adrenaline research inc.

Primary SIC and add'l.: 3728 3625

CIK No: 0000108312

Subsidiaries: Baker Electrical Products, Inc., Woodward (Tianjin) Controls Company Limited, Woodward Controls (Suzhou) Co. Ltd. Suzhou, Woodward Controls International Trading (Shanghai) Co. Ltd., Woodward Controls, Inc1, Woodward FST, Inc., Woodward Governor (Japan) Ltd., Woodward Governor (Quebec) Inc., Woodward Governor (Reguladores) Limitada, Woodward Governor (U.K.) Limited, Woodward Governor Company Leonhard-Reglerbau GmbH, Woodward Governor de Mexico S.A. de C.V, Woodward Governor France S.A.R.L., Woodward Governor GmbH, Woodward Governor India LTD. 18 Subsidiaries included in the Index

Officers: Thomas A. Gendron/Dir., CEO, Pres., Steven J. Meyer/VP, Robert F. Weber/CFO, Treasurer, Chad R. Preiss/VP, Donald J. Bergholz/VP, Martin V. Glass/Group VP, Dennis M. Benning/Group VP, Gerhard Lauffer/Group VP, Christopher A. Fawzy/VP, General Counsel, Corp. Sec.

Directors: Thomas A. Gendron/Dir., CEO, Pres., John A. Halbrook/Chmn., Mary L. Petrovich/Dir., John D. Cohn/Dir., Paul Donovan/Dir., Michael H. Joyce/Dir., Larry E. Rittenberg/Dir., James R. Rulseh/Dir., Michael T. Yonker/Dir.

Owners: Michael H. Joyce, John D. Cohn, James R. Rulseh, Larry E. Rittenberg, Thomas A. Gendron, Martin V. Glass, Royce& Associates, LLC/12.80%, Paul Donovan, Robert F. Weber, Dennis M. Benning, Michael T. Yonker, John A. Halbrook/3.83%, Woodward Governor Company/12.50%, Gerhard Lauffer, Insiders/5.82% *(16 Owners included in Index)*

Financial Data: *Fiscal Year End:*09/30 *Latest Annual Data:* 9/30/2006

Year	Sales	Net Income
2006	$854,515,000	$69,900,000
2005	$827,726,000	$55,971,000
2004	$709,805,000	$31,382,000

Curr. Assets:	$381,234,000	**Curr. Liab.:**	$120,991,000	**P/E Ratio:**	24.87
Plant, Equip.:	$124,176,000	**Total Liab.:**	$256,808,000	**Indic. Yr. Divd.:**	$0.440
Total Assets:	$735,497,000	**Net Worth:**	$478,689,000	**Debt/ Equity:**	0.0920

Woori Finance Holdings Co Ltd

20 F, 203 Hoehyon-Dong, 1-Ga, Chung-Gu, Seoul; *PH:* 82-221252000; *Fax:* 82-221252000; *http://* www.woorifg.com; *Email:* woorifg@woorifg.com

General - Incorporation ....Korea	Stock- Price on:12/24/2007 ....$73.01
Employees..93	Stock Exchange...NYSE
Auditor ....Deloitte Anjin LLC	Ticker Symbol...WF
Stk Agt.................Korean Securities Depository	Outstanding Shares 268,670,000
Counsel...NA	E.P.S...$9.83
DUNS No..NA	Shareholders..NA

Business: The group operates through its subsidiaries whose principle activity is to provide financial services. The groups service includes leasing loan for car. The group operates from United States.

Primary SIC and add'l.: NA

CIK No: 0001264136

Subsidiaries: P.T. Bank Woori Indonesia, Woori America Bank, Woori Capital Advisors Asset Management, Woori Credit Information, Woori F&I, Woori Finance Information System, Woori Investment Bank, Woori Securities

Officers: Byongwon Bahk/Chmn., CEO

Directors: Byongwon Bahk/Chmn., CEO, Pyoung-Wan Har/Dir., Woon-Youl Choi/Dir., Bong-Soo Park/Dir., Kwang-Dong Kim/Dir., In-Bong Ha/Dir., Myoung-Soo Choi/Dir.

Owners: KDIC/77.97%

Financial Data: Fiscal Year End:12/31   Latest Annual Data: 12/31/2006

Year	Sales	Net Income
2006	$12,968,644,000	$2,145,739,000
2005	$9,124,767,000	$1,805,895,000
2004	$8,876,265,000	$2,256,164,000

Curr. Assets:	$22,474,974,000	Curr. Liab.:	$147,056,141,000	P/E Ratio:	31.70
Plant, Equip.:	$2,453,131,000	Total Liab.:	$203,120,396,000	Indic. Yr. Divd.:	NA
Total Assets:	$214,589,298,000	Net Worth:	$11,468,903,000	Debt/ Equity:	NA

WordLogic Corp

650 W Georgia St., Ste. 2400, Vancouver, BC, V6B 4N9; *PH:* 1-604-257-3660; *http://* www.wordlogic.com; *Email:* getinfo@wordlogic.net

General - Incorporation ....NV	Stock- Price on:12/24/2007 ....$0.39
Employees...NA	Stock Exchange..OTC
Auditor ....Cordovano & Honeck LLP	Ticker Symbol..WLGC
Stk Agt...NA	Outstanding Shares ....NA
Counsel...NA	E.P.S..NA
DUNS No..NA	Shareholders..NA

Business: The group's principal activity is to research, develop, market, license and sell intellectual property including wordlogictm predictive keyboard, one patent for 'data entry for personal computing devices' and five additional pending patents. The group recently developed wordlogictm predictive keyboard software that is used in computing and communications devices. The software is compact and compressible and operates effectively in small handheld devices such as personal digital assistants, cell phones, smart phones, tablet computers as well as other touch screen devices. The software is marketed in seven languages to consumers using an online commerce engine powered by handango inc. In addition to this, the group has made available the trial versions of the software on international websites.

Primary SIC and add'l.: 6794 7372

CIK No: 0001139614

Subsidiaries: 602531 British Columbia

Officers: Frank R. Evanshen/Chmn., CEO, David Stirling/Exec. VP, Peter Knaven/Sr. VP, Mark Dostie/CTO, Allen T. Rose/Dir., CFO, Justin Lees/Mgr. - Information Systems, Robert Asconi/VP - Sales, Marketing

Directors: Frank R. Evanshen/Chmn., CEO, Allen T. Rose/Dir., CFO

Owners: Allen T. Rose/2.60%, Frank R. Evanshen/39.10%, MCC Meridian Capital Corp./2.60%, Insiders/48.30%, Harold Gunn/20.50%

Financial Data: Fiscal Year End:12/31   Latest Annual Data: 12/31/2006

Year	Sales	Net Income
2006	$18,000	-$2,215,000
2005	$12,000	-$1,222,000
2004	$8,000	$935,000

Curr. Assets:	$31,000	Curr. Liab.:	$347,000		
Plant, Equip.:	$20,000	Total Liab.:	$1,235,000	Indic. Yr. Divd.:	NA
Total Assets:	$51,000	Net Worth:	-$1,185,000	Debt/ Equity:	NA

Workstream Inc

2600 Lake Lucien Dr., Ste. 410, Maitland, FL, 32751; *PH:* 1-407-475-5500; *Fax:* 1-866-953-8800; *http://* www.workstreaminc.com

General - Incorporation ....Canada	Stock- Price on:12/24/2007 ....$1.07
Employees...210	Stock Exchange..NDQ
Auditor ....PricewaterhouseCoopers LLP	Ticker Symbol...WSTM
Stk Agt.....American Stock Transfer & Trust Co.	Outstanding Shares 51,530,000
Counsel...NA	E.P.S...-$0.24
DUNS No..NA	Shareholders..NA

Business: The group's principle activity is to provide human capital management solutions to do business with all four stakeholders in the employment relationship, which fulfill the needs of corporate hr professionals, their suppliers, third party recruiters and job seekers, by offering seamless management of the full employment process with a combination of high-tech and high-touch platforms and services. The group operates from United States.

Primary SIC and add'l.: 7361 7372 7375

CIK No: 0001095266

Subsidiaries: 6FigureJobs.com, Inc., OMNIpartners, Inc., Paula Allen Holdings, Inc., Workstream USA Inc.

Officers: Deepak Gupta/Dir., CEO, Michael Mullarkey/40/Exec. Chmn., Kevin Dobbs/Sr. VP - Sales - Marketing, Michael Gioja/CIO, Exec. VP - Products, Services, Joe Terry/Sr. VP - Sales, Gary Damiano/Sr. VP - Marketing, Philip Oreste/CFO

Directors: Deepak Gupta/Dir., CEO, Michael Mullarkey/40/Exec. Chmn., Thomas Danis/61/Dir., Michael Gerrior/Dir., John Oltman/63/Dir., Mitch Tuchman/61/Dir.

Owners: Deepak Gupta/3.13%, Thomas Danis, Stephen Lerch, Morgan Stanley/6.60%, Magnetar Capital LLC/6.10%, Michael A. Gerrior, Janus Capital Management LLC/10.30%, Mitch Tuchman, Insiders/13.10%, CCM Master Qualified Fund, Ltd./6.10%, Michael Mullarkey/8.84%, John Oltman

Financial Data: Fiscal Year End:05/31   Latest Annual Data: 5/31/2006

Year	Sales	Net Income
2006	$28,121,000	-$12,986,000
2005	$26,819,000	-$15,159,000
2004	$17,167,000	-$5,537,000

Curr. Assets:	$7,981,000	Curr. Liab.:	$14,496,000		
Plant, Equip.:	$2,715,000	Total Liab.:	$15,474,000	Indic. Yr. Divd.:	NA
Total Assets:	$58,661,000	Net Worth:	$43,187,000	Debt/ Equity:	NA

World Acceptance Corp

108 FreDr.ick St., Greenville, SC, 29607; *PH:* 1-864-298-9800; *http://* www.worldacceptance.com

General - Incorporation ....SC	Stock- Price on:12/24/2007 ....$41.97
Employees..2,594	Stock Exchange..NDQ
Auditor ....KPMG LLP	Ticker Symbol...WRLD
Stk Agt ....Wachovia Bank N.A	Outstanding Shares 17,520,000
Counsel........Robinson, Bradshaw & Hinson P.A.	E.P.S...$2.60
DUNS No......................................04-493-9098	Shareholders..NA

Business: The group's principal activities are to provide short-term loans, medium-term larger loans, related credit insurance and ancillary products and services to individuals. The group provides standardized installment loans of between $130 to $3,000. As of 30-Jun-2004, the group operated through 544 offices located in South Carolina, Georgia, Texas, Oklahoma, Louisiana, Tennessee, Illinois, Missouri, New Mexico, Kentucky and Alabama. The group also offers income tax return preparation services and refund anticipation loans. As an agent for an unaffiliated insurance company, the group markets and sells credit life, credit accident and health, credit property and unemployment insurance in connection with its loans. The company also markets automobile club memberships to its borrowers as an agent for an unaffiliated automobile club. Club memberships entitle members to automobile breakdown and towing insurance and related services.

Primary SIC and add'l.: 7374 6411 6141

CIK No: 0000108385

Subsidiaries: ParaData Financial Systems

Officers: Alexander A. McLean/55/Dir., CEO/$1,212,652.00

Directors: Alexander A. McLean/55/Dir., CEO, Charles D. Walters/65/Chmn., William S. Hummers/58/Dir., Ken R. Bramlett/44/Dir., James R. Gilreath/62/Dir., Charles D. Way/51/Dir.

Owners: Alexander A. McLean/1.30%, Mark C. Roland, Clinton D. Dyer, Columbia Wanger Asset Management L.P./14.50%, Charles D. Way, Goldman Sachs Asset Management, L.P./7.20%, Kelly M. Malson, William S. Hummers, James R. Gilreath, James Daniel Walters, Insiders/4.00%, Ken R. Bramlett, Barclays Global Investors, N.A./5.10%, Charles D. Walters/1.10%, Charles F. Gardner

Financial Data: Fiscal Year End:03/31   Latest Annual Data: 3/31/2007

Year	Sales	Net Income
2007	$292,318,000	$47,896,000
2006	$243,272,000	$38,515,000
2005	$210,758,000	$33,990,000

Curr. Assets:	$5,779,000	Curr. Liab.:	$24,423,000	P/E Ratio:	16.14
Plant, Equip.:	$14,310,000	Total Liab.:	$195,623,000	Indic. Yr. Divd.:	NA
Total Assets:	$411,116,000	Net Worth:	$215,493,000	Debt/ Equity:	NA

World Airways Inc

The Hlh Bldg., 101 World Dr., Peachtree City, GA, 30269; *PH:* 1-770-632-8002; *http://* www.worldair.com

General - Incorporation ....DE	Stock- Price on:12/24/2007 ....$12.01
Employees..2,104	Stock Exchange...NA
Auditor ....KPMG LLP	Ticker Symbol...NA
Stk Agt ....Continental Stock Transfer & Trust Co	Outstanding Shares 24,240,000
Counsel...NA	E.P.S...$0.48
DUNS No......................................00-691-0202	Shareholders..NA

Business: The group's principal activity is to operate as an air carrier in the air transportation industry. The group provides long range passenger and cargo air transportation service. The customers of the group include major international air carriers, U.S. Government, international passenger and cargo air carriers, tour operators, international freight forwarders and cruise ship companies. As of Dec 31, 2003, the group operated eleven md-11 and seven dc-10-30 aircraft. The md-11 fleet includes eight passenger aircraft and three freighter aircraft. The dc-10-30 fleet includes four freighter aircraft and three passenger aircraft.

Primary SIC and add'l.: 4512

CIK No: 0000949240

Subsidiaries: North American Airlines, Inc., World Airways Parts Company, LLC, World Airways, Inc., World Risk Solutions, Ltd.

Officers: Randy J. Martinez/52/CEO, Steve Forsyth/Dir. - Corporate Communications, Renee Skinner/VP, Controller, George Wilson/VP - Flight Operations, Charlie McDonald/COO, Ann Aktabowski/VP - Customer Services, Larry Montford/VP - Technical Operations, Jenny Poole/VP - In, Flight Services, Jeffrey L. MacKinney/51/Dir., Pres., Charles H.J. Addison/47/CIO, Robert R. Binns/43/Chief Marketing Officer, Mark M. McMillin/53/General Counsel, Corp. Sec., Michael W. Towe/52/CFO

Directors: Ronald R. Fogleman/65/Chmn., Madeline E. Hamill/48/Dir., Daniel J. Altobello/66/Dir., Russell L. Ray/72/Dir., Peter M. Sontag/64/Dir., Jeffrey L. MacKinney/51/Dir., Pres.

Owners: Robert R. Binns, Air Transportation Stabilization Board/8.69%, Russell L. Ray, Clinton Group, Inc./6.00%, Scott A. Andrews, Daniel J. Altobello, Peter M. Sontag, Michael W. Towe, Joel H. Cowan, Nicholas Applegate Capital Management LLC/5.43%, Virginia G. Clark, General Ronald R. Fogleman, Randy J. Martinez, Insiders/6.40%, Jeffrey W. Wehrenberg (*17 Owners included in Index*)

Financial Data: Fiscal Year End:12/31   Latest Annual Data: 12/31/2005

Year	Sales	Net Income
2005	$787,138,000	$31,628,000
2004	$503,900,000	$25,587,000
2003	$474,850,000	$15,321,000

Curr. Assets:	$156,182,000	Curr. Liab.:	$148,000,000	P/E Ratio:	25.02
Plant, Equip.:	$33,726,000	Total Liab.:	$173,808,000	Indic. Yr. Divd.:	NA
Total Assets:	$260,646,000	Net Worth:	$86,838,000	Debt/ Equity:	NA

World Energy Solutions Inc

3900A 31st St. N, St. Petersburg, FL, 33714; *PH:* 1-727-525-5552; *Fax:* 1-727-526-2990; *http://* www.worldenergysolutionsinc.com; *Email:* info@worldenergysolutionsinc.com

General - Incorporation	FL	Stock - Price on:12/24/2007	$0.65
Employees	NA	Stock Exchange	OTC
Auditor	Ferlita, Walsh & Gonzalez, PA	Ticker Symbol	WEGY
Stk Agt	Computershare Trust Co	Outstanding Shares	30,320,000
Counsel	NA	E.P.S.	-$0.2
DUNS No.	NA	Shareholders	NA

Business: The groups principle activities include marketing multi product package to commercial, industrial and residential facilities in order to lower overall cost of electric, gas and water. In August 2005, a old World Energy Solutions, Inc. merged with Advanced 3D Ultrasound, Inc., In November 2005, the group acquired Professional Technical Systems, Inc. and In October 2006, Pure Air Technologies, Inc. The group operates from the United States. The group's quarterly revenue for Sep '07 was 0.15 millions of USD.

Primary SIC and add'l.: 4911 6221 4924

CIK No: 0001058307

Officers: Benjamin C. Croxton/59/Dir., CEO, CFO, Mike Prentice/Chmn., Pres., Peter James/Dir., Consultant, Paula Scott/Contact - Investor Relations

Directors: Benjamin C. Croxton/59/Dir., CEO, CFO, Mike Prentice/Chmn., Pres., Peter James/Dir., Consultant, Keith Drucker/Dir.

Owners: Rachel Steele/14.12%, Mike Prentice/17.98%, Robert C. Kratz/6.50%, Insiders/48.42%, Benjamin C. Croxton/23.30%

Financial Data: Fiscal Year End:12/31   Latest Annual Data: 12/31/2006

Year	Sales	Net Income
2006	$555,000	-$8,531,000
2005	$471,000	-$1,205,000
2004	NA	-$406,000

Curr. Assets:	$873,000	Curr. Liab.:	$325,000	P/E Ratio:	13.41
Plant, Equip.:	$67,000	Total Liab.:	$325,000	Indic. Yr. Divd.:	NA
Total Assets:	$1,002,000	Net Worth:	$677,000	Debt/ Equity:	NA

World Fuel Services Corp

9800 NW 41st St., Ste 400, Miami, FL, 33178; *PH:* 1-305-428-8001; *http://* www.wfscorp.com; *Email:* information@wfscorp.com

General - Incorporation	FL	Stock - Price on:12/24/2007	$41.26
Employees	743	Stock Exchange	NYSE
Auditor	PricewaterhouseCoopers LLP	Ticker Symbol	INT
Stk Agt	American Stock Transfer & Trust Co.	Outstanding Shares	28,530,000
Counsel	Shutts & Bowen	E.P.S.	$2.28
DUNS No.	13-150-4342	Shareholders	NA

Business: The groups principle activity is to provide marine, aviation and land fuels products and services. In the year 2007, the group acquired AVCARD. The group operates from United States.

Primary SIC and add'l.: 5172

CIK No: 0000789460

Subsidiaries: Advance Petroleum Inc., AirData Limited, Atlantic Fuel Services S.A., Baseops Europe Ltd., Baseops International S.A., Baseops Mexico S.A. de C.V., Bunkerfuels UK Limited, Casa Petro S.A., IRC Oil Technics Inc., Marine Energy Arabia Co. LLC, Marine Energy Arabia Establishment Ltd., Norse Bunkers AS, Oil Shipping B.V., Oil Shipping Bunkering B.V., Oil Shipping Hong Kong Ltd. 63 Subsidiaries included in the Index

Officers: Paul H. Stebbins/Chmn., CEO/$3,787,416.00, Francis X. Shea/Exec. VP, Chief Risk, Administrative Officer/$1,174,356.00, Alexander R. Lake/General Counsel, Corp. Sec., Michael J. Kasbar/Dir., COO, Pres./$3,795,273.00, Michael Clementi/Pres. - World Fuel Services, Inc/$1,985,649.00, Paul M. Nobel/Chief Accounting Officer, Sr. VP/$352,496.00, Ira M. Birns/CFO, Exec. VP

Directors: Paul H. Stebbins/Chmn., CEO, Ken Bakshi/Dir., Richard A. Kassar/Dir., Thomas J. Presby/Dir., Myles Klein/Dir., John R. Benbow/76/Dir., Jerome Sidel/73/Dir., Michael J. Kasbar/Dir., COO, Pres., Stephen K. Roddenberry/Dir., Joachim Heel/Dir.

Owners: Barclays Entities/7.20%, John R. Benbow, Richard A. Kassar, Paul H. Stebbins/3.30%, Ken Bakshi, Paul Nobel, J. Thomas Presby, Jerome Sidel, Francis X. Shea, FMR Corp./7.80%, Robert S. Tocci, Michael S. Clementi, Insiders/8.70%, Myles Klein, Kayne Anderson Rudnick Investment Management, LLC/6.00% *(16 Owners included in Index)*

Financial Data: Fiscal Year End:12/31   Latest Annual Data: 12/31/2006

Year	Sales	Net Income
2006	$10,785,136,000	$63,948,000
2005	$8,733,947,000	$39,609,000
2004	$5,654,373,000	$28,559,000

Curr. Assets:	$1,196,091,000	Curr. Liab.:	$826,761,000	P/E Ratio:	18.75
Plant, Equip.:	$26,730,000	Total Liab.:	$851,431,000	Indic. Yr. Divd.:	0.150
Total Assets:	$1,277,400,000	Net Worth:	$425,969,000	Debt/ Equity:	0.0466

World Heart Corp

7799 Pardee Ln, Oakland, CA, 94621; *PH:* 1-510-563-5000; *http://* www.worldheart.com; *Email:* news@worldheart.com

General - Incorporation	Canada	Stock - Price on:12/24/2007	NA
Employees	117	Stock Exchange	NDQ
Auditor	PricewaterhouseCoopers LLP	Ticker Symbol	WHRT
Stk Agt	CIBC Mellon Trust CO.	Outstanding Shares	NA
Counsel	White & Case LLP	E.P.S.	-$1.56
DUNS No.	25-494-3764	Shareholders	NA

Business: The group's principal activity is to develop artificial heart technologies. The group is focused on two technologies, novacor lvas and the heartsaver ventricular assist device (heartsaver). Novacor technology is currently in commercial production and the heartsaver technology is currently

under development. This technology is being developed from licensed artificial heart and related technologies developed by the cardiovascular devices division (cvd) of the ottawa heart institute research corporation. The operations of the group are carried out in oakland, California, the United States, ottawa, ontario and Canada.

Primary SIC and add'l.: 3845 8731

CIK No: 0001024520

Subsidiaries: 2007262 Ontario Inc, World Heart B.V., World Heart Inc

Officers: Jal S. Jassawalla/Dir., CEO, Pres./$358,205.00, Pratap Khanwilkar/VP - Rotary Systems - Business Development, Piet Jansen/Chief Medical Officer/$267,187.00, John Marinchak/VP - Marketing - Sales/$265,125.00, Phillip J. Miller/VP - Research - Development/$171,051.00, Richard Juelis/60/VP - Finance/$200,923.00, John Vajda/VP - Manufacturing, David Pellone/VP - Finance, CFO

Directors: Jal S. Jassawalla/Dir., CEO, Pres., Ian C. Ross/Chmn., Robert J. Majteles/Dir., William C. Garriock/Dir., Gary Goertz/Dir.

Owners: Jal S. Jassawalla/1.90%, Maverick Venture Management, LLC/24.30%, Ian C. Ross, Phil Miller, Richard A. Juelis, Piet Jansen, Entities affiliated with BC Advisors, LLC/9.60%, Robert J. Majteles, Insiders/4.30%, John Marinchak, William C. Garriock, Austin W. Marxe/28.90%, SF Capital Partners Ltd/9.40%

Financial Data: Fiscal Year End:12/31   Latest Annual Data: 12/31/2006

Year	Sales	Net Income
2006	$8,616,000	-$20,085,000
2005	$11,646,000	-$52,834,000
2004	$9,576,000	-$22,807,000

Curr. Assets:	$18,306,000	Curr. Liab.:	$5,791,000		
Plant, Equip.:	$950,000	Total Liab.:	$5,791,000	Indic. Yr. Divd.:	NA
Total Assets:	$20,498,000	Net Worth:	$14,706,000	Debt/ Equity:	NA

World Information Technology Inc

Rockefeller Ctr, 7th Fl., 1230 Ave. Of The Americas, New York, NY, 10020; *PH:* 1-212-745-1382; *http://* www.eztravellv.com

General - Incorporation	NV	Stock - Price on:12/24/2007	NA
Employees	NA	Stock Exchange	NA
Auditor	LL Bradford & Co	Ticker Symbol	NA
Stk Agt	Holladay Stock Transfer, Inc.	Outstanding Shares	NA
Counsel	NA	E.P.S.	NA
DUNS No.	NA	Shareholders	NA

Business: The group's principle activity is to establish a business to provide facilities for booking cruise tours, hotels, air travel and car rentals to its clients. It also intends on providing other travel activities including, receptions and services for organized groups and individuals. On 19-May-2003, it acquired world information technology inc. The group operates from United States.

Primary SIC and add'l.: 4724

CIK No: 0001170422

World Ventures Inc

102 Piper Crescent, Nanaimo, BC, T4P 1L5; *PH:* 1-250-756-0291; *http://* www.worldventuresinc.net

General - Incorporation	Canada	Stock - Price on:12/24/2007	$0.22
Employees	NA	Stock Exchange	OTC
Auditor	Smythe Ratcliffe LLP	Ticker Symbol	WVNTF
Stk Agt	Smythe Ratcliffe	Outstanding Shares	NA
Counsel	NA	E.P.S.	NA
DUNS No.	24-898-0575	Shareholders	NA

Business: The group's principal activities are to develop resort properties and to explore natural resource properties.

Primary SIC and add'l.: 1099 1041

CIK No: 0000861398

Subsidiaries: World Ventures (Nevada) Inc

Officers: Ray Carson/Dir., CEO, Pres., Gary Van Norman/Dir., VP, John Curry/Dir., VP - Sales - Marketing, Stewart Jackson/Dir., VP - Explorations

Directors: Ray Carson/Dir., CEO, Pres., Gary Van Norman/Dir., VP, John Curry/Dir., VP - Sales - Marketing, Stewart Jackson/Dir., VP - Explorations

Owners: Cede & Co./37.70%, Stewart A. Jackson/2.00%, Insiders/1.24%, CDS & Co./14.80%, Brisas Atlantico S.A./6.20%, Curitiba S.A./7.70%, Investors First S.A./11.30%, Financial Pacific./15.70%

Financial Data: Fiscal Year End:10/31   Latest Annual Data: 10/31/2006

Year	Sales	Net Income
2006	NA	-$190,000
2005	NA	-$490,000
2004	NA	-$173,000

Curr. Assets:	$18,000	Curr. Liab.:	$245,000		
Plant, Equip.:	$1,000	Total Liab.:	$245,000	Indic. Yr. Divd.:	NA
Total Assets:	$19,000	Net Worth:	-$226,000	Debt/ Equity:	NA

World Waste Technologies Inc

13520 Evening Creek Dr. N, Ste 130, San Diego, CA, 92128; *PH:* 1-858-393-3400; *http://* www.worldwasteintl.com; *Email:* information@worldwasteintl.com

General - Incorporation	CA	Stock - Price on:12/24/2007	$0.95
Employees	13	Stock Exchange	OTC
Auditor	Stonefield Josephson	Ticker Symbol	WDWT
Stk Agt	Chadbourn & Laird Q. Cagan	Outstanding Shares	26,260,000
Counsel	NA	E.P.S.	-$1.41
DUNS No.	NA	Shareholders	NA

Business: The group's principal activity is to process and convert solid waste into usable commodities. The group holds U.S. License with respect to patented technology, which enables it to convert municipal solid waste into usable commodities. This patented process is known as pressurized steam classification. This process extracts both sanitized cellulose material containing papermaking fiber

that can be sold after a conventional screening and cleaning process for use in making paperboard and inorganic, recyclable materials such as aluminium, steel and plastic products. The customers of the group include taormina industries, llc, a wholly-owned subsidiary of republic services inc. The group is in its development stage and operates solely in the United States of America.

Primary SIC and add'l.: 4953

CIK No: 0000890447

Subsidiaries: World Waste of America, Inc., World Waste of Anaheim, Inc., World Waste of California, Inc., World Waste Operations, Inc.

Officers: John Pimentel/Chmn., CEO/$176,539.00, Thomas L. Collins/Sr. Advisor/$221,846.00, David Rane/CFO/$224,000.00, Fred Lundberg/Sr. Advisor/$200,057.00, Tom Beck/Sr. Marketing Advisor, Lee Torrens/Sr. Development Advisor, Member - Technical Advisory Board, Bill Farone/Sr. Scientific Advisor, Member - Technical Advisory Board, Michael Fatigati/VP - Engineering, Project Management, Matthew Lieb/COO

Directors: John Pimentel/Chmn., CEO, James Ferris/Dir., Ross M. Patten/Dir., Sam Pina Cortez/Dir., Dave Gutacker/Dir.

Owners: Laird Q. Cagan/8.92%, David A. Rane/2.37%, One World Zero Waste, LLC/8.80%, James L. Ferris, Steven Racoosin/8.80%, Sam P. Cortez, John Pimentel/5.75%, Ross M. Patten, David Gutacker, Insiders/11.60%

Financial Data: Fiscal Year End:12/31   Latest Annual Data: 12/31/2006

Year	Sales		Net Income
2006	$94,000		-$24,957,000
2005	NA		-$3,079,000
2004	NA		-$2,474,000
Curr. Assets:	$14,518,000	**Curr. Liab.:**	$932,000	
Plant, Equip.:	$9,268,000	**Total Liab.:**	$1,012,000	**Indic. Yr. Divd.:** NA
Total Assets:	$25,088,000	**Net Worth:**	$9,569,000	**Debt/ Equity:** 0.0106

World Wrestling Entertainment Inc

1241 E Main St., Stamford, CT, 06902; **PH:** 1-203-353-5066; **http://** www.corporate.wwe.com

General - Incorporation	DE	**Stock**- Price on:12/24/2007	$16.59
Employees	560	Stock Exchange	NYSE
Auditor	Deloitte & Touche LLP	Ticker Symbol	WWE
Stk Agt	American Stk Trnsfer c/o Joe Alicia	Outstanding Shares	71,150,000
Counsel	NA	E.P.S.	$0.62
DUNS No.	NA	Shareholders	NA

Business: The group's principal activities are to develop, produce and market television program, pay-per-view program and live events. It also provides branded merchandise that consists of licensing and sale of branded consumer products featuring world wrestling entertainment brand. It is an independent producer of television programming, which relies primarily on in-house production capabilities. Raw, smackdown !, sunday night heat, velocity, after burn and the wwe experience are programmes which are aired on spiketv and upn channels.

Primary SIC and add'l.: 7999 2721

CIK No: 0001091907

Subsidiaries: Condemned Productions Australia Pty Ltd, Condemned Productions, Inc., Event Services, Inc., Eye Scream Man Productions Australia Pty Ltd, Eye Scream Productions, Marine Productions, Marine Productions Australia Pty Ltd, Stephanie Music Publishing, Inc., TSI Realty Company, WCW, Inc., World Wrestling Entertainment (International) Limited, World Wrestling Entertainment Canada, Inc., WWE Films Development, Inc, WWE Films, Inc., WWE Libraries, Inc.

Officers: Linda E. McMahon/Dir., CEO/$22,013.00, Frank G. Serpe/CFO, Donna Goldsmith/Exec. VP - Consumer Products, Gary Davis/Contact - US Media Inquiries, Michael Weitz/Investor Relation, Dawn Dwyer/Contact - Canadian Media Inquiries, Christine Wypy/Contact - International Media Inquiries, Joe Villa/Contact - Media Credentials US Events, Thomas N. Barreca/Exec. VP - WWE Enterprises, Kevin Dunn/Exec. VP - Television Production/$1,025,636.00, Edward L. Kaufman/Exec. VP, General Counsel, Michael Sileck/Dir., COO/$1,156,986.00, Shane B. McMahon/Exec. VP - Global Media, Joel Simon/Pres. - WWE Films/$624,964.00, John Laurinaitis/Sr. VP - Talent Relations (20 Officers included in Index)

Directors: Linda E. McMahon/Dir., CEO, Vincent K. McMahon/Chmn., Michael B. Solomon/Dir., Michael Sileck/Dir., COO, Robert A. Bowman/Dir., David Kenin/Dir., Lowell P. Weicker/Dir., Joseph Perkins/Dir.

Owners: Kurt M. Schneider, Robert A. Bowman, Michael B. Solomon, Renaissance Technologies Corp./8.40%, Vincent K. McMahon/98.80%, Clearbridge Advisors, LLC/5.30%, Joseph H. Perkins, Invemed Catalyst Fund, L.P./11.10%, Barclays Global Investors Japan Limited/5.70%, Joel Simon, Linda E. McMahon/1.20%, Michael Sileck, Lowell P. Weicker, Kevin Dunn, Insiders/68.00% (16 Owners included in Index)

Financial Data: Fiscal Year End:04/30   Latest Annual Data: 4/30/2006

Year	Sales		Net Income
2006	$400,051,000		$47,047,000
2005	$366,431,000		$39,147,000
Curr. Assets:	$362,018,000	**Curr. Liab.:**	$76,828,000	**P/E Ratio:** 26.33
Plant, Equip.:	$67,570,000	**Total Liab.:**	$83,209,000	**Indic. Yr. Divd.:** $0.960
Total Assets:	$479,390,000	**Net Worth:**	$396,181,000	**Debt/ Equity:** 0.0144

World-Am Inc

Ste 104, 1400 W 122nd Ave., Westminster, CO, 80234; **PH:** 1-303-452-0022; **http://** www.world-am.com; **Email:** ir@world-am.com

General - Incorporation	NV	**Stock**- Price on:12/24/2007	$0.0065
Employees	10	Stock Exchange	OTC
Auditor	LL Bradford & Co	Ticker Symbol	WDAM
Stk Agt	Island Stock Transfer	Outstanding Shares	623,070,000
Counsel	NA	E.P.S.	$0.02
DUNS No.	NA	Shareholders	NA

Business: The group's principal activities are to design, develop, manufacture and distribute automated passage control and security devices. The group's activities are carried on through its wholly owned subsidiaries isotec inc and technology development international inc. Isotec inc develops, manufactures and distributes automated passage control and secutiy devices. Technology developments international inc acquires, develops and distributes innovative component products. It operates in the United States.

Primary SIC and add'l.: 7380

CIK No: 0001107522

Subsidiaries: Isotec, Inc., Senz-It

Officers: Robert A. Hovee/Chmn., CEO, David J. Barnes/Dir., CFO, James R. Largent/Dir., Sec.

Directors: Robert A. Hovee/Chmn., CEO, David J. Barnes/Dir., CFO, James R. Largent/Dir., Sec.

Financial Data: Fiscal Year End:12/31   Latest Annual Data: 12/31/2006

Year	Sales		Net Income
2006	$245,000		-$4,376,000
2005	$213,000		-$601,000
2004	$467,000		-$1,860,000
Curr. Assets:	$226,000	**Curr. Liab.:**	$1,921,000	
Plant, Equip.:	$4,000	**Total Liab.:**	$4,572,000	**Indic. Yr. Divd.:** NA
Total Assets:	$259,000	**Net Worth:**	-$4,313,000	**Debt/ Equity:** NA

WorldGate Communications Inc

3190 Tremont Ave., Trevose, PA, 19053; **PH:** 1-215-354-5100; **http://** www.wgate.com

General - Incorporation	DE	**Stock**- Price on:12/24/2007	$0.61
Employees	70	Stock Exchange	OTC
Auditor	Marcum & Kliegman, LLP	Ticker Symbol	WGAT
Stk Agt	American Stock Transfer & Trust Co.	Outstanding Shares	43,360,000
Counsel	NA	E.P.S.	$0.46
DUNS No.	NA	Shareholders	NA

Business: The group's principal activities are providing interactive television entertainment products and services to the cable television industry. The group designs, assembles, installs and maintains the equipment and computer software necessary to provide itv applications. Services include enhanced television applications such as broadcast data services, access to the Internet over television, news headlines, sports scores, stock quotes, shopping links, e-mail and chat. In addition, the service interfaces with other applications including video on demand and a variety of ipgs and t-commerce features.

Primary SIC and add'l.: 7372 7375

CIK No: 0001030058

Subsidiaries: Ojo Services LLC, WorldGate Acquisition Corp, WorldGate Finance, Inc, WorldGate Service, Inc

Officers: Hal M. Krisbergh/Chmn., CEO, Joel I. Boyarski/Sr. VP, CFO, Randall J. Gort/Sr. VP - CLO, Sec., James McLoughlin/Sr. VP - Sales, Marketing, Business Development, Rich Westerfer/COO, Sr. VP

Directors: Hal M. Krisbergh/Chmn., CEO, Jeff Morris/Dir., Martin Jaffe/Dir., Larry Irving/Dir., Lemuel A. Tarshis/Dir., Steve Davidson/Dir., Clarence L. Irving/52/Dir., David Tomasello/Dir.

Owners: Martin Jaffe, Lemuel Tarshis, Antonio Tomasello/17.48%, James McLoughlin/1.27%, Steven C. Davidson, Insiders/37.27%, David Tomasello/18.20%, Joel Boyarski/1.41%, Richard Westerfer/1.76%, Randall J. Gort/1.98%, Clarence L. Irving, Jeff Morris, Hal M. Krisbergh/11.92%

Financial Data: Fiscal Year End:12/31   Latest Annual Data: 12/31/2006

Year	Sales		Net Income
2006	$2,776,000		-$17,608,000
2005	$1,558,000		-$6,851,000
2004	$231,000		-$19,425,000
Curr. Assets:	$13,179,000	**Curr. Liab.:**	$11,398,000	
Plant, Equip.:	$1,266,000	**Total Liab.:**	$12,423,000	**Indic. Yr. Divd.:** NA
Total Assets:	$14,566,000	**Net Worth:**	$2,002,000	**Debt/ Equity:** NA

WorldSpace Inc

8515 Georgia Ave. Silver, Silver Spring, MD, 20910; **PH:** 1-301-960-1200; **Fax:** 1-301-960-2200; **http://** www.worldspace.com; **Email:** customerservice@worldspace.com

General - Incorporation	DE	**Stock**- Price on:12/24/2007	$4.96
Employees	NA	Stock Exchange	NDQ
Auditor	Grant Thornton LLP	Ticker Symbol	WRSP
Stk Agt	American Stock Transfer & Trust Co.	Outstanding Shares	39,870,000
Counsel	NA	E.P.S.	$3.56
DUNS No.	NA	Shareholders	NA

Business: The groups principle activity is to provide digital radio service. The groups service is digital audio radio service. The groups product is WorldSpace System. The group opeartes from the United States, France, Kenya, South Africa, Singapore, India and other.

Primary SIC and add'l.: 4832 4899 4899

CIK No: 0001315054

Subsidiaries: AfriSpace Kenya Ltd., AfriSpace, Inc., AsiaSpace Limited, Viatis Satellite Radio Europe SAS, Viatis Satellite Radio Holdings ApS, WorldSpace Asia Pte Ltd., WorldSpace Caribbean Limited, WorldSpace China, WorldSpace France, WorldSpace India Private Limited, WorldSpace Italia SpA, WorldSpace Satellite Company, WorldSpace Southern Africa (Pty) Ltd., WorldSpace Systems Corporation, WorldSpace UK Ltd.

Officers: Noah A. Samara/Chmn., CEO, Benoit Chereau/CEO - Europe, Vincent Loiacono/Chief Accounting Officer, Sr. VP, Stephen Horn/Chief Marketing Officer, Donald J. Frickel/General Counsel, Sec., Sridhar Ganesan/CFO, Gregory B. Armstrong/Co - COO, Alexander P. Brown/Co - COO, Judith Pryor/Sr. VP - Corporate Affairs

Directors: Noah A. Samara/Chmn., CEO, Donald J. Frickel/General Counsel, Sec., Kassahun Kebede/Dir., Jack Kemp/72/Dir., James R. Laramie/Dir., Charles McMathias/Dir., Michael Nobel/Dir., William Schneider/Dir., Frank-Jurgen Richter/Dir.

Owners: Insiders, Yenura Pte. Ltd., Michael Nobel, Noah A. Samara, James R. Laramie, Donald J. Frickel, William Schneider, Highbridge International LLC, Jack Kemp, Aletheia Research and Management, Inc., Charles C. Mathias, Alexander P. Brown, Sridhar Ganesan, Gregory B. Armstrong, Citadel Limited Partnership (17 Owners included in Index)

Financial Data: Fiscal Year End:12/31   Latest Annual Data: 12/31/2006

Year	Sales		Net Income
2006	$15,611,000		-$128,603,000
2005	$11,660,000		-$79,863,000
2004	$8,581,000		-$577,387,000
Curr. Assets:	$183,329,000	**Curr. Liab.:**	$76,036,000	
Plant, Equip.:	$17,745,000	**Total Liab.:**	$2,172,304,000	**Indic. Yr. Divd.:** NA
Total Assets:	$568,645,000	**Net Worth:**	-$1,603,659,000	**Debt/ Equity:** NA

Worldstar Energy Corp

1177 W Hastings St., Ste. 1901, Vancouver, BC, V6E 2K3; **PH:** 1-604-434-5256

Worthington Industries Inc (continued)

General	- Incorporation	NV
Employees		NA
Auditor	Pannell Kerr Forster Of Texas, P.c.	
Stk Agt	Pacific Stock Transfer Company	
Counsel		NA
DUNS No.		NA

Stock	- Price on:12/24/2007	$2.95
Stock Exchange		OTC
Ticker Symbol		WSTR
Outstanding Shares		NA
E.P.S.		NA
Shareholders		NA

Business: The groups principal activity is conducted an automotive communications business offering online and point of purchase marketing, commerce and customer relationship systems to auto dealerships. The group operates from Canada.

Primary SIC and add'l.: 1000

CIK No: 0001093677

Officers: Richard Tay/Dir., CEO, Pres., Michael W. Kinley/57/Dir., CFO

Directors: Richard Tay/Dir., CEO, Pres., Michael W. Kinley/57/Dir., CFO

Owners: Taj Mohammed/32.69%

Financial Data: Fiscal Year End:12/31   Latest Annual Data: 12/31/2006

Year	Sales	Net Income
2006	NA	-$381,000
2005	NA	-$212,000
2004	NA	-$134,000

Curr. Assets:	NA	Curr. Liab.:	$106,000		
Plant, Equip.:	NA	Total Liab.:	$106,000	Indic. Yr. Divd.:	NA
Total Assets:	NA	Net Worth:	-$106,000	Debt/ Equity:	NA

WorldTradeShow.com Inc

9449 Balboa Ave, Ste. 103, San Diego, CA, 92123; *PH:* 1-858-292-9637; *http://* www.worldtradeshow.com

General	- Incorporation	NV
Employees		NA
Auditor	Chang G. Park, CPA	
Stk Agt	First American Stock Transfer, Inc.	
Counsel		NA
DUNS No.		NA

Stock	- Price on:12/24/2007	NA
Stock Exchange		OTC
Ticker Symbol		BVNI
Outstanding Shares		NA
E.P.S.		-$0.04
Shareholders		NA

Business: The group's principle activity is to capture a lucrative online trade show production market by implementing the latest Virtual Trade show experience via the Internet. The group offers global show producers, exhibitors, businesses, and attendees a comprehensive database of updated trade shows, conventions, and fairs online. In addition, the interactive multimedia web portal features live virtual trade shows, complete with real-time registration, 3-D floor plans, conference news, chat forum, live web casting, and listing of show participants hyper-linked to their emails or web sites. Online reservations for hotels, travel services, along with destination information are also available for visitors to access. The group operates from United States.

Primary SIC and add'l.: 7389

CIK No: 0001084370

Officers: Sheldon Siverman/Chmn., CEO, Pres., Carlos Rosette/54/Dir., Dir. - Sales, Marketing in Mexico, Lee Johnson/Member - Advisory Board, CTO, Robert Malasek/40/CFO

Directors: Sheldon Siverman/Chmn., CEO, Pres., Carlos Rosette/54/Dir., Dir. - Sales, Marketing in Mexico, Lee Johnson/Member - Advisory Board, CTO, Juan Saldinas/Member - Advisory Board, Lai Nguyen Tuong/Member - Advisory Board, John Baca/Member - Advisory Board, Jen-Loup Bitterlin Geffroy/Member - Advisory Board, Gregg Lindquist/Member - Advisory Board

Owners: Sheldon Silverman/3.48%, Carlos Rosette/0.19%, Lee Johnson/59.40%, Robert Malasek/0.25%, Insiders/63.06%

Financial Data: Fiscal Year End:04/30   Latest Annual Data: 04/30/2007

Year	Sales	Net Income
2007	NA	-$1,384,000
2006	NA	-$623,000

Curr. Assets:	$59,000	Curr. Liab.:	$3,973,000		
Plant, Equip.:	NA	Total Liab.:	$3,973,000	Indic. Yr. Divd.:	NA
Total Assets:	$1,309,000	Net Worth:	-$2,664,000	Debt/ Equity:	NA

WorldWater & Power Corp

Formerly: Worldwater Corp
55 Rte. 31 S, Pennington, NJ, 08534; *PH:* 1-609-818-0700; *http://* www.worldwater.com

General	- Incorporation	NV
Employees		45
Auditor	Amper, Politziner & Mattia P.C	
Stk Agt	Computershare Trust Co	
Counsel		NA
DUNS No.		13-165-1366

Stock	- Price on:12/24/2007	$1.075
Stock Exchange		OTC
Ticker Symbol		WWAT
Outstanding Shares		165,370,000
E.P.S.		NA
Shareholders		NA

Business: The group's principal activities are to design, develop and market proprietary technology relating to solar energy and water engineering, including solar power products and international water management consulting. Primary products of the group are cost effective power systems which works on solar energy like water pumps. The major customers for the group's products are developing countries where there is lack of electricity and water.

Primary SIC and add'l.: 3561

CIK No: 0000811271

Subsidiaries: dba Quantum Energy Group, Philippine corporation., WorldWater (Phils) Inc, WorldWater Holdings Inc.

Officers: Quentin T. Kelly/Chmn., CEO/$268,000.00, Guido Delgado/CEO - Worldwater, Philippines Inc, Douglas L. Washington/60/Exec. VP - Sales, Larry Crawford/CFO, Exec. VP/$184,516.00, Frank Smith/COO, Exec. VP, James S. Brown/52/Exec. VP - Project Finance/$147,894.00, Anand Rangarajan/CTO, Exec. VP/$150,486.00, John Herrman/Pres. - Worldwater, Philippines Inc

Directors: Quentin T. Kelly/Chmn., CEO, Hong Hou/Dir., Harrison W. Wellford/Dir., Davinder Sethi/Dir., Joseph Cygler/Dir., Lange Schermerhorn/Dir., Reuben Richards/Dir.

Owners: Anand Rangarajan/0.10%, EMCORE Corporation/22.40%, Harrison Wellford/0.80%, Quercus Trust/19.50%, Quentin T. Kelly/3.10%, Larry L. Crawford/0.10%, Insiders/5.60%, Frank Smith, Hong Hou, James S. Brown/0.50%, Davinder Sethi/0.20%, Joseph Cygler/0.60%, Reuben Richards, Lange Schermerhorn/0.30%

Financial Data: Fiscal Year End:12/31   Latest Annual Data: 03/31/2007

Year	Sales	Net Income
2007	NA	NA
2006	$17,334,000	-$8,243,000
2005	$2,031,000	-$10,214,000

Curr. Assets:	$16,206,000	Curr. Liab.:	$5,653,000		
Plant, Equip.:	$196,000	Total Liab.:	$6,007,000	Indic. Yr. Divd.:	NA
Total Assets:	$17,268,000	Net Worth:	-$1,624,000	Debt/ Equity:	NA

Worldwide Biotech & Pharmaceutical CO

4 Fenghui S Rd., Jie Zuo Mansion, 15th Fl., A10-11501, Xi'an, Shaanxi, 710075;
PH: 86-2988193338; *Fax:* 86-2988193318; *http://* www.worldwidebio.com;
Email: wwbp@worldwidebio.com

General	- Incorporation	DE
Employees		NA
Auditor	Zhong Yi (hong Kong) C.P.A. Co. Ltd.	
Stk Agt	American Stock Transfer & Trust Co.	
Counsel		NA
DUNS No.		NA

Stock	- Price on:12/24/2007	$0.06
Stock Exchange		OTC
Ticker Symbol		WWBP
Outstanding Shares		NA
E.P.S.		NA
Shareholders		NA

Business: The groups principle activity is set up the in vitro intact HCV virus culturing system, which could continuously replicate the HCV virus in vitro. In January 2006, the group acquired Hunan Hua Yang Pharmaceutical Co. Ltd. The group operates from China. The group's quarterly revenue for Sep '07 was 0.04 millions of USD.

Primary SIC and add'l.: 5140

CIK No: 0000095302

Subsidiaries: Glory Dragon Investment Limited, Hunan Hua Yang Pharmaceutical Co. Ltd., Shaanxi Allied Shine Internationals Ltd., Shaanxi Daiying Medicine Distribution Co., Ltd, Yangling Daiying Biotech & Pharmaceutical Group Co., Ltd.

Officers: Wenxia Guo/40/Dir., CEO, Pres., Peiyi Tian/45/Dir., CFO, Sr. VP, Treasurer, Yuhui Liu/36/Sec., Xiaohong Bai/43/VP - Production, Xing Wei/35/VP - Operation

Directors: Wenxia Guo/40/Dir., CEO, Pres., Peiyi Tian/45/Dir., CFO, Sr. VP, Treasurer, Huimin Zhang/56/Dir.

Owners: Zeng Fu Lee/6.30%, Shaanxi Da Ze Movie & T.V./6.60%, Insiders/20.20%, Wenxia Guo/20.20%, Liu Qiuling/6.30%, Coast to Coast Equity Group, Inc./8.50%, Xian JinHao Sci-Tech/12.60%

Financial Data: Fiscal Year End:12/31   Latest Annual Data: 03/31/2007

Year	Sales	Net Income
2007	NA	NA
2006	$387,000	-$3,433,000
2005	$26,000	-$3,683,000

Curr. Assets:	NA	Curr. Liab.:	NA		
Plant, Equip.:	NA	Total Liab.:	NA	Indic. Yr. Divd.:	NA
Total Assets:	NA	Net Worth:	NA	Debt/ Equity:	NA

Worldwide Manufacturing USA Inc

1142 Cherry St., San Bruno, CA, 94066; *PH:* 1-650-794-9865; *http://* www.wwmusa.com;
Email: sales@wwmusa.com

General	- Incorporation	CO
Employees		206
Auditor	Child, Van Wagoner & Bradshaw, PLLC	
Stk Agt	Computershare Trust Co	
Counsel		NA
DUNS No.		NA

Stock	- Price on:12/24/2007	$5.35
Stock Exchange		OTC
Ticker Symbol		WWMU
Outstanding Shares		2,030,000
E.P.S.		$0.40
Shareholders		NA

Business: The group's principal activities are manufacturing and contract manufacturing as an engineering firm. Its products are manufactured in China. The contract manufacturer hires subcontractors that provide the plant, equipment, manufacturing working capital and factory labor. The group's goal is to timely deliver high quality components at manufacturing costs that what worldwide's customers would pay for similar parts in the United States. Its role is to ensure that the parts meet specifications and quality standards imposed by our customers. The group operates in two segments namely, contract manufacturing service & intech which are carried in the state of California and the peoples republic of China. It provides its services to several companies in the United States, primarily in the aerospace, automotive, and electronics industries. On 08-Sep-2004, the group acquired chuan lin precision die casting co. Ltd.

Primary SIC and add'l.: 8741

CIK No: 0001111816

Subsidiaries: Changchun Chengde Automobile Air-Conditioner Co., Chengde Science & Technology Co., Ltd, Intech Electro-Mechanical Products Co., Ltd, Intech Precision Machinery Co., Ltd, Worldwide USA

Officers: Jimmy Wang/52/Chmn., CEO, Pres., Mindy Wang/50/Corp. Sec., John Ballard/CFO, James Liu/Sales, Operation Mgr., Philip Zhang/48/VP - Operations, GM, Jim Painter/Investor Relations Officer, Andrew S. Hua/Technology, Asia Focus, Equity Research Team

Directors: Jimmy Wang/52/Chmn., CEO, Pres., Mindy Wang/50/Corp. Sec.

Owners: Jimmy Wang/79.82%, Insiders/87.25%, Mindy Wang/79.82%, John Ballard/4.08%, Philip Zhang/3.35%

Financial Data: Fiscal Year End:12/31   Latest Annual Data: 12/31/2006

Year	Sales	Net Income
2006	$11,409,000	$969,000
2005	$8,713,000	$581,000
2004	$6,701,000	$521,000

Curr. Assets:	$6,599,000	Curr. Liab.:	$3,563,000	P/E Ratio:	10.29
Plant, Equip.:	$493,000	Total Liab.:	$4,085,000	Indic. Yr. Divd.:	$0.010
Total Assets:	$7,128,000	Net Worth:	$3,043,000	Debt/ Equity:	NA

Worthington Industries Inc

200 Old Wilson Bridge Rd. , Columbus, OH, 43085; *PH:* 1-614-840-3133;
http:// www.worthingtonindustries.com; *Email:* contactir@worthingtonindustries.com

General - Incorporation .... OH
Employees 8,200
Auditor .... KPMG LLP
Stk Agt............ National City Bank
Counsel .... NA
DUNS No. 00-431-2401

Stock- Price on:12/24/2007 .... $20.67
Stock Exchange .... NYSE
Ticker Symbol .... WOR
Outstanding Shares 84,460,000
E.P.S. $0.93
Shareholders .... NA

Business: The groups principle activity is to process steel and manufacture metal products. The groups products include metal framing, pressure cylinders and automotive past-model service stampings. The group operates from United States.

Primary SIC and add'l.: 3312 3443 3999 3444 3593 3442

CIK No: 0000108516

Subsidiaries: Aegis Metal Framing, LLC, B. Alloy Corporation, Buckeye Energy Company, Inc., Buckeye International Development, Inc., Di Tai Light Steel Building Systems Consulting (Shanghai) Co. Ltd., Dietrich Building Systems, Inc., Dietrich Construction Group Companies, LLC, Dietrich Design Group Ltd., Dietrich Design Group, Inc., Dietrich Industries, Inc., Dietrich Metal Framing Canada, Inc., Dietrich Residential Construction, Inc., Dietrich Residential Construction, LLC, Dietrich Ventures, LLC, Dietrich/NOVA, LLC 57 Subsidiaries included in the Index

Officers: John P. McConnell/Chmn., CEO/$2,467,076.00, John S. Christie/Dir., CFO, Pres./$1,474,547.00, George P. Stoe/COO, Exec. VP/$1,419,521.00, Eric M. Smolenski/VP - Human Resources, Richard G. Welch/Controller, Virgil L. Winland/Sr. VP - Manufacturing, Ralph V. Roberts/Sr. VP - Marketing, Dale T. Brinkman/VP - Administration, General Counsel, Sec., Cathy M. Lyttle/VP - Communications, Robert A. Mowery/VP - Purchasing, Robert J. Richardson/CIO, Harry A. Goussetis/Pres. - Worthington Cylinder Corporation/$907,892.00, Mark A. Russell/Pres. - Worthington Steel, Allison McFerren Sanders/Dir. - Investor Relations, Lester V. Hess/53/Treasurer

Directors: John P. McConnell/Chmn., CEO, John S. Christie/Dir., CFO, Pres., John B. Blystone/Dir., William S. Dietrich/Dir., Michael J. Endres/Dir., Peter Karmanos/Dir., John R. Kasich/Dir., Carl A. Nelson/Dir., Sidney A. Ribeau/Dir., Mary F. Schiavo/Dir.

Owners: Insiders/4.90%, Michael J. Endres, Sidney A. Ribeau, John P. McConnell/3.10%, Capital Research and Management Company/5.20%, Snow Capital Management, L.P./7.70%, John R. Kasich, Carl A. Nelson, John S. Christie, Columbia Wanger Asset/5.70%, George P. Stoe, William S. Dietrich, Peter Karmanos, Mary Schiavo, John B. Blystone *(17 Owners included in Index)*

Financial Data: *Fiscal Year End:*05/31 *Latest Annual Data:* 05/31/2007

Year	Sales	Net Income
2007	$2,971,808,000	$113,905,000
2006	$2,897,179,000	$145,990,000
2005	$3,078,884,000	$179,412,000

Curr. Assets:	$996,241,000	**Curr. Liab.:**	$490,786,000	**P/E Ratio:**	15.78
Plant, Equip.:	$546,904,000	**Total Liab.:**	$955,091,000	**Indic. Yr. Divd.:**	$0.680
Total Assets:	$1,900,397,000	**Net Worth:**	$945,306,000	**Debt/ Equity:**	0.2726

WP Stewart & Co Ltd

527 Madison Ave., 20th Fl., New York, NY, 10022; *PH:* 1-212-750-8585; *Fax:* 1-212-980-8039; *http://* www.wpstewart.com; *Email:* info@wpstewart.com

General - Incorporation .... Bermuda
Employees 113
Auditor .... PricewaterhouseCoopers LLP
Stk Agt............ EquiServe Trust Co N.A
Counsel............ Dorsey & Whitney LLP
DUNS No. .... NA

Stock- Price on:12/24/2007 .... $10.39
Stock Exchange .... NYSE
Ticker Symbol .... WPL
Outstanding Shares 47,570,000
E.P.S. .... -$0.1
Shareholders .... NA

Business: The groups principle activity is to provide research-intensive equity investment management services. The group operates from United States.

Primary SIC and add'l.: 6282

CIK No: 0000750443

Subsidiaries: Cribewell Investments, NS Money Management Ltd., TPR Curacao N.V, TPRS Services N.V, W.P. Stewart & Co. (Europe), Ltd., W.P. Stewart & Co., Inc., W.P. Stewart Asset Management (Curacao), N.V, W.P. Stewart Asset Management (Europe), Ltd., W.P. Stewart Asset Management (Europe), N.V, W.P. Stewart Asset Management (NA), Inc., W.P. Stewart Asset Management Ltd., W.P. Stewart Asset Management, Inc., W.P. Stewart Fund Management Limited, W.P. Stewart Fund Management S.A, W.P. Stewart Securities Limited 17 Subsidiaries included in the Index

Officers: William P. Stewart/Chmn., CEO, Mark A. Henderson/Deputy MD, Co - Chmn. - WP Stewart Asset Management - Europe, Ltd, Rocco Macri/MD, COO, Michael W. Stamm/Deputy MD, General Counsel, Samantha Epstein/Analyst, Portfolio Mgr., Sr. VP, Edward C. Butler/CIO, Debra Randall/Sec., Frederick M. Ryan/Deputy MD - Investor Relations, Jack Mahler/Analyst, Portfolio Mgr., Sr. VP, Robert Kahn/Analyst, Portfolio Mgr., Dev Chakrabarti/Analyst - Europe, Stacey Brodbar/Analyst, Robert G. Gebhart/Analyst, Portfolio Mgr., Sr. VP, Robert Sterr/Analyst, Thomas M. Valenzuela/Analyst, Portfolio Mgr., Pres. *(49 Officers included in Index)*

Directors: William P. Stewart/Chmn., CEO, Mark A. Henderson/Deputy MD, Co - Chmn. - WP Stewart Asset Management - Europe, Ltd, Henry B. Smith/Dep. Chmn., Angus S. King/Dir., Jeremy W. Sillem/Dir., John C. Russell/Dir., Richard D. Spurling/Dir., Jan J. Spiering/Dir., Heinrich Spangler/Dir., Alfred J. Mulder/Dir., Dominik M.F. Brunner/Dir.

Owners: William P. Stewart/8.70%, Peter Jan P. Rubingh/1.59%, WPS II, Inc./40.10%, Van Den Berg Management/17.50%, Insiders

Financial Data: *Fiscal Year End:*12/31 *Latest Annual Data:* 12/31/2006

Year	Sales	Net Income
2006	$142,131,000	$37,475,000
2005	$147,855,000	$40,053,000
2004	$152,321,000	$63,149,000

Curr. Assets:	$48,394,000	**Curr. Liab.:**	$18,552,000		
Plant, Equip.:	$3,381,000	**Total Liab.:**	$33,785,000	**Indic. Yr. Divd.:**	$0.600
Total Assets:	$146,552,000	**Net Worth:**	$112,766,000	**Debt/ Equity:**	NA

WPCS International Inc

One E Uwchlan Ave., Ste. 301, Exton, PA, 19341; *PH:* 1-610-903-0400; *Fax:* 1-610-903-0401; *http://* www.wpcs.com; *Email:* info@wpcs.com

General - Incorporation .... DE
Employees 204
Auditor .... J.H. Cohn LLP
Stk Agt............ Interwest Transfer Company, Inc.
Counsel .... NA
DUNS No. .... NA

Stock- Price on:12/24/2007 .... $12.18
Stock Exchange .... NDQ
Ticker Symbol .... WPCS
Outstanding Shares 6,660,000
E.P.S. $0.72
Shareholders .... NA

Business: The groups principle activities include designing and deploying wireless networks services. The groups services include site design, spectrum analysis, engineering, trenching, electrical work, structured cabling, product integration, testing and project management. The groups operates through two segments namely specialty communication systems and wireless infrastructure services. In the year 2006, the group acquired New England Communication Systems, Inc. and Southeastern Communication Service, Inc. Specific customers of the group include CALTRANS, Amtrak, the New Jersey State Police and the State of New York, Mohegan Sun Hotel and Casino, and The Seminole Indian Nation. The group operates from the United States. The group's quarterly revenue in october 2007 was 28.11 millions of USD.

Primary SIC and add'l.: 7382 7389 3663 4812 3669 3661 4899

CIK No: 0001086745

Subsidiaries: Clayborn Contracting Group, Inc., Heinz Corporation, Invisinet, Inc., Quality Communications & Alarm Company, Inc., Walker Comm, Inc.

Officers: Andrew Hidalgo/Chmn., CEO/$238,800.00, Joseph Heater/CFO/$180,000.00, James Heinz/Exec. VP/$175,244.00, Richard Schubiger/Exec. VP/$247,829.00, Donald Walker/Exec. VP/$289,648.00, Brian Chang/Exec. VP, Charles Madenford/Exec. VP

Directors: Andrew Hidalgo/Chmn., CEO, Norm Dumbroff/Dir., Neil Hebenton/Dir., Gary Walker/Dir., William Whitehead/Dir.

Owners: Insiders/11.56%, Joseph Heater/1.45%, James Heinz/1.51%, Charles Madenford, William Whitehead, Special Situations Fund III QP, L.P./18.61%, SF Capital Partners Ltd./6.82%, Andrew Hidalgo/5.55%, Neil Hebenton, Gary Walker, Norm Dumbroff/1.33%, Richard Schubiger, Special Situations Private Equity Fund, L.P./13.75%

Financial Data: *Fiscal Year End:*04/30 *Latest Annual Data:* 4/30/2006

Year	Sales	Net Income
2006	$52,145,000	-$1,624,000
2005	$40,148,000	$1,329,000
2004	$22,076,000	-$124,000

Curr. Assets:	$27,433,000	**Curr. Liab.:**	$7,257,000		
Plant, Equip.:	$1,352,000	**Total Liab.:**	$11,559,000	**Indic. Yr. Divd.:**	NA
Total Assets:	$44,122,000	**Net Worth:**	$32,563,000	**Debt/ Equity:**	0.1003

WPP Group Plc

125 Pk. Ave., New York, NY, 10017; *PH:* 1-212-632-2200; *Fax:* 1-212-632-2222; *http://* www.wpp.com; *Email:* enquiries@wpp.com

General - Incorporation .... UK
Employees 98,000
Auditor .... Deloitte & Touche LLP
Stk Agt ..... American Stock Transfer & Trust Co.
Counsel............ Davis & Gilbert
DUNS No. 21-718-7160

Stock- Price on:12/24/2007 .... $72.93
Stock Exchange .... NDQ
Ticker Symbol .... WPPGY
Outstanding Shares 248,120,000
E.P.S. .... NA
Shareholders .... NA

Business: The group's principal activity is the provision of communications services. It operates in four divisions namely advertising & media investment management, information & consultancy, public relations/affairs and branding & identity, healthcare & specialist communications. The first division specialises in planning, creation and production of advertising for clients from radio commercials and posters to print, TV commercials and media research. Information & consultancy includes consumer, media, corporate communication and policy research. Public relations/affairs provides advice on corporate and financial communications. And the last division includes marketing services, corporate identity & design, audio-visual & multimedia communications. The group has 70,000 people working in 1,400 offices in 106 countries.

Primary SIC and add'l.: 8743 7311 8732 7389

CIK No: 0000806968

Subsidiaries: 10B Propaganda Ltda, 141 (Cambodia) Ltd, 141 (Hong Kong) Ltd, 141 Blue Skies Ltd, 141 Camarote SL, 141 France SA, 141 LLCChicago, 141 Worldwide Boomerang Inc., 141 Worldwide Pte Ltd, 141 Worldwide, SA de CV, 4D Communications Ltd, 85four Limited, A. Eicoff& Company, Inc., ABC Public Relations SA, Ablea Inc. 2663 Subsidiaries included in the Index

Officers: Richard Oldworth/CEO - Buchanan Communications, Claire Elliot/Contact, Chris Sweetland/Deputy Group Dir. - Finance, Fran Butera/Dir. - Investor Relations, Feona McEwan/Group Communications Dir., Kevin McCormack/US Press Relations, Martin Sorrell/Chief Executive, Mark Read/Strategy Dir., Paul Richardson/Dir. - Finance

Directors: Philip Lader/Non Exec. Chmn., Colin Day/52/Non Exec. Dir., Jeffrey Rosen/Non Exec. Dir., Christopher MacKenzie/Non Exec. Dir., Timothy Shriver/Non Exec. Dir., Lubna Olayan/52/Non Exec. Dir., Orit Gadiesh/57/Non Exec. Dir., David H. Komansky/69/Non Exec. Dir., Koichiro Naganuma/63/Non Exec. Dir., John Quelch/56/Non Exec. Dir., Stanley Morten/Non Exec. Dir., Paul Spencer/Non Exec. Dir., Esther Dyson/56/Non Exec. Dir.

Owners: MFS Investment Management/4.80%, WPP ESOPs/4.20%

Financial Data: *Fiscal Year End:*12/31 *Latest Annual Data:* 12/31/2006

Year	Sales	Net Income
2006	$11,573,971,000	$679,808,000
2005	$9,247,063,000	$432,609,000
2004	$37,757,507,000	$287,641,000

Curr. Assets:	$13,642,389,000	**Curr. Liab.:**	$15,837,364,000	**P/E Ratio:**	31.70
Plant, Equip.:	$813,614,000	**Total Liab.:**	$21,317,947,000	**Indic. Yr. Divd.:**	NA
Total Assets:	$29,931,913,000	**Net Worth:**	$8,613,967,000	**Debt/ Equity:**	NA

WPT Enterprises Inc

1041 N Formosa Ave., Formosa Bldg, Ste. 99, West Hollywood, CA, 90046; *PH:* 1-323-330-9900; *http://* www.worldpokertour.com; *Email:* wpt@worldpokertour.com

General - Incorporation .... DE
Employees 88
Auditor .... Piercy, Bowler, Taylor & Kern
Stk Agt .... NA
Counsel .... NA
DUNS No. .... NA

Stock- Price on:12/24/2007 .... $4.14
Stock Exchange .... NDQ
Ticker Symbol .... WPTE
Outstanding Shares 20,380,000
E.P.S. $0.09
Shareholders .... NA

Business: The group's principal activity is to develop, produce and market television programs and live events. The group is also engaged in licensing and sale of consumer entertainment products. The groups operates in three units, wpt studios, wpt consumer products and wpt corporate alliances. Wpt studios provides licensing of broadcast and telecast rights and membership fees from casinos and cardrooms that host the televised world poker tour events. Wpt consumer products provides licensing and direct sale of merchandise of world poker tour brand, and wpt corporate alliances provide corporate sponsorships that include elements of on-air visibility, corporate live event sponsorship, promotional sponsorships and corporate hospitality events.

Primary SIC and add'l.: 7812

CIK No: 0001283843

Officers: Steven Lipscomb/Founder, CEO, Pres., Peter Hughes/COO, Adam Pliska/General Counsel, Scott A. Friedman/CFO, Linda Johnson/Poker Relations Consultant, Mike Sexton/Television Commentator, Poker Relations Consultant, Robyn Moder/Exec. VP - WPT Studios

Directors: Steven Lipscomb/Founder, CEO, Pres., Lyle Berman/65/Chmn.

Owners: Michael Beindorff, Mimi Rogers, Steven Lipscomb, Scott A. Friedman, Lakes Entertainment, Inc., Peter Hughes, Glenn Padnick, Joseph S. Carson, Lyle Berman, Ray M. Moberg, Insiders, Galleon Management L.P., Robyn Moder, Bradley Berman, Timothy J. Cope

Financial Data: Fiscal Year End:01/01   Latest Annual Data: 12/31/2006

Year	Sales		Net Income
2006	$29,261,000		$7,769,000
2005	$17,557,000		$752,000
Curr. Assets:	$44,433,000	Curr. Liab.: $8,089,000	P/E Ratio: 46.00
Plant, Equip.:	$3,375,000	Total Liab.: $8,089,000	Indic. Yr. Divd.: NA
Total Assets:	$51,340,000	Net Worth: $43,251,000	Debt/ Equity: NA

WQN Inc

509 Madison Ave., Ste. 1510, New York, NY, 10022; **PH:** 1-212-774-3655; **http://** www.wqn.com; **Email:** support@wqn.com

General - Incorporation	DE	**Stock** - Price on:12/24/2007	$0.151
Employees	2	Stock Exchange	OTC
Auditor	Grant Thornton LLP	Ticker Symbol	WQNI
Stk Agt	Securities Transfer Corp	Outstanding Shares	6,880,000
Counsel	NA	E.P.S.	$0.04
DUNS No.	NA	Shareholders	NA

Business: The group's principal activity is to sell virtual prepaid calling cards through its Internet Website and transmits long distance calls through its Internet and traditional networks. It markets an intelligent address book and calendar that enables customers to make domestic and international phone calls from anywhere in the world through its Website. It also provides a Web service that enables customers to send money and personalized messages from the United States, Canada and the United Kingdom to India, sri lanka, the Philippines and Russia. In Sept 2002, the group began selling a new multi-purpose stored-value card, the worldquest cashcard, which can be used to withdraw money or check balances at ATM's worldwide and to pay for merchandise at any location associated. On 12-Apr-2004, the group acquired valucom(tm).

Primary SIC and add'l.: 4813 7375

CIK No: 0001089932

Subsidiaries: buyindiaonline.com, Inc., Park Ave. Assoc. LLC

Financial Data: Fiscal Year End:12/31   Latest Annual Data: 12/31/2005

Year	Sales		Net Income
2005	NA		$280,000
2004	$15,264,000		-$3,174,000
2003	$9,915,000		-$3,345,000
Curr. Assets:	$6,279,000	Curr. Liab.: $4,061,000	P/E Ratio: 3.78
Plant, Equip.:	$10,000	Total Liab.: $4,061,000	Indic. Yr. Divd.: NA
Total Assets:	$22,278,000	Net Worth: $18,217,000	Debt/ Equity: NA

Wright Express Corp

97 Darling Ave., South Portland, ME, 04106; **PH:** 1-207-773-8171; **http://** www.wrightexpress.com

General - Incorporation	DE	**Stock** - Price on:12/24/2007	$33.07
Employees	685	Stock Exchange	NYSE
Auditor	Deloitte & Touche LLP	Ticker Symbol	WXS
Stk Agt	American Stock Transfer & Trust Co.	Outstanding Shares	39,940,000
Counsel	Wilmer Cutler Pickering H & D LLP	E.P.S.	$1.66
DUNS No.	NA	Shareholders	NA

Business: The groups principle activity is to provide payment processing and information management services to the vehicle fleet industry. The group operates through two segments namely, fleet and master card. The group operates from the United States. The groups quarterly revenue for September 2007 was 87.65 millions of USD.

Primary SIC and add'l.: 7375 7374 7389

CIK No: 0001309108

Subsidiaries: Wright Express Canada, Inc., Wright Express Financial Services Corporation, Wright Express Fueling Solutions, Inc., Wright Express UK Limited

Officers: Michael E. Dubyak/Dir., CEO, Pres., Melissa D. Smith/CFO, Exec. VP - Finance, Operations, David D. Maxsimic/Exec. VP - Sales, Marketing, Robert C. Cornett/Sr. VP - Human Resources, Chief People Officer, Hilary A. Rapkin/Sr. VP, General Counsel, Corp. Sec., Jamie Morin/Sr. VP - Client Services Organization, George Hogan/CIO, Sr. VP

Directors: Michael E. Dubyak/Dir., CEO, Pres., Rowland T. Moriarty/Chmn., Shikhar Ghosh/Dir., Ronald T. Maheu/Dir., Larry McTavish/Dir., Kirk Pond/Dir., Regina O. Sommer/Dir., Jack A. Vanwoerkom/Dir.

Owners: Tod A. Demeter, Kirk P. Pond, David D. Maxsimic, Insiders, Jack VanWoerkom, Wellington Management Company, LLP/6.30%, Neuberger Berman LLC/7.00%, Michael E. Dubyak, Melissa D. Smith, Rowland T. Moriarty, TimesSquare Capital Management, LLC/7.40%, Katherine M. Greenleaf, Munder Capital Management/5.50%, Regina O. Sommer

Financial Data: Fiscal Year End:12/31   Latest Annual Data: 12/31/2006

Year	Sales		Net Income
2006	$291,247,000		$74,609,000
2005	$241,333,000		$18,653,000
2004	$189,100,000		$51,219,000
Curr. Assets:	$837,225,000	Curr. Liab.: $784,075,000	P/E Ratio: 29.58
Plant, Equip.:	$39,970,000	Total Liab.: $1,357,888,000	Indic. Yr. Divd.: NA
Total Assets:	$1,551,015,000	Net Worth: $183,127,000	Debt/ Equity: NA

Wright Medical Group Inc

5677 Airline Rd. , Arlington, TN, 38002; **PH:** 1-908-867-9971; **http://** www.wmt.com; **Email:** investorrelations@wmt.com

General - Incorporation	DE	**Stock** - Price on:12/24/2007	$25.31
Employees	1,060	Stock Exchange	NDQ
Auditor	KPMG LLP	Ticker Symbol	WMGI
Stk Agt	American Stock Transfer & Trust Co.	Outstanding Shares	35,430,000
Counsel	Baker, Donelson, Bearman & Caldwell	E.P.S.	$0.29
DUNS No.	NA	Shareholders	NA

Business: The group's principal activity are to design, manufacture and market reconstructive joint devices and bio-orthopaedic materials. The reconstructive joint devices are used to replace knee, hip and other joints that have deteriorated through disease or injury. The bio-orthopaedic materials are used to replace damaged or diseased bone and to stimulate natural bone growth. The group focuses on the higher-growth sector of advanced knee implants, bone-conserving hip implants, revision replacement implants and extremity implants, as well as on the integration of bio-orthopaedic products into reconstructive joint procedures.the group operates in the United States, Europe, Canada, Japan and other foreign countries. In Mar 2003, the group acquired certain assets from gliatech inc.

Primary SIC and add'l.: 3842

CIK No: 0001137861

Subsidiaries: 2Hip Holdings SAS, Cremascoli Ortho SA, Wright Cremascoli Ortho NV, Wright Medical Capital, Inc., Wright Medical Europe Manufacturing SA, Wright Medical Europe SA, Wright Medical Europe Trading SNC, Wright Medical France SAS, Wright Medical Germany GmbH, Wright Medical Italy Srl, Wright Medical Japan, K.K., Wright Medical Netherlands, B.V., Wright Medical Technology Canada Ltd., Wright Medical Technology, Inc., Wright Medical UK Limited

Officers: Gary D. Henley/Dir., CEO, Pres./$864,739.00, Barry F. Bays/Executive Chmn./$1,686,731.00, Eric A. Stookey/VP - North American Sales, Steve Gitlelis/Physician - Chicago, IL, Jonathan Garino/Physician - Philadelphia, PA, John S. Woodward/Physician - Englewood, CO, Harris Yett/Physician - Brookline, MA, John R. Treace/Exec. VP - North American Sales, Rich Rosa/Physician - West Orange, NJ, Chris Leslie/Physician - Camdenton, MO, Paul Beaule/Physician - Los Angeles, CA, Benjamin Bierbaum/Physician - Brookline, MA, Frederick V. Coville/Physician - Englewood, CO, John K. Davis/Physician - Englewood, CO, Dan Daluga/Physician - Lafayette, IN *(54 Officers included in Index)*

Directors: Gary D. Henley/Dir., CEO, Pres., Barry F. Bays/Executive Chmn., Martin J. Emerson/Dir., Thomas E. Timbie/Dir., Robert J. Quillinan/Dir., David D. Stevens/54/Dir., James T. Treace/Dir., Lawrence W. Hamilton/Dir., John L. Miclot/Dir.

Owners: Wellington Management Company, LLP/6.30%, Neuberger Berman Inc./6.10%, David D. Stevens, John R. Treace, Beverly A. Huss, James T. Treace, Gary D. Henley, T. Rowe Price Associates, Inc./6.40%, BlackRock, Inc./12.00%, Barry F. Bays, Thomas E. Timbie, Insiders/4.80%, Martin J. Emerson, Jason P. Hood, John K. Bakewell *(16 Owners included in Index)*

Financial Data: Fiscal Year End:12/31   Latest Annual Data: 12/31/2006

Year	Sales		Net Income
2006	$338,938,000		$14,411,000
2005	$319,137,000		$21,065,000
2004	$297,539,000		$24,022,000
Curr. Assets:	$279,722,000	Curr. Liab.: $59,416,000	P/E Ratio: 58.86
Plant, Equip.:	$86,265,000	Total Liab.: $73,578,000	Indic. Yr. Divd.: NA
Total Assets:	$409,402,000	Net Worth: $335,824,000	Debt/ Equity: 0.0017

WSFS Financial Corp

838 Market St., Wilmington, DE, 19801; **PH:** 1-302-792-6000; **http://** www.wsfsbank.com

General - Incorporation	DE	**Stock** - Price on:12/24/2007	$63.98
Employees	573	Stock Exchange	NDQ
Auditor	KPMG LLP	Ticker Symbol	WSFS
Stk Agt	American Stock Transfer & Trust Co.	Outstanding Shares	6,290,000
Counsel	NA	E.P.S.	$4.52
DUNS No.	36-445-9602	Shareholders	NA

Business: The group's principal activity is to provide banking services in the United States. The group provides residential and commercial real estate, commercial and consumer lending services, retail deposit and cash management services. The group conducts operations from its main office, two operations centers and 21 retail banking offices located in northern Delaware and southeastern Pennsylvania. The group accepts various deposit programs, which include savings account, demand deposits, interest-bearing demand deposits, money market deposit and certificate of deposits. The group sold wilmington finance, inc. In jan-2003.

Primary SIC and add'l.: 6035 6712

CIK No: 0000828944

Officers: Mark A. Turner/Dir., CEO, Pres./$549,017.00, Stephen A. Fowle/CFO/$331,604.00, Deborah A. Powell/49/Exec. VP, Dir. - Human Resources/$297,168.00, Karl L. Johnston/57/COO, Chief Lending Officer/$504,237.00, Rodger Levenson/Exec. VP, Dir. - Commercial Banking, Richard M. Wright/Exec. VP, Dir. - Retail Banking, Barbara J. Fischer/Exec. VP, Chief Administrative Officer, Peggy Eddens/Exec. VP, Dir. - Human Capital Management, Cynthia A. Cole/Exec. VP, Dir. - Marketing, Robert F. Mack/Sr. VP, Controller

Directors: Mark A. Turner/Dir., CEO, Pres., Charles G. Cheleden/Vice Chmn., Marvin N. Schoenhals/58/Chmn., Claibourne D. Smith/Dir., John F. Downey/Dir., Joseph R. Julian/Dir., Calvert A. Morgan/Dir., Eugene W. Weaver/Member - Advisory Board, Dennis E. Klima/Dir., David E. Hollowell/Dir., Thomas P. Preston/Dir., Linda C. Drake/Dir., Scott E. Reed/Dir., Ted R. Weschler/Dir., Dale E. Wolf/Member - Advisory Board

Owners: JPMorgan Chase & Co./5.45%, Wellington Management Company, LLP/5.51%, Barclays Global Investors, NA/6.22%, Private Capital Management/10.16%

Financial Data: Fiscal Year End:12/31   Latest Annual Data: 12/31/2006

Year	Sales		Net Income
2006	$219,463,000		$30,441,000
2005	$171,280,000		$27,856,000
2004	$136,060,000		$25,900,000
Curr. Assets:	$280,693,000	Curr. Liab.: $2,640,032,000	P/E Ratio: 14.22
Plant, Equip.:	$30,606,000	Total Liab.: $2,785,337,000	Indic. Yr. Divd.: $0.400
Total Assets:	$2,997,396,000	Net Worth: $212,059,000	Debt/ Equity: 0.7192

WSI Industries Inc

213 Chelsea Rd. , Monticello, MN, 55362; **PH:** 1-763-295-9202; **http://** www.wsci.com

General - Incorporation .... MN
Employees 62
Auditor .... Schechter Dokken Kanter
Stk Agt.......... Wells Fargo Shareowner Services
Counsel .... NA
DUNS No. 00-625-3041

Stock- Price on:12/24/2007 .... $4.74
Stock Exchange .... NDQ
Ticker Symbol .... WSCI
Outstanding Shares 2,700,000
E.P.S. $0.27
Shareholders .... NA

Business: The group's principal activity is to manufacture metal components in medium to high volumes requiring tolerances as close as one ten-thousandth of an inch. The tools are manufactured in accordance with the customer specifications. These components are used in aerospace, avionics industry and recreational vehicles market. The group's major customers include deer & co, rockwell collins, inc and polaris industries, inc.

Primary SIC and add'l.: 3599

CIK No: 0000104897

Officers: Mike Pudil/CEO, Pres., Michael J. Pudil/Chmn., CEO, Pres. , Paul D. Sheely/VP, Treasurer

Directors: Michael J. Pudil/Chmn., CEO, Pres. , Thomas C. Bender/Dir., Burton F. Myers/54/Dir., Paul Baszucki/Dir., Melvin L. Katten/Dir., George J. Martin/Dir., Eugene J. Mora/73/Dir.

Owners: George J. Martin/1.20%, Insiders/6.00%, Eugene J. Mora, Paul Baszucki, Michael J. Pudil/1.90%, Paul D. Sheely, Melvin L. Katten/1.70%

Financial Data: **Fiscal Year End:**08/28 **Latest Annual Data:** 8/27/2006

Year	Sales	Net Income
2006	$16,092,000	$573,000
2005	$15,654,000	$335,000
2004	$11,525,000	$49,000

Curr. Assets:	$3,267,000	**Curr. Liab.:**	$1,511,000	**P/E Ratio:**	18.96
Plant, Equip.:	$3,839,000	**Total Liab.:**	$4,124,000	**Indic. Yr. Divd.:**	$0.150
Total Assets:	$11,193,000	**Net Worth:**	$7,069,000	**Debt/ Equity:**	0.3501

WVS Financial Corp

9001 Perry Hwy, Pittsburgh, PA, 15237; *PH:* 1-412-364-1911; *http://* www.wvsbank.com; *Email:* info@wvsbank.com

General - Incorporation .... PA
Employees 36
Auditor .... S R Snodgrass, A.C
Stk Agt.......... Registrar & Transfer Co
Counsel.......... Bruggeman & Linn
DUNS No. 82-743-3582

Stock- Price on:12/24/2007 .... $16.4
Stock Exchange .... NDQ
Ticker Symbol .... WVFC
Outstanding Shares 2,320,000
E.P.S. $1.63
Shareholders .... NA

Business: The group's principal activity is to provide community banking services to individuals and businesses. It operates through its subsidiary west view savings bank. The group provides single-family and multi-family residential real estate loans, commercial real estate loans, construction loans and consumer loans. In addition, it also provides land acquisition and development loans, drive up banking facilities and automated teller machine services. The group operates six offices located in the north hills suburbs of pittsburgh.

Primary SIC and add'l.: 6035 6712

CIK No: 0000910679

Subsidiaries: West View Savings Bank

Officers: David J. Bursic/46/Dir., CEO, Pres./$302,806.00, Keith A. Simpson/51/Treasurer, Chief Accounting Officer, VP, Principal Accounting Officer/$76,223.00, Bernard P. Lefke/57/VP, Jonathan D. Hoover/40/Sr. VP

Directors: David J. Bursic/46/Dir., CEO, Pres., Lawrence M. Lehman/56/Dir., David L. Aeberli/71/Dir., Arthur H. Brandt/Dir., Donald E. Hook/79/Dir., Margaret Vonderau/68/Dir., John W. Grace/65/Dir.

Owners: Keith A. Simpson/0.80%, Donald E. Hook/1.20%, John W. Grace/0.20%, Arthur H. Brandt/2.00%, Margaret VonDerau/4.90%, David J. Bursic/7.80%, David L. Aeberli/1.90%, Lawrence M. Lehman/0.30%, Insiders/20.50%, WVS Financial Corp. Employee/10.00%

Financial Data: **Fiscal Year End:**06/30 **Latest Annual Data:** 06/30/2007

Year	Sales	Net Income
2007	$24,936,000	$3,646,000
2006	$22,953,000	$2,846,000
2005	$18,866,000	$2,909,000

Curr. Assets:	$4,117,000	**Curr. Liab.:**	$176,314,000	**P/E Ratio:**	10.45
Plant, Equip.:	$864,000	**Total Liab.:**	$392,324,000	**Indic. Yr. Divd.:**	$0.640
Total Assets:	$421,742,000	**Net Worth:**	$29,418,000	**Debt/ Equity:**	4.3455

WWA Group Inc

2465 W 12th St., Ste. 2, Tempe, AZ, 85281; *PH:* 1-480-505-0070; *http://* www.wwagroup.com

General - Incorporation .... NV
Employees 39
Auditor .... Williams & Webster, P.S
Stk Agt.......... Interwest Transfer Company, Inc.
Counsel.......... Robert N. Wilkinson Esq
DUNS No. .... NA

Stock- Price on:12/24/2007 .... $0.79
Stock Exchange .... OTC
Ticker Symbol .... WWAG
Outstanding Shares 17,220,000
E.P.S. $0.07
Shareholders .... NA

Business: The group is in its development stage. In 2002, the group abandoned the breast implant business. At present, the group is considering business opportunities either through merger or acquisition. Currently the group does not have any operations. On 08-Aug-2003, the group acquired world wide auctioneers ltd.

Primary SIC and add'l.: 9999

CIK No: 0001036478

Subsidiaries: World Wide Auctioneers, Ltd

Officers: Eric Montandon/Chmn., CEO, Young Yong/VP - Business Development, Keith Lupton/Dir., VP - Sales, Digamber Naswa/Dir., CFO, Robert N. Wilkinson/Corporate Legal Counsel, Chris Bettinson/48/Dir., GM, James Jackson/Contact - International Investor Relations

Directors: Eric Montandon/Chmn., CEO, Digamber Naswa/Dir., CFO, Keith Lupton/Dir., VP - Sales, Yogesh Saxena/Dir., Chris Bettinson/48/Dir., GM

Owners: Insiders/4.12%, Asia8, Inc./3.96%, Adderley Davis & Associates/5.10%, Eric Montandon/41.20%, Digamber Naswa

Financial Data: **Fiscal Year End:**12/31 **Latest Annual Data:** 12/31/2006

Year	Sales	Net Income
2006	$17,622,000	$1,180,000
2005	$16,313,000	$1,128,000
2004	$10,976,000	$774,000

Curr. Assets:	$8,976,000	**Curr. Liab.:**	$10,482,000	**P/E Ratio:**	13.17
Plant, Equip.:	$4,275,000	**Total Liab.:**	$10,571,000	**Indic. Yr. Divd.:**	NA
Total Assets:	$14,813,000	**Net Worth:**	$4,241,000	**Debt/ Equity:**	0.0146

Wyeth

5 Giralda Farms, Madison, NJ, 07940; *PH:* 1-973-660-5000; *http://* www.wyeth.com

General - Incorporation .... DE
Employees 50,060
Auditor .... PricewaterhouseCoopers LLP
Stk Agt .... Bank of New York
Counsel.......... NA
DUNS No. 00-131-7130

Stock- Price on:12/24/2007 .... $58.46
Stock Exchange .... NYSE
Ticker Symbol .... WYE
Outstanding Shares 1,350,000,000
E.P.S. $3.26
Shareholders .... NA

Business: The groups principle activity is to provide pharmaceutical and health care products that improve lives and deliver outstanding value to our customers and shareholders.The groups products include Advil(R), Alavert(R) and Anbesol(R). The group operates from United States.

Primary SIC and add'l.: 2879 2833 2834

CIK No: 0000005187

Subsidiaries: A H Investments LTD., AC Acquisition Holding Company, AHP Finance Ireland Limited, AHP Manufacturing B.V., Ayerst-Wyeth Pharmaceuticals Incorporated, Berdan Insurance Company, CICL Corporation, Dimminaco AG, Genetics Institute, LLC, John Wyeth& Brother Limited, Laboratorios Wyeth-Whitehall Ltda., Route 24 Holdings, Inc., Wyeth Australia Pty. Limited, Wyeth Canada , Wyeth Consumer Healthcare Inc. 32 Subsidiaries included in the Index

Officers: Robert Essner/Chmn., CEO/$32,846,960.00, Kenneth J. Martin/53/Vice Chmn., CFO/$10,726,220.00, Bernard J. Poussot/Vice Chmn., COO, Pres./$14,408,850.00, Joseph M. Mahady/54/Sr. VP, Pres. - Global Business, Wyeth Pharmaceuticals/$8,379,986.00, Lawrence V. Stein/58/Sr. VP, General Counsel, Thomas E. Corcoran/60/Pres. - Fort Dodge Animal Health Division, Mary Katherine Wold/55/Sr. VP - Finance, Robert R. Ruffolo/57/Sr. VP/$8,587,811.00, Kevin Wiggins/Contact - Media, International, Greg Norden/CFO, Sr. VP, Jeffrey E. Keisling/VP - Corporate Information Services, CIO, James J. Pohlman/VP - Corporate Strategic Initiatives, Steven A. Tasher/VP - Environmental Affairs, Facilities Operations, Assoc. General Counsel, Justin R. Victoria/VP - Investor Relations, Ulf Wiinberg/49/Sr. VP *(30 Officers included in Index)*

Directors: Robert Essner/Chmn., CEO, Bernard J. Poussot/Vice Chmn., COO, Pres., Frances D. Fergusson/Dir., Ivan G. Seidenberg/Dir., Walter V. Shipley/Dir., Robert M. Amen/Dir., Raymond J. McGuire/Dir., John D. Feerick/Dir., John R. Torell/Dir., John P. Mascotte/Dir., Victor F. Ganzi/Dir., Robert Langer/Dir., Mary Lake Polan/Dir., Gary L. Rogers/Dir.

Owners: Joseph M. Mahady, Robert Langer, Victor F. Ganzi, Robert Essner, Walter V. Shipley, Bernard Poussot, Kenneth J. Martin, John P. Mascotte, John R. Torell, Frances D. Fergusson, Robert R. Ruffolo, Mary Lake Polan, John D. Feerick, Ivan G. Seidenberg, Gary L. Rogers *(17 Owners included in Index)*

Financial Data: **Fiscal Year End:**12/31 **Latest Annual Data:** 12/31/2006

Year	Sales	Net Income
2006	$20,350,655,000	$4,196,706,000
2005	$18,755,790,000	$3,656,298,000
2004	$17,358,028,000	$1,233,997,000

Curr. Assets:	$17,514,241,000	**Curr. Liab.:**	$7,221,848,000	**P/E Ratio:**	18.44
Plant, Equip.:	$10,146,259,000	**Total Liab.:**	$21,825,960,000	**Indic. Yr. Divd.:**	NA
Total Assets:	$36,478,715,000	**Net Worth:**	$14,652,755,000	**Debt/ Equity:**	0.7537

Wyndham Worldwide Corp

Seven Sylvan Way, Parsippany, NJ, 07054; ; *http://* www.wyndhamworldwide.com

General - Incorporation .... DE
Employees 30,100
Auditor .... Deloitte & Touche LLP
Stk Agt .... Mellon Investor Services LLC
Counsel.......... NA
DUNS No. .... NA

Stock- Price on:12/24/2007 .... $36.6
Stock Exchange .... NYSE
Ticker Symbol .... WYN
Outstanding Shares 182,300,000
E.P.S. $2.10
Shareholders .... NA

Business: The groups principle activity is to provide management services. The group operates through four segments namely, luxury, upscale, midscale and economy. The group operates from the United States, Europe, the Middle East and Africa, Australia and Netherlands. The group's quarterly revenue for September 2007 was 1,216.00 millions of USD.

Primary SIC and add'l.: 7011

CIK No: 0001361658

Subsidiaries: EMEA Holdings C.V., RCI Global Vacation Network, Inc., Resorts, Inc., Wyndham Consumer Finance, Inc., Wyndham Hotel Group, LLC, Wyndham Resort Development, Wyndham Vacation Ownership, Inc., Wyndham Vacation Resorts, Inc., Wyndham Worldwide Corporation

Officers: Stephen P. Holmes/Chmn., CEO/$11,482,620.00, Franz S. Hanning/CEO, Pres. - Wyndham Vacation Ownership/$4,288,844.00, Kenneth N. May/57/CEO, Pres. - RCI Global Vacation Network/$3,022,116.00, Steven A. Rudnitsky/CEO, Pres. - Wyndham Hotel Group/$3,322,508.00, Virginia M. Wilson/CFO, Exec. VP/$3,073,549.00, Scott G. McLester/Exec. VP, General Counsel, Tom Anderson/Chief Real Estate Development Officer, Exec. VP, Mary R. Falvey/Chief Human Resources Officer, Exec. VP, Nicola Rossi/Chief Accounting Officer, Sr. VP, Lynn A. Feldman/Sr. VP, Deputy General Counsel, Corp. Sec.

Directors: Stephen P. Holmes/Chmn., CEO, Myra J. Biblowit/Dir., James E. Buckman/Dir., George Herrera/Dir., Brian Mulroney/Dir., Pauline D.E. Richards/Dir., Michael H. Wargotz/Dir.

Owners: Myra J. Biblowit, Pauline D.E. Richards, George Herrera, Michael H. Wargotz, Barclays Global Investors, N.A./6.39%, Kenneth N. May, Steven A. Rudnitsky, The Right Honourable Brian Mulroney, Virginia M. Wilson, Franz S. Hanning, James E. Buckman, Insiders/1.11%, Stephen P. Holmes

Financial Data: **Fiscal Year End:**12/31 **Latest Annual Data:** 03/31/2007

Year	Sales	Net Income
2007	NA	NA
2006	$3,842,000,000	$287,000,000

Curr. Assets:	$2,052,000,000	**Curr. Liab.:**	$1,977,000,000		
Plant, Equip.:	$1,350,000,000	**Total Liab.:**	$5,961,000,000	**Indic. Yr. Divd.:**	$0.160
Total Assets:	$9,520,000,000	**Net Worth:**	$3,559,000,000	**Debt/ Equity:**	NA

Wynn Resorts Ltd

3131 Las Vegas Blvd. S, Las Vegas, NV, 89109; **PH:** 1-702-770-7555; **Fax:** 1-702-697-5009; **http://** www.wynnresorts.com; **Email:** investorrelations@wynnresorts.com

General - Incorporation	NV	**Stock**- Price on:12/24/2007	$90.97
Employees	15,500	Stock Exchange	NDQ
Auditor	Ernst & Young, LLP	Ticker Symbol	WYNN
Stk Agt	American Registrar & Transfer Co	Outstanding Shares	101,970,000
Counsel	Skadden, Meagher & Flom LLP	E.P.S	$7.46
DUNS No.	NA	Shareholders	NA

Business: The group's principal activities are to own and operate wynn las vegas a preeminent luxury hotel and destination casino resort in las vegas. The resort features approximately 2,700 luxurious guest-rooms, a casually elegant approximately 111,000 square foot casino, 18 distinctive dining outlets, an exclusive on-site 18-hole championship golf course and a new water-based entertainment production.

Primary SIC and add'l.: 5812 7011

CIK No: 0001174922

Subsidiaries: B/W Clothiers, LLC, Kevyn, LLC, Las Vegas Jet, LLC, PW Automotive, LLC, Rambas, LLC, Toasty, LLC, Valvino Lamore, LLC, World Travel G-IV, LLC, World Travel, LLC, Worldwide Wynn, LLC, Wynn Coati Holding Company, Ltd., Wynn Completion Guarantor, LLC, Wynn Design & Development, LLC, Wynn Gallery, LLC, Wynn Golf, LLC 29 Subsidiaries included in the Index

Officers: Stephen A. Wynn/Chmn., CEO, Andrew Pascal/Pres., COO - Wynn Las Vegas, LLC, Ronald J. Kramer/Dir., Pres., John Strzemp/CFO, Exec. VP, Deruyter O. Butler/Exec. VP - Architecture, Wynn Design, Development, LLC, Marc D. Schorr/COO, Roger P. Thomas/Exec. VP - Design, Wynn Design, Development, LLC, Grant R. Bowie/50/Pres. - Wynn Resorts, Macau, SA, David R. Sisk/Sr. VP, Matt Maddox/Treasurer, Linda Chen/Pres. - Wynn International Marketing, Ltd, Kim Sinatra/Sr. VP, General Counsel, Sec., Ian Coughlan/Pres. - Wynn Resorts, Macau, SA, Maurice Wooden/COO - Wynn Las Vegas, LLC

Directors: Stephen A. Wynn/Chmn., CEO, Kazuo Okada/Vice Chmn., Elaine P. Wynn/Dir., John A. Moran/Dir., Ronald J. Kramer/Dir., Pres., Allan Zeman/Dir., Alvin V. Shoemaker/Dir., Robert J. Miller/Dir., Boone D. Wayson/Dir.

Owners: Allan Zeman, Linda Chen, Marc D. Schorr, Robert J. Miller, Baron Capital Group, Inc., Kazuo Okada, Stanley R. Zax, T. Rowe Price Associates, Inc., Boone D. Wayson, Marsico Capital Management, LLC, Insiders, Elaine P. Wynn, Aruze USA, Inc., Alvin V. Shoemaker, John A. Moran *(18 Owners included in Index)*

Financial Data: *Fiscal Year End:*12/31 *Latest Annual Data:* 12/31/2006

Year	**Sales**	**Net Income**
2006	$1,432,257,000	$628,728,000
2005	$721,981,000	-$90,836,000
2004	$195,000	-$205,586,000

Curr. Assets:	$1,095,791,000	**Curr. Liab.:**	$511,087,000	**P/E Ratio:**	14.58
Plant, Equip.:	$3,157,622,000	**Total Liab.:**	$3,014,595,000	**Indic. Yr. Divd.:**	NA
Total Assets:	$4,660,180,000	**Net Worth:**	$1,645,585,000	**Debt/ Equity:**	1.3597

X-Change Corp

710 Century Pkwy., Ste. 110, Allen, TX, 75002; **PH:** 1-972-747-0051; **Fax:** 1-972-359-6334; **http://** www.x-changecorp.com

General - Incorporation	NV	**Stock**- Price on:12/24/2007	$0.2
Employees	14	Stock Exchange	OTC
Auditor	Robison, Hill & Co	Ticker Symbol	XCHC
Stk Agt	Signature Stock Transfer, Inc.	Outstanding Shares	29,960,000
Counsel	NA	E.P.S	-$0.08
DUNS No.	84-979-7501	Shareholders	NA

Business: The group's principle activities include developing, marketing and hosting an Internet accessible trading market for securities that are currently quoted on the otc bulletin board. Upon establishment of the company's trading market, the company intends to offer access to its Web site on a subscription basis and intends to charge transaction fees for all transactions that are processed through the system. The group operates from United States.

Primary SIC and add'l.: 9999

CIK No: 0000054424

Subsidiaries: AirGATE Technologies, Inc., OIL ID Systems, Inc

Officers: Michael L. Sheriff/Chmn., CEO, Pres., Scott R. Thompson/45/Dir., Treasurer, Sec., Ivan Chow/CTO, Sr. VP - Software Solutions, Robert Barbee/VP - Operations, Kathleen Hanafan/Dir., COO, George Decourcy/CFO, Mike Sheriff/Contact - Investor Relations, Frank Kwong/CIO

Directors: Michael L. Sheriff/Chmn., CEO, Pres., Scott R. Thompson/45/Dir., Treasurer, Sec., Kathleen Hanafan/Dir., COO, David Friedman/Dir.

Owners: Frank Kwong/5.40%, Michael Sheriff/23.31%, Insiders/24.18%, Scott R. Thompson/0.88%

Financial Data: *Fiscal Year End:*12/31 *Latest Annual Data:* 12/31/2006

Year	**Sales**	**Net Income**
2006	$1,155,000	-$1,036,000
2005	$567,000	-$364,000
2004	$37,000	-$74,000

Curr. Assets:	$195,000	**Curr. Liab.:**	$549,000		
Plant, Equip.:	$69,000	**Total Liab.:**	$1,359,000	**Indic. Yr. Divd.:**	NA
Total Assets:	$483,000	**Net Worth:**	-$876,000	**Debt/ Equity:**	NA

X-Rite Inc

3100 44th St. SW, Grandville, MI, 49418; **PH:** 1-616-534-7664; **http://** www.xrite.com; **Email:** info@xrite.com

General - Incorporation	MI	**Stock**- Price on:12/24/2007	$14.86
Employees	968	Stock Exchange	NDQ
Auditor	Ernst & Young LLP	Ticker Symbol	XRIT
Stk Agt	Computershare Investor Services LLC	Outstanding Shares	29,070,000
Counsel	Varnum, Riddering	E.P.S	-$0.61
DUNS No.	00-602-6553	Shareholders	NA

Business: The group's principal activity is to develop, manufacture and sell technically sophisticated instrumentation and software solutions for color, and shape measurement applications. The group's products include micro-spot spectrodensitometer, auto tracking densitometer, integrated spheres and instruments that use tunable laser technology. Micro-spot spectrodensitometer is used to read color bars and related micro sized color control elements in printed inks in graphic arts applications. Spectrophotometers are used in color formulation for materials such as plastics, paints, inks, ceramics and metals. Auto tracking densitometer designed for newspaper presses to evaluate and adjust gray balance in newspaper production. In 2003, the group acquired the colorx(R) spectrophotometer product line and related assets of thermo electron corporation, ccdot meter product line of centurfax ltd and assets of monaco systems incorporated of andover and moniga gremmo s.r.l in 2004

Primary SIC and add'l.: 3565 3559 3826 3861

CIK No: 0000790818

Subsidiaries: Labsphere Ltd., Labsphere, Inc., Monaco Acquisition Company, OTP, Incorporated, X-Rite Asia Pacific Limited, X-Rite Asia Pacific PTE, X-Rite Europe, B.V., X-Rite Global, Incorporated., X-Rite GmbH, X-Rite Holdings, Incorporated, X-Rite International, Inc., X-Rite Ltd., X-Rite MA, Incorporated, X-Rite Mditerrane SARL, X-Rite, (Shanghai) International Trading Co. Ltd. 18 Subsidiaries included in the Index

Officers: Thomas J. Vacchiano/Dir., CEO, Pres./$210,276.00, Mary E. Chowning/CFO/$684,660.00, Francis Lamy/CTO, Bernard J. Berg/Sr. VP - Engineering/$448,937.00, Jeffrey L. Smolinski/Sr. VP - Operations/$484,051.00

Directors: Thomas J. Vacchiano/Dir., CEO, Pres., John E. Utley/Chmn., Stanley W. Cheff/Dir., Mark D. Weishaar/Dir., Gideon Argov/Dir., Mario Fontana/Dir., Peter L. Frieder/Dir., Massimo S. Lattmann/Dir., Paul R. Sylvester/Dir.

Owners: John E. Utley, Mark D. Weishaar, Paul R. Sylvester, Thomas J. Vacchiano, Mary E. Chowning, Massimo S. Lattmann, Lord, Abbett& Co. LLC/8.09%, Daruma Asset Management, Inc./7.28%, Michael C. Ferrara, Barclays Global Investors NA/5.01%, Jeffrey L. Smolinski, Insiders/4.62%, Bernard J. Berg, L.Peter Frieder, Stanley W. Cheff *(20 Owners included in Index)*

Financial Data: *Fiscal Year End:*12/31 *Latest Annual Data:* 12/30/2006

Year	**Sales**	**Net Income**
2006	$179,803,000	-$25,491,000
2005	$130,939,000	$11,052,000

Curr. Assets:	$76,633,000	**Curr. Liab.:**	$19,640,000		
Plant, Equip.:	$23,672,000	**Total Liab.:**	$20,053,000	**Indic. Yr. Divd.:**	$0.100
Total Assets:	$147,635,000	**Net Worth:**	$127,582,000	**Debt/ Equity:**	0.9065

X-Terra Resources Corp

Formerly: Canadian Empire Exploration Corp
675 W Hastings St., Ste. 1205, Vancouver, BC, V6B 1N2; **PH:** 1-604-687-4951; **http://** www.canadianempire.com

General - Incorporation	BC	**Stock**- Price on:12/24/2007	$0.085
Employees	NA	Stock Exchange	OTC
Auditor	PricewaterhouseCoopers LLP	Ticker Symbol	CXPJF
Stk Agt	Computershare Trust Co of Canada	Outstanding Shares	NA
Counsel	Reed Smith Crosby Heafey LLP	E.P.S	NA
DUNS No.	25-387-2493	Shareholders	NA

Business: The group's principle activity is to provide exploration services for precious metals, primarily gold and silver ores in Mexico. The group operates from United States.

Primary SIC and add'l.: 1041 1044

CIK No: 0001025761

Subsidiaries: Minera Reina Isabel, Minera Tatemas

Officers: Laurent Halle/Dir., CEO, Pres., Sebastien Plouffe/Dir., VP, Sec.

Directors: Laurent Halle/Dir., CEO, Pres., Lawrence P. Page/Dir., Sebastien Plouffe/Dir., VP, Sec., Xin Zhao/Dir.

XA Inc

875 N Michigan Ave. No. 2626, Chicago, IL, 60611; **PH:** 1-312-397-9100; **Fax:** 1-312-573-1515; **http://** www.experientialagency.com; **Email:** info@expagency.com

General - Incorporation	NV	**Stock**- Price on:12/24/2007	$0.45
Employees	28	Stock Exchange	OTC
Auditor	Pollard-Kelley Auditing Services, Inc	Ticker Symbol	XAIN
Stk Agt	Transfer Online, Inc.	Outstanding Shares	3,950,000
Counsel	NA	E.P.S	-$0.41
DUNS No.	NA	Shareholders	NA

Business: The groups principle activity is engage in the business of providing due diligence and administrative services for real estate syndications. The group operates through two segments namely business communications and event management, and meeting, conferences and trade shows. The group operates from the United States.

Primary SIC and add'l.: 7389

CIK No: 0001132034

Subsidiaries: Fiori XA, Inc., The Experiential Agency, Inc., XA Interactive, Inc., XA Scenes, Inc.

Officers: Joseph Wagner/42/Chmn., CEO, Pres., Sec., Jean Wilson/47/Dir., CFO, COO, Treasurer

Directors: Joseph Wagner/42/Chmn., CEO, Pres., Sec., Jean Wilson/47/Dir., CFO, COO, Treasurer, Christopher Spencer/39/Dir.

Owners: Insiders/36.20%, Frank Goldstin/21.50%, Sands Brothers Venture Capital IV LLC/9.40%, Sands Brothers Venture Capital III LLC/24.30%, Vision Opportunity Master Fund, Ltd./9.90%, Joe Wagner/20.40%, Chris Spencer/2.50%, David M. Loev/9.90%, Jean Wilson/13.20%, Mastodon Ventures, Inc./4.90%

Financial Data: *Fiscal Year End:*12/31 *Latest Annual Data:* 12/31/2006

Year	**Sales**	**Net Income**
2006	$9,825,000	-$1,992,000
2005	$10,913,000	-$110,000
2004	$8,545,000	-$838,000

Curr. Assets:	$1,275,000	**Curr. Liab.:**	$3,038,000		
Plant, Equip.:	$1,104,000	**Total Liab.:**	$4,350,000	**Indic. Yr. Divd.:**	NA
Total Assets:	$3,530,000	**Net Worth:**	-$820,000	**Debt/ Equity:**	NA

Xanser Corp

2435 N Central Expy., Richardson, TX, 75080; **PH:** 1-972-699-4000; **http://** www.xanser.com

General - Incorporation	DE	**Stock**- Price on:12/24/2007	NA
Employees	1,047	Stock Exchange	NA
Auditor	Grant Thornton LLP, KPMG LLP	Ticker Symbol	NA
Stk Agt	American Stock Transfer & Trust Co.	Outstanding Shares	NA
Counsel	NA	E.P.S	NA
DUNS No.	00-793-1868	Shareholders	NA

Business: The group's principle activities are to provide technical services and information technology services. These services are mainly provided through the group's subsidiaries, furmanite worldwide and xtria corporation. The technical services provided to customers include pulp and paper industries, refineries, pharmaceutical plants, petrochemical and chemical plants, pipelines, offshore drilling and production platforms, steel mills, food and drink processing facilities, power generation, and other process industries. The group also offers engineering solutions. The group's information technology services segment provides consulting services, hardware sales and other related information management and processing services to governmental, healthcare, insurance and financial institutions. The group's quartarterly revenue for September 2007 was 74.19 millions of USD.

Primary SIC and add'l.: 7375 8711 8748 9999

CIK No: 0000054441

Subsidiaries: Furmanite Holding BV, Furmanite Limited, Furmanite Offshore Services, Inc., Furmanite Worldwide, Inc., Xtria LLC

Officers: John R. Barnes/63/Chmn., CEO, Pres./$953,356.00, Michael L. Rose/69/Pres., Chief Operating/$573,156.00, Howard C. Wadsworth/63/Sr. VP - Treasur, Sec./$558,356.00, Joseph E. Milliron/53/COO - Furmanite/$498,531.00, Daryl L. Conner/44/Controller - Furmanite/$12,740.00

Directors: John R. Barnes/63/Chmn., CEO, Pres., Sangwoo Ahn/69/Dir., Charles R. Cox/65/Dir., Hans Kessler/58/Dir.

Owners: GAMCO Investors, Inc./6.00%, Howard C. Wadsworth, Jeffrey L. Gendell/7.70%, Royce & Associates, LLC/6.70%, Hans Kessler, Michael L. Rose, Charles R. Cox/1.40%, John R. Barnes/5.60%, Franklin Resources, Inc/7.90%, Sangwoo Ahn

XATA Corp

151 E Cliff Rd. , Ste 10, Burnsville, MN, 55337; ***PH:*** 1-612-894-3680; ***http://*** www.xata.com; ***Email:*** info@xata.com

General - Incorporation	MN	**Stock**- Price on:12/24/2007	$3.79
Employees	101	Stock Exchange	NDQ
Auditor	Grant Thornton LLP	Ticker Symbol	XATA
Stk Agt	Wells Fargo Bank Minnesota N.A	Outstanding Shares	8,500,000
Counsel	Moss & Barnett P.A	E.P.S	-$0.99
DUNS No.	13-073-2670	Shareholders	NA

Business: The group's principal activities are to design, develop, distribute and service fully integrated mobile information systems for the fleet trucking segment of the transportation industry in the United States of America and Canada. The group's systems utilize proprietary software, onboard touch-screen computers, and related hardware components and accessories to capture, analyze, and communicate operating information that assists fleet management in improving productivity and profitability. The major customers of the group are the kroger company. The group's operations are based in the United States. The group's patents and trademarks are xata, opcenter, smartcom, position plus, yard express and xatanet. The group installed systems in over 30,000 commercial trucks at over 1,000 customer locations. The group's customers include Fortune 500 companies and other large organizations.

Primary SIC and add'l.: 7372

CIK No: 0000854398

Officers: John J. Coughlan/Chmn., CEO, Pres., James C. Griffin/Exec. VP - Research, Development, Diane Hendricks/Human Resources Mgr., David Gagne/Exec. VP - Sales, Marketing, Thomas N. Flies/Sr. VP - Product Management, Peter A. Thayer/CTO, Mark E. Ties/CFO, Thomas L. Schlick/COO

Directors: John J. Coughlan/Chmn., CEO, Pres., Christopher P. Marshall/Dir., Roger W. Kleppe/Dir., Stephen A. Lawrence/Dir., Charles R. Stamp/Dir., Carl M. Fredericks/Dir.

Owners: Linda Flies, John Deere Special Technologies Group, Inc, John J. Coughlan, Thomas L. Schick, Stephen A. Lawrence, Christopher P. Marshall, Carl M. Fredericks, Trident Capital, Inc., Insiders, Roger W. Kleppe, Mark E. Ties, Thomas N. Flies

Financial Data: ***Fiscal Year End:***09/30 ***Latest Annual Data:*** 09/30/2007

Year	Sales	Net Income
2007	$30,676,000	-$6,808,000
2006	$30,629,000	-$1,743,000
2005	$19,302,000	-$5,980,000

Curr. Assets:	$17,529,000	***Curr. Liab.:***	$11,184,000		
Plant, Equip.:	$2,507,000	***Total Liab.:***	$16,533,000	***Indic. Yr. Divd.:***	NA
Total Assets:	$21,723,000	***Net Worth:***	$5,190,000	***Debt/ Equity:***	0.0082

Xcel Energy Inc

800 Nicollet Mall, Minneapolis, MN, 55402; ***PH:*** 1-612-330-5500; ***http://*** www.xcelenergy.com

General - Incorporation	MN	**Stock**- Price on:12/24/2007	$21.45
Employees	9,735	Stock Exchange	NYSE
Auditor	Deloitte & Touche LLP	Ticker Symbol	XEL
Stk Agt	Bank of New York	Outstanding Shares	408,920,000
Counsel	NA	E.P.S	$1.22
DUNS No.	00-696-2419	Shareholders	NA

Business: The groups principle activities include generating and distributing electricity and natural gas. The group operates from United States.

Primary SIC and add'l.: 4939 4931 4925

CIK No: 0000072903

Subsidiaries: Cheyenne Light, Fuel and Power Co., Eloigne Co., Northern States Power Co., Planergy International Inc., Public Service Co. of Colorado, Seren Innovations,Inc., Southwestern Public Service Co., Utility Engineering Corp., WestGas InterState Inc., Xcel Energy Communications Group Inc., Xcel Energy Foundation, Xcel Energy International Inc., Xcel Energy Markets Holdings Inc., Xcel Energy O&M Services Inc., Xcel Energy Retail Holdings Inc. 19 Subsidiaries included in the Index

Officers: Patricia K. Vincent/CEO, Pres. - Public Service Company, Colorado/$2,651,582.00, Michael L. Swenson/57/CEO, Pres. - NSP, Wisconsin, David M. Sparby/53/Dir., Exec. VP, Acting CEO, Pres. - NSP, Minnesota, Richard C. Kelly/Chmn., CEO, Pres./$11,200,880.00, Paul A. Johnson/MD - Investor Relations, Michael C. Connelly/VP, General Counsel, Benjamin G. Fowke/CFO, VP, Cathy J. Hart/VP - Corporate Services, Corp. Sec., Jack E. Nielsen/Dir. - Investor Relations, Cindy A. Hoffman/Sr. Analyst, Investor Relations, Dianne Perry/Mgr. - Shareholder Services, Raymond E. Gogel/VP - Customer, Enterprise Solutions, Chief Administrative Officer, David L. Eves/47/Dir., Pres., Paul J. Bonavia/Pres. - Utilities Group/$3,369,130.00, David M. Wilks/Pres. - Energy Supply *(19 Officers included in Index)*

Directors: Richard C. Kelly/Chmn., CEO, Pres., Richard H. Truly/Dir., David A. Westerlund/Dir., Timothy V. Wolf/Dir., Margaret R. Preska/Dir., Coney C. Burgess/Dir., Fredric W. Corrigan/Dir., Richard K. Davis/50/Dir., Roger R. Hemminghaus/Dir., Barry A. Hirschfeld/Dir., Douglas W. Leatherdale/Dir., Albert F. Moreno/Dir., Patricia A. Sampson/Dir.

Owners: Albert F. Moreno, David A. Westerlund, Margaret R. Preska, Paul J. Bonavia, Richard H. Truly, Douglas W. Leatherdale, Barry A. Hirschfeld, Roger R. Hemminghaus, Patricia K. Vincent, Benjamin G.S. Fowke, Patricia A. Sampson, Fredric W. Corrigan, Richard C. Kelly, Pictet Asset Management SA, Gary R. Johnson *(19 Owners included in Index)*

Financial Data: ***Fiscal Year End:***12/31 ***Latest Annual Data:*** 12/31/2006

Year	Sales	Net Income
2006	$9,840,304,000	$571,754,000
2005	$9,625,477,000	$512,972,000
2004	$8,345,259,000	$355,961,000

Curr. Assets:	$2,634,186,000	***Curr. Liab.:***	$2,865,281,000	***P/E Ratio:***	16.76
Plant, Equip.:	$15,548,658,000	***Total Liab.:***	$16,034,984,000	***Indic. Yr. Divd.:***	$0.920
Total Assets:	$21,958,346,000	***Net Worth:***	$5,921,802,000	***Debt/ Equity:***	1.2093

Xechem International Inc

100 Jersey Ave. E, Bldg B Ste. 310, New Brunswick, NJ, 08901; ***PH:*** 1-908-247-3300; ***http://*** www.xechem.com; ***Email:*** info@Xechem.com

General - Incorporation	DE	**Stock**- Price on:12/24/2007	$0.0205
Employees	80	Stock Exchange	OTC
Auditor	Moore Stephens, P.C	Ticker Symbol	XKEM
Stk Agt	Continental Stock Transfer & Trust Co	Outstanding Shares	1,640,000,000
Counsel	Mitchell D. Goldsmith, Esq	E.P.S	-$0.009
DUNS No.	86-132-6551	Shareholders	NA

Business: The group's principal activity is to conduct research and development and limited production of niche generic and proprietary drugs from natural sources. The group extracts, isolates and purifies technology to the production and manufacture of paclitaxel. The research and development of the group is focussed primarily on antifungal, anticancer, antiviral and anti-inflammatory compounds, antiaging and memory enhancing compounds. The group also provides technical and analytical laboratory services including the testing of chemicals, cosmetics, food, household and pharmaceutical products on a contract basis. It also offers consulting services for development and pilot-plant production of pharmaceuticals for companies on a contract basis. In 2004, the group acquired ceptor inc.

Primary SIC and add'l.: 8731 2834

CIK No: 0000919611

Subsidiaries: Xechem (India) Pvt. Ltd., Xechem Laboratories, Xechem UK Ltd, XetaPharm, Inc.

Officers: Ramesh C. Pandey/69/Chmn., CEO, Sec., Treasurer, Stephen F. Burg/70/Dir., Assist. Sec., Bhuwan C. Pandey/66/VP - International Operations, Howard Becker/48/VP - Operations, Renuka Misra/Member - Scientific Advisory Board, Dir. - Natural Products

Directors: Ramesh C. Pandey/69/Chmn., CEO, Sec., Treasurer, Renuka Misra/Member - Scientific Advisory Board, Dir. - Natural Products, Wayman J. Henry/Member - Sickle Cell Research, Efficacy, Awareness, Marketing Advisory Board, Federico Arcamone/Member - Scientific Advisory Board, Stephen F. Burg/70/Dir., Assist. Sec., Dakota Pippins/Member - Sickle Cell Research, Efficacy, Awareness, Marketing Advisory Board, Vincent A. Carter/Member - Sickle Cell Research, Efficacy, Awareness, Marketing Advisory Board, Geoffrey A. Cordell/Member - Scientific Advisory Board, Marcy Street/Member - Sickle Cell Research, Efficacy, Awareness, Marketing Advisory Board, Sukh Dev/Member - Scientific Advisory Board, Marcellus Grace/Member - Sickle Cell Research, Efficacy, Awareness, Marketing Advisory Board, William T. Bradner/Member - Scientific Advisory Board, Otto J. Plescia/Member - Scientific Advisory Board, Wallye Inese Holloway/Member - Sickle Cell Research, Efficacy, Awareness, Marketing Advisory Board, Stephen H. Kolison/Member - Sickle Cell Research, Efficacy, Awareness, Marketing Advisory Board *(31 Directors included in Index)*

Owners: Insiders/3.90%, Insiders/100.00%, Ramesh C. Pandey, Ramesh C. Pandey/100.00%, Stephen F. Burg/0.93%, Insiders/100.00%, Adesoji Adelaja, Bhuwan Pandey/2.35%, Ramesh C. Pandey/100.00%

Financial Data: ***Fiscal Year End:***12/31 ***Latest Annual Data:*** 12/31/2006

Year	Sales	Net Income
2006	$5,099,000	$314,000
2005	$4,525,000	$576,000
2004	$3,831,000	$405,000

Curr. Assets:	$1,012,000	***Curr. Liab.:***	$6,806,000		
Plant, Equip.:	$2,677,000	***Total Liab.:***	$9,790,000	***Indic. Yr. Divd.:***	NA
Total Assets:	$3,720,000	***Net Worth:***	-$6,070,000	***Debt/ Equity:***	NA

Xedar Corp

8310 South Valley Highway, Ste. 200, Englewood, CO, 80112; ***PH:*** 1-303-377-0033; ***http://*** www.xedarinc.com

General - Incorporation	CO	**Stock**- Price on:12/24/2007	NA
Employees	NA	Stock Exchange	OTC
Auditor	Ehrhardt Keefe Steiner & Hottman P.C	Ticker Symbol	XDRC
Stk Agt	Corporate Stock Transfer	Outstanding Shares	NA
Counsel	NA	E.P.S	-$0.15
DUNS No.	NA	Shareholders	NA

Business: The groups principle activity is to provide information technology systems and enterprise assurance and security analysis services to various federal government agencies. In January 2007, the group acquired Land Links Company Ltd. The group operates from the United States.

Primary SIC and add'l.: 6770

CIK No: 0000108770

Subsidiaries: Fugen, Inc., Land Links Company Ltd., PDS GIS/LIS, Inc., Premier Data Systems, Inc.

Officers: Richard Souders/CEO, Pres. - Premier Data Services/$282,500.00, Hugh H. Williamson/66/Dir., CEO, Pres./$45,000.00, Don Rakestraw/CEO - Atlantic Systems, Point One, Brad Taggart/Dir. - Software Development, Premier Data Services, Jeffrey Grime/Pres. - Atlantic

Systems, Point One, Chuck Killpack/Pres. - Geospatial Division, Glen Thurow/Dir. - Land Links Company, David King/Dir. - Land Links Company, Michelle Beiga/VP - Human Resources, Mitchell Gross/VP - Consulting Services, Fugen, Steve M. Bragg/CFO, Treasurer/$174,325.00, Marty Terwilliger/Pres. - Fugen, Bob Johnson/Sr. VP - Premier Data Services

Directors: Hugh H. Williamson/66/Dir., CEO, Pres., Jack Howard Jacobs/62/Dir., Samuel John Camarata/Dir., Trusten Allan McArtor/Dir., Roger John Steinbecker/Dir., Craig Andrew Parker/Dir., John Patrick Moreno/Dir.

Owners: John P. Moreno, Underwood Family Partners, Ltd./7.00%, Insiders/33.50%, Craig A. Parker, Jack H. Jacobs, Jeffrey R. Grime/5.05%, Roger J. Steinbecker, Richard V. Souders/5.80%, Hugh H. Williamson/26.70%, Steven M. Bragg, Samuel J. Camarata, Trusten A. McArtor, Don W. Rakestraw/6.90%

Financial Data: *Fiscal Year End:*12/31 *Latest Annual Data:* 12/31/2006

Year	Sales	Net Income
2006	$6,055,000	-$610,000
2005	NA	-$19,000
2000	$390,000	-$85,000

Curr. Assets:	$2,061,000	Curr. Liab.:	$1,520,000			
Plant, Equip.:	$289,000	Total Liab.:	$1,520,000	Indic. Yr. Divd.:	NA
Total Assets:	$3,597,000	Net Worth:	$2,077,000	Debt/ Equity:	NA

XELR8 Holdings Inc

Formerly: VitaCube Systems Holdings Inc
480 S Holly St., Denver, CO, 80246; *PH:* 1-303-316-8577; *http://* www.v3s.com

General - Incorporation	NV	Stock - Price on:12/24/2007	$1.55
Employees	16	Stock Exchange	AMEX
Auditor	Gordon, Hughes & Banks LLP	Ticker Symbol	PRH
Stk Agt	Corporate Stock Transfer, Inc.	Outstanding Shares	NA
Counsel	NA	E.P.S	NA
DUNS No.	NA	Shareholders	NA

Business: The group's principle activities include operates, develops, markets and sells a line of nutrition and sports supplement products supported by customer education and a packaging delivery system intended to make those products convenient to use. The group markets its products, through network marketing, sales through personal care providers and primary care physician referrals, e-commerce marketing and retail chain store sales. Network marketing is conducted through vitacube networking inc., a wholly owned subsidiary. The group has developed a line of nutritional supplements that consists of vitamins, minerals, amino acids, and proteins. Its vitamin mineral complexes are organized into systems of nutrition called vitacubes that explicitly tell the consumer what supplements to take and when to take them. The group has also developed a high-quality meal replacement beverage called the vitapro nutrition shake.

Primary SIC and add'l.: 2099

CIK No: 0001134765

Subsidiaries: VitaCube Systems Inc., XELR8, Inc

Officers: John Pougnet/CEO, CFO/$255,769.00, Timothy Transtrum/VP - Operations/$127,434.00, Doug Ridley/Pres./$163,814.00, Teresa Simoneau/Dir. - Communications, Sanjeev R. Javia/VP - Business Development/$107,936.00, John Hutchinson/VP - Information Technology, Web

Directors: John B. McCandless/Chmn., Anthony Digiandomenico/Dir., Sanford D. Greenberg/Founder, Anthony Petrelli/Dir., A. J. Robbins/Dir., Daniel Rumsey/Dir.

Owners: AJ Robbins, Douglas Ridley/1.70%, Timothy Transtrum, Anthony DiGiandomenico/3.20%, Anthony Petrelli, Insiders/11.30%, Sanjeevkumar Javia/2.20%, John B. McCandless, Sanford D. Greenberg/24.20%, John D. Pougnet/1.50%, Daniel Rumsey, John Hutchinson

Xeno Transplants Corp

Formerly: Icon Development Inc
1066 W Hastings St., Ste. 2610, Vancouver, BC, V6E 3X2; *PH:* 1-604-684-4691

General - Incorporation	NV	Stock - Price on:12/24/2007	$1.397
Employees	NA	Stock Exchange	OTC
Auditor	Davidson & Co. LLP	Ticker Symbol	XENO
Stk Agt	NA	Outstanding Shares	NA
Counsel	NA	E.P.S	NA
DUNS No.	NA	Shareholders	NA

Business: The groups principal activity is to commercialize enterprise information portal and related software applications. Services of the group include customer relations, support activities, marketing, documenting and data management. The group operates from the United States.

Primary SIC and add'l.: 6552

CIK No: 0001333077

Officers: Elliot Lebowitz/Dir., CEO, Wayne Smith/Dir., CFO, David Sachs/Dir., Chief Scientific Advisor, Deeda Blair/Advisor, Samuel M. Eisenstat/Advisor, Edwin H. Gordon/Advisor, Michael McClain/Advisor, Anne Peters/Advisor

Directors: Elliot Lebowitz/Dir., CEO, Michael S. Perry/Chmn., James L. Beckner/Dir., Wayne Smith/Dir., CFO, Milton Datsopoulos/Dir., David Sachs/Dir., Chief Scientific Advisor

Owners: Milton Datsopoulos, Elliot Lebowitz/22.40%, David Sachs, Ken Swaisland/17.40%, EMI Opportunity Fund/5.60%, Michael Perry, Insiders/23.30%

Financial Data: *Fiscal Year End:*06/30 *Latest Annual Data:* 6/30/2006

Year	Sales	Net Income
2006	NA	-$47,000

Curr. Assets:	$0	Curr. Liab.:	$13,000		
Plant, Equip.:	$1,000	Total Liab.:	$13,000	Indic. Yr. Divd.:	NA
Total Assets:	$1,000	Net Worth:	-$13,000	Debt/ Equity:	NA

Xenogen Corp

860 Atlantic Ave., Alameda, CA, 94501; *PH:* 1-510-291-6100; *http://* www.xenogen.com

General - Incorporation	DE	Stock - Price on:12/24/2007	$4.57
Employees	550	Stock Exchange	NA
Auditor	Deloitte & Touche LLP	Ticker Symbol	NA
Stk Agt	EquiServe Trust Co N.A	Outstanding Shares	47,170,000
Counsel	Wilson Sonsini Goodrich & Rosati	E.P.S.	-$0.84
DUNS No.	96-324-9982	Shareholders	NA

Business: The group's principal activities are to develop and manufacture products and technologies for acquiring, analyzing and managing complex image data from live animals. The group combines systems biology and low-light optical imaging to create powerful new biophotonic imaging technology that advances the ability of scientists to explore genes, proteins, pathogens and tumor cells in living animals in real time, providing predictive data that is designed to substantially improve the success rate in drug development. The biophotonic imaging technology is used to provide more accurate and previously unavailable data intended to result in the ability to make more timely and cost-effective decisions at every step in the drug development process.

Primary SIC and add'l.: 2835 3829

CIK No: 0001116449

Subsidiaries: Xenogen Biosciences Corporation

Financial Data: *Fiscal Year End:*12/31 *Latest Annual Data:* 12/31/2006

Year	Sales	Net Income
2006	$107,871,000	-$28,934,000
2005	$87,009,000	-$14,457,000
2004	$80,127,000	-$31,556,000

Curr. Assets:	$76,790,000	Curr. Liab.:	$49,938,000		
Plant, Equip.:	$13,182,000	Total Liab.:	$67,644,000	Indic. Yr. Divd.:	NA
Total Assets:	$225,053,000	Net Worth:	$157,409,000	Debt/ Equity:	0.0570

Xenomics Inc

420 Lexington Ave., Ste. 1701, New York, NY, 10170; *PH:* 1-212-297-0808; *Fax:* 1-212-297-1888; *http://* www.xenomics.com; *Email:* info@xenomics.com

General - Incorporation	FL	Stock - Price on:12/24/2007	NA
Employees	NA	Stock Exchange	OTC
Auditor	Lazar, Levine & Felix, LLP	Ticker Symbol	XNOM
Stk Agt	NA	Outstanding Shares	NA
Counsel	NA	E.P.S.	NA
DUNS No.	NA	Shareholders	NA

Business: The groups principal activity is to develop an on line marketplace for used car parts. The group effort to develop that business, entered into a contract with a web hosting service on a month to month basis to provide storage for website development and transaction processing. The group operates from the United States.

Primary SIC and add'l.: 8731

CIK No: 0001213037

Subsidiaries: Xenomics Sub

Officers: Gianluigi Longinotti-Buitoni/Executive Chmn., Subhash Patel/VP - Regulatory Affairs, Samuil R. Umansky/Chief Scientific Officer, Co - Founder, Frederick Larcombe/CFO, David Robbins/VP - Product Development, Hovsep Melkonyan/Co - Founder, VP - Research, Development

Directors: Gianluigi Longinotti-Buitoni/Executive Chmn., Donald Picker/Dir., Samuil R. Umansky/Chief Scientific Officer, Co - Founder, Hovsep Melkonyan/Co - Founder, VP - Research, Development, David Sidransky/Dir., John P. Brancaccio/Dir.

Owners: Randy V. White/1.60%, Samuil Umansky/9.70%, Panetta Partners, Ltd./5.10%, Christoph Bruening, Donald Picker, Hovsep Melkonyan/5.30%, Gabriele M. Cerrone/10.20%, David L. Tomei/9.90%, Insiders/32.80%

Curr. Assets:	$3,942,000	Curr. Liab.:	$235,000		
Plant, Equip.:	$122,000	Total Liab.:	$640,000	Indic. Yr. Divd.:	NA
Total Assets:	$4,121,000	Net Worth:	$3,481,000	Debt/ Equity:	NA

Xenonics Holdings Inc

2236 Rutherford Rd., Ste. 123, Carlsbad, CA, 92008; *PH:* 1-760-438-4004; *http://* www.xenonics.com; *Email:* IR@Xenonics.com

General - Incorporation	NV	Stock - Price on:12/24/2007	$2.4799
Employees	15	Stock Exchange	AMEX
Auditor	Singer Lewak Greenbaum & Goldstein	Ticker Symbol	XNN
Stk Agt	Interwest Transfer Company, Inc.	Outstanding Shares	18,510,000
Counsel	NA	E.P.S.	-$0.03
DUNS No.	NA	Shareholders	NA

Business: The group's principle activities include designing, manufacturing and marketing intensity portable illumination products. The group products include NightHunter, NightHunterII and NightHunter(EXT). Specific customers of the group include U.S. Navy SEALs, USMC FAST and the U.S. Army Rangers. The group operates from the United States. The group's quarterly revenue for September 2007 was 1.40 millions of USD.

Primary SIC and add'l.: 3699 3812 3629 3648

CIK No: 0001289550

Subsidiaries: Xenonics, Inc.

Officers: Richard J. Naughton/61/Dir., CEO, Charles Hunter/CEO, Donna G. Lee/49/Corp. Sec., Jeffrey P. Kennedy/Dir., COO, Pres., Richard S. Kay/CFO

Directors: Richard J. Naughton/61/Dir., CEO, Alan P. Magerman/Chmn., Jeffrey P. Kennedy/Dir., COO, Pres., Robert E. Petersen/Dir., Robert Buie/Dir., Eli Shapiro/Dir.

Owners: Eli Shapiro/2.83%, Richard J. Naughton/1.44%, Gemini Master Fund/8.37%, Jeffrey P. Kennedy/4.79%, Alan P. Magerman/5.44%, Robert Petersen/0.13%, Insiders/17.98%, Robert F. Buie/3.14%, Donna G. Lee/0.19%

Financial Data: *Fiscal Year End:*09/30 *Latest Annual Data:* 9/30/2006

Year	Sales	Net Income
2006	$4,833,000	-$1,488,000
2005	$4,434,000	-$5,004,000
2004	$11,927,000	$1,476,000

Curr. Assets:	$2,994,000	Curr. Liab.:	$665,000		
Plant, Equip.:	$46,000	Total Liab.:	$665,000	Indic. Yr. Divd.:	NA
Total Assets:	$3,065,000	Net Worth:	$2,400,000	Debt/ Equity:	NA

XenoPort Inc

3410 Central Expy., Santa Clara, CA, 95051; *PH:* 1-408-616-7200; *http://* www.xenoport.com; *Email:* info@XenoPort.com

General - Incorporation ... DE
Employees ... 141
Auditor ... Ernst& Young LLP
Stk Agt ... Mellon Investor Services LLC
Counsel ... NA
DUNS No. ... NA

Stock- Price on:12/24/2007 ... $43.99
Stock Exchange ... NDQ
Ticker Symbol ... XNPT
Outstanding Shares ... 24,800,000
E.P.S ... $0.28
Shareholders ... NA

Business: The groups principle activity is to develop portfolio of internally discovered product candidates. The group operates from the United States. The group's quarterly revenue for September 2007 was 35.42 millions of USD.

Primary SIC and add'l.: 2834

CIK No: 0001130591

Officers: Ronald W. Barrett/Dir., CEO/$840,906.00, William J. Rieflin/Pres./$654,232.00, William G. Harris/CFO, Sr. VP - Finance/$462,390.00, Kenneth C. Cundy/Sr. VP - Preclinical Development/$458,334.00, Mark A. Gallop/Sr. VP - Research/$444,230.00, David R. Savello/Sr. VP - Development/$638,303.00, Pierre V. Tran/48/Sr. VP, Chief Medical Officer, Martyn J. Webster/VP - Finance

Directors: Ronald W. Barrett/Dir., CEO, Paul L. Berns/Dir., John G. Freund/Dir., Jeryl L. Hilleman/Dir., Kenneth J. Nussbacher/Dir., Bryan Roberts/Dir., Gary D. Tollefson/Dir., Wendell Wierenga/Dir., Catherine J. Friedman/Dir.

Owners: Venrock Associates/5.80%, Gary D. Tollefson, Jeryl L. Hilleman, Mark A. Gallop/1.00%, John G. Freund/3.50%, Paul L. Berns, Insiders/15.50%, Wendell Wierenga, Maverick Capital, Ltd./9.80%, William J. Rieflin/1.00%, Robert A. Reed, Kenneth J. Nussbacher, David R. Savello, Kenneth C. Cundy, William G. Harris *(18 Owners included in Index)*

Financial Data: **Fiscal Year End:**12/31 **Latest Annual Data:** 12/31/2006

Year	Sales	Net Income
2006	$10,606,000	-$64,313,000
2005	$4,753,000	-$42,909,000
2004	$9,955,000	-$31,242,000

Curr. Assets:	$122,982,000	**Curr. Liab.:**	$21,455,000		
Plant, Equip.:	$3,532,000	**Total Liab.:**	$45,380,000	**Indic. Yr. Divd.:**	NA
Total Assets:	$128,665,000	**Net Worth:**	$83,285,000	**Debt/ Equity:**	NA

Xerium Technologies Inc

14101 Capital Blvd., Ste. 201, Youngsville, NC, 27596; *PH:* 1-919-556-7235; *Fax:* 1-919-556-2432; *http://* www.xerium.com

General - Incorporation ... DE
Employees ... 3,821
Auditor ... Ernst& Young LLP
Stk Agt ... American Stock Transfer & Trust Co.
Counsel ... NA
DUNS No. ... NA

Stock- Price on:12/24/2007 ... $7.48
Stock Exchange ... NYSE
Ticker Symbol ... XRM
Outstanding Shares ... 43,430,000
E.P.S ... NA
Shareholders ... NA

Business: The groups principle activities include manufacturing and supplying consumable products include clothing and roll covers. The groups products marketed under the brand names Huyck, Wangner, Weavexx, Stowe Woodward, Mount Hope and Robec. In the year 2006, the group acquired Coldwater Covers, Inc. and PMA Shoji Co. Ltd. The group operates from the United States. The group's quarterly revenue for September 2007 was 153.59 millions of USD.

Primary SIC and add'l.: 2221

CIK No: 0001287151

Subsidiaries: Huyck (UK) Limited, Huyck Argentina Sociedad Annima, Huyck Australia Pty. Limited, Huyck Austria GmbH, Huyck Italia SpA, Huyck Japan Limited, Huyck Licensco Inc, Robec Brazil LLC, Robec Walzen GmbH, Stowe Woodward AG, Stowe Woodward Finland Oy, Stowe Woodward France SAS, Stowe Woodward Licensco LLC, Stowe Woodward LLC, Stowe Woodward Mxico, SA De C.V. 38 Subsidiaries included in the Index

Officers: Thomas Gutierrez/Dir., CEO, Pres., Douglas Milner/Pres. - Stowe Woodward Rolls Worldwide, Joan Badrinas Ardevol/Pres. - Clothing Europe, Cheryl Diuguid/Pres. - Xerium Asia, Michael ODonnell/Dir., CFO, Exec. VP, David Pretty/Pres. - Weavexx, Miguel Quinonez/Pres. - Xerium South America, Michael J. Stick/Exec. VP, General Counsel, Josef Mayer/Exec. VP - Business Development

Directors: Thomas Gutierrez/Dir., CEO, Pres., John S. Thompson/Chmn., Michael Phillips/Dir., John Saunders/Dir., Michael ODonnell/Dir., CFO, Exec. VP, Donald P. Aiken/Dir., Edward Paquette/Dir.

Owners: John B. Saunders, Donald P. Aiken, Michael ODonnell, Michael ODonnell, Apax Europe IV GP Co. Ltd./53.00%, Michael Phillips, Thomas Gutierrez, Apax Europe IV GP Co. Ltd., Brandywine Global Investment Management, LLC/5.60%, Brandywine Global Investment Management, LLC, Thomas Gutierrez, Donald P. Aiken, John S. Thompson, John S. Thompson, Michael Phillips/53.00% *(26 Owners included in Index)*

Financial Data: **Fiscal Year End:**12/31 **Latest Annual Data:** 12/31/2006

Year	Sales	Net Income
2006	$601,439,000	$29,544,000
2005	$582,420,000	-$2,094,000

Curr. Assets:	$254,062,000	**Curr. Liab.:**	$109,033,000		
Plant, Equip.:	$375,179,000	**Total Liab.:**	$874,146,000	**Indic. Yr. Divd.:**	NA
Total Assets:	$990,726,000	**Net Worth:**	$116,580,000	**Debt/ Equity:**	5.4587

Xerox Corp

PO Box 1600, Stamford, CT, 06904; *PH:* 1-203-968-3000; *http://* www.xerox.com

General - Incorporation ... NY
Employees ... 53,700
Auditor ... PricewaterhouseCoopers LLP
Stk Agt ... Computershare Trust Co
Counsel ... NA
DUNS No. ... 04-959-1852

Stock- Price on:12/24/2007 ... $19.28
Stock Exchange ... NYSE
Ticker Symbol ... XRX
Outstanding Shares ... 937,350,000
E.P.S ... $1.27
Shareholders ... NA

Business: The groups principle activities include developing, manufacturing and finance document-processing products. The groups products line includes printer, copier and other software products. The group operates through three segments namely production, office, and developing markets operations. In the year 2007, the group acquired Advectis, Inc. The group operates from United States.

Primary SIC and add'l.: 6159 7359 3579 3577 5111

CIK No: 0000108772

Subsidiaries: 79861 Ontario Inc., 832667 Ontario Inc., AMTX, Inc., Bessemer Insurance Limited, Bessemer Trust Limited, Bipolar Limited, Carmel Valley, Inc., City Paper Limited, Continua Limited, Continua S.A., Continua Sanctum Limited, CREDITEXAluguer de Equipamentos S.A., Delphax Systems GmbH, dpiX, FairCopy Services Inc. 208 Subsidiaries included in the Index

Officers: Anne M. Mulcahy/Chmn., CEO/$10,694,730.00, Armando Zagalo De Lima/Corp Sr. VP, Pres. - Xerox Europe, Thomas J. Dolan/Corp Sr. VP, Pres. - Xerox Global Accounting Operations, Jean-Noel MacHon/Corp Sr. VP, Pres. - Developing Markets Operations/$3,528,556.00, Michael C. Mac Donald/Corporate Sr. VP - Pres. - Marketing Operations, John McDermott/Corporate VP, Chief Information Officert, Len Parker/55/VP, Chief Engineer, Jane M. Hollen/53/CIO - Xerox North America, James H. Lesko/Corp VP, VP - Investor Relations, Hector J. Motroni/Chief Staff Officer, Chief Ethics Officer, Rhonda L. Seegal/Corp VP, Treasurer, Michael J. Farren/55/VP - External, Legal Affairs, General Counsel, Corp. Sec., Gary Kabureck/Corp VP, Chief Accounting Officer, Michael D. Brannigan/Corp VP, Pres. - US Solutions Group, Ursula M. Burns/Pres./$3,374,579.00 *(52 Officers included in Index)*

Directors: Anne M. Mulcahy/Chmn., CEO, Glenn A. Britt/Dir., Stephen Robert/Dir., Robert McDonald/Dir., Richard J. Harrington/Dir., William Curt Hunter/Dir., Vernon E. Jordan/Dir., Hilmar Kopper/Dir., Ralph S. Larsen/Dir., N. J. Nicholas/Dir., Ann N. Reese/Dir., Mary Agnes Wilderotter/53/Dir.

Owners: State Street Bank and Trust Company, as Trustee under/6.70%, BlackRock, Inc./5.20%, Insiders, Neuberger Berman Inc./5.40%, FMR Corp./5.60%, Brandes Investment Partners, L.P./5.10%, Dodge &. Cox/12.30%

Financial Data: **Fiscal Year End:**12/31 **Latest Annual Data:** 12/31/2006

Year	Sales	Net Income
2006	$15,895,000,000	$1,210,000,000
2005	$15,701,000,000	$978,000,000
2004	$15,722,000,000	$859,000,000

Curr. Assets:	$8,754,000,000	**Curr. Liab.:**	$4,698,000,000	**P/E Ratio:**	15.18
Plant, Equip.:	$2,008,000,000	**Total Liab.:**	$14,629,000,000	**Indic. Yr. Divd.:**	NA
Total Assets:	$21,709,000,000	**Net Worth:**	$7,080,000,000	**Debt/ Equity:**	0.7613

Xerox Credit Corp

100 First Stamford Pl., Stamford, CT, 06904; *PH:* 1-203-325-6600

General - Incorporation ... DE
Employees ... NA
Auditor ... PricewaterhouseCoopers LLP
Stk Agt ... Computershare
Counsel ... NA
DUNS No. ... 09-975-9318

Stock- Price on:12/24/2007 ... NA
Stock Exchange ... NA
Ticker Symbol ... NA
Outstanding Shares ... NA
E.P.S ... NA
Shareholders ... NA

Business: The group's principle activity is to finance long term accounts receivables arising from installment sales and sales-type leases originated by the domestic marketing operations of the parent company. The group raises debt in the capital markets to fund purchases of these receivables. The terms on the purchased contract receivable range primarily from three to five years. The group is a wholly owned subsidiary of xerox financial services inc which is in turn wholly owned by xerox corporation.

Primary SIC and add'l.: 6159

CIK No: 0000351936

Subsidiaries: Xerox Canada Capital Limited, Xerox Corporation, Xerox Financial Services, Inc

Officers: Gary R. Kabureck/Dir., CEO, Pres., Robert J. Sorrentino/VP, Controller, John F. Rivera/Dir., VP, Treasurer, CFO

Directors: Gary R. Kabureck/Dir., CEO, Pres., Rhonda L. Seegal/Chmn., John F. Rivera/Dir., VP, Treasurer, CFO

XETA Technologies Inc

1814 W Tacoma, Broken Arrow, OK, 74012; *PH:* 1-918-664-8200; *http://* www.xeta.com

General - Incorporation ... OK
Employees ... 309
Auditor ... Tullius Taylor Sartain & Sartain LLP
Stk Agt ... UMB Bank, N.A.
Counsel ... Barber & Bartz
DUNS No. ... 06-236-4732

Stock- Price on:12/24/2007 ... $3.06
Stock Exchange ... NDQ
Ticker Symbol ... XETA
Outstanding Shares ... 10,210,000
E.P.S ... $0.12
Shareholders ... NA

Business: The group's principal activities are to provide voice and data networking services. The operations of the group are carried out through three segments: installation and services, commercial system and lodging system. The group sells avaya's definity(R) guestworkstm systems, hitachi's 5000(R) series digital communications systems and the nortel networks' product line to the hospitality industry under nationwide, non-exclusive dealer agreements. It also sells communication systems and software for commercial enterprises including voice over ip ("Voip"), call centers, customer relationship management, wireless, and messaging systems. Installation and service segment installs and maintains systems for customers in both the commercial and lodging segments. The registered trademarks are xeta, xetaxcel, xact, xpert, xpert+, xl, xpander and virtual xl. On 02-Aug-2004, the group acquired bluejack systems llc.

Primary SIC and add'l.: 3661 4813 7371

CIK No: 0000742550

Subsidiaries: Xetaplan, Inc

Officers: Greg Forrest/CEO, COO, Pres., Tom Luce/Executive Dir. - Managed Services, Larry Patterson/Executive Dir. - Operations, Don Reigel/Executive Dir. - Avaya Sales, Robert Wagner/CFO, Executive Dir. - Operations, Cheryl Moll/Investor Relations Contact, Scott Davis/Executive Dir. - Nortel Sales

Directors: Jack R. Ingram/64/Chmn., Donald T. Duke/58/Dir., Ronald L. Siegenthaler/64/Dir., Ron B. Barber/53/Dir., Robert D. Hisrich/63/Dir.

Owners: Robert B. Wagner, Jon A. Wiese/5.37%, Ronald L. Siegenthaler/10.92%, Ron B. Barber/1.16%, Greg D. Forrest, Insiders/26.05%, Donald T. Duke, Jack R. Ingram/10.23%, Robert D. Hisrich, FMR Corp./9.55%, Larry N. Patterson/1.53%

Financial Data: **Fiscal Year End:**10/31 **Latest Annual Data:** 10/31/2006

Year	Sales	Net Income
2006	$59,965,000	$719,000
2005	$58,003,000	$494,000
2004	$58,827,000	$1,608,000

Curr. Assets:	$18,725,000	Curr. Liab.:	$12,414,000	P/E Ratio:	25.50
Plant, Equip.:	$10,485,000	Total Liab.:	$18,028,000	Indic. Yr. Divd.:	NA
Total Assets:	$55,913,000	Net Worth:	$37,885,000	Debt/ Equity:	0.0375

Xethanol Corp

1185 Ave. of the Americas, 20th Fl., New York, NY, 10036; **PH:** 1-303-825-4570;
http:// www.xethanol.com

General - Incorporation	DE	Stock - Price on:12/24/2007	$1.23
Employees	34	Stock Exchange	AMEX
Auditor	Imowitz Koenig & Co. LLP	Ticker Symbol	XNL
Stk Agt	Corporate Stock Transfer, Inc.	Outstanding Shares	28,610,000
Counsel	NA	E.P.S.	-$0.943
DUNS No.	NA	Shareholders	NA

Business: The group's principle activity is to manufacture pottery kiln for resale to the public under the name zen raku kiln. The kiln is suitable for firing most varieties of pottery which may be produced individually. The company markets its products to the customer who makes pottery on an individual basis and not using mass production techniques. The group operates from United States.

Primary SIC and add'l.: 3559
CIK No: 0001145061
Subsidiaries: Xethanol BioFuels, Xethanol One, LLC
Officers: David R. Ames/Dir., CEO, Pres., Larry Bellone/Dir., Exec. VP - Corporate Development, Franz A. Skryanz/VP, Sec., Treasurer, Robin Buller/VP - Strategic Development, Tom J. Endres/COO, Jim Stewart/VP - Plant Operations, GM - Xethanol Biofuels, Blairstown, Mark Austin/Chief Technology Strategist, Gary Flicker/CFO, Exec. VP, Sec., Richard Wilson/Exec. VP - Communications, Technology Affairs
Directors: David R. Ames/Dir., CEO, Pres., William P. Behrens/Non - Exec. Chmn., Christopher Darnaud-Taylor/Dir., Larry Bellone/Dir., Exec. VP - Corporate Development, Richard Ditoro/Dir., Gil Boosidan/Dir., Robert L. Franklin/Dir., Edwin L. Klett/Dir.
Owners: David R. Ames/5.40%, Edwin L. Klett, Insiders/16.80%, Robert L. Franklin, William P. Behrens/1.10%, Gary Flicker, Lawrence S. Bellone/2.70%, Gil Boosidan, Richard D. Ditoro/1.00%, Thomas J. Endres, Christopher dArnaud-Taylor/4.90%

Financial Data: Fiscal Year End: 12/31   **Latest Annual Data:** 12/31/2006

Year	Sales	Net Income
2006	$11,029,000	-$20,179,000
2005	$4,343,000	-$11,377,000
2004	$38,000	-$32,000

Curr. Assets:	$20,000	Curr. Liab.:	$13,000		
Plant, Equip.:	NA	Total Liab.:	$13,000	Indic. Yr. Divd.:	NA
Total Assets:	$20,000	Net Worth:	$6,000	Debt/ Equity:	0.0071

Xfone Inc

2506 Lakeland Dr., Ste. 100, Jackson, MS, 39232; **PH:** 1-601-983-3800; **Fax:** 1-601-983-3801;
http:// www.xfone.com

General - Incorporation	NV	Stock - Price on:12/24/2007	$2.9
Employees	139	Stock Exchange	AMEX
Auditor	Stark Winter Schenkein & Co., LLP	Ticker Symbol	XFN
Stk Agt	Transfer Online, Inc.	Outstanding Shares	11,520,000
Counsel	NA	E.P.S	$0.09
DUNS No.	NA	Shareholders	NA

Business: The group operates through its subsidiaries whose principle activity is to provide international voice, video and data communications services. The groups services include local, long distance and international telephony services, prepaid and postpaid calling cards, cellular services, Internet services, messaging services and Cyber-Number. The group operates from the United Kingdom, the United States and Israel. The group's quarterly revenue for September 2007 was 12.14 millions of USD.

Primary SIC and add'l.: 4899
CIK No: 0001126216
Subsidiaries: Auracall Limited, Equitalk.co.uk Limited, eXpeTel Communications, Inc., Gulf Coast Utilities, Inc., Story Telecom (Ireland) Limited, Story Telecom Limited, Story Telecom, Inc., Swiftnet Limited, Xfone 018 Ltd., Xfone USA, Inc
Officers: Guy Nissenson/Dir., CEO, Pres., Wade Spooner/Pres. - Xfone USA, John Burton/MD - Swiftnet, Ted Parsons/Dir., Exec. VP, Chief Marketing Officer, Bosmat Houston/CTO, Iddo Keinan/Commercial Dir. - Swiftnet Ltd, Xfone Inc, Alon Reisser/General Counsel, Sec., John Nesbett/Institutional Marketing Services, IMS, Zvi Rabin/Kwan Communications, Niv Krikov/CFO, Roni Haliva/MD - Xfone 018
Directors: Guy Nissenson/Dir., CEO, Pres., Abraham Keinan/Chmn., Itzhak Almog/Dir., Aviu Ben-Horrin/Dir., Shemer Schwartz/Dir., Eyal J. Harish/Dir., Israel Singer/Dir., Morris Mansour/Dir., Ted Parsons/Dir., Exec. VP, Chief Marketing Officer
Owners: Mercantile Discount - Provident Funds/6.11%, Insiders/52.86%, Crestview Capital Master LLC/10.36%, Guy Nissenson/20.76%, Aviu Ben-Horrin, Shemer S. Schwartz, Abraham Keinan/37.45%, Eyal J. Harish, Itzhak Almog, MCG Capital Corporation/8.76%

Financial Data: Fiscal Year End: 12/31   **Latest Annual Data:** 12/31/2006

Year	Sales	Net Income
2006	$37,914,000	$661,000
2005	$24,346,000	$45,000
2004	$21,867,000	$77,000

Curr. Assets:	$10,291,000	Curr. Liab.:	$11,221,000		
Plant, Equip.:	$4,466,000	Total Liab.:	$13,555,000	Indic. Yr. Divd.:	NA
Total Assets:	$33,027,000	Net Worth:	$19,472,000	Debt/ Equity:	0.0849

XFormity Technologies Inc

14333 Proton Rd. , Dallas, TX, 75244; **PH:** 1-972-661-1200; http:// www.xformity.com;
Email: info@xformity.com

General - Incorporation	CO	Stock - Price on:12/24/2007	$0.135
Employees	9	Stock Exchange	OTC
Auditor	Altschuler, Melvoin & Glasser LLP	Ticker Symbol	XFMY
Stk Agt	Corporate Stock Transfer, Inc.	Outstanding Shares	40,080,000
Counsel	NA	E.P.S	-$0.02
DUNS No.	NA	Shareholders	NA

Business: The group's principal activity is to develop proprietary xml-based solutions for the Internet-based economy with a focus on e-commerce and the conversion of data from legacy formats to xml (extensible markup language). The products include goxml transform, goxml registry, goxml messaging & goxml db. Goxml transform xml data mapping can be easily managed with an environment that includes two main components: a gui for creating mapping templates and a server-side transformation engine, both written in java. Goxml registry is an enterprise registry platform based on goxml db, native xml database, and employs goxml transforms using commonly accepted standards, protocols & methodologies including ebxml & uddi. Goxml messaging delivers & messages ebxml messages. Goxml db is a native xml database and query engine. The customers of the group are information builders, inc and engineering, management and integration, inc. On 27-Sep-2004, the group acquired xformity, inc.

Primary SIC and add'l.: 7372
CIK No: 0001048501
Officers: Chris Ball/CEO, Mark Haugejorde/53/Chmn., Pres., Jack Rabin/CFO, Drew Seale/CTO
Directors: Michael Shahsavari/59/Chmn., Mark Haugejorde/53/Chmn., Pres., Paul Dwyer/48/Dir., Shawn Taylor/48/Dir.
Owners: Shawn Taylor/2.87%, Insiders/6.01%, Mark Haugejorde/5.00%, Paradigm Group II, LLC/4.22%, Jack Rabin/0.81%, Chris Ball/2.27%, Homayoun Aminmadani/7.34%, Paradigm Millennium Fund, LP/17.79%, Donald Ghareeb/15.74%, Drew Seale/2.07%, Farzin Ferdowsi/10.26%, Michael Shahsavari/0.86%

Financial Data: Fiscal Year End: 06/30   **Latest Annual Data:** 06/30/2007

Year	Sales	Net Income
2007	$1,076,000	-$1,436,000
2006	$724,000	-$2,970,000
2005	$457,000	-$2,167,000

Curr. Assets:	$130,000	Curr. Liab.:	$2,550,000		
Plant, Equip.:	$51,000	Total Liab.:	$2,753,000	Indic. Yr. Divd.:	NA
Total Assets:	$185,000	Net Worth:	-$2,568,000	Debt/ Equity:	NA

Xilinx Inc

2100 Logic Dr., San Jose, CA, 95124; **PH:** 1-408-559-7778; http:// www.xilinx.com

General - Incorporation	DE	Stock - Price on:12/24/2007	$27.22
Employees	3,353	Stock Exchange	NDQ
Auditor	Ernst & Young LLP	Ticker Symbol	XLNX
Stk Agt	Computershare Trust Co	Outstanding Shares	297,890,000
Counsel	NA	E.P.S.	NA
DUNS No.	11-816-8293	Shareholders	NA

Business: The groups principle activities include designing, developing and marketing programmable logic solutions. The groups solutions include advanced integrated circuits (ICs), software design tools, predefined system functions delivered as intellectual property (IP) cores, design services, customer training, field engineering and technical support solutions. The group operates from United States.

Primary SIC and add'l.: 3674 7372 7371
CIK No: 0000743988
Subsidiaries: AccelChip, Inc., Hier Design Inc., Xilinx AB, Xilinx Antilles N.V., Xilinx Asia Pacific Pte. Ltd., Xilinx Benelux B.V.B.A., Xilinx Canada Co., Xilinx Development Corporation, Xilinx GmbH, Xilinx Holding Five Limited, Xilinx Holding Four Limited, Xilinx Holding Seven, Xilinx Holding Six Limited, Xilinx Holding Three Ltd., Xilinx Holding Two Limited 23 Subsidiaries included in the Index
Officers: Willem P. Roelandts/Chmn., CEO, Pres./$4,444,887.00, Sandeep Vij/VP - Worldwide Marketing, Bruce Talley/VP, GM, Lisa Washington/Contact - Worldwide Public Relations, Corporate, Exec. Programs, Patrick Little/VP - Worldwide Sales, Services/$1,232,799.00, Paul McCambridge/VP - Xilinx International, Jon Olson/CFO, Sr. VP/$1,225,036.00, Kevin Cooney/CIO, VP, William G. Howard/Dir. - Consultant, Michael J. Patterson/Dir. - Consultant, Silvia Gianelli/Contact - Worldwide Public Relations Corporate, Vertical, Horizontal Markets, Customer Success, Bruce Fienberg/Contact - Worldwide Public Relations, High Performance Platform, Virtex, DSP, Embedded, Christelle Moraga/Public Relations, Europe, Scott Hover-Smoot/VP, General Counsel, Sec., Keith A. Chanroo/Sec. (26 Officers included in Index)
Directors: Willem P. Roelandts/Chmn., CEO, Pres., Elizabeth W. Vanderslice/Dir., John L. Doyle/Dir. - Consultant, Jerald G. Fishman/Dir., Philip T. Gianos/Dir., William G. Howard/Dir. - Consultant, Michael J. Patterson/Dir. - Consultant, Marshall C. Turner/Dir. - Consultant
Owners: UBS AG/10.30%, Michael J. Patterson, Omid Tahernia, Willem P. Roelandts, T. Rowe Price Associates, Inc./12.30%, Boon C. Ooi, John L. Doyle, Insiders/1.40%, Richard W. Sevcik, Marshall C. Turner, Capital Research and Management Company/14.60%, William G. Howard, Capital Group International, Inc./12.50%, Jerald G. Fishman, Elizabeth W. Vanderslice (19 Owners included in Index)

Curr. Assets:	$1,301,552,000	Curr. Liab.:	$381,130,000	P/E Ratio:	25.68
Plant, Equip.:	$335,114,000	Total Liab.:	$454,411,000	Indic. Yr. Divd.:	NA
Total Assets:	$2,937,473,000	Net Worth:	$2,483,062,000	Debt/ Equity:	0.5638

Xinhua China Ltd

PO Box 15, 505 Burrard St., Ste. 1880, Vancouver, BC, V1Y 7N3; **PH:** 1-86-1085656588;
http:// www.xinhuachina.com.cn; **Email:** info2@xinhuachina.com.cn

General - Incorporation	NV	Stock - Price on:12/24/2007	$0.043
Employees	NA	Stock Exchange	OTC
Auditor	Samuel H. Wong & Co., LLP	Ticker Symbol	XHUA
Stk Agt	Pacific Stock Transfer Company	Outstanding Shares	NA
Counsel	NA	E.P.S	NA
DUNS No.	NA	Shareholders	NA

Business: The group's principle activities include acquiring, exploring and developing mining properties. The company is in its exploration stage. The company maintains its offices in las vegas, Nevada and in vancouver, british columbia. The company in its first phase conducts research of the available geologic literature, personal interviews with geologists, mining engineers and others familiar with the prospect sites. In its second phase, it involves an initial examination of the underground characteristics of the vein structure that was identified by first phase of exploration. The group operates from United States.

Primary SIC and add'l.: 1041
CIK No: 0001104904
Subsidiaries: Beijing Boheng Investments and Management Co., Ltd., Beijing Joannes Information Technology Co. Lt, Pac-Poly and Boheng, Pac-Poly Investment Ltd
Officers: Xianping Wang/47/Dir., CEO, Pres.

Directors: Xianping Wang/47/Dir., CEO, Pres.

Owners: Derrick Luu/10.38%, Jianmin Zhou/16.03%, Hongxing Li/8.88%, Insiders/19.02%, Xianping Wang/19.00%, Lily Wang/12.40%

Financial Data: *Fiscal Year End:*06/30 *Latest Annual Data:* 6/30/2006

Year	Sales	Net Income
2006	$37,627,000	-$10,838,000
2005	$15,497,000	-$5,652,000
2004	NA	-$7,000

Curr. Assets:	$1,389,000	Curr. Liab.:	$2,554,000		
Plant, Equip.:	$14,000	Total Liab.:	$8,693,000	Indic. Yr. Divd.:	NA
Total Assets:	$2,028,000	Net Worth:	-$6,665,000	Debt/ Equity:	NA

XL Capital Ltd

XL Reinsurance America, Seaview House 70, Seaview Ave., Stamford, CT, 06902; *PH:* 1-203-964-5200; *Fax:* 1-203-964-0763; *http://* www.xl-capital.com

General - Incorporation	Cayman Islands	Stock- Price on:12/24/2007	$82.83
Employees	3,772	Stock Exchange	NYSE
Auditor	PricewaterhouseCoopers LLP	Ticker Symbol	XL
Stk Agt	Mellon Investor Services LLC	Outstanding Shares	175,150,000
Counsel	Hunter & Hunter	E.P.S	$10.51
DUNS No.	87-564-7240	Shareholders	NA

Business: The group's principal activities are to provide insurance and reinsurance coverage and financial products and services. The group's activities are carried out through three segments: insurance, reinsurance and financial products and services. The insurance division underwrites general liability, directors and officers' liability, professional and employment practices liability, environmental liability, property, program business, marine and energy, aviation and satellite and other product lines. The reinsurance division provides casualty, property, accident and health, other specialty reinsurance and life products. The financial products and services division provides insurance, reinsurance and derivative solutions for complex financial risks including financial guaranty insurance and reinsurance, weather and energy risk management products and institutional life products.

Primary SIC and add'l.: 6361 6331 6321 6311 6351

CIK No: 0000875159

Subsidiaries: 37 Lambert Road LLC, Baltusrol Holdings Limited, Brockbank Holdings Limited, Brockbank Personal Lines Limited (Dormant), Brockbank Syndicate Services Limited, Cassidy Brockbank Limited - (Dormant), ClearWater Opportunity Fund Ltd., County Down Limited, Cumberland California, Inc., Cumberland Holdings, Inc., Cumberland New York, Inc., Cybersettle Financial Services LLC, Cybersettle Insurance Brokerage Services LLC, Cybersettle, Inc., Denham Direct Underwriters Ltd 154 Subsidiaries included in the Index

Officers: Brian M. Ohara/Dir., CEO, Pres./$8,850,751.00, James H. Veghte/Exec. VP, Chief Executive - Reinsurance Operations, CEO - XL Reinsurance America Inc/$3,068,334.00, Sarah E. Street/Exec. VP, Chief Investment Officer/$3,451,143.00, Kirstin Romann Gould/Exec. VP, General Counsel, Sec., Michael Lobdell/Exec. VP, Brian Nocco/CFO, Exec. VP, Clive R. Tobin/Exec. VP, Chief Executive - Insurance Operations/$5,675,642.00, Anthony E. Beale/Exec. VP - Human Resources, Jerry M. De St Paer/Exec. VP/$3,510,393.00, Fiona E. Luck/Exec. VP, Chief - Staff, Henry C.V. Keeling/COO, Exec. VP/$5,170,416.00, Charles F. Barr/Exec. VP, General Counsel

Directors: Brian M. Ohara/Dir., CEO, Pres., Michael P. Esposito/Chmn., Robert R. Glauber/Dir., Herbert Haag/Dir., Joseph Mauriello/Dir., Dale R. Comey/Dir., Eugene M. McQuade/Dir., Alan Z. Senter/Dir., Ellen E. Thrower/Dir., Robert S. Parker/Dir., John T. Thornton/Dir., Cyril E. Rance/Dir.

Owners: Dale R. Comey, Cyril Rance, Alan Z. Senter, Robert Glauber, Insiders/2.71%, Henry C. V. Keeling, Joseph Mauriello, Pzena Investment Management, LLC/6.80%, Herbert Haag, Michael P. Esposito, Christopher V. Greetham, Jerry de St. Paer, AXA Assurances I.A.R.D. Mutuelle, AXA Assurances Vie Mutuelle,/8.80%, Franklin Resources, Inc./8.80%, Eugene M. McQuade *(25 Owners included in Index)*

Financial Data: *Fiscal Year End:*12/31 *Latest Annual Data:* 12/31/2006

Year	Sales	Net Income
2006	$9,833,195,000	$1,762,767,000
2005	$11,285,415,000	-$1,251,976,000
2004	$10,028,460,000	$1,166,613,000

Curr. Assets:	$15,466,412,000	Curr. Liab.:	$8,865,407,000	P/E Ratio:	7.52
Plant, Equip.:	NA	Total Liab.:	$49,177,704,000	Indic. Yr. Divd.:	$1.520
Total Assets:	$59,308,870,000	Net Worth:	$10,131,166,000	Debt/ Equity:	0.2977

XLR Medical Corp NEW

602 Deming Pl., Chicago, IL, 60614; *PH:* 1-360-201-0400; *Fax:* 1-773-871-0171; *http://* www.exelarmedical.com; *Email:* info@exelarmedical.com

General - Incorporation	NV	Stock- Price on:12/24/2007	$0.22
Employees	NA	Stock Exchange	OTC
Auditor	Manning Elliott LLP	Ticker Symbol	XLRM
Stk Agt	Pacific Stock Transfer Company	Outstanding Shares	NA
Counsel	NA	E.P.S	-$0.22
DUNS No.	NA	Shareholders	NA

Business: The groups principal activity is to focus on the acquisition, exploration and development of mineral properties. The group operates from the United States and Canada.

Primary SIC and add'l.: 1040

CIK No: 0001138608

Officers: Logan B. Anderson/54/CEO, CFO, Pres., Sec., Treasurer, Dir., Leonard Reiffel/Chmn., CTO, Robert J. Morton/Sr. Consultant Regulatory, Quality Assurance Matter, Roger Wheatley/Consultant

Directors: Logan B. Anderson/54/CEO, CFO, Pres., Sec., Treasurer, Dir.

Owners: Reg C. Handford/5.10%, Logan B. Anderson/2.40%

Financial Data: *Fiscal Year End:*12/31 *Latest Annual Data:* 1/31/2007

Year	Sales	Net Income
2007	NA	-$108,000
2006	NA	$681,000
2005	NA	-$2,246,000

Curr. Assets:	$0	Curr. Liab.:	$21,000		
Plant, Equip.:	NA	Total Liab.:	$21,000	Indic. Yr. Divd.:	NA
Total Assets:	$625,000	Net Worth:	$604,000	Debt/ Equity:	NA

XM Satellite Radio Holdings Inc

1500 Eckington Pl NE, Washington, DC, 20002; *PH:* 1-202-380-4000; *http://* www.xmradio.com

General - Incorporation	DE	Stock- Price on:12/24/2007	$10.84
Employees	860	Stock Exchange	NDQ
Auditor	KPMG LLP	Ticker Symbol	XMSR
Stk Agt	Bank Boston EquiServe	Outstanding Shares	306,080,000
Counsel	Dara F. Altman	E.P.S	-$2.48
DUNS No.	NA	Shareholders	NA

Business: The group's principal activity is to design and develop the xm radio system, which was formed for the purpose of operating a digital audio radio service (dars). The group provides audio entertainment and information programming for reception by vehicle, home and portable radios through its high-power satellites rock and roll. These satellites offer 100 channels which cover music, news, talk, sports and children's programs with clear sound and coast-to-coast coverage. Xm radios are available under the brand names sony, pioneer and alpine. The group also provides music formats and delivers a wide range of ethnic and informational programming. The group owns two fcc licenses to provide a satellite digital radio service in the United States. Radio services are transmitted through the commercial satellites.

Primary SIC and add'l.: 4832 4899

CIK No: 0001091530

Subsidiaries: Interoperable Technologies LLC, XM 1500 Eckington LLC, XM Capital Resources Inc., XM EMall Inc., XM Equipment Leasing LLC, XM Innovations Inc., XM Investments LLC, XM Orbit LLC, XM Radio Inc., XM Satellite Radio Inc.

Officers: Nathaniel A. Davis/Dir., CEO, Pres., Joseph Titlebaum/General Counsel, Sec., Joseph J. Euteneuer/CFO, Exec. VP/$1,871,186.00, Eric Logan/Exec. VP - Programming/$1,982,283.00, Dara F. Altman/Exec. VP - Business, Legal Affairs, Steve Cook/Exec. VP - Automotive Marketing, Vernon Irvin/Exec. VP, Chief Marketing Officer, Dan Murphy/Exec. VP - Retail Aftermarket Distribution, Stell Patsiokas/Exec. VP - Technology, Engineering, Joe Zarella/Exec. VP - Business Operations

Directors: Nathaniel A. Davis/Dir., CEO, Pres., Gary M. Parsons/Chmn., Thomas J. Donohue/Dir., Chester A. Huber/Dir., Hugh Panero/52/Dir., Jarl Mohn/Dir., Jack Shaw/Dir., Eddy W. Hartenstein/Dir., John W. Mendel/Dir., Jeffrey D. Zients/Dir., Joan Amble/Dir.

Owners: Jack Shaw, Hugh Panero, Insiders/2.40%, Jarl Mohn, Stelios Patsiokas, Nathaniel Davis, American Honda Motor Co., Inc./6.70%, Goldman Sachs Asset Management, L.P./5.60%, Eddy W. Hartenstein, Gary M. Parsons, Capital Research and Management Company/5.00%, Erik Logan Toppenberg, AXA Assurances I.A.R.D. Mutuelle/10.20%, Joan L. Amble, Rowe T. Price/8.60% *(18 Owners included in Index)*

Financial Data: *Fiscal Year End:*12/31 *Latest Annual Data:* 12/31/2006

Year	Sales	Net Income
2006	$933,417,000	-$718,872,000
2005	$558,266,000	-$666,715,000
2004	$244,443,000	-$642,368,000

Curr. Assets:	$432,658,000	Curr. Liab.:	$694,322,000		
Plant, Equip.:	$975,711,000	Total Liab.:	$2,238,498,000	Indic. Yr. Divd.:	NA
Total Assets:	$1,840,618,000	Net Worth:	-$397,880,000	Debt/ Equity:	NA

Xm Satellite Radio Inc

1500 Eckington Pl Ne, Washington, DC, 20002; *PH:* 1-202-380-4000; *Fax:* 1-202-380-4500; *http://* www.xmradio.com; *Email:* listenercare@xmradio.com

General - Incorporation	DE	Stock- Price on:12/24/2007	NA
Employees	710	Stock Exchange	Nasdaq
Auditor	KPMG LLP	Ticker Symbol	NA
Stk Agt	Bank Boston EquiServe	Outstanding Shares	NA
Counsel	Dara F. Altman	E.P.S	NA
DUNS No.	NA	Shareholders	NA

Business: The group's principle activity is to design and develop the xm radio system which was formed for the purpose of operating a digital audio radio service (dars). The group provides audio entertainment and information programming for reception by vehicle, home and portable radios through its high-power satellites rock and roll. These satellites offers 100 channels which covers music, talk, sports and children's programs with clear sound and coast-to-coast coverage. Xm radios are available under the brand names sony, pioneer and alpine. The group also provides music formats and delivers a wide range of ethnic and informational programming. The group owns two fcc licenses to provide a satellite digital radio service in the United States. The group transmits radio services through the commercial satellites. The group's quarterly revenue for September 2007 was 287.46 millions of USD.

Primary SIC and add'l.: 4832 4899

CIK No: 0001116317

Subsidiaries: Interoperable Technologies LLC, XM Capital Resources Inc., XM EMall Inc., XM Equipment Leasing LLC, XM Innovations Inc.

Officers: Hugh Panero/Dir., CEO, Nathaniel A. Davis/Dir., Interim CEO, Pres., Joseph Titlebaum/General Counsel, Sec., Eric Logan/Exec. VP - Programming, Stell Patsiokas/Exec. VP - Technology, Engineering, Dara F. Altman/Exec. VP - Business, Legal Affairs, Steve Cook/Exec. VP - Automotive Marketing, Joseph J. Euteneuer/CFO, Exec. VP, Vernon Irvin/Exec. VP, Chief Marketing Officer, Dan Murphy/Exec. VP - Retail Aftermarket Distribution, Joe Zarella/Exec. VP - Business Operations

Directors: Hugh Panero/Dir., CEO, Nathaniel A. Davis/Dir., Interim CEO, Pres., Gary Parsons/Chmn., Thomas J. Donohue/Dir., Chester A. Huber/Dir., Jack Shaw/Dir., Eddy W. Hartenstein/Dir., John Mendel/Dir., Jarl Mohn/Dir., Jeffrey D. Zients/Dir., Joan Amble/Dir.

XO Communications Inc

11111 Sunset Hills Rd., Reston, VA, 20190; *PH:* 1-703-547-2000; *http://* www.xo.com

General - Incorporation	DE	Stock- Price on:12/24/2007	$4.36
Employees	NA	Stock Exchange	OTC
Auditor	KPMG LLP	Ticker Symbol	XOHO
Stk Agt	KPMG LLP, Ernst & Young LLP	Outstanding Shares	182,010,000
Counsel	Willkie Farr & Gallagher LLP	E.P.S	NA
DUNS No.	NA	Shareholders	NA

Business: The group's principal activity is to provide telecommunication services. The services include local and long distance voice, Internet access, private data networking and hosting services. Voice services include conferencing, domestic and international toll free services and voicemail, and transaction processing services for prepaid calling cards. Internet access services include Internet access, digital subscriber line and dial access. Private data networking services provides virtual private network services

and ethernet services. Hosting services include Web site services, Web hosting services and server collocation and management and customer support services. Customer base of the group includes small and medium businesses to multi-location businesses, large enterprises and wholesale customers. During Jun 2002 the group filed for chapter 11 proceedings and emerged from such proceedings in jan 2003. During Jun 2004, the group acquired allegiance telecom inc.

Primary SIC and add'l.: 4813

CIK No: 0001111634

Subsidiaries: 50% Interest in Telecommunications of Nevada, LLC, 99% Interest in XO Asia Limited, Coast to Coast Telecommunications, Inc., LHP Equipment, Inc., LMDS Holdings, Inc., Nextlink Global ApS, V & K Holdings., XO Asia Limited, XO Communications Services, Inc., XO Communications, LLC, XO Communications, LLC., XO Data Services, LLC., XO Global Communications, Inc, XO Holdings, Inc., XO Interactive, Inc. 29 Subsidiaries included in the Index

Officers: Carl J. Grivner/Dir., CEO/$1,465,106.00, Terri Burke/VP - Human Resources, Wayne Rehberger/COO/$665,600.00, Heather Burnett Gold/Sr. VP - Government Relations/$415,500.00, Simone Wu/Sr. VP, General Counsel, Ron Scott/Sr. VP - XO Communications, Group Pres. - XO Interactive, XO Hosting, XO One, Robert Geller/CIO/$445,600.00, Ernie Ortega/Pres. - XO Carrier Services, William Garrahan/Sr. VP - Corporate Development, Strategy, Gregory W. Freiberg/CFO/$340,269.00, Tom Cady/Pres. - XO Business Services

Directors: Carl J. Grivner/Dir., CEO, Carl C. Icahn/Chmn., Keith Meister/Dir., Robert Knauss/Dir., Peter K. Shea/56/Dir., Vincent Intrieri/Dir., Adam Dell/Dir., Fredrik Gradin/Dir.

Owners: Heather Burnett Gold, Insiders/59.40%, Wayne M. Rehberger, Robert Knauss, Robert Geller, JPMorgan Chase& Co./7.90%, Gregory Freiberg, Third Point LLC/6.10%, Carl C. Icahn/58.80%, Amalgamated Gadget, L.P./8.10%, Carl J. Grivner/1.10%

Financial Data: Fiscal Year End:12/31 Latest Annual Data: 12/31/2006

Year	Sales	Net Income
2006	$1,411,616,000	-$130,344,000
2005	$1,433,622,000	-$146,505,000
2004	$1,300,420,000	-$405,543,000

Curr. Assets:	$333,010,000	Curr. Liab.:	$319,641,000		
Plant, Equip.:	$678,233,000	Total Liab.:	$945,263,000	Indic. Yr. Divd.:	NA
Total Assets:	$1,116,111,000	Net Worth:	$170,848,000	Debt/ Equity:	2.3505

Xoma Ltd

2910 7th St., Berkeley, CA, 94710; **PH:** 1-510-204-7200; **Fax:** 1-510-644-0537; http:// www.xoma.com

General - Incorporation	Bermuda	**Stock** - Price on:12/24/2007	$3.34
Employees	255	Stock Exchange	NDQ
Auditor	Ernst & Young LLP	Ticker Symbol	XOMA
Stk Agt	Mellon Investor Services LLC	Outstanding Shares	131,690,000
Counsel	Cahill Gordon & Reindel LLP	E.P.S.	-$0.444
DUNS No.	05-134-0339	Shareholders	NA

Business: The group's principal activity is to develop and manufacture recombinant antibodies and other protein products to treat cancer, immunological and inflammatory disorders and infectious diseases. The group's products are presently in various stages of development and all are subject to regulatory approval before the group or its collaborators can commercially introduce any products. Current strategic alliances of the group include baxter healthcare corporation, genentech inc., millennium pharmaceuticals, inc. And onyx pharmaceuticals, inc.

Primary SIC and add'l.: 2834 8731

CIK No: 0000791908

Subsidiaries: XOMA (Bermuda) Ltd., Xoma (us) LLC, XOMA Ireland Limited, XOMA Technology Ltd.

Officers: John L. Castello/Chmn., CEO, Pres./$923,598.00, Christopher J. Margolin/VP, General Counsel, Sec./$450,115.00, Patrick J. Scannon/Dir., Exec. VP, Chief Biotechnology Officer/$498,581.00, David J. Boyle/VP - Finance, CFO/$359,998.00, Robert S. Tenerowicz/VP - Operations/$439,015.00, Calvin L. McGoogan/VP - Quality, Facilities, Daniel P. Cafaro/VP - Regulatory Affairs, Mark L. White/VP - Cell, Analytical Development, Mary Haak-Frendscho/VP - Preclinical Research, Development, Charles C. Wells/VP - Human Resources, Information Technology

Directors: John L. Castello/Chmn., CEO, Pres., James G. Andress/Dir., Patrick J. Scannon/Dir., Exec. VP, Chief Biotechnology Officer, Peter Barton Hutt/Dir., William K. Bowes/Dir., Denman W. Van Ness/Dir., Patrick J. Zenner/Dir., Charles J. Fisher/Dir.

Owners: Patrick J. Scannon, William K. Bowes, David J. Boyle, Christopher J. Margolin, Wells Fargo & Company/4.80%, Arthur Kornberg, Patrick J. Zenner, Peter Barton Hutt, Insiders/1.50%, Denman W. Van Ness, Platinum Asset Management Limited/6.00%, QVT Financial LP/5.00%, James G. Andress, John L. Castello, Robert S. Tenerowicz (17 Owners included in Index)

Financial Data: Fiscal Year End:12/31 Latest Annual Data: 12/31/2006

Year	Sales	Net Income
2006	$29,498,000	-$51,841,000
2005	$18,669,000	$2,779,000
2004	$3,665,000	-$78,942,000

Curr. Assets:	$65,888,000	Curr. Liab.:	$22,667,000		
Plant, Equip.:	$22,434,000	Total Liab.:	$129,651,000	Indic. Yr. Divd.:	NA
Total Assets:	$91,478,000	Net Worth:	-$38,173,000	Debt/ Equity:	NA

Xpention Genetics Inc

10965 Elizabeth Dr., Conifer, CO, 80433; ; http:// www.xpention.com;
Email: davidkittrell@xpention.com

General - Incorporation	NV	**Stock** - Price on:12/24/2007	$0.051
Employees	NA	Stock Exchange	OTC
Auditor	Stark Winter Schenkein & Co., LLP	Ticker Symbol	XPNG
Stk Agt	Holladay Stock Transfer, Inc.	Outstanding Shares	57,730,000
Counsel	NA	E.P.S.	-$0.004
DUNS No.	NA	Shareholders	NA

Business: The groups principal activity is primarily engaged in the development of technology acquired under license for detection of cancer tumors. The group operates from the United States.

Primary SIC and add'l.: 8731

CIK No: 0001223533

Subsidiaries: Xpention, Inc

Officers: David Kittrell/57/Dir., CEO, CFO, Pres., Murray Fleming/Contact - Catalyst Investor Relations, Zbigniew Walaszek/Chief Scientific Officer

Directors: David Kittrell/57/Dir., CEO, CFO, Pres.

Owners: David Kittrell/23.80%, Zbigniew Walaszek, James Coutris/19.60%, Insiders/24.00%

Financial Data: Fiscal Year End:05/31 Latest Annual Data: 05/31/2007

Year	Sales	Net Income
2007	NA	-$206,000
2006	NA	-$976,000
2005	NA	-$157,000

Curr. Assets:	$25,000	Curr. Liab.:	$496,000		
Plant, Equip.:	NA	Total Liab.:	$496,000	Indic. Yr. Divd.:	NA
Total Assets:	$25,000	Net Worth:	-$471,000	Debt/ Equity:	NA

XRAYMEDIA Inc

555 Hastings St., Vancouver, BC, V6B 1M1; **PH:** 1-888-777-0658; http:// www.xraymedia.com;
Email: info@xraymedia.com

General - Incorporation	MN	**Stock** - Price on:12/24/2007	$0.0005
Employees	NA	Stock Exchange	OTC
Auditor	Bedinger & Co	Ticker Symbol	TWCI
Stk Agt	First American Stock Transfer, Inc.	Outstanding Shares	NA
Counsel	Michael J. Morrison	E.P.S.	NA
DUNS No.	NA	Shareholders	NA

Business: The group's principal activity is to operate and market a general media Internet Website portal. The group has software called the xraymedia live media marketplace. The Website xraymedia.com assists media buyers and sellers to register, list media buy and sell orders, track inventory changes, add private members to their personal groupings, negotiate and close deals in an online, real-time dynamically streaming marketplace. It also provides services such as print ad design services, public relations and investor relation services. The group is in development stage.

Primary SIC and add'l.: 7375 7389

CIK No: 0001097068

Subsidiaries: Xray and XRAYMEDIA refers to XRAYMEDIA, Inc.

Financial Data: Fiscal Year End:12/31 Latest Annual Data: 12/31/2004

Year	Sales	Net Income
2004	$70,000	-$15,634,000
2003	$0	-$2,013,000
2002	$0	-$1,680,000

Curr. Assets:	$29,000	Curr. Liab.:	$1,923,000		
Plant, Equip.:	$60,000	Total Liab.:	$1,923,000	Indic. Yr. Divd.:	NA
Total Assets:	$90,000	Net Worth:	-$1,833,000	Debt/ Equity:	NA

XRG Inc

601 Cleveland St., Ste 501-13, Clearwater, FL, 33755; **PH:** 1-727-475-3060; http:// www.xrginc.com;
Email: info@xrginc.com

General - Incorporation	DE	**Stock** - Price on:12/24/2007	$0.005
Employees	NA	Stock Exchange	OTC
Auditor	Mahoney Cohen & Co. CPA, P.C	Ticker Symbol	XRGI
Stk Agt	Florida Atlantic Stock Transfer, Inc.	Outstanding Shares	NA
Counsel	NA	E.P.S.	NA
DUNS No.	NA	Shareholders	NA

Business: The group's principal activities were to provide administrative services for invoicing, collections, regulatory compliance, credit reviews, processing payments and commissions. The group is in the development stage and is focused on acquiring and operating both asset and non-asset based truck-load carriers throughout the United States. The group acquired on 13-Apr-2004 highbourne corp & highway transport inc. On 04-May-2004, the group acquired express freight systems, inc and on 07-Jun-2004, carolina truck connection inc.

Primary SIC and add'l.: 4213 8748

CIK No: 0001168375

Subsidiaries: Express Freight Systems, Inc, R&R Express Intermodal, Inc., RSV, Inc., Xrg G&a, Inc., XRG Logistics, Inc.

Financial Data: Fiscal Year End:03/31 Latest Annual Data: 3/31/2005

Year	Sales	Net Income
2005	$39,353,000	-$14,237,000
2004	$4,682,000	-$4,450,000
2003	$686,000	-$830,000

Curr. Assets:	$5,638,000	Curr. Liab.:	$10,412,000		
Plant, Equip.:	$1,621,000	Total Liab.:	$11,262,000	Indic. Yr. Divd.:	NA
Total Assets:	$7,938,000	Net Worth:	-$3,324,000	Debt/ Equity:	NA

XStream Beverage Group Inc

2 S University Dr., Ste. 220, Plantation, FL, 33324; **PH:** 1-954-473-0850; http:// www.xbev.com

General - Incorporation	NV	**Stock** - Price on:12/24/2007	$0.021
Employees	4	Stock Exchange	OTC
Auditor	Sherb & Co. LLP	Ticker Symbol	XBVG
Stk Agt	Interwest Transfer Company, Inc.	Outstanding Shares	57,910,000
Counsel	NA	E.P.S.	-$0.043
DUNS No.	NA	Shareholders	NA

Business: The group's principal activity is to develop new age beverages. It has developed a non-alcoholic energy drink yohimbe. The raw materials utilized in the formulation of this drink are readily available from suppliers throughout the United States. Currently, the group is operating in the domestic market. It also intends to acquire candidates in the new age beverage field and develop an integrated network of regionally based branded bottlers whose brands, production capabilities and distribution outlets can be effectively leveraged. In 2004, it acquired historic squeeze soda brand, Pacific Rim natural juice company inc, maui juice company, ayer beverage and assets & certain liabilities of master distributors inc.

Primary SIC and add'l.: 2095 2099

CIK No: 0000853833

Subsidiaries: Beverage Network of Connecticut, Inc., Beverage Network of Hawaii, Inc., XStream Beverage Network, Inc., Xstream Brands

Officers: Theodore Farnsworth/46/Chmn., CEO, Pres., Principal Financial Officer, Barry Willson/60/Vice Chmn., Chief Scientific Officer, Sec., Treasurer

Directors: Theodore Farnsworth/46/Chmn., CEO, Pres., Principal Financial Officer, Barry Willson/60/Vice Chmn., Chief Scientific Officer, Sec., Treasurer, Foster Devereux/Member - Advisory Board, Elizabeth Dunn/Member - Advisory Board, Richard Q. Armstrong/Member - Advisory Board

Owners: Theodore Farnsworth/100.00%, Insiders/8.40%, Theodore Farnsworth/3.20%, Barry Willson/5.20%, Theodore Farnsworth/100.00%, Insiders/100.00%, Insiders/100.00%, Broadlawn Master Fund/12.60%

Financial Data: Fiscal Year End:12/31 **Latest Annual Data:** 12/31/2006

Year	Sales	Net Income
2006	$284,000	-$26,513,000
2005	$10,226,000	-$1,954,000
2004	$8,584,000	-$9,556,000

Curr. Assets:	$3,110,000	**Curr. Liab.:**	$17,725,000		
Plant, Equip.:	$16,000	**Total Liab.:**	$22,505,000	**Indic. Yr. Divd.:**	NA
Total Assets:	$4,077,000	**Net Worth:**	-$18,428,000	**Debt/ Equity:**	NA

Xstream Mobile Solutions Corp

Formerly: Netchoice Inc

14422 Edison Dr., Unit D, New Lenox, IL, 60451; **PH:** 1-708-205-2222

General - Incorporation	DE	Stock - Price on:12/24/2007	$2
Employees	1	Stock Exchange	NA
Auditor	Bagell, Josephs, Levine & Co. LLC	Ticker Symbol	NA
Stk Agt	Florida Atlantic Stock Transfer, Inc.	Outstanding Shares	11,760,000
Counsel	NA	E.P.S.	-$0.19
DUNS No.	15-187-6935	Shareholders	NA

Business: The group's principle activity is to provide environmental drilling which has been discontinued since 31-Dec-2001. The group sold its real estate, office equipment and drilling assets and ceased operation. Prior to 31-Dec-2001, the group provided environmental drilling, primarily environmental monitoring and testing in South Carolina and Georgia. The drilling activities included drilling for soil and water samples, drilling and installation of ground water monitoring wells, drilling and installation of recovery wells , and drilling and installation of water supply production wells. The group operates from United States.

Primary SIC and add'l.: 1781

CIK No: 0000842919

Financial Data: Fiscal Year End:09/30 **Latest Annual Data:** 9/30/2005

Year	Sales	Net Income
2005	NA	-$18,000
2004	NA	-$271,000
2003	NA	-$169,000

Curr. Assets:	NA	**Curr. Liab.:**	$263,000		
Plant, Equip.:	NA	**Total Liab.:**	$263,000	**Indic. Yr. Divd.:**	NA
Total Assets:	NA	**Net Worth:**	-$263,000	**Debt/ Equity:**	NA

XsunX Inc

65 Enterprise, Aliso Viejo, CA, 92656; **PH:** 1-949-330-8060; **Fax:** 1-949-330-8061;
http:// www.xsunx.com

General - Incorporation	CO	Stock - Price on:12/24/2007	$0.46
Employees	5	Stock Exchange	OTC
Auditor	Jaspers + Hall, PC	Ticker Symbol	XSNX
Stk Agt	Mountain Share Transfer	Outstanding Shares	157,020,000
Counsel	NA	E.P.S.	-$0.014
DUNS No.	NA	Shareholders	NA

Business: The groups principle activities include developing and marketing proprietary solar cell designing and core solar cell manufacturing systems, enabling licensees to manufacture advanced thin film solar devices on various substrates. The group operates from the United States.

Primary SIC and add'l.: 3674

CIK No: 0001039466

Officers: Tom M. Djokovich/Dir., CEO, Pres., Joseph Grimes/COO, Jeff Huitt/CFO

Directors: Tom M. Djokovich/Dir., CEO, Pres., John Moore/Chmn. - Scientific Advisory Board, Richard K. Ahrenkiel/Member - Scientific Advisory Board, Thomas Anderson/Dir., Edward T. Yu/Member - Scientific Advisory Board, Michael A. Russak/Member - Scientific Advisory Board

Owners: Joseph Grimes, Thomas Anderson, Tom Djokovich/11.39%

Financial Data: Fiscal Year End:09/30 **Latest Annual Data:** 9/30/2006

Year	Sales	Net Income
2006	$8,000	-$3,442,000
2005	NA	-$1,401,000
2004	NA	-$1,509,000

Curr. Assets:	$4,654,000	**Curr. Liab.:**	$589,000		
Plant, Equip.:	$398,000	**Total Liab.:**	$589,000	**Indic. Yr. Divd.:**	NA
Total Assets:	$6,884,000	**Net Worth:**	$6,296,000	**Debt/ Equity:**	NA

XTL Biopharmaceuticals Ltd

750 Lexington Ave., 20th Fl., New York, NY, 10022; **PH:** 1-212-531-5960; **Fax:** 1-212-531-5961;
http:// www.xtlbio.com

General - Incorporation	Israel	Stock - Price on:12/24/2007	$2.56
Employees	40	Stock Exchange	NDQ
Auditor	Kesselman & Kesselman	Ticker Symbol	XTLB
Stk Agt	NA	Outstanding Shares	22,010,000
Counsel	Kantor & Co	E.P.S.	-$1.02
DUNS No.	NA	Shareholders	NA

Business: The group's principle activities include acquiring, developing and commercializing of pharmaceutical products for the treatment of infectious diseases, particularly the prevention and treatment of hepatitis B and C. The company has three products under development including HepeX-B or HBV that will prevent re-infection with hepatitis B in liver transplant patients, XTL-6865 or HCV to prevent hepatitis C virus re-infection following a liver transplant and XTL-2125 from the HCV-SM small molecule development program which is a small molecule non-nucleoside polymerase inhibitor for the treatment of chronic hepatitis C. The group operates from United States.

Primary SIC and add'l.: 2834

CIK No: 0001023549

Subsidiaries: Biotest AG, ZLB Behring, Israeli tax, Israeli taxes, Ventures Ltd, XTL Biopharmaceuticals, Inc (Delaware), XTL Biopharmaceuticals, Inc.

Officers: Ron Bentsur/CEO, Bill Kessler/Dir. - Finance

Directors: Michael Weiss/Chmn., William Kennedy/Non Exec. Dir., Ido Seltenreich/Non Exec., External Dir., Vered Shany/Non Exec., External Dir., Ben Zion Weiner/Non Exec. Dir.

Financial Data: Fiscal Year End:12/31 **Latest Annual Data:** 12/31/2006

Year	Sales	Net Income
2006	$454,000	-$15,132,000
2005	$3,197,000	-$14,015,000

Curr. Assets:	$26,096,000	**Curr. Liab.:**	$3,402,000		
Plant, Equip.:	$490,000	**Total Liab.:**	$4,140,000	**Indic. Yr. Divd.:**	NA
Total Assets:	$26,900,000	**Net Worth:**	$22,760,000	**Debt/ Equity:**	NA

XTO Energy Inc

810 Houston St., Ste 2000, Fort Worth, TX, 76102; **PH:** 1-817-870-2800;
http:// www.crosstimbers.com

General - Incorporation	DE	Stock - Price on:12/24/2007	$62.45
Employees	1,939	Stock Exchange	NYSE
Auditor	KPMG LLP	Ticker Symbol	XTO
Stk Agt	Mellon Investor Services LLC	Outstanding Shares	368,370,000
Counsel	NA	E.P.S.	$3.51
DUNS No.	15-155-0084	Shareholders	NA

Business: The group's principle activities include acquiring, developing, exploiting and exploring of producing oil and gas properties. The group also processes, markets and transports oil and natural gas. The group operates from United States.

Primary SIC and add'l.: 1311 4924

CIK No: 0000868809

Subsidiaries: Barnett Gathering, LP, Cross Timbers Energy Services, Inc., Cross Timbers Trading Company, Ringwood Gathering Company, TimberlandGathering& ProcessingCompany,Inc., TrendGathering&Treating,LP, WTW Properties, Inc., X Landmark LLC, XTO Barnett LLC, XTO Resources I GP, LLC, XTO Resources I LP, LLC, XTO Resources I, LP

Officers: Bob R. Simpson/Chmn., CEO/$52,063,100.00, Frank G. McDonald/Sr. VP, General Counsel, Assist. Sec., Edwin S. Ryan/Sr. VP - Land Administration, Timothy L. Petrus/Dir., Exec. VP - Acquisitions, Advisory Dir./$2,166,942.00, Mark J. Pospisil/VP - Geology, Geophysics, Michael R. Tyson/VP - Financial Reporting, Douglas C. Schultze/Sr. VP - Midcontinent Operations, Nina C. Hutton/VP - Environmental, Health, Safety, Joy T. Webster/VP - Facilities, Bennie G. Kniffen/Sr. VP, Controller, Robert C. Myers/VP - Human Resources, Kenneth F. Staab/Sr. VP - Engineering, Terry F. Perkins/VP - Reservoir Engineering, Robert B. Gathright/Assist. Controller, Dir. - Budget and Planning, Kyle M. Hammond/VP - Operations, Permian Division, Alaska (33 Officers included in Index)

Directors: Bob R. Simpson/Chmn., CEO, Timothy L. Petrus/Dir., Exec. VP - Acquisitions, Advisory Dir., Lane G. Collins/Dir., William H. Adams/Dir., Phillip R. Kevil/Dir., Jack P. Randall/Dir., Scott G. Sherman/Dir., Herbert D. Simons/Dir., Louis G. Baldwin/Dir, CFO, Exec. VP, Advisory Dir., Vaughn O. Vennerberg/Dir., Sr. Exec. VP, Chief - Staff, Keith A. Hutton/Dir., Pres.

Owners: Louis G. Baldwin, Lane G. Collins, William H. Adams, Insiders/6.90%, Keith A. Hutton, Bob R. Simpson/2.68%, Vaughn O. Vennerberg, Timothy L. Petrus, Herbert D. Simons, Phillip R. Kevil, Scott G. Sherman, Jack P. Randall

Financial Data: Fiscal Year End:12/31 **Latest Annual Data:** 12/31/2006

Year	Sales	Net Income
2006	$4,578,000,000	$1,860,000,000
2005	$3,519,000,000	$1,152,000,000
2004	$1,947,601,000	$507,882,000

Curr. Assets:	$1,585,000,000	**Curr. Liab.:**	$1,240,000,000	**P/E Ratio:**	14.46
Plant, Equip.:	$10,824,000,000	**Total Liab.:**	$7,020,000,000	**Indic. Yr. Divd.:**	$0.480
Total Assets:	$12,885,000,000	**Net Worth:**	$5,865,000,000	**Debt/ Equity:**	0.6073

Xvariant Inc

2f-b, Xieton Bldg., No. 2 Gaoxin 2 Rd., New And Hi-tech Industry Zone Xian, Shaanxi, Shaanxi, 710000;

General - Incorporation	NV	Stock - Price on:12/24/2007	NA
Employees	NA	Stock Exchange	NA
Auditor	Moore & Assoc., Chartered	Ticker Symbol	NA
Stk Agt	Interwest Transfer Company, Inc.	Outstanding Shares	NA
Counsel	NA	E.P.S.	$0.00
DUNS No.	NA	Shareholders	NA

Business: The group's principal activities are to design, develop an Internet based referral system for the residential real estate industry. The technology enhances the use of the Internet in the home-buying process. The technology allows potential homebuyers to search for real estate properties from all participating real estate brokers listings. The group designs Web sites for real estate brokers. The group was incorporated as almost unique productions, inc., formed to produce and market music. In Nov 2000 the company discontinued its music production business and completed the acquisition of real estate federation, inc. (ref). The group changed its name to xvariant, inc. In Aug,2001. During fiscal 2002 the group acquired 360house.com, inc.

Primary SIC and add'l.: 7375

CIK No: 0001034764

Officers: Reed L. Benson/62/Dir., CEO, CFO

Directors: Reed L. Benson/62/Dir., CEO, CFO

Owners: Reed L. Benson/8.40%, Insiders/8.40%, Calico, Ltd./45.70%

Financial Data: Fiscal Year End:09/30 **Latest Annual Data:** 9/30/2002

Year	Sales	Net Income
2002	$1,383,000	-$1,460,000
2001	$266,000	-$1,298,000
2000	$0	-$20,000

Curr. Assets:	NA	**Curr. Liab.:**	$65,000		
Plant, Equip.:	NA	**Total Liab.:**	$65,000	**Indic. Yr. Divd.:**	NA
Total Assets:	NA	**Net Worth:**	-$65,000	**Debt/ Equity:**	NA

Xyratex Ltd

2031 Concourse Dr., San Jose, CA, 95131; *PH:* 1-408-325-7200; *Fax:* 1-408-894-0880;
http:// www.xyratex.com; *Email:* info@us.xyratex.com

General - Incorporation................Bermuda	*Stock*- Price on:12/24/2007 ....$22.06
Employees...1,557	Stock Exchange...NDQ
Auditor ....PricewaterhouseCoopers LLP	Ticker Symbol...XRTX
Stk Agt.....Computershare Investor Services LLC	Outstanding Shares 28,930,000
Counsel...NA	E.P.S...$2.08
DUNS No. 22-055-9095	Shareholders...NA

Business: The groups principle activity is to provide enterprise class data storage subsystems and network technology. The groups products include raid system and HP storage connectivity. The group operates from United States.

Primary SIC and add'l.: NA

CIK No: 0001284823

Subsidiaries: Xyratex (Malaysia) Sdn Bhd, Xyratex Holdings Inc., Xyratex International Inc., Xyratex Technology Limited

Officers: Steve Barber/47/Dir., CEO, Richard Pearce/Dir., CFO, Adam Wray/Exec. VP, Todd Gresham/Exec. VP

Directors: Steve Barber/47/Dir., CEO, Andrew Sukawaty/Chmn., Jonathan Brooks/Dir., Richard Pearce/Dir., CFO, Ernest Sampias/Dir., Steve Sanghi/Dir., Mike Windram/Dir.

Owners: Richard Pearce/0.46%, Ernest Sampias/0.01%, Adam Wray/0.31%, Andrew Sukawaty/0.37%, Steve Barber/2.44%, Steve Thompson/0.60%, Insiders/4.19%

*Financial Data: Fiscal Year End:*11/30   *Latest Annual Data:* 11/30/2006

Year	Sales	Net Income
2006	$983,633,000	$58,178,000
2005	$679,609,000	$42,169,000
2004	$459,014,000	-$135,169,000

Curr. Assets:	$267,506,000	*Curr. Liab.:*	$138,186,000	*P/E Ratio:*	10.61
Plant, Equip.:	$34,471,000	*Total Liab.:*	$141,186,000	*Indic. Yr. Divd.:*	NA
Total Assets:	$375,680,000	*Net Worth:*	$234,494,000	*Debt/ Equity:*	0.3433

Yahoo Inc

701 1st Ave., Sunnyvale, CA, 94089; *PH:* 1-408-349-3300; *Fax:* 1-408-349-3301;
http:// www.yahoo.com

General - Incorporation.............................DE	*Stock*- Price on:12/24/2007 ....$27.63
Employees...11,400	Stock Exchange...NDQ
Auditor ....PricewaterhouseCoopers LLP	Ticker Symbol...YHOO
Stk Agt.......................Computershare Trust Co	Outstanding Shares 1,340,000,000
Counsel................................Venture Law Group	E.P.S...$0.51
DUNS No. 88-436-4530	Shareholders...NA

Business: The group's principle activity is to provide Internet products and services to consumers and businesses through a network of online properties. The properties and services for consumers and businesses currently reside in four areas: search and marketplace; information and content; communications and consumer services and affiliate services. The products and service offerings are available without charge and revenues are generated from marketing and listing services and also offer fee-based premium services that provide the users access to additional content or services. The offices of the group are located in the United States, Europe, Asia, Latin America, Australia and Canada. The group's quarterly revenue for September 2007 was 1,767.51 millions of USD.

Primary SIC and add'l.: 7372 7375

CIK No: 0001011006

Subsidiaries: Alta Vista Internet Holdings Limited, Alta Vista Internet Operations Limited, Alta Vista Internet Solutions Limited, Arthas.com, Inc., Aurora I, LLC, AV-RB Holdings, Inc., C2B Technologies, Inc., del.icio.us, Inc., E-com Management NV, eGroups International (Thailand) Company Limited, eGroups International Ltda., eGroups International, Inc., eGroups, Inc., eScene Networks, Inc., Farechase Israel Ltd. 140 Subsidiaries included in the Index

Officers: Jerry Yang/Dir., CEO, Chief, Susan Decker/Pres./$15,959,720.00, Farzad Nazem/46/Head - Technology Group, CTO/$12,433,200.00, Marco Boerries/Sr. VP - Connected Life Division, Qi Lu/Sr. VP - Engineering Search, Search Marketing, Gregory Coleman/Exec. VP - Global Sales, Ash Patel/Exec. VP - Platforms, Infrastructure Division, Cammie Dunaway/Chief Marketing Officer, Head - Customer Experience Division, Robert Kotick/Dir., Presiding Dir., Usama Fayyad/Chief Data Officer, Sr. VP - Research, Strategic Data Solutions, Libby Sartain/Chief People, Jeff Weiner/Exec. VP - Network Division, Blake Jorgensen/CFO, Jill Nash/Chief Communications Officer, Hilary Schneider/Exec. VP - Global Partnership Solutions Division *(16 Officers included in Index)*

Directors: Jerry Yang/Dir., CEO, Chief, Terry Semel/Chmn., Roy Bostock/Dir., Maggie Wilderotter/Dir., Ronald W. Burkle/Dir., Eric Hippeau/Dir., Vyomesh Joshi/Dir., Arthur Kern/Dir., Edward Kozel/Dir., Gary Wilson/Dir., David Filo/Co - Founder

Owners: Jerry Yang/4.00%, Arthur H. Kern, Gary L. Wilson, Terry S. Semel/1.50%, Eric Hippeau, Legg Mason Capital Management, Inc/5.90%, Daniel L. Rosensweig, Susan L. Decker, Vyomesh Joshi, Roy J. Bostock, Edward R. Kozel, Ronald W. Burkle, Michael J. Callahan, Insiders/12.10%, David Filo/6.00% *(17 Owners included in Index)*

*Financial Data: Fiscal Year End:*12/31   *Latest Annual Data:* 12/31/2006

Year	Sales	Net Income
2006	$6,425,679,000	$751,391,000
2005	$5,257,668,000	$1,896,230,000
2004	$3,574,517,000	$839,553,000

Curr. Assets:	$3,750,142,000	*Curr. Liab.:*	$1,473,994,000		
Plant, Equip.:	$1,101,379,000	*Total Liab.:*	$2,352,998,000	*Indic. Yr. Divd.:*	NA
Total Assets:	$11,513,608,000	*Net Worth:*	$9,160,610,000	*Debt/ Equity:*	0.0848

Yak Communications Inc

300 Consilium Pl., Ste. 500, Toronto, ON, M1H 3G2; *PH:* 1-647-722-2752; *http://* www.yak.com

General - Incorporation.................................FL	*Stock*- Price on:12/24/2007 ....NA
Employees...NA	Stock Exchange...NA
Auditor ....Ernst & Young, LLP	Ticker Symbol..NA
Stk Agt......American Stock Transfer & Trust Co.	Outstanding Shares ....NA
Counsel...NA	E.P.S...NA
DUNS No. ....NA	Shareholders..NA

Business: The group's principal activity is to provide discount long distance telecommunication services. Telecommunication services are provided to residential, small and medium business enterprises. The group offers dial-around service known as casual calling. This allows customers to dial-around their existing long distance carrier on any call by entering a few digits. The group also provides long distance services to international destinations referred to as international calls. The services are provided in ottawa, quebec city, kitchener, london, edmonton, calgary and victoria. On 02-Jul-2003, the group acquired contour telecom inc and argos telecom inc.

Primary SIC and add'l.: 4813 6719 4899

CIK No: 0001084544

Subsidiaries: Contour Telecom Inc., Yak Canada Communications Corp., Yak Canada Local Exchange Carrier Inc., Yak Communications (America), Inc., Yak Communications (Canada) Inc.

Yamana Gold Inc

150 York St., Ste. 1102, Toronto, ON, M5H 3S5; *PH:* 1-416-815-0220; *Fax:* 1-416-815-0021;
http:// www.yamana.com; *Email:* investor@yamana.com

General - Incorporation....................Canada	*Stock*- Price on:12/24/2007 ....$13.07
Employees...NA	Stock Exchange...AMEX
Auditor ....Deloitte & Touche LLP	Ticker Symbol..AUY
Stk Agt.....................CIBC Mellon Trust CO.	Outstanding Shares 353,840,000
Counsel...NA	E.P.S...$0.32
DUNS No. ....NA	Shareholders...NA

Business: The groups principal activity is to explore minerals. In the year 2006, the group acquired RNC Gold Inc., Desert Sun Mining Corp. and Viceroy Explorations Ltd. The group operates from the United Stat and Canada.56. 'ASIA AUTOMATIVE (0001332552) filing not found.

Primary SIC and add'l.: 1021 1041

CIK No: 0001264089

Officers: Peter Marrone/Dir., CEO, Antenor Silva/Dir., COO, Pres., Charles Main/CFO, VP - Finance, Greg Mcknight/Sr. VP - Business Development, Evandro Cintra/VP - Technical Services, Daniel Kivari/VP - Operations, Mike Hoffman/VP - Special Projects, Jacqueline Jones/VP, General Counsel, Assist. Corp. Sec., Betty Soares/Corporate Controller, Ludovico Costa/VP - Operations, Mark Bennett/Corp. Sec., Ana Lucia Martins/VP - Safety, Health, Environment, Community, Darrin Rohr/VP - Human Resources, Arao Portugal/VP - Administration, Darcy Marud/Sr. VP - Exploration *(17 Officers included in Index)*

Directors: Peter Marrone/Dir., CEO, Victor Bradley/Chmn., Juvenal Mesquita Filho/Dir., Antenor Silva/Dir., COO, Pres., Bruce Humphrey/Dir., Nigel C. Lees/Dir., Dino Titaro/Dir., Patrick Mars/Dir., John Begeman/Dir., Richard Graff/Dir., Robert Horn/Dir., Carl Renzoni/Dir.

Owners: Greg McKnight, Charles Main, Peter Marrone, Seiti Nakamura, Evandro Cintra, Juvenal Mesquita Filho, Antenor Silva

*Financial Data: Fiscal Year End:*12/31   *Latest Annual Data:* 12/31/2006

Year	Sales	Net Income
2006	$169,206,000	-$88,072,000
2005	$46,038,000	-$12,911,000
2004	$32,298,000	-$636,000

Curr. Assets:	$153,460,000	*Curr. Liab.:*	$100,461,000		
Plant, Equip.:	$1,848,734,000	*Total Liab.:*	$461,680,000	*Indic. Yr. Divd.:*	$0.040
Total Assets:	$2,139,205,000	*Net Worth:*	$1,677,525,000	*Debt/ Equity:*	NA

Yang Holding Co

999 Brickell Ave., Ste. 600, Miami, FL, 33131; *PH:* 1-305-810-2898

General - Incorporation ....FL	*Stock*- Price on:12/24/2007 ....NA
Employees...NA	Stock Exchange...NA
Auditor ....Berenfeld Spritzer Shechter & Sheer	Ticker Symbol..NA
Stk Agt..NA	Outstanding Shares ....NA
Counsel...NA	E.P.S...NA
DUNS No. 11-296-5454	Shareholders..NA

Business: The group's principle activity is to commence business on telemarketing and sale of business or consumer products. The company has not commenced active business operations.

Primary SIC and add'l.: 9999 7389

CIK No: 0000878788

Yanzhou Coal Mining Co Ltd

40 Fushan Rd. , Zoucheng, Shandong, 273500; *PH:* 86-5375383489;
http:// www.yanzhoucoal.com.cn; *Email:* YZC@www.yanzhoucoal.com.cn

General - Incorporation ....China	*Stock*- Price on:12/24/2007 ....$73
Employees...39,785	Stock Exchange...NYSE
Auditor ....Deloitte & Touche LLP	Ticker Symbol..YZC
Stk Agt...........................Bank of New York	Outstanding Shares 100,100,000
Counsel...NA	E.P.S...$2.10
DUNS No. 65-428-4686	Shareholders...NA

Business: The group's principle activities are underground coal mining, coal preparation, sales and railway transportation service of coal. It operates six coal mine; the Xinglongzhuang coal mine, Baodian coal mine, Nantun coal mine, Dongtan coal mine, Jining ii coal mine ("Jining Ii") and Jining iii coal mine ("Jining Iii") as well as a regional railway network that links these mines with the national railway grid. Its major customers are mainly from Japan, South Korea, East China and Taiwan.

Primary SIC and add'l.: 1222

CIK No: 0001048098

Subsidiaries: Austar, Heze Nenghua, Yancoal, Yanmei Shipping, Yulin, Zhongyan Trade Co., Ltd.

Officers: Yang Deyu/Vice Chmn., GM, Zhang Shengdong/51/Supervisor, Wu Yuxiang/Dir., The CFO, Shi Chengzhong/45/Deputy GM, Xu Bentai/49/Supervisor, Liu Weixin/57/Supervisor, He Ye/51/Deputy GM, Lai Cunliang/48/Sr. Engineer, Jin Tai/53/Deputy GM, Zhang Yingmin/54/Executive Deputy GM, Tian Fengze/52/Deputy GM, Qu Tianzhi/46/Deputy General Manger, Ni Xinghua/51/Chief Engineer, Wang Xinkun/56/Dir., Deputy GM, Zhang Baocai/Dir., Sec. *(16 Officers included in Index)*

Directors: Yang Deyu/Vice Chmn., GM, Wang Xin/Chmn., Geng Jiahuai/58/Vice Chmn., Wu Yuxiang/Dir., The CFO, Shi Xuerang/53/Dir., Cui Jianmin/75/Dir., Wang Xiaojun/54/Dir., Wang Quanxi/53/Dir., Wang Xinkun/56/Dir., Deputy GM, Chen Changchun/55/Dir., Dong Yunqing/53/Dir., Sr. Administrative Officer, Pu Hongjiu/72/Dir.

Owners: Insiders, HKSCC Nominee Limited/39.72%

Financial Data: Fiscal Year End:12/31 Latest Annual Data: 12/31/2006

Year	Sales	Net Income
2006	$1,659,416,000	$308,418,000
2005	$1,543,431,000	$371,344,000
2004	$1,279,588,000	$395,970,000

Curr. Assets:	$1,265,579,000	Curr. Liab.:	$490,756,000	P/E Ratio:	10.61
Plant, Equip.:	$1,505,446,000	Total Liab.:	$541,110,000	Indic. Yr. Divd.:	$0.780
Total Assets:	$2,837,585,000	Net Worth:	$2,296,475,000	Debt/ Equity:	NA

Yardville National Bancorp

2465 Kuser Rd. , Hamilton, NJ, 08690; *PH:* 1-609-585-5100; *http://* www.yanb.com

General		Stock	
Incorporation	NJ	Price on:12/24/2007	$34.81
Employees	408	Stock Exchange	NA
Auditor	KPMG LLP	Ticker Symbol	NA
Stk Agt	Registrar & Transfer Co	Outstanding Shares	11,080,000
Counsel	NA	E.P.S	$0.29
DUNS No.	00-891-3840	Shareholders	NA

Business: The group's principal activity is to offer general, commercial and retail banking business services. The categories of loans offered include commercial, real estate and consumer loans to individuals and small and medium size businesses. It also provides automated teller machines (ATM) and automated clearing house (ach) services, which are used to process direct deposit activities inclusive of payrolls. In addition, the group also markets non-deposit financial products and services. The other financial services include financial planning, investment and insurance products. The operations are conducted through thirteen full-service banking offices located in mercer county, New Jersey, hamilton, ewing, hopewell, lawrence, east windsor and trenton.

Primary SIC and add'l.: 6021 6712

CIK No: 0000787849

Subsidiaries: Brendan, Inc., Jim Mary, Inc., Kuser Capital Corporation, Kuser Investment Corporation, Nancy Beth, Inc., The Yardville National Bank, Yardville Capital Trust, Yardville Capital Trust II, Yardville Capital Trust III, Yardville Capital Trust IV, Yardville Capital Trust V, Yardville Capital Trust VI, Yardville National Investment Corporation, YNB Capital Development, Inc., YNB Financial Services, Inc. 17 Subsidiaries included in the Index

Officers: Patrick M. Ryan/Dir., CEO, Kevin F. Tylus/Dir., COO, Pres., Howard N. Hall/Sr. VP, Investments Officer, Brian K. Gray/Sr. VP, Retail Banking, Marketing Officer, Daniel J. O'Donnell/Exec. VP, Chief Legal Officer, Sec., Patrick L. Ryan/Sr. VP, Strategic Planning Officer, John P. Samborski/Sr. VP, Sr. Lending Officer, Joanne C. O'Donnell/Sr. VP, Chief Credit Administration Officer, Stephen F. Carman/CFO, Exec. VP, Timothy J. Losch/Exec. VP - Marketing, Community Development Officer, Stephen R. Walker/CIO, Exec. VP, Edward J. Dietzler/Sr. VP - Capital Markets

Directors: Patrick M. Ryan/Dir., CEO, Jay G. Destribats/Chmn., Elbert G. Basolis/Vice Chmn., Kevin F. Tylus/Dir., COO, Pres., James E. Bartolomei/Dir., Anthony M. Giampetro/Dir., Gilbert W. Lugossy/Dir., Samuel D. Marrazzo/Dir., Louis R. Matlack/Dir., George D. Muller/Dir., Martin Tuchman/Dir., Robert L. Workman/Dir.

Owners: George D. Muller, Elbert G. Basolis, Anthony M. Giampetro, Stephen F. Carman, Louis R. Matlack, Patrick M. Ryan/3.71%, Kevin F. Tylus/2.06%, Robert L. Workman, Lawrence B. Seidman/8.97%, Insiders/14.65%, Jay G. Destribats/1.74%, Daniel J. ODonnell, Private Capital Management/5.00%, Samuel D. Marrazzo, James E. Bartolomei *(18 Owners included in Index)*

Financial Data: Fiscal Year End:12/31 Latest Annual Data: 12/31/2006

Year	Sales	Net Income
2006	$196,812,000	$5,265,000
2005	$177,757,000	$20,934,000
2004	$147,843,000	$18,525,000

Curr. Assets:	$65,978,000	Curr. Liab.:	$2,337,283,000	P/E Ratio:	120.03
Plant, Equip.:	$12,452,000	Total Liab.:	$2,434,637,000	Indic. Yr. Divd.:	$0.460
Total Assets:	$2,620,731,000	Net Worth:	$186,094,000	Debt/ Equity:	0.3296

Yellow Roadway Corp

10990 Roe Ave., Overland Park, KS, 66211; *PH:* 1-913-696-6100; *http://* www.yellowroadway.com

General		Stock	
Incorporation	DE	Price on:12/24/2007	$37.23
Employees	66,000	Stock Exchange	NDQ
Auditor	KPMG LLP	Ticker Symbol	NA
Stk Agt	Computershare Trust Co., N.A.	Outstanding Shares	57,500,000
Counsel	NA	E.P.S	$2.49
DUNS No.	10-710-1248	Shareholders	NA

Business: The groups principle activity is to provide transportation services. The group operates through four segments namely yellow transportation, roadway express, new penn and meridian iq. The group operates from United States and Canada.

Primary SIC and add'l.: 6719 4213 4731

CIK No: 0000716006

Subsidiaries: 3727484 Manitoba Ltd., Express Lane Service, Inc., Globe.com Lines, Inc., GPS Logistics (Cambodia) Ltd., GPS Logistics (EU) Limited, GPS Logistics Bangladesh Limited, GPS Logistics Group Limited (Bermuda), GPS Logistics Lanka (Private) Ltd., GPS Worldwide Malaysia Sdn Bhd, IMUA Handling Corporation, Integres Global Logistics, Inc., Meridian IQ (EU) B.V., Meridian IQ (Singapore) Holdings Pte Ltd., Meridian IQ (Thailand) Limited, Meridian IQ (UK) Limited 92 Subsidiaries included in the Index

Officers: James D. Ritchie/CEO, Pres. - YRC Logistics, Michael J. Smid/CEO, Pres. - YRC Regional Transportation/$1,074,068.00, William D. Zollars/Chmn., CEO, Pres./$4,483,554.00, Donald G. Barger/Special Advisor to The CEO/$1,352,303.00, Paul F. Liljegren/53/VP, Controller, Chief Accounting Officer - YRC Worldwide, Todd M. Hacker/VP - Investor Relations, Treasurer, Michael J. Naatz/Exec. VP, Stephen L. Bruffett/CFO, Exec. VP, Gregory A. Reid/Exec. VP - Enterprise Solutions Group, Chief Marketing Officer, Michael K. Rapken/CIO, Exec. VP, Daniel J. Churay/Sr. VP, General Counsel, Sec., Steven T. Yamasaki/Exec. VP - Human Resources, James D. Staley/57/Pres. - YRC Regional Transportation/$2,144,737.00

Directors: William D. Zollars/Chmn., CEO, Pres., Dennis E. Foster/Dir., Carl W. Vogt/Dir., William L. Trubeck/Dir., Howard M. Dean/Dir., Cassandra C. Carr/Dir., Michael T. Byrnes/Dir., Mark A. Schulz/Dir., Phillip J. Meek/Dir., John C. McKelvey/Dir., John F. Fiedler/69/Dir.

Owners: Insiders, William D. Zollars, John F. Fiedler, Michael J. Smid, Carl W. Vogt, James D. Staley, Phillip J. Meek, Barclays Global Investors, NA/8.56%, Dennis E. Foster, Donald G. Barger, Letko, Brosseau & Associates Inc./7.72%, Howard M. Dean, John C. McKelvey, Cassandra C. Carr, William L. Trubeck *(16 Owners included in Index)*

Financial Data: Fiscal Year End:12/31 Latest Annual Data: 12/31/2006

Year	Sales	Net Income
2006	$9,918,690,000	$276,632,000
2005	$8,741,557,000	$288,130,000
2004	$6,767,485,000	$184,327,000

Curr. Assets:	$1,591,091,000	Curr. Liab.:	$1,360,469,000	P/E Ratio:	10.89
Plant, Equip.:	$2,269,846,000	Total Liab.:	$3,759,688,000	Indic. Yr. Divd.:	NA
Total Assets:	$5,952,237,000	Net Worth:	$2,192,549,000	Debt/ Equity:	NA

Yi Wan Group Inc

101 E 52 St., 9th Fl., New York, NY, 10022; *PH:* 1-212-752-9700; *http://* www.yiwangroup.com

General		Stock	
Incorporation	FL	Price on:12/24/2007	$0.045
Employees	NA	Stock Exchange	OTC
Auditor	Moore Stephens Wurth F & T LLP	Ticker Symbol	USNT
Stk Agt	NA	Outstanding Shares	NA
Counsel	NA	E.P.S	NA
DUNS No.	NA	Shareholders	NA

Business: The group's principal activity is to provide lodging, food and beverage and entertainment products and services. It also manufactures telecommunications equipment and components. The group's operations are carried out through its subsidiaries, jiaozuo yi wan hotel co., ltd, qinyang yi wan hotel co., ltd, yi wan maple leaf high technology agriculture developing ltd. Co and shun de yi wan communication equipment plant co., ltd. The group's hotel division manages and operates an upscale hotel conference and entertainment facility in jiaozuo city, henan province. This includes lodging, food and beverage, entertainment, and conference and meeting products and services. The telecommunications division designs and manufactures telephone network switching component parts for use in telephone main distribution frames and assembled telephone main distribution frames. In 2002, the group sold its agriculture subsidiary.

Primary SIC and add'l.: 7011 3661 5812

CIK No: 0001157667

Subsidiaries: Jiaozuo Yi Wan Hotel Co., Ltd, Qinyang Yi Wan Hotel Co., Ltd., Shun De Yi Wan Communication Equipment Plant Co. Ltd., YI WanN Beijing Hotel Management Co., LTD.

Financial Data: Fiscal Year End:12/31 Latest Annual Data: 12/31/2004

Year	Sales	Net Income
2004	$11,217,000	$691,000
2003	$12,495,000	$1,596,000
2002	$13,901,000	$998,000

Curr. Assets:	$7,886,000	Curr. Liab.:	$7,834,000		
Plant, Equip.:	$17,366,000	Total Liab.:	$7,834,000	Indic. Yr. Divd.:	NA
Total Assets:	$30,232,000	Net Worth:	$20,374,000	Debt/ Equity:	NA

YM Biosciences Inc

5045 Orbitor Dr., Bldg. 11, Ste. 400, Mississauga, ON, L4W 4Y4; *PH:* 1-905-629-9761; *http://* www.ymbiosciences.com; *Email:* ir@ymbiosciences.com

General		Stock	
Incorporation	Canada	Price on:12/24/2007	$1.8
Employees	NA	Stock Exchange	AMEX
Auditor	Ernst & Young LLP	Ticker Symbol	YMI
Stk Agt	Mellon Trust Co	Outstanding Shares	55,840,000
Counsel	Heenan Blaikie LLP	E.P.S	-$0.46
DUNS No.	NA	Shareholders	NA

Business: The groups principle activities include identifying, developing and commercializing differentiated products for treatment of cancer. The groups products include nimotuzumab and AeroLEF(TM). The group operates from Canada. .

Primary SIC and add'l.: NA

CIK No: 0001178347

Subsidiaries: CIMYM BioSciences Inc, CIMYM Inc, YM BioSciences U.S. Operations Inc

Officers: David G.P. Allan/Chmn., CEO, David A. Kennard/Dir. - European Operations, Scott Bentham/Assoc. Dir. - Clinical Product Development, Paul M. Keane/Dir. - Medical Affairs, Niclas Stiernholm/Member - Scientific Advisory Board, Lorne J. Brandes/Member - Scientific Advisory Board, Lisa V. Deluca/VP - Global Regulatory Affairs YM Biosciences USA Inc, Gary Floyd/VP - Operations, YM Biosciences USA Inc, Jose Cevallos/Clinical Operations Mgr., Diana Pliura/Exec. VP - Aerolef, Vincent Salvatori/Exec. VP - YM Biosciences Inc, Pres. - Cimym Biosciences Inc, Jennifer Seibert/Sr. Dir. - Technology Assessment, Intellectual Property, German Roges/Country Mgr., Dir. - Operations, Sean Thompson/Dir. - Corporate Development, Igor A. Sherman/Dir. - Clinical Research *(17 Officers included in Index)*

Directors: David G.P. Allan/Chmn., CEO, Mark Vincent/Dir. - Investigational Oncology, Chmn. - Scientific Advisory Board, John Friedman/Dir., Mark Entwistle/Dir., Gilbert Wenzel/Dir., Thomas Allen/Dir., Henry Friesen/Dir., Julius Vida/Dir., James Barrett/Dir., Gail Schulze/Dir., Robert S. Kerbel/Member - Scientific Advisory Board, Daniel Von Hoff/Member - Scientific Advisory Board, Tryon Williams/Dir.

Owners: John Friedman, Tryon M. Williams, David G.P. Allan/1.20%, Sean Thompson, Paul M. Keane, James Barrett/2.40%

Financial Data: Fiscal Year End:06/30 Latest Annual Data: 6/30/2006

Year	Sales	Net Income
2006	$2,276,000	-$23,535,000
2005	$1,182,000	-$16,511,000
2000	$258,000	-$5,328,000

Curr. Assets:	$81,160,000	Curr. Liab.:	$3,980,000		
Plant, Equip.:	$272,000	Total Liab.:	$10,207,000	Indic. Yr. Divd.:	NA
Total Assets:	$89,353,000	Net Worth:	$79,146,000	Debt/ Equity:	NA

Yocream International Inc

5858 NE 87th Ave., Portland, OR, 97220; *PH:* 1-503-256-3754; *http://* www.yocream.com; *Email:* info@yocream.com

General		Stock	
Incorporation	OR	Price on:12/24/2007	NA
Employees	NA	Stock Exchange	NA
Auditor	Grant Thornton LLP	Ticker Symbol	NA
Stk Agt	Computershare Trust Co	Outstanding Shares	NA
Counsel	NA	E.P.S	NA
DUNS No.	08-442-5537	Shareholders	NA

Business: The group's principal activities are to manufacture, market and distribute frozen yogurt, sorbet, cultured soy, smoothie, coffee latte and ice cream products. The products are sold under the brand names yocream, dannon/yocream and yogurt stand. The products of the group include yocream frozen yogurt, dannon/yocream frozen yogurt, yocream frozen custard, yocream blender smoothies, yocream dispenser smoothies, yocream coffee latte freeze, soft scoop by yocream and yogurt stand frozen yogurt. The group's products are sold to convenience stores, restaurants, hospitals, school districts, food distributors, military installations, yogurt shops, fast food chains, discount club warehouses, business and industry locations and other outlets. International markets for the products include Canada, Mexico, Puerto Rico, Taiwan, Korea, Italy, Germany and other countries.

Primary SIC and add'l.: 2038 2024

CIK No: 0000821572

Officers: Tyler Bargas/Dir. - Sales, Suzanne Gardner/Dir. - Marketing, Military Sales, David Hahn/Business Development Mgr., Terry Lusetti/Dir. - Investor Relations, Julie Cosner/Inside Sales Mgr. - Customer Service, Lori Lusetti/Business Development Mgr., Tom English/Business Development Mgr., Matt Hanna/Custom Manufacturing, Copacking, Terry Oftedal/Operations, Vendor Relations, Gabby McClintock/Key Accounting Mgr., Barbara Rhoades/Key Accounting Mgr. - California, Kelly Stanphill/Inside Sales Mgr., Monica Zebryk/Key Accounting Mgr.

York International Corp

631 S Richland Ave, York, PA, 17403; *PH:* 1-717-771-7890; *http://* www.york.com

General - Incorporation	DE	**Stock** - Price on:12/24/2007	$114.17
Employees	136,000	Stock Exchange	NA
Auditor	KPMG LLP	Ticker Symbol	NA
Stk Agt	Chase Mellon Shareholder Services LLC	Outstanding Shares	197,300,000
Counsel	Wachtell Lipton Rosen & Katz	E.P.S	$5.76
DUNS No.	19-656-1252	Shareholders	NA

Business: The group's principal activity is to design, manufacture, sell and service heating, ventilation and air conditioning systems for residential and commercial markets. The group operates through three business segments. Hvac&r segment designs, produces, services, and sells hvac&r solutions worldwide. Their products include air-cooled and water-cooled chillers, large packaged rooftop units, indoor and outdoor air handling and ventilating equipment, variable air volume units, underfloor air distribution systems and mini-split and room air conditioning units. Unitary products group produces heating and air conditioning solutions designed for use in residential and light commercial applications and distributes proprietary and non-proprietary parts to the aftermarket. Bristol compressors manufactures reciprocating and scroll compressors for our use and for sale to original equipment manufacturers and wholesale distributors.

Primary SIC and add'l.: 3585

CIK No: 0000842662

Subsidiaries: AfroCool Ltd., Aircon GmbH, Alliancefroid S.A.S., Arduman Klima Sanayi Servisi AS, Arduman Mumessillik Klima Sanayi ve Ticaret AS, BMK Kaelte and Energie - Technik Gmbh, Bristol Compresors Properties LLC, Bristol Compressors Purchasing, Inc., Bristol Compressors Stock Holding Corporation, Bristol Compressors, Inc., Bristol Scroll Compressors Co. LLC, CBAW S.r.l., Codorus Acceptance Corp., Coil Services, Inc., Duplan Engineering S.A.S. 133 Subsidiaries included in the Index

Financial Data: *Fiscal Year End:*12/31 *Latest Annual Data:* 9/30/2006

Year	Sales	Net Income
2006	$32,235,000,000	$1,028,000,000
2005	$27,479,400,000	$909,400,000
2004	$26,553,400,000	$817,500,000

Curr. Assets:	$9,264,000,000	*Curr. Liab.:*	$8,146,000,000	*P/E Ratio:*	20.80
Plant, Equip.:	$3,968,000,000	*Total Liab.:*	$14,437,000,000	*Indic. Yr. Divd.:*	$1.320
Total Assets:	$21,921,000,000	*Net Worth:*	$7,355,000,000	*Debt/ Equity:*	0.4560

York Water Co

130 E Market St., York, PA, 17405; *PH:* 1-717-845-3601; *Fax:* 1-717-845-3792; *http://* www.yorkwater.com

General - Incorporation	PA	**Stock** - Price on:12/24/2007	$17.5801
Employees	106	Stock Exchange	NDQ
Auditor	Beard Miller Co. LLP	Ticker Symbol	YORW
Stk Agt	American Registrar & Transfer Co	Outstanding Shares	11,220,000
Counsel	NA	E.P.S	$0.58
DUNS No.	00-791-8154	Shareholders	NA

Business: The group's principal activity is to impound, purify and distribute water within its franchised territory situated in york country, Pennsylvania. The Pennsylvania public utility commission (ppuc) regulates the group in the areas of billing, payment procedures, dispute processing, terminations, service territory and rate setting. The group obtains water supply from the south branch and east branch of the codorus creek. The main pumping station of the group is located in spring garden township on the south branch of the codorus creek. The group caters to industries manufacturing fixtures and furniture, electrical machinery, food products, paper, textile products, air conditioning and barbells,

Primary SIC and add'l.: 4941

CIK No: 0000108985

Officers: Jeffrey S. Osman/65/Dir., CEO, Pres., Bruce C. McIntosh/VP - Human Resources/$122,875.00, Vernon L. Bracey/46/VP - Customer Service, Kathleen M. Miller/CFO, Treasurer/$113,426.00, Bonnie Rexroth/Assist. Corp. Sec., Jeffrey R. Hines/46/COO, Sec./$153,425.00, Duane R. Close/62/VP - Operations/$192,764.00

Directors: Jeffrey S. Osman/65/Dir., CEO, Pres., William T. Morris/70/Chmn., Irvin S. Naylor/72/Vice Chmn., John L. Finlayson/67/Dir., Chloe R. Eichelberger/73/Dir., Thomas C. Norris/69/Dir., George W. Hodges/57/Dir., George Hay Kain/59/Dir., Michael W. Gang/57/Dir.

Owners: Insiders/3.53%, Jeffrey R. Hines/0.21%, Thomas C. Norris/0.15%, William T. Morris/0.40%, Duane R. Close/0.10%, George W. Hodges/0.97%, Bruce C. McIntosh/0.01%, Vernon L. Bracey, George Hay Kain/0.38%, John L. Finlayson/0.15%, Irvin S. Naylor/0.76%, Chlo R. Eichelberger/0.09%, Michael W. Gang/0.07%, Jeffrey S. Osman/0.21%, Kathleen M. Miller/0.03%

Financial Data: *Fiscal Year End:*12/31 *Latest Annual Data:* 6/30/2006

Year	Sales	Net Income
2006	$13,630,000	$2,725,000
2005	$26,805,000	$5,833,000

Curr. Assets:	$5,911,000	*Curr. Liab.:*	$29,251,000	*P/E Ratio:*	30.31
Plant, Equip.:	$162,721,000	*Total Liab.:*	$129,629,000	*Indic. Yr. Divd.:*	$0.470
Total Assets:	$181,373,000	*Net Worth:*	$51,744,000	*Debt/ Equity:*	1.3105

Youbet.com Inc

5901 De Soto Ave., Woodland Hills, CA, 91367; *PH:* 1-818-668-2100; *http://* www.youbet.com; *Email:* playerservices@youbet.com

General - Incorporation	DE	**Stock** - Price on:12/24/2007	$2.67
Employees	447	Stock Exchange	NDQ
Auditor	Piercy, Bowler, Taylor & Kern	Ticker Symbol	UBET
Stk Agt	American Stock Transfer & Trust Co.	Outstanding Shares	42,030,000
Counsel	Christensen, Miller, Fink, Jacobs	E.P.S	-$0.11
DUNS No.	09-560-4566	Shareholders	NA

Business: The group's principal activity is to provide online live event sports entertainment, wagering and other forms of online gaming services. The group wagers on live events such as horse racing, car racing, soccer, football and other sporting events. The group currently provides its customers with the ability to receive interactive, real-time audio video broadcasts directly into their computers, access a comprehensive database of handicapping information and wagers on a wide selection of United States, Canadian and australian horse races.

Primary SIC and add'l.: 7999

CIK No: 0000814055

Subsidiaries: International Racing Group N.V, IRG Holdings Curacao, N.V., IRG Services, Inc, Irg U.s. Holdings Corp., Youbet Oregon, Inc.

Officers: Charles F. Champion/Chmn., CEO, Pres./$942,932.00, Gary W. Sproule/COO/$535,394.00, James A. Burk/CFO

Directors: Charles F. Champion/Chmn., CEO, Pres., David M. Marshall/Co - Founder, Vice Chmn., Joseph F. Barletta/Dir., Governor James Edgar/Dir., Jack Liebau/Dir., Gary Adelson/Dir., Steven C. Good/Dir., Doug R. Donn/Dir., James Edgar/Dir., Michael Brodsky/Dir., Jay R. Pritzker/43/Dir.

Owners: James Edgar/0.40%, New World Opportunity Partners I, LLC/9.30%, Charles F. Champion/4.00%, Insiders/19.60%, Douglas R. Donn, David M. Marshall/3.70%, Scott Solomon/0.40%, JPMorgan Chase & Co./6.50%, Jack F. Liebau, Steven C. Good, Gary W. Sproule/1.00%, Michael Brodsky/9.30%, Gary Adelson/0.20%, Joseph F. Barletta/0.30%

Financial Data: *Fiscal Year End:*12/31 *Latest Annual Data:* 12/31/2006

Year	Sales	Net Income
2006	$136,683,000	-$2,031,000
2005	$88,837,000	$5,691,000
2004	$65,249,000	$4,631,000

Curr. Assets:	$45,226,000	*Curr. Liab.:*	$40,207,000		
Plant, Equip.:	$30,110,000	*Total Liab.:*	$52,831,000	*Indic. Yr. Divd.:*	NA
Total Assets:	$105,605,000	*Net Worth:*	$52,774,000	*Debt/ Equity:*	0.2464

Young Broadcasting Inc

599 Lexington Ave., New York, NY, 10022; *PH:* 1-212-754-7070; *http://* www.youngbroadcasting.com; *Email:* invest@youngbroadcasting.com

General - Incorporation	DE	**Stock** - Price on:12/24/2007	$3.83
Employees	1,023	Stock Exchange	NDQ
Auditor	Ernst & Young LLP	Ticker Symbol	YBTVA
Stk Agt	American Stock Transfer & Trust Co.	Outstanding Shares	22,220,000
Counsel	Sonnenschein Nath & Rosenthal LLP	E.P.S	-$3.04
DUNS No.	18-317-4127	Shareholders	NA

Business: The group's principal activities are to own and operate television stations. The group has ten network affiliated stations (six with abc, three with cbs, and one with nbc) and one independent commercial television broadcasting station. These television stations are located in lansing, Michigan, green bay, Wisconsin, lafayette, Louisiana, rockford, Illinois, nashville and knoxville, Tennessee, albany, New York, richmond, Virginia, davenport, Iowa, sioux falls, South Dakota and san francisco, California. Each of the group's stations is owned and operated by a direct or indirect subsidiary.

Primary SIC and add'l.: 4833 7313

CIK No: 0000929144

Subsidiaries: Adam Young Inc., Fidelity Television, Inc., Honey Bucket Films, Inc., Klfy, L.p., LAT, INC., Wate, G.p., Winnebago Television Corporation, Wkrn, G.p., YBK, INC., YBT, INC., Young Broadcasting Of Albany, Inc., Young Broadcasting Of Davenport, Inc., Young Broadcasting Of Green Bay, Inc., Young Broadcasting Of Knoxville, Inc., Young Broadcasting Of Lansing, Inc. 23 Subsidiaries included in the Index

Officers: Vincent J. Young/Chmn., CEO/$3,369,439.00, Deborah A. McDermott/Dir., Pres./$1,406,725.00, Brian Greif/VP - News, James A. Morgan/Dir., Exec. VP, Sec., CFO/$1,363,915.00, Daniel R. Batchelor/VP - Sales, Robert Peterson/VP - Business Development, Peter Grazioli/VP - Information Technology, CIO, Stephen J. Baker/VP, Controller - Assist. Secy

Directors: Vincent J. Young/Chmn., CEO, Alfred J. Hickey/Dir., David C. Lee/Dir., Deborah A. McDermott/Dir., Pres., Leif Lomo/Dir., Richard C. Lowe/Dir., Reid Murray/46/Dir., James A. Morgan/Dir., Exec. VP, Sec., CFO, Alexander T. Mason/Dir.

Owners: Insiders, James A. Morgan, Eric Semler/6.70%, Adam Young 2003 Trust, Spray-V Limited Partnership, James A. Morgan, Mario J. Gabelli and various related entities/17.40%, Alfred J. Hickey, Leif Lomo, Vincent J. Young, Adam Young 2003 Trust, Spray-V Limited Partnership, David C. Lee, Westport Asset Management,Inc./5.00%, Vincent J. Young *(20 Owners included in Index)*

Financial Data: *Fiscal Year End:*12/31 *Latest Annual Data:* 12/31/2006

Year	Sales	Net Income
2006	$225,152,000	-$56,641,000
2005	$197,478,000	-$91,347,000
2004	$223,908,000	-$44,276,000

Curr. Assets:	$169,577,000	*Curr. Liab.:*	$66,125,000		
Plant, Equip.:	$67,591,000	*Total Liab.:*	$946,892,000	*Indic. Yr. Divd.:*	NA
Total Assets:	$794,702,000	*Net Worth:*	-$152,190,000	*Debt/ Equity:*	NA

Young Innovations Inc

13705 Shoreline Ct. E, Earth City, MO, 63045; *PH:* 1-314-344-0010; *http://* www.ydnt.com; *Email:* info@ydnt.com

General - Incorporation	MO	**Stock** - Price on:12/24/2007	$27.47
Employees	400	Stock Exchange	NDQ
Auditor	KPMG LLP	Ticker Symbol	YDNT
Stk Agt	UMB Bank, N.A.	Outstanding Shares	9,140,000
Counsel	McDermott Will & Emery	E.P.S	$1.43
DUNS No.	00-630-9355	Shareholders	NA

Business: The group's principal activities are to develop, manufacture and market equipment used by dentists, dental hygienists, dental assistants and consumers. The group operates in two segments: professsional dental equipment segment and retail segment. The group product includes disposable and metal prophy angles, prophy cups and brushes, panoramic X-ray machines, dental handpieces drills and related components. It markets product to retail outlets, including mass merchandisers, drug stores and super markets. Some of the brand names of the group's are Procare, D-lish and Festival. Major customers of the group are Henry Schein Inc and Patterson Dental Company the group's manufacturing and distribution facilities are located in Missouri, California, Indiana, Colorado, Tennessee and Texas. The group markets its products in Canada, Europe, South America, Central America and the Pacific Rim. The group acquired Obtura Spartan in 2004.

Primary SIC and add'l.: 3841 3843

CIK No: 0000949874

Subsidiaries: YI Ventures LLC

Officers: Alfred E. Brennan/Vice Chmn., CEO/$407,260.00, Christine R. Boehning/VP, Sec., CFO/$204,749.00, Arthur L. Herbst/Pres./$314,615.00, Daniel J. Tarullo/VP/$181,864.00, Stephen Yaggy/VP/$134,200.00

Directors: Alfred E. Brennan/Vice Chmn., CEO, George E. Richmond/Chmn., Brian F. Bremer/Dir., Patrick J. Ferrillo/Dir., Richard J. Bliss/Dir.

Owners: Brian F. Bremer, Insiders/45.00%, Daniel J. Tarullo, Arthur L. Herbst/4.00%, Royce & Associates, LLC/6.00%, FMR Corp./10.00%, Neuberger Berman, Inc./9.00%, George E. Richmond/36.00%, Stephen T. Yaggy, Christine R. Boehning, Eaton Vance Corp./8.00%, Patrick J. Ferrillo, Alfred E. Brennan/4.00%

Financial Data: Fiscal Year End:12/31   **Latest Annual Data:** 12/31/2006

Year	Sales	Net Income
2006	$90,805,000	$14,779,000
2005	$84,766,000	$15,338,000
2004	$79,201,000	$13,934,000

Curr. Assets:	$33,731,000	Curr. Liab.:	$7,749,000	P/E Ratio:	17.95
Plant, Equip.:	$29,178,000	Total Liab.:	$39,090,000	Indic. Yr. Divd.:	$0.160
Total Assets:	$156,588,000	Net Worth:	$117,498,000	Debt/ Equity:	0.1856

YouthStream Media Networks Inc

Pmb No. 358, 244 Madison Ave., New York, NY, 10016; **PH:** 1-212-883-0083; *http://* www.youthstream.com

General - Incorporation	DE	Stock - Price on:12/24/2007	$0.21
Employees	146	Stock Exchange	OTC
Auditor	Weinberg & Co. P.A	Ticker Symbol	ALJJ
Stk Agt	American Stock Transfer & Trust Co.	Outstanding Shares	39,400,000
Counsel	Proskauer Rose	E.P.S.	$0.44
DUNS No.	NA	Shareholders	NA

Business: The group's principle activity is to provide retail services through its beyond the wall subsidiary. The retail segment services includes on-campus, online and retail store poster sales. The subsidiary operated a chain of 18 retail stores operating in 12 states nationwide, including the district of columbia.

Primary SIC and add'l.: 7331 7375

CIK No: 0001103926

Subsidiaries: Atacama KES Holding Corporation, KES Acquisition Company, LLC, YouthStream Acquisition Corp

Financial Data: Fiscal Year End:09/30   **Latest Annual Data:** 9/30/2005

Year	Sales	Net Income
2005	$69,182,000	-$3,431,000
2004	NA	-$2,366,000
2003	$9,203,000	-$3,128,000

Curr. Assets:	$35,716,000	Curr. Liab.:	$34,636,000	P/E Ratio:	0.51
Plant, Equip.:	$5,568,000	Total Liab.:	$89,635,000	Indic. Yr. Divd.:	NA
Total Assets:	$41,922,000	Net Worth:	-$79,600,000	Debt/ Equity:	NA

YPF

Avenida Pte. R. Senz Pea, C. 1035 Aac, Buenos Aires, 777; **PH:** 34-913488100; *http://* www.repsolypf.com

General - Incorporation	AR	Stock - Price on:12/24/2007	$46.48
Employees	10,574	Stock Exchange	NYSE
Auditor	Deloitte & Co. S.R.L.	Ticker Symbol	YPF
Stk Agt	Bank of New York	Outstanding Shares	393,310,000
Counsel	NA	E.P.S.	$3.00
DUNS No.	97-078-8808	Shareholders	NA

Business: The group's principal activities are studying, exploring and operating liquid and/or gaseous hydrocarbons and other minerals. It also industrializes, transports, and markets these products and its derived products, including petroleum and chemical products. The group also generates energy from hydrocarbons.

Primary SIC and add'l.: 1311 2911

CIK No: 0000904851

Subsidiaries: YPF Holdings

Officers: Enrique Locutura/Vice Chmn., CEO, Javier Macian Perez/ED Human Resources, Luis Suarez De Lezo Mantilla/Dir., Sec., Antonio Gomis/ED YPF, Jesus Guinea/Dir. - Refining, Logistic, Rafael Lopez Revuelta/Dir. - Chemicals, Manuel Hermogenes Rollano/Dir. - Communication Services, William Gartland/Deputy Dir. - Internacional Media Relations, Begona Elices Garcia/Corp. Dir. - External Relations, Santiago Moreno Hueyo/Coordinator, Media Relations, Clara Velasco alvarez/Contact - Investor Relations, Vidal Larrad Cuadrillero/Back Office Mgr., Teresa Gil Aldea/Contact - Invester Relations, Fernando Ramirez Mazarredo/ED Finance, Corporate Services, Jaume Giro Ribas/44/ED Communication, Head - Chairmans Office *(26 Officers included in Index)*

Directors: Enrique Locutura/Vice Chmn., CEO, Antonio Brufau Niubo/60/Chmn., Jorge Mercader Miro/65/Vice Chmn., Luis Fernando Del Rivero Asensio/Vice Chmn., Alejandro Almarza/Alternate Dir., Juan Abello Gallo/Dir., Carmelo De Las Morenas Lopez/68/Dir., Javier Monzon/Dir., Antonio Hernandez-gil alvarez-Cienfuegos/55/Dir., Miguel Madanes/Dir., Eduardo Elsztain/Dir., Luis Pagani/Dir., Alejandro Quiroga Lopez/Dir., Paulina Beato Balanco/Dir., Artur Carulla Font/60/Dir. *(35 Directors included in Index)*

Financial Data: Fiscal Year End:12/31   **Latest Annual Data:** 12/31/2006

Year	Sales	Net Income
2006	$8,367,264,000	$1,196,909,000
2005	$7,545,880,000	$1,694,289,000
2004	$6,708,775,000	$1,409,008,000

Curr. Assets:	$3,652,090,000	Curr. Liab.:	$2,051,098,000	P/E Ratio:	10.61
Plant, Equip.:	$7,348,243,000	Total Liab.:	$3,636,096,000	Indic. Yr. Divd.:	$3.870
Total Assets:	$12,201,158,000	Net Worth:	$8,565,062,000	Debt/ Equity:	NA

YTB International, Inc

560 Sylvan Ave., Englewood Cliffs, NJ, 07632; **PH:** 1-201-567-8500; *http://* www.rezconnect.com

General - Incorporation	DE	Stock - Price on:12/24/2007	$4.35
Employees	144	Stock Exchange	NA
Auditor	UHY LLP	Ticker Symbol	NA
Stk Agt	American Stock Transfer & Trust Co.	Outstanding Shares	38,650,000
Counsel	NA	E.P.S.	-$0.28
DUNS No.	11-824-1694	Shareholders	NA

Business: The group's principal activity is using technology and the Internet for franchise chain and the retail consumer online. The group is also a full-service provider of discount travel products and services to the leisure and small business traveler. The group operates under the trade names travel network, global travel network and travel network vacation central as well as Web sites such as etravnet.com, hagglewithus.com, and rezconnect.com. In addition, the group offers its customers the ability to make reservations on over 424 airlines, at more than 35,000 hotels and with most major car rental companies, cruise lines and tour package operators.

Primary SIC and add'l.: 7375 4724

CIK No: 0000852766

Subsidiaries: REZconnect Technologies Inc, YourTravelBiz.com, YTB Travel Network Division.

Officers: Scott J. Tomer/CEO, Founder/$530,820.00, Kim J. Sorensen/56/CEO, Founder, Pres. - YTB Travel Network, Andrew F. Cauthen/Corp. Sec. - YTB International, Inc, CEO, Pres. - Yourtravelbizcom, Inc/$226,447.00, John D. Clagg/CFO, Corporate Treasurer/$182,649.00, Shelly Coppersmith/VP - Marketing, YTB Travel Network, Josh Tomer/Dir. - Marketing Services

Directors: Scott J. Tomer/CEO, Founder, Kim J. Sorensen/56/CEO, Founder, Pres. - YTB Travel Network, Lloyd J. Tomer/Chmn., Harold L. Kestenbaum/Dir., Clay Winfield/Dir., Andrew Wilder/Dir., Timothy Kaiser/Dir., John Simmons/Dir., Lou Brock/Dir.

Owners: Clay Winfield, Andrew Cauthen, John D. Clagg, Insiders, Harold L. Kestenbaum, Timothy Kaiser, John D. Simmons, Andrew Wilder, Lloyd J. Tomer, Scott J. Tomer, Lou Brock, Kim J. Sorensen, Michael Y. Brent

Financial Data: Fiscal Year End:12/31   **Latest Annual Data:** 12/31/2006

Year	Sales	Net Income
2006	$50,897,000	-$5,976,000
2005	$21,593,000	-$8,453,000
2004	$3,193,000	-$2,193,000

Curr. Assets:	$17,991,000	Curr. Liab.:	$30,637,000		
Plant, Equip.:	$6,191,000	Total Liab.:	$30,907,000	Indic. Yr. Divd.:	NA
Total Assets:	$28,890,000	Net Worth:	-$2,016,000	Debt/ Equity:	0.0342

Yucheng Technologies Ltd

105 W 13th St., Ste. 7A, New York, NY, 10011; ; *http://* www.yuchengtech.com

General - Incorporation British Virgin Islands	Stock - Price on:12/24/2007	NA
Employees	NA	Stock Exchange	OTC
Auditor	NA	Ticker Symbol	YCHTF
Stk Agt	Continental Stock Transfer & Trust Co	Outstanding Shares	NA
Counsel	NA	E.P.S.	NA
DUNS No.	NA	Shareholders	NA

Business: The groups principle activity is to provide recruiting services. The groups service area includes the research and development, engineering, marketing, sales, information technology and manufacturing industries. The group operates from United States.

Primary SIC and add'l.: 7371

CIK No: 0001356462

Officers: Weidong Hong/Dir., CEO, Wei Peng/Investor Relations Officer - Beijing, China, Shuo Zeng/Dir., COO, Peter Li/CFO, Jim Preissler/Dir. - Investor Relations, In USA, Graubard Miller/Legal Counsel

Directors: Weidong Hong/Dir., CEO, Chih T. Cheung/Non - Exec. Chmn., Shuo Zeng/Dir., COO

Owners: Shuo Zeng, Chih T. Cheung, Elite Concord International Limited, Jack Silver, Sihitech Company Limited, Mega Capital Group Services Limited, Insiders, Peter Li, Weidong Hong, James Z. Li, Profit Loyal Consultants Limited

Curr. Assets:	$39,168,000	Curr. Liab.:	$18,085,000		
Plant, Equip.:	$827,000	Total Liab.:	$18,763,000	Indic. Yr. Divd.:	NA
Total Assets:	$49,834,000	Net Worth:	$31,072,000	Debt/ Equity:	NA

Yukon Gold Corp Inc

55 York St., Ste. 401, Toronto, ON, M5J 1R7; **PH:** 1-416-865-9790; **Fax:** 1-416-865-1250; *http://* www.yukongoldcorp.com; **Email:** info@yukongoldcorp.com

General - Incorporation	DE	Stock - Price on:12/24/2007	$0.5
Employees	NA	Stock Exchange	OTC
Auditor	Schwartz Levitsky Feldman LLP	Ticker Symbol	YGDC
Stk Agt	CIBC Mellon Trust CO.	Outstanding Shares	NA
Counsel	Macleod Dixon	E.P.S.	NA
DUNS No.	NA	Shareholders	NA

Business: The groups principal activity is to explore and, if warranted and feasible, to develop ore reserves on the mineral claims located in the Mayo Mining District of the Yukon Territory. The group operates from Canada.

Primary SIC and add'l.: 1000

CIK No: 0001280396

Subsidiaries: Yukon Gold Corp.

Officers: Paul Gorman/Dir., CEO, Rakesh Malhotra/CFO, Macleod Dixon/Legal Counsel, Stewart L. Fumerton/VP - Exploration

Directors: Paul Gorman/Dir., CEO, J. L. Guerra/Chmn., Howard Barth/Dir., Kenneth P. Hill/Dir., Chet Idziszek/Dir., Robert Van Tassell/Dir.

Owners: Warren W. Holmes, Paul Gorman, Jose L. Guerra/7.66%, Insiders/8.44%, Howard Barth

Yum! Brands Inc

1900 Colonel Sanders Ln., Louisville, KY, 40213; **PH:** 1-502-874-8300; *http://* www.yum.com

General		Stock	
General - Incorporation	NC	Stock- Price on:12/24/2007	$66.92
Employees	53,200	Stock Exchange	NYSE
Auditor	KPMG LLP	Ticker Symbol	YUM
Stk Agt	American Stock Transfer & Trust Co.	Outstanding Shares	261,900,000
Counsel	NA	E.P.S.	$1.65
DUNS No.	17-929-4467	Shareholders	NA

Business: The groups principle activities include operating, developing, franchising and licensing traditional restaurants and non-traditional restaurants. The groups products include chicken (R), kfc (R), pizza hut (R), long john silver's(R) and taco bell(R). The group operates from United States.

Primary SIC and add'l.: 5812 6794

CIK No: 0001041061

Subsidiaries: 3018538 Nova Scotia Company, A&W Restaurants, Inc., A.c.n. 002 543 286 Pty. Ltd., A.c.n. 002 812 151 Pty. Ltd. , A.c.n. 054 055 917 Pty. Ltd., A.c.n. 054 121 416 Pty. Ltd., A.c.n. 084 994 374 Pty. Ltd. , A.c.n. 101 355 772 Pty. Ltd., Acn 085 239 961 Pty. Ltd. (sa1), Acn 085 239 998 Pty. Ltd. (sa2), American Restaurants Sp. z o.o., American Restaurants SRO , Amrest Holdings N.V., Ashton Fried Chicken Pty. Ltd., Beijing Pizza Co., Ltd. 271 Subsidiaries included in the Index

Officers: David C. Novak/Chmn., CEO, Pres./$12,432,090.00, Richard T. Carucci/CFO/$2,301,721.00, Harvey Brownlee/COO - KFC, Jonathan D. Blum/Sr. VP - Public Affairs, Gregg R. Dedrick/Pres., Chief Concept Officer - KFC, Samuel Su/Pres. - Yum! China Division, Graham D. Allan/Pres. - Yum! Restaurants International/$2,860,436.00, Greg Creed/Pres., Chief Concept Officer - Taco Bell, Anne P. Byerlein/Chief People Officer, Peter R. Hearl/Chief Operating, Development Officer, Emil J. Brolick/Pres. - US Brand Building/$3,388,282.00, Rob Savage/COO - Taco Bell, Jing-Shyh S. Su/Pres. - China Division/$3,829,848.00, Tim Jerzyk/Sr. VP - Investor Relations, Treasurer, Scott Bergren/Pres., Chief Concept Officer - Pizza Hut *(19 Officers included in Index)*

Directors: David C. Novak/Chmn., CEO, Pres., Massimo Ferragamo/Dir., Thomas C. Nelson/Dir., Thomas M. Ryan/Dir., David W. Dorman/Dir., David J. Grissom/Dir., Kenneth G. Langone/Dir., Jonathan S. Linen/Dir., Jackie Trujillo/Dir., Bonnie G. Hill/Dir., Robert Holland/Dir., Robert J. Ulrich/Dir.

Owners: David W. Dorman, Bonnie G. Hill, Robert Holland, Thomas C. Nelson, Jonathan Linen, Jing-Shyh S. Su, Thomas M. Ryan, Graham D. Allan, Emil J. Brolick, Insiders, Richard T. Carucci, Jackie Trujillo, David C. Novak, David J. Grissom, Massimo Ferragamo *(19 Owners included in Index)*

Financial Data: Fiscal Year End:12/31 Latest Annual Data: 12/30/2006

Year	Sales	Net Income
2006	$9,561,000,000	$824,000,000
2005	$9,349,000,000	$762,000,000
2004	$9,011,000,000	$740,000,000

Curr. Assets:	$837,000,000	Curr. Liab.:	$1,605,000,000	P/E Ratio:	42.62
Plant, Equip.:	$3,356,000,000	Total Liab.:	$4,249,000,000	Indic. Yr. Divd.:	$0.600
Total Assets:	$5,698,000,000	Net Worth:	$1,449,000,000	Debt/ Equity:	1.5133

Yummies Inc

1981 E Murray-holladay Rd., Salt Lake City, UT, 84117; **PH:** 1-801-272-9294

General		Stock	
General - Incorporation	NV	Stock- Price on:12/24/2007	NA
Employees	NA	Stock Exchange	OTC
Auditor	Burnham & Schumm	Ticker Symbol	YUMM
Stk Agt	Interwest Transfer Company, Inc.	Outstanding Shares	NA
Counsel	NA	E.P.S.	NA
DUNS No.	NA	Shareholders	NA

Business: The group's principle activity is to seek new businesses. The only activity of the company is to manage its current limited assets. The group operates from United States.

Primary SIC and add'l.: 9999

CIK No: 0001073748

Officers: Dianne Hatton-Ward/50/Dir., CEO, CFO, Pres., Sec., Treasurer

Directors: Dianne Hatton-Ward/50/Dir., CEO, CFO, Pres., Sec., Treasurer

Owners: Insiders/63.90%, Dianne Hatton-Ward/63.90%

YzApp International Inc

666 Burrard St., Ste. 500, Vancouver, BC, V6C 3P6; **PH:** 1-604-868-0264

General		Stock	
General - Incorporation	NV	Stock- Price on:12/24/2007	$0.12
Employees	NA	Stock Exchange	OTC
Auditor	N.I. Cameron Inc	Ticker Symbol	YZPI
Stk Agt	Pacific Stock Transfer Company	Outstanding Shares	NA
Counsel	NA	E.P.S.	NA
DUNS No.	NA	Shareholders	NA

Business: The groups principal activities include development of software allowing the Company to act as an application service provider acting as a conduit between retailers and financial institutions. The group operates from Canada.

Primary SIC and add'l.: 7372

CIK No: 0001273385

Officers: Brian Jaggard/47/Dir., CEO, CFO, Pres., Douglas Dunn/48/Dir., COO

Directors: Brian Jaggard/47/Dir., CEO, CFO, Pres., Douglas Dunn/48/Dir., COO, Sec., Carl Lacey/60/Dir.

Owners: Carl Lacey, Douglas Dunn/7.50%, Brian Jaggard/45.50%

Z-Trim Holdings Inc

Formerly: Circle Group Holdings Inc
1011 Campus Dr., Mundelein, IL, 60060; **PH:** 1-847-549-6002; **Fax:** 1-847-549-6146; *http://* www.crgq.com; **Email:** investorrelations@crgq.com

General		Stock	
General - Incorporation	IL	Stock- Price on:12/24/2007	$1.03
Employees	33	Stock Exchange	AMEX
Auditor	Spector & Wong LLP	Ticker Symbol	ZTM
Stk Agt	American Stock Transfer & Trust Co.	Outstanding Shares	63,690,000
Counsel	NA	E.P.S.	NA
DUNS No.	NA	Shareholders	NA

Business: The group's principal activity is to commercialize z-trim, a corn-based fat replacement developed by the agricultural research service of the United States department of agriculture. Z-trim can be used decrease fat and calories and increase insoluble healthy fiber in foods. The group operates through four segments: food product development, e-tailer, business consulting and security training and products. The food product development segment owns license to z-trim. The e-tailer segment distributes pillows, blankets and other bedding products. The business consulting segment develops distinctive Web sites and provides business-consulting services for the group's wholly owned subsidiaries. The security training and products segment offers self-defense training courses and products. The group operates solely in the United States.

Primary SIC and add'l.: 7389 2392 2399

CIK No: 0001052257

Subsidiaries: Fiber-Gel Technologies, Inc., On-Line Bedding Corp., thebraveway.com, Inc., Z-Amaize Technologies, Inc.

Officers: Triveni Shukla/65/Exec. VP - Marketing, Technology, Dir. Nominee

Directors: Randal Hoff/56/Dir., Mark Hershhorn/59/Dir., Harvey Rosenfeld/51/Dir., Michael Donahue/51/Dir., Brian S. Israel/51/Dir.

Owners: Insiders/41.23%, Michael J. Theriault/3.11%, Gregory J. Halpern/26.30%, Steve J. Cohen/2.12%, Stan J. Levin/1.10%, Alan G. Orlowsky/1.21%, Steven H. Salgan/1.69%, Dana L. Dabney/5.65%

Financial Data: Fiscal Year End:12/31 Latest Annual Data: 03/31/2007

Year	Sales	Net Income
2007	NA	NA
2006	NA	NA
2005	$515,000	-$6,026,000

Curr. Assets:	$1,082,000	Curr. Liab.:	$596,000		
Plant, Equip.:	$6,263,000	Total Liab.:	$596,000	Indic. Yr. Divd.:	NA
Total Assets:	$7,509,000	Net Worth:	$6,913,000	Debt/ Equity:	NA

Zab Resources Inc

Formerly: Lucky 1 Enterprises Inc
1255 W Pender St., Ste. 100, Vancouver, BC, A1 V6E 2V1; ; *http://* www.bronxventures.com

General		Stock	
General - Incorporation	Canada	Stock- Price on:12/24/2007	NA
Employees	2,100	Stock Exchange	NYSE
Auditor	Smythe Ratcliffe LLP	Ticker Symbol	NA
Stk Agt	Computershare Trust Co	Outstanding Shares	NA
Counsel	Anfield Sujir Kennedy & Durno	E.P.S.	NA
DUNS No.	24-557-9644	Shareholders	NA

Business: The group's principal activity is to acquire, explore and develop natural resource properties relating to minerals. At present the group's interest in resource properties include five groups of prospects containing lithium mineralization which are located in the province of ontario, Canada. The subsidiary of the group is blue rock mining, inc.

Primary SIC and add'l.: 1081 1382 1481

CIK No: 0000825171

Subsidiaries: Blue Rock Mining, Inc

Officers: Bedo H. Kalpakian/62/Dir., CEO, CFO, Pres., Jacob H. Kalpakian/40/Dir., VP, Penilla Klomp/46/Corp. Sec.

Directors: Bedo H. Kalpakian/62/Dir., CEO, CFO, Pres., Jacob H. Kalpakian/40/Dir., VP, Gregory T. McFarlane/40/Dir., Wayne J. Murton/71/Dir.

Owners: Jacob H. Kalpakian/24.90%, Bedo H. Kalpakian/28.80%

Curr. Assets:	$1,407,000	Curr. Liab.:	$82,000		
Plant, Equip.:	$25,000	Total Liab.:	$82,000	Indic. Yr. Divd.:	NA
Total Assets:	$1,440,000	Net Worth:	$1,358,000	Debt/ Equity:	NA

Zaldiva Inc

2805 E Oakland Pk. Blvd., No. 376, Fort Lauderdale, FL, 33306; **PH:** 1-877-925-3482; *http://* www.Zaldiva.com

General		Stock	
General - Incorporation	FL	Stock- Price on:12/24/2007	$0.77
Employees	4	Stock Exchange	OTC
Auditor	Mantyla McReynolds LLC	Ticker Symbol	ZLDV
Stk Agt	Atlas Stock Transfer Corp	Outstanding Shares	7,170,000
Counsel	NA	E.P.S.	-$0.05
DUNS No.	NA	Shareholders	NA

Business: The group's principle activity is to operate as an on-line shopping center known as zaldiva.com, which features products from retailers through the Internet. Zaldiva has two strategic business units: one, which sells cigars, accessories and other goods and one that offer Internet products and facilitates on-line shopping. Zaldiva cigars are hand-made by cuban tobacconists, featuring cameroon wrap and binder with dominican longleaf filler from cuban seed. The company sells zaldiva cigars and accessories through its e-commerce Web site as well as through direct sales to establishments in the United States, Germany, Australia and Japan. The company performs upscale Web site development and hosting and has developed and maintained Web sites for approximately 40 clients.

Primary SIC and add'l.: 5993 5194 5961

CIK No: 0001168325

Officers: Christopher Ebersole/40/CFO

Directors: Nicole Leigh Van Coller/Dir.

Owners: John A. Palmer/7.40%, Robert B. Lees/6.10%, Nicole Leigh Van Coller/7.40%, Christopher Ebersole/5.00%, Jeremy I. Van Coller/7.30%

Financial Data: Fiscal Year End:09/30 Latest Annual Data: 9/30/2006

Year	Sales	Net Income
2006	$78,000	-$195,000
2005	$74,000	-$252,000
2004	$490,000	$36,000

Curr. Assets:	$166,000	**Curr. Liab.:**	$20,000		
Plant, Equip.:	$602,000	**Total Liab.:**	$20,000	**Indic. Yr. Divd.:**	NA
Total Assets:	$769,000	**Net Worth:**	$749,000	**Debt/ Equity:**	NA

Zale Corp

901 W Walnut Hill Ln, Irving, TX, 75038; ***PH:*** 1-972-580-4000; ***http://*** www.zalecorp.com; ***Email:*** ir@zalecorp.com

General - Incorporation	DE	**Stock**- Price on:12/24/2007	$24.93
Employees	16,900	Stock Exchange	NYSE
Auditor	KPMG LLP	Ticker Symbol	ZLC
Stk Agt	Bank of New York	Outstanding Shares	49,030,000
Counsel	Troutman Saunders LLP	E.P.S	$1.16
DUNS No.	00-792-8757	Shareholders	NA

Business: The groups principle activity is to operate retail jewelry stores. The group operates through three business segments namely fine jewelry, kiosk jewelry and all other. The groups products are sold under the brand names Piercing Pagoda, Plumb Gold, Silver and Gold Connection. The group operates from United States.

Primary SIC and add'l.: 5944

CIK No: 0000109156

Subsidiaries: DDCC, Inc., Dobbins Jewelers, Inc., FINCO Holding, LP, FINCO Partnership, LP, Jewel Re-Insurance Ltd., Jewelers Credit Corporation, Jewelers Financial Services, Inc., TXDC, LP, Zale Canada Co., Zale Canada Diamond Sourcing, Inc., Zale Canada Holding, LP, Zale Delaware, Inc, Zale Employees Child Care Association, Inc, Zale Indemnity Company, Zale International, Inc. 18 Subsidiaries included in the Index

Officers: Mary E. Burton/55/Dir., CEO, Stephen R. Lang/40/Group Sr. VP, Chief Merchandise Officer, Rodney Carter/50/Exec. VP, Chief Administrative Officer, CFO, David H. Sternblitz/VP, Treasurer, Investor Relations Officer, Susann C. Mayo/56/Sr. VP - Supply Chain, Gilbert P. Hollander/55/Exec. VP, Chief Sourcing, Supply Chain Officer, Cynthia T. Gordon/44/Sr. VP, Controller, Mary A. Doran/52/Sr. VP - Human Resources, Charles E. Fieramosca/60/Corporate Sr. VP, Pres. - Bailey Banks, Biddle, Stephen C. Massanelli/52/Sr. VP - Real Estate, Hilary Molay/54/Sr. VP, General Counsel, Sec., George J. Slicho/59/Sr. VP - Loss Prevention, Steven Larkin/50/Sr. VP - E, Commerce, Sterling Pope/53/Sr. VP - Store Operations, Mark A. Stone/50/CIO, Sr. VP

Directors: Mary E. Burton/55/Dir., CEO, Richard C. Marcus/Chmn., Glen J. Adams/Dir., George R. Mihalko/Dir., Thomas C. Shull/Dir., Charles M. Sonsteby/54/Dir., Chuck Sonsteby/Dir., John B. Lowe/Dir., David M. Szymanski/Dir.

Owners: Glen J. Adams, Mary E. Burton, David M. Szymanski, Artisan Partners L.P./10.96%, Charles M. Sonsteby, First Pacific Advisors, Inc./8.84%, Thomas C. Shull, S.A.C. Capital Advisors/5.06%, George R. Mihalko, Harris Associates L.P./5.08%, John A. Zimmermann, Hayground Cove Asset Management, L.L.C./5.58%, Charles E. Fieramosca, Gilbert P. Hollander, U.S. Trust Corporation/6.09% *(23 Owners included in Index)*

Financial Data: ***Fiscal Year End:***07/31 ***Latest Annual Data:*** 7/31/2006

Year	Sales	Net Income
2006	$2,438,977,000	$53,622,000
2005	$2,383,066,000	$106,775,000
2004	$2,304,440,000	$106,473,000

Curr. Assets:	$1,172,318,000	**Curr. Liab.:**	$374,458,000	**P/E Ratio:**	40.21
Plant, Equip.:	$304,396,000	**Total Liab.:**	$711,373,000	**Indic. Yr. Divd.:**	NA
Total Assets:	$1,613,946,000	**Net Worth:**	$902,573,000	**Debt/ Equity:**	NA

Zandaria Ventures Inc

2300 Palm Beach Lakes Blvd., Ste. 218, West Palm Beach, FL, 33409; ***PH:*** 1-561-697-8751

General - Incorporation	NV	**Stock**- Price on:12/24/2007	NA
Employees	NA	Stock Exchange	OTC
Auditor	Pollard-kelley Auditing Services, Inc	Ticker Symbol	ZDVN
Stk Agt	Empire Stock Transfer Inc.	Outstanding Shares	NA
Counsel	NA	E.P.S	NA
DUNS No.	NA	Shareholders	NA

Business: The groups principal activity is in the exploration stage. The group operates from the United States and Canada.

Primary SIC and add'l.: 1000

CIK No: 0001334589

Officers: Jason Smart/28/Dir., CEO, Pres., Sec.

Directors: Jason Smart/28/Dir., CEO, Pres., Sec.

Owners: Insiders/32.20%, Steven Cozine/32.20%

Zanett Inc

635 Madison Ave., 15th Fl., New York, NY, 10022; ***PH:*** 1-212-759-5700; ***http://*** www.zanett.com; ***Email:*** ABayme@Zanett.com

General - Incorporation	DE	**Stock**- Price on:12/24/2007	$1.336
Employees	227	Stock Exchange	NDQ
Auditor	Amper, Politziner & Mattia P.c	Ticker Symbol	ZANE
Stk Agt	American Stock Transfer & Trust Co.	Outstanding Shares	29,740,000
Counsel	NA	E.P.S	-$0.078
DUNS No.	92-847-8064	Shareholders	NA

Business: The group's principal activity is to provide specialized it solutions. The services are provided to Fortune 500 corporations, middle market companies and large government agencies. The group operates through two segments: commercial solutions and government solutions. The commercial solutions provides services to initiate, develop and implement e-business systems. The government solutions provides software and satellite engineering services with domain area expertise on government and aerospace and it infrastructure contracts. The group acquired paragon dynamics inc on 31-Jan-2003 and deltadata inc on 04-Dec-2003.

Primary SIC and add'l.: 8742 7371 6794 6719 7389 7372

CIK No: 0001133872

Subsidiaries: Back Bay Technologies, Inc., Delta Communications Group, Inc, INRANGE Consulting Corporation, Paragon Dynamics, Inc, Whitbread Technology Partners, Inc, Zanett Commercial Solutions, Inc.

Officers: David McCarthy/CEO, Douglas L. Hartmann/CEO - Paragon Dynamics, Inc/$186,832.00, Dennis Harkins/CFO/$125,000.00, David Deboisblanc/Sr. VP - Sales, Claudio M. Guazzoni/Dir., Pres./$10,530.00, Jack Rapport/54/Pres./$235,000.00, Pierre-Georges Roy/Chief Legal Officer, Robert Wise/Dir. - Business Development, Vince Vickers/Sr. VP - Delivery, PMP, Jim Napier/VP - Marketing, John Schmitz/VP - Finance, CPA, Katie Reed/VP - Human Resources, Sphr, Chuck Deskins/46/Pres. - ZCS

Directors: Claudio M. Guazzoni/Dir., Pres., Jay W. Kelly/Dir., Scott L. Perry/Dir., William H. Church/Dir., Leoanrd Goldstein/Dir., Evans R. Hineman/Dir.

Owners: Doug Hartmann/1.22%, Jay W. Kelley, Leonard G. Goldstein, Claudio Guazzoni/55.75%, Evans R. Hineman, Insiders/60.10%, Bruno Guazzoni/29.20%, William H. Church, Jack M. Rapport/0.90%, Scott L. Perry

Financial Data: ***Fiscal Year End:***12/31 ***Latest Annual Data:*** 12/31/2006

Year	Sales	Net Income
2006	$45,258,000	-$1,768,000
2005	$34,892,000	-$13,207,000
2004	$29,873,000	-$253,000

Curr. Assets:	$11,166,000	**Curr. Liab.:**	$12,735,000		
Plant, Equip.:	$918,000	**Total Liab.:**	$23,207,000	**Indic. Yr. Divd.:**	NA
Total Assets:	$31,153,000	**Net Worth:**	$7,946,000	**Debt/ Equity:**	1.1149

Zann Corp

1403 US Hwy. 27 S, Clermont, FL, 34714; ***PH:*** 1-352-394-6629; ***Fax:*** 1-810-714-3524; ***http://*** www.zanncorp.com; ***Email:*** ir@zanncorp.com

General - Incorporation	NV	**Stock**- Price on:12/24/2007	$0.003
Employees	3	Stock Exchange	OTC
Auditor	Russell Bedford Stefanou Mirchandani	Ticker Symbol	ZNNC
Stk Agt	Corporate Stock Transfer, Inc.	Outstanding Shares	33,950,000
Counsel	NA	E.P.S	-$0.087
DUNS No.	NA	Shareholders	NA

Business: The group is a development stage company. Currently the company's purpose is to seek, investigate and, if such investigation warrants, acquire an interest in business opportunities presented to them by persons or firms who or which desire to seek the perceived advantages of a corporation which is registered under the securities exchange act of 1934. The company does not restrict their search to any specific business, industry or geographical location and may participate in a business venture of virtually any kind or nature. On 10-Aug-2004, the group acquried blue kiwi inc.

Primary SIC and add'l.: 4899

CIK No: 0001098329

Subsidiaries: Blue Kiwi Inc.

Financial Data: ***Fiscal Year End:***12/31 ***Latest Annual Data:*** 12/31/2005

Year	Sales	Net Income
2005	$1,000	-$2,937,000
2004	$1,000	-$10,565,000
2003	NA	$1,629,000

Curr. Assets:	$0	**Curr. Liab.:**	$1,523,000		
Plant, Equip.:	NA	**Total Liab.:**	$1,523,000	**Indic. Yr. Divd.:**	NA
Total Assets:	$0	**Net Worth:**	-$1,523,000	**Debt/ Equity:**	NA

ZAP

501 Fourth St., Santa Rosa, CA, 95401; ***PH:*** 1-707-525-8658; ***http://*** www.zapworld.com; ***Email:*** zap@zapworld.com

General - Incorporation	CA	**Stock**- Price on:12/24/2007	$0.98
Employees	50	Stock Exchange	OTC
Auditor	Odenberg, Muranishi & Co. LLP	Ticker Symbol	ZAAP
Stk Agt	Continental Stock Transfer & Trust Co	Outstanding Shares	45,610,000
Counsel	NA	E.P.S	-$0.6
DUNS No.	NA	Shareholders	NA

Business: The group's principal activities are to manufacture and market electric automobiles, motorcycles, bicycles and scooters. The group operates through the following segments: car outlet; electric products; rental outlets and car dealership.the group's principal activities are to manufacture and market electric automobiles, motorcycles, bicycles and scooters. It also markets personal watercraft, hovercraft, neighborhood electric vehicles and commercial vehicles. It also produces an electric scooter, known as the zappy(R), using parts manufactured by various contractors. It sells its electric vehicles to retail customers, international distributors, law enforcement agencies, electric utility companies and bicycle dealerships. The group established a rental program to rent neighborhood electric cars through agencies. Zap(R), electricruizer(R), zappy(R), powerbike(R), zapworld.com, zap electric vehicle outlet(R) and zero air pollution(R) are the trademarks of the group.

Primary SIC and add'l.: 4741 3751

CIK No: 0001024628

Subsidiaries: RAP Group, Inc., Voltage Vehicles, ZAP Manufacturing Inc., ZAP Stores Inc., ZAP World Outlet Inc.

Officers: Steven Schneider/Dir., CEO/$557,556.00, Renay Cude/Dir., Corp. Sec./$515,556.00, William Hartman/CFO/$232,800.00, Amos Kazzaz/COO, Michael Ringstad/Operations Controller

Directors: Steven Schneider/Dir., CEO, Gary Starr/Chmn., Raymond F. Byrne/59/Dir., Renay Cude/Dir., Corp. Sec., Peter H. Scholl/61/Dir.

Owners: Jeffrey G. Banks/13.20%, Daka Development Ltd./5.90%, Renay Cude/6.10%, Gary Starr/15.50%, Fusion Capital Fund II, LLC/5.60%, Peter Scholl/1.30%, William Hartman/2.10%, Steven Schneider/27.90%, Sunshine 511 Holdings/6.70%

Financial Data: ***Fiscal Year End:***12/31 ***Latest Annual Data:*** 12/31/2006

Year	Sales	Net Income
2006	$10,830,000	-$11,915,000
2005	$3,602,000	-$23,501,000
2004	$4,772,000	-$27,834,000

Curr. Assets:	$5,895,000	**Curr. Liab.:**	$5,966,000		
Plant, Equip.:	$4,466,000	**Total Liab.:**	$7,806,000	**Indic. Yr. Divd.:**	NA
Total Assets:	$10,816,000	**Net Worth:**	$3,010,000	**Debt/ Equity:**	0.5543

Zap Com Corp

100 Meridian Ctr., Ste 350, Rochester, NY, 14618; *PH:* 1-585-987-2800; *http://* www.zap.com

General - Incorporation	NV	**Stock**- Price on:12/24/2007	$0.18
Employees	2	Stock Exchange	OTC
Auditor	PricewaterhouseCoopers LLP	Ticker Symbol	ZPCM
Stk Agt	American Stock Transfer & Trust Co.	Outstanding Shares	NA
Counsel	NA	E.P.S	$0.00
DUNS No.	NA	Shareholders	NA

Business: The group's principle activity is to develop a global network of independently owned Website to provide a platform for advertising. The company currently does not have any existing business operations, other than maintaining its status as a public entity. The company's principal activities are expected to be exploring methods to enhance stockholder value. The company has developed zapbox, a proprietary Web application that can be made available in various forms of media, like graphics, animations and sound and community features like chat rooms and e-mail. The group operates from United States.

Primary SIC and add'l.: 7372

CIK No: 0001083243

Subsidiaries: Zapata.

Officers: Avram Glazer/Chmn., CEO, Pres., Gordon E. Forth/Corp. Sec. - Zapata Corp, Leonard Disalvo/VP - Finance, CFO

Directors: Avram Glazer/Chmn., CEO, Pres., Warren Gfeller/Dir., Bryan Glazer/Dir., Darcie Glazer/Dir., Edward Glazer/Dir., John Halldow/Dir., Robert Leffler/Dir.

Owners: Zapata Corporation/97.90%, Insiders, Avram Glazer, Leonard DiSalvo

Financial Data: ***Fiscal Year End:***12/31 ***Latest Annual Data:*** 12/31/2006

Year	Sales	Net Income
2006	NA	-$49,000
2005	NA	-$78,000
2004	NA	-$142,000

Curr. Assets:	$1,728,000	**Curr. Liab.:**	$53,000		
Plant, Equip.:	NA	**Total Liab.:**	$53,000	**Indic. Yr. Divd.:**	NA
Total Assets:	$1,728,000	**Net Worth:**	$1,676,000	**Debt/ Equity:**	NA

Zapata Corp

100 Meridian Ctr., Ste 350, Rochester, NY, 14618; *PH:* 1-585-242-2000; *http://* www.zapatacorp.com

General - Incorporation	NV	**Stock**- Price on:12/24/2007	$6.8
Employees	9	Stock Exchange	NYSE
Auditor	PricewaterhouseCoopers LLP	Ticker Symbol	ZAP
Stk Agt	American Stock Transfer & Trust Co.	Outstanding Shares	19,180,000
Counsel		E.P.S	-$0.19
DUNS No.	00-793-3328	Shareholders	NA

Business: The group's principal activities are to process, market and distribute fish meal and fish oil products and supplies automotive airbag fabric, cushions and technical fabrics. The group is a holding company with two operating companies: safety components international inc and omega protein corporation. Safety components international inc supplies automotive airbag fabric, cushions and technical fabrics with operations in North America and Europe. It manufactures value-added technical fabrics used in niche industrial and commercial applications such as fire service apparel, ballistics material for luggage, filtration and military tents. Omega protein corporation produces and sells protein and oil products, processes fish meal, fish oil and fish solubles. Its products are primarily used as a protein ingredient in animal feed for swine, cattle, aquaculture and household pets. On 23-Sep-2003, the group acquired 83% of safety components international inc.

Primary SIC and add'l.: 2394 6719 2077 7375 7371

CIK No: 0000109177

Subsidiaries: Charged Productions, Inc., Omega Protein Corporation, Zap.Com Corporation

Officers: Avram A. Glazer/Chmn., CEO, Pres./$605,738.00, Leonard Disalvo/CFO, VP - Finance/$276,421.00, Gordon Forth/Corp. Sec.

Directors: Avram A. Glazer/Chmn., CEO, Pres., Warren Gfeller/Dir., Bryan Glazer/Dir., Darcie Glazer/Dir., Edward Glazer/Dir., John Halldow/Dir., Robert Leffler/Dir.

Owners: Avram A. Glazer, Darcie S. Glazer, Linda Glazer/51.80%, Malcolm I. Glazer/51.80%, Edward S. Glazer, Leonard DiSalvo/1.40%, Warren H. Gfeller, Donald Smith& Co., Inc./8.40%, Insiders/3.50%, Royce& Associates, LLC/10.40%, River Road Asset Management, LLC/6.70%, Bryan G. Glazer, John R. Halldow, Robert V. Leffler, Dimensional FundAdvisors LP/5.70%

Financial Data: ***Fiscal Year End:***12/31 ***Latest Annual Data:*** 12/31/2006

Year	Sales	Net Income
2006	NA	-$4,663,000
2005	$109,896,000	-$9,176,000
2004	$367,528,000	$3,733,000

Curr. Assets:	$152,713,000	**Curr. Liab.:**	$2,223,000		
Plant, Equip.:	$3,000	**Total Liab.:**	$4,463,000	**Indic. Yr. Divd.:**	NA
Total Assets:	$163,731,000	**Net Worth:**	$159,268,000	**Debt/ Equity:**	NA

Zareba Systems Inc

Formerly: Waters Instruments Inc

13705 26th Ave. N, Ste. 102, Minneapolis, MN, 55441; *PH:* 1-763-551-1125; *http://* www.wtrs.com

General - Incorporation	MN	**Stock**- Price on:12/24/2007	$6
Employees	137	Stock Exchange	NDQ
Auditor	Virchow, Krause & Co. LLP	Ticker Symbol	NA
Stk Agt	Wells Fargo Bank, N.A.	Outstanding Shares	2,430,000
Counsel	Fredrikson & Byron	E.P.S	$1.26
DUNS No.	00-625-1631	Shareholders	NA

Business: The group's principal activities are to design, manufacture and market electric fence systems, local area network connectivity and medical products. The operations are carried out through three units: zareba systems, waters medical systems (wms) and waters network systems (wns). Zareba systems designs, manufactures and sells electric fence systems used for the control or containment of livestock, horses, predators, pets and lawn and garden pets. Waters medical systems (wms) designs, manufactures and markets electronic medical instruments for cardiovascular and organ preservation used in laboratories, clinics and hospitals. Waters network systems manufactures and markets connectivity products for local area networks (lans), which include various families of ethernet switches and media converters. The group discontinued waters network systems in 2004. On 27-Sep-2004, the group acquired rutland electric fencing company ltd.

Primary SIC and add'l.: 7373 3699 7379 7376 3678 5047

CIK No: 0000104987

Subsidiaries: Waters Medical Systems, Inc, Zareba Security, Inc, Zareba Systems Europe Limited, Zareba Systems of Canada Ltd.

Officers: Jerry W. Grabowski/Dir., CEO, Pres./$386,415.00, Elaine D. Beckstrom/Dir. - Marketing, Investor Relations, Donald G. Dalland/VP - Manufacturing/$208,177.00, John W. Frederick/Exec. VP - Sales, Business Development/$200,165.00, Jeff Matheisen/CFO/$223,088.00, Ron W. Oblizajek/Information Systems Dir., Simon Ragdale/MD - Rutland Electric Fencing Co, Kelly Spaulding/Dir. - Human Resources

Directors: Jerry W. Grabowski/Dir., CEO, Pres., Eugene W. Courtney/72/Dir., William R. Franta/Dir., John A. Grimstad/Dir., Dale A. Nordquist/Dir.

Owners: William John Frederick, Heartland Advisors, Inc./9.30%, Woodland Investment Company/10.50%, Jerry W. Grabowski/5.10%, John A. Grimstad/1.90%, Donald J. Dalland, Jerry W. Grabowski/5.10%, Insiders/10.60%, Duane Schiefelbein/7.60%, Nicole F. Kohl Gift Trust/5.50%, Dale A. Nordquist, Eugene W. Courtney, William R. Franta/1.40%

Financial Data: ***Fiscal Year End:***06/30 ***Latest Annual Data:*** 6/30/2006

Year	Sales	Net Income
2006	$34,418,000	-$301,000
2005	$32,607,000	$850,000
2004	$24,186,000	$1,964,000

Curr. Assets:	$17,322,000	**Curr. Liab.:**	$9,052,000	**P/E Ratio:**	24.00
Plant, Equip.:	$3,777,000	**Total Liab.:**	$18,209,000	**Indic. Yr. Divd.:**	NA
Total Assets:	$31,837,000	**Net Worth:**	$13,628,000	**Debt/ Equity:**	0.1854

Zarlink Semiconductor Inc

400 March Rd., Ottawa, ON, K2K 3H4; *PH:* 1-613-592-0200; *http://* www.zarlink.com; *Email:* corporate@zarlink.com

General - Incorporation	Canada	**Stock**- Price on:12/24/2007	$1.74
Employees	747	Stock Exchange	NYSE
Auditor	Ernst & Young LLP	Ticker Symbol	ZL
Stk Agt	Computershare Investor Services LLC	Outstanding Shares	127,350,000
Counsel	Rubinbaum LLP	E.P.S	-$0.15
DUNS No.	20-747-5054	Shareholders	NA

Business: The group's principle activities are to manufacture and distribute microelectronic components. The group operates in two segments: communication and medical. Communications business specializes in broadband connectivity solutions over wired, wireless and optical media. Products include network access products that provide connectivity to the network's core backbone, such as feeder, aggregation and transmission applications, and those that address the multi-protocol physical and network layers. Medical business provides asic solutions for applications such as pacemakers, hearing aids and portable instruments. The group's quarterly revenue for September 2007 was 49.60 millions of USD.

Primary SIC and add'l.: 3674 3661 3695 3679 5063

CIK No: 0000352435

Subsidiaries: Zarlink Semiconductor (Asia) Pte. Ltd., Zarlink Semiconductor (Barbados) Ltd., Zarlink Semiconductor (U.S.) Inc., Zarlink Semiconductor AB, Zarlink Semiconductor GmbH, Zarlink Semiconductor Japan KK, Zarlink Semiconductor Limited, Zarlink Semiconductor SA, Zarlink Semiconductor V.N. Inc., Zarlink Semiconductor XIC B.V.

Officers: Kirk K. Mandy/Dir., CEO, Pres., Stan Swirhun/Sr. VP, GM - Optical Communications, Mike McGinn/VP - Marketing Communications - Investor Relations, Scott Milligan/Sr. VP - Finance, CFO, Tony Gallagher/Sr. VP - Worldwide Operations, Simon Krelle/Contact - Europe, Middle East, Africa, EMEA, Press Office, Peter Burke/Sr. VP, GM - Network Communications, Jeff Crocker/Sr. VP - Worldwide Sales, Spencer J. Lanthier/Dir. - Management Consultant, Steve Swift/Sr. VP, GM - Ultra Low, Power Communications, Simon Flatt/Dir. - Europe, Middle East, Africa, EMEA, Press Office, Adam Chowaniec/Dir. - Semiconductor Industry Advisor, Edward Goffin/Contact - Corporate, US, Asia Pacific, Press Office

Directors: Kirk K. Mandy/Dir., CEO, Pres., Henry Simon/Chmn., Jules Meunier/Dir., Dennis A. Roberson/Dir., Adam Chowaniec/Dir. - Semiconductor Industry Advisor, Oleg Khaykin/Dir., Hubert T. Lacroix/Dir., Andre Borrel/Dir., Spencer J. Lanthier/Dir. - Management Consultant

Financial Data: ***Fiscal Year End:***03/31 ***Latest Annual Data:*** 3/31/2006

Year	Sales	Net Income
2006	$144,900,000	$43,400,000
2005	$214,200,000	-$20,800,000
2004	$198,500,000	-$38,600,000

Curr. Assets:	$173,000,000	**Curr. Liab.:**	$36,700,000	**P/E Ratio:**	15.82
Plant, Equip.:	$26,400,000	**Total Liab.:**	$50,900,000	**Indic. Yr. Divd.:**	NA
Total Assets:	$205,000,000	**Net Worth:**	$136,000,000	**Debt/ Equity:**	NA

Zaxis International Inc

115 E 57th St., Ste. 1118, New York, NY, 10022; *PH:* 1-646-202-9679

General - Incorporation	DE	**Stock**- Price on:12/24/2007	$0.01
Employees	NA	Stock Exchange	OTC
Auditor	Michael F. Cronin, CPA	Ticker Symbol	ZAXS
Stk Agt	Standard Registrar & Transfer Co Inc.	Outstanding Shares	92,930,000
Counsel	NA	E.P.S	-$0.001
DUNS No.	NA	Shareholders	NA

Business: The groups principal activities include manufacturing and distributing products that were used in a molecular separation process known as electrophoresis, a procedure used in research, industrial and clinical laboratories. The group operates from the United States.

Primary SIC and add'l.: 7379

CIK No: 0000797542

Officers: Ivo Heiden/41/Chmn., CEO, CFO

Directors: Ivo Heiden/41/Chmn., CEO, CFO

Owners: Juergen Heiden/7.75%, Ivo Heiden/69.51%, Insiders/69.51%

Financial Data: ***Fiscal Year End:***12/31 ***Latest Annual Data:*** 12/31/2006

Year	Sales	Net Income
2006	NA	-$61,000
2005	NA	-$9,000
2004	NA	$0

Curr. Assets:	$0	**Curr. Liab.:**	$46,000	**P/E Ratio:**	123.33
Plant, Equip.:	NA	**Total Liab.:**	$46,000	**Indic. Yr. Divd.:**	NA
Total Assets:	$0	**Net Worth:**	-$46,000	**Debt/ Equity:**	NA

Zebra Technologies Corp

333 Corporate Woods Pkwy, Vernon Hills, IL, 60061; *PH:* 1-847-634-6700; *http://* www.zebra.com

General - Incorporation	DE	Stock - Price on:12/24/2007	$39.12
Employees	2,800	Stock Exchange	NDQ
Auditor	Ernst & Young, LLP	Ticker Symbol	ZBRA
Stk Agt	Mellon Investor Services LLC	Outstanding Shares	69,080,000
Counsel	Katten Muchin Rosenman LLP	E.P.S.	$1.45
DUNS No.	04-901-5696	Shareholders	NA

Business: The group's principal activities are to design, manufacture and support direct thermal and thermal transfer bar code label printers, receipt printers, plastic card printers, related accessories and support software. The products are marketed mainly to manufacturing and service organizations for use in automatic identification, data collection and personal identification systems. These products are distributed world-wide through a multi-channel network of resellers, distributors and end users representing a wide cross section of industrial, service and government organizations. The group has operations in the United States, Europe, Middle East, Africa, Latin America and Asia. On 17-Nov-2003, the group acquired atlantek inc.

Primary SIC and add'l.: 3577
CIK No: 0000877212
Subsidiaries: Zebra Atlantek Inc, Zebra Technologies Asia Pacific, LLC, Zebra Technologies B.V., Zebra Technologies Europe Limited, Zebra Technologies Europe Sales Company, LLC, Zebra Technologies France, Zebra Technologies International, LLC, Zebra Technologies Latin America, LLC, ZIH Corp.
Officers: Anders Gustafsson/CEO, Mark Thomson/Zebra, Card Printer Solutions, Europe, Middle East, Africa, Asia Pacific, Douglas A. Fox/Dir. - Investor Relations, Bruce R. Ralph/VP - Human Resources, Leslie Brigham/Zebra, Card Printer Solutions, North America, Todd R. Naughton/VP, Controller, Noel Elfant/VP, General Counsel, Sec., Veraje Anjargolian/VP, GM/$687,750.00, Philip Gerskovich/Sr. VP - Corporate Development/$668,316.00, Hugh K. Gagnier/Sr. VP - Business Development, Operations, Specialty Printer Solutions Business Unit/$741,313.00, Gerhard Cless/Exec./VP, Michael H. Terzich/Sr. VP - Global Sales, Marketing, Specialty Printer Solutions, Charles R. Whitchurch/CFO, Treasurer/$593,050.00
Directors: Michael A. Smith/Chmn., Edward L. Kaplan/Dir., Ross W. Manire/Dir., Christopher G. Knowles/Dir., Robert J. Potter/Dir.
Owners: Edward L. Kaplan/1.60%, Ruth I. Cless/3.10%, Veraje Anjargolian, Ross W. Manire, Charles R. Whitchurch, Neuberger Berman Inc/8.30%, Hugh K. Gagnier, Oppenheimer Capital LLC/5.20%, Christopher G. Knowles, Insiders/5.40%, Gerhard Cless/3.10%, Carol K. Kaplan/1.60%, Philip Gerskovich, Michael A. Smith, Robert J. Potter *(16 Owners included in Index)*

Financial Data: *Fiscal Year End:*12/31 *Latest Annual Data:* 12/31/2006

Year	Sales	Net Income
2006	$759,524,000	$70,946,000
2005	$702,271,000	$111,603,000
2004	$663,054,000	$120,643,000

Curr. Assets:	$479,690,000	Curr. Liab.:	$74,854,000		
Plant, Equip.:	$57,431,000	Total Liab.:	$85,461,000	Indic. Yr. Divd.:	NA
Total Assets:	$963,142,000	Net Worth:	$877,681,000	Debt/ Equity:	NA

Zena Capital Corp

750 W Pender St., Ste. 640, Vancouver, BC, V6C 2T8; *PH:* 1-604-689-0188; *http://* www.zendagold.com

General - Incorporation	BC	Stock - Price on:12/24/2007	NA
Employees	NA	Stock Exchange	OTC
Auditor	Morgan & Co	Ticker Symbol	ZCCOF
Stk Agt	Pacific Corporate Trust Co	Outstanding Shares	NA
Counsel	NA	E.P.S.	NA
DUNS No.	NA	Shareholders	NA

Business: The group's principle activity is to explore minerals. The company is setting up for property acquisition and exploration or development. The group operates from United States.

Primary SIC and add'l.: 1400
CIK No: 0001295547
Subsidiaries: Rock Creek Minerals Inc.
Officers: Terry M. Amisano/53/Dir., CEO, Pres., Roy Brown/64/CFO, Sec.
Directors: Terry M. Amisano/53/Dir., CEO, Pres., Kevin R. Hanson/51/Dir., Alan Crawford/53/Dir.
Owners: Global Capital Group Ltd./5.90%, Terry Amisano/17.50%, Insiders/53.80%, Kevin Hanson/16.30%, Roy Brown/0.40%, Alan Crawford/12.50%, Greg Burnett/12.00%

Zenith National Insurance Corp

21255 Califa St., Woodland Hills, CA, 91367; *PH:* 1-818-713-1000; *http://* www.znic.com

General - Incorporation	DE	Stock - Price on:12/24/2007	$48.4
Employees	1,750	Stock Exchange	NYSE
Auditor	PricewaterhouseCoopers LLP	Ticker Symbol	ZNT
Stk Agt	Mellon Investor Services LLC	Outstanding Shares	37,040,000
Counsel	NA	E.P.S.	$7.44
DUNS No.	06-777-1048	Shareholders	NA

Business: The group's principle activity is to manage insurance and investment risk. The group operates in three segments: worker's compensation, reinsurance and investment. Workers' compensation provides coverage for the statutory benefits that employers are required to provide to their employees injured in the course of employment. Reinsurance is a transaction between insurance companies in which an original insurer or ceding company remits premiums to a reinsurer or assuming company as payment for the reinsurer's assumption of a portion of the risk. Reinsurance operation participates in assumed reinsurance transactions in which the reinsurance coverage being purchased by the ceding company is shared among a number of assuming companies. Investments department invests the funds available by our capital and the cash flows from our insurance operations. The group's quarterly revenue for September 2007 was 215.37 millions of USD.

Primary SIC and add'l.: 6321 1531 6513 6331
CIK No: 0000109261
Subsidiaries: 1390 Main Street LLC, Zenith Development Corp., Zenith Insurance Company, Zenith National Insurance Capital Trust I, Zenith National Insurance Corp., Zenith of Nevada,Inc.

Officers: Stanley R. Zax/Chmn., CEO, Pres./$4,938,693.00, Jack D. Miller/Exec. VP/$1,642,042.00, Keith E. Trotman/Exec. VP/$1,389,205.00, Hyman J. Lee/VP, Sec., Robert E. Meyer/Sr. VP/$1,339,392.00, Michael E. Jansen/Exec. VP, General Counsel, Davidson M. Pattiz/Exec. VP, Kari L. Van Gundy/CFO, Sr. VP/$544,297.00
Directors: Stanley R. Zax/Chmn., CEO, Pres., Alan I. Rothenberg/Dir., Catherine B. Reynolds/Dir., Max M. Kampelman/Dir., Leon E. Panetta/Dir., Michael Wm. Zavis/Dir., William S. Sessions/Dir., Robert J. Miller/Dir., Gerald Tsai/Dir.
Owners: Insiders/2.90%, Michael Wm. Zavis, Jack D. Miller, Max M. Kampelman, Robert E. Meyer, Leon E. Panetta, Catherine B. Reynolds, Barclays Global Investors, NA, et. al./5.60%, FMR Corp/7.70%, William S. Sessions, Gerald Tsai, Gilder, Gagnon, Howe & Co. LLC/13.70%, Alan I. Rothenberg, LSV Management/5.30%, Kari L. Van Gundy *(19 Owners included in Index)*

Financial Data: *Fiscal Year End:*12/31 *Latest Annual Data:* 12/31/2006

Year	Sales	Net Income
2006	$1,063,888,000	$258,700,000
2005	$1,280,124,000	$157,700,000
2004	$1,044,880,000	$119,000,000

Curr. Assets:	$955,514,000	Curr. Liab.:	$71,008,000	P/E Ratio:	6.51
Plant, Equip.:	NA	Total Liab.:	$1,826,833,000	Indic. Yr. Divd.:	$1.680
Total Assets:	$2,767,553,000	Net Worth:	$940,720,000	Debt/ Equity:	0.0601

ZEVEX International Inc

4314 Zevex Pk. Ln., Salt Lake City, UT, 84123; *PH:* 1-801-264-1001; *http://* www.zevex.com

General - Incorporation	DE	Stock- Price on:12/24/2007	NA
Employees	158	Stock Exchange	NA
Auditor	Ernst & Young LLP	Ticker Symbol	NA
Stk Agt	National City Bank Invst Srvcs	Outstanding Shares	NA
Counsel	Jones, Waldo, Holbrook & McDonough	E.P.S.	NA
DUNS No.	61-274-6933	Shareholders	NA

Business: The group's principal activity is to design, manufacture and distribute advanced medical devices. The group operates in three business segments namely, the therapeutics, the physical evaluation, and the applied technology. The therapeutics includes feeding pumps, disposable sets and feeding tubes used by patients who require direct gastrointestinal nutrition therapy. The physical evaluation includes the sale of stand-alone and computerized products that measure isolated muscle strength, joint ranges of motion and sensation. In the applied technology the group provides design and manufacturing services to global medical device leaders who, in turn, sell the group's components and systems under private labels or incorporate them into their products. The group's major trademark is enteralite(r).

Primary SIC and add'l.: 3841 8711 3674
CIK No: 0000827056
Subsidiaries: Ernst & Young LLP, JTech Medical Industries, Inc., ZEVEX, Inc.
Officers: David J. McNally/Dir., CEO, Pres., Phillip L. McStotts/Dir., CFO, Sec., Treasurer
Directors: David J. McNally/Dir., CEO, Pres., John T. Lemley/Chmn., Richard L. Shanaman/Dir., Dan Robertson/Dir., Phillip L. McStotts/Dir., CFO, Sec., Treasurer, Bradly A. Oldroyd/Dir., David B. Kaysen/Dir.
Owners: Michael Henderson, Dan M. Robertson, Richard L. Shanaman/1.10%, John T. Lemley/2.10%, David J. McNally/10.30%, David B. Kaysen, Philip Eggers, Bradly A. Oldroyd/1.40%, Insiders/21.90%, Timothy Govin, Phillip L. McStotts/7.60%, Wedbush, Inc./7.00%

Zhone Technologies Inc

7001 Oakport St., Oakland, CA, 94621; *PH:* 1-510-777-7000; *http://* www.zhone.com;
Email: info@zhone.com

General - Incorporation	DE	Stock - Price on:12/24/2007	$1.43
Employees	514	Stock Exchange	NDQ
Auditor	KPMG LLP	Ticker Symbol	ZHNE
Stk Agt	Computershare Trust Co	Outstanding Shares	149,460,000
Counsel	NA	E.P.S.	-$0.1
DUNS No.	03-674-2062	Shareholders	NA

Business: The group's principal activities are to design, develop and market, intelligent optical switching solutions that enable network service providers to deliver new high-speed services. Intelligent optical switches are products that are installed in telecommunications networks to manage the flow of optical signals, which are beams of light transmitted over fiber optic cables. The optical switches and software provide the following key benefits to service providers: improved network design, simplified delivery of new services, fast provisioning of new services, easy network expansion, cost effectiveness, compatibility with existing networks and flexible products.

Primary SIC and add'l.: 4899 3669
CIK No: 0001101680
Subsidiaries: Ark Electronic Products, Inc., Astarte Fiber Networks, Inc., Communications Equipment Corporation, Osicom Technologies Europe Limited, Paradyne Canada, LTD, Paradyne Corporation, Paradyne Finance Corp., Paradyne Networks do Brazil LTDA, Paradyne Networks, Inc., Paradyne Shanghai, LTD, Paradyne Worldwide Corporation, PDP Acquisition Corp., Premisys Communications Ltd., Premisys Communications, Inc., R-Net International, Inc. 42 Subsidiaries included in the Index
Officers: Morteza Ejabat/Chmn., CEO, Pres/$2,244,081.00, Hakim Alhusan/Europe, The Middle East, Dubai, Middle East, Africa Headquarters, Ulrich Sickelmann/Europe, The Middle East, Central Europe, Doug North/North America, Sales Offices, Canada, Antonio Jonusas/Caribbean, Latin America, Miami, Max Gaitan/Caribbean, Latin America, Colombia, Umberto Bertelli/Europe, The Middle East, Italy, Southern Europe, Vince Kerr/Europe, The Middle East, United Kingdom, Alex Baber/Caribbean, Latin America, Puerto Rico, Jorge Rivadulla/Caribbean, Latin America, Brazil, Peter Michalski/Europe, The Middle East, Eastern Europe, Ramy Abdallah/Europe, The Middle East, Egypt, Raymond Chiu/Asia, Pacific Region, Hong Kong, Jun Li/Asia, Pacific Region, China, Mathew Tan/Asia, Pacific Region, Singapore *(24 Officers included in Index)*
Directors: Morteza Ejabat/Chmn., CEO, Pres., Michael Connors/Dir., James Coulter/Dir., Robert Dahl/Dir., James H. Greene/57/Dir., Richard C. Kramlich/Dir., Steven Levy/Dir., James Timmins/Dir.
Owners: Michael Fischer, James Timmins, KKR entities/6.00%, Morteza Ejabat/2.90%, Robert Dahl, James Coulter, Kirk Misaka, New Enterprise Associates entities/9.80%, Michael Scheck, Insiders/25.90%, Richard C. Kramlich, Michael Connors, Steven Levy, Texas Pacific Group entities/6.00%, David Misunas *(16 Owners included in Index)*

Financial Data: *Fiscal Year End:*12/31 *Latest Annual Data:* 12/31/2006

Year	Sales	Net Income
2006	$194,344,000	-$142,666,000
2005	$151,828,000	-$126,891,000
2004	$97,168,000	-$35,646,000

Curr. Assets:	$145,026,000	Curr. Liab.:	$61,154,000	
Plant, Equip.:	$23,704,000	Total Liab.:	$82,578,000	Indic. Yr. Divd.: NA
Total Assets:	$240,182,000	Net Worth:	$157,604,000	Debt/ Equity: NA

Zhongpin Inc

C/O PRYOR CASHMAN SHERMAN & FLYNN LLP, 410 Pk. Ave., New York, NY, 10022;
PH: 1-86-3746216633; *http://* www.zhongpin.com

General - Incorporation............................ DE
Employees ....NA
Auditor Child, Van Wagoner & Bradshaw, PLLC
Stk Agt.......................Securities Transfer Corp
Counsel...NA
DUNS No. ....NA

Stock- Price on:12/24/2007 ....$9.3
Stock Exchange.......................................OTC
Ticker Symbol......................................ZHNP
Outstanding Shares ....NA
E.P.S. ....NA
Shareholders..NA

Business: The groups principal activity is engage in the meat and food processing. Products of the group include chilled pork, frozen pork, pig by products and prepared meats, which are sold on a wholesale basis and on a retail basis. The group operates through two segments namely pork and pork products, and vegetables and fruits. In January 2006, the group acquired Falcon Link. The group operates from the United States.

Primary SIC and add'l.: 2011
CIK No: 0001277092
Subsidiaries: Anyang Zhongpin Food Company Limited, Deyang Zhongpin Food Company Limited, Heilongjiang Zhongpin Food Company Limited, Henan Zhongpin Business Development Company Limited, Henan Zhongpin Fresh Food Logistics Company Limited, Henan Zhongpin Imports and Exports Trade Company Limited, Henan Zhongpin Industry Company Limited, Zhumadian Zhongpin Food Company Limited

Officers: Xianfu Zhu/44/Chmn., CEO, Yuanmei Ma/36/CFO/$93,335.00, Baoke Ben/44/Exec. VP, Sec., Rui Chen/39/VP

Directors: Xianfu Zhu/44/Chmn., CEO, Xinyu Li/Dir., Yunchun Wang/33/Dir.

Owners: Pinnacle China Fund, L.P/9.90%, Insiders/56.80%, Jayhawk China Fund Ltd/9.90%, Entities Affiliated with Atlas Capital L.P/5.90%, Capital Group, Inc/9.50%, Southwell Partners, L.P/5.40%, Xianfu Zhu/46.60%, Private Equity Fund, L.P/8.80%, Yunchun Wang/4.10%, Vision Opportunity Master Fund, Ltd/5.30%

Financial Data: *Fiscal Year End:*12/31 *Latest Annual Data:* 12/31/2006

Year	Sales	Net Income
2006	$143,812,000	$6,359,000
2005	NA	$46,000

Curr. Assets:	NA	Curr. Liab.:	NA	
Plant, Equip.:	NA	Total Liab.:	NA	Indic. Yr. Divd.: NA
Total Assets:	$0	Net Worth:	NA	Debt/ Equity: 0.0330

Zi Corp

2100, 840 - 7 Ave. SW, Calgary, AB, T2P 3G2; *PH:* 1-403-233-8875; *http://* www.zicorp.com;
Email: info@zicorp.com

General - Incorporation.......................Canada
Employees 78
Auditor ....Ernst & Young, LLP
Stk Agt................................Olympia Trust Co
Counsel.....................Armstrong Perkins Hudson
DUNS No. 24-809-7511

Stock- Price on:12/24/2007 ....$1.24
Stock Exchange.......................................NDQ
Ticker Symbol.......................................ZICA
Outstanding Shares 50,530,000
E.P.S. ....-$0.17
Shareholders..NA

Business: The group's principle activity is the delivery of intelligent interface solutions to enhance the user experience of wireless and consumer technologies. The group's core product, ezitext, is a predictive text input solution that connects people to short messaging, e-commerce, e-mail, Web browsing and similar applications in almost any written language. The group's service division provides engineering design in bluetooth, and voice over Internet protocol (volp). The group's e-learning division oztime is China's first Web-based education service provider. The group's quarterly revenue for September 2007 was 3.38 millions of USD.

Primary SIC and add'l.: 7372 7371 8711
CIK No: 0000922658
Subsidiaries: 845162 Alberta Ltd., Archer Education Group, Inc., Asia Translation & Telecommunications Limited, Beijing Oztime Education & Network Technology Co. Ltd., Canadian International College of Business and English Inc. (5), Diamond Institute of Business and Computer Technology Inc. (5), English Practice Inc. (5), Huayu Zi Software Technology (Beijing) Co., Ltd.(2), Huayu Zi Software Technology Limited.(1), Languages International (Toronto) Inc. (5), Magic Lantern Group, Inc.(3), Multi-Corp International Ltd., Telecom Technology Corporation Limited, The Language Circle Inc. (5), TMBJ Holdings Ltd. (5) 28 Subsidiaries included in the Index

Officers: Milos Djokovic/Dir., CEO, Pres., Derrick R. Armstrong/Corp. Sec., Roland Williams/Sr. VP - Intellectual Property, Blair Mullin/CFO, Axel Bernstorff/VP - Global Sales, Brandon Mensinga/Dir. - Qix, Corneil Goud/Dir. - Predictive Text, Jill Bertotti/Investor Relations Officer

Directors: Milos Djokovic/Dir., CEO, Pres., Richard D. Tingle/Chmn., Donald P. Moore/Dir., Michael E. Lobsinger/Dir., Donald H. Hyde/Dir., Andrew M. Gertler/Dir., Robert Stefanski/Dir.

Owners: Thompson MacDonald, Derrick R. Armstrong, Richard D. Tingle, Michael E. Lobsinger/12.00%, Milos Djokovic/1.10%, Roland Williams, Howard Balloch, Axel Bernstorff, Michael Mackenzie, Robert P. Stefanski, Donald H. Hyde, Donald P. Moore, Marty Steinberg/40.00%

Financial Data: *Fiscal Year End:*12/31 *Latest Annual Data:* 12/31/2006

Year	Sales	Net Income
2006	$11,836,000	-$10,995,000
2005	$11,385,000	-$5,317,000
2004	$13,403,000	-$2,388,000

Curr. Assets:	$10,219,000	Curr. Liab.:	$9,729,000	
Plant, Equip.:	$906,000	Total Liab.:	$9,729,000	Indic. Yr. Divd.: NA
Total Assets:	$14,547,000	Net Worth:	$4,818,000	Debt/ Equity: NA

Zila Inc

5227 N 7th St., Phoenix, AZ, 85014; *PH:* 1-602-266-6700; *http://* www.zila.com;
Email: inquiries@zila.com

General - Incorporation .... DE
Employees 116
Auditor ....BDO Seidman, LLP
Stk Agt.......................Computershare Trust Co
Counsel...........Quarles & Brady Streich Lang
DUNS No. 01-422-4182

Stock- Price on:12/24/2007 ....$1.43
Stock Exchange.......................................NDQ
Ticker Symbol...ZILA
Outstanding Shares 62,330,000
E.P.S. ....-$0.38
Shareholders..NA

Business: The group's principal activities are to manufacture and market of pharmaceutical, nutraceutical and biotechnology products. The group operates in three segments namely: nutraceuticals, consumer pharmaceuticals and professional pharmaceuticals. The nutarceutical group manufactures and distributes a patented form of vitamin c under the trademark ester-c(R) and a line of saw palmetto products under the palmettx(R) trademark. Consumer pharmaceutical group consists of over-the-counter and prescription products including the zilactin (r). The professional pharmaceutical group includes peridex(R) prescription mouth rinse and oratest (R), an oral cancer diagnostic system.

Primary SIC and add'l.: 3861 5047 6719 2834 5122
CIK No: 0000827156
Subsidiaries: Zila Biotechnology, Inc, Zila Limited, Zila Nutraceuticals, Inc, Zila Pharmaceuticals, Inc, Zila Technical, Inc

Officers: David R. Bethune/Exec. Chmn., Diane Klein/VP - Finance, Treasurer, Gary Klinefelter/VP, General Counsel, Frank J. Bellizzi/Pres. - Zila Pharmaceuticals, Inc

Directors: David R. Bethune/Exec. Chmn., Leslie H. Green/Dir., Steven J. Garrett/Dir., David Goldman/64/Dir., O. B. Parrish/Dir., George J. Vuturo/58/Dir.

Owners: Timothy S. Rose, Leslie H. Green, Hazel L. Myer, Douglas D. Burkett, Royce & Associates, LLC/8.00%, Gary V. Klinefelter, David Sidransky, MicroCapital LLC/12.00%, Diane E. Klein, Lawrence A. Gyenes, Christopher D. Johnson, David R. Bethune, Frank J. Bellizzi, Kurt R. Krauss, Visium Asset Management, LLC/8.00% *(18 Owners included in Index)*

Financial Data: *Fiscal Year End:*07/31 *Latest Annual Data:* 7/31/2006

Year	Sales	Net Income
2006	$28,188,000	-$29,346,000
2005	$44,325,000	$1,099,000
2004	$49,428,000	-$4,337,000

Curr. Assets:	$22,970,000	Curr. Liab.:	$29,824,000	
Plant, Equip.:	$8,411,000	Total Liab.:	$33,113,000	Indic. Yr. Divd.: NA
Total Assets:	$56,364,000	Net Worth:	$23,251,000	Debt/ Equity: NA

ZiLOG Inc

532 Race St., San Jose, CA, 95126; *PH:* 1-408-558-8500; *http://* www.zilog.com

General - Incorporation .... CA
Employees 550
Auditor ....Armanino Mckenna LLP
Stk Agt.........Computershare Shareholder Ser Inc
Counsel...............Pillsbury, Madison & Sutro
DUNS No. 07-631-4459

Stock- Price on:12/24/2007 ....$5.9
Stock Exchange.......................................NDQ
Ticker Symbol...ZILG
Outstanding Shares 16,790,000
E.P.S. ....-$0.61
Shareholders..NA

Business: The group's principal activity is to design, manufacture and market semiconductor micro-logic devices for use in the embedded control and communications markets. The group provides semiconductor devices that its customers design into their end products. The group's devices, which often include related application software, typically combine microprocessor and digital signal processor, memory and input and output functions on a single semiconductor. The group's primary product focus is on 8-bit and 16-bit microcontrollers and microprocessors. Microcontroller products include a broad range of standard products for use in hundreds of embedded control applications. Microprocessor products are higher performance products addressing the high-end 8-bit and 16-bit microprocessor and microcontroller markets. Major customers of the group are echostar, emerson, hypercom, philips, samsung, thomson consumer electronics and tyco.

Primary SIC and add'l.: 3672 3674
CIK No: 0000319450
Subsidiaries: ZiLOG Asia Ltd., ZiLOG Electronic Philippines,Inc., ZiLOG India Electronics Private Ltd., ZiLOG International Pte. Ltd., ZiLOG Japan K.K., ZiLOG MOD III,Inc, ZiLOG Philippines,Inc., ZiLOG UK, Ltd.

Officers: Darin G. Billerbeck/Dir., CEO, Pres./$200,009.00, Keith Bladen/VP, Marketing Interim VP - World Wide Sales, Perry J. Grace/Exec. VP - Administration, CFO, Principal Accounting Officer/$430,947.00, Norm Sheridan/Exec. VP - Technology, Operations/$406,107.00, Stew Chalmers/Investor Relations Contact, David Hedley/Contact - Sales Office, Alabama, Nancy Kochanski/Contact - Sales Office, Alaska, Mark Sprague/Contact - Sales Office, Arizona, Dave Coulson/Contact - Sales Office, Connecticut

Directors: Darin G. Billerbeck/Dir., CEO, Pres., Federico Faggin/Chmn., Richard L. Sanquini/Dir., Robin A. Abrams/Dir., David G. Elkins/Dir.

Owners: Capital Research& Management Company and related parties/15.70%, Federico Faggin, Riley Investment Partners Master Fund, L.P./5.00%, UBS AG/11.80%, Richard L. Sanquini, Insiders/4.80%, Perry J. Grace/1.60%, Norman G. Sheridan, David G. Elkins, James M. Thorburn/1.10%, Robin A. Abrams, Litespeed Management LLC/8.40%

Financial Data: *Fiscal Year End:*03/31 *Latest Annual Data:* 03/31/2007

Year	Sales	Net Income
2007	$82,000,000	-$9,000,000
2006	$78,800,000	-$16,800,000
2004	$95,600,000	-$18,500,000

Curr. Assets:	$46,800,000	Curr. Liab.:	$23,900,000	
Plant, Equip.:	$9,300,000	Total Liab.:	$29,800,000	Indic. Yr. Divd.: NA
Total Assets:	$71,600,000	Net Worth:	$41,800,000	Debt/ Equity: NA

Zim Corp

150 Isabella St., Ste. 150 , Ottawa, ON, K1S 1V7; *PH:* 1-613-727-1397; *http://* www.zim.biz;
Email: info@zim.biz

General - Incorporation ....Canada
Employees ....NA
Auditor ....Raymond Chabot Grant Thornton LLP
Stk Agt.............Corporate Stock Transfer, Inc.
Counsel...NA
DUNS No. ....NA

Stock- Price on:12/24/2007 ....$0.05
Stock Exchange.......................................OTC
Ticker Symbol.....................................ZIMCF
Outstanding Shares ....NA
E.P.S. ....NA
Shareholders..NA

Business: The groups principle activities include providing mobile messaging and data services. Services of the group include sms messages and other content, such as ringtones and wallpapers. The group also has a database product known as Zim IDE that is used by companies in the management of information databases. The group operates through two segments namely mobile applications and enterprise software. In April 2006, the group acquired Advanced Internet Inc. The group operates from the Canada, North and South America, Great Britain and Europe.

Primary SIC and add'l.: 4812

CIK No: 0001124160

Subsidiaries: Advanced Internet Inc, PCI Merge, Inc, ZIM Technologies do Brazil Ltda

Officers: Michael C.J. Cowpland/Dir., CEO, CFO, Pres., Phil Scavo/VP - Business Development, Yovav Meydad/Member - Advisory Board, Chief - Product Management, Roberto Campagna/VP - Sales, Marketing/$117,128.00

Directors: Michael C.J. Cowpland/Dir., CEO, CFO, Pres., Jim Stechyson/Chmn., Stephen Wrigh/Member - Advisory Board, Yovav Meydad/Member - Advisory Board, Chief - Product Management, Donald Gibbs/Dir., Steve Houck/Dir., Charles Saikaley/Dir.

Owners: James Stechyson/1.00%, Phil Scavo/1.10%, Roberto Campagna/1.10%, Michael Cowpland/64.00%, Insiders/66.20%, Steven Houck, Advanced Telecom Services/11.90%, Donald Gibbs

Zimmer Holdings Inc

345 E Main St., Warsaw, IN, 46580; **PH:** 1-219-267-6131; **http://** www.zimmer.com

General - Incorporation	DE	Stock - Price on:12/24/2007	$85.991
Employees	6,900	Stock Exchange	NYSE
Auditor	PricewaterhouseCoopers LLP	Ticker Symbol	ZMH
Stk Agt	Bank of New York	Outstanding Shares	236,780,000
Counsel	NA	E.P.S.	$3.71
DUNS No.	NA	Shareholders	NA

Business: The groups principle activity is to provide joint replacement solutions for knee pain and hip pain, and comprehensive spine care solutions for acute and chronic back pain. The group also provides a broad range of trauma, dental implant and orthopaedic surgical products. The group operates from United States.

Primary SIC and add'l.: 3842

CIK No: 0001136869

Subsidiaries: Magellan Petroleum (Belize) Limited, Magellan Petroleum (N.T.) Pty. Ltd., Magellan Petroleum (W.A.) Pty. Ltd., Magellan Petroleum Australia Limited, Paroo Petroleum (Holdings), Inc., Paroo Petroleum (USA), Inc., Paroo Petroleum Pty. Ltd.

Officers: David C. Dvorak/45/Dir., CEO, Pres./$2,897,895.00, Bruno A. Melzi/59/Chmn. - Europe, Africa, Middle East/$3,347,698.00, Laura C. O'Donnell/35/Chief Compliance Officer, Stephen H.L. Ooi/54/Pres. - Asia Pacific, Cheryl R. Blanchard/Sr. VP - Research, Development, Chief Scientific Officer, Sean F. O'Hara/Mgr. - Investor Relations, Chad F. Phipps/37/Sr. VP, General Counsel, Sec., Sam R. Leno/61/CFO, Exec. VP - Finance, Corporate Services/$4,225,885.00, Derek Davis/39/VP - Finance, Corporate Controller, Chief Accounting Officer, Jon E. Kramer/Pres. - US Sales, Renee Rogers/57/VP - Global Human Resources, James T. Crines/CFO, Exec. VP - Finance, Sheryl L. Conley/Group Pres. - Americas, Global Marketing, Chief Marketing Officer/$2,631,640.00, Richard C. Stair/VP - Global Operations, Logistics

Directors: David C. Dvorak/45/Dir., CEO, Pres., Raymond J. Elliott/59/Chmn., Stuart M. Essig/Dir., Larry C. Glasscock/Dir., Augustus A. White/Dir., Arthur J. Higgins/Dir., John L. McGoldrick/Dir.

Owners: Sam R. Leno, Larry C. Glasscock, John L. McGoldrick, Augustus A. White, Bruno A. Melzi, J. Raymond Elliott, Stuart M. Essig, Sheryl L. Conley, Insiders/1.40%, David C. Dvorak

Financial Data: Fiscal Year End:12/31   Latest Annual Data: 12/31/2006

Year	Sales	Net Income
2006	NA	$2,700,000
2005	NA	$2,300,000
2004	NA	$7,100,000

Curr. Assets:	$1,746,200,000	Curr. Liab.:	$628,200,000	P/E Ratio:	24.20
Plant, Equip.:	$807,100,000	Total Liab.:	$1,053,900,000	Indic. Yr. Divd.:	NA
Total Assets:	$5,974,400,000	Net Worth:	$4,920,500,000	Debt/ Equity:	0.0195

Zindart Ltd

Unit 711 - 717, 7/f., Tower A, New Mandarin Plz., 14 Science Museum Rd., Tst E, Kowloon, Hong Kong; ; **http://** www.zindart.com

General - Incorporation	Hong Kong	Stock - Price on:12/24/2007	$5.65
Employees	5,759	Stock Exchange	NDQ
Auditor	Eisner LLP	Ticker Symbol	NA
Stk Agt	Bank of New York	Outstanding Shares	1,700,000
Counsel	Cooley Godward LLP	E.P.S.	-$5.28
DUNS No.	66-299-3419	Shareholders	NA

Business: The group's principal activities are the manufacture of high-quality die-cast, injection molded and paper products that require a significant degree of engineering and hand-assembly expertise to produce. Some of its products include die-cast collectibles, collectible holiday ornaments and toys, hand-made books and other paper products.

Primary SIC and add'l.: 3089 5113 3999 2679

CIK No: 0001028637

Subsidiaries: Bassett Lowke (Railways) Ltd., Bassett Lowke Ltd., Blow-ko Ltd., Corgi Classics Holdings Ltd., Corgi Classics Inc., Corgi Classics Ltd., Corgi Collectors Ltd., Corgi Sales Ltd., Corgi Toys Ltd., Dongguan Xinda Giftware Co. Ltd., Guangzhou Jin Yi Advertising Co. Ltd., Hua Yang Holdings Co. Ltd., Hua Yang Printing Holdings Co. Ltd., Icon Collectibles Ltd., Lledo Collectibles Ltd. 21 Subsidiaries included in the Index

Officers: Michael Cookson/52/Dir., CEO, Denis Horton/57/MD - Europe, Paul Doran/Sr. VP - Operations, Bob Esterbrook/62/Dir. - Finance, Europe, K. H. Li/Sr. VP - Technical Services, Development VP - Technical Services, Development, Franki Lee/VP - Marketing, Sales, Trevor Hayes/61/VP - Global Product Development, Cynthia Chan/33/Internal Audit Dir. - Hong Kong, Darren Epstein/36/Dir., Exec. VP, Chief Strategy Officer, Jack Lawrence/47/CFO, COO, GM - US

Directors: Michael Cookson/52/Dir., CEO, Carrick John Clough/60/Chmn., Leo Paul Koulos/75/Dir., Daniel Widdicombe/42/Dir., Charles Carroll McGettigan/63/Dir., Darren Epstein/36/Dir., Exec. VP, Chief Strategy Officer, Timothy Steel/56/Dir.

Owners: Lagunitas Partners LP/5.04%, Jordan Schwartz/6.28%, Royal Capital Management LLC/10.29%, Consor Capital LLC/10.58%, Gruber & McBaine Capital Management LLC/8.62%, Knott Partners Offshore Fund, L.P./10.91%, Special Situations Private Equity Fund, L.P./9.90%

Financial Data: Fiscal Year End:03/31   Latest Annual Data: 03/31/2007

Year	Sales	Net Income
2007	$35,497,000	-$13,263,000
2006	$76,394,000	-$35,355,000
2005	$43,214,000	-$7,103,000

Curr. Assets:	$25,693,000	Curr. Liab.:	$32,323,000		
Plant, Equip.:	$16,457,000	Total Liab.:	$32,542,000	Indic. Yr. Divd.:	NA
Total Assets:	$60,029,000	Net Worth:	$27,487,000	Debt/ Equity:	0.0013

Zingo Inc

420 N Nellis Blvd., Ste. A3-146, Las Vegas, NV, 89110; **PH:** 1-877-779-4646; **http://** www.zingotel.com; **Email:** info@zingotel.com

General - Incorporation	NV	Stock - Price on:12/24/2007	NA
Employees	12	Stock Exchange	OTC
Auditor	Haynie & Co.	Ticker Symbol	ZNGO
Stk Agt	Nevada Agency & Trust Company	Outstanding Shares	115,000,000
Counsel	NA	E.P.S.	-$0.01
DUNS No.	NA	Shareholders	NA

Business: The groups principle activity is engaged in providing highly reliable and advanced telecommunications services through VoIP system that utilizes the Internet. The group operates from the United States.

Primary SIC and add'l.: 8742

CIK No: 0001230524

Subsidiaries: ZingoTel, Inc.

Officers: Holly Roseberry/57/Dir., CEO, Pres., Mehboob Charania/52/Dir., Treasurer, Sec.

Directors: Holly Roseberry/57/Dir., CEO, Pres., Mehboob Charania/52/Dir., Treasurer, Sec.

Owners: Udaya Madanayake/8.69%, Hybrid Technologies, Inc./69.56%, Chen Wu/8.69%

Financial Data: Fiscal Year End:12/31   Latest Annual Data: 03/31/2007

Year	Sales	Net Income
2007	$306,000	-$318,000
2006	$949,000	-$2,003,000
2005	$106,000	-$958,000

Curr. Assets:	$90,000	Curr. Liab.:	$3,176,000		
Plant, Equip.:	$85,000	Total Liab.:	$3,176,000	Indic. Yr. Divd.:	NA
Total Assets:	$215,000	Net Worth:	-$2,961,000	Debt/ Equity:	NA

Zions BanCorp

One S Main St., Ste 1134, Salt Lake City, UT, 84111; **PH:** 1-800-524-4787; **http://** www.zionsbank.com; **Email:** info@zionsbank.com

General - Incorporation	UT	Stock - Price on:12/24/2007	$80.54
Employees	10,618	Stock Exchange	NDQ
Auditor	Ernst & Young LLP	Ticker Symbol	ZION
Stk Agt	Zions First National Bank	Outstanding Shares	108,100,000
Counsel	NA	E.P.S.	$5.52
DUNS No.	05-503-8228	Shareholders	NA

Business: The groups principle activity is to provide banking services. The group also provides online banking loan services. The group operates from United States.

Primary SIC and add'l.: 6712 6021

CIK No: 0000109380

Subsidiaries: Amegy Corporation, California Bank & Trust, Cash Access, Inc., CSBI Capital Trust I, GB Capital Trust, Great Western Financial Corporation, MP Technology, Inc., National Bank of Arizona, NetDeposit, Inc., Nevada State Bank, Providus Software Solutions, Inc., The Commerce Bank of Oregon, The Commerce Bank of Washington, Vectra Bank Colorado, Zions Capital Trust B 20 Subsidiaries included in the Index

Officers: Bruce K. Alexander/CEO, Exec. VP - Vectra Bank Colorado, Harris H. Simmons/Chmn., CEO, Pres./$2,296,100.00, David E. Blackford/CEO, Exec. VP - California Bank, Trust, Aldon Scott Anderson/CEO, Exec. VP - Zions First National Bank, Danne L. Buchanan/CEO, Exec. VP - Netdeposit, Paul B. Murphy/CEO, Exec. VP - Amegy Bank, Texas/$1,813,025.00, Dallas E. Haun/CEO, Exec. VP - Nevada State Bank, Keith D. Maio/CEO, Exec. VP - National Bank, Arizona, Doyle L. Arnold/Vice Chmn., CFO/$1,503,874.00, Thomas E. Laursen/Exec. VP, General Counsel, John T. Itokazu/CIO, Exec. VP, Dean L. Marotta/Exec. VP - Risk Management, Nolan X. Bellon/Sr. VP, Controller, Scott J. McLean/Exec. VP, Pres. - Amegy Bank, Texas/$1,372,217.00, David W. Hemingway/Exec. VP - Capital Markets, Investments (21 Officers included in Index)

Directors: Harris H. Simmons/Chmn., CEO, Pres., Doyle L. Arnold/Vice Chmn., CFO, David J. Heaney/59/Dir., Laurence E. Simmons/Dir., Shelley Thomas Williams/Dir., Don R. Cash/Dir., James David Heaney/Dir., Stephen D. Quinn/Dir., Steven C. Wheelwright/Dir., Jerry C. Atkin/Dir., Patricia Frobes/Dir., Roger Blaine Porter/Dir.

Owners: Jerry C. Atkin, Shelley Thomas Williams, Steven C. Wheelwright, Harris H. Simmons/2.21%, L. E. Simmons/1.75%, Doyle L. Arnold, Roger B. Porter, Patricia Frobes, Paul B. Murphy, Stanley D. Savage, Stephen D. Quinn, David J. Heaney, R. D. Cash, Scott J. McLean, Insiders/3.90%

Financial Data: Fiscal Year End:12/31   Latest Annual Data: 12/31/2006

Year	Sales	Net Income
2006	$3,369,330,000	$583,125,000
2005	$2,350,411,000	$480,121,000
2004	$1,932,766,000	$405,987,000

Curr. Assets:	$2,371,522,000	Curr. Liab.:	$38,477,627,000	P/E Ratio:	14.59
Plant, Equip.:	$618,722,000	Total Liab.:	$41,983,203,000	Indic. Yr. Divd.:	$1.720
Total Assets:	$46,970,226,000	Net Worth:	$4,987,023,000	Debt/ Equity:	0.4773

Ziopharm Oncology Inc

1180 Ave. Of The Americas, New York, NY, 10036; **PH:** 1-646-214-0700; **Fax:** 1-646-214-0711; **http://** www.ziopharm.com

General - Incorporation: DE
Employees: 28
Auditor: Vitale, Caturano & Company, Ltd
Stk Agt: American Stock Transfer & Trust Co.
Counsel: NA
DUNS No.: NA

Stock - Price on:12/24/2007: $4.74
Stock Exchange: NDQ
Ticker Symbol: ZIOP
Outstanding Shares: 21,180,000
E.P.S: -$1.3
Shareholders: NA

Business: The groups principal activities include licensing and developing drug. The group operates from the United States.

Primary SIC and add'l.: 2834

CIK No: 0001107421

Subsidiaries: ZIO Acquisition Corp., ZIOPHARM, Inc.

Officers: Jonathan Lewis/Executive Chmn., CEO/$903,757.00, Brian Schwartz/Sr. VP - Medical, Regulatory, Chief Medical Officer, Barbara Wallner/Sr. VP - Technical Operations, CTO, Bob Morgan/VP - Regulatory Affairs, Quality, Contract Counsel, John Amedio/VP - Manufacturing, Process Development, Dick Bagley/Dir., COO, Pres., Treasurer

Directors: Jonathan Lewis/Executive Chmn., CEO, Timothy McInerney/Dir., Michael Weiser/Dir., James O. Armitage/Member - Medical Advisory Board, Murray Brennan/Dir., James A. Cannon/Dir., Senator Wyche Fowler/Dir., Gary S. Fragin/Dir., Joseph R. Bertino/Member - Medical Advisory Board, George Demetri/Member - Medical Advisory Board, Lawrence Einhorn/Member - Medical Advisory Board, Alan Houghton/Member - Medical Advisory Board, Alberto Pappo/Member - Medical Advisory Board, John F. Smyth/Member - Medical Advisory Board, David Spriggs/Member - Medical Advisory Board

Owners: Michael Weiser, Procific/Abu Dhabi Investment Authority/6.53%, Richard E. Bagley/1.19%, Millennium Partners, L.P./5.08%, PTV Sciences II, L.P./8.55%, ProQuest Investments III, LP/6.53%, Murray Brennan, Essex Woodlands Health Ventures Fund VI LP/10.65%, LBI Group, Inc./5.24%, James Cannon, Timothy McInerney/1.08%, Insiders/6.24%, Jonathan Lewis/2.87%, Lindsay A. Rosenwald/7.31%, Gary S. Fragin *(17 Owners included in Index)*

Financial Data: *Fiscal Year End:*12/31 *Latest Annual Data:* 12/31/2006

Year	Sales	Net Income
2006	NA	-$17,857,000
2005	NA	-$9,517,000
2004	NA	-$39,000

Curr. Assets:	$28,873,000	Curr. Liab.:	$2,938,000		
Plant, Equip.:	$451,000	Total Liab.:	$2,979,000	Indic. Yr. Divd.:	NA
Total Assets:	$29,512,000	Net Worth:	$26,533,000	Debt/ Equity:	NA

ZipRealty Inc

2000 Powell St., Ste. 300, Emeryville, CA, 94608; *PH:* 1-866-947-4663; *Fax:* 1-510-735-2850; *http://* www.ziprealty.com; *Email:* team@zipRealty.com

General - Incorporation: DE
Employees: 2,014
Auditor: PricewaterhouseCoopers LLP
Stk Agt: American Stock Transfer & Trust Co.
Counsel: NA
DUNS No.: NA

Stock - Price on:12/24/2007: $7.3601
Stock Exchange: NDQ
Ticker Symbol: ZIPR
Outstanding Shares: 22,490,000
E.P.S: -$1.09
Shareholders: NA

Business: The groups principle activity is to provide residential real estate brokerage services. The groups services include multiple listing service and home listings data. The group products sold under the trade name ZipRealty, ZipAgent, ZipNotify, Real-Estate.com and REALTORS(R). The group operates from the United States.

Primary SIC and add'l.: 6531 6531

CIK No: 0001142512

Subsidiaries: Highline Insurance Services, LLC, ZipRealty Title Holdings, LLC

Officers: Patrick Lashinsky/Dir., CEO, Pres./$358,139.00, William C. Sinclair/Exec. VP - Operations, Business Development/$304,572.00, David Rector/Sr. VP, CFO, Genni Combes/Sr. VP - Planning, Operations, Jim Beard/VP - Real Estate Sales, Joe Pucillo/VP - New Marketing Development, Joe Trifoglio/CIO, VP, Leslie Tyler/VP - Marketing, Scott Bekemeyer/VP - Business Development

Directors: Patrick Lashinsky/Dir., CEO, Pres., Donald F. Wood/Chmn., Elisabeth Demarse/Dir., Richard Sommer/Dir., Robert C. Kagle/Dir., Stanley M. Koonce/Dir., Gary A. Wetsel/Dir.

Owners: Pyramid Technology Ventures, Jeffrey G. Wagoner, William C. Sinclair, Marc L. Cellier, Eric A. Danziger, Vanguard Ventures, Passport Management, LLC, Juan F. Mini, Benchmark Capital Partners, Insiders, Elisabeth H. DeMarse, Stanley M. Koonce, Gary M. Beasley, Ronald C. Brown, Robert C. Kagle *(18 Owners included in Index)*

Financial Data: *Fiscal Year End:*12/31 *Latest Annual Data:* 12/31/2006

Year	Sales	Net Income
2006	$95,387,000	-$20,594,000
2005	$93,405,000	$20,467,000
2004	$62,288,000	$3,184,000

Curr. Assets:	$93,769,000	Curr. Liab.:	$9,975,000		
Plant, Equip.:	$4,114,000	Total Liab.:	$10,488,000	Indic. Yr. Divd.:	NA
Total Assets:	$98,357,000	Net Worth:	$87,869,000	Debt/ Equity:	NA

Zix Corp

2711 N Haskell Ave., Ste 2300, Lb 36, Dallas, TX, 75204; *PH:* 1-214-370-2000; *http://* www.zixcorp.com; *Email:* ps_info@zixcorp.com

General - Incorporation: TX
Employees: 156
Auditor: Whitley Penn LLP
Stk Agt: Computershare Investor Services LLC
Counsel: Hughes & Luce LLP
DUNS No.: 17-777-7794

Stock - Price on:12/24/2007: $1.84
Stock Exchange: NDQ
Ticker Symbol: ZIXI
Outstanding Shares: 60,340,000
E.P.S: -$0.24
Shareholders: NA

Business: The group's principal activities are to design, develop and market products and services that enhance privacy, security and convenience over the Internet. The group offers a range of solutions to protect organizations from viruses, spam and electronic attack, as well as enabling secure electronic communications, such as email encryption, e-prescribing, online doctor visits and electronic viewing of medical laboratory test results. The products and services include zixvpm, zixport, zixmail, zixauditor, message inspector and Web inspector. The group operates in the United States and Canada. On 22-Jul-2003, the group acquired pocketscript, inc & elron software, inc on 02-Sep-2003.

Primary SIC and add'l.: 7372

CIK No: 0000855612

Subsidiaries: Anacom Communications, Inc, PocketScript, Inc, ZixCorp Canada, Inc

Officers: Rick D. Spurr/Chmn., CEO, COO/$1,459,142.00, Peter Wilensky/VP - Corporate Communications/$172,498.00, Barry W. Wilson/59/CFO, Treasurer, Russell J. Morgan/VP - Client Services/$256,434.00, David J. Robertson/VP - Engineering/$267,694.00, Nigel Johnson/VP - Business Development, Product Management, Brent H. Sanders/VP - Sales, Marketing, Ronald A. Woessner/Sr. VP, General Counsel, Sec./$354,895.00, William J. Kadonsky/VP - Business Operations, Jim Lesniak/VP - Sales, Marketing, Kirk Paul Kirkman/VP - Physician Recruitment, Retention

Directors: Rick D. Spurr/Chmn., CEO, COO, Robert C. Hausmann/Dir., Paul E. Schlosberg/Dir., Charles N. Kahn/Dir., Antonio R. Sanchez/Dir., James S. Marston/Dir.

Owners: Russell J. Morgan, David J. Robertson, Robert C. Hausmann, H&Q Capital Management LLP/6.60%, Benjamin Streetman, Ronald A. Woessner, Richard D. Spurr/2.30%, Charles N. Kahn, Barry W. Wilson, James S. Marston, George W. Haywood/7.50%, Antonio R. Sanchez/1.20%, Insiders/6.20%, Bradley C. Almond, Paul E. Schlosberg

Financial Data: *Fiscal Year End:*12/31 *Latest Annual Data:* 12/31/2006

Year	Sales	Net Income
2006	$18,358,000	-$19,508,000
2005	$13,964,000	-$43,596,000
2004	$14,127,000	-$42,040,000

Curr. Assets:	$15,707,000	Curr. Liab.:	$16,604,000		
Plant, Equip.:	$2,404,000	Total Liab.:	$19,439,000	Indic. Yr. Divd.:	NA
Total Assets:	$20,366,000	Net Worth:	$927,000	Debt/ Equity:	1.2236

Zkid Network Co

18/f Metro Plz. Tower Ii, 223 Hing Fong Rd., Kwai Chung, New Territories; *PH:* 852-358-61383

General - Incorporation: NV
Employees: NA
Auditor: Gruber & Co., LLC
Stk Agt: Benfleet Essex UK
Counsel: NA
DUNS No.: NA

Stock - Price on:12/24/2007: NA
Stock Exchange: NA
Ticker Symbol: NA
Outstanding Shares: NA
E.P.S: -$0.83
Shareholders: NA

Business: The group's principal activities are to develop proprietary software, creating a completely animated and safe Internet environment for children aged 4-12. This software program is called kidskeep, 'the home of the safe Internet for children'. The zkid network is specifically designed for children and their needs. The network provides the following network services: intranet, safe chat, intranet safe-email with parental gateway, intranet content (videos, cartoons and games written and produced by zkid network) and access to the Internet Web content though safesurf gateway. The kidskeep client software provides graphically assisted interface to the zkid network vpn using animated characters. On 03-May-2004, the group acquired Web safe technologies inc.

Primary SIC and add'l.: 7372 7375

CIK No: 0001109153

Officers: Gerald Lau/50/Dir., CEO, Pres., Eddie Chou/37/Dir., Principal Financial Officer, CTO, Sec., Treasurer

Directors: Gerald Lau/50/Dir., CEO, Pres., Edwin Chan/42/Dir., Hillary Chu/31/Dir., Ricky Chiu/37/Dir., Eddie Chou/37/Dir., Principal Financial Officer, CTO, Sec., Treasurer

Owners: Ricky Chiu/10.60%, Insiders/78.30%, Gerald Lau/60.30%, Cede & Co./9.00%, Eddie Chou/7.40%

Financial Data: *Fiscal Year End:*12/31 *Latest Annual Data:* 12/31/2006

Year	Sales	Net Income
2006	$2,000	-$1,150,000
2005	NA	-$1,913,000
2004	$5,000	-$4,079,000

Curr. Assets:	$15,000	Curr. Liab.:	$998,000		
Plant, Equip.:	$206,000	Total Liab.:	$998,000	Indic. Yr. Divd.:	NA
Total Assets:	$320,000	Net Worth:	-$678,000	Debt/ Equity:	NA

Znomics Inc

Formerly: Pacific Syndicated
15239 92nd Ave., Surrey, BC, V3R 0A8; *PH:* 1-604-785-1827

General - Incorporation: NV
Employees: NA
Auditor: Dale Matheson Carr-Hilton LaBonte LLP
Stk Agt: Signature Stock Transfer, Inc.
Counsel: NA
DUNS No.: NA

Stock - Price on:12/24/2007: NA
Stock Exchange: OTC
Ticker Symbol: PSRI
Outstanding Shares: NA
E.P.S: $0.00
Shareholders: NA

Business: The groups principal activity is in the exploration of mineral properties. The group operates from Canada.

Primary SIC and add'l.: 2834

CIK No: 0001371473

Officers: Darrel Woronchak/45/Dir., CEO, CFO, Pres., Principal Accounting Officer, Sec., Treasurer

Directors: Darrel Woronchak/45/Dir., CEO, CFO, Pres., Principal Accounting Officer, Sec., Treasurer

Owners: Dwight A. Sangrey/6.72%, Richard A. Sessions/8.01%, Stephen E. Kurtz/6.87%, Insiders/29.49%, Wenbiao Chen/6.61%, Roger D. Cone/8.21%

Financial Data: *Fiscal Year End:*12/31 *Latest Annual Data:* 05/31/2007

Year	Sales	Net Income
2007	NA	-$21,000

Curr. Assets:	$7,000	Curr. Liab.:	$6,000	P/E Ratio:	34.60
Plant, Equip.:	NA	Total Liab.:	$6,000	Indic. Yr. Divd.:	NA
Total Assets:	$7,000	Net Worth:	$1,000	Debt/ Equity:	NA

ZOLL Medical Corp

269 Mill Rd. , Chelmsford, MA, 01824; *PH:* 1-978-421-9655; *http://* www.zoll.com; *Email:* info@zoll.com

General - Incorporation	MA
Employees	1,080
Auditor	Ernst & Young LLP
Stk Agt	Computershare Shareholder Ser Inc
Counsel	Goodwin, Procter & Hoar
DUNS No	05-536-3428

Stock - Price on:12/24/2007	$21
Stock Exchange	NDQ
Ticker Symbol	ZOLL
Outstanding Shares	20,390,000
E.P.S.	$0.81
Shareholders	NA

Business: The group's principal activities are to design, manufacture and market integrated line of proprietary, non-invasive cardiac resuscitation devices, external defibrillators, pacemakers, disposable electrodes and accessories. These are used for the emergency resuscitation of cardiac arrest victims. The group also designs and markets software, which automates the collection and management of both clinical and non-clinical data for emergency medical service providers. It also provides training, installation, consulting and maintenance product support services. The group operates in the United States, the United Kingdom, Canada, Germany, France, Australia and the Netherlands. On 17-Mar-2004, the group acquired infusion dynamics inc.

Primary SIC and add'l.: 3845 7376

CIK No: 0000887568

Subsidiaries: Bio-Detek, Incorporated., ZMI France, S.A.R.L., ZOLL Circulation, Inc. , ZOLL Data Systems, Inc., ZOLL International Holding BV., ZOLL Medical (U.K.) Ltd., ZOLL Medical Australia, Pty. Limited., ZOLL Medical Bermuda Limited., ZOLL Medical Canada, Inc., ZOLL Medical Deutschland (GmbH)., ZOLL Medical New Zealand Pty. Limited., ZOLL Medical sterreich, GmbH., ZOLL Securities Corporation.

Officers: Richard A. Packer/Chmn., CEO, Pres., Edward T. Dunn/VP - Operations, Alex N. Moghadam/VP - International Operations, Ernest A. Whiton/VP - Administration, CFO, Steven K. Flora/VP - North America Sales, Donald R. Boucher/VP - Research, Development, John P. Bergeron/VP, Corporate Treasurer, Ward M. Hamilton/VP - Marketing, Stephen Korn/VP, General Counsel, Sec.

Directors: Richard A. Packer/Chmn., CEO, Pres., James W. Biondi/Dir., Thomas M. Claflin/Dir., Daniel M. Mulvena/Dir., Benson F. Smith/Dir., Robert J. Halliday/Dir., John J. Wallace/Dir.

Owners: Richard A. Packer/1.35%, Insiders/3.81%, Daniel M. Mulvena, Robert J. Halliday, James W. Biondi, Thomas M. Claflin, Benson F. Smith

Financial Data: Fiscal Year End:10/02   Latest Annual Data: 09/30/2007

Year	Sales	Net Income
2007	$309,451,000	$16,662,000
2006	$248,849,000	$11,140,000
2005	$211,340,000	$1,963,000

Curr. Assets:	$149,023,000	Curr. Liab.:	$34,238,000	P/E Ratio:	28.00
Plant, Equip.:	$24,221,000	Total Liab.:	$36,246,000	Indic. Yr. Divd.:	NA
Total Assets:	$207,192,000	Net Worth:	$170,946,000	Debt/ Equity:	NA

Zoloto Resources Ltd

Formerly: Sutcliffe Resources Ltd
420 - 625 Howe St., Vancouver, BC, V6C 2T6; **PH:** 1-604-608-0223;
http:// www.sutcliferesources.com

General - Incorporation	Canada
Employees	NA
Auditor	BDO Dunwoody LLP., Gordon K.w.Gee Ltd.
Stk Agt	Computershare Trust Co of Canada
Counsel	NA
DUNS No	NA

Stock - Price on:12/24/2007	$1.61
Stock Exchange	NA
Ticker Symbol	NA
Outstanding Shares	NA
E.P.S.	NA
Shareholders	NA

Business: The group's principal activity is acquiring of mining properties and participating in mining properties and mineral exploration projects. The group operates in Canada. The group has acquired options to pursue interests in the Harrison Lake Nickel-Copper Massive Sulphide Project and in the Beale Lake Property in British Columbia and is in the process of searching for interests in other exploration properties and projects.

Primary SIC and add'l.: 1081

CIK No: 0001341313

Officers: Laurence Stephenson/60/Chmn., CEO, Pres., Susan Wong/60/CFO

Directors: Laurence Stephenson/60/Chmn., CEO, Pres., Glen Indra/60/Dir., Robert Maddigan/45/Dir., John Tichotsky/42/Dir., Patrick Downey/48/Dir.

Owners: Laurence Stephenson/2.57%, John Tichotsky/0.24%, Firebird/10.36%, Patrick Downey/0.30%, Insiders/9.48%, Robert Maddigan/3.79%, Glen Indra/2.54%, Susan Wong/0.42%

Zoltek Cos Inc

3101 McKelvey Rd., Bridgeton, MO, 63044; **PH:** 1-314-291-5110; **Fax:** 1-314-291-8536;
http:// www.zoltek.com

General - Incorporation	MO
Employees	1,025
Auditor	Grant Thornton, LLP
Stk Agt	Computershare Trust Co., N.A.
Counsel	Thompson Coburn LLP
DUNS No	12-260-5041

Stock - Price on:12/24/2007	$41.6
Stock Exchange	NDQ
Ticker Symbol	ZOLT
Outstanding Shares	29,290,000
E.P.S.	-$0.09
Shareholders	NA

Business: The group's principal activity is to develop, manufacture and market carbon fibers used in aircraft brakes and other composite materials. The group's operations consist of three business segments: carbon fibers, technical fibers and specialty products. Carbon fibers & technical fibers segments manufacture low-cost carbon fibers. These are used as reinforcement material in composites, oxidized acrylic fibers for heat/fire barrier applications and aircraft brakes, carbon fiber composite products and filament winding equipment used in the composite industry. This segment sells carbon fibers under the panex trade name and its heat and fire resistant fibers under the pyron trade name. Carbon fiber & technical fibers segments are located geographically in the us and hungary. Specialty products segment manufactures and markets acrylic and nylon products and fibers primarily to the textile industry and is located in hungary.

Primary SIC and add'l.: 3624 2824

CIK No: 0000890923

Subsidiaries: Engineering Technology Corporation, Zoltek Corporation, Zoltek Properties Inc., Zoltek Rt.

Officers: Zsolt Rumy/Chmn., CEO, Pres., Kevin Schott/CFO, George E. Husman/62/CTO

Directors: Zsolt Rumy/Chmn., CEO, Pres., Charles A. Dill/68/Dir., Linn H. Bealke/63/Dir., John L. Kardos/68/Dir., James W. Betts/70/Dir., Michael D. Latta/66/Dir.

Owners: Insiders/26.30%, Michael D. Latta, Kevin Schott, Zsolt Rumy/23.10%, James W. Betts, Linn H. Bealke/1.30%, Charles A. Dill/1.00%, John L. Kardos

Financial Data: Fiscal Year End:09/30   Latest Annual Data: 09/30/2007

Year	Sales	Net Income
2007	$150,880,000	-$2,517,000
2006	$92,357,000	-$65,802,000
2005	$60,204,000	-$40,393,000

Curr. Assets:	$63,081,000	Curr. Liab.:	$43,039,000		
Plant, Equip.:	$122,284,000	Total Liab.:	$76,023,000	Indic. Yr. Divd.:	NA
Total Assets:	$187,684,000	Net Worth:	$111,661,000	Debt/ Equity:	0.0649

Zomax Inc

5353 Nathan Ln., Plymouth, MN, 55442; **PH:** 1-763-553-9300; http:// www.zomax.com

General - Incorporation	MN
Employees	NA
Auditor	Deloitte & Touche LLP
Stk Agt	Wells Fargo Shareowner Services
Counsel	Fredrikson & Byron
DUNS No	80-844-6215

Stock - Price on:12/24/2007	NA
Stock Exchange	NA
Ticker Symbol	NA
Outstanding Shares	NA
E.P.S.	NA
Shareholders	NA

Business: The group's principle activities are to market and sell outsourced supply chain services to industry leading customers in a variety of markets. The group's services are: outsourcing solutions which enhances the process of sourcing, production, and fulfillment through a modular suite of supply chain services that enable customers to select the combination of services that best meet their unique needs. Customer contact: to support customers' revenue growth. Sourcing: material management services to decrease cost and ensure quality. Production: media replication, manufacturing, and print services for consistent products and scalable supply. Fulfillment: physical or electronic distribution to ensure timely delivery to the channel, retailer or end-customer and similar services like returns management services and assembly/kitting services. The customers of the group include microsoft(R), dell(R), aol(R), logitech(R), apple(R) and hewlett packard(r).

Primary SIC and add'l.: 7379

CIK No: 0001010788

Subsidiaries: Zomax Ireland

Officers: Ellis Kern/CEO, Melodie Gee/COO, David Silvon/CFO

Zond Windsystem Partners LTD Series 85-C

1221 Lamar St., Ste. 1600, Houston, TX, 77010; **PH:** 1-713-853-0530

General - Incorporation	CA
Employees	NA
Auditor	Hein & Assoc. LLP
Counsel	NA
DUNS No	NA

Stock - Price on:12/24/2007	NA
Stock Exchange	NA
Ticker Symbol	NA
Outstanding Shares	NA
E.P.S.	NA
Shareholders	NA

Business: The groups principle activities include purchasing, owning and operating system of 200 Vestas V-17 wind turbine electric generators. The group operates from United States.

Primary SIC and add'l.: 4911

CIK No: 0000783041

Subsidiaries: Enron Renewable Energy Corp.

Zone 4 Play Inc

103 Foulk Rd., Wilmington, DE, 19803; **PH:** 1-302-691-6177; **Fax:** 1-302-652-8667;
http:// www.zone4play.com; **Email:** info.us@zone4play.com

General - Incorporation	NV
Employees	61
Auditor	Ziv Haft
Stk Agt	NA
Counsel	NA
DUNS No	NA

Stock - Price on:12/24/2007	$0.095
Stock Exchange	OTC
Ticker Symbol	ZFPI
Outstanding Shares	32,320,000
E.P.S.	-$0.13
Shareholders	NA

Business: The groups principle activities include developing and providing software to companies that service the interactive gaming industry. The group also delivering cross platform systems that are built for mass participation gaming over mobile devices, TV and the Internet. The group operates from the United States.

Primary SIC and add'l.: 7372

CIK No: 0001175442

Subsidiaries: Gaming Ventures Plc, Get21 (Israel) Ltd, Get21 Ltd, MixTV Ltd, RNG gaming Ltd, Zone4Play (Israel) Ltd, Zone4Play (UK) Ltd, Zone4Play, Inc

Officers: Ronen Stein/CEO, CFO

Directors: Adiv Baruch/Chmn., Shimon Citron/Founder, Dir., Michael Chill/Dir., Niv Zilberstein/Dir., Steve Baker/Dir.

Owners: Smithfield Fiduciary LLC/6.40%, Shlomo Rothman, Insiders/16.90%, Shimon Citron/15.30%, Ronen Zadok, Dave Games Invest Corporation Inc./8.20%, Walham Investments Group Inc/8.20%, Liron Edrey, Oded Zucker, Pini Gershon/8.40%, Sedna Capital/5.80%, Orinda Capital/14.30%, Adiv Baruch

Financial Data: Fiscal Year End:12/31   Latest Annual Data: 12/31/2006

Year	Sales	Net Income
2006	$1,656,000	-$6,425,000
2005	$1,062,000	-$3,965,000
2004	$769,000	-$1,921,000

Curr. Assets:	$4,189,000	Curr. Liab.:	$1,432,000		
Plant, Equip.:	$699,000	Total Liab.:	$1,967,000	Indic. Yr. Divd.:	NA
Total Assets:	$5,434,000	Net Worth:	$3,466,000	Debt/ Equity:	NA

Zones Inc

1102 15th St. SW, Ste 102, Auburn, WA, 98001; **PH:** 1-253-205-3000; http:// www.zones.com;
Email: customerservice@zones.com

General - Incorporation	WA	**Stock**- Price on:12/24/2007	$9
Employees	661	Stock Exchange	NDQ
Auditor	Grant Thornton LLP	Ticker Symbol	ZONS
Stk Agt	Mellon Investor Services LLC	Outstanding Shares	13,130,000
Counsel	Gray, Cary, Ware & Freidenrich	E.P.S	$0.83
DUNS No.	19-559-0237	Shareholders	NA

Business: The group's principle activities are single-source, multi-vendor direct reseller of name-brand information technology products to the fast growing small to medium sized business market, enterprise and government and education accounts. The group sells these products through outbound and inbound account executives, specialty print and e-catalogs and the Internet. The group offers products through catalogs, trade publications and a telemarketing sales team. The group markets more than 150,000 products, which include printers, monitors, keyboards, modems, scanners and desktop. These products are supplied by manufactures such as apple, compaq, hewlett-packard, IBM, microsoft and toshiba. The group conducts its business in the United States under the service marks the PC zone(R) and the mac zone(R) registered with the United States. On 01-Apr-03, it acquired corporate PC source, inc.

Primary SIC and add'l.: 5045

CIK No: 0001013786

Subsidiaries: Mac Zone, Inc, Zones Corporate Solutions, Inc, Zones Government Solutions

Officers: Firoz H. Lalji/61/Chmn., CEO, Pres./$726,341.00, Ronald McFadden/Sr. VP, CFO, Sec./$460,336.00, Anwar Jiwani/CIO, Sr. VP/$440,495.00, Christina Corley/COO, Pres./$896,715.00, Sean Hobday/Exec. VP - Sales/$742,895.00, Patrick Sean Hobday/Exec. VP - Sales, Tom Ducatelli/Exec. VP - Business Development

Directors: Firoz H. Lalji/61/Chmn., CEO, Pres., Kenneth Kirkpatrick/54/Dir., Cathi Hatch/58/Dir., John H. Bauer/67/Dir., William Keiper/57/Dir.

Owners: Insiders/59.00%, John H. Bauer, Firoz H. Lalji/55.60%, Anwar Jiwani/1.60%, Cathi Hatch, Kinderhook Partners, LP/5.60%, Christina M. Corley/1.10%, Patrick Sean Hobday/1.90%, William C. Keiper, Ronald P. McFadden/1.70%, Kenneth M. Kirkpatrick, Dimensional Fund Advisors, LP/5.30%

Financial Data: *Fiscal Year End:*12/31 *Latest Annual Data:* 12/31/2006

Year	Sales	Net Income
2006	$577,027,000	$9,685,000
2005	$566,553,000	$6,051,000
2004	$495,563,000	$4,652,000

Curr. Assets:	$111,380,000	**Curr. Liab.:**	$69,705,000	**P/E Ratio:**	11.25
Plant, Equip.:	$3,771,000	**Total Liab.:**	$71,213,000	**Indic. Yr. Divd.:**	NA
Total Assets:	$120,695,000	**Net Worth:**	$49,482,000	**Debt/ Equity:**	NA

Zoom Technologies Inc

207 S St., Boston, MA, 02111; *PH:* 1-44-1252582000; *http://* www.zoom.com; *Email:* sales@zoom.com

General - Incorporation	DE	**Stock**- Price on:12/24/2007	$1.38
Employees	69	Stock Exchange	NDQ
Auditor	UHY LLP	Ticker Symbol	ZOOM
Stk Agt	U.S. Stock Transfer Corp	Outstanding Shares	9,350,000
Counsel	NA	E.P.S	$0.23
DUNS No.	08-421-6316	Shareholders	NA

Business: The group's principal activities are to design, produce and market dial-up and broadband modems, wireless local area network products and other communications products. The group's dial-up modems connect personal computers and other devices to the local telephone line for transmission of data, fax, voice and video. The products of the group facilitate communication of data through the Internet. The dial-up modems and integrated services digital network modems link pcs and portable information devices through the telephone network and connected networks, including the Internet and local area networks. The products are marketed through retailers, distributors, personal computer manufacturers and other original equipment manufacturers. The major customers of the group are staples, best buy and dixon group.

Primary SIC and add'l.: 3661

CIK No: 0000822708

Subsidiaries: Tribe Acquisition Corporation, Zoom Telephonics Foreign Sales Corporation, Zoom Telephonics, Inc., Zoom Telephonics, Ltd.

Officers: Frank B. Manning/59/Chmn., CEO, Pres./$316,376.00, Peter R. Kramer/56/Dir., Exec. VP/$258,979.00, Robert Crist/VP - Finance, CFO/$228,594.00, Deena Randall/VP - Operations/$215,244.00, Terry Manning/VP - Sales, Marketing/$198,919.00

Directors: Frank B. Manning/59/Chmn., CEO, Pres., Peter R. Kramer/56/Dir., Exec. VP, Bernard Furman/78/Dir., Ronald J. Woods/72/Dir., Joseph J. Donovan/58/Dir.

Owners: Deena Randall, Frank B. Manning/7.69%, Terry Manning/1.46%, Robert A. Crist, Insiders/18.19%, J. Ronald Woods, Peter R. Kramer/7.06%, Joseph J. Donovan, Bernard Furman

Financial Data: *Fiscal Year End:*12/31 *Latest Annual Data:* 12/31/2006

Year	Sales	Net Income
2006	$18,322,000	$1,030,000
2005	$25,551,000	-$2,117,000
2004	$31,412,000	-$3,072,000

Curr. Assets:	$15,999,000	**Curr. Liab.:**	$3,570,000	**P/E Ratio:**	6.00
Plant, Equip.:	$249,000	**Total Liab.:**	$3,927,000	**Indic. Yr. Divd.:**	NA
Total Assets:	$16,249,000	**Net Worth:**	$12,322,000	**Debt/ Equity:**	NA

Zoran Corp

3112 Scott Blvd, Ste 255, Santa Clara, CA, 95054; *PH:* 1-408-919-4111; *http://* www.zoran.com; *Email:* sales@zoran.com

General - Incorporation	DE	**Stock**- Price on:12/24/2007	$21.96
Employees	1,191	Stock Exchange	NDQ
Auditor	PricewaterhouseCoopers LLP	Ticker Symbol	ZRAN
Stk Agt	American Stock Transfer & Trust Co.	Outstanding Shares	49,600,000
Counsel	Gray, Cary, Ware & Freidenrich	E.P.S	-$0.07
DUNS No.	10-211-0863	Shareholders	NA

Business: The group's principal activities are to develop and market integrated circuits, integrated circuit cores and embedded software. The group's products are used by original equipment manufacturers in digital video and audio products for commercial and consumer markets. The group also provides complete, copy-ready system reference designs, that help the customers to produce consumer and commercial products more quickly and cost-effectively. The integrated circuits of the group are used in digital versatile disc, players, film-less digital cameras, professional and consumer video editing systems and digital speakers and audio systems. As on 11-Aug-2003, the group acquired oak technology inc.

Primary SIC and add'l.: 6794 7372 3674

CIK No: 0001003022

Subsidiaries: Emblaze Ltd, Emblaze Semiconductor Ltd, Oak Technology, Inc.

Officers: Levy Gerzberg/Co - Founder, CEO, Pres./$3,293,178.00, Karl Schneider/Sr. VP - Finance, CFO/$1,254,515.00, Isaac Shenberg/Sr. VP - Business Development/$1,173,499.00

Directors: Levy Gerzberg/Co - Founder, CEO, Pres., Uzia Galil/82/Chmn., Philip M. Young/67/Dir., Raymond A. Burgess/Dir., James D. Meindl/74/Dir., James B. Owens/57/Dir., David Rynne/66/Dir., Arthur B. Stabenow/68/Dir.

Owners: James B. Owens, Isaac Shenberg, Karl Schneider, AXA and affiliated entities/6.07%, Barclays Global Investors, NA. and affiliated entities/6.46%, Arthur B. Stabenow, Uzia Galil, Philip M. Young, Raymond A. Burgess, Levy Gerzberg/2.48%, David Rynne, James D. Meindl, Insiders/5.53%, Dimensional Fund Advisors,Inc./4.72%

Financial Data: *Fiscal Year End:*12/31 *Latest Annual Data:* 12/31/2006

Year	Sales	Net Income
2006	$495,805,000	$16,328,000
2005	$395,758,000	-$26,971,000
2004	$378,864,000	-$47,354,000

Curr. Assets:	$394,639,000	**Curr. Liab.:**	$79,849,000		
Plant, Equip.:	$15,673,000	**Total Liab.:**	$92,633,000	**Indic. Yr. Divd.:**	NA
Total Assets:	$676,630,000	**Net Worth:**	$583,997,000	**Debt/ Equity:**	NA

Zumiez Inc

6300 Merrill Creek Pkwy., Ste. B, Everett, WA, 98203; *PH:* 1-425-551-1500; *http://* www.zumiez.net; *Email:* help@zumiez.com

General - Incorporation	WA	**Stock**- Price on:12/24/2007	$39.65
Employees	786	Stock Exchange	NDQ
Auditor	PricewaterhouseCoopers LLP	Ticker Symbol	ZUMZ
Stk Agt	Wachovia Bank N.A	Outstanding Shares	28,380,000
Counsel	NA	E.P.S	$0.828
DUNS No.	NA	Shareholders	NA

Business: The groups principal activity is to retailer of action sports related apparel, footwear, equipment and accessories. The group products sold under the trade names Zumiez, Free World, O-Three, ALab and Limelight. The groups services include skateboarding, surfing, snowboarding, BMX and motocross. The group operates from the United States. The net sale of the group for the year 2006 was $298,177 (thousands)

Primary SIC and add'l.: 2325 2339 3149 2389 2331 5091 5995 5139 5632 2369 5611 5137 5941 3949 3144 5999 5699 2353 3143 5661 5621 2321 5963 2337 2387 2329 5136

CIK No: 0001318008

Subsidiaries: Zumiez Nevada, LLC

Officers: Richard M. Brooks/48/Dir., CEO, Brenda I. Morris/43/CFO, Sec., Gerald F. Ryles/71/Dir. - Financial Expert, Lynn K. Kilbourne/45/General Merchandise Mgr.

Directors: Richard M. Brooks/48/Dir., CEO, Thomas D. Campion/59/Chmn., Co - Founder, Gerald F. Ryles/71/Dir. - Financial Expert, William M. Barnum/54/Dir., Matthew L. Hyde/45/Dir., James M. Weber/48/Dir.

Owners: Insiders/39.20%, FMR Corp./11.80%, Matthew L. Hyde, Richard M. Brooks/14.40%, Gerald F. Ryles, Brenda I. Morris, William M. Barnum, T. Rowe Price Associates, Inc./8.20%, Thomas D. Campion/23.60%, Lynn K. Kilbourne, James M. Weber

Financial Data: *Fiscal Year End:*01/28 *Latest Annual Data:* 2/3/2007

Year	Sales	Net Income
2007	$298,177,000	$20,856,000
2006	$205,589,000	$12,851,000
2005	$153,583,000	$7,267,000

Curr. Assets:	$104,501,000	**Curr. Liab.:**	$49,572,000	**P/E Ratio:**	53.58
Plant, Equip.:	$49,889,000	**Total Liab.:**	$62,482,000	**Indic. Yr. Divd.:**	NA
Total Assets:	$167,294,000	**Net Worth:**	$104,812,000	**Debt/ Equity:**	NA

Zunicom Inc

1720 Hayden Rd. , Carrollton, TX, 75006; *PH:* 1-469-892-1200; *http://* www.zunicom.com; *Email:* info@zunicom.com

General - Incorporation	TX	**Stock**- Price on:12/24/2007	$0.83
Employees	77	Stock Exchange	OTC
Auditor	KBA Group LLP	Ticker Symbol	ZNCM
Stk Agt	Securities Transfer Corp	Outstanding Shares	8,950,000
Counsel	NA	E.P.S	$0.78
DUNS No.	79-404-3109	Shareholders	NA

Business: The group's principal activity is to distribute battery assembly, distribution of computer components and battery. It operates through its subsidiaries computer components corporation, which does business as universal battery corporation and alphanet hospitality systems inc. The group operates in two segments: battery and third party fulfillment and facsimile and business center. Battery and third party fulfillment segment sells battery, battery assembly systems, kitting systems, passive electronic components, ac transformers, ceramic sound sources and battery chargers. Facsimile and business center provides in-room facsimile and business center services to the hotel industry for their business travelers through licensing agreement. The products include innfax(R), office(R) and innphone.

Primary SIC and add'l.: 5065 4822 7378

CIK No: 0000886912

Subsidiaries: AlphaNet Hospitality Systems, Inc., Universal Power Group Inc.

Officers: William Tan/Chmn., CEO, Pres., Julie Sansom-Reese/45/Treasurer, Mimi Tan/34/Dir. - Operations, Corp. Sec., John C. Rudy/VP, Dir., CFO

Directors: William Tan/Chmn., CEO, Pres., Ian C. Edmonds/Dir., John C. Rudy/VP, Dir., CFO, David Parke/Dir.

Owners: Insiders/30.18%, John C. Rudy, Kim Yeow Tan/7.90%, Ian Colin Edmonds/1.98%, William Tan/28.02%

Financial Data: *Fiscal Year End:*12/31 *Latest Annual Data:* 12/31/2006

Year	Sales	Net Income
2006	$94,337,000	$8,622,000
2005	$83,091,000	$1,740,000
2004	$69,147,000	-$348,000

Curr. Assets:	$8,384,000	Curr. Liab.:	$820,000	P/E Ratio:	0.94
Plant, Equip.:	$226,000	Total Liab.:	$4,644,000	Indic. Yr. Divd.:	$0.800
Total Assets:	$20,585,000	Net Worth:	$15,941,000	Debt/ Equity:	NA

Zupintra Corp Inc

Formerly: Digital Rooster.com Ltd
181 University Ave, Ste. 210, Toronto, ON, M5H 3M7; *PH:* 1-416-815-1771;
http:// www.phinder.com

General - Incorporation	ON	**Stock** - Price on:12/24/2007	NA
Employees	NA	Stock Exchange	OTC
Auditor	Mintz & Partners LLP	Ticker Symbol	ZUPC
Stk Agt	Heritage Trust Co	Outstanding Shares	NA
Counsel	NA	E.P.S.	NA
DUNS No.	NA	Shareholders	NA

Business: The group's principle activity is to operate online adult entertainment Internet Web sites through its wholly owned subsidiary Web dream inc ("Web Dream"), and license video, picture and other content from third party distributors, such as adults only video, pacific direct and cv productions, in addition to operate its own websites, license digitized video content to wholesae customers operating their own adult entertainment websites. New registrant. The group operates from United States.

Primary SIC and add'l.: 7371 7375 7812 5735

CIK No: 0001136386

Officers: John Alexander Van Arem/Chmn., CEO, Kevin Donahue/MD

Directors: John Alexander Van Arem/Chmn., CEO, Wayne Doss/53/Dir.

Owners: Wayne Doss, John Van Arem/9.20%, Insiders/9.70%

Financial Data: Fiscal Year End:03/31 Latest Annual Data: 03/31/2007

Year	Sales	Net Income
2007	$302,000	-$1,908,000
2006	$4,326,000	-$2,064,000
2005	$164,000	-$675,000

Curr. Assets:	$2,203,000	Curr. Liab.:	$2,805,000
Plant, Equip.:	$295,000	Total Liab.:	$3,275,000	Indic. Yr. Divd.: NA
Total Assets:	$3,293,000	Net Worth:	$18,000	Debt/ Equity: NA

Zygo Corp

Laurel Brook Rd. , Middlefield, CT, 06455; *PH:* 1-860-347-8506; *http://* www.zygo.com;
Email: inquire@zygo.com

General - Incorporation	DE	**Stock** - Price on:12/24/2007	$14.39
Employees	533	Stock Exchange	NDQ
Auditor	Deloitte & Touche, LLP	Ticker Symbol	ZIGO
Stk Agt	Continental Stock Transfer & Trust Co	Outstanding Shares	18,530,000
Counsel	Fulbright & Jaworski LLP	E.P.S.	$0.57
DUNS No.	05-253-6570	Shareholders	NA

Business: The group's principal activities are to design, develop, manufacture and market optics and on-line yield enhancement solutions for the semiconductor and industrial manufacturing markets. The group operates in two segments: semiconductor and industrial. Semiconductor devices manufacture high performance macro-optics components, optical coatings and optical system assemblies. Industrial manufacturing segment manufactures noncontact optical measurement instruments and related products. The group owns over 130 active patents in the United States and 75 foreign patents. The group's major customers include applied materials, awe, au optronics, bosch, canon, chengdu, dupont lawrence, livermore national laboratory, IBM, northrop grumman, kla-tencor, raytheon, nikon, siemens, samsung, toyota, zeiss and university of rochester.

Primary SIC and add'l.: 3829 3827 3674

CIK No: 0000730716

Subsidiaries: NexStar Corporation, Sight Systems, Inc., Six Brookside Drive, Syncotec Neue Technologien und Instrumente GmbH, Technical Instrument Company, TechniStar Corporation, Zygo KK, Zygo PTE, Zygo TeraOptix, Inc., ZygoLOT GmbH

Officers: Bruce J. Robinson/Chmn., CEO, Mike Mckay/Mgr. - Customer Education, Training, Carl A. Zanoni/Dir., Sr. VP - Technology, William H. Bacon/VP - Corporate Quality, Support Services, Brian J. Monti/Sr. VP - Display Solutions, Douglas J. Eccleston/VP - Precision Positioning Solutions, David J. Person/VP - Human Resources, Walter A. Shephard/VP - Finance, CFO, Treasurer, James R. Northup/Pres. - Metrology Solutions Division, John M. Stack/Pres. - Optical Systems Division

Directors: Bruce J. Robinson/Chmn., CEO, Carol P. Wallace/Dir., Youssef A. El-Mansy/Dir., Robert B. Taylor/Dir., Eugene G. Banucci/Dir., Seymour E. Liebman/Dir., Paul F. Forman/Dir., Robert G. McKelvey/Dir., Bruce W. Worster/Dir., Samuel H. Fuller/Dir.

Owners: T. Rowe Price Associates, Inc./5.30%, Samuel H. Fuller, Bruce W. Worster, Douglas J. Eccleston, Insiders/9.20%, Eugene G. Banucci, Robert B. Taylor, Royce & Associates LLC/5.60%, Canon Inc./6.50%, Robert G. McKelvey, Youssef A. El-Mansy, Barclays Global Investors NA/5.00%, Seymour E. Liebman, Carol P. Wallace, Brian J. Monti *(19 Owners included in Index)*

Financial Data: Fiscal Year End:06/30 Latest Annual Data: 6/30/2006

Year	Sales	Net Income
2006	$168,137,000	$14,485,000
2005	$141,349,000	$8,984,000
2004	$116,642,000	-$3,407,000

Curr. Assets:	$140,120,000	Curr. Liab.:	$32,286,000	P/E Ratio:	16.93
Plant, Equip.:	$36,349,000	Total Liab.:	$33,817,000	Indic. Yr. Divd.:	NA
Total Assets:	$211,594,000	Net Worth:	$177,777,000	Debt/ Equity:	NA

Zylorain Inc

1905 Juarez Ln., Redding, CA, 96003; *PH:* 1-530-356-8198

General - Incorporation	NV	**Stock** - Price on:12/24/2007	NA
Employees	NA	Stock Exchange	NA
Auditor	NA	Ticker Symbol	NA
Stk Agt	NA	Outstanding Shares	NA
Counsel	NA	E.P.S.	NA
DUNS No.	NA	Shareholders	NA

Business: The group's principle activity is to provide lawful corporate undertaking, including, without limitation, mergers and acquisitions with companies selected by the management of the Company for such business opportunities. In analyzing prospective business opportunities, we may consider such matters as: the available technical, financial and managerial resources; working capital and other financial requirements; history of operations, if any; prospects for the future; nature of present and expected competition; the quality and experience of management services which may be available and the depth of that management; the potential for further research, development, or exploration; specific risk factors not now foreseeable but which then may be anticipated to impact our proposed activities; the potential for growth or expansion; the potential for profit; the perceived public recognition or acceptance of products, services, or trades; name identification; and other relevant factors. The group operates from United States.

Primary SIC and add'l.: 9995

CIK No: 0001305725

ZymoGenetics Inc

1201 Elake Ave. E, Seattle, WA, 98102; *PH:* 1-206-442-6600; *http://* www.zymogenetics.com;
Email: business@zgi.com

General - Incorporation	WA	**Stock** - Price on:12/24/2007	$15.02
Employees	498	Stock Exchange	NDQ
Auditor	PricewaterhouseCoopers LLP	Ticker Symbol	ZGEN
Stk Agt	Mellon Investor Services LLC	Outstanding Shares	68,110,000
Counsel	Perkins Coie LLP	E.P.S.	-$2.06
DUNS No.	NA	Shareholders	NA

Business: The group's principle activities include discovering, developing, and commercializing therapeutic protein-based products for the treatment of human diseases. The company has generated proprietary product candidates and commercializes them through internal development, collaborations with biopharmaceutical partners or out-licensing of patents. The company has developed five recombinant protein products marketed by other companies from which it derives royalties. The products are novolin(R), novorapid(R), novoseven(R), regranex(R), glucagen(R) and cleactor(tm). The products are marketed by novo nordisk, ortho-mcneil pharmaceuticals, inc. And eisai co., ltd. The company has also out-licensed two products to third parties in return for milestone payments and royalties.

Primary SIC and add'l.: 2834 8731

CIK No: 0001129425

Subsidiaries: Ares Trading S.A. (Serono), Novo Nordisk, Novo Nordisk North America, Serono S.A.

Officers: Bruce L.A. Carter/Chmn., CEO, Pres./$2,433,217.00, Suzanne M. Shema/Sr. VP, General Counsel - Law, Compliance, Michael J. Dwyer/Sr. VP - Sales, Marketing, Vaughn B. Himes/Sr. VP - Technical Operations, James A. Johnson/Exec. VP, CFO, Treasurer/$839,171.00, Nicole Onetto/Sr. VP, Chief Medical Officer/$932,889.00, Douglas E. Williams/Chief Scientific Officer, Exec. VP/$1,554,278.00, Darren R. Hamby/Sr. VP - Human Resources

Directors: Bruce L.A. Carter/Chmn., CEO, Pres., James A. Harper/Dir., Lars Rebien Sorensen/Dir., David I. Hirsh/Dir., Judith A. Hemberger/Dir., Jonathan S. Leff/Dir., David H. MacCallum/Dir., Kurt Anker Nielsen/Dir., Edward E. Penhoet/Dir.

Owners: Lars Rebien Srensen/32.00%, Judith A. Hemberger, Novo Nordisk Biotech Holdings, Inc./32.00%, James A. Harper, Warburg, Pincus Equity Partners, L.P./10.60%, Bruce L.A. Carter/1.90%, Insiders/45.10%, Wellington Management Company, LLP/9.70%, David I. Hirsh, James A. Johnson, David H. MacCallum, Jonathan S. Leff/10.70%, Douglas E. Williams, Kurt Anker Nielsen, Jan K. hrstrm *(17 Owners included in Index)*

Financial Data: Fiscal Year End:12/31 Latest Annual Data: 12/31/2006

Year	Sales	Net Income
2006	$25,380,000	-$130,002,000
2005	$42,909,000	-$78,027,000
2004	$35,694,000	-$88,756,000

Curr. Assets:	$267,390,000	Curr. Liab.:	$27,958,000		
Plant, Equip.:	$71,542,000	Total Liab.:	$111,320,000	Indic. Yr. Divd.:	NA
Total Assets:	$347,004,000	Net Worth:	$235,684,000	Debt/ Equity:	0.3178

1-800 Contacts Inc

66 E Wadsworth Pk. Dr., 3rd Fl., Draper, UT, 84020; *PH:* 1-801-924-9800;
http:// www.1800contacts.com; *Email:* legal@1800contacts.com

General - Incorporation	DE	**Stock** - Price on:12/24/2007	$23.75
Employees	1,101	Stock Exchange	NA
Auditor	KPMG LLP	Ticker Symbol	NA
Stk Agt	American Stock Transfer & Trust Co.	Outstanding Shares	14,010,000
Counsel	NA	E.P.S.	-$0.82
DUNS No.	92-697-3645	Shareholders	NA

Business: The group's principal activity is to market replacement contact lenses through toll-free telephone number and Internet. The group offers substantially all of the soft and hard contact lenses produced by the contact lens manufacturers, including johnson and johnson, ciba vision, bausch and lomb, ocular sciences and coopervision. The products are marketed through Internet, direct mail, cooperative mail programs and cable and networks television. The group's wholly owned subsidiary, clearlab, manufactures injection cast molded soft contact lenses on a contract basis for various contact lens manufacturers. On 30-Jan-2003, the group acquired certain assets and assumed certain liabilities of lens express llc and camelot ventures and on 24-Feb-2004, visiontec (clearlab UK).

Primary SIC and add'l.: 5048

CIK No: 0001050122

Subsidiaries: 1-800 Contacts Japan, KK, 1-800 Lens Now, Inc., CL I, Inc., CL II, Inc., CL III, Inc., ClearLab, ClearLab Europe Ltd., ClearLab International Pte Ltd., ClearLab UK Ltd., Evision, Inc., Lens 1st Holding Company, Shayna Ltd.

Officers: Jonathan C. Coon/Chmn., CEO/$265,911.00, Kevin K. McCallum/Sr. VP - Marketing, Operations/$434,158.00, John F. Nichols/46/Co - Founder, Dir., VP - Trade Relations, Robert G. Hunter/CFO/$285,736.00, Brian W. Bethers/Pres./$868,884.00, John R. Murray/CIO, Max Neves/VP - Human Resources, Joe R. Zeidner/General Counsel, Sec./$471,607.00

Directors: Jonathan C. Coon/Chmn., CEO, Stephen L. Key/64/Dir., Bradley T. Knight/48/Dir., Dean Edward Butler/63/Dir., Thomas Hale Boggs/66/Dir., Frank Lagrange Johnson/Dir., John F. Nichols/46/Co - Founder, Dir., VP - Trade Relations, Garth T. Vincent/45/Dir.

Owners: Joe R. Zeidner, Frank LaGrange Johnson/12.00%, Dean E. Butler, John F. Nichols/7.00%, Thomas H. Boggs, Stephen L. Key, Mario Cibelli/8.50%, Robert G. Hunter, Perry Corp/10.90%, Brian W. Bethers/1.20%, Artisan Partners Limited Partnership/9.00%, Kevin K. McCallum/1.10%, Insiders/44.90%, Jonathan C. Coon/21.50%, Garth T. Vincent *(17 Owners included in Index)*

Financial Data: *Fiscal Year End*:12/31 *Latest Annual Data:* 12/30/2006

Year	Sales	Net Income
2006	$248,676,000	-$22,459,000
2005	$237,950,000	-$2,605,000

Curr. Assets: $33,544,000 **Curr. Liab.:** $25,817,000
Plant, Equip.: $29,705,000 **Total Liab.:** $57,728,000 **Indic. Yr. Divd.:** NA
Total Assets: $114,945,000 **Net Worth:** $57,217,000 **Debt/ Equity:** 0.8038

1-800-Flowers Com Inc

1 Old Country Rd., Carle Place, NY, 11514; *PH:* 1-516-237-6087; *Fax:* 1-516-237-6101; *http://* ww22.1800flowers.com

General - Incorporation .... DE
Employees 3,700
Auditor .... Ernst & Young LLP
Stk Agt .... NA
Counsel .... NA
DUNS No. .... NA

Stock- Price on:12/24/2007 .... $9.06
Stock Exchange .... NDQ
Ticker Symbol .... FLWS
Outstanding Shares 62,480,000
E.P.S. $0.29
Shareholders .... NA

Business: The group's principal activity is to market gifts such as flowers, plants, gourmet foods, candies and gift baskets via the Internet, telephone, catalogs and retail stores. Through its subsidiaries, it also markets home decor and garden merchandise, popcorn, specialty food gifts and children's toys and games. The group maintains strategic online relationships with aol time warner, yahoo!, microsoft corporation and American greetings corporation. As of 29-Jun-2003, the group had a database of 21.3 million customers. Brands of the group include 1-800-flowers (R), plow & hearth (R), the popcorn factory (R), greatfood.com (R), hearthsong (R), magic cabin (r).

Primary SIC and add'l.: 7375 5963 5992 5399 5947

CIK No: 0001084869

Subsidiaries: 1-800-Flowers Retail, Inc., 1-800-Flowers Seasonal Team, Inc., 1-800-Flowers Service Support Center, Inc., 1-800-Flowers Team Services, Inc., 1-800-Flowers.Com Franchise Co., Inc., 800-flowers, Inc., Amalgamated Consolidated Enterprises, Inc., Bloomlink Systems, Inc., BloomNet Exchange, Inc., Cheryl & Co., Conroy's Inc., Fannie May Confections Brands Inc, Fannie May Confections, Inc, Floranet Iberia S.L., FMCB Acquisition Co., Inc. 27 Subsidiaries included in the Index

Officers: James F. McCann/Chmn., CEO, Christopher G. McCann/Dir., Pres., Stephen J. Bozzo/53/CIO, Sr. VP, Gerard M. Gallagher/Sr. VP, General Counsel, Sec., Vincent J. McVeigh/Sr. VP - Business Gift Services, William E. Shea/Sr. VP - Finance, Administration, Treasurer, CFO, Thomas G. Hartnett/COO, Sr. VP - Consumer Floral Brand, Monica L. Woo/Pres. - Consumer Floral Brand, Timothy J. Hopkins/Pres. - Specialty Brands, Mark Nance/Pres. - Bloomnet, Charles Fraas/Sr. VP - Business Process Improvement

Directors: James F. McCann/Chmn., CEO, Guy T. Minetti/50/Vice Chmn., Jan L. Murley/Dir., Christopher G. McCann/Dir., Pres., Lawrence Calcano/Dir., Leonard J. Elmore/Dir., John J. Conefry/Dir., Jeffrey C. Walker/Dir., James A. Cannivino/Dir.

Owners: RLR Capital Partners, LP/5.10%, Royce & Associates LLC/6.20%, AXA/7.00%, Christpher G. McCann/8.50%, Bear Stearns Asset Management, Inc/12.00%, The TCW Group, Inc./5.00%, Leonard J. Elmore/0.30%, Christpher G. McCann/6.40%, Awad Asset Management, Inc./7.60%, Timothy J. Hopkins/0.30%, John J. Conefry/0.20%, Insiders/99.70%, Monica L. Woo/0.40%, William E. Shea/1.40%, Insiders/12.80% *(20 Owners included in Index)*

Financial Data: *Fiscal Year End*:07/03 *Latest Annual Data:* 07/01/2007

Year	Sales	Net Income
2007	$912,598,000	$17,118,000
2006	$781,741,000	$3,187,000
2005	$670,679,000	$7,849,000

Curr. Assets: $101,410,000 **Curr. Liab.:** $59,718,000 **P/E Ratio:** 34.85
Plant, Equip.: $50,474,000 **Total Liab.:** $65,618,000 **Indic. Yr. Divd.:** NA
Total Assets: $251,952,000 **Net Worth:** $186,334,000 **Debt/ Equity:** 0.3664

1-900 Jackpot Inc

3-3838 Raymert Dr., Las Vegas, NV, 89122; *PH:* 1-604-575-0050; *http://* www.1900jackpot.com; *Email:* contact@1900jackpot.com

General - Incorporation ....
Employees 2
Auditor .... NA
Stk Agt .... Computershare Trust Co
Counsel .... NA
DUNS No. .... NA

Stock- Price on:12/24/2007 .... $42
Stock Exchange .... OTC
Ticker Symbol .... ONJP
Outstanding Shares 14,170,000
E.P.S. $0.00
Shareholders .... NA

Business: The groups principal activity is to provide license the operation of proprietary lottery products to lottery operators. The group operates from the United States.

Primary SIC and add'l.: 7990

CIK No:

Subsidiaries: Pultronex Corporation of Alberta

Owners: Fletcher& Associates/13.80%, Umbrella Asset Management, Inc/85.30%

Financial Data: *Fiscal Year End*:NA *Latest Annual Data:* 08/31/2006

Year	Sales	Net Income
2006	NA	-$180,000
2001	$2,620,000	-$1,304,000

180 Connect Inc

Formerly: Ad.Venture Partners Inc
6501 East Belleview, Englewood, CO, 80111; *PH:* 1-303-395-6001; *http://* www.adventurepartners.net

General - Incorporation .... DE
Employees .... NA
Auditor .... Eisner LLP
Stk Agt .... Valiant Trust Co.
Counsel .... NA
DUNS No. .... NA

Stock- Price on:12/24/2007 .... $5.78
Stock Exchange .... OTC
Ticker Symbol .... CNCT
Outstanding Shares 11,250,000
E.P.S. .... NA
Shareholders .... NA

Business: The group formed for the purpose of acquiring, through a merger, capital stock exchange, asset acquisition or other similar business combination, one or more operating businesses in the technology, media or telecommunications industries. The group operates from United States.

Primary SIC and add'l.: 8732

CIK No: 0001323639

Owners: Lawrence J. Askowitz, Andrew M. Weiss/11.03%, Shlomo Kalish, Howard S. Balter/31.90%, Ilan M. Slasky/20.93%, Insiders/47.22%, The Baupost Group, L.L.C./9.93%, Entities affiliated with Fir Tree, Inc./8.96%

Financial Data: *Fiscal Year End*:12/31 *Latest Annual Data:* 3/31/2007

Year	Sales	Net Income
2007	NA	$5,378,000
2006	NA	-$4,255,000

Curr. Assets: $269,000 **Curr. Liab.:** $9,068,000
Plant, Equip.: $3,000 **Total Liab.:** $19,608,000 **Indic. Yr. Divd.:** NA
Total Assets: $52,610,000 **Net Worth:** $33,002,000 **Debt/ Equity:** NA

1st Centennial Bancorp

218 E State St., Redlands, CA, 92373; *PH:* 1-909-798-3611; *Fax:* 1-909-335-2363; *http://* www.1stcent.com

General - Incorporation .... CA
Employees 125
Auditor .... Hutchinson & Bloodgood LLP
Stk Agt .... U.S. Stock Transfer Corp
Counsel .... NA
DUNS No. .... NA

Stock- Price on:12/24/2007 .... $27.4
Stock Exchange .... OTC
Ticker Symbol .... FCEN
Outstanding Shares 4,840,000
E.P.S. $1.57
Shareholders .... NA

Business: The group's principal activity is to serve as a holding company for redlands, palomar and other banking or banking related subsidiaries. The group provides banking services in redlands, brea and surrounding communities, as well as small business administration loans to customers in san bernardino, los angeles and orange counties. The banking services include a broad range of deposit instruments like, checking, savings, money market and time certificates of deposit for both business and personal accounts. The group operates three full-service branch office in southern California,one in escondido, in san diego county and one in brea, in orange county. The other services include a credit card program for merchants, international banking services, commercial and standby letters of credit, cash management services, balance reporting, check reconciliation service, electronic funds transfer services, lock box and courier services.

Primary SIC and add'l.: 6022 6712

CIK No: 0001097081

Subsidiaries: Centennial Capital Trust I, Centennial Capital Trust II, Centennial Capital Trust III

Officers: Thomas E. Vessey/Dir., CEO, Pres./$668,739.00, Bob Pavlik/Sr. VP, Mgr. - Religious Lending Division, Joe Flores/VP, Regional Mgr. - Escondido, Wayne Stair/VP, Regional Mgr. - Redlands, Harry Miller/VP, Regional Mgr. - Brea, Bill Schroeder/VP, Regional Mgr. - Irwindale, Katherine Bailey/VP, Regional Mgr. - Temecula, Richard S. Levenson/Sr. VP, Jon Enochs/VP, HOA Division Mgr., Beth Sanders/CFO, Exec. VP/$311,237.00, Suzanne Dondanville/Sr. Management Exec. VP, COO/$344,230.00, John P. Lang/Exec. VP, Chief Credit Officer/$281,922.00, Susie Fierro/VP, Operations Administrator, Sheri Passerino/VP - Human Relations, Cliff Schoonover/Sr. VP, Mgr. - Real Estate Division *(16 Officers included in Index)*

Directors: Thomas E. Vessey/Dir., CEO, Pres., Patrick J. Meyer/Chmn., Bruce J. Bartells/Vice Chmn., Carole H. Beswick/Dir., Ronald J. Jeffrey/Dir., James R. Appleton/Dir., William A. McCalmon/Dir., Stan C. Weisser/Dir., Douglas F. Welebir/Dir., Larry Frank Jacinto/Dir.

Owners: Insiders/25.12%, Douglas F. Welebir/2.63%, Bruce J. Bartells/2.10%, Larry Jacinto/4.19%, Stanley C. Weisser/1.41%, Suzanne Dondanville/1.16%, Thomas E. Vessey/1.38%, Ronald J. Jeffrey/2.47%, James R. Appleton/1.72%, Carole H. Beswick/2.31%, Beth Sanders/2.68%, William A. McCalmon/1.91%, Patrick J. Meyer/2.79%

Financial Data: *Fiscal Year End*:12/31 *Latest Annual Data:* 03/31/2007

Year	Sales	Net Income
2007	NA	NA
2006	$43,767,000	$7,427,000
2005	$37,652,000	$5,083,000

Curr. Assets: $27,676,000 **Curr. Liab.:** $486,895,000
Plant, Equip.: $3,152,000 **Total Liab.:** $508,930,000 **Indic. Yr. Divd.:** NA
Total Assets: $551,127,000 **Net Worth:** $42,197,000 **Debt/ Equity:** 0.4338

1st Colonial Bancorp Inc

1040 Haddon Ave., Collingswood, NJ, 08108; *PH:* 1-856-858-1100; *Fax:* 1-856-858-9255; *http://* www.1stcolonial.com; *Email:* info@1stcolonial.com

General - Incorporation .... US
Employees .... NA
Auditor .... KPMG LLP
Stk Agt .... StockTrans, Inc.
Counsel .... NA
DUNS No. .... NA

Stock- Price on:12/24/2007 .... $8.25
Stock Exchange .... OTC
Ticker Symbol .... FCOB
Outstanding Shares 2,860,000
E.P.S. $0.29
Shareholders .... NA

Business: The group's principal activity is to provide commercial and consumer financial services to businesses and individuals. It is a holding company and operates through its wholly owned subsidiary, 1st colonial national bank. The bank's deposit services include business and individual demand and time deposit accounts, now accounts, money market accounts, individual retirement accounts and holiday accounts. The lending services include real estate loans, residential mortgage loans, home equity loans, lines of credit, auto loans and other credit products. The group also provides direct payroll and social security deposit services, bank-by-mail services, automated teller machine network, safe deposit boxes, night depository facilities, notary services and travelers checks. The operations are conducted through an office located in collingswood, New Jersey.

Primary SIC and add'l.: 6021 6712

CIK No: 0001168230

Subsidiaries: Scottsdale Diecast, Inc

Officers: Gerard M. Banmiller/Dir., CEO, Pres., James E. Strangfeld/Sr. Lending Officer, Exec. VP, Robert C. Faix/Sr. VP, CFO, Irene H. Clark/Sr. VP - Operations, Robert P. Hawkins/VP - Branch Administration

Directors: Gerard M. Banmiller/Dir., CEO, Pres., Linda M. Rohrer/Chmn., Mary R. Burke/Dir., Letitia G. Colombi/Dir., John J. Donnelly/Dir., Michael C. Haydinger/Dir., Stanley H. Molotsky/Dir., Thomas A. Clark/Dir., Gerald J. Defelicis/Dir., Eduardo F. Enriquez/Dir., Harrison Melstein/Dir.

Financial Data: *Fiscal Year End*:12/31 *Latest Annual Data:* 12/31/2004

Year	Sales	Net Income
2004	$5,706,000	$625,000
2003	$5,063,000	$500,000
2002	$4,287,000	$495,000

Curr. Assets:	$4,287,000	Curr. Liab.:	$118,458,000	
Plant, Equip.:	$949,000	Total Liab.:	$118,574,000	Indic. Yr. Divd.: NA
Total Assets:	$135,973,000	Net Worth:	$17,399,000	Debt/ Equity: NA

1st Constitution Bancorp

2650 Rte. 130, Cranbury, NJ, 08512; *PH:* 1-609-655-4500; *Fax:* 1-609-655-5653; *http://* www.1stconstitution.com; *Email:* main@1stconstitution.com

General - Incorporation	NJ	Stock- Price on:12/24/2007	$17.46
Employees	90	Stock Exchange	NDQ
Auditor	Grant Thornton LLP	Ticker Symbol	FCCY
Stk Agt	Registrar & Transfer Co	Outstanding Shares	3,730,000
Counsel	NA	E.P.S.	-$0.27
DUNS No.	NA	Shareholders	NA

Business: The group's principal activity is to provide commercial banking and related financial services through its subsidiary, 1st constitution bank. The group accepts demand, savings and time deposits and provides commercial and consumer and installment loans. The federal deposit insurance corporation insures the deposits up to applicable legal limits. Loans consist of term loans, lines of credit, equipment loans, receivable financing loans and loans for the acquisition, development and construction of residential subdivisions. The group serves through a main office and nine branches in the counties of middlesex, mercer and somerset counties, New Jersey. It mainly caters to individuals, small businesses and not-for-profit organizations.

Primary SIC and add'l.: 6712 6022

CIK No: 0001141807

Subsidiaries: 1st Constitution Bank, 1st Constitution Capital Trust I, 1st Constitution Investment Company, FCB Assets Holdings, Inc.

Officers: Robert F. Mangano/62/Dir., CEO, Pres./$968,728.00, William M. Rue/60/Dir., Corp. Sec., Joseph M. Reardon/55/Sr. VP, Treasurer/$250,838.00

Directors: Robert F. Mangano/62/Dir., CEO, Pres., Charles S. Crow/58/Chmn., David C. Reed/57/Dir., William M. Rue/60/Dir., Corp. Sec., Frank E. Walsh/41/Dir.

Owners: Charles S. Crow, Joseph M. Reardon, David C. Reed, Robert F. Mangano/4.84%, Insiders/14.12%, Frank E. Walsh/4.56%, William M. Rue/3.47%

Financial Data: Fiscal Year End:12/31 Latest Annual Data: 12/31/2006

Year	Sales	Net Income
2006	$29,996,000	$5,333,000
2005	$24,247,000	$4,560,000
2004	$19,573,000	$3,838,000

Curr. Assets:	$12,597,000	Curr. Liab.:	$316,569,000	P/E Ratio: 12.04
Plant, Equip.:	$3,034,000	Total Liab.:	$357,481,000	Indic. Yr. Divd.: NA
Total Assets:	$392,678,000	Net Worth:	$35,197,000	Debt/ Equity: 1.0645

1st Enterprise Bank CA

818 W 7th St. Ste. 220, Los Angeles, CA, 90017; *PH:* 1-213-430-7000; *http://* www.1stenterprisebank.com

General - Incorporation		Stock- Price on:12/24/2007	$19.75
Employees	NA	Stock Exchange	OTC
Auditor	NA	Ticker Symbol	FENB
Stk Agt	U.S. Stock Transfer Corp	Outstanding Shares	NA
Counsel	NA	E.P.S.	NA
DUNS No.	NA	Shareholders	NA

Business: The groups principal activity is to provide banking services. The services of the group include personal and business banking, deposit accounts, certificates of deposit, loans and online banking. The group operates from California in the United States.

Primary SIC and add'l.: 6029

CIK No:

Officers: John C. Black/Dir., CEO, Brian K. Horton/Dir., Pres., Jeffrey McGraa/Exec. VP, Chief Credit Officer, Reginald R. Prout/Sr. VP, CFO, Benjamin E. Loveless/Sr. VP, Dir. - Operations, David Kohn/VP - Los Angeles Region, Keith Cerwinski/Sr. VP - Los Angeles Region, Mark Cislo/VP - Los Angeles Region, David Plourde/VP - Orange County Region, Matt West/Sr. VP - Orange County Region, Marlon Osorto/VP - Operations, Christine Mesropyan/New Accounting Specialist - Customer Service, Sylvia Longoria/Operations Officer - Customer Service, Gabriel Gomez/Operations Officer - Customer Service, Suzie Flores/Sr. Operations Specialist - Customer Service *(16 Officers included in Index)*

Directors: John C. Black/Dir., CEO, David C. Holman/Chmn., Frank Ferri/Dir., Brian K. Horton/Dir., Pres., Jeffrey J. Leitzinger/Dir., Charles Beaureguard/Dir., Adriana Boeka/Dir., Peter Csato/Dir., Jeffrey Levine/Dir., Brian Stone/Dir., Richard A. Trueblood/Dir.

1st Franklin Financial Corp

213 E Tugalo St., Toccoa, GA, 30577; *PH:* 1-706-886-7571; *Fax:* 1-706-886-7953; *http://* www.1ffc.com

General - Incorporation	GA	Stock- Price on:12/24/2007	$16
Employees	49	Stock Exchange	NA
Auditor	Deloitte & Touche LLP	Ticker Symbol	NA
Stk Agt	NA	Outstanding Shares	1,680,000
Counsel	Jones Day	E.P.S.	$0.50
DUNS No.	04-583-5923	Shareholders	NA

Business: The group's principle activity is to provide consumer finance to individuals for short periods and first and second mortgage loans on real estate for long periods. The group acquires and services direct cash loans, real estate loans and sales finance contracts through 190 branch offices. The business is operated through 104 branch offices in Georgia, 32 in Alabama, 32 in South Carolina, 19 in Mississippi and 16 in Louisiana. The group also writes credit insurance as an agent for a nonaffiliated company specializing in such insurance. Two of group's subsidiaries reinsure the life, the accident and health and the property insurance written by the group.

Primary SIC and add'l.: 6331 6153 6141 6321

CIK No: 0000038723

Subsidiaries: Frandisco Life Insurance Company of Georgia, Frandisco Property and Casualty Insurance Company, Franklin Securities, Inc., T & T Corporation

Officers: Ben F. Cheek/71/Chmn., CEO, Roger A. Guimond/53/Dir., CFO, Exec. VP, Virginia C. Herring/44/Pres., Lynn E. Cox/50/VP, Sec., Treasurer, Michael C. Haynie/53/Exec. VP - Human Resources, Karen S. Lovern/49/Exec. VP - Strategic, Organization, Michael J. Culpepper/COO, Exec. VP

Directors: Ben F. Cheek/71/Chmn., CEO, Ben F. Cheek/46/Vice Chmn., Keith D. Watson/50/Dir., Jack D. Stovall/71/Dir., Robert E. Thompson/75/Dir., Roger A. Guimond/53/Dir., CFO, Exec. VP, John G. Sample/51/Dir., Dean C. Scarborough/53/Dir.

Owners: Virginia C. Herring/11.00%, Ben F. Cheek/10.59%, Insiders/89.41%, Virginia C. Herring/10.59%, Ben F. Cheek/11.00%, Insiders/0.34%, David W. Cheek/10.59%, Ben F. Cheek, Ben F. Cheek/68.24%

Financial Data: Fiscal Year End:12/31 Latest Annual Data: 12/31/2006

Year	Sales	Net Income
2006	$19,934,000	$1,357,000
2005	$16,016,000	$1,240,000
2004	$14,830,000	$673,000

Curr. Assets:	$8,949,000	Curr. Liab.:	$231,179,000	P/E Ratio: 20.78
Plant, Equip.:	$4,492,000	Total Liab.:	$305,888,000	Indic. Yr. Divd.: $0.360
Total Assets:	$332,039,000	Net Worth:	$25,746,000	Debt/ Equity: 2.7266

1st Independence Financial Group Inc

8620 Biggin Hill Ln., Louisville, KY, 40250; *PH:* 1-502-897-5880; *Fax:* 1-502-897-9208; *http://* www.1stindependence.com; *Email:* bank@1stindependence.com

General - Incorporation	DE	Stock- Price on:12/24/2007	$16.7
Employees	85	Stock Exchange	NDQ
Auditor	BKD LLP	Ticker Symbol	FIFG
Stk Agt	NA	Outstanding Shares	1,990,000
Counsel	NA	E.P.S.	$0.47
DUNS No.	NA	Shareholders	NA

Business: The group's principal activity is to provide banking services. The group is the holding company of first financial bank, a federally chartered stock savings bank and for citizens financial bank inc, a state-chartered commercial bank. First financial bank operates savings bank business, attracting deposit accounts from the general public and using those deposits to originate and invest in loans secured by one to four family residential real estate, non-residential real estate, and commercial loans. Citizens financial bank operates as a commercial bank, attracting deposit accounts from the general public and using these deposits, to originate residential and non-residential, commercial and consumer loans.

Primary SIC and add'l.: 6035 6712 6022

CIK No: 0000946738

Subsidiaries: 1st Independence Bank, Inc., Harrodsburg Statutory Trust I, Independence Bancorp Statutory Trust I

Officers: Alan D. Shepard/46/Exec. VP, Chief Credit Officer

Owners: Lowell H. Wainwright, Matthew C. Chalfant/2.90%, William N. White/1.90%, Stephen R. Manecke/1.10%, Tontine Financial Partners, L.P./8.90%, Insiders/17.50%, Thomas Les Letton/1.20%, 1st Independence Employee Stock Ownership/7.90%, Charles L. Moore/4.10%, Jack L. Coleman, Dudley W. Shryock, Ronald L. Receveur/2.20%

Financial Data: Fiscal Year End:12/31 Latest Annual Data: 12/31/2006

Year	Sales	Net Income
2006	$24,381,000	$1,940,000
2005	$25,559,000	$4,481,000
2004	$4,328,000	$240,000

Curr. Assets:	$27,568,000	Curr. Liab.:	$292,224,000	P/E Ratio: 31.51
Plant, Equip.:	$8,322,000	Total Liab.:	$302,503,000	Indic. Yr. Divd.: $0.320
Total Assets:	$342,806,000	Net Worth:	$40,303,000	Debt/ Equity: 0.5028

1st NRG Corp

Formerly: Naptau Gold Corp
1941 Lake Whatcom Blvd, Ste. 212, Bellingham, WA, 98229; *PH:* 1-360-384-4390

General - Incorporation	DE	Stock- Price on:12/24/2007	NA
Employees	NA	Stock Exchange	OTC
Auditor	Peterson Sullivan PLLC	Ticker Symbol	NPTUE
Stk Agt	Liberty Transfer Co	Outstanding Shares	NA
Counsel	NA	E.P.S.	NA
DUNS No.	NA	Shareholders	NA

Business: The groups principal activities include acquiring and developing projects related to the base metal sectors of the mining industry and finding opportunities in the hospitality, real estate, and hotel sectors. The group operates from the United States and Canada.

Primary SIC and add'l.: 1041

CIK No: 0000949268

Officers: J. Greig/Chmn., Chief Strategic Officer, CEO, Edward D. Renyk/Dir., Sec., Treasurer, CFO

Directors: J. Greig/Chmn., Chief Strategic Officer, CEO, Edward D. Renyk/Dir., Sec., Treasurer, CFO, Larry Fix/Dir.

Owners: Edward D. Renyk/10.00%, Insiders/75.56%, J. Greig/65.48%, Larry Fix

1st Source Corp

PO Box 1602, South Bend, IN, 46601; *PH:* 1-574-235-2000; *http://* www.1stsource.com

General - Incorporation	IN	Stock- Price on:12/24/2007	$24.82
Employees	1,200	Stock Exchange	NDQ
Auditor	Ernst & Young LLP	Ticker Symbol	SRCE
Stk Agt	NA	Outstanding Shares	22,510,000
Counsel	Barnes & Thornburg	E.P.S.	$1.32
DUNS No.	06-157-4109	Shareholders	NA

Business: The group's principal activities are to provide a broad range of commercial banking, personal banking and trust services through its banking subsidiary 1st source bank. It provides consumer and commercial banking services through its lending operations, retail branches and fee based operations. The group also provides various depository services and financing services. It finances automobile fleets in the rental and leasing industries, privately owned aircraft for businesses and individuals, heavy duty

trucks, step vans, construction and environmental equipment. Other services offered include trust services, mortgage loan services, general property and casualty insurance agency services. The operations are conducted through a network of 60 branches in 15 counties located in Indiana and Michigan. It offers banking services through 68 automatic teller machines, bank by phone services and on-line personal and business financial products.

Primary SIC and add'l.: 6022 6712

CIK No: 0000034782

Subsidiaries: 1st Source Bank, 1st Source Capital Corporation, 1st Source Capital Trust II, 1st Source Capital Trust III, 1st Source Capital Trust IV, 1st Source Corporation Investment Advisors, Inc, 1st Source Funding, LLC, 1st Source Insurance, Inc, 1st Source Intermediate Holding, LLC, 1st Source Leasing, Inc., 1st Source Specialty Finance, Inc, Michigan Transportation Finance Corporation, SFG Commercial Aircraft Leasing, Inc, SFG Equipment Leasing Corporation I, SFG Equipment Leasing, Inc 16 Subsidiaries included in the Index

Officers: Christopher J. Murphy/61/Chmn., CEO, Pres./$1,555,290.00, Michael T. Arnett/City Pres., VP - Personal Banking Group, Wellington D. Jones/63/Dir., Exec. VP/$548,811.00, Robert W. Hirsch/Employee Benefit Administrator II - Retirement Plan Services, John Borkowski/Small Business Banking Officer - Personal Banking Division, William B. Burton/Regional Mgr., VP - Personal Banking Group, Joe B. Hunting/City Pres., Assist. VP - Community Banking Division, Richard Q. Stifel/66/Exec. VP, Chief Credit Officer - Commercial Banking Division/$466,613.00, Sean Kearns/Relationship Mgr., VP - Commercial Banking, Robert L. Jamieson/Mgr. - Certified Relationship, VP - Commercial Banking Division, Joe Kuzmitz/Sr. VP - Commercial Banking Division, Mgr. - Business Banking Group, Mgr. - Certified Relationship, Thomas J. Brown/Employee Benefits Administration III, Eugene Cavanaugh/Mgr. - Commercial Mortgage, VP - Commercial Banking Division, Julianna Herring/Small Business Banking Officer - Small Business Banking Division, Connie K. Lemler/Commercial Banking Regional Pres., VP - Ag Division *(61 Officers included in Index)*

Directors: Christopher J. Murphy/61/Chmn., CEO, Pres., Wellington D. Jones/63/Dir., Exec. VP, John B. Griffith/50/Dir., Sr. VP, General Counsel, Sec., Lawrence E. Hiler/62/Dir., Rex Martin/56/Dir., Timothy K. Ozark/58/Dir., John F. Affleck-Graves/57/Dir., Terry L. Gerber/67/Dir., William P. Johnson/65/Dir., Craig A. Kapson/57/Dir., John T. Phair/58/Dir., Mark D. Schwabero/55/Dir., Daniel B. Fitzpatrick/50/Dir., Dane A. Miller/62/Dir., Toby S. Wilt/63/Dir.

Owners: Family Trust/7.40%, Wendy W. Meyers/4.80%, Insiders/82.90%, Cyril J. Welter/3.40%, Wayne B. Welter/5.50%, William J. Welter Irrevocable Trust/22.30%, Charles P. Welter/3.20%, Donna D. Welter/36.30%, First Bankers Trust Services, Inc./8.50%

Financial Data: *Fiscal Year End:*12/31 *Latest Annual Data:* 12/31/2006

Year	Sales	Net Income
2006	$285,579,000	$39,297,000
2005	$237,065,000	$33,751,000
2004	$218,889,000	$24,965,000

Curr. Assets:	$183,110,000	**Curr. Liab.:**	$3,335,628,000	**P/E Ratio:**	14.95
Plant, Equip.:	$113,636,000	**Total Liab.:**	$3,438,411,000	**Indic. Yr. Divd.:**	$0.560
Total Assets:	$3,807,315,000	**Net Worth:**	$368,904,000	**Debt/ Equity:**	0.2736

21st Century Holding Co

3661 West Oakland Park Blvd., Lauderdale Lakes, FL, 33311; *PH:* 1-954-581-9993; *Fax:* 1-954-316-9201; *http://* www.21stcenturyholding.com

General - Incorporation	FL	**Stock**- Price on:12/24/2007	$11.1674
Employees	122	Stock Exchange	NDQ
Auditor	De Meo, Young, Mcgrath	Ticker Symbol	TCHC
Stk Agt	Registrar & Transfer Co	Outstanding Shares	8,020,000
Counsel	Broad & Cassel	E.P.S.	$1.12
DUNS No.	NA	Shareholders	NA

Business: The group's principal activities are to provide insurance underwriting, distribution and claims services through its subsidiaries. The operations are carried on through two segments insurance and financing. The insurance segment sells primarily standard and nonstandard personal automobile insurance, as well as homeowners and mobile home property and casualty insurance and includes substantially all aspects of the insurance, distribution and claims process. The financing segment offers premium financing and consumer loans to its own and third party insurers through its wholly owned subsidiary. The products are marketed and distributed in south Florida, through a network of 23 agencies, 40 franchised agencies and approximately 125 independent agents.

Primary SIC and add'l.: 6719 6331

CIK No: 0001069996

Subsidiaries: American Vehicle Insurance Company, Assurance Managing General Agents Inc., Attorney on Call Inc., Fed USA Inc., Federated Agency Group Inc., Federated Funding Corporation, Federated National Insurance Company, Federated Premium Finance Inc., FedFirst Corp., Reliable Towing and Rental Inc., RPA Financial Corporation, Superior Adjusting Inc.

Officers: Edward J. Lawson/Chmn., CEO/$341,803.00, Rebecca L. Campillo/Corp. Sec., Peter J. Prygelski/CFO, Gordon J. Jennings/Chief Accounting Officer/$153,912.00, Stephen C. Young/Pres.

Directors: Edward J. Lawson/Chmn., CEO, Bruce Simberg/Dir., Richard W. Wilcox/Dir., Charles B. Hart/Dir., Carl Dorf/Dir., Michael H. Braun/Dir., Anthony C. Krayer/Dir.

Owners: Richard W. Wilcox, Peter J. Prygelski, Edward J. Lawson/9.90%, Charles B. Hart, Insiders/15.40%, Bruce F. Simberg/2.10%, Carl Dorf/1.00%, Gordon J. Jennings, Michele V. Lawson/9.90%, Michael H. Braun, First Wilshire Securities Management, Inc./10.50%

Financial Data: *Fiscal Year End:*12/31 *Latest Annual Data:* 12/31/2006

Year	Sales	Net Income
2006	$103,915,000	$13,896,000
2005	$94,669,000	$12,116,000
2004	$76,571,000	-$10,858,000

Curr. Assets:	$64,853,000	**Curr. Liab.:**	$21,862,000	**P/E Ratio:**	8.86
Plant, Equip.:	$1,296,000	**Total Liab.:**	$145,941,000	**Indic. Yr. Divd.:**	$0.720
Total Assets:	$212,134,000	**Net Worth:**	$66,193,000	**Debt/ Equity:**	0.0468

21st Century Insurance Group

6301 Owensmouth Ave., Ste. 700, Woodland Hills, CA, 91367; *PH:* 1-818-704-3700; *http://* www.21st.com

General - Incorporation	CA	**Stock**- Price on:12/24/2007	$21.76
Employees	2,900	Stock Exchange	NA
Auditor	PricewaterhouseCoopers LLP	Ticker Symbol	NA
Stk Agt	American Stock Transfer & Trust Co.	Outstanding Shares	87,920,000
Counsel	Cardinal Investment Advisors, LLC	E.P.S.	$1.01
DUNS No.	06-668-6395	Shareholders	NA

Business: The group's principal activities are direct marketing and underwriting of private passenger automobile, homeowners and personal umbrella insurance. The group offers insurance coverage for private passenger automobiles which includes bodily injury liability, property damage, medical payments, uninsured and underinsured motorist, rental reimbursement, uninsured motorist property damage and collision deductible, towing, comprehensive and collision. The personal umbrella policy provides liability coverage with a limit of $1,000,000 in excess of the underlying automobile and homeowners liability coverage. The group operates in the United States.

Primary SIC and add'l.: 6719 6331

CIK No: 0000100331

Subsidiaries: 20th Century Insurance Services, Inc, 21st Century Casualty Company, 21st Century Insurance Company, 21st Century Insurance Company of the Southwest, i21 Insurance Services

Owners: Michael T. Ray, Jeffrey L. Hayman, Insiders, Steven J. Bensinger, American Home Assurance Company, American Union Insurance Company, Insiders, Scott R. Foster, John B. DeNault, Keith W. Renken, Steven P. Erwin, Michael J. Cassanego, National Union Fire Insurance Company, Commerce & Industry Insurance Company, Insiders *(25 Owners included in Index)*

Financial Data: *Fiscal Year End:*12/31 *Latest Annual Data:* 12/31/2006

Year	Sales	Net Income
2006	$1,375,287,000	$97,228,000
2005	$1,419,128,000	$87,426,000
2004	$1,383,332,000	$88,225,000

Curr. Assets:	$170,547,000	**Curr. Liab.:**	$43,611,000	**P/E Ratio:**	21.54
Plant, Equip.:	$174,247,000	**Total Liab.:**	$1,053,148,000	**Indic. Yr. Divd.:**	NA
Total Assets:	$1,951,697,000	**Net Worth:**	$898,549,000	**Debt/ Equity:**	0.1211

24/7 Real Media Inc

132 W 31st St., New York, NY, 10001; *PH:* 1-212-231-7100; *http://* www.247realmedia.com

General - Incorporation	DE	**Stock**- Price on:12/24/2007	$11.7
Employees	390	Stock Exchange	NA
Auditor	Goldstein Golub Kessler LLP	Ticker Symbol	NA
Stk Agt	Bank of New York	Outstanding Shares	51,000,000
Counsel	NA	E.P.S.	-$0.02
DUNS No.	01-745-2397	Shareholders	NA

Business: The group's principal activity is to provide interactive marketing and technology solutions. It operates in two segments: integrated media solutions and technology solutions. The integrated media solutions segment provides customized online marketing strategies that combine premier brands, content targeting and mass reach. The group also provides search engine optimization, online media representation which helps to connect Internet marketers with the consumers. Technology solutions provides advertising delivery and management for Web sites, ad agencies and advertisers; integrated marketing solutions which includes audience management and e mail delivery service. The group has operations in the United States, Canada and Europe. The group acquired certain assets of insight first inc and disposed certain assets of ipromotions inc in 2003. On 08-Jan-2004, the group acquired real media Korea ltd. On 19-Aug-2004, the group acquired decide interactive.

Primary SIC and add'l.: 7319 7311

CIK No: 0001062195

Subsidiaries: 24/7 Canada,Inc., 24/7 Media Canada Holding Company, 24/7 Real Media Europe Holding S.A., 24/7 Real Media France SARL, 24/7 Real Media Germany Gmbh, 24/7 Real Media Italy S.R.L., 24/7 Real Media Pty Limited, 24/7 Real Media Technology S.A., 24/7 Real Media UK Ltd, 24/7 Real Media US,Inc., 24/7 Real Media,Inc., Decide Holdings Pty Limited, K.k. 24-7 Search, Real Media Scandinavia, Real Media Spain

Officers: David J. Moore/Chmn., CEO, Jonathan Hsu/Exec. VP, CFO, COO, Jae Woo Chung/Pres., Mark E. Moran/Sr. VP, General Counsel, Ari Bluman/Sr. VP - North American Sales, Operations, Jack Smith/Sr. VP - Product Strategy, Oleg Vishnepolsky/CTO, Anthony Borruso/Chief Infrastructure Officer, Ian Leuchars/Sr. VP - Search Marketing Services

Directors: David J. Moore/Chmn., CEO, Robert J. Perkins/Dir., Tony Schmitz/Dir., Valentine J. Zammit/61/Dir., Arnie Semsky/Dir., Brian Silva/Dir.

Owners: PubliGroupe USA Holdings/4.92%, Driehaus Capital Management LLC and Richard H. Driehaus/8.19%, Valentine J. Zammit, Robert J. Perkins, Tony Schmitz, Pequot Capital Management, LLC/6.29%, T. Rowe Price Associates, Inc./11.88%, Brian Silva, Arnie Semsky, Wellington Management Company, LLP/9.76%, Insiders/6.21%, Jonathan K. Hsu, Mark E. Moran/1.34%, David J. Moore/3.60%, Mellon Financial Corporation/6.12%

Financial Data: *Fiscal Year End:*12/31 *Latest Annual Data:* 12/31/2006

Year	Sales	Net Income
2006	$200,243,000	-$8,622,000
2005	$139,794,000	$38,000
2004	$85,255,000	-$3,155,000

Curr. Assets:	$117,567,000	**Curr. Liab.:**	$63,051,000		
Plant, Equip.:	$8,072,000	**Total Liab.:**	$71,327,000	**Indic. Yr. Divd.:**	NA
Total Assets:	$176,658,000	**Net Worth:**	$103,658,000	**Debt/ Equity:**	0.0696

24Holdings Inc

Cyberia House, Church St., Basingstoke, RG21 7QN ; *PH:* 973-635-4047; *http://* www.24store.com

General - Incorporation	DE	**Stock**- Price on:12/24/2007	$0.51
Employees	NA	Stock Exchange	OTC
Auditor	Sherb & Co. LLP	Ticker Symbol	TWFH
Stk Agt	American Stock Transfer & Trust Co.	Outstanding Shares	1,240,000
Counsel	NA	E.P.S.	-$0.04
DUNS No.	19-139-6266	Shareholders	NA

Business: The group's principle activity is to provide computer hardware, software and other electronic products primarily to the business sector. The group operates from United States.

Primary SIC and add'l.: 5731 5734 6719

CIK No: 0001025315

Subsidiaries: 24Store

Officers: Arnold P. Kling/49/Dir., Pres., Treasurer, Principal Executive Officer, Kirk M. Warshaw/49/Dir., CFO, Sec.

Directors: Arnold P. Kling/49/Dir., Pres., Treasurer, Principal Executive Officer, Kirk M. Warshaw/49/Dir., CFO, Sec.

Owners: Arnold P. Kling, Moyo Partners, LLC, Insiders, Kirk M. Warshaw, R&R Biotech Partners, LLC

Financial Data: *Fiscal Year End:*12/31 *Latest Annual Data:* 12/31/2006

Year	Sales	Net Income
2006	NA	-$76,000
2005	NA	-$128,000
2004	NA	-$486,000

Curr. Assets:	$30,000	**Curr. Liab.:**	$15,000		
Plant, Equip.:	NA	**Total Liab.:**	$15,000	**Indic. Yr. Divd.:**	NA
Total Assets:	$30,000	**Net Worth:**	$15,000	**Debt/ Equity:**	NA

3COM Corp

350 Campus Dr., Marlborough, MA, 01752; ***PH:*** 1-508-323-5000; ***Fax:*** 1-508-323-1111; ***http://*** www.3com.com; ***Email:*** investor_relations@3com.com

General - Incorporation .... DE
Employees 5,572
Auditor .... Deloitte & Touche LLP
Stk Agt...... American Stock Transfer & Trust Co.
Counsel .... NA
DUNS No. 09-995-6906

Stock- Price on:12/24/2007 .... $4.35
Stock Exchange .... NDQ
Ticker Symbol .... COMS
Outstanding Shares 398,730,000
E.P.S .... -$0.24
Shareholders .... NA

Business: The group's principal activity is to provide data and voice networking products and solutions as well as support and customer services to private and public enterprises. The group's products include LAN switches, ip telephony, network security, routers and gateways, wireless LAN, network jack and intellijacktm switches, connectivity products,network management software and other customer support services. The major customers include ingram micro, inc. And tech data corporation.

Primary SIC and add'l.: 3661 3669 7373

CIK No: 0000738076

Subsidiaries: 3Com APR Pte Ltd., 3Com Europe Ltd, Hangzhou Huawei-3Com Technology Co., Ltd, Huawei-3Com Co., Ltd

Officers: Edgar Masri/Dir., CEO, Pres./$4,986,498.00, Jerry Kelly/CIO, Jay Zager/CFO, Exec. VP, Shusheng Zheng/COO - H3C, Daniel Beck/Sr. VP - Operations, Robert Dechant/Sr. VP - Worldwide Sales, Marketing, Neal Goldman/Sr. VP - Management Services, General Counsel, Sec./$2,287,313.00, James Hamilton/Pres. - Tippingpoint Division/$1,495,788.00, Marc Willebeek-Lemair/CTO, Sr. VP - Product Operations/$2,117,784.00

Directors: Edgar Masri/Dir., CEO, Pres., Eric A. Benhamou/Chmn., Robert Mao/Dir., Dominique Trempont/Dir., Gary Dicamillo/Dir., James R. Long/Dir., Raj Reddy/Dir., Paul G. Yovovich/Dir.

Owners: Jay Zager, Dominique Trempont, Insiders/3.10%, Entities and individuals related to Citadel Limited Partnership/9.70%, James R. Long, Raj Reddy, Donald M. Halsted, Edgar Masri, Entities related to Barclays Global/5.00%, Eric A. Benhamou/1.20%, Gary T. DiCamillo, Shusheng Zheng, Marc Willebeek-LeMair, James Hamilton, Neal D. Goldman

Financial Data: ***Fiscal Year End:***06/02 ***Latest Annual Data:*** 06/01/2007

Year	Sales	Net Income
2007	$1,267,481,000	-$88,589,000
2006	$794,807,000	-$100,675,000
2005	$651,244,000	-$195,686,000

Curr. Assets:	$1,249,345,000	**Curr. Liab.:**	$471,281,000		
Plant, Equip.:	$89,109,000	**Total Liab.:**	$485,069,000	**Indic. Yr. Divd.:**	NA
Total Assets:	$1,861,361,000	**Net Worth:**	$1,202,362,000	**Debt/ Equity:**	NA

3D Systems Corp

333 Three D Systems Cir., Rock Hill, SC, 29730; ***PH:*** 1-803-326-4080; ***http://*** www.3dsystems.com; ***Email:*** moreinfo@3dsystems.com

General - Incorporation .... DE
Employees 351
Auditor .... BDO Seidman LLP
Stk Agt .... U.S. Stock Transfer Corp
Counsel .... Akin, Gump, Strauss, Hauer & Feld LLP
DUNS No. 17-357-4161

Stock- Price on:12/24/2007 .... $23.42
Stock Exchange .... NDQ
Ticker Symbol .... TDSC
Outstanding Shares 19,140,000
E.P.S .... -$0.71
Shareholders .... NA

Business: The group's principal activity is to design, manufacture, market and support solid imaging systems and related materials. Solid imaging systems are designed to rapidly produce 3-dimensional physical objects from digital data using computer aided design and manufacturing, or computer-aided design, software utilities and related computer applications. The products include the mjm (multi-jet modeling) product line, the sla(R) (stereolithography apparatus) product line, the sls(R) (selective laser sintering) product line, the dcm (direct composite manufacturing) product line, and the accura(R) material line. The customers include major corporations in a broad range of industries including manufacturers of automotive, aerospace, computer, electronic, consumer, appliance, footwear, toy, power tool and medical products.

Primary SIC and add'l.: 7373 7372

CIK No: 0000910638

Subsidiaries: 3D Canada Company, 3D Capital Corporation, 3D European Holdings Ltd., 3D Holdings, LLC, 3D Systems Asia Pacific, Ltd., 3D Systems Europe Ltd., 3D Systems France SARL, 3D Systems GmbH, 3D Systems Italia S.r.l., 3D Systems Japan K.K., 3D Systems S.A., 3D Systems Solid Imaging S.A., 3D Systems,Inc., OptoFormLLC

Officers: Abe N. Reichental/Dir., CEO, Pres./$1,279,654.00, Gerald J. Pribanic/64/Interim VP, Charles W. Hull/Co - Founder, CTO, Exec. VP/$284,121.00, Kevin P. McAlea/VP, Robert M. Grace/VP, General Counsel, Sec., Ray R. Saunders/59/VP, Cary J. Love/43/VP, Stephen M. Goddard/VP, Brian K. Fraser/VP, William Tennison/VP, Controller, Chief Accounting Officer, Damon Gregoire/CFO

Directors: Abe N. Reichental/Dir., CEO, Pres., Walter G. Loewenbaum/Dir., Jim D. Kever/Dir., Daniel S. Van Riper/Dir., Kevin S. Moore/Dir., Miriam V. Gold/Dir.

Owners: Insiders/26.90%, The Clark Estates, Inc./11.60%, Fred R. Jones, St. Denis J. Villere & Company, L.L.C/17.10%, Walter G. Loewenbaum/7.90%, Kevin S. Moore/11.70%, Daniel S. Van Riper, Kevin P. McAlea, Richard C. Spalding, Abraham N. Reichental/2.90%, T. Rowe Price Associates, Inc./14.10%, Jim D. Kever, Robert M. Grace, Miriam V. Gold, Charles W. Hull/2.30% *(16 Owners included in Index)*

Financial Data: ***Fiscal Year End:***12/31 ***Latest Annual Data:*** 12/31/2006

Year	Sales	Net Income
2006	$134,820,000	-$29,280,000
2005	$139,670,000	$10,083,000
2004	$125,379,000	$2,561,000

Curr. Assets:	$86,628,000	**Curr. Liab.:**	$69,293,000		
Plant, Equip.:	$23,763,000	**Total Liab.:**	$96,525,000	**Indic. Yr. Divd.:**	NA
Total Assets:	$166,194,000	**Net Worth:**	$69,669,000	**Debt/ Equity:**	0.3522

3M Co

3M Ctr., St. Paul, MN, 55144; ***PH:*** 1-888-364-3577; ***Fax:*** 1-651-733-9973; ***http://*** www.mmm.com

General - Incorporation .... DE
Employees 75,333
Auditor .... PricewaterhouseCoopers LLP
Stk Agt .... Wells Fargo Bank Minnesota N.A
Counsel .... NA
DUNS No. 00-617-3082

Stock- Price on:12/24/2007 .... $87.41
Stock Exchange .... NYSE
Ticker Symbol .... MMM
Outstanding Shares 720,200,000
E.P.S $5.99
Shareholders .... NA

Business: The groups principle activity is to provide innovative products.The group's products include 3M(TM)computer filters, and wall display and projectors. The group's products are sold under the brand names Scotch(R), Scotch Brite(R) and Scotch guard (TM).The group operates from United States.

Primary SIC and add'l.: 3996 3993 2821 2891 5085 3842 3291

CIK No: 0000066740

Subsidiaries: 3M (East) A.G., 3M (New Zealand) Limited, 3M (Schweiz) A.G., 3M A/S, 3M Argentina S.A.C.I.F.I.A., 3M Australia Pty. Limited, 3M Belgium S.A./N.V., 3M Canada Company, 3M China Limited, 3M Corporate Services B.V., 3M Deutschland GmbH, 3M do Brasil Limitada, 3M Espana, S.A., 3m Espe Ag, 3M Europe S.A. 63 Subsidiaries included in the Index

Officers: George W. Buckley/Chmn., CEO, Pres./$16,578,100.00, Thomas A. Boardman/Assist. Sec., Moe S. Nozari/66/Exec. VP - Consumer, Office Business/$4,329,041.00, Hak Cheol Shin/51/Exec. VP - Industrial, Transportation Business, Jean Lobey/56/Exec. VP - Safety, Security, Protection Services Business, Brad T. Sauer/49/Exec. VP - Health Care Business, Herman E. Nauwelaerts/VP - Europe, Middle East, Africa, Joe E. Harlan/49/Exec. VP - Electro, Communications Business, Janet L. Yeomans/VP, Treasurer, Robert D. MacDonald/58/Sr. VP - Marketing, Sales, Richard F. Ziegler/59/Sr. VP - Legal Affairs, General Counsel/$2,306,576.00, Frederick J. Palensky/58/Exec. VP - Research, Development/$2,930,959.00, Inge G. Thulin/55/Exec. VP - International Operations, John K. Woodworth/Sr. VP - Corporate Supply Chain Operations, Steven J. Beilke/Assist. Sec. *(25 Officers included in Index)*

Directors: George W. Buckley/Chmn., CEO, Pres., Kevin W. Sharer/Dir., Linda G. Alvarado/Dir., Vance D. Coffman/Dir., Michael L. Eskew/Dir., James W. Farrell/Dir., Edward M. Liddy/Dir., Aulana L. Peters/Dir., Rozanne L. Ridgway/Dir., Robert S. Morrison/Dir., Herbert L. Henkel/60/Dir.

Owners: Linda G. Alvarado, Edward M. Liddy, Patrick D. Campbell, Robert S. Morrison, Vance D. Coffman, Michael L. Eskew, Richard F. Ziegler, Moe S. Nozari, Rozanne L. Ridgway, Insiders, State Street Bank and Trust/7.50%, Aulana L. Peters, James W. Farrell, George W. Buckley, Kevin W. Sharer *(16 Owners included in Index)*

Financial Data: ***Fiscal Year End:***12/31 ***Latest Annual Data:*** 12/31/2006

Year	Sales	Net Income
2006	$22,923,000,000	$3,851,000,000
2005	$21,167,000,000	$3,199,000,000
2004	$20,011,000,000	$2,990,000,000

Curr. Assets:	$8,946,000,000	**Curr. Liab.:**	$7,323,000,000		
Plant, Equip.:	$5,907,000,000	**Total Liab.:**	$11,057,000,000	**Indic. Yr. Divd.:**	$1.920
Total Assets:	$21,294,000,000	**Net Worth:**	$9,959,000,000	**Debt/ Equity:**	NA

3Si Holdings Inc

19 N Tejon, Ste. 100, Colorado Springs, CO, 80903; ***PH:*** 1-719-302-3500; ***Fax:*** 1-719-623-0162; ***http://*** www.3si.com; ***Email:*** info@3si.com

General - Incorporation .... WY
Employees .... NA
Auditor .... Gordon Hughes & Banks LLP
Stk Agt .... American Securities T & T Inc.
Counsel .... NA
DUNS No. 03-753-8378

Stock- Price on:12/24/2007 .... $0.015
Stock Exchange .... OTC
Ticker Symbol .... TSIH
Outstanding Shares .... NA
E.P.S .... NA
Shareholders .... NA

Business: The group's principal activities are to develop and distribute Internet-based customer support products and provide application services. The group is comprised of two entities. Ikew inc. Provides Internet-based content management, community portal and support capabilities commonly known as isupport. 3si inc serves as a master reseller and application service provider for the group's family of products. The products are sold under the ikew family product name and are designed to provide maximum distribution, ease of use, accessibility, immediate response time, scalability and a rapid development cycle. The services provided by the group help the customers to create, manage and exchange information as they participate and compete in the global marketplace.

Primary SIC and add'l.: 7373 6719 7372

CIK No: 0000317889

Subsidiaries: 3Si Inc., KEWi.net Inc.

Financial Data: ***Fiscal Year End:***06/30 ***Latest Annual Data:*** 6/30/2005

Year	Sales	Net Income
2005	$321,000	-$706,000
2004	$1,100,000	-$70,000
2003	$1,148,000	-$63,000

Curr. Assets:	$17,000	**Curr. Liab.:**	$520,000		
Plant, Equip.:	$77,000	**Total Liab.:**	$865,000	**Indic. Yr. Divd.:**	NA
Total Assets:	$94,000	**Net Worth:**	-$771,000	**Debt/ Equity:**	NA

4 Kids Entertainment Inc

1414 Ave. of the Americas, New York, NY, 10019; ***PH:*** 1-212-758-7666; ***http://*** www.4kidsentertainmentinc.com

General - Incorporation .... NY
Employees 209
Auditor .... Eisner LLP
Stk Agt .... Continental Stock Transfer & Trust Co
Counsel .... Kaye, Scholer LLP
DUNS No. 05-674-5367

Stock- Price on:12/24/2007 .... $15.65
Stock Exchange .... NYSE
Ticker Symbol .... KDE
Outstanding Shares 13,180,000
E.P.S $1.32
Shareholders .... NA

Business: The group's principal activity is to license the commercial rights to television and film properties, personalities and product concepts. The group operates through three segments: licensing, television and film production/distribution and advertising media and broadcast. Licensing provides licensing of properties including toys, electronic games, trading cards, food, toiletries, apparel,

housewares, footwear and publishing rights. Television and film production/distribution produces and adapts animated and live-action television programs and theatrical motion pictures for distribution to the television, home video and theatrical markets. Advertising media and broadcast provides media planning and buying services for both print and broadcast media.

Primary SIC and add'l.: 7812 6794

CIK No: 0000058592

Subsidiaries: 4Kids Ad Sales, Inc., 4Kids Entertainment Home Video, Inc., 4Kids Entertainment International, Ltd., 4Kids Entertainment Licensing, Inc., 4Kids Entertainment Music, Inc., 4Kids Productions, Inc., 4Kids Technology, Inc., The Summit Media Group, Inc.

Officers: Brian Lacey/Exec. VP, Bruce R. Foster/CFO, Exec. VP, Samuel R. Newborn/Dir., Exec. VP - Business Affairs, General Counsel, Carlin V. West/Exec. VP - Acquistion, Development, Stephen Gould/Co - MD, Olivia Mellett/Co - MD, Sandra Vauthier - Cellier/Co - MD

Directors: Michael Goldstein/Dir., Jay Emmett/Dir., Samuel R. Newborn/Dir., Exec. VP - Business Affairs, General Counsel

Owners: Brian Lacey, Jay Emmett, Richard Block, Samuel Newborn/1.03%, Royce & Associates, LLC/5.41%, Norman Grossfeld/1.14%, Alfred R. Kahn/15.47%, William Blair & Company, L.L.C./5.99%, Randy O. Rissman, West Coast Asset Management, Inc./5.97%, Michael Goldstein, Bruce Foster, The TCW Group, Inc./7.83%, Dimensional Fund Advisors LP/8.14%, Insiders/20.29%

Financial Data: Fiscal Year End:12/31 **Latest Annual Data:** 12/31/2006

Year	Sales	Net Income
2006	$71,781,000	-$1,006,000
2005	$86,662,000	$5,069,000
2004	$103,306,000	$12,730,000

Curr. Assets:	$152,347,000	**Curr. Liab.:**	$25,887,000		
Plant, Equip.:	$2,126,000	**Total Liab.:**	$26,658,000	**Indic. Yr. Divd.:**	NA
Total Assets:	$181,395,000	**Net Worth:**	$154,737,000	**Debt/ Equity:**	NA

4net Software Inc

100 Mill Plain Rd., Danbury, CT, 06811; **PH:** 1-203-748-6500; *http://* www.4netsoftware.com

General - Incorporation	DE	**Stock**- Price on:12/24/2007	$0.12
Employees	1	Stock Exchange	OTC
Auditor	Carlin, Charron & Rosen LLP	Ticker Symbol	FNSI
Stk Agt	American Stock Transfer & Trust Co.	Outstanding Shares	8,960,000
Counsel	NA	E.P.S.	$0.00
DUNS No.	15-207-4100	Shareholders	NA

Business: The group's principle activity is to provide software, Internet consulting and Web design and maintenance services for the business-to-business market. The company also provides Web site development services to small and middle-sized companies. The company's 4net software's flagship product and 4netmanager bridges the gap between content creation and content delivery by giving non-technical users the ability to update and maintain their own Web site. This functionality reduces the cost of Web site maintenance, and improves the process of sustaining a dynamic online presence. The group operates from United States.

Primary SIC and add'l.: 7371 7372 7378

CIK No: 0000812149

Officers: Steven N. Bronson/42/Chmn., CEO, Pres.

Directors: Steven N. Bronson/42/Chmn., CEO, Pres., Leonard Hagan/55/Dir., Alan Rosenberg/38/Dir.

Owners: Insiders/62.00%, Leonard Hagan, Steven N. Bronson/62.00%, Alan Rosenberg

Financial Data: Fiscal Year End:09/30 **Latest Annual Data:** 9/30/2006

Year	Sales	Net Income
2006	NA	-$27,000
2005	NA	-$30,000
2004	$2,000	-$35,000

Curr. Assets:	$27,000	**Curr. Liab.:**	$8,000		
Plant, Equip.:	NA	**Total Liab.:**	$8,000	**Indic. Yr. Divd.:**	NA
Total Assets:	$27,000	**Net Worth:**	$19,000	**Debt/ Equity:**	NA

51143 Inc

2320 Walsh Ave., Santa Clara, CA, 95051; **PH:** 1-408-562-0021

General - Incorporation	DE	**Stock**- Price on:12/24/2007	NA
Employees	NA	Stock Exchange	NA
Auditor	Gately & Assoc. LLC	Ticker Symbol	NA
Stk Agt.	NA	Outstanding Shares	NA
Counsel	NA	E.P.S.	NA
DUNS No.	NA	Shareholders	NA

Business: The group provide a method for a foreign or domestic private company to become a reporting (public) company whose securities are qualified for trading in the United States secondary market. There are certain perceived benefits to being a reporting company with a class of publicly- traded securities. These are commonly thought to include the following the ability to use registered securities to make acquisitions of assets or businesses; increased visibility in the financial community; the facilitation of borrowing from financial institutions; improved trading efficiency; shareholder liquidity; greater ease in subsequently raising capital; compensation of key employees through stock options for which there may be a market valuation; enhanced corporate image; a presence in the United States capital market.

Primary SIC and add'l.: 6770

CIK No: 0001317834

51144 Inc

201 Post St., Ste. 1101, San Francisco, CA, 94108; **PH:** 1-415-394-3401

General - Incorporation	DE	**Stock**- Price on:12/24/2007	NA
Employees	NA	Stock Exchange	NA
Auditor	Gately & Assoc. LLC	Ticker Symbol	NA
Stk Agt.	NA	Outstanding Shares	NA
Counsel	NA	E.P.S.	NA
DUNS No.	NA	Shareholders	NA

Business: The group's principal activity is to engage in lawful corporate undertaking, but not limited to, selected mergers and acquisitions. It has been formed to provide a method for a foreign or domestic private company to become a reporting company whose securities are qualified for trading in the United States secondary market. The company is in the developmental stage and has been issuing shares to their original shareholders.

Primary SIC and add'l.: 6770

CIK No: 0001317835

51149 INC

1250 Long Beach Ave., Apt 111, Los Angeles, CA, 90021; **PH:** 1-310-490-4582

General - Incorporation	DE	**Stock**- Price on:12/24/2007	NA
Employees	NA	Stock Exchange	NA
Auditor	Gately & Assoc. LLC	Ticker Symbol	NA
Stk Agt	Corporate Stock Transfer, Inc.	Outstanding Shares	NA
Counsel	NA	E.P.S.	NA
DUNS No.	NA	Shareholders	NA

Business: The group's principal activities are to engage in any lawful corporate undertaking, including selected mergers and acquisitions. The company has been in the developmental stage since its inception and has no operations to date other than issuing shares to their original shareholders. The group has been formed to provide a method for a foreign or domestic private company to become a reporting ("public") company whose securities are qualified for trading in the United States secondary market.

Primary SIC and add'l.: 6770

CIK No: 0001317841

51job Inc

21st Floor, Wen Xin Plz., 755 Wei Hai Rd, Shanghai, 200041; **PH:** 86-2132014888; *http://* www.51job.com; **Email:** beijing@51job.com

General - Incorporation	Cayman Islands	**Stock**- Price on:12/24/2007	$18.08
Employees	2,311	Stock Exchange	NDQ
Auditor	PricewaterhouseCoopers	Ticker Symbol	JOBS
Stk Agt	National Registered Agents Inc	Outstanding Shares	NA
Counsel	Prc Legal System	E.P.S.	NA
DUNS No.	NA	Shareholders	NA

Business: The groups principle activity is to provide human resource solutions. The groups services include campus recruiting and training service. The group operates from United States.

Primary SIC and add'l.: NA

CIK No: 0001295484

Subsidiaries: 51net Beijing, 51net HR, 51net.com Inc., Advertising Co., Ltd.), Beijing Qian Cheng Si Jin Advertising Co., Ltd., Beijing Run An Information Consultancy Co., Ltd., Chongqing Qian Cheng Wu You Advertising Co., Ltd., Culture Communication Co., Ltd.), Dalian Mei Hao Qian Cheng Advertising Co., Ltd., Hangzhou Meijin Advertising Co., Ltd., Hefei Wu You Culture Communication Co., Ltd., Kunming Mei Hao Qian Cheng Advertising Co., Ltd., Ningbo Qianjin Culture Advertising Co., Ltd., Qian Cheng Wu You Network Information Technology (Beijing) Co., Ltd., Qianjin Network Information Technology (Shanghai) Co., Ltd. 21 Subsidiaries included in the Index

Officers: Rick Yan/Dir., CEO, Pres., Kathleen Chien/Co - Founder, CFO, Sr. VP, Tao Wang/VP, Norman Lui/Co - Founder, VP, David Weimin Jin/Sr. VP, Jones Haijun Yu/VP, Linda Chien/Investor Relations Officer

Directors: Rick Yan/Dir., CEO, Pres., Donald L. Lucas/Chmn., Norman Lui/Co - Founder, VP, Kathleen Chien/Co - Founder, CFO, Sr. VP, David K. Chao/Dir., Hiroyuki Honda/Dir., Shan Li/44/Dir., Xiao Yue Chen/Dir.

Owners: Recruit Co., Ltd./20.10%, Rick Yan/28.70%, Kathleen Chien/3.00%, Jones Haijun Yu, Insiders/54.90%, Entities affiliated with DCM/17.30%, Hiroyuki Honda, Norman Lui/5.00%, David K. Chao/18.10%, Tao Wang, David Weimin Jin, Donald L. Lucas, Shan Li

Financial Data: Fiscal Year End:12/31 **Latest Annual Data:** 12/31/2005

Year	Sales	Net Income
2005	$69,642,000	$7,611,000
2004	$55,110,000	$7,388,000
2003	$33,845,000	$3,939,000

Curr. Assets:	$117,832,000	**Curr. Liab.:**	$17,821,000		
Plant, Equip.:	$24,899,000	**Total Liab.:**	$17,836,000	**Indic. Yr. Divd.:**	NA
Total Assets:	$144,490,000	**Net Worth:**	$126,654,000	**Debt/ Equity:**	NA

5G Wireless Communications Inc

2771 Plz. Del Amo, Ste.No. 805, Torrance, CA, 90503; **PH:** 1-310-328-0493; **Fax:** 1-310-328-0498; *http://* www.5gwireless.com; **Email:** support@5gwireless.com

General - Incorporation	NV	**Stock**- Price on:12/24/2007	$0.03
Employees	11	Stock Exchange	OTC
Auditor	Squar, Peterson, LLP	Ticker Symbol	FGWIE
Stk Agt	Holladay Stock Transfer, Inc.	Outstanding Shares	43,970,000
Counsel	NA	E.P.S.	-$0.039
DUNS No.	NA	Shareholders	NA

Business: The group's principal activity is to design, build, market and service compatible wireless broadband systems. The group's integrated hardware and software solutions offer significant improvements in distance, performance, throughputs and security while servicing both line of sight and non-line of sight applications. The group's products are used to create large and efficient wireless local area networks, or lans, and wide area networks, or wans, at competitive costs. The customers include universities, businesses, governments, municipalities and wireless Internet service providers.

Primary SIC and add'l.: 7375

CIK No: 0001100748

Subsidiaries: 5G Wireless Solutions, Inc., Wireless Think Tank, Inc.

Officers: Jerry Dix/Chmn., CEO, Don F. Boudewyn/Dir., Exec. VP, Sec., Treasurer, Andrew D. McCormac/44/CFO

Directors: Jerry Dix/Chmn., CEO, Don F. Boudewyn/Dir., Exec. VP, Sec., Treasurer

Owners: Longview Equity Fund, LP/6.75%, Insiders/100.00%, Jerry Dix, Jerry Dix, Longview Fund, LP/5.93%, Castellum Investments/9.61%, Don Boudewyn, Olaf Tagge/9.57%, Montgomery Equity Partners/33.93%, Karl Heinz Bruno Sartor,/9.57%, Insiders/92.00%, Don Boudewyn

Financial Data: Fiscal Year End:12/31 **Latest Annual Data:** 12/31/2006

Year	Sales	Net Income
2006	$782,000	-$6,127,000
2005	$1,619,000	-$4,025,000
2004	$651,000	-$4,989,000

Curr. Assets:	$323,000	Curr. Liab.:	$7,568,000		
Plant, Equip.:	$139,000	Total Liab.:	$7,568,000	Indic. Yr. Divd.:	NA
Total Assets:	$760,000	Net Worth:	-$6,808,000	Debt/ Equity:	NA

7-Eleven Inc

PO Box 711, Dallas, TX, 75221; **PH:** 1-972-828-7011; **Fax:** 1-972-828-7848; **http://** www.7-eleven.com

General - Incorporation	TX	Stock - Price on:12/24/2007	$26.45
Employees	7,250	Stock Exchange	NYSE
Auditor	PricewaterhouseCoopers LLP	Ticker Symbol	NA
Stk Agt	NA	Outstanding Shares	631,830,000
Counsel	NA	E.P.S.	NA
DUNS No.	00-734-7602	Shareholders	NA

Business: The group's principal activity is the operating, franchising and licensing of convenience food stores. The broad array of product offered by the group include tobacco, beverages, beer/wine, candy/snacks, fresh foods, dairy products, prepaid products, gasoline and other non-foods. In addition to a variety of products, the stores offer a number of services to its customers including sale of lottery tickets. The group has 5,200 ATMs in its United States stores and an additional 500 in Canada. The group operates, franchises or licenses more than 26,000 stores worldwide. The group operates stores in the United States and Canada.

Primary SIC and add'l.: 5541 5411 5451

CIK No: 0000092344

Subsidiaries: 7-Eleven Beverage Company, Inc., 7-Eleven Canada, Inc., 7-Eleven International, Inc., 7-Eleven of Idaho, Inc., 7-Eleven of Massachusetts, Inc., 7-Eleven of Nevada, Inc., 7-Eleven of Virginia, Inc., 7-Eleven Sales Corporation, 7-Eleven Stores Sales Corporation, Bawco Corporation, Bev of Vermont, Inc., Brazos Comercial E Empreendimentos Ltda., Cityplace Center East L.P., Cityplace Nevada LLC, Melin Enterprises, Inc. 23 Subsidiaries included in the Index

Officers: Joseph De Pinto/CEO, Pres., Jeffrey Schenck/Sr. VP - National Franchise, Joseph M. Strong/VP - Chesapeake Division, Don Thomas/VP, Tim Donegan/VP - Canada, Allen Pack/VP - Central Division, John Harris/Sr. VP - Store Operations, Bryan F. Smith/VP - Great Lakes Division, Mike Blair/VP - Mid, Pacific Division, Bob Jenkins/VP - International, Domestic Licensing, Shiro Ozeki/VP, Treasurer, Dennis Phelps/VP - Fresh Foods, Sharon Stufflebeme/CIO, Sr. VP, Ken Wakabayashi/VP - Store Support, Denis Wojcik/VP - Enterprise Procurement *(40 Officers included in Index)*

8x8 Inc

3151 Jay St., Santa Clara, CA, 95054; **PH:** 1-408-727-1885; **Fax:** 1-408-980-0432; **http://** www.8x8.com; **Email:** p8sales@packet8.net

General - Incorporation	DE	Stock - Price on:12/24/2007	$1.39
Employees	139	Stock Exchange	NDQ
Auditor	PricewaterhouseCoopers LLP	Ticker Symbol	EGHT
Stk Agt	Computershare Trust Co	Outstanding Shares	61,600,000
Counsel	NA	E.P.S.	-$0.12
DUNS No.	NA	Shareholders	NA

Business: The group's principal activity is to design, develop and market telecommunication technology for Internet protocol, telephony and video applications. The group has three product lines: Internet protocol telephone devices, Internet communication services and software that implements the functionality of a private branch exchange over data networks. The service is marketed under the brand name packet8. The group operates through its subsidiaries, netergy microelectronics inc and centile. Netergy microelectronics inc develops and markets a range of technology products, including semiconductors and embedded software. Centile develops and markets a hosted ipbx, which is a software-driven telephony solution. The group has operations in Europe, Japan, Taiwan and other countries. The group sold centile Europe sa on 01st jul 2003.

Primary SIC and add'l.: 3661 6794 3674 7372

CIK No: 0001023731

Subsidiaries: 8x8 (Hong Kong) Limited, 8x8 Europe SARL, Netergy Microelectronics, Inc., Netergy Networks Canada Holding Company, UForce Holding Company, Visit, Inc.

Officers: Bryan R. Martin/Chmn., CEO/$360,013.00, Marc Petit-Huguenin/CTO/$319,399.00, Kumaravel Chinnappan/VP - Engineering, Huw Rees/VP - Sales, Marketing/$337,663.00, Richard Murray/Pres./$391,081.00, Ramprakash Narayanaswamy/VP - Engineering, Joan Citelli/Contact - Media Relations, Dan Weirich/CFO/$276,807.00, Garth Judge/VP - Research, Development, Mehdi Salour/VP - Service Delivery, Support

Directors: Bryan R. Martin/Chmn., CEO, Barry Andrews/Vice Chmn., Guy L. Hecker/75/Dir., Christopher McNiffe/47/Dir., Joe Parkinson/63/Dir., Donn Wilson/72/Dir.

Owners: Dan Weirich, Huw Rees, Insiders/7.40%, Donn Wilson, Christopher McNiffe, Guy L. Hecker, Bryan R. Martin/2.30%, Marc Petit-Huguenin, Riverview Group LLC/5.60%, Joe Parkinson/1.80%

Financial Data: Fiscal Year End:03/31 Latest Annual Data: 03/31/2007

Year	Sales	Net Income
2007	$53,130,000	-$9,930,000
2006	$31,892,000	-$24,139,000
2005	$11,475,000	-$19,148,000

Curr. Assets:	$23,815,000	Curr. Liab.:	$10,957,000		
Plant, Equip.:	$3,071,000	Total Liab.:	$11,027,000	Indic. Yr. Divd.:	NA
Total Assets:	$31,120,000	Net Worth:	$20,093,000	Debt/ Equity:	NA

99 Cent Stuff Inc

1801 Clint Moore Rd., Ste. 205, Boca Raton, FL, 33487; **PH:** 1-561-999-9815; **Fax:** 1-561-999-9817; **http://** www.99centstuff.com; **Email:** customer.relations@99centstuff.com

General - Incorporation	FL	Stock - Price on:12/24/2007	NA
Employees	NA	Stock Exchange	OTC
Auditor	Daszkal Bolton LLP	Ticker Symbol	NNCT
Stk Agt	Registrar & Transfer Co	Outstanding Shares	NA
Counsel	NA	E.P.S.	NA
DUNS No.	NA	Shareholders	NA

Business: The group's principle activity is to operate retail outlets. The company is a specialty, single-priced retailer that targets individuals and small businesses with one-stop shopping for food, produce, consumable hard lines, health and beauty aids, novelty and impulse items. As of 31-Dec-2003, it operates 11 retail stores south Florida. The group operates from United States.

Primary SIC and add'l.: 7372 7375

CIK No: 0001176435

Officers: Raymond Zimmerman/Chmn., CEO, Barry Bilmes/CFO, Russ Field/VP - Information Technology, Oscar Martinez/Dir. - Warehouse, Distribution, Leo Milewicz/Sr. Management - Buyer

Directors: Raymond Zimmerman/Chmn., CEO, Nathan R. Light/Dir., Kevin R. Keating/Dir.

Curr. Assets:	$4,148,000	Curr. Liab.:	$5,064,000		
Plant, Equip.:	$3,327,000	Total Liab.:	$22,493,000	Indic. Yr. Divd.:	NA
Total Assets:	$7,637,000	Net Worth:	-$14,856,000	Debt/ Equity:	NA

99 Only Stores

4000 Union Pacific Ave., City of Commerce, CA, 90023; **PH:** 1-323-980-8145; **http://** www.99only.com; **Email:** contact1@99only.com

General - Incorporation	CA	Stock - Price on:12/24/2007	$5.24
Employees	9,690	Stock Exchange	NYSE
Auditor	BDO Seidman, LLP	Ticker Symbol	NA
Stk Agt	American Stock Transfer & Trust Co.	Outstanding Shares	69,980,000
Counsel	Akin, Gump, Strauss, Hauer & Feld LLP	E.P.S.	$0.08
DUNS No.	09-443-5237	Shareholders	NA

Business: The group's principal activity is to market and distribute consumable general merchandise on retail and wholesale basis. The group operates in two segments: retail operations and wholesale distribution. Retail operations segment provides close-out merchandise and regularly available consumable products including food and beverages, health, stationary, pet products, clothing, baby products, toys, gifts and household supplies. Wholesale distribution segment sells merchandise at prices below normal wholesale levels to retailers, distributors and exporters. Registered trademarks of the group are '99 cents only stores', '99 cents', 'rinso' and 'halsa'. As of 12-Mar-2004, the group operated 194 retail stores in California, Texas, Arizona and Nevada.

Primary SIC and add'l.: 5331 5399

CIK No: 0001011290

Officers: Eric Schiffer/CEO/$119,232.00, David Gold/Chmn., Executive Officer, Jeff Gold/COO, Pres./$121,367.00, Howard Gold/Exec. VP - Special Projects/$121,540.00, Robert Kautz/CFO, Exec. VP/$893,880.00

Directors: David Gold/Chmn., Executive Officer, Jennifer Holden Dunbar/45/Dir., Peter Woo/58/Dir.

Owners: Au Zone Investments #3, LLC, Eric and Karen Schiffer, Lawrence Glascott, Peter Woo, Sherry Gold, Marvin Holen, Akre Capital Management, LLC, Robert Kautz, Primecap Management Company, Jeff Gold, Insiders, David Gold, Dimensional Fund Advisors LP, Howard Gold, Eric Flamholtz

Financial Data: Fiscal Year End:12/31 Latest Annual Data: 03/31/2007

Year	Sales	Net Income
2007	$1,104,696,000	$9,762,000
2006	$1,023,589,000	$11,422,000
2004	$972,173,000	$27,831,000

Curr. Assets:	$310,536,000	Curr. Liab.:	$109,061,000	P/E Ratio:	32.75
Plant, Equip.:	$259,334,000	Total Liab.:	$127,182,000	Indic. Yr. Divd.:	NA
Total Assets:	$628,708,000	Net Worth:	$501,526,000	Debt/ Equity:	0.0012

Company Index

Officers & Directors Index

2056 - Officers & Directors Index **THE CORPORATE DIRECTORY - Walker's 2008**

Augier, Mie *Lecg Corp* 1063
Augsburger, Blake *Harman International Industries Inc* 847
Augur, Harrison H. *Pure Cycle Corp* 1490
August, Arthur A. *Helen of Troy Ltd* 866
August, Glenn R. *iStar Financial Inc* 992
August, Thomas J. *Unigene Laboratories Inc* 1850
August, Tom *Brandywine Realty Trust* 274
August, Tom *Brandywine Operating PArtnership LP* 274
Auguste, Georges *STMicroelectronics* 1706
Augusti, Mark *Smith & Nephew Plc* 1647
Augustin, Jeffrey G. *Johnson Controls Inc* 1009
Augustine, Charles *FTI Consulting Inc* 752
Augustine, Cynthia *Scholastic Corp* 1592
Augustine, Merlin *Baldor Electric Co* 201
Augustine, Norman R. *ConocoPhillips* 469
Augustine, Norman R. *Procter & Gamble* 1472
Augustine, Norman R. *Black & Decker Corp* 252
Augustine, Richard J. *U.S. Energy Systems Inc* 1840
Augusto, Nelson Rocha *Brazilian Petroleum Corp* 276
Augustson, Jim *Tandy Leather Factory Inc* 1748
Augustsson, Tommy R. *General Dynamics Corp* 770
Augustyn, Julie *Office Depot Inc* 1329
Aukerman, Arlie C. *Georgia Bancshares Inc* 781
Aukward, John *Delmar Bancorp* 538
Aulaya, Rakesh *NCR Corp* 1256
Auld, David *D.R. Horton Inc* 522
Auld-Susott, Evan *Spectrum Sciences & Software Hldgs Corp* 1678
Aulds, Chris A. *Crosstex Energy Inc* 503
Auletta, Patrick V. *Park Ohio Holdings Corp* 1386
Ault, John L. *Sherwin Williams Co* 1619
Ault, Lee A. *Anworth Mortgage Asset Corp* 129
Ault, Lee A. *Office Depot Inc* 1329
Ault, Mike *Quest Software Inc* 1500
Ault, Mike *American Ecology Corp* 90
Ault, Mimi *Outdoor Channel Holdings Inc* 1364
Aumack, Nancy E. *FPB Bancorp Inc* 742
Auman, Adrian *Orbotech Ltd* 1354
Aumiller, Judy R. *Juniata Valley Financial Corp* 1013
Aune, Brian J. *Teck Cominco Ltd* 1760
Aune, Geir *Ocean Rig* 1326
Aur, Jing-Shan *Siliconware Precision Industries Co Ltd* 1631
Auran, Mitchell D. *Micrus Endovascular Corp* 1183
Aurelio, Richard A. *Varian Semiconductor Equipment Associates Inc* 1889
Aurelio, Richard A. *Fairchild Semiconductor International Inc* 676
Aurelio, Roger L. *A.J. Smith Federal Savings Bank* 2
Auriana, Lawrence *Mediware Information Systems Inc* 1155
Auriemma, Sam M. *MSC.Software Corp* 1223
Ausburn, Kent *Tournigan Gold Corp* 1806
Ausfeld, Robert J. *Regent Communications Inc* 1526
Ausick, Richard M. *Brown Shoe Co Inc* 288
Ausiello, Dennis A. *Pfizer Inc* 1420
Ausikaitis, Joseph P. *Competitive Technologies Inc* 459
Ausley, Dubose *TECO Energy Inc* 1761
Ausley, Dubose *Huron Consulting Group Inc* 901
Ausman, Gregory S. *Sun Life Financial Inc* 1718
Ausman, James I. *Somanetics Corp* 1655
Ausman, Sheldon I. *Superior Industries International Inc* 1727
Ausonio, Andrew P. *Pacific Valley Bank CA* 1374
Aussenberg, Przemyslaw *Stream Communications Netwrk & Media Inc* 1712
Aust, Bruce E. *Nasdaq Stock Market Inc (The)* 1236
Aust, Robert D. *Premier Svc Bank CA* 1461
Austen, Frank K. *CV Therapeutics Inc* 515
Austen, Gerald W. *Abiomed Inc* 7
Austen, William F. *Bemis Co Inc* 230
Austen, William F. *Tennant Co* 1775
Austill, Laura *First National Bancshares Inc/SC* 712
Austill, Laura *First National Bancshares Inc/FL* 712
Austin, Anthony *Winn-Dixie Stores Inc* 1967
Austin, Bernard *U.S. Global Investors Inc* 1840
Austin, Cathie *SCBT Financial Corp* 1590
Austin, Edward H. *Kinder Morgan Inc* 1030
Austin, Edward L. *Wendy's International Inc* 1945
Austin, Gary *Claimsnet.com Inc* 418
Austin, Gary S. *Beach First National Bancshares Inc* 224
Austin, George L. *Matrix Service Co* 1132
Austin, Glenn S. *Post Properties Inc* 1451
Austin, Glenn T. *Triad Guaranty Inc* 1823
Austin, Glenn T. *Homebanc Corp* 887
Austin, Holly A. *Northwest Bancorporation Inc* 1305
Austin, James M. *Southern First Bancshares Inc* 1666
Austin, Jeff *Castle Arch Real Estate Investment Co LLC* 343
Austin, John D. *Performance Food Group Co* 1412
Austin, John H. *Coventry Health Care Inc* 491
Austin, Josiah T. *Goodrich Petroleum Corp* 811
Austin, Karen A. *Sears Holdings Corp* 1600
Austin, Kevin G. *TRX Inc* 1831
Austin, Lisa J. *Beverly National Corp* 235
Austin, Mark *Xethanol Corp* 1986
Austin, Michael *Scottish Re Group Ltd* 1596
Austin, Michael *O2micro International Ltd* 1323
Austin, Nic *Accelrys Inc* 10
Austin, Paul *Sonic Environmental Solutions Inc* 1657
Austin, Phyllis R. *Crawford & Co* 495
Austin, Rob *Expressjet Holdings Inc* 672
Austin, Robin *Emulex Corp* 627
Austin, Roxanne S. *Abbott Laboratories* 5
Austin, Roxanne S. *Target Corp* 1749
Austin, Roxanne S. *Teledyne Technologies Inc* 1766
Austin, Sean J. *Westside Energy Corp* 1953
Austin, Sharon *Old Dominion Electric Cooperative* 1333
Austin, Stephen *AngloGold Ashanti Ltd* 124
Austin, Stephen G. *Avanir Pharmaceuticals* 185
Austin, Thomas W. *Ferro Corp* 687
Auston, John S. *Eldorado Gold Corp* 611
Auston, John S. *Cameco Corp* 315
Austrian, Neil R. *Office Depot Inc* 1329
Austrian, Neil R. *DIRECTV Group Inc (The)* 561
Austrian, Robert *Handheld Entertainment Inc* 842
Ausura, Maureen K. *Lowe's Cos Inc* 1096
Auten, Joseph *ViewCast Corp* 1905
Auten, Harrell J. *Waste Industries USA Inc* 1934
Authur, Janelle K. *Federal Home Loan Bank of Boston* 682
Automovilista, Mutua Madrilena *Banco Santander S.A* 205
Auton, Sylvia *Time Warner Inc* 1795
Autor, Robert S. *Slm Corp* 1644
Autran, Brigitte *Transgene* 1816
Autry, Barry C. *Franklin Bank Corp* 743
Autry, Cindy *Sound Banking Company* 1661
Autry, Henry *Hyperion Solutions Corp* 905
Autry, Robert K. *First M & F Corp* 709
Autz, Will *Sirona Dental Systems Inc* 1639
Auvil, Paul *Quantum Corp* 1498
Auwers, Linda S. *ABM Industries Inc* 7
Avallet, Stephanie *A T Cross Co* 1
Avallone, Ronald J. *Asbury Automotive Group Inc* 157
Avant, Clifton *Entergy Louisiana Holdings Inc* 641
Avant, Jerry *Copart Inc* 479
Avants, Brett W. *MEMC Electronic Materials Inc* 1158
Avara, Michael T. *Horizon Lines Inc* 890
Avdasseva, Oxana *ST Online Corp* 1687
Avdeev, Sergei M. *Vimpel-Communications Company* 1907
Avedon, Marcia J. *Merck & Co Inc* 1162
Avedon, Marcia J. *Ingersoll Rand Co Ltd* 943
Avelar, Rui *Angiotech Pharmaceuticals Inc* 124
Aveleyra, Alberto *Santander BanCorp* 1583
Avellani, Anthony M. *Southern Connecticut Bancorp Inc* 1666
Aven, Peter *CTC Media Inc* 510
Aven, Petr *Golden Telecom Inc* 807
Avendt, Anthony *Grubb & Ellis Co* 827
Aveni, Joseph T. *Ourpets Co* 1364
Avera, Stephen R. *Flowers Foods Inc* 728
Averbach, Sergio *Korn Ferry International* 1041
Averback, Paul *Nymox Pharmaceutical Corp* 1321
Averett, Claire *Nu Skin Enterprises Inc* 1314
Averett, Devron R. *Anadys Pharmaceuticals Inc* 119
Averette, Teresa *Peoples BancTrust Co Inc* 1407
Averill, Barry W. *Universal American Financial Corp* 1866
Averill, Howard *Time Warner Inc* 1795
Averill, Twila *Coast Financial Holdings Inc* 431
Averitt, Richard G. *Raymond James Financial Inc* 1516
Aversano, Nina *New Jersey Resources Corp* 1272
Avery, Arnold *Peoples BancTrust Co Inc* 1407
Avery, Charles *Sun Bancorp Inc* 1717
Avery, Christopher J. *Home Diagnostics Inc* 885
Avery, Edwin A. *Paradigm Holdings Inc WY* 1383
Avery, James J. *Pruco Life Insurance Co* 1482
Avery, James J. *American Skandia Life Assurance Corp* 102
Avery, James H. *San Luis Trust Bank FSB* 1580
Avery, James *Saigon National Bank* 1576
Avery, James P. *San Diego Gas & Electric Co* 1579
Avery, Jim *American Bank Inc* 85
Avery, Julian *Aspen Insurance Holdings Ltd* 162
Avery, Keith *Express-1 Expedited Solutions Inc* 671
Avery, Kenny *Delta & Pine Land Co* 539
Avery, Michael L. *Waddell & Reed Inc* 1928
Avery, Nathan M. *Cameron International Corp* 315
Avery, Paul E. *OSI Restaurant Partners Inc* 1362
Avery, R. T. *Village Bank & Trust Financial Corp* 1906
Avery, Robert *Atmel Corp* 174
Avery, William J. *Rohm & Haas Co* 1557
Avery, William J. *Lincoln National Corp* 1081
Aveson, Kent D. *Golden Phoenix Minerals Inc* 806
Avet, Ray *Gulf Island Fabrication Inc* 834
Avey, Chris *Baker Boyer Bancorp* 200
Avezzu, Stefano *FSI International Inc* 752
Avgiris, Catherine *Comcast Corp* 444
Avi, Cheifetz *Israel Bank of Agriculture Ltd* 992
Avia, Kenneth *AEP Industries Inc* 36
Avice, Patrick *Euro Disney SCA* 662
Avidan, Guy *MRV Communications Inc* 1223
Aviezer, David *Orthodontix Inc* 1360
Avigael, Lester *International Bancshares Corp* 967
Avigdor, Gelem *Israel Bank of Agriculture Ltd* 992
Avila, Eduardo *Tortuga Mexican Imports Inc* 1805
Avila, Joseph A. *Quanta Services Inc* 1497
Avila, Joseph A. *Energy Conversion Devices Inc* 635
Avila, Juan Rafael Gutierrez *CorpBanca* 483
Avila, Kathleen L. *First State BanCorp* 717
Avila, Luis *Scientific-Atlanta Inc* 1594
Avila, Scott T. *Steakhouse Partners Inc* 1697
Avila, Vanessa *Tortuga Mexican Imports Inc* 1805
Aviles, Martha *SigmaTel Inc* 1627
Aviles, Mike *Vignette Corp* 1906
Aviles, Walter *Novint Technologies Inc* 1311
Avingu, Hanneli *Lawson Software Inc* 1060
Aviram, Gadi *BVR Systems (1998) Ltd* 298
Avis, Gregory M. *Rightnow Technologies Inc* 1545
Avis, Gregory M. *Ditech Communications Corp* 563
Avishai, Dagan *Shamir Optical Industry Ltd* 1616
Avita, Reuven *Neoprobe Corp* 1260
Aviv, Haim *Pharmos Corp* 1423
Avner, Brett *Coldwater Creek Inc* 438
Avner, Carmela *NICE Systems Ltd* 1285
Avner, David *Partner Communications Co Ltd* 1389
Avner, Emanuel *Partner Communications Co Ltd* 1389
Avni, Hillel *Elbit Vision Systems Ltd* 611
Avniel, Amir *Rosetta Genomics Ltd* 1559
Avramovich, Daniel W. *Kansas City Southern de Mexico, S.A. de C.V.* 1018
Avramovich, Daniel W. *Kansas City Southern* 1018
Avramovich, Michael *CTI Industries Corp* 510
Avril, Vicki L. *Greif Inc* 825
Avril, Vicki *IPSCO Inc* 987
Avrin, William N. *Cytec Industries Inc* 520
Awad, Atif *Forbes Medi-Tech Inc* 734
Awad, Azmy *Bio Reference Laboratories Inc* 240
Awad, George *Citicorp* 411
Awad, Jim *WP Stewart & Co Ltd* 1979
Awamleh, Khaldoun *Sonoran Energy Inc* 1659
Awang, Mohd Nor *Secured Digital Applications Inc* 1602
Awata, Toshio *Mitsui & Co Ltd* 1201
Awerkamp, Ted T. *Mercantile Bancorp Inc* 1160
Awmack, Henry *Rimfire Minerals Corp* 1546
Awram, David *Silver Wheaton Corp* 1632
Aws, Sheri *Innova Robotics & Automation Inc* 948
Aws, Sheri *Innova Robotics and Automation Inc* 948
Ax, Peter L. *Meritage Homes Corp* 1164
Ax, Robert T. *1st Source Corp* 2005
Axel, Richard *Genentech Inc* 768
Axelbank, Ernest *Artificial Life Inc* 155
Axelman, Klas *Swedish Export Credit Corp* 1732
Axelman, Mats *Swedish Export Credit Corp* 1732
Axelrod, Beth *eBay Inc* 597
Axelrod, Elizabeth L. *eBay Inc* 597
Axelrod, Michael E. *Pediatric Services of America Inc* 1400
Axelrod, Norman *Maidenform Brands Inc* 1113
Axelrod, Robert *Pangea Petroleum Corp* 1381
Axelrod, Todd M. *Gallery of History Inc* 759
Axelson, Thomas H. *Left Behind Games Inc* 1065
Axelson, Thomas H. *Left Behind Games* 1064
Axelsson, Agne I. *Digital Recorders Inc* 557
Axelsson, Anders *Echelon Corp* 598
Axford, John Stewart *Mannatech Inc* 1119
Axinn, Donald E. *Brandywine Realty Trust* 274
Axinn, Donald E. *Brandywine Operating PArtnership LP* 274
Axon, Thomas J. *Franklin Credit Mgmt Corp* 744
Axson, Harry B. *Northrop Grumman Corp* 1303
Axtell, Nancy *American Physicians Capital Inc* 99
Axworthy, Anne Marie *Avista Corp* 190
Ayad, Victor *Wilson Holdings Inc* 1964
Ayala, Agustin R. *Plaza Bank WA* 1440
Ayala, Orlando *Microsoft Corp* 1182
Ayalon, Eliyahu *Ceva Inc* 369
Ayalon, Eliyahu *DSP Group Inc* 578
Ayasli, Yalcin *Hittite Microwave Corp* 881
Ayat, Simon *Schlumberger Ltd* 1591
Aycock, Charles *Grubb & Ellis Co* 827
Aycock, Joey *Cytation Corp* 520
Aydelott, Jim *LifeSpan Inc* 1076
Ayelsworth, Andy *International Electronics Inc* 968
Ayento, Eva *Park Bancorp Inc* 1385
Ayer, Anne *Sappi Ltd* 1585
Ayer, Dan *CD&I Inc* 350
Ayer, Michael L. *First Farmers & Merchants Corp* 704
Ayer, Ramani *Hartford Life Inc* 850
Ayer, Ramani *Hartford Life Insurance Co* 851
Ayer, Ramani *Hartford Financial Services Group Inc* 850
Ayer, William S. *Puget Energy Inc* 1488
Ayer, William S. *Alaska Air Group Inc* 51
Ayer, William S. *Alaska Airlines Inc* 52
Ayers, Christopher L. *Precision Castparts Corp* 1458
Ayers, E. J. *Community Bankshares Inc SC* 453
Ayers, Fred D. *Ingles Markets Inc* 944
Ayers, Greg *SCBT Financial Corp* 1590
Ayers, Gregory M. *HemoSense Inc* 868
Ayers, Jason C. *FullNet Communications Inc* 754
Ayers, Jeffrey D. *NovaStar Financial Inc* 1309
Ayers, Jonathan W. *IDEXX Laboratories Inc* 917
Ayers, Richard H. *Applera Corp* 134
Ayers, Robert L. *Watts Water Technologies Inc* 1937
Ayers, Walter B. *Berry Petroleum Co CA* 234
Ayerza, Abel *Grupo Financiero Galicia* 828
Aylesworth, Art *Carmanah Technologies Corp* 335
Aylesworth, Derek W. *Baytex Energy Trust* 222
Aylesworth, Winsor H. *Friedman Billings Ramsey Group Inc* 749
Ayling, John R. *Leisure Direct Inc* 1067
Ayling, Peter *Cape Systems Group Inc* 322
Ayling, Victoria *Cape Systems Group Inc* 322
Aylor, Ron *American Retirement Corp* 100
Aylor, Timothy J. *Knobias Inc* 1036
Aylor, Wayne K. *BOE Financial Services of Virginia Inc* 262
Aylsworth, John S. *President Casinos Inc* 1462
Aylsworth, Laurie E. *Northeast Utilities* 1301
Aylward, George R. *Phoenix Cos Inc* 1425
Aynilian, Nicholas J. *Global Gold Corp* 793
Ayo, Dennis H. *MTS Medication Technologies Inc* 1225
Ayotte, Richard G. *WaterChef Inc* 1936
Ayoub, Alaa *RAESystems* 1510
Ayre, David *Nike Inc* 1287
Ayre, John C. *FNB Corp/FL* 730
Ayre, Michael C. *CanArgo Energy Corp* 319
Ayres, Arthur J. *MIGENIX Inc* 1188
Ayres, Jed *MTM Technologies Inc* 1224
Ayres, Merribel S. *CMS Energy Corp* 427
Ayres, Merribel S. *Consumers Energy Co* 474
Ayres, Merribel S. *Alliance Resource Partners LP* 62
Ayres, W. Dillaway *Harris & Harris Group Inc* 848
Ayscue, Dan *Alliance Bank & Trust NC* 60
Ayub, Arturo Elias *Telefonos de Mexico SA de CV* 1767
Ayub, Elias Uauy *Distribution & Service D&S* 562
Ayub, Mario *Mexoro Minerals Ltd* 1174
Ayvas, Theodore *Aceto Corp* 14
Ayyob, Muhammad *Infosmart Group Inc* 941
Azab, Mohammad *Chemokine Therapeutics Corp* 381
Azam, Syed Aamer *Migo Software, Inc.* 1189
Azam, Usman *Aspreva Pharmaceuticals Corp* 163
Azar, Alex M. *Eli Lilly & Co* 616
Azar, David *Grubb & Ellis Co* 827
Azar, James R. *Alfa Corp* 56
Azar, Michael C. *Noble International Ltd* 1292
Azar, Wilfred T. *CommerceFirst Bancorp Inc* 448
Azare, Monica *LHC Group Inc* 1072
Azartash, Mir *Actel Corp* 17
Azcarraga, Emilio Fernando *Grupo Televisa, S.A.B.* 829
Azcarraga, Laura Diez Barroso *Grupo Aeroportuario Del Pacifico S.A. de C.V.* 828
Azcona, Angela *Telefonica of Argentina Inc* 1767
Azel, Agustin M. *NxStage Medical Inc* 1320
Azem, Lina *Minrad International Inc* 1196
Azema, Jean *Veolia Environnement* 1894
Azevedo, Antonio Carlos *Unibanco Holdings* 1848
Azevedo, Celso *Tvia Inc* 1837
Azhar, Shariq *Omega Navigation Enterprises Inc* 1336
Azimi, Saeed *Marvell Technology Group Ltd* 1128
Azimi, Sam *Marvell Technology Group Ltd* 1128
Aziz, Asmadi *Andrew Corp* 122
Aziz, Mahmoud S. *Grand Peak Capital Corp* 814
Aziz, Stewart *Panavision Inc* 1381
Azizov, Esther *Berkshire Bancorp Inc* 232
Azlein, James G. *BPI Energy Holdings Inc* 272
Aznar, Enrique Used *Telefonica of Argentina Inc* 1767
Aznar, Jose Maria *News Corp Ltd (The)* 1281
Azoulay, David *On Track Innovations Ltd* 1340
Azoulay, Prosper *Viropro Inc* 1911
Azria, Rene-Pierre *Jarden Corp* 1004
Azulay, Idit *Internet Gold-Golden Lines Ltd* 974
Azuma, Haruki *Broadcom Corp* 284
Azuma, Kazunori *Ricoh Co Ltd* 1544
Azumi, Toru *NTT DoCoMo Inc* 1313
Azzara, Daniel C. *Hershey Co (The)* 872
Azzara, Michael W. *Hudson City Bancorp Inc* 896
Azzarelli, Kim K. *Avon Products Inc* 192
Azzarello, Peter J. *Inhibitex Inc* 944
Azzata, Joseph *Medical Connections Holdings Inc* 1151
Azzi, Antonio Carlos *Unibanco Holdings* 1848
Azzopardi, Evan *IPSCO Inc* 987
Baab, Carlton H. *Raining Data Corp* 1511
Baalbergen, Arie *Brilliant Technologies Corp* 280
Baalmann, Richard F. *Cass Information Systems Inc* 656
Baan, Adri *Imperial Chemical Industries Plc* 929
Baan, Adri *International Power Plc* 971

THE CORPORATE DIRECTORY - Walker's 2008

THE CORPORATE DIRECTORY - Walker's 2008 Officers & Directors Index - 2111

Clark, Leroy *Primedex Health Systems Inc* 1466
Clark, Lincoln *Heritage Financial Group* 871
Clark, Llloyd A. *Dejour Enterprises Ltd* 536
Clark, Lora D. *South Street Financial Corp* 1663
Clark, M. T. *Ohio Edison Co* 1330
Clark, M. T. *Metropolitan Edison Co* 1173
Clark, Mark *Liberty Property Trust* 1074
Clark, Mark T. *FirstEnergy Corp* 719
Clark, Martha A. *Howard Bancorp MD* 894
Clark, Mary *American Bank Inc* 85
Clark, Matthew Gordon *American Capital Strategies Ltd* 87
Clark, Maura J. *Elizabeth Arden Inc* 617
Clark, Maxine *Build-A-Bear Workshop Inc* 294
Clark, Maxine K. *J.C. Penney Co Inc* 998
Clark, Melissa *Community National Corp* 455
Clark, Michele H. *Auto Underwriters of America Inc* 181
Clark, Murray J. *Indiana Business Bancorp* 934
Clark, Nigel *ClickSoftware Technologies Ltd* 424
Clark, Patrick M. *Praxair Inc* 1458
Clark, Paul *Smithtown Bancorp* 1649
Clark, Paul *Micron Technology Inc* 1180
Clark, Paul *National City Corp* 1239
Clark, Paul W. *Independent Bank Corp* 933
Clark, Paul N. *Agilent Technologies Inc* 43
Clark, Paul *Canadian Pacific Railway Ltd* 318
Clark, Peter F. *SEMCO Energy Inc* 1606
Clark, Philip J. *Epoch Holding Corp* 651
Clark, Rachel *Greenhill & Co Inc* 824
Clark, Ralph W. *Leggett & Platt Inc* 1067
Clark, Rand R. *Northwest Pipeline Corp* 1306
Clark, Randall L. *Taylor Devices Inc* 1753
Clark, Ranjana B. *Wachovia Corp* 1928
Clark, Richard P. *Corriente Resources Inc* 485
Clark, Richard *Brookfield Asset Mgmt Inc* 286
Clark, Richard E. *Reader's Digest Association Inc* 1517
Clark, Richard F. *Old Point Financial Corp* 1334
Clark, Richard T. *Merck & Co Inc* 1162
Clark, Richard B. *Monsanto Co* 1213
Clark, Richard B. *Brookfield Properties Corp* 286
Clark, Robert J. *Storm Cat Energy Corp* 1708
Clark, Robert Charles *Omnicom Group Inc* 1338
Clark, Robert C. *Time Warner Inc* 1795
Clark, Robert D. *Tripos Inc* 1827
Clark, Robert J. *Evergreen Energy Inc* 665
Clark, Robert G. *Labarge Inc* 1047
Clark, Rod J. *Teekay Corp* 1761
Clark, Roddy J.H. *Emageon Inc* 619
Clark, Rodney *United Bancorp Inc/MI* 1855
Clark, Roger *Mediware Information Systems Inc* 1155
Clark, Ronald K. *Potomac Electric Power Co* 1452
Clark, Ross G. *Tercica Inc* 1777
Clark, Russell T. *Shumate Industries Inc* 1623
Clark, Sarah P. *Parkway Properties Inc* 1388
Clark, Sheila *Choiceone Financial Services Inc* 401
Clark, Sherry L. *Primedex Health Systems Inc* 1466
Clark, Sonia *Align Technology Inc* 57
Clark, Stanley L. *Amphenol Corp* 115
Clark, Stephan R. *Jinpan International Ltd* 1008
Clark, Stephen H. *South Jersey Industries Inc* 1663
Clark, Stephen *Sonesta International Hotels Corp* 1656
Clark, Stephen H. *Hughes Communications Inc* 898
Clark, Steve *Heinz Co* 866
Clark, Steven K. *Flanders Corp* 723
Clark, Stuart J. *Interactive Data Corp* 960
Clark, Susan *Potomac Bancshares Inc* 1452
Clark, Susan *Farmers & Merchants Bancorp* 679
Clark, Terri *AMAG Pharmaceuticals Inc* 76
Clark, Terry L. *MFB Financial Corp* 1175
Clark, Thomas D. *Dynegy Inc* 586
Clark, Thomas D. *Endeavour International Corp* 631
Clark, Thomas A. *1st Colonial Bancorp Inc* 2004
Clark, Thomas B. *First Merchants Corp* 710
Clark, Thomas E. *Harleysville Group Inc* 846
Clark, Thomas A. *FirstEnergy Corp* 719
Clark, Timothy G. *Ameriana Bancorp* 83
Clark, Todd *United Bancorp Inc/MI* 1855
Clark, Todd *Megola Inc* 1157
Clark, Tom *ICP Solar Technologies Inc* 913
Clark, Tom *GATX Corp* 764
Clark, Trippy *Community Trust Bancorp Inc* 456
Clark, Van *First National Bancshares Inc/FL* 712
Clark, Vernon *Grant Prideco Inc* 816
Clark, Vernon E. *Raytheon Co* 1516
Clark, Walter *Air T Inc* 46
Clark, Wesley *Argyle Security Acquisition Corp* 147
Clark, Wesley K. *Immtech Pharmaceuticals Inc* 927
Clark, Wesley K. *Summit Global Logistics Inc* 1717
Clark, Wesley *GlobalOptions Group Inc* 799
Clark, Wesley K. *Nutracea* 1317
Clark, William J. *Clarkston Financial Corp* 419
Clark, William E. *Realty Income Corp* 1519
Clark, William E. *Simmons First National Corp* 1634
Clark-Caruso, Karen R. *Bank of Granite Corp* 209
Clark-Flory, Tracy *Salon Media Group Inc* 1578
Clark-Johnson, Sue *Gannett Co Inc* 761
Clark-Mantle, Necia *Skywest Inc* 1643
Clark-Pierson, Sara *Firstbank Corp* 718
Clarke, Alan *BioProgress Plc* 246
Clarke, Alison *United Utilities Plc* 1864
Clarke, Andrew C. *Pacer International Inc* 1370
Clarke, Andy *Inter Parfums Inc* 960
Clarke, Anthony *Amarin Corp Plc* 77
Clarke, Boyd C. *QLT Inc* 1493
Clarke, Catherine *RCM Technologies Inc* 1517
Clarke, Charles *Travelers Property Casualty Corp* 1818
Clarke, Charles *St Paul Travelers Cos Inc* 1687
Clarke, Chester C. *Exponent Inc* 671
Clarke, Chris *United Bancorp Inc/MI* 1855
Clarke, David *FUSA Capital Corp* 755
Clarke, David *Advance Nanotech Inc* 27
Clarke, David F. *Standard Register Co* 1691
Clarke, David H. *Celsia Technologies Inc* 356
Clarke, David *IPSCO Inc* 987
Clarke, Donna Mae *IPC Holdings Ltd* 987
Clarke, Doug *Western Massachusetts Electric Co* 1950
Clarke, Edward J. *Oneida Financial Corp* 1342
Clarke, Ernest *China Huaren Organic Products Inc* 391
Clarke, Heath *Local.com Corp* 1090
Clarke, Hubert P. *Peapack Gladstone Financial Corp* 1399
Clarke, James *Sensient Technologies Corp* 1610
Clarke, Janet M. *eFunds Corp* 607
Clarke, Janet M. *Expressjet Holdings Inc* 672
Clarke, Janet M. *Gateway Inc* 764
Clarke, Janet M. *Asbury Automotive Group Inc* 157
Clarke, Janice *Stellar Pharmaceuticals Inc* 1699
Clarke, Jeff W. *Dell Inc* 537
Clarke, Jeffrey R. *Dell Inc* 537
Clarke, Jeffrey J. *UTStarcom Incorporated* 1881
Clarke, Joan *Bank McKenney* 208
Clarke, John *Banro Corp* 215
Clarke, John J. *WaterChef Inc* 1936
Clarke, John J. *Centrix Bank & Trust* 364
Clarke, John U. *Harvest Natural Resources Inc* 852
Clarke, John G. *American Express Co* 91
Clarke, John *Alnylam Pharmaceuticals Inc* 69
Clarke, John U. *Natco Group Inc* 1237
Clarke, John K. *Momenta Pharmaceuticals Inc* 1209
Clarke, John *GlaxoSmithKline Plc* 789
Clarke, John A. *Nevsun Resources Ltd* 1269
Clarke, John K. *Visicu Inc* 1913
Clarke, Joseph W. *FMS Financial Corp* 729
Clarke, Karyn R. *Rainier Pacific Financial Group Inc* 1510
Clarke, Kenneth *British American Tobacco Industries Plc* 282
Clarke, Kevin J. *Quebecor World Inc* 1499
Clarke, Mairtin *CRH Plc* 500
Clarke, Mark C. *Mission Energy Holding Co* 1199
Clarke, Max *Firearms Training Systems Inc* 694
Clarke, Michael J. *Simon Property Group Inc* 1634
Clarke, Michael A. *Coca-Cola Co* 433
Clarke, Michael J. *Mills Ltd Partnership* 1193
Clarke, Michael *Tenneco Automotive Inc* 1775
Clarke, Michael W. *Access National Corp* 11
Clarke, Neil *Liberty Property Trust* 1074
Clarke, Pat *Allied Irish Banks Plc* 65
Clarke, Patrick *A T Cross Co* 1
Clarke, Peter J. *Northeast Utilities* 1301
Clarke, Peter *Fairfax Financial Holdings Ltd* 676
Clarke, Peter J. *Connecticut Light & Power Co* 469
Clarke, Peter M. *Introgen Therapeutics Inc* 980
Clarke, Richard A. *Good Harbor PTR CL A* 810
Clarke, Richard A. *Universal Guardian Holdings Inc* 1869
Clarke, Richard A. *Good Harbor PTR CL B* 810
Clarke, Robert G. *Cardtrend International Inc* 333
Clarke, Robert L. *First Investors Financial Svcs Group Inc* 708
Clarke, Robert G. *Central Vermont Public Service Corp* 363
Clarke, Robert F. *Ormat Technologies Inc* 1359
Clarke, Robert L. *Stewart Information Services Corp* 1705
Clarke, Robert M. *First Chester County Corp* 699
Clarke, Robert G. *TD Banknorth Inc* 1755
Clarke, Sean *Primedex Health Systems Inc* 1466
Clarke, Steve *Lecg Corp* 1063
Clarke, Terry G. *Scor Holding (Switzerland) Ltd* 1595
Clarke, Thomas J. *Thestreet.com* 1787
Clarke, Thomas E. *Nike Inc* 1287
Clarke, Thomas E. *Newell Rubbermaid Inc* 1278
Clarke, Tim *AES Corp* 38
Clarke, Tim *Mitchells & Butlers Plc* 1200
Clarke, Tony *Amarin Corp Plc* 77
Clarke, Tracey *United Community Financial Corp* 1858
Clarke, Troy A. *General Motors Corp* 772
Clarke, Virginia A. *Medical Properties Trust Inc* 1152
Clarke, William S. *GeoGlobal Resources Inc* 780
Clarkeson, John S. *Cabot Corp* 301
Clarkson, Andrew M. *GTx Inc* 832
Clarkson, Brian M. *Moody's Corp* 1214
Clarkson, Gary D. *Circuit Research Labs Inc* 408
Clarkson, James R. *HCSB Financial Corp* 856
Clarkson, John G. *Noven Pharmaceuticals Inc* 1311
Clarkson, Jonathan M. *Edge Petroleum Corp* 603
Clarkson, Lawrence W. *Avnet Inc* 191
Clarkson, Robert T. *Symmetricom Inc* 1735
Clarkson, Ross G. *TransGlobe Energy Corp* 1816
Clarno, Beverly *Prineville Bancorp* 1468
Claro, Jaime *Embotelladora Andina S.A.* 620
Claro, Juan *Andina Bottling Co Inc* 121
Clarot, Timothy L. *Matrixx Initiatives Inc* 1132
Clary, Cheryl L. *Southwest Water Co* 1670
Clary, Edward J. *Haverty Furniture Companies Inc* 853
Clary, Robert E. *SuffolkFirst Bank* 1715
Clary, Tom *Affiliated Computer Services Inc* 39
Clasen, Robert B. *NTN Communications Inc* 1313
Clasen, Robert B. *Path 1 Network Technologies Inc* 1390
Classen, David C. *First Consulting Group Inc* 703
Classon, Rolf *Millipore Corp* 1193
Classon, Rolf *Auxilium Pharmaceuticals Inc* 184
Classon, Rolf A. *PharmaNet Development Group Inc* 1423
Classon, Rolf *Enzon Pharmaceuticals Inc* 648
Classon, Rolf A. *Hillenbrand Industries Inc* 879
Claudio, Cecilia *Sybase Inc* 1733
Claudy, Guy *Merisel Inc* 1164
Claunch, Jerry B. *Citizens National Corp KY* 414
Claus, Eric *Great Atlantic & Pacific Tea Co Inc* 818
Claus, Matthew *eSpeed Inc* 657
Clausen, Claus *Statoil* 1696
Clausen, Henrik *Neose Technologies Inc* 1260
Clausen, Jorgen M. *Sauer Danfoss Inc* 1586
Clausen, Susan P. *MiddleBrook Pharmaceuticals Inc* 1185
Clauser, Paul R. *Dillard's Inc* 558
Claussen, Carsten P. *Qiagen* 1492
Clauw, Daniel J. *Cypress Bioscience Inc* 519
Claux, Augusto *Clear Channel Outdoor Holdings Inc* 422
Claverie, Pierre *Spansion Inc* 1673
Clavijo, James *Dor Biopharma Inc* 570
Clavijo, Jesus Olmos *Endesa* 631
Clawges, John *Roebling Financial Corp Inc New* 1556
Clawson, Chad *American Capital Strategies Ltd* 87
Clawson, Curtis J. *Hayes Lemmerz International Inc* 855
Clawson, John G. *Non-Invasive Monitoring Systems Inc* 1293
Clawson, Matt *Moventis Capital Inc* 1220
Clawson, Matt *Endocare Inc* 632
Clawson, Matt *BioLife Solutions Inc* 244
Claxton, Robert C. *Big Lots Inc* 238
Clay, Blaise *Barnwell Industries Inc* 217
Clay, Catesby W. *Churchill Downs Inc* 404
Clay, George H. *Alabama National Bancorp* 50
Clay, Herb *AFP Imaging Corp* 41
Clay, Jennifer *SKECHERS USA* 1640
Clay, John R. *Americredit Corp* 108
Clay, Kendall O. *FNB Corp* 730
Clay, Kendall O. *FNB Corp/VA* 730
Clay, Kendall O. *FNB United Corp* 731
Clay, Kirsty *Lloyds TSB Group Plc* 1088
Clay, Landon *Golden Queen Mining Co Ltd* 806
Clay, Nicholas *DTS Inc* 579
Clay, Robert N. *PNC Financial Services Group Inc* 1442
Clay, Wendy F. *CPAC Inc* 493
Clay, William A. *Acxiom Corp* 20
Claybaugh, H. C. *Primedex Health Systems Inc* 1466
Clayborn, Kevin *Circuit Research Labs Inc* 408
Claybrook, Robert *Bed Bath & Beyond Inc* 227
Claycomb, Val *Republic Bancorp Inc/KY* 1534
Clayden, Paul F. *Navigators Group Inc (The)* 1253
Claydon, Lynn *Crawford & Co* 495
Clayman, Mark *NaviSite Inc* 1253
Claypool, Jeffrey C. *Sealy Corp* 1600
Claypool, William D. *ViroPharma Incorporated* 1911
Clayton, Annette K. *Polaris Industries Inc* 1444
Clayton, Bret *Rio Tinto Ltd* 1546
Clayton, Bret K. *Ivanhoe Mines Ltd* 995
Clayton, Bret *Rio Tinto Plc* 1547
Clayton, Bruce R. *Genuine Parts Co* 778
Clayton, Danny *Boots & Coots Intl Well Control Inc* 266
Clayton, Dawn *MTR Gaming Group Inc* 1225
Clayton, Gail *Suncor Energy Inc* 1720
Clayton, Garrick *Forster Drilling Corp* 737
Clayton, James H. *Federal Home Loan Banks* 684
Clayton, Jim *Fisher Communications Inc* 721
Clayton, John *First Industrial Realty Trust Inc* 708
Clayton, John M. *Matrixx Initiatives Inc* 1132
Clayton, Joseph P. *Sirius Satellite Radio Inc* 1638
Clayton, Joseph P. *Transcend Services Inc* 1815
Clayton, Karen *Tower Financial Corp* 1807
Clayton, Kerry J. *Assurant Inc* 165
Clayton, Kevin T. *Ruby Tuesday Inc* 1566
Clayton, Larry *Centerpoint Energy Inc* 359
Clayton, Michael *StarTek Inc* 1694
Clayton, Morrie *Badger Meter Inc* 199
Clayton, Paul E. *Jamba Inc* 1002
Clayton, Paul *Veeco Instruments Inc* 1892
Clayton, Richard *First Bancorp* 696
Clayton, Robert L. *Spherix Inc* 1680
Clayton, Robin *Republic Bancorp Inc/KY* 1534
Clayton, Robyn *Southwest Gas Corp* 1669
Clayton, Ronald W. *Hecla Mining Co* 864
Clayton, Russell G. *Discovery Laboratories Inc* 562
Clayton, Sharon *Equus Total Return Inc* 654
Clayton, Shirley Liu *Metrocorp Bancshares Inc* 1172
Clayton, Timothy C. *Adesa Inc* 24
Claytor, Preston J. *Railamerica Inc* 1510
Cleal, Dorothy *Telkonet Inc* 1770
Clear, Geoff *IRobot Corp* 988
Clearman, John F. *Esterline Technologies Corp* 659
Clearman, Stephen J. *Target Logistics Inc* 1750
Cleary, Dermott *Nike Inc* 1287
Cleary, Henry *Bank of Ireland (The)* 209
Cleary, James J. *El Paso Corp* 609
Cleary, James J. *El Paso Natural Gas Co* 610
Cleary, James J. *Colorado Interstate Gas Co* 441
Cleary, James F. *MWI Veterinary Supply Inc* 1229
Cleary, Loughlin *Federal Home Loan Bank of Boston* 682
Cleary, M. *Merck & Co Inc* 1162
Cleary, Martin D. *Electro-Optical Sciences Inc* 613
Cleary, Megan *Fox & Hound Restaurant Group* 741
Cleary, Patricia K. *International Lease Finance Corp* 970
Cleary, Raymond E. *Beach First National Bancshares Inc* 224
Cleary, Susan J. *CNB Corp MI* 428
Cleave, Ernest *Grandview Gold Inc* 815
Cleave, James H. *HSBC USA Inc* 895
Cleaveland, Becky *United Parcel Service Inc* 1861
Cleaver, Julie *General Growth Properties Inc* 771
Cleberg, Anthony S. *CNA Surety Corp* 427
Clees, John A. *Heritage Financial Corp* 871
Clegg, Al *AXS-One Inc* 196
Clegg, Andrea M. *NightHawk Radiology Holdings Inc* 1286
Clegg, Brian *CHC Helicopter Corp* 378
Clegg, Christopher R. *Aleris International Inc* 55
Clegg, Frank *Advanced Micro Devices Inc* 30
Clegg, Jackie M. *Blockbuster Inc* 255
Clegg, Jackie *Chicago Mercantile Exchange Holdings Inc* 384
Clegg, Jackie M. *Cardiome Pharma Corp* 333
Clegg, Jackie M. *Brookdale Senior Living Inc* 285
Clegg, Tim *Community Business Bank CA* 453
Cleghorn, John E. *Molson Coors Brewing Co* 1209
Cleghorn, John E. *Canadian Pacific Railway Ltd* 318
Cleghorn, Jon G. *First Federal Bankshares Inc* 704
Clein, Mark P. *Psychiatric Solutions Inc* 1485
Clelland, Alan *Iteris Inc* 993
Clem, Dave *Amcon Distributing Co* 80
Clem, Gail *Coast Financial Holdings Inc* 431
Clem, John *Stamps.com Inc* 1689
Clem, Kathryn O. *UDR Inc* 1844
Clem, Kevin *Huron Consulting Group Inc* 901
Clemedtson, Peter *LM Ericsson Telephone Co* 1089
Clemens, Alan R. *Southwestern Energy Co* 1670
Clemens, Alvin H. *Health Benefits Direct Corp* 857
Clemens, James *Espey Mfg & Electronics Corp* 657
Clemens, Kevan *Kosan Biosciences Inc* 1041
Clemens, Kevan *Chelsea Therapeutics International Ltd* 380
Clemens, Mark A. *Massey Energy Co* 1129
Clemens, Paul F. *First Midwest Bancorp Inc* 711
Clemens, Peter A. *Acura Pharmaceuticals Inc* 20
Clemens, Peter J. *Caremark Rx Inc* 334
Clemens, Philip A. *Harleysville Savings Financial Corp* 847
Clemens, Will *Advent Software Inc* 33
Clemensen, Tim *Woize International Ltd* 1973
Clemensen, Tim *mPhase Technologies Inc* 1221
Clemensen, Tim *Sulphco Inc* 1715
Clemensen, Tim *Vistula Communications Services Inc* 1915
Clemenson, Jim *Jones Soda Company* 1011
Clement, Albert E. *VeriSign Inc* 1896
Clement, Bond J. *Petroquest Energy Inc* 1418
Clement, Christopher G. *Savient Pharmaceuticals Inc* 1587
Clement, Cor J. *Rural/Metro Corp* 1567
Clement, Dale *Napco Security Systems Inc* 1235
Clement, Dallas S. *Simtrol Inc* 1635
Clement, Frank H. *Redhook Ale Brewery Inc* 1521
Clement, Hayes D. *Piedmont Natural Gas Co Inc* 1429
Clement, Jacob J. *MIGENIX Inc* 1188
Clement, Julie *Gevity HR Inc* 784
Clement, Philip B. *Aon Corp* 129
Clement, Phillip *International Electronics Inc* 968
Clement, Tracy *Enterprise Bancorp Inc* 642
Clement, Troy *Arkona Inc* 149

Donnan, John M. *Kaiser Aluminum Corp* 1016
Donnarumma, Stephen *Assured Guaranty Ltd* 165
Donnell, Barry *Cavalier Homes Inc* 346
Donnell, Curtis R. *Hallmark Financial Services Inc* 839
Donnell, Cydney C. *American Campus Communities Inc* 87
Donnell, Joe H. *Inergy LP* 936
Donnell, Jon *VistaCare Inc* 1915
Donnell, Thomas B. *Fifth Third Bancorp* 691
Donnelley, James R. *Sierra Pacific Resources* 1626
Donnelly, Barbara *American Riviera Bank* 101
Donnelly, Brian *ADA-ES Inc* 21
Donnelly, Charlene *ADA-ES Inc* 21
Donnelly, George J. *Parker Drilling Co* 1387
Donnelly, Howard W. *Vital Signs Inc* 1917
Donnelly, Howard W. *Angiodynamics Inc* 123
Donnelly, John L. *Citicorp* 411
Donnelly, John J. *1st Colonial Bancorp Inc* 2004
Donnelly, John L. *Citigroup Inc* 411
Donnelly, John *Grubb & Ellis Co* 827
Donnelly, John T. *Sun Life Financial Inc* 1718
Donnelly, Joseph M. *Comcast Corp* 444
Donnelly, Kevin *Rambus Inc* 1512
Donnelly, Michael J. *S&T Bank* 1570
Donnelly, Michael *IAMGOLD Corp* 908
Donnelly, Michael J. *Kroger Co* 1043
Donnelly, Patrick L. *Sirius Satellite Radio Inc* 1638
Donnelly, Patrick *Aon Corp* 129
Donnelly, Peter P. *General American Investors Inc* 769
Donnelly, Phil *Finova Group Inc* 694
Donnelly, Richard M. *Oshkosh Truck Corp* 1361
Donnelly, Richard G. *Aspenbio Inc* 163
Donnelly, Scott C. *General Electric Co* 770
Donnelly, Susan *MWI Veterinary Supply Inc* 1229
Donnelly, Tad *Airxcel Inc* 48
Donnelly, Thomas *Digital River Inc* 557
Donnelly, Timothy J. *American Vanguard Corp* 106
Donnelly, Vincent T. *PMA Capital Corp* 1441
Donnelly, William P. *Mettler-Toledo International Inc* 1173
Donnelly, William *Vocus Inc* 1920
Donnelly, Yvonne *Beverly National Corp* 235
Donnenberg, Milton *Wilshire Enterprises Inc* 1964
Donnenfeld, Eric D. *Insite Vision Inc* 951
Donnenwirth, Scott M. *First Citizens Banc Corp* 700
Donner, Fred R. *RenaissanceRe Holdings Ltd* 1530
Donner, Richard W. *First Citizens Bancshares Inc/TN* 701
Donnini, David A. *Commach Corp* 437
Donnini, David A. *Syniverse Holdings Inc* 1738
Donnini, David A. *Prestige Brand Holdings Inc* 1463
Donnino, Michael F. *Granite Construction Inc* 815
Donofrio, John *Visteon Corp* 1915
Donofrio, Katherine A. *North Shore Gas Co* 1299
Donofrio, Lawrence *Advanced Oxygen Technologies Inc* 31
Donofrio, Nicholas M. *Bank of New York Co Inc* 210
Donofrio, Nicholas M. *IBM Corp* 909
Donofrio, Thomas A. *Penns Woods Bancorp Inc* 1404
Donoghue, Bernard *WNS (Holdings) Ltd* 1972
Donoghue, Craig W. *Buffalo Wild Wings* 293
Donoghue, James W. *Nacco Industries Inc* 1232
Donoghue, John P. *Cyberkinetics Neurotechnology Systems Inc* 516
Donoho, Elisa *Noble Energy Inc* 1291
Donohoe, Christopher *Brandywine Realty Trust* 274
Donohoe, Patricia *Medical Staffing Network Holdings Inc* 1152
Donohoe, Seamus *MBI Mortgage Services Ltd* 1138
Donohue, Anne M. *SRA International Inc* 1685
Donohue, Ben *Axcess International Inc TX* 194
Donohue, Bertha *Jeffersonville Bancorp* 1006
Donohue, Craig S. *Chicago Mercantile Exchange Holdings Inc* 384
Donohue, Dan *GTECH Holdings Corp* 832
Donohue, James J. *Charles River Assoc Inc* 374
Donohue, Jody *Primedex Health Systems Inc* 1466
Donohue, Lilly *Newcastle Investment Corp* 1277
Donohue, Mark *Dow Jones & Co Inc* 573
Donohue, Paul E. *Main Street Trust Inc* 1114
Donohue, Richard R. *Midwestone Financial Group Inc* 1188
Donohue, Sean P. *United Air Lines Inc* 1854
Donohue, Sean P. *UAL Corp/DE* 1842
Donohue, Thomas J. *XM Satellite Radio Holdings Inc* 1987
Donohue, Thomas J. *Xm Satellite Radio Inc* 1987
Donohue, Thomas J. *Sunrise Senior Living Inc* 1723
Donohue, Thomas J. *Union Pacific Corp* 1852
Donoso, Jose Cox *Lan Airlines* 1052
Donoughue, Peter C. *John Wiley & Sons Inc* 1009
Donovan, Alfred L. *Independent Bank Corp* 933
Donovan, Bill *Guardian Technologies International Inc* 833
Donovan, Dan *Panavision Inc* 1381
Donovan, Daniel P. *Star Gas Partners LP* 1693
Donovan, Denis *Bank of Ireland (The)* 209
Donovan, Donna M. *Jacksonville Bancorp Inc FL* 1001
Donovan, Edmund D. *First Valley Bancorp Inc CT* 718
Donovan, Fred C. *Southern Co* 1666
Donovan, Fred C. *Gulf Power Co* 835
Donovan, James L. *IRIDEX Corp* 988
Donovan, John M. *VeriSign Inc* 1896
Donovan, John *Vermilion Energy Trust* 1897
Donovan, John *Emrise Corp* 627
Donovan, John *NII Holdings Inc* 1287
Donovan, John *Bank Holdings* 208
Donovan, Joseph J. *Zoom Technologies Inc* 2002
Donovan, Joseph *RAM Holdings Ltd* 1512
Donovan, Kevin *Bottomline Technologies (DE) Inc* 269
Donovan, Melinda N. *Cambridge Bancorp* 313
Donovan, Michael E. *United Surgical Partners International Inc* 1863
Donovan, Michael *Nexstar Broadcasting Group Inc* 1283
Donovan, Michael J. *Summit State Bank* 1717
Donovan, Michael J. *HCC Insurance Holdings Inc* 856
Donovan, Michael P. *HealthExtras Inc* 860
Donovan, Nancy S. *Lee Enterprises Inc* 1064
Donovan, Patrick W. *Mueller Industries Inc* 1226
Donovan, Paul Michael *China Mobile Hong Kong Ltd* 392
Donovan, Paul *Boston Scientific Corp* 268
Donovan, Paul *Amcore Financial Inc* 80
Donovan, Paul *CLARCOR Inc* 418
Donovan, Paul *Woodward Governor Co* 1974
Donovan, Paul *Vodafone Group Plc* 1920
Donovan, Paul *Syntel Inc* 1740
Donovan, Robert *Ambac Financial Group Inc* 78
Donovan, Scott R. *Odyssey Re Holdings Corp* 1329
Donovan, Stephen M. *Lattice Semiconductor Corp* 1058
Donovan, Steve *Sunrise Telecom Inc* 1723
Donovan, Sue *Pinnacle Bank Of OR* 1431
Donovan, Timothy R. *Tenneco Automotive Inc* 1775
Donovan, Timothy R. *Allied Waste Industries Inc* 66
Donovan, Timothy *Boston Communications Group Inc* 267
Donovan, Timothy R. *John B Sanfilippo & Son Inc* 1008
Donovan, William T. *Grey Wolf Inc* 825
Donovan, William M. *Hingham Institution for Savings* 880
Donovan, William J. *Nortel Networks Corp* 1296
Donovan Hart, Sharon E. *State Street Corp* 1696
Donze, Martha *Axcan Pharma Inc* 194
Doo, Lim Ah *PT Indosat Tbk* 1485
Doodchenko, Sergei *Klondike Star Mineral Corp* 1033
Doody, Don *IEC Electronics Corp* 918
Doody, Gregory L. *Calpine Corp* 311
Doody, Joseph G. *Casella Waste Systems Inc* 341
Doody, Joseph G. *Staples Inc* 1692
Doody, Paul *Union Trust Company* 1852
Doody, Rachelle *Medivation Inc* 1155
Doody, Susan *Beverly National Corp* 235
Doody, William *Grubb & Ellis Co* 827
Doogan, Declan *Amarin Corp Plc* 77
Doolan, Elizabeth A. *BankFinancial Corp* 213
Doolan, Victor H. *Sonic Automotive Inc* 1656
Dooley, Chuck *Western Massachusetts Electric Co* 1950
Dooley, Greg J. *Federal Home Loan Bank of Cincinnati* 683
Dooley, Joseph F. *Procter & Gamble* 1472
Dooley, Richard G. *Kimco Realty Corp* 1029
Dooley, Richard G. *Jefferies Group Inc* 1005
Dooley, Thomas E. *Viacom Inc* 1902
Dooley, Timothy *Republic Airways Holdings Inc* 1534
Dooley, William N. *American General Finance Inc* 92
Dooley, William N. *International Lease Finance Corp* 970
Doolin, James P. *Hangman Productions Inc* 844
Doolin, Wallace B. *BUCA Inc* 291
Doolin, Wallace B. *Caribou Coffee Company Inc* 334
Doolittle, Barbara *North State Bank Inc* 1300
Doolittle, James A. *Alliance Financial Corp NY* 61
Doolittle, Lea Anne *Northwest Natural Gas Co* 1306
Dooner, Marlene S. *Comcast Corp* 444
Doorley, Thomas L. *Natrol Inc* 1248
Doornink, Ron *Activision Inc* 19
Doot, Carl L. *EMC Insurance Group Inc* 621
Dopfner, Mathias *Time Warner Inc* 1795
Dopfner, Mathias *Bayer Schering Pharma Aktiengesellschaft* 221
Dopp, Natalie *Giant Industries Inc* 785
Dopp, Pierce *Mid Wisconsin Financial Services Inc* 1183
Doppler, Stephen B. *Aurelio Resource Corp* 178
Dor, Boaz *Security Devices International Inc* 1604
Dor, Mony Ben *Pharmos Corp* 1423
Dor, Nir *BVR Systems (1998) Ltd* 298
Dor, Tal *AudioCodes Ltd* 178
Dorais, Jose P. *Aeterna Zentaris Inc* 38
Doran, Harold G. *Kentucky Investors Inc* 1024
Doran, James J. *Columbia Bancorp OR* 442
Doran, James E. *Spansion Inc* 1673
Doran, James *Suntron Corp* 1724
Doran, Jeff *Veeco Instruments Inc* 1892
Doran, Jim J. *Columbia Bancorp OR* 442
Doran, Jim *Suntron Corp* 1724
Doran, Jim J. *Columbia Bancorp* 442
Doran, Mary A. *Zale Corp* 1995
Doran, Paul *Zindart Ltd* 1999
Doran, Shelly J. *Simon Property Group Inc* 1634
Doran, Theresa *Lamar Advertising Company* 1051
Doran, Vincent *ResCare Inc* 1535
Doran, Wayne S. *Glimcher Realty Trust* 790
Dordell, Timothy P. *Toro Co* 1804
Dordelman, William E. *Comcast Corp* 444
Dore, Clayton *Sunrise Telecom Inc* 1723
Dore, James J. *Global Industries Ltd* 794
Dore, James P. *Bitstream Inc* 251
Dore, Jim *Servidyne Inc* 1614
Dore, Kathleen *CanWest Global Communications Corp* 321
Dore, Mark *Grubb & Ellis Co* 827
Dore, Paule *CGI Group Inc* 370
Dore, William J. *Global Industries Ltd* 794
Dore-Falcone, Carol *GeoPharma Inc* 781
Doremus, George H. *Stolt Offshore* 1706
Doremus, George H. *Acergy S.A.* 14
Dorer, Benno *Clorox Co (The)* 425
Dorer, Lori *Kendle International Inc* 1022
Doretti, Robert *eDiets.com Inc* 604
Dorey, Norma J. *Towne Bank VA* 1808
Dorey, William G. *Granite Construction Inc* 815
Dorf, Carl *21st Century Holding Co* 2006
Dorflinger, Peter G. *Benchmark Electronics Inc* 231
Dorfman, Jack P. *Cyber Digital Inc* 516
Dorfman, Mark A. *DRS Technologies Inc* 577
Dorfman, Scott *Innotrac Corp* 947
Dorgan, David M. *Rockwell Automation Inc* 1554
Doria, Joseph G. *Lincoln Electric Holdings Inc* 1080
Doria, Robert G. *Pamrapo Bancorp Inc* 1380
Dorian, James *Discovery Bancorp CA* 561
Dorian, Michael V. *Dearborn Bancorp Inc* 533
Dorig, Rolf *Adecco* 23
Dorin, George *Moventis Capital Inc* 1220
Doring, Michael *Ceradyne Inc* 367
Doris, Jason *Omtool Ltd* 1339
Doris, Robert J. *Sonic Solutions* 1658
Dorit, Helmaliah *Israel Bank of Agriculture Ltd* 992
Dority, Norm *Denia Enterprises Inc* 542
Dorland, Gary A. *Mantech International Corp* 1120
Dorlaque, Mark *LMI Aerospace Inc* 1089
Dorman, Brett *Farmer Bros Co* 678
Dorman, Daniel J. *Sheffield Pharmaceuticals Inc* 1618
Dorman, Daniel J. *Sandston Corp* 1581
Dorman, David W. *Motorola Inc* 1219
Dorman, David W. *Yum! Brands Inc* 1994
Dorman, Diane *First South Bancorp Inc/VA* 717
Dorman, Harry *New Hampshire Thrift Bancshares Inc* 1272
Dorman, James H. *Transmeridian Exploration Inc* 1816
Dorman, James H. *Platinum Energy Resources Inc* 1438
Dorman, Janet L. *Virginia National Bank* 1911
Dorman, Jodi *Chubb Corp* 403
Dorman, Joe B. *North American Technologies Group Inc* 1297
Dorman, Margaret K. *Smith International Inc* 1648
Dorman, Mitzi *LHC Group Inc* 1072
Dorman, Robin Boss *A T Cross Co* 1
Dorman, Ronald J. *Telos Corp* 1771
Dorman, Tim *Korn Ferry International* 1041
Dormann, Juergen *IBM Corp* 909
Dormann, Juergen *ABB Ltd* 5
Dormann, Jurgen *Adecco* 23
Dormann, Jurgen *BG Group Plc* 236
Dormann, Jurgen *Sanofi Aventis* 1582
Dormer, Stephen G. *Provident New York Bancorp* 1481
Dorminey, Leonard O. *Heritage Financial Group* 871
Dorn, Andrew W. *Great Lakes Bancorp Inc* 819
Dorn, Eric C. *Cardica Inc* 330
Dorn, Erik J. *Burke & Herbert Bank & Trust Company* 296
Dorn, Randy *Covenant Transport Inc* 491
Dorn, Richard A. *First Interstate BancSystem Inc* 708
Dorn, Robert R. *American Healthchoice Inc* 93
Dorn, Thomas Jeff *Southeastern Bank Financial Corp* 1664
Dornau, Gregor M. *Ocean Bio Chem Inc* 1326
Dornau, Peter G. *Ocean Bio Chem Inc* 1326
Dornbush, Darwin C. *Levitt Corp* 1070
Dornbush, Darwin C. *Benihana Inc* 231
Dornbush, Darwin C. *Cantel Medical Corp* 320
Dornemann, Michael *Access Worldwide Communications Inc* 12
Dornemann, Michael *Take Two Interactive Software Inc* 1745
Dorner, Kimberly Ann *Prudential Bancorp Inc of Pennsylvania* 1482
Dorney, Kevin *Maximus Inc* 1136
Dorny, Matthew D. *Nu Skin Enterprises Inc* 1314
Dorofte, Luc *Richmont Mines Inc* 1543
Doron, Eli *Radvision Ltd* 1509
Doron, Rami *Sapiens International Corp* 1584
Dorosz, Wanda *Visiphor Corp* 1914
Dorpinghaus, Tim *Colorado Interstate Gas Co* 441
Dorr, Andrew *Lpath Inc* 1097
Dorr, Kristen *Vicon Industries Inc* 1903
Dorr, Marjorie W. *WellPoint Inc* 1944
Dorr, Richard A. *Summit State Bank* 1717
Dorrance, Bennett *Insight Enterprises Inc* 951
Dorrance, Bennett *Campbell Soup Co* 316
Dorrance, Bob *Toronto-Dominion Bank* 1804
Dorrance, David *Bio-Solutions International Inc* 241
Dorrance, Robert E. *Toronto-Dominion Bank* 1804
Dorrepaal, Karin *Bayer Schering Pharma Aktiengesellschaft* 221
Dorris, Jennifer H. *Express-1 Expedited Solutions Inc* 671
Dorris, Jim *Astec Industries Inc* 166
Dorris, Richard J. *Astec Industries Inc* 166
Dorrough, Jayme *Techlabs Inc* 1757
Dorsa, Caroline *Public Service Enterprise Group Inc* 1487
Dorsa, Caroline *Public Service Enterprise Group Incorporated* 1487
Dorsa, Caroline *Avaya Inc* 187
Dorsaisamy, Durga *Puget Energy Inc* 1488
Dorsch, Michael R. *iStar Financial Inc* 992
Dorschner, Diane *Hawkins Inc* 854
Dorsett, Herbert F. *Radiation Therapy Services Inc* 1507
Dorsey, Brian T. *Somaxon Pharmaceuticals Inc* 1655
Dorsey, James *ENGlobal Corp* 638
Dorsey, Jeremiah E. *Cardiotech International Inc* 333
Dorsey, Michael *Questar Assessment Inc* 1501
Dorsey, Patrick B. *Tiffany & Co* 1793
Dorsky, Steven M. *Developers Diversified Realty Corp* 547
Dorsman, Peter A. *Applied Industrial Technologies Inc* 135
Dorsman, Peter *NCR Corp* 1256
Dorst, James W. *Aethlon Medical Inc* 38
Dort, Thomas *Polymer Group Inc* 1446
Dorto, Joseph A. *Towne Bank VA* 1808
Dorval, Bernie *Toronto-Dominion Bank* 1804
Dorwart, Frederic *BOK Financial Corp* 263
Dorwart, Mark A. *Aeropostale Inc* 37
Dos Santos, Agenor Azevedo *Perdigao S.A.* 1411
Dos Santos, Alvaro Avelino Carvalho *Tele Norte Leste Participacoes* 1764
Dos Santos, Antonio Cardoso *Brazil Telecom Co* 275
Dos Santos, Antonio Cardoso *Brasil Telecom Participacoes S.A.* 274
Dos Santos, Everaldo Nigro *Sadia* 1572
Dos Santos, Francelino Pereira *Comp En De Mn Cemig ADS* 457
Dos Santos, Jamie *Terremark Worldwide Inc* 1779
Dos Santos, Maria Virginia Bastos *EDP Energias De Portugal SA* 605
Dos Santos, Milton Luciano *CPFL Energy Inc* 493
Dos Santos, Sergio Assenco Tavares *Vivo Participacoes S.A.* 1919
Dos Santos Diniz, Joao Paulo Falleiros Dos *Companhia Brasileira de Distribuicao* 457
Dos Santos Diniz, Joaopaulo Falleiros *Brazilian Distribution Co Companhia Brasileira De Distr CBD* 276
Dos Santos Diniz, Pedro Paulo Falleiros Dos *Brazilian Distribution Co Companhia Brasileira De Distr CBD* 276
Dos Santos Diniz, Pedro Paulo Falleiros Dos *Companhia Brasileira de Distribuicao* 457
Dos Santos Diniz DAvila, Anamaria Falleiros *Brazilian Distribution Co Companhia Brasileira De Distr CBD* 276
Dosanjh, Kam *Algoma Steel Inc* 56
Dosanjh, Paramjit *Mission Bancorp CA* 1198
Dosch, Michelle *Bridge Bancorp Inc* 278
Doshi, Jitendra N. *Caraco Pharmaceutical Laboratories Ltd* 329
Doski, Vicky L. *First Citizens Banc Corp* 700
Dosland, Michael W. *First Federal Bankshares Inc* 704
Dosoretz, Daniel E. *Radiation Therapy Services Inc* 1507
Doss, Galal P. *A T Cross Co* 1
Doss, James *Golden Valley Bank CA* 807
Doss, Keith *Gasco Energy Inc* 763
Doss, Michael P. *Graphic Packaging Corp* 816
Doss, Wayne *Zupintra Corp Inc* 2003
Dossche, Yves *Remedent USA Inc* 1529
Dossey, Michael T. *Frontier Oil Corp* 751
Dostal, David G. *FC Banc Corp* 681
Dostarty, Thomas J. *Massey Energy Co* 1129
Doster, Brian R. *Checkers Drive In Restaurants Inc* 378
Doster, Thomas *IMPSAT Fiber Networks Inc* 931
Dostie, Mark *WordLogic Corp* 1975
Doswell, Mary C. *Performance Food Group Co* 1412
Doswell, Mary C. *Dominion Resources Inc VA* 568
Dotan, Barak *Cimatron Ltd* 406
Dotan, Barak *Nexus Telocation Systems Ltd* 1284
Doti, James L. *Standard Pacific Corp* 1690
Doti, James L. *First American Corp* 695
Doti, James L. *Fleetwood Enterprises Inc* 724
Doti, Lynne Pierson *Plaza Bank CA* 1439
Doto, Robert *Technest Holdings Inc* 1757
Dotoli, Gustave T. *mPhase Technologies Inc* 1221
Dotson, Connie M. *E Trade Financial Corp* 588
Dotson, Garner W. *Kinder Morgan Inc* 1030
Dotson, Garner W. *Kinder Morgan Management LLC* 1030
Dotson, Garner W. *Kinder Morgan Energy Partners LP* 1030
Dotson, George S. *Atwood Oceanics Inc* 177
Dotson, Jerrold D. *Calypte Biomedical Corp* 312

Faulkner, Kenneth L. *Steak N Shake Co* 1697
Faulkner, Larry R. *Temple Inland Inc* 1773
Faulkner, Mikel D. *HKN Inc* 881
Faulkner, Peter *Metal Storm Ltd* 1169
Faulling, Ralph F. *Community Bankshares Inc SC* 453
Faulstich, Lance M. *Bank Holdings* 208
Faulstick, Luke T. *DJO Incorporated* 565
Faupel, Mark L. *Spectrx Inc* 1679
Faure, Michel *Air France-KLM* 45
Faure, Patrick *Air Products & Chemicals Inc* 46
Faurer, Lincoln D. *Analex Corp* 119
Faurer, Lincoln D. *Saflink Corp* 1574
Faurot, Barbara *Genworth Financial Inc* 779
Fausel, Peter *ID Systems Inc* 914
Fausett, Frank *Atlas Mining Co* 173
Fauske, Daniel R. *Federal Home Loan Bank of Seattle* 683
Faust, Joe *BNSF Railway Co* 261
Faust, John *Community Health Systems Inc* 454
Faust, Joseph *Burlington Northern Santa FE Corp* 296
Faust, Molly *American Express Co* 91
Faust, Thomas E. *Eaton Vance Corp* 596
Faust, William *Crystallex International Corp* 507
Fauster, John U. *First Defiance Financial Corp* 704
Fausti, Cameron *Integrity Bancshares Inc* 958
Fausti, Luigi *Telecom Italia SpA* 1765
Faux, Richard J. *BSD Medical Corp* 290
Favaro, Paul *Nordstrom Credit Inc* 1294
Favaro, Paul *Nordstrom Inc* 1294
Favati, Vittorio *EGL Inc* 608
Favero, Flavio L. *Sadia* 1572
Favero, Pamela *A.J. Smith Federal Savings Bank* 2
Favi, Morris *Cooper Tire & Rubber Co* 478
Favorite, Melissa M. *FPB Bancorp Inc* 742
Favorito, Joe *Paligent Inc* 1378
Favre, Michel Alain Maurice *Brazilian Distribution Co Companhia Brasileira De Distr CBD* 276
Favre, Michel Alain Maurice *Companhia Brasileira de Distribuicao* 457
Favreau, Philippe *Carmanah Technologies Corp* 335
Favrot, James P. *IBERIABANK Corp* 908
Favuzza, Steven P. *UIL Holdings Corp* 1845
Fawaz, Marwan *Charter Communications Inc* 376
Fawaz, Ramzi R. *Shell Canada Ltd* 1618
Fawcett, Amelia C. *State Street Corp* 1696
Fawcett, Gayle P. *Berkshire Hills Bancorp Inc* 233
Fawcett, James *Acorda Therapeutics Inc* 15
Fawcett, John *Capital Corp of the West* 324
Fawcett, Robert A. *Rurban Financial Corp* 1568
Fawcett, William W. *Travelstar Inc* 1818
Fawns, Denise *Golden Valley Bank CA* 807
Fawzy, Christopher A. *Woodward Governor Co* 1974
Fawzy, Ibrahim *Quality Systems Inc* 1496
Fay, Amy *Dillard's Inc* 558
Fay, Chris *Anglo American Plc* 124
Fay, Debbie *Charter Oak Bank CA* 376
Fay, Eric *Mer Telemanagement Solutions Ltd* 1160
Fay, George R. *CNA Financial Corp* 427
Fay, George R. *CAN Financial Corp* 316
Fay, John F. *Instinet Group Inc* 953
Fay, Mary *Sun Life Assurance Company of Canada US* 1718
Fay, Mary M. *Sun Life Financial Inc* 1718
Fay, Mary M. *Sun Life Insurance and Annuity Company of New York* 1719
Fay, Maureen A. *Kelly Services Inc* 1022
Fay, William F. *Digital Recorders Inc* 557
Fayard, Gary P. *Coca-Cola Co* 433
Fayard, Gary *Coca-Cola FEMSA* 433
Fayard, Gary P. *Coca-Cola Enterprises Inc* 433
Faye, Peter *North Valley Bancorp* 1300
Fayet, Arnaud *Transgene* 1816
Fayhee, Patrick D. *First Ottawa Bancshares Inc* 714
Fayyad, Usama *Yahoo Inc* 1990
Fazal, Lookman *Avaya Inc* 187
Fazekas, David *IPSCO Inc* 987
Fazekas, Franz *Neurochem Inc* 1267
Fazenbaker, Wheeler *Colonial Bankshares Inc* 440
Fazio, Albert *Intel Corp* 958
Fazio, George J. *St Jude Medical Inc* 1687
Fazio, John A. *Heidrick & Struggles International Inc* 865
Fazio, Roy *Liberty Bell Bank NJ* 1073
Fazio, Susan *Command Security Corp* 446
Fazio, Victor H. *Northrop Grumman Corp* 1303
Fazio, William J. *Hexcel Corp* 874
Fazzini, John P. *Goldfield Corp (The)* 807
Fazzolari, Salvatore D. *Harsco Corp* 849
Feagan, Brian G. *Santarus Inc* 1584
Feagan, Carole Sue *Telzuit Medical Technologies Inc* 1772
Fealey, Tim *Martek Biosciences Corp* 1126
Fealing, Burt M. *Supervalu Inc* 1728
Fealy, Robert L. *Churchill Downs Inc* 404
Fearer, Paul E. *UnionBanCal Corp* 1853
Fearnley, Mark *Wako Logistics Group Inc* 1929
Fearon, Richard H. *Polyone Corp* 1446
Fearon, Richard H. *Eaton Corp* 596
Fears, Alan *O Reilly Automotive Inc* 1322
Fears, Alfred D. *First Georgia Community Corp* 707
Fears, Douglas E. *Helmerich & Payne Inc* 867
Feasson, Philippe *Ventana Medical Systems Inc* 1893
Feather, Frank *Claxson Interactive Group Inc* 420
Feather, Jeffrey P. *KNBT Bancorp Inc* 1034
Featheringill, William W. *Biocryst Pharmaceuticals Inc* 242
Featherman, John A. *First Chester County Corp* 699
Featherstone, Diane L. *Edison International* 604
Featherstone, Mark A. *Quaker Chemical Corp* 1495
Featherstone, Michael *Cell Wireless Corp* 356
Featherstone, Robert *Mother Lode Bank CA* 1218
Feazle, Kim P. *Reliance Steel & Aluminum Co* 1528
Febbo, Albert J. *Titan International Inc* 1796
Febbo, William J. *MCF Corp* 1140
Fecht, Paul *Badger Meter Inc* 199
Fechter, George A. *US Helicopter Corp* 1877
Fechtner, Robert D. *Catalyst Pharmaceutical Partners Inc* 344
Feczko, Joe *Pfizer Inc* 1420
Fedak, Charles Z. *Molina Healthcare Inc* 1208
Fedde, Chris *Safenet Inc* 1573
Fedderly, Sanford *Tri City National Bank* 1821
Feddersen, Hinrich *Allianz* 63
Feddersen, Ron *Devine Entertainment Corp* 547
Feder, Ben *Take Two Interactive Software Inc* 1745
Feder, Franklin L. *Alcoa Inc* 54
Feder, Michael A. *Bally Total Fitness Holding Corp* 203
Féder, Roz *Schering Plough Corp* 1591
Feder, Steven J. *Safeguard Scientifics Inc* 1573
Federbush, Alexander P. *Mueller Industries Inc* 1226
Federici, William J. *West Pharmaceutical Services Inc* 1948
Federico, Anthony M. *Xerox Corp* 1985
Federico, Charles W. *Orthofix International* 1360
Federico, Charles W. *SRI Surgical Express Inc* 1685
Federico, Charles *BioMimetic Therapeutics Inc* 245
Federico, Chery J. *First Litchfield Financial Corp* 709
Federico, Corrado *Hot Topic Inc* 892
Federico, Nino *GSI Group Inc* 831
Federico, Richard L. *Jamba Inc* 1002
Federico, Richard L. *P.F. Chang's China Bistro Inc* 1368
Federko, Terry *IPSCO Inc* 987
Federle, Louis A. *Commercial Metals Co* 448
Federle, Michael *Grubb & Ellis Co* 827
Federman, Irwin *Sandisk Corp* 1581
Federman, Irwin *Check Point Software Technologies Ltd* 378
Federman, Jay L. *Escalon Medical Corp* 656
Federman, John *Art Technology Group Inc* 153
Federmann, David *Elbit Systems Ltd* 610
Federmann, Michael *Elbit Systems Ltd* 610
Federspiel, John *PDI-Inc* 1397
Fedida, Andre *Bradley Pharmaceuticals Inc* 272
Fedida, Michael *Bradley Pharmaceuticals Inc* 272
Fedida, Michael J. *Watson Pharmaceuticals Inc* 1937
Fedier, Jurg *Ciba Specialty Chemicals Holding Inc* 404
Fedor, Bruce G. *Marco Community Bancorp Inc* 1121
Fedor, Richard T. *GameTech International Inc* 760
Fedoroff, Nina V. *Sigma Aldrich Corp* 1627
Fedoruk, Marion Joseph *Exponent Inc* 671
Fedt, Darin *Verasun Energy Corp* 1894
Fedun, Greg *Shadow Marketing Inc* 1616
Fedus, Ronald C. *Enzo Biochem Inc* 648
Fedyszyn, Sascha P. *Senesco Technologies Inc* 1609
Fedyunin, Vladimir *Knewtrino Inc* 1035
Fee, Douglas F. *UDR Inc* 1844
Fee, Jay *Varsity Group Inc* 1889
Fee, Phil F. *Community Bank of Santa Maria* 452
Feehan, Daniel R. *RadioShack Corp* 1508
Feehan, Daniel R. *Cash America International Inc* 341
Feehan, Daniel R. *AZZ Inc* 197
Feeler, Jeffrey R. *American Ecology Corp* 90
Feeley, Irene A. *National Investment Managers Inc* 1243
Feeley, Paul S. *Central Bancorp Inc* 361
Feely, Doug *Intrawest Corp* 979
Feemster, Tim *Grubb & Ellis Co* 827
Feeney, Carole *Community Bank of Bergen County NJ* 452
Feeney, Gerard T. *Wave Systems Corp* 1938
Feeney, James *CoActive Marketing Group Inc* 430
Feeney, James *Shore Community Bank* 1622
Feeney, John F. *Lincoln Park Bancorp* 1081
Feeney, Maggie *Inhibitex Inc* 944
Feeney, Margaret *Cache Inc* 302
Feeney, Nancy O. *LCC International Inc* 1061
Feeney, Patrick *Grubb & Ellis Co* 827
Feeney, Paul M. *AEP Industries Inc* 36
Feeney, Robert J. *NeoGenomics Inc* 1259
Feeney, William F. *Dole Food Co Inc* 567
Feeny, Curtis F. *CB Richard Ellis Group Inc* 347
Feeny, Kathy F. *Pacificare Health Systems Inc* 1375
Feerick, John D. *Wyeth* 1981
Fees, John A. *McDermott International Inc* 1140
Feese, Kelly D. *Fidelity National Information Services Inc* 690
Fegan, Mike *Edmonds 1 Inc* 604
Fegely, Susan *East Penn Financial Corp* 593
Fegen, Joseph *Grubb & Ellis Co* 827
Fegtly, Donald C. *Con-way Incorporated* 465
Feher, William E. *Emcor Group Inc* 621
Fehlman, Paul W. *Flowserve Corp* 728
Fehlman, Robert A. *Simmons First National Corp* 1634
Fehr, Brian *Tandy Leather Factory Inc* 1748
Fehr, Rick *Dean Foods Co* 533
Fehr, Timothy D. *Raser Technologies Inc* 1515
Fehrenbach, Franz *Allianz* 63
Fehrenbach, Fred P. *Dime Community Bancshares Inc* 558
Fehringer, Carrie *Wells Gardner Electronics Corp* 1944
Fehrman, William J. *Midamerican Energy Co* 1184
Fehsenfeld, Fred M. *Calumet Specialty Products Partners LP* 312
Fehsenfeld, William S. *Calumet Specialty Products Partners LP* 312
Fei, Mike *PacificNet Inc* 1376
Feichtner, Eugene W. *ITT Educational Services Inc* 995
Feick, John E. *Vintage Petroleum Inc* 1908
Feick, John E. *Occidental Petroleum Corp* 1325
Feick, Terry A. *Camco Financial Corp* 314
Feidelberg, Geoffrey F. *CompuDyne Corp* 461
Feierstein, Ted *Ari Network Services Inc* 147
Feiertag, James E. *Twin Disc Inc* 1837
Feig, Ephraim *Kintera Inc* 1032
Feigal, David *Elan Corp Plc* 610
Feigal, David *Renovo Holdings* 1531
Feigal, David *Aspect Medical Systems Inc* 162
Feigel, Breanne *Canadian Pacific Railway Ltd* 318
Feigel, G. A. *Canadian Pacific Railway Ltd* 318
Feiger, George M. *Zions BanCorp* 1999
Feiger, Mitchell *Calamos Asset Management Inc* 305
Feiger, Mitchell *MB Financial Inc MD* 1137
Feigh, Brent T. *American Dental Partners Inc* 89
Feighan, Edward F. *Procentury Corp* 1471
Feighner, Mark S. *Dobson Communications Corp* 566
Feigin, Barbara S. *VF Corp* 1901
Feigin, Barbara S. *Circuit City Stores Inc* 408
Feil, Doug *Command Center Inc* 446
Feiler, Bill *American Vanguard Corp* 106
Feiler, William A. *Jamba Inc* 1002
Feilke, Chad *Cohn & Steers Inc* 437
Feilmeier, Keith R. *Gabriel Technologies Corp* 758
Feimann, Anthony V. *ParaFin Corp* 1384
Fein, Lee Anne *American Retirement Corp* 100
Fein, Scott *Bio Reference Laboratories Inc* 240
Fein, Seymour *Delcath Systems Inc* 536
Fein, Steve *Hewitt Assoc Inc* 874
Feinberg, David M. *Allegheny Energy Inc* 58
Feinberg, David M. *Allegheny Generating Co* 58
Feinberg, Henry J. *Eloyalty Corp* 618
Feinberg, Larry N. *Oracle Health ACQ* 1351
Feinberg, Lee *Orbit International Corp* 1353
Feinberg, Robert *Penton Media Inc* 1406
Feinberg, Stephen L. *ProLogis* 1475
Feinblum, Barnet M. *Gaiam Inc* 758
Feindert, Johann *GATX Corp* 764
Feiner, Barry *Protein Polymer Technologies Inc* 1478
Feiner, Peter *Hungarian Telephone & Cable Corp* 899
Feiner, Phillip *Cano Petroleum Inc* 320
Feiner, Richard *Capital Gold Corp* 324
Feingold, Pat *Bank of Marin* 210
Feingold, Stan *Peace Arch Entertainment Group Inc* 1398
Feinknopf, Abigail M. *WesBanco Bank Inc* 1946
Feinsand, Howard L. *Duke Realty Corp* 580
Feinsilver, Alan D. *Equus Total Return Inc* 654
Feinsilver, Alan D. *ACR Group Inc* 16
Feinsod, Michael *Ameritrans Capital Corp* 111
Feinstein, Jacob *U.S. Energy Systems Inc* 1840
Feinstein, Jeffrey L. *Bed Bath & Beyond Inc* 227
Feinstein, Joel *Starmed Group Inc* 1694
Feinstein, Leonard *Bed Bath & Beyond Inc* 227
Feinstein, Louie *Grill Concepts Inc* 826
Feinstein, Mark R. *Bancorp Rhode Island Inc* 206
Feinstein, Martin D. *Reynolds American Inc* 1541
Feinstein, Michael A. *NOCOPI Technologies Inc* 1292
Feinstein, Michelle *Grill Concepts Inc* 826
Feinstein, Paul M. *Delcath Systems Inc* 536
Feinstein, Richard S. *Bed Bath & Beyond Inc* 227
Feinstein, Richard L. *Edgar Online Inc* 603
Feinstein, Robert *Friedman Billings Ramsey Group Inc* 749
Feintuch, Richard D. *PGT Inc* 1421
Feir, Henry I. *FormFactor Inc* 736
Feiring, Jens Olav *ASA Eksportfinans* 156
Feisel, Lyle *RAESystems* 1510
Feist, Howard N. *Congoleum Corp* 468
Feist, Howard N. *American Biltrite Inc* 86
Feist, Katrina *VistaCare Inc* 1915
Feist, Ronald L. *Granite Community Bank* 815
Feitel, David M. *Martek Biosciences Corp* 1126
Feiten, Joseph B. *American Oil & Gas Inc* 98
Feitler, Robert *Strattec Security Corp* 1711
Feitler, Robert *Weyco Group Inc* 1955
Feiwell, Murray J. *Rio Vista Energy Partners LP* 1547
Feiwus, Bernard D. *J.C. Penney Co Inc* 998
Fekete, Frank L. *Provident Financial Services Inc* 1481
Fekete, Georg *Shuffle Master Inc* 1622
Feketekuty, Zsolt *Resin Systems Inc* 1536
Felando, Phil A. *Qlogic Corp* 1493
Felberg, Craig *Staar Surgical Co* 1688
Felch, David N. *Maine & Maritimes Corp* 1114
Felch, Donna *Female Health Co* 686
Felcht, Utz-Hellmuth *CRH Plc* 500
Felcht, Utz-Hellmuth *SGL Carbon* 1615
Felcht, Utz-Hellmuth *Ciba Specialty Chemicals Holding Inc* 404
Felcyn, Gloria H. *Patriot Scientific Corp* 1392
Feld, Alan D. *Clear Channel Communications Inc* 421
Feld, Charlie *Electronic Data Systems Corp* 614
Feld, Dmitry *AlphaTrade.com* 71
Feld, Gregory K. *CryoCor Inc* 506
Feld, Jeffrey S. *Able Energy Inc* 7
Feld, Joseph *Enterprise Financial Services Corp* 642
Feld, Peter A. *Sharper Image Corp* 1617
Feldbaum, Carl B. *Exelixis Inc* 668
Feldberg, Harley *Avnet Inc* 191
Feldberg, Meyer *Macys Inc* 1108
Feldberg, Meyer *Revlon Inc* 1540
Feldberg, Meyer *Revlon Consumer Products Corp* 1539
Feldberg, Meyer *PRIMEDIA Inc* 1466
Feldberg, Meyer *Sappi Ltd* 1585
Feldenkreis, George *Perry Ellis International Inc* 1414
Feldenkreis, Oscar *Perry Ellis International Inc* 1414
Felder, Stephanie *Brooke Corp* 285
Felder, William D. *SWS Group Inc* 1733
Felderer, Christian *Scor Holding (Switzerland) Ltd* 1595
Feldesman, Walter *Sterling Bancorp* 1702
Feldhake, Robert J. *Plaza Bank CA* 1439
Feldhaus, David *Chicago Federal Home Loan Bank* 384
Feldman, Alan *MGM MIRAGE* 1176
Feldman, Alan F. *Resource Capital Corp* 1537
Feldman, Alan F. *Resource America Inc* 1536
Feldman, Alan D. *Midas Inc* 1184
Feldman, Alan *Foot Locker Inc* 733
Feldman, Allan *Alberta Star Development Corp* 53
Feldman, Arthur Michael *I-trax Inc* 906
Feldman, Bruce *Interactive Systems Worldwide Inc* 961
Feldman, Carol A. *Central Jersey Bancorp* 362
Feldman, Daniel Caleb *Big Sky Energy Corp* 238
Feldman, David *QMed Inc* 1493
Feldman, Fred *Bentley Pharmaceuticals Inc* 232
Feldman, Fredric J. *Orthologic Corp* 1360
Feldman, Greg S. *Dave & Busters Inc* 529
Feldman, J. M. *Magna Lab Inc* 1111
Feldman, Jerome I. *GSE Systems Inc* 830
Feldman, Jerome I. *GP Strategies Corp* 813
Feldman, Lawrence H. *Feldman Mall Properties Inc* 686
Feldman, Lynn A. *Wyndham Worldwide Corp* 1981
Feldman, Maria *MediciNova Inc* 1153
Feldman, Matthew R. *Chicago Federal Home Loan Bank* 384
Feldman, Max *TC PipeLines LP* 1754
Feldman, Michael *GSE Systems Inc* 830
Feldman, Michel J. *Watson Pharmaceuticals Inc* 1937
Feldman, Moses *Commercial Metals Co* 448
Feldman, Ned *Management Network Group Inc* 1117
Feldman, Patrick *Thornburg Mortgage Inc* 1790
Feldman, Paul *Law Enforcement Assoc Corp* 1059
Feldman, Roger L. *Onvia Inc* 1345
Feldman, Sheila B. *Arch Coal Inc* 143
Feldman, Steve *Delia's Inc* 537
Feldman, Steven R. *Photomedex Inc* 1427
Feldman, Steven G. *BAB Inc* 198
Feldman, Steven *Crown Media Holdings Inc* 505
Feldman, Stuart *Google Inc* 811
Feldman, Tamara S. *HNI Corp* 882
Feldman, Thomas E. *Varsity Group Inc* 1889
Feldman, Tuvia *Ness Technologies Inc* 1261
Feldman, William M. *SeaBright Insurance Holdings Inc* 1598
Feldman, Zeev *Shamir Optical Industry Ltd* 1616
Feldmann, Cynthia L. *Steris Corp* 1702
Feldmann, Cynthia *Hayes Lemmerz International Inc* 855
Feldmann, Cynthia *Hanger Orthopedic Group Inc* 843
Feldmann, Gregory W. *FNB Corp* 730
Feldmann, Gregory W. *FNB United Corp* 731
Feldmann, Gregory W. *FNB Corp/VA* 730
Feldmann, John *BASF* 218
Feldmann, Klaus A. *Modine Manufacturing Co* 1206
Feldmann, Lutz *E On AG* 587

2190 - Officers & Directors Index THE CORPORATE DIRECTORY - Walker's 2008

Grier, Harold N. *Abington Community Bancorp Inc* ... 6
Grier, Mark B. *Prudential Financial Inc* ... 1483
Grierson, Donald K. *Parametric Technology Corp* ... 1385
Gries, Charles J. *MB Financial Inc MD* ... 1137
Gries, Louis *James Hardie Industries* ... 1003
Griesedieck, Joe *Korn Ferry International* ... 1041
Griesel, Dian *Digi International Inc* ... 554
Griesemer, Daniel *Coldwater Creek Inc* ... 438
Grieshaber, Joseph A. *Kroger Co* ... 1043
Griesheimer, Kristine *Oak Valley Community Bank CA* ... 1323
Griess, Bret *CSG Systems International Inc* ... 508
Griesser, Gerard F. *Willow Financial Bancorp Inc* ... 1963
Griesser, Gerard F. *Willow Grove Bancorp Inc* ... 1963
Grieve, James *Scor* ... 1595
Grieve, Pierson M. *Mair Holdings Inc* ... 1115
Grieve, Robert B. *Heska Corp* ... 873
Grieve, Tim *Salon Media Group Inc* ... 1578
Grieves, Robert *ACE Ltd* ... 13
Griffeth, Lesley *Southern First Bancshares Inc* ... 1666
Griffin, Abbie J. *Navistar International Corp* ... 1253
Griffin, Alice B. *Beverly National Corp* ... 235
Griffin, Alison G. *Dynex Capital Inc* ... 586
Griffin, Allison *Nashville BK & TR TN* ... 1237
Griffin, Archie M. *Abercrombie & Fitch Co* ... 6
Griffin, Barbara A. *Parkway Properties Inc* ... 1388
Griffin, Bill *Temecula Valley Bancorp Inc* ... 1773
Griffin, Bobby J. *Ryder System Inc* ... 1570
Griffin, Bobby J. *Hanesbrands Inc* ... 843
Griffin, Brian C. *Celerity Systems Inc* ... 354
Griffin, Brian T. *Medco Health Solutions Inc* ... 1148
Griffin, David W. *Lecg Corp* ... 1063
Griffin, David F. *BOK Financial Corp* ... 263
Griffin, Donald W. *Eastman Chemical Co* ... 595
Griffin, Donald W. *Olin Corp* ... 1334
Griffin, Donald W. *Barnes Group Inc* ... 216
Griffin, Eric J. *Protection One Inc* ... 1477
Griffin, Eric *Monroe Bancorp* ... 1213
Griffin, Faith *Enherent Corp* ... 638
Griffin, Frank *Grubb & Ellis Co* ... 827
Griffin, Gale L. *EMC Insurance Group Inc* ... 621
Griffin, Gerald D. *Comarco Inc* ... 444
Griffin, Greg *Tower Financial Corp* ... 1807
Griffin, Guy *OP-TECH Environmental Services Inc* ... 1345
Griffin, Jack *Meredith Corp* ... 1162
Griffin, James M. *BTU International Inc* ... 291
Griffin, James C. *XATA Corp* ... 1983
Griffin, James M. *Lecg Corp* ... 1063
Griffin, Jennifer *Beverly National Corp* ... 235
Griffin, Jerry C. *Sciele Pharma Inc* ... 1593
Griffin, Jerry C. *CryoCor Inc* ... 506
Griffin, Joel C. *First South Bancorp Inc* ... 717
Griffin, John *Delta Apparel Inc* ... 539
Griffin, John Andrew *Stallion Group (The)* ... 1688
Griffin, John Andrew *Lexaria Corp* ... 1070
Griffin, John J. *Charles River Assoc Inc* ... 374
Griffin, John R. *Exponent Inc* ... 671
Griffin, Joseph *Hiland Partners LP* ... 878
Griffin, Joseph *Hiland Holdings GP LP* ... 878
Griffin, Julian *Capital Bank Corp* ... 323
Griffin, Julie *Micros Systems Inc* ... 1181
Griffin, Karen *Petroleum Development Corp* ... 1417
Griffin, Kent R. *Biomed Realty Trust* ... 244
Griffin, Liam K. *Skyworks Solutions Inc* ... 1644
Griffin, Mark *Telos Corp* ... 1771
Griffin, Mark *Nuveen Investments Inc* ... 1319
Griffin, Mark J. *Green Energy Group Inc* ... 822
Griffin, Mark W. *Genworth Financial Inc* ... 779
Griffin, Mark J. *Cenveo Inc* ... 366
Griffin, Marshall W. *Simclar Inc* ... 1633
Griffin, Michael V. *Hill International Inc* ... 878
Griffin, Mikka *Fox & Hound Restaurant Group* ... 741
Griffin, Monty J. *Sherwin Williams Co* ... 1619
Griffin, Randall M. *Corporate Office Properties Trust* ... 484
Griffin, Richard *Grant Prideco Inc* ... 816
Griffin, Robert G. *Leggett & Platt Inc* ... 1067
Griffin, Robert C. *Builders FirstSource Inc* ... 294
Griffin, Robert T. *Firstbank Corp* ... 718
Griffin, Robert *Isle of Capri Casinos Inc* ... 991
Griffin, Robert *Escalade Inc* ... 656
Griffin, Robert C. *Commercial Vehicle Group Inc* ... 449
Griffin, Sam *South Street Financial Corp* ... 1663
Griffin, Scot A. *Tessera Technologies Inc* ... 1780
Griffin, Shelvy *Mercantile Bank Corp* ... 1160
Griffin, Stacy *LifeSpan Inc* ... 1076
Griffin, Steve *Gemstar-TV Guide International Inc* ... 766
Griffin, Terence J. *Applied Imaging Corp* ... 135
Griffin, Thomas N. *Santa Cruz CTY BK CA* ... 1583
Griffin, Thomas J. *United States Cellular Corp* ... 1862
Griffin, Timothy J. *Northeast Utilities* ... 1301
Griffin, Timothy J. *Northwest Airlines Corp* ... 1304
Griffin, Wallace W. *Pac-West Telecomm Inc* ... 1369
Griffin, William K. *Lexaria Corp* ... 1070
Griffin, William E. *Hudson Valley Holding Corp* ... 897
Griffin, William K. *Stallion Group (The)* ... 1688
Griffin, William A. *First Community Bank Corp of America* ... 702
Griffin, William D. *InsWeb Corp* ... 953
Griffing, Bruce *Kulicke & Soffa Industries Inc* ... 1045
Griffing, John *Northrop Grumman Corp* ... 1303
Griffing, Robert *Suffolk Bancorp* ... 1715
Griffith, Ann M. *Friedman Billings Ramsey Group Inc* ... 749
Griffith, Benjamin W. *Security Bank Corp* ... 1603
Griffith, Blake L. *Community First BanCorp* ... 454
Griffith, Charles L. *Caribou Coffee Company Inc* ... 334
Griffith, David L. *Qualstar Corp* ... 1496
Griffith, David *Iomega Corp* ... 984
Griffith, Dennis M. *Cardinal Financial Corp* ... 331
Griffith, Gary R. *Knight Capital Group Inc* ... 1035
Griffith, Geoffrey L. *Adams Resources & Energy Inc* ... 22
Griffith, Greg *OM Group Inc* ... 1335
Griffith, Gregory J. *OM Group Inc* ... 1335
Griffith, Harry *FNBH Bancorp Inc MI* ... 731
Griffith, Harry *FNBH Bancorp Inc* ... 731
Griffith, Hope *Pomeroy IT Solutions* ... 1447
Griffith, Irwin *ViRexx Medical Corp* ... 1910
Griffith, James W. *Timken Co* ... 1796
Griffith, James W. *Goodrich Corp* ... 810
Griffith, Jan *Idaho Bancorp ID* ... 915
Griffith, Jeff *Dolby Laboratories Inc* ... 566
Griffith, Jerry *MBT Financial Corp* ... 1138
Griffith, Jim *National Bancshares Corp OH* ... 1238
Griffith, Joanne Adams *Viacom Inc* ... 1902
Griffith, Jody W. *Southeastern Bank Financial Corp* ... 1664
Griffith, John A. *American Italian Pasta Co* ... 95
Griffith, John D. *Target Corp* ... 1749
Griffith, John B. *1st Source Corp* ... 2005
Griffith, Kathleen *Northwestern Corp* ... 1306
Griffith, Kevin *IDI Global Inc* ... 917
Griffith, Lisa L. *Fidelity Bancorp Inc* ... 689
Griffith, Luther T. *Lifecore Biomedical Inc* ... 1076
Griffith, Luther T. *Theragenics Corp* ... 1785
Griffith, Mark *BJ's Restaurants Inc* ... 251
Griffith, Marshall *Wilson Bank & Trust* ... 1964
Griffith, Mary H. *National City Corp* ... 1239
Griffith, Michael *StarTek Inc* ... 1694
Griffith, Michael *Activision Inc* ... 19
Griffith, Michael *Communications Systems Inc* ... 451
Griffith, Mike *Moller International Inc* ... 1208
Griffith, Patricia *FNBH Bancorp Inc MI* ... 731
Griffith, Patricia *FNBH Bancorp Inc* ... 731
Griffith, Robert *Grubb & Ellis Co* ... 827
Griffith, Robert C. *Navigant International Inc* ... 1253
Griffith, Robyn *Tandy Leather Factory Inc* ... 1748
Griffith, Ronald C. *Genelabs Technologies Inc* ... 768
Griffith, Ronald H. *Allied Defense Group Inc* ... 64
Griffith, Sanders G. *Total System Services Inc* ... 1806
Griffith, Sanders G. *Synovus Financial Corp* ... 1739
Griffith, Susan Patricia *Progressive Corp* ... 1474
Griffith, Thomas W. *Nuveen Investments Inc* ... 1319
Griffith, Wade A. *Americanwest BanCorp* ... 107
Griffith-Jones, Peter *Amazing Technologies Corp* ... 77
Griffiths, Andrew M. *Fleetwood Enterprises Inc* ... 724
Griffiths, Anthony F. *Crum & Forster Holdings Corp* ... 506
Griffiths, Anthony F. *Odyssey Re Holdings Corp* ... 1329
Griffiths, Anthony F. *Fairfax Financial Holdings Ltd* ... 676
Griffiths, Anthony F. *Vitran Corp Inc* ... 1918
Griffiths, Anthony F. *Russel Metals Inc* ... 1568
Griffiths, Anthony F. *IMI International Medical Innovations Inc* ... 927
Griffiths, Anthony F. *Alliance Atlantis Communications Inc* ... 60
Griffiths, Arthur *Wavelit Inc* ... 1938
Griffiths, David K. *Amerityre Corp* ... 111
Griffiths, Francis *National Instruments Corp* ... 1243
Griffiths, Gareth *International Power Plc* ... 971
Griffiths, Gary A. *Rackable Systems Inc* ... 1506
Griffiths, Jeff *Huron Consulting Group Inc* ... 901
Griffiths, Jeffrey *THQ Inc* ... 1790
Griffiths, Lloyd Cromwell *British Airways Plc* ... 282
Griffiths, Lord Brian *Herman Miller Inc* ... 872
Griffiths, Martin *Maguire Properties Inc* ... 1112
Griffiths, Peter *Cognos Inc* ... 436
Griffiths, Phillip A. *GSI Group Inc* ... 831
Griffiths, Richard *Hybrid Technologies Inc* ... 903
Griffiths, Robert P. *PrivateBancorp Inc* ... 1470
Griffiths, Scott A. *Copano Energy LLC* ... 478
Griffiths, Sheena *GFI Group Inc* ... 785
Griffiths, William C. *Champion Mortgage* ... 372
Griffiths, William C. *Wolverine Tube Inc* ... 1973
Griffo, Kevin *Cordia Corp* ... 480
Grigg, Charles W. *Breeze-Eastern Corp* ... 277
Grigg, David G. *First Bancorp* ... 696
Grigg, R. R. *Toledo Edison Co* ... 1800
Grigg, Richard R. *FirstEnergy Corp* ... 719
Grigg, Richard R. *Cleveland Electric Illuminating Co* ... 423
Grigg, Richard R. *Pennsylvania Electric Co* ... 1404
Grigg, Steven A. *Republic Property Trust* ... 1534
Grigg, William H. *Cato Corp (The)* ... 346
Griggs, Bradley P. *BRE Properties Inc* ... 276
Griggs, Brent E. *Protective Life Insurance Co* ... 1478
Griggs, Brent E. *Protective Life Corp* ... 1477
Griggs, Dale L. *Craftmade International Inc* ... 494
Griggs, Douglas *Venoco Inc* ... 1893
Griggs, Franky *Nucor Corp* ... 1315
Griggs, Jackie A. *First Citizens Banc Corp* ... 700
Griggs, Kathleen M. *J2 Global Communications Inc* ... 999
Griggs, Malcolm D. *Fifth Third Bancorp* ... 691
Griggs, Noah J. *CKE Restaurants Inc* ... 417
Griggs, Stacey *Post Properties Inc* ... 1451
Griggs, Stewart *Unity Holdings Inc* ... 1866
Grigioni, Carlo *UBS* ... 1843
Grigone, Butch *Union Pacific Corp* ... 1852
Grigoriadis, Dimitri E. *Neurocrine Biosciences Inc* ... 1267
Grigorian, Artem *Gold Fields Ltd* ... 803
Grigsby, Amy *Republic Bancorp Inc/KY* ... 1534
Grigsby, Charles T. *Boston Private Financial Holdings Inc* ... 268
Grigsby, Fred R. *Canadian National Railway Co* ... 317
Grigsby, James A. *Cytogen Corp* ... 520
Grigsby, Jennifer M. *Chesapeake Energy Corp* ... 383
Grigsby, Lane L. *Shaw Group Inc (The)* ... 1618
Grigsby, Samuel F. *Community National Bank of the Lakeway Area* ... 455
Grijalva, Ernesto *Pricesmart Inc* ... 1464
Grijalva, Victor E. *Dynegy Inc* ... 586
Grijalva, Victor E. *Transocean Inc* ... 1817
Grilk, Thomas S. *Brooks Automation Inc* ... 287
Grill, Donald L. *Fentura Financial Inc* ... 687
Grill, Laurence K. *Large Scale Biology Corp* ... 1055
Grillet, Robert J. *International Paper Co* ... 971
Grilli, Enzo *Telecom Italia SpA* ... 1765
Grillo, Adelaide *Janel World Trade Ltd* ... 1003
Grillo, Anthony *Littelfuse Inc* ... 1086
Grillo, Anthony *Silicon Graphics Inc* ... 1629
Grillo, Grace *CCI Group Inc* ... 350
Grillo, Jeffrey A. *Manor Care Inc* ... 1119
Grillo-Lopez, Antonio J. *Point Therapeutics Inc* ... 1444
Grillo-Lopez, Antonio J. *Onyx Pharmaceuticals Inc* ... 1345
Grillo-Lopez, Antonio J. *Favrille Inc* ... 681
Grillone, Lisa R. *ISTA Pharmaceuticals Inc* ... 992
Grillot, Cynthia M. *Barnwell Industries Inc* ... 217
Grills, Joe *Kimco Realty Corp* ... 1029
Grim, Charles *ING Life Insurance & Annuity Co* ... 943
Grim, Gregory *Patapsco Bancorp Inc* ... 1389
Grima, Joan-David *Banco Santander S.A* ... 205
Grimaldi, Andy *Qualmark Corp* ... 1496
Grimaldi, John *Navigators Group Inc (The)* ... 1253
Grimaldi, Michael A. *General Motors Corp* ... 772
Grimaud, Dennis L. *Tennessee Commerce Bank* ... 1775
Grime, Jeffrey *Xedar Corp* ... 1983
Grime, Mike A. *Australia & New Zealand Banking GRP* ... 180
Grimes, Brian F. *Coast Financial Holdings Inc* ... 431
Grimes, Claymon C. *South Financial Group Inc* ... 1663
Grimes, David W. *Gaming Partners International Corp* ... 760
Grimes, Fred D. *Mission Oaks Bancorp* ... 1199
Grimes, Greg *Dillard's Inc* ... 558
Grimes, James A. *Sanderson Farms Inc* ... 1580
Grimes, John F. *Capital Bank Corp* ... 323
Grimes, Joseph *XsunX Inc* ... 1989
Grimes, Kirk D. *Fluor Corp* ... 728
Grimes, Lee *Union Pacific Corp* ... 1852
Grimes, Patricia P. *Weststar Financial Services Corp* ... 1954
Grimes, Pearl E. *GammaCan International Inc* ... 760
Grimes, Perley H. *First Litchfield Financial Corp* ... 709
Grimes, Richard A. *Firstbank Financial Services Inc* ... 719
Grimes, Robert S. *Autobytel Inc* ... 181
Grimes, Thomas L. *Mid-America Apartment Communities Inc* ... 1184
Grimes, Vickie *River Valley Bancorp* ... 1549
Grimes, Virginia F. *Carolina Bank Holdings Inc* ... 336
Grimes, Warren L. *Four Oaks Fincorp Inc* ... 741
Grimes, William J. *ACE COMM Corp* ... 13
Grimley, Jason W. *IR BioSciences Holdings Inc* ... 988
Grimm, Donald W. *Invitrogen Corp* ... 983
Grimm, John *Debt Resolve Inc* ... 534
Grimm, Michael K. *Energy Transfer Partners LP* ... 636
Grimm, Ray W. *ACTIS Global Ventures Inc* ... 18
Grimm-Marshall, Barbara *Tejon Ranch Co* ... 1762
Grimme, Paul E. *Freescale Semiconductor Inc* ... 747
Grimmer, Linda *OP-TECH Environmental Services Inc* ... 1345
Grimoldi, Alberto L. *Wolverine World Wide Inc* ... 1973
Grimshaw, Eric *ONEOK Partners LP* ... 1343
Grimshaw, Eric *Oneok Inc* ... 1343
Grimshaw, Stuart *Commonwealth Bank of Australia* ... 449
Grimsley, Michael J. *Regent Communications Inc* ... 1526
Grimsley, Robert J. *A.C. Moore Arts & Crafts Inc* ... 1
Grimsrud, Knut S. *Intel Corp* ... 958
Grimstad, Carl A. *iPayment Inc* ... 986
Grimstad, Erlend *Statoil* ... 1696
Grimstad, John A. *Zareba Systems Inc* ... 1996
Grimston, Hugo *Greenhill & Co Inc* ... 824
Grinalds, John S. *Mid-America Apartment Communities Inc* ... 1184
Grinberg, Efraim *Movado Group Inc* ... 1220
Grinberg, Gedalio *Movado Group Inc* ... 1220
Grinberg, Paul *Encore Capital Group Inc* ... 630
Grinberg, Paul *BofI Holding Inc* ... 263
Grindle, Kelly T. *Johnson Outdoors Inc* ... 1010
Grindle, Leslye L. *Southern Community Bancshares Inc* ... 1666
Grindley, Peter C. *Lecg Corp* ... 1063
Grindstaff, Kurt D. *Suntron Corp* ... 1724
Grindstaff, Nicholas M. *Quanta Services Inc* ... 1497
Grinenco, Sergio *Grupo Financiero Galicia* ... 828
Grinfas, Zvi *Vishay Intertechnology Inc* ... 1913
Gring, James *Lockheed Martin Corp* ... 1090
Gringer, Donald H. *Hills Bancorp* ... 879
Grinnan, Richard R. *Massey Energy Co* ... 1129
Grinnell, Charles W. *Clean Diesel Technologies Inc* ... 421
Grinnell, Charles W. *Fuel Tech* ... 753
Grinney, Jay *HealthSouth Corp* ... 861
Grinsfelder, Gary S. *TXCO Resources Inc* ... 1838
Grinsfelder, Gary *Royale Energy Inc* ... 1563
Grinstein, Gerald *Delta Air Lines Inc* ... 539
Grinstein, Keith D. *F5 Networks Inc* ... 674
Grinstein, Keith D. *Nextera Enterprises Inc* ... 1283
Grinstein, Keith D. *Coinstar Inc* ... 438
Grinstein, Keith D. *Labor Ready Inc* ... 1048
Grint, Paul C. *Illumina Inc* ... 923
Grint, Paul *Multicell Technologies Inc* ... 1227
Grinten, Pete Vander *Badger Meter Inc* ... 199
Grinter, Jon *Information Architects Corp* ... 940
Grion, Sergio *Veritas DGC Inc* ... 1896
Griot, Denis *Freescale Semiconductor Inc* ... 747
Gripekoven, Sage *Grill Concepts Inc* ... 826
Grippo, John T. *Splinternet Holdings Inc* ... 1682
Grippo, John *Element 21 Golf Co* ... 615
Gripsborn, Jan *Advanced Analogic Technologies Inc* ... 28
Grisanti, Scott *eResearchTechnology Inc* ... 654
Grisar, Robert *REGI U.S. Inc* ... 1526
Grisar, Robert *Reg Technologies Inc* ... 1523
Griscelli, Claude *Viropro Inc* ... 1911
Grischow, Donald K. *Nacco Industries Inc* ... 1232
Grischow, K. Donald *Nacco Industries Inc* ... 1232
Grise, Cheryl W. *Dana Corp* ... 525
Grise, Cheryl W. *Pall Corp* ... 1378
Grise, Cheryl W. *Metlife Inc* ... 1171
Grise, Cheryl W. *Northeast Utilities* ... 1301
Grise, Sarah G. *Citizens First Corp* ... 414
Grishakov, Max *Wm Wrigley Jr Co* ... 1972
Grisham, Carole J. *EvergreenBancorp Inc* ... 665
Grisham, Jon *Acadia Realty Trust* ... 9
Grisham, Terry *Union Tank Car Co* ... 1852
Grisik, John J. *Goodrich Corp* ... 810
Grisius, Michael J. *Allied Capital Corp* ... 64
Grisko, Jerome P. *Century Business Services Inc* ... 365
Grisolia, Edoardo *Eni SpA* ... 639
Grissen, David *Good Times Restaurants Inc* ... 810
Grissen, David J. *Marriott International Inc* ... 1125
Grissom, David J. *Yum! Brands Inc* ... 1994
Grissom, David J. *Churchill Downs Inc* ... 404
Grissom, Douglas C. *Cbeyond Inc* ... 348
Grissom, Steve D. *Waste Industries USA Inc* ... 1934
Grissom, Taylor B. *Monarch Financial Holdings Inc* ... 1210
Grist, John *Clean Power Technologies Inc* ... 421
Gristi, Jean-Paul *France Telecom* ... 743
Griswell, Barry J. *Herman Miller Inc* ... 872
Griswell, Barry J. *Principal Financial Group Inc* ... 1468
Griswold, Benjamin H. *W. P. Carey & Co LLC* ... 1926
Griswold, Benjamin H. *Flowers Foods Inc* ... 728
Griswold, Benjamin H. *Black & Decker Corp* ... 252
Griswold, David W. *Carolina Bank Holdings Inc* ... 336
Griswold, Farrell *Service 1st Bancorp* ... 1613
Griswold, James B. *Keithley Instruments Inc* ... 1021
Griswold, Paul J. *SR Telecom Inc* ... 1684
Griswold, Scott A. *Dole Food Co Inc* ... 567
Gritz, Cecil D. *Galaxy Energy Corp* ... 758
Gritz, Richard *Primedex Health Systems Inc* ... 1466
Grivner, Carl J. *XO Communications Inc* ... 1987
Grizzard, Brian K. *Village Bank & Trust Financial Corp* ... 1906
Grizzard, Ken *Astec Industries Inc* ... 166
Grizzell, Dwight *Mountain National Bancshares Inc* ... 1219
Grizzle, David *Continental Airlines Inc* ... 475
Grizzle, Jerry W. *AMS Health Sciences Inc* ... 116
Grizzle, Robert D. *Navidec Financial Services Inc* ... 1252
Grizzle, Sam *Lockheed Martin Corp* ... 1090
Grizzle, Victor D. *Valmont Industries Inc* ... 1887
Groberg, Eric L. *Allied Capital Corp* ... 64
Grobicki, T. S.A. *Harmony Gold Mining Co Ltd* ... 847

Maher, Tom *Amarin Corp Plc* ... 77
Maher, Tony Denis *Wimm-Bill-Dann Foods OJSC* ... 1965
Maheras, Thomas G. *Citigroup Inc* ... 411
Maheswaran, Mohan *Semtech Corp* ... 1608
Maheu, Ronald T. *Wright Express Corp* ... 1980
Maheu, Ronald T. *Charles River Assoc Inc* ... 374
Mahieu, Gary *Smart Online Inc* ... 1646
Mahindroo, Sandeep *Infosys Technologies Ltd* ... 941
Mahl, Amy *Ecology & Environment Inc* ... 600
Mahl, Cindy *Western Reserve Bank* ... 1951
Mahl, Larry *Wells Gardner Electronics Corp* ... 1944
Mahlab, David *Scopus Video Networks Ltd* ... 1595
Mahle, Stephen H. *Medtronic Inc* ... 1156
Mahle, Stephen *ATMI Inc* ... 174
Mahler, Armando *Freeport McMoRan Copper & Gold Inc* ... 747
Mahler, Jack *WP Stewart & Co Ltd* ... 1979
Mahler, Joseph G. *FuelCell Energy Inc* ... 753
Mahler, Michael *First Federal of Northern Michigan Bancorp Inc* ... 705
Mahler, Peter *Coles Myer Ltd* ... 438
Mahler, Ron *Elbit Vision Systems Ltd* ... 611
Mahler, Solveigh *Qiagen* ... 1492
Mahler, Stephen P. *Partners Trust Financial Group Inc* ... 1389
Mahlke, Kent F. *Kimball International Inc* ... 1029
Mahlke, Thomas K. *C.H. Robinson Worldwide Inc* ... 300
Mahloele, Tshepo *Telkom Sa Ltd* ... 1770
Mahlstedt, Brian C. *First National Community Bancorp Inc* ... 712
Mahmarian, Richard E. *Emrise Corp* ... 627
Mahmood, Salman *Averox Inc* ... 188
Mahmoud, Adel A.F. *Becton Dickinson & Co* ... 227
Mahmoud, Adel A.F. *Merck & Co Inc* ... 1162
Mahnke, Greg *infoUSA Inc* ... 942
Mahnken, Alexandra *Huron Consulting Group Inc* ... 901
Mahomed, Yousuf *Medicalcv Inc* ... 1153
Mahomes, William *Kent Financial Services Inc* ... 1024
Mahon, Casey D. *United Fire & Casualty Co* ... 1858
Mahon, Cherrie *Document Security Systems Inc* ... 566
Mahon, Kenneth J. *Dime Community Bancshares Inc* ... 558
Mahon, Paul A. *United Therapeutics Corp* ... 1864
Mahone, Glenn R. *Matthews International Corp* ... 1133
Mahoney, Bob *Northwest Pipe Co* ... 1306
Mahoney, Bob *On Semiconductor Corp* ... 1340
Mahoney, Charles J. *Fibernet Telecom Group Inc* ... 688
Mahoney, Christopher T. *Moody's Corp* ... 1214
Mahoney, Cornelius D. *Berkshire Hills Bancorp Inc* ... 233
Mahoney, David L. *Corcept Therapeutics Inc* ... 479
Mahoney, David *Symantec Corp* ... 1734
Mahoney, David C. *Applix Inc* ... 137
Mahoney, David L. *Tercica Inc* ... 1777
Mahoney, Dennis L. *Aon Corp* ... 129
Mahoney, George R. *Family Dollar Stores Inc* ... 677
Mahoney, George L. *Media General Inc* ... 1149
Mahoney, James E. *Micron Technology Inc* ... 1180
Mahoney, James J. *Aspect Medical Systems Inc* ... 162
Mahoney, James R. *IndyMac Bancorp Inc* ... 936
Mahoney, James M. *Meadowbrook Insurance Group Inc* ... 1145
Mahoney, Jerome R. *SpeechSwitch Inc* ... 1679
Mahoney, Jerome *MM2 Group Inc* ... 1203
Mahoney, Jerome *Trey Resources Inc* ... 1821
Mahoney, Jerome *iVoice Inc* ... 996
Mahoney, John *Advo Inc* ... 34
Mahoney, John J. *Staples Inc* ... 1692
Mahoney, John J. *Chico's FAS Inc* ... 385
Mahoney, Joseph *L. B. Foster Co* ... 1046
Mahoney, Kathleen M. *Nash Finch Co* ... 1236
Mahoney, Kerstin *Optelecom Inc* ... 1348
Mahoney, Kevin P. *Sonoco Products Co* ... 1658
Mahoney, Kevin V. *Crompton Corp* ... 502
Mahoney, Kevin F. *A T Cross Co* ... 1
Mahoney, Laura *Algoma Steel Inc* ... 56
Mahoney, Megan L. *SE Financial Corp PA* ... 1597
Mahoney, Michael J. *Level 3 Communications Inc* ... 1069
Mahoney, Robert W. *Timken Co* ... 1796
Mahoney, Robert W. *Sherwin Williams Co* ... 1619
Mahoney, Robert W. *Cincinnati Bell Inc* ... 406
Mahoney, Robert L. *Northwest Pipe Co* ... 1306
Mahoney, Rosemary K. *National Consumer Cooperative Bank* ... 1240
Mahoney, Sean M. *Diamondrock Hospitality Company* ... 552
Mahoney, Thomas P. *Newmont Mining Corp* ... 1279
Mahoney, Thomas *Trans Lux Corp* ... 1812
Mahoney, Walt *Nanogen Inc* ... 1234
Mahony, Emon A. *Alltel Corp* ... 69
Mahood, Scott *FNB Corp/FL* ... 730
Mahowald, Christopher W. *Capstead Mortgage Corp* ... 328
Mahre, Michael D. *Building Materials Holding Corp* ... 294
Mahurin, Steven L. *Truserv Corp* ... 1831
Mahuson, William E. *Performance Technologies Inc* ... 1412
Mahy, Rohan *Counterpath Corp* ... 489
Mai, Falco *GigaMedia Ltd* ... 786
Mai, Mark F. *Dresser-Rand Group Inc* ... 575
Mai, Quentin *International Tower Hill Mines Ltd* ... 973
Mai, Quentin *Cardero Resource Corp* ... 330
Mai, Troy *Advanced Energy Industries Inc* ... 29
Maia, Michael *MoSys Inc* ... 1217
Maibach, Howard *EpiCept Corp* ... 650
Maida, Anthony E. *Spectrum Pharmaceuticals Inc* ... 1678
Maidique, Modesto A. *National Semiconductor Corp* ... 1246
Maidique, Modesto A. *Carnival Corp* ... 336
Maidique, Modesto A. *Carnival Plc* ... 336
Maidment, Karen E. *Bank of Montreal* ... 210
Maidy, Shane *MPLC Inc* ... 1221
Maier, Allen *Bucs Financial Corp* ... 293
Maier, Barbara *Community Bank of Bergen County NJ* ... 452
Maier, Blanche F. *Frisch's Restaurants Inc* ... 750
Maier, Craig F. *Frisch's Restaurants Inc* ... 750
Maier, Eric *Gulf Island Fabrication Inc* ... 834
Maier, Franz *Matritech Inc* ... 1131
Maier, Gary S. *Tower Group Inc* ... 1807
Maier, Gerald J. *Willbros Group Inc* ... 1960
Maier, Jeff *Union Pacific Corp* ... 1852
Maier, Jeffrey L. *Neuberger Berman Inc* ... 1266
Maier, Jim *L. B. Foster Co* ... 1046
Maier, Karen F. *Frisch's Restaurants Inc* ... 750
Maier, Oliver *Fresenius Medical Care Corp* ... 749
Maier, Russell W. *FirstEnergy Corp* ... 719
Maier, Stuart *Gulfport Energy Corp* ... 836
Maier, Tim *L. B. Foster Co* ... 1046
Maiese, Russell L. *Ameripath Inc* ... 109
Maietta, Lawrence F. *United Guardian Inc* ... 1859
Maietta, Rosanna *Washington Post Co* ... 1933
Maihofer, John *First Sound Bank WA* ... 716
Maikranz, Jim *IONA Technologies Plc* ... 985
Mailloux, Dominique S. *Sun Life Financial Inc* ... 1718
Mailloux, Mary R. *TWL Corp* ... 1837
Mailman, Allen J. *Journal Register Co* ... 1011
Maiman, Joseph *Eltek Ltd* ... 618
Maiman, Yosef A. *Ampal American Israel Corp* ... 115
Maimon, Jackob *Isramco Inc* ... 992
Maimon, Yossi *Orthodontix Inc* ... 1360
Main, Alan J. *Lexicon Pharmaceuticals Inc* ... 1070
Main, Charles *Yamana Gold Inc* ... 1990
Main, Hanne *Gartner Inc* ... 762
Main, Rebecca R. *Greene County Bancorp Inc* ... 823
Main, Richard W. *Enterprise Bancorp Inc* ... 642
Main, Robert B. *Jacksonville Bancorp Inc FL* ... 1001
Main, Susan L. *Teledyne Technologies Inc* ... 1766
Main, Timothy L. *Jabil Circuit Inc* ... 999
Maimardi, Pablo *Arauco & Constitution Pulp Inc* ... 141
Mainas, George *Public Media Works Inc* ... 1486
Maindonald, Greg *IPSCO Inc* ... 987
Maine, Douglas L. *Rockwood Holdings Inc* ... 1555
Maine, Douglas L. *Alliant Techsystems Inc* ... 63
Mainello, Greg *Copart Inc* ... 479
Maingot, Lawrence C. *Bairnco Corp* ... 199
Mainland, Alexis *New York Times Co* ... 1277
Mainstain, Peter *House of Taylor Jewelry Inc* ... 893
Mainwaring, Brenda *Union Pacific Corp* ... 1852
Mainz, Barry *Wind River Systems Inc* ... 1966
Maio, Keith D. *Zions BanCorp* ... 1999
Maiola, Elizabeth W. *New Hampshire Thrift Bancshares Inc* ... 1272
Maiolini, Nitza *Latin American Export Bank* ... 1058
Maiorano, Frank M. *Nuveen Investments Inc* ... 1319
Mair, Buff *Cryo-Cell International* ... 506
Mair, Lothar *FormFactor Inc* ... 736
Mair, Merri Buff *Cryo-Cell International* ... 506
Mair, Tom *Golden Star Resources Ltd* ... 806
Maira, Arun *Patni Computer Systems Ltd* ... 1391
Maire, Dulcia *PDG Environmental Inc* ... 1397
Mairs, Jonathan *Knight Capital Group Inc* ... 1035
Mais, Stephen M. *Hubbell Inc* ... 896
Maisch, Paul *Provident New York Bancorp* ... 1481
Maisel, David *Marvel Entertainment Inc* ... 1128
Maisto, Mark *FPL Group Inc* ... 742
Maitland, Alister *Lihir Gold Ltd* ... 1078
Maitland, Bill *ACR Group Inc* ... 16
Maitland, Peter K. *USG Corp* ... 1880
Maitland-Lewis, Stephen *Daily Journal Corp* ... 523
Maitra, Mandeep *HDFC Bank Ltd* ... 856
Maitre, Philippe M. *Oscient Pharmaceuticals Corp* ... 1361
Maixner, William *Cypress Bioscience Inc* ... 519
Maiz, Jose A. *Intel Corp* ... 958
Maizel, Issac *Shelron Group Inc* ... 1619
Maizel, Jacob V. *Alfacell Corp* ... 56
Maizes, Michael H. *NuVim Inc* ... 1319
Maiztegui, Ricardo *Millicom International Cellular* ... 1193
Majcher, William *Evolving Gold Corp* ... 666
Majchrzak, Janina *Harvey Electronics Inc* ... 852
Majczan, John *Great Atlantic & Pacific Tea Co Inc* ... 818
Majendie, Dominic J. *Composite Technology Corp* ... 460
Majeres, Richard *Petrosearch Energy Corp* ... 1418
Majerik, Michael *Magellan Health Services Inc* ... 1109
Majernik, Robert *Cordia Corp* ... 480
Majerus, Michael *Qimonda AG* ... 1493
Majeski, Carrie *Art's Way Manufacturing Co Inc* ... 154
Majeski, Peter *Latin American Export Bank* ... 1058
Majewski, David G. *Kodiak Oil & Gas Corp* ... 1037
Majewski, Theodore A. *Harleysville Group Inc* ... 846
Majewski, Thomas A. *Dataram Corp* ... 528
Majidimehr, Amir *Microsoft Corp* ... 1182
Majlis, Arturo *Andina Bottling Co Inc* ... 121
Majoor, C. H.S. *Calgon Carbon Corp* ... 307
Major, Chris *LHC Group Inc* ... 1072
Major, Frederick W. *Petco Animal Supplies Inc* ... 1415
Major, Jo *Avanex Corp* ... 185
Major, John *Tektronix Inc* ... 1763
Major, John E. *Lennox International Inc* ... 1068
Major, John E. *Littelfuse Inc* ... 1086
Major, John *Broadcom Corp* ... 284
Major, Joseph *Hemcure Inc* ... 868
Major, Sean D. *Joy Global Inc* ... 1012
Majoros, Matthew J. *Tapestry Pharmaceuticals Inc* ... 1749
Majors, Alvin L. *First Pactrust Bancorp Inc* ... 714
Majors, Charles H. *American National Bankshares Inc* ... 98
Majors, Jackie *American Physicians Service Group Inc* ... 99
Majteles, Robert J. *Macrovision Corp* ... 1108
Majteles, Robert J. *Adept Technology Inc* ... 23
Majteles, Robert J. *Unify Corp* ... 1849
Majteles, Robert J. *World Heart Corp* ... 1976
Majumder, Bobby I. *Tri-Isthmus Group Inc* ... 1822
Mak, Camon *Frontier Development Group* ... 750
Mak, Chris *Cardima Inc* ... 331
Mak, John *Rinker Group Ltd* ... 1546
Mak, Kin Kwong *China Gentech Corp Ltd* ... 390
Mak, Margaret *Western Union Company (The)* ... 1952
Mak, Michael *Asia Global Holdings Corp* ... 160
Mak, Peter *Dragon Pharmaceuticals Inc* ... 574
Mak, Peter *New Dragon Asia Corp* ... 1270
Mak, Peter S.O. *i-CABLE Communications Ltd* ... 906
Mak, Tak W. *EntreMed Inc* ... 645
Makadon, Arthur *RAIT Financial Trust* ... 1511
Makamson, April *Merrimac Industries Inc* ... 1166
Makanoeich, Robert *Parkway Bank* ... 1388
Makar, Ralph *Bioject Medical Technologies Inc* ... 243
Makarewicz, Stephen E. *Ryerson Tull Inc* ... 1570
Make, Barry J. *Resmed Inc* ... 1536
Makela, Mary E. *Art Technology Group Inc* ... 153
Makes, Brigid *Bioject Medical Technologies Inc* ... 243
Makey, Charlie *Merchants Group Inc* ... 1161
Maki, Atsushi *Amanasu Technologies Corp* ... 76
Maki, Atsushi *Amanasu Environment Corp* ... 76
Maki, Corinne A. *HomeFed Corp* ... 887
Maki, Craig A. *Transaction Systems Architects Inc* ... 1813
Maki, John *Suffolk Bancorp* ... 1715
Maki, Mark A. *Enbridge Energy Management LLC* ... 628
Maki, Mary *Suffolk Bancorp* ... 1715
Maki, Valerie C. *Emmis Communications Corp* ... 624
Makihara, Minoru *IBM Corp* ... 909
Makihara, Minoru *Millea Holdings Inc* ... 1191
Makimoto, Tsugio *Chartered Semiconductor Mfg Ltd* ... 376
Makings, Dean *Colorado Interstate Gas Co* ... 441
Makino, Masashi *Matsushita Electric Industrial Co Ltd* ... 1132
Makinson, John *Pearson Plc* ... 1399
Makinson, John C. *Interactive Data Corp* ... 960
Makita, Takae *Matsushita Electric Industrial Co Ltd* ... 1132
Makkiya, Ann B. *Smith & Wesson Holding Corp* ... 1648
Makleff, Amir *BackWeb Technologies Ltd* ... 199
Makler, Harry M. *Lecg Corp* ... 1063
Makov, Efrat *Alvarion Ltd* ... 75
Makov, Israel *Given Imaging Ltd* ... 788
Makovsky, Evan *Cobiz Financial Inc* ... 432
Makowiecki, Peter F. *First Horizon National Corp* ... 707
Makowka, Leonard *Wellstar International Inc* ... 1945
Makowka, Leonard *Universal Detection Technology* ... 1867
Makowski, Brian *Kingsway Financial Services Inc* ... 1031
Makowski, Paul *Doral Financial Corp* ... 570
Makrides, Andrew *Bovie Medical Corp* ... 269
Makris, George A. *Simmons First National Corp* ... 1634
Makris, N. *Taylor Devices Inc* ... 1753
Maksud, Michel *VisualMED Clinical Solutions Corp* ... 1916
Makuch, Anthony P. *FNX Mining Co Inc* ... 731
Malabannan, Derick *Amis Holdings Inc* ... 113
Malachowski, Robert *First Aviation Services Inc* ... 696
Malachowsky, Chris A. *Nvidia Corp* ... 1319
Malafronte, Michael W. *Bresler & Reiner Inc* ... 277
Malagodi, Richard *Action Products International Inc* ... 17
Malagon, Lisa *Pinnacle West Capital Corp* ... 1432
Malamed, Adam *Ladenburg Thalmann Financial Svcs Inc* ... 1049
Malan, Pedro Sampaio *Unibanco Holdings* ... 1848
Malandro, Edward *Sun Bancorp Inc* ... 1717
Malanga, Annette *Peapack Gladstone Financial Corp* ... 1399
Malanga, Michael *Starbucks Corp* ... 1693
Malaro, Magie *Primedex Health Systems Inc* ... 1466
Malasek, Robert *WorldTradeShow.com Inc* ... 1978
Malashenko, Natalia *UPM-Kymmene Group* ... 1872
Malatesta, Gino *L-3 Communications Holdings Inc* ... 1046
Malayil, Tom *Macerich Company (The)* ... 1106
Malburg, Robert W. *Capital Bank Corp* ... 323
Malchione, Robert M. *Avery Dennison Corp* ... 188
Malchow, Scott *Aon Corp* ... 129
Malcolm, Andrew L. *Sysco Corp* ... 1742
Malcolm, Rob *Diageo Plc* ... 549
Malcolm, Steven J. *Williams Cos Inc* ... 1961
Malcolm, Steven J. *Transcontinental Gas Pipe Line Corp* ... 1815
Malcolm, Steven J. *BOK Financial Corp* ... 263
Malcolm, Steven J. *Northwest Pipeline Corp* ... 1306
Malcolm, Steven J. *Williams Partners LP* ... 1962
Malcom, Robert *Logitech International SA* ... 1092
Malcynsky, Jay F. *Federal Home Loan Bank of Boston* ... 682
Malden, Guy *Mitcham Industries Inc* ... 1200
Malden, Nicholas *Ventana Medical Systems Inc* ... 1893
Maldonado, Freddy *W Holding Co Inc* ... 1926
Maldonado, Henry *Washington Post Co* ... 1933
Maldonado, Jaime *Liberty Property Trust* ... 1074
Maldonado, Santiago Perdomo *Latin American Export Bank* ... 1058
Male, Jeff *Cascade Corp* ... 339
Male, Jeffrey N. *PVF Capital Corp* ... 1490
Male, John R. *PVF Capital Corp* ... 1490
Male, Marie-Jospeh *Air France-KLM* ... 45
Maleh, Paul A. *Charles River Assoc Inc* ... 374
Malek, Brian *Owens & Minor Inc* ... 1365
Malek, Frederic V. *Northwest Airlines Corp* ... 1304
Malek, Frederic V. *Automatic Data Processing Inc* ... 183
Malek, Frederic V. *CB Richard Ellis Group Inc* ... 347
Malekian, Peter E. *MCG Capital Corp* ... 1141
Malempati, Krishna M. *Community Trust Bancorp Inc* ... 456
Malenbaum, William *IT Group Holdings Inc* ... 992
Malenfant, Matthew *Safeguard Scientifics Inc* ... 1573
Malenick, Donal H. *Max & Ermas Restaurants Inc* ... 1134
Malenka, Robert C. *Renovis Inc* ... 1531
Malerba, Marilynn *Mohegan Tribal Gaming Authority* ... 1207
Malesardi, Michael *AES Corp* ... 38
Maleska, Martin E. *VCampus Corp* ... 1891
Maleska, Martin E. *Questar Assessment Inc* ... 1501
Malet, Michael *Medcom USA Inc* ... 1148
Maley, Michael P. *Fuel Tech* ... 753
Maley, Patrick J. *Temple Inland Inc* ... 1773
Maley, Patrick A. *Verdant Technology Group* ... 1895
Malfitano, Ricardo S. *Praxair Inc* ... 1458
Malguzzi, Alfredo *Benetton Group SpA* ... 231
Malhotra, Ashwani Kumar *Dr Reddy's Laboratories Ltd* ... 574
Malhotra, Rakesh *Security Devices International Inc* ... 1604
Malhotra, Rakesh *Yukon Gold Corp Inc* ... 1993
Malhotra, Sanjeev *iPass Inc* ... 986
Malia, Stephen P. *Owens Illinois Inc* ... 1366
Malik, Aslam *American Pacific Corp* ... 99
Malik, Joseph A. *Pacific Financial Corp* ... 1372
Malik, Kenneth E. *Lawson Products Inc* ... 1059
Malik, Maren C. *Greenbrier Cos Inc* ... 823
Malik, Musadik *Charles River Assoc Inc* ... 374
Malik, Nadim *American Capital Strategies Ltd* ... 87
Malik, Rajesh K. *Adherex Technologies Inc* ... 24
Malik, Rajiv *Mylan Laboratories Inc* ... 1230
Malik, Shahid *Great Plains Energy Inc* ... 820
Malik, Shahzad *Emergent Biosolutions Inc* ... 622
Malik, Zia *PDF Solutions* ... 1397
Malin, Richard J. *Sensient Technologies Corp* ... 1610
Malin, Robert *A B Watley Group Inc* ... 1
Malina, Brian *Verizon Communications Inc* ... 1897
Malinconico, Nancy L. *Central Jersey Bancorp* ... 362
Malinen, Eino *Nestor-Partners* ... 1261
Malinen, Heikki *UPM-Kymmene Group* ... 1872
Malinkevich, Yuri *Electro-Optical Sciences Inc* ... 613
Malino, Gary M. *Realty Income Corp* ... 1519
Malinoski, Frank *Medimmune Inc* ... 1154
Malinowski, Eugene V. *Center Bancorp Inc* ... 358
Malinowski, Eugene P. *Tasty Baking Co* ... 1752
Malinowski, Richard *Intel Corp* ... 958
Malins, Annette *Merrimac Industries Inc* ... 1166
Malis, Ira H. *OneBeacon Insurance Group Ltd* ... 1342
Malis, Jerry L. *Valley Forge Scientific Corp* ... 1886
Malis, Oleg *Golden Telecom Inc* ... 807
Malis, Oleg A. *Vimpel-Communications Company* ... 1907
Malis, Oleg *Turkcell Iletisim Hizmetleri* ... 1835
Malits, Ida Keidar *Saifun Semiconductors Ltd* ... 1576
Malizia, Samuel J. *Mercer Insurance Group Inc* ... 1160
Maljers, Floris A. *Air France-KLM* ... 45
Malkiel, Burton *Theravance Inc* ... 1785
Malkin, Allison *J. Crew Group Inc* ... 998
Malkin, Allison *New York & Company Inc* ... 1276
Malkin, Allison *Cache Inc* ... 302
Malkin, Hamish *Entree Gold Inc* ... 644
Malkin, Hamish *Argentex Mining Corp* ... 146
Malkin, Roy K. *Cantel Medical Corp* ... 320

McDonald, Peter D. *United Air Lines Inc* 1854
McDonald, Peter D. *UAL Corp/DE* 1842
McDonald, Philip *Perfectenergy International Ltd* 1411
McDonald, Randal B. *VTEX Energy Inc* 1924
McDonald, Ray A. *Devcon International Corp* 546
McDonald, Rebecca *BHP Billiton Ltd* 237
McDonald, Rebecca A. *Granite Construction Inc* 815
McDonald, Richard *Lyris Inc* 1103
McDonald, Robert K. *Commonwealth Edison Co* 450
McDonald, Robert *Xerox Corp* 1985
McDonald, Robert J. *Firstbank Financial Services Inc* 719
McDonald, Robert A. *Versar Inc* 1898
McDonald, Robert A. *Procter & Gamble* 1472
McDonald, Ross G. *Corriente Resources Inc* 485
McDonald, Ross G. *Miranda Gold Corp* 1197
McDonald, Scott W. *Atmospheric Glow Technologies Inc* 175
McDonald, Scott C. *Castelle* 342
McDonald, Sean C. *Respironics Inc* 1537
McDonald, Stephen D. *Bank of Nova Scotia (The)* 211
McDonald, Sterling *Evolution Petroleum Corp Inc* 666
McDonald, Steven D. *Central Valley Community Bancorp* 363
McDonald, Stuart D. *Cumberland Resources Ltd* 512
McDonald, Tom *SkillSoft* 1641
McDonald, Walter T. *Security Bank of CA* 1603
McDonald, Wayne *American States Water Co* 104
McDonald, Wesley S. *Kohl's Corp* 1038
McDonald, William E. *Martin Marietta Materials Inc* 1127
McDonald, William J. *Humana Inc* 899
McDonald, Williams J. *Tenet Healthcare Corp* 1774
McDonald, Williams J. *Belo Corp* 230
McDonell, Donald L. *Ciprico Inc* 408
McDonell, Horace G. *Ethan Allen Interiors Inc* 660
McDonie, Patrick *ONEOK Partners LP* 1343
McDonie, Patrick *Oneok Inc* 1343
McDonnell, Archie *Citizens National Bancorp DE* 414
McDonnell, Brendan R. *Hollis-Eden Pharmaceuticals Inc* 882
McDonnell, David V. *Harleysville Group Inc* 846
McDonnell, Guy *Korn Ferry International* 1041
McDonnell, John F. *Boeing* 262
McDonnell, John J. *DealerTrack Holdings Inc* 533
McDonnell, Karl *Strayer Education Inc* 1712
McDonnell, Mark *OneBeacon Insurance Group Ltd* 1342
McDonnell, Michael R. *MCG Capital Corp* 1141
McDonnell, Michael R. *HealthExtras Inc* 860
McDonnell, Patrick J. *Material Sciences Corp* 1130
McDonnell, Patrick J. *First Midwest Bancorp Inc* 711
McDonnell, Paul I. *United Rentals Inc* 1861
McDonnell, Robert J. *Comm Bancorp Inc* 445
McDonnell, Sean *CRM Holdings Ltd* 501
McDonnell, Sean *Ace Marketing & Promotions Inc* 13
McDonnell, Sherry *Entergy Arkansas Inc* 641
McDonnell, Stephen J. *Holly Energy Partners LP* 883
McDonnell, Stephen J. *Holly Corp* 883
McDonnell, Thomas A. *Euronet Worldwide Inc* 663
McDonnell, Thomas A. *Commerce Bancshares Inc* 446
McDonnell, Thomas A. *DST Systems Inc* 578
McDonnell, Thomas A. *Garmin Ltd* 762
McDonnell, Thomas A. *Kansas City Southern* 1018
McDonnell, Thomas A. *Kansas City Southern de Mexico, S.A. de C.V.* 1018
McDonnell, Vincent *CanArgo Energy Corp* 319
McDonnell, William A. *AMF Bowling Centers Inc* 112
McDonough, Dennis *FullCircle Registry Inc* 754
McDonough, Douglas H. *Hanover Insurance Group Inc* 844
McDonough, George *Royal Bancshares of Pennsylvania Inc* 1561
McDonough, John P. *Cytyc Corp* 522
McDonough, John *Tomkins Plc* 1801
McDonough, Joseph E. *Analog Devices Inc* 119
McDonough, Kathleen A. *Ambac Financial Group Inc* 78
McDonough, Kevin *Mentor Graphics Corp* 1159
McDonough, Kevin *RLI Corp* 1550
McDonough, Mark V. *Taylor Devices Inc* 1753
McDonough, Marsha A. *LSB Corp* 1097
McDonough, Paul H. *OneBeacon Insurance Group Ltd* 1342
McDonough, Robert J. *Union Bankshares Corp* 1850
McDonough, Thomas R. *TII Network Technologies Inc* 1793
McDonough, Thomas *Enterprise Financial Services Corp* 642
McDonough, Thomas P. *Coventry Health Care Inc* 491
McDonough, Tom *Equity One Inc* 653
McDonough, William J. *Merrill Lynch & Co Inc* 1165
McDorman, Al *F & M Bank Corp* 674
McDorman, John A. *Cash America International Inc* 341
McDougal, Bill *Metalico Inc* 1169
McDougal, Melissa L. *First Citizens Banc Corp* 700
McDougal, Robert D. *Searchlight Minerals Corp* 1600
McDougal, Robert D. *Ireland Inc* 988
McDougal, Rubin J. *CNH Global* 429
McDougal, Scot *Circuit Research Labs Inc* 408
McDougal, Tim *Temecula Valley Bancorp Inc* 1773
McDougal, Timothy S. *Temecula Valley Bancorp Inc* 1773
McDougal, Tom M. *T Bancshares Inc* 1743
McDougald, James *Medianews Group Inc* 1150
McDougall, Barbara J. *Bank of Nova Scotia (The)* 211
McDougall, Bernard *Micron Enviro Systems Inc* 1180
McDougall, Duane C. *Cascade Corp* 339
McDougall, Duane C. *Greenbrier Cos Inc* 823
McDougall, Duane C. *West Coast Bancorp* 1947
McDougall, Mike *Bausch & Lomb Inc* 220
McDougall, Stanley E. *QSound Labs Inc* 1494
McDougall, Wendy *EnCana Corp* 629
McDoulett, Bob *Valley Community Bank CA* 1886
McDow, Ira *Calavo Growers Inc* 306
McDowell, Alex *United BanCorp of Alabama Inc* 1856
McDowell, Charles *University Bank* 1871
McDowell, Dave *ICP Solar Technologies Inc* 913
McDowell, David C. *Nucryst Pharmaceuticals Corp* 1316
McDowell, Dennis H. *Newnan Coweta Bancshares Inc* 1279
McDowell, Eric *Alaska Pacific Bancshares Inc* 52
McDowell, Frank C. *Eagle Hospitality Properties Trust Inc* 590
McDowell, John H. *Tower Bancorp Inc* 1807
McDowell, Julie *Teleflex Inc* 1766
McDowell, Larry T. *CEC Entertainment Inc* 352
McDowell, Mark *UpSnap Inc* 1872
McDowell, Mary T. *Nokia Corp* 1292
McDowell, Mary *Citigroup Inc* 411
McDowell, Mary *Citicorp* 411
McDowell, Paul H. *Feldman Mall Properties Inc* 686
McDowell, Paul *CapLease Inc* 328
McDowell, Richard E. *Northwest Bancorp Inc* 1305
McDowell, Robert S. *Sunesis Pharmaceuticals Inc* 1721
McDowell, Ron W. *Atmos Energy Corp* 175
McDowell, Virginia *Isle of Capri Casinos Inc* 991
McDowell, William *Federal Home Loan Bank of Indianapolis* 683
McDuffie, Anthony D. *Harrah's Entertainment Inc* 848
McEleney, John *Dassault Systemes* 526
McElhatton, Jerry *Electronic Clearing House Inc* 614
McElhinney, Robert *China Wireless Communications Inc* 398
McElraft, Harold F. *Hanover Capital Mortgage Holdings Inc* 844
McElrea, Charles H. *Bluelinx Holdings Inc* 259
McElreath, Vicki *Piedmont Natural Gas Co Inc* 1429
McElroy, Bernard K. *Pep Boys* 1409
McElroy, Deborah L. *Smithtown Bancorp* 1649
McElroy, George S. *Diamond Hill Investment Group Inc* 551
McElroy, James C. *Whitney Holding Corp* 1958
McElroy, Kevin M. *California United Bank* 309
McElroy, Roderick O. *Sonic Environmental Solutions Inc* 1657
McElroy, Ted E. *Pogo Producing Co* 1443
McElroy, Terry L. *Pantry Inc* 1382
McElroy, Thomas J. *Hughes Communications Inc* 898
McElvain, Ken *Synplicity Inc* 1740
McElveen, Jack W. *Carolina National Corp* 336
McElwain, Douglas R. *Champion Industries Inc* 371
McElwee, Andrew A. *Chubb Corp* 403
McElwee, Andrew *Carpenter Technology Corp* 337
McElwee, Arthur H. *Old National Bancorp* 1333
McElwee, James B. *DTS Inc* 579
McElwee, Melissa *International Barrier Technology Inc* 967
McElwrath, Michael R. *Far East Energy Corp* 678
McEnallay, Patrick *Panavision Inc* 1381
McEnaney, Michael F. *TLC Vision Corp* 1798
McEnany, Patrick J. *Catalyst Pharmaceutical Partners Inc* 344
McEnany, Patrick J. *Thermogenesis Corp* 1786
McEneny, Nancy *LifeSpan Inc* 1076
McEnroe, John T. *Schawk Inc* 1590
McEntee, Charles *Greene County Bancorp Inc* 823
McEntee, James J. *Alesco Financial Inc* 55
McEntee, James J. *Bancorp Bank Inc (The)* 206
McEntee, Robert E. *Valley National Bancorp* 1886
McEntee, William J. *Interep National Radio Sales Inc* 963
McEntire, R. C. *Carolina National Corp* 336
McEntire, Thomas T. *Oyo Geospace Corp* 1367
McErlane, James E. *Willow Grove Bancorp Inc* 1963
McErlane, James E. *Willow Financial Bancorp Inc* 1963
McErlean, Paul D. *Mendocino Brewing Co Inc* 1159
McEvilly, Michael *Helix Energy Solutions Group Inc* 866
McEvily, Arthur J. *SunOpta Inc* 1722
McEvoy, John D. *McLeodUSA Inc* 1142
McEvoy, Kevin M. *Oceaneering International Inc* 1327
McEvoy, Thomas J. *Embarq Corp* 619
McEvoy, Timothy G. *Wilson Greatbatch Technologies Inc* 1964
McEwan, Alastair *Averion International Corp* 188
McEwan, Allan *InterContinental Hotels Group* 962
McEwan, Feona *WPP Group Plc* 1979
McEwan, Ross *Commonwealth Bank of Australia* 449
McEwan, Trisha *Telecom Corp of New Zealand Ltd* 1765
McEwen, Brian *Buffalo Gold Ltd* 293
McEwen, Brian *Centrasia Mining Corp* 364
McEwen, Bruce S. *Corcept Therapeutics Inc* 479
McEwen, Rob *U.S. Gold Corp* 1841
McFadden, Alex *TransAlta Corp* 1813
McFadden, Bruce A. *Cascade Microtech Inc* 340
McFadden, Charles B. *Scana Corp* 1589
McFadden, John J. *Advanced Battery Technologies Inc* 28
McFadden, Leslie *Cecil Bancorp Inc* 353
McFadden, Nancy E. *Pacific Gas & Electric Co* 1372
McFadden, Nancy E. *PG&E Corp* 1420
McFadden, Patrick F. *UIL Holdings Corp* 1845
McFadden, Ronald *Zones Inc* 2001
McFadyen, Hector *Harvest Energy Trust* 852
McFadyen, John *New Century Bancorp Inc* 1270
McFadyen, Stewart *First Bancorp* 696
McFall, Andrew M. *Peoples Bancorporation Inc* 1407
McFall, Shane *ResCare Inc* 1535
McFall, Shaun *Stratex Networks Inc* 1710
McFall, Tom *O Reilly Automotive Inc* 1322
McFarlan, Douglas *Edison International* 604
McFarlan, Warren F. *Computer Sciences Corp* 462
McFarlan, Warren F. *INVESTools Inc* 982
McFarland, Brenda *Centerpoint Energy Inc* 359
McFarland, Bruce D. *BreitBurn Energy Partners LP* 277
McFarland, Clifford E. *Teletouch Communications Inc* 1769
McFarland, Clyde E. *Towne Bank VA* 1808
McFarland, Cole *Novagold Resources Inc* 1308
McFarland, Duncan M. *NYSE Group Inc* 1322
McFarland, Duncan M. *Gannett Co Inc* 761
McFarland, J. C. *Venoco Inc* 1893
McFarland, James W. *Stewart Enterprises Inc* 1704
McFarland, James W. *Newpark Resources Inc* 1280
McFarland, John S. *Pitney Bowes Inc* 1434
McFarland, John *Baldor Electric Co* 201
McFarland, Julie *Coast Financial Holdings Inc* 431
McFarland, Kevin M. *Flagstar Bancorp Inc* 723
McFarland, Loren L. *Mentor Corp Minn* 1159
McFarland, Packy *International Commercial Television Inc* 968
McFarland, Robert N. *Ezenia Inc* 673
McFarland, Stuart A. *Newcastle Investment Corp* 1277
McFarland, Ted *L-3 Communications Holdings Inc* 1046
McFarland, William J. *Atheros Communications Inc* 170
McFarland Farthing, Linda *Stein Mart Inc* 1699
McFarland Rub, Jenny *Pride International Inc* 1465
McFarlane, Christine L. *California Water Service Group* 309
McFarlane, Don *CorVel Corp* 486
McFarlane, Dorcas H. *Calavo Growers Inc* 306
McFarlane, Gregory T. *Zab Resources Inc* 1994
McFarlane, Gregory T. *Las Vegas From Home Com Entertainmnt Inc* 1056
McFarlane, James G. *Cohu Inc* 437
McFarlane, John *Australia & New Zealand Banking GRP* 180
McFarlane, John S. *Exar Corp* 667
McFarlane, Paul D. *Brookfield Properties Corp* 286
McFarlane, Robert G. *TELUS Corp* 1772
McFarlane, Sara *Crown Media Holdings Inc* 505
McFarlin, Brian *Huron Consulting Group Inc* 901
McFarlin, Whitney A. *Possis Medical Inc* 1451
McFarren, Paul D. *United Retail Group Inc* 1861
McFate, Carol Ann *Xerox Corp* 1985
McFaul, David *Boston Scientific Corp* 268
McFaul, William *PS Business Parks Inc* 1483
McFayden, Shannon W. *Wachovia Corp* 1928
McFee, Dorothy *FNB Corp/VA* 730
McFeeley, Beth *General Growth Properties Inc* 771
McFeely, Anthony *ABB Ltd* 5
McFeeters, Paul *Open Text Corp* 1346
McFeetors, Raymond L. *Great-West Life & Annuity Insurance Co* 821
McFerran, Jim *First Financial Service Corp* 706
McFerran, Michael *KKR Financial Corp* 1033
McFerren Sanders, Allison *Worthington Industries Inc* 1978
McFerrin, Gene *Chicago Federal Home Loan Bank* 384
McFerrin, Michael E. *Chicago Federal Home Loan Bank* 384
McFie, Bill *Sonoran Energy Inc* 1659
McGaha, Gary D. *Southern Community Bancshares Inc* 1666
McGaha, John R. *Entergy Corp* 641
McGahan, Patrick *United Retail Group Inc* 1861
McGahn, Dan *American Superconductor Corp* 104
McGahran, Kathleen T. *Adams Express Company (The)* 21
McGalla, Susan P. *American Eagle Outfitters Inc* 90
McGann, Joseph E. *Benjamin Franklin Bancorp Inc* 231
McGannon, Ed *Western Reserve Bank* 1951
McGannon, John L. *Document Sciences Corp* 566
McGarey, Patrick H. *Baseline Oil & Gas Corp* 218
McGarity, Ciara *Jones Lang Lasalle Inc* 1010
McGarity, Jon W. *Cypress Bioscience Inc* 519
McGarity, Kevin *Altera Corp* 72
McGarity, Kevin J. *Fairchild Semiconductor International Inc* 676
McGarity, Michael H. *PPG Industries* 1456
McGarraugh, Eddie *Smarts Oil & Gas Inc* 1647
McGarry, Barbara L. *PSB Holdings Inc* 1484
McGarry, Brian T. *Tri City National Bank* 1821
McGarry, Diane E. *Omnova Solutions Inc* 1339
McGarry, Helen V.W. *FNBH Bancorp Inc* 731
McGarry, Helen V.W. *FNBH Bancorp Inc MI* 731
McGarry, James M. *Farmer Bros Co* 678
McGarry, Joe *National Investment Managers Inc* 1243
McGarry, Judith *Shutterfly Inc* 1623
McGarry, Kathleen K. *First Litchfield Financial Corp* 709
McGarry, Randy *Republic First Bancorp Inc* 1534
McGarry, William J. *St Jude Medical Inc* 1687
McGarvey, David *Pharmaxis Ltd* 1423
McGarvie, Blythe J. *Accenture Ltd* 11
McGarvie, Blythe J. *Travelers Property Casualty Corp* 1818
McGarvie, Blythe J. *Pepsi Bottling Group Inc* 1409
McGarvie, Blythe J. *St Paul Travelers Cos Inc* 1687
McGarvie, Blythe J. *Viacom Inc* 1902
McGary, Elsa *Northeast Bancorp* 1300
McGauchie, Donald *James Hardie Industries* 1003
McGauchie, Donald G. *Telstra Corp Ltd* 1771
McGaughey, Frank S. *Haverty Furniture Companies Inc* 853
McGaughey, William H. *Temecula Valley Bancorp Inc* 1773
McGaughy, Kent R. *Genitope Corp* 776
McGavock, Daniel M. *Charles River Assoc Inc* 374
McGeary, Roderick C. *Dionex Corp* 560
McGeary, Roderick C. *Cisco Systems Inc* 409
McGeary, Roderick C. *BearingPoint Inc* 226
McGee, Allen R. *Petro Resources Corp* 1415
McGee, Brian T. *Generex Biotechnology Corp* 773
McGee, Brian T. *Hydrogen Corp* 903
McGee, Harold *Senomyx Inc* 1609
McGee, Harry S. *Boeing* 262
McGee, Henry *Time Warner Inc* 1795
McGee, Henry W. *Amerisourcebergen Corp* 110
McGee, Hugh E. *Lehman Brothers Holdings Inc* 1067
McGee, Jerry E. *First Charter Corp* 699
McGee, Jerry *Ambassadors International Inc* 79
McGee, Jim *Cooperative Bankshares Inc* 478
McGee, Joseph A. *Jabil Circuit Inc* 999
McGee, Julie A. *DeVry Inc* 547
McGee, Liam E. *Bank of America Corp* 208
McGee, Lillian *Verizon Communications Inc* 1897
McGee, Michael V. *PS Business Parks Inc* 1483
McGee, Michael V. *Weyerhaeuser Co* 1955
McGee, Mike *Patapsco Bancorp Inc* 1389
McGee, Paula H. *Timeline Inc* 1795
McGee, Woody M. *Coinmach Corp* 437
McGeehan, Thomas M. *United America Indemnity Ltd* 1854
McGeehan, Timothy D. *Best Buy Co Inc* 234
McGeeney, John R. *Sypris Solutions Inc* 1741
McGeeney, Patrick A. *MBI Mortgage Services Ltd* 1138
McGehee, Charles A. *Colonial Properties Trust* 440
McGehee, Don M. *IBERIABANK Corp* 908
McGehee, James E. *Pinnacle Airlines Corp* 1430
McGehee, Robert B. *Florida Power Corp* 727
McGehee, Robert B. *Progress Energy Inc* 1474
McGehee, Robert B. *Carolina Power & Light Co* 337
McGeoch, Rod *Telecom Corp of New Zealand Ltd* 1765
McGeorge, Don W. *Kroger Co* 1043
McGeorge, Scott W. *Simmons First National Corp* 1634
McGettigan, Charles Carroll *Zindart Ltd* 1999
McGettigan, Charles C. *Modtech Holdings Inc* 1206
McGettrick, Mark F. *Dominion Resources Inc VA* 568
McGhan, Donald K. *Medicor Ltd* 1153
McGhan, Jim J. *Medicor Ltd* 1153
McGhee, Bob *Target Logistics Inc* 1750
McGhee, Erin *Cray Inc* 495
McGhee, Geoff *New York Times Co* 1277
McGhee, James E. *Community Trust Bancorp Inc* 456
McGhee, Joe *Diamond Powersports Inc* 551
McGhee, Lynne *California Water Service Group* 309
McGhee, William T. *Delta Apparel Inc* 539
McGibbon, Leslie *InterContinental Hotels Group* 962
McGill, Archibald J. *CIBER Inc* 405
McGill, Brendan J. *Harleysville Savings Financial Corp* 847
McGill, Chris *Rollins Inc* 1557
McGill, Cindy *PNM Resources Inc* 1443
McGill, Daniel K. *FirstMerit Corp* 720
McGill, Glen *Lloyds TSB Group Plc* 1088
McGill, James W. *Eaton Corp* 596
McGill, James C. *Addvantage Technologies Group Inc* 23
McGill, John J. *Borgwarner Inc* 266
McGill, Joseph *Fort Dearborn Income Securities Inc* 737
McGill, Leonard J. *Fleetwood Enterprises Inc* 724
McGill, Lisa *Foundry Networks Inc* 740
McGill, Mark *Carbo Ceramics Inc* 330
McGill, Melissa A. *Home Federal Bancorp* 885
McGill, Rick *Downey Financial Corp* 573
McGill, Rick *Federal Home Loan Bank of San Francisco* 683
McGill, Rick *Broadway Financial Corp* 284
McGill, Robert J. *Aerosonic Corp* 37
McGill, Robert *L-3 Communications Holdings Inc* 1046
McGill, S. R. *Exxon Mobil Corp* 673
McGill, Sarah *PepsiCo Inc* 1410
McGill, Sarah *Wolseley Plc* 1973
McGill, Stephen J. *American Medical Systems Holdings Inc* 96

Richardson, Marvin R. *Arcadia Resources Inc* 142
Richardson, Mary-Ann *Kendle International Inc* 1022
Richardson, Matthew L. *Host Hotels & Resorts Inc* 892
Richardson, Max A. *First Community Corp/TN* 702
Richardson, Michael A. *American Consumers Inc* 89
Richardson, Michael *Reis Inc* 1527
Richardson, Michael R. *Caseys General Stores Inc* 341
Richardson, Nigel *Atwood Oceanics Inc* 177
Richardson, Pat J. *Biomet Inc* 245
Richardson, Paul *WPP Group Plc* 1979
Richardson, Paul *Balchem Corp* 201
Richardson, Peter *Colgate Palmolive Co* 439
Richardson, Peter C. *MannKind Corp* 1119
Richardson, Randy *Talbots Inc* 1746
Richardson, Rick P. *Huttig Building Products Inc* 902
Richardson, Rick *Portola Packaging Inc* 1450
Richardson, Robert J. *Lyndonbank VT* 1102
Richardson, Robert *Primal Solutions Inc* 1465
Richardson, Robert *Kentucky Bancshares Inc* 1024
Richardson, Robert J. *Applied Signal Technology Inc* 137
Richardson, Robert *Kentucky First Federal Bancorp* 1024
Richardson, Robert J. *Worthington Industries Inc* 1978
Richardson, Robyn *Metalico Inc* 1169
Richardson, Ruth M. *Lecg Corp* 1063
Richardson, Sally K. *Molina Healthcare Inc* 1208
Richardson, Sam *Entergy Louisiana Holdings Inc* 641
Richardson, Sheri B. *Dillard's Inc* 558
Richardson, Tammy *Genworth Financial Inc* 779
Richardson, Thad G. *Lyndonbank VT* 1102
Richardson, Thomas L. *American Consumers Inc* 89
Richardson, Tim *IXYS Corp* 997
Richardson, Tommy *First Federal Bancshares of Arkansas Inc* 704
Richardson, Travis *Metwood Inc* 1174
Richardson, William C. *Exelon Corp* 668
Richardson, William J. *Ameristar Casinos Inc* 110
Richardson, William C. *Bank of New York Co Inc* 210
Richardson, William *Pharmaceutical Product Development Inc* 1422
Richardson, William C. *CSX Corp Inc* 509
Richardson, Yvonne *Anesiva Inc* 122
Richart, Debbie *Corning Inc* 483
Richart, Ralph M. *International Isotopes Inc* 970
Richartz, Georg *CNH Global* 429
Richbourg, Scott C. *Financial Security Assurance Holdings Ltd* 692
Riche, Pamela W. *Centerpoint Energy Inc* 359
Riche, Randal *Centerpoint Energy Inc* 359
Richelieu, William A. *KB Home* 1020
Richels, John *Devon Energy Corp* 547
Richenhagen, Martin *AGCO Corp* 42
Richer, Lynne D. *Avid Technology Inc* 190
Richerson, Elmer H. *Wilson Bank & Trust* 1964
Richerson, Timothy J. *Interleukin Genetics Inc* 964
Richert, Melanie *Rockwell Collins Inc* 1554
Richert, Rick *American Capital Strategies Ltd* 87
Richeson, H. E. *Bank Of Virginia* 212
Richey, Albert L. *Kayne Anderson Energy Development Company* 1020
Richey, Albert L. *Anadarko Petroleum Corp* 118
Richey, Daniel R. *Alabama National Bancorp* 50
Richey, Gregg *Windstream Corp* 1966
Richey, Jerome P. *CONSOL Energy Inc* 470
Richey, Joseph B. *Steris Corp* 1702
Richey, Joseph B. *Invacare Corp* 981
Richey, Thomas B. *Cedar Shopping Centers Inc* 353
Richey, Van L. *Wachovia Corp* 1928
Richey, Victor L. *ESCO Technologies Inc* 657
Richgels, William P. *FirstMerit Corp* 720
Richie, John A. *Rogers Corp* 1557
Richie, Leroy C. *Infinity Energy Resources Inc* 938
Richie, Robert *Capital Bank Corp* 323
Richieri, Kenneth A. *New York Times Co* 1277
Richieri, Richard *Peregrine Pharmaceuticals Inc* 1411
Richings, Michael B. *Vista Gold Corp* 1914
Richins, Paul O. *Utah Medical Products Inc* 1880
Richkus, William A. *Versar Inc* 1898
Richli, Remo *Origin Agritech Ltd* 1357
Richlovsky, Thomas A. *National City Corp* 1239
Richman, Doug *Kaiser Aluminum Corp* 1016
Richman, Doug *Kaiser Aluminum & Chemical Corp* 1016
Richman, Douglas *Adventrx Pharmaceuticals Inc* 33
Richman, Douglas D. *Anadys Pharmaceuticals Inc* 119
Richman, Douglas D. *Vical Inc* 1903
Richman, Douglas D. *Monogram Biosciences Inc* 1212
Richman, Eric I. *Lev Pharmaceuticals Inc* 1069
Richman, Jordan *Grubb & Ellis Co* 827
Richman, Matt *Incentra Solutions Inc New* 932
Richman, Michael S. *Pharmafrontiers Corp* 1422
Richman, Michael S. *Cougar Biotechnology Inc* 488
Richman, Peter *Secured Diversified Investment Ltd* 1602
Richman, Ross *Bed Bath & Beyond Inc* 227
Richman, Steven *Liberty Property Trust* 1074
Richmond, Albert F. *Champion Communication Services Inc* 371
Richmond, Alexander E. *Civitas Bankgroup Inc* 417
Richmond, Barney A. *Swap & Shop.net Corp* 1732
Richmond, Barney A. *MyZipSoft Inc* 1231
Richmond, Barney A. *Green Energy Group Inc* 822
Richmond, Barney A. *American Capital Holdings Inc* 87
Richmond, Barney A. *Diamond Energy Partners Inc* 550
Richmond, Barney A. *USAS Digital Inc* 1879
Richmond, Barney A. *Classified Ad Inc* 420
Richmond, Barney A. *Super Deal.com Inc* 1725
Richmond, Barney A. *eSecureSoft CO* 657
Richmond, Barry *Energroup Holdings Corp* 634
Richmond, Brad *Darden Restaurants Inc* 525
Richmond, Brent E. *WesBanco Bank Inc* 1946
Richmond, Craig S. *Huron Consulting Group Inc* 901
Richmond, George R. *Walter Industries Inc* 1930
Richmond, George E. *Young Innovations Inc* 1992
Richmond, Graham *Makemusic Inc* 1115
Richmond, Heather *General Growth Properties Inc* 771
Richmond, Janet D. *PSB Holdings Inc* 1484
Richmond, Jeffrey L. *Astec Industries Inc* 166
Richmond, Kent *American Pacific Corp* 99
Richmond, Kimberly S. *Huron Consulting Group Inc* 901
Richmond, Laurence M. *Genworth Financial Inc* 779
Richmond, Merrill *Town Sports International Holdings Inc* 1808
Richmond, Michael *Landrys Restaurants Inc* 1054
Richmond, Robert *Steelcloud Inc* 1698
Richmond-Coggan, Martin *Applix Inc* 137
Richtarich, Thomas P. *Nayna Networks Inc* 1255
Richter, Alice M. *G & K Services Inc* 757
Richter, Alice *West Marine Inc* 1947
Richter, David *DivX Inc* 564
Richter, David L. *Hill International Inc* 878
Richter, Diane *Norwood Financial Corp* 1307
Richter, Frank-Jurgen *WorldSpace Inc* 1977
Richter, George H. *Smithfield Foods Inc* 1649
Richter, Glenn R. *Nuveen Investments Inc* 1319
Richter, Irvin E. *Hill International Inc* 878
Richter, Jacob *Orbotech Ltd* 1354
Richter, James M. *Regency Energy Partners LP* 1525
Richter, Jerome *Penn Octane Corp* 1402
Richter, John *US 1 Industries Inc* 1875
Richter, Julia *TB Wood's Corp* 1753
Richter, Kirk *Sigma Aldrich Corp* 1627
Richter, Maria C. *Pantry Inc* 1382
Richter, Maria *National Grid Transco Plc* 1241
Richter, Norman B. *Textron Inc* 1783
Richter, Pat *Anchor Bancorp Wisconsin Inc* 120
Richter, Razia *Petco Animal Supplies Inc* 1415
Richter, Richard O. *Exponent Inc* 671
Richter, Robert S. *Lin Tv Corp* 1079
Richter, Sharon *Copart Inc* 479
Richter, Stephen C. *Weingarten Realty Investors* 1943
Richter, Stuart S. *Hill International Inc* 878
Richter, Terry *Atlantic Pacific Bank* 171
Richter, Udo *DaimlerChrysler AG* 523
Richter, Yochai *Orbotech Ltd* 1354
Richtman, Ana Maria Linhares *Companhia de saneamento Basico Do Estado De Sao Paulo - Sabesp* 457
Rick, Ball *Standard Register Co* 1691
Rick, Roseleen P. *Central Virginia Bankshares Inc* 364
Rickabaugh, Melissa *Beach Business Bank CA* 224
Rickabaugh, Sandy *National Realty* 1245
Rickard, Candice J. *Old National Bancorp* 1333
Rickard, David B. *Harris Corp* 849
Rickard, David B. *Jones Lang Lasalle Inc* 1010
Rickard, Gary P. *Norwood Financial Corp* 1307
Rickard, James D. *Community Bank Shares of Indiana Inc* 452
Rickard, Scott *Norwood Financial Corp* 1307
Rickards, James S. *Community Valley Bancorp* 456
Rickel, John C. *Group 1 Automotive Inc* 826
Ricken, Norman *Forward Industries Inc* 739
Rickenbach, Bruce *Questar Gas Co* 1501
Rickenbacher, Joe *UBS* 1843
Rickenbaker, Tom *Family Dollar Stores Inc* 677
Ricker, Carl H. *Capital Bank Corp* 323
Ricker, Deb *Northeast Bancorp* 1300
Ricker, Jon J. *DSW Inc* 578
Ricker, Jonathan *Mass Megawatts Wind Power Inc* 1129
Rickershauser, Peter J. *Burlington Northern Santa FE Corp* 296
Rickershauser, Peter J. *BNSF Railway Co* 261
Rickertsen, Carl J. *Microstrategy Inc* 1182
Rickertsen, Carl J. *UAP Holding Corp* 1843
Rickertson, Carl J. *Convera Corp* 476
Ricketts, James *El Capitan Precious Metals Inc* 609
Ricketts, James F. *Ingram Micro Inc* 944
Ricketts, Jerald L. *North Valley Bancorp* 1300
Ricketts, Joe J. *Ameritrade Holding Corp* 110
Ricketts, Lawrence G. *One Liberty Properties Inc* 1341
Ricketts, Michael J. *Cano Petroleum Inc* 320
Ricketts, Peter J. *Ameritrade Holding Corp* 110
Ricketts, Stefan *BG Group Plc* 236
Ricketts, Thomas S. *Ameritrade Holding Corp* 110
Rickey, David M. *Netlist Inc* 1263
Rickey, David *Cytori Therapeutics Inc* 521
Rickey, Victoria L. *Nacco Industries Inc* 1232
Ricklef, Linda J. *Post Properties Inc* 1451
Ricklefs, Henry K. *Plum Creek Timber Company Inc* 1440
Rickman, John H. *Pacific Continental Corp* 1371
Rickman, Paul *Baldwin Technology Co Inc* 201
Ricks, Jay E. *TNS Inc* 1799
Ricks, Richard *Computer Sciences Corp* 462
Ricks, Ron *Southwest Airlines Co* 1669
Ricks, Thomas G. *Newfield Exploration Co* 1278
Rickwood, Robert *Radvision Ltd* 1509
Rico, Valeria *Herbalife Ltd* 870
Ridall, John H. *Comcast Corp* 444
Ridd, Brian V. *Huntsman Corp* 900
Ridd, Russell L. *Norwood Financial Corp* 1307
Riddell, David *Davey Tree Expert Co (The)* 529
Riddell, Edwin O. *Enova Systems Inc* 639
Ridder, Anthony P. *Sun Microsystems Inc* 1719
Ridder, Anthony P. *McClatchy Co* 1139
Ridder, Greg W. *Owens Illinois Inc* 1366
Ridder, Paul D. *Tasty Baking Co* 1752
Ridder, Wolfram *Mercer International Inc* 1161
Riddick, Frank A. *GrafTech International Ltd* 813
Riddick, Steve *National Bancshares Corp OH* 1238
Riddiford, David T. *Vicor Corp* 1903
Riddiford, David T. *Datawatch Corp* 529
Riddle, Craig J. *Community First Bancorp Inc* 454
Riddle, David *Amis Holdings Inc* 113
Riddle, Dennis *Archer-Daniels-Midland Co* 143
Riddle, Don E. *CommerceFirst Bancorp Inc* 448
Riddle, Ernest J. *Danka Business Systems Plc* 525
Riddle, Freeman E. *Southern Michigan Bancorp Inc* 1666
Riddle, Glynn L. *Advocat Inc* 34
Riddle, Greg *Eastman Chemical Co* 595
Riddle, James E. *Airnet Systems Inc* 47
Riddle, Matthew C. *Amylin Pharmaceuticals Inc* 118
Riddle, Raymond D. *AGL Resources Inc* 43
Riddle, Raymond D. *Atlantic American Corp* 170
Riddle, Richard A. *Salem Communications Corp* 1576
Riddle, Robert L. *Old Point Financial Corp* 1334
Riddle, Ron *Tandy Leather Factory Inc* 1748
Rideaux, Damon *International Lease Finance Corp* 970
Ridenour, Dean P. *Holly Energy Partners LP* 883
Ridenour, Dean P. *Holly Corp* 883
Ridenour, Eric *DaimlerChrysler AG* 523
Ridenour, Tom *VuBotics Inc* 1925
Ridens, J. C. *Forest Oil Corp* 735
Rider, Alton J. *First Financial Service Corp* 706
Rider, Lars *Echelon Corp* 598
Rider, Randall C. *Northeast Indiana Bancorp Inc New* 1300
Rider, Shawn *HopFed Bancorp Inc* 889
Ridge, Garry O. *WD-40 Company* 1939
Ridge, Malcom *Vicon Industries Inc* 1903
Ridge, Martin *TransAlta Corp* 1813
Ridge, Robert A. *ConocoPhillips* 469
Ridge, Thomas J. *Vonage Holdings Corp* 1922
Ridge, Thomas J. *Exelon Corp* 668
Ridgeway, Alan *CCE Spinco Inc* 349
Ridgeway, Dennis *Media Sciences International Inc* 1149
Ridgeway, Kellie *United BanCorp of Alabama Inc* 1856
Ridgeway, Riggie R. *Peoples Bancorporation Inc* 1407
Ridgeway, Susan *Apartment Investment and Management Company* 130
Ridgill, Pressley A. *LSB Bancshares Inc* 1097
Ridgley, Lorraine *HopFed Bancorp Inc* 889
Ridgway, Ben *CNA Financial Corp* 427
Ridgway, Corey *United Surgical Partners International Inc* 1863
Ridgway, Rozanne L. *Conmed Healthcare Management Inc* 468
Ridgway, Rozanne L. *Sara Lee Corp* 1585
Ridgway, Rozanne L. *3M Co* 2007
Ridgway, Rozanne L. *Emerson Electric Co* 623
Ridgway, Rozanne L. *Manpower Inc* 1119
Ridgway, Rozanne L. *Boeing* 262
Ridgway, Simon T. *Radius Explorations Ltd* 1508
Ridings, Barry *New Valley Corp* 1275
Ridings, James R. *Craftmade International Inc* 494
Ridings, Thomas *W. P. Carey & Co LLC* 1926
Ridler, Gregory L. *Sky Financial Group Inc* 1642
Ridley, Barry *Providence Resources Inc* 1480
Ridley, Clarence H. *Crawford & Co* 495
Ridley, Clarence H. *Haverty Furniture Companies Inc* 853
Ridley, Doug *XELR8 Holdings Inc* 1984
Ridlon, Dean *Avid Technology Inc* 190
Ridnour, Brad *ING Life Insurance & Annuity Co* 943
Ridout, Robert R. *E I Du Pont De Nemours & Co* 587
Rieb, Jennifer *BASF* 218
Riebel, Bjorn *Citrix Systems Inc* 415
Riebel, Philippe *UPM-Kymmene Group* 1872
Riebesell, Bambi *Bank of Marin* 210
Rieck, Kim A. *Glimcher Realty Trust* 790
Rieck, Thomas W. *Sigmatron International Inc* 1628
Ried, Fernando Gardeweg *Enersis* 637
Riedel, Craig *Nucor Corp* 1315
Riedel, Craig *Multi Fineline Electronix Inc* 1226
Riedel, George *Nortel Networks Corp* 1296
Riedel, Gerard E. *Momenta Pharmaceuticals Inc* 1209
Riedel, Linda *Leesport Financial Corp* 1064
Riedel, Norbert G. *Baxter International Inc* 220
Riedel, Norbert G. *Oscient Pharmaceuticals Corp* 1361
Rieder, Bob *Inovio Biomedical Corp* 949
Rieder, Robert W. *Inovio Biomedical Corp* 949
Rieder, Robert W. *Cardiome Pharma Corp* 333
Riederer, Richard K. *Cleveland Cliffs Inc* 423
Riederer, Richard K. *American Municipal Income Portfolio Inc* 98
Riediker, Martin *Ciba Specialty Chemicals Holding Inc* 404
Riedl, George J. *Walgreen Co* 1929
Riedl, Robert E. *Consumer Portfolio Services Inc* 473
Riedler, Al *St. Bernard Software Inc* 1688
Riedman, James R. *Phoenix Footwear Group Inc* 1426
Riedman, James R. *Harris Interactive Inc* 849
Riedman, John R. *Brown & Brown Inc* 288
Riedman, Suzanne M. *Kindred Healthcare Inc* 1030
Riedy, Mark J. *Biomed Realty Trust* 244
Riefer, Tina *LMI Aerospace Inc* 1089
Riefler, Linda *Morgan Stanley* 1215
Rieflin, William J. *XenoPort Inc* 1985
Riegel, David L. *Crossroads Systems Inc* 503
Riegel, Gregory *Liberty Property Trust* 1074
Riegelhaupt, Loren *Forest City Enterprises Inc* 735
Rieger, Ed *Cohn & Steers Inc* 437
Rieger, Victor H. *Bay National Corp (Maryland)* 221
Riegert, Richard W. *Shell Canada Ltd* 1618
Riegle, Donald W. *WellPoint Inc* 1944
Riegle, Donald W. *Stillwater Mining Co* 1705
Riegler, Bernhard *Sappi Ltd* 1585
Riegler, Richard R. *Aqua America Inc* 138
Riehemann, Walter E. *Adams Respiratory Therapeutics Inc* 22
Riehl, Peter *Stellar Pharmaceuticals Inc* 1699
Riehle, Nick J. *Chelsea Therapeutics International Ltd* 380
Riehs, Steven P. *DeVry Inc* 547
Riek, Jonathan *VirtualScopics Inc* 1912
Rieke, Kurt W. *Prospect Capital Corp* 1476
Riel, Marie-Annick *Manaris Corp* 1117
Riel, Pierre *Costco Wholesale Corp* 488
Rieland, William G. *CONSOL Energy Inc WY* 470
Rieley, John F. *J2 Global Communications Inc* 999
Rielly, J. P. *Hess Corp* 873
Rielly, Thomas J. *Javo Beverage Company Inc* 1004
Rieman, Deborah D. *Corning Inc* 483
Rieman, Deborah *Keynote Systems Inc* 1026
Rieman, Deborah D. *Kintera Inc* 1032
Rieman, Deborah D. *Tumbleweed Communications Corp* 1834
Rieman, Kendall W. *Croghan Bancshares Inc* 502
Riemann, Gunnar *Bayer Schering Pharma Aktiengesellschaft* 221
Riemenschneider, Gerd *Pfeiffer Vacuum Technology* 1419
Riemer, Joseph *Sono Tek Corp* 1658
Riemer, Neil B. *Sally Beauty Holdings Inc* 1578
Riemer, Wesley N. *VIASYS Healthcare Inc* 1903
Riendeau, Brenda *Old Dominion Electric Cooperative* 1333
Riepe, James S. *Nasdaq Stock Market Inc (The)* 1236
Riepe, James S. *Genworth Financial Inc* 779
Riepenhausen, Peter *A.P. Pharma Inc* 3
Riepl, Jochen *Mercer International Inc* 1161
Ries, Catherine E. *Unisource Energy Corp* 1853
Ries, Eric *Rambus Inc* 1512
Ries, Timothy R. *Koppers Inc* 1040
Rieschel, Gary *THQ Inc* 1790
Riese, Phillip J. *Hypercom Corp* 905
Riesenbach, James *Autobytel Inc* 181
Riesenfeld, Stefan C. *Learning Tree International Inc* 1063
Rieser, Kim *Portola Packaging Inc* 1450
Riesner, Detlev H. *Qiagen* 1492
Riess, Michele *Gartner Inc* 762
Riess, Richard K. *Raymond James Financial Inc* 1516
Riester, Derik *Cascade Corp* 339
Riesterer, Charles C. *First Citizens Banc Corp* 700
Rieth, Blair A. *Hillenbrand Industries Inc* 879
Rieth, Brian *Riviera Tool Co* 1550
Rieth, Kenneth K. *Riviera Tool Co* 1550
Rietheimer, Albert R. *Cambridge Bancorp* 313
Rietveldt, John *American Standard Companies Inc* 103
Rieveley, Cheryl A. *Biotech Holdings Ltd* 248
Rieveley, Robert B. *Biotech Holdings Ltd* 248
Rieveley -, Greg R. *Harry Winston Diamond Corp* 849
Riewold, Ronald L. *Paincare Holdings Inc* 1377
Rife, John A. *QCR Holdings Inc* 1492
Rife, John A. *United Fire & Casualty Co* 1858
Rifelli, Ero F. *Hudson Valley Holding Corp* 897

Owners Index

James G. McClure *Capital Bank Corp* 323
James G. McFarlane *Cohu Inc* 437
James G. Moore *Amerityre Corp* 111
James G. Murphy *BioMimetic Therapeutics Inc* 245
James G. Murphy *Immunicon Corp* 928
James G. OConnor *Ashworth Inc* 159
James G. Orie *FNB Corp/FL* 730
James G. Petcoff *North Pointe Holdings Corp* 1299
James G. Pratt *Heartland Express Inc* 863
James G. Pratt *Hills Bancorp* 879
James G. Rakes *National Bankshares Inc* 1239
James G. Reindl *Techprecision Corp* 1760
James G. Roche *Orbital Sciences Corp* 1354
James G. Schuetzle *Integral Systems Inc* 954
James G. Shennan *P.F. Chang's China Bistro Inc* 1368
James G. Shennan *Starbucks Corp* 1693
James G. Shiel *W. R. Berkley Corp* 1927
James G. Sippl *Navarre Corp* 1252
James G. Spencer *Allion Healthcare Inc* 66
James G. Stewart *VIA Pharmaceuticals Inc* 1901
James G. Tatum *Independence Holding Co* 933
James G. Tatum *Aristotle Corp (The)* 148
James G. Thomasch *PLC Systems Inc* 1440
James G. Townsend *Holly Energy Partners LP* 883
James G. Vetter *Pilgrims Pride Corp* 1430
James G. Wake *Midwestone Financial Group Inc* 1188
James Gordon *Audiovox Corp* 178
James Grant *Shire Plc* 1620
James Gunton *Redpoint Bio Corp* 1522
James H. & Constance Haddox *Quanta Services Inc* 1497
James H. Baillie *Mine Safety Appliances Co* 1194
James H. Barnhardt *TSB Financial Corp* 1832
James H. Bason *Carver Bancorp Inc* 339
James H. Berglund *Accredited Home Lenders Co* 12
James H. Bingham *Centerstate Banks of Florida Inc* 359
James H. Blanchard *Synovus Financial Corp* 1739
James H. Blanchard *Total System Services Inc* 1806
James H. Bloem *Humana Inc* 899
James H. Bloem *Rotech Healthcare Inc NEW* 1560
James H. Bond *Central Parking Corp* 363
James H. Brandi *Energy East Corp* 635
James H. Bromley *CSS Industries Inc* 509
James H. Bugbee *Chicopee Bancorp Inc* 385
James H. Bullock *Matrix Bancorp Inc* 1131
James H. Burton *Leesport Financial Corp* 1064
James H. Burton *Leesport Financial Corp* 1064
James H. Butler *First Pulaski National Corp* 715
James H. Carey *ABX Air Inc* 8
James H. Carey *Midland Co* 1187
James H. Carll *Cybex International Inc* 518
James H. Cavanaugh *MiddleBrook Pharmaceuticals Inc* 1185
James H. Cheek *Genesco Inc* 773
James H. Clardy *Microtune Inc* 1182
James H. Clark *Shutterfly Inc* 1623
James H. Cleave *HSBC USA Inc* 895
James H. Click *Banco Bilbao Vizcaya Argentaria* 204
James H. Coleman *Cortex Pharmaceuticals Inc* 485
James H. Collins *iLinc Communications Inc* 922
James H. Craig *Tower Bancorp Inc* 1807
James H. Dahl *ASV Inc* 168
James H. Dallas *Key Corp* 1025
James H. Davis *Human Genome Sciences Inc* 899
James H. Dawson *First Potomac Realty Trust* 715
James H. DeGraffenreidt *WGL Holdings Inc* 1955
James H. Delaney *Ryerson Tull Inc* 1570
James H. DeVries *Quixote Corp* 1504
James H. Diffendorfer *Hydrogen Power Inc* 904
James H. Dorman *Platinum Energy Resources Inc* 1438
James H. Dorman *Transmeridian Exploration Inc* 1816
James H. Dorton *NN Inc* 1290
James H. Drennan *Foothills Resources Inc* 733
James H. Dunsdon *IFF Inc* 919
James H. Dusenbury *Coastal Financial Corp* 432
James H. Everest *Sport Haley Inc* 1683
James H. Feeney *CoActive Marketing Group Inc* 430
James H. Ferebee *Gateway Financial Holdings Inc* 764
James H. Foglesong *Horizon Bancorp* 889
James H. Garner *First Bancorp* 696
James H. Geers *Cooper Tire & Rubber Co* 478
James H. Gentile *Microsemi Corp* 1181
James H. Graass *Eagle Materials Inc* 590
James H. Graves *Hallmark Financial Services Inc* 839
James H. Graves *Cash America International Inc* 341
James H. Greene *Accuride Corp* 12
James H. Greene *Zhone Technologies Inc* 1997
James H. Greer *Americredit Corp* 108
James H. Grogan *Chestatee Bancshares Inc* 383
James H. Hance *Cousins Properties Inc* 490
James H. Hance *Rayonier Inc* 1516
James H. Hartung *N Viro International Corp* 1231
James H. Holdrege *Hickory Tech Corp* 876
James H. Hoppel *Chart Industries Inc* 375
James H. Horne *Hancock Holding Co* 842
James H. Hudson *C&F Financial Corp* 299
James H. Hunter *Downey Financial Corp* 573
James H. Ingraham *Brooke Corp* 285
James H. Kauffman *Cash America International Inc* 341
James H. Kelly *Stem Cell Innovations Inc* 1700
James H. Keyes *LSI Corp* 1098
James H. Keyes *Pitney Bowes Inc* 1434
James H. Keyes *Navistar International Corp* 1253
James H. Kropp *PS Business Parks Inc* 1483
James H. Langmead *Eagle Bancorp Inc* 589
James H. Lee *Forest Oil Corp* 735
James H. Lee *Frontier Oil Corp* 751
James H. Limmer *Consolidated Graphics Inc TX* 471
James H. Lytal *Enterprise GP Holdings LP* 643
James H. Lytal *Enterprise Products Partners LP* 643
James H. Mayes *Financial Federal Corp* 691
James H. Maynard *BB&T Corp* 222
James H. McCroy *Nexxus Lighting Inc* 1284
James H. McGuire *Digital Insight Corp* 556
James H. McKnight *Baker Michael Corp* 200
James H. Meade *Avalon Pharmaceuticals Inc* 184
James H. Miller *Fidelity Southern Corp* 690
James H. Miller *Georgia Power Co* 782
James H. Miller *New Hampshire Thrift Bancshares Inc* 1272
James H. Moar *Graco Inc* 813
James H. Moore *GB&T Bancshares Inc* 765
James H. Moore *Mines Mgmt Inc* 1195
James H. Moore *Heritage Financial Group* 871
James H. Mulligan *Frontier Financial Corp* 751
James H. Ozanne *Distributed Energy Systems Corp* 562
James H. Patterson *Middleburg Financial Corp* 1185
James H. Perry *United Industrial Corp* 1859
James H. Reynolds *Multi Color Corp* 1226
James H. Richardson *Alexandria Real Estate Equities Inc* 55
James H. Roberts *Granite Construction Inc* 815
James H. Ross *McGraw-Hill Companies Inc* 1141
James H. Ross *SWS Group Inc* 1733
James H. Rourke *Mueller Industries Inc* 1226
James H. Rubenstein *Radiation Therapy Services Inc* 1507
James H. Sabry *Cytokinetics Inc* 521
James H. Sanford *Alabama Power Co* 50
James H. Schultz *Comfort Systems USA Inc* 445
James H. Schultz *Goodman Global Inc* 810
James H. Serrone *Torotel Inc* 1804
James H. Sexton *Southcoast Financial Corp* 1664
James H. Shaw *Cato Corp (The)* 346
James H. Shelton *Intrepid Holdings Inc* 979
James H. Simons *Franklin Electronic Publishers Inc* 744
James H. Smith *MidCarolina Financial Corp* 1185
James H. Smith *Pomeroy IT Solutions* 1447
James H. Steane *Standard Mgmt Corp* 1690
James H. Stever *Washington Mutual Inc* 1933
James H. Stone *Stone Energy Corp* 1707
James H. Strosahl *Glacier Bancorp Inc* 788
James H. Thornton *DNB Financial Corp* 565
James H. Thrall *E-Z-EM Inc* 588
James H. Van Horn *Nelnet Inc* 1258
James H. Vandenberghe *Lear Corp* 1062
James H. Vandenberghe *DTE Energy Co* 579
James H. Veghte *XL Capital Ltd* 1987
James H. Warren *First Georgia Community Corp* 707
James H. Welch *Rigel Pharmaceuticals Inc* 1545
James H. Wells *Asure Software* 168
James H. Willeke *Delta & Pine Land Co* 539
James H. Winston *Stein Mart Inc* 1699
James H. Winston *Patriot Transportation Holding Inc* 1392
James H. Wyckoff *Financial Institutions Inc* 692
James Hamilton *3COM Corp* 2007
James Heinz *WPCS International Inc* 1979
James I. Ausman *Somanetics Corp* 1655
James I. Cash *Wal-Mart Stores Inc* 1929
James I. Cash *Phase Forward Inc* 1424
James I. Cash *Phase Forward Inc* 1424
James I. Cash *Microsoft Corp* 1182
James I. Cash *Chubb Corp* 403
James I. Cash *General Electric Co* 770
James I. Freeman *Dillard's Inc* 558
James I. Golla *Altair Nanotechnologies Inc* 72
James I. Healy *InterMune Inc* 965
James I. Healy *Novacea Inc* 1308
James I. K. Murray *Wolseley Plc* 1973
James I. Rotenstreich *Golden Enterprises Inc* 805
James I. Thomson *EuroBancshares Inc* 662
James I. Tims *First M & F Corp* 709
James Iman *Sense Technologies Inc* 1610
James J . Burke *Standard Motor Products Inc* 1690
James J. Abel *Lamson & Sessions Co (The)* 1052
James J. Antal *SIGA Technologies Inc* 1627
James J. Antal *Centerstate Banks of Florida Inc* 359
James J. Antal *Cleveland BioLabs Inc* 423
James J. Barber *Metabolix Inc* 1168
James J. Barnes *Tollgrade Communications Inc* 1801
James J. Barnett *ValueVision Media Inc* 1888
James J. Bellinghausen *SAIA Inc* 1575
James J. Bender *Williams Partners LP* 1962
James J. Bennett *Bio Rad Laboratories Inc* 240
James J. Bennett *Bio Rad Laboratories Inc* 240
James J. Blosser *Levitt Corp* 1070
James J. Bookout *TXCO Resources Inc* 1838
James J. Bowes *Liberty Property Trust* 1074
James J. Brennan *BankFinancial Corp* 213
James J. Brownson *QCR Holdings Inc* 1492
James J. Bryja *Foundation Coal Holdings Inc* 740
James J. Burke *Lincoln Educational Services Corp* 1080
James J. Burke *Anntaylor Stores Corp* 126
James J. Burns *One Liberty Properties Inc* 1341
James J. Burns *Cedar Shopping Centers Inc* 353
James J. Burns *Reis Inc* 1527
James J. Byrne *Lennox International Inc* 1068
James J. Byrne *HealthAxis Inc* 859
James J. Byrnes *Tompkins Financial Corp* 1801
James J. Cahill *Branded Media Corp* 274
James J. Carpenter *New York Community Bancorp Inc* 1276
James J. Casey *Expeditors International of Washington Inc* 670
James J. Cerna *Lucas Energy Inc* 1099
James J. Clark *AAR Corp* 4
James J. Cleary *Colorado Interstate Gas Co* 441
James J. Cleary *El Paso Natural Gas Co* 610
James J. Cotter *Reading International Inc* 1518
James J. Cotter *Reading International Inc* 1518
James J. Cotter *Reading International Inc* 1518
James J. Cramer *Thestreet.com* 1787
James J. Cullers *Park National Corp* 1386
James J. Dal Porto *I-Flow Corp* 906
James J. Didion *GenCorp Inc* 767
James J. Doran *Columbia Bancorp OR* 442
James J. Dor *Global Industries Ltd* 794
James J. Doud *First Mutual Bancshares Inc* 711
James J. Dowling *K-Sea Transportation Partners LP* 1015
James J. Duderstadt *Unisys Corp* 1853
James J. Ellis *Merit Medical Systems Inc* 1164
James J. Ellis *Jack Henry & Assoc Inc* 1000
James J. Ensell *Virage Logic Corp* 1909
James J. Ferris *CH2M HILL Companies Ltd* 370
James J. Florio *Trump Hotels & Casino Resorts Inc* 1830
James J. Ford *New Hampshire Thrift Bancshares Inc* 1272
James J. Forese *Spherion Corp* 1680
James J. Forese *Anheuser-Busch Companies Inc* 124
James J. Forese *Suntron Corp* 1724
James J. Fuchs *Praxair Inc* 1458
James J. Fuller *Citizens South Banking Corp* 415
James J. Gaffney *Beacon Roofing Supply Inc* 225
James J. Gaffney *Pool Corp* 1447
James J. Gaffney *Imperial Sugar Co* 930
James J. Galvin *Brightec Inc* 279
James J. Gaynor *Lightpath Technologies Inc* 1078
James J. Gosa *American Woodmark Corp* 107
James J. Greed *inTEST Corp* 978
James J. Hinnendael *Marten Transport Ltd* 1127
James J. Hohman *Omnova Solutions Inc* 1339
James J. Hoolihan *Allete Inc* 60
James J. Howard *Honeywell International Inc* 888
James J. Howard *Walgreen Co* 1929
James J. Judge *Analogic Corp* 119
James J. Judge *NSTAR* 1313
James J. Keil *NeoMedia Technologies Inc* 1259
James J. Kim *Gamestop Corp* 759
James J. Kim *Amkor Technology Inc* 114
James J. Kim Family Control Group *Amkor Technology Inc* 114
James J. Koegel *DNB Financial Corp* 565
James J. Kohn *Nevada Gold & Casinos Inc* 1269
James J. Kropid *Southwest Gas Corp* 1669
James J. Landy *Hudson Valley Holding Corp* 897
James J. Leitzinger *CNB Financial Corp* 428
James J. Leto *GTSI Corp* 832
James J. Liguori *Morgan's Foods Inc* 1216
James J. Lillis *Anthracite Capital Inc* 128
James J. Lindsay *Law Enforcement Assoc Corp* 1059
James J. Logothetis *Merrimac Industries Inc* 1166
James J. Lott *ACNB Corp* 15
James J. Loughlin *Celgene Corp* 355
James J. Loughlin *Alfacell Corp* 56
James J. Loughlin *Datascope Corp* 528
James J. Lynch *Sovereign Bank* 1671
James J. Maguire *Philadelphia Consolidated Holding Corp* 1425
James J. Maguire *Philadelphia Consolidated Holding Corp* 1425
James J. Mahoney *Aspect Medical Systems Inc* 162
James J. Mahoney *PolyMedica Corp* 1445
James J. Malvaso *Graham Corp* 814
James J. Marino *Pharmacopeia Drug Discovery Inc* 1422
James J. Martell *Express-1 Expedited Solutions Inc* 671
James J. Mastriani *Velocity Asset Management Inc* 1892
James J. Mauzey *Pozen Inc* 1456
James J. McCaskey *Middlefield Banc Corp* 1186
James J. McEntee *Bancorp Bank Inc (The)* 206
James J. McEntee *Alesco Financial Inc* 55
James J. McGonigle *Factset Research Systems Inc* 675
James J. McGonigle *Corporate Executive Board Co* 484
James J. McGuire *Everlast Worldwide Inc* 666
James J. McNulty *NYSE Group Inc* 1322
James J. McSwiggan *Royal Bancshares of Pennsylvania Inc* 1561
James J. Meenaghan *Arch Capital Group Ltd* 143
James J. Monnat *Gehl Co* 765
James J. Morgan *Megadata Corp* 1157
James J. Morgan *Bertucci's Corp* 234
James J. Mulva *ConocoPhillips* 469
James J. Murren *MGM MIRAGE* 1176
James J. Noble *Curagen Corp* 513
James J. O'Donnell *Hines Horticulture Inc* 880
James J. O'Neill *Medialink Worldwide Inc* 1149
James J. OBrien *Ashland Inc* 159
James J. OConnor *Smurfit-Stone Container Enterprises Inc* 1650
James J. OConnor *Smurfit Stone Container Corp* 1650
James J. OConnor *UAL Corp/DE* 1842
James J. OConnor *Corning Inc* 483
James J. ODonovan *New York Community Bancorp Inc* 1276
James J. Padilla *Ford Motor Co* 734
James J. Padilla *Ford Motor Co* 734
James J. Pallota *Petrohawk Energy Corp* 1416
James J. Patterson *Schawk Inc* 1590
James J. Peoples *Peoples Educational Holdings Inc* 1408
James J. Peterson *SimpleTech Inc* 1634
James J. Peterson *Microsemi Corp* 1181
James J. Peveler *American Pacific Corp* 99
James J. Pieczynski *Capitalsource Inc* 327
James J. Postl *Cooper Industries Ltd* 477
James J. Postl *Centex Corp* 360
James J. Pryor *First Valley Bancorp Inc CT* 718
James J. Puplava *Kimber Resources Inc* 1029
James J. Reilly *Innovative Solutions & Support Inc* 948
James J. Ritchie *KMG America Corp* 1034
James J. Ritchie *Quanta Capital Holdings Ltd* 1497
James J. Roach *Summit Environmental Corp Inc* 1716
James J. Roberts *Newell Rubbermaid Inc* 1278
James J. Rothenbach *Bank of Montreal* 210
James J. Sanfilippo *John B Sanfilippo & Son Inc* 1008
James J. Scardino *CRM Holdings Ltd* 501
James J. Schiro *PepsiCo Inc* 1410
James J. Schweiger *Nyer Medical Group Inc* 1320
James J. Sclafani *Bristol West Holdings Inc* 282
James J. Spilker *Radyne Comstream Inc* 1510
James J. Steffek *American Access Technologies Inc* 84
James J. TerBeest *Crdentia Corp* 495
James J. Tietjen *C-COR Incorporated* 299
James J. Truchard *National Instruments Corp* 1243
James J. Unger *American Railcar Industries Inc* 100
James J. Veneruso *Hudson Valley Holding Corp* 897
James J. Vincenzo *Theater Xtreme Entertainment Group Inc* 1785
James J. Volk *Suncom Wireless Holdings Inc* 1720
James J. Volker *Whiting Petroleum Corp* 1958
James J. Walsh *EasyLink Services Corp* 596
James J. Woodcock *Teton Energy Corp* 1780
James Jay Seirmarco *SourceForge Inc* 1662
James Jensen *New Ulm Telecom Inc* 1275
James Jianzhang Liang *Ctrip.com International Ltd* 510
James Jianzhang Liang *Home Inns & Hotels Management Inc* 886
James K. Abcouwer *Trans Energy Inc* 1812
James K. Anderson *Everlast Worldwide Inc* 666
James K. Bass *TTM Technologies Inc* 1833
James K. Blackburn *First Pulaski National Corp* 715
James K. Browne *Freedom Financial Group Inc* 746
James K. Cummings *Hypertension Diagnostics Inc* 905
James K. Cummings *Hypertension Diagnostics Inc* 905
James K. Cummings *Hypertension Diagnostics Inc* 905
James K. Duff *Little Squaw Gold Mining Co* 1086
James K. Ehlen *Angeion Corp* 122
James K. Ehlen *Health Fitness Corp* 858
James K. Harlan *Ionatron Inc* 985
James K. Hilger *Davita Inc* 530
James K. Hunt *Primus Guaranty Ltd* 1467
James K. Jennings *Building Materials Holding Corp* 294
James K. Johnson *Alloy Inc* 67
James K. Klyman *NGAS Resources Inc* 1285
James K. Lowder *Colonial Properties Trust* 440
James K. Lowder *Alabama Power Co* 50
James K. McHugh *N Viro International Corp* 1231
James K. Murray *Sykes Enterprises Inc* 1734
James K. Norwood *Texas Pacific Land Trust* 1782
James K. Parsons *Decorize Inc* 534
James K. Price *Turbochef Technologies Inc* 1835

2586 - Owners Index THE CORPORATE DIRECTORY - Walker's 2008

James K. Price *Turbochef Technologies Inc* ... 1835
James K. Scott *Hawaiian Electric Industries Inc* ... 854
James K. Sims *Electronic Data Systems Corp* ... 614
James K. T. Lu *Diamond Entertainment Corp* ... 551
James K. T. Lu *Diamond Entertainment Corp* ... 551
James K. Toomey *Coast Financial Holdings Inc* ... 431
James K. Vizanko *Allete Inc* ... 60
James Keegan *Lions Gate Entertainment Corp* ... 1084
James Kernan *Quintek Technologies Inc* ... 1504
James Kopperson *Colombia Goldfields Ltd* ... 440
James L. Alexandre *Voxware Inc* ... 1923
James L. Anderson *American States Water Co* ... 104
James L. Bailey *First Farmers & Merchants Corp* ... 704
James L. Bareuther *Brown Forman Corp* ... 288
James L. Barksdale *Time Warner Inc* ... 1795
James L. Barksdale *Sun Microsystems Inc* ... 1719
James L. Barksdale *Fedex Corp* ... 685
James L. Bergey *Univest Corp of Pennsylvania* ... 1871
James L. Bicksler *Kent International Holdings Inc* ... 1024
James L. Bowen *Wheeling Pittsburgh Corp* ... 1956
James L. Breeden *K-Fed Bancorp* ... 1014
James L. Brill *Onvia Inc* ... 1345
James L. Broadhead *Brinks Co* ... 281
James L. Bryan *Anadarko Petroleum Corp* ... 118
James L. Busby *Cubic Energy Inc* ... 511
James L. Camaren *FPL Group Inc* ... 742
James L. Carino *S&T Bank* ... 1570
James L. Czech *Gottschalks Inc* ... 812
James L. Dewar *PAB Bankshares Inc* ... 1369
James L. DiStefano *Healthcare Services Group Inc* ... 860
James L. Dolan *Cablevision Systems Corp* ... 301
James L. Dolan *CSC Holdings Inc* ... 508
James L. Donald *Starbucks Corp* ... 1693
James L. Donovan *IRIDEX Corp* ... 988
James L. Doti *Standard Pacific Corp* ... 1690
James L. Doti *First American Corp* ... 695
James L. Doti *Fleetwood Enterprises Inc* ... 724
James L. Duggins *Centerline Holding Co* ... 358
James L. Dunn *iLinc Communications Inc* ... 922
James L. Easton *Ambassadors International Inc* ... 79
James L. Einstein *Rock Tenn Co* ... 1553
James L. Ellis *Willamette Valley Vineyards Inc* ... 1960
James L. Fares *Questcor Pharmaceuticals Inc* ... 1501
James L. Ferris *World Waste Technologies Inc* ... 1976
James L. Foght *Orchestra Therapeutics Inc* ... 1354
James L. Fox *Rock of Ages Corp* ... 1552
James L. Francis *Highland Hospitality Corp* ... 877
James L. Fraser *Boardwalk Bancorp Inc* ... 261
James L. Gallagher *Versar Inc* ... 1898
James L. Gallogly *ConocoPhillips* ... 469
James L. Gardner *Penn Virginia Resource Partners LP* ... 1403
James L. Gray *Moog Inc* ... 1215
James L. Green *Peco II Inc* ... 1399
James L. Hambrick *Lubrizol Corp (The)* ... 1099
James L. Hamling *Mikron Infrared Inc* ... 1189
James L. Heppell *Inovio Biomedical Corp* ... 949
James L. Herbert *Neogen Corp* ... 1258
James L. Heskett *Limited Brands Inc* ... 1079
James L. Holbrook *EMAK Worldwide Inc* ... 619
James L. Jadlos *Access National Corp* ... 11
James L. Katz *E-Z-EM Inc* ... 588
James L. Kempner *Intersections Inc* ... 976
James L. Kirtley *Satcon Technology Corp* ... 1585
James L. Koenig *Amacore Group Inc* ... 75
James L. Koley *Dover Corp* ... 572
James L. Lambert *Dot Hill Systems Corp* ... 571
James L. Lawson *Bell Industries Inc* ... 229
James L. Lemley *Georgia-Carolina Bancshares Inc* ... 782
James L. Lester *GB&T Bancshares Inc* ... 765
James L. Logan *Spartan Motors Inc* ... 1674
James L. Loomis *Bottomline Technologies (DE) Inc* ... 269
James L. Luikart *W&T Offshore Inc* ... 1926
James L. Mandel *CorVu Corp* ... 486
James L. Mandel *Multiband Corp* ... 1227
James L. Markos *Camden National Corp* ... 314
James L. Markos *Union Trust Company* ... 1852
James L. Martineau *Pinnacle Entertainment Inc* ... 1431
James L. Martineau *Apogee Enterprises Inc* ... 132
James L. McCulloch *GlobalSantaFe Corp* ... 799
James L. Mercer *Flanders Corp* ... 723
James L. Mertes *Amerigon Inc* ... 108
James L. Milinazzo *Massbank Corp* ... 1129
James L. Moore *CT Communications Inc* ... 509
James L. Morice *HSBC USA Inc* ... 895
James L. Murdy *Federated Investors Inc* ... 685
James L. North *Adtran Inc* ... 26
James L. Packard *CLARCOR Inc* ... 418
James L. Packard *Manitowoc Co Inc* ... 1118
James L. Packard *Regal Beloit Corp* ... 1523
James L. Pate *Coastal Banking Co Inc* ... 431
James L. Payne *BJ Services Co* ... 251
James L. Payne *Global Industries Ltd* ... 794
James L. Payne *Nabors Industries Ltd* ... 1232
James L. Peeler *Telkonet Inc* ... 1770
James L. Pickles *InsWeb Corp* ... 953
James L. Pierce *Esterline Technologies Corp* ... 659
James L. Purcell *Las Vegas Sands Corp* ... 1056
James L. Rathmann *Vermillion Inc* ... 1897
James L. Rawlings *Millennium Cell Inc* ... 1192
James L. Reissner *Rimage Corp* ... 1545
James L. Reissner *Magstar Technologies Inc* ... 1112
James L. Reissner *Winland Electronics Inc* ... 1967
James L. Rittenhouse *Harleysville Savings Financial Corp* ... 847
James L. Robinson *Financial Institutions Inc* ... 692
James L. Robo *Hunt J B Transport Services Inc* ... 900
James L. Robo *FPL Group Inc* ... 742
James L. Rohrs *First Defiance Financial Corp* ... 704
James L. Rossi *City Holding Co* ... 416
James L. Rowe *First Financial Holdings Inc* ... 706
James L. Saner *Mainsource Financial Group Inc* ... 1114
James L. Seward *Wilber Corp* ... 1959
James L. Shaub *Pinnacle Financial Partners Inc* ... 1432
James L. Sherman *Standard Register Co* ... 1691
James L. Sherman *Standard Register Co* ... 1691
James L. Simonton *Core Molding Technologies Inc* ... 480
James L. Singleton *WESCO International Inc* ... 1946
James L. Singleton *Williams Scotsman International Inc* ... 1962
James L. Sivils *Guaranty Federal Bancshares Inc* ... 833
James L. Speros *Braintech Inc* ... 273
James L. Stanley *Heritage Financial Group* ... 871
James L. Stewart *Rocky Shoes & Boots Inc* ... 1556
James L. Turley *Patriot Scientific Corp* ... 1392
James L. Vandeberg *IAS Communications Inc* ... 908
James L. Vincent *Alnylam Pharmaceuticals Inc* ... 69
James L. Wainscott *AK Steel Holding Corp* ... 48
James L. Wieser *Northwest Indiana Bancorp* ... 1305
James L. Wilcox *Immunicon Corp* ... 928
James L. Wold *Quantum Corp* ... 1498
James L. Wolohan *Citizens Republic Bancorp Inc* ... 415
James L. Zech *Max Capital Group Ltd* ... 1134
James L. Zech *Eastern Insurance Holdings Inc* ... 594
James L. Ziemer *Harley-Davidson Inc* ... 846
James L. Ziemer *Textron Inc* ... 1783
James L.D. Roser *Qualmark Corp* ... 1496
James L.K. Wang *Expeditors International of Washington Inc* ... 670
James Laier *American TonerServ Corp* ... 105
James Lee Witt *GlobalOptions Group Inc* ... 799
James LLC *Markland Technologies Inc* ... 1124
James M. Alic *Advanstar Inc* ... 32
James M. Anderson *Mainsource Financial Group Inc* ... 1114
James M. Augur *iDNA Inc* ... 918
James M. Austin *Southern First Bancshares Inc* ... 1666
James M. Barrett *Pharmion Corp* ... 1423
James M. Barrett *Iomai Corp* ... 984
James M. Barrett *Inhibitex Inc* ... 944
James M. Bethmann *Telecommunication Systems Inc* ... 1765
James M. Brophy *Chad Therapeutics Inc* ... 370
James M. Brostowitz *Harley-Davidson Inc* ... 846
James M. Cain *Whitney Holding Corp* ... 1958
James M. Callahan *Sonic Innovations Inc* ... 1657
James M. Campbell *FNB United Corp* ... 731
James M. Chadwick *Airnet Systems Inc* ... 47
James M. Chadwick *Meade Instruments Corp* ... 1144
James M. Chirico *Seagate Technology* ... 1599
James M. Clements *Imperial Petroleum Inc* ... 930
James M. Cohen *New York Times Co* ... 1277
James M. Coogan *Hudson Valley Holding Corp* ... 897
James M. Cornelius *Given Imaging Ltd* ... 788
James M. Cornelius *DIRECTV Group Inc (The)* ... 561
James M. Corroon *InsWeb Corp* ... 953
James M. Cracchiolo *American Express Financial Corp* ... 91
James M. Craig *Varsity Group Inc* ... 1889
James M. Crooks *Emclaire Financial Corp* ... 621
James M. Curry *Chestatee Bancshares Inc* ... 383
James M. Damian *Buffalo Wild Wings* ... 293
James M. DeAngelis *Commodore Applied Technologies Inc* ... 449
James M. Delaney *Associated Estates Realty Corp* ... 164
James M. Denny *Gilead Sciences Inc* ... 787
James M. Dubin *Carnival Corp* ... 336
James M. Edwards *Ameriserv Financial Inc* ... 110
James M. Emanuel *SRI Surgical Express Inc* ... 1685
James M. Ferguson *Superior Industries International Inc* ... 1727
James M. Fitzgibbons *Bill Barrett Corp* ... 239
James M. Frates *Alkermes Inc* ... 57
James M. Fricke *Hollis-Eden Pharmaceuticals Inc* ... 882
James M. Froisland *Material Sciences Corp* ... 1130
James M. Funk *Superior Energy Services Inc* ... 1726
James M. Furey *Penns Woods Bancorp Inc* ... 1404
James M. Fusaro *Amkor Technology Inc* ... 114
James M. Gasior *Cortland Bancorp* ... 485
James M. Gerlach *American Equity Investment Life Hldg Co* ... 90
James M. Goodrich *Roberts Realty Investors Inc* ... 1551
James M. Gould *Build-A-Bear Workshop Inc* ... 294
James M. Gower *Cell Genesys Inc* ... 355
James M. Gower *Rigel Pharmaceuticals Inc* ... 1545
James M. Griffin *BTU International Inc* ... 291
James M. Guyette *PrivateBancorp Inc* ... 1470
James M. Guyette *Priceline.com Inc* ... 1464
James M. Harrison *Amscan Holdings Inc* ... 117
James M. Harwell *Reliability Inc* ... 1528
James M. Healey *Jacksonville Bancorp Inc FL* ... 1001
James M. Heyer *Penn Treaty American Corp* ... 1403
James M. Hinton *Camden Property Trust* ... 314
James M. Hoak *Pier 1 Imports Inc* ... 1429
James M. Hoak *Chaparral Steel Co* ... 374
James M. Holland *Atwood Oceanics Inc* ... 177
James M. Ingram *Parkway Properties Inc* ... 1388
James M. Jenness *Kimberly Clark Corp* ... 1029
James M. Johnson *Southwest Bancorp Inc* ... 1669
James M. Judge *Mission Community Bancorp* ... 1199
James M. Kalustian *Ambassadors Group Inc* ... 78
James M. Kaney *Coast Bancorp* ... 431
James M. Kennedy *THQ Inc* ... 1790
James M. Kilts *Procter & Gamble* ... 1472
James M. Kilts *Metlife Inc* ... 1171
James M. Kilts *Meadwestvaco Corp* ... 1145
James M. Kitterman *Swift Energy Co* ... 1732
James M. Knowlton *VSE Corp* ... 1924
James M. Kolisch *Ocean Bio Chem Inc* ... 1326
James M. Kratochvil *BPC Holding Corp* ... 272
James M. Lapeyre *ION Geophysical Corp* ... 984
James M. Lee *AMS Health Sciences Inc* ... 116
James M. Levine *Pinnacle West Capital Corp* ... 1432
James M. Lewis *Miscor Group Ltd* ... 1198
James M. Link *Teledyne Technologies Inc* ... 1766
James M. Link *Dewey Electronics Corp* ... 548
James M. Link *Superior Bancorp* ... 1726
James M. Litvack *Delphi Financial Group Inc* ... 538
James M. Loree *Stanley Works* ... 1692
James M. Lynch *Universal Insurance Holdings Inc* ... 1869
James M. Mahoney *Meadowbrook Insurance Group Inc* ... 1145
James M. Martell *Champions Biotechnology Inc* ... 372
James M. Matthew *Empire Financial Holding Co* ... 625
James M. McClenahan *Apac Customer Services Inc* ... 130
James M. McCluney *Emulex Corp* ... 627
James M. McCormick *Synchronoss Technologies Inc* ... 1737
James M. McNeill *Pediatric Services of America Inc* ... 1400
James M. McTaggart *Blyth Inc* ... 259
James M. Michener *Assured Guaranty Ltd* ... 165
James M. Mullendore *IBT Bancorp Inc/MI* ... 909
James M. Murphy *Pennichuck Corp* ... 1404
James M. O'Connell *Landauer Inc* ... 1053
James M. OHara *Netratings Inc* ... 1264
James M. Oates *Stifel Financial Corp* ... 1705
James M. Osterhoff *GenCorp Inc* ... 767
James M. Outlaw *Trustmark Corp* ... 1831
James M. Pagos *Transwitch Corp* ... 1818
James M. Papada *Technitrol Inc* ... 1758
James M. Parker *First Citizens Bancshares Inc/DE* ... 700
James M. Powers *iLinc Communications Inc* ... 922
James M. Pusey *Orthologic Corp* ... 1360
James M. Raines *Waddell & Reed Inc* ... 1928
James M. Raines *Clear Channel Outdoor Holdings Inc* ... 422
James M. Rallo *Liquidity Services Inc* ... 1085
James M. Reed *Enpath Medical Inc* ... 639
James M. Reninger *Ben Franklin Financial Inc* ... 230
James M. Ringler *FMC Technologies Inc* ... 729
James M. Ringler *Autoliv Inc* ... 182
James M. Ringler *NCR Corp* ... 1256
James M. Rosser *Southern California Edison Co* ... 1665
James M. Rosser *Edison International* ... 604
James M. Rutledge *Clean Harbors Inc* ... 421
James M. Schmidt *Buffalo Wild Wings* ... 293
James M. Schneider *Lockheed Martin Corp* ... 1090
James M. Schneider *Gap Inc* ... 761
James M. Schneider *General Communication Inc* ... 769
James M. Schneiderf *Dell Inc* ... 537
James M. Seed *Fischer-Watt Gold Company* ... 721
James M. Shapiro *Hansen Medical Inc* ... 845
James M. Sheehan *Tellabs Inc* ... 1770
James M. Shelger *Service Corp International* ... 1614
James M. Shuler *National Bankshares Inc* ... 1239
James M. Simon *GeoEye Inc* ... 780
James M. Smaha *Sirf Technology Holdings Inc* ... 1638
James M. Smith *EDO Corp* ... 604
James M. Smith *Anntaylor Stores Corp* ... 126
James M. Spiezio *Beacon Power Corp* ... 225
James M. Stolze *Stereotaxis Inc* ... 1701
James M. Strickland *ImaRx Therapeutics Inc* ... 925
James M. Sullivan *Integra Lifesciences Holdings Corp* ... 954
James M. Sullivan *Marriott International Inc* ... 1125
James M. Thorburn *ZiLOG Inc* ... 1998
James M. Thorburn *IXYS Corp* ... 997
James M. Tidwell *T 3 Energy Services Inc* ... 1743
James M. Tidwell *Pioneer Drilling Co* ... 1433
James M. Tory *Cognos Inc* ... 436
James M. Townsend *Vestin Realty Mortgage I Inc* ... 1900
James M. Townsend *Vestin Realty Mortgage II Inc* ... 1901
James M. Treat *Stericycle Inc* ... 1701
James M. Usdan *Metro One Telecommunications Inc* ... 1172
James M. Weaver *X-Rite Inc* ... 1982
James M. Weber *Zumiez Inc* ... 2002
James M. Weichert *Peapack Gladstone Financial Corp* ... 1399
James M. Welch *Express-1 Expedited Solutions Inc* ... 671
James M. Wells *Suntrust Banks Inc* ... 1724
James M. Will *Columbia Banking System Inc* ... 442
James M. Williams *Monterey Gourmet Foods Inc* ... 1214
James M. Zemlyak *Stifel Financial Corp* ... 1705
James Mailon Kent *Superior Bancorp* ... 1726
James Manfredonia *Assured Pharmacy Inc* ... 165
James McCubbin *WidePoint Corp* ... 1959
James McKeever *United Energy Corp* ... 1858
James Meese *Smart Online Inc* ... 1646
James Meier *Full House Resorts Inc* ... 754
James Michael Johnston *Charter Communications Inc* ... 376
James Michael Kelley *Siena Technologies Inc* ... 1625
James Michael ODwyer *Metal Storm Ltd* ... 1169
James Mitarotonda *SIELOX Inc* ... 1624
James Monroe *Globalstar Inc* ... 799
James Monroe Capital Corp. *Originally New York Inc* ... 1358
James Muir Drummond *Andover Medical Inc* ... 121
James Murdakes *Image Sensing Systems Inc* ... 924
James N. Alexander *Williams Scotsman International Inc* ... 1962
James N. Bailey *Getty Images Inc* ... 784
James N. Bailey *Apartment Investment and Management Company* ... 130
James N. Ball *Westborough Financial Services Inc* ... 1949
James N. Fernandez *Tiffany & Co* ... 1793
James N. Fernandez *Dun & Bradstreet Corp* ... 580
James N. Hallene *MB Financial Inc MD* ... 1137
James N. Jannello *Janel World Trade Ltd* ... 1003
James N. Land *Riviera Holdings Corp* ... 1550
James N. Lane *Artistdirect Inc* ... 156
James N. Little *MFIC Corp* ... 1175
James N. Meehan *Delphi Financial Group Inc* ... 538
James N. Meehan *Bristol West Holdings Inc* ... 282
James N. Meek *Sterling Mining Company* ... 1704
James N. Moriarty *Bertucci's Corp* ... 234
James N. Perry *Cbeyond Inc* ... 348
James N. Plato *HealthMarkets Inc* ... 861
James N. Reynolds *United Bancshares Inc/OH* ... 1856
James N. Stanard *RenaissanceRe Holdings Ltd* ... 1530
James N. Topper *La Jolla Pharmaceutical Co* ... 1047
James N. White *Shutterfly Inc* ... 1623
James N. Wilson *Amylin Pharmaceuticals Inc* ... 118
James N. Wilson *Corcept Therapeutics Inc* ... 479
James N.B. Rucker *MarketAxess Holdings Inc* ... 1123
James Nave *Western Alliance Bancorp.* ... 1950
James Neil Aitken *Wealthcraft Systems Inc* ... 1940
James O. Armitage *MGI Pharma Inc* ... 1176
James O. Ellis *Level 3 Communications Inc* ... 1069
James O. Futterknecht *Dura Automotive Systems Inc* ... 581
James O. Harp *Hornbeck Offshore Services Inc* ... 891
James O. McCash *Alfacell Corp* ... 56
James O. Rollans *Advanced Medical Optics Inc* ... 30
James O. Rollans *Flowserve Corp* ... 728
James O. Woodward *Gottschalks Inc* ... 812
James P. Abel *Nelnet Inc* ... 1258
James P. Allen *NCI Inc* ... 1256
James P. Avery *Southern California Gas Co* ... 1665
James P. Avery *Pacific Enterprises* ... 1372
James P. Avery *San Diego Gas & Electric Co* ... 1579
James P. Bouchard *Wheeling Pittsburgh Corp* ... 1956
James P. Brannen *FBL Financial Group Inc* ... 681
James P. Breslawski *Henry Schein Inc* ... 869
James P. Bryce *IPC Holdings Ltd* ... 987
James P. Burke *Dun & Bradstreet Corp* ... 580
James P. Burra *Semtech Corp* ... 1608
James P. Clark *Oregon Pacific Bancorp* ... 1355
James P. Coleman *MFB Financial Corp* ... 1175
James P. Craig *Janus Capital Group Inc* ... 1003
James P. Creel *Coastal Financial Corp* ... 432
James P. Day *Northeast Bancorp* ... 1300
James P. DeBlasio *Internap Network Services Corp* ... 966
James P. Dolan *Peoples Educational Holdings Inc* ... 1408
James P. Dollive *Hartmarx Corp* ... 851
James P. Dollive *Kraft Foods Inc* ... 1042
James P. Doolin *Hangman Productions Inc* ... 844
James P. Dore *Bitstream Inc* ... 251
James P. Dugan *Central Jersey Bancorp* ... 362
James P. Flaherty *NBTY* ... 1255
James P. Foley *Lake Shore Bancorp Inc* ... 1050
James P. Fortescue *Annaly Capital Management Inc* ... 125

THE CORPORATE DIRECTORY - Walker's 2008 **Owners Index - 2637**

Mike Duff *Poly-Pacific International Inc* 1445
Mike Foster *NextWave Wireless WI* 1284
Mike H. Kwon *Axesstel Inc* 194
Mike J. Homer *Opsware Inc* 1348
Mike J. Walker *Dril-Quip Inc* 576
Mike K. Sayama *Central Pacific Financial Corp* 363
Mike Moses *SWS Group Inc* 1733
Mike P. Taylor *Americanwest BanCorp* 107
Mike Prentice *World Energy Solutions Inc* 1976
Mike R. Bowlin *FMC Technologies Inc* 729
Mike R. Bowlin *Edwards LifeSciences Corp* 606
Mike S. Zafirovski *Boeing* 262
Mike W. Baggett *Frozen Food Express Industries Inc* 751
Mikel D. Faulkner *HKN Inc* 881
Mikhail I. Vishnyakov *Wimm-Bill-Dann Foods OJSC* 1965
Mikhail Segal *Dynegy Inc* 586
Mikhail V. Dubinin *Wimm-Bill-Dann Foods OJSC* 1965
Mikkalya W. Murray *Harleysville National Corp* 847
Mikls Konkoly-Thege *Danaos Corp* 525
Milacron Geier Foundation *Milacron Inc* 1190
Milam Randolph Pharo *St Mary Land & Exploration Co* 1687
Milan Mandaric *NatureWell Inc* 1251
Milan Mehta *Integrated Healthcare Holdings Inc* 956
Milan Puskar *Centra Financial Holdings Inc* 360
Milburn E. Honeycutt *Powell Industries Inc* 1453
Mildred C. Joyner *DNB Financial Corp* 565
Mildred Lange Ranzini *University Bank* 1871
Mildred S. Christian *Pro Pharmaceuticals Inc* 1470
Miles A. McIntosh *Peco II Inc* 1399
Miles Berger *Innkeepers USA Trust* 946
Miles D. White *Motorola Inc* 1219
Miles E. Kilburn *Global Cash Access Holdings Inc* 791
Miles L. Berger *Universal Health Realty Income Trust* 1869
Miles L. Marsh *Whirlpool Corp* 1956
Miles O. Pollard *IBERIABANK Corp* 908
Miles R. Armentrout *Oak Hill Financial Inc* 1323
Miles R. Gilburne *SRA International Inc* 1685
Miles R. Gilburne *Pharmacyclics Inc* 1422
Miles S. Nadal *MDC Partners Inc* 1142
Miles W. McHugh *R.R. Donnelley & Sons Co* 1506
Milford A. Weaver *Mainstreet Bankshares Inc* 1115
Millard E. Morris *Amerisafe Inc* 109
Millard J. Younkers *TIB Financial Corp* 1791
Millard R. Bowen *Chestatee Bancshares Inc* 383
Millard S. Drexler *J. Crew Group Inc* 998
Millard S. Drexler *Apple Computer Inc* 134
Milledge A. Hart *Home Depot Inc* 884
Millenco *Orchid Cellmark Inc* 1355
Millenco, L.L.C. *National Medical Health Card Systems Inc* 1244
Millenco, L.L.C. *Flotek Industries Inc* 727
Millenco, L.L.C. *James River Coal Co* 1003
Millenco, L.L.C. *Gentium SpA* 778
Millenco, L.L.C. *Cold Spring Capital Inc* 438
Millenco, L.L.C. *Global Telecom & Technology Inc* 798
Millenco, L.L.C. *Global Svcs PTR CL B* 797
Millenco, L.L.C. *Global Svcs PTR* 797
Millenco, L.P. *REMEC Inc* 1529
Millenco, L.P. *MVC Capital Inc* 1229
Millenco, LLC *Cougar Biotechnology Inc* 488
Millenco, LLC *Tutogen Medical Inc* 1836
Millenco, LLC *Equity Media Holdings Corp* 653
Millenium Management, L.L.C *Lone Star Steakhouse & Saloon Inc* 1093
Millenium Partners, LP *Northern Oil & Gas Inc* 1301
Millennium Global High Yield Fund Limited *Radiant Logistics Inc* 1507
Millennium Global High Yield FundLimited *Touchstone Resources USA Inc* 1806
Millennium Global Investments Limited *Rancher Energy Corp* 1513
Millennium Global Investments Limited *Gran Tierra Energy Inc* 814
Millennium group *MiddleBrook Pharmaceuticals Inc* 1185
Millennium International Pension Plan *Gem Solutions Inc* 766
Millennium International Pension Plan *Gem Solutions Inc* 766
Millennium Management *Auxilium Pharmaceuticals Inc* 184
Millennium Management L.L.C. *Lecroy Corp* 1063
Millennium Management L.L.C. *Global Svcs PTR CL B* 797
Millennium Management L.L.C. *Global Svcs PTR* 797
Millennium Management LLC *Caliper Life Sciences Inc* 309
Millennium Management, L.L.C. *Consumer Portfolio Services Inc* 473
Millennium Management, L.L.C. *CRM Holdings Ltd* 501
Millennium Management, L.L.C. *Rhapsody Acquisition Corp* 1543
Millennium Management, L.L.C. *Cold Spring Capital Inc* 438
Millennium Management, L.L.C. *Gentium SpA* 778
Millennium Partners II, L.P. *Brigham Exploration Co* 279
Millennium Partners, L.P. *Ziopharm Oncology Inc* 1999
Millennium Partners, L.P. *Langer Inc* 1054
Millennium Partners, L.P. *MIV Therapeutics Inc* 1201
Millennium Partners, L.P. *Medicalcv Inc* 1153
Millennium Partners, L.P. *iBasis Inc* 908
Millennium Partners, LP *American Basketball Association Inc* 86
Miller M. Gorrie *Colonial Properties Trust* 440
Miller Ratner *Forest City Enterprises Inc* 735
Miller Ratner *Forest City Enterprises Inc* 735
Miller S. Williams *Elec Communications Corp* 611
Miller S. Williams *Willbros Group Inc* 1960
Millerworks, Limited Partnership *Exactech Inc* 667
Millicent W. West *Middleburg Financial Corp* 1185
Milo Finance, S.A *Heritage Worldwide Inc* 872
Milton A. Alpern *Applix Inc* 137
Milton B. Kidd *Midsouth Bancorp Inc* 1187
Milton Cooper *Kimco Realty Corp* 1029
Milton Corporation Limited *Westpac Banking Corp* 1953
Milton Cox *Altus Exploration Inc* 74
Milton D. Jernigan *CommerceFirst Bancorp Inc* 448
Milton D. Kniss *Dura Automotive Systems Inc* 581
Milton E. Cooper *Applied Signal Technology Inc* 137
Milton E. Magee *First Citizens Bancshares Inc/TN* 701
Milton G. Silva-Craig *Technology Solutions Co* 1759
Milton J. Childress *EnPro Industries Inc* 640
Milton J. Wallace *Imperial Industries Inc* 930
Milton J. Wallace *Catalyst Pharmaceutical Partners Inc* 344
Milton J. Walters *Sun Healthcare Group Inc* 1718
Milton J. Walters *Movie Star Inc* 1221
Milton L. Cohen *Lifetime Brands Inc* 1076
Milton L. Lohr *Ceradyne Inc* 367
Milton L. Scott *Sterling Construction Co Inc* 1703
Milton L. Scott *W-H Energy Services* 1926
Milton M. Segal *Kronos Advanced Technologies Inc* 1043
Milton R. Geilmann *Computerized Thermal Imaging Inc* 463
Milton Stanley Goggins *Firstbank Financial Services Inc* 719
Milton Steele *FMC Corp* 729
Milton W. Jones *Canyon Bancorp CA* 321
MiltonHersheySchoolTrust *Hershey Co (The)* 872
MiltonHersheySchoolTrust *Hershey Co (The)* 872
Min H. Kao *Garmin Ltd* 762
Min J. Kim *Nara Bancorp Inc* 1235
Minden Bancorp, Inc. *Minden Bancorp Inc LA* 1194
Minden Mutual Holding Company *Minden Bancorp Inc LA* 1194
Mindes Family Limited Partnership *Interactive Systems Worldwide Inc* 961
Mindy A. Horowitz *First Montauk Financial Corp* 711
Mindy J. Allport-Settle *Generex Biotechnology Corp* 773
Mineola Holdings Corporation *Veridien Corp* 1895
Minerva Group, L.P. *Reliability Inc* 1528
Ming Fen Liu *China Sun Group High-Tech Co* 396
Ming S. Liu *Qiagen* 1492
Ming S. Liu *eGene Inc* 607
Ming Tung Chok *Soyo Group Inc* 1672
Ming Wai Anthea Chung *Solar EnerTech Corp* 1653
Ming-yi Hwang *Surgilight Inc* 1729
Mingjuan Tan *Wintech Digital System Technology Corp* 1969
Mingrong Li *Wintech Digital System Technology Corp* 1969
Mingshi Qiu *Asia Biotechnology Group Inc* 160
MiniDoc AB *Etrials Worldwide Inc* 661
Ministerio del Poder Popular para la Infraestructura *Compania Anonima Nacional Telefonos de Venezuela* 458
Ministerio del Poder Popular para la Infraestructura *National Telephone Co of Venezuela* 1247
Ministry of Economy and Finance *Eni SpA* 639
Minneapolis Portfolio Management Group, LLC *HEI Inc* 865
Minnie Merchants, Inc. *Siclone Industries Inc* 1624
Minor M. Shaw *Delta Apparel Inc* 539
Minor M. Shaw *Piedmont Natural Gas Co Inc* 1429
Mir B. Ghaderi *Exar Corp* 667
Miretzky Holdings Ltd. *M-WISE Inc* 1104
Miriam Kidron *Oramed Pharmaceuticals Inc* 1352
Miriam L. Haas *Levi Strauss & Co* 1069
Miriam V. Gold *3D Systems Corp* 2007
Mirian M. Graddick-Weir *Harleysville Group Inc* 846
Miro I. Bergman *Euronet Worldwide Inc* 663
Miro Wikgren *MobiVentures.com* 1205
Mirus Oportunistic Fund *Juma Technology Corp* 1012
MiTAC International Corporation *SYNNEX Corp* 1738
Mitch Francis *Tix Corp* 1798
Mitch G. Mattingly *Parkway Properties Inc* 1388
Mitch Tuchman *Workstream Inc* 1975
Mitchel Sayare *Immucell Corp* 927
Mitchel Sayare *ImmunoGen Inc* 928
Mitchell A. Derenzo *American River Bankshares* 101
Mitchell A. Johnson *Federal Agricultural Mortgage Corp* 682
Mitchell A. Kosh *Polo Ralph Lauren Corp* 1444
Mitchell A. Rinek *American Physicians Capital Inc* 99
Mitchell A. Ring *Hain Celestial Group Inc* 838
Mitchell A. Saltz *Smith & Wesson Holding Corp* 1648
Mitchell A. Solomon *P & F Industries Inc* 1367
Mitchell A. Thaw *TNR Technical Inc* 1799
Mitchell B. Briskin *Technical Communications Corp* 1758
Mitchell B. Kleinman *KBW Inc* 1020
Mitchell B. Lewis *Euramax International Inc* 661
Mitchell B. Owens *Medtox Scientific Inc* 1156
Mitchell Binde *Orbit International Corp* 1353
Mitchell C. Rock *UFP Technologies Inc* 1844
Mitchell C. Waycaster *Renasant Corp* 1531
Mitchell E. Appel *Value Line* 1887
Mitchell E. Fadel *Rent A Center Inc* 1532
Mitchell E. Norville *Boston Properties Inc* 268
Mitchell E. Weatherly *Pier 1 Imports Inc* 1429
Mitchell G. Holthus *Brooke Corp* 285
Mitchell G. Lynn *United Panam Financial Corp* 1860
Mitchell G. Tyson *Photronics Inc* 1428
Mitchell H. Caplan *E Trade Financial Corp* 588
Mitchell H. Freeman *Medis Technologies Ltd* 1155
Mitchell H. Friedlaender *Insite Vision Inc* 951
Mitchell H. Gold *Dendreon Corp* 542
Mitchell H. Saranow *Lawson Products Inc* 1059
Mitchell H. Saranow *Telephone and Data Systems Inc* 1768
Mitchell H. Watson *Community Health Systems Inc* 454
Mitchell Hart *Terra Systems Inc* 1778
Mitchell I. Quain *Strategic Distribution Inc* 1709
Mitchell I. Quain *Magnetek Inc* 1111
Mitchell I. Quain *Hardinge Inc* 846
Mitchell I. Quain *Titan International Inc* 1796
Mitchell J. Blutt *DJO Incorporated* 565
Mitchell J. Collins *Equity Inns Inc* 653
Mitchell J. Krebs *Annapolis Bancorp Inc* 125
Mitchell J. Slater *CKX Inc* 418
Mitchell K. Dauerman *Ultimate Software Group Inc* 1845
Mitchell K. Fogelman *International Aluminum Corp* 966
Mitchell L. Hollin *Heartland Payment Systems Inc* 864
Mitchell L. Morgan *Royal Bancshares of Pennsylvania Inc* 1561
Mitchell M. Willoughby *First Community Corp/SC* 702
Mitchell Metzman *Jaguar Acquisition Corp* 1002
Mitchell O. Smith *Heritage Financial Group* 871
Mitchell P. Rales *Danaher Corp* 525
Mitchell Partners L.P. *Ameritrans Capital Corp* 111
Mitchell Partners L.P. *Ameritrans Capital Corp* 111
Mitchell Pindus *Lucy's Cafe Inc* 1099
Mitchell R. Little *Microchip Technology Inc* 1176
Mitchell Rosen *Neutron Enterprises Inc* 1268
Mitchell Rubenstein and Laurie S. Silvers *Hollywood Media Corp* 883
Mitchell S. Bregman *Exide Technologies* 669
Mitchell S. Karlan *Scpie Holdings Inc* 1597
Mitchell S. Klipper *Barnes & Noble Inc* 216
Mitchell S. Presser *Casual Male Retail Group Inc* 343
Mitchell S. Segal *Walker Financial Corp* 1929
Mitchell S. Wortzman *Medicis Pharmaceutical Corp* 1153
Mitchell Statham *Standard Microsystems Corp* 1690
Mitchell W. Legler *Stein Mart Inc* 1699
Mitsubishi Development Pty Ltd *BHP Billiton Ltd* 237
Mitsubishi UFJ Financial Group *Makita Corp* 1116
Mitsubishi UFJ Financial Group *Makita Corp* 1116
Mitsubishi UFJ Financial Group *Makita Corp* 1116
Mitsubishi UFJ Financial Group *Makita Corp* 1116
Mitsubishi UFJ Financial Group *Makita Corp* 1116
Mitsubishi UFJ Financial Group, Inc *Bank of Tokyo-Mitsubishi* 212
Mitsubishi UFJ Financial Group, Inc. *Bank of Tokyo-Mitsubishi* 212
Mitsubishi UFJ Financial Group, Inc. *Bank of Tokyo-Mitsubishi* 212
Mitsubishi UFJ Financial Group, Inc. *Kyocera Corp* 1045
Mitsubishi UFJ Financial Group, Inc. and its joint holders *Wacoal Holdings Corp* 1928
Mitsubishi UFJ Trust and Banking *Bank of Tokyo-Mitsubishi* 212
Mitsui & Co *United Auto Group Inc* 1855
Mitsui Life Insurance Company Limited *Mitsui & Co Ltd* 1201
Mitsui Sumitomo Insurance Co., Ltd. *Matsushita Electric Industrial Co Ltd* 1132
Mitsui& Co Venture Partners *MicroMed Cardiovascular Inc* 1180
Miura Global Management, LLC *UTStarcom Incorporated* 1881
Mivtach Shamir Finance Ltd. *Gilat Satellite Networks Ltd* 787
Mizuho Bank, Ltd. *Kubota Corp* 1044
Mizuho Corporate Bank, Ltd. *Kubota Corp* 1044
Mizuho Corporate Bank, Ltd. *Millea Holdings Inc* 1191
Mizuho Corporate Bank, Ltd. *Mitsui & Co Ltd* 1201
Mizuho Corporate Bank, Ltd. *Canon Inc* 320
Mizuho Financial Strategy *Mizuho Financial Group Inc* 1201
MJG Associates *Lin Television Corp* 1079
ML Global Private Equity Fund, L.P. *Hertz Global Holdings Inc* 873
ML Global Private Equity Fund, L.P. *Hertz Corp* 873
ML Hertz Co-Investor, L.P. *Hertz Global Holdings Inc* 873
MLC Consultants, LLC *Cedric Kushner Promotions Inc* 354
MLF Investments *Ambassadors International Inc* 79
MLF Investments, LLC and related parties *La Z Boy Inc* 1047
MLF Offshore Portfolio Company, L.P. *Sirva Inc* 1639
MM&B Holdings *GammaCan International Inc* 760
MMA Capital, LLC *Dynamic Leisure Corp* 584
MMC Norilsk Nickel *Stillwater Mining Co* 1705
MMCAP International Inc. SPC and MM Asset Management Inc. *Image Entertainment Inc* 924
MMI Investments, L.P. *Unisys Corp* 1853
MMI Investments, L.P. *Paxar Corp* 1394
MMI Investments, L.P. *Brinks Co* 281
Moab Partners LP *Morgan's Foods Inc* 1216
Mobius Risk Group, LLC *Medical Discoveries Inc* 1151
Mobius Venture Capital *Proxim Wireless* 1482
MOCHELLE A. STETTNER *Superior Uniform Group Inc* 1727
Modern Delta Holdings Ltd. *China Digital Media Corp* 388
Modern Delta Holdings Ltd. *China Digital Media Corp* 388
Modesto A. Maidique *National Semiconductor Corp* 1246
Modesto A. Maidique *Carnival Corp* 336
Moe S. Nozari *3M Co* 2007
Mogens C. Bay *Valmont Industries Inc* 1887
Mogens C. Bay *ConAgra Foods Inc* 465
Mohamed Abdulmohsin Al Kharafi & Sons W.L.L. *Krispy Kreme Doughnuts Inc* 1043
Mohamed Yousif Ahmed Saleh Sulaiman *Calypte Biomedical Corp* 312
Mohammad Azab *Chemokine Therapeutics Corp* 381
Mohammad Salem ben Mahfouz c/o National Commercial Bank *Arabian American Development Co* 140
Mohammed K. Al-Sada *Omagine Inc* 1335
Mohan N. Reddy *Brush Engineered Materials Inc* 290
Mohan N. Reddy *Keithley Instruments Inc* 1021
Mohan R. Maheswaran *Semtech Corp* 1608
Mohan S. Gyani *UnionBanCal Corp* 1853
Mohan S. Misra *Ascent Solar Technologies Inc* 158
Mohana Krishnan *Smart Modular Technologies (WWH) Inc* 1646
Mohanbir Gyani *Sirf Technology Holdings Inc* 1638
Mohanbir Sawhney *ExlService Holdings Inc* 669
Mohandas T.V. Pai *Infosys Technologies Ltd* 941
Mohnish Pabrai *Delta Financial Corp* 539
Mohr, Davidow Ventures *Shutterfly Inc* 1623
Mohsen M. Sohi *Steris Corp* 1702
Moiz M. Beguwala *Sirf Technology Holdings Inc* 1638
Moiz M. Beguwala *Skyworks Solutions Inc* 1644
Molina Marital Trust *Molina Healthcare Inc* 1208
Molina Siblings Trust *Molina Healthcare Inc* 1208
Mollie B. Williford *Oneok Inc* 1343
Mollie H. Carter *Westar Energy Inc* 1949
Mollie Hale Carter *Archer-Daniels-Midland Co* 143
Molly Henderson *VirtualScopics Inc* 1912
Molly J. Coye *Aetna Inc* 39
Molly Maloney Evangelisti *McClatchy Co* 1139
Molly Shi Boren *Dollar Thrifty Automotive Group Inc* 567
Moloco Capital Partners LLC *Avalon Holdings Corp* 184
Momentum Employee and Consultant Trust *Tonga Capital Corp* 1802
Monadnock Community Bank *Monadnock Bancorp Inc* 1209
Monahan Corporation, N.V. *T H Lehman & Co Inc* 1744
Monarch Capital Fund Ltd. *Analytical Surveys Inc* 120
Monarch Community Bancorp, Inc *Monarch Community Bancorp Inc* 1210
Monarch Pointe Fund, LP *Interactive Brand Development Inc* 960
Monarch Pointe Fund, Ltd *Interactive Television Networks Inc* 961
Monarch Pointe Fund, LTD *Multicell Technologies Inc* 1227
Monarch Pointe Fund, Ltd. *Medical Discoveries Inc* 1151
Monarch Pointe Fund, Ltd. *Diametrics Medical Inc* 550
Monarch Pointe Fund, Ltd. *Cardinal Communications* 331
Mondrian Investment Partners Limited *Telecom Corp of New Zealand Ltd* 1765
Mondrian Investment Partners Ltd *Latin American Export Bank* 1058
Monetta R. Dembosz *Plumas Bancorp* 1441
Monica A. Bowlin *Bowlin Travel Centers Inc* 270
Monica A. Underwood *Granite City Food & Brewery Ltd* 815
Monica Alfaro Welling *Hythiam Inc* 905
Monica C. Holmes *Fremont Michigan Insuracorp Inc* 748
Monica C. Lozano *Bank of America Corp* 208
Monica C. Lozano *Walt Disney Co* 1930
Monica Eisinger *MIND CTI Ltd* 1194
Monica G. Noether *Charles River Assoc Inc* 374
Monica L. Woo *1-800-Flowers Com Inc* 2004
Monica M. Gaudiosi *Southern Union Co* 1668
Monica Tsang *Techne Corp* 1757
Monish Kundra *Skyterra Communications Inc* 1643
Monroe Bank & Trust *MBT Financial Corp* 1138
Monroe J. Carell *Central Parking Corp* 363
Monroe W. Robertson *Cimarex Energy Co* 406
Monroe W. Robertson *Basic Earth Science Systems Inc* 218
Mons Bolin *Aries Maritime Transport Ltd* 148
Monsun, AS *CytoCore Inc* 520
Monsun, AS *Molecular Diagnostics Inc* 1207
Montague A. Miller *Georgia-Carolina Bancshares Inc* 782
Montague H. Hackett *Empire Petroleum Corp* 625
Monte E. Ford *Moneygram International Inc* 1211
Monte E. Taylor *GeneLink Inc* 768
Monte H. Thornton *Mohawk Industries Inc* 1206
Monte J. Barrow *Education Realty Trust Inc* 606
Monte J. Miller *Kirby Corp* 1032

Standard Industrial Classification (SIC) Code Index

Standard Industrial Classification
(SIC) Code Index

29   Petroleum & Coal Products

30   Rubber & Misc. Plastics Products

38 Instruments & Related Products

VirtualScopics Inc	1912
VNUS Medical Technologies Inc	1920

3822 Environmental Controls

Environmental Tectonics Corp	647
Honeywell International Inc	888
Johnson Controls Inc	1009
LSB Industries Inc	1097
Measurement Specialties Inc	1145
Misonix Inc	1198
MPM Technologies Inc	1222
Rentech Inc	1532

3823 Process Control Instruments

Advanced Energy Industries Inc	29
Ametek Inc	112
Badger Meter Inc	199
Biosphere Medical Inc	247
Braintech Inc	273
BTU International Inc	291
Calgon Carbon Corp	307
CECO Environmental	353
Cognex Corp	435
Crane Co	494
Dionex Corp	560
Eaton Corp	596
Elbit Vision Systems Ltd	611
Electric & Gas Technology Inc	612
Electro-Sensors Inc	613
Emerson Electric Co	623
Environmental Tectonics Corp	647
ESCO Technologies Inc	657
FARO Technologies Inc	680
FoxHollow Technologies Inc	742
Graco Inc	813
Honeywell International Inc	888
Innovative Solutions & Support Inc	948
iSECUREtrac Corp	990
JDS Uniphase Corp	1005
K-Tron International Inc	1015
Law Enforcement Assoc Corp	1059
MachineTalker Inc	1106
Measurement Specialties Inc	1145
Mesa Laboratories Inc	1166
Metso Corp	1173
Mettler-Toledo International Inc	1173
MFIC Corp	1175
MFRI Inc	1175
Micro Imaging Technology Inc	1178
Microwave Filter Co Inc NY	1183
Millipore Corp	1193
MKS Instruments Inc	1202
MTS Systems Corp	1225
Natco Group Inc	1237
New Century Equity Holdings Corp	1270
OI Corp	1331
Powell Industries Inc	1453
Powersecure International Inc	1455
Pro-Dex Inc	1470
Publicard Inc	1487
Qualmark Corp	1496
RadiSys Corp	1508
REMEC Inc	1529
Roper Industries Inc	1558
Rudolph Technologies Inc	1567
SGL Carbon	1615
Siemens	1625
Somerset International Group Inc	1656
Sono Tek Corp	1658
Sutron Corp	1731
Sypris Solutions Inc	1741
Teradyne Inc	1776
Transcat Inc	1814
Tyco International Ltd	1838
United Utilities Plc	1864
Veeco Instruments Inc	1892
Victory Energy Corp	1904
W-H Energy Services	1926

3824 Fluid Meters & Counting Devices

Honeywell International Inc	888
Itron Inc	994
Lowrance Electronics Inc	1096
Measurement Specialties Inc	1145
Power Technology Inc	1454
Powersecure International Inc	1455
Technitrol Inc	1758

3825 Instruments to Measure Electricity

Adeza Biomedical Corp	24
Aehr Test Systems	35
Aeroflex Inc	37
Aetrium Inc	39
Agilent Technologies Inc	43
Analog Devices Inc	119
Analogic Corp	119
Axcess International Inc TX	194
Cascade Microtech Inc	340
Catapult Communications Corp	345
Conectisys Corp	467
Credence Systems Corp	496
Danaher Corp	525
Digimarc Corp	555
Eagle Test Systems Inc	591
Electroglas Inc	613
FEI Co	686
Frequency Electronics Inc	748
Giga-tronics Inc	786
Honeywell International Inc	888
Itron Inc	994
JDS Uniphase Corp	1005
JMAR Technologies Inc	1008
Keithley Instruments Inc	1021
Lecroy Corp	1063
LTX Corp	1098
Mentor Graphics Corp	1159
Mesa Laboratories Inc	1166
Micro Component Technology Inc	1178
Micronetics Inc	1180
Mirae Corp	1197
Nextest Systems Corp	1284
Northrop Grumman Corp	1303
ORBIT/FR Inc	1354

Perkinelmer Inc	1413
Photon Dynamics Inc	1427
Plexus Corp	1440
Powersecure International Inc	1455
Rada Electronic Industries Ltd	1506
Reliability Inc	1528
SI Industries Inc	1644
Sonic Environmental Solutions Inc	1657
Sunrise Telecom Inc	1723
Synopsys Inc	1739
Taiwan Semiconductor Mfg Co Ltd	1745
Technology Research Corp	1759
Tektronix Inc	1763
Textron Inc	1783
Verigy Ltd	1895
Wireless Telecom Group Inc	1970

3826 Analytical Instruments

Accentia Biopharmaceuticals Inc	10
AcuNetx Inc	20
Aethlon Medical Inc	38
Affymetrix Inc	41
Agilent Technologies Inc	43
Applera Corp	134
Applied Imaging Corp	135
Avalon Pharmaceuticals Inc	184
Avitar Inc	191
Bayer	221
Beckman Coulter Inc	227
Bio Rad Laboratories Inc	240
Biosite Inc	247
Biosphere Medical Inc	247
Bruker Biosciences Corp	289
Caliper Life Sciences Inc	309
Cell Robotics International Inc	355
Cepheid	367
Cerus Corp	368
China Medical Technologies Inc	392
Clinical Data Inc	425
Cyberkinetics Neurotechnology Systems Inc	516
Cyberoptics Corp	517
Cytyc Corp	522
Dade Behring Holdings Inc	523
Dionex Corp	560
FUJIFILM Holdings Corp	754
Giga-tronics Inc	786
Harvard Bioscience Inc	851
IDEXX Laboratories Inc	917
Illumina Inc	923
Immunicon Corp	928
Infinity Pharmaceuticals Inc	938
KLA-Tencor Corp	1033
Lecroy Corp	1063
LTX Corp	1098
Mechanical Technology Inc	1145
Mettler-Toledo International Inc	1173
Millipore Corp	1193
MWI Veterinary Supply Inc	1229
Nanogen Inc	1234
Nuvelo Inc	1319
OSI Systems Inc	1362
Oyo Geospace Corp	1367
Pfeiffer Vacuum Technology	1419
Pressure Biosciences Inc	1463
pSivida Ltd	1485
Qiagen	1492
Spectrum Laboratories Inc	1678
Synthetech Inc	1740
Transgenomic Inc	1816
Valpey Fisher Corp	1887
Varian Inc	1889
Verigy Ltd	1895
Vermillion Inc	1897
Waters Corp	1936
X-Rite Inc	1982

3827 Optical Instruments & Lenses

AcuNetx Inc	20
Advanced Medical Optics Inc	30
APA Enterprises Inc	130
August Technology Corp	178
Bausch & Lomb Inc	220
Canon Inc	320
Coherent Inc	436
Cooper Companies Inc (The)	477
Cyberoptics Corp	517
Cymer Inc	518
DRS Technologies Inc	577
Dynasil Corp of America	585
Excel Technology Inc	667
FUJIFILM Holdings Corp	754
KLA-Tencor Corp	1033
Kyocera Corp	1045
Lasersight Inc	1058
Lightpath Technologies Inc	1078
Meade Instruments Corp	1144
Microvision Inc WA	1183
Nanometrics Inc	1234
Novamed Inc	1308
Opt-Sciences Corp	1348
OSI Systems Inc	1362
Photonic Products Group Inc	1427
Senior Optician Service Inc	1609
StockerYale Inc	1706
Surgilight Inc	1729
TLC Vision Corp	1798
View Systems Inc	1905
Vision-Sciences Inc	1913
Zygo Corp	2003

3829 Measuring & Controlling Devices NEC

AcuNetx Inc	20
Advantest Corp	33
Affymetrix Inc	41
ALR Technologies Inc	72
American Science & Engineering Inc	101
Argon St Inc	146
Astrata Group Inc	167
Axcess International Inc TX	194
Bio Rad Laboratories Inc	240
Biosynergy Inc	248
Bolt Technology Corp	264
Bonso Electronics International Inc	264

Catapult Communications Corp	345
Channell Commercial Corp	373
Checkpoint Systems Inc	379
Cygnus Inc	518
DexCom Inc	548
DexCom Inc	548
Digital Angel Corp	555
Dynatronics Corp	586
Elron Electronic Industries Ltd	618
Enpath Medical Inc	639
Esterline Technologies Corp	659
Falcon Ridge Development Inc	677
FLIR Systems Inc	726
Frequency Electronics Inc	748
Giga-tronics Inc	786
HemoSense Inc	868
HemoSense Inc	868
Hickok Inc	876
Hitachi Ltd	880
Hypertension Diagnostics Inc	905
ICOS Vision Systems Corp	913
ICU Medical Inc	914
Image Sensing Systems Inc	924
Immunicon Corp	928
InkSure Technologies Inc	944
Inmedica Development Corp	945
Integral Vision Inc	954
ION Geophysical Corp	984
JMAR Technologies Inc	1008
Keithley Instruments Inc	1021
KLA-Tencor Corp	1033
L.S. Starrett Co (The)	1046
LMS Medical Systems Inc	1090
Material Technologies Inc	1130
Measurement Specialties Inc	1145
Mechanical Technology Inc	1145
Mikron Infrared Inc	1205
Mocon Inc	1205
MTS Systems Corp	1225
Nanometrics Inc	1234
NanoSensors Inc	1234
Newport Corp	1280
North American Scientific Inc	1297
Oyo Geospace Corp	1367
Perkinelmer Inc	1413
PPT VISION Inc	1457
Publicard Inc	1487
RAESystems	1510
Raven Industries Inc	1515
Remotemdx Inc	1530
RF Monolithics Inc	1542
Rockwell Automation Inc	1554
Sierra Monitor Corp	1626
Sonosite Inc	1659
StockerYale Inc	1706
Stronghold Technologies Inc	1713
Sunrise Telecom Inc	1723
Tektronix Inc	1763
Tollgrade Communications Inc	1801
Transcat Inc	1814
Trimble Navigation Ltd	1824
Universal Detection Technology	1867
Veeco Instruments Inc	1892
Veri-Tek International Corp	1895
View Systems Inc	1905
Viscount Systems Inc	1912
Visualant Inc	1916
W-H Energy Services	1926
Winland Electronics Inc	1967
Xenogen Corp	1984
Z-Trim Holdings Inc	1994
Zygo Corp	2003

3841 Surgical & Medical Instruments

Abbott Laboratories	5
Abiomed Inc	7
AcuNetx Inc	20
Advanced Neuromodulation Systems Inc	30
Advanced Refractive Technologies Inc	31
AFP Imaging Corp	41
Akorn Inc	49
Aksys Ltd	49
Alcon Inc	54
Allied Healthcare Products Inc	64
Alpha Innotech Corp	70
Alpha Pro Tech Ltd	70
Alphatec Holdings Inc	71
Alphatec Holdings Inc	71
Altana AG	72
American Medical Systems Holdings Inc	96
Analogic Corp	119
Angeion Corp	122
Ansell Ltd	126
Arcadia Resources Inc	142
Arrow International Inc	153
Arthrocare Corp	155
Asthmatx Inc	166
AtriCure Inc	176
Atrion Corp	176
Baxter International Inc	220
Beckman Coulter Inc	227
Becton Dickinson & Co	227
Bio Rad Laboratories Inc	240
BioCurex Inc	242
Bioject Medical Technologies Inc	243
BioLife Solutions Inc	244
Biomerica Inc	245
Biomet Inc	245
BioMimetic Therapeutics Inc	245
Biophan Technologies Inc	246
Biosphere Medical Inc	247
Biosynergy Inc	248
Biotel Inc	248
Biovest International Inc	249
Boston Scientific Corp	268
Bovie Medical Corp	269
C. R. Bard Inc	299
Callisto Pharmaceuticals Inc	310
Calypte Biomedical Corp	312
Cantel Medical Corp	320
Cardiac Science Corp	330
Cardica Inc	330
Cardima Inc	331

6029 Commercial Banks NEC

65   Real Estate

6512 Nonresidential Building Operators

6513 Apartment Building Operators

6514 Dwelling Operators Except Apartments

6515 Mobile Home Site Operators

6517 Railroad Property Lessors

6519 Real Property Lessors NEC

6531 Real Estate Agents & Managers

6541 Title Abstract Offices

6552 Subdividers & Developers NEC

6553 Cemetery Subdividers & Developers

67   Holding & Other Invest. Offices

6712 Bank Holding Companies

7373 Computer Integrated Systems Design

7381 Detective & Armored Car Services

7382 Security Systems Services

7383 News Syndicates

7384 Photofinishing Laboratories

7389 Business Services NEC

88   Private Households

89   Services Not Elsewhere Class.

8999 Services NEC

91   Executive, Legislative & Gen'l

9199 General Government NEC

92   Justice, Public Order & Safety

9223 Correctional Institutions

9224 Fire Protection

---

94   Admin. of Human Resources

9411 Administration of Educational Programs

9441 Administration of Social and Manpower Programs

95   Environmental Quality & Housing

9511 Air, Water & Solid Waste Management

9532 Urban & Community Development

96   Admin of Economic Programs

9651 Regulation of Miscellaneous Commercial Sectors

9661 Space Research & Technology

97   National Security & Int'l Affairs

9711 National Security

99   Nonclassifiable Establishments

9999 Nonclassifiable Establishments

Subsidiary/Parent Index

Advance Homestead Title, Inc. *Stewart Information Services Corp* 1705
Advance Medical Supply Company Limited *DSG International Ltd* 578
Advance Merchandising Company, Inc. *Advance Auto Parts Inc* 27
Advance Mortgage *Wells Fargo & Co* 1944
Advance Nanotech Ltd. *Advance Nanotech Inc* 27
Advance Nanotech Singapore Pte. Ltd. *Advance Nanotech Inc* 27
Advance Petroleum Inc. *World Fuel Services Corp* 1976
Advance SC LLC *Duke Energy Corp* 580
Advance Stores Company, Incorporated *Advance Auto Parts Inc* 27
Advance Title Company *Stewart Information Services Corp* 1705
Advance Trucking Corporation *Advance Auto Parts Inc* 27
Advance Tubular de Ecuador S.A. *Maverick Tube Corp* 1134
Advance Tubular de Venezuela ATV, C.A. *Maverick Tube Corp* 1134
Advancecare Gesto de Servios de Sade, SA *Espirito Santo Financial Group* 658
AdvanceCo LP *Maverick Tube Corp* 1134
Advanced Absorbent Products Holdings Limited *Tyco International Ltd* 1838
Advanced Analog, Inc. *International Rectifier Corp* 971
Advanced Analogic Technologies *Advanced Analogic Technologies Inc* 28
Advanced Analogic Technologies *Advanced Analogic Technologies Inc* 28
Advanced Analogic Technologies Corporation *Advanced Analogic Technologies Inc* 28
Advanced Analogic Technologies (France) SARL *Advanced Analogic Technologies Inc* 28
Advanced Analogic Technologies Holdings, Inc. *Advanced Analogic Technologies Inc* 28
Advanced Analogic Technologies Japan *Advanced Analogic Technologies Inc* 28
Advanced Analogic Technologies(Hong Kong)Ltd. *Advanced Analogic Technologies Inc* 28
Advanced Answers on Demand Holding Corporation *Magic Software Enterprises Ltd* 1110
Advanced Beverage Solutions, LLC *Lancer Corp TX* 1053
Advanced Bio-Mechanics, Inc. *Hanger Orthopedic Group Inc* 843
Advanced Bionics Corporation *Boston Scientific Corp* 268
Advanced Bionics GmbH *Boston Scientific Corp* 268
Advanced Bionics Japan Company Ltd. *Boston Scientific Corp* 268
Advanced Bionics NV *Boston Scientific Corp* 268
Advanced Bionics SARL *Boston Scientific Corp* 268
Advanced Bionics SL *Boston Scientific Corp* 268
Advanced Bionics UK Ltd. *Boston Scientific Corp* 268
Advanced Biotherapy, Inc *Advanced Biotherapy Inc* 28
Advanced Business Fulfillment, LLC *HLTH Corp* 881
Advanced CAE Technology, Inc. *Moldflow Corp* 1207
Advanced Cardiovascular Systems, Inc. *Guidant Corp* 834
Advanced Casino Systems Corporation *Bally Technologies Inc* 202
Advanced Circuit Technology,Inc. *Amphenol Corp* 115
Advanced Coiled Tubing, Inc. *Complete Production Services Inc* 460
Advanced Collateral Solutions, LLC *First American Corp* 695
Advanced Communications Corporation *Black Box Corp* 252
Advanced Component Systems LLC *Universal Forest Products Inc* 1868
Advanced Conductor Technologies, Inc *Element 21 Golf Co* 615
Advanced Cyber Security, Inc *Manakoa Services Corp* 1117
Advanced Data Services, Inc. *IDT Corp* 918
Advanced Delivery & Chemical Systems Holdings, LLC *ATMI Inc* 174
Advanced Delivery & Chemical Systems Manager, Inc. *ATMI Inc* 174
Advanced Delivery & Chemical Systems Nevada, Inc. *ATMI Inc* 174
Advanced Delivery & Chemical Systems Operating, LLC *ATMI Inc* 174
Advanced Design Concepts GmbH *Dow Chemical Co* 573
Advanced Digital Optics, Inc. *JDS Uniphase Corp* 1005
Advanced Distributor Products LLC *Lennox International Inc* 1068
Advanced Egress Systems, Inc. *Goodrich Corp* 810
Advanced ElectroMagnetics, Inc. *ORBIT/FR Inc* 1354
Advanced Energy Systems, Inc. *NSTAR* 1313
Advanced Energy Technologies, Inc. *Unisource Energy Corp* 1853
Advanced Energy Technology Inc. *GrafTech International Ltd* 813
Advanced Engineering & Sciences Division *ITT Corp* 994
Advanced Environmental Technical Services, LLC *Waste Management Inc* 1934
Advanced Exercise Equipment, LLC *Brunswick Corp* 289
Advanced Fabricating Technology, LLC *A M Castle & Co* 1
Advanced Fibre Communications (HK) Limited *Tellabs Inc* 1770
Advanced Fibre Communications International GmbH *Tellabs Inc* 1770
Advanced Fibre Communications International Limited *Tellabs Inc* 1770
Advanced Fibre Communications Mexico S. de R.L. de C.V. *Tellabs Inc* 1770
Advanced Fibre Communications U.K. Limited *Tellabs Inc* 1770
Advanced Fibre Technology Communications (HK) Limited *Tellabs Inc* 1770
Advanced Filtration Systems Inc. *Caterpillar Inc* 345
Advanced Financial Solutions LLC *Marshall & Ilsley Corp* 1126
Advanced Financial Solutions, Inc. *Marshall & Ilsley Corp* 1126
Advanced Financial Technology, Inc. *Centex Corp* 360
Advanced Forming Technology, Inc. *Precision Castparts Corp* 1458
Advanced Heat Transfer LLC *Lennox International Inc* 1068
Advanced Hyperbaric Industries, Inc *Global Resource Corp* 797
Advanced ID Asia Engineering Co. Ltd *Advanced ID Corp* 29
Advanced Independent Monitoring Limited *Tyco International Ltd* 1838
Advanced Infusion Systems Inc. *Kindred Healthcare Inc* 1030
Advanced Inhalation Research, Inc. *Alkermes Inc* 57
Advanced Input Devices (UK) Ltd. *Esterline Technologies Corp* 659
Advanced Input Devices, Inc. *Esterline Technologies Corp* 659
Advanced Insurance Coverages, Inc. *Fiserv Inc* 721
Advanced Interconnect, Inc. *Woodhead Industries Inc* 1974
Advanced Internet Inc *Zim Corp* 1998
Advanced Internet Services, Inc. *Sitestar Corp* 1639
Advanced Internet Technologies, LLC *Beard Co* 226
Advanced Land Title of Lexington, LLC *Stewart Information Services Corp* 1705
Advanced Logic Research, Inc. *Gateway Inc* 764
Advanced Management Technology, Inc. *Tetra Tech Inc* 1780
Advanced Manufacturing and Development, Inc. *Avista Corp* 190
Advanced Materials Processing Inc. *AK Steel Holding Corp* 48
Advanced Measurement Technology, Inc. *Ametek Inc* 112
Advanced Medical Diagnostics, LLC *Global Concepts Ltd* 792
Advanced Medical Optics Australia Pty Ltd. *Advanced Medical Optics Inc* 30
Advanced Medical Optics India Private Limited *Advanced Medical Optics Inc* 30
Advanced Medical Optics Norden AB *Advanced Medical Optics Inc* 30
Advanced Medical Optics Norway ASA *Advanced Medical Optics Inc* 30
Advanced Medical Optics Spain S.L. *Advanced Medical Optics Inc* 30
Advanced Medical Optics Uppsala AB *Advanced Medical Optics Inc* 30
Advanced Medicine East, Inc. *Theravance Inc* 1785
Advanced Micro Devices Belgium N.V. *Advanced Micro Devices Inc* 30
Advanced Micro Devices (Canada) Limited *Advanced Micro Devices Inc* 30
Advanced Micro Devices (China) Co. Ltd. *Advanced Micro Devices Inc* 30
Advanced Micro Devices Export Sdn. Bhd. *Advanced Micro Devices Inc* 30
Advanced Micro Devices GmbH *Advanced Micro Devices Inc* 30
Advanced Micro Devices S.A.S. *Advanced Micro Devices Inc* 30
Advanced Micro Devices S.p.A. *Advanced Micro Devices Inc* 30
Advanced Micro Devices Sdn. Bhd. *Advanced Micro Devices Inc* 30
Advanced Micro Devices (Singapore) Pte. Ltd. *Advanced Micro Devices Inc* 30
Advanced Micro Devices (U.K.) Limited *Advanced Micro Devices Inc* 30
Advanced Micro Devices, AB *Advanced Micro Devices Inc* 30
Advanced Micro Electronics AS *OSI Systems Inc* 1362
Advanced Micro Ltd. *Advanced Micro Devices Inc* 30
Advanced Molded Packaging LLC *Citigroup Inc* 411
Advanced Motion Controls AB *Danaher Corp* 525
Advanced Motion Controls AB *Shanda Interactive Entertainment Ltd* 1616
Advanced Network Technologies, Inc. *Black Box Corp* 252
Advanced Neuromodulation Systems *St Jude Medical Inc* 1687
Advanced Neuromodulation Systems Australia Pty Limited *St Jude Medical Inc* 1687
Advanced Neuromodulation Systems Australia Pty Limited *Advanced Neuromodulation Systems Inc* 30
Advanced Neuromodulation Systems France S.A.S *St Jude Medical Inc* 1687
Advanced Neuromodulation Systems, Inc *St Jude Medical Inc* 1687
Advanced Orthopaedics of South Florida II, Inc. *Paincare Holdings Inc* 1377
Advanced Packaging Systems *Tyco International Ltd* 1838
Advanced Performance Consulting Group, Inc. *ICF International Inc* 911
Advanced Polymer Technology, Inc. *Franklin Electric Co Inc* 744
Advanced Power Technology Colorado, Inc. *Advanced Power Technology Inc* 31
Advanced Power Technology Europe SAS *Advanced Power Technology Inc* 31
Advanced Power Technology RF Pennsylvania, Inc. *Advanced Power Technology Inc* 31
Advanced Power Technology RF, Inc. *Advanced Power Technology Inc* 31
Advanced Products NV *Parker-Hannifin Corp* 1387
Advanced Products UK Ltd. *Parker-Hannifin Corp* 1387
Advanced Public Safety, Inc. *Trimble Navigation Ltd* 1824
Advanced Radio Corporation *Mercury Computer Systems Inc* 1162
Advanced Receivables Strategy, Inc. *Perot Systems Corp* 1413
Advanced Refining Technologies GmbH *W. R. Grace & Co* 1927
Advanced Refining Technologies K.K. *W. R. Grace & Co* 1927
Advanced Refining Technologies LLC *W. R. Grace & Co* 1927
Advanced Respiratory, Inc. *Hillenbrand Industries Inc* 879
Advanced Risk Management Techniques, Inc. *Aon Corp* 129
Advanced Sciences Integradas S.A *Commodore Applied Technologies Inc* 449
Advanced Sciences Integrated Mexico, S.A. de C.V *Commodore Applied Technologies Inc* 449
Advanced Security Installations Limited *Tyco International Ltd* 1838
Advanced Semiconductor Materials *ASM International* 161
Advanced Settlements, Inc. *National Financial Partners Corp* 1241
Advanced Sleep Products *Sealy Corp* 1600
Advanced Software Technologies, Inc. *Embarcadero Technologies Inc* 619
Advanced Sports Technologies, Inc. *Odyssey Oil & Gas Inc* 1329
Advanced Staffing International, Inc. *International Imaging Systems Inc* 970
Advanced Stent Technologies, Inc. *Boston Scientific Corp* 268
Advanced Sterilization Products Services Inc. *Johnson & Johnson* 1009
Advanced Systems Limited *Sybase Inc* 1733
Advanced Technologies and Installation Corporation *Quanta Services Inc* 1497
Advanced Technology Group GmbH *WPP Group Plc* 1979
Advanced Technology Marketing, Inc. *Learning Tree International Inc* 1063
Advanced Technology Materials, Inc. *ATMI Inc* 174
Advanced TelCom, Inc. *Eschelon Telecom Inc* 656
Advanced Telecomm of Maryland, Inc. *Applied Digital Solutions Inc* 135
Advanced Telecomm of Pittsburgh *Applied Digital Solutions Inc* 135
Advanced Telecommunications, Inc. *Applied Digital Solutions Inc* 135
Advanced Thermal Hydronics, Inc. *Mestek Inc* 1167
Advanced Thermal Sciences Corporation *BE Aerospace Inc* 223
Advanced Thermal Sciences Korea *BE Aerospace Inc* 223
Advanced Thermal Sciences Shanghai Corporation *BE Aerospace Inc* 223
Advanced Thermal Sciences Taiwan Corporation *BE Aerospace Inc* 223
Advanced Thermodynamics Inc. *Teleflex Inc* 1766
Advanced Title Holding Company, LLC *Stewart Information Services Corp* 1705
Advanced Title, LLC *Stewart Information Services Corp* 1705
Advanced Urology Services, LLC *HealthTronics Inc* 862
Advanced Wirecloth, Inc. *National Oilwell Inc* 1244
AdvancedDigitalImagingResearch,LLC *IRIS International Inc* 988
Advancel Logic Corporation *NCT Group Inc* 1256
AdvanceMed Corporation *Computer Sciences Corp* 462
AdvancePatriot, Inc. *Advance Auto Parts Inc* 27
AdvancePCS Holding Corporation *Caremark Rx Inc* 334
Advanmechatec Co., Ltd. *Advantest Corp* 33
Advanstar Communications Inc *Advanstar Inc* 32
Advanstar Holdings Corporation *Advanstar Inc* 32
Advanstar IH, Inc *Advanstar Inc* 32
Advanstar.com, Inc. *Advanstar Inc* 32
Advanta 101 GP Corp. *Advanta Corp* 32
Advanta Advertising, Inc. *Advanta Corp* 32
Advanta Auto Finance Corporation *Advanta Corp* 32
Advanta Auto Receivables Corp. I *Advanta Corp* 32
Advanta Bank Corp. *Advanta Corp* 32
Advanta Business Receivables Corp. *Advanta Corp* 32
Advanta Business Services Corp. *Advanta Corp* 32
Advanta Business Services Holding Corp. *Advanta Corp* 32
Advanta Capital LLC *Advanta Corp* 32
Advanta Corp. *Advanta Corp* 32
Advanta Finance Corp. *Advanta Corp* 32
Advanta GCF GP Corp. *Advanta Corp* 32
Advanta GP Corp. *Advanta Corp* 32
Advanta GP II Corp. *Advanta Corp* 32
Advanta Growth Capital Fund LP *Advanta Corp* 32
Advanta Information Services, Inc. *Advanta Corp* 32
Advanta Insurance Agency Inc. *Advanta Corp* 32
Advanta Insurance Company *Advanta Corp* 32
Advanta International Corporation I *Advanta Corp* 32
Advanta International Corporation II *Advanta Corp* 32
Advanta Investment Corp. *Advanta Corp* 32
Advanta Investment Corp. II *Advanta Corp* 32
Advanta Leasing Receivables Corp. VI *Advanta Corp* 32
Advanta Life Insurance Company *Advanta Corp* 32
Advanta Mortgage Corp. USA *Advanta Corp* 32
Advanta Mortgage Holding Company *Advanta Corp* 32
Advanta National Bank *Advanta Corp* 32
Advanta National Corp. *Advanta Corp* 32
Advanta Partners 101 LP *Advanta Corp* 32
Advanta Partners LP *Advanta Corp* 32
Advanta Service Corp. *Advanta Corp* 32
Advanta Shared Services Corp. *Advanta Corp* 32
Advanta UK *Advanta Corp* 32
Advantage Bank *Camco Financial Corp* 314
Advantage Behavioral Systems,Inc. *Magellan Health Services Inc* 1109
Advantage Belgium *Interpublic Group of Companies Inc* 975
Advantage Capital Corporation *American International Group Inc* 94
Advantage Diagnostics Corporation *Inverness Medical Innovations Inc* 981
Advantage Energy, Inc. *Wisconsin Public Service Corp* 1971
Advantage Entertainment Distribution Limited *Activision Inc* 19
Advantage Finance, Inc. *Commercial Bancshares Inc* 448
Advantage Health Corporation *HealthSouth Corp* 861
Advantage Health Harmarville Rehabilitation Corporation *HealthSouth Corp* 861
Advantage Holdings Pty (Australia)pty Ltd *Interpublic Group of Companies Inc* 975
Advantage Home Mortgage, LLC *Wells Fargo & Co* 1944
Advantage Insurers, Inc. *Habersham Bancorp* 838
Advantage Intl Holdings, Inc. *Interpublic Group of Companies Inc* 975
Advantage Learning Systems India Private Limited *Renaissance Learning Inc* 1530
Advantage Logistics - Southeast, Inc. *Supervalu Inc* 1728
Advantage Logistics PA LLC *Supervalu Inc* 1728
Advantage Logistics Southwest, Inc. *Supervalu Inc* 1728
Advantage Logistics USA East LLC *Supervalu Inc* 1728
Advantage Logistics USA West LLC *Supervalu Inc* 1728
Advantage Logistics USA, Inc. *Supervalu Inc* 1728
Advantage Mortgage Partners, LLC *Wells Fargo & Co* 1944
Advantage National Bank *Wintrust Financial Corp* 1969
Advantage Payroll Services, Inc. *Paychex Inc* 1394
Advantage Professional Management Group, Inc. (APMG) *American Leisure Holdings Inc* 95
Advantage R&D, Inc. *Weatherford International Ltd* 1940
Advantage Rehabilitation Clinics, Inc. *HealthSouth Corp* 861
Advantage Soccer Limited *Interpublic Group of Companies Inc* 975
Advantage Sponsorship Canada Limited *Interpublic Group of Companies Inc* 975
Advantage Sponsorship Pty Ltd *Interpublic Group of Companies Inc* 975
Advantage Sports Media Limited *Interpublic Group of Companies Inc* 975
Advantage Television Limited *Interpublic Group of Companies Inc* 975
Advantage Title LLC *Stewart Information Services Corp* 1705
Advantage Title& Insurance, LLC *Realogy Corp* 1518
Advantage Wire & Cable and Cable Management Services Inc *Houston Wire & Cable Company* 893
AdvantageWare, Inc. *Capital Title Group Inc* 326
AdvantEdge Credit Management Services Inc. *HMI Industries Inc* 882
Advantennis Corp. *Advanta Corp* 32
Advantest America, Inc. *Advantest Corp* 33
Advantest Customer Support Corporation *Advantest Corp* 33
Advantest DI Corporation *Advantest Corp* 33
Advantest (Europe) GmbH *Advantest Corp* 33
Advantest Finance Inc. *Advantest Corp* 33
Advantest Korea Co., Ltd. *Advantest Corp* 33
Advantest Laboratories Ltd. *Advantest Corp* 33
Advantest Manufacturing, Inc. *Advantest Corp* 33
Advantest (Singapore) Pte. Ltd. *Advantest Corp* 33
Advantest (Suzhou) Co., Ltd. *Advantest Corp* 33
Advantest Taiwan Inc. *Advantest Corp* 33
ADVANTICA CORPORATE VENTURES LIMITED *National Grid Transco Plc* 1241
ADVANTICA LIMITED *National Grid Transco Plc* 1241
ADVANTICA PTY LIMITED *National Grid Transco Plc* 1241
ADVANTICA, INC. *National Grid Transco Plc* 1241
Advantis Technologies, Inc. *Rockwood Holdings Inc* 1555
Advatech, LLC. *URS Corp* 1875
Advaxis Inc *Advaxis Inc* 33
Advent 3B2 Inc. *Parametric Technology Corp* 1385
Advent Denmark AS *Advent Software Inc* 33
Advent Europe Limited *Advent Software Inc* 33
Advent Guaranty Corporation *National City Corp* 1239
Advent Netherlands BV *Advent Software Inc* 33
Advent Norway AS *Advent Software Inc* 33
Advent Sweden AB *Advent Software Inc* 33
Advent Switzerland AG *Advent Software Inc* 33
Adventa Hospice of Louisiana *Amedisys Inc* 81
Adventa Hospice, Inc., A Florida Corporation *Amedisys Inc* 81
Adventist Midwest Health/USP Surgery Centers, LLC *United Surgical Partners International Inc* 1863
Adventrx (europe) Ltd. *Adventrx Pharmaceuticals Inc* 33
Adventure Four S.A *FreeSeas Inc* 747
Adventure of the Seas Inc. *Royal Caribbean Cruises Ltd* 1562
Adventure Sport Events Ltd. *CCE Spinco Inc* 349
Adventure Three S.A. *FreeSeas Inc* 747
Adventure Two S.A. *FreeSeas Inc* 747

THE CORPORATE DIRECTORY - Walker's 2008
Subsidiary/Parent Index - 2875

Boss Solutions Limited *MAI Systems Corp* 1113
Bosshardt Financial Services, LLC *Suntrust Banks Inc* 1724
BOSSIER OUTPARCEL, L.P. *General Growth Properties Inc* 771
Bosspak Pty Limited *Robbins & Myers Inc* 1551
Bostads Ab Drott *Stena AB* 1700
Bostco LLC *Wisconsin Electric Power Co* 1970
Bostco LLC *Wisconsin Energy Corp* 1970
Bostek, Inc. *Applied Digital Solutions Inc* 135
Boston Administradora de Fondos de Inversion S.A. *Bank of America Corp* 208
Boston Administradora General de Fondos S.A. *Bank of America Corp* 208
Boston Asesores de Seguros, S.A. *Bank of America Corp* 208
Boston Beer Corporation *Boston Beer Co Inc* 267
Boston Beer Corporation Canada Inc. *Boston Beer Co Inc* 267
Boston Biomedica, Inc *Seracare Life Sciences Inc* 1612
Boston Brewing Company, Inc. *Boston Beer Co Inc* 267
Boston Capital Southern Cone S.A. (d/b/a BancBoston Capital Southern Cone) *Bank of America Corp* 208
Boston Centros de Inversion S.A. *Bank of America Corp* 208
Boston Comercial e Participacoes Ltda. *Bank of America Corp* 208
Boston Corporate Finance SpA *Bank of America Corp* 208
Boston Design Center, L.L.C. *Vornado Realty Trust* 1923
Boston Directo S.A. *Bank of America Corp* 208
Boston Edison Company *NSTAR* 1313
Boston Equity General Partner LLC *American Express Financial Corp* 91
Boston Gas Company *Keyspan Corp* 1027
Boston Globe Electronic Publishing, LLC *New York Times Co* 1277
Boston Globe Marketing, LLC *New York Times Co* 1277
Boston Insurance Trust, Inc. *Principal Financial Group Inc* 1468
Boston International Holdings Corporation *Bank of America Corp* 208
Boston Inversiones Servicios y Administracion S.A. *Bank of America Corp* 208
Boston Investment Group S.A., The *Bank of America Corp* 208
Boston Latin America Finance Company *Bank of America Corp* 208
Boston Life Sciences International, Inc. *Boston Life Sciences Inc* 267
Boston Management and Research *Eaton Vance Corp* 596
Boston Market Corporation *McDonald's Corp* 1140
Boston Negocios e Participacoes Ltda. *Bank of America Corp* 208
Boston Opera House Development, LLC *CCE Spinco Inc* 349
Boston Overseas Financial Corporation *Bank of America Corp* 208
Boston Overseas Financial Corporation S.A. *Bank of America Corp* 208
Boston Overseas Holding Corporation *Bank of America Corp* 208
Boston Overseas Private Equity LLC *Bank of America Corp* 208
Boston Piano Company *Steinway Musical Instruments Inc* 1699
Boston Piano GmbH *Steinway Musical Instruments Inc* 1699
Boston Playhouse Realty, Inc. *CCE Spinco Inc* 349
Boston Previdencia Privada S.A. *Bank of America Corp* 208
Boston Private Bank& Trust Company *Boston Private Financial Holdings Inc* 268
Boston Private Value Investors Inc. *Boston Private Financial Holdings Inc* 268
Boston Probes, Inc. (10) *Applera Corp* 134
Boston Properties Limited Partnership *Boston Properties Inc* 268
Boston Properties LLC *Boston Properties Inc* 268
Boston Properties Management, Inc. *Boston Properties Inc* 268
Boston Properties Office Value-Added Fund, L.P. *Boston Properties Inc* 268
Boston Properties TRS, Inc. *Boston Properties Inc* 268
Boston Putford Offshore Safety Ltd. *Seacor Holdings Inc* 1599
Boston RE Ltd. *Credit Suisse Group* 497
Boston Scientific (2001) Ltd. *Boston Scientific Corp* 268
Boston Scientific AG *Boston Scientific Corp* 268
Boston Scientific Argentina S.A. *Boston Scientific Corp* 268
Boston Scientific Asia Pacific Pte. Ltd. *Boston Scientific Corp* 268
Boston Scientific B.V. *Boston Scientific Corp* 268
Boston Scientific Benelux B.V. *Boston Scientific Corp* 268
Boston Scientific Benelux NV *Boston Scientific Corp* 268
Boston Scientific Bulgaria EOOD *Boston Scientific Corp* 268
Boston Scientific Capital Japan Nin-I Kumiai *Boston Scientific Corp* 268
Boston Scientific Capital (UK) *Boston Scientific Corp* 268
Boston Scientific Ceska republika s.r.o. *Boston Scientific Corp* 268
Boston Scientific Colombia Limitada *Boston Scientific Corp* 268
Boston Scientific Cork Limited *Boston Scientific Corp* 268
Boston Scientific Corporation Northwest Technology Center, Inc. *Boston Scientific Corp* 268
Boston Scientific Danmark ApS *Boston Scientific Corp* 268
Boston Scientific de Costa Rica, S.R.L. *Boston Scientific Corp* 268
Boston Scientific de Mexico, S.A. de C.V. *Boston Scientific Corp* 268
Boston Scientific de Venezuela, C.A. *Boston Scientific Corp* 268
Boston Scientific del Caribe, Inc. *Boston Scientific Corp* 268
Boston Scientific Distribution Company *Boston Scientific Corp* 268
Boston Scientific Distribution Ireland Limited *Boston Scientific Corp* 268
Boston Scientific do Brasil Ltda. *Boston Scientific Corp* 268
Boston Scientific Eastern Europe B.V. *Boston Scientific Corp* 268
Boston Scientific Europe S.P.R.L. *Boston Scientific Corp* 268
Boston Scientific Far East B.V. *Boston Scientific Corp* 268
Boston Scientific Foundation, Inc. *Boston Scientific Corp* 268
Boston Scientific Funding Corporation *Boston Scientific Corp* 268
Boston Scientific Ges.m.b.H. *Boston Scientific Corp* 268
Boston Scientific Glens Falls Corp. *Boston Scientific Corp* 268
Boston Scientific Hellas S.A.Minimally Invasive Medical Instruments *Boston Scientific Corp* 268
Boston Scientific Holland B.V. *Boston Scientific Corp* 268
Boston Scientific Hong Kong Limited *Boston Scientific Corp* 268
Boston Scientific Hungary Trading Limited Liability Company *Boston Scientific Corp* 268
Boston Scientific Ibrica, S.A. *Boston Scientific Corp* 268
Boston Scientific International B.V.) *Boston Scientific Corp* 268
Boston Scientific International Distribution Limited *Boston Scientific Corp* 268
Boston Scientific International Finance Limited *Boston Scientific Corp* 268
Boston Scientific International Holding B.V. *Boston Scientific Corp* 268
Boston Scientific International S.A. *Boston Scientific Corp* 268
Boston Scientific Ireland Limited *Boston Scientific Corp* 268
Boston Scientific Israel Limited *Boston Scientific Corp* 268
Boston Scientific Japan K.K. *Boston Scientific Corp* 268
Boston Scientific Korea Co., Ltd. *Boston Scientific Corp* 268
Boston Scientific Latin America B.V. *Boston Scientific Corp* 268
Boston Scientific Latin America B.V. (Chile) Limitada *Boston Scientific Corp* 268
Boston Scientific Lebanon SAL *Boston Scientific Corp* 268
Boston Scientific Limited *Boston Scientific Corp* 268
Boston Scientific Limited *Boston Scientific Corp* 268
Boston Scientific Ltd. *Boston Scientific Corp* 268
Boston Scientific (Malaysia) Sdn. Bhd. *Boston Scientific Corp* 268
Boston Scientific Medizintechnik GmbH *Boston Scientific Corp* 268
Boston Scientific Miami Corporation *Boston Scientific Corp* 268
Boston Scientific Middle East SAL (Off Shore) *Boston Scientific Corp* 268
Boston Scientific Mountain View Corp. *Boston Scientific Corp* 268
Boston Scientific New Zealand Limited *Boston Scientific Corp* 268
Boston Scientific Norge AS *Boston Scientific Corp* 268
Boston Scientific Panama S.A. *Boston Scientific Corp* 268
Boston Scientific Philippines, Inc. *Boston Scientific Corp* 268
Boston Scientific Polska Sp. z o.o. *Boston Scientific Corp* 268
Boston Scientific Pty. Ltd. *Boston Scientific Corp* 268
Boston Scientific S. r.l. *Boston Scientific Corp* 268
Boston Scientific S.A. *Boston Scientific Corp* 268
Boston Scientific S.p.A. *Boston Scientific Corp* 268
Boston Scientific Santa Rosa Corp. *Boston Scientific Corp* 268
Boston Scientific Scimed, Inc. *Boston Scientific Corp* 268
Boston Scientific (South Africa) (Proprietary) Limited *Boston Scientific Corp* 268
Boston Scientific Suomi Oy *Boston Scientific Corp* 268
Boston Scientific Sverige AB *Boston Scientific Corp* 268
Boston Scientific Technologie Zentrum GmbH *Boston Scientific Corp* 268
Boston Scientific (Thailand) Ltd. *Boston Scientific Corp* 268
Boston Scientific TIP Gerecleri Limited (Turkey) Sirketi *Boston Scientific Corp* 268
Boston Scientific Tullamore Limited *Boston Scientific Corp* 268
Boston Scientific (UK) Limited *Boston Scientific Corp* 268
Boston Scientific Uruguay S.A. *Boston Scientific Corp* 268
Boston Scientific Wayne Corporation *Boston Scientific Corp* 268
Boston Scientific (Zurich) GmbH *Boston Scientific Corp* 268
Boston Securities S.A. Sociedad de Bolsa *Bank of America Corp* 208
Boston Securitizadora S.A. *Bank of America Corp* 208
Boston Suites TRS, Inc. *Eagle Hospitality Properties Trust Inc* 590
Boston Technology Foreign Sales Corp. *Comverse Technology Inc* 465
Boston Technology International, Inc. *Comverse Technology Inc* 465
Boston Technology Mexico, Inc. *Comverse Technology Inc* 465
Boston Whaler, Inc. *Brunswick Corp* 289
Boston World Holding Corporation *Bank of America Corp* 208
Bostrom Europe *Commercial Vehicle Group Inc* 449
Bostrom International Limited *Commercial Vehicle Group Inc* 449
Bostrom Investments Limited *Commercial Vehicle Group Inc* 449
Bostrom Limited *Commercial Vehicle Group Inc* 449
Bostrom Specialist Engineering Limited *Commercial Vehicle Group Inc* 449
Bostrom Vehicle Components Limited *Commercial Vehicle Group Inc* 449
BOT Lease Co., Ltd. *Mitsubishi Tokyo Financial Group Inc* 1200
BOTAC, Inc. *J.P. Morgan Chase & Company* 999
Botalia Pharmaceutical, Inc. *Hain Celestial Group Inc* 838
Botanic Building S.A. *Allianz* 63
BOTJ Investment Group, Inc. *Bank of the James Financial Group Inc* 212
Botsel Limited *Cabot Corp* 301
Botswana Oxygen Company (Pty) Limited *BOC Group Plc* 262
Botswana Steel Engineering (Pty) Limited *BOC Group Plc* 262
Bott Equipment Company, Inc. *Convergence Ethanol Inc* 476
Bottarini S.p.A. *Gardner Denver Inc* 762
Bottling Enterprises Management *Coca-Cola Enterprises Inc* 433
Bottling Enterprises Management Inc. *Coca-Cola Enterprises Inc* 433
Bottling Great Britain Ltd. (BGB) *Coca-Cola Enterprises Inc* 433
Bottling Group Espana, S.L. *Pepsi Bottling Group Inc* 1409
Bottling Group Holdings, Inc. *Phase Forward Inc* 1424
Bottling Group Holdings, Inc. *Pico Holdings Inc* 1429
Bottling Group Holdings, Inc. *Pepsi Bottling Group Inc* 1409
Bottling Group Servicios Centrales SL *Pepsi Bottling Group Inc* 1409
Bottling Group, LLC *Pico Holdings Inc* 1429
Bottling Group, LLC *Phase Forward Inc* 1424
Bottling Group, LLC *Pepsi Bottling Group Inc* 1409
Bottling Holding Company (BHC) *Coca-Cola Enterprises Inc* 433
Bottling Holding France (BHF) *Coca-Cola Enterprises Inc* 433
Bottling Holdings (Canada) ULC *Coca-Cola Enterprises Inc* 433
Bottling Holdings (International) Inc. (BHI) *Coca-Cola Enterprises Inc* 433
Bottling Holdings Investment (Luxembourg) *Coca-Cola Enterprises Inc* 433
Bottling Holdings (Luxembourg) (BHL) *Coca-Cola Enterprises Inc* 433
Bottling Holdings (Luxembourg) Commandite (BHLC) *Coca-Cola Enterprises Inc* 433
Bottling Holdings (Netherlands) B.V. (BHN) *Coca-Cola Enterprises Inc* 433
Bottling Investment Chile *PepsiCo Inc* 1410
Bottling Investments Corporation *Coca-Cola Co* 433
Bottling Investments (Netherlands) B.V. *Coca-Cola Enterprises Inc* 433
Bottling Realco Nova Scotia ULC *PepsiCo Inc* 1410
Bottomline Mortgage, Inc *Bottomline Home Loan Inc* 269
Bottomline Technologies Europe Limited *Bottomline Technologies (DE) Inc* 269
Bottomline Technologies Limited *Bottomline Technologies (DE) Inc* 269
Bottomline Transactional Services Limited *Bottomline Technologies (DE) Inc* 269
Botway Print Advert., Inc. *Interpublic Group of Companies Inc* 975
Boudeuse Limited *Barclays Plc* 216
Boulangerie Chez Tim Inc. *Wendy's International Inc* 1945
Boulder City LLC *Capitalsource Inc* 327
Boulder Creek Apartments LP *Edison International* 604
Boulder Creek Apartments LP *Edison International* 604
Boulder Creek Resort Company *Blue Ridge Real Estate Co* 257
Boulder Natural Foods, Inc. *The Inventure Group Inc* 1784
Boulder Publishing Company *E.W. Scripps Co (The)* 589
Boulder Station,Inc. *Station Casinos Inc* 1696
Boulder/Beaver, LLC *Vail Resorts Inc* 1883
BOULEVARD ASSOCIATES *General Growth Properties Inc* 771
Boulevard Communications *North Pittsburgh Systems Inc* 1299
BOULEVARD MALL I LLC *General Growth Properties Inc* 771
BOULEVARD MALL II LLC *General Growth Properties Inc* 771
BOULEVARD MALL, INC. *General Growth Properties Inc* 771
Boulevard Services Pvt. Ltd. *Vornado Realty Trust* 1923
BouncyNet, Inc. and subsidiary *Grupo Televisa, S.A.B.* 829
Boundless Racing, Inc *Dirt Motor Sports Inc* 561
Bounds Funeral Home, Inc. *Stewart Enterprises Inc* 1704
Bountiful Psychiatric Hospital, Inc. *Psychiatric Solutions Inc* 1485
Bountiful Surgery Center, LLC *HCA Inc* 855
Bounty Investment Inc. *Danaos Corp* 525
Bouquet Canyon Seniors LP *Edison International* 604
Bourbon Community Hospital, LLC *Lifepoint Hospitals Inc* 1076
Bourbon Physician Practice, LLC *Lifepoint Hospitals Inc* 1076
Bourbon Street Holding Company,Inc. *Harrah's Entertainment Inc* 848
Bourbon Warehouse Netherlands B.V. *Fortune Brands Inc* 738
Bourbon Warehouse Receipts, Inc. *Fortune Brands Inc* 738
Bourgeot-etiqso-lesbats Sa *Chesapeake Corp* 382
Bourne Security Limited *BB Holdings Ltd* 222
Bourque Printing, Inc. *Champion Industries Inc* 371
Bouwbedrijf Boven Winden, N.V. *Devcon International Corp* 546
Bouyer Elektronic GmbH *Tyco International Ltd* 1838
Bouyer S.A.S *Tyco International Ltd* 1838
Bow Lane Nominees Pty Ltd *Citigroup Inc* 411
Bow Physical Therapy & Spine *U.S. Physical Therapy Inc* 1841
Bow Tie Music, Inc. *Anheuser-Busch Companies Inc* 124
Bowater Alabama Inc. *Bowater Inc* 269
Bowater America Inc. *Bowater Inc* 269
Bowater Asia Pte Ltd. *Bowater Inc* 269
Bowater Canada Finance Corporation *Bowater Inc* 269
Bowater Canada Inc. *Bowater Inc* 269
Bowater Canadian Forest Products Inc. *Bowater Inc* 269
Bowater Canadian Holdings Incorporated *Bowater Inc* 269
Bowater Canadian Limited *Bowater Inc* 269
Bowater Europe Limited *Bowater Inc* 269
Bowater Finance Company Inc. *Bowater Inc* 269
Bowater Funding Inc. *Bowater Inc* 269
Bowater Maritimes Inc.(1) *Bowater Inc* 269
Bowater Mersey Paper Company Limited *Washington Post Co* 1933
Bowater Mersey Paper Company Limited(2) *Bowater Inc* 269
Bowater Mississippi LLC *Bowater Inc* 269
Bowater Nuway Inc. *Bowater Inc* 269
Bowater S. America Ltda. *Bowater Inc* 269
Bowater-Korea Co., Ltd. *Bowater Inc* 269
Bowden Building Corporation *BFC Financial Corp (B)* 236
Bowditch Insurance Corporation *South Financial Group Inc* 1663
Bowen Building, L.P. *Vornado Realty Trust* 1923
Bowen Development Company *Walgreen Co* 1929
Bowen Downhole LLC *National Oilwell Inc* 1244
Bowen Downhole, Inc. *National Oilwell Inc* 1244
Bowers & Merena Galleries, LLC *Escala Group Inc* 656
Bowers Eclipse Equipment Shanghai Co. Limited *Spear & Jackson Inc* 1676
Bowers Group plc *Spear & Jackson Inc* 1676
Bowers Metrology Limited *Spear & Jackson Inc* 1676
Bowers Metrology (UK) Limited *Spear & Jackson Inc* 1676
Bowery CBNA Loan Funding LLC *Citigroup Inc* 411
Bowery CFPI Loan Funding LLC *Citigroup Inc* 411
Bowes & Company, Inc., of New York *Aon Corp* 129
Bowes Publishers Limited *Sun Media Corp* 1719
Bowker Consultants Pte. Ltd. *Manpower Inc* 1119
Bowl America Duke Inc. *Bowl America Inc* 270
Bowl America of Florida Inc. *Bowl America Inc* 270
Bowl America Shirley Inc. *Bowl America Inc* 270
Bowler Housing L.P. *Wachovia Corp* 1928
Bowling Green Associates Intermediate, LLC *GMH Communities Trust* 802
Bowling Green Associates, LLC *GMH Communities Trust* 802
Bowling Green Medical Clinic - Greenview, LLC *HCA Inc* 855
Bowling Green Radiation Therapy Associates, LLP *Universal Health Services Inc* 1869
Bowmar/A.L.I., Inc. *White Electronic Designs Corp* 1957
Bowne Business Communications, Inc. *Bowne & Co Inc* 270
Bowne Enterprise Solutions, LLC *Bowne & Co Inc* 270
Bowne International de Mexico, S.A. de C.V. *Bowne & Co Inc* 270
Bowne International Holdings GmbH *Bowne & Co Inc* 270
Bowne International, LLC *Bowne & Co Inc* 270
Bowne International, Ltd. *Bowne & Co Inc* 270
Bowne International, SAS *Bowne & Co Inc* 270
Bowne Japan& Co, Inc. *Bowne & Co Inc* 270
Bowne Litigation Solutions, LP *Bowne & Co Inc* 270
Bowne MBC, LLC *Bowne & Co Inc* 270
Bowne of Atlanta, Inc. *Bowne & Co Inc* 270
Bowne of Boston, Inc. *Bowne & Co Inc* 270
Bowne of Canada, Ltd. *Bowne & Co Inc* 270
Bowne of Chicago, Inc. *Bowne & Co Inc* 270
Bowne of Cleveland, Inc. *Bowne & Co Inc* 270
Bowne of Dallas Limited Partnership *Bowne & Co Inc* 270
Bowne of Europe, B.V *Bowne & Co Inc* 270
Bowne of Gibraltar B.V *Bowne & Co Inc* 270
Bowne of Los Angeles, Inc. *Bowne & Co Inc* 270
Bowne of New York City, LLC *Bowne & Co Inc* 270
Bowne of Phoenix, Inc. *Bowne & Co Inc* 270
Bowne of South Bend, Inc. *Bowne & Co Inc* 270
Bowne of the Netherlands B.V *Bowne & Co Inc* 270
Bowne Solutions, LLC *Bowne & Co Inc* 270
Bowne Technology Enterprise, LLC *Bowne & Co Inc* 270
Bowne& Co., Inc. *Bowne & Co Inc* 270
Bowring and Minet (Swaziland) (Pty) Ltd. *Aon Corp* 129
Bowring (Bermuda) Investments Ltd. *Marsh & McLennan Cos Inc* 1125
Bowring Marine Limited *Marsh & McLennan Cos Inc* 1125
Bowring Risk Management Limited (In Liquidation) *Marsh & McLennan Cos Inc* 1125
BowSteel Corporation *Ceragon Networks Ltd* 367
BowSteel Corporation *Sba Communications Corp* 1588
BowSteel Corporation *RTI International Metals Inc* 1565
BowSteel of Texas Corporation *Sba Communications Corp* 1588
BowSteel of Texas Corporation *RTI International Metals Inc* 1565
BowSteel of Texas Corporation *Ceragon Networks Ltd* 367
BowTex Energy, Inc. *Calpine Corp* 311
Bowthorpe EMP Limited *Tyco International Ltd* 1838
Bowthorpe Industries Limited *Tyco International Ltd* 1838
Bowyang Nominees Pty Limited *Citigroup Inc* 411
Box Brothers Realty Investments Company *Helix Energy Solutions Group Inc* 866
Box Church Gas Gathering LLC. *St Mary Land & Exploration Co* 1687
Box Resources, Inc. *Helix Energy Solutions Group Inc* 866
Boxcarrier (No.1) Corp. *Danaos Corp* 525
Boxcarrier (No.2) Corp. *Danaos Corp* 525
Boxcarrier (No.3) Corp. *Danaos Corp* 525
Boxcarrier (No.4) Corp. *Danaos Corp* 525
Boxcarrier (No.5) Corp. *Danaos Corp* 525
Boxer Building LLC *Wachovia Corp* 1928
Boxer Cross, Inc. *Applied Materials Inc* 136
Boxmore Cape (pty) Limited *Chesapeake Corp* 382
Boxmore Cleland Ltd *Chesapeake Corp* 382
Boxmore Emballage Sa *Chesapeake Corp* 382
Boxmore International Ltd *Chesapeake Corp* 382
Boxmore Packaging Limited *Chesapeake Corp* 382

Dana World Trade Corporation *Dana Corp* 525
Dana (Wuxi) Technology Co. Ltd. *Dana Corp* 525
Dana-Albarus Industria E Comercio De Autopecas Ltda. *Dana Corp* 525
Danaflex Packaging Corporation Limited *Alcan Inc* 54
Danaher Canada Partners Inc. *Danaher Corp* 525
Danaher Canadian Finance LP *Danaher Corp* 525
Danaher Canadian Holdings LP *Danaher Corp* 525
Danaher Corporation *Danaher Corp* 525
Danaher Dental Technology Investments, Inc. *Danaher Corp* 525
Danaher Evolution GmbH *Danaher Corp* 525
Danaher Finance APS *Danaher Corp* 525
Danaher Finance Company *Danaher Corp* 525
Danaher Finance Company AB *Danaher Corp* 525
Danaher Finance Company LTD *Danaher Corp* 525
Danaher Finance Company, LLC *Danaher Corp* 525
Danaher Foundation *Danaher Corp* 525
Danaher GbR *Danaher Corp* 525
Danaher Holding B.V. *Danaher Corp* 525
Danaher Holding Company ApS *Danaher Corp* 525
Danaher Holding GmbH *Danaher Corp* 525
Danaher Hong Kong Finance Ltd *Danaher Corp* 525
Danaher Hong Kong Ltd. *Danaher Corp* 525
Danaher Iceland Finance Company EHF *Danaher Corp* 525
Danaher ICG Japan Co. LTD. *Danaher Corp* 525
Danaher Industrial Controls GmbH *Danaher Corp* 525
Danaher Insurance Company *Danaher Corp* 525
Danaher Linear GmbH *Danaher Corp* 525
Danaher Luxembourg Sarl *Danaher Corp* 525
Danaher Motion GmbH& Co. KG *Danaher Corp* 525
Danaher Motion i Flen AB *Danaher Corp* 525
Danaher Motion Inc. *Danaher Corp* 525
Danaher Motion India *Danaher Corp* 525
Danaher Motion Israel Ltd. (Servotech) *Danaher Corp* 525
Danaher Motion Japan Co. Ltd. *Danaher Corp* 525
Danaher Motion LLC *Danaher Corp* 525
Danaher Motion S.A. *Danaher Corp* 525
Danaher Motion S.r.l. *Danaher Corp* 525
Danaher Motion s.r.o *Danaher Corp* 525
Danaher Motion SARL *Danaher Corp* 525
Danaher Motion Saro AB *Danaher Corp* 525
Danaher Motion Stockholm AB *Danaher Corp* 525
Danaher Motion Technology, LLC *Danaher Corp* 525
Danaher Power Solutions, LLC *Danaher Corp* 525
Danaher Setra-ICG (Tianjin) Co. Ltd. *Danaher Corp* 525
Danaher Tax Administration ApS *Danaher Corp* 525
Danaher Tool Group *Danaher Corp* 525
Danaher Tool Shandong Co. Ltd. *Danaher Corp* 525
Danaher Tool (Shanghai) Ltd. *Danaher Corp* 525
Danaher UK Finance Inc. *Danaher Corp* 525
Danaher UK Industries Ltd. *Danaher Corp* 525
Danaher UK Partners *Danaher Corp* 525
Danaher Verwaltungs GmbH *Danaher Corp* 525
Danaven Rubber Products, C.A. *Dana Corp* 525
Danayai ve Ticaret AS [aka Solectron Turkey] *Solectron Corp* 1653
DANB Texas, Inc. *Dave & Busters Inc* 529
Danbury Auto Partnership *United Auto Group Inc* 1855
DANBURY MALL LLC *Macerich Company (The)* 1106
DANBURY MALL ASSOCIATES *Macerich Company (The)* 1106
DANBURY MALL SPC INC *Macerich Company (The)* 1106
Danbury Printing & Litho, Inc. *Banta Corp* 215
Danbury Suites, LLC *Hersha Hospitality Trust* 872
Danbury Surgical Center, Inc. *HealthSouth Corp* 861
Danby Pty Limited *Tyco International Ltd* 1838
Dance Nation Productions Inc. *CKX Inc* 418
Dandorr LLC *Dana Corp* 525
Dandy A/S *Cadbury Schweppes Plc* 302
Danel Naarra, S.A *Fluor Corp* 728
Danel nternatonal Corporaton *Fluor Corp* 728
Danforth Apartment Owners, LLC *Tarragon Corp* 1751
Danforth Hospital, Inc. *HCA Inc* 855
Danger Productions Inc *Viacom Inc* 1902
Danger Productions Inc. *CBS Corp* 349
Daniel Automation Company *Emerson Electric Co* 623
Daniel Communication, Inc. *Global Imaging Systems Inc* 794
Daniel Electrical Contractors, Inc. *Integrated Electrical Services Inc* 956
Daniel Electrical of Treasure Coast, Inc. *Integrated Electrical Services Inc* 956
Daniel En-Fab Systems, Inc. *Emerson Electric Co* 623
Daniel Europe Limited *Emerson Electric Co* 623
Daniel Industrial, Inc. *Emerson Electric Co* 623
Daniel Industries Canada Inc. *Emerson Electric Co* 623
Daniel Industries Limited *Emerson Electric Co* 623
Daniel Industries, Inc. *Emerson Electric Co* 623
Daniel Integrated Technologies, Inc. *Integrated Electrical Services Inc* 956
Daniel International Limited *Emerson Electric Co* 623
Daniel Island HPR, LLC *First Citizens BanCorp Inc* 700
Daniel M. Friedman & Associates, Inc. *Steven Madden Ltd* 1704
Daniel Measurement and Control, Inc. *Emerson Electric Co* 623
Daniel Measurement and Control, S. de R.L. de C.V. *Emerson Electric Co* 623
Daniel Measurement Services, Inc. *Emerson Electric Co* 623
Daniel Medical Systems, Inc. *Rotech Healthcare Inc NEW* 1560
Daniel Woodhead Company *Woodhead Industries Inc* 1974
Daniels Corporate Advisory Company, Inc. *INfe Human Resources Inc* 937
Daniels Pharmaceuticals Limited *Cardinal Health Inc* 332
Danielson Holding Corporation *Covanta Holding Corp* 491
Danjan (Pty) Ltd *BHP Billiton Ltd* 237
Danjan (Pty) Ltd *BHP Billiton Plc* 237
Danjan (Pty) Ltd *Bayer Schering Pharma Aktiengesellschaft* 221
Danka Australasia Pty Ltd. *Danka Business Systems Plc* 525
Danka Australia Pty Ltd. *Danka Business Systems Plc* 525
Danka Austria GmbH *Danka Business Systems Plc* 525
Danka Belgium NV/SA *Danka Business Systems Plc* 525
Danka Business Finance Ltd. *Danka Business Systems Plc* 525
Danka Canada, Inc. *Pitney Bowes Inc* 1434
Danka Danmark A/S *Danka Business Systems Plc* 525
Danka Danmark Holding A/S *Danka Business Systems Plc* 525
Danka Datakey Pty Ltd. *Danka Business Systems Plc* 525
Danka Deutschland Holding GmbH *Danka Business Systems Plc* 525
Danka Deutschland Leasing GmbH *Danka Business Systems Plc* 525
Danka Distribution BV *Danka Business Systems Plc* 525
Danka Distributors Pty Ltd. *Danka Business Systems Plc* 525
Danka Equipment Rentals Limited *CIT Group Inc* 410
Danka Europe BV *Danka Business Systems Plc* 525
Danka Europe BV (Netherlands) *Danka Business Systems Plc* 525
Danka France SA *Danka Business Systems Plc* 525
Danka Group BV *Danka Business Systems Plc* 525
Danka Holding Company *Danka Business Systems Plc* 525
Danka Holding France Sarl *Danka Business Systems Plc* 525
Danka Holdings Belgium NV/SA *Danka Business Systems Plc* 525
Danka Holdings BV *Danka Business Systems Plc* 525
Danka Holdings Iberia SA *Danka Business Systems Plc* 525
Danka Holdings New Zealand Ltd. *Danka Business Systems Plc* 525
Danka Holdings SA *Danka Business Systems Plc* 525
Danka Holdings Sarl *Danka Business Systems Plc* 525
Danka Holdings SpA *Danka Business Systems Plc* 525
Danka Holdings Sweden AB *Danka Business Systems Plc* 525
Danka Imaging Distribution, Inc. *Danka Business Systems Plc* 525
Danka Investment Holdings Ltd. *Danka Business Systems Plc* 525
Danka Italia SpA *Danka Business Systems Plc* 525
Danka Japan k.k. *Danka Business Systems Plc* 525
Danka Luxembourg Sarl *Danka Business Systems Plc* 525
Danka Management Company, Inc. *Danka Business Systems Plc* 525
Danka Management II Company, Inc *Danka Business Systems Plc* 525
Danka Miet& Leasing GmbH *Danka Business Systems Plc* 525
Danka Netherlands BV *Danka Business Systems Plc* 525
Danka New Zealand Ltd. *Danka Business Systems Plc* 525
Danka Norge AS *Danka Business Systems Plc* 525
Danka Office Imaging BV *Danka Business Systems Plc* 525
Danka Office Imaging Company *Danka Business Systems Plc* 525
Danka Office Imaging (Europe) Ltd. *Danka Business Systems Plc* 525
Danka Office Imaging Ireland Branch *Danka Business Systems Plc* 525
Danka Office Imaging Japan Branch *Danka Business Systems Plc* 525
Danka Office Imaging Ltd. *Danka Business Systems Plc* 525
Danka Office Imaging SA *Danka Business Systems Plc* 525
Danka Office Products BV *Danka Business Systems Plc* 525
Danka Services International BV *Danka Business Systems Plc* 525
Danka Services International Ltd. *Danka Business Systems Plc* 525
Danka Services International NV *Danka Business Systems Plc* 525
Danka Services International SA *Danka Business Systems Plc* 525
Danka Servicios SA (Venezuela) *Danka Business Systems Plc* 525
Danka Suisse SA *Danka Business Systems Plc* 525
Danka Sverige AB *Danka Business Systems Plc* 525
Danka Systems Pty Ltd. *Danka Business Systems Plc* 525
Danka Tower Australia Pty Ltd. *Danka Business Systems Plc* 525
Danka UK Holdings Ltd. *Danka Business Systems Plc* 525
Danka UK PLC *Danka Business Systems Plc* 525
Dankalux Sarl *Danka Business Systems Plc* 525
Dankalux Sarl& Co. SCA (Partnership) *Danka Business Systems Plc* 525
DanMar Transmission LLC *Edison International* 604
DanMar Transmission LLCLP *Edison International* 604
DanMar Transmission LLCLP *Edison International* 604
DanMar Transmission LLCLP *Edison International* 604
DanMar Transmission LLCLP *Edison International* 604
DanMar Transmission LLCLP *Edison International* 604
Danmasa S.A. de C.V. *Emerson Electric Co* 623
Danner, Inc. *Lacrosse Footwear Inc* 1049
Danop Ltd. *Chiquita Brands International Inc* 400
Dansommer A/ S *Avis Budget Group Inc* 190
Dante Coal Company *Brinks Co* 281
Dantean (Thailand) Company, Limited *Dana Corp* 525
Dantor S.A. *Becton Dickinson & Co* 227
Dantorque A/S *Emerson Electric Co* 623
Dantz Development (UK), Limited. *EMC Corp* 620
Danube Ltd. *ConocoPhillips* 469
Danube Shipping LLC *Omi Corp Marshall Islands* 1337
Danube Travel Limited *Sabre Holdings Corp* 1572
Danvers-DCII, Inc *Group 1 Automotive Inc* 826
Danvers-DCIII, Inc *Group 1 Automotive Inc* 826
Danvers-N, Inc *Group 1 Automotive Inc* 826
Danvers-NII, Inc *Group 1 Automotive Inc* 826
Danvers-S, Inc *Group 1 Automotive Inc* 826
Danvers-SB, Inc *Group 1 Automotive Inc* 826
Danvers-SU, LLC *Group 1 Automotive Inc* 826
Danvers-T, Inc *Group 1 Automotive Inc* 826
Danvers-TII, Inc *Group 1 Automotive Inc* 826
Danvers-TIII, Inc *Group 1 Automotive Inc* 826
Danvers-TL, Inc *Group 1 Automotive Inc* 826
Danville Community Development Corporation *Wachovia Corp* 1928
Danville Place I, LLC *Brookdale Senior Living Inc* 285
Danville Place Special Management, LLC *Brookdale Senior Living Inc* 285
Danville Regional Medical Center, LLC *Lifepoint Hospitals Inc* 1076
Danville Surgery Center, LP *HealthSouth Corp* 861
Danville, Pennsylvania 17821 *Fulton Financial Corp* 754
Danzansky-Goldberg Memorial Chapels, Inc. *Service Corp International* 1614
DAP Holdings, LLC *RPM International Inc* 1564
DAP Products Inc. *RPM International Inc* 1564
DAP Technologies Corp. *Roper Industries Inc* 1558
DAP Technologies Limited *Roper Industries Inc* 1558
DAP Technologies SARL *Roper Industries Inc* 1558
DAP Technologies, Ltd. *Roper Industries Inc* 1558
DAP Trucking, Inc. *LKQ Corp* 1088
DAP Trucking, LLC *LKQ Corp* 1088
Daploma International A/S *Applied Digital Solutions Inc* 135
Dapper Tire Co., Inc. *Goodyear Tire & Rubber Com (The)* 811
DAPT 51 Corp *Franklin Credit Mgmt Corp* 744
Daqing Oilfield Company Limited *PetroChina Co Ltd* 1416
Daqing Yu Shu Lin Oilfield Company Limited *PetroChina Co Ltd* 1416
Daquing Computalog Rainbow Geotechnical Development Corp. Ltd. *Weatherford International Ltd* 1940
Darby Asia Investors (HK), Ltd. *Franklin Resources Inc* 745
Darby Asia Investors, Ltd. *Franklin Resources Inc* 745
Darby CEE Founder Partner II, LLC *Franklin Resources Inc* 745
Darby Converging Europe founder Partner, L.P. *Franklin Resources Inc* 745
Darby Development Corp. *Vornado Realty Trust* 1923
Darby Development, L.L.C. *Vornado Realty Trust* 1923
Darby Emerging Markets Income Investments LLC *Franklin Resources Inc* 745
Darby Emerging Markets Income Investments, Ltd. *Franklin Resources Inc* 745
Darby Emerging Markets Investments, LDC *Franklin Resources Inc* 745
Darby Europe Mezzanine Management *Franklin Resources Inc* 745
Darby Global SICAV Managers, LLC *Franklin Resources Inc* 745
Darby Holdings, Inc. *Franklin Resources Inc* 745
Darby Latin American Mezzanine Investments *Franklin Resources Inc* 745
Darby Navigation Corp. *TBS International Ltd* 1754
Darby Overseas Investments, Ltd. *Franklin Resources Inc* 745
Darby Overseas Partners, L.P. *Franklin Resources Inc* 745
DARBY TOWNHOUSES ASSOCIATES *Apartment Investment and Management Company* 130
DARBY TOWNHOUSES LIMITED PARTNERSHIP *Apartment Investment and Management Company* 130
DARBY TOWNHOUSES PRESERVATION GENERAL PARTNER, L.L.C. *Apartment Investment and Management Company* 130
Darby-BBVA Latin American Investors, Ltd. *Franklin Resources Inc* 745
Darcom International, L.p. *Newpark Resources Inc* 1280
Darcy-Joliet, LLC *Lennar Corp* 1068
Darden Financial Services, L.p. *Centex Corp* 360
Dare Limited *Morgan Stanley* 1215
Darex CIS LLC *W. R. Grace & Co* 1927
Darex Puerto Rico, Inc. *W. R. Grace & Co* 1927
Darex UK Limited *W. R. Grace & Co* 1927
Dari Valdai *Wimm-Bill-Dann Foods OJSC* 1965
Darien Compania Armadora S.A. *Diana Shipping Inc* 552
Darien Lake Management Company Inc. *Six Flags Inc* 1640
Darien Lake Theme Park and Camping Resort, Inc. *Six Flags Inc* 1640
Darilor Sociedad Anonima *Eli Lilly & Co* 616
Darius International Inc. *Quigley Corp* 1503
Darley Investments Limited *Ryanair Holdings Plc* 1569
Darlington Inc. *EDO Corp* 604
Darlington Raceway of South Carolina, LLC *International Speedway CL B* 972
Darnay B.V. *Barclays Plc* 216
Darnelle Enterprises Ltd *Reading International Inc* 1518
Dart de Venezuela, C.A. *Tupperware Brands Corp* 1834
Dart do Brasil Industria e Comercio Ltda. *Tupperware Brands Corp* 1834
Dart Far East Sdn. Bhd. *Tupperware Brands Corp* 1834
Dart Industries Hong Kong Limited *Tupperware Brands Corp* 1834
Dart Industries Inc. *Tupperware Brands Corp* 1834
Dart Industries (New Zealand) Limited *Tupperware Brands Corp* 1834
Dart Resorts Inc. *Altria Group Inc* 74
Dart, S.A. de C.V. *Tupperware Brands Corp* 1834
Darta Saving Life Assurance Ltd. *Allianz* 63
Dartco Manufacturing Inc. *Tupperware Brands Corp* 1834
Dartek Corporation *Systemax Inc* 1742
Dartmouth Petroleum, Ltd. *Barnwell Industries Inc* 217
Darwin Grey Ltd *WPP Group Plc* 1979
Darwin Group, Inc. *Alleghany Corp* 58
Darwin LNG Pty. Ltd. *ConocoPhillips* 469
Darwin National Assurance Company *Alleghany Corp* 58
Darwin Precisions (L) Corp *AU Optronics Corp* 177
Darwin Precisions (Suzhou) Corp. *AU Optronics Corp* 177
Darwin Professional Underwriters, Inc. *Alleghany Corp* 58
Darwin Select Insurance Company *Alleghany Corp* 58
Darwish Consulting Engineers *Arcadis* 142
DAS Agricultural Investment Holding Company Ltd. *Dow Chemical Co* 573
Das Beste aus Readers Digest AG/Selection du Readers Digest SA/Selzione dal Readers *Reader's Digest Association Inc* 1517
DAS Holdings Inc. *Omnicom Group Inc* 1338
DAS Productions Ltd. *News Corp Ltd (The)* 1281
DAS Productions, Inc. *News Corp Ltd (The)* 1281
Dascit/White& Winston, Inc. *National Financial Partners Corp* 1241
Daser Agro SA *Dow Chemical Co* 573
DASH Limited *Morgan Stanley* 1215
DashAmerica, Inc. *Nautilus Inc* 1252
Dashiell Holdings Corporation *InfraSource Services Inc* 942
Dashiell Ltd *InfraSource Services Inc* 942
Dasibi Environmental Corp *Universal Detection Technology* 1867
DASIS ASSOCIATES LLC *Lexington Realty Trust* 1071
DASIS MANAGER LLC *Lexington Realty Trust* 1071
Dassault Data Services *Dassault Systemes* 526
Dassault Systmes KK *Dassault Systemes* 526
Dassault Systmes Services LLC *Dassault Systemes* 526
Dasytec Usa Incorporated *National Instruments Corp* 1243
DAT Productions, Inc. *News Corp Ltd (The)* 1281
Data Analysis & Research (DAR) LTD *Pharmaceutical Product Development Inc* 1422
Data Broadcasting Corp. *Interactive Data Corp* 960
Data Broadcasting Corporation *Pearson Plc* 1399
Data Communications 2000, Inc. *Black Box Corp* 252
Data Concepts International,Inc. *Bally Technologies Inc* 202
Data Dialog, Inc. *Dialog Group Inc* 549
Data Distilleries Gmbh *SPSS Inc* 1684
Data Distilleries United Kingdom Ltd *SPSS Inc* 1684
Data Entry International Limited *R.R. Donnelley & Sons Co* 1506
Data General Argentina S.A. *EMC Corp* 620
Data General BVI, Ltd. *EMC Corp* 620
Data General do Brasil Ltda. *EMC Corp* 620
Data General Gesellschaft m.b.H. *EMC Corp* 620
Data General Hong Kong Limited *EMC Corp* 620
Data General International, Inc. *EMC Corp* 620
Data I/O Canada Corporation *Data I/O Corp* 526
Data I/O China, Ltd *Data I/O Corp* 526
Data I/O Electronics (Shanghai) Co. Ltd *Data I/O Corp* 526
Data I/O FSC International, Inc. *Data I/O Corp* 526
Data I/O GmbH *Data I/O Corp* 526
Data I/O Programacao de Sistemas Ltda *Data I/O Corp* 526
Data Information Management Systems, Inc. *Diebold Inc* 554
Data Management & Research, Inc *HealthStream Inc* 862
Data Management Consultants, Inc. *MPS Group Inc* 1222
Data Niche Associates, Inc. *IMS Health Inc* 931
Data On Call, Inc. *J2 Global Communications Inc* 999
Data Pathing Incorporated *NCR Corp* 1256
Data Pathing LLC *NCR Corp* 1256
Data Processing Printing and Supplies Limited *NCR Corp* 1256
Data Recorders Incorporated *Danaher Corp* 525
Data Recovery Services *First American Corp* 695
Data Research Technologies, Inc. *Fair Isaac Corp* 675
Data Trace Abstractor Services, LLC *First American Corp* 695
Data Trace Information Services II LLC *First American Corp* 695
Data Trace Information Services LLC *First American Corp* 695
Data Trace LLC *First American Corp* 695
Data Transfer Systems, Inc. *GTECH Holdings Corp* 832
Data Tree LLC *First American Corp* 695
Data Ventures, LLC *Coca-Cola Bottling Co Consolidated* 433
Data-Chain Solutions, Inc. *Fiserv Inc* 721
Data-Link Systems, LLC *Fiserv Inc* 721
Data-Tronics Corp. *Arkansas Best Corp* 149
Database Tools Development (Proprietary) Limited *NetIQ* 1263
Databeacon Inc. *Cognos Inc* 436
Datac Ltd.1 *H.B. Fuller Co* 837

Durham-Mudd Insurance Agency, Inc *Porter Bancorp Inc* ... 1449
Durlacher Nominees Limited *Barclays Plc* ... 216
Durmed Phrmceuticl Sles Corp. *Barr Pharmaceuticals Inc* ... 217
Durmed Phrmceuticls Inc. *Barr Pharmaceuticals Inc* ... 217
Durmed Reserch Inc. *Barr Pharmaceuticals Inc* ... 217
Duro Enzyme Solutions Inc. *EAPI Entertainment Inc* ... 591
Duro Enzyme Solutions Inc. *EAPI Entertainment Inc* ... 591
Duro Metal Manufacturing, Inc. *Leggett & Platt Inc* ... 1067
Durocraft International, Inc. *Craftmade International Inc* ... 494
Durrett Sheppard Steel Co. Inc. *Reliance Steel & Aluminum Co* . 1528
DUSA Acquisition Corp. *Dusa Pharmaceuticals Inc* ... 582
DUSA Pharmaceuticals New York, Inc. *Dusa Pharmaceuticals Inc* ... 582
Duska Scientific Co. *Duska Therapeutics Inc* ... 582
Dusty Corporation *Harrah's Entertainment Inc* ... 848
Dutch American Manufacturers (D.A.M.) B.V. *Cardinal Health Inc* ... 332
Dutch Hill Realty Corp. *U.S.B. Holding Co Inc* ... 1842
Dutch Housing, Inc *Champion Mortgage* ... 372
Dutch Private Limited Liability Company *Luminex Corp* ... 1100
Dutch Valley Food Company, Inc. *Weis Markets Inc* ... 1943
Dutch, Inc. *W-H Energy Services* ... 1926
Dutchess Mall Sewage Plant, Inc. *J.W. Mays Inc* ... 999
Dutchess Resource Management, Inc. *Viacom Inc* ... 1902
Dutchess Resource Management, Inc. *CBS Corp* ... 349
Dutchmen Manufacturing, Inc. *Thor Industries Inc* ... 1790
DutchWest Oil Company *Crimson Exploration Inc* ... 500
Dutonorte Investimentos Ltda *El Paso Corp* ... 609
Dutton, Inc. *Stewart Enterprises Inc* ... 1704
Duvalpilot Equipment Outfitters, LLC *Terex Corp* ... 1777
Duvanska Industrija Nis (DIN) *Altria Group Inc* ... 74
Duvir Holdings Pty Ltd *News Corp Ltd (The)* ... 1281
Duxford Escrow, Inc *Fidelity National Financial Inc* ... 690
Duxford Escrow, Inc. *William Lyon Homes* ... 1960
Duxford Financial, Inc. *William Lyon Homes* ... 1960
Duxford Title Reinsurance Company *William Lyon Homes* ... 1960
Duxford, LLC *Equity Residential* ... 654
Duxtech Pty Ltd. *Thermadyne Holdings Corp* ... 1786
Duyvis B.v. *Sara Lee Corp* ... 1585
Duyvis Production B.v. *Sara Lee Corp* ... 1585
DVA Healthcare Nephrology Partners, Inc. *Davita Inc* ... 530
DVA Healthcare of Maryland, Inc. *Davita Inc* ... 530
DVA Healthcare of Massachusetts, Inc. *Davita Inc* ... 530
DVA Healthcare Of New London, LLC *Davita Inc* ... 530
DVA Healthcare of Norwich, LLC *Davita Inc* ... 530
DVA Healthcare of Pennsylvania, Inc. *Davita Inc* ... 530
DVA Healthcare Of Tuscaloosa, LLC *Davita Inc* ... 530
DVA Healthcare Procurement Services, Inc. *Davita Inc* ... 530
DVA Healthcare Renal Care, Inc. *Davita Inc* ... 530
DVA Healthcare-Southwest Ohio, LLC *Davita Inc* ... 530
DVA Laboratory Services, Inc. *Davita Inc* ... 530
DVA Nephrology Partners, Inc. *Davita Inc* ... 530
DVA Nephrology Services, Inc. *Davita Inc* ... 530
DVA of New York, Inc. *Davita Inc* ... 530
DVA Renal Healthcare, Inc. *Davita Inc* ... 530
DVA Supply Corp. *Davita Inc* ... 530
DVA/Washington University Healthcare of Greater St. *Davita Inc* ... 530
DVDO, Inc. *Silicon Image Inc* ... 1630
Dvega Limited *GFI Group Inc* ... 785
DVGM & Associates *Penton Media Inc* ... 1406
DVL Acquisition Sub, Inc. *C. R. Bard Inc* ... 299
DVL Mortgage Holdings, LLC *DVL Inc* ... 582
DVREX, Inc. *Miller Industries Inc* ... 1192
DVS Electronics Pvt. Ltd. *Digital Video Systems Inc* ... 557
DVS Electronics, Inc *Digital Video Systems Inc* ... 557
DVS Korea Co., Ltd *Digital Video Systems Inc* ... 557
DVT Corporation *Cognex Corp* ... 435
DVUA Massachusetts, Inc. *United America Indemnity Ltd* ... 1854
DVUA North Carolina, Inc. *United America Indemnity Ltd* ... 1854
DVUA of New Jersey, Inc. *United America Indemnity Ltd* ... 1854
DVUA of New York, Inc. *United America Indemnity Ltd* ... 1854
DVUA of Ohio, Inc. *United America Indemnity Ltd* ... 1854
DVUA Pittsburgh, Inc. *United America Indemnity Ltd* ... 1854
DVUA South Carolina, Inc. *United America Indemnity Ltd* ... 1854
DVUA Virginia, Inc. *United America Indemnity Ltd* ... 1854
DVUA West Virginia, Inc. *United America Indemnity Ltd* ... 1854
DW Administrators Inc. *Morgan Stanley* ... 1215
DW Aviation Co *Pulte Homes Inc* ... 1489
DW Dexco Investment LLC *Dow Chemical Co* ... 573
DW Holding, LLC *Woodhead Industries Inc* ... 1974
DW Homebuilding Co *Pulte Homes Inc* ... 1489
Dw Technologies, Inc. *Interpublic Group of Companies Inc* ... 975
DW Window Coverings Holding, Inc. *Morgan Stanley* ... 1215
DWA Finance I L.L.C. *Dreamworks Animation SKG Inc* ... 575
DWD Construction Services, Inc. *Hamptons Luxury Homes Inc* ... 841
DWFC, LLC *Deerfield Triarc Capital Corp* ... 535
Dwights Acquisition Corp. *IHS Inc* ... 921
DWM (Hong Kong) Holdings Ltd. *Prudential Financial Inc* ... 1483
DWN Properties, Inc. *Stewart Enterprises Inc* ... 1704
DWP Bates Technology LLC *WPP Group Plc* ... 1979
DWP/USI of Southern California Insurance Agency, Inc. *USI Holdings Corp* ... 1880
DWT Gateway I, LLC *Duke Realty Corp* ... 580
DWT Gateway II, LLC *Duke Realty Corp* ... 580
DX Company, Inc. *Alloy Inc* ... 67
DXP Acquisition, Inc. *DXP Enterprises Inc* ... 583
Dy 4, Inc. *Curtiss-Wright Corp* ... 514
DY&R Ltd *WPP Group Plc* ... 1979
Dyadic International (USA), Inc. *Dyadic International Inc* ... 583
Dyadic International, Spo ka z orgraniczon odpwiedzialno ci *Dyadic International Inc* ... 583
Dyadic Nederland BV *Dyadic International Inc* ... 583
Dyadic Real Estate Holdings, Inc. *Dyadic International Inc* ... 583
Dyax B.V. *Dyax Corp* ... 583
Dyax Holdings B.V. *Dyax Corp* ... 583
Dyax S.A. *Dyax Corp* ... 583
Dycom Aviation, LLC *Dycom Industries Inc* ... 583
Dycom Capital Management, Inc. *Dycom Industries Inc* ... 583
Dycom Corporate Identity, Inc. *Dycom Industries Inc* ... 583
Dycom Identity, LLC *Dycom Industries Inc* ... 583
Dycom Investments, Inc. *Dycom Industries Inc* ... 583
Dye Candy Company *Chase General Corp* ... 377
Dyelights, Inc. *Payless Shoesource Inc* ... 1394
Dyersburg Clinic Corp. *Community Health Systems Inc* ... 454
Dyersburg Hospital Corporation *Community Health Systems Inc* ... 454
DYHP Acquisitions, Inc. *Dynamic Health Products Inc* ... 584
Dyhr / Hagen A/S *WPP Group Plc* ... 1979
Dymax Corporation *C. R. Bard Inc* ... 299
Dymo Holdings SPRL *Newell Rubbermaid Inc* ... 1278
Dyn Network Management, Inc. *Computer Sciences Corp* ... 462
Dyn Specialty Contracting, Inc. *Emcor Group Inc* ... 621
Dyna Drill Technologies, Inc. *W-H Energy Services* ... 1926
Dyna-Drill Technologies Canada LP *W-H Energy Services* ... 1926
Dyna-Drill Technologies Canada Ltd. *W-H Energy Services* ... 1926
Dynacare - Gamma Medical Laboratories *Laboratory Corp of America Holdings* ... 1048
Dynacare - Kasper Medical Laboratories *Laboratory Corp of America Holdings* ... 1048
Dynacare Canada Inc. *Laboratory Corp of America Holdings* ... 1048
Dynacare Company *Laboratory Corp of America Holdings* ... 1048
Dynacare G.P. Inc. *Laboratory Corp of America Holdings* ... 1048
Dynacare Gamma Institutional Laboratory Services Limited *Laboratory Corp of America Holdings* ... 1048
Dynacare Holdco LLC *Laboratory Corp of America Holdings* ... 1048
Dynacare International Inc. *Laboratory Corp of America Holdings* ... 1048
Dynacare Kasper Medical Laboratories Inc. *Laboratory Corp of America Holdings* ... 1048
Dynacare Kasper Medical Laboratories (Northern Alberta) Inc. *Laboratory Corp of America Holdings* ... 1048
Dynacare Kasper Medical Sales Inc. *Laboratory Corp of America Holdings* ... 1048
Dynacare Laboratories, Inc. *Laboratory Corp of America Holdings* ... 1048
Dynacare Louisiana, LLC *Laboratory Corp of America Holdings* ... 1048
Dynacare Northwest Inc. *Laboratory Corp of America Holdings* ... 1048
Dynacare Realty Inc. *Laboratory Corp of America Holdings* ... 1048
Dynacare Southwest Laboratories, Inc. *Laboratory Corp of America Holdings* ... 1048
Dynacare US Financing LLC *Laboratory Corp of America Holdings* ... 1048
Dynacare X-Ray Services Limited *Laboratory Corp of America Holdings* ... 1048
Dynaf Bolivia S.A. *El Paso Corp* ... 609
Dynal Biotech ASA *Invitrogen Corp* ... 983
Dynal Biotech (Beijing) Ltd. *Invitrogen Corp* ... 983
Dynal Biotech Diagnostics AS *Invitrogen Corp* ... 983
Dynal Biotech Holding AS *Invitrogen Corp* ... 983
Dynal Biotech Inc. *Invitrogen Corp* ... 983
Dynal Biotech LLC *Invitrogen Corp* ... 983
Dynal Biotech Ltd. *Invitrogen Corp* ... 983
Dynal Biotech Pty. Ltd. *Invitrogen Corp* ... 983
Dynal Biotech S.A. *Invitrogen Corp* ... 983
Dynalco Controls Corporation *Crane Co* ... 494
Dynalex, Inc. *Alltel Corp* ... 69
Dynamet Incorporated *Carpenter Technology Corp* ... 337
Dynamex Canada Holdings, Inc. *Dynamex Inc* ... 584
Dynamex Fleet Services, Inc. *Dynamex Inc* ... 584
Dynamex Franchise Holdings, Inc. *Dynamex Inc* ... 584
Dynamex Operations East Inc. *Dynamex Inc* ... 584
Dynamex Operations West Inc. *Dynamex Inc* ... 584
Dynamex Provincial Couriers, Inc. *Dynamex Inc* ... 584
Dynamex Resources Corporation *Resource Finance & Investment Ltd* ... 1537
Dynamic Assets Limited *Payless Shoesource Inc* ... 1394
Dynamic Automation Systems Pty. Ltd. *Caterpillar Inc* ... 345
Dynamic Aviation, LLC(Indiana) *Steel Dynamics Inc* ... 1698
Dynamic Controls *Invacare Corp* ... 981
Dynamic Controls, Inc. *Catalina Marketing Corp* ... 344
Dynamic Decisions Pty. Ltd. *Applix Inc* ... 137
Dynamic Details, Incorporated (Dynamic Details) *DDi Corp* ... 532
Dynamic Europe Ltd *Invacare Corp* ... 981
Dynamic Financial Consultants, LLC *Dynamic Health Products Inc* ... 584
Dynamic Graphics International, Limited *Jupitermedia Corp* ... 1014
Dynamic Graphics, Inc. *Jupitermedia Corp* ... 1014
Dynamic Healthtech Inc. *SKF Inc* ... 1641
Dynamic Leisure Group North America, Inc., *Dynamic Leisure Corp* ... 584
Dynamic Life Products, Inc. *Dynamic Health Products Inc* ... 584
Dynamic Logic Inc. *WPP Group Plc* ... 1979
Dynamic Maritime Co. *Aries Maritime Transport Ltd* ... 148
Dynamic Marketing I, Inc. *Dynamic Health Products Inc* ... 584
Dynamic Marketing Services Inc *WPP Group Plc* ... 1979
Dynamic Seals, Inc. *Parker-Hannifin Corp* ... 1387
Dynamic Services, Inc. *Fonar Corp* ... 732
Dynamic Soap, Inc. *Viacom Inc* ... 1902
Dynamic Soap, Inc. *CBS Corp* ... 349
Dynamic Telecommunications, Inc. *PCTEL Inc* ... 1396
Dynamicon B.V. *Arcadis* ... 142
Dynamics Corporation of America *CTS Corp* ... 511
dynamicsoft Inc. *Cisco Systems Inc* ... 409
Dynamit Nobel GmbH *Rockwood Holdings Inc* ... 1555
Dynamit Nobel Unterstützungsfonds GmbH *Rockwood Holdings Inc* ... 1555
Dynamo Acquisition Corporation *C&D Technologies Inc* ... 299
Dynapar Corporation *Danaher Corp* ... 525
Dynasol Elastmeros, S.A. *Repsol YPF* ... 1533
Dynasol Elastmeros, S.A. de C.V. *Repsol YPF* ... 1533
Dynasol Gestin, S.A. *Repsol YPF* ... 1533
Dynasol LLC *Repsol YPF* ... 1533
Dynasty Three Limited *Citigroup Inc* ... 411
Dynasty Three Ocean (Tianjin) Real Estate Co., Ltd. *Citigroup Inc* ... 411
Dynasty Two Limited *Citigroup Inc* ... 411
Dynasty Two Ocean (Tianjin) Real Estate Co., Ltd. *Citigroup Inc* ... 411
Dynatech Hong Kong Limited *JDS Uniphase Corp* ... 1005
Dynavax Asia Pte. Ltd. *Dynavax Technologies Corp* ... 586
Dynavest Nova Scotia Company *Applied Industrial Technologies Inc* ... 135
Dynavision Electronics Pte Ltd *Tyco International Ltd* ... 1838
DynCorp *Computer Sciences Corp* ... 462
DynCorp *Dyncorp International Inc* ... 586
DynCorp International LLC *Dyncorp International Inc* ... 586
DynCorp of Colorado, Inc. *Computer Sciences Corp* ... 462
Dync-A-Pak *Smurfit Stone Container Corp* ... 1650
DynEco International, Inc. *Dynamic Leisure Corp* ... 584
Dynegy Administrative Services Company *Dynegy Inc* ... 586
Dynegy Catlin Member *Dynegy Inc* ... 586
Dynegy Holdings Inc. *Dynegy Inc* ... 586
Dynegy Midwest Generation, Inc. *Dynegy Inc* ... 586
Dynegy Northeast Generation, Inc. *Dynegy Inc* ... 586
Dynegy Power Marketing, Inc. *Dynegy Inc* ... 586
Dyneon GmbH *3M Co* ... 2007
Dyneon LLC *3M Co* ... 2007
Dynex Commercial Services, Inc *Dynex Capital Inc* ... 586
Dynex Securities, Inc. *Dynex Capital Inc* ... 586
DynKePRO LLC *Computer Sciences Corp* ... 462
DynMcDermott Petroleum Operations Company *Computer Sciences Corp* ... 462
DynMeridian Corporation *Computer Sciences Corp* ... 462
DynPort Vaccine Company LLC *Computer Sciences Corp* ... 462
DynTek Canada,Inc. *Dyntek Inc* ... 587
DynTek Services,Inc. *Dyntek Inc* ... 587
Dyo Printing Inks A.S. *Akzo Nobel* ... 49
Dyoser Investments SL *Western Union Company (The)* ... 1952
Dyson Creek Coal Company, LLC *Peabody Energy Corp* ... 1398
DZA Brands, LLC *Delhaize Group* ... 537
E & C Pub, Inc. *Elephant & Castle Group Inc* ... 616
E & E Budapest Kft. *Ecology & Environment Inc* ... 600
E & E Drilling and Testing Co., Inc. *Ecology & Environment Inc* ... 600
E & E Umwelt-Beratung GmbH *Ecology & Environment Inc* ... 600
E & P Investment Corporation *Republic Services Inc* ... 1534
E Com Ventures, Inc. *Parlux Fragrances Inc* ... 1388
E Comrcio de Embalagens Ltda. *Bemis Co Inc* ... 230
E Commerce Group Products Inc. *First Data Corp* ... 703
E Commerce Group Products Inc. *Western Union Company (The)* ... 1952
E Commerce Group, Inc. *Western Union Company (The)* ... 1952
E Commerce Group, Inc. *First Data Corp* ... 703
E Cubed Technology, Inc. *Signature Leisure Inc* ... 1629
E Engineering Inc. *NTT DoCoMo Inc* ... 1314
E Engineering Kansai, Inc. *NTT DoCoMo Inc* ... 1314
E Engineering Kyushu Inc. *NTT DoCoMo Inc* ... 1314
E Engineering Tokai, Inc. *NTT DoCoMo Inc* ... 1314
E Entertainment UK Limited *Comcast Corp* ... 444
E Incorporated *Paragon Technologies Inc* ... 1384
E L Management LLC *Eli Lilly & Co* ... 616
E Leasing Company, LLC *Allied Waste Industries Inc* ... 66
E O W S Midland Company *Primeenergy Corp* ... 1467
E Pointe Properties I, Ltd. *RAIT Financial Trust* ... 1511
E Representacoes, Limitada *Owens Illinois Inc* ... 1366
E TRADE Nordic AB *E Trade Financial Corp* ... 588
E TRADE Nordic AB *FARO Technologies Inc* ... 680
E TRADE Sverige AB *FARO Technologies Inc* ... 680
E TRADE Sverige AB *E Trade Financial Corp* ... 588
E TRADE Systems India Private Limited *FARO Technologies Inc* ... 680
E TRADE Systems India Private Limited *E Trade Financial Corp* ... 588
E! Entertainment Europe BV *Comcast Corp* ... 444
E! Entertainment Hong Kong Limited *Comcast Corp* ... 444
E! Entertainment Television International Holdings, Inc. *Comcast Corp* ... 444
E! Entertainment Television, Inc. *Comcast Corp* ... 444
E! Networks Productions, Inc. *Comcast Corp* ... 444
E! Networks Sales & Distribution, Inc. *Comcast Corp* ... 444
E&C Capital, LLC *Elephant & Castle Group Inc* ... 616
E&C San Francisco, LLC *Elephant & Castle Group Inc* ... 616
E&N Railway Company (1998)LTD. *Railamerica Inc* ... 1510
E&P Financing Limited Partnership *Supertel Hospitality Inc* ... 1727
E&P Reit Trust *Supertel Hospitality Inc* ... 1727
e-Auction Global Trading Inc. *Aucxis Corp* ... 177
E-Babylon, Inc. *ValueClick Inc* ... 1888
e-Banc Holding Corp. *Science Applications International Corp* . 1593
E-Birchtree, LLC *Williams Cos Inc* ... 1961
E-business *Banco Bilbao Vizcaya Argentaria* ... 204
E-Business Solutions.com, Inc. *Covansys Corp* ... 491
E-Business Strategy Ltd *WPP Group Plc* ... 1979
E-business Strategy (Mauritius) Ltd *WPP Group Plc* ... 1979
E-ClassicSystems, Inc. *Jack Henry & Assoc Inc* ... 1000
E-com Management NV *Yahoo Inc* ... 1990
E-Commerce Exchange, Inc. *iPayment Inc* ... 986
E-Commerce International Ltd. *Global Sources Ltd* ... 797
E-Commerce Latina S.A. *Alto Palermo* ... 74
E-Con Gas *Energy Transfer Partners LP* ... 636
e-CRM Central, LLC *Marriott International Inc* ... 1125
E-Cypress, LLC *Enterprise Products Partners LP* ... 643
E-Cypress, LLC *Enterprise GP Holdings LP* ... 643
e-Deliveries (Pty) Limited *UTi Worldwide Inc* ... 1881
E-Direct Inc. *Atlantis Business Development Corp* ... 172
e-DMEC Corporation *Diamond Entertainment Corp* ... 551
E-Doction, Inc. *First Data Corp* ... 703
E-Focus West LLC *ImageWare Systems Inc* ... 924
e-Future (Beijing) Tornado Information Technology Inc. *E-Future Information Technology Inc* ... 588
E-Health Solutions Group, Inc. *Proassurance Corp* ... 1471
e-Lab Technology Ventures Ltd. *MDC Partners Inc* ... 1142
E-Loan Auto Fund Two, LLC *Popular Inc* ... 1448
E-Loan, Inc. *Popular Inc* ... 1448
E-Lodge Associates Limited Partnership *Equity Residential* ... 654
E-Mind S.A. *Liberty Global Inc* ... 1074
E-Next A Equipment Leasing Company, LLC *Black Hills Corp* .. 253
E-Nutraceuticals, Inc. *Vital Living Inc* ... 1917
E-Oaktree, LLC *Enterprise GP Holdings LP* ... 643
E-Oaktree, LLC *Enterprise Products Partners LP* ... 643
E-OIR Technologies, Inc. *Technest Holdings Inc* ... 1757
E-ONE Canada, Ltd. *Federal Signal Corp* ... 684
E-One, Inc *Federal Signal Corp* ... 684
E-Pago Fcil SA *Western Union Company (The)* ... 1952
e-pay Australia Holdings Pty Ltd *Euronet Worldwide Inc* ... 663
e-pay Australia Pty Ltd *Euronet Worldwide Inc* ... 663
e-pay Holdings Limited *Euronet Worldwide Inc* ... 663
e-pay Limited *Euronet Worldwide Inc* ... 663
e-pay Malaysia Sdn Bhd *Euronet Worldwide Inc* ... 663
e-pay New Zealand Pty Ltd *Euronet Worldwide Inc* ... 663
E-Pet Services *Petco Animal Supplies Inc* ... 1415
E-Pet Services, LLC *Petco Animal Supplies Inc* ... 1415
e-Pilot Group *On Track Innovations Ltd* ... 1340
E-platform Venture Partners Empreendimentos E Participaess.a.9 *Unibanco Holdings* ... 1848
E-Plus Mobilfunk GmbH & Co.KG *Royal KPN N.V.* ... 1563
E-Plus Mobilfunk GmbH& Co.KG *Koninklijke Kpn* ... 1039
E-Port Internet Services Pty. Limited *News Corp Ltd (The)* ... 1281
E-r Rule Company Of Puerto Rico, Inc. *L.S. Starrett Co (The)* ... 1046
E-Sea Biomedical Engineering Co. International Ltd *Eternal Technologies Group Inc* ... 660
E-shop California *Quantum Co Inc* ... 1498
E-shop Nevada *Quantum Co Inc* ... 1498
E-Sil Components Ltd. *Vishay Intertechnology Inc* ... 1913
E-Site Technologies, Inc. *Online Holdings Inc* ... 1343
E-Tech Testing Services,Inc. *Quixote Corp* ... 1504
e-Tenants LLC *Brandywine Operating PArtnership LP* ... 274
E-Tenants LLC *Brandywine Realty Trust* ... 274
e-Tenants.com Holding *Brandywine Operating PArtnership LP* .. 274
E-Tenants.com Holding, L.P *Brandywine Realty Trust* ... 274
E-Top-Pics, Inc *Searchhelp Inc* ... 1600
E-Trend Networks, Inc. *China Pharmaceuticals International Corp* ... 394
e-Valuate, LP *Lehman Brothers Holdings Inc* ... 1067
e-Village Nordic AB *Tele2 AB* ... 1764
E-vision LLC *Shamir Optical Industry Ltd* ... 1616
e-Wise Solutions of Australia *ViryaNet Ltd* ... 1912

Famous Daves Ribs of Texas, Inc. *Famous Dave's of America Inc* ... 678
Famous Daves Ribs of Texas, LP *Famous Dave's of America Inc* ... 678
Famous Daves Ribs, Inc. *Famous Dave's of America Inc* ... 678
Famous Daves Ribs-U, Inc. *Famous Dave's of America Inc* ... 678
Famous Fixins, Inc *Warning Mgmt Services Inc* ... 1931
Famous Footwear *Brown Shoe Co Inc* ... 288
Famous Pawn, Inc. *First Cash Financial Services Inc* ... 699
Famous Players Investments B.V. *Viacom Inc* ... 1902
Famous Players Investments B.V. *CBS Corp* ... 349
FAN Company, LLC *Abercrombie & Fitch Co* ... 6
Fanacif Products Argentina S.A. *Dana Corp* ... 525
Fanal S.A. de C.V. *Stanley Works* ... 1692
Fanbase Co.UK Limited *CCE Spinco Inc* ... 349
FanBuzz Retail, Inc. *ValueVision Media Inc* ... 1888
FanBuzz, Inc. *ValueVision Media Inc* ... 1888
FANEUIL HALL BEVERAGE, LLC *General Growth Properties Inc* ... 771
FANEUIL HALL MARKETPLACE, LLC *General Growth Properties Inc* ... 771
Fanfourtwo Productions, Inc. *News Corp Ltd (The)* ... 1281
Fannie May Confections Brands Inc *1-800-Flowers Com Inc* ... 2004
Fannie May Confections, Inc *1-800-Flowers Com Inc* ... 2004
Fannin Regional Hospital, Inc. *Community Health Systems Inc* ... 454
Fannin Regional Orthopaedic Center, Inc. *Community Health Systems Inc* ... 454
Fantasia Confections, Inc. *J.M. Smucker Co (The)* ... 998
Fantasia Cruising Inc. *Royal Caribbean Cruises Ltd* ... 1562
Fantasy Sports, Inc. *Silverstar Holdings Ltd* ... 1633
Faplac S.A. *Arauco & Constitution Pulp Inc* ... 141
Far East Energy (Bermuda), Ltd *Far East Energy Corp* ... 678
Far East Energy (BVI), Inc. *Far East Energy Corp* ... 678
Far East Freight, Inc. *Ryder System Inc* ... 1570
Far East Holdings Inc *WPP Group Plc* ... 1979
Far East International Petroleum Company (FEIPCO) *Heartland Oil and Gas Corp* ... 864
Far East National Bank *Entrx Corp* ... 646
Far Eastern Industrial Gases Company Limited *BOC Group Plc* ... 262
Far West Division, Inc. *HCA Inc* ... 855
Faraday Reinsurance Company Ltd. *Berkshire Hathaway Inc* ... 233
Faraday Underwriting Limited *Berkshire Hathaway Inc* ... 233
Faradyne Motors LLC *ITT Corp* ... 994
FARADYNE Motors LLC *Pentair Inc* ... 1405
FARADYNE Motors (Suzhou) Co., Ltd *Pentair Inc* ... 1405
Farat Shipping Company Limited *DryShips Inc* ... 577
Faraway Maritime Shipping Inc. *Golar LNG Ltd* ... 803
Farechase Israel Ltd. *Yahoo Inc* ... 1990
FareChase, Inc. *Yahoo Inc* ... 1990
Fareham Developments (One) Limited *Staples Inc* ... 1692
Fareham Developments (Two) Limited *Staples Inc* ... 1692
Farewell Beteillgungages Mbh & Co. Kg *Interpublic Group of Companies Inc* ... 975
Farewell Gmbh *Interpublic Group of Companies Inc* ... 975
Fargo Acquisition Company *Fresh Del Monte Produce Inc* ... 749
Fargo Iron and Metal Company *Gerdau Ameristeel Corp* ... 783
Farlington Company *Morgan Stanley* ... 1215
Farm and City Insurance Company *EMC Insurance Group Inc* ... 621
Farm Bureau Life Insurance Company *FBL Financial Group Inc* ... 681
Farm Folly LLC *Parke Bancorp Inc* ... 1386
Farm Plan Corporation *Deere & Co* ... 535
Farm Produce (Australia) Pty. Ltd. *PepsiCo Inc* ... 1410
Farm (The) Associates LP *Edison International* ... 604
Farmaas B.V. *Akzo Nobel* ... 49
Farmaceutici Gellini S.R.L. *Akzo Nobel* ... 49
Farmacox-Companhia Farmaceutica, Lda *Merck & Co Inc* ... 1162
Farmasix-Produtos Farmaceuticos, Lda *Merck & Co Inc* ... 1162
Farmec SpA *AGCO Corp* ... 42
Farmer Jack Pharmacies, Inc. *Great Atlantic & Pacific Tea Co Inc* ... 818
Farmer Jack's Of Ohio, Inc. *Great Atlantic & Pacific Tea Co Inc* ... 818
Farmer LP Gas Co. *Inergy Holdings LP* ... 936
Farmer LP Gas Co. *Inergy LP* ... 936
Farmer Mac Securities Corporation *Federal Agricultural Mortgage Corp* ... 682
Farmers Landfill, Inc. *Waste Management Inc* ... 1934
Farmers & Merchants Bank *F & M Bank Corp* ... 674
Farmers & Merchants Bank of Central California *Farmers & Merchants Bancorp* ... 679
Farmers & Merchants Financial Services *F & M Bank Corp* ... 674
Farmers & Merchants Investment Corporation *Farmers & Merchants Bancorp* ... 679
Farmers & Merchants Life Insurance Company *Farmers & Merchants Bancorp Inc* ... 679
Farmers & Merchants State Bank *Farmers & Merchants Bancorp Inc* ... 679
Farmers and Mechanics Bank *FMS Financial Corp* ... 729
Farmers and Merchants Insurance Company *OneBeacon Insurance Group Ltd* ... 1342
Farmers and Merchants Trust Company of Chambersburg *Franklin Financial Services Corp* ... 744
Farmers Bank & Capital Trust Co. *Farmers Capital Bank Corp* ... 679
Farmers Bank and Trust Company *Farmers Capital Bank Corp* ... 679
Farmers Bank Realty Co *Farmers Capital Bank Corp* ... 679
Farmers Capital Bank Trust I *Farmers Capital Bank Corp* ... 679
Farmers Capital Bank Trust II *Farmers Capital Bank Corp* ... 679
Farmers Capital Insurance Corporation *Farmers Capital Bank Corp* ... 679
Farmers Casualty Insurance Company *State Auto Financial Corp* ... 1695
Farmers Crop Insurance Alliance, Inc. *American Financial Group Inc* ... 91
Farmers Deposit Bank *Premier Financial Bancorp Inc* ... 1460
Farmers Fidelity Insurance Agency, LLP *Farmers Capital Bank Corp* ... 679
Farmers National Bank of Canfield *Farmers National Banc Corp* ... 680
Farmers National Bank of Emlenton *Emclaire Financial Corp* ... 621
Farmers State Bank of Breckenridge *IBT Bancorp Inc/MI* ... 909
Farmers/Merchants Corp. *Farmers & Merchants Bancorp* ... 679
FARMINGDALE-OXFORD ASSOCIATES LIMITED PARTNERSHIP *Apartment Investment and Management Company* ... 130
Farmington Casualty Company *Travelers Property Casualty Corp* ... 1818
Farmington Casualty Company *St Paul Travelers Cos Inc* ... 1687
Farmington Properties, Inc. *Dominion Resources Inc VA* ... 568
Farmington Tarragon, LLC *Tarragon Corp* ... 1751
Farmington, Incorporated *Wachovia Corp* ... 1928
Farminova Produtos Farmaceuticos de Inovacao, Lda *Pfizer Inc* ... 1420
Farmitalia Carlo Erba Limited *Pfizer Inc* ... 1420
Farmland Distribution Inc. *Smithfield Foods Inc* ... 1649
Farmland Foods, Inc. *Smithfield Foods Inc* ... 1649
Farmogene Productos Farmaceuticos Lda *Pfizer Inc* ... 1420
Farmovs Parexel Ltd *Parexel International Corp* ... 1385
Farms Sewer Company, Inc. *United States Steel Corp* ... 1863
Farms Water Company, Inc. *United States Steel Corp* ... 1863
Farnham Limited *Tyco International Ltd* ... 1838
Faroudja Laboratories, Inc. *Genesis Microchip Inc* ... 774
Faroudja, Inc. *Genesis Microchip Inc* ... 774
Farr Associates, Inc. *BB&T Corp* ... 222
FARRAGUT REMAINDER I LIMITED PARTNERSHIP *Lexington Realty Trust* ... 1071
FARRAGUT REMAINDER II LIMITED PARTNERSHIP *Lexington Realty Trust* ... 1071
Farrells Ice Cream Parlour Restaurants LLC *Host Hotels & Resorts Inc* ... 892
Farrington American Express Travel Services Limited (37% owned) *American Express Co* ... 91
Farris Engineering Ltd. *Emerson Electric Co* ... 623
Farros Blatter AG *Metso Corp* ... 1173
Faru Ltd. *Phelps Dodge Corp* ... 1424
FAS S.r.l. *Praxair Inc* ... 1458
Fas-Gas Retail Services Co. of Texas *ConocoPhillips* ... 469
Fascel Limited *Hutchison Telecommunications International Ltd* ... 902
FASCO Asia Pacific Ltd. *Tecumseh Products Co* ... 1761
FASCO Australia Pty. Ltd. *Tecumseh Products Co* ... 1761
FASCO Industries, Inc. *Tecumseh Products Co* ... 1761
FASCO Motors, Ltd *Tecumseh Products Co* ... 1761
FASCO Motors, Ltd. *Tecumseh Products Co* ... 1761
FASCO Yamabishi Co., Ltd. *Tecumseh Products Co* ... 1761
Faserwave Inc. *MB Tech Inc* ... 1138
Fashion Angels Enterprises, Inc *Small World Kids Inc* ... 1645
Fashion Barn of Florida, Inc. *Big Lots Inc* ... 238
Fashion Barn of Georgia, Inc. *Big Lots Inc* ... 238
Fashion Barn of Indiana, Inc. *Big Lots Inc* ... 238
Fashion Barn of Missouri, Inc. *Big Lots Inc* ... 238
Fashion Barn of New Jersey, Inc. *Big Lots Inc* ... 238
Fashion Barn of North Carolina, Inc. *Big Lots Inc* ... 238
Fashion Barn of Ohio, Inc. *Big Lots Inc* ... 238
Fashion Barn of Oklahoma, Inc. *Big Lots Inc* ... 238
Fashion Barn of Pennsylvania, Inc. *Big Lots Inc* ... 238
Fashion Barn of South Carolina, Inc. *Big Lots Inc* ... 238
Fashion Barn of Texas, Inc. *Big Lots Inc* ... 238
Fashion Barn of Vermont, Inc. *Big Lots Inc* ... 238
Fashion Barn of Virginia, Inc. *Big Lots Inc* ... 238
Fashion Barn of West Virginia, Inc. *Big Lots Inc* ... 238
Fashion Barn, Inc. *Big Lots Inc* ... 238
Fashion Barn, Inc. *Big Lots Inc* ... 238
Fashion Bonanza, Inc. *Big Lots Inc* ... 238
Fashion Bug of California, Inc. *Charming Shoppes Inc* ... 375
Fashion Bug Retail Companies, Inc. *Charming Shoppes Inc* ... 375
Fashion Center Associates of Illinois No. 1 (MLP) Limited Partnership *Mills Ltd Partnership* ... 1193
Fashion Center Corp. *Mills Ltd Partnership* ... 1193
Fashion Center LLC *Mills Ltd Partnership* ... 1193
Fashion Development Corp. *Polo Ralph Lauren Corp* ... 1444
Fashion House, Inc *The Fashion House Holdings Inc* ... 1784
Fashion Outlets Corp. *Big Lots Inc* ... 238
FASHION PLACE, LLC *General Growth Properties Inc* ... 771
Fashion Resource (TCL), Inc. *Tarrant Apparel Group* ... 1751
Fashion Seal Corporation *Superior Uniform Group Inc* ... 1727
Fashion Service Corp. *Charming Shoppes Inc* ... 375
Fashion Service Fulfillment Corporation *Charming Shoppes Inc* ... 375
Fashion Service Protection Corporation *Charming Shoppes Inc* ... 375
Fashion Services Limited *Sally Beauty Holdings Inc* ... 1578
FASHION SHOW MALL LLC *General Growth Properties Inc* ... 771
Fashions Outlet of America, Inc. *Polo Ralph Lauren Corp* ... 1444
Fashions Outlet of Florida, LLC. *Polo Ralph Lauren Corp* ... 1444
Fasnet International S.A. *Ternium S.A.* ... 1777
Fasson Canada Inc. *Avery Dennison Corp* ... 188
Fasson Portugal Produtos Auto-adesivos Lda. *Avery Dennison Corp* ... 188
Fast & Fluid Management Iberica S.a. *IDEX Corp* ... 917
Fast & Fluid Management S.r.l. *IDEX Corp* ... 917
Fast & Fluid Management U.k. Limited *IDEX Corp* ... 917
FAST and FLUID MANAGEMENT FRANCE SARL *IDEX Corp* ... 917
Fast Forward Solutions, LLC *Airnet Systems Inc* ... 47
Fast Freedom, Inc. *Empire District Electric Co (The)* ... 624
Fast Plus Limited *News Corp Ltd (The)* ... 1281
Fast Srl *WPP Group Plc* ... 1979
Fast Video Security GmbH *NICE Systems Ltd* ... 1285
Fast Video Security (UK) Ltd. *NICE Systems Ltd* ... 1285
Fast4wd Ogilvy Limited *WPP Group Plc* ... 1979
Fastbridge Ab *Interpublic Group of Companies Inc* ... 975
Fastcash Limited *Dollar Financial Corp* ... 557
Fastclick, Inc. *ValueClick Inc* ... 1888
FASTCO (Shanghai) Trading Co., Ltd. *Fastenal Co* ... 680
Fastenal Asia Pacific, Limited. *Fastenal Co* ... 680
Fastenal Canada Company *Fastenal Co* ... 680
Fastenal Company Leasing *Fastenal Co* ... 680
Fastenal Company Purchasing1 *Fastenal Co* ... 680
Fastenal Europe, B.V. *Fastenal Co* ... 680
Fastenal IP Company *Fastenal Co* ... 680
Fastenal Mexico S. de R.L. de C.V. *Fastenal Co* ... 680
Fastenal Mexico Services S. de R.L. de C.V. *Fastenal Co* ... 680
Fastenal Singapore P.T.E. Ltd. *Fastenal Co* ... 680
Fasteners & Tools, Ltd. *Black & Decker Corp* ... 252
FastenMaster Corporation,Inc. *Strategic Distribution Inc* ... 1709
FastForward Networks, Inc. *Yahoo Inc* ... 1990
FastFunds Financial Corporation *Hydrogen Power Inc* ... 904
FastFunds International, Inc. *Fastfunds Financial Corp* ... 680
Fastighets Ab 7035 I Stockholm *Stena AB* ... 1700
Fastighets Ab Majng *Stena AB* ... 1700
Fastighets Ab Malmhus *Stena AB* ... 1700
Fastighets Ab Nimbo *Stena AB* ... 1700
Fastighets Ab Rnnebo *Stena AB* ... 1700
Fastighets Ab Skansen *Stena AB* ... 1700
Fastighets AB Stockvik *Akzo Nobel* ... 49
Fastighets Ab Tribune *Stena AB* ... 1700
Fastighetsbolaget Bardunen Hb *Stena AB* ... 1700
Fastlane Technologies Corporation *Quest Software Inc* ... 1500
Fastlane Technologies GmbH *Quest Software Inc* ... 1500
Fastlane Technologies (UK) Limited *Quest Software Inc* ... 1500
Fastnaparts Limited *Anixter International Inc* ... 125
FASTNET CALOOSAHATCHEE COMMUNICATIONS LIMITED *National Grid Transco Plc* ... 1241
FastObjects,Inc. *Versant Corp* ... 1898
Fastorq, LLC *Superior Energy Services Inc* ... 1726
Fastrak Limited *Virgin Media Inc* ... 1910
Fastrealty.com f/k/a First American Loan Servicing Corporation *First American Corp* ... 695
Fastrieve,Inc. *SOURCECORP* ... 1662
FastStart Real Estate Services (California), Inc. *HouseValues Inc* ... 893
FastStart Real Estate Services (Canada) Corporation *HouseValues Inc* ... 893
FastStart Real Estate Services, LLC *HouseValues Inc* ... 893
Fasttrack Insurance Ltd. *MTR Corp Ltd* ... 1225
Fasttrack Integrated Marketing Communications, Inc. *Interpublic Group of Companies Inc* ... 975
Fastwell Technology Limited *Premiere Global Services Inc* ... 1461
Fathom Business Systems, Inc *Franchise Capital Corp* ... 743
FATS Canada, Inc. *Firearms Training Systems Inc* ... 694
FATS, Inc. *Firearms Training Systems Inc* ... 694
Fattorie Osella S.p.A. *Altria Group Inc* ... 74
Fattorie Osella S.p.A. *Kraft Foods Inc* ... 1042
Faucheux S.A.S. (9) *Alamo Group Inc* ... 51
Fauji Kabirwala Power Company Limited *El Paso Corp* ... 609
Faulding Pharmaceutical Co. *Tapestry Pharmaceuticals Inc* ... 1749
Faulkner Hinton Suburban I, LLC *Health Care Property Investors Inc* ... 857
Faulkner Hinton Suburban III, LLC *Health Care Property Investors Inc* ... 857
Fauquier Bank Services, Inc *Fauquier Bankshares Inc* ... 681
Fauquier Landfill Gas, LLC *Delmarva Power & Light Co* ... 538
Fauquier Statutory Trust I *Fauquier Bankshares Inc* ... 681
Favarosi Asvanyviz es Uditoipari Reszvenytarsasag *Pepsiamericas Inc* ... 1410
Favorit Kommunikation AB *WPP Group Plc* ... 1979
Favorite Food Products Limited *Kellogg Co* ... 1021
Favorite Products Company, Ltd. *Oil-Dri Corp of America* ... 1332
favour of Bank of America, National Association (Canada Branch) *EMS Technologies Inc* ... 627
Fawcett Memorial Hospital, Inc. *HCA Inc* ... 855
Fawndeck Ltd. *Anixter International Inc* ... 125
FaxNet Acquisition Corp. *Critical Path Inc* ... 501
Faxton Leasing, LLC *Radiation Therapy Services Inc* ... 1507
Fayco Network Technology Development (Shenzhen) Co. Ltd. *Sina Corp* ... 1636
Fayette County Propane *Energy Transfer Partners LP* ... 636
Fayette Development Property, LLC *CBL & Associates Properties Inc* ... 348
Fayette Enterprises, Inc. *Furniture Brands International Inc* ... 755
FAYETTE-OXFORD ASSOCIATES LIMITED PARTNERSHIP *Apartment Investment and Management Company* ... 130
FAYETTE-OXFORD CORPORATION *Apartment Investment and Management Company* ... 130
FAYETTEVILLE BLACK INVESTMENT INC *Developers Diversified Realty Corp* ... 547
FAYETTEVILLE EXCHANGE LLC *Developers Diversified Realty Corp* ... 547
Fayetteville Health Associates Limited Partnership *Health Care Property Investors Inc* ... 857
Fayetteville Lithotripters Limited PartnershipArizona I *HealthTronics Inc* ... 862
Fayetteville Lithotripters Limited PartnershipArkansas I *HealthTronics Inc* ... 862
Fayetteville Lithotripters Limited PartnershipLouisiana I *HealthTronics Inc* ... 862
Fayetteville Lithotripters Limited PartnershipSouth Carolina II *HealthTronics Inc* ... 862
Fayetteville Lithotripters Limited PartnershipVirginia I *HealthTronics Inc* ... 862
FAYETTEVILLE MORGANTON ROAD ASSOCIATES LIMITED PARTNERSHIP *Developers Diversified Realty Corp* ... 547
Fayetteville Motel Enterprises, Inc. *Lodgian Inc* ... 1091
Fayetteville MSA Limited Partnership *Alltel Corp* ... 69
Fayetteville Open MRI, LLC *HealthSouth Corp* ... 861
Faygo Beverages, Inc. *National Beverage Corp* ... 1239
Fayser S.R.L. *Tyco International Ltd* ... 1838
FB Apparel, Inc. *Charming Shoppes Inc* ... 375
FB Australia Pty Limited *Bristow Group Inc* ... 282
FB Clothing, Inc. *Charming Shoppes Inc* ... 375
Fb Company Ab *Interpublic Group of Companies Inc* ... 975
FB Distro SM, Inc. *Charming Shoppes Inc* ... 375
FB Distro, Inc. *Charming Shoppes Inc* ... 375
FB Heliservices Limited *Bristow Group Inc* ... 282
FB Leasing Limited *Bristow Group Inc* ... 282
FB Statutory Trust II *Fidelity Bancorp Inc* ... 689
FBB Anadarko Corporation *Meridian Resource Corp* ... 1164
FBC Finance Co., a California corporation *Farmer Bros Co* ... 678
Fbc (futurebrand Consumer) Limited *Interpublic Group of Companies Inc* ... 975
Fbc (futurebrand Digital) Limited *Interpublic Group of Companies Inc* ... 975
Fbc (futurebrand Group)limited *Interpublic Group of Companies Inc* ... 975
FBC Holdings, LLC. *Franklin Bank Corp* ... 743
FBC Sub, Inc. *News Corp Ltd (The)* ... 1281
FBC, Inc *Cardinal Bankshares Corp* ... 331
FBD Consulting, Inc. *National Financial Partners Corp* ... 1241
FBF Insurance Agency, Inc. *Bank of America Corp* ... 208
FBIC, Inc. *Fidelity Bancorp Inc* ... 689
FBL Financial Group Capital Trust *FBL Financial Group Inc* ... 681
FBL Financial Group, Inc *American Equity Investment Life Hldg Co* ... 90
FBL Financial Services, Inc. *FBL Financial Group Inc* ... 681
FBL Leasing Services, Inc. *FBL Financial Group Inc* ... 681
FBM Dallas, Inc. *InterContinental Hotels Group* ... 962
FBM Houston, Inc. *InterContinental Hotels Group* ... 962
Fbm 1-10e, Inc. *InterContinental Hotels Group* ... 962
FBR Asset Management Holdings, Inc. *Friedman Billings Ramsey Group Inc* ... 749
FBR Bancorp, Inc. *Friedman Billings Ramsey Group Inc* ... 749
FBR Capital Markets Holdings, Inc. *Friedman Billings Ramsey Group Inc* ... 749
Fbr Ccp, Ltd. *Friedman Billings Ramsey Group Inc* ... 749
FBR Fund Advisers, Inc. *Friedman Billings Ramsey Group Inc* ... 749
FBR Investment Management, Inc. *Friedman Billings Ramsey Group Inc* ... 749
FBR Investment Services, Inc. *Friedman Billings Ramsey Group Inc* ... 749
FBR Investments LLC *Warner Music Group Corp* ... 1931
FBR Investments, LLC *Friedman Billings Ramsey Group Inc* ... 749
FBR NIM Investments, LLC *Friedman Billings Ramsey Group Inc* ... 749
FBR Securitization, Inc. *Friedman Billings Ramsey Group Inc* ... 749
FBR TRS Holdings, Inc. *Friedman Billings Ramsey Group Inc* ... 749

3008 - Subsidiary/Parent Index THE CORPORATE DIRECTORY - Walker's 2008

FBR Trust Investments, LLC *Friedman Billings Ramsey Group Inc* 749
FBRC, Ltd. *Friedman Billings Ramsey Group Inc* 749
FBS CBNA Loan Funding LLC *Citigroup Inc* 411
FBS CFPI Loan Funding LLC *Citigroup Inc* 411
FBS Communications, L.P. *Black Box Corp* 252
FBS Limited *Bristow Group Inc* 282
FBTC Statutory Trust I *First Banctrust Corp* 697
FBV Friseurbetriebe-Verwaltungsgesellschaft mbH *Procter & Gamble* 1472
FBV Service GmbH & Co. Beteiligungs-OHG *Procter & Gamble* 1472
FBV Service GmbH & Co. Holding OHG *Procter & Gamble* 1472
FC 2 Corp. *Foundation Coal Holdings Inc* 740
FC Acquisition Corp *Astea International Inc* 166
FC Ashton Mill Master Lessee, LLC *Wachovia Corp* 1928
FC Assets Corp *FirstCity Financial Corp* 719
FC Assets Five Corp. *FirstCity Financial Corp* 719
FC Assets Four Corp. *FirstCity Financial Corp* 719
FC Assets One Corp. *FirstCity Financial Corp* 719
FC Assets Six Corp. *FirstCity Financial Corp* 719
FC Assets Three Corp. *FirstCity Financial Corp* 719
FC Basketball, Inc. *Forest City Enterprises Inc* 735
FC Capital Corp *FirstCity Financial Corp* 719
Fc Consolidated Master Lessee, LLC *Wachovia Corp* 1928
FC East Fork Crossing LLC, *Sun Communities Inc* 1718
FC Energy Finance I, Inc. *J.P. Morgan Chase & Company* 999
FC Energy Finance II, Inc. *J.P. Morgan Chase & Company* 999
FC France Acquisition Sarl *Ferro Corp* 687
FC Funding Corp *FirstCity Financial Corp* 719
FC Glen Laurel LLC, *Sun Communities Inc* 1718
FC Meadowbrook LLC, *Sun Communities Inc* 1718
FC Pebble Creek LLC, *Sun Communities Inc* 1718
FC Properties Five,Ltd. *FirstCity Financial Corp* 719
FC Properties Four,Ltd. *FirstCity Financial Corp* 719
FC Properties One,Ltd. *FirstCity Financial Corp* 719
FC Properties Six,Ltd. *FirstCity Financial Corp* 719
FC Properties Three,Ltd. *FirstCity Financial Corp* 719
FC Properties,Ltd. *FirstCity Financial Corp* 719
FC River Ranch Limited Partnership, *Sun Communities Inc* 1718
FC Stonebridge Limited Partnership, *Sun Communities Inc* 1718
FC Summit Ridge Limited Partnership, *Sun Communities Inc* 1718
FC Sunset Ridge Limited Partnership, *Sun Communities Inc* 1718
FC Washington GP LLC *FirstCity Financial Corp* 719
FC Washington I LP *FirstCity Financial Corp* 719
FC1031 Limited *IAC/InterActiveCorp* 961
FCA Acquisition Corp. *flexSCAN Inc* 725
FCA Company, LLC *Bank of America Corp* 208
FCA Construction Company, LLC *Life Time Fitness Inc* 1075
FCA of Ohio, Inc. *Jo-Ann Stores Inc* 1008
FCA Real Estate Holdings, LLC *Life Time Fitness Inc* 1075
FCA Restaurant Company, LLC *Life Time Fitness Inc* 1075
Fcb / Honduras *Interpublic Group of Companies Inc* 975
Fcb Activ (pty)ltd *Interpublic Group of Companies Inc* 975
Fcb Advertising Limited *Interpublic Group of Companies Inc* 975
Fcb Africa (pty)limited *Interpublic Group of Companies Inc* 975
Fcb Asia (holding)ltd. *Interpublic Group of Companies Inc* 975
FCB Assets Holdings, Inc. *1st Constitution Bancorp* 2005
Fcb Cape Town (pty)limited *Interpublic Group of Companies Inc* 975
Fcb De Costa Rica, S.a. *Interpublic Group of Companies Inc* 975
Fcb Durban (pty)limited *Interpublic Group of Companies Inc* 975
Fcb Eduador *Interpublic Group of Companies Inc* 975
Fcb El Salvador Publicidad, S.a. De C.v. *Interpublic Group of Companies Inc* 975
Fcb Espa Oy *Interpublic Group of Companies Inc* 975
Fcb Events & Pr Gmbh *Interpublic Group of Companies Inc* 975
Fcb Frankfurt Gmbh *Interpublic Group of Companies Inc* 975
Fcb Fuze (pty)ltd *Interpublic Group of Companies Inc* 975
FCB Heritage 1901 Redevelopment LLC *Synovus Financial Corp* 1739
Fcb Japan Inc. *Interpublic Group of Companies Inc* 975
Fcb Jonssons (pty)limited *Interpublic Group of Companies Inc* 975
Fcb Kobza Werbeagentur Gmbh *Interpublic Group of Companies Inc* 975
Fcb Korea Inc. *Interpublic Group of Companies Inc* 975
Fcb Leutenegger Krull Ag *Interpublic Group of Companies Inc* 975
Fcb London Limited *Interpublic Group of Companies Inc* 975
FCB Mortgage, LLC *National City Corp* 1239
Fcb Plato Healthcare Promotions (pty)limited *Interpublic Group of Companies Inc* 975
Fcb Publicidad Guatemala Sa *Interpublic Group of Companies Inc* 975
Fcb Publicidad S.a. *Interpublic Group of Companies Inc* 975
Fcb Publicidad, C.a. *Interpublic Group of Companies Inc* 975
FCB Real Estate, Inc. *First Charter Corp* 699
Fcb Reklam Hizmetleri A.s. *Interpublic Group of Companies Inc* 975
Fcb Retail Consulting & Werbeges M.b.h. *Interpublic Group of Companies Inc* 975
FCB Services, Inc. *Farmers Capital Bank Corp* 679
Fcb South Africa 2004 (pty)limited *Interpublic Group of Companies Inc* 975
Fcb South Africa Holding (pty)limited *Interpublic Group of Companies Inc* 975
Fcb South Africa Properties (pty)limited *Interpublic Group of Companies Inc* 975
Fcb South Africa (pty)limited *Interpublic Group of Companies Inc* 975
FCB Statutory Trust I *FCB Bancorp CA* 681
Fcb Taiwan Ltd *Interpublic Group of Companies Inc* 975
Fcb Worldwide Colombia S.a. *Interpublic Group of Companies Inc* 975
Fcb Worldwide Inc. *Interpublic Group of Companies Inc* 975
Fcb Worldwide (japan)k.k. *Interpublic Group of Companies Inc* 975
Fcb Worldwide (puerto Rico), Inc. *Interpublic Group of Companies Inc* 975
Fcb Worldwide S.a. De C.v. *Interpublic Group of Companies Inc* 975
Fcb Worldwide Sa *Interpublic Group of Companies Inc* 975
Fcb Worldwide (thailand)ltd. *Interpublic Group of Companies Inc* 975
Fcb Worldwide, Inc. *Interpublic Group of Companies Inc* 975
Fcb Worldwide, LLC *Interpublic Group of Companies Inc* 975
Fcb-ulka Advertising Limited *Interpublic Group of Companies Inc* 975
FCB/NC Capital Trust I *First Citizens Bancshares Inc/DE* 700
FCB/NC Capital Trust II *First Citizens Bancshares Inc/DE* 700
FCB/SC Capital Trust I *First Citizens BanCorp Inc* 700
FCB/SC Capital Trust II *First Citizens BanCorp Inc* 700
Fcb/tapsa Barcelona, S.a. *Interpublic Group of Companies Inc* 975
Fcb/wilkens Gmbh *Interpublic Group of Companies Inc* 975
FCBDE Holdings, Inc. *Synovus Financial Corp* 1739
FCBi DEUTSCHLAND GMBH *Interpublic Group of Companies Inc* 975
Fcbi Interactive Consulting & Werbeges M.b.h. *Interpublic Group of Companies Inc* 975
Fcbi London Limited *Interpublic Group of Companies Inc* 975
Fcbi Relationship Marketing Ltda *Interpublic Group of Companies Inc* 975
FCC Acquisition Corp. *Lubrizol Corp (The)* 1099
FCC Equipment Financing, Inc. *Caterpillar Inc* 345
FCC Holdoco I, Inc. *Leucadia National Corp* 1068
FCC Receivables Corp. *Franklin Resources Inc* 745
FCC Resort LLC *Finova Group Inc* 694
FCC-PR, Inc *Wachovia Corp* 1928
FCD (Canada) Inc. *SPX Corp* 1684
Fcfs Mi, Inc. *First Cash Financial Services Inc* 699
Fcfs Mo, Inc. *First Cash Financial Services Inc* 699
Fcfs Ok, Inc. *First Cash Financial Services Inc* 699
Fcfs Sc, Inc. *First Cash Financial Services Inc* 699
Fcg Csi, Inc. *First Consulting Group Inc* 703
FCG Investment Company, Inc. *First Consulting Group Inc* 703
FCG Software Services *First Consulting Group Inc* 703
FCG Ventures, Inc. *First Consulting Group Inc* 703
FCH/DT BWI Holdings, L.P. *FelCor Lodging Trust Inc* 686
FCH/DT BWI Hotel, L.L.C. *FelCor Lodging Trust Inc* 686
FCH/DT Holdings, L.P. *FelCor Lodging Trust Inc* 686
FCH/DT Hotels, L.L.C. *FelCor Lodging Trust Inc* 686
FCH/DT Leasing, L.L.C. *FelCor Lodging Trust Inc* 686
FCH/HHC Hotels, L.L.C. *FelCor Lodging Trust Inc* 686
FCH/HHC Leasing, L.L.C. *FelCor Lodging Trust Inc* 686
FCH/IHC Atlanta Hotels, LLC *Interstate Hotels & Resorts Inc* 976
FCH/IHC Atlanta Leasing, LLC *Interstate Hotels & Resorts Inc* 976
FCH/IHC Dallas Holdings, LLC *Interstate Hotels & Resorts Inc* 976
FCH/IHC Dallas Hotels, LP *Interstate Hotels & Resorts Inc* 976
FCH/IHC Dallas Leasing, LLC *Interstate Hotels & Resorts Inc* 976
FCH/IHC Dallas Leasing, LP *Interstate Hotels & Resorts Inc* 976
FCH/IHC Hotels, L.P. *FelCor Lodging Trust Inc* 686
FCH/IHC Hotels, LP *Interstate Hotels & Resorts Inc* 976
FCH/IHC Houston Holdings, LLC *Interstate Hotels & Resorts Inc* 976
FCH/IHC Houston Hotels, LP *Interstate Hotels & Resorts Inc* 976
FCH/IHC Houston Leasing GP, LLC *Interstate Hotels & Resorts Inc* 976
FCH/IHC Houston Leasing, LP *Interstate Hotels & Resorts Inc* 976
Fch/ihc I-10 Holdings, LLC *Interstate Hotels & Resorts Inc* 976
Fch/ihc I-10 Hotels, Lp *Interstate Hotels & Resorts Inc* 976
Fch/ihc I-10 Leasing Gp, LLC *Interstate Hotels & Resorts Inc* 976
Fch/ihc I-10 Leasing, Lp *Interstate Hotels & Resorts Inc* 976
FCH/IHC Leasing, L.P. *FelCor Lodging Trust Inc* 686
FCH/IHC Leasing, LP *Interstate Hotels & Resorts Inc* 976
FCH/IHC Scottsdale Hotels, LLC *Interstate Hotels & Resorts Inc* 976
FCH/IHC Scottsdale Leasing, LLC *Interstate Hotels & Resorts Inc* 976
FCH/JVEIGHT Leasing, L.L.C. *FelCor Lodging Trust Inc* 686
FCH/PSH, L.P. (f/k/a Rouse & Associates-SHS) *FelCor Lodging Trust Inc* 686
FCH/SH Leasing II, L.L.C. *FelCor Lodging Trust Inc* 686
FCH/SH Leasing, L.L.C. *FelCor Lodging Trust Inc* 686
FCI Liquidations, Inc. *Tyco International Ltd* 1838
FCI Servicios de Mexico, S.A. de C.V. *BB Holdings Ltd* 222
FCI Servisistema S.A. de C.V. *BB Holdings Ltd* 222
FCL Ship Fifteen, Inc. *J.P. Morgan Chase & Company* 999
FCL Ship Fourteen, Inc. *J.P. Morgan Chase & Company* 999
FCL Ship One, Inc. *Citigroup Inc* 411
FCL Ship Three, Inc. *Citigroup Inc* 411
FCL Ship Two, Inc. *Citigroup Inc* 411
Fcmc 2000 C *Franklin Credit Mgmt Corp* 744
Fcmc 2000 D Corp *Franklin Credit Mgmt Corp* 744
Fcmc 2000b Corp *Franklin Credit Mgmt Corp* 744
Fcmc 2001 A Corp *Franklin Credit Mgmt Corp* 744
Fcmc 2001 B Corp *Franklin Credit Mgmt Corp* 744
Fcmc 2001 C Corp *Franklin Credit Mgmt Corp* 744
Fcmc 2001 D Corp *Franklin Credit Mgmt Corp* 744
Fcmc 2001 E Corp *Franklin Credit Mgmt Corp* 744
Fcmc 2001 F Corp *Franklin Credit Mgmt Corp* 744
Fcmc 2002 A Corp *Franklin Credit Mgmt Corp* 744
Fcmc 2002 B Corp *Franklin Credit Mgmt Corp* 744
Fcmc 2002 C Corp *Franklin Credit Mgmt Corp* 744
Fcmc 2002 D Corp *Franklin Credit Mgmt Corp* 744
Fcmc 2002 E Corp *Franklin Credit Mgmt Corp* 744
Fcmc 2002 F Corp *Franklin Credit Mgmt Corp* 744
Fcmc 2002 G Corp *Franklin Credit Mgmt Corp* 744
Fcmc 2002 H Corp *Franklin Credit Mgmt Corp* 744
Fcmc 2003 A Corp *Franklin Credit Mgmt Corp* 744
Fcmc 2003 B Corp *Franklin Credit Mgmt Corp* 744
Fcmc 2003 C Corp *Franklin Credit Mgmt Corp* 744
Fcmc 2003 D Corp *Franklin Credit Mgmt Corp* 744
Fcmc 2003 E Corp *Franklin Credit Mgmt Corp* 744
Fcmc 2003 F Corp *Franklin Credit Mgmt Corp* 744
Fcmc 2003 G Corp *Franklin Credit Mgmt Corp* 744
Fcmc 2003 H Corp *Franklin Credit Mgmt Corp* 744
Fcmc 2003 I Corp *Franklin Credit Mgmt Corp* 744
Fcmc 2004 A Corp *Franklin Credit Mgmt Corp* 744
Fcmc 2004 B Corp *Franklin Credit Mgmt Corp* 744
Fcmc 2004 C Corp *Franklin Credit Mgmt Corp* 744
Fcmc 2004 D Corp *Franklin Credit Mgmt Corp* 744
Fcmc 2004 E Corp *Franklin Credit Mgmt Corp* 744
Fcmc 2004 F Corp *Franklin Credit Mgmt Corp* 744
Fcmc 2004 G Corp *Franklin Credit Mgmt Corp* 744
Fcmc 2004 H Corp *Franklin Credit Mgmt Corp* 744
Fcmc 2004 I Corp *Franklin Credit Mgmt Corp* 744
Fcmc 2004 J Corp *Franklin Credit Mgmt Corp* 744
Fcmc 2004 K Corp *Franklin Credit Mgmt Corp* 744
Fcmc 2005 A Corp *Franklin Credit Mgmt Corp* 744
Fcmc 2005 B Corp *Franklin Credit Mgmt Corp* 744
Fcmc 2005 C Corp *Franklin Credit Mgmt Corp* 744
Fcmc 2005 D Corp *Franklin Credit Mgmt Corp* 744
Fcmc 2005 E Corp *Franklin Credit Mgmt Corp* 744
Fcmc 2005 F Corp *Franklin Credit Mgmt Corp* 744
Fcmc 2005 G Corp *Franklin Credit Mgmt Corp* 744
Fcmc 2005 H Corp *Franklin Credit Mgmt Corp* 744
Fcmc 2005 I Corp *Franklin Credit Mgmt Corp* 744
Fcmc 2005 J Corp *Franklin Credit Mgmt Corp* 744
Fcmc 2005 K Corp *Franklin Credit Mgmt Corp* 744
Fcmc 2005 L Corp *Franklin Credit Mgmt Corp* 744
Fcmc 2005 M Corp *Franklin Credit Mgmt Corp* 744
Fcmc 2005 N Corp *Franklin Credit Mgmt Corp* 744
Fcmc 2005 O Corp *Franklin Credit Mgmt Corp* 744
Fcmc 2005 P Corp *Franklin Credit Mgmt Corp* 744
Fcmc 2005 Q Corp *Franklin Credit Mgmt Corp* 744
Fcmc 2005 R Corp *Franklin Credit Mgmt Corp* 744
Fcmc B-1 2004 A Corp *Franklin Credit Mgmt Corp* 744
Fcmc B-1 2004 B Corp *Franklin Credit Mgmt Corp* 744
Fcmc B-1 2004 C Corp *Franklin Credit Mgmt Corp* 744
Fcmc B-1 2004 D Corp *Franklin Credit Mgmt Corp* 744
Fcmc B-1 2004 E Corp *Franklin Credit Mgmt Corp* 744
FCNH, Inc. *Steiner Leisure Ltd* 1699
FCP Enterprises Inc *Texas New Mexico Power Co* 1782
FCP Enterprises Inc *PNM Resources Inc* 1443
FCR Camden, LLC *Casella Waste Systems Inc* 341
FCR Florida, LLC *Casella Waste Systems Inc* 341
FCR Greensboro, LLC *Casella Waste Systems Inc* 341
FCR Greenville, LLC *Casella Waste Systems Inc* 341
FCR Morris, LLC *Casella Waste Systems Inc* 341
FCR Redemption, LLC *Casella Waste Systems Inc* 341
FCR Tennessee, LLC *Casella Waste Systems Inc* 341
FCR, LLC *Casella Waste Systems Inc* 341
FCRF X *Franklin Credit Mgmt Corp* 744
FCRF XII *Franklin Credit Mgmt Corp* 744
FCRF XIX *Franklin Credit Mgmt Corp* 744
Fcrf Xviii / Xx *Franklin Credit Mgmt Corp* 744
Fcs 525, Inc. *Finova Group Inc* 694
FCS Com, Inc *Moog Inc* 1215
FCS Control Systems BV *Moog Inc* 1215
FCS Kelsey Limited *Moog Inc* 1215
FCS Las Vegas Mining Claims, LLC *Rinker Group Ltd* 1546
FCS Simulator Systems BV *Moog Inc* 1215
FCT Atlantic Limited *First American Corp* 695
FCT Holdings Company Ltd. *First American Corp* 695
FCT Insurance Company Ltd. *First American Corp* 695
FCT Insurance Services Inc. *First American Corp* 695
FCT Valuation Services, Inc. *First American Corp* 695
FCTC Transfer Services, L.P. *Affiliated Computer Services Inc* 39
FD Archtects & Engneers Corporaton *Fluor Corp* 728
FD Direct Limited *Marsh & McLennan Cos Inc* 1125
FD Management, Inc. *Elizabeth Arden Inc* 617
FD Mexco, nc. *Fluor Corp* 728
FD/MK Limited Liability Company *Washington Group International Inc* 1932
FD/MK Lmited Lablty Company *Fluor Corp* 728
FDA Properties of Texas, LP *Famous Dave's of America Inc* 678
FDA Properties, Inc. *Famous Dave's of America Inc* 678
FDC Acquisition, Inc. *Marsh & McLennan Cos Inc* 1125
FDC Australia (Acquisitions) Pty Limited *First Data Corp* 703
FDC International Inc. *First Data Corp* 703
FDC Land Holdings, LLC *Florida East Coast Industries Inc* 726
FDC Offer Corporation *First Data Corp* 703
FDEE Consultng, nc. *Fluor Corp* 728
FDFS Holdings, LLC *First Data Corp* 703
FDGS Holdings, LLC *First Data Corp* 703
FDGS Holdings, LP *First Data Corp* 703
FDHM, nc. *Fluor Corp* 728
FDI Merchant Services Holding CV *Western Union Company (The)* 1952
FDI Merchant Services Holding (Netherlands) B.V. *First Data Corp* 703
FDI Merchant Services Holding (Netherlands) C.V. *First Data Corp* 703
FDM Holdings Limited *Fresh Del Monte Produce Inc* 749
FDMS Mexico Holdings Inc. *First Data Corp* 703
FDR Financial Group, Inc. *National Financial Partners Corp* 1241
FDR (First Data Resources) Europe B.V. *First Data Corp* 703
FDR Interactive Technologies Corporation *First Data Corp* 703
FDR Ireland Limited *First Data Corp* 703
FDR Limited *First Data Corp* 703
FDR Missouri Inc. *First Data Corp* 703
FDR Signet Inc. *First Data Corp* 703
FDR Singapore PTE Ltd. *First Data Corp* 703
FDR Subsidiary Corp. *First Data Corp* 703
Fdr U.k. Limited *First Data Corp* 703
FDS Bank *Macys Inc* 1108
Fds Liquidation Corporation *Southwest Community Bank* 1669
FDS Thrift Holding Co., Inc. *Macys Inc* 1108
FDT, Ltd. (Design Time, Ltd.) *Fossil Inc* 739
FDWR Parent LLC *GMH Communities Trust* 802
Fe & Fefh Holding, Inc. *Core Laboratories* 480
FE Acquisition Corp *Metropolitan Edison Co* 1173
FE Acquisition Corp *Ohio Edison Co* 1330
FE Acquisition Corp. *Jersey Central Power & Light Co* 1006
FE Acquisition Corp. *Pennsylvania Electric Co* 1404
FE Acquisition Corp. *Cleveland Electric Illuminating Co* 423
FE Acquisition Corp. *Toledo Edison Co* 1800
Fear of Flying Productions Inc. *Lions Gate Entertainment Corp* 1084
Fearing Manufacturing Co., Inc. *Digital Angel Corp* 555
Fearing Manufacturing Co., Inc. *Applied Digital Solutions Inc* 135
Fearless Shipco LLC *Quintana Maritime Ltd* 1503
Feather River Community Rentals, L.P. *Equity Residential* 654
Feather River Disposal, Inc. *Waste Management Inc* 1934
Feather River G.P. Corp. *Equity Residential* 654
Featherlite Aviation Company *Featherlite Inc* 682
Featherlite Chemicials Holdings, LLC *Featherlite Inc* 682
Feats Venture Capital Corp. *Massey Energy Co* 1129
FEBC-ALT Holdings Inc. *Brookdale Senior Living Inc* 285
FEBC-ALT Investors LLC *Brookdale Senior Living Inc* 285
FEC Highway Services, Inc. *Florida East Coast Industries Inc* 726
FECO, Inc. *Park Ohio Holdings Corp* 1386
Fed USA Franchising, Inc. *Affirmative Insurance Holdings Inc* 40
Fed USA Inc. *21st Century Holding Co* 2006
Fed USA Retail, Inc. *Affirmative Insurance Holdings Inc* 40
Fedders Addison Company, Inc *Fedders Corp* 682
Fedders Air Treatment Research and Development *Fedders Corp* 682
Fedders Eubank Company, Inc *Fedders Corp* 682
Fedders International Air Conditioning Pvt., Ltd. *Fedders Corp* 682
Fedders International, Inc. *Fedders Corp* 682
Fedders Investment Corporation *Fedders Corp* 682
Fedders Islandaire, Inc *Fedders Corp* 682
Fedders Koppel, Inc. *Fedders Corp* 682
Fedders North America, Inc. *Fedders Corp* 682
Fedders Shanghai Co., Ltd *Fedders Corp* 682
Fedders Suning (Nanjing) Co. Ltd *Fedders Corp* 682
Fedders (Suzhou) Indoor Air Quality Co. Ltd *Fedders Corp* 682
Fedders Xinle Co. Ltd. *Fedders Corp* 682
Fedea S.A. *Dow Chemical Co* 573
Federa S.A. *Cardinal Health Inc* 332
Federal APD do Brasil *Federal Signal Corp* 684
Federal APD, Inc. *Federal Signal Corp* 684
Federal Cartridge Company (in New York, d/b/a Federal Cartridge Company Inc.) *Alliant Techsystems Inc* 63
Federal Communications Group, Inc. *Integrated Electrical Services Inc* 956
Federal Deposit Insurance Corporation *Pacifica Bancorp Inc* 1375
Federal Deposit Insurance Corporation *Columbia Bancorp* 442

3030 - Subsidiary/Parent Index THE CORPORATE DIRECTORY - Walker's 2008

Fusion Technology International, Inc. *Axcelis Technologies Inc* ... 194
Fusion Telco S.A. *Fusion Telecommunications International Inc* ... 756
Fusion Turkey, LLC. *Fusion Telecommunications International Inc* ... 756
Fusion VoIP Acquisition Corp. *Fusion Telecommunications International Inc* ... 756
Fusite Corporation *Emerson Electric Co* ... 623
Fusite Land Company *Emerson Electric Co* ... 623
Fusite, B.V. *Emerson Electric Co* ... 623
Futaba Tenneco UK Ltd. *Tenneco Automotive Inc* ... 1775
Futaba-Walker U.K. Limited. *Tenneco Automotive Inc* ... 1775
FUTAC Group Limited *Intac International Inc* ... 953
Futbol del Distrito Federal, S.A. de C.V. *Grupo Televisa, S.A.B.* ... 829
Futura Natural Gas LLC *Macquarie Infrastructure Company Trust* ... 1107
Future Aviation, Inc *HEICO Corp* ... 865
Future Brand Israel Ltd *Interpublic Group of Companies Inc* ... 975
Future Brand Menu *Interpublic Group of Companies Inc* ... 975
Future Brands LLC *Fortune Brands Inc* ... 738
Future Communications Software *Flextronics International Ltd* ... 725
Future Communications Software Limited *Flextronics International Ltd* ... 725
Future Developments America, Inc. *MSGI Security Solutions Inc* ... 1223
Future Industrial and Welding Supplies Limited *BOC Group Plc* ... 262
Future Lab Business Group A/S *WPP Group Plc* ... 1979
Future Metals, Inc. *Union Tank Car Co* ... 1852
Future Mortgages 1 Limited *Citigroup Inc* ... 411
Future Mortgages Limited *Citigroup Inc* ... 411
Future Motorsport Concepts Pty Ltd *Interpublic Group of Companies Inc* ... 975
Future Net S.A. *Bancolombia* ... 205
Future Networks, Inc. *Tellabs Inc* ... 1770
Future Planning Associates, Inc. *USI Holdings Corp* ... 1880
Future Software Limited *Flextronics International Ltd* ... 725
Future Vision Media, Inc. *WPP Group Plc* ... 1979
Futurebrand Ag *Interpublic Group of Companies Inc* ... 975
Futurebrand Ag *Interpublic Group of Companies Inc* ... 975
Futurebrand Bc&h Ltda. *Interpublic Group of Companies Inc* ... 975
Futurebrand Fha Pty Ltd *Interpublic Group of Companies Inc* ... 975
Futurebrand Gio Rossi Associati Spa *Interpublic Group of Companies Inc* ... 975
Futurebrand Hong Kong Limited *Interpublic Group of Companies Inc* ... 975
Futurebrand Inc *Interpublic Group of Companies Inc* ... 975
Futurebrand Malaysia Sdn Bhd *Interpublic Group of Companies Inc* ... 975
Futurebrand Mexico, S.a. De C.v. *Interpublic Group of Companies Inc* ... 975
Futurebrand S.a. *Interpublic Group of Companies Inc* ... 975
Futurebrand S.a. *Interpublic Group of Companies Inc* ... 975
Futurebrand S.a. *Interpublic Group of Companies Inc* ... 975
Futurebrand S.a. *Interpublic Group of Companies Inc* ... 975
Futurebrand Singapore Pte Ltd *Interpublic Group of Companies Inc* ... 975
FutureCom Interactive AG *WPP Group Plc* ... 1979
FutureCom (Portugal) - Marketing, Telemarketing e Sistemas de Informacao Lda *WPP Group Plc* ... 1979
Futurecom-Imagination *WPP Group Plc* ... 1979
FutureGard Reinsurance Ltd. *Best Buy Co Inc* ... 234
FutureGen Industrial Alliance, Inc. *CONSOL Energy Inc* ... 470
FutureGen Industrial Alliance, Inc. *CONSOL Energy Inc WY* ... 470
Futuremedia America Inc. *Futuremedia Plc* ... 756
Futuremedia (BVI) Ltd *Futuremedia Plc* ... 756
Futuremedia Group *Futuremedia Plc* ... 756
Futuremedia Interactive Ltd. *Futuremedia Plc* ... 756
Futuremedia Sverige AB *Futuremedia Plc* ... 756
FutureSmart Systems, Inc. *Lifestyle Innovations Inc* ... 1076
FutureSource Capital Corp. *MDU Resources Group Inc* ... 1144
Futurestep (Australia) Pty Ltd *Korn Ferry International* ... 1041
Futurestep (Hong Kong) Ltd *Korn Ferry International* ... 1041
Futurestep (Japan) K.K. *Korn Ferry International* ... 1041
Futurestep (New Zealand) Ltd *Korn Ferry International* ... 1041
Futurestep (Singapore) Pte Ltd *Korn Ferry International* ... 1041
Futurestep (UK) Limited *Korn Ferry International* ... 1041
Futurestore Food Markets, Inc. *Great Atlantic & Pacific Tea Co Inc* ... 818
Futuretel S.A. *Citigroup Inc* ... 411
Futuro Familiar, S.a. De C.v. *Banco Bilbao Vizcaya Argentaria* ... 204
Fuvanka Industries Limited *Sun Motor International Inc* ... 1719
Fuyang Golden Autumn Chemicals Company Limited *Rockwood Holdings Inc* ... 1555
Fuzhou Focus Culture Communication Company Ltd. *Focus Media Holding Ltd* ... 732
Fuzhou Heng Ding Union Media Co., Ltd. *Focus Media Holding Ltd* ... 732
FV Commons, LLC *Regency Centers Corp* ... 1524
FV Fredericksburg, L.P. *Suntrust Banks Inc* ... 1724
FV Leasing Company *Transport Corp of America Inc* ... 1817
FV PEF GmbH *Allianz* ... 63
FV Productions Ltd. *News Corp Ltd (The)* ... 1281
FV SPE, LLC *Brookdale Senior Living Inc* ... 285
FV Steel and Wire Company *Keystone Consolidated Industries Inc* ... 1027
FV-I, Inc. *Morgan Stanley* ... 1215
FVB Capital Trust I *First Valley Bancorp Inc CT* ... 718
FVC Management Co.,Inc *Fleetwood Enterprises Inc* ... 724
FVEST.JOE, Inc. *Five Star Quality Care Inc* ... 722
FW Allenbeth GP, LLC *Regency Centers Corp* ... 1524
FW Bowie Plaza GP, LLC *Regency Centers Corp* ... 1524
FW CA-Auburn Village, LLC *Regency Centers Corp* ... 1524
FW CA-Bay Hill Shopping Center, LLC *Regency Centers Corp* ... 1524
FW CA-Brea Marketplace Member, LLC *Regency Centers Corp* ... 1524
FW CA-Brea Marketplace, LLC *Regency Centers Corp* ... 1524
FW CA-Five Points Shopping Center, LLC *Regency Centers Corp* ... 1524
FW CA-Granada Village, LLC *Regency Centers Corp* ... 1524
FW CA-Laguna Niguel Plaza, LLC *Regency Centers Corp* ... 1524
FW CA-Lake Forest Village, LLC *Regency Centers Corp* ... 1524
FW CA-Mariposa Gardens Shopping Center, LLC *Regency Centers Corp* ... 1524
FW CA-Navajo Shopping Center, LLC *Regency Centers Corp* ... 1524
FW CA-Pleasant Hill Shopping Center, LLC *Regency Centers Corp* ... 1524
FW CA-Point Loma Plaza, LLC *Regency Centers Corp* ... 1524
FW CA-Rancho San Diego Village, LLC *Regency Centers Corp* ... 1524
FW CA-Silverado Plaza, LLC *Regency Centers Corp* ... 1524
FW CA-Snell& Branham Plaza, LLC *Regency Centers Corp* ... 1524
FW CA-Stanford Ranch Village, LLC *Regency Centers Corp* ... 1524
FW CA-Twin Oaks Shopping Center, LLC *Regency Centers Corp* ... 1524
FW CA-Ygnacio Plaza, LLC *Regency Centers Corp* ... 1524
FW CT-Corbins Corner Shopping Center, LLC *Regency Centers Corp* ... 1524
FW DC-Spring Valley Shopping Center, LLC *Regency Centers Corp* ... 1524
FW Elkridge Corners GP, LLC *Regency Centers Corp* ... 1524
FW Energie B.V. *Foster Wheeler Ltd* ... 740
FW Energie Holdings Spain S.L. *Foster Wheeler Ltd* ... 740
FW Europe B.V. *Foster Wheeler Ltd* ... 740
FW European E&C Ltd. *Foster Wheeler Ltd* ... 740
FW First Colony GP, LLC *Regency Centers Corp* ... 1524
FW Gayton Holding, LLC *Regency Centers Corp* ... 1524
FW Hungary Licensing Limited Liability Company *Foster Wheeler Ltd* ... 740
FW IL-Brentwood Commons, LLC *Regency Centers Corp* ... 1524
FW IL-Civic Center Plaza, LLC *Regency Centers Corp* ... 1524
FW IL-Mallard Creek, LLC *Regency Centers Corp* ... 1524
FW IL-McHenry Commons Shopping Center, LLC *Regency Centers Corp* ... 1524
FW IL-Riverside/Rivers Edge, LLC *Regency Centers Corp* ... 1524
FW IL-Riverview Plaza, LLC *Regency Centers Corp* ... 1524
FW IL-Stonebrook Plaza, LLC *Regency Centers Corp* ... 1524
FW IL-The Oaks Shopping Center, LLC *Regency Centers Corp* ... 1524
FW Lake Forest Holding, LLC *Regency Centers Corp* ... 1524
FW Management Operations Ltd. *Foster Wheeler Ltd* ... 740
FW Management Operations (U.K.) Limited,International Management Systems Limited *Foster Wheeler Ltd* ... 740
FW MCW-Reg II Holding Company Two, LLC *Regency Centers Corp* ... 1524
FW MCW-Reg II Holdings, LLC *Regency Centers Corp* ... 1524
FW MD-Clinton Square, LLC *Regency Centers Corp* ... 1524
FW MD-Rosecroft Shopping Center, LLC *Regency Centers Corp* ... 1524
FW Memorial GP, LLC *Regency Centers Corp* ... 1524
FW NC-Shoppes of Kildaire, LLC *Regency Centers Corp* ... 1524
FW Netherlands C.V. *Foster Wheeler Ltd* ... 740
FW Newark, LLC *Regency Centers Corp* ... 1524
FW NJ-Westmont Shopping Center, LLC *Regency Centers Corp* ... 1524
FW Northway GP, LLC *Regency Centers Corp* ... 1524
FW OR-Greenway Town Center, LLC *Regency Centers Corp* ... 1524
FW Overseas Operations Limited *Foster Wheeler Ltd* ... 740
FW Penn Station GP, LLC *Regency Centers Corp* ... 1524
FW Pharma Systems *Parexel International Corp* ... 1385
FW Preferred Capital Trust I *Foster Wheeler Ltd* ... 740
FW Southside Marketplace GP, LLC *Regency Centers Corp* ... 1524
FW The Oaks Holding, LLC *Regency Centers Corp* ... 1524
FW TX-First Colony Marketplace, L.P. *Regency Centers Corp* ... 1524
FW TX-Memorial Collection, L.P. *Regency Centers Corp* ... 1524
FW TX-Weslyan Plaza, L.P. *Regency Centers Corp* ... 1524
FW TX-Westheimer Marketplace, L.P. *Regency Centers Corp* ... 1524
FW TX-Woodway Collection, L.P. *Regency Centers Corp* ... 1524
FW VA-601 Kings Street, LLC *Regency Centers Corp* ... 1524
FW VA-Ashburn Farm Village Center, LLC *Regency Centers Corp* ... 1524
FW VA-Brafferton Shopping Center, LLC *Regency Centers Corp* ... 1524
FW VA-Centre Ridge Marketplace, LLC *Regency Centers Corp* ... 1524
FW VA-Fox Mill Shopping Center, LLC *Regency Centers Corp* ... 1524
FW VA-Gayton Crossing Shopping Center, LLC *Regency Centers Corp* ... 1524
FW VA-Greenbriar Pad, LLC *Regency Centers Corp* ... 1524
FW VA-Kings Park Shopping Center, LLC *Regency Centers Corp* ... 1524
FW VA-Laburnum Square, LLC *Regency Centers Corp* ... 1524
FW VA-Saratoga Shopping Center, LLC *Regency Centers Corp* ... 1524
FW VA-The Village Shopping Center, LLC *Regency Centers Corp* ... 1524
FW Valley Centre GP, LLC *Regency Centers Corp* ... 1524
FW WA-Aurora Marketplace, LLC *Regency Centers Corp* ... 1524
FW WA-Eastgate Plaza, LLC *Regency Centers Corp* ... 1524
FW WA-Overlake Fashion Plaza, LLC *Regency Centers Corp* ... 1524
FW Weslyan GP, LLC *Regency Centers Corp* ... 1524
FW Westheimer GP, LLC *Regency Centers Corp* ... 1524
FW WI Racine Centre, LLC *Regency Centers Corp* ... 1524
FW WI-Cudahy Center, LLC *Regency Centers Corp* ... 1524
FW WI-Whitnall Square, LLC *Regency Centers Corp* ... 1524
FW Woodholm GP, LLC *Regency Centers Corp* ... 1524
FW Woodway GP, LLC *Regency Centers Corp* ... 1524
FWA Productions, Inc. *News Corp Ltd (The)* ... 1281
FWC Beverages Corp. *BJ's Wholesale Club Inc* ... 252
FWCC Merger Corp *US Global Nanospace Inc* ... 1877
FWJ Inc. *American Standard Companies Inc* ... 103
FWPI Ltd. *Foster Wheeler Ltd* ... 740
FWPS Group Ltd *Parexel International Corp* ... 1385
FWPS Specialty Products Inc. *Foster Wheeler Ltd* ... 740
Fx Drilling Company, Inc. *FX Energy Inc* ... 756
Fx Energy Netherlands B.v. *FX Energy Inc* ... 756
Fx Energy Netherlands Partnership C.v. *FX Energy Inc* ... 756
Fx Energy Poland Sp. Zo.o *FX Energy Inc* ... 756
FX Holdings, Inc. *Frozen Food Express Industries Inc* ... 751
FX Networks, LLC *News Corp Ltd (The)* ... 1281
Fx Producing Company, Inc. *FX Energy Inc* ... 756
FX Unlimited Inc. *Mad Catz Interactive Inc* ... 1108
FXF Logistica de Mexico, S. de R.L. de C.V. *Fedex Corp* ... 685
FXT Productions Ltd. *News Corp Ltd (The)* ... 1281
FYL CORP. *F5 Networks Inc* ... 674
FYL CORP. *General Mills Inc* ... 772
FYNRE *Millenium Holding Group Inc* ... 1191
Fyrcia HB *Pfizer Inc* ... 1420
Fyrnetics (Hong Kong) Limited *United Technologies Corp* ... 1863
FZN Marbaise LS Sp. z.o.o. *Emerson Electric Co* ... 623
G & C Business Services, Inc. *Century Business Services Inc* ... 365
G & I III Colony Woods, LLC *Colonial Properties Trust* ... 440
G & I III Madison, LLC *Colonial Properties Trust* ... 440
G & I III Meadows, LLC *Colonial Properties Trust* ... 440
G & I IV Cunningham LP *Colonial Properties Trust* ... 440
G & I V Riverchase LLC *Colonial Properties Trust* ... 440
G & K Propane *Energy Transfer Partners LP* ... 636
G C Limited Partners I, Inc. *W. R. Grace & Co* ... 1927
G C Management, Inc. *W. R. Grace & Co* ... 1927
G C Peru S.R.L. *Global Crossing Ltd* ... 792
G Judd and Rose Caterers Limited *Yum! Brands Inc* ... 1994
G L Baker (Transport) Limited *BOC Group Plc* ... 262
G Link Solutions, LLC *GlobeTel Communications Corp* ... 800
G Televisa-D, S.A. de C.V. *Grupo Televisa, S.A.B.* ... 829
G Too, LLC *Too Inc* ... 1802
G Van Dongen Holding BV *BOC Group Plc* ... 262
G Van Dongen Transportbedrjf Dirksland BV *BOC Group Plc* ... 262
G Whiz Entertainment Inc. *WPP Group Plc* ... 1979
G&C Venezuela. S.A. *Aon Corp* ... 129
G&G Medical, Inc. *Rotech Healthcare Inc NEW* ... 1560
G&K Properties Pty Ltd *Layne Christensen Co* ... 1060
G&K Services Canada Inc. *G & K Services Inc* ... 757
G&K Services, Co. *G & K Services Inc* ... 757
G&L Motion Control Inc. *Danaher Corp* ... 525
G&L Sign Manufacturing Corp. *Viacom Inc* ... 1902
G&L Sign Manufacturing Corp. *CBS Corp* ... 349
G&p Development, Inc. *Waste Connections Inc* ... 1934
G&W Leasing Company *Viacom Inc* ... 1902
G&W Leasing Company *CBS Corp* ... 349
G&W Natural Resources Company, Inc. *CBS Corp* ... 349
G&W Natural Resources Company, Inc. *Viacom Inc* ... 1902
G-Connect, Ltd. *ADC Telecommunications Inc* ... 22
G-TV Guide, LLC *Gemstar-TV Guide International Inc* ... 766
G. C. Leasing, Inc. *Wachovia Corp* ... 1928
G. D. Searle & Co. Limited *Pfizer Inc* ... 1420
G. D. Searle International Capital LLC *Pfizer Inc* ... 1420
G. D. Searle Land Corporation *Pfizer Inc* ... 1420
G. D. Searle LLC *Pfizer Inc* ... 1420
G. D. Searle (Philippines) Inc *Pfizer Inc* ... 1420
G. D. Searle South Africa Pty) Ltd *Pfizer Inc* ... 1420
G. D. Searle (Thailand) Limited *Pfizer Inc* ... 1420
G. E. Freeman Insurance Agency Limited *Marsh & McLennan Cos Inc* ... 1125
G. H. Bass Franchises Inc. *Phillips Van Heusen Corp* ... 1425
G. Kox en Zoon B.V. *Akzo Nobel* ... 49
G. Leblanc SNC *Steinway Musical Instruments Inc* ... 1699
G. M. Fabricators, L.P *Gulf Island Fabrication Inc* ... 834
G. stervig-Molex A/S *Molex Inc* ... 1208
G. Triad Development Corp. *Computer Horizons Corp* ... 462
G. Van Dyken Disposal Inc. *Allied Waste Industries Inc* ... 66
G.a. Love Foods Inc. *Great Atlantic & Pacific Tea Co Inc* ... 818
G.a.m.e., LLC *CCE Spinco Inc* ... 349
G.B. Import Sales & Service, LLC *Autonation Inc FL* ... 183
G.C. Evans (Holdings) Limited *SPX Corp* ... 1684
G.C. St. Croix Company, Inc. *Global Crossing Ltd* ... 792
G.E.M. Environmental Management, Inc. *Republic Services Inc* ... 1534
G.E.T. (Holdings) Limited *Gaming & Entertainment Group Ltd* ... 760
G.G. Canada, Inc. *Gartner Inc* ... 762
G.G. Credit, Inc. *Gartner Inc* ... 762
G.G. Properties, Ltd. *Gartner Inc* ... 762
G.G. Realty Corp., Ltd. *Toys R US Inc* ... 1809
G.G. West Corporation *Gartner Inc* ... 762
G.H. Bass Caribbean LLC *Phillips Van Heusen Corp* ... 1425
G.H.Y. Capital B.V. *Morgan Stanley* ... 1215
G.H.Y. Capital II B.V. *Morgan Stanley* ... 1215
G.I. Industries *Waste Management Inc* ... 1934
G.I.C. Uslugi Finansowe Sp. z o.o. *GTECH Holdings Corp* ... 832
G.I.S. Statewide Pty Limited (in liquidation) *Willis Group Holdings Ltd* ... 1962
G.I.T. Uniphnix *Allianz* ... 63
G.L. Insurance Corporation *Host Hotels & Resorts Inc* ... 892
G.m.a.c. Comercio E Aluguer De Veiculos, Lta. *General Motors Corp* ... 772
G.m.a.c. Financiera De Colombia S.a. Compania De Financiamiento Comercial *General Motors Corp* ... 772
G.M.A.C. Financiera de Colombia S.A. Compania de Financiamiento Comercial *GMAC LLC* ... 801
G.M.A.C. Comercio e Aluguer de Veiculos, Lda. *GMAC LLC* ... 801
G.N. Metal Products, Inc. *Servotronics Inc* ... 1614
G.P. Associates Holding Corp. *Independence Holding Co* ... 933
G.P. MUNICIPAL HOLDINGS, L.L.C. *Apartment Investment and Management Company* ... 130
G.P. Royalty Distribution Corporation *CVF Technologies Corp* ... 515
G.S. Blodgett Corporation *Middleby Corp* ... 1185
G.S. Blodgett International, LTD *Middleby Corp* ... 1185
G.S. North,Ltd *Tenet Healthcare Corp* ... 1774
G.s.p., LLC *Olympic Steel Inc* ... 1335
G.u.i.c. Insurance Company *Midland Co* ... 1187
G.W.M. Holdings, Inc. *Supervalu Inc* ... 1728
G.Z. Holdings Pte. Ltd. *Dow Chemical Co* ... 573
G/C Waterside Associates, L.L.C. *Crescent Real Estate Equities Company* ... 499
G1440 Holdings, Inc. *Sinclair Broadcast Group Inc* ... 1636
G1440, LLC *Sinclair Broadcast Group Inc* ... 1636
G2 Advertising Inc. *WPP Group Plc* ... 1979
G2 Agency Ltd (formerly GI Data Ltd) *WPP Group Plc* ... 1979
G2 Chile S.A. *WPP Group Plc* ... 1979
G2 Ltd *WPP Group Plc* ... 1979
G2 Oslo AS *WPP Group Plc* ... 1979
G2 Pty Ltd (fka Grey Direct Pty Ltd) *WPP Group Plc* ... 1979
G2 Srl (former Grey Direct Srl) *WPP Group Plc* ... 1979
G2 Stockholm AB *WPP Group Plc* ... 1979
G2 Taiwan *WPP Group Plc* ... 1979
G2 Worldwide Inc. *WPP Group Plc* ... 1979
G2.Grey Comunicaao e Marketing Ltda. (fka Alfaiataria de Marketing Ltda) *WPP Group Plc* ... 1979
G3 Communications Pvt. Ltd. *WPP Group Plc* ... 1979
G3 Worldwide Mail N.V. *TNT N.V.* ... 1800
G4 Holding Company *Comcast Corp* ... 444
G4 Media, Inc. *Comcast Corp* ... 444
Ga Holding Corp. *Metlife Inc* ... 1171
GA Landfills, Inc. *Waste Management Inc* ... 1934
GAB Investment Center, Inc. *German American Bancorp* ... 783
GAB Investment Company, Inc. *German American Bancorp* ... 783
GAB Investments, LLC *German American Bancorp* ... 783
GAB Mortgage Corp *German American Bancorp* ... 783
GABA Holding A.G. *Colgate Palmolive Co* ... 439
GABA Holdings Delaware, LLC *Colgate Palmolive Co* ... 439
Gabauer Funeral Home, Inc. *Service Corp International* ... 1614
Gabbay, LTD *Pharmaceutical Product Development Inc* ... 1422
Gabelli & Company, Inc. *Gabelli Asset Mgmt Inc* ... 757
Gabelli & Partners LLC *Gabelli Asset Mgmt Inc* ... 757
Gabelli Advisers, Inc. *Gabelli Asset Mgmt Inc* ... 757
Gabelli Asset Management (UK) Limited *Gabelli Asset Mgmt Inc* ... 757
Gabelli Convertible Holdings, LLC *Gabelli Asset Mgmt Inc* ... 757
Gabelli Direct, Inc. *Gabelli Asset Mgmt Inc* ... 757
Gabelli Fixed Income Distributors, Inc. *Gabelli Asset Mgmt Inc* ... 757
Gabelli Fixed Income LLC *Gabelli Asset Mgmt Inc* ... 757
Gabelli Fixed Income, Inc. *Gabelli Asset Mgmt Inc* ... 757
Gabelli Funds, LLC *Gabelli Asset Mgmt Inc* ... 757
Gabelli Securities, Inc. *Gabelli Asset Mgmt Inc* ... 757
Gabetti Holding SpA *Barclays Plc* ... 216
Gables Indiana, Inc. *Associated Estates Realty Corp* ... 164

3086 - Subsidiary/Parent Index THE CORPORATE DIRECTORY - Walker's 2008

Indiamalt Private Limited *Lubrizol Corp (The)* ... 1099
Indian Creek Investors, LLC *First Potomac Realty Trust* ... 715
Indian Gaming Corporation *Butler National Corp* ... 298
Indian Harbor Insurance Company *XL Capital Ltd* ... 1987
Indian Head Banks, Inc. *Bank of America Corp* ... 208
Indian Hill Company *Peabody Energy Corp* ... 1398
Indian Market Research Bureau Ltd *WPP Group Plc* ... 1979
Indian Oil Company *Castle Energy Corp* ... 343
Indian Path Hospital, Inc. *HCA Inc* ... 855
Indian Path Rehabilitation Center, Inc. *HCA Inc* ... 855
Indian Path, LLC *HCA Inc* ... 855
Indian Refining & Marketing I Inc. *Castle Energy Corp* ... 343
Indian Region Broadcasting Limited *News Corp Ltd (The)* ... 1281
Indian River Capital Trust I *Alabama National Bancorp* ... 50
Indian River IGCC LLC *NRG Energy Inc* ... 1312
Indian River National Bank *Alabama National Bancorp* ... 50
Indian River Operations Inc. *NRG Energy Inc* ... 1312
Indian River Power LLC *NRG Energy Inc* ... 1312
Indian River Surgery Center, Ltd. *HealthSouth Corp* ... 861
Indian River Title Company, LLC *Alabama National Bancorp* ... 50
Indian Run Limited Partnership *Wachovia Corp* ... 1928
Indian Springs at Woodlands, Ltd. *Regency Centers Corp* ... 1524
Indian Springs GP, LLC *Regency Centers Corp* ... 1524
Indiana & Ohio Rail Corp. *Railamerica Inc* ... 1510
Indiana & Ohio Railway Company *Railamerica Inc* ... 1510
Indiana Avenue LLC *HRPT Properties Trust* ... 894
Indiana Broadcasting LLC *Lin Television Corp* ... 1079
Indiana Broadcasting LLC *Lin Tv Corp* ... 1079
Indiana Gaming Company, L.P. *Penn National Gaming Inc* ... 1402
Indiana Gaming Holding Company *Penn National Gaming Inc* ... 1402
Indiana Gaming II, L.P. *Penn National Gaming Inc* ... 1402
Indiana Gas Company, Inc. *Vectren Corp* ... 1892
Indiana Glass Company *Lancaster Colony Corp* ... 1052
Indiana Harbor Coke Company *Sunoco Inc* ... 1721
Indiana Harbor Coke Corporation *Sunoco Inc* ... 1721
Indiana Interactive, LLC *NIC Inc* ... 1285
Indiana Lessor - Jeffersonville, Inc. *Omega Healthcare Investors Inc* ... 1336
Indiana Lessor - Wellington Manor, Inc. *Omega Healthcare Investors Inc* ... 1336
Indiana Newspapers, Inc. *Gannett Co Inc* ... 761
Indiana Parks, Inc. *Six Flags Inc* ... 1640
Indiana Pickling and Processing Company *Illinois Tool Works Inc* ... 922
Indiana Precision, Inc. *Kaydon Corp* ... 1019
Indiana Psychiatric Institutes, LLC *Psychiatric Solutions Inc* ... 1485
Indiana Recycling, LLC *Republic Services Inc* ... 1534
Indiana Residential Nominee Services, LLC *Fidelity National Financial Inc* ... 690
Indiana Residential Nominee Services, LLC *Fidelity National Information Services Inc* ... 690
Indiana Royalty Trustory, LLC *Aurora Oil & Gas Corp* ... 179
INDIANA RSA # 4, INC. *United States Cellular Corp* ... 1862
Indiana Rsa # 4, Inc. *Telephone and Data Systems Inc* ... 1768
Indiana Rsa # 5, Inc. *Telephone and Data Systems Inc* ... 1768
INDIANA RSA # 5, INC. *United States Cellular Corp* ... 1862
INDIANA RSA NO. 4 LIMITED PARTNERSHIP *United States Cellular Corp* ... 1862
Indiana Rsa No. 4 Limited Partnership *Telephone and Data Systems Inc* ... 1768
Indiana Rsa No. 5 Limited Partnership *Telephone and Data Systems Inc* ... 1768
INDIANA RSA NO. 5 LIMITED PARTNERSHIP *United States Cellular Corp* ... 1862
Indiana Southern Railroad, Inc. *Railamerica Inc* ... 1510
Indiana Southwestern Railway Co. *Pioneer Railcorp* ... 1433
Indiana Title Insurance Co., LLC *Mutualfirst Financial Inc* ... 1228
Indiana Title Insurance Company, LLC *Ameriana Bancorp* ... 83
Indiana Veterinary Diagnostic Lab, Inc. *VCA Antech Inc* ... 1891
Indiana-Kentucky Electric Corporation *Columbus Southern Power Co* ... 443
Indianapolis Campus Energy, Inc. *AES Corp* ... 38
Indianapolis Data Link, Inc. *Cincinnati Gas & Electric Co* ... 407
Indianapolis Data Link, Inc. *Union Light Heat & Power Co* ... 1852
Indianapolis Health Systems,Inc. *Tenet Healthcare Corp* ... 1774
Indianapolis Hospital Partner, LLC *HCA Inc* ... 855
Indianapolis Life Insurance Company *Amerus Group Co* ... 112
Indianapolis Power & Light Company *AES Corp* ... 38
Indianapolis Power & Light Company *IPALCO Enterprises Inc* ... 986
Indianapolis Real Estate, LLC. *Universal Forest Products Inc* ... 1868
Indianapolis Store No. 16, LLC *Agree Realty Corp* ... 44
Indianapolis TPP LLC *Host Hotels & Resorts Inc* ... 892
Indianhead Communications Corporation *Hector Communications Corp* ... 864
Indianhead Telephone Company *Hector Communications Corp* ... 864
Indiantown Project Investment Partnership, L.P. *Dana Corp* ... 525
IndiaWorld Communications Limited *Sify Technologies Ltd* ... 1627
Indie Built, Inc. *Take Two Interactive Software Inc* ... 1745
Indigo Acquisition Corporation *Yahoo Inc* ... 1990
Indigo America,Inc. *Hewlett-Packard Company* ... 874
Indigo Blue S.A. *Warnaco Group Inc* ... 1930
Indigo Development Inc *Consolidated Tomoka Land Co* ... 472
Indigo Entertainment Inc. *WPP Group Plc* ... 1979
Indigo Entertainment, Inc. *Playboy Enterprises Inc* ... 1439
Indigo Group Inc *Consolidated Tomoka Land Co* ... 472
Indigo Hewitson-Walker Limited *BB Holdings Ltd* ... 222
Indigo International Inc *Consolidated Tomoka Land Co* ... 472
Indigo Pointe Management, LLC *Suntrust Banks Inc* ... 1724
Indigo Pointe, L.P. *Suntrust Banks Inc* ... 1724
Indigo Selection Holdings PTY Limited *BB Holdings Ltd* ... 222
Indigo Selection Limited *BB Holdings Ltd* ... 222
Indigo Selection PTY Limited *BB Holdings Ltd* ... 222
Indigo Systems Corporation. *FLIR Systems Inc* ... 726
Indigo Technology Services, Inc. *Softnet Technology Corp* ... 1652
Indigosquare Limited (in liquidation 15.02.2006) *Barclays Plc* ... 216
INDIO GARDENS AFFORDABLE, L.P. *Apartment Investment and Management Company* ... 130
Indio Jackson, LLC *Regency Centers Corp* ... 1524
Indo-Pacific Energy Australia Pty Limited *Austral Pacific Energy Ltd* ... 180
Indo-Pacific Oil & Gas, Inc. *Fortune Oil & Gas Inc* ... 738
Indo-Pacific Resources Java Ltd. *Fortune Oil & Gas Inc* ... 738
Indoco International B.V. *Universal Corp* ... 1867
Indonesia Fuel Oil Capital Co., Ltd. *Mitsui & Co Ltd* ... 1201
Indonesia Power Holdings Limited *BOC Group Plc* ... 262
Indoor Air Quality Services, Inc *Searchhelp Inc* ... 1600
Indopco Inc *Imperial Chemical Industries Plc* ... 929
Indosat Finance Company B.V *PT Indosat Tbk* ... 1485
Indosat International Finance Company B.V *PT Indosat Tbk* ... 1485
Indosat Singapore Pte Ltd *PT Indosat Tbk* ... 1485
INDSPEC Chemical Corporation *Occidental Petroleum Corp* ... 1325
INDSPEC Holding Corporation *Occidental Petroleum Corp* ... 1325
INDSPEC Technologies, Ltd. *Occidental Petroleum Corp* ... 1325
Inductis India Private Limited *ExlService Holdings Inc* ... 669
Inductis LLC *ExlService Holdings Inc* ... 669
Inductis (Singapore) PTE Ltd. *ExlService Holdings Inc* ... 669
Inductis, Inc. *ExlService Holdings Inc* ... 669
Indugas N.V. *Praxair Inc* ... 1458
Indumentaria Andina S.A. *Hanesbrands Inc* ... 843
Indura Argentina S.A. *BOC Group Plc* ... 262
Indura Panama S.A. *BOC Group Plc* ... 262
Indura S.A. (Peru) *BOC Group Plc* ... 262
Indura S.A. Sucursal Peru *BOC Group Plc* ... 262
Indura S.A., Industria y Comercio *BOC Group Plc* ... 262
Indurisk Rckversicherungs-AG *BASF* ... 218
Industra-Comercio de Equipamentos Industriais, SA *Tyco International Ltd* ... 1838
Industrade AG *Arrow Electronics Inc* ... 152
Industri-Filter A/S *SPX Corp* ... 1684
Indstria Aeronutica Neiva Ltda. Neiva *Empresa Brasileira de Aeronautica S.A.* ... 625
Industria AG *Universal Corp* ... 1867
Industria Centroamericana de Sanitarios, Sociedad Anonima (Incesa - Guatemala) *American Standard Companies Inc* ... 103
Industria Ceramica Centroamericana, S.A. (Incesa-Nicaragua) *American Standard Companies Inc* ... 103
Industria Ceramica Costarricense S.A. (INCESA- Costa Rica) *American Standard Companies Inc* ... 103
Industria Ceramica Del Centro, S. A. de C. V. *American Standard Companies Inc* ... 103
Industria Composizioni Stampate, Spa *Exide Technologies* ... 669
Industria De Ejes Y Transmissiones S.A. *Dana Corp* ... 525
Industria de Materias Primas S.A. *Owens Illinois Inc* ... 1366
Industria de Refrescos Del Noreste, S.R.L. *Pepsi Bottling Group Inc* ... 1409
Industria de Refrescos, S.R.L. *Pepsi Bottling Group Inc* ... 1409
Industria del Alcali, S.A. de C.V. *Vitro* ... 1918
Industria Farmaceutica Serono S.p.A. *Serono* ... 1613
Indstria Nacional de Aos Laminados *National Steel Corp* ... 1247
Industria Paraguaya de Gases S.A. *Praxair Inc* ... 1458
Industria S. A. *CIRCOR International Inc* ... 408
Industria Textileras del Este, S. de R.L. *Hanesbrands Inc* ... 843
Industrial & Automotive Associates, Inc. *Standard Motor Products Inc* ... 1690
Industrial & Welding Management Limited *BOC Group Plc* ... 262
Industrial & Welding Supplies (North West) Limited *BOC Group Plc* ... 262
Industrial Airsystems, Inc. *Modine Manufacturing Co* ... 1206
Industrial Automation, Inc. *Powersecure International Inc* ... 1455
Industrial Blaju, S.A. de C.V. *TB Wood's Corp* ... 1753
Industrial Building Services LLC *Lennox International Inc* ... 1068
Industrial Capacitors (Wrexham) Ltd. *Tech Ops Sevcon Inc* ... 1756
Industrial Chill Servicing Private Ltd. *American Standard Companies Inc* ... 103
Industrial Cleaners (UK) Limited *Tyco International Ltd* ... 1838
Industrial Conveyors Sdn Bhd *Terex Corp* ... 1777
Industrial De Marcas Ltda *Avery Dennison Corp* ... 188
Industrial Electric Services, LLC *Industrial Electrical Services Inc* ... 935
Industrial Fastener Supplies Ltd. *Anixter International Inc* ... 125
Industrial Fasteners Ltd. *Anixter International Inc* ... 125
Industrial Fasteners, Inc. *Danaher Corp* ... 525
Industrial Gases Inc. *StealthGas Inc* ... 1697
Industrial Gases (Pvt) Limited *BOC Group Plc* ... 262
Industrial Group Metran *Emerson Electric Co* ... 623
Industrial Helvetia S.A. *Kimberly Clark Corp* ... 1029
Industrial Holding Group, Inc *Eline Entertainment Group Inc* ... 616
Industrial Investment Corporation *Bank of America Corp* ... 208
Industrial Investments Limited *Royal & Sun Alliance Insurance Group Plc* ... 1560
Industrial Leasing Corporation of Fitchburg, Inc. *Bank of America Corp* ... 208
Industrial Leasing Corporation of Massachusetts, Inc. *Bank of America Corp* ... 208
Industrial Leasing Corporation of Springfield, Inc. *Bank of America Corp* ... 208
Industrial Machine Co., Inc. *Sonoco Products Co* ... 1658
Industrial Machinery Company (liquidation in progress) *Textron Inc* ... 1783
Industrial Materials Inc. *StealthGas Inc* ... 1697
Industrial Mimosa S.A. *Kimberly Clark Corp* ... 1029
Industrial Minerals Canada, Inc. *Industrial Minerals Inc* ... 935
Industrial Molding GP, LLC *NN Inc* ... 1290
Industrial Molding LP *NN Inc* ... 1290
Industrial Molding LP,LLC *NN Inc* ... 1290
Industrial National Leasing Corporation *Bank of America Corp* ... 208
Industrial Plating Enterprise Co. *American Ammunition Inc FL* ... 84
Industrial Products of New England, Inc. *Big Lots Inc* ... 238
Industrial Research and Development (Pty) Limited *BOC Group Plc* ... 262
Industrial Sensors, Inc. *Danaher Corp* ... 525
Industrial Specialty Company Incorporated *MSC Industrial Direct Co Inc* ... 1223
Industrial Specialty Company,Inc. of Tupelo *MSC Industrial Direct Co Inc* ... 1223
Industrial Tectonics Bearings Corporation *RBC Bearings Inc* ... 1517
Industrial Tectonics Inc *Kaydon Corp* ... 1019
Industrial Valley Real Estate Co *Wachovia Corp* ... 1928
Industrial Waste Management Inc. *Perma Fix Environmental Services Inc* ... 1413
Industrial Y Minera Nortena S. A. *American Standard Companies Inc* ... 103
Industrias Alcan Packaging Enocap Limitada *Alcan Inc* ... 54
Industrias Arga, S.A. de C.V. *Hillenbrand Industries Inc* ... 879
Industrias Carlisil, S.A. *Dow Chemical Co* ... 573
Industrias Citrcolas de Montemorelos, S.A. de C.V. *Del Monte Foods Co* ... 536
Industrias Cousin Freres, S.L. *Lear Corp* ... 1062
Industrias De Carnes Nobre, S.a. *Sara Lee Corp* ... 1585
Industrias Del Tabaco, Alimentos Y Bebidas S.A. *Altria Group Inc* ... 74
Industrias Forestales S.A. *Arauco & Constitution Pulp Inc* ... 141
Industrias Frigorificas, S.A. de C.V. *Ingersoll Rand Co Ltd* ... 943
Industrias Fronterizas HLI, S.A. de C.V. *Hayes Lemmerz International Inc* ... 855
Industrias Hecla S.A. de C.V. *Hecla Mining Co* ... 864
Industrias Hudson S.A. de C.V. *Teleflex Inc* ... 1766
Industrias Internacionales de San Pedro S. de R.L. de C.V. *Hanesbrands Inc* ... 843
Industrias John Deere Argentina S.A. *Deere & Co* ... 535
Industrias Kativo de Nicaragua, S.A. *H.B. Fuller Co* ... 837
Industrias Lancermex, S.A. de C.V. *Lancer Corp TX* ... 1053
Industrias Lanier De Honduras S. de R.L. *Oxford Industries Inc* ... 1366
Industrias Lear de Argentina SrL *Lear Corp* ... 1062
Industrias Medina S.A. de C.V. *Flowserve Corp* ... 728
Industrias Metalicas Castello S.a. *Alcan Inc* ... 54
Industrias Mexicanas S.A. *SKF Inc* ... 1641
Industrias Modernas, S.A. *Procter & Gamble* ... 1472
Industrias National Supply C.A. *National Oilwell Inc* ... 1244
Industrias Oxford de Merida, S.A. de CV *Oxford Industries Inc* ... 1366
Industrias Polioles S.A. de C.V. *BASF* ... 218
Industrias Quimicas Falcon de Mexico, SA de CV *Dr Reddy's Laboratories Ltd* ... 574
Industrias Regard *Illinois Tool Works Inc* ... 922
Industrias Reliance S.A. de C.V. *Rockwell Automation Inc* ... 1554
Industrias Reunidas de Plastico e Mineracao S. A. *Praxair Inc* ... 1458
Industrias Royer, S.A. de C.V. *Cooper Industries Ltd* ... 477
Industrias Spartech de Mexico, S.R.L. de C.V. *Spartech Corp* ... 1675
Industrie Assekuranz GmbH *Willis Group Holdings Ltd* ... 1962
Industrie Assekuranz Gmbh *Aon Corp* ... 129
Industriepark Nienburg GmbH *Akzo Nobel* ... 49
Industries Universales Unidas de Mexico, S.A. *Superior Industries International Inc* ... 1727
Industrieservice Ges.m.b.H. *Rockwood Holdings Inc* ... 1555
Industrivej 30 Pandrup APS *Flextronics International Ltd* ... 725
Industry Land Development Company *St Paul Travelers Cos Inc* ... 1687
Industry Land Development Company *Travelers Property Casualty Corp* ... 1818
Industry Partners *Travelers Property Casualty Corp* ... 1818
Industry Partners *St Paul Travelers Cos Inc* ... 1687
Industry Research Collective, L.L.C. *Vornado Realty Trust* ... 1923
IndustryBrains, LLC *Marchex Inc* ... 1121
IndustryClick Corp. *PRIMEDIA Inc* ... 1466
Indy Preferred Mortgage, LLC *Suntrust Banks Inc* ... 1724
Indy Restaurant Concepts, Inc. *VCG Holding Corp* ... 1891
Indya.com Portal Private Limited *News Corp Ltd (The)* ... 1281
IndyMac ABS, Inc. *IndyMac Bancorp Inc* ... 936
IndyMac Bank, F.S.B. *IndyMac Bancorp Inc* ... 936
Ineen, Inc. *Counterpath Corp* ... 489
Inensur Brunete, S.l. *Banco Bilbao Vizcaya Argentaria* ... 204
INEO *Suez* ... 1715
Inergy Canada Company *Inergy LP* ... 936
Inergy Canada Company *Inergy Holdings LP* ... 936
Inergy Finance Corp. *Inergy Holdings LP* ... 936
Inergy Finance Corp. *Inergy LP* ... 936
Inergy Gas Marketing, LLC *Inergy LP* ... 936
Inergy Gas Marketing, LLC *Inergy Holdings LP* ... 936
Inergy GP, LLC *Inergy Holdings LP* ... 936
Inergy Midstream, LLC *Inergy Holdings LP* ... 936
Inergy Midstream, LLC *Inergy LP* ... 936
Inergy Partners, LLC *Inergy Holdings LP* ... 936
Inergy Propane, LLC *Inergy Holdings LP* ... 936
Inergy Propane, LLC *Inergy LP* ... 936
Inergy Sales& Service, Inc. *Inergy LP* ... 936
Inergy Sales& Service, Inc. *Inergy Holdings LP* ... 936
Inergy Services *Inergy Holdings LP* ... 936
Inergy Services *Inergy LP* ... 936
Inergy Stagecoach II, LLC *Inergy LP* ... 936
Inergy Stagecoach II, LLC *Inergy Holdings LP* ... 936
Inergy Storage, Inc. *Inergy Holdings LP* ... 936
Inergy Storage, Inc. *Inergy LP* ... 936
Inergy Transportation, LLC *Inergy LP* ... 936
Inergy Transportation, LLC *Inergy Holdings LP* ... 936
Inergy, L.P. *Inergy Holdings LP* ... 936
Inertial Airline Services, Inc. *HEICO Corp* ... 865
Inesco Corporation *Cimarex Energy Co* ... 406
iNest Realty of Minnesota, Inc. *IAC/InterActiveCorp* ... 961
iNest Realty, Inc. *IAC/InterActiveCorp* ... 961
Inet ATS, Inc. *Instinet Group Inc* ... 953
INET Centric Finance Inc. *CNET Networks Inc* ... 429
INET Clearing, LLC *Nasdaq Stock Market Inc (The)* ... 1236
Inet Futures Exchange, LLC *Nasdaq Stock Market Inc (The)* ... 1236
Inet Holding Company LLC *Nasdaq Stock Market Inc (The)* ... 1236
Inet Stock Exchange, LLC *Nasdaq Stock Market Inc (The)* ... 1236
Inet Technologies International, Inc. *Tektronix Inc* ... 1763
Inet Technologies Netherlands BV *Tektronix Inc* ... 1763
INET Technology Services, LLC *Nasdaq Stock Market Inc (The)* ... 1236
INET, Mexico *Pac-West Telecomm Inc* ... 1369
Ineto Services, Inc. *Siebel Systems Inc* ... 1624
InetrContinental Hotels Group (New Zealand) Limited *InterContinental Hotels Group* ... 962
iNetWorks Corporation *Irvine Sensors Corp* ... 990
INEWS GmbH *Avid Technology Inc* ... 190
Inews Ltd. *Avid Technology Inc* ... 190
Inews, LLC *Avid Technology Inc* ... 190
Inex Alternative Programs, Inc. *USI Holdings Corp* ... 1880
INEX Corporation *Speedway Motorsports Inc* ... 1680
Infast Automotive Ltd. *Anixter International Inc* ... 125
Infast Group Limited *Anixter International Inc* ... 125
Infast Ltd. *Anixter International Inc* ... 125
Infast Manufacturing Ltd. *Anixter International Inc* ... 125
Infast Subsidiary No. 2 Ltd. *Anixter International Inc* ... 125
INFCO Network Inc. *Viacom Inc* ... 1902
INFCO Network Inc. *CBS Corp* ... 349
Inference Corporation *eGain Communications Corp* ... 607
Infernet Limited *Yahoo Inc* ... 1990
InfiKnowledge, ULC *Traffix Inc* ... 1811
Infineer Ltd. *Publicard Inc* ... 1487
Infineer, Inc. *Publicard Inc* ... 1487
Infineon Technologies Flash Ltd. *Qimonda AG* ... 1493
infiNET Integrated Solutions, Inc. *Nelnet Inc* ... 1258
Infineum Holdings B.V. (5) *Exxon Mobil Corp* ... 673
InfiniteSpace.com, Corp. *Clearstory Systems Inc* ... 423
Infiniti *LaPolla Industries Inc* ... 1055
Infinitive Speech Systems Corp. *Visteon Corp* ... 1915
Infinitive Speech Systems U.K. Limited *Visteon Corp* ... 1915
Infinity Agency of Texas, Inc. *Infinity Property & Casualty Corp* ... 938
Infinity Consulting Group, Inc. *Answerthink Inc* ... 127
Infinity Inc. *Royal Caribbean Cruises Ltd* ... 1562
Infinity Information Network, Inc. *First American Corp* ... 695
Infinity Insurance Company *Infinity Property & Casualty Corp* ... 938
Infinity Mortgage Corporation *Popular Inc* ... 1448
Infinity National Insurance Company *Infinity Property & Casualty Corp* ... 938
Infinity Oil & Gas of Kansas, Inc. *Infinity Energy Resources Inc* ... 938
Infinity Oil & Gas of Wyoming, Inc. *Infinity Energy Resources Inc* ... 938
Infinity Oil and Gas of Texas, Inc. *Infinity Energy Resources Inc* ... 938
Infinity Outdoor of Florida Holding Co. *Viacom Inc* ... 1902
Infinity Outdoor of Florida Holding Co. *CBS Corp* ... 349
Infinity Outdoor of Florida Inc. *CBS Corp* ... 349
Infinity Outdoor of Florida Inc. *Viacom Inc* ... 1902
Infinity Property and Casualty Services, Inc. *Infinity Property & Casualty Corp* ... 938

KCMB Nova Scotia Corp.   *Fortune Brands Inc* 738
Kcms Ii LLC   *Marsh & McLennan Cos Inc* 1125
KCMS, Inc.   *Marsh & McLennan Cos Inc* 1125
KCOP Television, Inc.   *News Corp Ltd (The)* 1281
KCP Beneficiary Services, LLC   *Kenneth Cole Productions Inc* .1023
KCP Consulting (Dongguan), Co. Ltd.   *Kenneth Cole Productions Inc* 1023
KCP Innovative Services Inc   *Capital Reserve Canada Ltd* .. 325
KCP Trust, LLC   *Kenneth Cole Productions Inc* 1023
KCP,Inc   *Level 3 Communications Inc* 1069
KCPR, LLC   *HealthTronics Inc* 862
KCS Energy Services, Inc.   *KCS Energy Inc* 1020
KCS Holding Co.   *Windstream Corp* 1966
KCS Investment I, Ltd.   *Kansas City Southern* 1018
KCS Resources, Inc.   *KCS Energy Inc* 1020
KCSRC y Compania, S, de N.C. de C.V.   *Kansas City Southern* .1018
KCYT-FM License Corp.   *Univision Communications Inc* 1871
KD Hazel Dell 1031, INC.   *Kimco Realty Corp* 1029
KD Longview 1029, INC.   *Kimco Realty Corp* 1029
KD Medical, Inc.   *Calbatech* 306
KD Mortgage, LLC   *Wells Fargo & Co* 1944
KDAC (Thailand) Company Limited   *Delphi Corp* 538
KDB Homes, Inc.   *D.R. Horton Inc* 522
KDC Busch Boulevard LLC   *CapLease Inc* 328
KDC LLC   *Synovus Financial Corp* 1739
KDC Norman Woods Business Trust   *CapLease Inc* .. 328
KDF Malabar LP   *Edison International* 604
KDF Malabar LP   *Edison International* 604
KDF Malabar LP   *Edison International* 604
KDF Malabar LP   *Edison International* 604
KDF Malabar LP   *Edison International* 604
KDF Malabar LP   *Edison International* 604
KDF Malabar LP   *Edison International* 604
KDF Malabar LP   *Edison International* 604
KDF Malabar LP   *Edison International* 604
KDF Park Glenn LP (Park Glenn)   *Edison International*...... 604
KDF Park Glenn Seniors LP   *Edison International* 604
KDF Santa Paula LP   *Edison International* 604
KDFW License, Inc.   *News Corp Ltd (The)* 1281
KDFW Television, Inc.   *News Corp Ltd (The)* 1281
KDI Precision Products, Inc.   *L-3 Communications Holdings Inc* 1046
KDIS Distribution   *Goodyear Tire & Rubber Com (The)* 811
KDL Holdings, LLC   *Cincinnati Gas & Electric Co* 407
KDL Holdings, LLC   *Union Light Heat & Power Co* 1852
KDNLLicensee,LLC   *Sinclair Broadcast Group Inc* 1636
KDPC Lmted   *Fluor Corp* 728
KDS Company, Ltd.   *Delphi Corp* 538
KDS Corporation   *Lodgian Inc* 1091
KDS, Inc.   *Harvard Bioscience Inc* 851
KDSM,LLC   *Sinclair Broadcast Group Inc* 1636
KDSMLicensee,LLC   *Sinclair Broadcast Group Inc* 1636
KDTV License Partnership, G.P.   *Univision Communications Inc* 1871
Kean and Scott Limited   *Tyco International Ltd* 1838
Keane Stud LLC   *Tarragon Corp* 1751
Keane Stud Management LLC   *Tarragon Corp* 1751
Kearns-Tribune, LLC, (The Salt Lake Tribune)   *Medianews Group Inc* 1150
Kearny Federal Investment Corp.   *Kearny Financial Corp* .. 1021
Kearny Financial Securities, Inc.   *Kearny Financial Corp* 1021
Kearny 39 Corp   *Franklin Credit Mgmt Corp* 744
Kearny 61 Corp   *Franklin Credit Mgmt Corp* 744
Kearny Federal Savings Bank   *Kearny Financial Corp* 1021
Kearny Federal Savings Bank   *Labopharm Inc* 1047
Kearny Holding VF, L.L.C.   *Vornado Realty Trust* 1923
Kearny Leasing VF, L.L.C.   *Vornado Realty Trust* 1923
Kearsarge Telephone Company   *Telephone and Data Systems Inc* 1768
Keatherly, Inc.   *Supervalu Inc* 1728
Keating Gravure Corporation   *Sonoco Products Co* 1658
Keating Gravure LLC   *Sonoco Products Co* 1658
KECO Industries,Inc.   *DRS Technologies Inc* 577
KECS-FM License Corp.   *Univision Communications Inc* 1871
KEDC Holdings Corp.   *Keyspan Corp* 1027
Keddem Bioscience Ltd.   *Compugen Ltd* 461
Kee Trans, Inc.   *Roundys Supermarkets Inc* 1560
Keeb Canada Inc.   *Kellogg Co* 1021
Keebler Company   *Kellogg Co* 1021
Keebler Company Subsidiaries   *Kellogg Co* 1021
Keebler Foods Company   *Kellogg Co* 1021
Keebler Foods Company Subsidiaries   *Kellogg Co* 1021
Keebler Foreign Sales Corporation   *Kellogg Co* 1021
Keebler Holding Company   *Kellogg Co* 1021
Keebler Holding Corp Subsidiaries   *Kellogg Co* 1021
Keebler USA   *Kellogg Co* 1021
Keefe& Keefe Ambulette, Ltd.   *Rural/Metro Corp* 1567
Keefe& Keefe, Inc.   *Rural/Metro Corp* 1567
Keefe, Bruyette & Woods Limited   *KBW Inc* 1020
Keefe, Bruyette & Woods, Inc.   *KBW Inc* 1020
Keen General Limited (KG)   *New Dragon Asia Corp* 1270
Keen Personal Media, Inc.   *Western Digital Corp* 1950
Keen Personal Technologies, Inc.   *Western Digital Corp* 1950
Keen Rose Technology Group Limited   *Cincinnati Gas & Electric Co* 407
Keen Rose Technology Group Limited   *Union Light Heat & Power Co* 1852
Keene Gas   *Energy Transfer Partners LP* 636
Keene Road Landfill, Inc.   *Waste Management Inc* 1934
Keeper Holdings LLC   *Citigroup Inc* 411
Keepier Investments   *Barclays Plc* 216
KEG I Associates, LLC   *Boston Properties Inc* 268
Keil Elektronik GmbH   *ARM Holdings Plc* 150
Keil Software, Inc   *ARM Holdings Plc* 150
Keith C. Winters & Associates, LTD.   *Merchants & Manufacturers Bancorp Inc* 1161
Keith Littlewood Associates Limited   *Interpublic Group of Companies Inc* 975
Keith Monument Company LLC   *Rock of Ages Corp* 1552
Keith Rayment & Associates Ltd.   *Aon Corp* 129
Keith Wilson Limited   *Dentsply International Inc* 543
Keithen Limited (in liquidation)   *BHP Billiton Ltd* 237
Keithen Limited (in liquidation)   *BHP Billiton Plc* 237
Keithley Instruments BV   *Keithley Instruments Inc* 1021
Keithley Instruments GmbH   *Keithley Instruments Inc* 1021
Keithley Instruments International Corporation   *Keithley Instruments Inc* 1021
Keithley Instruments KK   *Keithley Instruments Inc* 1021
Keithley Instruments Ltd   *Keithley Instruments Inc* 1021
Keithley Instruments S.A.   *Keithley Instruments Inc* 1021
Keithley Instruments SARL   *Keithley Instruments Inc* 1021
Keithley Instruments Sdn Bhd   *Keithley Instruments Inc*...... 1021
Keithley Instruments SRL   *Keithley Instruments Inc* 1021

Keiyo Teisan Ltd   *BOC Group Plc* 262
Keiyo Toshi Service Co., Ltd.   *Mitsui & Co Ltd* 1201
Kelarg, Inc.   *Kellogg Co* 1021
Kelcone Limited   *Kellogg Co* 1021
Kelcorn Limited   *Kellogg Co* 1021
Kelf Limited (UK)   *Kellogg Co* 1021
Kelian Pty Limited   *Rio Tinto Plc* 1547
Kelian Pty Limited   *Rio Tinto Ltd* 1546
Kelko Quaker Chemical, S.A.   *Quaker Chemical Corp* 1495
Kelkoo AB Sweden   *Yahoo Inc* 1990
Kelkoo AS (Denmark)   *Yahoo Inc* 1990
Kelkoo France SA   *Yahoo Inc* 1990
Kelkoo (AS) Norway   *Yahoo Inc* 1990
Kelkoo GmbH (Germany)   *Yahoo Inc* 1990
Kelkoo Holdings BV (NL)   *Yahoo Inc* 1990
Kelkoo Holdings SAS   *Yahoo Inc* 1990
Kelkoo Ltd (UK)   *Yahoo Inc* 1990
Kelkoo NL BV (koopwitjzer)   *Yahoo Inc* 1990
Kelkoo SL (Spain)   *Yahoo Inc* 1990
Kelkoo srl (Italy)   *Yahoo Inc* 1990
Keller Booth Sumners JV   *Clear Channel Outdoor Holdings Inc* 422
Keller Booth Sumners JV   *Clear Channel Communications Inc*.....421
Keller Boulevard Associates Intermediate, LLC   *GMH Communities Trust* 802
Keller Boulevard Associates, LLC   *GMH Communities Trust* ...802
Keller Canyon Landfill Company   *Allied Waste Industries Inc*.... 66
Keller Drop Box, Inc.   *Allied Waste Industries Inc* 66
Keller Mortgage, LLC   *Wells Fargo & Co* 1944
Kelley Communication Company, Inc   *Siena Technologies Inc* ...1625
Kelley Company FSC, Inc.   *SPX Corp* 1684
Kelley International Limited   *SPX Corp* 1684
Kelley Technologies   *Siena Technologies Inc* 1625
Kellogg Argentina S.A.   *Kellogg Co* 1021
Kellogg Asia Co., Ltd   *Kellogg Co* 1021
Kellogg Asia Co., Ltd.   *Kellogg Co* 1021
Kellogg Asia Inc.   *Kellogg Co* 1021
Kellogg Asia Marketing Inc.   *Kellogg Co* 1021
Kellogg Asia Sdn. Bhd.   *Kellogg Co* 1021
Kellogg (Aust.) Pty. Ltd.   *Kellogg Co* 1021
Kellogg (Aust.) Pty. Ltd. Subsidiaries   *Kellogg Co* 1021
Kellogg Australia Holdings Pty Ltd   *Kellogg Co* 1021
Kellogg Benelux (Kellogg Produits Alimentaires, S.A.S. branch)   *Kellogg Co* 1021
Kellogg Brasil & CIA   *Kellogg Co* 1021
Kellogg Brasil, Inc.   *Kellogg Co* 1021
Kellogg Brown & Root Holdings Limited   *Halliburton Co* 839
Kellogg Brown & Root Holdings (U.K.) Limited   *Halliburton Co* 839
Kellogg Brown & Root Limited   *Halliburton Co* 839
Kellogg Brown & Root LLC   *Halliburton Co* 839
Kellogg Brown & Root Services, Inc.   *Halliburton Co* 839
Kellogg Canada Inc.   *Kellogg Co* 1021
Kellogg Canada Inc.   *Kellogg Co* 1021
Kellogg Caribbean Inc.   *Kellogg Co* 1021
Kellogg Caribbean Services Company, Inc.   *Kellogg Co* 1021
Kellogg Chile Inc.   *Kellogg Co* 1021
Kellogg Chile Limited   *Kellogg Co* 1021
Kellogg (China)   *Kellogg Co* 1021
Kellogg Company Mexico, S. de R.L. de C.V.   *Kellogg Co* 1021
Kellogg Company Mexico, S. de R.L. de C.V.   *Kellogg Co* 1021
Kellogg Company of Great Britain Limited   *Kellogg Co* 1021
Kellogg Company of Ireland, Limited   *Kellogg Co* 1021
Kellogg Company of Ireland, Ltd.   *Kellogg Co* 1021
Kellogg Company of South Africa (Pty) Limited   *Kellogg Co* 1021
Kellogg de Centro America, S.A.   *Kellogg Co* 1021
Kellogg de Colombia, S.A.   *Kellogg Co* 1021
Kellogg de Mexico, S.A. de C.V.   *Kellogg Co* 1021
Kellogg de Peru, S.A.C.   *Kellogg Co* 1021
Kellogg (Deutschland) GmbH   *Kellogg Co* 1021
Kellogg (Deutschland) GmbH Subsidiaries   *Kellogg Co* 1021
Kellogg El Salvador S. de R.L. de C.V.   *Kellogg Co* 1021
Kellogg Energy Services, Inc.   *Halliburton Co* 839
Kellogg Espana, S.L.   *Kellogg Co* 1021
Kellogg Espana, S.L. Subsidiaries   *Kellogg Co* 1021
Kellogg Europe Company Limited   *Kellogg Co* 1021
Kellogg Europe Company Limited Subsidiaries   *Kellogg Co* 1021
Kellogg Europe Trading Limited   *Kellogg Co* 1021
Kellogg Europe Trading Limited Subsidiaries   *Kellogg Co* 1021
Kellogg Fearn, Inc.   *Kellogg Co* 1021
Kellogg Group Limited   *Kellogg Co* 1021
Kellogg Group S.a.r.l.   *Kellogg Co* 1021
Kellogg Holding Company Limited   *Kellogg Co* 1021
Kellogg Holding Company Limited Subsidiaries   *Kellogg Co* ...1021
Kellogg India Private Limited   *Kellogg Co* 1021
Kellogg International Holding Company   *Kellogg Co* 1021
Kellogg International Holding Company Subsidiaries   *Kellogg Co* 1021
Kellogg Irish Holding Company Limited Subsidiaries   *Kellogg Co* 1021
Kellogg IT Services Company   *Kellogg Co* 1021
Kellogg Italia S.p.A.   *Kellogg Co* 1021
Kellogg (Japan) K.K.   *Kellogg Co* 1021
Kellogg Latin America Finance, LLC   *Kellogg Co* 1021
Kellogg Lux I S.ar.l.   *Kellogg Co* 1021
Kellogg Lux I S.a.r.l. Subsidiaries   *Kellogg Co* 1021
Kellogg Lux II S.a.r.l.   *Kellogg Co* 1021
Kellogg Lux III S.a.r.l.   *Kellogg Co* 1021
Kellogg Lux III S.a.r.l. Subsidiaries   *Kellogg Co* 1021
Kellogg Malaysia Manufacturing SDN BHD   *Kellogg Co* 1021
Kellogg Malta Limited   *Kellogg Co* 1021
Kellogg Management Services (Europe) Limited   *Kellogg Co* ...1021
Kellogg Management Services Espana, S.L.   *Kellogg Co* 1021
Kellogg Manchester Limited   *Kellogg Co* 1021
Kellogg Manufacturing GmbH & Co. KG- Limited Partnership   *Kellogg Co* 1021
Kellogg Marine, Inc.   *Brunswick Corp* 289
Kellogg Marketing and Sales Company (UK)Limited   *Kellogg Co* 1021
Kellogg Minerals, Inc   *Idaho General Mines Inc* 915
Kellogg (N.Z.) Limited   *Kellogg Co* 1021
Kellogg Norge   *Kellogg Co* 1021
Kellogg North America Company   *Kellogg Co* 1021
Kellogg (Osterreich) GmbH   *Kellogg Co* 1021
Kellogg (Poland) Sp. Zo.o   *Kellogg Co* 1021
Kellogg Portugal   *Kellogg Co* 1021
Kellogg Sales Company   *Kellogg Co* 1021
Kellogg Sales Company Subsidiaries   *Kellogg Co* 1021
Kellogg (Schweiz) GmbH   *Kellogg Co* 1021
Kellogg Services GmbH-Bremen   *Kellogg Co* 1021
Kellogg Services GmbH-limited partner   *Kellogg Co* 1021
Kellogg Servicios, S.C.   *Kellogg Co* 1021

Kellogg Superannuation Pty. Ltd.   *Kellogg Co* 1021
Kellogg Supply Services (Europe) Limited Manchester, England   *Kellogg Co* 1021
Kellogg Sverige   *Kellogg Co* 1021
Kellogg Talbot Limited   *Kellogg Co* 1021
Kellogg Talbot Limited Subsidiaries   *Kellogg Co* 1021
Kellogg (Thailand) Limited   *Kellogg Co* 1021
Kellogg (Thailand) Limited   *Kellogg Co* 1021
Kellogg U.K. Holding Company Limited   *Kellogg Co* 1021
Kellogg U.K. Holding Company Limited Subsidiaries   *Kellogg Co* 1021
Kellogg UK Minor Limited   *Kellogg Co* 1021
Kellogg USA Inc Subsidiaries   *Kellogg Co* 1021
Kellogg USA Inc.   *Kellogg Co* 1021
Kelloggs Produits Alimentaires, S.A.S.   *Kellogg Co* 1021
Kelloggs Produits Alimentaires, S.A.S. Subsidiaries   *Kellogg Co* 1021
Kellway Corporation   *CabelTel International Corp* 301
Kelly & Cohen Appliances, Inc.(1)   *Rex Stores Corp* 1540
Kelly Administratiekantoor B.V.   *Kelly Services Inc* 1022
Kelly Company World Group, Inc   *Instacare Corp* 952
Kelly Home Care Services, Inc.   *Kelly Services Inc* 1022
Kelly Lynch Physical Therapy   *U.S. Physical Therapy Inc* ...1841
Kelly Managed Services (Nederland) B.V.   *Kelly Services Inc* .. 1022
Kelly Management Group Inc.   *Interpublic Group of Companies Inc* 975
Kelly Management Services, Srl.   *Kelly Services Inc* 1022
Kelly Payroll Services Limited   *Kelly Services Inc* 1022
Kelly Properties, Inc.   *Kelly Services Inc* 1022
Kelly Receivables Services, LLC   *Kelly Services Inc* 1022
Kelly Run Sanitation, Inc.   *Waste Management Inc* 1934
Kelly Services AB   *Kelly Services Inc* 1022
Kelly Services (Australia), Ltd.   *Kelly Services Inc* 1022
Kelly Services (Canada), Ltd.   *Kelly Services Inc* 1022
Kelly Services CIS, Inc.   *Kelly Services Inc* 1022
Kelly Services Consulting GmbH   *Kelly Services Inc* 1022
Kelly Services Deutschland GmbH   *Kelly Services Inc* 1022
Kelly Services Empleo Empresa de Trabajo Temporal, S.L.   *Kelly Services Inc* 1022
Kelly Services France, S.A.S.   *Kelly Services Inc* 1022
Kelly Services Hong Kong Limited   *Kelly Services Inc* 1022
Kelly Services Hungary Staffing Limited Liability Company   *Kelly Services Inc* 1022
Kelly Services India Private Limited   *Kelly Services Inc* 1022
Kelly Services Insan Kaynaklari ve Danismanlik Ltd. Sti.   *Kelly Services Inc* 1022
Kelly Services Interim (Belgium) S.A., N.V.   *Kelly Services Inc* . 1022
Kelly Services Interim, S.A.S.   *Kelly Services Inc* 1022
Kelly Services (Ireland), Ltd.   *Kelly Services Inc* 1022
Kelly Services Italia Srl   *Kelly Services Inc* 1022
Kelly Services Japan, Inc.   *Kelly Services Inc* 1022
Kelly Services Luxembourg S.A.R.L.   *Kelly Services Inc* 1022
Kelly Services (Malaysia) SDN. BHD.   *Kelly Services Inc* 1022
Kelly Services Mexico, S.A. de C.V.   *Kelly Services Inc* 1022
Kelly Services (Nederland), B.V.   *Kelly Services Inc* 1022
Kelly Services (New Zealand), Ltd.   *Kelly Services Inc* 1022
Kelly Services Norge A.S.   *Kelly Services Inc* 1022
Kelly Services of Denmark, Inc.   *Kelly Services Inc* 1022
Kelly Services Personal Marketing GmbH   *Kelly Services Inc*... 1022
Kelly Services Seleccion y Formacion, S.L.   *Kelly Services Inc* .. 1022
Kelly Services Select (Belgium) S.A., N.V.   *Kelly Services Inc* .. 1022
Kelly Services (Singapore) Pte. Ltd.   *Kelly Services Inc* 1022
Kelly Services Staffing (Thailand) Co. Ltd.   *Kelly Services Inc* .. 1022
Kelly Services (Suisse) S.A.   *Kelly Services Inc* 1022
Kelly Services Training GmbH   *Kelly Services Inc* 1022
Kelly Services (UK), Ltd.   *Kelly Services Inc* 1022
Kelly Services Zeitarbeit GmbH& Co. OHG   *Kelly Services Inc* . 1022
Kelly Staff Leasing, Inc.   *Kelly Services Inc* 1022
Kelly, Luttmer & Associates Limited   *Sykes Enterprises Inc* ... 1734
Kelly-Springfield Puerto Rico, Inc.   *Goodyear Tire & Rubber Com (The)* 811
Kelly-Springfield Tyre Co. (Australia) Pty. Ltd.   *Goodyear Tire & Rubber Com (The)* 811
Kelly-Springfield Tyre Company Ltd.   *Goodyear Tire & Rubber Com (The)* 811
KellyServices(Societadifornituradilavorotemporaneo)SpA   *Kelly Services Inc* 1022
Kelmax Lopez Manufacturing, S.A. de C.V.   *Leggett & Platt Inc* 1067
Kelmill Limited   *Kellogg Co* 1021
Kelmscott Communications LLC   *Consolidated Graphics Inc TX* 471
Kelnic II JV   *Clear Channel Communications Inc* 421
Kelnic II JV   *Clear Channel Outdoor Holdings Inc* 422
Kelpac Limited   *Kellogg Co* 1021
Kelsan Holdings, Inc.   *Portec Rail Products Inc* 1449
Kelsan Technologies Corp.   *Portec Rail Products Inc* 1449
Kelsan Technologies (Europe) Limited   *Portec Rail Products Inc* 1449
Kelsan Technologies (USA), LLC   *Portec Rail Products Inc* 1449
Kelsar S.A. de C.V.   *Tyco International Ltd* 1838
Kelsey-Hayes Canada Limited   *TRW Automotive* 1831
Kelsey-Hayes Company   *TRW Automotive* 1831
Kelsey-Hayes Heerlen Inc   *TRW Automotive* 1831
Kelsey-Hayes Holdings Inc   *TRW Automotive* 1831
Kelsey-Hayes Netherlands Inc   *TRW Automotive* 1831
Kelstar International Inc.   *Altana AG* 72
Keltatim Publishing Company, Inc.   *Knight Ridder Inc* 1035
Keltic Oil Tools Limited   *Weatherford International Ltd* 1940
Keltsch Bros., Inc.   *Supervalu Inc* 1728
Kelvin Finance Company Limited   *Praxair Inc* 1458
Kem Manufacturing Corporation   *Crompton Corp* 502
Kema Nord AB   *Akzo Nobel* 49
KemaNord Kraft AB   *Akzo Nobel* 49
Kemax BV   *Tetra Technologies Inc* 1780
Kemberly, Inc.   *Dura Automotive Systems Inc* 581
Kemberly, LLC   *Dura Automotive Systems Inc* 581
Kemerovo Mobile Communications   *Tele2 AB* 1764
KEMET de Mexico, S.A. de C.V.   *Kemet Corp* 1022
KEMET Electronics Asia Limited   *Kemet Corp* 1022
KEMET Electronics Asia Pacific Pte Ltd.   *Kemet Corp* 1022
KEMET Electronics (Canada) Limited   *Kemet Corp* 1022
KEMET Electronics Corporation   *Kemet Corp* 1022
KEMET Electronics GMBH   *Kemet Corp* 1022
KEMET Electronics Greater China Limited   *Kemet Corp*...... 1022
KEMET Electronics Japan Co., Ltd.   *Kemet Corp* 1022
KEMET Electronics Ltd.   *Kemet Corp* 1022
KEMET Electronics Marketing (S)Pte Ltd.   *Kemet Corp* 1022
KEMET Electronics Pty Ltd.   *Kemet Corp* 1022
KEMET Electronics SARL   *Kemet Corp* 1022
KEMET Electronics (Shanghai) Co., Ltd.   *Kemet Corp* 1022
KEMET Electronics (Suzhou) Co., Ltd.   *Kemet Corp* 1022
KEMET Electronics, S.A.   *Kemet Corp* 1022

THE CORPORATE DIRECTORY - Walker's 2008 Subsidiary/Parent Index - 3129

Lattice Semiconductor SRL *Lattice Semiconductor Corp* 1058
Lattice Semiconductor UK Limited *Lattice Semiconductor Corp* 1058
LATTICE TELECOM FINANCE (NO 1) LIMITED *National Grid Transco Plc* 1241
LATTICE TELECOMMUNICATIONS ASSET DEVELOPMENT COMPANY LIMITED *National Grid Transco Plc* 1241
Latvia Snacks Ltd. *PepsiCo Inc* 1410
Latvija Statoil SIA *Statoil* 1696
Latvijas Mobilais Telefons SIA *TeliaSonera* 1769
Laubman And Pank Pty Ltd *Luxottica Group SpA* 1101
Lauderdale Clinical Services,Inc. *Tenet Healthcare Corp* 1774
LAUDERDALE TOWERS-REO, LIMITED PARTNERSHIP *Apartment Investment and Management Company* 130
Laughlin Funeral Home, Ltd. *Service Corp International* 1614
Laughton, LLC *Williams Cos Inc* 1961
Lauhoff Finance Corporation *Bunge Ltd* 295
Launch Media Inc. *Yahoo Inc* 1990
Launch Networks, Inc. *Yahoo Inc* 1990
Launch Radio Networks, Inc. *Yahoo Inc* 1990
Launchchange Holding Company *Danaher Corp* 525
Launchchange Inc. *Danaher Corp* 525
Launchchange Instrumentation Ltd. *Danaher Corp* 525
Launchchange Limited *Danaher Corp* 525
Lauraan Corp. *Lifestyle Innovations Inc* 1076
Laureate Capital, LLC *BB&T Corp* 222
Laureate Education International, Ltd. *Laureate Education Inc* 1059
Laureate Education, Inc. *Laureate Education Inc* 1059
Laureate Homes of Arizona, Inc. *Lennar Corp* 1068
Laureate I BV *Laureate Education Inc* 1059
Laureate International BV *Laureate Education Inc* 1059
Laureate International Costa Rica, Srl *Laureate Education Inc* 1059
Laureate OnLine Education BV *Laureate Education Inc* 1059
Laureate Partners LLC *Lennar Corp* 1068
Laureate Pharma, Inc. *Safeguard Scientifics Inc* 1573
Laurel Bay Petroleum Limited *Petsec Energy Ltd* 1419
Laurel Creek Associates, LLC *William Lyon Homes* 1960
Laurel Creek Co., Inc. *Foundation Coal Holdings Inc* 740
Laurel Entertainment LLC *CBS Corp* 349
Laurel Entertainment LLC *Viacom Inc* 1902
LAUREL GARDENS, A PARTNERSHIP IN COMMENDAM *Apartment Investment and Management Company* 130
Laurel Health Resources, Inc. *Genesis HealthCare Corp* 774
Laurel Highlands Landfill, Inc. *Waste Management Inc* 1934
Laurel Highlands, LLC *Hovnanian Enterprises Inc* 894
Laurel Hill Memorial Park LLC *StoneMor Partners LP* 1707
Laurel Hill Memorial Park Subsidiary, Inc. *StoneMor Partners LP* 1707
Laurel Hill Private Sewer Treatment Facility, LLC *AvalonBay Communities Inc* 184
Laurel Hills Mortgage, LLC *Wells Fargo & Co* 1944
Laurel Hotel Associates LLC *MHI Hospitality Corp* 1177
Laurel Lake Health and Rehabilitation LLC *Kindred Healthcare Inc* 1030
Laurel Mountain Medical Supply, Inc. *Air Products & Chemicals Inc* 46
Laurel Networks BV *ECI Telecom Ltd* 599
Laurel Networks GmbH *ECI Telecom Ltd* 599
Laurel Networks Holdings Corporation *ECI Telecom Ltd* 599
Laurel Networks Ltd. *ECI Telecom Ltd* 599
Laurel Oak Realty Corporation *Sunoco Inc* 1721
Laurel Park Apartments, Ltd. *Wachovia Corp* 1928
Laurel Park Retail Holding LLC *CBL & Associates Properties Inc* 348
Laurel Park Retail Properties LLC *CBL & Associates Properties Inc* 348
Laurel Physical Therapy *U.S. Physical Therapy Inc* 1841
Laurel Pipe Line Company, L.P. *Buckeye GP Holdings LP* 292
Laurel Pipe Line Company, L.P. *Buckeye Partners LP* 292
Laurel Pointe II, LLC *Wachovia Corp* 1928
Laurel Pointe of Salisbury Limited Partnership *Wachovia Corp* 1928
Laurel Pointe, LLC *Wachovia Corp* 1928
Laurel Racing Assoc.,Inc. *Magna Entertainment Corp* 1111
Laurel Racing Association Limited Partnership *Magna Entertainment Corp* 1111
Laurel Ridge Landfill, LLC *Waste Management Inc* 1934
Laurel Run Mining Company *CONSOL Energy Inc* 470
Laurel Run Mining Company *CONSOL Energy Inc WY* 470
Laurel Shipping LLC *Omi Corp Marshall Islands* 1337
Laurel Technologies Partnership *DRS Technologies Inc* 577
LAUREL-OXFORD ASSOCIATES LIMITED PARTNERSHIP *Apartment Investment and Management Company* 130
Laurelwood Associates Trust *Horizon Health Corp* 890
Laurelwood Associates, Inc. *Horizon Health Corp* 890
Laurelwood Cemetery LLC *StoneMor Partners LP* 1707
Laurelwood Cemetery Subsidiary LLC *StoneMor Partners LP* 1707
Laurelwood Center, Inc. *Psychiatric Solutions Inc* 1485
Laurelwood Holding Company *StoneMor Partners LP* 1707
Laurelwood Properties Inc. *Goodyear Tire & Rubber Com (The)* 811
Lauren Land Company *Massey Energy Co* 1129
Lauren Shipping LLC *Omi Corp Marshall Islands* 1337
Laurence's Orthotics & Prosthetics, Inc. *Hanger Orthopedic Group Inc* 843
Laurens County Landfill, LLC *Waste Industries USA Inc* 1934
LAURENS VILLAS, A LIMITED PARTNERSHIP *Apartment Investment and Management Company* 130
Laurentis B.v. *Sara Lee Corp* 1585
Laurentis UK Limited *Sara Lee Corp* 1585
Laurenton Diamonds Inc. *Tiffany & Co* 1793
Laurenton Diamonds Inc. *Tiffany & Co* 1793
Laurenton Diamonds Vietnam Ltd. *Tiffany & Co* 1793
Laurier Indemnity Company *Extendicare Canada Inc* 672
Laurier Indemnity Company, Ltd. *Extendicare Canada Inc* 672
Laurier, Inc. *BE Semiconductor Industries N.V.* 224
Laurila, Kauriala & Grig Ltd. *Aon Corp* 129
Laurit Limited *Lincoln National Corp* 1081
Laurtrust Limited *Lincoln National Corp* 1081
Laurus Master Fund, Ltd. (Laurus). *Implant Sciences Corp* 931
Lausor No. 1 Limited *Royal & Sun Alliance Insurance Group Plc* 1560
Lausor No. 2 Limited *Royal & Sun Alliance Insurance Group Plc* 1560
Lava Records LLC *Warner Music Group Corp* 1931
Lava Systems *Open Text Corp* 1346
Lava Trademark Holding Company LLC *Warner Music Group Corp* 1931
Lava Trading Inc. *Citigroup Inc* 411
Lava Trading Limited *Citigroup Inc* 411
LavaFlow, Inc. *Citigroup Inc* 411
Lavair Cogeneration Limited Partnership *TXU Corp* 1838
Laval Agricultural Company *Tejon Ranch Co* 1762
Laveen Properties, Inc *ILX Resorts Inc* 923
Lavell Village Associates LP *Edison International* 604
Law 1111 Limited *Applied Micro Circuits Corp* 136
Law 2299 Ltd. *NCR Corp* 1256
Law and Business Economics Limited *Marsh & McLennan Cos Inc* 1125
Law Enforcement Associates, Inc. *Law Enforcement Assoc Corp* 1059
Law Productions Ltd. *News Corp Ltd (The)* 1281
LAWNDALE SQUARE-REO LIMITED PARTNERSHIP *Apartment Investment and Management Company* 130
LawNet, Inc. *Western Union Company (The)* 1952
LawNet, Inc. *First Data Corp* 703
Lawnside VF, L.L.C. *Vornado Realty Trust* 1923
Lawnwood Medical Center, Inc. *HCA Inc* 855
Lawnwood Neurosurgery, LLC *HCA Inc* 855
Lawnwood Pavilion Physician Services, LLC *HCA Inc* 855
Lawnwood Regional Cancer Center Limited Partnership *HCA Inc* 855
Lawrence Amdeco, LLC *HCA Inc* 855
Lawrence Hospitality Associates, LP *Lodgian Inc* 1091
Lawrence Hydroelectric Associates LP *Enel SpA* 633
Lawrence Laboratories *Bristol Myers Squibb Co* 281
Lawrence Medical Equipment, Inc. *Rotech Healthcare Inc NEW* 1560
Lawrence Medical, LLC *HCA Inc* 855
Lawrence Savings Bank *LSB Corp* 1097
Lawrence Street Partners, LLC *Equity Residential* 654
Lawrence Tankers LDC *Knightsbridge Tankers Ltd* 1036
Lawrence-Curlew Medical Centre Inc. *Laboratory Corp of America Holdings* 1048
Lawrenceburg Dialysis, LLC *Davita Inc* 530
Lawrenceburg National Bank *Farmers Capital Bank Corp* 679
Lawrenceville Surgery Center, LLC *United Surgical Partners International Inc* 1863
Lawson Mardon Fibrenyle Ltd. *Alcan Inc* 54
Lawson Mardon Flexible Limited *Alcan Inc* 54
Lawson Mardon Group International Limited *Alcan Inc* 54
Lawson Mardon Northern Limited *Alcan Inc* 54
Lawson Mardon Packaging Ltd. *Alcan Inc* 54
Lawson Mardon Packaging Overseas (bristol) Limited *Alcan Inc* 54
Lawson Mardon Packaging Sales Ltd. *Alcan Inc* 54
Lawson Mardon Reading Ltd. *Alcan Inc* 54
Lawson Mardon Smith Brothers Ltd. *Alcan Inc* 54
Lawson Mardon Thermoplastics Ltd. *Alcan Inc* 54
Lawson Mardon Trentesaux Sa *Alcan Inc* 54
Lawson Products de Mexico S. de RL. de C.v. *Lawson Products Inc* 1059
Lawson Products, Inc. *Lawson Products Inc* 1059
Lawson Products, Inc. *Lawson Products Inc* 1059
Lawson Products, Inc. *Lawson Products Inc* 1059
Lawson Products, Inc. *Lawson Products Inc* 1059
Lawson Products, Inc. (Ontario) *Lawson Products Inc* 1059
Lawson Software Benelux, B.V. *Lawson Software Inc* 1060
Lawson Software France SARL *Lawson Software Inc* 1060
Lawson Software GmbH *Lawson Software Inc* 1060
Lawson Software Limited *Lawson Software Inc* 1060
Lawson Software USA,Inc. *Lawson Software Inc* 1060
Lawson Technologies,Inc. *Lawson Software Inc* 1060
Lawson, Noble& Webb,Inc. *Arcadis* 142
Lawter International Products, Pte. Ltd. *Eastman Chemical Co* 595
Lawyers Mortgage and Title Company, Inc. *First American Corp* 695
Lawyers Mortgage Network Inc. *Stewart Information Services Corp* 1705
LAX Properties, LLC *Marriott International Inc* 1125
Laxare, Inc. *Massey Energy Co* 1129
Laycable Shipping Limited Partnership *Barclays Plc* 216
Layne Christensen Australia Pty Limited *Layne Christensen Co* 1060
Layne Christensen Canada Limited *Layne Christensen Co* 1060
Layne de Bolivia S.R.L. *Layne Christensen Co* 1060
Layne de Mexico, S.A. de C.V. *Layne Christensen Co* 1060
Layne Drilling Pty Ltd (f/k/a Glindemann & Kitching Pty Ltd) *Layne Christensen Co* 1060
Layne Energy Cherryvale Pipeline, LLC *Layne Christensen Co* 1060
Layne Energy Cherryvale, LLC *Layne Christensen Co* 1060
Layne Energy Dawson Pipeline, LLC *Layne Christensen Co* 1060
Layne Energy Dawson, LLC *Layne Christensen Co* 1060
Layne Energy Illinois Pipeline, LLC *Layne Christensen Co* 1060
Layne Energy Illinois, LLC *Layne Christensen Co* 1060
Layne Energy Marketing, LLC *Layne Christensen Co* 1060
Layne Energy Operating, LLC *Layne Christensen Co* 1060
Layne Energy Osage, LLC *Layne Christensen Co* 1060
Layne Energy Pipeline, LLC *Layne Christensen Co* 1060
Layne Energy Production, LLC *Layne Christensen Co* 1060
Layne Energy Resources, Inc. *Layne Christensen Co* 1060
Layne Energy Sycamore Pipeline, LLC *Layne Christensen Co* 1060
Layne Energy Sycamore, LLC *Layne Christensen Co* 1060
Layne Energy, Inc. *Layne Christensen Co* 1060
Layne Texas, Incorporated *Layne Christensen Co* 1060
Layne Water Development and Storage, LLC *Layne Christensen Co* 1060
Laypipeline Shipping Limited Partnership *Barclays Plc* 216
Laysan Company Limited *Brown Shoe Co Inc* 288
Layton Homes Corp *Skyline Corp* 1643
Lazard & Co. Srl* *Lazard Ltd* 1060
Lazard & Co., Holdings Limited *Lazard Ltd* 1060
Lazard & Co., Limited *Lazard Ltd* 1060
Lazard Asset Management LLC *Lazard Ltd* 1060
Lazard Frres & Co. LLC *Lazard Ltd* 1060
Lazard Frres Banque SA *Lazard Ltd* 1060
Lazard Frres Gestion *Lazard Ltd* 1060
Lazard Frres SAS *Lazard Ltd* 1060
Lazard Funding Limited LLC *Lazard Ltd* 1060
Lazard Group LLC *Lazard Ltd* 1060
Lazare Kaplan Africa Inc. *Lazare Kaplan International Inc* 1060
Lazare Kaplan Belgium, N.V. *Lazare Kaplan International Inc* 1060
Lazare Kaplan Europe Inc. *Lazare Kaplan International Inc* 1060
Lazare Kaplan Japan Inc. *Lazare Kaplan International Inc* 1060
Lazenby Services Limited *Global Sources Ltd* 797
Lazer-Tek Designs *Crystalix Group International Inc* 507
Lazka HV Cable Installation,Inc. *InfraSource Services Inc* 942
Laznar Acquisition Corporation *Answerthink Inc* 127
LAZY HOLLOW PARTNERS *Apartment Investment and Management Company* 130
Lb 745 LLC *Lehman Brothers Holdings Inc* 1067
LB Asia Issuance Company Ltd. *Lehman Brothers Holdings Inc* 1067
LB Beta Finance Cayman Limited *Lehman Brothers Holdings Inc* 1067
LB Center, Inc. *Berman Center Inc* 233
LB Delta (Cayman) No 1 Ltd. *Lehman Brothers Holdings Inc* 1067
LB Delta Funding *Lehman Brothers Holdings Inc* 1067
LB Europe Limited *E I Du Pont De Nemours & Co* 587
LB Funding Corporation *Legacy Bancorp Inc* 1065
LB I Group Inc. *Lehman Brothers Holdings Inc* 1067
LB Investments (UK) Limited *Lehman Brothers Holdings Inc* 1067
LB Property, LLC *Marsh Supermarkets Inc* 1125
LB Tower Company, LLC *Cincinnati Gas & Electric Co* 407
LB Tower Company, LLC *Union Light Heat & Power Co* 1852
LB&P Ecologisch Advies B.V. *Arcadis* 142
LB-NL Holdings I Inc. *Lehman Brothers Holdings Inc* 1067
LB-NL Holdings L.P. *Lehman Brothers Holdings Inc* 1067
Lb-nl U.s. Investor Inc *Lehman Brothers Holdings Inc* 1067
LB-UBS Commercial Mortgage Trust 2004-C2 *Anthracite Capital Inc* 128
LB/L-Duc II Franceschi, LLC *Standard Pacific Corp* 1690
LBA Funding (Cayman) Limited *Lehman Brothers Holdings Inc* 1067
LBAC Holdings I Inc. *Lehman Brothers Holdings Inc* 1067
LBASC LLC *Lehman Brothers Holdings Inc* 1067
LBC Limited *Bank of America Corp* 208
LBC MergerSub, Inc *Berman Center Inc* 233
LBC-Digital Realty Trust Germany 1 GmbH & Co. KG (limited partnership) *Digital Realty Trust Inc* 556
LBCCA Holdings I Inc. *Lehman Brothers Holdings Inc* 1067
LBCCA Holdings II Inc. *Lehman Brothers Holdings Inc* 1067
LBG Financial Advisors, Inc. *National Financial Partners Corp* 1241
LBH, Inc. *Charming Shoppes Inc* 375
LBHK Funding (Cayman) No. 1 Ltd. *Lehman Brothers Holdings Inc* 1067
LBHK Funding (Cayman) No. 2 Ltd. *Lehman Brothers Holdings Inc* 1067
LBHK Funding (Cayman) No. 4 Ltd. *Lehman Brothers Holdings Inc* 1067
LBI Brands, Inc. *Leading Brands Inc* 1061
LBI, Inc *Amacore Group Inc* 75
LBP Partnership *CPI Corp* 493
Lbro Realty, Inc. *Great Atlantic & Pacific Tea Co Inc* 818
LBTW I,Inc. *Liberty Media LLC* 1074
LBTW II,Inc. *Liberty Media LLC* 1074
LBTW III,Inc. *Liberty Media LLC* 1074
LBX Company LLC *CNH Global* 429
LC Acquisition Corp *Burlington Coat Factory Warehouse Corp* 296
LC Bermuda No. 2 LLP *Aercap Holdings N.V.* 36
LC (Bermuda) No. 2 Limited *Aercap Holdings N.V.* 36
LC Billboard L.L.C. *Lamar Advertising Company* 1051
LC Investment Corporation *Fidelity National Financial Inc* 690
LC Limited *Harris Corp* 849
LC Portland, LLC, *Glimcher Realty Trust* 790
LC Productions Corp. *Lions Gate Entertainment Corp* 1084
LC/N Horsham Limited Partnership *Brandywine Operating PArtnership LP* 274
LC/N Horsham Limited Partnership *Brandywine Realty Trust* 274
LC/N Keith Valley Limited Partnership I *Brandywine Realty Trust* 274
LC/N Keith Valley Limited Partnership I *Brandywine Operating PArtnership LP* 274
LCA Holdings, LLC *Taubman Centers Inc* 1752
LCA-Vision (Canada) Inc. *LCA-Vision Inc* 1061
LCA-Vision (Ohio) Inc. *LCA-Vision Inc* 1061
LCB - Chicago Beverages, LLC *Career Education Corp* 334
LCB - Chicago Group, LLC *Career Education Corp* 334
LCB Culinary Schools, LLC *Career Education Corp* 334
LCB Educational Heritage, LLC *Career Education Corp* 334
Lcb France *CCE Spinco Inc* 349
LCB LIMITED PARTNERSHIP *Lexington Realty Trust* 1071
LCC Algeria LLP *LCC International Inc* 1061
LCC Asia Pacific LTD PTE *LCC International Inc* 1061
LCC China Services, LLC *LCC International Inc* 1061
LCC Deployment Services UK, Limited *LCC International Inc* 1061
LCC Design and Deployment Services. Ltd. *LCC International Inc* 1061
LCC Design Services, LLC *LCC International Inc* 1061
LCC do Brazil Ltda. *LCC International Inc* 1061
LCC Egypt *LCC International Inc* 1061
LCC Espana *LCC International Inc* 1061
LCC Europe AS *LCC International Inc* 1061
LCC India, Private Limited *LCC International Inc* 1061
LCC International Consulting (Shanghai) Ltd. *LCC International Inc* 1061
LCC International GMBH *LCC International Inc* 1061
LCC Italia Srl *LCC International Inc* 1061
LCC Middle East FZ-LLC *LCC International Inc* 1061
LCC Middle East Holdings, Inc. *LCC International Inc* 1061
LCC Southern Europe Holdings S.R.L. *LCC International Inc* 1061
LCC Telecom Management Services, Inc. *LCC International Inc* 1061
LCC Wireless Communications Espana, S.A. *LCC International Inc* 1061
LCC Wireless Design Services LLC *LCC International Inc* 1061
LCC Wireline, Inc. *LCC International Inc* 1061
LCC, United Kingdom, Ltd. *LCC International Inc* 1061
Lcd Communications LLC *Centex Corp* 360
Lcf&I, Inc. *Interpublic Group of Companies Inc* 975
LCH Acquisition, Inc. *Landrys Restaurants Inc* 1054
LCH Opportunities, LLC *Leucadia National Corp* 1068
LCHLN, Inc. *Landrys Restaurants Inc* 1054
Lci (h.k.) Limited *RC2 Corp* 1517
LCI Shipholdings, Inc. *International Shipholding Corp* 972
LCIE-Landauer, Ltd. *Landauer Inc* 1053
Lcni Ii, Inc. *Comcast Corp* 444
Lco Viii, LLC *First American Corp* 695
LCP Holding *Tyco International Ltd* 1838
LCP Truck Equipment, Inc. *Leggett & Platt Inc* 1067
LCP, Inc. *Tyco International Ltd* 1838
LCPI Properties Inc. *Lehman Brothers Holdings Inc* 1067
LCPS Acquisition, LLC *Omnicare Inc* 1338
LCR Telecom Group Ltd. *Primus Telecommunications Group Inc* 1467
LCR Telecom (Kenya) Limited *Primus Telecommunications Group Inc* 1467
LCR Telecom Limited *Primus Telecommunications Group Inc* 1467
LCR Telecom Offshore (Holdings) Limited *Primus Telecommunications Group Inc* 1467
LCS Services, Inc. *Waste Management Inc* 1934
Lct Insurance Co. *Tiffany & Co* 1793
LD Realty, Inc. *Drew Industries Inc* 576
LDA Group *American Community Properties Trust* 89
LdB O&M (Gronigen) B.V. *WPP Group Plc* 1979
LDG Insurance Agency Incorporated *HCC Insurance Holdings Inc* 856

Mechel Trading House (MTH) *Mechel OAO* 1146
Mechel Zeljezara (MZ) *Mechel OAO* 1146
Mechelenergo *Mechel OAO* 1146
MECIA Espana SA *WPP Group Plc* 1979
Mecklenburg County Recycling,Inc. *Casella Waste Systems Inc* 341
MECKLENBURG MILL ASSOCIATES, LIMITED PARTNERSHIP *Apartment Investment and Management Company* 130
Mecklenburg Park, Inc. *Bank of America Corp* 208
Mecklenburg Securities Corporation *Wachovia Corp* 1928
Mecklenburg Surgical Land Development, Ltd. *HCA Inc* 855
Meco Equipment Engineers B.V. *BE Semiconductor Industries N.V.* 224
Meco Equipment Engineers (Far East) Pte Ltd. *BE Semiconductor Industries N.V.* 224
MECO Holding Company *Thermadyne Holdings Corp* 1786
Meco International B.V. *BE Semiconductor Industries N.V.* 224
Med 4 Home Inc. *Lincare Holdings Inc* 1079
Med City Dallas Outpatient Surgery Center, L.P. *HCA Inc* 855
Med Close Corp *CPC of America Inc* 493
Med Corp., Inc. *HCA Inc* 855
Med Enclosure LLC *CPC of America Inc* 493
Med Group - Southern Hills Hospitalists, LLC *HCA Inc* 855
Med Plus of El Paso, Inc. *HCA Inc* 855
Med Properties Asset Group, L.L.C. *Health Care REIT Inc* 857
MED Resins, Inc. *Wellman Inc* 1943
Med Travelers, Inc. *AMN Healthcare Inc* 114
Med Travelers, LLC *AMN Healthcare Inc* 114
MED Urological, Inc *Pfizer Inc* 1420
Med World Acquisition Corp. *Omnicare Inc* 1338
Med-Center Hosp./Houston, Inc. *HCA Inc* 855
Med-Emerg Health Centres Inc. *Med-Emerg International Inc* 1146
Med-Emerg Inc. *Med-Emerg International Inc* 1146
Med-Point of New Hampshire, Inc. *HCA Inc* 855
Med-Safe Systems, Inc. *Becton Dickinson & Co* 227
Med-Staff, Inc. (f/k/a Cross Country Nurses, Inc.) *Cross Country Healthcare Inc* 503
Med-Tech Environmental (MA), Inc *Stericycle Inc* 1701
Med-Tech Environmental, Inc *Stericycle Inc* 1701
Med-Vine, Inc. *Sun Bancorp Inc* 1717
MedAire Limited. *MedAire Inc* 1147
Medallion Bank *Medallion Financial Corp* 1147
Medallion Business Credit, LLC *Medallion Financial Corp* 1147
Medallion California Properties Company *KCS Energy Inc* 1020
Medallion Capital, Inc. *Medallion Financial Corp* 1147
Medallion Foods, Inc. *Ralcorp Holdings Inc* 1511
Medallion Funding Corp. *Medallion Financial Corp* 1147
Medallion Hamptons Holding LLC *Medallion Financial Corp* 1147
Medam B.A. S.R.L. *Stericycle Inc* 1701
Medam S.A. de C.V *Stericycle Inc* 1701
Medarex *Abgenix Inc* 6
MedaSorb Acquisition Inc., *MedaSorb Technologies Corp* 1147
Medbloc, Inc. *Invacare Corp* 981
MEDC Limited *Cooper Industries Ltd* 477
Medcap HCPI Development, LLC *Health Care Property Investors Inc* 857
MedCap Holding II, LLC *Health Care Property Investors Inc* 857
Medcap Holding III, LLC *Health Care Property Investors Inc* 857
MedCap Holding IV, LLC *Health Care Property Investors Inc* 857
MedCap Properties I, LLC *Health Care Property Investors Inc* 857
MedCap Properties II, LLC *Health Care Property Investors Inc* 857
Medcap Properties, LLC *Health Care Property Investors Inc* 857
MedCath Cardiology Consulting & Management, Inc. *Medcath Corp* 1148
MedCath Diagnostics, LLC *Medcath Corp* 1148
MedCath Finance Company, LLC *Medcath Corp* 1148
MedCath Holdings Corp. *Medcath Corp* 1148
MedCath Incorporated *Medcath Corp* 1148
MedCath Nuclear Services, LLC *Medcath Corp* 1148
MedCath of Arkansas, Inc. *Medcath Corp* 1148
MedCath of Little Rock, LLC *Medcath Corp* 1148
MedCath of McAllen, L.P. *Medcath Corp* 1148
MedCath of New Jersey Cardiac Testing Centers, LP *Medcath Corp* 1148
MedCath of Texas, Inc. *Medcath Corp* 1148
MedCath of Tucson, LLC *Medcath Corp* 1148
Medcenter Management Services, Inc. *United Surgical Partners International Inc* 1863
MedChem Products, Inc. *C. R. Bard Inc* 299
MedChem, Limited *Sigma Aldrich Corp* 1627
Medco at Home, LLC *Medco Health Solutions Inc* 1148
Medco Containment Insurance Company of New Jersey *Medco Health Solutions Inc* 1148
Medco Containment Insurance Company of New York *Medco Health Solutions Inc* 1148
Medco Containment Life Insurance Company *Medco Health Solutions Inc* 1148
Medco de Mexico Managed Care S. de R.L. de C.V. *Merck & Co Inc* 1162
Medco Health New York Independent Practice Association, LLC *Medco Health Solutions Inc* 1148
Medco Health Puerto Rico, LLC *Medco Health Solutions Inc* 1148
Medco Health Receivables, LLC *Medco Health Solutions Inc* 1148
Medco Health Solutions of Columbus North, Ltd. *Medco Health Solutions Inc* 1148
Medco Health Solutions of Columbus West, Ltd. *Medco Health Solutions Inc* 1148
Medco Health Solutions of Fairfield, LLC *Medco Health Solutions Inc* 1148
Medco Health Solutions of Franklin Lakes, LLC *Medco Health Solutions Inc* 1148
Medco Health Solutions of Henderson, Nevada, LLC *Medco Health Solutions Inc* 1148
Medco Health Solutions of Hidden River, L.C. *Medco Health Solutions Inc* 1148
Medco Health Solutions of Las Vegas, Inc. *Medco Health Solutions Inc* 1148
Medco Health Solutions of Netpark, LLC *Medco Health Solutions Inc* 1148
Medco Health Solutions of North Versailles, LLC *Medco Health Solutions Inc* 1148
Medco Health Solutions of Richmond, LLC *Medco Health Solutions Inc* 1148
Medco Health Solutions of Sabal Park, L.C. *Medco Health Solutions Inc* 1148
Medco Health Solutions of Spokane, Inc. *Medco Health Solutions Inc* 1148
Medco Health Solutions of Texas, LLC *Medco Health Solutions Inc* 1148
Medco Health Solutions of Willingboro, LLC *Medco Health Solutions Inc* 1148
Medco Health, LLC *Medco Health Solutions Inc* 1148
Medco Holdings S. de R.L. de C.V. *Merck & Co Inc* 1162
Medco Professional Services, Corp. *Rotech Healthcare Inc NEW* 1560
Medco Services Puerto Rico, Inc. *Medco Health Solutions Inc* 1148
Medco Servicios de Mexico, S. de R.L. de C.V. *Merck & Co Inc* 1162
Medco Supply Company, Inc. *Patterson Cos Inc* 1393
medcohealth.com, LLC *Medco Health Solutions Inc* 1148
Medcon S.A. *Cardinal Health Inc* 332
MedCorp International, Inc. *Rotech Healthcare Inc NEW* 1560
Meddig Medizintechnik Vertriebs-GmbH *Teleflex Inc* 1766
MedE America Corporation *HLTH Corp* 881
MedE America Corporation of Ohio *HLTH Corp* 881
Medefield Pty Limited *Tyco International Ltd* 1838
Medefile, Inc. *Bio-Solutions International Inc* 241
MedElite, Inc *eFoodSafety.com Inc* 607
MedEquities Inc. *Kindred Healthcare Inc* 1030
Medesta Associates, LLC *Cardinal Health Inc* 332
Medevac Medical Response, Inc. *Emergency Medical Services Corp* 622
Medevac MidAmerica, Inc. *Emergency Medical Services Corp* 622
Medex, Inc. *Clark Inc* 419
MedFirst, Inc. *HCA Inc* 855
MedFocus, LLC *inVentiv Health* 981
Medfor (L)Ltd. *Pride International Inc* 1465
Medfor S.A.S. *Pride International Inc* 1465
Medford Coca-Cola Bottling Company *Coca-Cola Enterprises Inc* 433
Medford Ready Mix, Inc. *MDU Resources Group Inc* 1144
MEDgenesis Inc *Bioscrip Inc* 247
MEDI *Mediscience Technology Corp* 1155
Medi Flight of Oklahoma, LLC *HCA Inc* 855
Medi, Inc. *HLTH Corp* 881
Medi-Cab of Georgia, Inc. *Rural/Metro Corp* 1567
Medi-Car Ambulance Service, Inc. *Emergency Medical Services Corp* 622
Medi-Car Systems, Inc. *Emergency Medical Services Corp* 622
Medi-Health of Florida,Inc. *Tenet Healthcare Corp* 1774
Medi-Photonics Development LLC *Mediscience Technology Corp* 1155
Medi-Rents Business Trust *Praxair Inc* 1458
Medi-Rents of Maine, Inc. *Praxair Inc* 1458
Medi-Rents, Inc. *Praxair Inc* 1458
Medi-Speed Natal (Pty) Limited *BOC Group Plc* 262
Media Accounting Services Limited *Electronic Data Systems Corp* 614
Media Acquisition Corporation *Belo Corp* 230
Media Acquisition Partners, L.P. *Belo Corp* 230
Media Admin AB *WPP Group Plc* 1979
Media Assets (Cayman) Limited *News Corp Ltd (The)* 1281
Media Audits Ltd *Accenture Ltd* 11
Media Audits North America *Accenture Ltd* 11
Media Bridge Entertainment, Inc. *Interpublic Group of Companies Inc* 975
Media Buying Company (Ontario Partnership) *WPP Group Plc* 1979
Media by Storm (Pty) Ltd *WPP Group Plc* 1979
Media Capitol, a.s. *Central European Media Enterprises Ltd* 361
Media Central Acquisition, LLC *PRIMEDIA Inc* 1466
Media Central IP Corp. *PRIMEDIA Inc* 1466
Media Central LLC *PRIMEDIA Inc* 1466
Media Centre 1 *WPP Group Plc* 1979
Media Centre 2 *WPP Group Plc* 1979
Media Centre Auto *WPP Group Plc* 1979
Media Centre Inkoop *WPP Group Plc* 1979
Media Chips *Opti Inc* 1348
Media Club SpA *WPP Group Plc* 1979
Media Com Ltd *WPP Group Plc* 1979
Media Computer Technologies, Inc. *LSI Corp* 1098
Media Consortium, LLC *New York Times Co* 1277
Media Consultancy YH *News Corp Ltd (The)* 1281
Media Cybernetics Inc. *Roper Industries Inc* 1558
Media Data Systems Pte Ltd *Global Sources Ltd* 797
Media Debt Collections Limited *News Corp Ltd (The)* 1281
Media Discovery Ltd *WPP Group Plc* 1979
Media Edge Comunicaciones Chile Limitada *WPP Group Plc* 1979
Media Edge:CIA (Portugal)-Servicios Publiciatorios Lda *WPP Group Plc* 1979
Media Exposure BV *WPP Group Plc* 1979
Media First International Inc. *Interpublic Group of Companies Inc* 975
Media General Broadcasting of South Carolina Holdings, Inc. *Media General Inc* 1149
Media General Communications, Inc. *Media General Inc* 1149
Media General Operations, Inc. *Media General Inc* 1149
Media House d.o.o. *Central European Media Enterprises Ltd* 361
Media Ida Vision Inc. *Interpublic Group of Companies Inc* 975
Media Inform LLC *News Corp Ltd (The)* 1281
Media Initiative (proprietary)limited *Interpublic Group of Companies Inc* 975
Media Initiative (zimbabwe)pty Ltd *Interpublic Group of Companies Inc* 975
Media Insight GIE *WPP Group Plc* 1979
Media Insight Ltd *WPP Group Plc* 1979
Media Insight Polske Sp zoo *WPP Group Plc* 1979
Media Insight Srl *WPP Group Plc* 1979
Media Insight Srl *WPP Group Plc* 1979
Media Insight Sweden A.B. *WPP Group Plc* 1979
Media Insight/Outdoor Ltd *WPP Group Plc* 1979
Media Insikt AB *WPP Group Plc* 1979
Media Instruments S.r.l. (IT Italia) *WPP Group Plc* 1979
Media Investment S.A. *Liberty Global Inc* 1074
Media Logic USA, LLC. *Trans World Entertainment Corp* 1812
Media Marketing GmbH, Hannover *WPP Group Plc* 1979
Media Motor GmbH, Hannover *WPP Group Plc* 1979
Media Networks Per S.A.C. *Telefnica del Per* 1767
Media Networks, Inc *Time Warner Inc* 1795
Media Online Services, Inc. *Opentv Corp* 1346
Media Online Services,Inc. *Liberty Media LLC* 1074
Media Overseas *Vivendi* 1918
Media Partnership Corporation *Interpublic Group of Companies Inc* 975
Media Planning Group Sa. *Havas* 853
Media Planning Ltd *Havas* 853
Media Plus Ltd *WPP Group Plc* 1979
Media Pro International S.A. *Central European Media Enterprises Ltd* 361
Media Productions Ltd. *Global Sources Ltd* 797
Media Qualitat *WPP Group Plc* 1979
Media Research Inc *WPP Group Plc* 1979
Media Sciences UK Limited *Media Sciences International Inc* 1149
Media Sciences, Inc. *Media Sciences International Inc* 1149
Media Solutions Group *WPP Group Plc* 1979
Media Support AB *WPP Group Plc* 1979
Media Support Scandanavian AB *WPP Group Plc* 1979
Media Support Services Limited *News Corp Ltd (The)* 1281
Media Technology Corporation *TDK Corp* 1755
Media Tele SA *Tele2 AB* 1764
Media Trend S.R.L. *Viacom Inc* 1902
Media Trend S.R.L. *CBS Corp* 349
Media Vest Worldwide *Publicis Groupe* 1488
Media Vision S.R.L. *Central European Media Enterprises Ltd* 361
Media Zone, LTD *Broadcaster Inc* 283
Media+ S.A. *WPP Group Plc* 1979
Media/Professional Insurance Agency Limited *Aon Corp* 129
Media24 Limited *Naspers Ltd* 1237
Mediabroker A/S *WPP Group Plc* 1979
Mediabroker AB *WPP Group Plc* 1979
MediaBrokers Ltd. *Aquantive Inc* 139
MediaBruk Skandanavien AB *WPP Group Plc* 1979
Mediacom Arizona LLC *Mediacom Communications Corp* 1149
MediaCom B.V. *WPP Group Plc* 1979
MediaCom Bratislava *WPP Group Plc* 1979
Mediacom Broadband Corporation *Mediacom Communications Corp* 1149
Mediacom Broadband LLC *Mediacom Communications Corp* 1149
Mediacom California LLC *Mediacom Communications Corp* 1149
Mediacom Canada Ltd *WPP Group Plc* 1979
Mediacom Capital Corporation *Mediacom Communications Corp* 1149
MediaCom CIS GMBH *WPP Group Plc* 1979
MediaCom Danmark A/S *WPP Group Plc* 1979
Mediacom Delaware LLC *Mediacom Communications Corp* 1149
MediaCom GmbH *WPP Group Plc* 1979
MediaCom GMBH Vienna *WPP Group Plc* 1979
MediaCom Group (formerly The Media Business Group plc) Ltd *WPP Group Plc* 1979
MediaCom Holding Central Europe GMBH *WPP Group Plc* 1979
MediaCom Holdings Ltd (formerly MediaCom TMBG Ltd) *WPP Group Plc* 1979
Mediacom Iberia SA *WPP Group Plc* 1979
Mediacom Iberia Sucursal em Portugal *WPP Group Plc* 1979
Mediacom Illinois LLC *Mediacom Communications Corp* 1149
Mediacom (India) Pvt Ltd *WPP Group Plc* 1979
Mediacom Indiana Holdings, L.P. *Mediacom Communications Corp* 1149
Mediacom Indiana LLC *Mediacom Communications Corp* 1149
Mediacom Indiana Partnerco LLC *Mediacom Communications Corp* 1149
MediaCom Interacive *WPP Group Plc* 1979
Mediacom Iowa LLC *Mediacom Communications Corp* 1149
Mediacom Japan Inc *WPP Group Plc* 1979
Mediacom LLC *Mediacom Communications Corp* 1149
Mediacom Ltd *WPP Group Plc* 1979
Mediacom Minnesota LLC *Mediacom Communications Corp* 1149
MediaCom (New Zealand) Ltd. *WPP Group Plc* 1979
Mediacom Nordic A/S *WPP Group Plc* 1979
Mediacom Nordic AB *WPP Group Plc* 1979
Mediacom Nordic Group A/S (fka Dot Zero Holding A/S: ETP Holding A/S) *WPP Group Plc* 1979
MediaCom Norge AS *WPP Group Plc* 1979
Mediacom North Ltd *WPP Group Plc* 1979
Mediacom Paris SA *WPP Group Plc* 1979
MediaCom Praha s.r.o. *WPP Group Plc* 1979
MediaCom Romania Srl *WPP Group Plc* 1979
Mediacom S.A. *WPP Group Plc* 1979
Mediacom Scotland Ltd (formerly MediaCom Scotland TMB Ltd) *WPP Group Plc* 1979
MediaCom Service Hamburg GmbH *WPP Group Plc* 1979
MediaCom Service Mnchen GmbH *WPP Group Plc* 1979
Mediacom Services AB *WPP Group Plc* 1979
Mediacom Southeast LLC *Mediacom Communications Corp* 1149
MediaCom UK Ltd (formerly The Media Business Ltd) *WPP Group Plc* 1979
MediaCom Warsawa *WPP Group Plc* 1979
Mediacom Wisconsin LLC *Mediacom Communications Corp* 1149
Mediacom Worldwide Canada Ltd *WPP Group Plc* 1979
Mediacom Worldwide Inc. *WPP Group Plc* 1979
Mediacommunication Gteborg AB *WPP Group Plc* 1979
Mediacommunication I Visby AB *WPP Group Plc* 1979
Mediacommunication Interactive AB *WPP Group Plc* 1979
Mediacommunication resund AB *WPP Group Plc* 1979
Mediacommunication Services Sverige AB *WPP Group Plc* 1979
Mediacommunication Stockholm AB *WPP Group Plc* 1979
Mediacommunications Sverige I Stockholm AB *WPP Group Plc* 1979
Mediacompany Communications Ltd *WPP Group Plc* 1979
Mediacompete (Proprietary) Ltd *WPP Group Plc* 1979
MediaCompete Pty Ltd. *WPP Group Plc* 1979
Mediacompete Sdn. Bhd. *WPP Group Plc* 1979
Mediacompete Singapore Pte Ltd *WPP Group Plc* 1979
Mediacore Communications Ltd *WPP Group Plc* 1979
MediaDefender *Artistdirect Inc* 156
Mediaedge Cia Ltda (fka The Media Edge Ltda) *WPP Group Plc* 1979
Mediaedge CIA SA *WPP Group Plc* 1979
Mediaedge:cia *WPP Group Plc* 1979
Mediaedge:CIA Asia Pacific Holdings Pte Ltd *WPP Group Plc* 1979
Mediaedge:CIA Baltic *WPP Group Plc* 1979
Mediaedge:CIA BV *WPP Group Plc* 1979
Mediaedge:CIA Denmark AS *WPP Group Plc* 1979
Mediaedge:CIA Finland OY *WPP Group Plc* 1979
Mediaedge:CIA France SAS *WPP Group Plc* 1979
Mediaedge:CIA Germany Holding GmbH *WPP Group Plc* 1979
Mediaedge:cia GmbH *WPP Group Plc* 1979
Mediaedge:cia GmbH& Co. KG *WPP Group Plc* 1979
Mediaedge:cia India Pvt Ltd *WPP Group Plc* 1979
Mediaedge:CIA International Ltd *WPP Group Plc* 1979
Mediaedge:CIA Italy Holdings Srl *WPP Group Plc* 1979
Mediaedge:CIA Italy Srl *WPP Group Plc* 1979
Mediaedge:CIA LLC *WPP Group Plc* 1979
Mediaedge:cia Medianetwork Hellas *WPP Group Plc* 1979
Mediaedge:CIA Medianetwork Hong Kong Ltd *WPP Group Plc* 1979
Mediaedge:cia Medianetwork Singapore Pte Ltd *WPP Group Plc* 1979
Mediaedge:CIA Norway AS *WPP Group Plc* 1979
Mediaedge:CIA Norway Holdings AS *WPP Group Plc* 1979
Mediaedge:CIA Pacific Holdings Pte Ltd *WPP Group Plc* 1979
Mediaedge:cia Pacific Singapore Pte Ltd *WPP Group Plc* 1979
Mediaedge:cia Pty Ltd *WPP Group Plc* 1979
Mediaedge:CIA (Pty) Ltd *WPP Group Plc* 1979
Mediaedge:cia Radiokonsulterna AB *WPP Group Plc* 1979
Mediaedge:cia Sweden AB *WPP Group Plc* 1979
Mediaedge:CIA Sweden Direct AB *WPP Group Plc* 1979
Mediaedge:CIA Sweden Holdings AB *WPP Group Plc* 1979
Mediaedge:CIA Switzerland AG *WPP Group Plc* 1979

Mensi, Inc. *Trimble Navigation Ltd* 1824
Mensi, KK *Trimble Navigation Ltd* 1824
Mensi, S.A. *Trimble Navigation Ltd* 1824
Mental Health Outcomes, Inc. *Horizon Health Corp* 890
Mental Healthsource, LLC *Magellan Health Services Inc* ... 1109
Mentor Aesthetics B.V. *Mentor Corp Minn* 1159
Mentor Benelux B.V. *Mentor Corp Minn* 1159
Mentor Biologics, Inc. *Mentor Corp Minn* 1159
Mentor Biopharmaceuticals, Inc. *Mentor Corp Minn* 1159
Mentor Biopolymers Limited *Mentor Corp Minn* 1159
Mentor Design Systems Pte. Ltd. *Mentor Graphics Corp* ... 1159
Mentor Deutschland GmbH *Mentor Corp Minn* 1159
Mentor Excess and Surplus Lines Insurance Company *Murphy Oil Corp* 1228
Mentor Graphics (Asia) Pte Ltd *Mentor Graphics Corp* ... 1159
Mentor Graphics (Canada) Limited *Mentor Graphics Corp* .. 1159
Mentor Graphics Denmark, Filial af Mentor Graphics (Ireland) Limited *Mentor Graphics Corp* 1159
Mentor Graphics Denmark, Filial af Mentor Graphics (Scandinavia) AB, Sverige *Mentor Graphics Corp* 1159
Mentor Graphics (Deutschland) GmbH *Mentor Graphics Corp* . 1159
Mentor Graphics Development (Ireland) Ltd *Mentor Graphics Corp* 1159
Mentor Graphics Development Services Limited *Mentor Graphics Corp* 1159
Mentor Graphics (Egypt) *Mentor Graphics Corp* 1159
Mentor Graphics (Espana) SL *Mentor Graphics Corp* 1159
Mentor Graphics (Finland) Oy *Mentor Graphics Corp* 1159
Mentor Graphics (France) Sarl *Mentor Graphics Corp* 1159
Mentor Graphics (France) Sede Italiania *Mentor Graphics Corp* 1159
Mentor Graphics (Holdings) Limited *Mentor Graphics Corp* . 1159
Mentor Graphics (Hong Kong) Limited *Mentor Graphics Corp* . 1159
Mentor Graphics (Hungary) *Mentor Graphics Corp.* 1159
Mentor Graphics (India) Private Ltd. *Mentor Graphics Corp.* . 1159
Mentor Graphics Ireland Limited, fillal Sweden *Mentor Graphics Corp* 1159
Mentor Graphics (Ireland) Limited *Mentor Graphics Corp.* . 1159
Mentor Graphics (Ireland), Austria Branch *Mentor Graphics Corp* 1159
Mentor Graphics (Ireland), Finnish Branch *Mentor Graphics Corp* 1159
Mentor Graphics (Ireland), French Branch *Mentor Graphics Corp* 1159
Mentor Graphics (Ireland), German Branch *Mentor Graphics Corp* 1159
Mentor Graphics (Ireland), Taiwan Branch *Mentor Graphics Corp* 1159
Mentor Graphics (Ireland), UK Branch *Mentor Graphics Corp.* . 1159
Mentor Graphics (Israel) Limited *Mentor Graphics Corp* . 1159
Mentor Graphics (Japan) Co. Ltd. *Mentor Graphics Corp* . 1159
Mentor Graphics Ltd Bermuda *Mentor Graphics Corp* 1159
Mentor Graphics (Netherlands Antilles) N.V. *Mentor Graphics Corp* 1159
Mentor Graphics (Netherlands) B.V. *Mentor Graphics Corp.* . 1159
Mentor Graphics (NOIDA) Pvt. Ltd. *Mentor Graphics Corp.* . 1159
Mentor Graphics Polska *Mentor Graphics Corp.* 1159
Mentor Graphics Sales and Services *Mentor Graphics Corp.* . 1159
Mentor Graphics Scandinavia AB, Danish Branch *Mentor Graphics Corp* 1159
Mentor Graphics (Scandinavia) AB *Mentor Graphics Corp.* . 1159
Mentor Graphics (Schweiz) AG *Mentor Graphics Corp.* .. 1159
Mentor Graphics Shanghai Electronic Technology Co. *Mentor Graphics Corp* 1159
Mentor Graphics (Taiwan) Limited *Mentor Graphics Corp* . 1159
Mentor Graphics (UK) Limited *Mentor Graphics Corp* ... 1159
Mentor Holding Corporation *Murphy Oil Corp* 1228
Mentor Insurance and Reinsurance Company *Murphy Oil Corp.* . 1228
Mentor Insurance Company (U.K.) Limited *Murphy Oil Corp* . 1228
Mentor Insurance Limited *Murphy Oil Corp* 1228
Mentor International Holdings Alpha, Inc. *Mentor Corp Minn.* . 1159
Mentor International Holdings Beta, Inc. *Mentor Corp Minn.* . 1159
Mentor International Holdings Camda, Inc. *Mentor Corp Minn.* . 1159
Mentor International Holdings Delta, Inc. *Mentor Corp Minn* . 1159
Mentor Korea Company, Limited *Mentor Graphics Corp* . 1159
Mentor Medical Inc. *Mentor Corp Minn.* 1159
Mentor Medical Italia, S.r.l. *Mentor Corp Minn* 1159
Mentor Medical Systems B.V. *Mentor Corp Minn* 1159
Mentor Medical Systems (Canada), Inc. *Mentor Corp Minn.* . 1159
Mentor Medical Systems Ltd. *Mentor Corp Minn* 1159
Mentor Medical Systems Pty. Ltd. *Mentor Corp Minn* .. 1159
Mentor Medical Systems, C.V. *Mentor Corp Minn* 1159
Mentor Medical Systems, France, S.A. *Mentor Corp Minn* . 1159
Mentor Medical Systems, Iberica, S.L. *Mentor Corp Minn* . 1159
Mentor Minnesota Inc. *Mentor Corp Minn* 1159
Mentor Texas GP, LLC *Mentor Corp Minn.* 1159
Mentor Texas LP *Mentor Corp Minn.* 1159
Mentor Underwriting Agents (U.K.) Limited *Murphy Oil Corp.* . 1228
Mentorix Technologies, Inc *Lionbridge Technologies Inc.* . 1083
MenuLink Computer Solutions, Inc. *Radiant Systems Inc.* . 1507
Menvier CSA Srl *Cooper Industries Ltd* 477
Menvier Group Limited *Cooper Industries Ltd* 477
Menvier Overseas Holdings Limited *Cooper Industries Ltd* . 477
Menyc, LLC *Marriott International Inc* 1125
Menza Grundstcks-Verwaltungsgesellschaft mbH *Allianz* .. 63
Menza Grundstcks-Verwaltungsgesellschaft mbH& Co. KG *Allianz* 63
Meow Mix Decatur Production I LLC *Del Monte Foods Co.* . 536
Meow Mix Holdings, Inc. *Del Monte Foods Co* 536
MEP Marine AS *Emerson Electric Co.* 623
MER Fifth Avenue Realty Inc. *Mer Telemanagement Solutions Ltd.* 1160
Meragon Financial Services, Inc. *IAC/InterActiveCorp* . 961
Merant BV *Serena Software Inc* 1612
Merant Holdings *Serena Software Inc* 1612
Merant Inc. *Serena Software Inc* 1612
Merant Limited *Serena Software Inc* 1612
Merant SA *Serena Software Inc* 1612
Merant Trustees Limited *Serena Software Inc* 1612
Merban Equity *Credit Suisse Group* 497
Mercadeo Deportivo de Mxico, SA de CV *WPP Group Plc* . 1979
Mercado Gas Services Inc *Oneok Inc* 1343
Mercados Y Analisis, S.A. *IMS Health Inc* 931
Mercantil de Importaciones y Exportaciones Ltda. *Tyco International Ltd.* 1838
Mercantile Bank *South Financial Group Inc* 1663
Mercantile Bank Capital Trust I *Mercantile Bank Corp* . 1160
Mercantile Bank Mortgage Company, LLC *Mercantile Bank Corp* 1160
Mercantile Bank of Michigan *Mercantile Bank Corp* ... 1160
Mercantile Bank Real Estate Co., LLC *Mercantile Bank Corp* . 1160
Mercantile Credit Company Limited *Barclays Plc* 216
Mercantile Housing LLC *Edison International* 604

Mercantile Indemnity Company Ltd. *Unitrin Inc* 1865
Mercantile Industrial Leasing Limited *Barclays Plc* .. 216
Mercantile Insurance Center, Inc *Mercantile Bank Corp* . 1160
Mercantile Leasing Administration Limited *Barclays Plc.* . 216
Mercantile Leasing Company (No.132) Limited *Barclays Plc* . 216
Mercantile Leasing Company (No.144) Limited *Barclays Plc* . 216
Mercantile Leasing Company (No.147) Limited *Barclays Plc* . 216
Mercantile Leasing Company (No.150) Limited *Barclays Plc* . 216
Mercantile Logistics Company, Inc. *Dillard's Inc* 558
Mercantile Mortgage, LLC *Wells Fargo & Co.* 1944
Mercantile National Bank *National Mercantile Bancorp* . 1244
Mercantile Operations, Inc. *Dillard's Inc* 558
Mercantile U.K. Limited *Willis Group Holdings Ltd* .. 1962
MERCATOR DEVELOPMENTS LIMITED *National Grid Transco Plc* 1241
Mercator Energy Incorporated *Powersecure International Inc* . 1455
Mercator Shipping Inc. *Danaos Corp* 525
Merced Area Investment and Development, Inc. *Capital Corp of the West* 324
MERCED COMMONS *Apartment Investment and Management Company* 130
MERCED COMMONS II *Apartment Investment and Management Company* 130
Mercedes-Benz Manhattan, Inc. *DaimlerChrysler AG* ... 523
Mercedes-Benz USA, LLC *DaimlerChrysler AG* 523
Mercer Asesores de Seguros SA *Marsh & McLennan Cos Inc* . 1125
Mercer Australia Limited *Marsh & McLennan Cos Inc* .. 1125
Mercer Broking SA *Marsh & McLennan Cos Inc* 1125
Mercer Consulting Group Verwaltungs GmbH *Marsh & McLennan Cos Inc* 1125
Mercer Consulting Holdings Sdn. Bhd. *Marsh & McLennan Cos Inc* 1125
Mercer Consulting Limited *Marsh & McLennan Cos Inc* . 1125
Mercer Corredores de Seguros Ltda. *Marsh & McLennan Cos Inc* 1125
Mercer Corretora de Seguros Ltda *Marsh & McLennan Cos Inc.* . 1125
Mercer County Surgery Center, LLC *Amsurg Corp* 117
Mercer Delta Consulting Limited *Marsh & McLennan Cos Inc* . 1125
Mercer Delta Consulting Limited *Marsh & McLennan Cos Inc* . 1125
Mercer Delta Consulting LLC *Marsh & McLennan Cos Inc* . 1125
Mercer Delta Consulting SAS *Marsh & McLennan Cos Inc* . 1125
Mercer Employee Benefit Services Limited *Marsh & McLennan Cos Inc* 1125
Mercer Employee Benefits OY *Marsh & McLennan Cos Inc* . 1125
Mercer Employee BenefitsMediacao de Seguros, Lda. *Marsh & McLennan Cos Inc* 1125
Mercer Financial Services in Mercer *Northwest Bancorp Inc* . 1305
Mercer Global Investments, Inc. *Marsh & McLennan Cos Inc.* . 1125
Mercer Health & Benefits LLC *Marsh & McLennan Cos Inc* . 1125
Mercer Holdings 2002 Business Trust *BJ's Wholesale Club Inc* . 252
Mercer Holdings Canada, Inc. *Marsh & McLennan Cos Inc* . 1125
Mercer Holdings, Inc. *Marsh & McLennan Cos Inc* 1125
Mercer HR Services, LLC *Marsh & McLennan Cos Inc* .. 1125
Mercer Human Resource Consulting a.s. *Marsh & McLennan Cos Inc* 1125
Mercer Human Resource Consulting A/S *Marsh & McLennan Cos Inc* 1125
Mercer Human Resource Consulting and Insurance Brokers Limited *Marsh & McLennan Cos Inc* 1125
Mercer Human Resource Consulting AS *Marsh & McLennan Cos Inc* 1125
Mercer Human Resource Consulting B.V. *Marsh & McLennan Cos Inc* 1125
Mercer Human Resource Consulting (EB) Limited *Marsh & McLennan Cos Inc* 1125
Mercer Human Resource Consulting GmbH *Marsh & McLennan Cos Inc* 1125
Mercer Human Resource Consulting GmbH *Marsh & McLennan Cos Inc* 1125
Mercer Human Resource Consulting Korea Ltd. *Marsh & McLennan Cos Inc* 1125
Mercer Human Resource Consulting Lda. *Marsh & McLennan Cos Inc* 1125
Mercer Human Resource Consulting Limited *Marsh & McLennan Cos Inc* 1125
Mercer Human Resource Consulting Limited *Marsh & McLennan Cos Inc* 1125
Mercer Human Resource Consulting Limited *Marsh & McLennan Cos Inc* 1125
Mercer Human Resource Consulting Limited *Marsh & McLennan Cos Inc* 1125
Mercer Human Resource Consulting LLC *Marsh & McLennan Cos Inc* 1125
Mercer Human Resource Consulting Ltd *Marsh & McLennan Cos Inc* 1125
Mercer Human Resource Consulting Ltd *Marsh & McLennan Cos Inc* 1125
Mercer Human Resource Consulting Ltd. *Marsh & McLennan Cos Inc* 1125
Mercer Human Resource Consulting Ltda *Marsh & McLennan Cos Inc* 1125
Mercer Human Resource Consulting Ltda. *Marsh & McLennan Cos Inc* 1125
Mercer Human Resource Consulting of Puerto Rico, Inc. *Marsh & McLennan Cos Inc* 1125
Mercer Human Resource Consulting OY *Marsh & McLennan Cos Inc* 1125
Mercer Human Resource Consulting Pty Ltd *Marsh & McLennan Cos Inc* 1125
Mercer Human Resource Consulting Pvt Ltd *Marsh & McLennan Cos Inc* 1125
Mercer Human Resource Consulting (S) Pte Ltd *Marsh & McLennan Cos Inc* 1125
Mercer Human Resource Consulting S.A. *Marsh & McLennan Cos Inc* 1125
Mercer Human Resource Consulting S.A. de C.V. *Marsh & McLennan Cos Inc* 1125
Mercer Human Resource Consulting SA *Marsh & McLennan Cos Inc* 1125
Mercer Human Resource Consulting SA *Marsh & McLennan Cos Inc* 1125
Mercer Human Resource Consulting SA-NV *Marsh & McLennan Cos Inc* 1125
Mercer Human Resource Consulting Sdn. Bhd. *Marsh & McLennan Cos Inc* 1125
Mercer Human Resource Consulting SP. Z.O.O. *Marsh & McLennan Cos Inc* 1125
Mercer Human Resource Consulting Srl *Marsh & McLennan Cos Inc* 1125
Mercer Human Resource Consulting, Inc. *Marsh & McLennan Cos Inc* 1125
Mercer Human Resource Consulting, S.L. *Marsh & McLennan Cos Inc* 1125

Mercer Inc. *Marsh & McLennan Cos Inc* 1125
Mercer Insurance Company *Mercer Insurance Group Inc* . 1160
Mercer Insurance Company of New Jersey, Inc. *Mercer Insurance Group Inc* 1160
Mercer Investment Consulting Limited *Marsh & McLennan Cos Inc* 1125
Mercer Investment Consulting, Inc. *Marsh & McLennan Cos Inc* 1125
Mercer Investment Nominees Ltd *Marsh & McLennan Cos Inc.* . 1125
Mercer Ireland Holdings Limited *Marsh & McLennan Cos Inc.* . 1125
Mercer Legal (NSW) Pty Ltd *Marsh & McLennan Cos Inc* . 1125
Mercer Limited *Marsh & McLennan Cos Inc* 1125
Mercer Management Consulting AG *Marsh & McLennan Cos Inc* 1125
Mercer Management Consulting GmbH *Marsh & McLennan Cos Inc* 1125
Mercer Management Consulting Group GmbH & Co. KG *Marsh & McLennan Cos Inc* 1125
Mercer Management Consulting Holding GmbH *Marsh & McLennan Cos Inc* 1125
Mercer Management Consulting Limited *Marsh & McLennan Cos Inc* 1125
Mercer Management Consulting Limited *Marsh & McLennan Cos Inc* 1125
Mercer Management Consulting S.L. *Marsh & McLennan Cos Inc* 1125
Mercer Management Consulting Servicios, S. DE RL. DE CV *Marsh & McLennan Cos Inc* 1125
Mercer Management Consulting SNC *Marsh & McLennan Cos Inc* 1125
Mercer Management Consulting Sociedade Unipessoal, Lda *Marsh & McLennan Cos Inc* 1125
Mercer Management Consulting, Inc. *Marsh & McLennan Cos Inc* 1125
Mercer Management Consulting, Ltd. *Marsh & McLennan Cos Inc* 1125
Mercer Mortgage Holdings, Inc. *BJ's Wholesale Club Inc* . 252
Mercer Oliver Wyman Actuarial Consulting, Inc *Marsh & McLennan Cos Inc* 1125
Mercer Oliver Wyman Consulting Limited *Marsh & McLennan Cos Inc* 1125
Mercer Oliver Wyman Corporate Risk Consulting, Inc. *Marsh & McLennan Cos Inc* 1125
Mercer Oliver Wyman Limited *Marsh & McLennan Cos Inc* . 1125
Mercer Oliver Wyman Pty Ltd *Marsh & McLennan Cos Inc* . 1125
Mercer Pensionsraadgivning A/S *Marsh & McLennan Cos Inc.* . 1125
Mercer Personenversicherungs-makler GmbH *Marsh & McLennan Cos Inc* 1125
Mercer SAS *Marsh & McLennan Cos Inc* 1125
Mercer Securities, Inc. *Marsh & McLennan Cos Inc* ... 1125
Mercer Sweden AB *Marsh & McLennan Cos Inc* 1125
Mercer Tax Agents Pty Ltd *Marsh & McLennan Cos Inc* . 1125
Mercer Trust Company *Marsh & McLennan Cos Inc* 1125
Mercer Trustees Limited *Marsh & McLennan Cos Inc* .. 1125
Mercer UK Limited *Marsh & McLennan Cos Inc* 1125
Mercer Zainal Consulting Sdn Bhd *Marsh & McLennan Cos Inc* 1125
MercerHR.com LLC *Marsh & McLennan Cos Inc* 1125
MercerHR.com, Inc. *Marsh & McLennan Cos Inc* 1125
Mercers Debt Collections Limited *Barclays Plc* 216
Mercerville Associates of New Jersey, L.P. *Genesis HealthCare Corp.* 774
Merchandise Credit, LLC *Saks Inc* 1576
Merchandise Mart Enterprises, Inc. (Canada) *Vornado Realty Trust* 1923
Merchandise Mart First Mezzanine Borrower L.L.C. *Vornado Realty Trust* 1923
Merchandise Mart Properties, Inc. *Vornado Realty Trust* . 1923
Merchandise Mart Second Mezzanine Borrower L.L.C. *Vornado Realty Trust* 1923
Merchandise Mart Third Mezzanine Borrower L.L.C. *Vornado Realty Trust* 1923
Merchandise Mart, L.L.C. *Vornado Realty Trust* 1923
Merchant & Partners Australia Proprietary Limited *Interpublic Group of Companies Inc* 975
Merchant Bankers, Inc. *Regions Financial Corp* 1526
Merchant Energy-Petroleum Company *EL Paso CGP Co LLC* . 609
Merchant Services U.S.A., Inc. *Global Payments Inc* . 796
Merchant's, Incorporated *TBC Corp.* 1754
Merchant-Link, LLC *First Data Corp* 703
Merchants 450 LLC *Ramco-Gershenson Properties Trust* . 1512
Merchants and Farmers Bank *First M & F Corp* 709
Merchants and Farmers Bank Securities Corporation *First M & F Corp* 709
Merchants Bank *Merchants Bancshares Inc* 1161
Merchants Crossing of Jackson, Inc. *Servidyne Inc* .. 1614
Merchants Crossing of North Fort Myers, Inc. *Servidyne Inc* . 1614
Merchants Crossing, Inc. *Servidyne Inc* 1614
Merchants Financial Services Group, LLC *First M & F Corp* . 709
Merchants Insurance Company of New Hampshire, Inc. *Merchants Group Inc* 1161
Merchants Merger Corp. *Merchants & Manufacturers Bancorp Inc* 1161
Merchants New Merger Corp. *Merchants & Manufacturers Bancorp Inc* 1161
Merchants New York Commercial Corp. *Valley National Bancorp* 1886
Merchants Properties, Inc. *Merchants Bancshares Inc* . 1161
Merchants Trust Company *Merchants Bancshares Inc* ... 1161
MERCHANTWIRED LLC *Macerich Company (The)* 1106
Mercian Fast Foods Limited *Yum! Brands Inc* 1994
Merck and Company, Incorporated *Merck & Co Inc* 1162
Merck Borinquen Holdings, Inc. *Merck & Co Inc* 1162
Merck Capital Resources, Inc. *Merck & Co Inc* 1162
Merck Capital Ventures, LLC *Merck & Co Inc* 1162
Merck Cardiovascular Health Company *Merck & Co Inc* . 1162
Merck Electronic Chemicals Ltd. *BASF* 218
Merck Enterprises Canada, Ltd. *Merck & Co Inc* 1162
Merck Finance Co., Inc. *Merck & Co Inc* 1162
Merck Foreign Sales Corporation Ltd. *Merck & Co Inc.* . 1162
Merck Frosst Canada Ltd. *Merck & Co Inc* 1162
Merck Frosst Company *Merck & Co Inc* 1162
Merck Frosst Finco LP *Merck & Co Inc* 1162
Merck Hamilton, Inc. *Merck & Co Inc.* 1162
Merck Holdings II Corp. *Merck & Co Inc* 1162
Merck Holdings, Inc. *Merck & Co Inc* 1162
Merck Institute for Vaccinology *Merck & Co Inc* 1162
Merck Investment Co., Inc. *Merck & Co Inc* 1162
Merck Liability Management Company *Merck & Co Inc* .. 1162
Merck LMC Cash Management (Bermuda) Ltd. *Merck & Co Inc* 1162
Merck LMC Cash Management, Inc. *Merck & Co Inc* 1162
Merck Oncology Holdings, Inc. *Merck & Co Inc* 1162

Mgm Mirage Manufacturing Corp. *MGM MIRAGE* 1176
Mgm Mirage Marketing, Ltd. *MGM MIRAGE* 1176
Mgm Mirage Online Holdings Guernsey, Limited *MGM MIRAGE* 1176
Mgm Mirage Online Isle Of Man, Ltd. *MGM MIRAGE* 1176
Mgm Mirage Online Services United Kingdom, Ltd. *MGM MIRAGE* 1176
Mgm Mirage Online United Kingdom, Ltd. *MGM MIRAGE* 1176
Mgm Mirage Online, LLC *MGM MIRAGE* 1176
Mgm Mirage Operations, Inc. *MGM MIRAGE* 1176
Mgm Mirage Retail *MGM MIRAGE* 1176
Mgm Mirage Uk Holding Company, Inc. *MGM MIRAGE* 1176
MGM Well Services, Inc. *Complete Production Services Inc* 460
MGMM Insurance Company *MGM MIRAGE* 1176
MGMM International Holdings, Ltd. *MGM MIRAGE* 1176
MGMM Macau, Ltd. *MGM MIRAGE* 1176
MGN Technologies UK Limited *MGN Technologies Inc* 1177
MGP Holding SAS *Triumph Group Inc* 1828
MGP Ingredients of Illinois, Inc. *MGP Ingredients Inc* 1177
MGRC Management Limited *Marriott International Inc* 1125
MGRC Marketing Limited *Marriott International Inc* 1125
MGS Marketing Services, Inc. *Energysouth Inc* 636
MGS Storage Services, Inc. *Energysouth Inc* 636
MGT Services, Inc. *Midland Co* 1187
MGV Energy Inc. *Quicksilver Resources Inc* 1502
MH I LP *Edison International* 604
MH I LP *Edison International* 604
MH II LP *Edison International* 604
MH II LP *Edison International* 604
MH III LP *Edison International* 604
MH III LP *Edison International* 604
MH IV LP *Edison International* 604
MH IV LP *Edison International* 604
MH Kapalua Venture, LLC *Marriott International Inc* 1125
Mh Pictures, Inc. *Playboy Enterprises Inc* 1439
MH V LP *Edison International* 604
MH V LP *Edison International* 604
Mh, Inc., Dba Shadow Creek *MGM MIRAGE* 1176
MHA Allied Consulting, Inc. *AMN Healthcare Inc* 114
MHA IPA,Inc. *Tenet Healthcare Corp* 1774
MHB *Millenia Hope Inc* 1191
MHB Tower Rentals of America, LLC *American Tower Corp* 105
MHC Encore Holdings, LLC *Equity Lifestyle Properties Inc* 653
MHC Financing Limited Partnership *Equity Lifestyle Properties Inc* 653
MHC Financing Limited Partnership Two *Equity Lifestyle Properties Inc* 653
MHC I, Inc. *Friedman Billings Ramsey Group Inc* 749
MHC Inc. *Lyondell Chemical Co* 1102
MHC Inc. *Midamerican Energy Holdings Co* 1184
MHC Inc. *Midamerican Energy Co* 1184
MHC Investment Company *Midamerican Energy Holdings Co* 1184
Mhc Ltra, Inc. *Equity Lifestyle Properties Inc* 653
Mhc Nac, Inc. *Equity Lifestyle Properties Inc* 653
MHC Operating Limited Partnership *Equity Lifestyle Properties Inc* 653
MHC Stagecoach, LLC *Equity Lifestyle Properties Inc* 653
MHC TT Leasing Company, LLC *Equity Lifestyle Properties Inc* 653
MHC TT, Inc. *Equity Lifestyle Properties Inc* 653
MHC-DeAnza Financing Limited Partnership *Equity Lifestyle Properties Inc* 653
Mhcdc, LLC *Champion Mortgage* 372
MHFSCO, Ltd. *McGraw-Hill Companies Inc* 1141
MHG HR Acquisition Corp *Morgans Hotel Group Company* 1216
MHG Scottsdale Holdings LLC *Morgans Hotel Group Company* 1216
MHHP Acquisition Company LLC *Omnicare Inc* 1338
MHI GP LLC *MHI Hospitality Corp* 1177
MHI Hollywood LLC *MHI Hospitality Corp* 1177
MHI Hospitality TRS Holding, Inc. *MHI Hospitality Corp* 1177
MHI Hospitality TRS, LLC *MHI Hospitality Corp* 1177
MHI Hospitality, L.P. *MHI Hospitality Corp* 1177
MHI Insurance Ltd. *Matria Healthcare Inc* 1131
MHI Jacksonville LLC *MHI Hospitality Corp* 1177
MHI Laurel West LLC *MHI Hospitality Corp* 1177
MHI-Rugby Road, LLC *WCI Communities Inc* 1939
Mhical 94 Company *Edison International* 604
Mhical 94 Lp *Edison International* 604
Mhical 95 Company *Edison International* 604
Mhical 95 Lp *Edison International* 604
Mhical 95 Lp *Edison International* 604
Mhical 96 Company *Edison International* 604
Mhical 96 Lp *Edison International* 604
Mhical 96 Lp *Edison International* 604
Mhical 96 Lp *Edison International* 604
Mhical 97 Company *Edison International* 604
Mhical 97 Lp *Edison International* 604
Mhical 97 Lp *Edison International* 604
Mhical 97 Lp Lp *Edison International* 604
Mhifed 94 Lp *Edison International* 604
Mhifed 95 Lp *Edison International* 604
Mhifed 96a Lp *Edison International* 604
MHJ,Inc. *Tenet Healthcare Corp* 1774
MHM Resources, Inc. *Century Business Services Inc* 365
MHM Retirement Plan Solutions, LLC *Century Business Services Inc* 365
MHN Government Services, Inc. *Health Net Inc* 858
MHN Services (CA) *Health Net Inc* 858
MHN Services IPA, Inc. (NY) *Health Net Inc* 858
MHN Services of the Northeast, Inc. *Health Net Inc* 858
MHN Services of Wisconsin, Inc. (WI) *Health Net Inc* 858
MHNR, Inc. *Genesis HealthCare Corp* 774
MHO Holdings, LLC *M/I Homes Inc* 1104
MHO PARTNERS, LIMITED *Apartment Investment and Management Company* 130
Mho, LLC, A Florida Limited Liability Company *M/I Homes Inc* 1104
MHP Acquisition Corp. *Host Hotels & Resorts Inc* 892
MHP II Acquisition Corp. *Host Hotels & Resorts Inc* 892
MHR International Inc *Willis Group Holdings Ltd* 1962
MHR Limited *Sally Beauty Holdings Inc* 1578
MHS Ambulatory Surgery Center, Inc. *Triad Hospitals Inc* 1823
MHS Consulting Corporation *Centene Corp* 357
MHS Guam, Inc. *Marriott International Inc* 1125
MHS Partnership Holdings JSC, Inc. *HCA Inc* 855
MHS Partnership Holdings SDS, Inc. *HCA Inc* 855
MHS Realty Sales, Inc. *Marriott International Inc* 1125
MHS SC Partner, LLC *HCA Inc* 855
MHS Surgery Centers, L.P. *HCA Inc* 855
Mhsfr Ii, Inc. *Marriott International Inc* 1125
MHSFR, Inc. *Marriott International Inc* 1125
MHSI Conference Centers of Texas, Inc. *Marriott International Inc* 1125
MHSI Hawaii, Inc. *Marriott International Inc* 1125
MHV Joint Venture *FelCor Lodging Trust Inc* 686
MI Bachelor Gulch, LLC *Marriott International Inc* 1125
MI Boston Leaseco, LLC *Marriott International Inc* 1125
Mi Casa Publications, Inc. *Univision Communications Inc* 1871
MI CBM Investor, LLC *Marriott International Inc* 1125
MI Developments (America) Inc. *MI Developments Inc* 1177
MI Developments Austria GmbH *MI Developments Inc* 1177
MI Distribution, LLC *Marriott International Inc* 1125
MI European Holdings CV *Molex Inc* 1208
MI Finance Company *Marriott International Inc* 1125
MI Fulfillment Services, LLC *Marriott International Inc* 1125
MI Georgia Credits, LLC *Marriott International Inc* 1125
MI Holding, L.P. *Marriott International Inc* 1125
MI Hotels of Las Vegas, Inc. *Marriott International Inc* 1125
MI Hotels of Massachusetts, Inc. *Marriott International Inc* 1125
MI Insurance (Barbados) Ltd. *R.R. Donnelley & Sons Co* 1506
MI Investments I Ltd. *Marriott International Inc* 1125
MI Member, LLC *Marriott International Inc* 1125
MI Myrtle Beach, LLC *Marriott International Inc* 1125
MI Procurement Holdings, LLC *Marriott International Inc* 1125
MI RacingInc. *Magna Entertainment Corp* 1111
MI Seattle, LLC *Marriott International Inc* 1125
MI Tenant LLC *Marriott International Inc* 1125
Mi Th4 Investor, LLC *Marriott International Inc* 1125
MI Tucson, LLC *Marriott International Inc* 1125
MI Western Investment, LLC *Marriott International Inc* 1125
Mi-Tech Steel, Inc. *Steel Technologies Inc* 1698
Mialot Lagadic SAS *IDEXX Laboratories Inc* 917
Miami Airport Complex, LLC *Host Hotels & Resorts Inc* 892
Miami Beach EFL Imaging Center, LLC *HCA Inc* 855
Miami Beach Healthcare Group, Ltd. *HCA Inc* 855
Miami Dade Health and Rehabilitation Services, Inc *Continucare Corp* 476
Miami International Commerce Center *PS Business Parks Inc* 1483
Miami International University of Art& Design, Inc. *Education Mgmt Corp* 605
Miami Lakes GP One LLC, *Sun Communities Inc* 1718
Miami Lakes GP Two LLC, *Sun Communities Inc* 1718
Miami Lakes QRS, Inc *Sun Communities Inc* 1718
Miami Lakes Surgery Center, Ltd. *HCA Inc* 855
Miami Lakes Venture Associates, *Sun Communities Inc* 1718
Miami Power Corporation *Union Light Heat & Power Co* 1852
Miami Power Corporation *Cincinnati Gas & Electric Co* 407
Miami River Park Associates, Ltd. *Wachovia Corp* 1928
Miami Speedway Corp., *International Speedway CL B* 972
Miami Subs Corporation *Nathan's Famous Inc* 1238
Miami Subs of Delaware, Inc. *Nathan's Famous Inc* 1238
Miami Subs Real Estate Corp. *Nathan's Famous Inc* 1238
Miami Subs USA, Inc. *Nathan's Famous Inc* 1238
Miami Television Station WBFS Inc. *CBS Corp* 349
Miami Television Station WBFS Inc. *Viacom Inc* 1902
Miami Theatre LLC *IMAX Corp* 926
Miami Valley Insurance Company *DPL Inc* 574
Mianyang Brilliance Ruian Automotive Components Co., Ltd. *Brilliance China Automotive Holdings Ltd* 280
Mianyang Xinchen Engine Co., Ltd. *Brilliance China Automotive Holdings Ltd* 280
Miavita, Inc. *Matria Healthcare Inc* 1131
MIBRAG B.V. *NRG Energy Inc* 1312
Mibrag B.V. *Washington Group International Inc* 1932
MIBRAG Industriekraftwerke Betriebs GmbH *NRG Energy Inc* 1312
MIBRAG Industriekraftwerke GmbH & Co. KG *NRG Energy Inc* 1312
MIBRAG Industriekraftwerke Vermogensverwaltungs-und *NRG Energy Inc* 1312
MIBRAG Industriekraftwerke Vertriebs GmbH *NRG Energy Inc* 1312
Mibsa Investments (Namibia) (Pty) Limited *Aon Corp* 129
MIC European Financing Sarl *Macquarie Infrastructure Company Trust* 1107
MIC Financial, Inc. *Midwestone Financial Group Inc* 1188
MIC General Insurance Corporation *GMAC LLC* 801
MIC Property and Casualty Insurance Corporation *GMAC LLC* 801
Mic-Mac Investments, Inc. *Epicus Communications Group Inc* 650
MICA Energy Systems *Caterpillar Inc* 345
MICB, Inc. *Regions Financial Corp* 1526
Micc Spe I Corp. *Marriott International Inc* 1125
MICC(California), LLC *Marriott International Inc* 1125
Michael Adams Securities, Inc. *Macreport Net Inc* 1107
Michael Baker Architects/Engineers, P.C. *Baker Michael Corp* 200
Michael Baker de Mexico S.A. de C.V. *Baker Michael Corp* 200
Michael Baker Global, Inc. *Baker Michael Corp* 200
Michael Baker International, Inc. *Baker Michael Corp* 200
Michael Baker Jr. Company *Baker Michael Corp* 200
Michael Baker Jr., Inc. *Baker Michael Corp* 200
Michael Chevrolet-Oldsmobile, Inc. *United Auto Group Inc* 1855
Michael Electric, Inc. *Black Box Corp* 252
Michael G. Penney Insurance, Inc. *National Financial Partners Corp* 1241
Michael G. Rudelson and Company *National Financial Partners Corp* 1241
Michael Vagedes GmbH *WPP Group Plc* 1979
Michaels Finance Company, Inc. *Michael S Stores Inc* 1177
Michaels of Canada, ULC *Michael S Stores Inc* 1177
Michaels Stores Card Services, LLC *Michael S Stores Inc* 1177
Michaels Stores Procurement Company *Michael S Stores Inc* 1177
Michiana College Education Corporation *Education Mgmt Corp* 605
Michiana Easy Livin Country, LLC *Coachmen Industries Inc* 430
Michiana Gas *Energy Transfer Partners LP* 636
Michiana Metronet Inc. *Centennial Communications Corp* 358
Michigan & Western Railroad Company *Anixter International Inc* 125
Michigan ASC Partners, LLC *United Surgical Partners International Inc* 1863
Michigan banking corporation *Mercantile Bank Corp* 1160
Michigan Consolidated Gas Company *DTE Energy Co* 579
Michigan Coral Rock, LLC *Dana Corp* 525
Michigan Dairy, LLC *Kroger Co* 1043
Michigan Electric Transmission Company, LLC. *ITC Holdings Corp* 993
Michigan Environs, Inc. *Waste Management Inc* 1934
Michigan Gas Utilities Corporation *Wisconsin Public Service Corp* 1971
Michigan International Speedway, Inc., *International Speedway CL B* 972
Michigan Investment Corp. *Altria Group Inc* 74
Michigan Licenses, LLC *CCE Spinco Inc* 349
Michigan limited *Meritage Hospitality Group Inc* 1165
Michigan limited liability company *Mercantile Bank Corp* 1160
Michigan Local Interactive, LLC *NIC Inc* 1285
Michigan Logos, Inc. *Lamar Advertising Company* 1051
MICHIGAN MEADOWS LIMITED PARTNERSHIP *Apartment Investment and Management Company* 130
Michigan Medical Supply, Inc. *Rotech Healthcare Inc NEW* 1560
Michigan Psychiatric Services, Inc. *Psychiatric Solutions Inc* 1485
Michigan Racing,Inc. *Magna Entertainment Corp* 1111
Michigan Redevelopment Gp, LLC *Valero Energy Corp* 1884
Michigan Redevelopment, L.p. *Valero Energy Corp* 1884
Michigan Reutilization, LLC *Valero Energy Corp* 1884
Michigan RSA #9 Limited Partnership *Alltel Corp* 69
Michigan Rubber Products, Inc. *Myers Industries Inc* 1229
Michigan Southern Railroad Company *Pioneer Railcorp* 1433
Michigan Transco Holdings, LP. *ITC Holdings Corp* 993
Michigan Transportation Finance Corporation *1st Source Corp* 2005
Michigans Adventure, Inc. *Cedar Fair LP* 353
Mickey Thompson Performance Racing Inc. *Cooper Tire & Rubber Co* 478
Micogen Limited Partnership *El Paso Corp* 609
Micon Bedrijfsadviseurs Milieu B.V. *Arcadis* 142
Micrel Semiconductor *Micrel Inc* 1178
Micro (Beijing) Co., Ltd *O2micro International Ltd* 1323
Micro (Bermuda), Ltd. *Microsemi Corp* 1181
Micro Bio-Medical Waste Systems *Crown Partners Inc* 505
Micro (Chengdu) Co., Ltd *O2micro International Ltd* 1323
Micro (China) Co., Ltd *O2micro International Ltd* 1323
Micro Clever Consulting *Bally Technologies Inc* 202
Micro Companies Alliance, Inc. *Synovis Life Technologies Inc* 1739
Micro Component Technology Asia Pte. Ltd *Micro Component Technology Inc* 1178
Micro Components International Incorporated *Applied Digital Solutions Inc* 135
Micro Computer Store, Inc. *Interpharm Holdings Inc* 975
Micro Controle Finance Holding 1 (indirect) *Newport Corp* 1280
Micro Controle Finance Holding 2 (indirect) *Newport Corp* 1280
Micro Controle Italia S.r.l. *Newport Corp* 1280
Micro Controle Spectra-Physics S.A. *Newport Corp* 1280
Micro Craft Inc. *Alliant Techsystems Inc* 63
Micro Electronics, Inc *O2micro International Ltd* 1323
Micro Express Holdings Inc *Sterling Group Ventures Inc* 1703
Micro Express Ltd *Sterling Group Ventures Inc* 1703
Micro Flo Company LLC *BASF* 218
Micro Gauge, Inc. *Mueller Industries Inc* 1226
Micro General, LLC *Fidelity National Financial Inc* 690
Micro Imaging Technology *Micro Imaging Technology Inc* 1178
Micro International Japan Limited *O2micro International Ltd* 1323
Micro Medical Ltd. *VIASYS Healthcare Inc* 1903
Micro Motion, Inc. *Emerson Electric Co* 623
Micro Nano Plus Technology Co. *SKF Inc* 1641
Micro Networks Corporation *Integrated Device Technology Inc* 955
Micro Power Systems, Inc. *Exar Corp* 667
Micro PTE Limited-Singapore *O2micro International Ltd* 1323
Micro Robotics Systems, Inc. *Newport Corp* 1280
Micro Sensor Technologies, Inc. *China America Holdings Inc* 386
Micro Sistemas S.A. (2) *Telecom Argentina* 1764
Micro Sistemas SA *Nortel Investments Inc* 1296
Micro Tempus Corporation. *Optimal Group Inc* 1349
Micro Tempus GmbH. *Optimal Group Inc* 1349
Micro WaveSys, Inc. *Microsemi Corp* 1181
Micro, Inc. *O2micro International Ltd* 1323
Micro-Filtration, Inc. *Emerson Electric Co* 623
Micro-Med Industries, Inc *Stericycle Inc* 1701
Micro-Med of Georgia, Inc *Stericycle Inc* 1701
Micro-Med of North Carolina, Inc *Stericycle Inc* 1701
Micro-Med of Tennessee, Inc *Stericycle Inc* 1701
Micro-Swiss Limited Israel *Kulicke & Soffa Industries Inc* 1045
Microanalytics Instrumentation Corp. *Mocon Inc* 1205
Microcell Corporation *Delmarva Power & Light Co* 538
Microchip Technology (Barbados) Incorporated *Microchip Technology Inc* 1179
Microchip Technology (Thailand) Co., Ltd. *Microchip Technology Inc* 1179
MicroCor, Inc. *Inmedica Development Corp* 945
Microcosm Communications Ltd. *Mindspeed Technologies Inc* 1194
Microdot Connectors Europe Limited *Tyco International Ltd* 1838
Microdyne Communications Technologies Incorporated *L-3 Communications Holdings Inc* 1046
Microdyne Corporation *L-3 Communications Holdings Inc* 1046
Microdyne Ltd. *L-3 Communications Holdings Inc* 1046
Microdyne Outsourcing Incorporated *L-3 Communications Holdings Inc* 1046
MicroEdge, Inc. *Advent Software Inc* 33
Microelectronica Espanola S.A.U. *Msystems Ltd* 1224
Microflex 2001 LLC *IAC/InterActiveCorp* 961
Microflow Engineering S.A. *Aptargroup Inc* 138
Microfluidics Corporation *MFIC Corp* 1175
MicroGas Ltd. *VIASYS Healthcare Inc* 1903
Microgauge Machining, Inc. *Mueller Industries Inc* 1226
Micrografx B.V. *Corel Corp* 481
Micrografx (Europe) AG *Corel Corp* 481
Micrografx Italia S.r.L. *Corel Corp* 481
Micrografx Technology N.V. *Corel Corp* 481
Microgy, Inc *Environmental Power Corp* 646
microHelix Acquisition Corp. *Microhelix Inc* 1179
Microinvest S.a. Sociedade De Crdito Ao Microempreendedor *Unibanco Holdings* 1848
MicroIslet, Inc. *MicroIslet Inc* 1179
Micromass B.V. *Waters Corp* 1936
Micromass Holdings Ltd. *Waters Corp* 1936
Micromass International Ltd. *Waters Corp* 1936
Micromass Investments Ltd. *Waters Corp* 1936
Micromass Ltd. *Waters Corp* 1936
Micromass UK Ltd. *Waters Corp* 1936
MicroMed Technology, Inc. *MicroMed Cardiovascular Inc* 1180
Micromedia S.A. *Woodhead Industries Inc* 1974
MicroMedical Deutschland GmbH *VIASYS Healthcare Inc* 1903
Micromem Technologies B.V *Micromem Technologies Inc* 1180
Micromem Technologies S.p.A. *Micromem Technologies Inc* 1180
Micron Customs Brokerage Services, Inc. *Micron Technology Inc* 1180
Micron Electronics Asia-Pacific Holdings, Inc. *Web.com Inc* 1940
Micron Electronics Asia-Pacific Operations, Inc. *Web.com Inc* 1940
Micron Electronics Asia-Pacific Trading, Ltd. *Web.com Inc* 1940
Micron Electronics (H.K.) Limited *Web.com Inc* 1940
Micron Electronics International, Inc. *Web.com Inc* 1940
Micron Electronics Overseas Trading, Inc. *Web.com Inc* 1940
Micron Europe Limited *Micron Technology Inc* 1180
Micron Japan, Ltd. *Micron Technology Inc* 1180
Micron Milling and Packaging Company Ltd *American United Gold Corp* 105
Micron Products, Inc. *Arrhythmia Research Technology Inc* 152

Middle East Real Estate Services, LLC *Grubb & Ellis Co* 827
Middle Georgia Hospital, LLC *HCA Inc* 855
Middle Tennessee Ambulatory Surgery Center, L.P. *United Surgical Partners International Inc* 1863
Middle Tennessee Development, LLC *Regency Centers Corp* 1524
Middle Tennessee Medical Services Corporation *HCA Inc* 855
Middleburg Bank *Middleburg Financial Corp* 1185
Middleburg Bank Service Corporation *Middleburg Financial Corp* 1185
Middleburg Investment Advisors, Inc. *Middleburg Financial Corp* 1185
Middleburg Investment Group, Inc. *Middleburg Financial Corp* 1185
Middleburg Trust Company *Middleburg Financial Corp* 1185
Middleby China Corporation *Middleby Corp* 1185
Middleby Espana SL *Middleby Corp* 1185
Middleby Marshall Holdings, LLC *Middleby Corp* 1185
Middleby Marshall, Inc. *Middleby Corp* 1185
Middleby Mexico SA de CV *Middleby Corp* 1185
Middleby Philippines Corporation *Middleby Corp* 1185
Middleby Worldwide Korea Co., LTD *Middleby Corp* 1185
Middleby Worldwide Philippines *Middleby Corp* 1185
Middleby Worldwide (Taiwan) Co., LTD *Middleby Corp* 1185
Middleby Worldwide, Inc. *Middleby Corp* 1185
Middlesex Assurance Company Limited *Johnson & Johnson* 1009
Middlesex Cable Limited *Virgin Media Inc* 1910
Middlesex Dialysis Center, LLC *Davita Inc* 530
Middlesoft, Inc. *Macromedia Inc* 1107
Middleton and Wilson Corporation *Yum! Brands Inc* 1994
Middleton Pest Control, Inc. *Sunair Services Corp* 1720
Middletown & New Jersey Railway Company, Inc *Chartwell International Inc* 377
Middletown Finance, Inc. *Bank of America Corp* 208
Middletown Hotel Associates Limited Partnership *Interstate Hotels & Resorts Inc* 976
Middletown Manufacturing Company *Leggett & Platt Inc* 1067
Middletown Oxygen Company, Inc. *Air Products & Chemicals Inc* 46
Middletown Power LLC *NRG Energy Inc* 1312
Middletown (RI) Associates of Rhode Island, L.P. *Genesis HealthCare Corp* 774
Middletown VF, L.L.C. *Vornado Realty Trust* 1923
MIDDLETOWN-OXFORD LIMITED PARTNERSHIP *Apartment Investment and Management Company* 130
Middlewich Limited *Wellman Inc* 1943
Midgard Energy Co. *Repsol YPF* 1533
Midiman Ltd *Avid Technology Inc* 190
Midkiff Development Drilling Program, L.P. (1) *St Paul Travelers Cos Inc* 1687
Midkiff Development Drilling Program, L.P.(3) *Travelers Property Casualty Corp* 1818
Midkiff Development Drilling Program, Ltd. *Pioneer Natural Resources Co* 1433
Midland Acquisition Corporation *Encore Capital Group Inc* 630
Midland Bottling Co. *PepsiCo Inc* 1410
Midland Brake, Inc. *Dana Corp* 525
Midland Capital Holdings Corporation *Midland Capital Holdings Corp* 1186
Midland Cogeneration Venture Expansion, LLC *CMS Energy Corp* 427
Midland Cogeneration Venture Expansion, LLC *El Paso Corp* 609
Midland Cogeneration Venture Limited Partnership *El Paso Corp* 609
Midland Cogeneration Venture Limited Partnership *CMS Energy Corp* 427
Midland Concerts Promotions Group Ltd. *CCE Spinco Inc* 349
Midland Credit Management, Inc. *Encore Capital Group Inc* 630
Midland Escrow Services, Inc. *Midamerican Energy Holdings Co* 1184
Midland Federal Savings and Loan Association *Midland Capital Holdings Corp* 1186
Midland Federal Service Corporation *Midland Capital Holdings Corp* 1186
Midland Finance Co. *Consumer Portfolio Services Inc* 473
Midland Financial Group, Inc. *Oshkosh Truck Corp* 1361
Midland Financial Group, Inc. *Progressive Corp* 1474
Midland Funding 98-A Corporation *Encore Capital Group Inc* 630
Midland Funding LLC *Encore Capital Group Inc* 630
Midland Funding NCC-1 Corporation *Encore Capital Group Inc* 630
Midland Funding NCC-2 Corporation *Encore Capital Group Inc* 630
Midland Grocery of Michigan, Inc. *Roundys Supermarkets Inc* 1560
Midland Heating and Air Conditioning LLC *Lennox International Inc* 1068
Midland Holland Ltd. *Grand Peak Capital Corp* 814
Midland Housing Industries Corp. *Lennar Corp* 1068
Midland Hunter Petroleum Limited Liability Company *Cimarex Energy Co* 406
Midland Investment Corporation *Lennar Corp* 1068
Midland Mall LLC *CBL & Associates Properties Inc* 348
Midland Manufacturing Company, Inc. *Patterson Cos Inc* 1393
Midland Manufacturing Corporation *Dover Corp* 572
Midland Odessa Properties, Inc.* *American Realty Investors Inc* 100
Midland Odessa Properties, Inc.** *Transcontinental Realty Investors Inc* 1815
Midland Path Forward, Inc. *ElkCorp* 617
Midland Pharmacies, Inc. *Cardinal Health Inc* 332
Midland Pipeline Corp. *Dow Chemical Co* 573
Midland Portfolio Services, Inc. *Encore Capital Group Inc* 630
Midland Realty Investment Corporation *Municipal Mortgage & Equity LLC* 1227
Midland Receivables 98-1 Corporation *Encore Capital Group Inc* 630
Midland Receivables 99-1 Corporation *Encore Capital Group Inc* 630
Midland Research Laboratories UK Limited *Ecolab Inc* 600
Midland Research Laboratories, Inc. *Ecolab Inc* 600
Midland Risk Services, Inc. *Progressive Corp* 1474
Midland Risk Services, Inc. *Oshkosh Truck Corp* 1361
Midland Surgical Partners, Ltd. *U.S. Physical Therapy Inc* 1841
Midland Technical Crafts, Inc. *MDU Resources Group Inc* 1144
Midland Title Security, Inc. *First American Corp* 695
Midland Venture Limited Partnership *CBL & Associates Properties Inc* 348
Midland-Guardian Co. *Midland Co* 1187
Midlands Hydrocarbons (Bangladesh) Limited *Cincinnati Gas & Electric Co* 407
Midlands Hydrocarbons (Bangladesh) Limited *Union Light Heat & Power Co* 1852
Midlothian Energy Limited Partnership *International Power Plc* 971
MidNet Canada, Inc. *MidNet Inc* 1187
MidNet USA, Inc *MidNet Inc* 1187
MidOhio Data, Inc. *National City Corp* 1239
MIDPARK DEVELOPMENT CO. *Apartment Investment and Management Company* 130
MidPlains, LLC *Triad Hospitals Inc* 1823
Midrange Open Computing Alliance, Inc. *Arrow Electronics Inc* 152
MidSouth Bank, N.A. *Midsouth Bancorp Inc* 1187
MidSouth Statutory Trust I *Midsouth Bancorp Inc* 1187
MidSouth Statutory Trust II *Midsouth Bancorp Inc* 1187
Midstream Gas Services, L.P. *Eagle Rock Energy Partners LP* 591
MidTex Gas Storage Company, LLP *Kinder Morgan Energy Partners LP* 1030
Midtex LP Gas *Inergy Holdings LP* 936
Midtex LP Gas *Inergy LP* 936
Midtown ID Clinic, LLC *HCA Inc* 855
Midtown Insurance Company *New York Times Co* 1277
MIDTOWN PLAZA ASSOCIATES *Apartment Investment and Management Company* 130
Midtown Redevelopment Partners, LLC *Colonial Properties Trust* 440
Midtown Square, L. P. *Wachovia Corp* 1928
Midtown Square, L.P. *Wachovia Corp* 1928
Midway Amusement Games, LLC *Midway Games Inc* 1187
Midway Australia Holdings Pty Ltd *Midway Games Inc* 1187
Midway CBNA Loan Funding LLC *Citigroup Inc* 411
Midway Chevrolet, Inc. *Autonation Inc FL* 183
Midway Development Company, Inc. *Allied Waste Industries Inc* 66
Midway Entertainment, Ltd. *Fox & Hound Restaurant Group* 741
Midway Games Australia Pty Ltd *Midway Games Inc* 1187
Midway Games Canada Corp. *Midway Games Inc* 1187
Midway Games (Europe) GmbH *Midway Games Inc* 1187
Midway Games GmbH *Midway Games Inc* 1187
Midway Games Limited *Midway Games Inc* 1187
Midway Games Sales Corporation *Midway Games Inc* 1187
Midway Games SAS *Midway Games Inc* 1187
Midway Games West Inc. *Midway Games Inc* 1187
Midway Holdings Ltd. *Procter & Gamble* 1472
Midway Home Entertainment Inc. *Midway Games Inc* 1187
Midway Home Studios Inc. *Midway Games Inc* 1187
Midway Hospital Medical Center,Inc. *Tenet Healthcare Corp* 1774
Midway Insurance Company of Illinois *Allianz* 63
Midway Interactive Inc. *Midway Games Inc* 1187
Midway Mills Partners, L.P. *Tarragon Corp* 1751
Midway Sales Company, LLC *Midway Games Inc* 1187
Midway Studios Austin Inc. *Midway Games Inc* 1187
Midway Studios Australia Pty Ltd *Midway Games Inc* 1187
Midway Studios Los Angeles Inc. *Midway Games Inc* 1187
Midway Studios Newcastle Limited *Midway Games Inc* 1187
Midway Studios Development Australia Pty Ltd *Midway Games Inc* 1187
Midway Telephone Company, LLC *Telephone and Data Systems Inc* 1768
Midway Water Utilities,Inc. *Southwest Water Co* 1670
Midway-Sunset Cogeneration Company, LP *Edison International* 604
Midwesco Filter Resources, Inc. *MFRI Inc* 1175
Midwest Affordable Housing 1997-1, LLC *Bank of America Corp* 208
Midwest Agri-Commodities Company *American Crystal Sugar Co* 89
Midwest Airlines, Inc. *Midwest Air Group Inc* 1188
Midwest Ambulance Management Company *Emergency Medical Services Corp* 622
Midwest Anesthesia, Inc. *HealthSouth Corp* 861
MidWest Ash Disposal, Inc. *Reliant Energy Inc* 1528
Midwest Bank and Trust Company *Midwest Banc Holdings Inc* 1188
Midwest Bank Insurance Services, LLC *Midwest Banc Holdings Inc* 1188
Midwest Building Products & Contractor Services, LLC *Hovnanian Enterprises Inc* 894
Midwest Cable Communications, Inc. *Charter Communications Inc* 376
Midwest Cambridge Inc., *HealthTronics Inc* 862
Midwest Capital Group, Inc. *Midamerican Energy Co* 1184
Midwest Capital Group, Inc. *Midamerican Energy Holdings Co* 1184
Midwest Cardiovascular & Thoracic Surgery, LLC *HCA Inc* 855
Midwest Cellular Associates *McLeodUSA Inc* 1142
Midwest City H.M.A., Inc. *Health Management Associates Inc* 858
Midwest Coal Acquisition Corp. *Peabody Energy Corp* 1398
Midwest Coal Reserves of Illinois, LLC *Peabody Energy Corp* 1398
Midwest Coal Reserves of Indiana, LLC *Peabody Energy Corp* 1398
Midwest Coal Resources, LLC *Peabody Energy Corp* 1398
Midwest Coca-Cola Bottling Company *Coca-Cola Enterprises Inc* 433
Midwest Communications Technologies, Inc. *Black Box Corp* 252
Midwest Construction Services, Inc. *Otter Tail Corp* 1363
Midwest Corporate Tax Credit Fund *Ameriana Bancorp* 83
Midwest Division - ACH, LLC *HCA Inc* 855
Midwest Division - BLMC, LLC *HCA Inc* 855
Midwest Division - CMC, LLC *HCA Inc* 855
Midwest Division - IRHC, LLC *HCA Inc* 855
Midwest Division - LRHC, LLC *HCA Inc* 855
Midwest Division - LSH, LLC *HCA Inc* 855
Midwest Division - MCI, LLC *HCA Inc* 855
Midwest Division - MII, LLC *HCA Inc* 855
Midwest Division - MMC, LLC *HCA Inc* 855
Midwest Division - OPRMC, LLC *HCA Inc* 855
Midwest Division - PFC, LLC *HCA Inc* 855
Midwest Division - RBH, LLC *HCA Inc* 855
Midwest Division - RMC, LLC *HCA Inc* 855
Midwest Division - RPC, LLC *HCA Inc* 855
Midwest Division - TLM, LLC *HCA Inc* 855
Midwest Division, Inc. *HCA Inc* 855
Midwest Electric Power Inc. *Illinois Power Co* 922
Midwest Electric Power Inc. *Ameren Corp* 82
Midwest Electric Power Inc. *Union Electric Co* 1851
Midwest Electric Power Inc. *Cilcorp Inc* 405
Midwest Electric Power Inc. *Central Illinois Public Service Co* 362
Midwest Electronics and Communications, Inc. *Black Box Corp* 252
Midwest Express Services Kansas City, Inc. *Midwest Air Group Inc* 1188
Midwest Express Services Omaha, Inc *Midwest Air Group Inc* 1188
Midwest Finance Corp. *Edison International* 604
Midwest Finance Corp. *Mission Energy Holding Co* 1199
Midwest Financial and Investment Services, Inc. *Midwest Banc Holdings Inc* 1188
Midwest Framing, LLC *Universal Forest Products Inc* 1868
Midwest Generation EME, LLC *Mission Energy Holding Co* 1199
Midwest Generation Eme, LLC *Edison International* 604
Midwest Generation Energy Services, LLC *Edison International* 604
Midwest Generation Energy Services, LLC *Mission Energy Holding Co* 1199
Midwest Generation, LLC *Mission Energy Holding Co* 1199
Midwest Generation, LLC *Edison International* 604
Midwest Grain Pipeline, Inc. *MGP Ingredients Inc* 1177
Midwest Holdings, Inc. *HCA Inc* 855
Midwest Housing Investments J.V., Inc. *Dana Corp* 525
Midwest Ice Cream Company *Dean Foods Co* 533
Midwest Infectious Disease Specialists, LLC *HCA Inc* 855
Midwest Loan Services, Inc. *University Bank* 1871
Midwest Material Management, Inc. *Republic Services Inc* 1534
Midwest Medicine Associates, LLC *HCA Inc* 855
Midwest Microwave Inc. *Emerson Electric Co* 623
Midwest Microwave International Limited *Emerson Electric Co* 623
Midwest Microwave Limited *Emerson Electric Co* 623
Midwest Multispeciality Physicians Group, Inc. *HCA Inc* 855
Midwest N-Viro, Inc. *N Viro International Corp* 1231
Midwest Newborn Care, LLC *HCA Inc* 855
Midwest of Cannon Falls Canada *Blyth Inc* 259
Midwest of Cannon Falls,Inc. *Blyth Inc* 259
Midwest One Land Corporation *Waste Management Inc* 1934
Midwest Peaker Holdings, Inc. *Mission Energy Holding Co* 1199
Midwest Physician Services Lab, LLC *HCA Inc* 855
Midwest Portfolio Holdings, LP *Capital Senior Living Corp* 325
Midwest Racing, Inc. *Dover Motorsports Inc* 572
Midwest Security Administrators, Inc. *Unitedhealth Group Inc* 1864
Midwest Security Care, Inc. *Unitedhealth Group Inc* 1864
Midwest Security Holding, Inc. *Unitedhealth Group Inc* 1864
Midwest Security Life Insurance Company *Unitedhealth Group Inc* 1864
Midwest Title Company *Fidelity National Financial Inc* 690
Midwest Title Guarantee Company of Florida, LLC *Stewart Information Services Corp* 1705
Midwest Title Insurance Company *First American Corp* 695
Midwest Trauma Services, LLC *HCA Inc* 855
Midwest Uncuts, Inc. *Novamed Inc* 1308
Midwest Urologic Stone Unit, Limited Partnership *HealthTronics Inc* 862
Midwest Zinc Corporation *Aleris International Inc* 55
Midwest/Northwest Properties Inc. *Burlington Northern Santa FE Corp* 296
Midwestern Gas Marketing Company *ONEOK Partners LP* 1343
Midwestern Gas Transmission Company *ONEOK Partners LP* 1343
Midwestern Home Products Company, Ltd. *Big Lots Inc* 238
Midwestern Home Products, Inc. *Big Lots Inc* 238
Midwestern Insurance Company *OneBeacon Insurance Group Ltd* 1342
MidwestOne Bank *Midwestone Financial Group Inc* 1188
MidWestOne Bank& Trust *Midwestone Financial Group Inc* 1188
MidWestOne Investment Services, Inc. *Midwestone Financial Group Inc* 1188
Midwinter Offshore Holdings Ltd *Copa Holdings S.A.* 478
Mifala Holdings (Vanuatu) Ltd. *InterContinental Hotels Group* 962
MIFAM Teeth Sp. Z o. o. *Sybron Dental Specialties Inc* 1734
Mifflin Valley, Inc. *Lakeland Industries Inc* 1050
MIG II Realty Advisors, Inc. *Associated Estates Realty Corp* 164
MIG Production Company Limited *BOC Group Plc* 262
MIGENIX Corp *MIGENIX Inc* 1188
Migliori Inversiones, S.L. *Pepsi Bottling Group Inc* 1409
Mih (bvi) Limited *Naspers Ltd* 1237
MIH Holdings Limited *Naspers Ltd* 1237
MIH Investments (Proprietary) Limited *Naspers Ltd* 1237
MII Conference Center, Inc. *Marriott International Inc* 1125
MII Financial Corporation *Mueller Industries Inc* 1226
Mikasu Corporation *Akzo Nobel* 49
Mike Canada Productions Ltd. *News Corp Ltd (The)* 1281
Mike Hall Chevrolet, Inc. *Autonation Inc FL* 183
Mike Shad Chrysler Plymouth Jeep Eagle, Inc. *Autonation Inc FL* 183
Mike Shad Ford, Inc. *Autonation Inc FL* 183
Mike Smith Automotive-H, Inc *Group 1 Automotive Inc* 826
Mike Smith Automotive-N, Inc *Group 1 Automotive Inc* 826
Mike Smith Autoplaza, Inc *Group 1 Automotive Inc* 826
Mike Smith Autoplex Buick, Inc *Group 1 Automotive Inc* 826
Mike Smith Autoplex Dodge, Inc *Group 1 Automotive Inc* 826
Mike Smith Autoplex, Inc *Group 1 Automotive Inc* 826
Mike Smith Autoplex-German Imports, Inc *Group 1 Automotive Inc* 826
Mike Smith GM, Inc *Group 1 Automotive Inc* 826
Mike Smith Imports, Inc *Group 1 Automotive Inc* 826
Mike Smith Motors, Inc *Group 1 Automotive Inc* 826
Miken Sports LLC *K2 Inc* 1015
Miko Distributors, Inc. *Adsouth Partners Inc* 26
Mikohn Europe B.V. *Mikohn Gaming Corp* 1189
Mikohn Gaming Australasia Pty. Ltd. *Mikohn Gaming Corp* 1189
Mikohn Holdings, Inc. *Mikohn Gaming Corp* 1189
Mikohn International, Inc. *Mikohn Gaming Corp* 1189
Mikohn Nevada *Mikohn Gaming Corp* 1189
Mikom GmbH *Andrew Corp* 122
Mikron Europe *Mikron Infrared Inc* 1189
Mikron Europe GmbH *Mikron Infrared Inc* 1189
Mikron Industries,Inc. *Quanex Corp* 1497
MIL Overseas Limited *Moneygram International Inc* 1211
Milacron Assurance Ltd. *Milacron Inc* 1190
Milacron B.V *Milacron Inc* 1190
Milacron Canada, Inc. *Milacron Inc* 1190
Milacron Capital Holdings B.V *Milacron Inc* 1190
Milacron Equipamentos Plasticos Ltd. *Milacron Inc* 1190
Milacron France SAS *Milacron Inc* 1190
Milacron Industrial Products, Inc. *Milacron Inc* 1190
Milacron International *Milacron Inc* 1190
Milacron Investments B.V *Milacron Inc* 1190
Milacron Kunststoffmaschinen *Milacron Inc* 1190
Milacron Marketing Company *Milacron Inc* 1190
Milacron Nederland B.V *Milacron Inc* 1190
Milacron Plastics Iberica S.L *Milacron Inc* 1190
Milacron Plastics Machinery (Jiangyin) Ltd. *Milacron Inc* 1190
Milacron Plastics Technologies Group Inc. *Milacron Inc* 1190
Milacron U.K. Ltd. *Milacron Inc* 1190
Milacron-Holdings Mexico S.A. de C.V. *Milacron Inc* 1190
Milacron-Mexicana Sales S.A. de C.V. *Milacron Inc* 1190
Milan Holding Inc. *Mylan Laboratories Inc* 1230
MiLAN Technology Corporation *Communications Systems Inc* 451
Milano Gestioni, Srl. *Banco Bilbao Vizcaya Argentaria* 204
Milano& Grey S.P.A. *WPP Group Plc* 1979
Milar, S.A. de C.V. *Grupo Televisa, S.A.B.* 829
Milazzo Residences LLC *UDR Inc* 1844
Milbank Insurance Company *State Auto Financial Corp* 1695
Milbro, Inc. *Staples Inc* 1692

THE CORPORATE DIRECTORY - Walker's 2008 Subsidiary/Parent Index - 3179

MOB/GP 90 of Texas, LLC *Health Care Property Investors Inc* 857
MOB/GP 91 of Texas, LLC *Health Care Property Investors Inc* 857
MOB/GP 93 of Texas, LLC *Health Care Property Investors Inc* 857
MOB/GP 97 of Texas, LLC *Health Care Property Investors Inc* 857
MOB/GP of Plano, LLC *Health Care Property Investors Inc* 857
MOB/GP of Texas City, LLC *Health Care Property Investors Inc* 857
MOB/GP of Texas, LLC *Health Care Property Investors Inc* 857
MOB/GP Texas City 1 of Texas, LLC *Health Care Property Investors Inc* 857
MOB/LP of Plano, LLC *Health Care Property Investors Inc* 857
MOB/LP of Texas City, LLC *Health Care Property Investors Inc* 857
MOB/LP of Texas, LLC *Health Care Property Investors Inc* 857
MOB/LP Texas Holding, LLC *Health Care Property Investors Inc* 857
Mobeira, SARL *Seaboard Corp* 1597
Moberly Hospital, Inc. *Community Health Systems Inc* 454
Moberly Medical Clinics, Inc. *Community Health Systems Inc* 454
Moberly Physicians Corp. *Community Health Systems Inc* 454
Mobi Espace SARL *Viacom Inc* 1902
Mobi Espace SARL *CBS Corp* 349
MobiClear, Ltd. *MobiClear Inc* 1203
Mobifon S.a. *Telesystem International Wireless Inc* 1769
Mobil Argentina S.A. *Exxon Mobil Corp* 673
Mobil Australia Resources Company Pty Limited *Exxon Mobil Corp* 673
Mobil California Exploration& Producing Asset Company *Exxon Mobil Corp* 673
Mobil Caspian Pipeline Company *Exxon Mobil Corp* 673
Mobil Cerro Negro, Ltd. *Exxon Mobil Corp* 673
Mobil Corporation *Exxon Mobil Corp* 673
Mobil Equatorial Guinea Inc. *Exxon Mobil Corp* 673
Mobil Erdgas-Erdoel GmbH *Exxon Mobil Corp* 673
Mobil Exploration Indonesia Inc. *Exxon Mobil Corp* 673
Mobil North Sea Limited *Exxon Mobil Corp* 673
Mobil Oil Australia Pty Ltd *Exxon Mobil Corp* 673
Mobil Oil Exploration& Producing Southeast Inc. *Exxon Mobil Corp* 673
Mobil Oil New Zealand Limited *Exxon Mobil Corp* 673
Mobil Pipe Line Company *Exxon Mobil Corp* 673
Mobil Producing Nigeria Unlimited *Exxon Mobil Corp* 673
Mobil Producing Texas& New Mexico Inc. *Exxon Mobil Corp* 673
Mobil Refining Australia Pty Ltd *Exxon Mobil Corp* 673
Mobil Services (Bahamas) Limited *Exxon Mobil Corp* 673
Mobil Yanbu Petrochemical Company Inc. *Exxon Mobil Corp* 673
Mobil Yanbu Refining Company Inc. *Exxon Mobil Corp* 673
Mobilans B.V. *Manpower Inc* 1119
Mobile - SC, LTD. *HealthSouth Corp* 861
Mobile Apartment Assoc, Ltd *Equity Residential* 654
Mobile Attic Franchising Company *National Security Group Inc* 1246
Mobile Automation, Inc. *iPass Inc* 986
Mobile Bay Lithotripsy Partners *HealthTronics Inc* 862
Mobile Broadcasting A/S *EuroTrust* 663
Mobile Consultants, Inc. *FirstMerit Corp* 720
Mobile Corps., Inc. *HCA Inc* 855
Mobile Energy Products, Inc. *Electro Energy Inc* 612
Mobile Enterprises, Inc. *Comcast Corp* 444
Mobile Gas *Energy Transfer Partners LP* 636
Mobile Gas Service Corporation *Energysouth Inc* 636
Mobile Group Inc *Advanced Oxygen Technologies Inc* 31
Mobile Imaging Services, LLC *Tenet Healthcare Corp* 1774
Mobile Kidney Stone Centers of Calif. II, L.P. *HealthTronics Inc* 862
Mobile Kidney Stone Centers of Calif., III, L.P. *HealthTronics Inc* 862
Mobile Kidney Stone Centers, Ltd. *HealthTronics Inc* 862
Mobile Medic Ambulance Service, Inc. *Emergency Medical Services Corp* 622
Mobile Medical Transportation, Inc. *Rural/Metro Corp* 1567
Mobile Mini Holdings, Inc. *Mobile Mini Inc* 1204
Mobile Mini I, Inc. *Mobile Mini Inc* 1204
Mobile Mini of Ohio LLC *Mobile Mini Inc* 1204
Mobile Mini Texas Limited Partnership, LLP *Mobile Mini Inc* 1204
Mobile Mini, LLC *Mobile Mini Inc* 1204
Mobile Mini, LLC *Mobile Mini Inc* 1204
Mobile Modular Management Corporation *McGrath Rentcorp* 1141
Mobile P.E.T. Systems (UK) Limited *Molecular Imaging Corp* 1207
Mobile Position AB *Openwave Systems Inc* 1346
Mobile River Terminal Company *United States Steel Corp* 1863
Mobile Satellite Services B.V. *Globalstar Inc* 799
Mobile Spine and Rehabilitation *U.S. Physical Therapy Inc* 1841
Mobile Surgical Technologies, Inc *Trimedyne Inc* 1825
Mobile USA Insurance Company *Philadelphia Consolidated Holding Corp* 1425
MobileAria, Inc. *Delphi Corp* 538
MobileGuardian LLC *Numerex Corp* 1316
MobileHelix, Inc. *iGATE Corp* 919
MobileMail Limited *MobiVentures.com* 1205
MobileMedia Communications, Inc. *USA Mobility Inc* 1878
MobileTech Solutions, Inc. *Trimble Navigation Ltd* 1824
Mobiliario Urbano de Nueva Leon SA de CV *Clear Channel Outdoor Holdings Inc* 422
Mobility 2001 Limited *Mobility Electronics Inc* 1204
Mobility California, Inc. *Mobility Electronics Inc* 1204
Mobility Idaho, Inc. *Mobility Electronics Inc* 1204
Mobility Texas, Inc. *Mobility Electronics Inc* 1204
Mobility, Inc. *Consolidated Graphics Inc TX* 471
Mobilized Systems,Inc. *DRS Technologies Inc* 577
Mobipay International, S.a. *Banco Bilbao Vizcaya Argentaria* 204
Mobitec AB *Digital Recorders Inc* 557
Mobitec Brasil Ltda *Digital Recorders Inc* 557
Mobitec GmbH *Digital Recorders Inc* 557
Mobitec Mobilitatshilfen Ges.m.b.H. - Tiefgraben *Invacare Corp* 981
Mobitec Pty Ltd. *Digital Recorders Inc* 557
Mobitec Rehab AG - Wurenlos *Invacare Corp* 981
Mobitec S.a.r.l. - Venissieux *Invacare Corp* 981
Mobitel, S.A. Unitel *Portugal Telecom* 1450
Mobizzo, Inc. *News Corp Ltd (The)* 1281
Moblan Investments, B.V. *Dura Automotive Systems Inc* 581
Mobley Park Apartments, L.C. *Bank of America Corp* 208
Mobrey AB *Emerson Electric Co* 623
Mobrey GmbH *Emerson Electric Co* 623
Mobrey Group PLC *Emerson Electric Co* 623
Mobrey Limited *Emerson Electric Co* 623
Mobrey Overseas Sales Limited *Emerson Electric Co* 623
Mobrey S.A./N.V. *Emerson Electric Co* 623
Mobrey SA *Emerson Electric Co* 623
Mobrey Sp. Z.o.o. *Emerson Electric Co* 623
Mobrey Transducers Limited *Emerson Electric Co* 623
Mobrey Trustee Company Limited *Emerson Electric Co* 623
Mobrey, Inc. *Emerson Electric Co* 623
MOC Administration LLC *Marathon Oil Corp* 1121
Moc D.c., LLC *Smith & Wollensky Restaurant Group Inc* 1648
MOC Holdco I, LLC *Comcast Corp* 444
MOC Holdco II, Inc. *Comcast Corp* 444
MOC Holding Company *La Quinta Corp* 1047
MOC of Miami, LLC *Smith & Wollensky Restaurant Group Inc* 1648
MOC Portfolio Delaware, Inc. *Marathon Oil Corp* 1121
Mocoh Gas Madagascar Sarl *BOC Group Plc* 262
Mocoh Trading Mauritius Limited *BOC Group Plc* 262
MOD-PAC Pilot CORP *Mod Pac Corp* 1205
Mod-U-Kraf Homes, LLC *Coachmen Industries Inc* 430
Modcomp, Inc *CSP Inc* 508
Mode 1 Communications, Inc. *Connecticut Light & Power Co* 469
Mode 1 Communications, Inc. *Western Massachusetts Electric Co* 1950
Mode 1 Communications, Inc. *Northeast Utilities* 1301
Mode 1 Communications, Inc. *Public Service of New Hampshire* 1487
Mode Plastics, Inc. *Tyco International Ltd* 1838
Model Dairy, LLC *Dean Foods Co* 533
Modeland International Holdings Inc *Dow Chemical Co* 573
Modeland International Holdings Inc. *Dow Chemical Co* 573
Modem Media UK Limited *Digitas Inc* 558
Modem Media, Inc. *Digitas Inc* 558
Modern Abstract Corporation *First American Corp* 695
Modern Alarms Limited *Tyco International Ltd* 1838
Modern Alarms (Scotland) Limited *Tyco International Ltd* 1838
Modern Automatic Alarms Limited *Tyco International Ltd* 1838
Modern Gas *Inergy Holdings LP* 936
Modern Gas *Inergy LP* 936
Modern Hairdressing Supplies (Pty) Ltd. *Procter & Gamble* 1472
Modern Holdings Incorporated *Dag Media Inc* 523
Modern Holdings (Pty) Ltd. *Procter & Gamble* 1472
Modern Industrial Products FZE *Procter & Gamble* 1472
Modern Industries Company Dammam *Procter & Gamble* 1472
Modern Industries Company Jeddah *Procter & Gamble* 1472
Modern Integrated Systems Limited *Tyco International Ltd* 1838
Modern Mark International Limited *Avery Dennison Corp* 188
Modern Masters Inc. *RPM International Inc* 1564
Modern Medical Imaging at Atrium, LLC *Modern Medical Modalities Corp* 1205
Modern Medical Imaging Centers, LLC *Modern Medical Modalities Corp* 1205
Modern Metals, LLC *BE Aerospace Inc* 223
Modern Mind Technology Limited *ChipMOS Technologies (Bermuda) Ltd* 400
Modern Molded Products Limited *Eaton Corp* 596
Modern Molded Products, Inc. *Eaton Corp* 596
Modern Panache, Inc. *Sally Beauty Holdings Inc* 1578
Modern Park Development LLC *StoneMor Partners LP* 1707
Modern Park Development Subsidiary, Inc. *StoneMor Partners LP* 1707
Modern Portfolio Management, Inc. *National Financial Partners Corp* 1241
Modern Products Company Jeddah *Procter & Gamble* 1472
Modern Propane Gas *Energy Transfer Partners LP* 636
Modern Security Systems (IOM) Ltd. *Tyco International Ltd* 1838
Modern Security Systems Limited *Tyco International Ltd* 1838
Modern Security Systems (Private Unlimited Company) *Tyco International Ltd* 1838
Modern Security Systems (Products) Limited *Tyco International Ltd* 1838
Modern Services Group, Inc. *Midland Co* 1187
Modern Woman Catalog, Inc. *Charming Shoppes Inc* 375
Modern Woman Holdings, Inc. *Charming Shoppes Inc* 375
Modern Woman Specialty, Inc. *Charming Shoppes Inc* 375
Modern Woman, Inc. (Delaware) *Charming Shoppes Inc* 375
Modern Woman, Inc. (MI) *Charming Shoppes Inc* 375
Modern Wood Products, Inc. *Hillenbrand Industries Inc* 879
Modern-Mallard Energy, LLC *Waste Management Inc* 1934
Modern-Mallard Energy, LLC *Republic Services Inc* 1534
Moderna Noble e Associados *WPP Group Plc* 1979
Modesto Garbage Co., Inc. *Waste Management Inc* 1934
Modgold 68 Corp *Franklin Credit Mgmt Corp* 744
Modine Austria GmbH *Modine Manufacturing Co* 1206
Modine Automobiltechnik GmbH *Modine Manufacturing Co* 1206
Modine Climate Systems GmbH *Modine Manufacturing Co* 1206
Modine Climate Systems Inc. *Modine Manufacturing Co* 1206
Modine Delaware, LLC *Modine Manufacturing Co* 1206
Modine Europe GmbH *Modine Manufacturing Co* 1206
Modine Export Sales Corp. *Modine Manufacturing Co* 1206
Modine Grundstucksverwaltungs GmbH *Modine Manufacturing Co* 1206
Modine Holding GmbH *Modine Manufacturing Co* 1206
Modine Holding GmbH *Modine Manufacturing Co* 1206
Modine Holding Ltda. *Modine Manufacturing Co* 1206
Modine Hungaria Kft. *Modine Manufacturing Co* 1206
Modine Jackson, Inc. *Modine Manufacturing Co* 1206
Modine Japan K.K. *Modine Manufacturing Co* 1206
Modine Kirchentellinsfurt GmbH *Modine Manufacturing Co* 1206
Modine Korea, LLC *Modine Manufacturing Co* 1206
Modine Manufacturing Company Foundation, Inc. *Modine Manufacturing Co* 1206
Modine Montage GmbH *Modine Manufacturing Co* 1206
Modine Neuenkirchen GmbH *Modine Manufacturing Co* 1206
Modine of Puerto Rico, Inc. *Modine Manufacturing Co* 1206
Modine Pontevico S.r.l. *Modine Manufacturing Co* 1206
Modine Transferencia de Calor, S.A. de C.V. *Modine Manufacturing Co* 1206
Modine Tubingen GmbH *Modine Manufacturing Co* 1206
Modine Uden B.V. *Modine Manufacturing Co* 1206
Modine UK Dollar, Limited *Modine Manufacturing Co* 1206
Modine, Inc. *Modine Manufacturing Co* 1206
Modis Consulting Partners, Inc. *MPS Group Inc* 1222
Modis International Co. *MPS Group Inc* 1222
Modis International Limited *MPS Group Inc* 1222
Modis of Georgia, Inc. *MPS Group Inc* 1222
Modis Professional Services, Inc. *MPS Group Inc* 1222
Modis, Inc. *MPS Group Inc* 1222
Modis/Computer Action, Inc. *MPS Group Inc* 1222
Modoc Engineering Corporation *BE Aerospace Inc* 223
Modoc Rsa Limited Partnership *Alltel Corp* 69
Modular Brasil Participaes Ltda. *Smart Modular Technologies (WWH) Inc* 1646
Modular Data, Inc. *Global Payments Inc* 796
Modular Energy Devices, Inc. *Enersys* 637
Moduline Industries (Canada) Ltd. *Champion Mortgage* 372
Moduline International, Inc *Champion Mortgage* 372
Modus Media International Documentation Services (Ireland) Ltd. *CMGI Inc* 426
Modus Media International Dublin *CMGI Inc* 426
Modus Media International Financial Services Ltd. *CMGI Inc* 426
Modus Media International (Ireland) Limited *CMGI Inc* 426
Modus Media, Inc. *CMGI Inc* 426
ModusLink Angers S.A.S. *CMGI Inc* 426
Moduslink Australia Pty. Ltd. *CMGI Inc* 426
ModusLink B.V. *CMGI Inc* 426
ModusLink (China) Co. Ltd. *CMGI Inc* 426
ModusLink Corporation *CMGI Inc* 426
ModusLink Czech Republic s.r.o. *CMGI Inc* 426
ModusLink Electronic Technology (Shenzhen) Co. Ltd. *CMGI Inc* 426
ModusLink France S.A.S. *CMGI Inc* 426
ModusLink (Hong Kong) Pte. Ltd. *CMGI Inc* 426
ModusLink Ireland Holdings *CMGI Inc* 426
ModusLink Japan KK *CMGI Inc* 426
ModusLink Kildare *CMGI Inc* 426
ModusLink (Kunshan) Co. Ltd. *CMGI Inc* 426
ModusLink Leinster Unlimited *CMGI Inc* 426
ModusLink Limited *CMGI Inc* 426
ModusLink (M)Sdn. Bhd. *CMGI Inc* 426
ModusLink Mexico S.A. de C.V. *CMGI Inc* 426
ModusLink Packaging Hungary Limited Liability Company *CMGI Inc* 426
ModusLink Pte. Ltd. *CMGI Inc* 426
ModusLink (Pudong) Co., Ltd. *CMGI Inc* 426
ModusLink Services Europe *CMGI Inc* 426
ModusLink (Shanghai) Co. Ltd. *CMGI Inc* 426
ModusLink Software (Shenzhen) Co. Ltd. *CMGI Inc* 426
ModusLink Solution Services Pte. Ltd. *CMGI Inc* 426
ModusLink (SongJiang) Co. Ltd. *CMGI Inc* 426
ModusLink Tilburg B.V. *CMGI Inc* 426
MOE Offshore Corporation *Contango Oil & Gas Co* 474
Moes Beverage, Inc. (Moes) *Mills Ltd Partnership* 1193
Moen Guangzhou Faucet Co., Ltd. *Fortune Brands Inc* 738
Moen Incorporated *Fortune Brands Inc* 738
Moen, Inc. *Fortune Brands Inc* 738
Moes & Caviet Last bv *Aon Corp* 129
MOF Adshel Ltd. *Clear Channel Outdoor Holdings Inc* 422
Mof Adshel Ltd. *Clear Channel Communications Inc* 421
Moffett Iberica S.A. *Terex Corp* 1777
Moffett Meadows Partners, LLC *Lennar Corp* 1068
Mofia Ltd. *Phelps Dodge Corp* 1424
Mogul Electronics, Ltd. *Arrow Electronics Inc* 152
Mohaka Vineyard Partnership *Constellation Brands Inc* 473
Mohave Imaging Center, LLC *Community Health Systems Inc* 454
Mohave Transportation Captive Insurance Company *Swift Transportation Co Inc* 1732
Mohawk Brands, Inc. *Mohawk Industries Inc* 1206
Mohawk Canada Corporation *Mohawk Industries Inc* 1206
Mohawk Carpet Distribution, L.P *Mohawk Industries Inc* 1206
Mohawk Carpet Transportation of Georgia, LLC *Mohawk Industries Inc* 1206
Mohawk Commercial, Inc. *Mohawk Industries Inc* 1206
Mohawk Cutting Tools Sales, Limited *Precision Castparts Corp* 1458
Mohawk ESV, Inc. *Mohawk Industries Inc* 1206
Mohawk Europa, Limited *Precision Castparts Corp* 1458
Mohawk Factoring, Inc. *Mohawk Industries Inc* 1206
Mohawk Global Investments S.r.l *Mohawk Industries Inc* 1206
Mohawk International (China) Ltd *Mohawk Industries Inc* 1206
Mohawk International (Europe) S.r.l *Mohawk Industries Inc* 1206
Mohawk International FSC, Inc. *Mohawk Industries Inc* 1206
Mohawk International Holdings (DE) Corporation *Mohawk Industries Inc* 1206
Mohawk International Holdings S.r.l *Mohawk Industries Inc* 1206
Mohawk International (India) Ltd *Mohawk Industries Inc* 1206
Mohawk Management, LLC *Empire Resorts Inc* 625
Mohawk Mills, Inc. *Mohawk Industries Inc* 1206
Mohawk Resources, Inc. *Mohawk Industries Inc* 1206
Mohawk Rock Holdings Limited *Mohawk Industries Inc* 1206
Mohawk Servicing, Inc. *Mohawk Industries Inc* 1206
Mohed Emballage AB *Stora Enso Oyj* 1708
Mohegan Basketball Club LLC *Mohegan Tribal Gaming Authority* 1207
Mohegan Commercial Ventures PA, LLC *Mohegan Tribal Gaming Authority* 1207
Mohegan Hill Development, LLC *Tarragon Corp* 1751
Mohegan Hill Development/Wilson, LLC *Tarragon Corp* 1751
Mohegan Hill Tarragon, LLC *Tarragon Corp* 1751
Mohegan Ventures-NW *Mohegan Tribal Gaming Authority* 1207
MOHR Development, Inc. *Siebel Systems Inc* 1624
MOHS Corporation *Host Hotels & Resorts Inc* 892
MOIL Corporation *Bank of America Corp* 208
Moinho Jauense Industria e Comercio de Alimentos Ltda. *Bunge Ltd* 295
Mojarra Costa Afuera, S.de R.L. de C.V *Horizon Offshore Inc* 891
Mojave Foods Corporation *McCormick & Co Inc* 1139
Mojave Pipeline Company *El Paso Corp* 609
Mojave Pipeline Operating Company *El Paso Corp* 609
Mojo Acquisition Corp. *IAC/InterActiveCorp* 961
Mojo Concerts B.V. *CCE Spinco Inc* 349
Mojo Esp Cv (fka -?- Capetown Events Cv) *CCE Spinco Inc* 349
Mojo Theater B.V. *CCE Spinco Inc* 349
Mojo Works B.V. *CCE Spinco Inc* 349
Mojonnier do Brasil Industria e Commercio de Equipamentos Ltda. *Tyco International Ltd* 1838
Mokejimo Korteliu Sistemos UAB *First Data Corp* 703
Mokpo Pty Limited *Huntsman Corp* 900
Mokume Software,Inc. *Versant Corp* 1898
MOL Automotive Lda *Molex Inc* 1208
MOL Corporation *Microsoft Corp* 1182
Moldcell S.A. *Turkcell Iletisim Hizmetleri* 1835
Molde Produksjonssenter AS *National Oilwell Inc* 1244
Molded Solutions *Myers Industries Inc* 1229
Moldflow B.V. *Moldflow Corp* 1207
Moldflow (Europe) Ltd. *Moldflow Corp* 1207
Moldflow France *Moldflow Corp* 1207
Moldflow (Guangzhou) Ltd. *Moldflow Corp* 1207
Moldflow Iberica S.L. *Moldflow Corp* 1207
Moldflow International Pty. Ltd. *Moldflow Corp* 1207
Moldflow Ireland, Ltd. *Moldflow Corp* 1207
Moldflow Italia S.r.l *Moldflow Corp* 1207
Moldflow Japan KK *Moldflow Corp* 1207
Moldflow Korea Ltd. *Moldflow Corp* 1207
Moldflow Merger Corp. *Moldflow Corp* 1207
Moldflow Pty. Ltd. *Moldflow Corp* 1207
Moldflow Scandinavia AB *Moldflow Corp* 1207
Moldflow Securities Corp. *Moldflow Corp* 1207
Moldflow Singapore Pte. Ltd. *Moldflow Corp* 1207

OTS Finance and Management Ltd. *Baker Michael Corp* 200
OTS International Training Services Ltd. *Baker Michael Corp* 200
OTSG, Inc. *Caterpillar Inc* 345
OTT France S.a.r.l. *Danaher Corp* 525
OTT Hydrometria, S.L. *Danaher Corp* 525
OTT Hydrometrie A.G. *Danaher Corp* 525
OTT Hydrometry LTD *Danaher Corp* 525
OTT Latinoamerica, C.A. *Danaher Corp* 525
OTT Messtechnik GmbH& Co. KG *Danaher Corp* 525
OTT Messtechnik Verwaltungs GmbH *Danaher Corp* 525
OTT Southern Africa PTY LTD *Danaher Corp* 525
Ottauquechee Hydro Company Inc. *Enel SpA* 633
Ottawa County Landfill, Inc. *Allied Waste Industries Inc* 66
Ottawa Gas *Inergy LP* 936
Ottawa Gas *Inergy Holdings LP* 936
Ottawa Money Mart II *Dollar Financial Corp* 567
Ottawa Properties, Inc. *Dana Corp* 525
Ottawa Savings Bank *Ottawa Savings Bancorp Inc IL* 1363
Ottawa Shipping LLC *Omi Corp Marshall Islands* 1337
Ottawa-Kent Title Agency, LLC *Fidelity National Financial Inc* 690
Ottaway National Publishing, Inc. *Dow Jones & Co Inc* 573
Ottaway Newspapers of Delaware, SMLLC *Dow Jones & Co Inc* 573
Ottaway Newspapers of Pennsylvania Management, Inc. *Dow Jones & Co Inc* 573
Ottaway Newspapers of Pennsylvania, L.P. *Dow Jones & Co Inc* 573
Ottaway Newspapers, Inc. *Dow Jones & Co Inc* 573
Otter Gold Mines Pty Ltd *Newmont Mining Corp* 1279
Otter Gold Pty Ltd *Newmont Mining Corp* 1279
Otter Tail Assurance Limited *Otter Tail Corp* 1363
Otter Tail Energy Services Company, Inc. *Otter Tail Corp* 1363
Otter Tail Valley Railroad Company, Inc. *Railamerica Inc* 1510
Otto Redanz Funeral Home, Inc. *Stewart Enterprises Inc* 1704
Otto Vogeli Industriearmaturen GmbH *Precision Castparts Corp* 1458
OU Connection, Inc. *Hector Communications Corp* 864
Ouachita Coca-Cola Bottling Company *Coca-Cola Enterprises Inc* 433
Ouest Electro Service S.A.R.L. *Emerson Electric Co* 623
Oulu Shipping Ltd *Stora Enso Oyj* 1708
OUM & Associates of New York, A Corporation *Aon Corp* 129
Our Glass, Inc. *Basset Enterprises Inc* 219
Our Home Productions Inc. *Viacom Inc* 1902
Our Home Productions Inc. *CBS Corp* 349
OurChart.com LLC *CBS Corp* 349
Out of the Blue Productions, LLC *Graymark Productions Inc* 817
Outback & Carrabba's of New Mexico, Inc. *OSI Restaurant Partners Inc* 1362
Outback Catering, Inc. *OSI Restaurant Partners Inc* 1362
OutBack Resource Group, Inc. *GoAmerica Inc* 802
Outback Shipping Co., Inc. *OSI Restaurant Partners Inc* 1362
Outback Sports, LLC *OSI Restaurant Partners Inc* 1362
Outback Steakhouse International, Inc. *OSI Restaurant Partners Inc* 1362
Outback Steakhouse of Florida, Inc. *OSI Restaurant Partners Inc* 1362
Outback Steakhouse Partners, Inc. *OSI Restaurant Partners Inc* 1362
Outdoor Advertising BV *Clear Channel Outdoor Holdings Inc* 422
Outdoor Advertising BV *Clear Channel Communications Inc* 421
Outdoor Advertising Group *Interpublic Group of Companies Inc* 975
Outdoor Advertising Professionals India Pvt Ltd *WPP Group Plc* 1979
Outdoor CCWI BV *Clear Channel Communications Inc* 421
Outdoor Exchange BV *CCE Spinco Inc* 349
Outdoor Focus Ltd *WPP Group Plc* 1979
Outdoor Images Limited *Viacom Inc* 1902
Outdoor Images Limited *CBS Corp* 349
Outdoor International Holdings BV *Clear Channel Outdoor Holdings Inc* 422
Outdoor International Holdings BV *Clear Channel Communications Inc* 421
Outdoor Life Network, LLC *Comcast Corp* 444
Outdoor Life Products B.V. *Universal Corp* 1867
Outdoor LLC *News Corp Ltd (The)* 1281
Outdoor Management Funeral Network, Inc. *CBS Corp* 349
Outdoor Management Network, Inc. *Viacom Inc* 1902
Outdoor Management Services, Inc. *Clear Channel Communications Inc* 421
Outdoor Management Services, Inc. *Clear Channel Outdoor Holdings Inc* 422
Outdoor Marketing LLC *News Corp Ltd (The)* 1281
Outdoor Marketing Region LLC *News Corp Ltd (The)* 1281
Outdoor Marketing Systems, Inc. *Lamar Advertising Company* 1051
Outdoor Marketing Systems, L.L.C. *Lamar Advertising Company* 1051
Outdoor Media Displays Posters, Inc. *CBS Corp* 349
Outdoor Media Displays Posters, Inc. *Viacom Inc* 1902
Outdoor Media Management LLC *News Corp Ltd (The)* 1281
Outdoor MediaCom Ltd *WPP Group Plc* 1979
Outdoor Promotions West, LLC *Lamar Advertising Company* 1051
Outdoor Resorts Motorcoach Country Club Inc. *Monaco Coach Corp* 1209
Outdoor Resorts of Las Vegas Inc. *Monaco Coach Corp* 1209
Outdoor Resorts of Naples Inc. *Monaco Coach Corp* 1209
Outdoor Services S.a. *Interpublic Group of Companies Inc* 975
Outdoor Systems Electrical Corp. *Viacom Inc* 1902
Outdoor Systems Electrical Corp. *CBS Corp* 349
Outdoor Systems Limited *News Corp Ltd (The)* 1281
Outdoor Systems (New York), Inc. *CBS Corp* 349
Outdoor Systems (New York), Inc. *Viacom Inc* 1902
Outdoor TDI LLC *Viacom Inc* 1902
Outdoor TDI LLC *CBS Corp* 349
Outerbay Technologies Inc. *Hewlett-Packard Company* 874
OuterLink Corporation *Applied Digital Solutions Inc* 135
OuterLink Corporation *Digital Angel Corp* 555
Outland Center Drive LP *Weingarten Realty Investors* 1943
Outlet Division Management Co., Inc. *Charming Shoppes Inc* 375
Outlet Division Store Co., Inc. *Charming Shoppes Inc* 375
Outlet Networks Inc. *Viacom Inc* 1902
Outlet Networks Inc. *CBS Corp* 349
Outlet Retail Stores, Inc *Lifetime Brands Inc* 1076
Outlet Stores, Inc. *Warnaco Group Inc* 1930
Outlook Foods, Inc. *Outlook Group Corp* 1364
Outlook Label Systems, Inc *Outlook Group Corp* 1364
Outlook&BluePhoenix Ltd. *BluePhoenix Solutions Ltd* 259
Outpatient Cardiovascular Center of Central Florida, LLC *HCA Inc* 855
Outpatient GP, LLC *HCA Inc* 855
Outpatient LP, LLC *HCA Inc* 855
Outpatient Medical Network, Inc. *American Homepatient Inc* 93
Outpatient Services - LAD, LLC *HCA Inc* 855
Outpatient Services - River Oaks Imaging - Clear Lake, L.P. *HCA Inc* 855
Outpatient Services - River Oaks Imaging - Conroe, L.P. *HCA Inc* 855
Outpatient Services - River Oaks Imaging - East Houston, L.P. *HCA Inc* 855
Outpatient Services - River Oaks Imaging - Houston, L.P. *HCA Inc* 855
Outpatient Services - River Oaks Imaging - Humble, L.P. *HCA Inc* 855
Outpatient Services - River Oaks Imaging - Medical Center, L.P. *HCA Inc* 855
Outpatient Services - River Oaks Imaging - Pasadena, L.P. *HCA Inc* 855
Outpatient Services - River Oaks Imaging - Sugar Land, L.P. *HCA Inc* 855
Outpatient Services - River Oaks Imaging - West Houston, L.P. *HCA Inc* 855
Outpatient Services - River Oaks Imaging - Willowbrook, L.P. *HCA Inc* 855
Outpatient Services - River Oaks Imaging, L.P. *HCA Inc* 855
Outpatient Services Holdings, Inc. *HCA Inc* 855
Outpatient Surgery Center of Lakewood, L.P. *HCA Inc* 855
Outpatient Surgery Center of The Woodlands, Ltd. *HealthSouth Corp* 861
Outpatient Surgical Services, Ltd. *HCA Inc* 855
Outpatient Women's and Children's Surgery Center, Ltd. *HCA Inc* 855
Outrider AB *WPP Group Plc* 1979
Outrider Ltd *WPP Group Plc* 1979
Outrider North America Inc *WPP Group Plc* 1979
Outrider North America LLC *WPP Group Plc* 1979
Outrider SA *WPP Group Plc* 1979
Outside Counsel Solutions, Inc. *IDT Corp* 918
Outsourced Administrative Systems, Inc. *Affiliated Computer Services Inc* 39
Outsourcing de Servicios y Manufactura, S.A. de C.V. *Kelly Services Inc* 1022
Outsourcing Investments Pty. Limited *Citigroup Inc* 411
Outsourcing Unlimited, Inc. *Scansource Inc* 1590
Outstanding Media I Norge AS *Clear Channel Communications Inc* 421
Outstanding Media I Norge AS *Clear Channel Outdoor Holdings Inc* 422
Outstanding Media Stockholm AB *Clear Channel Outdoor Holdings Inc* 422
Outstanding Media Stockholm AB *Clear Channel Communications Inc* 421
Ovako Couplings Holding AB *SKF Inc* 1641
Ovako Steel Holding AB, in liquidation *SKF Inc* 1641
Ovako Tube AB *SKF Inc* 1641
Oval Financial Leasing Ltd *Copa Holdings S.A.* 478
Ovations Fanfare, L.P. *Comcast Corp* 444
Ovations Food Services, Inc. *Comcast Corp* 444
Ovations Food Services, L.P. *Comcast Corp* 444
Ovations Ontario Food Services, Inc. *Comcast Corp* 444
Ovations Ontario Food Services, LP *Comcast Corp* 444
Ovations, Inc. *Unitedhealth Group Inc* 1864
OVB Foreclosed Properties, Inc. *BB&T Corp* 222
OVERBROOK PARK, LTD. *Apartment Investment and Management Company* 130
Overdrive Limited *Manpower Inc* 1119
Overland Mechanical Services, Inc. *Otter Tail Corp* 1363
Overland Park AL, LLC *Health Care Property Investors Inc* 857
Overland Park Cardiovascular, Inc. *HCA Inc* 855
Overland Pass Pipeline Company LLC. *ONEOK Partners LP* 1343
Overland Pass Pipeline Company, LLC *Williams Cos Inc* 1961
Overland R.N.C. Inc. *Lennox International Inc* 1068
Overland Storage (Europe) Ltd. *Overland Storage Inc* 1365
Overland Storage Export Limited *Overland Storage Inc* 1365
Overland Storage GmbH *Overland Storage Inc* 1365
Overland Storage SARL *Overland Storage Inc* 1365
Overland Trail Transmission, LLC *Duke Energy Corp* 580
Overlook at Brook Run Associates, L.P. *Wachovia Corp* 1928
Overlook at Brook Run II Associates, L. P. *Wachovia Corp* 1928
Overlook I & Ii, LLC *St Joe Co* 1686
Overnite Corporation *United Parcel Service Inc* 1861
Overseas Drilling Ltd. *Transocean Inc* 1817
Overseas Finance Co. *Owens Illinois Inc* 1366
Overseas Internet Properties, Inc. *Banks.com Inc* 214
Overseas Leasing Five FSC, Ltd. *HSBC Finance Corp* 895
Overseas Leasing Four FSC, Ltd. *HSBC Finance Corp* 895
Overseas Leasing One FSC, Ltd. *HSBC Finance Corp* 895
Overseas Leasing Twp FSC, Ltd. *HSBC Finance Corp* 895
Overseas Lending Corporation *Bank of America Corp* 208
Overseas LNG H1 Corporation *Overseas Shipholding Group Inc* 1365
Overseas LNG H2 Corporation *Overseas Shipholding Group Inc* 1365
Overseas LNG S1 Corporation *Overseas Shipholding Group Inc* 1365
Overseas LNG S2 Corporation *Overseas Shipholding Group Inc* 1365
Overseas Petroleum Corp. *Mitsui & Co Ltd* 1201
Overseas Reinsurance Corporation Limited *Unitrin Inc* 1865
Overseas Services B.V. *Viacom Inc* 1902
Overseas Services B.V. *CBS Corp* 349
Overseas Shipping (GR) Ltd. *Overseas Shipholding Group Inc* 1365
Overseas Technical Services (Harrow) Ltd. *Baker Michael Corp* 200
Overseas Technical Services International, Ltd. *Baker Michael Corp* 200
Overseas Technical Services (Middle East) Ltd. *Baker Michael Corp* 200
Overseas, Inc. *Boots & Coots Intl Well Control Inc* 266
Overstock Mexico, S. de R.L. de C.V. *Overstock Com Inc* 1365
Overstreet Orlando Mitigation Team, LLC *Ecology & Environment Inc* 600
Overstreet-Hughes, Co., Inc. *Mueller Industries Inc* 1226
Overton Distributors, Inc. *Sysco Corp* 1742
Overton Partners, L.P. *Southwestern Energy Co* 1670
Overture do Brasil Servicos de Busca na Internet Ltda *Yahoo Inc* 1990
Overture International Inc. *Yahoo Inc* 1990
Overture K.K. *Yahoo Inc* 1990
Overture Marketing Services Limited *Yahoo Inc* 1990
Overture S.A.R.L. *Yahoo Inc* 1990
Overture Search Services (Asia) Limited *Yahoo Inc* 1990
Overture Search Services Holdco (Ireland) Limited *Yahoo Inc* 1990
Overture Search Services (Ireland) Limited *Yahoo Inc* 1990
Overture Services Australia Pty, Ltd. *Yahoo Inc* 1990
Overture Services (Canada) Inc. *Yahoo Inc* 1990
Overture Services Europe BV *Yahoo Inc* 1990
Overture Services Europe, Ltd. *Yahoo Inc* 1990
Overture Services GmbH *Yahoo Inc* 1990
Overture Services Hong Kong Limited *Yahoo Inc* 1990
Overture Services IP (Cayman) Ltd. *Yahoo Inc* 1990
Overture Services Japan Y.K. *Yahoo Inc* 1990
Overture Services Limited *Yahoo Inc* 1990
Overture Services YH *Yahoo Inc* 1990
Overture Services, Inc. *Yahoo Inc* 1990
Overture Services, SRL *Yahoo Inc* 1990
Overture Spain S.L. *Yahoo Inc* 1990
OVH, Inc. *Odyssey Marine Exploration Inc* 1328
Oviedo HMA, Inc. *Health Management Associates Inc* 858
Ovion Inc. *American Medical Systems Holdings Inc* 96
Ovonic Battery Company, Inc. *Energy Conversion Devices Inc* 635
Ovonic Fuel Cell Company LLC *Energy Conversion Devices Inc* 635
Ovonic Hydrogen Systems LLC *Energy Conversion Devices Inc* 635
OVS Inc. *Orleans Homebuilders Inc* 1359
OW Corp. *WebMD Health Corp* 1941
OW Corp. *HLTH Corp* 881
OWA Hoken (UK) Limited *Aon Corp* 129
OWA Insurance Services Austria Gesellschaft mbH *Aon Corp* 129
OWA Insurance Services Austria GmbH & Co. KG *Aon Corp* 129
Owen Compliance Services, Inc. *Core Laboratories* 480
Owen de Mexico S.A. de C.V. *Core Laboratories* 480
Owen Electric Steel Company of South Carolina *Commercial Metals Co* 448
Owen Industrial Products, Inc. *Commercial Metals Co* 448
Owen Oil Tools Argentina, S.A. *Core Laboratories* 480
Owen Oil Tools de Mexico, S.A. de C.V. *Core Laboratories* 480
Owen Oil Tools de Venezuela, C.A. *Core Laboratories* 480
Owen Oil Tools L.P. *Core Laboratories* 480
Owen Oil Tools (U.K.) Ltd. *Core Laboratories* 480
Owen Shared Services, Inc. *Cardinal Health Inc* 332
Owens Supermarket *Kroger Co* 1043
Owens Corning (Anshan) Fiberglass Co., Ltd. *Owens Corning* 1366
Owens Corning Argentina Sociedad de Responsabilidad *Owens Corning* 1366
Owens Corning Australia Pty Limited *Owens Corning* 1366
Owens Corning Automotive (UK) Ltd. *Owens Corning* 1366
Owens Corning BM (Korea), Ltd. *Owens Corning* 1366
Owens Corning Building Materials Espana, S.A. *Owens Corning* 1366
Owens Corning Canada Inc. *Owens Corning* 1366
Owens Corning Cayman (China) Holdings *Owens Corning* 1366
Owens Corning (China) Investment Company, Ltd. *Owens Corning* 1366
Owens Corning Commercial Insulation Systems, LLC *Owens Corning* 1366
Owens Corning Composites Italia S.r.l. *Owens Corning* 1366
Owens Corning Composites SPRL *Owens Corning* 1366
Owens Corning Enterprise (India) Pvt. Ltd. *Owens Corning* 1366
Owens Corning Espana SA *Owens Corning* 1366
Owens Corning Fiberglas A.S. Limitada *Owens Corning* 1366
Owens Corning Fiberglas S.A. *Owens Corning* 1366
Owens Corning (Guangzhou) Fiberglas Co., Ltd. *Owens Corning* 1366
Owens Corning HT, Inc. *Owens Corning* 1366
Owens Corning Integrated Acoustic Systems, LLC *Owens Corning* 1366
Owens Corning (Japan) Ltd. *Owens Corning* 1366
Owens Corning (Jiangyin) Building Materials Co., Ltd. *Owens Corning* 1366
Owens Corning Korea *Owens Corning* 1366
Owens Corning Mexico, S.A. de C.V. *Owens Corning* 1366
Owens Corning (Nanjing) Foamular Board Co. Ltd. *Owens Corning* 1366
Owens Corning NRO II Inc. *Owens Corning* 1366
Owens Corning NRO Inc. *Owens Corning* 1366
Owens Corning Remodeling Systems, LLC *Owens Corning* 1366
Owens Corning Sales Company, S.A. de C.V. *Owens Corning* 1366
Owens Corning (Shanghai) Composites Co. Ltd. *Owens Corning* 1366
Owens Corning (Shanghai) International Trade Co., Ltd. *Owens Corning* 1366
Owens Corning (Shanghai) Trading Co., Ltd. *Owens Corning* 1366
Owens Corning (Singapore) Pte Ltd. *Owens Corning* 1366
Owens Corning (Tianjin) Building Materials Co., Ltd. *Owens Corning* 1366
Owens Corning Trading (Korea) Co., Ltd. *Owens Corning* 1366
Owens Corning VF Holdings Inc. *Owens Corning* 1366
Owens Country Foods, Inc. *BOB Evans Farms Inc* 262
Owens Country Sausage, Inc. *BOB Evans Farms Inc* 262
Owens Foods, Inc. *BOB Evans Farms Inc* 262
Owens Insurance, Ltd. *Owens Illinois Inc* 1366
Owens& Minor Distribution, Inc. *Owens & Minor Inc* 1365
Owens& Minor Medical, Inc. *Owens & Minor Inc* 1365
Owens-Brockway Glass Container Inc. *Owens Illinois Inc* 1366
Owens-Brockway Glass Container Trading Co. *Owens Illinois Inc* 1366
Owens-Brockway Packaging,Inc. *Owens Illinois Inc* 1366
Owens-Corning Britinvest Limited *Owens Corning* 1366
Owens-Corning Capital Holdings I, Inc. *Owens Corning* 1366
Owens-Corning Capital Holdings II, Inc. *Owens Corning* 1366
Owens-Corning Capital LLC *Owens Corning* 1366
Owens-Corning Cayman Limited *Owens Corning* 1366
Owens-Corning Fiberglas Deutschland GmbH *Owens Corning* 1366
Owens-Corning Fiberglas Espana, S.A. *Owens Corning* 1366
Owens-Corning Fiberglas France S.A. *Owens Corning* 1366
Owens-Corning Fiberglas (G.B.) Ltd. *Owens Corning* 1366
Owens-Corning Fiberglas Norway A/S *Owens Corning* 1366
Owens-Corning Fiberglas Sweden Inc. *Owens Corning* 1366
Owens-Corning Fiberglas Technology Inc. *Owens Corning* 1366
Owens-Corning Fiberglas (U.K.) Pension Plan Ltd. *Owens Corning* 1366
Owens-Corning FSC, Inc. *Owens Corning* 1366
Owens-Corning Funding Corporation *Owens Corning* 1366
Owens-Corning Holdings Limited *Owens Corning* 1366
Owens-Corning (India) Limited *Owens Corning* 1366
Owens-Corning Overseas Holdings, Inc. *Owens Corning* 1366
Owens-Corning Real Estate Corporation *Owens Corning* 1366
Owens-Corning (Shanghai) Fiberglas Co., Ltd. *Owens Corning* 1366
Owens-Corning Sweden AB *Owens Corning* 1366
Owens-Corning Veil Netherlands B.V. *Owens Corning* 1366
Owens-Corning Veil U.K. Ltd. *Owens Corning* 1366
Owens-Illinois (Australia) Pty. Ltd. *Owens Illinois Inc* 1366
Owens-Illinois Closure Inc. *Owens Illinois Inc* 1366
Owens-illinois Closures de Mexico, S. de R.L. de C.V. *Owens Illinois Inc* 1366
Owens-Illinois de Venezuela, C. A. *Owens Illinois Inc* 1366
Owens-Illinois do Brasil S.A. *Owens Illinois Inc* 1366

Pagebank (Digital Storage) Limited *Yahoo Inc* 1990
Pageflex, Inc. *Bitstream Inc* 251
PageMill Corporation *Varian Medical Systems Inc* 1889
Pageon Shipping Company Limited *Top Tankers Inc* 1803
Paget Holdings GmbH *Unitrin Inc* 1865
Paget Reinsurance International Ltd. *ACE Ltd* 13
Paging Network Canadian Holdings, Inc. *USA Mobility Inc* 1878
Pagoda International Corporation do Brazil, LTDA *Brown Shoe Co Inc* 288
Pagoda International Footwear Limited *Brown Shoe Co Inc* 288
Pagoda Leather Limited *Brown Shoe Co Inc* 288
Pagoda Shipping LLC *Omi Corp Marshall Islands* 1337
Pagoda Trading North America, Inc. *Brown Shoe Co Inc* 288
PAH-Cambridge Holdings, LLC *Interstate Hotels & Resorts Inc* 976
PAH-Hilltop GP, LLC *Interstate Hotels & Resorts Inc* 976
Pahrump Valley Truss, Inc. *Hesperia Holding Inc* 873
PAI Acquisition Corp *Healthcare Acquisition Corp* 859
Pain and Rehabilitation Network, Inc. *Paincare Holdings Inc* 1377
PainCare Acquisition Company IX, Inc. *Paincare Holdings Inc* 1377
PainCare Acquisition Company V, Inc. *Paincare Holdings Inc* 1377
PainCare Acquisition Company VI, Inc. *Paincare Holdings Inc* 1377
PainCare Acquisition Company VIII, Inc. d/b/a Bone and Joint Surgical Clinic *Paincare Holdings Inc* 1377
PainCare Acquisition Company X, Inc. *Paincare Holdings Inc* 1377
PainCare Acquisition Company XI, Inc. *Paincare Holdings Inc* 1377
PainCare Acquisition Company XII, Inc. *Paincare Holdings Inc* 1377
PainCare Acquisition Company XIII, Inc. *Paincare Holdings Inc* 1377
PainCare Acquisition Company XIX, Inc. *Paincare Holdings Inc* 1377
PainCare Acquisition Company XV, Inc. *Paincare Holdings Inc* 1377
PainCare Acquisition Company XVII, Inc. *Paincare Holdings Inc* 1377
PainCare Acquisition Company XVIII, Inc. *Paincare Holdings Inc* 1377
PainCare Acquisition Company XX, Inc. *Paincare Holdings Inc* 1377
PainCare Acquisition Company XXI, Inc. *Paincare Holdings Inc* 1377
PainCare Acquisition Company XXII, Inc. *Paincare Holdings Inc* 1377
PainCare Acquisition Company XXIII, Inc. *Paincare Holdings Inc* 1377
PainCare Acquisition Company XXIV, Inc. *Paincare Holdings Inc* 1377
PainCare Acquisition Company XXIX, Inc. *Paincare Holdings Inc* 1377
PainCare Acquisition Company XXV, Inc. *Paincare Holdings Inc* 1377
PainCare Acquisition Company XXVI, Inc. *Paincare Holdings Inc* 1377
PainCare Acquisition Company XXVII, Inc. *Paincare Holdings Inc* 1377
PainCare Acquisition Company XXVIII, Inc. *Paincare Holdings Inc* 1377
PainCare Acquisition Company XXX, Inc. *Paincare Holdings Inc* 1377
PainCare Intraoperative Services, Inc. *Paincare Holdings Inc* 1377
PainCare Management Services, Inc. *Paincare Holdings Inc* 1377
PainCare Neuromonitoring I, Inc. *Paincare Holdings Inc* 1377
PainCare Reorganization Corp I Inc. *Paincare Holdings Inc* 1377
PainCare Reorganization Corp II Inc. *Paincare Holdings Inc* 1377
PainCare Reorganization Corp III Inc. *Paincare Holdings Inc* 1377
PainCare Reorganization Corp IV Inc. *Paincare Holdings Inc* 1377
PainCare Reorganization Corp V Inc. *Paincare Holdings Inc* 1377
PainCare Reorganization Corp VI Inc. *Paincare Holdings Inc* 1377
PainCare Surgery Centers I, Inc. *Paincare Holdings Inc* 1377
PainCare Surgery Centers II, Inc. *Paincare Holdings Inc* 1377
PainCare Surgery Centers III, Inc. *Paincare Holdings Inc* 1377
PainCare Surgery Centers, Inc. *Paincare Holdings Inc* 1377
PainCare, Inc. *Paincare Holdings Inc* 1377
PaineWebber Capital Inc *UBS* 1843
Paint Creek Terminals, Inc. *Arch Coal Inc* 143
Paint'r B.V. *Akzo Nobel* 49
Paintball Incorporated and ILM, Inc. *American Sports Development Group Inc* 103
Paintball, Inc. *American Sports Development Group Inc* 103
Paintbrush Residences, LLC *Crescent Real Estate Equities Company* 499
Painted Post LLC *Emeritus Corp* 623
Painted Post Properties, Inc. *Emeritus Corp* 623
Paintsville HMA Physician Management, Inc. *Health Management Associates Inc* 858
Paintsville Hospital Company *Health Management Associates Inc* 858
Paiton Power Investment Co., Ltd. *Mitsui & Co Ltd* 1201
Paiute Pipeline Company *Southwest Gas Corp* 1669
Paiva, Inc. *Finish Line Inc* 693
Pajaro Court Associates LP *Edison International* 604
Pajingo Gold Mine Pty Ltd *Newmont Mining Corp* 1279
Pak N Save, Inc. *Safeway Stores* 1574
Pakenso Sweden Holding AB *Stora Enso Oyj* 1708
Pakistan PTA Ltd *Imperial Chemical Industries Plc* 929
Pakon, Inc. *Eastman Kodak Co* 595
Pala Village Investments, Inc. *Standard Pacific Corp* 1690
Palabora Holdings Limited *Rio Tinto Ltd* 1546
Palabora Holdings Limited *Rio Tinto Plc* 1547
Palace Place Limited Partnership *Citigroup Inc* 411
Palace Station Hotel& Casino,Inc. *Station Casinos Inc* 1696
Palace Suite,Inc. *Regal Entertainment Group* 1523
Palace Theatre Operating Group, LLC *CCE Spinco Inc* 349
Palacio Associates LLC *Wachovia Corp* 1928
Paladin Academy LLC *Nobel Learning Communities Inc* 1291
Paladin Reinsurance Corporation *Aon Corp* 129
Palafox Joint Venture *Regency Energy Partners LP* 1525
Palamerican Corporation *Marsh & McLennan Cos Inc* 1125
Palange Productions Ltd. *News Corp Ltd (The)* 1281
Palange Productions, Inc. *News Corp Ltd (The)* 1281
Palco Trading Company *Thermadyne Holdings Corp* 1786
Palembang Coastal Technology (Singapore) Pte Ltd. *El Paso Corp* 609
PaleoTechnology Australia Pty Ltd. *PetroHunter Energy Corp* 1417
PaleoTechnology Inc. *PetroHunter Energy Corp* 1417
Palermo Invest *IRSA Investments and Representations Inc* 989
Palermo Italian Foods, LLC *Nascent Wine Company Inc* 1236
Palisades 14th Street, L.L.C. *Vornado Realty Trust* 1923
Palisades A/V Company, L.L.C. *Vornado Realty Trust* 1923
Palisades Acquisition I, LLC *Asta Funding Inc* 166
Palisades Acquisition II, LLC *Asta Funding Inc* 166
Palisades Acquisition IV, LLC *Asta Funding Inc* 166
Palisades Acquisition IX, LLC *Asta Funding Inc* 166
Palisades Acquisition V, LLC *Asta Funding Inc* 166
Palisades Acquisition VI, LLC *Asta Funding Inc* 166
Palisades Acquisition VII, LLC *Asta Funding Inc* 166
Palisades Acquisition VIII, LLC *Asta Funding Inc* 166
Palisades Acquisition X, LLC *Asta Funding Inc* 166
Palisades Collection, LLC *Asta Funding Inc* 166
Palisades Drive Associates Intermediate, LLC *GMH Communities Trust* 802
Palisades Drive Associates, LLC *GMH Communities Trust* 802
Palisades Park East Tarragon LLC *Tarragon Corp* 1751
Palisades Park West Tarragon LLC *Tarragon Corp* 1751
Pall - PASS US, Inc. *Pall Corp* 1378
Pall Acquisition LLC *Pall Corp* 1378
Pall Aeropower Corporation *Pall Corp* 1378
Pall Asia International Ltd. *Pall Corp* 1378
Pall Austria Filter GmbH *Pall Corp* 1378
Pall Biomedical, Inc. *Pall Corp* 1378
Pall (Canada) Limited *Pall Corp* 1378
Pall Corporation Filtration and Separations (Thailand) Ltd. *Pall Corp* 1378
Pall Deutschland Beteiligungs GmbH *Pall Corp* 1378
Pall Deutschland Holding GmbH & Co. KG Partnership (c) *Pall Corp* 1378
Pall Espana S.A. *Pall Corp* 1378
Pall Europe Limited (a) *Pall Corp* 1378
Pall Filter (Beijing) Co., Ltd. *Pall Corp* 1378
Pall Filtration Pte. Ltd. *Pall Corp* 1378
Pall France S.A. *Pall Corp* 1378
Pall India Private Ltd. *Pall Corp* 1378
Pall Industrial Membranes LLC *Pall Corp* 1378
Pall International Corporation *Pall Corp* 1378
Pall Italia S.R.L. *Pall Corp* 1378
Pall Korea Ltd. *Pall Corp* 1378
Pall Netherlands B.V. (a), (d) *Pall Corp* 1378
Pall New Zealand Limited *Pall Corp* 1378
Pall Norden AB *Pall Corp* 1378
Pall Norge AS *Pall Corp* 1378
Pall Puerto Rico, Inc. *Pall Corp* 1378
Pall (Schweiz) A.G. *Pall Corp* 1378
Pall Singapore Taiwan Branch Holding Company Pte. Ltd. *Pall Corp* 1378
Palladian Holdings, LLC *Alpha Natural Resources Inc* 70
Palladian Lime, LLC *Alpha Natural Resources Inc* 70
Palladian Mortgage, LLC *Suntrust Banks Inc* 1724
Palladio S.A. *Ingersoll Rand Co Ltd* 943
Pallas Marsh Corretagem de Seguros Ltda. *Marsh & McLennan Cos Inc* 1125
Palliser Nominees Limited *Citigroup Inc* 411
PALM AIRE-ISLAND CLUB APARTMENTS PARTNERS, L.P. *Apartment Investment and Management Company* 130
PALM AIREISLAND CLUB APARTMENTS, L.P. *Apartment Investment and Management Company* 130
Palm Asia Pacific Limited *Palm Inc* 1379
Palm Australasia Pty Limited *Palm Inc* 1379
Palm Auto Plaza, Inc. *United Auto Group Inc* 1855
Palm Beach County Black Business Investment Corporation *Bank of America Corp* 208
Palm Beach EFL Imaging Center, LLC *HCA Inc* 855
Palm Beach Entertainment, Inc. *International Thoroughbred Breeders Inc* 973
Palm Beach Florida Hotel and Office Building Limited Partnership *Ashford Hospitality Trust Inc* 158
Palm Beach Gardens Community Hospital,Inc. *Tenet Healthcare Corp* 1774
Palm Beach Gourmet Coffee, Inc *Viropro Inc* 1911
Palm Beach GP LLC *Ashford Hospitality Trust Inc* 158
Palm Beach Healthcare System, Inc. *HCA Inc* 855
Palm Beach Hospitalists Program, LLC *HCA Inc* 855
Palm Beach Neurosurgery, LLC *HCA Inc* 855
Palm Beach Physician Practices, Ltd. *HCA Inc* 855
Palm Beach Princess, Inc *International Thoroughbred Breeders Inc* 973
Palm Beach Rail Holding, Inc. *Railamerica Inc* 1510
PALM BEACH-OXFORD LIMITED PARTNERSHIP *Apartment Investment and Management Company* 130
Palm Benelux B.V. *Palm Inc* 1379
Palm Canada Inc. *Palm Inc* 1379
Palm Chile Limitada *Palm Inc* 1379
Palm Coast Forest, LLC *Allete Inc* 60
Palm Coast Holdings, Inc *Allete Inc* 60
Palm Coast Land, LLC *Allete Inc* 60
Palm Coast Marina *Centex Corp* 360
Palm Colombia Limitada *Palm Inc* 1379
Palm Comrcio de Aparelhos Eletrnicos Ltda. *Palm Inc* 1379
Palm Computing Mexico S.A. de C.V. *Palm Inc* 1379
Palm Court Apartment Owners, Inc. *Tarragon Corp* 1751
Palm Drive Hospital, L.P. *Triad Hospitals Inc* 1823
Palm Drive Medical Center, LLC *Triad Hospitals Inc* 1823
Palm Europe Limited *Palm Inc* 1379
Palm France *Palm Inc* 1379
Palm Geneva SARL *Palm Inc* 1379
Palm Germany GmbH *Palm Inc* 1379
Palm Global Operations Ltd. *Palm Inc* 1379
Palm Grove Gardens, Ltd. *Tarragon Corp* 1751
Palm Harbor Albemarle, LLC *Palm Harbor Homes Inc* 1379
Palm Harbor G.P., Inc. *Palm Harbor Homes Inc* 1379
Palm Harbor GenPar, LLC *Palm Harbor Homes Inc* 1379
Palm Harbor Holding, Inc. *Palm Harbor Homes Inc* 1379
Palm Harbor Homes I, L.P. *Palm Harbor Homes Inc* 1379
Palm Harbor Insurance Agency of Texas, Inc. *Palm Harbor Homes Inc* 1379
Palm Harbor Manufacturing, L.P. *Palm Harbor Homes Inc* 1379
Palm Harbor Marketing, Inc. *Palm Harbor Homes Inc* 1379
Palm Haven Insurance Agency of Florida, Inc. *Palm Harbor Homes Inc* 1379
Palm Ireland Investment *Palm Inc* 1379
Palm Italy S.r.l. *Palm Inc* 1379
PALM LAKE ASSOCIATES, LTD. *Apartment Investment and Management Company* 130
Palm Latin America, Inc. *Palm Inc* 1379
Palm Meadows Estates,LLC *Magna Entertainment Corp* 1111
Palm Nordic AB *Palm Inc* 1379
Palm Point Ltd. *Retalix Ltd* 1538
Palm Resort Group, Inc. *Avis Budget Group Inc* 190
Palm River Development Co., Inc. *BankAtlantic Bancorp Inc* 213
Palm River Development Co., Inc. *BFC Financial Corp* 236
Palm River Development Co., Inc. *BFC Financial Corp (B)* 236
Palm Singapore Pte. Ltd. *Palm Inc* 1379
Palm South America, Inc. *Palm Inc* 1379
Palm Springs FBO Two, LLC *Macquarie Infrastructure Company Trust* 1107
Palm Springs Productions Inc. *Lions Gate Entertainment Corp* 1084
PALM SPRINGS SENIOR AFFORDABLE, L.P. *Apartment Investment and Management Company* 130
PALM SPRINGS SENIOR CITIZENS COMPLEX LIMITED PARTNERSHIP *Apartment Investment and Management Company* 130
Palm Station, LLC *Station Casinos Inc* 1696
Palm Trademark Holding Company, LLC *Palm Inc* 1379
Palm Vacation Group *Avis Budget Group Inc* 190
Palm Valley Golf Club, Inc. *Arizona Public Service Co* 148
Palm Valley Golf Club, Inc. *Pinnacle West Capital Corp* 1432
Palm Valley Professional Plaza, LLC *Arizona Public Service Co* 148
Palmar Maritime Ltd. *Overseas Shipholding Group Inc* 1365
Palmas Country Club, Inc. *Maxxam Inc* 1136
Palmas del Mar Properties, Inc *Maxxam Inc* 1136
Palmer & Cay Holdings, Inc. *Wachovia Corp* 1928
Palmer & Cay Insurance Agency of Massachusetts *Wachovia Corp* 1928
Palmer & Cay Investment Services, Inc. *Wachovia Corp* 1928
Palmer & Cay of Arkansas, LLC *Wachovia Corp* 1928
Palmer & Cay of Colorado, LLC *Wachovia Corp* 1928
Palmer & Cay of Connecticut, LLC *Wachovia Corp* 1928
Palmer & Cay of District of Columbia, LLC *Wachovia Corp* 1928
Palmer & Cay of Florida, LLC *Wachovia Corp* 1928
Palmer & Cay of Georgia, LLC *Wachovia Corp* 1928
Palmer & Cay of Illinois, LLC *Wachovia Corp* 1928
Palmer & Cay of Kansas, LLC *Wachovia Corp* 1928
Palmer & Cay of Kentucky, LLC *Wachovia Corp* 1928
Palmer & Cay of Louisiana, LLC *Wachovia Corp* 1928
Palmer & Cay of Maryland, LLC *Wachovia Corp* 1928
Palmer & Cay of Michigan, LLC *Wachovia Corp* 1928
Palmer & Cay of Minnesota, LLC *Wachovia Corp* 1928
Palmer & Cay of Mississippi, LLC *Wachovia Corp* 1928
Palmer & Cay of Missouri, LLC *Wachovia Corp* 1928
Palmer & Cay of New York, LLC *Wachovia Corp* 1928
Palmer & Cay of North Carolina, LLC *Wachovia Corp* 1928
Palmer & Cay of Ohio, LLC *Wachovia Corp* 1928
Palmer & Cay of Pennsylvania, LLC *Wachovia Corp* 1928
Palmer & Cay of South Carolina, LLC *Wachovia Corp* 1928
Palmer & Cay of Tennessee, LLC *Wachovia Corp* 1928
Palmer & Cay of Texas, LLC *Wachovia Corp* 1928
Palmer & Cay of Virginia, LLC *Wachovia Corp* 1928
Palmer & Cay of Wisconsin, LLC *Wachovia Corp* 1928
Palmer & Cay Real Estate, Inc. *Wachovia Corp* 1928
Palmer & Cay Reinsurance Services, LLC) *Wachovia Corp* 1928
Palmer & Cay Securities Corporation *Wachovia Corp* 1928
Palmer & Cay, Inc. *Wachovia Corp* 1928
Palmer & Shelley Limited *Commercial Vehicle Group Inc* 449
Palmer Apartments Associates Limited Partnership *American Community Properties Trust* 89
Palmer Heights, LLC *Edison International* 604
Palmer Hill & Co. Limited *Royal & Sun Alliance Insurance Group Plc* 1560
Palmer Hill (Insurance Services) Limited *Royal & Sun Alliance Insurance Group Plc* 1560
Palmer House LP *Edison International* 604
Palmer Lane Golf, Inc. *American Realty Investors Inc* 100
Palmer Medical Center, LLC *HCA Inc* 855
Palmer-Wasilla Health System, LLC *Triad Hospitals Inc* 1823
PALMETTO APARTMENTS, A LIMITED PARTNERSHIP *Apartment Investment and Management Company* 130
Palmetto Assurance, Ltd. *Dun & Bradstreet Corp* 580
Palmetto Behavioral Health Solutions, LLC *Psychiatric Solutions Inc* 1485
Palmetto Behavioral Health System, LLC *Psychiatric Solutions Inc* 1485
Palmetto Bluff Club, LLC *Duke Energy Corp* 580
Palmetto Bluff Development, LLC *Duke Energy Corp* 580
Palmetto Bluff Investments, LLC *Duke Energy Corp* 580
Palmetto Bluff Lodge, LLC *Duke Energy Corp* 580
Palmetto Bluff Real Estate Company, LLC *Duke Energy Corp* 580
Palmetto Bluff Uplands, LLC *Duke Energy Corp* 580
Palmetto Capital Inc *Palmetto Bancshares Inc* 1379
Palmetto Lowcountry Behavioral Health, LLC *Psychiatric Solutions Inc* 1485
Palmetto Pee Dee Behavioral Health, LLC *Psychiatric Solutions Inc* 1485
Palmetto Physician Practices,Inc. *Tenet Healthcare Corp* 1774
Palmetto Products, Inc. *Owens Corning* 1366
Palmetto Radiation Associates, LLC *Radiation Therapy Services Inc* 1507
Palmetto Seed Captal Ltd. Partnershp *Fluor Corp* 728
Palmetto Womens Care, LLC *Triad Hospitals Inc* 1823
Palms Insurance Company, Limited *Florida Power & Light Co* 726
Palms Insurance Company, Limited *FPL Group Inc* 742
Palms of Pasadena Pathology, Inc. *Ameripath Inc* 109
Palms West Hospital *HCA Inc* 855
Palms West Pediatric Neurosurgery, Inc. *HCA Inc* 855
Palms West Radiation Therapy, LLC *Radiation Therapy Services Inc* 1507
Palms West Surgery Center, Ltd. *HCA Inc* 855
Palmstierna International AB *Flowserve Corp* 728
Palmtree Acquisition Corporation *ProLogis* 1475
Palmweb Inc. *CDC Corp* 351
Palmyra Park GP, Inc. *HCA Inc* 855
Palmyra Park Hospital, Inc. *HCA Inc* 855
Palmyra Park, Limited Partnership *HCA Inc* 855
Palmyra Professional Fees, LLC *HCA Inc* 855
Palmyra Village, LLC *Orleans Homebuilders Inc* 1359
Palo Alto Research Center Incorporated *Xerox Corp* 1985
Palo Alto Sanitation Company *Waste Management Inc* 1934
Palo Co. Ltd. *Procter & Gamble* 1472
Palo Verde 1-PNM August50 Corporation *J.P. Morgan Chase & Company* 999
Palo Verde 1-PNM December75 Corporation *J.P. Morgan Chase & Company* 999
Palo Verde Leasing Corporation *J.P. Morgan Chase & Company* 999
Palo Vista College of Nursing & Allied Health Sciences, Inc. *Washington Post Co* 1933
Paloma Asset Corp *FirstCity Financial Corp* 719
Paloma Realty,Ltd. *FirstCity Financial Corp* 719
Palomar Medical Products, Inc. *Palomar Medical Technologies Inc* 1379
Palomar Medical Technologies, Inc. *Palomar Medical Technologies Inc* 1379
Palomar Precision Tubes, Inc. *Tyco International Ltd* 1838
Palomar Products, Inc. *Esterline Technologies Corp* 659
Palomar Transfer Station, Inc. *Allied Waste Industries Inc* 66
Palomar Transit Mix Co. *Legacy Vulcan Corp* 1066
Palomino Park Owners Association *Reis Inc* 1527
Palomino Park Public Improvements Corp. *Reis Inc* 1527
Palomino Park Telecom L.L.C. *Reis Inc* 1527

Radica Technology (Shenzhen) Co. Ltd. *Radica Games Ltd* 1508
Radica UK Ltd *Radica Games Ltd* 1508
Radiel Bobinage S.A.R.L. *Emerson Electric Co* 623
Radin GmbH *Mercury Computer Systems Inc* 1162
Radio 103 BV *News Corp Ltd (The)* 1281
Radio Austin Management, LLC *Emmis Communications Corp* 624
Radio Broadcasting Australia Pty Ltd. *Clear Channel Communications Inc* 421
Radio Centro Publicidad, S.A. de C.V. *Grupo Radio Centro* 828
Radio City Networks Holdings I, LLC *CSC Holdings Inc* 508
Radio City Networks Holdings I, LLC *Cablevision Systems Corp* 301
Radio City Networks Holdings Ii, LLC *Cablevision Systems Corp* 301
Radio City Networks Holdings Ii, LLC *CSC Holdings Inc* 508
Radio City Networks LLC *CSC Holdings Inc* 508
Radio City Networks LLC *Cablevision Systems Corp* 301
Radio City Productions LLC *Cablevision Systems Corp* 301
Radio City Productions LLC *CSC Holdings Inc* 508
Radio City Trademarks, LLC *CSC Holdings Inc* 508
Radio City Trademarks, LLC *Cablevision Systems Corp* 301
Radio Comerciales, S.A. de C.V. . *Grupo Televisa, S.A.B.* 829
Radio Componentes de Mexico, S.A. de S.V. *SMTC Corp* 1650
Radio Components Sweden AB *Tele2 AB* 1764
Radio Data Group, Inc. *Viacom Inc* 1902
Radio Llamadas Panama, S.A. *Brinks Co* 281
Radio Melodia, S.A. de C.V. . *Grupo Televisa, S.A.B.* 829
Radio Modern LLC *News Corp Ltd (The)* 1281
Radio Movil Digital Argentina S.A. *NII Holdings Inc* 1287
Radio Natsionalnoi Sluzhbi Novostei *News Corp Ltd (The)* 1281
Radio Non Stop Ltd. *Blue Square Israel Ltd* 257
Radio Nostalgia LLC *News Corp Ltd (The)* 1281
Radio One Cable Holdings, Inc. *Radio One Inc* 1508
Radio One Licenses, LLC *Radio One Inc* 1508
Radio One Media Holdings, LLC *Radio One Inc* 1508
Radio One of Atlanta, LLC *Radio One Inc* 1508
Radio One of Boston, Inc. *Radio One Inc* 1508
Radio One of Charlotte, LLC *Radio One Inc* 1508
Radio One of Indiana, L.P *Radio One Inc* 1508
Radio One of Texas, L.P. *Radio One Inc* 1508
Radio Pro S.R.L *Central European Media Enterprises Ltd* 361
Radio Productions London Ltd *News Corp Ltd (The)* 1281
Radio Red, S.A. de C.V. *Grupo Radio Centro* 828
Radio Red-FM, S.A. de C.V. *Grupo Radio Centro* 828
Radio Sistema Mexicano, S.A. *Grupo Radio Centro* 828
Radio Tapatia, S.A. de C.V. . *Grupo Televisa, S.A.B.* 829
Radio Television, S.A. de C.V. *Grupo Televisa, S.A.B.* 829
Radio TV Riedo AG *Liberty Global Inc* 1074
Radio Veronica 103 FM BV *News Corp Ltd (The)* 1281
Radio X Network, Inc. *Aventura Holdings Inc* 187
Radio-Active Media, Inc. *Clear Channel Communications Inc* 421
Radiodetection Australia Pty Limited *SPX Corp* 1684
Radiodetection B.V. *SPX Corp* 1684
Radiodetection (Canada) Ltd. *SPX Corp* 1684
Radiodetection (China) Limited *SPX Corp* 1684
Radiodetection GmbH Ortungstechnik i.L. *SPX Corp* 1684
Radiodetection Holdings Limited *SPX Corp* 1684
Radiodetection JV Sdn Bhd *SPX Corp* 1684
Radiodetection Limited *SPX Corp* 1684
Radiodetection Limited *SPX Corp* 1684
Radiodetection S.L. *SPX Corp* 1684
Radiodetection Sarl *SPX Corp* 1684
Radiodetection Sp z.o.o. *SPX Corp* 1684
Radiodetection Srl *SPX Corp* 1684
Radiodetection Srl *SPX Corp* 1684
Radiodifusion Red, S.A. de C.V. *Grupo Radio Centro* 828
Radiofone, Inc. *Alltel Corp* 69
Radiokonsulterna AB *WPP Group Plc* 1979
Radiology Diagnostic Centers, Inc. *HealthSouth Corp* 861
Radiometer A/S *Danaher Corp* 525
Radiometer America Inc. *Danaher Corp* 525
Radiometer Analytical, S.A.S. *Danaher Corp* 525
Radiometer Basel AG *Danaher Corp* 525
Radiometer Canada *Danaher Corp* 525
Radiometer Corporate Development Ltd. *Danaher Corp* 525
Radiometer Danmark A/S *Danaher Corp* 525
Radiometer Finans A/S *Danaher Corp* 525
Radiometer GmbH *Danaher Corp* 525
Radiometer Iberica S.A. *Danaher Corp* 525
Radiometer Inc. *Danaher Corp* 525
Radiometer Ireland Ltd. *Danaher Corp* 525
Radiometer K.K. *Danaher Corp* 525
Radiometer Ltd. *Danaher Corp* 525
Radiometer Medical ApS *Danaher Corp* 525
Radiometer Medical Equipment (Shanghai) Co. Ltd. *Danaher Corp* 525
Radiometer Nederland B.V. *Danaher Corp* 525
Radiometer Pacific Ltd. *Danaher Corp* 525
Radiometer Pacific Pty. Ltd. *Danaher Corp* 525
Radiometer RSCH GmbH *Danaher Corp* 525
Radiometer S.A.S. *Danaher Corp* 525
Radiometer Spolka z.o.o. *Danaher Corp* 525
Radiometer Trading K.K. *Danaher Corp* 525
Radiometer (UK) LTD. *Danaher Corp* 525
Radiomovil Dipsa, S.A. de C.V. *America Movil* 83
Radionet Nordic Ab *Airspan Networks Inc* 47
Radionet Oy, Limited *Airspan Networks Inc* 47
Radionet Works Oy, Limited *Airspan Networks Inc* 47
Radiophone S.A. de C.V. *NII Holdings Inc* 1287
Radioplant of Beregovo/Beregivskiy Radiozavod *Flextronics International Ltd* 725
Radiotelefonia Movil Metropolitana, S.A. de C.V. *Grupo Televisa, S.A.B.* 829
Radiotelevisora de Mexicali, S.A. de C.V. *Grupo Televisa, S.A.B.* 829
Radiotelevisora de Mexico Norte, S.A. de C.V. . *Grupo Televisa, S.A.B.* 829
RadiSys B.V. *RadiSys Corp* 1508
RadiSys GmbH *RadiSys Corp* 1508
RadiSys Ireland Limited *RadiSys Corp* 1508
RadiSys Israel Ltd. *RadiSys Corp* 1508
RadiSys Systems Technology (Shanghai) Co. Ltd. *RadiSys Corp* 1508
RadiSys Technology (Ireland) Limited *RadiSys Corp* 1508
RadiSys UK Limited *RadiSys Corp* 1508
Radius (Cayman) Inc. *Radius Explorations Ltd* 1508
Radius (Cayman) Inc. and Pavon (Cayman) Inc. *Radius Explorations Ltd* 1508
Radius Panam Corporation, Weltern Resources Corp *Radius Explorations Ltd* 1508
Radius Partners, Inc. *Fundtech Ltd* 755
Radix Technologies, Inc. *Argon St Inc* 146
Radlan Computer Communications Ltd. *Marvell Technology Group Ltd* 1128
Radlan,Inc. *Marvell Technology Group Ltd* 1128
Radlan,Inc. *Marvell Technology Group Ltd* 1128
Radly Petroleum, Inc. *Chancellor Group Inc* 373
Radman, Inc. *Modine Manufacturing Co* 1206
RadMex S.A. de C.V. *Radica Games Ltd* 1508
RadNet Managed Imaging Services, Inc. *Primedex Health Systems Inc* 1466
Radnet Management I, Inc. *Primedex Health Systems Inc* 1466
Radnet Management II, Inc. *Primedex Health Systems Inc* 1466
RadNet Management, Inc. *Primedex Health Systems Inc* 1466
Radnet Sub, Inc. *Primedex Health Systems Inc* 1466
Radnor Center Associates *Brandywine Realty Trust* 274
Radnor Center Associates *Brandywine Operating PArtnership LP* 274
Radnor Corporation *Sunoco Inc* 1721
Radnor Funding Corp. *Airgas Inc* 47
Radnor GP *Brandywine Operating PArtnership LP* 274
Radnor GP, L.L.C *Brandywine Realty Trust* 274
Radnor GP-200 RC *Brandywine Operating PArtnership LP* 274
Radnor GP-200 RC, L.L.C *Brandywine Realty Trust* 274
Radnor GP-201 KOP *Brandywine Operating PArtnership LP* 274
Radnor GP-201 KOP, L.L.C *Brandywine Realty Trust* 274
Radnor GP-555 LA, L.L.C *Brandywine Realty Trust* 274
Radnor GP-SDC *Brandywine Operating PArtnership LP* 274
Radnor GP-SDC, L.L.C *Brandywine Realty Trust* 274
Radnor Homes, Inc *Pulte Homes Inc* 1489
Radnor Properties Associates-II *Brandywine Operating PArtnership LP* 274
Radnor Properties Associates-II, L.P *Brandywine Realty Trust* 274
Radnor Properties-200 RC *Brandywine Operating PArtnership LP* 274
Radnor Properties-200 RC Holdings *Brandywine Operating PArtnership LP* 274
Radnor Properties-200 RC Holdings, L.P *Brandywine Realty Trust* 274
Radnor Properties-200 RC, L.P *Brandywine Realty Trust* 274
Radnor Properties-201 KOP *Brandywine Operating PArtnership LP* 274
Radnor Properties-201 KOP, L.P *Brandywine Realty Trust* 274
Radnor Properties-555 LA *Brandywine Operating PArtnership LP* 274
Radnor Properties-555 LA, L.P *Brandywine Realty Trust* 274
Radnor Properties-SDC *Brandywine Operating PArtnership LP* 274
Radnor Properties-SDC, L.P *Brandywine Realty Trust* 274
Radnor/California Service Corporation *Sunoco Inc* 1721
Radnor/Credit Corporation *Sunoco Inc* 1721
Radnor/Dutton Mill Corporation *Sunoco Inc* 1721
Radnor/Edgewater, Inc. *Sunoco Inc* 1721
Radnor/Frederick Corporation *Sunoco Inc* 1721
Radnor/Investment Corporation *Sunoco Inc* 1721
Radnor/Loudoun Corporation *Sunoco Inc* 1721
Radnor/Murrieta Corporation *Sunoco Inc* 1721
Radnor/North Corporation *Sunoco Inc* 1721
Radnor/Spring Ridge Corporation *Sunoco Inc* 1721
Radnor/Vail Ranch Corporation *Sunoco Inc* 1721
Radnor/Victorville Corporation *Sunoco Inc* 1721
Radnor/Yorba Linda-I Corporation *Sunoco Inc* 1721
RADS Holding Corp. *Radiant Systems Inc* 1507
Radsource, LLC *United Surgical Partners International Inc* 1863
Radtke Physical Therapy *U.S. Physical Therapy Inc* 1841
RadView Software AB *Radview Software Ltd* 1509
RadView Software GmbH *Radview Software Ltd* 1509
RadView Software (UK) Ltd. *Radview Software Ltd* 1509
RadView Software, Inc. *Radview Software Ltd* 1509
Radvision B.v. *Radvision Ltd* 1509
Radvision Communication Development (beijing) Co. Ltd. *Radvision Ltd* 1509
Radvision France S.a.r.l *Radvision Ltd* 1509
Radvision (hk) Ltd. *Radvision Ltd* 1509
Radvision Inc. *Radvision Ltd* 1509
Radvision Japan Kk *Radvision Ltd* 1509
Radvision (uk) Ltd. *Radvision Ltd* 1509
Radware Australia Pty. Ltd. *Radware Ltd* 1509
Radware Canada Inc. *Radware Ltd* 1509
Radware France *Radware Ltd* 1509
Radware GmbH *Radware Ltd* 1509
Radware GmbH *Radware Ltd* 1509
Radware Inc *Radware Ltd* 1509
Radware Korea Ltd. *Radware Ltd* 1509
Radware Singapore Pte. Ltd. *Radware Ltd* 1509
Radware Srl *Radware Ltd* 1509
Radware UK Limited *Radware Ltd* 1509
Radwiz, Inc. *Terayon Communication Systems Inc* 1776
RAE France *RAESystems* 1510
RAE Systems (Asia) Limited *RAESystems* 1510
RAE Systems Europe ApS *RAESystems* 1510
RAE Systems (Hong Kong) Limited *RAESystems* 1510
RAE Systems Inc. *RAESystems* 1510
RAE Systems (Shanghai) Incorporated *RAESystems* 1510
RAE United Kingdom Limited *RAESystems* 1510
Rae-klh (beijing) Co. Ltd *RAESystems* 1510
Raeford Green Associates Limited Partnership *Wachovia Corp* 1928
Raekwon Productions Ltd. *News Corp Ltd (The)* 1281
Raekwon Productions, Inc. *News Corp Ltd (The)* 1281
Rael Handelsgmbh *Lear Corp* 1062
Rafael Benitez Carrillo Inc. *Applied Industrial Technologies Inc* 135
Rafael Development Corporation Ltd. *Elron Electronic Industries Ltd* 618
Raft River Energy I, LLC *US Geothermal Inc* 1877
Ragelite Limited *Aramark Corp* 140
Rags Productions, Inc. *News Corp Ltd (The)* 1281
Ragtime NY LLC *CCE Spinco Inc* 349
Ragus Holdings, Inc. *Imperial Sugar Co* 930
RAH Canada Limited Partnership *Ralcorp Holdings Inc* 1511
Rah Of Florida, Inc. *M.D.C Holdings Inc* 1104
Rah Of Texas, Lp *M.D.C Holdings Inc* 1104
Rah Texas Holdings, LLC *M.D.C Holdings Inc* 1104
Rahaxi Processing Oy *FreeStar Technology Corp* 747
Rahway Leasing, L.L.C. *Vornado Realty Trust* 1923
Rahway River Land LLC *Kinder Morgan Energy Partners LP* 1030
RAI Financial, Inc. *Resource America Inc* 1536
RAI Ventures, Inc. *Resource America Inc* 1536
Raianna Productions Inc. *Viacom Inc* 1902
Raianna Productions Inc. *CBS Corp* 349
Raider Beverage Corporation *Fox & Hound Restaurant Group* 741
Raider Motor Corporation *Jarden Corp* 1004
Rail Bearing Service Corporation *Timken Co* 1796
Rail Car Associates Limited Partnership *Union Tank Car Co* 1852
Rail Cycle North Ltd. *Waste Management Inc* 1934
Rail Line Holdings #1, Inc. *Railamerica Inc* 1510
Rail Line Holdings #2, Inc. *Railamerica Inc* 1510
Rail Link, Inc. *Genesee & Wyoming Inc* 773
Rail Partners Limited Partnership *Genesee & Wyoming Inc* 773
Rail Project, s r.o *Trinity Industries Inc* 1826
Rail Sourcing Solutions (International) Limited *MTR Corp Ltd* 1225
Rail Sourcing Solutions (UK) Limited *MTR Corp Ltd* 1225
Rail Switching LLC *Genesee & Wyoming Inc* 773
Rail Systems, Inc. *Kirby Corp* 1032
Rail4Chem Eisenbahnverkehrsgesellschaft mbH *BASF* 218
RailAmerica Australia Finance Pty Ltd. *Railamerica Inc* 1510
RailAmerica Australia II, LLC *Railamerica Inc* 1510
RailAmerica Australia, Pty, Ltd. *Railamerica Inc* 1510
RailAmerica Canada Corp. *Railamerica Inc* 1510
RailAmerica de Chile, S.A. *Railamerica Inc* 1510
RailAmerica Equipment Corp. *Railamerica Inc* 1510
RailAmerica Intermodal Services, Inc. *Railamerica Inc* 1510
RailAmerica Luxembourg S.R.L. *Railamerica Inc* 1510
RailAmerica Operations Support Group, Inc. *Railamerica Inc* 1510
RailAmerica Switching Services, Inc. *Railamerica Inc* 1510
RailAmerica Transportation Corp. *Railamerica Inc* 1510
Railcar Investment, LLC *Wachovia Corp* 1928
Railcar Services Corporation *Anixter International Inc* 125
RAILHEAD ASSOCIATES LLC *Macerich Company (The)* 1106
RaiLink Acquisition, Inc. *Railamerica Inc* 1510
RaiLink Canada, Ltd. *Railamerica Inc* 1510
Railroad Avenue Disposal, LLC *Waste Connections Inc* 1934
Railroad Friction Products Corporation *Westinghouse Air Brake Technologies Corp* 1952
Railroad Investments, Inc. *Reading International Inc* 1518
Railroad Pass Investment Group, dba Railroad Pass Hotel and Casino *MGM MIRAGE* 1176
Railroad Track Construction Corporation *Florida East Coast Industries Inc* 726
Railroad Y L.P. *Wachovia Corp* 1928
Railroads of Hawaii, d/b/a Lahaina Kaanapali & Pacific *Railamerica Inc* 1510
Railserve Inc. *Union Tank Car Co* 1852
Railserve, Inc. *Union Tank Car Co* 1852
RailTex Canada, Inc. *Railamerica Inc* 1510
RailTex Distribution Services, Inc. *Railamerica Inc* 1510
RailTex International Holdings, Inc. *Railamerica Inc* 1510
RailTex, Inc. *Railamerica Inc* 1510
Raimsa, S.A. de C.V. *Federal Mogul Corp* 684
Rain City C.V. *Starbucks Corp* 1693
Rain Forest Products Group, Inc. *Margo Caribe Inc* 1122
Rain Shipping LLC *Omi Corp Marshall Islands* 1337
Rainbow Advertising Holdings LLC *CSC Holdings Inc* 508
Rainbow Advertising Holdings LLC *Cablevision Systems Corp* 301
Rainbow Advertising Sales Corporation *Cablevision Systems Corp* 301
Rainbow Advertising Sales Corporation *CSC Holdings Inc* 508
Rainbow Casino *Bally Technologies Inc* 202
Rainbow Cinemas LLC *CSC Holdings Inc* 508
Rainbow Cinemas LLC *Cablevision Systems Corp* 301
Rainbow Concert Productions, Inc. *CCE Spinco Inc* 349
Rainbow Dbs Company LLC *Cablevision Systems Corp* 301
Rainbow Dbs Company LLC *CSC Holdings Inc* 508
Rainbow Dbs Company LLCDoing Business As: *CSC Holdings Inc* 508
Rainbow Dbs Holdings, Inc. *CSC Holdings Inc* 508
Rainbow Dbs Holdings, Inc. *Cablevision Systems Corp* 301
Rainbow Film Holdings LLC *Cablevision Systems Corp* 301
Rainbow Film Holdings LLC *CSC Holdings Inc* 508
Rainbow Garden Corp. *CSC Holdings Inc* 508
Rainbow Garden Corp. *Cablevision Systems Corp* 301
Rainbow Hd Holdings LLC *Cablevision Systems Corp* 301
Rainbow Hd Holdings LLC *CSC Holdings Inc* 508
Rainbow Hill Ltd. *Deswell Industries Inc* 545
Rainbow Information Technologies (Taiwan) Co., Ltd. *Safenet Inc* 1573
Rainbow Information Technology Co. Ltd. *Safenet Inc* 1573
Rainbow Media Enterprises, Inc. *CSC Holdings Inc* 508
Rainbow Media Enterprises, Inc. *Cablevision Systems Corp* 301
Rainbow Media Holdings LLC *Cablevision Systems Corp* 301
Rainbow Media Holdings LLC *CSC Holdings Inc* 508
Rainbow Multimedia Group, Inc. *THQ Inc* 1790
Rainbow Mvdds Company LLC *CSC Holdings Inc* 508
Rainbow Mvdds Company LLC *Cablevision Systems Corp* 301
Rainbow National Services LLC *Cablevision Systems Corp* 301
Rainbow National Services LLC *CSC Holdings Inc* 508
Rainbow National Sports Holdings LLC *CSC Holdings Inc* 508
Rainbow National Sports Holdings LLC *Cablevision Systems Corp* 301
Rainbow Natural Foods,Inc. *United Natural Foods Inc* 1860
Rainbow Network Communications *Cablevision Systems Corp* 301
Rainbow Network Communications *CSC Holdings Inc* 508
Rainbow News 12 Company *CSC Holdings Inc* 508
Rainbow News 12 Company *Cablevision Systems Corp* 301
Rainbow News 12 Company Doing Business As: *CSC Holdings Inc* 508
Rainbow Programming Holdings LLC *CSC Holdings Inc* 508
Rainbow Programming Holdings LLC *Cablevision Systems Corp* 301
Rainbow Regional Holdings LLC *Cablevision Systems Corp* 301
Rainbow Regional Holdings LLC *CSC Holdings Inc* 508
Rainbow Regional Holdings Sub LLC *CSC Holdings Inc* 508
Rainbow Regional Holdings Sub LLC *Cablevision Systems Corp* 301
Rainbow Resources, Inc. *Williams Cos Inc* 1961
Rainbow Satellite Group, LLC *Multiband Corp* 1227
Rainbow Technologies C.I. L.P. *Safenet Inc* 1573
Rainbow Technologies GmbH *Safenet Inc* 1573
Rainbow Technologies International GmbH *Safenet Inc* 1573
Rainbow Technologies Ltd. *Safenet Inc* 1573
Rainbow Technologies North America, Inc. *Safenet Inc* 1573
Rainbow Terrace Apartments, Inc. *Associated Estates Realty Corp* 164
Rainbow Travel, Inc. *Cablevision Systems Corp* 301
Rainbow Travel, Inc. *CSC Holdings Inc* 508
Rainee Resources Ltd. PTR Resources Ltd. *Enterra Energy Trust* 643
Raines Electric Co., Inc. *Integrated Electrical Services Inc* 956
Raines Electric LP *Integrated Electrical Services Inc* 956
Raines Holdings II LLC *Integrated Electrical Services Inc* 956
Raines Holdings LLC *Integrated Electrical Services Inc* 956
Raines Management LLC *Integrated Electrical Services Inc* 956
Rainey Kelly Cambell Roalfe Trustees Ltd *WPP Group Plc* 1979
Rainey Kelly Campbell Roalfe Ltd *WPP Group Plc* 1979
Rainey Land Title Services LLC *Stewart Information Services Corp* 1705
Rainfinity GmbH *EMC Corp* 620
Rainfinity Singapore Pte. Ltd. *EMC Corp* 620
Rainfinity UK Limited *EMC Corp* 620

THE CORPORATE DIRECTORY - Walker's 2008 Subsidiary/Parent Index - 3269

RC CA Santa Barbara, LLC *Regency Centers Corp* 1524
RC Georgia Holdings, LLC *Regency Centers Corp* 1524
RC Holdings I, LLC *Resources Connection Inc* 1537
RC Holdings II, LLC *Resources Connection Inc* 1537
RC Hotel Holding Company Limited *Marriott International Inc* 1125
RC Hotels (Virgin Islands), Inc. *Marriott International Inc* 1125
RC Management Group, LLC *Resources Connection Inc* 1537
RC Marriott II, Inc. *Marriott International Inc* 1125
RC Marriott III, Inc. *Marriott International Inc* 1125
RC Marriott, Inc. *Marriott International Inc* 1125
RC Miller Enterprises, Inc. *Allied Waste Industries Inc* 66
RC Miller Refuse Service, Inc. *Allied Waste Industries Inc* 66
RC Paradise Valley Development, LLC *Marriott International Inc* 1125
RC Rose Island Hotel Company Limited *Marriott International Inc* 1125
RC Royalty Sub LLC *Alkermes Inc* 57
RC Verwaltungs- und Beteiligungsgesellschaft mbH *Allianz* 63
RC-UK, Inc. *Marriott International Inc* 1125
RC06 Menomonee Falls WI LLC *Gladstone Commercial Corp* 789
RC2 Australia Pty. Ltd. *RC2 Corp* 1517
RC2 Brands, Inc. *RC2 Corp* 1517
RC2 Canada Corporation *RC2 Corp* 1517
RC2 Deutschland GmbH *RC2 Corp* 1517
Rc2 (h.k.) Limited *RC2 Corp* 1517
RC2 South, Inc. *RC2 Corp* 1517
RCAC, LLC *Triarc Cos Inc* 1823
RCBK Mortgage Corp. *New York Community Bancorp Inc* 1276
RCC Atlantic Licenses, LLC *Rural Cellular Corp* 1567
RCC Atlantic, Inc. *Rural Cellular Corp* 1567
RCC Commercial, Inc. *Resource Capital Corp* 1537
RCC Commercial, Inc. *Resource America Inc* 1536
RCC Georgia Investor LLC *Marriott International Inc* 1125
RCC Manager LLC *Centerline Holding Co* 358
RCC Minnesota, Inc. *Rural Cellular Corp* 1567
RCC Real Estate SPE II, LLC *Resource Capital Corp* 1537
RCC Real Estate SPE, LLC *Resource Capital Corp* 1537
RCC Real Estate, Inc. *Resource Capital Corp* 1537
RCC Real Estate, Inc. *Resource America Inc* 1536
RCC Transport, Inc. *Rural Cellular Corp* 1567
RCCM Limited *Willis Group Holdings Ltd* 1962
RCE Holdings, LLC *RC2 Corp* 1517
Rce Humbug Productions LLC *Cablevision Systems Corp* 301
Rce Humbug Productions LLC *CSC Holdings Inc* 508
RCG Information Services Corporation *Rotech Healthcare Inc NEW* 1560
RCG, LP *Resources Connection Inc* 1537
RCH Financial Services, Inc. *National Financial Partners Corp* 1241
RCH, LLC *HCA Inc* 855
RCI Acquisition Corp. *Premiere Global Services Inc* 1461
RCI Argentina, Inc. *Avis Budget Group Inc* 190
RCI Billing, Inc. *Rick's Cabaret International Inc* 1544
RCI Brasil Ltda. *Avis Budget Group Inc* 190
RCI Call Centre (Ireland) Limited *Avis Budget Group Inc* 190
RCI Canada, Inc. *Avis Budget Group Inc* 190
RCI Chile, Inc. *Avis Budget Group Inc* 190
RCI Colombia, Inc. *Avis Budget Group Inc* 190
RCI Construction, LLC *Building Materials Holding Corp* 294
RCI Consulting, Inc. *Avis Budget Group Inc* 190
RCI Dating Services, Inc. *Rick's Cabaret International Inc* 1544
RCI Debit Services, Inc. *Rick's Cabaret International Inc* 1544
RCI Entertainment (Ft. Worth), Inc. *Rick's Cabaret International Inc* 1544
RCI Entertainment (Minnesota), Inc. *Rick's Cabaret International Inc* 1544
RCI Entertainment (New York), Inc. *Rick's Cabaret International Inc* 1544
RCI Entertainment (North Carolina), Inc. *Rick's Cabaret International Inc* 1544
RCI Entertainment (San Antonio), Inc. *Rick's Cabaret International Inc* 1544
RCI Entertainment Texas, Inc. *Rick's Cabaret International Inc* 1544
RCI Europe *Avis Budget Group Inc* 190
RCI General Holdco2, Inc. *Avis Budget Group Inc* 190
RCI Global Vacation Network, Inc. *Wyndham Worldwide Corp* 1981
RCI Hawaii No.1, LLC *Avis Budget Group Inc* 190
RCI Hawaii No.2, LLC *Avis Budget Group Inc* 190
RCI Holdings, Inc. *Rick's Cabaret International Inc* 1544
RCI Holdings, Inc. *Kinder Morgan Energy Partners LP* 1030
RCI Hudson, Inc. *Waste Management Inc* 1934
RCI India Pvt. Ltd. *Avis Budget Group Inc* 190
RCI Internet Holding, Inc. *Rick's Cabaret International Inc* 1544
RCI Internet Services, Inc. *Rick's Cabaret International Inc* 1544
RCI Kiawah Island, LLC *Avis Budget Group Inc* 190
RCI Medical Corp. *Rotech Healthcare Inc NEW* 1560
RCI Pacific Pty. Ltd. *Avis Budget Group Inc* 190
RCI Pty Ltd. *James Hardie Industries* 1003
RCI Rewards LLC *Avis Budget Group Inc* 190
RCI Technology Corp. *Avis Budget Group Inc* 190
RCI Tourism Development (India) Ltd. *Avis Budget Group Inc* 190
Rci/rms, LLC *Regal Entertainment Group* 1523
RCL Holdings LLC *Bank of America Corp* 208
RCL Properties, LLC *Macquarie Infrastructure Company Trust* 1107
Rcl (uk) Ltd. *Royal Caribbean Cruises Ltd* 1562
RCM Capital Management LLC *Allianz* 63
RCM Distributors LLC *Allianz* 63
Rcm (uk) Ltd. *Allianz* 63
RCM US Holdings LLC *Allianz* 63
RCMD Financial Services, Inc. *Nationwide Financial Services Inc* 1248
RCMO Advertising Centre of Moscow Region LLC *News Corp Ltd (The)* 1281
RCN Telecom Services of Massachusetts, Inc *RCN Corp* 1517
RCN-BecoCom LLC *RCN Corp* 1517
RCOM Canada, Corp. *Register Com Inc* 1527
RCP Albuquerque Manager, Inc. *Resource America Inc* 1536
RCP Avalon Manager, Inc. *Resource America Inc* 1536
RCP Capital, LLC *Citigroup Inc* 411
RCP Chinoe Creek Manager, Inc. *Resource America Inc* 1536
RCP Cuestas Manager, Inc. *Resource America Inc* 1536
RCP Falls at Duraleigh Manager, Inc. *Resource America Inc* 1536
RCP Fountains GP, Inc. *Resource America Inc* 1536
RCP Holdco I Manager, Inc. *Resource America Inc* 1536
RCP Nittany Pointe Manager, Inc. *Resource America Inc* 1536
RCP Portland Courtyard Manager, Inc. *Resource America Inc* 1536
RCP Reserves HoldCo I Manager, Inc. *Resource America Inc* 1536
RCP Sage Canyon Manager, Inc. *Resource America Inc* 1536
RCP Summer View Manager, Inc. *Resource America Inc* 1536
RCR Vail, LLC *Vail Resorts Inc* 1883
RCS HOLDING CORP. *Kimco Realty Corp* 1029
RCS Managers *Allianz* 63
RCS Title Agency, LLC *Stewart Information Services Corp* 1705
RCS, Inc. *Allied Waste Industries Inc* 66
RCSB Corporation *New York Community Bancorp Inc* 1276
RCSH Holdings, Inc. *Ruth's Chris Steak House Inc* 1569
RCSH Management, Inc. *Ruth's Chris Steak House Inc* 1569
RCSH Operations, Inc. *Ruth's Chris Steak House Inc* 1569
RCSH Operations, LLC *Ruth's Chris Steak House Inc* 1569
RCSH Promotions, LLC *Ruth's Chris Steak House Inc* 1569
RCTC *Resources Connection Inc* 1537
RCTC LLC *Resources Connection Inc* 1537
RCTC Wholesale Corporation *Alltel Corp* 69
RCW of Edmond, Inc. *Universal Health Services Inc* 1869
RD Abington Associates Limited Partnership *Acadia Realty Trust* 9
RD Absecon Associates, L.P. *Acadia Realty Trust* 9
RD Absecon, Inc. *Acadia Realty Trust* 9
RD Bloomfield Associates Limited Partnership *Acadia Realty Trust* 9
RD Branch Associates L.P. *Acadia Realty Trust* 9
RD Columbia Associates, L.P. *Acadia Realty Trust* 9
RD Elmwood Associates, L.P. *Acadia Realty Trust* 9
RD Hobson Associates, L.P. *Acadia Realty Trust* 9
RD Large Edition, Inc. *Reader's Digest Association Inc* 1517
RD Magazine Value Partners, Inc. *Reader's Digest Association Inc* 1517
RD Member Services Inc. *Reader's Digest Association Inc* 1517
RD Methuen Associates Limited Partnership *Acadia Realty Trust* 9
RD Publications Limited *Reader's Digest Association Inc* 1517
RD Publications, Inc. *Reader's Digest Association Inc* 1517
RD Recruit Limited *BB Holdings Ltd* 222
RD Smithtown, LLC *Acadia Realty Trust* 9
RD Technologies, Inc. *Remote Dynamics Inc* 1530
RD Trade Shows, Inc. *Reader's Digest Association Inc* 1517
RD Village Associates Limited Partnership *Acadia Realty Trust* 9
RD Walking, Inc. *Reader's Digest Association Inc* 1517
RD Whitegate Associates, L.P. *Acadia Realty Trust* 9
RD Woonsocket Associates Limited Partnership *Acadia Realty Trust* 9
RDEN Management, Inc. *Elizabeth Arden Inc* 617
RDG Resource Dealer Group (Canada) Inc. *Aon Corp* 129
RDI UbiComs Limited *Answerthink Inc* 127
RDK Investments Company *Ruddick Corp* 1566
Rdl Coal LLC *General Mills Inc* 772
RDP Royal Palm Hotel Ltd. *InterContinental Hotels Group* 962
RDS *Portfolio Recovery Assoc Inc* 1449
RDS Acquisition Corp. *REMEC Inc* 1529
RDS Detroit,Inc. *Rite Aid Corp* 1548
RDS Ricerca Dati Servize R.r.l. *Dun & Bradstreet Corp* 580
RDT2M *Plangraphics Inc Colorado* 1437
RE Components Inc. *Goodrich Corp* 810
RE Holdings, Inc. *South Financial Group Inc* 1663
RE Retail Receivables, LLC *Reliant Energy Inc* 1528
RE'LEM Public Benefit Company *Energizer Holdings Inc* 634
RE-AA *Allianz* 63
Re-cy-co, Inc. *Waste Management Inc* 1934
re:Member Data Services, Inc. *Open Solutions Inc* 1345
Re:Source Americas Enterprises, Inc. *Interface Inc* 963
Reach Media, Inc. *Radio One Inc* 1508
React-NTI LLC *Northern Technologies International Corp* 1302
Reactine S.r.l *Pfizer Inc* 1420
Reaction Force Guards (Pty) Ltd *Tyco International Ltd* 1838
Reaction Force Patrols (Pty) Ltd *Tyco International Ltd* 1838
Read-Poland Inc. *WPP Group Plc* 1979
Read-Rite International *Western Digital Corp* 1950
Read-Rite (Malaysia) Sdn. Bhd. *Western Digital Corp* 1950
Read-Rite Philippines, Inc. *Western Digital Corp* 1950
READS,Inc. *Rite Aid Corp* 1548
Reader's Digest Asia Pte. Ltd. *Reader's Digest Association Inc* 1517
Readers Digest Aktiebolag *Reader's Digest Association Inc* 1517
Readers Digest Argentina, SRL *Reader's Digest Association Inc* 1517
Readers Digest Asia, Ltd. *Reader's Digest Association Inc* 1517
Readers Digest Association Far East Limited *Reader's Digest Association Inc* 1517
Readers Digest (Australia) Pty. Ltd. *Reader's Digest Association Inc* 1517
Readers Digest Book and Home Entertainment (India) Private Limited *Reader's Digest Association Inc* 1517
Readers Digest Brasil Ltda. *Reader's Digest Association Inc* 1517
Readers Digest Central & Eastern Europe Limited *Reader's Digest Association Inc* 1517
Readers Digest Childrens Publishing Limited *Reader's Digest Association Inc* 1517
Readers Digest Childrens Publishing, Inc. *Reader's Digest Association Inc* 1517
Readers Digest (China) Direct Marketing Services Co., Ltd. *Reader's Digest Association Inc* 1517
Readers Digest Consumer Services, Inc. *Reader's Digest Association Inc* 1517
Readers Digest Deutschland Holding GmbH *Reader's Digest Association Inc* 1517
Readers Digest (East Asia) Limited *Reader's Digest Association Inc* 1517
Readers Digest Entertainment, Inc. *Reader's Digest Association Inc* 1517
Readers Digest EOOD *Reader's Digest Association Inc* 1517
Readers Digest Europe Limited *Reader's Digest Association Inc* 1517
Readers Digest European Shared Services B.V. *Reader's Digest Association Inc* 1517
Readers Digest European Systems *Reader's Digest Association Inc* 1517
Readers Digest Financial Services Limited *Reader's Digest Association Inc* 1517
Readers Digest Financial Services, Inc. *Reader's Digest Association Inc* 1517
Readers Digest Global Advertising Ltd. *Reader's Digest Association Inc* 1517
Readers Digest (Guangzhou) Direct Mail Service Co. Ltd. *Reader's Digest Association Inc* 1517
Readers Digest Hellas Publications Company Limited *Reader's Digest Association Inc* 1517
Readers Digest Holdings Limited *Reader's Digest Association Inc* 1517
Readers Digest Kiado KFT *Reader's Digest Association Inc* 1517
Readers Digest Magazine Limited *Reader's Digest Association Inc* 1517
Readers Digest (Malaysia) Sdn. Bhd *Reader's Digest Association Inc* 1517
Readers Digest Mexico, S.A. de C.V. *Reader's Digest Association Inc* 1517
Readers Digest N.V.-S.A. *Reader's Digest Association Inc* 1517
Readers Digest (Philippines) Inc. *Reader's Digest Association Inc* 1517
Readers Digest Przeglad Sp.z o.o. *Reader's Digest Association Inc* 1517
Readers Digest Sales and Services, Inc. *Reader's Digest Association Inc* 1517
Readers Digest Secilmis Yayincilik Dagitim Pazarlama Ticaret Limited Sirketi *Reader's Digest Association Inc* 1517
Readers Digest Selecciones S.A. *Reader's Digest Association Inc* 1517
Readers Digest Selected Publishing Distribution Trade Ltd Company *Reader's Digest Association Inc* 1517
Readers Digest Sub Eight, Inc. *Reader's Digest Association Inc* 1517
Readers Digest Sub Nine, Inc. *Reader's Digest Association Inc* 1517
Readers Digest (Thailand) Limited *Reader's Digest Association Inc* 1517
Readers Digest Vyber s.r.o. *Reader's Digest Association Inc* 1517
Readers Digest Vyber Slovensko, s.r.o. *Reader's Digest Association Inc* 1517
Readers Digest World Services, S.A. *Reader's Digest Association Inc* 1517
Readers Digest Young Families, Inc. *Reader's Digest Association Inc* 1517
Readibank Investment Corporation *Massbank Corp* 1129
Readibank Properties, Inc. *Massbank Corp* 1129
Reading & Bates Coal Co., LLC *Transocean Inc* 1817
Reading & Bates-Demaga Perfuracoes Ltda. *Transocean Inc* 1817
Reading Acquisitions Pty Ltd *Reading International Inc* 1518
Reading Ambulatory Surgery Center, L.P. *United Surgical Partners International Inc* 1863
Reading Arthouse Distribution Ltd *Reading International Inc* 1518
Reading Arthouse Ltd *Reading International Inc* 1518
Reading Capital Corporation *Reading International Inc* 1518
Reading Center Development Corporation *Reading International Inc* 1518
Reading Cinemas Courtenay Central Ltd *Reading International Inc* 1518
Reading Cinemas NJ, Inc. *Reading International Inc* 1518
Reading Cinemas of Puerto Rico, Inc. *Reading International Inc* 1518
Reading Cinemas Pty Ltd *Reading International Inc* 1518
Reading Cinemas Puerto Rico LLC *Reading International Inc* 1518
Reading Cinemas USA LLC *Reading International Inc* 1518
Reading Cinemas, Inc. *Reading International Inc* 1518
Reading Colac Pty Ltd *Reading International Inc* 1518
Reading Company *Reading International Inc* 1518
Reading Courtenay Central Ltd *Reading International Inc* 1518
Reading Elizabeth Pty Ltd *Reading International Inc* 1518
Reading Entertainment Australia Pty Ltd *Reading International Inc* 1518
Reading Exhibition Pty Ltd *Reading International Inc* 1518
Reading Festival Ltd. *CCE Spinco Inc* 349
Reading Holdings, Inc. *Reading International Inc* 1518
Reading International Cinemas LLC *Reading International Inc* 1518
Reading Investment Company, Inc. *Reading International Inc* 1518
Reading Licenses Pty Ltd *Reading International Inc* 1518
Reading Melton Pty Ltd *Reading International Inc* 1518
Reading New Zealand Ltd *Reading International Inc* 1518
Reading Pacific LLC *Reading International Inc* 1518
Reading Properties Pty Ltd *Reading International Inc* 1518
Reading Queenstown Ltd *Reading International Inc* 1518
Reading Real Estate Company *Reading International Inc* 1518
Reading Resources, Inc. *Reading International Inc* 1518
Reading Royal George, LLC *Reading International Inc* 1518
Reading Scientific Services Ltd *Cadbury Schweppes Plc* 302
Reading Sunbury Pty Ltd *Reading International Inc* 1518
Reading Theaters, Inc. *Reading International Inc* 1518
Reading Transportation Company *Reading International Inc* 1518
Reading Wellington Properties Ltd *Reading International Inc* 1518
Readington Investments, Inc. *Merck & Co Inc* 1162
Ready Mix Concrete Company of Knoxville *U.S. Concrete Inc* 1840
Ready Mix, Inc. *Meadow Valley Corp* 1144
Readymix Cement Pty Ltd *Rinker Group Ltd* 1546
Readymix Emoleum Services Pty Ltd *Rinker Group Ltd* 1546
Readymix Materials Holdings, LLC *Rinker Group Ltd* 1546
Readymix Properties Pty Ltd *Rinker Group Ltd* 1546
Readymix Roads Group Pty Ltd *Rinker Group Ltd* 1546
Readysquare Ltd *WPP Group Plc* 1979
Readysquaretwo Ltd *WPP Group Plc* 1979
Reagan Holdings, Inc. *Findex.com Inc* 693
Real Estate Advisory Services, Inc *Peoples Bancorp of North Carolina Inc* 1407
REAL ESTATE ASSOCIATES LIMITED *Apartment Investment and Management Company* 130
REAL ESTATE ASSOCIATES LIMITED II *Apartment Investment and Management Company* 130
REAL ESTATE ASSOCIATES LIMITED III *Apartment Investment and Management Company* 130
REAL ESTATE ASSOCIATES LIMITED IV *Apartment Investment and Management Company* 130
REAL ESTATE ASSOCIATES LIMITED V *Apartment Investment and Management Company* 130
REAL ESTATE ASSOCIATES LIMITED VI *Apartment Investment and Management Company* 130
Real Estate Business Headquarters *Orix Corp Ads* 1358
Real Estate Collateral Management Company *HSBC Finance Corp* 895
Real Estate Consultants of the South, Inc. *Wachovia Corp* 1928
Real Estate Delivery, Inc. *BancWest Corp* 207
Real Estate Development *Horizon Financial Corp* 890
Real Estate Development Co. Ltd. *Empire Global Corp* 625
REAL ESTATE EQUITY PARTNERS INC. *Apartment Investment and Management Company* 130
REAL ESTATE EQUITY PARTNERS, L.P. *Apartment Investment and Management Company* 130
Real Estate Finance Headquarters *Orix Corp Ads* 1358
Real Estate Financial *Wells Fargo & Co* 1944
Real Estate Holdings, Inc. *Autonation Inc FL* 183
Real Estate Index, Inc. *Fidelity National Financial Inc* 690
Real Estate Investment Trust *United Security Bank* 1862
Real Estate Investment Trust *SVB Financial Group* 1731
Real Estate Investments, Inc *Westfield Financial Inc* 1952
Real Estate Investors, LLC *CabelTel International Corp* 301
Real Estate Links, LLC *Midamerican Energy Holdings Co* 1184
Real Estate Private Equity Inc *Lehman Brothers Holdings Inc* 1067
Real Estate Referral Network, Inc. *Midamerican Energy Holdings Co* 1184
Real Estate Referral, Inc. *Realogy Corp* 1518
Real Estate Referrals, Inc. *Realogy Corp* 1518
Real Estate Russia Z.A.O. *Benetton Group SpA* 231

THE CORPORATE DIRECTORY - Walker's 2008 Subsidiary/Parent Index - 3283

Rolling Green Memorial Park Subsidiary LLC *StoneMor Partners LP* ... 1707
Rolling Hills Landfill Gas, LLC *Delmarva Power & Light Co* ... 538
Rolling Hills LFG, LLC *Duquesne Light Co* ... 581
Rolling Hills Memorial Park *Carriage Services Inc* ... 337
Rolling Hills Resources LLC *Uranerz Energy Corp* ... 1873
Rolling Meadows Landfill, Inc. *Waste Management Inc* ... 1934
Rollins Western Real Estate Holding LLC *Rollins Inc* ... 1557
Rollins Continental,Inc. *Rollins Inc* ... 1557
Rollins Expansion,Inc. *Rollins Inc* ... 1557
Rollins Heath Korea Co. Ltd. *Aon Corp* ... 129
Rollins Hudig Hall & Co. (N.S.W.) Pty. Ltd. *Aon Corp* ... 129
Rollins Hudig Hall Associates B.V. *Aon Corp* ... 129
Rollins Hudig Hall (Hong Kong) Ltd. *Aon Corp* ... 129
Rollins Hudig Hall (Nederland) Limited *Aon Corp* ... 129
Rollins Hudig Hall Services Limited *Aon Corp* ... 129
Rollins Hudig Hall Singapore Pte. Ltd. *Aon Corp* ... 129
Rollins Supply,Inc. *Rollins Inc* ... 1557
Rollway Bearing International Ltd. *Emerson Electric Co* ... 623
Rollway Bearing N.V. *Emerson Electric Co* ... 623
ROM Holdings Pty. Limited *Pitney Bowes Inc* ... 1434
ROM Securities Pty. Limited *Pitney Bowes Inc* ... 1434
Roma Bank *Roma Financial Corp* ... 1557
Roma Capital Investment Corporation *Roma Financial Corp* ... 1557
Roma Servizi Informatici S.p.A. *Electronic Data Systems Corp* ... 614
Romaco A.G. *Robbins & Myers Inc* ... 1551
Romaco Australia Pty Ltd. *Robbins & Myers Inc* ... 1551
Romaco Bosspak *Robbins & Myers Inc* ... 1551
Romaco do Brazil *Robbins & Myers Inc* ... 1551
Romaco Holdings U.K. Limited *Robbins & Myers Inc* ... 1551
Romaco Immobilienverwaltungs GmbH *Robbins & Myers Inc* ... 1551
Romaco Inc. *Robbins & Myers Inc* ... 1551
Romaco International B.V. *Robbins & Myers Inc* ... 1551
Romaco Limited *Robbins & Myers Inc* ... 1551
Romaco Machinery Limited *Robbins & Myers Inc* ... 1551
Romaco Machinery, S.A. *Robbins & Myers Inc* ... 1551
Romaco Pharmatechnik GmbH *Robbins & Myers Inc* ... 1551
Romaco S.A. *Robbins & Myers Inc* ... 1551
Romaco S.a.r.l. *Robbins & Myers Inc* ... 1551
Romaco S.r.l. *Robbins & Myers Inc* ... 1551
Romaco UK Limited *Robbins & Myers Inc* ... 1551
Roman Brandgroup LLC *WPP Group Plc* ... 1979
Roman Entertainment Corporation of Indiana *Harrah's Entertainment Inc* ... 848
Roman Entertainment Corporation of Texas *Harrah's Entertainment Inc* ... 848
Roman Financial Press (Holdings) Limited *R.R. Donnelley & Sons Co* ... 1506
Roman Holding Corporation of Indiana *Harrah's Entertainment Inc* ... 848
Roman Philadelphia Management,Inc. *Harrah's Entertainment Inc* ... 848
Romance Du Jour, Inc. *Kellwood Co* ... 1022
Romanian Branch *Marriott International Inc* ... 1125
Romanian Entity *Hungarian Telephone & Cable Corp* ... 899
Romano Rehabilitation Hospital, Inc. *HealthSouth Corp* ... 861
ROMANOS OF ANNAPOLIS, INC. *Brinker International Inc* ... 281
Romantica (East) Ltd. *Liberty Global Inc* ... 1074
Romax Uitlaatsysteme B.V. *Arvinmeritor Inc* ... 156
Rombo Compaia Financiera *Banco Bilbao Vizcaya Argentaria* ... 204
Rombo Compaa Financiera S.A. *BBVA Banco Frances* ... 223
Rome Bureau S.r.l. *New York Times Co* ... 1277
Rome Coca-Cola Bottling Company *Coca-Cola Enterprises Inc* ... 433
Rome Imaging Center Limited Partnership *HCA Inc* ... 855
Rome Rental Housing, L.P. *Wachovia Corp* ... 1928
Rome Research Corporation *Par Technology Corp* ... 1383
Romeo Shipping Company Limited *Tsakos Energy Navigation Ltd* ... 1832
Romet Corp. *Yum! Brands Inc* ... 1994
Romintco Investments B.V. *Barclays Plc* ... 216
Romix 1990 Trustee Limited *PepsiCo Inc* ... 1410
Romney Health Care Center Ltd., Limited Partnership *Genesis HealthCare Corp* ... 774
Romtec UK Limited *Harris Interactive Inc* ... 849
Ron Jon Surf Shop Sawgrass Mills, LLC *Mills Ltd Partnership* ... 1193
Ron Jon Surf Shop Southern California, LLC *Mills Ltd Partnership* ... 1193
Rons Electric, Inc., dba IES North Plains *Integrated Electrical Services Inc* ... 956
Ronald Luke and Associates, Inc. *BB&T Corp* ... 222
Ronald Marley Associates Limited *American Standard Companies Inc* ... 103
Ronco Marketing Corporation *Ronco Corp* ... 1558
Rondonia Power Company *El Paso Corp* ... 609
Rondout Iron & Metal Company, LLC *Metal Mgmt Inc* ... 1169
Rondout Iron & Metal Company, LLC, *Metal Management Inc* ... 1168
Ronevsorg Hotel Operating Company Limited *Marriott International Inc* ... 1125
Ronkas Inversiones, S.L. *Pepsi Bottling Group Inc* ... 1409
Ronnberg Mccann Ab *Interpublic Group of Companies Inc* ... 975
Ronseal (Ireland) Limited *Sherwin Williams Co* ... 1619
Ronseal Limited *Sherwin Williams Co* ... 1619
Ronson Aviation, Inc. *Ronson Corp* ... 1558
Ronson Consumer Products Corporation (RCPC) *Ronson Corp* ... 1558
Ronson Corporation of Canada Ltd. *Ronson Corp* ... 1558
Ronsonol lighter fluid *Ronson Corp* ... 1558
Rontarca Prima, Willis, C.A. *Willis Group Holdings Ltd* ... 1962
Rontarca-Prima Consultores C.A. *Willis Group Holdings Ltd* ... 1962
Rontext 1617 Corp *Franklin Credit Mgmt Corp* ... 744
Ronwood Investments Ltd *Reading International Inc* ... 1518
ROO Broadcasting Limited *ROO Group Inc* ... 1558
ROO Media (Australia) Pty Ltd. *ROO Group Inc* ... 1558
ROO Media Corporation *ROO Group Inc* ... 1558
ROO TV Pty Ltd. *ROO Group Inc* ... 1558
Rood Nominees Ltd *Allianz* ... 63
Rooihoogte Suid Farm (Pty) Ltd. *Fresh Del Monte Produce Inc* ... 749
RoomFinders, Inc. *Expedia Inc* ... 670
Roomijsfabriek de Hoop B.v. *Interpublic Group of Companies Inc* ... 975
Rooney Life Insurance Company *Unitedhealth Group Inc* ... 1864
Roosevelt Associates *Allied Waste Industries Inc* ... 66
Roosevelt Associates, L.P. *Pennsylvania Real Estate Investment Trust* ... 1405
Roosevelt Equity Corporation *UTG Inc* ... 1881
Roosevelt Family Care, LLC *HCA Inc* ... 855
ROOSEVELT GARDENS APARTMENTS II LIMITED PARTNERSHIP *Apartment Investment and Management Company* ... 130
ROOSEVELT GARDENS LIMITED PARTNERSHIP *Apartment Investment and Management Company* ... 130
Roosevelt II Associates, L.P. *Pennsylvania Real Estate Investment Trust* ... 1405
Roosevelt Landfill Gas Recovery, LLC *Duquesne Light Co* ... 581
Ropak, Inc. *Roundys Supermarkets Inc* ... 1560
Ropeco Pty Ltd. *Aon Corp* ... 129
Ropepath Limited *Willis Group Holdings Ltd* ... 1962
Roper Canada Holdings, Inc. *Roper Industries Inc* ... 1558
Roper Canada Partners Inc. *Roper Industries Inc* ... 1558
Roper Capital Deutschland GmbH *Roper Industries Inc* ... 1558
Roper Engineering s.r.o *Roper Industries Inc* ... 1558
Roper Fundings KG *Roper Industries Inc* ... 1558
Roper Georgia, Inc. *Roper Industries Inc* ... 1558
Roper Holdings, Inc. *Roper Industries Inc* ... 1558
Roper Holdings, Limited *Roper Industries Inc* ... 1558
Roper Industrial Products Investment Company *Roper Industries Inc* ... 1558
Roper Industries B.V *Roper Industries Inc* ... 1558
Roper Industries Denmark ApS *Roper Industries Inc* ... 1558
Roper Industries Deutschland GmbH *Roper Industries Inc* ... 1558
Roper Industries (Europe) Limited *Roper Industries Inc* ... 1558
Roper Industries Limited *Roper Industries Inc* ... 1558
Roper Industries Manufacturing (Shanghai) Co. Ltd. *Roper Industries Inc* ... 1558
Roper International Products, LTD *Roper Industries Inc* ... 1558
Roper Luxenbourg S.a.r.l *Roper Industries Inc* ... 1558
Roper Marketing India Private Ltd. *Roper Industries Inc* ... 1558
Roper Mex, L.P. *Roper Industries Inc* ... 1558
Roper OOO *Roper Industries Inc* ... 1558
Roper Pump Company *Roper Industries Inc* ... 1558
Roper Pump Europe GmbH *Roper Industries Inc* ... 1558
Roper Scientific B.V *Roper Industries Inc* ... 1558
Roper Scientific GmbH *Roper Industries Inc* ... 1558
Roper Scientific SARL *Roper Industries Inc* ... 1558
Roper Scientific SAS *Roper Industries Inc* ... 1558
Roper Scientific, Inc. *Roper Industries Inc* ... 1558
Roper Southeast Asia LLC *Roper Industries Inc* ... 1558
RoperASW LLC *United Business Media Plc* ... 1857
Ropintassco 1, LLC *Roper Industries Inc* ... 1558
Ropintassco 2, LLC *Roper Industries Inc* ... 1558
Ropintassco 3, LLC *Roper Industries Inc* ... 1558
Ropintassco 4, LLC *Roper Industries Inc* ... 1558
Ropintassco 5, LLC *Roper Industries Inc* ... 1558
Ropintassco 6, LLC *Roper Industries Inc* ... 1558
Ropintassco 7, LLC *Roper Industries Inc* ... 1558
Ropintassco Holdings, L.P. *Roper Industries Inc* ... 1558
Rorke Data Italy s.r.l. *Bell Microproducts Inc* ... 229
Rorke Data, Inc. *Bell Microproducts Inc* ... 229
RRTNGEN 10 HB *Stena AB* ... 1700
ROS Mojave Desert, LLC *Wachovia Corp* ... 1928
Rosado Propane *Inergy Holdings LP* ... 936
Rosado Propane *Inergy LP* ... 936
Rosalyn Tanker Corporation *Overseas Shipholding Group Inc* ... 1365
Rosaria Grundst.-Vermietungs GmbH& Co (Ettlingen) *Stora Enso Oyj* ... 1708
Rosaria Grundst.-Vermietungs GmbH& Co (Heimstetten) *Stora Enso Oyj* ... 1708
Rosaria Grundst.-Vermietungs GmbH& Co (Saarbrucken) *Stora Enso Oyj* ... 1708
RosCaseMash *CNH Global* ... 429
Rose Ambulatory Surgery Center, L.P. *HCA Inc* ... 855
Rose Bay Trading Pty Limited *Citigroup Inc* ... 411
Rose City HMA, Inc. *Health Management Associates Inc* ... 858
Rose City Press *Champion Industries Inc* ... 371
Rose Corporation *Brunswick Corp* ... 289
Rose Harbor Limited Partnership *Wachovia Corp* ... 1928
Rose Haven Funeral Home & Cemetery, Inc. *Stewart Enterprises Inc* ... 1704
Rose Health Partners, LLC *HCA Inc* ... 855
Rose Healthcare, Inc. *Genesis HealthCare Corp* ... 774
Rose Hill Associates, LLC *Post Properties Inc* ... 1451
Rose Hill Burial Park, a Trust *Service Corp International* ... 1614
Rose Hill Securities Company *Service Corp International* ... 1614
Rose Lawn Cemeteries LLC *StoneMor Partners LP* ... 1707
Rose Lawn Cemeteries Subsidiary, Incorporated *StoneMor Partners LP* ... 1707
Rose Medical Plaza, Ltd. *HCA Inc* ... 855
Rose Merge Sub, Inc. *Charming Shoppes Inc* ... 375
Rose POB, Inc. *HCA Inc* ... 855
Rose View Manor, Inc. *Genesis HealthCare Corp* ... 774
Rosea Grundst.-Vermietungs GmbH& Co (Genshagen) *Stora Enso Oyj* ... 1708
Rosebank Meadows Subdivision, LLC *Bank of America Corp* ... 208
Rosebel Gold Mines N.V *Cambior Inc* ... 313
Rosebel Mine *Cambior Inc* ... 313
Rosebloom Associates LP *Edison International* ... 604
Rosecrans Holdings, LLC *Autonation Inc FL* ... 183
Rosecrans Investments, LLC *Autonation Inc FL* ... 183
Rosecreek Senior Living LP *Edison International* ... 604
Rosedale Cemetery Company *Service Corp International* ... 1614
Rosedale Corporate Plaza Condominium, Inc. *HRPT Properties Trust* ... 894
Rosedale Funeral Chapel, Inc. *Service Corp International* ... 1614
Rosedale General Partner, LLC *Bank of America Corp* ... 208
Rosedale II, LLC *Wachovia Corp* ... 1928
Rosedale Properties Limited Liability Company *HRPT Properties Trust* ... 894
Rosedale Properties Trust *HRPT Properties Trust* ... 894
Rosedale Properties, Inc. *HRPT Properties Trust* ... 894
Rosedale Terrace Limited Partnership *Bank of America Corp* ... 208
Rosedale Wallcoverings & Fabrics Inc. *Rosedale Decorative Products Ltd* ... 1559
Rosedale Wilsons, Inc. *Wilsons The Leather Experts Inc* ... 1965
Rosefield Finance Ltd. *Unibanco Holdings* ... 1848
Rosehill West Associates Limited Partnership *Wachovia Corp* ... 1928
Roselat Developments Limited *Laboratory Corp of America Holdings* ... 1048
Roselawn Development LLC *StoneMor Partners LP* ... 1707
Roselawn Development Subsidiary Corporation *StoneMor Partners LP* ... 1707
Roselectrocenter *Wimm-Bill-Dann Foods OJSC* ... 1965
Roselle Park VP, LLC *AvalonBay Communities Inc* ... 184
Rosemar Limited *Overseas Shipholding Group Inc* ... 1365
Rosemary Beach Cottage Rental Company *Leucadia National Corp* ... 1068
Rosemary Beach Land Company *Leucadia National Corp* ... 1068
Rosemary Beach Realty, Inc. *Leucadia National Corp* ... 1068
Rosemont Consulting, Inc. *CCE Spinco Inc* ... 349
Rosemont Manor Ltd. *Wachovia Corp* ... 1928
Rosemont Pharmaceuticals Limited *Savient Pharmaceuticals Inc* ... 1587
Rosemount Aerospace GmbH *Goodrich Corp* ... 810
Rosemount Aerospace Inc. *Goodrich Corp* ... 810
Rosemount Aerospace Limited *Goodrich Corp* ... 810
Rosemount Aerospace Properties Limited *Goodrich Corp* ... 810
Rosemount Aerospace S.A.R.L. *Goodrich Corp* ... 810
Rosemount Analytical Inc. *Emerson Electric Co* ... 623
Rosemount China Inc. *Emerson Electric Co* ... 623
Rosemount Corporation *Procter & Gamble* ... 1472
Rosemount Inc. *Emerson Electric Co* ... 623
Rosemount Nuclear Instruments, Inc. *Emerson Electric Co* ... 623
Rosenberg, Ltd. *Weingarten Realty Investors* ... 1943
Rosenblatt-klauber Group Canada Inc. *IMS Health Inc* ... 931
Rosenblatt-klauber Group, Inc. *IMS Health Inc* ... 931
Rosenbloom Group Inc. *Smurfit Stone Container Corp* ... 1650
Rosenbluth France Holdings, S.A.R.l. *American Express Co* ... 91
Rosenbluth Germany GMBH *American Express Co* ... 91
Rosenbluth Holding Company *American Express Co* ... 91
Rosenbluth International B.V. *American Express Co* ... 91
Rosenbluth International France, S.A.R.I. *American Express Co* ... 91
Rosenbluth International GMBH *American Express Co* ... 91
Rosenbluth International Hong Kong Ltd. *American Express Co* ... 91
Rosenbluth International Ireland Limited *American Express Co* ... 91
Rosenbluth International (Israel) Ltd. *American Express Co* ... 91
Rosenbluth International Limited *American Express Co* ... 91
Rosenbluth International Mexico *American Express Co* ... 91
Rosenbluth International Netherlands B.V. *American Express Co* ... 91
Rosenbluth International Reisebur GMBH Austria *American Express Co* ... 91
Rosenbluth International (Russia) Ltd. *American Express Co* ... 91
Rosenbluth International Travel, Ltd. *American Express Co* ... 91
Rosenbluth International U.K. Limited *American Express Co* ... 91
Rosenheim Automation Systems Corporation *Dover Corp* ... 572
Rosenthal AG *Waterford Wedgwood Plc* ... 1936
Roseridge Development, LLC *Lennar Corp* ... 1068
Rosetta Genomics Inc. *Rosetta Genomics Ltd* ... 1559
Rosetta Inpharmatics LLC *Merck & Co Inc* ... 1162
Rosetta Resources Holdings, LLC *Rosetta Resources Inc* ... 1559
Rosetta Resources Offshore, LLC *Rosetta Resources Inc* ... 1559
Rosetta Resources Operating GP, LLC *Rosetta Resources Inc* ... 1559
Rosetta Resources Operating LP *Rosetta Resources Inc* ... 1559
Rosetta Shipping LLC *Omi Corp Marshall Islands* ... 1337
Roseville Motor Corporation *Autonation Inc FL* ... 183
Roseville Schools, LLC *Lennar Corp* ... 1068
Roseville Surgery Center, L.P. *United Surgical Partners International Inc* ... 1863
ROSEWOOD APARTMENTS CORPORATION *Apartment Investment and Management Company* ... 130
Rosewood Indemnity, Ltd. *Simon Property Group Inc* ... 1634
Rosewood Medical Center, Inc. *HCA Inc* ... 855
Rosewood Professional Building, Ltd. *HCA Inc* ... 855
Roshco, Inc *Lifetime Brands Inc* ... 1076
Rosignano Energia Spa *Suez* ... 1715
Roslyn National Mortgage Corp. *New York Community Bancorp Inc* ... 1276
Roslyn Real Estate Asset Corp. *New York Community Bancorp Inc* ... 1276
Ross Bros. Waste & Recycling Co. *Allied Waste Industries Inc* ... 66
Ross Chemical& Storage Company Limited *Valero LP* ... 1884
Ross Chemical& Storage Company Limited *NuStar GP Holdings LLC* ... 1316
Ross Screw Ltd. *Anixter International Inc* ... 125
Ross Shipping Co., Inc. *CIT Group Inc* ... 410
Ross Systems, Inc. *CDC Corp* ... 351
Ross University Management, Inc.(6), a St. Lucia Corporation *DeVry Inc* ... 547
Ross University School of Medicine(7), a Dominica Corporation *DeVry Inc* ... 547
Ross University School of Veterinary Medicine(7), a St.KittsCorporation *DeVry Inc* ... 547
Ross University Services, Inc. *DeVry Inc* ... 547
Rossal *Telkom Sa Ltd* ... 1770
Rossal No 103 (Pty) Ltd *Goodyear Tire & Rubber Com (The)* ... 811
Rossal No 65 (Pty) Limited *Telkom Sa Ltd* ... 1770
Rosserv LLC *News Corp Ltd (The)* ... 1281
Rossford Development LLC *Ramco-Gershenson Properties Trust* ... 1512
Rossignol Lange SRL *Quiksilver Inc* ... 1503
Rossignol Osterreich GMBH *Quiksilver Inc* ... 1503
Rossignol SCI SRL *Quiksilver Inc* ... 1503
Rossignol Ski AG *Quiksilver Inc* ... 1503
Rossignol Ski Company, Inc. *Quiksilver Inc* ... 1503
Rossignol Ski Deutschland GMBH *Quiksilver Inc* ... 1503
Rossignol Ski Poles SRL *Quiksilver Inc* ... 1503
Rossman Sanitary Service, Inc. *Allied Waste Industries Inc* ... 66
Rossmar& Graham Community Association Management,Inc. *FirstService Corp* ... 721
Rost Inc. *Veridien Corp* ... 1895
Rost Medical Development, Inc. *Veridien Corp* ... 1895
Rostel Industries Ltd. *Precision Drilling Trust* ... 1459
Rosti (UK) Ltd. *In Veritas Medical Diagnostics Inc* ... 932
Rostov Cellular Communications *Tele2 AB* ... 1764
Rostov Grain Terminal LLC *Bunge Ltd* ... 295
Rostron Hancock Ltd. *Aon Corp* ... 129
Roswell Center for Foot and Ankle Surgery, LLC *Sanmina Sci Corp* ... 1582
Roswell Center for Foot and Ankle Surgery, LLC *Symbion Inc* ... 1735
Roswell Clinic Corp. *Community Health Systems Inc* ... 454
Roswell Community Hospital Investment Corporation *Community Health Systems Inc* ... 454
Roswell Corners Holdings LLC *Weingarten Realty Investors* ... 1943
Roswell Home Medical, Inc. *Rotech Healthcare Inc NEW* ... 1560
Roswell Hospital Corporation *Community Health Systems Inc* ... 454
Roswell Insurance & Surety Agency, Inc. *Brown & Brown Inc* ... 288
Roswell Medical Ventures,Inc. *Tenet Healthcare Corp* ... 1774
Roswell Surgery Center, LLC *United Surgical Partners International Inc* ... 1863
Roswell Therapy Services, LLC *Brookdale Senior Living Inc* ... 285
Roszel Advisors, LLC *Merrill Lynch & Co Inc* ... 1165
Rotac, Inc. *Lone Star Technologies Inc* ... 1093
Rotam Boxmore Packaging Company Limited *Chesapeake Corp* ... 382
Rotary Engine Technologies, Inc. *Encompass Holdings Inc* ... 629
Rotational Molding, Inc. *Rotonics Manufacturing Inc* ... 1560
Rotator AS *Oceaneering International Inc* ... 1327
Rotec Czech s.r.o. *Day International Group Inc* ... 530
Rotec Hulsensysteme GmbH & Co. KG *Day International Group Inc* ... 530
Rotec Verwaltungs GmbH *Day International Group Inc* ... 530
Rotech Employee Benefits Corporation *Rotech Healthcare Inc NEW* ... 1560
Rotech Home Medical Care, Inc. *Rotech Healthcare Inc NEW* ... 1560
Rotech Oxygen and Medical Equipment, Inc. *Rotech Healthcare Inc NEW* ... 1560
Rotenberg & Co. LLP *Corning Natural Gas Corp* ... 483
Roth Medical, Inc. *Rotech Healthcare Inc NEW* ... 1560

SafeNet Canada, Inc. *Safenet Inc* 1573
SafeNet China Ltd. *Safenet Inc* 1573
SafeNet Consultancy Limited *Safenet Inc* 1573
SafeNet France SARL *Safenet Inc* 1573
SafeNet Information Technologies Pvt. Ltd. *Safenet Inc* 1573
SafeNet Japan KK *Safenet Inc* 1573
SafeNet Pte. Ltd. *Safenet Inc* 1573
SafeNet Systems Pvt. Ltd. *Safenet Inc* 1573
SafeNet Technologies B.V. *Safenet Inc* 1573
SafeNet UK Limited *Safenet Inc* 1573
Safequest, LLC *BOC Group Plc* 262
SAFErealestate, Inc. *First American Corp* 695
SafeScience Products, Inc. *GlycoGenesys Inc* 801
Safeskin (B.V.I.) Limited *Kimberly Clark Corp* 1029
Safeskin Corporation (Malaysia) Sdn. Bhd. *Kimberly Clark Corp* 1029
Safeskin Corporation (Thailand) Limited *Kimberly Clark Corp* 1029
Safeskin Industries (Thailand) Limited *Kimberly Clark Corp* 1029
Safeskin Latex (Thailand) Limited *Kimberly Clark Corp* 1029
Safeskin Medical& Scientific (Thailand) Limited *Kimberly Clark Corp* 1029
SafeSpending Inc. *Sungold International Holdings Corp* 1721
Safety First Insurance Company *Delphi Financial Group Inc* 538
Safety Gas (Pty) Limited *BOC Group Plc* 262
Safety Harbor Physical Therapy *U.S. Physical Therapy Inc* 1841
Safety Indemnity Insurance Company *Safety Insurance Group Inc* 1574
Safety Insurance Company *Safety Insurance Group Inc* 1574
Safety National Casualty Corporation *Delphi Financial Group Inc* 538
Safety National Re SPC *Delphi Financial Group Inc* 538
Safety Scan Technology, Inc *HydroFlo Inc* 903
Safety Shop Co. U.K. Limited *Brady Corp* 273
Safety Shop Limited *Brady Corp* 273
Safety Syringe Corporation *Specialized Health Products Intl Inc* 1676
Safety Systems UK Limited *Tyco International Ltd* 1838
Safety Tech International, Inc. *TVI Corp* 1836
Safety, Claims & Litigation Services, Inc. *National Interstate Corp* 1243
Safety, Claims & Litigation Services, LLC. *National Interstate Corp* 1243
Safetylogic.com, Inc. *Aon Corp* 129
Safeway Australia Holdings, Inc. *Safeway Stores* 1574
Safeway Canada Holdings, Inc. *Safeway Stores* 1574
Safeway Claim Services, Inc. *Safeway Stores* 1574
Safeway Corporate, Inc. *Safeway Stores* 1574
Safeway Dallas, Inc. *Safeway Stores* 1574
Safeway Denver, Inc. *Safeway Stores* 1574
Safeway Foreign Sales Limited *Safeway Stores* 1574
Safeway Holdings I, Inc. *Safeway Stores* 1574
Safeway Intl Finance Corp. of Canada Ltd. *Safeway Stores* 1574
Safeway Leasing, Inc. *Safeway Stores* 1574
Safeway Liquor Stores, Inc. *Safeway Stores* 1574
Safeway New Canada, Inc. *Safeway Stores* 1574
Safeway of Western Nebraska, Inc. *Safeway Stores* 1574
Safeway Ontario Finance Corporation *Safeway Stores* 1574
Safeway Philtech Holdings, Inc. *Safeway Stores* 1574
Safeway Philtech Inc. *Safeway Stores* 1574
Safeway Products Inc. *Goodrich Corp* 810
Safeway Richmond, Inc. *Safeway Stores* 1574
Safeway Select Gift Source, Inc. *Safeway Stores* 1574
Safeway Southern California, Inc. *Safeway Stores* 1574
Safeway Stores 18, Inc. *Safeway Stores* 1574
Safeway Stores 26, Inc. *Safeway Stores* 1574
Safeway Stores 28, Inc. *Safeway Stores* 1574
Saffeway Stores 31, Inc. *Safeway Stores* 1574
Safeway Stores 42, Inc. *Safeway Stores* 1574
Safeway Stores 43, Inc. *Safeway Stores* 1574
Safeway Stores 44, Inc. *Safeway Stores* 1574
Safeway Stores 45, Inc. *Safeway Stores* 1574
Safeway Stores 46, Inc. *Safeway Stores* 1574
Safeway Stores 47, Inc. *Safeway Stores* 1574
Safeway Stores 48, Inc. *Safeway Stores* 1574
Safeway Stores 49, Inc. *Safeway Stores* 1574
Safeway Stores 50, Inc. *Safeway Stores* 1574
Safeway Stores 58, Inc. *Safeway Stores* 1574
Safeway Stores 59, Inc. *Safeway Stores* 1574
Safeway Stores 64, Inc. *Safeway Stores* 1574
Safeway Stores 67, Inc. *Safeway Stores* 1574
Safeway Stores 68, Inc. *Safeway Stores* 1574
Safeway Stores 69, Inc. *Safeway Stores* 1574
Safeway Stores 70, Inc. *Safeway Stores* 1574
Safeway Stores 71, Inc. *Safeway Stores* 1574
Safeway Stores 72, Inc. *Safeway Stores* 1574
Safeway Stores 73, Inc. *Safeway Stores* 1574
Safeway Stores 74, Inc. *Safeway Stores* 1574
Safeway Stores 75, Inc. *Safeway Stores* 1574
Safeway Stores 76, Inc. *Safeway Stores* 1574
Safeway Stores 77, Inc. *Safeway Stores* 1574
Safeway Stores 78, Inc. *Safeway Stores* 1574
Safeway Stores 79, Inc. *Safeway Stores* 1574
Safeway Stores 80, Inc. *Safeway Stores* 1574
Safeway Stores 82, Inc. *Safeway Stores* 1574
Safeway Stores 85, Inc. *Safeway Stores* 1574
Safeway Stores 86, Inc. *Safeway Stores* 1574
Safeway Stores 87, Inc. *Safeway Stores* 1574
Safeway Stores 88, Inc. *Safeway Stores* 1574
Safeway Stores 89, Inc. *Safeway Stores* 1574
Safeway Stores 90, Inc. *Safeway Stores* 1574
Safeway Stores 91, Inc. *Safeway Stores* 1574
Safeway Stores 92, Inc. *Safeway Stores* 1574
Safeway Stores 96, Inc. *Safeway Stores* 1574
Safeway Stores 97, Inc. *Safeway Stores* 1574
Safeway Stores 98, Inc. *Safeway Stores* 1574
Safeway Stores 99, Inc. *Safeway Stores* 1574
Safeway Stores, Incorporated *Safeway Stores* 1574
Safeway Supply, Inc. *Safeway Stores* 1574
Safeway Trucking, Inc. *Safeway Stores* 1574
Saffire Alarm Systems Limited *Tyco International Ltd* 1838
Saffire Extinguishers Limited *Tyco International Ltd* 1838
Saffron Acquisition Corporation *BPC Holding Corp* 272
Safir Publicite *Clear Channel Communications Inc* 421
Safir Publicite SAS *Clear Channel Outdoor Holdings Inc* 422
Safire Private Ltd. *ACE Ltd* 13
Saflink Corporation *Wave Systems Corp* 1938
Safti-Cell, Inc. *Cryo-Cell International* 506
Safway Services, Inc *Dayton Superior Corp* 531
SAG Software Private Limited *Washington Post Co* 1933
Saga Air, LLC *Saga Communications Inc* 1574
Saga Broadcasting, LLC *Saga Communications Inc* 1574
Saga Communications of Arkansas, LLC *Saga Communications Inc* 1574
Saga Communications of Charlottesville, LLC *Saga Communications Inc* 1574
Saga Communications of Illinois, LLC *Saga Communications Inc* 1574
Saga Communications of Iowa, LLC *Saga Communications Inc* 1574
Saga Communications of Michigan, LLC *Saga Communications Inc* 1574
Saga Communications of Milwaukee, LLC *Saga Communications Inc* 1574
Saga Communications of New England, LLC *Saga Communications Inc* 1574
Saga Communications of New Hampshire, LLC *Saga Communications Inc* 1574
Saga Communications of North Carolina, LLC *Saga Communications Inc* 1574
Saga Communications of South Dakota, LLC *Saga Communications Inc* 1574
Saga Communications of Tuckessee, LLC *Saga Communications Inc* 1574
Saga Quad States Communications, LLC *Saga Communications Inc* 1574
Sagami I.G.S. Ltd *BOC Group Plc* 262
Sagamiko Picnic-land Co., Ltd. *Mitsui & Co Ltd* 1201
Sagamore Insurance Company *Baldwin & Lyons Inc* 201
Sagamore Shipping Corp. *B+H Ocean Carriers Ltd* 198
Sagamore Street Associates, L.P. *Wachovia Corp* 1928
Sagane, S.A. *Repsol YPF* 1533
SagaX Inc. *MIV Therapeutics Inc* 1201
Sage Creek Coal Ltd *BHP Billiton Plc* 237
Sage Creek Coal Ltd *BHP Billiton Ltd* 237
Sage Partners, LLC *Lehman Brothers Holdings Inc* 1067
Sage Realty, LLC *Tarragon Corp* 1751
Sage Residential Services, Inc. *Tarragon Corp* 1751
SAGE SARL *Allianz* 63
Sage, Inc. *Genesis Microchip Inc* 774
Sagebrush Asset Management, Inc. *Wells Fargo & Co* 1944
Sagebrush Holdings Inc. *First Data Corp* 703
SAGEFI Socit Antillaise de Gestion Financire, SA *Espirito Santo Financial Group* 658
Sagent Inc. (Taiwan) *Pitney Bowes Inc* 1434
Sagent (Indonesia) Pte Ltd. *Pitney Bowes Inc* 1434
Sagent (Malaysia) Sdn Bhd *Pitney Bowes Inc* 1434
Sagent (Singapore) Pte Ltd. *Pitney Bowes Inc* 1434
Sagent UK, Ltd. *Pitney Bowes Inc* 1434
Sagetown Holdings Inc. *First Data Corp* 703
Sageville Holdings LLC *First Data Corp* 703
Sagia Productions Inc. *Viacom Inc* 1902
Sagia Productions Inc. *CBS Corp* 349
Saginaw Bay Cellular Company *Alltel Corp* 69
Saginaw Hospitality, LP *Lodgian Inc* 1091
Saginaw Valley Sport and Spine *U.S. Physical Therapy Inc* 1841
SAGINAW VILLAGE LIMITED PARTNERSHIP *Apartment Investment and Management Company* 130
Sagis Investments Limited *BB Holdings Ltd* 222
SAGO Grnstucks-Verwaltungsgesellschaft mbH *CAE Inc* 304
SAGO Grnstucks-Verwaltungsgesellschaft mbH & Co. KG *CAE Inc* 304
Sagres Discovery, Inc. *Chiron Corp* 401
SagresSociedade de Titularizacao de Creditos, S.A. *Citigroup Inc* 411
Sagrocry, Inc. *Publicard Inc* 1487
Saguaro Asset Management, Inc. *Wells Fargo & Co* 1944
Saguaro Electronica, S.a. De C.v. *Telex Communications Inc* 1769
Saguaro National Captive Insurance Company *Allied Waste Industries Inc* 66
Saguaro Power Company, a Limited Partnership *NRG Energy Inc* 1312
Saguaro Power LLC *NRG Energy Inc* 1312
Sah Limited *Interpublic Group of Companies Inc* 975
SAH, Inc. *Penson Worldwide Inc* 1405
SAHAC Corp. *Archon Corp* 144
Sahara Petroleum Exploration Corp *Global Environmental Energy Corp* 793
Sahara Imports, Inc. *Autonation Inc FL* 183
Sahara Las Vegas Corp *Archon Corp* 144
Sahara Las Vegas Corp. *Archon Corp* 144
Sahara LLC *Big Lots Inc* 238
Sahara Nevada Corp. *Archon Corp* 144
Sahara Nissan, Inc. *Autonation Inc FL* 183
Sahara Outpatient Surgery Center, Ltd. *HCA Inc* 855
Sahara Resorts *Archon Corp* 144
Sahelconsult Sarl, Ouagadougou *Arcadis* 142
SAHF FUNDING CORP. *Apartment Investment and Management Company* 130
SAHF II LIMITED PARTNERSHIP *Apartment Investment and Management Company* 130
Sahlman Holdings, Inc. *Katy Industries Inc* 1019
SAHP130 Holdings, Inc. *J.P. Morgan Chase & Company* 999
SAI Holdings, Inc. *Penson Worldwide Inc* 1405
SAI Productions Ltd. *News Corp Ltd (The)* 1281
Saia Motor Freight Line, Inc *SAIA Inc* 1575
Saia Title Company, Inc. *First American Corp* 695
Saian Microsystems, Inc. *Hifn Inc* 876
Saibos Akogep SNC *Technip* 1758
SAIC (Bermuda) Ltd. *Science Applications International Corp* 1593
SAIC Engineering of North Carolina, Inc. *Science Applications International Corp* 1593
SAIC Engineering of Ohio, Inc. *Science Applications International Corp* 1593
SAIC Engineering, Inc. *Science Applications International Corp* 1593
SAIC Europe Limited *Science Applications International Corp* 1593
SAIC Global Technology Corporation *Science Applications International Corp* 1593
SAIC Japan Ltd. *Science Applications International Corp* 1593
SAIC Limited *Science Applications International Corp* 1593
SAIC Merger Sub, Inc. *Science Applications International Corp* 1593
SAIC No.2 Pty Limited *Science Applications International Corp* 1593
SAIC Pty Limited *Science Applications International Corp* 1593
SAIC Services, Inc. *Science Applications International Corp* 1593
SAIC Venture Capital Corporation *Science Applications International Corp* 1593
SAIC, Inc. *Science Applications International Corp* 1593
SAIC-Frederick, Inc. *Science Applications International Corp* 1593
Saifun (BVI) Limited *Saifun Semiconductors Ltd* 1576
Saifun Semiconductors USA, Inc. *Saifun Semiconductors Ltd* 1576
Saifun Ventures Ltd *Saifun Semiconductors Ltd* 1576
Sail2save Bv *Stena AB* 1700
Sailfish Pipeline Company, L.L.C. *Enterprise GP Holdings LP* 643
Sailfish Pipeline Company, L.L.C. *Enterprise Products Partners LP* 643
Sailgold Limited *Willis Group Holdings Ltd* 1962
Sailview Properties, LLC *Duke Energy Corp* 580
SAIM, LLC *Delta Apparel Inc* 539
Saime SAS *Resmed Inc* 1536
Saint Barnabas / HealthSouth Rehab Center LLC *HealthSouth Corp* 861
Saint Fons *Ciba Specialty Chemicals Holding Inc* 404
Saint Francis Surgery Center, LLC *Tenet Healthcare Corp* 1774
Saint Jean Composants Moteurs S.A.S. *TRW Automotive* 1831
SAINT LOUIS GALLERIA ANCHOR ACQUISITION, LLC *General Growth Properties Inc* 771
SAINT LOUIS GALLERIA HOLDING L.L.C. *General Growth Properties Inc* 771
SAINT LOUIS GALLERIA L.L.C. *General Growth Properties Inc* 771
SAINT LOUIS LAND L.L.C. *General Growth Properties Inc* 771
Saint Lukes Pathology Associates, P.A. *Ameripath Inc* 109
Saint Thomas Campus Surgicare, L.P. *United Surgical Partners International Inc* 1863
Saint Thomas/USP Baptist Plaza, LLC *United Surgical Partners International Inc* 1863
Saint Thomas/USP Surgery Centers II, LLC *United Surgical Partners International Inc* 1863
Saint Thomas/USP Surgery Centers, LLC *United Surgical Partners International Inc* 1863
Saint Vincent Healthcare System,Inc. *Tenet Healthcare Corp* 1774
Saint Vincent Hospital, Inc *Tenet Healthcare Corp* 1774
Saint Vincent Hospital, LLC *Tenet Healthcare Corp* 1774
Saint-Barth Assurances S.A.R.L. *Allianz* 63
Saint-Girons Industries S.N.C. *Schweitzer Mauduit International Inc* 1592
Saipem SA *Eni SpA* 639
Saipem SpA *Eni SpA* 639
Saipol S.A.S. *Bunge Ltd* 295
Saitec S.A. *Distribution & Service D&S* 562
Saiwan Industries Limited *Highway Holdings Ltd* 877
Sakata Rice Snacks Australia Proprietary Limited *PepsiCo Inc* 1410
SAKDC-DaVita Dialysis Partners, L.P. *Davita Inc* 530
Sakertrax, Inc. *Tyco International Ltd* 1838
Sakhalin Bristow Air Services Limited *Bristow Group Inc* 282
Sakhalin Holding, LLC *Tidewater Inc* 1792
Sakhalin Offshore Marine, LLC *Tidewater Inc* 1792
Sako Kiinteistt Oy *Metso Corp* 1173
Sakonnet Shipping Ltd. *B+H Ocean Carriers Ltd* 198
Saks Direct, Inc. *Saks Inc* 1576
Saks Fifth Avenue Distribution Company *Saks Inc* 1576
Saks Fifth Avenue Food Corporation *Saks Inc* 1576
Saks Fifth Avenue of Texas, Inc. *Saks Inc* 1576
Saks Fifth Avenue Texas, L.P. *Saks Inc* 1576
Saks Fifth Avenue, Inc. *Saks Inc* 1576
Saks Holdings, Inc. *Saks Inc* 1576
Saks Wholesalers, Inc. *Saks Inc* 1576
Saks& Company *Saks Inc* 1576
SakSat, LLC *Alltel Corp* 69
SakSat-Georgia, Ltd. (an LLC) *Alltel Corp* 69
Sakura *Liberty Global Inc* 1074
Sakura Transport Corp. *Overseas Shipholding Group Inc* 1365
Sakura, Inc. *Oneida Ltd* 1342
SAL Petrochemical (Zhangjiagang) Company Limited *Dow Chemical Co* 573
Salaisons du Douesy SASU *Sara Lee Corp* 1585
Salamis / SGB Limited *Harsco Corp* 849
Salant Holding, LLC, a Delaware limited liability *Perry Ellis International Inc* 1414
Salcombe Securities Limited *News Corp Ltd (The)* 1281
Saldanha Cooperatieve U.A. *Morgan Stanley* 1215
Sale Point Posters, Inc., an *Entravision Communications Corp* 644
Salem 1 NQF, LLC *Exelon Corp* 668
Salem 2 NQF, LLC *Exelon Corp* 668
Salem Clinic Corp. *Community Health Systems Inc* 454
Salem Communications Acquisition Corporation AcquisitionCo *Salem Communications Corp* 1576
Salem Communications Corporation *Salem Communications Corp* 1576
SALEM COURTHOUSE, L.P. *Apartment Investment and Management Company* 130
SALEM GP, L.L.C. *Apartment Investment and Management Company* 130
Salem Hospital Corporation *Community Health Systems Inc* 454
Salem Lafayette Urban Renewal Associates, LP *Edison International* 604
SALEM MALL, LLC *General Growth Properties Inc* 771
SALEM MANOR OREG. LTD. *Apartment Investment and Management Company* 130
Salem Medical Professionals, P.C. *Community Health Systems Inc* 454
Salem Run Associates II, L.P. *Wachovia Corp* 1928
Salem Run Associates, L.P. *Wachovia Corp* 1928
Salem Surgery Center, Limited Partnership *HCA Inc* 855
Salem Surgery Center, Ltd. *HealthSouth Corp* 861
Salem Telephone Company *Telephone and Data Systems Inc* 1768
SALEM-OXFORD ASSOCIATES LIMITED PARTNERSHIP *Apartment Investment and Management Company* 130
Sales and Service Training Center Inc. *Pitney Bowes Inc* 1434
Sales de Magnesio Ltda. *Rockwood Holdings Inc* 1555
Sales Offices *Hitachi Ltd* 880
Sales Support Services, Inc. *Harte-Hanks Inc* 850
Sales.com, Inc. *Siebel Systems Inc* 1624
SalesCom GmbH *WPP Group Plc* 1979
Salesdesk Limited *Interpublic Group of Companies Inc* 975
Salesdirect123.com *Diamond Entertainment Corp* 551
Salesedge GmbH *WPP Group Plc* 1979
SalesLink de Mexico S De RL De CV *CMGI Inc* 426
SalesLink Hungary Kft. *CMGI Inc* 426
SalesLink International (Malaysia) Sdn. Bhd. *CMGI Inc* 426
SalesLink LLC *CMGI Inc* 426
SalesLink Mexico Holding Corp. *CMGI Inc* 426
SalesLink Servicios, S. de R.L. de C.V. *CMGI Inc* 426
SalesLink Solutions International Ireland Limited *CMGI Inc* 426
Salesplus Ltd *WPP Group Plc* 1979
Salesplus Sdn Bhd *WPP Group Plc* 1979
Salespoint Pty Ltd *WPP Group Plc* 1979
Salespower Limited *Manpower Inc* 1119
SalesRepsOnline, Inc. *Siebel Systems Inc* 1624
SALI Acquisition 1-A/GP, LLC *Brookdale Senior Living Inc* 285
SALI Acquisition 1-A/LP, LLC *Brookdale Senior Living Inc* 285
SALI Acquisition III/GP, LLC *Brookdale Senior Living Inc* 285
SALI Acquisition III/LP, LLC *Brookdale Senior Living Inc* 285
SALI Assets, LLC *Brookdale Senior Living Inc* 285
SALI Management Advisors, LLC *Brookdale Senior Living Inc* 285

TMK/INLAND AURORA VENTURE LLC *Inland Real Estate Corp* 945
TML LLC *Lennox International Inc* 1068
TMM Logistics, S.A. de C.V. (Logistics) *Grupo TMM* 829
TMN Telecomunicaes Mveis Nacionais, S.A. *Portugal Telecom* 1450
TMNG Strategy, Inc *Management Network Group Inc* 1117
TMNG.com, Inc. *Management Network Group Inc* 1117
TMNI International Inc. *Rewards Network Inc* 1540
Tmol Cs-uk Ltd. *IAC/InterActiveCorp* 961
TMP Hungary *WPP Group Plc* 1979
TMP Personnel Select s.r.o (Slovakia) *Hudson Highland Group Inc* 896
TMRG, Inc. *Viacom Inc* 1902
TMRG, Inc. *CBS Corp* 349
TMS Corporation of the Americas *Tierone Corp* 1793
TMS License California, Inc. *Univision Communications Inc* 1871
TMS Special Holdings, Inc. *Wachovia Corp* 1928
TMS Student Holdings, Inc. *Wachovia Corp* 1928
TMSF REIT, Inc *TMSF Holdings Inc* 1799
TMT Motoco, Ltd. *Tecumseh Products Co* 1761
TMW Marketing Company, Inc *Men's Wearhouse Inc* 1159
TMW Merchants LLC *Men's Wearhouse Inc* 1159
TMW Pramerica Real Estate Investors Luxembourg S.A. *Prudential Financial Inc* 1483
TMW Purchasing LLC *Men's Wearhouse Inc* 1159
TMW Real Estate Group, LLC *Prudential Financial Inc* 1483
TMW Realty Inc. *Men's Wearhouse Inc* 1159
TMW Texas General LLC *Men's Wearhouse Inc* 1159
TMX Administracion S.A. de C.V. *Swift Transportation Co Inc* 1732
TMX Realty Corporation *Introgen Therapeutics Inc* 980
TMXI RESOURCES S.A. DE C.V. *Tumi Resouces Ltd* 1834
TN Home Builders *Stewart Information Services Corp* 1705
Tn Media Limited *Interpublic Group of Companies Inc* 975
Tn Media S.a. De C.v. *Interpublic Group of Companies Inc* 975
Tn Media, Inc. *Interpublic Group of Companies Inc* 975
Tn Medios Publicidad, Ca *Interpublic Group of Companies Inc* 975
Tn Technologies, Inc. *Interpublic Group of Companies Inc* 975
TNA International Ltd. *CCE Spinco Inc* 349
TNA Tour I (USA)Inc. *CCE Spinco Inc* 349
TNA Tour II (USA)Inc. *CCE Spinco Inc* 349
TNA Tour M3 (USA), Inc. *CCE Spinco Inc* 349
TNA (USA)Inc. *CCE Spinco Inc* 349
TNB Financial Services Inc. *Thomasville Bancshares Inc* 1789
TNBANK *Tennessee Valley Financial Holdings Inc* 1775
TNC *Ohio Power Co* 1331
TNC *AEP Generating Co* 36
TNC Holdings Pte. Ltd. *Ansell Ltd* 126
Tni Partners *Gannett Co Inc* 761
TNI Partners *Lee Enterprises Inc* 1064
TNL Contax S.A. *Contax Holding Co* 474
TNL Flight Services, Inc *Trimble Navigation Ltd* 1824
Tnl Pcs S.a. *Tele Norte Leste Participacoes* 1764
TNL Pension Trustees Limited *News Corp Ltd (The)* 1281
TNL Singapore Components Holdings Pte. Ltd. *Technitrol Inc* 1758
TNP Enterprises, Inc. *Texas New Mexico Power Co* 1782
TNP Enterprises, Inc. *PNM Resources Inc* 1443
TNP Operating Company *TNMP* 1799
TNS Transline, LLC *TNS Inc* 1799
Tns-va, LLC *Quanta Services Inc* 1497
TNT Sands, Inc. *Waste Management Inc* 1934
TNT-NL Eurolease I, Ltd. *Northern Trust Corp* 1302
TNT-NL Eurolease II, Ltd. *Northern Trust Corp* 1302
TNT-NL Leasing I, Inc. *Northern Trust Corp* 1302
To-ricos Distribution, Ltd. *Pilgrims Pride Corp* 1430
To-ricos, Inc. *Pilgrims Pride Corp* 1430
To-ricos, Ltd. *Pilgrims Pride Corp* 1430
Toastmaster, Inc. *Salton Inc* 1578
Toasty, LLC *Wynn Resorts Ltd* 1982
Toba Pharma Inc. *Abbott Laboratories* 5
Tobacco Development Company Ltd *Alliance One International Inc* 62
Tobacco Row Phase II Associates, L.P. *Wachovia Corp* 1928
Tobacco Trading International, Inc. *Universal Corp* 1867
Tobaccoland Automatengesellschaft mbH & Co. KG (63.9%) *Gallaher Group Plc* 759
Tobaccoland Handels GmbH & Co. KG *Gallaher Group Plc* 759
Tobaccor S.A.S *Imperial Tobacco Group Plc* 930
Tobacna Ljubljana d.o.o. *Imperial Tobacco Group Plc* 930
Tobago Snack Holdings, LLC *PepsiCo Inc* 1410
Tobago Unlimited *BG Group Plc* 236
Tobal Products Incorporated *Abbott Laboratories* 5
Tobelan S.A. *Marsh & McLennan Cos Inc* 1125
TOBH,Inc. *Liberty Media LLC* 1074
Tobras Distribuidora de Combustivrs Ltda. *World Fuel Services Corp* 1976
Tobrooke Holdings Ltd *Reading International Inc* 1518
Toby Restaurants Ltd *Mitchells & Butlers Plc* 1200
Toc-ds Company *Valero Energy Corp* 1884
Tocco de Mexico S.A. de C.V. *Park Ohio Holdings Corp* 1386
Tocco, Inc. *Park Ohio Holdings Corp* 1386
Tocop Sarl *VeriSign Inc* 1896
Todagco *American Vanguard Corp* 106
Todays Teachers Technology and Culture Ltd. *China Education Resources Inc* 389
Todays Staffing, Inc. *CDI Corp* 351
Todays Staffing, Ltd. *CDI Corp* 351
Todays Way Manufacturing, LLC *Industrial Enterprises of America Inc* 935
TODCO Americas Inc. *TODCO* 1800
TODCO International Inc. *TODCO* 1800
TODCO Management Services Inc. LLC *TODCO* 1800
TODCO Mexico Inc. *TODCO* 1800
TODCO Trinidad Ltd. *TODCO* 1800
Todd Campus, Ltd. *Transgenomic Inc* 1816
Todd Communications, Inc. *Black Box Corp* 252
Todd Pacific Shipyards Corporation (Todd Pacific). *Todd Shipyards Corp* 1800
Todd SCP L.P. *Wachovia Corp* 1928
Todd Tenant, L. P. *Wachovia Corp* 1928
Todd-AO, Espana *Discovery Holding Co* 561
TOE Acquisition Corporation. *Fonix Corp* 733
Toe-To-Toe Productions Inc. *Viacom Inc* 1902
Toe-to-Toe Productions Inc. *CBS Corp* 349
Tofino Investment Limited *Applica Inc* 135
Tofteland Windfarm, LLCLP *Edison International* 604
Tofuku Shoji K.K. *Abbott Laboratories* 5
Together Reklamebrya A.S. *WPP Group Plc* 1979
Tohatsu Marine Corporation *Brunswick Corp* 289
Toho Bussan Kaisha, Ltd. *Mitsui & Co Ltd* 1201
Toho Kagaku Kenkyusho Co., Ltd. *E-Z-EM Inc* 588
Tohoku Pioneer Corporation *Pioneer Corp* 1433
Tohoku Rental Service Co., Ltd. *Caterpillar Inc* 345
Tohoku Ricoh Co., Ltd. *Ricoh Co Ltd* 1544
TOI, LLC *Technical Olympic USA Inc* 1758
Toitot S.A.S. *Akzo Nobel* 49
Tojan Holding Co (Pty) Ltd *BHP Billiton Plc* 237
Tojan Holding Co (Pty) Ltd *BHP Billiton Ltd* 237
Tokai Gas United Ltd *BOC Group Plc* 262
Tokai Wacoal Sewing Corp. *Wacoal Holdings Corp* 1928
Tokio Marine Asia Pte. Ltd. *Millea Holdings Inc* 1191
Tokio Marine Asset Management Company, Limited *Millea Holdings Inc* 1191
Tokio Marine Brasil Seguradora S.A. *Millea Holdings Inc* 1191
Tokio Marine Europe Insurance Limited *Millea Holdings Inc* 1191
Tokio Marine Financial Solutions Ltd. *Millea Holdings Inc* 1191
Tokio Marine Global Limited *Millea Holdings Inc* 1191
Tokio Marine Global Re Limited *Millea Holdings Inc* 1191
Tokio Marine& Nichido Career Service Co., Ltd. *Millea Holdings Inc* 1191
Tokio Marine& Nichido Facilities, Inc. *Millea Holdings Inc* 1191
Tokio Marine& Nichido Financial Life Co., Ltd. *Millea Holdings Inc* 1191
Tokio Marine& Nichido Fire Insurance Co., Ltd. *Millea Holdings Inc* 1191
Tokio Marine& Nichido Life Insurance Co., Ltd. *Millea Holdings Inc* 1191
Tokio Millennium Re Ltd. *Millea Holdings Inc* 1191
Tokyo Daisan Engineering Ltd *BOC Group Plc* 262
Tokyo Financial Services Corporation *Toyota Motor Corp* 1808
Tokyo Medical Gas Ltd *BOC Group Plc* 262
Tokyo Mitsubishi Bank *Dot Hill Systems Corp* 571
Tokyo Realty Investment Company *Morgan Stanley* 1215
Tokyo Realty Investment Company II *Morgan Stanley* 1215
Tokyo Rental Co., Ltd. *Caterpillar Inc* 345
Tokyo Sales Headquarters *Orix Corp Ads* 1358
Tokyo Toyo-Pet Motor Sales Co., Ltd. *Toyota Motor Corp* 1808
Tokyo Transport Corp. *Overseas Shipholding Group Inc* 1365
Tokyo, Japan branch *St Jude Medical Inc* 1687
Tolan Shipping Company Limited *DryShips Inc* 577
Toledo Holdings Corporation *Mirant Corp* 1197
Toledo MSA Limited Partnership *Alltel Corp* 69
Toledo Pharmacy Co. *Cardinal Health Inc* 332
Toledo Power Co. *Mirant Corp* 1197
Toledo Shipping Corporation *Fresh Del Monte Produce Inc* 749
Toledo Technologies Inc. *GenTek Inc* 777
Toledo Technologies Management LLC *GenTek Inc* 777
Toledo Technologies Manufacturing LLC *GenTek Inc* 777
Toledo, Peoria & Western Railway Corp. *Railamerica Inc* 1510
Toll Architecture Inc *Toll Brothers Inc* 1801
Toll Arizona LP Company Inc *Toll Brothers Inc* 1801
Toll Arizona-II LP Company Inc *Toll Brothers Inc* 1801
Toll Associates, LLC *Nasdaq Stock Market Inc (The)* 1236
Toll AZ GP Corp *Toll Brothers Inc* 1801
Toll Bros Inc *Toll Brothers Inc* 1801
Toll Bros Inc *Toll Brothers Inc* 1801
Toll Bros Inc *Toll Brothers Inc* 1801
Toll Bros of Arizona Inc *Toll Brothers Inc* 1801
Toll Bros of North Carolina II Inc *Toll Brothers Inc* 1801
Toll Bros of North Carolina III Inc *Toll Brothers Inc* 1801
Toll Bros of North Carolina Inc *Toll Brothers Inc* 1801
Toll Bros of Tennessee Inc *Toll Brothers Inc* 1801
Toll Brothers AZ Construction Company *Toll Brothers Inc* 1801
Toll Brothers Finance Corp *Toll Brothers Inc* 1801
Toll Brothers Real Estate Inc *Toll Brothers Inc* 1801
Toll CA GP Corp *Toll Brothers Inc* 1801
Toll California LP Company Inc *Toll Brothers Inc* 1801
Toll CO GP Corp *Toll Brothers Inc* 1801
Toll Colorado LP Company Inc *Toll Brothers Inc* 1801
Toll Connecticut LP Company Inc *Toll Brothers Inc* 1801
Toll Connecticut-II LP Company Inc *Toll Brothers Inc* 1801
Toll Corp *Toll Brothers Inc* 1801
Toll Delaware LP Company Inc *Toll Brothers Inc* 1801
Toll Delaware-II LP Company Inc *Toll Brothers Inc* 1801
Toll Development Company Inc *Toll Brothers Inc* 1801
Toll Finance Corp *Toll Brothers Inc* 1801
Toll FL GP Corp *Toll Brothers Inc* 1801
Toll Florida LP Company Inc *Toll Brothers Inc* 1801
Toll Florida-II LP Company Inc *Toll Brothers Inc* 1801
Toll Holdings Inc *Toll Brothers Inc* 1801
Toll IL GP Corp *Toll Brothers Inc* 1801
Toll Illinois LP Company Inc *Toll Brothers Inc* 1801
Toll Land Corp No 10 *Toll Brothers Inc* 1801
Toll Land Corp No 20 *Toll Brothers Inc* 1801
Toll Land Corp No 43 *Toll Brothers Inc* 1801
Toll Land Corp No 45 *Toll Brothers Inc* 1801
Toll Land Corp No 46 *Toll Brothers Inc* 1801
Toll Land Corp No 47 *Toll Brothers Inc* 1801
Toll Land Corp No 48 *Toll Brothers Inc* 1801
Toll Land Corp No 49 *Toll Brothers Inc* 1801
Toll Land Corp No 50 *Toll Brothers Inc* 1801
Toll Land Corp No 51 *Toll Brothers Inc* 1801
Toll Land Corp No 52 *Toll Brothers Inc* 1801
Toll Land Corp No 53 *Toll Brothers Inc* 1801
Toll Land Corp No 55 *Toll Brothers Inc* 1801
Toll Land Corp No 56 *Toll Brothers Inc* 1801
Toll Land Corp No 58 *Toll Brothers Inc* 1801
Toll Land Corp No 59 *Toll Brothers Inc* 1801
Toll Land Corp No 6 *Toll Brothers Inc* 1801
Toll Land Corp No 60 *Toll Brothers Inc* 1801
Toll Management AZ Corp *Toll Brothers Inc* 1801
Toll Management VA Corp *Toll Brothers Inc* 1801
Toll Manhattan I Inc *Toll Brothers Inc* 1801
Toll Maryland LP Company Inc *Toll Brothers Inc* 1801
Toll Maryland-II LP Company Inc *Toll Brothers Inc* 1801
Toll Massachusetts LP Company Inc *Toll Brothers Inc* 1801
Toll Massachusetts-II LP Company Inc *Toll Brothers Inc* 1801
Toll MD Builder Corp *Toll Brothers Inc* 1801
Toll MI GP Corp *Toll Brothers Inc* 1801
Toll Michigan LP Company Inc *Toll Brothers Inc* 1801
Toll Michigan-II LP Company Inc *Toll Brothers Inc* 1801
Toll Mid-Atlantic LP Company Inc *Toll Brothers Inc* 1801
Toll Mid-Atlantic Note Company Inc *Toll Brothers Inc* 1801
Toll Midwest LP Company Inc *Toll Brothers Inc* 1801
Toll Midwest Note Company Inc *Toll Brothers Inc* 1801
Toll MN GP Corp *Toll Brothers Inc* 1801
Toll NC GP Corp *Toll Brothers Inc* 1801
Toll Nevada LP Company Inc *Toll Brothers Inc* 1801
Toll New Hampshire LP Company Inc *Toll Brothers Inc* 1801
Toll New Hampshire-II LP Company Inc *Toll Brothers Inc* 1801
Toll New Jersey LP Company Inc *Toll Brothers Inc* 1801
Toll New Jersey-II LP Company Inc *Toll Brothers Inc* 1801
Toll New York LP Company Inc *Toll Brothers Inc* 1801
Toll New York-II LP Company Inc *Toll Brothers Inc* 1801
Toll NH GP Corp *Toll Brothers Inc* 1801
Toll NJ Builder Corp *Toll Brothers Inc* 1801
Toll NJX III Corp *Toll Brothers Inc* 1801
Toll NJX IV Corp *Toll Brothers Inc* 1801
Toll NJX-I Corp *Toll Brothers Inc* 1801
Toll NJX-II Corp *Toll Brothers Inc* 1801
Toll North Carolina LP Company Inc *Toll Brothers Inc* 1801
Toll North Carolina-II LP Company Inc *Toll Brothers Inc* 1801
Toll Northeast LP Company Inc *Toll Brothers Inc* 1801
Toll Northeast Note Company Inc *Toll Brothers Inc* 1801
Toll NV GP Corp *Toll Brothers Inc* 1801
Toll OH GP Corp *Toll Brothers Inc* 1801
Toll Ohio LP Company Inc *Toll Brothers Inc* 1801
Toll Ohio-II LP Company Inc *Toll Brothers Inc* 1801
Toll PA Builder Corp *Toll Brothers Inc* 1801
Toll PA GP Corp *Toll Brothers Inc* 1801
Toll PA II GP Corp *Toll Brothers Inc* 1801
Toll Pennsylvania LP Company Inc *Toll Brothers Inc* 1801
Toll Pennsylvania-II LP Company Inc *Toll Brothers Inc* 1801
Toll Peppertree Inc *Toll Brothers Inc* 1801
Toll Philmont Corporation *Toll Brothers Inc* 1801
Toll Realty Holdings Corp I *Toll Brothers Inc* 1801
Toll Realty Holdings Corp II *Toll Brothers Inc* 1801
Toll Realty Holdings Corp III *Toll Brothers Inc* 1801
Toll Rhode Island LP Company Inc *Toll Brothers Inc* 1801
Toll Rhode Island-II LP Company Inc *Toll Brothers Inc* 1801
Toll RI GP Corp *Toll Brothers Inc* 1801
Toll SC GP Corp *Toll Brothers Inc* 1801
Toll South Carolina LP Company Inc *Toll Brothers Inc* 1801
Toll South Carolina-II LP Company Inc *Toll Brothers Inc* 1801
Toll Southeast LP Company Inc *Toll Brothers Inc* 1801
Toll Southeast Note Company Inc *Toll Brothers Inc* 1801
Toll Southwest LP Company Inc *Toll Brothers Inc* 1801
Toll Southwest Note Company Inc *Toll Brothers Inc* 1801
Toll Texas LP Company Inc *Toll Brothers Inc* 1801
Toll Texas-II LP Company Inc *Toll Brothers Inc* 1801
Toll TN GP Corp *Toll Brothers Inc* 1801
Toll Turf Inc *Toll Brothers Inc* 1801
Toll TX GP Corp *Toll Brothers Inc* 1801
Toll VA GP Corp *Toll Brothers Inc* 1801
Toll VA Member Two Inc *Toll Brothers Inc* 1801
Toll Virginia LP Company Inc *Toll Brothers Inc* 1801
Toll Virginia-II LP Company Inc *Toll Brothers Inc* 1801
Toll WestCoast LP Company Inc *Toll Brothers Inc* 1801
Toll WestCoast Note Company Inc *Toll Brothers Inc* 1801
Toll Wood Corporation *Toll Brothers Inc* 1801
Toll WV GP Corp *Toll Brothers Inc* 1801
Toll YL Inc *Toll Brothers Inc* 1801
Tollin/Robbins Management, LLC *CCE Spinco Inc* 349
Tollo Linear AB *Danaher Corp* 525
Tolo Incorporated *Goodrich Corp* 810
Tolukuma Gold Mines Limited *DRDGold Ltd* 575
Tom Allen Construction Company *Quanta Services Inc* 1497
Tom Lucianos Disposal Service, Inc. *Allied Waste Industries Inc* 66
TOM Oil Broking Limited *World Fuel Services Corp* 1976
TOM Oil Limited *World Fuel Services Corp* 1976
Tom Snyder Productions, Inc. *Scholastic Corp* 1592
Tom Thumb Food Stores *Kroger Co* 1043
Toma Metals Inc. *Reliance Steel & Aluminum Co* 1528
Tomago Aluminium Company Pty Ltd *Alcan Inc* 54
Tomago Aluminium Joint-venture *Alcan Inc* 54
Tomahawk Railway LP *Genesee & Wyoming Inc* 773
Tomal AB *SPX Corp* 1684
Tomark Sports Inc. *Sport Supply Group Inc* 1683
Tombigbee Transport Corporation *Masco Corp* 1128
Tombo Aviation Inc. *Mitsui & Co Ltd* 1201
Tombo Capital Corporation *Mitsui & Co Ltd* 1201
Tomillo Ltd. *Solectron Corp* 1653
Tomisato Shoji Kabushiki Kaisha *Northwest Airlines Corp* 1304
Tommy Bahama Beverages, LLC *Oxford Industries Inc* 1366
Tommy Bahama Group, Inc. *Oxford Industries Inc* 1366
Tommy Bahama R&R Holdings, Inc. *Oxford Industries Inc* 1366
Tommy Bahama Texas Beverages, LLC *Oxford Industries Inc* 1366
Tommy Boy Music, Inc. *Warner Music Group Corp* 1931
Tommy Hilfiger Footwear, Inc. *Stride Rite Corp* 1713
Tommy Valando Publishing Group, Inc. *Warner Music Group Corp* 1931
Tomoka Holdings, LLC *Allete Inc* 60
Tomorrow Films Ltd. *News Corp Ltd (The)* 1281
Tomorrows Telecom Limited *Tyco International Ltd* 1838
TomoSeis Corporation *Core Laboratories* 480
Tompkins Insurance Agencies, Inc. *Tompkins Financial Corp* 1801
Tompkins Real Estate Holdings, Inc. *Tompkins Financial Corp.* 1801
TOMPKINS TERRACE ASSOCIATES LIMITED PARTNERSHIP *Apartment Investment and Management Company* 130
TOMPKINS TERRACE, INC. *Apartment Investment and Management Company* 130
Toms River Surgery Center, LLC *United Surgical Partners International Inc* 1863
Toms River Veterinary Hospital, P.A. *VCA Antech Inc* 1891
Tomsk Holdings Limited *BJ Services Co* 251
Tomusinsk Group Processing Plant (TGPP) *Mechel OAO* 1146
Tomusinsk Open Pit Mine (TOPM) *Mechel OAO* 1146
Tona a.s. *Stanley Works* 1692
Tonawanda II, L.P. *Citigroup Inc* 411
Tondeo-Werk GmbH *Procter & Gamble* 1472
Tone Lease Co. *Caterpillar Inc* 345
Tonen Kagaku K.K. *Exxon Mobil Corp* 673
TonenGeneral Sekiyu K.K. *Exxon Mobil Corp* 673
Toney Fork LLC *Penn Virginia Resource Partners LP* 1403
Tong Yuan Asset Management Limited Liability Company *J.P. Morgan Chase & Company* 999
Tongling SIVA Insulating Materials Co. Ltd. *Altana AG* 72
Tongonan Power Investment, Inc. *Midamerican Energy Holdings Co* 1184
Tonic Software, Inc. *Altiris Inc* 73
Tonic Software, Ltd. *Altiris Inc* 73
TonicHealth Ltd *WPP Group Plc* 1979
Tonkin Springs Gold Mining Corporation *U.S. Gold Corp* 1841
Tonmet AG *BHP Billiton Plc* 237
Tonmet AG *BHP Billiton Ltd* 237
Tonopah Health Services, Inc. *Universal Health Services Inc* 1869
Tonopah, LLC *Bank of America Corp* 208
Tony Stephens Associates Limited *CCE Spinco Inc* 349
Tony Stone Associates Limited *Getty Images Inc* 784
Tony Stone Images/Canada, Inc. *Getty Images Inc* 784
Too Brands Investment, LLC *Too Inc* 1802
Too Brands, Inc. *Too Inc* 1802
Too G.C., LLC *Too Inc* 1802
Too Import, LLC *Too Inc* 1802
Too Retail & Sales Puerto Rico, Inc. *Too Inc* 1802
Too Sourcing Hong Kong Limited *Too Inc* 1802

THE CORPORATE DIRECTORY - Walker's 2008 Subsidiary/Parent Index - 3391

Valero Aruba Holdings International, Ltd. *Valero Energy Corp* . 1884
Valero Aruba Maintenance/operations Company N.v. *Valero Energy Corp* 1884
Valero Bonaire Fuels Company N.v. *Valero Energy Corp* 1884
Valero Burgos, LLC *Valero LP* 1884
Valero Canada Finance, Inc. *Valero Energy Corp* 1884
Valero Canada L.p. *Valero Energy Corp* 1884
Valero Capital Corporation *Valero Energy Corp* 1884
Valero Caribbean Services Company *Valero Energy Corp* 1884
Valero Chops Gp, LLC *Valero Energy Corp* 1884
Valero Chops I, L.p. *Valero Energy Corp* 1884
Valero Chops Ii, L.p. *Valero Energy Corp* 1884
Valero Claims Management, Inc. *Valero Energy Corp* 1884
Valero Coker Corporation Aruba N.v. *Valero Energy Corp* 1884
Valero Corporate Services Company *Valero Energy Corp* 1884
Valero Customs & Trade Services, Inc. *Valero Energy Corp* 1884
Valero Diamond Metro, Inc. *Valero Energy Corp* 1884
Valero Diamond, L.p. *Valero Energy Corp* 1884
Valero Energy Aruba I Company *Valero Energy Corp* 1884
Valero Energy Aruba Ii Company *Valero Energy Corp* 1884
Valero Energy Corporation (parent) *Valero Energy Corp* 1884
Valero Finance L.p. I *Valero Energy Corp* 1884
Valero Finance L.p. Ii *Valero Energy Corp* 1884
Valero Finance L.p. Iii *Valero Energy Corp* 1884
Valero Gp Holdings, LLC *Valero Energy Corp* 1884
Valero GP, Inc. *Valero LP* 1884
Valero GP, LLC *NuStar GP Holdings LLC* 1316
Valero Gp, LLC *Valero Energy Corp* 1884
Valero Holdings, Inc. *Valero Energy Corp* 1884
Valero Internacional, S de R.L. de C.V. *Valero LP* 1884
Valero Javelina, Inc. *Valero Energy Corp* 1884
Valero Javelina, L.p. *Valero Energy Corp* 1884
Valero L.p. *Valero Energy Corp* 1884
Valero Logistics Operations, L.P. *Valero LP* 1884
Valero Marketing & Supply-aruba N.v. *Valero Energy Corp* 1884
Valero Marketing And Supply Company *Valero Energy Corp* 1884
Valero Natural Gas Pipeline Company *Valero Energy Corp* 1884
Valero Omega Company, LLC *Valero Energy Corp* 1884
Valero Pipeline Corporation *Valero Energy Corp* 1884
Valero Producing Company *Valero Energy Corp* 1884
Valero Refining And Marketing Company *Valero Energy Corp*. 1884
Valero Refining Company-aruba N.v. *Valero Energy Corp* 1884
Valero Refining Company-california *Valero Energy Corp* 1884
Valero Refining Company-louisiana *Valero Energy Corp* 1884
Valero Refining Company-new Jersey *Valero Energy Corp* 1884
Valero Refining Company-oklahoma *Valero Energy Corp* 1884
Valero Refining-new Orleans, LLC *Valero Energy Corp* 1884
Valero Refining-texas, L.p. *Valero Energy Corp* 1884
Valero Security Systems, Inc. *Valero Energy Corp* 1884
Valero Services, Inc. *Valero Energy Corp* 1884
Valero Terminaling And Distribution Company *Valero Energy Corp* 1884
Valero Uk Ltd *Valero Energy Corp* 1884
Valero Ultramar Holdings Inc. *Valero Energy Corp* 1884
Valero Unit Investments, LLC *Valero Energy Corp* 1884
Valeron Strength Films B.V.B.A. *Illinois Tool Works Inc* 922
Valertex, Inc. *Comcast Corp* 444
Valex Corp. *Reliance Steel & Aluminum Co* 1528
Valex Insurance Agency, Inc. *Aon Corp* 129
Valiant Packaging (Holdings) Limited *R.R. Donnelley & Sons Co* 1506
VALIC Retirement Services Company *American International Group Inc* 94
Valicert B.V. *Tumbleweed Communications Corp* 1834
Valicert Japan K.K. *Tumbleweed Communications Corp* 1834
Valimanda Pty. Limited *News Corp Ltd (The)* 1281
Valkyrie Commissioning Services, Inc. *Weatherford International Ltd* 1940
Valkyrie de Mexico S. de R.L. de C.V. *Weatherford International Ltd* 1940
Valkyrie Services S. de R.L. de C.V. *Weatherford International Ltd* 1940
Valle del Sol Associates Limited Partnership *American Community Properties Trust* 89
Valle Del Sol Energy, LLC *Edison International* 604
Valle Del Sol Energy, LLC *Mission Energy Holding Co* 1199
Valle Vista Hospital Partners, LLC *Psychiatric Solutions Inc* 1485
Valle Vista, LLC *Psychiatric Solutions Inc* 1485
Valley 747 Acquisition, LLC *Valley National Bancorp* 1886
Valley Ambulatory Surgery Center, L.P. *Symbion Inc* 1735
Valley Asset Management, Inc. *Wells Fargo & Co* 1944
Valley Bank *Banco Bilbao Vizcaya Argentaria* 204
Valley Bank *First Valley Bancorp Inc CT* 718
Valley Bank *Valley Bancorp* 1885
Valley Bank of Helena *Glacier Bancorp Inc* 788
Valley Behavioral Health Network, LLC(33.33% owned) *Psychiatric Solutions Inc* 1485
Valley Chevrolet, LLC *Autonation Inc FL* 183
Valley Coca-Cola Bottling Company *Coca-Cola Enterprises Inc* 433
Valley Commerce Trust I *Valley Commerce Bancorp CA* 1885
Valley Commercial Capital, LLC *Valley National Bancorp* 1886
Valley Communications, Inc. *Lynch Interactive Corp* 1102
Valley Corporation *American Realty Investors Inc* 100
Valley CT Management, LC *Complete Production Services Inc* 460
Valley Financial Corporation. *Valley Bank* 1885
Valley Financial (VA) Statutory Trust I *Valley Bank* 1885
Valley Financial (VA) Statutory Trust II *Valley Bank* 1885
Valley Fire Service, Inc. *Rural/Metro Corp* 1567
Valley First Community Bank *Capitol Bancorp Ltd* 327
Valley Forge Conservation Holding GP Corp *Toll Brothers Inc* . 1801
Valley Forge Enterprises, Ltd. *National Investment Managers Inc* 1243
Valley Forge Technical Information Services GmbH *SPX Corp* . 1684
Valley Forge (UK) Limited *SPX Corp* 1684
Valley Garbage and Rubbish Company, Inc. *Waste Management Inc* 1934
Valley Gas Transmission, LLC *Kinder Morgan Energy Partners LP* 1030
Valley Health System, LLC *Universal Health Services Inc* 1869
VALLEY HILLS MALL L.L.C. *General Growth Properties Inc* 771
VALLEY HILLS MALL, INC. *General Growth Properties Inc* .. 771
Valley Hospital Medical Center, Inc. *Universal Health Services Inc* 1869
Valley Irrigation South Africa,(PTY) Ltd. *Valmont Industries Inc* 1887
Valley Landfills, Inc. *Allied Waste Industries Inc* 66
Valley Laser Eye Center LLC *TLC Vision Corp* 1798
Valley Machining, Inc. *Ladish Co Inc* 1049
Valley Medical Equipment, Inc. *Rotech Healthcare Inc NEW* 1560
Valley Medical Services, Inc. *Genesis HealthCare Corp* 774
Valley Mortgage Company,Inc. *Texas Regional Bancshares Inc* 1782
Valley Mortgage Services, LP *National City Corp* 1239
Valley National Title Services, Inc. *Valley National Bancorp* 1886
Valley Network Partnership *Ntelos Holdings Corp* 1313
Valley Network Partnership *Embarq Corp* 619
Valley of California, Inc. *Realogy Corp* 1518
Valley of California, Inc. *Avis Budget Group Inc* 190
Valley Operating, Inc. *Kinder Morgan Inc* 1030
Valley Outpatient Surgery Center, L.P. *HealthSouth Corp* 861
Valley Park Apartments, LTD *Essex Property Trust Inc* 659
Valley Park South Partnership *Home Properties Inc* 886
VALLEY PLAZA ANCHOR ACQUISITION, LLC *General Growth Properties Inc* 771
Valley Pond, Sarl *Pepsi Bottling Group Inc* 1409
Valley Properties Corporation *HSBC Finance Corp* 895
Valley Race Park Inc. *Maxxam Inc* 1136
Valley Rail Service, Inc. *Pilgrims Pride Corp* 1430
Valley Shamrock, Inc. *Valero Energy Corp* 1884
Valley Sleep Centers, LLC *Symbion Inc* 1735
Valley Supply, Inc. *ACR Group Inc* 16
Valley Surgery Center, L.P. *Universal Health Services Inc* 1869
Valley Surgical Center, Ltd. *Symbion Inc* 1735
Valley Telephone Co., LLC *Knology Inc* 1036
Valley Transport Ambulance Service, Inc. *Genesis HealthCare Corp* 774
Valley View Coal, Inc. *Williams Cos Inc* 1961
Valley View Mall, LLC *CBL & Associates Properties Inc* 348
Valley View Surgery Center, L.P. *HealthSouth Corp* 861
Valley View Surgicare Partners, Ltd. *United Surgical Partners International Inc* 1863
Valley Wealth Management Services, Inc. *Valley Bank* 1885
Valley-Dynamo, L.P. *Brunswick Corp* 289
Valleybrooke Land Holdings *Brandywine Operating PArtnership LP* 274
Valleybrooke Land Holdings, Inc *Brandywine Realty Trust* 274
Valleydale, LLC *Regency Centers Corp* 1524
Valleyfield Vineyard Partnership *Constellation Brands Inc* 473
Valleylab (Australia) Pty Limited *Tyco International Ltd* 1838
Valleylab Holding Corporation *Tyco International Ltd* 1838
Valleylab Inc *Tyco International Ltd* 1838
Valleythorn Limited *Yum! Brands Inc* 1994
Vallis Leasobjekt GmbH *Aptargroup Inc* 138
Valmark Industries, Inc *Jordan Industries Inc* 1011
Valmed Pharmaceutical Inc. *Andrx Corp* 122
Valmed Pharmaceutical, Inc. *Andrx Corp* 122
Valmet Automotive Oy *Metso Corp* 1173
Valmet Converting Inc. *Metso Corp* 1173
Valmet Converting PLC *Metso Corp* 1173
Valmet Defibrator A/S *Metso Corp* 1173
Valmet Dura Oy *Metso Corp* 1173
Valmet Dura USA Inc. *Metso Corp* 1173
Valmet Ltd *Metso Corp* 1173
Valmont Australia Pty. Ltd. *Valmont Industries Inc* 1887
Valmont Coatings, Inc. *Valmont Industries Inc* 1887
Valmont Credit Corporation *Valmont Industries Inc* 1887
Valmont Formet S. de R.L. de C.V. *Valmont Industries Inc* 1887
Valmont France S.A.S. *Valmont Industries Inc* 1887
Valmont Iberica S.A. *Valmont Industries Inc* 1887
Valmont Industria e Comercio, Ltda. *Valmont Industries Inc* 1887
Valmont Industries (China) Co.,Ltd. *Valmont Industries Inc* 1887
Valmont Industries de Argentina S.A. *Valmont Industries Inc* 1887
Valmont Industries (Guangdong), Ltd. *Valmont Industries Inc* 1887
Valmont Industries Holland B.V. *Valmont Industries Inc* 1887
Valmont International Corp. *Valmont Industries Inc* 1887
Valmont International, LLC *Valmont Industries Inc* 1887
Valmont Investimentos Ltda. *Valmont Industries Inc* 1887
Valmont Mastbau Verwaltung *Valmont Industries Inc* 1887
Valmont Mastbau, GmbH & Co., KG *Valmont Industries Inc* 1887
Valmont Middle East FZE *Valmont Industries Inc* 1887
Valmont Nederland B.V. *Valmont Industries Inc* 1887
Valmont Northwest, Inc. *Valmont Industries Inc* 1887
Valmont Polska Sp.z oo *Valmont Industries Inc* 1887
Valmont S.A. *Valmont Industries Inc* 1887
Valmont Sarl *Valmont Industries Inc* 1887
Valmont Service Centers, Inc. *Valmont Industries Inc* 1887
Valmont Singapore Pte. Ltd. *Valmont Industries Inc* 1887
Valmont Structures, Inc. *Valmont Industries Inc* 1887
Valmont (UK) Limited *Valmont Industries Inc* 1887
Valmont Wind Energy, Inc. *Valmont Industries Inc* 1887
Valmorisco Communications, S.a. *Interpublic Group of Companies Inc* 975
Valmy SAS *Marriott International Inc* 1125
Valois Deutschland GmbH *Aptargroup Inc* 138
Valois Dispray S.A. *Aptargroup Inc* 138
Valois Espaa S.A. *Aptargroup Inc* 138
Valois India Private Ltd. *Aptargroup Inc* 138
Valois (Ireland) Limited *Aptargroup Inc* 138
Valois Italiana S.r.l. *Aptargroup Inc* 138
Valois S.A.S. *Aptargroup Inc* 138
Valois U.K. Limited *Aptargroup Inc* 138
Valor Telecommunications Corporate Group, LP *Windstream Corp* 1966
Valor Telecommunications Enterprises Finance Corp. *Windstream Corp* 1966
Valor Telecommunications Enterprises II, LLC *Windstream Corp* 1966
Valor Telecommunications Enterprises, LLC *Windstream Corp* . 1966
Valor Telecommunications Equipment, LP *Windstream Corp* .. 1966
Valor Telecommunications Investments, LLC *Windstream Corp* 1966
Valor Telecommunications of Texas., LP *Windstream Corp* 1966
Valor Telecommunications Services, LP *Windstream Corp* 1966
Valor Telecommunications Southwest II, LLC *Windstream Corp* 1966
Valor Telecommunications Southwest LLC *Windstream Corp* ... 1966
Valor Telecommunications, LLC *Windstream Corp* 1966
Valores Bermuda S.R.L. *PepsiCo Inc* 1410
Valores Mapumar *PepsiCo Inc* 1410
Valores Universales S.A. de CV *Smurfit Stone Container Corp* .. 1650
Valser Trading AG *Coca-Cola Co* 433
Valso, S.A. *7-Eleven Inc* 2009
Valspar Coatings Finance Corporation *Valspar Corp* 1887
Valspar Finance Corporation *Valspar Corp* 1887
Valspar Inc. *Valspar Corp* 1887
Valspar Industries GmbH *Valspar Corp* 1887
Valspar Mexicana, S.A. de C.V. *Valspar Corp* 1887
Valspar Refinish, Inc. *Valspar Corp* 1887
Valspar Rock Co., Ltd. *Valspar Corp* 1887
Valspar Sourcing, Inc. *Valspar Corp* 1887
Valta Tractors (A&NZ) PTY Ltd. *AGCO Corp* 42
Valtek Registros, Ltda. *Flowserve Corp* 728
Valtimet Sas *Titanium Metals Corp* 1797
Valto Systems, Inc. *Macromedia Inc* 1107
Valtra Argentina Tractors SA *AGCO Corp* 42
Valtra Danmark AS *AGCO Corp* 42
Valtra Deutschland GmbH *AGCO Corp* 42
Valtra do Brazil Ltda. *AGCO Corp* 42
Valtra Eastern Ventures OY *AGCO Corp* 42
Valtra GsmbH *AGCO Corp* 42
Valtra International BV *AGCO Corp* 42
Valtra Norge AS *AGCO Corp* 42
Valtra OY *AGCO Corp* 42
Valtra SPZOO *AGCO Corp* 42
Valtra Tracteurs S.A.S. *AGCO Corp* 42
Valtra Tractores SA *AGCO Corp* 42
Valtra Tractors (UK) Ltd. *AGCO Corp* 42
Valtra Vertriebs GmbH *AGCO Corp* 42
Valtra Voukraus OY *AGCO Corp* 42
Valtractor SA *AGCO Corp* 42
Valtractors Mexico SA de CV *AGCO Corp* 42
Valu Ventures, Inc. *Supervalu Inc* 1728
Valuation Information Technology, LLC *First American Corp* 695
Value Added Bakery Holding Company *Ralcorp Holdings Inc* .. 1511
Value Care, Inc. *Rotech Healthcare Inc NEW* 1560
Value City Department Stores Charitable Foundation *Retail Ventures Inc* 1538
Value City Department Stores LLC *Retail Ventures Inc* 1538
Value City Department Stores Services, Inc. *Retail Ventures Inc* 1538
Value City of Michigan, Inc. *Retail Ventures Inc* 1538
Value Fair, Inc. *Advo Inc* 34
Value Global International Limited *China Finance Inc* 389
Value Health Care Services, Inc. *Omnicare Inc* 1338
Value Health Holdings, Inc. *HCA Inc* 855
Value Health Management, Inc. *HCA Inc* 855
Value Health, Inc. *Express Scripts Inc* 671
Value Investments, Inc. *Broadcaster Inc* 283
Value Line Distribution Center, Inc *Value Line* 1887
Value Line Publishing, Inc. *Value Line* 1887
Value Line Securities, Inc. *Value Line* 1887
Value Network Service Inc. *FTD Group Inc* 752
Value Pharmacy, Inc. *Omnicare Inc* 1338
Value Plus Marketing *Diversified Financial Resources Corp* 563
ValueClick Europe Ltd. *ValueClick Inc* 1888
ValueClick GmbH *ValueClick Inc* 1888
ValueClick Sarl *ValueClick Inc* 1888
Valued Services Acquisitions Company II, LLC *CompuCredit Corp* 461
Valued Services Acquisitions Company, LLC *CompuCredit Corp* 461
Valued Services Financial Holdings, LLC *CompuCredit Corp* 461
Valued Services Holdings, LLC *CompuCredit Corp* 461
Valued Services Intellectual Property Funding, Inc. *CompuCredit Corp* 461
Valued Services Intellectual Property Holdings, Inc. *CompuCredit Corp* 461
Valued Services Intellectual Property Licensing, Inc. *CompuCredit Corp* 461
Valued Services Intellectual Property Management, Inc. *CompuCredit Corp* 461
Valued Services Intellectual Property Management, Inc. II *CompuCredit Corp* 461
Valued Services Investments, LLC *CompuCredit Corp* 461
Valued Services Management, LLC *CompuCredit Corp* 461
Valued Services of Alabama, LLC *CompuCredit Corp* 461
Valued Services of Arizona *CompuCredit Corp* 461
Valued Services of Arkansas, LLC *CompuCredit Corp* 461
Valued Services of California, LLC *CompuCredit Corp* 461
Valued Services of Colorado, LLC *CompuCredit Corp* 461
Valued Services of Florida, LLC *CompuCredit Corp* 461
Valued Services of Georgia, LLC *CompuCredit Corp* 461
Valued Services of Kansas, LLC *CompuCredit Corp* 461
Valued Services of Kentucky, LLC *CompuCredit Corp* 461
Valued Services of Louisiana, LLC *CompuCredit Corp* 461
Valued Services of Michigan, LLC *CompuCredit Corp* 461
Valued Services of Mississippi, LLC *CompuCredit Corp* 461
Valued Services of Missouri, LLC *CompuCredit Corp* 461
Valued Services of Nevada, LLC *CompuCredit Corp* 461
Valued Services of New Mexico, LLC *CompuCredit Corp* 461
Valued Services of North Carolina, LLC *CompuCredit Corp* 461
Valued Services of Ohio, LLC *CompuCredit Corp* 461
Valued Services of Oklahoma, LLC *CompuCredit Corp* 461
Valued Services of South Carolina, LLC *CompuCredit Corp* 461
Valued Services of Tennessee, LLC *CompuCredit Corp* 461
Valued Services of Texas, LLC *CompuCredit Corp* 461
Valued Services of Texas, LP *CompuCredit Corp* 461
Valued Services of Utah, LLC *CompuCredit Corp* 461
Valued Services of Virginia, LLC *CompuCredit Corp* 461
Valued Services of Washington DC, LLC *CompuCredit Corp* 461
Valued Services of Washington, LLC *CompuCredit Corp* 461
Valued Services of West Virginia, LLC *CompuCredit Corp* 461
Valued Services of Wisconsin, LLC *CompuCredit Corp* 461
Valued Services VFS, LLC *CompuCredit Corp* 461
Valued Services, LLC *CompuCredit Corp* 461
Valuedrive Investments Limited *Wachovia Corp* 1928
ValueLink, LLC *First Data Corp* 703
Valuepark Terneuzen Beheer BV *Dow Chemical Co* 573
Valuepark Terneuzen CV *Dow Chemical Co* 573
ValueRx of Michigan, Inc. *Express Scripts Inc* 671
Values Financial Network *Regan Holding Corp* 1524
ValueVision Direct Marketing Company, Inc. *ValueVision Media Inc* 1888
ValueVision Interactive, Inc. *ValueVision Media Inc* 1888
ValueVision Media Acquisitions, Inc. *ValueVision Media Inc* ... 1888
ValueVision Retail, Inc. *ValueVision Media Inc* 1888
ValuTree Real Estate Services, LLC *Suntrust Banks Inc* 1724
Valvcon Corporation *Metso Corp* 1173
Valvino Lamore, LLC *Wynn Resorts Ltd* 1982
Valvoline (Australia) Pty. Limited *Ashland Inc* 159
Valvoline (Deutschland) GmbH & Co. Kg *Ashland Inc* 159
VAMHC, Inc. *Vail Resorts Inc* 1883
Van American Insurance Services, Inc. *First Mercury Financial Corp* 710
van Ameringen-Haebler, Inc. *IFF Inc* 919
Van Blommestein Powalky B.V. *Akzo Nobel* 49
Van Buren County Landfill, LLC *Waste Industries USA Inc* 1934
Van Buren H.M.A., Inc. *Health Management Associates Inc* 858
Van Buren Holding, Inc. *Wilshire Enterprises Inc* 1964
Van Buren Pipe Corporation *Westlake Chemical Corp* 1953
Van Buren, LLC *Wilshire Enterprises Inc* 1964
Van der Horst U.S.A., Inc. *Weatherford International Ltd* 1940
Van der Moolen Effecten Specialist B.V. Amsterdam *Van der Moolen Holdings* 1888
Van der Moolen Effecten Specialist B.V. Cologne Branch *Van der Moolen Holdings* 1888

THE CORPORATE DIRECTORY - Walker's 2008 Subsidiary/Parent Index - 3395

VGL Properties, LLC *CCE Spinco Inc* 349
VGR Holding LLC *Vector Group Ltd* 1891
VH Holdco, Inc. *HCA Inc* 855
VH Holdings, Inc. *HCA Inc* 855
VHC Holdings, LLC *Triad Hospitals Inc* 1823
VHC Medical, LLC *Triad Hospitals Inc* 1823
VHG, Inc. *Allied Waste Industries Inc* 66
VHPM *Allianz* 63
VHSC Plantation, LLC *HCA Inc* 855
VHSC Pompano Beach, LLC *HCA Inc* 855
VI (C.I.) Limited *Las Vegas Sands Corp* 1056
VI Services Corporation *CBS Corp* 349
VI Services Corporation *Viacom Inc* 1902
Via Afrika Limited *Naspers Ltd* 1237
VIA Aircraft Management Inc. *Viacom Inc* 1902
Via Pierre 1 *Allianz* 63
Va Red Servicios Logsticos, S.A. *Repsol YPF* 1533
Via Spiga *Brown Shoe Co Inc* 288
Via-Sac Music Inc. *Viacom Inc* 1902
ViaCell BC Corp. *ViaCell Inc* 1901
ViaCell Endocrine Science, Inc. *ViaCell Inc* 1901
ViaCell Neuroscience, Inc. *ViaCell Inc* 1901
ViaCell Securities Corporation *ViaCell Inc* 1901
ViaCell Singapore Pte Ltd. *ViaCell Inc* 1901
Viacom A.G. *Viacom Inc* 1902
Viacom Broadcasting West Inc. *Viacom Inc* 1902
Viacom Canada Inc. *Viacom Inc* 1902
Viacom Communications Services Inc. *Viacom Inc* 1902
Viacom Corporate Services Inc. *Viacom Inc* 1902
Viacom DBS Inc. *Viacom Inc* 1902
Viacom Employee Services Inc. *Viacom Inc* 1902
Viacom Enterprises Canada Ltd. *Viacom Inc* 1902
Viacom Executive Services Corporation *Viacom Inc* 1902
Viacom Film Funding Company Inc. *Viacom Inc* 1902
Viacom Finanz AG *Viacom Inc* 1902
Viacom First Run Development Company Inc. *Viacom Inc* 1902
Viacom First Run Limited *Viacom Inc* 1902
Viacom Foundation Inc. *CBS Corp* 349
Viacom Foundation Inc. (not for profit corporation) *Viacom Inc* 1902
Viacom Holdings (Germany) B.V. *Viacom Inc* 1902
Viacom Holdings (Germany) II B.V. *Viacom Inc* 1902
Viacom IDA Inc. *Viacom Inc* 1902
Viacom International Canada Ltd. *Viacom Inc* 1902
Viacom International Holdings B.V. *Viacom Inc* 1902
Viacom International (Netherlands) B.V. *Viacom Inc* 1902
Viacom International Pty. Limited *Viacom Inc* 1902
Viacom Investments Inc. *Viacom Inc* 1902
Viacom IRB Acquisition Inc *Viacom Inc* 1902
Viacom Japan Inc. *Viacom Inc* 1902
Viacom K-Band Inc. *Viacom Inc* 1902
Viacom Middle East Holdings VOF *Viacom Inc* 1902
Viacom Networks Inc. *Viacom Inc* 1902
Viacom Outdoor Advertising Limited *Viacom Inc* 1902
Viacom Outdoor (Beijing) Ltd. *Viacom Inc* 1902
Viacom Outdoor (Beijing) Ltd. *CBS Corp* 349
Viacom Outdoor BV *Viacom Inc* 1902
Viacom Outdoor Holding Srl *Viacom Inc* 1902
Viacom Outdoor Limited *Viacom Inc* 1902
Viacom Outdoor Limited *Viacom Inc* 1902
Viacom Outdoor Mexico S De RL de CV *Viacom Inc* 1902
Viacom Outdoor Mexico S de RL de CV *CBS Corp* 349
Viacom Outdoor Norte SL *CBS Corp* 349
Viacom Outdoor Norte SL *Viacom Inc* 1902
Viacom Outdoor SA *Viacom Inc* 1902
Viacom Outdoor Sports Marketing Inc. *Viacom Inc* 1902
Viacom Outdoor Srl *Viacom Inc* 1902
Viacom Phoenix Inc. *Viacom Inc* 1902
Viacom Pictures Inc. *Viacom Inc* 1902
Viacom Pictures Movie Music LLC *Viacom Inc* 1902
Viacom Pictures Overseas Inc. *Viacom Inc* 1902
Viacom Pictures Songs Inc. *Viacom Inc* 1902
Viacom PNW Sports Inc. *Viacom Inc* 1902
Viacom Productions LLC *Viacom Inc* 1902
Viacom Receivables Funding II Corporation *Viacom Inc* 1902
Viacom Receivables Funding III Corporation *Viacom Inc* 1902
Viacom Retail Stores, Inc. *Viacom Inc* 1902
Viacom Satellite News Inc. *Viacom Inc* 1902
Viacom Services Inc. *Viacom Inc* 1902
Viacom Shopping Inc. *Viacom Inc* 1902
Viacom UK Limited *Viacom Inc* 1902
Viacom World Wide Ltd. *Viacom Inc* 1902
Viacom/Westinghouse of PA Inc. *Viacom Inc* 1902
Viacord, Inc. *ViaCell Inc* 1901
Viad Holding GmbH *Viad Corp* 1902
Viad Service Companies Limited *Viad Corp* 1902
Viagra Ltd *Pfizer Inc* 1420
Vialattea LLC *Citigroup Inc* 411
viaLink Operations, Inc. *Prescient Applied Intelligence Inc* 1462
Viance Limited *Rockwood Holdings Inc* 1555
Viance LLC *Rockwood Holdings Inc* 1555
Viance Oy *Rockwood Holdings Inc* 1555
Vianova Resins Germany Management GmbH *Cytec Industries Inc* 520
Viansa *Knightsbridge Fine Wines Inc* 1035
ViaSat Australia PTY Limited *Viasat Inc* 1902
ViaSat Canada Company *Viasat Inc* 1902
ViaSat China Services Inc. *Viasat Inc* 1902
ViaSat Europe Limited *Viasat Inc* 1902
ViaSat Europe S.r.l. *Viasat Inc* 1902
ViaSat Foreign Sales Corporation *Viasat Inc* 1902
ViaSat India Pvt. Ltd. *Viasat Inc* 1902
ViaSat Worldwide Limited *Viasat Inc* 1902
Viastar Distribution Group, Inc. *Pop3 Media Corp* 1448
VIASYS Healthcare GmbH *VIASYS Healthcare Inc* 1903
VIASYS Healthcare Hong Kong Limited *VIASYS Healthcare Inc* 1903
VIASYS Healthcare Inc. *VIASYS Healthcare Inc* 1903
VIASYS Healthcare Island ehf *VIASYS Healthcare Inc* 1903
VIASYS Healthcare Italy SpA *VIASYS Healthcare Inc* 1903
VIASYS Healthcare S.A.R.L. *VIASYS Healthcare Inc* 1903
VIASYS Healthcare Spain SA *VIASYS Healthcare Inc* 1903
VIASYS Healthcare UK Ltd. *VIASYS Healthcare Inc* 1903
VIASYS Holdings Inc. *VIASYS Healthcare Inc* 1903
VIASYS International Corporation *VIASYS Healthcare Inc* 1903
VIASYS Manufacturing Inc. *VIASYS Healthcare Inc* 1903
VIASYS MedSystems Inc. *VIASYS Healthcare Inc* 1903
Viasys Network Services, Inc. *Charys Holding Co Inc* 377
VIASYS NeuroCare BV *VIASYS Healthcare Inc* 1903
VIASYS NeuroCare France SAS *VIASYS Healthcare Inc* 1903
VIASYS NeuroCare Inc. *VIASYS Healthcare Inc* 1903
VIASYS NeuroCare Manufacturing Inc. *VIASYS Healthcare Inc* 1903
VIASYS NeuroCare Nederlands BV *VIASYS Healthcare Inc* 1903
VIASYS Polymer Products LLC *VIASYS Healthcare Inc* 1903
VIASYS Respiratory Care Inc. *VIASYS Healthcare Inc* 1903
Viasys Services, Inc. *Charys Holding Co Inc* 377
Viatis Satellite Radio Europe SAS *WorldSpace Inc* 1977
Viatis Satellite Radio Holdings ApS *WorldSpace Inc* 1977
Vibes Technologies, Inc. *Black Box Corp* 252
Vibrant Health Inc *Optigenex Inc* 1349
Vibration Sales & Service Limited *SPX Corp* 1684
Vibration Technology, Inc. *Layne Christensen Co* 1060
VIC,Inc. *Capital Trust Inc* 326
VICAN ASSOCIATES *Lexington Realty Trust* 1071
VICAN I LIMITED PARTNERSHIP *Lexington Realty Trust* 1071
VICAN II LIMITED PARTNERSHIP *Lexington Realty Trust* 1071
Vicar Operating, Inc. *VCA Antech Inc* 1891
Vicarious Visions, Inc. *Activision Inc* 19
Viceroy Australia Pty Ltd. *Quest Capital Corp* 1499
Viceroy Gold Corporation *Quest Capital Corp* 1499
Viceroy, Inc. *General Electric Co* 770
Vick International Corporation *Procter & Gamble* 1472
Vickers International Inc. *Eaton Corp* 596
Vickers Systems Asia Pacific Pte. Ltd. *Eaton Corp* 596
Vickers Systems International Ltd. *Eaton Corp* 596
Vickers Systems Limited *Eaton Corp* 596
Vickers Systems Limited *Eaton Corp* 596
Vickers Systems Pty. Ltd. *Eaton Corp* 596
Vickery Environmental, Inc. *Waste Management Inc* 1934
Vickerys Limited *Kadant Inc* 1016
Vicksburg Diagnostic Services, L.P. *HCA Inc* 855
Vicksburg Healthcare, LLC *Triad Hospitals Inc* 1823
Vicksburg Mall Associates, Ltd. *CBL & Associates Properties Inc* 348
Vicksmetal/Armco Associates *AK Steel Holding Corp* 48
Vicon Industries, Limited *Vicon Industries Inc* 1903
Vicor B.V *Vicor Corp* 1903
Vicor Development Corporation *Vicor Corp* 1903
Vicor France SARL *Vicor Corp* 1903
Vicor GmbH *Vicor Corp* 1903
Vicor Hong Kong Ltd *Vicor Corp* 1903
Vicor Italy SRL *Vicor Corp* 1903
Vicor Japan Company, Ltd *Vicor Corp* 1903
Vicor U.K. Ltd *Vicor Corp* 1903
VICR Securities Corporation *Vicor Corp* 1903
Vict. Th. Engwall& Co., Inc. *Altria Group Inc* 74
Vict. Th. Engwall& Co.,Inc. *Kraft Foods Inc* 1042
Victor Capital Group, L.P. *Capital Trust Inc* 326
Victor Company of Japan, Ltd. *Matsushita Electric Industrial Co Ltd* 1132
Victor Equipment Company *Thermadyne Holdings Corp* 1786
Victor Equipment de Mexico, S.A. de C.V. *Thermadyne Holdings Corp* 1786
Victor Huber GmbH *Teleflex Inc* 1766
Victor Industrial Equipment Ltd. *Federal Signal Corp* 684
Victor Industries, Ltd. *Federal Signal Corp* 684
Victor O. Schinnerer & Company Limited *Marsh & McLennan Cos Inc* 1125
Victor O. Schinnerer & Company, Inc. *Marsh & McLennan Cos Inc* 1125
Victor O. Schinnerer of Illinois, Inc. *Marsh & McLennan Cos Inc* 1125
Victor Products USA Inc. *Federal Signal Corp* 684
Victor Reinz Valve Seals LLC *Dana Corp* 525
Victor Ridder GmbH *Illinois Tool Works Inc* 922
VICTOR SQUARE SPE I LLC *Developers Diversified Realty Corp* 547
VICTOR SQUARE SPE LLC *Developers Diversified Realty Corp* 547
Victor V. Desrosier, Inc. *Stewart Enterprises Inc* 1704
Victoria + Co Ltd. *Jones Apparel Group Inc* 1010
VICTORIA ARMS APARTMENTS LIMITED PARTNERSHIP *Apartment Investment and Management Company* 130
Victoria Beverage Company Limited *China Food & Beverage Co* 390
Victoria Cellular Corporation *Telephone and Data Systems Inc* 1768
VICTORIA CELLULAR CORPORATION *United States Cellular Corp* 1862
Victoria Coca-Cola Bottling Company *Coca-Cola Enterprises Inc* 433
Victoria Functional Assessment & Restoration Center, Ltd. *Triad Hospitals Inc* 1823
Victoria Hills, LC *Tarragon Corp* 1751
Victoria Hospital, LLC *Triad Hospitals Inc* 1823
Victoria Hotels (Christchurch) Ltd. *InterContinental Hotels Group* 962
Victoria Investments, LLC *Wells Fargo & Co* 1944
Victoria Landfill TX, LP *Allied Waste Industries Inc* 66
Victoria Lumber *Victoria Industries Inc* 1904
Victoria Manor Associates, L.P. *Brookdale Senior Living Inc* 285
Victoria of Texas, L.P. *Triad Hospitals Inc* 1823
Victoria Park Mortgage, Inc. *St Joe Co* 1686
Victoria Park Real Estate, Inc. *St Joe Co* 1686
Victoria Partners, dba Monte Carlo Resort and Casino *MGM MIRAGE* 1176
Victoria Place Apartments, LLC *Bresler & Reiner Inc* 277
Victoria Properties, Inc. *Barnwell Industries Inc* 217
Victoria Regional Medical Center, Inc. *Universal Health Services Inc* 1869
Victoria Resource Corporation (Victoria) *Bema Gold Corp* 230
Victoria Resources, Inc. *Victoria Industries Inc* 1904
Victoria Siberian Wood *Victoria Industries Inc* 1904
VICTORIA WARD CENTER L.L.C. *General Growth Properties Inc* 771
VICTORIA WARD ENTERTAINMENT CENTER L.L.C. *General Growth Properties Inc* 771
VICTORIA WARD SERVICES, INC. *General Growth Properties Inc* 771
VICTORIA WARD, LIMITED *General Growth Properties Inc* 771
Victorias Secret Direct, LLC *Limited Brands Inc* 1079
Victorias Secret Stores Brand Management, Inc. *Limited Brands Inc* 1079
Victorias Secret Stores, LLC *Limited Brands Inc* 1079
Victorian Land Holdings Pty. Ltd *Global Wireless Satellite Ntwrks USA Inc* 798
Victorian Land Holdings Pty. Ltd. *Global Realty Development Corp* 797
Victory Beauty Systems, Inc. *Alberto Culver Co* 53
Victory Distributors, Inc. *Delhaize Group* 537
Victory Energy Partners, LLC *Range Resources Corp* 1514
Victory Environmental Services, Inc. *Republic Services Inc* 1534
Victory Exploration Inc. *Vista Gold Corp* 1914
Victory Faith S.A. *Tsakos Energy Navigation Ltd* 1832
Victory Gold Inc. *Vista Gold Corp* 1914
Victory Ltd. *Arlington Tankers Ltd* 150
Victory Mare S.A. *Tsakos Energy Navigation Ltd* 1832
Victory Medical Limited *Orthofix International* 1360
Victory Shipholding Inc. *Danaos Corp* 525
Victory Spirit S.A. *Tsakos Energy Navigation Ltd* 1832
VICTORY SQUARE APARTMENTS LIMITED PARTNERSHIP *Apartment Investment and Management Company* 130
Victory State Bank *VSB Bancorp Inc* 1924
Victory Waste Incorporated *Republic Services Inc* 1534
Vicuron Pharmaceuticals Inc *Pfizer Inc* 1420
Vicuron Pharmaceuticals Italy S.r.l *Pfizer Inc* 1420
Vicuron Pharmaceuticals, Inc *Oscient Pharmaceuticals Corp* 1361
Vida Herbal Suplementos Alimenticios, C.A *Herbalife Ltd* 870
Vida Network Sade Ltda. 35 *Unibanco Holdings* 1848
Vida Publishers L.L.C. *News Corp Ltd (The)* 1281
Vidacos Nominees Limited *Citigroup Inc* 411
Vidal (oyp) S.a. *United Business Media Plc* 1857
Vidal Sassoon Co. *Procter & Gamble* 1472
Vidal Sassoon (Shanghai) Academy *Procter & Gamble* 1472
Vidamed International Limited *Medtronic Inc* 1156
Vidapass, Sociedad Annima de Capital Variable *Citigroup Inc* 411
Video 2000 *Liberty Global Inc* 1074
Video Display (Europe), Ltd. *Video Display Corp* 1904
Video Domain Technologies Ltd. *Crow Technologies 1977 Ltd* 504
Video Injection S.A. *Insituform Technologies Inc* 952
Video Jukebox Network Europe, Ltd. *Liberty Media LLC* 1074
Video Tutorial Service, Inc *Multi Media Tutorial Services Inc* 1226
Video TV, Inc. *Gemstar-TV Guide International Inc* 766
Videocine, S.A. de C.V. *Grupo Televisa, S.A.B.* 829
Videoconferencing Systems, Inc *Simtrol Inc* 1635
Videojet Guangzhou Packaging Equipment Co LTD *Danaher Corp* 525
Videojet K.K. *Danaher Corp* 525
Videojet Technologies B.V. *Danaher Corp* 525
Videojet Technologies Canada L.P. *Danaher Corp* 525
Videojet Technologies Europe B.V. *Danaher Corp* 525
Videojet Technologies Gesellschaft mbH *Danaher Corp* 525
Videojet Technologies GmbH *Danaher Corp* 525
Videojet Technologies Inc. *Danaher Corp* 525
Videojet Technologies Kodlama ve Etiketleme Danismanlik ve Ticaret LTD.STI *Danaher Corp* 525
Videojet Technologies LTD *Danaher Corp* 525
Videojet Technologies Pte Ltd (Asia HQ) *Danaher Corp* 525
Videojet Technologies PTE. LTD. (Asia HG) *Danaher Corp* 525
Videojet Technologies PTE. LTD. (Singapore) *Danaher Corp* 525
Videojet Technologies S.A. *Danaher Corp* 525
Videojet Technologies S.L. *Danaher Corp* 525
Videojet Technologies SP z.o.o. *Danaher Corp* 525
Videojet Technologies Trading Co. Ltd. (Shanghai) *Danaher Corp* 525
Videoserpel, Ltd. *Grupo Televisa, S.A.B.* 829
VideoSite, Incorporated *GTECH Holdings Corp* 832
Videosys Ltd. *MDI Inc* 1143
Videotek, Inc. *Harris Corp* 849
VideOvation, Inc. *Reader's Digest Association Inc* 1517
VideoWare, Inc *ViewCast Corp* 1905
VidiAd *MGM MIRAGE* 1176
Vidriera Guadalajara, S.A. de C.V. *Vitro* 1918
Vidriera Los Reyes, S.A. de C.V. *Vitro* 1918
Vidriera Mexico, S.A. de C.V. *Vitro* 1918
Vidriera Monterrey, S.A. de C.V. *Vitro* 1918
Vidriera Queretaro, S.A. de C.V. *Vitro* 1918
Vidriera Toluca, S.A. de C.V. *Vitro* 1918
Vidrieria Fenicia *Owens Illinois Inc* 1366
Vidrieria Rovira, S. L. *Owens Illinois Inc* 1366
Vidrio Lux, S.A. *Vitro* 1918
Vidrio Plano de Mexico, S.A. de C.V. *Vitro* 1918
Viejo Energy Company *Mission Energy Holding Co* 1199
Viejo Energy Company *Edison International* 604
Vienna Operations Inc. *NRG Energy Inc* 1312
Vienna Power LLC *NRG Energy Inc* 1312
Viento II LLC *Morgan Stanley* 1215
Viento III LLC *Morgan Stanley* 1215
Viento IV LLC *Morgan Stanley* 1215
Viento IX LLC *Morgan Stanley* 1215
Viento LLC *Morgan Stanley* 1215
Viento V LLC *Morgan Stanley* 1215
Viento VI LLC *Morgan Stanley* 1215
Viento VII LLC *Morgan Stanley* 1215
Viento VIII LLC *Morgan Stanley* 1215
Viento X LLC *Morgan Stanley* 1215
Viento XI LLC *Morgan Stanley* 1215
Viento XII LLC *Morgan Stanley* 1215
Viento XIII LLC *Morgan Stanley* 1215
Viento XIV LLC *Morgan Stanley* 1215
Vierundzwanzigste Gamma Trans Leasing Verwaltungs GmbH& Co. Finanzierungs-Management KG *Citigroup Inc* 411
Vierzehnte FraM Beteiligungs GmbH *Allianz* 63
Vietnam Wacoal Corp. *Wacoal Holdings Corp* 1928
View Pointe Homeowners Association *Essex Property Trust Inc* 659
View Tanker Corporation *Overseas Shipholding Group Inc* 1365
Viewbridge, Inc. *Harris Corp* 849
ViewCast Online Solutions, Inc *ViewCast Corp* 1905
Viewgrove Holdings Ltd. *Orient Express Hotels Ltd* 1356
Viewmont Surgery Center, LLC *Tenet Healthcare Corp* 1774
Viewpoint Digital, Inc. *Viewpoint Corp* 1905
Viewpointe Archive Services, LLC *Bank of America Corp* 208
Viewsoft, Inc. *Citrix Systems Inc* 415
Viewsonics do Brasil, Ltda. *Emerson Electric Co* 623
Viewsonics Mexico S.A. de C.V. *Emerson Electric Co* 623
Viewtel Corporation *Vimicro International Corp* 1907
Vifor International, Ltd *Rockwell Medical Technologies Inc* 1555
Vigeland Metal Refinery A/s *Alcan Inc* 54
Vigelands Brug A/s *Alcan Inc* 54
Vigil Games, LLC *THQ Inc* 1790
Vigilant Insurance Company *Chubb Corp* 403
Vigilant Networks Canada Inc. *GenTek Inc* 777
Vigilant Networks LLC *GenTek Inc* 777
Vigindustries, Inc. *Mosaic Company (The)* 1217
Viginti NV *Delhaize Group* 537
Vigitec, S.a. *Allied Defense Group Inc* 64
Vignette Asia Pte Ltd. *Vignette Corp* 1906
Vignette B.V. (formerly known as OnDisplay Benelux B.V.) *Vignette Corp* 1906
Vignette Canada Corporation *Vignette Corp* 1906
Vignette de Mexico S. de R.L. de C. V. *Vignette Corp* 1906
Vignette Deutschland GmbH *Vignette Corp* 1906
Vignette do Brasil Ltda. *Vignette Corp* 1906
Vignette Europe Limited *Vignette Corp* 1906
Vignette Holdings LLC *Vignette Corp* 1906

THE CORPORATE DIRECTORY - Walker's 2008 Subsidiary/Parent Index - 3413

WF-AC TAX CREDIT FUND I, LLC *Apartment Investment and Management Company* 130
Wf-kw, LLC *Wells Fargo & Co* 1944
WF/TW Mortgage Venture, LLC *Wells Fargo & Co* 1944
WFAA Holdings, Inc. *Belo Corp* 230
WFAA of Texas, Inc. *Belo Corp* 230
Wfaa-tv, L.p. *Belo Corp* 230
WFB 83 Corp *Franklin Credit Mgmt Corp* 744
WFB Funding Corporation *Cabelas Inc* 300
WFB Funding, LLC *Cabelas Inc* 300
WFB Limitada *Willis Group Holdings Ltd* 1962
WFC Holdings Corporation *Wells Fargo & Co* 1944
WFC Inc. *Beverly Hills Bancorp Inc* 235
WFD Servicios S.A. de C.V. (Willis Europe BV 40%) *Willis Group Holdings Ltd* 1962
WFF Auto Hawaii, Inc. *Wells Fargo & Co* 1944
WFG Associates, Inc. *National Financial Partners Corp* 1241
WFG Liquidation Corporation *Service Corp International* 1614
WFGXLicensee,LLC *Sinclair Broadcast Group Inc* 1636
WFI Asesoria En Administracion SC *Kratos Defense & Security Solutions* 1042
WFI Asesoria En Telecommunicaciones SC *Kratos Defense & Security Solutions* 1042
WFI de Mexico S. de R.L. de C.V. *Kratos Defense & Security Solutions* 1042
WFI FSC Inc. *Kratos Defense & Security Solutions* 1042
WFI India Pvt. Ltd. *Kratos Defense & Security Solutions* 1042
WFI Insurance Agency Montana, Inc. *Wells Fargo & Co* 1944
WFI Insurance Agency Washington, Inc. *Wells Fargo & Co* 1944
WFI Insurance Agency Wyoming, Inc. *Wells Fargo & Co* 1944
WFI Network Management Services Corp. *Kratos Defense & Security Solutions* 1042
WFI NMC Corp. *Kratos Defense & Security Solutions* 1042
Wfi Nmc Lp *Kratos Defense & Security Solutions* 1042
WFI Scandinavia AB *Kratos Defense & Security Solutions* 1042
WFI Services de Mexico S.A. de C.V. *Kratos Defense & Security Solutions* 1042
WFI Spain SL *Kratos Defense & Security Solutions* 1042
WFI Telekomunikasyon Servis Ltd. *Kratos Defense & Security Solutions* 1042
WFI UK Ltd. *Kratos Defense & Security Solutions* 1042
WFLB License Limited Partnership *Beasley Broadcast Group Inc* 226
WFLC Subsidiary, LLC *Wells Fargo & Co* 1944
WFM Beverage Corp. *Whole Foods Market Inc* 1959
WFM Beverage Holding Company *Whole Foods Market Inc* 1959
WFM Cobb Property Investments, LLC *Whole Foods Market Inc* 1959
WFM Gift Card, Inc. *Whole Foods Market Inc* 1959
WFM IP Investments, Inc. *Whole Foods Market Inc* 1959
WFM IP Management, Inc. *Whole Foods Market Inc* 1959
WFM Private Label Management, Inc. *Whole Foods Market Inc* 1959
WFM Private Label, L.P. *Whole Foods Market Inc* 1959
WFM Procurement Investments, Inc. *Whole Foods Market Inc* 1959
WFM Purchasing Management, Inc. *Whole Foods Market Inc* 1959
WFM Purchasing, L.P. *Whole Foods Market Inc* 1959
WFM Select Fish, Inc. *Whole Foods Market Inc* 1959
WFM Southern Nevada, Inc. *Whole Foods Market Inc* 1959
Wfmy Television Corp. *Gannett Co Inc* 761
WFP 53 State Street Co. L.P. *Brookfield Properties Corp* 286
WFP 75 State Street Co. L.P. *Brookfield Properties Corp* 286
WFP Argentina S.R.L. *Hawk Corp* 854
WFP Tower A Co. L.P. *Brookfield Properties Corp* 286
WFP Tower B Co. L.P. *Brookfield Properties Corp* 286
WFP Tower D Co. L.P. *Brookfield Properties Corp* 286
WFS Liquids Company *Williams Cos Inc* 1961
WFS NGL Pipeline Company, Inc. *Williams Cos Inc* 1961
WFS Pipeline Company *Williams Cos Inc* 1961
WFS Agencia de Naves SA *World Fuel Services Corp* 1976
WFS Enterprises, Inc. *Williams Cos Inc* 1961
WFS Gathering Company, LLC *Williams Cos Inc* 1961
Wfs Ii LLC *Weyerhaeuser Co* 1955
WFXT, Inc. *News Corp Ltd (The)* 1281
WFXU Corporation *Pegasus Communications Corp* 1401
WFXU License Corporation *Pegasus Communications Corp* 1401
WG Holdings of Pennsylvania, L.L.C. *Pennsylvania Real Estate Investment Trust* 1405
WG Holdings, L.P. *Pennsylvania Real Estate Investment Trust* 1405
WG Investors Trust *CapLease Inc* 328
WG Maritime Plaza I, Inc. *WGL Holdings Inc* 1955
WG Park Anchor B, LLC *Pennsylvania Real Estate Investment Trust* 1405
WG Park General, L.P. *Pennsylvania Real Estate Investment Trust* 1405
WG Park Limited, L.P. *Pennsylvania Real Estate Investment Trust* 1405
WG Park, L.P. *Pennsylvania Real Estate Investment Trust* 1405
WG Park-Anchor B, LP *Pennsylvania Real Estate Investment Trust* 1405
Wg-4511 Mi, LLC *Wachovia Corp* 1928
Wg-5278 Mo, LLC *Wachovia Corp* 1928
Wg-5825 Il, LLC *Wachovia Corp* 1928
Wg-5873 Mo, LLC *Wachovia Corp* 1928
Wg-5885 Ia, LLC *Wachovia Corp* 1928
Wg-6138 Ga, LLC *Wachovia Corp* 1928
Wg-6329 Tx, LLC *Wachovia Corp* 1928
Wg-6458 Oh, LLC *Wachovia Corp* 1928
Wg-6478 Ks, LLC *Wachovia Corp* 1928
Wg-6920 Ks, LLC *Wachovia Corp* 1928
Wg-7060 Ks, LLC *Wachovia Corp* 1928
Wg-7428 Mo, LLC *Wachovia Corp* 1928
Wg-7683 Oh, LLC *Wachovia Corp* 1928
Wg-7817 Ks, LLC *Wachovia Corp* 1928
Wg-7865 Oh, LLC *Wachovia Corp* 1928
WGAC License, LLC *Beasley Broadcast Group Inc* 226
Wgal Hearst-argyle Television, Inc. *Hearst Argyle Television Inc* 862
WGBO License Partnership G.P. *Univision Communications Inc* 1871
WGCI,Inc. *Washington Group International Inc* 1932
WGGB,Inc. *Sinclair Broadcast Group Inc* 1636
WGGBLicensee,LLC *Sinclair Broadcast Group Inc* 1636
WGH, Inc. *HCA Inc* 855
WGH, Inc. *News Corp Ltd (The)* 1281
WGHP License, Inc. *News Corp Ltd (The)* 1281
WGI Asia Pacific Pte. Ltd. *Washington Group International Inc* 1932
WGI Asia,Inc. *Washington Group International Inc* 1932
WGI Global Inc. *Washington Group International Inc* 1932
WGI Inc *WPP Group Plc* 1979
WGI Industrial Services, Ltd. *Washington Group International Inc* 1932
WGI Middle East Inc. *Washington Group International Inc* 1932
WGI Middle East (UK) Ltd. *Washington Group International Inc* 1932
WGI Netherlands B.V. *Washington Group International Inc* 1932
WGL Holdings, Inc. *WGL Holdings Inc* 1955
WGL Intermediate Holdings, Inc. *Wilson Greatbatch Technologies Inc* 1964
WGME Licensee,LLC *Sinclair Broadcast Group Inc* 1636
WGME,Inc. *Sinclair Broadcast Group Inc* 1636
WGOR License, LLC *Beasley Broadcast Group Inc* 226
WGP Enterprises, Inc. *Williams Cos Inc* 1961
WGP Gulfstream Pipeline Company, LLC *Williams Cos Inc* 1961
WGP International Canada, Inc. *Williams Cos Inc* 1961
WGP LLC *K2 Inc* 1015
WGTKTC1 Limited *Applied Materials Inc* 136
WH Capital Corporation, *Herbalife Ltd* 870
WH Holdings (Cayman Islands) Ltd *Herbalife Ltd* 870
WH Inc. of Illinois *Whitehall Jewellers Inc* 1957
WH Intermediate Holdings Ltd *Herbalife Ltd* 870
WH Land I, Inc. *Hovnanian Enterprises Inc* 894
WH Luxembourg CM S..R.L, *Herbalife Ltd* 870
WH Luxembourg Holdings S..R.L, *Herbalife Ltd* 870
WH Luxembourg Intermediate Holdings, *Herbalife Ltd* 870
WH One, LLC *Woodhead Industries Inc* 1974
WH Properties, Inc. *Hovnanian Enterprises Inc* 894
WH Two, LLC *Woodhead Industries Inc* 1974
Whalen & Company, Inc. *Tetra Tech Inc* 1780
Whalen Service Corps Inc. *Tetra Tech Inc* 1780
Whalen/Sentrex LLC *Tetra Tech Inc* 1780
Wharf Holding, LLC *Equity Residential* 654
Wharf Resources Ltd. *Goldcorp Inc* 804
Wharf Resources (U.S.A.) Inc. *Goldcorp Inc* 804
Wharf Ventures Limited *Barclays Plc* 216
Wharfdome Limited *Royal & Sun Alliance Insurance Group Plc* 1560
Wharton Medco, LLC *Triad Hospitals Inc* 1823
WhatIfSports.com, Inc. *News Corp Ltd (The)* 1281
WHBC Holdings, LLC *Williams Cos Inc* 1961
WHBC, LLC *Williams Cos Inc* 1961
WHC Holdings Limited *Tyco International Ltd* 1838
WHC, Ltd. *MDU Resources Group Inc* 1144
Whc805, LLC *Red Lion Hotels Corp* 1520
WHD Enterprises, LLC *Williams Cos Inc* 1961
Wheat First Butcher Singer Private Equity Fund *Wachovia Corp* 1928
Wheatley Meadows Associates, LLC *Orleans Homebuilders Inc* 1359
Wheaton Bank and Trust Company *Wintrust Financial Corp* 1969
Wheaton Land Investment, LLC *AvalonBay Communities Inc* 184
Wheaton Minerals Asia pacific Pty Limited *Goldcorp Inc* 804
Wheaton River (Cayman Islands) Ltd. *Goldcorp Inc* 804
Wheaton River Cayman pampas Ltd. *Goldcorp Inc* 804
Wheaton Trading (Caymans) Ltd *Silver Wheaton Corp* 1632
Wheaton Uk Ltd. *Alcan Inc* 54
Wheel Assemblies Inc. *Goodyear Tire & Rubber Com (The)* 811
Wheel to Wheel Parts.com, LLC *Quantum Fuel Systems Techs Worldwide Inc* 1498
Wheel to Wheel Powertrain, LLC *Quantum Fuel Systems Techs Worldwide Inc* 1498
Wheel to Wheel, LLC *Quantum Fuel Systems Techs Worldwide Inc* 1498
Wheelabrator Baltimore LLC *Waste Management Inc* 1934
Wheelabrator Baltimore, L.P. *Waste Management Inc* 1934
Wheelabrator Bridgeport, L.P. *Waste Management Inc* 1934
Wheelabrator Cedar Creek Inc. *Waste Management Inc* 1934
Wheelabrator Claremont Company, L.P. *Waste Management Inc* 1934
Wheelabrator Concord Company, L.P. *Waste Management Inc* 1934
Wheelabrator Concord Inc. *Waste Management Inc* 1934
Wheelabrator Connecticut Inc. *Waste Management Inc* 1934
Wheelabrator Culm Services Inc. *Waste Management Inc* 1934
Wheelabrator Environmental Systems Inc. *Waste Management Inc* 1934
Wheelabrator Falls Inc. *Waste Management Inc* 1934
Wheelabrator Frackville Energy Company Inc. *Waste Management Inc* 1934
Wheelabrator Frackville Properties Inc. *Waste Management Inc* 1934
Wheelabrator Fuel Services Inc. *Waste Management Inc* 1934
Wheelabrator Gloucester Company, L.P. *Waste Management Inc* 1934
Wheelabrator Gloucester Inc. *Waste Management Inc* 1934
Wheelabrator Guam Inc. *Waste Management Inc* 1934
Wheelabrator Hudson Energy Company Inc. *Waste Management Inc* 1934
Wheelabrator Hudson Falls LLC *Waste Management Inc* 1934
Wheelabrator Land Resources Inc. *Waste Management Inc* 1934
Wheelabrator Lassen Inc. *Waste Management Inc* 1934
Wheelabrator Lisbon Inc. *Waste Management Inc* 1934
Wheelabrator Martell Inc. *Waste Management Inc* 1934
Wheelabrator McKay Bay Inc. *Waste Management Inc* 1934
Wheelabrator Millbury Inc. *Waste Management Inc* 1934
Wheelabrator New Hampshire Inc. *Waste Management Inc* 1934
Wheelabrator New Jersey Inc. *Waste Management Inc* 1934
Wheelabrator NHC Inc. *Waste Management Inc* 1934
Wheelabrator North Andover Inc. *Waste Management Inc* 1934
Wheelabrator North Broward Inc. *Waste Management Inc* 1934
Wheelabrator North Shore Inc. *Waste Management Inc* 1934
Wheelabrator Norwalk Energy Company Inc. *Waste Management Inc* 1934
Wheelabrator Penacook Inc. *Waste Management Inc* 1934
Wheelabrator Pinellas Inc. *Waste Management Inc* 1934
Wheelabrator Putnam Inc. *Waste Management Inc* 1934
Wheelabrator Ridge Energy Inc. *Waste Management Inc* 1934
Wheelabrator Saugus Inc. *Waste Management Inc* 1934
Wheelabrator Shasta Energy Company Inc. *Waste Management Inc* 1934
Wheelabrator Sherman Energy Company, G.P. *Waste Management Inc* 1934
Wheelabrator Sherman Station LLC *Waste Management Inc* 1934
Wheelabrator Sherman Station One Inc. *Waste Management Inc* 1934
Wheelabrator South Broward Inc. *Waste Management Inc* 1934
Wheelabrator Spokane Inc. *Waste Management Inc* 1934
Wheelabrator Technologies Inc. *Waste Management Inc* 1934
Wheelabrator Technologies International Inc. *Waste Management Inc* 1934
Wheelabrator Westchester, L.P. *Waste Management Inc* 1934
Wheeler Insurance, Ltd. *Pitney Bowes Inc* 1434
Wheeler Manor Associates LP *Edison International* 604
Wheeling Gateway Coal Co. *Repsol YPF* 1533
Wheeling Land Development Corp *Wheeling Island Gaming Inc* 1956
Wheeling Machine Products, L.P. *Lone Star Technologies Inc* 1093
Wheeling-Pittsburgh Steel Corporation *Wheeling Pittsburgh Corp* 1956
Where@Risk Limited *Yahoo Inc* 1990
Where2 LLC *Google Inc* 811
WHEREAS *Peoples Bancorp* 1406
Whereonearth Limited *Yahoo Inc* 1990
Whereonearth.com Inc. *Yahoo Inc* 1990
Whereonearth.com Limited *Yahoo Inc* 1990
Wherify California, Inc *Wherify Wireless Inc* 1956
Wherify Wireless, Inc. *Wherify Wireless Inc* 1956
Whessoe Piping Systems Limited *Shaw Group Inc (The)* 1618
Whessoe Vapour Control Limited *Tyco International Ltd* 1838
Whessoe Varec Company, The *Tyco International Ltd* 1838
Wheway Corporate Services Limited *SPX Corp* 1684
Wheway Hampshire Limited *SPX Corp* 1684
Wheway plc *SPX Corp* 1684
Wheway Secretarial Services Limited *SPX Corp* 1684
WHF INC. *Developers Diversified Realty Corp* 547
WHG Medical, LLC *HCA Inc* 855
WHGMH Realty, L.P. *GMH Communities Trust* 802
WHI-Republic, LLC *Hovnanian Enterprises Inc* 894
WHICH Belgium S.A. *Tyco International Ltd* 1838
Whidbey Island Bank *Washington Banking Co* 1932
Whippany Venture I, LLC *Shaw Group Inc (The)* 1618
Whippet Funding, LLC *Wells Fargo & Co* 1944
Whirlpool Canada LP *Whirlpool Corp* 1956
Whirlpool do Brasil Ltda. *Whirlpool Corp* 1956
Whirlpool Europe B.V. *Whirlpool Corp* 1956
Whirlpool Manufacturing Corporation *Whirlpool Corp* 1956
Whirlpool Mexico, S.A. de C.V. *Whirlpool Corp* 1956
Whirlpool Patents Company *Whirlpool Corp* 1956
Whirlpool Properties, Inc. *Whirlpool Corp* 1956
Whiskey Bay Gas Company *Energy Transfer Partners LP* 636
Whiskey Bay Gathering Company, Ltd. *Energy Transfer Partners LP* 636
Whisper Ridge of Staunton, LLC *Psychiatric Solutions Inc* 1485
Whisper RidgeInc. *American SkIIng Co* 102
Whispering Pines Landfill TX, LP *Allied Waste Industries Inc* 66
Whispering Wind Acres, LLCLP *Edison International* 604
Whistler *Gaylord Entertainment Co* 765
Whistler Chalets Holding Corp. *Gaylord Entertainment Co* 765
Whistler Lodging Company Ltd. *Gaylord Entertainment Co* 765
Whistling Pines Funding LLC *Bank of America Corp* 208
Whitaker Corporation, The *Tyco International Ltd* 1838
Whitbread Technology Partners, Inc *Zanett Inc* 1995
Whitby Entertainment Holdings, Inc. *Entertainment Properties Trust* 643
Whitcomb AB *Forrester Research Inc* 737
Whitcomb Investments, Inc. *Forrester Research Inc* 737
White and Associates/First Citizens Insurance, LLC *First Citizens Bancshares Inc/TN* 701
White Buck Coal Company *Massey Energy Co* 1129
White Caps Windfarm, LLCLP *Edison International* 604
WHITE CLIFF APARTMENTS LIMITED PARTNERSHIP *Apartment Investment and Management Company* 130
White Commercial Real Estate *Grubb & Ellis Co* 827
White County Coal, LLC *Alliance Holdings GP LP* 62
White County Coal, LLC *Alliance Resource Partners LP* 62
White County Physician Services, Inc. *Community Health Systems Inc* 454
White Eagle Assurance Company *Helmerich & Payne Inc* 867
White Flame Energy, Inc. *Alpha Natural Resources Inc* 70
White Group Electronics Limited *Tyco International Ltd* 1838
White Hall Mall Venture (partnership) *Pennsylvania Real Estate Investment Trust* 1405
White Haven Music,Inc. *CKX Inc* 418
White Holding, B.V. *DIRECTV Group Inc (The)* 561
White House | Black Market Inc. *Chico's FAS Inc* 385
White Ice Ventures Limited *Bema Gold Corp* 230
White Knight Gold (U.S.) Inc *White Knight Resources Inc* 1957
White Knob Mining Company *Mueller Industries Inc* 1226
White Lake Landfill, Inc. *Waste Management Inc* 1934
White Line Plant Ltd. *Bucyrus International Inc* 293
White Marsh Distribution, LLC *Charming Shoppes Inc* 375
WHITE MARSH GENERAL PARTNERSHIP *General Growth Properties Inc* 771
WHITE MARSH LIMITED PARTNERSHIP *General Growth Properties Inc* 771
WHITE MARSH MALL ASSOCIATES *General Growth Properties Inc* 771
WHITE MARSH MALL, LLC *General Growth Properties Inc* 771
WHITE MARSH PHASE II ASSOCIATES *General Growth Properties Inc* 771
White Martins de Camacari S.A. *Praxair Inc* 1458
White Martins e Companhia - Comrcio e Servios *Praxair Inc* 1458
White Martins e White Martins Comrcio e Servios *Praxair Inc* 1458
White Martins Gases Industriais do Nordeste S.A. *Praxair Inc* 1458
White Martins Gases Industriais do Norte S.A. *Praxair Inc* 1458
White Martins Gases Industriais Ltda. *Praxair Inc* 1458
White Martins Investimentos Ltda. *Praxair Inc* 1458
White Martins Participacoes Ltda. *Praxair Inc* 1458
White Mountain Apache LP *Edison International* 604
White Mountain Cable Construction, LLC *Dycom Industries Inc* 583
White Mountain Insurance Company *Tyco International Ltd* 1838
White Mountain Physical Therapy *U.S. Physical Therapy Inc* 1841
White Mountain Titanium Corporation *White Mountain Tianium Corp* 1957
White Mountains Advisors, LLC *White Mountains Insurance Group Ltd* 1957
White Mountains Holdings Bermuda Ltd. *White Mountains Insurance Group Ltd* 1957
White Mountains International S.a.r.l. *White Mountains Insurance Group Ltd* 1957
White Mountains (luxembourg) S.a.r.l. *White Mountains Insurance Group Ltd* 1957
White Mountains Re Financial Services, Ltd. *White Mountains Insurance Group Ltd* 1957
White Mountains Re Group, Ltd. *White Mountains Insurance Group Ltd* 1957
White Mountains Re Holdings, Inc. *White Mountains Insurance Group Ltd* 1957
White Mountains Underwriting (bermuda) Limited *White Mountains Insurance Group Ltd* 1957
White Mountains Underwriting Limited *White Mountains Insurance Group Ltd* 1957
White Nights Advertising Limited *News Corp Ltd (The)* 1281
White Oak Merger Corp. *Tellabs Inc* 1770
White Oak Royalty Company *Metlife Inc* 1171
White One Asset Securitization Specialty Limited *Citigroup Inc* 411
White Plains Galleria Investors, L.P. *Mills Ltd Partnership* 1193

Geographic Index

FLORIDA

3200 to 3299 ZIP Codes

3300 to 3399 ZIP Codes

OKLAHOMA

UTAH

Stock Exchange/Ticker Symbol Index

American Stock Exchange(AMS)

NASDAQ / Non - Nat 'l Market System (NDQ)

New York Stock Exchange(NYSE)